WORLD CHRISTIAN ENCYCLOPEDIA

WORLD CHRISTIAN ENCYCLOPEDIA

A comparative survey of churches and religions in the modern world

SECOND EDITION

David B. Barrett
George T. Kurian
Todd M. Johnson

Volume 1:
The world by countries:
religionists, churches, ministries

OXFORD
UNIVERSITY PRESS

2001

OXFORD
UNIVERSITY PRESS

Oxford New York
Athens Auckland Bangkok Bogotá Buenos Aires Calcutta
Cape Town Chennai Dar es Salaam Delhi Florence Hong Kong Istanbul
Karachi Kuala Lumpur Madrid Melbourne Mexico City Mumbai
Nairobi Paris São Paulo Shanghai Singapore Taipei Tokyo Toronto Warsaw

and associated companies in
Berlin Ibadan

Published by Oxford University Press, Inc.,
198 Madison Avenue, New York, New York 10016
www.oup.com

Library of Congress Cataloging-in-Publication Data

World Christian encyclopedia : a comparative survey of churches
and religions in the modern world / David B. Barrett,
George T. Kurian, Todd M. Johnson.—2nd ed.
p. cm.
Includes bibliographical references and index.
1. Christianity. 2. Christian sects. 3. Ecclesiastical geography. 4. Christianity—Statistics.
I. Barrett, David B. II. Kurian, George Thomas. III. Johnson, Todd M.
BR157 .W67 2000 230'.003—dc21 99-057323
ISBN 0-19-507963-9 (set)
ISBN 0-19-510318-1 (vol. 1)
ISBN 0-19-510319-X (vol. 2)

1 3 5 7 9 8 6 4 2

Printed in the United States of America
on acid-free paper

TABLE OF CONTENTS

Volume 1. THE WORLD BY COUNTRIES: RELIGIONISTS, CHURCHES, MINISTRIES

Volume 2. THE WORLD BY SEGMENTS: RELIGIONS, PEOPLES, LANGUAGES, CITIES, TOPICS

Preface to the Second Edition

This encyclopedia describes empirical Christianity—those facts about the world Christian movement that are measurable. It does this by setting out summaries of the survey data produced every year by a vast decentralized investigation quietly undertaken by churches and religious workers across the world.

In fact, for over 150 years now, most of the Christian world's denominations and agencies have been conducting an annual census which is probably the world's largest single detailed enumeration. In it some 10 million church leaders, clergy, and other Christian workers of every description are invited or instructed by their agencies to compile an annual report and to fill out sizable statistical questions. Soon after, these 10 million completed questionnaires are received in home offices and headquarters. After limited circulation to senior staff, most are then placed in archives. Only occasionally are scholars or researchers invited to analyze this enormous gold mine of new data and information. Meanwhile, year by year the data continue to pour in, accumulating at ever-increasing rates, justifying the whole endeavor being described as a megacensus.

The present encyclopedia has had access to much of this documentation, leading to this attempt to set out the survey data country by country in the global context.

Over the years the churches have built up a vast inventory of different numerical measurements of their activities, numbering at least 1,020 different significant measures often referred to as 'instruments'. A scientific approach to these phenomena not only records these raw survey data but also remembers that the Latin word for "measurement" was and is *dimensio.* This ancient word is translated today as "dimension" in English, French, and Spanish (and as *Dimension* in German and *dimensão* in Portuguese). Often 2 measurements open up a new dimension. Thus 'The dimension for speed is length divided by time' (Webster's). Providing one sticks close to actual measurements, the reader can begin to discern dimensions emerging and thus can make sense of this vast sea of new information year by year. In Ecclesiastical Latin, *dimensio* had the additional meaning of 'reasoning' or 'judgment'—accentuating the relationship between measurement and knowledge.

This annual megacensus costs the Christian world a little over US $1.1 billion, which is 0.4% of organized global Christianity's total annual income. It is not however a single coordinated endeavor. It consists in fact of many thousands of separate, decentralized, uncoordinated censuses. Many, paradoxically, are global censuses portraying their own denomination as either the main one in the world, or the most significant one, or even in several cases the only one.

Nor is this encyclopedia the megacensus' authorized report. Compiling the encyclopedia has been possible because the megacensus is backed up by scores of other major sources—not least the massive volume of 4.5 million separate and distinct book titles on Christianity and religion available to the reader on the shelves of the world's 50,000 largest libraries.

The subject matter of the census is the previous year's activities, its events, its demographics, its achievements, its failures, its numbers, and its statistics. It covers a vast range of contexts—from the local, national, continental, global, ethnic, ethnocultural, linguistic, and urban-rural, to the specifically religious and Christian contexts.

As an example one may take the questionnaire in Latin and its translation into a score of other lingua francas sent out by the Vatican's Central Statistics Office of the Church, Secretariat of State, to 3,500 bishops early in each year. In Latin it is entitled 'Universalis Ecclesiae Annuus Census'; its English version reads 'Annual General Statistical Questionnaire'. With 11 separate pages and 21 sheets (including carbons) it asks 20 descriptive questions and no less than 141 distinct statistical questions. Return rate is 95% within 2 months.

Parallel endeavors are undertaken by most of the world's 34,000 other Christian denominations and 50,000 large agencies. Questions are asked about the whole range of numerical variables such as 'How many hours a month have you been spending on (a) preaching, (b) Scripture exposition, (c) personal evangelism, and (d) preparation of catechumens for baptism?'

After being completed and mailed back, these questionnaires remain year by year at headquarters throughout the world, at various stages toward becoming treated as closed archival data. There is however no insurmountable difficulty in gaining access to study these materials if one is a serious researcher, journalist, doctoral candidate, or other investigator.

Volume 1: Summary data at country and world levels

In this present encyclopedia, Part 1 "World summary" sets out an overview of the data at various levels: global, continental, national, confessional. It presents the world picture in very abbreviated form describing a large number of these measurements or dimensions.

Part 2 "Glossary" then describes the technical terms and neologisms employed. Part 3 "Codebook" permits presenting the data in condensed form by giving the codes later used for shorthand purposes. Thus in several tables countries are listed by means of the first four letters of their anglicized names to enable the reader to rapidly identify countries on any list.

With Part 4 "Countries" the heart of this survey is reached. It contains a country-by-country description, in a standardized format, of the detailed data produced in the megacensus. This describes each country's life, liberty, religions, Christianity, churches, and their prospects. Part 4 thus contains the core of the Encyclopedia's research in the shape of a comparative listing, enumeration, and description of the globe's 34,000 Christian denominations. Each country's article follows a standard pattern and sequence to enable rapid comparisons from any countries to any others. Assisting this rapid comparison is a visual representation of the data in each country's standardized Great Commission Instrument Panel with its 6 instruments measuring 6 major features of each country's empirical situation.

Part 5 "CountryScan" summarizes the 167 most useful numerical variables describing each of the world's 238 countries. Volume 1 then concludes with Part 6 "Atlas". This 24-page atlas gives geographico-political color maps of each country overlaid with a number of environmental factors including population density, land usage, location of minerals, megacities, airports and the like. A smaller section of 16 global maps illustrates specific religious findings from the annual census.

Volume 2: Survey data under 9 segments or topics

This volume now goes into greater detail below the country level. For each country, data are given for 5 kinds of subdivision or segment—its religions and religionists, its ethnocultural peoples, its languages, its cities, and its major civil divisions—and for 4 additional approaches: dictionary topics, bibliography, directory, and indexes.

Part 7 "Religiometrics" begins by defining and setting out one-line profiles of the 270 largest of the 10,000 distinct religions worldwide. A complete listing of these 10,000, each described under 20 measurements or dimensions, is forthcoming on the related electronic version to assist readers wanting to construct their own tables, graphics, diagrams, or to conduct their own analyses, explanations, or interpretations.

In similar vein, Part 8 "EthnoSphere" sets out over 12,600 profiles—each given one line across 2 facing pages—describing the world's racial and ethnic cultures in each country. Part 9 "LinguaMetrics" does the same for languages, giving demographics of mother-tongue speakers, church members, religious adherents, names for God, and Scriptures for 13,500 language profiles. Likewise with Part 10 "MetroScan" showing the world's metropolises by means of 7,000 city profiles, one line with 10 variables for each city.

The last of these country subdivisions listed here is surveyed in Part 11 "ProvinceScan". This sets out survey profiles of the world's 3,030 major civil divisions. This term, abbreviated as MCDs, is used and quantified by the United Nations to designate each country's provinces, states, or other civil subdivisions.

Part 12 "Dictionary" introduces current usage of topical survey terms for

Christianity and religions in their global context. Part 13 "Bibliography" offers a selective world catalogue of 1,330 major books describing Christianity and religions, in addition to the 6,000 items describing Christianity in a single country each, listed in Part 4.

Part 14 "Directory" then provides evidence of the geographical spread of religion by means of a directory of 82 topics anchoring Christianity and religion on the worldwide scene with names, addresses, phone and fax numbers, e-mail addresses, for a representative selection of organizations. Lastly, Part 15 "Indexes" locates topics, in particular abbreviations, initials and acronyms in daily use around the world.

Readers should not be put off by this survey's practice of giving many totals to the last digit. This is not a claim to any unrealistic or phony precision. The reason is that the survey is often totalling lists combining both rounded totals of large churches with unrounded totals to the last digit published by very small churches. Rather than lose these details, in most cases here the totals are left unrounded. The United Nations' extensive demographic databases, their disks and their printouts and their published versions, including projections to AD 2050 for every country, follow this same procedure. Readers can then round any figure they need to the nearest hundred, or thousand, or million, or billion as suits their immediate requirements.

In passing, the reader should be assured that the total number of Christians in the world at AD 2000's midyear, which this survey puts at 1,999,563,000—or, when rounded, at 2,000 million—is a coincidental total arising as the end product of complex computerized subtotaling and totaling. No manipulation of any kind produced this startling figure, which indeed was only noticed by the authors shortly before publication. Knowing the many margins of error involved, little or no significance should be seen in this strange coincidence.

Survey data in electronic form

To assist the reader wanting to have ready access to this mass of survey data in some easily useable form, a related electronic version is forthcoming under the title *World Christian database*. This permits rapid navigation across this sea of new data and allows readers to conduct their own investigations.

Information, not interpretation

Analysis and interpretation of this mass of grassroots data is undeniably a formidable task. This is therefore not being undertaken in the present encyclopedia but will be handled in a forthcoming separate work.

The authors apologize for the almost indigestible nature of this mass of new survey data but they invite readers to assist them in their purpose of doing justice to, and making sense of, the labors of the 10 million collaborators and their new data year by year.

Richmond, Virginia, 2000 David B. Barrett

Preface to the First Edition

In 1968, a group of church demographers met and decided that the time was ripe to undertake, for possibly the first time in Christian history, a comprehensive survey of all branches of global Christianity. It was expected that the task of compiling this resulting encyclopedia would take about three years; in the event, it has taken twelve years. The reason for this lengthy period was that all those originally involved, including the editor, seriously underestimated the immense size and complexity of the Christian world. The number of denominations was found to be four times as numerous as the estimate made in 1968. Vast areas of Christian activity proved to be undocumented in the literature and had to be surveyed by means of visits to every country in the world. The survey proceeded through such visits, through an extensive correspondence, and through the part-time investigations of a modest network of specialists in every country.

Perhaps the first impression to strike the reader will be of the enormous diversity and fragmentation of Christianity. The proliferation of 20,800 denominations is sure to cause unfavourable comment. Some will see it as sectarianism run riot. But here several points to the contrary can be noted. Diversity—divergences in faith and practice from one denomination to another—is not divisiveness; it is what we would expect when Christianity is being spread among some 8,900 peoples speaking 7,010 languages in the modern world. Amongst other things, this diversity has made it far more difficult for hostile regimes to comprehend the phenomenon of Christianity in order to control it, suppress it, or eradicate it.

Fragmentation—multiplicity of denominations—seems to be more obviously wrong, even disastrous. But our response as Christians cannot be censorious. The United Nations' *Universal Declaration of Human Rights* (1948) states that every human being has the right to embrace the religion or belief of his choice, including no religion. In consequence, Christians should respect this human right by granting and showing genuine religious toleration to, at the least, all other expressions of faith in Christ, including those expressed in deviations. Such toleration does not, of course, imply that Christians should deny their convictions about Christ and his church, or abandon proclamation, evangelism or conversion; it means only that we recognize the right of others to adhere to whatever religion they choose, although we may believe those religions false or inadequate and may attempt to win them to faith in Jesus Christ as we understand it.

Again, the problem of fragmentation recedes when members of this great variety of denominations find themselves working together on a common task. In our case, Christians of every persuasion willingly co-operated in collecting accurate data about their own co-religionists. Fragmented they may be still, but these widely scattered individual believers, several thousand in number, have helped to produce a survey in which global Christianity emerges as a single whole, even as the Body of Christ.

The reader's second impression may well be of vast numbers confronting him at every turn. There are two pitfalls that we should avoid in interpreting large demographic tables and totals involving Christians. The first is triumphalism. We are well aware that a survey which describes church statistics as being startlingly larger than most currently-held stereotypes can easily be labeled by the superficial reader (whether he be Christian, secularist or atheist) as mere triumphalism. Massive church growth is often misinterpreted in this way. Spectacular growth or numerical success do not in themselves spell spiritual depth or significant progress. We need therefore continually to disavow any vestige of triumphalism, and to replace it by service in the name of Christ. As Hans Küng has put it, 'The Church must not conquer but serve the world religions'. Neither should we fall into the trap of equating the fortunes of organized Christianity and institutionalized religion with the fortunes of the Kingdom of God.

The other pitfall when examining these tables is to regard them as depersonalizing, and to allege that they treat human beings as mere cyphers of little individual worth. One must admit that statistics of enormous numbers of people, well into the billions, have a numbing effect on many of us. We need to remember Jesus' teaching that God's love for every individual is proved by his counting every last detail about us: 'Even the hairs of your head have all been counted' (Matthew 10:30). It is salutary therefore to view the statistical tables given here as vignettes or portraits of a scene in which every one of us features personally. If you belong to a church whose members are here given as 72,836, you are included in that total; without you the total would be 72,835. If you are a pastor in a country with 75 ordained ministers, you are one of the 75; without you it would have been 74. In fact, if you are a Christian of any sort, you personally appear (as a single digit, to be sure) in some 760 distinct absolute numbers (excluding percentages) in this encyclopedia's statistics. Every Christian also appears, though not as obviously as one digit, in some 570 percentages, and also in around 450 further derived figures (averages, etc). In several tables, you as a Christian of a particular type are included in over 100 numbers and percentages in each table. If you and your family are Charismatic Christians (or Evangelicals, or a similar tradition), you all feature in a total of 780 absolute numbers here. If in addition you are a Christian worker, you feature as an individual in an additional 35 sets of absolute numbers. If you are a worker in a foreign land, you feature in a further 20. And so on. Since you and I permeate these statistical tables to that extent, they cannot be so impersonal after all.

Nairobi, 1981 David B. Barrett

NATIONS AND COUNTRIES

Shortened, formal, full, alternate, earlier, popular, and official names for all countries

1. Short names. Names in bold capitals below form this Encyclopedia's definitive alphabetized geographical listing in English of all 238 sovereign and non-sovereign nations, countries, and territories in the world, as existing in AD 2000, with a handful of territories whose status has recently been in dispute (Palestine, Sahara, Timor, et alia). Territories that are uninhabited are excluded. This list is based on the official listing utilized by the United Nations, in most cases using the official terminology requested of the UN by each member country; but it modifies this terminology by changing nations alphabetized by the UN under 'Republic of . . .' or 'Democratic . . .' or 'Socialist . . .' to their recognized or normally-employed short geographical terms. Full details of names, including official names in their own languages, are given under SECULAR DATA at the start of each country's article in Part 4 on the page indicated below. In addition to the official UN names in English, all UN members also have official names in the other 5 of the 6 official UN languages (Arabic, Chinese, English, French, Russian, Spanish). All are given in full detail in the UN's *Terminology bulletin No. 347: country names*, 1995 and biennial updates.

2. Standard codes. To the left of each bold capital name is this Encyclopedia's standardized 4-letter code or abbreviation for the country (in almost every case its first 4 letters). This is used to save space in many tables in different Parts. This code may also be used to search for and access data on any table contained in the related electronic *World Christian database.*

3. Page numbers below. These refer only to the main article on each country, found in Part 4 "Countries" in Volume 1. Further extensive data on each country can be found, arranged alphabetically, in Part 5 "CountryScan", in Part 14 "Directory", and elsewhere. A full listing of all country variables and varieties of data by country in given on the first verso page at the start of Part 4.

4. Convenience names. All member countries of the United Nations are here given their definitive shortened names (shown in capitals), which are the shortest English official forms agreed to with the UN by the countries concerned. The only exceptions are a handful of countries which require the UN to use their full titles but which here, in the interests of standardization and ease of reference, are reduced to their normally-employed geographical terms, as follows: Britain, Brunei, Iran, Ivory Coast, Laos, Libya, North Korea, South Korea, Tanzania, Viet Nam, Yemen, Yugoslavia. Sometimes readers are referred to such names by the word 'here'.

5. Fuller names. Words in upper/lowercase following a capitalized short name, after a comma, form the rest of the full, formal, or official name in English of the country concerned (anglicized after UN usage, except words in parentheses). If there are no such additional words (as e.g. for Ukraine), this indicates that for UN purposes the full official name is the same as the shortest official form.

6. Alternative names. Words in upper/lowercase following a capitalized name, after a semi-colon, form the full official name and indicate that it has formal priority over the shortest official form (e.g. France is officially called The French Republic, Greece is The Hellenic Republic, Switzerland is The Swiss Confederation, etc.).

7. Parenthetic names. Names in parentheses are not part of official titles but have widespread popular use. Details of other names in use are given for each country under its SECULAR DATA.

8. Entries below not in capitals but in upper/lower case only do not form part of this definitive listing of countries; they are alternative forms of title, popular names, older names still in use, smaller parts of countries at one time considered eligible for such lists, or names of territories which are, or have now become part of some larger unit, to all of which the reader is referred.

9. The word 'see' refers the reader from an abbreviation or alternative or popular or widely-used or incorrect name to the fuller or correct or shortest official form of the name or its geographical equivalent as employed in this listing; or, in the case of 'see Antarctica' to the numerous footholds treated by agreement under that single entity.

10. The word 'now' indicates that although an older name is still in use in some international or national circles, correctly or incorrectly, the newer name indicated has now officially replaced it.

11. The word 'under' indicates that a territory is or is now part of the larger nation or country indicated.

code	*Name of country or territory*	*page in Vol 1*
	Aden, under Yemen	
	Admiralty Islands, under Papua New Guinea	
	Afars & Issas, now Djibouti	
afgh	**AFGHANISTAN,** The Islamic State of	49
	Agalaga Islands, under Mauritius	
alba	**ALBANIA,** The Republic of	51
alge	**ALGERIA,** The People's Democratic Republic of	55
amer	**AMERICAN SAMOA,** The Territories of	58
	Andaman Islands, under India	
ando	**ANDORRA,** The Principality of	60
ango	**ANGOLA,** The Republic of	61
angu	**ANGUILLA,** The Dependency of	66
anta	**ANTARCTICA,** The Continent of	68
anti	**ANTIGUA & BARBUDA,** The Realm of	69
arge	**ARGENTINA;** The Argentine Republic	71
	Argentinian Antarctic Territory, see Antarctica	
arme	**ARMENIA,** The Republic of	76
arub	**ARUBA,** The Territory of	79
aust	**AUSTRALIA,** The Commonwealth of	81
	Australian Antarctic Territory, see Antarctica	
ausz	**AUSTRIA,** The Republic of	86
	Azores, under Portugal	
azer	**AZERBAIJAN,** The Azerbaijani Republic	90
baha	**BAHAMAS,** The Commonwealth of the	93
bahr	**BAHRAIN,** The State of	95
	Balearic Islands, under Spain	
bang	**BANGLADESH,** The People's Republic of	97
barb	**BARBADOS,** The Realm of	101
	Basutoland, now Lesotho	
	Bechuanaland, now Botswana	
	Belarus, here Belorussia	
	Belau, now Palau	
	Belgian Antarctic Territory, see Antarctica	
belg	**BELGIUM,** The Kingdom of	103
beli	**BELIZE,** The Realm of	107
belo	**BELORUSSIA;** The Republic of Belarus	110
beni	**BENIN,** The Republic of	112
berm	**BERMUDA;** The Colony of the Bermuda Islands	115
bhut	**BHUTAN,** The Kingdom of	117
	Biafra, under Nigeria	
boli	**BOLIVIA,** The Republic of	119
bosn	**BOSNIA HERZEGOVINA,** The Republic of	123
	Bonin Islands, under Japan	
	BophuthaTswana, under South Africa	
bots	**BOTSWANA,** The Republic of	126
boug	**BOUGAINVILLE,** The Republic of	129
braz	**BRAZIL,** The Federative Republic of	130
	Brazilian Antarctic Territory, see Antarctica	
brit	**BRITAIN;** The United Kingdom of Great Britain and Northern Ireland (UK of GB & NI)	138
	British Antarctic Territory, see Antarctica	
	British Guiana, now Guyana	
	British Honduras, now Belize	
briy	**BRITISH INDIAN OCEAN TERRITORY,** The Crown Colony of the	148
	British Solomon Islands, now Solomon Islands	
briz	**BRITISH VIRGIN ISLANDS,** The Territory of the	149
brun	**BRUNEI;** The State of Brunei Darussalam	151
bulg	**BULGARIA,** The Republic of	153
burk	**BURKINA FASO,** The Democratic Republic of	157
	Burma, now Myanmar	
buru	**BURUNDI,** The Republic of	159
	Byelorussian SSR, now Belorussia	
	Cabinda, under Angola	
camb	**CAMBODIA,** The Kingdom of	162
came	**CAMEROON,** The Republic of	165
cana	**CANADA,** The Dominion of	169
	Canal Zone, under Panama	
	Canary Islands, under Spain	
	Canton & Enderbury Islands, under Kiribati	
cape	**CAPE VERDE,** The Republic of	175
	Caroline Islands, now Micronesia	
caym	**CAYMAN ISLANDS,** The Crown Colony of the	177
	Central African Empire, now Central African Republic	
cent	**CENTRAL AFRICAN REPUBLIC,** The	179
	Ceylon, now Sri Lanka	
chad	**CHAD,** The Republic of	181
chan	**CHANNEL ISLANDS,** The Crown Dependency of the	183
chil	**CHILE,** The Republic of	185
	Chilean Antarctic Territory, see Antarctica	
chin	**CHINA,** The People's Republic of	191
	China, The Republic of, see Taiwan	
	Chinese Antarctic Territory, see Antarctica	
chri	**CHRISTMAS ISLAND,** The Territory of	198
	Ciskei, under South Africa	
coco	**COCOS (KEELING) ISLANDS,** The Territory of	200
colo	**COLOMBIA,** The Republic of	201
como	**COMOROS,** The Islamic Federal Republic of the	206
cong	**CONGO (BRAZZAVILLE);** The Republic of the Congo	208
conz	**CONGO-ZAIRE;** The Democratic Republic of Congo	211
cook	**COOK ISLANDS,** The Territory Overseas of the	217
cost	**COSTA RICA,** The Republic of	218
	Côte d'Ivoire, see Ivory Coast	
croa	**CROATIA,** The Republic of	222
cuba	**CUBA,** The Republic of	225
	Curaçao, under Netherlands Antilles	
cypr	**CYPRUS,** The Republic of	229
	Czechoslovakia, now Czech Republic, Slovak Republic	
czec	**CZECH REPUBLIC,** The	232
	Dahomey, now Benin	
	Danish West Indies, see Virgin Islands of the US	
	Democratic Kampuchea, now Cambodia	
	Democratic People's Republic of Korea, see North Korea	
	Democratic Yemen, now Yemen	
denm	**DENMARK,** The Kingdom of	236
djib	**DJIBOUTI,** The Republic of	239
domi	**DOMINICA,** The Commonwealth of	241
domr	**DOMINICAN REPUBLIC,** The	243
	Dutch Guiana, now Suriname	
	East Berlin, under Germany	
	East Germany, under Germany	
	East Malaysia, under Malaysia	
	East Pakistan, now Bangladesh	
	East Timor, see Timor	
	Eastern Republic of Uruguay, see Uruguay	
	Eastern Samoa, see American Samoa	
ecua	**ECUADOR,** The Republic of	246
egyp	**EGYPT,** The Arab Republic of	250
	Eire, see Ireland	
	Ellice Islands, now Tuvalu	
elsa	**EL SALVADOR,** The Republic of	255
	England, under Britain	
equa	**EQUATORIAL GUINEA,** The Republic of	259
erit	**ERITREA,** The State of	261
esto	**ESTONIA,** The Republic of	263
ethi	**ETHIOPIA,** The Federal Democratic Republic of	265
faer	**FAEROE ISLANDS,** The	270
falk	**FALKLAND ISLANDS,** The Crown Colony of the	272
	Fernando Poo, under Equatorial Guinea	
fiji	**FIJI;** The Sovereign Democratic Republic of the Fiji Islands	274
finl	**FINLAND,** The Republic of	277
	Formosa, see Taiwan	
fran	**FRANCE;** The French Republic	280
freg	**FRENCH GUIANA,** The Department of	287
frep	**FRENCH POLYNESIA,** The Overseas Territory of	289
	French Republic, see France	
	French Somailand, now Djibouti	
	French Southern & Antarctic Territories, see Antarctica	
	French Territory of the Afars & Issas, now Djibouti	
	Friendly Islands, see Tonga	
gabo	**GABON,** The Gabonese Republic	291
gamb	**GAMBIA,** The Republic of the	294
	Gaza Strip, under Palestine	
	Gazankulu, under South Africa	
geor	**GEORGIA,** The Republic of	296
	German Antarctic Territory, see Antarctica	
	German Democratic Republic, under Germany	
germ	**GERMANY,** The Federal Republic of	298
ghan	**GHANA,** The Republic of	307
	Gilbert Islands, now Kiribati	
gibr	**GIBRALTAR,** The Colony of	312
	Great Britain, under Britain	
gree	**GREECE;** The Hellenic Republic	313
grel	**GREENLAND**	319
gren	**GRENADA,** The Realm of	321
guad	**GUADELOUPE,** The Department of	323
guam	**GUAM,** The United States Territory of	325
guat	**GUATEMALA,** The Republic of	326
guin	**GUINEA,** The Republic of	331
gunb	**GUINEA-BISSAU,** The Republic of	333
guya	**GUYANA,** The Co-operative Republic of	336
hait	**HAITI,** The Republic of	339
	Hashemite Kingdom of Jordan, see Jordan	
	Hellenic Republic, see Greece	
	Holland, see Netherlands	
holy	**HOLY SEE,** The (Vatican City State)	342
hond	**HONDURAS,** The Republic of	349
	Hong Kong, now under China	
hung	**HUNGARY,** The Republic of	353
icel	**ICELAND,** The Republic of	357
	Ifni, under Morocco	
indi	**INDIA,** The Republic of	359
	Indian Antarctic Territory, see Antarctica	
indo	**INDONESIA,** The Republic of	371
iran	**IRAN,** The Islamic Republic of	378
iraq	**IRAQ,** The Republic of	382
	Ireland, Northern, under Britain	
irel	**IRELAND,** The Republic of	386
	Irish Republic, see Ireland	
isle	**ISLE OF MAN,** The Crown Dependency of the	389
isra	**ISRAEL,** The State of	391
	Italian Republic, see Italy	
ital	**ITALY;** The Italian Republic	396
ivor	**IVORY COAST,** The Republic of Côte d'Ivoire	405
jama	**JAMAICA,** The Realm of	408
japa	**JAPAN**	412
	Japanese Antarctic Territory, see Antarctica	
	Jibuti, see Djibouti	
	Johnston Island, under USA	
jord	**JORDAN,** The Hashemite Kingdom of	419
	Kampuchea, now Cambodia	

AUTHORS, EDITORS, AND CONSULTANTS

Authors:

David B. Barrett, MA, BD, STM, PhD, Research Professor of Missiometrics, Regent University; Hon. Research Adviser, United Bible Societies
George T. Kurian, Founder & President, Society of Encyclopedists
Todd M. Johnson, MA, PhD, YWAM, Director, World Evangelization Research Center; Adjunct Professor, Trinity Evangelical Divinity School

Editor Emeritus:

Sir Kenneth Grubb, CMG, LLD

Editorial Associates:

Christopher & Jeanine Guidry, March for Jesus International
E. Michael Jaffarian, CBInternational
Peter Crossing, Sydney Centre for World Mission, Australia
Kimberly D. Doyle, Assemblies of God
Justin D. Long, Network for Strategic Missions

Global Consultants:

Tad de Bordenave, Director, Anglican Frontier Missions
David T.M.P. Dalby, PhD, Director, Language Watch
Paul Eshleman, Director, 'Jesus' Film Project
V. David Garrison, PhD, Associate Vice-President, International Mission Board, SBC
David M. Goodenough, European Charismatic Consultation; Founding Director, Cultural Television International
Joseph Hale, DD, World Methodist Council; past Chairman, Conference of Christian World Communions
Maurice Harvey, Photojournalist, United Bible Societies
Willi Henkel OMI, PhD, Vatican Missions Librarian, Pontificia Universita Urbaniana
Patrick J. St G. Johnstone, *Operation World,* WEC International
John S. Mbiti, PhD, *Evangelische Lexikon für Kirchen;* University of Bern
J. Gordon Melton, PhD, Director, Institute for the Study of American Religion
Samuel H. Moffett, PhD, Emeritus Professor of Missions, Princeton Theological Seminary
Bishop Stephen C. Neill, DD, Universities of Hamburg, Nairobi, and Oxford
H. Vinson Synan, PhD, Professor & Dean of Divinity, Regent University

Systems Analysts:

Peter Crossing, Justin D. Long, Glyn Roberts PhD, O. W. Shumaker

Chief Photographers:

Maurice Harvey, David B. Barrett

Bibliographers:

Stuart Baskin PhD, Mark Dubis PhD

Data Entry & Administration:

Judy Alexanian, Carol Vanlandingham, Sondra Stephens, Leah Haney, Emily Haney, Lana Moussa

Research and compilation by:

World Evangelization Research Center (WERC, begun Nairobi, 1965)
Global Evangelization Movement (GEM, begun Richmond, Virginia, 1985)

COLLABORATORS AND CONTRIBUTORS

This listing acknowledges the collaboration and contribution of a large number of experts or specialists indicated by their area of specialization or contribution given in parenthesis. It excludes the Encyclopedia's global consultants and production staff who have been listed on the previous page. The listing below, alphabetically by surname, includes all those assisting with the World Christian encyclopedia project at any stage from 1970 to AD 2000. Many (listed in the First Edition) contributed to that edition, many others to the Second Edition, and a fair number to both.

Names of collaborators and contributors listed below are followed in most cases by initials of their organization or style at the time of their contribution (see Index of Christian Abbreviations, Acronyms and Initials), or their profession, and in parentheses the country or countries of their contribution, expertise or residence, or in a few cases their subject. The listing excludes a number of experts who have requested anonymity, but includes a few requested pseudonyms.

Bishop I.A. Adetosoye, NAAC Aladura (Nigeria)
Dr Tokunboh Adeyemo, AEA (Nigeria)
Patience Ahmed, CAPRO (Nigeria)
S. Vasantharaj Albert, CGRC (India)
Rev. Dr Jean Albertini, Aumonier Militaire (Niger)
Rev. Canon Roger G. Allison, MBE (Israel)
Bishop Oliver C. Allison, CMS (Sudan)
Rev. Dr Johannes Althausen (German DR)
Rev. S. G. Andrews (Fiji)
Susan H. Andrews, CPA (Finance)
Rev. Charles Antoine, DIAL (Brazil)
Paul Arnold (France)
Rev. Dr A. G. Baan, OFM (Indonesia)
Rev. Brian H. Baily, BCC (Botswana)
Gary Baldridge, CBF (Azerbaijan)
J. F. Bango, sociologist (Hungary, Romania)
Rev. E. E. Barde, EEM (Morocco)
Dr John Barrett (UK)
Pam Barrett (Kenya)
Rev. P. Basile, OFM Cap (Comoros)
Albert Bastenier, CRSR (Belgium)
Peter Bayes, FEBA (UK)
Bertha Beachy, EMBMC (Somalia)
Nadia Benjamin, GICC (Grenada)
Dr Walter W. Benjamin (USA)
Rev. Joseph-Roger de Benoist, WF (Benin)
Rev. Augusto Beuzeville F. (Peru)
Rev. William E. Biernatzki, SJ (N. & S. Korea)
Dr R. Biernazek (Poland)
Gordon Bishop (Niger)
Rev. Joseph L. Blackett (Belize)
Dr C. Boeke, Interreligio (Netherlands)
Dr Hugo Bogensberger, IKS (Austria)
Rev. A. Boland (Laos, Thailand)
Jean-Charles Bonenfant (Canada)
Professor David J. Bosch, UNISA (South Africa)
Rev. Wallace Boulton, CMS (UK)
Rev. Dr Michael A. Bourdeaux, Keston College
Msgr J. E. Bourke, FCEO (Australia)
Rev. Malcolm R. Bradshaw, OMF (Singapore)
Rev. W. G. M. Brandful, CCG (Ghana)
Dr Rodolphe A. Bréchet, SAM (Angola)
Huguette Breil (Morocco)
Rev. H. Briand, FMI (St Lucia)
Leslie Brierley, IRRO/WEC (Guinea Bissau)
Helen Brown, TWR (UK)
Rev. Canon Jean Bruls, *Eglise Vivante*
Craig Buchanan (Internet)
Rev. Elden M. Buck, UCC (Pacific Islands)
Dr. Allan Buckman, LCMS (Missiology)
Dr Aldo Büntig (Argentina)
Professor Stanley Burgess (NIDPCM)
Rev. Canon Samuel R. Burgoyne, UMN (Nepal)
Dr Edgar H. Burks, SBC (Nigeria)
Rev. Palle Burla (Faeroe Islands)
Rev. A. J. Butler (Botswana)
Rev. James Byrne, SMA (Liberia)
Rev. Pierre Cadier, PEMS (Dahomey/Benin)
Rev. Giuseppe Caffaratto (Italy)
Bishop Michel Callens, WF (Tunisia)
Rev. Michael Campbell-Johnston, SJ (Guyana)
Rev. Humberto Capo, CEE (Spain)
Bishop Edmund M. H. Capper, CPSA (St Helena)
Archdeacon Jack Cattell (Bermuda)
Rev. Dr Rafael Cepeda, CIEC (Cuba)
Rev. Carlos Manuel de Cespedes, CEC (Cuba)
Rev. Ricardo Cetrulo, SJ, CER (Uruguay)
Rev. Marc Chambron, LWF (France)
Dr Maxwell Charlesworth, ANU (Australia)
Rev. F. E. Charman (St Kitts-Nevis-Anguilla)
Carlos Chiesa (Argentina)
Jose Chipenda, WSCF (Angola)
Franco Chittolina, sociologist (Italy)
Msgr. Damian Ciacci (Saudi Arabia, Gulf)
Sister Peter Claver, OP, CARA (USA)
William Cleveland, *Encyclopaedia Britannica*
Steve and Elisabeth Cochrane, YWAM (India)
Geraldine Coldham, BFBS (Names for God)
Rev. Tom S. Colvin, CSC/CCM (Malawi)
Calvin and Carol Conkey, YWAM (Indonesia)
Rev. W. H. Conrad (Costa Rica)
Dr Frank L. Cooley, DGI (Indonesia)
Rev. Jean Corbon (Lebanon)
Rev. Richard G. Cote, OMI (Lesotho)
Rev. J. B. D. Cotter (Bahrain)
Very Rev. W. Frank Curtis, C of E (UK)
Rev. Dr Marthinus L. Daneel, AICC (Zimbabwe)
Bishop Michel Darmancier, SM (Wallis & Futuna Is)
Nabih Kamel David (Egypt)
Brother Joseph M. Davis, SM, NOBC (USA)
Edward R. Dayton, MARC
John Dean, UBS (Scripture distribution)
Rev. M. Defresne (Japan)
Rev. Natale Del Mistro (Iran)
Rev. Dr Raymond Deniel, INADES (Upper Volta)
Georges Deroy, FERES (Louvain)
Dr Duncan Derrett (India)
Rev. M. Dhavamony, SJ (India)
Dr F. Dingjan (Netherlands)
Rev. Max Dominique, CSSp (Central African Rep)
Bep Donatz, YWAM (Research)
Rev. T. F. Doust, MMS (Benin)
Rev. du Noyer, BLASC (Madagascar)
Rev. Willehad Paul Eckert (FR Germany)
Bishop Sigurbjörn Einarsson (Iceland)
Mercedes Massi Elizalde (Argentina)
Edward A. Elliott, Living Bibles (USA)
M. F. Elliott-Binns, General Synod C of E (UK)
Rev. Edgar J. Elliston, CMF (Ethiopia)
Rev. Eulogio V. Enrique, SJ, CBIES (Philippines)
Dr Juan Estruch (Spain)
Rev. Gareth M. Evans, *Sobornost* (UK)
Paul Filidis, YWAM (Research)
Rev. John B. Finger (Bahamas)
Rev. Guillermo Flores (Guatemala)
Msgr. Jean Foradaris (Cyprus)
Rev. A. D. Fowler (Brunei)
Dr David A. Fraser, MARC
Bishop Hendrik Hubert Frehen, SMM (Iceland)
Joachim W. H. Freitag, WEC (Mauritania)
Gregory Fritz, Caleb Project (Logistics)
L. Andrew Friend (Mozambique)
Rev. Paul D. Fueter (Switzerland)
Ledo. Euclides J. Fuguet, CEV (Venezuela)
Bishop Hyancinthe Gad (Greece)
George Gallup, Jr., AIPO (Polls)
Rev. Anthony M. Gann, USPG (Lesotho)
Jay Gary (Futuristics)
Bishop Manuel J. Gaxiola, CINCOMEX (Mexico)
Helmut Geller, sociologist (FR Germany)
Pastor Dr Roswith Gerloff (UK Black churches)
Rev. Jean-Paul Gladu, CSC (Haiti)
Randy Gloyd, CCCI (Logistics)
Dr Walter Goddijn (Netherlands)
Bishop William Gomes (India)
Rev. Dr José-Maria Gonzalez-Ruiz, SJ (Spain)
Lee Grady, *Charisma Magazine*
D. Bruce Graham (India)
Rev. P. Grégoire, OP (Denmark)
Rev. Paul Grillou, WF, ISTR (France)
Sir Kenneth Grubb, CMG, LLD
Rev. Guilbert Guérin, SJ (China/Taiwan)
Bishop R. L. Guilly, SJ (Guyana)
Dr Berndt Gustafsson, RIS (Sweden)
Graeme Hackworth, YWAM (India)
Rev. Dr J. Harry Haines, UMC (PR China)
Rev. Joseph Hajjar, Melkite Patriarchate (Syria)
Stefan Hall, YWAM (Systems)
Rev. Richard Haller (Switzerland)
Rev. E. I. Hamelberg, CSSp (Sierra Leone)
Rev. Clive Handford, JEM (Syria)
Dr W. E. Ted Haney, FEBC (USA)
Rev. James T. Hardyman, LMS (Madagascar)
Rev. Patricia J. Harrison, CRC (Australia)
Robert W. Harvie, UPCUSA (India)
Bishop Ralph P. Hatendi, UBS (Zambia)
Paul Hattaway, AMO (China)
Rev. Stephen Hayes, CPSA (Namibia)
Bishop Edward G. Haynsworth, ECUSA (Nicaragua)
Archdeacon F. M. M. Haythornthwaite (Namibia)
Rev. Roger E. Hedlund, CBFMS/CBI (Italy, India)
Rev. André Heiderscheid (Luxembourg)
Rev. Jean Heinrichs, SJ (Sikkim)
Dr Guy Hermet (Spain)
Javier Solis Herrera (Costa Rica)
Dr Horst Herrmann (FR Germany)
John Hickey, sociologist (UK)
Rev. John A. Hinchey, SJ (Cayman Islands)
Bishop H. Hofmann, OFM Cap (Djibouti)
Nanci K. Hogan, YWAM (Cambodia)
Dr Sibenda M. Holsteyn, CCN (Netherlands)
Dr James D. Holway, Islam in Africa
Rev. Dr T. Floyd Honey, CCC (Canada)
Rev. Dr Norman A. Horner, UPCUSA (Lebanon)
Rev. John F. Hotchkin, NCCB (USA)
Rev. Dr François Houtart, FERES (Louvain)
Dr Mary Linda Hronek, WERC (Kenya)
Rev. C. Hulsen, SMA (Ghana)
Rev. Robert A. Humphreys (Australia)
Dr R. G. W. Huysmans (Netherlands)
Rev. Dr David Hynd, CBE (Swaziland)
Rev. Xavier Jacob, AA (Turkey)
Rev. Gustavo Amigo Jansen, SJ (Dominican Rep)
S. J. Jegasothy, NCCSL (Sri Lanka)
Rev. Alfred E. Johnson, WEC (Venezuela)
R. Boyd Johnson, MARC (USA)
Rev. Bernard Joinet, WF, TPRI (Tanzania)
Rev. Enrique Jorda, SJ, ISET (Bolivia)
François Joyaux (PR China)
Rev. Jean Julien (Martinique)
Basile Jultsis (Greece)
Janet Kalven (USA)

Lusanga Kanyinda (Zaire)
Rev. John Kelly (St Helena)
Rev. Jospeh Kelly, CSSp, AMECEA (Kenya)
Dr Jocelyn C. Kelsey (UK)
Oberkirchenrat Claus Kemper, EKD (FR Germany)
Sister Anne Marie Kernéis, UISG (Italy)
Rev. Pierre Kerzoncuf, OMI (Channel Islands)
Rev. John Key, MCC (Papua New Guinea)
Dr A. Khoury (FR Germany)
Pastor R. Buana Kibongi, EEC (Congo)
Rev. Karlo Kjaer, ELFD (Denmark)
Dr A. M. J. Kloosterman (Cook Islands)
Sydney Knightley, CMS (layout)
Josip Kolanovic (Yugoslavia)
Dr Elfriede Kreuzeder, ECCA (Austria)
Rev. Philip F. Kurts, SJ (Papua New Guinea)
Rev. Oscar Lacroix (Guadeloupe)
Rev. Victor A. Lamont (UK; photographic)
Dr Aldo Landi (Italy)
Gordon Landreth, EAGB (UK)
Rev. Gilles Langevin, SJ (Canada)
Bishop Neville Langford-Smith, CMS (Australia)
Rev. Bill Lasley (Senegal)
Rev. Professor René Laurentin, OP (Evangelization)
Rev. Angelo S. Lazzarotto, PIME (PR China)
Roger Lee, SDA (Macau)
Rev. A. Lemaire, OP (Finland)
Raymond Lemieux, CRSR (Canada)
Rev. James Lennon, RDU (Ireland)
Rev. David Chia-En Liao (Taiwan)
Archdeacon Ralph A. Lindley, ECJME (Qatar, UAE)
Rev. Melvin T. Long (USA)
Emily Kalled Lovell (USA, Canada)
Arthur M. Lundblad, ECZ (Zaire)
Rev. P. Lunot (Mauritania)
Rev. Gilles Lussier, PME (Honduras)
Rev. Finn Lynge, OMI (Greenland)
Rev. Brian J. Macdonald-Milne (Solomon Islands)
Rev. Luiz Machado de Abreu (Mozambique)
Rev. W. Mackey, SJ (Bhutan)
Dr Enrique Miret Magdalena (Spain)
Msgr. J. P. Mahony (Isle of Man)
Eric Maillefer, AEAM (Kenya)
Rev. Canon Dr Josef Majka (Poland)
Rev. Carl Major (Antigua)
Hilkka Malaska, CoN (Finland)
George K. Mambo, AACC (Kenya)
Rev. Edward F. Mann, SJ (Nepal)
Adele Manzi (Lebanon)
Bishop Antonious Markos, OAIC (Egypt)
Jimmy K. Maroney, IMB (Logistics)
Rev. Bill F. Marsters, CICC (Cook Islands)
Dr Marie-Louise Martin, EJCSK (Zaire)
Rev. Antonio Martins (Portugal)
Jonathan Marzeki, ICC (Iran)
Rev. Louis Mascarenhas, OFM, IRSS (Pakistan)
Rev. Dr Joseph Masson, SJ (Missiology)
Kathleen Matchcett, CSRC (USSR)
Senator Gordon Matthews, WHC (Barbados)
Bishop François-Joseph Maurer, CSSp (St Pierre & M)
Rev. J. B. Mayté (Mali)
Rev. Professor John S. Mbiti, WCC (Uganda)
Rev. Professor Donald A. McGavran, SWM
Donald McGilchrist, The Navigators
Sister Janice McLaughlin, MM (Kenya)
Rev. Noel McNeill, ACOP (Canada)
Rev. Dr Malcolm J. McVeigh, UMC
Marion McVeigh, UMC (Canada)
Rev. Dr Otto Meinardus (Egypt, Greece)
Rev. Clifford S. Michelsen (Cameroon)
Rev. Dr David I. Mitchell (Trinidad & Tobago)
Rev. Dr Samuel H. Moffett (Korea)
Bishop Michael Moloney, CSSp (Gambia)
Lic. Vital H. Moreno G. (Panama)
Scott Morey, DAI (Sierra Leone)
Rev. Professor Charlie F. D. Moule, Cambridge U.
Rev. Roger Muller (FTAI)
Rev. José Miguel Munarriz, CEP (Paraguay)
Rev. Paul Munier, MEP (Malaysia, Singapore)
Rev. Edward F. Murphy (Colombia)
Msgr. Amédée Nagapen (Mauritius)
Rev. Albert Nambiaparambil, CMI (India)
Rev. Juhani Natri, FMS (Finland)
Rev. Louis de Nauriois (France)
Bishop Justin Ndandali, CPR (Rwanda)
William A. Needham, MARC (USA)
Bishop Stephen C. Neill, *World Christian Books*
Rev. Charles A. Nelson (US Virgin Islands)
Rev. Jean Nenonene, EET (Togo)
Dr Arnaldo Nesti (Italy)
Rev. Gilbert Nichols, SBC (Paraguay)
Dr Elisa Juan de Nieves (Puerto Rico)
Paul H. Nilson, ABS (Turkey)
Rev. Dr Loren E. Noren (Hong Kong)
John J. Nquku, LACS (Swaziland)
Rt. Rev. Ildefonso Obama Obono (Equatorial Guinea)
Professor W. R. O'Brien, SBC
Rev. Gilbert W. Olson (Sierra Leone)
Rev. Dr J. M. Ondra (Czechoslovakia)
Rev. Adolphe Ouédraogo, CEHV (Upper Volta)
T. John Padwick, OAIC (Kenya)
Rev. Michel de Paillerets, OP (Sweden)
Rev. Peyton Palmore, III, UCCJ (Japan)
Rev. Angelo Panigati (Afghanistan)
Archbishop Anthony Pantin, CSSp (Trinidad)
Balwant A. M. Paradkar (India)
Rev. Ramon Pardo, OMI (Sahara)
Julia Campos Parise (Uruguay)
Rev. Dr. Janos Pasztor (Hungary)
Rev. Celestin Patock, OSA (USSR)
Rev. Zdzislaw Pawlik (Poland)
Oreste Pesare, ICCRS (Vatican)
Dr Howard Peskett, OMF (Statistics)
Rt. Rev. W. L. A. Don Peter (Sri Lanka)
Cardinal Sergio Pignedoli, Roman Curia (Statistics)
Rev. Renato Poblete, SJ (Chile)
Rev. Dr Titus Presler (Zimbabwe)
Rev. John R. Pritchard, MMS (Ivory Coast)
Professor Paul A. Puchkov, Akademii Nauk SSSR
Rev. Pedro Puentes (Chile)
Rev. Roland Quesnel, CSSp (Propaganda data)
Thomas E. Quigley, USCC (USA)
Rev. Jean Rabemanahaka (Comoro Islands)
Rev. J. P. Ramanankilana (Madagascar)
Lic. Manuel R. Gonzalez Ramirez, SJ, IMES (Mexico)
Dr Michael Raske (FR Germany)
Bishop Derek A. Rawcliffe, CPM (New Hebrides)
Rev. Dr William R. Read, UPCUSA (Brazil)
Pastor Piere Regard (Belgium, Luxembourg)
Rev. Dr H. Diether Reimer, EZW (FR Germany)
Reginald E. Reimer, CMA (Viet Nam)
Bishop Charles Reiterer, MHM (Brunei)
Rev. Norman G. Riddle, EBCO (Zaire)
Rev. Istvan Rigo (Hungary)
Dr C. A. Rijk, SIDIC (Italy)
Rev.Antonio Rivera Rodriguez (Puerto Rico)
Jean Robert (pseudonym) (German Democratic Rep)
Rev. M. A. Z. Rolston, NCCI (India)
Pastor Jean de Rougemont, AdD (Upper Volta)
André Rousseau, sociologist (France)
François Routhier, CRSR (Canada)
Dr Michael Rowe, U of Glasgow (USSR)
Bishop Jean Rupp (Monaco)
William Ryna, USCC (USA)
Rev. Réginald de Sa, OP, IDEO (Egypt)
Professor Todor Sabev, WCC (Bulgaria)
Luis Alberto Saenz (Costa Rica)
George Salinas (Electronic data)
Sister M. B. Salmon, SIDIC (France)
Bishop Samuel, See of St Mark (Egypt)
Rev. Kirkley Caleb Sands (Turks & Caicos Is)
Msgr. Victor San Miguel, OCD (Kuwait)
Rev. Giuseppe Scapino (Italy)
Rev. Joseph B. Schuyler, SJ (Nigeria)
J. Sayer, sociologist (FR Germany)
Rev. Herbert Seignoret, CSSp, AEC (Jamaica)
Rev. E. R. Simmons (New Zealand)
Rev. Adrian B. Smith, WF (Zambia)
Gudrun Smith, WCC (Councils)
William W. Smith, FMB, CSI, IMB (China)
Rev. Erwin L. Spruth, LCMS (Papua New Guinea)
Rev. Harvey Staal, RCA (Kuwait, Oman)
Bishop Gunnar Stalsett, LWF (Norway)
Paul Stawasz, UBS (Scripture distribution)
Dr Roland C. Stevenson, UBS (Sudan)
Rev. Fred E. Stock (Pakistan)
Pastor Larry Stockstill (Bethany WPC)
Bishop Daniel Stuyvenberg, SM (Solomon Islands)
Rev. Lloyd Swantz, ELCT (Tanzania)
Dean Vinson Synan, NARSC (Pentecostalism)
Pastor K. Tabuariki, SDA (Gilbert & Ellice Is)
Rev. Norman W. Taggart, ICC (Ireland)
Rabbi Marc H. Tannenbaum (USA)
Cardinal Pio Taofinu'u, SM (Western Samoa)
Michael A. Tarrant, WEC (Guinea Bissau)
Rev. David M. Taylor NCCNZ (New Zealand)
Rev. Canon Ronald J. Taylor, CMSNZ (Tanzania)
Bishop Henri Teissier (Algeria)
Dr O. ter Reegen (Netherlands)
Pastor Randall L. Thetford (Guam)
Rev. John Thetgyi, BCC (Burma)
Harvey Thomas, NLEA (UK)
Dr Lars Thunberg (Sweden)
Dr Donald Tinder, New College (Book reviews)
Rev. Canon Benjamin Tonna, SEDOS (Malta)
Rev. Dr T. Michael Traber, WACC (Zimbabwe)
Dr Garry Trompf, Univ. of Sydney (Melanesia)
Rev. Dr Harold W. Turner, PRONERM (UK)
Mady Vaillant, WEC (Upper Volta)
Rev. Roger Velasquez Valle (El Salvador)
Rev. G. van den Asdonk (Malawi)
Larry Vanderaa (West Africa)
Rev. J. Van Hecken, CICM (Mongolia)
Rev. Juan Ramon Vega (El Salvador)
Rev. Rodney Venberg, CLB (Chad)
Dr Ad F. Vermeulen (Netherlands)
Rev. Canon Trevor Verryn, UNISA (South Africa)
Canon Jacques Verscheure, CISR (France)
Rev. Modeste Vesin (Seychelles)
Dr Ignacio Palacios Videla (Argentina)
Dr Ernst K. Vilaghy (Bulgaria)
Jeanne-Françoise Vincent, anthropologist (Congo)
Rev. Edvard Vogt (Norway)
Rev. Paul M. Volz, LCMS (Kenya)
Rev. Dr J. D. J. Waardenburg, WF (Netherlands)
Rev. Professor C. Peter Wagner (Bolivia)
Rev. Peter Wanko (Uganda)
Rick Ward, YWAM (Peoples)
Rev. Wichean Watakeecharoen, CCT (Thailand)
Rev. Stanford A. Webley (Jamaica)
Warren Webster, CBFMS/CBI
Dr Erika Wienzierl, IKZ (Austria)
Benjamin M. Weir (Lebanon)
Dr Martin E. West, SACC (South Africa)
Rev. Francis J. Westoff, MSC (Gilbert & Ellice Is)
Rev. Frank E. Wilcox, UMN (Nepal)
Dr Bryan R. Wilson, All Souls College, Oxford
Dr J. Christy Wilson, Jr. (Afghanistan)
Dr Ralph D. Winter, USCWM (Statistics)
Rev. W. Wipfler, NCCCUSA (Dominican Republic)
Rev. Joseph C. Wold (Liberia)
Rev. Canon James Yui Kok Wong (Singapore)
Chester Woodhall, CCGB (Zambia)
Jean Woods, CMS (Bibliography)
Prälat Wilhelm Wöste (FR Germany)
Sister Gertrude Wright, MMS (Gambia)
Akiko Yamaguchi, NCCJ (Japan)
Rev. Y. Yamatoa (Niue)
Archbishop A. Yannoulatos (Missiology)
Antonio Ybarra, sociologist (Nicaragua)
Msgr L. Zichem, CSSR (Surinam)
Bishop Antonio Silvio Zocchetta (Somalia)
Rev. Francisco Zuluaga, SJ, CIAS (Colombia)

Part 1

WORLD SUMMARY

The status of Christianity and religions in the modern world

The kingdom of God is like a grain of mustard seed, which is the smallest of all the seeds on earth, yet when it is sown it grows up and becomes the greatest of all shrubs.

—Mark 4:30-32, Revised Standard Version

Every year, at their churches' request some 10 million Christian workers take myriads of careful measurements on a vast variety of subjects depicting Christianity and its contributions to the welfare of the planet. This enumeration produces an annual gold mine of new data.

This part of the Encyclopedia sets out the bulk of these survey data observed at their global levels—the totals of these measurements obtained by adding up churches into denominations, denominations into countries, countries into continents, and continents into the world scene. This is done here by means of a sequence of 6 global diagrams interspersed with a sequence of 8 global statistical tables.

The status of Christianity and religions in the modern world

A GLOBAL OVERVIEW

Christianity over 20 centuries

The fortunes of Christianity as a global religion have fluctuated widely since the crucifixion and resurrection of Jesus Christ in AD 33. Over the first 19 centuries, it gradually increased its size and influence, in a series of 9 massive pulsations or epochs. Of these 5 were times of advance for the Christian faith and 4 were times of retreat. Already by AD 500, 22% of mankind were believers in Jesus Christ, but by AD 1500 the figure had fallen to 19%. Throughout 18 centuries, Christians were predominantly (over 90%) Caucasian by race, and from 1500-1900 were predominantly Whites (93-81%). By the year 1900, one third of humanity were Christians, and one half were aware of Christianity and had become influenced by it. Optimism for rapid completion of the task of global evangelization was high. From 1889-1914 the great Protestant and Anglican communions of Europe and North America promoted the Watchword that summarized this optimism in the objective 'The Evangelization of the World in This Generation'. In 1900, the pioneer of the modern ecumenical movement, John R. Mott, summed it all up in a masterly book of the same title.

The 20th century itself, however, has proved to be startlingly different from these expectations. Certainly the total of Christians has grown enormously, from 558 millions in 1900 to 2,000 millions by AD 2000. Certainly also, since 1900 Christianity has become massively accepted as the religion of developing countries in the so-called Third World, Africa in particular. But no-one in 1900 expected the massive defections from Christianity that subsequently took place in Western Europe due to secularism, in Russia and later Eastern Europe due to Communism, and in the Americas due to materialism.

Tables 1-1 and 1-2: Depicting the world

Equally startling is the actual situation of empirical Christianity—global Christianity as it in practice exists at the end of the 20th century, which means in AD 2000. Two tables help at this point to describe the overall situation. Table 1-1 elaborates on the one basic situation of the statistical size, across the 20th century and even beyond, of Christianity in the context of the non-Christian world and its world religions. And Table 1-2 which follows reduces the time scale to a more easily envisaged single day of 24 hours and shows how everything changes somewhat even during that moment of time.

Global Christianity today

At the beginning of the Third Millennium, Christians of all kinds number 2 billion, which is 33.0% of the world's population. This percentage Christian had increased rapidly during the Great Century from 1815-1914 at a rate of 1.2% per decade, then after 1914 reverted to a catastrophic decline of 0.4% per decade which by 1980 had worsened to 1.0% per decade. Despite this, the absolute number of Christians increases at 25 million a year. Table 1-1 gives the overall picture. Christianity has in fact surged ahead in the world's less-developed countries from 83 millions in 1900 to 1,120 millions by AD 2000. During the 20th century, in fact, Christianity has become the most extensive and universal religion in history. There are today Christians and organized Christian churches in every inhabited country on earth. The church is therefore now, for the first time in history, ecumenical in the literal meaning of the word: its boundaries are coextensive with the *oikumene*, the whole inhabited world.

In two-thirds of the world's 238 countries, Christians now form the majority (over 50%); in one third, the minority. This spread is very uneven, though. As is shown on Global Map 1 in Part 6 "Atlas", Christians number over 90% in 84 countries, less than 10% in 51 countries, less than 1% in 14 countries, and less than 0.5% in 8 countries: Afghanistan, Algeria, Bhutan, Maldives, Mauritania, Sahara, Somaliland, and Yemen.

Of all Christians, 1,888 millions are church members affiliated to 6 major ecclesiastico-cultural megablocs, also to some 300 different ecclesiastical traditions, and also to 33,820 distinct Christian denominations across the world.

VISUALIZING TODAY'S WORLD

Viewing past, present, and future

This is an interpretative commentary on the 6 kaleidoscopic global diagrams followed by the 7 more statistical tables, 1-3 to 1-8, in this Part 1.

For almost 2 millennia, disciples of Jesus Christ have attempted to follow him on his mission of redemption to the whole world. They have sought to obey his last command on Earth, known as the Great Commission: 'Go into all the world and make disciples of all peoples' (Matthew 28:19).

The series of 6 kaleidoscopic global diagrams that follows attempts to portray the current status of this Christian world ministry. They do this by bringing together 3 elements: (a) any global statistics relevant to the subject, that is all available figures at the all-inclusive world or worldwide level, describing the subject or in any demonstrable way relevant to understanding the status of the subject; (b) a diagrammatic illustration of the subject, usually via a globe or other representation of the totality of the world situation and the world task; and (c) a short introductory text setting the scene and interpreting the whole diagram.

Each diagram is packed with relevant statistics—both already-published global numbers, and also newly-computed global statistics. All figures have exact definitions, time reference ('today' usually meaning mid-1995 or mid-2000), and geographical reference.

Note here an important usage with these statistics. The 6 global diagrams are intended to be impressionistic approaches to their subjects, using a range of statistics as illustrations. These statistics do not all relate to one single point in time but instead relate to the whole period of 1990-2000, covering the last decade before the new Millennium.

Global Diagram 1: Human need

Before considering their own situation and needs, Christians have attempted in their annual megacensus to understand the needs of the world as a whole and hence the ministry to be undertaken. The first diagram shows its magnitude.

Some 46% of the world, 2.8 billion people, eke out a living in 26 countries each with a per capita income of under US$235 per year. In the world's 172 less developed countries, 780 million live in absolute poverty, a clearly-defined category that represents 'a condition of life so characterized by malnutrition, illiteracy and disease as to be beneath any reasonable definition of human decency' (World Bank, 1980). This total increases annually as the gap between affluence and poverty widens rapidly almost everywhere. Among the consequences are: permanently unsettled refugees, now 16 million, increase in number each year; 20% of the Third World, and 33% in several countries, suffer from severe protein-calorie malnutrition; 40% remain without adequate shelter; 80% do not have access to adequate water supply; 850 million have little or no access to schools; and 500 million exist on the edge of starvation. Altogether, some 1.5 billion human beings on earth are malnourished. A further consequence is seething unrest, anger, hatred towards the affluent world, and revolutionary goals.

Christians suffer along with others in this predicament. Some 109 million Christians live in the 26 poorest countries. In all developing countries, Christians living in absolute poverty number 260 million (24% of the 1.1 billion absolutely poor, or 13% of all Christians); half of them live in Latin America, a third in Africa, the rest in South and Southeast Asia. This is 'the church of the poor'. By the world's standards, they have nothing. They are far from being spiritual paupers, however. Some of the most dynamic forms of Christianity today, and the most rapid church growth, are found in these areas of material poverty and destitution.

It is not surprising, then, that the church, entrusted with the gospel of Christ's compassion for the poor, should have become heavily involved in correcting the injustices of poverty.

Global Diagram 2: Geopolitico-religious blocs

This diagram together with Table 1-1 sets out the fortunes of the world's 19 distinct major religions, religious systems or quasi-religions at the end of the 20th century. Almost all of these religions have expanded numerically during the 10 decades of that century. Most have also expanded geographically: thus, Muslims now form significantly large communities in 204 countries, Jews in 134 countries, Buddhists in 126 countries, and Hindus in 114 countries, whilst the much smaller community of Baha'is have planted their faith significantly in no less than 218 countries.

Erosion of Christianity's numerical strength

Table 1-1 also summarizes in statistical form the fortunes of Christianity in the 20th century in its total global context. It shows the enormous numerical increases of almost all categories of Christians—those professing in censuses (sometimes called 'confessing Christians'), those who are affiliated church members on the churches' rolls, and those who regularly practice their faith. But it also shows the static nature of these categories when expressed as percentages of the world's total population.

Decline within all world religions

This static nature of Christianity must however be seen in context. It is not Christianity alone which is static or in decline; it is the entire phenomenon of religion. All the other major world religions have suffered similarly, some catastrophically. At the same time, revivals of religion are taking place in widespread secularized areas. One must therefore be careful not to exaggerate the progress of secularization. The best way to portray the trends is to quote the actual figures, as obtainable from Table 1-1.

This table shows that the number of nonreligionists (nonreligious and atheists) throughout the 20th century has skyrocketed from 3.2 million in 1900, to 697 million in 1970, and on to 918 million in AD 2000. But the percentages tell a different story. Nonreligionists increased from 0.2% of the world in 1900, to 18.9% in 1970, but then, after the collapse of Communism in Europe, fell rapidly to 15.2% by 2000. By contrast, religionists—followers of any or all religions—fell from 99.8% of the world in 1900 (1,616 millions) to 81.1% in 1970 (2,999 millions), but then increased to 84.8% by 2000 (5,137 millions).

The persistence of ethnoreligions

Startling evidence of religion's power to survive in an anti-religious world can be found in the persistence since 1900 of what are termed here ethnoreligions—local or tribal religions, usually limited in membership to one single ethnic people each. These are the faiths which are also termed primal religions, traditional religions, or local religions, and which cover animism, shamanism, polytheism, and the like. The expectation in 1900 was that these religions, more than any oth-

Table 1–1. Global adherents of the world's 19 major distinct religions, with 48 related major religious blocs, and a grand total of some 10,000 distinct and different other religions, quantified at 7 points in time over the period AD 1900–2050 assuming current trends continue.

Religion / Year	1900 Adherents	%	1970 Adherents	%	mid-1990 Adherents	%	Annual change, 1990–2000 Natural	Conversion	Total	Rate	mid-1995 Adherents	%	mid-2000 Adherents	%	mid-2025 Adherents	%	mid-2050 Adherents	%	Countries
Christians	**558,131,572**	**34.5**	**1,236,373,744**	**33.5**	**1,747,461,964**	**33.2**	**22,708,799**	**2,501,396**	**25,210,195**	**1.36**	**1,877,425,923**	**33.1**	**1,999,563,838**	**33.0**	**2,616,670,052**	**33.4**	**3,051,564,342**	**34.3**	**238**
PROFESSION																			
crypto-Christians	3,571,077	0.2	59,195,326	1.6	102,600,880	1.9	1,408,763	703,798	2,112,561	1.89	111,095,011	2.0	123,726,489	2.0	190,490,250	2.4	246,319,348	2.8	63
professing Christians	**554,560,495**	**34.2**	**1,177,177,748**	**31.8**	**1,644,854,444**	**31.2**	**21,299,796**	**1,797,505**	**23,097,301**	**1.32**	**1,766,322,612**	**31.2**	**1,875,827,394**	**31.0**	**2,426,157,502**	**31.0**	**2,805,218,484**	**31.5**	**238**
AFFILIATION																			
unaffiliated Christians	36,488,512	2.3	106,268,111	2.9	101,889,253	1.9	1,305,142	-381,603	923,539	0.87	107,507,683	1.9	111,124,545	1.8	125,711,785	1.6	124,655,275	1.4	237
affiliated Christians	**521,643,060**	**32.2**	**1,130,105,633**	**30.6**	**1,645,572,711**	**31.2**	**21,403,655**	**2,883,011**	**24,286,666**	**1.39**	**1,769,918,240**	**31.2**	**1,888,439,293**	**31.2**	**2,490,958,267**	**31.8**	**2,926,909,067**	**32.9**	**238**
Roman Catholics	266,547,757	16.5	666,609,154	18.0	929,701,934	17.7	13,117,804	-355,181	12,762,623	1.29	994,152,689	17.5	1,057,328,093	17.5	1,361,965,255	17.4	1,564,603,495	17.6	235
Independents	7,930,940	0.5	95,604,774	2.6	301,536,352	5.7	4,495,891	3,925,017	8,420,908	2.49	346,542,889	6.1	385,745,407	6.4	581,642,120	7.4	752,842,240	8.5	221
Protestants	103,023,615	6.4	210,759,378	5.7	296,349,246	5.6	4,224,076	341,161	4,565,237	1.44	319,679,377	5.6	342,001,605	5.6	468,632,927	6.0	574,418,922	6.4	233
Orthodox	115,844,210	7.2	139,661,574	3.8	203,765,600	3.9	750,901	385,410	1,136,311	0.54	209,624,412	3.7	215,128,717	3.6	252,715,940	3.2	266,806,050	3.0	135
Anglicans	30,570,768	1.9	47,501,042	1.3	68,195,625	1.3	1,071,503	73,897	1,145,400	1.56	74,521,243	1.3	79,649,642	1.3	113,746,355	1.5	145,983,770	1.6	166
Marginal Christians	927,580	0.1	11,100,424	0.3	21,832,515	0.4	269,292	153,482	422,774	1.79	23,850,937	0.4	26,060,230	0.4	45,554,730	0.6	62,200,556	0.7	215
doubly-affiliated	-2,609,410	-0.2	-29,781,765	-0.8	-154,615,427	-2.9	-2,458,025	-1,558,424	-4,016,449	2.34	-174,354,009	-3.1	-194,779,901	-3.2	-308,401,610	-3.9	-413,843,966	-4.6	93
disaffiliated	-592,400	0.0	-11,348,948	-0.3	-21,193,134	-0.4	-67,786	-82,351	-150,137	0.69	-24,099,298	-0.4	-22,694,500	-0.4	-24,897,450	-0.3	-26,102,000	-0.3	11
Trans-megabloc groupings																			
Evangelicals	71,726,220	4.4	93,449,158	2.5	173,272,155	3.3	2,839,602	893,484	3,733,086	1.97	193,419,748	3.4	210,602,983	3.5	327,834,735	4.2	448,862,899	5.0	238
Pentecostals/Charismatics	981,400	0.1	72,222,920	2.0	425,486,472	8.1	7,016,903	2,812,254	9,829,157	2.10	477,377,916	8.4	523,777,994	8.7	811,551,594	10.4	1,066,318,949	12.0	238
Great Commission Christians	**77,931,100**	**4.8**	**277,152,485**	**7.5**	**560,665,961**	**10.6**	**6,180,025**	**2,535,490**	**8,715,515**	**1.46**	**603,063,619**	**10.6**	**647,820,987**	**10.7**	**887,578,895**	**11.3**	**1,097,449,417**	**12.3**	**238**
NON-CHRISTIANS	1,061,494,169	65.5	2,459,774,397	66.5	3,518,980,036	66.8	56,151,992	-2,451,050	53,650,481	1.43	3,788,934,277	66.9	4,055,485,162	67.0	5,207,032,948	66.6	5,857,530,658	65.7	238
Muslims	199,940,924	12.3	553,527,803	15.0	962,357,235	18.3	21,723,118	865,558	22,588,676	2.13	1,070,198,775	18.9	1,188,242,789	19.6	1,784,875,653	22.8	2,229,281,610	25.0	204
Sunnis	172,949,994	10.7	468,475,783	12.7	815,735,235	15.5	18,214,974	465,783	18,680,757	2.08	905,511,775	16.0	1,002,542,801	16.6	1,467,825,653	18.8	1,767,356,610	19.8	195
Hanafites	104,539,994	6.5	236,432,783	6.4	432,758,235	8.2	9,480,204	385,753	9,865,957	2.07	480,712,775	8.5	531,417,801	8.8	724,355,653	9.3	868,156,610	9.7	135
Shafiites	39,000,000	2.4	112,000,000	3.0	193,000,000	3.7	4,590,019	99,981	4,690,000	2.20	215,200,000	3.8	239,900,000	4.0	393,500,000	5.0	472,900,000	5.3	105
Malikites	27,000,000	1.7	114,186,000	3.1	182,000,000	3.5	3,925,302	64,698	3,990,000	2.00	201,000,000	3.5	221,900,000	3.7	346,600,000	4.4	408,700,000	4.6	65
Wahhabites	1,910,000	0.1	4,717,000	0.1	6,107,000	0.1	91,447	-2,147	89,300	1.37	6,514,000	0.1	7,000,000	0.1	9,668,000	0.1	13,350,000	0.1	10
Hanbalites	500,000	0.0	1,140,000	0.0	1,870,000	0.0	28,002	17,498	45,500	2.20	2,085,000	0.0	2,325,000	0.0	3,370,000	0.0	4,250,000	0.0	25
Sufis	80,000,000	4.9	138,100,000	3.7	202,200,000	3.8	3,027,781	492,219	3,520,000	1.62	219,500,000	3.9	237,400,000	3.9	356,200,000	4.6	445,000,000	5.0	204
Shias	26,000,000	1.6	79,500,000	2.2	135,500,000	2.6	3,029,003	313,863	3,460,000	2.30	151,800,000	2.7	170,100,000	2.8	286,000,000	3.7	410,000,000	4.6	75
Ithna-Asharis	22,250,000	1.4	65,270,000	1.8	109,570,000	2.1	2,540,722	167,778	2,708,500	2.23	122,353,000	2.2	136,655,000	2.3	229,178,000	2.9	333,175,000	3.7	70
Ismailis	2,300,000	0.1	9,700,000	0.3	18,212,000	0.3	472,710	83,290	556,000	2.70	20,807,000	0.4	23,772,000	0.4	40,950,000	0.5	55,200,000	0.6	45
Zaydis	1,200,000	0.1	3,760,000	0.1	6,406,000	0.1	95,925	67,675	163,600	2.30	7,177,000	0.1	8,042,000	0.1	13,192,000	0.2	17,775,000	0.2	10
Alawites	250,000	0.0	770,000	0.0	1,312,000	0.0	19,646	12,254	31,900	2.20	1,463,000	0.0	1,631,000	0.0	2,680,000	0.0	3,850,000	0.0	15
Islamic schismatics	990,930	0.1	5,592,020	0.2	11,125,000	0.2	296,588	85,912	382,500	3.00	12,900,000	0.2	14,950,000	0.2	27,700,000	0.4	47,725,000	0.5	110
Ahmadis	70,030	0.0	2,635,220	0.1	5,774,000	0.1	156,461	61,139	217,600	3.25	6,775,000	0.1	7,950,000	0.1	14,700,000	0.2	24,100,000	0.3	75
Other sectarian Muslims	500,000	0.0	1,500,000	0.0	1,888,000	0.0	58,271	18,329	76,600	3.46	2,244,000	0.0	2,654,000	0.0	5,697,000	0.1	13,267,000	0.1	30
Black Muslims	0	0.0	200,000	0.0	1,290,000	0.0	25,317	10,683	36,000	2.49	1,460,000	0.0	1,650,000	0.0	2,910,000	0.0	5,020,000	0.1	5
Karijites	320,000	0.0	780,000	0.0	1,329,000	0.0	26,901	3,799	30,700	2.10	1,475,000	0.0	1,636,000	0.0	2,620,000	0.0	3,145,000	0.0	10
Druzes	71,000	0.0	374,800	0.0	664,000	0.0	15,943	1,057	17,000	2.31	744,000	0.0	834,000	0.0	1,402,000	0.0	1,710,000	0.0	15
Yazidis	29,900	0.0	102,000	0.0	180,000	0.0	3,695	905	4,600	2.30	202,000	0.0	226,000	0.0	371,000	0.0	483,000	0.0	10
Hindus	203,003,440	12.5	462,597,720	12.5	685,998,940	13.0	13,194,111	-660,377	12,533,734	1.69	751,591,511	13.3	811,336,265	13.4	1,049,230,740	13.4	1,175,297,850	13.2	114
Vaishnavites	143,153,440	8.8	323,462,720	8.8	462,536,940	8.8	8,026,116	-478,522	8,704,638	1.74	508,916,511	9.0	549,583,323	9.1	708,160,740	9.1	791,806,850	8.9	90
Shaivites	52,800,000	3.3	115,946,000	3.1	182,712,000	3.5	3,435,964	-118,836	3,354,800	1.70	198,780,000	3.5	216,260,000	3.6	278,900,000	3.6	312,410,000	3.5	60
Saktists	6,700,000	0.4	13,932,000	0.4	21,740,000	0.4	325,539	72,461	398,000	1.70	23,650,000	0.4	25,720,000	0.4	33,150,000	0.4	37,132,000	0.4	35
Neo-Hindus	100,000	0.0	6,957,000	0.2	13,318,000	0.3	389,426	17,274	406,700	2.70	15,215,000	0.3	17,385,000	0.3	23,200,000	0.3	27,300,000	0.3	65
Reform Hindus	250,000	0.0	2,300,000	0.1	3,732,000	0.1	65,884	6,916	72,800	1.80	4,080,000	0.1	4,460,000	0.1	5,820,000	0.1	6,650,000	0.1	30
Nonreligious	3,023,630	0.2	532,095,567	14.4	707,117,959	13.4	6,639,206	-535,100	6,104,106	0.83	738,017,729	13.0	768,158,954	12.7	875,120,895	11.2	887,994,945	10.0	236
Chinese folk-religionists	380,006,038	23.5	231,865,233	6.3	347,651,252	6.6	3,801,126	-85,578	3,715,548	1.02	369,192,379	6.5	384,806,732	6.4	448,842,560	5.7	454,332,660	5.1	89
Buddhists	127,076,771	7.8	233,424,191	6.3	323,106,550	6.1	3,530,918	156,609	3,687,527	1.09	341,764,830	6.0	359,981,757	5.9	418,344,730	5.3	424,607,060	4.8	126
Mahayana	71,476,771	4.4	131,892,191	3.6	181,724,550	3.5	1,951,178	100,357	2,050,821	1.08	192,425,830	3.4	202,232,757	3.3	235,264,730	3.0	238,772,060	2.7	115
Theravada	48,100,000	3.0	87,700,000	2.4	122,139,000	2.3	1,372,933	40,933	1,412,000	1.10	129,006,000	2.3	136,259,000	2.3	158,200,000	2.0	160,575,000	1.8	30
Lamaists	7,500,000	0.5	13,832,000	0.4	19,263,000	0.4	207,381	15,319	222,700	1.10	20,346,000	0.4	21,490,000	0.4	24,980,000	0.3	25,380,000	0.3	30
Ethnoreligionists	117,558,485	7.3	160,278,357	4.3	200,035,408	3.8	4,098,003	-1,264,887	2,833,116	1.33	214,088,710	3.8	228,366,515	3.8	277,247,150	3.5	303,598,980	3.4	142
Animists	106,275,545	6.6	143,566,857	3.9	188,691,748	3.6	3,985,506	-1,238,592	2,746,914	1.37	202,190,060	3.6	216,160,890	3.6	263,990,700	3.4	290,789,380	3.3	142
Shamanists	11,283,040	0.7	16,711,500	0.5	11,383,660	0.2	122,433	-30,971	91,462	0.78	11,965,650	0.2	12,298,267	0.2	13,256,450	0.2	12,809,600	0.1	12
Atheists	226,120	0.0	165,400,320	4.5	145,718,604	2.8	1,315,322	-878,227	437,095	0.30	148,318,655	2.6	150,089,508	2.5	159,544,080	2.0	169,150,200	1.9	161
New-Religionists (Neoreligionists)	5,910,000	0.4	77,762,430	2.1	92,396,355	1.8	1,032,400	-36,405	995,995	1.03	97,699,635	1.7	102,356,297	1.7	114,720,210	1.5	118,845,140	1.3	60
Sikhs	2,962,300	0.2	10,617,700	0.3	19,332,080	0.4	363,677	28,961	392,638	1.87	21,226,480	0.4	23,258,412	0.4	31,377,860	0.4	37,058,960	0.4	34
Jews	12,292,210	0.8	14,763,420	0.4	13,188,955	0.3	194,962	-70,447	124,515	0.91	13,860,205	0.2	14,434,039	0.2	16,053,350	0.2	16,694,500	0.2	134
Ashkenazis	11,278,810	0.7	12,620,920	0.3	10,124,855	0.2	151,611	-56,103	95,508	0.91	10,654,105	0.2	11,079,939	0.2	12,321,550	0.2	12,811,700	0.1	120
Oriental Jews	700,000	0.0	1,520,000	0.0	2,172,000	0.0	32,524	-11,924	20,600	0.91	2,273,000	0.0	2,378,000	0.0	2,645,000	0.0	2,750,000	0.0	25
Sefardis	300,000	0.0	607,000	0.0	870,000	0.0	13,028	-4,828	8,200	0.90	910,000	0.0	952,000	0.0	1,060,000	0.0	1,105,000	0.0	80
Karaites	13,400	0.0	15,500	0.0	22,100	0.0	331	-131	200	0.87	23,100	0.0	24,100	0.0	26,800	0.0	27,800	0.0	5
Samaritans	500	0.0	500	0.0	500	0.0	7	-7	0	0.00	500	0.0	500	0.0	500	0.0	500	0.0	5
Spiritists	269,040	0.0	4,602,780	0.1	10,154,665	0.2	137,163	80,748	217,911	1.96	11,142,555	0.2	12,333,735	0.2	16,211,780	0.2	20,709,300	0.2	55
Afro-American spiritists	112,440	0.0	420,260	0.0	875,000	0.0	15,524	4,149	19,673	2.05	971,555	0.0	1,071,735	0.0	1,609,190	0.0	2,116,020	0.0	18
Afro-Brazilian cultists	97,000	0.0	1,320,000	0.0	3,700,000	0.1	65,460	22,224	87,684	2.15	4,051,000	0.1	4,576,844	0.1	6,100,000	0.1	8,000,000	0.1	1
High Spiritists	40,000	0.0	1,220,000	0.0	2,920,000	0.1	53,725	29,275	83,000	2.53	3,321,000	0.1	3,750,000	0.1	5,100,000	0.1	7,000,000	0.1	20
Afro-Caribbean religionists	100	0.0	10,500	0.0	77,600	0.0	1,162	1,818	2,980	3.30	92,600	0.0	107,397	0.0	183,800	0.0	256,100	0.0	5
Baha'is	9,535	0.0	2,657,349	0.1	5,671,687	0.1	117,158	26,333	143,491	2.28	6,273,880	0.1	7,106,420	0.1	12,062,150	0.2	18,000,900	0.2	218
Confucianists	640,050	0.0	4,759,200	0.1	5,855,540	0.1	55,739	-11,434	44,305	0.73	6,075,720	0.1	6,298,597	0.1	6,817,950	0.1	6,952,900	0.1	15
Jains	1,323,280	0.1	2,617,810	0.1	3,868,470	0.1	74,539	-39,588	34,951	0.87	3,894,120	0.1	4,217,979	0.1	6,115,650	0.1	6,732,770	0.1	10
Shintoists	6,720,000	0.4	4,175,000	0.1	3,081,790	0.1	8,534	-40,527	-31,993	-1.09	2,838,540	0.1	2,761,845	0.0	2,122,950	0.0	1,655,400	0.0	8
Taoists	375,000	0.0	1,734,000	0.0	2,402,090	0.0	25,397	-155	25,242	1.00	2,551,850	0.0	2,654,514	0.0	3,066,300	0.0	3,272,200	0.0	5
Zoroastrians	108,490	0.0	121,890	0.0	1,959,260	0.0	45,391	13,080	58,471	2.65	2,265,800	0.0	2,543,950	0.0	4,439,930	0.1	6,964,700	0.1	24
Mandeans	8,000	0.0	23,000	0.0	31,600	0.0	823	-85	738	2.12	35,000	0.0	38,977	0.0	58,000	0.0	76,000	0.0	2
Other religionists	41,115	0.0	761,100	0.0	931,971	0.0	9,189	471	9,660	0.99	982,550	0.0	1,028,519	0.0	1,442,430	0.0	1,861,820	0.0	76
doubly-counted religionists	0	0.0	-4,000,000	-0.1	-11,879,300	-0.2	-214,784	-50,346	-265,130	2.04	-13,083,000	-0.2	-14,530,637	-0.2	-20,665,000	-0.3	-25,516,000	-0.3	24
World A (unevangelized persons)	879,671,736	54.3	1,641,245,161	44.4	1,665,470,930	31.6	28,353,920	-31,963,512	-3,609,592	-0.22	1,678,204,817	29.6	1,629,374,957	26.9	1,845,405,668	23.6	1,806,052,390	20.3	238
World B (evangelized non-Christians)	181,822,433	11.2	818,529,236	22.1	1,853,509,106	35.2	27,798,072	29,462,116	57,260,188	0.27	2,110,729,460	37.3	2,426,110,205	40.1	3,361,627,280	43.0	4,051,478,268	45.5	238
World C (Christians)	558,131,572	34.5	1,236,373,744	33.5	1,747,461,964	33.2	22,708,799	2,501,396	25,210,195	1.36	1,877,425,923	33.1	1,999,563,838	33.0	2,616,670,052	33.4	3,051,564,342	34.3	238
Global population	**1,619,625,741**	**100.0**	**3,696,148,141**	**100.0**	**5,266,442,000**	**100.0**	**78,860,791**	**0**	**78,860,791**	**1.41**	**5,666,360,200**	**100.0**	**6,055,049,000**	**100.0**	**7,823,703,000**	**100.0**	**8,909,095,000**	**100.0**	**238**

ers, were doomed and would disappear completely within a generation, to be replaced by one or other of the universal or world religions. Not only would Christianity provide an irresistible alternative; secular advances also—in education, science, technology, colonialism, communications—would destroy the ethnoreligions in a decade or two. The prognosis of the World Missionary Conference (Edinburgh 1910) concerning the so-called primitive peoples was:

> Most of these peoples will have lost their ancient faiths within a generation, and will accept that culture-religion with which they first come into contact.

The ancient faiths did not disappear as expected. Despite secularization, and despite vast numbers of conversions from their ranks to Christianity, Hinduism and Islam, the absolute numbers of ethnoreligionists including shamanists increased markedly and regularly from 117 million in 1900 to 228 million by the year 2000.

The meteoric rise of secular quasireligions
Equally startling has been the meteoric growth of secularism in its religious forms. Two immense quasi-religious systems have emerged at the expense of the world religions: agnosticism (also termed secularism, materialism, non-religion, etc) and atheism (also termed anti-religion or irreligion). Variations include secularism, scientific materialism, atheistic communism, nationalism, nazism, fascism, Maoism, liberal humanism and numerous constructed or fabricated pseudo-religions. From a minuscule presence in 1900, a mere 0.2% of the globe, these systems have mushroomed to 20.8% of the globe by 1980. They are today increasing at the extraordinary rate of 8.5 million new converts each year, and are likely to reach one billion adherents soon. A large percentage of their members are the children, grandchildren or great-grandchildren of persons who in their lifetimes were practicing Christians. No Christian strategist in 1900 had envisaged such a massive rate of defection from Christianity within its 19th-century heartlands.

Global Diagram 3. Annual religious change
These tables depict a situation of enormous religious complexity in today's world. Moreover, the situation is anything but static. Every year millions of people are changing their religious profession or their Christian affiliation. Mass defections are occurring from stagnant majority religions to newer religions. Mass conversions under way in many countries are accruing primarily to missionary religions aggressively engaged in proselytism. These tables document the phenomena by analyzing in detail the decade 1990-2000, and by giving, for all religions and for the different categories of Christians, the annual numerical change divided into natural increase and conversion change.

To illustrate this dynamic, ever-changing character of the world of religions today, Table 1-2 shows the numerical changes that are happening every 24 hours, for 74 major descriptors.

Massive gains offset by massive losses.
From the Christian standpoint, the overall situation presents a mixed picture. On the one hand, Christianity has experienced massive gains across the Third World throughout the 20th century. In Africa, Christians have mushroomed from 9.9 million in 1900 (0.6% of the world's population then) to 360 million in AD 2000 (8.9%). The present net increase on that continent is 8.4 million new Christians a year (23,000 a day), of which 1.5 million are net new converts (converts minus defections or apostasies). Sizeable net conversions are also taking place in Asia (2.4 million a year). A major reason for this expansion across the continents of the Third World is the attracting power of the Christian gospel of justice and the love of God for the poor and oppressed.

But on the other hand, Christianity has experienced massive losses in the Western world over the last 60 years. In Europe and North America, net defections from Christianity—converts to other religions or to irreligion—are now running at 1,820,500 former Christians a year. This loss is much higher if one considers only church members: 2,224,800 a year (6,000 a day). It is even higher if one is speaking of only church attenders: every year, some 2,765,100 church attenders in Europe and North America cease to be practicing Christians within the 12-month period, an average loss of 7,600 every day.

Table 1-2. Today's globe each 24 hours: daily worldwide statistical changes in 75 major secular, religious, Christian, and non-Christian characteristics.

Over the next 24-hour period, these average increases will occur:

Category	*Amount*
WORLD POPULATION	
Births (new persons born)	340,500
Deaths (new persons dying)	144,000
Increase in population	196,000
International migrants	275,000
Households (families)	104,100
Literates	281,000
URBANIZATION	
Cities (over 50,000 pop.)	2
Metropolises (over 100,000)	1
Non-Christian urbanites	129,000
Urban dwellers (urbanites)	190,400
Rural dwellers	3,500
Deforestation (sq km destroyed)	2,600
Urban poor	77,000
Urban slumdwellers	38,000
WORLD RELIGIONS	
New non-Christian religions	2
Non-Christians	***147,000***
Atheists	1,200
Baha'is	400
Buddhists	10,600
Chinese folk-religionists	10,700
Confucianists	120
Ethnoreligionists	8,200
Hindus	37,000
Jains	100
Jews	350
Muslims	68,000
New-Religionists	2,800
Nonreligious	16,700
Shintoists	-90
Sikhs	1,100
Spiritists	600
Taoists	70
Zoroastrians	160
Christians	***69,000***
GLOBAL CHRISTIANITY	
New baptized church members	122,000
Christian deaths	50,000
Evangelicals	11,000
Urban Christians	61,000
Pentecostals/Charismatics/Neocharismatics	30,000
Great Commission Christians	25,500
Christian martyrs	470
ECCLESIASTICAL MEMBERSHIP	
Anglicans	3,400
Independents	26,000
Marginal Christians	1,200
Orthodox	3,200
Protestants	13,300
Roman Catholics	37,000
MEMBERSHIP BY CONTINENT	
Africa	24,500
Asia	19,400
Europe	2,200
Latin America	21,000
Northern America	5,000
Oceania	800
CHRISTIAN ORGANIZATIONS	
Worship centers	500
Denominations	0.5
Service agencies	3
Foreign-mission sending agencies	1
Standalone global monoliths	1
CHRISTIAN WORKERS	
Nationals (citizens)	300
Aliens (foreign missionaries)	20
Home missionaries	30
Short-term missionaries	50
CHRISTIAN FINANCE (in US$)	
Personal income of church members	$41 billion
Giving to Christian causes	$740 million
Churches' income	$296 million
Parachurch and institutional income	$444 million
Ecclesiastical crime (sums embezzled)	$44 million
Income of global foreign missions	$41 million
Cost-effectiveness at global level	$50
NEW TECHNOLOGY	
New Christian computer users	100,000
Christians joining the Internet	68,500
CHRISTIAN LITERATURE	
New commercial book titles	6
New books/articles on evangelization	7
SCRIPTURE DISTRIBUTION (all sources)	
Bibles	165,000
New Testaments	334,000
Gospels	1,000,000
Selections	11,200,000
CHRISTIAN BROADCASTING	
New regular listeners/viewers	210,000
CHRISTIAN EVANGELISM	
Evangelism-hours	500 million
Offers	2.6 billion
WORLD EVANGELIZATION	
Unevangelized persons	-9,900
Evangelized persons	206,000

At the global level, these losses from Christianity in the Western world slightly outweigh the gains in the Third World. This can be observed by examining the trends in percentages over the period 1900-2000. In 1900, Christians numbered 34.5% of the world (37.8%, if adults only are counted). This percentage has fallen gradually over the decades until Christians in 1980 numbered 33.4% of the world (36.0% of the world's adults), and in AD 2000, 33.0%.

Global Diagram 4. Megatypologies of Renewal
Over the last 20 centuries, Christianity has been characterized by a multifold series of renewals, minirenewals, and even several megarenewals. These can be grouped into 4 overall global typologies of empirical Christianity, termed here Megatypologies 1, 2, 3, and 4. All are distinct and separate, historically, but they do in fact overlap somewhat at a number of points. Global Diagram 4 shows each as a separate globe, with each's characteristics and statistics. One larger globe then has superimposed on it all 4 megatypologies, showing the areas of overlap and their statistics in AD 2000.

Global Diagram 5: Independency
By the end of the 16th century, the Christian world had become polarized into 4 major ecclesiastico-cultural global megablocs: *Orthodox, Roman Catholic, Anglican, Protestant*. In the 19th century, a 5th global megabloc emerged, repudiating mainline organized Christianity and placing itself on the periphery or margins of the 4 existing blocs—hence the term, *Marginal Christians*. The bloc is composed of Mormons, Jehovah's Witnesses, Christian Science, and a host of other bodies characterized by one or both of these traits: anti-trinitarian or non-trinitarian christology, and the claim to have a second source of divine revelation in addition to the Bible.

Far less known is the fact that in recent centuries a sixth global bloc has emerged: *Independent*, with its 2 synonymous alternate terms *Postdenominationalist*, and *Neo-Apostolic*. Global Diagram 5, and then Table 1-6 (on 2 facing pages), depict and explain this new megabloc in detail.

Global Diagram 6: Martyrdom
The most startling of this series relating to understanding the past is Global Diagram 6, enumerating the 70 million Christians killed for their faith across 20 centuries. The effect of martyrdom (a word that originates in the Greek word *martys*, a witness) on evangelization over the centuries has been profound. This diagram analyzes the phenomenon. The huge numbers involved year by year justify observers in saying that, although involuntary for its victims, martyrdom is the most significant and far-reaching of all the modes and methodologies of evangelization.

Religious freedom in a country may be quite different, de facto, to what the state professes about it and what it purports to guarantee in its constitution. In fact, in 79 countries some 2.2 billion people (50.6% of the world in 1980) live under restrictions on their religious freedom, despite the guarantees in those countries' constitutions and in the 1948 United Nations' *Universal Declaration of Human Rights*. The worst recent case of persecution has been the 1966-67 Great Proletarian Revolution in China. This was history's most systematic attempt ever, by a single nation, to eradicate and destroy Christianity and all religion. In this it failed.

The underground church
There are several different ways of enumerating the so-called 'underground' church, or the 'churches of silence', by which is meant Christians living under hostile or unfavorable regimes or circumstances.

As the World Council of Churches resolved at its 1975 Nairobi Assembly: 'No-one—imprisoned, tortured, harassed or persecuted—should escape the vigilance of the praying church'.

Tables 1-3 to 1-8: other survey data
After the global diagrams come 5 other tables setting out some aspects of the fortunes of global Christianity.

Tables 1-3, 1-4, and 1-5 subdivide the global totals in Table 1-1. Table 1-3 divides Christians into their 6 component megablocs—Orthodox, Roman Catholic, Anglican, Protestant, Independent, marginal

Concluded on page 12

Global Diagram 1. Today's global human need: poverty, slums, disasters, deprivation, rights abuses, illness, disease, addiction.

Human need is covered here in 2 consecutive diagrams. Global Diagram 1 focuses on the unfortunate victims involved (described by the detailed statistics below).

The globe below gives an overview of these 2 subjects. It is divided into 2 halves. The lower half depicts the world of the Poor (the so-called 'lower classes') divided into 2 main slices (with a megapoor minislice) and into several population segments. The 4 columns of statistics below the globe then detail today's global human need.

The upper half of the globe depicts the world of the Rich (the 'middle and upper classes'), divided into 3 main slices (with a megarich minislice) and into several population segments. The figures shown attached to this upper half briefly outline the so-called 'structures of sin'.

All statistics refer to the Decade of Evangelism, 1990-AD 2000. All monies are given in USA dollars. Note also that 'p.a.' means 'per annum', 'per year', 'a year', 'each year', 'every year'. These terms are used alternately to provide variety. Note further that the same global totals throughout these diagrams may be given rounded to 1,2,3, or 4 significant figures (e.g. world population is 6.1 billion, or 6,055 million, etc). Partial totals may not always add up to global totals or 100.0% because of rounding.

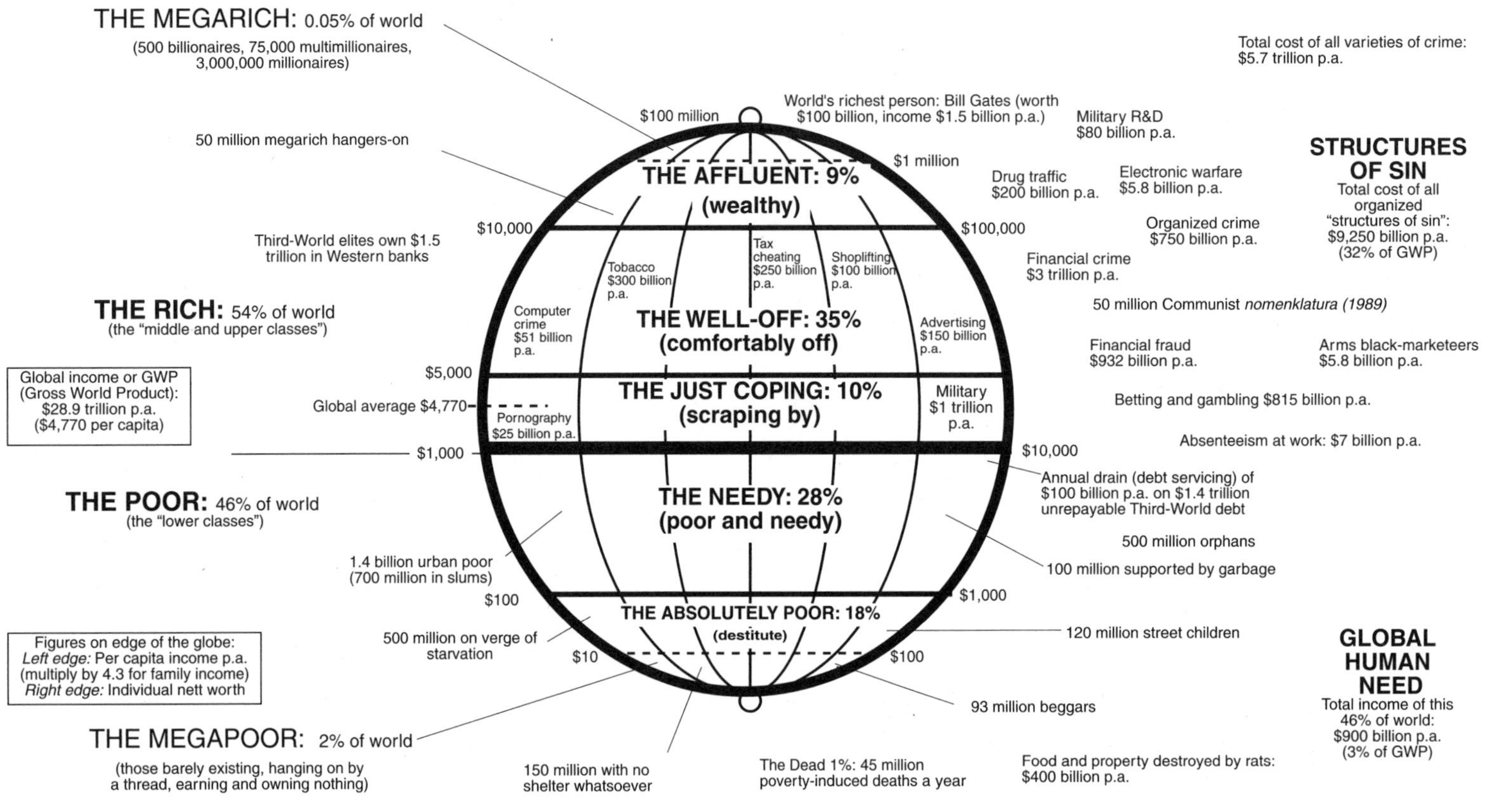

HUMANS ON THE GLOBE
6.1 billion population
71,600,000 population increase p.a. (1.2% p.a.; 93% in developing countries)
Median age 26.0 years
124.3 million births a year (2.05% p.a.)
52.7 million deaths a year (0.87% p.a.)
Life expectancy at birth 67.6 years

BASIC RIGHTS: FOOD, WATER, SHELTER, CARE
2 billion undernourished
1.2 billion hungry (inadequate food for active working life)
700 million severely malnourished
2.0 billion suffering from iron-deficiency anaemia
500 million on verge of starvation
15 million babies born malnourished p.a.
Infant mortality (deaths under 1 year old) 51.6 per 1000 live births
Maternal mortality 600,000 p.a.
18 million annual hunger-related deaths of under 5s
22 million starvation-related deaths p.a.
2.2 billion without safe water to drink
3.0 billion without adequate safe water supply
3.0 billion with unsafe water and bad sanitation
25,000 a day killed by dirty water
1.3 billion without adequate shelter
150 million with no shelter whatsoever
55 million cave-dwellers
1.5 billion without money to buy food
1.5 billion with scarce firewood
70 million abandoned children and infants
349 million homeless/family-less children
120 million megacity street children
500 million orphans
700 million slumdwellers or shanty-dwellers
New slumdwellers increase at 80 million p.a.
100 million supported by garbage collection/recycling
1.5 billion with no access to medical care
2.8 billion poor (46% of world)
1.4 billion urban poor (1.1 billion in Third World)
1.09 billion absolutely poor (in absolute poverty; 18%)
Poorest 20% of world gets 1.6% of GWP
Working-age population: 70 million more p.a.
Exploited child labor: 200 million
93 million beggars
1.0 billion unemployed workers
900 million underemployed labor
1.1 billion urban part-time street vendors
Physical quality of life index (global average): 68%
50 countries with less calorie supply than essential (2,600 per capita per day)

SOCIOPOLITICAL RIGHTS
10 million stateless (with no nationality)
14 million deportees (persons expelled) p.a.
4 billion unprotected from human rights abuses
Human rights: 45% violated
15 million permanently unsettled refugees
29 million emigrants/immigrants p.a.
154 countries not controlled by popular votes
2.8 billion disenfranchised (no control by vote; 54% of world)
991 million illiterate/nonliterate adults (23.3%)
1 billion orate (nonreader) adults unable to read or write (25%)
10 million more illiterate adults p.a.
300 million with language handicaps
3.7 billion without political freedom
1.96 billion in religious countries
2.40 billion in secular countries
1.5 billion under atheistic regimes
400 million under oppressive regimes
80 million under racist regimes
2.8 billion women denied full rights and equality
1.2 billion victims of corruption
850 million uneducated (no past schooling)
1.7 billion school-age children (ages 5-19)
1.2 billion with little or no access to schools (67% of those eligible)
670 million school-agers not in schools
410 million with no access to schools (24%)
28 million children reach school age p.a.
40% without access to electricity
43% without telephone access
43.5% without radio or TV
120 million prisoners in 12-month period
4.5 million political prisoners
1.2 million prisoners due to religion
1 million prisoners of conscience
2.2 billion denied freedom of religion
4.2 billion denied full political freedom and civil rights
2.2 billion in countries frequently employing torture
120,000 prisoners being tortured
151 million citizens killed by own governments since 1900
1,692,400 political executions, 1948-1977
50,000 executed by governments each year
35 million slaves (bought and sold, including bonded labor, involuntary servitude)
594 million victims of crime p.a.
386,000 murders a year
5.8 million child victims of pedophile racketeers p.a.
25 million child-abuse incidents p.a.
250 million persons abused in childhood

FUNDAMENTAL FREEDOMS
3 billion denied freedom to travel in own country
4 billion denied freedom to travel abroad
3 billion denied freedom to assemble
3 billion denied freedom to teach ideas

DISASTERS AND DESERTIFICATION
1,165,200 more desertification victims a year
11.6 million environmental refugees
1.0 billion at risk through desertification
1,800 major earthquakes, 1900-1985, killing 1.8 million
21,000 earthquake victims (deaths) a year
800 major floods, since 1960, killing 400,000
12,000 flood victims (deaths) a year
300 major cyclones, since 1960, killing 750,000
300,000 environmental disaster victims p.a.
1 million poisoned by pesticides p.a.
800 million live in areas with unhealthy air
25,000 pollution deaths a day
1.5 million killed in man-made disasters p.a.
Traffic deaths 3 persons per 100 million vehicle miles

ILLNESS/DISEASE
49 million legally blind
32.6 million totally blind (nonsighted)
120 million with river blindness (100 million at risk)
372 million partially deaf (hearing-impaired)
150 million severely deaf
23 million totally deaf
11.6 million dumb (deaf-mutes)
11.6 million with dracunculiasis
19.2 million leprosy sufferers (lepers)
145 million diabetics
450 million new malaria cases p.a.
3.2 billion live at risk of malaria
2.7 million malaria deaths p.a.
314 million with elephantiasis
250 million with schistosomiasis (700 million at risk)
1.2 million a year bitten by venomous snakes
50,000 deaths p.a. from venomous snake bites
10 million with Parkinson's disease
10 million with tuberculosis (TB: 2.9 million deaths p.a.)
542 million iron-deficiency anemic women
116 million with chemosensory (taste and smell) disorders
3.5 million persons worldwide with artificial implants (pacemakers, prostheses)
350,000 persons kept alive by artificial kidneys
65,000 organ transplants a year
3,500 heart transplants a year
75,000 awaiting organ donors
60 million psychotics
15 million schizophrenics
1 billion psychoneurotics
350 million arthritics
1 billion experiencing chronic pain
540 million disabled (handicapped)
340 million handicapped children
100 million severely handicapped children
3.4 million dwarfs (little people)
2.2 billion sick/ill persons (30% children)
Labor absenteeism: $7 billion p.a.
3.5 million children die p.a. from vaccine-preventable diseases
6 infectious diseases kill 4 million unimmunized children p.a.
4 billion persons not immunized
2.5 million diarrheal deaths of children under 5 p.a.
4 million children die of pneumonia p.a.
24 million prostitutes (9% male)
41 million AIDS carriers (growth rate 25% p.a.)
5 million AIDS cases
2.5 million AIDS-related deaths a year
500,000 suicides a year
700 million tobacco smokers
3 million tobacco-related deaths p.a.
198 million alcoholics
64 million drug addicts (illicit drug users)
Leading causes of 52.7 million deaths p.a.:
Parasitic diseases 19.0 million
Circulatory diseases 15.3 million
Cancer 6.2 million
Perinatal diseases 3.5 million
Injury and poisoning 2.7 million
Cardiovascular disease 5.8 million
150 million severely mentally-retarded
256,000 Downs-syndrome (mongoloid) births p.a.
30 million epileptics
303,000 hemophiliacs (all males)
524,000 albinos (homozygous persons)
100 million albino-gene carriers

FINANCE
Money needed to provide those in poverty with adequate food, water, education, health: $583 billion p.a.

Global Diagram 2. Today's geopolitico-religious blocs: 3 worlds, 3 megacontinents, 7 continents, 9 macro regions, 21 regions, 180 nations, 238 countries, 3,000 provinces, with the globe's 33 major religious and antireligious blocs.

The statistics below enumerate the main varieties of political and religious segmentation of the world's population in use today. The various basic segments listed here can be grouped or regrouped in different ways depending on one's requirements. The pie chart shows the world's major religious blocs or segments. All figures relate to the year AD 2000.

Indented categories are part of (included in) preceding unindented categories. Figures in parentheses with a % sign are in all cases annual change (% increase p.a., per year).

THE GLOBE IN MID-2000
6.06 billion persons
  13% in First (Western) world
  33% in Second (Communist-related) world
  55.3% in Third (Nonaligned) World
71 million more people a year (1.2% p.a.)
Land area: 151 million sq km

WORLDS
DEVELOPMENT
More developed regions: 49 countries
Less developed regions: 189 countries
1.15 billion in more developed regions
4.9 billion in less developed regions
Least developed countries (LDCs): 160
4.73 billion in least developed countries
GEOPOLITICAL WORLDS
Western world: 35 countries
Communist world: 30 countries
Third World: 173 countries
RELIGIOUS WORLDS
World A (unevangelized): 141 countries
World B (evangelized, non-Christian): 59 countries
World C (Christian): 38 countries

CONTINENTS AND REGIONS
3 megacontinents
7 continents
9 macro regions (continental areas)
21 regions

COUNTRIES
238 countries in world (3 under 1,000 population, 235 over)
145 sovereign nations (185 being UN members, including observer states)
43 nonsovereign countries (dependencies)
GOVERNMENT
82 multiparty democratic states
50 one-party states (30 Marxist)
35 military regimes
40 autocracies/dictatorships
39 dependencies/colonies (9.6 million population)
IDEOLOGY (1989)
113 religious countries
102 secular countries
30 atheistic countries
FREEDOM OR REPRESSION (adherence to UN Universal Declaration on Human Rights)
79 politically free countries
87 partially politically free
85 politically not free

ASSOCIATIONS OF COUNTRIES
  (number of member countries in each)
UN 185, FAO 170, GATT 125, IAEA 121,
IBRD 177, ICAO 180, IDA 177, IFAD 142,
IFC 161, ILO 168, IMF 179, IMO 149, ITU 166,
UNESCO 179, UNIDO 180, UPU 189,
WHO 189, WIPO 151, WMO 172 WTO 125.

PROVINCES
3,030 major civil divisions (MCDs)
MULTINATIONALS
11,500 transnational corporations (TNCs)
5,000 TNCs in association in Global T-Net
500 supranationals or intergovernmental organizations (IGOs)
4,000 international nongovernmental organizations (NGOs)
International electronic fund transfers $20 billion a day
International foreign exchange transactions p.a. $120 trillion
100 million internationals (persons living abroad)

WORLD COMMUNISM
Situation in mid-1989:
122 Communist, Leninist, or Marxist parties (in 130 countries)
88.7 million Communist party members
16 Communist-ruled (Leninist) states (with 83 million party members)
30 Marxist-ruled (including Communist-ruled) states
12 international Communist front organizations, with 1,400 affiliates (agencies)
1.7 billion persons under Marxist regimes

RELIGION (10,000 religions, analyzable into 33 major religious and antireligious blocs)

ADHERENCE TO RELIGION IN AD 2000
5.14 billion religionists (all religions) (annual increase 1.5% p.a.)
  2.5 billion popular-religionists
  500 million New Age/occult/neo-Hindu cultists
  838 million Christian popular-religionist-pietists
  80 million quasi-religionists, including 7.5 million Freemasons (males)
  918 million nonreligionists (0.7% p.a.)
  768 million nonreligious (0.8% p.a.)
  150 million atheists (0.3% p.a.)

ADHERENTS OF NON-CHRISTIAN RELIGIONS
3.2 billion non-Christian religionists (annual increase 1.6% p.a.)
GREAT WORLD RELIGIONS
1.2 billion Muslims (2.1% p.a.)
  1 billion Sunnis (2.1% p.a.)
  170 million Shias (Shiites) (2.3% p.a.)
  23.8 million Ismailis (2.7% p.a.)
  7.95 million Ahmadis (3.3% p.a.)
811.3 million Hindus (1.7% p.a.)
  550 million Vaishnavites (1.7% p.a.)
  216 million Shaivites (1.7% p.a.)
  26 million Saktists (1.7% p.a.)
  17 million Neo-Hindus (2.7% p.a.)
  4 million Reform Hindus (1.8% p.a.)
360 million Buddhists (1.1% p.a.)
  202 million Mahayana (1.1% p.a.)
  136 million Theravada (1.1% p.a.)
  21 million Tantrayana (Lamaists) (1.1% p.a.)
OTHER MAJOR RELIGIONS
228.4 million Ethnoreligionists (1.3% p.a.)
384.8 million Chinese folk-religionists (1.0% p.a.)
102.4 million Asian New-Religionists (1.0% p.a.)
MINOR RELIGIONS
14.4 million Jews (0.9% p.a.)
23.3 million Sikhs (1.9% p.a.)
12.3 million non-Christian Spiritists (2.0% p.a.)
7.1 million Baha'is (2.3% p.a.)
2.8 million Shintoists (-1.0% p.a.)
4.2 million Jains (0.9% p.a.)

CHRISTIANS AND NON-CHRISTIANS
2,000 million Christians (1.4% p.a.)
4,055 billion non-Christians (1.5% p.a.)

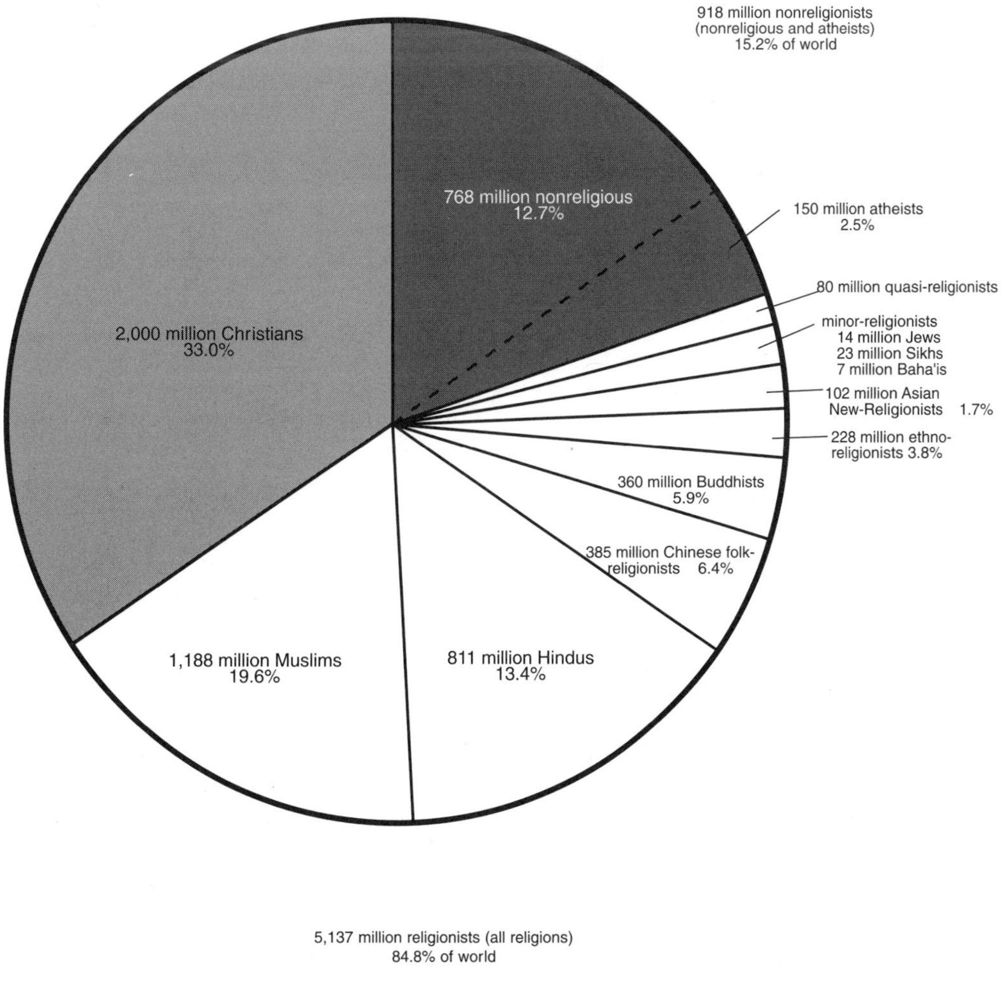

Global Diagram 3. The dynamics of global religious change: annual gains and losses in population, Christians, Non-Christians, evangelized and unevangelized persons, analyzed by Worlds A, B, and C in AD 2000.

Huge population movements and religious surges take place year by year on the surface of the globe. Causes are: births, deaths, conversions, defections, and evangelization under its 600 dimensions and varieties. The dynamics of these changes are portrayed below. The globe is analyzed from its top to its bottom into the 3 horizontal Worlds A, B, and C. Its populations are then shown moving through life from left to right. They are analyzed into 3 vertical segments of human life—births, change (from childhood to adult life to old age, with persons becoming evangelized or converts or defectors), and deaths.

Table A below gives the detailed statistics of these changes. It is arranged as 5 minitables and 27 lines or rows of figures. Each minitable (A,B,C,D,E) views the global scene from the standpoint of a different grouping and shows its demographic deployment in Worlds A, B, and C. The lines a-z' enumerate 27 categories of globe-wide change—gains, losses, increases, decreases. Lines are progressively derived or computed from earlier lines; column 3 shows how or whence. ('UN' refers to *World population prospects 1998.* Tables 1 refers to Part 4 "Countries".)

ANNUAL CHANGE

All figures on this illustration are of annual change (m=millions; p.a.=per annum, per year)

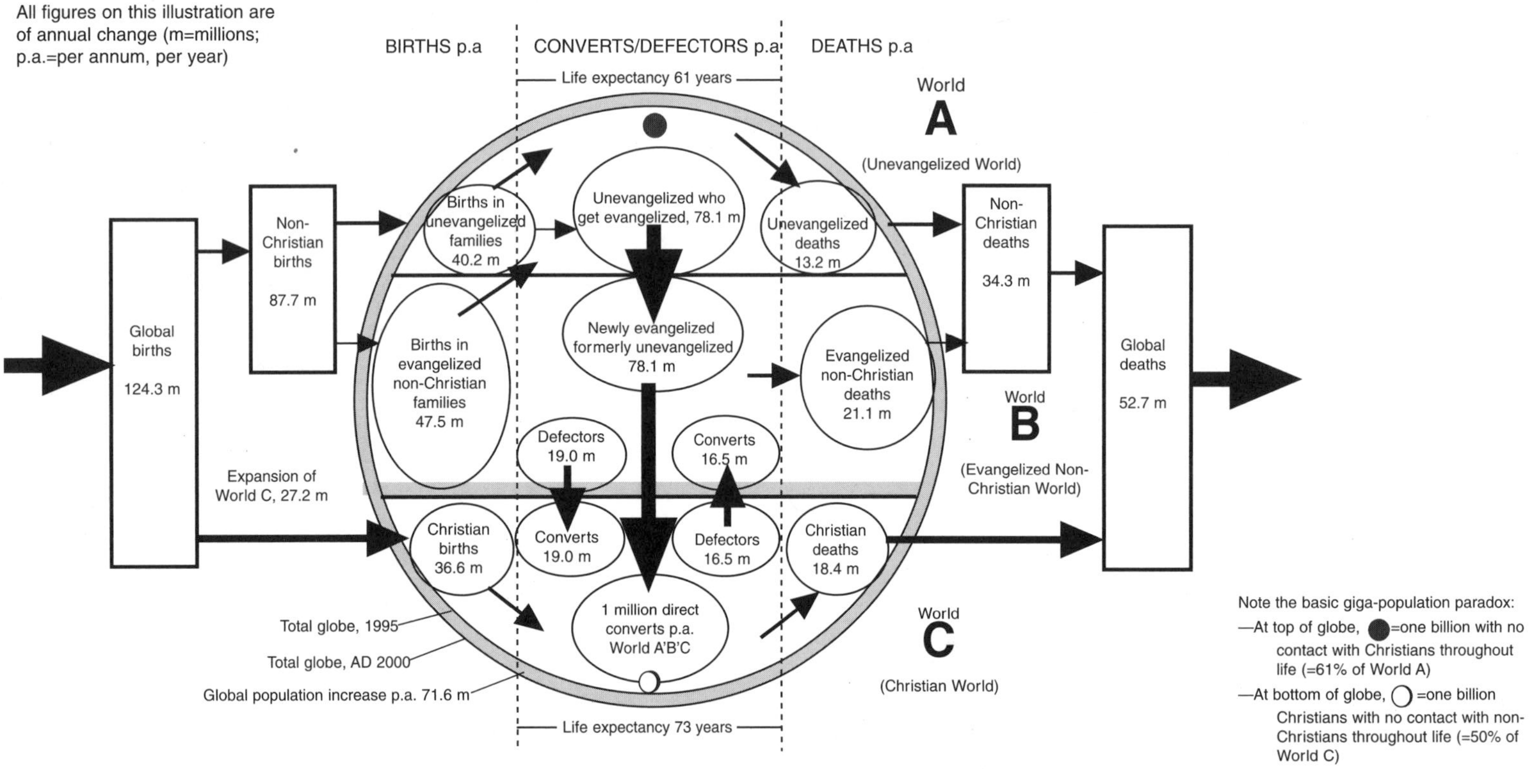

Table A. STATISTICS OF GLOBAL RELIGIOUS CHANGE.

Category of globe-wide change (column 1, 2)	Where located? Derivation (3)	GLOBE Global total per year (4)	per day (5)	Rate % p.a. (6)	WORLD A (Unevangelized individuals) (7)	WORLD B (Evangelized non-Christians) (8)	WORLD C (Christians) (9)
A. GLOBAL GROWTH OF POPULATION, AD 2000							
Total population		*6,055 m*			*1,629 m*	*2,426 m*	*2,000 m*
ANNUAL POPULATION GAINS							
a. Births, p.a.	UN	124.3 m	340,548	2.05	40.2 m	47.5 m	36.6 m
ANNUAL POPULATION LOSSES							
b. Deaths, p.a.	UN	52.7 m	144,384	0.87	13.2 m	21.1 m	18.4 m
ANNUAL INCREASE							
c. Natural increase of population (nett), p.a.	c=a-b	71.6 m	196,164	1.18	27.0 m	26.4 m	18.2 m
B. GLOBAL GROWTH OF CHRISTIANS, AD 2000							
Total Christians		*2,000m*			*0*	*0*	*2,000 m*
ANNUAL CHRISTIAN GAINS							
d. Births in Christian families, p.a.	Tables 1	36.6 m	100,274	1.83	0	0	36.6 m
e. Converts to Christianity, p.a.	Tables 1	19.0 m	52,055	0.95	0	0	19.0 m
f. New Christians, p.a.	f=d+e	55.6 m	152,329	2.78	0	0	55.6 m
g. Baptisms, p.a.	80% of f	44.5 m	121,918	2.23	0	0	44.5 m
ANNUAL CHRISTIAN LOSSES							
h. Deaths of Christians, p.a.	Tables 1	18.4 m	50,411	0.92	0	0	18.4 m
i. Defectors from Christianity, p.a.	Tables 1	16.5 m	45,210	0.83	0	0	16.5 m
ANNUAL CHRISTIAN INCREASE							
j. Nett increase in Christians, p.a.	j=f-h-i	20.7 m	56,710	1.04	0	0	20.7 m
C. GLOBAL GROWTH OF NON-CHRISTIANS, AD 2000							
Total non-Christians		*4,055 m*			*1,629 m*	*2,426 m*	*0*
ANNUAL NON-CHRISTIAN GAINS							
k. Births in non-Christian families, p.a.	k=a-d	87.7 m	240,274	2.16	40.2 m	47.5 m	0
l. Converts from Christianity, p.a.	l=i	16.5 m	45,210	0.41	0	16.5 m	0
m. New non-Christians, p.a.	m=k+l	104.2 m	285,480	2.57	40.2 m	64.0 m	0
ANNUAL NON-CHRISTIAN LOSSES							
n. Deaths of non-Christians, p.a.	n=b-h	34.3 m	93,973	0.85	13.2 m	21.1 m	0
o. Defectors to Christianity, p.a.	o=e	19.0 m	52,055	0.47	0	19.0 m	0
ANNUAL NON-CHRISTIAN INCREASE							
p. Nett increase in non-Christians, p.a.	p=m-n-o	50.9 m	139,450	1.26	27.0 m	23.9 m	0
D. GLOBAL GROWTH OF EVANGELIZED PERSONS, AD 2000							
Total evangelized individuals		*4,426 m*			*0*	*2,426 m*	*2,000 m*
q. Newly-evangelized persons, p.a.	q=r+s	114.7 m	314,247	2.59	0	78.1 m	36.6 m
r. —Former unevangelized persons, p.a.	Tables 1	78.1 m	213,973	1.76	0	78.1 m	0
s. —New Christian births, p.a.	s=d	36.6 m	100,274	0.83	0	0	36.6 m
t. Deaths of evangelized persons, p.a.	Tables 1	39.4 m	107,945	0.89	0	21.1 m	18.4 m
u. Nett increase in evangelized persons, p.a.	u=q-t	75.3 m	206,301	1.70	0	57.0 m	18.2 m
E. GLOBAL GROWTH OF UNEVANGELIZED PERSONS, AD 2000							
Total unevangelized individuals		*1,629 m*			*1,629 m*	*0*	*0*
v. Births of unevangelized persons, p.a.	v=k	87.7 m	240,274	5.38	87.7 m	0	0
w. —in unevangelized families, p.a.	Tables 1	40.2 m	110,137	2.47	40.2 m	0	0
x. —in evangelized non-Christian families, p.a.	Tables 1	47.5 m	130,137	2.92	47.5 m	0	0
y. Deaths of unevangelized persons, p.a.	Tables 1	13.2 m	36,164	0.81	13.2 m	0	0
z. Unevangelized persons becoming evangelized, p.a.	z=r	78.1 m	213,973	4.79	78.1 m	0	0
z'. Nett increase in unevangelized persons, p.a.	z'=v-y-z	-3.6 m	-9,863	-0.22	-3.6 m	0	0

Notes on lines at left
(to be read in conjunction with column 3).

c. *Population increase.* For analysis by countries and continents, see Table 17-A in *World population prospects 1998* (United Nations 1998:199-579). For definition by Worlds A,B,C, see Part 2: Glossary.

d. *Births.* Children born to Christian parents are enumerated as Christians (see evidence in *WCE* 1982:47-48).

e. *Converts.* Mainly from tribal religions, animism, shamanism.

g. *Baptisms.* 27% adult baptisms, 73% child baptisms. On average, 80% of all new Christians become baptized.

i. *Defectors.* Mainly to non-religion (agnosticism, secularism), atheism, also to Islam, New Religions, eastern cults; mostly due to marriage to non-Christians.

k. *Non-Christian births and deaths.* These occur as shown (lines k,n) both in World A and in World B.

q. *Newly-evangelized.* These are composed of (a) unevangelized persons who become evangelized for the first time in the course of the year, plus (b) children born to Christians.

v. The only way that individuals can become unevangelized is by birth—being born into a non-Christian family.

w. All children born to unevangelized families in World A start as unevangelized individuals themselves, at the worst disadvantage of any children on earth.

x. *Non-Christian births.* Children born to evangelized non-Christians in World B are reckoned to begin life unevangelized (and hence to immediately be located in World A).

Global Diagram 4. Four megatypologies of renewal for enumerating empirical global Christianity, AD 33-AD 2025.

This presentation depicts the 4 major ways in which Christians and their organizations measure and enumerate the empirical reality here termed global Christianity. The 4 megatypologies are first shown as the line of 4 separate schemes for segmentizing the globe. Under each of these 4 globes, 11 descriptors explain each megatypology. The 4 ways divide up global Christianity under 4 distinct and separate megatypologies of renewal—the never-ending struggle to revive and renew Christians worldwide and to cause them to obey and conform to Christ's original intentions concerning what his church should be.

However, the 4 schemes are not entirely divergent since they overlap at several points and in fact consist simply of differing arrangements of the same 7 basic building blocks or slices. These 7 are set out in the single large globe below. To the left of this globe, each slice is defined and enumerated. Above the globe, the major aggregate categories in this measuring of global Christianity are also enumerated. On the globe's right these categories are related to the 7 slices. Below the globe are described the 6 vertical segments which depict the 4 historical megablocs involved in ecumenical and evangelical conciliar Christianity (Orthodox, Roman Catholic, Anglican, Protestant) and the 2 mainly nonconciliar megablocs (Independent, Marginal Christian).

All statistics describing these components, for each of the world's peoples, languages, cities, provinces, countries, regions, continents, and for the whole globe, can be accessed via these codes on the related CD, the *World Christian database*.

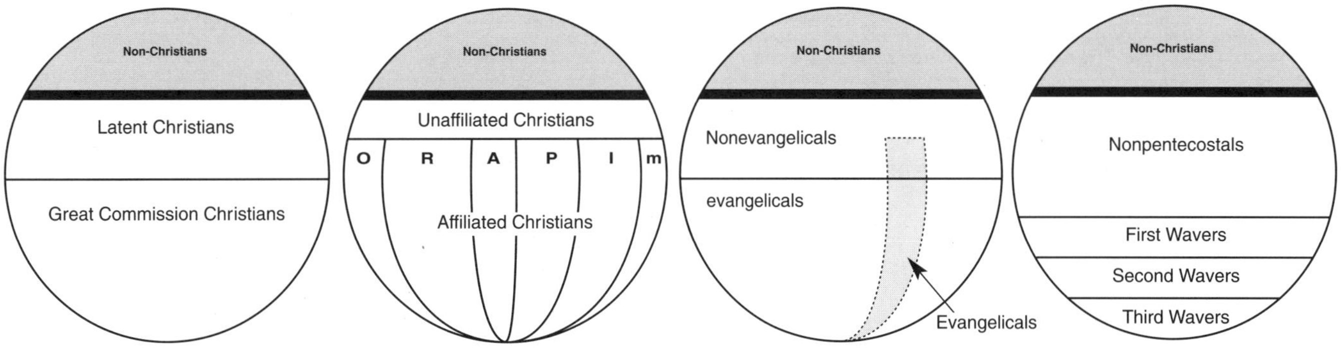

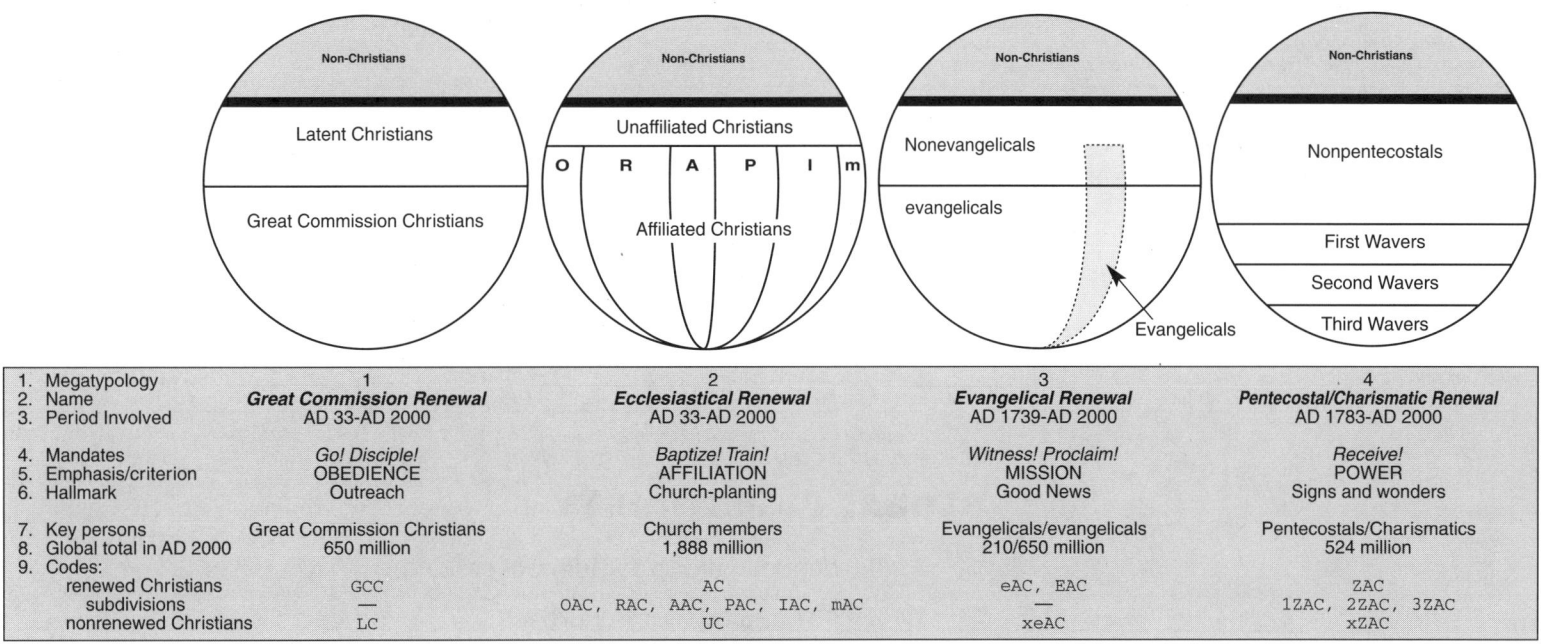

	1	2	3	4
1. Megatypology	1	2	3	4
2. Name	***Great Commission Renewal***	***Ecclesiastical Renewal***	***Evangelical Renewal***	***Pentecostal/Charismatic Renewal***
3. Period Involved	AD 33-AD 2000	AD 33-AD 2000	AD 1739-AD 2000	AD 1783-AD 2000
4. Mandates	*Go! Disciple!*	*Baptize! Train!*	*Witness! Proclaim!*	*Receive!*
5. Emphasis/criterion	OBEDIENCE	AFFILIATION	MISSION	POWER
6. Hallmark	Outreach	Church-planting	Good News	Signs and wonders
7. Key persons	Great Commission Christians	Church members	Evangelicals/evangelicals	Pentecostals/Charismatics
8. Global total in AD 2000	650 million	1,888 million	210/650 million	524 million
9. Codes:				
renewed Christians	GCC	AC	eAC, EAC	ZAC
subdivisions	—	OAC, RAC, AAC, PAC, IAC, mAC	—	1ZAC, 2ZAC, 3ZAC
nonrenewed Christians	LC	UC	xeAC	xZAC

HOW MAJOR AGGREGATE CATEGORIES OVERLAP (see arrows at below right)

Aggregate categories	*Groups of slices*		*Codes and their components*	*Total persons*
Non-Christians	0	=	X	4,055 million
Christians	1-6	=	C = UC + AC	2,000 million
Affiliated Christians	2-6	=	AC = OAC + RAC + AAC + PAC + IAC + mAC + 2AC	1,888 million
Great Commission Christians	3-6	=	GCC = pAC = eAC	650 million
Pentecostals/Charismatics	4-6	=	ZAC = 1ZAC + 2ZAC + 3ZAC	524 million
Charismatics	5-6	=	2ZAC + 3ZAC	460 million
Neocharismatics (Third-Wavers)	6	=	3ZAC	286 million
Nonpentecostals	1-3	=	xZAC	1,475 million
Evangelicals	7	=	EAC	210 million
evangelicals	3-6	=	eAC	650 million
Nonevangelicals	1-2	=	xeAC	1,349 million
Latent Christians	1-2	=	LC	1,349 million

MEANING OF EACH SLICE, 0 TO 7

Slice	*Code*	*Segments of the globe* *Meaning*	*Total persons*
0	X	Non-Christians	4,055 million
1	UC	Unaffiliated Christians	111 million
2	xpAC	Nonpracticing members	1,238 million
3	GCC - ZAC	Nonpentecostal GCCs	126 million
4	1ZAC	Pentecostals	64 million
5	2ZAC	Charismatics	173 million
6	3ZAC	Neocharismatics	286 million
7	EAC	Evangelicals (grey)	210 million

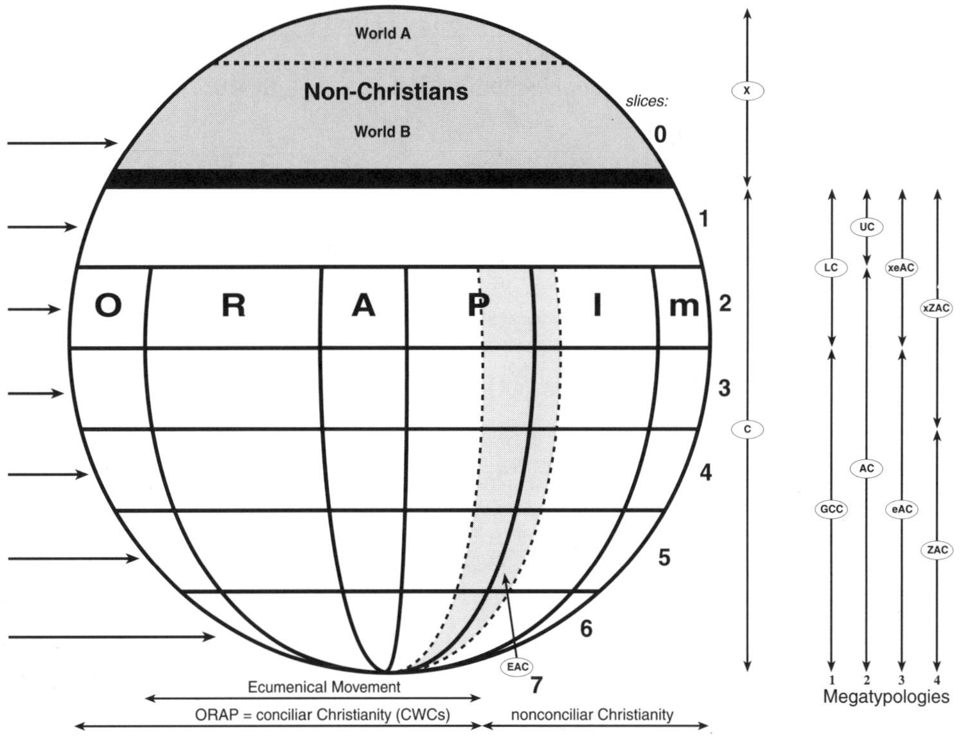

MEANING OF 6 VERTICAL MEGABLOCS (stretching from their code letters to the bottom)

Megabloc:	Orthodox	Roman Catholics	Anglicans	Protestants	Independents	Marginal Christians
Code:	O–	R–	A–	P–	I–	m–
Traditions:	40	20	25	100	200	30
Total affiliated:	215 million	1,057 million	80 million	342 million	386 million	26 million

Global Diagram 5. The rise of global Christianity across the 20th century showing the rise of global Independency out of global denominationalism, AD 1900-2025.

The rise and growth of global Independency is shown in the globes below covering the years 1900, 1970, 2000, and 2025 assuming current trends continue. Vertical slices represent the 6 megablocs (Orthodox, Roman Catholic, Anglican, Protestant, Independent, marginal Christian). The light grey balloon from 1970 to 2025 represents the size and ecclesiastical location of the whole Pentecostal/Charismatic/Neocharismatic Renewal in the Holy Spirit.

The table then analyzes the 6 totals for global Christianity shown at center below the globes. It does it for the year 1970, shown throughout by all numbers in light type. It does the same for the year AD 2000, shown throughout by all numbers in **black** type. This results in 91 pairs of figures showing AD 1970-2000 trends.

Next, the table dichotomizes the whole of Christianity into the *denominationalist* world (Christians organized into the 5 historic megablocs; shown in the lefthand half of the table), and the *postdenominationalist* world (the more recent Independent megabloc that rejects historic denominationalism; shown in the righthand half of the table). This results in 88 denominationalist/postdenominationalist comparisons.

Large-size percentage numbers are meant primarily to be compared horizontally (% meaning percent of each's global total at top). Small-size percentage numbers are meant primarily to be compared vertically (% meaning percent of nearest large-size number above each).

The table then gives 176 numbers which, when read horizontally analyze Christianity into 88 dichotomous pairs or parallels between the 1970 situation and the AD 2000 situation. These numbers can also be read vertically as 72 vertical comparisons arranged in 8 vertical trichotomies followed by 64 vertical dichotomies.

The bottom 5 lines enumerate the 3 Waves of the Pentecostal/ Charismatic/Neocharismatic Renewal by means of 40 different numbers. The first of these 5 lines gives 8 figures enumerating the whole Renewal (First and Second Waves on the left, Third Wave on the right). The following 2 pairs of 2 lines each analyze the Renewal in 16 horizontal dichotomies and 16 vertical dichotomies.

The rise of Renewal since 1900 (light grey balloon)

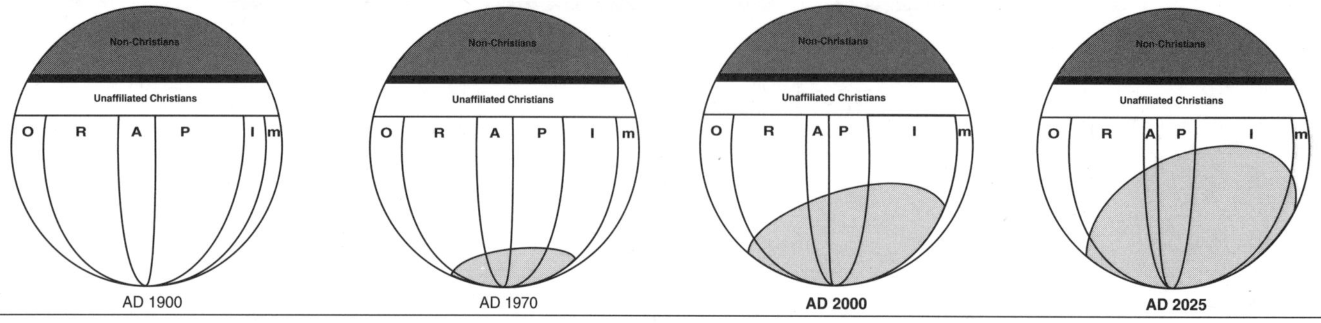

In the year 1970 (light figures in table below)
*In the year AD 2000 (**black** figures in table below)*

GLOBAL CHRISTIANITY

had
26,350 **33,820** denominations/paradenominations
with
1,391,020 **3,445,000** congregations/churches
composed of
1,130 million **1,888 million** affiliated Christians
dichotomized into
the 2 global categories below

1. DENOMINATIONALISM (in megablocs O,R,A,P,m)

1970	2000		%	%
		which had		
10,680	**11,830**	**traditional denominations**	41	**35**
		of which		
9,930	**7,100**	were clearcut denominationalist	93	**60**
530	**2,960**	were less markedly denominationalist	5	**25**
220	**1,770**	were borderline denominationalist/postdenominationalist	2	**15**
		all of which had		
975,620	**1,654,000**	**congregations/churches**	70	**48**
		of which		
965,860	**1,157,800**	were clearcut denominationalist	99	**70**
9,760	**496,200**	were borderline denominationalist	1	**30**
926,840	**1,405,900**	were affiliated to mainline denominations	95	**85**
48,780	**248,100**	were in minor minidenominations	5	**15**
83,100	**463,000**	were Pentecostal/Charismatic	10	**28**
892,520	**1,191,000**	were nonpentecostal/noncharismatic	90	**72**
		all of which had		
1,042 million	**1,502 million**	**Christians** (in O,R,A,P,m)	92	**80**
		of whom		
625 million	**451 million**	were personal denominationalists	60	**30**
416 million	**1,051 million**	were just Christians who happened to be there	40	**70**
1,011 million	**1,202 million**	were in mainline denominations	97	**80**
31 million	**300 million**	were in minor minidenominations	3	**20**
1,018 million	**1,265 million**	were nonpentecostal/noncharismatic Christians	97	**84**
24 million	**237 million**	were Pentecostals/Charismatics	2	**16**
		of this line above (which = the First & Second Waves)		
21 million	**64 million**	were Pentecostals (First-Wavers)	2	**4**
3 million	**173 million**	were Charismatics (Second-Wavers)	0	**12**
		and of that same line above		
1 million	**20 million**	also adopted Third-Wave identity	0	**1**
23 million	**217 million**	did not relate to Third-Wave activities	2	**15**

2. POSTDENOMINATIONALISM (in megabloc I)

1970	2000		%	%
		which had		
15,670	**21,990**	**paradenominations/networks**	59	**65**
		of which		
470	**1,760**	were clearcut apostolic networks	3	**8**
10,500	**5,500**	were looser groupings of churches	67	**25**
4,700	**14,730**	were postdenominationalist new denominations	30	**67**
		all of which had		
415,400	**1,791,000**	**congregations/churches**	30	**52**
		of which		
332,320	**1,773,000**	were clearcut postdenominationalist	80	**99**
83,080	**18,000**	were borderline postdenominationalist	20	**1**
170,310	**1,433,000**	were affiliated to independent networks	41	**80**
245,090	**358,000**	were independent single congregations	59	**20**
195,240	**1,522,000**	were clearly pentecostal/charismatic	47	**85**
220,160	**269,000**	were nonpentecostal/noncharismatic	53	**15**
		all of which had		
95 million	**386 million**	**Christians** (Independents, I)	8	**20**
		of whom		
38 million	**270 million**	were personal postdenominationalists	40	**70**
57 million	**116 million**	were just Christians who happened to be there	60	**30**
30 million	**293 million**	were in independent networks	32	**76**
65 million	**93 million**	were in independent single congregations	68	**24**
42 million	**100 million**	were nonpentecostals/noncharismatics	44	**26**
53 million	**286 million**	were independent pentecostals/charismatics/neocharismatics	56	**74**
		of this line above (which = the Third Wave, termed Neocharismatics)		
18 million	**91 million**	were personal pentecostals (Third-Wavers)	19	**24**
35 million	**195 million**	were personal charismatics (Third-Wavers)	37	**50**
		and of that same line above		
1 million	**31 million**	subsequently affiliated also to the First Wave	1	**8**
52 million	**255 million**	did not relate to First or Second Waves	55	**66**

Global Diagram 6. The phenomenon of martyrdom: 70 million Christians killed for their faith in 220 countries across 20 centuries.

At the heart of the Great Commission, the 3rd of the 7 Mandates is the command 'Witness!' Because living as a witness to Christ (NT Greek *martys*) often resulted in persecution and death, by the end of the 1st century AD, *martys* had taken on today's connotations of the 'martyr' who witnesses to Christ by his death.

Table 5-1 includes 2 columns (58, 59) that describe the whole extent of Christian martyrdom and its martyrs—defined by 5 criteria: believers in Christ, who have lost their lives, prematurely, in situations of witness, as a result of human hostility. These results are based on a 30-year research investigation into the extent of martyrdom in Christian history up to the present day, in every part of the world, and across all traditions of Christianity.

The diagram sets descriptive data on the phenomena of martyrdom onto a background diagram showing the expansion of Christianity in all its traditions over 20 centuries. History's 76 worst situations of mass martyrdom (over 100,000 each) are then shown as black crosses or dots, the latest being Amin's Uganda massacres in 1971, the Sudan holocaust of 1963-1999, and the Rwanda genocide of 1994. Numerous other equally dangerous situations have been averted because the persecutors have been alarmed by the prospect of international opprobrium.

Although 'martyr' on this page means almost exclusively a witness to Christ, the one exception is a single table below (bottom right) which puts Christian martyrs in the context of all persons regarded as martyrs by their own non-Christian religions—Islam, Hinduism, Buddhism, Judaism, et alia. All such martyrs share with Christian martyrs in this greatest of deprivations of human rights.

The effect of Christian martyrdom on evangelization over the centuries has been profound. Naturally, Christians have almost always insisted that martyrdom should not be deliberately sought for; but when it happens, the news spreads widely, and unbelievers including persecutors are converted. Martyrdom can be termed the final witness, the complete personal statement of faith in Christ, the ultimate proclamation of the gospel.

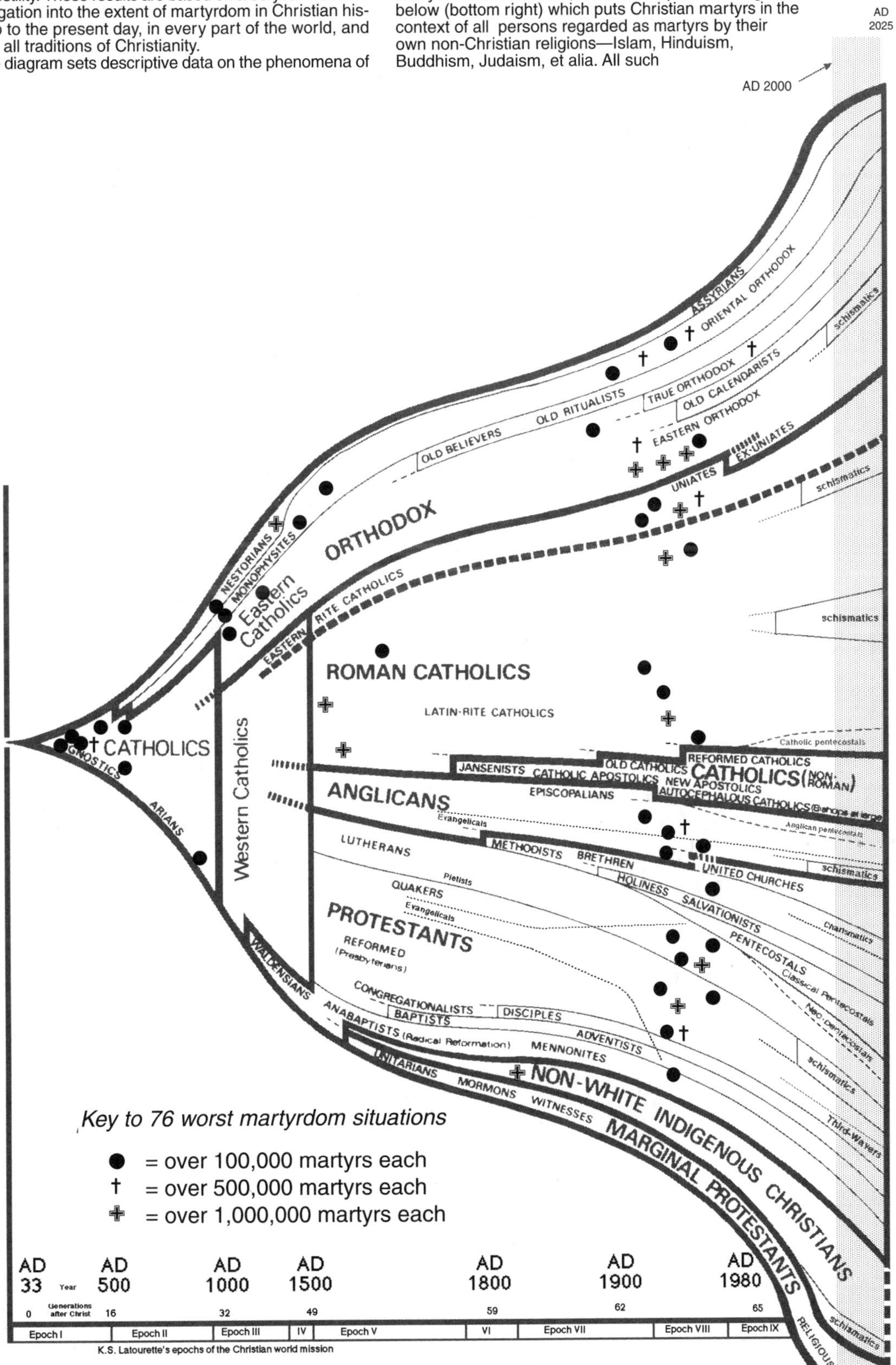

LONG-TERM EFFECT ON EVANGELIZATION
Countries with lengthy history of martyrs, now fully evangelized: 210
Countries with many martyrs, massive church growth today: 40
Countries with few or no martyrs, no church growth today: 30
Church leaders martyred over 20 centuries: 3,000
Workers martyred over 20 centuries: 400,000

For every martyr in history:
(no direct causation implied)
Persons on Earth: 531
Persons evangelized: 193
Christians converted: 127
Persons newly evangelized p.a. per martyr, 1990-2000: 690

AD 2000 AD 2025

TOTAL PERSONS, AD 33-2000
All persons born since AD 33: 36,831 million
All persons evangelized since AD 33: 13,366 million (36% of human race)
All Christians since AD 33: 8,816 million (24% of human race)
All martyrs killed since AD 33: 69,420,000
Martyrs as % all Christians ever: 0.8%
Martyrs among all Christian leaders ever: 2.0%

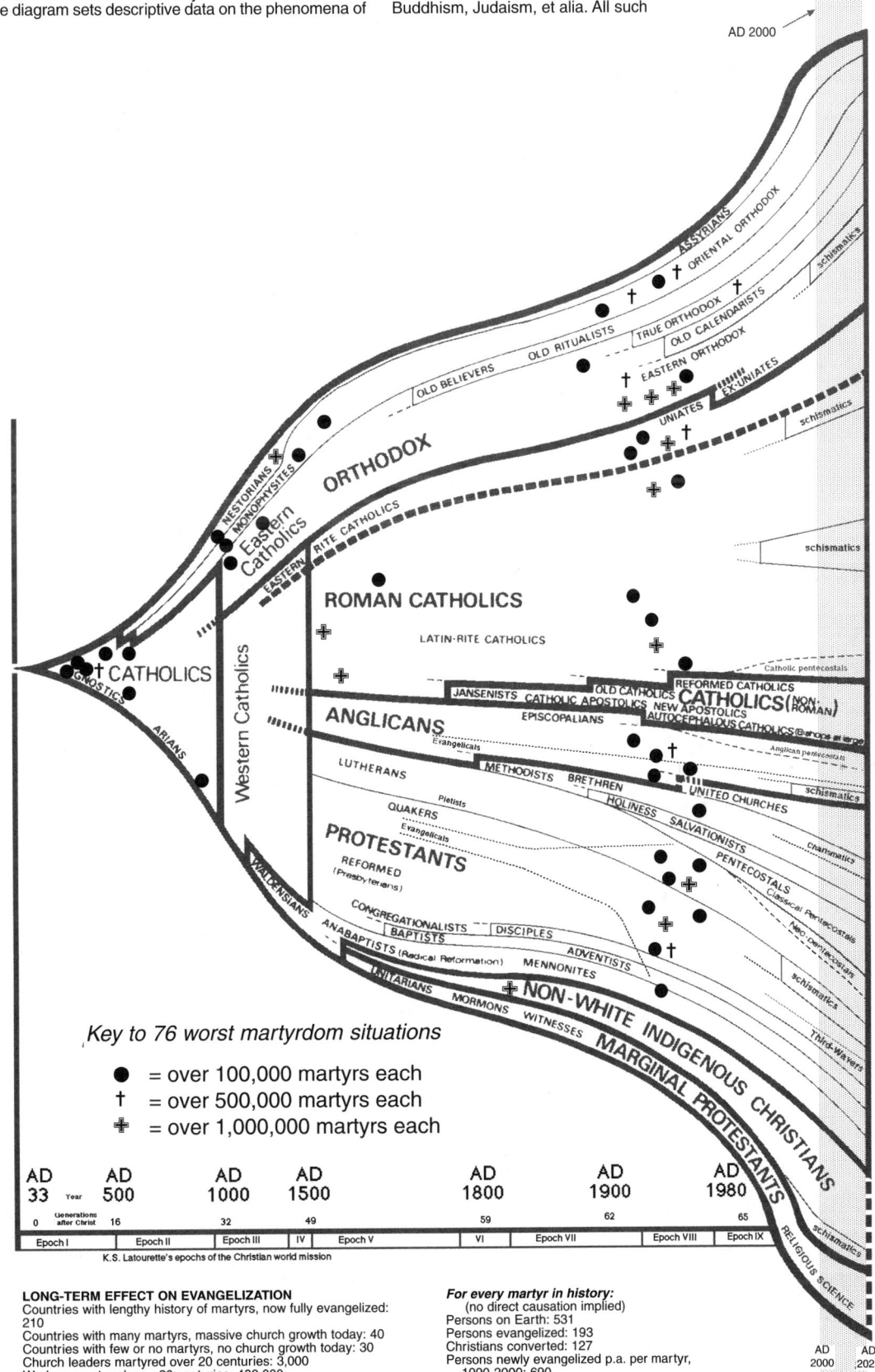

HISTORICAL OVERVIEW, AD 33-2000
600 major martyrdom situations over 20 centuries
76 with over 100,000 martyrs each
27 with over 500,000 martyrs each
15 with over 1 million martyrs each
Average martyrs per martyrdom situation: 115,000
Martyrdom loci: in 220 countries
Ecclesiastical traditions involved: all 300
Denominations with own martyrs: 4,000

CONFESSION OF VICTIMS, AD 33-2000
(total martyrs of each tradition)

Eastern Orthodox	37,444,000
East Syrians (Nestorians)	12,400,000
Roman Catholics (after AD 1000)	11,000,000
Protestants	3,170,000
Gregorians (Armenian Apostolic)	1,220,000
Coptic Orthodox	1,070,000
Anglicans	983,000
Catholics (before AD 1000)	838,000
Ethiopian Orthodox	651,000
West Syrians (Jacobites)	351,700
Maronites	153,000
Non-White indigenous Christians	140,000
Total all martyrs	69,420,000

PERSECUTORS AND THEIR VICTIMS, AD 33-2000

Persecutors responsible	*Martyrs*
Secular governments	55,597,000
Atheists (overlap with above)	31,519,000
Muslims	9,101,000
Ethnoreligionists (animists)	7,469,000
Roman Catholics	4,951,000
Quasi-Christians	2,711,000
Buddhists (Mahayana)	1,811,000
Hindus	676,000
Eastern Orthodox	600,000
Zoroastrians (Parsis)	384,000
Other non-Christians	250,000
Other Christians	220,000
SUBTOTALS:	
Non-Christian persecutors	64,100,000
Christian persecutors	5,320,000
Total all martyrs	69,420,000

SITUATION BY AD 2000 (p.a.= per year)
Martyrs in 20th century (1900-2000): 45,400,000
Martyrs since 1950: 13,300,000
Average annual martyrs since 1950: 278,000 p.a.
Recent annual martyrs: 171,000 p.a.
Current annual martyrs: 160,000 p.a.
Countries heavily involved in AD 2000: 50

CONFESSION OF VICTIMS, AD 2000
(average annual martyrdom rates)

Roman Catholics	100,000
Protestants	30,000
Orthodox	14,000
Non-White indigenous Christians	10,000
Marginal Protestants	5,000
Anglicans and Old Catholics	1,000
Total martyrs p.a	160,000

LIKELIHOOD (L%) OF BEING MARTYRED
(at current rates)

Full-time workers	*L%*	*Per year*
Bishops	5.0	15
Evangelists	4.0	133
Catechists	3.5	175
Foreign missionaries	3.0	131
Clergy	2.0	303
All Christian workers	2.0	1,700
Monks, brothers	1.9	63
Sisters, nuns	1.8	300
Other Christians		
Great Commission Christians	1.6	80,000
Christians (all kinds)	1.0	160,000

MARTYRDOM IN WORLD RELIGIONS SINCE ORIGIN (persons regarded as martyrs by their own religions)

Islam:	Muslim martyrs	80 million
Christianity:	Christian martyrs	70 million
Hinduism:	Hindu martyrs	20 million
Buddhism:	Buddhist martyrs	10 million
Judaism:	Jewish martyrs	9 million
Ethnoreligions	Ethnic martyrs	6 million
Others:	Other religious martyrs	5 million
Sikhism:	Sikh martyrs	2 million
Baha'i:	Baha'i martyrs	1 million

Continued from page 5

Christian. Each's totals of denominations, congregations (churches), adult members, and all affiliated adherents including children reveal a large number of significant trends across the 20th century, and, if present trends continue, well into the 21st century also.

Table 1-4 divides Table 1-1 and its religions by the 6 continents (nowadays termed 'major regions') of United Nations' usage. With 2 continents on each page this table is 3 pages long. A host of trends and minitrends can be observed.

Table 1-5 subdivides the 6 megablocs into their multitudes of Christian ecclesiastical traditions or families.

Table 1-6 is a 2-page chart showing the numerical growth of the Pentecostal/Charismatic/Neocharismatic Renewal in the Holy Spirit, which now encompasses 27.7% of the entire membership of global Christianity. In front of this table is a one-page text commenting on these survey data which arise from the annual megacensus and will be documented in detail on the forthcoming electronic version and forthcoming analytical publication.

Table 1-7 sums up the vast documentation from the megacensus to yield a financial statement of current annual income and expenditures of organized and unorganized global Christianity.

Lastly, Table 1-8 catalogues 93 stages in the translation, production, publication, and availability of the Christian Scriptures and enumerates how many of the world's 13,500 languages are at present situated at each stage.

Comments on statistical Tables 1-1 to 1-8

These Global Tables form a series of interconnected statistical presentations of data. They are derived from the computerized *World Christian database*, which covers all nations, languages, ethnolinguistic, cultures, religions, blocs, traditions, denominations and Christian activities. This database is available as a forthcoming electronic version.

Most figures in these tables are given to the nearest 1,000 or 100 or 10. Many, however, are given to the last digit. This latter should not be taken as implying any bogus claim to precision or exactitude. The reason they are given to the last digit is in order that all totals and sub-totals should add up exactly, and be seen to add up exactly, without which their comprehensibility and credibility would be less satisfactory. When using or quoting all such individual figures, therefore, especially for publication elsewhere, the reader is advised to round them off to the nearest 100 or 1,000, 10,000 or 100,000, or even million, as may best serve his or her purpose.

These tables are built on precisely defined and exactly delimited definitions, which should be carefully examined when particular figures are wanted or are to be used or quoted elsewhere. In particular, they set out a fundamental statistical distinction between 'global Christianity' (world total of all Christians of all categories) and 'global church membership' (world total of Christians affiliated to churches) which should be borne in mind throughout.

Also to be remembered throughout is that all figures, especially those of change or changing situations, report *net* totals of the categories concerned, i.e. births minus deaths, gains minus losses, immigrants minus emigrants, conversions minus defections, and so on.

Table 1-3. Organized Christianity: denominations and memberships on 6 continents in 6 ecclesiastical megablocs, AD 1900-2025.

Continent	Code	Megabloc	Congs 1970	Adults 1970	Congs 1995	Adults 1995	Affiliated, 1900-2025: 1900	1970	1990	1995	2000	2025	Denoms Total 1970	Denoms Total 1995	Countries
1	2	3	4	5	6	7	8	9	10	11	12	13	14	15	16
AFRICA															
		Total	247,100	63,193,000	551,700	151,866,000	8,756,000	117,070,000	255,621,000	294,507,000	335,116,000	600,527,000	5,622	11,496	60
	A	Anglicans	23,600	4,489,000	45,600	19,575,000	369,000	7,729,000	31,820,000	37,595,000	42,542,000	76,119,000	39	40	39
	I	Independent	60,500	9,066,000	213,500	35,555,000	39,000	17,944,000	62,602,000	73,779,000	83,841,000	139,813,000	4,460	9,603	59
	m	Marginal	5,300	380,000	12,600	749,000	1,000	1,004,000	1,811,000	2,098,000	2,427,000	5,547,000	113	183	53
	O	Orthodox	15,100	10,745,000	16,000	16,134,000	4,600,000	18,395,000	27,996,000	31,686,000	35,304,000	59,783,000	59	82	31
	P	Protestant	127,500	12,974,000	252,100	39,755,000	1,837,000	27,292,000	67,032,000	78,224,000	89,000,000	157,300,000	891	1,528	58
	R	Roman Catholic	15,100	25,737,000	11,900	57,522,000	1,910,000	45,073,000	90,655,000	105,622,000	120,386,000	228,295,000	60	60	60
	–	doubly-affiliated		-198,000		-16,377,000		-367,000	-26,295,000	-32,499,000	-38,384,000	-66,330,000			
	–	disaffiliated				-1,047,000				-1,998,000					
ASIA															
		Total	192,100	52,179,000	993,400	148,134,000	20,758,300	97,329,000	243,535,000	276,724,000	307,288,000	459,029,000	2,856	5,258	50
	A	Anglicans	1,200	202,000	1,700	388,000	709,000	361,000	598,000	677,000	727,000	946,000	33	33	32
	I	Independent	80,700	11,104,000	781,300	69,019,000	1,906,000	21,582,000	113,234,000	135,410,000	154,732,000	247,278,000	1,625	3,308	49
	m	Marginal	3,700	323,000	10,600	1,412,000	300	759,000	2,115,000	2,292,000	2,486,000	3,604,000	87	120	41
	O	Orthodox	3,500	5,406,000	6,500	8,041,000	6,864,000	8,967,000	13,926,000	14,351,000	14,113,000	17,351,000	131	191	36
	P	Protestant	89,000	10,398,000	150,800	25,486,000	1,916,000	21,745,000	41,640,000	45,956,000	49,970,000	73,270,000	930	1,555	49
	R	Roman Catholic	14,000	28,512,000	42,500	56,462,000	11,163,000	50,964,000	90,594,000	100,635,000	110,480,000	159,576,000	50	51	49
	–	doubly-affiliated		-3,766,000		-12,674,000	-1,800,000	-7,049,000	-18,572,000	-22,597,000	-25,220,000	-42,996,000			
EUROPE															
		Total	432,900	326,555,000	538,900	370,444,000	368,210,000	468,479,000	528,848,000	534,778,000	536,832,000	532,861,000	2,693	5,083	48
	A	Anglicans	22,200	14,386,000	20,700	13,226,000	24,902,000	29,468,000	26,302,000	26,592,000	26,637,000	26,410,000	29	30	26
	I	Independent	88,300	6,010,000	150,000	13,994,000	82,000	9,894,000	23,281,000	25,089,000	25,724,000	29,302,000	861	1,962	42
	m	Marginal	11,900	891,000	20,500	1,825,000	103,000	1,806,000	3,168,000	3,363,000	3,564,000	4,859,000	270	437	45
	O	Orthodox	55,200	74,990,000	65,100	102,631,000	103,954,000	107,126,000	155,120,000	156,451,000	158,105,000	165,804,000	212	319	40
	P	Protestant	112,800	54,906,000	123,600	52,554,000	59,487,000	82,132,000	76,377,000	76,867,000	77,529,000	77,089,000	1,271	2,285	46
	R	Roman Catholic	142,500	187,635,000	159,000	213,516,000	180,722,000	256,162,000	281,450,000	284,434,000	285,978,000	276,272,000	50	50	47
	–	doubly-affiliated		-5,851,000		-12,060,000	-529,000	-8,181,000	-17,140,000	-17,527,000	-19,737,000	-24,525,000			
	–	disaffiliated		-6,412,000		-15,242,000	-511,000	-9,928,000	-19,710,000	-20,491,000	-20,968,000	-22,350,000			
LATIN AMERICA															
		Total	128,200	149,654,000	419,000	246,880,000	60,026,000	263,595,000	404,399,000	440,039,000	475,660,000	635,271,000	2,814	5,324	46
	A	Anglicans	1,800	376,000	2,100	590,000	726,000	768,000	989,000	1,045,000	1,090,000	1,353,000	44	44	44
	I	Independent	32,500	4,807,000	115,100	19,086,000	29,000	9,242,000	32,902,000	36,357,000	39,706,000	60,022,000	1,174	2,719	44
	m	Marginal	5,600	433,000	28,100	2,368,000	4,000	847,000	5,014,000	5,739,000	6,595,000	13,212,000	165	264	46
	O	Orthodox	300	199,000	400	275,000	6,000	364,000	477,000	490,000	558,000	755,000	53	67	21
	P	Protestant	65,500	7,066,000	189,500	25,763,000	933,000	12,505,000	39,842,000	44,056,000	48,132,000	76,191,000	1,332	2,184	46
	R	Roman Catholic	22,500	143,689,000	83,800	241,369,000	58,689,000	251,791,000	391,772,000	426,725,000	461,220,000	606,059,000	46	46	46
	–	doubly-affiliated		-6,454,000		-41,600,000	-280,000	-11,156,000	-65,113,000	-72,762,000	-79,915,000	-119,774,000			
	–	disaffiliated		-462,000		-971,000	-81,000	-766,000	-1,484,000	-1,611,000	-1,726,000	-2,547,000			
NORTHERN AMERICA															
		Total	407,200	115,477,000	601,800	141,017,000	59,570,000	168,932,000	194,457,000	203,742,000	212,166,000	235,111,000	1,577	4,986	5
	A	Anglicans	10,800	2,824,000	9,100	2,243,000	2,172,000	4,395,000	3,354,000	3,318,000	3,244,000	2,923,000	3	3	3
	I	Independent	144,300	24,455,000	320,300	52,044,000	5,857,000	36,320,000	68,306,000	74,525,000	80,237,000	102,710,000	749	3,687	4
	m	Marginal	29,200	3,904,000	32,100	5,758,000	815,000	6,469,000	9,359,000	9,937,000	10,532,000	17,503,000	240	374	5
	O	Orthodox	1,700	2,995,000	2,600	3,272,000	415,000	4,539,000	5,660,000	6,015,000	6,342,000	7,962,000	54	67	2
	P	Protestant	197,100	44,012,000	209,800	48,994,000	37,300,000	62,812,000	65,135,000	67,732,000	69,978,000	74,765,000	526	850	5
	R	Roman Catholic	24,100	39,346,000	27,900	47,363,000	13,011,000	57,413,000	68,236,000	69,140,000	71,035,000	80,520,000	5	5	5
	–	doubly-affiliated		-2,059,000		-18,655,000		-3,016,000	-25,593,000	-26,925,000	-29,202,000	-51,272,000			
OCEANIA															
		Total	42,100	7,996,000	51,800	11,590,000	4,321,000	14,699,000	18,710,000	20,123,000	21,375,000	28,152,000	512	942	28
	A	Anglicans	10,800	2,052,000	12,500	2,369,000	1,692,000	4,781,000	5,132,000	5,294,000	5,409,000	5,996,000	18	18	18
	I	Independent	2,900	364,000	7,000	785,000	18,000	622,000	1,212,000	1,382,000	1,505,000	2,516,000	120	303	22
	m	Marginal	1,400	131,000	2,200	250,000	4,000	215,000	365,000	422,000	457,000	829,000	71	110	25
	O	Orthodox	200	188,000	300	407,000	4,000	271,000	586,000	631,000	706,000	1,060,000	24	38	3
	P	Protestant	23,800	2,244,000	27,000	3,952,000	1,551,000	4,273,000	6,323,000	6,843,000	7,392,000	10,015,000	252	446	27
	R	Roman Catholic	3,000	3,023,000	2,800	4,967,000	1,052,000	4,549,000	6,994,000	7,595,000	8,228,000	11,240,000	27	27	27
	–	doubly-affiliated		-6,000		-1,140,000		-12,000	-1,902,000	-2,044,000	-2,322,000	-3,504,000			
GLOBE															
		Total	1,449,600	715,054,000	3,156,600	1,069,933,000	521,641,300	1,130,104,000	1,645,570,000	1,769,913,000	1,888,437,000	2,490,951,000	16,074	33,089	237
	A	Anglicans	70,400	24,329,000	91,700	38,391,000	30,570,000	47,502,000	68,195,000	74,521,000	79,649,000	113,747,000	166	168	162
	I	Independent	409,200	55,806,000	1,587,200	190,483,000	7,931,000	95,604,000	301,537,000	346,542,000	385,745,000	581,641,000	8,989	21,582	220
	m	Marginal	57,100	6,062,000	106,100	12,362,000	927,300	11,100,000	21,832,000	23,851,000	26,061,000	45,554,000	946	1,488	215
	O	Orthodox	76,000	94,523,000	90,900	130,760,000	115,843,000	139,662,000	203,765,000	209,624,000	215,128,000	252,715,000	533	764	133
	P	Protestant	615,700	131,600,000	952,800	196,504,000	103,024,000	210,759,000	296,349,000	319,678,000	342,001,000	468,630,000	5,202	8,848	231
	R	Roman Catholic	221,200	427,942,000	327,900	621,199,000	266,547,000	665,952,000	929,701,000	994,151,000	1,057,327,000	1,361,962,000	238	239	234
	–	doubly-affiliated		-18,334,000		-102,506,000	-2,609,000	-29,781,000	-154,615,000	-174,354,000	-194,780,000	-308,401,000			
	–	disaffiliated		-6,874,000		-17,260,000	-592,000	-10,694,000	-21,194,000	-24,100,000	-22,694,000	-24,897,000			

Table 1-4. Adherents of all religions on 6 continents, AD 1900-2000.

1. This table is an expanded version of Table 1-1, adding, as a variable, continents as standardized by the United Nations. Corresponding world totals are given only in Table 1-1 and are not repeated below.
2. Indented rows are subdivisions of the unindented names, and are included in the latter's totals.
3. The order in which all rows are listed is in descending order of total adherents in AD 2000. The same applies to indented listings.
4. For exact definitions of all categories, see (a) Part 3 "Codebook" and/or Part 2 "Glossary" for brief definitions and (b) Part 12 "Dictionary" for expanded definitions.
5. The table is derived from the 238 Tables 1 presented in Part 4 for all countries.
6. Projections to AD 2025 are based on the assumption that current trends continue (for 7 alternate scenarios, see UN Demographic Database).

Continent	1900		mid-1970		1990		Annual change, 1990-2000				mid–1995		mid–2000		mid–2025		Coun
	Adherents	*%*	*Adherents*	*%*	*Adherents*	*%*	*Natural*	*Conversion*	*Total*	*Rate*	*Adherents*	*%*	*Adherents*	*%*	*Adherents*	*%*	*tries*
AFRICA																	
Christians	9,938,588	9.2	143,818,494	40.3	276,497,939	45.0	7,934,453	438,975	8,373,428	2.68	317,625,134	45.6	360,232,182	45.9	633,803,970	48.8	60
crypto-Christians	1,182,778	1.1	4,828,791	1.4	6,897,060	1.1	152,927	16,107	169,034	2.22	7,741,480	1.1	8,587,400	1.1	12,856,150	1.0	19
professing Christians	8,755,810	8.1	138,989,703	38.9	269,600,879	43.9	7,781,526	422,868	8,204,394	2.69	309,883,654	44.5	351,644,782	44.8	620,947,820	47.8	60
unaffiliated Christians	1,182,116	1.1	26,749,534	7.5	20,876,949	3.4	601,857	-177,906	423,951	1.87	23,118,061	3.3	25,116,432	3.2	33,277,700	2.6	60
affiliated Christians	8,756,472	8.1	117,068,960	32.8	255,620,990	41.6	7,332,594	616,885	7,949,479	2.74	294,507,073	42.3	335,115,750	42.7	600,526,270	46.3	60
Roman Catholics	1,909,812	1.8	45,072,986	12.6	90,655,340	14.7	2,754,331	218,760	2,973,091	2.88	105,621,883	15.2	120,386,235	15.3	228,294,600	17.6	60
Protestants	1,836,980	1.7	27,291,581	7.6	67,031,580	10.9	1,897,041	299,794	2,196,835	2.88	78,224,292	11.2	88,999,928	11.3	157,299,850	12.1	58
Independents	39,200	0.0	17,944,214	5.0	62,601,520	10.2	1,681,764	442,148	2,123,912	2.96	73,779,292	10.6	83,840,642	10.7	139,812,970	10.8	59
Anglicans	369,430	0.3	7,728,519	2.2	31,819,805	5.2	885,332	186,878	1,072,210	2.95	37,594,899	5.4	42,541,902	5.4	76,118,630	5.9	39
Orthodox	4,600,250	4.3	18,395,020	5.2	27,996,330	4.6	774,636	-43,852	730,784	2.35	31,685,766	4.6	35,304,168	4.5	59,783,200	4.6	31
Marginal Christians	800	0.0	1,004,113	0.3	1,811,015	0.3	51,883	9,671	61,554	2.97	2,097,874	0.3	2,426,550	0.3	5,547,290	0.4	53
doubly-affiliated	0	0.0	-367,473	-0.1	-26,294,600	-4.3	-712,389	-496,521	-1,208,910	3.86	-32,499,389	-4.7	-38,383,675	-4.9	-66,330,270	-5.1	59
Trans-megabloc groupings																	
Evangelicals	1,635,410	1.5	16,248,140	4.6	50,590,045	8.2	1,438,677	460,149	1,898,826	3.24	60,995,123	8.8	69,578,305	8.9	136,111,730	10.5	60
Pentecostals/Charismatics	901,000	0.8	17,049,020	4.8	93,703,065	15.2	2,589,538	642,277	3,231,815	3.01	110,454,194	15.9	126,021,202	16.1	227,819,720	17.6	60
Great Commission Christians	3,131,290	2.9	30,357,970	8.5	68,029,710	11.1	1,874,816	404,240	2,279,056	2.93	78,433,785	11.3	90,820,254	11.6	168,833,430	13.0	60
Muslims	34,485,292	32.0	143,095,965	40.1	251,066,766	40.8	6,500,296	130,471	6,630,767	2.37	282,641,990	40.6	317,374,423	40.5	519,347,830	40.0	58
Ethnoreligionists	62,685,865	58.2	67,429,897	18.9	79,519,748	12.9	2,345,361	-616,792	1,728,569	1.99	87,804,160	12.6	96,805,405	12.3	126,051,000	9.7	49
Nonreligious	7,210	0.0	583,740	0.2	3,588,570	0.6	90,144	53,373	143,517	3.42	4,329,925	0.6	5,023,704	0.6	10,575,560	0.8	60
Hindus	279,120	0.3	994,450	0.3	1,939,600	0.3	39,529	1,650	41,179	1.94	2,162,771	0.3	2,351,390	0.3	3,426,660	0.3	32
Baha'is	225	0.0	698,094	0.2	1,383,320	0.2	38,634	-3,679	34,955	2.28	1,546,330	0.2	1,732,816	0.2	3,396,180	0.3	58
Atheists	1,020	0.0	102,600	0.0	332,742	0.1	8,594	135	8,729	2.36	375,570	0.1	420,039	0.1	890,200	0.1	37
Jews	397,900	0.4	205,470	0.1	201,320	0.0	3,962	-2,686	1,276	0.62	205,960	0.0	214,055	0.0	234,100	0.0	22
Buddhists	3,400	0.0	11,650	0.0	107,640	0.0	2,764	-86	2,678	2.25	122,250	0.0	134,409	0.0	293,750	0.0	14
Jains	3,180	0.0	32,810	0.0	56,630	0.0	1,591	-648	943	1.55	60,750	0.0	66,061	0.0	94,650	0.0	5
Other religionists	1,000	0.0	28,750	0.0	54,350	0.0	1,410	-273	1,137	1.92	62,720	0.0	65,707	0.0	121,800	0.0	18
Sikhs	2,200	0.0	25,900	0.0	45,540	0.0	1,180	-425	755	1.54	49,980	0.0	53,076	0.0	100,900	0.0	9
Chinese folk-religionists	1,900	0.0	7,300	0.0	28,285	0.0	573	-166	407	1.35	30,910	0.0	32,351	0.0	57,490	0.0	9
New-Religionists	0	0.0	700	0.0	20,300	0.0	667	147	814	3.43	24,700	0.0	28,436	0.0	43,000	0.0	3
Spiritists	1,000	0.0	2,300	0.0	2,500	0.0	46	-45	1	0.04	2,630	0.0	2,509	0.0	4,400	0.0	2
Zoroastrians	200	0.0	480	0.0	720	0.0	20	-4	16	2.04	780	0.0	881	0.0	1,810	0.0	4
Confucianists	0	0.0	0	0.0	230	0.0	4	-3	1	0.51	240	0.0	242	0.0	500	0.0	1
doubly-professing	0	0.0	0	0.0	-76,300	0.0	-1,690	56	-1,634	1.96	-84,400	0.0	-92,652	0.0	-135,000	0.0	4
World A (unevangelized persons)	85,586,225	79.4	139,973,054	39.2	159,574,355	26.0	4,306,250	-2,584,202	1,722,048	1.03	168,839,893	24.2	176,794,822	22.5	241,415,415	18.6	60
World B (evangelized non-Christians)	12,283,287	11.4	73,247,052	20.5	178,773,906	29.1	4,726,835	2,145,487	6,872,062	3.31	210,581,773	30.2	247,510,682	31.6	423,224,415	32.6	60
World C (Christians)	9,938,588	9.2	143,818,494	40.3	276,497,939	45.0	7,934,453	438,975	8,373,428	2.68	317,625,134	45.6	360,232,182	45.9	633,803,970	48.8	60
CONTINENT'S POPULATION	107,808,100	100.0	357,038,600	100.0	614,846,200	100.0	16,967,538	0	16,967,538	2.47	697,046,800	100.0	784,537,686	100.0	1,298,443,800	100.0	60
ASIA																	
Muslims	156,139,610	16.3	391,407,279	18.2	676,677,775	21.2	15,156,918	463,200	15,620,118	2.10	751,779,485	21.8	832,878,936	22.5	1,219,867,350	25.7	50
Hindus	202,546,700	21.2	460,498,800	21.4	680,830,450	21.3	13,134,205	-705,258	12,428,947	1.69	745,833,820	21.6	805,119,915	21.8	1,040,588,600	21.9	30
Nonreligious	47,100	0.0	428,361,350	19.9	554,696,790	17.4	6,051,811	-662,047	5,389,764	0.93	581,093,525	16.9	608,594,416	16.5	702,802,500	14.8	50
Chinese folk-religionists	379,914,740	39.7	231,589,753	10.8	346,421,374	10.9	3,786,798	-88,160	3,698,638	1.02	367,875,620	10.7	383,407,747	10.4	447,120,300	9.4	23
Buddhists	126,619,501	13.2	232,239,001	10.8	318,863,450	10.0	3,494,084	84,715	3,578,799	1.07	336,973,085	9.8	354,651,462	9.6	408,835,280	8.6	37
Christians	21,897,519	2.3	101,394,552	4.7	248,728,290	7.8	4,046,396	2,365,720	6,412,116	2.32	281,908,145	8.2	312,849,430	8.5	464,800,100	9.8	50
crypto-Christians	2,388,299	0.3	18,185,055	0.9	93,838,820	2.9	1,255,122	754,905	2,010,027	1.96	102,163,531	3.0	113,939,089	3.1	176,334,100	3.7	45
professing Christians	19,509,220	2.0	83,209,197	3.9	154,885,130	4.9	2,791,188	1,610,678	4,401,866	2.53	179,739,214	5.2	198,903,786	5.4	288,451,700	6.1	49
unaffiliated Christians	1,138,810	0.1	4,065,302	0.2	5,194,370	0.2	67,929	-31,253	36,676	0.68	5,183,841	0.2	5,561,122	0.2	5,771,540	0.1	50
affiliated Christians	20,758,709	2.2	97,329,250	4.5	243,533,920	7.6	3,978,465	2,396,976	6,375,441	2.35	276,724,304	8.0	307,288,308	8.3	459,028,560	9.7	50
Independents	1,906,100	0.2	21,581,887	1.0	113,234,010	3.6	1,619,315	2,530,488	4,149,803	3.17	135,410,109	3.9	154,732,021	4.2	247,278,100	5.2	49
Roman Catholics	11,162,799	1.2	50,964,406	2.4	90,593,690	2.8	1,943,413	45,221	1,988,634	2.00	100,634,847	2.9	110,480,013	3.0	159,576,400	3.4	49
Protestants	1,916,480	0.2	21,745,218	1.0	41,639,670	1.3	689,419	143,564	832,983	1.84	45,955,800	1.3	49,969,501	1.4	73,269,600	1.5	49
Orthodox	6,864,220	0.7	8,967,132	0.4	13,926,370	0.4	97,226	-78,518	18,708	0.13	14,351,180	0.4	14,113,465	0.4	17,351,300	0.4	37
Marginal Christians	280	0.0	758,913	0.0	2,114,595	0.1	24,240	12,862	37,102	1.63	2,291,773	0.1	2,485,605	0.1	3,604,060	0.1	41
Anglicans	708,930	0.1	360,997	0.0	598,035	0.0	10,618	2,300	12,918	1.97	677,146	0.0	727,212	0.0	945,500	0.0	35
doubly-affiliated	1,800,100	-0.2	-7,049,303	-0.3	-18,572,450	-0.6	-405,766	-258,939	-664,705	3.11	-22,596,551	-0.7	-25,219,509	-0.7	-42,996,400	-0.9	50
Trans-megabloc groupings																	
Evangelicals	1,332,180	0.1	9,605,330	0.5	25,526,820	0.8	385,199	212,516	597,715	2.13	28,654,777	0.8	31,503,970	0.9	49,075,500	1.0	50
Pentecostals/Charismatics	4,300	0.0	10,144,120	0.5	108,921,565	3.4	1,690,301	906,496	2,596,797	2.16	122,696,550	3.6	134,889,530	3.7	217,550,606	4.6	50
Great Commission Christians	10,529,965	1.1	42,840,670	2.0	157,136,380	4.9	2,201,952	1,273,447	3,475,399	2.02	173,140,495	5.0	191,890,345	5.2	292,839,260	6.2	50
Ethnoreligionists	50,564,090	5.3	90,872,440	4.2	117,696,230	3.7	1,723,368	-663,140	1,060,228	0.87	123,190,410	3.6	128,298,498	3.5	147,975,620	3.1	35
Atheists	7,000	0.0	109,602,500	5.1	115,632,080	3.6	1,262,073	-630,754	631,319	0.53	119,570,720	3.5	121,945,250	3.3	135,461,900	2.9	43
New-Religionists	5,910,000	0.6	77,448,720	3.6	91,097,790	2.9	1,017,149	-62,994	954,155	1.00	96,191,135	2.8	100,639,356	2.7	112,430,400	2.4	21
Sikhs	2,959,900	0.3	10,378,800	0.5	18,645,520	0.6	357,406	20,107	377,513	1.86	20,465,290	0.6	22,420,618	0.6	30,206,460	0.6	17
Confucianists	640,050	0.1	4,758,050	0.2	5,823,610	0.2	55,441	-11,452	43,989	0.73	6,042,160	0.2	6,263,506	0.2	6,771,100	0.1	7
Jews	411,200	0.0	2,418,950	0.1	3,298,630	0.1	115,036	-1,975	113,061	2.99	3,924,295	0.1	4,429,230	0.1	5,811,500	0.1	29
Jains	1,320,100	0.1	2,585,000	0.1	3,806,840	0.1	72,900	-39,088	33,812	0.85	3,827,370	0.1	4,144,959	0.1	6,014,000	0.1	4
Baha'is	5,900	0.0	1,411,530	0.1	2,811,995	0.1	55,963	10,355	66,318	2.14	3,034,140	0.1	3,475,167	0.1	5,483,000	0.1	46
Shintoists	6,720,000	0.7	4,173,000	0.2	3,025,790	0.1	7,966	-40,662	-32,696	-1.14	2,778,340	0.1	2,698,820	0.1	2,042,950	0.0	6
Taoists	375,000	0.0	1,734,000	0.1	2,392,090	0.1	25,301	-172	25,129	1.00	2,541,250	0.1	2,643,380	0.1	3,052,800	0.1	4
Zoroastrians	108,290	0.0	121,000	0.0	1,895,530	0.1	44,723	12,066	56,789	2.66	2,193,650	0.1	2,463,407	0.1	4,311,140	0.1	14
Mandeans	8,000	0.0	23,000	0.0	31,600	0.0	823	-85	738	2.12	35,000	0.0	38,977	0.0	58,000	0.0	2
Other religionists	1,000	0.0	10,950	0.0	19,286	0.0	339	42	381	1.82	21,260	0.0	23,094	0.0	35,000	0.0	5
Spiritists	500	0.0	1,200	0.0	1,880	0.0	20	-16	4	0.21	1,900	0.0	1,919	0.0	3,000	0.0	1
doubly-professing	0	0.0	-4,000,000	-0.2	-11,803,000	-0.4	-213,094	-50,402	-263,496	2.04	-12,998,600	-0.4	-14,437,985	-0.4	-20,530,000	-0.4	20
World A (unevangelized persons)	781,294,400	81.7	1,455,175,150	67.7	1,472,841,080	46.1	23,976,662	-28,878,336	-4,901,674	-0.34	1,478,527,050	42.9	1,423,824,293	38.5	1,572,484,800	33.2	50
World B (evangelized non-Christians)	153,004,281	16.0	594,460,173	27.6	1,470,827,630	46.1	22,172,722	26,512,539	48,685,184	2.91	1,688,845,405	49	1,960,314,364	53	2,706,386,100	57.1	50
World C (Christians)	21,897,519	2.3	101,394,552	4.7	248,728,290	7.8	4,046,396	2,365,720	6,412,116	2.32	281,908,145	8.2	312,849,430	8.5	464,800,100	9.8	50
CONTINENT'S POPULATION	956,196,200	100.0	2,151,029,875	100.0	3,192,397,000	100.0	50,195,626	0	50,195,626	1.48	3,449,280,600	100.0	3,696,988,087	100.0	4,743,671,000	100.0	50

Continued overleaf

Table 1-4 continued

Continent	1900 Adherents	%	mid-1970 Adherents	%	1990 Adherents	%	Annual change, 1990-2000 Natural	Conversion	Total	Rate	mid–1995 Adherents	%	mid–2000 Adherents	%	mid–2025 Adherents	%	Countries
EUROPE																	
Christians	380,642,840	94.5	492,694,892	75.1	550,418,843	76.2	606,981	315,389	922,370	0.17	557,493,375	76.6	559,642,545	76.8	554,586,470	79.0	48
crypto-Christians	0	0.0	35,683,780	5.4	965,000	0.1	-4,138	-69,362	-73,500	-13.36	250,000	0.0	230,000	0.0	200,000	0.0	20
professing Christians	380,642,840	94.5	457,011,112	69.6	549,453,843	76.1	611,118	384,752	995,870	0.18	557,243,375	76.6	559,412,545	76.8	554,386,470	78.9	48
unaffiliated Christians	12,433,130	3.1	24,215,164	3.7	21,570,990	3.0	49,825	74,175	124,000	0.56	22,715,007	3.1	22,810,974	3.1	21,725,420	3.1	48
affiliated Christians	368,209,710	91.5	468,479,728	71.4	528,847,853	73.2	557,158	241,216	798,374	0.15	534,778,368	73.5	536,831,571	73.7	532,861,050	75.9	48
Roman Catholics	180,722,280	44.9	256,162,441	39.1	281,449,879	39.0	512,817	-60,025	452,792	0.16	284,434,435	39.1	285,977,773	39.2	276,272,080	39.3	47
Orthodox	103,954,150	25.8	107,125,809	16.3	155,120,280	21.5	-190,755	489,243	298,488	0.19	156,451,050	21.5	158,105,154	21.7	165,804,370	23.6	40
Protestants	59,486,600	14.8	82,131,881	12.5	76,376,594	10.6	232,580	-117,342	115,238	0.15	76,867,425	10.6	77,528,973	10.6	77,089,120	11.0	46
Anglicans	24,902,110	6.2	29,467,936	4.5	26,302,100	3.6	59,403	-25,865	33,538	0.13	26,591,699	3.7	26,637,479	3.7	26,410,100	3.8	26
Independents	81,880	0.0	9,894,261	1.5	23,280,700	3.2	-12,095	256,396	244,301	1.00	25,088,864	3.5	25,723,708	3.5	29,301,690	4.2	42
Marginal Christians	103,400	0.0	1,806,202	0.3	3,168,280	0.4	6,307	33,253	39,560	1.18	3,363,096	0.5	3,563,880	0.5	4,858,970	0.7	45
doubly-affiliated	-529,310	-0.1	-8,180,697	-1.3	-17,140,346	-2.4	-6,682	-252,993	-259,675	1.42	-17,527,431	-2.4	-19,737,096	-2.7	-24,525,280	-3.5	48
disaffiliated	-511,400	-0.1	-9,928,105	-1.6	-19,709,634	-2.7	-44,420	-81,447	-125,867	0.62	-20,490,770	-2.8	-20,968,300	-2.9	-22,350,000	-3.2	4
Trans-megabloc groupings																	
Evangelicals	32,357,300	8.0	22,026,770	3.4	20,899,286	2.9	36,546	27,884	64,430	0.30	21,385,735	2.9	21,543,577	3.0	22,043,420	3.1	48
Pentecostals/Charismatics	20,000	0.0	8,018,180	1.2	33,455,365	4.6	35,970	375,364	411,334	1.17	36,097,106	5.0	37,568,700	5.2	47,179,505	6.7	48
Great Commission Christians	49,767,490	12.4	128,476,980	19.6	185,297,970	25.7	305,743	410,668	716,411	0.38	189,712,000	26.1	192,462,065	26.4	198,404,720	28.3	48
Nonreligious	1,543,180	0.4	85,949,228	13.1	109,190,130	15.1	48,724	-283,602	-234,878	-0.22	108,755,640	14.9	106,841,391	14.7	86,237,350	12.3	47
Muslims	9,234,890	2.3	17,622,610	2.7	29,206,045	4.0	6,035	229,994	236,029	0.78	29,866,635	4.1	31,566,311	4.3	36,004,880	5.1	44
Atheists	205,300	0.1	53,915,110	8.2	25,883,952	3.6	-1,250	-294,909	-296,159	-1.21	24,030,535	3.3	22,922,349	3.1	16,767,600	2.4	41
Jews	9,926,800	2.5	4,283,800	0.7	2,654,830	0.4	1,654	-14,430	-12,776	-0.49	2,564,160	0.4	2,527,051	0.4	2,107,420	0.3	43
Buddhists	401,000	0.1	551,700	0.1	1,347,265	0.2	2,336	17,644	19,980	1.39	1,477,595	0.2	1,547,050	0.2	2,236,220	0.3	21
Hindus	60	0.0	243,390	0.0	1,243,370	0.2	1,133	16,115	17,248	1.31	1,343,165	0.2	1,415,843	0.2	1,706,770	0.2	15
Ethnoreligionists	619,500	0.2	586,100	0.1	1,213,860	0.2	-633	5,523	4,890	0.40	1,270,120	0.2	1,262,760	0.2	1,150,570	0.2	17
Chinese folk-religionists	0	0.0	60,000	0.0	228,650	0.0	662	2,004	2,666	1.11	243,450	0.0	255,310	0.0	350,600	0.1	11
Sikhs	0	0.0	200,000	0.0	228,200	0.0	508	574	1,082	0.46	233,560	0.0	239,021	0.0	281,300	0.0	3
Other religionists	23,770	0.0	209,650	0.0	222,180	0.0	765	583	1,348	0.59	231,310	0.0	235,660	0.0	294,600	0.0	17
New-Religionists	0	0.0	33,100	0.0	141,400	0.0	561	1,088	1,649	1.11	150,040	0.0	157,887	0.0	223,200	0.0	9
Spiritists	10,000	0.0	36,400	0.0	110,170	0.0	348	1,908	2,256	1.88	123,800	0.0	132,711	0.0	167,100	0.0	9
Baha'is	210	0.0	56,810	0.0	106,635	0.0	246	2,066	2,312	1.98	120,275	0.0	129,706	0.0	204,440	0.0	39
Confucianists	0	0.0	1,000	0.0	9,960	0.0	24	50	74	0.72	10,500	0.0	10,697	0.0	14,600	0.0	3
Zoroastrians	0	0.0	410	0.0	610	0.0	2	3	5	0.75	640	0.0	657	0.0	980	0.0	3
World A (unevangelized persons)	9,756,171	2.4	39,724,130	6.1	26,444,795	3.7	-5,200	-491,862	-497,062	-2.06	23,820,585	3.3	21,474,187	3.0	19,454,895	2.8	48
World B (evangelized non-Christians)	12,208,539	3.0	124,025,178	18.9	145,342,462	20.1	66,903	176,179	242,788	0.17	146,600,840	20.1	147,770,217	20.3	128,292,735	18.3	48
World C (Christians)	380,642,840	94.5	492,694,892	75.1	550,418,843	76.2	606,981	315,389	922,370	0.17	557,493,375	76.6	559,642,545	76.8	554,586,470	79.0	48
CONTINENT'S POPULATION	402,607,550	100.0	656,444,200	100.0	722,206,100	100.0	668,096	0	668,096	0.09	727,914,800	100.0	728,886,949	100.0	702,334,100	100.0	48
LATIN AMERICA																	
Christians	62,002,925	95.2	269,200,550	94.5	409,345,790	92.9	7,426,256	-250,598	7,175,658	1.63	445,272,855	92.8	481,102,373	92.7	641,115,950	92.0	46
crypto-Christians	0	0.0	497,700	0.2	900,000	0.2	4,852	2,148	7,000	0.75	940,000	0.2	970,000	0.2	1,100,000	0.2	1
professing Christians	62,002,925	95.2	268,702,850	94.4	408,445,790	92.7	7,421,404	-252,746	7,168,658	1.63	444,332,855	92.6	480,132,373	92.5	640,015,950	91.9	46
unaffiliated Christians	1,976,165	3.0	5,603,853	2.0	4,946,049	1.1	86,666	-36,923	49,743	0.96	5,232,160	1.1	5,443,473	1.1	5,845,230	0.8	46
affiliated Christians	60,026,760	92.2	263,596,697	92.6	404,399,741	91.8	7,339,592	-213,676	7,125,916	1.64	440,040,695	91.7	475,658,900	91.6	635,270,720	91.2	46
Roman Catholics	58,689,470	90.1	251,791,319	88.4	391,772,330	88.9	7,116,888	-172,120	6,944,768	1.65	426,725,018	88.9	461,220,001	88.8	606,059,020	87.0	46
Protestants	932,550	1.4	12,505,263	4.4	39,842,016	9.1	657,274	171,695	828,969	1.91	44,056,347	9.2	48,131,716	9.3	76,191,140	10.9	46
Independents	29,400	0.1	9,242,347	3.3	32,901,772	7.5	531,782	148,677	680,459	1.90	36,357,171	7.6	39,706,358	7.7	60,021,780	8.6	44
Marginal Christians	3,820	0.0	847,347	0.3	5,014,205	1.1	91,012	67,098	158,110	2.78	5,739,146	1.2	6,595,300	1.3	13,211,790	1.9	46
Anglicans	726,120	1.1	767,559	0.3	989,380	0.2	12,199	-2,177	10,022	0.97	1,045,447	0.2	1,089,611	0.2	1,352,770	0.2	44
Orthodox	6,400	0.0	364,263	0.1	477,000	0.1	7,470	580	8,050	1.57	490,315	0.1	557,500	0.1	755,170	0.1	21
disaffiliated	-81,000	-0.1	-765,843	-0.3	-1,483,500	-0.3	-23,366	-904	-24,270	1.53	-1,610,984	-0.3	-1,726,200	-0.3	-2,547,450	-0.4	6
doubly-affiliated	-280,000	-0.4	-11,155,558	-3.9	-65,113,462	-14.8	-1,053,669	-426,523	-1,480,192	2.07	-72,761,765	-15.2	-79,915,386	-15.4	-119,773,500	-17.2	46
Trans-megabloc groupings																	
Evangelicals	766,300	1.2	9,565,160	3.4	32,743,665	7.4	535,045	224,713	759,758	2.11	36,638,382	7.6	40,341,240	7.8	64,498,400	9.3	46
Pentecostals/Charismatics	10,000	0.0	12,621,450	4.4	118,629,420	26.9	1,994,890	285,456	2,280,346	1.77	130,166,167	27.1	141,432,880	27.2	202,277,880	29.0	46
Great Commission Christians	2,406,110	3.7	18,717,550	6.6	43,679,515	9.9	721,004	141,193	862,197	1.82	47,937,015	10.0	52,301,448	10.1	79,053,905	11.4	46
Nonreligious	372,340	0.6	5,842,940	2.1	12,657,905	2.9	175,515	151,524	327,039	2.32	14,489,910	3.0	15,928,252	3.1	25,799,710	3.7	46
Spiritists	257,040	0.4	4,557,880	1.6	9,902,865	2.3	135,393	78,217	213,610	1.97	10,863,185	2.3	12,038,942	2.3	15,836,080	2.3	38
Atheists	9,900	0.0	1,265,110	0.4	2,359,000	0.5	29,565	10,238	39,803	1.57	2,564,010	0.5	2,757,006	0.5	3,671,800	0.5	32
Muslims	57,710	0.1	488,630	0.2	1,373,320	0.3	20,296	9,572	29,868	1.99	1,546,300	0.3	1,672,011	0.3	2,638,130	0.4	40
Ethnoreligionists	2,244,540	3.5	1,150,610	0.4	1,094,475	0.3	21,914	-2,518	19,396	1.64	1,181,245	0.3	1,288,429	0.3	1,304,850	0.2	21
Jews	23,110	0.0	794,580	0.3	1,060,995	0.2	16,123	-7,974	8,149	0.74	1,094,265	0.2	1,142,465	0.2	1,227,360	0.2	33
Baha'is	0	0.0	299,350	0.1	657,845	0.2	14,700	6,795	21,495	2.87	763,205	0.2	872,757	0.2	1,577,280	0.2	46
Hindus	163,160	0.3	527,340	0.2	702,710	0.2	5,490	996	6,486	0.89	732,870	0.2	767,572	0.2	968,750	0.1	29
Buddhists	5,930	0.0	389,200	0.1	546,700	0.1	9,038	996	10,034	1.70	590,030	0.1	647,013	0.1	1,081,660	0.2	31
New-Religionists	0	0.0	167,910	0.1	518,835	0.1	7,907	2,406	10,313	1.83	578,025	0.1	621,961	0.1	982,860	0.1	16
Chinese folk-religionists	1,600	0.0	68,870	0.0	161,650	0.0	3,248	-21	3,227	1.84	176,085	0.0	193,932	0.0	281,920	0.0	29
Other religionists	4,045	0.0	40,530	0.0	81,210	0.0	1,301	378	1,679	1.89	89,995	0.0	97,974	0.0	149,850	0.0	29
Shintoists	0	0.0	2,000	0.0	6,000	0.0	90	-9	81	1.27	6,300	0.0	6,805	0.0	10,000	0.0	1
Confucianists	0	0.0	0	0.0	400	0.0	6	-2	4	1.05	420	0.0	444	0.0	600	0.0	1
World A (unevangelized persons)	1,762,315	2.7	4,906,660	1.7	2,020,630	0.5	28,229	-35,832	-7,603	-0.38	2,000,893	0.4	1,944,600	0.4	2,544,325	0.4	46
World B (evangelized non-Christians)	1,377,060	2.1	10,688,290	3.8	29,103,280	6.6	412,357	286,703	698,787	2.18	32,674,952	6.8	36,090,963	7	52,986,525	7.6	46
World C (Christians)	62,002,925	95.2	269,200,550	94.5	409,345,790	92.9	7,426,256	-250,598	7,175,658	1.63	445,272,855	92.8	481,102,373	92.7	641,115,950	92.0	46
CONTINENT'S POPULATION	65,142,300	100.0	284,795,500	100.0	440,469,700	100.0	7,866,842	0	7,866,842	1.66	479,948,700	100.0	519,137,936	100.0	696,646,800	100.0	46

Continued opposite

Table 1-4 concluded

Continent	1990 Adherents	%	mid-1970 Adherents	%	1990 Adherents	%	Annual change, 1990-2000 Natural	Conversion	Total	Rate	mid–1995 Adherents	%	mid–2000 Adherents	%	mid–2025 Adherents	%	Countries
NORTHERN AMERICA																	
Christians	78,811,550	96.6	211,419,760	91.3	240,458,450	85.3	2,354,524	-337,930	2,016,594	0.81	251,482,205	84.7	260,624,388	84.2	290,345,170	79.9	5
professing Christians	78,811,550	96.6	211,419,760	91.3	240,458,450	85.3	2,354,524	-337,930	2,016,594	0.81	251,482,205	84.7	260,624,388	84.2	290,345,170	79.9	5
unaffiliated Christians	19,241,860	23.6	42,487,820	18.4	46,001,485	16.3	449,770	-204,161	245,609	0.52	47,739,109	16.1	48,457,570	15.7	55,233,100	15.2	5
affiliated Christians	59,569,690	73.0	168,931,940	73.0	194,456,965	69.0	1,904,754	-133,768	1,770,986	0.88	203,743,096	68.7	212,166,818	68.5	235,112,070	64.7	5
Independents	5,856,800	7.2	36,320,074	15.7	68,305,890	24.2	656,301	536,822	1,193,123	1.62	74,525,264	25.1	80,237,120	25.9	102,710,220	28.3	4
Roman Catholics	13,011,300	15.9	57,413,009	24.8	68,235,790	24.2	681,677	-401,765	279,912	0.40	69,140,333	23.3	71,034,904	22.9	80,520,490	22.1	5
Protestants	37,299,590	45.7	62,811,885	27.1	65,135,355	23.1	634,364	-150,054	484,310	0.72	67,732,067	22.8	69,978,450	22.6	74,765,120	20.6	5
Marginal Christians	815,000	1.0	6,469,233	2.8	9,359,145	3.3	90,494	26,785	117,279	1.19	9,937,278	3.4	10,531,930	3.4	17,503,380	4.8	5
Orthodox	415,000	0.5	4,538,550	2.0	5,660,000	2.0	55,375	12,825	68,200	1.14	6,015,253	2.0	6,342,000	2.1	7,962,000	2.2	2
Anglicans	2,172,000	2.7	4,395,191	1.9	3,353,700	1.2	34,282	-45,232	-10,950	-0.33	3,318,042	1.1	3,244,200	1.1	2,922,700	0.8	3
doubly-affiliated	0	0.0	-3,016,002	-1.3	-25,592,915	-9.1	-247,737	-113,150	-360,887	1.33	-26,925,141	-9.1	-29,201,786	-9.4	-51,271,840	-14.1	5
Trans-megabloc groupings																	
Evangelicals	33,479,300	41.0	33,103,210	14.3	39,598,010	14.0	384,047	-24,867	359,180	0.87	41,725,462	14.1	43,189,810	14.0	50,365,020	13.9	5
Pentecostals/Charismatics	46,100	0.1	24,151,910	10.4	67,231,220	23.8	651,772	585,122	1,236,894	1.70	73,997,060	24.9	79,600,160	25.7	110,204,580	30.3	5
Great Commission Christians	11,562,270	14.2	52,335,120	22.6	98,657,250	35.0	970,387	293,187	1,263,574	1.21	105,328,980	35.5	111,292,984	35.9	136,413,220	37.5	5
Nonreligious	1,010,000	1.2	10,699,100	4.6	24,142,465	8.6	237,460	195,549	433,009	1.66	26,281,665	8.9	28,472,554	9.2	44,855,650	12.3	5
Jews	1,516,400	1.9	6,994,020	3.0	5,885,020	2.1	57,123	-43,203	13,920	0.23	5,980,020	2.0	6,024,219	2.0	6,560,040	1.8	3
Muslims	10,050	0.0	842,000	0.4	3,810,010	1.4	37,040	26,929	63,969	1.56	4,105,010	1.4	4,449,696	1.4	6,520,040	1.8	3
Buddhists	40,410	0.1	216,050	0.1	2,060,025	0.7	20,140	43,935	64,075	2.75	2,350,020	0.8	2,700,766	0.9	5,420,020	1.5	3
Atheists	2,000	0.0	300,000	0.1	1,190,000	0.4	12,431	36,601	49,032	3.51	1,435,000	0.5	1,680,320	0.5	2,250,000	0.6	2
Hindus	1,000	0.0	120,000	0.1	975,000	0.4	9,884	25,303	35,187	3.13	1,190,000	0.4	1,326,862	0.4	2,050,000	0.6	2
Chinese folk-religionists	75,120	0.1	120,000	0.1	756,000	0.3	8,938	851	9,789	1.23	807,000	0.3	853,886	0.3	945,000	0.3	2
New-Religionists	0	0.0	112,000	0.1	590,000	0.2	5,676	19,541	25,217	3.62	707,000	0.2	842,169	0.3	961,000	0.3	2
Baha'is	2,800	0.0	162,350	0.1	628,675	0.2	6,076	9,616	15,692	2.25	712,335	0.2	785,587	0.3	1,201,400	0.3	5
Other religionists	11,000	0.0	460,020	0.2	546,045	0.2	5,258	-197	5,061	0.89	568,445	0.2	596,648	0.2	830,080	0.2	3
Sikhs	0	0.0	8,000	0.0	400,000	0.1	4,427	8,326	12,753	2.81	462,300	0.2	527,533	0.2	760,000	0.2	2
Ethnoreligionists	145,170	0.2	82,500	0.0	289,460	0.1	2,785	12,654	15,439	4.37	395,970	0.1	443,860	0.1	506,300	0.1	3
Spiritists	0	0.0	4,000	0.0	130,650	0.1	1,274	726	2,000	1.43	144,300	0.1	150,653	0.1	192,200	0.1	3
Zoroastrians	0	0.0	0	0.0	61,400	0.0	634	990	1,624	2.37	69,530	0.0	77,638	0.0	124,000	0.0	2
Shintoists	0	0.0	0	0.0	50,000	0.0	478	144	622	1.18	53,900	0.0	56,220	0.0	70,000	0.0	1
Taoists	0	0.0	0	0.0	10,000	0.0	96	17	113	1.08	10,600	0.0	11,134	0.0	13,500	0.0	1
Jains	0	0.0	0	0.0	5,000	0.0	48	148	196	3.36	6,000	0.0	6,959	0.0	7,000	0.0	1
World A (unevangelized persons)	156,300	0.2	1,131,727	0.5	4,106,052	1.5	40,639	26,108	66,747	1.52	4,472,272	1.5	4,773,514	1.5	8,625,455	2.4	5
World B (evangelized non-Christians)	2,657,650	3.3	18,988,313	8.2	37,423,698	13.3	369,365	311,704	680,951	1.69	40,806,823	13.8	44,233,190	14.3	64,640,775	17.8	5
World C (Christians)	78,811,550	96.6	211,419,760	91.3	240,458,450	85.3	2,354,524	-337,930	2,016,594	0.81	251,482,205	84.7	260,624,388	84.2	290,345,170	79.9	5
CONTINENT'S POPULATION	81,625,500	100.0	231,539,800	100.0	281,988,200	100.0	2,764,292	0	2,764,292	0.94	296,761,300	100.0	309,631,092	100.0	363,611,400	100.0	5
OCEANIA																	
Christians	4,838,150	77.5	17,845,126	92.4	22,010,352	83.3	340,036	-30,117	309,919	1.33	23,641,309	83.0	25,109,520	82.6	32,010,392	80.7	28
professing Christians	4,838,150	77.5	17,845,126	92.4	22,010,352	83.3	340,036	-30,117	309,919	1.33	23,641,309	83.0	25,109,520	82.6	32,010,392	80.7	28
unaffiliated Christians	516,431	8.3	3,146,438	16.3	3,299,410	12.5	49,095	-5,535	43,560	1.25	3,519,505	12.4	3,734,974	12.3	3,858,795	9.7	27
affiliated Christians	4,321,719	69.2	14,698,688	76.1	18,710,942	70.8	290,939	-24,579	266,360	1.34	20,121,804	70.6	21,374,546	70.3	28,151,597	71.0	28
Roman Catholics	1,052,096	16.8	4,549,395	23.6	6,993,955	26.5	108,615	14,766	123,381	1.64	7,594,923	26.7	8,227,767	27.1	11,239,665	28.4	27
Protestants	1,551,415	24.8	4,273,450	22.1	6,323,401	23.9	113,356	-6,488	106,868	1.57	6,842,666	24.0	7,392,067	24.3	10,015,097	25.3	28
Anglicans	1,692,178	27.1	4,780,810	24.8	5,132,405	19.4	69,656	-42,004	27,652	0.53	5,293,760	18.6	5,408,938	17.8	5,996,255	15.1	18
Independents	17,560	0.3	621,951	3.2	1,211,960	4.6	18,791	10,499	29,290	2.19	1,381,589	4.9	1,504,858	5.0	2,515,860	6.4	22
Orthodox	4,190	0.1	270,800	1.4	585,600	2.2	6,948	5,132	12,080	1.89	630,828	2.2	706,400	2.3	1,059,800	2.7	3
Marginal Christians	4,280	0.1	214,616	1.1	365,275	1.4	5,356	3,813	9,169	2.26	421,770	1.5	456,965	1.5	829,240	2.1	25
doubly-affiliated	0	0.0	-12,334	-0.1	-1,901,654	-7.2	-31,782	-10,298	-42,080	2.02	-2,043,732	-7.2	-2,322,449	-7.6	-3,504,320	-8.8	28
Trans-megabloc groupings																	
Evangelicals	2,155,730	34.5	2,900,548	15.0	3,914,329	14.8	60,088	-6,911	53,177	1.28	4,020,269	14.1	4,446,081	14.6	5,740,665	14.5	28
Pentecostals/Charismatics	0	0.0	238,240	1.2	3,545,837	13.4	54,432	17,539	71,971	1.87	3,928,858	13.8	4,265,522	14.0	6,519,303	16.4	28
Great Commission Christians	533,975	8.6	4,424,195	22.9	7,865,136	29.8	106,123	12,755	118,878	1.42	8,511,344	29.9	9,053,891	29.8	12,034,360	30.4	28
Nonreligious	43,800	0.7	659,109	3.4	2,841,189	10.8	35,293	10,362	45,655	1.50	3,066,174	10.8	3,297,727	10.9	4,848,625	12.2	27
Atheists	900	0.0	215,000	1.1	320,830	1.2	3,909	462	4,371	1.29	342,820	1.2	364,544	1.2	502,580	1.3	6
Hindus	13,400	0.2	213,730	1.1	307,780	1.2	3,868	818	4,686	1.43	328,855	1.2	354,643	1.2	489,760	1.2	5
Muslims	13,372	0.2	71,309	0.4	223,279	0.9	2,790	5,012	7,802	3.04	259,295	0.9	301,292	1.0	497,223	1.3	8
Buddhists	6,530	0.1	16,580	0.1	181,450	0.7	2,555	9,405	11,960	5.19	251,830	0.9	301,027	1.0	477,700	1.2	19
Ethnoreligionists	1,299,320	20.8	156,810	0.8	221,635	0.8	5,131	-537	4,594	1.90	246,805	0.9	267,563	0.9	258,810	0.7	17
Baha'is	400	0.0	29,215	0.2	83,217	0.3	1,539	1,180	2,719	2.87	97,595	0.3	110,387	0.4	199,850	0.5	24
Jews	16,800	0.3	66,600	0.3	88,160	0.3	1,064	-179	885	0.96	91,505	0.3	97,019	0.3	112,930	0.3	4
New-Religionists	0	0.0	0	0.0	28,030	0.1	440	3,407	3,847	9.02	48,735	0.2	66,488	0.2	79,750	0.2	9
Chinese folk-religionists	12,678	0.2	19,310	0.1	55,293	0.2	907	-86	821	1.39	59,314	0.2	63,506	0.2	87,250	0.2	15
Confucianists	0	0.0	150	0.0	21,340	0.1	264	-27	237	1.06	22,400	0.1	23,708	0.1	31,150	0.1	3
Sikhs	200	0.0	5,000	0.0	12,820	0.1	156	379	535	3.55	15,350	0.1	18,164	0.1	29,200	0.1	3
Other religionists	300	0.0	11,200	0.1	8,900	0.0	116	-62	54	0.59	8,820	0.0	9,436	0.0	11,100	0.0	4
Spiritists	500	0.0	1,000	0.0	6,600	0.0	82	-42	40	0.59	6,740	0.0	7,001	0.0	9,000	0.0	2
Zoroastrians	0	0.0	0	0.0	1,000	0.0	12	25	37	3.18	1,200	0.0	1,367	0.0	2,000	0.0	1
World A (unevangelized persons)	1,116,325	17.9	334,390	1.7	483,818	1.8	7,327	621	7,948	1.53	543,904	1.9	563,298	1.9	880,428	2.2	28
World B (evangelized non-Christians)	291,875	4.7	1,130,623	5.9	3,917,705	14.8	50,917	29,437	80,295	1.88	4,303,534	15.1	4,720,574	15.5	6,756,500	17	28
World C (Christians)	4,838,150	77.5	17,845,126	92.4	22,010,352	83.3	340,036	-30,117	309,919	1.33	23,641,309	83.0	25,109,520	82.6	32,010,392	80.7	28
CONTINENT'S POPULATION	6,246,350	100.0	19,310,139	100.0	26,411,875	100.0	398,162	0	398,162	1.41	28,488,747	100.0	30,393,392	100.0	39,647,320	100.0	28

Table 1-5. Organized Christianity: global membership ranked by 6 major ecclesiastico-cultural megablocs and 300 major traditions, AD 1970-2025.

a. This table is derived from the 238 Country Tables 2 in Part 4 "Countries" for all countries.

b. All figures are given to the last digit in order that totals here, and in all other tables, shall add up exactly. When quoting any aggregate or global figures in these tables, therefore, they should be rounded, either to the nearest thousand, or ten thousand, or 0.1%, or 1% as may be appropriate to the reader's requirements.

c. *Meaning of columns.*

1. *Ecclesiastical bloc.* On these 6 lines are given the global statistical totals applicable to each bloc, and also, at the end of the table, for global church membership.

1-2. *Ecclesiastical tradition.* Under each of the 6 blocs are specified each's major constituent ecclesiastical traditions, listed in their codes' alphabetical order. First comes the 3-letter code as used in Tables 2, then the full name of each tradition. At the end of each listing for a bloc, the line 'Other' (whose code in Tables 2 is a blank space) then sums any smaller residual, aggregate or unspecified traditions in that bloc.

3-4. *Congregations* (worship centers) and adult church members (all referring to the year 1995). These two columns are totals derived directly by addition from columns in Country Tables 2 for all countries..

5-6. *Affiliated church members* (total Christian community) in 1970 and 1995.

7-12. *Denominations.* A denomination is defined in this Encyclopedia as an organized aggregate of worship centers or congregations of similar ecclesiastical tradition within a specific country; i.e as an organized Christian church or tradition or religious group or community of believers, within a specific country, whose component congregations and members are called by the same denominational name in different areas, regarding themselves as one autonomous Christian church distinct from other denominations, churches and traditions. As defined here, world Christianity consists of 6 major ecclesiastico-cultural blocs, divided into 300 major ecclesiastical traditions, composed of over 33, 000 distinct denominations in 238 countries, these denominations themselves being composed of over 3,400,000 worship centers, churches or congregations.

7-8. *Significant.* This word refers to those denominations which are significantly large, important or otherwise significant in a country's context for each to have its own single line in the country's Table 2.

9-12. *Total distinct denominations,* significant and less significant (or relatively insignificant), the latter being smaller bodies too small to each be enumerated with its own single line in Tables 2; for the years 1970, 1990, 1995, 2000, and 2025 assuming current trends continue.

13. *Countries.* Number of countries (out of 238) where this tradition exists.

MEGABLOC Tradition code 1	name 2	Congs 1995 3	Adults 1995 4	Affiliated 1970 5	Affiliated 1995 6	Denominations Sig 1970 7	Sig 1995 8	Total 1970 9	1995 10	2000 11	2025 12	Countries Count 13
ORTHODOX		90,900	130,759,000	139,662,000	209,624,000	431	466	533	764	781	887	133
O-Alb	Albanian/Greek-speaking (Orthodox)	600	221,000	198,000	537,000	6	6	6	6	6	6	4
O-Ara	Arabic- or Arabic/Greek-speaking Orthodox	1,100	722,000	777,000	1,380,000	31	31	31	31	31	31	29
O-Arm	Armenian Orthodox (Gregorian)	1,100	3,314,000	2,573,000	5,593,000	49	50	49	50	50	51	47
O-Bul	Bulgarian Orthodox	4,200	4,636,000	5,688,000	6,384,000	18	20	18	20	20	22	20
O-Bye	Byelorussian/Belorussian (White Russian/White Ruthenian)	900	3,177,000	4,528,000	4,854,000	7	7	7	7	7	7	6
O-Cop	Coptic Orthodox	2,500	5,403,000	6,180,000	9,234,000	20	24	20	24	25	28	24
O-Cze	Czech/Slavonic-speaking Orthodox	100	40,000	60,000	50,000	1	1	1	1	1	1	1
O-Est	Estonian Orthodox	100	130,000	277,000	209,000	5	5	5	5	5	5	5
O-Eth	Ethiopic, Ethiopian Orthodox, GeOez-speaking	13,100	10,647,000	11,932,000	21,902,000	13	15	13	15	15	17	15
O-Fin	Finnish/Slavonic-speaking Orthodox	40	44,000	58,000	65,000	2	2	2	2	2	2	2
O-Geo	Georgian Orthodox	600	1,156,000	1,268,000	2,589,000	9	9	9	9	9	9	9
O-Gre	Greek Orthodox	36,000	10,315,000	12,280,000	14,912,000	77	78	77	78	78	79	72
O-Hun	Hungarian/Slavonic-speaking Orthodox	40	30,000	40,000	50,000	1	1	1	1	1	1	1
O-Lav	Latvian Orthodox	100	200,000	200,000	250,000	1	1	1	1	1	1	1
O-Mac	Macedonian Orthodox	1,000	922,000	1,128,000	1,259,000	5	5	5	5	5	5	5
O-Mol	Moldavian Orthodox	200	902,000	1,151,000	1,303,000	2	3	2	3	3	4	3
O-Nes	Assyrian or Nestoran (East Syrian, Messihaye (Christians)	200	138,000	121,000	243,000	18	19	18	19	19	20	18
O-Pol	Polish/Slavonic-speaking Orthodox	400	642,000	547,000	1,021,000	2	2	2	2	2	2	2
O-Rum	Romanian Orthodox	8,300	13,135,000	16,108,000	19,271,000	21	23	21	23	23	25	23
O-Rus	Russian Orthodox	11,200	50,310,000	41,570,000	80,451,000	55	58	55	58	59	61	51
O-Ser	Serbian Orthodox	3,100	3,963,000	6,284,000	7,286,000	19	22	19	22	23	25	21
O-Slo	Slovak Orthodox	10	11,000	216,000	22,000	1	1	1	1	1	1	1
O-SyM	Syro-Malabarese (Eastern Syrian), Syriac/Malayalam-speaking	1,600	1,339,000	1,424,000	2,251,000	11	12	11	12	12	13	12
O-Syr	Syrian, Syriac-speaking Orthodox or Syro-Antiochian	700	449,000	208,000	1,018,000	17	24	17	24	25	31	24
O-Ukr	Ukrainian Orthodox	3,100	18,703,000	24,686,000	27,121,000	9	10	9	10	10	11	9
ROMAN CATHOLIC		328,000	621,200,000	665,954,000	994,154,000	239	240	239	240	242	245	235
R-Arm	Armenian (Eastern-rite Catholic)	100	98,000	189,000	151,000	–	–	–	–	–	–	15
R-Bul	Bulgarian (Byzantine rite)	30	12,000	7,000	20,000	–	–	–	–	–	–	1
R-Byz	Byzantine-rite (jurisdiction for more than one ethnic group)	100	112,000	190,000	154,000	–	–	–	–	–	–	3
R-Cha	Chaldean (Eastern Syrian rite)	100	178,000	281,000	312,000	–	–	–	–	–	–	9
R-Cop	Coptic (Alexandrian rite)	200	111,000	107,000	190,000	–	–	–	–	–	–	1
R-Eth	Ethiopic, Alexandrian rite	200	83,000	87,000	141,000	–	–	–	–	–	–	2
R-Gre	Greek (Byzantine rite)	10	2,000	3,000	2,000	–	–	–	–	–	–	2
R-Hun	Hungarian (Byzantine rite)	200	211,000	269,000	281,000	–	–	–	–	–	–	1
R-IAb	Italo-Albanian (Byzantine rite)	100	52,000	68,000	62,000	–	–	–	–	–	–	1
R-LEr	jurisdiction for both Latin-rite and Eastern-rite Catholics	600	782,000	2,110,000	1,599,000	36	37	36	37	38	40	9
R-Lat	Latin-rite Catholic	315,300	609,777,000	653,710,000	975,673,000	203	203	203	203	204	205	229
R-Mal	Malankara (Syro-Antiochian,Eastern Syrian), Syro-Malankarese	900	183,000	202,000	311,000	–	–	–	–	–	–	1
R-Mar	Maronite (Syro-Antiochian, Western Syrian)	1,000	1,802,000	1,030,000	2,976,000	–	–	–	–	–	–	11
R-Mel	Melkite (Byzantine, Greek Catholic; Arabic-speaking)	500	633,000	353,000	1,116,000	–	–	–	–	–	–	12
R-Ori	plural Oriental (jurisdiction for several Eastern rites)	40	172,000	129,000	255,000	–	–	–	–	–	–	3
R-Rum	Romanian Byzantine rite	1,600	1,509,000	1,563,000	2,012,000	–	–	–	–	–	–	2
R-Rus	Russian (Byzantine rite)	2	7,000	3,000	10,000	–	–	–	–	–	–	1
R-Rut	Ruthenian (Byzantine rite)	400	249,000	130,000	391,000	–	–	–	–	–	–	2
R-Slo	Slovak (Byzantine rite)	300	170,000	10,000	239,000	–	–	–	–	–	–	2
R-SyM	Syro-Malabarese (Eastern Syrian)	2,600	1,797,000	2,017,000	3,055,000	–	–	–	–	–	–	1
R-Syr	Syrian, Syriac-speaking (Syro-Antiochian, West Syrian)	100	61,000	75,000	111,000	–	–	–	–	–	–	7
R-Ukr	Ukrainian Byzantine rite	3,700	3,201,000	3,422,000	5,093,000	–	–	–	–	–	–	10
ANGLICAN		91,800	38,392,000	47,501,000	74,521,000	166	168	166	168	168	179	162
A-ACa	Anglo-Catholic	5,000	1,105,000	1,424,000	1,965,000	38	38	38	38	38	38	39
A-Cen	Central or Broad Church Anglican	5,500	5,094,000	10,204,000	9,292,000	31	31	31	31	31	32	32
A-Ecu	Ecumenical (Anglican/Protestant/Orthodox joint parishes)	700	80,000	0	120,000	0	1	0	1	1	1	1
A-Eva	Anglican Evangelical, Evangelical Anglican	18,500	7,841,000	5,355,000	15,345,000	11	11	11	11	11	14	12
A-Hig	High Church Anglican (Prayer Book Catholic)	12,800	3,452,000	5,805,000	7,604,000	31	31	31	31	31	33	30
A-Low	Low Church Anglican (Conservative Evangelical)	15,800	10,786,000	4,459,000	20,065,000	15	15	15	15	15	16	15
A-plu	Anglican, of plural or mixed traditions	33,500	10,034,000	20,254,000	20,129,000	40	41	40	41	41	45	41
PROTESTANT		947,000	195,757,000	210,037,000	318,027,000	2,933	3,399	5,198	8,844	8,973	9,490	231
P-Adv	Adventist	34,000	5,966,000	4,189,000	11,011,000	195	214	195	214	218	233	199
P-Bap	Baptist	125,400	31,520,000	27,726,000	48,133,000	266	313	266	313	322	360	163
P-CBr	Christian Brethren (Plymouth Brethren; Open only)	16,700	1,341,000	1,535,000	2,798,000	120	124	120	124	125	128	113
P-Con	Congregational, Congregationalist	11,500	1,385,000	1,893,000	2,438,000	81	85	81	85	86	89	55
P-Dis	Disciple, Restorationist, Restorationist Baptist, Christian	6,700	1,053,000	2,455,000	1,919,000	13	17	13	17	18	21	18
P-Dun	Dunker (Tunker), Dipper, German Baptist, Brethren	2,100	322,000	465,000	603,000	10	10	10	10	10	10	7
P-EBr	Exclusive Brethren (Plymouth Brethren, Closed, Strict)	2,500	107,000	175,000	211,000	20	20	20	20	20	20	18
P-Eva	Anglican Evangelical, Independent Evangelical	20,100	2,842,000	1,824,000	5,482,000	112	135	112	138	143	164	89
P-Fun	Fundamentalist	2,600	122,000	67,000	211,000	13	16	13	16	17	19	14
P-Hol	Holiness (Conservative Methodist, Wesleyan, Free Methodist)	43,600	3,978,000	4,111,000	7,387,000	283	339	283	339	350	395	117
P-LuR	Lutheran/Reformed united church or joint misssion	10,800	11,626,000	18,525,000	15,041,000	23	24	23	24	24	25	22
P-Lut	Lutheran	81,900	39,853,000	54,717,000	60,696,000	231	249	231	249	253	267	122
P-Men	Mennonite, Anabaptist (Left Wing or Radical Reformation)	9,500	1,166,000	1,117,000	2,009,000	99	123	99	123	128	147	59
P-Met	Methodist (mainline Methodist, United Methodist)	89,500	13,860,000	21,933,000	22,902,000	113	121	113	121	123	129	108
P-Mor	Moravian (Continental Pietist)	1,200	302,000	478,000	582,000	27	29	27	29	29	31	27
P-Non	Nondenominational (no church or anti-church groups)	11,800	1,938,000	886,000	3,434,000	125	142	166	191	196	216	76
P-Pe1	Oneness-Pentecostal or Unitarian-Pentecostal: Jesus Only	11,600	1,326,000	939,000	2,463,000	57	80	57	80	85	103	74
P-Pe2	Baptistic-Pentecostal or Keswick-Pentecostal	232,000	30,284,000	12,006,000	49,420,000	311	380	311	382	396	453	174
P-Pe3	Holiness-Pentecostal: 3-crisis-experience	28,800	3,219,000	2,322,000	5,650,000	167	233	167	233	246	299	118
P-PeA	Apostolic, or Pentecostal Apostolic (living apostles)	11,500	762,000	706,000	1,597,000	29	31	29	31	31	33	30
P-Pen	Pentecostal (Protestant; Classical Pentecostal	20	1,000	0	3,000	0	1	0	1	1	2	1
P-Qua	Friends (Quaker)	4,900	222,000	348,000	403,000	50	53	50	53	54	56	43
P-Ref	Reformed, Presbyterian	97,700	26,318,000	33,121,000	43,902,000	269	295	269	295	300	321	141
P-Sal	Salvationist (Salvation Army)	14,100	1,467,000	2,910,000	2,378,000	79	85	79	85	86	91	84
P-Uni	United church (union of bodies of different traditions)	50,300	12,348,000	13,608,000	22,266,000	49	53	49	53	54	57	45
P-Wal	Waldensian	200	31,000	37,000	41,000	2	2	2	2	2	2	2
P-com	community church or union congregation	50	12,000	19,000	20,000	19	19	20	23	24	26	18
INDEPENDENT		1,593,100	191,227,000	96,327,000	348,196,000	2,835	4,043	8,993	21,586	22,148	49,431	220
I-3aA	African Independent Apostolic	30,800	6,497,000	2,035,000	13,504,000	76	89	76	89	92	102	24
I-3aB	Black American Apostolic	200	19,000	16,000	31,000	3	4	3	4	4	5	2
I-3aF	Filipino Apostolic	20	1,000	1,000	1,000	1	1	1	1	1	1	1
I-3aI	Indian Apostolic	200	28,000	7,000	50,000	3	3	3	3	3	3	2
I-3aK	Korean Apostolic	20	4,000	0	7,000	0	1	0	1	1	2	1
I-3aL	Latin American Apostolic	800	178,000	49,000	271,000	13	14	13	14	14	15	6

Table 1-5 continued

Megabloc Tradition code 1	name 2	Congs 1995 3	Adults 1995 4	Affiliated 1970 5	Affiliated 1995 6	Denominations Sig 1970 7	Sig 1995 8	Total 1970 9	1995 10	2000 11	2025 12	Countries Count 13
I-3aO	Black American Oneness Apostolic	3,400	1,368,000	418,000	1,873,000	20	26	20	26	27	32	3
I-3aP	Pacific Apostolic	20	4,000	0	5,000	0	1	0	1	1	2	1
I-3aS	Arab Apostolic	30	1,000	1,000	4,000	1	2	1	4	5	7	2
I-3aU	Afro-Caribbean Apostolic	100	11,000	1,000	16,000	2	2	2	2	2	2	2
I-3aW	White-led Apostolic	1,000	132,000	22,000	199,000	4	18	4	18	21	32	4
I-3aX	New Apostolic, Catholic Apostolic (Irvingite), Old Apostolic	23,700	3,976,000	1,714,000	8,293,000	76	176	77	186	208	295	149
I-3cA	African Independent charismatic	12,400	1,041,000	98,000	1,935,000	9	68	57	517	609	977	30
I-3cB	Black American charismatic	100	360,000	80,000	500,000	1	1	1	1	1	1	1
I-3cC	Chinese charismatic	212,400	15,361,000	18,000	35,778,000	5	10	17	62	71	107	3
I-3cD	Black American Independent charismatic	200	89,000	63,000	137,000	3	5	3	5	5	7	2
I-3cE	Monoethnic charismatic	100	2,000	30	4,000	1	2	1	2	2	3	1
I-3cF	Filipino charismatic	1,700	640,000	0	1,289,000	0	5	0	54	65	108	2
I-3cI	Indian charismatic	6,800	528,000	8,000	971,000	16	44	18	399	475	780	5
I-3cK	Korean charismatic	200	35,000	5,000	72,000	1	2	1	2	2	3	1
I-3cL	Latin American charismatic	3,900	129,000	4,000	269,000	3	13	3	77	92	151	8
I-3cP	Pacific charismatic	500	27,000	1,000	64,000	1	9	4	42	50	80	6
I-3cQ	Japanese charismatic	300	19,000	6,000	28,000	7	14	11	30	34	49	1
I-3cS	Arab charismatic	900	33,000	7,000	61,000	5	13	10	87	102	164	9
I-3cU	Afro-Caribbean charismatic	40	2,000	0	4,000	0	5	0	8	10	16	3
I-3cW	White-led charismatic	111,900	10,406,000	548,000	17,478,000	30	152	118	2,400	2,856	4,682	43
I-3cY	Brazilian/Portuguese charismatic	1,400	360,000	42,000	651,000	4	6	4	6	6	8	2
I-3cZ	other Asian charismatic	200	53,000	0	94,000	0	11	0	15	18	30	6
I-3dW	White-led neocharismatic mainliners	20	10,000	0	15,000	0	1	0	1	1	2	1
I-3dZ	other Asian, doubly-affiliated mainliners	30	5,000	0	10,000	0	3	0	3	4	6	2
I-3fA	African Independent Full Gospel	1,900	264,000	157,000	517,000	8	17	8	17	19	26	12
I-3fB	Black American Full Gospel	30	11,000	0	15,000	0	3	0	3	4	6	1
I-3fC	Chinese Full Gospel	100	7,000	0	15,000	0	1	0	1	1	2	1
I-3fD	Black American charismatic Full Gospel	5,000	500,000	0	1,100,000	0	1	0	1	1	2	1
I-3fF	Filipino Full Gospel	3,300	1,225,000	9,000	2,050,000	2	5	2	5	6	8	4
I-3fG	Indonesian Full Gospel	1,200	362,000	51,000	603,000	1	2	1	2	2	3	2
I-3fI	Indian Full Gospel	6,300	390,000	31,000	631,000	7	10	7	10	11	13	1
I-3fK	Korean Full Gospel	700	180,000	4,000	308,000	1	5	1	5	6	9	5
I-3fL	Latin American Full Gospel	500	43,000	10,000	92,000	1	2	1	2	2	3	2
I-3fP	Pacific Full Gospel	200	6,000	4,000	13,000	3	3	3	3	3	3	3
I-3fW	White-led Full Gospel	9,200	1,730,000	519,000	2,537,000	21	43	21	192	226	363	6
I-3fY	Brazilian/Portuguese Full Gospel	300	15,000	0	30,000	0	1	0	1	1	2	1
I-3fZ	other Asian Full Gospel	40	16,000	0	27,000	0	5	0	5	6	10	4
I-3gL	Latin American grassroots	5,900	1,342,000	182,000	2,245,000	35	68	57	244	281	431	15
I-3gU	Afro-Caribbean grassroots	40	3,000	2,000	5,000	1	1	4	10	11	16	1
I-3gY	Brazilian grassroots	3,000	1,600,000	0	3,000,000	0	1	0	250	300	500	1
I-3hA	African house-church network	200	5,000	0	12,000	0	2	0	2	2	4	2
I-3hE	Monoethnic house-church network	20	1,000	20	2,000	1	1	1	1	1	1	1
I-3hG	Indonesian house-church network	300	9,000	0	20,000	0	1	0	1	1	2	1
I-3hI	Indian house-church network	11,500	106,000	0	304,000	0	4	0	4	5	8	3
I-3hK	Korean house-church network	22,000	330,000	10,000	672,000	1	3	1	3	3	5	2
I-3hL	Latin American house-church network	300	28,000	0	50,000	0	4	0	4	5	8	3
I-3hP	Pacific house-church network	600	21,000	0	52,000	0	3	0	3	4	6	3
I-3hS	Arab house-church network	1,100	12,000	1,000	18,000	1	1	1	1	1	1	1
I-3hV	Vietnamese house-church network	300	38,000	0	95,000	0	1	0	1	1	2	1
I-3hW	White-led house-church network	300	5,000	60	12,000	1	5	1	5	6	9	5
I-3hZ	other Asian house-church network	30	1,000	10	2,000	1	2	1	2	2	3	2
I-3jA	African healing network	100	27,000	20,000	43,000	5	9	5	9	10	13	3
I-3jW	White-led healing network	300	154,000	303,000	207,000	2	3	2	3	3	4	2
I-3kA	African cell-based network	100	15,000	0	45,000	0	1	0	1	1	2	1
I-3kB	Black American cell-based network	10	18,000	200	24,000	1	1	1	1	1	1	1
I-3kC	Chinese cell-based network	20	12,000	0	23,000	0	1	0	1	1	2	1
I-3kK	Korean cell-based network	100	790,000	23,000	1,100,000	1	2	1	2	2	3	1
I-3kL	Latin American cell-based network	100	97,000	1,000	235,000	1	2	1	2	2	3	2
I-3kW	White-led cell-based network	50	42,000	0	78,000	0	2	0	2	2	4	2
I-3kZ	other Asian cell-based network	800	15,000	0	36,000	0	1	0	1	1	2	1
I-3mA	Messianic African Independent	10	1,000	2,000	2,000	1	1	1	1	1	1	1
I-3mC	Messianic Chinese	2	70	0	150	0	1	0	1	1	2	1
I-3mH	Messianic Hindu temples	500	53,000	110,000	154,000	4	4	4	4	4	4	1
I-3mJ	Messianic Jewish	1,800	81,000	13,000	136,000	3	15	3	15	17	27	9
I-3mM	Messianic Muslim mosques	1,200	64,000	0	105,000	0	2	0	2	2	4	2
I-3nA	African Independent neocharismatic	17,800	4,684,000	3,842,000	8,730,000	6	19	12	33	37	54	13
I-3nB	Black American neocharismatic	4	0	1,000	1,000	1	1	3	7	8	11	1
I-3nC	Chinese neocharismatic	8,600	1,126,000	152,000	1,973,000	11	60	11	60	70	109	57
I-3nE	Monoethnic neocharismatic	400	18,000	14,000	60,000	1	1	1	1	1	1	1
I-3nF	Filipino neocharismatic	9,500	1,158,000	1,551,000	2,013,000	3	4	113	253	281	393	2
I-3nG	Indonesian neocharismatic	800	140,000	70,000	326,000	1	1	1	1	1	1	1
I-3nI	Indian neocharismatic	10,600	353,000	20,000	631,000	2	13	2	20	24	38	2
I-3nL	Latin American neocharismatic	32	1,000	150	4,000	1	2	1	2	2	3	2
I-3nN	Creole neocharismatic	300	32,000	6,000	63,000	2	2	20	45	50	70	2
I-3nP	Pacific neocharismatic	100	6,000	4,000	10,000	1	2	1	2	2	3	2
I-3nS	Arab neocharismatic	10	5,000	0	10,000	0	1	0	1	1	2	1
I-3nU	Afro-Caribbean neocharismatics	30	1,000	200	2,000	1	2	2	11	13	20	2
I-3nW	White-led neocharismatic	100	5,000	5,000	7,000	1	3	1	3	3	5	3
I-3nZ	other Asian neocharismatic	15,400	108,000	11,000	165,000	2	6	23	58	65	93	5
I-3oA	African Oneness pentecostal	4,300	408,000	83,000	707,000	7	28	7	81	96	155	15
I-3oC	Chinese Oneness pentecostal	4,000	455,000	71,000	1,084,000	12	12	12	12	12	12	11
I-3oF	Filipino Oneness pentecostal	700	41,000	3,000	99,000	3	6	3	35	41	67	1
I-3oG	Indonesian Oneness pentecostal	1,500	770,000	1,000,000	1,280,000	1	1	1	1	1	1	1
I-3oI	Indian Oneness pentecostal	200	121,000	5,000	232,000	1	3	1	42	50	83	1
I-3oL	Latin American Oneness pentecostal	5,100	647,000	467,000	1,136,000	19	26	19	30	32	41	14
I-3oO	Black American Oneness pentecostal	1,400	447,000	141,000	687,000	5	5	78	124	133	170	2
I-3oQ	Japanese Oneness pentecostal	600	361,000	65,000	435,000	2	3	2	12	14	22	2
I-3oU	Afro-Caribbean Oneness pentecostal	700	61,000	19,000	112,000	9	26	9	73	86	137	7
I-3oW	White-led Oneness pentecostal	6,300	469,000	135,000	796,000	14	21	14	85	99	156	8
I-3oY	Brazilian/Portuguese Oneness pentecostal	100	7,000	1,000	13,000	1	3	1	3	3	5	1
I-3oZ	other Asian Oneness pentecostal	10	200	110	300	1	1	1	1	1	1	1
I-3pA	African Independent pentecostal	55,900	8,998,000	4,339,000	18,943,000	169	219	2,234	4,860	5,385	7,486	41
I-3pB	Black American pentecostal	19,100	4,713,000	2,699,000	6,162,000	35	38	35	71	78	107	18
I-3pC	Chinese pentecostal	300	65,000	54,000	118,000	11	12	23	41	45	59	4
I-3pE	Monoethnic pentecostal	4,800	688,000	148,000	1,242,000	19	20	19	20	20	21	15
I-3pF	Filipino pentecostal	1,800	258,000	254,000	474,000	13	22	13	22	24	31	5
I-3pG	Indonesian pentecostal	10,700	1,253,000	1,462,000	3,347,000	12	12	77	160	177	243	2
I-3pI	Indian pentecostal	17,000	1,311,000	696,000	2,243,000	23	34	46	87	95	128	12
I-3pK	Korean pentecostal	600	232,000	21,000	420,000	4	7	4	7	8	10	5
I-3pL	Latin American pentecostal	27,300	3,281,000	2,264,000	6,027,000	161	192	333	592	644	851	22
I-3pN	Creole pentecostal	400	68,000	65,000	145,000	3	3	14	28	31	42	3
I-3pP	Pacific pentecostal	200	17,000	15,000	35,000	14	18	14	18	19	22	11
I-3pQ	Japanese pentecostal	300	30,000	64,000	56,000	11	11	11	11	11	11	1
I-3pR	Amerindian pentecostal	1,000	303,000	361,000	506,000	3	3	3	3	3	3	3
I-3pS	Arab pentecostal	100	11,000	10,000	22,000	8	10	8	16	18	24	7
I-3pU	Afro-Caribbean pentecostal	2,700	212,000	154,000	464,000	41	50	141	309	343	477	19
I-3pW	White-led pentecostal	28,900	3,816,000	2,436,000	6,553,000	131	172	207	712	813	1,217	55
I-3pY	Brazilian/Portuguese pentecostal	44,300	8,047,000	2,468,000	15,896,000	17	23	72	196	221	320	6
I-3pZ	other Asian pentecostal	600	27,000	6,000	50,000	7	13	9	27	31	45	10
I-3rA	African radio/TV believers	4,300	78,000	7,000	150,000	9	11	9	11	11	13	11
I-3rC	Chinese radio/TV believers	40,400	1,212,000	15,000	2,519,000	3	3	3	3	3	3	2
I-3rG	Indonesian radio/TV believers	15,000	300,000	66,000	500,000	1	1	1	1	1	1	1
I-3rI	Indian radio/TV believers	100,500	6,012,000	654,000	9,020,000	4	4	4	4	4	4	4
I-3rK	Korean radio/TV believers	600	69,000	8,000	80,000	1	1	1	1	1	1	1
I-3rL	Latin American radio/TV network	2,400	50,000	13,000	79,000	7	7	7	7	7	7	7
I-3rQ	Japanese radio/TV believers	8,000	300,000	165,000	500,000	1	1	1	1	1	1	1
I-3rS	Arab radio/TV network	20,700	557,000	121,000	963,000	18	19	18	19	19	20	19
I-3rV	Vietnamese radio/TV believers	2,000	60,000	13,000	100,000	1	1	1	1	1	1	1
I-3rW	European White radio/TV believers	83,900	3,262,000	1,599,000	5,128,000	11	11	11	11	11	11	11
I-3rY	Brazilian/Portuguese radio/TV believers	300	10,000	2,000	15,000	1	1	1	1	1	1	1
I-3rZ	other Asian radio/TV believers	12,500	369,000	137,000	602,000	10	13	10	13	14	16	13
I-3sA	African Independent Spiritual	8,300	586,000	475,000	1,186,000	29	29	315	418	439	521	8
I-3sU	Afro-Caribbean Spiritual	100	6,000	6,000	11,000	5	5	5	5	5	5	4

Continued overleaf

Table 1-5 concluded

Megabloc Tradition code 1	*name* 2	*Congs 1995* 3	*Adults 1995* 4	*Affiliated 1970* 5	*Affiliated 1995* 6	*Denominations Sig 1970* 7	*Sig 1995* 8	*Total 1970* 9	*1995* 10	*2000* 11	*2025* 12	*Countries Count* 13
I-3sW	White-led signs and wonders	40	2,000	0	6,000	0	3	0	3	4	6	3
I-3tW	White-led restorationist	1,600	132,000	0	280,000	0	10	0	10	12	20	1
I-3vA	African Independent deliverance	40	8,000	0	21,000	0	2	0	2	2	4	2
I-3vB	Black American deliverance pentecostal	30	83,000	25,000	100,000	1	1	1	1	1	1	1
I-3vW	White-led deliverance pentecostal	600	127,000	100,000	209,000	1	5	1	5	6	9	3
I-3wA	African Word of Faith/Prosperity	300	170,000	0	332,000	0	6	0	6	7	12	3
I-3wF	Filipino Word of Faith/Prosperity	40	15,000	0	25,000	0	1	0	1	1	2	1
I-3wP	Pacific Word-of-Faith/Prosperity	100	4,000	2,000	5,000	1	2	1	2	2	3	2
I-3wW	White-led Word of Faith/Prosperity	6,700	1,051,000	102,000	1,619,000	3	15	3	15	17	27	7
I-3xA	African neocharismatic of mixed traditions	4,200	950,000	850,000	1,500,000	1	1	1,333	3,000	3,333	4,667	1
I-3xK	Korean pentecostal of mixed traditions	3,000	50,000	30,000	140,000	1	1	67	150	167	233	1
I-3xL	Latin American neocharismatic of mixed traditions	30	15,000	0	19,000	0	1	0	1	1	2	1
I-3xW	European charismatic of mixed traditions	600	30,000	0	59,000	0	2	0	2	2	4	1
I-3zA	Zionist African Independent	12,200	4,067,000	999,000	10,140,000	41	49	93	147	158	201	6
I-3zU	Afro-Caribbean Zionist	400	21,000	35,000	37,000	1	1	1	1	1	1	1
I-ACa	Independent Anglo-Catholic	100	8,000	2,000	14,000	1	3	1	3	3	5	2
I-ARo	Anglo-Roman (schism ex Anglicanism in Roman direction)	500	43,000	83,000	80,000	18	18	18	18	18	18	13
I-Adv	Independent Adventist	1,100	71,000	91,000	141,000	22	25	22	25	26	28	19
I-Ang	schism ex Anglicanism in Protestant direction	4,500	721,000	875,000	1,460,000	40	40	44	59	62	74	14
I-Apo	apocalyptic, eschatological	100	2,000	2,000	4,000	2	3	2	3	3	4	2
I-Bap	Independent Baptist	97,900	21,314,000	17,048,000	27,547,000	184	238	192	258	271	324	95
I-BrI	British-Israelite	400	57,000	210,000	99,000	4	7	4	7	8	10	5
I-Bud	Hidden Buddhist believers in Christ	17,100	971,000	10,000	1,830,000	1	8	1	8	9	15	8
I-Bul	Independent Bulgarian Orthodox	200	200,000	0	500,000	0	1	0	1	1	2	1
I-Byz	Independent Byzantine-rite	30	3,000	0	6,000	0	1	0	1	1	2	1
I-CBr	Christian Brethren (Plymouth Brethren; Open only)	2,100	198,000	194,000	339,000	25	25	25	25	25	25	24
I-CCa	Conservative Catholic (schism ex Rome)	3,000	2,244,000	2,602,000	4,518,000	67	70	236	402	435	568	30
I-Con	Independent Congregational, Congregationalist	4,300	525,000	628,000	921,000	27	32	27	32	33	37	22
I-Dis	Independent Disciple, Restorationist, Christian	31,100	2,964,000	6,081,000	4,289,000	111	129	111	129	133	147	96
I-Dun	Independent Dunker (Tunker, Dipper)	600	80,000	70,000	115,000	3	3	3	3	3	3	1
I-EBr	Independent Exclusive Brethren (Closed, Strict)	400	21,000	30,000	42,000	5	7	5	7	7	9	5
I-Epi	episcopi vagantes (bishops-at-large) (under 100 members)	10	1,000	2,000	3,000	5	5	7	11	12	15	4
I-Est	Independent Estonian Orthodox	10	5,000	6,000	9,000	2	2	2	2	2	2	2
I-Eva	Anglican Evangelical, Independent Evangelical	6,800	684,000	461,000	1,357,000	67	88	67	88	92	109	48
I-Fun	Independent Fundamentalist	7,200	1,034,000	1,349,000	1,915,000	45	52	45	52	53	59	31
I-Gay	Gay/Lesbian homosexual tradition	300	121,000	30,000	154,000	1	2	1	2	2	3	2
I-Gre	Independent Greek Orthodox	20	11,000	13,000	16,000	2	2	2	2	2	2	1
I-Hin	Hidden Hindu believers in Christ	20,400	7,146,000	4,002,000	10,637,000	3	9	3	9	10	15	7
I-Hol	Holiness (Conservative Methodist, non-Pentecostal)	7,700	733,000	727,000	1,393,000	71	80	71	80	82	89	39
I-Hun	Independent Hungarian Orthodox	1	200	400	1,000	1	1	1	1	1	1	1
I-Jeh	Independent Jehovahs Witnesses (Jehovahs Christian Witnesses	1,200	198,000	111,000	323,000	8	8	8	8	8	8	7
I-Jew	Messianic, Jewish-Christian	200	20,000	50,000	30,000	1	1	1	1	1	1	1
I-Lat	Latin-rite Catholic	18,300	3,839,000	11,000	5,828,000	4	5	4	5	5	6	1
I-Lib	Liberal Catholic (Theosophical, Masonic, Gnostic)	300	55,000	87,000	106,000	27	27	27	27	27	27	18
I-LuR	Independent Lutheran/Reformed united church	10	1,000	2,000	2,000	1	1	1	1	1	1	1
I-Lut	Independent Lutheran	4,900	921,000	902,000	1,690,000	44	49	44	49	50	54	20
I-Mac	Independent Macedonian Orthodox	3	1,000	200	1,000	1	1	1	1	1	1	1
I-Men	Independent Mennonite, Anabaptist	800	70,000	71,000	130,000	6	10	6	10	11	14	7
I-Met	Independent Methodist	22,900	4,209,000	4,706,000	6,862,000	86	91	86	91	92	96	46
I-Mol	Independent Moldavian Orthodox	40	400,000	0	630,000	0	1	0	1	1	2	1
I-Mor	Independent Moravian (Continental Pietist)	1	100	200	200	1	1	1	1	1	1	1
I-Mus	Hidden Muslim believers in Christ	3,700	252,000	3,000	448,000	2	15	2	15	18	28	15
I-Nes	Independent Assyrian or Nestorian (East Syrian)	100	38,000	31,000	74,000	5	5	5	5	5	5	3
I-NoC	No-Church movement	100	2,000	3,000	3,000	2	2	2	2	2	2	2
I-Non	Nondenominational (no church or anti-church group)	15,200	1,188,000	1,091,000	2,109,000	179	206	188	228	236	268	71
I-OBe	Old Believer, Old Ritualist	3,300	1,135,000	2,631,000	1,957,000	23	24	23	25	25	27	19
I-OCa	Old Catholic	1,100	518,000	647,000	866,000	26	26	26	26	26	26	19
I-OCd	Old Calendarist, Authentic Orthodox	300	136,000	215,000	261,000	8	8	8	8	8	8	4
I-Ort	schism from Orthodoxy, in Protestant direction	300	58,000	50,000	95,000	6	6	11	25	28	39	6
I-Ose	Orthodox sect/sectarian	900	75,000	264,000	139,000	9	9	17	28	30	39	3
I-Qua	Independent Friends (Quaker)	200	22,000	40,000	37,000	2	2	2	2	2	2	2
I-ReA	Reformed Anglican	800	103,000	111,000	168,000	16	20	24	39	42	54	10
I-ReC	Reformed Catholic, retaining Roman Catholic claims	9,500	3,188,000	4,200,000	5,110,000	14	16	14	16	16	18	11
I-ReO	Reformed Orthodox (uncanonical reform movement)	1,800	641,000	420,000	1,023,000	22	23	22	23	23	24	15
I-Ref	Independent Reformed, Presbyterian	29,200	3,806,000	2,628,000	7,884,000	104	131	104	131	136	158	51
I-Rum	Independent Romanian Orthodox	100	73,000	67,000	110,000	3	3	3	3	3	3	3
I-Rus	Independent Russian Orthodox	700	610,000	219,000	921,000	27	31	27	31	32	35	30
I-Sal	Independent Salvationist	400	63,000	113,000	140,000	8	8	8	8	8	8	5
I-Ser	Independent Serbian Orthodox	50	20,000	17,000	34,000	4	5	4	5	5	6	5
I-Spi	Spiritualist, Spiritist (thaumaturgical), occult	200	61,000	107,000	114,000	3	3	3	3	3	3	1
I-TrA	Traditional Anglican, Traditionalist	100	7,000	0	10,000	0	1	0	1	1	2	1
I-Tru	True Orthodox (devoutly conservative Russian Orthodox)	8,100	185,000	259,000	358,000	6	6	6	6	6	6	4
I-Ukr	Independent Ukrainian Orthodox	3,400	3,238,000	661,000	6,324,000	20	23	20	23	24	26	18
I-Uni	United church (union of bodies of different traditions)	27,200	4,101,000	300,000	10,701,000	2	3	2	3	3	4	3
I-com	community church or union congregation	1	100	100	200	1	1	1	1	1	1	1
I-eth	ethnic or monoethnic denomination	6,700	451,000	52,000	1,092,000	15	15	161	214	225	267	2
I-ind	independent evangelical (dispensationalist)	1,700	228,000	304,000	380,000	2	3	2	3	3	4	2
I-mar	marginal independent Christian (Black/Third-World indigenous	4,500	599,000	2,017,000	1,211,000	54	76	59	90	96	121	48
I-rad	isolated radio churches (unorganized)	7,000	197,000	28,000	301,000	7	7	7	7	7	7	7
I-sin	single congregation(s): one single autonomous congregation	10,600	1,088,000	1,287,000	1,996,000	7	7	445	745	805	1,045	7
MARGINAL CHRISTIAN		106,200	12,362,000	11,100,000	23,851,000	493	545	946	1,488	1,596	2,030	215
m-Ade	Christadelphian	1,200	43,000	97,000	71,000	21	21	21	21	21	21	20
m-Apo	apocalyptic, eschatological	1	1,000	10,000	1,000	1	1	1	1	1	1	1
m-Div	Divine Science	20	1,000	0	1,000	0	1	0	1	1	2	1
m-Gno	Gnostic, esoteric, anthroposophical	200	58,000	53,000	70,000	5	5	5	5	5	5	3
m-HSA	Holy Spirit Assoc. for Unification of World Christianity	900	713,000	454,000	926,000	5	8	5	8	9	11	8
m-Jeh	Jehovah's Witnesses (Russellites)	70,500	4,466,000	4,017,000	11,305,000	204	222	204	222	226	240	212
m-LdS	Latter-day Saints (Mormons), including Mormon schismatics	20,000	5,117,000	3,111,000	7,985,000	88	116	88	116	122	144	102
m-Lib	Liberal Catholic (Theosophical, Masonic, Gnostic)	200	22,000	2,000	31,000	1	1	1	1	1	1	1
m-Ort	schism from Orthodoxy, in marginal direction	500	50,000	71,000	85,000	2	2	2	2	2	2	2
m-Pau	Paulician, Bogomil	30	4,000	5,000	6,000	2	2	2	2	2	2	2
m-Sci	metaphysical science, Divine Science, Religious Science	3,600	488,000	1,220,000	1,097,000	59	59	59	59	59	59	55
m-Spi	Spiritualist, Spiritist (thaumaturgical), psychic, occult	1,100	83,000	357,000	145,000	20	20	20	20	20	20	10
m-Swe	Swedenborgian (Church of the New Jerusalem; spiritualistic)	300	19,000	44,000	31,000	18	18	18	18	18	18	15
m-The	Theosophist, Theosophical, synthesist	100	3,000	6,000	5,000	3	3	3	3	3	3	3
m-Unt	Unitarian, Universalist, Free Christian, Liberal Christian	1,700	249,000	469,000	378,000	29	29	29	29	29	29	26
DOUBLY AFFILIATED / DISAFFILIATED			-119,766,000	-40,475,000	-198,453,000							237
2-Aff	Doubly-affiliated		-102,506,000	-29,781,000	-174,354,000							237
X-Aff	Disaffiliated		-17,260,000	-10,694,000	-24,099,000							11
WORLD TOTALS		**3,157,000**	**1,069,931,000**	**1,130,106,000**	**1,769,920,000**	**7,097**	**8,861**	**16,075**	**33,090**	**33,909**	**62,262**	**238**

THE PENTECOSTAL/CHARISMATIC RENEWAL

This aspect of empirical global Christianity has expanded with extreme rapidity throughout the 20th century. It is therefore described here in considerable detail, utilizing the large 2-page table that follows. First however an overall description will be given.

THREE WAVES OF RENEWAL

The table traces the expansion of this Renewal across 10 decades and two centuries, and also across 6 continents and the entire world. Historically, the Renewal can be seen to have arrived in 3 massive surges or waves whose origins are traced in Table 1-6a to the years 1886, 1907, and 1549 respectively. As with ocean waves they arrive at the shore sequentially but often can be seen originating far out to sea beforehand. The first wave is known today as Pentecostalism or the Pentecostal Renewal (line 4), the second wave as the Charismatic movement or the Charismatic Renewal (line 12), followed by a third wave of non-pentecostal, noncharismatic but neocharismatic renewal (line 21). (References are to numbered lines in the tables). The Pentecostals, Charismatics, and Neocharismatics who make up this Renewal today number 27.7% of organized global Christianity. They are here classified under 59 different categories (7 relating to Pentecostals, 8 to Charismatics, 44 to Neocharismatics).

Even with these 3 waves and 59 categories, an underlying unity pervades the movement. This survey views the Renewal in the Holy Spirit as one single cohesive movement into which a vast proliferation of all kinds of individuals and communities and cultures and languages have been drawn in a whole range of different circumstances. This explains the massive babel of diversity evident today.

These members are found in 740 Pentecostal denominations, 6,530 nonpentecostal mainline denominations with large organized internal Charismatic movements, and 18,810 independent Neocharismatic denominations and networks. Charismatics are now found across the entire spectrum of Christianity. They are found within all 150 traditional nonpentecostal ecclesiastical confessions, families, and traditions. Pentecostals/Charismatics (the shorthand generic term preferred here for the whole 3-Wave phenomenon) are found in 9,000 ethnolinguistic cultures, speaking 8,000 languages covering 95% of the world's total population.

The sheer magnitude and diversity of the numbers involved beggar the imagination. Table 1-6a documents an AD 2000 total of 523 million affiliated church members (line 66). Of these, 65 million are Pentecostals, 175 million are Charismatics, and 295 million are Third-Wavers. Some 29% of all members worldwide are White, 71% Non-White. Members are more urban than rural, more female than male, more children (under 18) than adults, more Third-World (66%) than Western world (32%), more living in poverty (87%) than affluence (13%), more family-related than individualist.

These totals of believers today are not however the whole story. They do not include believers who died yesterday, or last month, or last year, or earlier in the 20th century. A complete tally of all Renewal believers throughout the century must therefore include the 175 million former members who are no longer alive. The total of all Renewal believers since AD 1900 can thus now be seen to amount to 795 millions (see lines 81 and 82 in Table 1-6a-6b).

PERSECUTION AND DIVERSITY

Members are more harassed, persecuted, suffering, martyred than perhaps any other Christian tradition in recent history. They have been protected to some extent by the fact that their multiple cultures and vast diversity have made it virtually impossible for dictators, tyrants, archenemies, and totalitarian regimes to track them down and find them in order to liquidate them. Their incredible variety and diversity can be seen from the fact that to do justice to this diversity a whole variety of neologisms and new statistical categories has had to be created. Those described in the tables include: prepentecostals, quasi-pentecostals, indigenous pentecostals, ethnic pentecostals, isolated radio pentecostals, postpentecostals, non-Christian believers in Christ, postdenominationalists, neoapostolics, oneness apostolics, indigenous charismatics, grassroots neocharismatics, postcharismatics, crypto-charismatics, radio/TV charismatics, independent charismatics. Of these 16 categories only the last two have been universally recognized up to now as genuine pentecostals/charismatics. In this survey all of these categories are recognized and enumerated as part of the Renewal.

THE TIDE SURGES IN

All 3 waves are still continuing to surge in. Massive expansion and growth continue at a current rate of 9 million new members a year or over 25,000 a day. One-third of this is purely demographic (births minus deaths in the pentecostal/charismatic community); two-thirds are converts and other new members. In the early days of all 3 waves, annual rates of growth were enormous; now they have declined gradually to 2.7% per year for Pentecostals, 2.4% for Charismatics, 3.0% per year for Neocharismatics, and 3.2% per year for the Renewal as a whole (line 82). These overall figures hide a number of situations of saturation, some spheres of decline, and many situations of explosive, uncontrollable growth.

Charismatics greatly outnumber Pentecostals in numbers and in annual converts worldwide. They do, however, have a growing dilemma in that Charismatics in the nonpentecostal mainline Protestant and Catholic churches experience an average intense involvement of only two or three years—after this period as active weekly attenders at prayer meetings, they become irregular or nonattending, justifying the term postcharismatics (line 15). This 'revolving-door syndrome' results in an enormous annual turnover, a serious problem that has not yet begun to be adequately recognized or investigated.

PERMEATION OF GLOBAL CHRISTIANITY

Table 1-6a's lines 67-75 show the geographical spread of the Renewal today. Large numbers exist on every continent and in 236 countries. This table suggests the reason why Europe has always had the lowest response to Pentecostalism of any continent (less than 1%). Europeans rejected the First Wave because they were not prepared to leave the great state churches to become Pentecostals; since 1970, however, they have responded enormously as Charismatics *within* those churches. With 21 million Charismatics and 13 million Neocharismatics, Europe now has the highest ratio (6.6) of Charismatics to Pentecostals of all continents across the world.

At the other end of the spectrum from rejection to acceptance is Asia, whose Christians have become massively pentecostalized (line 70). This is due mainly to the phenomenal spread of the Renewal in Korea, India, the Philippines, Indonesia, and in mainland China.

All state churches and national denominations, with their myriads of agencies and institutions, are now rapidly becoming permeated with Charismatics. In addition, roughly 14% of Charismatics in these mainline churches have seceded or become independent each year since 1970. Altogether, White-led Independent charismatic churches across the world number over 100,000 loosely organized into 3,700 or so major denominations or networks (line 49).

The enormous force of the Renewal can be observed in many ways. One is that a majority of the fifty or so megachurches—the world's largest single congregations, each with over 50,000 members—are Pentecostal/Charismatic/Neocharismatic.

Another indication of its dynamic is the disproportionately high pentecostal/charismatic penetration of the media. Charismatics in particular have seized the global initiative in radio, television, movies, audio, video, publishing, literature, magazines, city-wide evangelistic campaigns (800 each year), and so on. Virtually all varieties of ministries engaged in by institutionalized Christianity worldwide have now been penetrated by stalwarts of the Renewal.

Finance, stewardship, and giving also have risen well above the global Christian average (lines 89-90). Personal annual income of church members in the Renewal has grown from $157 billion in 1970 to $1,550 billion by AD 2000 (line 89). Of this, $30 billion is donated to Christian causes (line 90). This means that the rank-and-file of the Renewal do not need to be further exhorted regarding stewardship. Its lay members are doing all they should, and more. There is, however, an almost universal failure by leaders of the Renewal to garner and organize these vast sums coherently for mission and ministry at the world level. In consequence, giving to global foreign missions per member per week is stuck at the minuscule figure of 15 US cents.

A further illustration of the permeation of global Christianity lies in the huge numbers of ordained pastors, priests, ministers, bishops, and other church leaders involved (lines 93-95). Over one-third of the world's full-time Christian workers (38%) are Pentecostals/Charismatics/Neocharismatics.

PENETRATION OF THE WORLD

Throughout the history of the Renewal, leaders have summoned members to the task of world evangelization. A favorite theme has been the saying of Jesus: 'The fields are white unto harvest.' The unharvested or unreached harvest field today consists of 1.6 billion unevangelized persons, who have never heard of Jesus Christ (line 101), in 3,000 unevangelized population segments (cities, peoples, countries). It includes 2,000 unreached ethnolinguistic peoples, 175 unreached megapeoples (of over 1 million population each), 140 unevangelized megacities, 300 unevangelized Islamic metropolises. The harvest force, or harvesters committed to harvesting, consists of 5.5 million full-time Christian workers: of these, 2.1 million are Pentecostals/Charismatics/Neocharismatics (38%; line no. 93).

Another indicator concerns global plans to evangelize the world (line 102). Of the world's 1,500 such plans since AD 30, some 12% have been definitively Pentecostal/Charismatic. Probably 20% altogether—300 plans—have had significant Charismatic participation. In the last twenty years, this percentage has risen markedly. Of the world's 24 current megaplans launched since 1960, 16, or 67%, are Pentecostal/Charismatic. So are 9 (64%) of the 14 current gigaplans (global plans to evangelize the world each spending over US $1 billion) launched since 1960.

New bodies are continually emerging. Over 100 new Charismatic mission agencies have recently been formed in the Western world, and over 300 more in the Third World. Many are taking on the challenge of unevangelized population segments in restricted-access countries by appointing nonresidential missionaries.

With Pentecostals/Charismatics/Neocharismatics now active in 80% of the world's 3,300 large metropolises, all in process of actively implementing networking and cooperation with Great Commission Christians of all confessions, a new era in world mission would clearly appear to have got under way.

Table 1-6a. The global expansion of the Pentecostal/Charismatic/Neocharismatic Renewal in the Holy Spirit, AD 1900–2025.

			Totals in AD 2000:		*PARTICIPANTS in:*				
Ref 1	*Category* 2	*Begun* 3	*Countries* 4	*Denoms* 5	*1900* 6	*1970* 7	*1995* 8	*2000* 9	*2025* 10
1.	**PERIPHERAL QUASI-PENTECOSTALS**								
2.	Prepentecostals	1739	100	2,600	2,500,000	3,824,000	5,000,000	7,300,000	18,800,000
3.	Postpentecostals	1950	80	509	0	1,000,000	6,000,000	10,500,000	33,000,000
4.	**FIRST WAVE: PENTECOSTAL RENEWAL**								
5.	**Pentecostals**	1886	225	740	20,000	15,382,330	57,424,520	65,832,970	97,876,000
6.	Denominational Pentecostals	1910	225	740	20,000	15,382,330	57,424,520	65,832,970	97,876,000
7.	Classical Pentecostals	1906	220	660	20,000	14,443,480	54,961,090	63,064,620	93,583,000
8.	Holiness Pentecostals	1886	170	240	15,000	2,322,430	5,650,230	6,315,790	9,644,000
9.	Baptistic Pentecostals	1906	210	390	5,000	11,415,390	47,713,650	54,973,310	81,272,000
10.	Apostolic Pentecostals	1904	29	30	0	705,660	1,597,210	1,775,520	2,667,000
11.	Oneness Pentecostals	1914	130	80	0	938,850	2,463,430	2,768,350	4,293,000
12.	**SECOND WAVE: CHARISMATIC RENEWAL**								
13.	**Charismatics**	1907	235	6,530	12,000	3,349,400	156,041,320	175,856,690	274,934,000
14.	Mainline active Charismatics	1960	225	6,990	12,000	3,349,400	100,841,320	114,029,250	179,969,000
15.	Mainline Postcharismatics	1973	150	3,540	0	0	55,200,000	61,827,440	94,965,000
16.	Anglican Charismatics	1907	163	130	1,000	509,900	15,980,520	17,562,110	25,470,000
17.	Catholic Charismatics	1967	234	236	10,000	2,000,000	104,900,000	119,912,200	194,973,000
18.	Protestant Charismatics	1959	231	6,460	1,000	824,100	32,208,900	35,200,000	50,156,000
19.	Orthodox Charismatics	1970	25	140	0	15,200	2,941,900	3,167,380	4,295,000
20.	Marginal Charismatics	1980	15	130	0	200	10,000	15,000	40,000
21.	**THIRD WAVE: NEOCHARISMATIC RENEWAL**								
22.	**Neocharismatics** (Independents, Postdenominationalists)	1549	225	18,810	949,400	53,490,560	254,726,840	295,405,240	460,798,000
23.	(a) *In 2 kinds of wholly Third Wave networks*	1656	220	17,125	949,300	36,854,370	217,689,150	253,936,540	401,173,000
24.	Non-White indigenous Neocharismatics	1783	210	13,425	919,300	29,379,360	174,221,530	203,270,400	327,515,000
25.	African indigenous pentecostals/charismatics	1864	60	9,300	890,000	12,569,300	56,520,100	65,310,530	99,263,000
26.	Afro-Caribbean pentecostals/charismatics	1783	38	420	10,000	217,610	649,670	736,080	1,168,000
27.	Arab/Assyrian/Semitic neocharismatics	1909	40	130	0	140,760	1,076,730	1,263,930	2,200,000
28.	Black American independent charismatics	1955	4	10	0	62,500	1,236,800	1,471,660	2,646,000
29.	Black American indigenous pentecostals	1889	20	90	15,000	2,820,540	6,832,460	7,634,850	11,647,000
30.	Black American Oneness Apostolics	1886	10	150	0	559,120	2,560,600	2,960,900	4,962,000
31.	Brazilian/Portuguese grassroots neocharismatics	1910	20	460	0	2,512,200	19,604,340	23,022,770	39,115,000
32.	Colored/Mixed-race indigenous charismatics	1931	4	70	0	71,000	207,500	234,800	371,000
33.	Ethnic (Monoethnic) pentecostal churches	1890	20	20	0	162,930	1,307,220	1,536,080	2,680,000
34.	Filipino indigenous pentecostals/charismatics	1913	25	380	0	1,818,020	5,950,340	6,776,800	10,909,000
35.	Han Chinese indigenous pentecostals/charismatics	1905	58	180	2,000	310,240	41,509,370	49,749,200	82,948,000
36.	Indian indigenous pentecostals/charismatics	1911	25	580	1,000	1,421,310	14,081,380	16,613,400	29,274,000
37.	Indonesian indigenous pentecostals	1920	5	170	0	2,649,780	6,076,000	6,761,240	10,187,000
38.	Japanese indigenous pentecostals	1930	15	50	0	298,650	1,016,140	1,159,640	1,877,000
39.	Korean indigenous pentecostals/charismatics	1910	30	170	500	100,700	2,799,030	3,338,700	6,037,000
40.	Latino-Hispanic grassroots believers	1909	24	990	0	2,988,090	10,427,650	11,915.560	17,355,000
41.	Messianic Hindu believers in Christ	1875	2	5	500	109,500	154,300	163,200	208,000
42.	Messianic Jewish believers in Christ	1894	14	20	100	13,000	136,000	160,600	284,000
43.	Messianic Muslim believers in Christ	1981	2	3	0	0	105,000	126,000	231,000
44.	Pacific/Oceanic indigenous charismatics	1917	20	70	0	25,730	183,100	214,570	372,000
45.	Red Indian/Amerindian neopentecostals	1870	3	4	0	361,000	506,300	535,360	681,000
46.	Vietnamese indigenous neocharismatics	1952	2	3	0	12,600	195,000	231,480	414,000
47.	other Asian indigenous neocharismatics	1948	40	130	100	153,780	986,500	1,153,050	1,986,000
48.	other Messianic non-Christian believers in Christ	1950	15	20	100	1,000	100,000	200,000	700,000
49.	White-led Independent Postdenominationalists	1805	210	3,700	30,000	7,475,010	43,467,620	50,666,140	73,658,000
50.	European/American White-led Neo-Apostolics	1805	200	3,510	10,000	5,760,760	35,174,210	41,056,900	60,470,000
51.	European White-led New Apostolics	1832	180	190	20,000	1,714,250	8,293,410	9,609,240	13,188,000
52.	(b) *as % of 7 kinds of non-Third-Wave denominations*	1549	200	925	100	16,636,190	37,037,690	41,468,700	59,625,000
53.	Independent Anglican neocharismatics	1925	80	30	0	10,000	1,595,000	1,716,000	2,321,000
54.	Independent Protestant neocharismatics	1920	180	450	0	11,832,690	18,642,360	20,489,290	25,724,000
55.	Independent Catholic neocharismatics	1724	30	60	0	700,000	1,187,260	1,314,800	1,953,000
56.	Independent Orthodox neocharismatics	1666	20	10	0	1,000	538,310	584,200	814,000
57.	Nonhistorical Independent neocharismatics	1549	100	90	0	1,000,000	3,200,000	3,500,000	5,000,000
58.	Isolated radio/TV neocharismatics	1930	30	5	0	30,000	159,100	188,100	333,000
59.	Hidden non-Christian believers in Christ	1800	70	280	100	3,062,500	11,715,660	13,676,310	23,480,000
60.	Hidden Hindu neocharismatics	1800	4	10	0	3,000,000	8,637,500	9,715,000	15,103,000
61.	Hidden Muslim neocharismatics	1930	15	10	0	2,000	348,560	417,790	764,000
62.	Hidden Buddhist neocharismatics	1950	17	10	0	10,000	1,829,600	2,193,520	4,013,000
63.	Hidden Jewish neocharismatics	1896	15	50	100	50,000	200,000	250,000	500,000
64.	Hidden other-religionist neocharismatics	1980	50	200	0	500	700,000	1,100,000	3,100,000
65.	doubly-counted First/Second/Third Wavers								
66.	**Global affiliated Pentecostals/Charismatics/Neocharismatics**		**236**	**21,080**	**981,400**	**72,223,000**	**477,378,000**	**523,767,390**	**811,551,600**
67.	**RENEWAL MEMBERS ON 7 CONTINENTS**								
68.	Renewal members in Africa	1830	60	9,990	901,000	17,049,020	110,409,270	126,010,200	227,819,720
69.	Renewal members in Antarctica	1980	1	0	2	0	300	400	600
70.	Renewal members in Asia	1870	50	2,690	4,300	10,144,120	122,691,990	134,889,530	217,550,600
71.	Renewal members in Europe	1805	48	1,870	20,000	8,018,180	36,097,050	37,568,700	47,179,500
72.	Renewal members in Latin America	1783	46	2,680	10,000	12,621,450	130,147,480	141,432,880	202,277,880
73.	Renewal members in Northern America	1889	5	3,520	46,100	24,151,910	73,997,060	79,600,160	110,204,580
74.	Renewal members in Oceania	1917	28	330	0	238,240	3,928,850	4,265,520	6,519,300
75.	Renewal members as % global church members	–	238	–	0.2	6.4	26.9	27.7	32.5
76.	**PERIPHERAL CONSTITUENTS**								
77.	Quasi-Pentecostals (Prepentecostals, Postpentecostals)	1739	110	2,700	2,500,000	4,824,000	11,000,000	17,800,000	51,800,000
78.	Unaffiliated believers professing Renewal	1950	230	2,000	210,000	5,300,000	52,000,000	78,327,510	120,000,000
79.	**WIDER GLOBAL TOTALS OF RENEWAL**								
80.	Total all Renewal believers alive at mid-year		236	26,565	3,691,400	82,346,270	529,597,680	619,894,900	961,000,000
81.	Renewal believers dying since AD 1900		236	11,565	–	34,657,900	146,743,000	175,728,800	270,000,000
82.	Total all Renewal believers ever, since AD 1900		236	29,500	3,691,400	117,004,170	676,340,680	795,623,700	1,231,000,000
83.	**CHURCHES, FINANCE, AGENCIES, WORKERS**								
84.	Pentecostal churches, congregations (1st Wave)		225	740	10	94,200	360,000	480,000	1,080,000
85.	Mainline Charismatic prayer groups (2nd Wave)		235	4,450	0	35,000	370,000	550,000	1,450,000
86.	Catholic Charismatic weekly prayer groups		234	239	0	2,185	143,000	160,000	245,000
87.	Anglican & Protestant Charismatic groups		231	3,700	0	32,815	200,000	250,000	500,000
88.	Independent congregations, house churches (3rd Wave)		–	–	15,000	138,970	450,000	591,000	1,296,000
89.	Personal income of all Renewal members, $ p.a.		–	–	250 million	157 billion	1,280 billion	1,550 billion	2,400 billion
90.	Renewal members' giving to all Christian causes, $ p.a.		–	–	7 million	3 billion	25 billion	30 billion	46 billion
91.	Renewal service agencies		–	–	20	600	3,400	4,000	7,000
92.	Renewal institutions		–	–	100	1,300	13,000	14,000	19,000
93.	All pentecostal/charismatic full-time workers		–	–	2,010	240,790	1,200,000	2,100,000	4,300,000
94.	Nationals: pastors, clergy, evangelists, et alii		–	–	2,000	237,000	1,060,000	1,933,000	3,900,000
95.	Aliens: foreign missionaries		–	–	100	3,790	140,000	167,000	400,000
96.	**THE CONTEXT OF WORLD EVANGELIZATION**								
97.	Global population		238	–	1,619,626,000	3,696,148,000	5,666,360,000	6,055,049,000	7,823,703,000
98.	Christians (all varieties)		238	33,800	558,132,000	1,236,374,000	1,877,426,000	1,999,564,000	2,616,670,000
99.	Affiliated church members (baptized)		238	33,800	521,576,500	1,130,106,000	1,796,918,000	1,888,439,000	2,490,958,000
100.	Non-Christians		238	–	1,061,494,000	2,459,774,000	3,788,934,000	4,055,485,000	5,207,033,000
101.	Unevangelized persons		230	–	879,672,000	1,641,245,000	1,678,205,000	1,629,375,000	1,845,406,000
102.	World evangelization global plans since AD 30		160	–	250	510	1,145	1,500	3,000

Table 1-6b. Codes and characteristics of each of the 95 generic categories and ministries of Pentecostals/Charismatics/Neocharismatics.

Ref Column 1	Category 2	Country Table codes Table 1 3	Table 2 4	Definitions, characteristics, examples of major significant bodies 5	Main country 6
1.	**PERIPHERAL QUASI-PENTECOSTALS:**	......	......	Table 1-5 divides all members into the 66 ecclesiastico-cultural categories below	
2.	Prepentecostals	0ZAC	......	Charismatic denominations not officially in Renewal: Salvationists, Holiness, Wesleyans	brit
3.	Postpentecostals	x1ZAC	......	Former Denominational Pentecostals who have left to join nonpentecostal churches	usa
4.	**FIRST WAVE: PENTECOSTAL RENEWAL**	......	......	Oldest part of Renewal, claiming name, history, experiences, and theology of Pentecostalism	usa
5.	Pentecostals	1ZAC	P-Pe	Churches of White origin (now 70% Non-White) requiring initial evidence of tongues-speaking	braz
6.	Denominational Pentecostals	P1ZAC	P-Pe	Members in the older, larger, more traditional Pentecostal denominations	cana
7.	Classical Pentecostals	CP1ZAC	P-Pe2/3	Self-designation of older White denominations, usually excluding Black Pentecostals	usa
8.	Holiness Pentecostals	......	P-Pe3	Those holding 3-fold Wesleyan experience of conversion, sanctification, infilling: IPHC	chil
9.	Baptistic Pentecostals	......	P-Pe2	Emphasizing 2-fold Pentecostal experience of conversion, Spirit-baptism: AoG, COG, ICFG	arge
10.	Apostolic Pentecostals	......	P-PeA	Denominations emphasizing Pentecostal church government by living apostles: ACG	ghan
11.	Oneness Pentecostals	OP1ZAC	P-Pe1	Denominations emphasizing baptism in name of 'Jesus Only'; anti-trinitarian: UPCI	colo
12.	**SECOND WAVE: CHARISMATIC RENEWAL**	......	*Formula*	Members of nonpentecostal mainline churches who experience Pentecostal phenomena	ital
13.	Charismatics	2ZAC	......	All who have experienced Spirit-baptism but remain within nonpentecostal mainline churches	mexi
14.	Mainline active charismatics	V2ZAC	......	All in nonpentecostal churches regularly attending Renewal activities	phil
15.	Mainline postcharismatics	x2ZAC	......	Charismatics who no longer attend Renewal activities but still regard selves as Charismatics	fran
16.	Anglican Charismatics	A2ZAC	%ΣA- .	Total Anglicans in Renewal, past and present, including children and infants	brit
17.	Catholic Charismatics	R2ZAC	%ΣR-	Total baptized RCs in CCR, past and present, including children and infants	braz
18.	Protestant Charismatics	P2ZAC	%ΣP- .	Total Protestants in Renewal, past and present, including children and infants	aust
19.	Orthodox Charismatics	O2ZAC	%ΣO-	Total Orthodox in Renewal, past and present, including children and infants	arme
20.	Marginal Charismatics	m2ZAC	%Σm- .	Total marginal Christians in Renewal, past and present, including children and infants	usa
21.	**THIRD WAVE: NEOCHARISMATIC RENEWAL**	......	......	Spirit-led Independents rejecting White Pentecostal/Charismatic denominationalism	chin
22.	Neocharismatics (Independents, Postdenominationalists).	3ZAC ..	I-3+I-	All baptised in the Holy Spirit in new churches independent of historic Christianity	
23.	(a) *In 2 kinds of wholly Third-Wave networks*	......	I-3	(1) *Non-White and (2) White-led Neocharismatics in wholly Third-Wave networks/churches*	
24.	Non-White indigenous Neocharismatics	N3ZAC	*End code*	Spirit-baptized Non-Whites in 26 varieties of indigenous, independent, apostolic churches	
25.	African indigenous pentecostals/charismatics	......	A.....	Most AICs are Zionist, Apostolic, Spiritual: ZCC, CCC, AICN, DLBC, AACJM, EJCSK	zimb
26.	Afro-Caribbean pentecostals/charismatics	......	U.....	West Indies churches of African origin: Spiritual Baptists/Shouters, Revival Zion, NESBC	trin
27.	Arab/Assyrian/Semitic neocharismatics	......	S.....	Arabic/Aramaean/Assyrian/Berber/Semitic charismatic churches: Tree of Life Chs, GPC	iraq
28.	Black American independent charismatics	......	D.....	African American independent charismatic bodies: Full Gospel Baptist Chs Fellowship	usa
29.	Black American indigenous pentecostals	......	B.....	Black Pentecostalism: Church of God in Christ, UHCA, Full Gospel Catholic Ch	usa
30.	Black American Oneness Apostolics	......	O.....	PAOW, AWCF, Bible Way Churches of Our Lord Jesus Christ WW, COLJCAF	usa
31.	Brazilian/Portuguese grassroots neocharismatics	......	Y.....	OBPC (Brazil for Christ Ev Ch), IURD/UCKG, CCB, IPF, IPDA	braz
32.	Colored/Mixed-race indigenous charismatics	......	N.....	Colored, Métis, mixed-race charismatics: Members in Christ Ch, Christen Gemeente	nami
33.	Ethnic (Monoethnic) pentecostal churches	......	E.....	Yi Churches, Miao Churches, Nagaland Christian Revival Churches, Gypsy Ev Movement	chin
34.	Filipino indigenous pentecostals/charismatics	......	F.....	Jesus is Lord Fellowship, CDCC, March of Faith, Ecclesiae Dei	phil
35.	Han Chinese indigenous pentecostals/charismatics	......	C.....	True Jesus Church, NBM/BAM, AHC(Little Flock), Han Chinese house churches	chin
36.	Indian indigenous pentecostals/charismatics	......	I.....	Indian Pentecostal Church of God, Believers' Chs of India, Christ Groups, IPA, MFGCM	indi
37.	Indonesian indigenous pentecostals	......	G.....	Indonesia Pentecostal Church (GPI), GBI, GBIS, GPPS, GBT, GUP	indo
38.	Japanese indigenous pentecostals	......	Q.....	Spirit of Jesus Church, Primitive Gospel Ch, Holy Ecclesia of Jesus, JJCC	japa
39.	Korean indigenous pentecostals/charismatics	......	K.....	Yoido FGC, Grace & Truth Ch, FGIGM, Korea Full Gospel Chs of America	souk
40.	Latino-Hispanic grassroots believers	......	L.....	Autochthonous grassroots (GR) churches, IMPC, IPP, IOAP, IEMP, IEPC	mexi
41.	Messianic Hindu believers in Christ	......	H.....	Messianic temples, organized Hindu-Christian chs: Hindu Ch of the Lord Jesus, SRM	indi
42.	Messianic Jewish believers in Christ	......	J.....	Messianic Jewish synagogues, Fellowship of Messianic Congregations, UMJC, IAMCS, JFJ	isra
43.	Messianic Muslim believers in Christ	......	M.....	Messianic Muslim mosques: Jesus Mosques, Jamaat	bang
44.	Pacific/Oceanic indigenous charismatics	......	P.....	Pacific indigenous churches: Christian Fellowship Ch, AGCFI, Samoan FGC	solo
45.	Red Indian/Amerindian neopentecostals	......	R.....	Amerindian neopentecostals: UIEI, Halleluja Church	mexi
46.	Vietnamese indigenous neocharismatics	......	V.....	Vietnamese churches: Good News house church movement	viet
47.	Other Asian indigenous neocharismatics	......	Z.....	Other Asian churches: Hope of God Churches of Thailand, Latter Rain Ch of Malaysia	thai
48.	Other Messianic non-Christian believers in Christ	......	T.....	Organized believers staying in Buddhism, Baha'i, Sikhism, &c	myan
49.	White-led independent postdenominationalists	W3ZAC	......	Spirit-baptized Whites in non-Pentecostal/Charismatic apostolic networks	brit
50.	European/American White-led Neo-Apostolics	......	W.....	AIGA, AVC, CEEC, COTRI, FCFI, IAOGI, ICCC, ICCEC, ICFCM, RBC-RMAI, UEC, VFM, &c	usa
51.	European White-led New Apostolics	......	X.....	Neuapostolische Kirche (NAK), begun as Universal Catholic Ch, and 30 schismatic bodies	germ
52.	(b) *as % of 6 kinds of non-Renewal denominations*	......	*Formula*	*Neocharismatics in non-pentecostal/charismatic (even anti-Renewal) denominations*	brit
53.	Independent Anglican neocharismatics.	A3ZAC	Σ%I-Ang	Neocharismatics within non-pentecostal/charismatic Independent Anglican bodies	brit
54.	Independent Protestant neocharismatics	P3ZAC	Σ%I-Bap	Neocharismatics within non-pentecostal/charismatic Independent Protestant bodies	nige
55.	Independent Catholic neocharismatics	R3ZAC	Σ%I-OCa	Neocharismatics within non-pentecostal/charismatic Independent Catholic bodies	neth
56.	Independent Orthodox neocharismatics	O3ZAC	Σ%I-OBe	Neocharismatics within non-pentecostal/charismatic Independent Orthodox bodies	russ
57.	Nonhistorical independent neocharismatics	I3ZAC	Σ%I-ind	Neocharismatics in other nonpentecostal Independent chs: PIC/IFI, NBCA	phil
58.	Isolated radio/TV neocharismatics	r3ZAC	Σ%I-rad	Neocharismatics among non-pentecostal/charismatic Independent radio believers	chin
59.	Hidden non-Christian believers in Christ.	......	......	Hindu, Muslim, Buddhist, Jewish, Sikh, Baha'i, New Religionist converts who stay hidden	indi
60.	Hidden Hindu neocharismatics	......	%I-Hin	Hindu believers in Christ (NBBCs) who have pentecostal/charismatic gifts	nepa
61.	Hidden Muslim neocharismatics	......	%I-Mus	Muslim believers in Christ (NBBCs) who have pentecostal/charismatic gifts	turk
62.	Hidden Buddhist neocharismatics	......	%I-Bud	Buddhist believers in Christ (NBBCs) who have pentecostal/charismatic gifts	myan
63.	Hidden Jewish neocharismatics	......	%I-Jew	Jewish believers in Christ who have pentecostal/charismatic gifts	isra
64.	Hidden other-religionist neocharismatics	......	%I-rel	Other religionist hidden believers in Christ who have pentecostal/charismatic gifts	japa
65.	doubly-counted First/Second/Third Wavers	4ZAC	......	Neocharismatics who join Pentecostal bodies; Charismatics who become Neocharismatics	souk
66.	**Global Pentecostals/Charismatics/Neocharismatics**	ZAC	......	Total all church members in the Pentecostal/Charismatic/Neocharismatic Renewal	
67.	**RENEWAL MEMBERS ON 7 CONTINENTS**	.....	.....	Renewal (which is 28% of globe) is: 12% Pentecostals, 33% Charismatics, 55% Neocharismatics.	
68.	Renewal members in Africa	......	......	12% Pentecostals, 25% Charismatics, 63% Neocharismatics.	
69.	Renewal members in Antarctica	......	......	1% Pentecostals, 95% Charismatics, 4% Neocharismatics.	
70.	Renewal members in Asia	......	......	5% Pentecostals, 16% Charismatics, 79% Neocharismatics.	
71.	Renewal members in Europe	......	......	8% Pentecostals, 56% Charismatics, 36% Neocharismatics.	
72.	Renewal members in Latin America	......	......	23% Pentecostals, 52% Charismatics, 24% Neocharismatics.	
73.	Renewal members in Northern America.	......	......	7% Pentecostals, 28% Charismatics, 65% Neocharismatics.	
74.	Renewal members in Oceania	......	......	14% Pentecostals, 63% Charismatics, 24% Neocharismatics.	
75.	Renewal members as % global church members.	......	......	Rising rapidly at first to 6% by 1970 and to 28% by AD 2000.	
76.	**PERIPHERAL CONSTITUENTS**				
77.	Quasi-Pentecostals (Prepentecostals, Postpentecostals)	......	......	Defined above for lines 2 and 3, not counted here as Renewal members but as Renewal believers.	
78.	Unaffiliated believers professing Renewal	......	......	Individual believers experiencing Holy Spirit gifts but remaining unrelated to Renewal bodies.	
79.	**WIDER GLOBAL TOTALS OF RENEWAL**				
80.	Total all Renewal believers alive at mid-year	......	......	Total of lines 66, 77, and 78.	
81.	Renewal believers dying since AD 1900.	......	......	Former members of Renewal who have died by the year indicated.	
82.	Total all Renewal believers ever, since AD 1900	......	......	Total of lines 80 and 81.	
83.	**CHURCHES, FINANCE, AGENCIES, WORKERS**				
84.	Pentecostal churches, congregations (1st Wave)	......	......	Mainly Assemblies of God buildings and properties.	
85.	Mainline Charismatic prayer groups (2nd Wave)	......	......	These groups' regular weekly attenders are known as the 'shock troops' of the Renewal.	
86.	Catholic Charismatic weekly prayer groups	......	......	Massive growth since origin in 1967, to 2,185 groups (1970), 12,000 (1980), 90,000 (1990), 160,000 (2000).	
87.	Anglican & Protestant Charismatic groups	......	......	Large-scale lay and clerical leadership from 1960 onwards.	
88.	Independent congregations, house churches (3rd Wave)	......	......	A huge number of smaller house groups, over half a billion.	
89.	Personal income of all Renewal members, $ p.a.	......	......	Enormous wealth but no organized finance or central bank accounts.	
90.	Renewal members' giving to all Christian causes, $ p.a.	......	......	Low at 2% of personal income given to Christian causes but higher than global Christian rates.	
91.	Renewal service agencies	......	......	A huge and variegated number of agencies (listed here in footnote).	
92.	Renewal institutions	......	......	Vast variety (listed here in footnote).	
93.	All pentecostal/charismatic full-time workers	......	......	Full-time church workers of all kinds: total of next 2 lines, 94 and 95.	
94.	Nationals: pastors, clergy, evangelists, et alii	......	......	Mostly well-documented by the major denominations and networks.	
95.	Aliens: foreign missionaries	......	......	Large and rapidly growing numbers serving abroad for shorter or longer terms.	
96.	**THE CONTEXT OF WORLD EVANGELIZATION**				
97.	Global population	......	......	Populations are shown at mid-year (30 June) for the years 1970, 1995, 2000, 2025.	
98.	Christians (all varieties)	......	......	Professing plus crypto-Christians; affiliated plus unaffiliated; Great Commission plus latent Christians.	
99.	Affiliated church members (baptized)	......	......	Baptized or other members of all the churches.	
100.	Non-Christians	......	......	Now over 4 billion and growing rapidly.	
101.	Unevangelized persons	......	......	All persons unaware of Christianity, Christ, and/or the gospel.	
102.	World evangelization global plans since AD 30	......	......	Distinct plans and proposals for completing world evangelization.	

Table 1-7. Current annual income and expenditures of both unorganized and organized global Christianity, with the latter viewed and analyzed under 3 standpoints.

Line 1	Category or item 2	% 3	Amount,US$ 4
1.	**GLOBAL CHRISTIANITY**		
2.	a. **GLOBAL INCOME per year**	100.0	15,300 billion
3.	Personal income of all church members (unorganized)	95.7	14,642 billion
4.	Personal income of all unaffiliated Christians	4.0	612 billion
5.	Institutional income from secular sources (state, industry, etc)	0.3	46 billion
6.	b. **GLOBAL EXPENDITURES per year**	100.0	15,300 billion
7.	Personal and family expenditures of all church members (unorganized)	94.04	14,418 billion
8.	Personal and family expenditures of unaffiliated Christians	4.0	612 billion
9.	Personal donations of Christians to secular or nonreligious causes	0.2	29 billion
10.	Collective expenditures of **organized global Christianity**	1.76	**270 billion**
11.	A. **MINISTRY AND MISSION of organized global Christianity**		
12.	This first standpoint views income and expenditures in terms of the Christian global apostolate.		
13.	a. **INCOME per year**	100.0	**270 billion**
14.	Direct regular live Christian income (donations from Christians, tithes, etc)	70.0	189 billion
15.	Indirect income from past Christians (legacies, endowments, etc)	20.0	54 billion
16.	Institutional investments (funds, properties)	7.0	19 billion
17.	Secular income from investments, state/political/business/commercial support	3.0	8 billion
18.	b. **EXPENDITURES per year**	100.0	**270 billion**
19.	Home pastoral ministry	82.6	223 billion
20.	Home missions	12.0	32 billion
21.	Monocultural home missions	9.0	24 billion
22.	Cross-cultural home missions	3.0	8 billion
23.	Foreign missions	5.4	15 billion
24.	1. Pastoral ministry in World C contexts	5.2	14 billion
25.	2. Evangelistic ministry in World B contexts	0.18	0.49 billion
26.	3. Outreach in World A contexts	0.02	0.054 billion
27.	B. **DONORS AND BENEFICIARIES in organized global Christianity**		
28.	This second standpoint begins to identify the populations involved.		
29.	a. **INCOME per year** (sums donated by individual Christians to churches, agencies)	100.0	**270 billion**
30.	(1) By Christians in these 6 major ecclesiastico-cultural megablocs:		
31.	Anglicans	3.6	10 billion
32.	Independents/Postdenominationalists	16.3	44 billion
33.	Marginal Christians	2.7	7 billion
34.	Orthodox	11.4	31 billion
35.	Protestants	20.0	54 billion
36.	Roman Catholics	45.9	124 billion
37.	(2) Or, in these 3 trans-bloc groupings (overlapping with the 6 megablocs):		
38.	Evangelicals	23.0	62 billion
39.	Pentecostals/Charismatics/Neocharismatics	25.7	69 billion
40.	Great Commission Christians	60.7	164 billion
41.	b. **EXPENDITURES** per year (recipients, who are thus the major beneficiaries)	100.0	**270 billion**
42.	1. Funds spent on Christians (World C persons)	96.8	261 billion
43.	2. Funds spent on Evangelized non-Christians (World B persons)	2.9	7.8 billion
44.	3. Funds spent on Unevangelized non-Christians (World A persons)	0.3	0.81 billion
45.	C. **CATEGORIES AND ITEMS within organized global Christianity**		
46.	This third standpoint itemizes expenditures under specific recognized categories.		
47.	a. **INCOME per year**	100.0	**270 billion**
48.	Denominations' and churches' income	36.0	108 billion
49.	Parachurch/service agencies' income	64.0	162 billion
50.	b. **EXPENDITURES** per year:	100.0	**270 billion**
51.	Ministry salaries:		
52.	5 million full-time Christian workers in full-time ministry	15.1	41 billion
53.	Workers in World C contexts	14.9	40 billion
54.	Ordained clergy and pastors	1.4	4 billion
55.	Workers in World B contexts	0.13	0.35 billion
56.	Workers in World A contexts	0.01	0.027 billion
57.	Pensions, retirement plans	0.3	0.81 billion
58.	Ministry expenses (pastoralia, equipment, secretarial)	3.0	8 billion
59.	Ministry programs:	5.0	14 billion
60.	Evangelistic mass campaigns (2,500 a year)	0.1	0.27 billion
61.	Earthkeeping (environmentalism)	1.0	3 billion
62.	Research	0.03	0.081 billion
63.	Academic scholarship (theology, Bible, history, religion)	0.01	0.027 billion
64.	Scriptures (translation, printing, distribution)	0.4	1.1 billion
65.	Films, audiovisuals	1.0	3 billion
66.	Other ministries	2.46	7 billion
67.	Ministry training: 1 million seminarians (4,600 seminaries)	4.0	11 billion
68.	Administration:	29.0	78 billion
69.	Honorary personnel (including 5 million unpaid or partly-paid treasurers)	0.5	1 billion
70.	Accounting and finance (loans, interest, fees, taxes)	5.0	14 billion
71.	Annual audits	0.3	0.81 billion
72.	Administrative salaries: 1 million accountants, accounts clerks	1.8	4.8 billion
73.	Property (buildings, plant, rents, taxes, fees)	2.0	5 billion
74.	New property (construction, new buildings)	3.0	8 billion
75.	Maintenance (upkeep, insurance, repairs)	3.0	8 billion
76.	Annual censuses	0.4	1.1 billion
77.	Legal affairs, litigation	2.5	7 billion
78.	Losses due to mismanagement	3.0	8 billion
79.	Ecclesiastical crime (embezzlements)	6.0	16 billion
80.	Other administrative expenses	1.8	4.8 billion
81.	Education (partial support):	14.0	38 billion
82.	Adult education	1.0	3 billion
83.	Health services (partial support):	3.3	9 billion
84.	Medical missions	0.1	0.27 billion
85.	Health plans	0.9	2.4 billion
86.	Communications (publishing, publications, media, advertising):	7.3	20 billion
87.	Broadcasting	2.7	7 billion
88.	Computers (hardware, software, updates, personnel)	4.5	12 billion
89.	Conferences, meetings	2.8	8 billion
90.	Travel	2.3	6 billion
91.	Miscellaneous ministry expenses	5.2	14 billion

Notes

This table describes and analyzes primarily the origins and usages of the sum of **US$270 billion**, which is the total collective income and expenditures of organized global Christianity each year, with particular reference to the year AD 2000. Of the table's 4 sections below, the first sets the background to the total amount of money circulating at the disposal of the Christian world, unorganized as well as organized into churches and agencies.

The remaining 3 sections analyze the $270 billion from 3 different standpoints: (A) ministry and mission, (B) donors and beneficiaries, and (C) categories and items widely used to track the flow of monies.

Column 3 shows the magnitude of all items, all expressed as percentages of the $270 billion. Groupings of these figures add to broader categories unindented above them. Column 4 then gives these magnitudes in billions of dollars.

Notes on specific lines

1. Defined as the total empirical Christian world of individuals, members, churches, denominations, agencies, and institutions.
2. Total amount of money circulating annually in the Christian world or available for Christian uses, or passing through Christians' hands and pockets each year.
3. Income of all church members, unorganized meaning before parts become organized by Christian churches or agencies.
4. Unaffiliated or nominal Christians are mostly unknown to the churches and have little or no financial interaction with them.
5. Income raised by Christian institutions from secular sources.
7. Church members on average donate 1.3% of their incomes to churches or agencies. The other 98.7% covers personal or family needs and activities.
8. Unaffiliated Christians spend income on personal and family interests, with little or nothing spent on organized Christian bodies.
9. Christians in the USA donate each year some $8 billion to secular or nonreligious causes (hospitals, schools, charities).
10. This is the major sum analyzed in this table. It does not follow exactly the format of a balance sheet since it deals only with annual income and expenditures and does not cover assets. These latter can however be estimated as follows: (1) global assets of individual Christians (total nett worth), $140,000 billion ($140 trillion); (2) global assets of Christian institutions and organizations, $2,700 billion ($2.7 trillion).

11. **MINISTRY AND MISSION**
12. Analysis from the standpoint of the Christian vocation to mission and ministry.
13. This total sum is handled through over 20 million separate and unrelated bank accounts, with no overall control, oversight, reporting, or even awareness.
14. Direct consequence of committed stewardship of money.
15. The figures represent current income from giving by Christians now dead, in the form of legacies, bequests, trusts, endowments, investments, stocks, foundations, and the like. Almost entirely in Europe and Northern America.
16. Income generated by Christian institutions themselves.
17. Many governments subsidize Christian schools, hospitals, broadcasting, and other Christian ministries.
20. All denominations with over a million members organize separate home and foreign mission agencies (the latter in line 23).

27. **DONORS AND BENEFICIARIES**
28. Who gives and who gets these sums of money? This second standpoint identifies the populations involved.
30. These 6 basic megablocs are as shown in Country Tables 1 & 2.
37. These 3 trans-bloc groupings are as defined in Part 2 "Glossary" and shown in all Country Tables 1.
39. The Renewal is regarded as composed of 3 distinct waves (First, Second, Third), as described in Tables 1-6a and 1-6b.
42. This line states that 96.8% of the entire income of all Christian organizations is spent on, and primarily benefits, other Christians at home or abroad.

45. **CATEGORIES AND ITEMS**
46. This third analysis lists the specific categories and items of payment each year. Most are widely understood and used in the churches' and agencies' own accounting.
48. This item has been declining in percentage annually since 1900 when it stood at 88%.
49. This item has been increasing in percentage annually since its 1900 value of 12%, and massively so since 1990.
61. This item is a recent and rapidly-growing aspect of global Christian concern, especially among African independent churches and in the worldwide ecumenical movement.
71. At 0.3% of income, this is the average cost of professional audits carried out by Christian bodies of all kinds.
74. The value of new construction of religious buildings in the USA alone rose from $900 million in 1970 to $5,000 million in AD 2000.
76. Every year Christian agencies and denominations instruct 10 million workers to fill out and return 10 million questionnaires detailing work and achievements in the previous year. These censuses cost on average $90 per questionnaire to compile, complete, return, process, analyze, report, and circulate or publish.
78. Mismanagement is here defined as losses due to incompetence and carelessness, rather than to criminal corruption. A recent example: in 1996 the Church Commissioners for England admitted losing £800 million of the Church of England's funds due to bad investments.
79. Embezzlement, defined here as criminal theft by treasurers or other top officials responsible for Christian monies, has risen markedly since 1900 and now stands at 6% of income. Although alarming, it represents a level of corruption considerably smaller than that existing in the secular worlds of national and international industry, commerce, business, and government.
81. Organized Christianity operates, but only partially pays for, a worldwide network of 190,000 schools, 1,500 universities and colleges.
83. Churches, mission agencies, and Christian organizations operate, but only partially pay for, 30,000 medical clinics and 5,000 hospitals worldwide.

Table 1-8. Scripture translation status: each language's status in translation, publication, provision, and availability: a chronological sequence of 93 stages giving totals of languages at each status.

The present status of scripture translation and publication into print in the entire world of languages is shown pinpointed below using a mutually-exclusive sequential time scale. On this scale, every language in the world at any given moment in time has one single unique numerical code value. Note that, for specific languages, individual steps or even whole sequences can be and in fact may have been bypassed or leapfrogged. In most cases, placing a language at a certain stage implies that it has passed through, or bypassed, all previous stages. In cases where a language could be construed as being at 2 points on the scale simultaneously, the more advanced stage and its code are always chosen here. Where multiple versions or translations or projects exist in a language, the code assigned always refers to this highest stage (most advanced development). The last 16 categories (codes 77–92) represent satisfactory completed Bibles; the last 11 (82–92) represent the most advanced types of Bible translation available today. Note that 'portions' (complete books of the Bible) here do not include 'selections' (short extracts or parts of complete books), and that 'Bibles' here can either include or (more usually) exclude the Deutero-Canonical Books (Apocrypha). It should further be observed that the values of this variable for a particular bibliglossonym in a specified script are the same whatever countries or contexts it is found in.

The second column of figures gives cumulative totals for each status from 0-92. Interpretation follows these lines: 'Only 30 languages out of 13,548 have reached the highest level (code 92)'; or, '1,943 languages have or can understand and use the whole Bible'; or, '6,638 languages have a portion or gospel they can understand and use'.

Note the 2 major levels describing scripture provision in any language:

(1) **SCRIPTURES ABSENT** (21 categories), and

(2) **SCRIPTURES PRESENT** (72 categories; this latter covers S = selections, P = portion (gospel, book), N = New Testament, and B = Bible).

Onto these 2 levels of availability are built the following 3 stages of translation work in the language:

(a) NO WORK IN PROGRESS (34 categories, describing work needed but not under way or not yet begun; or not needed, or contested; or extinct or obsolete).

(b) WORK IN PROGRESS (37 categories, with phrase 'under way', or 'in production/in press').

(c) WORK (ON NT OR BIBLE) COMPLETED (22 categories, representing a degree of finality or end of the current translation process).

Name of language:
Date for report below:
Code (sts) = scripture translation status, or status of language's speakers (0–92)
Total = total of languages at each level in AD 2000:
Total 1 = All languages benefitting directly from scriptures in closely-related languages.
Total 2 = Cumulative total of languages in Total 1, starting at the lower end at stage 92 and adding upwards.

Code		Total languages: 1	2
	NO SCRIPTURE ACCESS AT ALL		
0	No translations in this language, nor its cluster, nor its net	1,300	13,548
	SCRIPTURES ABSENT	**5,514**	
	NO WORK IN PROGRESS	**4,159**	
1	No translations in this language, need for survey stated	152	12,248
2	No translations yet, definite need, but nothing under way	700	12,096
3	No translations yet, probable need	234	11,396
4	No translations yet, possible need	1,980	11,162
5	No translations yet, unlikely or undetermined need	115	9,182
6	No translations; no need as bilingual in a scripture language	220	9,067
7	No translations; bilingual, but need contested	100	8,847
8	No translations; speakers nearly extinct, hence no need	455	8,747
9	No translations; speakers now extinct	199	8,292
	WORK IN PROGRESS	**1,355**	
10	First translating under way, selection (topical Scripture verses)	100	8,093
11	First translating of a portion (gospel) under way	40	7,993
12	First translating under way, whole of New Testament	360	7,953
13	First translating under way, whole of Old Testament	2	7,593
14	First translating under way, whole Bible	6	7,591
15	First translating under way, whole Bible with Apocrypha	6	7,585
16	First translating begun but later placed on hold	50	7,579
17	First translating begun but later suspended or dropped	40	7,529
18	Work on Braille version for the blind	117	7,489
19	Work on signed version for the deaf	25	7,372
20	Work on production of Luke's Gospel as 'Jesus' Film	609	7347
	SCRIPTURES PRESENT: SELECTION ONLY (a few verses)	**100**	
21	Selections in print, but no complete Book	100	6,738
	SCRIPTURES PRESENT: PORTION (gospel or complete book)	**1,963**	
	NO WORK IN PROGRESS	**1,691**	
22	Gospel or portion (complete book) in print (if since 1975)	242	6,638
23	Portion in print, but obsolescent (over 25 years ; latest 1951–1975)	217	6,396
24	Portion in print, but obsolete (over 50 years ; latest 1950 or earlier)	528	6,179
25	Portion in print, definite need for further translating, none under way	40	5,651
26	Portion in print, possible need for further translating, none under way	50	5,611
27	Portion in print; but speakers/readers now nearly extinct	24	5,561
28	Portion in print; but speakers now extinct	40	5,537
29	Portions available in Braille for blind persons	200	5,497
30	Portions available in sign/signed language for deaf persons	40	5,297
31	Audio portions available	200	5,257
32	Luke's Gospel available as 'Jesus' Film	110	5,057
	WORK IN PROGRESS	**272**	
33	Portion in print, additional portion under way	34	4,947
34	Portion in print, but new portion under way in new orthography	20	4,913
35	Portion in print, first translation of NT under way	125	4,893
36	Portion in print, first translation of OT under way	3	4,768
37	Portion in print, first translation of Bible under way	10	4,765
38	Portion in print, first translation of Bible with Apocrypha under way	10	4,755
39	First NT in production/in press (translated but not yet published)	50	4,745
40	First Bible in production/in press (translated but not yet published)	20	4,695
	SCRIPTURES PRESENT: NEW TESTAMENT ONLY	**2,897**	
	NO WORK IN PROGRESS	**1,220**	
41	NT in print, being first translation (if latest date is since 1975)	418	4,675
42	NT in print, but obsolescent (over 25 years ; latest 1951–1975)	440	4,257
43	NT in print, but obsolete (over 50 years ; latest 1950 or earlier)	177	3,817
44	NT in recent print, revision needed but not under way	118	3,640
45	NT in print; but speakers/readers now nearly extinct	32	3,522
46	NT in print; but speakers now extinct	35	3,490
	WORK IN PROGRESS	**412**	
47	NT in print, revision needed and under way	20	3,455
48	NT in print, new translation needed and under way	22	3,435
49	NT in revision in production (translated, not yet published)	60	3,413
50	NT in new translation in production (translated, not yet published)	30	3,353
51	NT in print, first translation of OT under way	130	3,323
52	NT in print, first translation of Bible under way	50	3,193
53	NT in print, first translation of Bible with Apocrypha under way	10	3,143
54	NT in print, first Bible in production (translated, not yet published)	90	3,133
	WORK ON NT COMPLETED	**1,100**	
55	NT in print, satisfactory or adequate (literal or formal translation)	200	3,043
56	NT in print (popular language translation)	30	2,843
57	NT in print (common-language, dynamic equivalent translation)	600	2,813
58	NT in Braille available	100	2,213
59	NT in special versions (children's NT, comics, etc) available	90	2,113
60	Audio NT available	80	2,023
	SCRIPTURES PRESENT: WHOLE BIBLE (with/without Apocrypha)	**1,943**	
	NO WORK IN PROGRESS	**749**	
61	Bible in print, being first translation (if since 1975), no further plans	200	1,943
62	Bible in print, but obsolescent (over 25 years ; latest 1951–1975)	120	1,743
63	Bible in print, but obsolete (over 50 years ; latest 1950 or earlier)	343	1,623
64	Bible in print, revision or new translation needed, not under way	20	1,280
65	Bible in print; but speakers/readers nearly extinct	40	1,260
66	Bible in print; but speakers now extinct	26	1,220
	WORK IN PROGRESS	**624**	
67	Bible in print, revision of NT needed and under way	20	1,194
68	Bible in print, new translation of NT needed and under way	59	1,174
69	Bible in print, revision of OT needed and under way	5	1,115
70	Bible in print, new translation of OT needed and under way	18	1,110
71	Revision of whole Bible under way	214	1,092
72	New translation of whole Bible under way	233	878
73	Revision of whole Bible with Apocrypha under way	20	645
74	New translation of whole Bible with Apocrypha under way	10	625
75	Bible in revision in production (translated, not yet published)	20	615
76	Bible in new translation in production (translated, not yet published)	25	595
	WORK ON BIBLE COMPLETED	**570**	
77	Bible in print, satisfactory or adequate (literal or formal translation)	30	570
78	Bible with Apocrypha in print, satisfactory or adequate	10	540
79	Bible in print (Union version), satisfactory or adequate	10	530
80	Bible in print (literary language or high-quality new translation)	15	520
81	Bible in print (popular language translation)	5	505
82	Bible in print (common-language, dynamic equivalent translation)	100	500
83	Bible in print (interconfessional CLT/DE translation)	30	400
84	Bible in Braille available	100	370
85	Bible available for handicapped (deaf, nonliterates, new literates)	20	270
86	Bible in print, concordance or dictionary also in print	40	250
87	Bible stories available as colored comics, or in children's Bible	30	210
88	Bible in print in special versions: study Bible, commentaries	30	180
89	Audio Bible available	20	150
90	Bible available in video	5	130
91	Bible available electronically on Internet	95	125
92	Bible available on Internet, full range electronic or web services	30	30
	All languages	**13,548**	

Part 2

GLOSSARY

Definitions of key variables and technical terms

We must not despise the science of numbers. That science is of eminent service to the careful interpreter.
—Augustine of Hippo, AD 400

Glossary: a list of difficult, technical, or foreign terms with definitions or translations.
—Webster's New World dictionary of the American language, 1984

Being defined as a collection of 'unusual terms', 'technical terms', 'terms limited to special areas of knowledge', or a list of 'difficult words requiring explanation' (*Webster's Third new international dictionary*), this glossary is designed to offer brief, definitive definitions of all such terms, especially of neologisms and new usages occurring throughout this Encyclopedia.

Definitions of key variables and technical terms

UNUSUAL TERMS, NEOLOGISMS, AND CONCEPTS EVOLVED IN THIS ENCYCLOPEDIA

(words in italics have their own entries alphabetically)

access. This variable measures the degree to which speakers of a language can read the Scriptures in a language they understand. There are 2 varieties: (1) *direct* access to Scripture is available when a translation has been made into a people's mother tongue; and (2) *indirect* access to Scripture is available when *near-scripture* (near-Bible, near-NT, etc) exists (translation in a language within the same cluster/outer language as the people's mother tongue).

action point. A sticking point or aspect holding up world evangelization which requires definite, specific action in order to overcome it.

adequacy. The quality or state of sufficiency of resources or activities to meet prior standards or promises, with special reference to meeting stated goals published by religious bodies.

adult. A person who is 15 years old or above.

advocacy. The process of championing a particular *unevangelized* population *segment*, especially if voiceless or neglected, and continually seeking opportunities to present its case for a larger share of Christian resources.

affiliated Christians. Church members: all persons belonging to or connected with organized churches, whose names are inscribed, written or entered on the churches' books, records, or rolls.

agencies-in-peoples. A measure of the widespread distribution of mission agencies across the world which quantifies one agency working in 50 peoples as 50 of these units.

agnostics. Persons who have no religion or do not believe in God but not militantly so.

alien Christian scale. Referring to a a specific people or other segment, this is a computed scale from 0-10 measuring culturally alien (non-indigenous) Christian and evangelistic influence on the people by estimating the number of Christians from other cultures who reside on its territory.

alien Christians. Christians who reside in or work on the territory of a different culture.

alternate future. A range of 2 or more future *scenarios* depicting possible future developments by means of trends and *statistics*, ranging from optimistic to pessimistic and covering all possible eventualities.

Apostolatus Copiae. (Latin: official translation into English: Workforce for the Apostolate). In Roman Catholic usage, the main statistical category for counting personnel (bishops, priests, deacons, monks, nuns, sisters, layworkers, catechists).

atheists. Militantly anti-religious or anti-Christian agnostics, secularists, or marxists.

audio gospel. A cassette or tape or recording of a complete Gospel.

audio scriptures. *Portions* (gospels) or *selections* on cassette, tape, or recording.

autoglossonym. Name for a people's own language as used by the people themselves in their own language; often with prefix or suffix meaning 'the language of'.

beachhead. The initial planting of indigenous fellowships in an otherwise *unreached* people or *unevangelized* population segment.

Bible. This term is always used to describe only the whole or complete Bible of 66 Books (sometimes plus Apocrypha).

Bibles in use. Number of Bibles in place in a country or population, allowing for the constant loss of copies due to wear and tear or other forms of attrition.

biblioglossonym. The name chosen by a Bible society by which a translation of the Bible, or part of it, is formally known; often the anglicized form (e.g. French, German, Russian), often the speakers' own *autoglossonym* (français, deutsch, russki).

bibliometrics. The science of measurement of books, libraries, cataloguing, publishing, use of books, analysis, future usage.

billion. 1,000 millions (American usage; British, French, and German usage is a million millions).

billionaire. An individual (or occasionally a family) worth one *billion* USA dollars or over.

bite-sized piece. Colloquial term for manageable population *segments* which, because of either their homogeneity or their moderate size, are capable of being monitored by a single nonresidential missionary or couple.

bivocational. Adjective describing a tentmaker or missionary with the dual vocation of (a) a secular profession in a restricted-access country, undertaken in order to exercise (b) part-time Christian *witness* or service or church planting.

black money. Banked profits from criminal enterprise.

Book. Any one of the 39 distinct books constituting the Christian Bible, or any set of them, which has been translated whole (at least one complete book), published, and distributed in a language; also termed a *scripture*, or a *portion* or a gospel; capitalized with a 'B' to distinguish it from other varieties of book, and as a parallel to 'Bible', 'Testament'.

book titles. Term used to refer to distinct and separate books, as in a library or bookstore, to avoid misunderstanding with copies or print runs of the same book.

bridge people. A variety of *people group* that can be regarded as a bridge for evangelistic ministry toward an otherwise unreachable or inaccessible target segment.

catechumen. A non-member of a church receiving instruction in Christian doctrine, ethics, and morality, prior to admission into the church through baptism.

chances. Used in the numerical analysis of distinct occasions or opportunities for persons to become disciples of Christ; synonymous with offers, invitations.

Charismatics. Baptized members affiliated to nonpentecostal denominations who have entered into the experience of being filled with the Holy Spirit; the Second Wave of the Pentecostal/Charismatic/Neocharismatic Renewal.

Christian. Followers of Jesus Christ as Lord, of all kinds, all traditions and confessions, and all degrees of commitment.

Christian safety index. An index, 0-100, with 100 as the safest, measuring the relative safety of Christians living in a particular country. The index measures a country's human suffering, murder rate, and religious liberty.

Christian World. In the *3-tier schema*, this is *World C*, consisting of all who individually are *Christians*.

Christopagans. Roman Catholics of Latin background, chiefly in Latin America, who combine traditional pre-Columbian ethnoreligion with popular Roman Catholic religiosity (images, shamans, incense, idols, nomenclature).

Classical Pentecostals. Denominational Pentecostals of North American or European origin, of 2 types: Baptistic Pentecostals, and Holiness Pentecostals, both being Trinitarian.

closed country. A country whose government or regime has closed it to some major form or forms of Christian ministry from outside, usually resident foreign missionaries, visiting evangelists, or freely distributed *scriptures*, Christian literature, tapes or videos or films, or other Christian influences from outside.

closed-country ministry. Legal or illegal modes of Christian mission and ministry, resident or *itinerant*, full-time or part-time, in countries otherwise closed to Christian activity.

closing country. A country still open to outside Christian influences but whose increasing restrictions suggest it may become closed within a few months or years.

closure. The concept that the mandate of the church for world mission can be completed in a measurable way by evangelizing or reaching all peoples on Earth; not effectively invoked unless attached to some sort of deadline, the usual one in the 1980s and 1990s being AD 2000.

cluster. *Language cluster* (qv); in religion, a grouping or family of related religions.

communion. A family of religions or denominations with many common ties and features.

comparative demographic evangelization. An index of the extent of evangelization among a population or population *segment*, as measured by a scale of 270 variables or indicators, and summed up as *E%*, the percentage of persons who have become evangelized.

complete Bibles. Copies of the whole Bible with 66 Books (sometimes plus Apocrypha).

continent. Defined by United Nations as one of 6 Major Regions/Macroregions.

continental area. UN definition of continent, now renamed *macro region*.

convergency. A concept describing the unstructured way in which the *world evangelization* thrusts of 7 major ecclesiastical traditions (Roman Catholic, Orthodox, Ecumenical, Evangelical, Catholic Charismatic, Pentecostal/Charismatic, and Fundamentalist) have converged since 1970 in stated aims, goals, terminology, theology, missiology, publications, periodicals, activities, cooperation, and programs, as a result of lay pressures and initiatives, and in many cases despite opposition from their own leaders.

conversion. A change in a person's allegiance or membership in one religion to allegiance or membership in another.

cosmoreligion. A universal (non-local) religion open to all, with over 200 million adherents.

cost-effectiveness. As a comparative measure, the total cost, to Christians in a country, of baptizing one person.

country. A term covering both (a) sovereign nations, and (b) nonsovereign territories (dependencies or colonies) which are not integral parts of larger parent nations.

covert evangelizers. Active Christians working anonymously or secretly.

cross-cultural missions scale. A computed scale from 0-16 measuring the influence of cross-cultural missionary presence and activity within a people or other *segment*.

crypto-Christians. Secret believers, hidden Christians, usually known to churches but not to state or secular or non-Christian religious society.

culture. Used here to signify a people and its total pattern of human behavior and its products.

Cursillistas. Roman Catholics since 1949, and Protestants since 1970, who have attended and completed a short course or retreat under the movement Cursillos de Cristianidad; including many early leaders of the Catholic Charismatic Renewal.

databasing. Use of a large collection of data (facts or figures) in a computer, organized so that it can be expanded, updated, and retrieved rapidly.

datacasting. The regular broadcasting of large quantities of computerized data over the airwaves for automatic reception and use by computer users, mainly with microcomputers.

denomination. Any agency consisting of a number of congregations or churches voluntarily aligning themselves with it. As a statistical unit in this Encyclopedia, a 'denomination' always refers to one single country. Thus the Roman Catholic Church, although a single organization, is described here as consisting of 236 denominations in the world's 238 countries.

denominationalism. The promoting of centralized agencies exercising control or oversight over their recognized congregations.

denominationalist. One who actively or aggressively promotes denominationalism.

dimension. Empirical characteristic of a measurement, size, magnitude, activity, quality, extent, scope, often assuming an explanatory function.

direct access. *Access* (qv) to Scripture in one's own mother tongue.

dirty money. Underground money, criminal profits, undeclared, unrecorded, untaxed, illegal monies of all kinds.

disaffiliated. One-time church members who later repudiate that membership, and in countries allowing it, obtain legal separation from their church.

disciple-opportunities. Chances or opportunities for individuals or groups to accept Christ as Savior and Lord.

discipleship scale. A computed scale from 0-10 measuring the evangelistic influence of Christian discipleship in a population *segment* by estimating the number of disciples.

distribution. In Bible society usage, term for measuring annual circulation or sale of scripture copies.

distribution goal. Any announced deadline some years into the future for reaching a firm numerical goal or objective.

doubly-affiliated Christians. Persons who are baptized members of 2 or more denominations at the same time.

doubly-counted Catholics. Catholics counted as members of an older diocese or jurisdiction who also get counted again as members of a newer diocese when it is divided off from its parent diocese.

doubly-counted religionists. Persons counted as belonging to 2 or more religions, hence counted twice in censuses.

E. A computed estimate of the percentage of persons in a particular population *segment* (world, country, people, city) who have become evangelized, by or at a particular date.

e-mail. Electronic mail (qv).

ecclesiastical crime. Criminal activity on the part of church officials; restricted in scope here to embezzlements of church funds by their top custodians (treasurers, presidents, et alii).

education rate. Percentage of the school-age population (aged 5-24) who are enrolled in schools.

electronic mail (e-mail). The regular sending and receiving of mail, letters, memos, and reports, over a computer network locally or worldwide.

engagement. An initial stage or first step in the process of a foreign mission agency formally beginning or taking responsibility for ministry in a foreign country where hitherto it has had no work; often focused on a particular people group or other *segment*.

ethnic non-users. Members of an ethnic group who do not use or understand its own mother-tongue language, preferring instead to learn and use a lingua franca.

ethnocultural people. An ethnic or racial population or people group defined by its ethnic and cultural behavior and features.

ethnolinguistic people. A distinct homogeneous ethnic

or racial group within a single country, speaking its own language (one single mother tongue). A large people spread across 2, 3, 4, or several countries is treated here as being 2, 3, 4, or several distinct ethnolinguistic peoples.

ethnoreligionists. Followers of a non-Christian or pre-Christian religion tied closely to a specific ethnic group, with membership restricted to that group; usually animists, polytheists, or shamanists. Older terminology: pagans, heathens, tribal religionists, traditional religionists.

ethnosphere. The world with its populations and cultures seen in terms of its ethnicity.

***euangelizo* (Greek).** This central biblical concept has 140 synonyms in biblical Greek and 700 meanings in current English centered around the English transliteration *evangelize*.

evangelicals. Church members of evangelical conviction, involved in Christ's mission on Earth; synonymous with Great Commission Christians.

Evangelicals. A subdivision mainly of Protestants consisting of all affiliated church members calling themselves Evangelicals, or all persons belonging to Evangelical congregations, churches or denominations; characterized by commitment to personal religion.

evangelism. The church's organized activity of spreading the gospel, in circumstances it can control, in contrast to *witness* which is the normal term for the informal, spontaneous, unorganized sharing of their faith by individual Christians in circumstances they do not control.

evangelism-hours. Amount of time in hours spent by evangelists among a specific population.

evangelistics. The science of, or the scientific study of, the growth and expansion of Christianity.

evangelization. (a)The whole process of spreading the good news of the Kingdom of God; (b) the extent to which the good news has been spread; (c) the extent of awareness of Christianity, Christ, and the gospel.

evangelize. To spread the good news of Christ, with signs following, in both supernatural power and compassionate deed, to preach, to persuade, to call to faith in Christ; and 700 other meanings in English.

Evangelized Non-Christian World. In the *3-tier schema*, this is *World B* which consists of all non-Christians who have nevertheless become evangelized.

evangelized person. An individual who has had adequate opportunity or opportunities to hear the gospel and to respond to it, whether he responds positively or negatively.

evangelizer. A Christian who is active regularly in *witness, evangelism*, and winning others to Christ.

expert system. A computer software program that encapsulates the expertise of a recognized human expert in some domain of knowledge; consisting of a knowledge base (facts and heuristics or rules of thumb), an inference engine or reasoning system, and a natural-language user interface.

exposure. Used as a measure of evangelism by numerous agencies (e.g. Campus Crusade for Christ): workers fill in statistical reports stating how many persons they have exposed to the Gospel in a presentation over the last month or year.

externally evangelized. Those persons in a people or population who have become evangelized as a result of persons or agencies or programs from outside their own people or population.

fax. Facsimile transmission of digitized pictures or text over telephone lines.

First World. In the post World War II terminology originated with Charles de Gaulle, the Western world (Europe, Northern America) in contrast to the communist world and the *Third World*.

First-Wavers. Denomination Pentecostals (Classical Pentecostals), members of mainline USA churches and their worldwide constituencies.

force for evangelism. The effective evangelizing nucleus in the church, made up of active *Great Commission Christians* who are engaged in some form of regular evangelizing.

force for evangelization. The total of all practicing church members, whose practice has various direct and indirect influences on *evangelization*.

foreign missionary. A full-time Christian worker who works in a country in which he or she is not a citizen but an alien.

foreign missions. Christian outreach carried out in any other countries than where a sending church or mission is based.

frontier missionary. A full-time foreign or cross-cultural missionary who works among an *unreached people*, an *unevangelized* population *segment* or in *World A*.

frontier missions. Missionary work among the unreached or unevangelized peoples of the world, i.e. World A.

frontier people. An alternate term for an *unreached* minipeople.

futures. Futurists usually speak of possible futures in the plural when discussing the future of a particular entity or concept, posing a range of 2 or 3 *scenarios* of the future instead of a more risky single future prediction.

futuristics (or, futurology). The professional study of the future employing a wide range of analytical tools and scientific procedures.

generation. The average period (about 30 years) between the birth of one generational group on Earth, and that of the next; a 30-year period.

giganetwork. An electronic network linking a vast number of computers, around one billion or more. The number of general-purpose computers in the world is likely to reach 700 million by AD 2000 and to pass one billion by AD 2004. The number of Christian-owned and operated general-purpose computers is likely to reach one billion by AD 2008.

global codes. Codes used in the analysis of Christianity and mission which have the same meaning across the whole area of statistical analysis.

global desk. A central office within a *Great Commission agency* charged with keeping the agency accountable to its global goals as they relate to the unevangelized world, networking with other *Great Commission Christians*, and maintaining a deliberate and regular electronic link with other global desks in other agencies across the world.

global diagram. A single-page analysis of a mission situation, concept, or term bringing together all relevant data, tables, graphics, diagrams, photographs.

global evangelization movement. A term describing the vast number of distinct agencies and plans directed towards *world evangelization* which have proliferated across the world since the year 1900.

global meganetwork. A *Great Commission* global *meganetwork* .

global mission. The mission of Jesus Christ as it involves the entire world.

global missions. Mission agencies with work in over 50 nations of the world or sends out over 5,000 foreign missionary personnel.

global network. A *Great Commission* global network.

global plans. A documented, christocentric plan, proposal, or program that starts with the Great Commission and articulates concern for evangelizing the world's entire population.

global statistics. Numbers, series of figures, and other varieties of *statistics* describing any aspect of the entire world, the Earth, our globe, its populations, its problems, its past, its present, and its future.

globalist. A specialist in *globalistics*, one who consistently takes the global view and emphasizes the big-picture approach to researching and understanding world problems.

globalistics. The professional study of the world in its entirety, with all its peoples, groupings, problems, and possibilities.

globalized evangelization. An organized pseudo-global attempt by a church or mission agency to reach the world by taking a successful local program of mission and *evangelism*, adding to it simply a veneer of global terminology, and then regarding it as certain to *evangelize* the whole world.

globalized mission. Pseudo-global missions, as initiated by mission agencies which profess to work for *global mission*, which propound a veneer of global or pseudo-global terminology, but which operate in budget-program isolation from other missions.

globalized missions. An impressionistic term for mission agencies whose publicity and propaganda continuously employs global mission terminology but whose actions in practice remain parochial.

globe. A term referring here to the entire population of Earth, used instead of 'world' to distinguish it from the usage *World A, World B, World C*.

glossozone (zone). One of 100 linguistic areas describing the whole world of 13,500 languages.

goals. An aim or set of objectives to accomplish a purpose, here relating to world evangelization, usually in a specified time or by a certain date.

gospel. (1) The Good News about God, Jesus Christ, salvation and discipleship. (2) When capitalized, one of the 4 Gospels (Matthew, Mark, Luke, John). (3) Not capitalized, a printed copy of one of the Gospels for mass distribution.

gray money. Dirty money or criminal profits laundered by banks.

Great Commission. The final commandment of Jesus Christ on Earth, to his disciples before his Ascension, ordering the evangelizing, discipling, baptizing, and training of all peoples as his followers.

Great Commission (used as an adjective). A descriptive term for persons or organizations or plans or activities of any nationality, denomination, or confession which are based on Christ's Great Commission and which are actively working to obey it, personally and corporately.

Great Commission agency. A church or parachurch or service agency which publicizes its raison d'dtre as obedience to Christ's Great Commission.

Great Commission Christians. Believers in Jesus Christ who are aware of the implications of Christ's Great Commission, who have accepted its personal challenge in their lives and ministries, are attempting to obey his commands and mandates, and who are seeking to influence the body of Christ to implement it.

Great Commission instrument panel. A standard panel of 6 *instruments* employed here in every country's descriptive article in Part 4 to indicate the status of religion, mission, and evangelization in that country.

Great Commission network. A Great Commission network is defined as any agency or organization or aggregate of contacts which (1) frequently articulates or refers back to the Commission, (2) centers on obedience to it, (3) utilizes a number of computers to make the network function every day, initially utilizing electronic mail, and (4) results in some kind of missionary sending endeavor.

harvest force. The cutting edge of all frontier use of Christian resources in mission to non-Christians—personnel, organizations, agencies deployed for *global mission*; also termed *Great Commission Christians* and groupings.

hearing impaired persons. Deaf and partially-deaf persons, able to converse by signing (use of a signed language).

heuristic. The use of empirical knowledge and rules of thumb in problem-solving by an expert or an *expert system*.

hidden Buddhist believers in Christ. NBBC, (q.v.).

hidden Hindu believers in Christ. NBBC, (q.v.).

hidden Muslim believers in Christ. NBBC, (q.v.).

hidden people. An alternate term for an *unreached minipeople*.

home missionary. A full-time missionary worker assigned to work in the country where he or she is a citizen.

household size. Standard size, for statistical purposes, of a family, composed of 2 spouses, 2 children (under 15), and one adult (15 or over).

human network. The linking together of people as nodes horizontally (as equals, without hierarchy or executive authority); the linking of numbers of individuals or organizations to address common interests or problems.

human rights. The whole range of the rights of individuals, families, communities, religious persons, as set out in the UN's 1948 Universal Declaration on Human Rights (especially the detailing of religious freedoms).

idiom. A language whose speech community regards it and its autoglossonym as their mother tongue and which shares less than 95% common vocabulary with any other idiom.

independency. The ecclesiastical position rejecting control of churches by centralized denominationalist headquarters; organizing churches and missions independent of historic Christianity.

Independents. One of Christianity's 6 ecclesiastico-cultural megablocs, separated from, uninterested in, and independent of historic denominationalist Christianity (the other 5 megablocs).

indirect access. *Access* (qv) to Scripture but only through a near-scripture in a language in the same *cluster*.

infobasing. Use of a large collection of useful, understandable, and easily retrieved information stored in a computer. Information is more useful than raw data (facts and figures) but less organized than knowledge (understanding, learning) or wisdom (superior understanding).

inner language. Alternative term for a *language* (qv) as utilized in this Encyclopedia.

instrument. Any measuring device (Websters); in missiological usage, any of the 1,200 means or methods employed by churches and missions to record the progress and status of Christianity,and so recorded and described in the present Encyclopedia.

instruments. As described here, these are measuring devices used by churches and missions to document progress or lack of it.

intercessors. Christians undertaking to pray daily for unreached peoples, for World A, for non-Christians; often in institutions (monasteries, converts, ashrams) or in other structured situations (prayerwalking, Praying through the Window).

interdenominational. Occurring between or among or common to several or many different denominations; accountable to several denominations, or partially or completely controlled by them.

internally evangelized. Those persons in a people or population who have become evangelized as a result of persons or agencies of their own people or population.

internationals. (1) Persons living abroad; workers, laborers, businessman, entrepreneurs, students, and many other categories of persons who live, reside, and work in a foreign country; excluding tourists or other transients. (2) Professionals working for United Nations-related agencies or parallel global organizations (as contrasted with national or regional bodies).

Internet. A network of computer networks which allows users to communicate using electronic mail, to retrieve data stored in databases, and to access the World Wide Web.

invitations. Clearcut opportunities for hearers to accept Christ and become disciples; synonymous with offers, chances.

isolated radio believers. Persons in isolated areas with no churches or missions who have become Christians through radio programs.

itinerant. Adjective describing an evangelist, missionary, or other church worker whose ministry involves being continually on the move from one city or people or country to the next.

kaleidoscopic. Multifaceted, many-featured, constantly changing.

knowledge base. A collection of data, rules, inferences, and procedures in a specific field of interest, organized to form the basis for an intelligent computer *expert system*.

language. A grouping of *idioms* or dialects whose speech communities share 85% or more common vocabulary.

language cluster. Also termed outer language, a grouping of languages with which it shares 80% or more lexical similarity (shared words).

language net. A grouping of languages sharing 70% or more common vocabulary.

language set. A grouping of *languages* sharing common vocabulary.

language user. Speakers of a specific language who can understand or use other languages within a cluster through sharing 80% common vocabulary.

language, inner. Technical name for the popularly used simplification *'language'*.

language, outer. Synonym for *language cluster*.

latent Christians. Christians, both church members and unaffiliated, who do not involve themselves in Christ's mission on Earth (and so are not counted here as *Great Commission Christians*).

lexicostatistics. The study of languages by comparing lexicons (word lists) and finding how many words, and what percentages of a standard word-list, are shared in common by 2 or more languages.

limited-access country. A country whose government or regime limits access by alien foreign missionaries wishing to reside, usually by small or decreasing quotas or progressively shorter residence permits; see *closing country*.

linguametrics. The scientific measurement and study of the whole world of languages (as distinct from linguistics).

literates. Adults over 15 years old who have learned how to read and write in a language, either their mother-tongue or lingua franca or other second language.

local religion. A single ethnoreligion or tribal religion restricted to a local tribe's, or people's, population.

macro region. United Nations' definition of continent, dividing the world into 6 such regions; previously named *continental area* now replaced by *major area*.

macro segment. A major population subgrouping which occupies a primary or significant place in a global taxonomy of populations, and which is used in detailing the remaining *unfinished task*.

macrodenomination. A Christian denomination in a country whose affiliated members number 10 million or more.

macroevangelistics. The scientific study of the propagation of Christianity at the macroscopic or global level.

macroreligion. A global or worldwide religion or family of religions, usually with from 20 to 100 million adherents.

macrozone. One of 10 global zones used in language classification.

major area. UN term used in statistical enumerations instead of the looser term 'continent'.

major civil division (MCD). United Nations' term for the next level of administrative or political subdivision in a country immediately below nationwide level.

Mandates. Seven basic commands, known collectively as the Great Commission, given by Christ to his disciples, namely the imperatives Receive! Go! Witness! Proclaim! Disciple! Baptize! Train!

marginal Christians. Members affiliated to bodies holding mainstream Christian doctrines except on the nature of Christ, and existence of the Trinity; also professing a second source of revelation in addition to the Bible.

martyr. A Christian martyr is a believer in Christ who loses his or her life, prematurely, in a situation of *witness*, as a result of human hostility.

martyrdom situation. Any description of mass or multiple martyrdoms at one point in Christian history.

martyrdom, intensity of. Christian martyrdom measured by the ratio of martyrs to local Christians in a given martyrdom situation.

martyrdom, magnitude of. Christian martyrdom measured by the sheer number of martyrs in a given martyrdom situation.

martyrology. The study of the phenomenon of martyrdom with particular reference to its demography.

matching up or matching. The process of linking or linking up a particular *unreached people* or *unevangelized* population *segment* with a specific ministry or mission agency or missionary; in particular, with a nonresidential missionary whose vocation it would be to see that the segment becomes evangelized.

maternal mortality rate. The annual number of deaths of women from pregnancy-related causes per 100,000 live births.

megabloc. One of 6 major ecclesiastico-cultural subdivisions of affiliated Christians and their churches.

megachurch. A very large local congregation or church, with membership in the range 1,000 to 1 million.

megacity. A *metropolis* or other city with a population of over one million persons.

megacommunion. A worldwide communion, world confessional family, or family of megatraditions, usually with over 10 million adherents.

megadenomination. A Christian denomination whose affiliated members in a country number one million or more.

megametrodwellers. Persons residing in cities with populations greater than a million.

megaministry. A specific global or other large-scale ministry reaching or evangelizing over one million persons a day, or (in earlier years) over 1% of the world's population every year.

megamissionary. A term coined for a missionary who is engaged in or working with a *megaministry*.

meganetwork. An electronic network linking a very large number of computers, around one million or more.

megapeople. An *ethnolinguistic people* speaking a single mother tongue whose population numbers over one million.

megareligion. A world religion or family of religions, usually with from one to 20 million adherents.

megarich. All *millionaires* of all kinds.

Messianic Jews. Jewish believers in Christ as Messiah who opt not to join mainline churches but form independent churches retaining much Hebrew terminology and Jewish traditions and customs.

metrodweller. A person residing in a city with a population greater than 50,000.

metropeople. An *ethnolinguistic people* or *sociopeople* resident in a *metropolis*, and forming a distinct homogenous group within it.

metropolis. The central city of a country or region or area, whether large or small (from the Greek for 'mother city').

metroscan. A statistical analysis of the world's metropolises, especially analyzing the presence or absence of Christians and evangelization.

micro segment. A minor population subgrouping which occupies only a minor or secondary place in a global taxonomy of populations, and which is used for local targeting in *evangelization*.

microevangelistics. The scientific study of the propagation of Christianity at the microscopic level of individuals, churches, peoples, countries.

micropeople. A small close-knit homogenous population *segment*.

millionaire. An individual (or occasionally a family) worth one million USA dollars or over.

minipeople. The largest *people group* within which the gospel can spread as a church-planting movement without encountering barriers of understanding or acceptance.

ministry option. One of a list of possible or potential ministries or missionary or evangelistic approaches that a noresidential missionary draws up, which he considers could be undertaken by a large variety of agents and agencies on behalf on his target segment.

missiological breakthrough. A term employed as a synonym to minimum mission achievement, which in turn rests on the basic, essential need for a *people movement* to Christ in a given culture.

missiology. Academic discipline or professional study of the church's task of spreading the Christian faith among nations of the world.

missiometrics. The science of mission with special reference to measurement, statistics, and analysis.

mission. The task, obligation, or commission adopted by the church to spread the Christian faith throughout the world.

monitoring. The process of regularly tracking and recording the progress of *evangelization* in a particular *unreached people* or *unevangelized* population *segment* with special reference to measuring the impact of all *Great Commission* activities and influences.

monovocational. In contrast to *bivocational* persons, monovocational persons describes missionaries whose main or only vocation and profession is full-time Christian service with particular emphasis on the ministry of evangelization and evangelism that results in churches.

mother tongue. Main language of a person's home or childhood; the first language spoken in an individual's home in his early or earliest childhood; one's first language or native language.

multichanneling. A mode of operation which accepts the present unsatisfactory multiplicity of *global plans* on the part of hundreds of mission agencies, recognizing that their *standalone* nature at least serves as insurance against multiple or overall failure.

multimillionaire. An individual worth many tens of millions of USA dollars.

name for God. In any people's scriptures, the major name used in those scriptures for God, the Supreme Being.

nation. A politically-organized nationality with independent, self-governing, autonomous existence as a sovereign *country* or nation-state, hence eligible for membership in the United Nations.

native language. Mother tongue (qv).

natural increase. Births in a population minus deaths within a fixed period, usually one year. Sometimes a figure for net immigration is added.

near-Bible. A Bible translation in a language in the same cluster as languages without translations but sufficiently close for speakers of the latter to utilize it.

near-gospel. A gospel translation in a language within the same cluster as several languages without, but which can use it because they share 80% common vocabulary.

near-NT. For a language without its own translation of the New Testament, any translation in a related-language within its cluster can be understood and used.

near-scriptures. Scriptures which can benefit a scripture-less language because the 2 languages concerned are within the same cluster.

Neo-Apostolic Reformation. Self-appellation of *Postdenominationalists/Independents.*

Neocharismatics. Members of the Third Wave of the Pentecostal/Charismatic Renewal characterized by the adjectives Independent, Postdenominationalist, and Neo-Apostolic.

Neopagans. New 20th-century attempts to revive long-dead traditional pre-Christian religion and beliefs.

networking. A term so widely used for any type of non-hierarchical communication that its value is best preserved by: (a) restricting it to mean computer networking or electronic networking involving the regular linking of 3 or more computers; and (b) using the term 'human networking' when all other kinds of non-electronic communication are meant.

new Christians. Totals of all who become Christians for the first time are larger than annual church growth because they equal annual increase in number of Christians plus annual deaths of Christians.

New Reader Scriptures. 1-, 4-, or 8- page Selections of texts, or whole Book translations of a gospel (New Reader Portions) prepared for newly literate reader, always illustrated.

New-Religionists. Adherents of Hindu or Buddhist sects or offshoots, or new syncretistic religious combining Christianity with Eastern religions, mostly in Asia.

newly baptized. Believers baptized within the last one-year period.

nomenklatura (Russian). Privileged bureaucratic elites in Communist or formerly-Communist countries.

non-baptized believers in Christ (NBBCs). Members of non-Christian religions who become converted to faith in Christ as Lord but choose not to join denominations but to remain in their religions as witnesses there to Christ.

Non-Christians. Generic term for describing all persons in the world who are not Christians.

non-native language. Any language understood by a people although not their mother tongue.

non-native speaker. Speakers of a language as a second or third language.

Non-White indigenous Christians. Independent believers, on every continent, who form their own autonomous churches, mostly pentecostal or charismatic in emphasis.

nondenominational. Of a parachurch agency, unrelated to any denomination or denominations, not accountable to any, outside their control.

nonreligious. Persons professing no religion, no interest in religion; secularists, materialists; agnostics, but not militantly antireligious or atheists.

nonreligionists. Term encompassing the 2 varieties of unbeliever: (a) *agnostics* or secularists or materialists, who are *nonreligious* but not hostile to religion, and (b) *atheists* or anti-religious/anti-religionists militantly opposed or hostile to religion.

nonsovereign country. A political entity or country which is not free of external control, hence not a nation but a colony or other dependent territory.

nonsighted persons. The blind.

offers. A scientific count producing numbers of concrete disciple-opportunities, invitations, chances to hear the gospel and become disciples of Christ.

Oneness Pentecostals. Denominational Pentecostals originating in the USA from 1910 onwards, now widespread worldwide, who emphasize baptism in the name of 'Jesus Only' and who oppose the doctrine of the Trinity.

online. Connecting through a network, modem, or high-speed cable to a computer service, usually accessing e-mail or the World Wide Web.

outer language. Alternative term for a *language cluster* (qv).

overt evangelizers. Evangelizing Christians who work openly without having to fear government spies or religious police in hostile lands.

p.a. Per annum, per year, each year, every year, annual, yearly, over the previous 12 months.

p.d. Per diem, per day, daily.

paradenomination. A recent network of churches that is becoming a new denomination but resisting denominationalist shortcomings.

people movement. The spread of the gospel among a people in such a way that all individuals in that group are presented with an opportunity to know Christ; usually accompanied by significant response.

people, people group. A significantly large grouping of individuals who perceive themselves to have a common affinity for one another because of their shared language, religion, ethnicity, residence, occupation, class or caste, situation, etc. or combination of these. The statistical unit 'people' in this Encyclopedia always refers to a people, or part thereof, in one single country.

persecution. Persecution of believers specifically on religious grounds, though this is often denied.

pluridenominational. A country's situation where denominations number over 1,000.

polytheists. Ethnoreligionists (q.v.) who worship several or many gods and deities.

popular-religionists. Practitioners of popularized versions of Christianity often combined with non-Christian features or superstitions.

Portions. Copies of a complete Book of the Bible, usually one of the 4 Gospels.

Postcharismatics. Formerly active Charismatics in mainline nonpentecostal denominations who still regard themselves as Charismatics though active in other different areas of church life.

Postdenominationalists. Independents and others who have replaced historic denominationalism by non-centralized lifestyle and church order.

Postpentecostals. Former members of classical Pentecostal denominations who leave to join nonpentecostal mainline churches but still regard themselves as Pentecostals.

Prepentecostals. Believers experiencing or manifesting marks of baptism in the Holy Spirit (glossolalia, healings) before the arrival of Denominational Pentecostalism.

prioritization. The science of setting priorities, especially as it relates the world's least evangelized population segments, e.g. peoples.

pseudo-religion. Undesirable or negative religious movement, usually with bad effects on persons under its influence.

quasi-religion. A secular movement which is partly or virtually a religion, but is also either antireligious or nonreligious or pseudo-religious.

quasipentecostal. Nonpentecostal or noncharismatic church members or churches which nevertheless are apparently/seemingly/largely pentecostal or semipentecostal in practice; especially strong in Third-World countries;not usually counted in Renewal enumerations.

R&D. Research and development, usually a budget item with a fixed percentage (1-10%) of a nation's or a large organization's annual income.

reached. Having heard the gospel, understanding it, and having had the opportunity to respond by joining an indigenous church or fellowship of one's own culture.

reached minipeople. A *minipeople* with a *viable indigenous church* capable of evangelizing the whole group, that is, with the resources and vision to reach out to the whole people.

reached people. An *ethnolinguistic people* with a *viable indigenous church* with the resources and vision to *evangelize* the whole people.

reached person. An individual who has had an adequate opportunity to hear the gospel and to respond to it, and also to contact a church of his own culture and to meet and join in fellowship with other believers.

region. UN term for statistical enumeration referring to a subdivision of a major area (continent).

religiometrics. The scientific measurement and analysis of religions and adherents, with special reference to description, analysis, trends.

religion. A religion is a grouping of persons with beliefs about God or gods, and defined by its adherents' loyalty to it, by their acceptance of it as unique and superior to all other religions, and by its relative autonomy.

religionists. Persons professing adherence to any religion, as contrasted with atheists or nonreligious persons.

religious liberty. Freedom to practice one's religion with the full range of religious rights specified in the UN's 1948 *Universal Declaration of Human Rights.*

religious libraries. A large library (over 100,000 volumes) specializing mainly in the study of religion.

Renewal. (1) Generic term for over 100 different current movements of revival or awakening or new spiritual life across the whole spectrum of global Christianity, involving 1,100 million Christians (68% of all affiliated church members). (2) Shorthand term for the entire Pentecostal/Charismatic/Neocharismatic Renewal in the Holy Spirit.

responsiveness of a population, R, a measure quantified as new church members baptized per year, per million evangelism-hours expended per year. Higher values indicate greater responsiveness to evangelism, lowest values signify small or even zero response.
restricted-access country. A country whose government or regime restricts access by foreign missionaries wishing to reside, foreign Christians wishing to visit, or foreign Christian literature, or broadcasting, or other Christian ministries or influences.
ruralites. Rural dweller, person residing in the countryside rather than in an urban area.
scenario. A description of one possible future situation with regard to a church or agency or person or population or country, developed by detailed compilation of likely trends and statistics. The study of the future of any such situation is best conducted by drawing up a range of 2 or 3 such scenarios, termed possible *alternate futures*, ranging from optimistic to pessimistic and covering all possible eventualities, good or bad.
Scripture (with capital 'S'). Holy Scripture, the Christian Scriptures, the Bible.
scripture (with small 's'). Printed copy or copies of the Bible, New Testament, Gospel, Portion, New Reader Portion, or any other Book (all the foregoing being capitalized to distinguish them from less specialized varieties of book or publication); or selection of Scripture texts.
Scripture language. A language in which some Scripture activity exists, either distribution of complete *scriptures* (complete *Books* of the Bible) in print, radio, audio, or video versions; or partial scriptures (ongoing translation and preparation of complete scriptures, or use of selections of texts in print, radio, or audio versions).
scripture translation status. A language's status with regard to translation, publication, provision and availability of its own Bible, New Testament, Portion (gospel), and Selection.
Second World. Formerly used of the Communist world, and still used now of the Communist/ex-Communist world.
second-language scriptures. Copies of Scripture used by persons without mother-tongue scriptures; usually in lingua francas.
Second-Wavers. Charismatics in the Renewal within mainline nonpentecostal churches.
segment. Any homogeneous subdivision of the world's population, made for purposes of understanding and analysis; the most generalized English translation of the biblical Greek word *ethnos* (usually translated "people").
segmentization. The process of dividing the world's population into meaningful small *segments,* usually countries, peoples, or cities in order to assist toward their *targeting* and *evangelization.*
Selections. 1-, 2-, 4-, or 8-page leaflets or booklets of Scripture texts on a topical theme, used in mass-distribute campaigns by Bible societies and churches in many lands.
Self-Religionists. Followers of varieties of religion centering on benefiting followers and helping them live prosperous lives.
service agency. Major national, international or countrywide bodies, parachurch organizations and agencies which assist or serve the churches but are not themselves denominations or church-planting missions.
shamanists. Ethnoreligionists with a hierarchy of shamans and healers.
short-term (short-service) missionary. Persons serving abroad as foreign missionary personnel under a recognized mission agency for a single period of from 3 to 24 months only.
slumdwellers. Persons residing in make-shift dwellings on the streets of the world's cities.
sociolect. An *idiom* or dialect differing from a standard only in pronunciation, accent, or special vocabulary.
sociopeople. A *people* or population group defined primarily by some sociological category such as class, caste, occupation, age, abode, for which a specific evangelistic strategy may be developed; sometimes regarded as a *bridge people* useful for initiating evangelism.
sovereign country. A *nation,* being an autonomous independent country free of external control.
standalone. This adjective as used here does not refer to individuals but to agencies or *global plans* which operate organizationally unrelated to the rest of the *Great Commission* world, i.e. with budget and program unrelated to those of other agencies; also used of a computer or network which serves only its immediate user without being linked or networked to other computers or other networks.
statistics. Facts or data of a numerical kind assembled, classified, and tabulated so as to present significant information about a given subject; the science of this process. Statistics are the shortest and most compact form of factual description with regard to a population or situation.
strategy coordinator. See nonresidential missionary.
structures of sin. The superstructure of organized human activity based on selfishness, greed, sin, evil, that keeps half the world's population in degrading poverty.
supercity. A city with over 4 million inhabitants.
supergiant. A city with over 10 million inhabitants.
target people. An ethnolinguistic people which is the evangelistic focus of a Christian worker, missionary, couple, or small team seeking to benefit that people in measurable ways.
targeting variable. Term from United Nations' usage denoting priority of measurable benefits: literacy, health care, famine or disaster relief (1-10, with 1=top priority).
teleporting. The transmission of very large quantities of digitized data by telecommunication round through teleports (specialized ground stations handling huge volumes daily).
Third World. Developing nations not politically aligned with either the Western (Capitalist) world (the First World) or the Communist/Marxist-related world (the Second World). The term is purely chronological (like "third child") and has never carried connotations of inferiority (as "third-rate" does). It is the standard term to use for the nonaligned world and should be used instead of popularized alternatives like "Two-Thirds World: a noncomparative term based only on population size".
Third-Wavers. Believers who have experienced baptism in the Holy Spirit but who do not affiliate with First-Wavers or Second-Wavers but who join Neocharismatic/Postdenominational congregations.
three (3) tier schema. A stylized schematic representation in which, to enhance the understanding of *world evangelization*, the globe is divided into 3 slices or tiers or worlds, and given the names *World A*, the *Unevangelized World; World B*, the *Evangelized Non-Christian World*; and *World C*, the *Christian World.*
tradition. An ecclesiastical family or type of denominations with many common features.
transient (noun). A person who is present in a country or area temporarily before moving on; usually a visitor, tourist, person on business, military personnel, refugee, displaced person.
tribal religionists. *Ethnoreligionists* (qv).
Trinitarianism. The Christian doctrine of the triune nature of the Godhead (Father, Son, and Holy Spirit). In the 20th century, this has become the major non-negotiable dogma of mainstream Christianity.
U. A computed estimate of the percentage of peoples in a particular population *segment* (world, country, person, city) who are unevangelized; equivalent to 100-E, as %.
unaffiliated Christians. Persons professing allegiance and commitment to Christ but who have no church affiliation.
unevangelized. Never having heard the Good News of Jesus Christ.
unevangelized persons. Individuals who have had no adequate opportunity to hear the gospel or respond to it; persons who are unaware of Christianity, Christ, and the gospel; those who have never heard the name of Jesus.
unevangelized World. In the *3-tier schema*, this is *World A*, consisting of all non-Christians who have not been evangelized.
unfinished task. The remaining task of evangelization, as the task of the Christian church on Earth, viewed as the church's responsibility usually viewed as completing the fulfillment of Christ's Great Commission.
unimax people. An alternate term for *minipeople* emphasizing the maximum size of people in which the gospel can spread before encountering barriers.
unreached. Never having heard the gospel nor having had the opportunity to contact an indigenous church or fellowship of one's own culture.
unreached minipeople. A *minipeople* with no *viable indigenous church.*
unreached people. An *ethnolinguistic people* which does not have its own *viable indigenous church.*
unreached person. Individuals who have, or have had, no adequate opportunity to hear the gospel, or to respond to it, or to meet and have fellowship with other believers.
urban dweller. *urbanites* (qv).
urbanites. Urban dwellers, persons residing in a city, town, or recognized urban area.
users of a language. All persons in a country who can understand a language since it belongs to a language cluster containing their own.
vehicular megalanguage. A language with a million or more speakers which acts a a trade language or lingua franca.
viable indigenous church. Within an *ethnolinguistic people* or *minipeople*, an indigenous community of believing Christians with adequate numbers and resources to evangelize their own *people group* without needing outside cross-cultural assistance.
visual gospel. (1) A film or movie of the life of Christ, either via video, or in an 8mm or 16mm presentation; or (2) a film strip based on a gospel, or (3) an art exhibit illustrating the Good News by works of art (paintings) or photographs.
volume of evangelism. A scientifically-derived computed estimate of the percentage of persons in a country or other population *segment* who have become influenced by evangelism to awareness of Christianity, Christ, and the gospel.
witness. The normal term used for the informal, spontaneous, unorganized sharing of their faith, by presence, word, or deed, by individual Christians in circumstances they do not control; as contrasted with organized *evangelism.*
Workforce for the Apostolate. Apostolatus Copiae (qv).
World A. In the *3-tier schema* or representation of the Earth, the *Unevangelized World*, i.e. the world of all unevangelized individuals.
World A countries. Countries in which evangelized individuals number under 50% of the population.
World A individuals. Unevangelized persons unaware of Christianity, Christ, or the gospel.
World A peoples. Ethnolinguistic peoples each with over 50% of population unevangelized.
World B. In the *3-tier schema* or representation of the Earth, the *Evangelized Non-Christian World*, i.e. all non-Christians who have nevertheless become evangelized.
World B countries. Countries in which evangelized persons number over 50% but Christians number less than 60%.
World B individuals. Non-Christians who have nevertheless become evangelized.
World B peoples. Ethnolinguistic peoples among whom evangelized persons number over 50% but Christians under 60%.
World C. In the *3-tier schema* or representation of the Earth, the *Christian World*, i.e. the world of all who individually are Christians.
World C countries. Countries in which Christians number 60% or more of the population.
World C individuals. Persons who are Christians.
World C peoples. Ethnolinguistic peoples among whom 60% or more of the population are Christian.
world evangelization. The term used for the goal of reaching the entire world with the gospel of Christ, or of giving every *people* and population on Earth the opportunity to hear the gospel with understanding and to become disciples of Christ.
World Wide Web. A hypermedia-based system for browsing Internet sites, housing millions of home pages, including most Christian organizations.
worship center. A church building or congregation's premises or other place for regular weekly services of Christian worship.
zone. In linguistic classification, a *glossozone* (qv).

Part 3

CODEBOOK

Quick-reference codebook for all statistical tables

Les chiffres sont les signes de Dieu—Statistics are signs from God.
—Prior Roger Schutz of Taizé Community, 1967

Part 3 gives all codes and meanings used throughout the Encyclopedia, with 2 exceptions. (1) The databases shown in Parts 7, 8, 9, 10, and 11 give their own codes in their own Parts immediately before the data appears. (2) So likewise does Part 6 "Atlas".

The pages that follow set out alphabetically or systematically, for quick reference, the meaning of the mainly mutually-exclusive classifications, categories, columns, codes, and abbreviations used in this Encyclopedia's statistical tables and in its related *World Christian database.* These summary tables of codes are as follows:

1. Table 3-1 lists countries and country codes used in many tables to save space.
2. Table 3-2 lists global codes used throughout, listed alphabetically by code.
3. Table 3-3 lists global codes used throughout, listed alphabetically by name.
4. Table 3-4 lists standard terms and codes for 85 categories of 'Christians' and 100 varieties of 'non-Christians'.

These are followed by detailed codes used in the 2 main tables for every country, which are shown in the main survey articles under Part 4 "Countries". These are arranged as follows:

5. Table 3-5 interprets ***Country Tables 1:*** Religion adherents in each country, AD 1900-2025.
6. Table 3-6 explains ***Country Tables 2:*** Organized churches and denominations in each country.
7. Table 3-7 gives codes for ***Part 5 "CountryScan", Table 5-1:*** Geopolitico-religious data and typologies for all countries and continents, AD 1900-2025.

A listing of all 167 variables is given here, but only those with codes are listed in detail.

8. ***Parts 7, 8, 9, 10, 11.*** These 5 Parts reproduce very large numbers of pages from source databases enumerating respectively the titles Religiometrics, EthnoSphere, LinguaMetrics, MetroScan, ProvinceScan.

Meanings of all columns and codes that they employ are given each within its Part immediately before its table of data. They are not therefore repeated here in this present Codebook.

Part 6 "Atlas". All scales, codes, symbols, and meanings used on the 16 Global Maps are explained each on its map's Key and under the map's title. Likewise the 18 Human Environment topographical maps that follow each has within it its detailed key with meanings.

Quick-reference codebook for all statistical tables

1. COUNTRIES LISTED BY CODE.

Table 3-1. **Standard short names for all 238 countries in the world, expanded official names (anglicized, after UN usage), and 4-letter codes.**

afgh	**AFGHANISTAN,** The Islamic State of
alba	**ALBANIA,** The Republic of
alge	**ALGERIA,** The People's Democratic Republic of
amer	**AMERICAN SAMOA,** The Territories of
ando	**ANDORRA,** The Principality of
ango	**ANGOLA,** The Republic of
angu	**ANGUILLA,** The Dependency of
anta	**ANTARCTICA,** The Continent of
anti	**ANTIGUA & BARBUDA,** The Realm of
arge	**ARGENTINA;** The Argentine Republic
arme	**ARMENIA,** The Republic of
arub	**ARUBA,** The Territory of
aust	**AUSTRALIA,** The Commonwealth of
ausz	**AUSTRIA,** The Republic of
azer	**AZERBAIJAN;** The Azerbaijani Republic
baha	**BAHAMAS,** The Commonwealth of the
bahr	**BAHRAIN,** The State of
bang	**BANGLADESH,** The People's Republic of
barb	**BARBADOS,** The Realm of
belg	**BELGIUM,** The Kingdom of
beli	**BELIZE,** The Realm of
belo	**BELORUSSIA;** The Republic of Belarus
beni	**BENIN,** The Republic of
berm	**BERMUDA;** The Colony of the Bermuda Islands
bhut	**BHUTAN,** The Kingdom of
boli	**BOLIVIA,** The Republic of
bosn	**BOSNIA & HERCEGOVINA,** The Republic of
bots	**BOTSWANA,** The Republic of
boug	**BOUGAINVILLE,** The Republic of
braz	**BRAZIL,** The Federative Republic of
brit	**BRITAIN;** The United Kingdom of Great Britain and Northern Ireland (UK of GB & NI)
briy	**BRITISH INDIAN OCEAN TERRITORY,** The Crown Colony of the
briz	**BRITISH VIRGIN ISLANDS,** The Territory of the
brun	**BRUNEI,** The State of Brunei Darussalam
bulg	**BULGARIA,** The Republic of
burk	**BURKINA FASO,** The Democratic Republic of
buru	**BURUNDI,** The Republic of
camb	**CAMBODIA,** The Kingdom of
came	**CAMEROON,** The Republic of
cana	**CANADA,** The Dominion of
cape	**CAPE VERDE,** The Republic of
caym	**CAYMAN ISLANDS,** The Crown Colony of the
cent	**CENTRAL AFRICAN REPUBLIC,** The
chad	**CHAD,** The Republic of
chan	**CHANNEL ISLANDS,** The Crown Dependency of the
chil	**CHILE,** The Republic of
chin	**CHINA,** The People's Republic of
chri	**CHRISTMAS ISLAND,** The Territory of
coco	**COCOS (KEELING) ISLANDS,** The Territory of
colo	**COLOMBIA,** The Republic of
como	**COMOROS,** The Islamic Federal Republic of the
cong	**CONGO (BRAZZAVILLE);** The Republic of the Congo
conz	**CONGO-ZAIRE;** The Democratic Republic of Congo
cook	**COOK ISLANDS,** The Territory Overseas of the
cost	**COSTA RICA,** The Republic of
croa	**CROATIA,** The Republic of
cuba	**CUBA,** The Republic of
cypr	**CYPRUS,** The Republic of
czec	**CZECH REPUBLIC,** The
denm	**DENMARK,** The Kingdom of
djib	**DJIBOUTI,** The Republic of
domi	**DOMINICA,** The Commonwealth of
domr	**DOMINICAN REPUBLIC,** The
ecua	**ECUADOR,** The Republic of
egyp	**EGYPT,** The Arab Republic of
elsa	**EL SALVADOR,** The Republic of
equa	**EQUATORIAL GUINEA,** The Republic of
erit	**ERITREA,** The State of
esto	**ESTONIA,** The Republic of
ethi	**ETHIOPIA,** The Federal Democratic Republic of
faer	**FAEROE ISLANDS,** The
falk	**FALKLAND ISLANDS,** The Crown Colony of the
fiji	**FIJI;** The Sovereign Democratic Republic of the Fiji Islands
finl	**FINLAND,** The Republic of
fran	**FRANCE,** The French Republic
freg	**FRENCH GUIANA,** The Department of
frep	**FRENCH POLYNESIA,** The Overseas Territory of
gabo	**GABON,** The Gabonese Republic
gamb	**GAMBIA,** The Republic of the
geor	**GEORGIA,** The Republic of
germ	**GERMANY,** The Federal Republic of
ghan	**GHANA,** The Republic of
gibr	**GIBRALTAR,** The Colony of
gree	**GREECE;** The Hellenic Republic
grel	**GREENLAND**
gren	**GRENADA,** The Realm of
guad	**GUADELOUPE,** The Department of
guam	**GUAM,** The United States Territory of
guat	**GUATEMALA,** The Republic of
guin	**GUINEA,** The Republic of
gunb	**GUINEA-BISSAU,** The Republic of
guya	**GUYANA,** The Co-operative Republic of
hait	**HAITI,** The Republic of
holy	**HOLY SEE,** The (Vatican City State)
hond	**HONDURAS,** The Republic of
hung	**HUNGARY,** The Republic of
icel	**ICELAND,** The Republic of
indi	**INDIA,** The Republic of
indo	**INDONESIA,** The Republic of
iran	**IRAN,** The Islamic Republic of
iraq	**IRAQ,** The Republic of
irel	**IRELAND,** The Republic of
isle	**ISLE OF MAN,** The Crown Dependency of the
isra	**ISRAEL,** The State of
ital	**ITALY;** The Italian Republic
ivor	**IVORY COAST;** The Republic of Côte d'Ivoire
jama	**JAMAICA,** The Realm of
japa	**JAPAN**
jord	**JORDAN,** The Hashemite Kingdom of
kaza	**KAZAKHSTAN,** The Republic of
keny	**KENYA,** The Republic of
kirg	**KIRGHIZIA;** The Kyrgyz Republic (Kyrgyzstan)
kiri	**KIRIBATI,** The Republic of
kuwa	**KUWAIT,** The State of
laos	**LAOS;** The Lao People's Democratic Republic
latv	**LATVIA,** The Republic of
leba	**LEBANON;** The Lebanese Republic
leso	**LESOTHO,** The Kingdom of
libe	**LIBERIA,** The Republic of
liby	**LIBYA;** The Libyan Arab Jamahiriya
liec	**LIECHTENSTEIN,** The Principality of
lith	**LITHUANIA,** The Republic of
luxe	**LUXEMBOURG,** The Grand Duchy of
mace	**MACEDONIA,** The Republic of
mada	**MADAGASCAR,** The Republic of
mala	**MALAWI,** The Republic of
malb	**MALAYSIA,** The Federation of
mald	**MALDIVES,** The Republic of
mali	**MALI,** The Republic of
malt	**MALTA,** The Republic of
mars	**MARSHALL ISLANDS,** The Republic of the
mart	**MARTINIQUE,** The Department of
maur	**MAURITANIA,** The Islamic Republic of
maus	**MAURITIUS,** The Republic of
mayo	**MAYOTTE,** The Territorial Collectivity of
mexi	**MEXICO;** The United Mexican States
micr	**MICRONESIA,** The Federated States of
mold	**MOLDAVIA;** The Republic of Moldova
mona	**MONACO,** The Principality of
mong	**MONGOLIA,** The State of
mont	**MONTSERRAT,** The Crown Colony of
moro	**MOROCCO,** The Kingdom of
moza	**MOZAMBIQUE,** The Republic of
myan	**MYANMAR,** The Union of
nami	**NAMIBIA,** The Republic of
naur	**NAURU,** The Republic of
nepa	**NEPAL,** The Kingdom of
neth	**NETHERLANDS,** The Kingdom of the
nets	**NETHERLANDS ANTILLES,** The
newc	**NEW CALEDONIA,** The Overseas Territory of
newz	**NEW ZEALAND,** The Dominion of
nica	**NICARAGUA,** The Republic of
niga	**NIGER,** The Republic of the
nige	**NIGERIA,** The Federal Republic of
niue	**NIUE ISLAND,** The Overseas Territory of
norf	**NORFOLK ISLAND,** The Territory of
nork	**NORTH KOREA;** The Democratic PR of Korea
norl	**NORTHERN CYPRUS,** The Turkish Republic of
norm	**NORTHERN MARIANA ISLANDS,** The Commonwealth of the
norw	**NORWAY,** The Kingdom of
oman	**OMAN,** The Sultanate of
paki	**PAKISTAN,** The Islamic Republic of
pala	**PALAU;** The Republic of Belau
pale	**PALESTINE;** The Palestine Authority
pana	**PANAMA,** The Republic of
papu	**PAPUA NEW GUINEA,** The Independent State of
para	**PARAGUAY,** The Republic of
peru	**PERU,** The Republic of
phil	**PHILIPPINES,** The Republic of the
pitc	**PITCAIRN ISLANDS,** The Colony of the
pola	**POLAND,** The Republic of
port	**PORTUGAL;** The Portuguese Republic
puer	**PUERTO RICO,** The Commonwealth of
qata	**QATAR,** The State of
reun	**REUNION,** The Department of
roma	**ROMANIA,** The Republic of
russ	**RUSSIA;** The Russian Federation
rwan	**RWANDA;** The Rwandese Republic
saha	**SAHARA;** The Sahara Arab Democratic Republic
saih	**SAINT HELENA,** The Colony of
saik	**SAINT KITTS & NEVIS,** The Federation of
sail	**SAINT LUCIA,** The Realm of
saip	**SAINT PIERRE & MIQUELON,** The Territorial Collectivity of
saiv	**SAINT VINCENT & THE GRENADINES,** The Realm of
samo	**SAMOA,** The Independent State of
sanm	**SAN MARINO,** The Republic of
saot	**SAO TOME & PRINCIPE,** The Democratic Republic of
saud	**SAUDI ARABIA,** The Kingdom of
sene	**SENEGAL,** The Republic of
seyc	**SEYCHELLES,** The Republic of
sier	**SIERRA LEONE,** The Republic of
sing	**SINGAPORE,** The Republic of
slok	**SLOVAKIA;** The Slovak Republic
slov	**SLOVENIA,** The Republic of
solo	**SOLOMON ISLANDS,** The Realm of the
soma	**SOMALIA;** The Somali Democratic Republic
somi	**SOMALILAND;** The Somaliland Republic
soua	**SOUTH AFRICA,** The Republic of
souk	**SOUTH KOREA;** The Republic of Korea
spai	**SPAIN,** The Kingdom of
span	**SPANISH NORTH AFRICA**
sril	**SRI LANKA,** The Democratic Socialist Republic of
suda	**SUDAN,** The Republic of the
suri	**SURINAME,** The Republic of
sval	**SVALBARD & JAN MAYEN ISLANDS**
swaz	**SWAZILAND,** The Kingdom of
swed	**SWEDEN,** The Kingdom of
swit	**SWITZERLAND;** The Swiss Confederation
syri	**SYRIA,** The Syrian Arab Republic
taiw	**TAIWAN;** The Republic of China
taji	**TAJIKISTAN,** The Republic of
tanz	**TANZANIA,** The United Republic of
thai	**THAILAND,** The Kingdom of
timo	**TIMOR**
togo	**TOGO;** The Togolese Republic
toke	**TOKELAU ISLANDS,** The Territory Overseas of
tong	**TONGA,** The Kingdom of
trin	**TRINIDAD & TOBAGO,** The Republic of
tuni	**TUNISIA,** The Republic of
turk	**TURKEY,** The Republic of
turm	**TURKMENISTAN,** The Republic of
turs	**TURKS & CAICOS ISLANDS,** The Crown Colony of the
tuva	**TUVALU,** The Realm of
ugan	**UGANDA,** The Republic of
ukra	**UKRAINE**
unia	**UNITED ARAB EMIRATES,** The
usa	**UNITED STATES OF AMERICA,** The
uuay	**URUGUAY,** The Eastern Republic of
uzbe	**UZBEKISTAN,** The Republic of
vanu	**VANUATU,** The Republic of
vene	**VENEZUELA,** The Republic of
viet	**VIET NAM,** The Socialist Republic of
virg	**VIRGIN ISLANDS OF THE US,** The
wall	**WALLIS & FUTUNA ISLANDS,** The Overseas Territory of
yeme	**YEMEN,** The Republic of
yugo	**YUGOSLAVIA,** The Federal Republic of
zamb	**ZAMBIA,** The Republic of
zimb	**ZIMBABWE,** The Republic of

2. GLOBAL CODES LISTED BY CODE.

Table 3-2. Global codes used throughout this Encyclopedia and related CD *World Christian database*, alphabetically by code.

Every distinct alphanumeric code listed below—whether one-letter, or from 2 to 8 characters—has meaning as a distinct variable that is being measured, and for which values, results, and meanings are presented at a variety of places in this Encyclopedia and its related CD, the *World Christian database*.

Each alphanumeric code thus used is a unique *global code* in that, wherever it occurs in this Encyclopedia's tables or in the related CD, it has in all cases only the *one global meaning*, as set forth below in this table of all such codes. Note that occasionally a single letter may have different meanings if considered in isolation. Thus 'P' means 'Protestant (Protestants, the Protestant megabloc)', whereas 'P..' means 'This people has portions of Scripture (gospels) in their own language, but no New Testament or Bible.' Hence to avoid ambiguity, the entire code must always be carefully extracted, exactly quoted, accurately keyboarded, interrogated, understood, and used.

Note carefully that this listing is of global variables and their codes, to enable users to locate identities and varieties of data instantly. This listing does not include local codes, by which is meant codes that are applicable to the various values of only one single variable (one global code). These local values or codes can be located at the points where variables are being described.

The table below lists all variables alphabetically by code. Table 3-3 which follows lists the same variables but alphabetically by name.

0ZAC	Prepentecostals
1ZAC	Pentecostals (First-Wavers)
2AC	doubly-affiliated Christians
2b	2nd-language Bible
2n	2nd-language NT
2p	2nd-language gospel
2PC	doubly-professing Christians
2r	doubly-counted religionists
2RAC	doubly-counted Catholics
2s	2nd-language scriptures
2ZAC	Charismatics (Second-Wavers)
3ZAC	Neocharismatics (Third-Wavers)
4ZAC	doubly-affiliated pentecostals
a	Atheists
A-	Anglican megabloc
A-C	Christians in World A countries
A-V	audio-visual ministries
a_1	Audio gospel, hearings per family
a_2	Audio gospel, hearings per adult
a_3	Audio gospel, hearings per capita
A3ZAC	Anglican Third-Wavers
AA	Audio gospel, hearers p.a. per 100
aAA	World A individuals in A peoples in A countries
aAB	World A individuals in A peoples in B countries
AAC	Anglicans (affiliated)
aAC	World A individuals in A peoples in C countries
aBA	World A individuals in B peoples in A countries
aBB	World A individuals in B peoples in B countries
aBC	World A individuals in B peoples in C countries
AC	affiliated Christians (church members), %
ACs	affiliated Christians (church members)
ACinc	personal income of church members, $ p.a.
aC	alien Christians, %
aCA	World A individuals in C peoples in A countries
aCB	World A individuals in C peoples in B countries
aCC	World A individuals in C peoples in C countries
Ad	adults (over 15) in a specific population
ad	adults (over 15) as % population
AHM	Ithna-Asharis
AIAC	Anglican Independents
AJ	Ashkenazi Jews
AL	Azali Babis
APC	Anglicans (professing)
Apop1	World A individuals
Apop2	population of World A peoples
Apop3	population of World A countries
AT	Animists
AU	Afro-American spiritists
au	audio scriptures
AV2ZAC	Anglican Charismatics (weekly adults)
Ax2ZAC	Anglican postcharismatics
AXM	Ahmadis
B	(if no statistics present) Bible, existence of
b	near-Bible
bap	baptisms
bappa	baptisms % per year
B-activity	earliest/latest Bible publication dates
B-C	Christians in World B countries
b_1	Bibles in use per family
b_2	Bibles in use per adult
b_3	Bibles in use per capita
B=	Buddhists (if statistics are present)
bAA	World B individuals in A peoples in A countries
bAB	World B individuals in A peoples in B countries
bAC	World B individuals in A peoples in C countries
BAT	Buddhist animists
BB	Bibles distributed p.a. per 100
bBA	World B individuals in B peoples in A countries
bBB	World B individuals in B peoples in B countries
bBC	World B individuals in B peoples in C countries
BBIAC	Isolated Buddhist believers in Christ
bCA	World B individuals in C peoples in A countries
bCB	World B individuals in C peoples in B countries
BCC	hidden Buddhist believers in Christ
bCC	World B individuals in C peoples in C countries
beds	hospital beds
Begun	year in which entity came into being
BIAC	Isolated non-Christian believers in Christ
BIHM	Bohoras
blind	nonsighted (blind) persons
BM3ZAC	Messianic Buddhists
bpop	births, % p.a.
Bpop1	World B individuals
Bpop2	population of World B peoples
Bpop3	population of World B countries
br	Braille scriptures for blind
Bs	complete Bibles distributed p.a.
BSM	Hanbalites
BU	Afro-Brazilian cultists
BXM	Black Muslims
C	Christians, %
C=	Roman Catholic religious institutes at work (clerics + brothers + sisters)
C-C	Christians in World C countries
C3ZAC	Catholic Third-Wavers
cAA	World C individuals in A peoples in A countries
CAAC	Anglican Charismatics
cAB	World C individuals in A peoples in B countries
cAC	World C individuals in A peoples in C countries
cBA	World C individuals in B peoples in A countries
CBB	culture barriers, total of
cBB	World C individuals in B peoples in B countries
cBC	World C individuals in B peoples in C countries
cc	congregations per million
CC	crypto-Christians (covert evangelizers)
cCA	World C individuals in C peoples in A countries
cCB	World C individuals in C peoples in B countries
cCC	World C individuals in C peoples in C countries
ce	cost-effectiveness, $ per baptism
CG	century's church growth, AD 1900-2000, p.a.
CIAC	Catholic Independents
cit-100	total cities of over 100,000
cit-50	total cities of over 50,000
CJ	Reconstructionist Jews
CMB	Chinese Buddhists
CN	Cargo cultists
code	4-letter identification code for a country
comp	computers (general purpose) in use
cou	total countries involved
CP1ZAC	Classical Pentecostals
CPAC	Protestant Charismatics
Cpop1	World C individuals
Cpop2	population of World C peoples
Cpop3	population of World C countries
CRAC	Catholic Charismatics
CRPC	Christopagans
CSI	Christian Safety Index
CU	Afro-Caribbean religionists
CX	contact of Christians with non-Christians
D	denominations
D=	Taoists
d	discipling stage, %
dd	denominations per million
deaf	hearing-impaired (deaf) persons
dev	more/less/least-developed countries
di	dialects
doct	doctors (physicians, surgeons)
dpop	deaths, % p.a.
ds	distinctiveness of statistics in totalling
DV	Digambara Jains
DXM	Druzes
E	extent of evangelization (persons evangelized), %
e	offers per capita per year
EAAC	Anglican Evangelicals
EAC	Evangelicals
eAC	evangelicals
EBB	evangelization barriers, total of
ed rate	education rate
EFL	Economic Freedom Level
EIAC	Independent Evangelicals
EJ	Oriental Jews
Enu	ethnic non-users of a language
enu	ethnic non-users as % group's population
EOAC	Orthodox Evangelicals
EP	total evangelized persons
EPAC	Protestant Evangelicals
ERAC	Catholic Evangelicals
ERPC	Evangelical Catholics
ET	Neopagans
ev	evangelicals, % of country
Ev	Evangelicals, % of AC
ext	extent or number of countries involved
fam	families (households)
F	Chinese folk-religionists
F=	(if a name) Founder
FB	Folk Buddhists
FEAC	Fundamentalists
FH	Folk/Popular Hindus
FM	Folk Muslims
FN	Self-Religionists
FS	Folk Shinto
g	growth of new Christians, % p.a.
G	numerical church growth, % p.a.
G=	Confucianists
GCC	Great Commission Christians, % country
GCCinc	personal income of GCCs, $ p.a.
GCCs	Great Commission Christians (GeoChristians)
GNPpc	gross national product, US$ p.a.p.c.
H	Hindus
hom	households (homes, families)
HAT	Hinduized animists
HBIAC	Isolated Hindu believers in Christ
HCC	hidden Hindu believers in Christ
HDI	Human Development Index
HFI	Human Freedom Index
HH	Vedantists
hi	hearing impaired/deaf/signed scriptures
HM	Shias
HM3ZAC	Messianic Hindus
home	household size (persons)
hosp	hospitals
HS	Shrine Shinto
HSI	Human Suffering Index
HSM	Hanafites
HU	High Spiritists
i	intercessors, intercession
I-	Independent megabloc
I3ZAC	Isolated non-Christian Neocharismatics
IAC	Independents/Postdenominationalists/Neo-Apostolics (affiliated)
IAT	Islamized animists
iC	indigenous Christians
ICC	isolated radio believers
IHM	Ismailis
IMB	Indian Buddhists
Inet	Internet users
IPC	Independents (professing)
IXM	Ibadis
J	Jews
JBIAC	Isolated Jewish believers in Christ
JCC	hidden Jewish believers in Christ
Jf	'Jesus' Film
JM3ZAC	Messianic Jews
JMB	Japanese Buddhists
K	Sikhs
KH	Saktists
KJ	Karaites
L	literary tradition
L=	Baha'is
lang	language code
LAT	Primal religionists
LAXM	Lahoris
LB	Tibetan Buddhists (Lamaists)
LBB	language barriers, total of
LC	latent (inactive) Christians
lepers	leprosy, sufferers from
LHM	Alawites
Lit	literacy, %
loc	main country or location involved
M	Muslims (if statistics are present)
m-	Marginal Christian megabloc
M3ZAC	Messianic Third-Wavers
M=	(without statistics) names of missions present
mAC	Marginal Christians (affiliated)
mar-sits	major martyrdom situations across 2,000 years
martyrs	martyrs for Christ (witness, hostility, death)
MB	Mahayana Buddhists
MBIAC	Isolated Muslim believers in Christ
MCC	hidden Muslim believers in Christ
me	mass evangelism
mega	total megacities (over 1 million each)
metro	metrodwellers (in cities over 1 million), %
mi	mission agencies, total (coded 0-5)
Mi	number of mission agencies
MIAC	Messianic non-Christian believers in Christ
MM	missionaries received per million population
MMM	missionaries received per million affiliated
MM3ZAC	Messianic Muslims
MMp	missionaries received per million affiliated
mPC	Marginal Christians (professing)
mpop	nett immigrants, % p.a.
MSM	Malikites
Mts	mother-tongue speakers (native speakers)
mts	mother-tongue speakers as % of country
murder	murder rate, per 1000 p.a.
mV2ZAC	Marginal Charismatics
MY	Mandeans
n	near-NT
N	New Testament, existence of
N=	Neoreligionists (New-Religionists)
N-activity	earliest and latest NT publication dates
n_1	NTs in use per family
n_2	NTs in use per adult
n_3	NTs in use per capita
N3ZAC	Non-White Third-Wavers
NB	nonreligious Buddhists
NBB	nationality barriers, total of
NCC	Messianic Neocharismatics
NH	Neo-Hindus
NIAC	Non-White indigenous Christians
NMB	Nichirenshu
NN	New Testaments distributed p.a. per 100
NN=	Nonsyncretist neoreligionists
nns	non-native speakers as % of country
Nns	non-native speakers (2nd-language)
npop	natural population increase, % p.a.

Continued opposite

Table 3-2 concluded

nr	New Reader Scriptures
nrp	New Reader Portions (gospels)
nrs	New Reader Selections
NTB	Neo-Buddhists
NTs	New Testaments distributed p.a.
NXM	Muslim Neo-Fundamentalists
NY	Quasi-Christians
O-	Orthodox megabloc
O3ZAC	Orthodox Third-Wavers
OAC	Orthodox (affiliated)
od	total offers p.d. (per day)
OEC	overt evangelizers
OIAC	Orthodox Independents
OJ	Orthodox Jews
ON	Occultists
oo	organizations per million
OP1ZAC	Oneness Pentecostals (White)
OPC	Orthodox (professing)
OV2ZAC	Orthodox Charismatics
p	near-portion, near-gospel
P	Portion (gospel), existence of
P-	Protestant megabloc
pa	per annum (per year)
p.a.	per capita (per person)
P-activity	earliest/latest gospel publication dates
p..	near-gospel only
P..	Portion (Gospel) only
p_1	Portions (gospels) placed per family
P1ZAC	Denominational Pentecostals (White)
p_2	Portions (gospels) placed per adult
p_3	Portions (gospels) placed per capita
P3ZAC	Protestant Third-Wavers
pAC	practising church members
PAC	Protestants (affiliated)
PAT	Polytheist animists
PC	professing Christians
p.d.	per diem (per day)
Peo	peoples in a country
people	ethnolinguistic or race code
PIAC	Protestant Independents
PMB	Pure Land (Amida)
PN.	gospel & NT only
pn.	near-NT only, for this people
PNB	gospel, NT, Bible
pnb	near-Bible only, for this people
Npop	country's population
pop	population (of a people, city, country, continent, world, globe)
PP	Portions (gospels) distributed p.a. per 100
PPC	Protestants (professing)
ppop	people as % of country
Ppop	population of an ethnolinguistic people
PPPC	Protestant popular-religionists
PRPC	Catholic popular-religionists
Ps	Portions (Gospels) distributed p.a.
PT	Polytheists
pub	published scriptures
PV2ZAC	Protestant Charismatics (weekly adults)
Px2ZAC	Protestant postcharismatics
pZ	Parsis
Q	Nonreligious
QAXM	Qadianis
QY	Quasireligionists
R	responsiveness: new church members p.a. per million offers
R-	Roman Catholic megabloc
R3ZAC	Isolated radio/TV Third-Wavers
ra	countries transmitting Christian radio
RAC	Roman Catholics (affiliated)
RBB	religion barriers, total of
re	response (baptisms per million offers)
religs	total distinct religions significantly present in country
RH	Reform Hindus
RIAC	Isolated radio/TV believers
RJ	Reformist Jews
RPC	Roman Catholics (professing)
Rs	ratio non-native speakers ÷ mother-tongue speakers, %
ru	ruralites (country-dwellers), % country
rural	ruralites (country-dwellers), %
RV2ZAC	Catholic Charismatics (weekly adults)
Rx2ZAC	Catholic postcharismatics
rY	other minor religionists
S	missionaries sent out per million affiliated
S=	Shintoists
s.	no scriptures in a second language
s_1	Selections sent out per family
s_2	Selections sent out per adult
s_3	Selections sent out per capita
sb	Bible in a second language
SBB	lifestyle barriers, total of
sB	other sectarian Buddhists
sc	script
SCC	secret church members
Sel	Selections, existence of
SF	Syncretist neoreligionists
sH	other sectarian Hindus
SH	Shaivites
sHM	other Shia sectarians
sJ	other Jewish movements
SJ	Sefardi Jews
SM	Sunnis
SN	Shinto New-Religionists
sn	New Testament in a second language
sp	gospel in a second language
SRPC	Spiritist Catholics
SS	missionaries sent abroad per million population
ss	second-language scriptures
SSS	Selections (1-8 page leaflets) p.a. per 100
sSM	other Sunni sectarians
SSM	Shafiites
sss	circulation of all scriptures, p.a.
sT	other ethnoreligionist sectarians
ST	Shamanists
SU	Afro-Surinamese religionists
sUM	other sectarian Sufis
SV	Svetambara Jains
sV	other sectarian Jains
sXM	other Islamic movements
T	Ethnoreligionists (Tribalists)
T-	targeting priority
TB	Theravada (Hinayana) Buddhists
TBB	total barriers to evangelization
TH	Tantrists (Tantrist Hindus)
TJ	Samaritans
TMB	Tendaishu
TS	Sect Shinto
tu	total users/speakers of a language, % of country
Tu	total users of a language (speakers, writers, readers)
ty	type or level of religion
U	Spiritists
U	unevangelized population, %
u	urbanites (city-dwellers), %
UC	unaffiliated Christians (nominal), %
UM	Sufis
UP	total unevangelized persons
ur	unevangelized remnant, %
urban	urbanites (city-dwellers)
V	volume of evangelization, %
V=	Jains
v1	Visual gospel, viewings per family
v2	Visual gospel, viewings per adult
V2ZAC	Mainline active charismatics (weekly)
v3	Visual gospel, viewings per capita
VB	Vajrayana (Tantrists)
VH	Vaishnavites
VN	Nativistic cultists
VV	Visual gospel, viewers p.a. per 100
W	Total religionists,%
W3ZAC	White-led Third-Wavers
wa	work among
WIAC	White-led Postdenominationalists
Wo	World (A, B, C)
WSM	Wahhabites
WT	Witchcraft eradicationists
WW	full-time citizen Christian workers in country
WW.	full-time citizen Christian workers p.m.a.
X	Non-Christians, %
x1ZAC	Postpentecostals
x2ZAC	Mainline postcharismatics
xAC	disaffiliated (former) church members
XBIAC	Isolated believers in Christ in other religions
xc	cross-cultural mission
XCC	Hidden other-religionist believers in Christ
XM	Islamic schismatics
XM3ZAC	other Messianic religionists
xpAC	nonpracticing church members
Y	other religionists
YB	Buddhayana
Z	GCC as % of AC (affiliated)
Z=	Zoroastrians
ZAC	Pentecostals/Charismatics/Neocharismatics
ZHM	Zaydis
ZMB	Zen

3. GLOBAL CODES LISTED BY NAME.

Table 3-3. Global codes used throughout this Encyclopedia and related CD *World Christian database*, alphabetically by name.

F=	(if a name) Founder
B	(if no statistics present) Bible, existence of
M=	(without statistics) names of missions present
2b	2nd-language Bible
2p	2nd-language gospel
2n	2nd-language NT
2s	2nd-language scriptures
code	4-letter identification code for a country
Ad	adults (over 15) in a specific population
ad	adults (over 15) as % population
AC	affiliated Christians (church members), %
ACs	affiliated Christians (church members)
AU	Afro-American spiritists
BU	Afro-Brazilian cultists
CU	Afro-Caribbean religionists
SU	Afro-Surinamese religionists
AXM	Ahmadis
LHM	Alawites
aC	alien Christians, %
CAAC	Anglican Charismatics
AV2ZAC	Anglican Charismatics (weekly adults)
EAAC	Anglican Evangelicals
AIAC	Anglican Independents
A-	Anglican megabloc
Ax2ZAC	Anglican postcharismatics
A3ZAC	Anglican Third-Wavers
AAC	Anglicans (affiliated)
APC	Anglicans (professing)
AT	Animists
AJ	Ashkenazi Jews
a	Atheists
AA	Audio gospel, hearers p.a. per 100
a_2	Audio gospel, hearings per adult
a_3	Audio gospel, hearings per capita
a_1	Audio gospel, hearings per family
au	audio scriptures
A-V	audio-visual ministries
AL	Azali Babis
L	Baha'is
bap	baptisms
bappa	baptism % per year
sb	Bible in a second language
BB	Bibles distributed p.a. per 100
b_2	Bibles in use per adult
b_3	Bibles in use per capita
b_1	Bibles in use per family
bpop	births, % p.a.
BXM	Black Muslims
BIHM	Bohoras
br	Braille scriptures for blind
YB	Buddhayana
BAT	Buddhist animists
B=	Buddhists (if statistics are present)
CF	Cargo cultists
CRAC	Catholic Charismatics
RV2ZAC	Catholic Charismatics (weekly adults)
ERAC	Catholic Evangelicals
CIAC	Catholic Independents
PRPC	Catholic popular-religionists
Rx2ZAC	Catholic postcharismatics
C3ZAC	Catholic Third-Wavers
CG	century's church growth, AD 1900-2000, p.a.
2ZAC	Charismatics (Second-Wavers)
CMB	Chinese Buddhists
F	Chinese folk-religionists
CSI	Christian Safety Index
A-C	Christians in World A countries
B-C	Christians in World B countries
C-C	Christians in World C countries
C	Christians, %
CRPC	Christopagans
sss	circulation of all scriptures, p.a.
CP1ZAC	Classical Pentecostals
Bs	complete Bibles distributed p.a.
comp	computers (general purpose) in use
G	Confucianists
cc	congregations per million
CX	contact of Christians with non-Christians
ce	cost-effectiveness, $ per baptism
ra	countries transmitting Christian radio
Npop	country's population
xc	cross-cultural mission
CC	crypto-Christians (covert evangelizers)
CBB	culture barriers, total of
dpop	deaths, % p.a.
P1ZAC	Denominational Pentecostals (White)
D	denominations
dd	denominations per million
di	dialects
DV	Digambara Jains
xAC	disaffiliated (former) church members
d	discipling stage, %
ds	distinctiveness of statistics in totalling
doct	doctors (physicians, surgeons)
2AC	doubly-affiliated Christians
4ZAC	doubly-affiliated pentecostals
2RAC	doubly-counted Catholics
2W	doubly-counted religionists
2PC	doubly-professing Christians
DXM	Druzes
N-activity	earliest and latest NT publication dates
B-activity	earliest/latest Bible publication dates
P-activity	earliest/latest gospel publication dates
EFL	Economic Freedom Level
ed rate	education rate
Enu	ethnic non-users of a language
enu	ethnic non-users as % group's population
people	ethnolinguistic or race code
T	Ethnoreligionists (Tribalists)
ERPC	Evangelical Catholics
EAC	Evangelicals
eAC	evangelicals
ev	evangelicals, % of country
Ev	Evangelicals, % of AC
EBB	evangelization barriers, total of
E	extent of evangelization (persons evangelized), %
ext	extent or number of countries involved
fam	families (households)
FB	Folk Buddhists
FM	Folk Muslims
FS	Folk Shinto
FH	Folk/Popular Hindus
WW	full-time citizen Christian workers in country
WW.	full-time citizen Christian workers p.m.a.
FEAC	Fundamentalists
Z	GCC as % of AC (affiliated)

Continued overleaf

Table 3-3 concluded

PN.	gospel & NT only
sp	gospel in a second language
PNB	gospel, NT, Bible
GCC	Great Commission Christians (GeoChristians), %
GCCs	Great Commission Christians (GeoChristians)
GNP	gross national product, US$ p.a.p.c.
g	growth of new Christians, % p.a.
HSM	Hanafites
BSM	Hanbalites
deaf	hearing impaired (deaf) persons
hi	hearing impaired/deaf/signed scriptures
BCC	hidden Buddhist believers in Christ
HCC	hidden Hindu believers in Christ
JCC	hidden Jewish believers in Christ
MCC	hidden Muslim believers in Christ
XCC	Hidden other-religionist believers in Christ
HU	High Spiritists
HAT	Hinduized animists
H	Hindus
beds	hospital beds
hosp	hospitals
home	household size (persons)
hom	households (homes, families)
HDI	Human Development Index
HFI	Human Freedom Index
HSI	Human Suffering Index
IXM	Ibadis
EIAC	Independent Evangelicals
I-	Independent megabloc
IPC	Independents (professing)
IAC	Independents/Postdenominationalists/Neo-Apostolics (affiliated)
IMB	Indian Buddhists
iC	indigenous Christians
i	intercessors, intercession
Inet	Internet users
XM	Islamic schismatics
IAT	Islamized animists
IHM	Ismailis
XBIAC	Isolated believers in Christ in other religions
BBIAC	Isolated Buddhist believers in Christ
HBIAC	Isolated Hindu believers in Christ
JBIAC	Isolated Jewish believers in Christ
MBIAC	Isolated Muslim believers in Christ
BIAC	Isolated non-Christian believers in Christ
I3ZAC	Isolated non-Christian Neocharismatics
ICC	isolated radio believers
RIAC	Isolated radio/TV believers
R3ZAC	Isolated radio/TV Third-Wavers
AHM	Ithna-Asharis
V	Jains
JMB	Japanese Buddhists
Jf	'Jesus' Film
J	Jews
KJ	Karaites
LBB	language barriers, total of
LAXM	Lahoris
lang	language code
LC	latent (inactive) Christians
lepers	leprosy, sufferers from
SBB	lifestyle barriers, total of
Lit	literacy, %
L	literary tradition
MB	Mahayana Buddhists
loc	main country or location involved
V2ZAC	Mainline active charismatics (weekly)
x2ZAC	Mainline postcharismatics
mar-sits	major martyrdom situations across 2,000 years
MSM	Malikites
MY	Mandeans
mV2ZAC	Marginal Charismatics
m-	Marginal Christian megabloc
mAC	Marginal Christians (affiliated)
mPC	Marginal Christians (professing)
martyrs	martyrs for Christ (witness, hostility, death)
me	mass evangelism
BM3ZAC	Messianic Buddhists
HM3ZAC	Messianic Hindus
JM3ZAC	Messianic Jews
MM3ZAC	Messianic Muslims
NCC	Messianic Neocharismatics
MIAC	Messianic non-Christian believers in Christ
M3ZAC	Messianic Third-Wavers
metro	metrodwellers (in cities over 1 million), %
mi	mission agencies, total (coded 0-5)
MM	missionaries received per million population
MMM	missionaries received per million affiliated
S	missionaries sent abroad per million affiliated
SS	missionaries sent abroad per million population
dev	more/less/least-developed countries
Mts	mother-tongue speakers (native speakers)
mts	mother-tongue speakers as % of country
murder	murder rate, per 1000 p.a.
NXM	Muslim Neo-Fundamentalists
M	Muslims (if statistics are present)
NBB	nationality barriers, total of
VN	Nativistic cultists
npop	natural population increase, % p.a.
b	near-Bible
pnb	near-Bible only, for this people
p..	near-gospel only, for this people
n	near-NT
pn.	near-NT only, for this people
p	near-portion, near-gospel
NTB	Neo-Buddhists
NH	Neo-Hindus
3ZAC	Neocharismatics (Third-Wavers)
ET	Neopagans
N	Neoreligionists (New-Religionists)
mpop	nett immigrants, % p.a.
nrp	New Reader Portions (gospels)
nr	New Reader Scriptures
nrs	New Reader Selections
sn	New Testament in a second language
N	New Testament, existence of
NTs	New Testaments distributed p.a.
NN	New Testaments distributed p.a. per 100
NMB	Nichirenshu
s.	no scriptures in a second language
X	Non-Christians, %
nns	non-native speakers as % of country
Nns	non-native speakers (2nd-language)
NIAC	Non-White indigenous Christians
N3ZAC	Non-White Third-Wavers
xpAC	nonpracticing church members
Q	Nonreligious
NB	nonreligious Buddhists
blind	nonsighted (blind) persons
NN	Nonsyncretist neoreligionists
n_2	NTs in use per adult
n_3	NTs in use per capita
n_1	NTs in use per family
Mi	number of mission agencies
G	numerical church growth, % p.a.
ON	Occultists
e	offers per capita per year
OP1ZAC	Oneness Pentecostals (White)
oo	organizations per million
EJ	Oriental Jews
OAC	Orthodox (affiliated)
OPC	Orthodox (professing)
OV2ZAC	Orthodox Charismatics
EOAC	Orthodox Evangelicals
OIAC	Orthodox Independents
OJ	Orthodox Jews
O-	Orthodox megabloc
O3ZAC	Orthodox Third-Wavers
sT	other ethnoreligionist sectarians
sXM	other Islamic movements
sJ	other Jewish movements
XM3ZAC	other Messianic religionists
rY	other religionists
sB	other sectarian Buddhists
sH	other sectarian Hindus
sV	other sectarian Jains
sUM	other sectarian Sufis
sHM	other Shia sectarians
sSM	other Sunni sectarians
OEC	overt evangelizers
pZ	Parsis
1ZAC	Pentecostals (First-Wavers)
ZAC	Pentecostals/Charismatics/Neocharismatics
ppop	people as % of country
Peo	peoples in a country
pa	per annum (per year)
p.d.	per diem (per day)
p.a.	per capita (per person)
ACinc	personal income of church members, $ p.a.
GCCinc	personal income of GCCs, $ p.a.
PAT	Polytheist animists
PT	Polytheists
pop	population (of a people, city, country, continent, world, globe)
Ppop	population of an ethnolinguistic people
Apop3	population of World A countries
Apop2	population of World A peoples
Bpop3	population of World B countries
Bpop2	population of World B peoples
Cpop3	population of World C countries
Cpop2	population of World C peoples
P..	Portion (Gospel) only
P	Portion (gospel), existence of
Ps	Portions (Gospels) distributed p.a.
PP	Portions (gospels) distributed p.a. per 100
p_2	Portions (gospels) placed per adult
p_3	Portions (gospels) placed per capita
p_1	Portions (gospels) placed per family
x1ZAC	Postpentecostals
pAC	practising church members
0ZAC	Prepentecostals
LAT	Primal religionists
PC	professing Christians
CPAC	Protestant Charismatics
PV2ZAC	Protestant Charismatics (weekly adults)
EPAC	Protestant Evangelicals
PIAC	Protestant Independents
P-	Protestant megabloc
PPPC	Protestant popular-religionists
Px2ZAC	Protestant postcharismatics
P3ZAC	Protestant Third-Wavers
PAC	Protestants (affiliated)
PPC	Protestants (professing)
pub	published scriptures
PMB	Pure Land (Amida)
QAXM	Qadianis
NY	Quasi-Christians
QY	Quasireligionists
Rs	ratio non-native speakers ÷ mother-tongue speakers, %
CJ	Reconstructionist Jews
RH	Reform Hindus
RJ	Reformist Jews
RBB	religion barriers, total of
re	response (baptisms per million offers)
R	responsiveness: new church members p.a. per million offers
C=	Roman Catholic religious institutes at work (clerics + brothers + sisters)
R-	Roman Catholic megabloc
RAC	Roman Catholics (affiliated)
RPC	Roman Catholics (professing)
ru	ruralites (country-dwellers), % country
rural	ruralites (country-dwellers), %
KH	Saktists
TJ	Samaritans
sc	script
ss	second-language scriptures
SCC	secret church members
TS	Sect Shinto
SJ	Sefardi Jews
SSS	Selections (1-8 page leaflets) p.a. per 100
s_2	Selections sent out per adult
s_3	Selections sent out per capita
s_1	Selections sent out per family
Sel	Selections, existence of
FN	Self-Religionists
SSM	Shafiites
SH	Shaivites
ST	Shamanists
HM	Shias
S	Shintoists
qN	Shinto New-Religionists
HS	Shrine Shinto
K	Sikhs
SRPC	Spiritist Catholics
U	Spiritists
UM	Sufis
SM	Sunnis
SV	Svetambara Jains
SN	Syncretist neoreligionists
TH	Tantrists (Tantrist Hindus)
D	Taoists
T-	targeting priority
TMB	Tendaishu
TB	Theravada (Hinayana) Buddhists
LB	Tibetan Buddhists (Lamaists)
TBB	total barriers to evangelization
cit-100	total cities of over 100,000
cit-50	total cities of over 50,000
cou	total countries involved
religs	total distinct religions significantly present in country
EP	total evangelized persons
mega	total megacities (over 1 million each)
od	total offers p.d. (per day)
W	Total religionists,%
UP	total unevangelized persons
Tu	total users of a language (speakers, writers, readers)
tu	total users/speakersof a language, % of country
ty	type or level of religion
UC	unaffiliated Christians (nominal), %
U	unevangelized population, %
ur	unevangelized remnant, %
u	urbanites (city-dwellers), %
urban	urbanites (city-dwellers)
VH	Vaishnavites
VB	Vajrayana (Tantrists)
HH	Vedantists
VV	Visual gospel, viewers p.a. per 100
v2	Visual gospel, viewings per adult
v3	Visual gospel, viewings per capita
v1	Visual gospel, viewings per family
V	volume of evangelization, %
WSM	Wahhabites
WIAC	White-led Postdenominationalists
W3ZAC	White-led Third-Wavers
WT	Witchcraft eradicationists
wa	work among
Wo	World (A, B, C)
Apop1	World A individuals
aAA	World A individuals in A peoples in A countries
aAB	World A individuals in A peoples in B countries
aAC	World A individuals in A peoples in C countries
aBA	World A individuals in B peoples in A countries
aBB	World A individuals in B peoples in B countries
aBC	World A individuals in B peoples in C countries
aCA	World A individuals in C peoples in A countries
aCB	World A individuals in C peoples in B countries
aCC	World A individuals in C peoples in C countries
Bpop1	World B individuals
bAA	World B individuals in A peoples in A countries
bAB	World B individuals in A peoples in B countries
bAC	World B individuals in A peoples in C countries
bBA	World B individuals in B peoples in A countries
bBB	World B individuals in B peoples in B countries
bBC	World B individuals in B peoples in C countries
bCA	World B individuals in C peoples in A countries
bCB	World B individuals in C peoples in B countries
bCC	World B individuals in C peoples in C countries
Cpop1	World C individuals
cAA	World C individuals in A peoples in A countries
cAB	World C individuals in A peoples in B countries
cAC	World C individuals in A peoples in C countries
cBA	World C individuals in B peoples in A countries
cBB	World C individuals in B peoples in B countries
cBC	World C individuals in B peoples in C countries
cCA	World C individuals in C peoples in A countries
cCB	World C individuals in C peoples in B countries
cCC	World C individuals in C peoples in C countries
Begun	year in which entity came into being
Z	Zoroastrians
ZHM	Zaydis
ZMB	Zen

4. STANDARD TERMS AND CODES FOR RELIGIONS.

Table 3-4. Standard terms and codes for 85 categories/varieties/meanings of the term 'Christians', also for 100 categories of non-Christians, and also for 9 major overall totals.

NOTES.

1. This Encyclopedia gives to each distinct religious category a unique alphanumeric code. The codes themselves are not employed in the print Encyclopedia but are used on the related *World Christian database* to facilitate rapid retrieval of wanted information. To assist the user to remember codes useful to him or her, for the most frequently-occurring categories each code in most cases consists of letters similar to the order of words in the category itself. Thus GCC = Great Commission Christians, AAC = Anglican affiliated Christians, AEAC = Anglican Evangelical affiliated Christians, and so on.

2. Categories and subcategories of Christians are not arranged below in alphabetical order, but in an ecclesiastically logical or chronological order. The 4 major Christian categories or standardized ways of enumerating Christians are shown here and in all other tables in boldface type: these are **Christians, professing Christians**, **affiliated Christians**, and **Great Commission Christians**. By contrast, major categories of non-Christians are however listed alphabetically, but with their subcategories listed in a logical order.

3. Indented categories form part of, and are included in, the unindented category above them. First indentations (indented once) are in all cases complete; their subcategories always add up to their parent category. Second indentations however, although usually complete, are in several cases selected subgroups not intended as a complete breakdown of their unindented parent subcategory.

4. A few subcategories are omitted in Country Tables 1 for countries in the print *WCE*, but are included in the total Table of all categories in the CD *World Christian database*. Three of them are exact repeats, repeated in order to clarify the overall scheme.

5. All other categories are omitted in the published Country Tables 1 where values are zero for the entire period 1900-2025. They all appear, however, in the CD in order to answer search questions like 'How many Orthodox Charismatics were there in this country in 1970?' (Answer: 'None').

6. All lines have statistics as shown in Country Tables 1, derived as shown in the last column below. Lines with no formulas there receive their totals from outside Country Tables 1 (mostly from censuses or Country Tables 2). Lines with formulas are secondary totals derived from other categories in Country Tables 1 or 2. A few are both, in which case the formulas serve as checks on the accuracy and consistency of the overall tables. Note that all the 'doubly-counted', 'doubly-affiliated', 'disaffiliated', and 'doubly-professing' items (2PC, 2AC, xAC, 2RAC, 4ZAC, and 2r) are shown in all tables as negative numbers because they represent a duplication (persons counted, or counting themselves, twice).

7. Non-Christian religions are coded into families and subfamilies. A specific sect in one of these may be identified by having the letter 'z' or 's' (for sect) added before the code.

ID	*Code*	*Category*	*Formulas (Definitions)*
1.	C	**Christians**	C = CC + PC = UC + AC = LC + GCC.
2.		*PROFESSION*	
3.	CC	crypto-Christians	CC = C - PC = SCC + ICC + NCC + HCC + MCC + BCC.
4.	SCC	Secret church members	SCC = CC - ICC - NCC - HCC - MCC - BCC.
5.	ICC	Isolated radio believers	ICC = RIAC.
6.	NCC	Messianic Neocharismatics	NCC = MIAC = M3ZAC.
7.	HCC	Hidden Hindu believers in Christ	HCC = HBIAC.
8.	MCC	Hidden Muslim believers in Christ	MCC = MBIAC.
9.	BCC	Hidden Buddhist believers in Christ	BCC = BBIAC.
10.	JCC	Hidden Jewish believers in Christ	JCC = JBIAC
11.	XCC	Hidden other religionist believers in Christ	
12.	PC	**professing Christians**	PC = APC + IPC + mPC + OPC + PPC + RPC + 2PC.
13.	APC	Anglicans	
14.	IPC	Independents	IPC = NIPC + PIPC.
15.	mPC	Marginal Christians	
16.	OPC	Orthodox	
17.	PPC	Protestants	
18.	PPPC	Popular-religionists	
19.	RPC	Roman Catholics	
20.	SRPC	Spiritist Catholics	
21.	CRPC	Christopagans	
22.	ERPC	Evangelical Catholics	
23.	PRPC	Popular-religionist Catholics	
24.	2PC	doubly-professing Christians	2PC = PC - (APC + IPC + mPC + OPC + PPC + RPC). This sum is always negative.
25.		*AFFILIATION*	
26.	UC	unaffiliated Christians	UC = C - AC.
27.	AC	**affiliated Christians** (church members)	AC = AAC + IAC + mAC + OAC + PAC + RAC + 2AC + xAC.
28.	pAC	practising church members	pAC = GCC = eAC.
29.	xpAC	nonpracticing church members	xpAC = AC - pAC.
30.	AAC	Anglicans	
31.	EAAC	Anglican Evangelicals	
32.	CAAC	Anglican Charismatics	CAAC = AV2ZAC + Ax2ZAC.
33.	IAC	Independents/Postdenominationalists/Neo-Apostolics	IAC = NIAC + OIAC + CIAC + AIAC + PIAC + WIAC + RIAC + MIAC + BIAC.
34.	EIAC	Independent Evangelicals	EIAC = IEAC
35.	NIAC	Non-White indigenous Christians	NIAC = N3ZAC + NNIAC.
36.	WIAC	White-led Postdenominationalists	WIAC = W3ZAC + WWIAC.
37.	OIAC	Independent Orthodox	
38.	CIAC	Independent Catholics	
39.	AIAC	Independent Anglicans	
40.	PIAC	Independent Protestants	
41.	RIAC	Isolated radio/TV believers	RIAC = R3ZAC + RRIAC.
42.	BIAC	Hidden non-Christian believers in Christ	BIAC = HBIAC + MBIAC + BBIAC + JBIAC + XBIAC.
43.	HBIAC	Hidden Hindu believers in Christ	HBIAC = I-Hin.
44.	MBIAC	Hidden Muslim believers in Christ	MBIAC = I-Mus.
45.	BBIAC	Hidden Buddhist believers in Christ	BBIAC = I-Bud.
46.	JBIAC	Hidden Jewish believers in Christ	JBIAC = I-Jew.
47.	XBIAC	Hidden other religionist believers in Christ	XBIAC = I-rel.
48.	mAC	Marginal Christians	
49.	EmAC	Marginal Evangelicals	
50.	m2ZAC	Marginal Charismatics	
51.	OAC	Orthodox	
52.	EOAC	Orthodox Evangelicals	
53.	COAC	Orthodox Charismatics	
54.	PAC	Protestants	
55.	EPAC	Evangelicals	
56.	1ZAC	Pentecostals	Defined below.
57.	CPAC	Protestant Charismatics	CPAC = PV2ZAC + Px2ZAC.
58.	RAC	Roman Catholics	
59.	ERAC	Catholic Evangelicals	
60.	CRAC	Catholic Charismatics	CRAC = RV2ZAC + Rx2ZAC.
61.	2RAC	doubly-counted Catholics	2RAC = RAC minus the sum of all members enumerated separately by dioceses. Sum is always negative.
62.	2AC	doubly-affiliated	2AC = AC - (AAC + IAC + mAC + OAC + PAC + RAC + xAC). This total is always negative.
63.	xAC	disaffiliated	Former Christians (still on church rolls) who now regard themselves as non-Christians or are dead. Negative.
64.		*Trans-megabloc groupings (also included above):*	
65.	eAC	evangelicals	eAC = GCC = pAC.
66.	EAC	Evangelicals	EAC = CEAC + FEAC + NEAC + LEAC + IEAC + mEAC.
67.	CEAC	Conservative Evangelicals	
68.	FEAC	Fundamentalists	
69.	NEAC	Neo-Evangelicals	
70.	LEAC	Conciliar Evangelicals	LEAC = ALEAC + OLEAC + PLEAC + RLEAC.
71.	ALEAC	Anglican Evangelicals	
72.	OLEAC	Orthodox Evangelicals	
73.	PLEAC	Protestant Evangelicals	
74.	RLEAC	Catholic Evangelicals	
75.	IEAC	Independent Evangelicals	
76.	mEAC	Marginal Evangelicals	

Continued overleaf

Table 3-4 continued

77.	ZAC	Pentecostals/Charismatics/Neocharismatics	ZAC = 0ZAC + 1ZAC + 2ZAC + 3ZAC + 4ZAC.
78.	0ZAC	Prepentecostals	
79.	1ZAC	Pentecostals (First-Wavers)	1ZAC = P1ZAC (= members of bodies in Country Tables 2 whose column 3 code begins 'P-Pe') + x1ZAC.
80.	P1ZAC	Denominational Pentecostals (White)	P1ZAC = CP1ZAC + OP1ZAC.
81.	CP1ZAC	Classical Pentecostals	CP1ZAC = Original, Trinitarian, largely-White bodies, whose column 3 code begins 'P-Pe' but excludes 'P-Pe1'.
82.	OP1ZAC	Oneness Pentecostals	OP1ZAC = Original, 'Jesus Only', largely-White bodies, whose column 3 code = 'P-Pe1'.
83.	x1ZAC	Postpentecostals	
84.	2ZAC	Charismatics (Second-Wavers)	2ZAC = V2ZAC + x2ZAC = A2ZAC + R2ZAC + O2ZAC + P2ZAC + m2ZAC.
85.	V2ZAC	Mainline active Charismatics	V2ZAC = AV2ZAC + RV2ZAC + mV2ZAC + OV2ZAC + PV2ZAC.
86.	AV2ZAC	Anglican Charismatics (active)	
87.	RV2ZAC	Catholic Charismatics (active)	
88.	mV2ZAC	Marginal Charismatics	
89.	OV2ZAC	Orthodox Charismatics	
90.	PV2ZAC	Protestant Charismatics (active)	
91.	x2ZAC	Mainline Postcharismatics	x2ZAC = Ax2ZAC + Px2ZAC + Rx2ZAC.
92.	Ax2ZAC	Anglican Postcharismatics	Ax2ZAC = CAAC - AV2ZAC.
93.	Px2ZAC	Protestant Postcharismatics	Px2ZAC = CPAC - PV2ZAC.
94.	Rx2ZAC	Catholic Postcharismatics	Rx2ZAC = CRAC - RV2ZAC.
95.	A2ZAC	Anglican Charismatics	A2ZAC = CAAC.
96.	R2ZAC	Catholic Charismatics	R2ZAC = CRAC.
97.	O2ZAC	Orthodox Charismatics	O2ZAC = COAC.
98.	P2ZAC	Protestant Charismatics	P2ZAC = CPAC.
99.	m2ZAC	Marginal Charismatics	
100.	3ZAC	Neocharismatics (Third-Wavers)	3ZAC = N3ZAC + O3ZAC + A3ZAC +P3ZAC + R3ZAC + W3ZAC + I3ZAC + r3ZAC + H3ZAC.
101.	N3ZAC	Non-White indigenous Neocharismatics	N3ZAC = bodies whose column 3 begins 'I-3', ends with capital A to V, Y, or Z; plus individual Neocharismatics.
102.		*Last code letter, A to Z:*	
103.	AN3ZAC	African indigenous pentecostals/charismatics	A
104.	UN3ZAC	Afro-Caribbean indigenous pentecostals/charismatics	U
105.	SN3ZAC	Arab/Assyrian/Semitic neocharismatics	S
106.	DN3ZAC	Black American independent charismatics	D
107.	BN3ZAC	Black American indigenous pentecostals	B
108.	ON3ZAC	Black American Oneness Apostolics	O
109.	YN3ZAC	Brazilian/Portuguese grassroots neocharismatics	Y
110.	NN3ZAC	Colored/Mixed-race indigenous charismatics	N
111.	EN3ZAC	Ethnic (Monoethnic) pentecostal churches	E
112.	FN3ZAC	Filipino indigenous pentecostals/charismatics	F
113.	CN3ZAC	Han Chinese indigenous pentecostals/charismatics	C
114.	IN3ZAC	Indian indigenous pentecostals/charismatics	I
115.	GN3ZAC	Indonesian indigenous pentecostals	G
116.	QN3ZAC	Japanese indigenous pentecostals	Q
117.	KN3ZAC	Korean indigenous pentecostals/charismatics	K
118.	LN3ZAC	Latino-Hispanic grassroots believers	L
119.	HN3ZAC	Messianic Hindu believers in Christ	H
120.	JN3ZAC	Messianic Jewish believers in Christ	J
121.	MN3ZAC	Messianic Muslim believers in Christ	M
122.	PN3ZAC	Pacific/Oceanic indigenous charismatics	P
123.	RN3ZAC	Red Indian/Amerindian neopentecostals	R
124.	VN3ZAC	Vietnamese indigenous neocharismatics	V
125.	ZN3ZAC	other Asian indigenous neocharismatics	Z
126.	TN3ZAC	other Messianic non-Christian believers in Christ	T
127.	W3ZAC	White-led Independent Postdenominationalists	W3ZAC = bodies whose column 3 begins 'I-3', ends with W or X; plus individuals in noncharismatic bodies.
128.	WW3ZAC	European/American White-led Neo-Apostolics	W
129.	XW3ZAC	European White-led New Apostolics	X
130.	O3ZAC	Independent Orthodox neocharismatics	
131.	R3ZAC	Independent Catholic neocharismatics	
132.	A3ZAC	Independent Anglican neocharismatics	
133.	P3ZAC	Independent Protestant neocharismatics	
134.	I3ZAC	Nonhistorical Independent neocharismatics	
135.	r3ZAC	Isolated radio/TV neocharismatics	
136.	H3ZAC	Hidden non-Christian believers in Christ	
137.	4ZAC	doubly-counted 1st-/2nd-/3rd-Wavers	4ZAC = ZAC - (0ZAC + 1ZAC + 2ZAC + 3ZAC). This sum is always negative.
138.		*MISSION*	
139.	LC	latent (inactive) Christians	LC = C - GCC = UC + xpAC.
140.	xpAC	nonpracticing church members	xpAC = AC - pAC.
141.	UC	unaffiliated Christians	UC = LC - xpAC.
142.	GCC	**Great Commission Christians** (GeoChristians)	GCC = eAC = pAC
143.	OEC	overt evangelizers	OEC = GCC - CC.
144.	CC	covert evangelizers	
145.		*CULTURE*	
146.	iC	indigenous Christians	
147.	aC	alien Christians	
148.		*GEOSTATUS*	
149.	A-C	World A Christians	A-C = CAA + CBA + CCA.
150.	B-C	World B Christians	B-C = CAB + CBB + CCB.
151.	C-C	World C Christians	C-C = CAC + CBC + CCC.
152.	X	**NON-CHRISTIANS**	
153.	a	Atheists	
154.	L	Baha'is	
155.	AL	Azali Babis	
156.	sL	other Baha'i sectarians	Note: s before a code refers to a specific sect of that code's religion
157.	B	Buddhists	B = MB + TB + LB + VB + BB + FB + NB + sB.
158.	MB	Mahayana Buddhists	MB = IMB + CMB + KMB + JMB.
159.	IMB	Indian Buddhists	
160.	CMB	Chinese Buddhists	
161.	KMB	Korean Buddhists	
162.	JMB	Japanese Buddhists	
163.	NJMB	Nichirenshu	
164.	TMB	Tendaishu	
165.	NMB	Nara	
166.	PMB	Pure Land (Amida)	
167.	ZMB	Zen	
168.	SMB	Shingon (Tantrists)	
169.	TB	Theravada (Hinayana) Buddhists	
170.	NTB	Neo-Buddhists	
171.	LB	Tibetan Buddhists (Lamaists)	
172.	VB	Vajrayana (Tantrists)	
173.	YB	Buddhayana	
174.	FB	Folk Buddhists	
175.	NB	nonreligious Buddhists	
176.	sB	other sectarian Buddhists	
177.	F	Chinese folk-religionists	
178.	G	Confucianists	
179.	T	Ethnoreligionists (Tribalists)	T = AT + NT + PT + ST + WT + sT.
180.	AT	Animists	AT = LAT + HAT + IAT + BAT + PAT.
181.	LAT	Primal religionists	

Continued opposite

Table 3-4–continued

182.	HAT	Hinduized animists	
183.	IAT	Islamized animists	
184.	BAT	Buddhistic animists	
185.	PAT	Polytheistic animists	
186.	ET	Neopagans	
187.	PT	Polytheists	
188.	ST	Shamanists	
189.	KST	Korean folk-religionists	
190.	WT	Witchcraft eradicationists	
191.	zT	other ethnoreligionist sectarians	
192.	H	Hindus	H = VH + SH + KH + NH + RH + FH + sH.
193.	HH	Vedantists	
194.	VH	Vaishnavites	
195.	SH	Shaivites	
196.	KH	Saktists	
197.	NH	Neo-Hindus	
198.	RH	Reform Hindus	
199.	TH	Tantrists (Tantrist Hindus)	
200.	FH	Folk/Popular Hindus	
201.	zH	other sectarian Hindus	
202.	V	Jains	V = DV + SV.
203.	DV	Digambara Jains	
204.	SV	Svetambara Jains	
205.	zV	other sectarian Jains	
206.	J	Jews	J = AJ + EJ + SJ + KJ + TJ + sJ.
207.	AJ	Ashkenazis	
208.	EJ	Oriental Jews	
209.	SJ	Sefardis	
210.	RJ	Reformists	
211.	OJ	Orthodox	
212.	CJ	Reconstructionists	
213.	KJ	Karaites	
214.	TJ	Samaritans	
215.	sJ	other Jewish movements	
216.	M	Muslims	M = SM + HM + UM + XM.
217.	SM	Sunnis	SM = HSM + SSM + MSM + BSM + WSM.
218.	HSM	Hanafites	
219.	SSM	Shafiites	
220.	MSM	Malikites	
221.	BSM	Hanbalites	
222.	WSM	Wahhabites	
223.	zSM	other Sunni sectarians	
224.	UM	Sufis	
225.	sUM	other sectarian Sufis	
226.	HM	Shias	HM = AHM + IHM + ZHM + LHM.
227.	AHM	Ithna-Asharis	
228.	IHM	Ismailis	
229.	BIHM	Bohoras	
230.	ZHM	Zaydis	
231.	LHM	Alawites	
232.	sHM	other Shia sectarians	
233.	XM	Islamic schismatics	XM = AXM + IXM + DXM + BXM + NXM + sXM.
234.	AXM	Ahmadis	
235.	LAXM	Lahoris	
236.	QAXM	Qadianis	
237.	IXM	Ibadis	
238.	DXM	Druzes	
239.	BXM	Black Muslims	
240.	MXM	Sabbateans	
241.	NXM	Neo-Fundamentalists	
242.	YXM	Yazidis	
243.	sXM	other Islamic sectarians	
244.	FM	Folk Muslims	
245.	N	Neoreligionists (New-Religionists)	N = SN + NN + FN.
246.	SN	Syncretist neoreligionists	
247.	NN	Nonsyncretist neoreligionists	
248.	ON	Occultists	
249.	VN	Nativistic cultists	
250.	CN	Cargo cultists	
251.	FN	Self-Religionists	
252.	Q	Nonreligious	
253.	S	Shintoists	
254.	HS	Shrine Shinto	
255.	TS	Sect Shinto	
256.	FS	Folk Shinto	
257.	K	Sikhs	
258.	U	Spiritists	
259.	AU	Afro-American spiritists	
260.	BU	Afro-Brazilian cultists	
261.	CU	Afro-Caribbean religionists	
262.	SU	Afro-Surinamese religionists	
263.	HU	High Spiritists	
264.	D	Taoists	
265.	Z	Zoroastrians	
266.	PZ	Parsis	
267.	Y	other religionists	
268.	MY	Mandeans	
269.	NY	Quasi-Christians	
270.	QY	Quasireligionists	
271.	rY	other minor religionists	
272.	2W	doubly-counted religionists	2W = W - (a + L + B + Y + G + T + H + V + J + M + N + Q + S + F + K + U + D + Z). Sum always negative.
273.		*TOTALS*	
274.	C	**Total Christians**	Defined as above.
275.	X	**Total Non-Christians**	X = a + L + B + Y + G + T + H + V + J + M + N + Q + S + F + K + U + D + Z + 2W.
276.	W	**Total religionists**	W = C + X - a - Q + 2W = pop - a - Q.
277.	pop	population	
278.	Ppop	A people's population	
279.	Npop	Country's population	
280.	Apop	World A population	
281.	Bpop	World B population	
282.	Cpop	World C population	
283.	Gpop	Total global population	
284.		*EVANGELIZATION*	
285.	EP	Total evangelized persons	
286.	UP	Total unevangelized persons	UP = pop - EP.

Continued overleaf

Table 3-4–concluded

287.		*GEOSTATUS*	
288.	Apop1	World A individuals	Apop1 = UP.
289.	Bpop1	World B individuals	Bpop1 = pop - UP - C.
290.	Cpop1	World C individuals	Cpop1 = C.
291.		*PEOPLES AND COUNTRIES*	
292.	Apop2	Population of World A peoples	
293.	Bpop2	Population of World B peoples	
294.	Cpop2	Population of World C peoples	
295.	Apop3	Population of World A countries	
296.	Bpop3	Population of World B countries	
297.	Cpop3	Population of World C countries	
298.		*LOCATION OF INDIVIDUALS*	
299.		First column letter in list below = World A, B, or C individuals (shown by lowercase letter a, b, or c)	
300.		Second column letter = who are also within World A/B/C peoples (shown by capital letter)	
301.		Third column letter = who are also within World A/B/C countries (shown by capital letter)	
302.	aAA	World A individuals in World A peoples in World A countries	
303.	aAB	World A individuals in World A peoples in World B countries	
304.	aAC	World A individuals in World A peoples in World C countries	
305.	aBA	World A individuals in World B peoples in World A countries	
306.	aBB	World A individuals in World B peoples in World B countries	
307.	aBC	World A individuals in World B peoples in World C countries	
308.	aCA	World A individuals in World C peoples in World A countries	
309.	aCB	World A individuals in World C peoples in World B countries	
310.	aCC	World A individuals in World C peoples in World C countries	
311.	bAA	World B individuals in World A peoples in World A countries	
312.	bAB	World B individuals in World A peoples in World B countries	
313.	bAC	World B individuals in World A peoples in World C countries	
314.	bBA	World B individuals in World B peoples in World A countries	
315.	bBB	World B individuals in World B peoples in World B countries	
316.	bBC	World B individuals in World B peoples in World C countries	
317.	bCA	World B individuals in World C peoples in World A countries	
318.	bCB	World B individuals in World C peoples in World B countries	
319.	bCC	World B individuals in World C peoples in World C countries	
320.	cAA	World C individuals in World A peoples in World A countries	
321.	cAB	World C individuals in World A peoples in World B countries	
322.	cAC	World C individuals in World A peoples in World C countries	
323.	cBA	World C individuals in World B peoples in World A countries	
324.	cBB	World C individuals in World B peoples in World B countries	
325.	cBC	World C individuals in World B peoples in World C countries	
326.	cCA	World C individuals in World C peoples in World A countries	
327.	cCB	World C individuals in World C peoples in World B countries	
328.	cCC	World C individuals in World C peoples in World C countries	

5. COUNTRY TABLES 1.

Table 3-5. Meanings of Country Tables 1. Religious adherents in each country, AD 1900-2025.

The term adherents refers to the whole de facto (present-in-area) resident population—men, women, children and infants, nationals and expatriates (citizens and aliens), armed services, alien troops, nomadic groups, refugees and so on.

Brief summary of the 17 columns
The columns are not numbered 1–17 in the tables themselves, but are numbered below here to assist in identifying particular columns. In the Table 1-1 (Part 1), 2 additional columns are added for the year AD 2050, and another for number of countries involved.

1. Major religions, listed in order of numerical size in AD 2000, with indented subdivisions
2. Adherents in the year 1900
3. Adherents in 1900 as % total population then
4. Adherents in mid-1970
5. Adherents in mid-1970 as % total population then
6. Adherents in mid-1990
7. Adherents in mid-1990 as % total population then

8-11. Annual change, 1990-2000; average long-term trend over the decade

8. Annual natural population increase among adherents, 1990-2000 (biological increase (births minus deaths) plus net immigration)
9. Annual conversion (or supranatural) increase (+ or -) to adherents, 1990-2000 (computed as col. 10 minus col. 8)
10. Total annual increase (+ or -) of adherents, 1990-2000 (= col. 8 plus col. 9) (computed as col. 14 minus col. 6, divided by 10)
11. Rate of change of adherents, 1990-2000, as % per year (= col. 10 divided by col. 12, times 100%)
12. Adherents in mid-1995
13. Adherents in mid-1995 as % total population then
14. Adherents in mid-2000
15. Adherents in mid-2000 as % total population then
16. Adherents in the year 2025 (assuming current trends continue)
17. Adherents in 2025 as % total population then

Definitions of various religious categories
Indented categories, in the listing below and in the tables, are sub-divisions of categories less indented.

Note our 3 basic equations concerning definitions of Christians:

(1) Total 'Christians'	=	professing Christians + crypto-Christians,
which also	=	affiliated Christians + unaffiliated Christians
(2) Total 'affiliated'	=	affiliated Roman Catholics + affiliated Protestants + affiliated Orthodox + affiliated Anglicans + affiliated marginal Christians + affiliated Independents, *minus* doubly-affiliated, *minus* disaffiliated.
(3) Total 'affiliated'	=	total practising Christians + non-practising Christians.

Note also that the first 9 categories below always (in Tables 1) refer to aggregate totals for all denominations of Christians (in all 6 major ecclesiastico-cultural megablocs: Roman Catholic, Protestant, etc) in the whole country.

Percentages. All columns headed % in Country Tables 1 refer to percentages of the total population of the country.
Footnotes. The notes below Country Tables 1 consist of (1) a note on columns and rows, (2) source data from any national population censuses of religion or public-opinion polls, and (3) NOTES ON RELIGIONS elaborating on, or giving additional data on, various categories in the table, these being listed in alphabetical order. If no footnote is given for a particular Christian category (e.g. 'Marginal Christians', 'Black/Third-World indigenous'), details of how the totals are arrived at may be studied in Country Table 2 for the country.

6. COUNTRY TABLES 2.

Table 3-6. Meanings of Country Tables 2. Organized churches and denominations in each country.

Brief summary of the 10 columns
In all Country Tables 2, the columns are always numbered 1-10.

Column:

1.	Name	Official name of church, denomination or diocese; names in boldface (heavy) type are churches each with over 10% of the country's affiliated Christians.
2.	Begun	Year when body was begun (or re-begun) permanently in this country (major significant date usually given).
3.	Type	Ecclesiastical type: major ecclesiastico-cultural megabloc, followed after hyphen by ecclesiastical tradition.
4.	Councils	Conciliarism: membership in councils (confessional, international, continental, regional, national).
5.	Congs	Congregations (places of regular worship), 1995 or latest available date.
6.	Adults	Adult church members (over 15 years) on rolls (communicants or full members, often with probationary or baptized non-communicant members), 1995.
7.	Aff 1970	Total affiliated church membership in 1970.
8.	Affiliated	Total church membership in 1995 (on average) or latest available date; total church member community, or inclusive membership, or total constituency (adults, children, infants, catechumens, adherents, members under discipline, etc) on the church's books or records, or known to the church (this column always includes those in column 6).
9.	G%	Church growth rate, % per year, over 25-year period 1970-1995, on exponential assumption.
10.	Notes	Names, notes and other statistics, covering descriptive data as available.

The following sections on 4 pages are the codes and abbreviations used in columns 1, 3, 4 and 10. The codes and statistics used in columns 3-7 are all mutually exclusive (i.e. each body belongs to only the type of council shown, and not to others; and individual congregations and Christians are enumerated only once in each Country Table 2, under a single body; in those cases where Christians are affiliated to 2 or more bodies, this is corrected by including them also in Doubly-affiliated).

Continued opposite

Table 3-6 continued

COLUMN 1: NAMES OF BODIES

(1) Abbreviations in names of bodies

In order to reduce names to a manageable length, the following standard abbreviations are used when necessary in the lists. In addition, the 3-letter abbreviations in column 3 may sometimes be employed (e.g. Bap, Met, Ref). All names are alphabetized in the listings on their unabbreviated versions.

Adv	Adventist
Apost, Ap	Apostolic, Apostolica
Asoc	Asociación
Assem	Assemblies
Assoc, As	Association
Autonom	Autonomous
Bapt	Baptist
Cath	Catholic
Ch	Church (in Italian, Chiesa)
Chr	Christian, Chrétien(ne), Christliche
Chs	Churches
Conf	Conference
Cong(r,s)	Congregation, Congregación
Conv	Convention, Convención
Cri	Cristiana
E, Egl(s)	Eglise(s) (=Church(es))
Epis	Episcopal
Ev	Evangelical, Evangélique(s), Evangelische(e,-er), Evangélica(s, -o, -os)
Ex	Exarchate
Fed	Federation, Federcion
Fell	Fellowship
Herm	Hermanos
Ig, Igl(s)	Igreja, Iglesia(s) (=Church(es))
Indep	Independent, Independiente(s)
Int	International
Intern(at)	International(e)
I(s)	Island(s); occasionally (in Spanish or Portuguese) Iglesia, Igreja
JC, J-C, CJ	Jesus Christ, Jésus-Christ, Jesu Cristo, Jesucristo, Cristo Jesus
K	Kirche (Church)
Luth	Lutheran, Lutherische(e), Luthérien(ne)
Meth	Methodist
Min	Ministries, Ministerial
Miss, Mis	Mission, Misión
Nac	Nacional
Orth	Orthodox(e)
Patr	Patriarchate
Pente	Pentecostal
Presb	Presbyterian, Presbiteriana
Ref	Reformed
Soc	Society
Syn	Synod
Syna	Synagogue(s)
Un	Union, Union

Other initials in names of bodies refer either to the country concerned (A = Austria, B = Belgium, etc), or to details explained at the end of the church's line in the table or in the notes beneath the table.

(2) Dioceses, jurisdictions and other sub-divisions.

AA	apostolic administration
AD	archdiocese
AN	abbey nullius
C	catholicate (catholicossate), diocese of catholicos
CD	church district
Co	Community (communauté) (used only in Zaire Table 2)
Con	conference
CR	conciliar region (regione conciliare)
D	diocese, eparchy
E	exarchate
EA	exarchate apostolic
EC	episcopal commissariat
EM	exarchical monastery
EP	ecumenical patriarchate
EPr	ecclesiastical province
EPi	episcopal area
J	jurisdiction
M	metropolitan archdiocese or see; metropolia (when superior to D)
MV	military vicariate or ordinariate
m	mission (sui juris)
O	ordinariate
P	patriarchate, patriarchal diocese
PA	prefecture apostolic
PE	patriarchal exarchate
PN	prelature (prelacy) nullius
Pro	province
R	region (apostolic or conciliar)
RN	priory nullius
S	synod
UD	united diocese
UDs	united dioceses
V	vicariate
VA	vicariate apostolic
VP	patriarchal vicariate
:	(at end of a name) composite body whose statistics are the total of its components shown below it
( )	jurisdiction based in another country, of which this body is a part

COLUMN 3: ECCLESIASTICAL TYPE (4 letter code)

1st letter: Megabloc (Stream) (definitions are given in Parts 2 or 12): A, O, R = Liturgical Pedobaptist (infant-baptizing); I, P, m = partly Non-Liturgical, partly Baptist (adult baptism only).

A	Anglican (Episcopalian)
I	Independent/Postdenominationalist/Neo-Apostolic (Non-White or Black/Third-World indigenous, White-led Postdenominationalist)
m	Marginal Christian (para-Christian of Western origin)
O	Orthodox (Eastern, Oriental, or Nestorian/Assyrian)
P	Protestant (sometimes called Evangelical)
R	Roman Catholic

2nd-4th letters (last 3 letters of column): Tradition (*major or dominant description*). (Note 1. Most of these codes are prefaced separately by only one megabloc code, but a number can be prefaced by 2 (such as P or I, or R or O). *Note 2.* All codes beginning '3' refer to Neocharismatic/Third-Wave paradenominations or networks, described separately by the last 2 letters of each: last letter = ethnic origin, middle letter = location on pentecostal/charismatic ecclesiastical spectrum).

ACa	Anglo-Catholic
Ade	Christadelphian (Adelphoi, Brothers of Christ, Unitarian Adventist)
Adv	Adventist
Alb	Albanian/Greek-speaking (Byzantine or Orthodox)
Ang	schism ex Anglicanism or Episcopalianism, in Protestant direction
Apo	apocalyptic, eschatological
Ara	Arabic- or Arabic/Greek-speaking (Orthodox)
Arm	Armenian (Orthodox (Gregorian) or Eastern-rite Catholic)
ARo	Anglo-Roman (schism ex Anglicanism in Roman direction)
Bap	Baptist
Brl	British-Israelite
Bud	Hidden Buddhist believers in Christ
Bul	Bulgarian (Orthodox or Byzantine rite)
Bye	Byelorussian/Belorussian (White Russian/White Ruthenian) (Orthodox or Byzantine)
Byz	Byzantine-rite (jurisdiction for more than one ethnic group)
Cat	other Independent Catholic bodies
CBr	Christian Brethren (Plymouth Brethren; Open only, not Exclusive); independent/fundamentalist/dispensationalist
CCa	Conservative Catholic (schism ex Rome, protesting liberal or updating trends)
Cel	Celtic (British)
Cen	Central or Broad Church Anglican (Prayer Book Liberal, Comprehensive, New Synod Group)
Cha	Chaldean (Eastern Syrian rite)
com	community church or union congregation (formed by 2 or more denominations), open to all denominations and races
Con	Congregational, Congregationalist
Cop	Coptic (Orthodox or Alexandrian-rite)
Cze	Czech/Slavonic-speaking (Orthodox)
Dis	Disciple, Restorationist, Restorationist Baptist, Christian (Restoration Movement Campbellites, Disciples, Churches of Christ)
Div	Divine Science
Don	Donatist
Dun	Dunker (Tunker), Dipper, German Baptist, Brethren (baptism by 3-fold immersion)
EBr	Exclusive Brethren (Plymouth Brethren, Closed, Strict; Darbyites); exclusive fundamentalist/dispensalionalist
Ecu	Ecumenical (Anglican/Protestant/Orthodox joint parishes)
Epi	episcopi-vagantes (bishops-at-large) (only those with 100 or under members)
Est	Estonian (Independent Orthodox)
eth	ethnic denomination, monoethnic
Eth	Ethiopic, Ethiopian Orthodox, Ge'ez-speaking, Alexandrian
Eva	Anglican Evangelical, Evangelical Anglican, Independent Evangelical
Fin	Finnish/Slavonic-speaking (Orthodox)
Fun	Fundamentalist
Gay	Gay/Lesbian homosexual tradition
Geo	Georgian Orthodox or Byzantine-rite Roman Catholic
Gno	Gnostic, esoteric, anthroposophical
Gre	Greek (Orthodox or Byzantine, Greek-speaking) (New Calendar)
Hig	High Church Anglican (Prayer Book Catholic)
Hin	Hidden Hindu believers in Christ
Hol	Holiness (Conservative Methodist, Wesleyan, Free Methodist, non-Pentecostal Perfectionist), 2-experience: conversion, entire sanctification; mainly schisms out of mainline Methodism differing chiefly on sanctification
HSA	Holy Spirit Association (Moon)
Hun	Hungarian/Slavonic-speaking (Byzantine or Orthodox)
IAb	Italo-Albanian (Byzantine)
ind	independent evangelical, often fundamentalist (dispensationalist), unrelated to other indigenous traditions, usually regarding itself as a denomination
Int	interdenominational evangelical Protestant (unaffiliated to any denomination, unrelated to any major tradition, or specifically interdenominational); faith mission
Ita	Italian (Byzantine)
Jeh	Jehovah's Witnesses (Jehovah's Christian Witnesses; Russellites) including Bible Student movement and other schismatics or dissidents
Jew	Messianic, Jewish-Christian, or Jewish crypto-Christian
Lat	Latin-rite Catholics
Lav	Latvian Orthodox
LdS	Latter-day Saints (Mormons), including Mormon schismatics or dissidents
LEr	jurisdiction for both Latin-rite and Eastern-rite Catholics
Lib	Liberal Catholic (deviant, Theosophical, Masonic, Gnostic)
Low	Low Church Anglican (Conservative Evangelical)
LuR	Lutheran/Reformed united church or joint misssion
Lut	Lutheran
Mac	Macedonian Orthodox
Mal	Malankara (Syro-Antiochian,Eastern Syrian), Syro-Malankarese
Mar	Maronite (Syro-Antiochian, Western Syrian)
mar	marginal (Black/Third-World indigenous churches, and Catholic schisms, of unorthodox or syncretistic christology, claiming a second or supplementary source of revelation in addition to the Bible)
Mel	Melkite (Byzantine, Greek Catholic; Arabic-speaking)
Men	Mennonite, Anabaptist (Left Wing or Radical Reformation), including other communal Anabaptist sects
Met	Methodist (mainline Methodist, United Methodist); English-speaking Pietist
Mol	Moldavian Orthodox
Mon	Montenegrin Orthodox
Mor	Moravian (Continental Pietist)
Mus	Hidden Muslim believers in Christ
NoC	No-Church movement
Nes	Assyrian or Nestoran (East Syrian, Messihaye (Christians), Syro-Chaldean; Dyophysite), including dissidents
Non	Nondenominational (no church or anti-church groups rejecting being described as a church)
Pau	Paulician/Bogomil
OBe	Old Believer, Old Ritualist
OCa	Old Catholic
OCd	Old Calendarist, Authentic Orthodox
Ori	plural Oriental (Roman Catholic jurisdiction for all or several Eastern rites together)
Ose	Orthodox sect/sectarian
Ort	schism from Orthodoxy, in Protestant direction
PeA	Apostolic, or Pentecostal Apostolic (stress on complex hierarchy of living apostles, prophets and other charismatic officials); White-originated or -led
Pen	Pentecostal (Protestant; Classical Pentecostal of unspecific type); charismatic, faithhealing (Classical Pentecostal sub-types include PeA, Pe1, Pe2, Pe3, Pe4)
Pe1	Oneness-Pentecostal or Unitarian-Pentecostal: 'Jesus only', sometimes unitarian, non- or anti-trinitarian; White-led
Pe2	Baptistic-Pentecostal or Keswick-Pentecostal: 2-crisis-experience (conversion, baptism of the Spirit); White-led, Classical
Pe3	Holiness-Pentecostal: 3-crisis-experience (conversion, sanctification, baptism of the Spirit); White-led, Classical
plu	Anglican, of plural or mixed traditions (no single tradition)
Pol	Polish/Slavonic-speaking (Orthodox)
Pro	ex-Protestant Catholic (movement out of Protestantism in a Catholic direction, receiving

Continued overleaf

Table 3-6 continued

	episcopacy and apostolic succession)
Qua	Friends (Quakers)
rad	isolated radio churches (unorganized isolated house congregations or cells of isolated radio believers brought into being by radio, mail and/or radiophonic evangelism)
ReA	Reformed Anglican
ReC	Reformed Catholic, retaining Roman Catholic claims
Ref	Reformed, Presbyterian (the latter originating in English-speaking areas, the former in continental Europe)
ReO	Reformed Orthodox (uncanonical reform movement out of Orthodoxy, retaining Orthodox claims)
Rum	Romanian (Orthodox or Byzantine)
Rus	Russian (Orthodox or Byzantine)
Rut	Ruthenian (Byzantine)
sAC	Anglican schism of Anglo-Catholic type, retaining Anglicans claims
Sal	Salvationist (Salvation Army)
Sci	metaphysical science, Divine Science, Religious Science, Christian Science, New Thought, magnetic healing, psychedelic
Ser	Serbian/Slavonic-speaking (Orthodox)
sin	single congregation(s): one single autonomous congregation, completely independent and unaffiliated to any denomination, nor claiming to be a denomination; or a defacto unstructured grouping of such congregations
Sla	Slavonic, Slavonic-speaking (Orthodox), members of several ethnic traditions
Slo	Slovak (Byzantine)
smi	Anglican schism of mixed types of churchmanship, retaining Anglican claims
Spi	Spiritualist, Spiritist (thaumaturgical), psychic, psychical, occult, mediumistic, of specifically Christian type
sub	sub-Orthodox Russian sect rejecting Orthodox ritual
Swe	Swedenborgian (Church of the New Jerusalem; spiritualistic)
SyM	Syro-Malabarese (Eastern Syrian), Syriac/Malayalam-speaking, Orthodox Syrian
Syr	Syrian, Syriac-speaking (Orthodox or Syro-Antiochian, West Syrian, Jacobite)
tel	TV (television) paradenomination, organized around regular worship telecasts
TrA	Traditional Anglican, Traditionalist
The	Theosophist, Theosophical, synthesist (combining philosophy and religions)
Tru	True Orthodox (devoutly conservative Russian Orthodox)
Ukr	Ukrainian (Orthodox or Byzantine)
Uni	United church (voluntary or involuntary unions of bodies of different traditions)
Unt	Unitarian, Universalist, Free Christian, Liberal Christian
Wal	Waldensian
Yug	Yugoslav (Byzantine)
All codes beginning '3' = Third-Wavers	
3aA	African Independent Apostolic
3aB	Black American Apostolic
3aF	Filipino Apostolic
3aK	Korean Apostolic
3aI	Indian Apostolic
3aL	Latin American Apostolic
3aO	Black American Oneness Apostolic
3aP	Pacific Apostolic
3aS	Arab Apostolic
3aU	Afro-Caribbean Apostolic
3aW	White-led Apostolic
3aX	New Apostolic, Catholic Apostolic (Irvingite) or Old Apostolic; sacramentalist, hierarchical
3cA	African Independent charismatic
3cB	Black American charismatic
3cC	Chinese charismatic
3cD	Black American Independent charismatic
3cE	Monoethnic charismatic
3cF	Filipino charismatic
3cI	Indian charismatic
3cK	Korean charismatic
3cL	Latin American charismatic
3cP	Pacific charismatic
3cQ	Japanese charismatic
3cS	Arab charismatic
3cU	Afro-Caribbean charismatic
3cW	White-led charismatic
3cY	Brazilian/Portuguese charismatic
3cZ	other Asian charismatic
3dW	White-led neocharismatic mainliners
3dZ	other Asian doubly-affiliated mainliners
3fA	African Independent Full Gospel
3fB	Black American Full Gospel
3fC	Chinese Full Gospel
3fD	Black American charismatic Full Gospel
3fF	Filipino Full Gospel
3fG	Indonesian Full Gospel
3fI	Indian Full Gospel
3fK	Korean Full Gospel
3fL	Latin American Full Gospel
3fP	Pacific Full Gospel
3fW	White-led Full Gospel
3fY	Brazilian/Portuguese Full Gospel
3fZ	other Asian Full Gospel
3gL	Latin American grassroots
3gU	Afro-Caribbean grassroots
3gY	Brazilian grassroots
3hA	African house-church network
3hE	Monoethnic house-church network
3hG	Indonesian house-church network
3hI	Indian house-church network
3hL	Latin American house-church network
3hP	Pacific house-church network
3hS	Arab house-church network
3hW	White-led house-church network
3hZ	other Asian house-church network
3hV	Vietnamese house-church network
3hK	Korean house-church network
3jA	African healing network
3jW	White-led healing network
3kA	African cell-based network
3kB	Black American cell-based network
3kC	Chinese cell-based network
3kK	Korean cell-based network
3kL	Latin American cell-based network
3kW	White-led cell-based network
3kZ	other Asian cell-based network
3mA	Messianic African Independent
3mC	Messianic Chinese
3mH	Messianic Hindu temples or individuals
3mJ	Messianic Jewish synagogues or individuals
3mM	Messianic Muslim mosques or individuals
3nA	African Independent neocharismatic
3nB	Black American neocharismatic
3nC	Chinese neocharismatic
3nE	Monoethnic neocharismatic
3nF	Filipino neocharismatic
3nG	Indonesia neocharismatic
3nI	Indian neocharismatic
3nL	Latin American neocharismatic
3nN	Creole neocharismatic
3nP	Pacific neocharismatic
3nS	Arab neocharismatic
3nU	Afro-Caribbean neocharismatic
3nW	White-led neocharismatic
3nZ	other Asian neocharismatic
3oA	African Oneness pentecostal
3oC	Chinese Oneness pentecostal
3oF	Filipino Oneness pentecostal
3oG	Indonesian Oneness pentecostal
3oI	Indian Oneness pentecostal
3oL	Latin American Oneness pentecostal
3oO	Black American Oneness pentecostal
3oQ	Japanese Oneness pentecostal
3oU	Afro-Caribbean Oneness pentecostal
3oW	White-led Oneness pentecostal
3oY	Brazilian/Portuguese Oneness pentecostal
3oZ	other Asian Oneness pentecostal
3pA	African Independent pentecostal
3pB	Black American pentecostal
3pC	Chinese pentecostal
3pE	Monoethnic pentecostal
3pF	Filipino pentecostal
3pG	Indonesian pentecostal
3pI	Indian pentecostal
3pK	Korean pentecostal
3pL	Latin American pentecostal
3pN	Creole pentecostal
3pP	Pacific pentecostal
3pQ	Japanese pentecostal
3pR	Amerindian pentecostal
3pS	Arab pentecostal
3pU	Afro-Caribbean pentecostal
3pW	White-led pentecostal
3pY	Brazilian/Portuguese pentecostal
3pZ	other Asian pentecostal
3rA	African radio/TV believers
3rC	Chinese radio/TV believers
3rG	Indonesian radio/TV believers
3rI	Indian radio/TV believers
3rK	Korean radio/TV believers
3rL	Latin American radio/TV network
3rQ	Japanese radio/TV believers
3rS	Arab radio/TV network
3rV	Vietnamese radio/TV believers
3rW	European White radio/TV believers
3rY	Brazilian/Portuguese radio/TV believers
3rZ	other Asian radio/TV believers
3sA	African Independent Spiritual
3sU	Afro-Caribbean Spiritual
3sW	White-led signs and wonders
3tW	White-led restorationist
3vA	African Independent deliverance
3vB	Black American deliverance pentecostal
3vW	White-led deliverance pentecostal
3wA	African Word of Faith/Prosperity
3wF	Filipino Word of Faith/Prosperity
3wP	Pacific Word-of-Faith/Prosperity
3wW	White-led Word of Faith/Prosperity
3xK	Korean pentecostal of mixed traditions
3xL	Latin American neocharismatic of mixed tradtions
3xW	European charismatic of mixed traditions
3zA	Zionist African Independent
3zU	Afro-Caribbean Zionist

COLUMN 4: CONCILIARISM, COLLEGIALITY, CONSULTATION, AND CHURCH ORGANIZATION (5-letter code)

Note on names. Most international bodies have official names in 2 or more major international languages. Almost all of these are given in Parts 2, 12, or 14, but in the interests of brevity names are given below only once in English (for international bodies with official names in several languages), or in the major European language in use followed by an English translation if widely used. Where a body uses varying sets of initials in its various languages, these are all given below in brackets separated by slashes.

Conference of Secretaries of Christian World Communions (until 1979 known as World Confessional Families). The 15 international confessional councils below followed by an asterisk* (making a total of 24 asterisks including duplications) are represented on this conference, begun in 1957; in addition, the following non-confessional international denominational bodies are participants: Church of the Brethren, Salvation Army, General Conference of Seventh-day Adventists, World Convention of Churches of Christ (Disciples).

Code	*Name of communion in English*
A	= Anglican Consultative Council (ACC)/Lambeth Conference/Anglican Primates Committee*
a	= Anglican Consultative Council: non-autonomous body*
B	= Sacred Congregation for Bishops*
b	= immediately subject to Holy See (under Sacred Congregation for Bishops)*
C	= canonical relationship with Ecumenical Patriarchate of Constantinople (also the other 3 Greek-speaking Orthodox patriarchates, and Panorthodox conference)*
c	= claimed but disputed relationship to Ecumenical Patriarchate of Constantinople
D	= canonical relationship with Syrian Orthodox (Jacobite) Patriarchate of Antioch (Damascus)
E	= Armenian Catholicate of Echmiadzin
e	= International Lutheran Conference (ILC)
F	= member of both WARC and RES (World Alliance of Reformed Churches, and Reformed Ecumenical Synod)*
G	= Mennonite World Conference (MWC)*
I	= Organization of African Instituted Churches (OAIC)
i	= International New Thought Alliance (INTA)
J	= Reformed Ecumenical Synod (RES)*
K	= International Federation of Free Evangelical Churches (IFFEC)
L	= Lutheran World Federation (LWF/FLM/LWB) (member, or congregation formally recognized by LWF)*
l	= permanent observer (but not member) relationship to Lutheran World Federation (LWF)*
M	= canonical relationship with Patriarchate of Moscow (in preference to Constantinople)*
N	= Coptic Orthodox Patriarchate of Alexandria
O	= Sacred Congregation for the Eastern Churches*
o	= immediately subject to Holy See (under Sacred Congregation for the Eastern Churches)*
P	= Sacred Congregation for the Evangelization of Peoples (Propaganda)*
p	= immediately subject to Holy See (under Propaganda)*
Q	= Friends World Committee for Consultation (FWCC)*
R	= World Alliance of Reformed Churches (Presbyterian and Congregational) (WARC)*
S	= Armenian Catholicate of Cilicia (Sis)
T	= Baptist World Alliance (BWA/ABM/BWB)*
U	= International Old Catholic Bishops Conference (Union of Utrecht)*
V	= World Methodist Council (WMC)*
W	= member of both WMC and WARC (World Methodist Council, and World Alliance of Reformed Churches)*
X	= Ukrainian Orthodox Church of the Free World
x	= quasi-confession (or non-confessional international denominational body), usually with world missionary outreach or, non-canonical Orthodox communion
Y	= canonical relationship with Ancient Assyrian Church of the East, Patriarchate of the East (Tehran) (Mar Dinkha IV)
y	= canonical relationship with Ancient Assyrian Church of the East, Patriarchate of Baghdad (Mar Addai)
Z	= Pentecostal World Conference (PWC)
C+M	= Great and Holy Council of the Orthodox Church*
D + E + N + S	= Oriental Orthodox Churches conference
.	= not a member of any confessional council, nor in communion with historical Orthodox/Anglican/Old Catholic/Roman Catholic churches; no international confessional links or membership of any kind.

Table 3-6 continued

Other international confessional councils, not coded here.
20 other non- or antitrinitarian heterodox communions, 20 schismatic communions ex Anglicanism, 25 Conservative networks hostile to historic confessions, 30 other meganetworks White-led Neo-Apostolic, 40 Independent Neocharismatic minicommunions, 50 major Protestant global denominations, African Apostolic Church of Johane Maranke (AACJM), Alliance World Fellowship (AWF), Ancient Assyrian Patriarchate of the East, Anglican Episcopal Council of Churches, Anglican Orthodox Communion, Apostolic World Christian Fellowship (AWCF), Assembly Hall Churches (Local Churches, Little Flock), Baptist Bible Fellowship International (BBFI), Brazil for Christ Evangelical Pentecostal Church (OBPC), Brazilian Catholic Apostolic Church (ICAB), Catholic Charismatic Renewal (CCR), Chaplaincy of Full Gospel Churches (CFGC), Christian Congregation of Brazil (CCB), Christian Holiness Association (CHA), Church of the Brethren, Church of Christ (Manalista), Church of Christ, Scientist, Church of God in Christ (CoGiC), Church of Jesus Christ of Latter-day Saints (CJCLdS), Coalition of Spirit-filled Churches (CSC), Consultation on Uniting and United Churches (CUUC), Confessional Lutheran Synod, Czechoslovak Hussite Church (CCH/CHC), Deeper Life Bible Church (DLBC), Disciples Ecumenical Committee for Consultation (DECC), Ethiopian Orthodox Patriarchate of Addis Ababa, Fellowship of French Evangelical and Reformed Churches (CEVAA) (a worldwide body), General Conference of Seventh-day Adventists (SDA), Gypsy Pentecostal Churches, India Pentecostal Church of God (IPCG), International Association for Religious Freedom (IARF), International Baptist Fellowsip, International Charismatic Consultation on World Evangelization (ICCOWE), International Communion of Charismatic Churches (ICCC), International Communion of the Charismatic Episcopal Church (ICCEC), International Conference of Reformed Churches (ICRC), International Congregational Fellowship (ICF), International Council of Unitarians and Universalists (ICUU), International Evangelical Congregational Union, International Fellowship of Charismatic Churches (IFCC), International League for Apostolic Faith and Order (ILAFO), International Moravian Church in Unity of Brethren, International Reformed Fellowship (IRF), Jehovah's Christian Witnesses, Ligue Oecuménique pour l'Unité Chrétienne, Malankara Orthodox Syrian Catholicossate of the East, Manna Church International, Mar Thoma Syrian Church of Malabar, New Apostolic Church (NAC/NAK), Old Ritualist Churches (Old Believers, Old Calendarists), Philippine Independent Church (IFI/PIC), Reformed Ecumenical Council (REC), Salvation Army (SA), True Jesus Church (TJC), Unification Church (Holy Spirit Association for Unification of World Christianity), Union of Messianic Jewish Congregations (UMJC), Universal Church of the Kingdom of God (UCKG/IURD), Willow Creek Association of Churches (WCAC), World Assemblies of God Fellowship (WAGF), World Convention of Churches of Christ (WCCC), World Fellowship of Reformed Churches (WFRC).

The codes for the next 4 letters apply to all denominations and churches including Roman Catholic local (nation-wide) churches, but not to dioceses or jurisdictions indented under churches (see code for 2nd-5th letters below).

2nd letter: World Conciliarism, Collegiality, and Consultation

- F = related or linked to World Evangelical Fellowship (WEF): church or mission related to Evangelical Foreign Missions Association (EFMA), hence tyo NAE (USA), hence to WEF
- G = church or mission related to Evangelical Missionary Alliance, UK (EMA), but not to EFMA or IFMA or WEF
- H = church or mission related to Australian Evangelical Alliance, but not to EFMA or IFMA or WEF
- M = church or mission related to Interdenominational Foreign Misssion Association (IFMA), but not to EFMA
- N = church or mission related to both IFMA and EFMA
- q = church related to EFMA, which has also applied to WCC for membership
- r = church related to IFMA, which has also applied to WCC for membership
- s = (diocese staffed by secular clergy: see under 2nd-5th letters, below)
- T = International Council of Christian Churches (ICCC), and The Associated Missions (TAM)
- t = former member of ICCC, or linked with it, but now withdrawn
- u = associate member of WCC (small churches in principle under 10,000 in membership)
- v = application for membership or enquiry made to WCC, but either withdrawn, rejected, delayed indefinitely, or otherwise not accepted by 2000
- W = World Council of Churches (WCC/COE/ORK)
- w = not a member of WCC in own right, but participating (e.g. as a foreign diocese or branch) through some larger confessional or ecclesiastical member grouping based in a different country
- x = Roman Catholic local (nation-wide) church with both a national consultative pastoral body, and also a national priests' organization
- y = Roman Catholic local (nation-wide) church with a national consultative pastoral body, but with no national priests' organization
- z = Roman Catholic local (nation-wide) church with a national priests' organization, but with no national consultative pastoral body
- . = (Protestant, Anglican, Orthodox) not a member of nor related to any world or international council; or (Roman Catholic) local church with neither a national priests' organization nor a naitonal consultative pastoral body

2nd letter (only for Roman Catholic and Orthodox dioceses and jurisdictions) STATUS AND STAFFING

- a = Orthodox diocese under an archbishop
- b = Orthodox diocese under a bishop
- e = Orthodox diocese under an exarch
- m = Orthodox diocese under a metropolitan
- p = Orthodox diocese under a patriarch or catholicos
- s = Roman Catholic diocese staffed by secular (diocesan) clergy (usually nationals and not expatriates)

2nd-5th letters: LOCAL/INTERNATIONAL STAFFING (only for Roman Catholic dioceses and jurisdictions)

sj and all other initials given here indicate the major Catholic religious or secular missionary institute serving a missionary jurisdiction (formerly, confided to the order). All may be identified from the Index of Abbreviations, Acronyms and Initials (Part 15).

3rd letter: Continental Conciliarism, Collegiality, and Consultation

- A = All Africa Conference of Churches (AACC/CETA)
- a = small foreign part of full member of AACC
- B = Consilium Conferentiarum Episcopalium Europae (CCEE) (Council of European Bishops' Conferences)
- C = Conference of European Churches (CEC/CEE/KEK)
- c = observer status in CEC; or, small foreign part of full member of CEC
- D = related to European Evangelical Alliance (EEA) through membership in affiliated national fellowship or council or alliance
- E = Christian Conference of Asia (CCA) (until 1973 East Asian Christian Conference, EACC)
- e = small foreign part of full member of CCA
- F = Federation of Asian Bishops' Conferences (FABC)
- G = related to Association of Evangelicals of Africa (AEA) through membership in affiliated national fellowship or council
- g = associate/special member of AEA
- H = related to Evangelical Association of the Caribbean (EAC) through membership in affiliated national fellowship or council
- I = Organization of African Independent churches (OAJC)
- i = member of OAIC, also member of AACC
- L = Consejo Episcopal Latinoamericano (CELAM) (LatinAmerican Ep[iscopal Council)
- M = Caribbean Conference of Churches (CCC)
- N = Caribbean Conference of Churches (CCC) and also member of CELAM
- O = Standing conference of Canonical Orthodox Bishops in the Americas (SCOBA)
- o = small foreign part of full member of SCOBA
- P = Pacific Conference of Churches (PCC)
- p = small foreign part of full member of PCC
- Q = member of CCC, also related to EAC
- S = Symposium of Episcopal Conferences of Africa and Madagascar (SECAM/SCEAM)
- T = continental council affiliated to ICCC (Latin American Alliance of Christian Churches (LAACC), Far Eastern Council of Christian Churches (FECCC), ICCC European Alliance, Caribbean Council of Christian Churches)
- U = Movimiento pro Unidad Evangelica Latinoamericana, (UNELAM) replaced from 1978 by Latin American Council of Churches (in formation) (CLAI)
- u = indirect member of UNELAM/CLAI through membership in a UNELAM/CLAI affiliated national council
- V = Caribbean Conference of Churches (CCC) and also member of UNELAM/CLAI
- X = member of CEC, also related to EEA
- x = related to EEA, also observer status in CEC
- Y = related to both Evangelical Association of the Caribbean (EAC) and ICCC
- . = not a member of nor related to any continental council

Other continental councils. These are numerous: e.g. Confraternidad Latinoamericana de Iglesias Reformadas (CLIR). There are also many other councils which are not coded here either because in formation only or because their members are not denominations but are national councils most of whom have members who in turn are not denominations but are local congregations or individuals. These include:Evangelical Fellowship of Asia (Association of Asian Evangelical Fellowships), and South East Asia Evangelical Alliance (in formation; both related to World Evangelical Fellowship, WEF).

Lower-case letters (a, c, e, o, p, u) indicate that a body belongs to the council concerned (A, C, E, O, P, U), not in its own right, but by belonging as a small part (e.g. as a small foreign diocese or branch) to some larger confessional or ecclesiastical grouping based in a different country; or, if listed above, observer status.

4th letter: Regional Conciliarism, Collegiality, and Consultation

- A = Council of the Church in East Asia (CCEA) (until 1975, CCSEA)
- B = Association des Conférences Episcopales du Congo/Republique Centrafricaine/Tchad (ACECCT) (formerly ACEACCAM)
- C = Consejo Anglicano Sud Americano (CASA) (Anglican Council for South America)
- D = Secretariado Episcopal de America Central y Panama (SEDAC)
- E = Association of Member Episcopal Conferences in Eastern Africa (AMECEA)
- e = regional fellowship or council of Evangelical churches (Fellowship of Middle East Evangelical Churches (FMEEC), Evangelical Fellowship/Alliance of the South Pacific (EFSP), Latin American Evangelical Fellowship (CONELA), North American Council of WEF)
- F = Conference Episcopale Regionale de l'Afrique Occidentale Francophone (CERAO) (Regional Episcopal Conference of French-speaking West Africa)
- G = Association of Episcopal Conferences of English-speaking West Africa (AECEWA)
- H = Conference Episcopale d'Afrique du Nord
- I = regional council of Black/Third-World or Non-White indigenous churches
- J = Asociacion Regional Episcopal del Norte de Sud America (ARENSA) (Anglican; part of CASA)
- K = South Pacific Anglican Council (SPAC)
- L = Conference des Evêques Latins dans les Regions Arabes (CELRA)
- M = Antilles Episcopal Conference (AEC)
- N = Middle East Council of Churches (MECC/CEMO) (until 1974 Near East Council of Churches, NECC/CEPO)
- O = regional council of Orthodox churches
- P = attached or partially attached to one of the 6 RC non-Latin Patriarchal Synods (Armenian, Chaldean, Coptic, Maronite, Melkite, Syrian)
- Q = Nordic Bishops' Conference (Scandinavian Bishops' Conference) (Nordiske Bispekonferanse)
- R = Anglican Council of North America and the Caribbean (ACNAC)
- S = Interterritorial (Inter-Regional) Meeting of Bishops in Southern Africa (IMBISA) (formerly Southern Africa Catholic Bishop' Conference)
- T = regional council affiliated to ICCC (Middle East Bible Council, Central Africa Christian of Bible Believing Christian Churches, Scandinavian Evangelical Council)
- U = member of both MECC and CAPA
- V = Conference/Council of the Anglican Provinces of Africa (CAPA)
- W = member of both AMECEA and CELRA
- X = Pentecostal Fellowship of North America (PENA)
- Y = Conference des Eveques du Pacifique (CEPAC) (Episcopal Conference of the Pacific)
- Z = Regional Conference of Chinese Bishops (Chung Kuo Chu-chiao T'uan)
- . = not a member of any regional council

Other regional councils, not coded here. These are confessional or denominational councils covering a region, together with a number whose names cover a continent but which in practice are only regional because that denomination's presence is not universal there . These include: Anglican Council of Latin America (CALA), Caribbean Assembly of Reformed Churches, Community of Latin American Evangelical Ministries, Conseil Methodiste de l'Quest/Council of the Methodist Church in West Africa, Council of Evangelical Methodist Churches in Latin Americ the Methodist Church in west Africa, Council of Evangelical Methodist Churches in Latin America (CIEMAL), Council of Reformed Churches in Central Africa, European Baptist Federation (EBF), European Pentecostal Fellowship (EPF), Federation of Evangelical Lutheran Churches of Southern Africa (FELCSA), Fellowhip of Evangelical Baptist Churches in Europe, Methodist Consultative Council of the Pacific (MCCP), North America Presbyterian and Reformed Council (NAPARC).

Continued overleaf

Table 3-6 continued

5th letter: National or Plurinational Conciliarism, Collegiality, and Consultation

All national (country-wide) councils are identified by name in the footnote under each country's Table 2, which also lists other national councils which do not have denominations as members.

- a = member of 2 national councils, one WCC-related and one Evangelical (WEF or AEAM or EAC)
- b = member of 2 national councils, one WCC-related and one Black/Third-World or Non-White indigenous
- C = national council (Protestant or Western) with no formal external international affiliations
- c = associate member of C (preceding line), or related for certain functions
- d = member of 2 national councils, one WCC-related and one unaffiliated (Protestant or Western)
- E = national Evangelical alliance or council, affiliated to WEF (World Evangelical Fellowship) and also to one of its regional associations or continental counterparts (AEAM, EAC, EEA, et alia) where existing
- e = national Evangelical alliance or council, affiliated to EEA (European Evangelical Alliance)
- F = national council including Roman Catholic, Protestant, Anglican and Independent churches, but with no formal external international affiliations
- f = formerly in the major national council, but has recently withdrawn
- G = national Evangelical council affiliated to AEAM but not to WEF
- H = national council of Pentecostal churches (Protestant)
- h = member of some other council (incompletely recorded in Table 2, though name and membership are given below it)
- I = national council of Black/Third-World or Non-White indigenous churches (predominantly)
- i = member of I (preceding line) and also of H
- J = national council of Black/Third-World or Non-White indigenous churches (different to I)
- K = national council of churches, or Christian council, in working relationship with WCC but not affiliated to it
- k = associate member of K (preceding line), or affiliated for certain services; or permanent observer member of K
- L = national Evangelical council affiliated to Evangelical Association of the Caribbean but not (in 1978) to WEF
- l = as L, but also affiliated to ICCC
- M = national council of foreign missionary societies (church represented through one or more of its mission bodies)
- N = national council of churches, or Christian council, affiliated to CWME or WCC (formerly to IMC)
- n = associate member of N (preceding line), or affiliated for certain services; or permanent observer member of N
- O = national council or liaison committee or Orthodox churches
- P = plurinational Roman Catholic episcopal or bishops' conferemce (covering 2 or 3 countries included in conference's name)
- Q = member of plurinational RC episcopal conference, also full membre of national council related to WCC
- q = as Q, but only observer or associate member of national council related to WCC
- R = national Roman Catholic episcopal or bishops' conference
- r = small diocese or church attached to RC national episcopal conference in another country (and so not included in conference's name)
- S = member of national RC episcopal conference, also full member of national council related to WCC
- s = as S, but only observer or associate member of national council related to WCC
- T = national council affiliated, or informally related, to ICCC
- t = former member of T (preceding line), now withdrawn; or, member of council formerly affiliated to ICCC, now withdrawn
- u = member in temporary or once-only national conference of churches in country where permanent council prohibited
- V = member of national RC episcopal conference, also full member of national council not related to WCC.
- v = As V, but only observer or associate member of national council not related to WCC
- W = national (ecumenical) council of churches, or Christian council, formally an associate council of WCC
- w = associate member of W (preceding line), or affiliated for certain services; or permanent observer member of W; or member of country-wide council associated with W
- x = member of 2 other national councils
- y = some other Black/Third-World or Non-White indigenous national council (different to I and J)
- Z = member of 3 national councils
- z = member of 3 national councils (one WCC-related, one Evangelical)
- . = not a member of any national council

COLUMN 10: NAMES, NOTES, AND OTHER STATISTICS

These descriptive notes include a selection of any significant data concerning some of the following elements (all items in italics are current initials, names, translations or expanded titles of the church's name in column 1): name in major national or local language (in italics), preceded by initials if commonly used (in italics), then geographical sub-title of the body if any (in italics), and wider geographical jurisdictions or entities to which the body belongs (not in italics), translation into English (in italics), alternate name(s) (in italics), former names (not in italics), foreign missionary society(ies) past and/or present, brief geographical or historical notes, ethnic or linguistic or national/expatriate (citizen/alien) composition of members (Christians) as % (in descending order of numerical size, or (single name) dominant ethnic or linguistic group), and any other statistics available.

Italicized abbreviations and initials (in italics) in column 10 are either (a) first initial of the country concercerned (A for Austria, B for Belgium, etc), or (b) local-language words in titles (e.g. in Indonesia, G = Gereja, church) identified in the notes under the table. Non-italicized letters are either (c) initials of co-operating missionary societies (listed in full in Index of Abbreviations, Acronyms and Initials), (d) jurisdictions, as listed above under column 1, or (e) abbreviations and codes common to all countries as set out below. In the listings of statistics in this column in the table, personnel are the first statistics shown, in the order C, n, x, m, w, Yy.

- A = year when church became autonomous (if significant)
- B = (at head of a sub-column) location in province or state
- b = parishes (as defined by the church concerned, if different from column 5)
- bc = Roman Catholic diocesan brothers' council
- C = Roman Catholic religious institutes (i.e. orders, congregations and societies) officially at work (foreign and local); the 3 figures given (e.g. C = 3 + 1 + 15) enumerate the number of distinct institutes of, respectively, *clerics* (priests mainly, occasionally also with some brothers and seminarians), + *brothers*, + *sisters*
- D = Roman Catholic diocesan councils of post-conciliar (Vatican II) type (Synod, PC, pc, bc, lc, se)
- d = monasteries (religious houses for men, monks, brothers)
- de = monasteries and convents
- dec = numerical decline or decrease in recent years compared to earlier larger following
- e = convents (religious houses for women, nuns, sisters)
- esp = especially
- et al = et alia (and other things), et alii (and other people)
- ex = schism (split, secession, breakoff) from or out of church or mission indicated
- f = foreign missionary personnel (aliens, expatriates), as defined by church or mission (lay and ordained, men and women, usually including only those active on the field, seconded or on furlough)
- G = annual growth rate of membership, % pa (% per year), over 25-year period 1970-1995 (G = 0 means zero growth; minus means decline)
- H = hospitals operated by church or mission (including leprosaria, sanatoria)
- HQ = location of headquarters, see city, episcopal residence, secretariat, denominational offices (usually only given here if not given in, or if not the same as, any location in title in column 1)
- h = clinics, dispensaries, maternity centres, mobile clinics, operated by church or mission
- i = mission stations (of foreign missionary societies)
- j = printing presses or publishing houses operated by church or mission
- k = bookshops run by church or mission
- L = (at head of a sub-column) official language used
- lc = Roman Catholic diocesan council of laity
- M = co-operating foreign missionary societies (with a local or national administration) in the past and/or present
- MS = Missionary Society (part of title or name)
- m = men lay workers, lay preachers, brothers, monks (full-time; nationals plus expatriates; Roman Catholic men religious (brothers as well as priests; members of men's religious institutes, nationals and expatriates) but excluding Roman Catholic lay catechists; Anglican or Orthodox brothers or monks, Protestants and Anglicans in church pastoral or evangelistic work (including nationals but not usually expatriates)
- mw = total full-time lay workers (Protestants, Anglicans, Orthodox), or (Roman Catholics) religious men plus women (= m + w)
- N = priests prevented from functioning by atheistic state
- n = national (citizen) clergy (ordained ministers, pastors, priests (secular and religious), deacons, deaconesses, ordained women, bishops); active only, excluding retired
- nm = total men workers, ordained and lay (= n + m)
- nx = total clergy or ministers, national plus expatriate (= n + x)
- P = practising Christians, % (those fulfilling their churches' minimum annual obligations of church attendance (e.g. Easter attenders or communicants), as % of affiliated Christians eligible to attend)
- PC = Roman Catholic diocesan pastoral council, for laity, religious, and clergy, with total members in parentheses ( ); if followed by 2 numbers in parentheses, these = priests/religious members, and lay members
- p = Bible schools, catechist training schools: Protestant Bible-training schools, usually for lay church workers, sometimes also for ordained; Roman Catholic catechist training schools, of primary or secondary level
- pc = Roman Catholic diocesan priests' council or senate, with total members in parentheses ( ); if followed by 3 numbers in parentheses, these = members nominated by bishop, members ex officio, and members elected by all priests
- pp = part-time preachers (unsalaried but officially-accredited volunteer spare-time local preachers, lay preachers, lay readers)
- q = religious seminaries (not secular or diocesan; Roman Catholic major seminaries for religious clergy)
- qv = quod vide, which see (i.e. refer elsewhere to the item just mentioned)
- R = radio letters (normal annual listeners' letters received from this country by all Christian radio stations or agencies, home or foreign)
- r = church-related or -operated colleges, teacher training colleges, major high or secondary schools, academies, technical or industrial schools, or other educational institutions of higher learning
- RE = Roman Catholic ecclesiastical region (in the USA only)
- S = active BCC students (enrolled in Bible correspondence courses)
- s = seminaries for preparation for the ordained ministry (major seminaries, theological colleges, Bible academies, Bible institutes, Bible colleges, officers' training schools, church-operated university faculties of theology; Roman Catholic secular/diocesan (but not religious/regular) major seminaries); sometimes followed in parentheses by number of seminarians (in training for the ordained ministy)
- sc = Roman Catholic diocesan sisters' council
- school = primary or middle schools (not secondary or higher)
- SS = Sunday-school enrolment
- ST = state: name or zip code abbreviation for secular or civil state or province co-terminous, or nearly so, with diocese
- Synod = Roman Catholic diocesan synod (climax of internal ecumenism)
- T = total or accumulated BCC enrolments (students in Bible correspondence courses now or in past)
- t = Sunday-schools, sabbath schools
- u = participation in a united seminary (sponsored by 2 or more denominations)
- V = BCC conversions (students enrolled in Bible correspondence courses who have professed conversion as a result)
- v = church-related or -operated universities
- W = attending Christians, or weekly church attenders, % (attenders each Sunday or Saturday as % of affiliated Christians eligible to attend)
- w = women lay workers, sisters, nuns (full-time; nationals plus expatriates; Roman Catholic women religious (members of women's religious institutes) but excluding Catholic lay women catechists; Anglican or Orthodox sisters or nuns, Protestants and Anglicans in church pastoral or evangelistic work)
- x = expatriate (alien, foreign, non-citizen) clergy (ordained ministers, pastors, priests (secular and religious), deacons, deaconesses, ordained women, bishops); active only, not retired
- Y, y = annual baptisms (new persons baptized in a recent year around 1995-2000); Y = adult baptisms, y = infant baptisms, Yy = adults + infants combined (or, if baptism not practised, Y = new adult members admitted)
- z = catechumens, baptismal candidates (these are always included in column 7; hence for the Roman Catholic Church, the number of baptized Catholics = column 7 minus catechumens)
- ( ) = number of students, monks, nuns, Sunday-school scholars, or pupils in the institutions referred to (e.g. 2s(20) means 2 seminaries with 20 seminarians training for the ordained ministry)
- % eth = percentage of Christian population belonging to various ethnic groups
- % RC = percentage of total population, in the area of a jurisdiction, who are RCs, Muslims, pagans, etc.

Continued opposite

Table 3-6 concluded

SUBTABLES IN COLUMN 10. For certain large denominations, almost always only the Roman Catholic Church, a subtable for all its dioceses may be given in column 10.
TOTALS FOR A CHURCH WITH DIOCESES. Statistics in column 10 for the first line of a denomination with indented component dioceses under it always include whatever statistics are shown for the dioceses below. Often the totals on the first line are greater than the totals of those below because the dioceses only show part of the breakdown and do not include non-diocesan staff.
DOUBLY-AFFILIATED. These are persons affiliated to or claimed by 2 denominations at once (as shown, defined and described in Country Tables 1; always a negative quantity).
DISAFFILIATED. Former Christians recently withdrawn from state or majority churches (as shown, defined and described in Tables 1); or, still on the churches rolls as members, but now dead.

7. PART 5 "COUNTRYSCAN"

Table 3-7. Meanings of Table 5-1. Geopolitico-religious data and typologies.

Up to this point, the Codebook has dealt with Country Tables 1 and 2 in Part 4. The same codes apply to several other Tables elsewhere in the Encyclopedia. The Codebook now deals with Table 5-1, labelled here as Table 3–7.

Table 5-1 has 167 columns of data for each of the 238 countries. The entire listing is shown below, followed by the 20 variables with coded values. If no code is given, the column reports statistics of the item described in the title.

Column	*Heading*	*Subject*
COUNTRY		
1.	*code*	4-letter country code
2.	*short name*	as in Table 3-1 or 5-1
3.	*UN*	UN major area and region
4.	*prov*	major civil divisions (provinces, states)
DEMOGRAPHICS		
5.	*pop 2000*	population, mid-AD 2000
6.	*pop 2010*	population, mid-AD 2010
7.	*pop 2025*	population, mid-AD 2025
8.	*adults*	population age 15 and over
9.	*apop*	adults as % population
10.	*bpop*	birth rate, % per year
11.	*dpop*	death rate, % per year
12.	*npop*	natural increase, % per year
13.	*life*	life expectancy, years
14.	*hom*	household size (adults, children)
15.	*spac*	floor area per person, sq. meters
16.	*den*	density of population per sq. kilometer
17.	*peop*	total ethnolinguistic peoples
18.	*langs*	official and national language(s)
GEOPOLITICAL TYPOLOGIES		
19.	*dev*	more/less/least-developed
20.	*HDI*	human development index
21.	*HFI*	human freedom index
22.	*HSI*	human suffering index
23.	*liter*	literacy as % population over 15
24.	*literates*	adult literates (over 15)
SOCIETY		
ECONOMICS		
25.	*GNP*	gross national product p.a. per capita
26.	*EFL*	economic freedom level
URBANIZATION		
27.	*rural*	ruralites, country-dwellers (millions)
28.	*urban*	urbanites, town/city dwellers (millions)
29.	*metro*	metropolitan urbanites (millions)
METROSCAN		
30.	*cit50*	cities over 50,000 persons
31.	*cit100*	cities over 100,000 persons
32.	*mega*	megacities over 1 million persons
HEALTH		
33.	*access*	people's access to health services, %
34.	*water*	people's access to safe water, %
35.	*mat-m*	maternal mortality, per 100,000 births
36.	*inf-m*	infant mortality, per 1000 live births
37.	*hosp*	hospitals
38.	*beds*	beds, per 10,000 population
39.	*doct*	doctors
40.	*blind*	nonsighted persons
41.	*deaf*	hearing-impaired persons
42.	*lepers*	persons with leprosy
43.	*murder*	murders per 100,000 per year
EDUCATION		
44.	*educ*	rate % school enrolments, female/male
45.	*schools*	elementary, secondary, high
46.	*univs*	degree-granting colleges, universities
COMMUNICATION		
47.	*news*	daily newspaper copies per 1000 persons
48.	*radios*	radio sets per 1000 persons
49.	*TVs*	TV sets per 1000 persons
50.	*fones*	telephones per 1000 persons
51.	*faxes*	fax machines per 1000 persons
52.	*computers*	general-purpose computers in use
53.	*Internet*	users of Internet, e-mail, www
GEORELIGIONS		
RELIGIONS		
54.	*religs*	total major religions in country
55.	*indig*	religions indigenous to this country
RELIGIOUS PERSECUTION		
56.	*liberty*	religious liberty or persecution
57.	*CSI*	Christian Safety Index, 0-100
58.	*martyrs*	martyrs ever (less background martyrs)
59.	*mar-sit*	major martyrdom situations (since AD 33)
CHURCH/STATE RELATIONS: state religion or philosophy		
60.	*1900*	situation in 1900
61.	*1970*	situation in 1970
62.	*1990*	situation in 1990
63.	*2000*	situation in AD 2000
BIBLIOGRAPHY		
64.	*items listed*	total listed in Part 4 after country's text
CHRISTIANITY		
CHURCH MEMBERS		
65.	*affiliated*	affiliated church members
66.	*AC*	affiliated church members, %
FOUR MEGATYPOLOGIES OF GEORENEWAL		
1. THE GREAT COMMISSION		
67.	*GCCs*	Great Commission Christians
68.	*GCC*	Great Commission Christians, % country
2. ECCLESIASTICAL GEORENEWAL: 6 MEGABLOCS		
69.	*Megabloc O*	Orthodox, affiliated
70.	*Megabloc R*	Roman Catholics, affiliated
71.	*Megabloc A*	Anglicans, affiliated
72.	*Megabloc P*	Protestants, affiliated
73.	*Megabloc I*	Independents, affiliated
74.	*Megabloc m*	Marginal Christians, affiliated
3. EVANGELICAL GEORENEWAL		
75.	*Evangelicals*	Evangelicals (linked to Ev councils)
76.	*evangelicals*	evangelicals (all varieties)
4. PENTECOSTAL/CHARISMATIC GEORENEWAL		
77.	*1st-Wavers*	Pentecostals (Classical denominations)
78.	*2nd-Wavers*	Charismatics (in non-Pentecostal churches)
79.	*3rd-Wavers*	Neocharismatics (Independents)
CHURCHES		
STRUCTURES		
80.	*denom*	denominations
81.	*p.m.*	denominations per million
82.	*worship*	worship centers (churches, congregations)
83.	*p.m.*	worship centers per million
GEOFINANCE, US$		
84.	*personal*	personal income p.a. of all Christians
85.	*church*	churches' income per year
86.	*parachurch*	parachurch income per year
87.	*ecc crime*	ecclesiastical crime p.a. (embezzlements)
MISSION		
STATUS OF MISSIONS		
88.	*stat*	current status of foreign missions, 1-7
89.	*misags*	foreign mission agencies present
90.	*all orgs*	all service agencies
91.	*p.m.*	all organizations per million
MISSION INSTITUTIONS		
92.	*major*	major institutions
93.	*p.m.*	major institutions per million
94.	*minor*	minor institutions
95.	*p.m.*	minor institutions per million
GEORESPONSE/GROWTH		
96.	*CG%*	annual church growth 1900-2000, % p.a.
97.	*g%*	new Christians per year, %
98.	*bapt p.a.*	newly baptized persons per year
99.	*resp R*	responsiveness to evangelism
100.	*cost-eff, $*	cost-effectiveness: $ cost per baptism
WORLDS A, B, and C		
101.	*A-individuals*	World A individuals
102.	*B-individuals*	World B individuals
103.	*C-individuals*	World C individuals
MINISTRIES		
104.	*peo-ags*	total agencies-in-peoples
CHRISTIAN PERSONNEL		
ALL WORKERS		
105.	*workers*	full-time Christian workers in country
106.	*w.p.m.*	Christian workers per million population
CITIZENS		
107.	*workers*	citizen Christian workers in country
108.	*citw p.m.*	citizen Christian workers per million
GLOBAL MISSION SHARING		
CITIZENS SENT ABROAD		
109.	*total*	citizen missionaries working abroad
110.	*p.m.a.*	citizen missionaries abroad, p.m. affiliated
ALIENS RECEIVED FROM ABROAD		
111.	*total*	aliens at work as missionaries
112.	*p.m.*	aliens at work as missionaries, p.m.
CHRISTIAN LITERATURE		
LIBRARIES		
113.	*total*	Christian or religious libraries
114.	*p.m.*	Christian or religious libraries, p.m.
BOOKS ON CHRISTIANITY IN EACH COUNTRY		
115.	*total*	all books describing this country's Christians
116.	*1970-99*	books published since 1970
117.	*p.a.*	books published per year in AD 2000
PERIODICALS		
118.	*total*	Christian periodicals
119.	*p.m.*	Christian periodicals, per million
GEOSCRIPTURES		
BIBLE DISTRIBUTION		
120.	*goal*	goal for all Bibles in place
121.	*goal p.a.*	required Bibles distributed p.a.
122.	*UBS p.a.*	UBS Bibles distributed p.a.
123.	*other p.a.*	all other Bibles distributed p.a.
124.	*total p.a.*	total all Bibles distributed p.a.
125.	*T/G%*	ratio Bible total (col 124) to goal (col 121), %
NEW TESTAMENT DISTRIBUTION		
126.	*goal*	goal for all NTs in place
127.	*goal p.a.*	required NTs distributed p.a.
128.	*UBS p.a.*	UBS NTs distributed p.a.
129.	*other p.a.*	all other NTs distributed p.a.
130.	*duplicates*	NTs distributed via Bibles p.a.
131.	*total p.a.*	total all NTs distributed p.a.
132.	*T/G%*	ratio NT total (col 131) to goal (col 127), %
PORTIONS DISTRIBUTION (GOSPELS)		
133.	*goal*	goal for all gospels in place
134.	*goal p.a.*	required gospels distributed p.a.
135.	*UBS p.a.*	UBS portions (gospels) distributed p.a.
136.	*other p.a.*	all other gospels distributed p.a.
137.	*duplicates*	gospels distributed via Bibles & NTs p.a.
138.	*total p.a.*	total all gospels distributed p.a.
139.	*T/G %*	ratio gospel total (col 138) to goal (col 134),%
SELECTIONS DISTRIBUTION		
140.	*goal*	goal for all selections in place
141.	*goal p.a.*	required selections distributed p.a.
142.	*UBS p.a.*	UBS selections distributed p.a.
143.	*other p.a.*	all other selections distributed p.a.
144.	*duplicates*	selections distributed via gospels,N or B p.a.
145.	*total p.a.*	total all selections distributed p.a.
146.	*T/G %*	ratio selection total (col 145) to goal (col 141),%
BROADCASTING		
RADIO/TV AUDIENCES		
147.	*cb aud*	regular audience for Christian programs, %
148.	*cstat*	audience via Christian stations, %
149.	*secstat*	audience via secular stations, %
EVANGELISM		
OFFERS VIA 45 MINISTRIES		
150.	*q per day*	offers (disciple-opportunities) per day
151.	*e p.a.p.c.*	offers per year per capita
EVANGELIZATION		
WHEN BEGUN		
152.	*year begun*	year first Christians resident
STATUS OF EVANGELIZATION, E		
153.	*1900*	E (% population evangelized), 1900
154.	*1970*	E (% population evangelized), 1970
155.	*1990*	E (% population evangelized), 1990
156.	*1995*	E (% population evangelized), 1995
157.	*2000*	E (% population evangelized), 2000
158.	*2025*	E (% population evangelized), 2025
SOURCE OF E IN AD 2000		
159.	*internal*	evangelized by population's Christians
160.	*external*	evangelized by Christians from outside
UNEVANGELIZED, AD 2000		
161.	*U*	U, % population unevangelized
162.	*total*	unevangelized persons
GEOSTRATEGIES		
163.	*World*	3-fold trichotomy: A, B, C
164.	*plans*	plans to evangelize globe (less 'other plans')
165.	*target*	total top priority target peoples (T=1)
FUTURES (CHRISTIAN FUTURISTICS)		
166.	*growth index*	growth relative to demographics
167.	*prospects*	outlook during 21st century (+2 to -2)

NON-STATISTICAL DATA AND TYPOLOGIES

COUNTRY

Column 1 Country's code
Column 3 Continent and region, as defined by UN

Code	*Continent and Region*
A	Africa
A1	Eastern Africa
A2	Middle Africa
A3	Northern Africa
A4	Southern Africa
A5	Western Africa
B	Antarctica
C	Asia
C1	Eastern Asia
C2	South-eastern Asia
C3	South-central Asia
C4	Western Asia
E	Europe
E1	Eastern Europe
E2	Northern Europe
E3	Southern Europe
E4	Western Europe
L	Latin America
L1	Caribbean
L2	Central America
L3	South America
N1	Northern America
P	Oceania
P1	Australia-New Zealand
P2	Melanesia
P3	Micronesia
P4	Polynesia

GEOPOLITICAL TYPOLOGIES

Column 19 Development

Code	
1	more developed (Europe, NAmerica, Aust-NZ, Japan, Russia, Temperate SAmerica)
2	less developed
3	least developed

Continued overleaf

Table 3-7 concluded

DEMOGRAPHICS

Column 18 Official state language(s), AD 2000: Languages are coded here as one-character variables, and include only those which are countrywide, i.e. official throughout their whole country. These are given in 2 listings: (1) at left below, a listing alphabetically by code, and (2) at right below, alphabetically by language.

Code	*Language*	Code	Language	Code	Language
A	Arabic	m	Malagasy	Y̲	Serbian
B	Bengali	n	Nepali	Z̲	Uzbek
C	Chinese (Mandarin)	o	Mongolian		
D	Dutch	p	Bislama	a̲	Armenian
E	English	q	Quechua	b̲	Monokutuba
F	French	r	Romansch	c̲	Chewa
G	German	s	Swedish	d̲	Marshallese
H	Hindi	t	Tamil	e̲	Lithuanian
I	Italian	u	Sinhalese	f̲	Divehi
J	Japanese	v	Somali	g̲	Guarani
K	Korean	w	Sotho	h̲	Haitian Creol
L	Amharic	x	Sango	i̲	Icelandic
M	Afrikaans	y	Rundi	j̲	Comorian
N	Persian	z	Dzongkha	k̲	Kirghiz
O	Filipino			l̲	Latin
P	Portuguese	A̲	Azerbaijani	m̲	Malay
Q	Serbo-Croatia	B̲	Belorussian	n̲	Nauruan
R	Russian	C̲	Croatian	o̲	Maltese
S	Spanish	D̲	Dari	p̲	Palauan
T	Turkish	E̲	Estonian	q̲	Tigrinya
U	Urdu	F̲	Catalan	r̲	Rwandese
V	Vietnamese	G̲	Georgian	s̲	Seselwa
W	Burmese	H̲	Greenlandic	t̲	Tok Pisin
X	Indonesian	I̲	Maori	u̲	Slovak
Y	Polish	J̲	Faeroese	v̲	Chamorro
Z	Thai	K̲	Kazakh	w̲	Samoan
		L̲	Latvian	x̲	Swazi
a	Albanian	M̲	Macedonian	y̲	Aymara
b	Bulgarian	N̲	Tahitian	z̲	Tongan
c	Czech	O̲	Luxemburgish		
d	Danish	P̲	Pushtu		
e	Hebrew	Q̲	Moldavian		
f	Finnish	R̲	Romanian		
g	Greek	S̲	Swahili		
h	Hungarian	T̲	Tajik		
i	Irish	U̲	Ukrainian		
j	Norwegian	V̲	Turkmen		
k	Khmer	W̲	Slovenian		
l	Lao	X̲	Tswana		

Language	*Code*	Language	Code	Language	Code
Afrikaans	M	Icelandic	i̲	Serbian	Y̲
Albanian	a	Indonesian	X	Serbo-Croatia	Q
Amharic	L	Irish	i	Seselwa	s̲
Arabic	A	Italian	I	Sinhalese	u
Armenian	a̲	Japanese	J	Slovak	u̲
Aymara	y̲	Kazakh	K̲	Slovenian	W̲
Azerbaijani	A̲	Khmer	k	Somali	v
Belorussian	B̲	Kirghiz	k̲	Sotho	w
Bengali	B	Korean	K	Spanish	S
Bislama	p	Lao	l	Swahili	S̲
Bulgarian	b	Latin	l̲	Swazi	x̲
Burmese	W	Latvian	L̲	Swedish	s
Catalan	F̲	Lithuanian	e̲	Tahitian	N̲
Chamorro	v̲	Luxemburgish	O̲	Tajik	T̲
Chewa	c̲	Macedonian	M̲	Tamil	t
Chinese (Mandarin)	C	Malagasy	m	Thai	Z
Comorian	j̲	Malay	m̲	Tigrinya	q̲
Croatian	C̲	Maltese	o̲	Tok Pisin	t̲
Czech	c	Maori	I̲	Tongan	z̲
Danish	d	Marshallese	d̲	Tswana	X̲
Dari	D̲	Moldavian	Q̲	Turkish	T
Divehi	f̲	Mongolian	o	Turkmen	V̲
Dutch	D	Monokutuba	b̲	Ukrainian	U̲
Dzongkha	z	Nauruan	n̲	Urdu	U
English	E	Nepali	n	Uzbek	Z̲
Estonian	E̲	Norwegian	j	Vietnamese	V
Faeroese	J̲	Palauan	p̲		
Filipino	O	Persian	N		
Finnish	f	Polish	Y		
French	F	Portuguese	P		
Georgian	G̲	Pushtu	P̲		
German	G	Quechua	q		
Greek	g	Romanian	R̲		
Greenlandic	H̲	Romansch	r		
Guarani	g̲	Rundi	y		
Haitian Creol	h̲	Russian	R		
Hebrew	e	Rwandese	r̲		
Hindi	H	Samoan	w̲		
Hungarian	h	Sango	x		

RELIGIOUS PERSECUTION

Column 56 Religious liberty

1. State propagates Christianity
2. Massive state subsidies to churches
3. Limited state subsidies to churches
4. State subsidizes schools only
5. Complete state non-interference
6. Limited political restrictions
7. Minorities discriminated against
8. State interference and obstruction
9. State hostility and prohibition
10. State suppression or eradication

Column 57 Christian Safety Index (CSI) computed as follows: [AC + (2 × HSI) + (5 × (100 – (10 × Religious liberty code))) + (2 × (100 – Murder Rate))]/10

Data in this column are percentages. Their meaning is illustrated here from the key of Global Map 7.

RELIGIOUS LIBERTY
Very safe (CSI > 85%)
Safe (CSI 80-85%)
Marginally safe (CSI 70-79%)
RELIGIOUS PERSECUTION
Some obstruction, harassment (CSI 60-69%)
Some persecution (CSI 50-59%)
MARTYRDOM SITUATIONS
Dangerous (CSI 40-49%)
Highly dangerous (CSI under 40%)

CHURCH/STATE RELATIONS

Columns 60-63
Global Christianity
State religion or philosophy

Code					
A	Atheistic	RH	Hindu	RC	Roman Catholic
S	Secular	RI	Islamic	RS	Shinto
R	Religious	RJ	Jewish	RT	Ethnoreligionist
RD	Adventist	RL	Lutheran	RX	Christian (unspecified)
RA	Anglican	RM	Methodist	R	Religious (unspecified)
RB	Buddhist	RO	Orthodox		
RG	Confucian	RR	Reformed		

MISSIONS

Column 88. Current status of foreign missions.

7 sharing
6 sending
5 receiving/sending
4 receiving
3 restricted
2 partially-closed
1 closed

FUTURES

Column 167. Prospects during 21st century.

Code
2 bright
1 fair
0 static
-1 dull
-2 bleak

8. PARTS 7, 8, 9, 10, 11

These 5 Parts reproduce sizable numbers of pages of data from their source databases, and so the codes for their columns are more appropriately placed there immediately before each table of data begins.

9. PART 6 "ATLAS"

The 16 Global Maps in this section utilize data and typologies from Table 5-1 and elsewhere, as indicated on each map under its title. In the process the exact definitions used on the maps differ in a few cases from those in Table 5-1. Thus Global Map 8 creates a more developed scale of foreign missions to utilize the explanatory potential of the mapping procedure. No contradictions are implied, but the reader should note that the scales and meanings of each key on a handful of global maps (especially Global Map 8) are not the same as those in the data in Table 5-1 (in this case, column 88).

Human Environment maps are explained on page 1:852.

Part 4

COUNTRIES

A country-by-country survey of each's life, liberty, religions, Christianity, churches, prospects

Beloved parish priests, pay attention, we beg you, to accurate and well-studied statistics. They are a very important task in governing a parish.

—John XXIII, Synod of the Diocese of Rome, 1960

DESCRIBING EACH OF 238 COUNTRIES

Part 4 comprises the greater part of this WCE Volume 1. It is preceded by its Codebook (Part 3), and followed by its statistical summary (167 variables, in Table 5-1) in Part 5 "CountryScan". It is then followed at the end of Volume 1 by its map section (Part 6 "Atlas").

Part 4 surveys in detail the life and activities of each of the world's 238 countries here described in alphabetical order. However, a large amount of additional information on each country is given elsewhere, in other Parts. The following 4 listings indicate (a) the standardized contents of Part 4, (b) where other varieties of data, for any country the reader is interested in, can be found; (c) where environmental data and comparative data on all countries can be seen on the color maps in "Atlas"; and (d) the item the reader should access to find the significantly more detailed databases from which this Encyclopedia has been derived. This means consulting the related CD, *World Christian database.*

At the end of Part 5 will be found technical notes on statistics.

(a) Standardized data layout in this Part 4, for every country

In the pages that follow, Part 4 sets out information describing each country in the same standardized order and layout, as follows:

1. *Identification*: masthead with standardized short reference name, at left a small map locator, and at right a facsimile of country's flag.
2. *Secular data* (referring to the year AD 2000), giving 61 items covering: state, major official name(s), government, cities, military, demography, peoples, languages, economy, education, health, literature, communication, refugees, human life and liberty.
3. *Country Table 1* listing major categories of Christians in the context of all other religious adherents, with statistics, percentages, and growth rates for the period AD 1900-AD 2025 (on current trends).
4. *Country Table 1's footnotes* listing censuses, and newer data on a selection of religions.
5. *Country status.* A brief sentence or two summarizing the country's role or significance.
6. *Main narrative text*, in 8 sections illustrated by a handful of photographs elaborating on statistical, descriptive, or other major features. The 8 sections are: human life and liberty, non-Christian religions, history of Christianity, description of the major churches by megablocs, church and state, broadcasting and media, interdenominational organizations, future trends and prospects (on current trends).
7. *Great Commission Instrument Panel*: a line of 6 minidiagrams, being 6 standard globes or graphs illustrating 6 new concepts evolved in this survey—sizes of Worlds A/B/C (=% of population), religions (=% of population), ecclesiastical megablocs (termed 'Ecclesiastical blocs' there; note especially: the numbers shown on this globe are % of *all affiliated Christians*), evangelization (=% of country's population), evangelistic offers per capita per year, cost-effectiveness in baptism.
8. *Country summary*, a thin box showing each country's totals of peoples (cultures), cities (metropolises), and provinces (major civil divisions, MCDs) divided under Worlds A, B, C.
9. *Photographs.* Captions refer these each to specific religions or denominations whose statistics have a line each in Country Tables 1 or 2.
10. *Bibliography.* Mostly books, with a handful of articles, describing the one country's Christians and other religionists.
11. *Country Table 2* listing all organized churches and denominations. Most data there are definitive and properly-sourced. Note however that one column (4) is provisional and under long-term compilation, to be available in the companion CD.
12. *125-year church growth.* Country Table 2 ends with 6-line totals of churches (congregations), adult members, affiliated Christians, related church growth rates per year, total denominations, denominations divided by the 6 megablocs, with all these given at 6 points in time during the period AD 1900-2025.
13. *Conciliarism,* being Country Table 2's footnotes on national Christian councils where they exist, and names of all other smaller denominations present in this country but not given a line each in the table.
14. *Map.* A color map showing each country's geographical, political, economic, urban, and human environment situations will be found in Part 6 "Atlas" at the end of Volume 1.

(b) Additional data on each country given elsewhere

	Volume and Part
Anglicans	1:1,1:5
Bibliography	2:13
Broadcasting	2:8
Catholic Charismatics	1:4
Charismatics	1:1
Christians located by metropolis	2:10
Cities	2:10
Cost-effectiveness in baptism	1:5
Directory: name, address, phone, fax, e-mail, www	2:14
Ecclesiastical crime	1:5
Embezzlement	1:5
Ethnolinguistic composition of country	2:8
Ethnolinguistic composition of Christians	2:8
Ethnolinguistic components of large religions	2:8
Ethnolinguistic components of other religions	2:8
Finance	1:1,1:6
Foreign mission agencies	1:4
Foreign missionaries (aliens from abroad)	1:5
Foreign missionaries (nationals sent abroad)	1:5
Future scenarios	1:5
Georeligions	2:7
Gross national product per capita	1:5
Identity as a World A, B, or C country	1:5
Income of church members	1:1,1:5,1:6
Income of Great Commission Christians	1:5,1:6
Languages	2:9
Literature on Christians in country	2:13
Major church history events	1:4
Major evangelistic events	1:4
Major institutions (church-operated)	2:14
Maps: human environment	1:6
Maps: religious situation	1:6
Martyrs	1:5,1:6
Martyrdom situations	1:5,1:6
Metropolises and each's basic data	2:10
Minor institutions (church-operated)	2:14
National (citizen) Christian workers	1:5
Neocharismatics	1:4
Non-Christian believers in Christ	1:4
Pentecostals	1:1,1:4
Peoples	2:8
Personnel	1:5
Periodicals, religious and/or Christian	1:5
Postdenominationalism	1:1
Provinces	2:11
Religions	2:7
Religious libraries	2:14
Response	1:5
Scripture density	1:5
Scripture distribution	1:5
Scripture translation languages	1:1
Service agencies, parachurch agencies	1:5
Strategies	1:5
Targeting	1:5
Urbanization, urban/rural, populations	2:10

(c) Visual data on each country in "Atlas"

	Human Environment Maps (HEM) or Global Map (GM)
Air traffic	HEM
Areas of rapid church growth	GM 2
Broadcasting	GM 9
Christian megalanguages	GM 1
Christians, % of country	GM 1
Church growth	GM 2
Coniferous forest	HEM
Cost-effectiveness	GM 13
Deciduous forest	HEM
Desert or sand	HEM
Environment, last quarter of 20th century	HEM
Evangelization, AD 1900	GM 3
Evangelization, AD 2000	GM 4
Farming	HEM
Finance	GM 12
Foreign missions	GM 8
Human environment	HEM
Marsh or bog	HEM
Martyrdom	GM 7
Megacities	GM 6
Metropolises	GM 6
Minerals	HEM
Mining	HEM
Other irrigation	HEM
Paddy	HEM
Persecution	GM 7
Population density (persons per sq. km)	HEM
Prospects	GM 16
Radio/TV stations	GM 9
Railways	HEM
Religious liberty	GM 7
Renewal	GM 14, 15
Roads	HEM
Savanna	HEM
Scripture distribution	GM 10
Tropical forest	HEM
Worlds A/B/C, in AD 1900	GM 3
Worlds A/B/C, in AD 2000	GM 4

(d) Background databases in CD: World Christian database

This electronic version contains most of the above data plus several hundred additional variables for countries, religions, denominations, peoples, cultures, languages, cities, provinces, agencies, institutions, et alia.

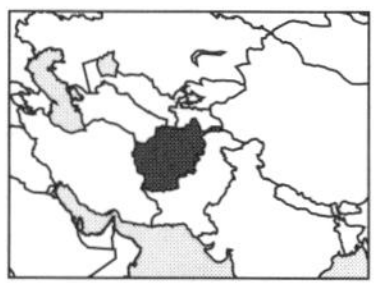

AFGHANISTAN

SECULAR DATA, AD 2000

STATE
Official name: Jamhuria Afghanistan (The Islamic Emirate of Afghanistan).
Short name: Afghanistan. **Adjective of nationality:** Afghan.
Flag: Black, red, and green tricolor, with coat of arms next to hoist.
Area: 652,225 sq. km. (251,825 sq. mi.).
Government: Islamic emirate, since 1991 (1747 absolute monarchy, 1881 British influence, 1919 Independence declared, 1964 limited constitutional monarchy, 1973 leftist military coup, 1978 Marxist military coup).
Legislature: Republican Revolutionary Council.
Official language: Pashto, Dari.
Monetary unit: 1 afghani (Af) = 100 puls (puli). **US$1=** Af 4,750.
Chief cities: KABOL (Kabul) 2,716,000; Kandahar (Qandahar) 419,654; Herat (Heroiva) 329,954; Baghlan 264,359; Tagab (Tageb) 254,590.
Political divisions: 29 provinces.
Armed forces: 45,000.

DEMOGRAPHY
Population: 22,720,000.
Population density: 34.8/sq. km. (90.2/sq. mi.).
Under 15 years: 9,938,000.
Growth rate p.a.: 4.85% (births 46.51, deaths 18.33).
Mortality: Infant, per 1,000: 142.8; **Maternal per 100,000:** 1,700.0.
Life expectancy: 47 (male 47, female 48).
Household size: 6.2. **Floor area per person, sq.m:** 2.0.
Major languages: Pushtu, Dari, Tadzhik, Uzbek, Turkoman, Baluchi, Arabic, Brahui, and about 45 smaller languages.
Urban dwellers: 22.18%. **Urban growth rate p.a.:** 4.88%.
Labor force: 30%.

ETHNOLINGUISTIC PEOPLES
47.5% Pathan (Pukhtun, Afghani); 17.9% Afghani Tajik (Tadzhik); 8.1% Hazara (Berberi); 8.0% Southern Uzbek; 3.3% Persian.

ECONOMY
National income p.a. per person: US$599; **per family:** US$3,719.

EDUCATION
Adult literacy: 31% (male 47%, female 15%). **Schools:** 2,605.
Universities: 5. **School enrolment:** female/male: 22%/49%.

HEALTH
Access to health services: 29%. **Access to safe water:** 12%.
Hospitals: 250 (3 beds per 10,000). **Doctors:** 2,233.
Blind: 200,000. **Deaf:** 1,535,500. **Murder rate:** 90. **Lepers:** 8,000.

LITERATURE
New book titles p.a.: 23 (1 p.a. per million). **Periodicals:** 147.
Newspapers: 15 dailies.

COMMUNICATION (per 1,000 people)
Phones: 1 (2% mobile). **Radios:** 73. **TV sets:** 10.
Daily newspaper circulation: 11. **Computers:** 1.

REFUGEES
Citizen refugees in other countries: 2,328,400.
Alien refugees from other countries: 18,400.
Internal displacement: 500,000.

HUMAN LIFE AND LIBERTY (optimum condition=100.0%)
HDI: 22.9. **HSI:** 11.0. **HFI:** 5.0. **EFL:** 2.0.

Country Table 1. Religious adherents in Afghanistan, AD 1900-2025.

Year	1900		1970		mid-1990		Annual change, 1990-2000				mid-1995		mid-2000		mid-2025	
Name	Adherents	%	Adherents	%	Adherents	%	Natural	Conversion	Total	Rate	Adherents	%	Adherents	%	Adherents	%
Muslims	5,070,700	99.4	13,500,780	99.1	14,452,370	98.0	780,164	4,168	784,332	4.43	19,284,810	98.1	22,296,095	98.1	44,153,400	98.3
Zoroastrians	0	0.0	0	0.0	191,800	1.3	10,354	911	11,265	4.73	260,000	1.3	304,454	1.3	675,000	1.5
Hindus	5,000	0.1	100,000	0.7	75,000	0.5	4,049	-3,597	452	0.59	80,000	0.4	79,521	0.4	50,000	0.1
Baha'is	0	0.0	400	0.0	19,500	0.1	1,053	-695	358	1.70	21,000	0.1	23,075	0.1	30,000	0.1
Christians	**300**	**0.0**	**8,020**	**0.1**	**7,000**	**0.1**	**378**	**-370**	**8**	**0.11**	**7,550**	**0.0**	**7,075**	**0.0**	**14,200**	**0.0**
PROFESSION																
crypto-Christians	0	0.0	200	0.0	2,000	0.0	108	-8	100	4.14	2,500	0.0	3,000	0.0	9,000	0.0
professing Christians	**300**	**0.0**	**7,820**	**0.1**	**5,000**	**0.0**	**270**	**-363**	**-93**	**-2.02**	**5,050**	**0.0**	**4,075**	**0.0**	**5,200**	**0.0**
AFFILIATION																
unaffiliated Christians	100	0.0	4,000	0.0	200	0.0	11	-13	-2	-1.16	150	0.0	178	0.0	400	0.0
affiliated Christians	**200**	**0.0**	**4,020**	**0.0**	**6,800**	**0.1**	**367**	**-357**	**10**	**0.14**	**7,400**	**0.0**	**6,897**	**0.0**	**13,800**	**0.0**
Independents	0	0.0	300	0.0	2,500	0.0	135	-85	50	1.84	3,000	0.0	3,000	0.0	10,000	0.0
Protestants	100	0.0	1,600	0.0	2,100	0.0	113	-123	-10	-0.49	2,300	0.0	2,000	0.0	2,000	0.0
Roman Catholics	100	0.0	2,000	0.0	1,600	0.0	86	-96	-10	-0.66	1,500	0.0	1,497	0.0	1,200	0.0
Marginal Christians	0	0.0	20	0.0	200	0.0	11	-11	0	0.00	200	0.0	200	0.0	400	0.0
Anglicans	0	0.0	100	0.0	200	0.0	11	-21	-10	-6.70	200	0.0	100	0.0	100	0.0
Orthodox	0	0.0	0	0.0	200	0.0	11	-21	-10	-6.70	200	0.0	100	0.0	100	0.0
Trans-megabloc groupings																
Evangelicals	10	0.0	400	0.0	500	0.0	27	3	30	4.81	795	0.0	800	0.0	800	0.0
Pentecostals/Charismatics	0	0.0	200	0.0	2,200	0.0	119	-109	10	0.45	2,475	0.0	2,300	0.0	5,000	0.0
Great Commission Christians	**200**	**0.0**	**3,000**	**0.0**	**3,600**	**0.0**	**194**	**-146**	**48**	**1.26**	**3,800**	**0.0**	**4,081**	**0.0**	**10,000**	**0.0**
Sikhs	0	0.0	2,000	0.0	3,000	0.0	162	-60	102	2.98	3,500	0.0	4,022	0.0	6,000	0.0
Ethnoreligionists	20,000	0.4	10,000	0.1	3,000	0.0	162	-160	2	0.05	3,200	0.0	3,016	0.0	600	0.0
Nonreligious	0	0.0	0	0.0	2,000	0.0	108	-32	76	3.28	2,400	0.0	2,763	0.0	4,500	0.0
Atheists	0	0.0	1,600	0.0	1,200	0.0	65	-159	-94	-14.21	400	0.0	259	0.0	200	0.0
Jews	4,000	0.1	200	0.0	130	0.0	7	-6	1	0.45	140	0.0	136	0.0	100	0.0
World A (unevangelized persons)	4,947,000	97.0	11,715,419	86.0	11,066,250	75.0	597,362	-103,921	493,441	3.76	14,354,053	73.0	15,994,880	70.4	29,207,100	65.0
World B (evangelized non-Christians)	152,700	3.0	1,899,141	13.9	3,681,750	24.9	198,762	104,291	303,053	6.20	5,301,483	27.0	6,718,045	29.6	15,712,700	35.0
World C (Christians)	300	0.0	8,020	0.1	7,000	0.1	378	-370	8	0.11	7,550	0.0	7,075	0.0	14,200	0.0
Country's population	**5,100,000**	**100.0**	**13,622,581**	**100.0**	**14,755,000**	**100.0**	**796,502**	**0**	**796,502**	**4.41**	**19,663,087**	**100.0**	**22,720,000**	**100.0**	**44,934,000**	**100.0**

COLUMNS, ROWS.
For meanings and definitions, see Codebook (Part 3). Note that, by definition, total 'Christians' = professing + crypto-Christians, which also = affiliated + unaffiliated Christians, and also = Great Commission Christians + latent Christians. Percentages may not always total exactly, due to rounding.

CENSUSES.
No population census has ever been taken.

NOTES ON RELIGIONS
ATHEISTS. Limited to Russians remaining after Soviet invasion (1979) and subsequent civil war.
BAHA'IS. From 4 local spiritual assemblies (1973), mostly Persians, Baha'is increased vastly as refugees from the Iranian revolution of 1979, when it began to launch violent attacks on the Baha'i Faith. Many subsequently converted to Islam.
CHRISTIANS. Many expatriate Christians have left since 1985. There is a growing number of indigenous believers in isolated radio churches.
CRYPTO-CHRISTIANS. Unorganized individual nationals in the recognized churches. In addition some 7,000 Muslims are believed to have recently become hidden or isolated believers in Christ as Lord.
JEWS. Rapid decline of traditional Bukharan resident community 1948-95 due to emigration (leaving only a few families in Kabul and Herat), offset by temporary expatriate personnel.
MUSLIMS. 90% Sunnis (mostly of the Hanafite rite), with 2 Sufi orders: Naqshabandiya and Qadiriya), 9% Shias (Twelvers among the Hazara, Kizilbash and other tribes; Neo-Ismailis among the Vokhani and Roshani); and a few Wahhabi reform movement centers in the northeast. There are 15,000 mosques. *Hajj pilgrims to Mecca.* (1969) 9,125; (1970) 13,663; (1971) 10,744; (1972) 17,447; (1973) 6,220; (1974) 6,299; (1975) 5,800; (1976) 8,309.
ETHNORELIGIONISTS. Nuristanis (called Kafirs, unbelievers) retaining ancient animistic religion despite 1890 conversion of tribes to Islam.
ZOROASTRIANS. Large numbers are known to be secret followers of this ancient historic faith of Persia.

Great Commission Instrument Panel: status of Afghanistan (for explanation see start of Part 4)

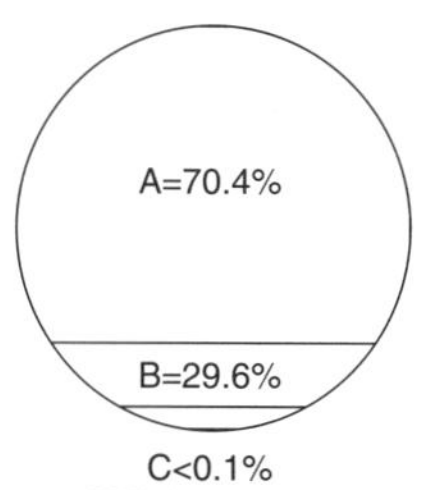

3 Worlds, AD 2000

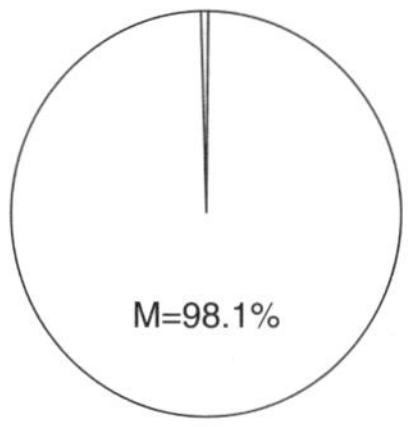

Religions, AD 2000

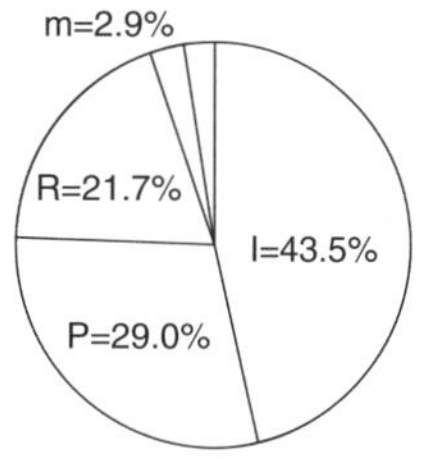

Ecclesiastical blocs

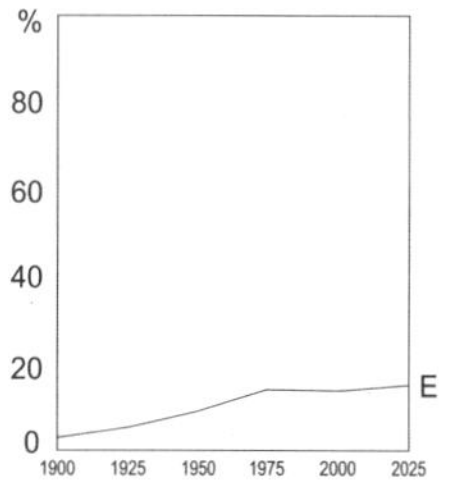

Evangelization, 1900-2025

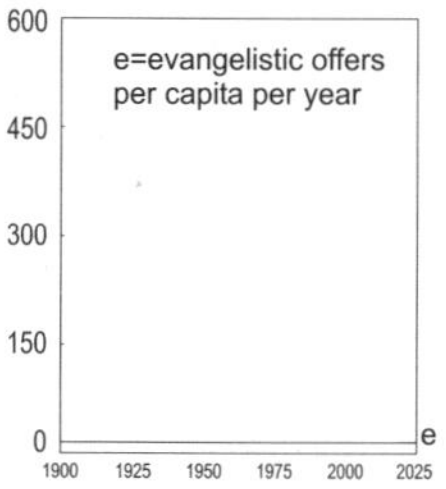

Offers, 1900-2025

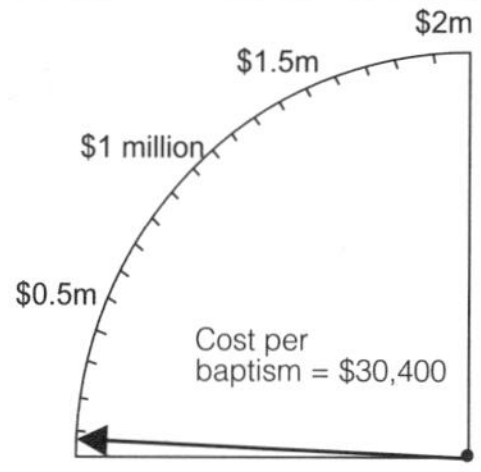

Cost-effectiveness, AD 2000

Country status. Afghanistan is a mountainous, landlocked country in Central Asia bordered by Iran, Pakistan, Turkmenistan, Tajikistan, and Uzbekistan. The climate is dry and its principal products are cotton, carpets, natural gas, and fruits.

HUMAN LIFE AND LIBERTY

Human need and development. After many decades of Communist rule followed by a bloody civil war, Afghanistan is a country in ruins where conditions of life have reverted to the 19th century. The infrastructure in the cities has been destroyed by the scorched earth policies of the rival political armies. Government, medical, and educational services have been suspended in many areas because there is no effective central government. Water, sanitation, and electricity supplies were limited even before the civil war, and have become scarcer since then. Thousands of Afghans were killed in the guerrilla wars and thousands more maimed and disabled

Country summary. **Worlds A, B, C by ethnolinguistic peoples, cities, and major civil divisions in Afghanistan.**

	PEOPLES							CITIES							CIVIL DIVISIONS						
World	*Num*	*Pop 2000*	*C%*	*Christians*	*E%*	*U%*	*Unevangelized*	*Num*	*Pop 2000*	*C%*	*Christians*	*E%*	*U%*	*Unevangelized*	*Num*	*Pop 2000*	*C%*	*Christians*	*E%*	*U%*	*Unevangelized*
A	65	22,715,628	0.02	3,625	30	70	16,000,188	10	4,853,998	0.11	5,367	33	67	3,244,251	29	22,720,414	0.03	6,897	30	70	16,000,406
B	1	1,363	31.03	423	84	16	218	0	0	0.00	0	0	0	0	0	0	0.00	0	0	0	0
C	4	3,424	83.15	2,847	100	0	5	0	0	0.00	0	0	0	0	0	0	0.00	0	0	0	0
Total	**70**	**22,720,415**	**0.03**	**6,895**	**30**	**70**	**16,000,411**	**10**	**4,853,998**	**0.11**	**5,367**	**33**	**67**	**3,244,251**	**29**	**22,720,414**	**0.03**	**6,897**	**30**	**70**	**16,000,406**

for life. The two million Afghan refugees who had fled to Pakistan have returned to their homes but with no means of subsistence or help. Only a few understaffed hospitals have survived and inadequate medical supplies and drugs have crimped whatever healthcare they can provide. Few homes destroyed during the war have been rebuilt as construction materials are difficult to obtain at any price. The nomads have escaped much of the misery but they continue to live a very austere life outside the cash economy. In the cities, where much of the conflict was centered, the narrow and winding thoroughfares have become impassable in places. Diet is generally adequate in quantity both in towns and villages, but of poor quality. Meat is a luxury among settled people. In the towns water is obtained from irrigation canals or canals feeding public tanks running alongside streets. These ditches also serve as receptacles for sewage and refuse since there are no sewer pipes. Epidemics are frequent, helped by the lack of proper vaccination programs, poor sanitation, and impure drinking water. Most Afghan doctors have fled the country, and foreign doctors are afraid to practice because of threats by militant fanatics.The World Bank has stopped reporting on the country, but it is believed to have the lowest literacy and life expectancy rates in the world.

Human rights and freedoms. Afghanistan has no constitution, no national judiciary, no effective central government and no national law enforcement agency. In such an anarchic environment, human rights have ceased to have any meaning. The local military commander or the controlling Islamic faction of an area determines who or what should survive. While some normalcy has returned to the north, central and eastern region, the capital is a cockpit under frequent fire from one faction or another. Looting, murder and rape are everyday occurrences. Hostage-taking is common, followed usually by summary execution. The coalition government that controls Kabul is believed to be holding thousands of political prisoners without trial. In the absence of a legal system, the Sharia is being administered in an impromptu manner by the leaders of the military factions. In some places, these factions are forcibly conscripting local men to serve in the militia as trench diggers and porters. Millions of land mines sown by the Soviet forces and by the resistance remain scattered on public thoroughfares, maiming and killing hundreds. Freedoms of the press and speech are not guaranteed and, in the absence of central authority, flouted by the authorities with impunity. Women and children are victims of the endemic violence, because they are unarmed and exposed to the penalties of the Sharia for even minor infractions of the strict Afghan code of conduct.

Muslims. In Kabul, devout Muslims observe the 5 obligatory times of prayer each day..

Human environment. Even rural areas have become wastelands following the civil war. Because the rebels and the government factions practice a scorched-earth policy, much of the natural vegetation has been permanently destroyed. The once-noted canal and irrigation networks have suffered irreversible damage. The war also has depleted livestock herds.

NON-CHRISTIAN RELIGIONS

Islam is the professed religion of virtually the entire populace, and the country is covered with mosques. Though Islam has been active in Afghanistan since the 9th century, it did not gain the allegiance of Nooristan until 1890. The majority are Sunnis of the Hanafite rite. Important Shia minorities include the Twelvers among the Hazara, Kizilbash and several other ethnic groups, and Neo-Ismailis in the northwest among the Vokhani and Roshani.

Other religions include 304,000 Zoroastrians (the historical religion), approximately 85,000 Hindu and Sikh Indians, and a small number of Nuristan inhabitants who retain their ancient animistic worship. Several communities of Afghani Jews remain in Kabul and Herat although most have emigrated recently to Israel, Europe and North America.

CHRISTIANITY

A bishop of Herat attended the Council of Seleucia in AD 424 and a Nestorian bishop was located at Kabul in the late Middle Ages, but Christian influence was terminated by Timur in the 14th century. A small Armenian church of about a dozen members existed in Kabul until 1898 when the church was destroyed and the group exiled, leaving no national Christians in the country. No missionaries, Catholic or Protestant, have been permitted inside Afghanistan. Since the penalty for apostasy from Islam is death, the few native Afghanis attracted to Christianity have in most cases left the country. The visible Christian community is therefore composed almost entirely of a few hundred foreign technicians, diplomats, and visitors, who form a fluctuating community. There are a few thousand Afghani crypto-Christians; 30 years ago there were none known.

CATHOLIC CHURCH. Catholics do not belong to a diocese but are termed the Work of Spiritual Assistance to Catholics of Afghanistan. Spiritual oversight has been given to Barnabite priests under the Roman Congregation for the Oriental Church, and there has been a priest in Kabul since 1932. A Barnabite priest with official status as chaplain at the Italian embassy serves the expatriate community. Catholics in 1974 were of 32 different nationalities. In 1996, 4 nuns were in Afghanistan serving in humanitarian work.

The Holy See has no diplomatic relations with Afghanistan in AD 2000.

OTHER CHURCHES. A small group of Jehovah's Witnesses have met secretly since 1957. The interdenominational Community Christian Church, which served the expatriate community, was responsible for construction of Afghanistan's first Protestant permanent church building in 1970, but this was demolished by government order in June 1973. Groups of expatriate Christians meet in homes in several cities across the country. A primarily German-speaking Lutheran congregation and an Anglican congregation have served the fluctuating communities from Germany and Britain.

Indigenous missions. The nascent indigenous Christian community of the 1990s is small and still under so many constraints that no mission effort exists.

CHURCH AND STATE

Under the monarchy, Islam of the Hanafite rite was the official religion. The king was its protector and was required to belong to this school, although individual Muslims could follow the rite of their choice. Non-Muslims were officially allowed freedom of worship in the constitution that was in effect from 1964-1973, however it has always been a capital offense for a Muslim to convert to Christianity. The military coup of 1973 began the rule by enacting numerous decrees, the first beginning as follows: 'Afghanistan is a republican state in accordance with the true spirit of Islam'. The pro-Marxist coup that came into power in 1978 and the subsequent 10-year Soviet occupation were ferocious in their persecution of all religion. The chaotic and anarchic situation since the fall of the communist regime in 1992 has allowed a measure of freedom for Christian presence in humanitarian service, but only in a context of great danger from many directions. The various factions, warlords, and guerillas that control various areas of the nation are without exception strongly Islamist, some to a violent extreme.

BROADCASTING AND MEDIA

Radio is extremely important in the life of Afghanistan. Nearly every village has a transistor radio whose broadcasts are shared by many. Although no Christian programming is permitted on broadcasts originating within the country, Afghanistan is blanketed by shortwave radio broadcasts from outside. The Russian language is heavily saturated with programs from the World By 2000 project and KNLS. There are also short daily and semi-daily broadcasts in the five largest languages (Pashto, Tajik, Hazara, Uzbek and Persian), which together are spoken by over 80% of the population. All but one of the World A megapeoples have programming available via shortwave radio.

The 'Jesus' Film has been shown and distributed in the Pashto language.

INTERDENOMINATIONAL ORGANIZATIONS

There are no ecumenical councils. An interdenominational body, the International Assistance (formerly Afghan) Mission begun in 1966, has 70 workers in the country from 10 different countries sponsored by 26 sending agencies. It seeks to serve the people of Afghanistan in the name and spirit of Christ; most of its work is medical assistance under the national government. Four other smaller Christian relief and development agencies are working in a similar way. Life is not easy for them. Relief workers have been threatened and even kidnapped, and facilities have been looted or destroyed.

FUTURE TRENDS AND PROSPECTS

No dramatic changes are expected in religious affiliation before AD 2025. Muslims, over 98% in AD 2000, will likely remain so for the next 25 years.

Christian Community Church of Kabul. *Top.* First permanent Protestant church building in Afghanistan, completed in 1971, destroyed at government order in 1973. *Bottom.* Its foundation stone.

The greatest growth in numbers is expected for Hinduism which could reach sizeable numbers after AD 2025. Later in the 21st century Christianity could also grow beyond 1% of the population but only if a significant movement occurs among indigenous peoples. Before AD 2050 the Christian message might reach one half of the population moving Afghanistan from World A into World B (>50% evangelized).

BIBLIOGRAPHY

Afghanistan. S. Jones. *World bibliographical series*, vol. 135. Oxford, UK: CLIO Press, 1992. 308p. (See especially 'Religion,' 143-5).

'Afghanistan: Islam and counter–revolutionary movements,' A. Ghani, in *Islam in Asia: religion, politics, & society*, p.79–96. J. L. Esposito (ed). New York: Oxford University Press, 1987.

Afghanistan: its people, its society, its culture. D. N. Wilber. New Haven, CT: HRAF Press, 1962. 320p.

Afghanistan: the forbidden harvest. C. Wilson Jr. Elgin, IL: David C. Cook, 1981. 130p.

Buddhism in Afghanistan and Central Asia. No. 14 in section 13, *Indian religions*, in *Iconography of religions*, S. Gaulier, R. Jera-Bezard & M. Maillard. Leiden: E. J. Brill, 1976. 2 vols.

Dictionary of Afghan wars, revolutions, and insurgencies. L. W. Adamec. Metuchen, NJ: Scarecrow Press, 1996.

Faction and conversion in a plural society: religious alignments in the Hindu Kush. R. L. Canfield. *Anthropological papers, Museum of Anthropology, University of Michigan*, 50. Ann Arbor: University of Michigan Press, 1973. 142p.

'Islam as a binding force in Afghan resistance,' Z. A. Mumtaz, *WUFA: quarterly journal of the Writers Union of Free Afghanistan*, 2, 2 (1987), 61–76.

'Notes on Afghan Sufi orders and Khanaqahs,' B. Utas, *Afghanistan journal*, 7, 2 (1980), 60–67.

Religiöse Funktionsträger in Nuristan. J. Frembgen. *Beiträge zur Zentralasienforschung*, Bd. 3. Sankt Augustin: VGH Wissenschaftsverlag, 1983. 215p.

Religiöses Volksbrauchtum in Afghanistan: Islamische Heiligenverehrung und Wallfahrtswesen im Raum Kabul. H. Einzmann. Leiden: E. J. Brill, 1977. 480p.

The Kirghiz and Wakhi of Afghanistan: adaptation to closed frontiers. M. N. M. Shahrani. *Publications on ethnicity and nationality of the School of International Studies, University of Washington*, 1. Seattle, WA: University of Washington Press, 1979. 287p.

The religions of the Hindukush. K. Jettmar. Wiltshire, UK: Aris & Phillips, 1986. 3 vols.

'The structure and position of Islam in Afghanistan,' D. N. Wilber, *Middle East journal*, 6, 1 (1952), 41–48.

'The Tajik of Afghanistan,' D. B. Barrett, *International journal of frontier missions*, 10 (April 1993), 93–94.

'The Uzbeks in Afghanistan,' E. Naby, *Central Asian Survey*, 3, 1 (1984), 1–21.

Träger medialer Begabung im Hindukusch und Karakorum. E. Friedl. *Acta Ethnologica et Linguistica*, 8. Vienna: Österreichische Ethnologische Gesellschaft, 1965. 127p.

Country Table 2. **Organized churches and denominations in Afghanistan.**

Official name (bold type = church with over 10% of all affiliated) 1	*Begun* 2	*Type* 3	*Counc* 4	*Congs* 5	*Adults* 6	*Affiliated 1970* 7	*Affiliated 1995* 8	*G%* 9	*Names, notes, and other statistics* (see Codebook, Part 3) 10
Anglican Church	c1970	A-Cen	aw...	1	100	100	200	2.81	*St Chrysostom's Church.* Expatriates. Services in Community Church. 1x.
Assemblies of God	1972	P-Pe2	Zf...	1	20	–	50	4.35	M=AoG(USA). Classical Pentecostals. Small medical mission begun. 2f.
Catholic Church	1933	R-Lat	O....	2	600	2,000	1,500	-1.14	*Work of Spiritual Assistance to Catholics of Afghanistan.* 2x,8w,W=25%,15Yy.
Community Christian Ch of Kabul	1952	P-com	.....	2	500	800	1,000	0.90	*Kalisa baroi Haregis.* Kabul church destroyed 1973. 4x,W=19%,1Y,3y.
German-speaking Protestant Church	c1960	P-Lut	.....	1	400	780	1,000	1.00	German expatriates, mainly Lutherans. Services in Community Church.
Isolated radio churches	c1960	I-rad	.....	30	2,000	300	3,000	9.65	Converts among numerous radio listeners.
Jehovah's Witnesses	1957	m-Jeh	x....	1	100	20	200	9.65	First expatriate residents 1957. Restricted activities, completely underground.
Russian Orthodox Church	1977	O-Rus	.....	2	100	–	200	5.56	Civilians remaining after lengthy Russian military occupation.
Seventh-day Adventist Church	c1960	P-Adv	x....	1	150	20	250	10.63	*SDA. Pakistan Union* (HQ Lahore). M=SDA(Philippine Union Mission). 2f.
Totals				**41**	**3,970**	**4,020**	**7,400**		

Churches, members, growth, 1900-2025	*Congs*	*Adults*	*Affiliated*	*G%*	*Total denominations*	*6 Megablocs:* O	R	A	P	I	m
Total churches, members, and denominations (mid-1900)	2	120	200	4.38	0	0	0	0	0	0	0
Total churches, members, and denominations (mid-1970)	36	2,370	4,020	4.38	7	0	1	1	3	1	1
Total churches, members, and denominations (mid-1990)	40	3,600	6,800	2.66	8	0	1	1	4	1	1
Total churches, members, and denominations (mid-1995)	41	3,970	7,400	1.71	9	1	1	1	4	1	1
Total churches, members, and denominations (mid-2000)	49	3,700	6,897	-1.40	9	1	1	1	4	1	1
Total churches, members, and denominations (mid-2025)	100	7,400	13,800	2.81	12	2	1	1	6	1	1

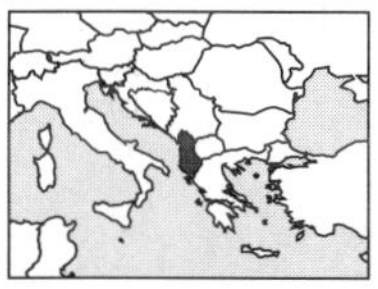

ALBANIA

SECULAR DATA, AD 2000

STATE
Official name: Republika e Shqipërisë (The Republic of Albania).
Short name: Albania. **Adjective of nationality:** Albanian.
Flag: Red field, black 2-headed eagle, gold-edged red star.
Area: 28,748 sq. km. (11,100 sq. mi.).
Government: Unitary multiparty republic with one legislature house since 1991 (1478 Turkish rule, 1912 Independence, 1925 republic, 1928 absolute monarchy, 1939 Italian rules, 1946 Communist republic).
Legislature: People's Assembly, 155 members.
Official language: Albanian (Tosk) (Shqip).
Monetary unit: 1 lek = 100 qindars. **US$1=** 147.15 leks.
Chief cities: TIRANE (Tirana) 266,700; Durres 92,634; Elbasan 90,393; Shkoder (Shkodra) 89,497; Vlore (Vlora) 80,312.
Political divisions: 26 provinces.
Armed forces: 73,000.

DEMOGRAPHY
Population: 3,113,000.
Population density: 108.3/sq. km. (280.4/sq. mi.).
Under 15 years: 918,000.
Growth rate p.a.: 0.62% (births 18.07, deaths 5.54).
Mortality: Infant, per 1,000: 26.6; **Maternal per 100,000:** 65.0.
Life expectancy: 74 (male 71, female 77).
Household size: 4.7. **Floor area per person, sq.m:** 8.0.
Major languages: Albanian (Gheg, Tosk), Greek, Macedonian, Chinese, Romany.
Urban dwellers: 39.14%. **Urban growth rate p.a.:** 1.88%.
Labor force: 57%.

ETHNOLINGUISTIC PEOPLES
82.5% Tosk Albanian; 9.1% Gheg Albanian (Scutari); 2.3% Greek; 1.8% Vlach Gypsy; 1.7% Aromanian (Armini).

ECONOMY
National income p.a. per person: US$670; **per family:** US$3,149.

EDUCATION
Adult literacy: 91% (male 95%, female 88%). **Schools:** 2,290.
Universities: 8. **School enrolment:** female/male: 79%/78%.

HEALTH
Access to health services: 45%. **Access to safe water:** 50%.
Hospitals: 895 (57 beds per 10,000). **Doctors:** 4,467.
Blind: 2,000. **Deaf:** 209,600. **Murder rate:** 50. **Lepers:** 500.

LITERATURE
New book titles p.a.: 620 (200 p.a. per million). **Periodicals:** 200.
Newspapers: 3 dailies.

COMMUNICATION (per 1,000 people)
Phones: 12 (3% mobile). **Radios:** 157. **TV sets:** 89.
Daily newspaper circulation: 54. **Computers:** 35.

HUMAN LIFE AND LIBERTY (optimum condition=100.0%)
HDI: 65.5. **HSI:** 53.0. **HFI:** 30.0. **EFL:** 31.0.

Country Table 1. **Religious adherents in Albania, AD 1900-2025.**

Year	*1900*		*1970*		*mid-1990*		*Annual change, 1990-2000*				*mid-1995*		*mid-2000*		*mid-2025*	
Name	*Adherents*	*%*	*Adherents*	*%*	*Adherents*	*%*	*Natural*	*Conversion*	*Total*	*Rate*	*Adherents*	*%*	*Adherents*	*%*	*Adherents*	*%*
Muslims	548,000	68.5	600,000	28.1	1,150,490	35.0	-6,156	11,881	5,725	0.49	1,151,475	36.3	1,207,737	38.8	1,505,500	39.4
Christians	**250,000**	**31.3**	**173,000**	**8.1**	**800,000**	**24.3**	**-4,281**	**34,404**	**30,123**	**3.25**	**1,060,000**	**33.4**	**1,101,230**	**35.4**	**1,680,000**	**44.0**
PROFESSION																
crypto-Christians	0	0.0	171,430	8.0	0	0.0	0	0	0	0.00	0	0.0	0	0.0	0	0.0
professing Christians	**250,000**	**31.3**	**1,570**	**0.1**	**800,000**	**24.3**	**-4,281**	**34,404**	**30,123**	**3.25**	**1,060,000**	**33.4**	**1,101,230**	**35.4**	**1,680,000**	**44.0**
AFFILIATION																
unaffiliated Christians	23,500	2.9	970	0.1	20,000	0.6	-107	1,191	1,084	4.43	27,519	0.9	30,840	1.0	40,000	1.1
affiliated Christians	**226,500**	**28.3**	**172,030**	**8.1**	**780,000**	**23.7**	**-4,174**	**33,213**	**29,039**	**3.22**	**1,032,481**	**32.5**	**1,070,390**	**34.4**	**1,640,000**	**42.9**
Roman Catholics	66,500	8.3	70,000	3.3	380,000	11.6	-2,033	16,172	14,139	3.21	492,201	15.5	521,390	16.8	773,000	20.2
Orthodox	160,000	20.0	101,000	4.7	375,000	11.4	-2,007	14,507	12,500	2.92	468,000	14.7	500,000	16.1	730,500	19.1
Protestants	0	0.0	530	0.0	5,000	0.2	-27	1,527	1,500	14.87	16,280	0.5	20,000	0.6	63,000	1.7
Independents	0	0.0	400	0.0	13,000	0.4	-70	470	400	2.72	46,283	1.5	17,000	0.6	35,000	0.9
Marginal Christians	0	0.0	100	0.0	7,000	0.2	-37	537	500	5.54	9,717	0.3	12,000	0.4	38,500	1.0
Trans-megabloc groupings																
Evangelicals	0	0.0	200	0.0	3,000	0.1	-16	316	300	7.18	5,252	0.2	6,000	0.2	40,000	1.1
Pentecostals/Charismatics	0	0.0	600	0.0	40,000	1.2	-214	6,214	6,000	9.60	82,544	2.6	100,000	3.2	250,000	6.5
Great Commission Christians	**21,600**	**2.7**	**42,700**	**2.0**	**444,000**	**13.5**	**-2,376**	**19,411**	**17,035**	**3.30**	**570,000**	**17.9**	**614,345**	**19.7**	**1,167,000**	**30.6**
Nonreligious	1,000	0.1	1,016,800	47.6	892,800	27.2	-4,778	-32,751	-37,529	-5.30	640,000	20.2	517,962	16.6	420,000	11.0
Atheists	0	0.0	348,000	16.3	443,400	13.5	-2,373	-13,917	-16,290	-4.48	320,000	10.1	280,496	9.0	200,000	5.2
Baha'is	0	0.0	0	0.0	2,000	0.1	-11	382	371	11.06	5,200	0.2	5,711	0.2	14,000	0.4
Jews	1,000	0.1	200	0.0	310	0.0	-2	1	-1	-0.36	325	0.0	299	0.0	500	0.0
World A (unevangelized persons)	488,000	61.0	1,411,080	66.0	799,227	24.3	-4,281	-30,308	-34,589	-5.51	600,381	18.9	454,498	14.6	351,440	9.2
World B (evangelized non-Christians)	62,000	7.7	553,920	25.9	1,689,773	51.4	-9,039	-4,006	-13,045	-0.81	1,516,241	47.7	1,557,272	50.0	1,788,560	46.8
World C (Christians)	250,000	31.3	173,000	8.1	800,000	24.3	-4,281	34,404	30,123	3.25	1,060,000	33.4	1,101,230	35.4	1,680,000	44.0
Country's population	**800,000**	**100.0**	**2,138,000**	**100.0**	**3,289,000**	**100.0**	**-17,601**	**0**	**-17,601**	**-0.55**	**3,176,623**	**100.0**	**3,113,000**	**100.0**	**3,820,000**	**100.0**

Continued overleaf

Country Table 1–concluded

COLUMNS, ROWS.
For meanings and definitions, see Codebook (Part 3). Note that, by definition, total 'Christians' = professing + crypto-Christians, which also = affiliated + unaffiliated Christians, and also = Great Commission Christians + latent Christians. Percentages may not always total exactly, due to rounding.

CENSUSES.
1938: 69.0% Muslims, 20.7% Orthodox, 10.3% Roman Catholics, 200 Jews. 1945: 68.9% Muslims, 19.2% Orthodox, 11.8% Roman Catholics. 1953 (estimate): 66.3% Muslims, 22.4% Orthodox, 11.2% Roman Catholics.

NOTES ON RELIGIONS
ATHEISTS. Reached apex of 17% in early 1980s; declining rapidly in post-Communist period.
BAHA'IS. After the collapse of Communism, Baha'i missionaries were welcomed and by mid-1996 had organized 42 LSAs (local spiritual assemblies).
CRYPTO-CHRISTIANS. In 1967 all Christians were forced underground. After the collapse of Communism, Christians were no longer under state pressure of needing to hide their profession.
MUSLIMS. Mainly Sunnis (80%; Hanafite rite) and 20% Bektashis (dervish monastic order, expelled from Turkey in 1925). Several thousand mosques were closed and secularized after 1965, and vast numbers of Muslims forced to apostatize. After 1990, large numbers returned to the faith and mosques were reopened.
UNAFFILIATED CHRISTIANS. Up to 1945 only, but expected to reemerge in the post-Communist period.
NONRELIGIOUS. Agnostics, indifferent to religion.
PROFESSING CHRISTIANS. These are nil from 1970 to about 1989 when Christians became free to declare their faith publicly.

Great Commission Instrument Panel: status of Albania (for explanation see start of Part 4)

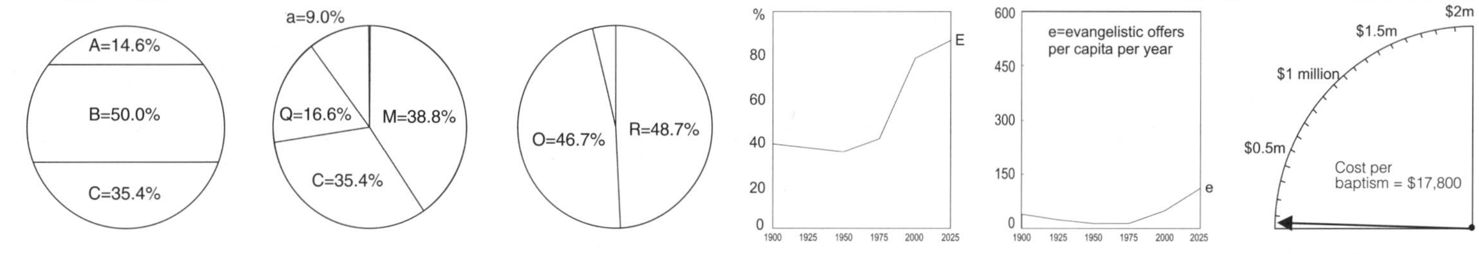

3 Worlds, AD 2000 | Religions, AD 2000 | Ecclesiastical blocs | Evangelization, 1900-2025 | Offers, 1900-2025 | Cost-effectiveness, AD 2000

Country status. Albania is a small Balkan country on the lower Adriatic coast. Though much of the land is mountainous, there are extensive forests and fertile valleys yielding products such as tobacco, cotton, and potatoes.

HUMAN LIFE AND LIBERTY

Human need and development. Albania has the dubious distinction of being the most undeveloped country in Europe. Its emergence into modern times has been delayed by its static Muslim-dominated culture, World War II, and then nearly 40 years of Communist rule. The Albanian brand of Communism under dictator Enver Hoxha stunted development by cutting off all links with the external world, including the Soviet Union and Yugoslavia. Because of the typically Marxist overemphasis on industrial growth, other sectors of the economy, particularly transportation, were neglected. There was some improvement in living conditions as a result of the elimination of many common ailments through mass inoculation campaigns and the expansion of medical services to the villages. The Communists also helped to electrify most of the country and to reduce chronic food shortages. However, the diet is still deficient in proteins and nutrients. Although the Communists claimed that they built over 200,000 houses, living quarters are crowded, and urban apartments generally lack central heating, separate kitchens, and bathroom facilities. Massive emigration attests to the country's continuing economic difficulties.

Human rights and freedoms. In 1993 the Albanian Parliament passed a human rights law, its first in history. It guarantees all basic freedoms and thus makes Albania a truly democratic state. However, freedoms of press and assembly are significantly restricted because of the persistence of Communist modes of bureaucratic behavior and also because of the pressures of ethnic divisiveness. The former secret police, the Sigurimi, has been disbanded and its files may be opened to the public in course of time. Parliament passed a press law which mandates 'responsible reporting' as a means of restricting criticism of the government. The rights of the 2 major minorities, Greeks and Vlachs, are fully protected, although the Greeks themselves often complain of discriminatory treatment.

Muslims. Long suppressed under atheistic regime, central mosque in Tirana central square.

Human environment. Because of its underdevelopment, Albania has not experienced environmental degradation of the kind found in its more advanced neighbors. Nevertheless, there is a distinct lack of environmental awareness in the country because none of the problems associated with pollution have reached serious dimensions.

NON-CHRISTIAN RELIGIONS

Islam. The oldest mosque in the country, in Berat, dates from 1380. The Turkish occupation began at the end of the 15th century, but the country remained largely Christian for centuries. Islam became the majority religion of Albania after a series of mass conversions in the 17th and 18th centuries, and remained the religion of the majority of the population (69%) up to 1945. Until 1967, when all forms of organized religion were abolished, there were 2 principal Muslim groups in Albania, Sunnis and Bektashis. Sunnis of the Hanafite rite were divided into 4 regions each under the authority of a grand mufti: Tiranë, Shkodër, Korçë, and Gjirokaster. They were found in all parts of the country but were strongest in the central region. The Bektashis were a dervish monastic order derived from the Sunnis, expelled from Turkey in 1925, whose head (baba) resided in Albania.

After 25 years of silence, the call of the muezzin once again echoed in the streets of Tiranë in 1992. The first legal Muslim prayer service in the country in decades, held in the Ethem Bey mosque at the heart of the city, was witnessed by15,000 onlookers gathered in the streets. When the national ban on religion was lifted in 1990, Muslims from Saudi Arabia, Sudan, Kuwait, and Egypt launched a massive effort to re-Islamize Albania. They sent missionaries, scholarships, and aid, and many Muslim nations stepped up diplomatic contact. Many Albanian youths were granted trips to Egypt and other countries for religious instruction. A re-building program for mosques, religious schools, and an Islamic cultural center began in 1991. Of the 1,050 mosques in the country before 1967, 800 survived to 1990. In 1992 there were 200 practicing imams.

Judaism. Albanian authorities in World War II refused to turn over to Germany the Jewish community of 300, which has continued since to be very small in number.

Baha'is have been active in the multi-religious context of Albania, and their missionary efforts have met with some success. In the early 1990s they claimed 4,000 members and obtained official recognition (which some Protestant groups at that time were unable to do, despite serious efforts).

CHRISTIANITY

Albania was successively under the Roman and Byzantine empires, Slavs, Bulgarians, Serbs, and the Ottoman Turkish empire until the 20th century. In its early years it was subject to missionary thrusts from both Constantinople (AD 200) and Rome (AD 385); but while under the Turks, most of the people became Muslims. During the 19th century, the country continually struggled for independence from neighboring powers and achieved it in 1913. Occupied by foreign forces during World War I, Albania became independent once again in 1918 but was taken over by Italy in 1939, with Communist partisans gaining control of the country at the end of World War II. Prior to World War II, Orthodox numbered 21% of the population and Catholics 11%, with only a few dozen Protestants. In 1959 there were about 700,000 Muslims, 200,000 Orthodox, and 100,000 Catholics out of a total population of 1,556,000. As an outward sign of the re-emergence of Christianity, the re-building of churches and Christian schools has been a constant and rigorous enterprise since 1991, at times with government aid. Catholics and Protestants launched separate projects to produce a new, more contemporary Bible for Albanians.

Orthodox Church. Archbishop Anastasios Yannoulatos confers ordination during liturgy.

ORTHODOX CHURCHES. The Orthodox have traditionally been strongest in the south among the Tosk. In 1923 the Orthodox Church of Albania made a unilateral declaration of autocephaly. Fan Noli, the first president of Albania (following independence in 1912), was the first archbishop. Only in 1937 was the Albanian Orthodox Church recognized by the Ecumenical Patriarch in Constantinople. Prior to 1967, it was composed of 4 dioceses: Tiranë (the capital), Berat, Gjirokaster, and Korçë. Because of the role played by Orthodox clergy during the Italo-German occupation in World War II, they were not harassed at first by the Communist regime, which came to power after resistance fighters had liberated the country in November 1944. However, by 1947 pressure began to build up against them, followed by detention of priests. Between 1949 and 1951, all 4 bishops were arrested and replaced by others more favorable to

Country summary. **Worlds A, B, C by ethnolinguistic peoples, cities, and major civil divisions in Albania.**

	PEOPLES							CITIES							CIVIL DIVISIONS						
World	Num	Pop 2000	C%	Christians	E%	U%	Unevangelized	Num	Pop 2000	C%	Christians	E%	U%	Unevangelized	Num	Pop 2000	C%	Christians	E%	U%	Unevangelized
A	4	6,788	22.95	1,558	44	56	3,807	0	0	0.00	0	0	0	0	0	0	0.00	0	0	0	0
B	2	2,855,330	30.30	865,145	84	16	445,476	6	690,775	36.75	253,866	90	10	71,950	26	3,113,434	34.38	1,070,390	85	15	454,107
C	6	251,316	81.05	203,687	98	2	4,823	0	0	0.00	0	0	0	0	0	0	0.00	0	0	0	0
Total	**12**	**3,113,434**	**34.38**	**1,070,390**	**85**	**15**	**454,106**	**6**	**690,775**	**36.75**	**253,866**	**90**	**10**	**71,950**	**26**	**3,113,434**	**34.38**	**1,070,390**	**85**	**15**	**454,107**

the regime. After the death of the primate, Paissi, the Holy Synod elected in 1966 the bishop of Gjirokaster, msgr Damianos Kokonesi as archbishop of Albania. The Serbian Orthodox Church had established a vicariate at Shkodër in the north in 1922 under the Patriarchate of Belgrade, but all relations with the Serbian Holy Synod were later forced to be cut. Orthodox priests from Greece serve the Greek-speaking faithful in the South. Before the Communist ban on religion, Albania had 224 Orthodox priests and 350 churches and monasteries. In January 1991 bishop Anastasios, a Greek, was appointed by the ecumenical patriarch of Constantinople as exarch for re-establishing the national Orthodox Church. When he was inaugurated archbishop of Tiranë in 1992, the celebratory sermon was disrupted by Albanians who opposed the inauguration of a 'foreigner'. Later in 1994, archbishop Anastasios issued an appeal for greater freedom for Orthodox Christians. He has also opposed the vigorous evangelistic work of Protestants. The first class from a re-opened seminary training priests for the Albanian Orthodox Church graduated in 1994.

Albanian Orthodox Church. New church building under construction in Tirana.

CATHOLIC CHURCH. The Catholic Church has been strongest in the north among the Ghegs. In 1944 there were 2 archdioceses: Durres (founded in the 13th century) and Shkodër (founded in AD 385). Shkodër had 3 suffragan dioceses: Leshe (since the 14th century), Pult (9th century), and Sape (AD 1062). The monastery of St Alexander of Ores was established in 1888, and the Apostolic Administration for Southern Albania in 1939. All these territories were under the supervision of Propaganda in Rome except the last which was administered by the Congregation for the Oriental Church. Especially because of the ambiguous situation under the Italian occupation and its attitude during this period, the Catholic Church began to experience from December 1944 an increasing number of repressive measures: expulsion of the apostolic delegate and detention of priests in 1945, expulsion of Italian religious priests and nuns in 1946, and a grim roster of imprisonments and executions following.

In the spring of 1971, there were only 14 Catholic priests left alive (12 in concentration camps, 2 in hiding), and of these one was executed in 1972 for baptizing a child in a prison camp. Nevertheless, there was considerable underground church activity. In particular the wearing of white wedding dresses, and local celebrations with traditionally religious overtones were used as deliberate protests.

Since the fall of Communism, the Roman Catholic Church has come to life once again. One important sign: in 1994 pope John Paul II created a new cardinal from Albania. In 1992 there were 30 priests in the country, in contrast to 300 in 1944. Their work has been helped by missionaries from India, the Philippines, Croatia, Austria, the Netherlands, and Ireland.

The Holy See has diplomatic relations with Albania and in AD 2000 is represented to government and the Catholic hierarchy by a nuncio residing in Tiranë.

Catholic Church in Albania. Pope John Paul II visits to establish post-Communist hierarchy.

PROTESTANT CHURCHES. Protestant activity has been very limited in Albania, restricted to the work of Seventh-day Adventists (originally related to their Greek Mission), Methodists (as part of their Yugoslavia Mission), and Baptists, all prior to the Italian occupation. These organizational contacts were broken for many years.

Many new churches have emerged since 1990 as a result of evangelistic activity by Evangelical Protestant mission agencies. Those with a history of work in Albania have returned, and many others have joined them. Within 18 months after the fall of Communism, 16 Evangelical agencies entered the nation, working in aid, evangelism, and church planting. By 1992 there were 1,000 Albanian Evangelicals worshipping in 36 new congregations and home groups. By 1995 there were more than 400 Evangelical missionaries active in Albania.

MARGINAL CHURCHES. Mormons and Jehovah's Witnesses have sent in many missionaries and distributed large volumes of literature—efforts that have been fruitful.

Indigenous missions. The Bogomil ('Friends of God') movement flourished in Albania in the 13th century and resulted in the sending of missionaries to all regions of the Balkans, to the Republic of Venice, to Genoa, and to the Provence and Languedoc regions of southern France. In those two latter regions it became the predominant faith. In the 1990s, the church in Albania is recuperating in the wake of the collapse of Communism. Widespread church growth, lack of pastoral and leadership training, and difficult economic conditions have led to a church only beginning to wake up to needs outside the country. However, the large number of Albanians abroad will likely become a target for monocultural foreign missions.

Word of Life Church. Relindja (Revival) Fellowship, one of many pentecostal congregations.

CHURCH AND STATE

The constitution of 1946 appeared liberal in its attitude towards religion. Article 18 called for the separation of church and state, freedom of conscience and religion, liberty of internal organization of religions and the material aid of the state to religious organizations. These were realities in the first years of the new republic. In 1949, modified again in 1963, religious communities were obliged to register their statutes with the government. Those of the Albanian Islamic community, the Albanian Bektashi community and the Albanian Orthodox Church were approved in 1950. The Catholic Church did not receive approval until 1951, because the first version of their request was refused by the government who then stipulated the necessity for a complete break of all ties with the Vatican.

A new anti-religious campaign was begun in 1964, followed by the Fifth Communist Party Congress of 1966, which set as its goal the total elimination of religion in Albania. According to the Albanian literary journal *Nendori*, 2,169 mosques, churches and convents were confiscated and secularized in 1967. At the same time, the clergy were abolished and priests were assigned to 'productive work'. In October 1967 Radio Tiranë proclaimed that Albania was the 'first atheist state of the world', and a few months later the Assembly of the People repealed all earlier decrees concerning religion, as part of the 'Cultural and Ideological Revolution'. Visitors to Albania found that organized religious life ceased to exist and all churches were closed. The last Catholic church, the cathedral of Tiranë, was closed in 1969.

In 1968 under government auspices Albanian youths spread throughout the country destroying places of worship, only a small number of edifices of artistic, cultural or historical value being spared. The entire operation lasted a year and a half. Thus at Shkoder in the north, the Catholic cathedral was transformed into a sports hall, the archbishop's house into a hotel for athletes, and the Great Mosque was razed to the ground. A museum of atheism was opened in the city, situated in the area where the anti-religious campaign encountered its greatest resistance. Even cemeteries were affected, all crosses and religious inscriptions being removed. In 1972 a 70-year old Catholic priest, Shtjefen Kurti, interned in the work camp of Lushnje was shot for having baptized an infant. The news of his execution was confirmed by official sources (Radio Tiranë, 29 April 1973), although the reason given was that he had engaged in espionage 'to the profit of the Vatican, Great Britain and the United States'. In November 1973, msgr Damian, head of the Albanian Orthodox Church and archbishop of Tiranë, died in prison at the age of 80 where he had been interned since 1967, also for alleged espionage.

The official publications of the Albanian Communist Party testified to the failure of the drive for atheism. The party ideological organ *Bashkimi* acknowledged in 1973: 'We have by no means achieved complete emancipation from the remnants of religious influences'. It especially deplored the increase in public and private acts of worship, and in certain regions, public celebration of religious feasts with illegal absence from work. It added that pilgrimages to ancient worship places still continued although the sanctuaries which are central to them had been destroyed, and that visits to parents and friends are used as a pretext to camouflage such manifestations. In 1976 a new clause drafted for the Albanian constitution clarified the position by stating that Albania 'recognizes no religion and supports and develops atheist propaganda for the purpose of implanting the scientific materialist world outlook'. At the same time the regime ordered a change of all citizens' names that were 'unsuitable from a political, ideological or moral viewpoint', including all Christian names.

In the 1980s the government was forced to admit that religion had survived. Official publications reported on, and railed against the implications of, a sociological study that showed 95% of young people were choosing spouses of the same religious background—possibly a stronger trend than before the anti-religious repression, and this in spite of official encouragement to the contrary. Cracks began to appear in the monolith of Albania's anti-religion campaign. In 1988 clergy were permitted to reenter the country and officiate at religious services. Mother Teresa, an internationally famous Christian figure and ironically the world's most well-known and loved Albanian, was permitted to visit Tiranë and was received by the foreign minister and the widow of the late president Hoxha.

In 1990, as Communism was rapidly collapsing in Central and Eastern Europe, and as Albania was forced to seek better relations with the West, the strict national ban on religion was lifted. The public and private practice of religion was legalized. As a result of a student-led revolt, the communist regime fell in 1991, and a democratic government came to power after a series of two free, multi-party elections, the nation's first. In that same year the president publicly admitted the quest for atheism was a mistake. Policies turned in the opposite direction, even encouraging religion—among other reasons, as an antidote to the national crime wave that accompanied freedom. In 1992 the government expressed its willingness to help with the rebuilding of Muslim, Orthodox, and Catholic buildings, perceiving these to be the three religions of Albania. The human rights law passed by parliament in 1993 guaranteed freedom of religion.

Under the post-Communist constitution, Albania is a secular state with full religious freedom for all. Controversy over a proposed law on religion erupted in 1993. The law required the leaders of all the 4 major recognized religious groups—Sunni Muslim, Bektashi, Catholic, and Orthodox—to be Albanian citizens and it was seen as a restriction on the activities of the Greek Orthodox Church which was headed by a Greek citizen. Religious activities are overseen by a secretariat of religions within the Ministry of Culture. The question of restoration of church property confiscated by the Hoxha regime is yet to be settled.

BROADCASTING AND MEDIA

Ironically, with the opening of Albania it has become possible to broadcast Christian programs on the government-owned Radio Tiranë, which was formerly used for the propagation of atheism. Albania's geographic position makes this a strategic transmitter. In 1992 TWR began using it to broadcast daily medium and short-wave programs in 19 languages, including the major European languages as well as Kurdish and Farsi. Moreover, Albania continues to be blanketed by shortwave radio programming by major broadcasters aiming generally at Europe; those from TWR (Monaco) and ECM (Italy) have both generated wide response. Listeners are followed-up from an office in Tiranë staffed by Albanian Christians.

Satellite TV and radio programs are received in English, Arabic, German and Italian. CBN's *700 Club* and *Another Life* programs can be seen on the national channel TVSH-1. CBN did a media 'blitz' with great response. The 'Jesus' Film has been seen by 43,800; more than 5,000 have responded.

INTERDENOMINATIONAL ORGANIZATIONS

The Albanian Encouragement Project began in 1991 as a coalition of 30 Evangelical Protestant missions and denominations. By 1995, 65 organizations and 300 long-term missionaries were included, almost all from the USA and Western Europe. An alliance of Evangelical churches in the nation has been formed under the sponsorship of the Evangelical Brotherhood, a denomination with roots reaching back to 1892, when it was founded by national hero and Evangelical preacher Gjerasim Qiriazi. The Albanian Orthodox Church has been a member of the World Council of Churches since 1992.

FUTURE TRENDS AND PROSPECTS

The collapse of the Communist regime in 1990 resulted in massive decline in nonreligious and atheists from a 1980 high of 74.1% to a projected 16.2% by 2025. These defections will probably be picked up by increases among Christians (44%) and Muslims (39%). High growth rates for Christians and Muslims in the 1990s are due to massive defections from nonreligious and atheist categories.

Sometime after 2025 Christianity could claim 60% of the population, but after that new Christians in Albania will have to come from defections from the Muslim community. Thus, it is expected that in the near future, Christianity and Islam will share the bulk of the inhabitants in a 60/40 ratio.

BIBLIOGRAPHY

Albania. W. B. Bland. *World bibliographical series*, vol. 94. Oxford, UK: CLIO Press, 1988. 328p. (See especially 'Religion,' 98-101).

'Albania: an atheist state,' B. Tonnes, *Religion in Communist lands*, 3, 1-3 (1975), 4–8.

Anfänge des albanischen Christentums: die frühe Bekehrung der Bessen und ihre langen Folgen. G. Schramm. *Rombach Wissenschaft Reihe Historiae*, Bd. 4. Freiburg im Breisgau: Rombach, 1994. 270p.

'Crypto–Christianity in the Balkan area under the Ottomons,' S. Skendi, *Slavic Review*, 26, 2 (1967), 227–46.

Islam in the Balkans: religion and society between Europe and the Arab World. H. T. Norris. Columbia, SC: University of South Carolina Press, 1993. 326p. (Deals with Bosnia, Albania, Macedonia).

'L'église catholique en Albanie (1945–1975),' R. Epp, *Revue des sciences religieuses*, 50, 1 (1976), 52–76.

'National minorities in Albania, 1919–1980,' S. M. Horak, in *East European national minorities: 1919–1980: a handbook*, p.309–313. S. M. Horak (ed). Littleton, CO: Libraries Unlimited, 1985.

Nazione e religione in Albania (1920–1944). R. Morozzo Della Rocca. Bologna: Il Mulino, 1990. 253p.

P. Giovanni Fausti, S.I., martire in Albania: un precursore del dialogo islamico–cristiano. A. Guidetti. Rome: Edizioni 'La Civiltà Cattolica', 1974. 233p.

'Persecution of religion in communist Albania,' R. Krasniqi, *ACEN news*, (Mar–Apr 1967), 17–20.

Populli mposht fenë. M. Xhafa. Tiranë: Shtëpia Botuese '8 Nëntori', 1978. 75p.

'Religion in Albania during the Ottoman rule,' S. Skendi, *Südost Forschungen*, 15 (1956), 311–27.

'Religious persecution in Albania,' B. Tonnes, *Religion in Communist lands*, 10, 3 (Autumn 1982), 242ff.

Skanderbegs Erben: Christen in Albanien. S. Jung. Uhldingen: Stephanus-Edition Verlags, 1990. 130p.

'The Catholic Church in Albania: from the time of the Apostles to the present,' *Albanian Catholic review*, 5 (1984), 4–25.

The fulfilled promise: a documentary account of religious persecution in Albania. G. Sinishta. Santa Clara, CA: Albanian Catholic Information Center, 1976. 234p.

The furtherance and afflictions of the gospel: evangelism, blessing and intolerance in Albania, 1935–1940. E. E. Jacques. : Albanian Evangelical Trust, 1988. 40p.

To Lykophos ton Theon stin Alvania (The twilight of the gods in Albania). Chicago: Panepirotic Federation of America and Canada, 1976. 72p.

Country Table 2. **Organized churches and denominations in Albania.**

Official name (bold type = church with over 10% of all affiliated) 1	*Begun* 2	*Type* 3	*Counc* 4	*Congs* 5	*Adults* 6	*Affiliated 1970* 7	*Affiliated 1995* 8	*G%* 9	*Names, notes, and other statistics* (see Codebook, Part 3) 10
Albanian Orthodox Church	c70	O-Alb	M....	600	144,000	100,000	400,000	0.05	Suppressed 1967, restored 1991. 4 Eparchies: Tirana, Berat, Gjirokastër, Korçë. Tosks in south.
Assemblies of God	c1960	P-Pe2	.....	15	1,200	400	2,400	7.43	20-year history of clandestine scripture distribution. M=AoG(USA, France, Italy, UK).
Baptist Churches	c1990	P-Bap	T....	5	2,100	–	3,000	20.00	Begun and supported by M=BUGB,SBC-IMB(USA).
Broadsheet Readers' Clubs	c1990	I-3nW	.....	21	400	–	1,000	20.00	Readers of Gospel Broadsheets produced by M=WEC(UK).
Catholic Church in Albania:	385	R-Lat	P....	83	260,000	70,000	492,201	0.06	Suppressed 1969, until 1991. Ghegs. 25n 33x 37m 150w 3595Yy
M Shkodre (Scutari)	385	R-Lat	P	27	120,000	29,300	240,000	0.06	Northwest border with Yugoslavia. 11n 10x 12m 39w 1180Yy
D Lezhe (Lesh)	c1350	R-Lat	P	10	24,000	7,000	42,000	7.43	North of Durres. 1n 0x 0m 0w 420Yy
D Pult (Pulati)	c850	R-Lat	Pofm	25	18,000	5,000	28,530	0.09	In far north adjoining Montenegro. 0n 1x 1m 0w 1150Yy
D Sape	1062	R-Lat	P	4	84,300	25,000	158,500	7.67	Adjoining Scutari to the south. 4n 2x 2m 3w 440Yy
AD Durres-Tirana	c1250	R-Lat	P	11	9,000	2,000	15,000	8.39	Port adjacent to capital, Tirana. 4n 15x 16m 62w 100Yy
AN Orosh	1939	R-Lat	P	1	4,000	1,500	7,050	6.39	*Shen Llezhri i Oroshit.* North central. 1n 0x 0m 0w 180Yy
AA Albania Meridionale	1939	R-Lat	Ofdp	5	700	200	1,121	7.14	Under Congregation for the Oriental South. 4n 5x 6m 46w 125Yy
Christ Groups	c1992	I-3hW	x....	6	300	–	1,000	33.33	Isolated believers as result of nationwide EHC campaign (Every Home for Christ).
Christian Brethren	1990	P-CBr	x....	6	350	–	550	20.00	M=Christian Ch of the Brethren, Italy. Plymouth (Open) Brethren.
Ch of Jesus Christ of Latter-day Saints	1990	m-LdS	x....	2	200	–	300	20.00	*Mormons.* M=CJCLdS(USA).
Church of the Evangelical Brotherhood	1938	I-Bap	.....	17	500	200	750	5.43	M=CBFMS. HQ=Korçe. Revived 1990.
Church of the Nazarene	c1990	P-Hol	.....	2	20	–	40	20.00	Social and evangelistic work after collapse of Communism. M=CON(USA),EHC.
Cornerstone Church	c1991	I-3cW	x....	10	800	–	2,000	25.00	Charismatic Mennonites. M=Cornerstone Mennonite Ch (USA).
Disciples of Jesus	c1990	I-3cW	.....	10	100	–	240	20.00	Sizeable involvement in every-home campaigns. M=FI,EHCA(EHCI).
Discipleship Church	c1985	I-3cW	.....	10	90	–	150	10.00	Evangelistic every-home ministries. M=OM,EHC.
Greek Orthodox Church	c1980	O-Gre	C....	30	21,000	–	35,000	6.67	Citizens, alien residents, and transients of Greek ethnicity.
Isolated radio churches	c1960	I-3rW	.....	30	500	200	1,000	6.65	Isolated radio believers following Protestant programs (TWR), Radio Vatican, OD, IBRA.
Jehovah's Witnesses	1925	m-Jeh	x....	25	5,250	100	9,417	19.94	Active witnessing by 1926. Forced underground. From 1990, aggressive resurgence. 273Y.
Methodist Church	c1920	P-Met	.....	1	70	100	150	1.64	Formerly in Yugoslav Mission, related to USA Methodism through C & S Europe CC.
New Apostolic Church	c1990	I-3aX	x....	10	500	–	1,560	20.00	*NAC,NAK.* M=Neuapostolische Kirche (HQ Zurich, Switzerland).
Romanian Orthodox Church	1990	O-Rum	C....	6	18,000	–	30,000	20.00	Citizens and aliens of Romanian ethnicity.
Serbian Orthodox Church: V Shkodër	1922	O-Ser	Cw...	2	1,800	1,000	3,000	4.49	*Srpska Pravoslavna Crkva.* Under P Belgrade. Diocese until 1939.
Seventh-day Adventist Church	1903	P-Adv	x....	1	30	30	90	4.49	*SDA*, formerly part of Greek Mission, Southern European Union Mission.
Way of Peace Church	c1970	P-Non	.....	1	20	–	50	16.94	*European Christian Mission.* M=ECM,EHC.
Word of Life Church	1981	I-3pW	.....	20	4,000	–	8,000	7.14	Rapidly-growing pentecostal bodies. M=SFM,NPY(Norway),Netherlands Pentecostals.
Other charismatic churches	1991	I-3cW	.....	50	15,000	–	30,000	25.00	Emmanual Church (M=Ichthus), Rebirth Church, Assembly Hall Churches (1 ch).
Other pentecostal churches	1991	I-3pW	.....	12	350	–	583	25.00	M=YWAM, Ichthus Fellowship (UK), other Swedish, USA, German Pentecostals, OM.
Other Protestant denominations	1990	P-	.....	30	4,000	–	10,000	20.00	Including: Church of God (Cleveland).
Totals				**1,005**	**480,580**	**172,030**	**1,032,481**		

Churches, members, growth, 1900-2025	*Congs*	*Adults*	*Affiliated*	*G%*	*Total denominations*	*6 Megablocs:* O	*R*	*A*	*P*	*I*	*m*
Total churches, members, and denominations (mid-1900)	300	133,000	226,500	-0.39	2	1	1	0	0	0	0
Total churches, members, and denominations (mid-1970)	619	101,130	172,030	-0.39	9	2	1	0	3	2	1
Total churches, members, and denominations (mid-1990)	900	363,000	780,000	7.85	13	4	1	0	4	3	1
Total churches, members, and denominations (mid-1995)	1,005	480,580	1,032,481	5.77	37	4	1	0	9	21	2
Total churches, members, and denominations (mid-2000)	1,010	498,000	1,070,390	0.72	51	4	1	0	15	27	4
Total churches, members, and denominations (mid-2025)	2,000	763,000	1,640,000	1.72	97	10	1	0	30	50	6

NOTES ON TABLE ABOVE
NATIONAL COUNCILS (Column 4, 5th letter).
C = Albanian Encouragement Project (begun 1991).
E = Albanian Evangelical Alliance (AEA).
R = Conferenza Episcopale dell'Albania (Episcopal Conference of Albania).

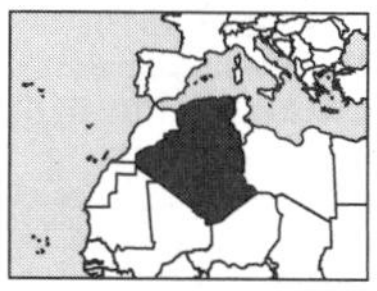

ALGERIA

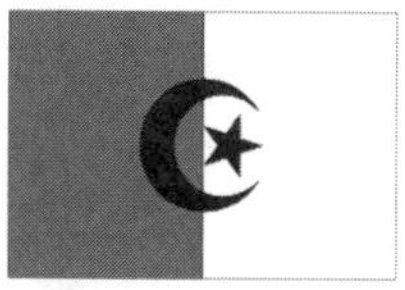

SECULAR DATA, AD 2000

STATE
Official name: Al-Jumhuriya al-Jazairiya ad-Dimuqratiya ash-Shabiya (The Democratic and Popular Republic of Algeria).
Short name: Algeria. **Adjective of nationality:** Algerian.
Flag: Green and white bars, centered red crescent enclosing red star.
Area: 2,381,741 sq. km. (919,595 sq. mi.).
Government: Multiparty republic with two legislative bodies since 1991 (c1500 Ottoman rule, 1848 French colony and later department, 1958 French military junta, 1962 Independence as republic, 1965 Socialist military junta).
Legislature: National People's Assembly, 380 members; Council of Nation, 144 members.
Official language: Arabic.
Monetary unit: 1 Algerian dinar (DA) = 100 centimes. **US$1=** DA 57.33.
Chief cities: EL DJAZAIR (Alger, Algiers) 4,447,000; Oran (Wahran, Ouahran) 1,042,905; Qacentina (Constantine) 593,997; Annaba (Bone, Bona) 411,670; Blida (El-Boulaida) 303,278.
Political divisions: 48 provinces.
Armed forces: 122,000.

DEMOGRAPHY
Population: 31,471,000.
Population density: 13.2/sq. km. (34.2/sq. mi.).
Under 15 years: 11,531,000.
Growth rate p.a.: 2.11% (births 26.72, deaths 5.08).
Mortality: Infant, per 1,000: 36.8; **Maternal per 100,000:** 160.0.
Life expectancy: 70 (male 69, female 72).
Household size: 6.9. **Floor area per person, sq.m:** 7.0.
Major languages: Arabic, French, Kabyle, Tuareg, Tamahaq, Russian, and 15 other languages.
Urban dwellers: 59.27%. **Urban growth rate p.a.:** 3.20%.
Labor force: 24%.

ETHNOLINGUISTIC PEOPLES
59.1% Algerian Arab; 6.9% Hamyan Bedouin; 6.1% Greater Kabyle (Western); 5.2% Shawiya (Chaouia); 4.1% Tajakant Bedouin.

ECONOMY
National income p.a. per person: US$1,600; **per family:** US$11,039.

EDUCATION
Adult literacy: 61% (male 73%, female 49%). **Schools:** 17,372.
Universities: 40. **School enrolment:** female/male: 79%/89%.

HEALTH
Access to health services: 98%. **Access to safe water:** 78%.
Hospitals: 284 (22 beds per 10,000). **Doctors:** 25,304.
Blind: 25,000. **Deaf:** 1,895,900. **Murder rate:** 1.
Lepers: 44,000. **Underweight prevalence under 5:** 13%.

LITERATURE
New book titles p.a.: 310 (10 p.a. per million). **Periodicals:** 67.
Newspapers: 6 dailies.

COMMUNICATION (per 1,000 people)
Phones: 42 (1% mobile). **Radios:** 125. **TV sets:** 71.
Daily newspaper circulation: 46. **Computers:** 7.

REFUGEES
Alien refugees from other countries: 120,000.

HUMAN LIFE AND LIBERTY (optimum condition=100.0%)
HDI: 73.7. **HSI:** 46.0. **HFI:** 20.0. **EFL:** 35.0.

Country Table 1. Religious adherents in Algeria, AD 1900-2025.

Year	1900		1970		mid-1990		Annual change, 1990-2000				mid-1995		mid-2000		mid-2025	
Name	Adherents	%	Adherents	%	Adherents	%	Natural	Conversion	Total	Rate	Adherents	%	Adherents	%	Adherents	%
Muslims	3,983,000	86.6	13,614,870	99.0	24,146,000	96.8	632,796	-3,258	629,538	2.34	27,134,420	96.7	30,441,669	96.7	44,667,300	95.8
Nonreligious	3,000	0.1	20,000	0.2	720,000	2.9	18,869	3,978	22,847	2.79	847,000	3.0	948,471	3.0	1,800,000	3.9
Christians	**563,000**	**12.2**	**105,430**	**0.8**	**78,400**	**0.3**	**2,055**	**-800**	**1,255**	**1.50**	**85,500**	**0.3**	**90,952**	**0.3**	**159,000**	**0.3**
PROFESSION																
crypto-Christians	0	0.0	30,000	0.2	50,000	0.2	1,310	690	2,000	3.42	60,000	0.2	70,000	0.2	130,000	0.3
professing Christians	**563,000**	**12.2**	**75,430**	**0.6**	**28,400**	**0.1**	**744**	**-1,489**	**-745**	**-3.00**	**25,500**	**0.1**	**20,952**	**0.1**	**29,000**	**0.1**
AFFILIATION																
unaffiliated Christians	5,700	0.1	0	0.0	130	0.0	3	-9	-6	-5.35	94	0.0	75	0.0	800	0.0
affiliated Christians	**557,300**	**12.1**	**105,430**	**0.8**	**78,270**	**0.3**	**2,051**	**-790**	**1,261**	**1.50**	**85,406**	**0.3**	**90,877**	**0.3**	**158,200**	**0.3**
Independents	0	0.0	20,500	0.2	47,000	0.2	1,232	568	1,800	3.30	56,040	0.2	65,000	0.2	125,000	0.3
Roman Catholics	544,000	11.8	76,500	0.6	25,000	0.1	655	-1,127	-472	-2.07	23,300	0.1	20,277	0.1	25,000	0.1
Protestants	13,000	0.3	4,850	0.0	3,950	0.0	104	-159	-55	-1.49	3,828	0.0	3,400	0.0	4,500	0.0
Orthodox	200	0.0	2,730	0.0	2,000	0.0	52	-72	-20	-1.05	1,900	0.0	1,800	0.0	2,500	0.0
Anglicans	100	0.0	800	0.0	200	0.0	5	-5	0	0.00	200	0.0	200	0.0	200	0.0
Marginal Christians	0	0.0	50	0.0	120	0.0	3	5	8	5.24	138	0.0	200	0.0	1,000	0.0
Trans-megabloc groupings																
Evangelicals	500	0.0	2,700	0.0	4,000	0.0	105	65	170	3.61	5,071	0.0	5,700	0.0	8,000	0.0
Pentecostals/Charismatics	0	0.0	21,500	0.2	41,000	0.2	1,074	326	1,400	2.98	45,505	0.2	55,000	0.2	100,000	0.2
Great Commission Christians	**40,000**	**0.9**	**50,000**	**0.4**	**55,000**	**0.2**	**1,441**	**-431**	**1,010**	**1.70**	**60,000**	**0.2**	**65,098**	**0.2**	**100,000**	**0.2**
Atheists	1,000	0.0	4,000	0.0	4,000	0.0	105	-109	-4	-0.11	4,000	0.0	3,958	0.0	3,000	0.0
Baha'is	0	0.0	700	0.0	2,000	0.0	52	29	81	3.44	2,500	0.0	2,806	0.0	6,000	0.0
Jews	50,000	1.1	1,000	0.0	600	0.0	16	-19	-3	-0.58	580	0.0	566	0.0	700	0.0
doubly-counted religionists	0	0.0	0	0.0	-15,000	-0.1	-393	179	-214	1.34	-16,000	-0.1	-17,144	-0.1	-25,000	-0.1
World A (unevangelized persons)	3,910,000	85.0	10,447,099	76.0	13,989,096	56.1	366,899	-179,298	187,601	1.27	14,842,876	52.9	15,892,855	50.5	21,021,561	45.1
World B (evangelized non-Christians)	127,000	2.8	3,193,654	23.2	10,868,504	43.6	284,546	180,098	464,644	3.60	13,129,991	46.8	15,487,193	49.2	25,430,439	54.6
World C (Christians)	563,000	12.2	105,430	0.8	78,400	0.3	2,055	-800	1,255	1.50	85,500	0.3	90,952	0.3	159,000	0.3
Country's population	**4,600,000**	**100.0**	**13,746,184**	**100.0**	**24,936,000**	**100.0**	**653,500**	**0**	**653,500**	**2.35**	**28,058,368**	**100.0**	**31,471,000**	**100.0**	**46,611,000**	**100.0**

COLUMNS, ROWS.
For meanings and definitions, see Codebook (Part 3). Note that, by definition, total 'Christians' = professing + crypto-Christians, which also = affiliated + unaffiliated Christians, and also = Great Commission Christians + latent Christians. Percentages may not always total exactly, due to rounding.

CENSUSES.
1856: 92.7% Muslims, 6.3% Christians, 1.0% Jews and others. **1876:** 87.7% Muslims, 11.2% Christians, 1.1% Jews. **1896:** 86.7% Muslims, 12.2% Christians, 1.1% Jews. **1906:** 86.8% Muslims, 12.1% Christians, 1.1% Jews. **1921:** 86.1% Muslims, 12.7% Christians, 1.2% Jews. **1931:** 86.4% Muslims, 12.4% Christians, 1.2% Jews. **1936:** 86.8% Muslims, 12.0% Christians, 1.2% Jews. **31.x.1948** (de jure, excluding military: 89.3% Muslims, 9.4% Christians, 1.3% Jews. **31.X.1954** (de jure): 89.6% Muslims, 9.1% Christians, 1.3% Jews. **15.IX.1960:** 89.7% Muslims, 9.0% Christians, 1.3% Jews.

NOTES ON RELIGIONS
INDEPENDENTS. Isolated radio believers (see Table 2); mainly Arabs, with some Berbers.
ATHEISTS. Mainly French expatriates. Algerian Communist Party (ACP) (proscribed 1962; pro-Soviet), succeeded by the Socialist Vanguard Party (SVP).
BAHA'IS. Expansion has been checked by waves of persecution and the expulsion of 16 Persian missionaries; all activity is still banned, since the 1970s.
COUNTRY'S POPULATION. Settlers from France began arriving after 1830, and numbered 7% of the population by 1856, 13% by 1900, and 10% in 1960; of these, 95% (850,000) returned to France in 1962. During the war years 1954-62, an estimated 1 million Algerians and 20,000 French soldiers were killed.
CRYPTO-CHRISTIANS. Arabs and Berbers. Unorganized individual nationals in the recognized churches, with many organized and unorganized isolated radio believers. In addition to the figure shown, some 17,000 Muslims are believed to have recently become hidden or isolated believers in Christ as Lord.
JEWS. In 1962, 125,000 of the 140,000 Algerian Jews of French nationality emigrated to France; most of the rest have subsequently left for Israel.
MUSLIMS. 99% Sunnis (of the Malikite rite, with some of Hanafite rite), 0.6% Ibadi (Kharijite) (in oasis of Mzab). Religious orders: Qadiriy, Shadhilzya, Rahmaniya, Alawiya, Darqawiya, Tijaniya, Hamalliya et alia. The Kabyle (Arabic for 'those who after lengthy resistance accepted Islam', 2.5 million, Berbers) were Christians before the 8th-century Muslims conquest, and are the only tribe in the once-Christian Maghreb to have in any way responded to the Christian faith in the present century; before the Franco-Algerian war and Independence in 1962, there were 200 Kabyle Protestants (mainly Methodists) and 3,000 Catholics. Over the past century the Kabyle have experienced waves of Muslim religious movements called zawiyas (confraternity, prayer house, mutual aid society). *Hajj pilgrims to Mecca.* (1970) 3,960; (1974) 49,028; (1975) 55,010; (1976) 34,150.
UNAFFILIATED CHRISTIANS. Before Independence in 1962, a small proportion of all French settlers were professing Catholics but unaffiliated to the Catholic Church.
PROFESSING CHRISTIANS. Mainly Europeans, both before and after Independence in 1962.
ROMAN CATHOLICS. In the year 1900, all were French except 811 indigenous baptized Catholics and 164 catechumens.

Great Commission Instrument Panel: status of Algeria (for explanation see start of Part 4)

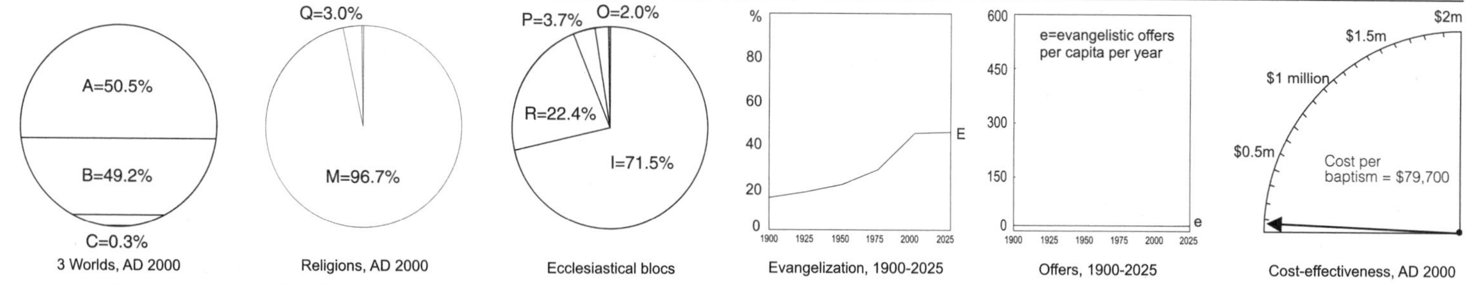

Country status. Algeria forms an integral part of a region called the Jazirat al Maghrib ('Island of the West') or the land between the 'Sea of Sand', i.e. the Sahara and the Mediterranean Sea. Algerians share common bonds of history, language, and religion with their Maghribi neighbors, Tunisians, and Moroccans.

HUMAN LIFE AND LIBERTY

Human need and development. Algeria's more than 31 million people are living in a period of rapid change. The population is made up of indigenous

Berber stock and Arabs, but the distinction between Arab and Berber is becoming less significant. The traditional extended family system is being replaced by the nuclear family, and the importance of traditional tribal values and organization is on the wane. The country's massive oil wealth has made little difference in the lives of the people. Chronic unemployment, high rate of illiteracy in the countryside, and limited industrialization have helped to create a large underclass whose discontents periodically erupt into political violence. The former safety valve of emigration to France has been closed for many years.

Human rights and freedoms. The 1989 Constitution was a democratic one which guaranteed basic human rights. Almost all these rights have been revoked following the suspension of the democratic government and the imposition of an authoritarian regime in 1992. Black Algerians face social discrimination at all levels of society and are forced into the most menial jobs. Historically, Berber ethnicity has been suppressed by the dominant Arabs. The teaching and propagation of Tamazight or Berber language is not allowed in schools. The nomadic Tuaregs in the southern desert region face economic and social difficulties and the disruption of their traditional mode of life. Women's rights are restricted by law, and they face discrimination in the workplace, home, and society. Women's rights are under constant attack from Islamic fundamentalists and from jurists. Under the 1984 family code women are 'perpetual minors', who, regardless of their age or civil status, remain under the legal guardianship of their husband or father. The code permits polygamy (which is more prevalent in the countryside than in the cities because of housing shortage), and makes it more difficult for a woman than for a man to obtain a divorce. Increasingly, women are pressured to wear Islamic headcovering (hidjab) and women in Western dress are occasionally spat upon in the streets. There are continued efforts to ban women's sports, women's swimming, coeducation, and to bar women from the workplace.

Ever since the death of Houari Boumedienne, Algerian society has been divided into 2 warring camps with the Islamic fundamentalists on one side and the secularists on the other. In the resulting violence, all human freedoms have suffered. During the State of Siege proclaimed by the High Security Council, thousands were arrested and detained, and a number of deaths were caused by the excessive use of police force. Press freedoms also have been curtailed. There is a formal state monopoly on the news through a holding company that owns all major newspapers and magazines. The Constitution provides for an independent judiciary, but this independence is largely circumvented in cases prosecuted under the State of Siege. There are no Islamic courts.

Human environment. Nearly 80% of Algeria is desert, wasteland, and mountains. The vast majority of the people live on the narrow coastal plain, 45% of them in the urban areas. Desertification has increased in recent years as a result of soil erosion, overgrazing and destruction of vegetation. Water is scarce and droughts are common. Sewage treatment is rare and tap water is not usually potable. As a result of water pollution, waterborne diseases are common. Industrial effluents are often dumped untreated into rivers or reservoirs. Unchecked migration into the cities has created a severe housing shortage. Rural migrants generally live in bidonvilles, so called because they are built of bidons or tin cans. The bidonville population of Algiers alone is estimated at over half a million. The most common rural dwelling is the gourbi which is built of mud and branches.

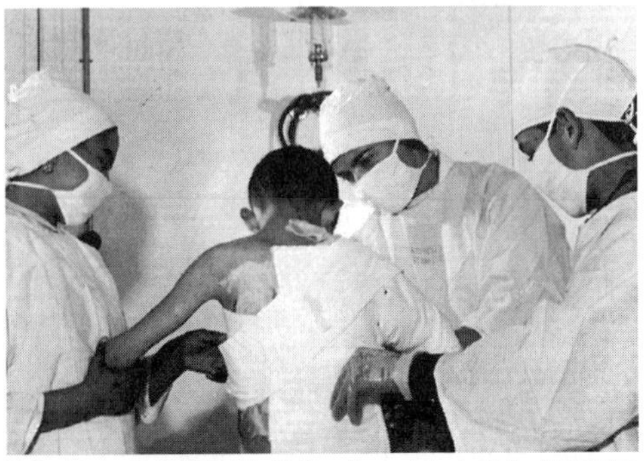

Eglise Protestante d'Algérie. Staff and burn victim in Methodist Il-Maten hospital begun 1964.

NON-CHRISTIAN RELIGIONS

Islam is now the predominant and official religion of Algeria. The overwhelming majority are Sunnis of the Malikite rite, except for a few elderly Turks and Moors, who are Hanafites. A small number (about 80,000) are Kharijite-Ibadites found mostly in the south. They maintain contact with the Kharjite islands of Africa (Djerba in Tunisia, Djebel Nefoussa in Libya) and Oman in Asia, who send their students to study at the Institute al-Haya (Life) of Guerara in Oasis province. For the last 8 centuries, Sunni religious brotherhoods have played an important part in the religious formation and islamization of the countryside. Their influence was considerably reduced by the efforts of reformers (especially those of the Association of Ulama founded in 1931), the progress of modern education, and changes resulting from the long struggle for national liberation (1954-1962). These 3 factors helped prepare the way for a renewal of Algerian Islam. Nonetheless, the Tijaniya brotherhood continues its influence in Black Africa. The FLN party, which ruled Algeria from independence until 1992, adopted for itself the reformist Islam credo, 'Islam is our religion, Arabic is our language, Algeria is our fatherland.' The spread of Muslim religious teaching and Arab-Muslim culture, hindered previously by the French administration, is today advanced by the national press, radio and television, by schools and mosques, by mass meetings, and in general by all national organizations including scouts and women's unions. The family and village nevertheless continue to play an important part in life, a fact which results in the persistence of many superstitions of agrarian origin, especially among Berber women. In 1970, the government secularized 3,000 mosques into 'centres of instruction' for adult literacy work. During 1974, 49,028 Muslim pilgrims from Algeria performed the Hajj to Mecca. Dissident voices, with both religious and political messages, were heard more and more in the 1970s. In the 1980s, fundamentalist Islam grew to be the nation's strongest political and social force. Women were harassed for not adhering to Muslim standards of dress. Restaurants and places selling alcohol were attacked. The government evicted certain imams from mosques and seminaries. In 1984 a fundamentalist guerilla movement began, and in 1989 the FIS (Front islamique du Salut or Islamic Salvation Front) was founded. After its stirring successes in elections in 1990 and 1991, martial law was declared, parliament was dissolved, a High Council of State began to rule, and Islam was at the center of a national catastrophe of social and political violence. The parts of the country controlled by the FIS are under strict fundamentalist observance.

Judaism came first from Palestine in Roman times, though most Jews in Algeria have been descendants of refugees from Spain in the 15th century. Before 1962 Algeria had 140,000 Jews, but then most migrated to Israel. By 1970 only 1000 were left, and by 1995, only 500. In 1977 the only remaining synagogue was ransacked by youths.

CHRISTIANITY

Christianity spread among the Latin-speaking people of Algeria's northern cities at the end of the 1st and the beginning of the 2nd centuries, and subsequently produced some of the church's most eminent theologians: Tertullian, Cyprian, and Augustine of Hippo (Annaba today). After Constantine, Christianity's favor was hindered by its association with Rome. Also, Augustine's attack on Donatism had the effect of turning many Berbers from Christianity, as they had identified themselves with this movement. Weakened by theological disputes and Berber revolts, the area fell before the Vandals in 429 and became subject to Arab Muslims in 702. The Moors extended their empire into Spain, with Ottoman Islamic forces halting the thrust of Spanish Christians pushing back into Africa in 1556. France entered Algeria in 1830, made northern Algeria a part of France in 1848, and French settlers rapidly increased in numbers. By 1900 the government had settled 200,000 Europeans, most of them Christian, in fertile lands and 400,000 in newly-founded towns and cities. Open revolt against French rule developed in 1954, and independence was achieved in 1962. During colonial rule, Christianity played an important role in Algeria, but few of the indigenous peoples became Christians. With the exodus of Europeans, Christian influence has been radically reduced.

This process was accelerated in 1964, when 60 expatriates were killed in the cross-fire of social and political strife. Most countries withdrew all of their citizens from Algeria. The sole Christian bookstore in the country was closed in 1994 due to threats.

CATHOLIC CHURCH. In 1838 Algeria became an episcopal see under Aix-en-Provence in France, but the French government forbade all Christian missionary activity among Muslims. Napoleon accepted the principle of religious freedom when Charles Lavigerie, founder of the White Fathers, became archbishop of Algeria in 1867, but missionary efforts achieved little permanent success.

In general one can now distinguish 5 kinds of Catholics: (1) former French colonials who have not yet emigrated (of the 950,000 such Catholics in 1961, about 90% had left the country by 1963); (2) Europeans working in national or foreign enterprises, living in Algeria for a limited period (90% French, with a growing number of other Europeans both Eastern and Western); (3) around 2,500 Europeans who have taken Algerian nationality (technicians, wives of Algerians, and also 5 of the 6 Catholic bishops); (4) several hundred native Algerians (many of the 10,000 who before 1954 emigrated to France); and (5) a growing number of Christians from the Middle East and political refugees from Black Africa and Latin America. Since independence in 1962, the Catholic Church has been drastically reduced numerically, but its new commitment to service in a Muslim milieu was widely noted. The personality and actions of the cardinal archbishop of Algiers, both during the war of liberation and subsequently, helped greatly towards the establishment of good Muslim-Christian relations for several years. In the 1970s, more than 1,000 clergy and nuns served the Algerian people and nation in a variety of fields, including medicine, engineering, architecture, and education. Diocesan schools all followed the arabization program of the government.

The Holy See has diplomatic relations with Algeria and in AD 2000 is represented to government and the Catholic hierarchy by a pro-nuncio residing in Algiers.

PROTESTANT CHURCHES. The first Protestant groups to enter Algeria were the French McCall Mission (1830) and the Basel Mission, but their work did not endure. The North Africa Mission was established in 1881 and continued to recent years. Other early missions include Open Brethren, Mission Rolland, Seventh-day Adventists and American Methodists.

Methodists carried on an effective youth hostel work as well as operating a dispensary at Les Ouaohias and a modern hospital at Il-Maten from 1964. In 1973 they united with the Reformed Church, which has been ministering mainly to French expatriates, to form the Protestant Church in Algeria. The Open Brethren and North Africa Mission concentrated on Bible correspondence courses. A number of independent faith missions began in various areas, but their influence was small.

Protestantism remains small, a presence and witness but little more. Of the few native Algerians to become Christians, most have been Kabyles; and of these the majority have emigrated to France since independence due to local hostility.

ORTHODOX CHURCHES. Although there are no priests, members of 4 different Orthodox churches are found in Algeria; 2 Chalcedonian (Greek and Russian) and 2 in the Oriental Monophysite tradition (Coptic and Jacobite). The Copts form the largest community.

Renewal movements. In the 1990s the Pentecostal/Charismatic Renewal continued to spread rapidly across most older churches, and numbered over 55,000 adherents (of whom 0% Pentecostals, 3% Charismatics, and 97% Independents).

Christians. Two renowned pioneers: *(left)* Augustine (AD 354-430) and *(center)* Charles de Foucauld.

Country summary. **Worlds A, B, C by ethnolinguistic peoples, cities, and major civil divisions in Algeria.**

	PEOPLES							CITIES							CIVIL DIVISIONS						
World	Num	Pop 2000	C%	Christians	E%	U%	Unevangelized	Num	Pop 2000	C%	Christians	E%	U%	Unevangelized	Num	Pop 2000	C%	Christians	E%	U%	Unevangelized
A	36	11,858,059	0.10	11,648	30	70	8,263,075	34	3,692,793	0.04	1,557	46	54	2,010,558	35	17,883,699	0.01	1,788	41	59	10,503,094
B	3	19,573,910	0.25	48,453	61	39	7,612,845	10	7,657,094	0.73	56,020	55	45	3,428,257	13	13,587,575	0.66	89,089	60	40	5,372,908
C	5	39,308	78.30	30,777	100	0	86	0	0	0.00	0	0	0	0	0	0	0.00	0	0	0	0
Total	**44**	**31,471,277**	**0.29**	**90,878**	**50**	**50**	**15,876,006**	**44**	**11,349,887**	**0.51**	**57,577**	**52**	**48**	**5,438,815**	**48**	**31,471,274**	**0.29**	**90,877**	**50**	**50**	**15,876,002**

Indigenous missions. Algerians are now spread throughout most of Europe, but there are very few Christians among them and very little cross-cultural mission to other peoples.

CHURCH AND STATE

Article 4 of the constitution of 8 September 1963 states that Islam is the state religion and that the republic 'guarantees to everyone respect for his opinions and beliefs and the free exercise of worship'.

Article 10, defining the fundamental objectives of the Algerian republic, mentions among these 'the struggle against all discrimination, especially that founded on race and religion'.

The Christian churches have no legal status in Algeria. Controversial questions are dealt with amicably by direct contact with the competent civil authorities. Nevertheless, the state has passed legislation of significance for Christians, including: (1) an order of 21 March 1968 concerning the status of private education, followed by a decree of 14 February 1970 defining the authorized categories of private institutions (all categories except those of higher education); (2) a decree of 6 December 1969 giving government allowances to all ministers of any religion who hold Algerian nationality; and (3) an official communique declaring Christian festivals as holidays for Christian personnel both Algerian and foreign.

The state is particularly vigilant in its efforts to preserve youth from influences considered incompatible with family traditions; national organizations alone may create movements or undertake educational campaigns. Certain Christian groups, notably the Methodist Church and Jehovah's Witnesses, have had leaders and faithful deported, allegedly for having infringed these principles.

BROADCASTING AND MEDIA

One out of 4 possess radio receivers, and radio programs have long been a useful method for presenting the Gospel. The national radio network permits Catholic and Protestant programs on major church festivals. From abroad, TWR (Monaco) transmits shortwave programs in Berber, Arabic and French; these are particularly effective among Berbers who value their radios highly. These programs receive contributions from 15 agencies and include music, Bible studies, apologetics, and dramas. IBRA broadcasts half-hour Arabic-language programs from Portugal; these are designed for college-age Muslims, and contain sermons, songs, dramas and testimonies. Arabic-language programs by HCJB and AWR can also be received. This concerted radio effort has yielded thousands of converts, and there is a wide partnership which has a comprehensive strategy of preparing radio programs, evangelistic and discipling literature, and follow-up programs.

Television receivers are not as common; nevertheless, results are still to be had. Satellite TV and radio programs are received in English, Arabic, German and Italian. Some examples include CBN's animated programs *Superbook* and *Micah's Christmas Treasure.*

The 'Jesus' Film has been shown on average 10 times daily to small groups. Chiefly through film teams (286,000), 796,000 have seen it. It was shown on television with an audience of 500,000. Some 7,000 have responded with decisions.

INTERDENOMINATIONAL ORGANIZATIONS

In 1940 an Evangelical Mission Council was established; but following its re-organization in 1964 as the Association of Protestant Churches and Institutions in Algeria, several member bodies left due to its connections with the World Council of Churches. In 1963 Protestant churches began a significant ecumenical social service project including reafforestation and school lunch programs, termed the Christian Committee for Service to Refugees (CCSR), which by 1972 had become the Christian Committee for Service in Algeria (CCSA). Staff were engaged in a number of development and social service activities, working under government auspices. Another cooperative activity also with Catholic support has been the Christian Centre for Maghrebine Studies in Algiers which has an extensive library. Prior to being closed indefinitely by the government after 1970, the center provided opportunities for a study of the religions of the Maghreb, offered courses for Christians studying Islam and facilitated Muslim-Christian dialogue.

FUTURE TRENDS AND PROSPECTS

Muslims are likely to maintain over 96% of population until after the year 2000 when churches among Algerian Arabs may begin to gain strength with the infusion of many radio believers. Muslims would then decline to 95% after 2025.

Nonetheless, with conditions for Christians in Algeria worsening in the near future it is difficult to assess the distant future other than to say that Christianity, in a strong Muslim context, is not expected to grow beyond 1%. However, steady church growth among groups like the Kabyle could elevate that percentage closer to 3-5%.

BIBLIOGRAPHY

Algeria. R. I. Lawless. *World bibliographical series*, vol. 19. Oxford, UK: CLIO Press, 1980. (No separate section on religion; see misc. entries under 'Politics' and 'History').

Algeria: assassination in the name of religion. London: Article 19 (International Centre Against Censorship), 1993. 14p.

Algérie et Sahara: Christianisme et Islam, Le Hoggar, Colomb–Béchar. R. Duvollet. Vesoul: R. Duvollet, [1982]. 260p.

Baal, Christ and Mohammed: religion and revolution in North Africa. J. K. Cooley. New York: Holt, Rinehart & Winston, 1965. 369p.

Chrétiens en Algérie: un souvenir de l'époque coloniale ou l'ébauche d'un nouveau visage de l'église dans le monde? J. J. Perennes. *Série Christianisme, cultures et idéologies.* Paris: Centre Lebret, 1977. 149p.

'Cultural resistance and religious legitimacy in colonial Algeria,' F. Colonna, *Economy and society*, 3, 3 (1974), 233–252.

'Donatism: the last phase,' R. A. Markus, in *Studies in church history*, p.118–126. C. W. Dugmore & C. Duggan (eds). London: Nelson, 1964.

Eglise en Islam: méditation sur l'existence Chrétienne en Algérie. H. Teissier. Paris: Centurion, 1984. 216p.

Islam et Chrétienté en Algérie. L. Lehuraux. Alger: Imprimerie Baconnier, [1957]. 198p.

Islam et nationalisme en Algérie d'après 'El Moudjahid,' organe central du FLN de 1956 à 1962. M. Gadant. *Collection histoire et perspectives méditerranéennes.* Paris: Editions L'Harmattan, 1988. 221p.

La Guerre d'Algérie et les Chrétiens. F. Bédarida & E. Fouilloux (eds). *Cahiers de l'Institut d'histoire du temps présent*, 9. Paris: Institut d'histoire du temps présent, 1988. 188p.

L'imitation des bourreaux de Jésus Christ. F. Mauriac. Paris: Desclée de Brouwer, 1984. 120p.

L'Islam algérien en l'an 1900. E. Doutté. Alger-Mustapha: Giralt, 1900. 181p.

L'Islam dans les cinq pays du maghreb arabe. L. Pruvost. *Dossiers de la C.R.R.M*, no. 6. : Commission pour les Relations Religieuses avec les Musulmans, Conseil Pontifical pour le Dialogue Interreligieux, 1993. 18p.

Missions des Pères Blancs en Tunisie, Algérie, Kabylie, Sahara. A. Philippe. Paris: Dillen, 1931. 146p.

'Muslim socialism in Algeria,' R. Vallin, in *Man, state and society in the contemporary Maghrib*, p.50–64. I. Zartman (ed). London: Pall Mall Press, 1973.

Religion and political structure: remarks on Ibadism in Oman and the Mzab (Algeria). T. Bierschenk. Bielefeld, Germany: University of Bielefeld, 1983. 27p.

Religion, rites et mutations: psychosociologie du sacré en Algérie. N. Toualbi. Alger: Entreprise Nationale du Livre, 1984. 291p.

'Religious dissent in the late Roman Empire: the case of North Africa,' P. R. L. Brown, *History*, 46 (1961), 83–101.

'Situation actuelle de l'Islam maghrébin,' *Maghreb*, 47 (September–October 1971), 30–46.

State and society in Algeria. J. P. Entelis & P. C. Naylor (eds). Boulder, CO: Westview Press, 1992.

The Algerians. P. Bordieu. Trans., A. C. M. Ross. Boston: Beacon Press, 1962.

Country Table 2. **Organized churches and denominations in Algeria.**

Official name (bold type = church with over 10% of all affiliated) 1	Begun 2	Type 3	Counc 4	Congs 5	Adults 6	Affiliated 1970 7	Affiliated 1995 8	G% 9	Names, notes, and other statistics (see Codebook, Part 3) 10
Armée du Salut	1934	P-Sal	xwa.c	3	100	500	300	-2.02	*Salvation Army*, under France Territory. In 5 cities. French officers until 1970.
Assemblées de Dieu	1950	P-Pe2	Z....	1	50	1,000	100	-8.80	*Assemblies of God.* M=Assemblées de Dieu (France). Loss by emigration since 1960.
Eglise Adventiste du Sèptieme Jour	c1905	P-Adv	x....	1	35	200	58	-4.83	*Seventh-day Adventists*, NAfrican Miss, Euro-Africa Div. 83% Arab, 17% Berber. 1x.
Eglise Anglicane (D Egypt)	c1910	A-plu	aw.U.	1	80	800	200	-5.39	*Anglican Church.* All expatriates (UK, USA, Arabs). 1 church in Algiers.
Eglise Catholique en Algerie:	1625	R-Lat	B.SH.	77	14,500	76,500	23,300	-4.64	*Catholic Ch.* 1% Algerians. C=5+2+34. 37n,W=10%. 75n 75x 99m 340w 13Yy
M El-Djezair (Alger, Algiers)	1838	R-Lat	Bs	38	13,000	50,000	21,000	-3.41	Mostly transient foreign workers. 500 Kabyles. 51n 30x 43m 191w 11Yy
D Constantine	1866	R-Lat	Bs	8	300	10,000	500	-11.29	Originally a diocese AD 150. Kabyles, Shawia. 15n 10x 11m 47w 2Yy
D Oran (Ouahran)	1866	R-Lat	Bsp	13	1,000	13,000	1,500	-8.28	Westernmost diocese; coast and Atlas range. 9n 13x 13m 55w 0Yy
D Laghouat	1901	R-Lat	pwf	18	200	3,500	300	-9.36	South, Sahara. Tamahaq area. 35 Algerians. 0n 22x 32m 47w 0Yy
Eglise Evangélique Copte	c1970	P-Ref	RWaN.	1	200	250	500	2.81	*Coptic Evangelical Ch.* Immigrant Egyptian workers. No pastors.
Eglise Neo-Apostolique	c1992	I-3aX	x....	1	28	–	40	33.33	*NAC, NAK.* M=Neuapostolische Kirche (HQ Zurich, Switzerland).
Eglise Orth Copte: D Afrique du Nord	c1965	O-Cop	NwaN.	1	1,000	2,000	1,500	-1.14	*Coptic Orthodox Ch.* Egyptian immigrant workers. No priests.
Eglise Orthodoxe Grecque	1940	O-Ara	Cw.N.	2	50	400	100	-5.39	*Greek Orthodox Ch.* 350 under P Antioch. 50 under P Alexandria. No priests.
Eglise Orthodoxe Russe	c1922	O-Rus	.....	1	50	30	100	4.93	*Russian Orthodox Ch.* White Russian exiles among 6,000 Russians in Algeria.
Eglise Orthodoxe Syrienne	1930	O-Syr	Dw.N.	1	100	300	200	-1.61	*Syrian Orthodox Ch (Jacobites).* Under P Antioch. Syrians. No priests.
Eglise Protestante d'Algérie	c1850	P-Uni	Wu.NC	13	300	1,500	750	-2.73	1908, M=UMC(USA). 1972 union Eglise Réformée de France. French, 200 Kabyles. 4x.
Eglises radiophoniques isolées	1958	I-3rS	.....	700	17,000	19,500	30,000	1.74	Isolated radio believers, most aged 12-25. R=2230 (TWR, RSB), T=103000 (NAM,GMU,ICI).
Frères Larges	c1887	P-CBr	x...C	3	100	100	200	2.81	*Open Brethren.* M=CMML(UK). Algiers, Kabylia, Bourg. 7f.
Hidden Muslim believers in Christ	c1970	I-Mus	.....	100	10,000	–	16,000	47.29	Muslims who accept Christ as Lord but remain in Islamic structures.
Mission Baptiste Evangélique	1950	P-Bap	x...f	2	50	100	100	0.00	M=Ev Baptist Missions (USA). Missionaries expelled in 1970.
Mission Biblique de Ghardaia	1956	P-Non	C	1	20	50	50	0.00	M=Biblical Mission of Ghardaia (France). Among poor nomadic tribes, Ghardaia oasis. lh.
Mission d'Afrique du Nord	1881	P-Eva	xMg.f	10	500	300	1,000	4.93	M=NAM/AWM. 200 Algerians. Bible courses from Marseilles (7000 enrolled). 15f,1Y.
Mission Evangélique au Sahara	1953	P-Eva	C	1	10	50	30	-2.02	M=Sahara Desert Mission (UK, France). At Tamanrasset oasis. Tuareg (Tamahaq).
Mission Evangélique de Médéa	1950	P-Non	C	1	10	50	20	-3.60	*Ev Mission of Medea.* An independent Swiss mission aided by Action Chrétienne en Orient.
Mission Evangélique du Sahara	c1950	P-Hol	C	1	10	50	20	-3.60	*Sahara Ev Mission.* M=Emmanuel Holiness Ch (UK). Tamanrasset oasis.
Mission Rolland	1908	P-Non	C	5	100	200	300	1.64	M=Rolland Mission (France). In Tizi-Ouzou (Kabylie). Kabyles only. 7f,1h.
Témoins de Jéhovah	c1950	m-Jeh	x....	2	55	50	138	4.14	*Jehovah's Witnesses.* First reported activity 1952. Missionaries expelled 1970. 4Y.
Other indigenous churches	c1960	I-3cS	.....	36	9,000	1,000	10,000	9.65	Mainly Kabyles, some Arabs. From visions, *'Jesus'* Film. Largely since 1980.
Other Protestant denominations	c1950	P-	.....	2	200	500	400	-0.89	Total about 8 (see list below); 250 Algerians, 100 Arabs.

Continued overleaf

Country Table 2–concluded

Official name (bold type = church with over 10% of affiliated) 1	*Begun* 2	*Type* 3	*Counc* 4	*Congs* 5	*Adults* 6	*Affiliated 1970* 7	*Affiliated 1995* 8	*G%* 9	*Names, notes, and other statistics* (see Codebook, Part 3) 10
Totals				**967**	**53,548**	**105,430**	**85,406**		

Churches, members, growth, 1900-2025	*Congs*	*Adults*	*Affiliated*	*G%*	*Total denominations*	*6 Megablocs:* O	R	A	P	I	m
Total churches, members, and denominations (mid-1900)	2,000	300,000	557,300	-2.35	4	0	1	0	3	0	0
Total churches, members, and denominations (mid-1970)	677	56,828	105,430	-2.35	26	4	1	1	17	2	1
Total churches, members, and denominations (mid-1990)	700	49,100	78,270	-1.48	35	4	1	1	22	6	1
Total churches, members, and denominations (mid-1995)	967	53,548	85,406	1.76	34	4	1	1	21	6	1
Total churches, members, and denominations (mid-2000)	1,100	57,000	90,877	1.25	33	4	1	1	20	6	1
Total churches, members, and denominations (mid-2025)	2,000	99,200	158,200	2.24	67	10	1	1	30	20	5

NOTES ON TABLE ABOVE
NATIONAL COUNCILS (Column 4, 5th letter).
C = Association des Eglises et Oeuvres Protestantes en Algérie (ADEOPA) (Association of Protestant Churches and activities in Algeria).
E = Evangelical alliance of Algeria.
f = formerly member of C, but withdrew about 1964.
OTHER PROTESTANT DENOMINATIONS. These include: Algeria Mennonite Mission (Mennonite Ch of North America), Communauté Evangélique Indépendante, Fellowship of Independent Missions (Morocco Evangelistic Fellowship) (1950), General Association of Regular Baptists (GARB), Southern Baptist Convention.

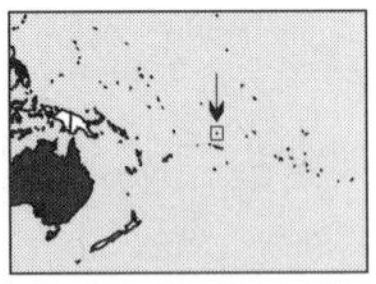

AMERICAN SAMOA

SECULAR DATA, AD 2000

STATE
Official name: The Territory of American Samoa.
Short name: American Samoa. **Adjective of nationality:** American Samoan.
Flag: Blue field, white triangle bordered with red with apex at midpoint of staff; American eagle at right side of triangle.
Area: 199 sq. km. (77 sq. mi.).
Government: Unorganized unincorporated territory of the USA administered under US Department of the Interior, since 1900 (1830 chiefdoms, 1889 monarchy).
Legislature: Senate, 18 members; House of Representatives, 20 members.
Official language: English.
Monetary unit: 1 US dollar = 100 cents. **US$1=** $1.20.
Chief cities: PAGO PAGO (Pango-Pango) 5,973.
Political divisions: 3 provinces.

DEMOGRAPHY
Population: 68,000.
Population density: 342.1/sq. km. (884.2/sq. mi.).
Under 15 years: 26,000.
Growth rate p.a.: 1.85% (births 27.33, deaths 4.64).
Mortality: Infant, per 1,000: 19.3; **Maternal per 100,000:** 30.0.
Life expectancy: 73 (male 71, female 75).
Household size: 7.0. **Floor area per person, sq.m:** 15.0.
Major languages: English, Samoan.
Urban dwellers: 52.70%. **Urban growth rate p.a.:** 3.54%.
Labor force: 30%.

ETHNOLINGUISTIC PEOPLES
80.8% Samoan; 10.0% Euronesian; 4.6% USA White; 1.6% Tongan; 1.0% Filipino.

ECONOMY
National income p.a. per person: US$2,599; **per family:** US$18,196.

EDUCATION
Adult literacy: 95% (male 95%, female 96%). **Schools:** 38.
Universities: 2. **School enrolment:** female/male: 95%/95%.

HEALTH
Access to health services: 80%.
Access to safe water: 80%.
Hospitals: 1 (27 beds per 10,000). **Doctors:** 34.
Blind: 50. **Deaf:** 3,800. **Murder rate:** 8. **Lepers:** 550.

LITERATURE
New book titles p.a.: 34 (500 p.a. per million). **Periodicals:** 10.
Newspapers: 1 daily.

COMMUNICATION (per 1,000 people)
Phones: 136 (10% mobile). **Radios:** 330. **TV sets:** 130.
Daily newspaper circulation: 51. **Computers:** 50.

HUMAN LIFE AND LIBERTY (optimum condition=100.0%)
HDI: 66.7. **HSI:** 75.0. **HFI:** 80.0. **EFL:** 50.0.

Country Table 1. **Religious adherents in American Samoa, AD 1900-2025.**

Year / *Name*	*1900 Adherents*	*%*	*1970 Adherents*	*%*	*mid-1990 Adherents*	*%*	*Annual change, 1990-2000 Natural*	*Conversion*	*Total*	*Rate*	*mid-1995 Adherents*	*%*	*mid-2000 Adherents*	*%*	*mid-2025 Adherents*	*%*
Christians	**5,700**	**100.0**	**27,030**	**99.1**	**45,120**	**96.0**	**2,016**	**-6**	**2,010**	**3.75**	**54,660**	**96.3**	**65,224**	**95.9**	**136,600**	**95.5**
PROFESSION																
professing Christians	**5,700**	**100.0**	**27,030**	**99.1**	**45,120**	**96.0**	**2,016**	**-6**	**2,010**	**3.75**	**54,660**	**96.3**	**65,224**	**95.9**	**136,600**	**95.5**
AFFILIATION																
unaffiliated Christians	60	1.1	410	1.5	5,880	12.5	263	147	410	5.44	8,100	14.3	9,984	14.7	25,200	17.6
affiliated Christians	**5,640**	**99.0**	**26,620**	**97.6**	**39,240**	**83.5**	**1,753**	**-153**	**1,600**	**3.48**	**46,560**	**82.0**	**55,240**	**81.2**	**111,400**	**77.9**
Protestants	5,340	93.7	18,400	67.5	25,460	54.2	1,138	-104	1,034	3.47	29,970	52.8	35,800	52.7	73,000	51.1
Roman Catholics	300	5.3	5,000	18.3	7,300	15.5	326	-109	217	2.64	8,500	15.0	9,470	13.9	17,000	11.9
Marginal Christians	0	0.0	2,450	9.0	5,100	10.9	228	62	290	4.60	6,448	11.4	8,000	11.8	16,000	11.2
Independents	0	0.0	670	2.5	1,240	2.6	55	-1	54	3.68	1,492	2.6	1,780	2.6	5,000	3.5
Anglicans	0	0.0	100	0.4	140	0.3	6	-1	5	3.10	150	0.3	190	0.3	400	0.3
Trans-megabloc groupings																
Evangelicals	1,000	17.5	4,200	15.4	4,200	8.9	188	-63	125	2.64	4,621	8.1	5,450	8.0	10,010	7.0
Pentecostals/Charismatics	0	0.0	1,600	5.9	6,100	13.0	273	107	380	4.96	8,003	14.1	9,900	14.6	23,000	16.1
Great Commission Christians	**570**	**10.0**	**7,000**	**25.7**	**20,300**	**43.2**	**907**	**89**	**996**	**4.07**	**24,900**	**43.9**	**30,261**	**44.5**	**64,350**	**45.0**
Nonreligious	0	0.0	70	0.3	800	1.7	36	19	55	5.40	1,000	1.8	1,354	2.0	3,300	2.3
Baha'is	0	0.0	200	0.7	630	1.3	28	8	36	4.62	780	1.4	990	1.5	2,000	1.4
Buddhists	0	0.0	0	0.0	200	0.4	9	15	24	8.18	300	0.5	439	0.7	900	0.6
Chinese folk-religionists	0	0.0	0	0.0	50	0.1	2	1	3	5.07	60	0.1	82	0.1	200	0.1
World A (unevangelized persons)	0	0.0	0	0.0	188	0.4	8	0	8	4.01	227	0.4	272	0.4	858	0.6
World B (evangelized non-Christians)	0	0.0	238	1.0	1,692	3.2	67	6	73	4.00	1,867	3.4	2,504	3.8	5,542	3.9
World C (Christians)	5,700	100.0	27,030	99.0	45,120	96.0	2,016	-6	2,010	3.75	54,660	96.3	65,224	95.9	136,600	95.5
Country's population	**5,700**	**100.0**	**27,268**	**100.0**	**47,000**	**100.0**	**2,091**	**0**	**2,091**	**3.76**	**56,755**	**100.0**	**68,000**	**100.0**	**143,000**	**100.0**

COLUMNS, ROWS.
For meanings and definitions, see Codebook (Part 3). Note that, by definition, total 'Christians' = professing + crypto-Christians, which also = affiliated + unaffiliated Christians, and also = Great Commission Christians + latent Christians. Percentages may not always total exactly, due to rounding.

CENSUSES.
25.IX.1956: 74.0% Protestants (69.6% Congregationalists, 4.0% Methodists). 15.4% Roman Catholics, 5.7 marginal Protestants, 4.9% other religionists. **1967:** 70.1% Protestants (59.0% Congregationalists, 4.7% Methodists, 3.5% Pentecostals, 2.2% Seventh-day Adventists), 18.3% Roman Catholics, 8.5% marginal Protestants (8.4% Mormons, 0.1% Jehovah's Witnesses), 2.1% Polynesian indigenous, 1.0% other religionists.

NOTES ON RELIGIONS
BAHA'IS. In 2 local spiritual assemblies (1973), increasing to 8 (1997).
INDEPENDENTS. Members of 2 Samoan indigenous churches in 1990 (see Country Table 2).

Great Commission Instrument Panel: status of American Samoa (for explanation see start of Part 4)

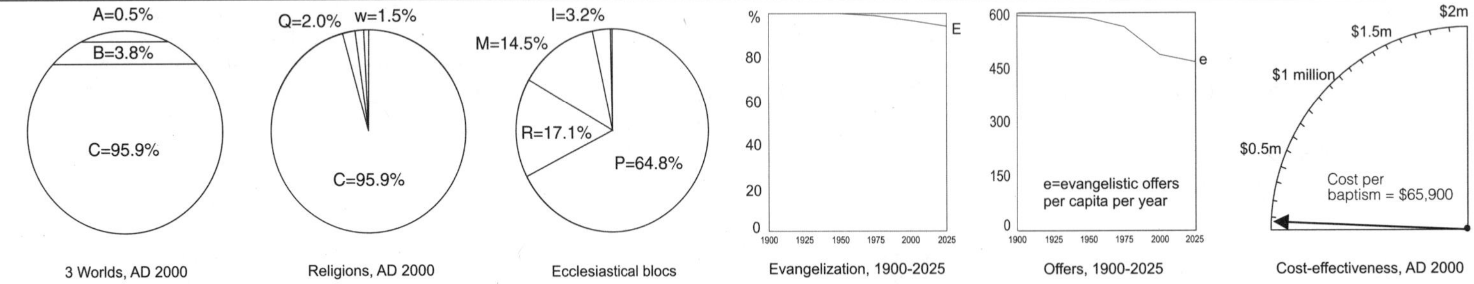

Country summary. **Worlds A, B, C by ethnolinguistic peoples, cities, and major civil divisions in American Samoa.**

	PEOPLES							CITIES							CIVIL DIVISIONS						
World	*Num*	*Pop 2000*	*C%*	*Christians*	*E%*	*U%*	*Unevangelized*	*Num*	*Pop 2000*	*C%*	*Christians*	*E%*	*U%*	*Unevangelized*	*Num*	*Pop 2000*	*C%*	*Christians*	*E%*	*U%*	*Unevangelized*
A	1	204	4.90	10	48	52	106	0	0	0.00	0	0	0	0	0	0	0.00	0	0	0	0
B	1	136	39.71	54	83	17	23	0	0	0.00	0	0	0	0	0	0	0.00	0	0	0	0
C	8	67,749	81.44	55,176	100	0	122	1	5,973	83.01	4,958	100	0	6	3	68,089	81.13	55,240	100	0	252
Total	**10**	**68,089**	**81.13**	**55,240**	**100**	**0**	**251**	**1**	**5,973**	**83.01**	**4,958**	**100**	**0**	**6**	**3**	**68,089**	**81.13**	**55,240**	**100**	**0**	**252**

Country status. American Samoa is made up of five volcanic islands and two coral atolls in the South Pacific Ocean administered as an overseas territory of the United States. Its chief exports are canned tuna and copra.

HUMAN LIFE AND LIBERTY

Human rights and freedoms. These remain a high standard, coming under American administration and courts. See the United States for discussion of human rights issues.

NON-CHRISTIAN RELIGIONS

Two small Baha'i congregations exist on Tutuila Island. Traditional religions have disappeared.

CHRISTIANITY

PROTESTANT CHURCHES. The history of Christianity in American Samoa is very similar to that in Western Samoa. Tahitian missionaries first arrived in 1830, under the London Missionary Society. By 1837 most of the islanders were Congregational Protestants. This has been the predominant denomination until recent decades. Although the Congregational Christian Church had 69.9% of the population in 1956, by 1967 it had declined to under 60% through losses to other churches.

By 1995 it held only 37% of the population. The second-largest denomination was the Catholic Church with 15% followed by the Church of Jesus Christ of Latter-day Saints (Mormons) with 8.7%, followed by the Assemblies of God with 4.7%.

Newer denominations also include the Church of Christ, United Pentecostal Church, and Church of the Nazarene, which have expanded due to the missionary activity of North American societies since World War II. While the Congregational Christian Church grew by 1.35% p.a. in the 25 years 1970-1995, several other denominations grew rapidly, often at their expense. In 1995 the young Baptist work included a Korean congregation, a Chinese congregation, a Samoan congregation, two Tongan congregations, and an English-speaking congregation.

CATHOLIC CHURCH. Catholic missionaries first arrived in 1845, but made little progress until 1965. American Samoa was formerly a part of the diocese of Apia based in Western Samoa. In 1982 the diocese of Samoa-Pago Pago was formed. In 1990 there were 7 parishes and one church. Catechists receive an extensive 4-year training course before being placed in village situations, and a number of Samoans have studied for the priesthood at the International Seminary in Suva, Fiji. The Samoan Islands are the most advanced in Catholic indigenous vocations of all the Pacific islands.

The Holy See has no diplomatic relations with American Samoa in AD 2000, but is represented there by an apostolic delegate for the Pacific Ocean residing in Wellington, New Zealand.

MARGINAL CHURCHES. Mormons, 5.6% of the population in 1956, and 11% a decade later, remained the third largest denomination in the country by 1995, with 8.7% of the population. In the 25 years 1970-1995 they grew by 3.0% p.a., passing the Assemblies of God at 2.38% p.a. growth. Jehovah's Witnesses also grew, to more than 500 affiliated by 1995.

Congregational Christian Church in Samoa. Church wedding for a Samoan nurse and guardsman in 1947.

INDIGENOUS CHURCHES. The Congregational Church of Jesus Christ, which was a schism from the Congregational Church as early as 1846, has followers in both Western and American Samoa and has attracted several hundred adherents.

There are scattered adherents of other independent groups also.

Indigenous missions. The internationalization of missions has led many Samoans to serve as foreign missionaries. They can now be found all over the world in denominational agencies such as the Franciscans and interdenominational ones such as Youth With A Mission (YWAM). In 1990 the local YWAM base had 33 staff.

CHURCH AND STATE

Since the island is a territory of the USA, the separation of church and state is more consciously observed than in many other islands of the Pacific. Private church-related schools are permitted, but they receive no subsidies from the government.

BROADCASTING AND MEDIA

Shortwave programs from HCJB (Ecuador), TWR (Antilles) and AWR (Costa Rica) can be easily received. FM and AM radio broadcasts from private Christian radio stations in the Caribbean can be heard. American Samoa is a member of UNDA.

Local churches have television broadcasts, and Christian programs can be viewed on television via satellite.

INTERDENOMINATIONAL ORGANIZATIONS

The National Council of Churches in American Samoa, which includes the Roman Catholics and nearly all the Protestant denominations, is an associate council of the WCC. These churches jointly observe the Week of Prayer for Christian Unity, and jointly lead a one-hour Sunday service on government-sponsored radio and TV.

FUTURE TRENDS AND PROSPECTS

Baha'is are expected to nearly double from 990 to 2,000 by AD 2025. With the nonreligious rising to 2.3% in the same period, Christians would still account for more than 95% of the population.

In the distant future, secularism is likely to continue to erode the Christian majority. Along with Baha'i growth and that of other religionists, Christians could drop below 90% as early as 2050. Additionally, the makeup within Christianity is likely to change dramatically as Marginal Christians and Independent bodies are on a trend to pass the 20% mark sometime in the mid 21st century.

BIBLIOGRAPHY

Amerika Soamoa: an anthropological photo essay. F. K. Sutter. Honolulu: University of Hawaii Press, 1984. 128p.

Bibliographies of the Kermadec Islands, Niue, Swains Island and the Tokelau Islands. W. G. Coppell. Honolulu, HI: Pacific Islands Studies Program, University of Hawaii, 1975. 102p.

Samoan village: then and now. L. D. Holmes & E. R. Holmes. 2nd ed. *Case studies in cultural anthropology.* Fort Worth, TX: Harcourt Brace Jovanovich College Publishers, 1992. 176p.

'The church in the New Testament as the basis of the church today: with special reference to the Congregational Christian Church in American Samoa.' E. M. Sopoaga. B.D. thesis, Pacific Theological College, Suva, Fiji, 1986. 139p.

Two Samoans: a cultural comparison. S. J. Burris. Hilo, HI: Samu Productions, 1984. (111 slide set with sound).

Country Table 2. **Organized churches and denominations in American Samoa.**

Official name (bold type = church with over 10% of all affiliated) 1	*Begun* 2	*Type* 3	*Counc* 4	*Congs* 5	*Adults* 6	*Affiliated 1970* 7	*Affiliated 1995* 8	*G%* 9	*Names, notes, and other statistics* (see Codebook, Part 3) 10
Anglican Church (D Polynesia)	c1950	A-Hig	awpKC	1	105	100	150	1.64	In D Polynesia, Ch of Province of New Zealand. 60% European, 35% part-Samoan.
Assemblies of God in Samoa	1926	P-Pe2	ZF...	20	1,800	1,500	2,700	2.38	M=AoG(USA). Based on Pago Pago. 1970, very rapid growth. 45n,1x,1r,W=67%.
Catholic Church: D Samoa-Pago Pago	1845	R-Lat	PzPYC	9	3,000	5,000	8,500	2.15	HQ Pago Pago. M=MM. 8 parishes, 2 schools Tutuila Is. 9n, 3x, 6m, 13w, 467Yy
Church of Christ	c1965	I-Dis	x....	2	50	35	77	3.20	M=CC(Non-Instrumental) (USA). Independents. In Pago Pago. 2f.
Church of God of Prophecy	1981	P-Pe3	Z....	2	28	–	70	7.14	M=CGP(USA). Holiness Pentecostals.
Ch of Jesus Christ of Latter-day Saints	1888	m-LdS	x....	23	2,990	2,370	4,950	2.99	*Mormons.* M=CJCLdS(USA). Many Samoans overseas as missionaries. 50f.
Church of the Nazarene	1960	P-Hol	xF...	10	180	150	250	2.06	M=CoN(USA). Holiness denomination. 143 Sunday-school children. 2n.
Community Christian Church	c1950	P-com	..p..	1	70	100	100	0.00	Union church in Pago Pago. Largely Protestant expatriates, mostly from USA.
Congregational Christian Ch in S	c1830	P-Con	RWP.C	22	6,500	15,000	21,000	1.35	Major part of church is in Western Samoa. M=LMS(UK).
Congregational Church of Jesus Christ	1846	I-Con	.....	2	400	540	900	2.06	*Ponesi's Ch. Ch of JC in Samoa.* Schism ex Congregational Christian Church.
Jehovah's Witnesses	1938	m-Jeh	x....	3	199	80	538	7.92	Placed under Australian branch in 1938. First active witnessing 1951. 2Y.
Methodist Church in Samoa	1827	P-Met	VuP.C	2	2,400	1,000	3,900	5.59	*Lotu Tonga (Church of Tonga). Tutuila Synod* (4 other synods are in Western Samoa).
New Apostolic Church	c1990	I-3aX	x....	3	100	–	224	20.00	*NAC.* M=NAK(Neuapostolische Kirche; HQ Zurich, Switzerland).
Samoan Full Gospel Church	c1965	I-3fP	.....	2	160	95	291	4.58	Indigenous pentecostal body. Samoans. Branch also in Western Samoa.
Seventh-day Adventist Church	1895	P-Adv	x...c	3	650	600	1,700	4.25	*SDA, Samoa Mission, Central Pacific Union Mission.* HQ Pago Pago.
United Pentecostal Church	c1965	P-Pel	x....	2	70	50	100	2.81	*Jesus Only Church.* M=UPC(USA). Unitarian Pentecostals. 2f.
Other marginal Protestants	c1970	m-	.....	10	480	–	960	31.61	Various groups for USA.
Other Protestant groups	c1970	P-Eva	.....	3	60	–	150	22.19	Including Christian Brethren, Church of Christ (Nashville)(50).
Totals				**120**	**17,392**	**26,620**	**46,560**		

Churches, members, growth, 1900-2025	*Congs*	*Adults*	*Affiliated*	*G%*	*Total denominations*	*6 Megablocs:* *O*	*R*	*A*	*P*	*I*	*m*
Total churches, members, and denominations (mid-1900)	20	3,000	5,640	2.24	6	0	1	0	3	1	1
Total churches, members, and denominations (mid-1970)	70	12,931	26,620	2.24	14	0	1	1	7	3	2
Total churches, members, and denominations (mid-1990)	100	15,000	39,240	1.96	19	0	1	1	10	3	4
Total churches, members, and denominations (mid-1995)	120	17,392	46,560	3.48	22	0	1	1	12	4	4
Total churches, members, and denominations (mid-2000)	130	20,000	55,240	3.48	25	0	1	1	13	5	5
Total churches, members, and denominations (mid-2025)	200	50,000	111,400	2.85	52	0	1	1	20	20	10

NOTES ON TABLE ABOVE
NATIONAL COUNCILS (Column 4, 5th letter).
W = National Council of Churches of American Samoa (NCCAS).
w = related to NCCAS.

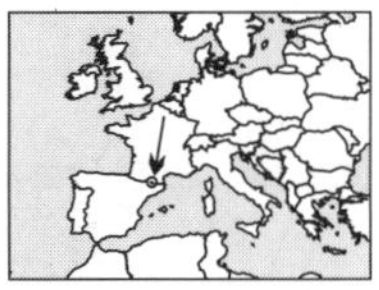

ANDORRA

SECULAR DATA, AD 2000

STATE
Official name: Principat d'Andorra (The Principality of Andorra).
Short name: Andorra. **Adjective of nationality:** Andorran.
Flag: Blue, yellow, and red bars, with coat of arms.
Area: 468 sq. km. (181 sq. mi.).
Government: Parliamentary coprincipality with one legislative house since 1993 (1278 autonomous principality, under joint suzerainty of 2 co-princes, the President of the French Republic and the Bishop of Urgel).
Legislature: General Council of the Valleys, 28 members.
Official language: Catalan.
Monetary unit: 1 franc (F) = 100 centimes, 1 peseta (Pta) = 100 céntimos. **US$1=** F 5.60.
Chief cities: ANDORRA LA VELLA 30,433.
Political divisions: 7 provinces.

DEMOGRAPHY
Population: 78,000.
Population density: 166.6/sq. km. (430.8/sq. mi.).
Under 15 years: 15,000.
Growth rate p.a.: 0.28% (births 11.85, deaths 9.51).
Mortality: Infant, per 1,000: 5.9; **Maternal per 100,000:** 10.0.
Life expectancy: 79 (male 75, female 83).
Household size: 3.0. **Floor area per person, sq.m:** 40.0.
Major languages: Catalan, Spanish, French.
Urban dwellers: 95.39%. **Urban growth rate p.a.:** 3.19%.
Labor force: 55%.

ETHNOLINGUISTIC PEOPLES
47.0% Spaniard; 28.4% Catalonian; 11.1% Portuguese; 7.5% French; ; 1.7% British.

ECONOMY
National income p.a. per person: US$16,195; **per family:** US$48,586.

EDUCATION
Adult literacy: 100% (male 100%, female 100%). **Schools:** 18.
Universities: 0. **School enrolment:** female/male: 90%/90%.

HEALTH
Access to health services: 95%. **Access to safe water:** 90%.
Hospitals: 1 (20 beds per 10,000). **Doctors:** 110.
Blind: 50. **Deaf:** 4,900. **Murder rate:** 1. **Lepers:** 0.

LITERATURE
New book titles p.a.: 70 (850 p.a. per million). **Periodicals:** 1.
Newspapers: 3 dailies.

COMMUNICATION (per 1,000 people)
Phones: 438 (29% mobile). **Radios:** 6. **TV sets:** 360.
Daily newspaper circulation: 63. **Computers:** 250.

HUMAN LIFE AND LIBERTY (optimum condition=100.0%)
HDI: 89.2. **HSI:** 80.0. **HFI:** 90.0. **EFL:** 45.0.

Country Table 1. **Religious adherents in Andorra, AD 1900-2025.**

Year	1900		1970		mid-1990		Annual change, 1990-2000				mid-1995		mid-2000		mid-2025	
Name	Adherents	%	Adherents	%	Adherents	%	Natural	Conversion	Total	Rate	Adherents	%	Adherents	%	Adherents	%
Christians	**4,980**	**99.6**	**18,430**	**99.9**	**48,870**	**94.0**	**2,444**	**-43**	**2,401**	**4.08**	**60,160**	**93.9**	**72,883**	**93.4**	**140,950**	**91.5**
PROFESSION																
professing Christians	**4,980**	**99.6**	**18,430**	**99.9**	**48,870**	**94.0**	**2,444**	**-43**	**2,401**	**4.08**	**60,160**	**93.9**	**72,883**	**93.4**	**140,950**	**91.5**
AFFILIATION																
unaffiliated Christians	480	9.6	430	2.3	1,800	3.5	90	-2	88	4.05	2,176	3.4	2,678	3.4	5,900	3.8
affiliated Christians	**4,500**	**90.0**	**18,000**	**97.6**	**47,070**	**90.5**	**2,354**	**-40**	**2,314**	**4.08**	**57,984**	**90.5**	**70,205**	**90.0**	**135,050**	**87.7**
Roman Catholics	4,500	90.0	17,900	97.0	46,700	89.8	2,335	-51	2,284	4.06	57,500	89.7	69,535	89.2	132,000	85.7
Marginal Christians	0	0.0	60	0.3	240	0.5	12	9	21	6.49	324	0.5	450	0.6	2,400	1.6
Protestants	0	0.0	40	0.2	80	0.2	4	2	6	5.76	100	0.2	140	0.2	500	0.3
Independents	0	0.0	0	0.0	50	0.1	3	0	3	4.81	60	0.1	80	0.1	150	0.1
Trans-megabloc groupings																
Evangelicals	0	0.0	10	0.1	10	0.0	1	0	1	7.18	13	0.0	20	0.0	100	0.1
Pentecostals/Charismatics	0	0.0	40	0.2	480	0.9	24	12	36	5.76	644	1.0	840	1.1	2,000	1.3
Great Commission Christians	**400**	**8.0**	**3,700**	**20.1**	**17,500**	**33.7**	**875**	**30**	**905**	**4.26**	**21,800**	**34.0**	**26,551**	**34.0**	**53,100**	**34.5**
Nonreligious	0	0.0	0	0.0	2,250	4.3	113	50	163	5.60	3,000	4.7	3,880	5.0	9,900	6.4
Muslims	0	0.0	0	0.0	170	0.3	9	23	32	11.26	330	0.5	494	0.6	1,500	1.0
Hindus	0	0.0	0	0.0	80	0.2	4	23	27	15.94	280	0.4	351	0.5	1,000	0.7
Jews	20	0.4	70	0.4	170	0.3	9	1	10	4.62	230	0.4	267	0.3	400	0.3
Baha'is	0	0.0	0	0.0	60	0.1	3	2	5	6.25	100	0.2	110	0.1	250	0.2
World A (unevangelized persons)	0	0.0	0	0.0	468	0.9	23	4	27	4.78	576	0.9	702	0.9	2,002	1.3
World B (evangelized non-Christians)	20	0.4	23	0.4	2,662	4.4	115	39	154	5.19	3,358	5.2	4,415	5.6	11,048	7.2
World C (Christians)	4,980	99.6	18,430	99.6	48,870	94.7	2,444	-43	2,401	4.08	60,160	93.9	72,883	93.5	140,950	91.5
Country's population	**5,000**	**100.0**	**18,453**	**100.0**	**52,000**	**100.0**	**2,582**	**0**	**2,582**	**4.14**	**64,095**	**100.0**	**78,000**	**100.0**	**154,000**	**100.0**

COLUMNS, ROWS.
For meanings and definitions, see Codebook (Part 3). Note that, by definition, total 'Christians' = professing + crypto-Christians, which also = affiliated + unaffiliated Christians, and also = Great Commission Christians + latent Christians. Percentages may not always total exactly, due to rounding.

CENSUSES.
The question on religion has not been asked.

NOTES ON RELIGIONS
BAHA'IS. In one organized LSA (local spiritual assembly).
COUNTRY'S POPULATION. In 1990, 75% of the population were foreign residents and only 25% were Andorrans.

Great Commission Instrument Panel: status of Andorra (for explanation see start of Part 4)

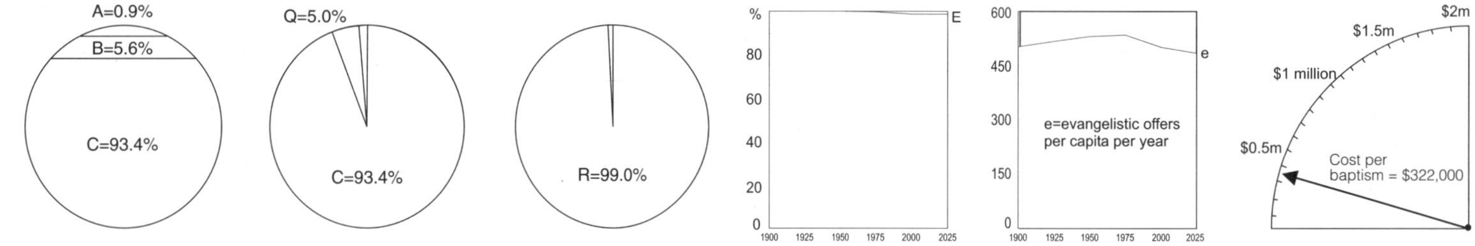

3 Worlds, AD 2000 | Religions, AD 2000 | Ecclesiastical blocs | Evangelization, 1900-2025 | Offers, 1900-2025 | Cost-effectiveness, AD 2000

Country status. Andorra is a small autonomous principality in the Southern Pyrenees between France and Spain. It consists of gorges, narrow valleys, and high mountain peaks but has excellent pasture lands for raising cattle and sheep as well as producing tobacco and fruit.

HUMAN LIFE AND LIBERTY

Human rights and freedoms. In 1989 the European Parliament concluded that human rights were generally respected in Andorra. However, it noted the lack of political parties, the lack of labor unions, and the absence of many social benefits common to other European countries. Much of this has changed with the approval in 1993 of a new Constitution, which includes human rights among its Basic Principles. Voting rights are limited to Andorran citizens who represent only 18% of the population. Only those born in Andorra of at least one Andorran parent, spouses of Andorran citizens, and long-term residents can become citizens.

NON-CHRISTIAN RELIGIONS

In AD 2000 there is a small Jewish community of 270 members in Andorra.

CHRISTIANITY

The great majority of the population are Roman Catholics. The church is part of the diocese of Urgel (Spain) with 8 parishes. A Catholic school, the College of St Ermengol, is administered by the national governing body, the General Council. In 1995 there were also more than 200 Jehovah's Witnesses in Andorra and less than 100 Protestants. There are no international denominational relations or organizations. There were two Protestant missionaries in 1995, and Evangelical groups have distributed literature from time to time.

Iglesia Católica (D Urgel). Renowned center, the Sanctuary of Meritxell.

CATHOLIC CHURCH. The Holy See has no diplomatic relations with Andorra in AD 2000.

Indigenous missions. Andorran missionaries are found primarily in the Catholic orders.

Country summary. **Worlds A, B, C by ethnolinguistic peoples, cities, and major civil divisions in Andorra.**

	PEOPLES							CITIES							CIVIL DIVISIONS						
World	*Num*	*Pop 2000*	*C%*	*Christians*	*E%*	*U%*	*Unevangelized*	*Num*	*Pop 2000*	*C%*	*Christians*	*E%*	*U%*	*Unevangelized*	*Num*	*Pop 2000*	*C%*	*Christians*	*E%*	*U%*	*Unevangelized*
A	3	1,139	1.14	13	41	59	668	0	0	0.00	0	0	0	0	0	0	0.00	0	0	0	0
B	0	0	0.00	0	0	0	0	0	0	0.00	0	0	0	0	0	0	0.00	0	0	0	0
C	8	76,845	91.34	70,190	100	0	67	1	30,433	90.00	27,390	99	1	231	7	77,986	90.02	70,205	99	1	735
Total	**11**	**77,984**	**90.02**	**70,203**	**99**	**1**	**735**	**1**	**30,433**	**90.00**	**27,390**	**99**	**1**	**231**	**7**	**77,986**	**90.02**	**70,205**	**99**	**1**	**735**

Iglesia Católica. A quarter of Andorra's postage stamps illustrate churches, Life of Christ scenes or other Christian topics; here, 3 of the Stations of the Cross

CHURCH AND STATE

Tradition holds that in the 8th century Charlemagne granted the Andorrans a charter for their support in his war against the Moors. His grandson made the Spanish count of Urgel overlord; and since 1278 the bishop of Urgel has been a co-prince of Andorra with the ruler (now president) of France as co-prince. The bishop of Urgel is in fact, along with the pope in Vatican City, the last Catholic bishop to retain official temporal power. However, this power was reduced in 1993 when a democratic government was instituted after more than 700 years of feudal rule. Official freedom of religion also began with the constitution of 1993, though the Catholic Church remains as the established church. Legislation is enacted by the 28-member General Council, which also names the state's administrators. Political factions include a liberal group leaning to France and a conservative group favoring Spain. France pays for some French-language schools while those near the Spanish border are church supported. The Catholic school is the only one teaching the national language of Catalan.

BROADCASTING AND MEDIA

Daily Catholic programs are broadcast by Radio Andorra. Shortwave broadcasts in a variety of languages can be received from HCJB (Ecuador), TWR (Monaco) and AWR (Costa Rica).

Satellite TV and radio programs are received in English, Arabic, German and Italian.

FUTURE TRENDS AND PROSPECTS

The rise of the nonreligious to 6.4% of the population by AD 2025 will probably be accompanied by a decline in Christianity to just above 91%.

Nonetheless, Andorra will most likely be both heavily Christian and heavily Catholic for many decades beyond 2025. The increasing role of the nonreligious may determine how long this lasts and could eventually account for more than 15% of the population at the end of the 21st century.

BIBLIOGRAPHY

Andorra. B. Taylor. *World bibliographical series*, vol. 167. Oxford, UK: CLIO Press, 1993. 136p. (Very short section on religion, 36-7; see also 'Folklore, festivals and customs,' 70-1).

Calendari de festes de Catalunya, Andorra i la Franja. M. D. Llopart et al. Barcelona: Alta Fulla, 1989. 627p.

Cants a Nostra Senyora de Meritxell, protectora de Canillo, patrona del Principat d'Andorra. 2nd ed. Canillo, Andorra: Unió Pro-Turisme de la Parròquia de Canillo, 1988. 103p.

Historia y novena de Nostra Senyora de Meritxell, patrona general de las Valls de Andorra, venerada en lo seu santuari situat en lo terme de la Parroquia de Canillo. [L. I. Fiter]. Barcelona: Tipografía Católica, 1874. 142p.

La religion populaire en Andorre: XVIe–XIXe siècles. J. Galinier-Pallerola. Paris: Editions du Centre national de la recherche scientifique, 1990. 209p.

Materials per una bibliografia d'Andorra. L. Armengol, M. Batlle & R. Gual. [Andorra]: Institut d'Estudis Andorrans, Centre de Perpinyà, 1978. 106p.

Country Table 2. **Organized churches and denominations in Andorra.**

Official name (bold type = church with over 10% of all affiliated) 1	*Begun* 2	*Type* 3	*Counc* 4	*Congs* 5	*Adults* 6	*Affiliated 1970* 7	*Affiliated 1995* 8	*G%* 9	*Names, notes, and other statistics* (see Codebook, Part 3) 10
Centro Biblico	1980	P-CBr	.....	1	15	–	30	6.67	*Free Brethren.* Noncharismatic. In Andorra La Vella.
Comunitat Cristiana d'Andorra	1990	I-3cW	.....	1	30	–	60	20.00	Spanish and Catalan. Multinationals from 12 countries.
Iglesia Adventista del Séptimo Día	c1960	P-Adv	x....	1	20	40	40	0.00	*SDA, Seventh-day Adventists*, in Spanish Church, Southern European Union Mission.
Iglesia Católica (D Urgel)	c360	R-Lat	B.B..	7	30,000	17,900	57,500	0.06	*Catholic Ch.* Part of diocese in Spain. (1995) 142 marriages p.a. , 12n, 7x, 15w, 369y, 18Yy
Iglesia de Jesu Cristo de los SUD	1992	m-LdS	x....	1	20	–	30	33.33	*Mormons.* M=CJCLdS(USA).
Iglesia Unificación	c1990	m-HSA	x....	1	25	–	40	20.00	*Holy Spirit Association for Unification of World Christianity. HSAUWC.*
Testigos de Jehová	c 1960	m-Jeh	x....	2	165	60	254	5.94	*Jehovah's Witnesses. Watch Tower.* Active witnessing first reported in 1963. 4Y.
Other Protestant churches	c1975	P-	.....	3	20	–	30	5.00	Including Apostolic Church (Switzerland); expatriates meeting informally.
Totals				**17**	**30,295**	**18,000**	**57,984**		

Churches, members, growth, 1900-2025	*Congs*	*Adults*	*Affiliated*	*G%*	*Total denominations*	*6 Megablocs:* O	R	A	P	I	m
Total churches, members, and denominations (mid-1900)	2	3,300	4,500	2.00	1	0	1	0	0	0	0
Total churches, members, and denominations (mid-1970)	10	13,143	18,000	2.00	3	0	1	0	1	0	1
Total churches, members, and denominations (mid-1990)	15	24,600	47,070	4.92	10	0	1	0	5	1	3
Total churches, members, and denominations (mid-1995)	17	30,295	57,984	4.26	10	0	1	0	5	1	3
Total churches, members, and denominations (mid-2000)	20	36,700	70,205	3.90	11	0	1	0	5	2	3
Total churches, members, and denominations (mid-2025)	50	70,600	135,050	2.65	32	1	1	0	10	10	10

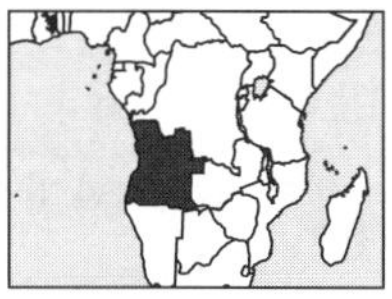

ANGOLA

SECULAR DATA, AD 2000

STATE
Official name: República de Angola (The People's Republic of Angola).
Short name: Angola. **Adjective of nationality:** Angolan.
Flag: Red and black stripes, yellow symbol of socialism, industry, agriculture.
Area: 1,246,700 sq. km. (481,354 sq. mi.).
Government: Unitary multiparty republic with one legislative house, since 1990 (14th century kingdom, 1483 Portuguese rule, 1975 Independence, 1975 one-party Communist state).
Legislature: National Assembly, 220 members.
Official language: Portuguese (Portugués).
Monetary unit: 1 readjusted Kwanza = 100 lwei. **US$1=** Kwanza 257,100.
Chief cities: LUANDA (Loanda) 2,665,000; Huambo (Nova Lisboa) 350,628; Benguela (Benguella) 267,721; Lobito 259,085; Namibe (Mocamedes, Mossamedes) 182,018.
Political divisions: 18 provinces.
Armed forces: 110,000.

DEMOGRAPHY
Population: 12,878,000.
Population density: 10.3/sq. km. (26.7/sq. mi.).
Under 15 years: 6,117,000.
Growth rate p.a.: 3.08% (births 45.63, deaths 16.47).
Mortality: Infant, per 1,000: 112.5; **Maternal per 100,000:** 1,500.0.
Life expectancy: 49 (male 47, female 51).
Household size: 4.8. **Floor area per person, sq.m:** 7.0.
Major languages: Portuguese, Mbundu, Kimbundu, Kongo (Kikongo), Chokwe, Luchazi, Spanish, and about 30 other tribal languages.
Urban dwellers: 34.20%. **Urban growth rate p.a.:** 4.89%.
Labor force: 40%.

ETHNOLINGUISTIC PEOPLES
25.2% Mbundu (Ovimbundu); 23.1% North Mbundu (Kimbundu); 10.0% Kongo; 8.1% Lwena (Luvale); 5.0% Chokwe (Kioko).

ECONOMY
National income p.a. per person: US$410; **per family:** US$1,967.

EDUCATION
Adult literacy: 41% (male 55%, female 28%). **Schools:** 6,308.
Universities: 1. **School enrolment:** female/male: 45%/45%.

HEALTH
Access to health services: 30%. **Access to safe water:** 32%.
Hospitals: 58 (12 beds per 10,000). **Doctors:** 662.
Blind: 12,000. **Deaf:** 766,800. **Murder rate:** 3. **Lepers:** 50,000.

LITERATURE
New book titles p.a.: 260 (20 p.a. per million). **Periodicals:** 38.
Newspapers: 4 dailies.

COMMUNICATION (per 1,000 people)
Phones: 5 **(12% mobile). Radios:** 39. **TV sets:** 51.
Daily newspaper circulation: 11. **Computers:** 10.

REFUGEES
Citizen refugees in other countries: 313,000.
Alien refugees from other countries: 10,900.
Internal displacement: 1,500,000.

HUMAN LIFE AND LIBERTY (optimum condition=100.0%)
HDI: 33.5. **HSI:** 14.0. **HFI:** 30.0. **EFL:** 13.0.

Country status. Angola is one of the African countries that remained longest under colonial rule. It became an independent state in 1975, after nearly five centuries of Portuguese colonial rule, but almost immediately entered a period of turmoil and insurgency that continued into the mid 1990s. Angola is one of the

Country Table 1. Religious adherents in Angola, AD 1900-2025.

Year	1900		1970		mid-1990		Annual change, 1990-2000				mid-1995		mid-2000		mid-2025	
Name	Adherents	%	Adherents	%	Adherents	%	Natural	Conversion	Total	Rate	Adherents	%	Adherents	%	Adherents	%
Christians	**17,000**	**0.6**	**4,564,350**	**81.7**	**8,636,000**	**93.6**	**341,342**	**6,589**	**347,931**	**3.44**	**10,307,930**	**93.9**	**12,115,308**	**94.1**	**24,441,100**	**97.4**
PROFESSION																
professing Christians	**17,000**	**0.6**	**4,564,350**	**81.7**	**8,636,000**	**93.6**	**341,342**	**6,589**	**347,931**	**3.44**	**10,307,930**	**93.9**	**12,115,308**	**94.1**	**24,441,100**	**97.4**
AFFILIATION																
unaffiliated Christians	4,300	0.1	1,415,344	25.3	1,090,300	11.8	43,092	-34,015	9,077	0.80	1,134,762	10.3	1,181,070	9.2	1,441,100	5.7
affiliated Christians	**12,700**	**0.4**	**3,149,006**	**56.4**	**7,545,700**	**81.8**	**298,231**	**40,623**	**338,854**	**3.78**	**9,173,168**	**83.6**	**10,934,238**	**84.9**	**23,000,000**	**91.6**
Roman Catholics	11,700	0.4	2,667,306	47.7	5,600,000	60.7	221,330	18,670	240,000	3.63	6,750,237	61.5	8,000,000	62.1	16,500,000	65.7
Protestants	1,000	0.0	417,500	7.5	1,300,000	14.1	51,380	11,644	63,024	4.03	1,632,615	14.9	1,930,238	15.0	4,100,000	16.3
Independents	0	0.0	61,200	1.1	570,000	6.2	22,528	8,472	31,000	4.44	697,516	6.4	880,000	6.8	2,062,000	8.2
Marginal Christians	0	0.0	1,000	0.0	73,000	0.8	2,885	1,815	4,700	5.10	89,400	0.8	120,000	0.9	330,000	1.3
Anglicans	0	0.0	2,000	0.0	2,700	0.0	107	23	130	4.01	3,400	0.0	4,000	0.0	8,000	0.0
Trans-megabloc groupings																
Evangelicals	1,000	0.0	400,000	7.2	830,000	9.0	32,804	6,896	39,700	3.99	1,009,654	9.2	1,227,000	9.5	3,066,000	12.2
Pentecostals/Charismatics	0	0.0	70,000	1.3	1,292,000	14.0	51,064	24,236	75,300	4.70	1,650,559	15.0	2,045,000	15.9	5,200,000	20.7
Great Commission Christians	**8,900**	**0.3**	**167,640**	**3.0**	**1,015,000**	**11.0**	**40,116**	**12,973**	**53,089**	**4.30**	**1,261,000**	**11.5**	**1,545,888**	**12.0**	**3,600,000**	**14.3**
Ethnoreligionists	2,953,000	99.4	1,017,810	18.2	513,020	5.6	20,276	-7,714	12,562	2.21	560,000	5.1	638,638	5.0	300,000	1.2
Nonreligious	0	0.0	5,000	0.1	60,000	0.7	2,371	1,122	3,493	4.69	79,500	0.7	94,929	0.7	300,000	1.2
Atheists	0	0.0	0	0.0	19,000	0.2	751	10	761	3.43	22,300	0.2	26,614	0.2	60,000	0.2
Baha'is	0	0.0	400	0.0	1,000	0.0	40	9	49	4.05	1,250	0.0	1,488	0.0	3,500	0.0
Buddhists	0	0.0	400	0.0	900	0.0	36	-16	20	2.04	930	0.0	1,101	0.0	2,200	0.0
Chinese folk-religionists	0	0.0	40	0.0	80	0.0	3	0	3	3.14	90	0.0	109	0.0	200	0.0
World A (unevangelized persons)	2,524,500	85.0	782,319	14.0	83,070	0.9	3,356	-2,723	633	0.72	87,779	0.8	90,146	0.7	125,535	0.5
World B (evangelized non-Christians)	428,500	14.4	241,325	4.3	510,930	5.5	20,121	-3,866	16,255	2.79	576,669	5.2	672,546	5.2	540,365	2.1
World C (Christians)	17,000	0.6	4,564,350	81.7	8,636,000	93.6	341,342	6,589	347,931	3.44	10,307,930	94.0	12,115,308	94.1	24,441,100	97.4
Country's population	**2,970,000**	**100.0**	**5,587,995**	**100.0**	**9,230,000**	**100.0**	**364,819**	**0**	**364,819**	**3.39**	**10,972,379**	**100.0**	**12,878,000**	**100.0**	**25,107,000**	**100.0**

COLUMNS, ROWS.
For meanings and definitions, see Codebook (Part 3). Note that, by definition, total 'Christians' = professing + crypto-Christians, which also = affiliated + unaffiliated Christians, and also = Great Commission Christians + latent Christians. Percentages may not always total exactly, due to rounding.

CENSUSES.
1940: 70.0% ethnoreligionists 22.0% Roman Catholics, 7.8% Protestants, 0.1% other religionists. **31.XII.1950:** 50.5% ethnoreligionists, 36.3% Roman Catholics, 13.1% Protestants, 0.1% nonreligious (Whites). **30.XII.1960:** 50.8% Roman Catholics, 32.5% ethnoreligionists, 16.6% Protestants, 0.1% nonreligious (Whites).

NOTES ON RELIGIONS
ATHEISTS. After Independence in 1975 a Communist party was formed based on the Movimento Popular de Libertação de Angola (MPLA). In 1977 the party was remodeled as a Marxist-Leninist party with membership initially restricted to around 5,000 hard-core revolutionaries. According to president Neto then, 'No party member can be a church member, and no church member can be a member of the party'.
BAHA'IS. In 1 local spiritual assembly (1973), mushrooming to 30 LSAs (1996).
COUNTRY'S POPULATION. Since 1975, about 1.5 million are thought to have been killed or died of starvation.
ETHNORELIGIONISTS. Tribes over 60% traditionalist (animist) in 1995: Hukwe Bushmen (80%), Aukwe (89%), Bakwe Pygmy (75%), Kung (90%), Kwadi (80%), Ndombe (60%). Almost all other tribes have a proportion of residual animists down to under 1% among the Bakongo.INDEPENDENTS. In 12 denominations in 1995 (see Table 2).
NONRELIGIOUS. Up to 1975, mainly Portuguese Whites (Brancos), with a few Macanese and other Chinese; after 1975, a growing number of Africans became nonreligious and a smaller number atheists.

Great Commission Instrument Panel: status of Angola (for explanation see start of Part 4)

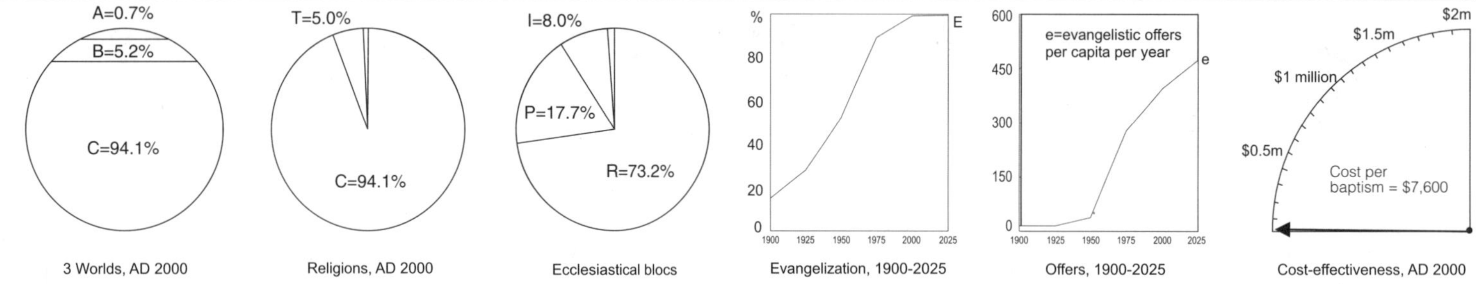

10 countries of the world where conditions of near anarchy have prevailed for over two decades since the 1970s.

HUMAN LIFE AND LIBERTY

Human need and development. Angola is one of the least developed of developing countries in Africa. It bears the scars of 5 centuries of colonialism as well as the ravages of slave trade for at least three centuries. Independence in 1975 brought neither peace nor prosperity, but rather increased violence and instability. Ethnic rivalries among the major groups, the Ovimbundu, Mbundu, and Bakongo, as well as between them and the Mesticos, have thrown society back to the Middle Ages. In spite of warfare and poor healthcare, the population has grown steadily. After independence, there have been dramatic changes in the structure of population. Urbanization has been disastrously rapid, increasing from 10.3% in 1960 to 34.2% in AD 2000. There also have been massive population shifts from the countryside to the coastal areas. With the onset of the Civil War, the Ovimbundu migrated to the central provinces, the Bakongo first fled to Zaire and then returned en masse, and others fled the central provinces into the cities. Displaced persons have tended to create unsettled conditions wherever they go. In Luanda, the destitute population, estimated at 600,000, live in shantytowns known as musseques. The literacy rate, although officially placed at 41%, is estimated to be no more than 20%. Primary school enrollment rate has actually declined since independence. Health conditions are poor even by African standards. Infectious and parasitic diseases are widely prevalent, particularly in refugee camps and shantytowns. Disease control programs are nonexistent and cholera epidemics periodically ravage the countryside.

Angola is one of the richest countries in Africa in its potential resources, yet it has remained one of the poorest. The Civil War has preempted all types of developmental efforts on the part of the government. Large scale destruction of the countryside was one of the strategic objectives of both the government and the UNITA (the armed opposition group) opposition. The exodus of trained Portuguese colonists, the mesticos and assimilados (educated Africans) also had a negative effect on development. During wartime, the writ of the Marxist-led government never ran beyond Luanda and the major urban centers. With the collapse of Angola's communist patrons, the government's socialist policies (never very successful to begin with) were formally abandoned. The UNITA insurgency had a far more negative impact on the country's development than state policies. Hundreds of thousands were displaced, and the work force was depleted through the conscription of the young adult population. The school and health systems suffered, and may take decades to return to normal levels.

Human rights and freedoms. Human rights are among the first casualties in a civil war and Angola has been no exception. In addition, the Marxist-Communist government that was in power from 1975 had scant regard for human rights, and neither did UNITA. Constitutional reforms enacted in May 1991 prepared the way for a multiparty and democratic government. The revised 1991 Constitution guarantees basic human rights, such as freedom of the press and right of free assembly. Meanwhile, the civil war has taken a heavy toll on the population. An estimated 1.9 million civilians were affected by the conflict; 500,000 were killed, 20,000 children orphaned, 50,000 persons lost their limbs in landmine explosions, and 430,000 persons fled the country as refugees. Political and extrajudicial killings, torture, disappearances, and arbitrary arrests and exile were commonplace. Angola had its first independent court system only in 1990. The Constitution bans all types of discrimination, but there is little information on the actual extent of discrimination in the country.

Angola has not known human freedom, either under its Portuguese masters or as an independent country. The post-1975 Marxist interlude followed the classic Stalinist model, and was characterized by a one-party rule in which all sectors of the economy and society were under state control. This posed an anomaly, not only because it ran counter to the cultural traditions of the country, but because it set the stage for a civil conflict in which the MPLA (Popular Movement for the Liberation of Angola) and UNITA had to seek foreign intervention and thus place the country's independence in jeopardy. The ground work for a new era in Angolan history is the revised 1991 Constitution which guarantees all basic rights, including free elections, freedom of assembly, freedom of speech and the press, and freedom of religion.

Human environment. Although Angola has rich agricultural farmland, it imports most of its food. Near famine conditions prevail in the countryside where the landmines have rendered fields unsafe. Safe drinking water is not available even in the cities. As a result, waterborne diseases are common. Soil erosion, deforestation, and overuse of pastures have led to the degradation of land. Indiscriminate deforestation has led to the deterioration of land quality and the loss of animal and plant species.

NON-CHRISTIAN RELIGIONS

Traditional religions have shown a progressive and rapid decline since World War II. In 1940 ethnoreligionists were 70.7% of the population, falling to 51% in 1950 and 33% in 1960. By 1995 they were estimated to be only 5.1%. The Hukwe, a small Bushman tribe on the southern border, are 80% tra-

Country summary. **Worlds A, B, C by ethnolinguistic peoples, cities, and major civil divisions in Angola.**

	PEOPLES							CITIES							CIVIL DIVISIONS						
World	Num	Pop 2000	C%	Christians	E%	U%	Unevangelized	Num	Pop 2000	C%	Christians	E%	U%	Unevangelized	Num	Pop 2000	C%	Christians	E%	U%	Unevangelized
A	7	51,325	17.08	8,764	43	57	29,315	0	0	0.00	0	0	0	0	0	0	0.00	0	0	0	0
B	11	216,064	38.63	83,456	80	20	42,605	0	0	0.00	0	0	0	0	0	0	0.00	0	0	0	0
C	42	12,610,799	85.97	10,842,019	100	0	19,306	6	3,885,862	87.93	3,416,742	100	0	13,835	18	12,878,186	84.91	10,934,238	99	1	91,224
Total	**60**	**12,878,188**	**84.91**	**10,934,239**	**99**	**1**	**91,226**	**6**	**3,885,862**	**87.93**	**3,416,742**	**100**	**0**	**13,835**	**18**	**12,878,186**	**84.91**	**10,934,238**	**99**	**1**	**91,224**

ditionalists; and their Bantu-speaking neighbors to the northeast, the Mbukushu, 70%. Other southeastern peoples with relatively high traditionalist percentages are the Mbwela (40%) and the Kwangali (50%). Of the large tribes, the Chokwe (554,000; 70%) have been the most resistant to Christianity. On the other hand, the Kongo of northern Angola (1.2 million) are only 1% traditionalist and the Mbundu (3.2 million) 30%. The 3 most common vernacular names for God in Angola are Nzambi in the north (Bakongo, Ambundu, Lunda, Chokwe), Suku in the center (Ovimbundu), and Kalunga in the south (Ambo, Kuanhama). Nevertheless, there is considerable intermixture of names, the term Kalunga also being used among the Ambundu, Lunda, Chokwe, and Nzambi or Ndiambi among southern peoples. The cult of ancestral spirits (Mahamba in Chokwe) exists as well as belief in the evil activity of witches (ndoki in Kikongo) and the beneficent function of medicine men (kimbanda in Kimbundu). During the 20th century a number of spirit possession cults, known by the generic term Mahamba, have arisen among the Luvale, Luchazi, Chokwe, Ovimbun-du, and Ndembu. The early forms mostly concerned troublesome ancestral spirits, but alien spirits were introduced as new Mahamba in 1925. One of the most important movements of the early 1930s was Tukuka Mahamba, which spread eastward among the Ndembu of Northern Rhodesia, and after World War II such other new Mahamba as Ndeke (aircraft) and Sitima (train) made their appearance.

Baha'i has been represented in Angola by a small community since the Baha'i World Crusade in Kampala in 1953.

CHRISTIANITY

CATHOLIC CHURCH. The first Catholic mission to the Congo kingdom arrived in 1491, centered on northern Angola's Sao Salvador. The initial group consisted of Franciscans, Dominicans, Canons of St John the Evangelist and secular priests and a widespread church was formed during the next century under the remarkable Christian king Afonso I. Afonso's son Henrique became the first Black African bishop in Catholic history, serving in North Africa. After a promising beginning, the ravages of the slave trade caused the disintegration of both kingdom and church. Jesuits arrived in 1548 and in 1560, accompanied by the first Portuguese expedition to the Ndongo kingdom inland on the Cuanza river. In 1576 Luanda was founded. By the end of the century, an episcopal see had been established and 4 monasteries built. Once again the slave trade acted as an impediment to the extension of the church. The Capuchins, mostly Italian, were the most important missionary force in the nation for many years. They first arrived in 1645 and were forced out in 1834. In spite of the activity of Capuchins, Franciscans and Carmelites at the coast, the 18th and 19th centuries witnessed the decline of Catholic missions. A reversal of this trend did not take place until 1865 when Propaganda was asked to assign Holy Ghost fathers to Angola. By 1890, 4 centers were established at Malange, Caconda, Cassina, and Huila, which served as bases for expansion into the interior. However, many areas were not effectively reached until after World War II. All missionary orders were suppressed during the intense anticlerical period of 1911-1919.

Catholicism has made remarkable progress in Angola since 1940 as revealed in government census statistics. In 1940, 22.0% of the population professed to be Catholics. By 1950 the figure had risen to 36.3% and to 60% in 1972. The estimate for 1990 is 73%. The church has its greatest strength among the Mbundu (Orimbundu) of central Angola. Because of limited penetration into the deeper interior, there are fewer Catholics in the east and southeast. The city of Huambo is two-thirds Catholic. In the late 1970s the dioceses of Angola were all reorganized, and most of them renamed. By 1988 there were 14 dioceses served by 1,348 missionaries—a figure that includes all priests, deacons, religious brothers and sisters, and lay missionaries. The number of priests in the country declined rapidly from 560 in 1975 to 335 in 1988. During about the same period the number of nuns grew from 158 to 331. Between independence and the early 1990s, 21 new religious orders for women entered the country, and one new order was created within Angola itself, the Congregation of the Sisters of Saint Catherine, an association of catechists. In 1967 a group of 9 young women were encouraged by their priest in their devotion and service of God, which eventually led to a new order, officially formed in 1982. By 1985 it included 51 sisters.

There were in 1995 15 dioceses including the 3 Archdioceses of Huambo, Luanda, and Lubango. The Catholic Church remained the dominant church of the country, with 78.6% of Angola's Christians, down from 89.8% in 1970.

The most serious problem for the Catholic church throughout most of its history in Angola has been its relationship with the Portuguese government. Portuguese Catholic missions have never played an independent role with regard to the Portuguese colonial system, whether in the realm of social action or in the face of Angola's principal social problem, forced labor, or in education. The educational system was designed primarily for the indigenous masses with emphasis on rudimentary training rather than on the development of leadership or an elite. The lack of African leadership is also evident in the church hierarchy. The first African bishop of the contemporary era, not only in Angola but for all of Portugal's colonies, was appointed in 1970 as auxiliary bishop of Luanda. In 1973 he was transferred to Malange as ordinary of the diocese. Following the change of regime in Portugal on 25 April 1974, the Holy See in August 1974 named a second African bishop as auxiliary of Luanda.

The Holy See has no diplomatic relations with Angola in AD 2000, but an apostolic delegate residing in Luanda.

PROTESTANT CHURCHES. Comity agreements have played a significant role in Angolan church history. Thus the major denominations have tended to restrict themselves to work among specific tribal groups, with very little overlapping even in urban areas.

The first to arrive were British Baptists, who opened a mission at Sao Salvador among the Bakongo of northern Angola in 1878. The Bakongo became the most christianized people in Angola in 1960 already 55.8% Catholic and 42.7% Protestant with only 1.5% remaining traditionalist. Two other smaller groups, founded by independent missionaries, have also worked among the Bakongo; the Angola Evangelical Mission (AEM) which arrived in Cabinda and the coastal area south of the Congo estuary in 1897, and the North Angola Mission which entered Uige (Carmona) in 1925. The latter body was founded by a missionary originally recruited by the AEM. The AEM was taken over by Canadian Baptists in 1957 as was the work begun in 1910 in Cabinda by the Christian and Missionary Alliance. The revolution which broke out in 1961 seriously affected the life of the Bakongo church. Following the opening of hostilities, more than 400,000 refugees fled from the area to nearby Zaire where they greatly strengthened local churches. Many churches in northern Angola continued to exist in villages hidden from Portuguese surveillance. Most missionaries were evacuated in 1961, 2 Canadian Baptist families remaining in Cabinda until 1964. However, after the Portugal coup d'etat of 1974 many of these refugees returned to northern Angola.

Methodists have worked among the Kimbundu-speaking people east of Luanda since 1885. In 1961 a number of Methodists took refuge in Zaire, and until 1974 many others continued to worship in hidden villages in the Dembos district. The Methodist church has been led by an Angolan bishop since 1972.

Several missions have been active among the Ovimbundu. The Evangelical Church of Central Angola unites the work originally begun by the American Board in 1880 and the United Church of Canada in 1886. This church is strongest on the Benguela plateau in the area of Nova Lisboa and Silva Porto as well as at Lobito on the coast. In addition to 60 primary and 3 secondary schools, it has the most highly developed medical program in the territory: 7 hospitals, 20 clinics, 3 leprosaria and an extensive rural public health service.

The region west of the plateau and extending south to Sa' da Bandeira is occupied by the Philafricaine Mission, which was begun in 1897 and since 1908 has been supported by the Swiss Reformed Churches. This church has 20 primary schools, 2 secondary schools, 4 hospitals, 6 clinics and 3 leprosaria. Pentecostals are active in the area of Novo Redondo and Gabela, north of Lobito. Adventists, who first appeared in 1922, are also found among the Ovimbundo although they have extensive work in the Moxico and Lunda of eastern Angola as well. Adventist institutions number 128 primary schools, 2 secondary schools, one hospital and 3 clinics. Brethren (CMML) missionaries have worked among

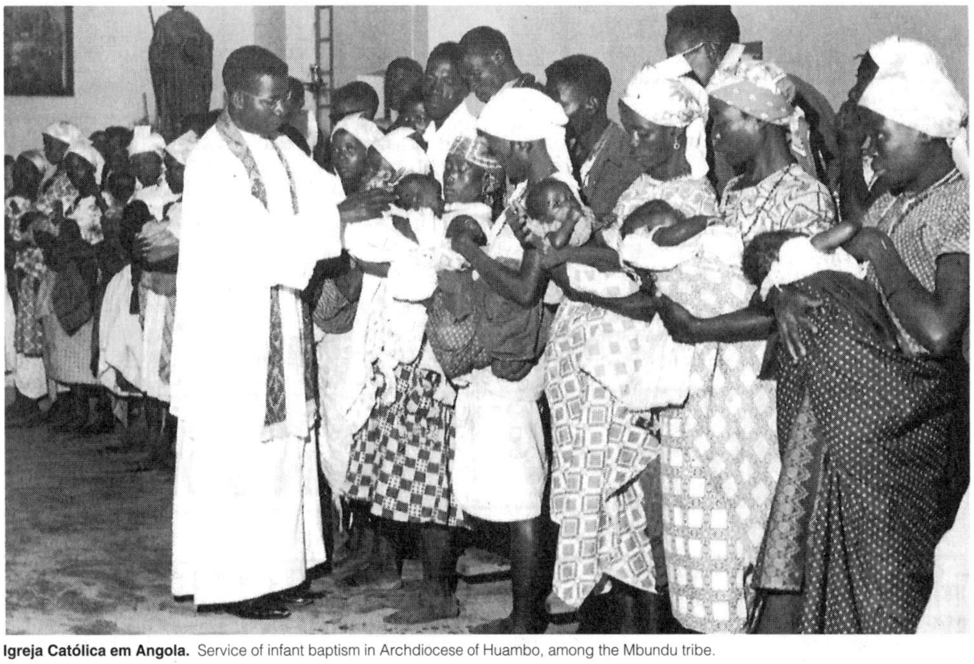

Igreja Católica em Angola. Service of infant baptism in Archdiocese of Huambo, among the Mbundu tribe.

the Chokwe and Lunda of the northeast since 1884, but these have shown themselves to be among the most resistant of Angola's peoples to Christian evangelization. The Brethren sponsor 6 primary schools, 2 hospitals and 2 leprosaria.

Southern Angola under comity was assigned to the African Evangelical Fellowship (AEF). Originally called the South African General Mission, the AEF is a faith mission which entered Angola in 1914. Southeastern Angola is virtually devoid of Protestants, and Protestant activity was actually prohibited in the Kwanyama area along the southern border from 1914 to 1960. The AEF is responsible for 2 primary schools, 2 hospitals and a leprosarium.

Although Portuguese (White) congregations exist in Angola's major cities, missionary outreach from metropolitan Portugal to the indigenous peoples has never been extensive. The only active body is a small Portuguese Baptist Mission near Nova Lisboa founded in 1936. Since 1968 Southern Baptist missionaries affiliated with the Portuguese Baptist Convention have been at work with Europeans in Luanda. In 1995 the largest Protestant denomination in Angola was the Evangelical Church of Central Angola, followed in order by the Christian Brethren, the United Methodist Church of Angola, the Evangelical Church of Southwest Angola (Filafricaine Mission), and the Seventh-day Adventist Church. The fastest growing denomination was the Assemblies of God, which grew from 3,000 in 1970 to more than 100,000 in 20 years.

INDIGENOUS CHURCHES. Angola is notable for the relative absence of African independent churches, due in part to government suppression of such movements. Kimbanguism, which began among the Bakongo of Zaire in 1921, has had its effect among the people of northern Angola as well. In Angola, Kimbanguism has manifested itself as Amicalismo (related to the Congo prophet Matswa Angre), the Igreja dos Negros (related to the Congo prophet Simon Mpadi) and the Movimento Tonsi (also related to Simon Mpadi); and more as an organized branch of the EJCSK in Zaire.

Another larger Bakongo group is that formed by the prophet Simao Toco in 1949. Although born in Maquela do Zombo, Toco was 'illuminated by the Holy Spirit' while working as a choir leader in a Baptist church in Kinshasa. Toco was expelled to Angola by the Belgian authorities in 1956, and the movement spread rapidly among Toco's own Bombo people. Portuguese attempts to suppress the sect by exiling its leader to other parts of Angola have also contributed to its expansion. Toco himself was exiled to Azores, but he continued to maintain contact with followers in Angola. As late as 1973 he was known to be seeking Christian literature for them from the Worldwide Evangelization Crusade (UK) and other bodies in Europe.

The Bakongo people of the Cabinda enclave have also had their prophets, the first being an ecstatic named Maiange in 1930. In 1953 an even larger group was gathered together by the Points Noire prophet, Simon Zepherin Lassy.

Lassyism, also called God of the Candle (Nzambi ya Bougie), continues to exert an important influence in both Cabinda and Congo.

In 1940 a movement called Muvungismo spread among the Yaka across the Kwango river from the Belgian Congo. A strongly anti-White split from the Unevangelized Tribes Mission, it was quickly stamped out by Belgians and Portuguese.

Although very little is known about them, at least 3 distinct independent groups are active in southern Angola: the Olosanto among the Mbundu, the Holy Spirit Group (Grupo do Espirito Santo), and the Bapostolo (Apostles) who owe their origin to the Apostolic Church of Johane Maranke in Zimbabwe. Overall, in 1990, those affiliated with the indigenous churches comprised only 5% of the Christians of Angola.

MARGINAL CHURCHES. Jehovah's Witnesses have been Angola's fastest-growing denomination in recent decades, growing to nearly 40,000 affiliated by 1990, despite being officially banned since March 1978.

Art and architecture. Angola has some of the oldest Catholic churches in southern Africa, dating back to the 17th century. They are typical of the colonial style of church architecture developed by the Portuguese in Africa as well as India and the Far East - simple, white buildings, with open verandas on either side, but with no ornamentation or steeples. They represent the most efficient use of local materials, such as baked bricks. Christian symbols are used extensively in art, but are heavily Africanized and mixed with indigenous motifs.

Renewal movements. In the 1990s the Pentecostal/Charismatic Renewal continued to spread rapidly across most older churches, and numbered over 2,045,000 adherents (of whom 20% Pentecostals, 38% Charismatics, and 41% Independents).

Indigenous missions. Three decades of war have kept the focus of Angolan Christians on their own survival. Thousands of young Christians were forcibly taken to Cuba for indoctrination. In the peace of the 1990s a few Angolans are beginning to participate in cross-cultural missions.

CHURCH AND STATE

Until Angola's independence in 1975, the Portuguese constitution guaranteed the free exercise of worship and the separation of church and state. Nevertheless, the Catholic Church enjoyed a special relationship with the Portuguese state as stipulated in the concordat, Missionary Agreement and Missionary Statue of 1940 and 1941. The major problem of religious liberty related to the failure of the Portuguese government to provide legal recognition for the Protestant community. The legal basis for this has existed since 1921, and de facto recognition was given, but Angolan Protestant organizations were unsuccessful in having their statutes approved. The effect of the Law on Religious Liberty of 22 July 1971, providing for the official recognition of religious associations and organizations other than the Catholic Church, was minimal.

Protestant activity in the Kwanyama area of the south was prohibited between 1914 and 1960, and other restrictions were evident through the years.

A Methodist attempt to open a new mission station and secondary school in the Dembos area during the 1950s for example never received government approval. Protestants were generally accused of denationalizing Angolans, and the criticism of existing conditions in 1961 by Baptist and Methodist missionaries led to imprisonment shortly after the outbreak of hostilities, and numerous Protestant pastors and teachers were killed by Portuguese soldiers and militia in the early days of the civil war. The fact that Protestants were prominent in the revolutionary movement also contributed to Portuguese hostility.

Individual Angolan Catholic priests were also imprisoned for alleged involvement in the revolutionary movement. Several were exiled to Portugal, including msgr Manuel Mendes das Neves, the former vicar general of the Luanda archdiocese, who was arrested in 1961 and died in exile in Portugal in 1967, and fr Joaquim Pinto de Andrade, former chancellor of the same diocese and brother of the nationalist writer Mario de Andrade, who was exiled to Portugal in 1960 and received a sentence of 3 years imprisonment in 1971 for 'belonging to the MPLA'. The MPLA had in fact named him honorary president of the movement.

The long duration of the war and the strengthening of nationalist aspirations among the Angolan population and the African priesthood led some foreign missionaries and a small minority of Portuguese clergy to raise questions regarding the colonial system and the war. In 1968, fr Adalberto Postima, professor of philosophy in the interdiocesan seminary of Luanda, was relieved of his functions by the archbishop of Luanda and returned to his homeland, Italy, for having suggested in an open letter to the archbishop the need of studying the right to self-determination according to the pontifical documents. In the same year, fr Waldo Garcia, a Spaniard and professor in the major seminary of Nova Lisboa, as well as being a member of the administration of the Catholic Institute, and 2 Portuguese priests, were expelled from Angola by the hierarchy for having organized colloquia dealing with pastoralia and for editing a book on ecumenism. The Catholic Institute for all practical purposes disappeared afterwards. In July 1970, in a letter addressed to the Episcopal Conference and made public a year later, 22 Portuguese Holy Ghost priests protested against the pastoral and indeed administrative role forced onto missionaries. They described the Angolan church as an 'official society intimately associated with the powers that be' and requested of the bishops permission to initiate a new mission experiment which, beginning with a critique of traditional mission, would seek for answers to the concrete situations created by the colonial regime. The Episcopal Conference refused approval and a number of these clergy were forced to leave Angola.

Until April 1974, the Angolan Catholic hierarchy continued unanimous in its support of the Lisbon regime and its colonial policies. On one side, there were declarations condemning African terrorists which were manifestly favorable towards the war carried on by the Portuguese army against the nationalists; and on the other hand, the episcopal documents of that time dealt with social, moral, and spiritual problems as if there were no war in Angola with its attendant repression, massacres, and brutality. At a time when the liberation war and Portugal's international isolation put pressure on the government to institute a degree of reform, the Angolan bishops published 2 pastoral letters, one in 1971 and the other in 1972, criticizing the 'social disequilibrium' and 'peace based on the domination of one class by another', without reference to Portuguese colonialism as a cause.

After the military coup in Portugal on 25 April 1974, the (Catholic) Episcopal Conference of Angola published a pastoral note in May and declaration in June manifesting their embarrassment over their previous position and also expressing somewhat awkwardly their acceptance of the new political orientation of the country. Their condemnation of the injustices of the previous regime was combined with warnings against a repetition of such injustices during the period of transition and by the future government of independent Angola. On the other hand, the pastoral letter published after the agreement of 15 January 1975 guaranteeing the independence of Angola showed a significant change. The bishops there renounced their previous political attitude, based on 'assimilation', in favor of an 'authentically African' church, which is 'derived of necessity by the apostolic requirements of our faith' and not from 'a spirit of calculation or tactics'. The 1974 Annual Conference of the United Methodist Church issued a document protesting that since 1961 Protestant Christians had suffered the detention and expulsion of missionaries, the destruction and burning of churches and chapels, pastors detained in prison without charges or trial, and the 'hideous massacre of many innocent Angolans'. It stated, 'the fact of someone belonging to the Protestant church was sufficient reason for an accusation in many places'. In the uncertain circumstances of the time, the document also called for calm and a climate of peace. An expression of hope for better times came from the General Synod of Evangelical Churches in Central Angola, which held an assembly in 1975, its first since 1961. These Protestant churches expressed their assumption that then, after independence, they would be able to expand their programs, and that they would enjoy the same privileges as the Catholic Church had before independence.

When president Agostinho Neto officially proclaimed independence in November 1975, in the same speech he declared the People's Republic of Angola to be a lay state, with complete separation of church and state. He promised that the new regime would respect all religions and protect all churches, places, and objects of worship. This immediately disestablished the Catholic Church. The new constitution sounded a more ominous note when it guaranteed freedom of religion 'so long as they (the churches) comply with the state laws'. The first serious confrontation between the churches and the new government came in December 1975 when all schools were nationalized. Church schools had been an important means for evangelization and Christian education, and the confiscation of school buildings and properties hurt more than the educational ministries of the churches. This was a very serious move, considering that the education of Africans in Angola had in 1940 been reserved as the exclusive responsibility of the (Catholic) missionaries, with all church activities subsidized by the state. In practice, Protestants had also been allowed to run schools so long as Portuguese was used as the medium of instruction.

The new constitution in 1976 proclaimed Angola as a secular state with the right of all to be either religious or nonreligious, freedom of conscience, religious belief and the right to worship, with all churches and missions having equal rights. Further, the churches' contribution to the building of the new society in Angola would be welcomed. However, shortly afterwards the regime indicated its true intentions, by silencing the Catholic radio station in Luanda, and by condemning as subversive both Jehovah's Witnesses and Our Lord the Bakongo Tokoist movement, the Church of Jesus Christ in the World. In 1978, the regime decreed the final nationalization of Rádio Eclésia and seizure of its property, abolished all religious holidays including Christmas, and began a ceaseless barrage of atheistic propaganda.

Still, not all leaders of the ruling MPLA were opposed to religion. Some of its activists were Catholics, even priests. The MPLA had received moral and possibly even financial help from the WCC during their liberation struggle. At the time of independence, the three leaders of the three main liberation movements (MPLA, FNLA, UNITA) had all been educated at Protestant missions.

In 1976 a number of Catholic and Protestant missionaries were imprisoned and expelled. Priests and a bishop were kidnapped in 1981-82. President Neto revealed more candidly his attitude toward religion when in 1977 he stated, 'Catholics and Protestants cannot be members of the (ruling Marxist-Leninist) party... and perhaps 50 years from now there will be no more churches in Angola'.

In 1978 the Ministry of Justice was instructed to start a process to register churches and religious groups. Also, churches were no longer allowed to construct new buildings without proper permits, and they lost their tax-exempt status. The first list of 'recognized' churches was not published until 1986, when it was issued by the National Office for Religious Subjects, which is within the Secretariat of State for Culture. They then told 19 denominations that they had not been approved. The 12 that were permitted to then begin the process of registry included the Evangelical Church of Southwest Angola, the Evangelical Congregational Church of Angola, the Catholic Church, the United Methodist Church, the Evangelical Baptist Church, the Evangelical Reformed Church, the Church of Jesus Christ on the Earth (Kimbanguist), the Pentecostal Assemblies of God, the Seventh-day Adventist Church, the Angola Baptist Convention, and the Union of Evangelical Churches of Angola.

Igreja Católica em Angola. Catholic station Radio Ecclesia in Luanda, begun 1954, silenced 1976, seized by the regime 1978.

In the late 1980s the government became more tolerant of religious organizations. One sign of this was that the banned Tokoist church was declared legal in 1988. When the elections of 1992 were held, both sides of the civil war reiterated the position that Angola should be a secular state.

BROADCASTING AND MEDIA

Receivers are not widely available, so results are limited. For shortwave listeners, HCJB carries programs in Kikongo and Portuguese, and TWR (Swaziland) has broadcasts in Umbundu, Kimbundu and Portuguese. AWR has English and French-language programs. Local AM and FM stations carry Christian programming, some of which comes from Angolan churches, and a large part from IBRA. Angola is a member of UNDA.

Television sets are rare: less than 1% of the residents own one, and there are no strategies aiming programs specifically at the country.

INTERDENOMINATIONAL ORGANIZATIONS

The Evangelical Alliance of Angola (Alianca Evangelica de Angola) was formed in 1922 and counts in its membership the main Protestant bodies working in the country, excepting the Adventists. Its effectiveness was hampered from 1961-1974 when its annual meetings were prohibited. Other cooperative ministries were similarly affected, including the Congress of Portuguese Language Camps and the Congress of Evangelical Youth. In addition to its involvement in regulating comity agreements between the churches, the Alliance helped to coordinate the missionary work of the Angola churches on the island of São Tomé. Another example of Protestant cooperation was the establishment of Emmanuel United Seminary in Dondi in 1957, a joint venture of Methodists and the Evangelical Church of Central Angola.

In 1974, the Alliance was re-formed with 6 member-denominations as the Association of Evangelicals of Angola, a member of the Association of Evangelicals of Africa and Madagascar (AEAM).

Eight denominations came together in 1977 to form the Angolan Council of Evangelical Churches (CAIE). This group, with ties to the WCC, immediately applied for membership in the All Africa Council of Churches (AACC).

Protestant-Catholic relations greatly improved after Vatican II, although there are still no formal organizations providing for dialogue or joint action. In July 1966 the first public Protestant-Catholic worship service took place in the College of Sao Jose de Cluny in Luanda with the Catholic archbishop and the bishops of the Portuguese Lusitanian and Methodist churches officiating. The (Catholic) Episcopal Conference of Angola and São Tomé (CEAST) has a commission on Ecumenism.

FUTURE TRENDS AND PROSPECTS

The gap between affiliated Christians (1970, 56.4%) and professing Christians (1970, 81.7%) should gradually close through 2025 (affiliated 91.6%, professing 97.4%).

Christianity will potentially decline in the 21st century due to the growth of secularism (the nonreligious and atheists). This will probably continue up to AD 2050 when Christianity may dip below 95%.

BIBLIOGRAPHY

'A history of the American Board Missions in Angola, 1880–1940.' F. Soremekun. Ph.D. dissertation, Northwestern University, Evanston, IL, 1965.

A igreja em Angola: um rio com várias correntes. L. W. Henderson. Lisbon: Além-Mar, 1990. 494p.

Among the primitive Bakongo: a record of thirty years close intercourse with the Bakongo and other tribes of equatorial Africa, with a description of their habits, customs, and religious beliefs. J. H. Weeks. London: Seely, Service & Co., 1914. 318p.

Angola. R. Black. *World bibliographical series*, vol. 151. Oxford, UK: CLIO Press, 1992. 206p. (See especially 'Religion,' 56-60, and 'Folklore and customs,' 138-9).

Angola awake. S. Gilchrist. Toronto: Ryerson, 1968. 123p.

Angola beloved. T. E. Wilson. Neptune, NJ: Loizeaux Bros, 1967. 254p.

Angola: cinco séculos de Cristianismo. M. N. Gabriel. Braga, Portugal: Literal, 1975. 647p.

Angola: the land of the blacksmith prince. J. T. Tucker. London: World Dominion Press, 1933. 180p. (Detailed Protestant survey).

Aspectos dos movimentos associativos na Africa Negra. J. M. da Silva Cunha. Lisbon: Junta de Investigações do Ultramar, 1958–59. 2 vols. (Lassismo and other cults).

Atlas missionário português. A. Rego & E. dos Santos. Lisbon: Junta de Investigações do Ultramar, 1964.

Boletim eclesiástico de Angola e São Tomé, 1963–64. Luanda: Missões Católicas Portuguesas, 1965. 239p.

Cry, Angola! L. Addicott. London: SCM Press, 1962. 144p.

'Do sincretismo mágico e religioso nos fundamentos ideológicos do terrorismo no noroeste de Angola,' E. dos Santos, *Garcia de Orta* (Lisbon), 10, 1 (1962).

Ilundu: espíritos e ritos angolanos. O. Ribas. [Lisbon]: União dos Escritores Angolanos, 1989. 205p.

L'Angola traditionelle: une introduction aux problèmes magico–religieux. M. L. Rodrigues de Areia. Coimbra, Portugal: Tipografia de Atlântida, 1974.

'L'eglise toko et le mouvement de libération de l'Angola,' *Le mois en Afrique*, (May, 1966), 80–97.

Les symboles divinatoires: analyse socio–culturelle d'une technique de divination des Cokwe d'Angola (Ngombo ya Cisuka). M. L. Rodrigues de Areia. Coimbra, Portugal: Instituto de Antropologia, Universidade de Coimbra, 1985. 555p.

Liturgia, Cristianismo e sociedade em Angola. A. F. Santos Neves. Angola: Editorial Coloquios, 1968. 192p.

'Nouvelles manifestations du prophétisme en Afrique équatoriale et en Angola,' C. Tastevin, *Comptes rendus de l'Académie des Sciences Coloniales* (Paris), 16, 3 (1956), 149–53.

'O Noroeste angolano e os movimentos profético–salvificos,' E. dos Santos, *Ultramar* (Lisbon), 17 (1964), 32–73.

One hundred years of Christian mission in Angola and Zaire, 1878–1978. London: Baptist Missionary Society, 1978. 50p.

Pequenas comunidades cristãs: o ondjango e a inculturação em Africa/Angola. J. Nunes. *Biblioteca humanística e teológica*, 3. Porto: Universidade Católica Portuguesa, 1991. 381p.

Quo vadis, Angola?: sobre a presença do cristianismo na Angola deste tempo. A. F. S. Neves. [Luanda]: Editorial Colóquios, 1974. 287p.

Religiões de Angola. E. dos Santos. *Estudos misionários*, 3. Lisboa: Junta de Investigações do Ultramar, 1969. 536p.

State and the church in Angola 1450–1980. G. Grohs & G. Czernik. *International studies on contemporary Africa*, 3. Geneva: Institut Universitaire de Hautes Études Internationales, 1983. 100p.

The church in Angola: a river of many currents. L. W. Henderson. Cleveland, OH: Pilgrim Press, 1992. 448p.

'The divining basket of the Ovimbundu,' L. Tucker, *Journal of the Royal Anthropological Institute*, 70, 2 (1940), 171–201.

The ethnography of southwestern Angola. C. Estermann. Trans. and ed., G. D. Gibson. New York: Africana, 1976. 3 vols.

The Kavango peoples. G. D. Gibson, T. J. Larson & C. R. McGurk. Wiesbaden, Germany: Franz Steiner Verlag, 1981. 275p. (Treats religion).

The Ovimbundu of Angola. Part 2 of *West Central Africa.* M. McCulloch. *Ethnographic survey of Africa*, D. Forde (ed). London: International African Institute, 1952. 50p.

The Ovimbundu of Angola. W. D. Hambly. *Field Museum of Natural History, Publication no. 329: Anthropological series*, 21, 2. Chicago: Field Museum of Natural History, 1934. 362p. (Treats religion).

The social responses of Christianity in Angola: selected issues. T. M. Okuma. Boston: Boston University Press, 1964. 277p.

Country Table 2. **Organized churches and denominations in Angola.**

Official name (bold type = church with over 10% of all affiliated) 1	*Begun* 2	*Type* 3	*Counc* 4	*Congs* 5	*Adults* 6	*Affiliated 1970* 7	*Affiliated 1995* 8	*G%* 9	*Names, notes, and other statistics* (see Codebook, Part 3) 10
Convenção Baptista de Angola	1936	P-Bap	T...G	85	15,470	1,000	20,900	12.93	*Angola Baptist Convention.* M=BCP(Portugal); 1968, SBC(USA); CBB(Brazil). Portuguese, 5n, 73Y
Igreja Adventista do Sétimo Dia	1922	P-Adv	x....	560	67,200	37,000	120,000	4.82	8 Missions in Angola UM. Mbundu. 49n,1H,3h,1j,2r,1S,812t(37515),2775Y.
Igreja Anglicana (D Damaraland)	1924	A-Hig	aWaV.	10	1,400	2,000	3,400	2.15	*Anglican Ch.* Part of D Damaraland (Namibia), CPSA. Ambo. Missionaries forbidden.
Igreja Apostolica Africana em A	c1980	I-3oA	.....	400	50,000	–	86,000	6.67	*African Apostolic Church in Angola.* HQ Luanda.
Igreja Baptista Livre en Angola	c1975	I-Bap	T....	28	15,290	–	25,000	5.00	*Free Baptist Church in Angola.*
Igreja Católica em Angola:	1491	R-Lat	P.SSP	278	3,845,000	2,667,306	6,750,237	3.78	*Catholic Ch in Angola. C=12+4+30.* 145n 221x 505m 1314w 111665Yy
M Huambo	1940	R-Lat	P	42	965,000	579,513	1,693,000	4.38	Formerly Archdiocese of Nova Lisboa, renamed 1977. 29n 22x 150m 196w 24250Yy
D Benguela	1970	R-Lat	P	47	456,000	374,748	800,000	3.08	Port area 300 miles south of capital 29n 23x 63m 244w 24875Yy
D Kwito-Bié	1940	R-Lat	P	27	213,000	349,613	373,000	0.26	Formerly D Silva Porto. Guerrilla disruption. 4n 4x 7m 33w 6284Yy
D Lwena	1963	R-Lat	P osb	12	29,000	31,000	51,538	2.05	Formerly D Luso, renamed 1979. 1n 7x 11m 5w 125Yy

Continued overleaf

Country Table 2–concluded

Official name (bold type = church with over 10% of all affiliated) 1	*Begun* 2	*Type* 3	*Counc* 4	*Congs* 5	*Adults* 6	*Affiliated 1970* 7	*Affiliated 1995* 8	*G%* 9	*Names, notes, and other statistics* (see Codebook, Part 3) 10
M Luanda	1940	R-Lat	P	26	606,000	710,000	1,064,000	1.63	Heavy fighting and destruction. 11n 61x 145m 319w 7788Yy
D Cabinda	1984	R-Lat	P	8	67,000	–	118,791	9.09	Northern enclave adjoining Congo. Oil. 15n 3x 3m 30w 1931Yy
D Malanje	1957	R-Lat	P	14	116,000	85,000	204,000	3.56	M=CSSp. 9n 15x 17m 113w 1196Yy
D Mbanza Congo	1984	R-Lat	Pofmc	6	80,000	–	140,000	9.09	Formerly in D Uije. M=OFMCap. 2n 11x 16m 20w 1369Yy
D Ndalatando	1990	R-Lat	Pofmc	8	114,000	–	200,000	20.00	Formerly in M Luanda. M=OFMCap,CSSp. 0n 16x 20m 33w 6550Yy
D Novo Redondo	1975	R-Lat	P	12	206,000	–	361,000	5.00	In Kwanza Sul. 4n 14x 18m 62w 4546Yy
D Saurimo	1975	R-Lat	P	8	37,000	–	65,000	5.00	Formerly D Henrique de Carvalho, renamed 1979. 5n 5x 7m 20w 1347Yy
D Uije	1967	R-Lat	P	15	254,000	128,388	446,005	5.11	Formerly D Carmona e São Salvador, renamed 1979. 8n 19x 24m 76w 12364Yy
M Lubango	1955	R-Lat	P	32	426,000	409,044	747,936	2.44	Formerly D Sá da Bandeira, renamed 1977. 17n 16x 19m 133w 13198Yy
D Menongue	1975	R-Lat	Pcssr	12	87,000	–	153,000	5.00	Formerly D Serpa Pinto, renamed 1979. M=CSsR. 7n 3x 3m 10w 3280Yy
D Ondijiva	1975	R-Lat	P	9	189,000	–	332,967	5.00	Formerly D Pereira de Eça, renamed 1979. 4n 2x 2m 20w 2562Yy
Igreja de Cristo do Angola	c1970	P-Dis	x....	33	5,000	–	7,690	43.03	*Ch of Christ in Angola.*
Igreja de Deus	1938	P-Pe3	ZF...	100	10,000	5,000	25,000	6.65	*Church of God.* M=CoG(Cleveland) (USA) until expelled 1957. Locally led,now part of ADPA.
Igreja de Lassy Zepherin	1953	I-3aA	.....	20	1,500	1,000	3,000	4.49	*Lassismo. Nzambi Bougie (God of the Candle).* In Cabinda, from Congo-Brazzaville.
Igreja do Arbusto	c1975	I-3cA	....	15	1,500	–	3,000	5.00	*Church of the Bush.*
Igreja do Nazareno	c1960	P-Hol	xF...	1	50	500	125	-5.39	*Ch of the Nazarene.* Immigrant Caboverdian farmers from Cape Verde Islands.
Igreja do Nosso Senhor Jesus Cristo	1949	I-3pA	.....	50	30,000	20,000	60,000	4.49	*Ebundu dia Mfumu eto Yeso Klisto. Red Star Cult.* Ex BMS. Persecuted, expanding.
Igreja Evangélica Baptista	1878	P-Bap	T.A.a	55	34,558	10,000	50,000	6.65	*Ev Baptist Ch.* M=BMS(UK). Northeast. 99% Kongo. 1961 war, most fled to Zaire. 1s.
Igreja Evangélica de Angola Central	1880	P-Uni	.W..K	1,077	140,000	204,000	380,000	2.52	*Ev Ch of Central Angola.* M=UCCan,UCC(USA). 98% Mbundu, 1% Kwanyama. 15f,10H,20h,1u.
Igreja Evangélica do Sudoeste de A	1897	P-Bap	...G	500	40,000	45,000	121,000	4.04	M=Filafricana (SEAM). 59% Mbundu. 20n,3x,421m,90w,7H,6h,1p,2r,W=40%,712Y,3899z.
Igreja Evangélica do Sul de Angola	1914	P-Eva	xM..G	148	13,800	10,000	38,000	5.49	*Ev Ch of South Angola.* M=AEF(SAGM). 50% Chokwe, 45% Ngonyelu. 15F,3H,1P,1S,250Y.
Igreja Evangélica dos Irmãos		P-CBr	x...G	1,200	125,000	20,000	278,000	0.05	*Christian Brethren* (Open). M=CMML(UK, USA). Chokwe, Luvale, Lunda. 17f,4H.
Igreja Ev Irmãos Menonita Renovada	1980	I-Men	G....	13	1,250	–	2,500	6.67	*Mennonite Church (Renewed).*
Igr Ev Pentecostal Assembleia de Deus	c1951	P-Pe3	....G	700	210,750	3,000	300,000	20.23	*ADPA.* Portuguese. Expelled 1957, returned 1970. Cuanza-Sul. 4n,1p. M=COGWM, AoG Brazil.
Igreja Ev Reformada de Angola	1925	P-Ref	.W...	300	40,000	6,000	70,000	10.33	*Ev Reformed Ch of Angola.* M=missions from UK, Switzerland. 120 pastors.
Igreja Evangélica Unida Angola	1897	P-Bap	T...a	197	15,000	2,000	25,000	10.63	1897 M=Angola Ev Mission; 1910 CMA; 1957 CBOMB(Canada). Cabinda, NW Angola; Kongo.
Igreja Kimbanguista	1927	I-3aA	IWi.K	425	106,000	30,000	320,000	9.93	*EJCSK* (Zaire). In north among Kongo tribe. Violent persecution until 1974.
Igreja Lusitana Católica Apostólica Ev	1965	I-ReC	uuc..	3	210	200	400	2.81	*Lusitanian Ch of Portugal.* In communion with Anglican Church. 1n.
Igreja Luterana de Angola	c1960	P-Lut	L....	68	4,760	1,000	11,900	10.41	Fast-growing small denomination.
Igreja Metodista Unida de Angola	1885	P-Met	Vw..K	2,400	120,000	70,000	179,000	3.83	*Africa CC, UMC.* 97% Kimbundu. 67n,386m,100w,1H,1p,1s,1u,W=70%,1000Y,1800y.
Igreja Nova Apostólica	c1970	I-3aX	x....	200	30,000	–	57,616	55.03	*NAC. New Apostolic Ch* (HQ Zurich, Switzerland).
Missão Ev Pentecostal de Angola	c1980	I-3pA	.W...	600	75,460	–	100,000	6.67	*Evangelical Pentecostal Mission of Angola.* Ex ADPA. *MEPA, IEPA.*
Testemunhas de Jeová	c1945	m-Jeh	x....	321	28,911	1,000	89,400	19.69	*Jehovah's Witnesses. Watch Tower.* Active witnessing by 1950. Banned 1976. 91Y. (1995) 3638Y.
Other African indigenous churches	c1940	I-3cA	.....	500	20,000	10,000	40,000	5.70	Total about 7 (see list below), including from Zaire, also IURD (Brazil), Manna Ch (Portugal).
Other Protestant denominations		P-	.....	150	4,000	3,000	6,000	0.05	Including Christian Ev Ch of Luanda, Ev Pentecostal Mission.
Totals				**10,437**	**5,052,109**	**3,149,006**	**9,173,168**		

Churches, members, growth, 1900-2025	*Congs*	*Adults*	*Affiliated*	*G%*	*Total denominations*	*6 Megablocs: O*	*R*	*A*	*P*	*I*	*m*
Total churches, members, and denominations (mid-1900)	30	7,000	12,700	8.19	6	0	1	0	5	0	0
Total churches, members, and denominations (mid-1970)	1,933	1,742,524	3,149,006	8.19	27	0	1	1	16	8	1
Total churches, members, and denominations (mid-1990)	6,000	4,156,000	7,545,700	4.47	40	0	1	1	20	17	1
Total churches, members, and denominations (mid-1995)	10,437	5,052,109	9,173,168	3.98	40	0	1	1	20	17	1
Total churches, members, and denominations (mid-2000)	11,000	6,022,000	10,934,238	3.57	42	0	1	1	21	18	1
Total churches, members, and denominations (mid-2025)	30,000	12,667,000	23,000,000	3.02	89	2	1	1	30	50	5

NOTES ON TABLE ABOVE

NATIONAL COUNCILS (Column 4, 5th letter).

d = member of AEA and CICA.

E = Aliança Evangélica de Angola (AEA) (Evangelical Alliance of Angola EAA) (formed 1922 as Alliança Evangélica de Angola; 1974, attempts to make it a council of churches; 1974, Associacção de Evangélicos de Angola formed).

P = Conferência Episcopal de Angola e São Tomé (CEAST) (Episcopal Conference of Angola & São Tomé).

W = Conselho de Igrejas Cristas em Angola (CICA, Council of Christian Churches in Angola), formed 1977.

OTHER AFRICAN INDIGENOUS CHURCHES. There are several other unorganized movements, including: Grupo do Espirito Santo (Holy Spirit Group), Igreja Apostolica de Angola; 1974, attempts to make it a council of churches; 1974, Associação de Evangélicos de Angola formed); Manna Church (Portugal) has also had vast attendances recently.

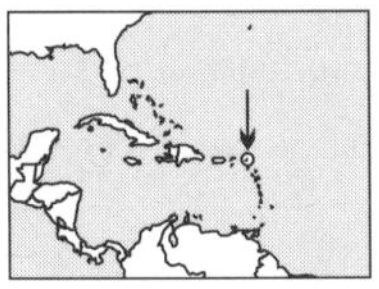

ANGUILLA

SECULAR DATA, AD 2000

STATE
Official name: The Colony of Anguilla.
Short name: Anguilla. **Adjective of nationality:** Anguillan.
Flag: British Blue Ensign with arms of the Colony in the fly.
Area: 91 sq. km. (35 sq. mi.).
Government: Self-governing colony or dependency of the United Kingdom (Britain), since 1976 (1650 British colony, ruled from St Kitts until 1967 revolt).
Legislature: House of Assembly, 13 members.
Official language: English.
Monetary unit: 1 Eastern Caribbean dollar (EC$) = 100 cents. **US$1=** EC$2.70.
Chief cities: THE VALLEY 1,281.
Political divisions: 1 province.

DEMOGRAPHY
Population: 8,000.
Population density: 91.3/sq. km. (237.4/sq. mi.).
Under 15 years: 2,000.
Growth rate p.a.: 1.19% (births 15.26, deaths 5.77).
Mortality: Infant, per 1,000: 7.8; **Maternal per 100,000:** 30.0.
Life expectancy: 78 (male 75, female 82).
Household size: 4.0. **Floor area per person, sq.m:** 18.0.
Major languages: English.
Urban dwellers: 12.0%. **Urban growth rate p.a.:** 3.6%.
Labor force: 60%.

ETHNOLINGUISTIC PEOPLES
89.8% West Indian Black; 8.0% Mulatto; 1.5% British; 0.5% Indo-Pakistani.

ECONOMY
National income p.a. per person: US$2,045; **per family:** US$8,183.

EDUCATION
Adult literacy: 90% (male 92%, female 88%). **Schools:** 7.
Universities: 0. **School enrolment:** female/male: 90%/90%.

HEALTH
Access to health services: 70%. **Access to safe water:** 90%.
Hospitals: 1 (50 beds per 10,000). **Doctors:** 10.
Blind: 10. **Deaf:** 500. **Murder rate:** 3. **Lepers:** 0.

LITERATURE
New book titles p.a.: 2 (200 p.a. per million). **Periodicals:** 4.
Newspapers: 0 dailies.

COMMUNICATION (per 1,000 people)
Phones: 350 **(1% mobile). Radios:** 700. **TV sets:** 500.
Daily newspaper circulation: <1. **Computers:** 1,000.

HUMAN LIFE AND LIBERTY (optimum condition=100.0%)
HDI: 85.0. **HSI:** 80.0. **HFI:** 70.0. **EFL:** 40.0.

Country status. Anguilla is the most northerly of the Leeward Islands in the West Indies and is a dependency of the United Kingdom where all basic human rights are respected. Its economy is dependent on tourism, fishing, and agriculture.

HUMAN LIFE AND LIBERTY

Human rights and freedoms. Anguilla is a dependency of the United Kingdom; all basic human rights are respected.

NON-CHRISTIAN RELIGIONS

There is one isolated group of Baha'is and several hundred Spiritists.

CHRISTIANITY

ANGLICAN CHURCH. The largest denomination in Anguilla is Anglicanism which is part of the diocese of Antigua in the Church of the Province of the West Indies. Antigua received its first Anglican priest in 1634, but Anguilla was not reached until later. Originally under the bishop of London, the Leeward Islands were placed in the bishopric of Barbados in 1824, with the diocese of Antigua being established in 1842. The Anglican community is today 95% Black.

PROTESTANT CHURCHES. Methodism is the principle Protestant body, having been brought back to Anguilla in 1813 by John Hodge, a local layman, after his visit to a nearby island. Hodge was ordained in 1822 and was the pioneer in the development of the early work. There are today 4 parishes which form part of the Leeward Islands District, Methodist Church in the Caribbean and the Americas.

Other small Protestant denominations, each with one congregation, are the Seventh-day Adventists, Church of God (Anderson), Brethren, Baptists, and Apostolic Faith.

CATHOLIC CHURCH. Catholicism is weak, consisting of one parish only without a resident priest. Anguilla belongs to the diocese of Saint John's and is served by Redemptorist priests stationed on St Kitts.

The Holy See has no diplomatic relations with Anguilla in AD 2000.

Indigenous missions. Christians on Anguilla have been isolated from the rest of the world but have had contact with various nationalities through tourism on the islands. The presence of Baha'is and Muslims has increased the church's awareness of world religions.

BROADCASTING AND MEDIA

The Caribbean Beacon is a local radio station broadcasting daily Christian programming over FM radio. Shortwave programs from HCJB (Ecuador), TWR (Antilles) and AWR (Costa Rica) can be easily received. LeSEA programming can be received from the World Harvest Satellite.

INTERDENOMINATIONAL ORGANIZATIONS

The Methodist and Anglican churches are members of the Anguilla Christian Council.

Country Table 1. **Religious adherents in Anguilla, AD 1900-2025.**

Year / Name	1900 Adherents	%	1970 Adherents	%	mid-1990 Adherents	%	Annual change, 1990-2000 Natural	Conversion	Total	Rate	mid-1995 Adherents	%	mid-2000 Adherents	%	mid-2025 Adherents	%
Christians	**4,200**	**100.0**	**5,850**	**95.9**	**6,730**	**96.1**	**95**	**-8**	**87**	**1.23**	**7,150**	**91.7**	**7,604**	**91.5**	**9,870**	**89.7**
PROFESSION																
professing Christians	**4,200**	**100.0**	**5,850**	**95.9**	**6,730**	**96.1**	**95**	**-8**	**87**	**1.23**	**7,150**	**91.7**	**7,604**	**91.5**	**9,870**	**89.7**
AFFILIATION																
unaffiliated Christians	300*	7.1	920	15.1	500	7.1	7	-15	-8	-1.78	487	6.3	418	5.0	70	0.6
affiliated Christians	**3,900**	**92.9**	**4,930**	**80.8**	**6,230**	**89.0**	**89**	**7**	**96**	**1.44**	**6,663**	**85.4**	**7,186**	**86.5**	**9,800**	**89.1**
Protestants	1,900	45.2	2,320	38.0	3,350	47.9	48	30	78	2.11	3,710	47.6	4,126	49.7	5,740	52.2
Anglicans	1,970	46.9	2,500	41.0	2,570	36.7	37	-29	8	0.31	2,600	33.3	2,650	31.9	3,200	29.1
Roman Catholics	30	0.7	100	1.6	230	3.3	3	5	8	3.03	263	3.4	310	3.7	520	4.7
Marginal Christians	0	0.0	10	0.2	80	1.1	1	1	2	2.26	90	1.2	100	1.3	340	3.1
Trans-megabloc groupings																
Evangelicals	1,000	23.8	800	13.1	760	10.9	11	-7	4	0.51	775	9.9	800	9.6	1,000	9.1
Pentecostals/Charismatics	0	0.0	150	2.5	830	11.9	12	9	21	2.28	932	12.0	1,040	12.5	1,550	14.1
Great Commission Christians	**90**	**2.1**	**60**	**1.0**	**880**	**12.6**	**13**	**9**	**22**	**2.24**	**975**	**12.5**	**1,098**	**13.2**	**1,650**	**15.0**
Spiritists	0	0.0	200	3.3	380	5.4	5	3	8	1.82	420	5.4	455	5.5	650	5.9
Nonreligious	0	0.0	0	0.0	80	1.1	1	1	2	2.46	95	1.2	102	1.2	200	1.8
Baha'is	0	0.0	50	0.8	70	1.0	1	1	2	2.08	80	1.0	86	1.0	160	1.5
Muslims	0	0.0	0	0.0	30	0.4	0	2	2	4.37	40	0.5	46	0.6	80	0.7
Hindus	0	0.0	0	0.0	10	0.1	0	1	1	5.45	15	0.2	17	0.2	40	0.4
World A (unevangelized persons)	0	0.0	0	0.0	14	0.2	0	0	0	2.72	15	0.2	16	0.2	55	0.5
World B (evangelized non-Christians)	0	0.0	250	4.1	256	7.6	7	8	15	4.03	632	8.1	680	8.3	1,075	9.8
World C (Christians)	4,200	100.0	5,850	95.9	6,730	92.2	95	-8	87	1.23	7,150	91.7	7,604	91.5	9,870	89.7
Country's population	**4,200**	**100.0**	**6,100**	**100.0**	**7,000**	**100.0**	**102**	**0**	**102**	**1.34**	**7,798**	**100.0**	**8,300**	**100.0**	**11,000**	**100.0**

COLUMNS, ROWS.
For meanings and definitions, see Codebook (Part 3). Note that, by definition, total 'Christians' = professing + crypto-Christians, which also = affiliated + unaffiliated Christians, and also = Great Commission Christians + latent Christians. Percentages may not always total exactly, due to rounding.

CENSUSES.
4.IV.1881: 51.5% Protestants (51.4% Methodists), 47.9% Anglicans, 0.6% Roman Catholics. **7.IV.1960:** 49.2% Protestants (43.4% Methodists, 3.3% SDAs, 1.8 Church of God), 49.2% Anglicans, 1.5% Roman Catholics, 0.1% marginal Protestants (Jehovah's Witnesses). **1992:** 47.2% Protestants (29.5% Methodists, 7.0% Baptists, 6.8% SDAs, 3.9% Church of God), 35.8% Anglicans, 5.6% Roman Catholics, 11.2% other (including Jehovah Witnesses). **1992:** 47.2% Protestants (29.5% Methodists, 7.0% Baptists, 6.8% SDAs, 3.9% Church of God), 35.8% Anglicans, 5.6% Roman Catholics, 11.2% other (including Jehovah's Witnesses).

Great Commission Instrument Panel: status of Anguilla (for explanation see start of Part 4)

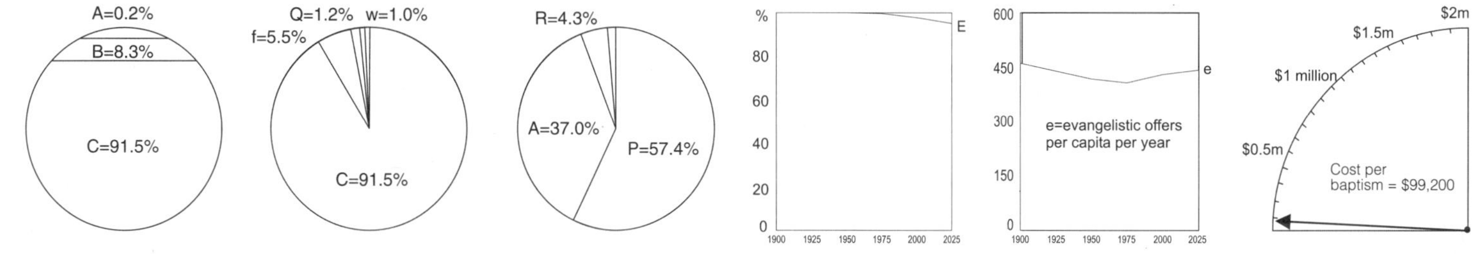

3 Worlds, AD 2000 — Religions, AD 2000 — Ecclesiastical blocs — Evangelization, 1900-2025 — Offers, 1900-2025 — Cost-effectiveness, AD 2000

Country summary. **Worlds A, B, C by ethnolinguistic peoples, cities, and major civil divisions in Anguilla.**

World	PEOPLES Num	Pop 2000	C%	Christians	E%	U%	Unevangelized	CITIES Num	Pop 2000	C%	Christians	E%	U%	Unevangelized	CIVIL DIVISIONS Num	Pop 2000	C%	Christians	E%	U%	Unevangelized
A	0	0	0.00	0	0	0	0	0	0	0.00	0	0	0	0	0	0	0.00	0	0	0	0
B	1	42	30.95	13	83	17	7	0	0	0.00	0	0	0	0	0	0	0.00	0	0	0	0
C	4	8,268	86.76	7,173	100	0	10	1	1,281	84.00	1,076	99	1	14	1	8,309	86.48	7,186	100	0	17
Total	**5**	**8,310**	**86.47**	**7,186**	**100**	**0**	**17**	**1**	**1,281**	**84.00**	**1,076**	**99**	**1**	**14**	**1**	**8,309**	**86.48**	**7,186**	**100**	**0**	**17**

Christians. A large number of the islands postage stamps, before its break with St Kitts-Nevis and after, portray Christ's Cross and Resurrection.

FUTURE TRENDS AND PROSPECTS

No dramatic changes are expected in Anguilla before AD 2025. The nonreligious and spiritists will likely constitute a significant minority into the first quarter of the 21st century.

Anguilla is expected to remain predominantly Christian (Anglican and Methodist) well up to AD 2050.

BIBLIOGRAPHY

A handbook history of Anguilla. C. L. Petty. [Anguilla, 1991]. 68p.

St. Kitts, Nevis, Anguilla archives. E. C. Baker. Mona, Jamaica: University of the West Indies, [1963]. 3 vols. (A catalogue of documents).

Country Table 2. **Organized churches and denominations in Anguilla.**

Official name (bold type = church with over 10% of all affiliated) 1	Begun 2	Type 3	Counc 4	Congs 5	Adults 6	Affiliated 1970 7	Affiliated 1995 8	G% 9	Names, notes, and other statistics (see Codebook, Part 3) 10
Anglican Church (D Antigua)	c1650	A-ACa	awMRC	5	1,040	2,500	2,600	0.16	In CPWI. M=USPG. 95% Blacks. 63% in Central Anguilla, 35% East End.
Baptist Church	c1970	P-Bap	.....	3	150	–	340	26.26	M=FMB-SBC(USA).
Catholic Church (D Saint John's)	1861	R-Lat	P.NM.	2	158	100	263	3.94	In D Saint John's (Antigua). M=CSSR,SVD. 46% in Central, 42% East End. No priest.
Christian Brethren	c1960	P-CBr	x....	1	10	20	20	0.00	One small group of Open Brethren or Plymouth Brethren. M=CMML(UK).
Church of God (Anderson)	1946	P-Hol	x....	2	40	100	120	0.73	M=CoG(Anderson) (USA). Holiness denomination. 50% in West End, 41% in Central.
Jehovah's Witnesses	c1960	m-Jeh	x....	1	24	10	90	9.19	*ISBA. Watch Tower.*
Meth Ch in Caribbean & Americas	1813	P-Met	VwM.C	4	1,050	2,000	2,090	0.18	In MCCA(1967 union), Leeward Islands District. M=MMS(UK). 75% in West End.
Seventh-day Adventist Church	c1960	P-Adv	x....	3	324	200	540	4.05	*SDA*, East Caribbean Conference, Caribbean Union Conference. 59% in East End.
Other Protestant churches	c1970	P-	.....	3	300	–	600	29.16	Total about 8 groupings.

Continued overleaf

Country Table 2–concluded

Official name (bold type = church with over 10% of affiliated) 1	*Begun* 2	*Type* 3	*Counc* 4	*Congs* 5	*Adults* 6	*Affiliated 1970* 7	*Affiliated 1995* 8	*G%* 9	*Names, notes, and other statistics* (see Codebook, Part 3) 10
Totals					**24**	**3,096**	**4,930**	**6,663**	

Churches, members, growth, 1900-2025	*Congs*	*Adults*	*Affiliated*	*G%*	*Total denominations*	*6 Megablocs:* O	R	A	P	I	m
Total churches, members, and denominations (mid-1900)	10	1,700	3,900	0.34	3	0	1	1	1	0	0
Total churches, members, and denominations (mid-1970)	12	2,195	4,930	0.34	7	0	1	1	4	0	1
Total churches, members, and denominations (mid-1990)	20	2,900	6,230	1.18	14	0	1	1	11	0	1
Total churches, members, and denominations (mid-1995)	24	3,096	6,663	1.35	16	0	1	1	13	0	1
Total churches, members, and denominations (mid-2000)	25	3,300	7,186	1.52	17	0	1	1	14	0	1
Total churches, members, and denominations (mid-2025)	40	4,600	9,800	1.25	36	0	1	1	20	10	4

NOTES ON TABLE ABOVE
NATIONAL COUNCILS (Column 4, 5th letter).
C = Anguilla Christian Council.

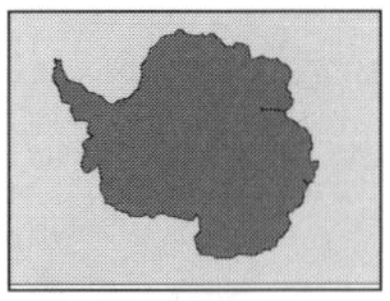

ANTARCTICA

SECULAR DATA, AD 2000

STATE
Official name: Antarctica.
Short name: Antarctica. **Adjective of nationality:** Antarctican.
Area: 15,500,000 sq. km. (5,980,000 sq. mi.).
Government: 1961 treaty signed by 39 countries.
Legislature: Treaty signers, 39 members.
Official language: English.
Monetary unit: 1 US dollar = 100 cents. **US$1=** $1.00.
Political divisions: 1 province.

DEMOGRAPHY
Population: 5,000.
Population density: 0.0/sq. km. (0.0/sq. mi.).
Under 15 years: 1,000.
Growth rate p.a.: 1.19% (births 19.05, deaths 7.78).
Mortality: Infant, per 1,000: 20.0; **Maternal per 100,000:** 10.0.
Life expectancy: 74 (male 71, female 78).
Household size: 2.0. **Floor area per person, sq.m:** 15.0.
Major languages: English, Russian, Spanish, Chinese.
Urban dwellers: 0.00%. **Urban growth rate p.a.:** 0.00%.
Labor force: 100%.

ECONOMY
National income p.a. per person: US$80,000; **per family:** US$160,000.

EDUCATION
Adult literacy: 100% (male 100%, female 100%). **Schools:** 0.
Universities: 0. **School enrolment:** female/male: 100%/100%.

HEALTH
Access to health services: 80%. **Access to safe water:** 100%.
Hospitals: 1 (20 beds per 10,000). **Doctors:** 20.
Blind: 10. **Deaf:** 300. **Murder rate:** 1. **Lepers:** 0.

LITERATURE
New book titles p.a.: 5 (1,000 p.a. per million). **Periodicals:** 0.
Newspapers: 0 dailies.

COMMUNICATION (per 1,000 people)
Phones: 200 (50% mobile). **Radios:** 2,000. **TV sets:** 200.
Daily newspaper circulation: <1. **Computers:** 2,000.

HUMAN LIFE AND LIBERTY (optimum condition=100.0%)
HDI: 80.0. **HSI:** 70.0. **HFI:** 80.0. **EFL:** 50.0.

Country Table 1. **Population and religious adherents in Antarctica, AD 1900-2025.**

Year / *Name*	*1900* *Adherents*	*%*	*1970* *Adherents*	*%*	*mid-1990* *Adherents*	*%*	*Annual change, 1990-2000* *Natural*	*Conversion*	*Total*	*Rate*	*mid-1995* *Adherents*	*%*	*mid-2000* *Adherents*	*%*	*mid-2025* *Adherents*	*%*
Christians	**0**	**0.0**	**370**	**74.0**	**2,300**	**76.7**	**110**	**0**	**110**	**3.99**	**2,900**	**74.4**	**3,400**	**68.0**	**8,000**	**80.0**
PROFESSION																
AFFILIATION																
affiliated Christians	**0**	**0.0**	**370**	**74.0**	**2,300**	**76.7**	**110**	**0**	**110**	**3.99**	**2,900**	**74.4**	**3,400**	**68.0**	**8,000**	**80.0**
Roman Catholics	0	0.0	200	40.0	950	31.7	45	0	45	3.95	1,250	32.1	1,400	28.0	3,000	30.0
Protestants	0	0.0	100	20.0	630	21.0	34	0	34	4.41	780	20.0	970	19.4	3,000	30.0
Independents	0	0.0	40	8.0	500	16.7	20	0	20	3.42	600	15.4	700	14.0	1,500	15.0
Anglicans	0	0.0	30	6.0	200	6.7	10	0	10	4.14	250	6.4	300	6.0	400	4.0
Orthodox	0	0.0	0	0.0	20	0.7	1	0	1	4.14	20	0.5	30	0.6	100	1.0
Trans-megabloc groupings																
Nonreligious	0	0.0	100	20.0	910	30.3	75	0	75	1.05	890	22.8	1,410	28.2	1,500	15.0
Muslims	0	0.0	10	2.0	40	1.3	8	0	8	11.61	60	1.5	120	2.4	200	2.0
Hindus	0	0.0	10	2.0	30	1.0	1	0	1	2.92	30	0.8	40	0.8	200	2.0
Buddhists	0	0.0	10	2.0	20	0.7	1	0	1	4.14	20	0.5	30	0.6	100	1.0
World A (unevangelized persons)	0	0.0	50	10.0	183	6.1	4	0	4	1.97	218	5.6	270	5.4	350	3.5
World B (evangelized non-Christians)	0	100.0	80	16.0	517	24.2	81	0	81	9.91	781	20.0	1,330	19.0	1,650	16.5
World C (Christians)	0	0.0	370	74.0	2,300	69.7	110	0	110	3.99	2,900	74.4	3,400	75.6	8,000	80.0
Country's population	**0**	**100.0**	**500**	**100.0**	**3,000**	**100.0**	**195**	**0**	**195**	**5.24**	**3,900**	**100.0**	**5,000**	**100.0**	**10,000**	**100.0**

Country status. Antarctica is an island continent with 39 nations having stakes on it of varying size, but all accepting internationally agreed limitations for the present and future (the Antarctic Treaty of 1959). There is no military or economic exploitation, leaving scientific research as the only viable activity.

HUMAN LIFE AND LIBERTY

Human rights and freedoms. Personnel of the different nations have achieved a high level of cooperation and respect for each other and assist each other at every turn. Determination to preserve the continent from political quarrels kept relations between the USA and USSR cordial and mutually assisting throughout the Cold War, 1945-1991. This camaraderie continues throughout the 1990s.

Protestants. Chapel of the Snows, used by all groups since 1958.

Human environment. The world's fifth largest continent, Antarctica has unique mineral and other resources, most notably its 14,700- foot thick ice cap which contains 75% of the Earth's water and 90% of its ice. Its greatest economic potential lies in carefully managed exploitation of the harvesting of krill in circumpolar waters.

NON-CHRISTIAN RELIGIONS

Religion has little role in activities or relations. The table above gives the de facto religious affiliation of scientists and support personnel resident there. Many express awe at the beauty and immensity of the Antarctic world and relate it to God's creative activity.

CHRISTIANITY

Most personnel are Christians and many have personal Christian convictions and practice. There are several informal discussion groups. Only one permanent church building exists, the Chapel of the Snows, served usually by one Protestant pastor and one Catholic chaplain.

BROADCASTING AND MEDIA

Many religious radio and TV programs are regularly accessed from the world's stations to the north.

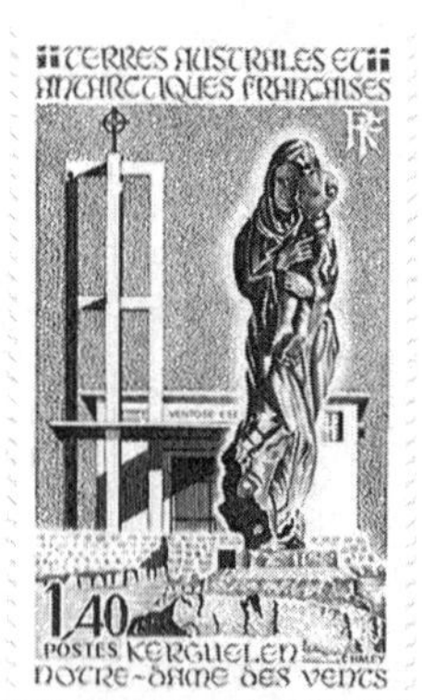

Roman Catholic. *Left.* Church on Kerguelen, Notre-Dame des Vents (Church of the Winds). *Right.* Pioneer worker, fr LeJay.

Left. **Christians.** Postage stamp showing 1953 Coronation oath administered by Archbishop of Canterbury.

FUTURE TRENDS AND PROSPECTS

With the vast biological, mineral, and other resources of Antarctica, and the unique political agreement about its development, the future of Antarctica is full of promise. At one time there was a proposal to build a semi-subterranean city there as the headquarters of the United Nations, and a name had even been proposed for it – Amundsen City.

BIBLIOGRAPHY

Antarctic bibliography. Washington, DC: Library of Congress, annual.

Antarctic diary. M. Buxton. : T. Dalton, 1988.

Antarctic journey: three artists in Antarctica. : AGPS, 1990. 50p.

Antarctica: an encyclopedia. J. Stewart. Jefferson, NC: McFarland, 1990. 1220p. in 2 vols.

Antarctica: an introductory guide. D. Galimberti. : Zagier Urruty, 1991. 160p.

Antarctica and the South Atlantic. R. Fox. London, 1985.

'Antarctica, the future of,' C. Joyner, in *Encyclopedia of the future*, p.211-26 (vol. 1). New York: Macmillan, 1996.

Antarctica: the next decade. A. Parsons (ed). *Studies in polar research*. Cambridge, UK: Cambridge University Press, 1987. 176p.

Antarctica's future: continuity or change? R. A. Hall, H. R. Hall & M. G. Howard (eds). Hobart: Australian Institute of International Affairs, 1990.

Australian Antarctic bibliography. R. W. Knight. Hobart, Australia: IASOS, 1987. 463p.

Chronological list of Antarctic expeditions and related historical events. R. K. Headland. , 1989.

South Georgia: the British Empire's subantarctic outpost: a synopsis of the history of the island. L. H. Matthews. Bristol, UK: John Wright & Sons, 1931. 163p.

The Antarctic. J. Meadows, W. Mills & H. G. R. King. *World bibliographical series*, 171. Oxford, UK: CLIO Press, 1994. 412p. (No separate section on religion).

The Antarctic Treaty system in world politics. A. Jorgensen-Dahl & W. Ostreng. London: St. Martin's Press, 1991. 400p.

'The desert continent that has no WCC member churches,' K. D. Suter, *One World*, 99 (1984), 8:10.

The island of South Georgia. R. K. Headland. Cambridge, UK: Cambridge University Press, 1984. 293p.

The South Sandwich Islands: 1. General description. M. W. Holdgate & P. E. Baker. *BAS scientific reports*, 91. Cambridge, UK: BAS, 1979. 76p.

Country Table 2. **Stations, populations, and Christians from 40 countries in Antarctica, AD 1995.**

Claimants, territories, stations	*Status of claim*	*Begun*	*Area sq. km*	*sq. mi.*	*Population*	*Christians*	*Megablocs*
1	*2*	*3*	*4*	*5*	*6*	*7*	*8*
Argentinian Antarctic Sector	Sovereignty claimed. Station in IGY 1957.	1903			50	40	Mainly Roman Catholics.
Australian Antarctic Territory	Sovereignty claimed. Station in IGY 1957.	1933	6,119,818	2,362,875	40	30	Anglicans and Roman Catholics.
Austria	Signatory only after 1965.	–	–	–	–	–	–
Belgium	Station in IGY 1957. Signatory 1959.	1957	–	–	–	–	–
Brazil	Signatory only, after 1965.	1983	–	–	–	–	–
British Antarctic Territory	Sovereign Crown Colony. Stations.	1908		475,025	350	250	Anglicans, some Protestants.
Bulgaria	Signatory only, after 1965.	–	–	–	–	–	–
Canada	Signatory only, after 1960.	–	–	–	–	–	–
Chilean Antarctic Territory	Sovereignty claimed. Big investments.	1940	1,269,723		1,550	1,320	Roman Catholics, also Independent pentecostals.
Chinese station (King George Is)	Signatory only, after 1965..	1984	–	–	60	10	Non-Christians.
Colombia	Signatory only, after 1965.	–	–	–	–	–	–
Cuba	Signatory only, after 1965.	–	–	–	–	–	–
Czech Republic	Signatory only, after 1965.	–	–	–	–	–	–
Denmark	Signatory only, after 1965.	–	–	–	–	–	–
Ecuador	Signatory only, after 1965.	–	–	–	–	–	–
Finland	Signatory only, after 1965.	–	–	–	–	–	–
French Southern & Antarctic Terrs	Sovereignty, as TAAF.	1938	7,557	2,918	330	100	Roman Catholics, several atheists.
German station	Signatory after 1965..	1981			40	30	Protestants and Catholics.
Greece	Signatory only, after 1965.	–	–	–	–	–	–
Hungary	Signatory only, after 1965.	–	–	–	–	–	–
Indian station	Signatory only, after 1965.	1983	–	–	60	10	Hindus, secularists.
Italian expedition	Signatory only, after 1965.	1975	–	–	–	–	–
Japanese stations	Station in IGY 1957. Signatory 1959.	1957	–	–	70	10	Buddhists, a few Catholics.
Netherlands	Signatory only, after 1965.	–	–	–	–	–	–
North Korea	Signatory only, after 1965.	–	–	–	–	–	–
Papua New Guinea	Signatory only, after 1965.	–	–	–	–	–	–
Peru	Signatory only, after 1965.	–	–	–	–	–	–
Polish station	Signatory only, after 1965.	1976	–	–	20	20	Roman Catholics.
Queen Maud Land (Norway)	Sovereignty claimed. A dependency.	1910	–	–	40	30	Protestants.
Romania	Signatory only, after 1965	–	–	–	–	–	–
Ross Dependency (NZ)	Sovereignty claimed. IGY. Signatory 1959.	1923	450,000	–	20	10	Protestants, Anglicans, nonreligious.
Russian station	No formal claim. Stations in IGY 1957-8	1950	–	–	10	5	Orthodox, secularists, atheists.
South African station	Station in IGY 1957. Signatory 1959	1950	–	–	10	5	Protestants, Independents.
South Georgia (Britain)	Annexed by captain James Cook.	1775	–	1,450	50	30	Anglicans, Protestants.
South Korea	Signatory only, after 1965.	–	–	–	–	–	–
Spain	Signatory only, after 1965.	–	–	–	–	–	–
Switzerland	Signatory only, after 1965.	–	–	–	–	–	–
Swedish exploration	Signatory only, after 1965.	1949	–	–	–	–	–
United States Antarctic Stations	No formal claim. Big base at McMurdo.	1928	–	–	1,200	1,000	Protestants, Catholics, Orthodox, Independents.
Uruguay	Signatory only, after 1965.	1975	–	–	–	–	–
Totals					*3,900*	*2,900*	

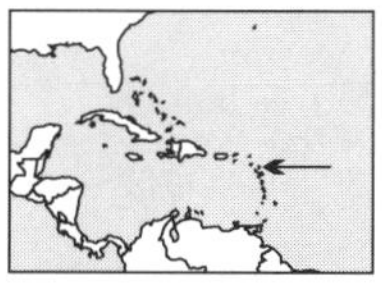

ANTIGUA & BARBUDA

SECULAR DATA, AD 2000

STATE
Official name: Antigua and Barbuda.
Short name: Antigua & Barbuda. **Adjective of nationality:** of Antigua and Barbuda.
Flag: Red triangles, white and blue bands with yellow sun on black.
Area: 442 sq. km. (171 sq. mi.).
Government: Republic, formerly self-governing state in association with the United Kingdom (Britain), since 1967 (1632 British colony, 1981 Independence).
Legislature: Bicameral, 34 members.
Official language: English.
Monetary unit: 1 Eastern Caribbean dollar (EC$) = 100 cents. **US$1=** EC$2.70.
Chief cities: ST JOHN'S CITY 27,766.
Political divisions: 7 provinces.
Armed forces: 200.

DEMOGRAPHY
Population: 68,000.
Population density: 152.8/sq. km. (395.0/sq. mi.).
Under 15 years: 16,000.
Growth rate p.a.: 1.19% (births 15.26, deaths 5.77).
Mortality: Infant, per 1,000: 7.8; **Maternal per 100,000:** 40.0.
Life expectancy: 78 (male 75, female 82).
Household size: 3.5. **Floor area per person, sq.m:** 25.0.
Major languages: English.
Urban dwellers: 36.82%. **Urban growth rate p.a.:** 1.5%.
Labor force: 45%.

ETHNOLINGUISTIC PEOPLES
82.4% West Indian Black; 12.0% USA White; 3.5% Mulatto; 1.3% British; 0.2% Indo-Pakistani.

ECONOMY
National income p.a. per person: US$7,696; **per family:** US$26,939.

EDUCATION
Adult literacy: 90% (male 94%, female 86%). **Schools:** 56.
Universities: 1. **School enrolment:** female/male: 90%/90%.

HEALTH
Access to health services: 90%. **Access to safe water:** 95%.
Hospitals: 2 (65 beds per 10,000). **Doctors:** 59.
Blind: 120. **Deaf:** 4,100. **Murder rate:** 4. **Lepers:** 200.

LITERATURE
New book titles p.a.: 17 (250 p.a. per million). **Periodicals:** 10.
Newspapers: 1 daily.

COMMUNICATION (per 1,000 people)
Phones: 311 (6% mobile). **Radios:** 778. **TV sets:** 419.
Daily newspaper circulation: 94. **Computers:** 100.

HUMAN LIFE AND LIBERTY (optimum condition=100.0%)
HDI: 89.2. **HSI:** 80.0. **HFI:** 70.0. **EFL:** 45.0.

Country status. Antigua and Barbuda is an independent state in the Caribbean Sea in the Leeward Islands of the West Indies. Though sugar dominated the economy in the past, tourism and other agricultural products such as cotton and fruit, contribute greatly to the country's livelihood.

HUMAN LIFE AND LIBERTY

Human rights and freedoms. Antigua and Barbuda is a small two-island parliamentary democracy and a member of the Commonwealth. The Constitution, on the British model, provides for all civil and political rights. However, the government dominates the electronic media and effectively denies access to the opposition parties. One son of the prime minister owns one of the two radio stations and another son owns the sole cable television company.

NON-CHRISTIAN RELIGIONS

Spiritism is represented here by Rastafarianism, an Afro-American cult from Jamaica. It has a growing following among unemployed young Blacks, and is now emphasizing development, thrift schemes, and the training of craftsmen living in community. There are also Muslims and Hindus among Asian immigrant communities. Afro-American spiritists now exceed 2,000.

CHRISTIANITY

ANGLICAN CHURCH. The Church of England has a long history in Antigua dating back to the 17th century. The population was 47.0% Anglican in 1900 and 34.2% in 1995. The diocese of Antigua, which covers Anglican work in the Leeward Islands, was formed in 1842 and is part of the Church of the Province of the West Indies.

Country Table 1. **Religious adherents in Antigua & Barbuda, AD 1900-2025.**

Year	1900		1970		mid-1990		Annual change, 1990-2000				mid-1995		mid-2000		mid-2025	
Name	Adherents	%	Adherents	%	Adherents	%	Natural	Conversion	Total	Rate	Adherents	%	Adherents	%	Adherents	%
Christians	**35,000**	**100.0**	**56,000**	**97.6**	**60,150**	**94.0**	**352**	**-23**	**329**	**0.53**	**61,770**	**94.0**	**63,441**	**93.9**	**69,500**	**92.7**
PROFESSION																
professing Christians	**35,000**	**100.0**	**56,000**	**97.6**	**60,150**	**94.0**	**352**	**-23**	**329**	**0.53**	**61,770**	**94.0**	**63,441**	**93.9**	**69,500**	**92.7**
AFFILIATION																
unaffiliated Christians	4,200	12.0	5,814	10.1	8,050	12.6	50	118	168	1.91	9,003	13.7	9,728	14.3	11,300	15.1
affiliated Christians	**30,800**	**88.0**	**50,186**	**87.4**	**52,100**	**81.4**	**326**	**-165**	**161**	**0.31**	**52,767**	**80.3**	**53,713**	**79.0**	**58,200**	**77.6**
Anglicans	16,450	47.0	22,000	38.3	22,400	35.0	140	-119	21	0.09	22,500	34.2	22,613	33.3	22,800	30.4
Protestants	13,300	38.0	21,886	38.1	21,200	33.1	133	-153	-20	-0.09	21,159	32.2	21,000	30.9	22,400	29.9
Roman Catholics	1,050	3.0	6,000	10.5	7,000	10.9	44	36	80	1.09	7,300	11.1	7,800	11.5	11,800	15.7
Independents	0	0.0	0	0.0	800	1.3	5	35	40	4.14	1,000	1.5	1,200	1.8	1,000	1.3
Marginal Christians	0	0.0	300	0.5	700	1.1	4	36	40	4.62	808	1.2	1,100	1.6	2,200	2.9
Trans-megabloc groupings																
Evangelicals	10,000	28.6	10,500	18.3	6,700	10.5	42	-12	30	0.44	6,842	10.4	7,000	10.3	7,700	10.3
Pentecostals/Charismatics	0	0.0	600	1.1	7,650	12.0	48	29	77	0.96	8,081	12.3	8,420	12.4	11,700	15.6
Great Commission Christians	**1,050**	**3.0**	**2,400**	**4.2**	**9,570**	**15.0**	**60**	**16**	**76**	**0.77**	**9,900**	**15.1**	**10,329**	**15.2**	**11,600**	**15.5**
Spiritists	0	0.0	700	1.2	2,000	3.1	13	9	22	1.06	2,100	3.2	2,223	3.3	3,300	4.4
Nonreligious	0	0.0	0	0.0	800	1.3	5	9	14	1.61	900	1.4	939	1.4	300	0.4
Baha'is	0	0.0	400	0.7	500	0.8	3	10	13	2.32	600	0.9	629	0.9	1,400	1.9
Muslims	0	0.0	300	0.5	300	0.5	2	-5	-3	-0.90	280	0.4	274	0.4	500	0.7
Hindus	0	0.0	0	0.0	50	0.1	0	0	0	0.77	50	0.1	54	0.1	100	0.1
World A (unevangelized persons)	0	0.0	57	0.1	128	0.2	1	0	1	0.46	131	0.2	136	0.2	225	0.3
World B (evangelized non-Christians)	0	0.0	1,346	2.3	3,722	5.5	22	23	45	1.74	3,831	5.8	4,423	5.9	5,275	7.2
World C (Christians)	35,000	100.0	56,000	97.6	60,150	94.3	352	-23	329	0.53	61,770	94.0	63,441	93.9	69,500	92.5
Country's population	**35,000**	**100.0**	**57,404**	**100.0**	**64,000**	**100.0**	**375**	**0**	**375**	**0.61**	**65,733**	**100.0**	**68,000**	**100.0**	**75,000**	**100.0**

COLUMNS, ROWS.
For meanings and definitions, see Codebook (Part 3). Note that, by definition, total 'Christians' = professing + crypto-Christians, which also = affiliated + unaffiliated Christians, and also = Great Commission Christians + latent Christians. Percentages may not always total exactly, due to rounding.

CENSUSES.
7.IV.1960 (de jure): 47.5% Anglicans, 42.9% Protestants, 9.6% Roman Catholics.

NOTES ON RELIGIONS
BAHA'IS. In 3 local spiritual assemblies (1973) and some expansion by 1997.
MUSLIMS. Mainly one Ahmadiya Mission community, since about 1955; Qadianis (world HQ Rabwah, Pakistan).
SPIRITISTS. Afro-American spiritists, mainly young Blacks, formerly nominal Anglicans or Protestants, who have in increasing numbers joined an Afro-American cult from Jamaica, the Ras Tafari Movement. The movement stresses self-reliance, development projects including literacy, art and handicrafts, thrift schemes, and the training of productive craftsmen living in community. Recently the government donated land, and CADEC (an arm of the Caribbean Conference of Churches) made a grant of funds.

Great Commission Instrument Panel: status of Antigua & Barbuda (for explanation see start of Part 4)

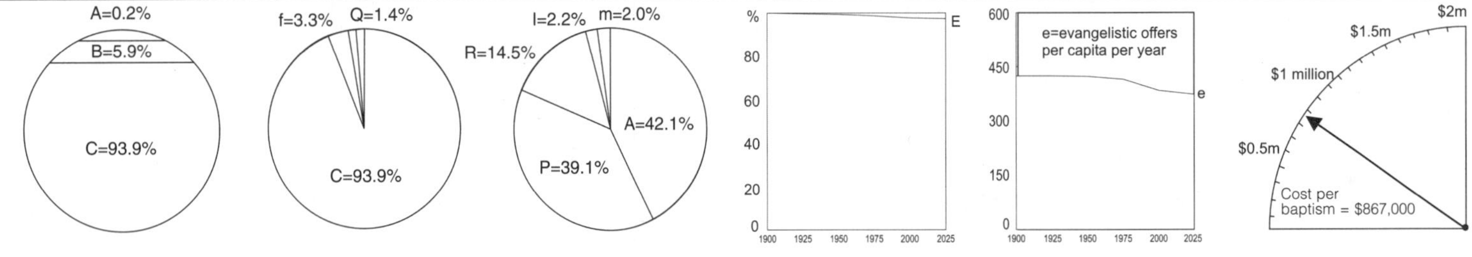

3 Worlds, AD 2000 | Religions, AD 2000 | Ecclesiastical blocs | Evangelization, 1900-2025 | Offers, 1900-2025 | Cost-effectiveness, AD 2000

PROTESTANT CHURCHES. The 2 largest Protestant bodies in Antigua are the Moravian Church (10.3% of the population in 1995) and the Methodist Church (6.1% of the population in 1995). Both owe their origin to influences from Europe in the 18th century. Zinzendorf's first Moravian missionaries arrived in the West Indies in 1732 and reached Antigua in 1756. Success was immediate, with a community of 7,000 Christians recorded by 1791. Methodism's beginning in the West Indies was at Antigua through the instrumentality of local plantation owner Nathaniel Gilbert, who was converted in 1760 at one of John Wesley's meetings in England. Upon his return, he built up a small congregation mostly of slaves, which at the time of his death in 1771 numbered 200. The work was carried on by John Baxter, grew to 2,000 members by 1786 and was further strengthened by the visit of Thomas Coke in the same year. Twentieth-century missionary bodies from North America include the Seventh-day Adventist and Wesleyan churches and several other smaller denominations.

CATHOLIC CHURCH. Antigua is only a part of the diocese of Saint John's based in Antigua, for it includes also St Kitts-Nevis, Anguilla, Montserrat, and the British Virgin Islands. In 1974 there were in Antigua 2 parishes, 4 stations, 4 priests including the bishop (a West Indian previously bishop in Ghana), 5 FSC brothers, and several missionary Sisters of the Immaculate Heart of Mary. Most of Antigua's Catholics are non-Black.

The Holy See has diplomatic relations with Antigua & Barbuda and in AD 2000 is represented to government and the Catholic hierarchy by a pronuncio residing in Port of Spain.

Indigenous missions. There has been little Christian mission from Antigua and Barbuda except through a few Protestant missionaries working in surrounding countries.

CHURCH AND STATE

Antigua was first settled in 1632. Although the French occupied the island at 2 different periods in the 17th and 18th centuries, their stay was brief which accounts for the relatively small Catholic population. Subsequently there has been no legal connection between any of the churches and the state; there is in fact no established church anywhere in the Leeward Islands, though the Anglican Church in Antigua and Barbuda is designated as the church of state.

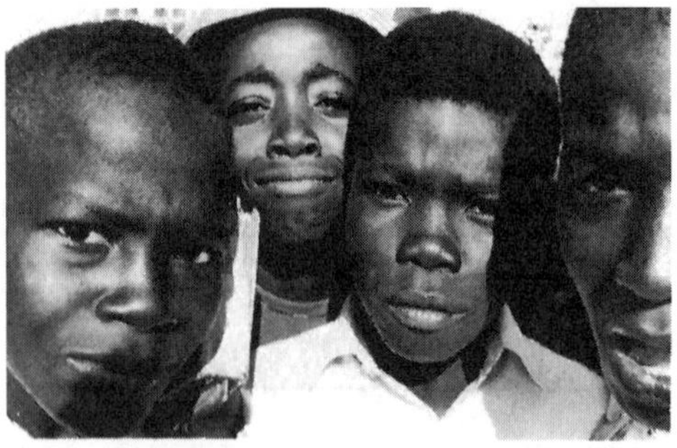

Anglican Church, Diocese of Antigua. School children at St Mary's, Old Road.

BROADCASTING AND MEDIA

The government's broadcasting service gives air time to both Protestant and Catholic programs, and there are several locally-produced private programs. Local radio station Caribbean Radio Lighthouse has daily radio broadcasts. From outside, shortwave broadcasts from TWR (Antilles), HCJB (Ecuador) and AWR (Costa Rica) can be received. Antigua is a member of UNDA.

CBN's *700 Club* and Christian soap opera *Another Life* are broadcast on ABS TV-10. LeSEA programming can be received from the World Harvest Satellite.

INTERDENOMINATIONAL ORGANIZATIONS

The Anglican, Catholic, Methodist, and Moravian churches and the Salvation Army are members of the Antigua Christian Council. Evangelical churches and missionaries have formed the United Evangelical Association.

FUTURE TRENDS AND PROSPECTS

Non-Christians, less than 2% of the population in 1900 are expected to rise to over 7% by AD 2025, with over 4% of these being spiritists.

Anglicans and Protestants are likely to represent over 70% of the population for the next half century but non-Christians could grow to over 10% of the population before AD 2050.

Christians. The country's postage frequently have Christian themes: Nativity, Madonna and Child.

BIBLIOGRAPHY

Antigua and Barbuda. R. Berleant-Schiller, S. Lowes & M. Benjamin. *World bibliographical series*, vol. 182. Oxford, UK: CLIO Press, 1995. 185p. (See especially 'Religion,' 93f).

Country summary. **Worlds A, B, C by ethnolinguistic peoples, cities, and major civil divisions in Antigua & Barbuda.**

	PEOPLES							CITIES							CIVIL DIVISIONS						
World	Num	Pop 2000	C%	Christians	E%	U%	Unevangelized	Num	Pop 2000	C%	Christians	E%	U%	Unevangelized	Num	Pop 2000	C%	Christians	E%	U%	Unevangelized
A	0	0	0.00	0	0	0	0	0	0	0.00	0	0	0	0	0	0	0.00	0	0	0	0
B	1	135	30.37	41	85	15	20	0	0	0.00	0	0	0	0	0	0	0.00	0	0	0	0
C	5	67,424	79.61	53,673	100	0	137	1	27,766	80.00	22,213	100	0	36	7	67,562	79.50	53,713	100	0	159
Total	**6**	**67,559**	**79.51**	**53,714**	**100**	**0**	**157**	**1**	**27,766**	**80.00**	**22,213**	**100**	**0**	**36**	**7**	**67,562**	**79.50**	**53,713**	**100**	**0**	**159**

Antigua archives. E. C. Baker. Mona, Jamaica: University of the West Indies, [1963]. 58p. (Covers the period 1725-1962).

'Antigua: Methodist shrine in the Caribbean,' M. Benjamin, *New world outlook*, (May 1986), 29–33. (Chronicles the founding of the Methodist church in Antigua).

'Caribbean clergywomen workshop–seminar 1987,' A. Spencer-Miller, *Caribbean journal of religious studies*, 9 (April 1988), 13–18. (Conference held in Antigua).

Out of the depths: papers presented at four missiology conferences held in Antigua, Guyana, Jamaica and Trinidad, 1975. I. Hamid (ed.). San Fernando, Trinidad: St. Andrew's Theological College, 1977. 261pp.

'Parties and priorities: the background to Anglican failure to evangelize the Negro population of Barbados and Antigua,' J. E. Pinnington, *Historical magazine of the Protestant Episcopal Church*, 42 (June 1973), 155–69.

The Hart sisters: early African Caribbean writers, evangelicals, and radicals. M. Ferguson (ed). Lincoln: University of Nebraska Press, 1993. 214p.

The influence of church and school upon the Antiguan society: a study of the first 50 years after emancipation. O. Flax. St. John's, Antigua: Antigua Archives Committee, 1984. 12p.

Three hundred years of witness. G. S. Baker. St. John's, Antigua, 1973. 71p.

Country Table 2. **Organized churches and denominations in Antigua & Barbuda.**

Official name (bold type = church with over 10% of all affiliated) 1	*Begun* 2	*Type* 3	*Counc* 4	*Congs* 5	*Adults* 6	*Affiliated 1970* 7	*Affiliated 1995* 8	*G%* 9	*Names, notes, and other statistics* (see Codebook, Part 3) 10
African Methodist Episcopal Zion Ch	c1970	I-Met	Vw...	1	370	–	500	28.22	*AMEZC.* Black American control.
Anglican Church: D Antigua	1634	A-ACa	AwMRK	8	16,200	22,000	22,500	0.09	Diocese 1842. In CPWI. M=USPG. 95% West Indian (90% Black).
Antigua Barbuda Baptist Association	1968	P-Bap	T....	3	200	20	600	14.57	M=FMB-SBC(USA).
Catholic Church: D Saint John's	c1950	R-Lat	P.NMK	10	4,820	6,000	7,300	0.79	*Diocese of Saint John's-Basseterre.* Suffragan of M Castries. M=SVD. C=1+1+2.
Christian Brethren	c1960	P-CBr	x....	4	180	300	360	0.73	*Plymouth Brethren. Open Brethren.* 1973, M=CMML(Canada).
Church of God (Cleveland)	1973	P-Pe3	x....	6	504	–	1,120	4.55	*General Assembly of the CoG (Antigua).* M=CoG(Cleveland) (USA). 8n,W=99%.
Church of God of Prophecy	1954	P-Pe3	Z....	5	300	500	857	2.18	M=CGP(USA). Schism in USA ex CoG (Cleveland). Holiness Pentecostals.
Ch of Jesus Christ of Latter-day Saints	c1970	m-LdS	x....	1	25	–	50	16.94	*Mormons.* M=CJCLdS(USA).
Church of the Nazarene	1973	P-Hol	x....	2	125	–	180	4.55	M=CON(USA).
Churches of Christ in Christian Union	1962	P-Hol	xF...	4	180	500	360	-1.31	*Christian Union Mission.* M=CCCU(USA). Holiness doctrines. HQ St. John's.
Jehovah's Witnesses	c1940	m-Jeh	x....	4	303	300	758	3.78	*Watch Tower. IBSA.* Active witnessing under way by 1948. HQ St John's. 25Y.
Methodist Ch in Caribbean & Americas	1760	P-Met	VWM.K	5	2,000	4,000	4,000	0.00	*MCCA*(1967 union), Leeward Islands District. HQ for MCCA. M=MMS(UK).
Moravian Church	1756	P-Mor	xwM.K	8	2,700	8,466	6,750	-0.90	*Antigua Conference*, Eastern West Indies Province, Unity of Brethren.
Salvation Army	c1950	P-Sal	xwM.K	4	430	600	652	0.33	*Antigua Region*, Caribbean & CAmerica Territory (HQ Jamaica). HQ St John's.
Seventh-day Adventist Church	1944	P-Adv	x....	15	1,700	3,500	2,320	-1.63	*SDA*, East Caribbean Conference, Caribbean Union Conference.
Wesleyan Church	1911	P-Hol	VF...	35	1,920	3,000	3,200	0.26	Before 1968, Pilgrim Holiness Ch. M=WC(USA). 15n,1j,1k,W=75%,92Y.
Other pentecostal bodies	c1975	I-3pU	.....	10	200	–	500	5.00	Smaller pentecostal groupings and missions.
Other Protestant denominations	c1950	P-	.....	13	380	1,000	760	-1.09	About 5, including: BMA(USA),BIM(arrived 1975).
Totals				**138**	**32,537**	**50,186**	**52,767**		

Churches, members, growth, 1900-2025	*Congs*	*Adults*	*Affiliated*	*G%*	*Total denominations*	*6 Megablocs:* O	R	A	P	I	m
Total churches, members, and denominations (mid-1900)	30	15,500	30,800	0.70	3	0	0	1	2	0	0
Total churches, members, and denominations (mid-1970)	106	25,230	50,186	0.70	14	0	1	1	11	0	1
Total churches, members, and denominations (mid-1990)	130	32,100	52,100	0.19	22	0	1	1	15	3	2
Total churches, members, and denominations (mid-1995)	138	32,537	52,767	0.25	24	0	1	1	16	4	2
Total churches, members, and denominations (mid-2000)	140	33,100	53,713	0.36	25	0	1	1	16	5	2
Total churches, members, and denominations (mid-2025)	200	35,900	58,200	0.32	47	0	1	1	20	20	5

NOTES ON TABLE ABOVE
NATIONAL COUNCILS (column 4, 5th letter).

E = United Evangelical Association of Antigua and Barbuda (UEAAB).

K = Antigua Christian Council.

ARGENTINA

SECULAR DATA, AD 2000

STATE
Official name: La República Argentina (The Argentine Republic).
Short name: Argentina. **Adjective of nationality:** Argentine.
Flag: Blue, white, and blue stripes, golden sun.
Area: 2,780,400 sq. km. (1,073,518 sq. mi.).
Government: Federal republic with two legislative houses, since 1994 (1516 Spanish rule, 1816 Independence, 1829 onwards a series of dictatorships and republics, 1971 republic, 1976 military rule, 1983, republic).
Legislature: Senate, 72 members; Chamber of Deputies, 257 members.
Official language: Spanish (Español/Castella).
Monetary unit: 1 peso (pl. pesos) (Arg$) = 100 centavos. **US$1=** Arg$1.00.
Chief cities: BUENOS AIRES 12,431,000; Cordoba (Gran Cordoba) 1,407,000; San Justo 1,246,342; Rosario (Gran Rosario) 1,228,000; Mendoza (Gran Mendoza) 943,000.
Political divisions: 24 provinces.
Armed forces: 73,000.

DEMOGRAPHY
Population: 37,027,000.
Population density: 13.3/sq. km. (34.4/sq. mi.).
Under 15 years: 10,264,000.
Growth rate p.a.: 1.19% (births 19.05, deaths 7.78).
Mortality: Infant, per 1,000: 20.0; **Maternal per 100,000:** 100.0.
Life expectancy: 74 (male 71, female 78).
Household size: 3.2. **Floor area per person, sq.m:** 20.0.
Major languages: Spanish, Italian, Galician, Quechua, Toba, Mataco, Yiddish, Irish, German, Polish, Ukrainian, Catalan, Portuguese, Arabic, English, Russian, Japanese, et alia.
Urban dwellers: 89.35%. **Urban growth rate p.a.:** 1.42%.
Labor force: 41%.

ETHNOLINGUISTIC PEOPLES
73.3% Argentinian White; 4.7% Italian; 4.0% Mestizo; 3.3% Levantine Arab; 2.6% Central Bolivian Quechua.

ECONOMY
National income p.a. per person: US$8,030; **per family:** US$25,695.

EDUCATION
Adult literacy: 96% (male 96%, female 96%). **Schools:** 31,735.
Universities: 1,540. **School enrolment:** female/male: 94%/93%.

HEALTH
Access to health services: 71%. **Access to safe water:** 64%.
Hospitals: 2,000 (44 beds per 10,000). **Doctors:** 88,800.
Blind: 14,300. **Deaf:** 2,221,800. **Murder rate:** 2.
Lepers: 40,000. **Underweight prevalence under 5:** 2%.

LITERATURE
New book titles p.a.: 10,740 (290 p.a. per million). **Periodicals:** 168.
Newspapers: 187 dailies.

COMMUNICATION (per 1,000 people)
Phones: 160 (27% mobile). **Radios:** 637. **TV sets:** 347.
Daily newspaper circulation: 138. **Computers:** 62.

HUMAN LIFE AND LIBERTY (optimum condition=100.0%)
HDI: 88.4. **HSI:** 61.0. **HFI:** 62.5. **EFL:** 47.0.

Country status. Argentina is the eighth largest country in the world, about one-fourth the size of Europe. Shaped like a giant cornucopia, it dominates the southern part of the continent. Culturally, it is one of the most homogeneous countries in the world, with a population that is predominantly Spanish and Catholic.

HUMAN LIFE AND LIBERTY

Human need and development. Argentina presents the paradox of a rich country perpetually on the brink of economic disaster. Although considered as a developing country, it shares many characteristic traits of a developed country. Its standard of living is one of the highest in South America, its density of population is one of the lowest and its natural resources are among the richest. Its problems are the product, rather, of political and economic mismanagement for many decades. The country's history, especially after Juan Peron, has been one of riots, bombings, strikes, and other disturbances as the military and civil rulers alternated in power. Argentine society is remarkable for the existence of a large middle class, the largest in South America. While the lower classes of other Latin American nations are composed largely of subsistence farmers, the Argentine lower class has three distinct segments: urban labor, rural labor, and the marginal poor, all of whom have conflicting interests. The marginal poor are the neediest segment of society, and are generally found in conventillos (inner city slums) or in suburban shantytowns known as villas miserias (misery towns). Because many of them are Indians or mestizos, they are called disparagingly cabecitas negras (blackheaded ones).

Although Argentina has become a byword for economic stagnation, it has one of the highest standards of living in South America, and more significantly, a more equal distribution of wealth than prevails in other parts of the continent. However, there is a heavy regional concentration of wealth in metropolitan Buenos Aires, the coastal area from La Plata to Rosario and in Santa Fe and Cordoba, so that there are sub-

Country Table 1. Religious adherents in Argentina, AD 1900-2025.

Year / *Name*	*1900* Adherents	%	*1970* Adherents	%	*mid-1990* Adherents	%	*Annual change, 1990-2000* Natural	Conversion	Total	Rate	*mid-1995* Adherents	%	*mid-2000* Adherents	%	*mid-2025* Adherents	%
Christians	**4,126,500**	**98.3**	**22,971,300**	**95.9**	**30,405,850**	**93.5**	**421,004**	**-21,589**	**399,415**	**1.24**	**32,337,335**	**93.0**	**34,399,998**	**92.9**	**43,311,300**	**91.9**
PROFESSION																
professing Christians	**4,126,500**	**98.3**	**22,971,300**	**95.9**	**30,405,850**	**93.5**	**421,004**	**-21,589**	**399,415**	**1.24**	**32,337,335**	**93.0**	**34,399,998**	**92.9**	**43,311,300**	**91.9**
AFFILIATION																
unaffiliated Christians	21,000	0.5	441,300	1.8	348,850	1.1	4,830	1,698	6,528	1.73	381,985	1.1	414,126	1.1	475,000	1.0
affiliated Christians	**4,105,500**	**97.8**	**22,530,000**	**94.0**	**30,057,000**	**92.4**	**416,144**	**-23,257**	**392,887**	**1.24**	**31,955,350**	**91.9**	**33,985,872**	**91.8**	**42,836,300**	**90.9**
Roman Catholics	4,132,800	98.4	22,431,530	93.6	29,800,000	91.6	412,586	-17,586	395,000	1.25	31,800,000	91.5	33,750,000	91.2	41,500,000	88.0
Protestants	40,000	1.0	576,136	2.4	1,900,000	5.8	26,306	13,194	39,500	1.91	2,128,450	6.1	2,295,000	6.2	3,500,000	7.4
Independents	0	0.0	339,796	1.4	1,650,000	5.1	22,845	17,155	40,000	2.19	1,918,382	5.5	2,050,000	5.5	3,200,000	6.8
Marginal Christians	1,000	0.0	63,774	0.3	325,000	1.0	4,500	13,000	17,500	4.40	402,133	1.2	500,000	1.4	900,000	1.9
Orthodox	3,000	0.1	112,000	0.5	138,000	0.4	1,911	89	2,000	1.36	134,670	0.4	158,000	0.4	220,000	0.5
Anglicans	1,000	0.0	13,200	0.1	17,500	0.1	242	-92	150	0.83	18,200	0.1	19,000	0.1	25,000	0.1
doubly-affiliated	-72,300	-1.7	-1,006,436	-4.2	-3,773,500	-11.6	-52,245	-49,018	-101,263	2.41	-4,446,485	-12.8	-4,786,128	-12.9	-6,508,700	-13.8
Trans-megabloc groupings																
Evangelicals	21,000	0.5	480,000	2.0	1,590,000	4.9	22,014	14,986	37,000	2.11	1,793,935	5.2	1,960,000	5.3	3,365,000	7.1
Pentecostals/Charismatics	0	0.0	479,000	2.0	7,220,000	22.2	99,962	18,038	118,000	1.53	7,839,328	22.6	8,400,000	22.7	11,550,000	24.5
Great Commission Christians	**210,000**	**5.0**	**1,677,000**	**7.0**	**2,380,000**	**7.3**	**32,951**	**3,037**	**35,988**	**1.42**	**2,560,000**	**7.4**	**2,739,882**	**7.4**	**4,243,500**	**9.0**
Nonreligious	5,000	0.1	210,000	0.9	620,000	1.9	8,584	15,874	24,458	3.38	760,000	2.2	864,583	2.3	1,582,000	3.4
Muslims	4,000	0.1	50,000	0.2	560,000	1.7	7,753	8,339	16,092	2.56	670,000	1.9	720,921	2.0	1,100,000	2.3
Jews	6,500	0.2	475,000	2.0	490,000	1.5	6,784	-6,786	-2	0.00	490,000	1.4	489,982	1.3	450,000	1.0
Atheists	5,000	0.1	140,000	0.6	220,000	0.7	3,046	2,751	5,797	2.37	255,000	0.7	277,968	0.8	370,000	0.8
Spiritists	1,000	0.0	50,000	0.2	70,000	0.2	969	725	1,694	2.19	78,000	0.2	86,943	0.2	100,000	0.2
Ethnoreligionists	50,000	1.2	30,000	0.1	50,000	0.2	692	158	850	1.58	54,800	0.2	58,496	0.2	60,000	0.1
New-Religionists	0	0.0	0	0.0	44,000	0.1	609	40	649	1.38	47,300	0.1	50,488	0.1	60,000	0.1
Buddhists	1,000	0.0	10,000	0.0	14,600	0.0	202	134	336	2.09	16,500	0.1	17,955	0.1	30,000	0.1
Baha'is	0	0.0	5,700	0.0	8,000	0.0	111	110	221	2.47	9,575	0.0	10,212	0.0	19,000	0.0
Hindus	0	0.0	0	0.0	4,800	0.0	66	-3	63	1.25	5,000	0.0	5,434	0.0	6,500	0.0
Confucianists	0	0.0	0	0.0	400	0.0	6	-2	4	1.05	420	0.0	444	0.0	600	0.0
Chinese folk-religionists	0	0.0	0	0.0	350	0.0	5	0	5	1.34	370	0.0	400	0.0	600	0.0
Other religionists	1,000	0.0	20,000	0.1	36,000	0.1	498	249	747	1.90	40,700	0.1	43,472	0.1	60,000	0.1
World A (unevangelized persons)	21,000	0.5	71,885	0.3	195,144	0.6	2,700	2,100	4,800	2.22	243,351	0.7	259,189	0.7	518,650	1.1
World B (evangelized non-Christians)	52,500	1.2	918,624	3.8	1,923,006	5.9	26,625	19,489	46,114	2.10	2,183,869	6.3	2,367,813	6.4	3,320,050	7.0
World C (Christians)	4,126,500	98.3	22,971,300	95.9	30,405,850	93.5	421,004	-21,589	399,415	1.24	32,337,335	93.0	34,399,998	92.9	43,311,300	91.9
Country's population	**4,200,000**	**100.0**	**23,961,810**	**100.0**	**32,524,000**	**100.0**	**450,329**	**0**	**450,329**	**1.31**	**34,764,556**	**100.0**	**37,027,000**	**100.0**	**47,150,000**	**100.0**

COLUMNS, ROWS.
For meanings and definitions, see Codebook (Part 3). Note that, by definition, total 'Christians' = professing + crypto-Christians, which also = affiliated + unaffiliated Christians, and also = Great Commission Christians + latent Christians. Percentages may not always total exactly, due to rounding.

CENSUSES.
1895 (excluding ethnoreligionists): 99.0% Roman Catholics, 0.7% Protestants, 0.2% Jews. **10.V.1947** (de jure): 94.3% Roman Catholics, 2.0% Evangelicals, 1.6% Jews, 1.5% nonreligious, 0.4% Orthodox, 0.1% Muslims, 0.1% other religionists. **30.IX.1960:** 93.3% Roman Catholics, 2.7% Evangelicals, 1.7% nonreligious and atheists, 1.6% Jews, 0.4% Orthodox, 0.1% Muslims, 0.2% other religionists. After 1960 the religion question was discontinued.

NOTES ON RELIGIONS
ATHEISTS. Partida Comunista Argentina (PCA) (outlawed 1966; pro-Soviet) and several rival parties. Includes Uruguayan settlers and Europeans.
BAHA'IS. Growth from 6 local spiritual assemblies (1964) to 38 (1973) and 54 (1993). Converts from Indian tribes include Chiriguano, Mapuche, Mataco, Tewelche, Toba.
BUDDHISTS. Japanese, Laotian, and Chinese immigrants, and about 500 Chinese.
INDEPENDENTS. In 70 indigenous denominations in 1995 (see Country Table 2).
DOUBLY-AFFILIATED. The term covers those affiliated to, or claimed by, both the Catholic Church and also a church termed Evangélica by the state (Protestant, Argentinian indigenous, Anglican or marginal Protestant) or other church, i.e. baptized Catholics who have recently become Evangelicals or others. Because their statistics represent a duplication, they are shown in the table as a negative quantity (with a minus sign).
ETHNORELIGIONISTS. Of the 100,000 tribal lowland Amerindians (or Aborigines) in 1995, mostly along the Paraguayan border, a proportion are still shamanists or animists, including a majority in the Chane (Guaná), Chulupi, and Mocovi. Guaraní shamans in particular occupy a respected healing role in society, and Guaraní mysticism remains the main agent for social cohesion.
JEWS. About 78% Ashkenazi, 22% Sefardi.
MUSLIMS. Including many Palestinian and other Arab immigrants.
OTHER RELIGIONISTS. Adherents of other non-Christian religions and cults, including Rosicrucians (AMORC, 8 centers), and others. ISKCON (Hare Krishna) also operates 1 centre, the Divine Light Mission, the Ramakrishna Mission and others.
PENTECOSTALS/CHARISMATICS. The largest component is the Catholic Charismatic Renewal, which began in 1972. By 1996 there were 3,000 local weekly prayer groups, 100,000 adult regular weekly attenders, 3 covenant communities, 500 involved priests and 5 bishops. One recent event drew 70,000 participants.
PROTESTANTS. In 1895, Evangelicals were 21% nationals and 79% expatriates.
ROMAN CATHOLICS. This line includes some 200,000 Christopagans, namely Amerindians whose syncretistic folk-Catholicism combines 17th-century Spanish Catholicism with their own traditional animism, concepts and world-views.
SPIRITISTS. Organized under the Confederación Espíritista Argentina (CEA). A number of lapsed Catholics and Protestants become spiritists each year, and by 1995 spiritism was recognized as a growing phenomenon.

Great Commission Instrument Panel: status of Argentina (for explanation see start of Part 4)

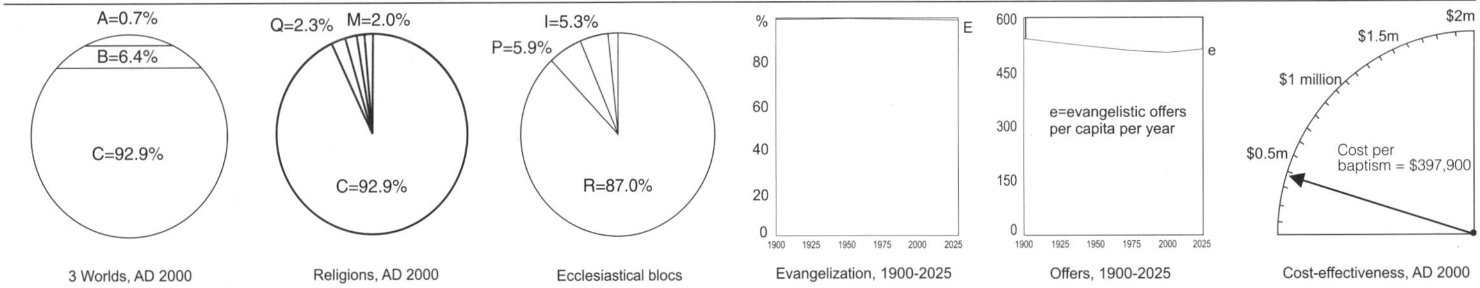

stantial inequalities of development between the capital and the more rural provinces. However, even the poorest Argentines have access to a relatively wide variety of goods and services. The national literacy rate is a high 96%. With beef as its mainstay, the national diet is one of the richest and most nutritious in the continent. There is a chronic housing shortage in the cities for the middle and lower income groups, but some 57% of the homes are owner-occupied, a percentage that is comparable to the United States. Healthcare is of high quality and is available, in the absence of a national health program, mostly through private hospitals. More than half of the working population is enrolled in the social security program.

Human rights and freedoms. Ever since the end of military rule in 1983, Argentina is generally considered a free country where basic human rights are constitutionally guaranteed and enforced. There have been two free elections since then and in the second one in 1989, Carlos Menem (a former Muslim of Syrian background who converted to Roman Catholicism as required by the Constitution) was elected president. However, legacies of the military rule persist to haunt the new administration. These include incidents of torture and extrajudicial killing by the police and intimidation of judges by rightist groups. The judicial system is generally fair and independent, although slow and cumbersome. There is constitutional protection against unreasonable search and seizure. The press is free and vigorous and is quite active in uncovering official corruption. The law prohibits discrimination based on sex, race, religion, language or social status. However, women continue to contend with sociocultural traditions that militate against them in the workplace. There has been an increase in sexual harassment cases brought before the courts.

Argentines enjoy a wide range of basic liberties. The Penal Code contains explicit guarantees of human freedoms and the Federal courts enforce them vigorously. Arrests require probable cause or a judicial order, and the law provides for judicial determination of the legality of detention. However, the legal limits on police powers are not always respected in practice. Most prisoners are held for several days without formal charges and are sometimes tortured. The legal system provides for the right to bail and free legal aid for indigents. Freedom of speech and press is unfettered. The media are active in uncovering official fraud and corruption, and the National Editors and Publishers Association has become one of the most influential organizations in the country.

Human environment. Argentina, like its neighbor Uruguay, is a very urban country with 89% of its people living in cities. Nevertheless, the rural population is fully integrated into the market economy and participates fully in national life. Except in Buenos Aires, density of population is light, and the vast pampa provides ample living space for its inhabitants. In the Rio de la Plata region, pollution is a severe problem. Also, improper land use practices and absence of flood controls contribute to heavy land erosion. Inflation, rather than poverty, is the central fact of life in Argentina. Inflation has had a profound influence on consumption patterns, encouraging people to spend as much as possible in the shortest possible time. A high proportion of the family budget is spent on food and apparel. Recreation occupies a prominent place in the lives of common people. Buenos Aires is believed to have more sports grounds than any other city in the world. Every city and town has numerous professional and amateur sports clubs.

Country summary. **Worlds A, B, C by ethnolinguistic peoples, cities, and major civil divisions in Argentina.**

World	*PEOPLES* Num	Pop 2000	C%	Christians	E%	U%	Unevangelized	*CITIES* Num	Pop 2000	C%	Christians	E%	U%	Unevangelized	*CIVIL DIVISIONS* Num	Pop 2000	C%	Christians	E%	U%	Unevangelized
A	1	18,514	0.01	2	36	64	11,847	0	0	0.00	0	0	0	0	0	0	0.00	0	0	0	0
B	13	1,775,019	29.21	518,479	88	12	212,418	0	0	0.00	0	0	0	0	0	0	0.00	0	0	0	0
C	50	35,233,764	94.99	33,467,389	100	0	18,732	43	22,732,622	90.86	20,655,767	99	1	166,889	24	37,027,286	91.79	33,985,872	99	1	242,988
Total	**64**	**37,027,297**	**91.79**	**33,985,870**	**99**	**1**	**242,997**	**43**	**22,732,622**	**90.86**	**20,655,767**	**99**	**1**	**166,889**	**24**	**37,027,286**	**91.79**	**33,985,872**	**99**	**1**	**242,988**

NON-CHRISTIAN RELIGIONS

Judaism is extremely strong. Argentina's Jewish community is in fact the largest in Latin America and the fifth in importance in the world, after Israel, USA, Russia, and France. Most of Argentina's Jews are descendants of immigrants from Russia in the 2nd half of the 19th century. Of the near 500,000 Jews in Argentina, about 100,000 are Sefardis, more than 350,000 inhabit Buenos Aires and its suburbs, and others are generally found in such larger centers as Cordoba, Rosario, and Santa Fe. The principal national organization of Jews is the Argentina Israelite Mutual Association (Asociación Mutual Israélita Argentina, AMIA) in Buenos Aires. An international Jewish organization with its headquarters in Buenos Aires is the International Council of Jewish Women, founded in Rome in 1912, with national branches in more than 20 countries of the world. The worst act of anti-Jewish violence in the nation's history was in 1994 when a Jewish community center was bombed and 96 people were killed.

Islam's influence and the Muslim population of Argentina multiplied 10-fold between 1970 and 1990, almost entirely through immigration. Islam is served by 3 institutions: the Centre for Islamic Studies (Centro de Estudios Islamicos) and the Islamic Centre (Centro Islamico), both in Buenos Aires; and the Arab Islamic Society in Mendoza.

Traditional Indian religions have largely disappeared although there are still some practitioners among the Chiriguano, as well Guarani-and Quechua- speaking Bolivians who work as laborers on the northern sugarcane plantations.

Baha'i , which grew from 6 assemblies in 1964 to 38 by 1973, has continued to expand in the 1990s.

Anglicans, Lutherans. *Upper.* Anglican priest of Mataco congregation, Chaco Mission. *Lower.* Lutheran pastor, Eldorando, Misiones.

CHRISTIANITY

CATHOLIC CHURCH. Argentina, originally inhabited by nomadic Indians, was first sighted by a Spanish navigator in 1516. Franciscan missionaries arrived in 1539 and the Jesuits in 1586, the latter developing their system of co-operative 'reduction' communities among the Indians in the north until their expulsion in 1767. After Independence in 1816, the new Argentine government, strongly anti-Spanish, attempted to establish a national church.

Spanish priests, poorly prepared for missionary work after the expulsion of the Jesuits, soon departed, leaving some 12 priests under 40 years of age to carry the burden of leadership in the face of a strong anticlerical ruling class and with religious ignorance and superstition rife among the people.

Political struggles continued between rural Argentina and the growing urban population, the latter increasingly coming under the influence of northern European countries through growing trade relations and immigration. In 1887 civil marriages were made obligatory, but efforts to legalize divorce did not succeed until the 1950s. Catholicism remains the religion of the majority, although its proportion is gradually declining. In 1895, the population was 99% Catholic, whereas by 1960 this was reduced to 93%. Catamarca still has the highest percentage (98%) because of its highly traditional Spanish culture. Misiones province in the north, on the other hand, where the immigration of Protestant and Orthodox has been relatively important, has the lowest proportion Catholics (82%). Between 1857 and 1950 over 4 million immigrants came to Argentina, 46% being Italian, 31% Spanish, and the rest from Ireland, Germany, Poland and other European countries. Ukrainian immigration to Misiones began about 1897, and there are today about 100,000 Ukrainian-rite Catholics in 3 centers: 50,000 in Buenos Aires, 30,000 in Apostoles (province of Misiones) and 20,000 in Saens Pena (province of Chaco); many are now assimilated Argentinians and no longer speak Ukrainian. For the past century the conservative sector of the upper class and a large portion of the middle class have identified themselves with the church. The middle class has furnished, and continues to furnish, almost all vocations to the priesthood and religious life, as well as contributing much to the effectiveness of lay apostolate movements. If rural Catholicism is the most solid and devotional, it is clearly in a minority position, since in 1995 87% of the population was urban. Sunday attendance reveals a wide range in practice. Only about 7% of those eligible to attend mass actually do so in the 12 parishes of greater Buenos Aires. In the lesser towns, between 8% and 20% attend. Argentina is a more secularized society than most in Latin America.

The Holy See has diplomatic relations with Argentina and in AD 2000 is represented to government and the Catholic hierarchy by a nuncio residing in Buenos Aires.

PROTESTANT CHURCHES. Early Protestant expansion in Argentina was due in large part to the immigration of peoples from Germany and Scandinavia at the end of the 19th century and the beginning of the 20th. Also important was the arrival of British executives, accompanied by their pastors, who came to work in the meat industry and on railroad construction. With a high urban population, Protestantism's literacy rate of 90% is the highest in Latin America. Although Protestants remain a minority of the population, Argentina is an important base for a number of Protestant missions that have spread throughout Latin America. Protestant membership is the fourth largest in Latin America, growing at a rate of 1.9% per year, in contrast to the Argentina population growth of 1.3% per year.

A Bible Society agent, James Thompson, who was to become the first Protestant missionary in numerous Latin American countries, began his work here in 1820. During his brief stay in Buenos Aires, he founded 100 schools. American Methodists arrived in 1836, but confined their work to European immigrants for several decades. The Methodist South American Annual Conference was organized in 1893; the Argentina Conference in 1954; and the church became autonomous in 1968. However, Methodist membership remains small considering the number of years the church has been at work. The presence of European Lutherans and Reformed in Argentina dates from 1843. In addition to the La Plata Evangelical Church, there are 8 Lutheran and 6 Reformed bodies, including the Waldensian Evangelical Church. The various Reformed denominations joined together to form the Association of Reformed Churches. European Baptists first entered Argentina in 1878, and American Southern Baptists followed in 1903. The Argentina Baptist Convention was organized in 1908. Today it is one of the largest churches in Argentina with most of its congregations self-supporting. Since 1940, 4 other Baptist missions entered Argentina. Other large constituencies begun at the end of the 19th century are those belonging to the Plymouth Brethren and Seventh-day Adventists. In spite of initial efforts as early as 1909, Pentecostals registered little growth prior to World War II. Even so, Pentecostalism has not shown a dynamic growth in Argentina equivalent to that in Brazil or Chile. The principal thrust has come from the USA, but Scandinavian and Canadian Pentecostals have also been influential. A charismatic movement, Movimiento de Renovacion, appeared among Plymouth Brethren in 1963, extending to over 20% of all members by 1973.

Iglesia Católica en la Argentina. Open-air mass celebrated by several bishops, with lifesize crucifix at center.

OTHER CHURCHES. Numerous independent Pentecostal churches have come into existence in recent years, the most important being the Christian Assemblies among descendants of Italian immigrants. The Evangelical Pentecostal Church of Chile, an indigenous body which has spread to Argentina from neighboring Chile, is also making a significant impact on the scene. In 1962 the Mennonite work among the Toba Indians experienced a Pentecostal outburst which transformed it into the independent Toba United Evangelical Church.

At least 9 different Orthodox churches have arisen, serving Orthodox immigrants from Armenia, Greece, Lebanon, Romania, Russia, Syria, Ukraine, and Yugoslavia.

The New Apostolic Church has built up a large following, mostly among German immigrants; and 5 Oriental and Eastern Orthodox traditions are represented in organized communities in the larger cities.

Anglicanism was first brought to Argentina in 1824 through the work of the South American Missionary Society among Patagonia Indians in the extreme south, and Anglicans are now also active among Indians in the northern Chaco and in urban slums.

Art and architecture. Argentine ecclesiastical architecture is essentially Iberian and heavily baroque. Some Indian influences have been incorporated in small churches in the interior. The best known work of art is the enormous figure of Christ of the Andes which towers over the border between Argentina and Chile. Until recently, Jesuit influences were particularly notable in music, art, and architecture. Many of the large churches, including those of San Ignacio, San Francisco, San Telmo and La Merced were designed by the Jesuit architects Juan Bautista Primoli and Andres Bianchi. Wood carvings of religious figures are made by craftsmen in the northern part of the country. There are a number of religious museums in the country, including Museum of Church History in Buenos Aires, Museum of Archeology and Religious Art in Catamarca, Juan de Tejeda Museum of Religious Art in Cordoba, the Jesuit Museum in San Ignacio, Museum of the Monastery of San Carlos in San Lorenzo, and Museum of the Monastery of San Francisco in Santa Fe.

Renewal movements. In the 1990s the Pentecostal/Charismatic Renewal continued to spread rapidly across most older churches, and numbered over 8,400,000 adherents (of whom 20% were Pentecostals, 55% Charismatics, and 25% Independents).

Indigenous missions. Roman Catholic Argentinians have been serving as missionaries since the early 1900s. Some serve as far away as Indonesia. A new development is a number of Argentinians (mainly Protestant) working among Muslims in North Africa and the Middle East.

CHURCH AND STATE

It may be said that the Catholic episcopate in Argentina is dependent on an historical past which made the church a real power, and that it is strongly attached to conserving a maximum of acquired rights, such as indissolubility of marriage, religious education in public schools, and the like. On its side, the state tends to consider the Catholic religion as a pillar of the established order. As a result, in December 1966 the government dedicated the republic 'to the Immaculate Heart of the Virgin Mary' in the presence of 14 of the most conservative bishops of the country, although other bishops declined to participate. Another example is the strong pressures put on the episcopate to control closely the alleged revolutionary activities of certain groups of priests and laymen.

An agreement between the Holy See and the Argentina republic, reached under the presidency of general Ongania in 1966, put to an end a regime of national patronage which had been incorporated in Articles 67 (paragraphs 19 and 20) and 86 (paragraphs 8 and 9) of the 1853 constitution. The agreement is a direct result of Vatican II, which requested that heads of state renounce their privilege of naming bishops. In the present case, it is nevertheless stipulated that bishops are to be citizens and that their nomination by the Holy See be subject to previous secret consultation with the government. Article 1 of the agreement states that the Argentina government recognizes and guarantees to the Roman Apostolic Catholic Church the freedom and full exercise of its spiritual power, the full public exercise of worship as well as jurisdiction within the limits of its competence to carry out its specific purposes.

The prior provision of Article 76, which required the president and vice-president to be members of the Catholic community, was resented by non-Catholics as discriminatory and was removed in 1994.

Freedom of worship is guaranteed for Argentina citizens in the constitution (Article 14) and for foreigners (Article 20). Administrative relations between the churches and the state are handled by the undersecretary of religion, Ministry of Foreign Relations and Religion (Subsecretaria de Culto, Ministerió de Relaciones Exteriores y Culto). Its most important functions include the distribution of subsidies to the Catholic Church (derived from Article 2 of the constitution), and the maintaining of a register of churches, where denominations and religions must be inscribed in order to conduct public activities in the country.

The return of democratic government has resulted by the 1990s in better church-state relations.

BROADCASTING AND MEDIA

State radio and television networks both accept religious programs. IBRA programs can be heard on 17 local stations. Southern Baptists produce several effective radio programs and have one of the largest Christian film libraries on the continent. Shortwave programs in a variety of languages, including Quichua, Spanish and Japanese, can be received from HCJB (Ecuador). Other programs aimed generally at Latin America from the Vatican, WYFR (USA), AWR (Costa Rica), KNLS and other international broadcasters have generated response. Argentina is a member of UNDA and Radio Cultura carries 4 hours of daily Catholic religious programming. There are 29 local Catholic radio stations.

The Spanish version of CBN's *700 Club* can be viewed daily on television and cable channels across the nation, reaching a potential audience of 15 million viewers. The ministry maintains four follow-up centers in Buenos Aires and other cities from which it conducts follow-up activities. The 'Jesus' Film has been shown to 12 million people, mainly through television (9.8 million) and film team presentations (1.7 million). TBN programming is aired on channel 60 in Mendoza.

Iglesia Católica en la Argentina. Virgin of Lujan (pilgrimage center), for 1st Interamerican Marian Congress, 1960.

INTERDENOMINATIONAL ORGANIZATIONS

The Argentina Federation of Evangelical Churches was founded as a separate entity in 1958, having earlier been part of the Confederation of Evangelical Churches of the River Plate (Argentina, Uruguay, Paraguay). It is a large body with 28 churches as full members and several others holding associate membership, and is affiliated to CWME of the WCC. The Episcopal Commission for Faith and Ecumenism of the Catholic Church has been set up to enter into dialogue with other churches. The Union of Latin American Ecumenical Youth (Union Latinoamericana de Juventudes Ecumenicas, ULAJE), founded in Lima in 1941 with its headquarters now in Buenos Aires, had 250,000 members in 16 countries in 1973. It sponsors training seminars and publishes pedagogical material with an aim to promoting justice, peace, and liberation. The River Plate Christian Study Centre (Centro de Estudios Cristianos del Rio de la Plata), founded in Buenos Aires in 1963, is an international center for study and dialogue, serving a wide group of churches in the River Plate area of Argentina and Uruguay. Also in Buenos Aires, Union Theological Seminary, considered one of the finest in Latin America, serves several churches. More recently, the Pentecostal Federation and the Christian Alliance of Evangelical Churches (Alianza Cristiana de las Iglesias Evangélias, ACIERA) have been formed.

The Catholic Church has a Jewish-Christian Confraternity and a research bureau on Jewish-Christian relations.

FUTURE TRENDS AND PROSPECTS

Due to the steady increases among the nonreligious and Muslims there will probably be a gradual decline of affiliated Christians through 2025.

Non-Christians, representing less than 2% of the population in 1900 are expected to grow over 10% by AD 2050. Atheists and nonreligious alone will likely pass 5% after 2025. Marginal Christians, virtually nonexistent in 1900 are expected to grow to 3% by 2050.

BIBLIOGRAPHY

500 años de cristianismo en Argentina. M. C. Liboreiro. Buenos Aires: CEHILA, [1992]. 526p.
'A description and evaluation of a church planting project among the middle class people of Buenos Aires, Argentina.' R. C. Bundy. D.Miss. thesis, Trinity Evangelical Divinity School, Deerfield, IL, 1991. 352p.
'A history of the Christian and Missionary Alliance in Argentina.' J. N. Shannon. D.Miss. thesis, Trinity Evangelical Divinity School, Deerfield, IL, 1989. 287p.
'Applying church growth principles in northwest Argentina.' D. Spruance. D.Min. thesis, Conservative Baptist Theological Seminary, [1981]. 425p.
'Argentina,' *Pro Mundi Vita* (Brussels), 27 (1969).
Argentina. A. Biggins. *World bibliographical series*, vol. 130. Oxford, UK: CLIO Press, 1991. 460p.
'Argentine pentecostalism: its history and theology.' J. N. Saracco. Ph.D. dissertation, University of Birmingham, 1989. 350p.
Catholicism and politics in Argentina, 1810–1960. A. Ivereigh. New York: St. Martin's Press, 1995. 289p.
'Catholicism and sociopolitical change in Argentina, 1943–1973.' R. McGeagh. Thesis, University of New Mexico, 1974. 382p.
Cry for me Argentina. R. E. Miller. Brentwood, UK: Sharon Publications, 1988. 160p.
El cristianismo en los cantares populares. J. A. Carrizo. [Buenos Aires]: Biblioteca Dictio, [1978]. 174p.
El Pentecostalismo en la Argentina. A. Frigerio. *Biblioteca política Argentina*, 459. Buenos Aires: Centro Editor de América Latina, 1994. 127p.
For God and fatherland: religion and politics in Argentina. M. A. Burdick. *SUNY series in religion, culture, and society.* Albany: State University of New York Press, 1995. 294p.
Foreign missionaries in Argentina, 1938–1962: a study of dependence. E. S. Sweeney. *Sondeos*, vol. 68. Cuernavaca, Mexico: Centro Intercultural de Documentacion, 1970. 361p.
Guía eclesiástica Argentina. Buenos Aires: Agencia Informativa Católica Argentina, [1988]. 160p.
Hablar de sectas en la Argentina y en América Latina. J. A. Gilles Marchand. *Colección Pistas de cambio Segunda serie.* Buenos Aires, Argentina: Ediciones Paulinas, [1989]. 186p.
Historia de la Iglesia en la Argentina. B. Cayetano. Buenos Aires: Editorial Don Bosco, 1966–69. 5 vols.
Iglesia Evangélica Metodista Argentina: 150 años anunciando lo que Cristo anunció, 1836–1986. Buenos Aires: Iglesia Evangélica Metodista Argentina, [1989]. 92p.
Kyrkan i Argentina. A. Ruuth. *Kyrkan i Latinamerika*, 3. [Stockholm]: Verbum, 1976. 68p.
La evangelización de la Patagonia y de la Tierra del Fuego. C. Bruno. Rosario: Ediciones 'Didascalia', 1992. 203p.
La evangelización del aborigen americano: con especial referencia a la Argentina. C. Bruno. Buenos Aires: Universidad Católica Argentina, El Derecho, 1988. 151p.
La Iglesia en Argentina. E. Amato. Buenos Aires: CIDOR/FERES, 1965. 253p. (Limits discussion to the Roman Catholic).
La Iglesia en la Argentina: cuatrocientos años de historia, del siglo XVI al siglo XIX. C. Bruno. *Estudios proyectos*, vol. 10. Buenos Aires: Centro Salesiano de Estudios San Juan Bosco, 1993. 720p.
La iglesia evangélica en la sociedad Argentina. R. Azzati. Buenos Aires, Argentina: The author, 1993. 122p.
'Leadership in churches of Christ in Argentina: expectations of national Christians for the use of power by church leaders.' W. A. Richardson. D.Min. thesis, Abilene Christian University, Abilene, TX, 1991. 312p.
Man, milieu and mission in Argentina. A. W. Enns. Grand Rapids, MI: Eerdmans, 1971. 258p.
'Marian piety as a sociocultural factor in Argentina.' J. H. Utter. Ph.D. dissertation, Columbia University, New York, 1981. 533p.
'Migration and church growth in Argentina.' P. A. Larson. D.Miss. thesis, Fuller Theological Seminary, Pasadena, CA, 1973. 524p.
'Miracles and promises: popular religious cults and saints in Argentina.' K. L. Figgen. Ph.D. dissertation, Indiana University, Bloomington, IN, 1990. 229p.
'Nationalism and religion in Argentina and Uruguay,' A. P. Whitaker, in *Religion, revolution, and reform: new forces for change in Latin America*, p.73–90. W. V. D'Antonio & F. B. Pike (eds). London: Burns and Oates, 1964.
Panorama estadistica de la Iglesia Argentina. N. Rosato. Buenos Aires: CAR y CONFER, 1976. 24p.
'Patterns of church growth within the Seventh–day Adventist Church in the River Platte Republics.' J. C. Viera-Rossano. M.A. thesis, Fuller Theological Seminary, Pasadena, CA, 1988. 165p. (Text in Spanish with extended summary in English).
'Quo Vadis IELU.' J. E. Hennesberger. Thesis, Fuller Theological Seminary, Pasadena, CA, 1968. 401p. (Iglesia Evangélica Luterana Unida).
Religiosidad popular y fe. G. T. Farrell & J. Lumerman. Buenos Aires: Editora Patria Grande, 1979. 157p.
'Religious innovation and the politics of Argentina: a study of the movement of priests for the third world.' J. M. Dodson. Indiana University, Bloomington, IN, 1973. 304p.
'Shamanism, illness and power in Toba church life,' J. A. Loewen, A. Buckwalter & J. Kratz, *Practical anthropology*, 12, 6 (1965), 250–80.
'The Argentine Church and politics, 1943–1976.' K. O. Dunlop. M.A. thesis, University of Virginia, Charlottesville, VA, 1989. 80p.
'The Brethren Church in Argentina: a church growth study.' H. R. Aspinall. M.A. thesis, Fuller Theological Seminary, Pasadena, CA, 1973. 135p.
The Church, society, and hegemony: a critical sociology of religion in Latin America. C. A. Torres. Westport, CT: Praeger, 1992. 238p.
The evangelical church in the River Plate republics: a study of the economic and social basis of the evangelical church in Argentina and Uruguay. J. M. Davis. New York: International Missionary Council, 1943. 119p.
'The influence of liberation theology on present day evangelism in Argentina.' R. H. Kasper. Th.M. thesis, Dallas Theological Seminary, Dallas, TX, 1979. 91p.
'The mission of the church in a country with a variety of cul-

tures.' J. E. Groh. D.Min. thesis, Concordia Theological Seminary, Fort Wayne, IN, 1989. 291p.

The River Plate republics: a survey of the religious, economic and social conditions in Argentina, Paraguay and Uruguay. W. E. Browning. London: World Dominion Press, 1928. 139p.

'The role of the Catholic Church in the revolution against President Juan D. Perón: (Argentina, 1954–1955).' R. J. De Hoyos. Ph.D. dissertation, New York University, 1970. 455p.

Ubicación del Metodismo en el Río de la Plata. D. P. Monti. Buenos Aires: Editorial La Aurora, 1976. 270p.

Witness to the truth: the complicity of Church and dictatorship in Argentina, 1976–1983. E. F. Mignone. Maryknoll, NY: Orbis Books, 1988. 190p.

Country Table 2. **Organized churches and denominations in Argentina.**

Official name (bold type = church with over 10% of affiliated) 1	*Begun* 2	*Type* 3	*Counc* 4	*Congs* 5	*Adults* 6	*Affiliated 1970* 7	*Affiliated 1995* 8	*G%* 9	*Names, notes, and other statistics* (see Codebook, Part 3) 10
Alianza Cristiana y Missionera	1897	P-Hol	xFu.N	59	4,331	4,100	12,482	4.55	*Christian & Missionary Alliance.* M=CMA(USA). 30n,9f,1s,W=33%,150Y.
Asamblea Cristiana Cultural		I-3pL	.....	64	3,200	4,000	8,000	0.05	*Cultural Christian Assemblies.* Local indigenous pentecostals. HZ Buenos Aires.
Asamblea Cristiana de Argentina	1916	I-3pL	..u.N	106	9,000	10,000	27,300	4.10	*Argentinian Christian Assemblies.* HQ Buenos Aires. 25n,7x,W=50%,700Y.
Asamblea Cristiana (Italiana)		I-3pL	.....	210	42,000	100,000	93,000	0.05	*Christian Assemblies (Italian).* Links with M=CCNA(USA). Argentinian pentecostals.
Asamblea de Dios	1941	I-3pL	.....	120	12,100	5,700	17,000	4.47	*Assembly of God.* Indigenous pentecostals. HQ Buenos Aires. 16n,2x,W=50%,310Y,100z.
Asamblea de Iglesias Cristianas	1965	I-3pL	x....	104	7,000	2,000	17,500	9.06	M=Assembly of Christian Churches, a Puerto Rican mission based in New York.
Asambleas Biblicas		I-3pL	.....	200	14,000	4,000	35,000	0.05	*Bible Assemblies.* Indigenous Argentinian pentecostals.
Asambleas de Dios	1910	P-Pe2	Z....	1,186	415,000	50,000	911,000	12.31	*Assemblies of God.* M=SFM(Sweden),NPY(Norway), Elim(Denmark). 65n,1500Y,600z.
Asambleas del Senor JC de Argentina	c1980	I-3oL	.....	30	3,000	–	5,000	6.67	*Assemblies of the Lord Jesus Christ in Argentina.* Oneness (member, AWCF), HQ Buenos Aires.
Asambleas Locales		I-3nC	.....	64	1,344	–	3,000	0.05	*Little Flock. Local Churches. Assembly Hall Churches.* Begun in China 1922.
Asoc de Igs Ev Cristianas	c1980	I-3gL	.....	17	500	–	1,250	6.67	Small grassroots network.
Asoc Ig Evan El Calvaro	c1960	I-3pL	.....	20	1,500	1,875	2,250	0.73	Older mini-denomination.
Asoc la Iglesia de Dios		I-3pL	.....	591	26,000	–	65,500	0.05	Large pentecostal body, *Church of God Association.*
Assoc of Baptists for World Evan	1978	I-Bap	.....	14	864	–	2,160	5.88	M=ABWE(USA).
Asociación de Iglesias Reformadas	1859	P-Ref	..u.N	84	6,460	13,960	20,850	1.62	*ADIRELA. Assoc. of Reformed Chs.*. Scottish, Hungarian, French, Swiss, Waldensian, Dutch.
Comunidad Cristiano		I-Con	.....	69	4,500	1,000	10,000	0.05	*Christian Community.*
Cong Crist de Goya		I-3gL	.....	30	2,300	–	5,110	0.05	Local grassroots churches.
Congr Cristiana Católica Apostólica	c1960	I-3aX	.v...	1	150	200	300	1.64	*Catholic Apostolic Christian Congr.* Buenos Aires. 1965, applied to join WCC, rejected.
Congregaciónes Messianicas	c1980	I-3mJ	.....	5	300	–	500	6.67	*Messianic Jewish Congregations.* Buenos Aires. 0.2% all Argentine Jews. M=JFJ,UMJC,IAMCS.
Convención Evangélica Bautista de A	1878	P-Bap	T.u.n	780	53,800	80,000	128,000	1.90	1878 Germans from Russia. 1903, M=SBC(USA). 160n,50x,85f,1s,W=59%,1177Y.
Ejército de Salvación	1889	P-Sal	xwu.N	96	14,200	15,000	20,000	1.16	*Salvation Army,* in South America East Territory. Division, 4 Districts. 100n,1s.
Fundacion Cristiana Ev de Santa Fe	1968	I-3gL	.....	8	1,500	50	3,000	17.79	*Ev Christian Foundation of Santa Fe.* Ladinos.
Grupos de Cristo	c1970	I-3hL	x....	62	1,500	–	4,000	39.34	*Christ Groups.* Isolated home churches after nationwide EHC campaign.
Iglesia Adventista del Séptimo Dia	1894	P-Adv	x....	261	60,000	60,000	92,300	1.74	*Seventh-day Adventists.* Austral UC: 2 Confs. 2x,4H,1j,20,3r,1s(60),1713Y.
Iglesia Anglicana	1824	A-Eva	AwuCn	70	10,000	13,200	18,200	1.29	*Anglican Ch of the Southern Cone.* 2 Dioceses. M=SAMS. Mataco Indians.32n,18x,61f,50Y,300y.
Igl Apostólica Armenia: D Argentina	c1880	O-Arm	Ewc..	4	4,000	5,000	6,670	1.16	*Armenian Apostolic Ch. Gregorians.* Refugees from USSR. Under C Echmiadzin. 8n.
Iglesia Bautista Biblica	1983	I-Bap	.....	9	1,000	–	1,670	8.33	*Bible Baptist Ch.* M=BIM(USA).
Iglesia Católica Americana Ortodoxa	c1968	I-CCa	.....	26	26,000	30,000	40,000	1.16	Schism ex Rome by RC priests, bishop. M=American Orthodox Catholic Ch (USA Slavs).
Iglesia Católica en la Argentina	1539	R-LEr	B.L.R	8,456	21,998,400	22,431,530	31,800,000	1.41	C=60+8+170. (1970: 5326nx,12486w,470504Yy). (1990)3116n2497x 4255m11716w 540625Yy
M Bahia Blanca	1934	R-Lat	Bs	199	396,000	480,000	572,000	0.70	PR: Comahue (PR=first of 8 Pastoral Regions). 49n 58x 85m 244w 9448Yy
D Alto Valle de Rio Negro	1993	R-Lat	Bsdb	18	158,000	–	227,612	50.00	In General Roca. 10n 18x 26m 42w 4077Yy
D Comodoro Rivadavia	1957	R-Lat	Bsdb	110	213,000	170,928	308,000	2.38	Patagonia. M=SDB. 23n 22x 25m 59w 4945Yy
D Río Gallegos	1961	R-Lat	Bsdb	45	140,000	85,000	202,000	3.52	Patagonia. 11n 33x 36m 67w 2164Yy
D San Carlos de Bariloche	1993	R-Lat	Bs	8	73,000	–	105,000	50.00	Rio Negro. 3n 12x 15m 17w 1495Yy
D Santa Rosa in Argentina	1957	R-Lat	Bs	27	156,000	165,000	226,000	1.27	Comahue. 11n 17x 19m 51w 2461Yy
D Viedma	1934	R-Lat	Bsdb	306	61,000	240,000	87,988	-3.93	Comahue. 15n 15x 15m 33w 2610Yy
M Buenos Aires	1582	R-Lat	Bs	442	2,284,000	2,675,200	3,299,000	0.84	Buenos Aires. 476n 570x 1100m 2620w 29500Yy
D Avellaneda	1961	R-Lat	Bs	24	262,000	907,000	379,000	-3.43	Buenos Aires. 20n 17x 28m 96w 3649Yy
D Lomas de Zamora	1957	R-Lat	Bs	221	1,187,000	885,000	1,713,836	2.68	Buenos Aires. 75n 69x 145m 378w 21192Yy
D Morón	1957	R-Lat	Bs	76	916,000	497,419	1,324,000	3.99	Buenos Aires. 91n 55x 143m 266w 19710Yy
D San Charbel (Maronite)	1990	R-Mar	Os	6	485,000	–	700,000	20.00	Arab Christians from Lebanon. 4n 16x 16m 20w 400Yy
D San Isidro	1957	R-Lat	Bs	218	770,000	842,572	1,112,000	1.12	Buenos Aires. 116n 45x 90m 310w 8200Yy
D San Justo	1969	R-Lat	Bsdb	136	953,000	630,000	1,377,000	3.18	Buenos Aires. 67n 57x 112m 191w 33600Yy
D San Martin	1961	R-Lat	Bs	68	624,000	1,173,000	901,000	-1.05	Buenos Aires. 33n 53x 81m 192w 8450Yy
D San Miguel	1978	R-Lat	Bs	100	498,000	–	720,000	5.88	Greatly reduced by 1997 to 125,000 Catholics. 29n 65x 155m 269w 8161Yy
D Santa Maria (Ukrainian)	1978	R-Ukr	Os	57	86,000	110,000	125,000	5.88	Ukrainian/Byzantine rite Catholics. 4n 12x 18m 84w 551Yy
M Córdoba	1570	R-Lat	Bs	411	1,026,000	1,100,000	1,482,000	1.20	Centro-Cuyo. 150n 204x 410m 1069w 26330Yy
D Cruz de Eje	1963	R-Lat	Bs	144	84,000	190,000	121,000	-1.79	Centro-Cuyo. 22n 7x 7m 87w 3340Yy
D Río Cuarto	1934	R-Lat	Bs	113	377,000	323,270	545,000	2.11	Centro-Cuyo. 69n 20x 23m 70w 6625Yy
D San Francisco	1961	R-Lat	Bs	82	166,000	166,600	240,000	1.47	Centro-Cuyo. 21n 10x 18m 42w 3207Yy
D Villa María	1957	R-Lat	Bs	48	291,000	360,000	420,000	0.62	Centro-Cuyo. 40n 13x 20m 74w 7815Yy
PN Deán Funes	1980	R-Lat	Bom	62	34,000	–	49,300	6.67	In Cordoba. M=OM(Mercedarians). 9n 1x 1m 6w 1002Yy
M Corrientes	1910	R-Lat	Bs	38	285,000	310,000	412,000	1.14	Nordeste. 40n 25x 30m 62w 9942Yy
D Goya	1961	R-Lat	Bs	22	182,000	216,781	263,000	0.78	Nordeste. 31n 9x 12m 51w 3370Yy
D Posadas	1957	R-Lat	Bsvd	419	304,000	418,082	439,000	0.20	Nordeste. M=Opus Dei. 20n 62x 69m 176w 10805Yy
D Puerto Iguazú	1986	R-Lat	Bsj	22	120,000	–	174,000	11.11	In Misiones. M=SJ,SVD. 12n 25x 50m 90w 4765Yy
D Santo Tomé	1979	R-Lat	Bs	94	87,000	–	126,400	6.25	M=Opus Dei. 15n 2x 1m 23w 3105Yy
M La Plata	1887	R-Lat	Bs	142	464,000	715,000	671,000	-0.25	La Plata. 96n 50x 93m 429w 7884Yy
D Azul	1934	R-Lat	Bs	291	271,000	311,757	392,000	0.92	La Plata. 53n 25x 51m 168w 6250Yy
D Chascomús	1980	R-Lat	Bs	82	165,000	–	239,000	6.67	Buenos Aires. 20n 9x 18m 53w 2877Yy
D Mar del Plata	1957	R-Lat	Bs	160	493,000	448,127	712,000	1.87	La Plata. 51n 37x 50m 197w 10135Yy
D Mercedes-Luján	1934	R-Lat	Bs	128	302,000	420,000	437,000	0.16	La Plata. 65n 37x 87m 168w 24313Yy
D Nueve de Julio	1957	R-Lat	Bs	127	255,000	299,377	369,000	0.84	La Plata. 40n 15x 26m 103w 6023Yy
D Quilmes	1976	R-Lat	Bsvd	235	756,000	–	1,092,000	5.26	Buenos Aires. M=SVD. 84n 37x 44m 253w 17751Yy
D Zarate-Campana	1976	R-Lat	Bs	124	277,000	–	400,000	5.26	Buenos Aires. M=CMF. 25n 20x 34m 130w 5522Yy
M Mendoza	1934	R-Lat	Bs	305	736,000	743,980	1,063,000	1.44	Centro-Cuyo. 72n 85x 109m 295w 22091Yy
D Neuquén	1961	R-Lat	Bsdb	107	246,000	150,000	354,900	3.50	Comahue. 27n 24x 29m 82w 5397Yy
D San Rafael	1961	R-Lat	Bs	26	197,000	155,000	284,000	2.45	Centro-Cuyo. 62n 85x 194m 126w 4759Yy
M Paraná	1859	R-Lat	Bs	257	300,000	350,000	434,000	0.86	Littoral. 80n 14x 24m 223w 10694Yy
D Concordia	1961	R-Lat	Bs	128	162,000	195,000	234,000	0.73	Littoral. 39n 2x 6m 97w 6329Yy
D Gualeguaychú	1957	R-Lat	Bs	34	183,000	225,000	265,000	0.66	Littoral. 56n 19x 36m 83w 4421Yy
M Resistencia	1939	R-Lat	Bs	29	256,000	227,000	370,000	1.97	In Chaco, Nordeste. 26n 32x 42m 101w 8100Yy
D Formosa	1957	R-Lat	Bafm	422	237,000	210,850	343,000	1.97	Nordeste. 13n 29x 37m 120w 6938Yy
D San Roque Saenz Peña	1963	R-Lat	Bs	22	270,000	251,000	390,000	1.78	Nordeste. 18n 22x 27m 194w 9872Yy
M Rosario	1934	R-Lat	Bs	318	638,000	1,200,000	921,000	-1.05	Littoral. 142n 118x 193m 455w 14123Yy
D San Nicolás de los Arroyos	1947	R-Lat	Bs	48	349,000	545,000	504,000	-0.31	Littoral. 69n 12x 20m 94w 6429Yy
D Venado Tuerto	1963	R-Lat	Bs	60	135,000	150,000	195,000	1.05	Littoral. 39n 6x 16m 30w 2599Yy
M Salta	1806	R-Lat	Bs	81	477,000	300,000	689,000	3.38	Nordoeste. 60n 26x 47m 99w 17352Yy
D Catamarca	1910	R-Lat	Bs	33	167,000	186,000	241,000	1.04	Nordoeste. 48n 15x 17m 44w 6884Yy
D Jujuy	1934	R-Lat	Bs	35	273,000	245,000	394,000	1.92	Nordoeste. 32n 19x 38m 131w 10344Yy
D Orán	1961	R-Lat	Bs	128	109,000	139,000	157,000	0.49	Nordoeste. 11n 10x 13m 55w 5243Yy
PN Cafayate	1969	R-Lat	Bosa	7	28,000	40,800	41,124	0.03	Nordoeste. 2n 12x 12m 12w 1207Yy
PN Humahuaca	1969	R-Lat	Bcmf	220	63,000	49,700	91,100	2.45	Nordoeste. 3n 14x 16m 13w 1945Yy
M San Juan de Cuyo	1834	R-Lat	Bs	66	380,000	379,974	549,115	1.48	Centro-Cuyo. 52n 14x 15m 64w 13373Yy
D La Rioja	1934	R-Lat	Bs	24	144,000	130,560	208,540	1.89	Centro-Cuyo. 20n 10x 15m 78w 6511Yy
D San Luis	1934	R-Lat	Bofmc	35	208,000	166,398	300,000	2.39	Centro-Cuyo. M=OFMCap. 42n 12x 16m 81w 6600Yy
M Santa Fe de la Vera Cruz	1897	R-Lat	Bs	240	489,000	498,080	707,000	1.41	Littoral. 86n 47x 64m 511w 11539Yy
D Rafaela	1961	R-Lat	Bs	126	169,000	180,000	244,000	1.22	Littoral. 35n 5x 8m 76w 4642Yy
D Reconquista	1957	R-Lat	Bs	158	125,000	152,760	180,000	0.66	Nordeste. 26n 8x 17m 82w 5476Yy
M Tucumán	1897	R-Lat	Bs	275	598,000	400,000	864,000	3.13	Nordoeste. 65n 75x 88m 209w 19931Yy
D Añatuya	1961	R-Lat	Bcssr	177	125,000	144,000	181,000	0.92	Nordoeste. 12n 15x 25m 146w 3654Yy
D Concepción	1963	R-Lat	Bomi	23	244,000	253,960	353,000	1.33	Nordoeste. 30n 3x 3m 23w 8399Yy
D Santiago del Estero	1907	R-Lat	Bs	41	411,000	370,355	594,000	1.91	Nordoeste. 48n 20x 23m 92w 13821Yy
EA America Lat e Messico (Armenian)	1968	R-Arm	Os	1	1,400	110,000	2,000	-14.81	Armenian-rite. Exarchate Apostolic.
O Argentina	1959	R-Ori	Os	3	76,000	122,000	110,000	-0.41	For all other Oriental rites. 1n 2x 2m 0w 209Yy
OM Argentina	1957	R-Lat	Bofm	222	30,000	20,000	60,000	4.49	*Ordinariato Militare (Military Jurisdiction).* All services. M=OFM. 236 bps. 46xmw. 1438Yy.
Doubly-counted Catholics	1980	R-Lat	.....	0	-1,029,000	–	-1,486,915		Catholics counted in older dioceses and newer dioceses formed out of them.
Ig Crist Casa de Misericordia		I-3pL	.....	17	1,600	500	5,330	0.05	House of Mercy Christian Church.
Ig Crist Evang de Quilmes		I-3pL	.....	60	1,800	600	4,500	0.05	Local grassroots churches.
Iglesia Cristiana Reformada	1930	P-Ref	JF...	15	900	1,850	2,000	0.31	*Christian Reformed Ch.* Calvinist doctrines. M=CRC(USA). 20f.
Iglesia de Dios Cristiana Pentecostal	1954	I-3pL	..u.N	200	19,000	7,500	63,300	8.91	*Christian Pentecostal Ch of God.* HQ Malaver, Buenos Aires. 30n,2x.
Iglesia de Biblia Abíerta	1962	I-3pW	.....	101	4,820	1,000	12,100	10.49	*Church of the Open Bible.* M=OBSC(USA).
Iglesia de Dios de la Profecía	1955	P-Pe3	Z....	33	924	500	1,850	5.37	*Ch of God of Prophecy.* M=CGP(USA). HQ San Jeronimo (Santa Fe).
Iglesia de Dios en la Argentina	c1930	P-Hol	x.u.N	405	17,000	2,000	28,300	11.18	*Ch of God.* M=CoG(Anderson)(USA). German immigrants before World War II. 10n,1s.
Iglesia de Jesucristo de los SUD	1935	m-LdS	x....	531	85,000	32,774	170,000	6.81	*Ch of JC of Latter-day Saints. Mormons.* M=CJCLdS(USA). Rapid growth, 9.4%pa. 400f.
Iglesia de los Hermanos Libres	1882	P-CBr	x.u.n	818	91,700	100,000	129,000	1.02	M=CMML(USA,UK). Many Syrians. 50n,20x,49f,4p,1s(200),W=50%,500Y.
Iglesia de los Hermanos (Ashland)	1948	P-Dun	xF...	17	500	1,000	1,200	0.73	*Brethren Ch.* M=BCMB(Ashland, USA). German Baptist origin. 6f.
Iglesia de los Hermanos (Grace)	1909	P-Dun	xF...	15	520	1,000	1,300	1.05	*Brethren Ch.* M=NFBC(Winona Lake, USA). In USA, 1939 split ex Ashland. 6f.
Iglesia del Evangelio Cuadrangular	1959	P-Pe2	ZFu.N	220	23,200	9,000	51,600	7.23	*International Ch of the Foursquare Gospel.* M=ICFG(USA). 65nm,2f,3p(51),W=95%,400Y.
Iglesia Ev Armenia de los Hermanos		I-CBr	x....	12	600	500	1,284	0.05	*Armenian Ev Spiritual Brethren.* Split ex Armenian Congregational Ev Ch. In capital.
Iglesia Ev Congregacionalista Armenia	c1930	P-Con	..u.N	1	500	500	700	1.35	*Armenian Congr Ev Ch.* Immigrants from Armenia, Turkey, Lebanon. HQ Buenos Aires.
Igl Ev Congregacionalista en la Rep A	1924	P-Con	..u.N	119	7,000	20,000	14,000	-1.42	*Congregational Ch.* Germans from Russia since 1870. 1964, M=UCBWM(USA). 20n,1s.

Continued overleaf

Country Table 2–concluded

Official name 1	Begun 2	Type 3	Counc 4	Congs 5	Adults 6	Affiliated 1970 7	Affiliated 1995 8	G% 9	Names, notes, and other statistics (see Codebook, Part 3) 10
Iglesia Evangélica del Nazareno	1919	P-Hol	xFu.N	83	6,138	4,000	10,900	4.09	*Ch of the Nazarene.* M=CoN(USA). 18n,12x,13m,23f,1s(70),56t(3556),125Y.
Iglesia Evangélica del Río de la Plata	1843	P-LuR	.Wu.N	62	27,500	60,000	38,610	-1.75	*La Plata Ev Ch.* Germans (10% Reformed). 50% nationals. 13n,32x,1s(8).
Iglesia Ev Discipulos de Cristo	1906	P-Dis	xuu.N	7	710	2,000	1,000	-2.73	*Disciples of Christ.* M=UCMS(USA). Several institutions. Decline since 1960. 8f.
Iglesia Evangélica Gracia y Gloria	c1950	I-3cL	.....	22	2,200	1,000	6,290	7.63	*Ev Ch of Grace and Glory.* USA & UK missions. HQ Formosa. Spanish; 2 Taba churches.
Iglesia Evangélica Luterana Argentina	1905	P-Lut	e....	241	20,000	22,816	30,000	1.10	*Ev Lutheran Ch in Argentina.* M=LC Missouri S(USA). German-speaking. 56n,1f,2s.
Iglesia Evangélica Luterana Unida	1908	P-Lut	Luu.N	34	5,360	5,565	7,653	1.28	*United Ev Luth Ch.* 1948, M=LCA(USA). A=1948. Diverse immigrants. 20n,6x,15f,2s.
Iglesia Evangélica Menonita Argentina	1917	P-Men	G.u.N	30	1,600	2,000	2,000	0.00	*Mennonite Ev Ch in A. Argentina Mennonite Conference.* M=MCNA(USA). 21f.
Iglesia Evangélica Metodista	1964	I-Hol	.TT.T	10	1,000	2,000	2,000	0.00	*Ev Methodist Ch. Bible Methodists.* M=EMC(USA). Korensa. HQ Buenos Aires. 6f.
Iglesia Evangélica Metodista Argentina	1836	P-Met	VWu.N	83	25,400	40,000	35,700	-0.45	*Ev Methodist Ch of A.* M=UMC(USA). 58n,14x,32f,1j,89t,1u,W=32%,244Yy.
Iglesia Ev Pentecostal Argentina	1917	P-Pe3	ZF...	235	21,278	20,000	42,600	3.07	*Pentecostal Ev Ch.* M=CoG(Cleveland), SFM. Some Toba Indians. 98n,1f,2p.
Iglesia Ev Pentecostal de Chile	c1940	I-3pL	x....	25	30,000	30,000	60,000	2.81	*Ev Pentecostal Ch of Chile.* Indigenous church from Chile. In all major cities.
Iglesia Ev Pentecostal Unida	1967	P-Pe1	x....	20	500	700	1,500	3.10	*United Pentecostal Ch.* M=UPC(USA). Oneness Pentecostals. 8n,6f,2p(35).
Iglesia Evangélica Unida Toba	1943	I-3pL	.....	190	50,100	15,000	70,400	6.38	Ex Mennonites(M=Chaco Mission). 1962, pentecostal split. 80% of all Toba Indians. 6f.
Iglesia Galesa	1865	P-Ref	.....	12	500	3,000	1,000	-4.30	*Welsh Ch.* Welsh immigrants in Patagonia (Chubut Valley). Declining. HQ Trelew.
Iglesia Luterana Danesa	1882	P-Lut	..u.N	5	1,100	3,000	2,600	-0.57	*Danish Lutheran Ch.* Danes from National Ch of Denmark. Begun 1882 in Tandil.
Iglesia Luterana Noruega		P-Lut	Lw...	1	370	825	680	0.05	*Norwegian Lutheran Ch. Norske Kirke.* Norwegians from national church of Norway.
Iglesia Nazarena Apostólica Cristiana	1958	P-Hol	x....	30	700	1,000	1,400	1.35	M=Apostolic Christian Ch (Nazarean) (USA). Swiss Mennonite origin. HQ Buenos Aires.
Iglesia Nueva Apostólica	c1930	I-3aX	x....	135	103,000	50,000	145,008	4.35	*NAK. New Apostolic Ch.* German immigrants. World HQ Dortmund (Germany).
Iglesia Ondas de Amor & Paz	1985	I-3gL	.....	110	275,000	–	400,000	10.00	*Waves of Love and Peace Ch.* Vast congregation in Buenos Aires. Daily services. 5,000 workers.
Iglesia Ortodoxa Arabe	c1890	O-Ara	Cwo..	20	24,000	30,000	35,000	0.62	*D Buenos Aires.* Under Antiochian Orth Ch (USA) and P Antioch. Syrians, Lebanese.
Iglesia Ortodoxa Griega	c1870	O-Gre	Cwo..	23	17,000	25,000	30,000	0.73	In 10th Archdiocesan District, Greek Orthodox AD N&SAmerica. Greeks. 1 bishop, 16n.
Iglesia Ortodoxa Romana	c1950	O-Rum	Cwc..	1	7,000	10,000	12,000	0.73	*Romanian Orthodox Ch. Biserica Ortodoxa Romana.* Immigrants from Romania.
Iglesia Ortodoxa Russa	c1880	O-Rus	Mwo..	6	12,000	15,000	17,000	0.50	*Russian Orthodox Ch.* In D SAmerica, Orth Ch in America (USA). Russian bishop,2n.
Iglesia Ortodoxa Russa: D Argentina	c1925	I-Rus	x....	10	6,000	10,000	12,000	0.73	*Russian Orthodox Ch Outside of Russia* (HZ New York). Refugees. Ultra-conservative.
Iglesia Ortodoxa Serba	c1950	O-Ser	Cwc..	2	3,000	7,000	8,000	0.54	*Serbian Orthodox Ch. Srpska Pravoslavna Crkva.* Under P Belgrade. Serbs, Albanians.
Iglesia Ortodoxa Syriana	c1970	O-Syr	D....	2	1,000	–	2,000	35.53	*Syrian Orthodox Ch, Patriarchal Vicariate* (under P Antioch).
Iglesia Ortodoxa Ucrania	c1920	O-Ukr	X....	6	15,000	20,000	24,000	0.73	*Ukrainian Autocephalous Orthodox Ch in Argentina.* Branch of UOC of the USA. 4n.
Iglesia Santa Pentecostés	c1930	P-Pe3	ZF...	79	7,800	7,000	19,500	4.18	*Pentecostal Holiness Ch.* M=PHC(USA). 3-stage Pentecostals. 37nm,14f.
Iglesia Sueca		P-Lut	Lw...	2	670	2,500	2,200	0.05	*Swedish Ch. Svenska Kyrkan.* Swedes from state church of Sweden. HQ Buenos Aires.
Iglesias Bautistas Ev del Norte A	1957	P-Bap	xF...	26	1,120	200	2,300	10.26	*Baptist Chs of Northern Argentina.* M=BGC(USA). HQ Jujuy. 14f.
Iglesias de Cristo	1958	I-Dis	x....	7	150	300	400	1.16	M=Churches of Christ (Non-Instrumental) (USA). In Buenos Aires, Mendoza. 10f.
Misión Bautista Conservador	1946	I-Bap	xF...	79	4,630	6,071	7,720	0.97	*Gen Assoc of Bapt Chs in N Arg.* M=CBFMS(1900 San Pedro Mission). 3n,43f,W=57%,262Y.
Misión Crist Escudo del Fe		I-3pL	.....	45	4,500	1,000	11,300	0.05	A grassroots pentecostal body.
Misión Evangélica Emmanuel		P-Pe3	x....	12	1,500	1,000	5,000	0.05	*Emmanuel Holiness Ch.* M=EHC(USA). 3-stage Pentecostals. HQ Formosa.
Misíon Evangelica en Villa Real	1973	I-3gL	.....	24	1,120	–	2,000	4.55	*Evangelical Mission in the Royal City.* Araucanos, Criollos.
Misión Ig del Señor		I-3pL	.....	95	12,000	2,000	30,000	0.05	*Church of the Lord Mission.* Argentinian pentecostals.
Movimiento Cristiano y Misionero	1958	I-3pL	.....	10	12,000	6,000	25,000	5.87	*Christian & Missionary Movement.* Schism ex Assemblies of God (USA). HQ La Plata.
Sociedad de la Ciencia Cristiana		m-Sci	x....	10	500	1,000	1,000	0.05	*Ch of Christ, Scientist, Christian Science.* M=CCS(Boston, USA). 1m,15w.
Sociedad Protestante del Sud		P-Lut	L....	4	2,200	3,620	4,000	0.05	*Protestant Society in Southern Argentina.* Lutheran immigrants.
Testigos de Jehová	1924	m-Jeh	x....	1,459	96,780	30,000	231,133	8.51	*Jehovah's Witnesses.* . 1924, first missionary. 1976, banned. (1975)2481Y. (1995) 7479Y.
Union Evangelica	1956	P-Eva	.....	61	2,045	1,000	4,125	5.83	*Gospel Missionary Union.* M=GMU.
Unión Evangélica de Sud America	1887	P-Eva	xM...	26	7,200	8,000	10,100	0.94	First M=RBMU; 1956,EUSA(UK,USA). Primarily evangelistic in interior. 37f.
Unión Misionera Neotestamentaria	1904	P-Non	x....	70	49,800	4,000	70,000	12.13	*New Testament Chs.* M=NTMU(UK). HQ Temperley. Corrientes, Entre Rios, Misiones. 3f.
Unión Nac de las Asambleas de Dios	1909	P-Pe2	ZF..N	825	129,000	20,000	415,000	12.90	*Assemblies of God.* 1914,M=PAoC,AoG(USA). Slavs. 175n,10x,21f,1j,1s(80),934Y.
Unión Pent del Chubut		I-3pL	.....	53	3,500	1,500	9,210	0.05	*Chubut Pentecostal Union.* Local pentecostals.
Visión del Futuro	1965	I-3gL	.....	339	95,000	1,000	190,000	23.35	Large charismatic network. F=Omar Cabrera. In 160 towns; programs on 60 radio stations.
Other independent Oneness bodies	c1970	I-3oL	.....	100	5,000	–	9,000	43.94	Total 5: Assemblies of the Lord Jesus Christ of the of Apostolic Faith.
Other independent pentecostal chs	c1940	I-3pL	.....	1,500	50,000	40,000	100,000	3.73	Total about 30, begun by Argentinians, some Chileans, and IURD (Brazil).
Other charismatic churches	c1972	I-3gL	.....	1,000	300,000	–	400,000	4.35	Independent charismatic churches, usually termed grassroots churches.
Other indigenous churches	c1950	I-	.....	250	5,000	5,000	10,000	2.81	Total about 15 (see below), including Igreja Católica Apostólica Brasileira.
Other Protestant denominations	c1955	P-	.....	200	2,000	5,000	6,000	0.73	Total 20, including BBFI(1959),BMM(1987),BWM(1977).
Doubly-affiliated		2-aff			-3,078,155	-1,006,436	-4,446,485		Members of both an older denomination and a newer charismatic one.
Totals				**22,991**	**21,092,339**	**22,530,000**	**31,955,350**		

Churches, members, growth, 1900-2025	*Congs*	*Adults*	*Affiliated*	*G%*	*Total denominations*	*6 Megablocs:* O	R	A	P	I	m
Total churches, members, and denominations (mid-1900)	2,000	2,000,000	4,105,500	2.46	6	4	1	1	0	0	0
Total churches, members, and denominations (mid-1970)	7,483	15,260,664	22,530,000	2.46	109	7	1	1	45	52	3
Total churches, members, and denominations (mid-1990)	22,000	20,000,000	30,057,000	1.45	170	8	1	1	57	100	3
Total churches, members, and denominations (mid-1995)	22,991	21,092,339	31,955,350	1.23	180	8	1	1	57	110	3
Total churches, members, and denominations (mid-2000)	24,000	26,000,000	33,985,872	1.24	193	8	1	1	60	120	3
Total churches, members, and denominations (mid-2025)	27,000	30,000,000	42,836,300	0.93	347	20	1	1	70	250	5

NOTES ON TABLE ABOVE

NATIONAL COUNCILS (Column 4, 5th letter).

- E = Association of Evangelical Churches in Argentina (ACIERA).
- N = Federación Argentina de Iglesias Evangélicas (FAIE) (Argentina Federation of Evangelical Churches) (also called Concilio Evangélico de Iglesias Argentinas); 1955.
- n = associate member of FAIE.
- R = Conferencia Episcopal Argentina (CEA) (Argentina Episcopal Conference).
- T = Argentina Consultative Committee of the ICCC.

OTHER INDIGENOUS CHURCHES.

These number at least 20 pentecostal bodies and about 10 non-pentecostal (of which about 5 are members of FAIE), including: Argentina para Cristo, Asociación Cristiana Evangelistica, Concilio Ev de Iglesias, Corporación Cooperadores Evangélicos, Iglesia Cristiana Biblica, Iglesia Cristiana Ev de Mendoza, Iglesia Ev de Mar del Plata, Iglesia Ev Ingenio Ledesma, Iglesia Ev Japonesa, Iglesia Ev Pentecostal Apostólica Argentian, Iglesia Pentecostal de Argentina, Iglesia Pentecostal de la Trinidad (from Chile; 4 pastors), Misión Pentecostal (Indígenas), Testigos Presbiterianas do Brasil, Unión de los Cristianos de la Fe Ev, Unión Ev de la Argentina. There is also a missionary bishop of the Igreja Católica Apostólica Brasileira, from Brazil.

OTHER PROTESTANT DENOMINATIONS. Among the many small Protestant denominations and para-denominations are the following (with names in Spanish or English depending on which is better known): Alianza Cristiana Hebrea Americana, Alianza Misionera Evangélica, Baptist Bible Fellowship International (1959), Ch of Christ (Non-Instrumental), Dutch Reformed Ch of South Africa (NGK; Afrikaans-speaking Boer immigrants after 1918), Eastern Bolivian Mission, Evangelical Alliance Mission, Exclusive Brethren (Kelly-Continental), Friends of Israel Mission, German Mennonite Ch, Gospel Mission of South America (1971), Go-Ye Fellowship, Gypsy Ev Movement (France), Iglesia Presbiteriana de San Andrés, Independent Assemblies of God, Irish Baptist Foreign Mission (Baptist Union of Ireland), Misiof Israel MissiMisiGerman Mennonite Ch, Gospel Mission of South America (1971), Go-Ye Fellowship, Gypsy Ev Movement (France), Iglesia Presbiteriana de San Andrés, Independent Assemblies of God, Irish Baptist Foreign Mission (Baptist Union of Ireland), Misiof Israel Missist Reform Movement, Slavic Gospel Association, Sociedad Bautista Ev, Synod of Ev Lutheran Chs (1941), United World Mission (1965), World Gospel Mission (1969), World Mission Prayer League, World-Wide Missions (1971).

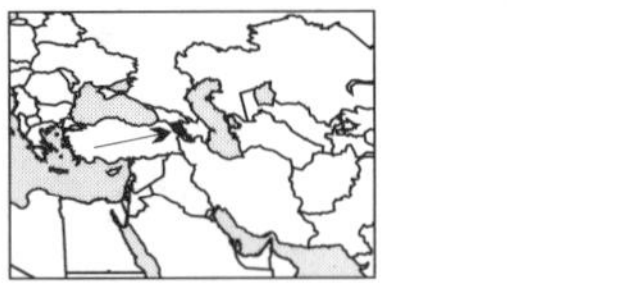

ARMENIA

SECULAR DATA, AD 2000

STATE
Official name: Hayastani Hanrapetoutium (The Republic of Armenia).
Short name: Armenia. **Adjective of nationality:** Armenian.
Flag: Mauve, blue, and mustard stripes.
Area: 29,800 sq. km. (11,500 sq. mi.).
Government: Unitary multiparty republic with single legislative body, since 1991 (1920 Soviet Socialist republic).
Legislature: National Assembly, 190 members.
Official language: Armenian.
Monetary unit: 1 dram = 100 lumas. **US$1=** 502.38 drams.
Chief cities: JEREVAN (Erevan, Yerevan) 1,322,000; Kirovakan (Karaklis) 196,852; Kumajri (Gumry, Gyumri) 137,859; Razdan 65,229; Ecmiadzin (Echmiadzin) 61,734.
Political divisions: 11 provinces.
Armed forces: 60,000.

DEMOGRAPHY
Population: 3,520,000.
Population density: 118.1/sq. km. (306.0/sq. mi.).
Under 15 years: 863,000.
Growth rate p.a.: 0.32% (births 13.98, deaths 7.92).
Mortality: Infant, per 1,000: 24.4; **Maternal per 100,000:** 50.0.
Life expectancy: 71 (male 68, female 75).
Household size: 4.7. **Floor area per person, sq.m:** 15.0.
Major languages: Armenian, Azerbaijani, Russian, Ukrainian, Kurdish.
Urban dwellers: 69.95%. **Urban growth rate p.a.:** 1.0%.
Labor force: 44%.

ETHNOLINGUISTIC PEOPLES
94.5% Armenian (Ermeni); 1.7% Northern Kurd; 1.5% Russian; ; 0.5% Azerbaijani (Azeri Turk); 0.2% Kurdish.

ECONOMY
National income p.a. per person: US$729; **per family:** US$3,430.

EDUCATION
Adult literacy: 98% (male 99%, female 98%). **Schools:** 1,443.
Universities: 14. **School enrolment:** female/male: 91%/82%.

HEALTH
Access to health services: 50%. **Access to safe water:** 60%.
Hospitals: 183 (83 beds per 10,000). **Doctors:** 14,000.
Blind: 3,000. **Deaf:** 219,700. **Murder rate:** 5.
Lepers: 1,000.

LITERATURE
New book titles p.a.: 280 (80 p.a. per million). **Periodicals:** 56.
Newspapers: 7 dailies.

COMMUNICATION (per 1,000 people)
Phones: 155 (1% mobile). **Radios:** 250. **TV sets:** 241.
Daily newspaper circulation: 23. **Computers:** 35.

REFUGEES
Citizen refugees in other countries: 185,000.
Alien refugees from other countries: 304,000.

HUMAN LIFE AND LIBERTY (optimum condition=100.0%)
HDI: 65.1. **HSI:** 55.0. **HFI:** 40.0. **EFL:** 25.0.

Country status. Armenia, a former republic of the Soviet Union, is an independent state in the South Caucasus in Western Asia. It is mountainous with many peaks over 10,000 feet yet produces cotton, tobacco, fruits, and rice. Armenia is currently a member of the Commonwealth of Independent States.

Country Table 1. **Religious adherents in Armenia, AD 1900-2025.**

Year	1900		1970		mid-1990		Annual change, 1990-2000				mid-1995		mid-2000		mid-2025	
Name	*Adherents*	*%*	*Adherents*	*%*	*Adherents*	*%*	*Natural*	*Conversion*	*Total*	*Rate*	*Adherents*	*%*	*Adherents*	*%*	*Adherents*	*%*
Christians	**470,800**	**89.0**	**858,000**	**34.1**	**2,400,000**	**67.7**	**-1,737**	**57,342**	**55,605**	**2.11**	**2,780,400**	**77.8**	**2,956,051**	**84.0**	**3,659,500**	**92.7**
PROFESSION																
crypto-Christians	0	0.0	374,000	14.8	0	0.0	0	0	0	0.00	0	0.0	0	0.0	0	0.0
professing Christians	**470,800**	**89.0**	**484,000**	**19.2**	**2,400,000**	**67.7**	**-1,737**	**57,342**	**55,605**	**2.11**	**2,780,400**	**77.8**	**2,956,051**	**84.0**	**3,659,500**	**92.7**
AFFILIATION																
unaffiliated Christians	5,300	1.0	1,550	0.1	2,200	0.1	-2	18	16	0.70	2,297	0.1	2,358	0.1	4,000	0.1
affiliated Christians	**465,500**	**88.0**	**856,450**	**34.0**	**2,397,800**	**67.6**	**-1,691**	**57,280**	**55,589**	**2.11**	**2,778,103**	**77.7**	**2,953,693**	**83.9**	**3,655,500**	**92.6**
Orthodox	464,500	87.8	854,000	33.9	2,280,000	64.3	-1,608	48,857	47,249	1.90	2,623,900	73.4	2,752,493	78.2	3,361,000	85.2
Roman Catholics	500	0.1	0	0.0	100,000	2.8	-71	6,071	6,000	4.81	130,000	3.6	160,000	4.6	210,000	5.3
Independents	0	0.0	2,100	0.1	13,000	0.4	-9	1,509	1,500	7.97	16,895	0.5	28,000	0.8	50,000	1.3
Protestants	500	0.1	150	0.0	4,500	0.1	-3	753	750	10.31	6,800	0.2	12,000	0.3	24,500	0.6
Marginal Christians	0	0.0	200	0.0	300	0.0	0	90	90	14.87	508	0.0	1,200	0.0	10,000	0.3
Trans-megabloc groupings																
Evangelicals	500	0.1	6,000	0.2	1,600	0.1	-1	31	30	1.73	1,740	0.1	1,900	0.1	3,000	0.1
Pentecostals/Charismatics	0	0.0	3,000	0.1	67,300	1.9	-47	1,007	960	1.34	71,709	2.0	76,900	2.2	125,500	3.2
Great Commission Christians	**28,000**	**5.3**	**12,600**	**0.5**	**337,000**	**9.5**	**-238**	**6,076**	**5,838**	**1.61**	**360,000**	**10.1**	**395,380**	**11.2**	**520,000**	**13.2**
Nonreligious	500	0.1	966,500	38.4	634,600	17.9	-448	-33,476	-33,924	-7.36	430,000	12.0	295,365	8.4	146,000	3.7
Atheists	0	0.0	580,000	23.0	359,000	10.1	-253	-18,454	-18,707	-7.10	240,000	6.7	171,934	4.9	55,000	1.4
Muslims	54,000	10.2	110,000	4.4	150,000	4.2	-106	-5,462	-5,568	-4.53	122,000	3.4	94,325	2.7	80,000	2.0
Baha'is	0	0.0	0	0.0	600	0.0	0	73	73	8.29	1,000	0.0	1,331	0.0	5,000	0.1
Jews	3,200	0.6	5,000	0.2	800	0.0	-1	-23	-24	-3.45	600	0.0	563	0.0	500	0.0
Ethnoreligionists	500	0.1	500	0.0	0	0.0	0	0	0	0.00	0	0.0	0	0.0	0	0.0
World A (unevangelized persons)	26,450	5.0	176,400	7.0	124,075	3.5	-87	-4,519	-4,606	-4.54	92,926	2.6	77,440	2.2	43,406	1.1
World B (evangelized non-Christians)	31,750	6.0	1,485,600	58.9	1,020,925	28.8	-721	-52,823	-53,544	-7.14	700,778	19.6	486,509	13.8	243,094	6.2
World C (Christians)	470,800	89.0	858,000	34.1	2,400,000	67.7	-1,737	57,342	55,605	2.11	2,780,400	77.8	2,956,051	84.0	3,659,500	92.7
Country's population	**529,000**	**100.0**	**2,520,000**	**100.0**	**3,545,000**	**100.0**	**-2,545**	**0**	**-2,545**	**-0.07**	**3,574,105**	**100.0**	**3,520,000**	**100.0**	**3,946,000**	**100.0**

COLUMNS, ROWS.
For meanings and definitions, see Codebook (Part 3). Note that, by definition, total 'Christians' = professing + crypto-Christians, which also = affiliated + unaffiliated Christians, and also = Great Commission Christians + latent Christians. Percentages may not always total exactly, due to rounding.

NOTES ON RELIGIONS
ATHEISTS. Over 20% of the population during Communist rule, declining rapidly after 1989.
BAHA'IS. By 1995 Baha'i had become organized into 9 LSAs (local spiritual assemblies) after decades of enforced inactivity under Communism.
JEWS. Steady emigration to Israel after 1985.
MUSLIMS. Mainly Kurds and Azerbaijanis.

Great Commission Instrument Panel: status of Armenia (for explanation see start of Part 4)

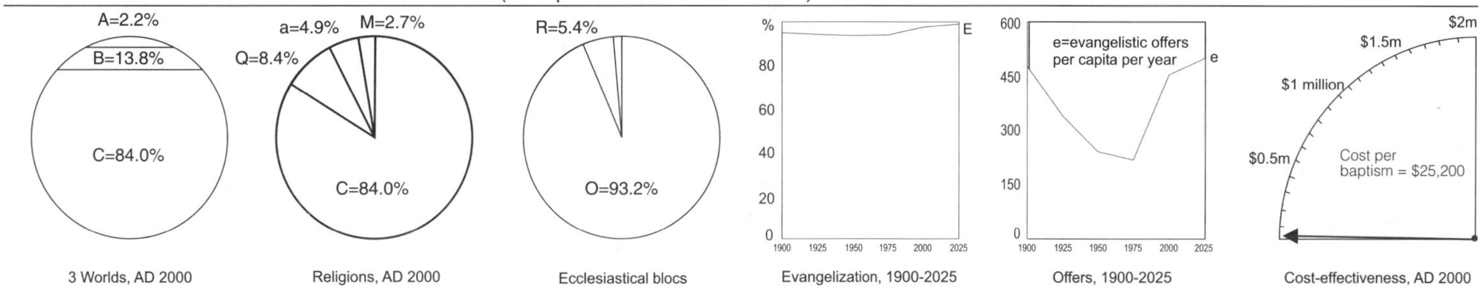

HUMAN LIFE AND LIBERTY

Human rights and freedoms. Since achieving independence from the Soviet Union in 1991 Armenia has been trying, with mixed results, to create a multiparty parliamentary democracy. Legislative power is vested in the parliament whose members were elected in a free, albeit Soviet-style, election. However, the parliament has been unable to adopt a constitution, particularly because of the ongoing conflict in Nagorno-Karabakh, an overwhelmingly ethnic Armenian enclave within Azerbaijan. Since 1988 when the enclave voted to secede from Azerbaijan and join Armenia, thousands have died or been injured and thousands more have fled to Armenia as refugees. A crippling Azerbaijani and Turkish embargo has strangled land-locked Armenia. In the absence of a constitution, the International Covenant on Civil and Political Rights adopted by the parliament in 1991 serves as the bastion of human rights. Armenia still relies on parts of the old Soviet constitution as well as the Soviet-era criminal code. Under this code, suspects may be held without bail for up to 72 hours, and judges are vulnerable to political pressures. The law on religion prohibits proselytization in deference to the Armenian Church.

Christians. Karekin I, late Supreme Patriarch and Catholicos of All Armenians, formally opens Bible Society of Armenia's center.

NON-CHRISTIAN RELIGIONS

Islam has a lengthy history of dominating Armenia, but in the 1990s the number of Muslims in Armenia was in sharp decline due to emigration related to the war with Azerbaijan over Nagorno Karabagh. The 70,000 Kurds of Armenia are mostly Muslim, but with significant minorities of Christians and Yazidis-the latter being a syncretic religion combining Zoroastrian, Manichean, Jewish, Nestorian Christian, and Islamic elements. The other large, predominantly-Muslim people are the Azerbaijanis. Some new religious movements and smaller religions, such as Transcendental Meditation, Hari Krishnas, Baha'is, the Unification Church, and a neopagan sun-worshipping group have made inroads into the country since independence in 1991. Some suffered sporadic attacks in the early 1990s, especially as a reaction against pacifism.

CHRISTIANITY

ORTHODOX CHURCH. The Armenian Apostolic Church, also called the Armenian Orthodox Church or the Gregorian Church, traces its roots to the witness of the two disciples of Christ, Bartholomew and Thaddeus. The national church remembers the names and honors the memory of a number of saints and martyrs who witnessed prior to 301. Armenia holds the distinction of being the first nation to become Christian as a nation. After converting in Cappadocia and returning to his homeland, Gregory the Illuminator was thrown in prison by king Tiridates III. Years later, when the king was suffering from a mortal illness, Gregory was called upon to pray, resulting in a miraculous healing. Tiridates was baptized and declared Armenia Christian in 301. Many Zoroastrian priests became Christian clergy, and some pagan shrines were converted to churches. Armenian bishops were unable to attend the council of Chalcedon, 451, and opposed its formula concerning the two natures of Christ. Since then the Armenian church has been in communion only with the other monophysite churches, of Egypt, Syria, and Ethiopia. The motivation behind this division of the Armenian Church from the Greek was as much political as doctrinal: the Armenians were at that time already resisting Greek domination. The survival of the Armenian Apostolic Church, and of the Armenians as a distinct people, was challenged in 653 when the region was ceded to the Arabs, in the 11th century by the invasions of the Byzantine Greeks and the Seljuk Turks, in 1375 when the Armenian kingdom of Cilicia fell to the Mamluk Turks, and in the 16th century when Armenia was divided between the Ottoman Turks and the Persians.

In 1933 the Armenian Church suffered a serious split, partly over the question of the church's relations with the Soviet state. This rift was formalized in 1956, with the catholicos of Echmidazin on one side and the catholicos of Cilicia, based in Antelias, Lebanon, on the other. There has been greater harmony since the late 1980s due to the Karabagh struggle, the 1988 earthquake, the fall of the USSR, and the elevation of the Cilician catholicos, Karekin I, to become the supreme patriarch and catholicos of all Armenians.

In a 1981 visit to Germany, Vasken I, then catholicos of all Armenians at Echmiadzin, reported that 60% of the people in Soviet Armenia attended church and 60% of all children were baptized. This was despite restrictions, such that in 1984 there were fewer than 90 churches open (vs. 1,500 in 1917), and only 200 active clergy.

Besides the Armenian Orthodox, in 1990 the country had 15,000 Russian Orthodox faithful and 5,400 Assyrian Orthodox.

In 1995 the history of schism was dramatically reversed when, after the death of Vasken I, the catholics of Sis (Lebanon) was elected catholicos of Echmiadzin, to universal acclaim.

CATHOLIC CHURCH. The Armenian kingdom of Cilicia (1080-1375), bordering on the Mediterranean Sea, had good relations with many of the Catholic crusaders. The Roman Catholic presence begun at that time was later strengthened through missionary work of Dominicans and Franciscans in the first half of the 15th century. The Dominicans set up a

Country summary. **Worlds A, B, C by ethnolinguistic peoples, cities, and major civil divisions in Armenia.**

	PEOPLES							CITIES							CIVIL DIVISIONS						
World	*Num*	*Pop 2000*	*C%*	*Christians*	*E%*	*U%*	*Unevangelized*	*Num*	*Pop 2000*	*C%*	*Christians*	*E%*	*U%*	*Unevangelized*	*Num*	*Pop 2000*	*C%*	*Christians*	*E%*	*U%*	*Unevangelized*
A	10	104,130	4.82	5,023	34	66	69,004	0	0	0.00	0	0	0	0	0	0	0.00	0	0	0	0
B	4	11,362	9.82	1,116	61	39	4,376	0	0	0.00	0	0	0	0	0	0	0.00	0	0	0	0
C	11	3,404,078	86.59	2,947,557	100	0	4,567	5	1,783,674	84.84	1,513,342	99	1	19,634	11	3,519,567	83.92	2,953,693	98	2	77,942
Total	**25**	**3,519,570**	**83.92**	**2,953,696**	**98**	**2**	**77,947**	**5**	**1,783,674**	**84.84**	**1,513,342**	**99**	**1**	**19,634**	**11**	**3,519,567**	**83.92**	**2,953,693**	**98**	**2**	**77,942**

Latin-Armenian brotherhood, Unitor. The Armenian Catholic congregation formed in Constantinople in 1701 moved in 1717 to the island of San Lazzaro in Venice, Italy, where the Mekhitarist Armenian Catholic order began. The Armenian Uniate Catholic Church patriarchate was moved in the 18th century from Aleppo to Bzommar in Lebanon. Catholic Armenians were recognized by the Ottoman government as a distinct 'Katolik' millet in 1830. Census figures of the dioceses roughly corresponding to Armenia today reported 28,000 Armenian Uniate Catholics before World War I; corresponding figures for 1954 reported none. This drop is due to emigration as well as to mass martyrdom. By 1995 there were 130,000 Catholics in Armenia, 100,000 of them ethnic Armenians.

The Holy See has diplomatic relations with Armenia and in AD 2000 is represented to government and the Catholic hierarchy by a nuncio residing in Tiflis, Georgia.

Catholicate of Echmiadzin. Armenian Apostolic procession into Echmiadzin cathedral for consecration of 4 new bishops.

PROTESTANT AND OTHER CHURCHES. The first permanent Protestant mission among the Armenians began in 1831 with the arrival in Constantinople of William Goodall of the American Board of Commissioners for Foreign Mission. In 1846 his new Armenian-Turkish New Testament was published and the first Armenian Evangelical Church was organized. In the next year the Ottoman government recognized a separate Protestant millet, or semi-autonomous community. Protestant missionaries in the 19th century evangelized, opened schools and seminaries, and performed humanitarian work. Though the first Protestant missionaries worked under the vision of bringing renewal to the ancient church, the Armenian Apostolic clergy opposed them and excommunicated their followers. In general, the impact of these missionary efforts on the life of the nation was small. Census figures of the dioceses roughly corresponding to the Armenia of 1991 reported 1,500 Armenian Protestants; corresponding figures for 1954 reported only 200. By 1996 there were 900 Baptists in 7 churches, up from only 400 in 1990. They also ran a well-attended Bible school.

Art and architecture. As a reaction against idolatry, early Armenian Christians melted down or destroyed all statues from the Classical era, and the Armenian Church has never since allowed statues, though it has its own extensive iconography. The Armenian countryside is dotted with khatchkars, stone memorial slabs with carved crosses, many of them reminiscent of Celtic patterns in their intricacy. Some of the finest illuminated manuscripts are Armenian. The Soviet-era manuscript museum in Yerevan contains a world-class collection of this beautiful Christian art form.

Renewal movements. In the 1990s the Pentecostal/Charismatic Renewal continued to spread rapidly across most older churches, and numbered over 76,900 adherents (of whom 77% were Charismatics, and 23% Independents).

Indigenous missions. Though under Soviet domination in recent decades, Armenia has a long unbroken record of foreign outreach since the introduction of Christianity. Much of this has been through the significant influence of the Armenian diaspora in over 100 nations.

CHURCH AND STATE

In 1903, in the part of Armenia controlled by Russia, Armenian Orthodox churches and schools were forcibly closed and church property confiscated. The clergy resisted, and Russian police occupied Holy Echmiadzin. In Soviet Armenia, the church suffered ridicule and a variety of pressures, though not as severe of treatment as that suffered by the church elsewhere in the USSR catholicos Vasken I was asked to address the first session of the new parliament of independent Armenia in 1991. When given the floor he was speechless with emotion, in light of Armenia's centuries of political and religious oppression, now suddenly ended. Finally he uttered the Lord's Prayer. The new national constitution guaranteed religious freedom, but recognized the Armenian Apostolic Church as the national church of the Armenian people, and as an important bulwark for the edification of its spiritual life and national preservation. The Armenian Orthodox Church enjoys a privileged position in the life of the country.

Due largely to pressure from Armenian Apostolic Church leaders, in 1993 a decree was issued criticizing unregistered religious groups as disruptive and claiming they opposed military service. This was a sensitive issue, due to the war against Azerbaijan over Nagorno Karabagh. Control over religious groups was increased, through the government Council for Religious Affairs. In 1995 the State Minister for Military Affairs came on TV and asked citizens to inform authorities about where religious sects met for worship. Local administrators were directed to draw up lists of people according to religious affiliation. Soon, 11 young men, Jehovahs Witnesses, were arrested. Officials invaded the Yerevan offices of the (Protestant) Armenian Missionary Association of America and harassed workers, but later returned and apologized. Police and border guards entered the Yerevan Evangelical Christian-Baptist church and threatened worshipers.

BROADCASTING AND MEDIA

TWR broadcasts in 8 languages from its station in Yerevan, and in Armenian from Cyprus and Tirana. Azeri programs can be received from FEBA (Seychelles). Some wealthy expatriate Armenians have been funding the installation of Christian radio stations to cover Armenia and surrounding countries.

Satellite TV programs are received mainly in Arabic. The 'Jesus' Film has been shown on national television, where 3 million are estimated to have watched it.

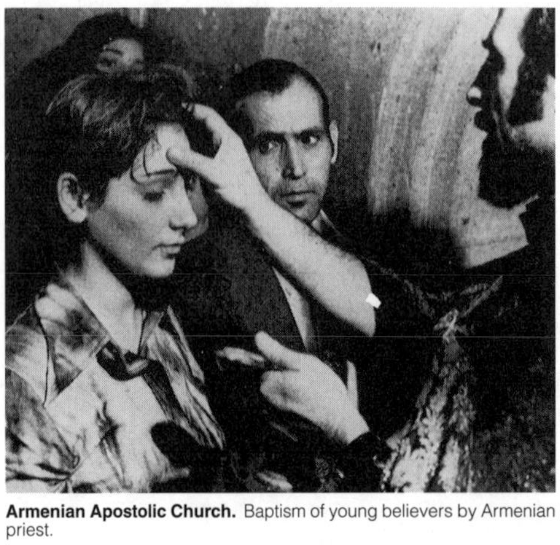

Armenian Apostolic Church. Baptism of young believers by Armenian priest.

INTERDENOMINATIONAL ORGANIZATIONS

No council of churches yet exist.

FUTURE TRENDS AND PROSPECTS

Atheists and nonreligious, representing over half of the population in 1970, are expected to decline to only 5% by AD 2025.

This decline among atheists and the nonreligious is expected to slow and then reverse by about the middle of the 21st century. Christians are expected to peak at about 95% in 2050. After this the Christian percentage should decline again, albeit very slowly. Consequently, Armenia, predominantly Christian since the 3rd century, is likely to remain so well over the next 50 years.

BIBLIOGRAPHY

A brief introduction to Armenian Christian literature. K. Sarkissian. : Michael Barbour, 1974. 83p.

A critical examination of Armenian Catholic communities in Transcaucasia: their late origins, historical development, and contemporary status. Armenian Church of America. New York: St. Vartan Press, 1994. 237p. (English and Armenian).

A history of Armenian Christianity from the beginning to our own time. L. Arpee. New York: Armenian Missionary Association of America, 1946. 386p.

A history of Eastern Christianity. A. S. Atiya. London: Methuen, 1968. 486p. (Chapter 4 on Armenian Church).

Armenia. V. Nersessian. *World bibliographical series*, vol. 163. Oxford, UK: CLIO Press, 1993. 330p. (Extensive section on religion, 112–36).

'Armenia: a Christian enclave in the Islamic Near East in the Middle Ages,' E. Schütz, in *Conversion and continuity: indigenous Christian communities in Islamic lands, eighth to eighteenth centuries*, p.217–36. M. Gervers & R. J. Bikhazi (eds). Toronto: University of Toronto, 1986.

Armenia: cradle of civilization. D. M. Lang. London: George Allen & Unwin, 1970. 320p. (Deals extensively with Christianity in Armenia).

Armenian Christology and evangelization of Islam: a survey of the relevance of the Christology of the Armenian Apostolic Church to Armenian relations with its Muslim environment. H. A. Chakmakjian. Leiden: E. J. Brill, 1965. 146p.

'Armenian nationalism and the ferment of faith,' V. Guroian, *Christian Century*, 108, 7 (February 27, 1991), 233–36.

Art in the Armenian Church: origins and teaching. G. Kochakian. New York: St. Vartan Press, 1995.

Die Kirche Armeniens: Eine Volkskirche zwischen Ost und West. F. Heyer (ed). *Der Reihe die Kirchen der Welt*, 18. Stuttgart, Germany: Evangelisches Verlagswerk, 1978. 231p.

Imperialism, evangelism, and the Ottoman Armenians, 1878–1896. J. Salt. London: Frank Cass and Co., 1993. 198p.

Les Arméniens, histoire d'un Chrétienté. G. Dédéyan (ed). Toulouse, France: The editor, 1990. 122p.

'Religion and nationalism in Soviet Georgia and Armenia,' S. F. Jones, in *Religion and nationalism in Soviet and East European politics*, p.171–195. P. Ramet (ed). 2nd ed. Durham, NC: Duke University Press, 1989.

Saints and feasts of the Armenian Church. T. Koushagian. Trans. and ed., H. Melkonian. New York: St Vartan, 1988. 62p.

Studies in Armenian literature and Christianity. R. W. Thomson. Altershot, UK: Variorum, 1994.

Summary topics of Armenian church history. T. Nersoyan. New Rochelle, NY: St. Nerses Armenian Seminary, 1986. 31p.

The Armenian church. P. C. Gulesserian. Trans., D. Poladian. New York: AMS, 1970. 61p.

The Armenian Evangelical Church. V. H. Tootikian. Southfield, MI: Armenian Heritage Committee, 1984. 322p.

The Armenian Evangelical Church on the crossroads. H. P. Aharonian. Beirut: Middle East Council of Churches, 1988. 335p.

The Armenian Evangelical movement: why needed, why separated: an inquiry. H. A. Chakmakjian. Fresno, CA: H.A. Chakmakjian, 1985. 161p.

The Armenian Evangelical reformation. G. H. Chopourian. New York: Armenian Missionary Association, 1972. 170p.

The Armenians in history and the Armenian question. E. Uras. Istanbul: Documentary Publications, 1988. 1064p.

The Church of Armenia: her history, doctrine, rule, discipline, liturgy, literature, and existing condition. M. Ormanian. Trans., G. M. Gregory, ed., D. Poladian. 2nd ed. London: A. R. Mowbray, 1955. 219p.

The conversion of Armenia: a retelling of Agathangelos' History. V. G. Zahirsky. *Armenian Church classics.* [New York]: St. Vartan Press, 1985. 48p.

The conversion of Armenia to the Christian faith. W. St. Clair-Tisdall. Oxford, UK: Horace Hart, 1897. 256p.

The Eastern Christian churches: a brief survey. R. G. Roberson. 3rd ed. Rome: Pontificum Studiorum Orientalium, 1990. 129p.

'The ferment of faith in post–Soviet Armenia,' V. Guroian, *Christian Century*, 109, 3 (January 22, 1992), 66–68.

The Mother Church and Roman Catholic missionary activity in a reborn Armenia: documents pertaining to the Armenian Uniate Patriarchate's design to proselytize in Armenia. Armenian Church of America. New York: St Vartan Press, 1993. 104p. (English and Armenian).

The origins of Caucasian civilization: the Christian component. R. W. Thomson. Washington, DC: The Wilson Center, Kennan Institute for Advanced Russian Studies, [1980]. 28p.

The Tondrakian Movement: religious movements in the Armenian Church from the fourth to the tenth centuries. V. Nersessian. *Princeton Theological monograph series*, 15. Allison Park, PA: Pickwick Publications, 1988. 145p.

Country Table 2. **Organized churches and denominations in Armenia.**

Official name (bold type = church *with over 10% of all affiliated)* 1	*Begun* 2	*Type* 3	*Counc* 4	*Congs* 5	*Adults* 6	*Affiliated 1970* 7	*Affiliated 1995* 8	*G%* 9	*Names, notes, and other statistics* (see Codebook, Part 3) 10
Ancient Ch of the East (P-Tehran)	c100	O-Nes	Yw...	5	3,000	1,000	5,400	6.98	*Assyrian Apostolic Ch of the East* (Nestorians). Eastern-Syriac-speaking Assyrians.
Armenian Apostolic Church	c35	O-Arm	EWc.u	100	1,430,000	850,000	2,600,000	0.05	*Catholicate of Echmiadzin.* 72 bishops. Charismatic renewal: Brotherhood of Lovers of the Ch.
Armenian Pentecostal Church	c1960	I-3pW	.....	1	100	100	250	3.73	Formerly in USSR's registered AUCECB, now independent.
Assembly Hall Churches	c1990	I-3nC	.....	2	70	–	200	20.00	*Little Flock. Local Churches.*
Baptist Churches	c1930	P-Bap	T....	25	1,900	150	3,800	13.80	Formerly AUCECB(HQ Moscow).
Catholic Church in Armenia:	1991	R-LEr	O....	7	80,000	–	130,000	25.00	Byelorussians, Poles, Lithuanians, Ukrainians. 7n 7x 9m 14w 1384Yy
O Eastern Europe	1991	R-Arm	Ormv	2	20,000	–	30,000	25.00	Ordinariate for Armenian-rite Catholics. M=CMV. 5n 5x 7m 6w 1384Yy
AA Caucasus	1993	R-Lat	Bs	5	60,000	–	100,000	50.00	Apostolic Administration, also in Georgia, Azerbaijan. 2n 2x 2m 8w 0Yy
Ch of Jesus Christ of Latter-day Saints	c1990	m-LdS	x....	1	100	–	200	20.00	*Mormons.*Slight influence.
Jehovah's Witnesses	c1940	m-Jeh	x....	2	200	200	308	1.74	Little progress since collapse of hostile Communist regime.
New Apostolic Church	c1990	I-3aX	x....	2	200	–	445	20.00	*NAC,NAK.* M=Neuapostolische Kirche (HQ Zurich, Switzerland).
Pentecostal Churches	c1940	I-3pW	.....	80	6,000	2,000	15,000	8.39	Related to unregistered CCECB in Russia and Ukraine.
Russian Orthodox Church	c1800	O-Rus	Mw...	3	7,500	3,000	15,000	6.65	Russians, Ukrainians, Byelorussians, Assyrians, some Armenians.
Other independent Orthodox chs	c1970	I-OBe	x....	4	500	–	1,000	31.83	Old Ritualist Churches (Old Believers).
Other Protestant churches	c1990	P-	.....	30	1,000	–	3,000	20.00	German Evangelical Lutheran Ch,SDA,CWE,CEF,ELCL,ERCL.
Other Orthodox churches	1971	O-	.....	6	2,500	–	3,500	4.17	Georgian Orthodox Ch, Greek OC, Romanian OC, Bulgarian OC.
Totals				**268**	**1,533,070**	**856,450**	**2,778,103**		

Churches, members, growth, 1900-2025	*Congs*	*Adults*	*Affiliated*	*G%*	*Total denominations*	*6 Megablocs:* *O*	*R*	*A*	*P*	*I*	*m*
Total churches, members, and denominations (mid-1900)	50	273,000	465,500	0.87	3	3	0	0	0	0	0
Total churches, members, and denominations (mid-1970)	45	502,750	856,450	0.87	7	3	0	0	1	2	1
Total churches, members, and denominations (mid-1990)	250	1,323,000	2,397,800	5.28	12	5	0	0	1	5	1
Total churches, members, and denominations (mid-1995)	268	1,533,070	2,778,103	2.99	24	7	1	0	8	6	2
Total churches, members, and denominations (mid-2000)	300	1,630,000	2,953,693	1.23	27	8	1	0	10	6	2
Total churches, members, and denominations (mid-2025)	400	2,017,000	3,655,500	0.86	66	15	1	0	15	30	5

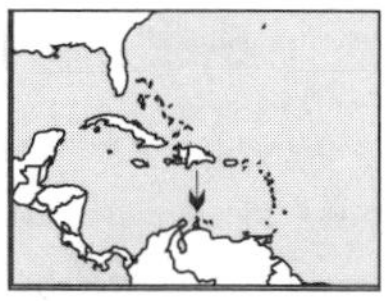

ARUBA

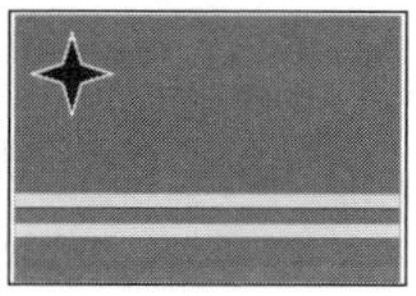

SECULAR DATA, AD 2000

STATE
Official name: The Territory of Aruba.
Short name: Aruba. **Adjective of nationality:** Aruban.
Flag: Light blue field, red star, two thin yellow stripes.
Area: 193 sq. km. (75 sq. mi.).
Government: Unicameral legislature since 1986 (1828 part of Dutch West Indies, 1845 part of Netherlands Antilles).
Legislature: Legislature, 21 members.
Official language: Dutch.
Monetary unit: Arubian florin (Af). **US$1=** Af 1.65.
Chief cities: ORANJESTAD 22,723.
Political divisions: 1 province.

DEMOGRAPHY
Population: 103,000.
Population density: 532.3/sq. km. (1,369.9/sq. mi.).
Under 15 years: 26,000.
Growth rate p.a.: 0.92% (births 15.32, deaths 6.11).
Mortality: Infant, per 1,000: 12.6; **Maternal per 100,000:** 30.0.
Life expectancy: 76 (male 73, female 79).
Household size: 3.6. **Floor area per person, sq.m:** 35.0.
Major languages: Papiamentu, English, Dutch.
Urban dwellers: 70.42%. **Urban growth rate p.a.:** 1.2%.
Labor force: 47%.

ETHNOLINGUISTIC PEOPLES
75.0% Antillean Creole; ; 5.0% Dutch; 0.3% Filipino; 0.3% Han Chinese; 0.2% Turk.

ECONOMY
National income p.a. per person: US$15,893; **per family:** US$57,216.

EDUCATION
Adult literacy: 95% (male 96%, female 94%). **Schools:** 56.
Universities: 1. **School enrolment:** female/male: 85%/85%.

HEALTH
Access to health services: 90%. **Access to safe water:** 90%.
Hospitals: 2 (44 beds per 10,000). **Doctors:** 74.
Blind: 60. **Deaf:** 4,400. **Murder rate:** 1.
Lepers: 0.

LITERATURE
New book titles p.a.: 70 (700 p.a. per million). **Periodicals:** 0.
Newspapers: 14 dailies.

COMMUNICATION (per 1,000 people)
Phones: 390 **(9% mobile). Radios:** 571. **TV sets:** 471.
Daily newspaper circulation: 757. **Computers:** 80.

HUMAN LIFE AND LIBERTY (optimum condition=100.0%)
HDI: 89.9. **HSI:** 90.0. **HFI:** 80.0. **EFL:** 46.0.

Country Table 1. **Religious adherents in Aruba, AD 1900-2025.**

Year	*1900*		*1970*		*mid-1990*		*Annual change, 1990-2000*				*mid-1995*		*mid-2000*		*mid-2025*	
Name	*Adherents*	*%*	*Adherents*	*%*	*Adherents*	*%*	*Natural*	*Conversion*	*Total*	*Rate*	*Adherents*	*%*	*Adherents*	*%*	*Adherents*	*%*
Christians	**14,000**	**100.0**	**58,850**	**97.0**	**61,360**	**95.9**	**3,924**	**-19**	**3,773**	**4.91**	**78,765**	**96.6**	**99,094**	**96.2**	**239,800**	**95.9**
PROFESSION																
professing Christians	**14,000**	**100.0**	**58,850**	**97.0**	**61,360**	**95.9**	**3,924**	**-19**	**3,773**	**4.91**	**78,765**	**96.6**	**99,094**	**96.2**	**239,800**	**95.9**
AFFILIATION																
unaffiliated Christians	700	5.0	7,780	12.8	1,360	2.1	83	166	249	10.98	2,925	3.6	3,853	3.7	5,300	2.1
affiliated Christians	**13,300**	**95.0**	**51,070**	**84.2**	**60,000**	**93.8**	**3,656**	**-132**	**3,524**	**4.73**	**75,840**	**93.1**	**95,241**	**92.5**	**234,500**	**93.8**
Roman Catholics	10,900	77.9	48,000	79.1	50,950	79.6	3,105	234	3,339	5.17	66,000	81.0	84,341	81.9	210,000	84.0
Protestants	2,400	17.1	2,240	3.7	6,260	9.8	381	-257	124	1.82	6,750	8.3	7,500	7.3	18,000	7.2
Independents	0	0.0	230	0.4	1,100	1.7	67	-42	25	2.07	1,233	1.5	1,350	1.3	2,500	1.0
Marginal Christians	0	0.0	300	0.5	1,090	1.7	66	-45	21	1.78	1,190	1.5	1,300	1.3	3,000	1.2
Anglicans	0	0.0	300	0.5	600	0.9	37	-22	15	2.26	667	0.8	750	0.7	1,000	0.4
Trans-megabloc groupings																
Evangelicals	1,200	8.6	2,400	4.0	3,340	5.2	204	-128	76	2.07	3,708	4.6	4,100	4.0	6,000	2.4
Pentecostals/Charismatics	0	0.0	200	0.3	5,080	7.9	310	27	337	5.22	6,657	8.2	8,450	8.2	24,000	9.6
Great Commission Christians	**420**	**3.0**	**1,200**	**2.0**	**3,050**	**4.8**	**186**	**49**	**235**	**5.88**	**4,075**	**5.0**	**5,402**	**5.2**	**17,500**	**7.0**
Nonreligious	0	0.0	650	1.1	800	1.3	49	15	64	6.07	1,100	1.4	1,442	1.4	5,000	2.0
Spiritists	0	0.0	350	0.6	600	0.9	37	4	41	5.29	800	1.0	1,005	1.0	2,000	0.8
Muslims	0	0.0	50	0.1	140	0.2	9	5	14	7.33	200	0.3	284	0.3	1,000	0.4
Atheists	0	0.0	100	0.2	160	0.3	10	0	10	4.85	170	0.2	257	0.3	600	0.2
Chinese folk-religionists	0	0.0	200	0.3	110	0.2	7	-2	5	4.07	115	0.1	164	0.2	400	0.2
Baha'is	0	0.0	50	0.1	70	0.1	4	4	8	7.77	100	0.1	148	0.1	400	0.2
Jews	0	0.0	250	0.4	110	0.2	7	-4	3	2.73	105	0.1	144	0.1	300	0.1
Buddhists	0	0.0	200	0.3	100	0.2	6	-3	3	2.82	95	0.1	132	0.1	300	0.1
Other religionists	0	0.0	0	0.0	50	0.1	3	0	3	4.41	50	0.1	77	0.1	200	0.1
World A (unevangelized persons)	0	0.0	60	0.1	256	0.4	15	8	23	6.63	407	0.5	515	0.5	1,500	0.6
World B (evangelized non-Christians)	0	0.0	1,765	2.9	2,384	3.0	117	11	128	3.59	2,330	2.9	3,391	3.1	8,700	3.5
World C (Christians)	14,000	100.0	58,850	97.0	61,360	96.6	3,792	-19	3,773	4.91	78,765	96.6	99,094	96.4	239,800	95.9
Country's population	**14,000**	**100.0**	**60,676**	**100.0**	**64,000**	**100.0**	**3,924**	**0**	**3,924**	**4.87**	**81,503**	**100.0**	**103,000**	**100.0**	**250,000**	**100.0**

COLUMNS, ROWS.
For meanings and definitions, see Codebook (Part 3). Note that, by definition, total 'Christians' = professing + crypto-Christians, which also = affiliated + unaffiliated Christians, and also = Great Commission Christians + latent Christians. Percentages may not always total exactly, due to rounding.

NOTES ON RELIGIONS
BUDDHISTS. Mainly Han Chinese.
MUSLIMS. Turkish and Arab immigrants.

Great Commission Instrument Panel: status of Aruba (for explanation see start of Part 4)

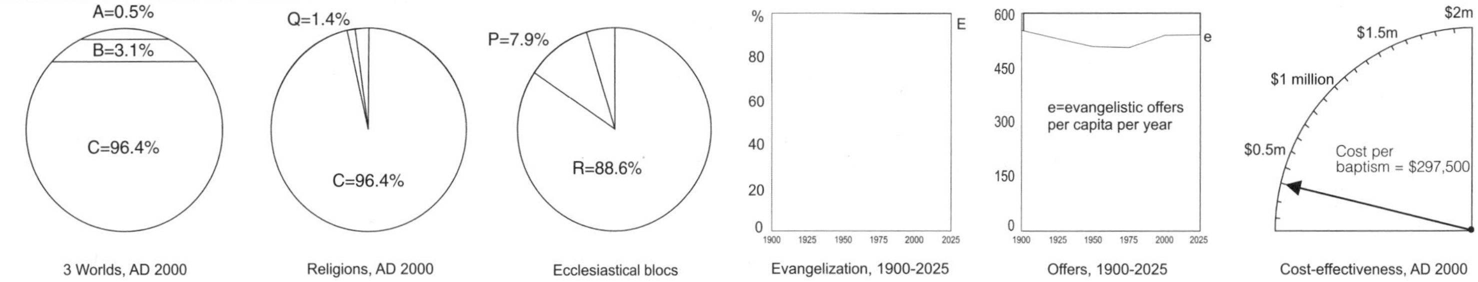

Country summary. **Worlds A, B, C by ethnolinguistic peoples, cities, and major civil divisions in Aruba.**

	PEOPLES							CITIES							CIVIL DIVISIONS						
World	*Num*	*Pop 2000*	*C%*	*Christians*	*E%*	*U%*	*Unevangelized*	*Num*	*Pop 2000*	*C%*	*Christians*	*E%*	*U%*	*Unevangelized*	*Num*	*Pop 2000*	*C%*	*Christians*	*E%*	*U%*	*Unevangelized*
A	2	349	0.00	0	30	70	243	0	0	0.00	0	0	0	0	0	0	0.00	0	0	0	0
B	1	329	10.03	33	50	50	165	0	0	0.00	0	0	0	0	0	0	0.00	0	0	0	0
C	4	102,068	93.28	95,207	100	0	67	1	22,723	92.00	20,905	99	1	148	1	102,747	92.69	95,241	100	0	475
Total	**7**	**102,746**	**92.69**	**95,240**	**100**	**0**	**475**	**1**	**22,723**	**92.00**	**20,905**	**99**	**1**	**148**	**1**	**102,747**	**92.69**	**95,241**	**100**	**0**	**475**

Country status. Aruba, formerly part of the Netherlands Antilles, is a Dutch island in the Caribbean Sea north of Venezuela. Its economy is almost entirely based on refining oil imported from Venezuela and on tourism.

HUMAN LIFE AND LIBERTY

Human rights and freedoms. Aruba, formerly part of the Netherlands Antilles, is a full and integral part of the Dutch realm. All basic human rights are respected.

NON-CHRISTIAN RELIGIONS

Most of the 2,000 non-Christians in Aruba in 1995 were nonreligious or Spiritists, with a small number of Buddhists, Chinese folk-religionist, Jews, and Muslims in non-Caribbean ethnic minorities.

Christians 11th World Council of YMCA meets in Aruba in 1988 on theme 'Your Will be Done on Earth'.

CHRISTIANITY

The Roman Catholic Church plays a dominant role among the Christians of Aruba, as well as playing a strong role in the life of the tiny country overall. Catholics comprise 85% of the Christians of the country, and 80.9% of the general population. Aruba's Dutch heritage is reflected in the presence of the Reformed Church in Aruba, the largest single Protestant group, with 1,500 affiliated in 1995. Other Protestant traditions represented include Anglicans, Pentecostals, Baptists, Church of Christ, Methodists, and Seventh-day Adventists. All these and others are the result of missionary work since World War II, with the exception of the Methodists (began c1930) and the Anglicans.

The Holy See has no diplomatic relations with Aruba in AD 2000.

Indigenous missions. Much of the outreach from this island has been through the Radio Victoria and Assemblies of God broadcasts in Papiamento and other languages.

BROADCASTING AND MEDIA

Local FM stations such as Radio Victoria carry Christian programming, some of which is produced by other agencies such as IBRA. These programs can be heard throughout the Caribbean. Shortwave programs from HCJB (Ecuador), TWR (Antilles) and AWR (Costa Rica) can be easily received.

LeSEA programming can be received from the World Harvest Satellite.

INTERDENOMINATIONAL ORGANIZATIONS

No council of churches yet exists.

FUTURE TRENDS AND PROSPECTS

Roman Catholics, 79.1% in 1970 are expected to grow to 84.0% by AD 2025. Otherwise, few changes are expected in the religious composition of Aruba.

Christianity is expected to remain well over 90% for the forseeable future.

BIBLIOGRAPHY

Bibliografie Nederlandse Antillen Aruba. S. R. Criens. Amsterdam: Universiteit van de Nederlandse Antillen, Stichting voor Culturele Samenwerking, Bibliotheek der Rijksuniversiteit Utrecht, 1989. (Contains 23,625 entries).

Iglesia di Aruba: 25 anja na caminda. Oranjestad, Aruba: Conseho pastoral di Aruba, 1984. 86p. (History of Roman Catholic Church).

Kerkgeschiedenis Aruba. W. M. Brada. Curaçao: [Paulus Drukkerij], 1946. 45p.

Netherlands Antilles and Aruba. K. Schoenhals. *World bibliographical series*, vol. 168. Oxford, UK: CLIO Press, 1993. 186p. (See especially 'Religion,' p.61–3).

'The adoption and execution of a training course for the Methodist Church of Aruba: 'Relational evangelism' and 'The gift of spirit'.' W. O. R. Worrell. Project report, Candler School of Theology, Emory University, Atlanta, 1991. 60p.

Country Table 2. **Organized churches and denominations in Aruba.**

Official name (bold type = church with over 10% of all affiliated) 1	*Begun* 2	*Type* 3	*Counc* 4	*Congs* 5	*Adults* 6	*Affiliated 1970* 7	*Affiliated 1995* 8	*G%* 9	*Names, notes, and other statistics* (see Codebook, Part 3) 10
Anglican Church of Aruba (D Antigua)	c1950	A-ACa	awMRK	1	490	300	667	3.25	In Church of the Province of the West Indies (CPWI). 90% Black.
Assemblies of God		P-Pe2	.....	4	700	100	1,000	0.05	M=AoG(USA).
Baptist Church in Aruba		P-Bap	.....	3	300	–	500	0.05	M=FMB-SBC.
Catholic Church (D Willemstad)	c1800	R-Lat	P....	5	48,900	48,000	66,000	1.28	*Rooms-Katholieke Kerk, Bisdom Willemstad.* Suffragan diocese of M Port of Spain.
Church of Christ in Aruba	c1970	I-Dis	.....	4	80	30	133	6.14	*Church of Christ (Non-Instrumental).*
Church of God in Aruba	1968	P-Pe3	ZF...	4	300	40	500	10.63	M=CoG(Cleveland) (USA). Holiness Pentecostals. Blacks.
Ch of God of Prophecy		P-Pe3	Z....	2	200	50	400	0.05	Earlier schism ex Ch of God (Cleveland).
Evangelical Church in Aruba	c1950	P-Eva	.....	5	450	200	750	5.43	M=TEAM(USA). Radio Victoria.
Jehovah's Witnesses	c1950	m-Jeh	x....	6	474	300	1,190	5.67	*Getuigen van Jehovah.* Watchtower. Mainly expatriates. 29Y.
Liberal Catholic Church		I-Lib	x....	2	150	200	200	0.05	*Vrije-Katholieke Kerk.* In Netherlands, UK, USA, Australia, New Zealand.
Methodist Church in Aruba	c1930	P-Met	VwM.K	3	320	500	800	1.90	Part of MCCA, Leeward Islands District.
Reformed Church in Aruba	c1940	P-Ref	.....	6	900	1,000	1,500	1.64	*Dutch Reformed Church.*
Seventh-day Adventist Church	c1940	P-Adv	x....	1	100	50	300	7.43	*Advent-Zendings Genootschap.*
United Protestant Ch of Aruba	c1930	P-LuR	.uM.K	2	200	200	500	3.73	*UPCA. Verenigde Protestantse Gemeente van Aruba.*
Other pentecostal churches	c1980	I-3pU	.....	12	450	–	900	6.67	About 4.
Other Protestant churches	c1950	P-	.....	5	200	100	500	6.65	Lutheran Ch of Christ (VKK), UPCC, Largo Community Ch, Salvation Army, Moravian Ch.
Totals				**65**	**54,214**	**51,070**	**75,840**		

Churches, members, growth, 1900-2025	*Congs*	*Adults*	*Affiliated*	*G%*	*Total denominations*	*6 Megablocs:* O	R	A	P	I	m
Total churches, members, and denominations (mid-1900)	10	8,300	13,300	1.94	1	0	1	0	0	0	0
Total churches, members, and denominations (mid-1970)	25	31,930	51,070	1.94	16	0	1	1	11	2	1
Total churches, members, and denominations (mid-1990)	60	42,900	60,000	0.81	23	0	1	1	15	5	1
Total churches, members, and denominations (mid-1995)	65	54,214	75,840	4.80	24	0	1	1	15	6	1
Total churches, members, and denominations (mid-2000)	90	68,100	95,241	4.66	25	0	1	1	15	7	1
Total churches, members, and denominations (mid-2025)	130	168,000	234,500	3.67	52	0	1	1	20	25	5

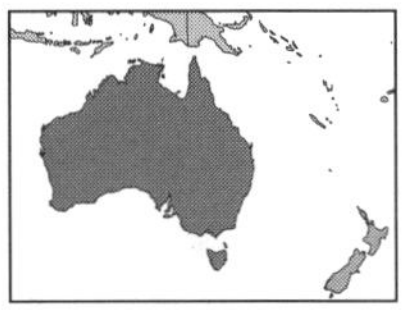

AUSTRALIA

SECULAR DATA, AD 2000

STATE
Official name: Commonwealth of Australia.
Short name: Australia. **Adjective of nationality:** Australian.
Flag: Blue field with Union Jack, white star, five smaller stars.
Area: 7,682,300 sq. km. (2,966,200 sq. mi.).
Government: Federal parliamentary state (also constitutional monarchy), since 1901 (1770 British possession, 1859 six colonies).
Legislature: Parliament: Senate, 76 members; House of Representatives, 148 members.
Official language: English.
Monetary unit: 1 Australian dollar ($A) = 100 cents. **US$1=** $A 1.70.
Chief cities: Sydney 3,665,000; Melbourne 3,188,000; Brisbane 1,591,000; Perth 1,313,000; Adelaide 1,063,000.
Political divisions: 8 provinces (6 States and 2 Territories).
Armed forces: 62,000.

DEMOGRAPHY
Population: 18,880,000.
Population density: 2.4/sq. km. (6.3/sq. mi.).
Under 15 years: 3,897,000.
Growth rate p.a.: 0.91% (births 12.57, deaths 7.65).
Mortality: Infant, per 1,000: 5.5; **Maternal per 100,000:** 9.0.
Life expectancy: 79 (male 76, female 82).
Household size: 3.0. **Floor area per person, sq.m:** 50.0.
Major languages: English, Italian, Greek, Cantonese, Arabic, Vietnamese, German, Mandarin, Spanish, Macedonian, Tagalog, Croatian, Polish, Maltese, Turkish and 260 Aboriginal languages.
Urban dwellers: 84.69%. **Urban growth rate p.a.:** 1.1%.
Labor force: 49%.

ETHNOLINGUISTIC PEOPLES
73.9% Anglo-Australian; 6.5% British; 2.2% Italian; 1.6% Greek; 1.5% Anglo-New Zealander.

ECONOMY
National income p.a. per person: US$18,720; **per family:** US$56,160.

EDUCATION
Adult literacy: 99% (male 99%, female 99%). **Schools:** 9,865.
Universities: 95. **School enrolment:** female/male: 96%/95%.

HEALTH
Access to health services: 90%. **Access to safe water:** 95%.
Hospitals: 1,071 (50 beds per 10,000). **Doctors:** 38,800.
Blind: 18,820. **Deaf:** 1,129,900. **Murder rate:** 1.
Lepers: 1,800.

LITERATURE
New book titles p.a.: 11,710 (620 p.a. per million). **Periodicals:** 364.
Newspapers: 69 dailies.

COMMUNICATION (per 1,000 people)
Phones: 510 (36% mobile). **Radios:** 1,152. **TV sets:** 641.
Daily newspaper circulation: 255. **Computers:** 525.

REFUGEES
Alien refugees from other countries: 75,000.

HUMAN LIFE AND LIBERTY (optimum condition=100.0%)
HDI: 93.1. **HSI:** 96.0. **HFI:** 82.5. **EFL:** 58.0.

Country Table 1. **Religious adherents in Australia, AD 1900-2025.**

Year	1900		1970		mid-1990		Annual change, 1990-2000				mid-1995		mid-2000		mid-2025	
Name	Adherents	%	Adherents	%	Adherents	%	Natural	Conversion	Total	Rate	Adherents	%	Adherents	%	Adherents	%
Christians	**3,640,300**	**96.6**	**11,639,850**	**92.9**	**13,632,500**	**80.8**	**161,204**	**-27,181**	**134,027**	**0.94**	**14,360,800**	**80.1**	**14,972,765**	**79.3**	**17,364,000**	**75.2**
PROFESSION																
professing Christians	**3,640,300**	**96.6**	**11,639,850**	**92.9**	**13,632,500**	**80.8**	**161,204**	**-27,181**	**134,027**	**0.94**	**14,360,800**	**80.1**	**14,972,765**	**79.3**	**17,364,000**	**75.2**
AFFILIATION																
unaffiliated Christians	419,200	11.1	2,047,722	16.3	2,162,500	12.8	25,579	-3,348	22,231	0.98	2,260,800	12.6	2,384,806	12.6	2,364,000	10.2
affiliated Christians	**3,221,100**	**85.4**	**9,592,128**	**76.5**	**11,470,000**	**67.9**	**135,673**	**-23,877**	**111,796**	**0.93**	**12,100,000**	**67.5**	**12,587,959**	**66.7**	**15,000,000**	**65.0**
Roman Catholics	840,000	22.3	3,037,589	24.2	4,685,000	27.8	55,416	16,084	71,500	1.43	5,043,881	28.1	5,400,000	28.6	6,800,000	29.5
Anglicans	1,357,200	36.0	3,775,000	30.1	4,010,000	23.8	47,432	-42,432	5,000	0.12	4,040,000	22.5	4,060,000	21.5	4,200,000	18.2
Protestants	1,017,900	27.0	1,911,027	15.3	2,480,000	14.7	29,335	-14,335	15,000	0.59	2,547,441	14.2	2,630,000	13.9	3,000,000	13.0
Independents	0	0.0	499,025	4.0	700,000	4.2	8,280	5,720	14,000	1.84	794,977	4.4	840,000	4.5	1,300,000	5.6
Orthodox	4,000	0.1	266,600	2.1	580,000	3.4	6,861	5,139	12,000	1.90	624,928	3.5	700,000	3.7	1,050,000	4.6
Marginal Christians	2,000	0.1	102,887	0.8	170,000	1.0	2,011	2,989	5,000	2.61	206,171	1.2	220,000	1.2	420,000	1.8
doubly-affiliated	0	0.0	0	0.0	-1,155,000	-6.8	-13,662	2,958	-10,704	0.89	-1,157,398	-6.5	-1,262,041	-6.7	-1,770,000	-7.7
Trans-megabloc groupings																
Evangelicals	1,562,000	41.4	1,804,608	14.4	2,397,386	14.2	28,357	-8,210	20,147	0.81	2,324,503	13.0	2,598,851	13.8	2,870,880	12.4
Pentecostals/Charismatics	0	0.0	60,000	0.5	2,130,000	12.6	25,195	7,305	32,500	1.43	2,309,523	12.9	2,455,000	13.0	3,460,000	15.0
Great Commission Christians	**377,000**	**10.0**	**3,383,000**	**27.0**	**5,757,000**	**34.1**	**68,096**	**4,780**	**72,876**	**1.20**	**6,153,000**	**34.3**	**6,485,759**	**34.4**	**8,300,000**	**35.9**
Nonreligious	38,000	1.0	561,750	4.5	2,385,000	14.1	28,211	7,812	36,023	1.42	2,557,200	14.3	2,745,229	14.5	4,025,000	17.4
Atheists	500	0.0	200,000	1.6	290,000	1.7	3,430	450	3,880	1.26	310,000	1.7	328,802	1.7	454,500	2.0
Buddhists	6,000	0.2	12,000	0.1	140,000	0.8	1,656	8,538	10,194	5.62	200,000	1.1	241,939	1.3	380,000	1.7
Muslims	10,000	0.3	25,000	0.2	160,000	1.0	1,893	5,044	6,937	3.67	191,000	1.1	229,369	1.2	400,000	1.7
Jews	15,200	0.4	62,500	0.5	83,000	0.5	982	-173	809	0.93	86,000	0.5	91,094	0.5	105,000	0.5
Hindus	0	0.0	0	0.0	46,000	0.3	544	879	1,423	2.73	52,000	0.3	60,226	0.3	91,000	0.4
New-Religionists	0	0.0	0	0.0	20,000	0.1	237	3,172	3,409	10.46	38,500	0.2	54,090	0.3	60,000	0.3
Ethnoreligionists	50,000	1.3	5,000	0.0	35,000	0.2	414	747	1,161	2.91	44,000	0.3	46,610	0.3	52,000	0.2
Baha'is	0	0.0	9,100	0.1	25,100	0.2	297	547	844	2.94	30,500	0.2	33,536	0.2	60,000	0.3
Chinese folk-religionists	10,000	0.3	5,000	0.0	24,000	0.1	284	-76	208	0.84	24,600	0.1	26,082	0.1	33,000	0.1
Confucianists	0	0.0	0	0.0	21,000	0.1	248	-26	222	1.01	22,000	0.1	23,219	0.1	30,000	0.1
Sikhs	0	0.0	1,800	0.0	8,000	0.1	95	351	446	4.53	10,000	0.1	12,460	0.1	20,000	0.1
Spiritists	0	0.0	0	0.0	5,400	0.0	64	-38	26	0.47	5,500	0.0	5,661	0.0	7,000	0.0
Zoroastrians	0	0.0	0	0.0	1,000	0.0	12	25	37	3.18	1,200	0.0	1,367	0.0	2,000	0.0
Other religionists	0	0.0	10,000	0.1	7,000	0.0	83	-75	8	0.11	6,700	0.0	7,076	0.0	7,500	0.0
World A (unevangelized persons)	30,160	0.8	62,661	0.5	236,362	1.4	2,792	4,405	7,197	2.70	287,039	1.6	302,080	1.6	531,093	2.3
World B (evangelized non-Christians)	99,540	2.6	829,847	6.6	3,014,138	17.8	35,658	22,772	58,430	1.81	3,292,104	18.3	3,605,155	19.1	5,195,907	22.5
World C (Christians)	3,640,300	96.6	11,639,850	92.9	13,632,500	80.8	161,204	-27,181	134,027	0.94	14,360,800	80.1	14,972,765	79.3	17,364,000	75.2
Country's population	**3,770,000**	**100.0**	**12,532,359**	**100.0**	**16,883,000**	**100.0**	**199,654**	**0**	**199,654**	**1.12**	**17,939,944**	**100.0**	**18,880,000**	**100.0**	**23,091,000**	**100.0**

COLUMNS, ROWS.
For meanings and definitions, see Codebook (Part 3). Note that, by definition, total 'Christians' = affiliated + unaffiliated Christians, and also = Great Commission Christians + latent Christians. Percentages may not always total exactly, due to rounding.

CENSUSES.
Official censuses prior to 1961 excluded Aborigines; they have therefore been adjusted to include Aborigines for the table above. **1891:** 39.7% Anglicans, 34.1% Protestants (12.8% Methodists, 11.3% Presbyterians, 2.3% Baptists), 23.0% Roman Catholics, 1.3% nonreligious, 0.5% Jews, 0.5% Chinese folk-religionists, 0.4% Muslims, 0.3% Buddhists, 0.2% tribal religionists, 0.1% marginal Protestants. **1901:** 40.3% Anglicans, 34.1% Protestants (13.6% Methodists, 11.5% Presbyterians, 2.4% Baptists), 23.1% Roman Catholics, 1.0% nonreligious, 0.4% Jews, 0.3% Chinese folk-religionists, 0.3% Muslims, 0.2% Buddhists, 0.1% tribal religionists, 0.1% marginal Protestants. **3.IV.1911:** 39.4% Anglicans, 36.5% Protestants (12.9% Presbyterians, 12.6% Methodists, 2.2% Baptists), 21.3% Roman Catholics, 0.6% nonreligious, 0.4% Jews, 0.4% Buddhists, Muslims and Chinese folk-religionists. **30.VI.1947** (excluding 47,000 full-blooded Aborigines): 74.5% Anglicans & Protestants, 23.2% Roman Catholics, 0.5% Jews, 0.4% nonreligious, 0.3% other religionists, 0.1% Orthodox. **30.VI.1954:** 72.7% Anglicans & Protestants, 25.4% Roman Catholics, 0.9% Orthodox, 0.6% Jews, 0.3% nonreligious, 0.1% other religionists. **30.VI.1961:** 39.0% Anglicans, 29.5% Protestants, 27.9% Roman Catholics, 1.6% Orthodox, 0.7% marginal Protestants, 0.7% nonreligious, 0.6% Jews. **30.VI.1966:** 36.2% Anglicans, 28.3% Roman Catholics 27.8% Protestants, 4.0% nonreligious, 2.4% Orthodox, 0.7% marginal Protestants, 0.6% Jews. **30.VI.1971:** 33.0% Anglicans, 28.7% Roman Catholics, 26.0% Protestants, 7.4% nonreligious and atheists, 2.8% Orthodox, 0.8% marginal Protestants, 0.5% Jews, 0.2% Muslims, 0.1% other religionists. **1991:** 27.3% Roman Catholics, 23.9% Anglicans, 12.9% nonreligious and atheists, 17.9% Protestants, 2.9% Orthodox, 0.6% Marginal Christians, 0.9% Muslims, 0.8% Buddhists, 0.4% Jews, 0.3% Hindus. **1996:** 27.0% Roman Catholics, 22.0% Anglicans, 18.2% Protestants, 16.6% nonreligious and atheists, 3.0% Orthodox, 0.7% Marginal Christians, 1.1% Muslims, 1.1% Buddhists, 0.4% Jews, 0.4% Hindus.

POLLS.
Numerous public-opinion polls of religion have been taken since 1940 (Gallup, Morgan Research Centre, Australian Community Survey,1998). The National Church Life Survey (1991 & 1996) and the Catholic Church Life Survey (1996) surveyed church attenders from Catholic, Anglican and 21 Protestant denominations.

NOTES ON RELIGIONS
ATHEISTS. Communist Party of Australia (CPA) and 3 rival parties. Many European immigrants.
BAHA'IS. Entered before 1921. Recent growth has been very rapid, from 32 local spiritual assemblies (1964) to 61 (1973; 3 in Tasmania) to 187 (1996). In Sydney, there is one of the world's 7 Baha'i temples. Large numbers of missionaries have been sent from Australia to Oceania.
BUDDHISTS. Chinese, Japanese, Tibetans and Thais, mainly in cities; including Buddhist Federation of Australia, Chinese Buddhist Society of NSW, Chinese Temple Society, Thai Buddhist students (Sydney). The Nan Tien temple (Wollongong) is the largest Buddhist temple in the Southern Hemisphere.
ETHNORELIGIONISTS. Aborigines declined in number from 300,000 in 1,000 bands in 1770, to 80,000 by 1900, when a majority still retained their traditional religion. By 1970 Aborigines numbered 138,000 (106,300 pure-blooded, though only 40,000 of full descent), and pagans had shrunk to less than 5%. Animistic peoples: Murngin (Wulamba; population 3,500), Gugu-Yalanji (500), Iwaidja (250), Yanyula (150).
EVANGELICALS. Consisting of 3 groupings: (1) Anglican Evangelicals, (2) Evangelicals, affiliated to Protestant denominations which are Conservative Evangelical in theology, and (3) Evangelicals (sometimes called Conciliar Evangelicals) who are affiliated to non-evangelical Protestant denominations usually within the Ecumenical Movement.
INDEPENDENTS. In about 30 denominations in 1995 (see Table 2).
JEWS. Orthodox and Liberal congregations and 1 Sefardi synagogue with 1,000 members.
MUSLIMS. The first Muslims were Afghan camel-drivers in the 1860s. There are now mosques in Canberra, Brisbane, Mareeba, Shepparton, Adelaide, Perth, Melbourne and Sydney; and there is an Australian Federation of Islamic Societies (HQ Victoria). Over 20,000 Muslims have immigrated from each of Lebanon and Turkey and over 5,000 each from Indonesia, Bosnia and Iran. There are 2 Druze communities (Adelaide, Sydney). There is also a small Ahmadiya Mission in Western Australia. *Hajj pilgrims to Mecca* (1976). 22.
ORTHODOX. Numbers have increased rapidly since 1950 by large-scale immigration from Europe and the Middle East.
OTHER RELIGIONISTS. There are a large and rapidly-growing number of adherents of other non-Christian religions and syncretistic cults: Eckankar, Ramakrishna Vedanta Society, et alia), Rosicrucians (10 AMORC Lodges in 1977, 1 centre (Adelaide) of Lectorium Rosicrucianum, and 2 independent bodies: Rosicrucian Fraternal Society, and Rosicrucian Fellowship, both in Sydney), Subud (300 adherents; a 1925 New Religion from Indonesia), Theosophists, Cao Dai temple in Sydney, and numerous others.
PENTECOSTALS/CHARISMATICS. The largest single group are Anglican Charismatics who number over a million. The Catholic Charismatic Renewal is much smaller. Beginning in 1970, in 1996 it had 404 weekly prayer groups in English and 70 in other languages; 3,000 regular adult attenders; 6 covenant communities; 160 involved priests and 4 bishops; and rallies of up to 13,000 participants.
SIKHS. In 2 organized groups with 1 temple at Woolgoolga (NSW).

Country status. The only country in the world that is also a continent, Australia is characterized by immense physical size and a disproportionately small population. An outpost of Anglo-Saxon civilization in the antipodes, Australia has made significant efforts in recent years to diversify its society and culture.

HUMAN LIFE AND LIBERTY

Human need and development. Australia is a developed country, although its physical location and small population have blunted its impact on the rest

Great Commission Instrument Panel: status of Australia (for explanation see start of Part 4)

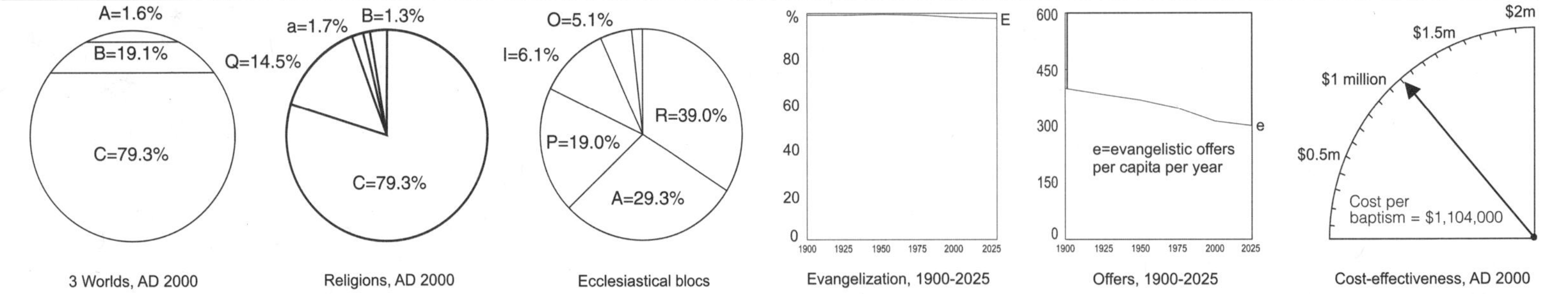

of the world. It is a very egalitarian society. Disparities in income are not as pronounced as in Europe or North America, and there are very few in dire need. Weighing on the national conscience, however, is the historic mistreatment of the Aboriginals and Torres Strait Islanders (ATSI) which has reduced the status of some to that of wards of state. The arrest rate of ATSI peoples is 29 times as high as that of other Australians, and many of them die in custody.

Australia is a highly developed country, whether judged by standards of buying power, food consumption, health, housing, or education. Moreover, the national income is distributed fairly evenly making extremes of wealth and poverty very rare. The socialist ideals of the labor governments that were in power for much of the 20th century also have helped to maintain a wide range of social services and welfare programs for the disadvantaged. The vast majority of Australians own the homes they live in, although apartment living has become quite fashionable in the cities.

Human rights and freedoms. All basic human rights are guaranteed by law and respected in practice. Australia does not have a bill of rights, but it is party to the International Covenant on Civil and Political Rights. The weakest link in the human rights chain is the disadvantaged status of the ATSI peoples whose conditions have deteriorated in recent years. Their standards of living, especially in health, education, housing, and employment, fall far short of those of other Australians. The Aboriginal and Torres Strait Islanders Commission established in 1989 is designed to give ATSI some voice in the administration of programs affecting them. Recent legislation has established the Council for Aboriginal Reconciliation, one of whose goal is to draw up a charter for Aboriginals to be promulgated during the centennial of the federation in 2001. On the land rights issue, Aboriginal land councils have gained control over four national parks in New South Wales, and 2,300 square kilometers in the Northern Territory, but lost a 13-year legal battle for the Cox Peninsula in the Northern Territory. The 11-volume report of the Royal Commission on Aboriginal Deaths in Custody is a landmark study of the relationship of ATSI people to the criminal justice system.

Australians enjoy all basic freedoms, including freedoms of press and speech, association, movement, and religion. Political power is effectively dispersed among the three major parties, each of which may be in power at any given time in the center or in one of the states. The federal constitution does not specify fundamental rights and freedoms, nor are these rights included in the state constitutions, except certain ones in the constitution of Tasmania. The premises of the constitution and political and government practices are based on British parliamentary conventions. Throughout Australian history, basic human rights have been considered as inviolable. Law and practice gives defendants the rights to due process, including a presumption of innocence, the right to confront witnesses, and the right to appeal. However, no free legal aid is available except in cases which satisfy a merit test. Violence or discrimination against women is prohibited by the Sex Discrimination Act of 1984 which is enforced by the Office of the Status of Women. Domestic violence involves as many as one in three families. The National Domestic Violence Education Program has conducted a campaign since 1989 to educate the public on the dimensions of the problem.

Human environment. Australia is an arid country and is the driest continent in the world. Its physical features, particularly the well watered coastal edges, have dictated the concentration of population along a narrow strip. Nearly two-thirds of the people live in the urban-suburban complexes that comprise the state capitals, and another one-third live in their hinterlands, making Australia the most urbanized of the world's countries. Like Canada, another large country with only a small arable area, Australia supports a small population. However, inhabited regions are subject to quick degradation because of overexploitation of resources. The loss of natural vegetation has led to soil salinity and the extinction of many rare species of animals peculiar to the continent. Costs of transportation are high because of the great distances between population centers in the east and west or north and south. The country's distance from the rest of the developed world also adds to a general sense of isolation.

Ethnoreligionists. Aborigines maintain many traditional beliefs and customs such as these totem poles in Arnhem Land, Northern Territory.

NON-CHRISTIAN RELIGIONS

Traditional Aboriginal religion is still a significant factor, although a majority of Aborigines now profess to be Christians. The key religious specialist is the medicine man (called kunki among the Dieri) who maintains contact with the spirits (Kutchi) and divinities (Mura-muras), the latter being the spirits of the early inhabitants of the region. Appeal with elaborate ceremonies is made to the Mura-muras in time of drought and during rites of passage, especially death. In addition there is a belief in a supreme being known by various tribes as Biamban, Bunjil, Mungangama, Nurelli and Nurrundere.

Muslims. The Auburn Mosque, Sydney, in Ottoman style, accomodates 5,500 of the 40,000 local Turks and Arabs.

Other religions include Judaism (0.5% of the population in AD 2000) Islam (1.2%), and Buddhists (1.3%) in addition to small groups of Baha'is in the larger urban centers. In 1971, 7.4% of the population stated that they had no religion; by 1996, this figure had risen to 16.6%.

Buddhists. 'Paradise of the Southern Hemisphere'/Nan Tien Temple, Wollongong (opened 1995) has 8,000 Buddha images; it is one of the global network of 110 pilgrimage centers founded by Fo Kuang Shan Monastery, whose HQ is in Taiwan.

CHRISTIANITY

In 1770 captain James Cook took possession of the east coast of Australia for Britain. The slow growth of the churches in the early days can be attributed in part to the fact that Australia was initially used as a penal colony for Britain, the first convicts and soldiers being sent to what is now Sydney in 1788. This practice continued until 1853 in Tasmania and 1868 in Australia itself. Another factor was the early tendency of the population to cluster into urban centers to which the European clergy were unaccustomed. The rest of the population on the other hand went either to sparsely-populated and inaccessible ranching areas, or to mining camps with a transient male population unprepared for settled church community life. Churches tend to be strongest in the south.

The discovery of gold in 1851 increased the flow of settlers and 6 colonies, including Tasmania, had been organized by 1859. These remained independent until a commonwealth was formed in 1901. Following World War II the government encouraged immigration to work in Australia's expanding industries, and 2 million immigrants had arrived by 1970. During this period arrivals came mainly from Southern Europe, resulting in an increase in the Catholic population in comparison to the early years when settlers were mostly from the British Isles and hence Anglicans or Protestants.

In 1995, 80.1% of the population claimed to be Christian, down from 91.7% in 1971. The 4 largest denominations (Roman Catholic, Anglican, Uniting Church of Australia, and Presbyterian Church of Australia Continuing) together have 77.7% of the nation's Christians. Australian Christianity reflects the independent spirit and immigrant heritage of the country, with 216 total denominations. Australian Christianity has tended to reproduce the denominational pattern of the British Isles, although more cosmopolitan in membership at the present time.

ANGLICAN CHURCH. Chaplains arrived in 1788 with the first convicts sent to Australia, and to Tasmania in 1804. Samuel Marsden, arriving in 1793, was responsible for much of the development of the church and accompanying social services throughout Australia and the South Pacific until his death in 1838. In 1823 Australia was placed under the bishopric of Calcutta; in 1836 a bishop was appointed for Australia, and the country was divided into 5 dioceses by 1847. In 1853 the discovery of gold in Victoria

Country summary. **Worlds A, B, C by ethnolinguistic peoples, cities, and major civil divisions in Australia.**

	PEOPLES							CITIES							CIVIL DIVISIONS						
World	*Num*	*Pop 2000*	*C%*	*Christians*	*E%*	*U%*	*Unevangelized*	*Num*	*Pop 2000*	*C%*	*Christians*	*E%*	*U%*	*Unevangelized*	*Num*	*Pop 2000*	*C%*	*Christians*	*E%*	*U%*	*Unevangelized*
A	17	43,648	2.96	1,294	37	63	27,519	0	0	0.00	0	0	0	0	0	0	0.00	0	0	0	0
B	40	956,432	20.75	198,480	76	24	225,663	0	0	0.00	0	0	0	0	0	0	0.00	0	0	0	0
C	76	17,879,446	69.39	12,407,068	100	0	54,789	25	13,824,653	65.01	8,986,904	99	1	179,773	8	18,879,521	66.68	12,587,959	98	2	307,965
Total	**133**	**18,879,526**	**66.78**	**12,606,842**	**98**	**2**	**307,971**	**25**	**13,824,653**	**65.01**	**8,986,904**	**99**	**1**	**179,773**	**8**	**18,879,521**	**66.68**	**12,587,959**	**98**	**2**	**307,965**

resulted in an increase in state funds which made possible grants to several denominations, about half going to the Anglican church. Both Victoria and South Australia were settled by non-convict immigrants, and 6 Anglican clergy were sent to South Australia when it became a diocese 11 years after the first settlers arrived. The only minister in Western Australia for many years was the Church of England chaplain at Perth, until the first British missionary arrived in 1836. In 1856 Perth became a separate diocese. Queensland, originally a part of New South Wales, received its first bishop in 1859 while Northern Australia with a large Aborigine population did not have a bishop until 1900.

Of all the denominations, the Anglican Church has carried out the most work among nomadic Aborigines, who were living throughout Australia in some 680 different groups when the first Europeans arrived. As Whites took over their land, Aborigines were pushed back and gradually declined from 300,000 to a third of that number by the end of the 19th century, although they began increasing again in the late 20th century. In Tasmania natives were completely exterminated. The CMS began work among Aborigines in New South Wales in 1826. The churches have generally found it difficult to build up congregations of baptized members among Aborigines.

In 1891 a mission was opened among the Kanaka laborers imported from the Pacific Islands between 1862 and 1904, who have been very receptive to Christianity. Anglican missions have also been established among Chinese, Jewish, and Syrian immigrants.

Although Anglican membership increased from 1851 to 1971, in proportion to the total population professing Anglicans have steadily declined, from 53% in 1851, to 40% in 1901, to 39% in 1947, and to 33% in 1971. This decrease was in part due to immigration from Britain being replaced by immigration from southern Europe and later from Asia. By 1990 Roman Catholics passed Anglicans as the largest Christian group in the country and in 1996 Anglicans made up 22% of the total population.

CATHOLIC CHURCH. Catholics in Australia are predominantly Irish in background, the result of early convicts from Ireland together with Irish immigrants following the Irish potato famine. The first Catholic priests were appointed in 1803. During the next 10 years a cathedral in Sydney and the first Catholic school were built. In the 1830s a vicar apostolic was appointed for Australia and another for Tasmania. Subsequent highlights in Catholic history include the International Eucharistic Congress of 1929 in Sydney, and the visit of pope Paul VI in 1970.

Professing Catholics as a percentage of the total population gradually increased, from 21% in 1947, to 27% in 1966, to 29% in 1971. Some of this increase was due to the large numbers of immigrants from predominantly Catholic countries including Italy, Malta, Croatia, and Poland, and also due to the Catholic birth-rate being higher than that in other denominations. By 1996 Catholics as a percentage of the total population had eased to 27%.

Religious care of migrants is the responsibility of the Federal Catholic Immigration Committee, established in 1974. A total of 137 priests from countries sending immigrants are employed as migrant chaplains, and at least 2 orders specialize in this work, namely Capuchin and Scalabrinian priests in South Australia and Victoria.

Among Aborigines, 26% were Catholics in 1966. The first Aborigine Catholic priest was ordained in 1975. The National Aboriginal & Torres Strait Islander Catholic Council (NATSICC) was formed in 1989.

The Irish influence in Australian Catholicism has remained dominant until very recently. The Irish bishops who came to Australia were mostly conservative products of Roman seminaries. This background is responsible for the pragmatism of Australian Catholicism, as shown in the building of churches, operating social services and comprehensive Catholic primary and secondary school systems, and there has been little interest in theological renewal.

The Holy See has diplomatic relations with Australia and in AD 2000 is represented to government and the Catholic hierarchy by a pro-nuncio residing in Canberra.

PROTESTANT CHURCHES. In 1809 settlers built a Presbyterian church and their first minister arrived in 1823. A dispute over whether state financial support ought to be accepted led to a division with 2 separate synods established in New South Wales in 1846, later united in 1864. Presbyterian services were also held in Tasmania in 1823. Australian Presbyterians maintained missions for Aborigines in addition to overseas stations in the New Hebrides, Korea, and India. Chinese Presbyterian churches are located in Sydney and Melbourne. Professing Presbyterians numbered 10% of the population in 1851, 11% in 1901, 10% in 1947 and 8% in 1971. In 1971 the church sponsored 33 schools (18,645 pupils), 9 hospitals, and 7 clinics.Methodists were among the early settlers in New South Wales, and through their efforts Samuel Leigh arrived from England in 1815 to serve them. He established the British and Foreign Bible Society in Australia and a home for the poor. In 1855 the first Australasian Conference was held in Sydney.

With the influx of settlers to Victoria following the discovery of gold, one out of every ten was Methodist by 1886. Methodism began in Tasmania about 1820 and by the 1840s had become self-supporting. In South Australia, Methodists were relatively more numerous in the early years. By 1876 they had nearly 5 times as many churches as Anglicans had and 30 times as many as Presbyterians. In Western Australia, Methodism remained weak, with no clergy appointed until 1840. Queensland was made a Methodist district in 1863. Methodists early became involved in work among Aborigines. In 1851 professing Methodists numbered 6% of the population, 13% in 1901, 12% in 1947 and 9% in 1971.

Through the efforts of the London Missionary Society, Congregationalists early had contact with Australia, but their first congregation was not organized until 1829. From 1963 negotiations were carried on by the Congregational, Methodist, and Presbyterian churches leading towards the creation in 1977 of the Uniting Church in Australia. The Uniting Church in 1995 was the third largest church in Australia, and is seeking solutions to declining attendance and an ageing population profile.

The first Baptist Church in New South Wales was organized in 1813, followed by the Churches of Christ in 1846, Salvation Army in 1881, and Seventh-day Adventists in 1885. The Lutheran Church, whose original missionaries came from Germany and from the USA Missionary Synod, has missions serving Aborigines. The Churches of Christ had stations among Aboriginal peoples, while Baptists missionaries also worked at some government stations. Most missions were opened between 1914 and 1937, and several which owe their origin to Christian initiative are now being administered by government. Recent apologies have been made for the church's role in the government policy of assimilation of aboriginals into white culture. The heartbreak of the 'stolen generation' of aboriginals, who were sometimes forcibly taken from their parents, is now being realized. A large number of other smaller Protestant denominations are also at work in Australia.

Charismatic Churches. Independents are growing very rapidly especially among young people; meetings in public places (forecourt of Sydney Opera House.).

ORTHODOX CHURCHES. In 1901 professing adherents of Orthodox churches numbered 2% of the population, decreasing to 1% in 1947. With the postwar increase in immigration from Southern Europe, by 1995 they made up 3.5% of the population, and were divided into 24 distinct communities, the most important being the Greek Orthodox Church.

INDIGENOUS CHURCHES. A variety of pentecostal groups exist among Aborigines, some initiated by trained pastors and some developing spontaneously.

Art and architecture. Australia has not developed an indigenous style of church architecture. Anglican cathedrals are built on the English abbey models with many Victorian features. The so-called Federal style, an uniquely Australian form, is used in some of the church buildings of the interwar years. Catholic churches are built on European models, the larger ones in granite. There are no major museums devoted to Christian art.

Renewal movements. In the 1990s the Pentecostal/Charismatic Renewal continued to spread rapidly across most older churches, and numbered over 2,455,000 adherents (of whom 6% Pentecostals, 72% Charismatics, and 22% Independents). In 1995 the fastest-growing churches were the Third-Wave Neocharismatic churches. Loosely organized in postdenominational networks, these are strongest in urban areas and emphasize contemporary praise and worship styles.

Indigenous missions. Australians serve all over the world as missionaries in Anglican, Pentecostal, Catholic, and other Protestant agencies. Protestant missionaries to Asia now outnumber those in the South Pacific and among Aborigines, however, missions giving and awareness has ebbed significantly in the past few decades. Many Australian faith missionaries find it extremely difficult to raise support and the vast majority of mission agency personnel remain resident in Australia.

CHURCH AND STATE

The Preamble to the Constitution of 9 July 1900, begins: 'Whereas the people . . . humbly relying on the blessing of Almighty God have agreed. . .' The Constitutional Convention in 1998 voted to retain this wording 'as a unifying statement for people of all religious faiths' with the word 'God' to be understood in the generic sense.

The only legal provision concerning church-state relations in Australia is Section 116 of the Australian constitution, modeled on the First Amendment of the constitution of the USA. The section is negative in intent and states simply that there should be no religious test or bar for the holding of public office. It has not been extended by legal interpretation to imply that Australia is formally and officially a secular state, nor that there is a clearly-demarcated wall of separation between the domains of church and state, as the First Amendment has been interpreted in the USA. Some secularists have claimed that Section 116 forbids the giving of financial aid by federal or state governments to such religious organizations as church schools, but this interpretation has not been upheld by the courts. There has been very little legal controversy over Section 116, and except for the question of religious education there has been little church-state conflict in Australia.

The Anglican Church in Australia has no special position or privileges under the law, nor has any other religious group. Clergy and students for the ministry are however exempt from military service. Members of pacifist Christian bodies including Quakers and Christadelphians are also exempt from military service.

Churches receive no direct financial aid from the federal or state governments, and clergy are not paid from government funds. Churches do however receive financial assistance for social services including orphanages, hospitals, and family welfare organizations. By virtue of a program to assist Aborigines in the Northern Territory, the Australian government gives a sizeable annual grant to missions run by Anglicans, Catholics, and Protestants. Further, church properties and funds are exempt from taxes.

In 1974 for the first time in the history of the country, the Australian government decided to provide subsidies to private schools. One of the required conditions was that interested schools renounce the use of entrance examinations in religion for students who enroll. Education is controlled by federal and state governments, and the syllabus of government schools is nonreligious in content, although religious instruction may be given on a voluntary basis from outside. Universities were all state institutions until recently (the handful of private universities now includes two operated by the Catholic church). There are however denominational colleges within universities which receive governmental subsidies, and facilities are also provided for chaplaincy work. There is no ministry or government department in charge of religious or ecclesiastical affairs. Churches are not required to register with either federal or state government.

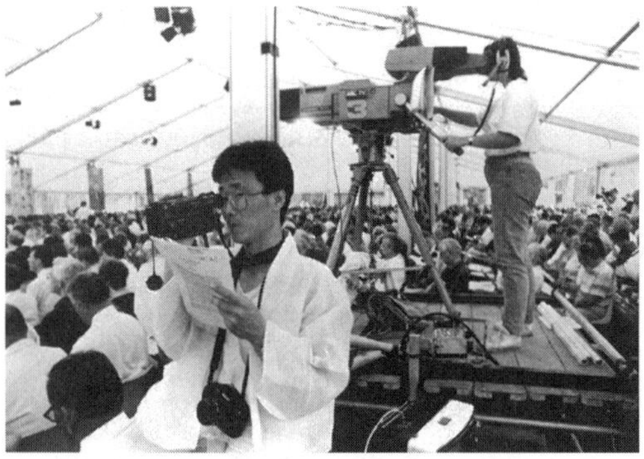

Ecumenism. At the WCC's 7th Assembly in Canberra (1991), television cameras film the new Lima liturgy.

BROADCASTING AND MEDIA

Australia has a national non-commercial system operated by the Australian Broadcasting Commission, which has a religious programs section. There are numerous licensed commercial radio stations which are required to provide time each week to religious material. Anglicans, Protestants, and Catholics each get a share of this time. Radio stations operated by Christians for ministry/evangelistic purposes have flourished since the 1980s and can be heard in most urban areas. Programming varies with station policy and may, or may not, include secular music, worship, teaching, advertising, prayer, talk-back shows and news. Music style also varies from classical and easy listening to rock. From outside the country, shortwave programs from HCJB (Ecuador), TWR (Guam) and KNLS can be received. AWR has a studio which produces English-language programs. Australia is a member of UNDA.

Like radio, commercial television stations are required to give a share of their viewing time to local church programs as well. Catholic activity in broadcasting has been considerable. Production centers include Catholic Radio and TV (Melbourne) which produces a weekly program; and a radio and TV center, founded in Sydney in 1962, which has several production studios. Lower budget 'community access' television has opened the way for Christian (and non-Christian) broadcasting in a range of community languages.

Over half the population has seen the 'Jesus' Film, most through viewing it on television, and 17,000 have responded.

INTERDENOMINATIONAL ORGANIZATIONS

In 1994 the Australian Council of Churches (ACC, 1946) became the National Council of Churches in Australia (NCCA) with 14 members including Catholic, Orthodox, Anglican and Protestant. Both the NCCA and its Commission on Mission grew out of worldwide student initiatives for world mission in the late 19th century. The National Missionary Council (1926) had previously (in 1965) become the ACC's Division of Mission.

The Australian Evangelical Alliance Missions Commission (Missions Interlink) is an active cooperation of denominational and non-denominational missionary sending organizations.

In 1988 a grass roots movement known as the 'Aussie Awakening' began as over 35,000 Christians surrounded the new parliament house in Canberra to offer prayer after it was announced that there would be no prayers at the official opening. Christians from across denominations continue to gather for prayer, community outreach and witness in events such as the Global March for Jesus.

The Ecumenical Office of the archdiocese of Melbourne is a Catholic body founded in 1933 which presents the Christian message according to the spirit of Vatican II and in co-operation with other churches wherever possible.

FUTURE TRENDS AND PROSPECTS

Australia has received large numbers of non-Christian immigrants in the 1990s. A gradual decline of professing Christians (from a high of 96.6% in 1900 to 75% by 2025) is expected due to secularism and the rise of non-Christian immigrants. Affiliated Christians will likely drop to 65% by 2025.

Although still the largest religious tradition in Australia, Christians will likely decline below 60% around AD 2050. The nonreligious could grow to over 25% of the population. Australia in the future may well be a country of four or five major religious (and nonreligious) traditions.

BIBLIOGRAPHY

A history of the Australian churches. I. Breward. St. Leonards, Australia: Allen & Unwin, 1993. 317p.

A place for strangers: towards a history of Aboriginal being. T. Swain. Melbourne: Cambridge University Press, 1993. 303p. (Concerned with Aboriginal religion).

Aboriginal Australians and Christian missions: ethnographic and historical studies. T. Swain & D. B. Rose. *Special studies in religions*, vol. 6. Bedford Park, SA, Australia: Australian Association for the Study of Religions, 1988. 498p.

Aboriginal religions in Australia: a bibliographical survey. T. Swain. *Bibliographies and indexes in religious studies*, no. 18. New York: Greenwood Press, 1991. 351p.

Amazing grace: Evangelicalism in Australia, Britain, Canada, and the United States. G. A. Rawlyk & M. A. Noll (eds). Grand Rapids, MI: Baker Books, 1993. 429p.

Australia. I. Kepars. 2nd ed. *World bibliographical series*, vol. 46. Oxford, UK: CLIO Press, 1994. 425p. (Complements first edition, focusing upon material from 1984; contains less than 10% of previous material from 1984 edition. See especially 'Religion and philosophy,' 70–3).

'Australia,' in *Western religion: a country by country sociological enquiry*, p.27-45. H. Mol. The Hague: Mouton, 1972.

Australian charismatic directory. Waverley, NSW: Temple Trust, 1975.

Australian Christian communes. J. McKnight. [Cobbity]: Trojan Head Press, [1990]. 240p.

Australian Christian life from 1788: an introduction and anthology. I. H. Murray. Edinburgh and Carlisle, PA: The Banner of Truth Trust, 1988. 375p.

Australian Christianity in outline: a statistical analysis and directory. D. Hynd. Rev. ed. Homebush West, NSW: Lancer Books, 1984. 150p.

Australian Christians in conflict and unity. F. G. Engel. Melbourne: Joint Board of Christian Education, 1984. 275p.

Australian Evangelical Alliance directory of missions, 1973. Mont Albert, Victoria: Australian Evangelical Alliance, 1973. 45p.

Australian sourcebooks: social sciences. B. Brady. Melbourne: ALIA/Thorpe, 1992. 193p. (Annotated bibliography).

Australian Aboriginal religion. R. M. Berndt. *Iconography of religions*, section 5: Australia. Leiden: E. J. Brill, 1974. 4 vols.

Being Christian, being Australian: contemporary Christianity down under. W. Lawton. *Moore Theological College lecture series.* Homebush West, NSW: Anzea Publishers, 1988. 128p.

Bringing Christ to Aboriginal Australia: a brief survey of the efforts of the church to reach the original inhabitants of this land with the gospel of the Lord Jesus Christ. I. Lindsay & H. Miles. Lawson, NSW: Mission Publications, 1989. 20p.

Buddhism in Australia 1848–1988. P. Coucher. Sydney: New South Wales University Press, 1989. 147p.

Build My Church: trends and possibilities for Australian churches. P. Kaldor et al, Adelaide: Openbook Publishers, 1999. 119p.

Called to be church in Australia: an approach to the renewal of local churches. D. Edwards. Homebush, NSW: St. Paul Publications, 1987. 110p.

Can God survive in Australia? B. Wilson. : Albatross, 1983. 224p.

Catholics in Australia: a social history. N. Turner. Melbourne: Collins Dove, 1992. 2 vols.

'Christianity and culture in colonial Australia: selected Catholic, Anglican, Wesleyan and Adventist perspectives, 1891–1900.' A. N. Patrick. Ph.D. dissertation, University of Newcastle, NSW, 1993. 319p.

Churches and people in Australia and New Zealand, 1860–1930. H. R. Jackson. Wellington, NZ: Allen & Unwin, 1987. 219p.

Directory of ethnic community organizations in Australia. Canberra: Department of Immigration, Local Government and Ethnic Affairs, 1993. 367p.

Evangelical Christianity in Australia: spirit, word, and world. S. Piggin. New York: Oxford University Press, 1996. 350p.

Faith without the church? nominalism in Australian Christianity. P. Bentley, T. Blombery & P. J. Hughes. Kew, Victoria: Christian Research Association, 1992. 118p.

'Growth in Australian churches.' D. F. Brookes. D.Min. thesis, Fuller Theological Seminary, Pasadena, CA, 1990. 166p.

Heart of fire: the story of Australian Pentecostalism. B. Chant. Adelaide, South Australia: Luke Publications, 1973. 212p.

Images of religion in Australian art. R. Crumlin. Kensington, NSW: Bay Books, 1988. 204p.

Many faiths one nation: a guide to the major faiths and denominations in Australia. I. Gillman (ed). Sydney: Collins, 1988. 416p.

Ministry among Aboriginal people: missiological overview of the church in Australia. M. J. Wilson. *Pastoral investigation of contemporary trends.* Melbourne: Collins Dove, 1988. 67p.

Official year book of the Catholic Church in Australia & Papua New Guinea, New Zealand & the Pacific Islands. Sydney: E. J. Dwyer, 1970. 544p.

One blood: 200 years of Aboriginal encounter with Christianity: a story of hope. J. Harris. Sydney: Albatross Books, 1990. 956p.

Orthodox and other Eastern churches in Australia. 2nd ed. Townsville, Queensland: Church of England in Australia, 1978. 21p.

Patterns of faith in Australian churches: report from the combined churches survey for faith and mission. P. J. Hughes & T. Blombery. Hawthorn, Victoria: Christian Research Association, 1990. 167p.

Religion: a view from the Australian census. P. J. Hughes. Kew, Victoria: Christian Research Association, 1993. 71p.

Religion and ethnic identity: an Australian study. I. W. Ata (ed). Richmond, Victoria: Spectrum Publications, 1988–1990. 3 vols.

Religion and multiculturalism in Australia: essays in honour of Victor Hayes. N. C. Habel (ed). Bedford Park, SA, Australia: Australian Association for the Study of Religions, 1992. 359p.

Religion in aboriginal Australia: an anthology. M. J. Charlesworth (ed). St. Lucia, Australia: University of Queensland Press, 1984. 470p.

Religion in Australia: a history. R. C. Thompson. *Australian retrospectives.* Melbourne: Oxford University Press, 1994. 175p.

Religion in Australia: a sociological investigation. H. Mol. Melbourne: Thomas Nelson, 1971. 398p.

Religion in Australia: sociological perspectives. A. W. Black (ed). Sydney: Allen & Unwin, 1991. 222p.

Religion in Australia: facts and figures: P.J. Hughes. Melbourne: Christian Research Association, 1997. 80p.

Religion in Australian life: a bibliography of social research. M. C. Mason (ed). Bedford Park, SA: Australian Association for the Study of Religions, 1982. 264p.

Religious bodies in Australia: a comprehensive guide. R. A. Humphries & R. S. Ward (eds). 3rd ed. Wantirna, Australia: New Melbourne Press, 1995. 431p. (1st ed., 1986; 2nd ed., 1988).

Religious broadcasting in Australia. K. McLennan. Melbourne: Uniting Church Historical Society (Victoria), 1990. 21p.

Religious life in the Australian church today. M. D. Whelan. Homebush, NSW: St. Paul Publications, 1985. 71p.

Some Scots were here: a history of the Presbyterian Church in South Australia, 1839–1977. R. J. Scrimgeour. Adelaide: Lutheran Publishing House, 1986. 239p.

South–land of the Holy Spirit: a Christian history of Australia. E. R. Kotlowski. Orange, NSW, Australia: Christian History Research Institute, 1994. 374p.

The Aborigines and the Church. H. Deakin. Melbourne: Catholic Archdiocese, 1975. 85p.

The Australian dictionary of evangelical biography. B. Dickey (ed). Sydney: Evangelical History Association, 1994. 438p.

The Catholic Church and community: an Australian history. P. J. O'Farrell. 3rd ed. Sydney: New South Wales University Press, 1992. 488p.

The gospel of good giving: stewardship in Australian churches. D. McDiarmid. Melbourne: Joint Board of Christian Education, 1990. 64p.

The Jews in Australia: a thematic history. H. Rubinstein & W. D. Rubinstein. Melbourne: Heinemann, 1991. 2 vols.

The sectarian strand: religion in Australian history. M. Hogan. Melbourne: Penguin Books, 1987. 316p.

The silent revolution: the effects of modernization on Australian aboriginal religion. E. Kolig. Philadelphia: Institute for the Study of Human Issues, 1981. 204p.

The state of the churches in Great Britain, Ireland, Australia and New Zealand, 1986. Peoria, AZ: Ecumenism Research Agency, 1987. 6 microfilm reels.

The sunburnt soul: Christianity in search of an Australian identity. D. Millikan. Homebush West, Australia: Anzea Publishers, 1981. 111p.

Tin mosques and Ghanatowns: a history of Afghan camel drivers in Australia. C. Stevens. Melbourne: Oxford University Press, 1989. 400p.

Under the Southern Cross: history of the Evangelical Lutheran Church of Australia. A. Braner. 1956; reprint, Adelaide: Lutheran Publishing House, 1985. 456p.

Country Table 2. **Organized churches and denominations in Australia.**

Official name (bold type = church with over 10% of all affiliated) 1	Begun 2	Type 3	Counc 4	Congs 5	Adults 6	Affiliated 1970 7	Affiliated 1995 8	G% 9	Names, notes, and other statistics (see Codebook, Part 3) 10
Aboriginal pentecostal congregations	1934	I-3pP	.....	38	2,300	2,000	4,600	3.39	No White aid. Northeast NSW. Bandjalang tribe and others. 3-stage initiation.
Australian Indigenous Ministries Chs	1905	P-Non	.H..E	24	12,300	15,000	15,700	0.18	*AIM Fellowship Ch.* NSW, NT, Queensland. 8n,113m,1p,W=80%,550Y,80z.
Ancient Assyrian Church of the East	c1930	O-Nes	Yw...	23	12,900	4,500	16,500	5.33	*Nestorians.* Assyrians. Related to Ch of the East in Iraq and USA. Sydney. 1 priest.
Anglican Catholic Church in Australia	1983	I-ACa	.....	15	2,000	–	5,000	8.33	*ACCA.* Schism ex C of E in A rejecting ordination of women, begun with 7 parishes.
Anglican Church of Australia	1788	A-plu	AWEAW	9,000	1,500,000	3,775,000	4,040,000	0.27	*Ch of England in Australia.* 23 Dioceses. 3528n; M=USPG,MTS,NZCMS.
Apostolic Church of Australia & NZ	1928	P-PeA	Z....	55	4,500	3,100	6,801	3.19	Work among Aborigines in west. M=Apostolic Ch (UK). 2s,23n,W=80%,146Y,351z.
Apostolic Church of Queensland	c1960	I-3aX	x....	30	2,000	2,000	3,000	1.64	Split ex New Apostolic Ch. In Vereinigung Apostolischer Christen (Switzerland).
Armenian Apostolic Church	c1850	O-Arm	Ewc.W	2	4,200	12,000	14,000	0.62	*Gregorians.* Under C Echmiadzin. Sydney, Melbourne. 5n.
Assemblies of God in Australia	1922	P-Pe2	Z...w	500	79,600	12,000	101,440	8.91	Slavs, Italians, Finnish; 1,500 Aborigines. M=AoG(USA). (1970) 175n. (1990) 1300n.
Assembly Hall Churches	c1980	I-3nC	.....	7	484	–	1,000	6.67	*Little Flock. Local Churches.* Begun 1922 in China by Watchman Nee. Chinese.
Associated Mission Chs of Australia	1952	I-3aW	x....	20	600	1,000	1,500	1.64	*Latter Rain Assemblies.* Radical Pentecostals (government through prophecy, &c). 1p.
Association of Vineyard Chs	c1990	I-3cW	.....	13	400	–	1,000	20.00	Assisted by M=AVC(USA). Signs and wonders emphasized.
Australian Aborigines Ev Mission	1949	P-Non	.H..E	15	1,500	2,000	3,000	1.64	*AAEM.* In Kundalee, Western Australia. 37 workers. Hostels for working youths.
Autocephalic GOC of America & Aust	c1960	I-Gre	.....	15	7,000	10,000	12,000	0.73	Ex Greek OC (AD Australia) by laity opposing hierarchy. In NSW, SA, Victoria.
Baptist Union of Australia	1813	P-Bap	T....	884	64,444	170,000	135,054	-0.92	*BUA.* HQ Melbourne. 673n,4x,5p,5s(250),W=85%,2147Y.
Bible Baptist Churches	1970	I-Bap	.....	15	1,200	600	1,710	4.28	M=BIM(USA). Fundamentalist mission from USA.
Bulgarian Orthodox Church	c1950	O-Bul	Mwc..	5	3,000	3,000	5,000	2.06	*Balgarskata Pravoslavna Crkva.* In AD N&S America, under P Sofia. Bulgarians. 2nx.
Byelorussian Autocephalic Orth Ch	c1950	O-Bye	x....	10	2,000	1,000	3,000	4.49	Refugees from White Russian church, suppressed 1922. HQ USA. 1 archbishop. 4n.
Catholic Apostolic Church	c1870	I-3aX	x....	1	50	500	100	-6.23	Irvingites from Britain. Declining rapidly from 976 in 1933, and 720 in 1947.
Catholic Church in Australia:	1803	R-LEr	B...s	1,540	3,530,300	3,037,589	5,043,881	2.05	From Italy, Poland, Croatia. C=29+8+67. W=61%. 2119n 1283x 2693m 7992w 75283Yy
M Adelaide	1842	R-Lat	Bs	87	185,000	193,137	264,839	1.27	SAustralia. Metropolitan. Many migrants. 1s. 96n 81x 120m 437w 4357Yy
D Darwin	1847	R-Lat	Bmsc	17	28,000	21,000	39,772	2.59	Northern Territory. Uninhabitable. Aborigines. 5n 25x 57m 93w 732Yy
D Port Pirie	1887	R-Lat	Bs	27	21,000	26,924	29,859	0.41	West, north of South Australia, Steel, metals. 29n 8x 14m 45w 545Yy
M Brisbane	1859	R-Lat	Bmsc	110	340,000	273,200	485,000	2.32	Tropical agriculture. Charismatics strong. 1s. M=MSC. 198n 101x 249m 947w 7835Yy
D Cairns	1887	R-Lat	Bs	24	42,000	33,210	59,649	2.37	Northern Queensland. Aborigines. Agriculture. 30n 4x 12m 69w 978Yy
D Rockhampton	1882	R-Lat	Bs	37	51,000	50,000	73,000	1.53	North of Brisbane. Mining. Many Aborigines. 52n 8x 24m 183w 1728Yy
D Toowoomba	1929	R-Lat	Bs	35	40,000	44,377	57,172	1.02	Southwest Queensland. Rich pastoral area. 48n 16x 30m 71w 1298Yy
D Townsville	1930	R-Lat	Bs	29	48,000	56,000	69,241	0.85	Coastal and back country. Minerals, sugar. 30n 7x 33m 121w 1176Yy
M Melbourne	1847	R-Lat	Bs	233	685,000	650,000	978,844	1.65	Southern part of Victoria. Commercial. 1s. 390n 300x 580m 1504w 14982Yy
D Ballarat	1874	R-Lat	Bs	55	69,000	78,628	97,971	0.88	Western part of Victoria. Agriculture, industry. 84n 22x 52m 250w 1641Yy
D Melbourne *(Ukrainian)*	1958	R-Ukr	Ocssr	9	24,000	22,850	35,000	1.72	Ukrainians, Ruthenians. Also Oceania, NZ. W=57%. 13n 3x 3m 12w 122Yy
D St Michael's of Sydney *(Melkite)*	1987	R-Mel	Obc	7	7,000	–	10,000	12.50	Greek Melkites. M=BC,BS. 6n 2x 2m 0w 167Yy
D St Maron of Sydney *(Maronite)*	1973	R-Mar	Osj	9	105,000	–	150,000	4.55	Maronites, from Lebanon (Arabs). 12n 0x 2m 22w 873Yy
D Sale	1887	R-Lat	Bs	29	52,000	48,537	74,772	1.74	EVictoria. Industry, pastoral, agriculture. 34n 11x 20m 53w 1539Yy
D Sandhurst	1874	R-Lat	Bs	41	63,000	61,389	89,486	1.52	Northern Victoria. Agriculture, light industry. 59n 11x 21m 103w 1538Yy
M Perth	1845	R-Lat	Bs	104	230,000	145,800	329,004	3.31	SAustralia, desert. Includes Cocos Is. 1s. 101n 122x 216m 626w 5000Yy
D Broome	1887	R-Lat	Bsac	20	5,000	3,800	7,051	2.50	Western Australia. Aborigines. 6n 6x 19m 38w 171Yy
D Bunbury	1954	R-Lat	Bs	26	29,300	29,000	41,800	1.47	Southwest of Western Australia. Agriculture. 23n 10x 15m 50w 629Yy
D Geraldton	1898	R-Lat	Bs	42	20,000	13,200	28,500	3.13	WAustralia. Uninhabitable. Mining. Aborigines. 15n 14x 32m 51w 479Yy
M Sydney	1842	R-Lat	Bs	136	571,000	740,927	815,000	0.38	NSW. City of Sydney, suburbs. 3s. 243n 288x 589m 1432w 7762Yy
D Armidale	1869	R-Lat	Bs	25	29,000	38,518	41,168	0.27	Inland northern NSW. Pastoral, agricultural. 30n 5x 12m 78w 821Yy
D Bathurst	1865	R-Lat	Bs	24	44,000	43,793	62,500	1.43	West of Blue Mountains. Agricultural. 44n 4x 12m 139w 1343Yy
D Broken Bay	1986	R-Lat	Bs	39	126,000	–	180,249	11.11	Gosford, NSW, coastal. North of Sydney. 49n 61x 111m 166w 2642Yy
D Lismore	1887	R-Lat	Bs	30	63,000	45,250	90,427	2.81	Northern NSW, coastal. Dairying, agricultural. 51n 9x 19m 171w 1589Yy
D Maitland	1847	R-Lat	Bs	53	94,000	88,360	134,218	1.69	Coastal NSW. Coal, industry, agriculture. 76n 15x 21m 300w 2443Yy
D Parramatta	1986	R-Lat	Bs	58	176,000	–	252,000	11.11	Western Sydney suburbs, including Blacktown. 75n 35x 178m 231w 4173Yy
D Wagga Wagga	1917	R-Lat	Bs	29	41,000	43,571	58,951	1.22	Southern NSW, along river Murray. Agriculture. 42n 7x 22m 136w 1330Yy
D Wilcannia-Forbes	1887	R-Lat	Bs	20	26,000	37,500	37,658	0.02	Remote west of NSW. Rural depopulation. 29n 0x 12m 45w 725Yy
D Wollongong	1951	R-Lat	Bs	35	111,000	85,000	158,448	2.52	Coastal strip south of Sydney. Steel, mining. 47n 37x 94m 204w 2783Yy
AD Canberra	1862	R-Lat	bs	62	107,000	97,000	152,806	1.83	Australian Capital Territory. Catholics 32%. 84n 44x 68m 227w 2229Yy
AD Hobart	1842	R-Lat	bs	42	63,000	64,618	89,496	1.31	State of Tasmania. Major ecumenical activity. 40n 27x 54m 188w 1238Yy
OM Australia	1969	R-Lat	Bs	46	35,000	2,000	50,000	13.74	*Catholic Military Ordinariate,* for armed services. 78n 0x 0m 0w 415Yy
Children of God International	c1969	I-mar	xv...	2	100	1,000	300	-4.70	From USA. Youth colonies: Melbourne, Sydney. 1973 applied to WCC, ACC(Australia).
Christadelphian Ecclesias	1866	m-Ade	x....	114	5,000	12,000	9,934	-0.75	*Australian Christadelphian Bible Mission.* 104 ecclesias (churches). Pacifist.
Christian & Missionary Alliance	1969	P-Hol	xF...	32	1,045	330	3,074	9.34	M=CMA(USA). Mostly in NSW, Victoria. HQ Chatswood, NSW. 6n,5x,10f,1s(14),29Y.
Christian Brethren	1870	P-CBr	x....	290	14,500	30,000	32,200	0.28	*Open Brethren.* Strong in Queensland; Aborigines' work. 90m,10f(NZ),1p.
Christian Brethren (Exclusive)	c1910	P-EBr	x....	257	9,000	15,000	13,800	-0.33	*Exclusive (Closed) Brethren.* Groups; Glanton, Raven Taylor, Kelly-Continental, &c.
Christian Israelite Church		I-Eva	.....	8	600	1,000	1,100	0.05	Small evangelical body. In Sydney and Strethfield (NSW), also in Indiana (USA).
Christian Outreach Centres	1974	I-3cW	.....	170	12,500	–	25,000	4.76	Recent charismatic groupings. Mainly in urban centers.
Christian Outreach Centers Intl	c1980	I-3cW	x....	40	2,000	–	5,000	6.67	*COCI.* Charismatic network based on HQ Brisbane. Overseas: 10 chs in USA, others in UK.
Christian Revival Crusade	1944	I-3pW	x...h	100	10,000	10,000	13,500	1.21	*CRC* (NRC until 1952, Commonwealth RC with 1958). 65n,2s,300Y.
Church of Christ, Scientist	c1900	m-Sci	x....	50	1,100	20,000	1,792	-9.20	*Christian Science.* M=CCS(Boston, USA). Growth 1933-47: 8,878 to 11,389. 16m,75w.
Church of God (Anderson)	1954	P-Hol	x....	3	132	500	220	-3.23	M=CoG(Anderson) (USA). Begun by German and USA immigrants. 1 Greek church. 2n.
Church of God of Prophecy	1956	P-Pe3	x....	6	90	100	300	4.49	M=CGP(USA). Split in USA ex Church of God (Cleveland).
Ch of Jesus Christ of Latter-day Saints	1851	m-LdS	x....	212	53,600	27,087	76,575	4.24	*Mormons.* M=CJCLdS(Utah, USA). HQ NSW. Growth: 2,501 (1933), 3,499 (1947). 200f.
Church of the Nazarene	1946	P-Hol	xF...	31	905	2,800	1,537	-2.37	3 Churches Greek-speaking. M=CoN(USA). HQ Thornleigh. 25n,1s,SS=2153.
Church of the New Jerusalem		m-Swe	x....	1	40	100	100	0.05	*Swedenborgian Church.* In Penshurst, NSW. Split in USA ex New Church.
Churches of Christ in Australia	1846	P-Dis	xWE.W	440	35,228	94,000	72,591	-1.03	*Federal Conf.* M=CCCC(Instrumental) (USA). 324n,4f,1H,3s(100),W=74%,1393Y.
Churches of Christ (Non-Instrumental)	1949	I-Dis	x....	100	4,000	3,000	6,000	2.81	M=CC(Non-Instrumental) (USA). Across nation. Several churches for the deaf. 28f.
Cooneyites (Go Preachers)	c1920	I-Fun	x....	500	60,000	150,000	110,000	-1.23	*Go-(Tramp-)Preachers.* Irish itinerants, in UK, USA, South Africa, Ireland. No books, no training.
Coptic Orthodox Church (P Alexandria)	c1960	O-Cop	Nwa.W	15	35,000	7,000	50,000	8.18	Egyptian immigrants since 1947. Churches in Sydney, Melbourne. 2n,2x.
Dawn Bible Students Association	c1940	m-Jeh	x....	10	250	500	600	0.73	Split ex Jehovah's Witnesses. World HQ New Jersey (USA). 15 classes (1 Polish).
Estonian Ev Lutheran Church in Exile	1944	P-Lut	Lwc..	5	2,000	1,000	3,000	4.49	St John's Ch, Sydney. USSR refugees, independent of ELCE (USSR). HQ Stockholm. 1n.
Estonian Orthodox Church in Exile	c1940	I-Est	C....	3	2,000	2,000	4,000	2.81	Estonian refugees after annexation of Estonia by USSR. Bishop in Sweden.
Ev Lutheran Congs of the Reformation		I-Lut	.....	10	200	225	400	0.05	Independent congregations with office in Kingaroy, Queensland.
Evangelical Presbyterian Church of A	c1958	I-Ref	.....	10	400	700	1,000	1.44	5 Baptist congregations which accepted Westminster Confession. 70% Tasmania. 5n.
Fellowship of Congregational Churches	1829	I-Con	RWE.W	29	3,300	7,500	4,250	-2.25	10% of denomination which refused to enter 1977 Uniting Ch in Australia. W=65%.
Fellowship of Evangelical Chs in A	1956	I-Eva	.....	30	3,000	4,000	4,500	0.47	*FECA.* Conservative fellowship of independent congregations. HQ Fitzroy, Victoria.
Finnish Evangelical Lutheran Church	1960	P-Lut	.....	6	400	475	600	0.94	*Melbournen Suomalainen.* Finns in Melbourne, Victoria, Tasmania. W=23%,23Yy,11z.
Free Reformed Churches of Australia		I-Ref	.....	5	800	1,500	2,000	0.05	Congregations in Launceston and Albany. WA. Calvinistic doctrines. 2n.
Free Serbian Orth Ch: D Aus & NZ	c1969	I-Ser	.....	20	10,000	12,000	16,000	1.16	Dissident Yugoslavs rejecting P Belgrade. USA links. One bishop, 9 priests.
Full Gospel Church in Australia	1962	I-3fP	.....	150	6,000	4,000	12,000	4.49	*Associated Full Gospel Chs.* Gospel Light Ministry. Split ex AoG. Many Aborigines.
Greater World Chr Spiritualist League		m-Spi	x....	2	160	200	200	0.05	Chr=Christian. *Greater World Sanctuary.* In Nowra and Oak Flats, NSW.
Greek Orthodox Church: AD Australia	1896	O-Gre	Cw..W	110	220,500	175,100	357,487	2.90	Greek immigrants and descendants. 1959 AD, also E all Oceania. 83nx,W=10%, 7000Yy.
Holy Ap Cath Assyrian Ch of the East	c1970	O-Nes	Y....	1	2,000	–	3,000	37.75	Assyrian immigrants from Iraq, Iran.
Independent Congregational Churches		I-Con	.....	20	4,000	–	6,323	0.05	Persons rejecting older Congregationalist denominations.
Independent Greek Orthodox Church	c1950	I-Gre	.....	6	3,500	3,000	4,000	1.16	Formed by 10 Greek Orthodox priests looking to Byelorussian AOC archbishop. NSW, SA.
Independent Russian Orthodox Church		I-Rus	.....	1	400	500	600	0.05	One church of Russian emigres, under Greek Orthodox Ch, AD Australia.
Internat Ch of the Foursquare Gospel	1923	P-Pe2	ZF...	43	3,600	2,000	5,000	3.73	*Gospel Lighthouse Chs.* M=ICFG(USA). Finns, Arabs, Swedes, &c. 39nm,2f,1s,W=60%,34Y.
Jehovah's Witnesses	1896	m-Jeh	x....	645	53,142	34,000	98,489	4.35	Branch formed 1904. Missions in Pacific. HQ Strathfield, NSW. (1975) 1808Y. (1995) 2373Y.
Latvian Ev Lutheran Church in Exile	1948	P-Lut	lw...	20	9,000	13,503	16,000	0.68	*Latvijas Ev Lut Baznica.* Melbourne and District. 11n,W=50%,126Yy,128z.
Liberal Catholic Church	1916	I-Lib	x....	5	200	2,000	657	-4.36	Theosophist. HQ Ryde. 4 churches in Sydney. 3 bishops. 36n,1s,W=13%,55Yy,35z.
Lutheran Church of Australia	1838	P-Lut	e...w	649	197,000	147,859	250,844	2.14	1966 union: ELCA, United ELCA. 10 lang. 336n,3x,1s(90),W=45%,3442Yy. M=LCMS.
Macedonian Orth Autocephalous Ch	1960	O-Mac	cv...	12	36,200	6,000	46,141	8.50	*Makedonska Pravoslavna Crkva.* Macedonian (Slav) immigrants from Yugoslavia. 7nx.
Messianic Jewish Congregations	c1980	I-3mJ	.....	10	200	–	300	6.67	New work beginning in Sydney, Melbourne. M=JFJ.
Methodist Ch of Australasia Continuing	1812	I-Met	VWE.W	300	30,000	75,000	50,000	-1.61	10% of denomination who refused to enter 1977 Uniting Ch in Australia.
National Revival Crusade	1952	I-3pW	Z....	10	500	2,000	1,000	-2.73	Split 1952 ex CRC with original name NRC. British Israelite. Rejoining CRC.
New Apostolic Church	c1900	I-3aX	x....	40	1,800	3,900	3,707	-0.20	Schism ex Catholic Apostolic Ch (Irvingites) in Europe. HQ Dortmund (Germany). 16n.
New Church in Australia		m-Swe	x....	3	310	500	400	0.05	*Sydney Society,* and others. Swedenborgians. Originally from UK.
New Testament Church of God	1976	P-Pe3	.....	17	884	–	2,000	5.26	M=CoG(Cleveland) (USA). Holiness Pentecostals.
Old Believers Russian Orthodox Ch		I-OBe	x....	10	600	300	1,000	0.05	*Old Ritualist Ch.* Schism in Russia 1667 ex Orth Ch. Russian emigres in Auburn. 1n.
Orthodox Catholic Church		I-CCa	.....	2	40	100	100	0.05	Links with American Catholic Ch (USA), OCC (UK). 2 priests.
Orthodox Church in America & Canada		O-Rus	Mw...	5	2,000	2,000	4,000	0.05	*OCA.* Linked with OCA (USA). Russians, other Slavs. HQ Sydney. 2nx.
People's Churches		I-Non	.TTTT	12	1,500	2,000	3,000	0.05	A number of independent congregations. Best-known: Kew and Reservoir (Victoria).
Presbyterian Ch of Australia Continuing	1809	I-Ref	JWE.W	768	36,176	150,000	70,000	-3.00	*PCA.* 30% refused to enter 1977 Uniting Ch in Australia. 356n. Abroad: 130f.
Presbyterian Ch of Eastern Australia	1846	I-Ref	J....	30	1,000	2,000	2,000	0.00	Schism ex PCA. M=Free Ch of Scotland. 3 Presbyteries. North coast of NSW. 15n.
Presbyterian Reformed Church of A	1968	I-Ref	.....	10	400	1,000	900	-0.42	Schism ex Presbyterian Ch of Australia after Geering heresy trial (in NZ). 13n,1p.
Reformed Churches of Australia	1951	P-Ref	J....	45	5,898	8,358	10,301	0.84	Immigrants from Europe, mainly Dutch. 6 Classis. Sydney. 29n,W=13%,15Yy.
Reformed Presbyterian Ch of Ireland		P-Ref	J....	2	100	200	300	0.05	*RPC. Australian Presbytery.* Part of Irish church. HQ MacKinnon. Victoria. 2x.
Religious Society of Friends in A	1832	P-Qua	Qv..W	42	1,077	1,154	1,876	1.96	*Australian Yearly Meeting.* A=1964. 7 regional meetings. 1r,W=50%.
Reorganized Ch of JC of LD Saints		m-LdS	x....	40	5,800	4,270	7,346	0.05	Schism ex CJCLdS(Mormons). 5 churches in Sydney. World HQ Independence, MO (USA).
Revival Centres International	1948	I-3pW	.....	200	16,000	500	24,671	16.88	Schism ex CRC. Water & Spirit baptism essential for salvation. Abroad: 50,000 in 15 countries.
Romanian Orthodox Church		O-Rum	Cwc..	5	4,000	5,000	6,000	0.05	*Biserica Orthodoxa Romana.* Under P Bucharest. Romanian immigrants in Melbourne. 4nx.
Russian Orthodox Ch Outside Russia	c1950	I-Rus	x...w	21	26,400	21,000	40,000	2.61	*Russkaya Pravoslavnaya Cerkov. D Australia & NZ.* 9 churches in Sydney. 17n,1e,1s.
Russian Orthodox Church (P Moscow)		O-Rus	M....	5	9,000	3,000	15,000	0.05	ROC in communion with Patriarchate of Moscow. Russians.
Salvation Army	1881	P-Sal	xwE.W	553	56,500	62,000	71,984	0.60	*SA, Eastern Territory, Southern Terr.* 16 Divisions. 110 institutions. 1898n,2s.
Self-Independent Macedonian Church		I-Mac	.....	3	500	200	1,000	0.05	Macedonian Orthodox immigrants in Fitzroy (Victoria). Slavs. 1 Bulgarian priest.
Serbian Orthodox Ch (D WEurope,)	c1960	O-Ser	Cwc.W	16	22,100	40,000	30,800	-1.04	*Srpska Pravoslavna Crkva.* Under P Belgrade. Yugoslav immigrants. Bishop, 10nx,1d(4).
Seventh-day Adventist Church	1885	P-Adv	x....	391	46,174	39,000	79,226	2.88	*Trans-Tasman/Commonwealth UCs.* 210n,2H,1j,1s,364t(33884),W=95%,1471Y.
SDA Reform Movement of Australia		I-Adv	x....	10	600	1,000	1,200	0.05	Schism ex Seventh-day Adventist Church; world HQ West Germany. HQ Auburn, NSW.
Sydney City Mission		P-Non	.....	20	2,000	2,000	3,000	0.05	18 centres including homes for children, aged, and soup kitchens.

Continued overleaf

Country Table 2–concluded

Official name 1	Begun 2	Type 3	Counc 4	Congs 5	Adults 6	Affiliated 1970 7	Affiliated 1995 8	G% 9	Names, notes, and other statistics (see Codebook, Part 3) 10
Syrian Antiochian Orthodox Church	1920	O-Ara	Cw.NW	10	29,300	5,000	45,000	9.19	Under Greek Orthodox P Antioch. Lebanese in NSW, Victoria. Bishop, 5 priests.
Syrian Orthodox Church		O-Syr	D....	3	6,000	–	9,000	0.05	Syrian Arab Christians (Jacobites), recent immigrants.
Ukrainian Autoceph Orth Ch in A & NZ	1948	I-Ukr	X....	25	15,000	15,000	25,000	2.06	*AD Aust & NZ, UOCUSA.* Factions: Metropolitan Diocese, United Diocese, Council-led. 14n.
Ukrainian OC (Autocephalic) of Aust		I-Ukr	X....	20	3,500	4,000	6,000	0.05	Ukrainian emigres rejecting USA links of UAOCANZ. Under UGOCC(Canada). 9 priests.
Unitarian & Liberal Christian Chs	1850	m-Unt	.....	4	300	2,000	735	-3.93	*Australian Assembly of OLCC.* In UFCC(UK), UUA(USA). Declining. HQ Geelong.
United Aborigines Mission of Australia	1895	P-CBr	.H..E	6	3,000	5,000	6,000	0.73	*UAM.* White mission to Aborigines. 75% in west, some churches in SA,NSW. 73 workers.
United Church in NA & the Territories		P-Uni	.....	100	6,000	10,000	12,000	0.05	Methodist, Presbyterian and Congregational churches in sparsely-populated NT. 1r.
United Pentecostal Church	1954	P-Pel	x....	40	6,000	4,000	10,000	3.73	*Jesus Only Church.* M=UPC(USA). Unitarian Pentecostals. 10n,3x,6f,1p,1s,W=50%,100Y.
Uniting Church of Australia	1809	P-Uni	WWE.W	3,236	600,000	1,194,088	1,387,646	0.60	*UCA.* 1977 union of Cong Union of A, Methodist Ch of A, Presbyterian Ch of A. 10H.
Universal World Church		I-3pP	x....	2	200	500	500	0.05	North Queensland and Brisbane. All Torres Strait Islanders. HQ Los Angeles (USA).
Welsh Calvinistic Methodist Church		P-Ref	Rw...	4	200	300	400	0.05	Parts of Presbyterian Church of Wales. 3 charges in Victoria. 3n.
Wesleyan Church	1945	P-Hol	VF...	60	1,231	960	1,547	1.93	M=WC(USA). Mostly in Victoria. 12n,1p,W=52%,27Yy.
Worldwide Church of God		I-BrI	x....	40	2,000	1,000	3,059	0.05	*WCG. Radio Ch of God.* M=WCG(Pasadena, USA). HQ North Sydney. By 1975, 2500 members.
Other Protestant denominations		P-	.....	300	200,000	74,300	300,000	0.05	Total about 80 (see list below), with numerous independent single congregations.
Other neocharismatic networks	1975	I-3cW	.....	600	200,000	–	300,000	5.00	Including Jesus is Lord Fellowship (Philippines), Manna Ch (Portugal).
Other Non-White indigenous churches		I-3cP	.....	200	8,000	1,000	15,000	0.05	Total over 5 (see below), including CoGiC.
Other marginal Protestant bodies		m-	.....	100	7,000	2,230	10,000	0.05	Total over 30 (see list below).
Other Orthodox churches		O-	.....	20	15,000	3,000	20,000	0.05	Polish, Russians, Spiritual Christians/Molokans.
Doubly-affiliated		2-aff			-647,000	0	-1,157,398		Members of both older denomination and newer Renewal body.
Totals				**23,715**	**6,760,960**	**9,592,128**	**12,100,000**		

Churches, members, growth, 1900-2025	*Congs*	*Adults*	*Affiliated*	*G%*	*Total denominations*	*6 Megablocs: O*	*R*	*A*	*P*	*I*	*m*
Total churches, members, and denominations (mid-1900)	4,000	1,686,000	3,221,100	1.57	28	4	1	1	9	7	6
Total churches, members, and denominations (mid-1970)	21,253	5,020,863	9,592,128	1.57	151	15	1	1	65	43	26
Total churches, members, and denominations (mid-1990)	22,500	6,409,000	11,470,000	0.90	253	20	1	1	111	75	45
Total churches, members, and denominations (mid-1995)	23,715	6,760,960	12,100,000	1.08	262	21	1	1	110	84	45
Total churches, members, and denominations (mid-2000)	24,000	7,034,000	12,587,959	0.79	267	22	1	1	112	85	46
Total churches, members, and denominations (mid-2025)	28,000	8,382,000	15,000,000	0.70	427	35	1	1	140	200	50

NOTES ON TABLE ABOVE

NATIONAL COUNCILS (Column 4, 5th letter).

- E = Australian Evangelical Alliance (AEA).
- h = Australian Pentecostal Fellowship.
- I = Uniting Aboriginal and Islander Christian Congress (UAICC).
- S = Australian Catholic Bishops' Conference, and also in NCCA.
- T = Australian Consultative Council of the ICCC.
- W = National Council of Churches in Australia (NCCA).
- w = associate member of NCCA.

Other national councils. Aboriginal and Islander Catholic Council (AICC) (1976, in Queensland only). Australian Assembly of Unitarian Churches (AAUC) (5 small denominations). *Local councils.* 7 state councils affiliated to NCCA.

OTHER PROTESTANT DENOMINATIONS. These include a large number of independent single congregations and independent house groups, as well as the following small denominations or groupings: American Baptist Association, Apostolic Christian Ch (Nazarean) (2 churches), Armenian Ev Spiritual Ch, Armenian Spiritual Brethren, Association of Baptists for World Evangelism (6 churches), Australian Baptist Independent Fellowship, Australian Ev Mission, Baptist Bible Fellowship International (1954) (7 churches), Baptist International Missions (1970), Baptist Mid-Missions (1968), Baptist Missionary Association of America, Bible Christian Ch, Bible Presbyterian Ch (Adelaide), Christian Catholic Ch in Zion, (USA; 2 churches), Christian Ch of North America, Christian Reformed Ch, Churches of God in the British Isles & Overseas (4 churches, 150 members), City Missions (Hobart, Launceston, et alia), Elim Foursquare Gospel Ch, Ev Baptist Mission, Evangelisation Society of South Australia, Faith Baptist Chs Fellowship of Congregational Chs (NSW; 22 churches), Fellowship of Independent Ev Chs of Australia (WA; 2 churches), Free Presbyterian Ch of Scotland (1 congregation, Grafton, NSW), German Ev Lutheran Ch (5 centres), House of David, Hungarian Reformed Ch (1 church), Independent Congregation Chs (14 churches), Italian Ev Christian Ch (Pentecostal, 300 members), Maranatha Baptist Mission, Melbourne Revival Centre, Missionary Baptist Chs, Norwegian Seamen's Mission Ch, 'Old Paths' Christadelphians, Reformed Baptists (USA: 4 churches), Reformed Presbyterian Ch (Evangelical Synod), Remnant Ch (Hebrew Christian sabbatarians), Scandinavian Seamen's Missions (3 pastors and churches), Slavic Ev Pentecostal Ch of Australia (3 churches, 400 members), Slavic Gospel Association, Strict & Particular Baptist Chs of Australia (Gospel Standard) (4 churches), United Gospel Mission, United Welsh Ch, Universal Fellowship of Metropolitan Community Churches (from USA; gay/homosexuals), Westminster Presbyterian Ch (4 churches, 200 adherents), World Baptist Fellowship Mission Agency (1969).

OTHER MARGINAL BODIES. These include Anthroposophical Society (Christian Community Ch), Branhamites (End Times Believers; HQ Jeffersonville, IN, USA; Jesus-Only Unitarians), British-Israel Federation, Ch of the Mystic Christ (3 churches), Ch of the New Faith Scientology (banned, and immigrants banned until 1974; rapid growth by 1976 to 30,000 members with 5 centres, 50 full-time ministers and 120 lay workers), Divine Science Federation International (2 churches), Good Samaritan Ch of Truth (1 church in Glen Iris, Victoria), Order of the Cross (3 groups), Seventh Ch, Spiritual Churches. Temple Society in Australia (5 centres; linked with Templegesellschaft in Germany in Germany begun 1861; Unitarian), Unity School of Christianity (3 centres, 2 ministers, 250 members); and about 64 spiritualist churches, many independent.

OTHER NON-WHITE INDIGENOUS CHURCHES. Several Third-World indigenous churches have opened branches in Australia, including in 1963 a Korean movement: Holy Spirit Association for the Unification of World Christianity (in 1977: 7 centres, 100 members). The Father Divine Peace Mission Movement (USA Blacks), formerly strong, has 3 remaining churches with under 30 members (HQ Sydney). From India, the Assemblies (Jehova Shammah) of Brother Bakht Singh have a Christian Fellowship Centre in Hurstville (NSW).

AUSTRIA

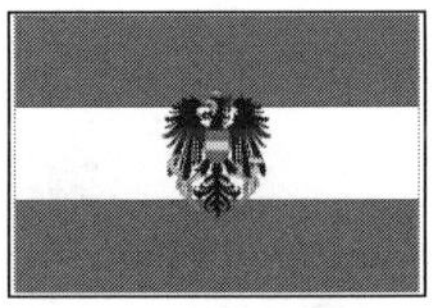

SECULAR DATA, AD 2000

STATE
Official name: Die Republik Österreich (The Republic of Austria).
Short name: Austria. **Adjective of nationality:** Austrian.
Flag: Red, white, and red stripes, black coat of arms.
Area: 83,858 sq. km. (32,378 sq. mi.).
Government: Federal republic, since 1918 (1282 Hapsburg empire).
Legislature: National Assembly: Federal Council (Bundesrat), 64 members; Nationalrat, 183 members.
Official language: German (Deutsch).
Monetary unit: 1 Austrian Schilling (S) = 100 Groschen. **US$1=** S 11.76.
Chief cities: WIEN (Vienna) 2,072,000; Linz 352,064; Graz 341,554; Salzburg 231,206; Innsbruck 194,423.
Political divisions: 9 provinces.
Armed forces: 51,000.

DEMOGRAPHY
Population: 8,211,000.
Population density: 97.9/sq. km. (253.5/sq. mi.).
Under 15 years: 1,396,000.
Growth rate p.a.: 0.27% (births 9.43, deaths 9.94).
Mortality: Infant, per 1,000: 5.9; **Maternal per 100,000:** 10.0.
Life expectancy: 78 (male 74, female 81).
Household size: 2.6. **Floor area per person, sq.m:** 55.0.
Major languages: German, Slovenian, Serbo-Croatian, Hungarian, Greek, Russian, Italian, Czech, Turkish, English.
Urban dwellers: 64.65%. **Urban growth rate p.a.:** 0.6%.
Labor force: 47%.

ETHNOLINGUISTIC PEOPLES
86.4% Bavarian Austrian; 3.9% German Swiss (Allemanic); 3.5% German; 0.9% Bosniac (Muslmani); 0.9% Turk.

ECONOMY
National income p.a. per person: US$26,890; **per family:** US$69,914.

EDUCATION
Adult literacy: 100% (male 100%, female 100%). **Schools:** 6,311.
Universities: 44. **School enrolment:** female/male: 104%/107%.

HEALTH
Access to health services: 95%. **Access to safe water:** 100%.
Hospitals: 324 (92 beds per 10,000). **Doctors:** 26,121.
Blind: 11,000. **Deaf:** 497,500. **Murder rate:** 2.
Lepers: 300.

LITERATURE
New book titles p.a.: 8,290 (1,010 p.a. per million). **Periodicals:** 3,534. **Newspapers:** 23 dailies.

COMMUNICATION (per 1,000 people)
Phones: 466 (22% mobile). **Radios:** 584. **TV sets:** 497.
Daily newspaper circulation: 465. **Computers:** 346.

REFUGEES
Alien refugees from other countries: 55,900.

HUMAN LIFE AND LIBERTY (optimum condition=100.0%)
HDI: 93.2. **HSI:** 94.0. **HFI:** 90.0. **EFL:** 59.0.

Country status. The modern Republic of Austria is the direct descendant of the Habsburg Empire, which collapsed in 1918. Much of this Central European country is mountainous with nearly half covered with forests. Its chief products include wheat, rye, fruit, timber, iron ore, and textiles with tourism playing an essential role.

HUMAN LIFE AND LIBERTY

Human need and development. After the Austrian State Treaty of 1955 and the removal of the four power occupation forces, Austrians have developed a sense of nationhood that had been comparatively lacking in the First Republic. Bound by a common language, race and religion, Austrians have not been subject to the divisive forces that have afflicted neighboring countries. With a prosperous economy that in many areas is comparable to that of Germany, and helped by an official policy of neutrality, Austria has emerged as a second Switzerland in the heart of Europe. With the decline of the nobility, class distinctions have come to be muted. However, an underclass is emerging in the form of guestworkers from foreign countries, especially Turkey, who are mostly engaged in menial work. Ghettoes where housing conditions are substandard are found in Vienna and other large cities.

Austria is a fully developed country with standards of living comparable to Germany. As in Germany, the government takes an active role in economic development and owns many public utilities, communications systems, and some industrial plants.

Human rights and freedoms. Human rights are highly respected in Austria, and over the years their scope has been expanded. Most cases of the arbitrary use of power result from police handling of refugees. Freedom of association is constitutionally guaranteed except in the case of pro-Nazi organizations. Religious freedom is complete, although the Treaty of St Germain restricts this freedom to religions 'compatible with public safety and morality.' In order to qualify as a religious group, registration is required.

Austria recognizes the competence of the European Human Rights Commission in Strasbourg and conforms to the European Convention on Human Rights. Discrimination against minorities and women is illegal both in law and in practice. Human rights of the Slovene minority in Carinthia has been an issue in past years, but is no longer an active problem.

Country Table 1. **Religious adherents in Austria, AD 1900-2025.**

Year / Name	1900 Adherents	%	1970 Adherents	%	mid-1990 Adherents	%	Annual change, 1990-2000 Natural	Conversion	Total	Rate	mid-1995 Adherents	%	mid-2000 Adherents	%	mid-2025 Adherents	%
Christians	**5,828,000**	**97.1**	**7,240,000**	**97.0**	**6,996,400**	**90.8**	**45,900**	**-8,532**	**37,368**	**0.52**	**7,209,020**	**90.1**	**7,370,078**	**89.8**	**7,123,630**	**87.0**
PROFESSION																
professing Christians	**5,828,000**	**97.1**	**7,240,000**	**97.0**	**6,996,400**	**90.8**	**45,900**	**-8,532**	**37,368**	**0.52**	**7,209,020**	**90.1**	**7,370,078**	**89.8**	**7,123,630**	**87.0**
AFFILIATION																
unaffiliated Christians	10,000	0.2	46,637	0.6	348,400	4.5	2,288	8,913	11,201	2.83	412,799	5.2	460,408	5.6	323,630	4.0
affiliated Christians	**5,818,000**	**96.9**	**7,193,363**	**96.3**	**6,648,000**	**86.3**	**43,659**	**-17,492**	**26,167**	**0.39**	**6,796,221**	**85.0**	**6,909,670**	**84.2**	**6,800,000**	**83.1**
Roman Catholics	5,500,000	91.6	6,613,278	88.6	6,000,000	77.9	39,403	-19,403	20,000	0.33	6,129,263	76.6	6,200,000	75.5	6,156,500	75.2
Protestants	160,000	2.7	455,510	6.1	420,000	5.5	2,758	-3,401	-643	-0.15	419,560	5.2	413,570	5.0	400,000	4.9
Orthodox	138,000	2.3	52,000	0.7	115,000	1.5	755	3,245	4,000	3.03	125,710	1.6	155,000	1.9	190,000	2.3
Independents	20,000	0.3	46,600	0.6	63,000	0.8	414	586	1,000	1.48	66,538	0.8	73,000	0.9	50,000	0.6
Marginal Christians	0	0.0	23,975	0.3	47,000	0.6	309	1,491	1,800	3.30	52,150	0.7	65,000	0.8	100,000	1.2
Anglicans	0	0.0	2,000	0.0	3,000	0.0	20	-10	10	0.33	3,000	0.0	3,100	0.0	3,500	0.0
Trans-megabloc groupings																
Evangelicals	20,000	0.3	37,300	0.5	42,380	0.6	278	84	362	0.82	45,008	0.6	46,000	0.6	45,800	0.6
Pentecostals/Charismatics	0	0.0	15,000	0.2	254,200	3.3	1,669	2,761	4,430	1.62	280,802	3.5	298,500	3.6	415,200	5.1
Great Commission Christians	**300,000**	**5.0**	**1,000,000**	**13.4**	**1,590,000**	**20.6**	**10,442**	**2,854**	**13,296**	**0.81**	**1,664,000**	**20.8**	**1,722,957**	**21.0**	**1,830,000**	**22.4**
Nonreligious	8,000	0.1	144,000	1.9	490,000	6.4	3,218	3,955	7,173	1.38	540,000	6.8	561,725	6.8	700,000	8.6
Muslims	0	0.0	18,000	0.2	139,370	1.8	915	3,428	4,343	2.75	160,000	2.0	182,797	2.2	240,000	2.9
Atheists	2,000	0.0	50,000	0.7	60,000	0.8	394	535	929	1.45	66,500	0.8	69,286	0.8	85,000	1.0
Jews	166,000	2.8	10,000	0.1	9,000	0.1	59	-99	-40	-0.45	8,700	0.1	8,604	0.1	8,000	0.1
Buddhists	0	0.0	1,000	0.0	1,500	0.0	10	358	368	13.20	5,000	0.1	5,181	0.1	9,000	0.1
Baha'is	0	0.0	2,000	0.0	2,500	0.0	16	112	128	4.22	3,200	0.0	3,780	0.1	5,000	0.1
Hindus	0	0.0	0	0.0	1,500	0.0	10	86	96	5.08	2,300	0.0	2,463	0.0	5,000	0.1
Chinese folk-religionists	0	0.0	0	0.0	570	0.0	4	69	73	8.60	1,200	0.0	1,301	0.0	2,200	0.0
New-Religionists	0	0.0	0	0.0	700	0.0	5	17	22	2.77	880	0.0	920	0.0	1,500	0.0
Sikhs	0	0.0	0	0.0	200	0.0	1	20	21	7.47	360	0.0	411	0.0	1,000	0.0
Confucianists	0	0.0	0	0.0	60	0.0	0	33	33	20.43	350	0.0	385	0.0	600	0.0
Ethnoreligionists	0	0.0	0	0.0	0	0.0	0	4	4	44.97	40	0.0	41	0.0	70	0.0
Other religionists	0	0.0	2,000	0.0	3,200	0.0	21	14	35	1.04	3,450	0.0	3,549	0.0	5,000	0.1
World A (unevangelized persons)	12,007	0.2	7,467	0.1	100,165	1.3	657	894	1,551	1.45	112,009	1.4	114,954	1.4	180,092	2.2
World B (evangelized non-Christians)	163,772	2.7	219,618	2.9	608,435	7.9	3,996	7,638	11,634	1.78	679,682	8.5	725,968	8.8	882,278	10.8
World C (Christians)	5,828,000	97.1	7,240,000	97.0	6,996,400	90.8	45,900	-8,532	37,368	0.52	7,209,020	90.1	7,370,078	89.8	7,123,630	87.0
Country's population	**6,003,780**	**100.0**	**7,467,086**	**100.0**	**7,705,000**	**100.0**	**50,553**	**0**	**50,553**	**0.64**	**8,000,712**	**100.0**	**8,211,000**	**100.0**	**8,186,000**	**100.0**

COLUMNS, ROWS.
For meanings and definitions, see Codebook (Part 3). Note that, by definition, total 'Christians' = professing + crypto-Christians, which also = affiliated + unaffiliated Christians, and also = Great Commission Christians + latent Christians. Percentages may not always total exactly, due to rounding.

CENSUSES.
1869: 96.2% Roman Catholics, 2.4% Protestants, 1.3 Jews. **1900:** 91.8% Roman Catholics (12.0% Greek Catholics), 2.8% Jews, 2.7% Protestants, 2.3% Greek Orthodox, 0.3% Old Catholics. **1923:** 91.1% Roman Catholics, 3.4% Protestants, 3.2% Jews. **1934:** 90.6% Roman Catholics, 4.5% Protestants, 2.8% Jews, 1.6% nonreligious, 0.5% Old Catholics. **1939:** 88.7% Roman Catholics, 5.2% Protestants, 1.2 Jews. **1.VI.1951** (de jure): 89.6% Roman Catholic, 6.2% Protestants, 3.8% nonreligious, 0.3% other religionists, 0.2% Jews. **21.III.1961** (de jure): 89.0% Roman Catholics, 6.2% Protestants, 3.8% nonreligious, 0.4% Old Catholics, 0.1% Jews. **12.V.1971** (adjusted): 89.3% Roman Catholics, 6.2% Protestants, 2.7% nonreligious (and atheists), 0.8% Orthodox, 0.4% Old Catholics, 0.2% Muslims, 0.1% Jews. **1991:** 78.0% Roman Catholics, 8.5% nonreligious & atheists, 2.1% Muslims, 0.3% Old Catholics, 0.2% Jews.

NOTES ON RELIGIONS
ATHEISTS. Kommunistische Partei Osterreichs (KPO) (split between USSR/China) and one small faction. Many European immigrants.
BAHA'IS. Entered before 1921. Growth from 7 local spiritual assemblies (1964) to 11 (1973) and to 30 (1997), and 48 other isolated centers or groups.
BUDDHISTS. Including about 900 Chinese.
EVANGELICALS. In German, Evangelikale (Conservative Evangelicals).
JEWS. Decline from over 200,000 in 1938 to 4,000 in 1945, rising to 10,000 in 1970, then again declining due to emigration to Israel. 80% Liberal, 20% Orthodox.
MUSLIMS. In 1995, 75,000 Bosnians, 55,000 Turks, 25,000 Kurds, 7,000 Arabs, 6,500 Iranians. All Sunnis, except for a small Ahmadiya mission begun in 1955 under its Swiss mission.
OTHER RELIGIONISTS. Adherents of smaller religions and cults, including Rosicrucians (3 AMORC centres).
PENTECOSTALS/CHARISMATICS. The Catholic Charismatic Renewal began in 1977. By 1997, there were 420 regular weekly prayer groups and 5 covenant communities with 6,600 regular adult attenders; 70 involved priests and 5 bishops.
ROMAN CATHOLICS. Defections of affiliated Catholics each year have gradually increased from 8,368 in 1958 to 23,833 (0.46% per year; mostly urban) in 1972; the former figure was less than the natural population increase among Catholics, but the latter figure (which with children and infants of defectors amounts to 28,000 a year) is nearly twice the natural increase during the period 1970-80 (averaging 15,743 per year), meaning that affiliated Roman Catholics have since about 1965 been gradually decreasing each year in absolute numbers as well as (since about 1955) as a percentage of the population. The analysis 'Annual change, 1990-2000' in the table above is based on an average defection rate. It should be noted that defection here refers to withdrawal of church affiliation with its legal implications; most defectors however still regard themselves as professing Catholics and are counted as such in the government population census.

Great Commission Instrument Panel: status of Austria (for explanation see start of Part 4)

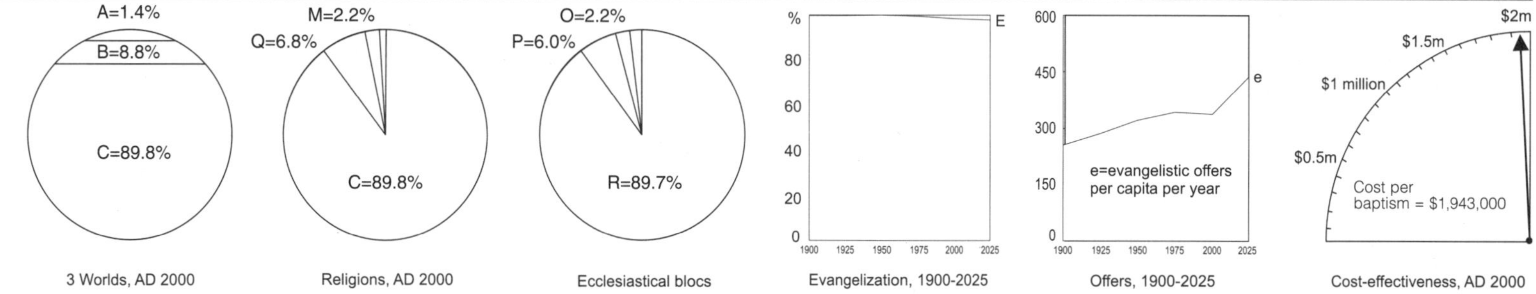

Human environment. Environmental movements have grown in Austria after the rise of the Green Party brought the environmental agenda to the fore. In 1985 the country introduced the most stringent exhaust standards for cars in Europe. Recycling has become universal, both in industry and in municipalities. There are 129 protected areas of natural reserves covering 20% of the country, and 302 plant species and 108 animal species protected by law.

NON-CHRISTIAN RELIGIONS

Islam increased rapidly from 1970-1995 to about 160,000 Muslims, mostly manual laborers from Turkey and the states of former Yugoslavia, the rest being embassy personnel, students and immigrants from Bosnia who have taken Austrian citizenship since World War II. Muslim Social Service (Muslimische Sozialdienst), founded in Vienna in 1964, is administered by expatriates sponsored by their respective governments. There are 3 Muslim prayer halls in Vienna.

Judaism suffered a catastrophic decrease from more than 200,000 Jews in 1938, the year of the Anschluss when Austria was absorbed in Hitler's Third Reich, to 4,000 in 1945. Following World War II, the Jewish community grew initially due to immigration from Hungary (especially in 1956), Romania, and Czechoslovakia. In 1995 there were only about 8,700 Jews in the country. The average age of Austria's Jews is extremely old, with high mortality and few replacements, since Jewish youth prefer to emigrate to Israel or to Western countries. Thus the Austrian Hebrew community is at present in decline. Jewish organizations and institutions include: (1) Association of Israelite Religious Communities (Verband der Osterreichischen Israelitischen Kultusgemeinden), which sponsors a home in Vienna, with a geriatric department; (2) Youth House (Haus der Jugend) in Vienna, which co-ordinates all Jewish youth organizations; and (3) the Vienna synagogue, which administers a kindergarten and 3 Talmud-Torah schools, and organizes religious courses. Orthodox Jews have their own prayer houses. Since 1965 the University of Vienna has maintained an Institute for Judaism (Institut fur Judaistik), which sponsors the Austrian Jewish Museum of Eisenstadt Association and provides expositions and annual meetings dedicated to the scientific study of Judaism in Austria.

Buddhism is active in Austria although the number of Buddhist groups remains small. Austria is a member of the European Buddhist Community. The Amidist sect Jodashin-shu has chosen Salzburg as the central headquarters for their work in all German-speaking countries. The OctopusVersandbuchhandlung in Vienna is an important Buddhist publishing house and also maintains a library. In addition Austrian Buddhists produce a trilingual journal serving the whole of Europe.

Official state postage stamp commemorating 1517 Reformation, with Bible as Rock, all-seeing Eye, and prayer 'Lord, preserve for us the Light of the Gospel'

CHRISTIANITY

The Austrian area of central Europe came under Roman rule at the beginning of the Christian era; Christianity was slowly introduced and earliest evidence of it comes from the year 174. During the next thousand years, central Europe experienced a series of invasions by Ostrogoths, Huns, Lombards, Avars

Country summary. **Worlds A, B, C by ethnolinguistic peoples, cities, and major civil divisions in Austria.**

	PEOPLES							CITIES							CIVIL DIVISIONS						
World	Num	Pop 2000	C%	Christians	E%	U%	Unevangelized	Num	Pop 2000	C%	Christians	E%	U%	Unevangelized	Num	Pop 2000	C%	Christians	E%	U%	Unevangelized
A	3	101,811	0.07	68	46	54	55,386	0	0	0.00	0	0	0	0	0	0	0.00	0	0	0	0
B	10	107,311	1.59	1,707	54	46	49,013	0	0	0.00	0	0	0	0	0	0	0.00	0	0	0	0
C	23	8,001,401	86.33	6,907,898	100	0	11,111	13	3,752,489	82.76	3,105,690	99	1	34,030	9	8,210,519	84.16	6,909,670	99	1	115,507
Total	**36**	**8,210,523**	**84.16**	**6,909,673**	**99**	**1**	**115,510**	**13**	**3,752,489**	**82.76**	**3,105,690**	**99**	**1**	**34,030**	**9**	**8,210,519**	**84.16**	**6,909,670**	**99**	**1**	**115,507**

and Slavs, with some unification achieved under Charlemagne. The bishop of Salzburg began sending missionaries eastward in 955. The duchy of Austria came under the rule of the Bavarian family of Babenberg in 973 and from then onwards gradually gained dominance over other central European duchies. The Hapsburg family was given added powers in 1282 and continued to rule when Austria became an archduchy, from 1438 to 1806. During the Middle Ages the only Christian centres throughout most of the land were the monasteries of different religious orders, and Vienna had no bishop until 1468. In 1519, the houses of Austria, Burgundy, Aragon, and Castile were united through marriage under Charles V, joined later by Bohemia and Hungary. By 1520 there were Protestants in Salzburg and possibly in Vienna. The Lutheran reform movement made progress in Austria and Bohemia prior to the Counter-Reformation which began with the entrance of the Jesuits into Vienna. In 1552 Lutherans were given some recognition, to the exclusion of Calvinists. Following the Thirty Years War, the Hapsburgs accorded no privileges to Protestants but rigidly enforced a united Catholicism in their part of Europe. In 1699 the Turks were defeated at Vienna, Hungary was added to Austria, and the country entered into what has been called Austria's Great Century. Joseph II sought to increase his powers at the expense of the church by destroying monasteries, establishing his own diocesan boundaries, controlling communication between Austria's bishops and Rome, and in 1781 he issued the Edict of Tolerance for Protestants and Orthodox. Following the destruction of Napoleon's advances, Austria became an empire in its own right. Revolutionary movements sought change, with greater religious freedom achieved in the constitution of 1861. Churches of the Augsburg and Helvetic confessions emerged into the open at this time, later to become united as the present Evangelical Church. In 1867 Hungary achieved equal status with Austria in the Austro-Hungarian Empire. In 1918 the defeated empire was dissolved and Austria was reduced in size to its present area, as a republic. While the country continued predominantly Catholic, new churches appeared, and in 1925 the Synods of the Augsburg and Helvetic Confessions began meeting together. In 1934 Austria signed a concordat with Rome to the disadvantage of the Evangelical Church, the latter suffering further by being incorporated into the German Evangelical Church at the time of the Nazi Anschluss.

CATHOLIC CHURCH. In Austria there has been a close interrelationship between church and state since the early days of christianization in the time of the Roman empire, but it was the Counter-Reformation which brought about a Catholic pattern of culture simultaneous with the foundation of such new religious congregations as the Jesuits and Capuchins. The establishment of the Catholic Church as the national church in the absolute welfare state of Joseph II was caused by the peculiarly Austrian form that the Enlightenment there took. Catholic doctrine with its values and norms dominated the prevailing culture until the 19th century, and the various competing currents of liberalism, nationalism, and socialism had a limited influence on social elites only.

The process of secularization was then initiated by the rise of industrialization and of economic, social, and political institutions independent of the church. The middle classes and the social democrats were the first to demand separation of church and state. However, the church maintained an influence in politics and society as a result of both the Christian democratic movement and the ruling Catholic House of Hapsburg. Major ideological controversies between Christian political parties on the one hand and socialists and nationalists on the other raged after the end of the Hapsburg monarchy. The church lost its influence, particularly with the working class, through the failure of the Catholic corporate state experiment of 1934-1938.

Between the 2 world wars a liturgical movement (Pius Parsch) arose which inspired a new conception of the church through its translations of the Bible into the vernacular. A spiritual renewal of the church and a change in its position in state society took place at the time of its persecution by the Nazi regime (1938-1945). During World War II, and thereafter, theological thought was also renewed through the writing of such men as K. Rahner and A. Jungmann, and new pastoral ideas were developed around the pastoral centers founded by K. Rudolf. Catholic organizations also were reshaped for the apostolate along the Italian and French model of Catholic Action, and Catholic priests largely withdrew from party politics to further dialogue with all groups in society.

In 1952, at the first national reunion of Catholics after the war, the Katholikentag, the Catholic Church finally gave up its claim to be the national church and its engagement in party politics, and in its Mariazell manifesto proclaimed a free church in a free society.

At present, most Austrians continue to maintain basic religious convictions. The great majority are baptized Catholics (89% in 1951; 83% in 1995) and practically all Catholic parents continue to have their children baptized. Catholic marriages decreased by 20% between 1955 and 1971, mainly because divorced Catholics may not remarry in the church; but 95% of all first marriages still follow Catholic rites. Almost all Catholics are buried with church rites.

The number of affiliated Catholics leaving the church each year steadily increased, from 833,368 persons in 1958 to 23,833 in 1972, a process which however only decreased the proportion of professing Catholics in the population by 1% in 20 years; and two-thirds of these persons lived in urban areas.

Regularly-practicing Catholics are a minority and are gradually decreasing in number. Major doctrines such as the resurrection are now accepted by only a minority of Catholics (33%), although a large majority (69%) believe in life after death. In 1949, Sunday mass attendance was 39%. In 1974, this had only declined slightly, and mass attendance (Catholics older than 13 years) was: 3% several times a week, 31% every Sunday and on church feast days, 17% at least once a month, 22% on feast days only, and 27% never or almost never. In certain urban areas, however, Sunday attendance declined much more (Innsbruck: 1950, 51%; 1970, 30%). But even regular churchgoers do not accept central doctrines; the resurrection is believed in by only 50% of Sunday mass attenders. Traditional Catholic religiosity (acceptance of, and compliance with, all church norms) is followed by only 20%.

The number of priests is steadily declining. In 1949 Austrian dioceses had 4,443 secular priests and 1,129 religious priests working in parishes (excluding contemplatives). By 1971 the number of secular priests had decreased (by 11%) to 3,987, whereas the number of religious priests in parishes remained approximately unchanged (1,106 in 1971). In 1945 there was one parish priest for 1,347 Catholics, while in 1971 the average priest had to serve 1,678 Catholics. From 1968 to 1974 ordinations of secular priests averaged 46 per year, whereas from 1961 to 1967 the average had been 93. For religious priests ordinations decreased from 67 to 47 a year. There is therefore now a disproportionate number of older priests. Recently, the church has tried to overcome the shortage by appointing lay theologians to teach religion in public schools and to work as pastoral assistants in parishes. Lastly, nuns in Austria declined from 16,356 in 1950 to 13,574 in 1972. And with regard to the laity, in 1974, 5% of all Catholics were members of one of the many Catholic organizations.

Diocesan synods have been held in most of the Austrian dioceses, continuing the Aggiornamento of Vatican II. The composition of the synodal councils (50% priests, 50% lay men and women) reflects the new theology of the laity as the People of God. Important decisions have been made concerning the functions of parishes in such areas as preaching, liturgy, and charity. This renewal of parish life has led to parish councils being formed to give lay persons a share in decision-making and responsibility. Following the diocesan synods, a National Synod for Austria was held from May 1973 to May 1974 to deal with the problems of shortage of personnel, church and society, education, and the mass media.

The Holy See has diplomatic relations with Austria and in AD 2000 is represented to government and the Catholic hierarchy by a nuncio residing in Vienna.

Katholische Kirche Österreichs, Diözese Feldkirch. One of 4 Roman Catholic churches in town of Dornbirn, Vorarlberg.

PROTESTANT CHURCHES. Although Austria is still predominantly Roman Catholic, the Protestant proportion of the population has increased since the period prior to World War II to more than 5%. This increase, unique in Europe, is due primarily to migration from Germany during 1938-1945 and the influx of refugees from central, southern, and eastern Europe after the war.

Some change of affiliation also occurred for political reasons at the time of the Catholic corporate state experiment (1934-1938) and following the absorption of Austria by Nazi Germany in 1938, in addition to other cases motivated by dissatisfaction over the Catholic attitude to divorce.

The principal Protestant body is the Evangelical Church, which is a loose union of the Helvetian (HB) Reformed and Augsburg (AB) Lutheran churches, the latter being by far the most significant in terms of membership. The general synod is the church's supreme authority and carries on its administrative functions through the AB and HB Church Council, with headquarters in Vienna. Protestants are strongest in the Alpine regions of Upper Austria, which were less accessible to suppression at the time of the Counter-Reformation, as well as in Burgenland, which was part of Hungary until 1918. New Protestant groups have been formed among refugees since World War II.

Only 2 other Protestant groups are officially recognized: Moravians, who were given legal status in 1880 but no longer have members or congregations in Austria, and Methodists, who have been active since 1870 and legally recognized since 1951. Austrian Methodists are related to the United Methodist Church in the USA.

A host of smaller Protestant groups continue to function without official recognition, including Adventists, Baptists, Brethren, Friends, Churches of Christ, and Pentecostals.

OTHER CHURCHES. The Old Catholic Church was founded in 1871 as a protest movement against the doctrine of papal infallibility promulgated at Vatican Council I, and was given legal recognition in Austria in 1877. This is now Austria's fifth largest denomination after the Roman Catholic, Lutheran, Jehovah's Witnesses and Orthodox churches. Another Catholic (non-Roman) body, the New Apostolic Church, with headquarters in Dortmund (Germany) has also built up a significant following in Austria.

Eastern Orthodoxy is represented by more than 8 branches: Armenian, Bulgarian, Coptic Greek, Romanian, Russian (2), and Serbian Orthodox Churches, as well as smaller immigrant groups. Anglicans serve a small mostly expatriate community in Vienna, in addition to maintaining seasonal chaplaincies in some of the resort areas. Among marginal Protestant groups, only Mormons have been granted legal recognition (in 1955), but Jehovah's Witnesses are much larger—by 1995 they ranked as the 4th largest denomination in the country, with almost 38,000 affiliated.

Art and architecture. The Christian heritage of Austria is most clearly evident in its art and architecture. From about the sixth century to the 19th, Austrian art and architecture were predominantly ecclesiastical. The first important architectural style was Romanesque, of which the most outstanding example is the Cathedral at Gurk, the Klosterneuberg Abbey near Vienna with its enameled goldwork altar and the carved wooden Madonna at Miriazell in Styria. Later the Gothic style supplanted the Romanesque when Vienna became the imperial capital under the Habsburgs. The Gothic style reached its acme with the Cathedral of St Stephen's, in the Cistercian monasteries at Heiligenkreuz and Zwettl, in St Augustine's, and in the Church of the Friars Minor in Vienna. After the Turkish threat ended there was a flurry of churchbuilding, this time in the Baroque style. The notable examples of this era are the Karlskirche in Vienna, the Abbey at Melk perched on a cliff over the Danube and the monastery of St Floria in Upper Austria. The Votive Church is the best architectural legacy of emperor Franz Josef. After World War II Clemens Holzmeister has designed many of the modern churches. The close association of the Vatican with the Habsburgs had a significant effect on artistic and intellectual development in Austria. In 1551 the pope authorized Spanish Jesuits to come to Austria to establish schools. The Jesuits played a great part in fostering the growth of both theater and music. One of the oldest theaters in the world is in the former Jesuit college in Vienna. Anton Brucker, the church musician, is ranked with Brahms and Hugo Wolf as among the greatest musical geniuses of his age.

Renewal movements. In the 1990s the Pentecostal/Charismatic Renewal continued to spread rapidly across most older churches, and numbered over 298,500 adherents (of whom 6% Pentecostals, 90% Charismatics, and 4% Independents).

Indigenous missions. Though heavily Christian, Austria has long been considered a mission field with over 60 foreign Protestant agencies engaged in evangelism and church planting. At the same time, Austrian Christians have long been engaged in foreign mission, primarily through the Catholic missionary orders.

CHURCH AND STATE

The federal constitution, revised in 1929, contains no stipulation concerning religions. Nevertheless, the Basic Law of 21 December 1867 (RGB1 No. 142) dealing with the general rights of nationals, which is considered a constitutional law by Article 149 of the federal constitution, guarantees freedom of conscience and belief (Article 14), the internal autonomy of the churches (Article 15), and freedom of religious instruction (Article 17). The State Treaty for the Re-establishment of an Independent and Democratic Austria (BGB1 No. 152), signed in 1955 by the 4 former occupying powers, also guarantees freedom of worship and non-discrimination on the grounds of religious belief (Article 6).

The legal status of religious communities is regulated by a law of 20 May 1874, which continues valid. According to this law, only legally-recognized religious communities may be granted a juridical personality, and their organizations and institutions enjoy a special penal protection.

Relations between the Austrian Republic and the Catholic Church are covered by the concordat with the Holy See signed on 5 June 1933. This concordat grants to the church, among other rights, the right to institute, administer, and supervise religious instruction for Catholic schools in all branches of the primary and middle educational system. The Catholic Church, its orders and congregations, have the right to open schools which enjoy all benefits of public schools as long as they respect general legal stipulations. The church enjoys full liberty in the administration of its affairs and property as well as in the public celebration of worship. Although the concordat also calls for recognition by the Republic of the civil juridical effects of marriages celebrated according to canon law, this latter stipulation was abolished by the law of 6 July 1938, still in force, concerning the unification of marriage and divorce in Austria and other territories of the German Third Reich, which made civil marriage obligatory.

The concordat has been extended by a series of agreements concluded with the Holy See. These include: (1) the agreements of 23 June 1960 concerning church property, resulting in the restitution to the church of its lands and buildings and commitment by the state to provide it with an annual subsidy of 100 million austrian shillings, and the apostolic administration of Burgenland, which was raised to the rank of diocese (Eisenstadt); (2) the agreement of 9 July 1962 regarding the educational question, by which the Austrian Republic agreed to subsidize Catholic schools for up to 60% of the cost of its teaching personnel (100% beginning in 1971); and (3) the agreements of 7 July 1964 and 7 October 1968 relating to the creation respectively of the dioceses of Innsbruck and Feldkirch.

Relations between the state and the Evangelical Lutheran and Reformed churches are regulated by the federal law of 6 June 1961. This law explicitly recognizes these churches both as separate entities and as an ecclesiastical federation. They are completely autonomous in their organization. Their parishes are at every echelon in the position of state-recognized corporations, which includes legal assistance by the authorities. Financial contributions from the state to the Old Catholic Church and Jewish religious communities were fixed in October 1960.

Concerning the right to collect ecclesiastical taxes, this was already affirmed for legally recognized churches in Article 15 of the fundamental law of 21 December 1867, but its effective application did not become operative until the promulgation of the German law of 1 May 1939 concerning the collection of ecclesiastical taxes in the 'Land' of Austria.

The Cultural Section of the Federal Ministry for Teaching and Art (Kultursektion des Bundesministeriums fur Unterricht und Kunst) is responsible for all matters relating to the churches and religious communities.

BROADCASTING AND MEDIA

The Religious Section of the government's Osterreichischer Rundfunk (ORF) broadcasts Catholic programs weekly on each of the 3 radio stations, including 3 hours of worship, preaching and education. IBRA and ERF programs can be heard on local radio stations. Shortwave radio programs from international broadcasters such as HCJB, FEBC, TWR and KNLS can be received and have generated response.

Satellite TV and radio programs are received in English, Arabic, German, and Italian. In particular, Arabic programming is received via SAT-7. Catholics broadcast 4 hours of weekly programming on two TV channels.

INTERDENOMINATIONAL ORGANIZATIONS

The Ecumenical Council of Churches in Austria (Okumenischer Rat der Kirchen in Osterreich), founded in Vienna in 1958, is the principal coordinating body for ecumenical activity in Austria. Members include the Lutheran, Reformed, Old Catholic, Methodist, Anglican, and Orthodox churches. Several other denominations and church-related organizations have observer status.

Two mixed commissions have been formed: the Joint Catholic/Evangelical Commission of Austria (Gemischte Katholische/Evangelische Kommission Osterreichs), founded in Vienna in 1966; and the Old Catholic/Roman Catholic Consultations (Altkatholische/Romisch-Katholische Konsultationen), also in Vienna.

Alt-katholische Kirche in Österreich. Assistant bishop (right) administers priests' communion in Vienna cathedral.

The Society for the Law of the Oriental Churches, founded in Vienna in 1969, is an international interconfessional body, providing for scientific collaboration between specialists in Eastern canon law and civil law concerning the Eastern churches. It unites representatives of Eastern Orthodox, Oriental Orthodox and Eastern-rite Catholic churches, as well as Western specialists.

Organizations dedicated to practical co-operation include 8 major ones: (1) Austrian Missionary Council (Osterreichischer Missionsrat), founded in Vienna in 1963, and affiliated to CWME of the WCC; (2) Ecumenical Youth Council in Austria (Okumenischer Jugendrat in Osterreich), founded in Vienna in 1960-1961, an independent multi-confessional youth organization including Catholics since 1967, which provides for studies and work projects on national and international levels; (3) Theological Work Circle of Vienna (Theologischer Abeitkreis in Wien); (4) Committee for Aid to Serbian Orthodox Immigrant Workers in Austria (Komitee zur Betreuung Serbisch-Orthodoxer Gastarbeiter in Osterreich) in Linz, (5) Working Group for Voluntary Social Service (Arbeitsge-meinschaft Freiwilliger Sozialer Dienste) in Vienna; (6) Women's Ecumenical Working Group (Okume-nischer Arbeits Kreis der Frauen) in Vienna; (7) International Christian Youth Exchange (Internationaler Christlicher Jugendaustausch), in Vienna; and (8) Telephonic Aid Services, sponsored by Catholics and Evangelicals in Vienna (Telephonseelorge) and Linz (Notrufdienst).

FUTURE TRENDS AND PROSPECTS

A gradual erosion of affiliated Christians is expected for the next 30 years, falling to a low mark of 83.1% in 2025. Muslims and the nonreligious together will likely pass 11% before 2025.

Non-Christians will probably claim more than 15% of Austria's population around AD 2030. In the decades that follow Christians are expected to continue to decline, perhaps falling as low as 75% by AD 2050.

BIBLIOGRAPHY

Alt–katholisches Jahrbuch 1964. Vienna: Alt-katholische Kirche Österreichs, 1964.

'An evaluation of different strategies for church planting in Austria which are transferable to the Roman Catholic European context.' D. W. Trefz. M.A. thesis, Columbia Biblical Seminary and Graduate School of Missions, Columbia, SC, 1991. 207p.

'Austria,' H. Bogensberger, in *Western religion: a country by country sociological enquiry*, p.47–66. H. Mol (ed). The Hague: Mouton, 1972.

Austria. D. Salt & A. F. Radley. *World bibliographical series*, vol. 66. Oxford, UK: CLIO Press, 1986. 319p. (See especially 'Religion,' 108-10).

'Buddhism in Austria,' *Austria Today*, 4 (1983), 41–42.

Christliches Handbuch für Österreich: Kirchen und Missionen. M. Lawson (ed). London: MARC Europe, 1991. 72p. (German and English).

Church, state, and religious dissent: a history of Seventh–day Adventists in Austria, 1890–1975. D. Heinz. Frankfurt: Lang, 1993. 206p.

Die Katholiken in Österreich: ein religionssoziologischer Uberblick. E. Bodzenta. Vienna: Herder, 1962.

Die Zukunft der Evangelischen Kirche in Wien: ein Managementkonzept für eine Non–Profit–Organization. R. Eschenbach, C. Horak & A. Weger (eds). Vienna: Evangelischer Presseverband im Österreich, [1993].

Jahrbuch für die Kirche von Wien, 1970. Vienna: Erzbischöflishen Pastoralamt im Wiener-Dom Verlag,

Kirche in Österreich 1918–1965. F. Klostermann et al. Vienna: Herder, 1966.

Modern Austria. K. Steiner, F. Fellner & H. Feichtlbauer (eds.). Palo Alto, CA: Society for the Promotion of Science and Scholarship, 1980. 507p.

Neue Wege der Nachfolge: katholische Intensivgemeinschaften und Erneuerungsbewegungen in Österreich. F. Valentin. Salzburg: St. Peter, 1981. 219p.

New move forward in Europe: growth patterns of German speaking Baptists in Europe. W. L. Wagner. South Pasadena, CA: William Carey Library, 1978. 362p.
'Priests, parish, and religious practice: a social history of Catholicism in the Archdiocese of Vienna, 1800–1870.' W. D. Bowman. Ph.D. dissertation, Johns Hopkins University, Baltimore, MD, 1990. 390p.
Protestanten in Österreich. G. Reingrabner. Vienna: Hermann Böhlau, 1981. 312p.
'Reaching the unreachable: using a market–sensitive approach to evangelism to reach nominal Christians in Austria.' T. L. Zimmerman. D.Min. thesis, Denver Conservative Baptist Seminary, Denver, CO, 1994. 183p.
Religions in Austria. Austria documentation. Vienna: Federal Press Service, 1990. 55p.
'Skills for intercultural relationships: the first two years of missionary service of Americans in Austria.' M. T. Wilson. D.Ed. thesis, Trinity Evangelical Divinity School, Deerfield, IL, 1993. 195p.
'The Catholic Church and the authoritarian regime in Austria, 1933–1938.' L. S. Gellott. Ph.D. dissertation, University of Wisconsin-Madison, 1982. 420p.
'The Church in Austria,' H. Bogensberger, *Pro Mundi Vita* (Brussels), (1984), 1–36.
The Greek Catholic Church and Ukrainian society in Austrian Galicia. J. Himka. *Millennium series.* Cambridge, MA: Ukrainian Studies Fund, Harvard University, 1986.
The Slovene minority of Carinthia. T. M. Barker with the collaboration of A. Moritsch. *East European Monographs*, no. 169. Boulder, CO: East European Monographs, 1984.
'Theological bridges for evangelism in Austria in light of Austrian history and culture.' D. G. Hotovec. Th.M. thesis, Western Conservative Baptist Seminary, 1992. 104p.
Where is the church heading? F. Koenig. Slough: St. Paul Publications, 1986. 122p.

Country Table 2. **Organized churches and denominations in Austria.**

Official name (bold type = church with over 10% of all affiliated) 1	*Begun* 2	*Type* 3	*Counc* 4	*Congs* 5	*Adults* 6	*Affiliated 1970* 7	*Affiliated 1995* 8	*G%* 9	*Names, notes, and other statistics* (see Codebook, Part 3) 10
Alt-Katholische Kirche in Österreich	1871	I-OCa	UWC.W	50	8,500	26,000	25,000	-0.16	*Old Catholic Ch of Austria.* 1925, Diocese of Vienna. 17n,1s,W=9%,178Yy.
Anglikanische Kirche (D Europe)	c1950	A-plu	awc.W	10	2,000	2,000	3,000	1.64	*Ch of England.* Christ Ch, Vienna; seasonal chaplaincies Innsbruck, Kitzbuhel. 1x.
Arb Mennonitischer Brudergemeinden	1953	P-Men	GF..w	7	300	1,000	450	-3.14	1953, M=Mennonite Brethren Ch of NAmerica. HQ Vienna. 6f.
Armenische Apostolische K: V Wien		O-Arm	Ewc.W	2	1,500	1,000	2,140	0.05	*Armenian Apostolic Ch (Gregorians).* Under C Echmiadzin (USSR). 1n.
Bulgarisch-Orthodoxe Kirche		O-Bul	Mwc.W	4	2,000	2,000	4,000	0.05	*Bulgarian Orthodox Ch. Balgarskata Pravoslavna Crkva.* Under P Sofia.
Bund der Baptisten-Gemeinden in Ö	1869	P-Bap	T.D.a	16	1,064	2,000	1,700	-0.65	*Baptist Union of Austria.* 1965, M=SBC(USA). HQ Vienna. 6n,5f,35Y.
Bund Evangelikaler Gemeinde in O	1991	I-Bap	....E	60	5,000	–	10,000	25.00	*Evangelical Association of Congregations in Austria.* M=Greater Europe Mission.
Christadelphianer		m-Ade	x....	1	20	100	50	0.05	*Christadelphian Ecclesias.* HQ Linz: 2 ecclesias (churches). Pacifist, adventist.
Christengemeinde/Offene Brüder	1919	P-CBr	x.D.e	29	379	1,000	500	-2.73	*Christian Brethren (Open). Plymouth-Brüder.* 10 missionaries from West Germany.
Christliche Wissenschaft		m-Sci	x....	2	160	200	200	0.05	*Christian Science. Church of Christ, Scientist.* M=CCS(Boston, USA). 1m,3w.
Evangelische Kirche AB in Österreich	1781	P-Lut	LWC.W	183	180,000	406,260	359,400	-0.49	*EKAB. Ev Luth Ch (Augsburg Confession).* Rapid growth from Catholics, refugees. 200n,1s.
Evangelische Kirche HB	1781	P-Ref	RWC.W	9	10,600	20,000	14,900	-1.17	*Ev Ch of the Helvetic Confession. Reformed Ch of Austria.* Linked to EKAB. 12n.
Ev Tschechisch-Brüderische Kirche		P-LuR	Rwc..	1	792	3,000	1,200	0.05	*Ceskobratrska Cirkev Evangelicka. Ev Ch of Czech Brethren.* Czechs, Slovaks.
Evangelische-Methodistenkirche	1870	P-Met	VwC.W	8	1,100	2,000	2,200	0.38	*Methodist Ch.* Provisional Annual Conf, C&S Europe Central Conf,UMC(USA). 8n,2f.
Freie Baptistenkirch in Österreichs	1967	I-Bap	xF...	4	57	100	95	-0.20	M=CBFMS(USA). 4f,1t(44),W=95%,2Y.
Freie Christengemeinden in Österreich	1920	P-Pe2	ZF..H	31	2,100	2,000	4,031	2.84	*Free Christians. Philadelphia Ch.* M=SFM(Sweden),AoG(UK,USA). 19n,4f,1s.
Gemeinde Christi	1950	I-Dis	x....	20	2,000	500	3,000	7.43	*Churches of Christ.* M=CC(Non-Instrumental) (USA). Mainly USA expatriates. 22f,1s.
Gemeinde Gottes		P-Hol	x....	3	200	100	500	0.05	M=Ch of God (Anderson) (USA). Small mission of holiness body from USA.
Gemeinschaft Evangelisch Taufgesinnter	1850	P-Hol	x....	10	400	50	600	10.45	*Apostolic Christian Ch (Nazarean).* Linked with same USA body. Mennonite origins.
Griechisch-Orth Kirche: D Österreich		O-Gre	Cwc.W	3	15,000	12,000	20,000	0.05	*Greek Orthodox Ch.* Also E Italy, Switzerland & Hungary. Under EP Constantinople.
Heilsarmee	1927	P-Sal	xwx.e	3	210	10,000	250	-13.72	*Salvation Army, Austria Region*, Switzerland & Austria Territory. HQ Vienna.
International Chapel of Vienna	c1970	P-Uni	.....	1	90	–	129	21.46	Union congregation.
Katholische Kirche Österreichs:	174	R-LEr	BzB.s	4,244	4,827,500	6,613,278	6,129,263	-0.30	*Catholic Ch of Austria.* C=47+3+65. 3q,7s. 2877n 1755x 2399m 7835w 75907Yy
M Salzburg	c 550	R-Lat	Bs	225	414,000	478,667	525,226	0.37	Workers: 40% industrial. 1s. 273n 125x 210m 579w 7140Yy
D Feldkirch	1964	R-Lat	Bs	145	217,000	244,514	275,326	0.48	Vorarlberg. High immigration. Tourism. M=Opus Dei. 164n 35x 50m 472w 3908Yy
D Graz-Seckau	1218	R-Lat	Bs	417	825,000	1,060,000	1,045,484	-0.06	Steiermark. Emigration south, east. 1s. 423n 171x 257m 874w 12809Yy
D Gurk	1071	R-Lat	Bs	987	373,000	459,925	471,855	0.10	Kärnten/Carinthia. Emigration, tourism. 221n 82x 95m 414w 5634Yy
D Innsbruck	1921	R-Lat	Bs	289	341,000	382,000	431,967	0.49	Workers: 40% industrial, 20% rural. 1s. 239n 237x 331m 924w 5465Yy
M Wien (Vienna)	1469	R-Lat	Bosb	931	1,118,000	2,072,510	1,416,822	-1.51	Capital. Immigration, industries. 1s. 607n 439x 683m 2443w 15438Yy
D Eisenstadt	1922	R-Lat	Bs	312	183,000	232,864	231,500	-0.02	Burgenland. Forests. Emigration. 1s. 155n 36x 44m 150w 2341Yy
D Linz	1785	R-Lat	Bosb	477	863,000	1,037,073	1,093,389	0.21	Oberösterreich. Some industry. 1s. 479n 392x 452m 1570w 15174Yy
D Sankt Pölten	1785	R-Lat	Bs	425	460,000	631,895	583,044	-0.32	Niederösterreich. Rural, emigration. 1s. 313n 238x 277m 408w 7905Yy
AN Wettingen-Mehrerau	1227	R-Lat	bsoc	3	300	30	325	10.00	Abbey nullius. In northwest Vorarlberg. M=OCist. 20 religious priests, 40 brothers.
O Österreich *(Byzantine)*	1945	R-Byz	Oosb	9	3,100	3,670	4,000	0.35	For all Catholics of Byzantine rite. 3n 0x 0m 1w 14Yy
AN Wettingen-Mehrerau	1227	R-Lat	bsoc	3	100	130	325	3.73	Abbey nullius. In northwest Vorarlberg.
OM Osterreich	1959	R-Lat	Bs	21	30,000	10,000	50,000	6.65	*Militärordinariat.* 109 n. catholic Military Ordinariate.
KJC der Heiligen der Letzten Tage	c1922	m-LdS	x....	9	3,030	2,675	4,100	1.72	*KJC=Kirche Jesus Christi. Latter-day Saints* (USA). *Mormons.* 60f.
Kinder Gottes	c1975	I-mar	.....	1	13	–	32	5.00	*Children of God.*
Koptische Orthodoxe Kirche	c1975	O-Cop	N....	15	1,800	–	2,570	5.00	*Coptic Orthodox Ch. Church of the Holy Virgin.* Egyptian Arabs.
Neuapostolische Kirche		I-3aX	x....	4	3,000	10,000	5,021	0.05	*NAK, Bezirk Schweiz. New Apostolic Ch*, Switzerland District. HQ Zurich.
Orthodoxe Kirche von Rumänien		O-Rum	Cwc.W	20	10,000	4,000	15,000	0.05	*Romanian Orthodox. Ch. Parohia Ortodoxa Romana din Viena.* Under P Bucharest. 1x.
Religiöse Gesellschaft der Freunde	1938	P-Qua	Q....	2	100	100	200	2.81	*Religious Society of Friends. Quakers.* M=FSC(UK). Work for peace, and refugees.
Russisch-Orth K ausserhalb Russlands	c1920	I-Rus	x....	60	15,000	10,000	20,000	2.81	1975: *D Austria, ROC Outside of Russia* (HQ New York). Anti-Moscow.
Russisch-Orth Kirche (PE Mitteleuropa)		O-Rus	Mwc.W	10	7,000	2,000	10,000	0.05	*Russian Orthodox Ch, D Vienna & Austria.* Patriarchal Exarchate of Moscow. 1 bishop.
Serbisch-Orthodoxe Kirche		O-Ser	Cwc.W	20	40,000	30,000	60,000	0.05	In D Western Europe, Serbian Orthodox Ch, P Belgrade. HQ London. Serbian laborers.
Siebenten-Tags-Adventisten	1947	P-Adv	x....	53	2,925	6,000	6,500	0.32	*SDA, Austrian Union of Chs.* 21n,66m,1j,1s,45t(3150),85Y.
Vereinigte Pfingstkirche	1971	P-Pel	x....	150	7,000	1,000	10,000	4.17	*United Pentecostal Ch. Jesus Only Ch.* M=UPC(USA). Unitarian Pentecostals. 2x,4f.
Volksmission	c1970	I-Non	.....	4	195	–	390	26.95	Small no-church grouping.
Zeugen Jehovas	c1910	m-Jeh	x....	252	18,891	20,000	37,800	2.58	*Jehovah's Witnesses.* Active witnessing under way by 1926. (1975) 716Y. (1995) 740Y.
Other charismatic bodies	c1980	I-3cW	.....	30	1,500	–	3,000	6.67	Including Association of Vineyard Chs (2 chs).
Other Protestant denominations		P-	.....	40	10,000	1,000	17,000	0.05	Total about 15 (see list below), including BIM,BMM.
Other marginal Protestant bodies		m-	.....	20	5,000	1,000	10,000	0.05	Total about 10 (see list below).
Other Orthodox churches		O-	.....	13	6,000	1,000	12,000	0.05	Refugees, including Eastern Apostolic Ch in Iraq (applied to join WCC, rejected).
Totals				**5,404**	**5,192,426**	**7,193,363**	**6,796,221**		

Churches, members, growth, 1900-2025	*Congs*	*Adults*	*Affiliated*	*G%*	*Total denominations*	*6 Megablocs:* *O*	*R*	*A*	*P*	*I*	*m*
Total churches, members, and denominations (mid-1900)	2,000	4,469,000	5,818,000	0.30	9	2	1	0	5	1	0
Total churches, members, and denominations (mid-1970)	4,285	5,525,888	7,193,363	0.30	43	7	1	1	21	5	8
Total churches, members, and denominations (mid-1990)	5,000	5,079,000	6,648,000	-0.39	68	10	1	1	30	12	14
Total churches, members, and denominations (mid-1995)	5,404	5,192,426	6,796,221	0.44	70	10	1	1	30	14	14
Total churches, members, and denominations (mid-2000)	5,400	5,279,000	6,909,670	0.33	70	10	1	1	30	14	14
Total churches, members, and denominations (mid-2025)	5,200	5,195,000	6,800,000	-0.06	107	15	1	1	40	30	20

NOTES ON TABLE ABOVE
NATIONAL COUNCILS (Column 4, 5th letter).
a = member of Austrian Evangelical Alliance, and also observer member of ECCA.
E = Oesterreichische Evangelische Allianz (OEA).
H = Independent Pentecostal Council of Austria
s = Osterreichische Bischofskonferenz (Bishops' Conference of Austria), and also observer in ECCA.
W = Okumenischer Rat der Kirchen in Osterreich (Ecumenical Council of Churches in Austria, ECCA), 1957.
w = associate member of ECCA.
OTHER PROTESTANT DENOMINATIONS. These include: Baptist Mid-Missions (1967), Bible Christian Union (1962), Christian Brethren (Exclusive), Christians Chs/Chs of Christ (1971; 12 missionaries), Estonian Ev Lutheran Ch in Exile (c1945), Evangelical Alliance Mission (TEAM) (1965), Fellowship of Independent Missions (1971), Gemeinde Bibelglaubiger Christen (Pentecostals), Gospel Missionary Union (1966), Vienna Community Ch (English-language).
OTHER MARGINAL PROTESTANT BODIES. These include: Amis de l'Homme (Sayerce Freytag), Anthroposophical Society (Christian Community Ch), General Conference of the New Ch (1 church, 42 members), Greater World Christian Spiritualist League (UK; church in Vienna), Reorganized Ch of JC of Latter-day Saints.

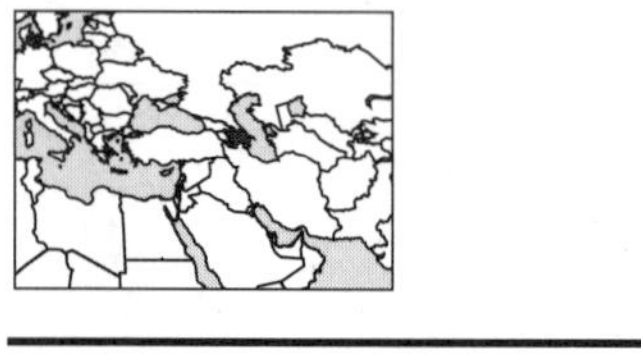

AZERBAIJAN

SECULAR DATA, AD 2000

STATE
Official name: Azarbaijchan Respublikasy (The Azerbaijani Republic).
Short name: Azerbaijan. **Adjective of nationality:** Azerbaijani.
Flag: Blue, red, and green stripes, with crescent moon and star.
Area: 86,600 sq. km. (33,400 sq. mi.).
Government: Federal multiparty republic with a single legislative body, since 1991 (1920 Soviet Socialist republic).
Legislature: National Assembly, 124 members.
Official language: Azerbaijani.
Monetary unit: 1 manat (A.M.) = 100 gopik. **US$1=** A.M. 3,950.
Chief cities: BAKU 1,946,000; Kirovabad (Gandzha, Gyandzha) 302,178; Sumgait 261,187; Mingecaur 100,516; Seki (Nucha) 69,885.
Political divisions: 4 provinces.
Armed forces: 66,000.

DEMOGRAPHY
Population: 7,734,000.
Population density: 89.3/sq. km. (231.5/sq. mi.).
Under 15 years: 2,213,000.
Growth rate p.a.: 0.77% (births 15.69, deaths 6.72).
Mortality: Infant, per 1,000: 32.2; **Maternal per 100,000:** 22.0.
Life expectancy: 71 (male 67, female 75).
Household size: 4.8. **Floor area per person, sq.m:** 12.3.
Major languages: Azerbaijani, Russian, Armenia, Ukrainian.
Urban dwellers: 57.26%. **Urban growth rate p.a.:** 1.4%.
Labor force: 45%.

ETHNOLINGUISTIC PEOPLES
85.6% Azerbaijani (Azeri Turk); 3.2% Armenian (Ermeni); 3.0% Russian; 2.3% Lezgian (Lezghi); 1.9% Talysh (Lenkoran).

ECONOMY
National income p.a. per person: US$479; **per family:** US$2,303.

EDUCATION
Adult literacy: 97% (male 98%, female 95%). **Schools:** 4,578. **Universities:** 23. **School enrolment:** female/male: 95%/98%.

HEALTH
Access to health services: 30%. **Access to safe water:** 50%. **Hospitals:** 749 (105 beds per 10,000). **Doctors:** 29,000. **Blind:** 7,000. **Deaf:** 469,700. **Murder rate:** 8. **Lepers:** 10,000. **Underweight prevalence under 5:** 10%.

LITERATURE
New book titles p.a.: 400 (52 p.a. per million). **Periodicals:** 69. **Newspapers:** 3 dailies.

COMMUNICATION (per 1,000 people)
Phones: 85 (7% mobile). **Radios:** 200. **TV sets:** 212. **Daily newspaper circulation:** 28. **Computers:** 20.

REFUGEES
Citizen refugees in other countries: 390,000. **Alien refugees from other countries:** 238,000. **Internal displacement:** 670,000.

HUMAN LIFE AND LIBERTY (optimum condition=100.0%)
HDI: 63.6. **HSI:** 25.0. **HFI:** 25.0. **EFL:** 6.0.

Country Table 1. **Religious adherents in Azerbaijan, AD 1900-2025.**

Year	1900		1970		mid-1990		Annual change, 1990-2000				mid-1995		mid-2000		mid-2025	
Name	Adherents	%	Adherents	%	Adherents	%	Natural	Conversion	Total	Rate	Adherents	%	Adherents	%	Adherents	%
Muslims	1,330,800	89.3	3,153,800	61.0	5,835,150	81.5	46,867	16,792	63,659	1.04	6,276,000	83.0	6,471,738	83.7	8,489,700	90.3
Nonreligious	500	0.0	999,500	19.3	887,250	12.4	7,126	-12,011	-4,885	-0.56	850,000	11.2	838,405	10.8	500,000	5.3
Christians	**148,700**	**10.0**	**263,200**	**5.1**	**352,500**	**4.9**	**2,832**	**-2,286**	**546**	**0.15**	**368,000**	**4.9**	**357,957**	**4.6**	**365,300**	**3.9**
PROFESSION																
crypto-Christians	0	0.0	150,000	2.9	55,080	0.8	442	-4,750	-4,308	-14.13	15,300	0.2	12,000	0.2	2,000	0.0
professing Christians	**148,700**	**10.0**	**113,200**	**2.2**	**297,420**	**4.2**	**2,389**	**2,465**	**4,854**	**1.52**	**352,700**	**4.7**	**345,957**	**4.5**	**363,300**	**3.9**
AFFILIATION																
unaffiliated Christians	5,000	0.3	0	0.0	620	0.0	5	-52	-47	-12.94	579	0.0	155	0.0	300	0.0
affiliated Christians	**143,700**	**9.6**	**263,200**	**5.1**	**351,880**	**4.9**	**2,826**	**-2,234**	**592**	**0.17**	**367,421**	**4.9**	**357,802**	**4.6**	**365,000**	**3.9**
Orthodox	142,700	9.6	250,200	4.8	340,000	4.8	2,731	-2,201	530	0.15	355,000	4.7	345,302	4.5	350,000	3.7
Roman Catholics	1,000	0.1	12,000	0.2	8,000	0.1	64	-114	-50	-0.64	8,000	0.1	7,500	0.1	8,000	0.1
Independents	0	0.0	0	0.0	2,500	0.0	20	90	110	3.71	3,041	0.0	3,600	0.1	5,000	0.1
Protestants	0	0.0	1,000	0.0	1,380	0.0	11	-9	2	0.14	1,380	0.0	1,400	0.0	2,000	0.0
Trans-megabloc groupings																
Evangelicals	0	0.0	800	0.0	440	0.0	4	-3	1	0.22	434	0.0	450	0.0	800	0.0
Pentecostals/Charismatics	0	0.0	100	0.0	7,900	0.1	63	147	210	2.39	8,751	0.1	10,000	0.1	13,000	0.1
Great Commission Christians	**14,900**	**1.0**	**72,400**	**1.4**	**114,500**	**1.6**	**920**	**315**	**1,235**	**1.03**	**122,500**	**1.6**	**126,853**	**1.6**	**145,700**	**1.6**
Atheists	0	0.0	750,000	14.5	55,000	0.8	442	-2,340	-1,898	-4.14	39,400	0.5	36,023	0.5	20,000	0.2
Jews	10,000	0.7	5,000	0.1	28,000	0.4	225	-179	46	0.16	28,300	0.4	28,461	0.4	25,000	0.3
Baha'is	0	0.0	500	0.0	1,100	0.0	9	24	33	2.67	1,300	0.0	1,432	0.0	3,000	0.0
World A (unevangelized persons)	1,221,800	82.0	3,879,000	75.0	4,739,258	66.2	38,071	-24,785	13,286	0.28	4,953,637	65.5	4,872,420	63.0	5,500,755	58.5
World B (evangelized non-Christians)	119,500	8.0	1,029,800	19.9	2,067,242	28.9	16,598	27,071	43,669	1.93	2,241,168	29.6	2,503,623	32.4	3,536,945	37.6
World C (Christians)	148,700	10.0	263,200	5.1	352,500	4.9	2,832	-2,286	546	0.15	368,000	4.9	357,957	4.6	365,300	3.9
Country's population	**1,490,000**	**100.0**	**5,172,000**	**100.0**	**7,159,000**	**100.0**	**57,501**	**0**	**57,501**	**0.78**	**7,562,806**	**100.0**	**7,734,000**	**100.0**	**9,403,000**	**100.0**

COLUMNS, ROWS.
For meanings and definitions, see Codebook (Part 3). Note that, by definition, total 'Christians' = professing + crypto-Christians, which also = affiliated + unaffiliated Christians, and also = Great Commission Christians + latent Christians. Percentages may not always total exactly, due to rounding.

NOTES ON RELIGIONS.
ATHEISTS. Mainly Russians, Armenians, and Ukrainians.
BAHA'IS. By 1996, Baha'i had become organized under 14 LSAs (local spiritual assemblies).
JEWS. Including 15,000 Caucasian mountain Jews and 6,000 Kurdish Jews.

Great Commission Instrument Panel: status of Azerbaijan (for explanation see start of Part 4)

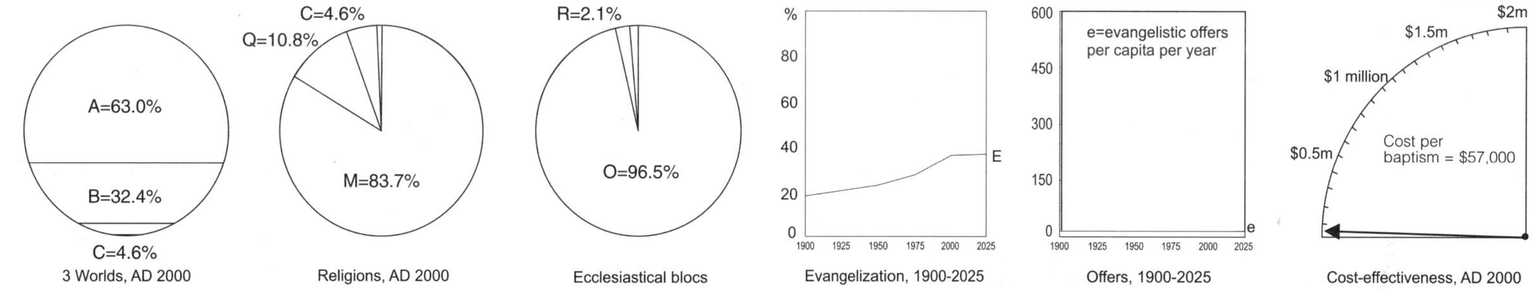

Country status. Azerbaijan, a former republic of the Soviet Union, is one of the world's oldest centers of oil production. Its strategic location in Western Asia between Iran, Russia, and Armenia have made it important in the region's history since ancient times. Other products include cotton, grain, rice, and fruit.

HUMAN LIFE AND LIBERTY

Human rights and freedoms. Azerbaijan has not made much progress toward achieving a parliamentary form of government or a democratic society. The loss of a large portion of the Nagorno-Karabakh Enclave to Armenian rebels led to the fall of the first democratically elected president, Abulfez Elcibey, and the rise of former Communist Party leader, Heydar Aliyev as president. Under Aliyev the old Ministry of National Security has been reactivated and its surveillance activities have resumed. Armenian offensives in the Nagorno-Karabakh Enclave led to the flight of over one million Azers to Azerbaijan. The war and the attendant social instability gave rise to many human rights violations. Under the state of emergency enacted in April 1993, press censorship was introduced, demonstrations banned, travel regulations tightened, and police were given permission to enter homes without warrants. President Aliyev has concentrated power into his own hands and suppressed political opposition. Armenian residents in Azerbaijan face inhuman conditions and are subjected to kidnapping and terrorism. The regime has instigated anti-Armenian hysteria in order to justify its seizure of power as well as its continued abuse of human rights.

NON-CHRISTIAN RELIGIONS

Zoroastrianism, mixed with pagan fire-worshipping practices, was the religion of Azerbaijan before the coming of Islam. Though Zoroastrianism is associated more with ancient Persia, Zoroaster/Zarathustra was born in what is now Azerbaijan in the 7th century BC. In the time of Alexander the Great, a certain rocky slope near Baku burned with continual flames of fire (from escaping methane) and Azerbaijani likely means land of fire. The Ateshgah fire-worship temple at Surakhany, on the Apsheron Peninsula near Baku, remains a tourist attraction today. Until the Soviets stopped the practice, Zoroastrian pilgrims visited it and other holy sites in Azerbaijan. Remnants of Zoroastrianism remain in Azerbaijani culture, notably the continuing celebration of the festival of Navroz on 21 March, which marks the start of the Zoroastrian new year.

Islam came to Azerbaijan with the Arab invasion in the 7th century, followed by the Turkish invasion in the 11th century. The country had at least 2,000 active mosques before the Soviet era. Most of them were closed in the repressive years of the 1930s, though some were re-opened during World War II. The old Shiite and Sunni leadership councils, disbanded by the Bolsheviks, were also restored then. In the 1980s only 18 official mosques remained open in the country, including 7 in Baku. The Djuma Mosque in the capital had become a Museum of Carpets and Folk Crafts. The country then had less than 100 legal clerics, and no religious schools or publications. But underground Islam was relatively strong, with a network of religious schools, more than 1,000 unofficial prayer houses, and about 300 holy places maintained for devotion.

Islam had for centuries been the traditional religion of the majority ethnic Azerbaijani people, who constituted about 83% of the national population in 1995. In the 20th century that position was challenged. Though in 1900 the nation was 89.3% Muslim, by 1970 Azerbaijan was only 61.0% Muslim—with the decline explained by communism, anti-religious propaganda, a departure from traditional Islamic education, and the secularizing forces of modernity. Soviet anti-religious propaganda was more successful in Azerbaijan than in the other predominantly-Muslim republics. Also, persecution was more severe. The Shiite Islam of Azerbaijan was led by an organized, visible hierarchy that posed a greater threat to the power of the state, and that presented an easier target.

Muslims. Meeting of religious leaders in Communist days. Most Muslims are Shias.

Country summary. **Worlds A, B, C by ethnolinguistic peoples, cities, and major civil divisions in Azerbaijan.**

	PEOPLES							CITIES							CIVIL DIVISIONS						
World	Num	Pop 2000	C%	Christians	E%	U%	Unevangelized	Num	Pop 2000	C%	Christians	E%	U%	Unevangelized	Num	Pop 2000	C%	Christians	E%	U%	Unevangelized
A	22	7,184,246	0.04	2,939	32	68	4,869,759	7	2,615,851	7.60	198,811	43	57	1,491,864	3	7,524,533	2.95	221,639	35	65	4,867,325
B	2	18,063	39.46	7,128	93	7	1,257	0	0	0.00	0	0	0	0	0	0	0.00	0	0	0	0
C	11	531,707	65.40	347,734	100	0	1,841	0	0	0.00	0	0	0	0	1	209,481	65.00	136,163	97	3	5,530
Total	**35**	**7,734,016**	**4.63**	**357,801**	**37**	**63**	**4,872,857**	**7**	**2,615,851**	**7.60**	**198,811**	**43**	**57**	**1,491,864**	**4**	**7,734,014**	**4.63**	**357,802**	**37**	**63**	**4,872,855**

The country experienced a resurgence of interest in Islam from the start of the Gorbachev era. Once again Korans were available, children received religious instruction, and mosques were re-opened. Thanks to the provision of Turkish teachers, the Koran was being taught throughout the Azerbaijani educational system. Without authorization, people removed locks from the doors of mosques, entered, and began praying. In 1988, 30 mosques were officially opened, and in 1989, 30 more. By 1994 about 200 mosques were functioning officially. In 1990 the government once again allowed flights to Mecca for the hajj, though few used the opportunity. Iran, Oman, and Saudi Arabia sent religious teachers and money for the building of new mosques. In 1991 a Muslim seminary was established. In 1995, 6 new Islamic centers were built with foreign funding. With the help of funding from Saudi Arabia, the small Islamic Institute of Baku was upgraded to an Islamic University with strong ties to its counterpart in Medina, expecting soon to be teaching 500 students. Thus with the fall of communism Islam became again an important symbol of national identity and citizens enjoyed a new freedom of worship, so that Islam returned to a position close to its former place of national dominance, claiming 83.0% of the population by 1995.

Islam is the national religion, the great majority being Shias. Although the state is secular, Islam has great influence.

Though many remained Sunni, the majority of Azerbaijanís Muslims have been Shiite since the 16th century. In 1995, the Muslims of Azerbaijan were about 70% Shiite and 30% Sunni. The Sheikh ul-Islam gives spiritual direction to the Muslim communities of Georgia, Armenia, and Azerbaijan. The incumbent in 1996, sheik Allahshukur Pashazade, had studied in Qum, Iran under the Ayatollah Shariat-madari. His deputy is Sunni. At independence in 1991, the former Muslim Spiritual Board of Transcaucasia in Baku became the Supreme Religious Council of the Caucasus Peoples, led by the Sheikh ul-Islam. The leading mosque of the Shiites in the capital is the Taza-Pir mosque, and for the Sunnis, the Azhdarbek mosque. But elsewhere in the country the two groups often share the same mosque and even join in the same religious ceremonies. This is extremely rare in the Muslim world - possibly unique. Shiites dominate the cities. The eastern, southern, and western districts tend to be more Shiite, and the central and northern districts Sunni. Sunnis are the majority in the cities of Kuba, Nukha, and Shemakha. Folk Islam is strong. Through the Communist era and since, Islam has remained stronger in the rural areas, where illegal Muslim clergy continued to serve, illegal shrines continued to be visited, and illegal religious practices endured—such as Shiite Muharram (bride price) and the fast of Ramadan. Soviet media railed against survivals of the past (= traditional Muslim practices) and the cult of holy places (= pir, usually tombs of important Muslim saints and martyrs). Thousands continue to make pilgrimages to these holy sites. Other rural people continue pre-Islamic shamanist or animist beliefs and practices, venerating certain sacred places, trees, and rocks. On one holiday (Su Jeddim) Azerbaijanis bathe in certain holy streams to seek communion with ancestors. The oak and iron trees are considered sacred and cannot be cut down. Pieces of bark from the iron tree are used for spiritual protection or power. Also in the countryside, sufi brotherhoods have been strong. Large public religious festivals are celebrated and dramas are staged.

Judaism. Azerbaijan was home to about 28,000 Jews in 1995.

CHRISTIANITY

As early as the 3rd century AD there were churches in present-day Azerbaijan. An isolated indigenous group, the Udin, numbering about 6,500 in 1995, were missed by the Muslim conquests and remain Christian. In 1900 almost all of the non-Muslims in the country were Orthodox - mainly ethnic Russians and Armenians. Christianity has endured persecution both from communists and Muslims. In Nagorno-Karabakh in 1931 there were 112 Armenian churches and 18 monasteries. Within 6 months, all were closed by the authorities. In 1988 directives from Moscow allowed a few to open, though this was forbidden from Baku. One of these, in Amaraz, was attacked by Azerbaijani troops 2 days after being officially opened. Since World War II there has been little Russian immigration into Azerbaijan, so the Russian Orthodox Church has been stable. Almost no Muslims have converted to Orthodoxy, nor Orthodox to Islam. Still in 1995 more than 90% of Azerbaijani Christians were Orthodox, and were ethnic Russians and Armenians. In the mid-1990s, most of the Armenians were living in the disputed area of Nagorno-Karabakh (which was actually controlled by Armenia, as a result of the war in the early 1990s).

PROTESTANT CHURCHES. The American Presbyterians began missionary work in Azerbaijan in 1834. They established a mission station at Urmla in 1872 and another at Tabriz in 1873. Their plan in Tabriz was to convert Armenians, but soon Muslims also came to their meetings. In 1893 they built a hospital in Tabriz. A fund was established in 1864 for the translation of the Bible into Azerbaijani and by 1893 the complete Bible was published. Still, the Protestant impact on the nation overall was extremely limited. In 1961 only one Soviet Baptist church (AUCECB) was known in Azerbaijan, in Baku, with 600 members. They were listed as an Initsiativniksi - Baptists who held to their right to evangelize and who thus were in confrontation with the state. Some Western Christians have entered Azerbaijan since the 1980s for humanitarian and educational work, most of them in Baku. The Ichthus Christian Fellowship of Britain has played a leading role in this. In the mid-1990s some older churches in the countryside were emerging from the underground, and new fellowships were starting. By 1995 there were a few hundred ethnic Azeri Christians in Protestant churches, notably in newer churches begun since independence. Christian Solidarity International in 1996 opened two rehabilitation centers for landmine victims in Karabakh. By 1996 there were 4 Protestant churches registered in Baku, and new fellowships in Ganja, the nations second city. One independent Evangelical church, begun in 1992 in Baku, by 1994 had 300 people attending and 200 enrolled in their evening Bible School. Services were held in English, Russian, and Azeri. Special evangelistic meetings in 1995 drew an attendance of 1,000 and a baptism of 50 in the Caspian Sea soon followed.

CATHOLIC CHURCH. The Holy See has diplomatic relations with Azerbaijan and in AD 2000 is represented to government and the Catholic hierarchy by a nuncio residing in Tiflis, Georgia.

Indigenous missions. The nascent Christian church in Azerbaijan has not yet formed missionary structures or sent out missionaries.

CHURCH AND STATE

In the 16th century Ismail I (reigned 1486-1524), the first shah of the Safavid dynasty, established Shia Islam as the state religion. In 1918 Muslim nationalists declared the 'Azerbaijan People's Democratic Republic', formed the 'Army of Islam', and defeated the Bolsheviks in Baku. This Islamic republic was short-lived, however, as the Ottoman Turks occupied the city later in the same year, followed soon by the British occupation that followed WWI. Most of Azerbaijan was incorporated into the Russian empire in 1806, and the entire country became part of the USSR in 1921. Prince Grigori Golitsyn, who ruled from 1896-1904, was pro-Islamic. In 1903 he ordered Armenian church lands confiscated. The violent Armenian reaction led to the restoration of church lands. In 1905 a new Russian court restored a pro-Armenian position, Muslim mullahs were brought under state control, and then, with the tables turned, Muslim religious properties were confiscated. The Russian Orthodox Church became active in evangelizing Muslims. In the Soviet era state operatives succeeded in infiltrating and compromising the Muslim clergy to the point that citizens were afraid to visit mosques for fear of being reported.

BROADCASTING AND MEDIA

The popularity of Islamic programming from Radio Tabriz (Iran) in Azerbaijan has proven radio can be an effective way to reach the country. Azeri-language broadcasts are beamed into the country from FEBA (Seychelles) with the help of Elam, a British Christian group. Armenian and Russian, the next two largest languages, are covered by TWR. IBRA programs originating in Malta can also be heard.

Satellite TV programs are received mainly in Arabic. The 'Jesus' Film has been shown on television, where it was watched by 2.5 million people.

INTERDENOMINATIONAL ORGANIZATIONS

In 1992 representatives from the WCC and CEC, on the invitation of the Sheik ul-Islam, met with the President of Azerbaijan and key advisors as part of an ecumenical effort to help end the war with Armenia. In 1994, Orthodox, Baptists, Seventh-day Adventists, and representatives from several mission organizations joined together to form the Bible Society of Azerbaijan. Many Protestant groups with an interest in assisting the national development of Azerbaijan have banded together in an informal alliance that met annually in the mid-1990s. In 1994, 40 representatives from 30 agencies involved in radio, literature, relief, and church planting met in Norway.

FUTURE TRENDS AND PROSPECTS

Following the collapse of Communism, Islam has expanded to fill the nonreligious and atheistic void. These gains will probably continue for Muslims until AD 2025 (80.3%), while Christians are expected to decline to only 3.9% by AD 2025.

After AD 2025 Christians will likely grow slowly perhaps reaching 5% by AD 2050. Islam will likely remain just under 90% well into the future.

BIBLIOGRAPHY

Azerbaijan: mosques, turrets, palaces. K. Gink & I. Turansky. Budapest: Kossuth Printing House, 1979.

Country profile: Azerbaijan. London: International Institute for the Study of Islam and Christianity, 1994. 119p.

Russian Azerbaijan, 1905–1920: the shaping of a national identity in a Muslim community. T. Swietochowski. Cambridge, UK: Cambridge University Press, 1985.

The Azerbaijani Turks: power and identity under Russian rule. A. L. Altstadt. Stanford, CA: Hoover Press, 1992. 330p.

'The forgotten factor: the Shi'ite mullahs of Azerbaijan,' A. L. Altstadt, in *Passé Turco-Tatar, Présent Soviétique.* C. Lemercier-Quelquejay, G. Veinstein & S. E. Wimbush (eds). Paris: Editions Peeters, 1986.

The Muharram mysteries among the Azerbeijan Turks of Caucasia: an academical dissertation. I. Lassy. Helsingfors, 1916. 288p.

Country Table 2. **Organized churches and denominations in Azerbaijan.**

Official name (bold type = church with over 10% of all affiliated) 1	*Begun* 2	*Type* 3	*Counc* 4	*Congs* 5	*Adults* 6	*Affiliated 1970* 7	*Affiliated 1995* 8	*G%* 9	*Names, notes, and other statistics* (see Codebook, Part 3) 10
Armenian Apostolic Church	60	O-Arm	E....	5	132,000	100,000	195,000	0.05	*Gregorians. Under C Echmiadzin. Most are in disputed region of Nagorno-Karabakh.*
Baptist Churches	c1950	P-Bap	T....	50	700	1,000	1,080	0.31	Remnant of Soviet-era AUCECB, mostly Russians, some Azeris. Ukrainians. M=SBC-IMB.
Catholic Church (AA Caucasus)	c1930	R-Lat	O....	2	4,640	12,000	8,000	-1.61	Latin rite, with concessions to other rites: Ukrainians, Armenians, et alia.
Georgian Orthodox Church	c1880	O-Geo	M....	10	6,000	10,200	10,000	-0.08	No churches remain.
Greater Grace Churches	1991	I-3cZ	.....	10	700	–	1,200	25.00	HQ Baltimore, MD (USA). Russians, many Azeris.
Icthus Fellowship	c1990	I-3cZ	x....	2	80	–	100	20.00	HQ in London (England). Based in second largest city Ganje. Azeri war refugees.
Independent Pentecostal Church	c1975	I-3pZ	.....	5	300	–	400	5.00	Formerly mostly Russians, now many Azaris.
New Apostolic Church	c1992	I-3aX	x....	4	200	–	341	33.33	*NAC,NAK.* M=Neuapostolische Kirche (HQ Zurich, Switzerland).
Russian Orthodox Church	c1850	O-Rus	.....	7	100,500	140,000	150,000	0.28	Rapid emigration.
Seventh-day Adventist Church		P-Adv	x....	2	60	–	100	0.05	*SDA.* Small number of immigrants from Russia.
Word of Life Church	1990	I-3cZ	.....	3	800	–	1,000	20.00	Large church in Baku. Baptisms in Caspian Sea. Swedish pastor.
Other Protestant churches	c1990	P-	.....	2	120	–	200	20.00	M=YWAM,SCI,Santal Mission, FI.
Totals				**102**	**246,100**	**263,200**	**367,421**		

Churches, members, growth, 1900-2025	*Congs*	*Adults*	*Affiliated*	*G%*	*Total denominations*	*6 Megablocs:* *O*	*R*	*A*	*P*	*I*	*m*
Total churches, members, and denominations (mid-1900)	20	89,900	143,700	0.87	4	3	0	0	1	0	0
Total churches, members, and denominations (mid-1970)	51	164,621	263,200	0.87	5	3	1	0	1	0	0
Total churches, members, and denominations (mid-1990)	100	236,000	351,880	1.46	11	3	1	0	6	1	0
Total churches, members, and denominations (mid-1995)	102	246,100	367,421	0.87	18	3	1	0	9	5	0
Total churches, members, and denominations (mid-2000)	100	240,000	357,802	-0.53	19	3	1	0	10	5	0
Total churches, members, and denominations (mid-2025)	110	244,000	365,000	0.08	54	15	1	0	15	20	3

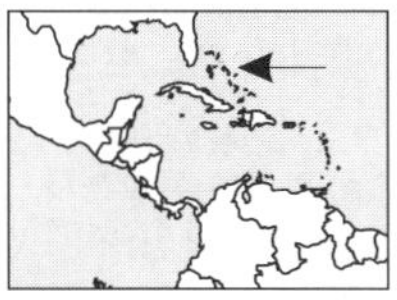

BAHAMAS

SECULAR DATA, AD 2000

STATE
Official name: The Commonwealth of the Bahamas.
Short name: Bahamas. **Adjective of nationality:** Bahamian.
Flag: Black triangle, 2 aquamarine stripes with central gold band.
Area: 13,939 sq. km. (5,382 sq. mi.).
Government: Parliamentary state (constitutional monarchy), since 1973 (1626 British colony, 1717 crown colony, 1964 self-government, 1973 Independence).
Legislature: House of Assembly, 40 members; Senate, 16 members.
Official language: English.
Monetary unit: 1 Bahamian dollar (B$) = 100 cents. **US$1=** B$1.00.
Chief cities: NASSAU 162,719.
Political divisions: 19 provinces.
Armed forces: 900.

DEMOGRAPHY
Population: 307,000.
Population density: 21.9/sq. km. (56.9/sq. mi.).
Under 15 years: 93,000.
Growth rate p.a.: 1.56% (births 20.64, deaths 5.01).
Mortality: Infant, per 1,000: 13.9; **Maternal per 100,000:** 100.0.
Life expectancy: 75 (male 72, female 78).
Household size: 3.8. **Floor area per person, sq.m:** 40.0.
Major languages: English, Bahamas Creole (Indo-European Creole), French Creole, Greek, Chinese.
Urban dwellers: 88.53%. **Urban growth rate p.a.:** 1.7%.
Labor force: 51%.

ETHNOLINGUISTIC PEOPLES
67.5% Black; 14.2% Mulatto; 12.0% British; 3.0% Haitian Black; 2.4% USA White.

ECONOMY
National income p.a. per person: US$11,940; **per family:** US$45,372.

EDUCATION
Adult literacy: 98% (male 98%, female 98%). **Schools:** 227.
Universities: 1. **School enrolment:** female/male: 99%/97%.

HEALTH
Access to health services: 95%. **Access to safe water:** 97%.
Hospitals: 5 (40 beds per 10,000). **Doctors:** 357.
Blind: 110. **Deaf:** 18,100. **Murder rate:** 17.
Lepers: 60.

LITERATURE
New book titles p.a.: 110 (350 p.a. per million). **Periodicals:** 17.
Newspapers: 3 dailies.

COMMUNICATION (per 1,000 people)
Phones: 277 **(6% mobile). Radios:** 282. **TV sets:** 233.
Daily newspaper circulation: 126. **Computers:** 250.

REFUGEES
Alien refugees from other countries: 200.

HUMAN LIFE AND LIBERTY (optimum condition=100.0%)
HDI: 89.4. **HSI:** 90.0. **HFI:** 90.0. **EFL:** 60.0.

Country Table 1. **Religious adherents in the Bahamas, AD 1900-2025.**

Year	*1900*		*1970*		*mid-1990*		*Annual change, 1990-2000*				*mid-1995*		*mid-2000*		*mid-2025*	
Name	*Adherents*	*%*	*Adherents*	*%*	*Adherents*	*%*	*Natural*	*Conversion*	*Total*	*Rate*	*Adherents*	*%*	*Adherents*	*%*	*Adherents*	*%*
Christians	**51,900**	**97.9**	**164,990**	**97.2**	**239,000**	**93.7**	**4,829**	**-408**	**4,421**	**1.71**	**261,000**	**93.1**	**283,205**	**92.3**	**375,500**	**90.5**
PROFESSION																
professing Christians	**51,900**	**97.9**	**164,990**	**97.2**	**239,000**	**93.7**	**4,829**	**-408**	**4,421**	**1.71**	**261,000**	**93.1**	**283,205**	**92.3**	**375,500**	**90.5**
AFFILIATION																
unaffiliated Christians	2,130	4.0	11,172	6.6	13,610	5.3	278	-4	274	1.85	15,396	5.5	16,354	5.3	17,150	4.1
affiliated Christians	**49,770**	**93.9**	**153,818**	**90.6**	**225,390**	**88.4**	**4,551**	**-405**	**4,146**	**1.70**	**245,604**	**87.6**	**266,851**	**86.9**	**358,350**	**86.4**
Protestants	20,140	38.0	85,780	50.5	137,000	53.7	2,794	223	3,017	2.01	151,204	53.9	167,171	54.5	231,000	55.7
Roman Catholics	5,030	9.5	33,220	19.6	42,500	16.7	867	-317	550	1.22	45,237	16.1	48,000	15.6	57,000	13.7
Anglicans	24,400	46.0	30,000	17.7	27,800	10.9	567	-617	-50	-0.18	27,500	9.8	27,300	8.9	25,000	6.0
Independents	200	0.4	3,341	2.0	14,000	5.5	285	215	500	3.10	17,133	6.1	19,000	6.2	35,000	8.4
Marginal Christians	0	0.0	1,014	0.6	3,700	1.5	75	55	130	3.06	4,140	1.5	5,000	1.6	10,000	2.4
Orthodox	0	0.0	463	0.3	390	0.2	8	-9	-1	-0.26	390	0.1	380	0.1	350	0.1
Trans-megabloc groupings																
Evangelicals	10,600	20.0	42,500	25.0	73,900	29.0	1,507	163	1,670	2.06	82,561	29.5	90,600	29.5	129,000	31.1
Pentecostals/Charismatics	0	0.0	10,000	5.9	39,000	15.3	795	205	1,000	2.31	43,974	15.7	49,000	16.0	72,000	17.4
Great Commission Christians	**530**	**1.0**	**15,300**	**9.0**	**32,300**	**12.7**	**659**	**165**	**824**	**2.30**	**35,800**	**12.8**	**40,536**	**13.2**	**57,000**	**13.7**
Nonreligious	0	0.0	2,600	1.5	10,450	4.1	213	367	580	4.51	12,890	4.6	16,246	5.3	30,000	7.2
Spiritists	1,000	1.9	1,700	1.0	3,600	1.4	73	41	114	2.78	4,000	1.4	4,736	1.5	6,500	1.6
Baha'is	0	0.0	230	0.1	1,000	0.4	20	4	24	2.18	1,100	0.4	1,241	0.4	1,800	0.4
Jews	100	0.2	480	0.3	800	0.3	16	-4	12	1.37	840	0.3	917	0.3	900	0.2
Chinese folk-religionists	0	0.0	0	0.0	150	0.1	3	0	3	2.06	170	0.1	184	0.1	300	0.1
World A (unevangelized persons)	106	0.2	169	0.1	765	0.3	13	9	22	2.99	841	0.3	921	0.3	1,660	0.4
World B (evangelized non-Christians)	994	1.9	4,587	2.8	15,235	6.0	312	399	711	4.15	18,544	6.5	22,874	7.3	37,840	9.1
World C (Christians)	51,900	97.9	164,990	97.1	239,000	93.7	4,829	-408	4,421	1.71	261,000	93.2	283,205	92.4	375,500	90.5
Country's population	**53,000**	**100.0**	**169,747**	**100.0**	**255,000**	**100.0**	**5,154**	**0**	**5,154**	**1.87**	**280,386**	**100.0**	**307,000**	**100.0**	**415,000**	**100.0**

COLUMNS, ROWS.
For meanings and definitions, see Codebook (Part 3). Note that, by definition, total 'Christians' = professing + crypto-Christians, which also = affiliated + unaffiliated Christians, and also = Great Commission Christians + latent Christians. Percentages may not always total exactly, due to rounding.

CENSUSES.
6.XII.1953: 55.1% Protestants, 24.1% Anglicans, 15.6% Roman Catholics, 4.7% other religionists, 0.5% nonreligious. **15.XI.1963** (de jure): 55.1% Protestants and Black indigenous, 24.2% Anglicans, 20.3% Roman Catholics, 0.4% marginal Protestants. **7.IV.1970** (de jure): 51.1% Protestants and Black indigenous, 22.7% Anglicans, 22.5% Roman Catholics, 2.5% nonreligious, 0.6% marginal Protestants, 0.3% Orthodox, 0.3% Jews.

NOTES ON RELIGIONS
BAHA'IS. Growth from 1 local spiritual assembly (1964) to 4 (1973), and to 6 (1996).
INDEPENDENTS. In 10 denominations in 1995 (see Table 2).
PROTESTANTS. Including many USA expatriates.
SPIRITISTS. Afro-American spiritists practice Obeah, syncretizing Christianity with African tribal religions. It is practiced by many including numerous church members. There are also Rastafarians, from Jamaica.

Country status. Bahamas is an island nation consisting of an archipelago of 700 islands off the coast of Florida, USA. It is linked to the United Kingdom by constitutional ties and a common sovereign. Tourism is the main industry.

HUMAN LIFE AND LIBERTY

Human need and development. Although a developing country, Bahamas has a strong economy based mostly on tourism and offshore banking. It has one of the highest per capita gross domestic product in the region and also one of the highest standards of living. Literacy is close to 98%, and life expectancy is 72 years for males and 78 for females.

Human rights and freedoms. The Constitution provides for the protection of fundamental human rights and freedom from discrimination on the basis of sex, race, religion, national origin, and political beliefs. The principal human rights problems are the abuse of detainees and prisoners by police and prison guards,

Great Commission Instrument Panel: status of the Bahamas (for explanation see start of Part 4)

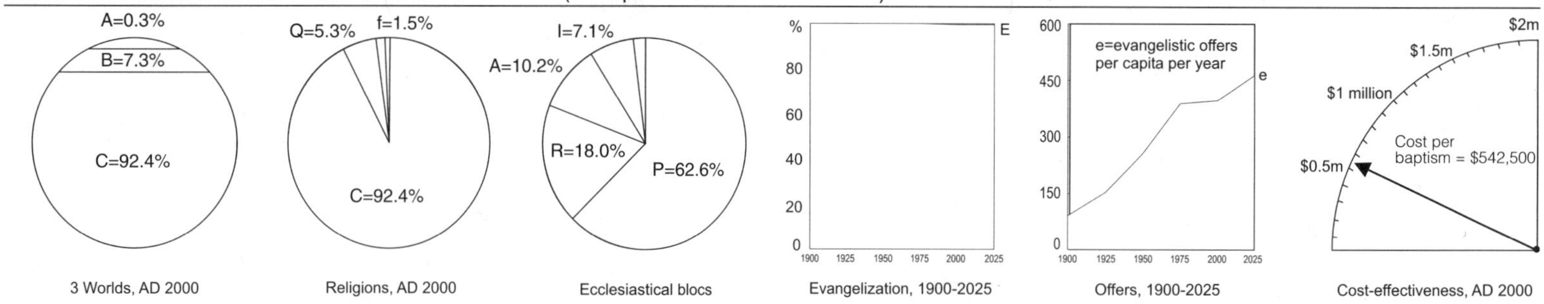

Country summary. **Worlds A, B, C by ethnolinguistic peoples, cities, and major civil divisions in the Bahamas.**																						
	PEOPLES							*CITIES*							*CIVIL DIVISIONS*							
World	*Num*	*Pop 2000*	*C%*	*Christians*	*E%*	*U%*	*Unevangelized*	*Num*	*Pop 2000*	*C%*	*Christians*	*E%*	*U%*	*Unevangelized*	*Num*	*Pop 2000*	*C%*	*Christians*	*E%*	*U%*	*Unevangelized*
A	1	920	0.22	2	48	52	476	0	0	0.00	0	0	0	0	0	0	0.00	0	0	0	0
B	1	613	50.08	307	100	0	3	0	0	0.00	0	0	0	0	0	0	0.00	0	0	0	0
C	7	304,997	87.39	266,543	100	0	381	1	162,719	86.00	139,938	100	0	553	19	306,531	87.06	266,851	100	0	861
Total	**9**	**306,530**	**87.06**	**266,852**	**100**	**0**	**860**	**1**	**162,719**	**86.00**	**139,938**	**100**	**0**	**553**	**19**	**306,531**	**87.06**	**266,851**	**100**	**0**	**861**

the miserable condition of the prison system, and the growing antagonism toward Haitian immigrants. Conditions at Fox Hill prison, Bahamas' only prison facility, are notorious with as many as 6 prisoners housed in 6 by 8 foot cells. Most prisoners at Fox Hill are illegal aliens. The Bahamas is not a party to the 1967 United Nations Protocol Relating to the Status of Refugees. Domestic violence against women is common despite a 1991 Sexual Offenses and Domestic Violence Act.

Human environment. The Bahamas is subject to considerable soil erosion as well as coastal pollution that does damage to its coral reefs.

NON-CHRISTIAN RELIGIONS

Small groups of Jews and Baha'is exist, and about 5% claim no religious allegiance. About 4,700 are Afro-American spiritists.

Labour Day parade in Nassau celebrating 1973 Independence with the words of Martin Luther King: 'Free at last, Great God Almighty, we are free at last'.

CHRISTIANITY

PROTESTANT CHURCHES.The largest denomination is the Bahamas Baptist Union, and in 1970, some 17% of the population professed to be Baptists. The Baptist Missionary Society of Great Britain sent its first missionaries to the Bahamas in the middle of the last century from which an autonomous church has been developed. New impulses from the USA have come since World War II, including the arrival of Southern Baptists in 1951, and of BIM in 1960.

After the Anglicans, the second-oldest denomination in the country are the Methodists. The pioneer Methodist was an ex-slave from the USA, Joseph Paul, who arrived in 1786, and the first British Methodist minister was sent from Barbados in 1800.

Several Pentecostal missions are found in the islands. Both the Church of God (Cleveland) and its splinter body, the Church of God of Prophecy, made the Bahamas their first overseas field, in 1910 and 1923 respectively, and the Assemblies of God are also active. Other significant bodies include the Church of God (Anderson), Church of God in Christ, Nazarenes, African Methodist Episcopal Zion Church, and the Brethren.

ANGLICAN CHURCH. The first English settlement was from Bermuda in the 17th century, served by Anglican chaplains, and for the next 200 years, the Church of England was virtually the only Christian body working in the islands. At the end of the 18th century, Anglican membership was increased by the arrival from the USA of many Loyalist settlers who opposed the American Revolution. The Anglican Church is the third largest denomination in the Bahamas.

CATHOLIC CHURCH. Benedictine priests of St John's Abbey, Minnesota (USA) began a mission in the Bahamas in 1891 and continue to support it.

A prefecture was erected in 1929 becoming a vicariate in 1941. A major part of the religious personnel and financial support continues to come from the USA and Canada. There are parishes on the following islands: New Providence, Andros, Harbour, Eleuthera, San Salvador, Long Island, Inagua, Cat, Grand Bahama, Bimini, Exuma, and Abaco.

The Holy See has diplomatic relations with Bahamas and in AD 2000 is represented to government and the Catholic hierarchy by a pro-nuncio residing in Port of Spain.

Indigenous missions. The number of Bahaman Christians in missions has been quite small but nearly all of the denominations are implementing plans to increase missions vision and commitment in their congregations.

CHURCH AND STATE

The Preamble to the constitution states: 'We... recognizing the Supremacy of God and believing in the Fundamental Rights and Freedoms of the Individual...' In Chapter III, Article 22(1), freedom of religion is defined in detail and is guaranteed.

Woman evangelist Rowena Rand featured on postage stamps during International Woman's Year 1975.

BROADCASTING AND MEDIA

Although there are no local Christian radio stations, FM programs from other Caribbean stations can be received. Shortwave programs are beamed into the area from HCJB (Ecuador), TWR (Antilles) and AWR (Costa Rica). The Bahamas are a member of UNDA.

LeSEA programming can be received from the World Harvest Satellite.

INTERDENOMINATIONAL ORGANIZATIONS

The Bahamas Christian Council, founded in 1948, is made up of an unusually broad denominational constituency: Adventists, Anglicans, Baptists, Brethren, Greek Orthodox, Lutherans, Methodists, Pentecostals, Roman Catholics, and Salvation Army. The Catholic diocese of Nassau also has an Ecumenical Commission.

FUTURE TRENDS AND PROSPECTS

Bahamas is becoming rapidly secularized with the nonreligious possibly growing from 1.5% in 1970 to 7.2% by AD 2025.

After 2025, Christianity is expected to continue to decline, falling below 85% before AD 2050.

BIBLIOGRAPHY

'A religious survey of the Bahama Islands, British West Indies.' V. M. Prozan. M.A. thesis, Columbia Bible College, Columbia, SC, 1961. 82p.

'A study of a strategy designed to produce numerical growth in the Maranatha Seventh–day Adventist Church of Nassau, Bahamas.' L. A. Johnson. D.Min. thesis, Reformed Theological Seminary, Orlando, FL, 1994. 125p.

'An annotated ethnographic bibliography of the Bahama Islands,' A. G. LaFlamme, *Behaviour science research*, 11, 1 (1976), 57–66.

Baptists in the Bahamas: an historical review. M. C. Symonette & A. Canzoneri. El Paso, TX: Baptist Spanish Publishing House, 1977. 79p.

'Church growth and renewal in the Bahamas.' R. W. Kay. Thesis, Fuller Theological Seminary, Pasadena, CA, 1972. 282p.

'Early history of Baptists in the Bahamas,' A. Canzoneri, *Journal of the Bahamas Historical Society*, 4 (October 1982), 9–16.

For love of mercy: missioned in Maine and Andros Island, Bahamas 1883–1983. M. R. Higgins. Portland, ME: Sisters of Mercy, 1995. 812p.

His light for an island nation: a missionary account of God's faithfulness to His Word in the Bahama Islands. E. Ford. Sayre, PA: Bible Lighthouse Press, 1982. 318p.

It's a natural fact: obeah in the Bahamas. B. C. Hedrick & J. E. Stephens. *Museum of Anthropology. Miscellaneous studies*, 39. Greeley, CA: University of Northern Colorado, Museum of Anthropology, 1977. 38p.

Religious songs and drums in the Bahamas. M. Stearns & H. Courlander. Washington, D.C.: Smithsonian Folkways Records, 1991. (Audio cassette).

'Research on the history of Baptists in the Bahamas,' A. Canzoneri, *Caribbean Archives*, 5 (1976), 41–50.

Ten, ten the Bible ten: obeah in the Bahamas. T. O. McCartney. Nassau: Timpaul, 1976. 192p.

The Bahamas. P. G. Boultbee. *World bibliographical series*, vol. 108. Oxford, UK: CLIO Press, 1989. 118p. (See especially 'Religion,' 96-9).

The Methodist contribution to education in the Bahamas (circa 1790 to 1975). C. Williams. Gloucester: A. Sutton, 1982. 256p.

The rise of the Seventh–day Adventist Church in the Bahamas and the Cayman Islands. J. K. Thompson. [Nassau, Bahamas], 1992. 193p.

Upon these rocks: Catholics in the Bahamas. C. J. Barry. Collegeville, MN: St. John's Abbey Press, 1973. 582p.

Ups and downs in a West Indian diocese. R. G. Shedden. London: A. R. Mowbray, 1927. 188p. (Deals with the Anglican diocese).

Country Table 2. Organized churches and denominations in the Bahamas.

Official name (bold type = church with over 10% of all affiliated) 1	Begun 2	Type 3	Counc 4	Congs 5	Adults 6	Affiliated 1970 7	Affiliated 1995 8	G% 9	*Names, notes, and other statistics* (see Codebook, Part 3) 10
African Methodist Episcopal Zion Ch	1877	I-Met	Vw...	15	765	1,000	1,500	1.64	M=AMEZC(Blacks from USA). 9 pastors and catechists.
Anglican Church: D Nassau & the B	c1670	A-ACa	AwMRK	96	11,600	30,000	27,500	-0.35	1861, Diocese in CPWI. Many islands. M=USPG(UK). 95% Black. 5% White. 26n,14x,2r.
Assemblies of Brethren	c1900	P-CBr	x...K	68	2,700	4,000	4,910	0.82	*Christian Brethren, Plymouth Brethren* (Open). M=CMML(USA). HQ Nassau. 2f.
Assemblies of God in the Bahamas	1928	P-Pe2	ZF...	23	5,500	2,000	8,750	6.08	Classical Pentecostals. M=AoG(USA). HQ Nassau. 12n,9x,2f,1p,W=71%,70Y.
Bahamas Faith Ministries	c1980	I-3cU	.....	4	250	–	700	6.67	F=Miles Munro. Local charismatic mission with international lines.
Bahamas National Baptist Union	c1830	P-Bap	T.M.K	215	55,150	39,000	77,000	2.76	Mainly Bahamians. c1850, M=BMS(UK); since 1951, M=SBC(USA). HQ Nassau. 11f.
Baptist International Missions	c1960	I-Bap	.....	16	3,500	231	5,390	13.43	M=BIM. In 1962 the churches were served by 26 missionaries.
Christian Brethren (Exclusive)	c1930	P-EBr	x....	12	800	2,000	1,330	-1.62	Exclusive (Closed) Plymouth Brethren. Groups: Booth, Ames, Kelly-Continental.
Catholic Church: D Nassau	1885	R-Lat	PxNMK	92	25,000	33,220	45,237	1.24	Suffragan of M Kingston. M=0SB,SFM,CSSp,SJ. C=7+0+11. (1990) 14n, 16x, 18m, 37w, 1328Yy
Church of Christ, Scientist	c1920	m-Sci	x....	2	50	200	150	-1.14	*Christian Science.* M=CCS(Boston, USA). Nassau, Freeport. 2w.
Church of God (Anderson)		P-Hol	x....	34	3,430	15,000	10,400	0.05	Holiness. M=CoG(Anderson) (USA).
Church of God in the Bahamas	1909	P-Pe3	ZF..K	72	4,264	4,000	8,530	3.08	*Jumpers.* M=CoG(Cleveland) (USA). Rapid growth. 76n,4f,1p,56Y,902z.
Church of God in Christ	c1950	I-3pB	Z....	10	2,000	1,000	4,000	5.70	Black pentecostals. M=CoGiC(Black mission from USA). HQ Nassau. 7nx.
Church of God of Prophecy	1923	P-Pe3	Z...K	52	3,600	3,000	7,200	3.56	M=CGP(USA), schism ex CoG(Cleveland). Holiness Pentecostals.
Ch of Jesus Christ of Latter-day Saints	1979	m-LdS	x....	2	128	–	200	6.25	*Mormons* (HQ Utah, USA).
Church of the Nazarene	1971	P-Hol	xF...	11	1,050	–	1,877	4.17	Holiness denomination. M=CoN(USA). 1n,2m,3t(125).
Churches of Christ	1952	I-Dis	x...K	4	140	110	220	2.81	M=Bahamas Chr M (CCCC Instrumental) (USA). Nassau, Clarence Town. 2n,4f,W=82%,18Y.
Evangelical Church of the West Indies	c1960	P-Eva	....	2	460	80	667	8.85	M=World Team.
Greek Orthodox Church	c1920	O-Gre	Cwo.K	1	156	463	390	-0.68	Ch of the Annunciation. Nassau. In Greek Orthodox AD North & South America.
Jehovah's Witnesses	1926	m-Jeh	x....	17	1,213	814	3,790	6.35	*Watch Tower.* IBSA. Active witnessing under way by 1932. HQ Nassau. (1975) 70Y. (1995) 76Y
Lutheran Church of Nassau	c1950	P-Lut	x...K	10	1,000	900	1,500	2.06	Small Lutheran community linked with Missouri Synod (USA).
Methodist Ch in Caribbean & Americas	1786	P-Met	VwM.K	69	5,416	6,800	7,000	0.12	*MCCA, Bahamas District.* M=MMS(UK). 80% Black. 10n,7x,17f,2,1s,W=43%,355Yy,162z.
New Apostolic Church	c1980	I-3aX	x....	5	200	–	323	6.67	*NAC.* M=Neuapostolische Kirche (HQ Zurich, Switzerland).
New Promise Community Church	1980	I-3cU	.....	3	700	–	1,000	6.67	In Nassau. Links with M=Willow Creek Association (USA).
Presbyterian Church	c1850	P-Ref	Rw..k	2	360	1,500	900	-2.02	Scots and British origin. M=Church of Scotland (UK). In Nassau. 2f.
Salvation Army	1931	P-Sal	xwM.K	3	800	2,000	1,140	-2.22	*Bahamas Region*, Caribbean & CAmerica Territory (HQ Jamaica). HQ Nassau. 4f.
Seventh-day Adventist Church	1909	P-Adv	x...K	37	11,000	3,500	15,700	6.19	*SDA, Bahamas Conference.* Expanding. 5n,3x,38mw,1r,31t(1980),W=80%,306Y,300z.
United Pentecostal Church	1988	P-Pe1	.....	3	300	–	500	14.29	M=UPC(USA). Oneness (Jesus Only) Pentecostals. 2f.
Other Protestant denominations		P-	.....	27	2,240	2,000	3,800	0.05	Total about 10 (see list below), including GMU.
Other Black indigenous churches		I-	.....	30	2,000	1,000	4,000	0.05	Including: AOC(USA), International City Mission, NBCUSA(1942), PAW.
Totals				**937**	**145,772**	**153,818**	**245,604**		

Churches, members, growth, 1900-2025	*Congs*	*Adults*	*Affiliated*	*G%*	*Total denominations*	*6 Megablocs:* O	*R*	*A*	*P*	*I*	*m*
Total churches, members, and denominations (mid-1900)	160	30,800	49,770	1.63	6	0	1	1	3	1	0
Total churches, members, and denominations (mid-1970)	745	95,273	153,818	1.63	29	1	1	1	17	7	2
Total churches, members, and denominations (mid-1990)	900	134,000	225,390	1.93	43	1	1	1	24	13	3
Total churches, members, and denominations (mid-1995)	937	145,772	245,604	1.73	45	1	1	1	25	14	3
Total churches, members, and denominations (mid-2000)	1,000	158,000	266,851	1.67	47	1	1	1	26	15	3
Total churches, members, and denominations (mid-2025)	16,000	213,000	358,350	1.19	87	4	1	1	35	40	6

NOTES ON TABLE ABOVE
NATIONAL COUNCILS (Column 4, 5th letter).
N = Bahamas Christian Council.

OTHER PROTESTANT DENOMINATIONS. These total about 10, including: American Lutheran Ch, Bahamas United Baptist Mission, Baptist Mid-Missions, Bethany Fellowship Missions (1968), Gospel Missionary Union (1956), West Indies Mission.

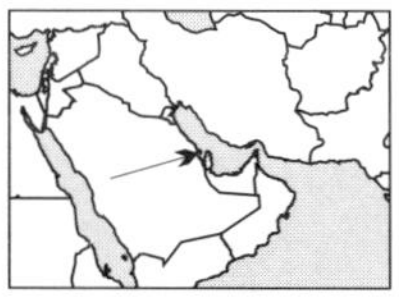

BAHRAIN

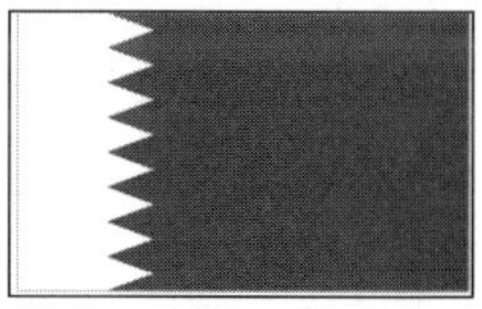

SECULAR DATA, AD 2000

STATE
Official name: Dawlat al Bahrayn (The State of Bahrain).
Short name: Bahrain. **Adjective of nationality:** Bahraini.
Flag: Scarlet, with white serrated border on hoist.
Area: 694 sq. km. (268 sq. mi.).
Government: Absolute monarchy, since 1975 (c1550 Portuguese possession, 1820 British protectorate, 1971 Independence, 1973 constitutional monarchy).
Legislature: Consultative Council, 40 members (advisory only).
Official language: Arabic.
Monetary unit: 1 Bahrain dinar (BD) = 1,000 fils. **US$1=** U.S.$2.65.
Chief cities: AL-MANAMAH (Manama) 376,456; Al-Muharraq 107,559; Jidd Hafs 66,190.
Political divisions: 12 provinces. **Armed forces:** 11,000.

DEMOGRAPHY
Population: 617,000.
Population density: 889.3/sq. km. (2,303.0/sq. mi.).
Under 15 years: 182,000.
Growth rate p.a.: 1.55% (births 16.08, deaths 3.76).
Mortality: Infant, per 1,000: 14.5; **Maternal per 100,000:** 60.0.
Life expectancy: 74 (male 72, female 76).
Household size: 6.5. **Floor area per person, sq.m:** 25.0.
Major languages: Arabic, Persian, English, Hindi, Urdu, Punjabi.
Urban dwellers: 92.24%. **Urban growth rate p.a.:** 1.9%.
Labor force: 45%.

ETHNOLINGUISTIC PEOPLES
63.9% Bahraini Arab; 13.0% Persian; 4.5% Filipino; 4.5% Urdu; 3.5% Malayali.

ECONOMY
National income p.a. per person: US$7,840; **per family:** US$50,960.

EDUCATION
Adult literacy: 85% (male 89%, female 79%). **Schools:** 118.
Universities: 4. **School enrolment:** female/male: 107%/104%.

HEALTH
Access to health services: 80%.
Access to safe water: 100%.
Hospitals: 12 (23 beds per 10,000). **Doctors:** 542.
Blind: 62. **Deaf:** 37,100. **Murder rate:** 1.
Lepers: 100. **Underweight prevalence under 5:** 7%.

LITERATURE
New book titles p.a.: 370 (600 p.a. per million). **Periodicals:** 4.
Newspapers: 3 dailies.

COMMUNICATION (per 1,000 people)
Phones: 242 (27% mobile). **Radios:** 542. **TV sets:** 442.
Daily newspaper circulation: 128. **Computers:** 70.

HUMAN LIFE AND LIBERTY (optimum condition=100.0%)
HDI: 87.0. **HSI:** 71.0. **HFI:** 30.0. **EFL:** 66.0.

Country status. Bahrain is an emirate in the Arabian Peninsula ruled by the Al Khalifa family. It consists of a group of islands in the Persian Gulf off the coast of Saudi Arabia. The economy is almost entirely based on oil. Bahrain has an autocratic government with no judicial or legislative check. The National Assembly was disbanded in 1975 and many provisions of the 1973 constitution remain suspended.

HUMAN LIFE AND LIBERTY

Human need and development. Oil wealth has enabled Bahrain to leap into the 20th century from the Middle Ages. Although actual wealth and power are in the hands of a few, mainly members and friends of the Al Khalifa family, the desert principality has all the outward material trappings of prosperity; modern buildings, hospitals, schools, good roads, airports, and communication systems.

Bahrain has a mixed economy with government ownership of many basic industries, including the oil industry, the main wealth producer. Some of this wealth has been used to build modern amenities. Medical and educational facilities are considered adequate, but are dependent on continued import of know-how from the West.

Human rights and freedoms. Civil rights have remained circumscribed since the early 1970s. Violations of human rights include arbitrary and incommunicado detention, as well as numerous restrictions on the right to a fair public trial, freedom of speech and press, freedom of association, women's rights, and workers' rights. Although the government does not release data, credible sources indicate that there are over 150 political prisoners in the country's jails. Police informer networks are extensive and telephone calls and correspondence are subject to monitoring. The electronic media are officially owned and the print media are subject to official watchdogs.

With some exceptions the Sunnis enjoy the status of a favored community and the Shias, who form two-thirds of the population, form an underclass. Sunnis receive preference for employment, particularly in the armed forces and in the public sector. Shias tend generally to be employed in more menial positions. Municipal and social services in Shia neighborhoods are inferior to those in Sunni communities. Women suffer the disabilities common to all Islamic societies, most markedly in the areas of inheritance, divorce, employment, and education. Violence against women is known to occur but is almost never reported or brought to public attention. Expatriate women, working as domestics, are often subject to severe physical abuse. Freedom of the press and speech is nominal. In the absence of a free press, most educated Bahrainis obtain their news from foreign news broadcasts. Although the Constitution affirms the right of free assembly, political organizations are prohibited. Social and sports clubs serve in their stead as forums for discreet political discussion.

Human environment. The major environmental problems are coastal degradation from oil spills and discharges from ruptured oil wells, growing desertification, and water scarcity. There is virtually no domestic agriculture because Bahrain has no surface water resources and only sparse rainfall. The present rate of groundwater extraction from wells has led to saltwater intrusion into underground aquifers.

NON-CHRISTIAN RELIGIONS

Islam is the religion of virtually all Bahraini citizens and immigrant Arabs. Sunnis predominate in urban centers while Shias are more influential in the rural areas. The two communities, which are ancient rivals, are about equal in size and importance.

Country Table 1. Religious adherents in Bahrain, AD 1900-2025.																	
Year	*1900*		*1970*		*mid-1990*		*Annual change, 1990-2000*				*mid-1995*		*mid-2000*		*mid-2025*	
Name	*Adherents*	*%*	*Adherents*	*%*	*Adherents*	*%*	*Natural*	*Conversion*	*Total*	*Rate*	*Adherents*	*%*	*Adherents*	*%*	*Adherents*	*%*
Muslims	64,800	99.7	208,970	95.2	410,020	83.7	10,647	-811	9,836	2.17	462,860	83.0	508,382	82.4	689,100	80.3
Christians	**200**	**0.3**	**8,230**	**3.8**	**48,800**	**10.0**	**1,265**	**303**	**1,568**	**2.82**	**56,400**	**10.1**	**64,475**	**10.5**	**97,000**	**11.3**
PROFESSION																
crypto-Christians	100	0.2	1,480	0.7	8,000	1.7	270	130	400	3.15	9,000	1.6	10,000	1.7	15,000	1.8
professing Christians	**100**	**0.2**	**6,750**	**3.1**	**40,800**	**8.3**	**995**	**173**	**1,168**	**2.55**	**47,400**	**8.5**	**54,475**	**8.8**	**82,000**	**9.5**
AFFILIATION																
unaffiliated Christians	0	0.0	0	0.0	2,080	0.4	54	-84	-30	-1.56	1,940	0.4	1,777	0.3	2,740	0.3
affiliated Christians	**200**	**0.3**	**8,230**	**3.8**	**46,720**	**9.5**	**1,211**	**387**	**1,598**	**2.99**	**54,460**	**9.8**	**62,698**	**10.2**	**94,260**	**11.0**
Independents	0	0.0	2,100	1.0	20,000	4.1	518	188	706	3.07	23,769	4.3	27,058	4.4	42,000	4.9
Roman Catholics	0	0.0	1,800	0.8	18,000	3.7	467	233	700	3.34	21,000	3.8	25,000	4.1	37,000	4.3
Protestants	100	0.2	1,300	0.6	3,900	0.8	101	19	120	2.72	4,549	0.8	5,100	0.8	7,400	0.9
Anglicans	100	0.2	2,500	1.1	2,800	0.6	73	-53	20	0.69	2,900	0.5	3,000	0.5	4,000	0.5
Orthodox	0	0.0	530	0.2	2,000	0.4	52	-2	50	2.26	2,220	0.4	2,500	0.4	3,800	0.4
Marginal Christians	0	0.0	0	0.0	20	0.0	1	1	2	7.18	22	0.0	40	0.0	60	0.0
Trans-megabloc groupings																
Evangelicals	100	0.2	1,000	0.5	2,450	0.5	64	61	125	4.21	2,996	0.5	3,700	0.6	6,500	0.8
Pentecostals/Charismatics	0	0.0	2,000	0.9	20,580	4.2	533	249	782	3.27	24,669	4.4	28,400	4.6	50,900	5.9
Great Commission Christians	**180**	**0.3**	**3,300**	**1.5**	**16,500**	**3.4**	**428**	**63**	**491**	**2.64**	**19,000**	**3.4**	**21,414**	**3.5**	**38,800**	**4.5**
Hindus	0	0.0	2,350	1.1	28,000	5.7	726	334	1,060	3.26	34,000	6.1	38,604	6.3	63,000	7.3
Nonreligious	0	0.0	0	0.0	1,400	0.3	36	144	180	8.63	2,500	0.5	3,204	0.5	5,000	0.6
Baha'is	0	0.0	300	0.1	1,000	0.2	26	12	38	3.27	1,200	0.2	1,379	0.2	2,400	0.3
Jews	0	0.0	150	0.1	500	0.1	13	-1	12	2.12	550	0.1	617	0.1	700	0.1
Buddhists	0	0.0	0	0.0	240	0.1	6	13	19	6.05	390	0.1	432	0.1	600	0.1
Ethnoreligionists	0	0.0	0	0.0	20	0.0	1	3	4	11.98	50	0.0	62	0.0	100	0.0
New-Religionists	0	0.0	0	0.0	20	0.0	1	3	4	11.98	50	0.0	62	0.0	100	0.0
World A (unevangelized persons)	59,215	91.1	131,521	59.9	229,810	46.9	5,981	-2,568	3,413	1.39	248,673	44.6	264,076	42.8	300,300	35.0
World B (evangelized non-Christians)	5,585	8.6	79,816	36.4	211,390	43.1	5,475	2,265	7,740	3.16	252,490	45.3	288,449	46.7	460,700	53.7
World C (Christians)	200	0.3	8,230	3.7	48,800	10.0	1,265	303	1,568	2.82	56,400	10.1	64,475	10.5	97,000	11.3
Country's population	**65,000**	**100.0**	**219,568**	**100.0**	**490,000**	**100.0**	**12,721**	**0**	**12,721**	**2.33**	**557,564**	**100.0**	**617,000**	**100.0**	**858,000**	**100.0**

COLUMNS, ROWS.
For meanings and definitions, see Codebook (Part 3). Note that, by definition, total 'Christians' = professing + crypto-Christians, which also = affiliated + unaffiliated Christians, and also = Great Commission Christians + latent Christians. Percentages may not always total exactly, due to rounding.

CENSUSES.
96.1% Muslims, 2.7% Christians, 0.9% Hindus, 0.3% Jews. **2.V.1959** (excluding foreign military and shipping personnel): 94.8% Muslims, 3.4% Christians, 0.9% Hindus, 0.7% other religionists, 0.2% Jews. **13.II.1965:** 95.3% Muslims, 3.2% Christians, 1.4% other religionists, 0.1% Jews. **3.IV.1971** (de jure): 95.7% Muslims, 3.0% Christians, 1.3% other religionists. **1981:** 85.0% Muslims, 7.3% Christians, 7.7% other religionists. **1991:** 81.8% Muslims, 8.5% Christians, 9.7% other religionists.

NOTES ON RELIGIONS
BAHA'IS. Growth from 1 local spiritual assembly (1964) to 3 (1973). In subsequent decades there has been little growth in organization though numbers have increased.
COUNTRY'S POPULATION. The totals include all categories of resident foreigner, including immigrant workers.
CRYPTO-CHRISTIANS. Local Arab Christians, secret believers in local churches, together with isolated Bahraini radio believers.
HINDUS. Expatriates from India, with a few temples.
INDEPENDENTS. South Indian and Arab indigenous congregations, in 6 denominations or groupings in 1995 (see Table 2).
MUSLIMS. 50% Sunnis (found in urban areas), 50% Shias (rural areas); Arabs (Bahraini and expatriate), with some Iranians and Pakistanis. *Hajj pilgrims to Mecca.* (1970) 2,418; (1975) 1,928; (1976) 1,989.
PROFESSING CHRISTIANS. Declining slightly in the 1990s due to replacement of expatriate technicians by Bahrainis.

Great Commission Instrument Panel: status of Bahrain (for explanation see start of Part 4)

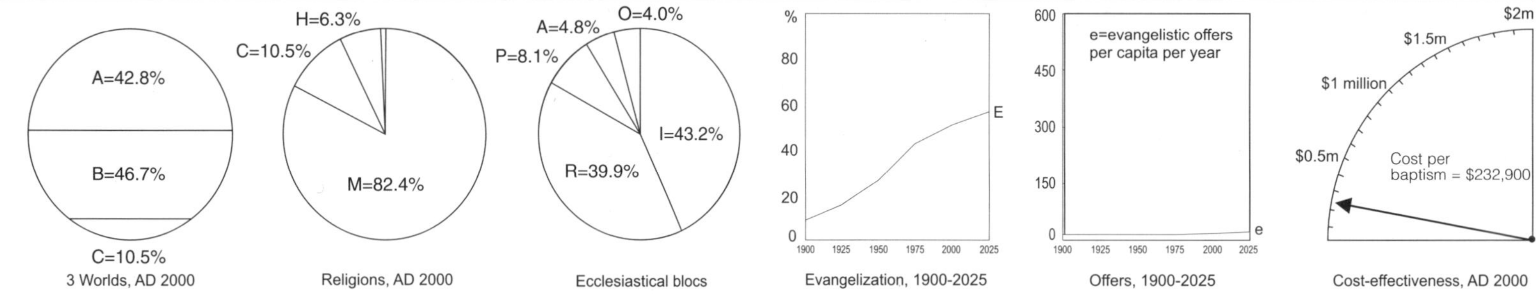

Hinduism exists among the large number of expatriate Indians working in the country.

Christians. Worship service in a Bahrain church; most Christians are expatriate.

CHRISTIANITY

In the 3rd century, a Christian bishopric was established in the Bahrain Islands. Christian communities existed along the borders of the Arabian peninsula during the 4th and 5th centuries but disappeared at the time of the Islamic invasion. In 1889, the Arabia Mission, sent out by the Reformed Church of America, opened work with an emphasis on schools and hospitals at the head of the Persian Gulf, later spreading out to other areas, including Bahrain. The Catholic vicariate of Arabia, with its see in Aden, was also erected in 1889. Most Christians in Bahrain are expatriates of Indian, British or USA nationality, although there are also some Arab Christians from Jordan, Palestine and Syria. No Bahraini nationals are acknowledged Christians, though secret believers are numerous. Most churches are located in Manama.

PROTESTANT CHURCHES. The majority of American and Arab Christians, plus a number of Indians, are members of the National Evangelical Church, which is reformed in tradition. This church sponsors a school and a hospital. Beginning as a dispensary in 1896, the first hospital was built in 1906, and a new installation was completed in 1960. The first predominantly Indian church, the Malayalee Christian Congregation, has been interdenominational in character since the beginning. Through the years, many members have left to form churches of their own home denomination with priests provided from India, although not uncommonly they have maintained an affiliation with the original body and attend services and special programs.

CATHOLIC CHURCH. Catholics in Bahrain form part of the vicariate apostolic of Arabia erected as a prefecture in 1875. There is one parish, Sacred Heart Church, founded in Manama in 1938.

The Holy See has no diplomatic relations with Bahrain in AD 2000, but an apostolic delegate residing in Lebanon.

OTHER CHURCHES. The Anglican community, which is mostly British with some expatriate Arabs, and like the Roman Catholics, operates its own school. It is part of the Episcopal Church in Jerusalem and the Middle East (formerly the Jerusalem Archbishopric). For many years, there was also a Church of England chaplaincy of the Royal Air Force (UK). Syrian Orthodox and Mar Thoma Christians from India are also organized into small communities.

Art and architecture. There is very little evidence of Christian art and architecture in Bahrain.

Renewal movements. In the 1990s the Pentecostal/Charismatic Renewal continued to spread rapidly across most older churches, and numbered over 28,400 adherents (of whom 0% Pentecostals, 8% Charismatics, and 92% Independents).

Indigenous missions. As much of the Christian force in Bahrain is made up of expatriates there has been little attempt to form indigenous mission efforts to other countries or peoples.

Bible Society's Resource Centre in Bahrain, staffed by volunteers.

CHURCH AND STATE

As is true of most Muslim countries in the Persian Gulf, there is a strong bias against Christianity. Islam is the official religion of the country, and all Bahraini citizens are counted as Muslims. No evangelistic work is allowed among them. Christian churches are permitted as a concession to the expatriate community, which is tending to diminish in size as more Bahrainis are trained in technical skills.

Country summary. **Worlds A, B, C by ethnolinguistic peoples, cities, and major civil divisions in Bahrain.**

	PEOPLES							CITIES							CIVIL DIVISIONS						
World	Num	Pop 2000	C%	Christians	E%	U%	Unevangelized	Num	Pop 2000	C%	Christians	E%	U%	Unevangelized	Num	Pop 2000	C%	Christians	E%	U%	Unevangelized
A	6	127,763	0.26	334	39	61	77,356	0	0	0.00	0	0	0	0	2	14,399	4.00	576	46	54	7,768
B	3	424,028	2.56	10,876	56	44	186,639	1	376,456	10.80	40,657	59	41	153,782	10	602,818	10.31	62,122	57	43	256,366
C	5	65,426	78.70	51,490	100	0	140	0	0	0.00	0	0	0	0	0	0	0.00	0	0	0	0
Total	**14**	**617,217**	**10.16**	**62,700**	**57**	**43**	**264,135**	**1**	**376,456**	**10.80**	**40,657**	**59**	**41**	**153,782**	**12**	**617,217**	**10.16**	**62,698**	**57**	**43**	**264,134**

BROADCASTING AND MEDIA

Bahrain is a Muslim state with no internal Christian broadcasting allowed. English and Arabic radio programs beamed in from outside have been very successful. FEBA provides over 2 hours of daily programming, including Bible studies and music. TWR provides an additional 2 hours with programs from 15 agencies. Voice of Hope has the longest Arabic-language schedule: 8.5 hours daily on AM, FM and shortwave; most of the program is music.

Christian television programs are available via satellite. 63,000 have seen the 'Jesus' Film, mainly through videocassettes. About 800 have responded.

INTERDENOMINATIONAL ORGANIZATIONS

Since 1970, the various Christian clergy of Bahrain have met monthly for informal discussion and fellowship.

FUTURE TRENDS AND PROSPECTS

Two factors will ultimately determine the future of Christianity in Bahrain. First, if the number of expatriates continues to grow, so will the number of Christians. Second, if indigenous Christianity grows, then more Christians will emerge from the Muslim majority. Current trends will likely result in 11% Christian affiliation by 2025 and Muslims would drop to 80% in the same period.

Given current trends, Bahrain could be 15-20% Christian by AD 2050. Expatriate Hindus could also grow to 10-15% in the same period.

BIBLIOGRAPHY

Analytical guide to the bibliographies on the Arabian Peninsula. C. L. Geddes. *Bibliographic series*, 4. Denver, CO: American Institute of Islamic Studies, 1974.

Bahrain. P. T. H. Unwin. *World bibliographical series*, vol. 49. Oxford, UK: CLIO Press, 1984. 300p.

Persian Gulf states: country studies. H. C. Metz (ed). 3rd ed. *Area handbook series.* Lanham, MD: Bernan, 1994. 501p.

'Present–day Christianity in the Gulf States of the Arabian Peninsula,' N. A. Horner, *Occasional bulletin of missionary research*, 2 (April 1978), 53–63.

Source book on Arabian Gulf States, Arabian Gulf in general, Kuwait, Bahrain, Qatar and Oman. S. Kabeel. Kuwait: Kuwait University, Libraries Department, 1975. 427p. (With over 3,000 item bibliography).

The Arab at home. P. W. Harrison. London: Hutchinson, 1924. 345p.

The golden milestone: reminiscences of pioneer days fifty years ago in Arabia. S. M. Zwemer & J. Cantine. New York: Revell, 1938. 157p. (Chapter 10 on Bahrain).

Country Table 2. **Organized churches and denominations in Bahrain.**

Official name (bold type = church with over 10% of all affiliated) 1	*Begun* 2	*Type* 3	*Counc* 4	*Congs* 5	*Adults* 6	*Affiliated 1970* 7	*Affiliated 1995* 8	*G%* 9	*Names, notes, and other statistics* (see Codebook, Part 3) 10
Anglican Church (D Cyprus & the Gulf)	1946	A-plu	aw...	10	1,740	2,500	2,900	0.60	In Episcopal Ch in Jerusalem & ME. British. Oil companies' support. 1 school(500),W=5%.
Assemblies (Jehova Shammah)	c1960	I-CBr	x....	30	120	100	300	4.49	Missionaries from India (Brother Bakht Singh); HQ Hyderabad, AP. Tamils.
Catholic Church (VA Arabia)	1938	R-Lat	P..L.	11	12,000	1,800	21,000	10.33	*Latini.* Expatriates (Indians, Americans, British). 3n,5w,1r,(954),W=90%.
Christian Brethren (Open)		P-CBr	x....	1	100	100	200	0.05	*Plymouth Brethren.* Expatriates, mostly British and Indians, but no Arabs.
Church of South India	c1950	P-Uni	.we..	1	200	200	500	3.73	*CSI.* Former members of Malayalee Christian Congregation. No Arabs. W=65%.
Coptic Orthodox Church	c1960	O-Cop	N....	1	800	300	2,000	7.88	Coptic Arabs from Egypt as migrant labor, mostly highly skilled.
Interdenominational Church		P-Non	.....	1	80	200	229	0.05	At Awali oil camp. Mostly USA expatriates. W=60%.
Isolated radio churches	c1950	I-3rS	.....	40	13,700	900	20,000	13.21	Isolated radio believers, mostly aged 12-25. R=140(FEBA), T=1000(ICI).
Jehovah's Witnesses	1979	m-Jeh	.....	2	12	–	22	6.25	*Watch Tower.* Handful of adherents though proscribed.
Malayalee Christian Congregation		I-3cI	.....	2	1,000	700	1,500	0.05	Serving Malayalam-speaking Indians until own denominations begun. W=80%.
Mar Thoma Syrian Ch (D Bahya Kerala)		I-ReO	xwe..	1	600	250	1,000	0.05	South Indians from Kerala. Congregation uses Anglican church building. 1x,W=90%.
National Evangelical Ch of Bahrain	1889	P-Ref	.....	18	972	700	1,620	3.41	Congs: English, Arab, Tamil, Telugu, Urdu. M=RCA(USA),DMS. 50 Arabs. 9f,1H,1k,W=70%.
New Apostolic Church	c1992	I-3aX	x....	1	40	–	69	33.33	*NAC.* M=Neuapostolische Kirche (HQ Zurich, Switzerland).
Orthodox Syrian Church of India	c1955	O-SyM	Dwe..	1	132	230	220	-0.18	Syrians from Kerala, South India, in D Bahya Keralam (Outside Kerala). W=80%.
Pentecostal congregations		I-3pI	.....	6	300	100	600	0.05	House groups for small Indian pentecostal groupings.
St Thomas Evangelical Church	c1965	I-ReO	.T...	1	100	50	300	7.43	1961 schism in Kerala from Mar Thoma Syrian Ch. Home meeting.
Other Protestant denominations	1932	P-	.....	40	1,450	100	2,000	12.73	Including USA military chaplaincy, Ch of God (1977), and USA Protestant house groupings.
Totals				**167**	**33,346**	**8,230**	**54,460**		

Churches, members, growth, 1900-2025	*Congs*	*Adults*	*Affiliated*	*G%*	*Total denominations*	*6 Megablocs:* O	R	A	P	I	m
Total churches, members, and denominations (mid-1900)	2	100	200	5.45	1	0	0	0	1	0	0
Total churches, members, and denominations (mid-1970)	44	4,320	8,230	5.45	17	2	1	1	7	6	0
Total churches, members, and denominations (mid-1990)	150	28,600	46,720	9.07	21	2	1	1	9	7	1
Total churches, members, and denominations (mid-1995)	167	33,346	54,460	3.11	21	2	1	1	9	7	1
Total churches, members, and denominations (mid-2000)	180	38,400	62,698	2.86	22	2	1	1	9	8	1
Total churches, members, and denominations (mid-2025)	280	57,700	94,260	1.64	47	10	1	1	12	20	3

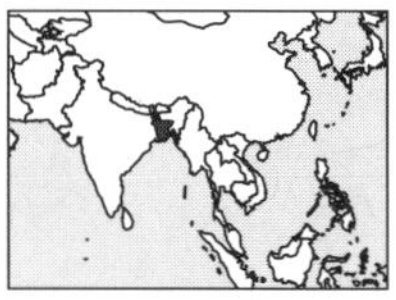

BANGLADESH

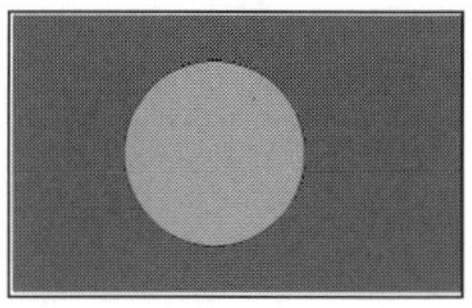

SECULAR DATA, AD 2000

STATE

Official name: Gana Prajatantri Bangladesh (The People's Republic of Bangladesh).
Short name: Bangladesh. **Adjective of nationality:** (of) Bangladesh, a Bangladeshi.
Flag: Orange circle on bottle green field.
Area: 147,570 sq. km. (56,977 sq. mi.).
Government: Unitary multiparty republic with one legislative house, since 1983 (c1200 Turkish rule, c1750 British rule, 1947 East Pakistan, 1971 Independence as republic, 1975 one-party state).
Legislature: Parliament, 330 members.
Official language: Bengali.
Monetary unit: 1 Bangladesh taka (Tk) = 100 paisa. **US$1=** Tk 47.10.
Chief cities: DHAKA (Dacca) 10,979,000; Chittagong (Chittagram) 2,906,000; Khulna 1,229,000; Narayanganj 602,870; Mirpur 518,836.
Political divisions: 6 provinces.
Armed forces: 121,000.

DEMOGRAPHY

Population: 129,155,000.
Population density: 875.2/sq. km. (2,266.7/sq. mi.).
Under 15 years: 45,359,000.
Growth rate p.a.: 1.69% (births 26.44, deaths 8.62).
Mortality: Infant, per 1,000: 67.0; **Maternal per 100,000:** 850.0.
Life expectancy: 61 (male 61, female 61).
Household size: 5.3. **Floor area per person, sq.m:** 5.0.
Major languages: Bengali, English, Urdu, Santali, Garo, Hindi, Lushai, Burmese, and over 30 smaller languages.
Urban dwellers: 21.18%. **Urban growth rate p.a.:** 4.5%.
Labor force: 47%.

ETHNOLINGUISTIC PEOPLES

79.0% Bengali; 11.7% Bengali (Hindu); 4.6% Sylhetti Bengali; 1.5% Bihari; 0.6% Urdu.

ECONOMY

National income p.a. per person: US$240; **per family:** US$1,271.

EDUCATION

Adult literacy: 38% (male 49%, female 26%). **Schools:** 62,433.
Universities: 1,046. **School enrolment:** female/male: 40%/51%.

HEALTH

Access to health services: 45%. **Access to safe water:** 83%.
Hospitals: 891 (3 beds per 10,000). **Doctors:** 21,749.
Blind: 200,000. **Deaf:** 7,698,600. **Murder rate:** 1.
Lepers: 700,000. **Underweight prevalence under 5:** 67%.

LITERATURE

New book titles p.a.: 520 (4 p.a. per million). **Periodicals:** 57.
Newspapers: 51 dailies.

COMMUNICATION (per 1,000 people)

Phones: 2 (4% mobile). **Radios:** 67. **TV sets:** 7.
Daily newspaper circulation: 6. **Computers:** 3.

REFUGEES

Citizen refugees in other countries: 48,000.
Alien refugees from other countries: 55,000.

HUMAN LIFE AND LIBERTY (optimum condition=100.0%)

HDI: 36.8. **HSI:** 32.0. **HFI:** 17.5. **EFL:** 27.0.

Country status. Bangladesh is the third most populous Muslim nation in the world, and it is the youngest of the nations that was carved out of the old British Indian Empire. It is also one of the world's poorest and most densely populated countries. Paradoxically, it is also among the world's fertile regions, well watered by two of the world's greatest rivers, and with the world's highest annual rainfall.

HUMAN LIFE AND LIBERTY

Human need and development. No country in the Indian subcontinent is as chronically on the verge of economic disaster as Bangladesh. Grinding poverty characterizes the life of all but a small segment of the population. Known as Sonar Bangla or golden Bangladesh, because of the lush paddyfields, the country was prosperous under the British, but the partition of the province in 1947 and the subsequent war of independence, natural disasters, and political mismanagement combined to ravage the economy. Unchecked population growth from about 28 million in 1900 to over 129 million by AD 2000 has depressed the quality of life to mere subsistence levels. It fares badly on all key indicators, but particularly in literacy, infant mortality, political and social equality, life expectancy, and school enrollment.

Country Table 1. Religious adherents in Bangladesh, AD 1900-2025.

Year	1900		1970		mid-1990		Annual change, 1990-2000				mid-1995		mid-2000		mid-2025	
Name	Adherents	%	Adherents	%	Adherents	%	Natural	Conversion	Total	Rate	Adherents	%	Adherents	%	Adherents	%
Muslims	18,806,750	65.6	54,663,508	82.0	93,588,350	85.5	1,683,435	42,630	1,726,033	1.71	101,852,330	85.9	110,848,684	85.8	155,923,600	87.2
Hindus	9,372,000	32.7	11,169,000	16.8	14,000,000	12.8	251,825	-52,366	199,459	1.34	14,700,000	12.4	15,994,593	12.4	19,500,000	10.9
Christians	**36,250**	**0.1**	**249,092**	**0.4**	**730,000**	**0.7**	**13,131**	**7,247**	**20,378**	**2.49**	**828,000**	**0.7**	**933,776**	**0.7**	**1,518,000**	**0.9**
PROFESSION																
crypto-Christians	5,250	0.0	44,828	0.1	250,000	0.2	4,497	5,503	10,000	3.42	300,000	0.3	350,000	0.3	550,000	0.3
professing Christians	**31,000**	**0.1**	**204,264**	**0.3**	**480,000**	**0.4**	**8,634**	**1,744**	**10,378**	**1.98**	**528,000**	**0.5**	**583,776**	**0.5**	**968,000**	**0.5**
AFFILIATION																
unaffiliated Christians	0	0.0	1,264	0.0	1,760	0.0	32	-4	28	1.47	1,764	0.0	2,036	0.0	2,600	0.0
affiliated Christians	**36,250**	**0.1**	**247,828**	**0.4**	**728,240**	**0.7**	**13,099**	**7,251**	**20,350**	**2.49**	**826,236**	**0.7**	**931,740**	**0.7**	**1,515,400**	**0.9**
Independents	50	0.0	50,855	0.1	400,000	0.4	7,195	6,405	13,600	2.97	468,398	0.4	536,000	0.4	950,000	0.5
Roman Catholics	18,000	0.1	120,392	0.2	200,000	0.2	3,597	-97	3,500	1.63	216,895	0.2	235,000	0.2	325,000	0.2
Protestants	13,000	0.1	76,281	0.1	128,000	0.1	2,302	947	3,249	2.29	140,697	0.1	160,490	0.1	240,000	0.1
Orthodox	200	0.0	200	0.0	160	0.0	3	-3	0	0.00	160	0.0	160	0.0	200	0.0
Marginal Christians	0	0.0	100	0.0	80	0.0	1	0	1	1.18	86	0.0	90	0.0	200	0.0
Anglicans	5,000	0.0	0	0.0	0	0.0	0	0	0	0.00	0	0.0	0	0.0	0	0.0
Trans-megabloc groupings																
Evangelicals	10,000	0.0	45,000	0.1	66,000	0.1	1,187	-587	600	0.87	67,245	0.1	72,000	0.1	100,000	0.1
Pentecostals/Charismatics	0	0.0	15,000	0.0	362,000	0.3	6,511	5,289	11,800	2.86	411,935	0.4	480,000	0.4	825,000	0.5
Great Commission Christians	**36,000**	**0.1**	**200,000**	**0.3**	**495,000**	**0.5**	**8,904**	**5,497**	**14,401**	**2.59**	**560,000**	**0.5**	**639,011**	**0.5**	**1,075,000**	**0.6**
Buddhists	157,000	0.6	450,000	0.7	700,000	0.6	12,591	-2,371	10,220	1.37	734,000	0.6	802,198	0.6	1,100,000	0.6
Ethnoreligionists	300,000	1.1	100,000	0.2	590,000	0.5	10,613	3,875	14,488	2.22	656,000	0.6	734,884	0.6	950,000	0.5
Nonreligious	0	0.0	20,000	0.0	62,000	0.1	1,115	2,055	3,170	4.22	76,000	0.1	93,696	0.1	130,000	0.1
Sikhs	1,000	0.0	6,000	0.0	18,000	0.0	324	7	331	1.70	19,500	0.0	21,307	0.0	29,000	0.0
Atheists	0	0.0	10,000	0.0	9,400	0.0	169	-88	81	0.83	9,300	0.0	10,211	0.0	10,000	0.0
Baha'is	0	0.0	3,200	0.0	7,000	0.0	126	8	134	1.77	7,600	0.0	8,341	0.0	10,000	0.0
Zoroastrians	0	0.0	200	0.0	250	0.0	4	1	5	1.74	270	0.0	297	0.0	400	0.0
doubly-counted religionists	0	0.0	0	0.0	-240,000	-0.2	-4,317	-966	-5,283	2.01	-267,000	-0.2	-292,834	-0.2	-420,000	-0.2
World A (unevangelized persons)	24,372,050	85.0	38,002,186	57.0	51,448,550	47.0	925,456	-543,668	381,788	0.72	53,377,066	45.0	55,278,340	42.8	67,925,380	38.0
World B (evangelized non-Christians)	4,264,700	14.9	28,419,224	42.6	57,286,450	52.3	1,030,429	536,453	1,566,850	2.45	64,410,636	54.3	72,942,884	56.5	109,307,620	61.1
World C (Christians)	36,250	0.1	249,092	0.4	730,000	0.7	13,131	7,247	20,378	2.49	828,000	0.7	933,776	0.7	1,518,000	0.9
Country's population	**28,673,000**	**100.0**	**66,670,503**	**100.0**	**109,465,000**	**100.0**	**1,969,016**	**0**	**1,969,016**	**1.67**	**118,615,703**	**100.0**	**129,155,000**	**100.0**	**178,751,000**	**100.0**

COLUMNS, ROWS.
For meanings and definitions, see Codebook (Part 3). Note that, by definition, total 'Christians' = professing + crypto-Christians, which also = affiliated + unaffiliated Christians, and also = Great Commission Christians + latent Christians. Percentages may not always total exactly, due to rounding.

CENSUSES.
1.III.1901 (present-day territory of Bangladesh): 65.7% Muslims, 32.7% Hindus, 1.0% animists, 0.5% Buddhists, 0.11% Christians (0.05% Roman Catholics, 0.04% Protestants, 0.01% Anglicans). **28.II.1951** (East Pakistan; excluding foreigners): 76.8% Muslims, 22.0% Hindus (12.0% scheduled castes), 0.2% Christians, 0.9% other religionists. **1.II.1961** (east Pakistan; excluding foreigners): 80.4% Muslims, 18.4% Hindus (9.8% scheduled castes), 0.7% Buddhists, 0.3% Christians (148,903 persons), 0.1% tribal religionists. **1974:** 85.4% Muslims, 13.5% Hindus, 1.1% other religionists. **1981:** 86.6% Muslims, 12.1% Hindus, 1.2% other religionists. **1991:** 88.3% Muslims, 10.5% Hindus, 0.6% other religionists.

NOTES ON RELIGIONS
ANGLICANS. One of the largest denominations, Anglicans disappeared as a separate entity in 1970 when they merged into the Protestant union, the Church of Bangladesh.
ATHEISTS. Communist Party of Bangladesh (CPBD) (banned 1954, legalized 1971; pro-Soviet) and 4 rival factions.
BAHA'IS. Numbers have mushroomed from 21 local spiritual assemblies (1973) to 700 LSAs (1996). A number of Baha'is are Persians; new converts are Tipera and Hill Tract tribes.
BUDDHISTS. Mainly in the Chittagong Hill Tracts, especially the Buddhist tribes Chakma, Chak, Magh and Mru; often syncretized with tribal animism.
CHRISTIANS. After 1975, most Christians were drawn from the Namasudra scheduled-caste Hindus, and the Garo tribe, also Santal, Oraon, Mahili, Tipera, Khasi and other tribes. Between 1961 and 1974 many Christians migrated to India and never returned.
COUNTRY'S POPULATION. In the world's worst natural catastrophe of the 20th century, on 13 November 1970, between 300,000 and 500,000 were killed by a massive cyclone and tidal wave. Thousands more were killed or massacred in the 1971 civil war; first 100,000 non-Bengalis (Urdu-speaking Biharis and others), then over 150,000 killed by the West Pakistan army; and 9 million refugees, mostly Hindus, fled to India, although most returned to Bangladesh within a year or two. In 1973, over 30,000 Biharis again fled.
CRYPTO-CHRISTIANS. Christians affiliated to churches, including isolated radio believers, but unknown as such publicly to state or society.
ETHNORELIGIONISTS. Animists among the Garos, Santals and Chittagong Hill tribes including the Khumi, Koch (population 47,000), Murung (Mru: 23,000), and Hajong (28,000).
HINDUS. 48% high-caste (Brahmin, Kshatriya, Vaishya, Sudra), 52% low-caste (formerly depressed classes or outcastes or untouchables, known since 1935 as scheduled castes; over 25 major castes). Hindus include the Tiperas (high-caste Hindus) and Piangs (low-caste). The 8 million who fled to India in 1971 and then lived in refugee camps largely abandoned any Hindu practice, and by 1975 were increasingly open to Christian evangelism. Since 1900 the Hindu community has declined in size relative to the Muslim community due to (1) emigration, (2) mass killings, and (3) lower Hindu fertility due to the prohibition of widow remarriage. The column 'Natural change' above embodies these losses, averaged over the decade 1990-2000.
INDEPENDENTS. In 10 groupings in 1995 (see Table 2).
MUSLIMS. Mostly Sunnis of the Hanafite rite, with a number of Wahhabi reform movement centres, and a small Shia minority in towns (descendants of Persian immigrants). Muslim society has 3 social groups: Ashraf (upper-class Muslim) including Mallik, Mughal, Pathan, Saiyed, Sheikh; Ajlaf (lower-class Muslim) with about 20 divisions; and Arzal (degraded-class) with over 7 groups. Another minority, hated and discriminated against are the 4 million Urdu-speaking Bihari Muslims originally from Bihar state (India) with a few from other parts of India. There are also 150,000 followers of the Ahmadiya Mission (Qadianis; enumerated here as Muslims though declared non-Muslim by Pakistan). *Hajj pilgrims to Mecca.* (1972) 6,595; (1973) 5,187; (1974) 2,921; (1976) 3,490.
PENTECOSTALS/CHARISMATICS. (1996) Including 13,000 Catholic Charismatics in 19 prayer groups (begun 1972; ICCRS). In 1994, 7,000 attended daily their Three Day's Mission on Healing entitled 'Meet the Father'.
PROTESTANTS. Since (1971 there have been large-scale conversions to Christianity in several areas. The most responsive have been the Santalis, among whom in 1972-73, 3,500 former animists were baptized in 20 months in Rajshahi and Dinajpur districts. In 1975, 32 new churches related to BMS (UK) were organized; and 1,200 Garos were baptized. Since 1971 also, about 2,000 Muslims and 2,000 Hindus each year have become Christians (45 Muslims in 1975 through a Bengali evangelist).

Great Commission Instrument Panel: status of Bangladesh (for explanation see start of Part 4)

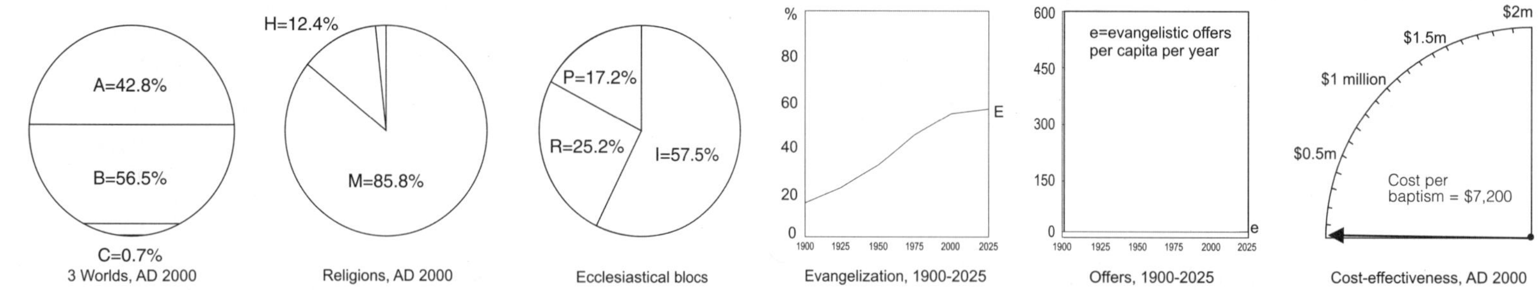

3 Worlds, AD 2000 — Religions, AD 2000 — Ecclesiastical blocs — Evangelization, 1900-2025 — Offers, 1900-2025 — Cost-effectiveness, AD 2000

A major social problem - people falling from overcrowded buses.

The almost universal absence of family planning and the lack of official efforts to curb population growth makes developmental activities meaningless in Bangladesh. Despite sustained foreign aid from the World Bank and other international agencies, the GNP per capita growth from 1965 to 1990 was only 0.7% and the literacy rate has risen from 23 to only 38%. Medical care is virtually nonexistent in the villages where 84% of Bangladeshis live.

Human rights and freedoms. Under military rule for most of the time since independence, Bangladesh has not known a regime that consistently promoted human rights. The new government that took office under the 1991 Constitution has made some progress in enforcing constitutional liberties and in curbing abuses. Nevertheless, there remain serious problems of arbitrary detention under the Special Powers Act, prisoner abuse, and restrictions on the rights of workers and women. Although the Constitution forbids torture and degrading punishment, prisoners are subjected to inhuman treatment. Under the Special Powers Act persons may be detained without a charge for up to 30 days. The most serious human rights violations occur in the Chittagong Hill Tracts where a tribal insurgent group known as Shanti Bahini has been engaged in a low-level conflict with the government since 1973. Religious differences between the predominantly non-Muslim tribals and the Muslim settlers is a contributory factor in this conflict. Under the new government freedoms of the press and speech are formally honored, and instances of overt censorship have become rare.

There are 3 classes of Bangladeshis who suffer some form of civil disabilities: the so-called Biharis, or persons who opted for Pakistan on independence, but who were not allowed to migrate, women, and tribals. The 250,000 Biharis face serious discrimination as noncitizens. By custom and local Islamic tradition women occupy a subordinate position in society, but their legal status has improved following the passage of such laws as the Dowry Prohibition Act, the Cruelty to Women Act, the Child Marriage Restraint

Country summary. **Worlds A, B, C by ethnolinguistic peoples, cities, and major civil divisions in Bangladesh.**

World	PEOPLES Num	Pop 2000	C%	Christians	E%	U%	Unevangelized	CITIES Num	Pop 2000	C%	Christians	E%	U%	Unevangelized	CIVIL DIVISIONS Num	Pop 2000	C%	Christians	E%	U%	Unevangelized
A	30	10,535,341	0.35	37,340	36	64	6,744,884	0	0	0.00	0	0	0	0	0	0	0.00	0	0	0	0
B	19	118,414,172	0.62	731,714	59	41	48,521,324	36	19,784,595	1.18	234,027	61	39	7,767,102	6	129,155,153	0.72	931,744	57	43	55,267,878
C	12	205,641	79.11	162,689	99	1	1,673	0	0	0.00	0	0	0	0	0	0	0.00	0	0	0	0
Total	**61**	**129,155,154**	**0.72**	**931,743**	**57**	**43**	**55,267,881**	**36**	**19,784,595**	**1.18**	**234,027**	**61**	**39**	**7,767,102**	**6**	**129,155,153**	**0.72**	**931,744**	**57**	**43**	**55,267,878**

Act, and the Illegal Trafficking in Women Act. Bangladesh became the second Islamic country in 1991 to have a woman as prime minister. The tribals are threatened with the loss of their distinct culture and institutions in the face of government neglect and incessant pressures from the dominant Muslim culture.

Human environment. Overpopulation has led to the deforestation of much of the land, even in the hilly areas to the northeast. Forests now cover less than 16% of the land area. Very little wildlife has survived. Industrial effluents and sewage pollute the rivers and few communities have access to potable water. Waterborne diseases combined with chronic malnutrition and inadequate health services result in an infant mortality rate of 6.7%.

NON-CHRISTIAN RELIGIONS

Islam is the main religion of the country. Muslims are mostly Sunnis with a small Shia minority concentrated in urban areas. The Muslim population increased from 77% in 1950 to 86% in 1995. In 1995, 5,000 Muslim pilgrims from Bangladesh performed the hajj to Mecca.

Hinduism is still the principal religious and ethnic minority in spite of a gradual decline from its 22 percent after partition in 1947 and in spite of severe losses from deaths and refugee movements during the 1971-72 civil war.

Buddhism has a very ancient history in the whole of the subcontinent, but the Buddhist population of Bangladesh has never been large and numbers under 1 percent.

Traditional tribal religions are still prevalent among the Santal, Koch, Oraon Sadri, and Chittagong Hill tribes.

CHRISTIANITY

Christians in Bangladesh form a very small minority and consist mostly of former low-caste Hindu peasants and members of certain tribes, including the Garo (now 90 percent Christian), Santal, Khasi, and Kurulel. The tribes have proved far more receptive to Christianity than the Bengalis, upon whom it has had little influence.

CATHOLIC CHURCH. Although Catholic missionaries were attached to Portuguese trading posts as early as the 16th century, the first of the present four dioceses was not erected until 1886. The Catholic Church is strongest in urban areas, notably Dacca, where the church has been able to attract many members of mixed Portuguese descent.

The Holy See has diplomatic relations with Bangladesh and in AD 2000 is represented to government and the Catholic hierarchy by a nuncio residing in Dhaka.

PROTESTANT CHURCHES. Baptists were the first to arrive and remain the strongest of the Protestant traditions. William Carey entered Calcutta in 1793 and within two years, work was opened at Dinajpur. Dacca was reached by 1816. Mass conversions took place in Mymensingh in the late 19th century, and growth is still considerable among the tribes of the Chittagong Hills.

The Baptist Sangha (formerly Baptist Union of Bangladesh) is the result of this early British activity, whereas the Bangladesh Baptist Fellowship combines work begun by missionaries from Australia, New Zealand and later Southern Baptists from the USA . The Mymensingh Garo Baptist Convention is an independent body which receives some aid from Australian Baptists.

Anglicans and Presbyterians, the latter owing their origin to English Presbyterian missionary activity, united in 1970 to form one of the dioceses of the Church of Pakistan, but all relations with Pakistan became difficult after the civil war of 1972. For all practical purposes, the Church of Bangladesh operates today as an autonomous body.

The Bangladesh Evangelical Lutheran Church grew out of the Santal Mission of the Northern Churches, which was begun in 1867 and has received support from Norwegian, Danish and American Lutheran societies. Before partition in 1947, the church had 40,000 members, but 80% of the church is now in India.

The Church of Sylhet was founded by Welsh Presbyterians, and a number of other smaller Protestant groups are also active.

Protestant churches sponsor an extensive medical and educational program and have been heavily involved in relief and rehabilitation following Bangladesh's various natural disasters as well as the civil war of 1971-72.

INDIGENOUS CHURCHES. Bangladesh is home to the world's largest movement of messianic mosques (Christian mosques). The large and fast-growing Jamaat movement retains most cultural elements of Islamic worship and practice around a core of Christian theology, faith, and commitment. At the same time, these believers in Christ remain within Islam, Muslim society and family, and have nothing to do with the regular churches.

Art and architecture. Most Christian traditions in Bangladesh have no distinctive architectural or artistic traditions. Most churches are unobtrusive buildings. There are no noted Christian artists or writers. The Jamaat movement holds promise for eventually developing a distinctive Christian mosque architecture and art.

Renewal movements. In the 1990s the Pentecostal/Charismatic Renewal continued to spread rapidly across most older churches, and numbered over 480,000 adherents (of whom 4% Pentecostals, 6% Charismatics, and 90% Independents).

Indigenous missions. In a country well-known for its opposition to Christians a surprisingly strong indigenous mission movement has grown. This is manifested primarily in two ways. First of all, the many heavily-Christian tribal groups have been sending evangelists and missionaries to other peoples. Second, Evangelical congregations have set goals to penetrate each sub-district and ethnic group with the gospel.

CHURCH AND STATE

Pakistan was created in 1947 when the Punjab and Bengal were partitioned, with the Muslim majority areas forming respectively West and East Pakistan. East Pakistan's substantial Hindu minority acted as a moderating influence against extremist Muslim elements. Nevertheless, the East was dominated by the Punjabi West, which was an increasing source of unrest and ultimately led to civil war. In 1956, largely due to Punjabi pressure, Pakistan was declared an Islamic republic, and there was further erosion of religious liberty during the 1960s. Shortly after independence in 1972, the first president of the republic declared that Bangladesh was a secular socialist state and that its government would commit itself to a policy of complete religious liberty.

Secularism is one of the principles affirmed in the Preamble of the 1972 constitution, promulgated on Nov. 4, 1972. Following the first military coup of 1975, the new regime immediately proclaimed Bangladesh to be once again an Islamic state. However, the regime subsequently tended to minimize the significance of that declaration.

By 1978, the future of foreign missionaries was in doubt. One government edict calling for the eviction of all Protestant missionaries during 1978 was only withdrawn under diplomatic pressure.

The amendment in 1988 that established Islam as the state religion has had a stronger impact than the declaration of 1975.

BROADCASTING AND MEDIA

Receivers are not common: less than 4% of the populace own a radio, and fewer still own a TV. FEBA (Seychelles), VERITAS and AWR all broadcast shortwave programs in (Bangla) and Bengali, and programs from FEBC (Philippines) and KNLS can also be received. AWR has a studio in Dhaka that produces Bangla-language programs. IBRA-produced programs broadcast from Radio Moscow in Tashkent can be heard. Bangladesh is represented in UNDA. A Christian Communication Centre run by Catholics offers media education from its center in Dhaka, and a course in mass communications is taught at the National Major Seminary.

There are several 'Jesus' Film teams regularly showing the film, but only 5% of the population has seen it. Response has been good: 1 out of 8 viewers have made a decision for Christ.

INTERDENOMINATIONAL ORGANIZATIONS

Founded in 1954 as the East Pakistan Christian Council, the Bangladesh National Council of Churches (BNCC) brings together eight Protestant churches and a number of missions and other agencies. In 1972, Bangladesh Ecumenical Relief and Rehabilitation Services was formed with BNCC, Catholic, and government support. A Christian Medical Association helps coordinate medical programs for the churches.

FUTURE TRENDS AND PROSPECTS

The continuation of Christian movements among Muslims will potentially result in 0.9% of Bangladesh affiliated with Christian churches in 2025, half of these being independents. Muslims are expected to rise to over 87% by 2025 with continuing declines in the Hindu population reaching an all-time low of 11% by 2025.

Demographic growth (births-deaths) is forecasted to remain strong in the general population over the next few decades. This means that seemingly large gains among Christians are often overshadowed by gains among Muslims. With this in mind it is most plausible that Christians will not grow past 2% until around AD 2050.

Church of Bangladesh. Anglican village school in 1962 supervised by CMS missionaries.

Independents. *Top.* New Covenant Church, founder at Lord's Supper *Below.* Indigenous Mission of Bangladesh teaching Santalis.

BIBLIOGRAPHY

'A cassette project in the development of lay leadership training in Bangladesh villages.' S. Sircar. D.Min. thesis, Southwestern Baptist Theological Seminary, Fort Worth, TX, 1985. 149p.

A study of Christian–Muslim relations in East Pakistan. W. B. Davis. , 1961. 59p.

'A study of the religious customs and practices of the Rajbangshis of North Bengal.' R. H. Clark. Ph.D. dissertation, Hartford Seminary Foundation, Hartford, CT, 1969.

Atlas of South Asia. A. K. Dutt & M. M. Geib. Boulder, CO, and London: Westview Press, 1987. 255p.

Bamladesa o Khrishta–mandali. Y. Rojario. [Cattagrama]: Yajaka-sammilani, Cattagrama Dharmapradesa, 1988.

Baptists in Bangladesh: an historical sketch of more than one hundred years' work of the Baptist Missionary Society in Bengal. G. Soddy. [Khulna, Bangladesh]: Literature Committee, National Council of Churches, Bangladesh, 1987. 228p.

British Christians, Indian nationalists, and the Raj. G. Studdert-Kennedy. Delhi: Oxford University Press, 1991. 284p.

Catholic directory of Bangladesh, 1973. Dacca: Catholic Bishops' Conference, 1974.

'Changing faces of nationalism in Bangladesh.' M. G. Kabir. Ph.D. dissertation, University of Pittsburgh, 1984. 310p.

Chapel address, March 10-11, 1992. J. McKinley. Missions emphasis week (Southern Baptist Theological Seminary, Louisville, Ky.) 1991-1992. Sound recording, 2 sides of sound tape reel, analog, 3 3/4 ips, mono, 7 inch. (Includes prayers and music).

Christ in Bangladesh. J. C. Hefley & M. Hefley. London: Coverdale House, 1973. 128p.

Christian mission in Bangladesh: a survey. A. K. Khan. Leicester: Islamic Foundation, [1982]. 30p.

Christianity in Bangladesh. South Asia ephemera collection Bangladesh, B-CLR-26.1. New Delhi Washington, D.C: Library of Congress Office Library of Congress Photoduplication Service, 1994. 5 microfiches(Collection of 1985-1993 pamphlets).

'Christianity in Bangladesh.' P. Parshall. Dacca, 1974. (Mimeographed).

Christianity in the north eastern hills of South Asia: social impact and political implications. F. A. Quarishi. Dhaka, Bangladesh: University Press, 1987. 86p.

'Church and mission: Sylhet District, Bangladesh 1893–1987: a study of the Presbyterian Church of Sylhet, Bangladesh, its growth and relation to two successive foreign missions.' J. V. Selle. Th.M. thesis, Fuller Theological Seminary, Pasadena, CA, 1991. 306p.

Crucial issues in Bangladesh: making missions more effective in the mosaic of peoples. P. McNee. South Pasadena, CA: William Carey Library, 1976. 304p.

Daktar. V. B. Olsen & J. W. Lockerbie. London: Hodder & Stoughton, 1974. 414p.

Directory of Christian work in East Pakistan. Dacca: East Pakistan Christian Council, 1960. 64p.

Gloria! a biography of Gloria Thurman, missionary to Bangladesh. B. Joiner. Birmingham, AL: Women's Missionary Union, Southern Baptist Convention, 1993. 146p.

Holy Cross priests in the Diocese of Dacca 1853–1981. E. N. Goedert. *Preliminary studies in the history of the Congregation of Holy Cross in America*, 3. Notre Dame, IN: Province Archives Center, 1983. 62p.

Identity, Islam, and human development in rural Bangladesh. D. Abecassis. Dhaka, Bangladesh: University Press, 1990. 143p.

'Islam and Pakistan: a descriptive study.' A. M. Williams. M.A. thesis, Columbia Bible College, Columbia, SC, 1953. 125p.

Islam in Bangladesh. R. A. Banu. *International studies in sociology and social anthropology*, vol. 58. Leiden: E. J. Brill, 1991.

Islam in Bangladesh: society, culture, and politics. R. Ahmed (ed). Dhaka: Bangladesh Itihas Samiti, 1983. 286p.

'Le syncrétisme religieux d'un village mog du territoire de Chittagong,' C. Levi-Strauss, *Revue d'histoire des religions*, 141 (1952), 202–37. (Animist and magico-religious syncretism among a Buddhist tribe, the Mog).

Muslim festivals in Bangladesh. A. Jafar. Dacca: Islamic Foundation, Bangladesh, 1980. 134p.

New horizon for dialogue = Samlapera nabadiganta. M. Eugenia & S. Garello (eds). *Samlapa*, 6. Dhaka, Bangladesh: Xaverian Centre for Inter-Religious Dialogue, 1991. 56p. (Deals with Roman Catholic interreligious dialogue in Bangladesh, in both English and Bengali).

Religion and politics in Bangladesh and West Bengal: a study of communal relations. S. Biswas. Tokyo: Institute of Developing Economies, 1993. 131p.

Religion, nationalism, and politics in Bangladesh. R. Ahmed (ed). New Delhi: South Asian Publishers, 1990. 213p.

Ripe mangoes: miracle missionary stories from Bangladesh. J. Walsh & P. C. Oviatt. Cherry Hill, NJ: Association of Baptists for World Evangelism, [1978]. 124p.

Social welfare services of the Christian missionaries and the foreign voluntary agencies in Bangladesh. A. B. M. Shamsuddoulah. Dacca: Great Eastern Books, 1979. 130p.

The Bauls of Bangladesh: a study of an obscure religious cult. A. S. M. Anwarul Karim. Kushtia: Lalan Academy, 1980. 212p.

The Catholic directory of Bangladesh, 1992. S. D. Rozario. 4th rev. ed. Dhaka: Catholic Bishops' Conference of Bangladesh, [1992]. 212p.

'The history and development of the Church among the Bawm tribe and the future plan for the evangelization of other tribes in Bangladesh.' P. B. Tlung. M.Div. thesis, Asian Center for Theological Studies and Mission, Seoul, Korea, 1987. 194p.

The Islamic syncretistic tradition in Bengal. A. Roy. Princeton, NJ: Princeton University Press, 1983. 336p.

'The laity in the local church in Bangladesh.' P. Costa. Ph.D. dissertation, Pontificia Università lateranense, Rome, 1983. 179p.

'The origins of secularism in the ideology of Bangladesh.' D. K. Ghosh. Ph.D. dissertation, University of Pennsylvania, Philadelphia, 1975. 319p.

The rise of Islam and the Bengal frontier, 1204–1760. R. M. Eaton. *Comparative studies on Muslim societies*, 17. Berkeley, CA: University of California Press, 1993. 386p.

Write the vision. J. Lockerbie. South Pasadena, CA: William Carey Library, 1989. 152p.

Country Table 2. **Organized churches and denominations in Bangladesh.**

Official name (bold type = church *with over 10% of all affiliated)* 1	*Begun* 2	*Type* 3	*Counc* 4	*Congs* 5	*Adults* 6	*Affiliated 1970* 7	*Affiliated 1995* 8	*G%* 9	*Names, notes, and other statistics* (see Codebook, Part 3) 10
All One in Christ Fellowship	1947	I-Bap	.....	113	9,000	15,000	22,500	1.64	*Namasudra Reform Movement.* Ex nominal Baptists. One-caste only. 32m.
Armenian Apostolic Church (D India)	c1800	O-Arm	Ewc..	1	80	200	160	-0.89	*Gregorians.* Under C Echmiadzin (USSR). Armenians in Dacca. Declining.
Assemblies of God	1945	P-Pe2	ZF..n	120	12,350	850	15,000	12.17	Begun by Muslim convert. M=AoG(USA). Ex Baptists. Ex Baptists. All Namasudras. 6n,9f,1p.
Assoc of Baptists for World Evangelism	1956	I-Bap	x....	73	1,600	1,150	3,000	3.91	Regular Baptists. M=ABWE(USA). Bengali, tribal Mru, Tipperah. 7n,35f,1H,2h.
Bangladesh Baptist Fellowship	1882	P-Bap	TH..N	242	7,281	2,276	20,000	9.08	*BBU.* M=ABMS(Australia),NZBMS,SBC(USA). Bengalis. 82 schools. 40f,1H,2h,5r,1s.
Bangladesh Baptist Sangha	1793	P-Bap	Tu..N	230	12,000	22,000	25,000	0.51	*BUB.* Formerly Baptist Union. M=BMS(UK); Liebenzell Mission. Namasudras, Mizos. 38f,1s.
Bangladesh Ev Lutheran Church	1867	P-Lut	....N	186	4,950	9,000	8,200	-0.37	*Bangladesh Mission of Northern Chs.* M=SM(Norway),WMPL. Santals. 13f,1h,1p,2100Y.
Bangladesh Lutheran Church		P-Lut	.....	174	1,920	–	3,205	0.05	Bengalis, Oraons.
Bengal Evangelistic Mission	1833	I-Eva	.....	10	500	400	1,000	3.73	Indigenous body founded in Gopalganj by an Indian. 2 schools. 1h.
Catholic Church in Bangladesh:	c1580	R-Lat	P.F.R	78	119,000	120,392	216,895	2.38	*Katholik Mondoli.* C=3+2+13. 258f,2p. 87n 118x 202m 691w 6476Yy
M Dhaka (Dacca)	1886	R-Lat	Pcsc	20	35,000	62,000	64,205	0.14	Bengali tribal Garos; many of Portuguese origin. 28n 45x 93m 308w 1333Yy
D Chittagong	1927	R-Lat	Pcsc	11	11,000	17,486	19,734	0.48	Urban and rural. Bengali, English spoken. M=CSC. 9n 13x 22m 60w 405Yy
D Dinajpur	1927	R-Lat	Pcsc	15	17,000	26,100	31,000	0.69	Rural, poor. Santal, Bengali spoken. M=CSC,PIME. 13n 16x 21m 88w 805Yy
D Khulna	1952	R-Lat	Psx	9	13,000	14,806	24,029	1.96	*Dharmapradesh Khulna.* Formerly D Jessore. 12n 24x 33m 84w 780Yy
M Mymensingh	1987	R-Lat	Pcsc	11	28,000	–	50,896	12.50	Formed out of M Dhaka. M=CSC. Mostly Garos. 13n 11x 13m 86w 1588Yy
D Rajshahi	1990	R-Lat	Pcsc	12	15,000	–	27,031	20.00	Formerly part of D Dinajpur. M=CSC. 12n 9x 20m 65w 1565Yy
Children of God	1970	I-mar	.....	1	26	–	28	14.26	Main body in USA, Australia, et al.
Christ Groups	c1980	I-3hI	x....	132	5,000	–	10,000	6.67	Isolated home churches for converts after nationwide EHC campaign (Every Home for Christ).
Christian Brethren	1961	P-CBr	x....	1	40	50	100	2.81	*Open Brethren.* Emmaus Bible Courses. M=CMML(UK). In Ramna, Dacca. 2f.
Christian Church of Bangladesh		I-Eva	.....	28	1,510	–	3,015	0.05	Recent independent body of Evangelical character.
Church of Bangladesh	1805	P-Uni	.uE.N	42	4,620	17,000	13,200	-1.01	1970 union Anglican D Dacca (M=CMS,OMC,PCE(M=CWM). Bengalis. 20n,22f4H,2h.
Church of God (Anderson)	1969	P-Hol	x...N	39	1,337	1,254	2,230	2.33	M=CoG. Remnant of India body. Lalmanirhat, Nilphimari. Khasis, Bengalis. 5n,2f.
Church of Sylhet	c1880	P-Ref	....N	84	3,360	5,000	6,000	0.73	*Sylhet Christiya Dharmosovar.* M=PCW,SM. Santali, Khasi, Lushai, Garo. 9n,8f.
Evangelical Christian Church	1918	I-Eva	....N	61	5,995	18,500	14,600	-0.94	M=NEIGM(IM). A=1965. Bawm, Mru, Tipperah, Pankho. 20m,1f,1p(20). Formerly Bawm ECC.
Evangelical Church of Bangladesh		I-Eva	.....	53	2,050	–	5,000	0.05	Small mission, recent growth.
Free Baptist Churches (New Life)	1980	I-Bap	.....	56	1,030	–	3,430	6.67	Mission on bridges of mainline Baptist work.
Garo Baptist Convention	1882	P-Bap	TH..N	140	9,844	15,000	19,637	1.08	Begun by M=BMS, then ABMS. Members 20% of all Garos. 3n,33f,1h,1p(5).
Hidden Hindu believers in Christ	c1970	I-Hin	.....	4,000	120,000	–	200,000	62.95	Converted believers in Christ who choose to remain as witnesses in Hinduism.
Hidden Muslim believers in Christ	c1970	I-Mus	.....	300	30,000	–	40,000	52.79	Muslims who accept Christ as Lord but witness within Islam.
International Christian Church	c1980	I-Non	.....	1	200	–	320	6.67	Small no-church congregation.
Isolated radio churches	1952	I-3rZ	.....	1,000	16,000	12,200	30,000	3.66	Believers mostly aged 12-25. R=250(FEBC,RVOG,HCJB),T=100000(ICF,Emmaus, ICI,VOP).
Jamaat (Messianic Muslims)	1981	I-3mM	.....	1,000	60,000	–	100,000	7.14	*Jesus Mosques.* M=Global Partners for Development. Most members joined 1982-1991.
Jehovah's Witnesses	c1932	m-Jeh	x....	1	37	100	86	-0.60	First missionaries about 1932; witnessing reported from 1947. Few converts. 10Y.
New Apostolic Church	c1974	I-3aX	x....	120	11,000	–	17,738	4.76	*NAC.* M=Neuapostolische Kirche (HQ Zurich, Switzerland).
New Covenant Church	1995	I-3cI	.....	30	3,000	–	10,000	298.11	*Christabda Paricharja.* Aided by Christian Aid Mission (USA).
Reformed Church of Bangladesh	c1985	P-Ref	.....	10	1,000	–	2,000	10.00	Mission, slight results.
Seventh-day Adventist Church	1906	P-Adv	x....	58	7,000	2,851	15,900	7.12	*SDA, Bangladesh Section*, Southern Asia Division. 3nx,88mw,1H,2h,2r,24Y.
SIM Church	c1980	P-Non	.....	2	90	–	225	6.67	M=SIM. Mission from USA now a global denomination.
Tribal Baptist Church	c1980	I-Bap	.....	20	1,230	–	2,467	6.67	Small number of converts.
United Christian Church SCMSS	1905	I-Hol	x...N	30	2,000	3,500	5,000	1.44	*Sanjukta Christiya Mandali Samuher Sangha. Church of God.* M=CGNA(USA). Bogra. 6n,92Y.
World Missionary Evangelism	c1970	I-3oZ	x....	5	200	105	300	4.29	*Mukti Bani Sangsta.*M=American Evangelistic Association. All Namasudras. 35nm.
Other Protestant denominations		P-	.....	20	5,000	1,000	10,000	0.05	Total about 5 (see list below).
Totals				**8,461**	**460,250**	**247,828**	**826,236**		

Churches, members, growth, 1900-2025	*Congs*	*Adults*	*Affiliated*	*G%*	*Total denominations*	*6 Megablocs:* *O*	*R*	*A*	*P*	*I*	*m*
Total churches, members, and denominations (mid-1900)	100	17,400	36,250	2.78	10	1	1	1	6	1	0
Total churches, members, and denominations (mid-1970)	1,117	118,701	247,828	2.78	22	1	1	0	12	7	1
Total churches, members, and denominations (mid-1990)	7,000	406,000	728,240	5.54	38	1	1	0	17	18	1
Total churches, members, and denominations (mid-1995)	8,461	460,250	826,236	2.56	40	1	1	0	18	19	1
Total churches, members, and denominations (mid-2000)	9,000	519,000	931,740	2.43	42	1	1	0	19	20	1
Total churches, members, and denominations (mid-2025)	17,000	844,000	1,515,400	1.96	84	3	1	0	25	50	5

NOTES ON TABLE ABOVE

NATIONAL COUNCILS (Column 4, 5th letter).

E = National Christian Fellowship of Bangladesh (NCFB).

N = Bangladesh National Council of Churches (BNCC) (Jatio Church Parisad, Bangladesh).

n = associate member of BNCC.

R = Catholic Bishops' Conference of Bangladesh (CBCB).

OTHER PROTESTANT DENOMINATIONS. These include: Indo-Burma Pioneer Mission (Bibles for the World), New Life Center (begun 1972 in Dacca; M=Orebro Mission, 4 missionaries), Salvation Army (1970), World Missions (1972).

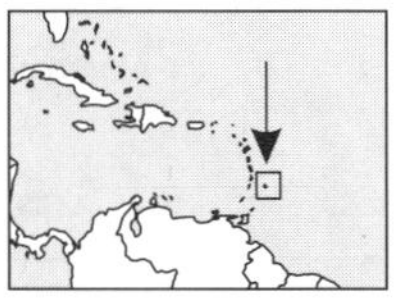

BARBADOS

SECULAR DATA, AD 2000

STATE
Official name: The Dominion of Barbados.
Short name: Barbados. **Adjective of nationality:** Barbadian.
Flag: Blue, gold, and blue bars, black trident.
Area: 430 sq. km. (166 sq. mi.).
Government: Parliamentary state (constitutional monarchy), since 1966 (1625 British possession, 1966 Independence).
Legislature: Senate, 21 members; House of Assembly, 28 members.
Official language: English.
Monetary unit: 1 Barbados dollar (BDS$) = 100 cents.
US$1= BDS$2.01.
Chief cities: BRIDGETOWN 123,682.
Political divisions: 11 provinces.
Armed forces: 600.

DEMOGRAPHY
Population: 270,000.
Population density: 628.9/sq. km. (1,629.2/sq. mi.).
Under 15 years: 57,000.
Growth rate p.a.: 0.43% (births 12.13, deaths 7.88).
Mortality: Infant, per 1,000: 10.9; **Maternal per 100,000:** 43.0.
Life expectancy: 77 (male 74, female 79).
Household size: 3.7. **Floor area per person, sq.m:** 30.0.
Major languages: English, Hindi, Greek.
Urban dwellers: 49.98%. **Urban growth rate p.a.:** 1.4%.
Labor force: 50%.

ETHNOLINGUISTIC PEOPLES
87.0% Barbadian Black; 6.0% Mulatto; 4.3% British; 1.2% USA White; 1.1% Indo-Pakistani.

ECONOMY
National income p.a. per person: US$6,559; **per family:** US$24,270.

EDUCATION
Adult literacy: 97% (male 98%, female 96%). **Schools:** 139.
Universities: 1. **School enrolment:** female/male: 88%/92%.

HEALTH
Access to health services: 90%. **Access to safe water:** 100%.
Hospitals: 10 (75 beds per 10,000). **Doctors:** 312.
Blind: 250. **Deaf:** 15,900. **Murder rate:** 6.
Lepers: 180. **Underweight prevalence under 5:** 6%.

LITERATURE
New book titles p.a.: 70 (250 p.a. per million). **Periodicals:** 73.
Newspapers: 2 dailies.

COMMUNICATION (per 1,000 people)
Phones: 345 (6% mobile). **Radios:** 1,132. **TV sets:** 284.
Daily newspaper circulation: 159. **Computers:** 90.

HUMAN LIFE AND LIBERTY (optimum condition=100.0%)
HDI: 90.7. **HSI:** 89.0. **HFI:** 80.0. **EFL:** 40.0.

Country Table 1. **Religious adherents in Barbados, AD 1900-2025.**

Year	1900		1970		mid-1990		Annual change, 1990-2000				mid-1995		mid-2000		mid-2025	
Name	*Adherents*	*%*	*Adherents*	*%*	*Adherents*	*%*	*Natural*	*Conversion*	*Total*	*Rate*	*Adherents*	*%*	*Adherents*	*%*	*Adherents*	*%*
Christians	**196,500**	**100.0**	**234,770**	**98.3**	**250,245**	**97.4**	**1,309**	**-146**	**1,163**	**0.46**	**256,585**	**97.1**	**261,875**	**97.0**	**284,200**	**95.7**
PROFESSION																
professing Christians	**196,500**	**100.0**	**234,770**	**98.3**	**250,245**	**97.4**	**1,309**	**-146**	**1,163**	**0.46**	**256,585**	**97.1**	**261,875**	**97.0**	**284,200**	**95.7**
AFFILIATION																
unaffiliated Christians	32,700	16.2	73,888	31.0	62,545	24.3	316	-69	247	0.39	64,111	24.3	65,017	24.1	60,600	20.4
affiliated Christians	**163,800**	**83.8**	**160,882**	**67.4**	**187,700**	**73.0**	**949**	**-33**	**916**	**0.48**	**192,474**	**72.8**	**196,858**	**72.9**	**223,600**	**75.3**
Protestants	16,280	8.3	50,582	21.2	80,000	31.1	405	111	516	0.63	83,421	31.6	85,158	31.5	105,000	35.4
Anglicans	146,600	75.0	90,000	37.7	79,300	30.9	401	-601	-200	-0.26	78,000	29.5	77,300	28.6	70,000	23.6
Independents	100	0.1	8,900	3.7	12,900	5.0	65	395	460	3.10	14,933	5.7	17,500	6.5	24,000	8.1
Roman Catholics	820	0.4	9,000	3.8	10,200	4.0	52	28	80	0.76	10,500	4.0	11,000	4.1	15,000	5.1
Marginal Christians	0	0.0	2,200	0.9	5,000	2.0	25	35	60	1.14	5,320	2.0	5,600	2.1	9,000	3.0
Orthodox	0	0.0	200	0.1	300	0.1	2	-2	0	0.00	300	0.1	300	0.1	600	0.2
Trans-megabloc groupings																
Evangelicals	10,000	5.1	74,000	31.0	78,400	30.5	397	-197	200	0.25	79,492	30.1	80,400	29.8	88,000	29.6
Pentecostals/Charismatics	0	0.0	14,000	5.9	45,000	17.5	228	162	390	0.83	47,057	17.8	48,900	18.1	65,000	21.9
Great Commission Christians	**2,000**	**1.0**	**12,000**	**5.0**	**45,200**	**17.6**	**229**	**243**	**472**	**1.00**	**47,520**	**18.0**	**49,919**	**18.5**	**59,400**	**20.0**
Baha'is	0	0.0	1,300	0.5	2,500	1.0	13	89	102	3.49	2,900	1.1	3,522	1.3	5,000	1.7
Muslims	0	0.0	400	0.2	1,750	0.7	9	18	27	1.45	1,800	0.7	2,021	0.8	3,200	1.1
Nonreligious	0	0.0	2,350	1.0	1,200	0.5	6	19	25	1.88	1,300	0.5	1,445	0.5	2,400	0.8
Hindus	0	0.0	100	0.0	800	0.3	4	5	9	1.09	860	0.3	892	0.3	1,150	0.4
Buddhists	0	0.0	0	0.0	100	0.0	1	0	1	0.77	100	0.0	108	0.0	150	0.1
Spiritists	0	0.0	0	0.0	50	0.0	0	0	0	0.77	50	0.0	54	0.0	90	0.0
Jews	0	0.0	30	0.0	30	0.0	0	0	0	0.65	30	0.0	32	0.0	60	0.0
Ethnoreligionists	0	0.0	0	0.0	25	0.0	0	0	0	1.14	25	0.0	28	0.0	50	0.0
Other religionists	0	0.0	50	0.0	300	0.1	2	15	17	4.61	350	0.1	471	0.2	700	0.2
World A (unevangelized persons)	0	0.0	477	0.2	1,799	0.7	9	29	38	1.95	2,114	0.8	2,160	0.8	2,970	1.0
World B (evangelized non-Christians)	0	0.0	3,508	1.6	4,956	1.9	26	117	143	1.87	5,606	2.0	5,965	2.4	9,830	3.3
World C (Christians)	196,500	100.0	234,770	98.2	250,245	97.4	1,309	-146	1,163	0.46	256,585	97.2	261,875	96.8	284,200	95.7
Country's population	**195,500**	**100.0**	**238,756**	**100.0**	**257,000**	**100.0**	**1,344**	**0**	**1,344**	**0.49**	**264,306**	**100.0**	**270,000**	**100.0**	**297,000**	**100.0**

COLUMNS, ROWS.
For meanings and definitions, see Codebook (Part 3). Note that, by definition, total 'Christians' = professing + crypto-Christians, which also = affiliated + unaffiliated Christians, and also = Great Commission Christians + latent Christians. Percentages may not always total exactly, due to rounding.

CENSUSES.
9.IV.1945: 58.0% Anglicans, 39.3% Protestants, 1.5% Roman Catholics, 0.5% marginal Protestants, 0.1% Orthodox. **7.IV.1960:** 57.6% Anglicans, 38.6% Protestants (7.9% Methodists, 4.8% Pentecostals, 2.0% SD Adventists), 2.8% Roman Catholics, 0.7% marginal Protestants (Jehovah's Witnesses), 0.1% Muslims. **7.IV.1970:** 53.1% Anglicans, 35.2% Protestants (8.6% Methodists, 7.2% Pentecostals, 2.6% SD Adventists), 5.0% Black indigenous, 3.9% Roman Catholics, 0.9% marginal Protestants, 0.8% nonreligious, 0.7% other religionists. **1990:** 35.7% Anglicans, 28% Protestants (12.7% Pentecostals, 5.9% Methodists, 4.5% SD Adventists), 7.1% Independents, 4.4% Roman Catholics, 1.8% Marginal Christians, 20.1% nonreligious, 2.9% other religionists.

NOTES ON RELIGIONS
BAHA'IS. Rapid growth of local spiritual assemblies: 1964, none; 1973, 9 By 1995 the total including many immigrants.
INDEPENDENTS. In 11 denominations in 1995 (see Table 2).
OTHER RELIGIONISTS. Including Rosicrucians (1 AMORC centre).
UNAFFILIATED CHRISTIANS. Since 1950 there has been a rapid decline of professing Anglicans and Protestants, and an even larger decline among affiliated Anglicans and Protestants, resulting in a sharp rise in the number of unaffiliated Christians in these churches, tapering off after AD 2000.

Great Commission Instrument Panel: status of Barbados (for explanation see start of Part 4)

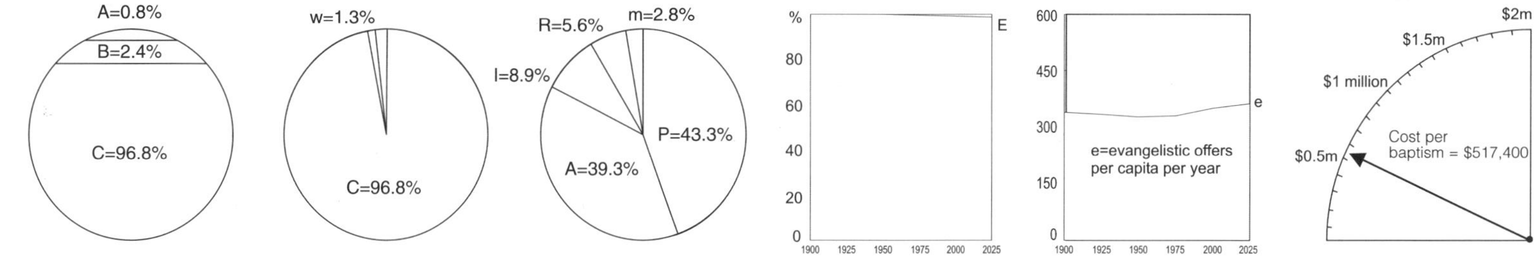

3 Worlds, AD 2000 | Religions, AD 2000 | Ecclesiastical blocs | Evangelization, 1900-2025 | Offers, 1900-2025 | Cost-effectiveness, AD 2000

Country status. Barbados is the most easterly of the Caribbean islands, just northeast of Venezuela. The population is 80% black, but a long tradition of racial harmony, begun under British rule, prevails. It has the distinction of having the third oldest elected parliament in the Western hemisphere.

HUMAN LIFE AND LIBERTY

Human need and development. Until recently the island had a sugar-based economy, but since the seventies light industry and tourism have become the largest revenue earners. It is an open economy, susceptible to external conditions and dependent on import. Nevertheless, the quality of life has not suffered during the global recession of the late 1980s, although it has not shown much improvement either. It does well in quality of life rankings, such as life expectancy and infant mortality rate.

Human rights and freedoms. All human rights are constitutionally guaranteed, and the government does not arbitrarily interfere in the private lives of its citizens. The legal system is based on the English model and prohibits arbitrary arrest and imprisonment. Freedoms of the press and speech as well as those of assembly and association are unrestricted; however, the only television service is state-owned. Women have made considerable progress in closing the gender gap in employment and in obtaining redress against abuse and exploitation. The close relationship between the Democratic Labor Party and the government in power since 1986 has ensured that the rights of workers do not suffer any abridgment.

Country summary. **Worlds A, B, C by ethnolinguistic peoples, cities, and major civil divisions in Barbados.**

	PEOPLES							CITIES							CIVIL DIVISIONS						
World	Num	Pop 2000	C%	Christians	E%	U%	Unevangelized	Num	Pop 2000	C%	Christians	E%	U%	Unevangelized	Num	Pop 2000	C%	Christians	E%	U%	Unevangelized
A	1	32	0.00	0	44	56	18	0	0	0.00	0	0	0	0	0	0	0.00	0	0	0	0
B	4	3,399	6.85	233	58	42	1,435	0	0	0.00	0	0	0	0	0	0	0.00	0	0	0	0
C	6	267,016	73.64	196,624	100	0	705	1	123,682	72.00	89,051	98	2	1,967	11	270,449	72.79	196,858	99	1	2,159
Total	**11**	**270,447**	**72.79**	**196,857**	**99**	**1**	**2,158**	**1**	**123,682**	**72.00**	**89,051**	**98**	**2**	**1,967**	**11**	**270,449**	**72.79**	**196,858**	**99**	**1**	**2,159**

Human environment. Despite a high density of population, Barbados has few serious environmental problems other than coastal pollution from oil slicks and soil erosion, especially in the hilly northeast. The government has a cabinet-level ministry dealing with the environment. Coral reefs surround most of the island and in some areas marine reserves have been established to protect them.

NON-CHRISTIAN RELIGIONS

Muslims make up about 0.7% of the population, and there are also over 3,000 Baha'is and several hundred East Indian Hindus. In addition, there is a larger group which claims no religious allegiance.

CHRISTIANITY

ANGLICAN CHURCH. Anglican clergy accompanied the first British settlers in 1626, and by 1637, the construction of six churches and 10 chapels had been completed. The diocese of Barbados, which is part of the Church of the Province of the West Indies, was created in 1824. In 1995, 37.6% of the population were professing Anglicans. Church institutions include 39 primary schools, 2 secondary schools, one preparatory school, 2 homes for the aged and one home for handicapped children.

PROTESTANT CHURCHES. The Protestant churches of Barbados are a mixture of long-established bodies (Methodists and Moravians) which owe their origin primarily to European efforts in the 18th century and a host of North American missions which have entered during the present century. The two largest churches at the present time are the New Testament Church of God, a Pentecostal group dating from World War I, and the older Methodist Church. Other important denominations include the Seventh-day Adventists, Wesleyan Church, Pentecostal Assemblies of the West Indies, Church of God (Anderson), and Church of the Nazarene.

CATHOLIC CHURCH. The diocese of Bridgetown-Kingstown, with headquarters in St Michael, was erected in 1970 and is responsible for work in the islands of Barbados and St Vincent. Catholicism has been less influential in Barbados than in most of the other islands of the West Indies.

The Holy See has diplomatic relations with Barbados and in AD 2000 is represented to government and the Catholic hierarchy by a pro-nuncio residing in Port of Spain.

BLACK INDIGENOUS CHURCHES. Five Black denominations from the USA are presently at work in Barbados, including one Baptist, one Methodist, one Orthodox and 2 Pentecostal bodies. The first to arrive was the African Methodist Episcopal Church in 1897. The Church of the First Born, on the other hand, spread to Barbados from Jamaica.

Renewal movements. In the 1990s the Pentecostal/Charismatic Renewal continued to spread rapidly across most older churches, and numbered over 48,900 adherents (of whom 64% Pentecostals, 22% Charismatics, and 14% Independents).

Indigenous missions. The majority of Christians sent overseas from Barbados have left to study in other lands. Very little direct missionary sending has taken place and most have ended up in Guyana and the United Kingdom.

CHURCH AND STATE

The Preamble to the constitution of 30 November 1966, states: 'The people of Barbados proclaim that they are a sovereign nation founded upon principles that acknowledge the supremacy of God.' In Article 11, among 'the fundamental rights and freedoms of the individual' is listed 'freedom of conscience and of assembly and association.' The constitutional protection of freedom of conscience is further explained in Article 19, which allows for complete freedom of religious belief and practice and prohibits any hindrance thereof, entitles religious communities to establish and maintain schools at their own expense and to provide for religious instructions in such schools while also exempting those who do not wish to participate and prohibits the administration of oaths contrary to a person's religious convictions.

The Anglican Church has been the established state church from early days. In 1969, an act of parliament (Anglican Church Act, 1969) was passed to repeal the Anglican Church Act, 1911, and to provide eventually for the church's complete disestablishment in 1977. Financial grants from the government have been reduced since at the rate of one-sixth annually and terminated entirely in 1977.

There is a governmental Ministry of Ecclesiastical Affairs which handles all matters relating to the churches. Churches desiring to perform marriages must be registered. There has been no tension over religious matters between church and state, but in 1975, the prime minister showed resentment over criticisms made by religious leaders.

Anglican Church, Diocese of Barbados. Anglican theological student at Codrington College.

BROADCASTING AND MEDIA

Shortwave programs from HCJB (Ecuador), TWR (Antilles), KNLS and AWR (Costa Rica) can be received. Barbados is a member of UNDA.

Christian television programming such as *CBN News* can be seen on local channels. Local television broadcasts have shown the 'Jesus' Film to 163,000 (54%). LeSEA programming can be received from the World Harvest Satellite.

INTERDENOMINATIONAL ORGANIZATIONS

The Barbados Ministerial Fraternal Association has for some time been an informal group of Conservative Evangelical and WCC-oriented clergy representing 16 different church traditions. In 1972, it crystallized out in the formation of the Barbados Council of Evangelical Churches, with 14 member denominations. Five churches also have since begun the process of forming the Barbados Christian Council in working relationship with the WCC. Christian Action for Development in the Caribbean (CADEC) is a project initiated through the WCC under Anglican, Methodist, Moravian, and Church of God sponsorship and is now an agency of the Caribbean Conference of Churches (CCC), with headquarters in Bridgetown, Barbados. CADEC is a member of CIDSE in Belgium and serves as an affiliate to Sodepax in the Caribbean.

FUTURE TRENDS AND PROSPECTS

Though professing Christians will likely remain above the 95% mark through 2025, affiliated Christians claim only 75%, continuing a trend since 1970.

Non-Christians are projected to claim close to 10% of Barbados' population by AD 2050. Within the Christian world, Marginal Christians could reach 6% in the same period.

BIBLIOGRAPHY

A history of the Moravian Church, Eastern West Indies province. G. O. Maynard. Port of Spain, Trinidad: Yuille's Printerie, 1968. 175p.

A missionary's cry from Barbados. R. W. Ives. Kingswood, KY: Missionary Office, [1928]. 72p.

A populous but unfruitful island: the origins of Methodism in Barbados. N. Titus. [Cave Hill, Barbados], 1986. 52p.

Barbados. R. B. Potter & G. M. S. Dann. *World bibliographical series*, vol. 76. Oxford, UK: CLIO Press, 1987. 357p. (See especially 'Religion,' 135–41).

'Christian political obedience.' J. D. Gibson. Th.M. thesis, Columbia Theological Seminary, Decatur, GA, 1983. 107p. (Church and state in Barbados).

'Church and society in Barbados in the eighteenth century,' K. Hunte, in *Social groups and institutions in the history of the Caribbean, paper presented to the VIth annual conference of Caribbean historians, Puerto Rico, April 7, 1974.* Association of Caribbean Historians, 1975.

Codrington chronicle: an experiment in Anglican altruism on a Barbados plantation, 1710–1834. F. J. Klingberg. Berkeley: University of California Press, 1949. 164p.

Cross and crown in Barbados: Caribbean political religion in the late 19th century. K. Davis. Frankfurt am Main: Peter Lang, 1983. 187p.

'Episcopacy, emancipation and evangelization: aspects of the history of the Church of England in the British West Indies.' J. Gilmore. Ph.D. dissertation, Sidney Sussex College, Cambridge University, Cambridge, UK, [1985]. 298p.

Historic churches of Barbados. B. Hill. Bridgetown, Barbados: Art Heritage Publications, 1984. 128p.

Methodism, 200 years in Barbados. F. Blackman. Bridgetown, Barbados: Caribbean Contact, 1988. 172p.

Over a century of Adventism, 1884–1991. G. O. Phillips. Barbados: East Caribbean Conference of Seventh–day Adventists, 1991. 166p.

'Parties and priorities: the background to Anglican failure to evangelize the Negro population of Barbados and Antigua,' J. E. Pinnington, *Historical magazine of the Protestant Episcopal Church*, 42 (June 1973), 155–69.

The African Methodist Episcopal Church in Barbados, 1892–1980. U. Hendricks. [St. John, Barbados, West Indies]: Caribbean Group for Social and Religious Studies, [1982]. 41p.

The church in Barbados in the seventeenth century. P. F. Campbell. The Garrison, St. Michael, Barbados: Barbados Museum and Historical Society, 1982. 188p.

The crown and mitre in 17th century Barbados. B. C. Ullyett. Bridgetown, Barbados: Lighthouse Communications, 1989. 54p.

The development of Methodism in Barbados, 1823–1883. N. Titus. Bern and New York: P. Lang, 1994. 302p.

The Moravian mission in Barbados, 1816–1886: a study of the historical context and theological significance of a minority church among an oppressed people. K. Lewis. Frankfurt: P. Lang, 1985. 273p.

'The Moravian mission in Barbados: historical sketch of the past hundred years,' *Journal of the Barbados Museum and Historical Society*, 31, 2 (May 1965), 73–78.

'The Rev. William Harte and attitudes to slavery in early nineteenth–century Barbados,' J. T. Gilmore, *Journal of ecclesiastical history*, 30 (October 1979), 461–74.

The revelations of Spiritual Baptists in Barbados: 30th anniversary. Sons of God Apostolic Spiritual Baptist Church. [Barbados, 1987]. 44p.

Country Table 2. **Organized churches and denominations in Barbados.**

Official name (bold type = church with over 10% of all affiliated) 1	*Begun* 2	*Type* 3	*Counc* 4	*Congs* 5	*Adults* 6	*Affiliated 1970* 7	*Affiliated 1995* 8	*G%* 9	*Names, notes, and other statistics* (see Codebook, Part 3) 10
African Methodist Episcopal Church	1897	I-Met	VwQ.L	3	105	200	300	1.64	*Windward Is Annual Conf*, 16th Episcopal Dist. M=AMEC. Begun from Bermuda. 5n,14w.
Anglican Church: D Barbados	1626	A-ACa	AwMRK	58	59,900	90,000	78,000	-0.57	CPWI. State church, 1626-1969. 96% Black, 4% White. 31n,30x,P=80%,1s,W=46%,2813y.
Barbados Baptist Convention	1972	P-Bap	T....	4	421	–	523	4.35	M=SBC(USA). Southern Baptist Missionaries.
Berean Bible Churches	1957	I-Non	xM...	20	600	500	1,000	2.81	Interdenominational. M=Berean Mission (USA). HQ Bridgetown. 5f.
Bible Missionary Church	1956	I-Hol	x....	2	80	200	133	-1.62	M=BMC(USA). Members West Indian Blacks. In Strathclyde. 1x,W=20%,6Y.
Catholic Ch: D Bridgetown	c1920	R-Lat	P.NMK	6	7,000	9,000	10,500	0.62	Diocese formed in 1989. C=3+2+4. (1990) 5n, 7x, 8m, 15w, 151Yy. , 5n, 7x, 8m, 15w, 151Yy
Christadelphian Ecclesia		m-Ade	x....	1	20	100	100	0.05	*Christadelphian Bible Mission (CMB)*. 1 ecclesia, linked with Birmingham (UK).
Christian Brethren		P-CBr	x....	8	500	1,000	1,300	0.05	*Brethren Assemblies. Open Brethren*. 1974, M=CMML(USA). 4f (Blacks).
Christian Union Church	1959	P-Hol	x.H.L	7	500	500	1,000	2.81	M=Chs of Christ in Christian Union (USA). HQ St Michael. 3n,2x,f,W=50%,35Y.
Church of Christ, Scientist		m-Sci	x....	1	60	100	120	0.05	*Christian Science*. M=CCS(Boston, USA). First Church, Bridgetown.
Church of God of Prophecy	1935	P-Pe3	Z....	16	700	500	1,940	5.57	M=CGP(USA). Holiness Pentecostals. Theocratic government. Emigration to UK.
Church of God (Anderson)	1912	P-Hol	x.H.L	24	2,800	3,000	7,000	3.45	*General Assembly of the CoG(Barbados)*. M=CoG(Anderson) (USA). 16n,1x,1k,1r.
Church of the First-Born		I-Non	x....	5	500	500	1,000	0.05	Indigenous evangelicals from Jamaica (HQ Kingston). Strict ethical standards.
Church of the Nazarene	1926	P-Hol	xFH.L	32	2,003	4,000	3,188	-0.90	*Barbados Dist*. M=CoN(USA). 99% Black. 7n,1x,19m,2f,35t(3023),132Y,115z.
Churches of Christ	1953	I-Dis	x....	10	600	100	1,000	9.65	M=CCCC(Instrumental) (USA). Independents. In Bridgetown. 5f.
Episcopal Orth Ch (Greek Communion)	c1940	I-Lib	x....	10	1,000	1,000	1,500	1.64	Black. Ex AOC(USA). Begun 1920 in Trinidad, 1921 Cuba, 1939 New York. 20mw,1s.
Fundamental Baptist Churches	1890	I-Bap	.....	9	1,500	3,000	3,000	0.00	M=South Atlantic Bapt Mission, NBCUSA(Blacks). Barbados Bapt Academy. 2n,5m,22w.
Greek Orthodox Church		O-Gre	Cw...	1	100	200	300	0.05	*Greek Orth Episcopal Church*, Silver Sands, Christ Ch. Greeks, Arabs. One priest.
Jehovah's Witnesses	1932	m-Jeh	x....	18	1,783	1,900	4,600	3.60	*Watch Tower. International Bible Students Association*. HQ Bridgetown. (1975) 85Y. (1995) 105Y.
Methodist Ch in Caribbean & Americas	1788	P-Met	VwQ.a	30	4,500	9,000	15,000	2.06	In *MCCA, South Caribbean District*. 6 Island Circuits. M=MMS. 6n,2x,514y.
Moravian Church	1765	P-Mor	xwQ.a	8	2,800	5,500	3,600	-1.68	*Barbados Conf, Eastern WI Prov, Unity of Brethren*. 99% Black. 3n,2f,W=48%,80Yy.
New Testament Church of God	1917	P-Pe3	ZFH.L	48	15,400	10,000	20,000	2.81	1935 joined by large Anglican pentecostal group. 1936,M=CoG(Cleveland). 70n,2f,1s.
Pentecostal Assemblies of the W Indies		P-Pe2	Z.H.L	20	4,589	500	7,400	0.05	2-stage Pentecostals. Emigration to UK. Formerly M=PAofC(Canada).
Pentecostal Assemblies of the World		I-3pU	x....	10	500	500	1,000	0.05	M=PAW(USA). Black pentecostal mission from USA. Jesus Only doctrine. 2f.
Presbyterian Church		P-Ref	R....	2	165	449	330	0.05	Small Reformed presence.
Salvation Army	1898	P-Sal	xwQ.a	8	611	3,000	940	-4.54	*Barbados Division*, Caribbean & CAmerica Territory. Many social projects. 19nx.
Seventh-day Adventist Church		P-Adv	x....	31	7,810	7,000	11,000	0.05	*SDA, East Caribbean Conference, Caribbean Union Conference*. HQ Bridgetown. 1r.
United Holy Church of America	1953	I-3pU	x.H.L	20	1,500	2,500	3,500	1.35	*Barbados District*. M=UHCA(USA Blacks). Spread to Trinidad, St Lucia. 10nx,1p.
Wesleyan Holiness Church	1911	P-Hol	VFH.L	72	3,600	5,133	7,200	1.36	Till 1968, M=Pilgrim Holiness, now WC. 14n,1x,2f,1s(25),W=45%,215Yy,128z.
World-Wide Missions of Barbados	c1965	I-Non	x....	6	200	300	500	2.06	M=World-Wide Missions (USA). Evangelicals linked to Pasadena, CA (USA).
Other Protestant denominations		P-	.....	25	2,000	1,000	3,000	0.05	Total about 12 (see list below).
Other Black indigenous churches		I-	.....	10	1,000	100	2,000	0.05	Including: AME Zion Ch (1971; Blacks from USA), Antioch Ch, Spiritual Baptists (Shouters).
Other marginal Protestant bodies		m-	.....	5	200	100	500	0.05	Including: Unity School of Christianity (2 churches, 8 associate ministers), from USA.
Totals				**530**	**125,047**	**160,882**	**192,474**		

Churches, members, growth, 1900-2025	*Congs*	*Adults*	*Affiliated*	*G%*	*Total denominations*	*6 Megablocs:* O	R	A	P	I	m
Total churches, members, and denominations (mid-1900)	420	74,100	163,800	-0.03	6	0	0	1	3	2	0
Total churches, members, and denominations (mid-1970)	418	72,790	160,882	-0.03	38	1	1	1	18	13	4
Total churches, members, and denominations (mid-1990)	400	122,000	187,700	0.77	52	1	1	1	26	17	6
Total churches, members, and denominations (mid-1995)	530	125,047	192,474	0.50	52	1	1	1	26	17	6
Total churches, members, and denominations (mid-2000)	550	128,000	196,858	0.45	52	1	1	1	26	17	6
Total churches, members, and denominations (mid-2025)	600	145,000	223,600	0.51	93	4	1	1	35	40	12

NOTES ON TABLE ABOVE
NATIONAL COUNCILS (Column 4, 5th letter).
a = member of both BCEC and Barbados Christian Council.
C = Barbados Christian Council.
E = Barbados Council of Evangelical Churches (BCEC).
OTHER PROTESTANT DENOMINATIONS. These include: Apostolic Church, Apostolic Faith, Christian Mission, Exclusive Brethren (groups: Raven-Taylor and Kelly-Continental), International Pentecostal Assemblies (in Black Rock St Michael), Missionary Ch, Streams of Power, West Indies Mission, Worldwide Evangelization Crusade.

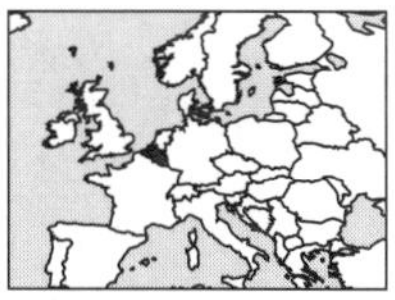

BELGIUM

SECULAR DATA, AD 2000

STATE
Official name: Le Royaume de Belgique/Koninkrijk België (The Kingdom of Belgium).
Short name: Belgium. **Adjective of nationality:** Belgian.
Flag: Bars of black, yellow, and red.
Area: 30,528 sq. km. (11,787 sq. mi.).
Government: Federal constitutional monarchy, since 1993 (1555 Spanish rule, 1797 French rule, 1830 Independence, 1830 constitutional monarchy).
Legislature: Parliament: Senate, 71 members; House of Representatives, 150 members.
Official language: Flemish (Vlaams), French.
Monetary unit: 1 Belgian franc (BF) = 100 centimes.
US$1= BF 34.47.
Chief cities: Antwerpen (Antwerp) 1,140,713; BRUXELLES (Brussels) 1,122,000; Liege (Luik) 777,759; Charleroi 497,765; Gent (Gand, Ghent) 482,210.
Political divisions: 11 provinces.
Armed forces: 63,000.

DEMOGRAPHY
Population: 10,161,000.
Population density: 332.8/sq. km. (862.0/sq. mi.).
Under 15 years: 1,741,000.
Growth rate p.a.: 0.02% (births 10.03, deaths 10.72).
Mortality: Infant, per 1,000: 6.4; **Maternal per 100,000:** 10.0.
Life expectancy: 78 (male 75, female 81).
Household size: 2.7. **Floor area per person, sq.m:** 50.0.
Major languages: 56.3% Flemish, 32.1% French, 0.6% German (along Eastern border), 11.0% bilingual; also Italian, Spanish, Dutch, English, Polish, Yiddish, Arabic, Greek, Russian, Turkish.
Urban dwellers: 97.35%. **Urban growth rate p.a.:** 0.2%.
Labor force: 42%.

ETHNOLINGUISTIC PEOPLES
53.6% Fleming (Flemish); 31.6% Walloon (French); 2.6% Italian; 2.0% French; 1.5% German.

ECONOMY
National income p.a. per person: US$24,709; **per family:** US$66,716.

EDUCATION
Adult literacy: 100% (male 100%, female 100%). **Schools:** 6,707. **Universities:** 21. **School enrolment:** female/male: 102%/101%.

HEALTH
Access to health services: 92%. **Access to safe water:** 89%.
Hospitals: 363 (76 beds per 10,000). **Doctors:** 37,792.
Blind: 4,780. **Deaf:** 615,400. **Murder rate:** 3.
Lepers: 200.

LITERATURE
New book titles p.a.: 14,230 (1,400 p.a. per million). **Periodicals:** 19,188. **Newspapers:** 32 dailies.

COMMUNICATION (per 1,000 people)
Phones: 458 (17% mobile). **Radios:** 500. **TV sets:** 464.
Daily newspaper circulation: 321. **Computers:** 405.

REFUGEES
Alien refugees from other countries: 16,400.

HUMAN LIFE AND LIBERTY (optimum condition=100.0%)
HDI: 93.2. **HSI:** 98.0. **HFI:** 87.5. **EFL:** 58.0.

Country status. Geographically, Belgium is a small nation in northeast Europe, between the Netherlands and France. But culturally there are 2 nations, Flemish and Walloon, siamesed by history, and preserved by a complex governmental system.

HUMAN LIFE AND LIBERTY

Human need and development. Belgium is a densely populated nation, with a high standard of living and an extensive social security system. However, an aging population and an influx of migrant labor have caused a crisis in the social security system.

Human rights and freedoms. All human rights and freedoms are guaranteed by the Constitution and enforced in practice. In recent years, these rights have been expanded beyond their traditional limits. These include the rights of privacy, rights of asylum seekers, and rights of women against harassment and abuse.

Violations of human rights occur primarily in official policy toward immigrants, many of whom are Turks and North Africans. Some 27% of the residents of Brussels are foreigners. Riots have occurred in Brussels by Moroccan and other immigrant youth to protest police brutality against them.

Human environment. Air and water pollution is a serious environmental problem. The Meuse supplies drinking water to 5 million people, yet it is highly polluted. The Escaut-Doel River has high concentration of nitrates. Air pollution has been significantly reduced, but, nevertheless, is worse than in France and Germany.

NON-CHRISTIAN RELIGIONS

Islam has entered Belgium through the massive immigration of manual workers characterizing many European countries in recent years. From the beginning of the 1960s, large number of workers have left Muslim Mediterranean countries to live and work in industrial zones of the country, especially in the provinces of Hainault, Liege and Limbourg, and in the Brussels region. In 1970, it was estimated that about 40,000 foreign Muslim workers were living in Belgium; 25,000 Moroccans; 10,000 Turks; 2,000 Algerians and 3,000 Tunisians, Libyans, and Egyptians. By 1995, over 350,000 nationals of Muslim countries lived in Belgium, including personnel and families of embassies, offices, and organizations. The General Council of the Islamic Community, and the Islamic Center of Muslim Culture, were created in 1863. In 1969 the Belgian government gave the Islamic Center a mosque and buildings in Brussels. Official recognition of the Islamic religion by the Belgian parliament in July 1974 has assisted the Muslim community financially, resulting in an increase in the number of imams.

Judaism has an ancient history in Belgium, dating back to the 13th century. At the time of Belgian independence in 1830, the Jewish population was 3,000 rising to 10,000 in 1900, 50,000 in 1914 and 85,000 in

Country Table 1. **Religious adherents in Belgium, AD 1900-2025.**

Year	1900		1970		mid-1990		Annual change, 1990-2000				mid-1995		mid-2000		mid-2025	
Name	*Adherents*	*%*	*Adherents*	*%*	*Adherents*	*%*	*Natural*	*Conversion*	*Total*	*Rate*	*Adherents*	*%*	*Adherents*	*%*	*Adherents*	*%*
Christians	**6,623,000**	**99.0**	**8,940,000**	**92.6**	**8,838,290**	**88.8**	**18,668**	**-5,577**	**13,091**	**0.15**	**8,932,780**	**88.6**	**8,969,202**	**88.3**	**8,478,570**	**85.5**
PROFESSION																
professing Christians	**6,623,000**	**99.0**	**8,940,000**	**92.6**	**8,838,290**	**88.8**	**18,668**	**-5,577**	**13,091**	**0.15**	**8,932,780**	**88.6**	**8,969,202**	**88.3**	**8,478,570**	**85.5**
AFFILIATION																
unaffiliated Christians	50,000	0.8	75,398	0.8	365,990	3.7	772	7,680	8,452	2.10	407,455	4.0	450,506	4.4	366,570	3.7
affiliated Christians	**6,573,000**	**98.2**	**8,864,602**	**91.8**	**8,472,300**	**85.1**	**17,879**	**-13,239**	**4,640**	**0.05**	**8,525,325**	**84.5**	**8,518,696**	**83.8**	**8,112,000**	**81.8**
Roman Catholics	6,518,000	97.4	8,654,602	89.6	8,200,000	82.4	17,305	-15,065	2,240	0.03	8,241,605	81.7	8,222,396	80.9	7,750,000	78.1
Protestants	25,000	0.4	78,980	0.8	117,000	1.2	247	553	800	0.66	120,322	1.2	125,000	1.2	150,000	1.5
Marginal Christians	20,000	0.3	50,540	0.5	64,500	0.7	136	614	750	1.11	68,850	0.7	72,000	0.7	100,000	1.0
Orthodox	1,000	0.0	55,000	0.6	49,200	0.5	104	-174	-70	-0.14	49,000	0.5	48,500	0.5	45,000	0.5
Independents	8,000	0.1	13,480	0.1	30,500	0.3	64	886	950	2.75	34,548	0.3	40,000	0.4	57,000	0.6
Anglicans	1,000	0.0	12,000	0.1	11,100	0.1	23	-53	-30	-0.27	11,000	0.1	10,800	0.1	10,000	0.1
Trans-megabloc groupings																
Evangelicals	7,000	0.1	19,300	0.2	25,900	0.3	55	125	180	0.67	27,575	0.3	27,700	0.3	35,800	0.4
Pentecostals/Charismatics	0	0.0	15,000	0.2	278,600	2.8	588	1,802	2,390	0.83	291,900	2.9	302,500	3.0	410,800	4.1
Great Commission Christians	**937,000**	**14.0**	**3,862,000**	**40.0**	**4,500,000**	**45.2**	**9,497**	**8,036**	**17,533**	**0.38**	**4,600,000**	**45.6**	**4,675,333**	**46.0**	**4,700,000**	**47.4**
Nonreligious	50,000	0.8	475,790	4.9	550,000	5.5	1,161	2,690	3,851	0.68	565,000	5.6	588,507	5.8	650,000	6.6
Muslims	0	0.0	90,000	0.9	335,000	3.4	707	2,246	2,953	0.85	358,000	3.6	364,534	3.6	500,000	5.0
Atheists	10,000	0.2	100,000	1.0	166,000	1.7	350	659	1,009	0.59	170,000	1.7	176,093	1.7	212,000	2.1
Buddhists	0	0.0	4,000	0.0	20,000	0.2	42	131	173	0.83	21,000	0.2	21,725	0.2	30,000	0.3
Jews	10,000	0.2	40,000	0.4	23,000	0.2	49	-215	-166	-0.75	21,800	0.2	21,338	0.2	20,000	0.2
Confucianists	0	0.0	1,000	0.0	8,000	0.1	17	11	28	0.35	8,200	0.1	8,281	0.1	10,000	0.1
Spiritists	0	0.0	800	0.0	3,400	0.0	7	10	17	0.48	3,500	0.0	3,567	0.0	5,000	0.1
Ethnoreligionists	0	0.0	500	0.0	3,000	0.0	6	14	20	0.65	3,100	0.0	3,201	0.0	4,000	0.0
Baha'is	0	0.0	1,800	0.0	2,200	0.0	5	11	16	0.70	2,300	0.0	2,358	0.0	4,000	0.0
New-Religionists	0	0.0	100	0.0	300	0.0	1	1	2	0.49	310	0.0	315	0.0	400	0.0
Zoroastrians	0	0.0	10	0.0	10	0.0	0	0	0	0.96	10	0.0	11	0.0	30	0.0
Other religionists	0	0.0	2,000	0.0	1,800	0.0	4	19	23	1.22	2,000	0.0	2,032	0.0	4,000	0.0
World A (unevangelized persons)	0	0.0	48,277	0.5	179,118	1.8	380	3,564	3,944	2.00	201,760	2.0	223,542	2.2	277,704	2.8
World B (evangelized non-Christians)	70,000	1.0	667,269	6.9	933,592	9.4	1,969	2,013	3,982	0.37	953,504	9.4	968,256	9.5	1,161,726	11.7
World C (Christians)	6,623,000	99.0	8,940,000	92.6	8,838,290	88.8	18,668	-5,577	13,091	0.15	8,932,780	88.6	8,969,202	88.3	8,478,570	85.5
Country's population	**6,693,000**	**100.0**	**9,655,547**	**100.0**	**9,951,000**	**100.0**	**21,017**	**0**	**21,017**	**0.21**	**10,088,045**	**100.0**	**10,161,000**	**100.0**	**9,918,000**	**100.0**

COLUMNS, ROWS.
For meanings and definitions, see Codebook (Part 3). Note that, by definition, total 'Christians' = professing + crypto-Christians, which also = affiliated + unaffiliated Christians, and also = Great Commission Christians + latent Christians. Percentages may not always total exactly, due to rounding.

CENSUSES.
The religion question has not been asked.

NOTES ON RELIGIONS
ATHEISTS. Parti Communiste Belge (PCB) (legal; split over Sino-Soviet dispute) and 2 rival groups. Communists are 80% French-speaking Walloons, in southern industrial and mining regions. Communists, and also those in the Socialist party, are almost all atheists. There is also the Ligue Humniste (Humanist League), which is in dialogue with the Protestant Federation of Belgium.
BAHA'IS. Growth from 4 local spiritual assemblies (1964) to 11 (1973), then stagnant to 11 again (1996).
BUDDHISTS. In 5 separate groups (4 in Brussels, 1 in Liège).
JEWS. Decline from 85,000 in 1940. Mainly urban, in Brussels and Antwerp; in 12 recognized communities, 10 Ashkenazi and 2 Sefardi. About 45% are religiously practicing.
MUSLIMS. Migrants, Algerian Arabs (18,000), Arabized Berbers (40,000), Egyptian Arabs (10,000), Kabyle (50,000), Kurds (26,000), Libyan Arabs (5,000), Moroccan Arabs (130,000), Persians (3,500), Tunisian Arabs (12,000), Turks (60,000). *Hajj pilgrims to Mecca.* (1976) 2.
OTHER RELIGIONISTS. Adherents of smaller religions and cults, including Rosicrucians (8 AMORC centers).
PENTECOSTALS/CHARISMATICS. The Catholic Charismatic Renewal began in 1970. In 1996, regular prayer groups numbered 250 French-speaking and 100 Flemish-speaking, with 14 charismatic covenant communities (ICCRS).

Great Commission Instrument Panel: status of Belgium (for explanation see start of Part 4)

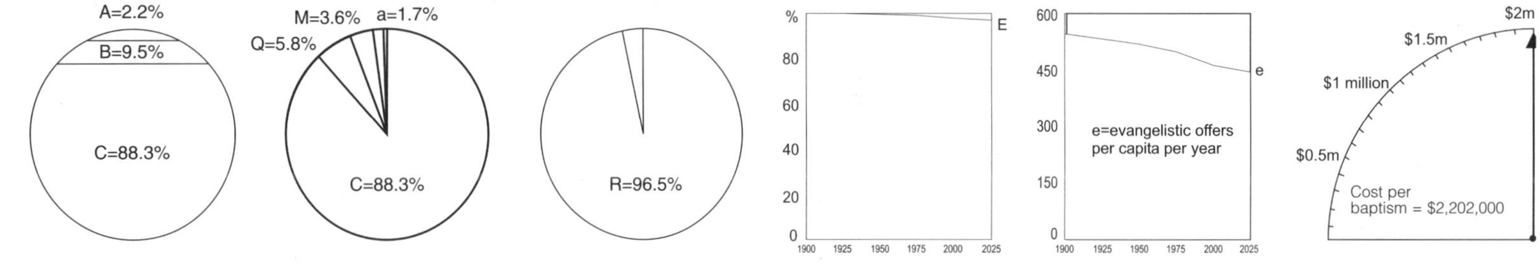

3 Worlds, AD 2000 — Religions, AD 2000 — Ecclesiastical blocs — Evangelization, 1900-2025 — Offers, 1900-2025 — Cost-effectiveness, AD 2000

1940 at the time of the German invasion. Following the war, however, there were only 30,000 left (1945). In 1970, they numbered 40,000, of whom many originally came from central and eastern Europe and who were concentrated mostly in urban areas including Brussels (18,000) and Antwerp (12,000). Today they form a stable population, socially and economically integrated into Belgian society. The number practicing their religion is estimated to be about 9,600 (45 percent). Belgian Jews are led by the Israelite Central Consistory of Belgium in Brussels, created the day following national independence. There are also a very large number of different Jewish organizations (cultural, philanthropic, political, zionist) which nourish the life of Belgium's Jewish community.

Buddhism is represented by 21,000 members divided into five different groups (four in Brussels and one in Liege), with no attempt at unification.

CHRISTIANITY

Christianity came to Belgium at the time of the Roman occupation. By the 4th century, the bishoprics of Tongres and Tournai had ben established, but these were destroyed during the Frankish invasion. The situation improved during the 6th century, 30 monasteries being built between 530 and 640. A period of consolidation and expansion ensued. The 10th century was characterized by the secularization of the church, but this was followed by the information of new religious institutes, including the Beguines (women living in common and engaging in social service without religious vows). The 15th century was influenced by the mysticism of John Ruysbroeck, Thomas A. Kempis and Denis Chartreus. The University of Louvain was founded in 1425, while the Reformation, led by Guy de Bres in Belgium, made its appearance a century later. The Peace of Westphalia of 1648 divided the Low Countries into religious spheres of influence, Calvinism in northern Holland and Catholicism in Belgium. The Catholic Hapsburgs ruled during 1715-1794 followed by France between 1794 and 1814. The Treaty of Vienna united the Netherlands and Belgium under one crown, and in 1830 Belgium was granted independence. Freedom of religion was proclaimed, and three religious communities (Catholic, Protestant and Jewish) were officially recognized at independence.

CATHOLIC CHURCH. The Catholic faith is closely linked to Belgian history in the sense that it was the common hostility of anticlerical liberals and Catholics to the Calvinist William I of Holland, which led to the creation of the state in 1830. The remarkable progress of Catholicism in Belgium during the 19th century is related to the fact that the bishops of that time used to the full liberties offered by the constitution (liberties of teaching, press, and association) and the attachment of the majority of the citizens to their religions. Since 1831, there has been a significant restoration of religious orders and a development of parish missions. Charitable institutions of all types have also been established, but primary attention has been given to schools. This blending of initiatives, crowned by the formation of a political party conceived as the defender of church interest, helped to create the strongly institutionalized Catholicism which still characterized Belgium.

The Catholic Church in Belgium is conceived traditionally as occupying a more important place than in other neighboring countries. This is due both to its massive presence (90 percent of the population were baptized Catholics in 1971) and the Catholic bias of many temporal institutions (Catholic trade unions, worker movements, hospitals, schools, and universities). Nevertheless, during the past decade, a growing number of Belgian Catholics have begun to question the pastoral conceptions which have prevailed until now and to ask whether the activity of the past has not given way now to passivity. These doubts are shared by a relatively important part of the clergy who through diverse informal groups support the tendency towards the increasing collaboration of Catholics and non-Catholics within pluralistic institutions. This is still a minority movement, but recent trends in Belgian society encourage its growth, such as the weakening of the Christian Social Party (which no longer has a monopoly of Christian votes), and decline in religious practice (from 45% Sunday mass attendance in 1964 to 42% in 1968 and 34% in 1972) and the fall in annual priestly vocations (from 156 in 1964 to 57 in 1973).

The powerful influence of the church and the Catholic world are not spread evenly across the country. A morphological analysis of Belgian Catholicism reveals a clear difference between the Flemish area of the north and the Wallon (Francophone) area of the south. The church thus, like the state, is split by cultural cleavage and experiences the tensions of the communal problem. At least two indicators reveal the religious significance of regional differences:

Country summary. **Worlds A, B, C by ethnolinguistic peoples, cities, and major civil divisions in Belgium.**

	PEOPLES							CITIES							CIVIL DIVISIONS						
World	Num	Pop 2000	C%	Christians	E%	U%	Unevangelized	Num	Pop 2000	C%	Christians	E%	U%	Unevangelized	Num	Pop 2000	C%	Christians	E%	U%	Unevangelized
A	2	158,514	0.43	686	47	53	83,590	0	0	0.00	0	0	0	0	0	0	0.00	0	0	0	0
B	15	292,946	5.26	15,416	58	42	123,726	0	0	0.00	0	0	0	0	0	0	0.00	0	0	0	0
C	17	9,709,702	87.57	8,502,595	100	0	12,128	17	4,731,578	83.29	3,940,833	98	2	104,360	11	10,161,163	83.84	8,518,696	98	2	219,443
Total	**34**	**10,161,162**	**83.84**	**8,518,697**	**98**	**2**	**219,444**	**17**	**4,731,578**	**83.29**	**3,940,833**	**98**	**2**	**104,360**	**11**	**10,161,163**	**83.84**	**8,518,696**	**98**	**2**	**219,443**

Sunday practice and the type of participation of Catholics in the diverse organizations and movements of the church. In both, Flemish Catholics show themselves to be significantly more active than French-speaking. The Germanic cultural context appears to furnish greater possibilities for the development of mass movements and structured organizations than Francophone society. This difference is not always fully evident given the often unified structures of these diverse movements, but the contrast becomes apparent on closer examination.

Catholic Charismatic Renewal. Cardinal Primate of Belgium, L.-J. Suenens (center), world leader of Catholic charismatics, celebrates at a charismatic liturgy.

In reality, it is increasingly difficult to speak of a single Catholic Church in Belgium. Although there is one Ecclesiastical province and one Episcopal conference, the fact is that there are 2 Catholic communities each with their own sensibilities and interests. The clearest proof of this was the 1966 conflict over the Catholic University of Louvain which resulted in the forced removal of the French section of the university to a French-speaking part of the country. Many observers believe that pastoral efficiency will ultimately require a restructuring of the church to conform to present reality.

Beyond the existence of presbyterial and pastoral councils in each diocese, there is also a Flemish Interdiocesan Pastoral Council (Interdiocesaan Pastooraal Beraad, IPB) which serves in part the function of a permanent synodal assembly for the Flemish part of the country and draws its inspiration from the Netherlands (although, unlike the Netherlands, it has never had to submit its statutes to Rome for approval).

The presence in Brussels of a large number of foreign officials and their families has led to the creation of a European Catholic center (Foyer Catholique Europeen) concerned to respond to the need for pastoral service of members of the European Economic Community and other international institutions.

The Holy See has diplomatic relations with Belgium and in AD 2000 is represented to government and the Catholic hierarchy by a nuncio residing in Brussels.

PROTESTANT CHURCHES. Though clearly a minority, Protestantism has a long history in Belgium. The country was reached early on by the Reformation and had its own reformer, Guy De Bres, who published in 1561 the *Confessio Belgica*. However, the political context did not enable Protestantism to survive, other than in a few centers. At the time of independence in 1830, there were only a few thousand Protestants among Belgium's three million inhabitants. At that time, Protestants, Catholics, and Jews were all officially recognized and accorded the same juridical and material privileges.

The Protestant community in 1995 is about 120,000 affiliated. They are distributed unevenly throughout the country, forming 1.2 percent of the total population, with more in the French than in the Flemish area. The provinces of Limbourg and Luxembourg are virtually devoid of Protestants.

The largest and oldest denomination is the Protestant Church of Belgium, which is popularly considered by other Protestants to be a national church because of its official recognition and financial support accorded by the state. In 1830, the scattered Protestant congregations then existing joined together to form the Evangelical Protestant Church of Belgium, and in 1969, this body merged with the Methodists to form the present church.

Belgium's second Protestant church both in size and age is the Reformed Church of Belgium, formed in 1837 among coal miners through the joint work of the Evangelical Free Church of Switzerland and the British and Foreign Bible Society. Between 1931 and 1969, it was known as the Belgian Christian Missionary Church.

Pentecostalism came to Belgium in 1931 with the arrival of the first missionaries of the Assemblies of God, and this remains the principal Pentecostal community. Nine smaller Pentecostal denominations are also present, as well as a number of fast-growing independent charismatic churches. Other major churches include the Union of Free Evangelical Churches; Reformed Churches of the Netherlands in Belgium; Adventists, 3 Baptist denominations, 3 Brethren, and 3 Lutheran or Lutheran Reformed.

ORTHODOX CHURCHES. The Orthodox community in Belgium is composed primarily of Russians and Greeks, with a relatively small number of Belgians, altogether totalling about 44,000. The Russian Orthodox, with about 11,000 affiliated, consists for the most part of families in exile since the revolution of 1917 and their descendants. They are divided into two groups, those under the Moscow Patriarchate and those belonging to the Russian Orthodox Church Outside of Russia with headquarters in New York. The Greeks, with 38,000 affiliated, have grown in recent decades through the influx of Greek migrant workers. They are under the Greek archbishop of London and, thus, are attached to the Patriarchate of Constantinople. Lacking the official recognition granted to other traditional denominations in Belgium, Orthodoxy receives no salary support for its ministers nor other financial aid from the state. Recently, several Catholic dioceses have put places of worship at the disposal of local Orthodox communities.

MARGINAL CHURCHES. Jehovah's Witnesses, who entered Belgium prior to World War I, have become the second-largest denomination in the country, surpassed only by the Roman Catholics. Their community is 25% larger than the largest Protestant Church. Other marginal bodies include Mormons, Christian Scientists, Unitarians and Apostolic Rosicrucians.

OTHER CHURCHES. The Anglican Church exists mainly for the sizeable English-speaking expatriate community. Nevertheless, there are also a few native Belgian members, and the Anglican Church is one of Belgium's officially-recognized religious communities. There are around 10 smaller Catholic (non-Roman) churches: The Belgian Old Catholic Church, which traces its origin to the Jansenist controversy of the early 18th century and is related to the Utrecht-based Old Catholic Church in the Netherlands; the Catholic Apostolic (Irvingite) Church, and its secession the New Apostolic Church; Antoinistes and several smaller bodies under bishops-at-large.

Art and architecture. Belgium has some of the finest cathedrals in Europe. Most impressive are the Gothic Cathedral of Our Lady in Antwerp, Church of Saint Gudule in Brussels, the Chapel of the Holy Blood in Bruges, the Church of Notre Dame in Bruges (which contains Michelangelo's Virgin and Child, one of his few paintings outside Italy), the Cathedral of Antwerp, the fourth largest in Europe, which contains three works of Rubens, Assumption of Our Lady over the High Altar and the two companion masterpieces, the Elevation of the Cross and Descent from the Cross, the Churches of St Augustine, St James and St Paul, which also contain works of Rubens, the Cathedral of Malines(or Mechelen), the seat of the Cardinal-Primate, which contains one of Van Dyck's masterpieces, an altarpiece of the Crucifixion, the Church of Notre Dame of Malines which contains Rubens's Miraculous Draught of Fishes, the Beguinage Church, the baroque Church of SaintPierre, and the simple shrine of St John Berchmans in the Jesuit church on Rue de Recollets in Louvain (or Leuven), and the Cathedral at Tournai. Many museums contain precious religious art and relics. Of these the most notable are the Treasury of the Church of Our Lady at Alsemberg, Museum of St Bernard's Abbey at Bornem, the Beguine's House, Cathedral Museum and Museum of the Holy Blood at Brugge, the Old Beguinage at Brussels, St Dymphne Museum at Geel, Museum of the Blessed Amandina at Herk-deStad, Treasury of the Collegiate Church of Notre Dame in Huy, Museum of Local History at Latour, Museum of Christian Art at Louvain, Diocesan Museum and Cathedral Treasury at Liege, Church Treasury at Maaseik, Collegiate Church of St Waudru and Iconographic Museum at Mons, Diocesan Museum at Namur, Abbey Museum at Stavelot, Cathedral Treasury at Tournai, Father Damien Museum at Tremelo, and Museum of the Portede-Bruxelles at Villers-La-Ville. Belgian painters of the Middle Ages have left a vast treasury of Christian art distributed throughout the major churches and museums.

Renewal movements. In the 1990s the Pentecostal/Charismatic Renewal continued to spread rapidly across most older churches, and numbered over 302,500 adherents (of whom 4% Pentecostals, 88% Charismatics, and 7% Independents).

Indigenous missions. Most of the missionaries from Belgium are sent out through the Catholic orders. Protestants now send nearly 10 times the number of missionaries to Belgium than are sent out.

CHURCH AND STATE

The constitution of 1831, still in force, guarantees freedom of religion and worship in its Articles 14 and 15, and the nonintervention of government in the appointment of clergy in Article 16. Although the constitution does not mention specifically the phrase 'recognized churches or religions,' 5 churches or denominations or religions are in fact recognized officially, which means that they are accorded juridical personality and receive the benefit of salaries and pensions from the government for heads of churches, bishops, priests, and vicars of parishes, as defined in Article 117. At the time of Belgian independence in 1830, official recognition was given to Catholics, Protestants, and Jews. This was extended to Anglicans in 1870 and to Muslims in July 1974. The Administrations of Religions of the Ministry of Justice is responsible for relations with these 5 recognized religious bodies, and churches or denominations wishing to benefit from the advantages offered by the Belgian constitution must be affiliated with one of these. Others are not legally registered as churches, although they may be registered as 'non-profit organizations' (in uniformity with the law of 21 June 1921), a solution little utilized, or they may receive official recognition as 'establishments for public use'.

The Catholic Church holds a position of unique importance within the Belgian context. Although the government has a definite Catholic stamp to it, there is no concordat with the Holy See, no state religion, nor official collaboration between church and state. It is a unique system which is neither one of union nor of separation but a reciprocal type of independence in which government recognizes the social usefulness of religion and accords it aid and protection. The constitution affirms the separation of the 2, but the administration is practically that of a regime with a concordat, bringing together the advantages of a union with the benefits of independence. In addition to the protection given to private and public exercise of worship and salaries for clergy guaranteed by the constitution, substantial material assistance is also provided for the upkeep of church buildings. The provincial and general laws of 1836 charged the administrative authorities with the responsibility of supplementing the insufficient resources of places of worship and of covering designated necessary expenses. In addition to regular subsidies, churches have also been able to obtain extra subsidies from government in certain cases determined by the law. From the fiscal point of view, churches benefit from other important advantages. Complete freedom of education is maintained, with all impediments removed, according to Article 17 of the constitution. There was nothing to prevent the Catholic Church from establishing a complete educational system, which was accomplished through generous support from the faithful and large government subsidies. In recent years, this assistance has been increased even more. Since 1930, the Catholic University of Louvain has received subsidies for the salaries of its scientific staff and equipment.

Eglise Catholique de Belgique. Cathedral, Diocese of Antwerp.

There is no doubt that this system of separation with reciprocal consideration has contributed greatly to the strength of the Catholic Church and that it is one of the reasons for the very institutionalized pattern of Catholicism in the country. It is also evident that the protection and assistance which the Catholic Church enjoys in Belgium has negative aspects, even if they do not appear very important at the legal level. These include the obligation to celebrate religious marriages after a civil marriage, and the legal offense involved if a clergyman, while exercising his priestly functions, attacks the government or any act of public authority. There exist also certain activities of religious authorities which produce effects within the civil order and so must first be submitted to government before being put into effect. The coherence of a system in which the church makes use of the government to its own advantage means in turn that it is also made use of through a system of informal ties, binding it to traditional and conservative political forces in the state. This has been in evidence throughout the history of the nation, although less noticeable in recent years. One manifestation of this was the creation and maintenance of a denominational political party called at first the Catholic Party but, since 1944, the Christian Social Party. Its mission was to defend the institutional interests of the church, and for many years, it received the open support of the hierarchy. The influence of the Christian Social Party and of the religious factor in Belgian public life declined after unpopular party involvement in a labor dispute in 1960. Finally in 1966, the intervention of the bishops concerning the maintenance of the French section of the University of Louvain provoked a massive Flemish reaction. With the archbishop's replacement by cardinal Suenens, the pastoral conceptions of the primate of Belgium no longer coincided with the ideas of the Christian Social Party.

Tensions between Flemish and Walloon have periodically arisen in the 1980s and 1990s also.

BROADCASTING AND MEDIA

Numerous 30 and 60-minute Christian programs are aired on local channels in French and Flemish. Radio Spes is a Catholic radio station broadcasting in Flemish. Shortwave programs from HCJB (Ecuador), TWR (Monaco), AWR (Slovakia), KNLS and the Vatican, as well as other international broadcasters, can be clearly received and cover most of the major European languages. Satellite TV and radio programs are received in English, Arabic, German and Italian.

For television, Radio Television Catholique Belge is a Catholic radio and TV production center. TELEPRO produces a Catholic magazine-format television show.

INTERDENOMINATIONAL ORGANIZATIONS

The Federation of Protestant Churches in Belgium was founded in 1923 and reorganized in 1969. It consists of 5 full member churches and one associate. The main Protestant communities train their pastors in the Protestant Faculty of Theology of Brussels.

For coordination of foreign missions, the Protestant Mission of Belgium (Mission Protestante de Belgique), which is affiliated to CWME of the WCC, was founded in 1910 through the efforts of the Reformed churches in Belgium. Originally, it was called the Belgian Society of Protestant Missions in the Congo (Société Belge des Missions Protestantes au Congo). The missionaries coordinated the activities of churches in Belgium, Switzerland, and the Netherlands in the cooperative work with the Evangelical Presbyterian Church in Rwanda.

The Catholic Episcopal Conference maintains a Commission for Ecumenism, and there is also an ecumenical commission attached to each diocese. In the diocese of Antwerp, the commission is itself ecumenical in membership.

Several transconfessional organizations have their headquarters in Belgium. (1) Academie Internationale des Sciences Religieuses, founded in Brussels in 1966, is an independent body consisting of theologians representing different denominations from European countries together with Egypt, Peru, and Brazil. Activities include conferences and publications. (2) Secrétariat Européen du Mouvement Chrétien pour la Paix (MCP), founded in Liege in 1923, includes within its membership Catholics, Protestants, Orthodox, and Anglicans, although it has no official link with the various church hierarchies. (3) Union Internationale Chretienne des Gerants d'Entreprise (UNIAPAC), founded in Brussels in 1931 as a Catholic organization, later became interdenominational. Its purpose is to study and promote Christian social teachings. (4) Confédération Mondiale du Travail (CMT), with headquarters in Brussels, also began as a Catholic organization but became interdenominational in 1968.

Three ecumenical centers are prominent. (1) The Monastère Bénédictin de Chèvetogne, founded in 1926, is dedicated to the development of spiritual ecumenism, scientific study, and dialogue, with special emphasis on relations between Catholics and Orthodox. In addition to an extensive ecumenical library, the center publishes the journal *Irenikon.* (2) Centre Oecuménique pour Eglise et Société, founded in Brussels in 1965, is recognized, supported, and guided by the Churches' Commission to the European Communities. This commission is composed of Christian councils or federations in nearly all the member countries of the European Economic Community. It maintains observers at the WCC and CEC (Conference of European Churches) in Switzerland and OCIPE in Belgium, in addition to publishing an information bulletin. (3) Foyer Oriental Chrétien 'Pro Russia,' founded in Brussels in 1954, is a Catholic center for ecumenical spirituality and dialogue which gives spiritual and material aid to Eastern Christians, especially Russian Orthodox.

The Comité Interecclésial Bruxellois, founded in 1971, groups together the parishes of the major Christian denominations in Brussels. The Institut d'Histoire du Christianisme, founded in 1965, is attached to the Faculty of Philosophy and Letters of the Free University of Brussels and offers nonconfessional courses, conferences, research, and publications.

Centers devoted to inter-religious study, research and dialogue include: (1) Fédération Internationale des Instituts de Recherches Socio-religieuses (FERES), founded in Louvain in 1958, with 40 affiliated centers and a regional secretariat for Latin America, which promotes socioreligious research on an international, interdenominational, and inter-religious basis and publishes the journal *Social Compass;* (2) Bureau de Decumentation sur les Relatinos Judéo-Chrétiennes, founded in Brussels by the Sisters of Our Lady of Zion, which disseminates information on Jewish-Christian relations; (3) Centre Nationale des Hautes Etudes Juives, founded in 1959 and attached to the Institute of Sociology of the Free University of Brussels, which engages in the scientific study of various aspects of contemporary Judaism, particularly in Belgium; and (4) Institut Belge des Hautes Etudes Bouddhiques, in Brussels, an independent institute engaging in Buddhist studies which works in close cooperation with the University of Louvain.

FUTURE TRENDS AND PROSPECTS

Roman Catholic affiliation is expected to continue a precipitous decline due to secularism, somewhat offset by gains among Protestants (affiliation rising from 0.8% in 1970 to 1.5% by 2025) and marginal Christians but total Christian affiliation is still likely to drop below 80% after 2025.

With current growth rates, atheists and the nonreligious will together represent more than 10% of the population by the middle of the 21st century. Adherents of non-Christian religions could also reach 10%. Thus, before AD 2050, it is possible that Christians will represent less than 80% of the population for the first time in nearly 1,300 years.

BIBLIOGRAPHY

150 ans de vie des Églises. R. Aubert. Brussels: P. Legrain, [1980]. 104p.

Aanzien kerk en godsdienst in Nederland en België 1945–1985. G. Klaasen. Utrecht: Spectrum, [1985]. 192p.

Anabaptism in Flanders 1530–1650: a century of struggle. A. L. E. Verheyden. Trans., M. Kuitse, J. Matthijssen & J. H. Yoder. Scottdale, PA: Herald, 1961. 136p.

Begie en zijn goden: kerken, religieuze groeperingen en lekenbewegingen: met Franse en Engelse samenvattingen. K. Dobbelaere et al. Leuven: Cabay, 1985. 503p.

Belgique: pays de Chrétienté? L. Halkin et al. *Cahiers de L'I.S.C.P.*, vol. 3. Liege: Editions ISCP-CDD, 1991. 150p.

'Belgium,' F. Houtart, in *Western religion: a country by country sociological enquiry*, p.67–82. H. Mol (ed). The Hague: Mouton, 1972.

Belgium. R. C. Riley. *World bibliographical series*, vol. 104. Oxford, UK: CLIO Press, 1989. (See especially 'Religion,' 95-7).

Foi, gestes et institutions religieuses aux 19e et 20e siècles. L. Courtois & J. Pirotte (eds). *Collection Cerfaux-Lefort*, vol. 9. Louvain-la-Neuve: Centre d'histoire des religions, 1992. 174p. (Papers from the 3rd congress of the Association des Cercles Francophones d'Histoire et Archéologie de Belgique held in Namur, Belgium on August 18-21,1988).

Handbook of French and Belgian Protestantism. L. S. Houghton. New York: Missionary Education Movement, 1919. 244p.

Histoire de l'Eglise en Belgique. E. d. Moreau. Brussels: Editions Universelles, 1949. 2 vols.

Histoire des religions pratiquées à Cuesmes à travers les siècles. H. Buslin & R. G. W. Mahieu. [Cuesmes]: R. G. W. Mahieu, 1977. 93p.

Histoire du mouvement ouvrier Chrétien en Belgique. E. Gerard & P. Wynants. *KADOC-studies*, vol. 16. Leuven: Leuven University Press, 1994. 2 vols.

Katholiek Jaarboek voor België/Annuaire Catholique de Belgique, 1971–72. Brussels: Centre Interdioésain, 1972.

Les sectes contemporaines. M. Mat-Hasquin. 2nd ed. Brussels: Editions de l'Université de Bruxelles, 1983. 119p.

Les sectes en Belgique et au Luxembourg. A. Lallemand. Brussels: Editions EPO, 1994. 238p.

Sociologische analyse van de katholiciteit. K. Dobbelaere. Antwerp: Standard, 1966.

The Beguines and Beghards in medieval culture with special emphasis on the Belgian scene. E. W. McDonnell. New York: Octagon, 1969. 643p.

Country Table 2. Organized churches and denominations in Belgium.

Official name (bold type = church with over 10% of all affiliated) 1	Begun 2	Type 3	Counc 4	Congs 5	Adults 6	Affiliated 1970 7	Affiliated 1995 8	G% 9	*Names, notes, and other statistics* (see Codebook, Part 3) 10
Armée du Salut	1889	P-Sal	xwc..	13	530	1,000	1,060	0.23	*Leger des Heils. Salvation Army, Belgium Command.* Officers 75, institutions 12.
Assemblée Chrétienne Evangélique		P-CBr	.....	11	700	2,000	1,000	0.05	*Christelijk Evangelische Vergaderingen. Ev Christian Assembly.* 60% Walloon.
Assemblée Evangélique Italienne		I-3pW	....H	1	50	130	100	0.05	*Assemblea Evangelica Italiana. Italian Ev Assembly.* 2p,1s(3),W=88%,6Y,13z.
Assemblées de Dieu de Belgique	1931	P-Pe2	ZF..H	86	6,065	7,000	9,000	1.01	*Gemeenten Gods. Assemblies of God.* M=AoG(UK,USA). 70% Walloon. 34n,11x,1s(47).
Assemblées des Frères		P-CBr	x....	22	1,300	2,000	1,730	0.05	*Vergadering der Broeders. Assembly of Brethren. Open Brethren.* 90% Walloon. 6f.
Association des Eglises de Siloam	1962	I-3pW	....H	6	200	500	600	0.73	*AES. Association of Churches of Siloam.* Based on Ghent. 1s.
Assoc Ev des Egls Baptistes Françaises	1924	P-Bap	TT...	1	100	200	333	2.06	*AEEB.* French-speaking Baptist Chs. French Bible Mission. Ex FEEBF. 1n,1x,1s,W=33%.
Conseil Mennonite Belge	1950	P-Men	G...k	4	40	400	85	-6.01	*Belgian Mennonite Mission.* M=MCNA(USA). Notable social work. 2n,3x,W=38%,15Y,12z.
Eglise Adventiste du Septième Jour	1897	P-Adv	x....	28	1,530	1,680	2,190	1.07	*SDA, Belgium-Luxembourg Conf.* 9n,1s,1j,1s(5),25t,W=75%,71Y,67z.
Eglise Anglicane (D Europe)	c1650	A-plu	awc..	10	3,300	12,000	11,000	-0.35	*Anglikaanse Kerk. Anglican Ch.* M=CCCS,PECUSA. Some Belgians. 3x,9f,W=38%,27Yy,40z.
Eglise Apostolique	1950	P-PeA	Z....	3	180	200	360	2.38	*Apostolische Kerk. Apostolic Ch.* Pentecostal body with links to UK and Germany churches.
Eglise Baptistê Indépendente	1978	I-Bap	.....	9	350	–	538	5.88	M=BIM. Fundamentalist mission from USA.
Eglise Catholique Apostolique	c1840	I-3aX	x....	2	50	200	100	-2.73	*Catholic Apostolic Ch. Irvingites.* 3 parishes in Belgium. Rapidly declining.
Egl Catholique Apostolique Gallicane	1870	I-CCa	.....	1	400	1,000	800	-0.89	*Catholic Apostolic Gallican Ch.* Ex Church of Rome. Branch of body in France.
Eglise Catholique de Belgique:	c 200	R-Lat	B.B.R	4,357	6,239,000	8,654,602	8,241,605	-0.20	*Katholieke Kerk.* C=41+14+350. 7p,11q,13s(619). 5848n 3499x 5166m19800w 93441Yy
M Malines-Bruxelles (Brussel)	1559	R-Lat	Bs	695	1,233,000	1,988,835	1,623,000	-0.81	Mechelen-Brussel. Bilingual Flemish/Walloon. 3s. 1158n 1175x 1705m 4280w 16997Yy
D Antwerpen (Anvers)	1559	R-Lat	Bs	405	994,000	1,202,000	1,308,733	0.34	Suppressed 1801. Flemish. Port (900,000), rural. 1s. 620n 529x 694m 3044w 11991Yy
D Brugge (Bruges)	1559	R-Lat	Bs	448	798,000	1,045,000	1,050,000	0.02	Flemish. Rural. Major foreign missions activity. 968n 364x 558m 3900w 13373Yy
D Gent (Gand) (Ghent)	1559	R-Lat	Bs	477	912,000	1,200,000	1,200,000	0.00	Flemish. Rural, expanding new industry. 1s. 785n 240x 550m 3430w 14422Yy
D Hasselt	1967	R-Lat	Bs	316	490,000	560,000	645,000	0.57	Flemish. 50% rural. Formerly in D Liege. 1s. 541n 360x 476m 1261w 8028Yy
D Liege (Luik, Lübtich)	c 350	R-Lat	Bs	635	570,000	835,000	750,000	-0.43	Walloon. Industry declining. Dechristianized. 1s. 559n 215x 277m 1055w 8809Yy
D Namur (Namen)	1559	R-Lat	Bs	745	452,000	596,057	594,872	-0.01	Walloon. Namur, Luxembourg, rural areas. 1s. 618n 391x 681m 1350w 7975Yy
D Tournai (Doornik)	c 550	R-Lat	Bs	584	760,000	1,197,710	1,000,000	-0.72	Walloon. Rural areas, declining industries. 2s. 599n 225x 225m 1480w 11511Yy
OM Belgique (Belgio)	1957	R-Lat	B....	52	30,000	30,000	70,000	3.45	*Military Ordinariate of Belgium,* all armed services. 20 bps, and ordinaries, 89 auxiliaries.335Yy.
Eglise de Dieu (Cleveland)	1973	P-Pe3	ZF...	4	514	–	857	4.55	M=Ch of God(Cleveland). Zairois immigrants.
Eglise de Dieu de Prophétie	1983	P-Pe3	.....	1	30	–	75	8.33	*Church of God of Prophecy.* M=CGP(USA).
Eglise de J-C des Saints des DJ	c1860	m-LdS	x....	33	3,340	3,340	4,400	1.11	*Kerk van JK Heiligen der Laatste Dagen. DJ=Dernières Jours. Latter-day Saints. Mormons.* 50f.
Eglise du Christ, Scientiste		m-Sci	x....	2	50	200	150	0.05	*Ch of Christ, Christian Scientist. Science.* M=CCS(Boston, USA). 3w.
Eglise Elim Pentecôtiste	1991	P-Pe2	Z....	9	270	–	415	25.00	*Belgische Christelijke Pintestergeimeenschap Elim.* M=Elim Pentecostal Ch (UK).
Eglise Ev Allemande en Belgique		P-LuR	....K	2	2,880	5,000	4,800	0.05	*Deutschsprachige Ev Kirche in Belgien.* German-speaking Ev Ch. In 4 regions. 4n.
Eglise Ev Luthérienne Belge	1950	P-Lut	Lv...	1	266	2,600	699	-5.12	*Belgian Ev Luth Ch of Augsburg Confession (BELCAC),* Holy Trinity Parish. Linked EPB.
Eglise Evangélique Peniel	1935	I-3pW	.....	10	660	1,000	800	-0.89	M=Peniel MK(UK). French, German, Dutch sections. 8n,1x,1p,W=86%,22Y,28z.
Eglise Ev Protestante Luthérienne de B	1927	P-Lut	.v...	1	100	100	300	4.49	*Synode de France et de Belgique.* HQ Strasbourg. Ex ERAL. M=LCMS(USA).1n,8z.
Eglise Neo-Apostolique	c1970	I-3aX	x....	4	400	–	674	29.76	*Nederlandse Bezirk (District), New Apostolic Ch.* Germans. HQ Zurich.
Eglise Orthodoxe Grecque: D Belgique	1920	O-Gre	Cwc..	14	27,700	40,000	38,000	-0.20	*D Belgique, Pays Bas & Luxembourg. Griekse Orthodoxe Kerk.* Cypriots. 6x,W=30%,310y.
Egl Orth Russe: D Brussel & België	c1922	O-Rus	MWc..	3	6,600	15,000	11,000	-1.23	*Russische Orthodoxe Kerk, PE WEurope. Belgische Orthodoxe Missie.* Russian bishop.
Eglise Orth Russe Hors-Frontières	c1922	I-Rus	x....	10	6,000	5,000	10,000	2.81	*In D Western Europe & Austria, Russian Orthodox Ch Outside of Russia.* HQ New York.
Eglise Protestante Unie de Belgique	1830	P-Uni	WWC.K	104	25,000	30,000	35,000	0.62	*Protestantse Kerk van België.* United Prot Ch. 1969 union Ev Prot Ch, UMC. 48% Walloon. 96n.
Eglise Protestante Libérale de Belgique	1888	m-Unt	.....	4	3,840	16,000	12,000	-1.14	*Liberal Protestant Ch. Free Christian Ch.* Unitarians. HQ Brussels. Walloons.
Eglise Réformée de Belgique	1837	P-Ref	RWC.K	40	32,900	12,000	40,000	4.93	*Hervormde Kerk van België.* Formerly BCMC. 93% Walloon. 20n,11x,15p,W=28%,75Yy.
Eglise Rosicrucienne Apostolique		I-Epi	.v...	1	20	50	40	0.05	*Apostolic Rosicrucian Ch.* Brussels. Miniscule Gnostic body under episcopi vagantes.
Eglise Vieille-Catholique Belge		I-OCa	Uv...	1	100	100	300	0.05	*Belgian Old Catholic Ch.* Brussells. Related to Old Catholic Ch (Netherlands).
Eglises du Christ	1956	I-Dis	x....	15	300	500	429	-0.61	*Kerk van Kristus. Ch of Christ.* M=CCCC(Instrumental) (USA). USA personnel. 3f.
Eglises Pentecôtistes	1936	P-Pe2	Z...H	14	680	1,000	1,450	1.50	*Pentecostal Chs.* M=SFM(Sweden),NPY(Norway). Namur, Brussels.
Fédération Evangélique Libre		I-3pW	.....	5	400	–	667	0.05	*Free Evangelical Federation.*
Frères Larges	1972	P-CBr	.....	23	1,035	–	1,725	4.35	*Christian Brethren* (Flemish).
Mission Mondiale Unie	1970	P-Non	.....	4	200	–	308	25.76	*United World Mission.* M=UWM(USA).
Société des Amis		P-Qua	Qw...	1	16	–	25	0.05	*Religious Society of Friends (Quakers).*
Société des Antoinistes	1888	I-mar	x....	20	2,000	4,000	3,000	-1.14	Begun by RC healer Père Antoine along Meuse. Coal-miners round Liège. In 15 nations.
Témoins de Jéhovah	1901	m-Jeh	x....	325	25,161	30,000	50,300	2.09	*Getuigen van Jehovah's Witnesses.* Witnessing under way 1926. (1975) 1666Y. (1995) 972Y.
Union des Eglises Ev Baptistes de B	1850	P-Bap	T...K	18	850	800	2,670	4.94	*UEEBB. Belgian Baptist Union.* 1967, M=SBC(USA). 60% Walloon. 3n,4x,W=42%,21Y.
Union des Eglises Ev Libres de B	1918	P-Eva	KM...	67	3,430	8,000	6,240	-0.99	*UEELB. Bond van Vrije Ev Gemeenten.* M=MEB(BGM)(USA). 54% Walloon. 9n,14x,W=60%.
Other independent charismatic chs	c1985	I-3cW	.....	100	10,000	–	15,000	10.00	Scattered networks: Manna Ch (Portugal), also EJCSK (Zaire).
Other Protestant denominations		P-	.....	70	5,000	5,000	10,000	0.05	Total about 25 (see list below), USA military chapels, Cornerstone Chs (M=GEM) in Brussels.
Other marginal Protestant bodies		m-	.....	40	1,000	1,000	2,000	0.05	Total about 6 (see list below).
Other independent Catholic churches		I-CCa	.....	20	1,000	1,000	1,500	0.05	Liberal Catholic Ch, Mariavite Ch, Vrai Eglise Catholique, 5 episcopi vagantes bodies.
Totals				**5,520**	**6,415,537**	**8,864,602**	**8,525,325**		

Churches, members, growth, 1900-2025	*Congs*	*Adults*	*Affiliated*	*G%*	*Total denominations*	*6 Megablocs:* O	R	A	P	I	m
Total churches, members, and denominations (mid-1900)	3,000	4,964,000	6,573,000	0.43	14	0	1	1	5	4	3
Total churches, members, and denominations (mid-1970)	4,691	6,694,390	8,864,602	0.43	54	2	1	1	27	16	7
Total churches, members, and denominations (mid-1990)	5,500	6,376,000	8,472,300	-0.23	94	2	1	1	46	34	10
Total churches, members, and denominations (mid-1995)	5,520	6,415,537	8,525,325	0.12	97	2	1	1	47	36	10
Total churches, members, and denominations (mid-2000)	5,500	6,411,000	8,518,696	-0.02	99	2	1	1	48	37	10
Total churches, members, and denominations (mid-2025)	5,000	6,104,000	8,112,000	-0.20	152	5	1	1	55	60	30

NOTES ON TABLE ABOVE

NATIONAL COUNCILS (Column 4, 5th letter).

E = Alliance Evangélique Francophone de Belgique (AEFB)/Evangelische Alliantie Vlaanderen (EAV) (Evangelical Alliance of French-speaking/Flemish-speaking Belgium).

H = Union des Eglises Evangéliques de Pentecôte Belge/Vereniging van der Evangelische Pinkster Kerken in België (Union of Belgian Pentecostal Churches); begun 1954.

N = Commission Missionnaire de l'Eglise Protestante Unie de Belgique (Missionary Commission of the United Protestant Church of Belgium), formerly Fédération des Eglises Protestantes de Belgique (FEPB)/Federatie der Protestantse Kerken van België (Federation of Protestant Churches in Belgium).

R = Conférence Episcopale de Belgique/Bisschoppenconferentie van België (Episcopal Conference of Belgium).

OTHER PROTESTANT DENOMINATIONS. Several state churches in Europe and Scandinavia have one or 2 congregations in Belgium for their expatriate members. In addition, there are a number of independent single congregations. The total includes: Baptist Bible Fellowship International (1962), Ch of Denmark, Ch of Norway, Eglise Ev Slave (Slavic Missionary Service), Eglise Luthérienne Libre, Enfants de Dieu (Children of God), Estonian Ev Lutheran Ch in Exile, European Evangelistic Society, Ev Ch of the Augsburg Confession in Poland in Exile, Ev Lutheran Ch of Finland, Exclusive Brethren (Kelly-Continental, and Continuing Tunbridge Wells), Gospel Missionary Union (1966), Nederlandse Hervormde Kerk, Strict Baptist Mission.

OTHER MARGINAL PROTESTANT BODIES. Including: Amis de l'Homme (Freytag, Sayerce), Eglise Chrétienne Universelle (Témoins du Christ Revenu), General Convention of the New Jerusalem.

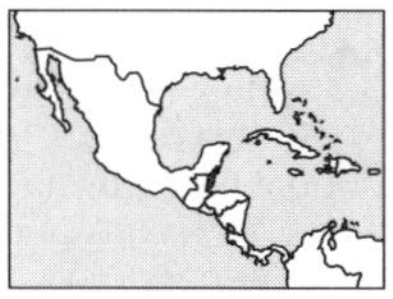

BELIZE

SECULAR DATA, AD 2000

STATE

Official name: The Colony of Belize.
Short name: Belize. **Adjective of nationality:** Belizean.
Flag: Blue with arms of the Colony surrounded by green garland on white disc.
Area: 22,965 sq. km. (8,867 sq. mi.).
Government: Constitutional monarchy with two legislative houses, since 1981 (1862 British colony, known as British Honduras until 1973, 1981 Independence).
Legislature: House of Representatives, 29 members; Senate, 8 members.
Official language: English.
Monetary unit: 1 Belize dollar (BZ$) = 100 cents. **US$1=** BZ$2.00.
Chief cities: Belize City (Belice) 56,581; BELMOPAN 6,817.
Political divisions: 6 provinces.
Armed forces: 1,000.

DEMOGRAPHY

Population: 241,000.
Population density: 10.4/sq. km. (27.1/sq. mi.).
Under 15 years: 96,000.
Growth rate p.a.: 2.09% (births 27.34, deaths 3.91).
Mortality: Infant, per 1,000: 26.2; **Maternal per 100,000:** 70.0.
Life expectancy: 76 (male 74, female 77).
Household size: 4.9. **Floor area per person, sq.m:** 18.0.
Major languages: English, Kekchi, Mopan, Yucateco, other Mayan, Spanish, Black Carib.
Urban dwellers: 46.51%. **Urban growth rate p.a.:** 2.6%.
Labor force: 33%.

ETHNOLINGUISTIC PEOPLES

35.4% Belizean Black; 22.0% Guatemalan Mestizo; 7.9% Mulatto; 6.6% Black Carib; 4.3% Kekchi.

ECONOMY

National income p.a. per person: US$2,629; **per family:** US$12,885.

EDUCATION

Adult literacy: 70% (male 75%, female 65%). **Schools:** 267.
Universities: 4. **School enrolment:** female/male: 91%/92%.

HEALTH

Access to health services: 70%. **Access to safe water:** 89%.
Hospitals: 7 (29 beds per 10,000). **Doctors:** 110.
Blind: 80. **Deaf:** 14,500. **Murder rate:** 33.
Lepers: 1,000. **Underweight prevalence under 5:** 6%.

LITERATURE

New book titles p.a.: 80 (330 p.a. per million). **Periodicals:** 11.
Newspapers: 4 dailies.

COMMUNICATION (per 1,000 people).

Phones: 134 (9% **mobile**). **Radios:** 140. **TV sets:** 167.
Daily newspaper circulation: 100. **Computers:** 50.

REFUGEES

Alien refugees from other countries: 8,650.

HUMAN LIFE AND LIBERTY (optimum condition=100.0%).

HDI: 80.6. **HSI:** 75.0. **HFI:** 70.0. **EFL:** 46.0.

Country Table 1. Religious adherents in Belize, AD 1900-2025.

Year	1900		1970		mid-1990		Annual change, 1990-2000				mid-1995		mid-2000		mid-2025	
Name	Adherents	%	Adherents	%	Adherents	%	Natural	Conversion	Total	Rate	Adherents	%	Adherents	%	Adherents	%
Christians	**34,950**	**94.5**	**116,100**	**94.6**	**170,620**	**91.2**	**4,897**	**-67**	**4,830**	**2.52**	**193,800**	**90.8**	**218,923**	**90.8**	**332,900**	**90.0**
PROFESSION																
professing Christians	**34,950**	**94.5**	**116,100**	**94.6**	**170,620**	**91.2**	**4,897**	**-67**	**4,830**	**2.52**	**193,800**	**90.8**	**218,923**	**90.8**	**332,900**	**90.0**
AFFILIATION																
unaffiliated Christians	5,950	16.1	8,227	6.7	14,920	8.0	431	255	686	3.86	18,838	8.8	21,784	9.0	30,900	8.4
affiliated Christians	**29,000**	**78.4**	**107,873**	**87.9**	**155,700**	**83.3**	**4,496**	**-352**	**4,144**	**2.39**	**174,962**	**82.0**	**197,139**	**81.8**	**302,000**	**81.6**
Roman Catholics	14,000	37.8	74,500	60.7	108,000	57.8	3,119	-225	2,894	2.40	121,918	57.2	136,939	56.8	200,000	54.1
Protestants	7,000	18.9	14,773	12.0	29,500	15.8	852	148	1,000	2.96	33,464	15.7	39,500	16.4	70,000	18.9
Anglicans	8,000	21.6	16,000	13.0	11,500	6.2	332	-432	-100	-0.91	11,000	5.2	10,500	4.4	9,000	2.4
Independents	0	0.0	1,600	1.3	3,500	1.9	101	69	170	4.04	4,770	2.2	5,200	2.2	12,000	3.2
Marginal Christians	0	0.0	1,000	0.8	3,200	1.7	92	88	180	4.56	3,810	1.8	5,000	2.1	11,000	3.0
Trans-megabloc groupings																
Evangelicals	5,200	14.1	7,000	5.7	12,900	6.9	373	47	420	2.86	14,898	7.0	17,100	7.1	30,000	8.1
Pentecostals/Charismatics	0	0.0	2,000	1.6	23,000	12.3	664	176	840	3.16	27,025	12.7	31,400	13.0	58,500	15.8
Great Commission Christians	**400**	**1.1**	**4,400**	**3.6**	**21,500**	**11.5**	**621**	**116**	**737**	**2.99**	**24,900**	**11.7**	**28,865**	**12.0**	**52,000**	**14.1**
Baha'is	0	0.0	2,900	2.4	5,300	2.8	153	11	164	2.73	6,100	2.9	6,941	2.9	12,000	3.2
Hindus	0	0.0	0	0.0	4,000	2.1	116	38	154	3.30	4,900	2.3	5,536	2.3	10,000	2.7
Jews	200	0.5	1,400	1.1	2,100	1.1	61	-11	50	2.16	2,300	1.1	2,600	1.1	2,800	0.8
Spiritists	750	2.0	1,500	1.2	1,600	0.9	46	-2	44	2.46	1,800	0.8	2,040	0.9	3,000	0.8
Nonreligious	0	0.0	100	0.1	1,300	0.7	38	32	70	4.38	1,700	0.8	1,996	0.8	5,000	1.4
Muslims	0	0.0	0	0.0	1,000	0.5	29	10	39	3.34	1,200	0.6	1,389	0.6	2,500	0.7
Buddhists	0	0.0	0	0.0	600	0.3	17	7	24	3.45	750	0.4	842	0.4	1,500	0.4
Ethnoreligionists	1,100	3.0	1,000	0.8	480	0.3	14	-18	-4	-0.87	450	0.2	440	0.2	300	0.1
World A (unevangelized persons)	370	1.0	1,226	1.0	3,740	2.0	110	26	136	3.10	4,479	2.1	5,061	2.1	9,990	2.7
World B (evangelized non-Christians)	1,680	4.5	5,343	4.6	12,640	6.8	364	41	405	3.02	15,052	6.9	17,016	6.9	27,110	7.3
World C (Christians)	34,950	94.5	116,100	94.4	170,620	91.2	4,897	-67	4,830	2.52	193,800	91.0	218,923	91.0	332,900	90.0
Country's population	**37,000**	**100.0**	**122,670**	**100.0**	**187,000**	**100.0**	**5,371**	**0**	**5,371**	**2.57**	**213,332**	**100.0**	**241,000**	**100.0**	**370,000**	**100.0**

COLUMNS, ROWS.
For meanings and definitions, see Codebook (Part 3). Note that, by definition, total 'Christians' = professing + crypto-Christians, which also = affiliated + unaffiliated Christians, and also = Great Commission Christians + latent Christians. Percentages may not always total exactly, due to rounding.

CENSUSES.
9.IV.1946: 99.7% Christians (59.6% Roman Catholics, 21.0% Anglicans, 18.9% Protestants (14.0% Methodists), 0.3% nonreligious. **7.IV.1960** (de jure): 62.3% Roman Catholics, 18.5% Anglicans, 17.4% Protestants (11.9% Methodists, 1.9% SDAs, 0.6% Baptists), 1.2% Jews, 0.5% marginal Protestants (Jehovah's Witnesses). **7.IV.1970:** 64.6% Roman Catholics, 14.8% Anglicans, 13.2% Protestants (8.9% Methodists, 2.1% SDAs, 0.7% Baptists), 1.2% Jews, 0.8% Black indigenous, 0.8% marginal Protestants. **1991:** 62.7% Roman Catholics, 21.4% Protestants (6.3% Pentecostals, 4.2% Methodists, 4.1% SD Adventists, 4.0% Mennonites), 7.9% Anglicans, 2.5% Hindus, 1.7% Marginal Christians, 0.1% Baha'is, 0.1% Muslims, 3.6% other religionists.

NOTES ON RELIGIONS
BAHA'IS. Rapid growth from 1 local spiritual assembly (1964) to 33 (1973), followed by decline to 15 LSAs (1996) largely due to reorganization of LSA coverage.
ETHNORELIGIONISTS. Amerindians.
INDEPENDENTS. In 4 denominations in 1995 (see Table 2).
SPIRITISTS. Afro-American spiritists performing Obeah (a form of magic syncretizing Christianity and African tribal religions). This is practiced among Black Caribs.

Great Commission Instrument Panel: status of Belize (for explanation see start of Part 4)

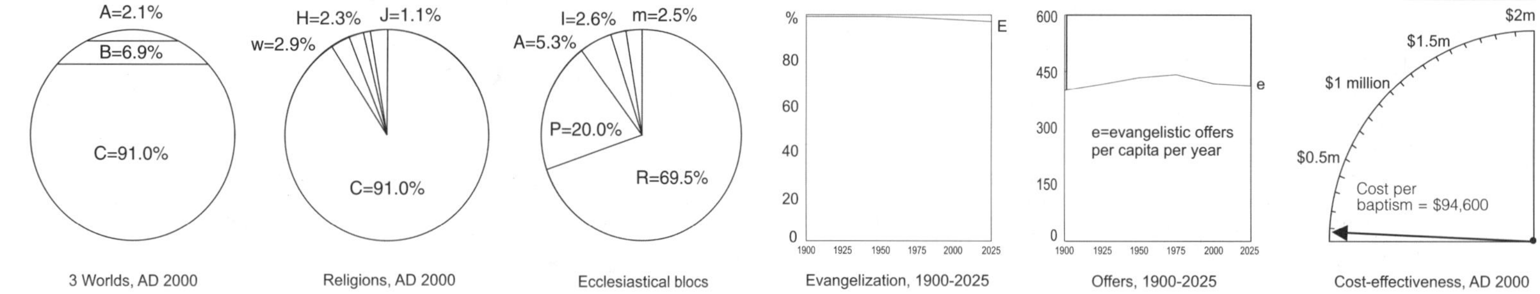

Country status. Belize is the second smallest country in Central America, and also the most sparsely populated. The population is extremely varied; about half are African; one-fifth is Carib, Mayan, or other Amerindian; another one-fifth is mixed local Indian and European, and the remaining 10% European, East Indian, Chinese, and Lebanese. A former British colony, named British Honduras until 1974, Belize has more in common with the Caribbean than with Spanish Central America.

HUMAN LIFE AND LIBERTY

Human need and development. Because of its small population and tourist potentials, Belize has achieved a better standard of living than comparable countries in the region. However, the economy is still agriculture-based, and the small market does not permit industrial growth.

Human rights and freedoms. Belize is a parliamentary democracy on the British model. Human rights and freedoms are constitutionally guaranteed and legally enforced. The major violations have occurred in regard to the 40,000 Central American illegal migrants. Many of them face widespread discrimination when competing for jobs with native Belizeans. Belizean women face some social and economic prejudices in the employment market, but the official Women's Bureau has worked hard to improve the status of women. Both the governor general and the president of the Senate are women.

Human environment. Belize possesses some unique environmental resources including the longest barrier reef in the world. Many of these natural features remain unspoiled because tourism is not highly developed and does not, as yet, pose a threat to the environment.

NON-CHRISTIAN RELIGIONS

Four religions each have as followers near or more than 1% of the population: Spiritism, Baha'i, Hinduism, and Judaism. The largest of these is Baha'i, with almost 7,000 affiliated in AD 2000.

CHRISTIANITY

CATHOLIC CHURCH. The territory's first 7,000 Catholics came from Yucatan, Mexico, following the Indian revolt of 1848. Catholics make up more than 60 percent of the population and are for the most part ethnically Blacks (African Negroes) and Indians, with a few Whites and natives of the East Indies. The church is served by diocesan and American Jesuit priests.

The Holy See has diplomatic relations with Belize and in AD 2000 is represented to government and the Catholic hierarchy by a pro-nuncio residing in Port of Spain.

The Nativity of Christ, often portrayed on the country's postage stamps.

ANGLICAN CHURCH. The Society for the Propagation of the Gospel was the first mission in Belize, coming originally to work with Black laborers from Jamaica. In 1995 Anglicans were third in size after the Catholic Church and the Adventists. The diocese of Belize, formed in 1891, is part of the Church of the Province of the West Indies.

PROTESTANT CHURCHES. British Methodists were the first to open Protestant work in Belize (1825). After their arrival in 1959, the Mennonites had the most numerous expatriate missionary staff, engaged mostly in service and development programs, but they also built up a sizeable Christian community. The largest Protestant denominations in 1995 were the Seventh-day Adventists, the Methodists, the Assemblies of God, and the Baptists.

OTHER CHURCHES. Two Black independent denominations are active in Belize: Church of God in Christ from the USA and International City Mission from Jamaica. Two marginal groups, Mormons and Jehovah's Witnesses, are relatively strong.

Indigenous missions. Though over 90% Christian, Belize is still considered by most traditions as a mission field rather than a mission sending country. There are only a handful of foreign missionaries sent out and fewer that truly have a cross-cultural focus.

CHURCH AND STATE

The former Spanish sovereignty over Belize was first challenged in 1786, and in 1840, it was formally declared a British colony.

Full internal self-government was granted in 1964. Belize is a secular state, and the churches enjoy equal status before the law.

Country summary. **Worlds A, B, C by ethnolinguistic peoples, cities, and major civil divisions in Belize.**

	PEOPLES							CITIES							CIVIL DIVISIONS						
World	*Num*	*Pop 2000*	*C%*	*Christians*	*E%*	*U%*	*Unevangelized*	*Num*	*Pop 2000*	*C%*	*Christians*	*E%*	*U%*	*Unevangelized*	*Num*	*Pop 2000*	*C%*	*Christians*	*E%*	*U%*	*Unevangelized*
A	1	2,889	0.10	3	47	53	1,529	0	0	0.00	0	0	0	0	0	0	0.00	0	0	0	0
B	3	9,846	11.94	1,176	66	34	3,305	0	0	0.00	0	0	0	0	0	0	0.00	0	0	0	0
C	15	227,973	85.96	195,960	100	0	320	2	63,398	83.11	52,688	99	1	659	6	240,709	81.90	197,139	98	2	5,155
Total	**19**	**240,708**	**81.90**	**197,139**	**98**	**2**	**5,154**	**2**	**63,398**	**83.11**	**52,688**	**99**	**1**	**659**	**6**	**240,709**	**81.90**	**197,139**	**98**	**2**	**5,155**

BROADCASTING AND MEDIA

The government station Radio Belize broadcasts Protestant programs for nine hours from Monday to Saturday, with three hours on Sunday, and a daily half-hour Catholic program. Many Protestant programs are produced locally. The Mennonite mission sponsors two radio programs over Radio Belize. Many Caribs follow the Mennonite program linked to followup Bible correspondence courses. Belize is a member of UNDA.

A Catholic TV station in Belize City broadcasts family TV programs in English and Spanish for 18 hours per day.

INTERDENOMINATIONAL ORGANIZATIONS

The Christian Social Council of Belize was founded in 1957 as the Church World Service Committee with Methodist, Presbyterian and Salvation Army membership. Adventists, Anglicans, Assemblies of God, Church of God in Christ, and Nazarenes joined in 1961, at which time it was reorganized under the name Christian Social Council. More recent changes in membership include the withdrawal of the Assemblies of God in 1968 and the addition of the Catholic Church in 1969. There are no subregional or local councils in Belize, but there is a Planning Commission of the Churches (consisting of Anglicans, Methodists, and Catholics) which undertakes educational, social, and economic projects as well as providing opportunities for ecumenical worship services on special occasions.

FUTURE TRENDS AND PROSPECTS

Insulated from much of the turbulence of the region, Belize's religious development may be smoother than that of any other country in Central America. Christianity will probably continue to hover just under 90% for the next thirty years.

After 2025, Christians in Belize are expected to experience a slow decline during the 21st century, possibly dipping below 85% for the first time since the 16th century. Baha'is could reach 5% shortly after AD 2050.

BIBLIOGRAPHY

A bishop amongst bananas. H. Bury. Milwaukee, WI: Young Churchman Co., 1911. 236p.

'A felt needs approach to evangelism in Corozal District, Belize.' W. H. Searcy. Ph.D. dissertation, Harding Graduate School of Religion, Memphis, TN, 1985. 277p.

A history of Christianity in Belize: 1776–1838. W. R. Johnson. New York: University Press of America, 1985. 279p.

A history of the Catholic Church in Belize. R. O. Buhler. Belize: BISRA, 1976. 96p.

Belize. P. Wright & B. E. Coutts. 2nd ed. *World bibliographical series,* vol. 21. Oxford, UK: CLIO Press, 1993. 334p. (Focuses on materials since 1979. See especially 'Religion,' 135-41).

'Belize: Black Caribs,' N. L. S. González, in *Witchcraft and sorcery of the American native peoples,* p.279–93. D. E. Walker Jr. (ed). Moscow, ID: University of Idaho Press, 1989.

Ethnic minorities in Belize: Mopan, Kekchi and Garifuna. R. Wilk & M. Chapin. Belize City: SPEAR, 1990. 43p.

Heart drum: spirit possession in the Garifuna communities of Belize. B. Foster. 2nd rev. ed. Belize: Cubola Productions, 1994. 59p.

La religiosidad contemporánea maya–kekchí. L. Pacheco. Quito, Ecuador: Ediciones Abya–Yala, 1992. 225p.

Like the seed of the mustard plant: the history of the Presbyterian Church in Belize. W. B. Gresham. , 1992. 95p.

'Mennonites in Belize,' J. C. Everitt, *Journal of cultural geography,* 3, 2 (1983), 82–93.

Methodist sesquicentennial brochure. Methodist Church in the Belize-Honduras District. Belize: Benex Press, 1975. 77p.

'Myths in politics and politics in religion: early state formation in Belize,' C. J. M. Gullick & J. Crane, in *Faith and polity: essays on religion and politics,* p.173–201. M. Bax, P. Kloos & A. Loster (eds). Amsterdam: Vrije University, 1992.

One God—two temples: schismatic process in a Kekchi village. J. Schackt. *Occasional papers,* no. 13. Oslo: University of Oslo, 1986. 206p. (Treats cargo system).

'Shadow and substance: a Mopan Maya view of human existence,' A. E. Fink, *Canadian journal of native studies,* 7, 2 (1987), 399–414.

'Spirit possession in southern Belize,' B. Foster, *Belizean studies,* 10, 2 (1982), 18–23.

'The Mayahac of the Kekchi Belizeans,' J. Cayetano, *Belizean studies,* 10, 2 (1982), 1–8.

Thy bread and water shall be sure: the story of Magdalena Young of Belize. H. Temple. Kansas City, MO: Beacon Hill Press, 1983. 124p.

To Belize with love. H. B. Lapp. Lawrenceville, VA: Brunswick Publishing Co., 1986. 295p.

'Una mayor recompensa en el cielo: actividades de misioneros entre los Amerindios de Belice,' N. L. González, *America Indígena,* 47, 1 (1987), 139–68.

Country Table 2. **Organized churches and denominations in Belize.**

Official name (bold type = church with over 10% of all affiliated) 1	*Begun* 2	*Type* 3	*Counc* 4	*Congs* 5	*Adults* 6	*Affiliated 1970* 7	*Affiliated 1995* 8	*G%* 9	*Names, notes, and other statistics* (see Codebook, Part 3) 10
Anglican Church: D Belize	1776	A-ACa	AwMRK	26	3,740	16,000	11,000	-1.49	In CPWI. 96% Creole, 2% Carib, 1% other Indians. M=USPG. 4n,12x,2r,W=25%,700y.
Assemblies of God	1946	P-Pe2	ZF..k	56	1,790	350	3,000	8.97	Classical Pentecostals (2-stage). M=AoG(USA). 3n,2f,1 day school (250).
Assembly Hall Churches	c1990	I-3nC	.....	5	221	–	400	20.00	*Little Flock. Local Churches.* Begun in China 1922.
Association of Evangelical Chs of Belize	1955	P-Hol	xM...	15	919	800	1,329	2.05	Holiness mission from North America. M=GMU(USA). 18f.
Baptist Association of Belize	1976	P-Bap	T....	48	1,850	–	2,590	5.26	M=SBC(USA). Southern Baptist missionaries.
Baptist Churches in Belize	1822	I-Bap	xF..C	6	400	400	533	1.15	Begun by BMS(UK); 1960, M=CBHMS(USA). 3 schools. HQ Belize City. 11n,5f,15Y.
Belize Mennonite Mission	1960	P-Men	G....	1	118	100	225	3.30	Begun by immigrants. M=Mennonite Ch of NAmerica (EMBMC). 24f.
Caribbean Light & Truth	1974	I-Men	.....	10	156	–	240	4.76	Small Independent Mennonite presence.
Catholic Ch: D Belize City	c1650	R-Lat	P.NMK	126	65,800	74,500	121,918	1.99	*D Belize City-Belmopan.* M=SJ. C=1+0+3. (1970).135Y,3327y. (1990)13n, 71x, 39m, 7w, 3324Yy
Christian Brethren	c1952	P-CBr	x....	6	280	400	467	0.62	*Open Brethren. Plymouth Brethren. Gospel Halls.* Numerous expatriates.
Church of God in Christ		I-3pB	Z...K	10	780	500	1,560	0.05	M=CoGiC(Black mission from USA). Black pentecostals.
Church of God (Cleveland)	1944	P-Pe3	ZF...	20	680	300	971	4.81	Holiness Pentecostals. M=CoG(Cleveland) (USA). 4 churches, 3 missions. 6n,2f.
Church of God of Prophecy	1980	P-Pe3	.....	6	120	–	200	6.67	Split ex COG in USA.
Ch of Jesus Christ of Latter-day Saints		m-LdS	.....	5	780	–	1,300	0.05	*Mormons.* M=CJCLdS(USA).
Church of the Nazarene	1934	P-Hol	xF..K	22	1,306	2,023	2,023	0.00	Holiness body. M=CoN(USA). 9n,35m,8f,3h,23t(2030),W=61%,36Y,21z.
Churches of Christ		I-Dis	.....	2	260	–	371	0.05	M=CC(Non-Instrumental).
Evangelical Bible Mission	1984	I-Eva	.....	1	25	–	38	9.09	Small mission presence.
Ev Mennonite Mission Conference		P-Men	G....	13	247	100	669	0.05	M=Ev Mennonite Mission Conference (HQ Winnipeg, Canada).
International City Mission	c1960	I-3pU	x....	7	300	500	600	0.73	From Jamaica (HQ Kingston). Also in Bahamas, Barbados, UK, USA. Women bishops.
Jehovah's Witnesses	1931	m-Jeh	x....	22	1,004	1,000	2,510	3.75	*Watch Tower. IBSA.* Active witnessing under way by 1940. (1975) 37Y. (1995) 80Y.
Mennonite Church in Belize	1959	P-Men	G....	4	500	4,000	625	-7.16	2,500 Old Colony Mennonites, 1,000 Kleingemeinde. Amish immigrants in farming.
Methodist Ch in Caribbean & Americas	1825	P-Met	VwM.K	5	1,672	3,000	5,000	2.06	*MCCA*(1967 union), *Honduras (Belize) District.* M=MMS(UK). 5n,4x,4r,252Yy.
Methodist Protestant Church		I-Fun	..T..	5	200	200	300	0.05	M=MPC(USA). Fundamentalist mission from North America. 2f.
New Apostolic Church	c1985	I-3aX	x....	10	300	–	561	10.00	*NAC.* M=Neuapostolische Kirche(HQ Zurich, Switzerland).
Pentecostal Church of God	1956	P-Pe2	Z....	40	600	300	1,000	4.93	Classical Pentecostals from North America. M=PCG(USA). 4f.
Presbyterian Church	c1840	P-Ref	Rw..K	7	260	200	371	2.50	*Church of Scotland.* Small group with Scots and British links in past.
Resurrection Churches & Ministries	1985	I-3pU	.....	5	100	–	167	10.00	Afro-Caribbean network.
Salvation Army	1915	P-Sal	xwM.K	1	120	200	171	-0.62	*Belize Region,* Caribbean & CAmerica Territory (HQ Jamaica). HQ Belize City.
Seventh-day Adventist Church	1927	P-Adv	x...K	45	8,600	2,500	12,300	6.58	*SDA, Belize Mission,* Central America Union Mission. 3nx,34mw,1r,34t(2088),174Y.
United Pentecostal Church	1985	P-Pel	.....	18	350	–	583	10.00	M=UPC (USA). Jesus Only Pentecostals.
Wesleyan Church		P-Met	.....	9	610	–	1,040	0.05	Mission from USA.
Other Protestant denominations		P-	.....	12	540	500	900	0.05	Total about 10 (see list below).
Totals				**568**	**94,628**	**107,873**	**174,962**		

Churches, members, growth, 1900-2025	*Congs*	*Adults*	*Affiliated*	*G%*	*Total denominations*	*6 Megablocs:* *O*	*R*	*A*	*P*	*I*	*m*
Total churches, members, and denominations (mid-1900)	100	15,500	29,000	1.89	5	0	1	1	2	1	0
Total churches, members, and denominations (mid-1970)	326	57,602	107,873	1.89	24	0	1	1	17	4	1
Total churches, members, and denominations (mid-1990)	400	84,200	155,700	1.85	39	0	1	1	26	9	2
Total churches, members, and denominations (mid-1995)	568	94,628	174,962	2.36	41	0	1	1	27	10	2
Total churches, members, and denominations (mid-2000)	600	107,000	197,139	2.42	43	0	1	1	28	11	2
Total churches, members, and denominations (mid-2025)	900	163,000	302,000	1.72	67	0	1	1	35	25	5

NOTES ON TABLE ABOVE

NATIONAL COUNCILS (Column 4, 5th letter).
C = Evangelical Association.
K = Belize Christian Council (BCC).
k = associate member of BCC.

OTHER PROTESTANT DENOMINATIONS. These include: Elim Fellowship (1967), Elim Missionary Assemblies, Lutheran Ch, Missionary Ch, Moravian Ch.

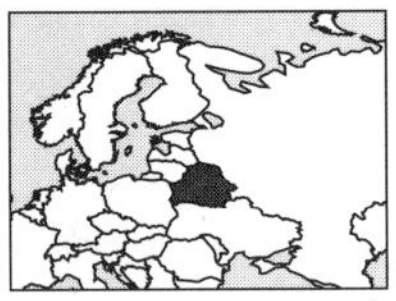

BELORUSSIA

SECULAR DATA, AD 2000

STATE
Official name: Respublika Belarus (The Republic of Belarus).
Short name: Belorussia. **Adjective of nationality:** Belorussian.
Flag: Red and green stripes with red pattern on left border.
Area: 207,595 sq. km. (80,153 sq. mi.).
Government: Unitary multiparty republic with two legislative bodies (1920 Soviet Socialist republic).
Legislature: Council of the Republic, 64 members; House of Representatives, 110 members.
Official language: Belarussian, Russian.
Monetary unit: rubel (Rbl; plural rubli). **US$1=** Rbl 177,500.
Chief cities: MINSK 1,862,000; Gomel' (Homei) 495,896; Mogil'ov (Mogilev, Mogilyov) 357,660; Vitebsk 356,182; Grodno (Gardinas) 280,610.
Political divisions: 6 provinces.
Armed forces: 93,000.

DEMOGRAPHY
Population: 10,236,000.
Population density: 49.3/sq. km. (127.7/sq. mi.).
Under 15 years: 1,914,000.
Growth rate p.a.: -0.30% (births 10.48, deaths 13.67).
Mortality: Infant, per 1,000: 21.3; **Maternal per 100,000:** 37.0.
Life expectancy: 68 (male 63, female 75).
Household size: 3.2. **Floor area per person, sq.m:** 19.5.
Major languages: Belorussian, Russian, Polish, Ukrainian.
Urban dwellers: 74.42%. **Urban growth rate p.a.:** 0.5%.
Labor force: 47%.

ETHNOLINGUISTIC PEOPLES
78.3% Byelorussian; 13.2% Russian; 4.1% Polish (Pole); 2.8% Ukrainian; 0.6% Jewish.

ECONOMY
National income p.a. per person: US$2,070; **per family:** US$6,624.

EDUCATION
Adult literacy: 97% (male 99%, female 96%). **Schools:** 5,047.
Universities: 38. **School enrolment:** female/male: 96%/94%.

HEALTH
Access to health services: 65%. **Access to safe water:** 80%.
Hospitals: 868 (122 beds per 10,000). **Doctors:** 45,000.
Blind: 9,000. **Deaf:** 617,100. **Murder rate:** 2.
Lepers: 300.

LITERATURE
New book titles p.a.: 3,890 (380 p.a. per million). **Periodicals:** 217.
Newspapers: 10 dailies.

COMMUNICATION (per 1,000 people).
Phones: 190 **(0% mobile). Radios:** 311. **TV sets:** 265.
Daily newspaper circulation: 187. **Computers:** 40.

REFUGEES
Alien refugees from other countries: 7,000.

HUMAN LIFE AND LIBERTY (optimum condition=100.0%)
HDI: 80.6. **HSI:** 50.0. **HFI:** 55.0. **EFL:** 29.0.

Country Table 1. **Religious adherents in Belorussia, AD 1900-2025.**

Year	1900		1970		mid-1990		Annual change, 1990-2000				mid-1995		mid-2000		mid-2025	
Name	Adherents	%	Adherents	%	Adherents	%	Natural	Conversion	Total	Rate	Adherents	%	Adherents	%	Adherents	%
Christians	**6,936,000**	**99.3**	**5,417,570**	**59.9**	**6,900,000**	**67.3**	**-1,596**	**30,703**	**29,107**	**0.41**	**7,105,000**	**68.4**	**7,191,068**	**70.3**	**8,107,000**	**85.4**
PROFESSION																
crypto-Christians	0	0.0	1,107,300	12.3	0	0.0	0	0	0	0.00	0	0.0	0	0.0	0	0.0
professing Christians	**6,936,000**	**99.3**	**4,310,270**	**47.7**	**6,900,000**	**67.3**	**-1,596**	**30,703**	**29,107**	**0.41**	**7,105,000**	**68.4**	**7,191,068**	**70.3**	**8,107,000**	**85.4**
AFFILIATION																
unaffiliated Christians	500,000	7.2	0	0.0	767,000	7.5	-179	-15,822	-16,001	-2.31	763,629	7.4	606,991	5.9	497,000	5.2
affiliated Christians	**6,436,000**	**92.2**	**5,417,570**	**59.9**	**6,133,000**	**59.8**	**-1,435**	**46,543**	**45,108**	**0.71**	**6,341,371**	**61.0**	**6,584,077**	**64.3**	**7,610,000**	**80.1**
Orthodox	4,224,500	60.5	4,508,300	49.9	4,750,000	46.3	-1,111	24,719	23,608	0.49	4,840,000	46.6	4,986,077	48.7	5,450,000	57.4
Roman Catholics	2,206,500	31.6	810,000	9.0	1,200,000	11.7	-281	15,281	15,000	1.18	1,302,000	12.5	1,350,000	13.2	1,570,000	16.5
Protestants	5,000	0.1	23,270	0.3	90,000	0.9	-21	4,021	4,000	3.75	101,100	1.0	130,000	1.3	320,000	3.4
Independents	0	0.0	75,000	0.8	90,000	0.9	-21	2,021	2,000	2.03	94,071	0.9	110,000	1.1	250,000	2.6
Marginal Christians	0	0.0	1,000	0.0	3,000	0.0	-1	501	500	10.31	4,200	0.0	8,000	0.1	20,000	0.2
Trans-megabloc groupings																
Evangelicals	4,000	0.1	18,000	0.2	23,600	0.2	-6	726	720	2.70	26,260	0.3	30,800	0.3	57,800	0.6
Pentecostals/Charismatics	0	0.0	16,000	0.2	80,600	0.8	-19	1,459	1,440	1.66	90,493	0.9	95,000	0.9	125,000	1.3
Great Commission Christians	**700,000**	**10.0**	**814,000**	**9.0**	**2,100,000**	**20.5**	**-491**	**6,748**	**6,257**	**0.29**	**2,150,000**	**20.7**	**2,162,574**	**21.1**	**2,350,000**	**24.8**
Nonreligious	20,000	0.3	2,208,430	24.4	2,520,420	24.6	-590	-6,092	-6,682	-0.27	2,550,400	24.5	2,453,603	24.0	1,136,750	12.0
Atheists	5,000	0.1	1,403,000	15.5	758,000	7.4	-177	-25,066	-25,243	-3.97	650,000	6.3	505,570	4.9	150,000	1.6
Jews	12,000	0.2	9,000	0.1	58,000	0.6	-14	49	35	0.06	59,000	0.6	58,346	0.6	60,000	0.6
Muslims	8,000	0.1	2,000	0.0	22,000	0.2	-5	400	395	1.66	25,000	0.2	25,949	0.3	40,000	0.4
Buddhists	1,000	0.0	0	0.0	980	0.0	0	4	4	0.44	1,000	0.0	1,024	0.0	1,500	0.0
Ethnoreligionists	2,000	0.0	0	0.0	500	0.0	0	1	1	0.26	500	0.0	513	0.0	600	0.0
Baha'is	0	0.0	0	0.0	100	0.0	0	1	1	0.58	100	0.0	106	0.0	150	0.0
World A (unevangelized persons)	6,984	0.1	198,869	2.2	153,900	1.5	-36	-6,674	-6,710	-5.56	93,521	0.9	92,124	0.9	75,968	0.8
World B (evangelized non-Christians)	41,016	0.6	3,423,061	37.9	3,206,100	31.2	-750	-24,029	-24,779	-0.82	3,192,805	30.7	2,952,808	28.8	1,313,032	13.8
World C (Christians)	6,936,000	99.3	5,417,570	59.9	6,900,000	67.3	-1,596	30,703	29,107	0.41	7,105,000	68.4	7,191,068	70.3	8,107,000	85.4
Country's population	**6,984,000**	**100.0**	**9,039,500**	**100.0**	**10,260,000**	**100.0**	**-2,382**	**0**	**-2,382**	**-0.02**	**10,391,327**	**100.0**	**10,236,000**	**100.0**	**9,496,000**	**100.0**

COLUMNS, ROWS.
For meanings and definitions, see Codebook (Part 3). Note that, by definition, total 'Christians' = professing + crypto-Christians, which also = affiliated + unaffiliated Christians, and also = Great Commission Christians + latent Christians. Percentages may not always total exactly, due to rounding.

NOTES ON RELIGION.
ATHEISTS. The number of militant nonreligious has declined rapidly after the 1970s.

Great Commission Instrument Panel: status of Belorussia (for explanation see start of Part 4)

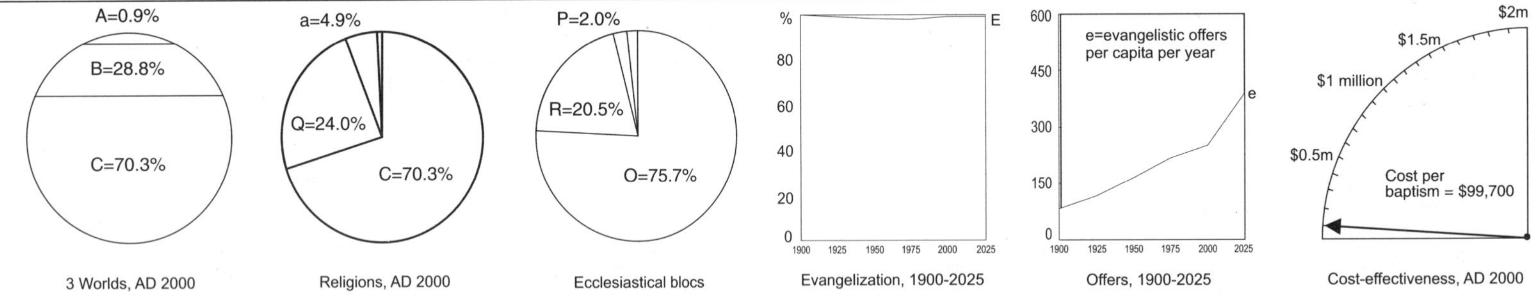

3 Worlds, AD 2000 | Religions, AD 2000 | Ecclesiastical blocs | Evangelization, 1900-2025 | Offers, 1900-2025 | Cost-effectiveness, AD 2000

Country status. Belorussia, a former republic of the Soviet Union, is an independent state on the plains of Eastern Europe, bordered by Poland, Russia, Ukraine, Lithuania, and Latvia. Farming, the principal economic activity, produces meat, dairy products, and flax. Belorussia is currently a member of the Commonwealth of Independent States.

HUMAN LIFE AND LIBERTY

Human rights and freedoms. Belorussia, which gained its independence from the Soviet Union in 1991, approved a new Constitution in March 1994. Its new form of government is a 260-member Assembly, and is headed by a President. Respect for human rights is mixed. Progress continued in some areas but flagged in others. The executive is slow in implementing political reforms, although there is no suppression of political activity. Freedom of the press is restricted through the state monopoly of the media. However, a 1992 Law on Freedom of Religious Beliefs and Organizations lifted most Soviet-era religious controls, although some bureaucratic impediments remain. State relations with the Roman Catholic Church eased somewhat and the first papal internuncio was accredited to Minsk. The Catholic seminary in Grodno has resumed its classes. The government continues to return church property seized during the Soviet era, but numerous legal disputes have slowed the process. During 1993 the government began to clamp down on Western Protestant missionaries, partly to allay the fears of the Orthodox Church. All foreign missionaries are required to have a local sponsor to visit or work in the country. Criminal procedures remain virtually unchanged and detainees may be kept in pretrial detention for up to three months. Because of the rapid spread of criminal gangs, police raids and swoops are frequent in certain areas. Demonstrations are discouraged through legal restrictions, but continue to occur. Citizens are free to travel within and without the country, but the government limits residence permits in Minsk and the five regional centers of Brest, Grodno, Mogilev, Vitebsk, and Gomel. The Belarus League of Human Rights, founded in 1992, is active in monitoring abuses of human rights and seeking legal redress.

NON-CHRISTIAN RELIGIONS

Judaism. Jews were first known in Belorussia in the 14th century and their numbers increased until the 20th century. By the late 1700s they were restricted to the Pale of Settlement and later to towns and cities

Country summary. **Worlds A, B, C by ethnolinguistic peoples, cities, and major civil divisions in Belorussia.**

	PEOPLES							***CITIES***							***CIVIL DIVISIONS***						
World	*Num*	*Pop 2000*	*C%*	*Christians*	*E%*	*U%*	*Unevangelized*	*Num*	*Pop 2000*	*C%*	*Christians*	*E%*	*U%*	*Unevangelized*	*Num*	*Pop 2000*	*C%*	*Christians*	*E%*	*U%*	*Unevangelized*
A	6	95,094	2.35	2,235	47	53	50,102	0	0	0.00	0	0	0	0	0	0	0.00	0	0	0	0
B	6	1,362,749	49.90	679,991	99	1	8,439	0	0	0.00	0	0	0	0	0	0	0.00	0	0	0	0
C	14	8,778,337	67.23	5,901,851	100	0	28,363	22	5,270,403	63.86	3,365,495	99	1	50,722	6	10,236,181	64.32	6,584,077	99	1	86,904
Total	**26**	**10,236,180**	**64.32**	**6,584,077**	**99**	**1**	**86,904**	**22**	**5,270,403**	**63.86**	**3,365,495**	**99**	**1**	**50,722**	**6**	**10,236,181**	**64.32**	**6,584,077**	**99**	**1**	**86,904**

within that Pale. In 1914 there were 1.3 million Jews in Belarus, and many towns and cities had a Jewish majority. Before 1917 there were 657 Jewish congregations in the country. During the three years of Nazi occupation the Jewish population was decimated by mass executions. The 1989 census found less than 1% of the national population to be Jewish, reflecting a terrible decrease due mainly to genocide but also to emigration. Many more have emigrated since. Still, since glasnost Jewish life in the country has revived. There were nearly 70 Jewish organizations active in the country in 1992, some of them functioning across the nation.

Islam. By the end of the 16th century more than 200,000 Tatars lived in Belorussia, descendants of the Golden Horde invaders who came between the 11th and mid-16th centuries. They soon lost their language but retained their Muslim faith. The main Tatar settlements were Hrodno, Minsk, Trakai, and Vilna. After 1569 when Belarus fell under Polish/Lithuanian control, Muslims were isolated and persecuted, and many emigrated. The number of Tatars declined even more after the country fell under Russian control in 1790. They suffered severely again under the wars and pogroms of the 20th century. In January 1994 a supreme administration for the Muslim community of Belorussia was re-established, after being banned since 1939. The 25,000 Muslims in the nation in 1995 included also many relatively recent immigrants from the former Soviet republics of Central Asia.

Atheism. Though the percentage of Belorussian SSR citizens who were members of the Communist Party was small relative to other republics, the withering Soviet campaign of pro-atheist, anti-religious propaganda won a measure of victory. By 1970 nearly 15% of the population was atheist and another 25% nonreligious—together almost half of the country. But in the 1990s hundreds of thousands of atheists and nonreligious returned to the Christian faith of their ancestors. By AD 2000, atheists and nonreligious together comprise less than 29% of Belorussia.

Orthodox. 12th century Cross of Ephosinia of Polotsk, on 1,000th anniversary of Orthodoxy in Belorussia.

CHRISTIANITY

Belorussia has never been strong enough to shake free from the cultural and religious domination of its larger neighbors. The 1,000-year history of Christianity in Belorussia has been influenced by the Orthodoxy of Russia to the east, the Latin-rite Catholicism of Poland to the west, and the Uniate Catholicism of Ukraine to the south.

ORTHODOX CHURCH. Since today's Belarus was part of Kievan Rus since the 9th century, it converted to Orthodox Christianity under Vladimir I in 988. The Belorussian Orthodox Church was organized under Greek jurisdiction in 1291 but later fell under the Russian Patriarchate of Moscow. Large numbers of the faithful turned to Catholicism during the centuries of Polish/Lithuanian rule. Civil and religious authorities favored the Latin-rite and Uniate Catholic churches, and persecuted the Orthodox church, supporting the Uniates in their efforts to wrest church properties. This was a factor in the great peasant rebellion of 1648-54, as the peasantry tended to remain Orthodox. The tides turned in the 1790s when Poland was partitioned and Belorussia became again a part of the Russian empire. In 1840 tsar Nicholas I instituted his heavy-handed program of Orthodoxy, Russianism, and Absolutism. On the one hand, this policy banned the term Belarussia and the use of the Belorussian language in schools, but on the other hand insisted that all whose ancestors had turned to Catholicism must now return to the Orthodox Church. This immediately boosted the number of Orthodox Christians, but was seen as foreign oppression and bitterly resented.

Belorussian Orthodox Church, Diocese of Minsk. Cathedral of the Holy Spirit.

By 1917 the Orthodox church was dominant in Belorussia, with 1,650 congregations vs. only 127 Roman Catholic ones. Metropolitan Melchizedek in 1922 led the Minsk Council of Clergy and Laity in establishing the Belarus Orthodox Church, independent from the Russian Orthodox Church of Moscow. This move was vigorously protested by ecclesiastical officials and severely punished by Bolshevik officials. The Orthodox Church, with the rest of the nation, suffered a great loss of numbers during World War II. In 1942, under Nazi occupation, the Belorussian Autocephalous Orthodox Church was restored. This revival was short-lived, however, as the territory was turned back to the USSR after World War II and the church was set under the Moscow patriarchate again. This took place in 1946 at a stage-managed 'Reunion Council' held on the 350th anniversary of the Council of Brest that gave birth to the Uniate church.

Under government repression Orthodoxy continued to decline until the early 1980s, when revival began and was then boosted by the millennial celebration of 1988. The autonomy affirmed and destroyed in 1922 was granted again in 1990 when the Moscow Patriarchate designated Belorussia as an exarchate. Some welcomed the new measure of independence this represented, while others emphasized the continuing reality of strong control from Moscow. Church institutions began to re-emerge: in the early 1990s there was a seminary, a monastery, and 3 convents; and a Belorussian theological academy opened in 1995. Sermons in the Orthodox Church are preached in Russian, as a result of the strong ethnic Russian presence in the church and the decline of the use of the Belorussian language. With more than 46% of the national population in 1995, the Orthodox Church has returned to its place as the majority faith of the country. In 1995, about 100,000 belonged to Orthodox churches other than the Russian Orthodox majority church, including 60,000 in the Old Ritualist Church founded in 1710.

CATHOLIC CHURCH. The blow of the Mongol invasion drove Belorussia into the protective arms of Lithuania to the north. The Kingdom of Poland and Lithuania was formed in 1385 by the Union of Krevo, which required grand duke Jogalia of Lithuania to convert from paganism to Roman Catholicism. In Belorussia, Polish replaced Belorussian as the official language, and Polish Catholic culture became the way of the envied classes. As usually happens in circumstances of foreign cultural imperialism, Belorussian reaction split in 2 directions: many responded to official and cultural pressure and converted to Roman Catholicism; the majority resisted and clung to Orthodoxy more tightly than ever.

The Holy See has diplomatic relations with Belarus and in AD 2000 is represented to government and the Catholic hierarchy by a nuncio residing in Minsk.

UNIATE CHURCH. The Belorussian Byzantine Catholic Church was instituted at the Council of Brest (1596). The new church recognized the supremacy of the pope and accepted Catholic doctrine, but retained its Orthodox rites, liturgical language, and a measure of freedom in nondoctrinal matters. Not only the Polish king, Sigismund III, but also many Orthodox bishops, priests, and members were pleased with the Uniate arrangement. A majority of Orthodox faithful were not pleased however, and both churches continued to exist side by side in the country, often at conflict with each other. The Uniate Church continued to grow and by 1839 claimed 75% of the population of Belorussia. That year the Uniate Church was abolished by tsar Nicholas I, and many Eastern-rite Catholics were reluctantly forced back into Orthodoxy. Most chose to pass to the Latin rite. In 1905 Nicholas II allowed greater religious freedom and 230,000 Belorussians identified themselves as Uniate Catholics. None were, however, allowed to worship in their own language, and still more passed to the Latin rite.

From 1920 to 1939, part of western Belorussia was under Polish control. A distinct community of 30,000 Belorussian Uniate Catholics quickly emerged. An exarch was appointed for them in 1940, even though in 1939 the territory was returned to Soviet control, under the Molotov-Ribbentrop Agreement. The Belorussian Uniate Church was again banned in 1946, when the Roman Catholic Church was denounced as a Polish imperialist imposition and condemned for 'siding with bloody Fascism'.

Still, after the Uniate Church was officially dead for a third of a century, the Soviet press continued to carry bitter articles about it, revealing continuing activity. Uniate Catholics, never tolerated by the Soviet state, in their turn never wanted nor requested registration from a state they considered to be the Antichrist. Soviet enmity against Roman Catholics was fueled by the Catholics' recognition of an outside authority, the pope, and by the historic ties between Catholics of Belarus and Poland.

In 1980 a Vatican synod invalidated the actions of the 1946 'Reunion Council,' thus reaffirming the separate validity of Belorussian Uniate Christianity. Glasnost in the late 1980s, and then independence, provided the opportunity for the Uniate Church to arise yet again, and thus for Christian worship in the Belorussian language to be restored. But this restoration has not captured the allegiance of many. Some otherwise nonreligious and nationalistic young people have turned to the Uniate Church because of its use of the Belorussian language, but by 1995 only 33,000 of Belorussians' 1.3 million Catholics were Uniate. In 1992 3 priests and 2 deacons were active.

LATIN RITE. Since the tsar's action in 1839, by far most Belorussian Catholics have worshipped in Latin-rite churches. In the early 1970s there were about 80 priests, serving 100 parishes, but no bishops. Efforts from Rome to fill this gap were futile. In 1989 freedom of religion was declared and the Belorussian Catholic Church was legalized. Inter-church struggles over previously nationalized church properties began almost immediately. Conflicts over certain churches and cathedrals were so sharp that both sides accused the other of using violence, though strife was not as severe in Belorussia as in Ukraine. The 5 official dioceses which had existed since World War II were reorganized into 5 dioceses and the archdiocese of Minsk and Mahilyow. One seminary was functioning in the early 1990s. Preaching in Belorussia's Catholic churches is generally in Polish. It has been reported that as many as 25% of the Catholics in Belorussia are ethnically Polish.

PROTESTANTS. The Protestant Reformation and the Counter-Reformation were known and hotly discussed in Belorussia as early as elsewhere, due to contact through trade relations and the attendance of Belorussians in Western universities. Protestantism has never been a strong force in the religious life of Belorussia, despite growth in recent decades. Before 1917 there were only 32 Protestant congregations in the country. Since independence in 1991, Protestant churches have grown and multiplied, but not to the same extent as in the Ukraine. Hindrances to Protestant growth have included difficulties with building permits for new churches, scarcity of building supplies, and a dearth of trained leaders. In 1993 there were 51 foreign mission organizations active in Byelorussia, most of them Protestant Evangelical and many of them Charismatic. In 1995 less than 2% of the population was Protestant, the largest groups being Pentecostal and Baptist.

Renewal movements. In the 1990s the Pentecostal/Charismatic Renewal continued to spread rapidly across most older churches, and numbered over 95,000 adherents (of whom 67% Pentecostals, 23% Charismatics, 10% Independents).

CHURCH AND STATE

Belorussia's periods of Polish/Lithuanian control have favored Catholicism, of Russian control have favored Orthodoxy, and of Soviet control have been friendly to no religion. All churches suffered under the decades of Communist repression, and each have contributed many martyrs. State interference by various foreign powers has established and encouraged the Belorussian Uniate Catholic Church, and then nearly destroyed it. Various attempts through many centuries to establish a distinct national Orthodox Church have been made and repulsed, and the sincerity of the 1990 action of the Moscow Patriarchate is doubted by many. The 1989 national declaration of freedom of religion, which preceded independence in 1991, opens the way for a new chapter to be written in the history of Christianity in Belorussia—new and completely unprecedented.

BROADCASTING AND MEDIA

Shortwave programs from HCJB (Ecuador), TWR (Monaco, Tirane), AWR (Slovakia), KNLS and the Vatican, as well as other international broadcasters, can be clearly received and cover most of the major European languages. TWR has production facilities in Belarus from which it develops programs in Russian and Belorussian. An English language program 'Bible Focus,' produced in England, is aired for 30 minutes each Tuesday evening.

The 'Jesus' Film has been shown on television, watched by 3.5 million people. Satellite TV programs are received mainly in Arabic.

FUTURE TRENDS AND PROSPECTS

The collapse of Communism is expected to have an influence on changing religious affiliation well into the 21st century. Most of the atheists and nonreligious from the pre-Communist period will probably have chosen Christianity before 2005. The nonreligious, nearly 25% in 1970, will be only 12% by 2025 and atheists, over 15% in 1970, are expected to fall below 2% by 2025.

Christianity, having experienced rapid growth at the beginning of the 21st century, will potentially level out at about 90% over the next five decades.

BIBLIOGRAPHY

A bibliographical guide to Belorussia. N. P. Vakar. *Russian Research Center studies*, 22. Cambridge, MA: Harvard University Press, 1956. 63p.

Belarus: at a crossroads in history. J. Zaprudnik. Boulder, CO: Westview Press, 1993. 299p.

'Belarus on the road to nationhood,' G. Sanford, *Survival* (London), 38 (Spring 1996), 131–53.

Children of Chernobyl: raising hope from the ashes. M. Carter. Minneapolis, MN: Augsburg, 1993. 236p.

Katolitsizm v Belorussii: traditsionalizm i prisposoblenie. Minsk: Nauka i tekhnika, 1987. 238p.

Purism and language: a study in modern Ukrainian and Belorussian nationalism (1840–1967). P. Wexler. Bloomington, IN: Indiana University Press, 1974. 446p.

'Rétablissement de la hiérarchie latine en Biélorussie,' T. Kondruziewicz, *Istina*, 35 (July–September 1990), 301–302.

'Standing room only: Christian resurgence in Belarus,' J. Rigsby, *Christian Century*, 111 (July 27–August 3, 1994), 709–711.

The eve of the Holocaust: Shtetl Jews under Soviet rule 1939–1941. B. Pinchuk. Oxford, UK and Cambridge, MA: Blackwell, 1990. 186p.

Women's monasteries in Ukraine and Belorussia to the period of suppressions. S. Senyk. *Orentalia Christiana Analecta*, no. 222. Rome: Pont. Institutum Studiorum Orientalium, 1983. 235p.

Country Table 2. **Organized churches and denominations in Belorussia.**

Official name (bold type = church with over 10% of all affiliated) 1	Begun 2	Type 3	Counc 4	Congs 5	Adults 6	Affiliated 1970 7	Affiliated 1995 8	G% 9	*Names, notes, and other statistics* (see Codebook, Part 3) 10
Adventist Church	c1900	P-Adv	.....	2	300	200	600	4.49	*SDA. Seventh-day Adventists.*
Belorussian Autocephalic Orthodox Ch	992	O-Bye	M....	25	15,000	4,000	34,000	0.10	*White Russian Ch*, begun 992 D Polotsk. Absorbed into ROC broke free. 1996, 15 BOC chs join.
Belorussian Orth Ch: D Minsk & B	1793	O-Bye	Ma	900	3,150,000	4,500,000	4,800,000	0.26	*D Minsk and Byelorussia.* Now 10 Dioceses, 10 bishops under P Moscow. 13% Russians.
Catholic Ch in Belarus:	c1600	R-Lat	B....	290	900,000	810,000	1,302,000	1.92	33,000 Uniates. 1995, 100 Polish priests expelled. 90n 86x 102m 173w 12384Yy
M Minsk-Mohilev	1783	R-Lat	B....	91	250,000	800,000	350,000	-3.25	Archdiocese is 5% Catholic 26n 23x 35m 77w 3653Yy
D Grodno	1991	R-Lat	B....	150	614,000	–	902,000	25.00	Heavily Catholic: 75%. 55n 51x 52m 79w 8105Yy
D Pinsk	1925	R-Lat	B....	49	36,000	10,000	50,000	6.65	Under an apostolic administration. 9n 12x 15m 17w 626Yy
Church of Christ (Disciples)	c1970	I-Dis	x....	30	1,000	–	2,000	35.53	Small congregations of former Disciples churches.
Jehovah's Witnesses	c1930	m-Jeh	.....	100	1,260	1,000	4,200	5.91	Moderate success (IBSA, Watch Tower).
Lutheran Church of Belarus	c1900	P-Lut	.....	3	500	200	1,000	6.65	Remnants of large Lutheran bodies now dispersed.
New Apostolic Church	c1990	I-3aX	x....	30	1,500	–	2,071	20.00	*NAC, NAK.* M=Neuapostolische Kirche (HQ Zurich, Switzerland).
Old Ritualist Church	1710	I-OBe	x...u	20	39,000	50,000	60,000	0.73	*Old Believers.* Widespread followings for Western Europe to Siberia.
Orthodox dissenting bodies	c1800	I-Ort	.....	200	19,500	25,000	30,000	0.73	Several smaller breakoff from Orthodoxy.
Pentecostal Churches	1961	P-Pe2	.....	38	3,000	4,000	10,000	3.73	Formerly illegal unregistered churches. M=Christ for the Nations.
Pentecostal Union	c1930	P-Pe2	.....	200	16,000	12,000	50,000	5.87	Mainline Pentecostal, with USA mission links.
Union of Ev Christian Baptists of B	c1860	P-Bap	T....	150	25,100	6,670	32,000	6.47	Formerly unregistered pentecostals.
Other Orthodox churches		O-	.....	20	3,600	4,300	6,000	0.05	Armenian Apostolic Ch, Georgian Orthodox Ch, Moldavian Orthodox Ch, Ukrainian O.C.
Other Protestant churches		P-	.....	30	3,000	200	7,500	0.05	About 10 groups.
Totals				**2,038**	**4,178,760**	**5,417,570**	**6,341,371**		

Churches, members, growth, 1900-2025	*Congs*	*Adults*	*Affiliated*	*G%*	*Total denominations*	*6 Megablocs:* O	*R*	*A*	*P*	*I*	*m*
Total churches, members, and denominations (mid-1900)	1,000	4,129,000	6,436,000	-0.25	8	4	1	0	1	2	0
Total churches, members, and denominations (mid-1970)	1,058	3,475,680	5,417,570	-0.25	19	6	1	0	9	2	1
Total churches, members, and denominations (mid-1990)	1,200	4,041,000	6,133,000	0.62	31	10	1	0	15	4	1
Total churches, members, and denominations (mid-1995)	2,038	4,178,760	6,341,371	0.67	31	10	1	0	15	4	1
Total churches, members, and denominations (mid-2000)	2,030	4,339,000	6,584,077	0.75	31	10	1	0	15	4	1
Total churches, members, and denominations (mid-2025)	2,300	5,015,000	7,610,000	0.58	64	13	1	0	25	20	5

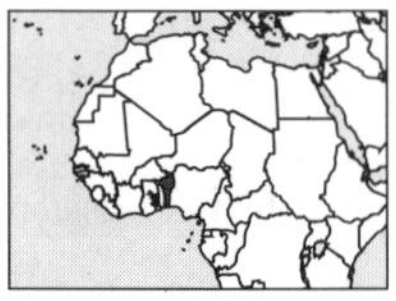

BENIN

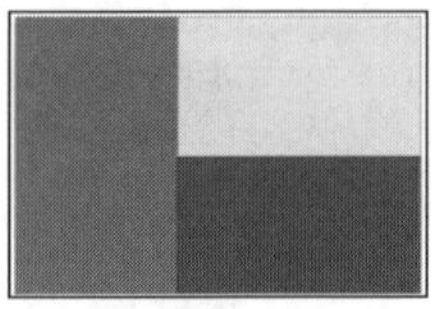

SECULAR DATA, AD 2000

STATE

Official name: La République du Bénin (The Republic of Benin).
Short name: Benin. **Adjective of nationality:** Beninese.
Flag: Green field with red star in upper hoist corner.
Area: 112,680 sq. km. (43,500 sq. mi.).
Government: Multiparty republic with one legislative house, since 1990 (1822 Kingdom, 1851 French rule, 1891 protectorate, 1904 in French West Africa, 1960 Independence as republic of Dahomey, 1963 military rule, 1974 Communist state).
Legislature: National Assembly, 83 members.
Official language: French (Français).
Monetary unit: 1 CFA franc (CFAF) = 100 centimes. **US$1=** CFAF 560.38.
Chief cities: Cotonou 773,183; PORTO-NOVO 265,276; Parakou 148,813; Abomey 85,729.
Political divisions: 6 provinces.
Armed forces: 5,000.

DEMOGRAPHY

Population: 6,097,000.
Population density: 54.1/sq. km. (140.1/sq. mi.).
Under 15 years: 2,793,000.
Growth rate p.a.: 2.63% (births 39.53, deaths 12.37).
Mortality: Infant, per 1,000: 80.7; **Maternal per 100,000:** 990.0.
Life expectancy: 54 (male 52, female 55).
Household size: 5.4. **Floor area per person, sq.m:** 6.0.
Major languages: Fon, Yoruba, Bariba, Gun, Fulani, Somba, French, Ewe, and about 20 other tribal languages.
Urban dwellers: 42.27%. **Urban growth rate p.a.:** 4.6%.
Labor force: 43%.

ETHNOLINGUISTIC PEOPLES

26.0% Fon (Fo, Dahomean, Fogbe); 7.1% Bariba (Nikki, Batonu); 6.7% Yoruba; 6.3% Adja; 6.1% Gun (Gu, Egun).

ECONOMY

National income p.a. per person: US$370; **per family:** US$1,998.

EDUCATION

Adult literacy: 37% (male 48%, female 25%). **Schools:** 3,048.
Universities: 13. **School enrolment:** female/male: 26%/54%.

HEALTH

Access to health services: 18%. **Access to safe water:** 50%.
Hospitals: 50 (10 beds per 10,000). **Doctors:** 323.
Blind: 5,000. **Deaf:** 373,300. **Murder rate:** 1.
Lepers: 100,000.

LITERATURE

New book titles p.a.: 300 (50 p.a. per million). **Periodicals:** 21.
Newspapers: 1 daily.

COMMUNICATION (per 1,000 people).

Phones: 5 (14% mobile). **Radios:** 73. **TV sets:** 73.
Daily newspaper circulation: 2. **Computers:** 15.

REFUGEES

Alien refugees from other countries: 2,500.

HUMAN LIFE AND LIBERTY (optimum condition=100.0%).

HDI: 36.8. **HSI:** 38.0. **HFI:** 32.5. **EFL:** 41.0.

Country Table 1. **Religious adherents in Benin, AD 1900-2025.**

Year	1900		1970		mid-1990		Annual change, 1990-2000				mid-1995		mid-2000		mid-2025	
Name	Adherents	%	Adherents	%	Adherents	%	Natural	Conversion	Total	Rate	Adherents	%	Adherents	%	Adherents	%
Ethnoreligionists	569,200	91.8	1,809,000	66.9	2,522,300	54.1	77,724	-15,935	61,799	2.22	2,792,800	52.3	3,140,286	51.5	4,594,000	41.4
Christians	**7,300**	**1.2**	**515,000**	**19.0**	**1,247,000**	**26.8**	**38,454**	**7,328**	**45,782**	**3.18**	**1,467,000**	**27.5**	**1,704,817**	**28.0**	**3,850,000**	**34.7**
PROFESSION																
professing Christians	**7,300**	**1.2**	**515,000**	**19.0**	**1,247,000**	**26.8**	**38,454**	**7,328**	**45,782**	**3.18**	**1,467,000**	**27.5**	**1,704,817**	**28.0**	**3,850,000**	**34.7**
AFFILIATION																
unaffiliated Christians	1,000	0.2	27,434	1.0	20,000	0.4	617	-555	62	0.31	19,535	0.4	20,622	0.3	20,000	0.2
affiliated Christians	**6,300**	**1.0**	**487,566**	**18.0**	**1,227,000**	**26.3**	**37,837**	**7,883**	**45,720**	**3.22**	**1,447,465**	**27.1**	**1,684,195**	**27.6**	**3,830,000**	**34.5**
Roman Catholics	5,200	0.8	393,813	14.6	950,000	20.4	29,295	2,325	31,620	2.91	1,101,287	20.6	1,266,195	20.8	2,700,000	24.3
Protestants	1,000	0.2	52,531	1.9	148,000	3.2	4,564	3,636	8,200	4.51	190,354	3.6	230,000	3.8	600,000	5.4
Independents	100	0.0	37,222	1.4	120,000	2.6	3,700	1,800	5,500	3.85	145,424	2.7	175,000	2.9	470,000	4.2
Marginal Christians	0	0.0	4,000	0.2	9,000	0.2	278	122	400	3.75	10,400	0.2	13,000	0.2	60,000	0.5
Trans-megabloc groupings																
Evangelicals	1,000	0.2	26,900	1.0	81,500	1.8	2,513	537	3,050	3.23	97,410	1.8	112,000	1.8	270,000	2.4
Pentecostals/Charismatics	0	0.0	47,000	1.7	243,500	5.2	7,509	2,341	9,850	3.46	289,972	5.4	342,000	5.6	900,000	8.1
Great Commission Christians	**4,300**	**0.7**	**216,500**	**8.0**	**712,000**	**15.3**	**21,956**	**7,302**	**29,258**	**3.50**	**838,400**	**15.7**	**1,004,584**	**16.5**	**2,400,000**	**21.6**
Muslims	43,500	7.0	376,000	13.9	870,000	18.7	26,828	8,272	35,100	3.45	1,050,000	19.7	1,221,003	20.0	2,580,000	23.2
Baha'is	0	0.0	3,400	0.1	8,000	0.2	247	260	507	5.03	10,800	0.2	13,074	0.2	40,000	0.4
Nonreligious	0	0.0	600	0.0	7,200	0.2	222	53	275	3.29	8,800	0.2	9,953	0.2	28,000	0.3
Atheists	0	0.0	0	0.0	3,100	0.1	96	-1	95	2.72	3,700	0.1	4,054	0.1	10,000	0.1
Other religionists	0	0.0	1,000	0.0	2,400	0.1	74	23	97	3.45	2,900	0.1	3,370	0.1	7,000	0.1
World A (unevangelized persons)	540,020	87.1	1,292,929	47.8	1,533,140	32.9	47,335	-43,429	3,906	0.25	1,552,726	29.1	1,573,026	25.8	2,255,127	20.3
World B (evangelized non-Christians)	72,680	11.7	896,943	33.2	1,879,860	40.3	57,866	36,009	93,967	4.14	2,316,103	43.4	2,819,157	46.2	5,003,873	45.0
World C (Christians)	7,300	1.2	515,000	19.0	1,247,000	26.8	38,454	7,328	45,782	3.18	1,467,000	27.5	1,704,817	28.0	3,850,000	34.7
Country's population	**620,000**	**100.0**	**2,704,873**	**100.0**	**4,660,000**	**100.0**	**143,655**	**0**	**143,655**	**2.72**	**5,335,830**	**100.0**	**6,097,000**	**100.0**	**11,109,000**	**100.0**

COLUMNS, ROWS.
For meanings and definitions, see Codebook (Part 3). Note that, by definition, total 'Christians' = professing + crypto-Christians, which also = affiliated + unaffiliated Christians, and also = Great Commission Christians + latent Christians. Percentages may not always total exactly, due to rounding.

CENSUSES.
25.V-30.IX.1961 (Africans over 14 years): 70.8% tribal religionists ('fetishists', animists), 13.6% Muslims, 12.3% Roman Catholics, 2.6% Protestants, 0.6% African indigenous.

NOTES ON RELIGIONS
ATHEISTS. No Communist party; atheists virtually nil, a few intellectuals only, until after 1970, mainly expatriate Europeans.
BAHA'IS. Growth from 1 local spiritual assembly (1964) to 23 (1973), then growing explosively to 66 LSAs (1996). Missionaries from Haiti (West Indies) are at work.
ETHNORELIGIONISTS. Traditional religion (also termed Vodoun (Voodoo) or fetishism remains very strong. In Abomey sub-division there are 257 fetishist monasteries. Tribes over 60% traditionalist (animist) in 1995: Burba (94%), Dompago (85%), Boko (80%), Ana (70%), Bariba (60%), Aizo (60%).
INDEPENDENTS. In 20 denominations in 1995 (see Table 2).
MUSLIMS. All Sunnis (of the Malikite rite). In the south, among the Nago, and spreading also among the Gun; in the north, Fulani, Dendi, Bariba (20% Muslim). The Dendi, long islamized, have helped spread Islam throughout the north, and Dendi is now the lingua franca of Muslims in the north. Orders: Qadiriya; Tijaniya; also Ahmadiya whose Qadiani mission begun from Nigeria in 1966 opened its first mosque, in Porto Novo, in 1974. Adherents are largely Yorubas. *Hajj pilgrims to Mecca.* (1970) 468; (1974) 527; (1975) 419; (1976) 545.
OTHER RELIGIONISTS. Including Rosicrucians (6 AMORC centers).

Great Commission Instrument Panel: status of Benin (for explanation see start of Part 4)

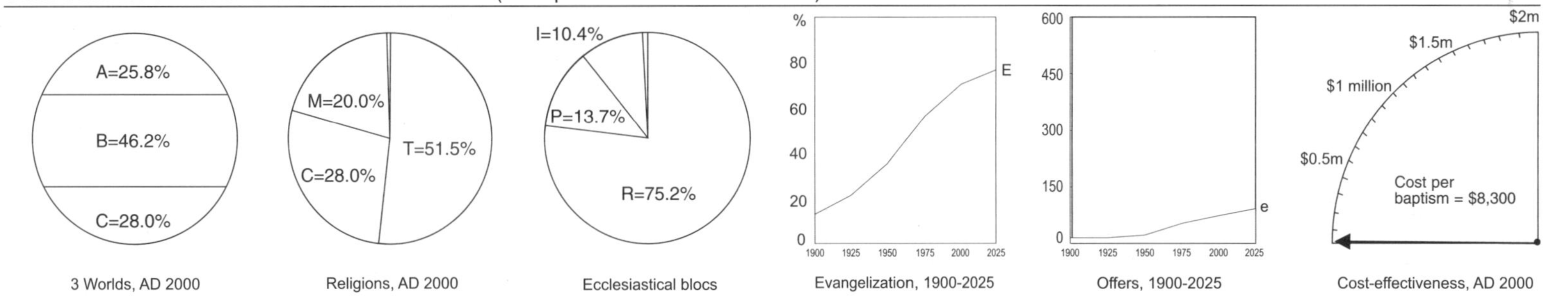

Country status. Benin lies on the south side of the West African bulge, formerly known as the Slave Coast, because it was one of the primary supply centers for slaves to the New World. It is a francophone country ruled until 1991 by a hardline Marxist government.

HUMAN LIFE AND LIBERTY

Human need and development. Benin is one of the world's 35 poorest countries with an economy largely based on subsistence agriculture. The economy grew worse during the Marxist rule when its external debt grew to intolerable levels, from $41 million in 1970 to $1.427 billion in 1991. The per capita GNP was about $370 in AD 2000. In order to reduce its bloated debt and debt-servicing charges, an austerity program under IMF auspices was launched by the new democratic government in 1991. Nevertheless an inefficient bureaucracy, tribal animosities, and widespread unemployment have served to slow development activities.

Human rights and freedoms. After free elections in 1991 led to the defeat of the 17-year-old Marxist government, the new rulers have set about to open Benin to a new era of human rights. All political prisoners have been released, and torture and inhuman treatment of prisoners have been prohibited in prisons. The new Constitution provides for the inviolability of private property and the home, and guarantees freedoms of the press and speech. There is no censorship of literary or artistic works. The primary threat to human rights arises from regional and ethnic rivalries. The regional rivalry is between southerners and northerners. The former Marxist president Mathieu Kerekou was a northerner and he favored northerners during his regime. After his fall, the southerners under president Nicephore Soglo have reasserted themselves. The southerners who prospered during French rule are themselves divided into various ethnic and religious groups. Women are generally discriminated against in education and public service. They suffer not only from widespread domestic violence but also from the rite of female circumcision historically practiced by some Beninese societies.

Human environment. During the 1980s Benin lost its forests at an average annual rate of 1.7%, or roughly 3 times the rate of loss in the rest of Africa. About 59% of the original forest cover has been lost. Many wildlife species are unprotected and illegal hunting threatens to reduce their stock. Unsafe drinking water is a major cause of disease, and 65% of the rural population lacks access to safe drinking water.

NON-CHRISTIAN RELIGIONS

Traditional African religions retain the allegiance of almost half the population and are active everywhere, especially in rural areas and among women. In spite of their diversity, they have, notably in the south, several common characteristics: a coherent yet mystical view of the universe; a concept of God (Mawu among the Ewe, Mawu-Lisa among the Fon); a desire for communion with the divinities in their various manifestations (Vodoun or Voodoo among the Fon, Orisha among the Yoruba); and a need to know the will of the divinities by consulting the Fa oracles. The Fon, who have been generally resistant to both Islam and Christianity, have traditionalist or fetishist convents in the region of Abomey, and their chief medicine-men play a not inconsiderable part politically in the degree to which they draw their clientele towards active participation in national life.

Islam has been introduced among the Nago of the Yoruba cluster in the south by the Yoruba and Hausa of Nigeria and among the Fulani, Dendi, and Bariba in the north by the Dendi of Niger. The Qadiriya and Tijaniya orders are active. Largely urban in orientation, many Muslims are merchants. Islam is growing; almost 20% of the population of Benin in AD 2000.

Eglise Catholique au Bénin. Cotonou cathedral.

CHRISTIANITY

CATHOLIC CHURCH. A chapel was built by the Portuguese at Ouidah (Whydah) in 1680 and was served by French and Portuguese priests during the 17th and 18th centuries. By 1830, there were 2,000 Catholics in Dahomey. However, active missionary work in the interior did not begin until 1860, when Dahomey was turned over to the African Missions of Lyons. A prefecture was erected in 1883. By 1900, there were 5,000 Catholics, and a seminary was opened in 1913. The first African priest was ordained in 1928.

The archdiocese of Cotonou was established in 1955 and the first African archbishop appointed in 1960. Strongly represented now in the cities and among the modern elite, Catholicism reaches primarily the populations of the southern half of the country, including the Fon, Mina, Adja, and Gun as well as Mulattoes descended from Portuguese sailors and merchants and repatriated slaves who returned from Brazil during the 19th century.

The Holy See has diplomatic relations with Benin and in AD 2000 is represented to government and the Catholic hierarchy by a nuncio residing in Accra.

PROTESTANT CHURCHES. Methodists, who are associated with the Methodist Church of Great Britain, were the first Protestant mission to enter, arriving in Abomey in 1843. They are by far the largest Protestant group and have concentrated their atten-

Country summary. **Worlds A, B, C by ethnolinguistic peoples, cities, and major civil divisions in Benin.**

	PEOPLES							*CITIES*							*CIVIL DIVISIONS*						
World	*Num*	*Pop 2000*	*C%*	*Christians*	*E%*	*U%*	*Unevangelized*	*Num*	*Pop 2000*	*C%*	*Christians*	*E%*	*U%*	*Unevangelized*	*Num*	*Pop 2000*	*C%*	*Christians*	*E%*	*U%*	*Unevangelized*
A	29	1,119,546	4.52	50,644	40	60	676,875	0	0	0.00	0	0	0	0	0	0	0.00	0	0	0	0
B	22	4,622,126	30.04	1,388,285	81	19	895,500	4	1,273,001	35.92	457,246	84	16	208,923	6	6,096,560	27.63	1,684,194	74	26	1,574,061
C	7	354,884	69.11	245,267	100	0	1,684	0	0	0.00	0	0	0	0	0	0	0.00	0	0	0	0
Total	**58**	**6,096,556**	**27.63**	**1,684,196**	**74**	**26**	**1,574,059**	**4**	**1,273,001**	**35.92**	**457,246**	**84**	**16**	**208,923**	**6**	**6,096,560**	**27.63**	**1,684,194**	**74**	**26**	**1,574,061**

Ethnoreligionists. 80% of the largest tribe, the Fon, are traditionalists (fetishists). *Above.* Pagan temple, with mud walls and mixed with blood of sacrificed slaves, in Fon capital of Abomey.

tion principally on the Gun of the southern coast. They also have work among the Fon around Abomey. The Assemblies of God are active in northwest among the Somba and Pilapila tribes, whereas EECOA or ECWA (served by the Sudan Interior Mission), is located in central and northcentral Benin. The latter have had their greatest success among the Logba and Bariba peoples. The extreme northeast and the region west of Djougou are relatively unevangelized areas.

INDIGENOUS CHURCHES. There are a number of small independent churches working in Benin. The most important are the Heavenly Christianity Church begun 1947 and which later spread to Nigeria as the Celestial Church of Christ, Cherubim and Seraphim who entered from Nigeria in 1933; and Eglise Methodiste Africaine (Elidja) which split from the Methodists in 1927.

Art and architecture. Outside the cathedrals of Porto Novo and Cotonou, most Christian churches are modest in appearance, built of wood and rough bricks.

Renewal movements. In the 1990s the Pentecostal/Charismatic Renewal continued to spread rapidly across most older churches, and numbered over 342,000 adherents (of whom 25% Pentecostals, 31% Charismatics, and 45% Independents).

Indigenous missions. Though over one fourth of Benin is Christian the ratio of missionaries received to those sent is still over 10 to 1. Thus only a few Benin Christians have been involved in foreign missions, mostly in neighboring African countries or in France.

CHURCH AND STATE

According to the constitution of March 1968, the republic is a secular state (Article 2), but the president takes his oath 'before God and the ancestors' (Article 29). Liberty of conscience and religion is assured.

Eglise du Christianisme Céleste du Bénin. Signpost to one of the denomination's 300 churches in Benin.

In practice, the fact that the republic is secular means that the state maintains a neutral stance before all religions, which are considered equal.

Legal holidays include the main Christian and Muslim festivals. Official ceremonies are accompanied by libations and offerings to the ancestors and divinities, as well as prayers in churches and mosques. In August 1970, the government organized at Cotonou a colloquium entitled, 'The Social Role of the Traditional African Religions.' Before 1974, the state subsidized education in denominational schools at a rate equivalent to 60% of the gross salary of public school teachers, all other charges being borne by the churches. In public schools, religion classes were normally integrated into the class schedule. On 10 September 1974, all Catholic and Protestant primary schools were taken over by government and state aid to denominational secondary and technical schools abolished.

The historic role played by the Catholic Church in the formation of an elite, by means of its schools, gives it a greater influence than the number of its adherents warrants. In the years 1945-51, such missionary personalities as Fr. Aupiais played an important part in the evolution of the colony, but since Independence, the Catholic hierarchy has forbidden priests to interfere in political life or to seek election to political posts.

From 1972-1991, Benin was led by a revolutionary military government (GMR), which stated on 10 November 1974, its choice of the socialist way to development 'on the basis of Marxism-Leninism'. In February 1975, 3 Catholic priests in senior posts were arrested together with a number of influential laymen. One of the priests was condemned to death, an action which provoked widespread attempts and appeals to prevent the application of the sentence. On 12 February 1975, the government warned the Catholic Church against the involvement of priests and laity in opposition to the present regime. In 1976, all schools were nationalized. Church-state tensions have eased since the establishment of democracy in 1991.

There is no government ministry in charge of religious affairs, but all churches must be registered with the Ministry of the Interior.

BROADCASTING AND MEDIA

Most families own a radio receiver. Benin is registered as a member of UNDA, and the government-owned Radio Benin broadcasts a Catholic mass and a Protestant service every Sunday morning, and a Catholic and Protestant news magazine during the week. Christian programs can be received from TWR (South Africa) and AWR (Slovakia), and could be received from ELWA (Liberia) as well until its destruction.

A Catholic service is televised each Sunday, but few families own a television set. The 'Jesus' Film has been shown to 2.2 million people, mostly on television (1.5 million) and through film team presentations (550,000).

INTERDENOMINATIONAL ORGANIZATIONS

There are no organizations which coordinate the work of Protestants and Catholics, nor is there a Protestant council to further Protestant cooperation. There is, however, an association of indigenous churches. The Evangelical pastoral school at Porto Novo trains pastors for the Evangelical Church of Togo and the Methodist Church of Benin-Togo, and the Christian Center for Lay Training attached to it serves all the churches.

Regarding Christian and Muslim relations, the Catholic Episcopal Conference has established an Episcopal Commission for Islam and Ecumenism.

FUTURE TRENDS AND PROSPECTS

Christian affiliation is expected to increase to 34.5% by 2025 primarily due to gradual decline of animism among peoples like the Fon and the Bariba.

Christianity, just over 1% of the population in 1900, is likely to rise to near 40% by AD 2030. Barring the entrance of other religions, Christians and Muslims will probably share a 75/25 percentage of Benin's population after mid-century.

BIBLIOGRAPHY

A travers les missions du Togo et du Dahomey. A. Boucher. Paris: Librairie P. Téqui, 1926. 164p.

An outline of Dahomean religious belief. M. J. Herskovits & F. S. Herskovits. *Memoirs of the American Anthropological Association*, no. 41. 1933; reprint, New York: Kraus, 1976. 77p.

Asen, iron altars of the Fon people of Benin: October 2–December 21, 1985, Emory University, Museum of Art and Archaeology, Michael C. Carlos Hall, Emory University, Atlanta, Georgia. E. G. Bay. Atlanta: The Museum, 1985. 48p.

Benin. Gerrards Cross, UK: Worldwide Evangelical Crusade, 1990. (1 transparency, map of Benin depicting the 38 language groups, the percentage of each group which is Evangelical Christian, and Evangelical missions working in each group).

Dieux en diaspora: les loa haitiens et les vaudou du Royaume d'Allada (Bénin). G. Montilus. *Cultures africaines.* Niamey: CELHTO, 1988. 143p.

Études sur l'Islam au Dahomey: le bas Dahomey, le haut Dahomey. P. Marty. Paris: E. Leroux, 1926. 295p.

Heviesso et le bon ordre du monde: approche d'une religion africaine. B. Gilli. *Studium combonianum*, 40. Lomé, Togo: Editions HAHO, [1987]. 230p.

Jalons pour une théologie africaine: essai d'une herméneutique Chrétienne du vodun dahoméen. B. Adoukonou. Paris: Lethielleux Culture et Vérité, 1980. 2 vols.

Le culte de Maria dans la spiritualité africaine au Dahomey en Afrique noire. J. Amoussou. Oudiah: Grand seminaire Saint Gall, 1974. 78p.

Le vodou fon dans le Royaume d'Allada (Bas–Dahomey): ses images et ses symboles. G. Montilus. Cotonou, 1972. 23p.

Le vodun sakpata: recherche sur le vodun sakpata à partir des noms individuels de ses vodunsi. P. Saulnier. Porto-Novo, 1974. 73p.

'Les sectes au Dahomey,' M. C. Merlo, in *Devant les sectes non-chrétiennes: rapports et compte rendu. Museum Lessianum. Section missiologique*, no. 42. [Paris]: Desclée de Brouwer, 1961.

'Les société–religieuses en Afrique occidentale,' E. G. Parrinder, *Présence africaine*, 17/18 (1958), 17–21.

Lumiere sur le monde de vodoun. P. E. Edah. Cotonou, Benin: Organisation Béninoise pour la Recherche et la Définition de la Tradition Divinatoire. 83p.

Mission catholique et choc des modèles culturels en Afrique: l'exemple du Dahomey, 1861–1928. C. Roussé-Grosseau. Paris: L'Harmattan, 1992. 390p.

Société et religion au Bénin. M. Palau. Paris: Maisonneuve et Larose, 1993. 314p. (Contains summaries in English and Catalan).

Yoruba religious carving: pagan and Christian sculpture in Nigeria and Dahomey. K. Carroll. London: G. Chapman, 1967. 184p.

Country Table 2. Organized churches and denominations in Benin.

Official name (bold type = church with over 10% of all affiliated) 1	*Begun* 2	*Type* 3	*Counc* 4	*Congs* 5	*Adults* 6	*Affiliated 1970* 7	*Affiliated 1995* 8	*G%* 9	*Names, notes, and other statistics* (see Codebook, Part 3) 10
Assemblées de Dieu	1938	P-Pe2	ZF..I	240	36,318	6,000	50,000	8.85	*Assemblies of God.* M=AoG(USA). Northwest. Sombas. HQ Cotonou. 38n,14f,1s(19).
Chérubin et Séraphin	1933	I-3aA	x.I.I	200	6,000	6,000	12,000	2.81	*Cherubim and Seraphim Society.* Nigerian indigenous pentecostals. Egba, Gun.
Eglise Adventiste du 7me Jour	c1970	P-Adv	x...I	1	316	–	527	28.49	*Seventh-day Adventist Church.* M=SDA(USA).
Eglise Apostolique du Nigérie	1950	P-PeA	ZG..I	170	8,500	7,000	17,000	3.61	M=Apost Ch of Nigeria (Lagos). 48 congs in Deve district. Yoruba, Gun, Adja, Mina.
Eglise Apostolique du Togo et Bénin	c1960	I-3aA	x.I.I	10	3,000	2,000	4,000	2.81	*Apostolic Ch of T & B. Divine Healer's Temple.* Begun 1951 in Togo. Apostle in Lomé.
Eglise Baptiste	1970	P-Bap	I	21	4,700	–	9,000	43.94	*Baptist Church.* M=SBC(USA).
Eglise Catholique au Bénin:	1680	R-Lat	P.SFR	146	616,600	393,813	1,101,287	4.20	*Catholic Ch.* Mainly south. C=2+2+20. 4p,1s(18). 207n 119x 145m 556w 44566Yy
M Cotonou	1883	R-Lat	Ps	29	196,000	139,433	351,032	3.76	Port, centre of nation. 33% urban. Fon. 51n 51x 62m 200w 14866Yy
D Abomey	1963	R-Lat	Ps	22	185,000	100,000	330,000	4.89	Fon Capital. Strong traditional religion. 43n 6x 10m 62w 9492Yy
D Kandi	1994	R-Lat	Ps	8	3,000	–	5,313	100.00	Formed out of D Parakou. M=SMA. 6n 7x 0m 19w 100Yy
D Lokossa	1968	R-Lat	Ps	21	36,000	24,314	63,950	3.94	Rural development, coastal fishing. 36n 1x 2m 43w 3389Yy
D Natitingou	1964	R-Lat	Psma	25	14,600	6,630	26,152	5.64	15% Somba, 15% Bariba, 15% Kabre. M=SMA. 16n 17x 22m 74w 1469Yy
D Parakou	1948	R-Lat	Psma	18	31,000	11,031	55,840	6.70	41% Muslim. South: 85% Fon, 10% Egba. M=SMA. 24n 33x 44m 94w 1796Yy
D Porto-Novo	1954	R-Lat	Ps	23	151,000	112,405	269,000	3.55	Densely populated (110/km2). 177 expatriates. 31n 4x 5m 64w 13454Yy
Eglise de Dieu de Prophétie	c1980	P-Pe3	.....	7	210	–	525	6.67	*Church of God of Prophecy.* Large mission from USA.
Eglise de l'Evangile et Foi	1976	I-3aA	I	21	3,000	–	5,000	5.26	*Gospel Faith Mission.* Begun in Nigeria (Ibadan: 1953). Mostly Yorubas.
Eglise du Christianisme Céleste du B	1947	I-3aA	xvI.I	300	40,000	20,000	60,000	4.49	*Celestial Ch of Christ. Heavenly Christianity Ch.* Schism ex Cherubim. Gun, Nago, Mina, Ewe.
Eglise Evangélique Baptiste	1970	P-Bap	.....	12	1,400	–	2,800	37.37	*Evangelical Baptist Mission.* M=EBM(USA).
Egl Ev Chrétienne de l'Ouest-Africain	1946	P-Eva	xM..I	124	5,200	3,335	10,000	4.49	*EECOA/ECWA*: M=SIM. 33% Bariba, 32% Logba, 13% Fulani, Nago. 11n,29f,1H,3h,3p(26).
Eglise Méthodiste Africaine (Eledja)	1927	I-Met	x.I.I	69	5,500	4,622	15,700	5.01	M=United Afr Meth Ch (Fishmongers) (HQ Lagos). 68% Gun, 32% Yoruba. 4n,W=64%,15Y,94y.
Eglise Neo-Apostolique	c1980	I-3aX	x....	100	10,000	–	14,524	6.67	*NAC. New Apostolic Church.* HQ Zurich (Switzerland).
Eglise Pentecôtiste Unie	1985	P-Pe1	x....	5	300	–	600	10.00	*United Pentecostal Church.* Oneness (Jesus Only) Pentecostals.
Eglise Protestante Méthodiste au Benin	1843	P-Met	VWA.I	357	46,900	35,696	90,000	3.77	*Protestant Meth Ch.* M=MMS, PEMS,AAC. 12n,4x,16f,3r,1s(4),W=50%,322Y,1971y,3021z.
Eglise Quadrangular	c1970	P-Pe2	I	29	961	–	2,402	36.53	*Church of the Foursquare Gospel.* M=ICFG(USA).
Eglise Union Africaine	1895	I-Met	x.I.I	20	1,000	2,000	2,200	0.38	*African Union Mission. Boda-Owa* (If it's good, come). In UNAC(Nigeria). Ex MMS. Yoruba.
Groupes du Christ	c1980	I-3hA	x....	43	800	–	2,000	6.67	*Christ Groups.* Isolated home churches for converts from nationwide EHC campaign.
Témoins de Jéhovah	c1935	m-Jeh	x....	81	2,904	4,000	10,400	3.90	*Jehovah's Witnesses..* Active witnessing by 1940s. HQ Cotonou. 154Y. (1995) 444Y.
Other African indigenous churches		I-3nA	I	150	20,000	2,600	30,000	0.05	Total 35, including: Christ Apostolic Ch (Nigeria), Eglise Christique Primitive.
Other Protestant denominations		P-	.....	50	3,000	500	7,500	0.05	Total: Ev Baptist Missions, Southern Baptist Convention, World-Wide Missions, Chs of Christ.
Totals				**2,156**	**816,609**	**487,566**	**1,447,465**		

Churches, members, growth, 1900-2025	*Congs*	*Adults*	*Affiliated*	*G%*	*Total denominations*	*6 Megablocs:* O	R	A	P	I	m
Total churches, members, and denominations (mid-1900)	100	3,500	6,300	6.41	3	0	1	0	1	1	0
Total churches, members, and denominations (mid-1970)	909	268,934	487,566	6.41	22	0	1	0	8	12	1
Total churches, members, and denominations (mid-1990)	1,900	692,000	1,227,000	4.72	42	0	1	0	18	22	1
Total churches, members, and denominations (mid-1995)	2,156	816,609	1,447,465	3.36	44	0	1	0	19	23	1
Total churches, members, and denominations (mid-2000)	2,400	950,000	1,684,195	3.08	46	0	1	0	20	24	1
Total churches, members, and denominations (mid-2025)	4,000	2,161,000	3,830,000	3.34	82	2	1	0	25	50	4

NOTES ON TABLE ABOVE
NATIONAL COUNCILS (Column 4, 5th letter).
C = Conseil Interconfessionelle Protestante du Benin.
E = Fédération des Eglises et Missions Evangéliques du Bénin (FEMEB) (Federation of Churches and Missions in Benin).
I = Association des Eglises Chrétiennes au Bénin (Association of Christian Churches).
R = Conférence Episcopale du Bénin (Episcopal Conference of Benin).

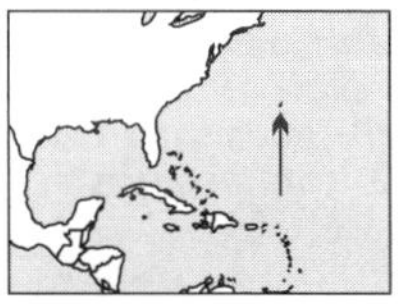

BERMUDA

SECULAR DATA, AD 2000

STATE
Official name: The Colony of the Bermuda Islands.
Short name: Bermuda. **Adjective of nationality:** Bermudan.
Flag: That of the UK (Britain).
Area: 54 sq. km. (21 sq. mi.).
Government: Self-governing dependency of United Kingdom, since 1968 (1684 British crown colony, 1968 internal autonomy).
Legislature: Legislative Council, 11 members; House of Assembly, 40.
Official language: English.
Monetary unit: Bermuda dollar. **US$1=** 1.00.
Chief cities: HAMILTON 17,441.
Political divisions: 10 provinces.
Armed forces: 700.

DEMOGRAPHY
Population: 65,000.
Population density: 1,196.1/sq. km. (3,075.7/sq. mi.).
Under 15 years: 20,000.
Growth rate p.a.: 1.56% (births 20.64, deaths 5.01).
Mortality: Infant, per 1,000: 13.9; **Maternal per 100,000:** 30.0.
Life expectancy: 75 (male 72, female 78).
Household size: 2.6. **Floor area per person, sq.m:** 45.0.
Major languages: English, Portuguese.
Urban dwellers: 100.00%. **Urban growth rate p.a.:** 0.6%.
Labor force: 60%.

ETHNOLINGUISTIC PEOPLES
50.3% West Indian Black; 29.0% British; 10.0% Mulatto; 6.0% USA White; 4.5% Portuguese.

ECONOMY
National income p.a. per person: US$31,862; **per family:** US$82,842.

EDUCATION
Adult literacy: 96% (male 96%, female 97%). **Schools:** 36.
Universities: 1. **School enrolment:** female/male: 75%/75%.

HEALTH
Access to health services: 95%. **Access to safe water:** 85%.
Hospitals: 2 (42 beds per 10,000). **Doctors:** 91.
Blind: 25. **Deaf:** 3,900. **Murder rate:** 5.
Lepers: 0.

LITERATURE
New book titles p.a.: 45 (700 p.a. per million). **Periodicals:** 42.
Newspapers: 1 daily.

COMMUNICATION (per 1,000 people)
Phones: 900 (15% mobile). **Radios:** 1,311. **TV sets:** 460.
Daily newspaper circulation: 254. **Computers:** 200.

HUMAN LIFE AND LIBERTY (optimum condition=100.0%)
HDI: 92.0. **HSI:** 95.0. **HFI:** 90.0. **EFL:** 50.0.

Country Table 1. Religious adherents in Bermuda, AD 1900-2025.

Year	*1900*		*1970*		*mid-1990*		*Annual change, 1990-2000*				*mid-1995*		*mid-2000*		*mid-2025*	
Name	*Adherents*	*%*	*Adherents*	*%*	*Adherents*	*%*	*Natural*	*Conversion*	*Total*	*Rate*	*Adherents*	*%*	*Adherents*	*%*	*Adherents*	*%*
Christians	**20,300**	**100.2**	**51,810**	**97.8**	**55,910**	**94.8**	**496**	**-64**	**432**	**0.75**	**58,100**	**93.7**	**60,230**	**92.7**	**69,110**	**90.9**
PROFESSION																
professing Christians	**20,300**	**100.2**	**51,810**	**97.8**	**55,910**	**94.8**	**496**	**-64**	**432**	**0.75**	**58,100**	**93.7**	**60,230**	**92.7**	**69,110**	**90.9**
AFFILIATION																
unaffiliated Christians	1,270	6.3	5,585	10.5	4,360	7.4	44	-24	20	0.44	4,431	7.2	4,555	7.0	5,110	6.7
affiliated Christians	**19,030**	**93.9**	**46,225**	**87.3**	**51,550**	**87.4**	**452**	**-38**	**413**	**0.77**	**53,669**	**86.6**	**55,675**	**85.7**	**64,000**	**84.2**
Anglicans	13,000	64.2	22,000	41.5	23,700	40.2	241	-191	50	0.21	24,500	39.5	24,200	37.2	22,700	29.9
Protestants	2,230	11.0	11,625	21.9	17,500	29.7	178	22	200	1.09	18,370	29.6	19,500	30.0	25,000	32.9
Roman Catholics	1,000	4.9	7,500	14.2	9,400	15.9	96	2	98	1.00	9,980	16.1	10,384	16.0	13,000	17.1
Independents	2,800	13.8	4,650	8.8	5,800	9.8	59	61	120	1.90	6,690	10.8	7,000	10.8	10,000	13.2
Marginal Christians	0	0.0	450	0.9	950	1.6	10	60	70	5.68	1,129	1.8	1,650	2.5	2,700	3.6
doubly-affiliated	0	0.0	0	0.0	-5,800	-9.8	-59	-67	-126	1.98	-7,000	-11.3	-7,059	-10.9	-9,400	-12.4
Trans-megabloc groupings																
Evangelicals	1,600	7.9	5,200	9.8	6,700	11.4	68	32	100	1.40	7,300	11.8	7,700	11.9	10,000	13.2
Pentecostals/Charismatics	0	0.0	1,200	2.3	11,100	18.8	113	117	230	1.90	12,251	19.8	13,400	20.6	16,800	22.1
Great Commission Christians	**1,200**	**5.9**	**5,900**	**11.1**	**10,000**	**17.0**	**102**	**31**	**133**	**1.25**	**10,700**	**17.3**	**11,327**	**17.4**	**15,000**	**19.7**
Nonreligious	0	0.0	1,000	1.9	1,850	3.1	19	57	76	3.49	2,300	3.7	2,606	4.0	3,500	4.6
Spiritists	0	0.0	0	0.0	1,150	2.0	12	7	19	1.54	1,200	1.9	1,340	2.1	2,200	2.9
Baha'is	0	0.0	100	0.2	300	0.5	3	0	3	0.80	315	0.5	325	0.5	650	0.9
Buddhists	0	0.0	50	0.1	25	0.0	0	0	0	-1.73	20	0.0	21	0.0	20	0.0
Jews	0	0.0	20	0.0	20	0.0	0	0	0	0.49	20	0.0	21	0.0	40	0.1
Other religionists	0	0.0	20	0.0	45	0.1	0	0	0	0.22	45	0.1	46	0.1	80	0.1
World A (unevangelized persons)	0	0.0	52	0.1	118	0.2	1	1	2	1.92	124	0.2	130	0.2	228	0.3
World B (evangelized non-Christians)	-39	0.0	1,113	2.1	2,972	5.5	33	63	96	4.56	3,776	6.1	4,640	6.5	6,662	8.3
World C (Christians)	20,300	100.0	51,810	97.8	55,910	94.3	496	-64	432	0.75	58,100	93.7	60,230	93.3	69,110	91.4
Country's population	**20,261**	**100.0**	**52,976**	**100.0**	**59,000**	**100.0**	**530**	**0**	**530**	**0.97**	**62,000**	**100.0**	**65,000**	**100.0**	**76,000**	**100.0**

Continued overleaf

Country Table 1–concluded

COLUMNS, ROWS.
For meanings and definitions, see Codebook (Part 3). Note that, by definition, total 'Christians' = professing + crypto-Christians, which also = affiliated + unaffiliated Christians, and also = Great Commission Christians + latent Christians. Percentages may not always total exactly, due to rounding.

CENSUSES.
1901 (Census of the British Empire) (excluding 707 foreign visitors): 67.3% Anglicans, 15.0% Black indigenous (AMEC), 11.5% Protestants (3.5% Presbyterians), 6.2% Roman Catholics. **22.X.1950:** 53.0% Anglicans, 24.4% Protestants (8.1% Methodists & Wesleyans, 3.3% Presbyterians, 2.0% Christian Brethren, 1.9% SDAs, 1.6% Salvation Army, 1.6% Pentecostals), 10.2% Black indigenous (AMEC), 10.0% Roman Catholics, 1.6% nonreligious, 0.4% marginal Protestants, 0.3% Buddhists, 0.1% Chinese folk-religionists. **23.X.1960** (excluding tourists and British and USA military and dependents): 48.4% Anglicans, 27.6% Protestants (7.2% Methodists & Wesleyans, 3.1% Presbyterians, 3.0% SDAs, 2.4% Christian Brethren 2.1% Salvation Army, 2.1% Pentecostals), 11.2% Black indigenous (AMEC), 10.4% Roman Catholics, 2.2% nonreligious, 0.1% marginal Protestants, 0.1% Buddhists. **25.X.1970:** 45.1% Anglicans, 26.6% Protestants (6.9% Methodists & Wesleyans, 3.6% SDAs, 3.4% Presbyterians, 2.1% Brethren), 14.6% Roman Catholics, 10.5% Black indigenous (AMEC), 2.0% nonreligious, 1.0% marginal Protestants, 0.2% other religionists. **1980:** 38.3% Anglicans, 29% Protestants (6% Methodists, 5% SDAs), 14% Roman Catholics, 13% Independents, 10% (AMEC), 1.2% Marginal Christians, 2.5% nonreligious, 2.0% other religionists. **1991:** 30% Anglicans, 31% Protestants (6% SDAs, 5% Methodists), 15% Roman Catholics, 15% Independents (12% AMEC), 2.0% Marginal Christians, 3.0% nonreligious, 4.0% other religionists.

NOTES ON RELIGIONS
BAHA'IS. In 2 local spiritual assemblies (1973), rising to 7 (1995).
INDEPENDENTS. In 4 denominations in 1995 (see Table 2).
OTHER RELIGIONISTS. Small groups of Hindus and Muslims.

Great Commission Instrument Panel: status of Bermuda (for explanation see start of Part 4)

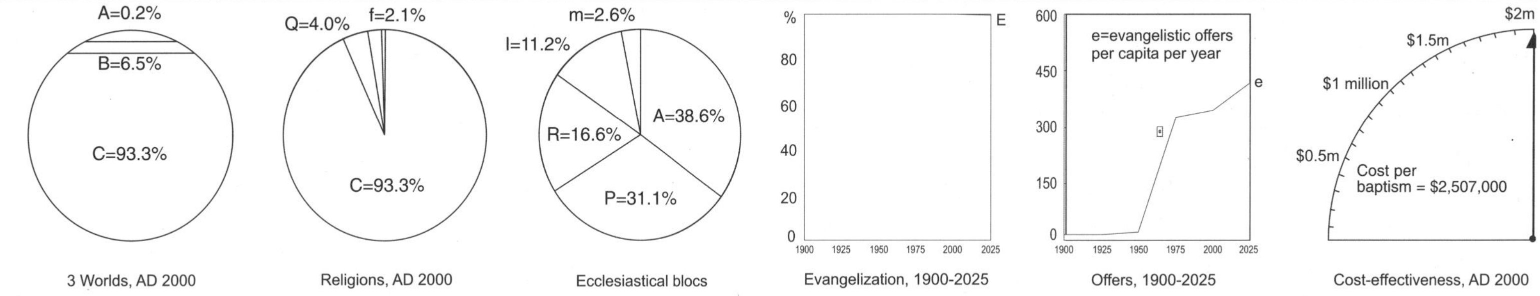

Country summary. **Worlds A, B, C by ethnolinguistic peoples, cities, and major civil divisions in Bermuda.**

World	PEOPLES Num	Pop 2000	C%	Christians	E%	U%	Unevangelized	CITIES Num	Pop 2000	C%	Christians	E%	U%	Unevangelized	CIVIL DIVISIONS Num	Pop 2000	C%	Christians	E%	U%	Unevangelized
A	1	21	0.00	0	43	57	12	0	0	0.00	0	0	0	0	0	0	0.00	0	0	0	0
B	1	65	36.92	24	68	32	21	0	0	0.00	0	0	0	0	0	0	0.00	0	0	0	0
C	5	64,504	86.28	55,652	100	0	89	1	17,441	86.20	15,034	100	0	33	10	64,590	86.20	55,675	100	0	121
Total	**7**	**64,590**	**86.20**	**55,676**	**100**	**0**	**122**	**1**	**17,441**	**86.20**	**15,034**	**100**	**0**	**33**	**10**	**64,590**	**86.20**	**55,675**	**100**	**0**	**121**

Country status. Bermuda is a British colony with internal self-government. It is the oldest self-governing colony in the Commonwealth. Bermuda is comprised of nearly 150 small islands in the western Atlantic off the coast of North Carolina, USA. Its primary industry is tourism.

HUMAN LIFE AND LIBERTY

Human need and development. Bermuda is a relatively prosperous country. Despite this prosperity and the small population, there are severe pressures on housing, and the distribution of income is uneven. However, ample job opportunities in tourism and retailing have ensured relative social stability.

Human rights and freedoms. All civil liberties are guaranteed by the Constitution of 1968. The government enjoys the support of both Blacks and Whites, and racial unrest is rare.

Human environment. The principal threat to the environment is coastal pollution from shipping and depletion of the natural vegetation as a result of overextended tourism.

NON-CHRISTIAN RELIGIONS

There are small groups of Baha'is, Buddhists, Jews, Hindus, and Muslims and a larger number with no religious profession. The number of nonreligious, though small, has nearly doubled between 1970 and 1995.

CHRISTIANITY

ANGLICAN CHURCH. Bermuda was first colonized in 1609, the original settlers being Anglicans from Great Britain. St Peter's church was built in 1619, and within a few years 9 parishes were established, each with a church of its own. Until 1813, Bermuda was under the diocese of London. Between 1813 and 1825, Episcopal supervision was provided from Nova Scotia, with the bishop of Newfoundland assuming responsibility from 1825 to 1917. During 1917-1925, the islands were without Episcopal oversight, but since 1925 Bermuda has been an extra-provincial diocese under the direct jurisdiction of the archbishop of Canterbury. Anglicanism is the principal denomination, professed by 30.1 percent of the population. Two-thirds of Anglicans are Black, but most of the clergy come from Britain.

PROTESTANT CHURCHES. Influences from both the Old World and the New World are responsible for Bermuda's Protestant community. From Europe, British Methodists have built up an important work, although Scottish Presbyterians, Brethren, and Salvation Army also have significant followings.

In addition, there is a Portuguese Evangelical church in Hamilton. From North America have come numerous denominations, the largest being Seventh-day Adventists. The majority of these churches are served by expatriate ministers.

CATHOLIC CHURCH. Prior to 1953, Bermuda formed part of the diocese of Halifax (Canada). At that time, it was made a prefecture confided to Resurrectionists, was elevated to a vicariate in 1956, and became the diocese of Hamilton in Bermuda in 1967 as a suffragan diocese of Kingston in Jamaica.

Professing Catholics grew from 10% of the population in 1960 to one sixth by 1995.

The Holy See has no diplomatic relations with Bermuda in AD 2000.

BLACK INDIGENOUS CHURCHES. The African Methodist Episcopal Church from the USA has the third largest Christian community in Bermuda, after the Anglican and Catholic churches.

Indigenous missions. Bermudans have initiated very little missionary effort.

CHURCH AND STATE

Until 1974, the Anglican Church was established by law, its legislation coming from the British colonial parliament. In 1693, by act of Parliament, the British government initiated payment of clergy stipends which continued to the end of the 19th century. The British Crown held the patronage of all livings until 1882, when after synodical government had been introduced in 1878, this was transferred to the synod. By a 1974 act of parliament and at the request of the diocesan synod, the former name Church of England in Bermuda was changed to Anglican Church of Bermuda, the synod becoming at the same time fully self-governing. The act thus had the effect of disestablishing Anglicanism in Bermuda. There is no government ministry or department dealing with the churches or religious affairs.

BROADCASTING AND MEDIA

Local radio station VSB carries Christian programs, including some produced by *Back to the Bible*. Shortwave programs from HCJB (Ecuador), TWR (Antilles) and AWR (Costa Rica) can be easily received. Bermuda is a member of UNDA.

LeSEA programming can be received from the World Harvest Satellite.

INTERDENOMINATIONAL ORGANIZATIONS

The Bermuda Ministerial Association, originally composed of Protestant clergy, and the Anglican Church came together in 1957 to form a cooperative body. Since the Catholic Church joined in 1966 this has been known as the Joint Committee of Churches.

FUTURE TRENDS AND PROSPECTS

The nonreligious and spiritists combined will potentially account for near 10% of the population by 2025. This means that Christianity would soon dip below 90% for the first time since it was introduced to the islands.

Christians are expected to decline thereafter, perhaps falling below 75% before AD 2050. Nonreligious persons could rise dramatically in the same period, reaching 20% before AD 2050.

BIBLIOGRAPHY

Bermuda in print: a guide to the printed literature on Bermuda. A. C. H. Hallett. Hamilton, Bermuda: A.C.H. Hallett, 1985. 210p.

Bermuda national bibliography. Bermuda Library Technical Services. (Quarterly).

'Expatriate ministry in Bermuda.' D. B. Paterson. D.Min. thesis, Lancaster Theological Seminary, Lancaster, PA, 1988. 157p.

Country Table 2. **Organized churches and denominations in Bermuda.**

Official name (bold type = church with over 10% of all affiliated) 1	*Begun* 2	*Type* 3	*Counc* 4	*Congs* 5	*Adults* 6	*Affiliated 1970* 7	*Affiliated 1995* 8	*G%* 9	*Names, notes, and other statistics* (see Codebook, Part 3) 10
African Methodist Episcopal Church	c1870	I-Met	Vw...	10	2,220	3,900	5,540	1.41	AMEC. Black mission from USA. Large work among Blacks, Mulattoes. HQ Harris Bay.
Anglican Ch of Bermuda (D Bermuda)	1609	A-Hig	aw..C	17	16,900	22,000	24,500	0.43	Under D Canterbury. 67% Black, 33% White (10% alien). 1n,14x,15pp,W=33%,8Y,475y.
Bermuda Baptist Fellowship	1956	P-Bap	T....	4	336	175	1,020	7.31	*First Baptist Ch.* Devonshire Parish. M=SBC(USA). 1x,4f,W=86%,33Y,3z.
Catholic Ch: D Hamilton in Bermuda	1953	R-Lat	P.NMC	8	6,930	7,500	9,980	1.15	M=CR. C=1+0+1 (Canadian). (1970) 9nx,11w,1r,13Y,196y. (1990) 1n,7x,7m,5w,105Yy.
Christian Brethren		P-CBr	x....	9	450	1,000	1,050	0.05	*Open (Plymouth) Brethren.* Many British; begun under British influence. Paget.
Church of Christ	1957	I-Dis	x....	2	100	50	200	5.70	M=CC(Non-Instrumental) (USA). One church in Devonshire.

Continued opposite

Country Table 2–concluded

Official name (bold type = church with over 10% of affiliated) 1	*Begun* 2	*Type* 3	*Counc* 4	*Congs* 5	*Adults* 6	*Affiliated 1970* 7	*Affiliated 1995* 8	*G%* 9	*Names, notes, and other statistics* (see Codebook, Part 3) 10
Church of Christ, Scientist		m-Sci	x....	1	40	100	100	0.05	*Christian Science.* M=CCS(Boston, USA). First Church, Hamilton. 1w.
Church of God of Prophecy	1955	P-Pe3	Z....	1	50	50	100	2.81	M=CGP(USA). Schism from CoG(Cleveland). Holiness Pentecostals. HQ Shelly Bay.
Church of God (Anderson)	1905	P-Hol	x....	2	100	300	300	0.00	*General Assembly of the CoG (Bermuda).* M=CoG(Anderson) (USA). 2n,2f,250z.
Ch of Jesus Christ of Latter-day Saints		m-LdS	x....	2	100	50	200	0.05	*Mormons.* M=CJCLdS(USA). Mostly North American Whites.
Church of the Nazarene	1961	P-Hol	xF...	1	15	150	50	-4.30	Attached to New York District, Ch of the Nazarene. M=CoN(USA). 1n,SS=110,W=50%.
Jehovah's Witnesses	1928	m-Jeh	x....	4	373	300	829	4.15	*Watch Tower. Int'l Bible Students Assoc.* Active witnessing by 1941. (1975) 2Y. (1995) 28Y.
Lutheran Church	1964	P-Lut	Lw...	3	100	150	300	2.81	*Peace Lutheran Ch.* Part of American Lutheran Ch (USA). Paget. 1x,W=63%,7y,15z.
Methodist Church		P-Met	Vw...	3	870	2,000	2,900	0.05	Begun by and related to British Methodism from UK. Based in Hamilton.
New Testament Church of God	1921	P-Pe3	ZF...	5	770	500	1,280	3.83	*Ch of God.* Holiness Pentecostals. M=CoG(Cleveland) (USA). In Pembroke. 10n.
Pentecostal Assemblies of the W Indies	1938	P-Pe2	Z....	2	440	500	733	1.54	Classical Pentecostals (2-stage). In Pentecostal Assemblies of Canada (PAoC).
Portuguese Evangelical Church		P-Eva	.....	3	200	300	500	0.05	Portuguese-speaking immigrants. In Paget, Hamilton.
Presbyterian Church	1896	P-Ref	Rw...	4	650	1,000	867	-0.57	Includes M=Ch of Scotland, and Presbyterian Ch in Canada. 1f,8Yy.
Reformed Episcopal Church	c1890	I-ReA	x....	1	100	200	300	1.64	*Reformed Ch of England.* M=REC(USA),FCE(UK). Mainly Black. In 1900, 64 adherents.
Salvation Army	1896	P-Sal	xw...	10	1,000	1,400	2,000	1.44	*Bermuda Division*, under Canada & Bermuda Territory. HQ Hamilton. W=57%,25z.
Seventh-day Adventist Church	1900	P-Adv	x....	8	2,496	1,800	3,670	2.89	*SDA, Bermuda Mission*, Atlantic UC, NAmerican Division. 5nx,16m,1r,6t(977),48Y.
United Church of Canada		P-Uni	Ww...	3	200	300	500	0.05	M=UCCanada. Small work related to home body in Canada. In Pembroke Parish.
United Holy Church of America		I-3pB	x....	1	60	100	100	0.05	Black pentecostals. M=UHCA(USA).
World-Wide Missions of Bermuda	1966	I-Non	x....	10	200	300	400	1.16	M=World-Wide Missions (USA). Evangelicals from California.
Other Protestant denominations		P-	.....	55	1,000	2,000	3,100	0.05	Total 40: USA missions, military chaplaincies; Exclusive Brethren (Raven-Taylor).
Other independent Catholic churches		I-Epi	.....	5	70	100	150	0.05	Small churches under bishops-at-large, usually visiting from UK or USA.
Doubly-affiliated		2-aff			-4,100	0	-7,000		Members of both an older and a younger denomination.
Totals				**174**	**31,670**	**46,225**	**53,669**		

Churches, members, growth, 1900-2025	*Congs*	*Adults*	*Affiliated*	*G%*	*Total denominations*	*6 Megablocs: O*	*R*	*A*	*P*	*I*	*m*
Total churches, members, and denominations (mid-1900)	50	11,000	19,030	1.28	5	0	0	1	2	2	0
Total churches, members, and denominations (mid-1970)	116	26,786	46,225	1.28	45	0	1	1	32	8	3
Total churches, members, and denominations (mid-1990)	150	30,400	51,550	0.55	71	0	1	1	54	12	3
Total churches, members, and denominations (mid-1995)	174	31,670	53,669	0.81	71	0	1	1	54	12	3
Total churches, members, and denominations (mid-2000)	190	32,800	55,675	0.74	71	0	1	1	54	12	3
Total churches, members, and denominations (mid-2025)	230	37,700	64,000	0.56	89	1	1	1	60	20	6

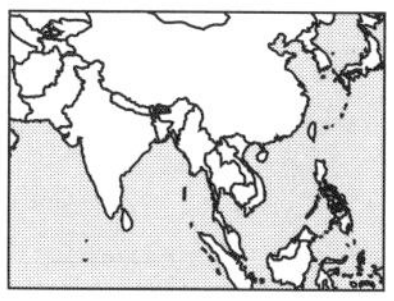

BHUTAN

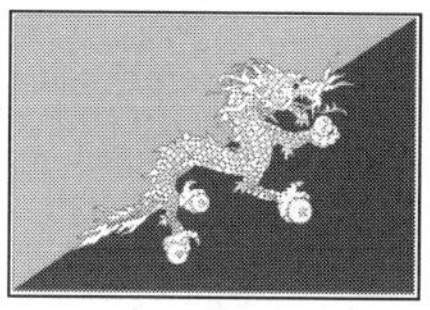

SECULAR DATA, AD 2000

STATE
Official name: Druk-Yul (The Kingdom of Bhutan).
Short name: Bhutan. **Adjective of nationality:** Bhutanese.
Flag: Yellow triangle above orange one, white dragon in center.
Area: 47,000 sq. km. (18,150 sq. mi.).
Government: Constitutional monarchy, since 1969 (1865 British rule, 1907 hereditary absolute monarchy).
Legislature: National Assembly (Tsogdu), up to 150 members.
Official language: Dzongkha.
Monetary unit: 1 ngultrum (Nu) = 100 chetrum. **US$1=** Nu 42.51.
Chief cities: THIMPHU (Thimbu) 17,156; Paro 4,352.
Political divisions: 17 provinces.
Armed forces: 4,000.

DEMOGRAPHY
Population: 2,124,000.
Population density: 45.1/sq. km. (117.0/sq. mi.).
Under 15 years: 904,000.
Growth rate p.a.: 2.65% (births 34.96, deaths 8.53).
Mortality: Infant, per 1,000: 53.6; **Maternal per 100,000:** 1,600.0.
Life expectancy: 63 (male 62, female 65).
Household size: 5.4. **Floor area per person, sq.m:** 5.0.
Major languages: Dzongkha, Shashap (in east), Nepali, Assamese, Hindi, English, Lepcha, Santali, Kebumtamp (Bhumtam), Tibetan, and numerous others.
Urban dwellers: 7.14%. **Urban growth rate p.a.:** 5.9%.
Labor force: 30%.

ETHNOLINGUISTIC PEOPLES
21.0% Central Bhutanese (Bhotia); 12.0% Nepalese (Paharia); 11.2% Eastern Bhutanese (Sharchop); 10.8% Western Bhutanese (Drukpa); 7.1% Sangla.

ECONOMY
National income p.a. per person: US$419; **per family:** US$2,267.

EDUCATION
Adult literacy: 42% (male 56%, female 28%). **Schools:** 187.
Universities: 2. **School enrolment:** female/male: 30%/30%.

HEALTH
Access to health services: 65%. **Access to safe water:** 58%.
Hospitals: 27 (12 beds per 10,000). **Doctors:** 141.
Blind: 10,000. **Deaf:** 121,900. **Murder rate:** 6.
Lepers: 9,000. **Underweight prevalence under 5:** 38%.

LITERATURE
New book titles p.a.: 42 (20 p.a. per million). **Periodicals:** 0.
Newspapers: 0 dailies.

COMMUNICATION (per 1,000 people)
Phones: 6 (2% mobile). **Radios:** 28. **TV sets:** 3.
Daily newspaper circulation: 6. **Computers:** 1.

REFUGEES
Citizen refugees in other countries: 118,600.

HUMAN LIFE AND LIBERTY (optimum condition=100.0%)
HDI: 33.8. **HSI:** 27.0. **HFI:** 10.0. **EFL:** 2.0.

Country Table 1. Religious adherents in Bhutan, AD 1900-2025.

Year / *Name*	*1900 Adherents*	*%*	*1970 Adherents*	*%*	*mid-1990 Adherents*	*%*	*Annual change, 1990-2000 Natural*	*Conversion*	*Total*	*Rate*	*mid-1995 Adherents*	*%*	*mid-2000 Adherents*	*%*	*mid-2025 Adherents*	*%*
Buddhists	241,800	79.0	704,950	66.6	1,223,370	72.1	30,869	3,913	34,782	2.53	1,351,090	73.2	1,571,194	74.0	2,953,500	75.7
Hindus	45,900	15.0	256,200	24.2	379,230	22.4	9,570	-3,902	5,668	1.40	394,450	21.4	435,909	20.5	750,000	19.2
Ethnoreligionists	15,300	5.0	41,000	3.9	65,000	3.8	1,640	-7	1,633	2.27	71,000	3.8	81,334	3.8	140,000	3.6
Muslims	3,000	1.0	55,700	5.3	17,000	1.0	429	69	498	2.60	18,300	1.0	21,983	1.0	40,000	1.0
Christians	**0**	**0.0**	**950**	**0.1**	**8,400**	**0.5**	**212**	**-87**	**125**	**1.40**	**8,910**	**0.5**	**9,649**	**0.5**	**14,500**	**0.4**
PROFESSION																
crypto-Christians	0	0.0	500	0.1	6,800	0.4	172	-82	90	1.25	7,100	0.4	7,700	0.4	12,500	0.3
professing Christians	**0**	**0.0**	**450**	**0.0**	**1,600**	**0.1**	**40**	**-5**	**35**	**1.99**	**1,810**	**0.1**	**1,949**	**0.1**	**2,000**	**0.1**
AFFILIATION																
affiliated Christians	**0**	**0.0**	**950**	**0.1**	**8,400**	**0.5**	**212**	**-87**	**125**	**1.40**	**8,910**	**0.5**	**9,649**	**0.5**	**14,500**	**0.4**
Independents	0	0.0	500	0.1	5,000	0.3	126	-41	85	1.58	5,330	0.3	5,849	0.3	8,000	0.2
Protestants	0	0.0	200	0.0	2,900	0.2	73	-43	30	0.99	3,040	0.2	3,200	0.2	5,500	0.1
Roman Catholics	0	0.0	250	0.0	500	0.0	13	-3	10	1.84	540	0.0	600	0.0	1,000	0.0
Trans-megabloc groupings																
Evangelicals	0	0.0	100	0.0	1,000	0.1	25	-15	10	0.96	1,029	0.1	1,100	0.1	2,000	0.1
Pentecostals/Charismatics	0	0.0	400	0.0	4,300	0.3	109	11	120	2.49	4,838	0.3	5,500	0.3	10,500	0.3
Great Commission Christians	**0**	**0.0**	**850**	**0.1**	**7,300**	**0.4**	**184**	**-47**	**137**	**1.73**	**7,600**	**0.4**	**8,666**	**0.4**	**13,000**	**0.3**
Nonreligious	0	0.0	0	0.0	2,500	0.2	63	12	75	2.67	2,700	0.2	3,254	0.2	5,000	0.1
Baha'is	0	0.0	200	0.0	500	0.0	13	2	15	2.61	550	0.0	647	0.0	1,000	0.0
World A (unevangelized persons)	306,000	100.0	894,741	84.5	1,373,760	81.0	34,645	-3,634	31,011	2.06	1,477,689	80.0	1,682,208	79.2	2,951,424	75.6
World B (evangelized non-Christians)	0	0.0	163,174	15.4	313,840	18.5	7,939	3,721	11,660	3.25	360,512	19.5	432,143	20.3	938,076	24.0
World C (Christians)	0	0.0	950	0.1	8,400	0.5	212	-87	125	1.40	8,910	0.5	9,649	0.5	14,500	0.4
Country's population	**306,000**	**100.0**	**1,058,866**	**100.0**	**1,696,000**	**100.0**	**42,796**	**0**	**42,796**	**2.28**	**1,847,112**	**100.0**	**2,124,000**	**100.0**	**3,904,000**	**100.0**

COLUMNS, ROWS.
For meanings and definitions, see Codebook (Part 3). Note that, by definition, total 'Christians' = professing + crypto-Christians, which also = affiliated + unaffiliated Christians, and also = Great Commission Christians + latent Christians. Percentages may not always total exactly, due to rounding.

NOTES ON RELIGIONS
BAHA'IS. Mostly Indians; in 1 local spiritual assembly (1973), remaining at 1 for many years (1996).
BUDDHISTS. The Bhutia (Bhute) ethnic group (of Tibetan extraction) in northern and central Bhutan are Buddhists, followers of Tibetan Lamaism syncretized with pre-Buddhist shamanism (Bon), Taoism and Lepcha traditional animistic beliefs and practices. There are over 6,000 monks. There are less strict Buddhists in eastern Bhutan, who are Bhote, Monpa and Sherdukpen, with fewer monasteries and lamas.
CRYPTO-CHRISTIANS. Unorganized individuals in the recognized churches, also a few isolated radio believers.
ETHNORELIGIONISTS. Animists among the hill tribes (Lepcha, et alii).
HINDUS. Nepali settlers (Rai, Gurung and Limbu ethnic groups, speaking Nepali, but Bhutanese citizens although further immigration has been prohibited since 1959). There are also some Hindu expatriate residents from India in southern and southwestern Bhutan.
MUSLIMS. Sunnis, mainly Indians.

Country status. Bordered by India and Tibet, Bhutan is a Himalayan mountain kingdom, known to its inhabitants as the Land of the Thunder Dragon. Subsistence farming is the principal activity of most of the population. Products include rice, fruit, and vegetables.

HUMAN LIFE AND LIBERTY

Human need and development. The 20th century has had little impact on Bhutan where life goes on

Great Commission Instrument Panel: status of Bhutan (for explanation see start of Part 4)

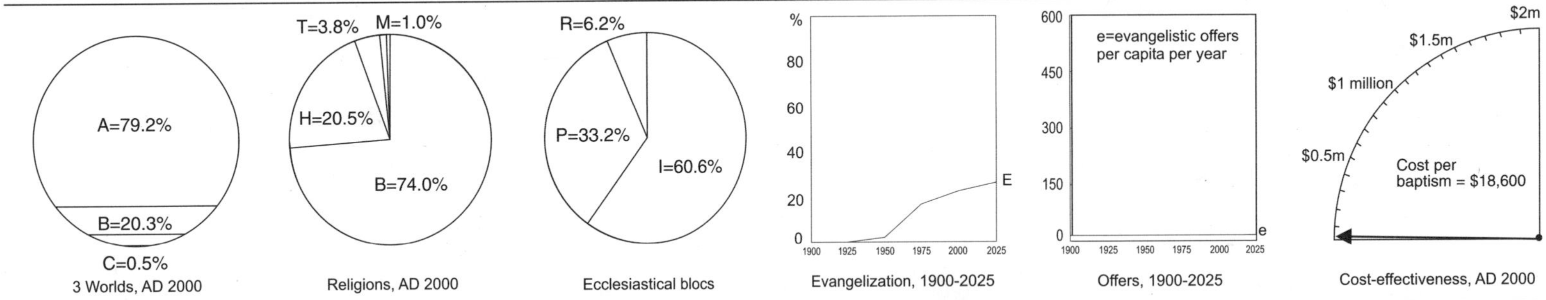

much as it has for centuries. Forces of change have been kept at bay by a combination of Buddhist spiritual traditions and royal authority. The society is almost entirely rural outside of the capital, Thimpu, and no towns in the modern sense exist. Nevertheless, neither grinding poverty nor great concentrations of wealth are found. On the whole Bhutanese eat and dress well and show little desire to possess the luxuries that seem to bedazzle non-Bhutanese. Currency plays only a small role in the economy where barter seems to be just as effective as a medium of commercial transactions. However, these estimates are subject to great error margins. The population may be only half the official estimate which means that the per capita income would actually rise to about par with India. Also, it is difficult to estimate per capita income in a noncash economy.

Human rights and freedoms. The principal human rights problem is that of 'Bhutanization' under which several thousand ethnic Nepalese Hindus have been expelled from the kingdom. The People's Forum on Human Rights (PFHR), an organization of ethnic Nepalese which operates inside Nepal, has alleged widespread killings, beatings, torture, rape and disappearances of Nepalese dissidents. Additional violations of human rights include denial of fair trial, and restrictions on freedom of speech and press, rights of association and workers' rights. Under a 1989 decree the wearing of the Drukpa national dress is compulsory for all citizens and violators may be fined $10 or sent to jail for one week. With an adult literacy rate of only 12% freedom of the press is a moot issue. A weekly newspaper, the Kuensel, is the country's only regular publication. There is no domestic television. A 1989 government order dismantled all television antennas to prevent foreign broadcasts from reaching the people. Criticism of the king is not permitted in the media. The use of Nepali language is banned, particularly in schools. There are few associations of any kind; political parties, private voluntary social associations and trade and professional groups are nonexistent. There is a strong climate of discrimination against non-Buddhist Bhutanese in land tenure and taxation.

Human environment. Bhutanese Buddhism is nature-friendly and discourages overexploitation of land and encourages austerity. There is a strong trend against tourism, expressed in the law limiting tourists to 3,000 annually. There is virtually no conspicuous consumption and no mining of natural resources. However, the land has a variety of physical and chemical constraints. Roughly half the land is on steep slopes susceptible to erosion and about 15% has shallow soils that are washed down the slopes during heavy rains. Only about one-fourth of the population has safe drinking water and only 7% has access to sanitation services. Medical services are meager; the country has only about 140 doctors.

State postage stamp with (right) the Buddha and (left) Christ with Mary (Pieta, by Michelangelo).

Buddhists. A senior Dupka or Red Hat (Unreformed) lama, one of over 6,000 Tantrayana bonzes (monks). Red Hat Lamaism is the official religion of Bhutan.

NON-CHRISTIAN RELIGIONS

Lamaism or ***Tantrayana*** (Tibetan or Tantric Buddhism) is the religion of the Bhotia, the Tibetan majority of the population. It is an unreformed type of Lamaism which is a mixture of Buddhist ethics and animistic practices. Bhutan's official Buddhist sect is the Dupka (Red Hat), which is part of Tibetan Lamaism. In Bhutan, this also includes an admixture of the pre-Buddhist shamanism known as Bon, also of Taoism and of traditional animistic beliefs and practices of the Pelcha people. There are numerous monasteries (Dzongs), mainly in central Bhutan, which also serve as administrative centers and storehouses, and the Dzong of Thimbu, the capital, houses the secretariat of the king and his ministers. The Buddhist clergy consists of over 6,000 lamas or bonzes (monks) serving under the authority of the Jey Khempo (chief of monks), whom protocol places on a level of equality with the king.

Hinduism is the religion of the Nepali settlers, a fifth of the population who predominate in southern and southwestern Bhutan. Although now Bhutanese citizens, they are prohibited from settling in central Bhutan, and further immigration of Nepalis has been forbidden since 1959. Hinduism also exists among many Assamese and other Indian residents, who total a sixth of the population.

CHRISTIANITY

CATHOLIC CHURCH. Bhutan comes within the Catholic diocese of Tezpur in India. In 1995, Bhutan had about 540 Catholics, all being Indians working on development projects or in schools. At government invitation, three state schools enrolling mainly Buddhist pupils have recently been opened by Catholic religious personnel and are supervised by them. These are the Don Bosco Technical School begun in 1965 by Salesians (SDB) on the border at Puntsholing, the Sherubtse Public School established in 1968 by Jesuits at Kanglung in eastern Bhutan and a school conducted by Jesuits in Punakha, the old religious and cultural center of western Bhutan. Sisters of St Joseph of Cluny are working in the two Jesuit schools, having joined the staffs in 1969. The Salesians in Puntsholing are also in charge of the country's only parish, begun in 1965.

The Holy See has no diplomatic relations with Bhutan in AD 2000.

PROTESTANT CHURCHES. Protestants are found mainly among the large number of Indians engaged in technical assistance to Bhutan, but they are not organized into any recognized church. Because of a prohibition against evangelistic work, Protestant missionary societies have tended to concentrate their attention on Bhutanese living across the border in East Bengal. The Scandinavian Alliance Mission opened its first center in Baksa Duar in 1892, and 2 other missions were active at an early date: the Santal Mission of the Northern Churches (Ebenezer Lutheran Church), and the Church of Scotland Mission later under the United Church of North India (now CNI). The latter body, known also as the Eastern Himalayan Church, is the only Protestant denomination resident and working within Bhutan itself, operating several village schools in the western region. Since 1959, the Free Church of Finland has carried on work among Bhutanese in the border area outside the country itself. In recent years Indian and Nepalese Evangelical missionaries from several agencies have been active, working from bases in India and Nepal.

Indigenous missions. Though very small, the Christian community in Bhutan, particularly ethnic Nepalis, has been involved in evangelistic outreach in Bhutan, Nepal and northern India.

CHURCH AND STATE

In 1907, the chief lama or priest-king was replaced as head of state by a maharajah or king as hereditary monarch combining both spiritual and temporal powers. The Dupka sect of Lamaistic Buddhism is the official religion. All evangelistic foreign missionary activity and proselytism are prohibited.

BROADCASTING AND MEDIA

Shortwave programming can be received from FEBA (Seychelles) in Tsangla and Nepali, and from TWR (Irkutsk) in Bhutanese.

FUTURE TRENDS AND PROSPECTS

There is likely to be a gradual increase of Christians due to conversion of Hindus in contact with Nepali Christians working in Bhutan. Muslims are expected to remain at about 1.0% through 2025.

Christians face a long uphill climb to claim 1% of the population which may happen before 2050. Buddhists, Hindus, and Muslims are expected to claim over 95% of the population in the future.

BIBLIOGRAPHY

A cultural history of Bhutan. B. Chakravarti. Chittaranjan: Hilltop, 1979–1980. 2 vols.

Ancient Bhutan: a study on early Buddhism in the Himalayas. B. C. Olschak. Zurich: Swiss Foundation for Alpine Research, 1979. 222p.

Atlas of South Asia. A. K. Dutt & M. M. Geib. Boulder, CO, and London: Westview Press, 1987. 255p.

Bhutan. R. C. Dogra. *World bibliographical series*, vol. 116. Oxford, UK: CLIO Press, 1991. 160p. (See especially 'Religion,' 46-52).

'Buddhism in Bhutan,' L. Nado, in *Buddhism's contribution to the world culture and civilization*, p.104–105. A. W. P. Guruge & D. C. Ahir (eds). New Delhi: Maha Bodhi Society of India, 1977.

History of Bhutan based on Buddhism. C. T. Dorji. Thimphu, Bhutan: Sangay Xam in collaboration with Prominent Publishers, 1994. 281p.

Incarnate Buddha kings of the dragon country: Buddhism in Bhutan. N. M. Gettelman & R. Sherburne. *Video-outlines of Asian religions*, vol. 5. Bellevue, WA: Video-Outlines, 1991. (37 min. videocassette).

Lands of the thunderbolt: Sikkim, Chumbi & Bhutan. L. J. L.

Country summary. **Worlds A, B, C by ethnolinguistic peoples, cities, and major civil divisions in Bhutan.**																						
	PEOPLES							**CITIES**							**CIVIL DIVISIONS**							
World	*Num*	*Pop 2000*	*C%*	*Christians*	*E%*	*U%*	*Unevangelized*	*Num*	*Pop 2000*	*C%*	*Christians*	*E%*	*U%*	*Unevangelized*	*Num*	*Pop 2000*	*C%*	*Christians*	*E%*	*U%*	*Unevangelized*
A	24	2,072,998	0.34	6,995	20	80	1,660,067	2	21,508	1.94	417	25	75	16,121	17	2,123,970	0.45	9,649	21	79	1,683,112
B	3	50,976	5.21	2,656	55	45	23,045	0	0	0.00	0	0	0	0	0	0	0.00	0	0	0	0
C	0	0	0.00	0	0	0	0	0	0	0.00	0	0	0	0	0	0	0.00	0	0	0	0
Total	**27**	**2,123,974**	**0.45**	**9,651**	**21**	**79**	**1,683,112**	**2**	**21,508**	**1.94**	**417**	**25**	**75**	**16,121**	**17**	**2,123,970**	**0.45**	**9,649**	**21**	**79**	**1,683,112**

Zetland. 1923; reprint, Berkeley, CA: Snow Lion Graphics, 1987. 316p.

Lepcha, my vanishing tribe. A. R. Foning. Delhi: Sterling, 1987. 314p. (Treats religion).

On the threshold of three closed lands: the guild outpost in the Eastern Himalayas. J. A. Graham. Edinburgh: T & T Clark, 1897. 166p. (Church of Scotland work in Tibet, Nepal, and Bhutan).

Rituals of the Drukpa order. J. Levy. *Tibetan Buddhist rites from the monasteries of Bhutan*, vol. 1. New York: Lyrichord. (Sound recording on compact disc with English translations inserted).

So close to heaven: the vanishing Buddhist kingdoms of the Himalayas. B. Crossette. New York: Knopf, 1995. 316p.

'Studies in Bhutanese history dealing with the structural organisation of the Bhutanese theocracy,' K. Frey, *Tibetan review*, 18, 4 (1983), 15–22.

The monasteries of the Himalayas: Tibet, Bhutan, Ladakh, Sikkim. S. Held. Italy: Edita, 1988. 150p.

The sacred dance–drama of Bhutan. M. R. Tulku. *Monographs on Asian music, dance and theater*, vol. 6. [New York: Asian Society's Performing Arts Program, 1979].

Tibetan Buddhist rites from the monasteries of Bhutan. New York: Lyrichord Discs, 1971. (Phonodisc).

Country Table 2. **Organized churches and denominations in Bhutan.**

Official name (bold type = church with over 10% of all affiliated) 1	*Begun* 2	*Type* 3	*Counc* 4	*Congs* 5	*Adults* 6	*Affiliated 1970* 7	*Affiliated 1995* 8	*G%* 9	*Names, notes, and other statistics* (see Codebook, Part 3) 10
Assemblies (Jehova Shammah)		I-CBr	x....	15	600	100	1,200	0.05	*El Shaddai.* Missionaries from HQ Kalimpong, India (Brother Bakht Singh). HQ Hyderabad, AP.
Catholic Church (D Tezpur)	1965	R-Lat	P.F..	3	450	250	540	3.13	HQ in India. Catholics all Indians in schools or projects. 5x,3m,4w; 3 schools.
Ch of God in Christ, India		I-3pI	x....	2	200	–	500	0.05	M=CoGiC(USA), largest USA Black pentecostal denomination.
Church of North India (D Darjeeling)	1890	P-Uni	Rwe..	10	900	50	1,300	13.92	*Eastern Himalayan Church.* Village schools in western region. M=CSM(UK).
Fellowship of Free Baptist Chs	c1985	P-Pe2	Z....	5	100	–	200	10.00	*Masihi Mandal. FFBC.* HQ Kalimpong. M=Orebro M (Sweden).
Indian New Life League	c1970	I-3nZ	.....	1	50	–	100	20.23	Along border with India. M=Gospel for Asia,India Evangelical Mission.
International Fellowship	c1974	P-Eva	.....	1	30	–	40	4.76	English-medium union congregation meeting in Thimphu, for expatriates.
Isolated radio churches	c1968	I-3rZ	.....	100	1,000	200	2,000	9.65	Isolated believers, mostly young people, across country, in small house-groups. R=30 (FEBA).
Nagaland Missionary Movement	c1990	I-3pI	.....	1	20	–	30	20.00	*NMM.* Indian Mission board just across border in India.
Northern Evangelical Lutheran Ch		P-Lut	.....	3	700	100	1,000	0.05	*NELC.* Mostly Santals from India. M=Santal Mission.
Other indigenous churches	c1965	I-3nI	.....	20	975	200	1,500	8.39	Mainly Indians in south: Nagaland Revival Ch, Himalayan Crusade, Christ Groups (EHC).
Other Protestant denominations	1892	P-	.....	20	200	50	500	9.65	From India: SDA, FC of Finland, CAF, AO, TEAM, WWM, TLM, IS, Norwegian Tibetan Mission.
Totals				**181**	**5,225**	**950**	**8,910**		

Churches, members, growth, 1900-2025	*Congs*	*Adults*	*Affiliated*	*G%*	*Total denominations*	*6 Megablocs: O*	*R*	*A*	*P*	*I*	*m*
Total churches, members, and denominations (mid-1900)	0	0	0	0.00	2	0	0	0	2	0	0
Total churches, members, and denominations (mid-1970)	26	570	950	15.00	16	0	1	0	12	3	0
Total churches, members, and denominations (mid-1990)	100	4,900	8,400	11.51	29	0	1	0	16	12	0
Total churches, members, and denominations (mid-1995)	181	5,225	8,910	1.19	31	0	1	0	17	13	0
Total churches, members, and denominations (mid-2000)	200	5,700	9,649	1.61	32	0	1	0	17	14	0
Total churches, members, and denominations (mid-2025)	400	8,500	14,500	1.64	67	1	1	0	25	40	0

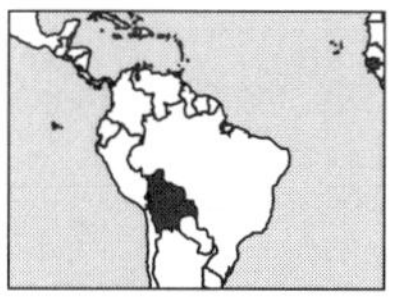

BOLIVIA

SECULAR DATA, AD 2000

STATE
Official name: La República de Bolivia (The Republic of Bolivia).
Short name: Bolivia. **Adjective of nationality:** Bolivian.
Flag: Stripes of red, gold, and green, coat of arms in centre.
Area: 1,098,581 sq. km. (424,164 sq. mi.).
Government: Military junta, most of period, since 1825 (1200 Inca empire, 1532 Spanish rule, 1825 Independence, many dictatorships).
Legislature: Chamber of Senators, 27 members; Chamber of Deputies, 130 members.
Official language: Spanish (Español/Castella).
Monetary unit: 1 boliviano (Bs) = 100 centavos. **US$1=** Bs 5.57.
Chief cities: LA PAZ 1,458,000; Santa Cruz 1,110,000; Cochabamba 523,713; Oruro 263,187; Potosí 152,184.
Political divisions: 9 provinces.
Armed forces: 34,000.

DEMOGRAPHY
Population: 8,329,000.
Population density: 7.5/sq. km. (19.6/sq. mi.).
Under 15 years: 3,300,000.
Growth rate p.a.: 2.15% (births 30.47, deaths 8.18).
Mortality: Infant, per 1,000: 55.6; **Maternal per 100,000:** 650.0.
Life expectancy: 63 (male 62, female 65).
Household size: 3.8. **Floor area per person, sq.m:** 7.0.
Major languages: Spanish, Quechua, Aymara, Guaraní, Japanese, Portuguese, Ryukyuan, and about 45 minor languages.
Urban dwellers: 64.84%. **Urban growth rate p.a.:** 3.2%.
Labor force: 39%.

ETHNOLINGUISTIC PEOPLES
37.2% Central Bolivian Quechua; 26.8% Bolivian Mestizo; 17.0% Central Aymara; 6.5% Southern Aymara; 4.5% Latin American White.

ECONOMY
National income p.a. per person: US$800; **per family:** US$3,040.

EDUCATION
Adult literacy: 83% (male 90%, female 76%). **Schools:** 10,529.
Universities: 10. **School enrolment:** female/male: 73%/81%.

HEALTH
Access to health services: 67%. **Access to safe water:** 55%.
Hospitals: 336 (15 beds per 10,000). **Doctors:** 3,392.
Blind: 1,070. **Deaf:** 499,700. **Murder rate:** 5.
Lepers: 6,500. **Underweight prevalence under 5:** 15%.

LITERATURE
New book titles p.a.: 500 (60 p.a. per million). **Periodicals:** 70.
Newspapers: 11 dailies.

COMMUNICATION (per 1,000 people)
Phones: 47 (17% mobile). **Radios:** 553. **TV sets:** 202.
Daily newspaper circulation: 69. **Computers:** 20.

REFUGEES
Alien refugees from other countries: 600.

HUMAN LIFE AND LIBERTY (optimum condition=100.0%)
HDI: 58.9. **HSI:** 32.0. **HFI:** 45.0. **EFL:** 45.0.

Country status. One of two landlocked countries in South America, Bolivia was created partly as a buffer between four of the most powerful states on the continent, Argentina, Brazil, Chile, and Peru. It is noted for its striking contrasts in terrain and climate as well as for the wealth of its natural resources and the poverty of its inhabitants.

HUMAN LIFE AND LIBERTY

Human need and development. Bolivia has been described as a beggar on a throne because few nations in South America have been endowed with so much natural wealth, yet have remained so poor. There are also glaring inequities in the distribution of wealth with the top 5% receiving about a third of the national wealth and the poorest 20% receiving 5%. This disparity prevails in the city as well as in rural areas. Development is hindered by geographical isolation, political instability, and vestiges of racial and social stratification which have persisted after the 1952 Revolution. The majority of the population is engaged in low-productivity agriculture with primitive tools. Although some of the worst endemic diseases have been brought under control, poor nutrition and lack of sanitation continue to depress the state of national health. A social security program provides extensive coverage, but the level of benefits is low and it excludes most rural workers. Only a fraction of the country's deaths are reported and even those reported are only sometimes defined by cause. About three-fourths or more of the population lack adequate housing. The traditional campesino houses, with designs that have remained essentially unmodified since Colonial days, are typically 10 feet by 12 feet adobe boxes about 6 feet high with steep gabled roofs of thatch.

Human rights and freedoms. Bolivia, like many of its neighbors, has emerged from a long period of military rule as a full-fledged democracy. Human rights guarantees are built into the Constitution and have been respected by the executive and the judiciary. Human rights abuses, when they occur, are generally limited to mistreatment of prisoners, societal discrimination against women, and discrimination against the indigenous Indians. Corruption and intimidation in the judicial system remains a serious problem. Although violence against women is a criminal offense and there is a progressive family code on the statute books, women suffer numerous disabilities and are exposed to violence and abuse in both rural and urban families. The Aymara and Quechua-speaking Indians remain an underclass, as they have been for centuries. The majority of them are illiterate and desperately poor.

Human environment. As a result of deforestation and unguided land settlements, Bolivia's rich natural habitats are under siege. Animal species are threatened by illegal traffic in hides and skins. The expansion of economic activity has created conflicts between new settlers and the older indigenous groups. Water pollution is a problem in arid and semiarid regions.

Country Table 1. **Religious adherents in Bolivia, AD 1900-2025.**

Year	1900		1970		mid-1990		Annual change, 1990-2000				mid-1995		mid-2000		mid-2025	
Name	Adherents	%	Adherents	%	Adherents	%	Natural	Conversion	Total	Rate	Adherents	%	Adherents	%	Adherents	%
Christians	**1,456,000**	**93.6**	**3,985,000**	**94.6**	**6,216,280**	**94.6**	**166,039**	**-4,147**	**161,892**	**2.34**	**6,989,550**	**94.3**	**7,835,201**	**94.1**	**12,153,700**	**92.6**
PROFESSION																
professing Christians	**1,456,000**	**93.6**	**3,985,000**	**94.6**	**6,216,280**	**94.6**	**166,039**	**-4,147**	**161,892**	**2.34**	**6,989,550**	**94.3**	**7,835,201**	**94.1**	**12,153,700**	**92.6**
AFFILIATION																
unaffiliated Christians	0	0.0	0	0.0	34,400	0.5	919	538	1,457	3.59	34,550	0.5	48,969	0.6	153,700	1.2
affiliated Christians	**1,456,000**	**93.6**	**3,985,000**	**94.6**	**6,181,880**	**94.1**	**165,120**	**-4,685**	**160,435**	**2.33**	**6,955,000**	**93.8**	**7,786,232**	**93.5**	**12,000,000**	**91.4**
Roman Catholics	1,455,000	93.5	3,963,492	94.1	5,840,000	88.9	156,018	-5,018	151,000	2.33	6,558,904	88.5	7,350,000	88.3	11,400,000	86.8
Protestants	1,000	0.1	183,914	4.4	400,000	6.1	10,686	2,314	13,000	2.85	499,238	6.7	530,000	6.4	1,100,000	8.4
Independents	0	0.0	24,210	0.6	103,000	1.6	2,752	1,448	4,200	3.48	124,393	1.7	145,000	1.7	270,000	2.1
Marginal Christians	0	0.0	7,752	0.2	91,000	1.4	2,431	1,969	4,400	4.02	105,600	1.4	135,000	1.6	300,000	2.3
Orthodox	0	0.0	2,000	0.1	2,900	0.0	77	-57	20	0.67	3,000	0.0	3,100	0.0	10,000	0.1
Anglicans	0	0.0	200	0.0	1,000	0.0	27	-17	10	0.96	1,040	0.0	1,100	0.0	1,400	0.0
doubly-affiliated	0	0.0	-196,568	-4.7	-256,020	-3.9	-6,840	-5,355	-12,195	3.97	-337,175	-4.6	-377,968	-4.5	-1,081,400	-8.2
Trans-megabloc groupings																
Evangelicals	1,000	0.1	147,400	3.5	276,000	4.2	7,373	2,527	9,900	3.11	322,038	4.3	375,000	4.5	800,000	6.1
Pentecostals/Charismatics	0	0.0	50,000	1.2	920,000	14.0	24,578	4,922	29,500	2.82	1,060,729	14.3	1,215,000	14.6	2,150,000	16.4
Great Commission Christians	**62,200**	**4.0**	**421,100**	**10.0**	**1,358,000**	**20.7**	**36,279**	**389**	**36,668**	**2.42**	**1,534,000**	**20.7**	**1,724,676**	**20.7**	**2,928,000**	**22.3**
Baha'is	0	0.0	94,000	2.2	200,000	3.0	5,343	1,582	6,925	3.02	230,000	3.1	269,246	3.2	525,000	4.0
Nonreligious	0	0.0	40,000	1.0	60,000	0.9	1,603	3,403	5,006	6.25	90,000	1.2	110,063	1.3	300,000	2.3
Ethnoreligionists	100,000	6.4	69,900	1.7	60,000	0.9	1,603	-837	766	1.21	63,000	0.9	67,658	0.8	70,000	0.5
Atheists	0	0.0	15,000	0.4	26,000	0.4	695	53	748	2.56	29,800	0.4	33,478	0.4	60,000	0.5
Buddhists	0	0.0	4,000	0.1	4,500	0.1	120	-37	83	1.71	4,750	0.1	5,329	0.1	9,000	0.1
Jews	0	0.0	2,000	0.1	2,600	0.0	69	-18	51	1.79	2,800	0.0	3,105	0.0	4,000	0.0
Muslims	0	0.0	500	0.0	1,100	0.0	29	28	57	4.24	1,400	0.0	1,666	0.0	4,000	0.0
New-Religionists	0	0.0	500	0.0	1,200	0.0	32	-10	22	1.68	1,300	0.0	1,418	0.0	3,500	0.0
Spiritists	0	0.0	1,000	0.0	1,000	0.0	27	-15	12	1.10	1,050	0.0	1,116	0.0	1,200	0.0
Chinese folk-religionists	0	0.0	100	0.0	320	0.0	9	-2	7	1.87	350	0.0	385	0.0	600	0.0
World A (unevangelized persons)	60,684	3.9	42,116	1.0	19,719	0.3	473	198	671	3.26	22,241	0.3	24,987	0.3	39,393	0.3
World B (evangelized non-Christians)	39,316	2.5	184,495	4.4	337,001	5.1	9,057	3,949	13,006	3.36	402,011	5.4	468,812	5.6	937,907	7.1
World C (Christians)	1,456,000	93.6	3,985,000	94.6	6,216,280	94.6	166,039	-4,147	161,892	2.34	6,989,550	94.3	7,835,201	94.1	12,153,700	92.6
Country's population	**1,556,000**	**100.0**	**4,211,612**	**100.0**	**6,573,000**	**100.0**	**175,569**	**0**	**175,569**	**2.40**	**7,413,803**	**100.0**	**8,329,000**	**100.0**	**13,131,000**	**100.0**

COLUMNS, ROWS.
For meanings and definitions, see Codebook (Part 3). Note that, by definition, total 'Christians' = professing + crypto-Christians, which also = affiliated + unaffiliated Christians, and also = Great Commission Christians + latent Christians. Percentages may not always total exactly, due to rounding.

CENSUSES.
1992: 88% Roman Catholics, 11% Evangelicals, 1% other religionists.

NOTES ON RELIGIONS
ATHEISTS. 3 rival parties of Muscovite, Maoist, or Trotskyite emphasis: Communist Party of Bolivia (Soviet-line) (PCB), Communist Party of Bolivia (Chinese-line), Revolutionary Workers Party (Trotskyite) (POR); all underground, proscribed since 1967. Other factions include Castroites.
BAHA'IS. La Fe Bajay. Since its origin, in 1956 there has been exceptionally rapid response and growth among Amerindians, from 91 local spiritual assemblies (1964) to 625 (1973). From April to August 1970, over 6,000 converts were enrolled. Interest however then peaked and by 1996 LSAs had dropped to 237, largely reorganized to cover wider areas.
BUDDHISTS.Several colonies of Japanese immigrants in Santa Cruz district, including 250 families of Ryukyuans (Okinawan-speaking) until the conversion of 60% to Catholicism by 1960.
DOUBLY-AFFILIATED. The term covers those affiliated to, or claimed by, both the Catholic Church and also a church termed Evangelical by the state (Protestant, Anglican, Bolivian indigenous, marginal Protestant), i.e. baptized Catholics who have recently become Evangelicals or others. Because their statistics represent a duplication, they are shown in the table as a negative quantity (with a minus sign).
ETHNORELIGIONISTS. Of the total of 99,800 tribal lowland or jungle Amerindians (from 20,000 Chiquitanos down to 7 persons in the Jorá group), a high proportion are still animists. Many Aymara are still openly animist.
INDEPENDENTS. In about 4 denominations or groupings in 1995 (see Table 2).
NEW-RELIGIONISTS. Japanese adherents of Soka Gakkai (350 converts) and other New Religions from Japan.
PENTECOSTALS/CHARISMATICS. Begun in 1969, the Catholic Charismatic Renewal in 1996 numbered 600 regular prayer groups and 5 covenant communities with 12,000 weekly attenders including 35 priests and 6 bishops (ICCRS).
SPIRITISTS. Mainly recent adherents among the upper classes.

Great Commission Instrument Panel: status of Bolivia (for explanation see start of Part 4)

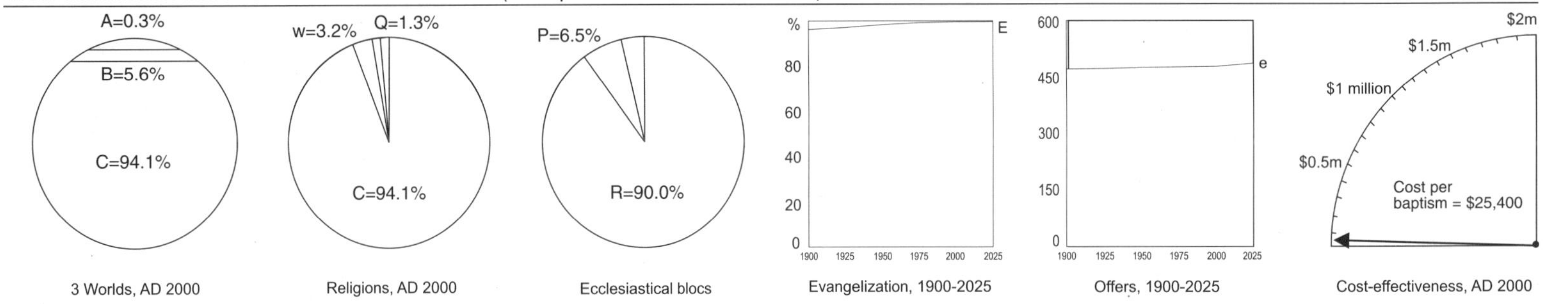

NON-CHRISTIAN RELIGIONS

Baha'i has experienced in Bolivia one of its greatest missionary expansions. Since its origin in 1956, response among Indians has been phenomenal, and Baha'is have grown from 91 local spiritual assemblies in 1964 to a sizeable number by 1995. By 1995, 230,000 Bolivians were Baha'i. It is particularly strong among the Quechua.

Traditional Indian religions continue to hold the allegiance of substantial numbers of the indigenous peoples and are strongest among the Guarani, Guayaru and Quechua, although many of these (especially the Quechua) are baptized Catholics at the same time. Aymara religion is also a mixture of traditional beliefs with later Inca and Catholic additions. The original name for the supreme being, Viracocha, who was recognized as creator, is no longer used, and Catholic ideas of God now take precedence. However, much more important in daily life is Ekeko, the divinity of good luck, whose carved image in the form of a dwarf is venerated and Pachamama, old Mother Earth, who plays an important role at the planting and harvesting seasons. For the forgiveness of sins, the blood of llamas and goats is sprinkled on stone alters and wooden crosses commonly found on hillsides, especially in the Carangas area of southwestern Bolivia. Aymaras believe that the earth is peopled by a multitude of spirits (Achachila): guardian spirits; spirits of hills, mountains, and lakes; spirits of such natural phenomena as lightning, wind, and hail; and a large number of evil spirits (Supaya). The diviner-medicine man continues to play an important role in Aymara society.

Other religions include small Jewish groups with synagogues and cemeteries in the major cities, some Buddhists in the newly-formed Japanese colonies and a renewed interest in spirits among the upper classes.

Independents. Worker with Serving Jesus Christ Mission aids church.

CHRISTIANITY

Bolivia became part of the Catholic diocese of Cuzco (Peru) in 1537, when a Christian community was established among the Parias and Charcas. During the 16th and 17th centuries, Franciscans established 17 Indian missions and Jesuits 31 *reductiones* (cooperative Indian villages) among the Moxos and Chiquitanos before the Society of Jesus was expelled from Spain and its colonies. Bolivia was one of the first Latin American colonies to revolt against Spain and one of the last to achieve independence. During the war for independence, bishops generally remained loyal to Spain, while some priests were involved in the rebellion and were later elected to the new legislative assembly. In the years of revolution during the 19th century, church-state relations were in constant turmoil, fluctuating from cordiality to outright hostility. Protestantism did not make its appearance until the end of the 19th century.

CATHOLIC CHURCH. About 86% of the Bolivian population has been baptized in the Catholic Church and are more or less attached to it. Bolivia is no exception to the Latin American phenomenon of popular folk-Catholicism, a mixture of 16th century Spanish Catholicism and indigenous religions at the time of the Conquest. Regions which remained outside the influence of Christianity or that were abandoned by missionaries retain much of the old religion and show this in syncretistic practices usually termed christo-paganism. In recent decades, the church has been giving more attention to the creative use of indigenous elements which offer hope for a more vital expression of the faith in the future. An example is the joint pastoral plan for the Aymara-speaking altiplano (high plateau). Also of significance are the over 50 prayer groups of pentecostal Catholics in Santa Cruz, Cochabamba, La Paz, and other centers. Bolivia is

Country summary. **Worlds A, B, C by ethnolinguistic peoples, cities, and major civil divisions in Bolivia.**

World	*PEOPLES* Num	Pop 2000	C%	Christians	E%	U%	Unevangelized
A	5	19,470	8.21	1,599	43	57	11,096
B	10	77,397	43.75	33,861	90	10	7,708
C	43	8,231,800	94.16	7,750,775	100	0	5,600
Total	**58**	**8,328,667**	**93.49**	**7,786,235**	**100**	**0**	**24,404**

World	*CITIES* Num	Pop 2000	C%	Christians	E%	U%	Unevangelized
A	0	0	0.00	0	0	0	0
B	0	0	0.00	0	0	0	0
C	8	3,795,867	92.83	3,523,754	100	0	10,328
Total	**8**	**3,795,867**	**92.83**	**3,523,754**	**100**	**0**	**10,328**

World	*CIVIL DIVISIONS* Num	Pop 2000	C%	Christians	E%	U%	Unevangelized
A	0	0	0.00	0	0	0	0
B	0	0	0.00	0	0	0	0
C	9	8,328,666	93.49	7,786,232	100	0	24,407
Total	**9**	**8,328,666**	**93.49**	**7,786,232**	**100**	**0**	**24,407**

one of several Latin American countries which depend heavily on foreign clergy. From 1912 to 1969, the proportion of Bolivians among the total of priests, both secular and religious, continued to decrease. In 1912, there were 641 Bolivians, and by 1960, this had fallen to 215 (29%), in 1964 to 198 (24%), and in 1969 to 197 (22%).

During the same period foreign clergy increased correspondingly: to 527 in 1960 (71%), 632 in 1964 (76%), and to 716 in 1969 (78%).

Since 1969, there has been a decrease in foreign clergy due in large part to the expulsion or voluntary exile of many following the repression that followed the military coup d'etat of 1971. Local clergy have also increased again.

The Holy See has diplomatic relations with Bolivia and in AD 2000 is represented to government and the Catholic hierarchy by a nuncio residing in La Paz.

PROTESTANT CHURCHES. Bolivia is unusual in Latin America for the relatively late arrival of Protestant missions. Although a Bible agent traveled through Bolivia in 1827, the first resident missionary, of the Brethren Assemblies, did not appear until 1895. Because of the strict requirements for membership, this church remained small and has not grown rapidly as it has in neighboring Argentina. Canadian Baptists arrived in 1898, but by 191, they had enrolled only 63 members, giving most of their attention to the Guatajata farm project and the development of schools. An increased rate of growth has taken place since 1960, although Baptists remain basically an urban middle-class church.

The first permanent Methodist missionary arrived in 1901. Initially, Methodists followed the Baptists' early emphasis on schools, both to develop educated leadership and to gain social acceptance, in addition to the establishment of agricultural and medical centers including the Pfeiffer Memorial Hospital in La Paz. More rapid growth has taken place since the early 1960s.

The Evangelical Christian Union, second among Protestants in membership, is the result of a merger of the Andes Evangelical Mission (1903) and the Evangelical Union of South America (1937) in 1959. Both missions were originally organized to reach the Quechua Indians, the older missions responsible for the Quechua translation of the New Testament and the development of several Bible institutes.

Iglesia Evangélica Metodista en Bolivia. In Altiplano's famine, drought, and floods, Methodists distribute relief.

Seventh-day Adventists, the largest Protestant church in Bolivia, began in 1907 but made little progress until after World War I. At that time, the Peruvian and Bolivian Aymaras in the region of Lake Titicaca requested them to provide schools, and the result was a mass movement into the church. Other early Protestant churches which have built up significant followings are the Nazarenes and Friends.

Pentecostals have not been as successful here as in many other Latin American countries, due in part to Bolivia's low degree of urbanization. Nevertheless, the Assemblies of God have grown since 1946 to be the third largest Protestant church. Pentecostals from Sweden, Chile, and Brazil have also been active and several indigenous pentecostal groups have been formed.

By the mid-1990s there were more than 25 Protestant seminaries, Bible colleges, and other training institutes. Korean missionaries have founded 2 of the nation's 3 Christian universities.

Art and architecture. Emiliano Lujan Sandoval is the country's only contemporary monumental sculptor. His bronze Sacred Heart of Jesus, done for Santa Cruz in 1961, is more than 60 feet tall. The cathedral treasury at Sucre and the church of Santa Clara contain masterpieces of Bolivian Christian art. The cathedral of San Miguel at Sucre is the oldest church in South America. Closed for over 120 years, it was lovingly restored with magnificent carved and painted ceilings. The font in the baptistry is made of silver and alabaster, and there is a painting by Viti, the first great painter of the New World and a student of Raphael. It was from San Miguel that Jesuit missionaries went south to convert Argentina, Uruguay, and Paraguay. Also in Sucre is the chapel of the jewel-encrusted Virgin of Guadalupe.

Renewal movements. In the 1990s the Pentecostal/Charismatic Renewal continued to spread rapidly across most older churches, and numbered over 1,215,000 adherents (of whom 12% Pentecostals, 78% Charismatics, and 10% Independents).

Indigenous missions. Large numbers of Bolivian Christians have served as foreign missionaries, primarily Roman Catholics in surrounding countries and in Spain and Italy. Some Protestants serve abroad but Bolivia is viewed more as a mission field (over 1,000 missionaries in 88 agencies).

CHURCH AND STATE

The constitution of 2 February 1967, affirms in Article 3 that: (1) the Catholic religion is the official religion of the state, but that public worship on the part of other religions is permitted; (2) relations between the state and the Catholic Church are to be regulated by concordats, although in fact none exist, but the one concluded on 29 May 1851, never having been put into effect; (3) the state supports the Catholic Church, subsidizing the salaries of bishops, canons, military chaplains, and charitable works.

The regulation of church-state relations is under the jurisdiction of the Ministry of Religion which is part of the Ministry of Foreign Affairs (Ministerio de Relaciones Exteriores y Culto). The Ministry of Religion was created expressly for the Catholic Church, but in actuality it is concerned with all churches and religions, since all are required to be registered.

Numerous legal and customary provisions continue to be applied to the Catholic Church, making it in many cases excessively dependent on the state. Catholic bishops are often considered as public officials, and as a result, the other religions enjoy greater freedom of action. Nevertheless, the Catholic Church enjoys certain advantages including economic aid and exemption from taxes. The church renewal of Vatican II and the coup d'etat of the extreme right wing which brought the Banzer regime to power in August 1971, created serious tensions between the progressive sector of the church on the one hand and the government and conservative sector of the church on the other. The repressive measures initiated by the regime, which proclaimed itself 'nationalistic and Christian,' were especially harsh on progressive Catholic circles. Campaigns were conducted against 'atheistic clergymen,' and both Bolivian and foreign priests and religious personnel were imprisoned or expelled. Catholic militants were arrested and police placed in convents and even in bishops' residences for surveillance. This campaign has resulted in weakening of the Catholic Church by the loss of a larger number of its most dynamic members. The episcopate was slow to react but finally published a declaration denouncing political repression and the consequent popular misery. However, the abstract tenor and prudence of this document failed to satisfy the Catholic opposition.

During 1974-75, the government came into conflict with Catholicism's Justice and Peace Commission which had organized an amnesty campaign for political prisoners and had denounced the killing of 200 peasants in the Cochabamba valley in 1974, of which the government only admitted to 13 killed. A number of foreign priests attached to the commission were expelled from Bolivia. The military government unceasingly called itself 'Christian' and had no interest in a test of strength with the Catholic Church, and for its part, the ecclesiastical hierarchy does not wish to lose its privileged status as the official religion, with its tax exemptions for the Catholic University, fiscal aid to the daily paper Presencia which is sponsored by the Episcopal conference and other benefits. Successive democratic governments since 1985 have returned peace and stability to church-state relations.

In the following 2 decades, tensions existed but also a relatively stable situation.

Over 180,000 attended Luis Palau Crusade in La Paz and 2 other cities (1978).

BROADCASTING AND MEDIA

IBRA-produced programs can be heard on several local stations in a variety of languages, including Mataco, Guarani, Aymara and Quechua. Shortwave programs from HCJB (Ecuador), TWR (Antilles), KNLS, and AWR (Costa Rica) can be easily received. Bolivia is a member of UNDA. Some stations feature occasional Catholic radio spots, and there are 15 local AM and FM Catholic radio stations broadcast daily in Spanish, Quechua, and Guarani.

Daily television broadcasts of CBN's *700 Club* can be seen in 34 cities and heard on three radio stations. Volunteers conduct follow-up in 8 cities. CBN worked in cooperation with Luis Palau's 'Bolivia 95' crusade, training new counselors before and conducting Bible studies for new converts afterward with the support of local pastors. There are also occasional Catholic TV programs. The 'Jesus' Film has been seen by 3.5 million (34%): 2.3 million on television and 811,000 through film team presentations. TBN programming is aired in 3 cities on channel 27.

INTERDENOMINATIONAL ORGANIZATIONS

The Association of Evangelicals in Bolivia, initially formed in 1966, has the largest interdenominational membership in the country. In the 1990s it sponsored a national DAWN program (Discipling A Whole Nation) with the goal of tripling Evangelicals and churches by AD 2000.Other Protestant interdenominational groups include the Bolivian Evangelical Social Action Commission (Comision Boliviana de Accion Social Evangelica, COMBASE), which offers social and medical assistance.

Several organizations provide opportunities for cooperation between Catholics and Protestants. Alfalit Boliviano, supported by Protestant churches, works on large-scale literacy campaigns in collaboration with the Catholic and other churches, using parish buildings as literacy centers. A charismatic movement called Spiritual Renewal (Renovacion Espiritual) also regularly brings together Protestants and Catholics for Bible study and prayer.

FUTURE TRENDS AND PROSPECTS

Roman Catholic affiliation will probably drop off slightly into the 21st century resulting in church membership of 87% by 2025. There is likely to be a marked resurgence among Protestants and also postdenominational churches.

Christians will probably decline below 90% before 2050. Nonreligious persons and Baha'is would then take their place jointly reaching 10% by then.

BIBLIOGRAPHY

'Aging, religion, and mastery style among the Quechua of Pocona, Bolivia.' T. L. Schemper. Ph.D. dissertation, Northwestern University, Evanston, IL, 1987. 176p.

Animistic Aymaras and church growth. Q. Nordyke. Newberg, OR: Barclay, 1970. 200p.

'Bolivia,' *Pro Mundi Vita* (Brussels), 8 (1965).

Bolivia. G. M. Yeager. *World bibliographical series*, vol. 89. Oxford, UK: CLIO Press, 1988. 230p. (See especially 'Religion,' 134f).

Bolivian Friends: from mission to yearly meeting. R. Chapman. Newberg, OR: Friends Missionary Literature Service, 1980. 85p.

Bolivien und Nicaragua: Modelle einer Kirche im Aufbruch. M. Hofmann. Münster: Edition Liberación, 1987. 364p.

Christianismo y religión quechua en la prelatura de Ayairril. T. Gair. Cusco, Bolivia: Instituto Pastoral Andina, 1972. 257p.

Commandos for Christ. B. Porterfield. New York: Harper, 1963. 238p.

'Conversion to Protestantism and social change in a Bolivian Aymara community.' D. C. Knowlton. M.A. thesis, University of Texas, Austin, TX, 1982. 261p.

'Distribution of the *mesa* in Latin America,' D. Sharon, *Journal of Latin America lore*, 2, 1 (1976), 71–95.

El cristianismo aymara: inculturación o culturización. L. Jolicoeur. Cochabamba: Universidad Católica Boliviana, 1994. 465p.

El desafio de las sectas. F. L. Damen. 3d ed. *Fe y compromiso*, 5. Oruro, Bolivia: Centro Diocesano de Pastoral Social, 1989. 107p.

Figuras eclesiásticas en Bolivia. J. R. Arze. La Paz: Editorial Los Amigos del Libro, 1985. 185p.

'From the Sun of the Incas to the Virgin of Copacabana,' S. G. MacCormack, *Representations*, 8 (1984), 30–60.

Gracias!: a Latin American journal. H. J. M. Nouwen. San Francisco: Harper & Row, 1983. 202p.

Guia de la Iglesia, Bolivia, 1970. La Paz: SNES, 1970. (Catholic).

History of the medical work of the United Methodist Church in Bolivia. B. D. Beck. , 1974. 89p.

La Iglesia Católica en Bolivia. J. M. Barnadas. La Paz: Libreria Editorial Juventud, 1976. 130p.

La Iglesia en Perú y Bolivia: estructuras eclesiásticas. I. Alonso et al. Madrid: Oficina Internacional de Investigaciones Sociales, 1961. 271p.

La tierra no da así nomás: los ritos agrícolas en la religión de los aymara–cristianos. H. van den Berg. La Paz: HISBOL, 1990. 352p.

L'univers religieux des Aymaras de Bolivie: observations recueillies dans les carangas: jalons de pastorale. J. Monast. *Sondeso No. 10.* Cuernavaca, Mexico: CIDOC, 1966. 300p.

Mitos, supersticiones y supervivencias populares de Bolivia. M. R. Paredes. 3rd ed. La Paz: Editorial Isla, 1964. 309p.

'Protestant Christianity in Bolivia: mission theory and practice in three mission churches.' W. T. Boots. Ph.D. dissertation, American University, Washington, DC, 1971. 348p.

'Protestant missionary activity and freedom of religion in Ecuador, Peru, and Bolivia.' P. E. Kuhl. Ph.D. dissertation, Southern Illinois University at Carbondale, 1982. 500p.

'Ritual and cultural lag: the feast of San Isidoro in Tiraque, Bolivia,' J. M. Torsa, *Social compass*, 19, 4 (1972).

Rituales en las regiones andinas de Bolivia y Peru. L. Girault. La Paz, Bolivia: Don Cosco, 1988. 467p.

Sincretismo religioso de los indigenas de Bolivia. J. Esch-Jakob. La Paz, Bolivia: HISBOL, 1994. 132p.

'The clergy in Bolivia, *Pro Mundi Vita* (Brussels), Special note 11 (1970).

The gospel according to Bolivia: analogies in Bolivian culture. H. L. Firestone. Cochabamba, Bolivia: Mobile Publishers, 1984. 197p.

'The kingdom at hand: religion and politics in highland Bolivia.' S. R. Nelson. Ph.D. dissertation, University of Michigan, 1984. 314p.

'The Old Colony Mennonites of Bolivia: a case study.' J. W. Lanning. Thesis, Texas A & M University, College Station, TX, 1972. 141p.

The Protestant movement in Bolivia. C. P. Wagner. South Pasadena, CA: William Carey Library, 1970. 240p.

Country Table 2. **Organized churches and denominations in Bolivia.**

Official name (bold type = church with over 10% of all affiliated) 1	*Begun* 2	*Type* 3	*Counc* 4	*Congs* 5	*Adults* 6	*Affiliated 1970* 7	*Affiliated 1995* 8	*G%* 9	*Names, notes, and other statistics* (see Codebook, Part 3) 10
Asamblea Ev de Dios (Riberalta)		I-3pL	.....	29	2,340	429	3,350	0.05	*Riberalta Evangelical Assembly of God.* M=SFM(Sweden).
Asambleas de Dios de Bolivia	1946	P-Pe2	ZF..C	842	65,865	20,000	95,268	6.44	*ADB.* M=AoG(USA). 50% Aymara. 151n,10x,14f,3s(129),W=83%,1100Y.
Asambleas de Dios Noruega		P-Pe2	Z...C	15	500	200	1,000	0.05	*ADN. Norwegian Assemblies of God.* M=NPY(Norway). In Beni, Pando, Cochabamba.
Asambleas Locales	c1980	I-3nC	.....	11	1,800	–	3,000	6.67	*Local Churches. Little Flock. Assembly Hall Ch.* Begun 1922 in China. Chinese missionaries.
Asociación de Igl de Dios Reformadas		I-3pL	.....	93	7,000	–	17,500	0.05	*Association of Reformed Churches of God.* Grassroots body.
Asociación de Iglesias Ev del Oriente		P-Eva	.....	17	1,000	–	2,500	0.05	*Association of Evangelical Churches of the East.*
Centro Crist Casa de Oracion	c1965	I-3gL	.....	48	1,200	500	2,670	6.93	*Christian House of Prayer Center.*
Concilio Bautista Maranata	1962	I-Bap	x....	5	400	500	800	1.90	*West Side Baptists.* M=Maranatha Baptist Mission (USA). Cochabamba department. 12f.
Convención Bautista Boliviana	1946	P-Bap	T....	29	2,178	1,000	3,630	5.29	*CBB. Bolivian Baptist Convention.* M=Brazilian Bapt Conv. 13n,2x,1s,W=79%.
Ejército de Salvación	1920	P-Sal	xw...	20	1,500	4,000	4,500	0.47	*Salvation Army, Bolivia Dist.* SAmerica West Territory. Aymaras. 4n,2x,1s,W=79%.
Ekklesia Bolivia	1973	I-3cL	.....	2	3,000	–	8,570	4.55	Founded by Julio Cesar Ruibal (martyred 1995). Also abroad (Cali, Colombia).
Fed de Iglesia Ev Luterana Alemana	1957	I-3cL	L....	14	2,100	2,500	3,000	0.73	*German-speaking Ev Lutheran Ch in Bolivia.* Recent immigrants, in La Paz. 1x,W=60%.
Hermanos Libres	1895	P-CBr	x....	145	5,949	2,500	11,000	6.11	*Free (Open) Brethren. Plymouth Brethren.* M=CMML(UK, Australia, NZ, USA). 3m,29f.
Iglesia Adventista del Séptimo Dia	1907	P-Adv	x....	119	30,800	50,000	68,361	1.26	*Seventh-day Adv. Bolivia Mission*, Inca UM. Aymaras. 1 plane. 18nx,1h,1s,379t(17208),1981Y.
Igl Alianza Cristiana y Misionera de B	c1980	P-Hol	.....	1	53	–	85	6.67	M=Christian & Missionary Alliance(USA).
Iglesia Anglicana (D Chile & Bolivia)	1926	A-Low	aw.C.	3	620	200	1,040	6.82	In ACSCA. Expatriate English. Student work. M=CMS(Australia). 2x,1Y,1y.
Iglesia Asamblea de Dios Boliviana		I-3pL	.....	1	100	100	200	0.05	*IADB, Assembly of God Ch in Bolivia.* Cochabamba, Sucre. Brazilian pentecostals.
Iglesia Católica en Bolivia:	1537	R-Lat	B.L.R	667	3,812,700	3,963,492	6,558,904	2.04	*Catholic Ch in Bolivia.* C=30+3+69. 6q,1s(121). 275n 620x 989m 1985w 224807Yy
M Cochabamba	1847	R-Lat	Bs	68	570,000	607,442	983,046	1.94	Spanish, Quechua. Recent industrialization. M=SDB. 54n 136x 268m 460w 33612Yy
D Oruro	1924	R-Lat	Bocd	39	171,000	270,000	294,157	0.34	Spanish, Aymara, Quechua. Mining town. M=OCD. 19n 24x 33m 86w 5824Yy
PN Aiquile	1961	R-Lat	Bofm	20	158,000	89,960	273,000	4.54	Quechua, Spanish. Entirely rural. M=OFM. 7n 11x 13m 55w 4878Yy
M La Paz	1605	R-Lat	Bofm	103	412,000	992,000	709,000	-1.33	Spanish, Aymara. 3 Pastoral Zones. M=OFM,OCD. 58n 119x 194m 320w 73658Yy
D Coroico	1958	R-Lat	Bofm	9	107,000	148,000	185,000	0.90	Aymara, Spanish. Tropical, rural. M=OFM. 9n 6x 9m 45w 1428Yy
D El Alto	1994	R-Lat	B sdb	46	384,000	–	662,414	100.00	M=SDB. Suffragan of La Paz. 17n 26x 49m 77w 5456Yy
PN Corocoro	1949	R-Lat	Bs	29	110,000	272,887	190,000	-1.44	Aymara, Spanish. Rural altiplano, mining. M=CP. 4n 9x 9m 20w 3020Yy
M Santa Cruz de la Sierra	1605	R-Lat	Bcssr	119	668,000	405,000	1,150,000	4.26	Spanish, Japanese, Guarani. Prosperous (gas). 9n 124x 173m 337w 25237Yy
D San Ignacio de Velasco	1930	R-Lat	Pofm	21	81,000	57,500	140,000	3.62	Chiquitano, Spanish, Ayore, Pauserna. M=OFM. 15n 21x 36m 87w 4550Yy
M Sucre	1552	R-Lat	Bofm	42	253,000	390,000	435,898	0.45	Spanish, Quechua. Old town, industrialization. 34n 24x 32m 180w 9984Yy
D Potosí	1924	R-Lat	Bs	74	400,000	878,294	689,540	-0.96	Spanish, Quechua. Mining population. M=OFM. 34n 31x 51m 65w 36642Yy
D Tarija	1924	R-Lat	Bs	14	173,000	105,900	298,000	4.23	Spanish only. Rural. Close links with Argentina. 10n 20x 27m 74w 7608Yy
VA Cuevo	1919	R-Lat	Pofm	21	58,000	67,000	100,100	1.62	Spanish, Mataco, Guarani, Guayaru, Canochana. 2n 16x 25m 43w 2385Yy
VA El Beni	1917	R-Lat	Pofm	25	72,000	90,000	124,100	1.29	Ignaciano, Trinitario, Baure, Jora, More, Cayuvana. 1n 17x 23m 39w 3670Yy
VA Nuflo de Chávez	1951	R-Lat	Pofm	15	42,700	28,000	73,649	3.94	Spanish, Siriono, Guayaru, Ayore, Chiquitano. P=45% 0n 15x 19m 36w 2152Yy
VA Pando	1942	R-Lat	Pmm	8	73,000	64,000	125,600	2.73	Pacahuara, Aroana, Chama, Spanish. P=15%. 1n 7x 8m 25w 2558Yy
VA Reyes	1942	R-Lat	Pcssr	13	50,000	30,000	85,400	4.27	In Beni. M=CSSR. 1n 14x 20m 36w 2145Yy
OM Bolivia	1961	R-Lat	Bs	1	30,000	10,000	40,000	5.70	*Bolivia Military Ordinariate.* M=CMF. 3 ordinaries, 52 auxiliaries.
Doubly-counted Catholics		R-Lat		0	0	-542,491	0		Persons counted in older diocese and also a newly-formed one.
Iglesia de Cristo en Bolivia		I-Dis	.....	4	300	–	500	0.05	*Church of Christ in Bolivia.* Disciples.
Iglesia de Dios	1960	P-Pe3	ZF...	38	2,272	500	5,680	10.21	*Ch of God.* M=CoG(Cleveland) (USA). 5 churches, 14 missions. HQ Sucre. 10n.
Iglesia de Dios Boliviana	1945	P-Hol	x...C	89	2,400	4,000	5,000	0.90	*IDB. Bolivian Ch of God.* M=CoGHoliness (Overland Park, USA). Aymaras. 7f,1s.
Iglesia de Dios de la Profecia	1974	P-Pe3	.....	72	2,500	–	7,140	4.76	M=CoGP. Church of God of Prophecy.
Iglesia de Dios Misión Boliviana		P-Pe2	.....	14	1,000	–	2,500	0.05	*Church of God Bolivian Mission.* Support from USA.
Iglesia de JC de los Santos de los UD	c1961	m-LdS	x....	157	35,900	5,752	69,000	10.45	*Ch of JC of LdS. Mormons.* M=CJCLdS(USA). Indians. Rapid growth, 13.8%pa. 70f.
Iglesia de la Puerta Abierta	1955	I-3pL	.TT.T	10	150	200	300	1.64	*IPA.* M=Ch of the Open Door (USA). Fundamentalist. HQ Cochabamba.
Iglesia del Evangelio Cuadrangular	1929	P-Pe2	ZF..C	51	1,380	2,000	2,294	0.55	M=Internat Ch of Foursquare Gospel (USA). Sirionos. 10nm,2s,1H,1p(8),W=68%,50Y.
Iglesia del Nazareno	1908	P-Hol	xF..C	137	10,055	8,000	14,517	2.41	M=Ch of the Nazarene (USA). Aymaras. 9n79m,12f,3h,1s(28),68t(4990),W=63%,161Y.
Iglesia Evangélica Anabautista	1973	P-Men	.....	3	153	–	240	4.55	Mennonites from other South American countries.
Iglesia Ev Asamblea de Dios		I-3pL	.....	17	610	75	1,472	0.05	*Evangelical Assembly of God.* M=SEM(Sweden).
Iglesia Evangélica Boliviana	1946	I-Ref	.TT.T	36	1,800	1,066	2,570	3.58	*Bolivian Ev Ch. Bible Presbyterians.* 90% Aymara. HQ La Paz. 3n,W=20%,89z.
Iglesia Ev de Dios Boliviana		I-3pL	.....	130	6,500	3,780	14,400	0.05	*Bolivian Evangelical Church of God.*
Iglesia Evangelica Boliviana de Santidad	1948	P-Hol	x...C	143	5,000	2,000	10,000	6.65	*IBS. Bolivian Holiness Ch.* M=Holiness Meth Chs (USA). 94% Aymara, 6% Quechua. 1s.
Iglesia Evangélica Independiente		I-Eva	.....	1	300	200	350	0.05	*IEI. Independent Ev Ch.* Indigenous Bolivian church in Cochabamba.
Iglesia Evangélica Los Amigos	1919	P-Qua	Q....	33	1,000	1,500	2,000	1.16	*IELA. Ev Ch of Friends.* M=BFHM(Central Yearly Meeting, USA). 15n,3x,5f,1p,1s(5).
Iglesia Ev Israelita del Nuevo Pacto		I-Adv	.....	10	1,000	–	2,000	0.05	*Ev Israelite Ch of the New Covenant.* Cabanistas (Tabernaclers). Ex SDA.
Iglesia Ev Luterana Boliviana	1938	P-Lut	L...C	120	7,200	6,000	24,000	5.70	*IELB. Ev Lutheran Ch of B.* M=World Mission Prayer League. Aymaras. 24f,3k,1s.
Iglesia Ev Menonita Boliviana	1970	P-Men	.....	5	125	–	329	26.09	*Bolivian Evangelical Mennonite Church.*
Iglesia Ev Metodista en Bolivia	1878	P-Met	VuU..	151	11,000	10,000	31,400	4.68	*IEMB. Ev Methodist Ch.* M=UMC(USA). A=1969. 36n,40m,37f,5H,4r,1s. Many projects.
Iglesia Evangélica Mundial	1943	P-Hol	xF..C	86	2,500	2,000	8,330	5.87	*IEM. World Gospel Church.* M=World Gospel Mission (USA). HQ Santa Cruz. 23f,1s.
Iglesia Evangélica National	1957	I-Eva	C	25	500	1,000	1,500	1.64	*National Ev Ch. Assembly of God.* Ex Bethesda Mission. Works with UWM. 2n,W=49%,45Y.
Iglesia Ev Pentecostal de Chile	c1935	I-3pL	x....	105	4,105	4,000	12,083	4.52	*IEPC: Ev Pentecostal Ch of Chile.* In Oruro, Chuquisaca, Potosí, Cochabamba, La Paz.
Iglesia Ev Pentecostal Nacional		I-3pL	.....	47	1,800	–	3,043	0.05	*National Pentecostal Ch.* M=SFM(Sweden).
Iglesia Ev Pentecostal Unida	1974	P-Pe1	x....	20	1,500	–	2,000	4.76	*United Pentecostal Church.* M=UPC(USA). Oneness Pentecostals. f4.
Iglesia Luterana Latinoamericana de B	1967	P-Lut	l.U..	1	770	489	1,300	3.99	*Latin American Lutheran Ch.* Ecumenical split ex WMPL, in La Paz. 2n,W=30%,7y.
Iglesia Menonita	1954	P-Men	G....	46	5,500	5,500	9,170	2.07	*Mennonite Ch in Bolivia. Old Colony Mennonites*, from Paraguay. German-speaking.
Iglesia Nacional Bethesda	1950	P-Non	x....	20	1,000	1,260	2,500	2.78	*INB. Bethesda National Ch.* M=Bethesda Mission (USA). 11n,4x,7f,1s(15),W=85%,25z.
Iglesia Nacional Ev de Los Amigos	1924	P-Qua	QF..C	292	14,000	7,000	21,900	4.67	*INELA. Friends National Ev Ch.* M=Oregon YM(USA). Aymaras. 35n,2x,6f,1s(30),W=99%.
Iglesia Nueva Apostolica	c1970	I-3aX	x....	40	2,000	–	3,065	37.87	*NAC. NAK.* M=Neuapostolische Kirche (HQ Zurich, Switzerland).
Iglesia Ortodoxa Griega	c1970	O-Gre	Cwo..	1	1,500	2,000	3,000	1.64	Part of XIth Archdiocesan District, Greek Orthodox AD of N&SAmerica. Greeks.
Iglesia Pentecostal Brasilera		I-3pY	.....	20	500	300	1,000	0.05	*Brazilian Pentecostal Ch.* From Brazil. In Santa Cruz, Cochabamba departments.
Iglesia Pentecostal Nacional		I-3pL	C	40	1,000	1,000	2,000	0.05	*National Pentecostal Ch.* Schism ex ICFG. HQ Trinidad. Indigenous pentecostals.
Iglesia Pentecostal Sueca	1920	P-Pe2	Z...C	23	2,500	1,000	4,170	5.88	*Swedish Pentecostal Ch.* M=SFM(Sweden). Cochabamba department. 1H,14mf.
Iglesia Presbiteriana en Bolivia		P-Ref	.....	12	1,000	750	2,500	0.05	*Presbyterian Church in Bolivia.*
Iglesia Unida Mundial	1936	P-Non	xF..C	5	900	500	1,500	4.49	*United World Ch.* M=UWM(USA). Santa Cruz. Mestizos. 2n,2x,1k,W=20%,20Y,10z.

Continued opposite

Country Table 2–concluded

Official name (bold type = church with over 10% of affiliated) 1	*Begun* 2	*Type* 3	*Counc* 4	*Congs* 5	*Adults* 6	*Affiliated 1970* 7	*Affiliated 1995* 8	*G%* 9	*Names, notes, and other statistics* (see Codebook, Part 3) 10
Iglesias radiofónicas solitarias	c1960	I-3rL	.....	30	1,200	350	2,000	7.22	Isolated radio believers, mostly young, in remote jungle areas. R=450 (HCJB,FEBC).
Misión Bautista Internacional	1967	I-Bap	x....	13	1,500	50	2,500	16.94	M=Baptist International Missions (Tennessee Temple School) (USA). HQ Cochabamba.6f.
Misión Bautista Leta	1950	P-Bap	.....	1	200	200	400	2.81	M=Latvian Baptist Mission(Brazil). Latvian colony in jungle. Rincon del Tigre.
Mision Bol de Santidad Amigos	1931	P-Qua	.....	200	12,000	3,000	20,000	7.88	*Friends Bolivian Holiness Mission.*
Misión del Seminario Biblico	1919	P-Qua	C	50	2,000	1,500	3,330	3.24	*MSB.* M=Union Bible Seminary (Westfield, Indiana, USA). Quakers. 1j,1s.
Mision Evangélica Bethesda		I-3pL	.....	17	1,000	–	2,500	0.05	*Bethesda Evangelical Mission.*
Misión Evangélica Bautista	1956	I-Bap	.....	7	200	50	400	8.67	*MEB. Ev Baptist Mission.* Independent group from USA. Central region. 1x,W=41%,5z.
Misión Llamamiento de Medianoche	1960	P-Non	x....	5	200	200	500	3.73	M=Midnight Cry Mission (Switzerland). Beni, Pando departments. Social projects.
Misión Luterana Norvega en Bolivia		P-Lut	.....	3	194	–	500	0.05	*Norwegian Lutheran Mission in Bolivia.*
Misión de la Fe Evangelica	1922	P-Eva	.N..C	19	290	500	694	1.32	*Mision de Fe.* M=South America Indian Mission (SAIM) (USA). Ayoré Indians. 19x,20f,15z.
Misiones Cristianas Bolivianas		I-Non	.....	74	5,949	–	11,900	0.05	*Bolivian Christian Missions.*
Misiones Mundiales de Bolivia	1961	I-Non	x....	11	950	2,000	2,110	0.21	M=World-Wide Missions (USA). Evangelical group from California.
Movi Cristiano y Misionero Boliviano		I-3pL	.....	40	3,000	–	4,500	0.05	*Christian Missionary World Movement.*
Movimiento Mundial Cris Misionera		I-3pL	.....	31	2,300	1,110	5,110	0.05	*World Christian Missionary Movement.*
Obra Evangélica Nacional	1942	P-Eva	x...C	36	5,900	1,615	10,000	7.57	*MNT.* M=New Tribes Mission (USA). Beni department: 6 Indian jungle tribes. 89f,W=15%,90Y.
Testigos de Jehová	1932	m-Jeh	x....	150	7,452	2,000	36,600	12.33	*Jehovah's Witnesses.* Witnessing under way by 1932. HQ La Paz. 271Y. (1995) 1429Y.
Unión Bautista Boliviana	1898	P-Bap	T....	170	16,200	6,000	30,000	6.65	*UBB. BBU. Bolivian Baptist Union.* M=CBOMB(Canada). Cochabamba. 90nm,37f,2r,3s.
Unión Biblica	1952	P-Non	.....	3	300	200	600	4.49	M=Seattle Bible Union (USA). Small independent Protestant mission. AQ Camiri.
Unión Cristiana Evangélica	1903	P-Eva	.M..C	437	30,120	28,000	66,900	3.55	*UCE. Ev Chr Union.* M=SIM(former Andes EM, USA), EUSA. A=1950. 148n,15x,76f,3s,360Yy.
Unión Misionera Neotestamentaria	1926	P-Non	x....	15	800	500	1,500	4.49	*NT Churches.* M=NTMU(USA, Canada). 1933 split ex SAIM. Puerto Suarez. 2f.
Other Bolivian indigenous churches		I-	.....	60	4,000	5,000	10,000	0.05	Total about 40 bodies (see below), mainly Aymara independent congregations.
Other Protestant denominations		P-	.....	200	14,000	12,000	20,000	0.05	Total about 15 smaller bodies (see list below).
Doubly-affiliated		2-aff			-193,000	-196,568	-337,175		Evangelicals who also are or were baptized Roman Catholics.
Totals				**5,637**	**3,987,580**	**3,985,000**	**6,955,000**		

Churches, members, growth, 1900-2025	*Congs*	*Adults*	*Affiliated*	*G%*	*Total denominations*	*6 Megablocs:* O	R	A	P	I	m
Total churches, members, and denominations (mid-1900)	1,000	840,000	1,456,000	1.45	4	0	1	0	3	0	0
Total churches, members, and denominations (mid-1970)	2,073	2,299,415	3,985,000	1.45	81	1	1	1	39	37	2
Total churches, members, and denominations (mid-1990)	5,000	3,544,000	6,181,880	2.22	123	1	1	1	51	67	2
Total churches, members, and denominations (mid-1995)	5,637	3,987,580	6,955,000	2.38	129	1	1	1	55	69	2
Total churches, members, and denominations (mid-2000)	7,000	4,464,000	7,786,232	2.28	131	1	1	1	56	70	2
Total churches, members, and denominations (mid-2025)	10,000	6,880,000	12,000,000	1.75	224	2	1	1	65	150	5

NOTES ON TABLE ABOVE

NATIONAL COUNCILS (Column 4, 5th letter).

E = Asociación Nacional de Evangélicos de Bolivia (ANDEB) (National Association of Evangelicals of Bolivia).

R = Conferencia Episcopal Boliviana (CEB) (Episcopal Conference of Bolivia).

T = Confederation of Fundamental Evangelical Churches of Bolivia.

OTHER BOLIVIAN INDIGENOUS CHURCHES. There are scores of Aymara independent congregations, mainly pentecostal, especially in La Paz. Among more organized denominations are: Iglesia Boliviana Los Pelegrinos (member of ICCC), and work (under a missionary bishop from Brazil) of the Igreja Católica Apostólica Brasileira.

OTHER PROTESTANT DENOMINATIONS. These include: Baptist Missionary Association of America, Children of God International (from USA; 1973, 500,000 letters distributed in Bolivia), Church of the Brethren (1942), Chs of Christ in Christian Union, Ev Methodist Ch (1956), Exclusive Brethren (Continuing Tunbridge Wells), United Ev Chs.

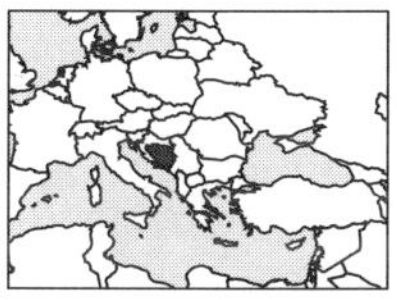

BOSNIA-HERZEGOVINA

SECULAR DATA, AD 2000

STATE

Official name: Republika Bosna i Hercegovina (The Republic of Bosnia and Herzegovina).
Short name: Bosnia and Herzegovina. **Adjective of nationality:** of Bosnia and Herzegovina.
Flag: White field with blue shield and yellow stars.
Area: 51,129 sq. km. (19,741 sq. mi.).
Government: Federal multiparty republic with bicameral legislature, since 1992 (1918 Kingdom of Serbs, Croats, and Slovenes, 1929 Yugoslavia).
Legislature: Senate, 15 members; House of Representatives, 42 members.
Official language: Serbo-Croatian.
Monetary unit: 1 marka (KM) = 100 pfenning. **US$1=** KM 1.67.
Chief cities: SARAJEVO 485,855; Banja Luka 196,392; Zenica 146,731; Tuzla 131,637; Mostar 117,941.
Political divisions: 8 provinces.
Armed forces: 40,000.

DEMOGRAPHY

Population: 3,972,000.
Population density: 77.6/sq. km. (201.2/sq. mi.).
Under 15 years: 748,000.
Growth rate p.a.: 1.28% (births 11.10, deaths 8.11).
Mortality: Infant, per 1,000: 14.0; **Maternal per 100,000:** 50.0.
Life expectancy: 74 (male 71, female 77).
Household size: 3.6. **Floor area per person, sq.m:** 12.0.
Major languages: Bosnian, Serbo-Croatian, Romani.
Urban dwellers: 43.14%. **Urban growth rate p.a.:** 1.2%.
Labor force: 23%.

ETHNOLINGUISTIC PEOPLES

52.5% Bosniac (Muslimani); 21.4% Serb; 11.8% Croat; 10.1% Vlach Gypsy (Gurbeti); 1.1% Rumelian Turk.

ECONOMY

National income p.a. per person: US$300; **per family:** US$1,080.

EDUCATION

Adult literacy: 86% (male 96%, female 76%). **Schools:** 2,443.
Universities: 44. **School enrolment:** female/male: 70%/70%.

HEALTH

Access to health services: 40%. **Access to safe water:** 50%.
Hospitals: 200 (46 beds per 10,000). **Doctors:** 6,929.
Blind: 4,000. **Deaf:** 260,300. **Murder rate:** 2.
Lepers: 500.

LITERATURE

New book titles p.a.: 400 (100 p.a. per million). **Periodicals:** 129.
Newspapers: 2 dailies.

COMMUNICATION (per 1,000 people)

Phones: 69 (7% mobile). **Radios:** 263. **TV sets:** 111.
Daily newspaper circulation: 131. **Computers:** 35.

REFUGEES

Citizen refugees in other countries: 905,500.
Internal displacement: 1,300,000.

HUMAN LIFE AND LIBERTY (optimum condition=100.0%)

HDI: 72.0. **HSI:** 20.0. **HFI:** 35.0. **EFL:** 10.0.

Country Table 1. **Religious adherents in Bosnia-Herzegovina, AD 1900-2025.**

Year	*1900*		*1970*		*mid-1990*		*Annual change, 1990-2000*				*mid-1995*		*mid-2000*		*mid-2025*	
Name	*Adherents*	*%*	*Adherents*	*%*	*Adherents*	*%*	*Natural*	*Conversion*	*Total*	*Rate*	*Adherents*	*%*	*Adherents*	*%*	*Adherents*	*%*
Muslims	450,000	39.5	1,400,000	39.3	1,972,550	45.8	-15,385	56,606	41,221	1.92	1,590,550	46.6	2,384,757	60.0	3,078,650	71.2
Christians	**684,000**	**60.1**	**1,650,000**	**46.3**	**2,060,000**	**47.8**	**-16,085**	**-50,837**	**-66,920**	**-3.85**	**1,599,000**	**46.8**	**1,390,802**	**35.0**	**1,110,000**	**25.7**
PROFESSION																
crypto-Christians	0	0.0	450,000	12.6	270,000	6.3	-2,106	-1,894	-4,000	-1.59	250,000	7.3	230,000	5.8	200,000	4.6
professing Christians	**684,000**	**60.1**	**1,200,000**	**33.7**	**1,790,000**	**41.6**	**-13,961**	**-48,959**	**-62,920**	**-4.24**	**1,349,000**	**39.5**	**1,160,802**	**29.2**	**910,000**	**21.1**
AFFILIATION																
unaffiliated Christians	6,000	0.5	14,678	0.4	5,500	0.1	-43	-15	-58	-1.11	5,396	0.2	4,917	0.1	4,600	0.1
affiliated Christians	**678,000**	**59.5**	**1,635,322**	**45.9**	**2,054,500**	**47.7**	**-16,024**	**-50,838**	**-66,862**	**-3.86**	**1,593,604**	**46.7**	**1,385,885**	**34.9**	**1,105,400**	**25.6**
Orthodox	488,000	42.8	1,011,721	28.4	1,100,000	25.5	-8,579	-31,421	-40,000	-4.42	820,000	24.0	700,000	17.6	600,000	13.9
Roman Catholics	190,000	16.7	620,500	17.4	950,000	22.1	-7,409	-19,478	-26,887	-3.27	768,912	22.5	681,135	17.2	500,000	11.6
Protestants	0	0.0	1,783	0.1	2,500	0.1	-19	39	20	0.77	2,617	0.1	2,700	0.1	3,000	0.1
Marginal Christians	0	0.0	338	0.0	1,200	0.0	-9	19	10	0.80	1,300	0.0	1,300	0.0	1,600	0.0
Independents	0	0.0	980	0.0	800	0.0	-6	1	-5	-0.64	775	0.0	750	0.0	800	0.0
Trans-megabloc groupings																
Evangelicals	0	0.0	400	0.0	300	0.0	-2	12	10	2.92	323	0.0	400	0.0	1,000	0.0
Pentecostals/Charismatics	0	0.0	500	0.0	34,500	0.8	-269	59	-210	-0.63	31,563	0.9	32,400	0.8	34,500	0.8
Great Commission Christians	**114,000**	**10.0**	**570,000**	**16.0**	**470,000**	**10.9**	**-3,666**	**-6,512**	**-10,178**	**-2.41**	**365,000**	**10.7**	**368,217**	**9.3**	**390,000**	**9.0**
Nonreligious	0	0.0	350,000	9.8	180,000	4.2	-1,404	-3,701	-5,105	-3.28	150,000	4.4	128,953	3.3	100,000	2.3
Atheists	0	0.0	164,000	4.6	95,000	2.2	-741	-2,069	-2,810	-3.45	75,000	2.2	66,905	1.7	35,000	0.8
Jews	5,000	0.4	0	0.0	450	0.0	-4	-1	-5	-1.27	450	0.0	396	0.0	350	0.0
World A (unevangelized persons)	399,789	35.1	1,247,536	35.0	1,262,244	29.3	-9,827	-11,601	-21,428	-1.85	969,976	28.4	1,044,636	26.3	1,098,296	25.4
World B (evangelized non-Christians)	55,211	4.8	666,853	18.7	985,756	22.9	-7,707	62,436	54,729	4.54	846,434	24.8	1,536,562	38.7	2,115,704	48.9
World C (Christians)	684,000	60.1	1,650,000	46.3	2,060,000	47.8	-16,085	-50,837	-66,920	-3.85	1,599,000	46.8	1,390,802	35.0	1,110,000	25.7
Country's population	**1,139,000**	**100.0**	**3,564,390**	**100.0**	**4,308,000**	**100.0**	**-33,619**	**0**	**-33,619**	**-0.81**	**3,415,411**	**100.0**	**3,972,000**	**100.0**	**4,324,000**	**100.0**

COLUMNS, ROWS.

For meanings and definitions, see Codebook (Part 3). Note that, by definition, total 'Christians' = professing + crypto-Christians, which also = affiliated + unaffiliated Christians, and also = Great Commission Christians + latent Christians. Percentages may not always total exactly, due to rounding.

NOTES ON RELIGIONS.

ORTHODOX. Mainly Serbs.

ROMAN CATHOLICS. Mainly Croats.

Great Commission Instrument Panel: status of Bosnia-Herzegovina (for explanation see start of Part 4)

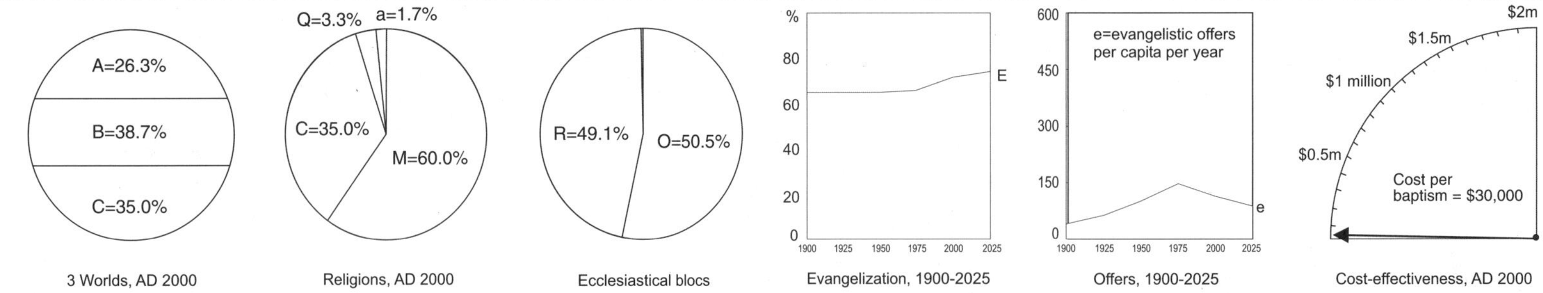

Country status. Bosnia-Herzegovina is a new state born in the aftermath of the disintegration of former Yugoslavia and is bordered by Croatia, Serbia, and Montenegro. Ethnic conflict between Muslims, Serbs, and Croats has characterized Bosnia since its independence in 1992.

HUMAN LIFE AND LIBERTY

Human rights and freedoms. Bosnia-Herzegovina has had a bloody and turbulent history from the first day of its existence when it identified itself as a Muslim state even though Muslims constituted only a plurality. Its legitimacy was derived from a 1992 referendum which was boycotted by the Serbs who constituted 31% of the population. The first government of the republic was dominated by Muslims who expressed their intention to make it the first Islamic state in Europe. The school curriculum was revised to include teaching of the Koran and Arabic even to non-Muslims. Fears raised by these actions led the pan-Serbian nationalists under Radovan Karadzic to form a breakaway state called Republika Srpska based on their right to ethnic autonomy. The Serb armed militia, BSA, then swept through northern and eastern Bosnia where the Serbs were in a majority to drive out non-Serbs. This effort, known in the media as ethnic cleansing, was characterized by brutal acts, including laying siege to cities, indiscriminately shelling civilian buildings and sites, strangling communities by withholding food, medical supplies and fuel oil, executing noncombatants, establishing concentration camps, executing and torturing prisoners, raping women, impeding international relief efforts, and razing villages. These acts were committed not only by the Bosnian Muslims and Serbs but also by the Croatians led by Croatian Defense Council (HVO). All the three groups are victimized by the violence and all violate the Geneva Conventions on the treatment of prisoners. The conflict has uprooted millions of civilians. However, the Bosnian Muslims managed to manipulate international media by covering up crime and atrocities committed by them and exaggerating those committed by their opponents. They also introduced foreign troops from Turkey, Saudi Arabia, Pakistan, and Malaysia into the conflict. These mercenaries have reportedly been responsible for some of the worst war crimes in the country, including the looting of churches, murder of Catholic and Orthodox priests, and the burning of crosses as well as systematic rape of Serbian and Croatian women.

All told, human life and liberty has been at its most atrocious in Bosnia's first years as a state.

NON-CHRISTIAN RELIGIONS

Islam. Bosnia-Herzegovina is Europe's only country with a Muslim majority. The Ottoman Turks first invaded Bosnia in 1386 and the country became a Turkish province in 1463. Through the late 15th and early 16th centuries, many Bosnians converted to Islam in a process that was mainly peaceful, voluntary, and slow. The census of 1489 counted 25,000 Christian hearths and 4,500 Muslim hearths; in a similar census between 1520 and 1530 the numbers were close to even. The growth of Islam was uneven by area—some places saw many conversions, other places few. The Austrian government in 1909 created the office of the Reis-ul-ulema, supreme leader of the Muslim religious community in the country.

World War II was a time of brutal suffering. Chetniks (nationalistic Serbian guerilla units) and Ustases (similar Croat groups) were formed, and in 1941-42, 2,000 Muslims were killed in a series of massacres. Another 10,000 were killed in a set of massacres in 1942-43. On the other side, 12,000 Muslim volunteers joined a Muslim SS division that in 1943 carried out bloody anti-Serb actions. In that war, 20% of the population of Bosnia was killed. Under the post-war Communist regime, Islam was not banned, but many Muslim places of worship and study were closed or converted to other purposes, and all religion came under persecution. Children could not be taught their religion, no Muslim teachers were allowed to be trained, no Islamic books could be published, and many practices were banned, including the wearing of the veil. In the 1950s and 1960s, Bosnia experienced an Islamic religious revival, tied to a growing Bosnian ethnic nationalism. This movement was especially strong among young people. The Muslim Bosnians are distinguished only by religion—in language and race they are indistinguishable from Serbs and Croats. In the civil war that began in 1992, both Serbs and Croats claimed Bosnians as their own ethnic brothers, as 'Muslim Serbs' or as 'Muslim Croats' respectively. Bosnian Muslims clinging to their separate identity, responded by reviving an old term for their self-designation, Bosniacs, which did not carry the label of their religion.

CHRISTIANITY

Christians are a minority in Bosnia-Herzegovina, in AD 2000 constituting 35.0% of the population. Orthodox are the largest confession, with 700,000 affiliated, followed by Roman Catholic with 680,000. The Protestant community is among the smallest in any European country.

ORTHODOX CHURCH. The ancestors of the Serbs became Christians in the 9th century, accepting the Eastern rites preached by Saints Cyril and Methodius. The east/west split of the Roman Empire was reflected in this borderland between the two states, with the Serbs looking for their religious capital to Constantinope and the Croats looking to Rome. Nearly all of the Serbs of Bosnia-Herzegovina are Orthodox, and vice-versa. One distinctive is their continued use of the Cyrillic alphabet.

CATHOLIC CHURCH. Missionaries from Rome brought Christianity to the ancestors of the Croats in the late 7th century, but Roman Catholicism was not fully accepted until the 9th century. Hungarians conducted a crusade in Bosnia-Herzegovina from 1235-1241. Approval was granted from Rome because Hungarian leaders convinced the pope of heresy in the country. Many have questioned whether in fact that was a valid accusation or if Hungary was merely seeking an excuse to dominate its smaller neighbor. In the Middle Ages missionaries from Rome preached in Croatia and Dalmatia. In the early 1900s Croatian Catholics in Bosnia organized politically to become a stronger, more unified force in national life. As with the Serbs and Orthodoxy, nearly all the Croats of the country are Roman Catholic and nearly all the Roman Catholics are Croat.

The Holy See has diplomatic relations with Bosnia-Hercegovina and in AD 2000 is represented to government and the Catholic hierarchy by a nuncio residing in the Vatican.

OTHER CHURCHES. In the Middle Ages, a distinctive Bosnian church arose, partly as a reaction against Hungarian (Catholic) domination, and partly as a result of limited contact with, and teaching from, the Christian churches of either east or west. In the mid-14th century a Franciscan mission sought to win the Bosnian Church to Roman Catholicism. As a result, most of Bosnia's rulers following 1318 were Catholic, though they also continued to be tolerant of the Bosnian church. In the mid-15th century, the Bosnian church was formally removed. The king forced all clergy to either convert to Catholicism or leave the country. Most converted; a minority left. Most members became either Catholic, Orthodox, or Muslim. In 1463, when the Ottomans were making their final drive to control Bosnia, many Bosnians aided the Turks, in hopes of gaining freedom from Catholicism and restoring their national Bosnian church.

The oldest Protestant denomination, the Evangelical Church, which began in Bosnia c1750, opened new work in 3 Bosnian cities following 1991. Seventh-day Adventists had more than 1,000 affiliated in 1995. Other churches in the country include the Old Catholic Church and Jehovah's Witnesses. There has been less Evangelical missionary activity in Bosnia than in other former Communist states post-1989 due to the civil war.

Indigenous missions. As a country Bosnia-Herzegovina has no real record of missionary sending. The Orthodox Church has focused on the rights of its citizens and little has been done to recruit Bosnian missionaries.

Religionists. Muslim minaret for call to prayer, and Catholic cathedral, in Sarajevo.

CHURCH AND STATE

Bosnia was under Turkish rule from 1463, under Austro-Hungarian rule from 1908, under Serbian rule following 1918, and was a part of Communist Yugoslavia following 1946 until the civil war that began in 1992. Each of these regimes left their mark on the religious life of the country, for Islam, Catholicism, Orthodoxy, and atheism respectively. The post-war Communist regime's persecution of Serbian Orthodoxy was harsher than that of Islam, and its persecution of Roman Catholicism was the most severe. A law on freedom of religion was passed in 1954. The civil war in 1992 brought a de facto partition of the country and chaotic circumstances in most state operations, including relations with religion. In December of 1995 the warring parties signed the

Country summary. **Worlds A, B, C by ethnolinguistic peoples, cities, and major civil divisions in Bosnia-Herzegovina.**

	PEOPLES							CITIES							CIVIL DIVISIONS						
World	*Num*	*Pop 2000*	*C%*	*Christians*	*E%*	*U%*	*Unevangelized*	*Num*	*Pop 2000*	*C%*	*Christians*	*E%*	*U%*	*Unevangelized*	*Num*	*Pop 2000*	*C%*	*Christians*	*E%*	*U%*	*Unevangelized*
A	3	56,002	0.23	129	46	54	29,990	0	0	0.00	0	0	0	0	4	842,025	14.39	121,179	48	52	437,601
B	4	2,173,377	0.76	16,473	53	47	1,012,044	6	1,194,818	34.00	406,254	74	26	314,521	4	3,129,789	40.41	1,264,706	81	19	608,117
C	13	1,742,434	78.58	1,369,283	100	0	3,686	0	0	0.00	0	0	0	0	0	0	0.00	0	0	0	0
Total	**20**	**3,971,813**	**34.89**	**1,385,885**	**74**	**26**	**1,045,720**	**6**	**1,194,818**	**34.00**	**406,254**	**74**	**26**	**314,521**	**8**	**3,971,814**	**34.89**	**1,385,885**	**74**	**26**	**1,045,718**

Dayton peace accords that established two distinct sections in the country: the Muslim-Croat Federation, holding about 51% of the former land, and the Serb Republic.

Cardinal Puljic presents copies of new Croatian children's Bible to church choir.

BROADCASTING AND MEDIA

Radio receivers are widely owned and used: 25% own at least one. Shortwave programming from HCJB (Ecuador) and other broadcasters can be received. IBRA-produced programs can be heard on local channels in Mostar, Tuzla, and Bihac.

The 'Jesus' Film was shown on television with an estimated audience of 10,000. Satellite TV and radio programs are received in English, Arabic, German and Italian.

INTERDENOMINATIONAL ORGANIZATIONS

There are no councils of churches.

FUTURE TRENDS AND PROSPECTS

The exodus of Orthodox and Catholic Christians from Bosnia will potentially result in a decline of total Christian affiliation below 26% by AD 2025. Islam will pick up almost all of the gains.

Bosnia would then increasingly become a predominately Muslim country after the year 2025 reaching perhaps 80% Muslim by AD 2050.

BIBLIOGRAPHY

'A history of Baptists in Yugoslavia, 1862–1962.' J. D. Hopper. Ph.D. dissertation, Southwestern Baptist Theological Seminary, Fort Worth, TX, 1977. 180p.

'A history of the Congregational and Methodist Churches in Bulgaria and Yugoslavia.' P. B. Mojzes. Ph.D. dissertation, Boston University, Boston, 1965. 674p.

'Bosnia–Herzegovina at war: relations between Moslems and non–Moslems,' Y. A. Jelinek, *Holocaust and Genocide studies*, 5, 3 (1990), 275–92.

'Bosnia's national–religious diversity: a comparative study of Croats, Muslims, Serbs and Yugoslavs in the Republic of Bosnia, 1989–90.' K. J. Hahn. M.A. thesis, University of Wyoming, 1994. 107p.

'Changing functions of religion in a socialist society: the case of Catholicism in Yugoslavia,' S. Vrcan, *Social compass*, 28, 1 (1981), 43–61.

Church and state in Yugoslavia since 1945. S. Alexander. Cambridge, UK: Cambridge University Press, 1979. 351p.

'Church–state relations in Yugoslavia since 1967,' S. Alexander, *Religion in Communist lands*, 4, 1 (Spring 1976), 18–27.

'Denominational affiliation in Yugoslavia, 1930–1989,' S. Flere, *East European quarterly*, 25 (June 1991), 145–65.

Die 'Bosnische Kirche' und das Islamisierungsproblem Bosniens und der Herzegowina in den Forschungen nach dem Zweiten Weltkrieg. S. M. Dzaja. *Beiträge zur Kenntnis Südosteuropas und des Nahen Orients*, 28. Munich: R. Trofenik, 1978. 145p.

In the claws of the red dragon: ten years under Tito's heel. W. Gruber. Toronto: St. Michaelswerk, 1988. 208p.

Islam in the Balkans: religion and society between Europe and the Arab World. H. T. Norris. Columbia, SC: University of South Carolina Press, 1993. 326p. (Deals with Bosnia, Albania, Macedonia).

'Islam in Yugoslavia today,' S. Ramet, *Religion in Communist lands*, 18, 3 (Autumn 1990), 226–35.

'La situación religiosa en Yugoslavia,' G. Canders, *Revista de estudios politicos*, 161 (1968), 259–67.

Medjugorje unfolds in peace and in war. R. Faricy & L. Rooney. 2nd ed. Leominster: Gracewing, 1993. 117p.

Nations and nationalities of Yugoslavia. K. Joncic (ed). Belgrade: Medjunarodna politika, 1974. 549p.

Opci sematizam katolicka crkve u Jugoslaviji, cerkerv Jugoslaviji, 1974 (General survey of the Catholic Church in Yugoslavia). Zagreb: Biskupska konferencija Jugoslavije, 1975. 1,166p. (Parts in Croat, Slovenian, Latin, English, French, German).

'Recent developments in church–state relations in Yugoslavia,' C. Criic, *Religion in Communist lands*, 1, 1 (Spring 1973), 6–8.

'Religion and nationality in Yugoslavia,' P. Ramet, in *Religion and nationalism in Soviet and East European politics*, p.299–327. P. Ramet (ed). 2nd ed. Durham, NC: Duke University Press, 1989.

'Religion et opinions chez les étudiants de l'Université Sarajevo,' J. Fisera & A. Fiamengo, *Archives de sociologie des religions*, 12 (1961), 145–55.

'Religion in Yugoslavia: the background,' J. Broun, *America*, 165 (November 30, 1991), 414–16.

Religions in Yugoslavia: historical survey, legal status, church in socialism, ecumenism, dialogue between Marxists and Christians, etc. Z. Frid (ed). Zagreb: Binoza, 1971. 168p.

Savez komunista i religija. I. Cvitkovic. Sarajevo: NISRO 'Osloboenje,' OOUR Izdavacka djelatnost, 1984. 218p.

'Some social expectations of Christians in Yugoslavia with primary emphasis on the Protestant churches,' N. G. Shenk, *Occasional papers on religion in Eastern Europe*, 1 (November 1981), 1–10.

The Bosniam Muslims: denial of a nation. F. Friedman. Boulder, CO, and Oxford, U.K.: Westview Press, HarperCollins, 1996. 304p.

The development of spiritual life in Bosnia under the influence of Turkish rule. I. Andric. 1924; Durham, NC, and London: Duke University Press, 1990. 147p. (Translation of: Die Entwicklung des geistigen Lebens in Bosnien unter der Einwirkung der türkischen Herrschaft.).

'The ethnic Moslems of Bosnia,' D. Dyker, *Slavonic and East European review*, 50, 2 (1972), 238–56.

'The Gypsy population of Yugoslavia,' T. P. Vukanovic, *Journal of the Gypsy Lore Society*, 42, 1/2 (1963), 10–27.

'The Islamic revival and the Muslims of Bosnia–Hercegovina,' Z. T. Irwin, *East European quarterly*, 17, 4 (1984), 437–58.

'The position of believers as second–class citizens in Socialist countries: the case of Yugoslavia,' Z. Roter, *Occasional papers on religion in Eastern Europe*, 9 (June 1989), 1–17.

The position of the Church in Yugoslavia. R. Vidic. Belgrade: Izdavac, 1962.

'The social role of religion in contemporary Yugoslavia.' N. G. Shenk. Ph.D. dissertation, Northwestern University, Evanston, IL, 1987. 264p.

'Yugoslavia,' A. Fiamengo, in *Western religion: a country by country sociological enquiry*, p.587–99. H. Mol (ed). The Hague: Mouton, 1972.

Yugoslavia. J. J. Horton. 2nd ed. *World bibliographical series*, vol. 1. Oxford, UK: CLIO Press, 1990. 304p. (See especially 'Religion,' p.72f, and 'Nationalities,' p.97–103).

Yugoslavia: a comprehensive English–language bibliography. F. Friedman (ed). Wilmington, DE: Scholarly Resources, Inc., 1993. 547p. (Section on 'Religion,' p.453–61).

Yugoslavia inferno: ethnoreligious warfare in the Balkans. P. Mojzes. , 1994.

Yugoslavia: the church and the state. London: Information Office, Embassy of the Federal People's Republic of Yugoslavia, 1953. 92p.

'Yugoslavie aujourd'hui: une église entre l'est et l'ouest,' *Information catholique internationale* (Paris), 400 (January 1972), 7–15.

Country Table 2. **Organized churches and denominations in Bosnia-Herzegovina.**

Official name (bold type = church with over 10% of all affiliated) 1	*Begun* 2	*Type* 3	*Counc* 4	*Congs* 5	*Adults* 6	*Affiliated 1970* 7	*Affiliated 1995* 8	*G%* 9	*Names, notes, and other statistics* (see Codebook, Part 3) 10					
Baptist Church	1875	P-Bap	.....	1	40	54	62	0.55	Local Baptists with relations to Croatia, Serbia.					
Catholic Church in Bosnia:	c550	R-Lat	B.B.R	293	529,000	620,500	768,912	0.07	Many aliens: 1,500 Arabs, 6,000 Gypsies.	157n	293x	388m	358w	9975Yy
M Sarajevo (Vrhbosna)	c650	R-Lat	P....	153	364,000	426,000	528,000	0.07	Violent civil war, 1992-96.	71n	118x	181m	84w	6644Yy
D Banja Luka	1881	R-Lat	P....	59	33,000	38,900	48,186	0.86	Civil war center for 4 years.	21n	45x	48m	79w	569Yy
D Mostar-Duvno	c550	R-Lat	P....	81	132,000	155,600	192,726	0.07	Includes D Trebinge-Mrban (founded AD c950).	65n	130x	160m	195w	2762Yy
Christian Brethren	c1965	P-CBr	.....	1	25	20	42	3.01	Small body with letter growth over 30 years.					
Ev Church in Croatia & B-H		P-Pe2	.....	10	200	–	300	0.05	Mainline Pentecostals.					
Evangelical Ch in Bosnia-H	c1750	P-Lut	LvC.W	2	385	571	550	-0.15	Lutherans with LWF contacts.					
New Apostolic Church	c1985	I-3aX	x....	2	100	–	175	10.00	*NAC. NAK.* M=Neuapostolische Kirche (HQ Zurich, Switzerland).					
Old Catholic Church in B-H	1965	I-OCa	U....	1	300	980	600	-1.94	*OCCBH.* Separate from the other 4 Old Catholic denominations in former Yugoslavia.					
Pentecostal Churches of Christ	c1920	P-Pe2	.....	2	80	108	123	0.52	Mainline Pentecostals, strong relations with Serbia.					
Serbian Orthodox Church:	c150	O-Ser	C....	331	633,000	1,011,721	820,000	-0.84	Remnant of original major denomination.					
M Dabar-Bosnia	1219	O-Ser	Cm	65	109,000	185,370	140,000	-1.12	HQ Sarajevo.					
D Banja Luka	1900	O-Ser	Cb	125	219,000	367,672	280,000	-1.08	HQ Banja Luka. Strong Muslim area.					
D Zahumlje-Herzegovina	1219	O-Ser	Cb	46	45,000	58,679	50,000	-0.64	Old diocese of Hum. HQ Mostar.					
D Zvornik-Tuzla	c1550	O-Ser	Cb	95	260,000	400,000	350,000	-0.53	Civil war zone, protracted fighting.					
Seventh-day Adventist Church	1909	P-Adv	x....	21	673	1,030	1,040	0.04	*SDA.* Relations with Serbia and world SDAs.					
United Jehovah's Witnesses	1925	m-Jeh	x....	9	452	338	1,300	5.54	*Watch Tower.* (1995) 161Y.					
Other Protestant churches	c1990	P-	.....	10	300	–	500	20.00	Total over 15, served by M=GEM,CAC,MCY,SA,COGY,PCCY,GGMS.					
Totals				**683**	**1,164,555**	**1,635,322**	**1,593,604**							

Churches, members, growth, 1900-2025	*Congs*	*Adults*	*Affiliated*	*G%*	*Total denominations*	*6 Megablocs:* O	R	A	P	I	m
Total churches, members, and denominations (mid-1900)	200	468,000	678,000	1.27	4	1	1	0	2	0	0
Total churches, members, and denominations (mid-1970)	737	1,128,095	1,635,322	1.27	9	1	1	0	5	1	1
Total churches, members, and denominations (mid-1990)	700	1,501,000	2,054,500	1.15	12	1	1	0	7	2	1
Total churches, members, and denominations (mid-1995)	683	1,164,555	1,593,604	-4.95	29	1	1	0	24	2	1
Total churches, members, and denominations (mid-2000)	700	1,013,000	1,385,885	-2.75	30	1	1	0	25	2	1
Total churches, members, and denominations (mid-2025)	500	808,000	1,105,400	-0.90	66	5	1	0	35	20	5

NOTES ON TABLE ABOVE

NATIONAL COUNCILS (Column 4, 5th letter).

R = Biskupska Konferencija Bosne i Hercegovine (BKBiH, Episcopal Conference of Bosnia-Herzogovina).

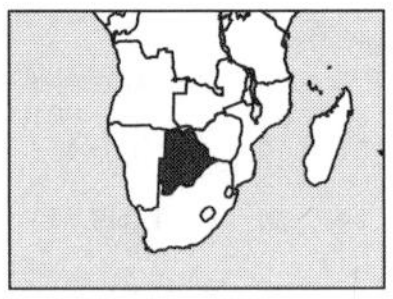

BOTSWANA

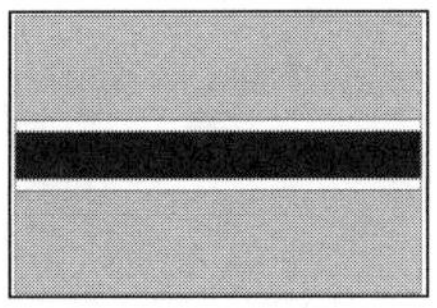

SECULAR DATA, AD 2000

STATE
Official name: The Republic of Botswana.
Short name: Botswana. **Adjective of nationality:** of Botswana.
Flag: Wide light-blue bands separated by central black band and narrow white stripes.
Area: 581,730 sq. km. (224,607 sq. mi.).
Government: Republic, since 1966 (chiefdom, 1885 Bechuanaland Protectorate of Britain, 1966 Independence).
Legislature: National Assembly, 46 members; House of Chiefs, 15 members.
Official language: English and Setswana.
Monetary unit: 1 pula (P) = 100 thebe. **US$1=** P 4.48.
Chief cities: GABORONE (Gaberone) 174,534; Francistown 84,828.
Political divisions: 19 provinces.
Armed forces: 8,000.

DEMOGRAPHY
Population: 1,622,000.
Population density: 2.7/sq. km. (7.2/sq. mi.).
Under 15 years: 684,000.
Growth rate p.a.: 1.19% (births 31.79, deaths 19.94).
Mortality: Infant, per 1,000: 58.7; **Maternal per 100,000:** 250.0.
Life expectancy: 41 (male 41, female 42).
Household size: 5.7. **Floor area per person, sq.m:** 8.0.
Major languages: Tswana, English, Kalanga, Afrikaans, Nguni (Ndebele), Lozi, Pedi, Xhosa, Sotho, Shona, and 10 Bushman languages.
Urban dwellers: 73.55%. **Urban growth rate p.a.:** 4.2%.
Labor force: 33%.

ETHNOLINGUISTIC PEOPLES
21.4% Ngwato Tswana; 14.8% Kalanga (Kalana); 10.5% Central Tswana (Beetjuans); 9.8% Kwena Tswana; 9.6% Ngwaketse Tswana.

ECONOMY
National income p.a. per person: US$3,019; **per family:** US$17,213.

EDUCATION
Adult literacy: 69% (male 80%, female 59%). **Schools:** 1,025.
Universities: 1. **School enrolment:** female/male: 93%/91%.

HEALTH
Access to health services: 89%. **Access to safe water:** 70%.
Hospitals: 30 (25 beds per 10,000). **Doctors:** 240.
Blind: 1,880. **Deaf:** 97,100. **Murder rate:** 12.
Lepers: 6,000. **Underweight prevalence under 5:** 15%.

LITERATURE
New book titles p.a.: 210 (130 p.a. per million). **Periodicals:** 20.
Newspapers: 2 dailies.

COMMUNICATION (per 1,000 people)
Phones: 41 (15% mobile). **Radios:** 206. **TV sets:** 24.
Daily newspaper circulation: 29. **Computers:** 15.

HUMAN LIFE AND LIBERTY (optimum condition=100.0%)
HDI: 67.3. **HSI:** 43.0. **HFI:** 65.0. **EFL:** 44.0.

Country Table 1. **Religious adherents in Botswana, AD 1900-2025.**

Year	1900		1970		mid-1990		Annual change, 1990-2000				mid-1995		mid-2000		mid-2025	
Name	Adherents	%	Adherents	%	Adherents	%	Natural	Conversion	Total	Rate	Adherents	%	Adherents	%	Adherents	%
Christians	**17,100**	**14.3**	**274,100**	**43.0**	**714,700**	**56.0**	**19,403**	**6,346**	**25,749**	**3.12**	**850,320**	**57.7**	**972,191**	**59.9**	**1,487,700**	**66.4**
PROFESSION																
professing Christians	**17,100**	**14.3**	**274,100**	**43.0**	**714,700**	**56.0**	**19,403**	**6,346**	**25,749**	**3.12**	**850,320**	**57.7**	**972,191**	**59.9**	**1,487,700**	**66.4**
AFFILIATION																
unaffiliated Christians	4,000	3.3	104,110	16.3	168,700	13.2	4,574	668	5,242	2.74	199,824	13.6	221,118	13.6	322,000	14.4
affiliated Christians	**13,100**	**10.9**	**169,990**	**26.7**	**546,000**	**42.8**	**14,805**	**5,702**	**20,507**	**3.24**	**650,496**	**44.1**	**751,073**	**46.3**	**1,165,700**	**52.0**
Independents	0	0.0	44,670	7.0	340,000	26.7	9,219	6,606	15,825	3.90	421,033	28.6	498,253	30.7	780,000	34.8
Protestants	13,000	10.8	96,568	15.2	146,460	11.5	3,971	-817	3,154	1.97	162,416	11.0	178,000	11.0	250,000	11.2
Roman Catholics	100	0.1	21,202	3.3	47,800	3.8	1,296	-76	1,220	2.30	54,854	3.7	60,000	3.7	115,000	5.1
Anglicans	0	0.0	7,000	1.1	9,500	0.7	258	-158	100	1.01	9,950	0.7	10,500	0.7	12,500	0.6
Marginal Christians	0	0.0	500	0.1	2,160	0.2	59	145	204	6.88	2,160	0.2	4,200	0.3	8,000	0.4
Orthodox	0	0.0	50	0.0	80	0.0	2	2	4	4.14	83	0.0	120	0.0	200	0.0
Trans-megabloc groupings																
Evangelicals	12,500	10.4	15,900	2.5	38,100	3.0	1,033	337	1,370	3.12	45,301	3.1	51,800	3.2	103,000	4.6
Pentecostals/Charismatics	0	0.0	50,000	7.9	370,000	29.0	10,033	6,467	16,500	3.76	465,837	31.6	535,000	33.0	820,000	36.6
Great Commission Christians	**7,200**	**6.0**	**70,000**	**11.0**	**270,000**	**21.2**	**7,321**	**4,088**	**11,409**	**3.59**	**330,000**	**22.4**	**384,089**	**23.7**	**700,000**	**31.2**
Ethnoreligionists	102,900	85.8	359,200	56.4	546,250	42.8	14,812	-6,507	8,305	1.43	605,300	41.1	629,301	38.8	714,500	31.9
Baha'is	0	0.0	3,400	0.5	9,400	0.7	255	47	302	2.82	11,000	0.8	12,417	0.8	22,000	1.0
Muslims	0	0.0	200	0.0	2,300	0.2	62	34	96	3.56	2,900	0.2	3,264	0.2	6,000	0.3
Nonreligious	0	0.0	0	0.0	1,400	0.1	38	50	88	4.98	2,000	0.1	2,277	0.1	5,000	0.2
Hindus	0	0.0	0	0.0	1,550	0.1	42	27	69	3.75	2,000	0.1	2,239	0.1	6,000	0.3
Jews	0	0.0	100	0.0	250	0.0	7	2	9	3.03	300	0.0	337	0.0	400	0.0
Sikhs	0	0.0	0	0.0	150	0.0	4	1	5	2.66	180	0.0	195	0.0	400	0.0
World A (unevangelized persons)	98,400	82.0	95,550	15.0	114,840	9.0	3,118	-6,285	-3,167	-3.17	103,194	7.0	82,722	5.1	89,680	4.0
World B (evangelized non-Christians)	4,500	3.7	267,350	42.0	446,460	35.0	12,102	-61	12,041	2.42	520,690	35.3	567,087	35.0	664,620	29.6
World C (Christians)	17,100	14.3	274,100	43.0	714,700	56.0	19,403	6,346	25,749	3.12	850,320	57.7	972,191	59.9	1,487,700	66.4
Country's population	**120,000**	**100.0**	**637,000**	**100.0**	**1,276,000**	**100.0**	**34,623**	**0**	**34,623**	**2.43**	**1,474,205**	**100.0**	**1,622,000**	**100.0**	**2,242,000**	**100.0**

COLUMNS, ROWS.
For meanings and definitions, see Codebook (Part 3). Note that, by definition, total 'Christians' = professing + crypto-Christians, which also = affiliated + unaffiliated Christians, and also = Great Commission Christians + latent Christians. Percentages may not always total exactly, due to rounding.

CENSUSES.
7.V.1946 (Bechuanaland): 73.9% tribal religionists, 23.9% Protestants (16.3% LMS, 4.3% DRC/NGK), 1.5% Anglicans, 0.7% Roman Catholics. No subsequent census has enumerated religion.

NOTES ON RELIGIONS
BAHA'IS. Growth from 12 isolated groups in 1964 to 23 local spiritual assemblies in 1973, but by 1995 LSAs still numbered 23 (due to boundary and area realignments) although substantial growth took place over the previous 3 decades. A major effort to convert Kalahari Bushmen had won 9 converts by 1972 and 80 by 1973 in 15 localities (with 2 all-Bushmen assemblies); and many more subsequently.
ETHNORELIGIONISTS. Found among all tribes, with only the 15 Bushmen tribes (25,000) still predominantly traditionalist (80%), in 1995.
INDEPENDENTS. In about 60 denominations in 1995 (see Table 2).
MUSLIMS. *Hajj pilgrims to Mecca.* (1976) 1.
PROTESTANTS. In the year 1900, 80% of all Christians belonged to the LMS mission under the Christian chief of the Bamangwato, Khama.
UNAFFILIATED CHRISTIANS. For a hundred years from 1830 the LMS church (UCCSA) was virtually the state church and no other church was allowed (as among the Bamangwato). As a result, large numbers profess to belong to the church still, although the church is only in touch with a small percentage of them. Further, as cattle-raisers many peoples are constantly on the move to cattle-posts around the Kalahari desert, where the church is unable to maintain contact with them. To a lesser extent, other denominations are out of touch with many of their professing members.

Great Commission Instrument Panel: status of Botswana (for explanation see start of Part 4)

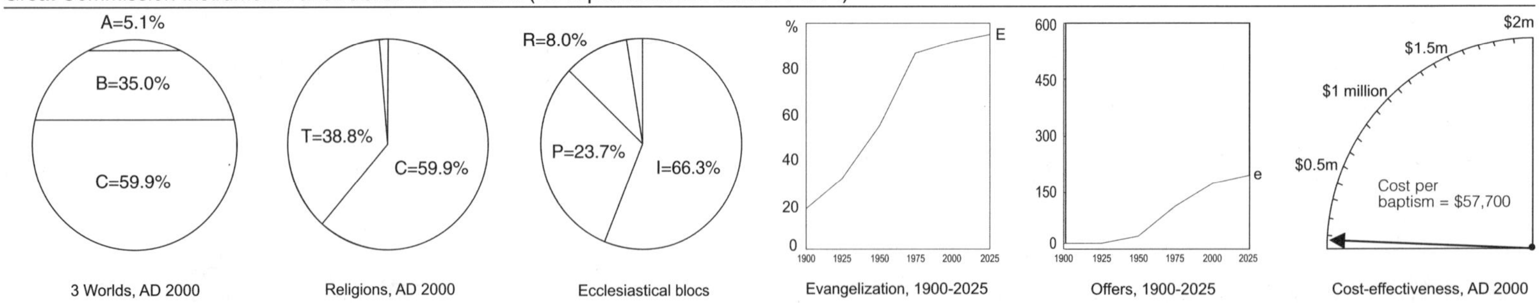

Country status. Botswana is a landlocked country in southern Africa and it is one of the few flourishing multiparty democracies in the continent. The chief products are agricultural in nature including cattle, corn, millet, and sorghum. More recently, copper, nickel, and diamond mines have become an important source of income.

HUMAN LIFE AND LIBERTY

Human need and development. Botswana has a prosperous economy based on the production of diamonds and the export of workers to South Africa. Its diamond lodes are among the richest in Africa. In addition Botswana has coal and copper-nickel deposits as well as gold mines. With a large cattle herd, the government operates the continent's largest abattoir in Lobatse. However, the rural people have not generally benefited from the growing revenues from mining and meat exports. Although the per capita income has grown from $69 at independence to $3,019 today, income distribution is heavily skewed with the top 20% earning two-thirds of the total income and and the bottom 50% earning less than one sixth. The population growth is high and is disproportionately concentrated in the east. Official development efforts have focused on health services, water supplies and primary education, in all of which Botswana fares better than comparable Black African nations.

Human rights and freedoms. Botswana has one of the best human rights records in the continent. The country's small minority of Whites and non-Africans participate freely in political and social life. The country has a strong indigenous democratic tradition,

Country summary. **Worlds A, B, C by ethnolinguistic peoples, cities, and major civil divisions in Botswana.**

	PEOPLES							CITIES							CIVIL DIVISIONS						
World	Num	Pop 2000	C%	Christians	E%	U%	Unevangelized	Num	Pop 2000	C%	Christians	E%	U%	Unevangelized	Num	Pop 2000	C%	Christians	E%	U%	Unevangelized
A	20	54,458	12.36	6,730	38	62	33,752	0	0	0.00	0	0	0	0	0	0	0.00	0	0	0	0
B	23	1,280,599	43.45	556,431	96	4	48,585	2	259,362	46.15	119,696	95	5	13,963	19	1,622,221	46.30	751,073	95	5	83,332
C	11	287,165	65.44	187,910	100	0	993	0	0	0.00	0	0	0	0	0	0	0.00	0	0	0	0
Total	**54**	**1,622,222**	**46.30**	**751,071**	**95**	**5**	**83,330**	**2**	**259,362**	**46.15**	**119,696**	**95**	**5**	**13,963**	**19**	**1,622,221**	**46.30**	**751,073**	**95**	**5**	**83,332**

harking back to the kgotlas or village councils in which the power of the elders was circumscribed. The legal system provides for a broad range of individual rights and freedoms, including freedom from arbitrary arrest and illegal detention, rights to due process and public trials, rights of privacy, and freedom of association. Opposition viewpoints and criticisms of the government are freely expressed in the media. The Kalanga minority, which constitutes 25% of the population, does not suffer any discrimination, although ethnic rivalries are not entirely absent. Women suffer a number of civil disabilities because of the prevalence of traditional codes regarding marriage and inheritance, but they are becoming increasingly active in politics and hold two posts in the cabinet, including that of the minister of external affairs. Married women are considered legal minors subject to the authority of their husbands. Abortion is legal in certain cases. Domestic violence against women is reported to be on the increase and so is the incidence of rape.

Human environment. The major environmental problem is overgrazing resulting from the growth of livestock population. Cattle outnumber human beings by almost 2 to one. As new grazing areas are opened in the west and north wildlife are driven from their natural habitats. Cordon fences established by ranchers also block wildlife migration paths. The growth in population has also reduced water levels, making water one of the scarcest resources in the country.

NON-CHRISTIAN RELIGIONS

African traditional religions continue to exert an influence on Botswana life. The people most resistant to Christian influences are the Bushmen who remain 90% traditionalist. They identify God by various names, the most important being Kaang in the southeast and Huwe in the north and west. Their mythology is richer than that of their Bantu neighbors, with emphasis on the role of certain animals (especially the praying mantis) and celestial bodies (sun, moon, morning star, and southern cross) as manifestations of divinity. Among the Tswana, the ancestors are called Badimo and God is Modimo. Distinctive Tswana features are the identification of God as mother and extreme reverence for the name Modimo, making its pronunciation taboo for most people. Modimo generally works through the Badimo, who also serve as intermediaries in the approach of men to God.

African indigenous churches. Service of thanksgiving for religious freedom held by some of the 60 indigenous denominations in Botswana. On left, Botswana minister of local government.

CHRISTIANITY

PROTESTANT CHURCHES. The Protestant churches have been a significant force in Botswana life since the early part of the 19th century, though very small for many years. The first British resident commissioner in 1885 was a missionary, and since Independence, the speakers of the Botswana parliament have been Christian missionaries. The major Protestant denomination is the United Congregational Church, a result of the pioneering efforts of the London Missionary Society. With work in all parts of the country, this has been considered as almost the established church of Botswana, but its growth has been slow in recent years, and there are large numbers of nominal adherents out of touch with it. Although a number of denominations (Methodists, Lutherans, Dutch Reformed) have been in Botswana longer, Seventh-day Adventists (1921) are the second largest Protestant church. Before Independence, all hospital and secondary school facilities were maintained by church organizations, most of which were Protestant prior to World War II, and church involvement in education, medical and social service continues to be extensive.

INDIGENOUS CHURCHES. African independent churches play a significant and increasing role on the Botswana scene, although all remain relatively small. The majority have come from neighboring South Africa, but since 1960, a number of new indigenous healing groups have arisen in the north.

CATHOLIC CHURCH. The first Catholic mission was founded in 1895, and until 1959, Botswana was divided into 3 different jurisdictions based in South Africa, Namibia, and Southern Rhodesia. With the establishment of one national jurisdiction in 1959 came a new sense of identity, and the church has been characterized by rapid growth over the past decade.

The Holy See has no diplomatic relations with Botswana in AD 2000.

Renewal movements. In the 1990s the Pentecostal/Charismatic Renewal continued to spread rapidly across most older churches, and numbered over 535,000 adherents (of whom 5% Pentecostals, 5% Charismatics, and 90% Independents).

Indigenous missions. There is little vision among Botswanan Christians for foreign missions.

CHURCH AND STATE

Under the rule of king Khama I (1872-1930), Congregationalism was virtually the state religion. No other church was allowed among the Bamangwato until recently.

Freedom of conscience and religious expression is guaranteed in Articles 11-12 of the 1966 constitution. The same articles give to religious communities the right to establish schools at their own expense and to offer religious instruction to those students wishing to participate. At the present time, religious teaching is included in the syllabus of all schools.

If a priest or pastor is licensed, he may solemnize marriage which thereby receives legal recognition. There is no governmental register for the churches, nor many separate ministry or department of religion. The Minister of Home Affairs has responsibility for all religious matters affecting government.

BROADCASTING AND MEDIA

One-fifth of the populace own a radio receiver. Botswana is a member of UNDA, and a topical 5-minute 'Thought for the Day' is broadcast over local radio stations in the early morning. A 30-minute worship service is broadcast each Sunday.

Some 27,000 (2%) have seen the 'Jesus' Film, mainly through mission agencies.

INTERDENOMINATIONAL ORGANIZATIONS

The Christian Council of Botswana (CCB) was formed in 1966. Seven churches are full members, including Catholics, and 4 others have observer status. It is now an associate council of the World Council of Churches.

The council carries on a significant program in urban and rural development through its service committee and urban-industrial mission. Another smaller ecumenical body, with 4 members some of whom also belong to the CCB, is the Evangelical Fellowship of Botswana. Further, Lutherans and Catholics sponsor a joint training program in local crafts.

FUTURE TRENDS AND PROSPECTS

Massive increase in church membership from 1970 (26.7%) to 2025 (52.0%) may be expected due to the massive decline of tribal religionists (from 56% in 1970 to 32% by 2025).

With little projected growth among non-Christians of all kinds Christians could claim over 75% of the population by AD 2050.

Spiritual Healing Church. Prophet Jacob M. Motswalese in 1953, 3 years after he founds largest indigenous church in Botswana.

BIBLIOGRAPHY

A bibliography of religion in Botswana. J. Amanze. Gaborone: Departments of Theology and Religious Studies, University of Botswana, 1990. 58p.

A guide to the registered churches in Botswana. T. T. Fako. Gaborone: University of Botswana, [1983]. 94p.

'A history of the Spiritual Healing Church in Botswana.' R. Friesen. Th.M. thesis, Toronto School of Theology, 1990. 118p.

Among the Bantu nomads: a record of forty years spent among the Bechuana, a numerous and famous branch of the Central South African Bantu, with the first full description of their ancient customs, manners, and beliefs. J. T. Brown. London: Seeley, Service & Co., 1926. 272p. (Treats religion).

An introduction to religion and churches in Botswana. L. Millar. Gaborone: Mennonite Central Committee, 1980. 13p.

Body of power, spirit of resistance: the culture and history of a South African people. J. Comaroff. Chicago: University of Chicago Press, 1985. 276p. (Treats Barolong boo Ratshidi people and Zion Christian Church).

Botswana. J. Wiseman. *World bibliographical series*, vol. 150. Oxford, UK: CLIO Press, 1992. 218p. (Contains short section on religion and ritual, p.84-6; but also see sections on history and peoples).

Botswana handbook of churches: a handbook of churches, ecumenical organisations, theological institutions and other world religions in Botswana. J. N. Amanze. Gaborone, Botswana: Pula Press, 1994. 327p.

'Bushmen of the Kalahari,' E. M. Thomas, *National Geographic*, (June, 1963), 866–88.

Empirical data on religion in Botswana: comparative studies of the objectives of 14 religious societies in Botswana. A. B. T. KyaruhangaAkiiki. : University of Botswana.

'Farm Bushmen and Mission Bushmen: socio–cultural change in a setting of conflict and pluralism of the San of the Ghanzi District, Republic of Botswana.' M. G. Guenther. Ph.D. dissertation, University of Toronto, 1973.

Great Lion of Bechuanaland: the life and times of Roger Price, missionary. E. W. Smith. London: Independent Press, 1957.

Hunters and herders of Southern Africa: a comparative ethnography of the Khoisan peoples. A. Barnard. Cambridge, UK: Cambridge University Press, 1992. 349p. (Treats religion).

Missionaries and western education in the Bechuanaland protectorate 1859–1904: the case of the Bangwato. P. T. Mgadla. *Studies on the church in southern Africa*, no. 2. Gaborone: University of Botswana, 1989. 47p.

Missionary labours and scenes in Southern Africa. R. Moffat. 1842; reprint, New York: Johnson Reprint, 1969. 655p.

'Muslims in Botswana,' S. N. Parratt, *African studies*, 48, 1 (1989), 71–82.

'Overcoming nominal Christianity in Botswana through spiritual warfare.' J. R. Baker. D.Min. thesis, Westminster Theological Seminary, Chestnut Hill, PA, 1994. 365p.

Rainmaking rites of Tswana tribes. I. Schapera. Cambridge, UK: African Studies Centre, 1971. 144p.

Religion and folklore amongst the Basarwa in Letlhakane, Botswana. L. M. Barnes. Gaborone: Republic of Botswana, 1980. 52p.

Robert Moffat: pioneer in Africa. C. Northcott. New York: Harper & Row, 1961.

'Sorcery and witchcraft in Bechuanaland,' I. Schapera, *African affairs*, 51, 202 (1952), 41–50. (On Tswana religion).

'Sorcery and witchcraft with the Bayei and Hambukushu: a cross cultural comparison,' T. J. Larson, *South African journal of ethnology*, 12, 4 (1989), 131–36.

'The conflict between new religious movements and the state in the Bechuanaland Protectorate prior to 1945.' D. Boschman. Th.M. thesis, Harvard University, Cambridge, MA, 1989. 103p.

The image of god among the Sotho–Tswana. G. M. Setiloane. Rotterdam, Netherlands: A. A. Balkema, 1976. 298p. (Treats Christianity among Sotho-Tswana).

The Kavango peoples. G. D. Gibson, T. J. Larson & C. R. McGurk. Wiesbaden, Germany: Franz Steiner Verlag, 1981. 275p. (Treats religion).

'The making of Christianity in a southern African kingdom: GammaNgwato, ca. 1870 to 1940.' P. S. Landau. Ph.D. dissertation, University of Wisconsin, Madison, WI, 1992. 589p.

The Naron: a Bushman tribe of the central Kalahari. D. F. Bleek. Cambridge, UK: University of Cape Town, Publications of the School of African Life and Language, 1928. 67p.

The origin and development of the Ecumenical Movement in Botswana, 1965–1994. J. N. Amanze. *Studies on the Church in Southern Africa*, vol. 4. Gaborone: Departments of Theology and Religious Studies, University of Botswana, 1994. 71p.

The pool that never dries up. R. Wynne. London: USPG, 1988. 129p. (Christian missions among the Hambukushu).

The realm of the Word: language, gender, and Christianity in a Southern African kingdom. P. S. Landau. *Social history of Africa.* Portsmouth, NH: Heinemann, 1995. 278p.

'The Seleka–Rolong and the Wesleyan Methodist missionaries, 1823–1884.' R. L. Watson. Ph.D. dissertation, Boston University, Boston, 1974. 237p.

The Tswana. I. Schapera. 2nd ed. London: International African Institute, 1976. 93p.

'They pray for you ...': independent churches and women in Botswana. L. Lagerwerf. Leiden: Interuniversitair Instituut voor Missiologie en Oecumenica, 1982. 138p.

Tswana religion vis–a–vis world religions. A. B. T. Byaruhanga-Akiiki. *Religion in Botswana project*, vol. 9. Gaborone: University of Botswana, 1985. 136p.

Country Table 2. **Organized churches and denominations in Botswana.**

Official name (bold type = church with over 10% of all affiliated) 1	*Begun* 2	*Type* 3	*Counc* 4	*Congs* 5	*Adults* 6	*Affiliated 1970* 7	*Affiliated 1995* 8	*G%* 9	*Names, notes, and other statistics* (see Codebook, Part 3) 10
Africa Evangelical Church	1969	P-Eva	xM...	15	1,500	115	2,000	12.10	M=AEF.
African Apost Ch of Johane Maranke	c1960	I-3pA	x....	21	3,800	4,000	7,600	2.60	*AACJM. VaPostori (Apostles).* Shona immigrants tinkers from Zimbabwe.
African Born Full Gospel Apostolic Ch	1979	I-3fA	I....	39	1,600	–	2,600	6.25	Split ex African Baptist Full Gospel Apostolic Ch in SA.
Apostolic Faith Mission of Africa	1958	P-Pe2	Z....	41	1,000	500	2,000	5.70	From South Africa.
African Gospel Church	c1960	I-3fA	.....	9	1,290	1,000	2,120	3.05	Schism ex Full Gospel Ch of God (HQ SAfrica). Zulu, Xhosa immigrants; also Tswana.
African Methodist Episcopal Church	1898	I-Met	VW..W	25	1,650	500	2,000	5.70	*AMEC.* In 18th Episcopal District, AME(USA, SAfrica). USA Black bishop.
Anglican Church: D Botswana	1899	A-Hig	AWaVW	12	2,990	7,000	9,950	1.42	In CPCA (D 1972). M=USPG. 50% Ngwato, 30% Kwena, 20% White. 5n,2x,1H,3h,35Y,130y.
Assemblies of God in Botswana	1963	P-Pe2	ZFG.a	45	11,056	2,000	14,977	8.39	Classical Pentecostals. M=AoG(USA). Gaborone, Francistown. 6n,4f,1s(10).
Baptist Convention of Botswana	1968	P-Bap	T.G.G	14	557	150	1,567	9.84	M=FMB-Southern Baptist Convention (USA). Francistown. Dental clinic. 8f,8Y.
Bethlehem City of Christ in Zion	1973	I-3zA	.....	24	2,160	–	2,500	4.55	From Swaziland (Jerusalem Bethsaida Ch).
Bethlehem Faith Mission	1948	I-3pA	.....	16	2,365	500	2,900	7.28	Begun 1935 in SA ex AoG.
Blackman's Mission		I-Lut	.....	11	2,240	4,700	5,600	0.05	Sizeable indigenous church.
Botswana Star Ch in Zion	1973	I-3zA	.....	7	1,400	–	2,000	4.55	M=Apostolic Jerusalem Ch in SA.
Botswana United Ch in Zion	c1960	I-3zA	.....	10	1,090	200	1,500	8.39	Ex Morian Episcopal Ch (South Africa).
Catholic Church: D Gaborone	1880	R-Lat	P.SSW	30	31,000	21,202	54,854	3.88	M=CP. C=1+0+3. (1970) 2n,21x,2m,33w. (1990) 5n,35x,41m,56w,1590Yy.
Christ the Word of God	1942	I-3pA	.....	20	1,500	100	1,800	12.26	Begun as Church of Christ (in Zimbabwe).
Christian Brethren	1968	P-CBr	x....	7	370	200	740	5.37	*Plymouth Brethren (Open).* M=CMML(UK). Small group with South Africa links. 2f,1h.
Church of God in Christ, Botswana	1935	I-3pB	Z...W	13	800	1,500	1,210	-0.86	M=CoGiC(USA Black pentecostals). 2 African bishops (Lobatse, Francistown). 6n.
Church of God of Prophecy	1958	P-Pe3	.....	17	1,220	1,440	2,850	2.77	M=CGP(USA), rival to Church of God (Cleveland).
Church of the Nazarene	1984	P-Hol	.....	2	31	–	65	9.09	M=CON(USA). Holiness body.
Deeper Christian Life Ministry	1991	I-3pA	.....	1	170	–	300	25.00	In Gaborone. Mission from large body headquartered in Lagos, Nigeria.
Dipesalema Ch of Botswana	1970	I-3cA	.....	15	3,200	–	4,000	39.34	*New National Apostolic Ch of God.*
Dutch Reformed Church in Botswana	1869	P-Ref	F.G.a	60	5,300	3,000	14,500	6.50	M=DRC(SA). Members Black, all Kgatla tribe. HQ Mochudi. 5n,1m,1H,4h.
Dutch Reformed Church (Mother Ch)	c1830	P-Ref	F....	20	2,000	2,000	3,600	2.38	*NGK. Nederduitse Gereformeerde Kerk (Moederkerk).* White Afrikaners.
Episcopal Apostolic Ch in Zion of SA	1967	I-3zA	.....	9	2,784	200	3,200	11.73	Split ex MEC in South Africa.
Ev Luth Ch in SA (Western Diocese)	1857	P-Lut	L...W	42	10,600	4,433	15,553	5.15	*ELCSA. Kereke ya Luthere ya Efangele, Afrika kwa Borwa.* M=HM(Germany). 27n,4m,1H,4h.
Ev Religious Protestant Unity Ch	1959	I-3sA	I....	24	900	100	1,250	10.63	Ex Spiritual Healing Ch.
Faith Gospel After Christ Ch	1949	I-3fA	.....	30	3,000	120	4,000	15.06	Schism ex African Baptist Full Gospel Apostolic Ch in SA.
First Apostolic Ch of St John	1962	I-3aA	.....	8	1,600	100	2,100	12.95	From South Africa.
Followers of Jesus Church	1954	I-3aA	I....	12	1,500	150	2,000	10.92	Originated in South Africa as Twelve Apostolic Ch of Christ.
Free Church of Botswana	1971	I-3pA	.....	26	2,700	–	3,500	4.17	Schism ex CoGiC.
Full Gospel Ch of God in Southern A	1968	P-Pe3	ZF...	19	400	1,500	851	-2.24	M=CoG(Cleveland) (USA). Holiness Pentecostals. Mochudi.
Galatia Church in Zion	1956	I-3zA	.....	23	2,300	100	2,900	14.42	From South African body of same name.
General Apostolic Church	1965	I-3aA	I....	19	1,100	120	1,600	10.92	Schism ex DRC, in South Africa.
Gospel of God Church	1959	I-3aA	.....	7	1,543	60	2,000	15.06	*Apostolic Ch of Johane Masowe*, from Zimbabwe.
Greek Orthodox Church		O-Gre	CW...	1	50	50	83	0.05	In D Ioannopolis (Johannesburg), under Patriarchate of Alexandria (Egypt). Greeks.
Head Mountain of God Ap Ch in Zion	1940	I-3zA	I....	52	2,079	150	2,600	12.09	Begun 1939 in South Africa ex Ch of Christ.
Healing Ch in Botswana	c1970	I-3jA	.....	25	1,200	–	1,700	34.65	Ex Morian Epis Ap Ch in Zion, in South Africa.
Herero Church	c1960	I-Lut	.....	5	900	1,000	1,800	2.38	*Oruuano (Community).* Mainly immigrant Hereros from Namibia. Several factions.
Hermon Church	1977	I-3zA	I....	14	3,500	–	4,000	5.56	Schism ex Head Mountain of God AC Zion.
Holiness Union Church of Botswana	1966	P-Hol	x.G.G	9	2,500	500	3,000	7.43	M=Swedish Holiness Union Mission, Swedish Zulu Mission. Begun by immigrant Zulus.
Holy Full Gospel Ap Ch in Zion of SA	1970	I-3zA	.....	17	8,795	–	11,000	45.10	By 1974, over 300 followers; rapid growth since.
Holy Zion Church in Botswana	1963	I-3zA	.....	21	1,180	200	1,500	8.39	From Holy Christian Apostolic Ch in Zion of South Africa.
International Pentecostal Holiness Ch	c1930	P-Pe3	Z....	27	2,097	1,480	3,500	3.50	M=IPHC(USA, SA). Spread from South Africa. 6n,8x.
Israel Church in Zion	1977	I-3zA	.....	10	2,000	–	2,600	5.56	Schism from Apostolic New Jerusalem in Zion Ch of SA.
Jehovah's Witnesses	c1945	m-Jeh	x....	19	777	500	2,160	6.03	*Watch Tower. IBSA.* Active witnessing under way by 1949. 7Y. (1995) 79Y.
Johane Church of God	1973	I-3pA	.....	5	5,000	–	7,000	4.55	Claimants as original followers of Johane Masowe.
Lambs Followers Apostles Church	1985	I-3aA	.....	31	2,000	–	4,000	10.00	Schism out of Church of Alfa.
Light of Hope Mission of Botswana	1962	P-Pe2	.....	10	1,500	200	2,100	9.86	M=AFM(Portland, Oregon).
Love of God Church	1979	I-3cA	.....	14	3,000	–	3,600	6.25	Ex Free Corner Stone Church (South Africa).
Lutheran Ch of Southern Africa	1971	P-Lut	.....	41	4,000	–	6,000	4.17	Free Lutherans. M=MELFC(Germany).
Messiah Ch of the Ten Commandments	1976	I-3zA	.....	6	1,280	–	1,600	5.26	Schism ex Zion Christian Ch (South Africa).
Methodist Church of Southern Africa	1836	P-Met	VWa.W	45	2,700	5,000	4,500	-0.42	*Botswana Circuit*, Mafeking District, MCSA(SA). In south. Rolong tribe. 2n.
Methodist Church, Zimbabwe Synod	1969	P-Met	VWa..	4	1,100	4,000	1,830	-3.08	In Plumtree District, Rhodesia Synod, Methodist Ch. White circuit in north.
Nazareth Church of Botswana	1972	I-3aA	I....	20	1,200	–	1,500	4.35	Schism ex Nation Twelve Ap New Nazareth Church in Zion.
New Apostolic Church	1961	I-3aX	x....	30	4,000	200	5,753	14.38	*NAC.* M=Neuapostolische Kirche (HQ Zurich, Switzerland).
New Apostolic Church in Zion	c1960	I-3zA	I....	9	2,010	300	2,500	8.85	F=Prophetess Jane Peter, in Tonota.
New Apostolic Prophets Church	1974	I-3aA	.....	20	1,800	–	2,300	4.76	Migrant laborers from South Africa.
New Foundation Ap Ch of Christ in Jerus	1978	I-3aA	.....	14	3,250	–	3,600	5.88	Schism ex LMS.
New Jerusalem Apostolic Ch in Zion	1958	I-3zA	I....	13	1,000	400	1,400	5.14	Offshoot of Morian Ap Ch in Zion (SA).
Old Apostolic Church	1961	I-3aX	x....	36	2,000	700	2,700	5.55	*Catholic Apostolic Ch* (UK, Germany, SA).
Pentecostal Protestant Church	c1960	I-3pW	x...G	24	3,500	1,670	4,000	3.56	*Pinkster Protestante Kerk.* Whites, split from AFMSA in 1959. HQ in Germiston, South Africa.
Persia Church in Zion of Botswana	1982	I-3zA	.....	20	1,800	–	2,500	7.69	Schism ex Holy Sun Ch, Nazareth Ch.
Reformed Apostolic Faith of Botswana	1959	I-3aA	.....	5	1,500	200	2,000	9.65	Branch of RAFMSA from South Africa.
Religious Society of Friends	1948	P-Qua	Q....	1	20	50	33	-1.65	In Southern Africa YM. M=FSC(UK). 1964-70 in Trinity Ch, Gaborone. 1f.
Revelation Blessed Peace Ch of B	1975	I-3jA	.....	27	3,000	–	3,600	5.00	Schism ex Spiritual Healing Ch (Botswana).
St Engenas Zion Christian Ch	1937	I-3zA	.....	25	18,000	700	22,000	14.79	Mission of Zion Christian Ch, in South Africa.
St Faith Holy Church	1958	I-3sA	I....	19	5,000	200	6,000	14.57	Schism ex Spiritual Healing Church.
St John's Apostolic Faith Mission of B	1986	I-3aA	I....	34	6,700	–	7,500	11.11	Schism from SJAFM of South Africa.
St John's Apost Faith Mission of SA	1956	I-3pA	x.I..	25	2,500	500	12,000	13.56	M=SJAFM(South Africa). In Mochudi, Maun, Rasesa.
St Mark's Service Church	1964	I-3aA	I....	18	1,100	100	1,600	11.73	Branch of St Andrew's Service Ch in South Africa.
St Matthew's Apostolic Faith Mission	1964	I-3aA	.....	21	1,600	200	2,100	9.86	Schism ex SJAFM of SA.
St Paul's Apostolic Faith Mission	1959	I-3pA	I....	55	6,200	500	9,500	12.50	One of many healing bodies. In Serowe, Sikwane, Mochudi, Francistown. M=SPAFMSA.
St Paul's Apostolic Faith Mission of SA	1957	I-3aA	.....	4	1,150	100	1,600	11.73	Branch of SPAFM of South Africa.
St Peter's Apostolic Faith Healing Ch	1952	I-3pA	I....	30	6,000	2,000	12,000	7.43	Schism ex St John's Apostolic Faith Mission of SA. HQ Mahalapye. 5Y.
St Philip's Faith Healing Church	1957	I-3jA	.....	22	5,800	100	6,300	18.02	Mission of: Salvation of Israel Ch in South Africa.
Seventh-day Adventist Church	1922	P-Adv	x...w	32	9,000	2,000	12,000	7.43	*Botswana Field*, Zambezi Union. 53% Tswana, 47% Lozi. 13nx,1H,6h,93t(6026),547Y.
Spiritual Healing Church	1950	I-3sA	.....	80	18,000	5,000	30,100	7.44	Begun by, and linked with, MBBRC(Lesotho). Tswana. Bishop and branch in Namibia.
Trinity Church, Gaborone	1964	P-com	....w	1	450	1,000	750	-1.14	Union congregation (Angl,Presb,Congr,Meth), linked to UCCSA. 90% African.
United Apostolic Faith Church	1952	I-3aA	x...w	16	4,000	1,000	8,000	8.67	M=UAFC(UK). British-Israelite Pentecostals; widespread missions, HQ Pretoria (SA).
United Congr Ch of Southern Africa	1816	P-Con	RWa.W	200	22,000	60,000	50,000	-0.73	*UCCSA Botswana Region.* M=CWM,UCBWM,UMC. 29% Ngwato. 8n,7x,24m,2H1,14h,3000Yy.
World Outreach Team Action	1995	I-3pA	.....	2	200	–	400	109.13	Mission from Zambia to Birwa Tswana. 6 workers.
Zion Christian Church of South Africa	1937	I-3zA	I....	78	18,000	1,000	30,000	14.57	Part of ZCC (Lekganyane) in SA. In Mochudi, Maun, Serowe.
Other African indigenous churches		I-3zA	.....	1,700	70,000	15,000	140,000	0.05	Total over 50 (see list below), rapidly spreading; including Protestant Unity Ch (Namibia).
Other Protestant denominations		P-	.....	100	10,000	7,000	20,000	0.05	Total over 40 (see list below), including BiCC; served by M=AFM,LCMS,YWAM,MBBRC; CC.
Totals				**3,730**	**388,654**	**169,990**	**650,496**		

Churches, members, growth, 1900-2025	*Congs*	*Adults*	*Affiliated*	*G%*	*Total denominations*	*6 Megablocs:* O	*R*	*A*	*P*	*I*	*m*
Total churches, members, and denominations (mid-1900)	100	6,800	13,100	3.73	8	0	1	1	5	1	0
Total churches, members, and denominations (mid-1970)	665	88,393	169,990	3.73	109	1	1	1	41	64	1
Total churches, members, and denominations (mid-1990)	2,500	326,000	546,000	6.01	189	1	1	1	70	115	1
Total churches, members, and denominations (mid-1995)	3,730	388,654	650,496	3.56	193	1	1	1	71	118	1
Total churches, members, and denominations (mid-2000)	3,900	449,000	751,073	2.92	196	1	1	1	72	120	1
Total churches, members, and denominations (mid-2025)	5,000	696,000	1,165,700	1.77	330	3	1	1	80	240	5

Continued opposite

Country Table 2–concluded

NOTES ON TABLE ABOVE
NATIONAL COUNCILS (Column 4, 5th letter).
a = member of both EFB and BCC.
E = Evangelical Fellowship of Botswana (EFB).
I = Botswana Spiritual Council of Churches (BSCC), begun 1971.
W = Botswana Christian Council (BCC, Lekgotla la Sekeresete la Botswana).
w = associated observer member of BCC.

Other national councils. Botswana Association of Inter-Spiritual Churches (1973 applied to WCC for associate council status; 20 member churches).

Local councils. In Francistown, Lobatse, and elsewhere.

OTHER AFRICAN INDIGENOUS CHURCHES. Many are branches of bodies centered in the republic of South Africa, with immigrant Shona bodies from Zimbabwe and immigrant Herero bodies from Namibia, but there is also a growing number of zionist and other congregations indigenous to Botswana. These include (within parentheses date of founding in Botswana, and present headquarters): African Mission Society Ch (member of CCB), Apostolic Ch of Johane Masowe (Shona immigrants), Apostolic Diphapha Ch-in-Zion (1959, Mosung Village, Serowe), Apostolic Spiritual Healing Ch (1969, Gaborone, Mochudi), Bakwena Lutheran Ch, Faith Healing Ch (1966, Francistown, Gaborone), Galatia Apostolic Ch (1961, Serowe, 2 churches), Holy Sarda Apostolic Christian Ch (1961, Serowe), Morians, Episcopal Apostolic Ch in Zion (1954, Serowe), National Ch of God in Christ (1960, Mahalapye), Nazirite Baptist Ch (Shembe) (from Zululand), New Apostolic-in-Zion Ch (1966, Tonota), Protestant Unity Ch (Hereros from Namibia), Revelation Healing Ch (1965, Mahalapye), St Apostolic Ch in South Africa (1957, Basimane-Serowe), St Matthew's Apostolic Faith Mission (1958), Serowe), St Philip's Healing Ch (Francistown), Spiritual Apostle Faith Healing Ch (1950, Serowe), United Pentecostal Ch of God in Christ (Molepolole), 11 Apostolic Healing Spirit Ch (1963, Maun), 17 Apostolic Spiritual Healing Ch (1950, Maun).

OTHER PROTESTANT DENOMINATIONS. These include: Apostolic Faith Mission (observer member of EFB), and other bodies from South Africa.

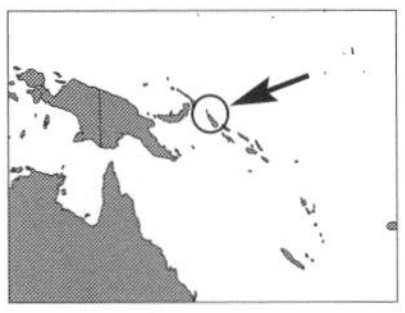

BOUGAINVILLE

SECULAR DATA, AD 2000

STATE
Official name: Bougainville.
Short name: Bougainville. **Adjective of nationality:** Bougainville Islanders.
Flag: That of Papua New Guinea.
Area: 10,050 sq. km. (3,880 sq. mi.).
Government: Papua New Guinea provincial rule but de facto secessionist movement, since 1975 (1884 British protectorate, 1906 Australian territory, 1973 self-government, 1975 Independence).
Legislature: Provincial government of Papua New Guinea.
Official language: English.
Monetary unit: 1 Solomon Islands dollar (SI$) = 100 cents. **US$1=** S$4.99.
Chief cities: Arawa 20,000.
Political divisions: 1 province.

DEMOGRAPHY
Population: 198,000.
Population density: 19.7/sq. km. (51.1/sq. mi.).
Under 15 years: 77,000.
Growth rate p.a.: 2.14% (births 30.39, deaths 9.00).
Mortality: Infant, per 1,000: 54.8; **Maternal per 100,000:** 20.0.
Life expectancy: 60 (male 59, female 61).
Household size: 4.0. **Floor area per person, sq.m:** 7.0.
Major languages: Nissan, Buin, Halia, Nasioi, Nagovisi.
Urban dwellers: 20.00%. **Urban growth rate p.a.:** 2.0%.
Labor force: 30%.

ETHNOLINGUISTIC PEOPLES
14.6% Buin (Uitai); 14.4% Halia (Tasi, Tulon); 7.7% Nasioi (Kieta, Naasioi); 7.7% Neo-Melanesian Papuan; 5.2% Nagovisi.

ECONOMY
National income p.a. per person: US$1,400; **per family:** US$5,602.

EDUCATION
Adult literacy: 80% (male 86%, female 74%). **Schools:** 140.
Universities: 0. **School enrolment:** female/male: 50%/50%.

HEALTH
Access to health services: 20%. **Access to safe water:** 30%.
Hospitals: 5 (20 beds per 10,000). **Doctors:** 15.
Blind: 200. **Deaf:** 11,900. **Murder rate:** 7. **Lepers:** 7,000.

LITERATURE
New book titles p.a.: 24 (120 p.a. per million). **Periodicals:** 0.
Newspapers: 0 dailies.

COMMUNICATION (per 1,000 people)
Phones: 8 (15% mobile). **Radios:** 72. **TV sets:** 163.
Daily newspaper circulation: 15. **Computers:** 10.

HUMAN LIFE AND LIBERTY (optimum condition=100.0%)
HDI: 47.8. **HSI:** 30.0. **HFI:** 30.0. **EFL:** 25.0.

Country Table 1. **Religious adherents in Bougainville, AD 1900-2025.**

Year	*1900*		*1970*		*mid-1990*		*Annual change, 1990-2000*				*mid-1995*		*mid-2000*		*mid-2025*	
Name	*Adherents*	*%*	*Adherents*	*%*	*Adherents*	*%*	*Natural*	*Conversion*	*Total*	*Rate*	*Adherents*	*%*	*Adherents*	*%*	*Adherents*	*%*
Christians	**1,920**	**4.0**	**99,600**	**93.1**	**155,300**	**94.1**	**3,157**	**131**	**3,288**	**1.94**	**174,880**	**94.8**	**188,176**	**95.0**	**273,800**	**95.7**
PROFESSION																
professing Christians	**1,920**	**4.0**	**99,600**	**93.1**	**155,300**	**94.1**	**3,157**	**131**	**3,288**	**1.94**	**174,880**	**94.8**	**188,176**	**95.0**	**273,800**	**95.7**
AFFILIATION																
unaffiliated Christians	680	1.4	1,274	1.2	2,300	1.4	46	9	55	2.15	2,500	1.4	2,845	1.4	3,800	1.3
affiliated Christians	**1,240**	**2.6**	**98,326**	**91.9**	**153,000**	**92.7**	**3,009**	**122**	**3,233**	**1.94**	**172,380**	**93.4**	**185,331**	**93.6**	**270,000**	**94.4**
Roman Catholics	740	1.5	87,000	81.3	124,820	75.7	2,496	-138	2,358	1.75	139,000	75.3	148,401	75.0	208,000	72.7
Protestants	500	1.0	11,226	10.5	18,000	10.9	360	105	465	2.32	20,700	11.2	22,650	11.4	37,500	13.1
Independents	0	0.0	5,000	4.7	10,000	6.1	200	200	400	3.42	12,500	6.8	14,000	7.1	24,000	8.4
Marginal Christians	0	0.0	100	0.1	180	0.1	4	6	10	4.52	180	0.1	280	0.1	500	0.2
doubly-affiliated	0	0.0	-5,000	-4.7	0	0.0	0	0	0	0.00	0	0.0	0	0.0	0	0.0
Trans-megabloc groupings																
Evangelicals	500	1.0	5,100	4.8	4,800	2.9	96	-56	40	0.80	5,140	2.8	5,200	2.6	5,700	2.0
Pentecostals/Charismatics	0	0.0	500	0.5	6,600	4.0	132	138	270	3.49	8,120	4.4	9,300	4.7	17,160	6.0
Great Commission Christians	**1,680**	**3.5**	**4,500**	**4.2**	**12,400**	**7.5**	**248**	**129**	**377**	**2.69**	**14,600**	**7.9**	**16,167**	**8.2**	**28,600**	**10.0**
Ethnoreligionists	46,080	96.0	6,800	6.4	7,200	4.4	144	-143	1	0.01	7,200	3.9	7,207	3.6	6,500	2.3
Nonreligious	0	0.0	500	0.5	2,000	1.2	40	16	56	2.49	2,400	1.3	2,557	1.3	5,000	1.8
Buddhists	0	0.0	100	0.1	500	0.3	10	-4	6	1.07	520	0.3	556	0.3	700	0.2
World A (unevangelized persons)	45,600	95.0	428	0.4	330	0.2	6	-9	-3	-1.24	369	0.2	198	0.1	286	0.1
World B (evangelized non-Christians)	480	1.0	6,973	6.5	9,370	5.7	188	-122	66	0.27	9,251	5.3	9,626	5.1	11,914	4.2
World C (Christians)	1,920	4.0	99,600	93.1	155,300	94.1	3,157	131	3,288	1.94	174,880	94.5	188,176	94.8	273,800	95.7
Country's population	**48,000**	**100.0**	**107,002**	**100.0**	**165,000**	**100.0**	**3,351**	**0**	**3,351**	**1.84**	**184,500**	**100.0**	**198,000**	**100.0**	**286,000**	**100.0**

COLUMNS, ROWS.
For meanings and definitions, see Codebook (Part 3). Note that, by definition, total 'Christians' = professing + crypto-Christians, which also = affiliated + unaffiliated Christians, and also = Great Commission Christians + latent Christians. Percentages may not always total exactly, due to rounding.

NOTES ON RELIGIONS
ETHNORELIGIONISTS. By 1995, 20% or less of most tribal groups followed traditional religions.

Great Commission Instrument Panel: status of Bougainville (for explanation see start of Part 4)

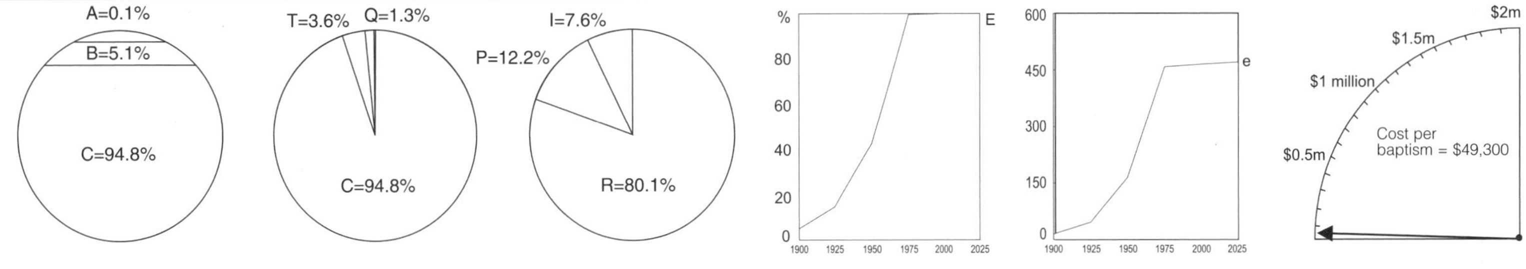

3 Worlds, AD 2000 — Religions, AD 2000 — Ecclesiastical blocs — Evangelization, 1900-2025 — Offers, 1900-2025 — Cost-effectiveness, AD 2000

Country status. Bougainville is the largest of the volcanic islands in the Solomon Islands in the South Pacific Ocean. In 1989 Melanesian nationalists declared independence and guerilla warfare since then has closed down the country's copper and gold mines.

HUMAN LIFE AND LIBERTY

Human rights and freedoms. Part of the national territory of Papua New Guinea, Bougainville has been for some years the scene of protracted fighting between government troops and secessionists led by the Bougainville Revolutionary Army (BRA). Both sides are responsible for violations of human rights of both civilians and combatants. The BRA, which controls parts of the island, has alleged that government troops engage in brutal executions of its leaders to strike terror into the people. Government has only limited access to BRA-controlled areas.

NON-CHRISTIAN RELIGIONS

Traditional religions continue to exert an influence in the Northern Solomons (Bougainville) as in

Country summary. **Worlds A, B, C by ethnolinguistic peoples, cities, and major civil divisions in Bougainville.**

	PEOPLES							CITIES							CIVIL DIVISIONS						
World	*Num*	*Pop 2000*	*C%*	*Christians*	*E%*	*U%*	*Unevangelized*	*Num*	*Pop 2000*	*C%*	*Christians*	*E%*	*U%*	*Unevangelized*	*Num*	*Pop 2000*	*C%*	*Christians*	*E%*	*U%*	*Unevangelized*
A	0	0	0.00	0	0	0	0	0	0	0.00	0	0	0	0	0	0	0.00	0	0	0	0
B	1	794	29.97	238	93	7	56	0	0	0.00	0	0	0	0	0	0	0.00	0	0	0	0
C	34	197,702	93.62	185,096	100	0	201	1	20,000	93.00	18,600	99	1	120	1	198,495	93.37	185,331	100	0	256
Total	**35**	**198,496**	**93.37**	**185,334**	**100**	**0**	**257**	**1**	**20,000**	**93.00**	**18,600**	**99**	**1**	**120**	**1**	**198,495**	**93.37**	**185,331**	**100**	**0**	**256**

the Solomon Islands and Papua New Guinea. As with the other areas, non-Christian cargo cults have also developed and played an important role in the islands; there have been 4 on Bougainville island and 5 on Buka.

CHRISTIANITY

CATHOLIC CHURCH. Catholicism has been represented in the Northern Solomons since the year 1900 and is now by far the principal religion of the territory. The diocese of Bougainville which continues to form part of the archdiocese of Rabaul in Papua New Guinea is at present served by 5 national and 34 expatriate priests, as well as brothers and sisters who are also predominantly expatriate.

The Holy See has no diplomatic relations with Bougainville in AD 2000.

PROTESTANT CHURCHES. Two Protestant churches are active. The United Church has its centre in Papua New Guinea and traces its origin to both New Zealand Methodists and native Christians from other Pacific islands. Tongan and Fijian missionaries are still at work there, although the church is controlled by local personnel. The other Protestants are Seventh-day Adventists, a more recent arrival (1929) but still with substantial membership.

OTHER CHURCHES. The Hahalis Welfare Society is a syncretistic sect formed among Catholic and Methodist Buka villagers in 1957, with a mixture of Christian elements combined with traditional and cargo cult emphases. Friday Religion is an ex-Catholic movement. There is also a small community of Jehovah's Witnesses.

CHURCH AND STATE

The Northern Solomons is a secular territory strongly influenced by Christianity, especially Catholicism. The Catholic Church and its bishops are known to have played a significant role in the move towards secession and the declaration in 1975 of independence for the Northern Solomons from Papua New Guinea.

INTERDENOMINATIONAL ORGANIZATIONS

The Bougainville Inter-Church Council (BICC), which had formerly been the Kieta Inter-Church Council, has 2 members, the Catholic and United Churches. The BICC is affiliated with the Melanesian Council of Churches with its headquarters in Port Moresby, Papua New Guinea.

FUTURE TRENDS AND PROSPECTS

Christianity will likely hover around 95% of the population for the next thirty years as losses by tribal religionists to Christianity are made up by losses of Christianity to the nonreligious.

After 2025, the nonreligious are expected to continue to grow with many defections from Christianity. By AD 2050 it is possible that Christians will represent less than 90% of the population.

BIBLIOGRAPHY

'Friday Religion.' B. H. Sipari. Catholic Education Office, Kieta, 1976.

'Le 'cargo cult' à Bougainville,' M. Lenormand, *Etudes melanésiennes*, n.s. no. 4 (July 1949), 82–83.

'Sorcellerie et civilisation européene aux Iles Salomon,' P. O'Reilly, in *La sorcellerie dans les pays de mission. Compte rendu de la XIVe Semaine de Missiologie de Louvain 1936*. Brussels: Desclee de Brouwer, 1937. (Account of an unsuccessful revolution in Buka).

Studies in the anthropology of Bougainville, Solomon Islands. D. L. Oliver. 1949; reprint, New York: Kraus Reprint Co, 1970.

'The continuity of the cults: Buka,' in *The trumpet shall sound: a study of cargo cults in Melanesia*, p.114–22. P. Worsley. New York: Schocken, 1968.

'The Hahalis Welfare Society,' H. Griffin, in *Melanesian and Judaeo-Christian traditions*, p.38f. G. W. Trompf (ed). Port Moresby, Papua New Guinea: University of PNG, 1976.

'The Hahalis Welfare Society of Buka.' M. R. Rimoldi. Ph.D. dissertation, Australian National University, Canberra, Australia, 1971.

Country Table 2. **Organized churches and denominations in Bougainville.**

Official name (bold type = church with over 10% of all affiliated) 1	*Begun* 2	*Type* 3	*Counc* 4	*Congs* 5	*Adults* 6	*Affiliated 1970* 7	*Affiliated 1995* 8	*G%* 9	*Names, notes, and other statistics* (see Codebook, Part 3) 10
Catholic Church: D Bougainville	1900	R-Lat	P...Q	70	89,133	87,000	139,000	1.89	Under M Rabaul. M=SM. Copper mines. C=1+3+3. 5n,34x,43m,87w,1p,P=54%,2601Yy,286z.
Friday Religion	1958	I-3pP	.....	40	1,741	500	2,000	5.70	Split ex RCC. HQ Pontana, in mountains. 6 Laws. Catholic liturgy.
Hahalis Welfare Society	1957	I-mar	.....	130	6,000	4,500	10,500	3.45	Syncretistic cargo cult ex RCC, Methodists. Began at Hahalis (Buka). Baby gardens.
Jehovah's Witnesses	1969	m-Jeh	x....	3	130	100	180	2.38	*Watch Tower. IBSA.* Rapid expansion after first arrival in 1969.
Seventh-day Adventist Church	1929	P-Adv	x....	30	4,000	3,226	5,000	1.77	*Bougainville Mission.* HQ Kastiorita, Inus. Highly organized. 3n,1x,4m,6w,4f.
United Ch in PNG & the Solomon Is	1922	P-Uni	.....	120	10,500	7,500	15,000	2.81	*Bougainville Region.* Bishop a Tongan. M=MMB(NZ). 6 Circuits. 10n,5x,41m,3w,4f.
Other Protestant denominations		P-	.....	20	500	500	700	0.05	Including Baptists in Kieta, and Campaigners for Christ (Everyman's Hut).
Doubly-affiliated		2-aff			0	-5,000	0		Persons claimed as affiliated by both United Church, Catholic Church, and Hahalis.
Totals				**413**	**112,004**	**98,326**	**172,380**		

Churches, members, growth, 1900-2025	*Congs*	*Adults*	*Affiliated*	*G%*	*Total denominations*	*O*	*R*	*A*	*P*	*I*	*m*
Total churches, members, and denominations (mid-1900)	30	570	1,240	6.45	1	0	1	0	0	0	0
Total churches, members, and denominations (mid-1970)	202	45,164	98,326	6.45	8	0	1	0	4	2	1
Total churches, members, and denominations (mid-1990)	300	99,400	153,000	2.24	9	0	1	0	5	2	1
Total churches, members, and denominations (mid-1995)	413	112,004	172,380	2.41	10	0	1	0	6	2	1
Total churches, members, and denominations (mid-2000)	430	120,000	185,331	1.46	11	0	1	0	7	2	1
Total churches, members, and denominations (mid-2025)	550	175,000	270,000	1.52	35	0	1	0	20	10	4

(*6 Megablocs:* O, R, A, P, I, m)

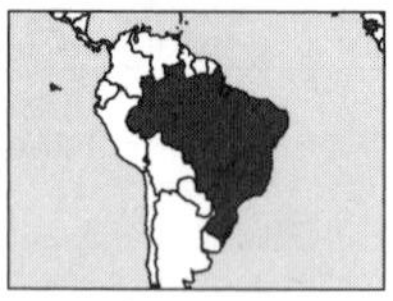

BRAZIL

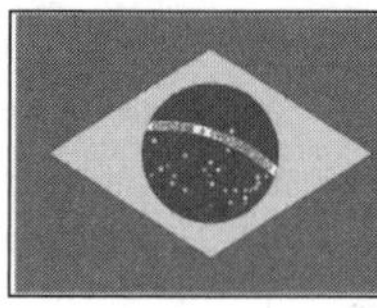

SECULAR DATA, AD 2000

STATE

Official name: La República Federativa do Brasil (The Federative Republic of Brazil).
Short name: Brazil. **Adjective of nationality:** Brazilian.
Flag: Green Field, centered yellow diamond with blue globe, 22 stars and motto.
Area: 8,547,404 sq. km. (3,300,171 sq. mi.).
Government: Multiparty federal republic with two legislative houses since, 1985 (1500 Portuguese rule, 1822 Independence as empire, 1889 United States of Brazil, 1964 military junta).
Legislature: National Congress: Senate, 81 members; Chamber of Deputies, 513 members.
Official language: Portuguese (Portugués).
Monetary unit: 1 real = 100 centavos. **US$1=** 1.18 reais.
Chief cities: Sao Paulo 17,711,000; Rio de Janeiro (Rio) 10,556,000; Belo Horizonte 4,160,000; Porto Alegre 3,699,000; Recife 3,307,000.
Political divisions: 27 provinces.
Armed forces: 337,000.

DEMOGRAPHY

Population: 170,115,000.
Population density: 19.9/sq. km. (51.5/sq. mi.).
Under 15 years: 49,078,000.
Growth rate p.a.: 1.20% (births 19.22, deaths 7.22).
Mortality: Infant, per 1,000: 38.3; **Maternal per 100,000:** 220.0.
Life expectancy: 68 (male 64, female 72).
Household size: 4.2. **Floor area per person, sq.m:** 10.0.
Major languages: Portuguese, German, French, English, Italian, Spanish, Japanese, Russian, Arabic, Polish, Chinese, and over 150 smaller languages.
Urban dwellers: 81.28%. **Urban growth rate p.a.:** 1.7%.
Labor force: 44%.

ETHNOLINGUISTIC PEOPLES

51.7% Brazilian White (Branco); 22.0% Brazilian Mulato; 12.0% Brazilian Mestico; 11.0% Brazilian Black; 0.8% Japanese.

ECONOMY

National income p.a. per person: US$3,640; **per family:** US$15,287.

EDUCATION

Adult literacy: 83% (male 83%, female 83%). **Schools:** 208,147.
Universities: 873. **School enrolment:** female/male: 96%/96%.

HEALTH

Access to health services: 45%. **Access to safe water:** 72%.
Hospitals: 35,701 (37 beds per 10,000). **Doctors:** 208,966.
Blind: 60,700. **Deaf:** 10,152,100. **Murder rate:** 12.
Lepers: 280,000. **Underweight prevalence under 5:** 7%.

LITERATURE

New book titles p.a.: 22,970 (135 p.a. per million). **Periodicals:** 5,295. **Newspapers:** 317 dailies.

COMMUNICATION (per 1,000 people)

Phones: 78 **(28% mobile). Radios:** 340. **TV sets:** 278.
Daily newspaper circulation: 45. **Computers:** 46.

REFUGEES

Alien refugees from other countries: 2,000.

HUMAN LIFE AND LIBERTY (optimum condition=100.0%)

HDI: 78.3. **HSI:** 50.0. **HFI:** 45.0. **EFL:** 31.0.

Country status. Brazil is the largest country in South America and also the largest Portuguese-speaking country in the world. Its population is one of the largest ethnic melting pots in the world with white, Indian, and black elements. One third of the world's remaining tropical rainforests are in the Amazon River Basin. The main source of income for Brazil is agriculture but minerals such as iron, gold, and phosphates are gradually gaining in importance.

HUMAN LIFE AND LIBERTY

Human need and development. Wide disparities between the rich and the poor have characterized Brazilian society throughout the centuries, but they have become more accentuated since World War II.

Country Table 1. **Religious adherents in Brazil, AD 1900-2025.**

Year	1900		1970		mid-1990		Annual change, 1990-2000				mid-1995		mid-2000		mid-2025	
Name	*Adherents*	*%*	*Adherents*	*%*	*Adherents*	*%*	*Natural*	*Conversion*	*Total*	*Rate*	*Adherents*	*%*	*Adherents*	*%*	*Adherents*	*%*
Christians	**17,319,000**	**96.3**	**91,628,000**	**95.4**	**136,496,000**	**92.3**	**2,046,011**	**-141,109**	**1,904,901**	**1.31**	**146,266,400**	**91.8**	**155,545,014**	**91.4**	**195,848,000**	**89.9**
PROFESSION																
professing Christians	**17,319,000**	**96.3**	**91,628,000**	**95.4**	**136,496,000**	**92.3**	**2,046,011**	**-141,109**	**1,904,901**	**1.31**	**146,266,400**	**91.8**	**155,545,014**	**91.4**	**195,848,000**	**89.9**
AFFILIATION																
unaffiliated Christians	0	0.0	120,740	0.1	78,000	0.1	1,169	-2,029	-860	-1.16	76,400	0.1	69,405	0.0	48,000	0.0
affiliated Christians	**17,319,000**	**96.3**	**91,507,260**	**95.3**	**136,418,000**	**92.2**	**2,044,795**	**-139,034**	**1,905,761**	**1.32**	**146,190,000**	**91.7**	**155,475,609**	**91.4**	**195,800,000**	**89.9**
Roman Catholics	17,200,000	95.6	85,119,393	88.7	134,000,000	90.6	2,008,551	-78,551	1,930,000	1.35	144,000,000	90.4	153,300,000	90.1	190,000,000	87.2
Protestants	200,000	1.1	7,225,746	7.5	25,600,000	17.3	383,723	76,277	460,000	1.67	27,904,085	17.5	30,200,000	17.8	45,000,000	20.7
Independents	3,000	0.0	5,092,510	5.3	21,500,000	14.5	322,267	77,733	400,000	1.72	23,534,690	14.8	25,500,000	15.0	36,000,000	16.5
Marginal Christians	1,000	0.0	262,611	0.3	1,050,000	0.7	15,739	21,261	37,000	3.06	1,206,360	0.8	1,420,000	0.8	3,000,000	1.4
Orthodox	2,000	0.0	109,000	0.1	135,000	0.1	2,024	1,476	3,500	2.33	143,000	0.1	170,000	0.1	220,000	0.1
Anglicans	300	0.0	45,000	0.1	95,000	0.1	1,424	1,576	3,000	2.78	105,000	0.1	125,000	0.1	170,000	0.1
doubly-affiliated	-87,300	-0.5	-6,347,000	-6.6	-45,962,000	-31.1	-688,933	-238,806	-927,739	1.86	-50,703,135	-31.8	-55,239,391	-32.5	-78,590,000	-36.1
Trans-megabloc groupings																
Evangelicals	180,000	1.0	6,000,000	6.3	22,940,000	15.5	343,852	137,048	480,900	1.92	25,396,887	15.9	27,749,000	16.3	42,236,000	19.4
Pentecostals/Charismatics	0	0.0	6,950,000	7.2	68,500,000	46.3	1,026,759	118,241	1,145,000	1.56	74,255,525	46.6	79,950,000	47.0	108,965,000	50.0
Great Commission Christians	**540,000**	**3.0**	**6,721,000**	**7.0**	**20,415,000**	**13.8**	**306,004**	**73,244**	**379,248**	**1.72**	**22,300,000**	**14.0**	**24,207,478**	**14.2**	**34,000,000**	**15.6**
Spiritists	137,000	0.8	2,540,000	2.7	6,620,000	4.5	99,228	71,456	170,684	2.32	7,372,000	4.6	8,326,844	4.9	11,200,000	5.1
Nonreligious	10,000	0.1	780,000	0.8	2,900,000	2.0	43,469	66,286	109,755	3.26	3,630,000	2.3	3,997,551	2.4	7,500,000	3.4
Atheists	1,000	0.0	200,000	0.2	490,000	0.3	7,345	1,138	8,483	1.61	530,000	0.3	574,829	0.3	850,000	0.4
New-Religionists	0	0.0	160,000	0.2	370,000	0.3	5,546	1,334	6,880	1.72	410,000	0.3	438,797	0.3	700,000	0.3
Buddhists	1,000	0.0	313,000	0.3	370,000	0.3	5,546	89	5,635	1.43	390,000	0.2	426,352	0.3	720,000	0.3
Jews	5,000	0.0	155,000	0.2	310,000	0.2	4,647	74	4,721	1.43	330,000	0.2	357,207	0.2	450,000	0.2
Ethnoreligionists	500,000	2.8	100,000	0.1	150,000	0.1	2,248	404	2,652	1.64	165,000	0.1	176,519	0.1	220,000	0.1
Muslims	10,000	0.1	90,000	0.1	150,000	0.1	2,248	69	2,317	1.45	161,000	0.1	173,173	0.1	270,000	0.1
Chinese folk-religionists	0	0.0	30,000	0.0	32,000	0.0	480	20	500	1.46	34,000	0.0	37,000	0.0	65,000	0.0
Baha'is	0	0.0	13,000	0.0	30,000	0.0	450	225	675	2.05	34,000	0.0	36,745	0.0	70,000	0.0
Hindus	0	0.0	5,000	0.0	8,000	0.0	120	62	182	2.07	9,000	0.0	9,820	0.0	15,000	0.0
Shintoists	0	0.0	2,000	0.0	6,000	0.0	90	-9	81	1.27	6,300	0.0	6,805	0.0	10,000	0.0
Other religionists	1,000	0.0	5,000	0.0	8,000	0.0	120	-39	81	0.96	8,300	0.0	8,806	0.0	12,000	0.0
World A (unevangelized persons)	305,728	1.7	480,103	0.5	443,820	0.3	6,676	-8,644	-1,968	-0.45	478,036	0.3	510,345	0.3	435,860	0.2
World B (evangelized non-Christians)	359,272	2.0	3,912,668	4.1	11,000,180	7.4	164,861	149,753	314,614	2.48	12,601,083	7.9	14,059,641	8.3	21,646,140	9.9
World C (Christians)	17,319,000	96.3	91,628,000	95.4	136,496,000	92.3	2,046,011	-141,109	1,904,901	1.31	146,266,400	91.8	155,545,014	91.4	195,848,000	89.9
Country's population	**17,984,000**	**100.0**	**96,020,772**	**100.0**	**147,940,000**	**100.0**	**2,217,547**	**0**	**2,217,547**	**1.41**	**159,345,520**	**100.0**	**170,115,000**	**100.0**	**217,930,000**	**100.0**

COLUMNS, ROWS.
For meanings and definitions, see Codebook (Part 3). Note that, by definition, total 'Christians' = professing + crypto-Christians, which also = affiliated + unaffiliated Christians, and also = Great Commission Christians + latent Christians. Percentages may not always total exactly, due to rounding.

CENSUSES.
31.XII.1890 (excluding jungle Indians): 98.9% Roman Catholics (14,179,615 persons), 1.0% Evangelicals (143,743 persons), 7,257 nonreligious, 1,327 positivists, 1,673 Orthodox, 300 Muslims. The religion question has been asked during several subsequent national population censuses, as follows. **1940:** 95.0% Roman Catholics, 2.6% Evangelicals (1,074,857 persons), 1.1% spiritists, 0.4% nonreligious. **1.VII.1950** (excluding jungle Indians): 93.7% Roman Catholics, 3.4% Evangelicals (1,741,430 persons), 1.6% spiritists, 0.5% nonreligious, 0.3% Buddhists, 0.1% Orthodox, 0.1% Jews, 0.3% other religionists. **1.IX.1970:** 91.8% Roman Catholics (including some spiritists), 5.2% Evangelicals (Protestants, Anglicans, marginal Protestants and Brazilian indigenous) (4,814,728 persons), 1.3% spiritists, 1.0% other religionists (including some classified in this survey as Brazilian indigenous), 0.8% nonreligious. **1.IX.1980:** 89.0% Roman Catholics, 6.6% Evangelicals, 1.3% Spiritists, 1.2% other religionists, 1.9% nonreligious. For many years, also, *Anuário estatístico do Brasil* has published statistics, but of affiliated Christians, i.e. Catholic and Evangelical communicant members gathered direct from municipios and counties, and thence from local churches, but not from church headquarters. Usually these compilations have omitted 10-30% of all Evangelical congregations. For 1933 this government publication listed 149,645 affiliated baptized Evangelical members in 730 local churches, with 13,486 annual baptisms.

NOTES ON RELIGIONS
AFFILIATED PROTESTANTS. In addition to communicants and their families, there are large numbers of adult attenders and adherents who cannot become communicants because of irregular marriages. In addition to Protestants and Evangelical Catholics as indicated above, there is also a large number of professing Roman Catholics sympathetic to Protestantism and committed to attendance in varying degrees. *Pentecostals.* Mostly of Mediterranean origin (Italian, Sicilian (half-Arab), Portuguese), and Mestico; very few Blacks (Negroes) are Pentecostals.
AFFILIATED ROMAN CATHOLICS. The total claimed by the church in 1990 (derived from Table 2) is somewhat higher than the government census of the same year because of double affiliation (see below).
ATHEISTS. Brazilian Communist Party (PCB) (pro-Soviet), Communist Party of Brazil (CPB) (pro-Chinese), (all communists proscribed 1947).
BAHA'IS. Entered before 1921. Recent rapid growth from 16 local spiritual assemblies (1964) to 87 (1973), with a huge leap to 198 LSAs (1996). Mainly in Bahia and northeastern states.
BUDDHISTS. Mostly Japanese (30% of all Japanese settlers and new immigrants), also Chinese and Koreans.
COUNTRY'S POPULATION. In the year 1800, 2.6 million (800,000 Whites, 1,800,000 Mulatto and Black slaves); 1860, 8.4 million; 1880, 11.7 million.
DOUBLY-AFFILIATED. The term covers those affiliated to, or claimed by, both the Catholic Church and also a church termed Evangélica by the state (Protestant, Independent, Anglican or marginal Protestant), i.e. baptized Catholics who have recently become Evangelicals or others. Because their statistics represent a duplication, they are shown in the table as a negative quantity (with a minus sign).
ETHNORELIGIONISTS. Jungle or lowland Amerindians, estimated at 2 million in the year 1500, had been reduced by massacres and assimilation to 500,000 in 230 tribes in 1900, to 200,000 in 1964, and in 1972 to 130,000 in only 140 tribes (91 in the Amazon basin, 35 in the center, 10 in the northeast, 4 in the south); of these in 1972, 36% were considered integrated into national life and 27% were marginally so. Many tribes retain traditional animism and have also produced modern reactionary cults.
EVANGELICALS. This English term, employed here as used and understood within the churches themselves (not as understood by the state), covers 3 main groupings: (1) Conservative Evangelicals, being all persons affiliated to Protestant denominations which are Conservative Evangelical in theology and emphasis; (2) Conciliar Evangelicals, affiliated to non-Evangelical Protestant denominations usually within the Ecumenical Movement; and (3) Fundamentalists, being all persons affiliated to Protestant denominations of fundamentalist emphasis usually affiliated to the ICCC.
HINDUS. A small number of communities, with a Samadhi Hindu Centre (Centro Hinduista Samadhi) in Rio de Janeiro, also 2 centers and a farm run by ISKCON (Hare Krishna), and others run by Ananda Marga.
INDEPENDENTS. In about 550 denominations in 1995 (see Table 2).
JEWS. Introduced first by immigrants from Germany and Central Europe, now with communities in Rio, São Paulo, Curitiba, Recife, and Belo Horizonte.
MARGINAL CHRISTIANS. As in most other majority-Catholic, Orthodox, Muslim, atheistic, and other non-Christian countries, marginal Protestants recorded in government censuses are considerably fewer than members known to those bodies.
MUSLIMS. In 1835 there was an unsuccessful revolt by the Muslim Males sect among African Negroes. Since 1948, many Palestinian, Lebanese, Syrian, Egyptian and other Arabs have immigrated from the Middle East. There were also Turks, and Yugoslavs, Pakistanis and others.
NEW-RELIGIONISTS. Japanese adherents and Brazilian converts of Soka Gakkai (centers in São Paulo and Rio de Janeiro, Seicho no Ie, Sekai Kyusei Kyo (Church of World Messianity; 70% being Whites), Tenrikyo, and other syncretistic New Religions from Japan.
OTHER RELIGIONISTS. Adherents of other non-Christian religions and cults, including Japanese Shintoists, Rosicrucians (97 AMORC Lodges and centers, 5 centers of Lectorium Rosicrucianum), et alii.
PENTECOSTALS/CHARISMATICS. Total adherents by AD 2000 number 80 million, which is some 15% of the entire global total.
In Brazil, the Catholic Charismatic Renewal began in 1971 and has subsequently mushroomed phenomenally. By 1996, there were 61,000 regular weekly prayer groups at parish level, with some 9 million regular adult attenders (60% or 5.4 million being young people under 25 years old). Also there were: 151 registered covenant communities, with more unregistered ones; 500 involved priests and 5 bishops. At one recent annual CCR meeting in São Paulo attenders numbered 120,000. Most large cities have an annual CCR rally at Pentecost with 20,000 to 40,000 attenders.
PROTESTANTS. In the year 1860, there were 25,000 Protestants; in 1900, 200,000 in 13 denominations.
SPIRITISTS. This term here, when used by itself alone, is restricted to non-Christian and non-Catholic followers of Kardecism or high spiritism (so named because of its emphasis on science, philosophy, and religion). In the census of 1.IX.1970, the number describing themselves as non-Christian spiritists (high or low) was 1.5 million of all ages including children. However, it is estimated that 30% of the nation's population has been affiliated at one time or another with organized spiritist activities, and 15% are estimated to be regularly and actively engaged in organized spiritism. Kardecism began in 1857 and became organized in 1884 as the Spiritist Federation of Brazil (Federação Espírita Brasileira, FEB); by 1958 it had 5,000 associations and a wide network of institutions including 31 hospitals, 77 homes, and 435 schools. Reincarnationist dogmas are also spread through the related movement of Rosicrucianism (AMORC, Fraternitas Rosa Crucis, Kabbalistic Order of Rosa Cruz, the Igreja Expectante).
SPIRITISTS. The term here is restricted to non-Catholic and non-Christian followers of Umbanda (White Magic), Quimbanda (Black Magic, or Kimbanda invoking Satan and malevolent spirits), and other Afro-Brazilian syncretistic religions including Batuque (in the south), Xangô (Shango, of Yoruba origin, in Pernambuco), Nago (of Maranhao), Catimbo (northeast), Pajelanca (in Amazonia), Macumba (a more violent form resembling Vodoun, with animal sacrifices), Candomblé (a form of Macumba in Bahia region, also called Afro-Amerindian fetishism), etc, all of which syncretize African and Amerindian traditional religions and animistic concepts with Catholicism, Kardecism, and oriental elements, and which are usually described collectively as low spiritism. Umbanda is not controlled centrally although there is a Confederation of Umbandist Spiritism; it is far more widespread throughout Brazil than Kardecism (high spiritism) and since 1973 has been expanding across Uruguay also. In addition to these non-Christian low spiritists, there are very large numbers of Roman Catholics involved, known as spiritist Catholics (see below). Adherents of low spiritism were, originally, African slaves, later mixed Blacks and Mulattoes, but now include large numbers of mixed blood and also Whites. The influence of these religions on the whole population is growing, and Macumba utilizes daily newspapers and radio/TV programs. Their extraordinary expansion is due to (1) opposition to spiritism within the Catholic Church and to the hierarchy's desire since Vatican II to purify Catholicism, as a result of which vast numbers of low spiritists have realized there can be no future for them in the church and now regard themselves as Catholics no longer; and (2) the influential role of medium religions in assisting rootless persons to adapt to urban mass life.
SPIRITIST CATHOLICS. This term is here restricted to Roman Catholics who are actively and regularly involved in the practice of the medium religions, high or low spiritism, mainly Afro-American low spiritists (Umbanda, Macumba, etc), as described above. In fact, however, a much larger proportion of all Catholics (around 30%, can be said to be affiliated to some degree with organized spiritism, and a large majority of all Catholics (over 60 million) defer to spiritist dogmas and participate from to time.

Great Commission Instrument Panel: status of Brazil (for explanation see start of Part 4)

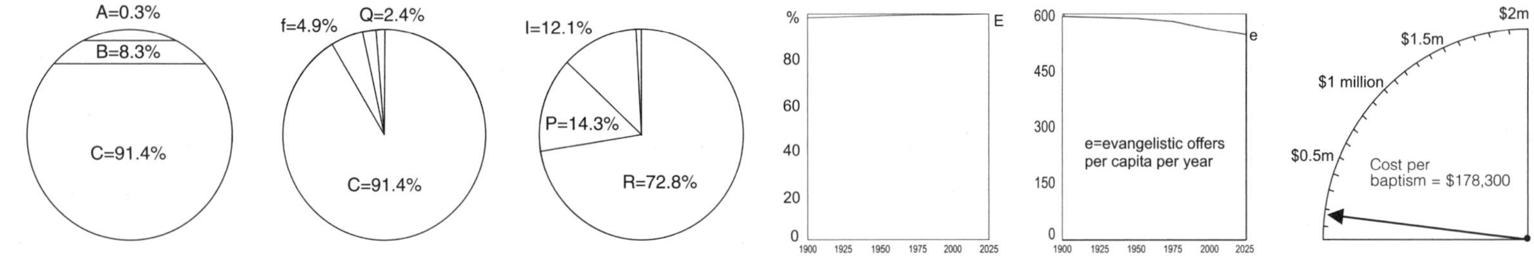

3 Worlds, AD 2000 | Religions, AD 2000 | Ecclesiastical blocs | Evangelization, 1900-2025 | Offers, 1900-2025 | Cost-effectiveness, AD 2000

Country summary. **Worlds A, B, C by ethnolinguistic peoples, cities, and major civil divisions in Brazil.**

World	PEOPLES Num	Pop 2000	C%	Christians	E%	U%	Unevangelized
A	16	80,991	4.48	3,630	47	53	42,719
B	91	1,034,503	18.77	194,212	76	24	250,548
C	117	168,999,959	91.88	155,277,779	100	0	132,458
Total	**224**	**170,115,453**	**91.39**	**155,475,621**	**100**	**0**	**425,725**

World	CITIES Num	Pop 2000	C%	Christians	E%	U%	Unevangelized
A	0	0	0.00	0	0	0	0
B	0	0	0.00	0	0	0	0
C	185	92,269,668	90.03	83,066,460	100	0	267,759
Total	**185**	**92,269,668**	**90.03**	**83,066,460**	**100**	**0**	**267,759**

World	CIVIL DIVISIONS Num	Pop 2000	C%	Christians	E%	U%	Unevangelized
A	0	0	0.00	0	0	0	0
B	0	0	0.00	0	0	0	0
C	27	170,115,516	91.39	155,475,609	100	0	425,777
Total	**27**	**170,115,516**	**91.39**	**155,475,609**	**100**	**0**	**425,777**

The slums of Rio and São Paulo have more in common with the slums of Bombay and Cairo than with urban settlements in the developed world. It is a world of stark poverty, illiteracy, murder and abuse of children, illegitimacy, crime, and drugs. Cheek by jowl with this world exists the rich and glittering world of high Brazilian society dedicated to conspicuous consumption and vacuous frivolities. Almost every Brazilian city has its slums, called favelas in Rio de Janeiro, corticos in São Paulo, malocas in Porto Alegre, and Belo Horizonte, macombos in Recife, alagados in Fortaleza, and cidade flutuante in Manaus. Some one-fourth of the country's population is believed to live in such slums. Other low-income families live in flophouses, called hospedarias, which rent beds nightly, or in rooming houses called cabecas de porco, single room cubicles occupied by entire families. Health hazards are directly related to poverty. Mortality rates and incidence of disease are higher in the poor southeast and northeast than elsewhere. Dietary deficiencies are a cause in the spread of parasitic diseases, the most significant cause of mortality. Endemic communicable diseases occur most frequently in the countryside and are then transferred by migrants into urban areas. In urban areas the most serious problem relates to abandoned children. With the breakdown of families, children are either evicted from their homes or tend to run away on their own, and end up in the streets as waifs. In São Paulo alone it is estimated that there are half a million abandoned children.

Human rights and freedoms. Brazil is a constitutional federal republic and the strength of its democratic commitment was demonstrated by the peaceful transfer of the presidency following the fall of Fernando Collor in 1992. The principal human rights problems are the high number of extrajudicial killings and death threats against rural activists by landowners and their agents, and against criminal suspects and minors in urban areas by vigilante groups. Human rights organizations have made credible charges that thugs are hired by policemen to deal rough and ready justice on the streets and on the farms. Among those killed are social activists, priests, union leaders, and human rights promoters. There are several cases of illegal and incommunicado detention without a judicial order. The judicial system is inefficient and has a serious backlog; many cases have not been tried for years. Lynchings of suspected criminals by irate citizens is an emerging problem. Discrimination on the basis of sex, race, religion, and nationality is unconstitutional and racial discrimination illegal. However, Black Brazilians encounter substantial de facto discrimination. About 40% to 60% of all Brazilians are of African and non-European ancestry, yet they are found in few positions of authority in public or private sectors or in the armed forces. There is strong discrimination in housing, education, the workplace and society at large. Blacks also bear the brunt of police brutality, and murder victims are predominantly black. Discrimination and violence against women are equally widespread. Several thousands of cases of violence against women are reported annually, especially in the major cities, and over 70% of such violence occur in the home. Indians number over 250,000, and their status has improved considerably in recent years, especially through the efforts of the National Foundation for the Indian (FUNAI). But land disputes between Indians and non-Indians have led to the murder of hundreds of Indians, the burning down of their houses and the destruction of their cattle. Illegal prospecting, aided by powerful local interest groups, continues on Indian lands. Indians receive little health care and must travel long distances to find healthcare facilities.

Human environment. The principal environmental problems are land degradation as a result of land erosion, widespread deforestation and the consequent loss of biodiversity, and water pollution as a result of the dumping of untreated sewage and industrial pollutants into the rivers. Brazil has the world's largest tropical forest which provides natural replacement for 15% or more of the world's oxygen. Land erosion is serious because of the poor soil cover in most regions. Where the forests have been cut down, the loss of top soil is estimated at 14 tons per acre annually.

Afro-American spiritists. During spiritist service in dishevelled Umbanda temple, girls prostrate themselves before spirit-possessed leader. Note altar, cross, sacred heart of Jesus, and other Christian symbols. Umbanda has some 33 million adherents in Brazil.

NON-CHRISTIAN RELIGIONS

Spiritism is still the principal non-Christian religion in Brazil. The term itself covers two distinct groups: non-Christian spiritists and spiritists who also regard themselves as Roman Catholics. Non-Christian spiritists were 1.8% of the population in 1940, increasing to 2.1% by 1950, and continued to grow to 5% by AD 2000. Introduced into Brazil in the middle of the 19th century, the French spiritism of Allan Kardec found a ready response and developed into an organized religion. It absorbed elements of popular Catholicism, in particular devotion to saints and the souls of the dead, as well as specific characteristics of cults of African origin. In addition to those who declare themselves spiritists in censuses, there are numerous others in high positions who regularly or occasionally attend spirit seances but who declare themselves to be Catholics. Not uncommonly, the term Catholic spiritists or spiritist Catholics is used to identify them. At present, spiritism again may be divided into two general categories: a high spiritism (*alto espiritismo*) adhering to Kardecist orthodoxy with a minority of adherents; and, low spiritism, syncretisms of Catholic and African elements including Umbanda with a larger popular following. In its purer form, Kardecism has been very active in the social welfare field, developing hospitals, schools, and other social service institutions.

Afro-American spiritism is the term used here to describe all forms of low spiritism. Of these, the best-known and most active is Umbanda. Each Umbanda center is autonomous. Voluntarily created, it recognizes no religious authority, doctrinal or ritual, which accounts for the plurality of its forms. Similarly to high spiritism, Umbanda sees no contradiction between its own practices and the beliefs of Catholicism. Most of its followers in fact regard themselves as Catholics. Today, its members are mostly urban, middle-class, with no racial distinctions. However, occasional members can also be found among the upper classes. Umbanda has resisted a concerted campaign of opposition from the Catholic Church for the past 50 years and displays great vitality, with centers multiplying throughout the country. There are also several other Afro-Brazilian religions known by different regional names. Candomblé in Bahia, Batuque in Pôrto Alegre, Xangô in Recife, and Macumba in Rio de Janeiro. Their greatest concentration, however, is in Bahia. These have all shown a remarkable capacity to adapt traditional African elements to the new conditions of life of modern Brazil.

Buddhism was introduced into Brazil by Japanese immigrants. Several temples, pagodas, and meditation centers for Buddhism's different denominations are located in the city and province of São Paulo. A Theravada Buddhist Center (*Centro Budista Theravada*) was established in Rio de Janeiro in 1968. **Judaism** was introduced into Brazil by Jewish immigrants from Germany and central Europe as well as by groups from the Near East. Judaism is represented by the Israelite Religious Association (*Associação Religiosa Israelita*) and councils connected with B'nai B'rith. Jewish communities are found in larger cities including Rio de Janeiro, São Paulo, Curitiba, Belo Horizonte, and Recife.

Amerindian tribal religions continue among the indigenous peoples including the Bororo, Nambi-kuara, and Yanomamo. In 1995, the Amerindian population was estimated at over 250,000 in 150 tribes, 91 being located in the Amazon basin, 35 in the central region of the country, 10 in the northeast and 4 in the south. Of the total, 35 tribes were then considered integrated into the national population, 34 tribes marginally, with the remainder more or less in touch with Whites but still preserving their own traditions. As in other South American countries, Indians have been victims of acts of genocide, and their numbers are decreasing rapidly. In reaction to this situation, a large number of Amerindian nativistic cults and movements have arisen from the 16th century up to the present.

Ethnoreligionists. Chief of the Gorotene tribe (a Kayapo language) and wife. This tribe is rapidly becoming extinct.

CHRISTIANITY

Little resistance was offered by Brazil's Indian tribes when in 1500 Pedro Alvares Cabral claimed the land in the name of Portugal, or later when sugar was introduced, in spite of the fact that large areas of land were allocated to a select number of Portuguese for its production. African slaves were brought in as Brazil became a major world source of sugar in the 17th century and a world supplier of gold and diamonds during the 18th century.

The first organized mission efforts among the Indians began in 1549 when Jesuits were sent to establish schools and churches. During the next century, cooperative Indian villages called reductions were established by the Jesuits in face of opposition by colonists and government. In 1580, 3 additional missionary congregations arrived, followed by 3 congregations of women in 1734 and, still later, the establishment of the first Brazilian religious congregation.

During the first half of the 17th century, intermittent warfare took place with the Dutch who were also seeking a foothold on the American continent. The fighting took on religious overtones with the Dutch being Protestants opposing the Catholic religion. Their partial introduction of Protestant worship was completely eliminated, as was true also of an earlier attempt by Huguenots in 1557 to introduce French Calvinism on Villegagnon island. During the 19th century, an increasing number of European immigrants entered Brazil. German Lutherans arrived in 1823 and established the first Protestant church in 1837. American Methodists appeared briefly in 1835 but did not remain. However, they returned again in 1885. The first continuous Protestant mission did not begin until 1855 with the arrival of LMS Scottish Presbyterians. American Presbyterians entered Brazil in 1859, and by 1888, the Presbyterian Church of Brazil was firmly established. Southern Baptists came in 1881, and in 1907, the Brazilian Baptist Convention was organized. The Anglican Church at first considered that this mission field should be left to Roman Catholics, but American Episcopalians began a mission there in 1889. Seventh-day Adventists came in 1902, and the Assemblies of God opened the first Pentecostal work in 1910. During this period, the Jesuits who had been expelled from Brazil in 1750 returned and new Catholic missions made their appearance. Some governmental reforms and secularization of institutions were initiated as Brazil's economy improved, with the country becoming a major producer of coffee and rubber. During the 1870s, the Catholic Church came increasingly under attack. Two bishops were imprisoned and Brazilians were forbidden to enter religious orders. The culmination of this movement was the separation of church and state as part of the inauguration of the republic in 1889. The 20th century has witnessed an extensive development of Catholic seminaries, primary and secondary schools, over 40 Brazilian religious congregations and the appearance of lay religious associations.

Spiritist Catholics. A large majority of Brazil's Roman Catholics, over 60 million, defer to spiritist dogmas and from time to time participate in such activities as (above) the Macumba feast of Iemanja. Yoruba goddess of the sea, symbol of fecundity, celebrated on many Brazilian beaches to start the new year, with offerings of flowers, candles et alia.

CATHOLIC CHURCH. While Catholicism continues to be the religion of the majority, its practice is uneven. In small towns Sunday mass attendance ranges from 60% to 70%; in rural areas slightly higher, although the celebration of mass is sporadic due to shortage of priests. In large cities and regions undergoing rapid social change, attendance averages 15%, and sometimes drops to 10%. The Catholicism practiced by the majority is a strongly individualistic religion, centered on devotion to saints and ancestral spirits, with the aim of seeking personal protection. For most of the faithful, it is perceived only marginally in relation to the church as an institution. The vast majority remain ignorant of Catholic doctrine. In recent years a new effort at renewal of Christian life has made its appearance as evidenced by the development of 2 national pastoral plans, the creation of ecclesial basic communities of variable size but localized in rural or poor urban areas, the adoption in 1972 of a 'sister churches' program whereby dioceses with more resources aid poorer diocese, and a greater concern for evangelization and social action aimed at humanization.

In terms of structure, the Catholic Church experienced a rapid growth in the number of jurisdictions, from 19 in 1900 to 114 in 1950, 154 in 1960, 200 in 1970, and 255 in 1990. The number of parishes increased from 4,455 in 1963 to 5,577 in 1970, and 35,598 in 1990.

Of special note is the large Japanese community in Brazil, rising to 700,000 by 1975 and to nearly 1.3 million by 1995, of whom more than 70% were Christians. There are in fact nearly twice as many Japanese Catholics in Brazil as in Japan itself.

A progressive Catholic minority is active in specialized Catholic Action movements and in the Basic Education Movement at the community level, movements which operate in opposition to a majority of the bishops and which were nearly destroyed by the military regime in the 1970s. Chaplains of these movements and priests supporting other allegedly subversive movements were imprisoned and tortured. In contrast, ultra-conservative groups have also been active, such as the Family Rosary Crusade and the Group for the Restoration of the Rosary, which contributed to the success of the Family Marches with God for Liberty which contributed to the fall of the democratic regime in 1964. In the 1990s, some leaders, concerned about the hundreds of thousands of members leaving the Roman Catholic church for Evangelical and especially Pentecostal churches, have supported the global 'Evangelization 2000' initiative and have promoted new and vigorous evangelistic and renewal activities. An Evangelical commentator asserted, 'They are imitating Assemblies of God worship, singing our songs, and studying how to recoup their losses'. In response, Catholic leaders emphasized their desire to stem the growing tide of secularism in the rapidly-changing society of modern Brazil.

Igreja Catolica em Brasil. Cathedral of archdiocese of Brasilia.

The Holy See has diplomatic relations with Brazil and in AD 2000 is represented to government and the Catholic hierarchy by a nuncio residing in Brasilia.

PROTESTANT CHURCHES. Protestantism may be classified in 3 categories: (1) traditional mainline denominations owing their origin to the missionary outreach of North American churches beginning in the second half of the 19th century; (2) Pentecostal groups which began with the arrival of the Assemblies of God (USA) in 1910; and (3) Conservative Evangelical bodies from the USA which have proliferated since World War II. Of these 3, Pentecostals are the largest and display the greatest growth and vitality. Professing Evangelicals as a whole increased from 2.6% of the population in 1940 to 16.0% by 1995. In the first category, the principal denominations are Baptists, Lutherans, Adventists, Presbyterians, and Methodists.

Among Protestant churches, the Brazilian Baptist Convention is second in size only to the Assemblies of God and is one of the fastest-growing of the non-Pentecostal churches

The large Evangelical Church of the Lutheran Confession has its strength among Germans in southern Brazil. It maintains fraternal relations with the Evangelical Lutheran Church in America. A schism in 1890 produced the Lutheran Evangelical Church of Brazil which is related to the Missouri Synod. Seventh-day Adventists have built up a large membership which continues to grow rapidly. Part of their success has been due to their emphasis on radio and correspondence courses. The Presbyterian Church of Brazil's first joint synod was held in 1888. In 1903, a schism occurred which resulted in the formation of the Independent Presbyterian Church. Other schisms have produced the Conservative Presbyterians in 1940 and the Fundamentalist Presbyterians in 1956. Methodists were among the earliest to begin evangelistic outreach in Brazil, but their growth has been slower than that of the other major denominations. The church has been autonomous since 1930. Small Free Methodist and Wesleyan groups also exist.

Although the membership of these churches is large in comparison to other Latin American countries, their growth has not kept pace with the enormous increase in Pentecostalism in recent years. The Pentecostal movement began with the arrival of two Swedish ministers from Chicago in 1910. From this early initiative has grown up a complex group of churches, some of which maintain relations with foreign missionary societies while others are completely independent. In the former category are the Assemblies of God, which today represent the largest non-Catholic denomination in the country. They have placed emphasis on the training of laymen at large central mother churches, who then go out to plant satellite churches in surrounding areas. In contrast to the historical denominations which have concentrated their attention on the south, the Assemblies of God are found in every state and actually have their greatest membership in the north and northeast.

Many Conservative Evangelical faith missions are now at work in Brazil, a large number of which have made their appearance since World War II. Most are small with leadership concentrated largely in the hands of foreign missionaries. Several are working exclusively with unevangelized Indian tribes in the interior.

INDIGENOUS CHURCHES. Except for the Brazilian Catholic Apostolic Church, which was a schism from Catholicism in 1945 by the former Catholic bishop of Botucatu, the major independent churches are postdenominationalist in nature. The most important are the Christian Congregation of Brazil, which originated in 1910 among Italian immigrants and now is widely spread in the states of Sao Paulo and Parana, and the Evangelical Pentecostal Church 'Brazil for Christ', which emerged out of the Assemblies of God in 1955. Most independent pentecostal churches have been formed since 1945.

The largest indigenous church in Brazil is the Universal Church of the Kingdom of God, with 4 million affiliated in 1995. It is noted for rapid growth, for its hangar-like main building, for extensive use of radio and TV, for support of political candidates, for extensive and diverse social ministry, for ecumenism, and for controversy. The mother church building in São Paulo seats 25,000 under an arched-girder roof with a 230-foot clear span and is declared to be the 'largest evangelical temple in the world'. Controversy came to a head in 1995 when a bishop of the church destroyed a statue of Brazil's patron saint, Our Lady of the Immaculate Conception, on TV, an event that sent the religious life of the nation into turmoil. The bishop was admonished and removed from his post by the church's founder and leader, Edir Macedo. Macedo himself has come under severe attack from Catholics and government agencies, suffering accusations ranging from tax evasion, to unethical fund-raising, to lewd behavior.

Art and architecture. Brazil's most famous Christian architectural monument is the Cathedral at Brasilia in the form of a Crown of Thorns. Also remarkable are the Church of Dom Bosco, the Igrejinha, built largely of blue glass, the Fatima Church in Asa Sul and the Chapel of Dom Bosco opposite the Alvorado. There are many attractive churches in Rio de Janeiro, most of them with serene exteriors and lavishly decorated interiors. The Cathedral Church of Sao Sebastiao in the Rua Primeiro de Marco was built between 1749 and 1770. In its crypt are the bones of Pedro Alvares Cabral, the discoverer of Brazil. The new cathedral is on the Avenida Republica de Chile.

Other churches include the Church of Sao Francisco de Paula built in 1759, the Church of Nossa Senhora de Candelaria, founded in 1610, the doubletowered church of Santa Luzia built in 1752, the Church of the Holy Military Cross built in 1781, the Nossa Senhora de Gloria do Outeiro, the favorite church of the imperial family and of Dom Pedro II, who was baptized here and the Church of Nossa Senhora de Penha, cut out of a rock. There are 2 old convents in the city: the Convent of Carmo and the Convent of Santo Antonio as well as the Monastery of Santo Bento, which contains the best of 17th and 18th century Brazilian religious art. The Cathedral of São Paulo, built in neo-Gothic style, is one of the largest cathedrals in South America, with a capacity of 8,000 worshippers. Salvador, the capital of Brazil until 1763, has over 70 churches, such as the Church of São Francisco de Assis, the Church of the Ordem Terceira, the Cathedral Terreiro de Jesus, Santa Casa de Misericordia, and the church and monastery of Nossa Senhora do Carmo. There are many old churches in Recife: São Francisco de Assis, São Pedro dos Clergios, Santo Antonio, Conceição dos Militares, Madre de Deus, Pilar Church, Igreja de Espirito Santo, Igreja de Santo Antonio, do Convento de Sao Francisco, and the Capela Dourada, or the Golden Chapel. Brazil also has some of the finest Christian museums in the world. Noteworthy are the Museum of Our Lady of Aparecida, the Archdiocesan Museum of Brusque, Museum of Imperial Chapel, Ecclesiastical Museum and 2 Museums of Religious Art in São Paulo, Museum of the Monastery of San Antonio and Museum of the Order of St Francis in Rio de Janeiro, Museum of the Carmelite Convent and two museums of religious art in Salvador, and diocesan museums and local museums of religious art at Vitoria, Sobral, Sant'ana do Parnaiba, Recife, Pirapora, Niteroi, Mariana, Maceio, Laguna, Lapa, Ilheus, Goias, Igaracu, Jaragua do Sul, Corupa, Cachoeira, Cajazeiras, and Campinas.

Renewal movements. In the 1990s the Pentecostal/Charismatic Renewal continued to spread rapidly across most older churches, and numbered over 79,950,000 adherents (of whom 32% Pentecostals, 42% Charismatics, and 27% Independents).

Indigenous missions. Several thousand foreign missionaries are sent out by the Catholic and Protestant churches of Brazil. However, the vast majority of these serve Brazilian expatriates in the United States and Europe. Recently, growing numbers of Brazilians are working among Muslims in North Africa.

CHURCH AND STATE

Though church and state are separate in law, the state still regards itself as religious, and the constitution of 1967 was promulgated by the National Congress 'invoking the protection of God'. In the introduction, it guarantees liberty of conscience and the free exercise of religious worship, on condition that these are not contrary to public order or good morals (Article 150.4).

Until 1889, Brazil was under a regime in which the state and the Catholic Church were united. The proclamation of the republic created a juridical separation which however only gradually brought about an alteration in relations between the 2, particularly between the Catholic hierarchy and government leaders. The traditional connection between church and state was reestablished in the 1934 constitution but was severed again in 1946.

In the 1960s there were many sharp instances of confrontation and conflict between the churches and the heavy-handed, dictatorial regime. There was no serious conflict between church and state at the constitutional or juridical level. Opposition was rather confined to individuals or groups of Catholics disturbed by the economic situation and government policies.

A survey of the first decade of the military regime in Brazil revealed that more than 500 priests were victims of a form of repression (imprisonment, torture, expulsion) and that thousands of lay militants of Catholic movements have suffered the same or an even more serious fate.

Nevertheless, the dominant note in church-state relations continues to be a desire for harmony and collaboration made possible by the systematic representation of the Catholic Church at official functions to the virtual exclusion of all other churches.

On 15 April 1974, for the first time in the history of the 'largest Catholic country in the world', a Protestant, general Ernesto Geisel, became president of the republic. Paradoxically, a certain relaxation of tension between the Catholic Church and the state followed, the principal reason being the assumption that the new president would adopt a less rigid political and social policy. The new president achieved a limited detente in relations with the Catholic Church, but police repression continued, especially of the Christian worker movement and social action in São Paulo.

In 1977, trouble arose for Protestant missions when 84 workers of Wycliffe Bible Translators were ordered out of Indian areas by end of the year.

By 1978, a temporary crisis had arisen concerning government refusal to grant entry visas for missionaries. Up to May 1977, 500 new missionaries or religious personnel had been admitted each year. Over the following 12 months, however, only 65 Catholic visas and six Protestant ones were issued.

In the early 1990s Brazil's Bureau of Indian Affairs continued to take actions that hindered the work of missionaries in the Amazon. Partly in response to the Brazilian Anthropologists Association, the Bureau issued a series of more and more restrictive and demanding rulings that made it virtually illegal for missionaries to enter tribes, even Brazilian missionaries or tribal Christians from other tribes.

BROADCASTING AND MEDIA

Brazil is saturated with a wealth of Christian broadcasting from both within and without. AWR has a studio which develops Portuguese-language programs. Brazil is a member of UNDA. There are two Catholic TV studios which produce local broadcasts, and 1,557 AM and 1,208 FM stations in the country, nearly all of which feature Catholic programs. Some programs are found on over 500 stations. There are 122 Catholic-owned stations, leaving no province uncovered. In addition, shortwave programs from HCJB (Ecuador), TWR (Antilles), KNLS and AWR (Costa Rica) can be easily received.

Portuguese versions of CBN's *700 Club* can be seen on 2 local channels each Wednesday. TBN programs are aired in 21 cities on several local TV stations.

The 'Jesus' film has been shown to 6 million people: mainly through television (4.2 million) and film teams (1.5 million). Mission agencies have used the film widely to reach 234,000 people.

INTERDENOMINATIONAL ORGANIZATIONS

There are a fair number of national councils and fellowships at work, but considerably fragmented.

FUTURE TRENDS AND PROSPECTS

Roman Catholic affiliation will probably drop off slightly into the 21st century resulting in church membership of 87% by 2025. A marked resurgence among Protestants and postdenominational churches is expected.

Christians will probably decline below 85% by 2050. Nonreligious persons and other non-Christians would then take their place jointly reaching 15% shortly after.

A missionary ship 'Light of the Amazon II' brings evangelism, scriptures, and a variety of aid and relief services.

BIBLIOGRAPHY

'A history of Protestant missions to Brazil, 1850–1914.' W. Wedemann. Thesis, Southern Baptist Theological Seminary, Louisville, KY, 1977. 292p.

'A history of the Christian Evangelical Church in Brazil.' E. P. Velasco. Th.M. thesis, Reformed Theological Seminary, 1992. 330p.

A Igreja no Brasil. A. Gregory. Louvain: FERES, 1965. 227p.

A mitología heroica de tribos indígenas do Brasil: ensaio etno–sociológico. E. Schaden. [Rio de Janeiro]: Ministerio da Educação e Cultura, [1959]. 183p. (Summary in English).

'A sociological analysis of the development of Brazilian Protestantism: a study in social change.' R. G. Frase. Thesis, Princeton Theological Seminary, Princeton, NJ, 1975. 605p.

A Umbanda no Brasil: orientação para os Católicos. B. Kloppenburg. Petropolis: Editôra Vozes, 1960. 263p.

'Afro–Brazilian religious cults,' K. Oberg, *Sociologia*, 21, 2 (1959), 131–41.

'An analytical history of the Church of Christ missions in Brazil.' H. R. Baird. D.Miss. thesis, Fuller Theological Seminary, Pasadena, CA, 1979. 162p.

Anuário Católico do Brasil, 1970–71. Rio de Janeiro: CERIS, 1972. 2292p.

Base Christian communities and social change in Brazil. W. E. Hewitt. Lincoln, NE: University of Nebraska Press, 1991. 166p.

Basic ecclesial communities in Brazil: the challenge of a new way of being church. M. de Carvalho Azevedo. *Studies in ethics.* Washington, DC: Georgetown University Press, 1987. 317p.

'Brasil para Cristo: the cultural construction of pentecostal networks in Brazil.' J. Page. Ph.D. dissertation, New York University, 1984. 525p.

Brazil 1980: the Protestant handbook: the dynamics of church growth in the 1950's and 60's, and the tremendous potential for the 70's. W. R. Read & F. A. Ineson. Monrovia, CA: MARC, [1973]. 435p.

'Brazil: the church in process of renewal,' *Pro Mundi Vita* (Brussels), 24 (1968).

'Capitalism and religion at the periphery: Pentecostalism and Umbanda in Brazil,' G. N. Howe, in *Perspectives on Pentecostalism*, p.125–41. S. D. Glazier (ed). Lanham, MD: University Press of America, 1980.

Catholic radicals in Brazil. E. de Kadt. London: Oxford University Press, 1970.

Católicos, Protestantes, Espíritas. C. P. F. de Camargo. Petropolis: Editôra Vozes, 1973.

Church and state in Dutch Brazil (1630–1654). F. L. Scalkwijk. Zoetermeer, Netherlands: Boekencentrum, 1988. 320p.

'Conflict and change in the Brazilian Catholic Church.' T. C. Bruneau. Ph.D. dissertation, University of California, Berkeley, 1970. 435p.

Coping with poverty: Pentecostals and Christian base communities in Brazil. C. L. Mariz. Philadelphia: Temple University Press, 1994. 204p.

'Essai de typologie du Catholicisme brésilien,' C. P. F. de Camargo, *Social compass* (Louvain), 14, 5-6 (1967), 399–422.

'Evangelical worship in Brazil: its origins and development.' C. J. Hahn. Thesis, University of Edinburgh, 1970. 600p.

Followers of the new faith: culture change and the rise of Protestantism in Brazil and Chile. E. Willems. Nashville, TN: Vanderbilt University Press, 1967. 290p.

Il sincretismo religioso afro–cattolico in Brasile. T. Sepilli. Bologna (Italy): N. Zanichelli, 1955. 2 parts.

Kardecismo e Umbanda: uma interpretação sociológica. C. P. F. de Camargo. São Paulo: Livraria Pioneira Editôa, 1961. 196p.

Kingdoms come: religion and politics in Brazil. R. Ireland. *Pitt Latin American series.* Pittsburgh, PA: University of Pittsburgh Press, 1991. 273p.

'La secte musulmane des Males au Brésil et leur revolte en 1835,' I. Etienne, *Anthropos*, 4 (1909), 99–105, 405–15. (A liturgical Negro Muslim sect).

Le Candomblé de Bahia (rite Nagó). R. Bastide. The Hague: Mouton, 1958. (Full bibliography on African religions in Brazil).

L'Eglise et la politique au Brésil. M. Moreira-Alves. Paris: Editions du Cerf, 1974. 263p.

Looking for God in Brazil: the progressive Catholic Church in urban Brazil's religious arena. J. Burdick. Berkeley, CA: University of California Press, 1993. 292p.

Lutherans in Brazil, 1990: history, theology, perspectives. G. Brakemeier & W. Altmann (eds). São Leopoldo: Post-Graduate Studies Institute of the IECLB, 1989. 102p.

'Messiahs in Brazil,' M. I. Pereira de Queiroz, *Past and present*, 31 (July, 1965), 62–86.

'Mormonism in Brazil: religion and dependency in Latin America.' M. L. Grover. Ph.D. dissertation, Indiana University, Bloomington, IN, 1985. 336p.

New patterns of church growth in Brazil. W. R. Read. Grand Rapids, MI: Eerdmans, 1965. 240p.

O Messianismo: no Brasil e no mundo. M. I. Pereira de Queiroz. São Paulo: Editôra da Universidade de São Paulo, 1965. 385p.

'Pastors, prophets and politicians: a study of the Brazilian Catholic Church, 1916–1945.' M. P. Todaro. Ph.D. dissertation, Columbia University, New York, 1971. 550p.

Pentecostais no Brasil. R. F. Cartaxo. Petropolis: Vozes, 1985.

'Pentecostalismo em São Paulo.' B. M. de Souza. Ph.D. dissertation, Universidade de Campinas, Campinas, Brazil, 1967. 169p.

'Persistence of spiritism in Brazil.' J. P. Wiebe. D.Miss. thesis, Fuller Theological Seminary, Pasadena, CA, 1979. 197p.

Promised land: base Christian communities and the struggle for the Amazon. M. Adriance. *SUNY series in religion, culture, and society.* Albany, NY: State University of New York

Press, 1995. 224p.
'Protestantism and politics in Chile and Brazil,' F. C. Turner, *Comparative studies in society and history*, 12, 2 (1970), 213–29.
Protestantism and repression: a Brazilian case study. R. Alves. Maryknoll, NY: Orbis Books, 1985.
Religion and politics in urban Brazil. D. D. U. Brown. Ann Arbor, MI: UMI Research Press, 1985.
'Religion and racial identity in the movimento negro of the Roman Catholic church in Brazil.' A. D. Myatt. Ph.D. dissertation, Iliff School of Theology and the University of Denver (Colorado Seminary), Denver, CO, 1995. 292p.
'Religion in Brazil: a sociological approach to religion and its integrative function in rural–urban migrant adjustment.' H. W. Melvin Jr. Ph.D. dissertation, Boston University, Boston, 1971. 358p.
Religionen in Brasilien. M. Gerbert. Berlin: Colloquium Verlag, 1970.
'Roman Catholicism in Brazil,' D. E. Mutchler, *Studies in comparative international development*, 1, 8 (1965), 103–117.
Spirits and scientists: ideology, spiritism, and Brazilian culture. D. J. Hess. University Park, PA: Pennsylvania State University Press, 1991. 272p.
The African religions in Brazil: toward a sociology of the interpenetration of civilizations. R. Bastide. Baltimore, MD: Johns Hopkins University Press, 1978. (Includes long lexicon of terms; see also 1960 French edition).
'The Brazilian popular church in crisis: local religion and global capitalism.' M. A. Vásquez. Ph.D. dissertation, Temple University, Philadelphia, 1994. 2 vols.
The Catholic church and politics in Brazil. S. Mainwaring. Stanford, CA: Stanford University Press, 1986.
'The Catholic Church in Brazil: a sociological perspective,' A. Gregory, in *Report of International Conference of Sociology of Religion*, p.143–64. Lille, France: 1973.
The expectation of the poor: Latin American base ecclesial communities in Protestant perspective. G. Cook. Maryknoll, NY: Orbis Books, 1985.
'The growth of Japanese churches in Brazil.' J. Mizuki. D.Miss. thesis, Fuller Theological Seminary, Pasadena, CA, 1976. 290p.
The political transformation of the Brazilian Catholic Church. T. C. Bruneau. London: Cambridge University Press, 1974. 270p.
'The religious heritage of Africa in Brazil,' J. G. Piepke, *Verbum SVD*, 33, 2 (1992), 165–84.
'The revival in Latvia during the 1920s and subsequent Baptist immigration to Brazil.' O. Bruvers. Ph.D. dissertation, Fuller Theological Seminary, Pasadena, CA, 1991. 297p.

Country Table 2. **Organized churches and denominations in Brazil.**

Official name (bold type = church with over 10% of all affiliated) 1	*Begun* 2	*Type* 3	*Counc* 4	*Congs* 5	*Adults* 6	*Affiliated 1970* 7	*Affiliated 1995* 8	*G%* 9	*Names, notes, and other statistics* (see Codebook, Part 3) 10
Aliança Biblica do Brasil	1958	P-Non	xM...	5	1,000	250	2,330	9.34	*Biblical Alliance.* M=Pan-American Mission (WIM) (USA). 1n,4x,14f,1s,W=90%,12Y,93z.
Aliança Cristã e Missionária	1962	P-Hol	xF...	13	629	300	1,573	6.85	M=Christian & Missionary Alliance (USA). 50% Japanese. 8x,10f,W=97%,13Y.
Aliança das Igrejas Cristãs Ev do Brasil	1931	P-Eva	xF...	434	8,700	20,000	22,900	0.54	*Alliance of Christian Ev Chs.* M=UFM(UK, USA). In north, 13m,138f,8h,1s,W=83%,80Y.
Alianca Evangelica Missionaria	1970	P-Eva	.....	12	300	–	500	28.22	*The Evangelical Alliance Mission.* M=TEAM.
Assembleias de Deus	1910	P-Pe2	ZF..N	85,000	14,400,000	4,000,000	22,000,000	7.06	*Assemblies of God.* 1934,M=AoG,SFM,NPY,FFFM. 30000n,27000mw,20f.
Assambleias Locales	c1970	I-3nC	.....	353	19,225	–	30,000	51.04	*Local Churches. Little Flock. Assembly Hall Chs.* Chinese (1922, China).
Assoc das Igs Congregaçionais Biblicas	1970	I-Con	.TT.T	40	4,000	2,000	8,890	6.15	*Association of Congregational Bible Chs of Brazil.* Ex IECC(EUSA). HQ São Paulo.
Associacão das Igrejas Luteranas Livres	1964	I-Lut	.....	12	480	350	800	3.36	*Association of Free Lutheran Churches.*
Ass dos Batistas Evangelismo Mundial	1942	I-Bap	x....	143	5,000	5,000	12,500	3.73	M=Assoc of Baptists for World Evangelism (ABWE) (USA). 74f,2s.
Ass Ev de Catequese dos Indios Caiuas	1928	P-Ref	.....	10	500	900	1,000	0.42	*Ev Association for Indian Teaching.* Works in Caiua tribe. 4n,W=50%,105Y,150z.
Associação Evangélica Menonita	1955	P-Men	G....	25	1,200	3,000	2,400	-0.89	*Ev Mennonite Association.* M=Brazil Mennonite Mission (MCNA); Araguacema. 2f.
Assoc Geral das Igs Batistas Regulares	1939	P-Bap	.TT.T	75	3,000	5,000	6,000	0.73	*General Assoc of Regular Baptist Chs.* Assisted by USA missionaries. 1n,W=50%.
Con Bras des Ig dos Irmãos Menonitas	1930	P-Men	GF...	23	1,800	5,000	2,500	-2.73	*AIIM. Mennonite Brethren Ch.* M=MBCNA. German-speaking ex-USSR immigrants. 134f,1p.
Congregação Cristã do Brasil	1910	I-3pY	.....	15,294	1,560,000	1,000,000	3,120,000	4.66	*Christian Congregation of B.* Italian origins. States: 53% in SPaulo, 30% Paraná.
Congregação da Ciéncia Cristã		m-Sci	x....	4	180	1,000	360	0.05	*Ch of Christ, Scientist. Christian Science.* M=CCS(Boston, USA). 2m,7w.
Congregação dos Missionários DSTS		I-ReC	.v...	10	1,500	2,000	3,000	0.05	*DSTS=Discipulos da Santíssima Trindade, Séde.* Ex RCC. HQ Caetés. 1970 applied to WCC.
Convenção Batista Brasileira	1881	P-Bap	T....	4,810	902,000	1,050,000	1,440,000	1.27	*Brazilian Baptist Conv.* M=SBC,BMS. Germans, Japanese. 1382n,320f,1H,77h,1j,30p,29690Y.
Convenção Batista Nacional	1967	I-3cY	T...I	900	200,000	20,000	360,000	12.26	*National Baptist Convention. Igreja do Renovaçoã.* Split ex Brazilian Baptist Convention.
Conv das Igs Ev Batistas Indep do B	1912	I-3pY	Z....	685	37,000	26,600	82,200	4.62	*Indep Bapt Chs.* M=Örebro (Sweden). 55n,44x,G=11%pa,1s,198t(9433),W=80%,928Y,11600z.
Cruzada de Evangelização do Acre e Am	1937	P-Bap	.....	36	1,500	800	3,000	5.43	*Am=Amazones. Missão Ev Amazonica.* M=Acre Gospel Mission (UK). 14f,W=80%,80Y,100z.
Cruzada Interamericana do Brasil	1914	P-Non	.....	20	3,500	1,500	7,500	6.65	*Interamerican Crusade of B.* M=SAIM(USA). Tribal Indians. (1990) 4n, 10x, 24f, 4h.
Cruzada Nacional de Evangelização	1946	P-Pe2	ZFu.b	2,641	389,266	200,000	607,567	4.54	National Evangelization Crusade. M=ICFG(USA). 800nm, 7f, 2p(81), W=72%, 8836Y
Exército de Salvação	1922	P-Sal	xwu.N	56	4,480	6,000	7,470	0.88	*Salvation Army, Brazil Territory.* 3 Divisions. Officers 127, institutions 15,1s.
Federação Ev Japonesa do Brasil		P-Dis	x....	27	4,100	5,000	5,690	0.05	*Japanese Ev Federation of Brazil.* M=UCMS(USA). Japanese immigrants.
Igreja Adventista da Promessa	c1958	I-3pY	I	2,727	150,000	15,000	333,000	13.20	A pentecostal split ex SDAs. Meetings changed from Saturdays to Sundays.
Igreja Adventista da Reforma	1947	I-Adv	x....	20	1,000	600	2,000	4.93	*SDA Reform Movement.* Schism from SDAs in Germany 1914, in Brazil since 1947.
Igreja Adventista do Sétimo Dia	1894	P-Adv	x....	1,634	482,065	300,000	900,000	4.49	*SDAs.* E,N,SBrazil. 10 launches, 2 planes. 306nx,56f,4H,6h,1j,8r,2s,2099t(177230),17036Y.
Igreja Apostólica Arménia: D Brasil		O-Arm	Ewc..	3	7,920	15,000	24,000	0.05	*Armenian Apostolic Ch (Gregorians).* Under C Echmiadzin (USSR). Armenians. 2nx.
Igreja Assoc das Igs Ev Menonita do B	1930	P-Men	G....	8	898	1,000	1,400	1.35	1954,M=Brazil MM(MCNA). USSR immigrants. 50% German, 50% Portuguese.
Igreja Batista do Sétimo Dia do Brasil		P-Bap	Tw...	156	7,000	3,000	23,300	0.05	*Seventh Day Baptist Ch of Brazil.* M=SDBC(USA). Sabbatarians with USA/UK links.
Igreja Batista Evangélica Restrita		P-Bap	x....	25	1,600	3,000	3,560	0.05	*Strict Baptist Church.* Links with Strict Baptists.
Igreja Batista Internacional	1967	I-Bap	x....	34	2,680	616	5,360	9.04	*Baptist International Missions.*
Igreja Brasileira	1961	I-CCa	.v...	8	800	2,000	1,600	-0.89	*Brazilian Ch.* Schism ex Rome. 6 bishops. Attempt to rejoin RCC as clergy; failed.
Igreja Católica Apostólica Brasileira	1945	I-CCa	.....	300	1,500,000	2,000,000	3,000,000	1.64	*ICAB.* Schism by RC ex-bishop of Botucatu. 12 Dioceses, 25 bishops. c1990 NNCM splits off.
Igreja Católica Livre no Brasil	1936	I-CCa	.....	20	2,000	3,000	4,000	1.16	*Free Catholic Ch.* Ex Rome; 1945, bishop consecrated through ICAB, rejoined RCC 1961.
Igreja Católica no Brasil:	1500	R-LEr	B.L.R	35,598	82,128,670	85,119,393	144,000,000	2.13	C=101+14+329. 7254n 6904x 12170m 35900w 2323767Yy
M Aparecida	1958	R-Lat	Bs	101	99,000	97,650	173,545	2.33	In São Paulo. M=OFM. 17n 58x 138m 152w 2356Yy
D Lorena	1937	R-Lat	Bs	209	153,000	190,000	268,000	1.39	M=SCI. 24n 21x 50m 45w 4493Yy
D São José dos Campos	1981	R-Lat	Bsci	30	297,000	–	520,000	7.14	M=SCI. 46n 11x 11m 209w 9347Yy
D Taubaté	1908	R-Lat	Bsci	223	252,000	480,356	442,000	-0.33	In São Paulo. M=SCI. 44n 35x 95m 307w 6801Yy
M Aracaju	1910	R-Lat	Bs	46	366,000	403,585	606,000	1.64	In SE. 39n 12x 13m 161w 16200Yy
D Estância	1060	R-Lat	Bs	16	216,000	265,000	378,000	1.43	In SE. 20n 0x 0m 57w 8204Yy
D Propriá	1960	R-Lat	Bcssr	27	136,000	196,000	238,000	0.78	M=CSSR. 13n 3x 5m 59w 2497Yy
M Belém do Pará	1720	R-Lat	Bcm	71	839,000	869,167	1,471,550	2.13	M=CM. 68n 105x 158m 335w 30339Yy
D Abaetetuba	1961	R-Lat	Bsx	12	121,000	160,000	213,000	1.15	M=SX. 5n 17x 20m 32w 5518Yy
D Bragança do Pará (Guamá)	1928	R-Lat	Bs	17	337,000	233,857	591,000	3.78	In PA. 19n 9x 15m 121w 10567Yy
D Conceição do Araguaia	1976	R-Lat	Bs	10	185,000	–	326,000	5.26	In PA. 8n 6x 6m 19w 2402Yy
D Macapá	1949	R-Lat	Bpime	39	142,000	107,108	249,000	3.43	M=PIME. 7n 33x 38m 21w 8467Yy
D Marabá	1911	R-Lat	Btor	23	277,000	50,000	486,000	9.52	M=TOR. 4n 18x 19m 45w 9200Yy
D Ponta de Pedras	1963	R-Lat	Bsj	226	48,000	67,500	84,000	0.88	M=SJ. 5n 2x 2m 14w 1548Yy
D Santarém	1903	R-Lat	Bofm	18	281,000	212,089	492,000	3.42	M=OFM. 12n 19x 43m 42w 8609Yy
PN Cametá	1952	R-Lat	Bcm	519	205,000	144,546	359,000	3.71	M=CM. 3n 12x 12m 45w 5123Yy
PN Itaituba	1988	R-Lat	Bofm	67	114,000	–	201,000	14.29	M=OFM. 1n 7x 8m 6w 1960Yy
PN Marajó	1928	R-Lat	Boar	358	123,000	140,000	215,000	1.73	M=OAR. 3n 12x 12m 7w 5582Yy
PN Obidos	1957	R-Lat	Bofm	6	101,000	105,272	178,000	2.12	M=OFM. 3n 8x 18m 14w 3722Yy
PN Xingu	1934	R-Lat	Bcpps	12	124,000	39,000	218,000	7.13	M=CPPS. 5n 16x 25m 46w 3323Yy
M Belo Horizonte	1921	R-Lat	Bs	1,470	1,543,000	1,509,497	2,705,353	2.36	M=SDB. 218n 262x 708m 2144w 52639Yy
D Divinópolis	1958	R-Lat	Bs	571	260,000	298,000	457,000	1.73	In MG. 38n 18x 27m 79w 8958Yy
D Luz (Aterrado)	1918	R-Lat	Bs	31	287,000	480,000	503,000	0.19	M=CM. 42n 20x 22m 73w 7711Yy
D Oliveira	1941	R-Lat	Bs	25	148,000	210,500	260,000	0.85	In MG. 22n 5x 12m 20w 4184Yy
D Sete Lagoas	1955	R-Lat	Bs	35	175,000	203,212	307,000	1.66	In MG. 31n 13x 13m 89w 4555Yy
M Botucatu	1908	R-Lat	Bs	55	385,000	380,000	675,000	2.32	In SP. 37n 27x 34m 187w 7063Yy
D Araçatuba	1994	R-Lat	Bs	36	222,000	–	390,000	100.00	In SP. 11n 17x 17m 20w 3000Yy
D Assis	1928	R-Lat	Bcss	32	136,000	270,000	239,000	-0.49	M=CSS. 21n 20x 27m 63w 11159Yy
D Bauru	1964	R-Lat	Bsj	28	208,000	209,598	365,000	2.24	M=SJ. 19n 29x 50m 127w 5162Yy
D Lins	1926	R-Lat	Bsdb	55	325,000	500,000	570,000	0.53	M=SDB. 57n 22x 31m 110w 22850Yy
D Marília	1952	R-Lat	Bs	59	334,000	501,000	586,000	0.63	M=OFMCap. 39n 29x 61m 219w 8689Yy
D Presidente Prudente	1960	R-Lat	Bs	278	218,000	318,732	380,000	0.71	In SP. 27n 7x 10m 47w 6374Yy
M Brasília	1960	R-Lat	Bs	183	791,000	545,000	1,386,000	3.80	M=SJ. 57n 92x 170m 380w 24031Yy
D Formosa	1956	R-Lat	Bsscc	29	100,000	115,000	175,000	1.69	M=SSCC. 10n 5x 7m 38w 4823Yy
D Luziânia	1989	R-Lat	Bofmc	8	212,000	324,000	372,000	16.67	M=OFMConv. 6n 11x 22m 23w 4395Yy
D Paracatu	1929	R-Lat	Bs	135	122,000	170,000	215,600	0.96	In MG. 11n 8x 8m 12w 5467Yy
D Uruaçu	1956	R-Lat	Bs	16	193,000	225,000	339,000	1.65	M=CMF. 11n 13x 14m 52w 3928Yy
M Campinas	1908	R-Lat	Bs	174	1,004,000	950,000	1,760,000	2.50	In SP. 83n 94x 166m 603w 21906Yy
D Bragança Paulista	1925	R-Lat	Bs	241	462,000	215,000	810,000	5.45	In SP. 59n 13x 13m w 8053Yy
D Limeira	1976	R-Lat	Bs	51	598,000	–	1,048,000	5.26	In SP. 49n 22x 23m 107w 8749Yy
D Piracicaba	1944	R-Lat	Bs	77	385,000	319,140	675,000	3.04	In SP. 33n 32x 96m 134w 7136Yy
D São Carlos (Pinhal)	1908	R-Lat	Bs	715	458,000	460,000	803,000	2.25	In SP. M=SSS. 76n 28x 34m 141w 13950Yy
M Campo Grande	1957	R-Lat	Bsdb	205	225,000	321,892	395,672	0.83	M=SDB. 21n 4x 81m 178w 4388Yy
D Corumbá	1910	R-Lat	Bdc	20	55,000	235,000	96,500	-3.50	M=DC. 4n 7x 9m 23w 2015Yy
D Dourados	1957	R-Lat	Bocar	36	378,000	380,000	663,000	2.25	M=OCar. 9n 57x 67m 74w 9325Yy
D Jardim	1981	R-Lat	Bsdb	137	105,000	–	184,000	7.14	In MS. M=SDB. 5n 6x 6m 35w 2635Yy
D Três Lagoas	1978	R-Lat	Bcm	24	81,000	–	142,000	5.88	M=CM. 5n 7x 8m 19w 2722Yy
PN Coxim	1978	R-Lat	Bofmc	11	82,000	–	144,000	5.88	M=OFMCap. 7n 12x 13m 22w 987Yy
M Cascavel	1978	R-Lat	Bosi	384	186,000	–	326,000	5.88	M=OSI. 19n 34x 44m 105w 6756Yy
D Foz do Iguaçu	1978	R-Lat	Bsvd	348	194,000	–	340,000	5.88	M=SVD. 5n 32x 34m 92w 5346Yy
D Palmas-Francisco Beltrão	1933	R-Lat	Bofmc	39	345,000	539,000	606,000	0.47	M=OFMCap. 25n 46x 114m 132w 11566Yy
D Toledo	1959	R-Lat	Bs	26	190,000	704,000	333,000	-2.95	27n 19x 45m 57w 4219Yy
M Cuiabá	1745	R-Lat	Bsdb	140	221,000	180,200	387,000	3.10	In PR. 11n 39x 46m 128w 9341Yy
D Barra do Garças	1982	R-Lat	Bsdb	15	71,000	–	124,000	7.69	M=SDB. 5n 17x 25m 74w 1913Yy
D Diamantino	1929	R-Lat	Bsj	74	107,000	65,000	187,000	4.32	M=SJ. 4n 16x 17m 40w 2401Yy
D Guiratinga	1914	R-Lat	Bsdb	12	71,300	115,000	125,000	0.33	M=SDB. 7n 10x 12m 31w 1541Yy
D Rondonópolis	1940	R-Lat	Bofm	17	140,000	170,000	246,000	1.49	M=OFM. 15n 14x 16m 53w 2803Yy
D São Luís de Cáceres	1910	R-Lat	Bs	17	137,000	140,000	240,000	2.18	M=TOR. 20n 6x 13m 78w 4472Yy
D Sinop	1982	R-Lat	Bsj	571	234,000	–	410,000	7.69	M=SJ. 11n 25x 29m 56w 4814Yy
PN São Félix	1969	R-Lat	Bcmf	22	31,000	54,000	54,000	0.00	M=CMF. 3n 6x 6m 8w 1271Yy

Continued overleaf

Country Table 2–continued

Official name (bold type = church with over 10% of all affiliated) 1	Begun 2	Type 3	Counc 4	Congs 5	Adults 6	Affiliated 1970 7	Affiliated 1995 8	G% 9	Names, notes, and other statistics (see Codebook, Part 3) 10
M Curitiba	1892	R-Lat	Bs	137	1,144,000	840,000	2,006,000	3.54	M=CM,CSS. 88n 344x 825m 1216w 30401Yy
D Guarapuava	1965	R-Lat	Bs	32	296,000	391,000	519,000	1.14	In PR. 31n 34x 37m 103w 9908Yy
D Paranaguá	1962	R-Lat	Bcssr	229	118,000	139,707	208,000	1.60	M=CSSR. 8n 12x 14m 40w 4044Yy
D Ponta Grossa	1926	R-Lat	Bsci	38	316,000	465,000	554,000	0.70	M=SCI. 25n 91x 146m 300w 7062Yy
D S João Batista em C (*Ukrainian*)	1962	R-Ukr	Oosbm	212	80,000	128,000	140,000	0.36	*C=Curitiba.* M=OSB. 16n 55x 87m 481w 3193Yy
D União da Vitória	1976	R-Lat	Bop	421	136,000	-	239,000	5.26	M=OP. 14n 19x 26m 43w 4161Yy
M Diamantina	1854	R-Lat	Bs	29	309,000	570,608	541,000	-0.21	M=SVD. 42n 8x 12m 115w 11800Yy
D Almenara	1981	R-Lat	Bofm	15	125,000	-	220,000	7.14	M=OFM. 2n 9x 21m 20w 3814Yy
D Araçuaí	1913	R-Lat	Bs	21	245,000	450,000	430,000	-0.18	In MG. 18n 6x 12m 34w 5260Yy
D Guanhães	1985	R-Lat	Bs	26	185,000	-	325,000	10.00	In MG. 20n 4x 4m 26w 5950Yy
D Januária	1957	R-Lat	Bmsf	16	236,000	271,479	415,000	1.71	M=MSF. 7n 13x 13m 13w 9489Yy
D Montes Claros	1910	R-Lat	Bopr	29	532,000	600,000	933,000	1.78	M=OPraem. 24n 21x 34m 110w 17592Yy
D Teófilo Otoni	1960	R-Lat	Bs	31	312,000	526,000	548,000	0.16	M=OFM. 29n 3x 4m 64w 4236Yy
M Florianópolis	1908	R-Lat	Bsci	61	465,000	528,731	815,000	1.75	M=SCI. 91n 74x 178m 563w 14807Yy
D Caçador	1968	R-Lat	Bs	22	222,000	248,000	390,000	1.83	In SC. 19n 21x 31m 98w 3379Yy
D Chapecó	1958	R-Lat	Bs	43	325,000	392,000	571,561	1.52	In SC. 29n 53x 80m 215w 15635Yy
D Joaçaba	1975	R-Lat	Bofm	22	160,000	-	281,000	5.00	M=OFM. 16n 26x 36m 50w 4301Yy
D Joinville	1927	R-Lat	Bs	518	467,000	295,000	820,000	4.17	In SC. 32n 64x 83m 263w 4049Yy
D Lages	1927	R-Lat	Bs	292	220,000	400,000	386,000	-0.14	In SC. 37n 20x 20m 209w 5811Yy
D Rio do Sul	1968	R-Lat	Bs	32	135,000	240,972	237,000	-0.07	In SC. 17n 38x 52m 176w 5717Yy
D Tubarão	1954	R-Lat	Bsdb	53	398,000	495,000	698,000	1.38	M=SDB. 81n 30x 36m 256w 9700Yy
M Fortaleza	1854	R-Lat	Bofm	115	1,255,000	1,202,650	2,200,000	2.45	M=OFM. 120n 581x 687m 2100w 80279Yy
D Crateús	1963	R-Lat	Bs	12	201,000	305,000	352,000	0.57	In CE. 8n 4x 5m 28w 8385Yy
D Crato	1914	R-Lat	Bs	306	514,000	554,520	902,000	1.97	In CE. 38n 13x 17m 104w 21946Yy
D Iguatu	1961	R-Lat	Bs	19	318,000	416,600	558,000	1.18	In CE. 15n 4x 7m 51w 8973Yy
D Itapipoca	1971	R-Lat	Bs	22	231,000	-	405,000	4.17	In CE. 21n 2x 7m 32w 10025Yy
D Limoeiro do Norte	1938	R-Lat	Bs	19	284,000	335,000	499,000	1.61	In CE. 17n 3x 8m 47w 8951Yy
D Quixadá	1971	R-Lat	Bpsdp	12	180,000	-	316,000	4.17	M=PSDP. 12n 6x 7m 65w 4192Yy
D Sobral	1915	R-Lat	Bs	24	407,000	509,966	713,000	1.35	In CE. 41n 3x 4m 83w 16631Yy
D Tianguá	1971	R-Lat	Boar	14	257,000	-	451,000	4.17	In CE. 20n 0x 0m 79w 10672Yy
M Goiânia	1956	R-Lat	Bs	222	768,000	498,700	1,346,000	4.05	In GO. 55n 89x 161m 329w 18303Yy
D Anápolis	1966	R-Lat	Bs	30	169,000	250,000	295,666	0.67	M=OFM. 31n 35x 129m 111w 5091Yy
D Goiás	1745	R-Lat	Bop	20	204,000	230,000	358,000	1.79	M=OP,OSB. 11n 10x 10m 38w 1759Yy
D Ipameri	1966	R-Lat	Bofmc	153	104,000	130,261	182,000	1.35	M=OFMCap. 11n 5x 5m 49w 1978Yy
D Itumbiara	1966	R-Lat	Bs	23	128,000	160,000	224,000	1.35	In GO. 12n 10x 11m 31w 2575Yy
D Jataí	1929	R-Lat	Bofm	125	208,000	225,000	364,000	1.94	M=OFM. 9n 17x 17m 58w 4170Yy
D Miracema do Tocantins	1966	R-Lat	Bcssr	18	106,000	120,000	186,000	1.77	M=CSSR. 9n 2x 3m 46w 2779Yy
D Porto Nacional	1915	R-Lat	Bop	22	178,000	178,000	312,000	2.27	M=OP. 17n 7x 7m 61w 5332Yy
D Rubiataba-Mozarlândia	1966	R-Lat	Bcssr	18	52,000	191,815	91,000	-2.94	M=CSSR. 8n 8x 16m 20w 1225Yy
D São Luís de Montes Belos	1961	R-Lat	Bcp	23	192,000	224,846	336,000	1.62	M=CP. 9n 14x 14m 59w 3923Yy
D Tocantinópolis	1954	R-Lat	Bfdp	21	251,000	210,000	441,000	3.01	M=FDP. 17n 12x 16m 26w 24370Yy
PN Cristalândia	1956	R-Lat	Bosb	13	110,000	92,000	193,000	3.01	M=OSB. 4n 8x 11m 44w 1632Yy
M Juiz de Fora	1924	R-Lat	Bofmc	716	275,000	540,000	482,000	-0.45	M=OFMCap. 72n 54x 124m 187w 9486Yy
D Leopoldina	1942	R-Lat	Bopr	236	246,000	328,835	431,000	1.09	M=OPraem. 30n 22x 22m 190w 8436Yy
D São João del Rei	1960	R-Lat	Bs	32	250,000	230,901	439,000	2.60	In MG. 39n 23x 24m 109w 3053Yy
M Londrina	1956	R-Lat	Bs	279	390,000	444,275	684,000	1.74	In PR. 29n 56x 101m 242w 10055Yy
D Apucarana	1964	R-Lat	Bcm	671	267,000	468,900	468,000	-0.01	M=CM. 44n 9x 9m 72w 6715Yy
D Cornélio Procópio	1973	R-Lat	Bsrd	23	114,000	-	200,000	4.55	M=SVD. 14n 16x 19m 35w 3260Yy
D Jacarezinho	1926	R-Lat	Bsac	631	246,000	686,451	432,000	-1.84	M=SAC. 56n 12x 17m 122w 8067Yy
M Maceió(Alagôas)	1900	R-Lat	Bsdb	45	512,000	790,096	898,000	0.51	M=SDB. 66n 18x 39m 289w 18336Yy
D Palmeira dos Indios	1962	R-Lat	Bs	186	321,000	385,000	563,000	1.53	In AL. 31n 0x 0m 58w 11407Yy
D Penedo	1916	R-Lat	Bs	26	416,000	436,000	730,000	2.08	M=OFM. 27n 2x 3m 31w 18790Yy
M Manaus (Amazonas)	1892	R-Lat	Bs	51	566,000	325,205	992,000	4.56	In AM. 27n 75x 125m 150w 10918Yy
D Alto Solimões	1910	R-Lat	Bofmc	8	52,000	46,866	92,200	2.74	M=OFMCap. 4n 9x 15m 15w 2097Yy
D Cruzeiro do Sul (Juruá)	1931	R-Lat	Bcssp	12	83,000	118,000	146,000	0.86	M=CSSp. 8n 16x 28m 85w 4138Yy
D Parintins	1955	R-Lat	Bpima	438	88,000	90,500	154,000	2.15	M=PIME. 5n 13x 17m 15w 4025Yy
D Rio Branco (Acre e Purus)	1919	R-Lat	Bosm	263	189,000	140,000	332,000	3.51	M=OSM. 13n 14x 15m 91w 11530Yy
D Roraima	1944	R-Lat	Bimc	12	75,000	40,000	132,000	4.89	M=IMC. 4n 21x 25m 34w 2695Yy
D S Gabriel da Cachoeira	1925	R-Lat	Bsdb	11	24,000	24,500	41,700	2.15	M=SDB. Rio Negro. 2n 12x 19m 38w 728Yy
PN Borba	1963	R-Lat	Btor	24	44,000	45,000	78,100	2.23	M=TOR. 5n 9x 9m 10w 1952Yy
PN Coari	1963	R-Lat	Bcssr	6	74,000	118,000	129,000	0.36	M=CSSR. 2n 10x 11m 15w 2857Yy
PN Itacoatiara	1963	R-Lat	Bsfm	236	71,000	70,000	125,000	2.35	M=SFM. 2n 9x 9m 20w 2272Yy
PN Tefé	1910	R-Lat	Bcssp	23	62,000	85,452	109,100	0.98	M=CSSp. 1n 15x 17m 21w 2665Yy
M Mariana	1745	R-Lat	Bsj	486	657,000	830,558	1,152,000	1.32	M=SJ. 140n 36x 43m 307w 31150Yy
D Caratinga	1915	R-Lat	Bs	42	438,000	780,560	768,000	-0.06	In MG. 28n 21x 43m 126w 9365Yy
D Governador Valadares	1956	R-Lat	Bs	32	252,000	481,700	442,000	-0.34	M=SSCC. 25n 17x 19m 33w 7162Yy
D Itabira-Fabriciano	1965	R-Lat	Bsds	38	451,000	400,000	791,000	2.76	M=SDS,CSSR. 24n 16x 19m 81w 7527Yy
M Maringá	1956	R-Lat	Bs	39	215,000	494,000	377,000	-1.08	In PR. 42n 6x 15m 124w 5318Yy
D Campo Mourão	1959	R-Lat	Bs	38	248,000	1,100,000	436,000	-3.63	In PR. 30n 21x 23m 37w 6241Yy
D Paranavaí	1968	R-Lat	Bs	25	162,000	240,000	284,000	0.68	In PR. 19n 12x 27m 61w 3380Yy
D Umuarama	1973	R-Lat	Bsac	431	207,000	-	363,000	4.55	M=SAC. 20n 28x 29m 73w 4910Yy
M Natal	1909	R-Lat	Bs	252	794,000	906,321	1,393,000	1.73	In RN. 52n 16x 29m 229w 30841Yy
D Caicó	1939	R-Lat	Bs	13	138,000	184,000	242,000	1.10	In RN. 19n 0x 0m 63w 5249Yy
D Mossoró	1934	R-Lat	Bs	20	399,000	389,178	699,000	2.37	In RN. 17n 12x 16m 69w 8320Yy
M Niterói	1892	R-Lat	Bs	66	1,113,000	970,000	1,952,000	2.84	M=CSSR. 53n 48x 58m 219w 21332Yy
D Campos	1922	R-Lat	Bsdb	72	438,000	692,250	769,000	0.42	M=SDB. 25n 20x 21m 53w 11708Yy
D Nova Friburgo	1960	R-Lat	Bop	533	235,000	350,000	412,000	0.65	M=OP,OSB. 26n 24x 39m 129w 5591Yy
D Petrópolis	1946	R-Lat	Bs	31	417,000	930,000	731,000	-0.96	In RJ. 41n 20x 76m 325w 13550Yy
M Olinda e Recife	1676	R-Lat	Boc	457	1,794,000	1,742,272	3,145,000	2.39	M=OC. 64n 109x 212m 950w 38164Yy
D Afogados da Ingazeira	1956	R-Lat	Bs	14	200,000	275,048	350,000	0.97	In PE. 14n 4x 5m 34w 4878Yy
D Caruaru	1948	R-Lat	Bs	26	411,000	465,473	720,000	1.76	In PE. 30n 8x 15m 50w 15400Yy
D Floresta	1964	R-Lat	Bcssr	105	146,000	199,500	256,000	1.00	M=CSSR. 8n 4x 6m 4w 4323Yy
D Garanhuns	1918	R-Lat	Bs	130	389,000	550,273	682,000	0.86	In PE. 17n 19x 26m 101w 8606Yy
D Nazaré	1918	R-Lat	Bs	26	458,000	700,816	803,200	0.55	In PE. 28n 8x 16m 74w 24303Yy
D Palmares	1962	R-Lat	Bs	16	190,000	280,000	334,000	0.71	In PE. 16n 6x 7m 83w 7113Yy
D Pesqueira	1910	R-Lat	Bs	22	247,000	307,750	434,000	1.38	In PE. 18n 10x 12m 30w 9020Yy
D Petrolina	1923	R-Lat	Bocar	17	335,000	313,212	587,000	2.54	M=OCarm. 14n 6x 9m 52w 15115Yy
M Paraíba	1892	R-Lat	Bs	38	517,000	989,500	906,000	-0.35	In PB. 44n 30x 44m 225w 18409Yy
D Cajazeiras	1914	R-Lat	Bs	288	264,000	460,000	463,000	0.03	In PB. 24n 4x 4m 54w 7505Yy
D Campina Grande	1949	R-Lat	Bs	37	410,000	370,000	720,000	2.70	In PB. 21n 19x 33m 138w 13100Yy
D Guarabira	1980	R-Lat	Bs	20	194,000	-	340,000	6.67	In PB. 16n 3x 3m 20w 4322Yy
D Patos	1959	R-Lat	Bs	23	217,000	218,000	380,000	2.25	In PB. 18n 6x 12m 33w 9723Yy
M Porto Alegre	1848	R-Lat	Bcssr	173	1,483,000	1,814,000	2,601,000	1.45	M=CSSR,OCD. 219n 199x 580m 1353w 60730Yy
D Bagé	1960	R-Lat	Bcs	17	236,000	305,000	415,000	1.24	M=CS. 17n 16x 18m 96w 5960Yy
D Cachoeira do Sul	1991	R-Lat	Bofmc	367	81,000	-	143,000	25.00	M=OFMCap. 18n 8x 15m 68w 2706Yy
D Caxias do Sul	1934	R-Lat	Bs	75	465,000	415,000	815,000	2.74	In RS. 95n 81x 178m 567w 11339Yy
D Cruz Alta	1971	R-Lat	Bs	31	239,000	-	420,000	4.17	In RS. 13n 29x 34m 146w 4654Yy
D Erexim	1971	R-Lat	Bs	27	138,000	-	241,900	4.17	In RS. 34n 16x 26m 155w 3536Yy
D Frederico Westphalen	1961	R-Lat	Bs	36	287,000	382,000	504,000	1.11	In RS. 34n 31x 32m 165w 6377Yy
D Novo Hamburgo	1980	R-Lat	Bofm	53	260,000	-	457,000	6.67	M=OFM. 53n 59x 138m 405w 12503Yy
D Passo Fundo	1951	R-Lat	Bs	773	246,000	380,000	431,000	0.51	In RS. 57n 65x 201m 420w 7258Yy
D Pelotas	1910	R-Lat	Bs	26	230,000	387,000	403,000	0.16	In RS. 37n 7x 24m 170w 3545Yy
D Rio Grande	1971	R-Lat	Bs	20	169,000	-	296,000	4.17	In RS. 12n 13x 18m 90w 3048Yy
D Santa Cruz do Sul	1959	R-Lat	Bs	881	253,000	317,287	444,462	1.36	In RS. 71n 15x 49m 278w 6660Yy
D Santa Maria	1910	R-Lat	Bs	50	259,000	410,000	454,000	0.41	M=IMC. 46n 58x 140m 444w 6065Yy
D Santo Angelo	1961	R-Lat	Bs	39	299,000	390,000	525,000	1.20	In RS. 65n 24x 54m 365w 4100Yy
D Uruguaiana	1910	R-Lat	Bs	13	200,000	280,000	350,000	0.90	In RS. 22n 3x 10m 127w 6560Yy
D Vacaria	1934	R-Lat	Bofmc	26	126,000	203,000	221,000	0.34	M=OFMCap. 24n 34x 46m 189w 3552Yy
M Porto Velho	1925	R-Lat	Bs	401	130,000	237,650	228,000	-0.17	M=SDB. 14n 26x 31m 50w 3224Yy
D Guajará-Mirim	1929	R-Lat	Bs	11	104,000	24,500	182,000	8.35	M=TOR. 5n 10x 12m 42w 1646Yy
D Humaitá	1961	R-Lat	Bsdb	62	43,000	45,200	76,700	2.14	M=SDB. 1n 7x 11m 15w 1130Yy
D Ji-Paraná	1978	R-Lat	Bsdb	29	246,000	-	432,000	5.88	M=SDB. 7n 36x 42m 67w 7379Yy
PN Lábrea	1925	R-Lat	Boar	4	41,000	42,600	71,900	2.12	M=OAR. 0n 11x 20m 7w 1912Yy
M Pouso Alegre	1900	R-Lat	Bs	743	314,000	426,000	551,000	1.03	In MG. 59n 21x 59m 208w 9396Yy
D Campanha	1907	R-Lat	Bsci	805	317,000	410,000	557,000	1.23	M=SCI. 66n 22x 27m 260w 12989Yy
D Guaxupé	1916	R-Lat	Bcss	61	355,000	432,854	622,000	1.46	M=CSS. 68n 19x 32m 116w 9926Yy
AN Claraval	1968	R-Lat	Bocis	17	5,600	12,096	9,900	-0.80	M=OCist. 0n 5x 8m 5w 242Yy
M Ribeirão Preto	1908	R-Lat	Bs	227	527,000	373,753	924,000	3.69	In SP. 37n 32x 66m 160w 27780Yy
D Barretos	1973	R-Lat	Bcssr	212	204,000	-	358,000	4.55	M=CSSR. 14n 12x 12m 92w 3409Yy
D Franca	1971	R-Lat	Bs	136	378,000	-	663,000	4.17	In SP. 26n 14x 41m 55w 7801Yy
D Jaboticabal	1929	R-Lat	Bs	161	206,000	455,000	361,000	-0.92	In SP. 32n 8x 17m 109w 5210Yy
D Jales	1959	R-Lat	Bs	24	227,000	360,000	399,000	0.41	In SP. 24n 6x 6m 7w 3698Yy
D Rio Preto	1929	R-Lat	Bs	426	411,000	445,000	720,000	1.94	In SP. 83n 15x 17m 102w 9822Yy

Continued opposite

Country Table 2–continued

Official name (bold type = church with over 10% of all affiliated) 1	*Begun* 2	*Type* 3	*Counc* 4	*Congs* 5	*Adults* 6	*Affiliated 1970* 7	*Affiliated 1995* 8	*G%* 9	*Names, notes, and other statistics* (see Codebook, Part 3) 10
D São João da Boa Vista	1960	R-Lat	Bs	645	189,000	280,000	331,000	0.67	In SP. 48n 27x 36m 136w 7572Yy
M São Luis do Maranhão	1677	R-Lat	Bs	29	396,000	1,500,000	694,000	-3.04	In MA. 30n 41x 85m 52w 14625Yy
D Bacabal	1968	R-Lat	Bofm	37	295,000	545,000	517,000	-0.21	M=OFM. 9n 14x 18m 43w 7207Yy
D Balsas (Santo Antonio)	1954	R-Lat	Bmcci	15	104,000	165,000	183,000	0.42	M=MCCI. 6n 11x 20m 45w 2912Yy
D Brejo	1971	R-Lat	Bsds	616	220,000	–	385,000	4.17	M=SDS. 9n 4x 4m 20w 14530Yy
D Carolina	1958	R-Lat	Bofmc	11	67,000	178,480	118,000	-1.64	M=OFMCap. 4n 2x 2m 12w 3151Yy
D Caxias do Maranhão	1939	R-Lat	Bofmc	105	359,000	456,999	630,000	1.29	M=OFMConv. 16n 3x 3m 30w 10313Yy
D Coroatá	1977	R-Lat	Bs	711	218,000	–	382,649	5.56	In MA. 17n 6x 15m 45w 9087Yy
D Grajaú	1922	R-Lat	Bofmc	11	204,000	230,000	358,000	1.79	M=OFMCap. 6n 13x 14m 26w 4636Yy
D Imperatriz	1987	R-Lat	Bs	19	251,000	–	441,000	12.50	In MA. 8n 14x 16m 54w 4993Yy
D Pinheiro	1939	R-Lat	Bmsc	490	174,000	200,000	306,000	1.72	M=MSC. 13n 7x 8m 52w 6630Yy
D Viana	1962	R-Lat	Bofmc	18	265,000	585,600	465,000	-0.92	M=OFMCap. 21n 9x 9m 27w 8700Yy
D Zé Doca (Cândido Mendez)	1961	R-Lat	Bimc	13	155,000	63,000	272,000	6.03	M=IMC. 12n 6x 13m 20w 6447Yy
M São Paulo	1745	R-Lat	Bofm	568	4,392,000	6,000,000	7,699,000	1.00	M=OFM,SVD. 292n 381x 847m 1786w 40985Yy
D Campo Limpo	1989	R-Lat	Bs	50	1,110,000	–	1,946,000	16.67	In SP. 36n 48x 58m 7w 17000Yy
D Guarulhos	1981	R-Lat	Bs	145	405,000	–	710,000	7.14	In SP. 34n 5x 16m 83w 8686Yy
D Mogi das Cruzes	1962	R-Lat	Bopr	325	386,000	530,000	677,000	0.98	M=OPraem. 32n 27x 54m 122w 8212Yy
D NS do Líbano (*Maronite*)	1971	R-Mar	Oolm	6	247,000	–	434,000	4.17	NS=Nossa Senhora. M=OLM. 4n 4x 4m 0w 412Yy
D NS do Paraíso (*Melkite*)	1971	R-Mel	Osmsp	6	221,000	–	388,000	4.17	M=SMSP. 6n 2x 4m 0w 661Yy
D Osasco	1989	R-Lat	Bs	296	912,700	–	1,600,000	16.67	In SP. 40n 42x 139m 243w 17887Yy
D Santo Amaro	1989	R-Lat	Bofm	47	1,303,000	–	2,284,000	16.67	M=OFM. 34n 60x 69m 153w 8632Yy
D Santo André	1954	R-Lat	Bofm	215	1,294,000	800,000	2,268,000	4.26	M=OFM. 61n 35x 58m 144w 37448Yy
D Santos	1924	R-Lat	Bs	213	628,000	726,201	1,101,000	1.68	In SP. 45n 35x 40m 214w 9707Yy
D São Miguel Paulista	1989	R-Lat	Bsdb	275	1,379,000	–	2,417,000	16.67	M=SDB. 52n 34x 45m 269w 24540Yy
M São Salvador da Bahia	1551	R-Lat	Bop	658	1,677,000	1,824,000	2,940,000	1.93	M=OP. 118n 116x 179m 663w 31579Yy
D Alagoinhas	1974	R-Lat	Bs	23	291,000	–	510,000	4.76	M=OSB. 20n 10x 10m 66w 8440Yy
D Amargosa	1941	R-Lat	Bs	23	310,000	480,000	544,000	0.50	In BA. 18n 6x 7m 25w 6842Yy
D Barra	1913	R-Lat	Bofmc	9	100,000	350,000	176,000	-2.71	M=OFMCap. 8n 6x 7m 40w 3650Yy
D Barreiras	1979	R-Lat	Bosb	144	157,000	–	275,000	6.25	M=OSB,SSCME. 10n 6x 6m 28w 5659Yy
D Bom Jesus da Lapa	1962	R-Lat	Bcssr	16	164,000	214,000	288,000	1.20	M=CSSR. 3n 2x 3m 29w 6700Yy
D Bonfim	1933	R-Lat	Bs	15	371,000	280,000	651,000	3.43	M=OSFS. 3n 21x 24m 72w 13273Yy
D Caetité	1913	R-Lat	Bcss	35	360,000	400,000	631,000	1.84	M=CSS. 16n 3x 3m 42w 14185Yy
D Feira de Santana	1962	R-Lat	Bofm	37	670,000	600,000	1,175,000	2.72	M=OFM. 31n 17x 18m 121w 14379Yy
D Ilhéus	1913	R-Lat	Bofm	30	344,000	900,000	603,000	-1.59	M=OFM. 33n 4x 6m 53w 5795Yy
D Irecê	1979	R-Lat	Bs	9	204,000	–	358,000	6.25	In BA. M=OSM. 4n 4x 4m 23w 9540Yy
D Itabuna	1978	R-Lat	Bs	37	299,000	–	525,000	5.88	M=OFMCap. 16n 17x 26m 42w 5100Yy
D Jequié	1978	R-Lat	Bs	255	266,000	–	466,000	5.88	In BA. 20n 8x 8m 19w 7139Yy
D Juazeiro	1962	R-Lat	Bcssr	12	173,000	165,000	303,000	2.46	M=CSSR. 7n 6x 6m 23w 1225Yy
D Livramento de Nossa Senhora	1967	R-Lat	Bcss	20	185,000	220,000	325,000	1.57	M=CSS. 6n 8x 8m 21w 6705Yy
D Paulo Afonso	1971	R-Lat	Bs	32	311,000	–	545,000	4.17	M=CSS. 28n 15x 15m 66w 9156Yy
D Ruy Barbosa	1959	R-Lat	Bs	16	238,000	475,000	418,000	-0.51	In BA. 10n 11x 19m 33w 6890Yy
D Teixeira de Freitas-Caravelas	1962	R-Lat	Bofmc	24	295,000	570,000	518,000	-0.38	M=OFMCap. 12n 19x 20m 35w 9694Yy
D Vitória da Conquista	1957	R-Lat	Bs	24	287,000	480,000	504,000	0.20	In BA. 18n 8x 8m 54w 9089Yy
M São Sebastião do Rio de Janeiro	1676	R-Lat	Bs	719	2,913,000	3,100,000	5,106,000	2.02	In RJ. Several assistant bishops. 239n 209x 326m 1863w 55535Yy
D Barra do Piraí-Volta Redonda	1922	R-Lat	Bs	325	429,000	300,000	752,000	3.74	In RJ. 27n 18x 41m 104w 8332Yy
D Duque de Caxias	1980	R-Lat	Bs	21	575,000	–	1,009,000	6.67	In RJ. 15n 18x 29m 71w 7880Yy
D Itaguaí	1980	R-Lat	Bocar	14	106,000	–	187,000	6.67	M=OCarm. 5n 16x 17m 52w 2419Yy
D Nova Iguaçu	1960	R-Lat	Bsvd	311	664,000	111,124	1,165,000	9.86	M=SVD. 31n 32x 38m 77w 18901Yy
D Valença	1925	R-Lat	Bofmc	26	191,000	156,230	335,000	3.10	M=OFMConv. 13n 9x 10m 97w 1798Yy
AN NS do Monserrate do Rio de J	1907	R-Lat	Bosb	1	70	70	90	1.01	NS=Nossa Senhorra. M=OSB. 0n 28x 41m 0w 529Yy
M Sorocaba	1924	R-Lat	Bcss	48	390,000	440,000	684,000	1.78	M=CSS. 55n 11x 26m 165w 10800Yy
D Itapeva	1968	R-Lat	Bs	542	218,000	256,003	382,000	1.61	In SP. 14n 20x 36m 21w 2820Yy
D Jundiaí	1966	R-Lat	Bs	238	344,000	350,000	603,000	2.20	In SP. 38n 26x 35m 196w 13846Yy
D Registro	1974	R-Lat	Bsvd	300	142,000	–	249,000	4.76	M=SVD. 4n 10x 18m 14w 2041Yy
M Teresina (Piauí)	1902	R-Lat	Bs	35	463,000	609,358	812,000	1.16	In PI. 52n 26x 56m 196w 16711Yy
D Bom Jesus do Gurguéia	1920	R-Lat	Bodm	153	90,000	110,500	158,500	1.45	M=OdeM. 11n 8x 9m 20w 3995Yy
D Campo Maior	1975	R-Lat	Bodm	21	268,000	–	470,000	5.00	M=OdeM. 23n 1x 1m 38w 5256Yy
D Oeiras-Floriano	1944	R-Lat	Bmsc	10	169,000	427,198	297,000	-1.44	M=MSC,OFM. 13n 8x 8m 27w 5420Yy
D Parnaíba	1944	R-Lat	Bs	17	282,000	413,149	495,000	0.73	In PI. 17n 10x 12m 55w 8947Yy
D Picos	1974	R-Lat	Bs	12	189,000	–	331,000	4.76	In PI. 13n 2x 2m 27w 5156Yy
D São Raimundo Nonato	1960	R-Lat	Bodm	106	116,000	130,000	204,000	1.82	M=OdeM. 9n 4x 4m 18w 4056Yy
M Uberaba	1907	R-Lat	Bs	32	223,000	275,293	391,000	1.41	In MG. 32n 12x 21m 185w 4889Yy
D Ituiutaba	1982	R-Lat	Bs	22	134,000	–	235,000	7.69	In MG. 11n 20x 23m 43w 4418Yy
D Patos de Minas	1955	R-Lat	Bs	349	436,000	398,000	765,000	2.65	M=OFMCap. 31n 17x 20m 48w 7481Yy
D Uberlândia	1961	R-Lat	Bcss	23	279,000	200,000	489,000	3.64	M=CSS. 29n 21x 22m 54w 6847Yy
M Vitória	1895	R-Lat	Bsvd	42	710,000	550,000	1,245,000	3.32	M=SVD. 36n 35x 49m 95w 9388Yy
D Cachoeiro de Itapemirim	1958	R-Lat	Bsscc	33	220,000	332,100	385,000	0.59	M=SSCC. 25n 23x 26m 62w 5073Yy
D Colatina	1990	R-Lat	Bs	20	209,000	–	366,000	20.00	In ES. 17n 11x 17m 46w 6700Yy
D São Mateus	1958	R-Lat	Bmcci	632	262,000	320,000	459,000	1.45	M=MCCI. 12n 14x 16m 43w 5194Yy
O Brasile (*Oriental-rite*)	1951	R-Lat	Bs	3	6,000	80,000	10,000	-7.98	*Ordinariato per i fedeli di rito orientale.* 2n 2x 2m 3w 30Yy
OM Brasile	1950	R-Lat	Bs	124	160,000	75,000	280,000	5.41	*Ordinariato Militare.* 15 ordinaries, 90 auxiliaries, 54 religious. 6670Yy.
Doubly-counted Catholics		R-Lat	.....	0	-3,095,000		-5,426,848		Catholics counted in 2 dioceses or jurisdictions when creations of new dioceses are frequent.
Igreja Cristã Apostólica	1962	P-Hol	x....	20	1,000	2,000	3,000	1.64	*Corporação Igreja Nazareno. Apostolic Christian Ch.* M=ACC(Nazarean) (USA).
Igreja Cristã Batista Bíblica	1952	I-Bap	xTT.T	10	1,600	1,000	3,000	4.49	*Baptist Bible Christian Church.* M=BBFI(USA). HQ São Paulo. 42f,2s.
Igreja Cristã Pentecostal da Bíblia	1958	I-3pY	I	30	3,000	4,000	6,000	1.64	*Pentecostal Christian Ch of the Bible. Cruzada Bíblica Sagrada.* Schism ex IPI.
Igreja Cristã Primitiva		I-Non	.....	20	1,500	2,000	2,500	0.05	*Primitive Christian Church.* Small indigenous independent grouping.
Igr Cristã Reformada do Brazil	1932	P-Ref	RW...	12	8,550	9,000	19,000	3.03	*Christian Reformed Ch.* M=Ref Ch of Hungary, CRC(USA). A=1945. Hungarians. 5n,8f.
Igreja da Bíblia Abierto	1982	I-3pW	.....	3	118	–	215	7.69	*Open Bible Standard Church.* M=OBSC(USA).
Igreja da Restauração		I-3cY	I	280	70,000	15,000	156,000	0.05	*Church of the Restoration.* Schism ex Brazilian Baptist Convention. 15n,40m.
Igreja de Cristianismo Decidido		P-Non	.....	20	500	500	700	0.05	*Assoc of Churches of Committed Christians.* M=Marburger Mission (Germany).
Igreja de Cristo	1948	I-Dis	x....	200	16,000	10,000	32,000	4.76	*Ch of Christ.* M=Brazil Christian Mission (CCCC Instrumental) (USA). 8n,15x,125f,250Y.
Igreja de Cristo Jesus	1958	I-3pY	I	59	10,000	5,000	22,200	6.14	*Ch of Jesus Christ.* Schism ex Independent Presbyterian Ch. HQ São Paulo. 8n,20m.
Igreja de Cristo Pentecostal do Brasil	1937	P-Pe3	x....	625	77,700	30,000	114,000	5.49	*Pentecostal Ch of Christ of B.* M=PCC(USA). 27n,2x,W=60%700Y,500z.
Igreja de Deus de Profecia	1965	P-Pe3	Z....	48	1,440	5,000	3,600	-1.31	*Ch of God of Prophecy.* M=CGP(USA), split ex CoG(Cleveland).
Igreja de Deus do Brasil	1923	P-Hol	x....	37	6,000	3,000	13,600	6.23	*Ch of God.* M=CoG(Anderson) (USA). 1923, German immigrants to Santa Catarina. 20n.
Igreja de Deus do Brasil (Cleveland)	1935	P-Pe3	ZF...	152	11,957	5,000	26,600	6.91	*Ch of God.* M=CoG(Cleveland) (USA). 59 churches, 92 missions. 79n,10f,1p.
Igreja de Deus em Cristo		P-Men	.....	3	211	100	352	0.05	*Church of God in Christ, Mennonite.* M=Ch of God in Christ, Mennonite (USA).
Igreja de Deus Pentecostal do Brasil	c1955	P-Pe2	Z....	100	3,000	2,300	5,000	3.15	*Pentecostal Ch of God.* Classical Pentecostals. M=PCG(USA). 19n,1x,6f,150Y.
Igr de JC dos Santos dos Ultimos Dias	c1925	m-LdS	x....	567	220,000	41,776	302,000	8.23	*Mormons.* M=Ch of JC of Latter-day Saints (USA). 70% in South Brazil. 730f.
Igreja de Nosso Senhor Jesus Cristo	1943	I-3pY	.....	35	2,000	2,000	3,000	1.64	*Ch of Our Lord Jesus Christ.* Founded by a Black evangelist in São Paulo.
Igreja de Nova Vida	1960	I-3pY	.....	50	5,000	2,000	10,000	6.65	*INV. Churches of New Life.* Network of charismatic chs (HQ Rio de Janeiro) in IEC and ICCC.
Igreja de Reavivamento Bíblico	c1950	I-3pY	I	55	5,500	5,000	11,000	3.20	*Ch of Biblical Revival.* Ex Methodist. Early pentecostal body. HQ São Paulo.
Igreja do Nazareno do Brasil	1934	P-Hol	xFu.N	92	7,512	2,500	8,675	5.10	*Ch of the Nazarene.* M=CoN(USA). 2n,6x,22m,12f,2s(38),41t(2098),W=80%,158Y.
Igreja do Spirito Jesus		I-3oQ	x....	60	3,000	2,000	5,000	0.05	*Iesu No Mitama Kyokai. Spirit of Jesus Church.* Indigenous church from Japan.
Igreja dos Irmãos	1949	P-Dun	xF...	30	500	800	1,200	1.64	M=NFBC(Brethren Ch, Grace) (USA). German Baptist tradition. 6n,6x,17f,58Y.
Igreja dos Wesleyanos	1960	P-Hol	VF...	16	528	382	715	2.54	M=Wesleyan Church (USA). Holiness denomination. 3x,6f,1p,W=47%,12Yy,20z.
Igreja Episcopal do Brasil	1810	A-Cen	AWuCN	276	68,700	45,000	105,000	3.45	*Episcopal Ch.* 7 Dioceses. M=PECUSA,SAMS. A=1964. 96n,3x,14m13f,97pp,1s,W=50%,2039y.
Igreja Evangélica Arabe do Brasil		P-Ref	..u.N	10	1,600	500	3,000	0.05	*Arab Ev Ch of Brazil.* Immigrants from Lebanon and Syria Protestant bodies.
Igreja Ev Apostolica do Brasil	c1960	I-3oY	.....	20	3,000	500	5,000	9.65	*Apostolic Evangelical Church of Brazil.* Oneness body in AWCF. HQ Rio de Janeiro.
Igreja Ev Congregaçional Cristã	1855	P-Con	Rru.N	350	42,000	75,000	70,000	-0.28	*Uniã das Igr Ev Cong.* M=EUSA,UCC(USA). 119n,3x,35f,1j,2s,W=75%,1000Yy.
Igr Ev da Confissão Luterana no Brasil	1823	P-Lut	LWu.N	2,204	595,000	628,690	950,000	1.67	*IECLB.* Lutheran Confession, Germans. M=ALC. 183n,106x,34f,1s(90),14012Yy.
Igreja Evangélica Holiness do Brasil	1925	P-Hol	xFu.N	75	1,500	4,000	3,750	-0.26	M=Japan Holiness Ch,OMS(USA). A=1933. Japanese. 5n,9x20f,1s,W=38%,70Y.
Igreja Evangélica Independente	1958	I-Eva	x....	10	680	350	1,000	4.29	*Ev Independent Ch.* M=Bethesda Mission (USA). 1x,7f,W=80%.
Igreja Evangélica Luterana do Brasil	1890	I-Lut	e.u.N	1,426	128,000	186,200	216,000	0.60	*Ev Lutheran Ch of Brazil.* 1890 split ex IECLB. 1899, M=LC Missouri Synod (USA). 394n,6f,1s.
Igreja Evangélica Neo-Testamentaria	1904	P-Eva	x....	80	13,600	3,000	20,000	7.88	*Ev Ch of the New Testament. NT Churches.* M=NTMU(UK). In interior. 3f.
Igreja Evangélica Pentecostal Elim	1960	P-Pe2	Z....	16	368	3,000	920	-4.62	*Elim Pentecostal Church.* M=EMS(UK). 2-stage Pentecostals. 4n,W=82%,50z.
Igreja Evangélica Pentecostal Unida	1955	I-3pY	I	252	37,000	30,000	112,000	5.41	*United EPC.* Union: IE Cristã Unida, IE de Povo, IP Maravilhas de Jesus. 35n.
Igreja Ev Pente 'O Brasil para Cristo'	1955	I-3pY	ZWu.b	5,000	1,000,000	1,000,000	2,000,000	2.81	*OBPC. Brazil for Christ.* Ex AoG. Church seating 40,000 in São Paulo. Left WCC. In Costa Rica.
Igreja Evangélica Reformada do Brasil	1933	P-Ref	F....	4	690	1,457	1,530	0.20	*Ev Reformed Ch.* M=Ref Chs in Netherlands. A=1963. 1n,6x,W=85%,50Yy,803z.
Igreja Evangélica Suica		P-Ref	Rw...	5	500	500	1,000	0.05	*Swiss Reformed Ch.* 3 parishes only. Mostly immigrants from Switzerland.
Igreja Messiânica Mundial do Brasil		I-3pY	.....	30	1,500	2,000	2,500	0.05	*World Messianic Church of Brazil,* small Brazilian independent grouping.
Igreja Metodista do Brasil	1835	P-Met	VWu.N	1,580	79,000	93,600	132,000	1.38	6 Conferences. M=UMC(USA). A=1935, 300n,30x,83f,1j,3p,1s,W=60%,2843Yy.
Igreja Metodista Livre do Brasil	1928	P-Hol	VFu.N	30	8,200	5,000	12,000	3.56	M=Free Methodist Ch (USA). Japanese. 12n,12x,10f,1s(65),W=30%,212Y,544z.
Igreja Metodista Wesleyana	1967	I-3pY	.....	611	55,000	22,000	78,600	5.23	*Wesleyan Meth Ch.* Pentecostal split ex Igreja Metodista. 42n,W=70%,1914Yy.
Igreja Missionária do Brasil	1962	P-Hol	xF...	44	4,271	1,614	8,540	6.89	*United Missionary Ch of Brazil.* M=OMS(IAMS),WGM,MC(USA), 11n,5x,228Y.
Igreja Nacional Independente do B	c1975	I-3oY	.....	25	4,000	–	7,000	5.00	*National Independent Church of Brazil.*
Igreja Nova Apostólica	c1930	I-3aX	x....	140	35,000	50,000	54,985	0.38	*NAC. New Apostolic Ch.* Many German immigrants. World HQ Zurich.
Igreja Orthodoxa Arabe: D São Paulo		O-Ara	Cwo..	25	15,000	20,000	30,000	0.05	In Antiochian Orthodox Christian AD New York (USA), & Greek P Antioch. Arabs. 1 bishop.
Igreja Ort Grega: AD N&S América		O-Gre	Cwo..	7	3,500	5,000	7,000	0.05	In 11th Archdiocesan District, Greek Orthodox Archdiocese of N&S America. Greeks.
Igreja Ortodoxa Romana		O-Rum	Cwo..	4	6,600	9,000	11,000	0.05	*Parohia Ortodoxa Romana.* Under Romanian Orthodox Missionary Episcopate (USA). 1x.
Igreja Ortodoxa Russa		O-Rus	Mwo..	11	22,000	50,000	55,000	0.05	Russian Orthodox, with bishop. In D SAmerica, Orthodox Ch in America (USA).
Igreja Ortodoxa Russa: D Brasil		I-Rus	x....	13	12,600	15,000	18,000	0.05	*Russian Orthodox Ch Outside of Russia.* M=ROCOR(USA). Ultra-conservative Russians.
Igreja Ortodoxa Ucrania		I-Ukr	x....	12	6,000	10,000	12,000	0.05	*Ukrainian Autocephalous Orthodox Ch.* Branch of UOC of USA. Refugees from USSR. 7n.

Continued overleaf

Country Table 2–concluded

Official name (bold type = church with over 10% of all affiliated) 1	*Begun* 2	*Type* 3	*Counc* 4	*Congs* 5	*Adults* 6	*Affiliated 1970* 7	*Affiliated 1995* 8	*G%* 9	*Names, notes, and other statistics* (see Codebook, Part 3) 10
Igreja Pedra Fundamental	c1970	I-3pY	.....	2,000	1,000,000	–	2,400,000	79.97	*Cornerstone Gospel Ch.* 7th largest in Brazil (after RCC,AoG,CCB, IURD,ICAB, God is Love).
Igreja Pentecostal da Nova Vida	1960	P-Pe2	Z....	75	4,000	5,000	10,000	2.81	*Cruzada da Nova Vida. New Life Pente Ch.* M=PAoC(Canada). 28n,8f,1p(64),W=53%,285Y.
Igreja Pentecostal da Oração	1950	I-3pY	.....	20	500	2,000	1,000	-2.73	*Pentecostal Church of Prayer.* Independents. Declined since 1955.
Igreja Pentecostal Deus e Amor		I-3pY	x....	3,200	1,600,000	50,000	2,670,000	0.05	*God is Love Pentecostal Ch.* Huge in big cities: drab. Many chs abroad (Cape Verde, USA, &c).
Igreja Pentecostal Unida do Brasil	1952	P-Pe1	x....	150	12,000	8,000	20,000	3.73	*United Pentecostal Ch. Jesus Only.* M=UPC(USA). Unitarian. HQ São Paulo. 50n,11f,2p'(44).
Igreja Presb Conservadora do Brasil	1940	I-Ref	.TT.T	110	2,000	2,000	3,000	1.64	*Conservative Presbyterian Ch.* Schism ex IPI opposing modernism. 3 Presbyteries. 1s.
Igreja Presbiteriana do Brasil	1859	P-Ref	R.u.N	1,232	190,630	623,995	480,000	-1.04	*IPB, Presbyterian Ch.* 65 Presbyteries. M=UPUSA,PCUS. 574n,155f,2H,2h,2s,2063t(169097).
Igreja Presbiteriana Renovada		I-3cY	.....	175	35,000	5,000	54,700	0.05	*Renewed Presbyterian Church.*
Igreja Presbitertana Unida do Brasil	1978	P-Ref	.....	61	20,000	–	33,300	5.88	*United Presbyterian Ch of Brazil.*
Igreja Presb Fundamentalista do Brasil	1956	I-Fun	.TT.T	20	500	800	1,000	0.90	*Fundamental Presbyterian Ch.* Schism ex IPB opposing modernism. HQ Recife. 1s.
Igreja Presby Independente do Brasil	1903	I-Ref	Rvu.N	420	55,000	180,000	91,700	-2.66	*IPI. Independent Presbyterian Ch.* Schism ex IPB. 1946, M=IBPFM(USA). 235n1s,W=80%,35Yy.
Igreja Unicista	c1980	I-3oY	.....	5	200	–	500	6.67	Oneness pentecostals, small following.
Igreja Universal do Reino de Deus	1977	I-3pY	x....	10,000	2,000,000	–	4,000,000	5.56	*Universal Ch of the Kingdom of God. IURD/UCKG.* 2000n. In 50 countries (Portugal, Angola & c)
Igrejas de Cristo	1952	I-Dis	x....	110	8,800	2,000	14,700	8.31	M=Chs of Christ (Non-Instrumental) (USA). Independent group of congregations. 52f.
Igrejas Paz	1977	I-3fY	.....	300	15,000	–	30,000	5.56	*Full Gospel Peace Churches.* Amazon. HQ Santarem. M=Vineyard Chs, GSMA(USA).
Igrejas radiofónicas isoladas	c1950	I-3rY	.....	300	10,000	2,000	15,000	8.39	Isolated radio believers in remote jungle areas. R=49700 (HCJB,TWR,FEBC,Radio Vatican).
Irmãos Cristãos	c1905	P-CBr	x....	420	40,000	25,000	80,000	4.76	*Christian (Plymouth, Open) Brethren. Gospel Halls.* M=CMML(UK,USA.Australia). 47f.
Missão Amazonas	1949	P-Non	.....	30	1,000	600	2,000	4.93	M=Amazon Mission (USA). Pioneer work between Rio Negro and Amazon rivers.
Missão Batista Conservadora	1946	I-Bap	xF...	60	4,804	5,494	9,240	2.10	*North & South Brazil Missions.* M=CBFMS(USA). 4n,10m,59f,2s,W=39%,178Y.
Missão Batista Livre do Brasil	1958	P-Bap	xF...	9	290	658	579	-0.51	*Brazil Free Will Baptist Mission.* M=NAFWB(USA). 3n,12x,22f,W=88%,33Y,40z.
Missão de Evangelização Mundial	1957	P-Non	xF...	10	270	500	400	-0.89	*M=WEC,WEK(UK,USA,Germany). HQ Belo Horizonte. Declining. 11f,W=75%,40Y,12z.*
Missão Ev Independente do Brasil	1965	P-Bap	.....	20	680	550	1,000	2.42	M=Evangelical Free Ch (USA). Congregationalist, Baptist. 3n,5x,W=64%,22Y.
Missão Interior do Brasil	1954	P-CBr	.....	25	400	350	600	2.18	M=Brazil Inland Mission. Open Brethren tradition. 7n,2x,W=99%,38Y,20z.
Missão Mundial Unida	1960	P-Non	.....	3	500	300	1,000	4.93	*United World Mission.* M=UWM.
Missão Novas Tribos do Brasil	1946	P-Fun	x....	95	4,750	5,000	11,900	3.53	M=New Tribes Mission (USA). Work among Amerindian jungle tribes. 181f,2h,1s.
Renascer em Cristo	1988	I-3cY	.....	31	50,000	–	70,000	14.29	*Born Again in Christ.* Rock concerts, massive radio/TV. 80% under 27 years. In Spain, France.
Sociedade Betânia do Brasil	1963	P-Lut	xF...	15	1,500	1,000	2,000	2.81	M=Bethany Fellowship (USA). Independents. 1n,2x,48f,1H,2s,W=87%,50Y,15z.
Sociedade Cristã Missionaria	1957	P-Hol	.....	7	202	100	300	4.49	*Christian Missionary Fellowship.* M=CMF(USA).
Sociedade Evangelizadora Biblica	1950	I-Eva	.....	40	1,500	2,000	2,500	0.90	*Bible Evangelizing Society.* Independents. 1n,17x,1p(14),159Y.
Testemunhas de Jeová	1920	m-Jeh	x....	5,332	335,039	169,835	779,000	6.28	*Jehovah's Witnesses.* 70 Korean churches. (1970) 2270n,98x,7451Y,64921z. (1995) 35760Y.
União Batista Evangélica	1957	P-Bap	xF...	70	2,000	2,000	3,000	1.64	*Ev Baptist Union.* M=Baptist General Conference (USA). HQ São Paulo. 18f,1s.
União Missionaria Evanhelo	1931	P-Hol	.....	44	1,434	1,000	2,134	3.08	Gospel Missionary Union. M=GMU. 29f.
Other independent charismatic chs	1970	I-3gY	.....	3,000	1,600,000	–	3,000,000	81.59	Grassroots (GR) churches: Rio has 984 GR chs, São Paulo 1,468 chs with 650,000; NNCM.
Other indigenous nonpentecostal chs		I-	.....	4,000	500,000	100,000	1,000,000	0.05	Total over 400 (see list below).
Other Protestant denominations		P-	.....	2,000	270,000	70,000	818,000	0.05	Total about 500 (see list below).
Other indigenous pentecostal churches		I-3pY	.....	800	232,000	300,000	450,000	0.05	Total over 115 (see list below).
Other marginal Protestant bodies		m-	.....	300	51,200	50,000	125,000	0.05	Total over 100, including New Ch (UK), RCJCLdS (USA).
Other Orthodox churches		O-	.....	100	8,000	10,000	16,000	0.05	Total about 20 (see list below), including Syrian Orthodox (Patriarchal Vicariate).
Doubly-affiliated		2-aff			-28,969,000	-6,347,000	-50,703,135		Evangelicals/Pentecostals who also are or were baptized Roman Catholics.
Totals				**200,534**	**83,526,117**	**91,507,260**	**146,190,000**		

Churches, members, growth, 1900-2025	*Congs*	*Adults*	*Affiliated*	*G%*	*Total denominations*	*6 Megablocs:* *O*	*R*	*A*	*P*	*I*	*m*
Total churches, members, and denominations (mid-1900)	20,000	9,882,000	17,319,000	2.41	28	3	1	1	20	3	0
Total churches, members, and denominations (mid-1970)	46,415	52,214,316	91,507,260	2.41	636	14	1	1	278	290	52
Total churches, members, and denominations (mid-1990)	160,000	77,943,000	136,418,000	2.02	1,506	25	1	1	556	810	113
Total churches, members, and denominations (mid-1995)	200,534	83,526,117	146,190,000	1.39	1,554	25	1	1	558	856	113
Total churches, members, and denominations (mid-2000)	220,000	88,831,000	155,475,609	1.24	1,581	25	1	1	560	880	114
Total churches, members, and denominations (mid-2025)	300,000	111,871,000	195,800,000	0.93	3,367	35	1	1	700	2500	130

NOTES ON TABLE ABOVE

NATIONAL COUNCILS (Column 4, 5th letter).

b = member of both CEB and CPB.
C = Confederação Evangélico Brasileira (CEB) (Evangelical Federation of Brazil).
E = Associaçao Evangélica Brasileira (AEB).
I = Confederação Pentecostal do Brasil (CPB) (Brazil Pentecostal Federation) (an indigenous council begun in 1959, with about 20 members).
R = Conferência Nacional dos Bispos do Brasil (CNBB) (National Bishops' Conference of Brazil).
T = Confederação das Igrejas Evangélicas Fundamentalistas (CIEF) (Evangelical Federation of Fundamental Churches of Brazil).
W = Conselho Nacional de Igrejas Cristas do Brasil (CONIC, National Council of Christian Churches in Brazil).

Other national councils. Federação Evangélica Japonesa do Brasil (Japanese Evangelical Federation of Brazil): members include Igreja Evangélica Holiness do Brasil.

OTHER INDIGENOUS CHURCHES (pentecostal and non-pentecostal). Smaller bodies begun by Brazilians (or other Third-World Christians, e.g. Chinese and Japanese) number at least 155 (115 pentecostal, 40 non-pentecostal), and include the following: Assembleia Cristã, Assembleia de Deus (Missão Batista), Assembly Hall Ch (Chinese), Associação das Igrejas de Cristianismo Decidido, Associação das Igrejas Ev Independentes do Brasil (member of ICCC), Gospel of Jesus Ch (Iesu Fukuin Kyodan), Igreja Adventista Apostólica, Igreja Adventista da Reforma Completa, Igreja Apostólica Brasileira, Igreja Apostólica Ev Tenda de Deus pro Salvação e Cura Divina, Igreja Apostólica Pentecostal, Igreja Batista de Parque das Nações, Igreja Batista Revelação, Igreja Cristã Ev Independente, Igreja Cristã Pentecostal do B, Igreja Cristo Jesus, Igreja Ev Aposólica, Igreja Ev de Povo, Igreja Ev do Avivamento Biblico, Igreja Ev do Espírito Santo, Igreja Ev dos Primogênitos Hebreus, Igreja Ev Maravilhas de Jesus, Igreja Ev Pentecostal, Igreja Ev Pentecostal Livre, Igreja Jesus Fonte de Agua Viva, Igreja Pentecostal Independente, Igreja Pentecostal Jesus Nazareno, Igreja Viva Jesus, Irmandade Metodista Ortodoxa, Korean Presbyterian Ch of São Paulo (member of ICCC), Ordem Católica Apostólica dos Missionários da Santa Cruz (1970 applied to join WCC), Renovação Espiritual, True Jesus Ch (Chinese).

OTHER PROTESTANT DENOMINATIONS. This list includes 53 of the around 100 smaller denominations and recently-arrived foreign Protestant faith missions, most of the latter having under 5 missionaries each (names are given in Portuguese unless the English (or German, or Spanish) name is more used): Acampamento Biblico Pioneiro (Pioneer Bible Mission), Aliança Missionária do Brasil (Missionary & Soul-Winning Fellowship), Apostolic Ch of Pentecost (Canada, 2 missionaries), Asas (Alas) de Socorro (Mission Aviation Fellowship; several congregations), Baptist Faith Missions (1923), Baptist International Missions (1965), Baptist Mid-Missions (1936), Baptist Missionary Association of America, Baptist Missionary Society (UK, 1953; 33 missionaries), Berean Mission (1967), Brazil Gospel Fellowship Mission (1939), Brazilian Bible Mission, Children of God International (USA), Christian Bible Mission, Christian Missionary Fellowship (1957), Christian Nationals Evangelism Commission (1969), Congregational Holiness Ch (1972), Convenção Batista do Japão, Darbistas (Exclusive Brethren: Kelly-Continental), Deutsche Indianer Pionier Mission, Emmanuel Association, Federação de Igrejas Batistas do Nordeste do Brasil (member of ICCC), Fellowship of Independent Missions (1964), Gospel Fellowship Missions, Go-Ye Fellowship of Brazil, Iglesia Ev ApostContinental), Deutsche Indianer Pionier Mission, Emmanuel Association, Federação de Igrejas Batistas do Nordeste do Brasil (member of ICCC), Fellowship of Independent inheiros (Scandinavian Sailors' Ch), Fellowship of Independent a Bíblica do Brasil, Missão da Amaz, Igreja Eslavá Brasileira Pentecostal, Igreja Ev Armenia, Igreja Ev Batista, Independent Bible Baptist Mission (1954), Instituto Apostde Igrejas Batistas do Nordeste do Brasil (member of ICCC), Fellowship of Independent , Sociedade União Cristã (Gnadauer Verband), United Missions, United World Mission (1961), Voz Bíblica Brasileira (Independent Faith Mission), World Gospel Mission (1966), World Missions (1964), World-Wide Missions (1963).

OTHER ORTHODOX CHURCHES. These include: Coptic Orthodox Ch, Old Believers Russian Orthodox Ch (Old Ritualist Ch, Priestless) (1958-61 from China and Turkey), Orthodox Syrian Ch, Serbian Orthodox Ch, Syrian Orthodox Ch.

OTHER CATHOLIC (NON-ROMAN) CHURCHES. Including Antoinists (from Belgium and France), and miniscule episcopal churches under bishops-at-large (episcopi vagantes).

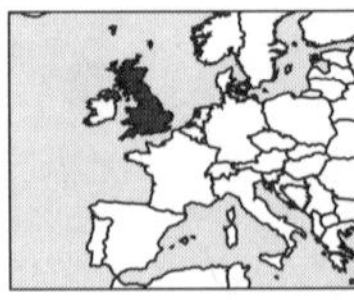

BRITAIN (UK OF GB & NI)

SECULAR DATA, AD 2000

STATE

Official name: The United Kingdom of Great Britain and Northern Ireland.
Short name: Britain. **Adjective of nationality:** of the United Kingdom of Great Britain and Northern Ireland, British.
Flag: Union Jack: red-on-white crosses of St George of England and St Patrick of Ireland, and white-on-blue cross of St Andrew of Scotland.
Area: 244,110 sq. km. (94,251 sq. mi.).
Government: Parliamentary constitutional monarchy, since 1690 (c500 kingdoms, 1215 parliamentary monarchy, 1649 commonwealth, 1660 monarchy, 1690 constitutional monarchy, 1801 United Kingdom formed).
Legislature: Parliament: House of Lords, 1,075 members; House of Commons, 635 members.
Official language: English.
Monetary unit: 1 pound sterling (£) = 100 new pence. **US$1=** £ 0.59.
Chief cities: LONDON (Greater London) 7,640,000; Birmingham-West Midlands 2,271,000; Manchester (Greater Manchester) 2,252,000; Glasgow 1,850,508; Leeds-Bradford (West Yorkshire) 1,433,000.
Political divisions: 64 provinces.
Armed forces: 254,000.

DEMOGRAPHY

Population: 58,830,000.
Population density: 241.0/sq. km. (624.1/sq. mi.).
Under 15 years: 11,072,000.
Growth rate p.a.: 0.11% (births 11.09, deaths 10.70).
Mortality: Infant, per 1,000: 6.6; **Maternal per 100,000:** 9.0.
Life expectancy: 78 (male 75, female 81).
Household size: 2.7. **Floor area per person, sq.m:** 50.0.
Major languages: English, Irish, Welsh (26% in Wales), French, Italian, Greek, Polish, Gaelic, Punjabi, Gurajati, Bengali, Chinese (Cantonese), German, Arabic, Ukrainian, Russian, Romany, Spanish, Maltese.
Urban dwellers: 89.48%. **Urban growth rate p.a.:** 0.2%.
Labor force: 49%.

ETHNOLINGUISTIC PEOPLES

74.7% English (British); 9.5% Scottish (British); 2.4% Irish; 1.9% Welsh; 1.8% Ulster Irish.

ECONOMY

National income p.a. per person: US$18,700; **per family:** US$50,490.

EDUCATION

Adult literacy: 94% (male 95%, female 94%). **Schools:** 28,169.
Universities: 820. **School enrolment:** female/male: 104%/103%.

HEALTH

Access to health services: 95%. **Access to safe water:** 100%.
Hospitals: 2,423 (54 beds per 10,000). **Doctors:** 87,000.
Blind: 116,414. **Deaf:** 3,500,200. **Murder rate:** 2.
Lepers: 500.

LITERATURE

New book titles p.a.: 111,780 (1,900 p.a. per million). **Periodicals:** 8,971. **Newspapers:** 103 dailies.

COMMUNICATION (per 1,000 people)

Phones: 502 (31% mobile). **Radios:** 1,109. **TV sets:** 612.
Daily newspaper circulation: 351. **Computers:** 441.

REFUGEES

Alien refugees from other countries: 44,000.

HUMAN LIFE AND LIBERTY (optimum condition=100.0%)

HDI: 93.1. **HSI:** 84.0. **HFI:** 80.0. **EFL:** 61.0.

Country Table 1. **Religious adherents in Britain (UK of GB & NI), AD 1900-2025.**

Year	*1900*		*1970*		*mid-1990*		*Annual change, 1990-2000*				*mid-1995*		*mid-2000*		*mid-2025*	
Name	*Adherents*	*%*	*Adherents*	*%*	*Adherents*	*%*	*Natural*	*Conversion*	*Total*	*Rate*	*Adherents*	*%*	*Adherents*	*%*	*Adherents*	*%*
Christians	**37,125,000**	**97.4**	**49,298,000**	**88.6**	**48,083,500**	**83.5**	**106,022**	**-56,306**	**49,716**	**0.10**	**48,409,000**	**83.0**	**48,580,660**	**82.6**	**47,904,500**	**79.9**
PROFESSION																
professing Christians	**37,125,000**	**97.4**	**49,298,000**	**88.6**	**48,083,500**	**83.5**	**106,022**	**-56,306**	**49,716**	**0.10**	**48,409,000**	**83.0**	**48,580,660**	**82.6**	**47,904,500**	**79.9**
AFFILIATION																
unaffiliated Christians	998,600	2.6	5,345,559	9.6	8,883,500	15.4	19,585	44,816	64,401	0.70	9,259,000	15.9	9,527,509	16.2	9,904,500	16.5
affiliated Christians	**36,126,400**	**94.8**	**43,952,441**	**79.0**	**39,200,000**	**68.1**	**86,421**	**-101,106**	**-14,685**	**-0.04**	**39,150,000**	**67.1**	**39,053,151**	**66.4**	**38,000,000**	**63.4**
Anglicans	24,536,400	64.4	29,058,547	52.2	25,960,000	45.1	57,232	-25,432	31,800	0.12	26,240,380	45.0	26,278,000	44.7	26,000,000	43.4
Roman Catholics	2,429,000	6.4	5,553,431	10.0	5,600,000	9.7	12,346	-10,346	2,000	0.04	5,612,480	9.6	5,620,000	9.6	5,650,000	9.4
Protestants	9,144,000	24.0	7,713,411	13.9	5,195,000	9.0	11,453	-25,953	-14,500	-0.28	5,102,986	8.8	5,050,000	8.6	4,800,000	8.0
Independents	5,000	0.0	833,164	1.5	1,990,000	3.5	4,387	10,613	15,000	0.73	2,076,288	3.6	2,140,000	3.6	3,000,000	5.0
Marginal Christians	10,000	0.0	477,688	0.9	525,000	0.9	1,157	1,343	2,500	0.47	536,615	0.9	550,000	0.9	750,000	1.3
Orthodox	2,000	0.0	316,200	0.6	345,000	0.6	761	1,739	2,500	0.70	353,400	0.6	370,000	0.6	500,000	0.8
doubly-affiliated	0	0.0	0	0.0	-415,000	-0.7	-915	-53,070	-53,985	8.69	-772,149	-1.3	-954,849	-1.6	-2,700,000	-4.5
Trans-megabloc groupings																
Evangelicals	18,669,000	49.0	11,960,880	21.5	11,369,000	19.8	25,064	-5,964	19,100	0.17	11,497,387	19.7	11,560,000	19.7	11,350,000	18.9
Pentecostals/Charismatics	0	0.0	2,480,000	4.5	5,600,000	9.7	12,346	9,654	22,000	0.39	5,719,011	9.8	5,820,000	9.9	7,820,000	13.0
Great Commission Christians	**13,335,000**	**35.0**	**16,689,000**	**30.0**	**20,435,000**	**35.5**	**45,051**	**23,535**	**68,586**	**0.33**	**20,816,000**	**35.7**	**21,120,856**	**35.9**	**21,885,000**	**36.5**
Nonreligious	720,000	1.9	4,400,400	7.9	6,498,000	11.3	14,326	27,946	42,272	0.63	6,760,700	11.6	6,920,719	11.8	8,100,000	13.5
Muslims	0	0.0	635,000	1.1	1,050,000	1.8	2,315	12,417	14,732	1.32	1,095,000	1.9	1,197,316	2.0	1,400,000	2.3
Atheists	10,000	0.0	300,000	0.5	720,000	1.3	1,587	5,833	7,420	0.99	760,000	1.3	794,203	1.4	1,000,000	1.7
Hindus	0	0.0	220,000	0.4	375,000	0.7	827	4,584	5,411	1.36	405,000	0.7	429,113	0.7	500,000	0.8
Jews	235,000	0.6	450,000	0.8	310,000	0.5	683	-1,456	-773	-0.25	300,000	0.5	302,269	0.5	275,000	0.5
Sikhs	0	0.0	200,000	0.4	225,000	0.4	496	536	1,032	0.45	230,000	0.4	235,321	0.4	275,000	0.5
Buddhists	0	0.0	30,000	0.1	120,000	0.2	265	4,192	4,457	3.21	155,000	0.3	164,571	0.3	250,000	0.4
Spiritists	10,000	0.0	20,000	0.0	55,000	0.1	121	1,259	1,380	2.26	63,000	0.1	68,802	0.1	85,000	0.1
Chinese folk-religionists	0	0.0	15,000	0.0	35,000	0.1	77	377	454	1.23	37,000	0.1	39,539	0.1	45,000	0.1
Baha'is	0	0.0	13,600	0.0	26,000	0.1	57	406	463	1.65	28,000	0.1	30,628	0.1	40,000	0.1
New-Religionists	0	0.0	0	0.0	13,500	0.0	30	220	250	1.71	15,000	0.0	16,002	0.0	38,500	0.1
Ethnoreligionists	0	0.0	0	0.0	6,000	0.0	13	93	106	1.64	6,500	0.0	7,060	0.0	8,000	0.0
Other religionists	0	0.0	50,000	0.1	44,000	0.1	97	-101	-4	-0.01	43,800	0.1	43,957	0.1	40,000	0.1
World A (unevangelized persons)	38,100	0.1	278,160	0.5	1,036,098	1.8	2,315	4,383	6,698	0.62	1,107,854	1.9	1,117,770	1.9	1,379,103	2.3
World B (evangelized non-Christians)	936,900	2.5	6,055,840	10.9	8,441,402	14.7	18,579	51,923	70,502	0.79	8,791,287	15.1	9,131,570	15.5	10,677,397	17.8
World C (Christians)	37,125,000	97.4	49,298,000	88.6	48,083,500	83.5	106,022	-56,306	49,716	0.10	48,409,000	83.0	48,580,660	82.6	47,904,500	79.9
Country's population	**38,100,000**	**100.0**	**55,632,000**	**100.0**	**57,561,000**	**100.0**	**126,916**	**0**	**126,916**	**0.22**	**58,308,142**	**100.0**	**58,830,000**	**100.0**	**59,961,000**	**100.0**

COLUMNS, ROWS.
For meanings and definitions, see Codebook (Part 3). Note that, by definition, total 'Christians' = professing + crypto-Christians, which also = affiliated + unaffiliated Christians, and also = Great Commission Christians + latent Christians. Percentages may not always total exactly, due to rounding.

CENSUSES.
The question on religious profession has never been asked in government censuses of the whole of Great Britain. *England and Wales.* The only national census of religion in England and Wales was taken on Sunday, **30.III.1851.** A total of 10,896,066 attendances was recorded, by (since 50% went twice) 7,261,032 individuals (3,526,900 Anglicans, 3,478,500 Protestants (Free Churches), 255,600 Roman Catholics). Since Sunday-school children were excluded, and since at that time about 30% of the population (ten 16.9 million) were under 15 years old, this means that 61.4% of the total adult population were weekly Sunday attenders. Assuming that weekly attendance was 90% for Protestants but only 50% for Anglicans and Catholics, and that nominal Christians were less than 1%, this gives the following proportions for both professing and affiliated Christians in England and Wales in 1851: 62.0% Anglicans, 33.0% Protestants, 5.0% Roman Catholics; and also a figure of about 90% for annually practicing Christians as defined in this Encyclopedia. *Northern Ireland* (Ulster). **8.IV.1951:** 65.0% Anglicans & Protestants, 34.4% Roman Catholics, 0.5% nonreligious, 0.1% Jews. **23.IV.1961:** 39.7% Protestants, 35,6% Roman Catholics, 24.7% Anglicans. Similar results are obtained annually from religion questions asked in secular polls.

NOTES ON RELIGIONS
ATHEISTS. Communist Party of Great Britain (CPGB) (legal; pro-Soviet): Communist voters (election of 1922) 52,000, (election of VII.1945) 102,780 (4% of all votes), (18.VI.1970) 37,996 (0.1% of all votes), (111.1974) 32,741 (0.1%). In the 30 major trade unions, 150 of the 900 senior posts (17%) are held by communists or their open sympathizers. In the UK, communists are mainly in London, Glasgow and south Wales.
BAHA'IS. Entered Britain in 1905. Recent growth from 49 local spiritual assemblies in 1964 to 91 in 1973 (England 69, Scotland 11, Wales 6, Northern Ireland 5) and 434 other isolated centers and groups; and by 1995 to 184 LSAs (England 143, Scotland 18, Wales 10, Northern Ireland 13).
BUDDHISTS. In 1970 about 50% Chinese, 50% from Sri Lanka, also Thai monks, and Tibetans in Wales. After 1970, however, there were massive numbers of British converts during 1971-77, including at least 20,000 men who became bhikkus (monks). By 1995 all Buddhists were 50% followers of Tibetan Buddhism, 25% of Theravada, and 25% of Zen; with 12 main Buddhist centers, 45 affiliated groups, and 12 priests.
EVANGELICALS. This category as used in the churches covers the following 4 groupings, in order of size: (1) Anglican Evangelicals, i.e. Evangelicals affiliated to Anglican churches, mostly in the Church of England and the Church of Ireland, with a few (4,600) in Anglican free or dissident churches; (2) Conservative Evangelicals, here enumerated as all persons affiliated to Protestant denominations which are Conservative Evangelical in theology and emphasis; (3) Conciliar Evangelicals, namely Evangelicals within non-Evangelical or conciliar Protestant denominations usually within the Ecumenical Movement; and (4) Fundamentalists, being all persons affiliated to Protestant denominations of fundamentalist theology, usually linked with the ICC or other fundamentalist councils. The definition as used here does not include Black indigenous church members. *Anglican Evangelicals.* After the Evangelical Revival from 1739 onwards, by 1800 about 5% of all clergy and a higher percentage of the laity in the Church of England were avowed Evangelicals; by 1853, 41% of all clergy were High Church, 21% Broad Church, and 38% Low Church (W.J. Conybeare); the latter then rose rapidly until by 1900 around 53% were Evangelicals or Low Churchmen of one kind or another. After the year 1900, the proportion of Evangelicals in the Church of England (including the large proportion of Low Churchmen) declined rapidly to around 20% by 1948, but since 1950 a gradual numerical resurgence has been underway, especially during the 1970s, accompanied by a spiritual, theological and ecclesiological renewal, and stimulated to a considerable extent by the Anglican charismatic renewal, of whose members a majority in England are Evangelicals. By 1977 it had become clear that the Church of England as a whole was steadily assuming a distinctly Evangelical character. (a) *Parishes.* In 1975, of the Church of England's 14,400 parishes, 14% regarded themselves as High Church in churchmanship, 48% as Central or Broad Church (or non-Evangelical), 34% as Evangelical (of whom 21% were Conservative Evangelical or Low Church Evangelical), and 4% as Low Church but not Evangelica. With regard to foreign mission support, 58% of all parishes in 1977 supported USPG (High/Central; 21% also supporting CMS), 51% supported CMS (Evangelical; 21% also supporting USPG, and 12% also SAMS, BCMS or RCMS), 15% supported SAMS, 5% BCMS and 4% Ruanda CMS (the latter 3, Conservative Evangelical); these figures total to over 100% because, as indicated, many parishes support 2 or more of these major societies. (b) *Clergy.* With regard to clergy, in 1977 some 35% of the Church of England's 17,500 active clergy regarded themselves as Evangelicals (16% Conservative Evangelicals). (The results of our present survey gave Evangelical clergy as from 25% to 40% depending on the exact definition followed). By 1975 the formerly-strong Liberal Evangelicals, as represented by clergy in the Anglican Evangelical Group Movement, had virtually disappeared. These percentages had all increased considerably over the preceding 25 years; and in 1977, 45% of all ordinands for the Church of England were in training in the 6 Evangelical theological colleges, and about 25% of newly-ordained clergy were Conservative Evangelicals. (c) *Laity.* With regard to the laity, around 28% regarded themselves as Evangelicals in 1975, rising gradually each year from around 20% in 1948. (The results of our present survey gave lay Evangelicals as from 25% to 35% depending on the exact definition followed). As can be seen from the column 'Conversion' above, over half of the annual increase in Evangelicals comes from the increase in Anglican pentecostals. (d) *Anglican Evangelical organizations and conferences.* These include: AEGM, BCMS, CEEC (Church of England Evangelical Council), Climbers, CMJ, CMS, CPAS, Church Society, CWN, CYFA (Church Youth Fellowship Association/ 494 groups), Diocesan Evangelical Fellowships, Eclectics, ECOC, Explorers, FEC, FECOF, Islington Clerical Conference, Lee Abbey, NEAC (National Evangelical Anglican Congress, 1977), Pathfinders, RCMS, SAMS, SEAC (Senior Evangelical Anglican Clergy Conference), Simeon's Trustees.
HINDUS. Originally Indian immigrants, the vast majority Gujaratis from central and southern Gujarat, mostly of the Vaisya (merchant) caste. The column 'Natural change' above consists of biological increase annually and new immigrants each year. Unlike Muslims and Sikhs, Hindus have not built or opened more than a handful of orthodox temples in the UK because of the prohibition of such activity outside India. The total includes a number of sects: 30,000 followers of the Swaminarayan Hindu Mission, the Ramakrishna Mission, Eckankar, Auroville International, Meher Baha Association (Oceanic Limited), and several sects with widespread White followings and annual White converts; Divine Light Mission (DLM), begun in India in 1960 and in England in 1971; 3,000 members of Hare Krishna (International Society for Krishna Consciousness, ISKCON), which reached the UK in 1968; Spiritual Regeneration Movement (SRM) or Transcendental Meditation, a yoga therapy introduced around 1965; 1,000 adherents (170 committed disciples) of the Bengali movement Sri Chimnoy Centre; Ananda Marga; et alia.
INDEPENDENTS. In over 300 distinct denominations in 1995 (see Table 2), increasing each year. In addition, there are a large number of other Black and Black-led churches with dominant West Indian membership which are not classified here as Third-World indigenous because they are part of, or affiliated to, White Protestant churches based in the USA or the UK; the largest are the New Testament Church of God, Seventh-day Adventist Church, Church of God of Prophecy, Moravian Church, Church of God Fellowship (Welsh Latter Rain Movement), Seventh Day Baptist Church, United Pentecostal Church, et alia, with over 60,000 affiliated Black members.JEWS. 77% belong to the United Synagogue (Orthodox), 8% Liberal, 7% Reform, 8% no synagogue. There are 350 synagogues in Britain. Over half of all Jews live in the London area. Attendance at synagogue: of all Jews, 26% attend weekly, 6% fortnightly, 8% monthly, 19% quarterly, 20% less often, 21% never. Liberal and Reform Jews attend less regularly than United.
MUSLIMS. Over 80% are immigrants since 1950 from Pakistan and other British Commonwealth Muslim countries and areas with their dependants. The column 'Natural change' above consists of biological increase annually and new immigrants each year. In 1995 the majority of Muslims were Sunnis from Pakistan (including Bengalis from Bangladesh), with about 200,000 Sunnis from India (mainly Gujaratis), around 20,000 Arabs and Middle Easterners (including 30,000 Moroccans), 30,000 Turkish Cypriots (Sunnis), 50,000 from Malaysia, 20,000 from East Africa, 10,000 from West Africa, 10,000 Ismaili Shias, 30,000 Yemenis, 7,000 Somalis, 15,000 Eritreans, some Shias, and 8,000 in the Ahmadiya Mission. *Muslim temporary residents* (excluded from Table 1). (1980) 500,000. *Mosques.* (1980) About 1,200. *Quranic schools.* (1980) 5,000. *Hajj pilgrims to Mecca.* (1974) 1,254; (1976) 757.
NONRELIGIOUS. Among these are followers of the over 91 humanist groups, most affiliated to one of the national bodies.
OTHER RELIGIONISTS. There is a large number of smaller non-Christian religious groupings. These include 10,000 militant supporters of Moral Re-Armament (MRA) with 100,000 sympathizers or adherents most of whom belong to Christian churches; about 30,000 practice occultism and black magic in England; many adherents of African, Asian and Afro-American non-Christian and syncretistic religions, including non-Christian Rastafarians from Jamaica; 1,200 adherents of Soka Gakkai (Nichiren Shoshu) from Japan, Rosicrucians (AMORC with 16 Lodges and centers, also Lectorium Rosicrucianum and other orders); Druidism and Neo-Paganism; Atlanteans and followers of other New Age cults; and other groupings. Some of the 1 million Freemasons in the British Isles practice it as a non-Christian religion, although most are either professing or nominal Anglicans or Protestants, or nonreligious.
PENTECOSTALS/CHARISMATICS. The largest bloc of followers in this category are Anglican Charismatics, who in Britain in AD 2000 number more than 3 million.

Among Roman Catholics, the Catholic Charismatic Renewal began in 1968. By 1997 there were 250 regular weekly prayer groups in the dioceses in England, with 5,500 regular adult attenders, 120 involved priests and 6 bishops, 12 covenant communities, and a total Catholic Charismatic community including children of over 300,000.
ROMAN CATHOLICS. Annual converts (adult baptisms) have declined (as a % of all Catholics) from 1911-90: there were 7,700 in 1911, a peak of 13,735 in 1959, a plateau of 12,000 from 1960-62, then a decline to 3,700 in 1990. Nominal Catholics (alienated to the extent of not using church offices for baptisms, marriages or funerals) increased from 4% of all professing Catholics in 1958 to 23% in 1970 and to 30% by 1990. In England, the Roman Catholic Church recognizes that it is out of touch with around 30% of all Catholics, who are either unknown to the church and clergy, or lapsed, or non-practicing, or practicing elsewhere.
SIKHS. Immigrants from India; Punjabis, mainly from 2 districts in the Punjab: Jullundur and Hoshiarpur. There are over 38 temples in the British Isles. In the 1990s there was still a small annual immigration (included in the column 'Natural change' above).
SPIRITISTS. Non-Christian adherents of several varieties of specifically non-Christian Spiritism and mediumistic religions, which nevertheless hold some basic Christian tenets and assign a leading role to Christ, and hence also claim numerous Christian adherents; including White Eagle Lodge (begun 1936; in 120 groups in UK, USA, Netherlands, Sweden, Norway, Switzerland and over 30 other countries; HQ at White Temple, Liss, UK).

Country status. Britain is the shorthand name for the countries of England, Scotland, Wales, and Ulster, located on two large islands to the northwest of the European mainland. The first three together form 'Great Britain', and all four form the United Kingdom of Great Britain and Northern Ireland. Due to immigration, the population has become greatly diversified particular with large numbers of immigrants from South Asia.

HUMAN LIFE AND LIBERTY

Human need and development. The United Kingdom is a developed country and one of the leaders of the industrialized world. Despite the loss of empire, it is still a major financial and technological power and its cultural influence extends to every

Great Commission Instrument Panel: status of Britain (UK of GB & NI) (for explanation see start of Part 4)

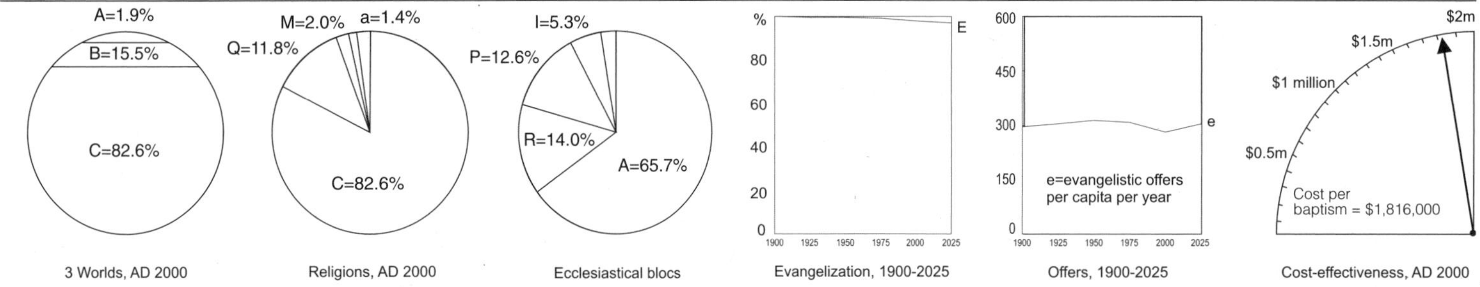

part of the globe. Although the economy is driven by the private sector there is a strong but diminishing public sector. Since the end of World War II, it has developed into a welfare state providing its citizens with a broad range of welfare services, including free healthcare.

Human rights and freedoms. The only blot on the human rights situation in the United Kingdom is Northern Ireland, where, until 1994, an insurgency raged with much violence and bloodshed. Both the Provisional Irish Republican Army and the Unionists or Loyalists have engaged in indiscriminate slaughter to which the British government troops also have occasionally contributed. Both the Helsinki Watch and the U. N. Committee Against Torture have complained about the torture of IRA prisoners and the use of confessions obtained under duress. Some of the historic safeguards against arbitrary arrest and prolonged detention have been removed under the Northern Ireland (Emergency Provisions) Act (EPA) of 1991 and the Prevention of Terrorism (Temporary Provisions) Act of 1989 both of which are directed against the IRA. Under the EPA, police or military personnel may enter private premises without warrant and arrest and detain persons suspected of having committed or being about to commit an offense. Such detainees may be denied legal representation or judicial review. In 1988 the European Court of Human Rights found that this practice violated the European Human Rights Convention. The rising crime rates in the kingdom have prompted a series of proposals to reform the criminal justice system and make it easier to convict criminals. These proposals permit judges to instruct juries to draw 'inference of guilt' from the defendant's refusal to answer questions during interrogation or trial, end bail for serious or repeated offenses, and create new categories of terrorism-related offenses. The right to trial by jury has been suspended for terrorism-related offenses in favor of the so-called Diplock Courts in which a single judge presides over a trial without a jury. Security checks carried by military forces in Northern Ireland are directed particularly against the Catholic community and are viewed by them as a form of harassment and intimidation. The abridgment of civil liberties also affects the freedom of the press and freedom of assembly. The Official Secrets Act prohibits the disclosure of a broad range of national security and foreign policy information. Radio and television are prohibited from broadcasting the voices of members of proscribed terrorist organizations such as the Provisional IRA and the Sinn Fein, as well as the voices of those who 'solicit, support or invite support for such organizations'. The Public Order Act of 1986 gives police broad powers to restrict or ban public demonstrations, marches or assemblies when they deem that violence or vandalism is likely to result. Although the law prohibits discrimination based on race or religion, persons of African and South Asian origin face substantial discrimination in the criminal justice system as well as in housing, employment, and other areas. These minorities are often the victims of racial insults and skinhead violence. In Northern Ireland Catholics face overt discrimination in public employment and housing.

Human environment. As the cradle of the Industrial Revolution, United Kingdom suffered considerable environmental damage until the late 1970s. Since then, conditions have ameliorated to the extent that the air is cleaner and the salmon have returned to the Thames. However, it still remains one of the main polluters of the North Sea where 17% of its sewage and 20% of its industrial wastes are dumped. Even with strong emission controls, it is responsible for about 10% of the acid rain that falls on Norway and other Scandinavian countries.

NON-CHRISTIAN RELIGIONS

Judaism has a long history in Britain, and its Jewish community is among the most important in the world. Jews first came to England during the Norman conquest, but a 13th-century edict by Edward I resulted in their expulsion. The present Anglo-Jewish community, one of the largest in Europe, dates from 1656 and its composed of 2 branches, Ashkenazi (originally from Germany and eastern Europe) and Sefardi (from Spain and Portugal), both divided into Orthodox and Reformed schools of thought. About 90% of all practicing Jews are Orthodox, the chief rabbi being the head of the Ashkenazis, the principal group, and the haham, the leader of the Sefardis. Reformed Judaism began in 1840 and was succeeded by the liberal Jewish movement in 1901. There are at present hundreds of synagogues in the UK, and recent years have witnessed a marked growth in Jewish schools. A survey in 1992 found that about one-third of British Jews claimed to go to synagogue weekly, while almost 50% claimed to go once a year.

International Jewish organizations with their headquarters in London include the World Sefardi Federation, World Union of Jewish Students, World Zionist organization, Institute of Jewish Affairs, Conference of European Rabbis, and Jewish Colonization Association.

Among the many national Jewish organizations may be mentioned the following: the Chief Rabbinate, Reform Synagogues of Great Britain, Union of Liberal and Progressive Synagogues, Central Council for Jewish Social Service, Federation of Jewish Relief Organizations, Jewish Agency for Israel, Zionist Federation of Great Britain and Ireland, Federation of Women Zionists of Great Britain and Ireland, Central Council for Jewish Religious Education, Institute of Jewish Studies, Association for Jewish Yough, Hillel Foundation, Inter-University Jewish Federation of Great Britain and Ireland, Association of Jewish Women's Organizations in the United Kingdom, and League of Jewish Women.

Islam has the largest following among Asian religions in Britain due to immigration, amounting to 1.9% of the population in 1995. The Central Mosque and Islamic Cultural Centre in London serve as headquarters for the orthodox Muslim community, while mosques and centers also exist in Liverpool, Manchester, Cardiff, Bradford, and other cities. The 1991 census reported less than 1,000 Muslims in Northern Ireland. Not many are in Wales or Scotland. About half of Britain's Muslims live in or near London, and then mainly in 8 of the city's 42 wards. The majority are Sunnis but several Shia sects are also present. An international Muslim organization with its headquarters in London is the Islamic Council of Europe. Three national organizations based in London are the Union of Muslim Organizations of UK and Eire, Islamic Cultural Centre, and Muslim Students Society; while the Islamic Foundation has its center in Leicester.

Hinduism. New Swaminarayan temple in London, largest outside India.

Hinduism has the next largest following, 0.7% of the population in 1995. For decades the Hindus of Britain built no temples, but now scores of temples are found in all major East Indian communities. Among the first temples was the East London Hindu Centre which opened a temple in London in 1970. By 1995 there were about 130 temples in Britain, most of them well attended. In addition to traditional Hindu sects, there are many White converts to new sects of which the largest are the Divine Light Mission (8,000), the Hare Krishna movement (3,000), and the Spiritual Regeneration Movement (TM).

Sikhism amounted to 0.4% of the population in 1995. Most Sikh families are from the Punjab, with many also from East Africa. The British Sikh community is the world's largest outside its south Asian homeland. Most live in Birmingham, Bradford, Cardiff, Coventry, Glasgow, Leeds, Leicester, Wolverhampton, and Southall in London. The first gurdwara was opened in 1911; by 1995 there were 180 in Britain, each serving not only as a place of worship but also as a significant community and cultural center. That functional mix is also generally the case for Muslim mosques and Hindu temples.

Buddhism has a long history in the UK going back to the 19th century, although there were only about 150,000 adherents in the country in 1995. The Buddhist Society, founded in London in 1924, maintains a shrine room and one of Europe's finest Buddhist libraries, and includes as members most of Buddhism's numerous local associations, in Aberdeen, Devon, Dover, and Edinburgh, to cite only a few. These groups are often small but very active and characterized by independence with regard to the variety of Buddhist practices. Later Tibetan schools established centers of meditation, and the Theravada school of Thailand opened a temple (Buddhapadipa Temple) in East Sheen, London which is much used for daily meditation. The Buddhist Society belongs to the Buddhist Community of Europe, based in France. Since 1971, massive numbers of British converts have been won, including more than 20,000 men who have become bhikkus (monks).

Other religions include various organized and informal groups of neo-pagan worshippers who have revived pre-Christian beliefs and practices. One estimate in 1995 reckoned there were 5,000 who regularly took part in Druid ceremonies, with as many as 40,000 attending major events. Neo-pagan observances are often closely linked with ecological and feminist sensibilities. The Council of British Druid Orders serves as a point of unity and functions as a political lobbying group.

CHRISTIANITY

The definitive introduction of Christianity into Britain may be put at around the end of the first century, the first church according to tradition having been erected at Glastonbury in AD 61. In AD 314, 3 English bishops attended the Council of Arles in France. From about 350 the Celtic church in Britain was cut off from the rest of Christendom, finally becoming absorbed by the church of the Romans during 632-777. In 563, Columba left Ireland to found a monastery of Iona (Scotland), and Augustine was sent by the Roman pope in 596 to England, which had become a virtually heathen country again; he became the first bishop of Canterbury. During the next century Wilfred and Theodore of Tarsus completed the evangelization of England and the organization of the British church, and Willibrord and Boniface were sent out as missionaries to Holland, Germany, and Denmark. Norwegian and Swedish kings educated in

Country summary. **Worlds A, B, C by ethnolinguistic peoples, cities, and major civil divisions in Britain (UK of GB & NI).**

	PEOPLES							CITIES							CIVIL DIVISIONS						
World	*Num*	*Pop 2000*	*C%*	*Christians*	*E%*	*U%*	*Unevangelized*	*Num*	*Pop 2000*	*C%*	*Christians*	*E%*	*U%*	*Unevangelized*	*Num*	*Pop 2000*	*C%*	*Christians*	*E%*	*U%*	*Unevangelized*
A	9	581,711	0.13	746	41	59	346,001	0	0	0.00	0	0	0	0	0	0	0.00	0	0	0	0
B	22	1,928,651	6.44	124,136	69	31	597,576	0	0	0.00	0	0	0	0	0	0	0.00	0	0	0	0
C	64	56,319,793	69.12	38,928,269	100	0	173,402	111	36,832,070	64.02	23,579,556	98	2	889,252	64	58,830,161	66.38	39,053,150	98	2	1,116,977
Total	**95**	**58,830,155**	**66.38**	**39,053,151**	**98**	**2**	**1,116,979**	**111**	**36,832,070**	**64.02**	**23,579,556**	**98**	**2**	**889,252**	**64**	**58,830,161**	**66.38**	**39,053,150**	**98**	**2**	**1,116,977**

England in their turn introduced Christianity to their own countries before the year 1000. British kings and nobles were involved in the Crusades during the 13th century, and universities and mendicant orders were developed during this period of the Middle Ages. The 14th and 15th centuries were a time of secular disillusionment and religious dissatisfaction with current Christian practices, voiced by John Wycliffe and the Lollards, who stressed the importance of the Bible, the practice of poverty, and personal spirituality.

Britain severed its relationship with Rome during the 16th century, the Church of England becoming autonomous through Henry VIII's Supremacy Act of 1534, making the British monarch head of the church. In 1534 the English Bible was placed in all parish churches. Persecution of Catholics was widespread under Edward VI (1549-53), and of Protestants under Mary (1553-58). In 1560 the Church of Scotland was reformed. Congregationalists arose in 1580, and the next century saw the rise of Baptists and Friends.

Reaction against nonconformists set in under Charles II, with the passage of the Uniformity Act of 1662 through which 2,000 clergymen were displaced because of their refusal to accept the Book of Common Prayer. During this period foreign missionary activity was begun by the Society for the Propagation of the Gospel in New England in 1649, the Society for the Promotion of Christian Knowledge in 1698 and the Society for the Propagation of the Gospel in Foreign Parts in 1701.

The most notable development of the 18th century was the Wesleyan Revival and the formation of the Methodist Church which also helped to spark a renewal of interest in missions and the creation of new bodies: Baptist Missionary Society in 1792, London Missionary Society in 1795, Scottish and Glasgow Missionary Societies in 1796, Church Missionary Society in 1799, and British and Foreign Bible Society in 1804. The 19th century was characterized not only by the creation of many new Protestant denominations, including the Brethren and Salvation Army, but also by a new tolerance towards Roman Catholicism. Civil rights were restored to Roman Catholics in 1829, and thousands of Irish Catholics migrated to Britain following the potato famine of 1846. The Roman Catholic hierarchy was restored in England in 1850, Scotland following suit in 1878. The Oxford Movement, with attention focused on reunion with Rome, resulted in a number of prominent Anglicans becoming Roman Catholics. The 20th century has witnessed the arrival of new holiness and pentecostal groups and the growth of secularism, accompanied by a massive numerical decline of Anglican and mainline Protestant churches. The Scotland Census of the Churches in 1984 found that church attendance on a typical Sunday for most denominations fell far below membership. For the Church of Scotland attendance was only 29% of membership, for the Roman Catholic Church, 35%, and for the Scottish Episcopal, 40%. In contrast, Baptist attendance was 107% of attendance and attendance among what were classified as 'Independent churches' was at 76% of membership. An extensive but unofficial English Church Census of 1989 produced even more marked results. It found adult church attendance on a typical Sunday to include only 9.55% of the national adult population, a 7% decline from 1979, otherwise translating to about 1,000 per week. The English 9.55% compared to 17% in Scotland in 1984, and 13% in Wales in 1982.

ANGLICAN CHURCHES. The major tradition in the United Kingdom is that of the Anglican Communion, which exists as 4 distinct churches corresponding to the main geographical divisions of England, Wales, Scotland, and Ireland. These churches go back to the earliest days of Christianity in Britain, as their claimed dates of origin (given in Country Table 2 below) attest. The smaller of these churches will be briefly described first.

The Episcopal Church in Scotland is the smallest of the 4 and the most uniformly in the High Church tradition of churchmanship (including both Prayer Book Catholic and Anglo-Catholic). In 1970 it had 335 parishes divided into 7 dioceses with a total community of just under 90,000. By 1995 it had declined to 300 parishes with 53,000 affiliated. The church is governed by the Episcopal Synod, Consultative Council on Church Legislation, and Representative Church Council. Anglican strength in Scotland is concentrated in the east, northeast and Perthshire, its membership being upper middle class with a large number of landed aristocrats.

The Church of Ireland consists of 2 provinces, Dublin and Armagh, Dublin being entirely in the republic of Ireland while Armagh is mostly in Ulster (Northern Ireland). The church in Eire is traditionally Low Church (also Evangelical) in ritual. It continues to lose members by emigration to the north whose 475 parishes in 5 dioceses has about 600,000 Anglicans in 1990. The General Synod consists of a House of Bishops and a House of Representatives, the latter composed of both clergy and laity.

The Church in Wales, with 1,600 parishes in 6 dioceses and a community of 1,300,000 in 1995, is in the High Church tradition. Its dioceses are co-terminous with the geographical boundaries of Wales and Monmouthshire (now Gwent). Central legislative functions are carried out by the Governing Body consisting of bishops, clergy and laity, with financial and administrative control exercised by the church's Representative Body.

In terms of membership and significance, the Church of England is the major Anglican church in the world. It is divided into 2 provinces, Canterbury and York, with more than 16,000 parishes in 42 dioceses and a baptized community of nearly 24 million in 1995. In 1995 the number of priests was about 6,000 and new ordinations were well below the level needed for replacement. The archbishop of Canterbury is the primate of all England and is also

Anglicans. Representing 55 million across world, 396 bishops convene for 1978 Lambeth conference.

recognized as the leader and focus of unity for the entire world-wide Anglican Communion.

Although the Anglican Church is omnipresent in England, there is a considerable geographical variation in its strength. Anglicans play a more important role in rural areas with small populations than in urban areas. Carlisle and Hereford, which have the lowest population densities of all English dioceses, manifest also the highest church-going. Allegiance is lowest in the urban areas of London, Birmingham, northeast Midlands and the Potteries; whereas Anglican influence is greatest in the west (West Midlands, West Country except for Cornwall, and the northwest generally), East Anglia, Lincolnshire, Oxford and portions of the southern coastal region.

Anglicanism in England represents a wide diversity of traditions of churchmanship existing within the one church without serious conflict. The major traditions and their respective emphases are: Low Church, sometimes called Conservative Evangelical (emphasizing conservative theology and simplicity of faith and ritual), Evangelical (emphasizing the importance of the Bible, evangelism, holy communion, and foreign missions), Central or Broad Church (Prayer Book worship, liberal theology), High Church or Prayer Book Catholic and Anglo-Catholic (accepting much of Roman Catholic ritual and dogma but without the supremacy of the pope). Many parishes in England follow predominantly one or other of these traditions. At the diocesan level, the traditions are far more intermingled, although individual bishops may be known as Evangelicals or High Churchmen. In a 1970 poll, 14% of Anglicans in Great Britain described themselves as of High Churchmanship, 70% of Low (including 'Central) churchmanship, and 16% of no particular views on

Church of England. Governing body, 1969: Convocations of Canterbury and York, in Church House, Westminster, voting on Anglican-Methodist reunion scheme.

the subject. Evangelicals numbered 10 million laity and 5,000 clergy in 1975.

The Church of England was the originator of the worldwide Anglican Communion, and is still the largest of its national member Churches which in 1990 were in 162 countries of the world. Since 1867 the bishops of the entire Communion have met in Lambeth Palace, London, for the 10-yearly Lambeth Conferences. At the 1968 Conference, a body representative of laity and clergy as well as bishops was formed, the Anglican Consultative Council with headquarters in London, which has around 50 delegates and meets biennially. Although most Anglican Churches overseas are now autonomous, there are still several detached dioceses which come under the metropolitical jurisdiction of the archbishop of Canterbury.

PROTESTANT CHURCHES. The principal Protestant tradition in the United Kingdom is Presbyterianism, the main bodies being the Church of Scotland, Presbyterian Church in Ireland, Presbyterian Church of Wales, and United Reformed Church, the latter resulting from a 1972 merger of the Presbyterian and Congregational churches in England. A number of smaller Presbyterian denominations are also active, particularly in Scotland: Free Church of Scotland, Free Presbyterian Church of Scotland, Reformed Presbyterian Church of Scotland and United Free Church of Scotland. The Church of Scotland is the largest and most significant body in the Reformed tradition, with about 1,220,000 Christians in 1995. Tracing its history back through the Scottish Reformation of 1560 to the 4th century, the Church of Scotland was re-united in 1929 with the United Free Church, which came into existence in 1900 following schisms in 1843 and 1893. The church's central legislative body is the General Assembly.

Methodism is the second most important Protestant tradition in Britain, owing its origin to the 18th-century Wesleyan revival. Five Methodist denominations exist: the Free Methodist Church, Wesleyan Reform Union, Independent Methodist Connexion, Methodist Church in Ireland, and Methodist Church of Great Britain, the latter being by far the largest with about 9,000 churches and chapels and a Christian community of 1.2 million. The result of a merger in 1932 of United, Primitive, and Wesleyan Methodists, the present Methodist Church of Great Britain has its strength in the southwestern counties of Cornwall and Devon, the Isle of Wight, the eastern counties of Yorkshire and Lincolnshire and the northern counties of Cumberland, Durham, and Northumberland.

Baptists first came to England as immigrants from Holland at the beginning of the 16th century, but the emergence of the General Baptists (moderates rejecting Calvinism) as an organized movement did not take place until 1611. A stricter Calvinistic Particular Baptist group began to form after 1633, followed by a new body, the General Baptists of the New Connexion in 1770. By 1813 the first attempt had been made to form a Baptist Union. At the present time the Baptist tradition in the United Kingdom is organized into 4 different unions with some overlapping of membership, plus about 500 unaffiliated churches. There are also small groups of Seventh-day and Strict Baptists. Baptists are strongest in the counties north of London, in the area of the Bristol Channel and to a lesser extent in the southeast. Few are found in northern England.

The Salvation Army owes its origin to William Booth, a minister of the Methodist New Connexions, who began work in east London in 1865. Booth's Christian Revival Association, later called the Christian Mission, continued to develop and spread; in 1878 the name was changed to the Salvation Army and it became a world-wide movement. The Salvation Army is noted for its vast proliferation of social service activities, as well as for its evangelistic work.

The Brethren movement was begun in Dublin through an Anglican clergyman, John Darby, in 1827 and in Britain also in 1828. An early important center was at Plymouth, England (1831) from which the popular name Plymouth Brethren was derived, although this name has never been accepted by the membership. In 1848 a conservative faction split off to form the Exclusive or Closed Brethren, and in 1889 another schism among the Open Brethren produced the Churches of God in the British Isles and Overseas.

Congregationalists, dating from the Reformation period, formed about 70% of the membership of the United Reformed Church at its inauguration in 1972. Other Congregational groups include the Union of Welsh Independents, Congregational Union of Scotland, and the Congregational Union of Ireland.

Pentecostals have not been particularly successful among the British. The largest denominations are the Assemblies of God, Elim Pentecostal Church and the Apostolic Church.

Other small but active groups include Adventists,

Catholic Church in England & Wales. Roman Catholic churches overlap, parallel, or duplicate Anglican churches almost everywhere; above, Anglican neo-Gothic Liverpool Cathedral (4th largest cathedral in the world) dominates the skyline of Liverpool (left), but so does Roman Catholic ultramodern circular Metropolitan Cathedral of Archdiocese of Liverpool (center).

Disciples, Lutherans, Moravians, Quakers, and several holiness churches.

CATHOLIC CHURCH. Several Catholic dioceses in Britain go back to the early centuries, as their claimed dates of origin (given in Table 2 below) attest: 4th century in Ireland, 5th century in Scotland, 7th century in England and Wales. These 3 churches will now be considered separately.

(1) *England and Wales*. During the reign of Henry VIII, through Acts passed by the Reformation Parliament of 1530-36, papal authority over the Church of England was formally repudiated and the established Church of England continued as an institution separate from Rome. For almost 3 centuries, with one short break during the reign of Mary Tudor (1553-58), Catholics who maintained allegiance to the pope were penalized in a variety of ways. The Roman Catholic population gradually dwindled until by the middle of the 18th century it was restricted to a number of upper-class and aristocratic families and a small minority of farmers living mainly in the north of England. In 1767, Roman Catholics in England and Wales numbered 80,000.

From the last part of the 18th century and throughout the 19th century the Roman Catholic population increased considerably, largely due to the influx of immigrants from Ireland who came to England and Wales seeking employment. From 70,000 in 1780 (0.9% of the total population of England and Wales), Catholics increased to 580,000 in 1840 (4%) and to 2,500,000 in 1880 (8%). Most of the Irish settled in the rapidly developing urban areas, and by 1850 their numbers were sufficient to warrant the re-establishment of the Roman Catholic hierarchy, which was now possible after the Catholic Emancipation Act of 1829, which finally removed almost all the disabilities under which Roman Catholics had suffered. Subsequently the Roman Catholic Church in England and Wales developed until by 1975 it consisted of 5 provinces and 19 dioceses.

In 1975 the impact of Irish immigration was still being strongly felt. It is this which accounts for the geographical division of the Catholic Church in England into 2 parts, the large western cities including Liverpool on the one hand and the London conurbation on the other, the latter representing the most important concentration of English Catholics, although always less than one third of the population. The majority of Catholic priests in Great Britain continue to be Irish immigrants, with only a few English and Welsh clergy. Between 1965 and 1970, 209 priests were ordained in Ireland for service in the dioceses of Great Britain.

For many years after 1850 the Roman Catholic urban population remained isolated; since 1950, however, this isolation has been breaking down and Catholics are increasingly becoming more socially mobile and more easily assimilated within the wider society.

One major field of activity since the re-establishment of the hierarchy is that of education. Considerable effort has been put into building up a very wide-ranging system of schools for all age groups. In this the church has received, for most of the 20th century, financial support from the state. At the present time the state provides 80% of the capital cost of building schools and colleges and accepts responsibility for maintenance of buildings and payment of teachers' salaries.

(2) *Scotland*. On 24 August 1560 there came into force legislation enacted by the Scottish parliament under which the Catholic religion and papal authority were abolished, celebration of mass declared illegal and Protestantism established as the state religion. But as the events of the next 3 centuries were to show, the Presbyterian reformation in Scotland was never complete. Catholicism survived in the southwest and northeast, the highlands and the islands; and Episcopalianism also continued active in the northeast. Nevertheless, by the end of the 18th century Catholicism in Scotland was at its lowest ebb. Apart from general religious persecution since the reformation, the attachment of the Catholic Church to the fortunes of the Stuart family brought inevitable repression after the failure of the rebellions of 1715 and 1745. To add further to their suffering, the beginning of the highland clearances in the second half of the 18th century forced many Catholics to leave Scotland or to join the highland regiments which were then being formed for service in foreign wars. By the year 1800 the Catholic population of Scotland numbered only about 30,000, less than 2% of the total population then.

The 19th century however witnessed a dramatic increase in the number of Catholics in Scotland. The prime cause of this was firstly immigration from Ireland caused by the failure of the Irish rebellion of 1798, and secondly massive immigration after the failure of the Irish potato crops in 1845 and succeeding years. In 1851 Catholics numbered 145,860 (5% of the population), and in 1878 the Catholic hierarchy was restored. Irish immigration continued for the rest of the 19th century, although by 1908 it had been reduced to insignificant numbers. Since the end of World War II in 1945, immigration of English, Polish, Ukrainian and German Catholics has increased significantly.

Ecclesiastically, the Scottish Catholic community is conservative and has been little affected by the spirit of Vatican II. This is especially true of Glasgow and the western part of the country. Aberdeen and northeastern Scotland on the other hand display a style of Catholicism which is more open and tolerant.

(3) *Northern Ireland*. The Catholic Church in Ulster is the largest single denomination, although Catholics form only one third of the population. There is in reality only one church for the whole of Ireland served by one episcopal conference located in Eire. The archdiocese of Armagh is found entirely in Ulster as is its suffragan diocese of Down & Connor. The other dioceses of Clogher, Derry, and Dromore cover parts of both Ulster and Eire.

The Holy See has diplomatic relations with Britain and in AD 2000 is represented to government and the Catholic hierarchy by a nuncio residing in London.

INDEPENDENT CHURCHES. There is a large number of these bodies, of all varieties. The postdenominationalist House Church movement experienced rapid growth in the 1970s and 1980s. The English Church Census of 1989 showed 144% growth in the prior 10 years. This movement began in the late 1960s and early 1970s. Groups first met in homes, and though they outgrew them quickly, the name has remained. These young churches tended to be informal, contemporary in music, innovative, evangelistic, and charismatic. Most who attended were dissatisfied members from other churches, a cause for inter-church friction at times.

CATHOLIC INDEPENDENT CHURCHES. Catholic (non-Roman) churches include the English Catholic Church, Liberal Catholic Church, Old Catholic Church of England, and Old Roman Catholic Church (English Rite). Over the last century there has also been in England a proliferation of bishops-at-large (episcopi vagantes) as the heads of autocephalous Catholic churches most of which have very small lay memberships.

True Jesus Church. A Chinese indigenous church, TJC has bought up unused church buildings (in Edinburgh).

THIRD-WORLD INDIGENOUS CHURCHES. There are over 108 predominantly Black denominations in the UK, most of which were brought to Britain by immigrants from the West Indies, especially Jamaicans and Guyanas. Most average 1,000 members each. Some of these are entirely independent while others maintain ties with mother churches in the USA and the Caribbean. The largest of these is the First United Church of Jesus Christ (Apostolic) from Jamaica. Several West African indigenous churches are also active, the most important being the Church of the Lord (Aladura) and the Church of the Cherubim and Seraphim, both based in Nigeria.

MARGINAL CHURCHES. The main marginal churches in the UK include Spiritualists, Jehovah's Witnesses, Mormons, Christian Scientists, Unitarians, and Swedenborgians. Those registering the most significant gains in recent years are Mormons and Jehovah's Witnesses.

ORTHODOX CHURCHES. Orthodox churches in the UK include the Armenian, Assyrian, Belorussian, Bulgarian, Coptic, Estonian, Greek, Polish, Romanian, Russian (3 groups), Serbian, Syrian, and Ukrainian churches. The Greek Orthodox Archdiocese for Western Europe, under the Ecumenical Patriarchate of Constantinople, has its headquarters in London.

Renewal movements. In the 1990s the Pentecostal/Charismatic Renewal continued to spread rapidly across most older churches, and numbered over 5,820,000 adherents (of whom 5% Pentecostals, 70% Charismatics, and 25% Independents).

Indigenous missions. Britain, a mission-receiving country in the first century, quickly became a mission sending country with some of the world's great missionaries over nearly 2 millennia. Major contributions include Patrick's evangelization of Ireland (400s), Celtic peregrini (500-600s), Boniface to Germany, the conversion of the Vikings (800-900s), the Crusades (1100-1200s), and William Carey and the modern worldwide Protestant and Anglican missionary movement (1792-onward).

Church of England. In Guilford Cathedral, 3,000 Anglican Charismatics sing praises to God.

CHURCH AND STATE

The British constitution has never been formulated as a single written document. The rules governing Britain's political institutions are found in several areas: in written laws known as statutes or acts of Parliament, in judicial decisions interpreting both these laws and also common law, and in unwritten but definitive conventions. In all of these, the part played by religion and ecclesiastical authorities is considerable.

There are 2 established or state churches in the UK. The Church of England is the established church in England, and the Church of Scotland (Presbyterian) is established in Scotland; the sovereign is the head of both. The Church of Ireland and the Church in Wales, both Anglican, were disestablished respectively by the Irish Church Act of 1869 and the Welsh Church Acts of 1914 and 1919.

The close relations of the Church of England with the state date back to the 6th century. A millennium later in the reign of Henry VIII, by various acts of Parliament between 1532 and 1534, the church repudiated papal jurisdiction and separated itself from Rome. The former position was temporarily restored under Mary I, a Roman Catholic, but the legislation of Henry VIII was reinstated by the Act of Supremacy in 1558, the first year of the reign of Elizabeth I.

In the UK, the British sovereign is the supreme governor of the church under God, and during the coronation service is crowned by the archbishop of Canterbury. Parliament has authority to pass legislation on church affairs, such as sanction for the Book of Common Prayer which was authorized by the Act of Uniformity in 1662. Since 1965 the church may authorize services that do not conform to the 1662 pattern. Through the Submission of the Clergy Act of 1533, the ancient Convocations of Canterbury and York received permission to pass canons subject to certain restrictions, and by the Church of England (Assembly) Powers Act of 1919 the then newly-created Church Assembly was given authority to pass measures having the force of acts of Parliament and the right to repeal or amend them. Measures required the simple assent of both Houses of Parliament but could not be amended by them; they also required the royal assent. The Synodical Government Measure of 1969 substituted the General Synod for the Church Assembly, and this body now passes both measures and canons.

According to the Appointment of Bishops Act of 1533, diocesan bishops are chosen by the sovereign on the advice of the prime minister after careful consultation with the church. In 1974, General Synod voted that the decisive voice should be that of the church, and more acceptable procedures were evolved which came into operation in 1977. The 26 senior bishops are entitled to sit as members in the House of Lords. A recognized system of ecclesiastical courts was formed through the Ecclesiastical Jurisdiction Measure of 1963. Incumbents (clergy in charge of parishes) have a pastoral relationship with their parishioners, and marriages conducted by the church are recognized in their own right.

The Church of Scotland also dates from early times, being reformed in 1560-67 at which time it also separated from the Church of Rome. In 1592 the church was recognized as Presbyterian and became self-governing except that secular courts have always been recognized as having jurisdiction in matters of property and civil rights. The General Assembly is the governing body. The main purpose of the Church of Scotland Act of 1921, which has appended to it declaratory articles setting out the position of the church, was to reunite the church following the schism of 1843 over the question of lay patronage subsequently abolished.

The other churches and denominations in the UK have no special links with the state but the major Protestant denominations are governed by constitutions defined and promulgated by themselves which have been ratified by private acts of Parliament. The Toleration Act of 1688 largely freed Protestant nonconformists from disabilities, and none now exist. Roman Catholics were in the past subject to penal legislation, and a few traces of little importance still survive. Churches are not registered as such, but church buildings of non-established churches may be registered under the Places of Worship Registration Act of 1855, from which certain financial advantages are derived.

Under the Education Act (England and Wales) of 1944, schools and colleges of education for teacher training may be formed by church bodies. All maintenance costs, including staff salaries, are paid from public funds, as well as 80% of capital expenditures. In Scotland with its quite different educational system, the religious issue in the schools was settled by the (Scottish) Education Act of 1918, which accepted the principle of denominational schools and established a broadly-based national system of primary, secondary and further education leading to higher study. The effect of this was to relieve the churches of the financial burden of maintaining their own parochial schools through the assumption of responsibility by government for administrative control and financial upkeep of church schools. For their part, the churches were granted specific safeguards concerning the belief and character of the teachers appointed to their schools and also given control of the religious instruction taught in them.

A major source of contention within the UK is the long-drawn-out sectarian conflict or civil war in Northern Ireland. This has not been merely a church-state problem or even a Protestant-Catholic issue, since there are many political, social, and economic factors involved. Nevertheless, this is clearly an area where religion has become unrest within the body politic.

Christian worship services have been broadcast and televised every day since 1921.

BROADCASTING AND MEDIA

Britain has numerous Christian radio programs and stations. Every week, about 11 million people in Britain hear a religious program via BBC radio.

Salvation Army. A worldwide body famed for its social services and militant evangelism.

Shortwave radio broadcasts from KNLS, HCJB (Ecuador), TWR (Monaco) and AWR have generated responses. Satellite TV and radio programs are received in English, Arabic, German and Italian.

INTERDENOMINATIONAL ORGANIZATIONS

The British Council of Churches (BCC) was founded in 1942, uniting the Council on the Christian Faith and the Common Life (1937), the Commission of the Churches for International Friendship and Social Responsibility (1937), and the British Section of the World Conference on Faith and Order. In 1977, new members included the first Black church, the Holy Order of Cherubim & Seraphim Church, and also the Congregational Federation, and the Russian Orthodox Church (under Moscow). The Catholic Church already belongs to most of the main city councils of churches including Sheffield, Liverpool, and Bristol, as well as 73% of the 720 local councils of churches in the UK which are associated councils of the British Council of Churches.

Two other sub-national or local councils are the Scottish Churches' Council, founded in 1964, and the Council of Churches for Wales (Cyngor Eglwysi Cymru), with 8 member and 3 observer churches, which was formed in 1955 building on the work begun in 1930 by the Committee for Mutual Cooperation and Understanding between Christian Communions in Wales, and which has over 60 affiliated local councils of churches.

The Conference for World Mission (CFWM), known up to 1978 as the Conference of Missionary Societies in Great Britain and Ireland (CBMS), was founded in 1912 as an association of organizations dedicated to the propagation of the gospel overseas in partnership with churches in other lands. The Conference is affiliated to CWME/WCC and works in association with the BCC. The Sodepax program for England comes under the Churches' Action for World Development.

Other Anglican and Protestant interdenominational councils and societies include the British and Foreign Bible Society (BFBS, formed in 1804), Evangelical Alliance of Great Britain (1846), Free Church Federal Council, National Christian Education Council (1803), and the United Society for Christian Literature (USCL, 1799). There are also a number of smaller interdenominational councils of churches.

The 2 Catholic episcopal conferences (England and Wales; Scotland) each sponsor an ecumenical commission. In September 1972, the Catholic Church of England and Wales and the Catholic Church of Scotland, for the first time officially participated to the full extent in a Church Leaders Conference at Birmingham, thus bringing together all the major Christian denominations of the UK.

In addition to 2 international commissions which are of particular interest in Great Britain (Anglican/Roman Catholic and Methodist/Roman Catholic), there are several national joint working groups between Anglicans and Protestants on the one hand and Catholics on the Other: (1) the Joint Commission between the Church of England and Catholic Church in England (began 1971); (2) English Roman Catholic/Methodist Committee (began 1968, reorganized 1972); (3) British Council of Churches/Roman Catholic Joint Working Group (begun 1967); (4) Church in Wales (Anglican)/Roman Catholic Church Joint Working Group (begun 1971);

and (5) the Roman Catholic/Church of Scotland Joint Commission on Marriage.

A council of Black or Black-led churches was formed in 1977, the Afro-West Indian United Council of Churches (or, Afro-Caribbean United Church Council), but with as members only 9 Black denominations out of the 110 Third-World and a dozen Protestant Black churches.

International associations based in the UK are very numerous, and include: (1) the World Association for Christian Communication (WACC), founded in London in 1963, which provides for cooperation concerning all means of communication and organizes every 2 years with UNDA in Switzerland the International Christian Television Festival; (2) the Ecumenical Satellite Commission (ECUSAT), founded in London in 1970, which was created jointly by Catholics (UNDA and UCIP in Switzerland; OCIC in Belgium) and Protestants (WACC) for the purpose of informing the churches concerning communications by satellite and to place the latter at the service of man in a Christian perspective; (3) the International Ecumenical Fellowship, founded in London in 1952 and reorganized in 1967, an interdenominational international association of Christians who, by prayer, study and action, aim to foster the visible unity of all Christians; and (4) International Hebrew Christian Alliance (IHCA), founded in London in 1925 and now located in Ramsgate, Kent, with national branches in 13 countries on 5 continents, whose purpose is to unite Christians of Jewish background who recognize their origin but remain Christian and continue to bear Christian witness within the Jewish community.

A very large number of national ecumenical associations and centers for dialogue and co-operation exist.

Several national and international organizations in Britain are dedicated to the promotion of inter-religious dialogue. International bodies with headquarters in London include: (1) World Congress of Faiths (WCF), founded in London in 1936 with its membership composed of individuals and branches in 25 countries, whose aim is to promote a spirit of fellowship among mankind through religion and to awaken and develop a world loyalty while allowing complete freedom for the diversity of men, nations and faiths; (2) Standing Conference of Jews, Christians and Muslims in Europe (JCM), founded in London in 1971 with local branches in West Berlin (West Germany) and the Netherlands (in addition to a local British branch), which seeks to promote respect for the theological, political, and national differences of the 3 religions, to remove misunderstanding between them and to enlarge common areas of religious awareness; (3) International Council of Christians and Jews, with its international secretariat in London and some 12 branches throughout the world (including a local British affiliate known as the Council of Christians and Jews), whose purposes are to establish dialogue between Christians and Jews on the basis of religious and human concerns, to promote freedom of conscience and respect for the convictions and rights of others and to work for the abolition of discrimination from which Judaism has suffered; and (4) World Spiritual Council, founded in Ashford, Kent in 1946, with autonomous national branches in 4 countries (Denmark, France, Holland and UK) and individual members in others countries, which seeks to establish contacts between all the great religions, as well as esoteric schools, artists, and writers.

National London-based Catholic organizations dealing with Christian-Jewish relations are the Study Centre for Christian-Jewish Relations, and the Commission to Implement the Vatican Declaration on the Jews, both of which are sponsored by the Sisters of Our Lady of Zion.

FUTURE TRENDS AND PROSPECTS

An increase of non-Christian immigrants and a rise in secularism and non-religion both contribute to a continuing decline of church affiliation which could reach a millennial low of 63.4% by 2025. The nonreligious would then grow to over 13% by 2025 and Muslims to 2.3%.

With the long-term influences of immigration and secularization, Christianity will probably dip below 60% of the population before AD 2050. Minority religions, such as Islam, Hinduism, and Sikhism, may grow to over 10% by AD 2050. The nonreligious could grow to 25% in the same period.

A number of detailed studies of the possible futures of Christianity in Britain have been published, as listed below. All envisage new and revitalized forms of church life and witness in the near future.

BIBLIOGRAPHY

A century of British Christianity: historical statistics 1900–1985 with projections to 2000. MARC monograph, no. 14. Bromley, UK: MARC Europe, [1989]. 101p.

A church history of Scotland. J. H. S. Burleigh. London: Oxford University Press, 1960. 456p.

A directory of the religious life: for the use of those concerned with the administration of the religious life in the Church of England. 4th ed. London: Advisory Council on the Relations of Bishops and Religious Communities, 1990. 55p.

A historical account of the belief in witchcraft in Scotland. C. K. Sharpe. East Ardesley, UK: E. P. Publishing, 1972. 268p.

A history of religion in Britain: practice and belief from pre–Roman times to the present. S. Gilley & W. J. Sheils (eds). Oxford, UK: Blackwell, 1994. 603p.

A history of the Church in Wales. D. Walker (ed). Penarth, Wales: Church in Wales Publications, 1976.

A history of the Church of Ireland, 1691–1996. A. Acheson. Dublin: Columba Press.

A history of the Jews in England. C. Roth. 3rd ed. London: E. J. Brill, 1978. 328p.

A history of the Scottish Reformation. J. D. Mackie. Edinburgh: Church of Scotland Youth Committee, 1960. 175p.

A plea for British black theologies: the Black Church Movement in Britain in its transatlantic cultural and theological interaction. R. I. H. Gerloff. Frankfurt am Main: Peter Lang, 1992. 1130p in 2 vols.

A short history of the Episcopal church in Scotland: from the Restoration to the present time. F. Goldie. 2nd ed. Edinburgh: Saint Andrew Press, 1976. 181p.

A sociology of English religion. D. Martin. London: Heinemann, 1967. 158p.

Amazing grace: Evangelicalism in Australia, Britain, Canada, and the United States. G. A. Rawlyk & M. A. Noll (eds). Grand Rapids, MI: Baker Books, 1993. 429p.

Anglican religious communities yearbook, 1999. Norwich, UK: Canterbury Press, 1998.

'Aspects of the Roman Catholic Church in England,' *Pro Mundi Vita* (Brussels), 70 (January–February 1978), 1–36.

Belonging to Britain: Christian perspectives on religion and identity in a plural society. R. H. Hooker & J. Sargant (eds). London: CCBI Publications for the Committee for Relations with People of Other Faiths, [1991]. 179p.

Beyond the Kingdom. A. Walker. London: Hodder & Stoughton, 1992. (New Churches).

'Black Christian communities in Britain, with special reference to the Birmingham area.' R. Gerloff. Ph.D. dissertation, University of Birmingham, 1978.

Catholic directory of England and Wales, 1975. London: Associated Catholic Newspapers, 1975. (1970 edition: 808p).

Catholicism in England: portrait of a minority, its culture and tradition. D. Mathew. London: Eyre & Spottiswoode, 1955.

Changing perspectives: Christian culture and morals in England today. R. Osmond. London: Darton, Longman & Todd, 1993. 142p.

'Christian' England: what the English Church Census reveals. P. Brierley. London: MARC Europe, 1991. 278p.

Christian voluntarism in Britain and North America: a bibliography and critical assessment. W. H. Brackney. *Bibliographies and indexes in religious studies*, no. 35. Westport, CT: Greenwood Press, 1995. 320p.

Christianity and other faiths in Britain. A. G. Hunter. London: SCM, 1985. 192p.

Christians in Britain today. D. Cush, C. Miles & M. Stylianides. London: Hodder & Stoughton, 1991. 191p.

Church and politics today: essays on the role of the Church of England in contemporary politics. G. Moyser (ed). Edinburgh: T. & T. Clark, 1985. 357p.

Church and society in England, 1770–1970: a historical study. E. R. Norman. Oxford, UK: Clarendon, 1976. 507p. (With full bibliography).

Church and state: report of the Archbishops' Commission. London: Church Information Office, 1970. 120p.

Churches and churchgoers: patterns of church growth in the British Isles since 1700. R. Currie, A. Gilbert & L. Horsley. Oxford, UK: Clarendon, 1977. 244p. (Statistical time series for major denominations).

Conflict and Christianity in Northern Ireland. B. Mawhinney & R. Wells. Grand Rapids, MI: Eerdmans, 1975. 126p.

Crockford's clerical directory, 1977. London: Oxford University Press, 1977. (Bibliographical details of all Anglican clergy. Biennial).

Dictionary of Celtic mythology. P. B. Ellis. New York: Oxford University Press, 1992; paperback, 1994. 232p.

Dictionary of Scottish church history and theology. N. M. de S. Cameron (ed). Edinburgh: T & T Clark, 1993; Downer's Grove, IL: InterVarsity Press, 1994. 906p.

Disestablishment in Ireland and Wales. P. M. H. Bell. London: SPCK, 1969. 400p.

England. A. Day. *World bibliographical series*, vol. 160. Oxford, UK: CLIO Press, 1993. 612p.

Evangelism and pagan England. J. E. Rattenbury. London: Epworth Press, 1954. 148p.

Facts and figures about the Church of England. R. F. Neuss (ed). London: Church Information Office, 1965. 96p.

God and greater Britain: religion and national life in Britain and Ireland, 1843–1945. J. Wolffe. London: Routledge, 1994. 336p.

God's people: West Indian Pentecostal sects in England. M. J. C. Calley. London: Oxford University Press, 1965. 182p. (Describes 13 sects).

Goodbye, beloved brethren. N. Adams. Aberdeen: Impulse, 1972. 162p.

'Great Britain: England,' D. Martin, in *Western religion: a country by country sociological enquiry*, p.229–47. H. Mol (ed). The Hague: Mouton, 1972.

'Great Britain: Scotland,' J. Highet, in *Western religion: a country by country sociological enquiry*, p.249–69. H. Mol (ed). The Hague: Mouton, 1972.

History of the Church of Scotland, beginning the Year of Our Lord 203, and continued to the end of the reign of King James VI. J. Spottiswood. London: E. J. Brill, 1978. 3 vols. (Originally published in London, 1847-51).

Islam in Britain: past, present and the future. M. S. Raza. Leicester: Volcano Press, 1991.

Islamic Britain: religion, politics and identity among British Muslims. P. Lewis. London and New York: I. B. Tauris, 1994. 256p.

Le Catholicisme contemporain en Grand Brétagne. J. Dingle. Paris: Spes, 1967.

Local councils of churches today: an interim report. London: British Council of Churches, 1971. 117p.

'New denominationalism: tendencies towards a new reformation of English Christianity.' A. J. Worsfold. Ph.D. dissertation, University of Hull, 1988. 355p.

Northern Ireland. M. O. Shannon. *World bibliographical series*, vol. 129. Oxford, UK: CLIO Press, 1990. 644p.

Patterns of sectarianism: organisation and ideology in social and religious movements. B. R. Wilson (ed). London: Heinemann, 1967. 416p. (Detailed studies of 9 British sects).

Prospects for the nineties: trends and tables from the English Church Census. P. Brierley. London: MARC Europe, 1991. 416p.

Rastaman: the Rastifarian movement in England. E. E. Cashmore. London: Unwin, 1983.

'Religion,' R. Currie & A. Gilbert, in *Trends in British society since 1900*, p.407–47. A. H. Halsey (ed). London: Macmillan, 1972.

Religion and society in industrial England: church, chapel, and social change, 1740–1914. A. D. Gilbert. London: Longmans, 1975. (Statistical sociology).

Religion in Britain since 1945: believing without belonging. G. Davie. *Making contemporary Britain.* Oxford, UK: Blackwell, 1994. 235p.

Religion in modern Britain. S. Bruce. *Oxford modern Britain.* Oxford, UK: Oxford University Press, 1995. 155p.

Religious institutions. J. Brothers. *Aspects of modern sociology*, The social structure of modern Britain. London: Longman, 1971. 112p.

Restoring the Kingdom. A. Walker. London: Hodder & Stoughton, 1985. (On the New Churches).

Scotland. E. G. Grant. *World bibliographical series*, vol. 34. Oxford, UK: CLIO Press, 1982. 430p.

Scotland: church and nation through sixteen centuries. G. Donaldson. 2nd ed. London: SCM Press, 1972. 128p.

Streams of renewal: the origins and early development of the Charismatic movement in Great Britain. P. Hocken. Devon, UK: Paternoster Pres, 1986. 288p.

The bitter harvest: church and state in Northern Ireland. A. J. Menendez. Washington, DC: R. B. Luce, 1973. 228p.

The British churches today. K. Slack. 2nd ed. London: SCM, 1970. 144p.

The British: their identity and their religion. D. Jenkins. London: SCM, 1975. 200p.

The British: their religious beliefs and practices, 1800–1986. T. Thomas (ed). *Library of religious beliefs and practices.* London: Routledge, 1988. 254p.

The Celtic Churches: a history, AD 200–1200. J. T. McNeill. Chicago: University of Chicago, 1974. 290p.

The Church of England, 1815–1948: a documentary history. R. P. Flindall (ed). London: SPCK, 1972. 512p.

The Church of England, 1900–1965. R. Lloyd. London: SCM, 1966. 623p.

The Church of England year book 1978. London: Church Information Office, 1978. 430p. (Annual).

The Church of Scotland year-book 1974. Glasgow: Department of Publicity and Publication, 1974. 430p. (Annual).

The church under Thatcher. H. Clark. London: SPCK, 1993. 166p.

The churches and the British Broadcasting Corporation, 1922–1956: the politics of broadcast religion. K. M. Wolfe. London: SCM Press, 1984. 663p.

The churches in England from Elizabeth I to Elizabeth II. K. Hyslon–Smith. London: SCM Press, 1998. 3 vols.

The deployment and payment of the clergy. L. Paul. London: Church Information Office, 1964. 311p. (Church of England).

The geography of religion in England. J. D. Gay. London: Duckworth, 1971. 334p.

The growth of religious diversity: Britain from 1945. G. Parsons (ed). London: Routledge, 1993–1994. 2 vols.

The kirk in Scotland. J. Bulloch. Edinburgh: Saint Andrew Press, 1960. 230p.

The making of post–Christian Britain: a history of the secularization of modern society. A. D. Gilbert. London: Longman, 1980.

The mirror and the cross: Scotland and the Catholic faith. G. Scott-Moncrieff. London: Burns & Oates, 1960. 168p.

The Oxford dictionary of saints. D. H. Farmer. 3rd ed. Oxford, UK and New York: Oxford University Press, 1992. 558p.

The Scottish church: a short study in ecclesiastical history. C. S. Black. Glasgow: Maclellan, 1952. 276p.

The Scottish churches: a review of their state 400 years after the Reformation. J. Highet. London: Skeffington, 1960. 224p.

The state of the churches in Great Britain, Ireland, Australia and New Zealand, 1986. Peoria, AZ: Ecumenism Research Agency, 1987. 6 microfilm reels.

The turn of the tide: Christian belief in Britain today. K. Ward. London: BBC, 1986. 176p.

UK Christian handbook. P. W. Brierley & H. Wraight (eds). 1996/97 ed. London: Christian Research Evangelical Alliance, 1995. 976p.

UK Protestant missions handbook: Vol 1, *Overseas:* Vol 2, *Home.* P. Brierley. London: EAGB, 1977 & 1978. 80p and 56p.

Wales. G. Huws & D. Roberts. *World bibliographical series,* vol. 122. Oxford, UK: CLIO Press, 1991. 266p.

Where do we go from here?: Protestants and the future of Northern Ireland. T. Kinahan. Blackrock: Columba Press, 1995. 93p.

Country Table 2. Organized churches and denominations in Britain (UK of GB & NI).

Official name (bold type = church with over 10% of all affiliated) 1	*Begun* 2	*Type* 3	*Counc* 4	*Congs* 5	*Adults* 6	*Affiliated 1970* 7	*Affiliated 1995* 8	*G%* 9	*Names, notes, and other statistics* (see Codebook, Part 3) 10
African Methodist Episcopal Church	1966	I-Met	Vw..I	8	300	220	700	4.74	In 16th Episcopal District, AMEC (USA). WIndians. London N7. New style ministries.
African Methodist Episcopal Zion Ch	c1960	I-Met	Vw...	32	2,600	3,500	4,000	0.54	In 1st Epis Dist, AMEZC(USA). In UK, pentecostal. Jamaicans, Guyana Asians. 11nx.
Aladura Internat Ch, UK & Overseas	1970	I-3aA	x.I.J	5	2,000	–	6,000	41.62	Nigerians, Ghanaians, West Indians. 95% students. M=C&S(Ibadan). London SW18. 7x.
Ancient Assyrian Church of the East	c1930	O-Nes	Yw...	5	3,000	1,000	6,200	7.57	*Holy Apostolic & Cath Ch of the East.* Nestorians. 200 Assyrian refugee families.
Ancient Orthodox Church	1970	I-Epi	.....	1	1,200	2,000	3,000	1.64	HQ Glasgow.
Anglican Catholic Church	1992	I-ACa	.....	60	3,000	–	5,000	33.33	Missionary Diocese of England & Wales. HQ Stoke-on-Trent.
Anglican Orthodox Free Church	1840	I-ACa	.....	60	2,500	2,200	4,000	2.42	Formerly Anglican Apostolic Episcopal Free Ch of England. HQ London SW17.
Anglo-West-Indian Assembly	1962	I-3oU	x....	2	200	250	500	2.81	*Ev Reformed Ch.* From Montserrat, St Kitts, Jamaica, ex PAoWI. HQ London E5. 2nx.
Antioch Ministries	1985	I-3cY	x....	5	100	–	300	10.00	M=Antioch Mission (Brazil). F=Derek Brown. In 60 countries.
Antiochian Orthodox Ch: P Antioch	c1930	O-Ara	C....	12	1,600	100	2,000	12.73	Arabic-speaking Patriarchate of Antioch. Bishop in Paris. 1 Deanery of ex Anglican clergy.
Apostolic Church of God	1973	I-3oU	.....	10	1,000	–	2,000	4.55	Jamaican pentecostals, schism ex PAW. M=Highway Ch of Christ of AF (USA). 4nx.
Apostolic Ch of God in Christ	c1970	I-3oU	.....	20	2,000	–	3,000	37.75	Oneness doctrine, member of AWCF. Afro-Caribbean members
Apostolic Church of Great Britain	1904	P-PeA	Z...H	145	6,100	40,000	9,390	-5.63	Formed 1916. HQ SWales. Centralized hierarchy of apostles, prophets. Rapid decline. 85n,1j,1s.
Apostolic Church of Jesus Christ	c1960	I-3oU	.....	25	3,000	4,000	8,000	2.81	West Indian Blacks. Third-largest West Indian immigrant church. 60% women.
Armenian Apostolic Ch: D England	c1850	O-Arm	Ewc..	20	13,000	20,000	21,000	0.20	*Gregorians.* Under C Echmiadzin (USSR). London, Manchester. 700 families. 2 bishops.
Assemblies of God in GB & Ireland	1924	P-Pe2	ZG..H	680	49,381	70,000	107,000	1.71	*AGGBI.* Originally Pentecostal Missionary Union, until 1924. HQ Nottingham. 950n,1s.
Assemblies of the First-Born	1960	I-3pU	.....	20	2,300	1,200	5,000	5.87	From St Kitts & Jamaica (HQ Kingston). HQ London SW8. Became pentecostals in UK. 28n.
Assembly Hall Churches	c1980	I-3nC	.....	8	225	–	500	6.67	*Little Flock. Local Churches.* Begun 1922 in China.
Associated Presb Chs of Scotland	1989	I-Ref	.....	30	3,000	–	3,500	16.67	HQ Inverness.
Association of Vineyard Churches	1987	I-3cW	.....	24	6,000	–	8,000	12.50	HQ London SW20.
Baptist Church of God	1972	I-3pU	.....	10	600	–	1,000	4.35	Jamaicans. Link with British Free Baptists, now pentecostal. HQ London NW10. 8nx.
Baptist Union of Great Britain	1611	P-Bap	TWC.W	2,130	484,000	600,000	600,000	0.00	*BUGBI* (1812). General & Particular Baptists. 2090n,7s(162),W=65%,4000Y.
Baptist Union of Ireland	1648	P-Bap	.....	101	8,500	19,000	24,300	0.99	Not in BUGBI. 7 more churches in republic of Ireland. 50n,1s(31),W=41%,400Y.
Baptist Union of Scotland	1750	P-Bap	Tv..W	172	16,212	60,000	40,500	-1.56	Not in BUGBI (except 10 churches). Member of WCC 1948-55. 130n,1x,1s(25),415Y.
Baptist Union of Wales	1649	P-Bap	Tw...	560	67,700	150,000	83,900	-2.30	*Undeb Bedyddwyr Cymru (1866). 43% in BUGBI. 80% Welsh. 216n,2s(33),W=68%.*
Bethany Fellowship of Great Britain	1979	I-3oA	.....	4	2,000	–	3,000	6.25	F=bp Prince Blackson (Ghana).
Bible Church of God	1964	I-3pU	x....	5	300	300	1,000	4.93	Jamaicans. M=CoG World HQ (Alabama, USA). 2 bishops: Birmingham, Nottingham.
Bible Pattern Church Fellowship	1939	I-3pW	.....	5	1,000	2,000	1,800	-0.42	Split ex Elim Foursquare Gospel Alliance by founder G. Jeffreys. British-Israelite. Declining.
Bible Way Chs of Our Lord JC WW	1958	I-3oO	x....	33	1,100	2,000	3,000	1.64	*WW=World Wide.* West Indians. M=BWCOLJCWW(USA). HQ London SE 13. Bishop, 18n.
Bridge Ministries	c1980	I-3cW	.....	2	200	–	400	6.67	F=David Day.
Bristol Christian Fellowship	c1983	I-3cW	.....	9	1,600	–	3,500	8.33	An early charismatic network.
Bulgarian Orthodox Church	c1950	O-Bul	Mwc..	1	300	1,600	500	-4.55	*Balgarskata Pravoslavna Crkva.* Under P Sofia. Bulgarians. No full-time priest.
Byelorussian Autocephalic Orth Ch	c1945	O-Bye	x....	3	970	1,500	1,200	-0.89	Refugees; White Russian Church begun AD 1291. HQ Brooklyn (USA). Linked Polish OC. 2n.
Calvary Church of God in Christ	1952	I-3pU	Z...I	100	6,000	5,000	9,000	2.38	First Jamaican pentecostals. M=CoGIC(USA Blacks). HQ London. Bishop, 28nx,20m,15w.
Catholic Apostolic Church	1832	I-3aX	x....	3	1,600	8,000	2,000	-5.39	*Irvingites.* Early pentecostals. No clergy left; 59 churches closed; almost extinct.
Catholic Ch in England & Wales:	c 678	R-LEr	B.B.s	3,163	3,243,900	4,142,905	4,228,796	0.08	C=55+12+352. P=75%,5s,W=43%. 50% Irish; 7% converts.
M Birmingham	1850	R-Lat	Bs	332	233,000	347,500	303,786	-0.54	Catholics mostly Irish in industry. Few rural. 1s. 284n 109x 186m 865w 7083Yy
D Clifton	1850	R-Lat	Bs	108	97,000	100,000	126,262	0.94	Mostly in Bristol; scattered rural Catholics. 127n 90x 108m 259w 2103Yy
D Shrewsbury	1850	R-Lat	Bs	117	153,000	192,000	199,241	0.15	Cheshire, Shrops, part Lancs, Derby. Largely rural. 161n 39x 57m 203w 3551Yy
M Cardiff	1850	R-Lat	Bs	82	66,000	103,476	85,726	-0.75	*Eglwys Catholig Rufeinig.* Irish, French. M=OFMCap. 82n 57x 63m 183w 1573Yy
D Menevia	1898	R-Lat	Bs	61	23,700	39,410	30,897	-0.97	Central and north Wales. HQ Wrexham. Rural. 37n 25x 37m 156w 621Yy
D Wrexham	1987	R-Lat	Bs	47	27,100	–	35,317	12.50	Inland city on Welsh border. 43n 35x 40m 192w 528Yy
M Liverpool	1850	R-Lat	Bs	223	390,000	515,644	508,257	-0.06	Seaport. Mainly Irish in city, industries. 318n 156x 220m 754w 8243Yy
D Hallam	1980	R-Lat	Bs	65	53,600	–	69,800	6.67	Suffragan diocese of Liverpool. 79n 17x 18m 125w 992Yy
D Hexham & Newcastle	678	R-Lat	Bs	180	186,000	277,742	242,000	0.08	Diocese AD 678. Northumberland, Durham. M=OSB. 241n 35x 67m 283w 4100Yy
D Lancaster	1924	R-Lat	Bs	109	90,000	129,688	116,731	-0.42	Cumbria, and Lancs south to Preston. Largely rural. 156n 57x 62m 242w 2166Yy
D Leeds	1878	R-Lat	Bs	128	143,000	262,753	186,000	-1.37	West Yorks. Catholics in industry and mining areas. 211n 14x 21m 285w 2779Yy
D Middlesbrough	1878	R-Lat	Bs	124	66,000	85,832	86,104	0.01	North Yorks, Humberside. Mostly in Middlesbrough. 122n 61x 87m 186w 1605Yy
D Salford	1850	R-Lat	Bs	204	238,000	358,684	310,650	-0.57	Salford, Blackburn. Urban manufacturing areas. 285n 78x 107m 411w 6420Yy
M Southwark	1850	R-Lat	Bs	286	290,000	364,900	378,220	0.14	London south of Thames, and Kent. M=OFMConv. 304n 147x 196m 945w 7568Yy
D Arundel & Brighton	1965	R-Lat	Bs	115	117,000	136,000	153,000	0.47	Sussex, Surrey. HQ Hove. Densely urban. 1s. 196n 90x 140m 765w 2511Yy
D Plymouth	1850	R-Lat	Bs	89	53,000	54,349	69,497	0.99	Cornwall, Devon, Dorset. Seaports, thin rural RCs. 95n 50x 76m 220w 536Yy
D Portsmouth	1882	R-Lat	Bs	117	147,000	147,813	192,200	1.06	Berks, Hants, IoW, Channel Is. Catholics urban. 122n 104x 178m 533w 2657Yy
M Westminster	1850	R-Lat	Bs	217	370,000	484,680	482,000	-0.02	Primatial see. London north of Thames. M=OSB. 401n 426x 543m 1671w 10847Yy
D Brentwood	1917	R-Lat	Bs	96	143,000	175,170	186,655	0.25	East London, Essex. Catholics mainly urban. 112n 50x 55m 370w 4000Yy
D East Anglia	1976	R-Lat	Bs	65	76,300	–	99,317	5.26	Recent diocese northeast of London. 67n 34x 34m 222w 1250Yy
D Northampton	1850	R-Lat	Bs	78	129,000	182,597	168,165	-0.33	Beds, Bucks, Cambs, Northants, Norfolk. Rural. 89n 41x 43m 250w 2737Yy
D Nottingham	1850	R-Lat	Bs	118	103,700	149,667	134,971	-0.41	Derby, Leics, Lincoln, Notts. Catholics in cities. 146n 64x 93m 290w 2403Yy
EA Great Britain (*Ukrainian*)	1957	R-Ukr	Os	67	11,500	25,000	15,000	-2.02	*Ukrainian Catholic Exarchate in GB.* M=CSSR. 12n 3x 3m 4w 78Yy
OM Great Britain	1953	R-Lat	Bs	135	37,000	10,000	49,000	6.56	*Military Ordinariate of Great Britain, Bishopric of the Forces.* 47 ordinaries, 8 auxiliaries, 9w.
Catholic Church in Ireland:	c 350	R-Lat	B.B.R	199	475,000	588,410	617,233	0.19	In Ulster. 82% of Church is in Eire. C=34+11+104. Border with Eire is nonexistent.
M Armagh	445	R-Lat	Bs	50	108,000	148,820	140,000	0.06	All in Ulster. HQ Armagh, Northern Ireland. 200n 50x 130m 350w 3000Yy
D Clogher	454	R-Lat	Bs	20	30,000	40,000	39,000	0.06	Other half of diocese is in Eire. HQ Monaghan (Eire). 50n 10x 10m 90w 600Yy
D Derry	1158	R-Lat	Bs	30	77,000	100,000	100,000	0.00	25% of diocese is in Eire. HQ Londonderry, NI. 95n 5x 10m 130w 2700Yy
D Down & Connor	c 470	R-Lat	Bs	84	230,000	259,590	299,233	0.57	All in Ulster. HQ Belfast. 1970-78 violence. 209n 93x 150m 369w 5487Yy
D Dromore	514	R-Lat	Bs	15	30,000	40,000	39,000	0.07	30% of diocese is in Eire. HQ Newry, NI. 40n 12x 20m 120w 880Yy
Catholic Church in Scotland:	c 400	R-Lat	B.B.s	478	588,600	822,116	766,451	-0.28	Hierarchy restored 1878. Many Irish. C=22+4+51. 2s. 683n 206x 310m 902w 11390Yy
M Glasgow	c 550	R-Lat	Bs	108	198,000	318,000	257,000	-0.85	D in 6th century. Glasgow, Dumbarton. Irish. 1s. 232n 52x 76m 283w 3527Yy
D Motherwell	1947	R-Lat	Bs	74	130,800	178,800	169,900	-0.20	Lanarkshire. Catholics 30% of total population. 115n 32x 41m 107w 2725Yy
D Paisley	1947	R-Lat	Bs	35	64,000	82,700	84,000	0.06	Renfrewshire. Catholics 23% of total population. 71n 3x 11m 122w 1421Yy
M St Andrews & Edinburgh	c 950	R-Lat	Bs	96	90,000	124,200	117,529	-0.22	D in 10th century. Berwick to St Andrews. 1s. 122n 60x 86m 210w 1827Yy
D Aberdeen	1125	R-Lat	Bs	52	13,000	10,347	17,000	2.01	D in AD 1125, vacant 1577-1878. Orkneys, Shetlands. 25n 33x 55m 40w 388Yy
D Argyll & the Isles	1200	R-Lat	Bs	24	8,800	11,769	11,476	-0.10	D in AD 1200, vacant 1579-1878. HQ Oban. 23n 2x 2m 20w 200Yy
D Dunkeld	1107	R-Lat	Bs	38	47,000	52,700	60,700	0.57	Created AD 1115, restored 1878. HQ Dundee. 40n 16x 21m 59w 597Yy
D Galloway	c 350	R-Lat	Bs	51	37,000	43,600	48,846	0.46	D in 4th century. Southwest. HQ Ayr. 55n 8x 18m 61w 705Yy
Catholic Tridentine Church	1976	I-CCa	x....	6	1,500	–	3,000	5.26	Ex Ch of Rome, supporting archbishop Lefebvre (Latin mass, &c). Also in USA, NZ, et alia.
Cherubim & Seraphim Council of Chs	1965	I-3pA	....W	30	2,870	300	6,000	12.73	Begun in Nigeria 1925. Nigerians (Yorubas), but 50% Afro-Caribbeans.
Christ Apostolic Church	1974	I-3pA	x.I..	14	2,500	–	5,000	4.76	*Bethel.* Nigerians. M=CAC(Ibadan, Nigeria). HQ London N8.
Christadelphian Ecclesias	c1848	m-Ade	x....	310	10,000	30,000	19,500	-1.71	*Birmingham Central Basis of Fellowship.* 342 ecclesias in 1970. Pacifist. Declining.
Christian Brethren (Exclusive, Closed)	1848	P-EBr	x....	860	40,000	60,000	70,000	0.62	*Kelly-Continental; Continuing Tunbridge Wells; Raven-Taylor; Glanton. Darbyites.*
Christian Brethren (Open)	1828	P-CBr	x....	1,537	63,200	140,000	126,000	-0.42	1831, Plymouth Brethren, 1848, J. N. Darby splits to form Exclusives. 25% in Scotland. 181m.
Christian Community, The (1685)	1685	P-Non	.....	9	810	900	1,000	0.42	Founded by French Huguenot refugees. Social and hospital services. W=30%,11Y.
Christian & Missionary Alliance	1973	P-Hol	x....	6	500	–	1,000	4.55	Formerly British Missionary Alliance. HQ Oxford.
Christian Outreach Centers Internat	c1980	I-3cW	x....	5	300	–	1,000	6.67	*COCI.* Charismatic network based on HQ Brisbane (Australia): also in USA.
Church in Wales	c 300	A-Hig	AWC.W	1,600	400,000	1,000,000	1,300,000	1.05	*Eglwys yng Nghymru.* State church until 1920. 6 Dioceses. 2s(50),1000Y. (1995) 671n.
Church of Christ, Scientist	1896	m-Sci	x....	210	10,500	50,000	25,000	-2.73	*Christian Science.* HQ Mother Church, Boston, USA. 413 practitioners.
Church of England:	c 100	A-plu	AWC.W	16,213	12,407,300	27,659,000	24,493,000	-0.49	Reformed 1558. 1960, Charismatic Renewal, now 12%. 100x,308m,2358w,23s (950). SEngland. Confirmees declining at 7% pa.
Province of Canterbury:	597	A-plu	A						
D Bath & Wells	909	A-Hig	A	575	253,000	436,000	386,000	0.09	Confirmees declining since 1965 at 7% pa.
D Birmingham	1905	A-plu	A	193	599,000	838,000	742,000	-0.49	Mainly urban, vast new housing estates. 2s.
D Bristol	1542	A-plu	A	205	305,000	427,000	378,000	-0.49	Urban. Confirmees: 2,195 (1966), 1,718 (1969). 2s.
D Canterbury	597	A-Cen	A	329	232,000	613,000	543,000	0.07	Archdeaconries: 2 rural, 1 urban. 1s.
D Chelmsford	1914	A-Eva	A	611	939,000	1,313,000	1,163,000	-0.48	Urban, suburban; vast housing estates. 498b.
D Chichester	1075	A-plu	A	514	329,000	680,000	602,000	-0.49	Rapid population growth in new towns. 1s.
D Coventry	1918	A-plu	A	240	362,000	506,000	448,000	-0.49	75% urban. Cathedral ministry to secular life.
D Derby	1927	A-plu	A	336	462,000	646,000	572,000	-0.49	Industry, mining, housing estates, villages.
D Ely	1109	A-plu	A	341	117,000	296,000	262,000	-0.49	Mainly rural. Confirmations 1,400 a year. 2s.
D Exeter	1050	A-ACa	A	619	286,000	515,000	456,000	-0.49	Rural, 494 parishes. Agriculture, tourism.
D Gloucester	1540	A-Hig	A	404	121,000	364,000	322,000	-0.49	Confirmees declining since 1965 at 8% pa. 1s.
D Guildford	1927	A-plu	A	216	165,000	535,000	474,000	-0.48	Confirmees: 3,296 (1966), 2,644 (1969).
D Hereford	676	A-plu	A	425	147,000	204,000	181,000	0.08	Rural. Confirmees: 1,639 (1966), 1,344 (1969).
D Leicester	1926	A-plu	A	330	127,000	418,000	370,000	-0.49	Diocese existed 7-8th centuries. 50% urban.
D Lichfield	664	A-Cen	A	580	1,130,000	1,581,000	1,400,000	0.08	Large industrial areas, vast overspill areas.
D Lincoln	1072	A-Hig	A	665	198,000	638,000	565,000	-0.48	Mainly rural. 42 deaneries, 505 parishes. 1s.
D London	180	A-plu	A	477	375,000	1,327,000	1,175,000	-0.49	Refounded 604. Urban, north of Thames.
D Norwich	1091	A-Low	A	650	161,000	439,000	389,000	-0.48	Formerly D Thetford. Rural. Many abbeys.
D Oxford	1542	A-plu	A	817	318,000	1,052,000	932,000	-0.48	Rapid industrialization; university. 12de,4s.
D Peterborough	1541	A-plu	A	380	133,000	329,000	291,000	-0.49	Partly rural, Corby new town development.
D Portsmouth	1927	A-plu	A	168	107,000	331,000	293,000	-0.49	Rapid urbanization. Tourism, Navy.
D Rochester	604	A-plu	A	264	206,000	752,000	666,000	0.07	30% urban, 30% suburban. Many new churches. 2s.
D Salisbury	1078	A-Cen	A	580	230,000	443,000	392,000	-0.49	Rural, Poole harbour. Many ancient churches. 1s.
D Southwark	1905	A-plu	A	386	307,000	953,000	844,000	-0.48	London south of Thames. Industrial mission. 1s.

Continued overleaf

Country Table 2–continued

Official name (bold type = church with over 10% of all affiliated) 1	*Begun* 2	*Type* 3	*Counc* 4	*Congs* 5	*Adults* 6	*Affiliated 1970* 7	*Affiliated 1995* 8	*G%* 9	*Names, notes, and other statistics* (see Codebook, Part 3) 10
D St Albans	1887	A-Cen	A	412	239,000	699,000	619,000	-0.49	Vast population & housing explosion (5% pa).
D St Edmundsbury & Ipswich	1914	A-Low	A	479	151,000	305,000	270,000	-0.49	Mainly rural. 500 West Indians. 146 schools.
D Truro	1876	A-Hig	A	314	100,100	197,000	174,000	-0.50	Rural. Cornwall is 25% Methodist, 50% Anglican.
D Winchester	662	A-Cen	A	409	200,200	566,000	501,000	0.08	Rural. In addition, covers Channel Islands.
D Worcester	679	A-Hig	A	283	132,000	433,000	383,000	0.08	180 parishes. Confirmees declining at 9% pa.
Province of York:	735	A-plu	A						NEngland. Confirmees declining at 6% pa.
D Blackburn	1926	A-Eva	A	286	260,000	656,000	581,000	-0.48	Industrial, rural, and residential areas.
D Bradford	1920	A-Cen	A	167	94,000	351,000	311,000	-0.48	Some Anglicans among huge Pakistani influx.
D Carlisle	1133	A-Hig	A	351	170,000	374,000	331,000	-0.49	Major problem building new churches required.
D Chester	1541	A-Cen	A	370	288,000	980,000	868,000	-0.48	Formed 1541 out of diocese of Lichfield.
D Durham	995	A-Cen	A	304	325,000	1,048,000	928,000	0.10	60% urban. Confirmees: 4,445 (1966), 3,892 (1969).
D Liverpool	880	A-Eva	A	256	301,000	1,050,000	930,000	0.09	Includes 250 West Indians. City 40% Catholic.
D Manchester	1848	A-Cen	A	371	367,000	1,265,000	1,120,000	-0.49	Densely-populated city. 250 church schools.
D Newcastle	1882	A-plu	A	251	131,000	475,000	421,000	-0.48	Seaport, many ethnic groups. High unemployment.
D Ripon	1836	A-Hig	A	267	143,000	448,000	397,000	-0.48	First founded 650. Leeds city and rural areas.
D Sheffield	1914	A-Cen	A	223	675,000	944,000	836,000	-0.48	Heavy industry (coal, steel). Industrial Mission.
D Southwell	1884	A-Cen	A	312	451,000	631,000	559,000	-0.48	Rural, coal-mining in Sherwood Forest.
D Wakefield	1888	A-Cen	A	241	523,000	732,000	648,000	-0.49	90% urban industrial (textiles, coal).
D York	625	A-plu	A	612	248,000	869,000	770,000	0.07	3 large urban areas, rest rural. 4 bishops.
Church of God Brethren	c1970	I-EBr	.....	65	1,500	–	2,000	35.53	Exclusive Brethren.
Church of God Fellowship	1967	I-3pU	.....	12	600	400	1,100	4.13	From Barbados, Grenada, Jamaica. Broke with NTCoG(UK). 1 overseer, 5nx,7m,6 deacons.
Ch of God Fellowship in GB World Wide	1943	I-3pU	.....	10	500	500	1,000	2.81	*Welsh Latter Rain movement*. 4 West Indian congregations. HQ. Trethomas.
Church of God in Christ	1948	I-3pB	Z....	20	5,700	5,000	7,000	1.35	Begun by Black USA troops. M=CoGiC, 1st British Jurisd. HQ Luton. Bishop,13nx,21w.
Church of God of Prophecy	1952	P-Pe3	Z...I	88	16,100	7,000	20,000	4.29	Jamaicans; 4 White, 2 Greek congs. M=CGP(USA). 269nx,64m,1f,3p,84t.
Church of God Pentecostal	1958	I-3pU	.....	10	2,000	2,000	3,000	1.64	Barbados, Jamaica, some White. M=CoG(Huntsville, USA). HQ East Ham. 4 bishops,29nx.
Church of God Reformation Movement	1894	I-3pU	.....	5	600	200	1,000	6.65	Afro-Caribbean. HQ London. N15.
Church of God Seventh-day	c1963	I-3pU	.....	8	600	500	1,000	2.81	Jamaicans. M=CoGSD(Denver, USA). Sabbatarians, now pentecostal. HQ SNorwood. 4nx.
Church of God (Anderson)	1900	P-Hol	x...I	5	200	350	400	0.54	M=CoG(Anderson) (USA). Anti-Pentecostal. 50% Black. Belfast, London, Liverpool. 1n.
Church of God (UK)	1958	I-3pU	.....	5	1,000	300	1,500	6.65	From Antigua, Barbados, Jamaica; some Whites. HQ London E7. 2 bishops. 10n,18m.
Church of Ireland	c 350	A-Low	AWc.W	475	90,000	313,196	274,280	-0.53	*Province of Armagh* only (of its 8 dioceses, 3 wholly in Eire, 3 partly).
Ch of Jesus Christ of Latter-day Saints	1837	m-LdS	x....	313	97,000	70,138	149,200	3.07	*Mormons.* Temple SLondon. Since 1992 declining. 1600f,W=66%,5115Yy,17675z.
Church of the Nations		I-3cW	.....	10	1,000	–	2,000	0.05	Recent charismatic network.
Church of Norway	1868	P-Lut	.....	6	480	600	1,000	2.06	Norwegian Lutherans from state church.
Ch of Our Lord JC of the Apostolic Faith	1964	I-3aU	.....	10	600	400	1,000	3.73	West Indians. Link with Greater Refuge Temple, NY (USA). HQ London SW16. Bishop,4n,15m.
Church of Scotland	397	P-Ref	RWC.W	1,668	752,719	2,500,000	1,220,000	0.06	Established 1560. 12 Synods. Declining. 1782n,6p,4s(160),35371Yy.
Church of Sweden	1710	P-Lut	.....	4	2,500	2,000	4,000	2.81	Swedish Lutherans. Swedes.
Church of the First-Born	1959	I-3pU	x....	7	500	500	1,000	2.81	From Barbados & Jamaica (HQ Kingston). Branches in USA, Canada. HQ Birmingham 23.
Church of the Living God	1962	I-3oO	.....	6	1,100	2,000	2,500	0.90	West Indian church brought by Black immigrants. Split ex Victorious Ch of God.
Church of the Lord (Aladura)	1964	I-3pA	xwI..	15	2,000	1,600	3,000	2.55	Nigerians, Ghanaians; Yoruba elites. M=CLA(Lagos). London SW4. Several UK schisms.
Church of the Nazarene	1906	P-Hol	xFD.E	112	4,140	10,000	10,076	0.03	M=CoN(USA). Ex Congr U of Scotland. Joined by IHM, Calvary Holiness Ch. 1963n,1s.
Churches of Christ in GB & Ireland	1842	P-Dis	xW..W	95	4,000	10,000	8,000	-0.89	*Disciples of Christ. Campbellites.* Ex Ch of Scotland. 26n,200m,1s,48Y.
Churches of Christ (Non-Instrumental)	1945	I-Dis	x....	37	3,250	6,000	8,000	1.16	M=CC(Non-Instrumental) (USA). Rapid growth. 55 churches in England. 44f,1s.
Churches of God in Ireland	c1980	I-3oW	.....	10	1,500	–	3,000	6.67	Oneness body, member of AWCF, HQ in Strandtown, Belfast, Northern Ireland.
Chs of God in the British I & Overseas	1889	P-EBr	x....	80	4,500	10,000	8,500	-0.65	*Luxmore Needed Truth, Green Pastures* (=periodicals). Ex Open Brethren. 250m.
Community Resources		I-3cW	.....	10	1,000	–	2,000	0.05	F=John Singleton.
Congregational Federation	1831	I-Con	....W	284	9,278	18,000	15,000	-0.73	Group of churches rejecting 1972 merger in United Reformed Church. 62n,206m.
Congregational Union of Ireland	c1600	P-Con	R....	25	2,500	5,360	4,000	-1.16	Union formed 1829. Declining. HQ Greenisland, Newtonabbey. 11n,W=70%,3617z.
Congregational Union of Scotland	1795	P-Con	RW..W	91	17,000	49,626	30,000	-1.99	1795, ex Ch of Scotland; 1812, Union. Declining 3.4%pa. 105n,1s(5),W=35%,1263Yy.
Cooneyites (Go Preachers)	1894	I-Fun	x....	50	6,000	10,000	11,000	0.38	*Two by Twos.* Tramp Preachers. Fundamentalists. In NI. Itinerants; in USA, Australia, S Africa.
Coptic Orthodox Church	c1965	O-Cop	Nwa..	7	3,500	4,300	6,000	1.34	Parishes: Kensington, Holborn. Under P Alexandria (Egypt). Egyptians. 1x.
Cornerstone Resources	1982	I-3tW	....E	35	12,500	–	27,000	7.69	Cornerstone Team. HQ Southampton. F=Tony Morton,Arthur Wallis. R-1 type. Abroad: 90 chs.
Countess of Huntingdon's Connexion	1777	P-Con	..D.E	24	900	2,000	1,200	-2.02	Schism ex CofE. Many congs also in United Ref Ch. Declining 3.2%pa. 12n,W=60%.
Covenant Ministries International	1968	I-3tW	.....	170	13,000	–	24,000	49.70	Harvestime Fellowship. 1969 Bradford. F=Bryn Jones. Restoration 1 (R-1). Abroad: 35 chs.
Deeper Life Bible Church	1985	I-3pA	x....	3	810	–	1,000	10.00	M=DLBC(Nigeria). Headquarters in Lahos.
Deliverance Ministries International	1983	I-3vW	.....	3	300	–	1,000	8.33	Victory charismatics.
Divine Prayer Society 1944	1960	I-3pA	.....	3	300	400	800	2.81	*Ch of Family of God & JC (HQ Accra).* Ghanaians, WIndians. Ex Aladura. Northampton. 8nx.
Eden Revival Church	1972	I-3pA	xv...	3	150	–	300	4.35	Split ex Ch of Universal Prayer Fellowship. M=EFC(Accra, Ghana). HQ London SE27.
Elim Pentecostal Church	1915	P-Pe2	Z...H	590	42,901	45,000	79,400	2.30	*Elim Foursquare Gospel Alliance.* Began as Elim Evangelistic Band. Schisms 1939-42. 620n.
Emmanuel Holiness Church	1916	P-Hol	.....	7	500	1,000	1,400	1.35	Holiness denomination. HQ Birkenhead. Mission in Morocco, Sahara. 13n,1j,1p,1s.
English Episcopal Church	1947	I-ReA	.....	2	350	1,000	600	-2.02	*Ch of England (Ev).* Ex Ev Ch of England. Use 1662 BCP. HQ Acton. West Indians.
Estonian Apostolic Orth Ch in Exile	c1950	I-Est	C....	5	2,500	4,000	5,000	0.90	London parishes. Estonian refugees. Under archbishop of Great Britain & Sweden.
Estonian Ev Lutheran Church in Exile	1944	P-Lut	LwC..	60	5,000	5,000	8,000	1.90	Refugees from Estonia after 1940. Independent of ELCE(USSR). World HQ Stockholm.
Eternal Sacred Order of Morning Star	1971	I-3pA	I	5	600	–	1,000	4.17	*...& St Michael Star Fountain of Life Mount Zion.* Ex Holy Order of C&S. Nigerians.
Ethiopian Orthodox Ch (P Addis Ababa)	1974	O-Eth	Nwa..	8	5,700	1,200	8,500	4.76	Under bishop of New York. Ethiopians, Eritreans, Jamaicans, other West Indians.
Evangelical Church of England	1922	I-ReA	.....	6	100	500	300	-2.02	Ex CofE opposing Anglo-Catholicism. Archbishop in Ferrette succession. Lancashire.
Evangelical Church of Germany	1904	P-LuR	.....	50	40,000	10,000	70,000	8.09	*EKD. Evangelische Kirche in Deutschland.* Expatriate Germans.
Ev Fellowship of Congregational Chs	1967	I-Con	C	132	6,200	10,000	12,000	0.73	*Ev Congregational Ch.* Group of congs rejecting 1972 merger in United Reformed Ch.
Evangelical Lutheran Ch of England	1896	P-Lut	e....	16	600	1,197	820	-1.50	Confessional Lutheranism. M=LC Missouri S (USA). 1n,13x,1s(5),W=48%,29y.
Ev Presbyterian Ch in England & Wales	1970	P-Ref	.....	10	1,000	–	2,000	35.53	Irish immigrants to EPCI in Northern Ireland.
Evangelical Presbyterian Ch of Ireland	1927	P-Ref	J...C	12	2,500	5,000	4,500	-0.42	*Irish Evangelical Ch.* Independent congregations in and around Belfast, NIreland.
Fellowship of Independent Ev Chs	1922	I-Eva	C	440	34,500	30,000	47,100	1.82	*FIEC. Peculiar People* (Essex). Growing as new autonomous congregations join. 400n.
First United Ch of Jesus Christ (Apost)	1955	I-3oU	.....	50	11,000	10,000	15,000	1.64	Jamaicans. Former Bethel Apost/Shilo Ch. M=FUCJCA(USA). (1970) 61nx,56m. (1990) 66n.
Forward in Faith	1996	I-TrA	.....	100	7,000	–	10,000	50.00	Anglican Traditionalists, ex C of E over ordination of women. 1,100 clergy.
Foursquare Gospel Ch of Great Britain	1988	P-Pe2	Z....	10	727	–	1,000	14.29	M=ICFG(USA). HQ Tring.
Free Church of England	1844	I-ReA	x.D.E	30	2,000	3,194	2,500	-0.98	*Reformed Episcopal Ch.* Linked with REC(USA). 2 Dioceses. Declining. 33n (5 bishops), 38m.
Free Church of Scotland	1843	I-Ref	JGD.x	232	20,000	30,000	29,200	-0.11	*Wee Frees.* Ex Ch of Scotland. 1900, most joined United Free C of S. 130n,1s.
Free Methodist Church in the UK	1959	I-Hol	VFD.E	23	3,300	2,500	4,100	2.00	Small branches in Wigan and Belfast. M=FMC(USA). Expanding. 14n,3p,W=48%,65Y,50z.
Free Presbyterian Church of Scotland	1893	P-Ref	.....	60	3,000	4,500	10,000	3.25	Ex Free Ch of Scotland. Presbyteries: Northern, Western, Southern, Outer Is. 36n.
Free Presbyterian Church of Ulster	1951	P-Ref	.TT.T	60	12,363	35,000	30,000	-0.61	Fundamentalist body, rejecting religious or political rapproachement with Catholics.
Free Protestant Episcopal Church	1897	I-ARo	x....	35	900	3,000	2,500	-0.73	Healing. Bishops. Branches: USA, Canada, West Indies, West Africa. HQ Tottenham.
General Church of the New Jerusalem	1890	m-Swe	x....	2	100	250	150	-2.02	*Swedenborgian Church.* Split ex New Church. 2 Societies: Colchester, London. 3n.
Gospel Standard Strict Baptist Societies	1872	I-Bap	.....	156	6,300	8,000	9,000	0.47	HQ Chippenham.
Grace Baptist Assembly	1620	P-Bap	.....	258	10,000	11,000	16,000	1.51	Particular or Strict Baptists.
Greater World Chr Spiritualist League	1852	m-Spi	x....	200	14,000	30,000	20,000	-1.61	1931, *GWCSL. GW Sanctuary.* Specifically Christian body of spiritualists. Urban.
Greek Orthodox Ch: AD Thyateira & GB	1815	O-Gre	Cwc.W	64	200,000	219,000	230,000	0.20	Under EP Constantinople. 90% Greek Cypriots. 8 bishops. 20n,41x,2d,1e,1600Yy.
Ground Level Ministries		I-3xW	.....	168	9,500	–	19,000	0.05	F=Dave Kitchen, Stuart Bell. Runs Grapevine. HQ Lincoln.
Gypsy Evangelical Movement	1975	I-3pE	x....	150	23,000	1,000	36,000	5.00	100% Gypsies, run by Gypsies. Caravan communities. M=GGMS(Switzerland), GFC(UK).
Healing Ch of God in Christ UK	1964	I-3pU	.....	2	200	150	500	4.93	Ex Ch of God in Christ Pentecostal. West Indians. HQ Forest Gate, E7. Bishop, 4nx.
Holiness Churches of God	1988	I-Hol	.....	4	480	–	600	14.29	Small independent Holiness body.
Holy Order of Cherubim & Seraphim Ch	1965	I-3pA	xvI.W	20	4,000	3,000	7,000	3.45	HQ Nigeria. Largest African body in UK. Rapid growth. Yoruba, WIndians. 60% men.
House-Church Movement/Restoration	1942	I-3xW	x....	450	20,000	–	40,000	52.79	*Ch of the Great Shepherd/Pyramid Ch.* In Chard, Bradford. M=CGM(USA). Strong in Yorks.
Ichthus Team Ministries	1961	I-3cW	x...E	129	8,500	–	20,000	48.61	Honour Oak Fellowship. F=Roger Forster. HQ Forest Hill. Missions abroad include Azerbaijan.
Independent Methodist Connexion	1805	I-Met	.v..W	103	3,416	16,000	8,000	-2.73	NWEngland. HQ Loughborough. Seatings 40000. Declining rapidly. 235n,140t(8000).
India Pentecostal Church	c1970	I-3pI	.....	20	1,700	–	3,000	37.75	*IPC.* Malayalis from huge indigenous church in India.
Int Assoc of Messianic Congs & Synag		I-3mJ	.....	35	1,500	–	2,700	0.05	*IAMCS.* S=Synagogues. Messianic Jews. M=CMJ,IAMCS(USA),JFJ.
International Churches of Christ	1982	I-Dis	x....	11	1,300	–	2,000	7.69	HQ Los Angeles (USA). Strict discipling and proselytizing on campuses.
International City Mission	1961	I-3pU	x....	10	600	700	1,000	1.44	Barbados, Jamaica (HQ Kingston); some Whites. Also in USA. Women bishops. 4nx,4f.
International Evangelistic Fellowship	c1960	I-3pU	.....	6	1,000	1,000	2,000	2.81	West Indian immigrants. Link with Swedish Pentecostals. HQ London SE24. 1n.
International Ministerial Association	1965	I-3oU	.....	20	1,100	900	1,800	2.81	Independent congregations of Jamaica Apostolics. M=IMA(Houston, USA). 15nx.
Internat Ministerial Council of GB	1968	I-3oU	.....	25	1,200	100	2,500	13.74	From St Kitts, Guyana, India, Jamaica (Apostolics). Ecumenical. HQ London N19. 10nx,1p.
International Pentecostal Holiness Ch	1978	P-Pe3	ZF...	10	300	500	800	5.88	*PHC, British Conference.* Holiness Pentecostals. HQ Bristol 6. M=IPHC(USA). 14n,7f.
Jamaica WI Hackney Pente Apost Ch	1968	I-3oU	I	10	1,100	1,000	2,000	2.81	*WI=West Indies.* Jamaican Apostolics. 22 congregations in WI. HQ London E8. 4n.
Jehovah's Witnesses	1881	m-Jeh	x....	1,362	120,611	200,000	241,000	0.75	Missionaries 1881, branch office 1900. HQ Brooklyn, USA. (1975) 5177Y. (1995) 4758Y.
Jesus Fellowship Army	1805	I-3cW	.....	88	2,100	1,000	4,000	5.70	*Jesus People.* Charismatic Baptists, excluded from EAGB,BUGB. F=Noel Stanton. Shepherding.
Kensington Temple Network	c1970	I-3pW	.....	200	10,000	–	14,000	46.50	Centered on Toronto Airport revival: big effect on London ch. Related to Elim Pentecostal Ch.
Kingdom Faith Ministries	1978	I-3fW	.....	3	700	–	1,000	5.88	Very large church at HQ Horsham (West Sussex). F=Colin Urquart.
Kingsway Int Christian Centre	c1970	I-3cA	.....	20	5,000	–	10,000	44.54	*KICC.* F=M. Ashimolowo (Nigeria). Africans, Asians. London,
Korean International Presbyterian Ch	1978	P-Ref	.....	6	450	–	900	5.88	Immigrant Koreans from large body in Korea.
Latvian Lutheran Church in Exile	1946	P-Lut	Lwc..	60	4,000	5,500	9,500	2.21	*Latvijas Evangeliska Luteriska Baznica.* Refugees from USSR. 7n,21Yy,55z.
Liberal Catholic Church	1915	I-Lib	xv...	17	1,200	2,500	1,500	-2.02	Split ex ORCC. HQ London. 1965, applied to WCC, rejected. 28n,2x,W=45%,31Yy,43z.
Life & Light Fellowship	1966	I-3pU	.....	4	500	250	1,000	5.70	Jamaicans. Large healing crusades. Mission to Jamaica. HQ Handsworth. 3nx,3m.
Local Ecumenical Project Churches		A-Ecu	.....	680	80,000	–	120,000	0.05	Growing by 1994 to over 900 Local Ecumenical Partnerships (multidenominational).
London City Mission	1835	P-Non	.....	34	1,500	5,000	3,000	-2.02	One of 50 city missions begun by D. Nasmith. LCM: 150 missionaries, 60 missions halls.
Lutheran Council of Great Britain	1669	P-Lut	l...W	160	11,000	16,500	15,000	-0.38	Joint Lutheran ministry to refugees, immigrants and diaspora congregations. 47nx.
Manchester City Mission	1837	P-Non	.....	15	900	2,000	1,900	-0.20	Second largest city mission. 20 missionaries and deaconesses, 16 mission halls.
Mar Thoma Syrian Church	1957	I-ReO	x....	3	1,500	1,000	2,000	2.81	*MTSC.* Immigrants from Kerala, India.
Methodist Church in Ireland	1795	P-Met	VWc.W	197	43,070	70,000	68,000	-0.12	Northern Ireland (8,000 others in Republic). 235n,328pp,1s,W=76%,1000Yy.
Methodist Church of Great Britain	1795	P-Met	VWC.W	9,000	408,000	2,000,000	1,200,000	-2.02	1795, ex CofE. 34 Districts. Declining 1.8%pa. 4167n,20652pp,1p,4s(141),43423Yy.
Moravian Church in GB & Ireland	1737	P-Mor	xWX.a	44	2,577	7,000	3,200	-3.08	*British Province.* Unity of Brethren. 5 Districts. Since 1961, 15% WIndians. 30n,17m.
National Church of Denmark	1692	P-Lut	.....	2	400	1,000	500	-2.73	Kanes in state Lutheran Church of Denmark.
Netherlands Reformed Church	1550	P-Ref	.....	25	16,000	15,000	25,000	2.06	*NRC. NGK. Dutch Reformed Ch.* Dutch expatriates, also Afrikaners from South Africa.
Network Ministries		I-3tW	.....	10	1,000	–	2,000	0.05	F=Peter Fenwick.
New Apostolic Church	1948	I-3aX	x....	42	0	2,000	2,031	0.06	*NAC, Canada Bezirk (District).* Ex Catholic Apost Ch. World HQ Zurich.

Continued opposite

Country Table 2–continued

Official name (bold type = church with over 10% of all affiliated) 1	*Begun* 2	*Type* 3	*Counc* 4	*Congs* 5	*Adults* 6	*Affiliated 1970* 7	*Affiliated 1995* 8	*G%* 9	*Names, notes, and other statistics (see Codebook, Part 3)* 10
New Church	1783	m-Swe	xv...	36	1,639	3,500	2,000	-2.21	*General Conference of the New Church. Swedenborgian Ch.* Overseas missions. 36n,1s.
New Covenant Church	1986	I-3pU	.....	11	600	–	1,000	11.11	Afro-Caribbean.
New Frontiers International	1980	I-3tW	....E	710	58,000	–	120,000	6.67	F=Terry Virgo. South Coast. Shepherding controversy. R-1 type. NFI missions abroad.
New Life Christian Churches	c1970	I-3tW	.....	40	5,000	–	10,000	44.54	Large neocharismatic denomination.
New Testament Assembly (England)	1962	I-3pU	....W	20	3,500	400	8,000	12.73	Jamaicans; Grenada, Trinidad, et al. Black. HQ Leyton, E10. Social work, 8nx,14m.
New Testament Church of God	1951	P-Pe3	ZF..i	110	24,200	22,000	30,000	1.25	Jamaicans, few Irish. M=CoG(Cleveland). HQ Handsworth. 260n,1p,W=60%,1323Y.
Non-Subscribing Presb Ch of Ireland	1725	P-Ref	.....	32	4,000	8,500	8,000	-0.24	Unitarian tendencies. Linked to General Assembly, UFCC. 20n,W=30%,100Yy,800z.
Old Baptist Union	1880	P-Bap	.....	13	500	600	1,000	2.06	HQ Sheffield.
Old Roman Catholic Ch (English Rite)	1950	I-CCa	.....	14	700	1,500	1,000	-1.61	Schism ex ORCC. 1963, large USA branch of 65,000 added (HQ Chicago).
Order of the Cross	1904	m-The	x....	30	1,000	3,000	2,000	-1.61	Theosophical. In England, Scotland, Wales, Ulster. Sacramentalist, vegetarian. 5 nations.
Orthodox Church of the British Isles	1866	I-Ort	.....	5	200	1,000	500	-2.73	Also called Catholic Apostolic Ch. HQ London SE7.
Outpouring Ministries		I-3cW	.....	7	1,000	–	2,500	0.05	F=Alan Vincent.
Orthodox Syrian Ch of the East	c1967	O-SyM	Dwa..	5	1,600	2,000	3,000	1.64	Immigrants from Kerala (South India), around southall, Middlesex.
Pentecostal Assemblies of the World	1969	I-3oU	x....	6	600	500	1,000	2.81	From St Kitts, Grenada, Jamaica. Ex FUCJCA. M=PAW,UPC(USA). HQ Battersea. 3nx.
Pentecostal Church of God	1956	I-3pU	.....	20	2,000	1,000	3,000	4.49	Trinidad, Jamaica. 3 districts. Missions: Nigeria, India. HQ Islington. 2 bishops,6n.
Pilgrim Wesleyan Holiness Church	1958	I-Hol	V...I	30	700	1,600	2,000	0.90	Blacks from Barbados,St Kitts,Trinidad,Jamaica. M=WC(USA). HQ Birmingham. 19n,36m.
Pioneer Peoples Network of Churches	I 1982	I-3tW	....E	360	25,000	–	58,000	0.05	*Pioneer Team.* F=Gerald Coates. Southwest London. Annual Global March for Jesus. R-2 type.
Plumbline Ministries	1985	I-3cW	.....	30	1,000	–	2,000	10.00	F=Simon Matthews. An apostolic network.
Polish Evangelical Lutheran Church	1943	P-Lut	e....	27	2,750	4,000	5,500	1.28	Exiles from Evangelical Church of the Augsburg Confession in Poland. M=LCMS.
Polish Orthodox Church Abroad	c1940	O-Pol	Cw...	7	16,000	20,000	21,000	0.20	5 parishes. Resettled Polish army refugees after 1940. Under GOC AD Thyateira. 7n.
Polish Reformed Church in Exile	c1940	P-Ref	.T...	4	1,200	2,000	2,500	0.90	Refugees from Polish church obliterated in World War II. 1956, M=IBPFM(USA).
Presbyterian Church in Ireland	1610	P-Ref	RW..W	456	253,700	396,216	330,000	-0.73	19 Presbyteries in NI. 475n,P=70%,2s(41),750t(70688),W=40%,6789Yy.
Presbyterian Church of Wales	1735	P-Ref	RW..W	1,012	59,815	145,309	83,000	-2.22	*Eglwys Bresbyteraidd Cymru. Calvinistic Meth Ch.* HQ Brecon. 368n,1s,601Yy.
Protestant Evangelical Ch of England	1989	I-ReA	.....	3	400	–	1,000	16.67	Schism ex Church of England.
Rainbow Churches	1991	I-3cW	.....	6	800	–	2,000	25.00	Affiliated to Pioneer Team. F=Adrian Hawkes.
Ras Tafari Melchizedek Orthodox Ch	1960	I-mar	x....	5	2,400	2,000	3,000	1.64	Ras Tafari=Haile Selassie of Ethiopia. Radical WIndian Black youths, some Whites.
Reformed Presbyterian Ch of Ireland	1763	P-Ref	J...C	40	2,500	8,000	6,000	-1.14	*RPC. Covenanters.* HQ Belfast. 30n,1s(6),W=90%,90Yy,100z.
Reformed Presbyterian Ch of Scotland	1743	P-Ref	J....	4	290	800	700	-0.53	*RPC. Modern Covenanters. Joint Reformed Presbyteries of Edinburgh & Glasgow.* 4n.
Religious Society of Friends	1652	P-Qua	Q...W	460	17,000	30,600	28,000	-0.35	*London Yearly Meeting. Quakers.* In Wales: *Cymdeithas y Cyfeillion.* Declining. 1s.
Religious Soc of Friends in Ireland	1654	P-Qua	Qv...	21	1,200	2,500	2,300	-0.33	*Ulster Quarterly Meeting*, Ireland Yearly Meeting (established 1669). Emigration.
Reorganized Ch of JC of L-d Saints	1863	m-LdS	xv...	22	560	2,500	1,765	-1.38	Schism in USA ex CJCLdS (Utah Mormons). Birmingham 13, Leicester, Gloucester.
Resurrected Church of God	1967	I-3pU	.....	6	300	250	600	3.56	Jamaicans. M=Resurrected CoG (Philadelphia, USA) (Black). HQ Wolverhampton. 6nx.
Reunited Brethren		I-EBr	.....	115	4,000	–	6,000	0.05	Exclusive Brethren.
Romanian Orthodox Church	c1955	O-Rum	Cwc..	2	1,900	2,500	3,000	0.73	*Biserica Ortodoxa Romana.* Under P Bucharest. Romanian immigrants, 400 families. 1x.
Russian Orth Ch: PE Western Europe	1500	O-Rus	Mwc.W	10	7,000	6,000	10,000	2.06	Under P Moscow. Russians, also some UK converts. 1 charismatic parish. 8nx,1d(5).
Russian Orthodox Church in Exile	1924	I-Rus	x....	20	20,000	20,000	30,000	1.64	*D Great Britain, ROC Outside of Russia* (HQ New York). Ultra-conservative. 1e(6).
Salt & Light Ministries	1985	I-3tW	....E	172	15,000	–	31,000	10.00	F=Barney Coombs. R-2 type. HQ Basingstoke.
Salvation Army	1865	P-Sal	xWC.W	923	242,000	500,000	300,000	-2.02	*SA, British Territory, Scotland Territory.* 31 Divisions. 2200n,2j,2s.
Scottish Episcopal Church	397	A-Hig	AWc.W	300	30,000	86,351	53,100	0.06	*Episcopal Church in Scotland.* Disestablished 1689. 7 Dioceses. 1s,25Y.
Serbian Orthodox Church	c1960	I-Ser	.....	1	600	1,000	1,100	0.38	Schismatic diocese under Libertyville (USA) opposing P Belgrade. Strong in Bradford.
Serbian Orth Ch: D WEurope, Australia	1952	O-Ser	Cwc..	25	6,000	9,000	10,000	0.42	Under jurisdiction of P Belgrade. Serbian immigrants after 1945. 4 parishes. 7x.
Seventh Day Baptist Church	1617	P-Bap	Tw...	5	200	200	500	3.73	In SDBC(USA). Began 1617 in UK, brought back 1966 by Jamaicans. HQ London N19. 4nx.
Seventh-day Adventist Church	1878	P-Adv	x...w	232	17,609	25,000	35,200	1.38	*British Union Conf.* 55% Blacks (Jamaicans,&c). 99nx,409mw,1H,1j,2r,188t (12330), 563Y.
Shaftesbury Society	1844	P-Non	.....	28	1,900	4,000	4,000	0.00	Care, education, accommodation for disabled or handicapped persons. HQ London SW19.
Shiloh Pentecostal Fellowship (UK)	1965	I-3pU	.....	8	400	500	1,000	2.81	From Trinidad, Montserrat, Grenada (work of PAoC); few Whites. HQ London E8. 5n,1p.
Shiloh United Ch of Christ Apostolic WW	1958	I-3oU	I	7	1,600	1,400	2,000	1.44	*World Wide.* From Jamaica, Trinidad, Barbados. Link, Int Ministerial Council of GB. 9nx,10mw.
Spiritualist Association of GB	1872	m-Spi	.....	15	6,000	10,000	8,000	-0.89	Originally Marylebone Spiritualist Association, till 1960. Psychic research. Urban.
Spiritualists National Union	1891	m-Spi	.....	450	15,000	30,000	26,000	-0.57	*SNU.* Former Spiritualists Nat Federation. Includes non-Christian spiritists. Urban.
Strict & Particular Baptist Churches	1620	P-Bap	.T..C	700	7,000	20,000	19,000	-0.20	*National Strict Baptist Assembly.* 3 regional Associations. Not in BUGBI. 74n.
Swiss Church in London	1762	P-Ref	.....	3	1,600	2,900	3,000	0.14	Swiss immigrants from Reformed Churches of Switzerland.
Team Spirit Ministries	1993	I-3tW	.....	10	400	–	1,000	50.00	F=Dave Tomlinson. Disbanded.
Teamwork Ministries	c1975	I-3tW	.....	50	1,000	–	2,000	5.00	F=David Bowlzer, apostle D. Tomlinson. R-1, then R-2 type.
The Family (Children of God)	c1967	I-mar	xv...	5	690	2,000	857	-3.33	The Family of Love. Communes. In 100 countries, particularly Australia. HQ Bromley.
The King's Churches		I-3tW	.....	15	1,500	–	5,000	0.05	F=Dereck Brown. Aldersboro area; loosely Restorationist (R-1).
The Vine Fellowship of Churches		I-3cW	.....	10	1,000	–	3,000	0.05	Small charismatic network.
The Way International	1955	I-3pW	x....	45	600	300	1,000	4.93	Ex Jesus Revolution. HQ New Knoxville, USA (begun 1953). UK HQ Altrincham, Chesire.
Triumphant Church of God	1959	I-3pU	.....	10	700	700	1,500	3.10	From Jamaica,Montserrat. Split ex CGP. Mission in USA. HQ West Bromwich. 4nx,8m.
True Jesus Church	c1965	I-3oC	x....	20	2,000	500	3,000	7.43	*TJC, World Conference* (HQ Taiwan). Chinese. 3 halls: London, Edinburgh, Newcastle.
Ukrainian Autocephalous Orthodox Ch	1947	I-Ukr	x....	16	1,500	2,000	3,000	1.64	*Sobornopravna* (Democratic). Linked to UOC (USA). Ukrainian refugees, 1945. 12n.
Ukrainian Orthodox Ch (P Kiev)	c1900	O-Ukr	.....	35	17,000	27,000	26,000	-0.15	Disagreement with ROC-P Moskva after Ukraine's independence.
Unaffiliated fundamentalist chapels		I-Fun	.....	2,800	300,000	500,000	600,000	0.05	Large de facto grouping. Expanding. Healing, foreign missions. 2000n.
Union of Evangelical Churches	1838	I-Eva	..D.x	20	535	2,000	1,100	-2.36	Independent congregations in East London and Essex. 56n,28m (local preachers).
Union of Messianic Jewish Congs		I-3mJ	.....	20	1,700	–	3,500	0.05	UMJC. Largest of 2 small Messianic Jewish networks in UK. M=UMJC(USA),CMJ,JFJ.
Union of Welsh Independents	1639	P-Con	.W..W	615	45,000	140,000	70,000	-2.73	*Undeb yr Annibynwyr Cymraeg* (1871). Welsh-speaking only. 235n,101m,2s.
Unitarian & Free Christian Churches	1645	m-Unt	.v..w	197	24,200	40,000	30,000	-1.14	*General Assembly of UFCC.* Unitarians. 1928 merger. Declining. 223n,2s.
United Apostolic Faith Church	c1910	P-Pe2	x...H	30	6,000	10,000	11,000	0.38	Pentecostals with British-Israel doctrines. HQ London N8. Missions in SAfrica.
United Church of God	1963	I-3pU	.....	5	700	300	1,000	4.93	Jamaica, Barbados. Ex NTCoG. M=Un Holiness Ch of Faith in Christ (USA Blacks). 1n,3m.
United Free Church of Scotland	1900	P-Ref	RW..W	73	7,457	19,753	10,100	-2.65	1929, majority rejoined Ch of Scotland. 5 Presbyteries. 77n,1u,346Yy.
United Holy Church of God	1961	I-3pB	x....	12	1,000	650	2,000	4.60	Jamaicans. M=UHCA(NJ,USA). 2 British Districts, HQ Paddington. 2 bishops,10nx.
United Pentecostal Church of GB & I	c1960	P-Pe1	x....	35	3,000	2,000	5,000	3.73	*Jesus Only Ch.* Jamaicans. M=UPC,PAW(USA). Also in Europe. HQ London SW2. 10n,4f.
United Pentecostal Church of God	1974	I-3pU	.....	4	200	–	400	4.76	Mainly Jamaicans. Split ex Triumphant Ch of God. HQ Birmingham 21. 1n.
United Reformed Church	1662	P-Ref	RWc.W	1,800	117,900	350,000	187,000	-2.48	1972 union Congr Ch in E&W (74%),Presb CofE (26%). 12 Provs. 2080n,6s,1u.
Universal Church of God	1965	I-Hol	.....	10	500	400	1,000	3.73	Mainly Jamaicans. Split ex CoG (Anderson) (USA). Anti-pentecostal. HQ Aston. 6nx.
Universal Fell of Metropolitan Com Chs		I-	x....	12	420	–	1,000	0.05	European & North Sea District.
Universal Pentecostal Church	c1965	I-3pI	Z....	20	1,100	2,000	2,500	0.90	M=Ceylon Pente Mission. Sri Lanka Tamil immigrants. London, Midlands, Wales, York.
Univ Pente Ch (Ghana & Overseas)	1973	I-3aA	.....	3	250	–	400	4.55	Ex Ch of the Lord (Battersea). Ghanaians, Sierra Leonians, WIndians. London SE13.
Universal Prayer Group Ministries	1962	I-3pA	.....	3	600	1,000	1,300	1.05	West African transients & students. Collective healing prayer, fasting, dreams.
Victorious Church of God	c1965	I-3pU	.....	5	2,000	2,000	3,000	1.64	Black (West Indian) pentecostal immigrants. Schism ex ch of God in Christ.
Wesleyan Holiness Church	1958	I-Hol	....W	20	700	400	1,100	4.13	Recent Holiness body without wider relations.
Wesleyan Reform Union	1849	P-Met	V.D.a	123	2,804	12,000	9,000	-1.14	Expelled ex British Wesleyan Methodism. Midlands, North. 22n,237m.
Worldwide Church of God	1953	I-BrI	x....	44	2,988	2,000	4,000	2.81	*WCG. Radio Church of God.* Radio, TV, Literature ministries. HQ Pasadena, CA (USA).
World-Wide Missions	1967	I-Non	x....	5	900	2,000	1,700	-0.65	M=World-Wide Missions (USA). Evangelicals based on Pasadena, CA (USA).
Other independent charismatic chs	c1975	I-3cW	.....	2,000	150,000	–	290,000	5.00	Many Restorationist (R-1, R-2), many non-Restorationist; also JILF.
Other independent Oneness bodies	c1970	I-3oU	.....	200	10,000	–	15,000	46.91	Total 10, mostly immigrating recently from Caribbean.
Other single independent churches	c1930	I-	.....	500	15,000	7,000	25,000	5.22	Many different bodies mainly in urban centers.
Other independent Baptist Churches		I-Bap	.....	30	2,000	–	3,000	0.05	Varieties of Baptists with no wider affiliations.
Other Protestant denominations	c1950	P-	.....	170	10,500	20,000	22,000	0.38	Total over 100 (see list below), including British Conference of Mennonites.
Other Third-World indigenous chs		I-3pA	.....	300	8,000	12,200	17,000	0.05	Total over 80 (see list below), mainly West Indians and West Africans, also UCKG/IURD (Brazil).
Other marginal Protestant bodies	c1900	m-	.....	100	6,000	8,300	12,000	1.49	Total about 30 bodies (see list below), and many independent congregations.
Other city missions	c1830	P-Non	.....	180	4,000	10,000	9,000	-0.42	In: Bristol, Chester, Edinburgh, Glasgow, Leeds, Liverpool, York & 40 other cities.
Other Orthodox churches	c1960	O-	.....	20	3,000	1,000	5,000	6.65	Total about 20, including Antiochian OC, Syrian OC, Albanian OC, Macedonian OC.
Other independent Anglican Churches	c1970	I-ReA	.....	20	3,000	–	5,000	40.59	Recent breakoffs or schisms from Anglican Communion; links in USA.
Other Afro-Caribbean independent chs		I-3pU	.....	1,700	100,000	50,000	250,000	0.05	Total over 100 more bodies.
Other independent Catholic churches	c1830	I-CCa	.....	60	900	3,000	2,900	-0.14	Total about 50 (see list below), including about 35 under bishops-at-large.
Doubly-affiliated		2-aff			-425,000	0	-772,149		Persons in a large denomination and also in newer Renewal body.
Totals				**66,422**	**21,528,796**	**43,952,441**	**39,150,000**		

Churches, members, growth, 1900-2025	*Congs*	*Adults*	*Affiliated*	*G%*	*Total denominations*	*6 Megablocs:* O	R	A	P	I	m
Total churches, members, and denominations (mid-1900)	20,000	18,860,000	36,126,400	0.28	123	4	3	4	70	30	12
Total churches, members, and denominations (mid-1970)	60,939	22,945,042	43,952,441	0.28	465	20	3	4	157	243	38
Total churches, members, and denominations (mid-1990)	66,000	21,557,000	39,200,000	-0.57	774	34	3	5	235	450	47
Total churches, members, and denominations (mid-1995)	66,422	21,528,796	39,150,000	-0.03	803	34	3	5	236	478	47
Total churches, members, and denominations (mid-2000)	66,000	21,476,000	39,053,151	-0.05	828	35	3	5	237	500	48
Total churches, members, and denominations (mid-2025)	61,000	20,897,000	38,000,000	-0.11	1,873	45	3	5	260	1500	60

NOTES ON TABLE ABOVE

NATIONAL COUNCILS (Column 4, 5th letter).

= Commission of the Covenanted Churches in Wales (ENFYS, with RCC as observer)
a = member of both BCC & EAGB.
C = British Evangelical Council (BEC).
E = Evangelical Alliance of the United Kingdom (EAUK).
H = British Pentecostal Fellowship (begun 1948).
I = Afro-West Indian United Council of Churches (Afro-Caribbean United Church Council) (begun 1977).
i = member of I (preceding line) and also of H.
J = Council of African & Allied Churches in the UK (begun 1979; 20 churches).
R = Episcopal Conference of Ireland (ECI).
s = Bishops' Conference of England & Wales (or Bishops' Conference of Scotland), also member of CCBI.
T = British Council of Protestant Christian Churches.
W = Churches Together in England (CTE); or Churches Together in Wales (CTW, CYTUN); or, Commission of the Covenanted Churches in Wales (ENFYS, with RCC as observer); or Action of Churches Together in Scotland (ACTS); or Churches Together in Man (CTM); all collectively being known as Council of Churches for Britain & Ireland (CCBI).
w = associate member of CCBI, or observer member.
x = member of both EAGB and BEC.

Other national councils. Council of Churches for Wales (Cyngor Eglwysi Cymru) = Baptist Union of GB & I, Baptist Union of Wales, Ch in Wales, Chs of Christ (observer), Methodist Ch, Presbyterian Ch of Wales, Religious Society of Friends (observer), Roman Catholic Ch (Consultant observer), Salvation Army, Union of Welsh Independents, United Reformed Ch. Free Church Federal Council (FCFC) = Baptist Union of GB & I, Churches of Christ in GB & I, Congregational Federation, Countess of Huntingdon's Connexion, Free Ch of England, Independent Methodist Connexion, Methodist Ch in GB, Moravian Ch, Presbyterian Ch of Wales, Salvation Army (joined 1974), Union of Welsh Independents, United Reformed Ch, Wesleyan Reform Union. Irish Council of Churches (ICC) = Ch of Ireland, Methodist Ch in Ireland, Moravian Ch, Non-Subscribing Presbyterian Ch of Ireland, Presbyterian Ch in Ireland, Religious Society of Friends, Salvation Army. Scottish Churches Council (SCC) = Baptist Union of Scotland, Churches of Christ, Ch of Scotland, Congregational Union of Scotland, Episcopal Ch in Scotland, Methodist Ch in Scotland, Religious Society of Friends, Salvation Army, United Free Ch of Scotland.

Continued overleaf

Country Table 2–concluded

Other local councils. The BCC has some 720 local (county, city, town or regional) Christian councils, or councils of churches, affiliated to it (some linked also with CCW, SCC or ICC). The EAGB has 46 area fellowships affiliated to it.

TRADITION (Column 3). *Types of Anglican churchmanship.* Almost all of the 61 Anglican dioceses in the UK have parish churches of every tradition of churchmanship, from Anglo-Catholic to Low Church, although former clearcut divisions are disappearing and the issue is increasingly seen as unimportant or even irrelevant. Nevertheless a descriptive typology is still possible and useful. In a 1970 public-opinion poll (NOP), Anglicans in Great Britain described themselves as: 14% High Church, 70% Low (including Central) Church, 16% no particular views. These percentages apply to the entire church, which is 99.9% laity; for clergy, the proportions are different. The type of Anglican churchmanship recorded here in column 3 gives each diocese's self-description, as seen from the diocesan office, of the main emphasis or predominant tradition of churchmanship found in the diocese. The *Church of Ireland* is traditionally Low Church in ritual, the *Episcopal Church in Scotland* is traditionally Anglo-Catholic, and the *Church in Wales* is High Church (Prayer Book Catholic). In the *Church of England* itself, these traditions are far more pluralistic or mixed, and it is often impossible to state a dominant tradition; the code above therefore gives only an impressionistic view of the major tradition in the diocese, as seen from the diocesan office, sometimes following the churchmanship or emphases of the incumbent bishops during 1970-75.

OTHER PROTESTANT DENOMINATIONS. In addition to the denominations listed in the denominations listed in the table, there are a large number of smaller groups (many from the USA since 1970), including the following: Apostolic Faith Church, Armenian Ev Ch (1 congregation at Bromley), Berean Forward Movement, Bible Fellowship Union (ex Jehovah's Witnesses), Calvary Holiness Ch (HQ Glamorgan), Calvinistic Independent Ch, Christian Israelite Ch, Ch of Denmark (begun 1689), Ch of Finland, Chs of Christ (Instrumental) (1958), Crown Covenanters Society, Dutch Reformed Ch (begun 1550), Ev Movement of Wales, Evangelistic Association, Evangelization Society, Free Presbyterian Ch of England, Free Salvationist Mission, Frichley Friends (schism ex Quakers), Gospels Halls (a large number of independent congregations across GB and NIreland), Greek Evangelical Ch (begun 1960), Hebrew Christian Movement, Hutterian Brethren (Wheathill Bruderhof, Salop), Independent Ch of God, Independent Holiness Ch, Independent Jesus Name, International Laymen's Bible Fellowship, Italian Christian Chs of North Europe (CCINE; Pentecostal), Italian Pentecostal Ch (1969), Kingdom Revival Crusade, Maranatha Convention, Mennonite Ch, Original Scottish Succession, Pentecostal Ch of the West Indies, Pillar of Fire (USA; 1922; holiness body with 2 churches), Polish Ev Lutheran Ch in Exile (6 pastors), Primitive Baptists, Railway Mission, Reformed Ch of France (begun 1550), Slavic & Baltic Missionary Society, Society of Dependents (1850 Loxwood, Sussex; Cogglers, Cokelers; 100 left), Spanish Evangelical Ch (1961), Swiss Reformed Ch. There are also USA military chaplaincies in addition to those already listed in the table above.

OTHER THIRD-WORLD INDIGENOUS CHURCHES. Numerous other Third-world immigrant groups have established branches of their home churches in the UK. Most were begun by West Indian Blacks, some by Indians, Sinhalese or Koreans, and some by Africans (including Nigerians who have begun Aladura (Praying churches). These additional bodies numbered over 80 by 1976 and included the following, all of which are operated by West Indian Blacks unless another national is indicated here in parentheses: African Orthodox Ch (USA Blacks), All Nations Ch of God, Apostolic Churches (several independent Jesus-Only pentecostal congregations in West Bromwich, Stafford, &c, from Apostolic movement in Jamaica; including Apostolic Church of God in Christ), Army of the Cross of Christ Ch (MDCC, from Ghana; church in London), Asian Ch of Jesus Christ (Pakistani and West Indian pentecostals; HQ Ilford), Bethel Apostolic Ch, Bible Truth Ch of God (HQ Brixton), Bible Way Pentecostal Ch, Celestial Ch of Christ (2 churches; from Benin and Nigeria), Cherubim & Seraphim Society (Nigeria; begun 1974; 110 members in 1976), Ch of God Assembly (begun 1974), Ch of God Holiness (Jamaicans, 2 congregations), Ch of God (Holiness) (Jamaicans, HQ Handsworth), Ch of Jesus (Jamaica), Ch of the Lord (Battersea) (Ghanaians), Ch of Universal Prayer Fellowship (1968 ex CLA (Nigeria); Ghanaians, Nigerians, Sierra Leonians), Deeper Last Day World Vision (Ev Ch of God), Emmanuel Ch of God, Emmanuel Pentecostal Faith Ch of God, Evangelical Touring Harmonizing Ch (HQ Peckham), Father Divine Peace Mission Movement (USA Blacks), Gospel of God Ch (Apostles of Johane Masowe, from Rhodesia/Zimbabwe), Holy Spirit Association for Unification of World Christianity (from South Korea; by 1976, 3,000 adherents in 20 communities), Holy Tabernacle of Christ Jesus, Latter Rain Outpouring Revival, Mount Carmel Ch of God (HQ Brixton), Mount Olivet Spiritual Baptist Ch, Mount Zion Sanctuary Assembly Seventh-day (Jamaicans, HQ Croydon), New Covenant Ch of God (HQ Brixton), People's Christian Fellowship, Recruit for Christ Evangelistic Crusade, Redeemed Ch of Christ (1968; ex Holy Order of C&S; Nigerians, Ghanaians, West Indians), Refuge Ch of God (1961; Jamaican pentecostals), Sacred Cherubim and Seraphim (Nigeria), Seventh Ch of Melchizedek (1975), Seventh Day Pentecostal Ch (Jamaica), Spiritual Baptist Ch (Trinidad), Universal Ch of the Lord (1975), Voice of Prophecy Ch; and at least 50 other Black denominations (1977). There are also numerous single congregations of revivalist type, including Miracle Ministry Mission (London E7), Miracle Revival Fellowship (London E17), Resurrection Revival Ministry (London E7).

OTHER MARGINAL PROTESTANT BODIES. Among the many small marginal bodies are the following: Bible Students (ex Jehovah's Witnesses), Branhamites (End Time Local Believers), British-Israel World Federation, Christian Science Parent Ch (c1920 split), Christian Spiritualist Ch, Ch of Scientology, Ch of the Good Shepherd (Chelsea; Spaxtonites; healing of animals), Divine Science Federation International (1 church), General Anthroposophical Society (Christian Community Ch), Goshen Fellowship (ex Jehovah's Witnesses), Maranatha Convention (ex Jehovah's Witnesses), Millennila Dawn Association, New Jerusalem Fellowship (ex British Israelites), New Thought, Olive Branch Ch, Progressive Spiritualist Ch, Religious Science Ch, United Ch of Religious Science (3 churches), Unity School of Christianity. Among the numerous independent congregations are around 180 unaffiliated spiritualist churches.

OTHER INDEPENDENT CATHOLIC CHURCHES. Minuscule unrecognized episcopal churches begun by bishops-at-large (episcopi vagantes) number over 30. In addition there are another 15 or so larger autocephalous Catholic churches, including: Ancient British Ch, Ancient Catholic Ch, English Catholic Ch, Free Catholic Ch, Old Holy Catholic Ch, Old Roman Catholic Ch, Polish Mariavite Ch, Reformed Catholic Ch (Utrecht Confession). For details of all these bodies, see table in Part 9. There are also other cults stemming from Roman Catholicism, including Antoinists (from Belgium and France). The totals given above exclude numerous other such bodies which were in existence earlier but are now defunct.

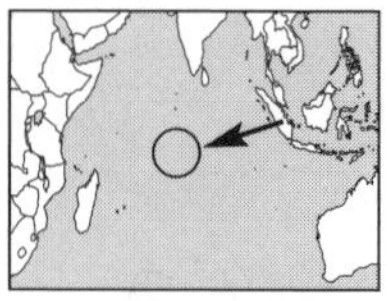

BRITISH INDIAN OCEAN TERRITORY

SECULAR DATA, AD 2000

STATE
Official name: The Crown Colony of the British Indian Ocean Territory.
Short name: British Indian Ocean Territory.
Adjective of nationality: of British Indian Ocean Territory.
Flag: That of the UK (Britain).
Area: 60 sq. km. (23 sq. mi.).
Government: Crown colony of the United Kingdom (Britain), formed 1965.
Legislature: One commissioner, one administrator.
Official language: English.
Monetary unit: 1 pound sterling (£) = 100 new pence. **US$1=** £ 0.59.
Chief cities: DIEGO GARCIA 1,000.
Political divisions: 1 province.
Armed forces: 1,000.

DEMOGRAPHY
Population: 2,000.
Population density: 33.3/sq. km. (86.9/sq. mi.).
Under 15 years: 1,000.
Growth rate p.a.: 0.83% (births 15.78, deaths 6.55).
Mortality: Infant, per 1,000: 13.9; **Maternal per 100,000:** 20.0.
Life expectancy: 73 (male 69, female 76).
Household size: 4.0. **Floor area per person, sq.m:** 16.0.
Major languages: English, Creole.
Urban dwellers: 100.00%. **Urban growth rate p.a.:** 0.00%.
Labor force: 50%.

ETHNOLINGUISTIC PEOPLES
91.7% Creole (Mulatto); 5.0% USA White; 2.0% British; 1.0% French.

ECONOMY
National income p.a. per person: US$5,000; **per family:** US$20,000.

EDUCATION
Adult literacy: 65% (male 70%, female 60%). **Schools:** 1.
Universities: 0. **School enrolment:** female/male: 80%/80%.

HEALTH
Access to health services: 75%. **Access to safe water:** 100%.
Hospitals: 1 (40 beds per 10,000). **Doctors:** 10.
Blind: 10. **Deaf:** 100. **Murder rate:** 2. **Lepers:** 0.

LITERATURE
New book titles p.a.: 1 (400 p.a. per million). **Periodicals:** 0.
Newspapers: 0 dailies.

COMMUNICATION (per 1,000 people)
Phones: 300 (20% mobile). **Radios:** 800. **TV sets:** 250.
Daily newspaper circulation: <1. **Computers:** 700.

HUMAN LIFE AND LIBERTY (optimum condition=100.0%)
HDI: 75.0. **HSI:** 75.0. **HFI:** 70.0. **EFL:** 40.0.

Country Table 1. **Religious adherents in the British Indian Ocean Territory, AD 1900-2025.**

Year	1900		1970		mid-1990		Annual change, 1990-2000				mid-1995		mid-2000		mid-2025	
Name	Adherents	%	Adherents	%	Adherents	%	Natural	Conversion	Total	Rate	Adherents	%	Adherents	%	Adherents	%
Christians	**200**	**40.0**	**900**	**45.0**	**900**	**45.0**	**0**	**3**	**3**	**0.27**	**919**	**46.0**	**925**	**46.3**	**970**	**48.5**
PROFESSION																
professing Christians	**200**	**40.0**	**900**	**45.0**	**900**	**45.0**	**0**	**3**	**3**	**0.27**	**919**	**46.0**	**925**	**46.3**	**970**	**48.5**
AFFILIATION																
unaffiliated Christians	0	0.0	300	15.0	0	0.0	0	2	2	37.97	19	1.0	25	1.3	40	2.0
affiliated Christians	**200**	**40.0**	**600**	**30.0**	**900**	**45.0**	**0**	**0**	**0**	**0.00**	**900**	**45.0**	**900**	**45.0**	**930**	**46.5**
Roman Catholics	150	30.0	500	25.0	700	35.0	0	0	0	0.00	700	35.0	700	35.0	720	36.0
Anglicans	50	10.0	100	5.0	200	10.0	0	0	0	0.00	200	10.0	200	10.0	210	10.5
Trans-megabloc groupings																
Evangelicals	0	0.0	0	0.0	10	0.5	0	0	0	0.00	10	0.5	10	0.5	20	1.0
Pentecostals/Charismatics	0	0.0	20	1.0	105	5.3	0	1	1	0.65	110	5.5	112	5.6	140	7.0
Great Commission Christians	**40**	**8.0**	**400**	**20.0**	**470**	**23.5**	**0**	**1**	**1**	**0.21**	**470**	**23.5**	**480**	**24.0**	**430**	**21.5**
Hindus	250	50.0	900	45.0	800	40.0	0	-4	-4	-0.45	771	38.6	765	38.3	720	36.0
Muslims	50	10.0	200	10.0	200	10.0	0	-3	-3	-1.33	185	9.3	175	8.8	150	7.5
Nonreligious	0	0.0	0	0.0	100	5.0	0	4	4	3.05	125	6.3	135	6.8	160	8.0
World A (unevangelized persons)	200	40.0	400	20.0	120	6.0	0	-5	-5	-4.59	90	4.5	76	3.8	60	3.0
World B (evangelized non-Christians)	100	20.0	700	35.0	980	49.0	0	2	2	0.19	991	49.5	999	49.9	970	48.5
World C (Christians)	200	40.0	900	45.0	900	45.0	0	3	3	0.27	919	46.0	925	46.3	970	48.5
Country's population	**500**	**100.0**	**2,000**	**100.0**	**2,000**	**100.0**	**0**	**0**	**0**	**0.00**	**2,000**	**100.0**	**2,000**	**100.0**	**2,000**	**100.0**

COLUMNS, ROWS.
For meanings and definitions, see Codebook (Part 3). Note that, by definition, total 'Christians' = professing + crypto-Christians, which also = affiliated + unaffiliated Christians, and also = Great Commission Christians + latent Christians. Percentages may not always total exactly, due to rounding.

CENSUSES.
No religion question has been asked.

Country status. The British Indian Ocean Territory is a group of islands with strategic importance in the middle of the Indian Ocean, mainly the Chagos Archipelago. There are no permanent residents but British and American naval personnel are stationed on Diego Garcia.

HUMAN LIFE AND LIBERTY

Human rights and freedoms. The situation of the original indigenous inhabitants was controversial for some years until its satisfactory resolution. Human rights are similar to those in Britain.

NON-CHRISTIAN RELIGIONS

The inhabitants of this territory are indigenous Indian Ocean peoples. Transient workers, they are mostly Hindu with a minority of Muslims. Neither group has any permanent facilities or organized events for worship.

Great Commission Instrument Panel: status of the British Indian Ocean Territory (for explanation see start of Part 4)

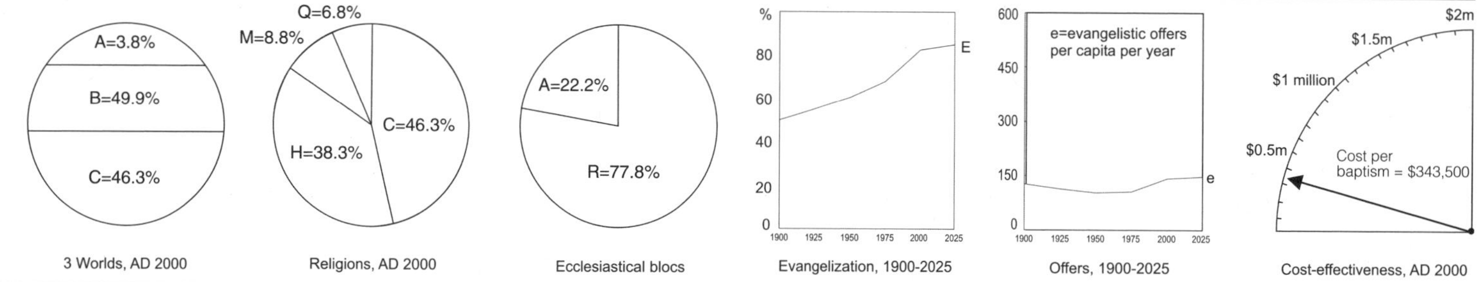

Country summary. **Worlds A, B, C by ethnolinguistic peoples, cities, and major civil divisions in the British indian Ocean Territory.**

World	PEOPLES Num	Pop 2000	C%	Christians	E%	U%	Unevangelized	CITIES Num	Pop 2000	C%	Christians	E%	U%	Unevangelized	CIVIL DIVISIONS Num	Pop 2000	C%	Christians	E%	U%	Unevangelized
A	0	0	0.00	0	0	0	0	0	0	0.00	0	0	0	0	0	0	0.00	0	0	0	0
B	2	1,840	42.01	773	96	4	74	1	1,000	45.00	450	96	4	38	1	2,000	45.00	900	96	4	75
C	3	160	79.38	127	100	0	0	0	0	0.00	0	0	0	0	0	0	0.00	0	0	0	0
Total	**5**	**2,000**	**45.00**	**900**	**96**	**4**	**74**	**1**	**1,000**	**45.00**	**450**	**96**	**4**	**38**	**1**	**2,000**	**45.00**	**900**	**96**	**4**	**75**

CHRISTIANITY

There are no resident clergy in the territory. The Anglican and Catholic communities are served by visiting priests. Most Christians are among the British and American military personnel, and none have this territory as their permanent home. The territory is administered under the Catholic diocese of Port Louis (Mauritius) and the Anglican diocese of Mauritius.

Indigenous missions. No indigenous mission has been undertaken by Christians in British Indian Ocean Territory.

FUTURE TRENDS AND PROSPECTS

There is little religious change expected in the next 30 years in British Indian Ocean Territory.

Beyond 2025, nonreligious persons are expected to increase and exceed 10% of the population by AD 2050.

BIBLIOGRAPHY

Limuria, the lesser dependencies of Mauritius. R. Scott. 1961; reprint, Westport, CT: Greenwood Press, 1976. 324p.
Peak of Limuria: the story of Diego Garcia. R. Edis. London: Bellew, 1993. 128p.

Crucifixion of Christ (Ethiopic manuscript) on Easter 1973 postage stamp.

Country Table 2. **Organized churches and denominations in the British Indian Ocean Territory.**

Official name (bold type = church with over 10% of all affiliated) 1	*Begun* 2	*Type* 3	*Counc* 4	*Congs* 5	*Adults* 6	*Affiliated 1970* 7	*Affiliated 1995* 8	*G%* 9	*Names, notes, and other statistics* (see Codebook, Part 3) 10
Anglican Church (D Mauritius)		A-Hig	aw...	2	100	100	200	0.05	Under Diocese of Mauritius, in CPIO. No resident clergy; periodic visits.
Catholic Church		R-Lat	P.S..	10	500	500	700	0.05	In D Port Louis (Mauritius), D Port Victoria (Seychelles). Annual visit by priest.
Totals				**12**	**600**	**600**	**900**		

Churches, members, growth, 1900-2025	*Congs*	*Adults*	*Affiliated*	*G%*	*Total denominations*	*6 Megablocs:* O	R	A	P	I	m
Total churches, members, and denominations (mid-1900)	1	120	200	1.58	1	0	0	1	0	0	0
Total churches, members, and denominations (mid-1970)	2	350	600	1.58	2	0	1	1	0	0	0
Total churches, members, and denominations (mid-1990)	10	600	900	2.05	2	0	1	1	0	0	0
Total churches, members, and denominations (mid-1995)	12	600	900	0.00	2	0	1	1	0	0	0
Total churches, members, and denominations (mid-2000)	12	600	900	0.00	2	0	1	1	0	0	0
Total churches, members, and denominations (mid-2025)	20	620	930	0.13	2	0	1	1	0	0	0
Total churches, members, and denominations (mid-2000)	12	600	900	0.00	2	0	1	1	0	0	0
Total churches, members, and denominations (mid-2025)	20	700	930	0.13	2	0	1	1	0	0	0

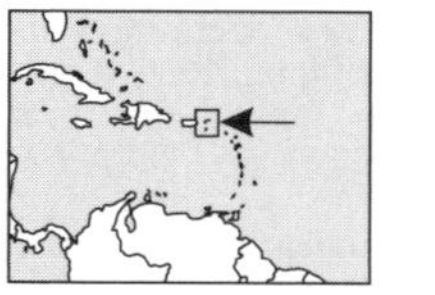

BRITISH VIRGIN ISLANDS

SECULAR DATA, AD 2000

STATE
Official name: The Colony of the British Virgin Islands.
Short name: British Virgin Islands.
Adjective of nationality: British Virgin Islanders.
Flag: British Blue Ensign with arms of the Colony in the fly.
Area: 153 sq. km. (59 sq. mi.).
Government: British colony, since 1956 (1666 British colony of Leeward Islands, 1956 separate colony).
Legislature: Executive Council, 6 members; Legislative Council, 10 members.
Official language: English.
Monetary unit: 1 pound sterling (£) = 100 new pence. **US$1=** £ 0.59.
Chief cities: ROAD TOWN 3,793.
Political divisions: 1 province.

DEMOGRAPHY
Population: 21,000.
Population density: 139.6/sq. km. (362.1/sq. mi.).
Under 15 years: 7,000.
Growth rate p.a.: 0.87% (births 19.95, deaths 5.62).
Mortality: Infant, per 1,000: 19.8; **Maternal per 100,000:** 10.0.
Life expectancy: 76 (male 74, female 78).
Household size: 4.0. **Floor area per person, sq.m:** 45.0.
Major languages: English, Portuguese, Hindi, Arabic.
Urban dwellers: 61.0%. **Urban growth rate p.a.:** 3.6%.
Labor force: 50%.

ETHNOLINGUISTIC PEOPLES
90.0% West Indian Black; 5.0% British; 2.0% USA White; 1.6% Mulatto; 0.7% Indo-Pakistani.

ECONOMY
National income p.a. per person: US$8,003; **per family:** US$32,013.

EDUCATION
Adult literacy: 93% (male 94%, female 92%). **Schools:** 18.
Universities: 1. **School enrolment:** female/male: 95%/95%.

HEALTH
Access to health services: 90%. **Access to safe water:** 90%.
Hospitals: 1 (50 beds per 10,000). **Doctors:** 60.
Blind: 20. **Deaf:** 1,300. **Murder rate:** 2. **Lepers:** 20.

LITERATURE
New book titles p.a.: 10 (450 p.a. per million). **Periodicals:** 3.
Newspapers: 0 dailies.

COMMUNICATION (per 1,000 people)
Phones: 370 (30% mobile). **Radios:** 625. **TV sets:** 234.
Daily newspaper circulation: 250. **Computers:** 300.

HUMAN LIFE AND LIBERTY (optimum condition=100.0%)
HDI: 87.7. **HSI:** 90.0. **HFI:** 90.0. **EFL:** 50.0.

Country status. The British Virgin Islands are 36 islands and islets, 16 of them inhabited, forming a British dependency in the northwest of the Lesser Antilles in the Caribbean Sea. The main industry is tourism with stone and gravel mining, and sugar cane as secondary activities.

HUMAN LIFE AND LIBERTY

Human rights and freedoms. The situation is parallel to that in Britain itself.

CHRISTIANITY

PROTESTANT CHURCHES. Methodism, which owes its origin to British missionary activity at the end of the 18th century, is the dominant Christian influence in the islands. Although many are not active members, the population in 1960 was 73% Methodist, the largest percentage for Methodism in many of the islands of the West Indies. By 1970, this had dropped to 52% and by 1990 to 32% due to non-Methodist immigration. Other Protestant denominations are Seventh-day Adventists, the Baptists, and the Church of God (Cleveland).

ANGLICAN CHURCH. Anglicans made up 16% of the population in 1960 and 14% in 1990, and are the principal denomination on Virgin Gorda. Since 1916, the islands have been served by the Protestant Episcopal Church in the USA The diocese of the Virgin Islands, which is part of PECUSA and includes both the British and US Virgin Islands, was formed in 1947.

Country Table 1. **Religious adherents in the British Virgin Islands, AD 1900-2025.**

Year / Name	1900 Adherents	1900 %	1970 Adherents	1970 %	mid-1990 Adherents	mid-1990 %	Annual change, 1990-2000 Natural	Conversion	Total	Rate	mid-1995 Adherents	mid-1995 %	mid-2000 Adherents	mid-2000 %	mid-2025 Adherents	mid-2025 %
Christians	**4,900**	**100.0**	**9,220**	**91.6**	**14,140**	**88.4**	**452**	**-20**	**432**	**2.70**	**16,230**	**87.0**	**18,461**	**87.9**	**31,130**	**84.1**
PROFESSION																
professing Christians	**4,900**	**100.0**	**9,220**	**91.6**	**14,140**	**88.4**	**452**	**-20**	**432**	**2.70**	**16,230**	**87.0**	**18,461**	**87.9**	**31,130**	**84.1**
AFFILIATION																
unaffiliated Christians	490	10.0	1,147	11.4	2,160	13.5	68	73	141	5.15	2,999	16.1	3,569	17.0	6,930	18.7
affiliated Christians	**4,410**	**90.0**	**8,073**	**80.2**	**11,980**	**74.9**	**384**	**-93**	**291**	**2.20**	**13,231**	**70.9**	**14,892**	**70.9**	**24,200**	**65.4**
Protestants	3,960	80.8	5,703	56.6	8,040	50.3	251	-76	175	1.99	8,791	47.1	9,792	46.6	16,100	43.5
Anglicans	440	9.0	1,500	14.9	2,300	14.4	72	-22	50	1.99	2,600	13.9	2,800	13.3	3,600	9.7
Independents	0	0.0	270	2.7	680	4.3	21	11	32	3.93	830	4.5	1,000	4.8	2,500	6.8
Roman Catholics	10	0.2	500	5.0	660	4.1	21	-17	4	0.59	680	3.6	700	3.3	900	2.4
Marginal Christians	0	0.0	100	1.0	300	1.9	9	21	30	7.18	330	1.8	600	2.9	1,100	3.0
Trans-megabloc groupings																
Evangelicals	2,500	51.0	1,600	15.9	2,750	17.2	86	4	90	2.87	3,192	17.1	3,650	17.4	5,700	15.4
Pentecostals/Charismatics	0	0.0	500	5.0	1,940	12.1	61	12	73	3.25	2,292	12.3	2,670	12.7	4,800	13.0
Great Commission Christians	**440**	**9.0**	**2,750**	**27.3**	**4,700**	**29.4**	**147**	**6**	**153**	**2.86**	**5,440**	**29.2**	**6,229**	**29.7**	**10,500**	**28.4**
Spiritists	0	0.0	700	7.0	1,350	8.4	42	3	45	2.89	1,570	8.4	1,795	8.6	3,200	8.7
Nonreligious	0	0.0	50	0.5	465	2.9	15	19	34	5.67	630	3.4	807	3.8	1,800	4.9
Baha'is	0	0.0	60	0.6	150	0.9	5	-1	4	2.50	170	0.9	192	0.9	400	1.1
Muslims	0	0.0	30	0.3	50	0.3	2	-1	1	1.67	55	0.3	59	0.3	80	0.2
Hindus	0	0.0	40	0.4	45	0.3	1	0	1	1.46	45	0.2	52	0.3	90	0.2
World A (unevangelized persons)	0	0.0	20	0.2	48	0.3	2	2	4	6.05	74	0.4	84	0.4	185	0.5
World B (evangelized non-Christians)	0	0.0	827	8.5	1,812	12.4	63	18	81	3.08	2,360	12.8	2,455	13.2	5,685	14.7
World C (Christians)	4,900	100.0	9,220	91.3	14,140	87.3	452	-20	432	2.70	16,230	86.8	18,461	86.4	31,130	84.8
Country's population	**4,900**	**100.0**	**10,068**	**100.0**	**16,000**	**100.0**	**517**	**0**	**517**	**2.76**	**18,665**	**100.0**	**21,000**	**100.0**	**37,000**	**100.0**

COLUMNS, ROWS.
For meanings and definitions, see Codebook (Part 3). Note that, by definition, total 'Christians' = professing + crypto-Christians, which also = affiliated + unaffiliated Christians, and also = Great Commission Christians + latent Christians. Percentages may not always total exactly, due to rounding.

CENSUSES.
7.IV.1960 (de jure): 81.5% Protestants (73.2% Methodists), 16.2% Anglicans, 1.0% Roman Catholics, 0.3% nonreligious, 1.0% other religionists. **7.IV.1970**: 69.6% Protestants (51.9% Methodists, 4.6% SDAs, 2.5% Baptists), 21.4% Anglicans, 6.1% Roman Catholics, 1.0% marginal Protestants, 0.5% nonreligious. **1981**: 63.5% Protestants (45.5% Methodists, 5.2% SDAs, 3.9% Baptists), 21.0% Anglicans, 6.1% Roman Catholics, 2.0% Marginal Christians, 3.1% nonreligious, 0.4% Hindus, 0.3% Muslims, 3.6% other religionists.

NOTES ON RELIGIONS
BAHA'IS. No local spiritual assemblies had been organized by 1995.
HINDUS. Indians.
MUSLIMS. Indo-Pakistanis, some Arabs.

Great Commission Instrument Panel: status of the British Virgin Islands (for explanation see start of Part 4)

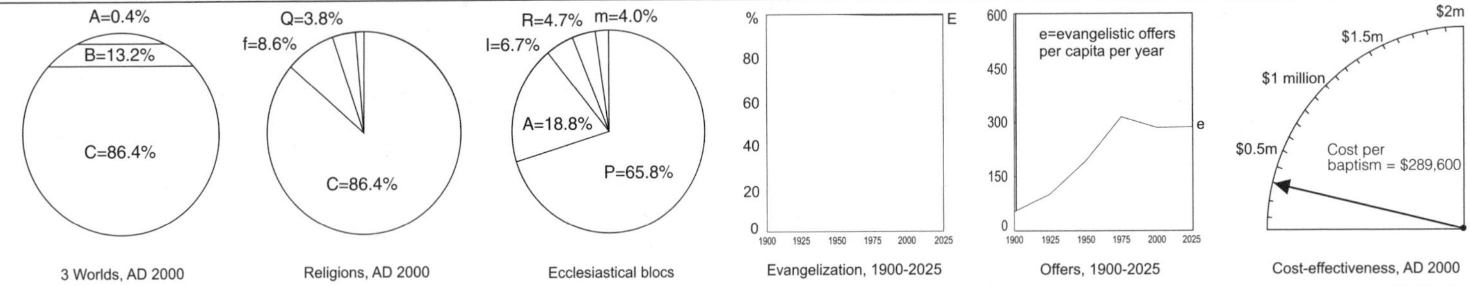

Country summary. **Worlds A, B, C by ethnolinguistic peoples, cities, and major civil divisions in the British Virgin Islands.**

World	PEOPLES Num	Pop 2000	C%	Christians	E%	U%	Unevangelized	CITIES Num	Pop 2000	C%	Christians	E%	U%	Unevangelized	CIVIL DIVISIONS Num	Pop 2000	C%	Christians	E%	U%	Unevangelized
A	0	0	0.00	0	0	0	0	0	0	0.00	0	0	0	0	0	0	0.00	0	0	0	0
B	3	235	41.70	98	89	11	27	0	0	0.00	0	0	0	0	0	0	0.00	0	0	0	0
C	5	21,130	70.01	14,794	100	0	64	1	3,793	70.00	2,655	100	0	5	1	21,366	69.70	14,892	100	0	90
Total	**8**	**21,365**	**69.70**	**14,892**	**100**	**0**	**91**	**1**	**3,793**	**70.00**	**2,655**	**100**	**0**	**5**	**1**	**21,366**	**69.70**	**14,892**	**100**	**0**	**90**

CATHOLIC CHURCH. This British territory has the smallest Catholic population of any of the islands of the West Indies. Originally, part of the prelature of the Virgin Islands, a suffragan of the archdiocese of Washington, D.C. (USA), in February 1971, it was transferred to the diocese of St John's in Antigua. The number of professing Catholics increased largely by immigration, from 80 in 1960 to 680 in 1995.

The Holy See has no diplomatic relations with British Virgin Islands in AD 2000.

Indigenous missions. There has been little mission outreach from the Christians in the British Virgin Islands.

Christian themes are frequent on postage stamps: *left*, Virgin & Child, by Pintorricchio; *right*, Holy Bible presented (*far right*) to Queen at 1953 Coronation.

CHURCH AND STATE

The islands have been a British possession since 1666. Freedom of religion has been the norm. There is no established church in the territory.

BROADCASTING AND MEDIA

Shortwave programs from HCJB (Ecuador), TWR (Antilles) and AWR (Costa Rica) can be easily received.

A wide variety of television programs can be received via satellite-equipped televisions.

INTERDENOMINATIONAL ORGANIZATIONS

Anglicans, Catholics, and Methodists cooperate in the Tortola Inter-Church Council.

FUTURE TRENDS AND PROSPECTS

Christians will probably represent a declining percentage (less than 85% by 2025) of the British Virgin Islands in direct proportion to an increase of nonreligious persons and spiritists (greater than 13% by AD 2025).

This trend is expected to continue into mid-century when Christians could represent less than 80% of the population. Within Christianity, Jehovah's Witnesses could reach 10% by that time.

BIBLIOGRAPHY

1980–1991 population census of the Commonwealth Caribbean: British Virgin Islands, volume one. Regional Census Co-ordinating Committee. : Caricom Council of Ministers, 1980. 101p.
Annual Synod, 1980. Methodist Church. Road Town, Tortola, BVI: British Virgin Islands Circuit, 1980. 32p. (Illustrations of places and people).
Caribbean Quakers. H. F. Durham. Hollywood, FL: Dukane, 1972. 133p. (Pages 57-78 deal with British Virgin Islands).
Christmas in the Virgin Islands. E. Burnett. East End, Tortola, BVI: E. & R. Burnett, 1983. 36p.
East End Methodist Church: 175th anniversary, 1810–1985. V. E. Moll. East End, Tortola, BVI: East End Methodist Church, 1985. 25p. (Oldest remaining Methodist church building in the Virgin Islands).
Methodism: two hundred years in the British Virgin Islands. F. W. Blackman. Bridgetown, Barbados: Methodist Church of British Virgin Islands, 1989. 160p.
'The church in the process of development in the British Virgin Islands.' D. G. Mason. S.T.M. thesis, Drew University, Madison, NJ, 1974. 104p.
The folklore of the British Virgin Islands. T. Bates. Cambridge, UK: Cambridge University Press. 509p.
Tortola: a Quaker experiment of long ago in the tropics. C. F. Jenkins. London: Friends Bookshop, 1923. 106p.
Virgin Islands. V. Moll. *World bibliographical series,* vol. 138.

Country Table 2. Organized churches and denominations in the British Virgin Islands.

Official name (bold type = church with over 10% of all affiliated) 1	Begun 2	Type 3	Counc 4	Congs 5	Adults 6	Affiliated 1970 7	Affiliated 1995 8	G% 9	Names, notes, and other statistics (see Codebook, Part 3) 10
Anglican Church (D Virgin Islands)	c1700	A-ACa	awMRC	1	1,700	1,500	2,600	2.22	Begun under Ch of England. 1963, in PECUSA. Major body on Virgin Gorda. School. 1f.
Baptist Church		I-Fun	x....	2	228	230	570	0.05	M=Baptist Missionary Association of America. Fundamentalist Baptists.
Baptist Convention	1976	P-Bap	T....	1	100	–	250	5.26	M=SBC(USA).
Catholic Church (D Saint John's)	1960	R-Lat	B.NMC	2	450	500	680	1.24	In D Saint John's (Antigua). One SVD priest. No institutions.
Church of God (Anderson)		P-Hol	x....	3	240	463	600	0.05	M=CoG(Anderson) (USA).
Church of God (Cleveland)		P-Pe3	ZF...	1	400	300	600	0.05	Holiness Pentecostals. M=CoG(Cleveland) (USA). 1 church on Tortola. 1n.
Church of the Nazarene	1961	P-Hol	xF...	9	260	200	520	3.90	M=CON(USA).
Jehovah's Witnesses	c1940	m-Jeh	x....	3	122	100	330	4.89	*Watch Tower. IBSA.* Active witnessing under way by 1947. (1975) 1Y. (1995) 14Y.
Methodist Ch in Carib & Americas	1789	P-Met	VwM.C	5	2,570	4,000	5,950	1.60	In MCCA (1967 union), Leeward Islands District. M=MMS(UK). 2 schools. 2n,1x,1w,1f.
Seventh-day Adventist Church		P-Adv	x....	2	540	440	771	0.05	*SDA, East Caribbean Conference, Caribbean Union Conference.*
Other Protestant denominations		P-	.....	2	60	300	100	0.05	About 4 denominations, including Moravian Ch (80 adherents), PCA(USA, 1995).
Other pentecostal denominations	c1920	I-3pU	.....	10	104	40	260	7.77	About 5 Black indigenous churches.
Totals				**41**	**6,774**	**8,073**	**13,231**		

Churches, members, growth, 1900-2025	*Congs*	*Adults*	*Affiliated*	*G%*	*Total denominations*	*6 Megablocs:* O	R	A	P	I	m
Total churches, members, and denominations (mid-1900)	10	2,000	4,410	0.87	2	0	0	1	1	0	0
Total churches, members, and denominations (mid-1970)	25	3,703	8,073	0.87	14	0	1	1	7	4	1
Total churches, members, and denominations (mid-1990)	35	6,100	11,980	1.99	19	0	1	1	10	6	1
Total churches, members, and denominations (mid-1995)	41	6,774	13,231	2.01	19	0	1	1	10	6	1
Total churches, members, and denominations (mid-2000)	45	7,600	14,892	2.39	19	0	1	1	10	6	1
Total churches, members, and denominations (mid-2025)	70	12,400	24,200	1.96	42	0	1	1	20	16	4

NOTES ON TABLE ABOVE
NATIONAL COUNCILS (Column 4 5th letter).
C = Tortola Inter-Church Council.

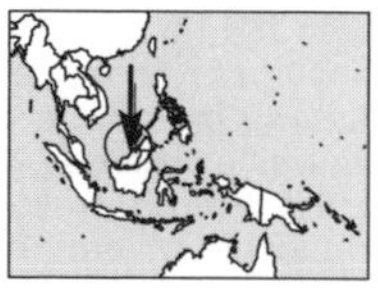

BRUNEI

SECULAR DATA, AD 2000

STATE
Official name: Negara Brunei Darussalam (The State of Brunei Abode of Peace).
Short name: Brunei. **Adjective of nationality:** of Brunei Darussalam.
Flag: Yellow filed, diagonal white and black stripes, with coat of arms in centre.
Area: 5,765 sq. km. (2,226 sq. mi.).
Government: Self-governing constitutional monarchy, since 1983 (16th century sultanate, 1888 British protectorate, 1963 opted not to join Malaysia, 1983 Independence).
Legislature: Legislative Council, 21 members.
Official language: Malay and English.
Monetary unit: 1 Brunei dollar (B$) = 100 cents. **US$1=** B$1.69.
Chief cities: BANDAR SERI BEGAWAN (Brunei town) 99,854.
Political divisions: 4 provinces.
Armed forces: 5,000.

DEMOGRAPHY
Population: 328,000.
Population density: 56.9/sq. km. (147.3/sq. mi.).
Under 15 years: 106,000.
Growth rate p.a.: 1.74% (births 18.77, deaths 3.19).
Mortality: Infant, per 1,000: 8.8; **Maternal per 100,000:** 60.0.
Life expectancy: 76 (male 74, female 79).
Household size: 5.8. **Floor area per person, sq.m:** 15.0.
Major languages: Malay, Chinese (Fukienese), English, Kedayan, Dusun, Melanau, Iban.
Urban dwellers: 72.22%. **Urban growth rate p.a.:** 2.4%.
Labor force: 43%.

ETHNOLINGUISTIC PEOPLES
44.9% Orang Bukit (Kedayan); 6.9% Dusun (Kadazan); 6.4% Southern Bisaya (Visayak); 5.7% Bisayan Tutong; 5.6% Han Chinese (Mandarin).

ECONOMY
National income p.a. per person: US$15,801; **per family:** US$91,645.

EDUCATION
Adult literacy: 88% (male 92%, female 82%). **Schools:** 187.
Universities: 4. **School enrolment:** female/male: 89%/89%.

HEALTH
Access to health services: 80%. **Access to safe water:** 90%.
Hospitals: 10 (36 beds per 10,000). **Doctors:** 197.
Blind: 300. **Deaf:** 19,500. **Murder rate:** 1.
Lepers: 500.

LITERATURE
New book titles p.a.: 60 (170 p.a. per million). **Periodicals:** 21.
Newspapers: 1 daily.

COMMUNICATION (per 1,000 people)
Phones: 240 (38% mobile). **Radios:** 417. **TV sets:** 609.
Daily newspaper circulation: 71. **Computers:** 80.

HUMAN LIFE AND LIBERTY (optimum condition=100.0%)
HDI: 88.2. **HSI:** 55.0. **HFI:** 40.0. **EFL:** 45.0.

Country Table 1. Religious adherents in Brunei, AD 1900-2025.

Year	*1900*		*1970*		*mid-1990*		*Annual change, 1990-2000*				*mid-1995*		*mid-2000*		*mid-2025*	
Name	*Adherents*	*%*	*Adherents*	*%*	*Adherents*	*%*	*Natural*	*Conversion*	*Total*	*Rate*	*Adherents*	*%*	*Adherents*	*%*	*Adherents*	*%*
Muslims	11,580	61.0	71,570	55.2	162,680	63.3	4,494	358	4,852	2.64	188,710	64.1	211,201	64.4	305,900	66.6
Ethnoreligionists	4,750	25.0	18,860	14.5	28,700	11.2	793	-2	791	2.46	33,000	11.2	36,606	11.2	50,000	10.9
Buddhists	1,330	7.0	15,960	12.3	24,800	9.7	685	-181	504	1.87	26,800	9.1	29,838	9.1	38,000	8.3
Christians	**100**	**0.5**	**11,800**	**9.1**	**21,050**	**8.2**	**590**	**-177**	**413**	**1.81**	**23,600**	**8.0**	**25,183**	**7.7**	**33,500**	**7.3**
PROFESSION																
crypto-Christians	0	0.0	570	0.4	4,400	1.7	122	-2	120	2.44	5,000	1.7	5,600	1.7	8,000	1.7
professing Christians	**100**	**0.5**	**11,230**	**8.7**	**16,650**	**6.5**	**468**	**-175**	**293**	**1.64**	**18,600**	**6.3**	**19,583**	**6.0**	**25,500**	**5.6**
AFFILIATION																
unaffiliated Christians	0	0.0	102	0.1	510	0.2	14	-6	8	1.48	538	0.2	591	0.2	800	0.2
affiliated Christians	**100**	**0.5**	**11,698**	**9.0**	**20,540**	**8.0**	**567**	**-162**	**405**	**1.82**	**23,062**	**7.8**	**24,592**	**7.5**	**32,700**	**7.1**
Independents	0	0.0	1,528	1.2	6,400	2.5	177	13	190	2.63	7,425	2.5	8,300	2.5	11,500	2.5
Protestants	0	0.0	1,650	1.3	4,800	1.9	133	-13	120	2.26	5,885	2.0	6,000	1.8	9,000	2.0
Roman Catholics	60	0.3	4,520	3.5	5,000	2.0	138	-78	60	1.14	5,300	1.8	5,600	1.7	7,000	1.5
Anglicans	40	0.2	4,000	3.1	4,300	1.7	119	-90	29	0.66	4,400	1.5	4,592	1.4	5,000	1.1
Marginal Christians	0	0.0	0	0.0	40	0.0	1	5	6	9.60	52	0.0	100	0.0	200	0.0
Trans-megabloc groupings																
Evangelicals	0	0.0	1,100	0.9	4,370	1.7	121	77	198	3.81	5,461	1.9	6,350	1.9	13,000	2.8
Pentecostals/Charismatics	0	0.0	600	0.5	6,200	2.4	171	94	265	3.62	7,540	2.6	8,850	2.7	15,300	3.3
Great Commission Christians	**95**	**0.5**	**7,000**	**5.4**	**14,000**	**5.5**	**387**	**33**	**420**	**2.66**	**16,100**	**5.5**	**18,199**	**5.6**	**25,700**	**5.6**
Chinese folk-religionists	1,140	6.0	9,980	7.7	9,860	3.8	272	-95	177	1.66	10,350	3.5	11,626	3.5	11,500	2.5
Confucianists	0	0.0	0	0.0	4,500	1.8	124	6	130	2.57	5,150	1.8	5,801	1.8	8,000	1.7
Nonreligious	0	0.0	0	0.0	2,600	1.0	72	70	142	4.45	3,050	1.0	4,017	1.2	6,000	1.3
Hindus	100	0.5	1,300	1.0	2,000	0.8	55	20	75	3.25	2,400	0.8	2,753	0.8	4,500	1.0
Baha'is	0	0.0	530	0.4	750	0.3	21	2	23	2.72	875	0.3	981	0.3	1,500	0.3
New-Religionists	0	0.0	0	0.0	60	0.0	2	-1	1	2.12	65	0.0	74	0.0	100	0.0
World A (unevangelized persons)	17,860	94.0	77,690	59.9	148,803	57.9	4,110	-986	3,124	1.92	164,245	55.8	180,072	54.9	219,861	47.9
World B (evangelized non-Christians)	1,040	5.5	40,209	31.0	87,147	33.9	2,408	1,163	3,571	3.48	106,501	36.2	122,745	37.4	205,639	44.8
World C (Christians)	100	0.5	11,800	9.1	21,050	8.2	590	-177	413	1.81	23,600	8.0	25,183	7.7	33,500	7.3
Country's population	**19,000**	**100.0**	**129,700**	**100.0**	**257,000**	**100.0**	**7,108**	**0**	**7,108**	**2.47**	**294,347**	**100.0**	**328,000**	**100.0**	**459,000**	**100.0**

COLUMNS, ROWS.
For meanings and definitions, see Codebook (Part 3). Note that, by definition, total 'Christians' = professing + crypto-Christians, which also = affiliated + unaffiliated Christians, and also = Great Commission Christians + latent Christians. Percentages may not always total exactly, due to rounding.

CENSUSES.
21.XI.1947: 67.1% Muslims, 17.2% Chinese folk-religionists and Buddhists, 10.9% tribal religionists, 4.3% Christians (2.3% Anglicans, 1.7% Roman Catholics, 0.3% Protestants), 0.5% other religionists. **9.VIII.1960**: 60.2% Muslims, 31.7% Chinese folk-religionists and Buddhists and tribal religionists, 8.1% Christians (6,796 persons). **1.IX.1971**: 62.2% Muslims, 13.5% Buddhists, 7.6% Christians, 7,5% Chinese folk-religionists, 8.8% other religionists. **1981:** 63.4% Muslims, 14.0% Buddhists, 9.7% Christians, 9.5% Free-Thinkers, 2.9% other faiths (including Baha'is). **1986:** 66.5% Muslims, 11.8% Buddhists, 9.1% Free-Thinkers, 8.9% Christians, 3.7% other faiths (including Baha'is). **1991:** 67.2% Muslims, 12.8% Buddhists, 10.0% Christians, 10.0% Christians, 10.0% other faiths (including Free-Thinkers and Baha'is).

NOTES ON RELIGIONS
BAHA'IS. In 2 local spiritual assemblies and 27 isolated groups (1964, 1973). Growth in 1997 has been far slower than was planned and anticipated by Baha'i leaders in 1964.
BUDDHISTS. Chinese (Mahayana), with a few Sinhalese (Theravada) from Sri Lanka.
ETHNORELIGIONISTS. Most of the Sea Dayaks, and also some Kedayans, Dusuns and Belaits, are animists or spirit-worshippers.
HINDUS. Indians.
INDEPENDENTS. In 10 groupings in 1995 (see Table 2): Chinese indigenous Christians, and isolated radio believers.
MUSLIMS. All the Malays (Shafite Sunnis), and all Tutongs (Melanau), are Muslims; also about 70% of Kedayans, Dusuns and Belaits; and a few Indo-Pakistanis. *Hajj pilgrims to Mecca.* (1975) 431; (1976) 11.

Great Commission Instrument Panel: status of Brunei (for explanation see start of Part 4)

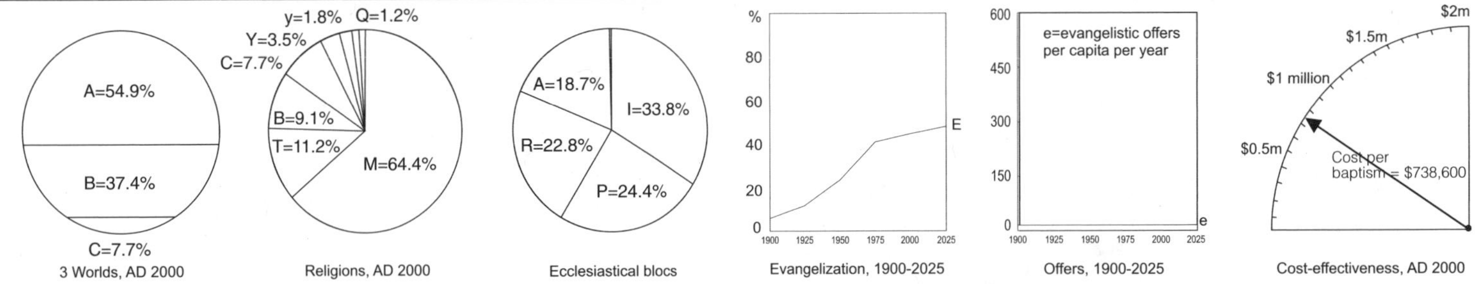

Country summary. **Worlds A, B, C by ethnolinguistic peoples, cities, and major civil divisions in Brunei.**

World	*PEOPLES* Num	Pop 2000	C%	Christians	E%	U%	Unevangelized
A	11	217,852	2.00	4,367	32	68	147,193
B	14	103,011	15.01	15,467	68	32	32,803
C	2	7,217	65.90	4,756	100	0	25
Total	**27**	**328,080**	**7.50**	**24,590**	**45**	**55**	**180,021**

World	*CITIES* Num	Pop 2000	C%	Christians	E%	U%	Unevangelized
A	1	99,854	9.00	8,987	50	50	50,296
B	0	0	0.00	0	0	0	0
C	0	0	0.00	0	0	0	0
Total	**1**	**99,854**	**9.00**	**8,987**	**50**	**50**	**50,296**

World	*CIVIL DIVISIONS* Num	Pop 2000	C%	Christians	E%	U%	Unevangelized
A	4	328,080	7.50	24,592	45	55	180,020
B	0	0	0.00	0	0	0	0
C	0	0	0.00	0	0	0	0
Total	**4**	**328,080**	**7.50**	**24,592**	**45**	**55**	**180,020**

Country status. Brunei is a small Muslim sultanate on the northeast coast of Borneo facing the South China Sea. The oil-rich country's principal exports are petroleum and natural gas. The Sultan of Brunei is the richest person in the world.

HUMAN LIFE AND LIBERTY

Human need and development. With a small population and massive oil wealth, Brunei is one of the richest nations in the world in per capita wealth. However, the bulk of the oil revenues goes into the sultan's coffers and does not trickle down to the people.

Human rights and freedoms. Brunei is a medieval country in terms of human rights. The sultan, who is also the prime minister, is an autocrat, who has suspended his own constitution 14 times since 1962. As Dar ul Islam, or House of Islam, Brunei has made the Sharia its effective legal code. Whipping is a mandatory punishment in many criminal cases. Women are treated as second class citizens and chattels, and are forced to wear the tudong, the traditional head covering. They are not permitted to hold permanent public office. Although there is a large Chinese minority, the Chinese are denied citizenship and access to government jobs.

Muslims. Omar Ali Saifuddin Mosque, Brunei.

NON-CHRISTIAN RELIGIONS

Islam is the official religion of Brunei, and 64% of the population, mostly Malays, are professing Muslims. Following a visit in AD 1425 to sultan Muhammed Shah (Parameswara) of Malacca, the Hindu ruler of Brunei, Awang Alak Betatar, became a Muslim. Arab scholars were later invited to carry on missionary work in the country which resulted in the conversion of the majority of the population to Islam. Conversions to Islam from tribal religions continued into the 1990s. Converts adopt Muslim names.

Other religions include Buddhism, Confucianism and Taoism among the Chinese, traditional animism among the Aboriginal peoples, and Baha'i.

CHRISTIANITY

CATHOLIC CHURCH. Brunei is part of the Catholic diocese of Miri, the other half of the diocese being formed by 2 of the 5 administrative divisions of Sarawak in eastern Malaysia. In 1995, there were 5,300 baptized members, mostly native Chinese, with Indian and European expatriates. In 1991, two-thirds of the Catholic priests and nuns were given one month to leave the country, and replacements were not allowed.

The Holy See has no diplomatic relations with Brunei AD 2000, but an apostolic delegate residing in Bangkok.

OTHER CHURCHES. Anglicans form the strongest of the non-Catholic churches.

Their membership is approximately 60% Chinese and 10% Iban, with 13% Indian and 13% European. About 40% are expatriates working for the Shell petroleum enterprise or for the government.

The Borneo Evangelical Mission is an Australian interdenominational faith mission working with Aboriginal peoples in the interior.

Methodism owes its origin to British missionary influence and is organized as part of the Sarawak Chinese and Iban Conferences of the Methodist Church in Malaysia and Singapore. Seventh-day Adventists are also active and growing. Protestant churches of ethnic Chinese were in 1991 served by 10 full-time pastoral workers. Three churches together sent out 22 Bruneian Chinese missionaries, 15 to Malaysia, 4 to Singapore, 2 to Africa, and one to South America.

The True Jesus Church was founded in mainland China in 1917 as a result of an indigenous revival movement. Entirely Chinese in membership, it has spread to a number of countries in the China diaspora since the Communist accession to power on the mainland in 1949.

Indigenous missions. A fledgling mission initiative among Brunei Christians was stifled in 1992 when contact with Christians from other countries was cut off by government edict.

CHURCH AND STATE

According to the constitution of 1959, which was amended in 1965, Islam is the state religion and the sultan is its head (Article 3, paragraphs 1 and 2), but the free practice of all other religions is guaranteed (paragraph 1). A senior government official in 1984 said to a reporter, 'We'd like to see Brunei become 100% Muslim'. In 1991, the sultan proclaimed a new order called Malay Muslim Monarchy (Melayu Islam Beraja or MIB) which established Islam to an even stronger and more dominant position than before. MIB links Malay culture and Islam tightly with national identity and stresses the monarch's role as a defender of the Muslim faith. Alcohol was banned, raising pigs became illegal, and religious instruction in the schools was increased. Buddhist temples and shrines were closed on the ground they were not legally registered. The only religious buildings permitted to be built are mosques. New churches applying for registration are generally ignored, and then face the accusation of conducting illegal meetings. It is illegal to import Christian literature, and contact between local and foreign Christians is banned.

BROADCASTING AND MEDIA

The 'Jesus' film has been shown to 14, 800, most in showings by film teams. Shortwave radio programs can be received.

FUTURE TRENDS AND PROSPECTS

Christianity is expected to decline from 8.2% in 1970 to 7.3% in 2025. Buddhists will likely hold steady at 11% respectively throughout the 30-year period.

Islam will claim over 66% of the population in 2025, and is expected to be the dominant religion of the distant future in Brunei. Tribal religionists, many converting to Islam, will likely diminish to less than 8% by mid-century. In the same period Christians could rise to 10% of the population.

BIBLIOGRAPHY

Borneo: the land of river and palm. E. Green. London: Society for the Propagation of the Gospel in Foreign Parts, 1912. 172p. (missionary account).
'Brunei,' P. Hsieh & R. Self, in *The Church of Asia*, p.96–100. D. E. Hoke (ed). Chicago: Moody Bible Institute of Chicago, [1975].
Brunei. S. C. E. Krausse & G. H. Krausse. *World bibliographical series*, vol. 93. Oxford, UK: CLIO Press, 1988. 296p. (See especially 'Religion,' p.162-7).
Drunk before dawn. S. Lees. Kent, UK: Overseas Missionary Fellowship, 1979. 215p.
In the shadow of Kinabalu. C. Alliston. London: Robert Hale, 1961. 191p.
Khabar Gembira (the Good News): A history of the Catholic Church in East Malaysia and Brunei. J. Rooney. London: Burns & Oates with Mill Hill Missionaries, 1981. 292p.
Pameran sejarah perkembangan Islam di Brunei. Bandar Seri Begawan: Dewan Bandaran, 1979. 46p.
'Singapore, Malaysia and Brunei: the Church in a racial melting pot,' J. R. Fleming, in *Christ and crisis in Southeast Asia*, p.81–106. G. H. Anderson (ed). New York: Friendship Press, 1968.
The pagan tribes of Borneo: a description of their physical, moral and intellectual condition, with some discussion of their ethnic relations. C. Hose & W. McDougall. London: Macmillan, 1912. 2 vols.
The pagans of North Borneo. O. Rutter. 1929; reprint, Oxford: Oxford University Press, 1985. 288p.

Country Table 2. **Organized churches and denominations in Brunei.**

Official name (bold type = church with over 10% of all affiliated) 1	*Begun* 2	*Type* 3	*Counc* 4	*Congs* 5	*Adults* 6	*Affiliated 1970* 7	*Affiliated 1995* 8	*G%* 9	*Names, notes, and other statistics (see Codebook, Part 3)* 10
Anglican Church (D Kuching)		A-Hig	aweA.	3	2,900	4,000	4,400	0.05	60% Chinese, 13% Indian, 13% English, 10% Iban. M=USPG,ABM.
Assembly Hall Churches	c1970	I-3nC	x....	3	137	33	400	10.49	*Chu Hui So. Little Flock.* Begun in China in 1926 by Watchman Nee. Mandarin.
Bethel Chapel	1964	I-CBr	x....	2	250	295	625	3.05	Small indigenous body with Brethren background.
Brunei Christian Fellowship	c1960	I-Non	.....	2	450	200	900	6.20	Independent body of no-church persuasion.
Catholic Church (VA Miri)	c1600	R-Lat	P.F..	3	2,970	4,520	5,300	0.64	Mainly Chinese; also Indians, some Europeans in petrol industry. M=MHM.
Evangelical Church of Borneo	1928	P-Eva	.H...	5	1,000	1,000	3,000	4.49	*Sidang Injil Borneo.* M=BEM(Australia). HQ Lawas, Saraak. Converts from animism.
Isolated radio churches	1952	I-3rZ	.....	100	3,000	50	4,000	19.16	Isolated radio believers (FEBC), mostly young people, across country. S=4(ICI).
Jehovah's Witnesses	1975	m-Jeh	.....	1	13	–	52	5.00	*Watch Tower.* Recently begun from abroad.
Korean Church	1970	P-Ref	.....	1	300	50	450	9.19	Expatriate workers from Korea. M=WOM.
Methodist Church		P-Met	Vwe..	1	63	100	90	0.05	Part of *Chinese and Iban Conferences*, Methodist Ch, Malaysia & Singapore.
Seventh-day Adventist Church	1961	P-Adv	x....	2	1,000	500	1,545	4.62	*SDAs.* In Sarawak Mission (SDA Ch of Sarawak), Southeast Asia Union Mission.
True Jesus Church	c1940	I-3oC	x....	3	350	500	500	0.00	Chinese indigenous church begun on mainland China. Strong in Sabah (Malaysia).
Other independent tribal chs	c1960	I-	.....	4	500	450	1,000	3.25	Several different groups.
Other Protestant denominations	c1980	P-	.....	6	500	–	800	6.67	Recent arrivals, including M=SAIM,BAS.
Totals				**136**	**13,433**	**11,698**	**23,062**		

Churches, members, growth, 1900-2025	*Congs*	*Adults*	*Affiliated*	*G%*	*Total denominations*	*6 Megablocs:* O	R	A	P	I	m
Total churches, members, and denominations (mid-1900)	1	55	100	7.04	1	0	0	1	0	0	0
Total churches, members, and denominations (mid-1970)	25	6,408	11,698	7.04	13	0	1	1	4	7	0
Total churches, members, and denominations (mid-1990)	120	12,000	20,540	2.85	20	0	1	1	5	12	1
Total churches, members, and denominations (mid-1995)	136	13,433	23,062	2.34	20	0	1	1	5	12	1
Total churches, members, and denominations (mid-2000)	140	14,300	24,592	1.29	20	0	1	1	5	12	1
Total churches, members, and denominations (mid-2025)	300	19,000	32,700	1.15	41	0	1	1	10	25	4

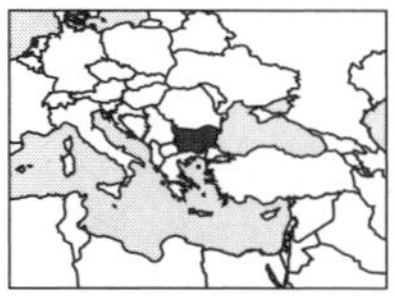

BULGARIA

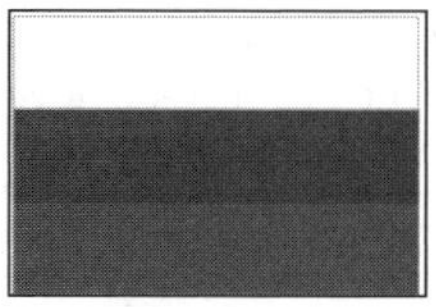

SECULAR DATA, AD 2000

STATE
Official name: Republika Bulgaria (The Republic of Bulgaria).
Short name: Bulgaria. **Adjective of nationality:** Bulgarian.
Flag: Stripes of white, green, and red, national coat of arms in top left corner.
Area: 110,994 sq. km. (42,855 sq. mi.).
Government: Unitary multiparty republic with one legislative body, since 1991 (1396 Ottoman rule, 1908 Independence as empire, 1945 Communist state).
Legislature: National Assembly, 240 members.
Official language: Bulgarian (Bulgarski).
Monetary unit: 1 lev (leva) = 100 stotinki. **US$1=** 1,673 leva.
Chief cities: SOFIJA (Sofia, Sophia, Sofiya) 1,188,000; Plovdiv 346,870; Varna 291,756; Burgas (Bourgas) 190,945; Ruse (Rousse, Russe) 181,664.
Political divisions: 9 provinces.
Armed forces: 102,000.

DEMOGRAPHY
Population: 8,225,000.
Population density: 74.1/sq. km. (191.9/sq. mi.).
Under 15 years: 1,335,000.
Growth rate p.a.: -0.59% (births 8.77, deaths 13.75).
Mortality: Infant, per 1,000: 14.8; **Maternal per 100,000:** 27.0.
Life expectancy: 72 (male 69, female 76).
Household size: 3.3. **Floor area per person, sq.m:** 17.0.
Major languages: Bulgarian, Turkish, Romany, Russian, Armenian, Yiddish, Greek, Macedonian, Gagauzi, and several others.
Urban dwellers: 70.08%. **Urban growth rate p.a.:** 0.0%.
Labor force: 46%.

ETHNOLINGUISTIC PEOPLES
79.8% Bulgar; 9.5% Rumelian Turk; 3.5% Bulgarian Gypsy; 2.5% Macedonian; 1.3% Arliski Balkan Gypsy.

ECONOMY
National income p.a. per person: US$1,329; **per family:** US$4,388.

EDUCATION
Adult literacy: 97% (male 98%, female 97%). **Schools:** 3,881.
Universities: 88. **School enrolment:** female/male: 80%/81%.

HEALTH
Access to health services: 75%. **Access to safe water:** 99%.
Hospitals: 287 (106 beds per 10,000). **Doctors:** 28,457.
Blind: 3,312. **Deaf:** 498,300. **Murder rate:** 5.
Lepers: 400.

LITERATURE
New book titles p.a.: 4,520 (550 p.a. per million). **Periodicals:** 1,043.
Newspapers: 17 dailies.

COMMUNICATION (per 1,000 people)
Phones: 306 (2% mobile). **Radios:** 437. **TV sets:** 359.
Daily newspaper circulation: 141. **Computers:** 77.

REFUGEES
Alien refugees from other countries: 500.

HUMAN LIFE AND LIBERTY (optimum condition=100.0%)
HDI: 78.0. **HSI:** 68.0. **HFI:** 10.0. **EFL:** 30.0.

Country Table 1. **Religious adherents in Bulgaria, AD 1900-2025.**

Year / *Name*	*1900* Adherents	%	*1970* Adherents	%	*mid-1990* Adherents	%	*Annual change, 1990-2000* Natural	Conversion	Total	Rate	*mid-1995* Adherents	%	*mid-2000* Adherents	%	*mid-2025* Adherents	%
Christians	**3,065,500**	**81.9**	**5,664,030**	**66.7**	**6,734,000**	**77.2**	**-38,077**	**31,077**	**-7,000**	**-0.10**	**6,789,000**	**79.9**	**6,664,003**	**81.0**	**5,888,200**	**83.8**
PROFESSION																
crypto-Christians	0	0.0	3,358,430	39.6	0	0.0	0	0	0	0.00	0	0.0	0	0.0	0	0.0
professing Christians	**3,065,500**	**81.9**	**2,305,600**	**27.2**	**6,734,000**	**77.2**	**-38,077**	**31,077**	**-7,000**	**-0.10**	**6,789,000**	**79.9**	**6,664,003**	**81.0**	**5,888,200**	**83.8**
AFFILIATION																
unaffiliated Christians	186,150	5.0	100	0.0	5,000	0.1	-28	133	105	1.93	5,837	0.1	6,053	0.1	8,200	0.1
affiliated Christians	**2,879,350**	**76.9**	**5,663,930**	**66.7**	**6,729,000**	**77.2**	**-38,049**	**30,944**	**-7,105**	**-0.11**	**6,783,163**	**79.8**	**6,657,950**	**81.0**	**5,880,000**	**83.7**
Orthodox	2,848,050	76.1	5,533,800	65.2	6,500,000	74.6	-36,757	-24,598	-61,355	-0.99	6,035,000	71.0	5,886,450	71.6	5,030,000	71.6
Independents	0	0.0	28,130	0.3	69,000	0.8	-390	51,490	51,100	23.73	576,313	6.8	580,000	7.1	620,000	8.8
Protestants	4,300	0.1	40,500	0.5	80,000	0.9	-452	1,952	1,500	1.73	86,190	1.0	95,000	1.2	115,000	1.6
Roman Catholics	27,000	0.7	57,000	0.7	75,000	0.9	-424	1,924	1,500	1.84	80,000	0.9	90,000	1.1	100,000	1.4
Marginal Christians	0	0.0	4,500	0.1	5,000	0.1	-28	178	150	2.66	5,660	0.1	6,500	0.1	15,000	0.2
Trans-megabloc groupings																
Evangelicals	4,000	0.1	40,000	0.5	87,000	1.0	-492	3,792	3,300	3.27	114,282	1.3	120,000	1.5	135,000	1.9
Pentecostals/Charismatics	0	0.0	49,000	0.6	120,000	1.4	-679	2,679	2,000	1.55	132,881	1.6	140,000	1.7	160,000	2.3
Great Commission Christians	**150,000**	**4.0**	**679,000**	**8.0**	**440,000**	**5.1**	**-2,488**	**7,818**	**5,330**	**1.15**	**470,000**	**5.5**	**493,299**	**6.0**	**470,000**	**6.7**
Muslims	642,500	17.2	934,000	11.0	1,016,000	11.7	-5,745	1,808	-3,937	-0.39	994,000	11.7	976,633	11.9	850,000	12.1
Nonreligious	3,000	0.1	1,184,870	14.0	633,140	7.3	-3,580	-18,421	-22,001	-4.18	482,000	5.7	413,134	5.0	200,000	2.9
Atheists	1,000	0.0	700,000	8.3	330,000	3.8	-1,866	-14,463	-16,329	-6.60	229,340	2.7	166,710	2.0	80,000	1.1
Jews	32,000	0.9	7,000	0.1	4,200	0.1	-24	-5	-29	-0.72	4,000	0.1	3,907	0.1	3,800	0.1
Baha'is	0	0.0	100	0.0	660	0.0	-4	4	0	-0.05	660	0.0	657	0.0	1,000	0.0
World A (unevangelized persons)	351,962	9.4	2,122,393	25.0	671,286	7.7	-3,813	-18,209	-22,022	-3.88	560,950	6.6	452,375	5.5	301,989	4.3
World B (evangelized non-Christians)	326,817	8.7	703,150	8.3	1,312,714	15.1	-7,406	-12,868	-20,274	-1.68	1,149,293	13.5	1,108,622	13.5	832,811	11.9
World C (Christians)	3,065,500	81.9	5,664,030	66.7	6,734,000	77.2	-38,077	31,077	-7,000	-0.10	6,789,000	79.9	6,664,003	81.0	5,888,200	83.8
Country's population	**3,744,280**	**100.0**	**8,489,574**	**100.0**	**8,718,000**	**100.0**	**-49,296**	**0**	**-49,296**	**-0.58**	**8,499,244**	**100.0**	**8,225,000**	**100.0**	**7,023,000**	**100.0**

COLUMNS, ROWS.
For meanings and definitions, see Codebook (Part 3). Note that, by definition, total 'Christians' = professing + crypto-Christians, which also = affiliated + unaffiliated Christians, and also = Great Commission Christians + latent Christians. Percentages may not always total exactly, due to rounding.

CENSUSES.
1887 (Kingdom of Bulgaria): 77.1% Orthodox (76.9% Bulgarian Orthodox, 0.2% Armenian Apostolic), 21.4% Muslims, 0.8% Jews, 0.6% Roman Catholics, 0.0% Protestants. **1892:** 78.9% Orthodox (78.7% Bulgarian, 0.2% Armenian), 19.4% Muslims, 0.9% Jews, 0.7% Roman Catholics, 0.1% Protestants. **1900:** 81.0% Orthodox (80.66% Bulgarian, 0.37% Armenian), 17.2% Muslims, 0.9% Jews, 0.8% Roman Catholics, 0.1% Protestants. **1905:** 83.1% Orthodox (82.90% Bulgarian, 0.31% Armenian), 15.0% Muslims, 0.9% Jews, 0.7% Roman Catholics, 0.1% Protestants. **1910:** 84.0% Orthodox, 13.9% Muslims, 2.1% other Christians and other religionists. **1934:** 84.8% Orthodox (84.4% Bulgarian, 0.4% Armenian), 13.5% Muslims, 0.9% Jews, 0.8% Roman Catholics, 0.1% Protestants. **31.XII.1946:** 85.2% Orthodox (84.9% Bulgarian Orthodox, 0.3% Armenian Apostolic), 13.3% Muslims, 0.6% Jews, 0.6% Roman Catholics, 0.2% nonreligious, 0.1% Protestants. **4.XII.1992:** 86.6% Christians, 13.1% Muslims, 0.3% others.

NOTES ON RELIGIONS
ATHEISTS. Bulgarian Communist Party (BCP) (pro-Soviet). Communist voters (election of 27.VI.1971) 6,154,082 (99.9% of all votes). Of Communist party members, about 25% are estimated to be militant atheists, the other 75% being nonreligious, with few or no Christians.
BAHA'IS. By 1997, 15 LSAs (local spiritual assemblies) had been organized.
CRYPTO-CHRISTIANS. (1970) Persons not professing to be Christians in polls, but who are affiliated to churches; mainly unorganized individuals including government officials who attend Orthodox activities irregularly or clandestinely; also members of illegal or underground churches.
JEWS. 3 synagogues, 7 rabbis.
MUSLIMS. Turks, 120,000 Gypsies, some 200,000 southeastern Bulgarians (Pomaks), and 5,000 Tatars; almost all Sunnis (of the Hanafite rite). In 1950, 250,000 Bulgarian Turks were forcibly returned to Turkey. Active Muslims numbered only 6.5% in 1962, but many others practice privately unknown to the state. In 1966, there were 1,180 mosques and 460 imams under a grand mufti. Muslims have been severely repressed by the state since 1950. By 1974, only 600 mosques were open.
NONRELIGIOUS. Agnostics, indifferent to religion. In addition, there is a further 39.5% (in 1970) of the population regarded as nonreligious by the state but who are affiliated to churches and hence are classified here as crypto-Christians.
PROFESSING CHRISTIANS. Persons known to the state through social scientists' surveys.

Great Commission Instrument Panel: status of Bulgaria (for explanation see start of Part 4)

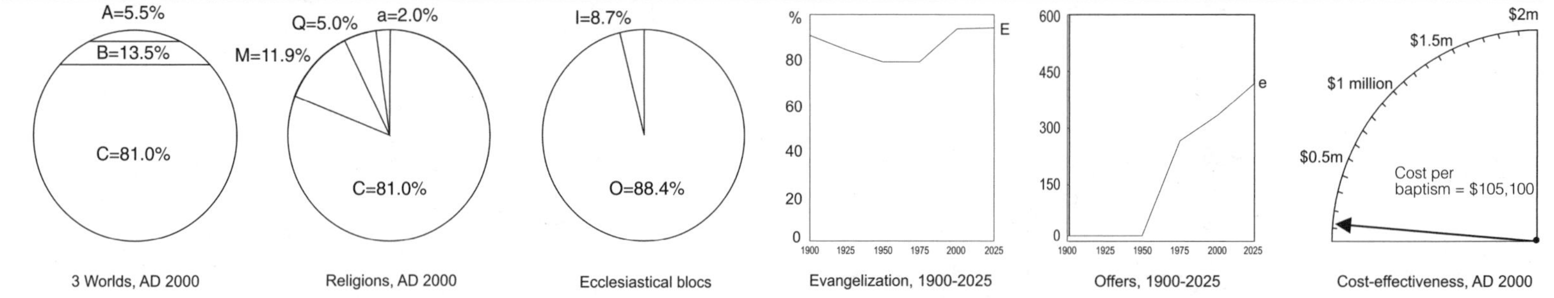

Country status. Bulgaria, a southeastern European nation on the Black Sea, was formerly Communist but is now a constitutional republic with a democratically-elected government. Engineering is the principal economic activity supplemented by agricultural products such as wheat, corn, and barley. Bulgaria is the fourth largest exporter of tobacco in the world.

HUMAN LIFE AND LIBERTY

Human need and development. Bulgaria, like other former Soviet satellites, has witnessed considerable economic turmoil as 'shock therapy' reforms were implemented to move it from a command system to a free market. There are chronic fuel and energy shortages and frequent blackouts in the winter. On the positive side, many state enterprises were privatized, agricultural land was returned to its prewar owners, and many small businesses began to flourish.

Human rights and freedoms. Bulgaria's overall human rights performance has continued to improve since 1990 when the country's first free elections in half a century were held. The dreaded security forces have been weakened, and the Interior Ministry which oversees the police has brought its practices into line with European human rights standards. Treatment of the Turkish minority poses some concerns. The issue of Turkish language instruction in the schools has sparked nationalist protests and counterprotests by ethnic Turks. However, many of the state ordinances during the forced assimilation drive of 1984-89 have been removed including those directed against the use of non-Slavic names, public practice of Muslim religious traditions, and the use of Turkish language in public. Censorship of the press is prohibited by the Constitution and nearly every political party publishes its own newspaper representing all shades of political opinion. The Constitution protects the right to free association, but forbids political parties formed along racial, religious or ethnic lines. However, minorities suffer discrimination in the job marketplace; Turks, Gypsies, and Pomaks claim that they are usually among the first to be laid off and are given the most menial jobs. Although the majority of the 13,000 Vietnamese guest workers have been repatriated to Vietnam, those remaining face much public hostility.

Human environment. Air pollution has damaged approximately one-quarter of Bulgaria's forests. Severe air pollution is experienced in Varna, Ruse, Burgas, Plovdiv as well as Sofia. Bulgaria is a heavy contributor of the industrial pollutants and raw sewage that flow into the Black Sea. Soils have been degraded by mining operations and dumping practiced by metallurgical factories.

NON-CHRISTIAN RELIGIONS

Islam has the major non-Christian religious community in the country. There are 3 main groups of Muslims: (1) Turks, by far the most numerous, living in enclosed communities in the districts of Schumen, Razgrad, Kerdschali, and Haskovo; (2) Gypsies (Tziganes) scattered in small groups, especially in towns; and (3) Bulgarians (known as Pomaks) in the southeast of the country near Mount Rhodopes, with about 120 mosques and 100 imams. Muslims along with Catholics were the religious communities most oppressed by the former Communist regime and most under attack from official atheistic propaganda, as a result of which large numbers no longer profess to be Muslims. Because many of the Muslims are Turks, there is a tendency to consider all Muslims as being under the influence of Turkey.

Atheism was widely professed in Bulgaria. In the early years of Communism, it was promulgated with fervor. By AD 2000, only 7% of the population was atheist or nonreligious, down from about 22% in 1970.

Judaism is nominally the religion of about 4,000 ethnic Jews (in 1995), but very few practice their religion. Under the Communist regime, the civil authorities showed a certain tolerance towards the Jewish community. In 1967, authorization was granted for the first time to publish a religious yearbook, Godichnik. As with the other religious communities of the nation, Judaism has experienced new freedom and growth since 1990.

CHRISTIANITY

By the 2nd century, churches had been founded at Anchialus and Debeltum near Burgas. During the first centuries of the Christian era, Goths, Huns, Slavs, Bulgars, Avars, and other barbarian tribes from the north surged into the Roman and Byzantine empires through the Balkan peninsula; yet throughout these invasions, Christian communities and diocesan structures continued to exist. The large number of Slavs entering in the 6th and 7th centuries adopted the language and culture of the land in which, under the rule of Constantinople, Christianity had become an intrinsic part. The Bulgars of Turkish origin next seized the peninsula and were in turn assimilated. The Latin church sent missionaries to the Slavs and Bulgars from the northwest and Byzantine rulers from the southeast. The Bulgarian king Boris was first baptized by Greek clergy, then turned to Rome, then returned again to Constantinople. In 870, he achieved his goal when a Bulgar was consecrated archbishop of Bulgaria. Bulgarian leaders began to send their sons to Constantinople to be educated, and the Greek missionaries Methodius and Constantine (Cyril) translated existing Christian literature into Slavonic as well as training Slav missionaries. In 889, Boris abdicated to enter a monastery, while his son, Simeon, left life as a monk to continue his father's ideal of substituting Slavonic for Greek in the church of the Bulgars. Under his leadership, the Bulgarian bishops declared the church autocephalous with a patriarch at its head, over Constantinople's opposition. Thus, by Simeon's death in 927, Bulgaria had become an independent Christian nation with its own autonomous church. With Bulgarian support, the Serbs to the west also adopted the Eastern Orthodox faith, then obtained the right to choose their own patriarch and became autocephalous.

In 1018 the Bulgarian kingdom fell to the Byzantine rulers and the Bulgarian patriarchate was suppressed. Bulgaria regained its independence in 1186 and the patriarchate was reestablished in 1235 following an ephemeral 30-year union with Rome. Finally in 1396 Bulgaria fell before a third wave of Muslim invaders, the Ottoman Turks.

For almost 500 years including the period when the Protestant Reformation was taking place from western Europe eastward to Hungary, the Turks controlled Bulgaria and the greek Orthodox controlled its church. In the Bulgarian revolt of 1876, Russia lent its support and brought about a treaty which gave Bulgaria independence. Other European nations, apprehensive of Russia's influence in the Balkans, revised the original treaty and divided Bulgaria into 3 parts under Turkish control. In 1908, Bulgaria was finally able to proclaim its full independence. In siding with Germany in World War I, Bulgaria lost much territory, which it attempted to regain by joining with Germany once again in World War II. At the end of the war, the country was occupied by the USSR.

ORTHODOX CHURCHES. In 1870, the Turkish sultan permitted the reestablishment of a national Bulgarian church which was promptly excommunicated by a Greek Orthodox council in 1872. After some efforts at reunion with Rome, reconciliation with the ecumenical patriarchate in Constantinople was effected in 1945.

Bulgarian Orthodox Church. WCC Executive Committee Meeting, 1971, with Patriarch Cyril.

The Bulgarian Orthodox Church was 11 dioceses under the authority of a patriarch and 11 diocesan bishops. For Bulgarians living in the USA, Canada and Australia, there are 3 other dioceses with seats in New York, Akron (Ohio), and Detroit. The Bulgarian church has priests and officials in both Constantinople and Moscow, and there are also churches and priests in Romania and Hungary. The Bulgarian monastery of St George on Mount Athos (Greece) is, however, under the authority of the patriarch of Constantinople.

Prior to World War II, Orthodox made up 85% of the population. A sociological survey conducted in 1962 estimated them to have declined to 27 percent of the population, although the church itself claimed an affiliated community of over 5 million (65%) in 1970.

Much property and many institutions were lost in 1945 following the war. All monasteries were expropriated, but after the church officially and formally pledged its loyalty to the Communist regime in

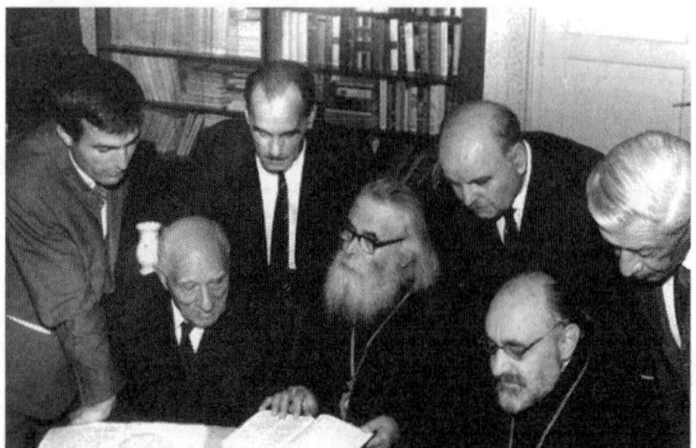

Bulgarian Orthodox Church. Faculty at Theological Academy completing translation of New Testament.

Country summary. **Worlds A, B, C by ethnolinguistic peoples, cities, and major civil divisions in Bulgaria.**

	PEOPLES							CITIES							CIVIL DIVISIONS						
World	*Num*	*Pop 2000*	*C%*	*Christians*	*E%*	*U%*	*Unevangelized*	*Num*	*Pop 2000*	*C%*	*Christians*	*E%*	*U%*	*Unevangelized*	*Num*	*Pop 2000*	*C%*	*Christians*	*E%*	*U%*	*Unevangelized*
A	6	804,831	0.12	997	49	51	412,401	0	0	0.00	0	0	0	0	0	0	0.00	0	0	0	0
B	4	92,952	10.09	9,375	62	38	35,085	0	0	0.00	0	0	0	0	0	0	0.00	0	0	0	0
C	25	7,327,264	90.72	6,647,579	100	0	6,593	27	3,932,377	77.78	3,058,695	92	8	296,880	9	8,225,044	80.95	6,657,950	94	6	454,078
Total	**35**	**8,225,047**	**80.95**	**6,657,951**	**94**	**6**	**454,079**	**27**	**3,932,377**	**77.78**	**3,058,695**	**92**	**8**	**296,880**	**9**	**8,225,044**	**80.95**	**6,657,950**	**94**	**6**	**454,078**

1953, these were returned to church control. After 1953 the church received financial aid from the government but remained relatively poor. Two institutions, Tcherepich Seminary near Vraca and the Sofia Theological Academy, remained open and served hundreds of students.

The Bulgarian Orthodox Church had an opportunity to regain a central role in the life of the nation after Communism fell in 1991. But that opportunity was destroyed by a noisy schism and accompanying atmosphere of strife that preoccupied the church in the early 1990s. A central issue had to do with the validity of high ecclesiastical appointments made by secular state authorities in the prior regime. At the height of it, a certain priest Hristofor Subev and his supporters repeatedly interrupted the liturgy at Alexander Nevsky Cathedral and denounced the hierarchs as Communists. The matter was resolved, at least on the legal level, when the new prime minister and representatives from the ecumenical patriarch in Istanbul endorsed the older patriarch and his synod at a liturgy celebrating the Epiphany in 1993.

The Armenian Apostolic Church has 12 congregations in Bulgaria served by 10 priests. Armenians first came to Bulgaria in the 5th century. The first church was built in Sofia in the 11th century and in Plovdiv a century later. Armenians and their churches are found principally in the cities of Sofia, Plovdiv, Varna, Ruse, Haskovo, and Sliven.

CATHOLIC CHURCH. From the 9th century to the 14th century, the Catholic Church of the Latin rite repeatedly sent missionaries into the Balkans from Germany and its other strongholds in northern Europe, and then through the Crusaders and the new Dominican and Franciscan missionary orders. The majority of Bulgarian Catholics today are descendants of Bogomils converted to Catholicism by Franciscans in the 17th century. In 1758, the vicariate of Sofia was established and, in 1789, the diocese of Nicopoli. From 1870 onwards, some Uniate groups were recognized by Rome, and in 1926, an exarchate of Sofia was created for Catholics of the Byzantine rite.

Catholics are widely dispersed across Bulgaria. Those of the Byzantine rite numbered about 20,000 in 1995 and are to be found in Sofia, Plovdiv, and along the Greek border. Those of the Latin rite were about 60,000 in the same year. Nikolaievo is one of the few towns that are entirely Catholic, along with a few found along the length of the Danube. The Catholic church in Sofia is attended by foreign diplomats and their families.

Until the end of World War II, the church in Bulgaria was under Propaganda, now the Congregation for the Evangelization of Peoples. As a result, it had no legal status and there were only missions established by religious orders (OFM, OFMCap, AA, CP, SJ). Over the period 1946-48, the church lost all its institutions and, apart from a few churches, all of its possessions, buildings, schools (including 9 colleges in 1944), and orphanages. Foreign religious personnel and priests were expelled in 1948. Most of the others were arrested and sentenced and many died in prison.

The Catholic Church survived despite such difficulties as the material poverty of priests, the aging of the faithful, and continuous pressures to prevent baptism of infants or church attendance. The Eastern-rite Catholics or Uniates include many Latin elements, and in contrast to what took place in Romania, they have not been forcibly reunited with the Orthodox Church, no doubt because of their small numbers. In 1971, the Catholic Church of the Byzantine rite had an apostolic exarch, with about 20 priests. There were also 2 religious communities, an order of Bulgarian origin (Eucharistines) and 7 cloistered Carmelites in Sofia. This situation, which would have been impossible in the 1950s, indicated the gradual amelioration of relations.

Until the visit of the Bulgarian president Zhivkov to the pope in Rome in 1975, the 2 Latin-rite jurisdictions had been without bishops since the execution of the bishop of Nicopoli in 1952. During his visit, Zhivkov agreed to let the Vatican fill these vacancies, and subsequently, there was a marked thaw in state relations with the Catholic Church. The end of Communism has brought a new era of freedom and growth.

The Holy See has diplomatic relations with Bulgaria and in AD 2000 is represented to government and the Catholic hierarchy by anuncio residing in Sofia.

PROTESTANT CHURCHES. Protestantism was introduced by American Congregationalist missionaries in 1856, American Methodists in 1857, and Baptists from Russia in 1865. Seventh-day Adventists arrived in 1891 as emigrants from the Russian Crimea and settled in northern Dobruja.

Pentecostalism was established in 1921 by Russian Pentecostals at Burgas. The 2 largest Pentecostal denominations in the 1990s were the Pentecostal Union and the Church of God. The former group chose to register under the communist regime, while the latter refused. These 2 groups together serve a greater Christian community than all other Protestants. Their numbers were boosted also by an unusual influx of several thousand Turkish converts from Islam in the early 1990s. Evangelical churches in general experienced unusual growth in the first years of that decade, sometimes seeing entire villages convert. The interdenominational Bulgarian Center for Christian Education in Sofia, also known as the Oasis of Love, began in 1991 with 150 students and soon had several hundred. The end of communism was immediately followed by extensive and high-profile evangelistic activity by Pentecostals especially, but also by Evangelical Protestants and others. Orthodox prelates protested to the minister of culture against a Swedish Pentecostal event, 'Heavenly Explosion', in Sofia's Vasil Levski stadium in 1992, attacking it as a crusade against the Orthodox church and against Bulgarians.

Art and architecture. Many of the great Christian churches of Bulgaria were destroyed during Turkish rule. Among those that have survived is the celebrated Monastery at Rila, typical of the National Revival Architecture of the 17th and 18th centuries. Its interior walls are covered with frescoes and its interior and exterior abound in carved wooden structural ornaments and other decorative details.

Renewal movements. In the 1990s the Pentecostal/Charismatic Renewal continued to spread rapidly across most older churches, and numbered over 140,000 adherents (of whom 40% Pentecostals, 3% Charismatics, and 57% Independents).

Independents. (*Lower*) Baptism of Christians from country churches. (*Upper*) Instruction of new converts.

Indigenous missions. Nascent mission efforts have been building since 1990 and many Bulgarian Christians are currently serving outside the country, with some in Muslim Central Asia.

CHURCH AND STATE

A new constitution promulgated in May 1971, stipulated in Article 53: '(1) Freedom of conscience and of religion is guaranteed to all citizens. They have the right to engage in both religious rites and antireligious propaganda. (2) The church is separated from the state. (3) The juridical status of religious communities and questions concerning their maintenance and right to be internally organized and administered are regulated by law. (4) Abusive acts which tend to place the church and religion at the service of political organizations of a religious background are forbidden. (5) Religion may not be used to justify refusal to carry out duties imposed by the constitution or the law'. All citizens are equal before the law (Article 35, items 1 and 2) and 'hating and humiliating a man' on account of his religious belief is forbidden (Article 35, item 4).

The law regulating the juridical status and internal organization of religious communities which went into effect in March 1949, is based on the stipulations of the constitution of 1947 and is called the Law concerning Religious Faiths (Official Journal, No. 48/1949). It declares: 'The Bulgarian Orthodox Church is the traditional faith of the Bulgarian people. It is bound up with their history and as such, by its structure, its nature and its spirit can be considered a church of the popular democracy'. (Article 3).

The Bulgarian Orthodox Church was more fortunate than others in Communist countries in that it was authorized to maintain its rural property and received from the state an annual subsidy of 700,000 levas (about US$400,000) for the construction and support of churches and for the salaries of its personnel. The state, thus, provided 17% of the church's financial requirements.

The Catholic Church suffered the most from the persecutions of the 1950s. Its last imprisoned priests were not freed until 1964.

The new national constitution of 1990 emphasized the separation of church from state but recognized Orthodox Christianity as the traditional religion of Bulgaria. All churches were required to register with the government, and registration was only permitted if all internal rules and procedures violated no state laws. The Holy Synod of the Bulgarian Orthodox Church, unlike other churches, refused to register. The fall of communism in 1991 brought many immediate and substantial changes in church-state relations, both *de facto* and *de jure*. The oppressive Committee for Church and Cult Affairs was replaced by the new Directorate of Religious Affairs. The regime of 1993 then dissolved the unpopular Directorate. A law of restoration mandated the return of property to Christian, Muslim, and Jewish believers, though after several years practical complications on a case-by-case basis hindered or blocked nearly all such transfers. By 1994, 30 religious organizations, mostly Protestant, had been refused registration with no clear reasons given, thus facing possible loss of property.

BROADCASTING AND MEDIA

Shortwave programming from KNLS, HCJB (Ecuador), TWR (Monaco), and the Vatican can be received in the major European languages.

Satellite TV programs are received mainly in Arabic.

INTERDENOMINATIONAL ORGANIZATIONS

Evangelical missionaries and church leaders representing many organizations met annually from 1990 in the Bulgarian Consultation. A smaller group of missions with an interest in the Turks of the country formed a Bulgarian-Turkish consultation. Representatives from Baptist, Church of God, Congregational, Methodists, and Pentecostal churches met in 1993 to form the United Evangelical Churches, partly as a response to anti-Evangelical allegations made by the Bulgarian Orthodox Church. This alliance, afraid that the legal status of their churches was threatened, was quick to declare, 'We are not a sect'.

FUTURE TRENDS AND PROSPECTS

The collapse of Communism in 1989-90 arrested decline in Christian affiliation, and a marked increase in church membership can be anticipated through 2025 to a high of 83.7%.

Christianity is then expected to steadily climb to and remain slightly over 85% by AD 2050.

BIBLIOGRAPHY

'A history of the Congregational and Methodist Churches in Bulgaria and Yugoslavia.' P. B. Mojzes. Ph.D. dissertation, Boston University, Boston, 1965. 674p.

American missionaries among the Bulgarians (1858–1912). T. Nestorova. *East European Monographs*, no. 218. New York: Columbia University Press, 1987.

Bulgaria. R. J. Crampton. *World bibliographical series*, vol. 107. Oxford, UK: CLIO Press, 1990. 268p. (See especially 'Religion,' p.77-81f).

'Bulgaria,' J. Ochavkov, in *Western religion: a country by country sociological inquiry*, p.83–99. H. Mol (ed). *Method and Theory in the Study and Interpretation of Religion*, vol. 2. The Hague: Mouton, 1972.

Bulgarian monasteries: monuments of history, culture, and art. G. Chavrukov. Sofia: Naouka i Izkoustvo, 1974. 371p. (Photographic collection).

'Bulgarian uniate bishop: problems of uniatism and autocephaly,' R. Popov, *Sobornost*, 6, 1 (1984), 46–60.

'Catholics in Bulgaria,' J. Broun, *Religion in Communist lands*, 11, 3 (Autumn 1983), 310–320.

Churches and religions in the People's Republic of Bulgaria. P. Stoyanov (ed). Sofia: Synodal Publishing House, 1975. 98p.

Die bulgarische orthodoxe Kirche, 1944–1956. D. Slijepcevic. Munich: R. Oldenbourg, 1957.

Document of darkness: a document of 35 years of atheist–communist terror against the Christians in the People's Republic of Bulgaria. M. Matheeff. St. Catherine's, Ontario: Mission 'Your Neighbor in Need' Bulgaria, 1980. 148p.

Feuergehen: psychologisch–physiologische und historisch–geographische Utersuchung des Nestinarentums in Bulgarien. E. Sharankov. Stuttgart: Hippokrates, 1980. 232p.

Icons from Bulgaria. K. P. Kabadayeva. Edinburgh: Scottish Arts Council & Coutauld Institute Galleries. 42p.

'Kirche und Staat in Bulgarien,' G. Podskalsky, *Stimmen der Zeit*, 97 (1972), 122–24.

Kirchen und religiöses Leben in Bulgarien. W. Oschlies. Cologne: Bundesinstitut für Ostwissenschaftliche und Internationale Studien, 1983. 37p.

'Man in the Middle Ages in Bulgaria,' D. Angelov, *Bulgarian Historical Review*, 8, 1 (1980), 38–52.

Monasteries in Bulgaria. L. Prashkov, E. Bakalova & S. Boyadjiev. Sofia: Spectrum, 1990. 286p.

'Nationalism and the Bulgarian Orthodox Church,' S. T. Raikin, in *Religion and nationalism in Soviet and East European politics*, p.352–77. P. Ramet (ed). 2nd ed. Durham, NC: Duke University Press, 1989.

'Pentecostal youth organizations and the Bulgarian Komsomol,' R. Homan, *Comparative Education*, 13, 3 (1977), 243–248.

'Religious survival in Bulgaria,' J. A. Broun, *America*, 153 (November 16, 1985), 323–327.

'Sotsiologichesko izsledvane na religioznostta na pulnoletnoto naselenie v Bulgaria,' *(Sociological survey of religiosity of the adult population of Bulgaria)*, J. Ochavkov, *Novo Vreme*, 5 (1964).

The Bogomil movement. D. S. Angelov. Sofia: Sofia Press, 1987. 54p.

The Bogomils: a study in Balkan Neo-Manichaeism. D. Obolensky. Cambridge, UK: Cambridge University Press, 1948. 319p.

The Bulgarians in the seventeenth century: Slavic Orthodox society and culture under Ottoman rule. D. P. Hupchick. Jefferson, NC: McFarland, 1993. 341p.

The history of the cult of Boris and Gleb. F. A. Sciacca. Ann Arbor, MI: University Microfilms, 1985. 2 vols.

Two conversions to Christianity, the Bulgarians and the Anglo–Saxons. H. Mayr-Harting. *Stenton lecture*, 1993. [Reading, UK]: University of Reading, 1994. 29p.

Country Table 2. **Organized churches and denominations in Bulgaria.**

Official name (bold type = church *with over 10% of all affiliated)* 1	*Begun* 2	*Type* 3	*Counc* 4	*Congs* 5	*Adults* 6	*Affiliated 1970* 7	*Affiliated 1995* 8	*G%* 9	*Names, notes, and other statistics* (see Codebook, Part 3) 10
Armenian Apostolic Ch: D Sofija	c1050	O-Arm	Ewc..	11	14,600	22,000	21,000	-0.19	*Gregorians.* Under C Echmiadzin. First Armenians in 5th century. In cities. 10n.
Baptist Union of Bulgaria	1865	P-Bap	T....	50	3,000	2,000	5,000	3.73	*Baptistka Crkve.* Begun 1865 in Lom through Baptists from Russia. HQ Sofia. 23n.
Broadsheet Readers' Clubs	c1990	I-3nW	.....	17	300	–	1,000	20.00	Readers of Gospel Broadsheets produced by M=WEC(UK).
Bulgarian Orthodox Church:	c 150	O-Bul	MWc..	4,040	4,438,000	5,499,800	6,000,000	0.35	*Balgarskata Pravoslavna Crkva.* 23 bps. 1785n,123de(200m,360w),1j,2s(330),W=13%.
P Sofija (Sofia)	870	O-Bul	Mp	800	876,000	1,085,000	1,184,000	0.09	Diocese of patriarch, in capital city. 1s (70 in theological academy).
D Dorostola Cerven		O-Bul	Mm	320	345,000	427,600	467,000	0.05	*Eparchija (Metropolia).* HQ Ruse. Political districts: Razgrad, Ruse, Silistra.
D Lovec		O-Bul	Mm	110	116,000	143,800	157,000	0.05	HQ (Seat) at Lovec. All dioceses are autonomous though loosely under Sofia.
D Nevrokope		O-Bul	Mm	160	163,000	201,900	220,000	0.05	HQ Blagoevgrad. Boundaries of dioceses are not exactly defined. Macedonians.
D Plodiv		O-Bul	Mm	810	906,000	1,122,400	1,224,000	0.05	HQ Plovdiv. Largest diocese. Political districts: Smolyan, Haskovo, Plovdiv et alia.
D Sliven		O-Bul	Mm	400	448,000	555,400	606,000	0.05	HQ Sliven. Dioceses do not follow political divisions exactly.
D Star Zagora		O-Bul	Mm	180	196,000	242,800	265,000	0.05	HQ Stara Zagora. Covers political district of Stara Zagora.
D Varna & Preslav		O-Bul	Mm	510	556,000	689,700	752,000	0.05	HQ Varna. Covers political districts of Tolboukhin and Turgovishte.
D Veliko Tarnovo	1186	O-Bul	Mm	330	365,000	452,700	494,000	0.35	HQ Veliko Tarnovo. Covers part of Pleven political district.
D Vidin		O-Bul	Mm	190	216,000	268,000	292,000	0.05	HQ Vidin, in extreme northwestern tip of country.
D Vraca (Vratza)		O-Bul	Mm	230	251,000	310,500	339,000	0.05	HQ Vraca. 1s (St John of Rila, Cherepich Monastery; 200 students).
Catholic Apostolic Church	c1900	I-3aX	x....	1	10	30	20	-1.61	One small congregation of Irvingites (begun 1832 in Britain) in Sofia.
Catholic Church in Bulgaria:	1565	R-LEr	O.B.R	54	62,300	57,000	80,000	1.37	*Rimo-Katoliceskata Crkva.* Bogomil descendants. 8n 24x 45m 60w 1075Yy
D Nicopoli	1789	R-Lat	Os	13	20,300	20,000	25,000	0.90	*Eparchija Nicopoli.* Bishop executed in 1952. 0n 11x 11m 8w 125Yy
D Sofija & Plovdiv	1758	R-Lat	Os	16	30,000	30,000	35,000	0.62	*Apostolski Vikarijat Sofija.* Violent persecutions 1952. 3n 8x 18m 17w 644Yy
EA Sofija *(Bulgarian-rite)*	1926	R-Bul	Os	25	12,000	7,000	20,000	4.29	*Uniates.* Catholics of Byzantino-Slav rite. M=AA. 5n 5x 16m 35w 306Yy
Children of God	1990	I-mar	.....	5	150	–	250	20.00	Marginal body from USA.
Christian Brethren		P-CBr	x....	150	4,500	5,000	7,500	0.05	*Plymouth (Open) Brethren.* Not legally recognized; meetings in homes.
Church of God	c1950	I-3pW	.....	40	15,000	28,000	45,000	1.92	*Petdesatnik Crkva.* Dissidents rejecting state registration. M=Ch of God Cleveland (USA).
Church of God (Anderson)		P-Hol	.....	3	120	–	150	0.05	Holiness denomination from USA.
Church of God Union	1991	I-3pW	.....	14	3,000	–	5,000	25.00	Indigenous body, White pentecostals of recent origin.
Ch of Jesus Christ of Latter-day Saints	1990	m-LdS	x....	2	210	–	300	20.00	*Mormons.* Small mission (USA) .
Church of Varna	1988	I-3cW	.....	12	340	–	600	14.29	Bulgarians, Gypsies (5 congregations).
Congregational Church in Bulgaria	1856	P-Con	.v...	54	5,000	5,000	6,250	0.90	*Soborna Congrezanska Crkva.* South. 32 congregations lost (12 to Pentecostals). 14n.
Evangelical Church in Varna	1990	I-3cW	.....	10	1,000	–	3,000	20.00	Bulgarians. Congregations: including 1 Turkish, 1 Gypsy.
Good News Christian Church	1990	I-3cW	.....	1	500	–	1,000	20.00	Small charismatic church with mixed congregation.
Isolated radio churches	c1954	I-3rW	.....	200	2,000	100	3,000	14.57	Isolated radio believers, mostly students and youths. R=92 (TWR,HCJB, Radio Vatican).
Jehovah's Witnesses	1922	m-Jeh	x....	6	900	1,000	1,060	0.23	Active witnessing under way by 1926. 1 pastor. Suppressed; completely underground. 53Y.
Jesus Mosques	c1988	I-3mM	.....	200	4,000	–	5,000	14.29	Messianic Muslims. Groups of Turkish Gypsy Muslims who have converted to Christ.
Methodist Church in Bulgaria	1857	P-Met	Vwc..	17	1,700	2,500	4,250	2.15	*Methodistka Crkva. Bulgaria Provisional Conf.* C&S Europe CC, UMC(USA). North.
New Apostolic Church	c1995	I-3aX	x....	2	100	–	193	80.76	*NAC. NAK.* M=Neuapostolische Kirche (HQ Zurich, Switzerland).
Orthodox Church of Bulgaria	1992	I-Bul	.....	200	200,000	–	500,000	33.33	Massive schism ex BOC by disaffected bishops and clergy.
Paulician Church (Bogomils)	c250	m-Pau	x....	20	3,300	3,000	4,000	0.06	A few groups, speaking Palityan (related to Bulgarian). Also in Hungary. Dualist, rejecting OT.
Pentecostal Union of Bulgaria	c1910	P-Pe2	Z....	330	36,000	20,000	53,000	3.98	*PEC. Petdesetna Evangelska Crkva.* Links with AoG(USA), EES(UK). 70n,600Y.
Romanian Orthodox Church		O-Rum	Cwc..	3	2,000	2,000	3,000	0.05	*Parohia Ortodoxa Romana din Sofia.* Romanians. Decline from 75,000 in 1900. 1x.
Seventh-day Adventist Church	1891	P-Adv	x....	75	4,500	5,000	8,040	1.92	*Adventisti. SDA, Bulgarian Church, Euro-Africa Division.* 9n,14mw,70t(2940).
Turkish indigenous churches	1985	I-3pZ	.....	130	4,000	–	7,000	10.00	A third of Turkish converts are in Pentecostal Union or in Ch of God. M=COG,WEC,OD,OM,IF.
Unitarian Church		m-Unt	.....	1	100	500	300	0.05	Decline from 862 in 1946. Links with Unitarians in Romania, Hungary, Czechoslovakia.
United Church of God	1991	I-3oW	.....	20	2,000	–	3,000	25.00	*Jesus Only Church.* Split ex Church of God
Other Orthodox churches	c1950	O-	.....	11	5,500	10,000	11,000	0.38	Including: Greek, Old Ritualist, Russian, Serbian, Albanian, Macedonian OC.
Other Protestant denominations		P-	.....	30	1,000	1,000	2,000	0.05	Including: Ch of Christ (Non-Instrumental), Reformed Ch, Assemblies of God.
Other pentecostal denominations		I-3pW	.....	7	700	–	1,080	0.05	About 8 groups of pentecostal Independents.
Other charismatic fellowships	c1980	I-3cW	.....	5	700	–	1,170	6.67	Small group of independent congregations.
Totals				**5,721**	**4,816,530**	**5,663,930**	**6,783,163**		

Churches, members, growth, 1900-2025	*Congs*	*Adults*	*Affiliated*	*G%*	*Total denominations*	*6 Megablocs:* *O*	*R*	*A*	*P*	*I*	*m*
Total churches, members, and denominations (mid-1900)	2,000	2,126,000	2,879,350	0.97	10	2	1	0	5	0	2
Total churches, members, and denominations (mid-1970)	4,294	4,182,373	5,663,930	0.97	23	7	1	0	9	3	3
Total churches, members, and denominations (mid-1990)	5,600	4,778,000	6,729,000	0.87	50	12	1	0	13	20	4
Total churches, members, and denominations (mid-1995)	5,721	4,816,530	6,783,163	0.16	53	12	1	0	13	23	4
Total churches, members, and denominations (mid-2000)	5,600	4,728,000	6,657,950	-0.37	54	12	1	0	13	24	4
Total churches, members, and denominations (mid-2025)	5,400	4,175,000	5,880,000	-0.50	88	20	1	0	20	40	7

NOTES ON TABLE ABOVE

NATIONAL COUNCILS (Column 4, 5th letter).

E = Bulgarian Evangelical Alliance (BEA), 1993.

R = Mejduritualnata Episcopska Konferenzia vav Balgaria (MEKB, Bulgarian Catholic Bishops' Conference).

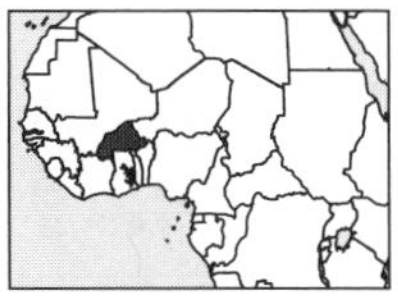

BURKINA FASO

SECULAR DATA, AD 2000

STATE
Official name: La République Démocratique Populaire de Burkina Faso (The Democratic Peoples' Republic of Burkina Faso).
Short name: Burkina Faso. **Adjective of nationality:** of Burkina Faso.
Flag: Black, white and red stripes.
Area: 274,400 sq. km. (105,946 sq. mi.).
Government: Multiparty republic with one advisory body, since 1991 (c1300 Mossi empire, 1896 French colony, 1958 autonomous territory, 1960 Independence as republic, 1966 military junta, 1970 republic, 1974 military junta).
Legislature: House of Representatives, 178 members; Assembly of People's Deputies, 111 members.
Official language: French (Français).
Monetary unit: 1 CFA franc (CFAF) = 100 centimes. **US$1=** CFAF 560.38.
Chief cities: OUAGADOUGOU (Wagadugu) 1,131,000; Bobo-Dioulasso 339,805; Koudougou 77,163; Ouahigouya 57,809.
Political divisions: 30 provinces.
Armed forces: 10,000.

DEMOGRAPHY
Population: 11,937,000.
Population density: 43.5/sq. km. (112.6/sq. mi.).
Under 15 years: 5,650,000.
Growth rate p.a.: 2.74% (births 44.32, deaths 16.88).
Mortality: Infant, per 1,000: 91.2; **Maternal per 100,000:** 930.0.
Life expectancy: 46 (male 45, female 47).
Household size: 6.2. **Floor area per person, sq.m:** 6.0.
Major languages: Mossi, French, Bobo, Senufo, Fulani, Grunshi, Lobi, Gurma, Busansi, Dogon, and 40 other tribal languages.
Urban dwellers: 18.46%. **Urban growth rate p.a.:** 5.6%.
Labor force: 51%.

ETHNOLINGUISTIC PEOPLES
46.3% Mossi (Moshi); 3.8% Bissa (Bisa); 3.4% Liptako Fula (Macina); 3.3% Gurma (Gourmance); 2.7% Black Bobo (Bobo Fing).

ECONOMY
National income p.a. per person: US$229; **per family:** US$1,425.

EDUCATION
Adult literacy: 19% (male 29%, female 9%). **Schools:** 2,936.
Universities: 9. **School enrolment:** female/male: 19%/31%.

HEALTH
Access to health services: 90%. **Access to safe water:** 78%.
Hospitals: 78 (5 beds per 10,000). **Doctors:** 341.
Blind: 90,000. **Deaf:** 723,400. **Murder rate:** 1.
Lepers: 450,000. **Underweight prevalence under 5:** 33%.

LITERATURE
New book titles p.a.: 6,800 (570 p.a. per million). **Periodicals:** 52.
Newspapers: 1 daily.

COMMUNICATION (per 1,000 people)
Phones: 2 (6% mobile). **Radios:** 48. **TV sets:** 4.
Daily newspaper circulation: 1. **Computers:** 2.

REFUGEES
Alien refugees from other countries: 21,000.

HUMAN LIFE AND LIBERTY (optimum condition=100.0%)
HDI: 22.1. **HSI:** 27.0. **HFI:** 15.0. **EFL:** 26.0.

Country Table 1. **Religious adherents in Burkina Faso, AD 1900-2025.**

Year	1900		1970		mid-1990		Annual change, 1990-2000				mid-1995		mid-2000		mid-2025	
Name	Adherents	%	Adherents	%	Adherents	%	Natural	Conversion	Total	Rate	Adherents	%	Adherents	%	Adherents	%
Muslims	140,000	10.0	1,884,000	34.7	4,376,500	48.3	138,976	2,985	141,961	2.85	5,080,000	48.8	5,796,106	48.6	12,370,000	53.0
Ethnoreligionists	1,260,000	90.0	3,023,700	55.8	3,181,300	35.1	101,022	-12,128	88,894	2.49	3,562,000	34.2	4,070,239	34.1	6,005,000	25.8
Christians	**0**	**0.0**	**515,362**	**9.5**	**1,450,000**	**16.0**	**46,027**	**7,818**	**53,845**	**3.21**	**1,701,000**	**16.3**	**1,988,446**	**16.7**	**4,760,000**	**20.4**
PROFESSION																
crypto-Christians	0	0.0	62,462	1.2	180,000	2.0	5,716	2,284	8,000	3.75	220,000	2.1	260,000	2.2	550,000	2.4
professing Christians	**0**	**0.0**	**452,900**	**8.4**	**1,270,000**	**14.0**	**40,311**	**5,524**	**45,845**	**3.13**	**1,481,000**	**14.2**	**1,728,446**	**14.5**	**4,210,000**	**18.1**
AFFILIATION																
unaffiliated Christians	0	0.0	0	0.0	4,400	0.1	140	-143	-3	-0.07	4,154	0.0	4,368	0.0	5,000	0.0
affiliated Christians	**0**	**0.0**	**515,362**	**9.5**	**1,445,600**	**16.0**	**45,905**	**7,943**	**53,848**	**3.22**	**1,696,846**	**16.3**	**1,984,078**	**16.6**	**4,755,000**	**20.4**
Roman Catholics	0	0.0	416,349	7.7	835,000	9.2	26,515	2,893	29,408	3.06	971,669	9.3	1,129,078	9.5	2,600,000	11.2
Protestants	0	0.0	95,863	1.8	570,000	6.3	18,100	4,800	22,900	3.43	677,491	6.5	799,000	6.7	2,000,000	8.6
Independents	0	0.0	3,100	0.1	39,000	0.4	1,238	262	1,500	3.31	45,886	0.4	54,000	0.5	150,000	0.6
Marginal Christians	0	0.0	50	0.0	1,600	0.0	51	-11	40	2.26	1,800	0.0	2,000	0.0	5,000	0.0
Trans-megabloc groupings																
Evangelicals	0	0.0	95,500	1.8	540,000	6.0	17,148	5,352	22,500	3.54	653,139	6.3	765,000	6.4	1,876,000	8.0
Pentecostals/Charismatics	0	0.0	85,700	1.6	572,000	6.3	18,164	9,036	27,200	3.97	698,035	6.7	844,000	7.1	2,100,000	9.0
Great Commission Christians	**0**	**0.0**	**416,000**	**7.7**	**1,062,000**	**11.7**	**33,724**	**12,258**	**45,982**	**3.66**	**1,255,000**	**12.1**	**1,521,822**	**12.8**	**3,980,000**	**17.1**
Nonreligious	0	0.0	500	0.0	50,000	0.6	1,588	1,283	2,871	4.64	69,100	0.7	78,710	0.7	180,000	0.8
Baha'is	0	0.0	338	0.0	1,800	0.0	57	40	97	4.39	2,400	0.0	2,767	0.0	5,000	0.0
Other religionists	0	0.0	100	0.0	400	0.0	13	2	15	3.29	500	0.0	553	0.0	1,000	0.0
World A (unevangelized persons)	1,400,000	100.0	2,999,527	55.3	4,031,700	44.5	128,004	-90,473	37,531	0.89	4,269,976	41.0	4,404,753	36.9	6,506,559	27.9
World B (evangelized non-Christians)	0	0.0	1,909,210	35.2	3,578,300	39.5	113,652	82,655	196,307	4.48	4,443,600	42.7	5,543,801	46.4	12,054,441	51.7
World C (Christians)	0	0.0	515,362	9.5	1,450,000	16.0	46,027	7,818	53,845	3.21	1,701,000	16.3	1,988,446	16.7	4,760,000	20.4
Country's population	**1,400,000**	**100.0**	**5,424,100**	**100.0**	**9,060,000**	**100.0**	**287,683**	**0**	**287,683**	**2.80**	**10,414,577**	**100.0**	**11,937,000**	**100.0**	**23,321,000**	**100.0**

COLUMNS, ROWS.
For meanings and definitions, see Codebook (Part 3). Note that, by definition, total 'Christians' = professing + crypto-Christians, which also = affiliated + unaffiliated Christians, and also = Great Commission Christians + latent Christians. Percentages may not always total exactly, due to rounding.

NOTES ON RELIGIONS
BAHA'IS. The Baha'i Faith has spread rapidly. By 1997 there were 37 LSAs (local spiritual assemblies) organized.

PENTECOSTALS/CHARISMATICS. The Catholic Charismatic Renewal began in 1977. By 1997, there were 100 regular weekly prayer groups at parish level with 10,000 regular adult attenders, including 40 involved priests and 1 bishop. A recent CCR meeting drew 20,000 attenders.

Great Commission Instrument Panel: status of Burkina Faso (for explanation see start of Part 4)

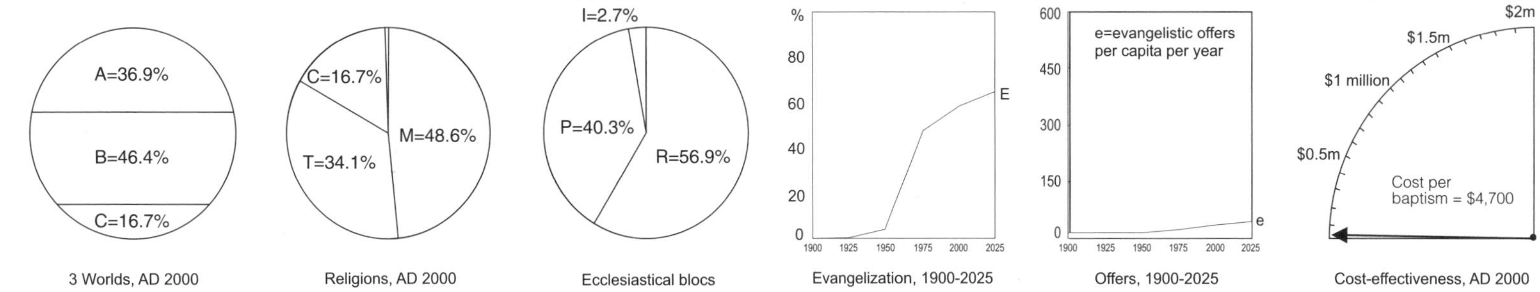

3 Worlds, AD 2000 — Religions, AD 2000 — Ecclesiastical blocs — Evangelization, 1900-2025 — Offers, 1900-2025 — Cost-effectiveness, AD 2000

Country status. Burkina Faso is a landlocked country in the Sahel in Western Africa. Much of the country verges on the Sahara Desert but the land in the south is quite fertile. Most of its people are subsistence farmers, producing millet, maize, and rice. Cotton, ground nuts, and sesame are grown for export.

HUMAN LIFE AND LIBERTY

Human need and development. Burkina Faso is one of the poorest countries in the world. Frequent droughts, weak transportation and communications facilities, political instability, and a low literacy rate have continued to depress the economy to bare subsistence levels. To escape the oppressive poverty, many Burkinabe flee to neighboring countries.

Human rights and freedoms. Burkina Faso has been continuously under military rule since 1980. The ruling junta is heavily leftist although it has tried to adopt the cloak of a moderate middle-of-the-road ideology since the collapse of Communism in Europe. Arrest, detention, and murder of political opponents are commonplace occurrences. Private newspapers and radio stations have been permitted since 1990, but the government resorts to intimidatory tactics to muzzle criticism. Although the Mossi form the racial majority, minority groups are represented in government. Women occupy a much lower social position in education, public service, property, and family rights. Violence against women occurs fairly frequently in rural areas as also the tribal practice of female genital mutilation.

Human environment. As a result of frequent drought, much of Burkina Faso is desert. But desertification has not arrested population growth, which in many areas is more than can be sustained by indigenous resources. The limited area of arable land has led to soil degradation.

NON-CHRISTIAN RELIGIONS

Traditional religions retain the allegiance of about one-third of the population. Ethnic groups which are more than 80% traditionalist include: Birifor 86%, Doghosie 85%, Lobi 85%, and Nunuma 62%. Names for God include Winnam among the Mossi, Na'angmin among the Lodagaa, and Amma among the Dogon.

Islam entered the area during the 18th century, with the building of the first mosque in Ouagadougou and the installation of the first imam dating from the end of the century. Under French colonial rule Islam experienced harassment, persecution, imprisonments,

Country summary. **Worlds A, B, C by ethnolinguistic peoples, cities, and major civil divisions in Burkina Faso.**

	PEOPLES	*CITIES*							*CIVIL DIVISIONS*													
World	*Num*	*Pop 2000*	*C%*	*Christians*	*E%*	*U%*	*Unevangelized*	*Num*	*Pop 2000*	*C%*	*Christians*	*E%*	*U%*	*Unevangelized*	*Num*	*Pop 2000*	*C%*	*Christians*	*E%*	*U%*	*Unevangelized*
A	62	3,808,815	5.00	190,316	38	62	2,344,325	1	339,805	5.00	16,990	46	54	181,898	12	4,161,819	6.63	275,926	45	55	2,284,844
B	15	8,094,704	21.85	1,768,416	75	25	2,061,914	3	1,265,972	37.19	470,773	87	13	164,503	18	7,775,004	21.97	1,708,152	73	27	2,121,470
C	3	33,304	76.10	25,346	100	0	79	0	0	0.00	0	0	0	0	0	0	0.00	0	0	0	0
Total	**80**	**11,936,823**	**16.62**	**1,984,078**	**63**	**37**	**4,406,318**	**4**	**1,605,777**	**30.38**	**487,763**	**78**	**22**	**346,401**	**30**	**11,936,823**	**16.62**	**1,984,078**	**63**	**37**	**4,406,314**

and executions. With Independence in 1960, Islam experienced a surge of conversions which has continued to the present day. Islam's greatest impact is felt in the large cities of Bobo Dioulasso and Ouagadougou and secondary commercial centers and villages situated along the main transportation arteries. The current migratory pattern of Upper Volta citizens to Ivory Coast is an important factor in islamization. Islam is spreading most rapidly among the urban masses, but rural areas are also affected. Almost completely islamized peoples are the Liptako (Fulani), Masina, Sia, Songhai, Udalan, Wala, and Zerma. In 1962 Muslims established a national association, called the Muslim Community (Communauté Musulmane), which maintains contact with the wider world of Islam and with Muslim groups in neighboring countries. Its purpose is to facilitate social, cultural, and religious activities.

Ethnoreligionists. Bobo Dancers, masked to impersonate tribal ancestors. The Bobo are still 62% pagans or animists.

CHRISTIANITY

CATHOLIC CHURCH. White Fathers entered what was then known as the Upper Volta in 1900 and established a mission at Ouagadougou the following year. The first baptisms were recorded in 1905 and were followed by severe persecution. In 1911 the work was strengthened by the arrival of White Sisters. The Grunshi were reached in 1912 and the Bobo and Samo in 1913. The vicariate of Ouagadougou was created in 1921 and became an archdiocese in 1955. An indigenous congregation of over 200 nuns, the Black Sisters of the Immaculate Conception, was formed in 1922, and the first indigenous priests were ordained in 1942. Catholicism is strongest among the Mossi, who make up half the population of the country and in 1995 were 23% Christian. Catholics are growing rapidly in numbers, with thousands of converts each year from traditional religions. Catholic laity are especially active through their organization, the Christian Community of Upper Volta (Communauté Chrétienne de Haute-Volta), which was first established in 1970.

The Holy See has diplomatic relations with Burkina Faso and in AD 2000 is represented to government and the Catholic hierarchy by a nuncio residing in Abidjan.

PROTESTANT CHURCHES. The Protestant pioneers in Burkina Faso both in date of arrival and extent of activity have been the Assemblies of God. Begun in 1919 by North American Pentecostal missionaries and followed later by their counterparts from France, the Assemblies of God have grown to be the most important Protestant church in the country. The church has been characterized by extensive Sunday-school and publishing programs as well as by widespread training of national leadership. A revival during a 4-year period in the 1960s resulted in a doubling of the Christian community. The church has been autonomous since 1955. By the mid-1990s it was recognized that possibly 50% of its nearly 280,000 community were Muslim converts, and the church was sending out its own Burkinabé missionaries to 4 other countries. Other groups include the churches supported by the CMA among the Bobo (1923), the SIM among the Gurma (1930), the WEC among the Lobi and Birifor (1937), and Canadian Pentecostals among the Nouna (1945).

Emperor of the Mossi, the Moro Naba, in ceremonies at end of Ramadan.

INDIGENOUS CHURCHES. Separatist churches are not a significant factor in the Upper Volta church life. In 1958 there was only one small independent congregation in Ougadougou, Temple Apostolique, which was joined in 1974 by 2 dissident congregations of the ECEHV among the Bobo. Called the Eglise Apostolique de Haute Volta, the group applied unsuccessfully to the WCC for membership in 1971.

Renewal movements. In the 1990s the Pentecostal/Charismatic Renewal continued to spread rapidly across most older churches, and numbered over 844,000 adherents (of whom 75% Pentecostals, 18% Charismatics, and 7% Independents).

Indigenous missions. Burkina Faso has its own vibrant foreign missionary force, Catholic and Protestant, with the vast majority sent out to surrounding countries.

CHURCH AND STATE

Until around 1950, the Mossi empire formed a large and powerful traditional religionist or animistic state which held islamization in check for several centuries. After Independence in 1960, the new state was proclaimed secular. The constitution of the second republic of the Upper Volta, adopted by referendum in 1970, guaranteed 'freedom of conscience, the profession and free practice of religion' (Article 14). The constitution was suspended on 8 February 1974 following a political crisis involving the military, but the rights affirmed in Articles 14 and 21 of the old constitution continued to be recognized and guaranteed, as with the other fundamental rights of man. The various dioceses, religious congregations, and denominations have administrative councils which are recognized by government as 'private moral persons, invested with a juridical personality'.

Subsequent years have seen a reduction in church-state tensions and a relatively stable climate.

BROADCASTING AND MEDIA

Two out of every 10 people own a radio. Burkina Faso is a member of UNDA, and a 30 minute Catholic program is broadcast each week on radio and television. Shortwave programming from international broadcasters can be received. AWR has programs in French and English. HCJB World Radio has helped to start local radio stations in cooperation with ministries like Youth for Christ, and IBRA-produced programs can be heard on some of these.

The 'Jesus' film has been shown to 890,000 people, most on television (500,000) and from missions using the film in outreach programs (294,000).

INTERDENOMINATIONAL ORGANIZATIONS

The Federation of Evangelical Churches and Missions in the Upper Volta (Fédération des Eglieses et Missions Évangéliques en Haute-Volta, FEME), formed in 1961, is a member of the Association of Evangelicals of Africa and Madagascar, based in Nairobi (Kenya). FEME provides common representation before government and co-operative endeavor in relief and development projects.

FUTURE TRENDS AND PROSPECTS

Tribal religionists are expected to continue to convert to either Islam or Christianity with resulting church membership of 20.4% in 2025. Tribal religionists accordingly decline to 25.8% by 2025, from the 1900 high of 90%. Muslims will likely increase to 53% by 2025.

By 2040, it is probable that Muslims and Christians will share two thirds and one third of the population respectively. One plausible scenario then is that evangelistic efforts by Christians will steadily erode Muslim dominance with both claiming 50% of the population by AD 2050.

BIBLIOGRAPHY

'An eye in the sky, one deep in the earth: elements of Zaose religion,' A. Roberts, in *Ethnologies: hommage à Marcel Griaule*, p.291–306. S. Ganay et al. (ed). Paris: Hermann, 1987.

Approche de la religion des Birifor. A. Erbs. Paris: Musée de l'Homme, 1975. 75p.

Burkina Faso. S. Decalo. *World bibliographical series*, vol. 169. Oxford, UK: CLIO Press, 1994. 154p. (Se especially chapters on 'The peoples,' and 'Religion,' p. 47-51).

Celebration de l'annee jubilaire du Diocese de Ouahigouya: 5 Fevrier 1983. [Ouahigouya, Upper Volta: Diocese de Ouahigouya], 1983. 94p.

'Christianity and Islam among the Mossi,' E. P. Skinner, *American anthropologist*, 60, 6 (1958), 1102–1119.

Croyances et pratiques religieuses traditionelles des Mossi. P. Ilboudo. *Etudes sur l'histoire et l'archéologie du Burkina Faso*, vol. 3. Stuttgart: Franz Steiner, 1990. 160p.

Croyances religieuses et vie quotidienne: Islam et Christianisme à Ouagadougou. R. Deniel. *Recherches Voltaïques*, no. 14. Paris: CNRS, 1970. 360p.

Die Kurumba von Lurum. A. Schweeger-Hefel & W. Staude. Vienna: Verlag A. Schendl, 1972. 532p.

Divination bei den Kafibele–Senufo: zur Aushandlung und Bewältigung von Alltagskonflikten. T. Förster. Berlin: Reimer, 1985. 370p.

Du gomdé au Verbe incarné: puissance de la parole. E. D. Wedraogo. Ouagadougou, Upper Volta, 1976. 160p.

Eglises et mouvements évangéliques au Burkina Faso. T. I. Flavien. [Burkina Faso]: Ouagadougou, 1990. 62p.

Gourmantche ethnoanthropology: a theory of human being. R. A. Swanson. Lanham, MD: University Press of America, 1985. 464p.

'Historique des missions Protestantes en Haute–Volta avec un etat de la formation actuelle des autochtones.' M. Vaillant. Thesis, Faculté Libre de Théologie Evangélique de Vaux-sur-Seine, 1975. 92p.

'Islam in Mossi society,' E. P. Skinner, in *Islam in tropical Africa*, p.350–73. I. M. Lewis (ed). London: Oxford University Press, 1966.

Kinkirsi, Boghoba, Saba: das Weltbild der Nyonyosi in Burkina Faso. A. Schweeger-Hefel. Vienna: A. Schendl, 1986. 436p.

Kunst und Religion der Lobi. P. Meyer. Zurich: Museum Rietberg, 1981. 184p.

'La religion musulmane: facteur d'intégration ou d'identification ethnique. Le cas des yarsé du Burkina Faso,' A. Kouanda, in *Les ethnies ont une histoire*, p.125–34. J. P. Chrétien & G. Prunier (eds). Paris: Karthala, 1989.

Le Chrétien dans l'église. Evêques de Haute-Volta. Bobo-Dioulasso: Savane, [1962]. 108p.

Le Noir du Yatenga: pays Mossi et Gourounsi. L. Tauxier. Paris: Larose, 1912. 796p. (Mossi, Gurunsi, and Fulani peoples, including their religion).

Le pouvoir du Bangré: enquête initiatique à Ouagadougou. K. Fidaali. Paris: Presses de la Renaissance, 1987. 222p.
'Le sens des limites: maladie, sorcellerie, religion et pouvoir chez les Winye, Gourounsi du Burkina Faso.' J. Jacob. Doctoral dissertation, Université de Neuchâtel, 1988. 384p.
'L'Eglise catholique en Haute–Volta,' B. Nouaille-Degorge, *Année africaine*, (1971), 361–80.
'Les activités religieuses des jeunes enfants chez les Bobo,' G. L. Moal, *Journal des Africanistes* (Paris), 51, 1–2 (1981), 235–50.
Les Assemblées de Dieu en Haute–Volta: 50e anniversaire. Ouagadougou, Upper Volta: Assemblées de Dieu, 1971. 40p.
Les Bobo: nature et fonction des masques. G. Le Moal. *Travaux et documents de l'ORSTOM*, no. 121. Paris: ORSTOM, 1980. 545p.
'L'état de la recherche sur l'Islam au Burkina,' A. Kouanda, *Islam et Sociétés du Sud du Sahara* (Paris), 2 (1988), 94–105.
L'évangile au pays Bobo. E. de Montjoye. [Bobo-Dioulasso, Haute-Volta: Diocése de Bobo-Dioulasso, 1980]. 103p.
L'intérieur des choses: maladie, divination et reproduction sociale chez les Bisa du Burkina. S. Fainzang. Paris: L'Harmattan, 1986. 204p.
Of water and the spirit: ritual, magic, and initiation in the life of an African shaman. M. P. Somé. New York: Putnam, 1994. 311p.
Sorciers, féticheurs et guérisseurs de la Côte d'Ivoire—Haute Volta. J. Kerharo & A. Bouquet. Paris: Vigot, 1950. 144p.
'The position of women in the Sisala divination cult,' E. L. Mendonsa, in *The new religions of Africa*, p.57–66. B. Jules–Rosette (ed). Norwood, NJ: Ablex Publishing, 1979.
'Tierce, Eglise, ma Mère: ou, la conversion d'une Communauté païenne au Christ.' A. T. Sanon. Thesis, Institut Catholique de Paris, 1970. 294p.
'Transformations of belief: Islam among the Dyula of Kongbougou from 1880 to 1970.' L. G. Quimby. Ph.D. dissertation, University of Wisconsin, 1972. 250p.
Trois ministères de puissance en Afrique. A. Brisset (ed). Collombey: Dépôt Pro-Africa, 1977. 98p.
'Un exemple d'indépendence et de résistance religieuse: les hommes et les dieux Lobi,' M. Cros, *Mondes et Développement* (Paris), 17, 65 (1989), 59–65.

Country Table 2. **Organized churches and denominations in Burkina Faso.**

Official name (bold type = church with over 10% of all affiliated) 1	*Begun* 2	*Type* 3	*Counc* 4	*Congs* 5	*Adults* 6	*Affiliated 1970* 7	*Affiliated 1995* 8	*G%* 9	*Names, notes, and other statistics* (see Codebook, Part 3) 10
Assemblées de Dieu en BF	1919	P-Pe2	ZFG.G	1,686	379,000	80,000	500,907	7.61	*Assemblies of God.* M=AoG(USA); 1947, AdD(France). A=1955. Mossi. 330n,22f,1j,1s(52).
Assoc des Eglises Evangéliques	1930	P-Eva	xMG.G	255	41,900	3,500	80,000	13.33	*AEEBF. Assoc of Ev Chs.* M=ECWA,EMS(Nigeria),SIM(USA).A=1962. Gurma. 6n,22f,1H,4h,1s.
Assoc des Egls Ev de Pentecôte en BF	1945	P-Pel	x.G.G	86	3,500	2,000	6,700	4.95	*MEP.* M=BFM(ACP,Canada). 64% Nouna, 11% Dian,11% Sissala,7% Birifor.10n,18f,55Y.
Assoc de la Convention Baptiste en BF	c1965	P-Bap	T....	88	7,920	200	11,300	17.51	*Baptist Ch.* M=NBC(Nigeria),FMB-SBC. Yoruba. Correspondence courses. 11f.
Eglise Adventiste du Septième Jour	1971	P-Adv	x....	1	72	–	181	4.17	*SDA. Seventh-day Adventists.*
Eglise Apostolique en BF	1958	I-3aA	.v...	80	3,150	1,500	9,000	7.43	Schism ex AoG in Ouagadougou, also 1974 ex CMA. M=AC(Ghana). Applied to WCC 1971.
Eglise Catholique en Burkina Faso:	1900	R-Lat	P.SFP	110	561,100	416,349	971,669	3.45	*Catholic Ch in BF.* M=FSC,WF,CSSR. C=4+4+19. 277n 156x 300m 795w 52040Yy
M Ouagadougou	1921	R-Lat	Ps	17	185,000	105,460	320,803	4.55	95% Mossi. 23,554 catechumens. M=WF. 71n 41x 116m 263w 20874Yy
D Bobo-Dioulasso	1927	R-Lat	Pwf	18	37,000	31,129	64,045	2.93	Potentially rich agricultural land. 17 tribes. 32n 28x 50m 149w 3165Yy
D Diebougou	1968	R-Lat	Ps	9	48,900	45,050	84,525	2.55	80% Dagari. Main tribe, Lobi, unevangelized. 32n 0x 6m 44w 1974Yy
D Fada N'Gourma	1959	R-Lat	Pcssr	13	17,000	10,966	29,440	4.03	70% Mossi, 29% Gurma, 1% Fulani (Liptako). 11n 22x 33m 75w 1825Yy
D Kaya	1969	R-Lat	Ps	6	20,600	9,015	35,600	5.65	Formed from M Ouagadougou, D Koupela. Mossi. 9n 10x 10m 32w 2651Yy
D Koudougou	1947	R-Lat	Ps	12	87,000	72,591	150,565	2.96	Small industrial town. Mossi, Grunsi. 26960z. 35n 10x 28m 80w 5850Yy
D Koupéla	1956	R-Lat	Ps	13	86,500	52,584	149,298	4.26	90% Mossi, also Busansi and Kusasi. 38n 12x 11m 55w 9497Yy
D Nouna-Dédougou	1947	R-Lat	Pwf	13	53,100	56,784	91,691	1.94	33% Samo, 23%Bobo, 11% Pana, 7% Marka. 27n 21x 30m 36w 3868Yy
D Ouahigouya	1958	R-Lat	Ps	9	26,000	32,770	45,702	1.34	96% Mossi, 4% Foulse(Lilse). M=WF. 18034z. 22n 12x 16m 59w 2073Yy
Eglise Chrétienne Evangélique en BF	1923	P-Hol	xFG.G	499	25,100	5,563	47,900	8.99	*ECEBF.* M=CMA. A=1964. 74% Bobo, 16% Samo.
Eglise de Dieu de Prophétie	1987	P-Pe3	x....	5	100	–	333	12.50	*Church of God of Prophecy.* M=CoGP(USA).
Eglise de la Mission Apostolique	1959	P-PeA	x....	88	5,650	600	14,120	13.47	*Apostolic Church.* M=ACP(MEP),Ghana.
Eglise Evangélique Reformée	c1980	P-Ref	.....	20	660	–	2,000	6.67	*Reformed Evangelical Church.* Mission from France.
Eglise Mennonite en BF	1978	P-Men	.....	4	130	–	250	5.88	*Mennonite Church in Burkina Faso.* M=AIMM,EMBC.
Eglise Neo-Apostolique	c1970	I-3aX	x....	200	12,000	–	18,886	48.27	*New Apostolic Church. NAC. ENA.* Mission from HQ Zurich (Switzerland).
Eglise Protestante Evangélique	1931	P-Eva	xFG.G	38	2,000	2,000	3,800	2.60	*MEAO.* 1931, M=Qua Iboe;1937,WEC(UK),WEK. Lobi, also Birifor, Dagari, Guin. 12f,1p.
Eglises radiophoniques isolées	c1960	I-3rA	.....	500	5,000	1,100	8,000	8.26	Isolated radio believers, mainly pupils and students aged 12-25. T=11000(ICI).
Témoins de Jéhovah	c1960	m-Jeh	x....	17	449	50	1,800	15.41	*Jehovah's Witnesses.* Active witnessing by 1962, then lapse until 1967. 6f. 83Y
Other Protestant denominations		P-	.....	30	6,000	2,000	10,000	0.05	Total about 4, including: World-Wide Missions (1965), Free Will Baptist Mission, CC.
Other African indigenous churches		I-3pA	.....	35	3,500	500	10,000	0.05	20 AICs from Ghana, Togo, Benin, Ivory Coast (Harrist Ch, 1984), Nigeria: C&S, COTLA, CAD.
Totals				**3,742**	**1,057,231**	**515,362**	**1,696,846**		

Churches, members, growth, 1900-2025	*Congs*	*Adults*	*Affiliated*	*G%*	*Total denominations*	*6 Megablocs:* *O*	*R*	*A*	*P*	*I*	*m*
Total churches, members, and denominations (mid-1900)	0	0	0	15.00	1	0	1	0	0	0	0
Total churches, members, and denominations (mid-1970)	1,255	282,742	515,362	10.00	21	0	1	0	9	10	1
Total churches, members, and denominations (mid-1990)	3,000	901,000	1,445,600	5.29	39	0	1	0	15	22	1
Total churches, members, and denominations (mid-1995)	3,742	1,057,231	1,696,846	3.26	39	0	1	0	15	22	1
Total churches, members, and denominations (mid-2000)	4,000	1,236,000	1,984,078	3.18	40	0	1	0	15	23	1
Total churches, members, and denominations (mid-2025)	7,000	2,963,000	4,755,000	3.56	82	1	1	0	26	50	4

NOTES ON TABLE ABOVE
NATIONAL COUNCILS (Column 4, 5th letter).
E = Fédération des Eglises et Missions Evangéliques du Burkina Faso (FEMEBF, Federation of Evangelical Churches and Missions in BF).
P = Conférence des Evêques de Burkina Faso et du Niger (CEBFN, Bishops' Conference of BF & N).

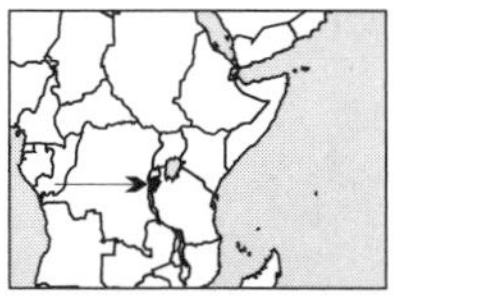

BURUNDI

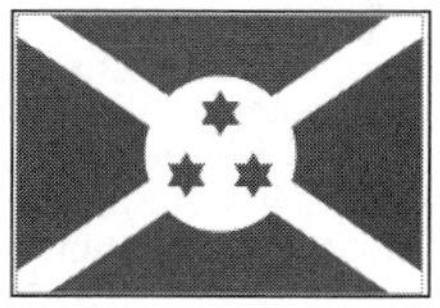

SECULAR DATA, AD 2000

STATE
Official name: Republika y'Uburundi (The Republic of Burundi).
Short name: Burundi. **Adjective of nationality:** of Burundi.
Flag: White diagonal cross, red quarters above and below, green quarters at sides, centered white circle with 3 red stars.
Area: 27,816 sq. km. (10,740 sq. mi.).
Government: Military junta, since 1966 (17th century Tutsi absolute monarchy, 1898 German rule, 1919 Belgian mandated territory, 1962 Independence as monarchy, 1966 military rule).
Legislature: National Assembly, 81 members.
Official language: Kirundi and French (Français).
Monetary unit: 1 Burundi franc (FBu) = 100 centimes. **US$1=** FBu 457.70.
Chief cities: BUJUMBURA 302,227; Gitega 146,423.
Political divisions: 15 provinces.
Armed forces: 19,000.

DEMOGRAPHY
Population: 6,695,000.
Population density: 240.6/sq. km. (623.3/sq. mi.).
Under 15 years: 3,104,000.
Growth rate p.a.: 2.57% (births 39.66, deaths 18.24).
Mortality: Infant, per 1,000: 109.8; **Maternal per 100,000:** 1,300.0.
Life expectancy: 44 (male 42, female 45).
Household size: 4.6. **Floor area per person, sq.m:** 7.0
Major languages: Rundi (Kirundi), Ruanda (Kinyarwanda), French, Swahili.
Urban dwellers: 8.96%. **Urban growth rate p.a.:** 5.9%.
Labor force: 53%.

ETHNOLINGUISTIC PEOPLES
80.8% Hutu; 14.0% Tutsi; 1.6% Lingala (Zairian); 1.6% Ruanda Tutsi; 1.0% Twa (Gesera) Pygmy.

ECONOMY
National income p.a. per person: US$159; **per family:** US$735.

EDUCATION
Adult literacy: 35% (male 49%, female 22%). **Schools:** 1,531.
Universities: 8. **School enrolment:** female/male: 35%/44%.

HEALTH
Access to health services: 80%. **Access to safe water:** 52%.
Hospitals: 264 (19 beds per 10,000). **Doctors:** 317.
Blind: 11,000. **Deaf:** 418,400. **Murder rate:** 3.
Lepers: 70,000. **Underweight prevalence under 5:** 37%.

LITERATURE
New book titles p.a.: 170 (25 p.a. per million). **Periodicals:** 18.
Newspapers: 1 daily.

COMMUNICATION (per 1,000 people)
Phones: 2 **(3% mobile). Radios:** 47. **TV sets:** 7.
Daily newspaper circulation: 3. **Computers:** 1.

REFUGEES
Citizen refugees in other countries: 290,000.
Alien refugees from other countries: 140,000.
Internal displacement: 300,000.

HUMAN LIFE AND LIBERTY (optimum condition=100.0%)
HDI: 24.7. **HSI:** 25.0. **HFI:** 20.0. **EFL:** 25.0.

Country status. Burundi is a small landlocked country in Central Africa, located on the highlands of the Congo-Nile Divide along the Western branch of the Great East African Rift Valley. It is one of the most densely populated countries in Africa, and also one of the last to be penetrated by Europeans. The country's chief products are coffee, tea, and bananas. Recent tribal conflict between Hutus and Tutsis has greatly crippled Burundi's economy.

HUMAN LIFE AND LIBERTY

Human need and development. Although Burundi is a very fertile country, high population density keeps its people chronically poor. Further, the country has been riven since independence by factional strife between the ruling Tutsi minority and the powerless Hutu majority. The pressure on land and resources is intensified by a growing cattle population. As in many other African countries, the cow is a status symbol and social institution. In rural areas each peasant family occupies a self-contained homestead on its own plot of land. These huts, shaped like beehives, are so small that most family activities are carried out in the open. Because the huts are invariably built on the crests and slopes of hills, much time is spent every day hauling water from the valleys. The deficiency of starch and proteins in the diet causes a number of health problems, such as kwashiorkor.

Human rights and freedoms. Burundi is a one-party authoritarian state in which power is vested in a Tutsi-dominated army command supported by the Tutsi-dominated UPRONA political party. Although some progress has been made in mitigating the harshness of the minority rule, some 10,000 people, mostly Hutu, were killed in 1988 in interethnic clashes and several thousands more at police hands in 1990 and

Country Table 1. **Religious adherents in Burundi, AD 1900-2025.**

Year	*1900*		*1970*		*mid-1990*		*Annual change, 1990-2000*				*mid-1995*		*mid-2000*		*mid-2025*	
Name	*Adherents*	*%*	*Adherents*	*%*	*Adherents*	*%*	*Natural*	*Conversion*	*Total*	*Rate*	*Adherents*	*%*	*Adherents*	*%*	*Adherents*	*%*
Christians	**100**	**0.0**	**2,579,000**	**73.4**	**4,931,800**	**90.4**	**111,994**	**8,590**	**120,584**	**2.21**	**5,626,000**	**91.4**	**6,137,639**	**91.7**	**10,851,000**	**93.8**
PROFESSION																
professing Christians	**100**	**0.0**	**2,579,000**	**73.4**	**4,931,800**	**90.4**	**111,994**	**8,590**	**120,584**	**2.21**	**5,626,000**	**91.4**	**6,137,639**	**91.7**	**10,851,000**	**93.8**
AFFILIATION																
unaffiliated Christians	66	0.0	277,300	7.9	783,600	14.4	17,793	2,327	20,120	2.31	899,136	14.6	984,798	14.7	1,576,500	13.6
affiliated Christians	**34**	**0.0**	**2,301,700**	**65.5**	**4,148,200**	**76.0**	**94,201**	**6,263**	**100,464**	**2.19**	**4,726,864**	**76.8**	**5,152,841**	**77.0**	**9,274,500**	**80.2**
Roman Catholics	34	0.0	2,107,500	60.0	3,200,000	58.7	72,669	-9,915	62,754	1.81	3,594,126	58.4	3,827,541	57.2	6,600,000	57.1
Protestants	0	0.0	146,600	4.2	580,000	10.6	13,171	8,829	22,000	3.27	668,870	10.9	800,000	12.0	1,600,000	13.8
Anglicans	0	0.0	45,000	1.3	350,000	6.4	7,948	7,052	15,000	3.63	443,000	7.2	500,000	7.5	1,000,000	8.6
Independents	0	0.0	1,500	0.0	16,500	0.3	375	275	650	3.38	19,064	0.3	23,000	0.3	70,000	0.6
Orthodox	0	0.0	1,000	0.0	1,000	0.0	23	17	40	3.42	1,000	0.0	1,400	0.0	2,500	0.0
Marginal Christians	0	0.0	100	0.0	700	0.0	16	4	20	2.54	804	0.0	900	0.0	2,000	0.0
Trans-megabloc groupings																
Evangelicals	0	0.0	45,000	1.3	620,000	11.4	14,080	8,920	23,000	3.21	733,945	11.9	850,000	12.7	1,900,000	16.4
Pentecostals/Charismatics	0	0.0	105,000	3.0	600,000	11.0	13,625	3,875	17,500	2.59	696,201	11.3	775,000	11.6	1,620,000	14.0
Great Commission Christians	**0**	**0.0**	**246,000**	**7.0**	**890,000**	**16.3**	**20,211**	**5,266**	**25,477**	**2.55**	**1,030,000**	**16.7**	**1,144,771**	**17.1**	**2,500,000**	**21.6**
Ethnoreligionists	1,007,900	99.8	903,000	25.7	440,000	8.1	9,992	-8,971	1,021	0.23	434,300	7.1	450,210	6.7	500,000	4.3
Muslims	2,000	0.2	30,000	0.9	72,000	1.3	1,635	392	2,027	2.51	82,000	1.3	92,274	1.4	190,000	1.6
Hindus	0	0.0	300	0.0	5,000	0.1	114	-52	62	1.18	5,300	0.1	5,624	0.1	10,000	0.1
Baha'is	0	0.0	1,600	0.1	4,000	0.1	91	50	141	3.07	4,900	0.1	5,414	0.1	10,000	0.1
Nonreligious	0	0.0	100	0.0	3,200	0.1	73	-9	64	1.84	3,500	0.1	3,840	0.1	8,000	0.1
World A (unevangelized persons)	1,008,990	99.9	70,270	2.0	60,016	1.1	1,363	-1,902	-539	-0.94	61,561	1.0	53,560	0.8	57,845	0.5
World B (evangelized non-Christians)	910	0.1	864,230	24.6	464,184	8.5	10,542	-6,688	3,854	0.82	468,635	7.6	503,801	7.5	660,155	5.7
World C (Christians)	100	0.0	2,579,000	73.4	4,931,800	90.4	111,994	8,590	120,584	2.21	5,626,000	91.4	6,137,639	91.7	10,851,000	93.8
Country's population	**1,010,000**	**100.0**	**3,513,500**	**100.0**	**5,456,000**	**100.0**	**123,899**	**0**	**123,899**	**2.07**	**6,156,197**	**100.0**	**6,695,000**	**100.0**	**11,569,000**	**100.0**

COLUMNS, ROWS.
For meanings and definitions, see Codebook (Part 3). Note that, by definition, total 'Christians' = professing + crypto-Christians, which also = affiliated + unaffiliated Christians, and also = Great Commission Christians + latent Christians. Percentages may not always total exactly, due to rounding.

NOTES ON RELIGIONS
BAHA'IS. In 1964, 3 local spiritual assemblies; 1973, 47 isolated groups: after years of civil war, by 1992 there were only 16 LSAs organized.
COUNTRY'S POPULATION. In 1972-73, about 4,000 Tutsis and later 150,000 Hutus were massacred.
ETHNORELIGIONISTS. Only the Twa pygmies (Gesara; 30,000) remain predominantly traditionalist or animist (90%). There are, however, still many Rundi animists.
INDEPENDENTS. In 7 groups in 1995 (see Table 2).
MUSLIMS. Africans are Sunnis (of the Malakite rite), with 400 Asian Shias (Ismailis) and Bohora, Ithna-Ashari and Kharijite minorities. Islam is growing gradually; many Rundi are converted to Islam in Bujumbura.
PENTECOSTALS/CHARISMATICS. Although the Renewal has spread throughout the country and virtually all the churches, the years of civil war have destroyed any organization of the Catholic Charismatic Renewal. In 1997 its coordinator knew of only one functioning regular weekly prayer group.

Great Commission Instrument Panel: status of Burundi (for explanation see start of Part 4)

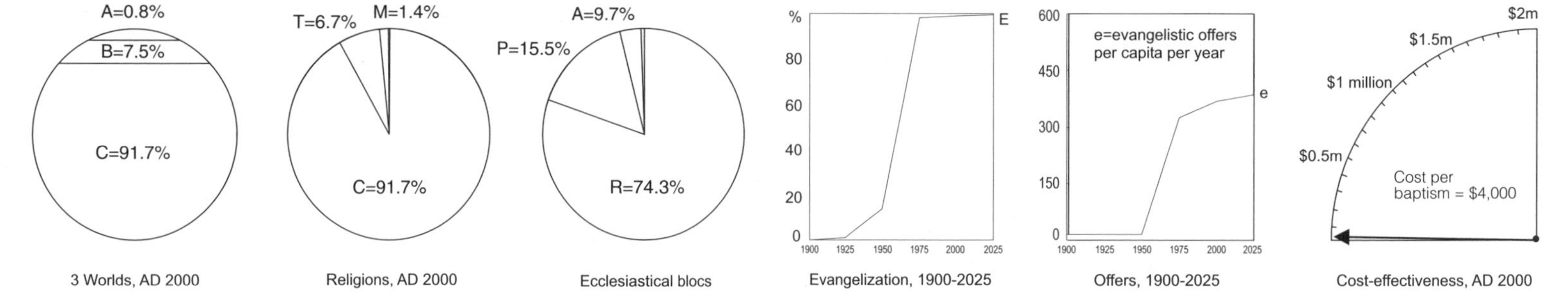

1991. Civil rights are significantly restricted, and detention and torture of prisoners are common. There are numerous reports of disappearances of political prisoners. Suspects may be detained without arrest warrant. Freedoms of the press and speech are circumscribed, and possession of opposition political tracts is a punishable offense. Both print and broadcast media are under state control. Although race-based discrimination is illegal, de facto discrimination against Hutus persists in almost all areas of public life, particularly in the military, economy, and civil service. The vast majority of the 150,000 Hutus who left Burundi following the 1972 civil conflict remain in Zaire or Rwanda. Women hold a secondary position in society based on their traditional subordination to men. While dowry and polygamy are outlawed and women may inherit property, a woman may not start a business without her husband's permission. Women generally are less educated and less represented in the professions than men. Violence against women is common in the home.

Human environment. Indiscriminate cutting of firewood has led to widespread deforestation. The originally fertile soils have been depleted over the years primarily because of the small size of the family plots and the nearly total use of farmland. Improper terracing encourages soil erosion. Pastureland is severely overgrazed by large cattle herds. Deforestation is also contributing to the degradation of the soils. Wildlife populations are losing in the competition for habitat, and many species are already extinct or in great danger.

NON-CHRISTIAN RELIGIONS

Traditional religions are followed by one-fifth of the population. The Twa pygmies, however, remain 90% traditionalist. The Barundi name for the creator God is Imana. He is normally invisible but sometimes visits his people in the form of a white lamb. Few prayers are addressed to Imana, Barundi attention being focused on the cult of a former human being Kiranga which originated in Rwanda where he is known as Ryangombe. The highly-organized Kiranga cult is attended by initiates of varying rank known as Abana b'Imana (children of Imana). Kiranga periodically possesses his highest-ranked initiate, to whom special honor is accorded. Although not himself God, Kiranga is able to enhance or prevent Imana's aid and, thus, serves as intermediary between God and man.

Islam accounts for less than 1.5% of the population. There are about 90,000 Muslims, most of whom work as merchants, fishermen, and artisans in centers on Lake Tanganyika. In Bujumbura, there are 16,000; including 13,000 Africans and 3,000 Asians; at Rumange 5,000 and 1,000 at Nyanza-Lac. Africans are Sunnis and Asians Ismailis, with Bohora, Ithna-Asheri and Kharijite minorities. Since they speak Swahili, they have difficulty in obtaining access to education although there are some Quranic schools. They maintain relations with Muslims in neighboring countries.

CHRISTIANITY

In the 15th century, tall pastoral Tutsi warriors migrated from Ethiopia to the Ruanda-Urundi area and established a feudal system over the Hutu and Twa pygmies. The Hutu, 85% of the population, became the serfs of the cattle-owning Tutsi and both tribes came to speak the same language. Europeans were late in arriving, the first being Speke and Burton in 1858 seeking the source of the Nile. Livingstone and Stanley also shared in this search in the 1870s. The White Fathers established their first mission in Burundi in 1879. In 1881, 2 priests and a lay helper were murdered, and they were not replaced until 1899. Burundi became part of German East Africa at the Berlin Conference in 1884, and in 1907, Bethel Lutherans sought to establish themselves in this area. Belgian troops from the Congo occupied the country in 1916 and German missions were forced to close. In 1923, Belgium received a mandate to administer Ruanda-Urundi. Belgian Protestant missions were too few in number to meet the request to take over German missions, and so other Protestant missions were allowed to enter.

Eglise Catholique au Burundi. A packed pontifical mass celebrated at Mugera in 1938 at height of mass movement into church in Urundi, when 1,000 a week were being baptized..

CATHOLIC CHURCH. In 1922, Burundi was made a vicariate apostolic, having at that time 5 stations, 18 missionaries and 14,356 Catholics. The first Murundi priest was ordained in 1925. In 1930, a mass movement into the church began to take place, with an average of 1,000 baptisms a week by 1935. By 1937, the Catholic population had risen to 250,000 baptized and 230,000 catechumens. In 1959, the first African bishop in Burundi was appointed to a new diocese, and the country became an ecclesiastical province. At that time, the number of baptized Catholics was 1,200,000 or 55% of the population. At territorial independence 3 years later, the number of baptized was 1,445,000 with 127,000 catechumens, and a fourth diocese was created. In 1971, there were 90 parishes averaging in size over 23,400 baptized and catechumens, each divided into central branches (with Sunday services and a complete cycle of cate-

Country summary. **Worlds A, B, C by ethnolinguistic peoples, cities, and major civil divisions in Burundi.**

	PEOPLES CITIES										*CIVIL DIVISIONS*										
World	*Num*	*Pop 2000*	*C%*	*Christians*	*E%*	*U%*	*Unevangelized*	*Num*	*Pop 2000*	*C%*	*Christians*	*E%*	*U%*	*Unevangelized*	*Num*	*Pop 2000*	*C%*	*Christians*	*E%*	*U%*	*Unevangelized*
A	3	16,738	0.29	48	41	59	9,881	0	0	0.00	0	0	0	0	0	0	0.00	0	0	0	0
B	1	66,950	8.00	5,356	56	44	29,458	0	0	0.00	0	0	0	0	0	0	0.00	0	0	0	0
C	10	6,611,316	77.86	5,147,439	100	0	15,272	2	448,650	83.02	372,474	100	0	1,291	15	6,694,999	76.97	5,152,841	99	1	54,609
Total	**14**	**6,695,004**	**76.97**	**5,152,843**	**99**	**1**	**54,611**	**2**	**448,650**	**83.02**	**372,474**	**100**	**0**	**1,291**	**15**	**6,694,999**	**76.97**	**5,152,841**	**99**	**1**	**54,609**

chetical instruction for adults and children), semi-central branches (with Sunday services and an incomplete cycle of catechetical instruction) and prayer huts (without Sunday services and with incomplete catechetical instruction). The lack of priests has necessitated that certain parishes be placed under lay responsibility. A variety of catechetical training centers have been developed, with catechists carrying much of the responsibility for the instruction of new converts.

The life of the church was deeply affected by the violence of the Hutu rebellion of 29 April 1972, in the Bururi region of southern Burundi and the Tutsi repression throughout the country which followed. Violence continued during 1973, provoked particularly by armed incursions of Hutu refugees from bordering countries. The initial rebellion cost 3,000 to 4,000 dead, mostly Tutsis but also some Hutus who tried to protect them or refused to join the rebels. The 100,000 killed (most Hutus, plus a few Tutsis favorable to the Hutu cause) in the Tutsi repression of 1972, accounted for 2.7% of the total population and 3.2% of the Hutu population of Burundi. Of these, 18 were priests (17 Hutus and one Tutsi), 7 male and female religious personnel, 2,100 catechists and teachers in Catholic schools (out of 4,580), a large number of nurses and Hutu medical assistants and in general the major portion of the Hutu intelligentsia. Some 100,000 Hutus (including some seminary students) became refugees: 50,000 in Tanzania, 40,000 in Rwanda and 10,000 in Zaire.

For the most part, the unity of the local Tutsi and Hutu clergy was not seriously threatened by these trials, although some Tutsi priests found themselves in opposition to missionary clergy who were often outspokenly critical of the repression. A number of missionaries were expelled from the country. In May and June 1972, a difference of opinion arose between the missionary religious superiors (both male and female) and the president of the Episcopal conference concerning the attitude of the hierarchy to the situation. A confidential note from the superiors to the bishops, dated 24 May 1972, stated, 'We desire that the hierarchy take a firm and unambiguous position concerning these events'. At the time, two of the bishops, including the archbishop of Gitega who also presided over the Episcopal conference, were Tutsis, 2 were Hutus and one was Belgian, although the latter withdrew in September 1973 and was replaced by an open-minded Tutsi.

By 1997 the situation had worsened for several years, with over 100,000 Hutus killed by the Tutsi army and clergy being openly targeted. In 1996 archbishop J. Ruhuna of Bijumbura was assassinated. No end to the carnage seemed in sight.

The Holy See has diplomatic relations with Burundi and in AD 2000 is represented to government and the Catholic hierarchy by a pro-nuncio residing in Bujumbura.

PROTESTANT CHURCHES. The Neukirchener Mission followed the Bethel Lutherans into Ruanda-Urundi and established 5 stations before being forced to leave at the time of the first World War. Seventh-day Adventists entered in 1921 and now operate two fields, West Burundi and East Burundi, which were organized respectively in 1936 and 1964. In 1928, Danish Baptist missionaries took over the work of 3 Neukirchener stations evacuated in 1916. A fourth Neukirchener mission was occupied by the Kansas Yearly Meeting of Friends in 1932, and the Friends have since developed 4 additional centers. American Free Methodists took over the fifth Neukirchener station in 1935 and later added 3 more. The Swedish Free Mission, a Pentecostal body, also began in 1935 in the region of Bururu, and they are now the largest Protestant community in Burundi, with 38 missionaries in the field. The World Gospel Mission entered in 1938.

Protestants are heavily involved in education, medical and social service. In 1970, Protestants and Anglicans were responsible for 275 primary schools (40,058 pupils, 22.2% of the total), 3 secondary schools (323 students, 9% of the total) and 3 teacher-training schools (395 students) in addition to technical, trade, agricultural, and domestic science institutions.

Eglise Protestante Episcopal. School at Anglican Mission HQ Ibuye.

ANGLICAN CHURCH. The Rwanda General and Medical Mission (CMS) entered Burundi in 1934. The East African Revival which began in Rwanda in 1927, swept through Burundi in the 1930s, having its greatest influence in Anglican churches. Most members were Tutsi, many of whom were later killed in tribal fighting. CMS medical facilities were particularly hard-pressed when 120,000 Tutsi refugees poured into Burundi with the first Hutu uprisings in Rwanda following its independence. The Anglican Church shares in sponsoring 2 teacher-training colleges in addition to Warner Theological College which provides training for priests and for other full-time workers. The first African bishop was consecrated in Burundi in 1965, and Burundi became an independent diocese within the Church of Uganda, Rwanda, and Burundi in 1966. During the Hutu uprising of 1972, and the massacres which followed, the clergy were reduced by half. Approximately 100 catechists lost their lives, leaving 350 untrained and badly-paid men to help the remaining pastors in the outchurches. Only 2 of the 17 clergy in 1974 had had secondary education, and the annual income of the church was reduced by half as a result of the country's internal troubles.

INDIGENOUS CHURCHES. In 1962, two-thirds of all Anglicans in southern Burundi seceded to form the Eglise de Dieu (Church of God). Although at one time numbering 20,000 members, it was accused of subversion in 1965 and suppressed. An earlier schismatic group broke away from the Friends in 1959, but it has also largely disappeared. There is one immigrant Kimbanguist congregation from Zaire.

Renewal movements. In the 1990s the Pentecostal/Charismatic Renewal continued to spread rapidly across most older churches, and numbered over 775,000 adherents (of whom 64% Pentecostals, 33% Charismatics, and 3% Independents).

Indigenous missions. A small number of Catholics, Anglican, and Protestant missionaries have been sent out by the Burundi churches, mainly to surrounding countries.

CHURCH AND STATE

Although the country became independent in 1962, it continued to be ruled by the Mwami (king), who governed with the assistance of Ganwa (princes). The Ganwa each administered a different province, each had his own court and army and frequently quarreled among themselves. In 1966, the monarchy and Ganwa system were overthrown by an army colonel Micombero who set up a military regime with himself as president. In 1969, discussions were held between the chief of state and representatives of the Catholic and Anglican churches, which were followed by a joint pastoral letter whose aim was to lessen ethnic tensions. Later that year, 25 alleged conspirators against the government were executed, and the number of Tutsi from the south within the government were increased. These events were then followed by the Hutu rebellion and Tutsi repression of 1972.

The churches in general play an important role in social action and education. The Catholic Church in particular is sufficiently strong for its declarations to be listened to with seriousness. As with the former Belgian colonial administration and private enterprise, the church has since the beginning tended to place more confidence in Tutsis than Hutus, the former being considered more open and dynamic, and thus, the church also contributed to the social and political cleavage of the country and to the fact that at Independence, the intellectual and political elite were for the most part Tutsis while the majority of the population were Hutus. The failure of the Catholic hierarchy to take a clear and vigorous position in the face of the evolving situation was evident both before and after the 1972 rebellion. During 1972-73, the Tutsi bishops were the only ones who could express themselves without constraint. Many Hutus and missionaries have complained about the failure of episcopal declarations to condemn the massacres and especially the failure to make any comment on the social and ethnic causes for the 1972 Hutu rebellion, although everyone is in agreement that the situation is extremely complex. A number of missionaries were expelled from Burundi in 1972 and 1973.

The constitution of 11 July 1974, states that 'Burundi is a unitary, indivisible, secular and democratic Republic' (Article 1); and that 'All Barundi have equal rights and responsibilities without distinction of sex, origin, race, religion and opinion: (Article 4). Article 9 reads, 'Freedom of thought and the practice of religion are guaranteed to all. Within the limits and conditions fixed by law, the State protects the free exercise of worship without intervening in its practice'. In Burundi, clergy and religious congregations have been exempted from taxes, and both Protestant and Catholic schools and dispensaries receive large government subsidies. The state university of Bujumbura was originally founded under Jesuit initiative and both the rector and faculty members are for the most part Catholic priests. Catholic religious personnel are employed in numerous state medical institutions.

In April 1977, the government expelled without warning or explanation 15 Catholic missionaries in the diocese of Bujumbura (14 Italians, one Mexican; most Verona priests).

In the 1980s and 1990s the same tensions between church and state continued and escalated several times to near anarchy.

BROADCASTING AND MEDIA

The 'Jesus' Film has been seen by more than 5 million people, chiefly through presentations by film teams. It has had an enormous response: 20% of viewers have made a decision for Christ.

INTERDENOMINATIONAL ORGANIZATIONS

The Alliance of Protestant Churches of Burundi, founded in 1935 as the Protestant Alliance, includes Baptists, Free Methodists, Anglicans, Friends, and World Gospel Missions, with Plymouth Brethren and Swedish Pentecostals maintaining a cooperative relationship. One division, Secours Protestant, has provided material assistance through contributions from overseas agencies. A series of ecumenical seminars providing opportunity for dialogue between Protestants and Catholics was begun by CERAS of Bujumbura, and several other such initiatives have been begun.

FUTURE TRENDS AND PROSPECTS

In the 21st century, a steady rise of church membership with attendant decline of animism among the majority Hutu people is expected. In 2025, affiliation at 80% may continue to lag behind profession at 94%.

Christians will possibly grow to over 95% after 2025 and remain there by 2050, unless Muslims, Baha'is, and the nonreligious are able to grow beyond 5%.

BIBLIOGRAPHY

Annuaire ecclésiastique, Burundi et Rwanda, 1970–1971. Bujumbura, Burundi: SECOREB, 1970. (Roman Catholic).
Banyarwanda et Barundi. R. Bourgeois. Brussels: Institut Royal Colonial Belge, 1954–58. 4 vols. (Vol.1 treats 'ethnology,' vol. 2 'custom,' and vol. 3 'religion and magic').
'Burundi,' *Pro Mundi Vita* (Brussels), 9 (1965).
Burundi. M. Daniels (comp). *World bibliographical series*, vol. 145. Oxford, UK: CLIO Press, 1992. 164p. (See especially 'Religion,' p.56-61).
Burundi et Rwanda, 1964–1968: plan quinquennal de développement. Usumbura, Burundi: COREB, 1963.
'Burundi: l'Eglise sous surveillance étatique,' C. Carrai, *La revue nouvelle* (Brussels), Ann. 42, vol. 83, 2 (1986), 144–56.
Burundi, recherche sur les prêtres: résultats du dépouillement des questionnaires individuels. Bujumbura: Centre de recherches socio-religieuses, 1971.
Church growth in Burundi. D. Hohensee. South Pasadena, CA: William Carey Library, 1978. 153p.
'Conflict in Burundi,' *Pro Mundi Vita*, Special note 25 (1973), 1–28.
Croyances et pratiques religieuses des Barundi. B. Zuure. Brussels: Editions de l'Essorial, 1929. 206p.
Eglise et développement: inventaire commenté de la contribution de l'Eglise au développement économique et social au Rwanda et au Burundi. W. Hilgers. Bujumbura, Burundi: Centre de recherches et d'animation sociale, [1967]. 109p.
'Eglise, pouvoir et culture: l'itinéraire d'une chrétienté africaine,' J. P. Chrétien, *Les quatre fleuves: cahiers de recherche et de réflexion religieuses*, 10 (1979), 33–55.
'L'Eglise au Burundi: un conflit peut en cacher un autre,' P. Chamay, *Etudes: revue mensuelle fondée par des Pères de la Compagnie de Jésus*, 366, 2 (1987), 159–70.
Les chemins de la sagesse: Imana et le Murundi. T. M. L. Musaniwabo. Louvain-la-Neuve, Belgium: Centre d'Histoire des Religions, 1979. 231p.
'Les communautés chrétiennes au Burundi, lieux d'éclosion de nouveaux ministères,' E. Ngoyagoyé, *Les quatre fleuves: cahiers de recherche et de réflexion religieuses*, 10 (1979), 57–68.
Les debuts de l'evangelisation au Burundi. R. Collart. Bologna: Editrice Missionaria Italiana, 1981. 2 vols.
'Les peuples de la République démocratique du Congo, du Rwanda et du Burundi,' A. Dorsinfang-Smets, in *Ethnologie régionale*, p.566–661, vol. 1. J. Poirier (ed). Paris: Gallimard, 1972.
Naissance d'une église: histoire du Burundi Chrétien. J. Perraudin. Usumbura: Presses Lavigerie, 1963. 228p.
Road to revival: the story of the Ruanda Mission. A. C. S. Smith. London: Church Missionary Society, 1946. 116p.
'Rundi worldview and contextualization of the gospel: a study in theologizing in terms of worldview themes.' D. W. Hohensee. D.Miss. thesis, Fuller Theological Seminary, Pasadena, CA, 1980. 280p.
The Church of Uganda, Rwanda and Burundi: survey on administration and finance of the Church in Uganda. J. Bikangaga. Kampala, Uganda: Uganda Bookshop, 1969.
'The doctrine of God in Ruanda–Urundi,' R. Guillebaud, in *African ideas of God: a symposium*, p.180–200. E. Smith (ed). London: Edinburgh House Press, 1950.
Une réflexion théologique sur les données de la religion traditionnelle du Rwanda et du Burundi. B. Muzungu. , [1975].

Country Table 2. **Organized churches and denominations in Burundi.**

Official name (bold type = church with over 10% of all affiliated) 1	*Begun* 2	*Type* 3	*Counc* 4	*Congs* 5	*Adults* 6	*Affiliated 1970* 7	*Affiliated 1995* 8	*G%* 9	*Names, notes, and other statistics* (see Codebook, Part 3) 10
Assemblée Evangélique		I-Eva	.....	5	500	–	909	0.05	*Evangelical Fellowship.*
Assemblées des Frères	1938	P-CBr	x...k	44	3,000	2,000	4,000	2.81	*Open Brethren.* From Zaire; M=WGT,CMML(USA, UK), Immanuel Mission (Zaire). 5m,5f,1h.
Assemblée Pentecôtiste Ev d'Afrique	c1950	P-Pe2	.....	75	9,000	7,400	18,000	3.62	*Pentecostal Evangelical Fellowship of Africa.* Elim. M=PEFA(Kenya, Tanzania).
Comm des Eglises de Pentecôte au B	1935	P-Pe2	Z...k	2,267	270,000	90,000	425,000	6.41	*CEPBU (formerly ADEEP). Chs of Pentecost.* M=SFM. 330n,2300 evangelists, 3p, 24400Y.
Eglise Adventiste du Septième Jour	1921	P-Adv	x....	81	23,969	20,000	43,600	3.17	*Seventh-day Adventists, E&W Burundi Fields.* 21n,4x,6f,1s,88t(18847),W=90%,1229Y.
Eglise Catholique au Burundi:	1879	R-Lat	P.S.P	115	2,048,700	2,107,500	3,594,126	2.16	*Catholic Ch.* C=9+6+30. 3p,1s(51). 250n 76x 227m 840w 113549Yy
M Gitega (Kitega)	1912	R-Lat	Pwf	23	441,000	579,200	773,678	1.16	84% Hutu. Rwandan refugee camp at Mugera. M=WF. 50n 12x 57m 227w 24488Yy
D Bubanza	1980	R-Lat	P	8	158,500	–	278,122	6.67	Formed out of D Bujumbura. 15n 3x 8m 44w 9877Yy
D Bujumbura	1959	R-Lat	Ps	22	462,300	517,000	811,000	1.82	Northwest. Only urban centre in nation. 1p,1s. 66n 29x 93m 217w 22874Yy
D Bururi	1961	R-Lat	Pwf	15	159,000	196,000	278,895	1.42	Extreme south. Rundi, 1% Bembe and Fulero. 31n 1x 7m 66w 9718Yy
D Muyinga	1968	R-Lat	Ps	13	243,100	288,200	426,468	1.58	Formed out of D Ngozi. Impoverished. 28n 15x 23m 94w 14427Yy
D Ngozi	1949	R-Lat	Ps	17	419,400	527,100	735,783	1.34	North centre. Highest population density. 2p. 37n 10x 25m 128w 21329Yy
D Ruyigi	1973	R-Lat	P	17	165,400	–	290,180	4.55	Formed out of M Gitega and D Bururi. 23n 6x 14m 64w 10836Yy
Eglise de Dieu		P-Pe3	.....	10	1,800	–	3,270	0.05	Church of God. M=CoG(Cleveland) USA.
Eglise de Dieu au Burundi	1962	I-Ang	.....	14	700	1,000	1,400	1.35	*Ch of God. Kinamaites.* Schism of 20,000 ex EAB(RCMS). 1966, suppressed.
Eglise Emmanuel		P-Hol	.....	33	5,000	4,200	10,000	0.05	*Emmanuel Church.*
Eglise Evangélique des Amis	1932	P-Qua	QF..K	60	6,500	4,000	9,500	3.52	*Burundi Quarterly Mtg.* M=Friends Africa Gospel Mission (Kansas YM). 20f,1H,3h,1s,225Y.
Eglise Evangélique Episcopale	1938	P-Hol	xF..K	160	20,000	2,000	40,000	12.73	*EEE,EEM.* M=World Gospel Mission (USA). East and southeast. Hutu. 30f,1H,3h,1j,1k,1p.
Eglise Kimbanguiste	c1968	I-3pA	xWi..	35	7,000	500	14,000	14.26	M=EJCSK. Mission from Kinshasa (Zaire).
Eglise Neo-Apostolique		I-3aX	x....	6	400	–	748	0.05	*NAC. New Apostolic Ch.* M=Neuapostolische Kirche (HQ Zurich, Switzerland).
Eglise Orthodoxe: AD Afrique Centrale	1958	O-Gre	CW...	6	500	1,000	1,000	0.00	*Orthodox Ch.* Under Greek P Alexandria (Egypt). Greek traders. 1 school. 2x.
Eglise Pentecôtiste Sanctité		P-Pe3	Z....	1	50	–	100	0.05	*International Pentecostal Holiness Church.* M=IPHC.
Egl Protestante Episcopale du Burundi	1934	A-Low	AwAVK	1,621	148,600	45,000	443,000	9.58	*EAB. Province of Burundi* (4 Dioceses). M=MAM-RCMS(UK). 92n,3x,31f,3H,3421Yy.
Eglise Unie du Saint-Esprit	1993	I-3pA	.....	20	2,000	–	4,000	50.00	*EUSE. United Church of the Holy Spirit.* Members from older Pentecostal bodies.
Eglise Vivante	c1995	I-3oA	.....	10	1,000	–	3,000	20.00	*EV. Living Church.* 'Jesus Only' doctrines. Mostly members ex CEPBU.
Fraternité de la Communauté de Christ		I-3cA	.....	10	1,000	–	2,000	0.05	Brotherhood of Christ Community.
Témoins de Jéhovah	c1960	m-Jeh	x....	50	450	100	804	8.70	*Jehovah's Witnesses. Watch Tower. IBSA.* First activity reported 1964. 15Y.
Union des Eglises Baptistes du Burundi	1911	P-Bap	T.A.K	87	32,527	6,000	40,400	7.93	*UEBB/Baptist Union.* 1911, Germans; 1928, M=DBM,FMB-SBC. 95% Hutu. 670m,1H,1r,223Y.
Union des Eglises Méthodistes	1935	P-Hol	VPA.K	244	37,298	10,000	70,000	8.09	*ELMB.* M=Free Methodist Ch (USA). 92% Rundi, 7% Bembe.
Other Protestant denominations		P-	.....	40	3,000	1,000	5,000	0.05	Total about 10 small denominations from neighboring countries.
Totals				**4,994**	**2,619,997**	**2,301,700**	**4,726,864**		

Churches, members, growth, 1900-2025	*Congs*	*Adults*	*Affiliated*	*G%*	*Total denominations*	*6 Megablocs: O*	*R*	*A*	*P*	*I*	*m*
Total churches, members, and denominations (mid-1900)	1	19	34	17.22	1	0	1	0	0	0	0
Total churches, members, and denominations (mid-1970)	2,039	1,293,570	2,301,700	17.22	19	1	1	1	13	2	1
Total churches, members, and denominations (mid-1990)	4,100	2,299,000	4,148,200	2.99	32	1	1	1	21	7	1
Total churches, members, and denominations (mid-1995)	4,994	2,619,997	4,726,864	2.65	32	1	1	1	21	7	1
Total churches, members, and denominations (mid-2000)	5,100	2,856,000	5,152,841	1.74	34	1	1	1	22	8	1
Total churches, members, and denominations (mid-2025)	7,900	5,141,000	9,274,500	2.38	65	1	1	1	31	30	1

NOTES ON TABLE ABOVE
NATIONAL COUNCILS (Column 4, 5th letter).
E = Evangelical Fellowship of Burundi.
K = Conseil National des Eglises du Burundi (CNEB, National Council of Churches of Burundi).
k = associated with AEPB for educational matters.
R = Conférence des Evêques Catholiques du Burundi (CECAB, Catholic Bishops' Conference of Burundi).

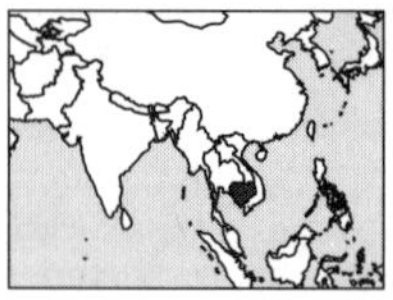

CAMBODIA

SECULAR DATA, AD 2000

STATE
Official name: Preah Reach Ana Pak Kampuchea (The Kingdom of Cambodia).
Short name: Cambodia. **Adjective of nationality:** Cambodian.
Flag: Red field with Angkor Wat pagoda in yellow.
Area: 181,916 sq. km. (70,238 sq. mi.).
Government: Constitutional monarchy with one legislative house, since 1993 (1863 French protectorate, 1947 constitutional monarchy, 1953 Independence, 1970 Khmer Republic, 1975 Communist state).
Legislature: National Assembly, 120 members.
Official language: Khmer.
Monetary unit: 1 riel = 100 sen. **US$1=** 3,800 riels.
Chief cities: PHNUM-PENH (Phnom Penh) 629,008; Batdambang 124,271; Siemreab 100,607; Kampong Saom 88,784; Sisophon 88,243.
Political divisions: 20 provinces.
Armed forces: 140,000.

DEMOGRAPHY
Population: 11,168,000.
Population density: 61.3/sq. km. (159.0/sq. mi.).
Under 15 years: 4,564,000.
Growth rate p.a.: 1.77% (births 29.66, deaths 12.00).
Mortality: Infant, per 1,000: 92.1; **Maternal per 100,000:** 900.0.
Life expectancy: 54 (male 52, female 56).
Household size: 5.6. **Floor area per person, sq.m:** 4.0.
Major languages: Khmer, French, Chinese, Vietnamese, Cham, Malay, Brao, Kui, Mnong, Pear, and numerous others.
Urban dwellers: 23.48%. **Urban growth rate p.a.:** 4.4%.
Labor force: 43%.

ETHNOLINGUISTIC PEOPLES
85.1% Central Khmer (Cambodian); 3.0% Vietnamese (Annamese); 2.5% Han Chinese (Teochew); 2.4% Western Cham (Cambodian); 2.0% Han Chinese (Cantonese).

ECONOMY
National income p.a. per person: US$269; **per family:** US$1,511.

EDUCATION
Adult literacy: 66% (male 79%, female 53%). **Schools:** 5,044.
Universities: 9. **School enrolment:** female/male: 65%/84%.

HEALTH
Access to health services: 53%. **Access to safe water:** 13%.
Hospitals: 188 (16 beds per 10,000). **Doctors:** 600.
Blind: 40,000. **Deaf:** 672,400. **Murder rate:** 70.
Lepers: 47,000. **Underweight prevalence under 5:** 40%.

LITERATURE
New book titles p.a.: 340 (30 p.a. per million). **Periodicals:** 4.
Newspapers: 2 dailies.

COMMUNICATION (per 1,000 people)
Phones: 1 (71% mobile). **Radios:** 150. **TV sets:** 8.
Daily newspaper circulation: 5. **Computers:** 1.

REFUGEES
Citizen refugees in other countries: 26,300.
Internal displacement: 55,000.

Country status. Cambodia lies in the southeastern part of the Indo-Chinese Peninsula on the Gulf of Thailand surrounded by Thailand, Laos, and Vietnam. The economy is based on the staple crop, rice. The country's history is one of the most tragic in all of modern history, Cambodia having been subjected to continuous civil strife and foreign invasion since the end of French colonial rule.

HUMAN LIFE AND LIBERTY

Human need and development. Between 1975 and 1979 when the Khmer Rouge held power in Cambodia, it compiled one of the worst human rights

Country Table 1. **Religious adherents in Cambodia, AD 1900-2025.**

Year / Name	1900 Adherents	1900 %	1970 Adherents	1970 %	mid-1990 Adherents	mid-1990 %	Annual change, 1990-2000 Natural	Conversion	Total	Rate	mid-1995 Adherents	mid-1995 %	mid-2000 Adherents	mid-2000 %	mid-2025 Adherents	mid-2025 %
Buddhists	2,137,590	85.5	6,038,131	87.0	7,283,800	84.2	211,784	5,989	217,773	2.65	8,447,880	84.6	9,461,526	84.7	13,988,900	84.7
Chinese folk-religionists	100,000	4.0	141,000	2.0	410,000	4.7	11,923	-508	11,415	2.49	470,000	4.7	524,153	4.7	750,000	4.5
Ethnoreligionists	175,000	7.0	250,000	3.6	430,000	5.0	12,504	-6,958	5,546	1.22	455,000	4.6	485,458	4.4	600,000	3.6
Nonreligious	100	0.0	150,000	2.2	200,000	2.3	5,816	509	6,325	2.79	234,000	2.3	263,249	2.4	470,000	2.8
Muslims	50,000	2.0	170,000	2.5	200,000	2.3	5,816	56	5,872	2.61	232,000	2.3	258,715	2.3	420,000	2.5
Christians	**37,310**	**1.5**	**35,269**	**0.5**	**72,200**	**0.8**	**2,100**	**2,540**	**4,640**	**5.09**	**91,020**	**0.9**	**118,600**	**1.1**	**231,100**	**1.4**
PROFESSION																
crypto-Christians	7,310	0.3	12,270	0.2	22,000	0.3	640	-1,040	-400	-1.99	20,000	0.2	18,000	0.2	10,000	0.1
professing Christians	**30,000**	**1.2**	**22,999**	**0.3**	**50,200**	**0.6**	**1,460**	**3,580**	**5,040**	**7.20**	**71,020**	**0.7**	**100,600**	**0.9**	**221,100**	**1.3**
AFFILIATION																
unaffiliated Christians	0	0.0	440	0.0	100	0.0	3	7	10	7.28	117	0.0	202	0.0	1,000	0.0
affiliated Christians	**37,310**	**1.5**	**34,829**	**0.5**	**72,100**	**0.8**	**2,097**	**2,533**	**4,630**	**5.09**	**90,903**	**0.9**	**118,398**	**1.1**	**230,100**	**1.4**
Independents	0	0.0	2,200	0.0	42,500	0.5	1,236	1,985	3,221	5.80	55,750	0.6	74,708	0.7	139,500	0.8
Roman Catholics	37,310	1.5	20,069	0.3	15,000	0.2	436	264	700	3.90	17,900	0.2	22,000	0.2	45,000	0.3
Protestants	0	0.0	12,360	0.2	14,500	0.2	422	278	700	4.02	17,120	0.2	21,500	0.2	45,000	0.3
Marginal Christians	0	0.0	0	0.0	70	0.0	2	6	8	7.92	100	0.0	150	0.0	500	0.0
Anglicans	0	0.0	200	0.0	30	0.0	1	0	1	2.92	33	0.0	40	0.0	100	0.0
Trans-megabloc groupings																
Evangelicals	0	0.0	12,000	0.2	14,800	0.2	430	90	520	3.06	17,233	0.2	20,000	0.2	40,000	0.2
Pentecostals/Charismatics	0	0.0	2,000	0.0	40,000	0.5	1,163	437	1,600	3.42	47,948	0.5	56,000	0.5	120,000	0.7
Great Commission Christians	**30,000**	**1.2**	**30,000**	**0.4**	**67,000**	**0.8**	**1,948**	**1,690**	**3,638**	**4.43**	**85,000**	**0.9**	**103,375**	**0.9**	**210,000**	**1.3**
New-Religionists	0	0.0	100,000	1.4	36,000	0.4	1,047	-1,185	-138	-0.39	33,000	0.3	34,620	0.3	36,000	0.2
Hindus	0	0.0	1,000	0.0	20,000	0.2	582	289	871	3.68	24,500	0.3	28,713	0.3	60,000	0.4
Atheists	0	0.0	30,000	0.4	25,000	0.3	727	-489	238	0.91	25,400	0.3	27,382	0.3	30,000	0.2
Baha'is	0	0.0	22,600	0.3	11,000	0.1	320	-134	186	1.58	11,700	0.1	12,862	0.1	15,000	0.1
doubly-counted religionists	0	0.0	0	0.0	-36,000	-0.4	-1,047	-109	-1,156	2.82	-42,500	-0.4	-47,558	-0.4	-75,000	-0.5
World A (unevangelized persons)	2,325,000	93.0	5,203,500	75.0	5,364,240	62.0	155,956	-123,800	32,156	0.58	5,500,110	55.1	5,684,512	50.9	6,494,718	39.3
World B (evangelized non-Christians)	137,690	5.5	1,699,231	24.5	3,215,560	37.2	93,516	121,260	214,776	5.25	4,390,920	44.0	5,364,888	48.0	9,800,182	59.3
World C (Christians)	37,310	1.5	35,269	0.5	72,200	0.8	2,100	2,540	4,640	5.09	91,020	0.9	118,600	1.1	231,100	1.4
Country's population	**2,500,000**	**100.0**	**6,938,000**	**100.0**	**8,652,000**	**100.0**	**251,572**	**0**	**251,572**	**2.59**	**9,982,051**	**100.0**	**11,168,000**	**100.0**	**16,526,000**	**100.0**

COLUMNS, ROWS.
For meanings and definitions, see Codebook (Part 3). Note that, by definition, total 'Christians' = professing + crypto-Christians, which also = affiliated + unaffiliated Christians, and also = Great Commission Christians + latent Christians. Percentages may not always total exactly, due to rounding.

NOTES ON RELIGIONS
ATHEISTS. People's Party (Pracheachon) (forced underground in 1962): also Cambodian People's Revolutionary Party (PRP) and Khmer Rouge.
BAHA'IS. Very rapid growth from 1 local spiritual assembly (1964) to 151 (1973), with 425 other isolated centers or groups. Many Vietnamese before 1974; but after the years of civil war and genocide, in 1996 there were only 20 LSAs remaining.
BUDDHISTS. Theravada (Hinayana, Little Vehicle), with 2 main religious orders: the aristocratic Thommayutt (Order of the Law), and Mohanikay (Great Order). Mainly Khmers with over 200,000 Chinese, also Vietnamese, Lao and others. From 1970-71, Communists destroyed 208 Buddhist temples and killed 40 monks; losses up to 1995 are far higher.
CRYPTO-CHRISTIANS. Christians affiliated to churches but unknown as such to state or society.
ETHNORELIGIONISTS. Animists among the Montagnard tribes (Khmer-Loeu, i.e. Upland Khmer) of the northeast adjoining the Laos border, including the Mnong, Brao, Stieng and Kui.
INDEPENDENTS. Chinese and Cambodian indigenous congregations and groups, mostly isolated radio believers (see Table 2).
MUSLIMS. Sunnis (of the Shafiite rite); mainly among the Cham-Malays (known as Khmer Islam) along the Mekong river.
NEW-RELIGIONISTS. Vietnamese followers of the Cao Daist syncretistic religion, mainly in Phnom Penh, Siem Reap and on the shores of the Tonlé´Sap lake.
NONRELIGIOUS. In the year 1900, French and other expatriates; by 1995, mostly Chinese.
ROMAN CATHOLICS. In the year 1900, 36,107 baptized Catholics and 1,200 catechumens. During the year 1970, Catholics fell from 60,000 to 20,000 by the expulsion or deaths in war of 40,000 Vietnamese Catholics, and continued to decline by 1,200 a year over the following 3 or 4 years.

Great Commission Instrument Panel: status of Cambodia (for explanation see start of Part 4)

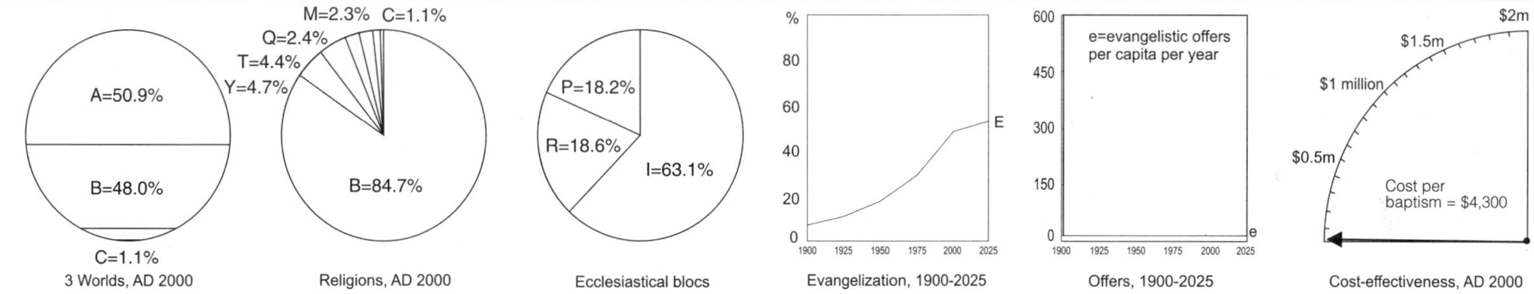

violations record of any modern government as a result of its brutal attempt to restructure Cambodian society. More than 2 million people out of a total of 7 million died during the process which ended only when the Vietnamese army invaded Cambodia and set up a puppet government. Although the excesses of the Khmer Jacobins were not repeated by the puppet regime, it maintained itself in power for the next 14 years through terror and mass repression. The result was that Cambodia almost ceased to exist as a nation. The monetary, education, industrial, agricultural, trade, transportation and other systems were in shambles and only through seeking refuge in Thailand or through illegal means were most Khmer able to survive. Hospitals were abandoned as their doctors were displaced. Whole towns disappeared as their inhabitants were forcibly relocated under Pot Pol.

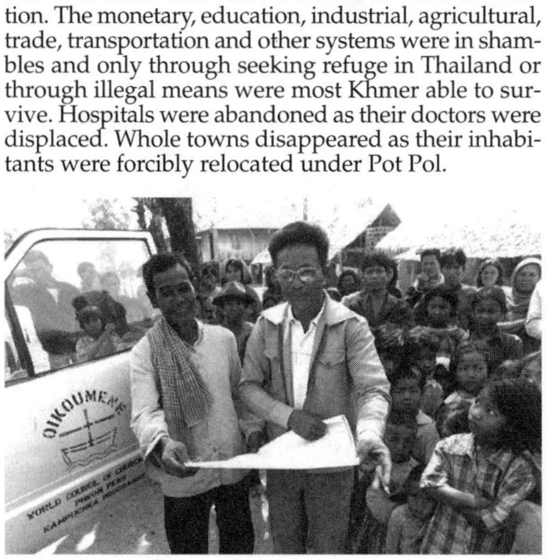

Agriculturalists lay plans for aid to village south of capital.

Human rights and freedoms. Cambodia has not known full human freedom since the establishment of the Khmer Rouge regime and the subsequent Vietnamese invasion. Civil society virtually ceased to exist as Pol Pot and his band embarked on their experiment to convert the nation into a slaughterhouse. In the areas controlled by the Phnom Penh regime, thousands remain in jail and the freedoms of the press, speech, association, and religion are largely absent. In the areas controlled by the Khmer Rouge rebels, executions and disappearances of political foes were common. Prisoners were subjected to inhuman treatment and physical abuse as well as torture. In the absence of a clearly defined legal structure, the interior ministry remained a law unto itself and exercised arbitrary power. All arrested suspects were sentenced irrespective of their guilt or innocence, and those charged with cooperation with the resistance were summarily incarcerated. Civilians were subject to extensive surveillance by an extensive network of informers. The militia and soldiers regularly extorted money from travelers. Mail was censored. Official permission is required for all marriages, and such permission may be withheld. The press and radio are still somewhat under official control and publications that 'do not express reality properly' are shut down. The only associations permitted to operate are those created to support the regime, and these are generally headed by ranking party or regime officials. In 1990 it was reported that there were over 1 million Vietnamese settlers in the country enjoying a privileged status. With the departure of Vietnamese troops many of them have left but the scars of their occupation remain.

Human environment. The environmental consequences of the pillage of Cambodia under the Khmer Rouge and the Vietnamese satellite regime are still felt. Largescale shifts of population have resulted in damage to the forests on the Annamite mountain range, loss of approximately three-fourths of wild life habitat and half of the wetlands, and destruction of the coastal mangrove swamps.

NON-CHRISTIAN RELIGIONS

Theravada Buddhism (or Hinayana) has been the predominant religion of Cambodia since the 14th century. There are 2 main religious orders whose doctrine and rules are similar: the Thommayutt (Order of the Law) which is by nature aristocratic, with 104 monasteries and 2,053 monks; and the Mohanikay (Great order), having wider support, with 2,722 monasteries and 66,092 monks. Buddhism has always played an important social role, with the clergy exercising an intermediary function between government and people. The majority of Cambodian boys at age 12 serve a period of several weeks in a monastery in order to learn Buddhism's main precepts and, when adult, often return for retreats. Annexed to the monasteries is a vast primary school network, in addition to the Buddhist lyceum and university in Phnom Penh. A hereditary caste of Brahmans, called Bakou, a witness to the survival of Brahmanic influence in Buddhism, exercised an important function among officials at the royal palace of former regimes.

Traditional tribal religion continues to exist among the Montagnard tribes (Khmer-Loeu) of the northeast

Country Summary. **Worlds A, B, C by ethnolinguistic peoples, cities, and major civil divisions in Cambodia.**

	PEOPLES	CITIES										CIVIL DIVISIONS										
World	Num	Pop 2000	C%	Christians	E%	U%	Unevangelized	Num	Pop 2000	C%	Christians	E%	U%	Unevangelized	Num	Pop 2000	C%	Christians	E%	U%	Unevangelized
A	25	10,032,116	0.68	68,604	47	53	5,267,374	5	456,472	0.37	1,692	46	54	247,734	13	7,555,087	0.53	40,258	47	53	3,985,263
B	10	1,131,136	4.10	46,335	63	37	418,178	1	629,008	2.30	14,467	52	48	301,106	7	3,612,633	2.16	78,140	53	47	1,700,301
C	2	4,467	77.50	3,462	100	0	10	0	0	0.00	0	0	0	0	0	0	0.00	0	0	0	0
Total	**37**	**11,167,719**	**1.06**	**118,401**	**49**	**51**	**5,685,562**	**6**	**1,085,480**	**1.49**	**16,159**	**49**	**51**	**548,840**	**20**	**11,167,720**	**1.06**	**118,398**	**49**	**51**	**5,685,564**

near the border with Laos, including the Mnong, Brao, Stieng, and Kui.

Islam was first introduced by Malays in 1550. Cambodian Muslims are Sunnis of the Shafite rite. Although strongest among the Cham-Malays who are descended from the people of the ancient kingdom of Cahmpa and who continue to perform its rites in Malay, Islam is fully integrated in Khmer society.

It is strongest along the banks of the Mekong river and its affluents, in the province of Kompong-Cham and the region of Phnom Penh, as well as at Battambang and Kampot. In addition to an active Muslim religious life, there are numerous Quranic schools.

Cao Dai, a syncretistic new religion composed of Buddhist, Christian and animistic elements, existed among the Vietnamese, especially at Phnom Penh, Siem Reap and along the banks of Lake Tonle Sap, until April 1970 when many were deported. Subsequently Cao Dai regained government favor.

Independents. Sunday worship in house church in Phnom Penh.

CHRISTIANITY

Evangelization began with the arrival of Jesuits and Dominicans in 1555, but permanent stations were not opened until the 17th century. By 1842, there were only 4 churches and 222 Catholics. The apostolic prefecture of Cambodia (Phnom Penh) was erected in 1850, and the territory was elevated to the rank of vicariate in 1924. Protestants began work in the country only after World War I.

CATHOLIC CHURCH. The events of 1970 and 1975 profoundly changed the situation of the Catholic church in Cambodia. In 1969, the church reported 62,000 baptized members, of which 55,000 (88%) were Vietnamese, 3,000 Khmers, 2,000 Chinese and 2,000 Europeans. The clergy were predominantly French (58) and Vietnamese (16), with only 5 Khmer priests out of 80, one of whom was resident in Paris. There was also one Chinese priest. The 4 Khmer priests resident in the country included a bishop (the Franco-Khmer apostolic prefect of Battambang), an OSB priest and 2 secular priests. Although the first ordination of a Vietnamese priest in Cambodia took place in 1888, the first Khmer was not ordained until 1957. Between 1888 and 1870, 163 local priests were ordained, 156 being Vietnamese, 5 Khmers and 2 Chinese. Of those enrolled in the major seminary of Phnom Penh in 1970, six were Vietnamese, 2 Laotians and one Khmer. There were also 2 training centers for catechists, one for Khmers and the other for Vietnamese. Other religious personnel included 27 Vietnamese and 2 Khmer brothers and 266 sisters (183 Europeans, 75 Vietnamese and 8 Khmers). In addition, the church maintained 50 primary and 4 secondary schools, 2 hospitals, a dispensary, 2 day nurseries, an orphanage, a home for the destitute, a training center for girls, a hostel for students, a co-operative and a community center.

The Catholic Church was primarily the church of the Vietnamese and Europeans and was little integrated into Khmer society. The languages commonly in use in the church were French and Vietnamese, only 14 priests being capable of preaching in Khmer. Catholic Vietnamese with Khmer citizenship were little integrated into Cambodian society and tended to form so-called Catholic villages along the Mekong river and its tributaries. In addition, the majority of Khmer Catholics were descendants of mixed Khmer-Portuguese and Khmer-Spanish people whose origins go back to the 17th century. Only a few Catholics were Khmers in the full sense of the term. The episcopate was slow in expressing concern about the situation, its joint pastoral letter of 3 September 1969, being the first serious attempt to call for the integration of the church into Khmer society. This letter was followed by a conference on missionary pastoralia conducted by the French sociologist canon Boulard, which proved to be the most important event in the life of the Cambodian Catholic church during this period.

Given Catholicism's particularly vulnerable situation in Cambodia, the anti-Vietnamese campaign which followed the coup d'etat of March 1970 by the Lon Nol faction proved to be a disaster for the church. In April 1970, thousands of resident Vietnamese were massacred and Catholic villages were among the first attacked. About 40,000 Catholics were killed while others escaped to Viet Nam. Missionaries were also involved; 5 were killed and a sixth disappeared in the area held by the Communist revolutionaries. Several churches in Phnom Penh were set on fire, and the new regime closed all private schools, which were for the most part Catholic and frequented by Vietnamese. Many MEP missionaries followed their members into South Viet Nam, to which also local Vietnamese feminine congregations fled en masse. Social and medical institutions and programs were severely restricted or completely abandoned although some were begun again later. Only the infirmary of the Chruy Changvar community center continued to function normally. The major seminary of Phnom Penh was also closed, due to a lack of Khmer students and was turned into a transit center for Vietnamese refugees. At the end of 1970, there remained in Cambodia only about 20,000 Catholics, 29 priests (12 Vietnamese and 4 Khmers, the rest being missionaries), 3 brothers and 54 sisters. Three years later, official statistics showed a decline to 16,835 Catholics, with 29 priests, 3 brothers and 68 sisters. The only priests left in the prefecture of Kompong Cham was the apostolic vicar, a Frenchman, while 2 (a Khmer, the apostolic vicar; and a French missionary) remained in the prefecture of Battambang. The figure of 16,835 also included Catholics living in liberated zones who had no contact with the rest of the church, as well as Khmers in the republican zone who chose after 1970 to keep their distance from a religion which they considered too Vietnamese. In 1974, another Khmer was ordained priest; and on 15 April 1975, (2 days before the fall of the capital), a Khmer priest was consecrated bishop of the vicariate of Phnom Penh.

On 17 April 1975, when Phnom Penh fell, the situation of the Catholic Church was as follows: (1) the prefecture of Kompong Cham had no religious personnel, although a few hundred Catholics remained; (2) the prefecture of Battambang had a Khmer bishop, a French OSB priest, a Khmer and 4 Vietnamese sisters and about 2,000 Vietnamese and Khmer Catholics; and (3) the vicariate of Phnom Penh had one Khmer and 2 French bishops, 3 Khmer and 10 French priests, 2 Khmer OSB brothers and five Khmer and 4 French sisters. Shortly after taking the city, the revolutionaries expelled all Europeans including religious personnel, while Khmer and Vietnamese were forced out of the cities into the countryside. Khmer bishops and priests were generally involved in leading Catholic groups during the exodus. In the whole of Cambodia, including zones held for a long time by the Communists, the Catholic population at the end of May 1975 was estimated to be not more than 15,000 widely dispersed.

The change from this chaotic historical situation to today's stable picture is illustrated by Country Table 2 below. Once again churches are thriving and growing.

The Holy See has diplomatic relations with Cambodia and in AD 2000 is represented to government and the Catholic hierarchy by a nuncio residing in Bangkok.

PROTESTANT CHURCHES. Protestant work in Cambodia has also suffered from the political events of the last decade. The major Protestant denomination in the country is the Eglise Evangelique Khmere which was created through the work of the Christian Missionary Alliance. Since its origins in 1922, the CMA has been strongest in the Phnom Penh area, while also gradually spreading its influence to other parts of the country. In addition to its work among Cambodians, Chinese, and Vietnamese, the church has opened work among the Mnong Biet and Kuoy (Kui) tribes of northeastern Cambodia. By 1964, it had established 13 churches in 9 of the 17 provinces. In 1961, it invited the Far Eastern Gospel Crusade to pioneer work in eastern Cambodia; but due to anti-American feeling, all missionaries except for one French couple were withdrawn in 1965. Because of a broader base among Cambodians, rather than Vietnamese, Protestants were not adversely affected by the events of 1970 and registered phenomenal membership growth during the early part of the decade.

Indeed, American CMA missionaries were allowed to return in 1970 and, during 1970-75 they were extensively involved in relief work as well as evangelistic activities. As with the Catholics, all foreign Protestant religious personnel were evacuated again in 1975. Prior to 1975, Cambodia's small Seventh-day Adventist Church was served by an Indonesian missionary.

During the massacres under the Pol Pot regime, it would have been difficult to foresee the remarkable recovery that the churches have experienced. Yet by 1997 they were again growing markedly.

Indigenous missions. The Cambodian church is only beginning to emerge from the 2 decades of oppression and violence. Nonetheless there have been attempts to evangelize the neighboring Vietnamese. The Khmer Christian diaspora is also involved in evangelistic efforts in the homeland.

Independents. Fellowship meal after Sunday service in house churches.

CHURCH AND STATE

The royal constitution of May 1947, which was further modified in January 1956, remained in effect until the coup d'etat of 18 March 1970. It proclaimed Buddhism the state religion and assured freedom of religion for all (Article 8). The Ministry of Religion (Krasuong Thommaka) dealt with all matters relating to religious observance, and leaders of the 2 Buddhist orders were nominated by the king. Higher clergy also participated in certain government activities. Buddhist monks were exempt from fiscal responsibilities and enjoyed other juridical privileges. The Ministry of Religion, working in close cooperation with the heads of the Buddhist orders, prepared legislation to cover religious matters and saw to its implementation. It organized and controlled Buddhist schools and provided lay diplomas for them. The king also nominated the supreme head of the Islamic community, and the Ministry of Religion controlled the appointment of mosque leaders (Hakem). Other religions were considered to be private affairs. The opening of new worship centers required the authorization (Prakas) of the Ministry of Religion, and any other acts of worship, beyond those of Catholics and Protestants, required the sanction of the king.

The republican government of Long Nol came to power in March 1970 and in its constitution of 30 April 1972, proclaimed Buddhism as the state religion. The government attempted to gain the support of Buddhist leaders and clergy through the Khmer Buddhist congress, but most monks remained faithful to prince Sihanouk. During this period, Sihanouk's revolutionary government-in-exile maintained a Ministry of Religion and continued to affirm its recognition of Buddhism as the state religion.

After the victory of the Communist forces on 17 April 1975, an important meeting was held in Phnom Penh (April 25-27) to define the major political policies of the new government. Among the 311 delegates were Buddhist monks representing the Buddhist clergy. The revolutionary government maintains a Ministry of Religious and Social Affairs, and the new authorities affirmed their desire to respect freedom of conscience and religion while insisting on the social role that the religions should play in the development of the country. This was also emphasized in the zones held by revolutionaries before the fall of Phnom Penh, where monks were forbidden to beg and instead were required to work. However, in practice, churches and religions have all suffered together in the reign of terror that followed in the next year, when an estimated 2 million persons were killed across the country.

The subsequent 2 decades have tended to be more favorable to Christians and Christian churches. These have now become stable and somewhat strong.

BROADCASTING AND MEDIA

IBRA-produced programs can be heard on local radio channels. Shortwave programs in Khmer are received from FEBC (Philippines).

Some 170,000 people (2%) have seen the 'Jesus' film, mostly through film team presentations.

INTERDENOMINATIONAL ORGANIZATIONS

Missions today cooperate more than in the past, with several strategic alliances under way.

FUTURE TRENDS AND PROSPECTS

The influx of Cambodian Christian refugees from abroad strengthened the existing church in the aftermath of Pol Pot and Vietnamese rule. Christians, 0.5% in 1970 are expected to nearly triple to 1.4% by AD 2025. After rising to 88% in 1975, Buddhists will probably decline to less than 85% by 2025.

If Christian growth is strong into the middle of the 21st century, Cambodia could be 3% Christian by 2050. Losses would be experienced mainly by Buddhists.

BIBLIOGRAPHY

1972 Mission directory of Thailand, Cambodia and Laos. B. Bray (ed). Bangkok: Newsasia, 1972.

'Cambodia: Buddha's burden,' R. Norton, *Far Eastern economic review,* (May 1971).

'Cambodia recognises the Christian church,' F. Corley, *Religion in Communist lands,* 18, 4 (Winter 1990), 363–364.

'Church and State in Cambodia,' J. C. Haughley, *America,* (October 1971).

Ethnic groups of French Indochina. L. Malleret. Washington, DC: US Joint Publications Research Service, 1962. 110p. (Translation of 1937 French edition).

'Foi Chrétienne et culture Bouddhiste au Cambodge: interview by G. Baguet,' F. Ponchaud, in *Le Christ et les cultures,* p.179–190. G. Langevin & R. Pirro (eds). Montreal: Bellarmin, 1991.

Killing fields, living fields: an unfinished portrait of the Cambodian church. D. Cormack. London: Monarch, 1998.

Les êtres surnaturels dans la religion populaire khmère. Ang Chouléan. Paris: Cedorek, 1986. 369p.

'New translation, new beginning: Christians in Cambodia,' R. L. Omanson, *Touchstone,* 12 (January 1994), 13–15. (Reprint from Christian Century 110 (November 3, 1993):1079-1080).

The Buddhism of Cambodia. A. Leclère. [New Haven, CT]: Human Relations Area Files, 1956. 204p. (Translation of books VII-X of *Le Buddhisme au Cambodge*. Paris, E. Leroux, 1899).

The Devaroaja cult. H. Kulke. Ithaca, NY: Southeast Asia Program, Dept. of Asian Studies, Cornell University, 1978. 68p.

'The way of the monk and the way of the world: Buddhism in Thailand, Laos and Cambodia,' J. Bunnag, in *The world of Buddhism: Buddhist monks and nuns in society and culture,* p.159–70. H. Bechert & R. Gombrich (eds). London: Thames & Hudson, 1984.

Country Table 2. **Organized churches and denominations in Cambodia.**

Official name (bold type = church with over 10% of all affiliated) 1	*Begun* 2	*Type* 3	*Counc* 4	*Congs* 5	*Adults* 6	*Affiliated 1970* 7	*Affiliated 1995* 8	*G%* 9	*Names, notes, and other statistics* (see Codebook, Part 3) 10
Assemblées de Dieu	1990	P-Pe2	.....	12	758	–	1,000	20.00	*Assemblies of God.* M=AoG(USA). Influential, strong, growing.
Association Baptiste du Cambodge	c1980	P-Bap	T....	45	1,500	–	3,000	6.67	*Baptist Association of Cambodia.* M=FMB-SBC/CSI.
Congrégations Chinoises indépendantes		I-Hol	.....	3	200	200	500	0.05	Independent congregations of Chinese, of CMA origin. Holiness doctrines.
Eglise Adventiste du Septième Jour	c1937	P-Adv	x....	1	50	200	100	-2.73	*SDA Seventh-day Adventists*, Southeast Asia Union Mission. 8f.
Eglise Anglicane (D Singapore)		A-Cen	awaA.	1	20	200	33	0.05	*Anglican Church. Trinity Congregation*, Phnom Penh. 60% USA, 40% British. W=27%.
Eglise Catholique au Cambodge:	1555	R-Lat	P.F.P	15	9,630	20,069	17,900	-0.46	*Catholic Ch.* C=2+0=1. Vietnamese, 3,000 Khmer. 3n 18x 22m 51w 486Yy
VA Phnom-Pénh (Phnum Penh)	1850	R-Lat	Pmep	2	5,380	6,569	10,000	1.70	50% Vietnamese, 30% Europeans, 15% Chinese. 1n 15x 17m 27w 0Yy
PA Battambang	1968	R-Lat	Ps	12	2,420	4,500	4,500	0.00	Thailand border. 70% Vietnamese, 20% Khmer. 1n 2x 2m 14w 286Yy
PA Kompóng Cham	1968	R-Lat	Pmep	1	1,830	9,000	3,400	-3.82	Viet-Nam border; forest. 90% Vietnamese. M=MEP. 1n 1x 3m 10w 200Yy
Eglise Apostolique Nouvelle	1990	I-3aX	x....	3	1,200	–	3,000	20.00	*New Apostolic Ch.* HQ Switzerland. M=NAC(Khmer members), from Canada; 47,955 by 1995.
Eglise Evangélique Khmère	1922	P-Hol	xF...	55	5,500	9,560	9,560	0.00	*Khmer Ev Ch.* M=ACM(France),CMA(USA). Tenfold expansion, 1971-73. 13n,9f,1p,1s.
Eglises Evangéliques	1961	P-Eva	xM...	50	2,000	2,000	3,000	1.64	Begun by M=Far Eastern Gospel Crusade; left 1965. 1971, M=OMF, rapid growth.
Eglises radiophoniques isolées	1952	I-3rZ	.....	1,500	6,000	2,000	10,000	6.65	Isolated radio believers, mostly youths, across nation. R=50 (FEBC),S=2000 (CMA).
Hidden Buddhist believers in Christ	c1970	I-Bud	.....	400	20,000	–	36,000	52.14	Converted Buddhists who chose to remain in Buddhist structures.
Témoins de Jehovah	c1995	m-Jeh	.....	1	50	–	100	58.49	*Jehovah's Witnesses.* In capital. Aggressive witnessing. (1995) 3Y.
Unorganized local churches	1979	I-	.....	61	2,500	–	6,250	6.25	From earlier M=CMA work, refugees converted in Thailand; new ministry after 1990.
Other Protestant denominations	1965	P-	.....	3	230	600	460	-1.06	Small French and USA missions, mostly Pentecostal/charismatic. M=YWAM.
Totals				**2,150**	**49,638**	**34,829**	**90,903**		

Churches, members, growth, 1900-2025	*Congs*	*Adults*	*Affiliated*	*G%*	*Total denominations*	*6 Megablocs:* *O*	*R*	*A*	*P*	*I*	*m*
Total churches, members, and denominations (mid-1900)	1,000	20,200	37,310	-0.10	1	0	1	0	0	0	0
Total churches, members, and denominations (mid-1970)	626	18,850	34,829	-0.10	8	0	1	1	4	2	0
Total churches, members, and denominations (mid-1990)	1,900	39,400	72,100	3.71	18	0	1	1	12	4	0
Total churches, members, and denominations (mid-1995)	2,150	49,638	90,903	4.74	21	0	1	1	13	5	1
Total churches, members, and denominations (mid-2000)	2,300	64,700	118,398	5.43	23	0	1	1	14	6	1
Total churches, members, and denominations (mid-2025)	4,000	126,000	230,100	2.69	50	0	1	1	20	25	3

NOTES ON TABLE ABOVE
NATIONAL COUNCILS (Column 4, 5th letter).
E = Evangelical Fellowship of Cambodia (EFC).
P = Conférence Episcopale du Laos et du Cambodge (CELC).

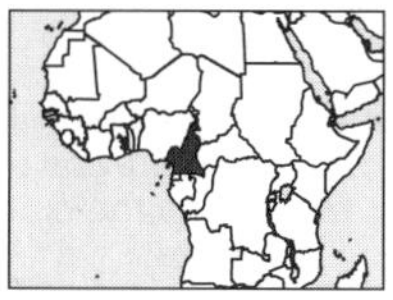

CAMEROON

SECULAR DATA, AD 2000

STATE

Official name: La République du Cameroun/The Republic of Cameroon.
Short name: Cameroon. **Adjective of nationality:** Cameroonian.
Flag: Tricolor of green, red, and yellow bars, centered yellow star.
Area: 475,442 sq. km. (183,569 sq. mi.).
Government: One-party republic, since 1960 (1884 German protectorate, 1918 under French and British, 1946 UN trust territory, 1960 Independence).
Legislature: National Assembly, 180 members.
Official language: French (Français) and English.
Monetary unit: 1 CFA franc (CFAF) = 100 centimes. **US$1=** CFAF 560.38.
Chief cities: Douala 1,672,000; YAOUNDE 1,446,000; Nkongsamba 182,891; Maroua 153,937; Garoua (Garua) 146,769.
Political divisions: 10 provinces.
Armed forces: 15,000.

DEMOGRAPHY

Population: 15,085,000.
Population density: 31.7/sq. km. (82.1/sq. mi.).
Under 15 years: 6,560,000.
Growth rate p.a.: 2.52% (births 37.75, deaths 12.59).
Mortality: Infant, per 1,000: 66.8; **Maternal per 100,000:** 550.0.
Life expectancy: 54 (male 53, female 55).
Household size: 5.2. **Floor area per person, sq.m:** 9.6.
Major languages: Bulu Fang, Bamileke, French, English, Douala, Pidgin English, Fulani, Hausa, and in addition over 180 other tribal languages.
Urban dwellers: 48.92%. **Urban growth rate p.a.:** 4.2%.
Labor force: 40%.

ETHNOLINGUISTIC PEOPLES

8.4% Adamawa Fulani (Fula); 8.1% Ewondo (Beti, Yaunde); 5.8% Cameroonian Creole; 4.0% Bulu Fang; 3.0% Bamileke-Bandjoun.

ECONOMY

National income p.a. per person: US$649; **per family:** US$3,379.

EDUCATION

Adult literacy: 63% (male 75%, female 52%). **Schools:** 6,763.
Universities: 5. **School enrolment:** female/male: 53%/63%.

HEALTH

Access to health services: 70%. **Access to safe water:** 41%.
Hospitals: 629 (27 beds per 10,000). **Doctors:** 945.
Blind: 15,630. **Deaf:** 907,700. **Murder rate:** 1.
Lepers: 200,000. **Underweight prevalence under 5:** 15%.

LITERATURE
New book titles p.a.: 2,560 (170 p.a. per million). **Periodicals:** 81. **Newspapers:** 1 daily.

COMMUNICATION (per 1,000 people)
Phones: 4 (5% mobile). **Radios:** 115. **TV sets:** 75. **Daily newspaper circulation:** 4. **Computers:** 2.

REFUGEES
Alien refugees from other countries: 2,000.

HUMAN LIFE AND LIBERTY (optimum condition=100.0%)
HDI: 46.8. **HSI:** 23.0. **HFI:** 20.0. **EFL:** 28.0.

Country Table 1. **Religious adherents in Cameroon, AD 1900-2025.**

Year	1900		1970		mid-1990		Annual change, 1990-2000				mid-1995		mid-2000		mid-2025	
Name	Adherents	%	Adherents	%	Adherents	%	Natural	Conversion	Total	Rate	Adherents	%	Adherents	%	Adherents	%
Christians	**9,500**	**0.4**	**3,136,600**	**47.4**	**6,038,000**	**52.6**	**190,160**	**23,406**	**213,566**	**3.07**	**7,010,000**	**53.2**	**8,173,659**	**54.2**	**16,043,000**	**60.6**
PROFESSION																
professing Christians	**9,500**	**0.4**	**3,136,600**	**47.4**	**6,038,000**	**52.6**	**190,160**	**23,406**	**213,566**	**3.07**	**7,010,000**	**53.2**	**8,173,659**	**54.2**	**16,043,000**	**60.6**
AFFILIATION																
unaffiliated Christians	1,780	0.1	745,225	11.3	483,800	4.2	15,236	-22,402	-7,164	-1.59	436,085	3.3	412,158	2.7	339,000	1.3
affiliated Christians	**7,720**	**0.3**	**2,391,375**	**36.2**	**5,554,200**	**48.4**	**174,924**	**45,806**	**220,730**	**3.40**	**6,573,915**	**49.9**	**7,761,501**	**51.5**	**15,704,000**	**59.3**
Roman Catholics	2,720	0.1	1,528,760	23.1	2,970,000	25.9	93,537	8,403	101,940	2.99	3,431,074	26.0	3,989,401	26.5	7,600,000	28.7
Protestants	4,000	0.2	717,215	10.8	2,140,000	18.7	67,397	30,603	98,000	3.84	2,598,044	19.7	3,120,000	20.7	6,500,000	24.5
Independents	1,000	0.0	124,400	1.9	400,000	3.5	12,598	6,402	19,000	3.96	492,897	3.7	590,000	3.9	1,400,000	5.3
Marginal Christians	0	0.0	20,000	0.3	43,000	0.4	1,354	346	1,700	3.39	50,000	0.4	60,000	0.4	200,000	0.8
Orthodox	0	0.0	1,000	0.0	1,200	0.0	38	-38	0	0.00	1,200	0.0	1,200	0.0	2,500	0.0
Anglicans	0	0.0	0	0.0	0	0.0	0	90	90	97.44	700	0.0	900	0.0	1,500	0.0
Trans-megabloc groupings																
Evangelicals	3,000	0.1	132,000	2.0	460,000	4.0	14,487	1,513	16,000	3.03	536,963	4.1	620,000	4.1	1,500,000	5.7
Pentecostals/Charismatics	0	0.0	90,000	1.4	655,000	5.7	20,629	11,871	32,500	4.11	788,953	6.0	980,000	6.5	2,250,000	8.5
Great Commission Christians	**8,000**	**0.3**	**826,000**	**12.5**	**1,880,000**	**16.4**	**59,209**	**91,648**	**150,857**	**6.07**	**2,240,000**	**17.0**	**3,388,574**	**22.5**	**5,561,000**	**21.0**
Ethnoreligionists	2,479,500	94.6	2,116,000	32.0	2,906,900	25.3	91,550	-24,085	67,465	2.11	3,260,700	24.7	3,581,551	23.7	4,000,000	15.1
Muslims	131,000	5.0	1,325,200	20.0	2,435,000	21.2	76,688	36	76,724	2.78	2,800,000	21.2	3,202,235	21.2	6,123,000	23.1
Baha'is	0	0.0	29,500	0.5	48,000	0.4	1,512	117	1,629	2.96	56,200	0.4	64,286	0.4	150,000	0.6
Nonreligious	0	0.0	5,000	0.1	31,000	0.3	976	507	1,483	3.99	40,000	0.3	45,829	0.3	140,000	0.5
Atheists	0	0.0	1,000	0.0	11,000	0.1	346	-23	323	2.61	12,400	0.1	14,228	0.1	22,000	0.1
Other religionists	0	0.0	700	0.0	2,100	0.0	66	42	108	4.24	2,700	0.0	3,181	0.0	6,000	0.0
World A (unevangelized persons)	2,211,280	84.4	2,314,737	35.0	2,523,840	22.0	79,554	-29,440	50,114	1.83	2,847,324	21.6	3,032,085	20.1	4,263,924	16.1
World B (evangelized non-Christians)	399,220	15.2	1,162,198	17.6	2,910,160	25.4	91,584	6,034	97,618	2.92	3,324,731	25.2	3,879,256	25.7	6,177,076	23.3
World C (Christians)	9,500	0.4	3,136,600	47.4	6,038,000	52.6	190,160	23,406	213,566	3.07	7,010,000	53.2	8,173,659	54.2	16,043,000	60.6
Country's population	**2,620,000**	**100.0**	**6,613,536**	**100.0**	**11,472,000**	**100.0**	**361,298**	**0**	**361,298**	**2.78**	**13,182,056**	**100.0**	**15,085,000**	**100.0**	**26,484,000**	**100.0**

COLUMNS, ROWS.
For meanings and definitions, see Codebook (Part 3). Note that, by definition, total 'Christians' = professing + crypto-Christians, which also = affiliated + unaffiliated Christians, and also = Great Commission Christians + latent Christians. Percentages may not always total exactly, due to rounding.

CENSUSES.
No census question on religion has been asked for the whole country. West Cameroon only, 1964: 43.9% Protestants, 28.7% tribal religionists (termed 'animists', 'pagans'), 25.1% Roman Catholics, 2.3% Muslims.

NOTES ON RELIGIONS
ATHEISTS. No Communist party; mainly intellectuals and expatriates.
BAHA'IS. One of the first pioneers was an African Baha'i from Uganda. Growth from 63 local spiritual assemblies (1964) to 197 (1973). By 1995, the number had stabilized at 189 LSAs. Particularly strong in Mamfe division, West Cameroon, attracting disaffected Presbyterians.
ETHNORELIGIONISTS. Over 50 tribes were in 1995 still over 60% traditionalist (animist). Although large numbers of traditionalists are being converted to Islam, there is also a steady trickle returning from Islam. In 1962, a large number of Mundang who had been Muslim converts abandoned Islam and returned to their traditional agrarian rites and ancestor worship; and there are similar more recent cases.
INDEPENDENTS. In over 60 denominations in 1995 (see Table 2).
MUSLIMS. All Sunnis (of the Malikite rite). Muslim tribes: Fulani, Bamum, Tikar, Kotoko, Mandara, and Shoa (Shuwa or Black Arabs). Under the German and French regimes, forced conversions to Islam lasted until the end of the 1930s. Since the 1930s, Islam has spread rapidly among the Kirdi (pagans of the north), especially the Mbum (now 60% Muslims), Duru (5%), Lakka, Kutin, Giddar, Fali (50,000; became 80% islamized in 2 generations), Mofu, Matakam (5%), Mundang (20%), Musgu (25%). *Sects.* Qadiriya (the oldest; HQ Garoua; declining), Tijaniya (introduced 1840; HQ Yola), Mahdism (strong among Fulani, producing a new mahdi every decade or so). The north is now 50% Muslim, 5% Christian. *Hajj pilgrims to Mecca.* (1970) 808; (1974) 4,422; (1975) 1,005; (1976) 779.
OTHER RELIGIONISTS. Including Rosicrucians (11 AMORC centers).
PROTESTANTS. In 1886, the Basel Mission had 203 converts, rising to 8,913 by 1926 and 20,307 by 1936. In 1913, Baptists had 3,000 converts and 3,000 pupils.
ROMAN CATHOLICS. In 1900, 2,457 baptized Catholics and 263 catechumens.

Great Commission Instrument Panel: status of Cameroon (for explanation see start of Part 4)

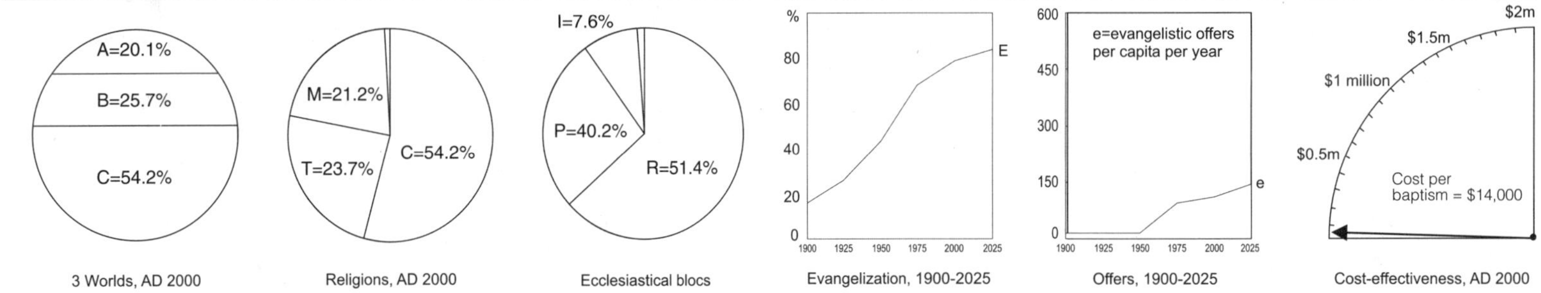

Country status. Cameroon, known as the hinge of Africa, is in the western-central region of the continent and extends like an irregular wedge northeastward from the Gulf of Guinea to Lake Chad. Its linguistic and ethnic diversity is remarkable even by African standards. It has over 230 tribes and languages and 3 European colonial traditions: German, French, and British. In this sense it represents the meeting place of anglophone and francophone Africa.

HUMAN LIFE AND LIBERTY

Human need and development. Living conditions are characterized by extreme regional differences. Lifestyles of wealthy Douala merchants would approximate that of their counterparts in the West, but in rural areas, peasants still wear goatskins, live in mud houses and on the average do not live beyond 49 years. Living conditions are harshest in the northern hills where standards of hygiene, diet, and housing are so inadequate that only one out of 3 children grow to maturity. Although the country is self-sufficient in food, diets are often deficient because of regional, seasonal, and cultural factors. Children, in particular, suffer from a variety of nutritional insufficiencies resulting in debilitating diseases. About 75% of the population suffer from one or more recurrent forms of kwashiorkor, schistosomiasis, and onchocerciasis. No area is free of malaria. In the countryside, medicine men are generally witch doctors or herbalists. Sanitation and good drinking water are available only in the large cities. In other areas, rivers, canals, stagnant pools, and wells polluted with human and animal waste serve for laundering, bathing, and drinking.

Human rights and freedoms. Cameroon is a one-party authoritarian state where the human rights situation has deteriorated sharply since 1991. Abuses of human rights have included extrajudicial killings, torture, harsh prison conditions, arbitrary arrests, and abridgments of women's and workers' rights. Public demonstrations are often met with brutal repression by security forces. Police commonly harass citizens suspected of anti-state activity and enter homes without warrants during periodic searches. Freedoms of the press and speech have long been restricted. Domestic newspapers are constantly censored and foreign newspapers opposed to the administration are seized. Police frequently stop travelers to check identification documents, vehicle registrations, and tax receipts as a security and immigration control measure. These roadblocks, sometimes as many as 10 within 8 miles, are employed to limit political demonstrations. Personnel manning the roadblocks often solicit bribes to speed passage. Anglophone Cameroonians complain of discrimination against them by the francophone Bamileke, who make up the largest ethnic group. The traditional subordination of women in Cameroonian society has persisted despite legal efforts to grant them equal rights with men. Polygamy is permitted by law. Women suffer legal disabilities in many areas, but particularly in regard to inheritance, divorce, and education.

Human environment. The forests and the wildlife habitats in Cameroon are disappearing at a fast rate as a result of poaching and logging. Drought and overgrazing by cattle have destroyed the semiarid rangelands of northern Cameroon. Water pollution in rivers and lakes is the principal reason for the continuing prevalence of malaria, which has been wiped out in most other parts of the world.

NON-CHRISTIAN RELIGIONS

Traditional religions are followed by around a fifth of the population. Those people who are more than 90% traditionalist include the following: Budugum, Duru, Gisei, Gisiga, Gude, Kotopo, Laka, Matakam, Musei, Podokwo, and Tigon. Others who are at least 60% traditionalist are the Adamawa, Fungom, Kapsiki, Kundu, Li, Mambila, Mundang, Namshi, Nen, Tuburi, Utange, and Wute. The traditional blacksmith, who serves equally as a diviner among several peoples, plays a significant role at birth and death, as well as during illness, pottery-

Country Summary. **Worlds A, B, C by ethnolinguistic peoples, cities, and major civil divisions in Cameroon.**

	PEOPLES CITIES							CIVIL DIVISIONS													
World	Num	Pop 2000	C%	Christians	E%	U%	Unevangelized	Num	Pop 2000	C%	Christians	E%	U%	Unevangelized	Num	Pop 2000	C%	Christians	E%	U%	Unevangelized
A	76	4,308,875	5.75	247,650	43	57	2,458,142	0	0	0.00	0	0	0	0	0	0	0.00	0	0	0	0
B	88	1,954,222	35.63	696,307	72	28	537,619	10	4,119,875	48.91	2,015,135	80	20	826,343	10	15,084,968	51.45	7,761,501	80	20	3,027,137
C	133	8,821,854	77.28	6,817,552	100	0	31,389	0	0	0.00	0	0	0	0	0	0	0.00	0	0	0	0
Total	**297**	**15,084,951**	**51.45**	**7,761,509**	**80**	**20**	**3,027,150**	**10**	**4,119,875**	**48.91**	**2,015,135**	**80**	**20**	**826,343**	**10**	**15,084,968**	**51.45**	**7,761,501**	**80**	**20**	**3,027,137**

making, and iron-smelting. The importance of sacrifices, especially of cattle, is also widely emphasized. Traditional names for the supreme being among Cameroonian peoples are Si (for the Bamileke), Njinyi (Bamum), Hoel (Banen), Mebee (Bulu), Loba (Duala), Osawa (Ekoi), Nzame (Fang), Lova (Kpe), Nyooly (Tikar), Buimulvong (Gisiga), Masing (Mundang), Bah (Tupuri), Zigile (Matakam), and Zigta (Mukulehe).

Muslims. Sultan of Meiganga with bodyguards and entourage armed with rifles, bows and arrows. Since the 1930's, Islam has spread rapidly in Northern Cameroon.

Islam was introduced in the 18th century by the Fulani (Peul) who entered northern Cameroon from Mali and Nigeria. At the beginning of the 19th century, the Fulani chiefs in the north began to impose their authority on the pagan peoples and formed the Fulani kingdoms, in which the temporal and religious leader is known as the lamido. Some local peoples submitted and adopted Islam, but the majority took refuge in the mountains and retained their traditional religions. The Fulani then set up a feudalistic system which has subsequently impeded economic and social development.

Apart from the Fulani, the principal islamized ethnic groups are the Bamum and the arabized Shoa. Islam is now the religion of 20% of the population, and in 1969, there were 25 Quranic schools with 2,755 pupils. The Qadiriya is the principal Muslim brotherhood. In 1974, 4,422 Muslim pilgrims from Cameroon performed the hajj to Mecca.

Baha'i has grown rapidly from 63 local spiritual assemblies in 1964 to 197 in 1973, then levelled off to 189 by 1996. It is particularly strong in West Cameroon.

CHRISTIANITY

The churches are strongest in southern Cameroon. In the central and northern parts of the country, Christians have faced stiff resistance from Islam, and their progress has been slower. In the region north of Ngaoundere and also in Bankim and Galim in central Cameroon, churches have experienced severe persecution. Chapels have been destroyed and authorization to open new work has often been refused. In the Rey Bouba area, there has been a recent exodus of Christians due to Muslim harassment. Catholic membership in the nation is nearly twice that of Protestants, although in west Cameroon Catholics number less than Protestants. Catholicism is strongest in urban areas whereas Protestant churches are more rural.

CATHOLIC CHURCH. Catholic missions were permanently introduced in 1890 in the south by German Pallotines, and by 1934, a mass movement into the Catholic Church was taking place. The population in the archdiocese of Yaounde has now passed 74% Catholic. In the north, Catholic evangelization did not begin until after World War II. The church has had its greatest success among the younger generation due to its extensive involvement in education. Easter communications are high, rising from 37% in Yaounde to over 70% or more in some rural dioceses.

A series of postage stamps showing (from top, left to right) Buea RC Cathedral, Yaoundé RC Cathedral, Garoua Mosque, Greek Orthodox Church in Yaoundé.

A major effort has been made recently to adapt the liturgy and religious teaching to the cultural and religious milieu of the country. In 1969, 2 associations of African priests were formed: Interdiocesan Association of Indigenous Priests (Association Interdiocesaine des Prêtres Indigenes, AIPI) in the dioceses of Nkongsamba and Bafoussam, which in spite of its small numbers exerts a significant influence in Bamileke country; and a group called Serve and Liberate (Servir et Liberer) in the diocese of Douala with 15 members in 1972. Aiming to promote the interests of priests and dioceses generally, these associations testify to uneasiness about existing Western structures in pastoral work and indicate the desire of clergy to indigenize the church. In 1970, the Episcopal Conference attempted to create a National Liaison Committee for Cameroonian Priests (Comite National de Liaison pour les Pretres Camerounais), but because of its imposition from the top, nothing came of the attempt. The 2 English-speaking dioceses (Bamenda and Buea) have organized a Catholic Convention, a kind of synod, beginning in 1967 and whose third and final session was held at Bamenda in 1972. Membership consisted of 150 delegates elected by the laity, priests, and male and female religious personnel.

In the 1980s and 1990s indigenization of the church proceeded apace, especially with Cameroonian clergy and bishops. By 1995 Catholics numbered 3.4 million.

The Holy See has diplomatic relations with Cameroon and in AD 2000 is represented to government and the Catholic hierarchy by a pro-nuncio residing in Yaounde.

PROTESTANT CHURCHES. The largest Protestant churches are the Evangelical Church of Cameroon (EEC), Presbyterian Church of Cameroon (EPC), and Presbyterian Church in West Cameroon. They have extensive educational programs, an increasing evangelistic outreach and large numbers of national workers.

The Evangelical Church of Cameroon and the Union of Baptist Churches (UEBC) both owe their origin to the Baptist Missionary Society (UK) from 1845 onwards. With the German occupation in 1884, part of the work was ceded to the Basel Mission and part to the Baptist Mission of Berlin. Although following World War I both were turned over to the Paris Mission, separate organizations were maintained and they remain autonomous denominations. In 1957, the EEC joined with the UEBC to form the Council of Baptist and evangelical Churches of Cameroon, with united efforts in the medical, social, educational, and evangelistic fields.

In 1879, the French-speaking Presbyterian Church of Cameroon was begun in the south through the instrumentality of Presbyterian missionaries from the USA, eventually leading to a first general assembly of the autonomous EPC organized in 1957.

The English-speaking Presbyterian Church in West Cameroon originated with Basel missionaries in 1884 and has now grown to be the largest church in West Cameroon. It became autonomous in 1957 although it continues to receive support from the Basel Mission.

In 1891, a missionary of the North American Baptist General Conference was sent to Cameroon under the auspices of the Baptist Mission of Berlin. Today, this work is organized separately from UEBC and, since 1954, has been called the Cameroon Baptist Convention. The church's strength is concentrated in the western region.

There are 2 Lutheran denominations in Cameroon. The Evangelical Lutheran Church of Cameroon is the union of 2 missions, the Sudan Mission supported by the American Lutheran Church and the Norwegian Mission Society, which arrived in 1925. The church became autonomous in 1960. The second group, the Church of the Lutheran Brethren in North Cameroon (Eglise Fraternelle Lutherienne au Cameroun), originated with the American mission of the same name in 1918 and became autonomous in 1964.

The Sudan United Mission (Swiss Branch) works in the extreme north where Swiss missionaries appeared in 1938. Other groups include the European Baptist Mission, which entered the north in 1954, and Seventh-day Adventists, who have been in Cameroon since 1928.

Eglise Baptiste Camerounaise. EBC begun 1884, largest of Cameroon's 28 indigenous denominations. The pastor of one of the largest of the 239 EBC congregations is shown.

INDIGENOUS CHURCHES. As a reaction to foreign missionary influence, secessions led by African Baptists began in Cameroon in 1864. They began again in 1888, when Duala Baptists left the Basel Mission to form ultimately the Native Baptist Church and the Eglise Baptiste Camerounaise, the latter being Cameroon's largest indigenous body. The first Presbyterian schism, the African Protestant Church, occurred in 1934 and includes half the entire Ngumba tribe. Numerous other secessions have taken place since then.

Renewal movements. In the 1990s the Pentecostal/Charismatic Renewal continued to spread rapidly across most older churches, and numbered over 980,000 adherents (of whom 10% Pentecostals, 57% Charismatics, and 33% Independents).

Indigenous missions. Both Catholics and Protestants have sent out missionaries, primarily to surrounding countries.

CHURCH AND STATE

The constitution of the united republic (1972) proclaims a secular state, assures the equality of all citizens before the law and affirms its acceptance of the fundamental liberties inscribed in the Universal Declaration of Human Rights (Preamble and Article 1). Law 67-LF-19 of 12 June 1967, which deals with 'freedom of association', stipulates that all religious and confessional associations and congregations must obtain legal recognition. This was decreed by the president of the republic after being proposed by the minister charged with territorial administration.

Before Independence in 1960, the opening of new missions or catechetical posts required prior authorization. This measure is no longer applied in the south but continues in vigor in the Muslim north, where such authorization is difficult to obtain. Religious youth movements have not been permitted since 1963, except for those which have accepted integration in government-controlled youth federations. Confessional trade unions have also been suppressed.

By Law 64-LF-11 of 26 June 1964, the state recognizes private denominational instruction and subsidizes it by providing a portion of teachers' salaries. The whole confessional system of education may, however, soon be taken over by the state. This transfer has the support of government and, for financial reasons, is also desired by some Catholic bishops. On the other hand, such action is feared by other bishops and by a number of priests, some of whom are found within the associations of Cameroonian priests, as well as by progressive missionaries who see confessional schools and associations as an obstacle to political totalitarianism. This tendency towards state control is also evident in medical institutions and, indeed in a general way, in all areas where the churches exercise a function parallel to or in place of that of the state.

The head of state since Independence in 1960 has been a Muslim, and the northern peoples exercise an important influence at the center of government. In spite of the often unjustified fears of Christians, especially Catholics, the problems of relations between the Christian churches and the state have been political rather than religious. Although the ideology of the regime, sometimes called 'the ethics of unity', implies a minimal and even restrictive definition of the role of religion, religious authorities at all levels do not hesitate to make personal interventions to protect the population from arbitrary measures and to call the attention of the government to the problems of disadvantaged ethnic and social groups. The exercise of the churches' prophetic ministry has created tensions and conflicts, but their gravity is limited by the fact that ecclesiastical authorities have never called in question the established political system.

The Catholic Church has strenuously opposed activities of the revolutionary movement Union of the Peoples of Cameroon (Union des Populations Camerounaises, UPC), which was very active among the Bamileke between 1955 and 1965, accusing it of being communist. In retaliation, UPC followers systematically destroyed Catholic missions. An added complication occurred when the Catholic bishop of Nkongsamba was implicated in a plot against the head of state with the UPC leader and both were sentenced to death, the latter being executed and the bishop's sentence eventually commuted to life imprisonment. On 17 May 1975, the bishop and 49 other persons imprisoned with him were pardoned by the president of the republic. Many UPC militants have had Protestant education and the movement itself has some support in Protestant circles, especially among the Presbyterian and Evangelical churches. This has resulted from an increasing lack of understanding between Protestant leaders and civil authorities. Likewise, relations between the state and the Catholic Church have also deteriorated. The Catholic Church has traditionally been more conservative than the Protestants and several bishops have actively supported a major political rival of the head of state.

Considering that in a developing country the number of public holidays should be limited, the Catholic hierarchy of Cameroon requested and obtained from Rome authorization to celebrate those feast days which fall during the week on the following Sunday, Christmas being the only exception.

BROADCASTING AND MEDIA

The wide distribution of receivers makes radio a useful strategy. AWR and other broadcasters beam French programs in via shortwave radio. The Lutheran World Federation maintains a radio studio in the country which produces programs in Fulfulde and French. Cameroon is a member of UNDA.

Some 1.5 million have seen the 'Jesus' film, chiefly through television broadcasts (950,000) and mission agency outreach programs (430,000).

INTERDENOMINATIONAL ORGANIZATIONS

The Federation of Protestant Churches and Missions in Cameroon (Federation des Eglises et Missions evangeliques du Cameroun, FEMEC), was established in 1970, replacing a wider regional federation include Rio Muni, Gabon, and Congo-Brazzaville formed in 1943. The Ecumenical Study circle (Cercle d'Etudes Oecumeniques, CEO) is an independent organization not officially recognized by the churches, but which receives support from the Catholic Episcopal conference and FEMEC. Founded in 1964, it consisted in 1972 of 100 members (40 active, 60 sympathizers), including priests, pastors, religious personnel and laymen, most being Europeans. Its activities include monthly meetings, organization of conferences, and other forms of ecumenical dialogue.

FUTURE TRENDS AND PROSPECTS

Church affiliation is expected to rise to near 60% by 2025, primarily by decline of tribal religions.

As tribal religionists continue in their decline it is plausible that by 2050 Christians and Muslims will share most of the country's population in a 70/30 ratio. Both of these religions could lose adherents to the nonreligious and atheism if these experience resurgence in the distant future.

BIBLIOGRAPHY

Album of the centenary, 1890–1990: the Catholic Church in Cameroon: 100 years of evangelization. E. Mveng & J. Messina. [Cameroon], 1990. 432p.

Alfred Saker: the pioneer of the Cameroons. E. M. Saker. London: Religious Tract Society, 1908. 224p.

An African trail. J. K. Mackenzie. West Medford, MA: Central Committee on the United Study of Foreign Missions, 1917. 222p. (Religion of Bulu of Cameroon).

'Bibliographie choisie d'écrits en sciences sociales et humaines sur le Cameroun,' H. F. Illy, in *Kamerun*, p.317–43. H. F. Illy (ed). Mainz, GFR: Hase and Koehler Verlag, 1974.

Cameroon. M. W. DeLancey & P. J. Schraeder. *World bibliographical series*, vol. 63. Oxford,: CLIO Press, 1986. 230p. (See especially 'Peoples,' p.16f, and 'Religion,' p. 56-61).

'Cameroons and Fernando Po.' J. J. Fuller. Unpublished manuscript, Baptist Missionary Society, London, 1887. 22p. (History of Baptists in Cameroon and Fernando Po).

Christians and Muslims in Cameroon. G. M. Okafor. *Religionswissenschaftliche studien*, 34. Würzburg: Echter, 1994. 144p.

Coastal Bantu of the Cameroons. E. Ardener. London: International African Institute, 1956. 116p.

Conquérants du Golfe de Guinée. H. Nicod. Lausanne: Secrétariat Romand de la Mission de Bâle, 1947. 306p.

'Contribution á l'étude du comportement religieux des Wodaabe Dageeja du Nord–Cameroun,' R. Labatut, *Journal des Africanistes*, 48, 2 (1978), 63–92.

'Crossing religious frontiers: Christianity and the transformation of Bulu society, 1892–1925.' P. R. Dekar. Ph.D. dissertation, University of Chicago, Chicago, IL, 1978. 392p.

Cry justice: the church in a changing Cameroon. Nyansako-ni-Nku (ed). [Buea, Cameroon: Presbyterian Church in Cameroon], 1993. 64p.

De la procuration à la conviction: cent ans d'évangélisation du Cameroun. B. Nkoé. Yaoundé, Cameroon: Editions SOPECAM, 1991. 196p.

'Education of the Christian clergy in the Cameroon since 1957: implications for and problems in religious reconstruction and nation–building.' M. Walters. Ph.D. dissertation, Loyola University of Chicago, 1991. 372p.

Ethno–sociologie religieuse des Duala et apparentés. R. Bureau. Yaoundé, Cameroon: Editions Clé, 1969. 149p.

Histoire de l'Eglise du Cameroun, 1841–1982. B. Omgba. [Cameroon, 1985]. 84p.

Histoire de l'église en Afrique (Cameroun). J. van Slageren. Yaoundé, Cameroon: Editions CLE, 1969. 149p.

Histoire des églises chrétiennes au Cameroun: les origines. E. Mveng. [Yaoundé, Cameroon]: E. Mveng, [1990]. 111p.

Histoire des forces religieuses au Cameroun: de la première guerre mondiale à l'indépendence (1916–1955). L. Ngongo. *Hommes et Sociétés.* Paris: Editions Karthala, 1982. 298p.

International influences and Baptist mission in West Cameroon: German–American missionary endeavor under international mandate and British colonialism. C. W. Weber. *Studies in Christian mission*, vol. 9. Leiden: E. J. E.J. Brill, 1993. 192p.

Inventaire ethnique du Sud–Cameroun. I. Dugast. *Populations*, no. 1. Yaoundé, Cameroon: l'Institut Français d'Afrique Noire, 1949. 159p.

Journey in faith: the story of the Presbyterian Church in Cameroon. Nyansako-ni-Nku (ed). Yaoundé, Cameroon: Buma Kor, 1982. 173p.

Kirche in Kamerun, Kirche der Hoffnung: zur Hundertjahrfeier der Gründung der katholischen Kirche in Kamerun. E. Dillinger. Friedrichsthal: CV-Afrika-Hilfe, 1991. 176p.

Le Catholicisme au Nord–Cameroun. D. Veillette-Santerre. Québec: Université Laval, 1979.

'Le Harrisme et le Bwiti: deux réactions Africaines à l'impact Chrétien,' R. Bureau, *Recherches de Sciences Religieuses*, 63, 1 (1975), 83–100.

Les églises chrétiennes face à la montée du nationalisme camerounais. E. Kengne Pokam. Paris: L'Harmattan, [1987]. 202p.

Les Gbaya. J. Hilberth. *Studia Ethnographica Upsaliensia*, 19. Uppsala: Studia Ethnographica Upsaliensia, 1962. 142p.

'Les missionnaires et le christianisme dans la littérature camerounaise: essai de sociologie africaine.' L. Laverdière. Thesis, Université Paris-Nord, [1979]. 425p.

Les origines de l'Eglise Evangélique du Cameroun: missions européennes et christianisme autochtone. J. van Slageren. Leiden: E. J. Brill, 1972. 298p.

Les populations païennes du Nord–Cameroun et de l'Adamaoua. B. Lembezat. Paris: Presses Universitaires de France, 1961. 252p.

Les rites beti au Christ: essai de pastorale liturgique sur quelques rites de nos ancêtres. I. Tabi. N.p., 1991. 31p.

L'Habitation des Fali: montagnards du Cameroun septentrional. J. Lebeuf. Paris: Librairie Hachette, 1961. 607p. (Includes Fali religion).

One hundred years of the Roman Catholic Church in Cameroon, 1890–1990. J. N. Dah. , 1989. 72p.

'Origine et développement d'une église indépendante africaine: l'Eglise Baptiste Camerounaise,' J. Brutsch, *Le monde non-chrétien* (Paris), n.s. no. 12 (October–December, 1949), 408–24.

Presbyterian Church in West Cameroon, Forest District: a survey, 1961. (Also Grassfield District, 1962).

'Protestant Christianity in West Cameroon, 1841–1886.' L. E. Kwast. D.Miss. thesis, Fuller Theological Seminary, Pasadena, CA, 1972. 417p.

Quatre vingts ans de christianisme en pays bamoun. J. Mfochivé, M. Lamère & R. Peshandon. [Yaoundé, Cameroon], 1986. 94p.

Spider divination in the Cameroons. P. Gebauer. *Publications in anthropology*, no. 10. Milwaukee, WI: Milwaukee Public Museum, 1964. 157p.

'Stewardship in traditional societies insights within the Evangelical Lutheran Church of Cameroon.' D. P. Mann. Th.M. thesis, Fuller Theological Seminary, Pasadena, CA, 1988. 236p.

The Catholic Church in Kom: its foundation and growth, 1913–1977. P. N. Nkwi. Yaoundé, Cameroon: Afo-A-Kom Publications, 1977. 23p.

The discipling of West Cameroon: a study of Baptist growth. L. E. Kwast. Grand Rapids, MI: Eerdmans, 1971. 205p.

'The Evangelical Lutheran Church of East Cameroun.' C. S. Michelsen. Thesis, Fuller Theological Seminary, Pasadena, CA, 1969. 226p.

'The Gbaya naming of Jesus: an inquiry into the contextualization of soteriological themes among the Gbaya of Cameroon.' T. G. Christensen. Th.D. thesis, Lutheran School of Theology, Chicago, 1984. 484p.

The history of the Presbyterian Church in West Cameroon. W. Keller. Buea, Cameroon: Radio and Literature Department of the Presbyterian Church, 1969. 154p.

The impact of Catholic Christianity on the Cameroonian society. T. H. Mbuy. Limbe, Cameroon: Cosmos Educational Publishers, 1991. 63p.

Tradition and Christianity in the Bakossi society: a lecture delivered in the Presbyterian Theological College, Nyasoso, 6 Jan. 1976. S. N. Ejedepang–Koge. N.p., 1976. 23p.

Un souffle venant d'Afrique: communautés chrétiennes au Nord–Cameroun. B. de Dinechin & Y. Tabart. Paris: Le Centurion, 1986. 190p.

Country Table 2. **Organized churches and denominations in Cameroon.**

Official name (bold type = church with over 10% of all affiliated) 1	Begun 2	Type 3	Counc 4	Congs 5	Adults 6	Affiliated 1970 7	Affiliated 1995 8	G% 9	*Names, notes, and other statistics* (see Codebook, Part 3) 10
Anglican Church of Cameroon	c1970	A-plu	A....	5	300	–	700	29.96	*Missionary Area of Cameroon*, in CP West Africa. Support also from Anglican Ch of Nigeria.
Cameroon Baptist Convention	1891	P-Bap	TF...	729	66,720	55,000	80,200	1.52	*CBC.* M=NABGMS(USA). 11 Fields. 53n,373m,76f,3H,5h,1s(104),W=75%,1390Y,4557z.
Cameroon Bible Mission	1949	I-Bap	.....	375	15,669	2,000	20,000	9.65	Peoples: Kundu, Bakwiri, Duala, Kenyang, Bamileke.
Cherubim and Seraphim	c1950	I-3aA	x....	24	4,800	5,000	12,000	3.56	Nigerian pentecostals. M=C&S(Nigeria). In many villages from Loum to Douala.

Continued opposite

Country Table 2–concluded

Official name (bold type = church with over 10% of affiliated) 1	*Begun* 2	*Type* 3	*Counc* 4	*Congs* 5	*Adults* 6	*Affiliated 1970* 7	*Affiliated 1995* 8	*G%* 9	*Names, notes, and other statistics* (see Codebook, Part 3) 10
Confédération Baptiste du Cameroun	1864	I-3cA	.v...	30	4,000	5,000	7,000	1.35	Ex first Baptists (now UEBC). HQ Bali, Duala. 1964, applied to join WCC; rejected.
Congrégation Baptiste du Cameroun	1963	I-3nA	.T...	10	2,000	2,000	3,000	1.64	*CBC. Baptist Congregation.* Schism ex EBC and EEC. Pentecostal. Duala. HQ Deido.
Eglise Adventiste du Septième Jour	1928	P-Adv	x....	494	39,279	25,000	74,100	4.44	*SDA.* Equatorial Africa UM. 56% Bulu. 19nx,6f,1H,6h,1j,1r,1s,283t(22564),1456Y.
Eglise Apostolique	1949	P-PeA	.....	143	10,000	7,140	20,400	4.29	M=Apostolic Church.
Eglise Baptiste Camerounaise	1884	I-Bap	TWA.K	142	55,936	35,000	106,000	4.53	*EBC. Cameroon Baptist Ch.* Schism ex BM. Duala tribe, spreading across nation. 49n.
Eglise Baptiste Suédoise	c1925	P-Pe2	Z....	135	27,000	20,000	45,000	3.30	Pentecostal Baptists, *Equatorial Africa UM.* 56% Bulu. 19nx,6f,1H,6h,1j,1r,1s,283t(22564),1456Y.
Eglise Catholique au Cameroun:	1883	R-Lat	P.S.R	1,160	1,872,600	1,528,760	3,431,074	3.29	*Catholic Ch.* C=14+8+65. 5p,2s(92). 536n 447x 952m 1509w 76341Yy
M Bamenda	1970	R-Lat	Ps	24	98,000	129,714	179,668	1.31	In west. English-speaking. 7 tribes. 1s. M=MH. 37n 40x 80m 97w 7072Yy
D Buea	1923	R-Lat	Pmhm	21	108,000	97,265	198,519	2.89	40 tribes: Kossi, Nsaw, Widekum, Dpe, Fut. M=MHM. 36n 25x 35m 58w 4882Yy
D Kumbo	1982	R-Lat	Ps	15	62,000	–	114,091	7.69	M=MHM. 22n 10x 15m 126w 3332Yy
M Bertoua	1983	R-Lat	Pcssp	81	31,000	–	56,857	8.33	M=CSSp. 12n 15x 25m 51w 3685Yy
D Batouri	1994	R-Lat	Pcicm	126	17,400	–	31,975	50.00	M=CICM.
D Doumé-Abong' Mbarg	1949	R-Lat	Psci	16	29,000	77,384	52,700	-1.52	M=SCI. 12n 8x 9m 43w 1044Yy
D Yokadouma	1991	R-Lat	Pomi	9	9,700	–	17,775	25.00	M=OMI. 3n 8x 13m 9w 472Yy
M Douala	1931	R-Lat	Ps	27	211,000	232,420	386,189	2.05	42% Koko, 32% Bamileke, 12% Fang, 8% Duala. 43n 23x 28m 89w 6331Yy
D Bafoussam	1970	R-Lat	Ps	35	142,000	135,055	260,010	2.65	Prosperous Bamileke farmers. 4 monasteries. 38n 28x 33m 92w 5832Yy
D Edea	1993	R-Lat	Ps	20	76,600	–	140,183	50.00	Created out of M Douala. 17n 2x 2m 7w 803Yy
D Eseka	1993	R-Lat	Ps	21	60,000	–	110,000	50.00	Diocese is 69% Catholic. 19n 1x 1m 25w 5000Yy
D Nkongsamba	1914	R-Lat	Ps	48	173,000	146,997	316,304	3.11	20% urban. Bamileke, Mbo. 1965, bishop jailed. 47n 6x 23m 58w 6081Yy
M Garoua	1947	R-Lat	Pomi	439	35,000	24,483	65,600	4.02	M=OMI. 14n 40x 43m 74w 2752Yy
D Maroua-Mokolo	1968	R-Lat	Pomi	28	12,500	9,628	22,900	3.53	M=PFV. 22n 19x 28m 102w 1612Yy
D Ngaoundere	1982	R-Lat	Pomi	18	16,700	–	30,486	7.69	M=OMI. 7n 29x 35m 42w 1590Yy
D Yagoua	1968	R-Lat	Pomi	22	19,100	19,154	35,000	2.44	M=OMI. 12n 31x 35m 70w 2107Yy
M Yaounde	1890	R-Lat	Ps	90	335,500	406,129	614,160	1.67	87% Fang (Ewondo, Eton), 4% Bamileke. 1s. 81n 124x 358m 349w 13453Yy
D Bafia	1965	R-Lat	Pcssp	16	90,000	59,480	165,000	4.17	M=CSSp. 12n 7x 16m 58w 1252Yy
D Ebolowa-Kribi	1991	R-Lat	Ps	24	87,300	–	159,860	25.00	Diocese is 53% Catholic. 31n 8x 8m 35w 2800Yy
D Mbalmayo	1961	R-Lat	Ps	27	92,600	101,751	169,500	2.06	Southeast of Yaounde. Rural. Beti tribe. 1p. 31n 6x 15m 31w 4240Yy
D Obala	1987	R-Lat	Ps	41	136,600	–	250,117	12.50	Created out of M Yaounde. 33n 10x 143m 50w 6383Yy
D Sangmelima	1963	R-Lat	Ps	12	29,600	89,300	54,180	-1.98	Rural. High % Protestant, 750 Orthodox. 1d. 7n 7x 7m 43w 1421Yy
Eglise de Dieu	1970	P-Pe3	ZF...	57	5,935	15,000	11,900	-0.92	Holiness Pentecostals (3-stage). M=Church of God (Cleveland) (USA). 35n,1p.
Eglise de Dieu de Prophétie	1985	P-Pe3	Z....	7	280	–	622	10.00	Church of God of Prophecy. M=CoGP.
Eglise Evangélique du Cameroun	1845	P-Ref	.WA.K	1,700	543,000	215,000	1,175,000	7.03	*EEC.* M=PEMS. 33% Bamileke. 91n,9x,911m,62w,67f,1s,1u,W=57%,8944Y,11832y,11098z.
Eglise Ev Luthérienne du Cameroun	1915	P-Lut	L...K	248	49,600	63,398	82,629	1.07	*EEL.* M=NMS,SM(ALC). A=1960. 28n,21x,57f,2H,1h,2p,1s(25),W=60%,1971Y,1557y,7471z.
Eglise Fraternelle Luthérienne au C	1918	P-Lut	x...K	808	18,514	22,325	49,433	3.23	M=CLB. 58% Mundang, 23% Masana. 20n,4x,15f,1H,2h,15p,1s(22),1001Yy,2592z.
Eglise Luthérienne	1969	P-Lut	I....	32	3,200	909	5,820	7.71	Lutheran Synod. M=Wisconsin Ev Lutheran Synod (USA).
Eglise Orthodoxe Grecque (D Accra)		O-Gre	Cw...	1	600	1,000	1,200	0.05	Under Greek P Alexandria, Egypt. 8 parishes in West Africa, 3 priests. HQ Yaound.
Eglise Pentecostale Unie	1971	P-Pe1	x....	24	2,880	–	5,240	4.17	*United Pentecostal Ch, Jesus Only Church.* M=UPC(USA). 5n,2f,1p(12).
Eglise Presbytérienne Camerounaise	1879	P-Ref	RWA.K	3,137	113,000	112,815	300,000	3.99	M=UPUSA. 26% Bulu. 136n,7x,37f,5H,24h,1p,1s(33),W=80%,5011Y,5713y,15208z.
Eglise Presb Camerounaise Orthodoxe	1967	I-Ref	.T...	700	78,600	20,000	100,000	6.65	Continuing Presbyterian Ch. Schism ex EPC by 13 pastors. Bulu. 1967, M=1BPFM(USA).
Eglise Protestante Africaine	1934	I-Ref	.uA.K	29	8,400	11,000	13,500	0.82	*EPA. African Protestant Ch.* Schism ex EPC(American M) over language policy. Ngumba tribe.
Eglises Chrétiennes		I-Dis	x....	100	3,000	2,000	5,000	0.05	*Christian Churches.* Independent congregations. M=CCCC(Instrumental) (USA). 2f.
Eglises du Christ	1957	I-Dis	x....	114	4,000	3,000	8,890	4.44	*Ch of Christ.* M=CC(Non-Instrumental) (USA). Missionaries in Kumba. 11f,1h,1s.
Free Prot Episcopal Ch (D West Africa)	1970	I-ARo	x....	10	900	900	1,200	1.16	M=FPEC(UK). Douala. 84% nationals, 16% Nigerians. 1n,6m,2w,1r,W=99%,70Y,175z.
Full Gospel Mission	1961	I-3fA	.....	387	29,275	5,000	35,774	8.19	M=AoG. Assemblies of God.
Global Frontier Church	c1960	I-3pA	x....	40	8,000	5,000	20,000	5.70	All over Forest in West. M=Wings of Healing (USA). Revival and healing campaigns.
Mission Baptiste Européenne	1954	P-Bap	x...K	60	1,000	1,060	2,000	2.57	*MBE.* M=EBMS. Link with UEBC. 26% Kola, 19% Gisiga, 11% Mofou. 2n,3x,19m.15f.
Mission Mondiale	1961	I-Non	x....	50	2,000	2,000	3,000	1.64	M=World-Wide Missions (USA). Evangelicals from California.
Native Baptist Church	1888	I-Bap	.....	10	400	500	1,000	2.81	Schisms among Kpe (Bakwiri) in 1888, 1898, 1917, 1960 opposing mission prohibitions.
New Apostolic Church	c1980	I-3aX	x....	40	3,000	–	4,533	6.67	*NAC.* M=Neuapostolische Kirche (HQ Zurich, Switzerland).
Presbyterian Church in Cameroon	1884	P-Ref	RWA.K	3,137	208,117	127,068	600,000	6.41	M=Basel M. 30% Widekum. 67n,16x,337m,40f,3H,7r,1s(12),W=90%,2866Y,10330y,5140z.
Témoins de Jéhovah	c1935	m-Jeh	x....	481	13,000	20,000	50,000	3.73	*Jehovah's Witnesses.* Strong in West. Banned 1970. (1975) 592Y. (1995) 2068Y.
Union Baptiste Camerounaise	1931	I-Bap	.....	30	1,000	1,000	2,000	2.81	*Cameroon Baptist Union.* Schism ex UEBC. M=Cooperation Ev Mondiale (Switzerland).
Union des Eglises Baptistes du C	1845	P-Bap	TWA.K	542	63,000	40,000	86,000	3.11	*UEBC. Union of Baptist Chs.* M=PEMS(France), BEFG. 27% in Douala. 40n,42f,1u.
Union des Eglises Ev au Nord C	1938	P-Eva	x...K	232	17,400	12,000	39,700	4.90	M=SUM(Swiss). Far north. Matakam, Kirdi. 56m,25f.
Other African indigenous churches		I-3pA	.....	730	70,000	25,000	150,000	0.05	Total about 50 AICs, including Celestial Ch of Christ, and many others from Nigeria.
Other Protestant denominations		P-	.....	286	10,000	500	20,000	0.05	Total about 15 missions, including Exclusive Brethren (Kelly-Continental), FMB/CSI-SBC.
Totals				**16,239**	**3,356,405**	**2,391,375**	**6,573,915**		

Churches, members, growth, 1900-2025	*Congs*	*Adults*	*Affiliated*	*G%*	*Total denominations*	*6 Megablocs:* O	R	A	P	I	m
Total churches, members, and denominations (mid-1900)	10	4,600	7,720	8.54	9	0	1	0	5	3	0
Total churches, members, and denominations (mid-1970)	7,933	1,429,205	2,391,375	8.54	61	1	1	0	21	37	1
Total churches, members, and denominations (mid-1990)	14,000	2,836,000	5,554,200	4.30	100	1	1	1	30	66	1
Total churches, members, and denominations (mid-1995)	16,239	3,356,405	6,573,915	3.43	101	1	1	1	31	66	1
Total churches, members, and denominations (mid-2000)	17,000	3,963,000	7,761,501	3.38	103	1	1	1	32	67	1
Total churches, members, and denominations (mid-2025)	29,000	8,018,000	15,704,000	2.86	197	2	1	1	40	150	3

NOTES ON TABLE ABOVE

Language. Names in column 1 are given in either French or English, depending on which is in major usage; the former work mainly in East Cameroon, the latter in West Cameroon.

NATIONAL COUNCILS (Column 4, 5th letter).

E = Evangelical Alliance of Cameroon.

K = Fédération des Eglises et Missions Evangéliques du Cameroun (FEMEC)/Federation of Protestant Churches & Missions in Cameroon.

R = Conférence Episcopale du Cameroun (CENC)/Episcopal Conference of Cameroon.

Other national councils. Conseil des Eglises Baptistes et Evangéliques du Cameroun (CEBC) (1957; members EEC and UEBC); Comité d'Union des Eglises du Cameroun.

OTHER AFRICAN INDIGENOUS CHURCHES. There are many pentecostal and other immigrant groups from Nigeria, particularly in the west. Others include: Apostolic Ch, Eglise Chrétienne, Spiritual Holiness Ch of Cameroon (archbishop, in West Cameroon).

CANADA

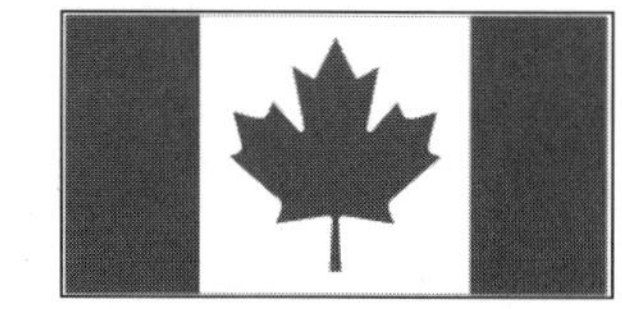

SECULAR DATA, AD 2000

STATE
Official name: The Dominion of Canada/Le Dominion du Canada.
Short name: Canada. **Adjective of nationality:** Canadian.
Flag: Red maple leaf on white field, with red bars at each side.
Area: 9,970,610 sq. km. (3,849,674 sq. mi.).
Government: Federal parliamentary state (also constitutional monarchy), since 1867 (1534 French rule, 1763 British rule, 1867 Dominion of Canada).
Legislature: Parliament: Senate, 104 members; House of Commons, 301 members.
Official language: English and French (Français).
Monetary unit: 1 Canadian dollar (Can$) = 100 cents. **US$1=** Can$1.51.
Chief cities: Toronto 4,657,000; Montreal 3,401,000; Vancouver 1,987,000; OTTAWA 1,085,000; Edmonton 913,000.
Political divisions: 12 provinces.
Armed forces: 78,000.

DEMOGRAPHY
Population: 31,147,000.
Population density: 3.1/sq. km. (8.0/sq. mi.).
Under 15 years: 5,899,000.
Growth rate p.a.: 0.88% (births 10.98, deaths 7.50).
Mortality: Infant, per 1,000: 5.9; **Maternal per 100,000:** 6.0.
Life expectancy: 79 (male 77, female 82).
Household size: 2.7. **Floor area per person, sq.m:** 50.0.
Major languages: English, French, German, Italian, Ukrainian, Dutch, Polish, Yiddish, Norwegian, Greek, Hungarian, Chinese, Swedish, Serbo-Croatian, Danish, Portuguese, Eskimo, and over 70 others.
Urban dwellers: 77.07%. **Urban growth rate p.a.:** 0.9%.
Labor force: 52%.

ETHNOLINGUISTIC PEOPLES
45.4% Anglo-Canadian; 23.4% French-Canadian; 3.4% Han Chinese; 3.3% British; 2.3% Punjabi.

ECONOMY
National income p.a. per person: US$19,380; **per family:** US$52,326.

EDUCATION
Adult literacy: 96% (male 97%, female 96%). **Schools:** 16,231.
Universities: 272. **School enrolment:** female/male: 104%/105%.

HEALTH
Access to health services: 95%. **Access to safe water:** 100%.
Hospitals: 1,079 (50 beds per 10,000). **Doctors:** 60,559.
Blind: 27,184. **Deaf:** 1,840,700. **Murder rate:** 5.
Lepers: 500.

LITERATURE
New book titles p.a.: 23,050 (740 p.a. per million). **Periodicals:** 1,960. **Newspapers:** 107 dailies.

COMMUNICATION (per 1,000 people)
Phones: 590 (22% mobile). **Radios:** 803. **TV sets:** 647.
Daily newspaper circulation: 189. **Computers:** 511.

REFUGEES
Alien refugees from other countries: 24,900.

HUMAN LIFE AND LIBERTY (optimum condition=100.0%)
HDI: 96.0. **HSI:** 97.0. **HFI:** 85.0. **EFL:** 60.0.

Country status. Canada is the world's second largest country, stretching across five time zones with a climate ranging from polar and sub-polar in the north to cool in the south. Efficient national transportation has played a major role in Canada's economic development.

HUMAN LIFE AND LIBERTY

Human need and development. Canada is a developed country with a prosperous and stable economy. It is also one of the major donor countries providing

Country Table 1. **Religious adherents in Canada, AD 1900-2025.**

Year / Name	1900 Adherents	1900 %	1970 Adherents	1970 %	mid-1990 Adherents	mid-1990 %	Annual change, 1990-2000 Natural	Conversion	Total	Rate	mid-1995 Adherents	mid-1995 %	mid-2000 Adherents	mid-2000 %	mid-2025 Adherents	mid-2025 %
Christians	**5,504,020**	**98.4**	**20,135,000**	**94.4**	**22,624,000**	**81.4**	**273,169**	**-59,370**	**213,799**	**0.91**	**23,778,000**	**80.3**	**24,761,988**	**79.5**	**28,864,000**	**76.2**
PROFESSION																
professing Christians	**5,504,020**	**98.4**	**20,135,000**	**94.4**	**22,624,000**	**81.4**	**273,169**	**-59,370**	**213,799**	**0.91**	**23,778,000**	**80.3**	**24,761,988**	**79.5**	**28,864,000**	**76.2**
AFFILIATION																
unaffiliated Christians	393,020	7.0	4,589,000	21.5	4,084,000	14.7	49,318	-5,297	44,021	1.03	4,378,000	14.8	4,524,210	14.5	4,864,000	12.8
affiliated Christians	**5,111,000**	**91.4**	**15,546,000**	**72.9**	**18,540,000**	**66.7**	**223,851**	**-54,073**	**169,778**	**0.88**	**19,400,000**	**65.5**	**20,237,778**	**65.0**	**24,000,000**	**63.3**
Roman Catholics	2,230,000	39.9	9,094,858	42.7	11,720,000	42.2	141,529	-11,734	129,795	1.06	12,408,837	41.9	13,017,945	41.8	15,500,000	40.9
Protestants	2,288,000	40.9	4,197,246	19.7	4,863,000	17.5	58,725	-10,025	48,700	0.96	5,149,272	17.4	5,350,000	17.2	5,700,000	15.0
Independents	4,000	0.1	670,800	3.2	1,400,000	5.0	16,906	11,094	28,000	1.84	1,575,319	5.3	1,680,000	5.4	2,700,000	7.1
Anglicans	559,000	10.0	1,176,914	5.5	880,000	3.2	10,627	-16,627	-6,000	-0.70	848,256	2.9	820,000	2.6	800,000	2.1
Orthodox	15,000	0.3	375,500	1.8	510,000	1.8	6,159	841	7,000	1.29	543,100	1.8	580,000	1.9	800,000	2.1
Marginal Christians	15,000	0.3	342,868	1.6	418,000	1.5	5,048	-1,848	3,200	0.74	433,668	1.5	450,000	1.4	500,000	1.3
doubly-affiliated	0	0.0	-312,186	-1.5	-1,251,000	-4.5	-15,107	-25,810	-40,917	2.87	-1,558,452	-5.3	-1,660,167	-5.3	-2,000,000	-5.3
Trans-megabloc groupings																
Evangelicals	1,405,000	25.1	1,578,000	7.4	2,240,000	8.1	27,050	2,950	30,000	1.26	2,402,166	8.1	2,540,000	8.2	3,145,000	8.3
Pentecostals/Charismatics	0	0.0	1,640,000	7.7	3,696,000	13.3	44,632	28,268	72,900	1.82	4,110,722	13.9	4,425,000	14.2	6,000,000	15.8
Great Commission Christians	**560,000**	**10.0**	**6,823,000**	**32.0**	**10,977,000**	**39.5**	**132,557**	**30,232**	**162,789**	**1.39**	**11,846,800**	**40.0**	**12,604,889**	**40.5**	**15,920,000**	**42.0**
Nonreligious	10,000	0.2	628,000	3.0	2,725,500	9.8	32,913	33,617	66,530	2.21	3,128,200	10.6	3,390,796	10.9	4,850,000	12.8
Chinese folk-religionists	5,120	0.1	30,000	0.1	680,000	2.5	8,212	1,327	9,539	1.32	730,000	2.5	775,389	2.5	880,000	2.3
Atheists	1,000	0.0	100,000	0.5	420,000	1.5	5,072	6,011	11,083	2.37	485,000	1.6	530,834	1.7	650,000	1.7
Jews	16,400	0.3	294,000	1.4	350,000	1.3	4,227	1,059	5,286	1.42	380,000	1.3	402,859	1.3	460,000	1.2
Muslims	50	0.0	42,000	0.2	250,000	0.9	3,019	3,759	6,778	2.43	280,000	1.0	317,776	1.0	600,000	1.6
Hindus	0	0.0	20,000	0.1	225,000	0.8	2,717	4,302	7,019	2.75	260,000	0.9	295,185	1.0	550,000	1.5
Sikhs	0	0.0	7,000	0.0	240,000	0.9	2,898	2,473	5,371	2.04	270,000	0.9	293,713	0.9	450,000	1.2
Buddhists	10,410	0.2	16,000	0.1	180,000	0.7	2,174	4,944	7,118	3.39	200,000	0.7	251,175	0.8	420,000	1.1
Baha'is	0	0.0	24,000	0.1	28,000	0.1	338	2	340	1.15	29,600	0.1	31,396	0.1	50,000	0.1
New-Religionists	0	0.0	2,000	0.0	15,000	0.1	181	1,450	1,631	7.64	17,000	0.1	31,310	0.1	31,000	0.1
Zoroastrians	0	0.0	0	0.0	19,000	0.1	229	363	592	2.75	22,000	0.1	24,917	0.1	40,000	0.1
Spiritists	0	0.0	4,000	0.0	9,500	0.0	115	25	140	1.39	10,300	0.0	10,901	0.0	15,000	0.0
Ethnoreligionists	44,000	0.8	12,000	0.1	9,000	0.0	109	-153	-44	-0.49	8,500	0.0	8,565	0.0	6,000	0.0
Other religionists	1,000	0.0	10,000	0.1	16,000	0.1	193	191	384	2.17	18,400	0.1	19,835	0.1	30,000	0.1
World A (unevangelized persons)	55,923	1.0	106,620	0.5	555,820	2.0	6,712	6,594	13,306	2.17	621,966	2.1	685,234	2.2	1,326,360	3.5
World B (evangelized non-Christians)	32,357	0.6	1,082,380	5.1	4,611,180	16.6	55,685	52,776	108,461	2.14	5,217,481	17.6	5,699,778	18.3	7,705,640	20.3
World C (Christians)	5,504,020	98.4	20,135,000	94.4	22,624,000	81.4	273,169	-59,370	213,799	0.91	23,778,000	80.3	24,761,988	79.5	28,864,000	76.2
Country's population	**5,592,300**	**100.0**	**21,324,000**	**100.0**	**27,791,000**	**100.0**	**335,566**	**0**	**335,566**	**1.15**	**29,617,448**	**100.0**	**31,147,000**	**100.0**	**37,896,000**	**100.0**

COLUMNS, ROWS.
For meanings and definitions, see Codebook (Part 3). Note that, by definition, total 'Christians' = professing + crypto-Christians, which also = affiliated + unaffiliated Christians, and also = Great Commission Christians + latent Christians. Percentages may not always total exactly, due to rounding.

CENSUSES.
1871 (Dominion of Canada only): 43.6% Protestants (16.3% Methodists, 16.2% Presbyterians, 6.8% Baptists), 41.7% Roman Catholics, 13.7% Anglicans, 1% Buddhists/Confucians/pagans, 0.0% Jews. **1901** (Dominion only): 44.0% Protestants, 41.7% Roman Catholics, 12.8% Anglicans, 1.2% Buddhists/Confucians/pagans, 0.3% Jews. Note: the 1900 column above is based on the separate 1901 censuses for the Dominion of Canada (5,371,315) plus Newfoundland & Labrador (220,984). **1911:** 43.9% Protestants, 39.4% Roman Catholics, 14.5% Anglicans, 1.2% Buddhists/Confucians/pagans, 1.0% Jews. **1921:** 41.3% Protestants, 38.7% Roman Catholics, 16.1% Anglicans, 1.9% Orthodox, 1.4% Jews, 0.3% marginal Protestants, 0.2% nonreligious, 0.1% Buddhists. **1931:** 39.8% Protestants (19.5% United Ch of Canada), 39.5% Roman Catholics, 15.8% Anglicans, 2.6% Orthodox, 1.5% Jews, 0.3% marginal Protestants, 0.2% nonreligious, 0.1% Buddhists. **1941:** 41.8% Roman Catholics, 38.1% Protestants (19.2% United Ch of Canada), 15.2% Anglicans, 2.6% Orthodox, 1.5% Jews, 0.3% marginal Protestants, 0.2% nonreligious, 0.1% Buddhists. **1.VI.1951** (de jure): 43.3% Roman Catholics, 36.9% Protestants (20.5% United Ch of Canada), 14.7% Anglicans, 2.6% Orthodox, 1.5% Jews, 0.5% marginal Protestants, 0.4% nonreligious, 0.1% Buddhists. **1.VI.1961** (de jure): 45.7% Roman Catholics, 35.5% Protestants (20.1% United Ch of Canada), 13.2% Anglicans, 2.7% Orthodox, 1.4% Jews, 0.8% marginal Protestants (0.4% Jehovah's Witnesses), 0.5% nonreligious, 0.1% Buddhists, 0.1% ethnoreligionists. **1.VI.1971** (de jure): 46.2% Roman Catholics, 32.0% Protestants (17.5% United Ch of Canada), 11.8% Anglicans, 4.3% nonreligious and atheists, 2.8% Orthodox, 1.3% Jews, 1.2% marginal Protestants (0.8% Jehovah's Witnesses), 0.1% Buddhists, 0.3% other religionists. The detailed census statistics of religion every decade from 1921-71 given in *Religious denominations, 1971 Census of Canada* (1973), p. 9-1, permit clear comparisons for all confessions except the Orthodox, whose census labels ('Greek Orthodox' and 'Ukrainian Catholic') are too imprecise to clearly enumerate the complex Catholic/Orthodox/Greek/Russian/Ukrainian/etc situation, as has here been done in our Table 2 below.

POLLS.
Numerous polls of profession, attendance and belief have been taken since 1940 (Gallup Poll of Canada, et alia).

NOTES ON RELIGIONS
ATHEISTS. 2 parties: Communist Party of Canada (CPC) (legal); and Communist Party of Canada Marxist-Leninist (CPCM/L) (legal; pro-Chinese).
BAHA'IS. Entered before 1921. Recent growth from 68 local spiritual assemblies (1964) to 160 (1973), including several on Indian reservations; to a total of 385 (1996)
BUDDHISTS. Japanese, Vietnamese, and Chinese followers of Mahayana Buddhism, with some White converts.
CHINESE FOLK-RELIGIONISTS. In 1900, these numbered 5,120 (called Confucians) out of a total of 17,300 Chinese. A blend of Confucianism, Taoism and Buddhism, folk religion is practiced by over a third of all Chinese in Canada.
ETHNORELIGIONISTS. Shamanists. In 1900, 44,000 out of a total of 108,000 Canadian Indians followed their tribal religion (the rest: 32% RCs, 14% Anglicans, 13% Protestants). After declining from 200,000 in the 16th century, the Indian population began to increase again in the 20th. By 1970 about 96% of all Indians were members of Christian churches.
HINDUS. Immigrants from India and (1972) Uganda Asians; also Canadian converts to new sects including Sri Chinmoy Centre (1,000 adherents, 200 committed disciples), Ananda Marga, and 90,000 members of various religions who are also followers of a movement with Hindu origins which claims to be a philosophy but not a religion: the Science of Creative Intelligence (SCI) or Transcendental Meditation (TM). ISKCON (Hare Krishna) operates 4 centers and a farm.
INDEPENDENTS. In over 50 denominations in 1995 (see Table 2).
JEWS. 170 Orthodox, 25 Conservative and 5 Reform congregations. The total 'Natural change' above includes immigration of about 2,000 a year.
MUSLIMS. In 1965 mostly Canadian-born, with immigrants after 1965 from Pakistan, India, Guyana, Uganda (20,000 Ismaili Asians), Malaysia, Indonesia, Iran, Turkey, Albania, Lebanon, Egypt and other Arab countries. Muslims live throughout Canada in urban and rural areas, and also in the isolated northern settled areas. Mosques: Ottawa, Edmonton. There is also a small Ahmadiya Mission based in Toronto. The total 'Natural change' above includes over 6,000 immigrants a year. *Hajj pilgrims to Mecca*. (1976) 22.
NEW-RELIGIONISTS. Adherents of various Asian syncretistic New Religions including 2,500 converts to Nichiren Shoshu (Soka Gakkai) from Japan.
NONRELIGIOUS. Mainly Whites.
OTHER RELIGIONISTS. Adherents of a variety of other non-Christian religions, including 1,200 Rastafarians (Blacks from Jamaica and other West Indies islands; 800 in Toronto; 600 allegedly with criminal records), and a host of syncretistic cults from the USA including Rosicrucians (27 AMORC centers), and I Am Religious Movement (in Calgary and Edmonton) and its offshoot the Church Universal and Triumphant (in BC, Ontario and Quebec).
PENTECOSTALS/CHARISMATICS. By contrast with developing countries, in Canada the Catholic Charismatic Renewal showed vast activity in the 1970s but appears to have peaked by the 1990s. Thus totals in January 1974 were about 10,000 involved adults. Totals (January 1974), were about 10,000 involved adults (over 15 years old) in 500 prayer groups; total charismatic community including children, 20,000. (Mid-1976) in Quebec alone, 35,000 involved adults including 10,000 in the movement's youth wing Youth Testimony; total community including children for all Canada, about 100,000. In June 1977, 50,000 attended a French-speaking renewal conference in Montreal. By 1995 numbers had shrunk to 253 anglophone weekly prayer meetings, and up to 3,300 attenders at the Catholic Charismatic Crusade 'Washed in the Blood' at Hamilton, Ontario, 31 May-2 June 1996.
SIKHS. First immigrants settled in Vancouver early in the 20th century.

Great Commission Instrument Panel: status of Canada (for explanation see start of Part 4)

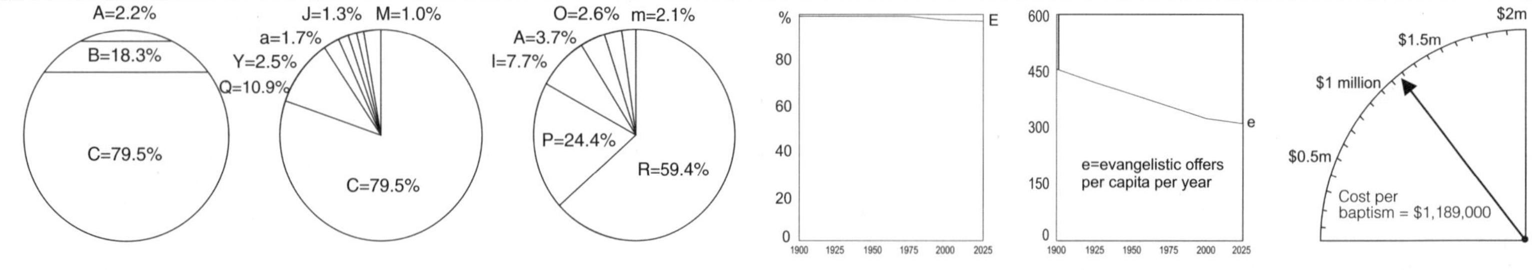

3 Worlds, AD 2000 | Religions, AD 2000 | Ecclesiastical blocs | Evangelization, 1900-2025 | Offers, 1900-2025 | Cost-effectiveness, AD 2000

aid to less developed countries of the world. Canadians enjoy a standard of living comparable to that of the United States, equal universal health coverage and extensive social security benefits.

Human rights and freedoms. Canadians enjoy in law and in practice a wide range of freedoms and individual rights enumerated in the Charter of Rights and Freedoms appended to the 1982 Constitution. Principal complaints in the field of human rights arise from occasional incidents involving nonwhite minorities, Aboriginals, and women. Native groups sometimes complain of cultural insensitivity and harassment by police officers. Minority language and cultural rights are protected by law. Freedom of press and speech is guaranteed in all circumstances except when it promotes racial hatred, pornography, or affects the rights of defendants in criminal trials involving grisly crimes.

Human environment. Canada is one of the least densely populated countries in the world. Outside the region bordering the United States, the land is virtually desolate. Pollution is therefore concentrated in this region which also suffers from acid rain, much of it of U. S. origin. Fish habitats are particularly affected by overexploitation. As one of the few countries with a National Green Plan, Canada has a goal of setting aside 12% of its land area as wilderness preserve.

NON-CHRISTIAN RELIGIONS

Judaism is the second largest non-Christian religious community in Canada. There are at present 170 Orthodox, 25 Conservative and 5 Reform con-

Country summary. **Worlds A, B, C by ethnolinguistic peoples, cities, and major civil divisions in Canada.**

	PEOPLES							CITIES							CIVIL DIVISIONS						
World	Num	Pop 2000	C%	Christians	E%	U%	Unevangelized	Num	Pop 2000	C%	Christians	E%	U%	Unevangelized	Num	Pop 2000	C%	Christians	E%	U%	Unevangelized
A	1	0	0.00	0	0	0	0	0	0	0.00	0	0	0	0	0	0	0.00	0	0	0	0
B	22	2,514,844	8.35	210,053	76	24	595,651	0	0	0.00	0	0	0	0	0	0	0.00	0	0	0	0
C	129	28,631,799	69.95	20,027,731	100	0	93,205	49	21,091,780	63.01	13,289,256	97	3	586,822	12	31,146,632	64.98	20,237,778	98	2	688,849
Total	**152**	**31,146,643**	**64.98**	**20,237,784**	**98**	**2**	**688,856**	**49**	**21,091,780**	**63.01**	**13,289,256**	**97**	**3**	**586,822**	**12**	**31,146,632**	**64.98**	**20,237,778**	**98**	**2**	**688,849**

gregations. Some 25 national organizations exist including: for Orthodox Judaism, the Rabbinical Council of America (Canadian section) and the Union of Orthodox Jewish Congregations; for Conservative Judaism, the Rabbinical Assembly (Canada Division); and for reform Judaism, the Council of Reform Synagogues. In addition, there is the Canadian Jewish Congress, founded in Montreal in 1919, which represents Canadian Jewry as a whole. Each synagogue is autonomous, choosing its own rabbi and administering its affairs. Many synagogues have schools for teaching Hebrew and the history of Judaism.

Islam is rapidly growing with the continuous arrival of immigrants from Pakistan, India, Guyana, Uganda (Asians) and some Arab countries. The Ottawa Muslim Association was founded in 1962, and funds have recently been collected for the construction of the first Canadian mosque in the capital. There is also a mosque in Edmonton, Alberta. Muslims often meet in rented halls and university students in their campus student union. The principal coordinating body since 1952 has been the Federation of Islamic Associations of the United States and Canada (FIA) with headquarters in the USA, and in 1973, a national organization was formed in Toronto, the Council of Muslim Communities of Canada. Various provincial Islamic associations and city chapters are affiliated with the council. The Muslim Students Association of USA and Canada is centered in Gary, Indiana (USA). The nonconfessional Institute of Islamic Studies was founded in 1952 at McGill University, Montreal, for research and the teaching of Islamics.

Baha'i is organized under the National Spiritual Assembly of the Baha'is of Canada with its headquarters in Willowdale, Ontario. A part of the Baha'i World Community centered in Haifa, Israel, there are 385 local spiritual assemblies or a thousand or so Baha'i centers throughout the country, several of which are found on Indian reservations. Baha'i schools include the National Teaching Institute in Fort Qu'Appelle, Saskatchewan and summer schools in Ontario, British Columbia, and Quebec.

Hinduism has continued to increase due to the influx of Asians from the Indian subcontinent and most recently from Uganda. Two Hindu organizations exist in Montreal: the Yoga Vedanta Sivananda Center and the Sound of India.

Buddhism has many adherents organized into 18 groupings called churches and organized under a national office in Toronto into 4 districts (Eastern, with seven churches, Manitoba with one church, Alberta with seven churches and British Columbia with seven churches). The Buddhist Churches of Canada belong to the Jodo Shin sect of Mahayana Buddhism. Buddhist strength is concentrated in the Japanese-Canadian community in western Canada. There is a Buddhist Center in Montreal.

Shamanism continues to influence the Eskimo peoples in spite of the formal conversion of most to Christianity. In the Yukon, sickness is believed to be caused by evil spirits (Aguiqtuq) who originate when the names of dead persons are not passed on to the new-born children of succeeding generations. Shamans or medicine men use 'helping' spirits in their role as intermediaries between the natural and supernatural worlds.

CHRISTIANITY

The first Catholic missionary, a French secular priest, arrived in 1608 and began work among the Micmac Indians, and he was followed shortly afterwards by a Jesuit party and 3 Recollet priests in 1615. Huguenot merchants from France and Anglican explorers and traders from Great Britain were early on the scene, but opposition to Protestantism in French Canada was strong. Regular Anglican services were not begun until 1700 in Newfoundland and a decade later in Nova Scotia. SPG missionaries arrived in Halifax in 1749, and the first Anglican bishop was named for Nova Scotia in 1787. Sometime after 1750, began the immigration of New England Congregationalists into Nova Scotia, and within the next decade, Ulster Irish Presbyterians (1763) and New England Baptists had also settled there.

Methodism came to Newfoundland from Great Britain in 1765. Yorkshire Methodists entered Nova Scotia in 1772, and the Bay of Quinte was reached by 1785. Anglicanism grew more rapidly following the American war of independence due to the influx of American Loyalists as well as through British immigration after the Napoleonic wars in Europe. These early patterns have continued to dominate the Canadian religious scene. While French Canada has remained overwhelmingly Catholic, English Canada has been influenced mostly by Anglican and Protestant groups from Britain and the USA.

CATHOLIC CHURCH. From the time of the British victory in Canada until the beginning of the 1960s, the Catholic Church was closely allied with French Canadian society and made a profound contribution to the development of Quebec identity. Beginning about 1960, a rapid and often violent movement for the deconfessionalization of Catholic institutions has gained force and contributed to the disintegration of existing Catholic ecclesial structures. According to the report of the Episcopal conference's Dumont Study Commission concerning laity and the church, this manifests itself in a decline in religious practice, a decrease in vocations (from 2,000 new priestly vocations in 1946 to 100 in 1970), the indifference of youth and the collapse of lay organization. A survey carried out during 1968-70 by CRSR (Laval University, Quebec) estimated the total number of Canadian priests to be 15,546, of which 1,541 were residents outside the country. The majority are French-speaking, 70.3% of the diocesan clergy and 74.1% of the regular clergy, while English-speaking clergy were respectively 27.8% and 20.5% and those with other mother tongues were 1.8% and 5.4%. A major finding was that every year since 1963, the number of young priests has diminished significantly in all categories, religious and secular as well as French- and English-speaking.

Ecclesial activity now manifests itself through new grass-roots communities, marginal groups and post-conciliar institutions. In recent years, Quebec has witnessed the creation of numerous religious life entities outside the formal structures of the church, some of which are informally related to the official church while others are not. Several different types of groups may be distinguished, such as parish communities, marginal communities, and extraecclesial religious groups.

Parish communities consist of groups of faithful within a parish or regional grouping of several parishes. They are usually organized by parish clergy and are dedicated to experimenting with new liturgical forms and missionary ventures. Although often of progressivist tendencies, they define their role in relationship to the universal church. Primarily an urban phenomenon, their principal problems revolve around their functional relationship to official parish structures. Their numerical importance is considerable since they numbered at least 150 communities by 1970.

In addition, marginal communities exist without ties to any official structures of the church. They express a similar intensity of Christian conviction as that evident in parish communities, but their participation is more limited. They are strongest in the urban milieu and manifest sectarian tendencies in some cases. Not uncommonly, they present themselves as study groups including non-Catholics, without the participation of clergy. Among these are extraecclesial religious bodies generally belonging to the Canadian revival movement and often influenced by Pentecostal and marginal groups, including Mormons and Jehovah's Witnesses. They are found exclusively in urban areas among the younger elements in the population. All of these new movements are found in the English-speaking as well as French-speaking Catholic areas.

The Holy See has diplomatic relations with Canada and in AD 2000 is represented to government and the Catholic hierarchy by a nuncio residing in Ottawa.

PROTESTANT CHURCHES. The largest Protestant denomination is the United Church of Canada which came into being in 1925, uniting the work of the Methodist, Congregational and nearly half the Presbyterian churches. In 1968, the Canadian Conference of the Evangelical United Brethren joined as well and church union discussions with the Anglican Church are continuing. The UCC is organized into 11 geographical conferences which are further subdivided into 93 presbyteries. The chief policy-making body is the General Council which meets every 2 years. United Church service agencies are organized into 5 divisions dealing with Communication; Finance; Ministry, Personnel and Education; Mission in Canada; and World Outreach.

The Presbyterian Church in Canada, the second largest Protestant body, was formed from those Presbyterian congregations which refused to go into union in 1925. National agencies include the Boards of World Missions, Christian Education, Stewardship and Budget, Evangelism and Social Action, and the Women's Missionary Society.

Canadian Baptists are found principally in the Baptist Federation of Canada whose member bodies are the Baptist Convention of Ontario and Quebec, Baptist Union of Western Canada, French Baptist

United Church of Canada. Pastoral visit by floatplane on part of UCC minister from Yellowknife in far North.

Union, and United Baptist Convention of the Atlantic Provinces. The federation carries on its work through 4 departments dealing with Canadian Missions, Christian Education, Ministry, and Overseas Missions. Of other bodies not forming part of the federation, the most important is the fellowship of Evangelical Baptist Churches. Other smaller groups include the Baptist General Conference, which was established through the efforts of swedish Missionaries from the USA; Canadian Baptist Conference, which is related to the Southern Baptist Convention of the USA; Convention of Regular Baptists; North American Baptist General Conference; and Primitive Baptist Conference of New Brunswick.

Over 15 distinct Pentecostal churches have been organized. Most are small and many have direct connections with similar groups in the USA. By far, the largest is the Pentecostal Assemblies of Canada which is the fourth largest Protestant denomination in Canada, is the Canadian counterpart to the USA Assemblies of God and which has widespread overseas missionary work.

Several Lutheran denominations are active, the most important being the Lutheran Church in American—Canada section, which consists of the 3 Canadian synods of the American church; the Lutheran Church—Canada, which has been autonomous since 1959 but retains fraternal ties with its parent body; the Lutheran Church—Missouri Synod in the U.S.A.; and the Evangelical Lutheran Church in Canada, which until 1967 was the Canada District of the American Lutheran Church. In addition, there is the small Latvian Evangelical Lutheran Church, which consists exclusively of refugees from eastern Europe.

Mennonites are widely dispersed across Canada. Of 14 distinct bodies, the Conference of Mennonites of Canada, General Conference Mennonite Church, and the Mennonite Brethren Churches of North America are the largest.

Anglican Church of Canada. Members include 80% of all Eskimos (shown at 1974 consecration of Bishop of The Arctic).

Other significant Protestant groups are the Salvation Army, Christian Reformed Churches in Canada, and the Seventh-day Adventist Church.

ANGLICAN CHURCH. The Anglican Church of Canada is organized into 28 dioceses in 4 provinces (British Columbia, Canada, Ontario and Rupert's Land), each under a metropolitan or archbishop, the head of the general synod bearing the title of primate. Service agencies of the church include 5 divisions (National and World Program, Parish and Diocesan Services, Communication, Planning, Pensions) in addition to the Missionary Society and the Department of Administration and Finance. Canadian Anglicanism has been autonomous for more than a century.

ORTHODOX CHURCHES. Immigration patterns have helped to create a wide variety of Orthodox churches of different traditions; Arab, Armenian, Bulgarian, Belorussian, Coptic, Estonian, Greek, Macedonian, Old Believer, Romanian, Serbian, Syrian, Russian, and Ukrainian. The largest body is the Ninth Archdiocesan District of the Greek Orthodox Archdiocese of North and South America, which is under the jurisdiction of the Ecumenical Patriarchate of Constantinople and whose primate resides in the USA.

Renewal movements. In the 1990s the Pentecostal/Charismatic Renewal continued to spread rapidly across most older churches, and numbered over 4,425,000 adherents (of whom 11% Pentecostals, 59% Charismatics, and 30% Independents).

Indigenous missions. The missionary movement in Canada dates from the mid-19th century, dramatically increasing in both Catholic and Protestant traditions at the end the 19th century. Catholic and mainline Protestant missions have been on the decline since the 1960s. Independent charismatic churches have taken up some of this slack in the late 1970s through early 1990s, sending hundreds of missionaries directly from their fellowships.

Greek Orthodox Archdiocese. At WCC 6th Assembly (1983) in Vancouver, Archbishop Iakovos.

CHURCH AND STATE

The churches have been separated from the state since 1852, the year when the Anglican Church, the official church at the time, became a voluntary association similar to Canada's other denominations. Freedom of religion was proclaimed at the same time which today is expressed in the following terms in the Law Digest of Quebec: 'The enjoyment and free exercise of worship of every religious profession without distinction or preference is permitted by the constitution and laws of this province, but in a manner which does not serve as an excuse for license neither authorizes practices which are incompatible with the peace and security of the province'. A similar situation exists in other provinces of Canada. Religious questions are not handled primarily by either provincial or federal authorities, but may come under the jurisdiction of either depending upon the issue in question. No public organization deals specifically with religious or ecclesiastical affairs.

Canadian public law is not specifically Christian, but throughout its history, it has accorded a place of honor to all forms of Christianity, particularly Catholicism in Quebec. Religious groups have often enjoyed privileges, notably tax exemptions. In some provinces, including Quebec, education is organized according to religious preference. However, for some years now, there has been an accelerated secularization of state institutions, and the separation of church and state, already a legal fact, has tended to become an increasing reality in practice. This evolution is especially evident in Quebec, which up to the early 1960s displayed under the Duplessis regime all the characteristics of a clerical state.

BROADCASTING AND MEDIA

There are numerous local Christian radio and television stations. Canada is a member of UNDA, and Canadian dioceses sponsor 16 programs, some daily and some weekly. Programs created by *Back to the Bible* and other producers are aired on more than 80 local stations. Shortwave programming from HCJB, TWR, KNLS and other international broadcasters can be received.

CBN's *700 Club* is seen daily on television channels covering Ontario, Manitoba, and Toronto. LeSEA's satellite network covers one-third of Canada with evangelistic programming. The 'Jesus' Film has been aired on national TV. There are 9 local Christian French programs aired, plus 2 on local cable networks. Vision TV is an English-language Catholic program producing pre-evangelistic programs over the Anik D2 satellite.

INTERDENOMINATIONAL ORGANIZATIONS

The Canadian Council of Churches (CCC) was founded in 1944, building on the foundations of many other prior organizations: Moral and Social Reform Council of Canada in 1907, Social service Council of Canada in 1914, Religious education Council of Canada in 1917, Committee on Evangelism in 1930, World Council of Churches Canadian Committee in 1938, Christian Social Council of Canada in 1939, University Christian Mission Committee in 1940, Inter-Church Committee on Missionary Education in 1941, Conference of Secretaries of Foreign Mission Boards in 1942, and Canadian Overseas Mission Council in 1944. Twenty-four regional and local ecumenical bodies work in cooperation with CCC. One such body which includes Catholic participation is the Joint Working Group of the Montreal Churches/Groupe de Travail des Eglises de Montreal, a bilingual body formed in 1970, consisting of 26 members officially appointed by the Catholic, United, Anglican, Presbyterian, Orthodox, Lutheran, and Baptist churches. The Group is open to all denominations and serves as an authentic Council of Churches for Montreal.

The Office National de'Oecumenisme (French sector), founded in 1963, and the National secretariat for Ecumenism (English sector), founded in 1966, are executive bodies of 2 ad hoc Catholic Episcopal commissions charged with the organization and coordination of ecumenical activity in Catholic dioceses. The Council of Ecumenism, consisting of 10 members, assists them in a consultative capacity.

The Joint Working Group CCC-CCC (Canadian Council of Churches and Canadian Catholic Conference) was founded in 1968 on the model of the Joint Working Group of the Roman Secretariat for Unity and the World Council of Churches. Consisting of 7 members from each organization, it inspires and coordinates the activities of the Canadian churches. The Joint CCC-CCC Steering Committee on Poverty Strategy has a similar composition, but its aims and objectives are more limited. The 2 CCCs have also together created the Canadian Coalition for Development, a bilingual body grouping together some 20 Christian and non-Christian organizations interested in all aspects of development.

There are a number of other ecumenical centers and bodies. The Canadian Liturgical Society is an interdenominational English-speaking group which engages in study and research for the churches in collaboration with the Joint Working Group CCC-CCC. The Center Oecumenique Diocesain of the Catholic archdiocese of Montreal, founded in 1960, handles information, dialogue and teaching on ecumenism. The Catholic Information Center, founded in Toronto in 1958 and directed by Paulists (CSP) and laymen, engages in adult training in theology with an ecumenical orientation, including preparation of couples for mixed marriages. The ecumenical Institute of Canada, founded in Toronto in 1963, and directed by the Canadian Council of Churches and the Canadian School of Missions, gives courses for theology students. The Center d'Information et d'Oecumenisme, in Montreal, is sponsored jointly by the Consistory of Montreal and the United Church of Canada and gives special attention to youth.

Of ecumenical significance also is the fact that the Catholic Church has 6 members on the bilingual and interdenominational Faith and Constitution Commission and is involved in official dialogue bilingually with Anglicans and in English with Lutherans.

FUTURE TRENDS AND PROSPECTS

Steady decline of church affiliation is expected to continue into 21st century falling to 63.3% by 2025. The nonreligious are expected to increase to 12.8% by 2025.

With the continued growth of non-Christian immigrant populations and the rising tide of secularism, it is probable that Christians will represent less than 70% of Canada's population by AD 2050. The nonreligious would be the main benefactor of this Christian decline with Muslims, Sikhs, atheists, Hindus, and other non-Christian religions all gaining considerably.

BIBLIOGRAPHY

A concise history of Christianity in Canada. T. Murphy. New York: Oxford University Press, 1996. 352p.

A history of Christianity in the United States and Canada. M. A. Noll. Grand Rapids, MI: Eerdmans, 1992. 592p.

A history of the churches in the United States and Canada. R. T. Handy. *Oxford history of the Christian Church.* Oxford, UK: Oxford University Press, 1977. 486p.

A pilgrimage of faith: the Mennonite Brethren Church in Russia and North America, 1860–1990. J. B. Toews. *Perspectives on Mennonite life and thought,* 8. Winnipeg: Kindred Press, 1993. 383p.

A solitary pillar: Montreal's Anglican church and the quiet revolution. J. Marshall. Montreal: McGill-Queen's University Press, 1995. 220p.

Amazing grace: Evangelicalism in Australia, Britain, Canada, and the United States. G. A. Rawlyk & M. A. Noll (eds). Grand Rapids, MI: Baker Books, 1993. 429p.

Anglican essentials: reclaiming faith within the Anglican Church of Canada. G. W. Egerton (ed). Toronto: Anglican Book Centre, 1995. 320p.

Anglican year book, 1972. Toronto: Anglican Church of Canada, 1972 (annual). 206p.

Annuaire/Directory, 1969–1970. Ottawa: Canadian Catholic Conference, 1970. (Roman Catholic).

Canada. E. Ingles. *World bibliographical series,* vol. 62. Oxford, UK: CLIO Press, 1990. 375p. (See especially 'Religion,' p.81-7).

Canadian churches and foreign policy. B. Greene (ed). Toronto: J. Lorimer, 1990. 234p.

Canadian evangelicalism in the twentieth century: an introduction to its character. J. G. Stackhouse. Toronto: University of Toronto Press, 1993. 345p.

Christian resources handbook: a directory of Christian organizations in Canada. 1986/87 ed. Mississauga, Ontario: MARC Canada, 1986. 452p.

Christianity and native traditions: indigenization and syncretism among the Inuit and Dene of the western Arctic. A. R. Gualtieri. Notre Dame, IN: Cross Roads Books, 1984. 186p.

Christianity in Canada: a bibliography of books and articles to 1985. J. Arndt. Waterloo, Ontario: Wilfrid Laurier University Library, 1987. 195p.

Church and Canadian culture. R. E. VanderVennen (ed). Lanham, MD: University Press of America, 1991. 231p.

Church and sect in Canada. S. D. Clark. Toronto: University of Toronto Press, 1965.

Creed and culture: the place of English–speaking Catholics in Canadian society, 1750–1930. T. Murphy & G. J. Stortz (eds). *McGill-Queen's studies in the history of religion,* 11. Montreal: McGill-Queen's University Press, 1993. 303p.

'Developing a Pentecostal missiology in the Canadian context (1867–1944): the Pentecostal Assemblies of Canada.' I. A. Whitt. D.Miss. thesis, Fuller Theological Seminary, Pasadena, CA, 1994. 458p.

Die religionen Nordeurasiens und der amerikanischen Arktis. I. Paulson, Å. Hultkrantz & K. Jettmar. *Die Religionen der Menschheit,* vol. 3. Stuttgart: W. Kohlhammer, 1962. 425p.

Directory of departments and programs of religious studies in North America. D. G. Truemper (ed). Valparaiso, IN: Council of Societies for the Study of Religion, 1994. 545p.

Eskimos: Greenland and Canada. No. 2 of section 8: *Arctic peoples,* of *Iconography of religions.* I. Kleivan & B. Sonne. Leiden: E. J. Brill, 1985. 52p.

Ethnographic bibliography of North America. G. P. Murdock. 3rd ed. New Haven, CT: Human Relations Area Files, 1960. 393p.

Ethnographic bibliography of North America, 4th edition. Supplement 1973–1987. M. M. Martin & T. J. O'Leary. New Haven, CT: Human Relations Area Files Press, 1990. 3 vols. (Previously published as *Ethnographic bibliography of North America.* G. P. Murdock, 1960, 1975.).

Guide to schools and departments of religion and seminaries in the United States and Canada: degree programs in religious studies. New York: Macmillan, 1987. 623p.

Indians of Northeastern North America. No. 7 of section 10, *North America,* of *Iconography of religions.* A. W. Geertz. Leiden: E. J. Brill, 1986. 50p.

Le Canada ecclésiastique/Catholic directory of Canada, 1971–72. Montreal: Librairie Beauchemin, 1971.

Les Saints Martyrs canadiens. G. Laflèche. Laval, Québec: Singulier, 1988–89. 2 vols.

Mennonites in Canada. T. D. Regehr. Toronto: University of Toronto Press. 3 vols. to date; in progress.

Muslims in America. Y. Y. Haddad (ed). Oxford, UK: Oxford University Press, 1991. 272p. (Includes both Canada and the U.S.A.).

Native and Christian: indigenous voices on religious identity in the United States and Canada. J. Treat (ed). New York: Routledge, 1996. 256p.

New religious movements in the United States and Canada: a critical assessment and annotated bibliography. D. Choquette. *Bibliographies and indexes in religious studies,* 5. Westport, CT: Greenwood, 1985. 235p.

Prairie and plains Indians. No. 2 of section 10, *North America,* of *Iconography of religions.* Å. Hultkrantz. Leiden: E. J. Brill, 1973. 46p.

Profiles in belief: the religious bodies of the United States and Canada. A. C. Piepkorn. New York: Harper & Row, 1977–79. 4 vols in 3.

Religion in Canadian society. S. Crysdale & L. Wheatcroft (eds). Toronto: Macmillan & MacLean Hunter, 1976.

Religion in native North America. C. Vecsey (ed). Moscow, ID: University of Idaho Press, 1990. 208p.

Religions of the circumpolar north. R. Minion. *BINS bibliographic series,* no. 15. Edmonton, Alberta: University of Alberta, Boreal Institute for Northern Studies, 1985. 92p.

Religious denominations, 1971 Census of Canada. Ottawa: Statistics Canada, 1973. (Detailed tables, maps).

Subjects or citizens? the Mennonite experience in Canada, 1870–1925. A. Ens. Ottawa: University of Ottawa Press, 1994. 276p.

The Anglican Church in Canada: a history. P. Carrington. Toronto: Collins, 1963. 320p.

The Brethren in Christ in Canada: two hundred years of tradition and change. E. M. Sider. [Hamilton, Ontario]: Canadian Conference, Brethren in Christ Church, 1988.

The Canadian Christian source book 1994/95. S. Froom (ed). 2d ed. Mississauga, Ontario: Genesis Publications, 1994. 245p.

The Canadian Protestant experience, 1760 to 1990. G. A. Rawlyk (ed). Montreal: McGill-Queen's University Press,

The changing church in Canada: beliefs and social attitudes of United Church people. S. Crysdale. Toronto: United Church of Canada, 1965. 125p.

The Christian church in Canada. H. H. Walsh. Toronto: Ryerson Press, 1956, 1968. 355p.

The church grows in Canada. D. Wilson. Toronto: Canadian Council of Churches, 1966. 224p.

'The Church in Canada'. P Furse. Toronto: Canadian Council of Churches, 1966 (A detailed historical map).

The churches and the Canadian experience: a Faith and Order study of the Christian tradition. J. W. Grant (ed). Toronto: Ryerson Press, 1963.

The contribution of Methodism to Atlantic Canada. C. H. H. Scobie (ed). : McGill-Queen's University Press, 1992. 290p.

The Mormon presence in Canada. B. Y. Card (ed). Logan, UT: Utah State University Press, 1990. 408p.

'The organizational dilemmas of ethnic churches: a case study of Japanese Buddhism in Canada,' M. R. Mullins, *Sociological Analysis,* 49, 3 (Fall 1988), 217–233.

The state of the churches in the U.S.A. and Canada, 1985, as shown in their own official yearbooks and other reports: a study resource. Sun City, AZ: Ecumenism Research Agency, 1985. 15 microfilm reels. (Listing of USA denominational yearbooks, minutes, and reports).

The Ukrainian religious experience: tradition and the Canadian cultural context. D. J. Goa (ed). Edmonton: Canadian Institute of Ukrainian Studies, University of Alberta, 1989. 257p.

This is your church: a guide to the beliefs, policies, and positions of the United Church of Canada. S. Chambers. 3d ed. Toronto: United Church Pub. House, 1993. 176p.

United Church of Canada year book, 1974. Toronto: UCC, 1974. 2 vols. (See especially volume I, Statistics).

Yearbook of American and Canadian churches, 1998. K. B. Bedell (ed). Nashville, TN: Abingdon Press, for the Communication Division of the National Council of Churches of Christ in the U.S.A., 1998. 300p. (Annual publication. 1998 edition is the 66th issue).

Country Table 2. Organized churches and denominations in Canada.

Official name (bold type = church with over 10% of affiliated) 1	*Begun* 2	*Type* 3	*Counc* 4	*Congs* 5	*Adults* 6	*Affiliated 1970* 7	*Affiliated 1995* 8	*G%* 9	*Names, notes, and other statistics* (see Codebook, Part 3) 10
African Methodist Episcopal Church	c1920	I-Met	Vw...	3	1,000	3,000	3,030	0.04	M=AMEC(USA). US Blacks. Canadian HQ Toronto, USA HQ New York.
African Orthodox Church	1921	I-ARo	x....	4	1,000	1,000	2,000	2.81	*AOC.* Begun 1919 in New York. Large Black community on east coast of Canada.
Anglican Church of Canada	1578	A-plu	AW.RW	1,767	529,943	1,176,914	848,256	-1.30	*Eglise Episcopale de Canada.* 95% English-speaking. 4 Provinces, 31 Dioceses. 3463n.
Antiochian Orth Archdiocese of Toledo	c1940	O-Ara	.....	10	1,000	500	2,000	5.70	In Greek P Antioch. HQ Toledo, Ohio (USA). Arabs. 1975 Reunited with AD New York. Inx.
Antiochian Orth Christian AD New York	c1910	O-Ara	Cwo.f	13	40,000	25,000	100,000	5.70	Formerly Syrian Antiochian Orth Ch. HQ Montreal. Under Greek P Antioch. Arabs. 22n.
Apostolic Christian Church (Nazarean)	c1920	P-Hol	x....	15	1,000	715	1,500	3.01	Swiss immigrants related to Mennonites. In 17 nations. 32n,31t(320).
Apostolic Church in Canada	1924	P-PeA	Z..X.	14	1,200	2,000	1,600	-0.89	Related to Apostolic Church (UK). HQ Toronto. Missions in West Africa.
Apostolic Ch of Pentecost in Canada	1921	P-Pe1	x....	126	50,000	30,000	70,000	3.45	Schism ex PAoC over Jesus-only teaching. Ukrainians, Germans, Scandinavians. In 15 nations.
Apostolic Faith Mission of Canada	1910	P-Pe3	x....	10	1,000	1,000	1,500	1.64	HQ Portland, Oregon (USA). Strongest in Alberta. 8n,W=75%,50Y.
Armenian Apostolic Church: D Canada	1930	O-Arm	Ewc.W	7	17,600	15,000	27,000	2.38	*Armenian Ch of N America.* Gregorians. Under jurisdiction C Echmiadzin (USSR). 4n.
Assembly Hall Churches	c1970	I-3nC	.....	17	2,056	–	4,000	39.34	*Little Flock. Local Church.* Begun 1922 in China by Watchman Nee.
Associated Gospel Churches	1922	P-CBr	.....	123	9,402	20,000	17,502	-0.53	Founded as Christian Workers Church of Canada. Plymouth Brethren. 167n,101t.
Association of Vineyard Churches	1985	I-3cW	.....	24	4,000	–	6,670	10.00	F=John Wimber. M=AVC(USA).
Assoc of Independent Holiness Chs	1958	P-Hol	.....	15	400	650	800	0.83	Small denomination in holiness tradition. 10n,1s(2),W=75%.
Assoc of Regular Baptist Churches of C	1926	I-Bap	.T..T	15	4,600	7,000	6,570	-0.25	Association of local congregations. Schism ex Baptist Conv of Ontario & Quebec.
Baptist General Conference of Canada	c1890	P-Bap	TF...	75	6,165	20,000	10,300	-2.62	*BGC.* In west, Swedes from USA. 3 conferences: Central, Alberta, Columbia. 30Y.
Bible Holiness Movement	1949	P-Hol	x....	29	688	300	1,060	5.18	HQ Vancouver. Work in USA, India, Nigeria, Philippines. 5n,W=49%.
Brethren in Christ Church	1788	P-Men	GF..E	36	3,069	3,500	6,820	2.70	*Canadian Conference. Tunkers.* Ontario, Saskatchewan. HQ Sherkston. 47n,27t(2806).
Bulgarian Orthodox Church	c1950	O-Bul	MwO..	10	10,000	7,000	15,000	3.10	Bulgarian immigrants. Under P Sofia. Parish and cathedral in Toronto.
Byelorussian Autocephalic Orth Ch in C	1948	O-Bye	x....	2	600	1,000	1,100	0.38	White Russians. 1922 attempt at autonomy in USSR crushed. 1 bishop, HQ USA.
Canadian Baptist Conference	1959	P-Bap	.....	110	6,304	5,000	12,600	3.77	In BC despite SBC(USA) agreement not to work in Canada. M=IMB-SBC.
Canadian Baptist Ministries	1944	P-Bap	Tv..W	1,082	38,000	250,800	92,000	-3.93	*Federation Baptists.* 4 bodies. Supports M=CBOMB. 874n,973t(54899),2899Y.
Catholic Church of Canada:	1534	R-LEr	Bz..W	6,054	8,401,800	9,094,858	12,408,837	1.25	L, B. *Eglise Catholique.* C=63+17+196. 11q,15s. 6176n 4098x 7064m 28026w 171759Yy
M Edmonton	1871	R-Lat	Bs	167	201,000	139,237	294,935	3.05	Eng Alb English-French, Polish, German. 81n 117x 148m 535w 4084Yy
D Calgary	1912	R-Lat	Bs	77	200,000	113,000	294,379	3.90	Eng Alb English-speaking. 87n 59x 71m 168w 3773Yy
D St Paul in Alberta	1948	R-Lat	Bs	72	27,000	21,049	40,034	2.60	Fre Alb French-speaking. 25n 1x 1m 50w 853Yy
M Gatineau-Hull	1963	R-Lat	Bs	65	150,000	139,497	220,023	1.84	Fre Que 95% French-speaking. 91% RC. D=PC. 55n 54x 66m 270w 2843Yy
D Amos	1938	R-Lat	Bs	70	71,600	95,719	105,050	0.37	Fre Que French-speaking, rural. 95% RC. D=pc. 39n 25x 38m 182w 1975Yy
D Mont-Laurier	1913	R-Lat	Bs	59	53,000	68,525	78,124	0.53	Fre Que French-speaking. Tourism. 98% RC. 46n 29x 61m 148w 1068Yy
D Rouyn-Noranda	1973	R-Lat	Bs	39	39,000	–	56,240	4.55	Fre Que On border with Ontario. 26n 12x 15m 112w 811Yy
M Grouard-McLennan	1862	R-Lat	Pomi	67	27,700	30,789	40,715	1.12	Fre Alb Very extended. 40% Indians, mixed. M=OMI. 5n 27x 28m 38w 783Yy
D Mackenzie-Fort Smith	1901	R-Lat	Pomi	16	15,200	18,927	22,300	0.66	Fre NWT Missionary diocese, 5 towns. M=OMI. 0n 15x 17m 23w 232Yy
D Prince George	1944	R-Lat	Pomi	20	40,000	26,000	58,700	3.31	Eng BC Missionary diocese. M=OMI. P=68%. 7n 17x 24m 27w 697Yy
D Whitehorse	1944	R-Lat	Pomi	24	5,300	5,910	7,876	1.16	Eng Yuk Mining area, cosmopolitan influx. M=OMI. 1n 13x 17m 8w 118Yy
M Halifax	1842	R-Lat	Bs	77	103,000	120,000	152,000	0.95	Eng NS Many charismatics, including archbishop. 69n 16x 17m 339w 1834Yy
D Antigonish	1844	R-Lat	Bs	129	89,800	124,684	131,700	0.22	Eng NS 8-parish industrial mission. D=pc,Synod. 152n 9x 17m 440w 2028Yy
D Charlottetown	1829	R-Lat	Bs	59	40,600	45,677	59,627	1.07	Eng PEI 1976: 1,000 charismatics (15 priests). 63n 2x 2m 180w 940Yy
D Yarmouth	1953	R-Lat	Bs	39	27,000	31,392	39,510	0.92	Fre NS Relative poverty and emigration. D=pc,sc. 18n 17x 20m 41w 381Yy
M Keewatin-Le Pas	1910	R-Lat	Pomi	52	25,200	23,000	36,951	1.91	Fre Man Missionary diocese, many Indians. M=OMI. 2n 24x 26m 30w 1151Yy
D Churchill-Baie d'Hudson	1925	R-Lat	Pomi	18	3,900	3,589	5,750	1.90	Fre Man Mainly Indians. M=OMI. P=49%. 0n 12x 13m 11w 187Yy
D Labrador City-Schefferville	1945	R-Lat	Pomi	25	8,800	18,366	12,900	-1.40	Fre Que 1,600 Indians and Eskimos. P=99%. 3n 10x 14m 30w 234Yy
D Moosonee	1938	R-Lat	Pomi	19	2,800	3,500	4,244	0.77	Fre Ont Indian work. M=OMI. P=44%. 2n 6x 10m 11w 135Yy
M Kingston	1826	R-Lat	Bs	52	70,000	54,337	102,650	2.58	Eng Ont English-speaking. D=PC. 71n 7x 9m 206w 1637Yy
D Alexandria-Cornwall	1890	R-Lat	Bs	34	40,000	54,000	59,000	0.35	Fre Ont English-French. D=pc. 43n 5x 10m 83w 916Yy
D Peterborough	1882	R-Lat	Bs	78	57,000	36,730	83,680	3.35	Eng Ont English-speaking. 86n 3x 3m 142w 1286Yy
D Sault Sainte Marie	1904	R-Lat	Bs	126	159,000	160,000	234,000	1.53	Eng Ont 60% English-,40% French-speaking. 101n 40x 46m 287w 2754Yy
M Moncton	1936	R-Lat	Bs	52	58,300	71,048	85,623	0.75	Fre NB 75% French, 25% English. D=pc,PC. 67n 32x 58m 323w 1118Yy
D Bathurst in Canada	1860	R-Lat	Bcsc	66	80,000	100,687	117,117	0.61	Fre NB All French-speaking. M=CSC. 62n 14x 20m 264w 1412Yy
D Edmundston	1944	R-Lat	Bs	33	36,400	49,569	53,525	0.31	Fre NB 92% French-speaking. D=pc. 36n 9x 11m 160w 719Yy
D St John, New Brunswick	1842	R-Lat	Bs	92	76,800	67,762	112,710	2.06	Eng NB All English-speaking. D=pc. 79n 12x 13m 189w 1584Yy
M Montréal	1836	R-Lat	Bs	291	1,000,900	1,665,000	1,556,055	-0.27	Fre Que Parishes: 212 French, 34 English. M=OSM. 707n 917x 1654m 6480w 19023Yy
D Joliette	1904	R-Lat	Bs	93	137,000	118,006	200,816	2.15	Fre Que French-speaking. 98% Catholic. D=pc. 85n 63x 205m 380w 2855Yy
D Saint-Jean-Longueuil	1933	R-Lat	Bs	93	380,000	310,000	557,000	2.37	Fre Que French. Urban. 84% RC. M=CSV. 137n 67x 158m 494w 6893Yy
D Saint-Jérôme	1951	R-Lat	Bs	71	229,000	175,290	335,807	2.63	Fre Que French. 29% RC. D=pc,PC: 137n 91x 177m 268w 5607Yy
D Valleyfield	1892	R-Lat	Bs	70	126,000	124,168	185,295	1.61	Fre Que French-speaking, with bilingual zones. 86n 34x 96m 241w 3034Yy
M Ottawa	1847	R-Lat	Bs	115	248,000	263,113	363,815	1.30	Fre Ont Parishes: 63 French, 29 English. M=SMM. 148n 208x 288m 972w 4129Yy

Continued overleaf

Country Table 2–continued

Official name (bold type = church with over 10% of affiliated) 1	*Begun* 2	*Type* 3	*Counc* 4	*Congs* 5	*Adults* 6	*Affiliated 1970* 7	*Affiliated 1995* 8	*G%* 9	*Names, notes, and other statistics (see Codebook, Part 3)* 10
D Hearst	1938	R-Lat	Bpme	36	20,000	31,914	29,868	-0.26	Fre Ont French-speaking half rural. M=PME. 27n 1x 1m 17w 236Yy
D Pembroke	1898	R-Lat	Bs	75	44,700	52,779	65,575	0.87	Eng Que Parishes: 65% English, 35% French. 81n 5x 9m 244w 1050Yy
D Timmins	1915	R-Lat	Bs	33	41,900	94,722	61,500	-1.71	Fre Que 90% English, 10% French. 27n 6x 15m 53w 849Yy
M Québec	1674	R-Lat	Bs	420	717,700	797,814	1,052,664	1.11	Fre Que French, urban. 99% RC. M=RSV. D=pc. 630n 400x 872m 4325w 11209Yy
D Chicoutimi	1878	R-Lat	Bs	103	182,600	254,568	267,948	0.21	Fre Que French. 99% RC. D=pc,PC,bc,sc,1c. 1s. 203n 62x 133m 759w 3817Yy
D Sainte Anne de-la-Pocatière	1951	R-Lat	Bs	54	59,500	90,252	87,320	-0.13	Fre Que French, rural. 100% RC. D=pc,PC,bc,1c. 131n 4x 13m 263w 1070Yy
D Trois-Rivières	1852	R-Lat	Bs	93	174,000	233,469	256,524	0.38	Fre Que French, urban. 98% RC. D=pc,Synod. 1s. 189n 84x 248m 842w 3009Yy
M Regina	1910	R-Lat	Bs	168	84,000	95,000	124,190	1.08	Eng Sas English-speaking. D=pc. 75n 25x 29m 169w 1745Yy
D Gravelbourg	1930	R-Lat	Bs	39	8,000	16,275	11,715	-1.31	Fre Sas French-speaking, rural. D=pc. 27n 2x 2m 63w 200Yy
D Prince-Albert	1907	R-Lat	Bs	92	31,300	40,988	45,916	0.46	Fre Sas Immigrants from Europe and east Canada. 28n 17x 19m 124w 789Yy
D Saskatoon	1933	R-Lat	Bs	62	43,800	39,336	64,300	1.99	Eng Sas 75% English, 5% French, 20% others. 35n 47x 50m 170w 1475Yy
AN Saint Peter-Muenster	1921	R-Lat	Bosb	20	7,500	12,900	11,000	-0.64	Eng Sas English-speaking, rural. 0n 23x 39m 76w 154Yy
M Rimouski	1867	R-Lat	Bs	122	105,000	165,305	154,335	-0.27	Fre Que French, half urban. 90% RC. D=Synod. 143n 59x 97m 819w 1907Yy
D Baie-Comeau (Hauterive)	1905	R-Lat	Bs	50	64,500	89,770	94,655	0.21	Fre Que French, 50% urban. Charismatics strong. 38n 19x 36m 131w 1311Yy
D Gaspé	1922	R-Lat	Bs	66	64,800	100,606	95,094	-0.23	Fre Que 90% French, rural. 89% RC. D=pc. 67n 18x 25m 195w 1212Yy
M Saint-Boniface	1847	R-Lat	Bs	106	69,500	74,125	101,920	1.28	Fre Man Half urban. D=pc. 1s. 78n 60x 120m 432w 1375Yy
M Saint John's, Newfoundland	1847	R-Lat	Bs	94	81,300	84,840	119,260	1.37	Eng New English, half in capital. M=CSC. D=pc. 37n 20x 31m 281w 1753Yy
D Grand Falls	1856	R-Lat	Bs	67	20,700	33,000	30,432	-0.32	Eng New English-speaking. 25n 1x 4m 34w 488Yy
D Saint George's	1904	R-Lat	Bs	56	28,700	40,723	42,108	0.13	Eng New English-speaking, half urban. 21n 1x 5m 43w 598Yy
M Sherbrooke	1874	R-Lat	Bs	142	193,000	196,038	283,377	1.48	Fre Que French-speaking. D=pc,PC. 93% RC. 243n 121x 235m 1280w 3082Yy
D Nicolet	1885	R-Lat	Bs	87	122,600	154,388	179,879	0.61	Fre Que French. D=pc,PC.99% RC. 169n 41x 163m 840w 2450Yy
D Saint-Hyacinthe	1852	R-Lat	Bwf	113	237,600	256,513	348,504	1.23	Fre Que French-speaking. M=WF. D=pc. 94% RC. 189n 91x 327m 1084w 4582Yy
M Toronto	1841	R-Lat	Bs	217	787,000	655,000	1,155,155	2.30	Eng Ont English, urban. Italian, Portuguese. 1s. 347n 503x 621m 1036w 23421Yy
D Hamilton	1856	R-Lat	Bs	123	261,000	223,700	382,898	2.17	Eng Ont English-speaking. D=pc. 137n 124x 153m 376w 7396Yy
D London	1856	R-Lat	Bs	175	246,000	278,286	361,013	1.05	Eng Ont English, French minority. D=pc,PC.1s. 223n 92x 106m 516w 7236Yy
D Saint Catharines	1958	R-Lat	Bs	50	105,600	93,893	154,850	2.02	Eng Ont English-speaking. 59n 34x 36m 79w 2109Yy
D Thunder Bay	1952	R-Lat	Bs	41	48,800	55,000	71,634	1.06	Eng Ont Missionary diocese. English. 29n 28x 31m 67w 1038Yy
M Vancouver	1890	R-Lat	Bomi	95	233,400	150,000	342,436	3.36	Eng BC Urban. English, with minorities. M=OMI. 96n 91x 113m 180w 3602Yy
D Kamloops	1945	R-Lat	Bcs	70	22,800	18,800	33,500	2.34	Eng BC English-speaking, half rural. M=CS. 14n 11x 16m 21w 442Yy
D Nelson	1936	R-Lat	Bs	53	43,200	33,798	63,370	2.55	Eng BC English-speaking, rural. 27n 18x 20m 38w 617Yy
D Victoria	1846	R-Lat	Bofm	56	53,600	33,000	78,706	3.54	Eng BC English. Missionary diocese. M=OFM. 27n 14x 18m 104w 778Yy
AD Winnipeg	1915	R-Lat	bs	149	116,000	97,500	170,590	2.26	Eng Man English-speaking. 54n 47x 49m 210w 2065Yy
M Winnipeg *(Ukrainian)*	1912	R-Ukr	Ocssr	132	30,700	60,000	45,000	-1.14	Eng Man Widespread use of Ukrainian. M=CSSR. 27n 11x 12m 45w 308Yy
D Edmonton *(Ukrainian)*	1948	R-Ukr	Os	109	23,800	51,985	35,000	-1.57	Eng Alberta, BC, Yukon, western NWT. 29n 14x 17m 15w 364Yy
D New Westminster	1974	R-Ukr	Os	23	2,000	–	3,000	4.76	Eng Sas Ukrainian-rite. 13n 3x 3m 3w 52Yy
D Saskatoon *(Ukrainian)*	1951	R-Ukr	Os	135	10,500	35,000	15,450	-3.22	Eng Sas French- and Ukrainian-speaking. 22n 15x 17m 28w 344Yy
D Toronto *(Ukrainian)*	1948	R-Ukr	Os	80	58,000	55,000	85,000	1.76	Eng Ontario, Quebec, NS, NB, Newfoundland. 82n 14x 24m 38w 620Yy
D Saint-Sauveur de Montréal	1980	R-Mel	Obs	10	27,000	–	40,000	6.67	Greek Melkites. M=Bs. 4n 7x 7m 0w 301Yy
D Saint-Maron de Montréal	1982	R-Mar	Oolm	12	31,000	–	45,000	7.69	Maronite rite Catholics. 6n 10x 10m 6w 341Yy
D SS Cyril & Methodius of Toronto	1980	R-Slo	Ocssr	30	20,400	–	30,000	6.67	Slovak (Byzantine) rite; only other, D Presov, Slovakia. 17n 0x 0m 0w 81Yy
OM Canada	1951	R-LEr	Bs	36	49,000	20,000	60,000	4.49	Catholic Chaplain Generalate. 56 ordinaries. 1129Yy.
Christadelphian Ecclesias in Canada	c1880	m-Ade	x....	20	800	2,000	1,000	-2.73	Loose relationship with Birmingham HQ (UK), 29 ecclesias (churches). Pacifist.
Christian & Missionary Alliance in C	1889	P-Hol	xF..E	327	26,794	21,355	74,290	5.11	CMA, HQ Nyack (USA). Members mostly in Alberta. 200n,G=1.7%pa.1s,178t(25951).
Christian Brethren	c1860	P-CBr	x....	600	30,000	20,000	50,000	3.73	*Open Brethren.* Mainly Ontario, BC, Quebec. 150 missionaries abroad. 185m.
Christian Brethren (Exclusive)	c1880	P-EBr	x....	338	6,000	5,000	11,000	3.20	Groups: Booth, Ames, Continuing Tumbridge Wells, Raven-Taylor, Kelly-Continental.
Christian Church (Disciples of Christ)	1813	P-Dis	xW..W	36	2,506	8,039	4,092	-2.66	*All Canada Committee.* Related to USA denomination. HQ Toronto. 47n,41t(2554).
Christian Churches & Chs of Christ	1820	I-Dis	x....	140	7,500	10,000	15,300	1.72	*Churches of Christ (Non-Instrumental).* No central organization. 56n,77t(3265).
Christian Congregation	c1900	P-Hol	.....	9	1,000	2,000	1,500	-1.14	From rural mountainous USA; HQ Monroe, North Carolina. Holiness body. 9n,9t(928).
Christian Reformed Churches in C	1908	P-Ref	.F...	235	50,927	70,747	88,892	0.92	Dutch immigrants from Holland. Schism in USA ex Reformed Ch in America. 149n.
Church of Christ, Scientist	c1910	m-Sci	x....	70	9,000	25,000	20,000	-0.89	*Christian Science.* M=CCS(Boston, USA). 41 churches in Ontario, 25 in BC. 24m,96w.
Church of God in Canada	1919	P-Pe3	ZF...	81	4,559	3,000	7,120	3.52	M=CoG(Cleveland) (USA). 2 Divisions: Eastern, Western. Holiness Pentecostals.
Church of God in Christ, Mennonite	c1880	P-Men	G....	35	4,110	4,000	7,470	2.53	Branch of USA Mennonite body. Immigrants over the years. 25n.
Church of God of Prophecy in Canada	1937	P-Pe3	Z....	50	2,705	1,150	6,760	7.34	Ex CoG(Cleveland). BC,Man,Alberta,Sask,Ont,Quebec. 42n,29t(1287),W=70%.
Church of God (Anderson)	c1920	P-Hol	x....	51	3,362	4,000	6,340	1.86	HQ Anderson, USA. Holiness denomination. Mainly in Alberta. 1x,46t(3515),W=80%.
Ch of Jesus Christ of Latter-day Saints	1832	m-LdS	x....	379	96,300	67,890	125,000	2.47	*Mormons.* 11 Stakes. Temple: Cardston. 1239n,740f,214t(29400),12000Y.
Church of the First-Born	c1960	I-3pU	x....	20	1,000	1,000	2,000	2.81	Blacks from Barbados & Jamaica (HQ Kingston). Branches in UK, USA. Strict ethics.
Church of the Lutheran Brethren	c1920	P-Lut	x....	7	300	500	800	1.90	Based on USA. HQ Fergus Falls, Manitoba.
Church of the Nazarene	1911	P-Hol	xF...	157	10,844	20,000	19,000	-0.20	Mainly in Alberta. HQ Calgary. World HQ in USA. 200n,1s.
Church of the New Jerusalem	1835	m-Swe	x....	3	100	500	200	-3.60	*Swedenborgian Ch.* USA-related. 2 Societies (Toronto, Kitchener), 2 Circles. 2n.
Chs of God in the British I & Overseas		P-EBr	x....	3	200	600	500	0.05	I=Isles. *Chs of God in the Fellowship of the Son of God.* Ex Open Brethren in UK.
Conf of Mennonites in Canada	c1880	P-Men	GF..E	156	28,994	30,000	60,400	2.84	*Canadian Conference.* Branches: USA, 14 nations. Russians. 252n,1j,4s,130t(18293).
Convention of Regular Baptists of BC		I-Bap	.....	22	600	1,000	1,200	0.05	Independent groupings of Regular Baptists. HQ Vancouver (British Columbia).
Cooneyites (Two-by-Two's)		I-Fun	x....	180	6,000	10,000	9,000	0.05	*Go-Preachers.* 1500 in Alberta. Itinerants. 300,000 others in UK, USA, Australia.
Coptic Orthodox Church in Canada	1961	O-Cop	NwaNw	12	28,800	25,000	45,000	2.38	Egyptian immigrants since 1965 in Montreal, Toronto, Ottawa. Rapid growth.
Estonian Evangelical Alliance Church	c1940	P-Eva	.....	30	1,000	500	2,000	5.70	Estonian refugees from USSR. HQ Vancouver, BC.
Estonian Ev Lutheran Church		P-Lut	.....	13	6,394	8,200	6,906	0.05	Lutheran Estonians, refugees from USSR and Germany.
Estonian Orthodox Church	c1940	O-Est	C....	5	2,000	1,000	4,000	5.70	Refugees from USSR. Parishes: Toronto, Montreal, Vancouver. HQ Los Angeles (USA).
Evangelical Church in Canada	c1850	I-Hol	....E	45	3,688	10,000	6,710	-1.58	*Northwest Canada Conference.* EUB members rejecting 1968 UCC merger. 62n,50t.
Evangelical Covenant Ch of Canada	1904	P-Con	K....	19	1,198	2,000	2,180	0.35	Branch of USA body. Ethnic Scandinavians. HQ Edmonton. 13n,21t(1751).
Evangelical Free Church of Canada	1917	P-Con	KF..E	124	6,358	500	16,700	15.07	Branch of Ev Free Ch of America. Especially in Western Canada. HQ Vancouver.
Evangelical Lutheran Church of C	1880	P-Lut	LW...	654	150,072	83,274	207,264	3.71	*ELCC.* Formerly in American LC. 242n,2p,1s(19),1895Yy. Merger in 1986.
Ev Mennonite Brethren Conference	c1880	P-Men	G....	21	2,100	3,000	3,820	0.97	*Defenseless Mennonites.* Branch of USA body. Immigrants from Russia. 25n.
Evangelical Mennonite Conference	1874	P-Men	GF...	50	6,089	6,000	8,700	1.50	*Kleingemeinde.* Branches in Mexico, Nicaragua, Paraguay. 70n,1p,144Y.
Ev Mennonite Mission Conference	1874	P-Men	G....	28	3,528	3,000	5,880	2.73	*Rudnerweide.* Dutch-German. Branch in Belize, CAmerica. 58n,2p,2p,40Y.
Fellowship of Christian Assemblies	1987	I-3pW	x....	62	3,100	–	5,170	12.50	*FOCA.* Pentecostal body with Latter Rain doctrines. Mostly White Charismatics.
Fellowship of Ev Baptist Churches in C	c1925	I-Bap	.....	492	60,566	110,000	110,000	0.00	Ex BCOQ; 1953 union Regular Baptists. Aided by CBHMS(USA). 335n,2s.
Fellowship of Ev Bible Chs	1985	I-Fun	.....	19	1,569	–	3,140	10.00	Fundamentalists with links in USA.
Foursquare Gospel Church of Canada	1934	P-Pe2	ZF.X.	45	2,250	15,000	4,500	-4.70	Branch of ICFG (Los Angeles, USA). In Western Canada. HQ Burnabe, Vancouver. 1s.
Free Methodist Church in Canada	1876	I-Hol	VF..E	135	6,767	15,000	13,395	-0.45	Strong in Alberta, West, Ontario. Schism, United Holiness Ch. W=71%,466z.
Free Reformed Ch of North America		I-Ref	.....	6	1,000	3,000	2,000	0.05	In independent Reformed traditions. 2 churches also in USA.
General Conf of Mennonite Brethren	c1880	P-Men	G....	317	27,751	30,000	43,452	1.49	*Conference of Mennonites in Canada.* (HQ USA). HQ Winnipeg. 300n,4s.
Glad Tidings Churches	c1940	P-Pe2	x....	30	3,000	2,000	4,000	2.81	HQ Vancouver. Missions in 7 nations, especially Uganda and China (Taiwan).
Gospel Missionary Association		P-Fun	x....	30	2,000	3,000	4,000	0.05	Fundamentalist churches. Mainly in Alberta. HQ Calgary.
Greek Ch of True Orthodox Christians	c1940	I-Tru	.....	3	2,500	3,000	3,500	0.62	Ex GOC, claiming restoration of authentic Orthodoxy. Parishes: Montreal, Toronto.
Greek Orthodox AD of N & S America	1922	O-Gre	CwO.W	39	140,000	210,000	230,000	0.36	*9th Archdiocesan District (Canada).* Under EP Constantinople. 124,000 Greeks. 28n.
Holy Cath Apost & Roman Renewed Ch	1960	I-CCa	.....	1	400	2,000	500	-5.39	*Eglise du Christ-Roi Rénovée. HQ Clémery (France). Papal claimant Clement XV.*
Hutterian Brethren	1918	P-Men	x....	265	9,800	14,100	24,000	2.15	*Hutterites.* Descendants of Swiss Brethren. Pacifists. Alberta, Manitoba, Saskatchewan.
Independent Assemblies of God, C	c1945	I-3pW	.....	200	4,000	5,500	7,000	0.97	Links with Pentecostal movement in Sweden. 165n,1s (Temple Bible College), 50t.
Independent Holiness Church	1938	I-Hol	.....	13	500	800	1,000	0.90	*Holiness Movement of Canada,* rejecting 1958 merger in Free Methodist Ch. 13n.
Internat Pentecostal Holiness Ch of C	1943	P-Pe3	ZF.X.	40	5,000	2,000	10,000	6.65	Holiness Pentecostals. HQ Toronto. World HQ USA. 53n.
Italian Pentecostal Church of Canada	1913	P-Pe2	...X.	21	3,300	3,000	5,000	2.06	Ex Italian Presbyterian Ch. Links with PAoC. Missions to Italy. 12n,10n,10t(1402).
Jehovah's Witnesses	1880	m-Jeh	x....	1,312	101,713	175,000	192,000	0.37	*Témoins de Jéhovah.* IBSA. 31 chs in Newfoundland (begun 1910). (1975) 3907Y. (1995) 4025Y.
Latter Rain Assemblies	1947	I-3pW	x....	10	300	500	600	0.73	Schism ex PAoC in Saskatoon, as a Pentecostal renewal. HQ North Battleford. 1s.
Latvian Ev Lutheran Ch Outside Latvia	1948	P-Lut	LW...	8	2,380	8,000	5,000	-1.86	*Latvijas Evangeliské Luteriské Baznica. From USSR. 15n,W=30%,57y,150z.*
Liberal Catholic Church	1925	I-Lib	xv...	10	800	1,000	1,500	1.64	Branch of LCC-USA. Ex ORCC. Theosophical. HQ London (UK). 1992, joins Christ Catholic Ch.
Lutheran Church-Canada	1854	P-Lut	e....	349	65,590	98,097	85,584	-0.54	*LC-C.* In LCMS(Missouri Synod) (St Louis, MO, USA). HQ Edmonton. 287n,337t(299037).
Macedonian Orthodox Church	c1940	O-Mac	cv...	2	2,000	1,000	3,000	4.49	Yugoslavs from Macedonia: canonical orthodoxy disputed. Overlea, Toronto.
Mennonite Church in Canada		P-Men	G....	90	18,039	14,000	33,100	0.05	Old Colony, Bergthaler, Chortitz, Reinland and Sommerfelder congregations.
Mennonite Church (Canada)	1898	P-Men	G....	108	10,200	13,000	14,729	0.50	*Region I* of MCNAmerica (HQ USA). HQ Kitchener, Ontario. 81n,67t(10004).
Missionary Church-Canada	1883	P-Hol	xF...	96	6,654	6,000	14,800	3.68	Districts Canada West, Ontario. Formerly Mennonite. 91n,2s,52t(6600),551Y.
Moravian Church in America	1771	P-Mor	xw..f	9	1,437	1,583	2,116	1.17	*Canadian District,* American Province North. Labrador Province, Unity of Brethren. 11n.
Native American Church of Canada	c1900	I-mar	x...I	200	40,000	40,000	80,000	2.81	*NAC.* From USA, among all American Indian tribes. Strict ethics: peyote eating.
Native Evangelical Fellowship of C	1967	I-	I	30	4,000	5,000	7,000	1.35	*NEF.* Founded as Indigenous Indian Fellowship within Northern Canada Ev Mission.
Netherlands Reformed Congs of NA	1907	P-Ref	.....	9	2,172	1,000	4,762	6.44	*NRC.* Based in Netherlands (162 congregations, 90,000 members).
New Apostolic Church	c1880	I-3aX	x....	769	9,000	200,000	11,534	-10.78	*Canada Church Bezirk* (also UK, Aisa, SAmerica). HQ Zurich. Germans. Declining.
New Testament Church of God	c1940	P-Pe3	ZF.X.	68	1,080	2,000	2,700	1.21	*Ch of God (Cleveland).* HQ USA. Includes many Jamaicans and other West Indians. 2s.
North American Baptist General Conf	1865	P-Bap	xF...	123	17,629	50,000	32,100	-1.76	German Baptist immigrants. USA body. HQ Winnipeg. 102n,92t(12570),413Y.
Old Believers Russian Orthodox Ch	c1940	I-OBe	x....	3	1,000	500	2,000	5.70	*Old Ritualist Ancient Orthodox Christians;* 1667 schism in Russia. USSR refugees.
Old Calendar Greek Orthodox Ch in NA	c1950	I-OCd	c....	2	1,500	3,000	3,000	0.00	1924 schism in Greece ex GOC rejecting New Calendar. 1974, D Montreal formed.
Old Order & Wisler Mennonite Chs	1886	P-Men	G....	65	2,000	3,000	3,100	0.13	Branch of USA Mennonite body (Ohio). Schism ex Mennonite Church. 15n.
Old Roman Catholic Church	c1960	I-CCa	.v...	2	600	1,000	1,200	0.73	*ORCC, Orthodox Orders.* HQ Havelock, Ontario. 1967 applied to join WCC and CCC.
Orthodox Ch in America: AD Canada	1926	O-Rus	MwO.	59	27,000	50,000	45,000	-0.42	*OCA.* Russian refugees. 1970, given autocephalous status by P Moscow. 18n,3x(USA).
Pentecostal Assemblies of Canada	1910	P-Pe2	ZF.XE	1,000	194,972	170,000	300,000	2.30	*PAoC.* 80% English, 8% Amerindian, 5% German. 4% Slav,2% French. 1150n,1H,5r,7s.
Pente Assemblies of Newfoundland	1925	P-Pe2	ZF.X.	160	15,707	24,000	31,719	1.12	Close co-operation with Pentecostal Assemblies of Canada. 50 schools. 287n,1j,2k.
People's Church, Toronto		I-Non	.....	4	4,000	6,000	7,000	0.05	Largest Protestant congregation and SS. Color TV services. 410 missionaries abroad. 1r(300).
Polish National Catholic Ch of Canada	1904	I-OCa	Uw...	20	6,000	8,000	11,000	1.28	1967, *Canadian Diocese,* PNCC(USA). Poles; schism ex RCC. 8n,10t,W=19%,150y.
Presbyterian Ch in America (Canadian)	c1900	P-Ref	x....	14	527	500	821	2.00	*Church of the Covenanters.* RPCEv Synod churches joined PCA in 1982. HQ Calgary.
Presbyterian Church in Canada	1875	P-Ref	RW..W	1,023	156,513	530,000	215,369	-3.54	Congregations (over 50%) rejecting 1925 merger in UCCanada. 866n,5868Yy.
Primitive Baptist Conf of N Brunswick	1874	P-Bap	.....	15	4,000	10,000	9,000	-0.42	Schism from Baptist group over offerings. Arminian, fundamentalist. 21n,15t(900).
Reformed Church in Canada	c1850	P-Ref	Rw..W	41	4,127	11,990	6,758	-2.27	*RCA, Classis of Ontario.* Part of USA denomination. HQ Woodstock. 24n,18t(1588).
Reformed Church of Quebec	1986	P-Ref	.....	20	2,000	–	5,000	11.11	New francophone body for French-speakers. M=PCA/USA,CRCN.
Reformed Episcopal Church	1873	I-ReA	x...f	3	284	300	400	1.16	Anti-sacramentarian. M=REC(Maryland, USA), Free Ch of England. HQ Victoria.
Reformed Mennonite Church	c1850	P-Men	G....	7	400	400	800	2.81	Branch of USA body. Nonresistant, pacifist, anti-political. Foot-washing.

Continued opposite

Country Table 2–concluded

Official name (bold type = church with over 10% of affiliated) 1	*Begun* 2	*Type* 3	*Counc* 4	*Congs* 5	*Adults* 6	*Affiliated 1970* 7	*Affiliated 1995* 8	*G%* 9	*Names, notes, and other statistics* (see Codebook, Part 3) 10
Reorganized Ch of JC of L-d Saints	1833	m-LdS	xv...	82	5,610	11,178	12,465	0.44	Schism in USA ex CJCLdS(Utah). Decline. HQ Guelph, Ontario. 942n,244Yy.
Religious Society of Friends	c1790	P-Qua	QW..W	96	1,146	2,000	2,550	0.98	*Canadian Yearly Meeting. Quakers.* M=FUM,FGC(USA). No clergy. 13t(215),W=60%.
Revival Fellowship Assemblies		I-3cW	.....	5	500	500	1,000	0.05	Independent revivalist congregations. Faith Temple, Toronto.
Romanian Orthodox Ch in America	1902	O-Rum	CwO..	21	11,700	15,000	18,000	0.73	*Missionary Episcopate*, HQ USA. Romanians. A=1950. HQ Windsor. 12n,8t(373).
Romanian Orth Episcopate of America	1929	I-Rum	Mwo..	10	5,000	10,000	10,000	0.00	1951 broke ex Orthodox Ch in Romania; under Orthodox Ch in America. 9n,10t(530).
Russian Orthodox Church in Canada	1897	O-Rus	MwO..	24	2,600	4,500	7,000	1.78	Patriarchal Exarchate, under P Moscow. Russians. Bishop, 15 clergy. HQ Edmonton.
Russian Orthodox Ch Outside Russia	c1950	I-Rus	x....	23	17,800	30,000	26,000	-0.57	*D Canada*, Refugees from USSR since World War II. HQ New York. Ultra-conservative.
Salvation Army in Canada	1882	P-Sal	xw..W	407	75,600	123,600	94,733	-1.06	*Armée du Salut. SA, Canada & Bermuda Territory.* 1735n,10H,40p,2s,W=41%.
Serbian Orth Ch (D East USA & C)	1963	O-Ser	CwO..	20	10,000	10,000	20,000	2.81	Immigrants from Yugoslavia. Under jurisdiction of P Belgrade. HQ Toronto. 10nx.
Seventh-day Adventist Church	1853	P-Adv	x....	317	40,047	28,000	57,200	2.90	*SDA, Canada Union Conf.* NAmerica Division. 137n,1552mw,2H,1j,4r,219t(19451),1149Y.
Standard Churches of America	1916	I-3pW	ZF.X.	70	6,000	10,000	11,000	0.38	*Canadian Section.* Branch of Open Bible Standard Chs (USA). HQ Brockville, Ont. 1p.
Syrian Orth Ch of Antioch: AD US & C	1895	O-Syr	Dw...	4	1,000	500	2,000	5.70	Under Syrian P Antioch, HQ Hackensack, NJ (USA). Archdiocese established 1957.
Ukrainian Greek-Orthodox Ch of C	1918	I-Ukr	X....	258	85,200	140,000	120,000	-0.61	Uniates, schism ex RCC in Canada. Largest UOC outside Ukraine. 3 Dioceses. 95n,1s.
Ukrainian Orthodox Church of America	c1930	O-Ukr	C.O..	20	2,000	2,000	4,000	2.81	*UOCA (Ecumenical Patriarchate)* (HQ Jamaica, LI USA). HQ Winnipeg. 10n.
Union of Spiritual Communities of Christ	1899	m-Ort	.....	40	10,000	21,300	30,000	1.38	*Orthodox Doukhobors (Spirit-Wrestlers).* Many factions. 17,000 in British Columbia. 8t(632).
Unitarian Universalist Association	1842	m-Unt	.....	40	4,800	15,000	6,003	-3.60	*Canadian Unitarian Council*, 3 of the 22 UUA districts (HQ Boston, USA). 23n.
United Brethren in Christ	1850	P-Hol	xF...	9	835	1,500	2,000	1.16	*Ontario Conference.* Part of United Brethren in Christ (USA). 14n,10t(875).
United Conf of Icelandic Chs in NA		m-Unt	.....	10	3,000	5,000	7,000	0.05	Unitarians, Liberal Christians. From Iceland. In Manitoba and Saskatchewan.
United Church of Canada	1765	P-Uni	WW..W	3,960	2,468,000	2,277,446	3,093,120	1.23	1925 union, declining since 1960. 11 Conferences. 4p,6s,W=35%.
United Pentecostal Church in Canada	c1930	P-Pel	x....	197	9,260	15,000	23,100	1.74	White Oneness Pentecostals. Linked with UPC(USA). HQ Picton, Ont. Strong missions abroad.
Universal Fell of Metro Comm Chs	1973	I-Gay	x....	16	1,500	–	2,000	4.55	*UFMCC.* Member of UFMCC(USA) and worldwide affiliates. Gays, lesbians.
Victory Protestant Church	1975	I-3wW	.....	20	10,000	–	20,000	5.00	Prosperity gospel teaching. HQ Edmonton. Abroad: work in 25 countries.
Wesleyan Methodist Ch of America in C	1889	P-Hol	VF...	82	2,000	8,000	4,956	-1.90	1968 union Wesleyan Methodist Ch, Pilgrim Holiness Ch; called Wesleyan Ch in USA.
West Indian C I Apostolic Fellowship	c1970	I-3oU	.....	25	3,000	–	6,000	41.62	*CI=Canadian International.* Oneness churches, members of AWCF. HQ Mississauga.
Wisconsin Ev Lutheran Synod	1870	P-Lut	.....	17	797	700	1,307	2.53	Ties with Wisconsin ELS(USA). Congregations in 3 Canadian provinces.
Worldwide Church of God	c1950	I-BrI	x....	30	3,000	7,000	5,000	-1.34	*WCG.* Radio Ch of God. Radio, TV. Originally Non-trinitarian. HQ Pasadena, CA (USA). 103nx.
Other independent charismatic chs	c1975	I-3cW	.....	5,000	600,000	–	1,000,000	5.00	Including Jesus is Lord Fellowship (Philippines), Manna Church (Portugal).
Other Protestant denominations		P-	.....	2,000	100,000	97,000	200,000	0.05	Total over 100 (see list below), including Elim Fellowship of Ev Chs (1984).
Other Non-White indigenous churches		I-	.....	300	20,000	25,000	45,000	0.05	Total over 20 (USA Blacks, West Indians, Amerindians, Koreans: see list below)
Other marginal Christian chs		m-	.....	50	30,000	20,000	40,000	0.05	Total over 20 smaller groups (see list below).
Other Orthodox churches		O-	.....	30	10,000	8,000	20,000	0.05	Total over 10, including: Sons of Freedom Doukhobors, Orthodox Syrian Ch of the East.
Other independent Catholic churches		I-CCa	.....	20	1,000	1,000	1,500	0.05	About 10: Antoinists, NAORCC, ORCC (English Rite), and bodies under bishops-at-large.
Other Anglican denominations		I-ReA	.....	10	600	200	1,000	0.05	Small schisms, rapidly expanding after 1975, including Anglican Catholic Ch in NAmerica (1977).
Doubly-affiliated		2-aff			-1,053,000	-312,186	-1,558,452		Members of an older denomination and also of a Renewal body.
Totals				**34,043**	**13,101,777**	**15,546,000**	**19,400,000**		

Churches, members, growth, 1900-2025	*Congs*	*Adults*	*Affiliated*	*G%*	*Total denominations*	*6 Megablocs:* *O*	*R*	*A*	*P*	*I*	*m*
Total churches, members, and denominations (mid-1900)	10,000	3,054,000	5,111,000	1.60	50	2	1	1	32	6	8
Total churches, members, and denominations (mid-1970)	32,997	9,289,001	15,546,000	1.60	220	20	1	1	119	57	22
Total churches, members, and denominations (mid-1990)	34,000	12,521,000	18,540,000	0.88	404	27	1	1	186	150	39
Total churches, members, and denominations (mid-1995)	34,043	13,101,777	19,400,000	0.91	453	27	1	1	187	198	39
Total churches, members, and denominations (mid-2000)	35,000	13,668,000	20,237,778	0.85	469	27	1	1	190	210	40
Total churches, members, and denominations (mid-2025)	40,000	16,209,000	24,000,000	0.68	727	35	1	1	230	400	60

NOTES ON TABLE ABOVE

NATIONAL COUNCILS (Column 4, 5th letter).

- E = Evangelical Fellowship of Canada (EFC)/Alliance Francophone des Protestants Evangéliques du Québec.
- f = former member of Canadian Council of Churches, now withdrawn (Moravian Church was in friendly association.
- I = Pan-Indian Ecumenical Association of the USA and Canada.
- R = Canadian Conference of Catholic Bishops (CCCB)/Conférence des Evângues Catholiques du Canada (CECC).
- T = Canadian Council of Evangelical Protestant Churches.
- W = Canadian Council of Churches (CCC)/Conseil Canadien des Eglises (CCE).
- w = associate member of Canadian Council of Churches.

Other national councils. The 3 largest Lutheran churches cooperate in the Lutheran Council in Canada (LCIC). Canadian Holiness Federation (members include Free Methodist Church in Canada). National Catholic Federation of Canada (Old Roman Catholic bodies). Alliance Francophone des Protestants Evangéliques du Québec.

Local councils. 22 local and 3 regional ecumenical councils cooperate with the Canadian Council of Churches.

OTHER PROTESTANT DENOMINATIONS. The number is very large because many USA denominations, and a number of European and Third-World denominations also, have small branches in Canada. Among these others are: American Baptist Association, Baptist Bible Fellowship International, Beachy Amish Mennonite Ch, Canadian Reformed Chs, Children of God International, Christ Assemblies, Christian Community in Canada, Christian Congregational Churches, Ch of God (Pentecostal), Community Ch of Canada, Deeper Walk, Ev Lutheran Synod, Fundamental Baptists (Maritimes), Independent Baptist Fellowship, Lutheran Free Ch, Manifested Sons of God (perfectionist Pentecostals), Members in Christ Assemblies (Toronto), Northern Canada Ev Mission, Old German Baptist Brethren in Canada, Old Mennonite Conference, Overcomers Ch, Pentecostal Missionary Fellowship (by 1976 a de facto schism ex United Pentecostal Ch), Reformed Baptist (USA), Reformed Presbyterian Ch of NA, The Way International, Ukrainian Baptist Chs, United Holiness Ch (schism ex Free Methodist Ch), Universal Christian Apostolic Ch, Waldensian Ch, Worldwide Christian Ev Mission of Canada. There are also several very large independent single congregations in Winnipeg, Toronto, et alia.

OTHER NON-WHITE INDIGENOUS CHURCHES. USA Black churches (including AME Zion Ch, Christian Union, Coloured Zion Ch, Father Divine Peace Mission), West Indian bodies, Unification Ch of Korea (1963), Amerindian groups, et alia.

OTHER MARGINAL PROTESTANT BODIES. The many small groups include: Branhamites (End Time Believers, Local Believers; HQ Edmonton; Jesus-Only Unitarians), Ch of Our Lord Jesus Christ (Bickertonites), Ch of Scientology (6,000 members), Divine Science Federation International, Eglise Humanitaire, Greater World Christian Spiritualist League (Hamilton, Ontario), United Ch of Religious Science (1 church), Unity Ch of Truth, Unity School of Christianity (9 churches, 8 ministers).

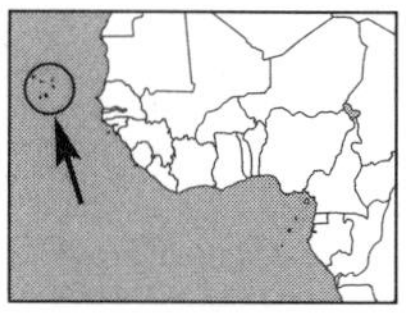

CAPE VERDE

SECULAR DATA, AD 2000

STATE
Official name: La República de Cabo Verde (The Republic of Cape Verde).
Short name: Cape Verde. **Adjective of nationality:** Cape Verdean.
Flag: Red vertical bar at hoist with black star and green corn stalks and yellow sea shell, 2 horizontal stripes yellow over green.
Area: 4,033 sq. km. (1,557 sq. mi.).
Government: Multi-party state, since 1990 (c1450 Portuguese rule, 1951 province of Portugal, 1975 Independence).
Legislature: National People's Assembly, 72 members.
Official language: Portuguese (Português).
Monetary unit: 1 escudo (C.Vsc.) = 100 centavos. **US$1=** C.V.Esc 99.69.
Chief cities: PRAIA 80,937; Mindelo (Porto Grande) 61,853.
Political divisions: 9 provinces.
Armed forces: 1,000.

DEMOGRAPHY
Population: 428,000.
Population density: 106.0/sq. km. (274.7/sq. mi.).
Under 15 years: 168,000.
Growth rate p.a.: 2.23% (births 29.21, deaths 5.57).
Mortality: Infant, per 1,000: 49.6; **Maternal per 100,000:** 100.0.
Life expectancy: 71 (male 67, female 73).
Household size: 5.1. **Floor area per person, sq.m:** 15.0.
Major languages: Portuguese, Portuguese Creole, Brava Island Creole, Fulani, Balante, Manjaco.
Urban dwellers: 62.21%. **Urban growth rate p.a.:** 4.0%.
Labor force: 35%.

ETHNOLINGUISTIC PEOPLES
43.3% Caboverdian Mestico; 26.2% Caboverdian Mestico; 12.2% Fulani; 10.0% Balanta (Brassa, Alante); 4.6% Mandyak (Manjaco).

ECONOMY
National income p.a. per person: US$960; **per family:** US$4,900.

EDUCATION
Adult literacy: 71% (male 81%, female 63%). **Schools:** 367.
Universities: 3. **School enrolment:** female/male: 81%/85%.

HEALTH
Access to health services: 80%. **Access to safe water:** 51%.
Hospitals: 75 (15 beds per 10,000). **Doctors:** 112.
Blind: 400. **Deaf:** 26,200. **Murder rate:** 7.
Lepers: 3,000. **Underweight prevalence under 5:** 19%.

LITERATURE
New book titles p.a.: 60 (150 p.a. per million). **Periodicals:** 6.
Newspapers: 1 daily.

COMMUNICATION (per 1,000 people)
Phones: 55 **(2% mobile). Radios:** 135. **TV sets:** 3.
Daily newspaper circulation: 40. **Computers:** 2.

HUMAN LIFE AND LIBERTY (optimum condition=100.0%)
HDI: 54.7. **HSI:** 70.0. **HFI:** 45.0. **EFL:** 31.2.

Country status. Cape Verde consists of an archipelago of 10 islands and 5 islets in the Atlantic Ocean off the coast of West Africa. It is a former Portuguese colony that gained independence in 1975. Corn and beans are the chief agricultural products and salt and limestone are important mineral resources.

HUMAN LIFE AND LIBERTY

Human need and development. Plagued by frequent drought and a high population density, Cape Verde has found its quality of life deteriorating after independence. The major safety valve was emigration, but opportunities for emigration are becoming fewer in Portugal and elsewhere. Most Cape Verdeans eke out an exiguous existence through fishing, and livestock raising.

Human environment. Degradation of vegetation and erosion are problems common to all islands, and desertification is a serious problem in the windward islands. In 1991 the islands experienced their worst drought in history, posing considerable threat to the economy.

NON-CHRISTIAN RELIGIONS

Traditional African religions have now ceased to have adherents. Some Cape Verdeans however have become Baha'is.

CHRISTIANITY

CATHOLIC CHURCH. The Cape Verde Islands were discovered by the Portuguese explorer Diogo Gomes in 1460, and within 2 years, Catholic clergy had arrived. Franciscan missionaries appeared in 1466, and in 1532, a diocese was erected which included the African coast between Gambia and Cape

Country Table 1. **Religious adherents in Cape Verde, AD 1900-2025.**

Year	1900		1970		mid-1990		Annual change, 1990-2000				mid-1995		mid-2000		mid-2025	
Name	Adherents	%	Adherents	%	Adherents	%	Natural	Conversion	Total	Rate	Adherents	%	Adherents	%	Adherents	%
Christians	**69,300**	**99.0**	**265,600**	**99.5**	**326,710**	**95.8**	**8,309**	**-292**	**8,017**	**2.22**	**362,500**	**95.3**	**406,880**	**95.1**	**637,450**	**95.0**
PROFESSION																
professing Christians	**69,300**	**99.0**	**265,600**	**99.5**	**326,710**	**95.8**	**8,309**	**-292**	**8,017**	**2.22**	**362,500**	**95.3**	**406,880**	**95.1**	**637,450**	**95.0**
AFFILIATION																
unaffiliated Christians	700	1.0	5,456	2.0	0	0.0	0	0	0	0.00	0	0.0	0	0.0	0	0.0
affiliated Christians	**68,600**	**98.0**	**260,144**	**97.5**	**326,710**	**95.8**	**8,309**	**-292**	**8,017**	**2.22**	**362,500**	**95.3**	**406,880**	**95.1**	**637,450**	**95.0**
Roman Catholics	68,600	98.0	251,394	94.2	332,000	97.4	8,470	30	8,500	2.31	371,500	97.6	417,000	97.4	650,000	96.9
Protestants	0	0.0	8,500	3.2	10,500	3.1	268	232	500	3.97	12,698	3.3	15,500	3.6	30,000	4.5
Independents	0	0.0	200	0.1	9,000	2.6	230	150	380	3.58	11,080	2.9	12,800	3.0	25,000	3.7
Marginal Christians	0	0.0	50	0.0	3,500	1.0	89	41	130	3.21	4,160	1.1	4,800	1.1	10,000	1.5
doubly-affiliated	0	0.0	0	0.0	-28,290	-8.3	-722	-771	-1,493	4.33	-36,938	-9.7	-43,220	-10.1	-77,550	-11.6
Trans-megabloc groupings																
Evangelicals	0	0.0	8,000	3.0	8,900	2.6	227	-27	200	2.05	9,905	2.6	10,900	2.6	17,000	2.5
Pentecostals/Charismatics	0	0.0	500	0.2	23,500	6.9	600	220	820	3.04	27,103	7.1	31,700	7.4	64,000	9.5
Great Commission Christians	**3,500**	**5.0**	**16,000**	**6.0**	**44,000**	**12.9**	**1,123**	**69**	**1,192**	**2.43**	**49,600**	**13.0**	**55,921**	**13.1**	**95,000**	**14.2**
Muslims	0	0.0	0	0.0	7,800	2.3	199	206	405	4.27	10,600	2.8	11,848	2.8	19,000	2.8
Ethnoreligionists	700	1.0	300	0.1	3,440	1.0	88	51	139	3.46	4,300	1.1	4,833	1.1	6,000	0.9
Nonreligious	0	0.0	1,000	0.4	2,600	0.8	66	19	85	2.88	3,000	0.8	3,453	0.8	7,000	1.0
Baha'is	0	0.0	100	0.0	400	0.1	10	16	26	5.06	550	0.1	655	0.2	1,500	0.2
Jews	0	0.0	0	0.0	50	0.0	1	0	1	0.96	50	0.0	55	0.0	50	0.0
World A (unevangelized persons)	70	0.1	266	0.1	341	0.1	4	-1	3	1.74	380	0.1	428	0.1	671	0.1
World B (evangelized non-Christians)	630	0.9	1,045	0.4	13,949	4.1	360	293	653	4.02	17,649	4.8	20,692	4.8	32,879	4.9
World C (Christians)	69,300	99.0	265,600	99.5	326,710	95.8	8,309	-292	8,017	2.22	362,500	95.1	406,880	95.1	637,450	95.0
Country's population	**70,000**	**100.0**	**266,912**	**100.0**	**341,000**	**100.0**	**8,673**	**0**	**8,673**	**2.30**	**380,530**	**100.0**	**428,000**	**100.0**	**671,000**	**100.0**

COLUMNS, ROWS.
For meanings and definitions, see Codebook (Part 3). Note that, by definition, total 'Christians' = professing + crypto-Christians, which also = affiliated + unaffiliated Christians, and also = Great Commission Christians + latent Christians. Percentages may not always total exactly, due to rounding.

CENSUSES.
15.XII.1950: 98.2% Roman Catholics, 1.0% Protestants, 0.2% other religionists.

NOTES ON RELIGIONS
BAHA'IS. Begun 1957. By 1995, 11 local spiritual assemblies organized.
COUNTRY'S POPULATION. In 1947-48 severe drought killed 30,000 persons. Since Independence there has been a major population exodus to Europe and North America; in particular, there is a large Cape Verdean population in southeastern New England (USA).

Great Commission Instrument Panel: status of Cape Verde (for explanation see start of Part 4)

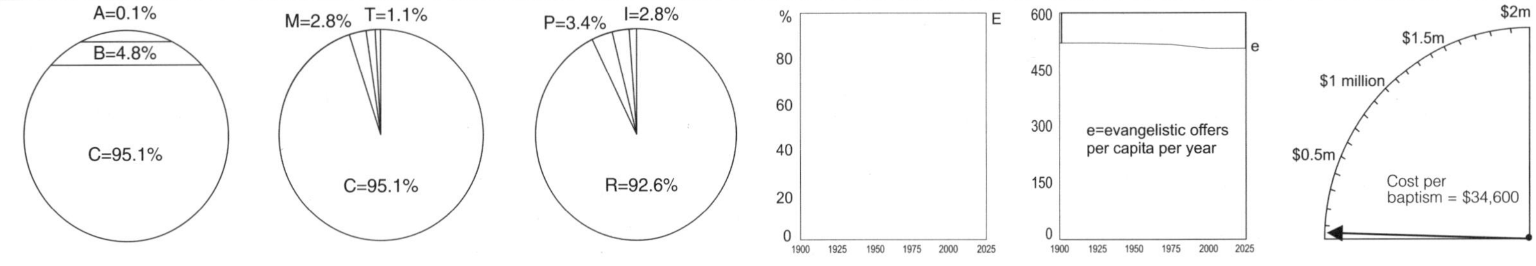

3 Worlds, AD 2000 — Religions, AD 2000 — Ecclesiastical blocs — Evangelization, 1900-2025 — Offers, 1900-2025 — Cost-effectiveness, AD 2000

Country summary. **Worlds A, B, C by ethnolinguistic peoples, cities, and major civil divisions in Cape Verde.**

	PEOPLES							CITIES							CIVIL DIVISIONS						
World	Num	Pop 2000	C%	Christians	E%	U%	Unevangelized	Num	Pop 2000	C%	Christians	E%	U%	Unevangelized	Num	Pop 2000	C%	Christians	E%	U%	Unevangelized
A	0	0	0.00	0	0	0	0	0	0	0.00	0	0	0	0	0	0	0.00	0	0	0	0
B	0	0	0.00	0	0	0	0	0	0	0.00	0	0	0	0	0	0	0.00	0	0	0	0
C	7	427,723	95.13	406,880	100	0	203	2	142,790	93.87	134,031	100	0	114	9	427,723	95.13	406,880	100	0	201
Total	**7**	**427,723**	**95.13**	**406,880**	**100**	**0**	**203**	**2**	**142,790**	**93.87**	**134,031**	**100**	**0**	**114**	**9**	**427,723**	**95.13**	**406,880**	**100**	**0**	**201**

Palmas. Jesuits were at work between 1604 and 1642, and the first Capuchins arrived in 1656. At present, the diocese is served by Holy Ghost and Capuchin priests and two congregations of sisters (Holy Ghost, Love of God). Although there are no local religious congregations, half the clergy are natives of the islands, many of the rest coming from Goa (India). In recent years, a process of marked dechristianization has been noticeable.

The Holy See has diplomatic relations with Cape Verde and in AD 2000 is represented to government and the Catholic hierarchy by a nuncio residing in Dakar.

PROTESTANT CHURCHES. Protestants are a small minority. Most are Nazarenes, who opened their first station on the islands in 1903. Seventh-day Adventists, with 8 congregations now, established the Cape Verde Islands Mission in 1935.

Indigenous missions. There is only a handful of citizen Roman Catholic missionaries serving outside of Cape Verde.

Igreja Catolica. Postage stamp commemorating 1951 Exposition of Sacred Missionary Art.

CHURCH AND STATE

Until 1975, relations between church and state were governed by the 1940 concordat between Portugal and the Holy See. After Independence from Portugal, a move towards secularization of the state was begun.

Igreja do Nazareno. Welcome being extended to visitors.

BROADCASTING AND MEDIA

Nearly every one has a radio. English-language shortwave programs can be received from from TWR (Swaziland). Cape Verde is a member of UNDA.

INTERDENOMINATIONAL ORGANIZATIONS

No councils of churches exist.

FUTURE TRENDS AND PROSPECTS

Muslims and the nonreligious are expected to remain constant at about 4% until 2025 with Christians hovering at 95% over the same period.

In the distant future, secularism and immigration could erode Christian affiliation resulting in Christians claiming less than 90% of the population by mid-century.

BIBLIOGRAPHY

A igreja de Cabo Verde e o desenvolvimento. P. L. Évora. [Praia]: Diocese de Cabo Verde, 1985. 20p. (Roman Catholic).
A primeira missão dos Capuchinhos em Cabo Verde. F. L. de Faria. Braga: Missões Franciscanas, 1954. 53p.
'Because we are the true Catholics: os rebelandos of the Cape Verde Islands.' S. L. Motley. M.A. thesis, University of California at Los Angeles, 1993. 47p.
Cabo Verde, subsídios para um levantamento cultural. J. Lopes Filho. Lisbon: Plátano Editora, [1981]. 150p.
Cape Verde. C. S. Shaw. *World bibliographical series,* vol. 123. Oxford, UK: CLIO Press, 1991. 210p. (See especially 'Religion,' p.70-3).
'Descobrimento povoamento evangelização do Archipélago de Cabo Verde,' A. Brásio, *Cabo Verde,* n.s. 14 (1963), 4–17.
Guinea–Bissau and Cape Verde Islands. J. M. McCarthy. *Garland Reference Library of Social Science,* no. 27. New York: Garland, 1977. 196p. (2,547 entries).
História da igreja de Cabo Verde: 450 anos da Igreja em Cabo Verde. F. Cerrone. São Vicente, Cape Verde: Gráfica do Mindelo, 1983. 75p. (Roman Catholic).
Ilhas de Cabo Verde: origem do povo caboverdiano e da diocese de Santiago de Cabo Verde. B. P. Vaschetto. Boston, MA: Edição Farol, 1987. 670p. (Roman Catholic).
Like a river flowing: the Church of the Nazarene in Africa and the Republic of Cape Verde. H. R. Friberg. *Missionary resource book,* 1982-83. Kansas City, MO: Nazarene Publishing House, 1982. 58p.
'Notes sur le catholicisme aux îles du Cap–vert,' N. E. Cabral, *Revue française d'études politiques africaines,* 14, 165-66 (1979), 108–117.
Os rebelados da Ilha de Santiago, de Cabo Verde: elementos para o estudo socio–religioso de uma comunidade. J. Monteiro Júnior. Centro de Estudos de Cabo Verde, 1974.
The people of the Cape Verde islands: exploitation and emigration. A. Carreira. London: C. Hurst, 1982. 233p. (Deals with emigration and immigration, including slave trade and slavery in Sao Tome and Principe).
The seed and the wind. E. Howard & J. de Barros. *Missionary reading books,* 1982-83. Kansas City, MO: Nazarene Publishing House, 1982. 84p.
Vangêle contód d'nôs móda. S. Frusoni. São Filipe, Cape Verde: Edição Terr Nova, 1979. 223p.

Country Table 2. Organized churches and denominations in Cape Verde.

Official name (bold type = church with over 10% of all affiliated) 1	Begun 2	Type 3	Counc 4	Congs 5	Adults 6	Affiliated 1970 7	Affiliated 1995 8	G% 9	Names, notes, and other statistics (see Codebook, Part 3) 10
Assembleias de Deus	1989	P-Pe2	.....	5	243	–	398	16.67	M=AoG(Brazil).
Igr de JC dos Santos dos Ultimos Dias	1989	m-LdS	x....	6	860	–	1,100	16.67	*Mormons.* M=Ch of JC of Latter-day Saints (USA).
Igreja Adventista do Sétimo Dia	1935	P-Adv	x....	27	1,309	1,000	3,190	4.75	*Seventh-day Adventists,* Portugal Mission. 1n,7mw,4t(417),W=80%,46Y,66z.
Igreja Católica: D Santiago de Cabo V	1462	R-Lat	P.B.r	31	241,000	251,394	371,500	1.57	96.2% of nation. M=CSSp,OFMCap,SDB. C=3+0+2. (1990) 13n,33x,42m,111w,11643Yy.
Igreja da Vida Profunda	1988	I-3cA	.....	2	58	–	63	14.29	*Deeper Life Bible Church.* M=DLC(Nigeria).
Igreja de Cristo Mana	1989	I-3cW	.....	1	18	–	52	16.67	*Mana Church of Christ.* M=Manna Church (Portugal).
Igreja do Nazareno	1903	P-Hol	xF...	23	5,300	7,500	9,110	0.78	*Nazarenes.* M=CoN(USA). 9n,2x,21m,6f,1j,1s(7),100t(6982),W=83%,73Y,224z.
Igreja Nova Apostolica	c1980	I-3aX	x....	1	5,000	–	10,360	6.67	*New Apostolic Church. NAC.*
Igreja Pentecostal Deus e Amor	1990	I-3pY	.....	5	200	–	345	20.00	*God is Love Church.* M=IPDA/GLC(Brazil).
Missão Baptista	1956	I-Bap	.....	1	130	200	260	1.05	*Baptist Mission Association.* M=BMAA(USA).
Testemunhas de Jeová	c1955	m-Jeh	x....	13	642	50	3,060	17.89	*Jehovah's Witnesses. Watch Tower. IBSA.* Active witnessing under way by 1962. (1995) 180Y.
Doubly-affiliated		2-aff			-23,600	0	-36,938		Baptized Roman Catholics who are also Evangelical members.
Totals				**115**	**231,160**	**260,144**	**362,500**		

Churches, members, growth, 1900-2025	*Congs*	*Adults*	*Affiliated*	*G%*	*Total denominations*	*6 Megablocs:*	*O*	*R*	*A*	*P*	*I*	*m*
Total churches, members, and denominations (mid-1900)	20	44,300	68,600	1.92	1		0	1	0	0	0	0
Total churches, members, and denominations (mid-1970)	92	167,828	260,144	1.92	5		0	1	0	2	1	1
Total churches, members, and denominations (mid-1990)	110	208,000	326,710	1.15	10		0	1	0	3	5	1
Total churches, members, and denominations (mid-1995)	115	231,160	362,500	2.10	11		0	1	0	3	5	2
Total churches, members, and denominations (mid-2000)	130	260,000	406,880	2.34	12		0	1	0	3	6	2
Total churches, members, and denominations (mid-2025)	210	407,000	637,450	1.81	33		0	1	0	7	20	5

NOTES ON TABLE ABOVE
NATIONAL COUNCILS (Column 4, 5th letter).
T = Conférence des Evêques du Sénégal, de la Mauritanie, du Cap-Vert, et de Guinée-Bissau (Bishops' Conference of S, M, CV, & G-B).

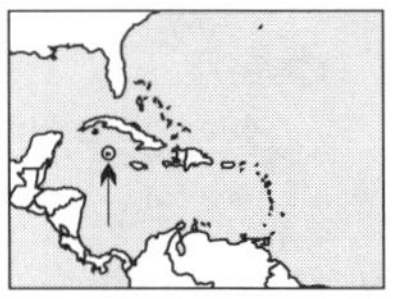

CAYMAN ISLANDS

SECULAR DATA, AD 2000

STATE
Official name: The Crown Colony of the Cayman Islands.
Short name: Cayman Islands. **Adjective of nationality:** Cayman Islanders.
Flag: British Blue Ensign with arms of the Colony in the fly.
Area: 259 sq. km. (100 sq. mi.).
Government: Crown colony of the United Kingdom (Britain), since 1959 (before 1959 ruled from Jamaica as a dependency).
Legislature: Legislative Assembly, 19 members Executive Council, 9 members.
Official language: English.
Monetary unit: Cayman Island dollar. **US$1=** 0.83.
Chief cities: GEORGETOWN 20,555.
Political divisions: 1 province.

DEMOGRAPHY
Population: 38,000.
Population density: 148.1/sq. km. (383.7/sq. mi.).
Under 15 years: 12,000.
Growth rate p.a.: 0.87% (births 19.95, deaths 5.62).
Mortality: Infant, per 1,000: 19.8; **Maternal per 100,000:** 10.0.
Life expectancy: 76 (male 74, female 78).
Household size: 4.0. **Floor area per person, sq.m:** 40.0.
Major languages: English, Hindi.
Urban dwellers: 100.00%. **Urban growth rate p.a.:** 2.7%.
Labor force: 60%.

ETHNOLINGUISTIC PEOPLES
51.5% Mulatto; 25.8% West Indian Black; 19.3% British; 1.9% Jewish; 0.3% Indo-Pakistani.

ECONOMY
National income p.a. per person: US$5,003; **per family:** US$20,015.

EDUCATION
Adult literacy: 93% (male 95%, female 91%). **Schools:** 20.
Universities: 1. **School enrolment:** female/male: 95%/95%.

HEALTH
Access to health services: 95%. **Access to safe water:** 90%.
Hospitals: 5 (65 beds per 10,000). **Doctors:** 50.
Blind: 10. **Deaf:** 2,200. **Murder rate:** 1. **Lepers:** 0.

LITERATURE
New book titles p.a.: 8 (200 p.a. per million). **Periodicals:** 4.
Newspapers: 1 daily.

COMMUNICATION (per 1,000 people)
Phones: 700 (10% mobile). **Radios:** 1,450. **TV sets:** 800.
Daily newspaper circulation: 700. **Computers:** 400.

HUMAN LIFE AND LIBERTY (optimum condition=100.0%)
HDI: 89.1. **HSI:** 90.0. **HFI:** 85.0. **EFL:** 60.0.

Country Table 1. Religious adherents in the Cayman Islands, AD 1900-2025.

Year	1900		1970		mid-1990		Annual change, 1990-2000				mid-1995		mid-2000		mid-2025	
Name	Adherents	%	Adherents	%	Adherents	%	Natural	Conversion	Total	Rate	Adherents	%	Adherents	%	Adherents	%
Christians	**4,800**	**100.0**	**9,240**	**91.5**	**20,815**	**80.1**	**956**	**-61**	**895**	**3.64**	**25,020**	**78.2**	**29,766**	**77.6**	**59,000**	**75.6**
PROFESSION																
professing Christians	**4,800**	**100.0**	**9,240**	**91.5**	**20,815**	**80.1**	**956**	**-61**	**895**	**3.64**	**25,020**	**78.2**	**29,766**	**77.6**	**59,000**	**75.6**
AFFILIATION																
unaffiliated Christians	480	10.0	389	3.9	2,545	9.8	117	23	140	4.48	3,224	10.1	3,946	10.3	8,000	10.3
affiliated Christians	**4,320**	**90.0**	**8,851**	**87.6**	**18,270**	**70.3**	**838**	**-83**	**755**	**3.52**	**21,796**	**68.1**	**25,820**	**67.3**	**51,000**	**65.4**
Protestants	4,280	89.2	7,200	71.3	14,500	55.8	669	-50	619	3.62	17,349	54.2	20,690	54.6	41,300	53.0
Independents	0	0.0	1,171	11.6	2,950	11.4	136	-26	110	3.22	3,512	11.0	4,050	10.6	7,800	10.0
Anglicans	0	0.0	100	1.0	320	1.2	15	3	18	4.56	400	1.3	500	1.3	900	1.2
Marginal Christians	0	0.0	130	1.3	300	1.2	14	-6	8	2.39	335	1.1	380	1.0	700	0.9
Roman Catholics	40	0.8	250	2.5	200	0.8	9	-9	0	0.00	200	0.6	200	0.5	300	0.4
Trans-megabloc groupings																
Evangelicals	3,400	70.8	1,800	17.8	3,950	15.2	182	-17	165	3.55	4,763	14.9	5,600	14.5	10,500	13.5
Pentecostals/Charismatics	0	0.0	100	1.0	4,300	16.5	198	22	220	4.22	5,358	16.7	6,500	17.0	14,000	18.0
Great Commission Christians	**300**	**6.3**	**1,000**	**9.9**	**4,900**	**18.9**	**226**	**27**	**253**	**4.25**	**6,080**	**19.0**	**7,430**	**19.3**	**15,970**	**20.5**
Spiritists	0	0.0	500	5.0	3,900	15.0	180	13	193	4.10	4,800	15.0	5,826	15.2	12,000	15.4
Nonreligious	0	0.0	110	1.1	780	3.0	36	48	84	7.55	1,250	3.9	1,615	4.2	5,000	6.4
Jews	0	0.0	200	2.0	480	1.9	22	-4	18	3.17	530	1.7	656	1.7	800	1.0
Baha'is	0	0.0	50	0.5	200	0.8	9	5	14	5.32	260	0.8	336	0.9	700	0.9
Hindus	0	0.0	0	0.0	75	0.3	3	-1	2	2.71	80	0.3	98	0.3	250	0.3
Muslims	0	0.0	0	0.0	50	0.2	2	0	2	4.00	60	0.2	74	0.2	150	0.2
World A (unevangelized persons)	0	0.0	10	0.1	468	1.8	21	8	29	5.00	608	1.9	760	2.0	1,794	2.3
World B (evangelized non-Christians)	0	0.0	849	8.4	4,717	19.1	231	53	284	4.71	6,372	19.9	7,474	20.4	17,206	22.0
World C (Christians)	4,800	100.0	9,240	91.5	20,815	79.1	956	-61	895	3.64	25,020	78.2	29,766	77.6	59,000	75.7
Country's population	**4,800**	**100.0**	**10,100**	**100.0**	**26,000**	**100.0**	**1,208**	**0**	**1,208**	**3.87**	**32,000**	**100.0**	**38,000**	**100.0**	**78,000**	**100.0**

COLUMNS, ROWS.
For meanings and definitions, see Codebook (Part 3). Note that, by definition, total 'Christians' = professing + crypto-Christians, which also = affiliated + unaffiliated Christians, and also = Great Commission Christians + latent Christians. Percentages may not always total exactly, due to rounding.

CENSUSES.
7.IV.1960 (de jure): 95.9% Protestants (37.4% Presbyterians, 26.4% Ch of God, 11.5% Pilgrim Holiness Ch), 2.2% Roman Catholics, 0.9% nonreligious, 0.7% Anglicans, 0.3% marginal Protestants. **7.IV.1970:** results invalidated because 16% were returned 'Not stated'.

Country status. The Cayman Islands form a small chain of 3 coral islands south of Cuba and northwest of Jamaica in the Caribbean Sea. They have been a British colony since 1670. Tourism and international finance are the main industries.

HUMAN LIFE AND LIBERTY

Human rights and freedoms. Cayman Islands is a United Kingdom dependency where UK laws fully protect all human rights.

NON-CHRISTIAN RELIGIONS

A small Jewish community exists, as well as isolated followers of other religions including the Ras Tafari cult (Jamaica), and a small number without religion.

Great Commission Instrument Panel: status of the Cayman Islands (for explanation see start of Part 4)

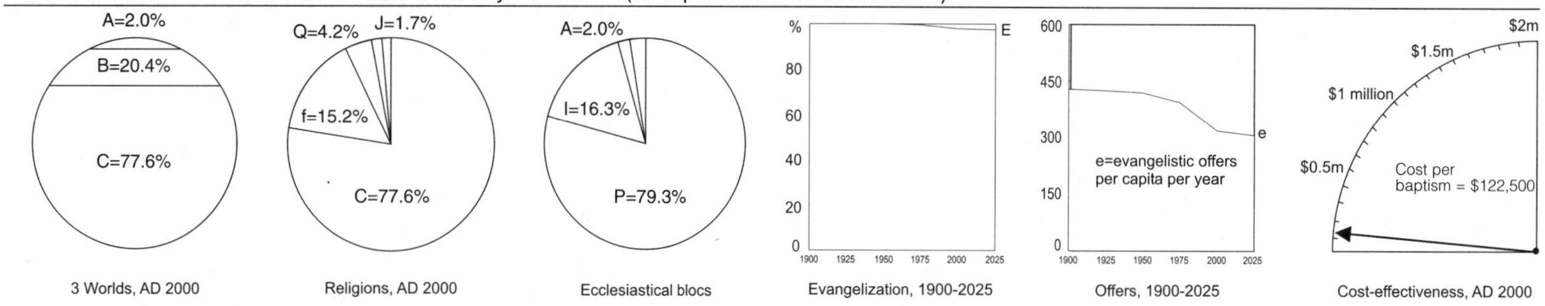

Country summary. **Worlds A, B, C by ethnolinguistic peoples, cities, and major civil divisions in the Cayman Islands.**

	PEOPLES							***CITIES***							***CIVIL DIVISIONS***						
World	*Num*	*Pop 2000*	*C%*	*Christians*	*E%*	*U%*	*Unevangelized*	*Num*	*Pop 2000*	*C%*	*Christians*	*E%*	*U%*	*Unevangelized*	*Num*	*Pop 2000*	*C%*	*Christians*	*E%*	*U%*	*Unevangelized*
A	1	729	0.96	7	49	51	373	0	0	0.00	0	0	0	0	0	0	0.00	0	0	0	0
B	2	575	22.09	127	54	46	262	0	0	0.00	0	0	0	0	0	0	0.00	0	0	0	0
C	3	37,067	69.30	25,687	100	0	114	1	20,555	67.30	13,834	98	2	399	1	38,371	67.29	25,820	98	2	749
Total	**6**	**38,371**	**67.29**	**25,821**	**98**	**2**	**749**	**1**	**20,555**	**67.30**	**13,834**	**98**	**2**	**399**	**1**	**38,371**	**67.29**	**25,820**	**98**	**2**	**749**

CHRISTIANITY

The Cayman Islands are unique among former British possessions in the West Indies in that the traditionally strong Catholic, Anglican, and Methodist churches have had little impact on the scene.

PROTESTANT CHURCHES. Presbyterianism, which owes its origin to Church of Scotland influences as early as 1800, is the most important tradition with more than one-third of the population. The Cayman Islands have been closely associated with Jamaica from earliest days and so were included in the union negotiations of Jamaican Presbyterians and Congregationists which resulted in 1965 in the United Church of Jamaica and Grand Cayman. On the Caymans there is also a small community related to the Reformed Presbyterian Church, Evangelical Synod (USA). The Baptist Church, with 1% of the population, is another Old-World Christian community whose origin dates back to the last century. Protestant missions from the USA have made considerable progress in the present century. The Church of God (Anderson) and Church of God (Holiness), both of which began work in the 1930s, claimed the allegiance of more than 25% of the population in 1960. The Pilgrim Holiness Church opened its first worship center in 1911, and the Adventist Cayman Islands Mission was organized in 1944.

CATHOLIC CHURCH. The Cayman Islands are a part of the diocese of Kingston in Jamaica. In 1972, the islands had 62 Catholic families, about two-thirds being Europeans, South Americans or Central Americans, the other third being of African or mixed-African descent. There is one parish in Grand Cayman with one Jesuit priest who periodically visits Little Cayman and Cayman Brac.

The Holy See has no diplomatic relations with Cayman Islands in AD 2000.

Indigenous missions. There is no missionary outreach from the Cayman Islands.

CHURCH AND STATE

The Cayman Islands were discovered in 1503 by Columbus but were never colonized by Spain. They were ruled from Jamaica as a British dependency until 1959 when they became a separate self-governing colony but reverted to British rule in 1962. There has never been an established church in the islands.

BROADCASTING AND MEDIA

Shortwave programs from HCJB (Ecuador), TWR (Antilles) and AWR (Costa Rica) can be easily received.

LeSEA programming can be received from the World Harvest Satellite. TBN broadcasts can be seen on channel 21 in Grand Caymans.

FUTURE TRENDS AND PROSPECTS

The nonreligious are expected to continue to grow steadily from 1.1% in 1970 to 6.4% by 2025. Christianity would then decline from 91.5% in 1970 to a low of under 75.6% in the same period.

The nonreligious will possibly grow beyond 10% of the population by mid-century. Christians, though still holding the majority of adherents, could fall below 60% in the same period.

The Resurrection of Christ, one of many Christian themes on the islands' postage stamps; here 'Noli me tangere' (Do not touch me) by Titian.

BIBLIOGRAPHY

Cayman emerges: a human history of long ago Cayman. S. O. Ebanks. : Northwester, [1983]. 80p.
Notes on the history of the Cayman Islands. G. S. S. Hirst. Grand Cayman: Hobbies and Books. 412p.
The people time forgot: [a photographic portrayal of the people of the Cayman Islands]. H. G. Nowak, R. Bodden & H. George. Grand Cayman: Cayman Free Press, [1987].
The rise of the Seventh–day Adventist Church in the Bahamas and the Cayman Islands. J. K. Thompson. [Nassau, Bahamas], 1992. 193p.

Country Table 2. **Organized churches and denominations in the Cayman Islands.**

Official name (bold type = church with over 10% of all affiliated) 1	*Begun* 2	*Type* 3	*Counc* 4	*Congs* 5	*Adults* 6	*Affiliated 1970* 7	*Affiliated 1995* 8	*G%* 9	*Names, notes, and other statistics* (see Codebook, Part 3) 10
Anglican Church (D Jamaica)		A-Cen	awMR.	3	200	100	400	0.05	*CPWI.* In Ch of the Province of the West Indies. Growing; support from Jamaica.
Baptist Church	c1870	P-Bap	.....	2	166	800	460	-2.19	Baptists related to Jamaica Baptist Union.
Baptist Convention	1977	P-Bap	.....	1	151	–	252	5.56	M=FMB-SBC(USA). Southern Baptist missionaries.
Bible Baptist Church		I-Bap	.....	6	300	71	429	0.05	M=BIM(USA). Fundamentalist mission from USA.
Catholic Church (M Kingston)		R-Lat	P.NM.	2	120	250	200	0.05	Under M Kingston (Jamaica). On Cayman Brac. 60% White, 40% Black. 1x(SJ),3w.
Christian Churches & Chs of Christ		I-Dis	x....	1	50	100	83	0.05	Independent Churches of Christ missionaries. M=CCCC(Instrumental) (USA). 2f.
Church of God (Anderson)	1930	P-Hol	x....	25	1,000	2,000	2,500	0.90	Holiness denomination. M=CoG(Anderson) (USA). 3n,1x,W=12%.
Church of God (Cleveland)	1971	P-Pe3	.....	2	232	–	387	4.17	M=CoG(Cleveland)(USA).
Church of God Holiness	1933	P-Hol	x....	15	1,000	500	2,000	5.70	M=CoG Holiness(Overland Park, Kansas, USA). Wesleyan doctrines. 2f.
Church of God of Prophecy	1978	P-Pe3	.....	1	20	–	80	5.88	M=CGP(USA). Holiness Pentecostals.
Jehovah's Witnesses	c1950	m-Jeh	x....	1	82	30	205	7.99	*Watch Tower.* IBSA. Active witnessing under way by 1956. 4Y.
Reformed Presb Ch, Evangelical Synod		P-Ref	x....	1	200	200	500	0.05	Reformed mission from North America. Calvinists. M=WPM(RPCES)(USA).
Reorganized Ch of Jesus Christ of LdS		m-LdS	x....	3	52	100	130	0.05	LsD=Latter-day Saints. Schism in USA ex Mormons claiming legal succession.
Seventh-day Adventist Church	1944	P-Adv	x....	7	931	700	1,550	3.23	*Cayman Islands Mission*, West Indies Union Conference. 2nx,11mw,1r,5T(484),129Y.
United Ch of Jam & Grand Cayman	c1800	P-Uni	RWM..	20	5,490	2,500	9,000	5.26	Formerly Presb Ch of J & Grand Cayman; 1965 union Congreg Union of Jamaica.
Wesleyan Church	1911	P-Hol	VF...	3	210	400	320	-0.89	Formerly Pilgrim Holiness Ch. Declining (977 in 1960). 2n,1x,2f,W=90%,13y.
Other independent bodies		I-	.....	50	2,000	1,000	3,000	0.05	Including: New Apostolic Church (23 members).
Other Protestant denominations		P-	.....	10	200	100	300	0.05	Total about 3, including: Ch of God(Cleveland), Disciples of Christ.
Totals				**153**	**12,404**	**8,851**	**21,796**		

Churches, members, growth, 1900-2025	*Congs*	*Adults*	*Affiliated*	*G%*	*Total denominations*	*6 Megablocs:* *O*	*R*	*A*	*P*	*I*	*m*
Total churches, members, and denominations (mid-1900)	20	2,700	4,320	1.03	3	0	0	1	2	0	0
Total churches, members, and denominations (mid-1970)	61	5,627	8,851	1.03	16	0	1	1	8	4	2
Total churches, members, and denominations (mid-1990)	130	10,400	18,270	3.69	23	0	1	1	12	7	2
Total churches, members, and denominations (mid-1995)	153	12,404	21,796	3.59	24	0	1	1	13	7	2
Total churches, members, and denominations (mid-2000)	160	14,700	25,820	3.45	25	0	1	1	14	7	2
Total churches, members, and denominations (mid-2025)	300	29,000	51,000	2.76	46	0	1	1	20	20	4

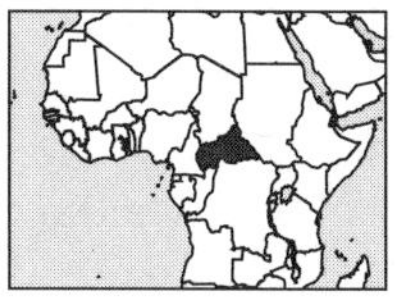

CENTRAL AFRICAN REPUBLIC

SECULAR DATA, AD 2000

STATE
Official name: La République Centrafricaine (The Central African Republic).
Short name: Central African Republic. **Adjective of nationality:** of the Central African Republic.
Flag: Blue, white, green, and yellow stripes crossed by vertical red bar: gold star in upper hoist corner.
Area: 622,436 sq. km. (240,324 sq. mi.).
Government: Republic, since 1979 (1894 French territory, 1905 colony in French Equatorial Africa, 1960 Independence as republic 1966 military dictatorship and empire).
Legislature: National Assembly, 85 members.
Official language: French (Français).
Monetary unit: 1 CFA franc (CFAF) = 100 centimes. **US$1=** CFAF 560.38.
Chief cities: BANGUI 697,104; Berberati 141,043; Bouar 73,928; Bambari 63,469.
Political divisions: 17 provinces.
Armed forces: 5,000.

DEMOGRAPHY
Population: 3,615,000.
Population density: 5.8/sq. km. (15.0/sq. mi.).
Under 15 years: 1,537,000.
Growth rate p.a.: 1.80% (births 36.34, deaths 18.36).
Mortality: Infant, per 1,000: 92.3; **Maternal per 100,000:** 700.0.
Life expectancy: 45 (male 43, female 47).
Household size: 4.7. **Floor area per person, sq.m:** 6.0.
Major languages: Branda, Baya, French, Sango, Mandja, Mbum, and over 45 other tribal languages.
Urban dwellers: 41.19%. **Urban growth rate p.a.:** 3.3%.
Labor force: 48%.

ETHNOLINGUISTIC PEOPLES
22.8% Baya (Gbaya); 10.3% Sango; 9.8% Banda; 6.4% Manja (Mandja); 3.3% Bororo Fulani.

ECONOMY
National income p.a. per person: US$339; **per family:** US$1,597.

EDUCATION
Adult literacy: 60% (male 68%, female 52%). **Schools:** 976.
Universities: 1. **School enrolment:** female/male: 31%/54%.

HEALTH
Access to health services: 45%. **Access to safe water:** 18%.
Hospitals: 133 (15 beds per 10,000). **Doctors:** 170.
Blind: 27,000. **Deaf:** 218,400. **Murder rate:** 1.
Lepers: 200,000. **Underweight prevalence under 5:** 27%.

LITERATURE
New book titles p.a.: 720 (200 p.a. per million). **Periodicals:** 17.
Newspapers: 1 daily.

COMMUNICATION (per 1,000 people)
Phones: 2 (6% mobile). **Radios:** 55. **TV sets:** 5.
Daily newspaper circulation: 1. **Computers:** 1.

REFUGEES
Alien refugees from other countries: 34,000.

HUMAN LIFE AND LIBERTY (optimum condition=100.0%)
HDI: 35.5. **HSI:** 27.0. **HFI:** 30.0. **EFL:** 22.0.

Country Table 1. **Religious adherents in the Central African Republic, AD 1900-2025.**

Year / Name	1900 Adherents	1900 %	1970 Adherents	1970 %	mid-1990 Adherents	mid-1990 %	Annual change, 1990-2000 Natural	Conversion	Total	Rate	mid-1995 Adherents	mid-1995 %	mid-2000 Adherents	mid-2000 %	mid-2025 Adherents	mid-2025 %
Christians	**50**	**0.0**	**1,184,500**	**64.1**	**1,953,000**	**66.4**	**44,703**	**5,021**	**49,724**	**2.29**	**2,205,000**	**67.1**	**2,450,244**	**67.8**	**4,066,000**	**71.3**
PROFESSION																
professing Christians	**50**	**0.0**	**1,184,500**	**64.1**	**1,953,000**	**66.4**	**44,703**	**5,021**	**49,724**	**2.29**	**2,205,000**	**67.1**	**2,450,244**	**67.8**	**4,066,000**	**71.3**
AFFILIATION																
unaffiliated Christians	0	0.0	475,414	25.7	713,500	24.3	16,322	-3,547	12,775	1.66	788,833	24.0	841,245	23.3	766,000	13.4
affiliated Christians	**50**	**0.0**	**709,086**	**38.3**	**1,239,500**	**42.1**	**28,381**	**8,569**	**36,950**	**2.64**	**1,416,167**	**43.1**	**1,608,999**	**44.5**	**3,300,000**	**57.9**
Roman Catholics	50	0.0	277,926	15.0	500,000	17.0	11,438	5,026	16,464	2.89	579,216	17.6	664,639	18.4	1,421,000	24.9
Protestants	0	0.0	222,960	12.1	404,000	13.7	9,242	2,438	11,680	2.57	454,280	13.8	520,800	14.4	1,050,000	18.4
Independents	0	0.0	203,100	11.0	330,000	11.2	7,549	1,251	8,800	2.39	377,141	11.5	418,000	11.6	820,000	14.4
Marginal Christians	0	0.0	5,100	0.3	5,500	0.2	126	-120	6	0.11	5,530	0.2	5,560	0.2	9,000	0.2
Trans-megabloc groupings																
Evangelicals	0	0.0	259,000	14.0	499,000	17.0	11,415	1,685	13,100	2.36	566,388	17.2	630,000	17.4	1,100,000	19.3
Pentecostals/Charismatics	0	0.0	100,000	5.4	382,000	13.0	8,738	1,562	10,300	2.42	434,393	13.2	485,000	13.4	850,000	14.9
Great Commission Christians	**40**	**0.0**	**222,000**	**12.0**	**550,000**	**18.7**	**12,582**	**13,582**	**26,164**	**3.97**	**657,600**	**20.0**	**811,638**	**22.5**	**1,440,000**	**25.3**
Muslims	3,000	0.4	86,000	4.7	455,000	15.5	10,408	496	10,904	2.17	510,000	15.5	564,040	15.6	920,000	16.1
Ethnoreligionists	766,950	99.6	575,000	31.1	503,000	17.1	11,506	-6,091	5,415	1.03	535,000	16.3	557,149	15.4	620,000	10.9
Nonreligious	0	0.0	0	0.0	23,000	0.8	526	374	900	3.36	28,000	0.9	32,000	0.9	70,000	1.2
Baha'is	0	0.0	3,500	0.2	8,000	0.3	183	200	383	3.99	10,000	0.3	11,833	0.3	28,000	0.5
World A (unevangelized persons)	769,230	99.9	399,447	21.6	541,328	18.4	12,376	-8,603	3,773	0.68	575,367	17.5	578,400	16.0	701,592	12.3
World B (evangelized non-Christians)	720	0.1	265,347	14.3	447,672	15.2	10,247	3,582	13,829	2.74	507,448	15.4	586,356	16.2	936,408	16.4
World C (Christians)	50	0.0	1,184,500	64.1	1,953,000	66.4	44,703	5,021	49,724	2.29	2,205,000	67.1	2,450,244	67.8	4,066,000	71.3
Country's population	**770,000**	**100.0**	**1,849,295**	**100.0**	**2,942,000**	**100.0**	**67,326**	**0**	**67,326**	**2.08**	**3,287,816**	**100.0**	**3,615,000**	**100.0**	**5,704,000**	**100.0**

COLUMNS, ROWS.
For meanings and definitions, see Codebook (Part 3). Note that, by definition, total 'Christians' = professing + crypto-Christians, which also = affiliated + unaffiliated Christians, and also = Great Commission Christians + latent Christians. Percentages may not always total exactly, due to rounding.

CENSUSES.
X.1960-IV.1961 (persons over 13 years): 41.8% Protestants, 28.1% Roman Catholics, 27.6% ethnoreligionists, 2.5% Muslims.

NOTES ON RELIGIONS
AFFILIATED. The column 'Conversion' above shows a net annual total (conversions minus defections) of 5,021 persons. Most of these converts receive adult baptism in the churches, as can be seen from baptism figures in column 8 in Table 2 below.
BAHA'IS. Growth from 1 local spiritual assembly (1964) to 21 (1973) mushrooming thereafter to 65 LSAs by 1995. Radio broadcasts over government radio began in 1973. Missionaries from Haiti (West Indies) are at work.
ETHNORELIGIONISTS. Tribes over 60% traditionalist (animist) in 1995: Binga Pygmies (90%), Monjombo (80%). Among several movements covered by this category is Nzapa ti Azande which is government-recognized as an authentic African religion.
INDEPENDENTS. In over 10 denominations in 1995 (see Table 2).
MUSLIMS. Strongest in towns among non-Africans (31%); also among Hausa and Bororo nomads in north. Mostly Sunnis (of the Malikite rite). There has been lengthy infiltration among the Gbaya (Baya), who are now somewhat islamized in some areas. *Hajj pilgrims to Mecca.* (1975) 390; (1976) 361.
UNAFFILIATED. The very large proportion of Christians who are nominal (professing in censuses, but not known to the churches) and who form a nominal fringe of over 840,000 around affiliated Christians, reflects a situation typical of rapid mass conversions of societies: vastly more persons regard themselves as having broken with non-Christian society, and having become believers, than the churches are capable of contacting, initiating by baptism, and discipling. Many have attended Christian-originated schools and regard themselves as Christians as a result.

Great Commission Instrument Panel: status of the Central African Republic (for explanation see start of Part 4)

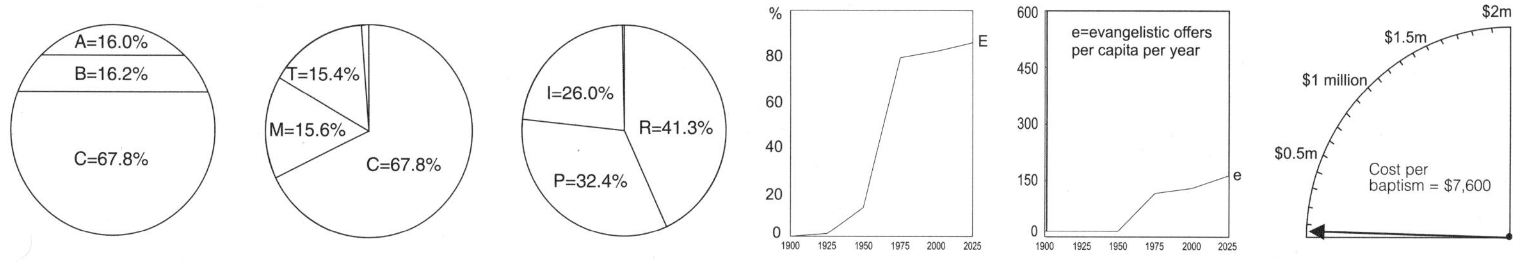

3 Worlds, AD 2000 | Religions, AD 2000 | Ecclesiastical blocs | Evangelization, 1900-2025 | Offers, 1900-2025 | Cost-effectiveness, AD 2000

Country status. The Central African Republic is a landlocked country in the Sahel region of central Africa. It is a former French colony that, after independence, became a monarchy for a few years under a misguided adventurer. Coffee and diamonds are the major source of income.

HUMAN LIFE AND LIBERTY

Human need and development. Central African Republic is a microcosm of Africa and typifies all the problems that face post-colonial African nations. Its economy is characterized by primitive infrastructure, little or no industry, subsistence agriculture, low literacy, and rudimentary medical facilities. Development efforts are hampered by poor planning and political mismanagement as well as ethnic rivalries. The country's landlocked position adds to the transportation costs and limits access to the rest of the continent. A further burden is the presence of over 10,000 refugees from the civil war in the Sudan and 1,600 refugees from Chad.

Human rights and freedoms. The Central African Republic has been under military dictatorship since 1981. During this period, human rights have suffered greatly as his government sought to suppress dissident movements and imprisoned their leaders. Many deaths have been reported as a result of police and military brutality. Political prisoners are held without charges being filed for long periods and they are denied fair trials or the benefit of procedural legal safeguards. In 1991, 2 judges, including the president of the Supreme Court, were removed from office because they had ruled against the government in certain cases. There is no freedom of speech or press as the government owns all newspapers, radio, and television, and does not permit the publication of any news unfavorable to the government. Although the Constitution mandates equal treatment of all ethnic groups, some are singled out for discrimination. These

Country summary. **Worlds A, B, C by ethnolinguistic peoples, cities, and major civil divisions in the Central African Republic.**

	PEOPLES							CITIES							CIVIL DIVISIONS						
World	*Num*	*Pop 2000*	*C%*	*Christians*	*E%*	*U%*	*Unevangelized*	*Num*	*Pop 2000*	*C%*	*Christians*	*E%*	*U%*	*Unevangelized*	*Num*	*Pop 2000*	*C%*	*Christians*	*E%*	*U%*	*Unevangelized*
A	19	438,690	3.98	17,451	31	69	301,722	0	0	0.00	0	0	0	0	0	0	0.00	0	0	0	0
B	51	2,667,409	46.55	1,241,660	90	10	266,426	4	975,544	50.08	488,568	92	8	73,947	17	3,615,268	44.51	1,608,999	84	16	578,730
C	25	509,165	68.72	349,892	98	2	10,584	0	0	0.00	0	0	0	0	0	0	0.00	0	0	0	0
Total	**95**	**3,615,264**	**44.51**	**1,609,003**	**84**	**16**	**578,732**	**4**	**975,544**	**50.08**	**488,568**	**92**	**8**	**73,947**	**17**	**3,615,268**	**44.51**	**1,608,999**	**84**	**16**	**578,730**

include the forest-dwelling Bayaka, commonly known as Pygmies, and the Muslim Mbororo. Although there are 80 ethnic groups in the country, power is concentrated in the Yakoma (to which President Kalingba belongs) who make up less than 5% of the population. Women face considerable discrimination, particularly in the rural areas where only 20% of them attend primary school. Violence against women, including genital mutilation, is widely prevalent despite being outlawed.

Human environment. The Central African Republic is one of the world's largest refuges of the African elephant, but poaching by herders and nomads has taken a heavy toll. The elephant population has dropped from 150,000 to 15,000 since independence. The environment suffers from the incursions of nomads from Chad and Sudan who use the grasslands for cattle grazing. The result is extensive devegetation and desertification.

NON-CHRISTIAN RELIGIONS

Traditional religions are still professed by a small minority of each of the main tribes, as well as by 99% of the Binga Pygmies. In 1960, 28% of the population was recorded as traditionalist with the following tribal breakdown: Banda 27%, Baya 35%, Mandja 25%, Sara 21%, Mbaka 23%, Mbum 17%, Nzakara 22% and Azande 13%. All these figures have since been substantially reduced, to 16% for the nation by 1975. The most common Baya name for God is So, although Zambi is also used. Meanwhile, the government has granted recognition to the Nzapa ti Azande movement as an authentic African religion.

Islam is strongest among the non-African population which in 1960 was 31% Muslim. The Banda then were only 0.4% Muslim, Baya 1.6% and Mandja 2.6%, making 2.5% for the whole population. Except for some Hausa and Bororo nomads in the north, Islam has had little impact on rural peoples and is primarily an urban phenomenon. In 1976, president Bokassa announced his conversion to Islam after a visit by president Gaddaffi of Libya.

CHRISTIANITY

Since territorial independence in 1959, the number of professing Christians rose dramatically from 42% Protestant and 28% Catholic (1960) to 47% Protestant and 32% Catholic (1975), making this mass influx one of the most dramatic in Africa.

PROTESTANT CHURCHES. The 2 largest Protestant denominations are the Baptist and Brethren churches, both of which were started by North American missionary societies following World War I. The first to arrive was Baptist Mid-Missions, coming in 1920 from Conga-Kinshasa and building their first center at Rafai among the Azande. They now have 12 stations concentrated primarily among the Banda, Mandja, and Nzakara. A year later followed the Church of the Brethren mission, which in addition to a large number of self-supporting congregations, sponsors a hospital, 16 dispensaries, several Bible schools, and a school of theology. Other denominations include those begun by Swedish and Swiss Pentecostals. Lutheran work was begun by the Sudan Mission in 1923, assisted later by the American Lutheran Church and the Church of Norway; its work extends over the border into Cameroon.

Union des Eglises. Baya-speaking Pentecostal church elders sweep up after service, with pastor and wife at far left.

CATHOLIC CHURCH. The first Catholic mission was opened at Bangui in 1894. A prefecture was erected in 1909, elevated to a vicariate in 1937. The Catholic Church is now organized into 5 dioceses under an African archbishop.

The Holy See has diplomatic relations with Central African Republic and in AD 2000 is represented to government and the Catholic hierarchy by a nuncio residing in Bangui.

Eglise Catholique à la RCA, Diocèse de Berberati. Postage stamp of 1971 consecration of Berberati Cathedral.

INDIGENOUS CHURCHES. A schism by Mandja tribesmen out of Baptist Mid-Missions in 1956 resulted in the Comité Baptiste, which has since received missionaries from Coopération Evangélique Mondiale (France, Switzerland); and a split from the Church of the Brethren by a Banda pastor at Bouca in 1960 resulted in the formation of the Eglise Centrafricaine. In addition, numerous white-robed adherents of independent churches from Zaire, including Kimbanguists, now live and work in Bangui and other centers.

Renewal movements. In the 1990s the Pentecostal/Charismatic Renewal continued to spread rapidly across most older churches, and numbered over 485,000 adherents (of whom 21% Pentecostals, 26% Charismatics, and 53% Independents).

Indigenous missions. There has been little missionary outreach from this country. There are less than a dozen citizen Catholic and Protestant missionaries sent out from the Central African Republic.

CHURCH AND STATE

The constitution was suspended in January 1966 and the country subsequently governed by decree. There are therefore no juridical provisions for relations between church and state. There are however de facto agreements recognized: (1) the Ministry of Social Affairs subsidizes church rural development projects and sometimes even the construction of church buildings; (2) all primary, secondary, and technical schools are run by government, although religious orders are allowed to operate schools in Bangui (Lyceum of The Rapids, by Marist brothers and Lyceum Pius XII, by Sisters of the Holy Spirit) as well as a number of primary schools outside the capital, and missions operate 2 recognized private schools (Protestants at Crampel and Catholics in the diocese of Bangui run by Sisters of the Holy Spirit); (3) although chaplains of lyceums have no legal status, religious instruction is permitted outside school hours; and (4) a small nominal tax is paid by clergy and religious personnel at the same rate as villagers. There is no government ministry in charge of religious affairs, but churches are required to keep the Ministry of the Interior informed about their activities in the country.

Catholic bishops have over the last few years tended to withdraw from their earlier close connections with the political authorities. In 1977, they and the Vatican refused to perform the coronation ceremony requested by the emperor.

In June 1977, the Central African Evangelical Baptist Church was decreed dissolved because it 'constitutes a danger to public order'.

Over the subsequent 2 decades, church-state relations stabilized and matured.

BROADCASTING AND MEDIA

One out of 5 own a radio receiver, so radio is a crucial strategy. AWR airs programs in French and English. English-language shortwave programs are broadcast from TWR (Swaziland). Central African Republic is a member of UNDA, and a 15-minute Catholic homily is broadcast each Sunday morning, and a 45-minute religious news program is aired each Monday.

Television programs reach fewer people due to the lack of widespread ownership of TV sets. A Catholic program is aired each third Saturday for 45 minutes. Virtually all have seen the 'Jesus' Film: film teams have had an aggregate viewing audience of 4.2 million. About 10% of viewers have responded.

INTERDENOMINATIONAL ORGANIZATIONS

There is no ecumenical council nor other organization. Most Protestants cooperate in the Association of Central African Evangelical Churches, organized in 1974 and a member of AEAM. Relations between all denominations are limited and are confined largely to Bible translation work. The AEAM however has sponsored, and in 1976 opened, the interdenominational Bangui Evangelical School of Theology (BEST), offering higher degrees in biblical theology and serving Protestants throughout francophone Africa.

FUTURE TRENDS AND PROSPECTS

Though the unaffiliated are expected to decline through 2025, Muslims are expected to grow to 16.1% in the same period with an increase to 71.3% for the overall Christian community.

With current trends, Christians will climb to about 80% and Muslims will represent the remaining 20% of the population by AD 2050.

BIBLIOGRAPHY

Album du Centenaire de l'Église Catholique en Centrafrique, 1894–1994. Bangui, C.A.R.: Commission du Centenaire de l'Eglise de Centrafrique, 1994. 36p.

Bibliographie centrafricaine. G. de Banville. Bangui, C.A.R.: Maison St. Charles, 1991. 102p.

Bibliographique signalétique sur les missions chrétiennes en Oubangui–Chari, des origines à nos jours. M. Amaye. Aix-en-Provence, France: Université d'Aix-en-Provence, IHPOM, 1981. 78p.

Central African Republic. P. Kalck. *World bibliographical series*, vol. 152. Oxford, UK: CLIO Press, 1993. 209p. (See especially 'Religion,' p.62-6).

Conquering Oubangui–Chari for Christ. O. Jobson. Winona Lake, IN, 1957. 159p.

Introduction au wanzanisme ou au culte ancestral. B. Lala. Bangui, C.A.R.: B. Lala, 1991. 19p.

'Les Bandas de l'Oubangui–Chari (Afrique Equatoriale Française),' R. P. J. Daigre, *Revue internationale d'ethnologie et de linguistiques anthrôpos*, 26 (1932) 647–95, and 27 (1933) 151–81.

Les Débuts de l'Eglise catholique en R.C.A: notes et documents. R. P. G. de Banville (ed). Bangui, C.A.R.: Maison Saint-Charles, 1988. 188p.

Les rites secrets des primitifs de l'Oubangui. A. Vergiat. Paris: Payot, 1936. 308p.

Nos pères dans la foi. Les anciens de la mission Saint Paul. R. P. L. Godart & C. Zoubé. Bangui, Central African Republic: Saint Paul, 1986. 196p.

'Teaching theology in the Ubangi.' K. Kuzuli. D.Miss. thesis, Trinity Evangelical Divinity School, Deerfield, IL, 1990. 198p.

'The christianization of the Central African Republic.' R. W. Hill. Thesis, Fuller Theological Seminary, Pasadena, CA, 1969. 301p.

'The Gbaya naming of Jesus: an inquiry into the contextualization of soteriological themes among the Gbaya of Cameroon.' T. G. Christensen. Th.D. thesis, Lutheran School of Theology, Chicago, 1984. 484p.

Twenty-five years in Oubangui–Chari (1921–1946). O. Jobson. Long Beach, CA, 1947. 220p.

Country Table 2. **Organized churches and denominations in the Central African Republic.**

Official name (bold type = church *with over 10% of all affiliated)* 1	*Begun* 2	*Type* 3	*Counc* 4	*Congs* 5	*Adults* 6	*Affiliated 1970* 7	*Affiliated 1995* 8	*G%* 9	*Names, notes, and other statistics* (see Codebook, Part 3) 10
Assoc des Egl Bapt Ev Centrafricaines	1973	I-Bap	.....	150	15,000	–	37,500	4.55	*AEBEC.* A=Association. Schism ex Eglises Baptistes de la RCA.
Action Apostolique	c1975	I-3aA	.....	100	15,000	–	25,000	5.00	*A.A. Apostolic Action.* M=Eglise du Chandelir (Church of the Candlestick, France).
Christianisme Prophétique en Afrique	c1970	I-3pA	.v...	10	495	300	1,500	6.65	*Prophetic Christianity in Africa.* Healings. HQ Bangui. 1973 applied to join WCC.
Comité Baptiste	1956	I-3pA	.....	5	1,000	7,000	3,000	-3.33	*Baptist Committee.* Schism ex BMM among Mandja. Initially aided by M=CEM(Switzerland),PO.
Cooperation Ev Centrafricaine	1956	I-3pA	.....	288	30,000	18,600	54,900	4.42	*Central Africa Evangelical Cooperation.* M=Coopération Ev Mondiale (Switzerland),PO.
Egl Baptiste de l'Ouest RCA	1923	P-Pe2	Z.G.G	712	50,553	50,000	95,400	2.62	*UEB.* M=Örebro M (Sweden). 90% Baya, 10% Mpimo. 38n,65f,1H,7h,1s(12),3563Y,10446z.
Eglise Adventiste du Septième Jour	1960	P-Adv	x....	40	2,400	1,800	4,180	3.43	*Seventh-day Adv, CAR Mission.* 60% Mbougou, 15% Baguiro, 15% Baya. 1x,1h,1s,123Y.
Eglise Catholique à la RCA:	1894	R-Lat	P.SBR	113	335,500	277,926	579,216	2.98	*Catholic Ch in CAR.* C=4+1+25. M=CSSp,OFMCap. 100n 147x 150m 198w 21008Yy
M Bangui	1909	R-Lat	Ps	35	146,000	115,618	252,169	3.17	45% Banda, 30% Baya, 8% Banziri. M=CSSp. 33n 48x 86m 2w 8655Yy
D Bambari	1965	R-Lat	Pcssp	13	36,000	41,150	62,200	1.67	Banda, Banziri. Formed out of M Bangui. 1p. 10n 10x 12m 28w 1697Yy
D Bangassou	1954	R-Lat	Pcssp	20	46,300	48,414	79,867	2.02	1964-73, 25,000 Sudanese refugees. 1p. 17n 20x 28m 31w 2754Yy
D Berbérati	1940	R-Lat	Pofmc	19	36,800	39,800	63,510	1.89	72% Baya, 19% Mbimou, 6% Pana, 3% Kare. 19n 11x 20m 24w 2340Yy
D Bossangoa	1959	R-Lat	Pofmc	15	32,100	32,944	55,418	2.10	Baya, Banda, Banziri. In northwest. 3p. 21n 20x 22m 46w 3469Yy
D Bouar	1978	R-Lat	Pofmc	11	38,300	–	66,052	5.88	M=OFMCap. 0n 38x 68m 69w 2093Yy
Eglise Centrafricaine	1960	I-Eva	.....	1	50	200	100	-2.73	*Central African Ch.* Schism ex EEF by Banda pastor at Bouca. Dying out.
Eglise Evangélique Centrafricaine	1924	P-Eva	xMG.E	267	22,800	5,000	40,000	8.67	M=AIM(USA). 90% Azanda, 3% Kare. 1964-73, many Sudanese refugees. 18f,4h.
Eglise Evangélique des Frères	1921	P-Dun	xPG.G	610	122,000	150,000	290,000	2.67	*EEF. Brethren Ch.* M=NFBC(USA). 70% Baya, 20% Mandja, 10% Karre. 56f,1H,16h,1r,2s.
Eglise Ev Luthérienne de la RCA	1923	P-Lut	L....	215	8,580	15,960	22,000	1.29	*EELRCA.* M=Sudan M,NMS,ALC(USA). 99% Baya. 3n,2x,65m,1p,600Y,447y,603z.
Eglise Evangélique du Réveil	c1960	I-3pA	.....	50	3,000	1,000	5,000	6.65	*ER. Evangelical Revival Church. M=SPM (Switzerland).*
Eglise Neo-Apostolique	c1980	I-3aX	x....	150	7,000	–	11,341	6.67	*NAC, NAK.* New Apostolic Church. M=Neuapostolische Kirche (HQ Zurich, Switzerland).
Eglise Protestante du Christ-Roi		P-Ref	.....	2	350	200	700	0.05	*Protestant Ch in Bangui.* Union church. Largely expatriates.
Eglises Baptistes de la RCA	1920	I-Fun	xT...	118	40,000	150,000	100,000	-1.61	*Baptist Chs of CAR.* M=BMM(USA). 70% Banda, 20% Mandja. 80f,1H,6h,12i,1j,2p,1s.
Mission Evangélique (Américaine)	1937	I-Eva	.....	50	4,000	5,000	6,000	0.73	*Ev Mission (American).* M=Central Africa Pioneer Mission (USA). HQ Carnot.
Témoins de Jéhovah	c1945	m-Jeh	x....	41	1,327	5,100	5,530	0.32	*Jehovah's Witnesses. Watch Tower.* Active witnessing by 1948. 10f. (1975) 103Y. (1995) 208Y.
Union des Eglises Ev Elim	1927	I-3pA	Z.G.G	400	48,000	20,000	70,300	5.16	M=Elim MA,SPM(Switzerland). 99% Banda. HQ Alindao. 59n,8x,1h,1s(33),W=65%,646Y.
Union Fédération Eglise Baptiste	1978	I-Bap	T....	141	12,900	–	22,500	5.88	*UFEB.* Schism ex Eglises Baptistes de la RCA.
Other African indigenous churches		I-3pA	.....	200	20,000	1,000	40,000	0.05	Several prophet groups from Zaire, EPC, EJCSK, and other AICs (see list below).
Other Protestant bodies	c1980	P-	.....	20	1,000	–	2,000	6.67	Several groups. Nigerians, ACT(Chad), EET(Chad), ECZ(Zaire), ICFG (USA, Nigeria).
Totals				**3,683**	**740,955**	**709,086**	**1,416,167**		

Churches, members, growth, 1900-2025	*Congs*	*Adults*	*Affiliated*	*G%*	*Total denominations*	*6 Megablocs:* O	R	A	P	I	m
Total churches, members, and denominations (mid-1900)	1	24	50	14.63	1	0	1	0	0	0	0
Total churches, members, and denominations (mid-1970)	2,024	344,164	709,086	14.63	27	0	1	0	6	19	1
Total churches, members, and denominations (mid-1990)	3,000	649,000	1,239,500	2.83	58	0	1	0	20	36	1
Total churches, members, and denominations (mid-1995)	3,683	740,955	1,416,167	2.70	60	0	1	0	21	37	1
Total churches, members, and denominations (mid-2000)	4,000	842,000	1,608,999	2.59	62	0	1	0	22	38	1
Total churches, members, and denominations (mid-2025)	7,500	1,727,000	3,300,000	2.91	136	1	1	0	30	100	4

NOTES ON TABLE ABOVE

NATIONAL COUNCILS (Column 4, 5th letter).

E = Association des Eglises Evangéliques Centrafricaines (AEEC) (Association of Central African Evangelical Churches).

R = Conférence Episcopale Centrafricaine (CECA) (Bishops' Conference of the CAR).

OTHER AFRICAN INDIGENOUS CHURCHES. These groups have come mostly from Zaire, including the EJCSK (Kimbanguist Church), Kanda Dia Kinzinga (People for Eternal Life; since 1945), Kitawala and Kolinga. There are also other bodies with some foreign mission connections: Assemblées de Dieu (6 churches in Bangui, related to AoG Kinshasa), Eglise Ev de Pentecôte (ex Elim), Eglise de la Fraternité Apostolique (ex AA), Eglise de la Fraternité Evangelique, Eglise du Chemin vers Jésus (Ch of the Way to Jesus), Eglise du Christ.

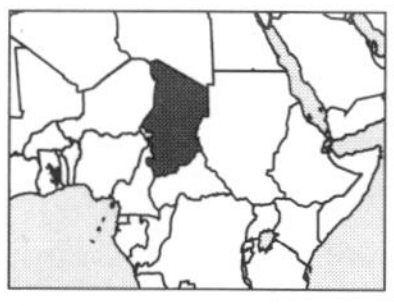

CHAD

SECULAR DATA, AD 2000

STATE

Official name: Jumhuriyah Tshad/La République du Tchad (The Republic of Chad).
Short name: Chad. **Adjective of nationality:** Chadian.
Flag: Blue, yellow, red bars.
Area: 1,284,000 sq. km. (495,755 sq. mi.).
Government: Military junta, since 1975 (1900 French military territory, 1910 colony in French Equatorial Africa, 1960 Independence as republic).
Legislature: National Assembly, 125 members.
Official language: Arabic, French.
Monetary unit: 1 CFA franc (CFAF) = 100 centimes. **US$1=** CFAF 560.38.
Chief cities: N'DJAMENA (Fort-Lamy) 1,044,000; Moundou 137,348; Sarh (Fort-Archambault) 105,531; Abeche 54,939.
Political divisions: 14 provinces.
Armed forces: 25,000.

DEMOGRAPHY

Population: 7,651,000.
Population density: 5.9/sq. km. (15.4/sq. mi.).
Under 15 years: 3,486,000.
Growth rate p.a.: 2.58% (births 41.92, deaths 16.17).
Mortality: Infant, per 1,000: 103.3; **Maternal per 100,000:** 1,500.0.
Life expectancy: 49 (male 47, female 50).
Household size: 3.9. **Floor area per person, sq.m:** 5.0.
Major languages: Sara, Sango, Arabic, French, Hausa, Fur, Kanuri, Berber, and about 100 other tribal languages.
Urban dwellers: 23.79%. **Urban growth rate p.a.:** 4.0%.
Labor force: 35%.

ETHNOLINGUISTIC PEOPLES

16.4% Shuwa (Chad Arab, Baggara); 9.9% Sara Gambai; 4.7% Daza; 3.2% Marfa; 3.0% Sara Majingai-Ngama (Sar).

ECONOMY

National income p.a. per person: US$179; **per family:** US$701.

EDUCATION

Adult literacy: 48% (male 62%, female 34%). **Schools:** 2,610.
Universities: 4. **School enrolment:** female/male: 20%/46%.

HEALTH

Access to health services: 30%. **Access to safe water:** 24%.
Hospitals: 40 (7 beds per 10,000). **Doctors:** 217.
Blind: 175,000. **Deaf:** 436,200. **Murder rate:** 45.
Lepers: 25,000.

LITERATURE

New book titles p.a.: 770 (100 p.a. per million). **Periodicals:** 14.
Newspapers: 1 daily.

COMMUNICATION (per 1,000 people)

Phones: <1 (3% mobile). **Radios:** 240. **TV sets:** 2.
Daily newspaper circulation: <1. **Computers:** 1.

REFUGEES

Citizen refugees in other countries: 16,000.

Country Table 1. **Religious adherents in Chad, AD 1900-2025.**

Year	*1900*		*1970*		*mid-1990*		*Annual change, 1990-2000*				*mid-1995*		*mid-2000*		*mid-2025*	
Name	*Adherents*	*%*	*Adherents*	*%*	*Adherents*	*%*	*Natural*	*Conversion*	*Total*	*Rate*	*Adherents*	*%*	*Adherents*	*%*	*Adherents*	*%*
Muslims	612,000	36.0	1,802,000	49.3	3,359,000	58.5	111,363	4,657	116,020	3.01	3,952,000	58.9	4,519,198	59.1	9,060,000	65.1
Christians	**0**	**0.0**	**864,000**	**23.7**	**1,327,000**	**23.1**	**43,993**	**-2,113**	**41,880**	**2.78**	**1,529,700**	**22.8**	**1,745,795**	**22.8**	**3,150,000**	**22.7**
PROFESSION																
professing Christians	**0**	**0.0**	**864,000**	**23.7**	**1,327,000**	**23.1**	**43,993**	**-2,113**	**41,880**	**2.78**	**1,529,700**	**22.8**	**1,745,795**	**22.8**	**3,150,000**	**22.7**
AFFILIATION																
unaffiliated Christians	0	0.0	391,455	10.7	261,200	4.6	8,660	-4,002	4,658	1.65	277,789	4.1	307,781	4.0	448,000	3.2
affiliated Christians	**0**	**0.0**	**472,545**	**12.9**	**1,065,800**	**18.6**	**35,333**	**1,888**	**37,221**	**3.04**	**1,251,911**	**18.7**	**1,438,014**	**18.8**	**2,702,000**	**19.4**
Protestants	0	0.0	209,634	5.7	585,000	10.2	19,395	381	19,776	2.95	688,037	10.3	782,756	10.2	1,350,000	9.7
Roman Catholics	0	0.0	231,111	6.3	370,000	6.4	12,267	949	13,216	3.10	433,326	6.5	502,158	6.6	950,000	6.8
Independents	0	0.0	31,700	0.9	110,000	1.9	3,647	553	4,200	3.29	129,621	1.9	152,000	2.0	400,000	2.9
Marginal Christians	0	0.0	100	0.0	800	0.0	27	3	30	3.24	927	0.0	1,100	0.0	2,000	0.0
Trans-megabloc groupings																
Evangelicals	0	0.0	239,000	6.5	500,000	8.7	16,577	-1,277	15,300	2.71	582,150	8.7	653,000	8.5	1,200,000	8.6
Pentecostals/Charismatics	0	0.0	7,000	0.2	170,000	3.0	5,636	2,364	8,000	3.93	210,053	3.1	250,000	3.3	670,000	4.8
Great Commission Christians	**0**	**0.0**	**255,000**	**7.0**	**500,000**	**8.7**	**16,577**	**5,238**	**21,815**	**3.69**	**600,000**	**9.0**	**718,153**	**9.4**	**1,517,000**	**10.9**
Ethnoreligionists	1,088,000	64.0	980,000	26.8	1,000,000	17.4	33,153	-3,154	29,999	2.66	1,155,000	17.2	1,299,990	17.0	1,538,000	11.1
Baha'is	0	0.0	5,000	0.1	56,000	1.0	1,857	611	2,468	3.72	66,000	1.0	80,683	1.1	150,000	1.1
Nonreligious	0	0.0	1,000	0.0	4,000	0.1	133	-1	132	2.88	4,300	0.1	5,315	0.1	10,000	0.1
World A (unevangelized persons)	1,700,000	100.0	2,008,578	55.0	2,987,920	52.0	98,963	-15,596	83,367	2.49	3,420,812	51.0	3,817,849	49.9	6,397,680	46.0
World B (evangelized non-Christians)	0	0.0	779,382	21.3	1,431,080	24.9	47,543	17,709	65,252	3.85	1,756,962	26.2	2,087,356	27.3	4,360,320	31.3
World C (Christians)	0	0.0	864,000	23.7	1,327,000	23.1	43,993	-2,113	41,880	2.78	1,529,700	22.8	1,745,795	22.8	3,150,000	22.7
Country's population	**1,700,000**	**100.0**	**3,651,960**	**100.0**	**5,746,000**	**100.0**	**190,499**	**0**	**190,499**	**2.90**	**6,707,475**	**100.0**	**7,651,000**	**100.0**	**13,908,000**	**100.0**

Continued overleaf

COLUMNS, ROWS.
For meanings and definitions, see Codebook (Part 3). Note that, by definition, total 'Christians' = professing + crypto-Christians, which also = affiliated + unaffiliated Christians, and also = Great Commission Christians + latent Christians. Percentages may not always total exactly, due to rounding.

CENSUSES.
XII.1963-VIII.1964 (de jure): 41.0% Muslims, 29.8% ethnoreligionists, 19.6% Roman Catholics (494,970 persons), 9.6% Protestants (241,370 persons). North): 95% Muslims, 4% ethnoreligionists, 4,260 Roman Catholics, 2,270 Protestants, (South): 47% ethnoreligionists, 32% Roman Catholics (490,710 persons), 16% Protestants (239,100 persons), 5% Muslims. (Urban centers): 39% Muslims, 29% Roman Catholics, 20% Protestants, 12% ethnoreligionists.

NOTES ON RELIGIONS
BAHA'IS. Rapid expansion to 50 local spiritual assemblies by 1973, with 3,500 active members and a school at Gassi. Thereafter, however, growth became explosive, rising by 1996 to 437 organized LSAs.
CHRISTIANS. By the time the first generation of Christian children had grown up (about 1960), a massive people movement began in southern Chad, which by 1970 had become about 16.5% Protestant.
ETHNORELIGIONISTS. Tribes over 60% traditionalist (animist) in 1995: Banana Marba (Masa) (65%), Bua (80%), Bon Gula (95%), Gkelendeng (80%), Jumam (90%).
INDEPENDENTS. In about 6 groupings in 1995 (see Table 2).
MUSLIMS. Islamization began in the 11th century with major waves in the 16th and 17th centuries; it is almost complete (over 95%) in the northern and eastern regions. Most are Sunnis (Shafiite and Malikite rites). Orders: Hamalliya (50% of all Muslims), Tijaniya (20% of all Muslims), Sanusiya, Qadiriya, Mahdiya, et alia. In the south, Islam is weak (5%), confined to the Fulani (Léré region) and the urban Bornu. *Hajj pilgrims to Mecca.* (1970) 2,034; (1974) 4,921; (1975) 965; (1976) 1,392.

Great Commission Instrument Panel: status of Chad (for explanation see start of Part 4)

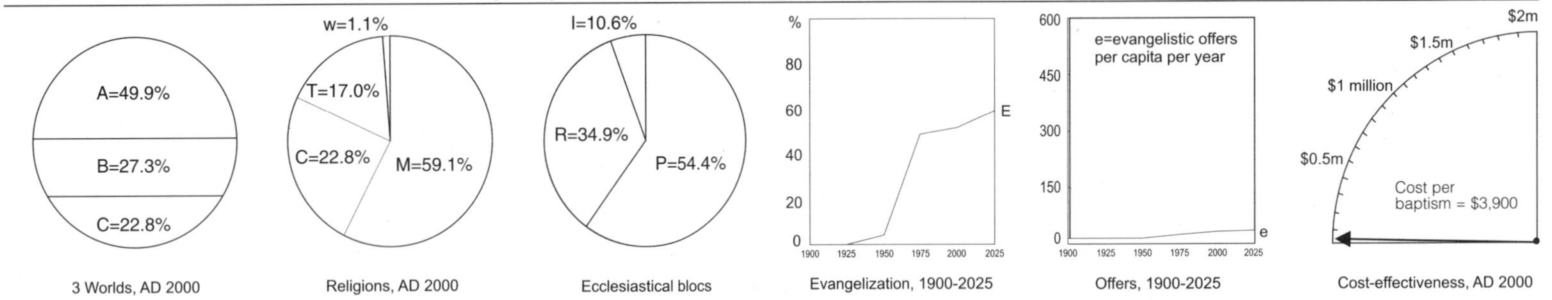

Country status. Chad is the largest country in both population and area of the countries of the former colonial federation of French Equatorial Africa. It is also one of the least developed nations in Africa in terms of natural resources. Its chances of growth have been permanently set back by a bloody civil war that pitted the Muslim north against the animist and Christian south.

HUMAN LIFE AND LIBERTY

Human need and development. Chad is one of the poorest countries in Africa with a per capita income of about $180 per year. The literacy rate is 48%, and 80% of the population is engaged in subsistence agriculture. The bulk of the budget and almost all foreign investment is obtained as French aid. The civil war which ended in 1990, after raging for over a decade, laid waste the country, and set back many villages to the stone age. The country is subject to periodic droughts, a particularly severe one visiting it in 1991. Few observers give Chad a reasonable chance of becoming a self-sufficient country or of its economy expanding beyond the subsistence level.

Human rights and freedoms. Until the end of the civil war in 1990, Chad was the scene of some of the worst human rights abuses in Africa. The transitional government headed by Idriss Deby that took office in 1990 declared the restoration of human rights among its primary objectives. However, because the new government has a narrow power base in the Zaghawa ethnic group, it still faces considerable hostility from other groups and, in turn, does not hesitate to use its power to suppress its opponents. For one of the poorest countries in Africa, it maintains a massive security force of 50,000 on which it spends a large part of the national budget. Armed groups loyal to the government or opposed to it roam and pillage the countryside settling interethnic scores. Torture, whippings, beatings and other inhuman practices are routine in prisons. The abrogation of the 1989 Constitution has left the citizens with no safeguards against arbitrary arrest or against detention without legal warrant. The dominant Zaghawa are able to flout justice with impunity and take the law into their own hands

Although private newspapers exist, the radio, television, and the national news agency are all state-owned. Members of the armed forces sometimes rough up journalists and vandalize newspaper offices in an effort to intimidate the press. Freedoms of assembly and association are circumscribed. Neither traditional law nor the penal code specifically protects women's rights. Women occupy a subordinate position in society and government.

Human environment. Chad is ecologically a desert, and even in the best of times suffers from drought and other disasters common to a desert environment. Its natural landscape has further suffered from the depredations of the long civil war and the absence of any developmental activities. Overgrazing by livestock has led to devegetation enabling the desert to take over formerly inhabited areas.

NON-CHRISTIAN RELIGIONS

Islam first penetrated Chad in the 11th century. Then in successive waves in the 16th and 17th centuries, it spread throughout the country. Chad is now about 60% Muslim. Islamization is almost complete in the northern and eastern regions which are geographically immense but sparsely populated with only 3 to 4 inhabitants per square kilometer. Islamic influence on the southern Black peoples is a more recent 20th century phenomenon. In Chad, one finds many different Islamic schools and brotherhoods, including Tijaniya, Sanusiya, Qadiriya, and Madhism. The number of Muslims from Chad who perform the hajj to Mecca each year rose rapidly from 2,034 in 1970 to 4,921 in 1974, after which it declined.

Traditional African religions are still significant south of the Chari river and are more generally found among the Black population living by agriculture and fishing. Tribes resistant to both Islam and Christianity include the Banana Marba (Masa), Bui, Gaberi, Mbai and Sara.

Eglise Catholique au Tchad. Church destroyed by fighting in the capital.

CHRISTIANITY

CATHOLIC CHURCH. Although an attempt was made to open work in Chad by Capuchins in 1663, the first permanent missions was not founded until 1929, when Holy Ghost priests from Bangui built a station at Kou. Nevertheless, it is only since 1947 that Catholic activity has become extensive and organized. It reaches the younger levels of the population but its effectiveness with urban adults is limited, especially those of the middle and upper classes. It is relatively strong in the southern territories but sporadic in the Muslim zones, except in the urban centers among Catholics who have emigrated from the south.

The Holy See has diplomatic relations with Chad and in AD 2000 is represented to government and the Catholic hierarchy by a nuncio residing in Bangui.

PROTESTANT CHURCHES. The work of the Sudan United Mission has been joined to that of the French Mennonites and the Worldwide Evangelization Crusade to form the largest Protestant church in the country, Eglises Evangéliques du Tchad. Its youth movement called Flambeau (Little Flame) is particularly effective in its evangelistic outreach. The total Protestant community is slightly larger than that of Roman Catholicism. Protestant service projects include a secondary school, hospital, and orphanage; 6 clinics; several adult literacy projects; and a rural development program Société Chrétienne Rurale.

Dr. Lydie Ngaba Kedigui, Vice-President, Bible Society in Chad.

INDIGENOUS CHURCHES. Christian independency has not been a significant factor in Chad. Although a few groups have emerged from time to time, the majority have returned to the mission churches, including a group encouraged by the Tombalbaye regime in 1974 in its attempt to force traditional customs back on the churches.

Renewal movements. In the 1990s the Pentecostal/Charismatic Renewal continued to spread rapidly across most older churches, and numbered over 250,000 adherents (of whom 7% Pentecostals, 60% Charismatics, and 33% Independents).

Indigenous missions. The missionary movement among Christians in Chad has been directed primarily at home missions—outreach to non-Christian peoples residing in Chad. Less than 10 Chadian missionaries are serving as foreign missionaries.

CHURCH AND STATE

The constitution of 14 April 1962, states in the Preamble that Chad is a secular republic which assures for all equality before the law without distinction of origin or religion (Article 3). Nevertheless, a strong sense of religion permeates political life; thus, in 1972, the Bureau Politique National (BPN) proclaimed that on November 28 every year, all Chadians must pray to God on behalf of Chad in the manner prescribed by their own religion.

Country summary. **Worlds A, B, C by ethnolinguistic peoples, cities ,and major civil divisions in Chad.**

	PEOPLES							CITIES							CIVIL DIVISIONS						
World	*Num*	*Pop 2000*	*C%*	*Christians*	*E%*	*U%*	*Unevangelized*	*Num*	*Pop 2000*	*C%*	*Christians*	*E%*	*U%*	*Unevangelized*	*Num*	*Pop 2000*	*C%*	*Christians*	*E%*	*U%*	*Unevangelized*
A	87	4,319,029	0.89	38,610	24	76	3,295,438	2	192,287	5.57	10,713	31	69	132,395	6	2,517,085	8.19	206,037	38	62	1,560,786
B	40	2,824,462	38.17	1,078,130	82	18	517,418	2	1,149,531	30.73	353,268	66	34	392,148	8	5,133,898	24.00	1,231,977	56	44	2,257,882
C	9	507,492	63.31	321,273	99	1	5,811	0	0	0.00	0	0	0	0	0	0	0.00	0	0	0	0
Total	**136**	**7,650,983**	**18.80**	**1,438,013**	**50**	**50**	**3,818,667**	**4**	**1,341,818**	**27.13**	**363,981**	**61**	**39**	**524,543**	**14**	**7,650,983**	**18.80**	**1,438,014**	**50**	**50**	**3,818,668**

Religious associations such as denominations and dioceses must be registered with government, thereby becoming legal entities with the rights which follow from it. Catholic and Protestant private education is recognized, controlled by the state and subsidized usually by about 50%.

The imam of the mosque in N'Djamena, the Catholic archbishop, and a Protestant representative have been members of the Economic and Social Council and commonly invited to official receptions. The president of the republic and members of government also attend important religious ceremonies.

Because of its developed organization, number of places of worship and the role of its educational and social work, the Catholic Church receives more consideration than its numbers warrant.

In November 1973, president Ngarta Tombalbaye launched an 'authenticity' or chaditude program requiring that all Chadians undergo the traditional Yondo initiation rites of his own Sara tribe and prohibited the use of foreign names. At the same time, 18 Baptist missionaries were expelled, 13 Chadian pastors imprisoned and all Baptist churches and schools serving the Sara people were closed. Some Christians who opposed the government decrees were forcibly initiated, others were harassed and still others killed. In the 12 months from November 1973, at least 130 Protestant African pastors were put to death, including the 13 leading Chadian Baptist pastors. Also, during 1974, the government was instrumental in helping to establish an independent church among dissident Sara Baptists. In February 1975, 9 Swedish Pentecostal missionaries (SFM) were expelled. On 13 April 1975, Tombalbaye was assassinated, and the new military regime later assured Christians that no one would thereafter be required to participate in any rites against his wishes. Both the new head of state and the chairman of the Supreme Council in 1975 were committed Protestants. On 3 May 1975, the government announced that all laws restricting religious freedom were repealed, affirmed once again that the Chadian state was secular and reinstated as public holidays the major Christian and Muslim festivals.

Although the 1980s and 1990s saw continued military activity and civil war, church-state relations did not deteriorate but, rather, matured and stabilized.

BROADCASTING AND MEDIA

The large number of receivers makes broadcasting an important evangelistic option. Chad is a member of UNDA, and Catholics broadcast a 15 minute meditation each Sunday in French, and a second 15 minute segment in various local languages. A Catholic program featuring stories and testimonies is aired for 13 minutes each week on television. From abroad, shortwave radio programs can be received from AWR (Italy, Slovakia), TWR (Monaco, Albania), and HCJB (Ecuador).

Mission agencies have used the 'Jesus' Film with moderate response: out of 268,000 viewers, 35,000 responded.

FUTURE TRENDS AND PROSPECTS

Christians are expected to remain about 23% through 2025 with conversions from ethnoreligionists being mainly to Islam.

After ethnoreligionists diminish to less than 10%, Muslims and Christians will potentially share Chad's population in a 75/25 ratio over subsequent decades.

BIBLIOGRAPHY

Jean Paul II au Chad: du 30 Janvier au 1er février 1990. Chad, [1990]. 68p.

Le dieu des autres. P. Teisserenc. Paris: Union Générale d'éditions, 1975. 318p.

'Le sacrifice ou la question du meurtre,' F. Dumas-Champion, *Anthropos*, 82, 1-3 (1987), 135–149.

Le symbolisme religieux dans l'ethnie Ngambay: approche culturelle de la religion. L. Draman Odial. St.–Paul, Ottawa: Université St.–Paul, 1975–1976. 100p.

Pilgrims in a strange land: Hausa communities in Chad. J. A. Works. New York: Columbia University Press, 1976. 294p.

'The Lutheran Brethren Church in Chad and Cameroun.' R. W. Venberg. Thesis, Fuller Theological Seminary, Pasadena, CA, 1970. 178p.

'The problem of a female deity in translation,' R. Venberg, *Bible Translator*, 35, 4 (October 1984), 415–417. (Translating the Bible for the Pévé tribe, southwestern Chad. Reprinted from *Bible Translator*, April 1971).

'The Sudanese 'Mahdiyya' and the Niger–Chad region,' S. Biobaku & M. al-Hajj, in *Islam in tropical Africa: studies presented and discussed at the Fifth International African Seminar, Ahmadu Bello University, Zaria, January 1964*, p.226–39. I. M. Lewis (ed). 2nd ed. Bloomington, IN: International African Institute in association with Indiana University Press, 1988.

Country Table 2. **Organized churches and denominations in Chad.**

Official name (bold type = church with over 10% of affiliated) 1	*Begun* 2	*Type* 3	*Counc* 4	*Congs* 5	*Adults* 6	*Affiliated 1970* 7	*Affiliated 1995* 8	*G%* 9	*Names, notes, and other statistics* (see Codebook, Part 3) 10
Assemblées Chrétiennes du Tchad	1921	P-CBr	x...C	600	82,400	60,000	230,000	5.52	*AdD.* Open Brethren. M=CMML. 63% Mbai, 12% Dai, 12% Kim, 6% Kado. 300m,150w,20f,200Y.
Assemblées de Dieu	c1960	P-Pe2	Z....	40	1,000	400	2,500	7.61	*ACT.Assemblies of God.* M=AdD(France). Formed ex EEF in Baibokoum. Medical work.
Eglise Adventiste du Septième Jour	c1962	P-Adv	x....	13	412	300	1,110	5.37	*SDA, Chad Mission.* Equatorial African Union Mission. 10nxm,7t(225),27Y.
Eglise Catholique au Tchad:	1929	R-Lat	P.SBR	98	238,600	231,111	433,326	2.55	*Catholic Ch.* M=SJ,OFMCap,OMI,MCCI. C=3+0+24. 61n 123x 173m 274w 14843Yy
M N'Djamena (Fort-Lamy)	1947	R-Lat	Psj	21	34,600	23,876	63,000	3.96	Capital (50% Muslim, 50% pagan). 33% White. 1p. 11n 26x 33m 63w 1714Yy
D Doba	1989	R-Lat	Pmcci	14	55,500	–	101,000	16.67	Formed out of D Moundou. M=MCCI. 10n 14x 36m 43w 2727Yy
D Moundou	1951	R-Lat	Pofmc	19	106,000	154,348	192,012	0.88	Oldest RC work (1928). Ngambais. 63% pagan. 14n 26x 30m 55w 6963Yy
D Pala	1956	R-Lat	Pomi	28	11,200	24,887	20,400	-0.79	87% pagan. Farmers, cattlemen, fishermen. 1p. 15n 23x 27m 48w 1050Yy
D Sarh (Fort-Archambault)	1961	R-Lat	Psj	16	31,300	28,000	56,914	2.88	EDT. Pagan farmers. Muslim cattlemen. 1p. 11n 34x 47m 65w 2389Yy
Eglise de Dieu	c1960	P-Pe3	ZF...	76	3,600	4,000	12,000	4.49	Ch of God. M=CoG(Cleveland) (USA). Between Ft-Lamy and Bongor. Orphanage. 16n,1p.
Eglise Dissidente du Tchad	1951	I-3pA	.....	10	1,000	1,000	2,000	2.81	*Independent Ch of Chad.* Schism ex BMM. M=La Porte Ouverte (France). Ngama, Sara.
Eglise Evangélique des Frères	1928	P-Dun	xF...	90	21,300	15,000	64,600	6.01	*EEF. Ev Ch of the Brethren.* M=NFBC(USA); begun from Central African Republic. 2f.
Eglise Evangélique du Tchad	1974	I-Eva	.....	20	2,000	–	5,000	4.76	*Ev Ch of Chad.* State church set up by government. Sara Protestants forced to join.
Egl Fraternelle Luthérienne au Tchad	1920	P-Lut	x...C	595	17,127	27,434	43,827	1.89	EFLT. M=CLB/LBWM(USA). 40% Mundang. 24n,3x,6f,20p,(1645),1s(22) 646Y,793y,2932z.
Eglise Neo-Apostolique	c1980	I-3aX	x....	400	25,000	–	33,321	6.67	*NAC. New Apostolic Church.* M=Neuapostolische Kirche (HQ Zurich, Switzerland).
Eglises Baptistes du Tchad	1925	I-Fun	xT..C	292	38,000	30,000	63,300	3.03	EBT. *Chad Baptist Chs.* M=BMM(USA). 1973 mission expelled. 25n,10x,57m,25f,1H,2h,2p,1r.
Eglises Evangéliques au Tchad	1926	P-Eva	xM..C	1,030	177,000	100,000	329,000	4.88	EET. *Ev Chs of Chad.* M=TEAM,SUM,WEC,EMEK,AIM. 47n,291mw,3k7f,1H,3h,1r,7s,1626Y.
Eglises radiophoniques isolées	1960	I-3rA	.....	300	4,000	200	6,000	14.57	Isolated radio believers, mostly aged 12-25 in north. S=1397(RSB Arabic courses).
Témoins de Jéhovah	c1945	m-Jeh	x....	11	278	100	927	9.32	*Jehovah's Witnesses. Watch Tower.* Active witnessing under way by 1948. 4f,5Y. (1995) 49Y.
Other Protestant denominations		P-	.....	40	3,000	2,500	5,000	0.05	Total 6: M=CEM(Switzerland),YWAM,SFM,MEDELU,EMS,SIM,FI.
Other African indigenous churches		I-3pA	.....	100	10,000	500	20,000	0.05	Several small schisms ex CMML,SUM,CLB, plus many AICs from Nigeria, Cameroon, CAR, Zaire.
Totals				**3,715**	**624,717**	**472,545**	**1,251,911**		

Churches, members, growth, 1900-2025	*Congs*	*Adults*	*Affiliated*	*G%*	*Total denominations*	*6 Megablocs:* *O*	*R*	*A*	*P*	*I*	*m*
Total churches, members, and denominations (mid-1900)	0	0	0	0.00	0	0	0	0	0	0	0
Total churches, members, and denominations (mid-1970)	1,340	251,005	472,545	15.00	28	0	1	0	10	16	1
Total churches, members, and denominations (mid-1990)	3,100	532,000	1,065,800	4.15	49	0	1	0	13	34	1
Total churches, members, and denominations (mid-1995)	3,715	624,717	1,251,911	3.27	50	0	1	0	13	35	1
Total churches, members, and denominations (mid-2000)	3,800	718,000	1,438,014	2.81	51	0	1	0	13	36	1
Total churches, members, and denominations (mid-2025)	7,100	1,348,000	2,702,000	2.56	97	1	1	0	20	70	5

NOTES ON TABLE ABOVE

NATIONAL COUNCILS (Column 4, 5th letter).

E = Entente des Eglises et Missions Evangéliques au Tchad (EEMET), formerly Fédération des Eglises Evangéliques du Tchad (FEET) (Federation of Evangelical Churches of Chad), a loose grouping of missions and some national churches.

R = Conférence Episcopale du Tchad (CET) (Chad Episcopal Conference).

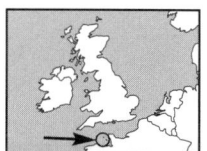

CHANNEL ISLANDS

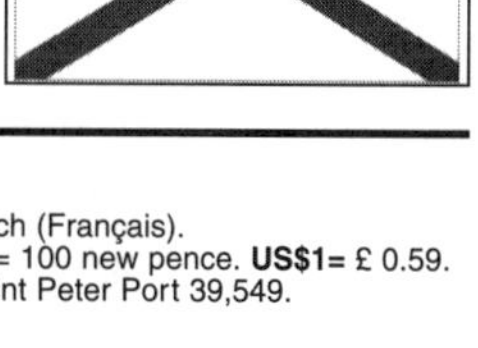

SECULAR DATA, AD 2000

STATE

Official name: Les Iles Anglo-Normandes/The Crown Dependency of the Channel Islands.
Short name: Channel Islands. **Adjective of nationality:** Channel Islanders.
Flag: White with a red saltire. Guernsey: White with a red cross.
Area: 194 sq. km. (75 sq. mi.).
Government: Self-governing British crown dependency, since 1066.
Legislature: Assemblies of the States: The States of Jersey, 57 members; The states of Deliberation (Guernsey), 60 members; and States of Election.
Official language: English and French (Français).
Monetary unit: 1 pound sterling (£) = 100 new pence. **US$1=** £ 0.59.
Chief cities: ST HELIER 49,423; Saint Peter Port 39,549.
Political divisions: 1 province.

DEMOGRAPHY
Population: 153,000.
Population density: 788.1/sq. km. (2,038.6/sq. mi.).
Under 15 years: 29,000.
Growth rate p.a.: 0.11% (births 11.09, deaths 10.70).
Mortality: Infant, per 1,000: 6.6; **Maternal per 100,000:** 10.0.
Life expectancy: 78 (male 75, female 81).
Household size: 2.0. **Floor area per person, sq.m:** 45.0.
Major languages: English, French.
Urban dwellers: 30.0%. **Urban growth rate p.a.:** 1.5%.
Labor force: 60%.

ETHNOLINGUISTIC PEOPLES
97.2% British; 2.0% French; ; 0.2% Norman; 0.1% Indo-Pakistani; 0.0% Jewish.

ECONOMY
National income p.a. per person: US$12,001; **per family:** US$24,002.

EDUCATION
Adult literacy: 98% (male 99%, female 97%). **Schools:** 50.
Universities: 2. **School enrolment:** female/male: 95%/95%.

HEALTH
Access to health services: 95%. **Access to safe water:** 90%.
Hospitals: 70 (50 beds per 10,000). **Doctors:** 230.
Blind: 120. **Deaf:** 9,200. **Murder rate:** 1.
Lepers: 0.

LITERATURE
New book titles p.a.: 230 (1,500 p.a. per million). **Periodicals:** 14.
Newspapers: 1 daily.

COMMUNICATION (per 1,000 people)
Phones: 700 **(30% mobile). Radios:** 900. **TV sets:** 500.
Daily newspaper circulation: 300. **Computers:** 250.

HUMAN LIFE AND LIBERTY (optimum condition=100.0%)
HDI: 92.3. **HSI:** 85.0. **HFI:** 85.0. **EFL:** 60.0.

Country Table 1. **Religious adherents in the Channel Islands, AD 1900-2025.**

Year	1900		1970		mid-1990		Annual change, 1990-2000				mid-1995		mid-2000		mid-2025	
Name	Adherents	%	Adherents	%	Adherents	%	Natural	Conversion	Total	Rate	Adherents	%	Adherents	%	Adherents	%
Christians	**82,170**	**99.0**	**115,900**	**95.0**	**125,005**	**88.0**	**958**	**-300**	**658**	**0.51**	**128,270**	**86.8**	**131,580**	**86.0**	**134,130**	**77.5**
PROFESSION																
professing Christians	**82,170**	**99.0**	**115,900**	**95.0**	**125,005**	**88.0**	**958**	**-300**	**658**	**0.51**	**128,270**	**86.8**	**131,580**	**86.0**	**134,130**	**77.5**
AFFILIATION																
unaffiliated Christians	1,660	2.0	12,120	9.9	26,645	18.8	206	209	415	1.46	28,470	19.3	30,799	20.1	29,540	17.1
affiliated Christians	**80,510**	**97.0**	**103,780**	**85.1**	**98,360**	**69.3**	**752**	**-510**	**242**	**0.24**	**99,800**	**67.6**	**100,781**	**65.9**	**104,590**	**60.5**
Anglicans	58,930	71.0	69,250	56.8	65,000	45.8	504	-253	251	0.38	66,500	45.0	67,511	44.1	70,000	40.5
Roman Catholics	8,300	10.0	20,500	16.8	22,000	15.5	170	-140	30	0.14	22,100	15.0	22,300	14.6	24,000	13.9
Protestants	13,280	16.0	13,600	11.2	10,900	7.7	84	-124	-40	-0.37	10,735	7.3	10,500	6.9	10,000	5.8
Marginal Christians	0	0.0	230	0.2	260	0.2	2	-1	1	0.38	265	0.2	270	0.2	350	0.2
Orthodox	0	0.0	200	0.2	200	0.1	2	-2	0	0.00	200	0.1	200	0.1	240	0.1
Trans-megabloc groupings																
Evangelicals	28,000	33.7	21,800	17.9	18,900	13.3	146	-36	110	0.57	19,543	13.2	20,000	13.1	21,500	12.4
Pentecostals/Charismatics	0	0.0	800	0.7	7,100	5.0	55	75	130	1.70	7,664	5.2	8,400	5.5	13,000	7.5
Great Commission Christians	**7,500**	**9.0**	**22,000**	**18.0**	**36,210**	**25.5**	**281**	**152**	**433**	**1.14**	**38,480**	**26.1**	**40,543**	**26.5**	**46,800**	**27.1**
Nonreligious	780	0.9	5,700	4.7	15,000	10.6	116	274	390	2.34	17,500	11.9	18,902	12.4	35,000	20.2
Atheists	0	0.0	110	0.1	1,300	0.9	10	15	25	1.75	1,400	1.0	1,547	1.0	2,200	1.3
Baha'is	10	0.0	200	0.2	400	0.3	3	9	12	2.66	500	0.3	520	0.3	1,000	0.6
Hindus	10	0.0	20	0.0	100	0.1	1	1	2	1.92	115	0.1	121	0.1	220	0.1
Muslims	10	0.0	20	0.0	100	0.1	1	1	2	1.75	110	0.1	119	0.1	230	0.1
Jews	20	0.0	50	0.0	90	0.1	1	0	1	1.36	100	0.1	103	0.1	200	0.1
Buddhists	0	0.0	0	0.0	5	0.0	0	0	0	0.00	5	0.0	5	0.0	20	0.0
World A (unevangelized persons)	83	0.1	122	0.1	568	0.4	4	18	22	3.70	590	0.4	765	0.5	1,211	0.7
World B (evangelized non-Christians)	747	0.9	6,003	4.9	16,427	11.6	128	282	410	2.32	18,864	12.9	20,655	13.4	37,659	21.8
World C (Christians)	82,170	99.0	115,900	95.0	125,005	88.0	958	-300	658	0.51	128,270	86.7	131,580	86.1	134,130	77.5
Country's population	**83,000**	**100.0**	**122,026**	**100.0**	**142,000**	**100.0**	**1,090**	**0**	**1,090**	**0.75**	**147,725**	**100.0**	**153,000**	**100.0**	**173,000**	**100.0**

COLUMNS, ROWS.
For meanings and definitions, see Codebook (Part 3). Note that, by definition, total 'Christians' = professing + crypto-Christians, which also = affiliated + unaffiliated Christians, and also = Great Commission Christians + latent Christians. Percentages may not always total exactly, due to rounding.

CENSUSES. The religion question has not been asked.

NOTES ON RELIGIONS
BAHA'IS. In 1 local spiritual assembly and 1 other center (1973); 1996, still one LSA.

Great Commission Instrument Panel: status of the Channel Islands (for explanation see start of Part 4)

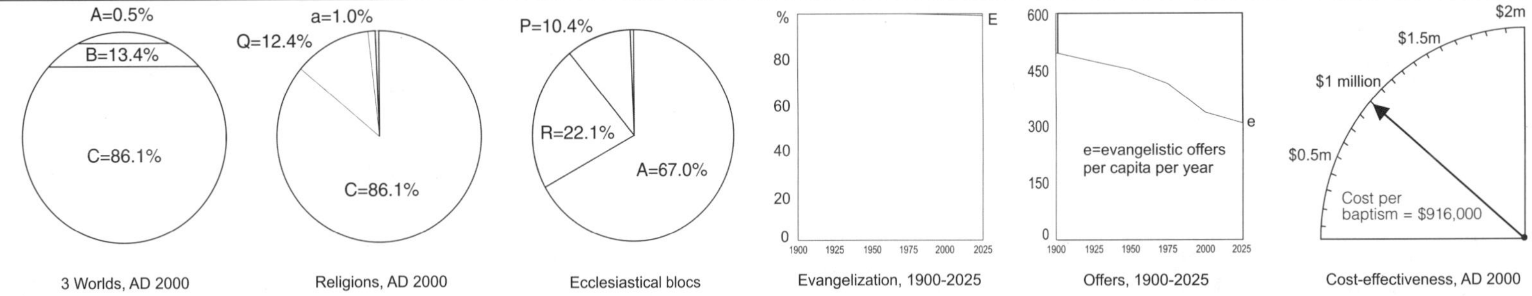

Country status. The Channel Islands is a domain of the British Crown in the English Channel off the northwest coast of France. The Jersey and Guernsey breeds of cattle originated here. Fruits, vegetables, and flowers are exported.

HUMAN LIFE AND LIBERTY

Human rights and freedoms. British laws applying to rights are fully observed.

NON-CHRISTIAN RELIGIONS

Several Asian families live on Jersey, of Muslim, Buddhist, and Hindu background. A few families of Jews live on Jersey and have recently opened a synagogue in the countryside. There are also two Baha'i centers. Those claiming to be without religion increased from 1% of the population in 1900 to 12.4% by AD 2000.

CHRISTIANITY

The Christian faith came to the Channel Islands with the Breton migration of the 6th century and was strongly influenced by the missionary activity of Helier (martyred 555) and Samson of Dol. Administratively, the islands were included in the Norman diocese of Coutances, and a large portion of their land was owned by Norman monasteries.

Calvinist refugees from France brought the 16th-century Reformation to the islands, organizing the first Presbyterian synod in 1564, and Presbyterianism dominated the islands during subsequent years.

ANGLICAN CHURCH. Anglicanism was first organized in Jersey in 1623 and in Guernsey in 1663 but made little progress prior to the 19th century. Forming part of the diocese of Winchester of the Church of England, the islands are now predominantly Anglican. There are 2 deaneries, one for Jersey with 21 parishes and the other for Guernsey with 15 parishes. Their deans exercise authority similar to but greater than that of archdeacons in England, including delegated Episcopal authority to institute clergy to parish livings.

CATHOLIC CHURCH. Catholic responsibility for the Channel Islands is invested in the diocese of Portsmouth of the Catholic Church in England and Wales. The church's strength is concentrated in Jersey which maintains its French language and traditions. Catholics are divided into 17 parishes served by 3 institutes: OMI, FSC, and FICP. The Catholic church sponsors 10 schools.

The Holy See has no diplomatic relations with Channel Islands in AD 2000.

PROTESTANT CHURCHES. The islands were strongly influenced by Wesleyan Methodism in the 18th and 19th centuries, and the Methodist Church of great Britain continues to play an important role. Its Channel Islands District consists of 3 circuits, with 30 congregations served by 22 ministers. Other Protestant groups include the Baptist Union, Elim Pentecostals, Friends (Quakers), United Reformed Church (formerly Congregationalists), and a Presbyterian church which did not join the URC at union.

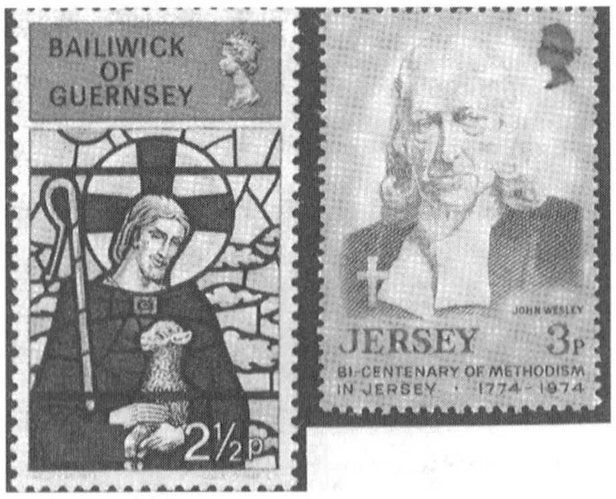

The Islands' postage stamps often illustrate Christian topics: *left*, Christ the Good Shepherd (in St-Michel du Valle); *right*, evangelist John Wesley.

CHURCH AND STATE

The Channel Islands are under the British Crown and are ecclesiastically part of the diocese of Winchester of the established Church of England, and so the Church of England is the established or state church in the islands. The Anglican dean of Jersey is an ex-officio member without vote of the legislative council known as the States of Jersey. A similar provision is however not made for the dean of Guernsey in Guernsey's States of Deliberation. The fabric of parish churches is maintained out of public funds, for which secular local authorities are respon-

Country summary. **Worlds A, B, C by ethnolinguistic peoples, cities, and major civil divisions in the Channel Islands.**

	PEOPLES							CITIES							CIVIL DIVISIONS						
World	*Num*	*Pop 2000*	*C%*	*Christians*	*E%*	*U%*	*Unevangelized*	*Num*	*Pop 2000*	*C%*	*Christians*	*E%*	*U%*	*Unevangelized*	*Num*	*Pop 2000*	*C%*	*Christians*	*E%*	*U%*	*Unevangelized*
A	0	0	0.00	0	0	0	0	0	0	0.00	0	0	0	0	0	0	0.00	0	0	0	0
B	2	367	2.45	9	55	45	165	0	0	0.00	0	0	0	0	0	0	0.00	0	0	0	0
C	4	152,531	66.07	100,772	100	0	554	2	88,972	62.44	55,558	99	1	605	1	152,898	65.91	100,781	100	0	719
Total	**6**	**152,898**	**65.91**	**100,781**	**100**	**0**	**719**	**2**	**88,972**	**62.44**	**55,558**	**99**	**1**	**605**	**1**	**152,898**	**65.91**	**100,781**	**100**	**0**	**719**

sible. There are therefore, in contrast to England, no parochial church councils (PCCs).

Measures passed by the Church Assembly and the British parliament in London and still in force as legislation in the Channel Islands are: Channel Islands (Representation) Measure, 1931; Channel Islands (Church Legislation) Measure, 1931, and its (Amendment) Measure, 1957.

BROADCASTING AND MEDIA

Programs for Western Europe are received by terrestrial and satellite TV and radio.

INTERDENOMINATIONAL ORGANIZATIONS

Two local church councils are active, the Guernsey Council of Churches and the Jersey Council of Churches. Both are associate members of the British Council of Churches. Ecumenism is comparatively strong in the islands.

FUTURE TRENDS AND PROSPECTS

The nonreligious are expected to reach 20.2% of the population by 2025 (from only 4.7% in 1970). Christianity may well experience steady decline over the same period.

With the rise of the nonreligious it is likely that Christians will fall to less than 75% by AD 2050 or perhaps below 70% as secularism expands.

BIBLIOGRAPHY

A short history of Guernsey. P. Johnston. 3d ed. : Guernsey Press Co, 1987. 96p.

Channel Island churches: a study of the medieval churches and chapels. J. McCormack. Chichester, UK: Phillimore, 1986. 360p.

Ecumenical procession, under auspices of Jersey Council of Churches, from St. Helier to Elizabeth Castle.

Country Table 2. **Organized churches and denominations in the Channel Islands.**

Official name (bold type = church with over 10% of all affiliated) 1	*Begun* 2	*Type* 3	*Counc* 4	*Congs* 5	*Adults* 6	*Affiliated 1970* 7	*Affiliated 1995* 8	*G%* 9	*Names, notes, and other statistics* (see Codebook, Part 3) 10
Baptist Union of GB & Ireland	1864	P-Bap	Twc.w	3	220	800	595	-1.18	3 Baptist churches on Guernsey, 1 on Jersey. Independent congregations.
Catholic Ch in E & W (D Portsmouth)	1802	R-Lat	B.B.s	19	16,600	20,500	22,100	0.30	E&W=England & Wales. 75% on Jersey. M=OMI(English & French),SJ,FSC,FICP. C=2+2+6.
Church of Christ, Scientist		m-Sci	x....	1	21	50	35	0.05	*Christian Science.* M=CCS(Boston, USA). Congregation in St Helier.
Church of England (D Winchester)	1111	A-Cen	awc.w	44	53,700	69,250	66,500	-0.16	2 Deaneries: Jersey (21 parishes), Guernsey (15 parishes). Also Alderney and Sark.
Ch of Jesus Christ of Latter-day Saints		m-LdS	x....	1	42	30	70	0.05	*Mormons.* M=CJCLdS(Utah, USA). On Jersey.
Elim Pentecostal Church		P-Pe2	Z...h	5	940	600	1,170	0.05	*Channel Islands Presbytery.* 3 on Guernsey, 1 on Jersey.
Greater World Christian Spiritualist Ch		m-Spi	x....	1	33	100	110	0.05	C=Church, *Greater World Sanctuary.* Specifically Christian spiritualists. St Helier.
Greek Orthodox Ch (AD Thyateira & GB)		O-Gre	Cwc.w	1	100	200	200	0.05	*Orthodox Community of St Andrew,* St Helier, Visiting priest from Bristol (UK).
Methodist Church of Great Britain	1774	P-Met	Vwc.w	18	2,800	10,000	7,570	-1.11	*Channel Islands District.* 3 Circuits: on all 4 islands. 22nx.
New Church		m-Swe	xv..w	1	30	50	50	0.05	*Jersey Society, General Conf of the New Ch* (Swedenborgian). St Helier. 1n.
United Reformed Church	1800	P-Ref	Rwc.w	2	100	400	200	-2.73	Formerly Congregationalists. 2 churches on Guernsey, 2 on Jersey.
Other Protestant denominations		P-	.....	20	600	1,800	1,200	0.05	Total about 10, including: Open Brethren, Presbyterian Ch, Quakers, Salvation Army.
Totals				**116**	**75,186**	**103,780**	**99,800**		

Churches, members, growth, 1900-2025	*Congs*	*Adults*	*Affiliated*	*G%*	*Total denominations*	*6 Megablocs:* O	R	A	P	I	m
Total churches, members, and denominations (mid-1900)	80	35,900	80,510	0.36	7	0	1	1	3	0	2
Total churches, members, and denominations (mid-1970)	116	46,320	103,780	0.36	15	1	1	1	8	0	4
Total churches, members, and denominations (mid-1990)	110	74,100	98,360	-0.27	21	1	1	1	14	0	4
Total churches, members, and denominations (mid-1995)	116	75,186	99,800	0.29	21	1	1	1	14	0	4
Total churches, members, and denominations (mid-2000)	120	75,900	100,781	0.20	22	1	1	1	15	0	4
Total churches, members, and denominations (mid-2025)	140	78,800	104,590	0.15	41	2	1	1	25	5	7

NOTES ON TABLE ABOVE

NATIONAL COUNCILS (Column 4, 5th letter).

h = British Pentecostal Fellowship.

s = in Bishops' Conference of England & Wales, also JCC, GCC.

w = Jersey Council of Churches (JCC), & Guernsey Council of Churches (GCC) (associated councils of the British Council of Churches for Britain and Ireland (CCBI).

Other councils. Jersey Free Church Federal Council (dissolved).

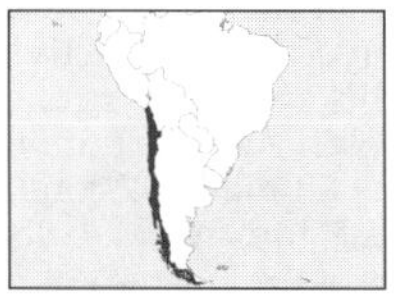

CHILE

SECULAR DATA, AD 2000

STATE

Official name: La República de Chile (The Republic of Chile).
Short name: Chile. **Adjective of nationality:** Chilean.
Flag: Stripes of white and red, blue square with white star.
Area: 756,626 sq. km. (292,135 sq. mi.).
Government: Multiparty republic with two legislative houses, since 1981 (1541 Spanish rule, 1810 Independence from Spain, military juntas, 1942 constitutional democracy, 1970 Marxist regime, 1973 military rule).
Legislature: Senate, 47 members; Chamber of Deputies, 120 members.
Official language: Spanish (Español/Castella).
Monetary unit: 1 peso (Ch$) = 100 centavos. **US$1=** Ch$469.55.
Chief cities: SANTIAGO (Gran Santiago) 5,261,000; Concepcion 826,443; Valparaiso 803,163; Santiago 576,545; Vina del Mar 327,201.
Political divisions: 13 provinces.
Armed forces: 95,000.

DEMOGRAPHY

Population: 15,211,000.
Population density: 20.1/sq. km. (52.0/sq. mi.).
Under 15 years: 4,328,000.
Growth rate p.a.: 1.18% (births 18.18, deaths 5.74).
Mortality: Infant, per 1,000: 11; **Maternal per 100,000:** 65.0.
Life expectancy: 76 (male 73, female 79).
Household size: 4.1. **Floor area per person, sq.m:** 14.4.
Major languages: Spanish, German, Mapuche, Italian, Quechua, Aymara, Greek, and over 10 other languages.
Urban dwellers: 84.59%. **Urban growth rate p.a.:** 1.4%.
Labor force: 39%.

ETHNOLINGUISTIC PEOPLES
72.3% Chilean Mestizo; 20.8% Chilean White; 3.5% Mapuche (Araucanian); 1.2% Huilliche (Veliche); 0.2% Jewish.

ECONOMY
National income p.a. per person: US$4,160; **per family:** US$17,056.

EDUCATION
Adult literacy: 95% (male 95%, female 95%). **Schools:** 8,626. **Universities:** 201. **School enrolment:** female/male: 89%/89%.

HEALTH
Access to health services: 97%. **Access to safe water:** 85%. **Hospitals:** 217 (32 beds per 10,000). **Doctors:** 15,015. **Blind:** 2,910. **Deaf:** 912,700. **Murder rate:** 11. **Lepers:** 1,000. **Underweight prevalence under 5:** 1%.

LITERATURE
New book titles p.a.: 2,050 (135 p.a. per million). **Periodicals:** 584. **Newspapers:** 32 dailies.

COMMUNICATION (per 1,000 people)
Phones: 132 (13% mobile). **Radios:** 317. **TV sets:** 280. **Daily newspaper circulation:** 99. **Computers:** 58.

REFUGEES
Alien refugees from other countries: 300.

HUMAN LIFE AND LIBERTY (optimum condition=100.0%)
HDI: 89.1. **HSI:** 63.0. **HFI:** 20.0. **EFL:** 51.0.

Country Table 1. **Religious adherents in Chile, AD 1900-2025.**

Year	*1900*		*1970*		*mid-1990*		*Annual change, 1990-2000*				*mid-1995*		*mid-2000*		*mid-2025*	
Name	*Adherents*	*%*	*Adherents*	*%*	*Adherents*	*%*	*Natural*	*Conversion*	*Total*	*Rate*	*Adherents*	*%*	*Adherents*	*%*	*Adherents*	*%*
Christians	**2,863,000**	**96.8**	**8,793,300**	**92.6**	**11,716,250**	**89.4**	**188,934**	**-4,243**	**184,691**	**1.47**	**12,690,000**	**89.3**	**13,563,164**	**89.2**	**17,246,000**	**88.2**
PROFESSION																
professing Christians	**2,863,000**	**96.8**	**8,793,300**	**92.6**	**11,716,250**	**89.4**	**188,934**	**-4,243**	**184,691**	**1.47**	**12,690,000**	**89.3**	**13,563,164**	**89.2**	**17,246,000**	**88.2**
AFFILIATION																
unaffiliated Christians	29,590	1.0	448,300	4.7	216,250	1.7	3,487	-4,630	-1,143	-0.54	210,000	1.5	204,824	1.4	146,000	0.8
affiliated Christians	**2,833,410**	**95.8**	**8,345,000**	**87.9**	**11,500,000**	**87.8**	**185,448**	**386**	**185,834**	**1.51**	**12,480,000**	**87.8**	**13,358,340**	**87.8**	**17,100,000**	**87.5**
Roman Catholics	2,812,110	95.0	7,793,958	82.1	10,200,000	77.9	164,458	-4,458	160,000	1.47	11,041,010	77.7	11,800,000	77.6	14,800,000	75.7
Independents	0	0.0	1,408,742	14.8	3,200,000	24.4	51,595	10,405	62,000	1.79	3,534,359	24.9	3,820,000	25.1	5,700,000	29.2
Marginal Christians	0	0.0	40,738	0.4	335,000	2.6	5,401	3,099	8,500	2.29	373,171	2.6	420,000	2.8	720,000	3.7
Protestants	30,000	1.0	200,953	2.1	324,000	2.5	5,224	576	5,800	1.66	352,808	2.5	382,000	2.5	700,000	3.6
Orthodox	300	0.0	23,500	0.3	23,650	0.2	381	-371	10	0.04	23,715	0.2	23,750	0.2	25,000	0.1
Anglicans	1,000	0.0	4,000	0.0	11,000	0.1	177	-77	100	0.87	11,500	0.1	12,000	0.1	15,000	0.1
doubly-affiliated	-10,000	-0.3	-1,126,891	-11.9	-2,593,650	-19.8	-41,818	-8,758	-50,576	1.80	-2,856,563	-20.1	-3,099,410	-20.4	-4,860,000	-24.9
Trans-megabloc groupings																
Evangelicals	29,000	1.0	108,000	1.1	200,000	1.5	3,225	1,775	5,000	2.26	228,789	1.6	250,000	1.6	500,000	2.6
Pentecostals/Charismatics	0	0.0	1,480,000	15.6	4,715,000	36.0	76,022	6,178	82,200	1.62	5,147,599	36.2	5,537,000	36.4	7,430,000	38.0
Great Commission Christians	**118,000**	**4.0**	**760,000**	**8.0**	**1,860,000**	**14.2**	**29,989**	**6,247**	**36,236**	**1.80**	**2,046,000**	**14.4**	**2,222,359**	**14.6**	**3,320,000**	**17.0**
Nonreligious	2,000	0.1	321,200	3.4	875,000	6.7	14,108	4,709	18,817	1.97	973,730	6.9	1,063,168	7.0	1,610,000	8.2
Atheists	1,900	0.1	240,000	2.5	325,000	2.5	5,240	552	5,792	1.65	355,000	2.5	382,923	2.5	480,000	2.5
Ethnoreligionists	90,000	3.0	100,000	1.1	122,000	0.9	1,967	-813	1,154	0.91	127,000	0.9	133,539	0.9	130,000	0.7
Jews	1,000	0.0	30,000	0.3	31,200	0.2	503	-285	218	0.68	31,700	0.2	33,381	0.2	32,000	0.2
Baha'is	0	0.0	7,800	0.1	15,000	0.1	242	52	294	1.81	16,700	0.1	17,943	0.1	25,000	0.1
Buddhists	0	0.0	500	0.0	4,500	0.0	73	21	94	1.91	5,000	0.0	5,437	0.0	7,500	0.0
Muslims	100	0.0	2,000	0.0	4,000	0.0	64	17	81	1.86	4,400	0.0	4,809	0.0	8,000	0.0
Chinese folk-religionists	0	0.0	0	0.0	250	0.0	4	4	8	2.69	300	0.0	326	0.0	500	0.0
Other religionists	1,000	0.0	1,200	0.0	5,800	0.0	94	-14	80	1.31	6,170	0.0	6,604	0.0	9,000	0.1
World A (unevangelized persons)	44,385	1.5	37,984	0.4	52,396	0.4	887	-274	613	1.06	56,841	0.4	60,844	0.4	58,644	0.3
World B (evangelized non-Christians)	51,615	1.7	664,718	7.0	1,330,354	10.2	21,408	4,517	25,925	1.78	1,463,571	10.3	1,586,992	10.4	2,243,356	11.5
World C (Christians)	2,863,000	96.8	8,793,300	92.6	11,716,250	89.4	188,934	-4,243	184,691	1.47	12,690,000	89.3	13,563,164	89.2	17,246,000	88.2
Country's population	**2,959,000**	**100.0**	**9,496,003**	**100.0**	**13,099,000**	**100.0**	**211,229**	**0**	**211,229**	**1.51**	**14,210,413**	**100.0**	**15,211,000**	**100.0**	**19,548,000**	**100.0**

COLUMNS, ROWS.
For meanings and definitions, see Codebook (Part 3). Note that, by definition, total 'Christians' = professing + crypto-Christians, which also = affiliated + unaffiliated Christians, and also = Great Commission Christians + latent Christians. Percentages may not always total exactly, due to rounding.

CENSUSES.
1907 (excluding Indians): 98.8% Roman Catholics, 1.1% Evangelicals, 0.1% nonreligious. **1920:** 95.8% Roman Catholics, 2.6% nonreligious, atheists and ethnoreligionists, 1.4% Evangelicals, 0.1% Jews. **1930:** 97.7% Roman Catholics, 1.5% Evangelicals, 0.7% nonreligious, atheists, and ethnoreligionists, 0.1% Jews. **1940:** 93.7% Roman Catholics, 3.5% nonreligious, atheists and ethnoreligionists, 2.5% Evangelicals, 0.2% Jews, 0.1% Orthodox. **24.IV.1952:** 92.3% Roman Catholics, 4.2% Evangelicals (Protestants, Anglicans, marginal Protestants, and Chilean indigenous), 3.2% nonreligious, atheists and ethnoreligionists, 0.2% Jews, 0.1% Orthodox. **29.XI.1960:** 89.2% Roman Catholics, 5.7% Evangelicals (Protestants, Anglicans, marginal Protestants and Chilean indigenous), 4.7% nonreligious, atheists and ethnoreligionists, 0.1% Orthodox, 0.1% Jews, 0.1% other religionists (Hindus, Buddhists). **1992:** (Population 14 years and older), 76.7% Roman Catholics, 12.4% Evangelicals, 0.8% Protestant, 5.8% nonreligious, 4.3% other religions.

NOTES ON RELIGIONS
ATHEISTS. Partido Comunista de Chile (PCCh) (in government until 1973 coup; pro-Soviet). A certain proportion of communists are practicing Evangelicals, pentecostals, and Catholics.
BAHA'IS. Growth from 8 local spiritual assemblies (1964) to 51 (1973), and 2 decades later to 86 (1996). Converts include Mapuche Indians.
BUDDHISTS. Chinese.
DOUBLY-AFFILIATED. The term covers those affiliated to, or claimed by, both the Catholic Church and also a church termed Evangélica by the state (Protestant, Chilean indigenous, Anglican or marginal Protestant), i.e. baptized Catholics who have recently become Evangelicals or others. Because their statistics represent a duplication, they shown in the table as a negative quantity (with a minus sign).
ETHNORELIGIONISTS. Of the 700,000 Amerindians in 1995 (Araucanian Indians, especially Mapuche, also Aymara and Quechua in the north), about 20% were non-Catholics still practicing animism, ancestor-veneration, polytheism, and shamanism.
EVANGELICALS. This English term is used in the sense understood within the churches (not as understood by the state) to mean: (a) Conservative Evangelicals, namely all persons affiliated to Protestant denominations of Conservative Evangelical theology, (b) Conciliar Evangelicals, affiliated to non-Evangelical Protestant denominations usually within the Ecumenical Movement, (c) Fundamentalists, namely all persons affiliated to Protestant denominations themselves affiliated to the ICCC or other fundamentalist councils, and (d) Anglican Evangelicals.
INDEPENDENTS. In over 200 indigenous denominations in 1995 (see Table 2). Leadership in the 2 major indigenous pentecostal bodies in mainly White (Italian, Spanish, especially former railway drivers or instructors) or Mestizo, but there are several Indian-speaking congregations with many Indian members.
OTHER RELIGIONISTS. Including spiritists, 56 Theosophists in 9 lodges, Rosicrucians (2 AMORC centers), et alii.
PENTECOSTALS/CHARISMATICS. From its beginnings in 1972 the Catholic Charismatic Renewal (CCR) grew steadily to, in 1997, 705 regular weekly prayer groups (averaging 30 attenders each week), 15 priests, and 2 bishops, 3 covenant communities. Largest single attendance at a CCR rally: 11,000.
PROTESTANTS. In 1907, 34% nationals and 66% expatriates; in 1920, 69% nationals, 31% expatriates.

Great Commission Instrument Panel: status of Chile (for explanation see start of Part 4)

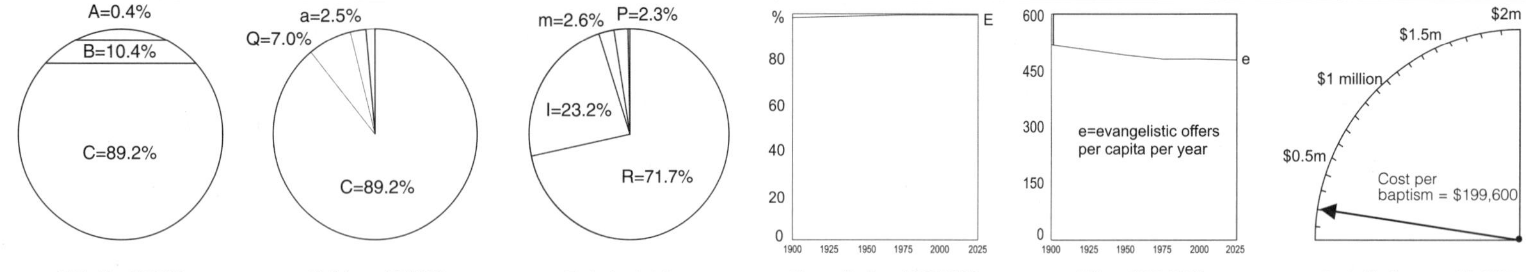

3 Worlds, AD 2000 | Religions, AD 2000 | Ecclesiastical blocs | Evangelization, 1900-2025 | Offers, 1900-2025 | Cost-effectiveness, AD 2000

Country status. Located on a ribbon of land extending along the west coast of South America for some 2,600 miles, Chile is compressed between the Andes and the South Pacific. Geographically, it is one of the most isolated countries in the world, far from all the major centers of civilization. Geographic isolation and the absence of large Indian groups have helped to make it one of the most ethnically homogeneous nations.

HUMAN LIFE AND LIBERTY

Human need and development. Living conditions in Chile are generally satisfactory and are comparable to those in developed countries. Predominantly rural in 1900, it grew to 85% urban by AD 2000 and consequently the largely backward society at the beginning of the century has been replaced by a mobile and dynamic one. Social distinctions, however, persist and these distinctions are characterized by different standards of life. The most visible variable is housing. While the well-to-do lived in spacious houses, the urban poor live in tenements called conventillo. On the fringes of cities are found squatter villages called callampa (mushroom), usually a one-room shanty devoid totally or partially of sanitary facilities. In rural areas, the houses are only slightly better, consisting of one or two rooms with rough boards or wattles and interstices filled with clay. In medical care Chile fares better than many advanced countries. It has one of the most comprehensive public health systems, virtually free for all but the very rich. The country also supports a comprehensive public welfare program

Human rights and freedoms. After more than 16 years of military rule, democracy was restored to Chile in 1990, and since then the principal thrust of human rights activists has been in seeking retroactive justice for victims of human rights violations in the past. Terrorists, however, continue to exact retribution on their own through extrajudicial killings and bomb attacks. There are credible reports of torture of leftists by the Carabinero. Some members of the judiciary, appointed by the former military regime, are unwilling to pursue human rights cases. President Patricio Aylwin has pardoned over 50 people who had been convicted of politically motivated crimes by the military regime and 9,500 Chileans who had fled the country under Augusto Pinochet have been permitted to return. Certain types of discrimination against women persist, but enormous strides have been made in closing the gender gap in education and society.

Country summary. **Worlds A, B, C by ethnolinguistic peoples, cities, and major civil divisions in Chile.**

World	*PEOPLES* Num	Pop 2000	C%	Christians	E%	U%	Unevangelized
A	1	37,090	0.10	37	49	51	18,879
B	4	94,851	36.20	34,337	74	26	24,931
C	20	15,079,354	88.36	13,323,962	100	0	17,322
Total	**25**	**15,211,295**	**87.82**	**13,358,336**	**100**	**0**	**61,132**

World	*CITIES* Num	Pop 2000	C%	Christians	E%	U%	Unevangelized
A	0	0	0.00	0	0	0	0
B	0	0	0.00	0	0	0	0
C	28	10,271,598	86.08	8,841,512	100	0	46,576
Total	**28**	**10,271,598**	**86.08**	**8,841,512**	**100**	**0**	**46,576**

World	*CIVIL DIVISIONS* Num	Pop 2000	C%	Christians	E%	U%	Unevangelized
A	0	0	0.00	0	0	0	0
B	0	0	0.00	0	0	0	0
C	13	15,211,296	87.82	13,358,340	100	0	61,136
Total	**13**	**15,211,296**	**87.82**	**13,358,340**	**100**	**0**	**61,136**

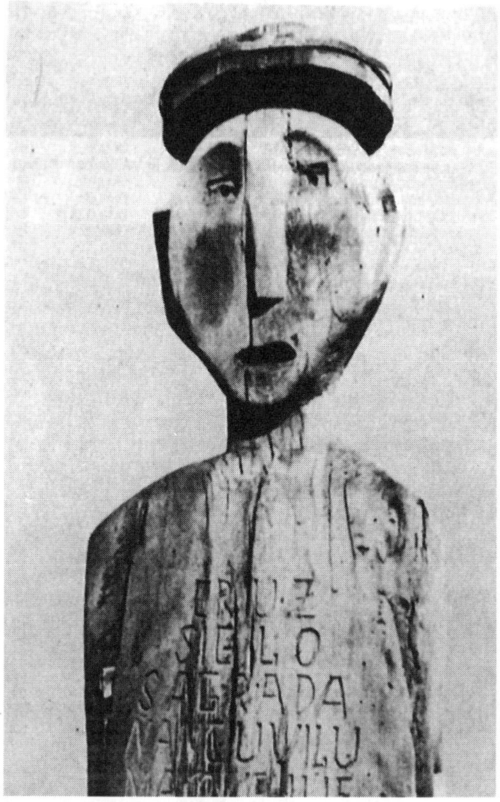

Ethnoreligionists. An ancient Amerindian wooden image from Araucania.

Human environment. Parts of Chile are very dry and competition for water use poses a serious environmental threat. This is exacerbated by steadily increasing watershed degradation. Untreated sewage is allowed to pollute water sources. Since the vast majority of Chileans live in urban areas, air pollution has approached danger levels. A thick smog covers Santiago on most days. Because of overexploitation, the rich fishing grounds are being depleted.

NON-CHRISTIAN RELIGIONS

Agnosticism has grown considerably over the last 25 years and the nonreligious form over 3% of the population, increasing annually in number.

Traditional Indian religions still account for a substantial 1% of the population. Arauca (Mapuche), Quechua, and Aymara Indians make up about 5% of the population. The Mapuche (People of the Land), who number 360,000, are polytheists who retain belief in a supreme being, Nenechen, who is head of a pantheon of divinities (sun, moon, thunder, stars, earth, sea), although there are no Mapuche temples. The divinity of thunder or volcanoes is called Pillan. Medicine men or shamans are active and fear of sorcerer-witches is prevalent, but the main focus of Mapuche religion is the ancestor cult.

Judaism is the religion of 0.2% of the population. The University of Chile in Santiago has a Department of Jewish Culture which is part of its Pedagogical Institute, and there are several other centers for Jewish culture and studies in the country.

CHRISTIANITY

CATHOLIC CHURCH. The first priest arrived in 1541, and in 1561, the diocese of Santiago was erected as a suffragan of Lima. A seminary was built in Santiago in 1584. Catholicism was recognized as the state religion when Chile became independent in 1810, but relations became increasingly strained after 1878, resulting finally in the separation of church and state in 1925.

Since 1960, the Catholic Church has experienced a significant renewal, of which there are 5 principal elements. (1) A carefully prepared national plan was launched in 1962, before the Second Vatican Council, to mobilize the various potential apostolates in the Catholic community. The plan included liturgical reform and reorganization of pastoral work to meet needs more adequately at diocesan, parish, and subparish levels. (2) Greater involvement of women's religious communities in diocesan pastoral work was obtained by abandoning a number of traditional activities (schools, clinics, homes for the aged) and concentrating instead on evangelization through small groups. (3) Synods were held in most dioceses throughout the country. The synod of the archdiocese of Santiago (1966-1969) was the first postconciliar synod both in Chile and anywhere in the world and has been one of the most open. It brought together some 500 persons, most of them elected at grassroots level. Members at the first session included 98 secular priests, 87 religious brothers, 5 seminarians, 9 lay brothers, 85 nuns and 209 lay persons. The themes of the synod were priority for evangelization, involvement of the church in the world, ecclesiastical institutions, the church and nonbelievers, ecumenism and Judeo-Christian dialogue. (4) Socioreligious surveys were widely conducted concerning religious attitudes and Sunday observance, especially in Santiago, Taca and Concepcion. Sunday mass attendance in Santiago was found to be 13% of those eligible. A comparison of the results of surveys made in 1960 and 1970 indicated a drop in Sunday observance of 50% during the decade for the age group 11-20 years. (5) Lastly, there has been a new understanding of the social and economic problems facing the country, as evidence by pastoral letters and actions concerning agrarian reform. In Chile, Catholicism has had a longer tradition of social concern and involvement than anywhere else in Latin America, dating back to 1910. Msgr. Larrain, bishop of Talca and the first president of CELAM, was the first Latin American prelate to distribute church agricultural land to workers who farmed it, and at Vatican II the progressive role of the Chilean church was pronounced. Chile was also one of the first countries in the world to organize a Christians for Socialism movement (1971). In April 1972, the first Latin American meeting of Christians for Socialism was held in Santiago, with 170 priests, 40 Protestant pastors, 30 religious personnel and 160 lay persons in attendance. The coming to power in 1970 of the Allende government from the communist and noncommunist left did not provoke the kind of disturbance among churchmen that would have occurred in others parts of the continent. In 1971, the Bellarmino Institute conducted a survey on attitudes held by clergy concerning Marxism. The sample consisted of 60% of all priests in chile, both national and foreign. Results indicated that 53% believed the practical attitude of Christians should express itself through 'friendly collaboration' without ignoring ideological differences; 37% were opposed to Marxism but wanted to maintain dialogue with Marxists; 3% believed Christian and Marxists should work closely together; 1% wanted to avoid all contact with them; and the remaining 5% indicated that it was necessary to fight Marxist doctrine as 'intrinsically perverse'.

The Holy See has diplomatic relations with Chile and in AD 2000 is represented to government and the Catholic hierarchy by a nuncio residing in Santiago.

Iglesia Católica en Chile. New bishop for Araucania with Amerindian population.

INDIGENOUS CHURCHES. Local Pentecostal groups have grown very rapidly in Chile as in Brazil. The movement in Chile can be dated to 1909 when a Methodist missionary, W. C. Hoover, received baptism in the Holy Spirit. Repudiated by his own church, he helped form the Methodist Pentecostal Church (IMP), which is distinguished by its retention of many Wesleyan traditions, including infant baptism, semi-authoritarian government, elected bishops, and a belief that the gift of tongues is not essential to baptism in the Spirit. Its rapid expansion has been influenced by centralized organization, freedom from foreign control and consequent ability to adapt to local conditions. In 1933, a schism in this church produced the Evangelical Pentecostal Church (IEP), which has also expanded enormously. The IMP and the IEP are now by far the largest non-Catholic churches in Chile. A large number of similar bodies also exist, though smaller in size. Taken together, there were over 1.3 million indigenous pentecostals affiliated to churches in Chile in 1970 (1.5 million in 1975) compared to only 200,000 persons in Protestant churches. The world's largest Evangelical congregation is the Jotabeche Pentecostal Church (IMP) in Santiago, which has 80,000 regular members. Of particular significance is that all of this pentecostal growth has been achieved with no financial support from outside.

Independent pentecostals. 6,000 members, assembled for week-long 30th annual Assembly, begin dancing in the Spirit.

PROTESTANT CHURCHES. The first Protestant missionary was an agent of the British and Foreign Bible Society, who established several schools in 1821 at the invitation of Chile's new president. The first resident missionary was David Trumbull in 1845, with a group of Christians from several traditions which became the nucleus for the work of the Presbyterian Church USA in 1873.

Efforts to train a national clergy met with misunderstandings almost from the beginning, which has greatly hindered Presbyterian expansion. More successful have been the Lutherans, who came in 1846, but they remain primarily German in membership.

In 1877, a Methodist, William Taylor, established self-supporting schools in that part of Bolivia which later was ceded to Chile. Emphasis on self-support, development of a lay ministry and the relatively low salaries of American missionaries, contributed to the very rapid growth of Methodism between 1893 and 1907. However, Methodists were badly divided by a schism in 1910 over Pentecostalism from which they never fully recovered.

Seventh-day Adventists arrived in 1890 and are now the largest Protestant church in Chile.

German immigrants founded the first Baptist church in 1892 followed by the organization of the Chilean Baptist Convention in 1908. In 1917, Southern Baptists sent their first missionaries from the USA to work with this developing church. Baptist history has been characterized by numerous schisms, but overall growth has not been significantly impaired. In some cases, membership has actually increased as a result of divisions. Of the major denominations, Baptists have been least affected by the expansion of Pentecostalism, largely due to the freedom and flexibility of Christian expression which is given to each local congregation. The church has maintained a steady growth of about 5% per year over the past decade.

Several foreign Pentecostal missions have recently entered Chile with the object of helping the rapidly-growing indigenous Pentecostal churches, but disagreements concerning doctrine have discouraged cooperation. The largest of these bodies is the Church of God (Cleveland).

Art and architecture. Chile's most famous ecclesiastical building is the Temple Votivo, a massive shrine near the village of Maipo built in honor of the Virgin in fulfillment of a vow by Bernard O' Higgins, the country's liberator. In the village of Ayquina, in the foothills of the Cordillera, is the ancient church housing the Virgin of Guadalupe. The massive Cathedral of Santiago contains a recumbent wooden statue of St. Francis Xavier. The most ancient church in Santiago is the red-spired church and monastery of San Francisco which houses the statue of the Virgin carried by Pedro de Valdivia, the founder of the city, when he rode from Peru to Chile. The church also has a museum of colonial arts.

Renewal movements. In the 1990s the Pentecostal/Charismatic Renewal continued to spread rapidly across most older churches, and numbered over 5.5 million adherents (of whom 2% Pentecostals, 30% Charismatics, and 69% Independents).

Indigenous missions. Both Catholics and Protestants have been involved in mission since before 1970. Though the highest percentage are sent out to neighboring countries more, Chilean missionaries are being sent to North Africa and Asia as a result of Redemptoris Missio for Catholics and COMIBAM for Protestants. Even the recently converted Mapuche are sending out foreign missionaries.

Ejercito de Salvación. Salvation Army officer in front of his church.

CHURCH AND STATE

The constitution of 1925, modified in 1970, guarantees freedom of conscience, and freedom of expression and practice for all religions. The text in Article 10 specified that 'Places of worship and related buildings are exempt from taxation'. The 1925 constitution put an end to the patronato or close relation between the Catholic Church and the state as defined in the 1833 constitution. Henceforth, no governmental ministry was responsible for religious or ecclesiastical affairs, and the government no longer officially subsidized churches, although it continued to aid their social and educational work. Numerous denominational colleges still receive government grants of up to 50% of the cost per pupil. In 1972, the Chilean congress granted to officials of all churches (priests, religious, rabbis, and pastors) the status of 'workers', thus procuring for them Social Security benefits for illness or retirement. Foreign priests who have worked at least 5 years in Chile are also beneficiaries. Churches and denominations enjoy a large measure of independence and are not required to register with government.

During and after the electoral campaign in 1970, which brought Allende to power, the Catholic episcopate maintained complete neutrality in spite of heavy pressures on them to take issue. In November 1970, the cardinal archbishop of Santiago was present at the installation of the government, which was considered to be a gesture of recognition of the leftist government by the church. In 1971 and 1982, the episcopate, following the cardinal's lead, continued this policy of providing practical support for government measures concerning the changing of social structures as well as support for constitutional legality and political pluralism.

The military coup d'etat of 11 November 1973, presented itself as a crusade to 'remove the Marxist cancer'. In this sense, it was applauded by the Christian Democratic party and a certain number of bishops.

In 1974, the prolongation of repression and the deterioration of the social situation provoked the Episcopal conference, also the cardinal and several individual bishops, to take a strong position concerning the rights of man.

Representatives of 32 Evangelical churches, in a full-page advertisement in the magazine El mercurio, published a declaration of unreserved support for the junta. A few months later, general Pinochet with other government leaders officially opened the new IMP cathedral (Jotabeche Pentecostal Church) in Santiago in the presence of 100,000 Chilean Pentecostals. Evangelicals and Pentecostals are thus reasserting the right of Christians to political expression long left to Catholics alone.

Similar sentiments and tensions have surfaced repeatedly in the following 2 decades.

Iglesia Metodista Pentecostal de Chile. *Above.* Earliest (1909) and largest of 200 Chilean indigenous churches. IMP's members in procession through Santiago, culminating (*below*) in rally.

BROADCASTING AND MEDIA

Daily and weekly 30-minute radio programs produced by IBRA can be heard on local radio stations in 9 different cities. Shortwave programs from KNLS, HCJB (Ecuador), TWR (Antilles) and AWR (Costa Rica) can be easily received. Chile is a member of UNDA. There are 27 local Catholic radio stations, broadcasting mainly in Spanish. ARCA is the national association of Catholic broadcasters.

CBN's television programs are seen on local cable channels 3 days a week. CBN maintains full-time follow up centers with evangelistic and discipleship activities and a video ministry. Christian television programming can also be received via satellite.

Some 2.7 million people (3%) have seen the 'Jesus' Film, chiefly through TV (1.1 million) and film teams (1.5 million).

INTERDENOMINATIONAL ORGANIZATIONS

The Evangelical Council of Chile, with 10 members, was begun in 1941, building on an earlier committee founded in 1916, but has in recent years split into 2 factions over relations with the World Council of Churches. The more conservative Confederation of Evangelical Fundamentalist Churches has 5 member bodies. The Evangelical Theological Community is an ecumenical training center sponsored by Methodists, Anglicans and some Pentecostal groups. The interdenominational Evangelical Audio-Visual Center, founded in 1967 by the Lutheran and Pentecostal churches, has developed programs of education and communications based on the psycho-social methods of Paulo Freire and engages in community development work with Pentecostal churches. Caritas and Evangelical Aid work together in the distribution of food in areas of need.

FUTURE TRENDS AND PROSPECTS

A slight decline of Christians from 92.6% in 1970 to 88.2% is expected by 2025 (primarily due to disaffiliation of individuals from the Roman Catholic Church).

The nonreligious of Chile will probably to continue growing well into the 21st century. As such, they might pass 10% by AD 2050. Christians, conversely, would then decline below 85% by mid-century.

Iglesia Metodista Pentecostal de Chile. Ordination by renowned pastor Humberto (*center*).

BIBLIOGRAPHY

'A critical study of Baptist church growth in Chile.' J. H. Bitner. Th.D. thesis, Southwestern Baptist Theological Seminary, Fort Worth, TX, 1975. 321p.

A study of the older Protestant missions and churches in Peru and Chile: with special reference to the problems of division, nationalism and native ministry. J. B. A. Kessler Jr. Goes, Netherlands: Oosterbaan & Le Cointre, 1967. 369p.

'A vision for church growth in Chile: a study of growth factors in Protestant churches in Chile with an analysis of the relationship between numerical growth and integral ministry.' R. B. Ramsay. D.Min. thesis, Westminster Theological Seminary, Chestnut Hill, PA, 1992. 518p.

A yankee reformer in Chile: the life and works of David Trumball. I. Paul. South Pasadena, CA: William Carey Library, 1973. 155p.

Alliance or compliance: implications of the Chilean experience for the Catholic Church in Latin America. V. M. Bouvier. *Foreign and comparative studies, Latin American series*, no. 3. Syracuse, NY: Syracuse University, 1983. 116p.

'Chile,' *Pro Mundi Vita* (Brussels), 49 (1974), 1–40.

Chile. H. Blakemore. *World bibliographical series*, vol. 97. Oxford, UK: CLIO Press, 1988. (See especially 'Religion,' 69-71).

Chile: la Vicaría de la Solidaridad. J. I. G. Fuente. Madrid: Alianza, 1986. 232p.

Chile: the role of the church. Life choices, no. 31. [Notre Dame, IN]: Golden Dome Productions, 1990. (29 min. videocassette produced by the University of Notre Dame).

Christian communities in Chile and Peru. M. Fleet. Notre Dame, IN: Helen Kellogg Institute for International Studies, University of Notre Dame, 1992. 40p.

El Protestantismo en Chile. I. Vergara. Santiago: Editorial del Pacifico, 1962. 261p.

Followers of the new faith: culture change and the rise of Protestantism in Brazil and Chile. E. Willems. Nashville, TN: Vanderbilt University Press, 1967. 290p.

Guia eclesiástica y parroquial de Chile, 1972. Santiago: Arzobispado de Santiago, 1973. (Roman Catholic).

Haven of the masses: a study of the Pentecostal movement in Chile. C. L. d'Epinay. London: Lutterworth Press, 1969. 263p.

Hawks of the sun: Mapuche morality and its ritual attributes. L. C. Faron. Pittsburgh, PA: University of Pittsburgh Press, 1964. 220p.

'Helping church planters to develop successful churches in Santiago, Chile.' V. A. Quezada. D.Min. thesis, Southern Baptist Theological Seminary, Louisville, KY, 1988. 111p.

Historia del Avivamiento pentecostal en Chile. W. C. Hoover. Santiago: Imprenta El Esfuerzo, 1931. 125p. (By the leader of the 1909 revival).

La evangelización de la Patagonia y de la Tierra del Fuego. C. Bruno. Rosario: Ediciones 'Didascalia', 1992. 203p.

La Iglesia chilena y los cambios sociopolíticos. M. A. Huerta & L. Pacheco Pastene. Santiago: Pehuén, 1988. 369p.

La Iglesia en Chile. I. Alonso, R. Robert & G. Garrido. Fribourg: FERES, 1962. 223p. (Roman Catholic).

'Les religions au Chili entre l'aliénation et le prise de conscience,' C. L. d'Epinay & J. Zylberberg, *Social compass*, 21, 1 (1974), 85–100.

Los cristianos por el socialismo en Chile. T. D. Loero. 3d ed. Santiago: Editorial Vaitea, 1976.

Los micromedios de iglesias cristianas en Chile: funcionamiento y discurso. M. Quezada & G. Riveri. Santiago: CENECA, 1984. 155p.

Maryknoll in Chile: the first fifty years. D. J. Molineaux & M. J. Ress. : Mosquito Editores, 1993. 456p.

'Popular religion, pastoral renewal, and national reconciliation in Chilean Catholicism.' T. G. Sanders. Report, American Universities Field Staff, Hanover, NH, 1981. 12p.

'Popular religious music in Chile: a discussion of practice and culture.' R. G. Magee. M.A. thesis, Vanderbilt University, Nashville, TN, 1991. 71p.

'Protestantism and politics in Chile and Brazil,' F. C. Turner, *Comparative studies in society and history*, 12, 2 (1970), 213–29.

Religion and politics in Chile: an analysis of religious models. O. Mella. *Studia sociologica Upsaliensia*, 27. Uppsala: Academiae Ubsaliensis, 1987. 202p.

Religiosidad popular en el norte de Chile. H. Tennekes. Iquique, Chile: Centro de Investigación de la Realidad del Norte, [1986]. 128p.

Religiosidad y cultura popular. A. A. Chazarreta. *Cuadernos de Iglesia y sociedad*, no. 7. Buenos Aires: Centro de Investigación y Orientación Social, 1982. 42p.

Sociología religiosa de Chile. H. M. Ramirez. Santiago: Ediciones Paulinas, 1957.

'The Catholic Church and political change in Chile, 1920–1978.' B. H. Smith. Ph.D. dissertation, Yale University, New Haven, CT, 1979. 765p.

'The challenge of growth for the Baptist Church in Chile.' V. A. Quezada. Th.M. thesis, Fuller Theological Seminary, Pasadena, CA, 1985. 126p.

The Chilean Catholic Church during the Allende and Pinochet regimes. T. G. Sanders & B. H. Smith. *American Universities Field Staff Field Staff reports*, vol. 23, no.1. [Hanover, NH]: American Universities Field Staff, 1976. 25p.

'The Chilean hierarchy and the political events of 1973–1975,' *Pro Mundi Vita* (Brussels), Special note 42 (1975), 1–20.

The Church and politics in Chile: challenges to modern Catholicism. B. H. Smith. Princeton, NJ: Princeton University Press, 1982. 396p.

The church and politics in the Chilean countryside. H. W. Stewart-Gambino. Boulder, CO: Westview Press, 1992. 207p.

The history, dynamic, and problems of the Pentecostal Movement in Chile. N. E. Johnson. Richmond, VA: Union Theological Seminary in Virginia, 1970. 132p.

The rise and fall of Chilean Christian democracy. M. Fleet. Princeton, NJ: Princeton University Press, 1985. 289p.

'Torture and eucharist in Pinochet's Chile.' W. Cavanaugh. Ph.D. dissertation, Duke University, Durham, NC, 1996.

Country Table 2. **Organized churches and denominations in Chile.**

Official name (bold type = church with over 10% of all affiliated) 1	*Begun* 2	*Type* 3	*Counc* 4	*Congs* 5	*Adults* 6	*Affiliated 1970* 7	*Affiliated 1995* 8	*G%* 9	*Names, notes, and other statistics* (see Codebook, Part 3) 10
Alianza Cristiana Pentecostal		I-3pL	.....	25	3,000	–	4,290	0.05	*Pentecostal Christian Alliance.*
Asambleas de Dios en Chilé	1941	P-Pe2	ZF...	445	25,000	10,000	34,000	5.02	*Assemblies of God.* M=AoG(USA). No aid to indigenous pentecostals. 74n,10f,3s(81).
Asambleas de Dios Autónomas	1925	I-3pL	Z....	60	12,000	10,000	18,500	2.49	*Misión Sueca. Autonomous Assemblies of God.* 1937, M=SFM(Sweden). 3n,156Y.113z.
Asambleas Locales	c1980	I-3nC	.....	47	1,365	–	3,000	6.67	*Little Flock. Local Churches. Assembly Hall Churches.*
Asoc Bautista para la Ev del Mondo	1952	I-Bap	x....	28	2,200	1,000	3,140	4.68	M=Association of Baptists for World Evangelism (USA). HQ Santiago. 22f,1h,1s.
Congr Ev de la Fe Apostólica del SD	1936	I-3aL	.....	68	27,000	15,000	40,300	4.03	SD=Séptimo Dia. *Ev Congr of the Apostolic Faith Seventh-day.* W=60%,300Y.
Conv Bautista Nac de Misión Chilena	c1970	I-Bap	T....	36	1,690	–	3,000	37.75	*National Convention of Baptist Chs of the Chilean Mission.*
Convención Ev Bautista de Chile	1892	P-Bap	T....	225	27,600	30,000	40,000	1.16	*Ev Baptist Convention of Chile.* 1917, M=SBC(USA). SS=12,334. 74n,53f,1h,1s,860Y.
Corporación Evangélica de Vitacura	1933	I-3pL	..u.N	187	14,000	10,000	28,000	4.20	*Ev Corporation of Vitacura* (Santiago). Ex IMP. M=AFM(Portland, USA). Mestizos.
Corporación Evangélica Pentecostal	1956	I-3pL	.....	100	12,000	20,000	18,000	-0.42	*Coronel. Ev Pentecostal Corporation.* Schism ex IEP, in Concepción province.
Corporación Iglesia del Señor	c1920	I-3pL	.....	250	20,000	15,000	28,600	2.62	*Ch of the Lord Corporation.* Schism ex Iglesia del Senor. Round Puerto Montt.
Ejército de Salvación	1909	P-Sal	xw...	100	8,000	5,451	13,300	3.63	*Salvation Army.* In South America West Territory. 47n,19x,1s,W=71%,161z.
Ejército Evangélico de Chile	1937	I-3gL	.....	722	65,000	15,000	92,900	7.57	*Ev Army of Chile.* Schism ex IMP. Until 1942, Ejército Ev Uniformado. Mestizos.
Ejército Evangélico Nacional	1942	I-3gL	..u.I	37	1,100	1,000	1,570	1.82	*National Evangelical Army.* Schism ex Ejército Ev de Chile. Mestizos.
El Aposento Alto	c1975	I-3gL	.....	25	2,000	–	2,860	5.00	*The Upper Room.* Relations with similar body in USA.
Hermanos Libres Nacionales	1928	P-CBr	x....	40	2,800	500	4,670	9.35	*Christian Brethren, Plymouth (Open) Brethren.* M=CMML(USA). 10f.
IEvMP Reunida en el Nombre de Jesús	1950	I-3gL	.....	200	65,000	100,000	105,000	0.20	*Ev Meth Pentecostal Ch Re-united in Name of Jesus.* Split ex IMP; O'Higgins province.
Iglesia Adventista del Séptimo Día	1890	P-Adv	x....	329	69,000	30,000	98,600	4.87	*Seventh-day Adventists, Chile UM* (2 Confs). 37nx,10f,1h,1r,1s, 186t(10826),1612Y.
Igl Adventista, Movimiento de Reforma	1929	I-Adv	x....	15	400	500	1,000	2.81	*SDA Movement of Reform.* Schism ex SDA church. World HQ Charlottenlund, Denmark.
Igl Aliancista Nacional de Sostén y GP	1929	I-Hol	.TT.T	65	6,500	5,000	9,290	2.51	GP=Gobierno Propio. *Self-support Self-governing Alliance Ch.* Schism ex CMA.
Iglesia Alianza Cristiana y Misionera	1897	P-Hol	xFu.N	185	11,117	12,000	33,350	4.17	*Christian & Missionary Alliance Ch.* M=CMA(USA). Over 4 schisms. 50n,19f,1j,1s.
Iglesia Anglicana: D Chile & Bolivia	1837	A-Low	Aw.C.	93	6,500	4,000	11,500	4.31	*Anglican Ch of the Southern Cone.* M=SAMS. 69% Araucanian, 22% UK, 9% Chilean. 16n,12x.
Iglesia Apostólica Armenia	c1910	O-Arm	Ew...	2	3,600	5,000	6,000	0.73	*Armenian Apostolic ch, D South America. Gregorians.* Refugees from USSR.
Iglesia Batista de la Misión Chilena	1940	I-Bap	.TT.T	533	16,000	1,000	22,900	13.34	*Misión Chilena.* Anti-mission schism ex Baptist Convention.
Iglesia Católica en Chile:	1541	R-Lat	BxL.R	4,512	6,597,700	7,793,958	11,041,010	1.40	Catholic Ch in Chile. C=49+4+136. 1090x,12p,3s. 937n 1188x 1869m 7048w 181280Yy
M Antofagasta	1928	R-Lat	Bs	66	128,500	212,500	217,128	0.09	Most northerly province. Pampa, desert, mining. 17n 26x 28m 79w 3503Yy
D Arica	1959	R-Lat	Bsj	27	83,700	90,000	141,342	1.82	In extreme north adjoining Peru and Bolivia. M=SJ. 18n 7x 7m 22w 1872Yy
D Iquique	1929	R-Lat	Bs	46	81,700	90,000	138,047	1.73	In extreme north, south of PN Arica. 12n 17x 18m 39w 2126Yy
PN Calama	1965	R-Lat	Bodm	56	72,800	100,000	123,000	0.83	In northeast, adjoining Argentina and Bolivia. M=OdM. 8n 4x 4m 16w 2029Yy
M Concepción	1564	R-Lat	Bs	363	357,000	688,000	602,525	-0.53	Central coastal diocese. M=OCD. 1p,1s. 58n 60x 67m 264w 9700Yy
D Chillan	1925	R-Lat	Bs	477	207,000	266,963	350,000	1.09	Central, bordering Argentina; Nuble province. 1p. 36n 12x 12m 109w 5061Yy
D Los Angeles	1959	R-Lat	Bs	187	150,000	198,604	254,000	0.99	In Bio-Bio civil province. M=Opus Dei. 24n 13x 18m 67w 4632Yy
D Temuco	1925	R-Lat	Bs	489	238,000	333,500	402,000	0.75	Protestant stronghold. Malleco, Cautin provinces. 1p. 35n 22x 30m 177w 5390Yy
D Valdivia	1944	R-Lat	Bs	156	125,000	191,720	211,000	0.38	Covers part of Valdivia civil province. 1p. 15n 22x 23m 60w 2626Yy
M La Serena	1840	R-Lat	Bs	290	201,000	289,776	340,000	0.64	Northern. In civil province of Coquimbo. 1p. 34n 35x 40m 173w 7372Yy
D Copiapó	1955	R-Lat	Bs	97	112,000	136,800	188,623	1.29	In Atacama civil province. 1p. 22n 7x 8m 109w 3702Yy
PN Illapel	1960	R-Lat	Bsvd	12	44,000	69,000	75,300	0.35	Southernmost area. M=OFM,SVD. 16n 4x 5m 38w 675Yy
M Puerto Montt	1939	R-Lat	Bosm	24	135,000	180,000	228,000	0.95	Southerly, including Tierra del Fuego. M=OSM. 28n 21x 25m 95w 4603Yy
D Osorno	1955	R-Lat	Bs	75	143,000	155,705	241,000	1.76	Northernmost diocese in ecclesiastical province. 15n 28x 37m 64w 3341Yy
D Punta Arenas	1916	R-Lat	Bsdb	50	85,000	93,000	143,000	1.74	In extreme south: half Tierra del Fuego. M=SDB. 6n 20x 22m 34w 1563Yy
D San Carlos de Ancud	1840	R-Lat	Bs	216	77,000	100,000	130,000	1.05	Chiloé and other southern islands. 13n 5x 7m 42w 2008Yy
M Santiago de Chile	1561	R-Lat	Bs	187	1,924,000	2,300,000	3,250,000	1.39	Decline from W=13%(1964) to 7% (1973). M=OLM. 238n 594x 1040m 4066w 57535Yy
D Linares	1925	R-Lat	Bs	457	218,000	251,300	368,000	1.54	Covers Linares and Maule civil provinces. 1p. 32n 20x 27m 114w 5432Yy
D Melipilla	1991	R-Lat	Bs	282	196,000	–	331,066	25.00	Halfway to the coast from Santiago. 24n 10x 30m 133w 7650Yy
D Rancagua	1925	R-Lat	Bsscc	727	344,000	495,000	581,000	0.64	In O'Higgins and Colchagua civil provinces. M=SSCC. 54n 55x 80m 164w 11732Yy
D San Bernardo	1987	R-Lat	Bs	27	298,000	–	504,000	12.50	M=SCI. 25n 17x 33m 190w 5650Yy
D San Felipe	1925	R-Lat	Bodm	30	135,000	156,104	228,000	1.53	Covers Aconcagua civil province. M=IPS,OdM. 32n 21x 34m 160w 4554Yy
D Talca	1925	R-Lat	Bs	42	234,000	390,000	396,178	0.06	Covers Curico and Talca civil provinces. 58n 29x 47m 214w 5657Yy
D Valparaíso	1925	R-Lat	Bs	67	519,000	520,000	877,000	2.11	Covers Valparaíso civil province 1p. 77n 103x 178m 353w 16163Yy
VA Araucanía	1901	R-Lat	Pofmc	31	206,000	338,986	348,000	0.11	Indians; also Easter Island (3500km west). P=18%,1p. 38n 21x 32m 233w 4819Yy
VA Aysén	1940	R-Lat	Posm	6	43,000	47,000	72,801	1.77	HQ Puerto Aisén. Very low practice: P=4%. Declining. 2n 15x 17m 33w 1885Yy

Continued overleaf

Country Table 2–concluded

Official name (bold type = church with over 10% of all affiliated) 1	*Begun* 2	*Type* 3	*Counc* 4	*Congs* 5	*Adults* 6	*Affiliated 1970* 7	*Affiliated 1995* 8	*G%* 9	*Names, notes, and other statistics* (see Codebook, Part 3) 10
OM Chile	1910	R-Lat	Bs	25	240,000	100,000	300,000	4.49	Military Ordinariate of Chile. 15 ordinaries, 36 auxiliaries. 4726Yy.
Iglesia Cristiana Apostólica	1929	I-3aL	..u.I	10	1,000	1,000	1,500	1.64	*Apostolic Christian Ch.* Schism ex Methodist Church. Mestizos. HQ Santiago.
Iglesia Cristiana de la Fe Apostólica	1933	I-3aL	x....	58	3,500	200	5,000	13.74	*Christian Ch of the Apostolic Faith.* Schism ex IEP. M=AFM(Portland, Oregon, USA).
Iglesia Cristiana Misionera	1989	I-Dis	.....	3	296	–	400	16.67	Christian Missionary Fellowship. M=CMF(USA).
Iglesia Cristiana Metodista Pentecostal		I-3pL	.....	10	2,000	1,430	2,860	0.05	*Christian Methodist Pentecostal Church.*
Iglesias de Biblia Abierta	1982	I-3pW	x....	15	756	–	1,080	7.69	*Open Bible Standard Churches.* M=OBSC(USA).
Iglesia de Cristo Evangélica Nacional	1946	I-3gL	.....	3	80	200	200	0.00	*National Ev Church of Christ.* Schism ex Iglesia Metodista Pentecostal. Mestizos.
Iglesia de Dios de la Profecía	1975	P-Pe3	Z....	31	1,090	–	1,550	5.00	*Ch of God of Prophecy.* M=CGP(USA), a split in USA ex CoG(Cleveland).
Iglesia de Dios en Chile	1951	P-Pe3	ZF...	196	14,324	15,000	20,500	1.26	*Ch of God. M=CoG(Cleveland) (USA). Opposed to indigenous pentecostals. 78n,1p,1s.*
Iglesia de Dios Pentecostal	1951	I-3pL	Z....	37	14,000	100,000	20,000	-6.23	*Pentecostal Ch of God.* Split ex Iglesia Ev Pentecostal. M=PCG(USA). Mestizos.
Iglesia de JC de los Santos de los UD	1956	m-LdS	x....	570	160,000	20,238	266,000	10.85	*Latter-day Saints. Mormons.* M=CJCLdS(USA). Rapid growth, 11.9%pa. 300f.
Iglesia del Evangelio Cuadrangular	1940	P-Pe2	ZF...	53	15,300	8,000	21,740	4.08	M=Int Ch Foursquare Gospel (USA). To 1959, Igl Cr Apost. 44nm,2f,1p(31),W=79%,203Y.
Iglesia del Nazareno	1962	P-Hol	xF...	38	1,660	1,500	2,937	2.72	*Ch of the Nazarene.* M=CoN(USA). HQ Santiago. 4n,10x,8f,1s(8),7t(1066).
Iglesia del Señor	1913	I-3pL	..u.N	58	35,000	15,000	50,000	4.93	*Church of the Lord.* Indigenous pentecostals. Schism ex IMP. Mestizos.
Iglesia Ev Autonoma Pentecostal		I-3pL	.....	20	1,600	714	2,290	0.05	*Autonomous Pentecostal Evangelical Church.*
Iglesia Evangélica Cristiana	1936	I-3pL	..u.I	35	2,000	2,000	3,000	1.64	*Ev Christian Church.* Schism ex IMP. Especially strong in Santiago. Mestizos.
Iglesia Evangélica de Dios Pentecostal		I-3pL	.....	80	20,000	7,140	28,600	0.05	*Pentecostal Evangelical Church of God.*
Iglesia Ev de la Nueva Jerusalem		I-3pL	.....	19	1,500	714	2,140	0.05	*Evangelical Church of the New Jerusalem.*
Iglesia Evangélica del Emanuel	1945	I-3pL	.....	1	80	200	180	-0.42	*Ev Ch of Emmanuel.* 1945 split ex Pentecostal Methodists. Mestizos.
Igl Ev el Pesebre Humilde de Cristo	1943	I-3pL	.....	2	150	400	300	-1.14	*Humble Manger of Christ Church.* 1943 split ex IMP. Mestizos.
Iglesia Ev Israelita del Nuevo Pacto	1948	I-Adv	.....	3	200	300	400	1.16	*Ev Israelite Ch of New Covenant. Cabañistas (Tabernaclers).* Old Testament rituals.
Iglesia Evangelica Luterana Alemana		P-Lut	.....	3	560	1,000	1,120	0.05	German Ev Lutheran Ch. Ethnic German Chs. Puerto Mont=900, Valparaiso=220.
Iglesia Evangélica Luterana en Chile	1846	P-Lut	LW...	10	1,620	25,687	2,700	-8.62	Germans, Swiss. A=1937. 1962, M=LCA. 1974, schism. 3n,12x,1u,W=15%,167Yy.
Iglesia Evangélica Metodista Pentecostal	1950	I-3pL	.....	1,500	120,000	20,000	171,000	8.96	*Evangelical Methodist Pentecostal Ch.* Schism ex IMP.
Iglesia Evangélica Mision Cristiana		I-3pL	.....	175	14,000	5,710	20,000	0.05	*Christian Evangelical Mission Church.*
Iglesia Evangélica Pentecostal de Chile	1933	I-3pL	x.u.N	1,680	400,000	400,000	571,000	1.43	*IEP. Ev Pentecostal Ch.* Split ex IMP. Many schisms. Missions in 5 nations. 109n,1j.
Iglesia Evangelica Presbiteriana en Chile	1943	P-Ref	xTT.T	15	600	1,500	1,090	-1.27	*National Presbyterian Ch.* Schism ex IPC. M=WPM(RPCES)(USA). HQ Quillota. 15f,1s.
Iglesia Evangelica Union Pentecostal		I-3pL	.....	100	8,000	1,430	11,400	0.05	*Pentecostal Evangelical Union Church.*
Iglesia Evangélica Universal	1940	I-3pL	..u.I	7	900	2,000	1,800	-0.42	*Universal Ev Ch.* Split ex CMA, in Concepción province. HQ Coronel. Mestizos.
Iglesia Evangélica Universal de Cristo	c1950	I-Hol	.....	2	100	300	300	0.00	*Universal Ev Church of Christ.* Split ex Iglesia Evangélica Universal. Mestizos.
Iglesia Hermanidad Pentecostal		I-3pL	.....	60	3,000	714	4,290	0.05	*Pentecostal Brotherhood Church.*
Iglesia La Voz de Cristo		I-3gL	.....	63	5,000	1,430	7,140	0.05	*Voice of Christ Church.*
Iglesia Luterana en Chile	1970	P-Lut	.....	10	6,000	17,000	12,000	-1.38	Lutheran Church in Chile.
Iglesia Luterana (Misuri)	1953	P-Lut	x....	3	200	115	400	5.11	M=Lutheran Ch, Missouri Synod (USA). Work begun at Valparaíso.
Iglesia Metodista Independiente	1950	I-3gL	.TT.T	5	400	1,000	1,000	0.00	*Independent Methodist Ch.* Schism ex Methodists. Mestizos.
Iglesia Metodista Nacional de Chile	1877	P-Met	VuV..	77	17,600	20,000	25,000	0.90	*Methodist Ch of Chile.* A=1969. M=UMC(USA). Many pentecostal splits. 44n,25f,4r,1u.
Iglesia Metodista Pentecostal de Chile	1909	I-3pL	..U.N	3,250	520,000	400,000	720,000	2.38	*IMP. Pentecostal Meth Ch.* Split ex Methodists; 20 schisms since. 1967, M=IPHC. 120n,1u.
Iglesia Mision Cristiana Pentecostal		I-3pL	.....	67	8,000	1,430	11,400	0.05	*Pentecostal Christian Mission Church.*
Iglesia Misión Pentecostal	1952	I-3pL	.Wu.N	109	24,000	25,000	34,300	1.27	*Misión Ev Pentecostal Chileana.* Ex IEP. Internal split 1971. In WCC 1961. 36n,1h,1p.
Iglesia Misión San Pablo	1942	I-3gL	.....	10	300	1,000	800	-0.89	*Church of St Paul's Mission.* Schism ex Iglesia Wesleyana Nacional Mestizos.
Iglesia Misionera de Cristo	1947	I-3gL	.....	3	500	1,500	1,000	-1.61	*Missionary Ch of Christ.* Schism ex Ejército Ev Nacional. Mestizos. Santiago area.
Iglesia Misionera Pentecostes	c1980	I-3pL	.....	53	4,200	–	6,000	6.67	*Missionary Church of Pentecostals.*
Iglesia Nueva Apostolica		I-3aX	x....	10	500	–	949	0.05	*New Apostolic Ch.* HQ Zurich (Switzerland).
Iglesia Orthodoxa Griega		O-Gre	Cwo..	7	7,100	15,000	13,000	0.05	Part of 10th Archdiocesan District, Greek Orthodox AD of N&S America. Greeks.
Iglesia Ortodoxa Russa	c1930	O-Rus	Mw...	1	250	500	625	0.90	*Russian Orthodox Ch.* Under Moscow Patriarchat. Russian immigrants. One bishop.
Iglesia Ortodoxa Russa: D Chile	c1940	I-Rus	x....	8	1,200	2,000	2,400	0.73	*Russian Orthodox Ch Outside of Russia* (HQ New York). Refugees. Ultra-conservative. 1e.
Iglesia Ortodoxa: D Santiago de Chile		O-Ara	Cwo..	3	2,700	3,000	4,090	0.05	Under Antiochian Orthodox Ch (USA), & Greek P Antioch. Arabs (Lebanese).
Iglesia Pentecostal Apostólica	1938	I-3aL	..u.N	41	24,500	20,000	35,000	2.26	*IPA. Apostolic Pentecostal Ch.* Schism ex IMP. Has itself suffered several splits.
Iglesia Pentecostal Apostolica de la Fe		I-3aL	.....	43	4,300	1,430	6,140	0.05	Apostolic Faith Pentecostal Church.
Iglesia Pentecostal Apostólica Libre	1943	I-3aL	..u.I	20	1,500	2,000	3,000	1.64	*Free Apostolic Pentecostal Ch.* Schism ex Iglesia Pentecostal Apostólica.
Iglesia Pentecostal de Chile	1946	I-3pL	ZWu.N	300	150,000	100,000	400,000	5.70	*IPC. Pentecostal Ch of Chile.* Schism ex IMP. 1961, joined WCC. 83n,2s,2459Y.
Iglesia Pentecostal de Chile Austral	1950	I-3pL	.....	200	18,000	20,000	27,000	1.21	*Pentecostal Ch of Southern Chile.* Schism ex IMP. Works with Iglesia Pentecostal de Chile.
Iglesia Pentecostal de la Trinidad	1965	I-3pL	.v...	313	25,000	20,000	35,700	2.34	*Pentecostal Ch of the Trinity.* Schism ex IPA. N&S Chile; also Argentina. HQ Temuco.
Iglesia Pentecostal Unida de Chile	1964	P-Pe1	x....	30	2,000	2,000	5,000	3.73	*United Pentecostal Ch. Jesus Only Church.* M=UPC(USA). HQ Santiago. 9n,2f.
Iglesia Pentecostal Evangélica Mision		I-3pL	.....	100	10,000	1,430	14,300	0.05	*Pentecostal Evangelical Mission Church.*
Iglesia Pentecoste Naciente		I-3pL	.....	1,500	120,000	4,290	171,000	0.05	*Pentecostal Church of New Birth.*
Iglesia Presbiteriana en Chile	1845	P-Ref	Rv...	129	4,500	10,000	15,000	1.64	*IPC. Presbyterian Ch of Chile.* M=UPUSA. A=1964. 1966 applied to join WCC. 18n,1u.
Iglesia Presbiteriana Fundamentalista	c1960	I-Fun	.TT.T	10	150	500	500	0.00	*Fundamentalist Presbyterian Ch.* Schism ex IPC. Mestizos. HQ Chillán.
Iglesia SIM	1986	P-Non	.....	1	15	–	21	11.11	M=Sudan Interior Mission(USA).
Iglesia Sionista	1945	I-Adv	.....	20	500	1,000	1,100	0.38	*Zionist Church. Cabañistas (Tabernaclers).* Ex SDA church. Old Testament customs.
Iglesia Unida Methodista Pentecostal		I-3pL	.....	245	49,000	10,000	70,000	0.05	*United Methodist Pentecostal Ch.* Split ex IMP and its own schisms.
Iglesia Unión de Centros Bíblicos	1923	I-Eva	.M...	333	5,000	3,000	7,140	3.53	*Union of Bible Centers.* M=Gospel Mission SA. 14n,45f,2h,1p,1s,W=75%,162Y.
Iglesia Unión Pentecostal El Templo		I-3pL	.....	138	11,000	2,860	15,700	0.05	*Temple Pentecostal Union Church.*
Iglesia Universal de Cristo	1938	I-3gL	.....	10	300	1,000	700	-1.42	*Universal Ch of Christ.* Ex Christian & Missionary Alliance Ch. HQ Curanilahue.
Iglesia Wesleyana Nacional	1928	I-3gL	..u.N	83	2,500	15,000	7,580	-2.69	*National Wesleyan Ch.* Members must be in trade unions and leftist politics. 1H.
Iglesias Cristianas	1949	I-Dis	x....	30	1,000	500	2,000	5.70	*Christian Chs & Chs of Christ.* M=CCCC(Instrumental) (USA). 10f.
Misión Cristiana Apostólica	1938	I-3aL	..u.N	107	16,000	500	22,900	16.53	*Apostolic Christian Mission.* Schism ex IMP. Mestizos. HQ Santiago.
Misión Cristiana, Igl Ev Pentecostal	1951	I-3pL	.....	2	150	200	250	0.90	*Christian Mission, Ev Pentecostal Ch.* Schism ex Methodists. Mestizos.
Mision Evangélica de America del Sur	1923	P-Eva	.....	70	5,600	6,000	9,330	1.78	M=Evangelical Mission of South America.
Sociedad de la Ciencia Cristiana	1937	m-Sci	x....	4	120	500	171	-4.20	*Ch of Christ, Scientist. Christian Science.* M=CCS (Boston, USA). In Santiago. 2w.
Sociedad Noruega de Evangelización	1948	P-Pe2	Z....	5	200	200	500	3.73	*Norwegian Society for Evangelism in Chile.* M=NPY(Norway). Radio ministry. 3n,2x.
Testigos de Jehová	1929	m-Jeh	x....	429	44,067	20,000	107,000	6.94	*Jehovah's Witnesses.* Begun 1929 by Argentina witnesses. (1975) 1141Y. (1995) 3495Y.
Unión de Iglesias Apostólicas		I-3aL	.....	138	11,000	4,290	15,700	0.05	*Union of Apostolic Churches.*
Unión Pentecostes de Iglesias Locales		I-3pL	.....	75	6,000	1,430	8,570	0.05	*Pentecost Union of Local Churches.*
Voz de Deserto	c1980	I-3oL	.....	300	40,000	–	70,000	6.67	*Voice in the Desert.* Oneness pentecostals.
Other Protestant denominations		P-	.....	60	4,000	5,000	10,000	0.05	Total about 20 (see list below).
Other independent charismatic chs	c1980	I-3gL	.....	900	300,000	–	500,000	6.67	Including Association of Vineyard Chs (3 chs).
Other indigenous pentecostal churches		I-3pL	.....	250	25,000	10,000	50,000	0.05	Total over 100 (see list below).
Other indigenous churches		I-	.....	50	2,000	3,000	5,000	0.05	Total about 30 (see list below).
Doubly-affiliated		2-aff			-1,733,000	-1,126,891	-2,856,563		Evangelicals who also are or were baptized Roman Catholics.
Totals				**22,738**	**7,572,240**	**8,345,000**	**12,480,000**		

Churches, members, growth, 1900-2025	*Congs*	*Adults*	*Affiliated*	*G%*	*Total denominations*	*O*	*R*	*A*	*P*	*I*	*m*
Total churches, members, and denominations (mid-1900)	2,300	1,663,000	2,833,410	1.56	9	0	1	1	7	0	0
Total churches, members, and denominations (mid-1970)	7,516	4,898,900	8,345,000	1.56	146	4	1	1	28	109	3
Total churches, members, and denominations (mid-1990)	20,000	6,977,000	11,500,000	1.62	154	4	1	1	40	105	3
Total churches, members, and denominations (mid-1995)	22,738	7,572,240	12,480,000	1.65	244	4	1	1	41	194	3
Total churches, members, and denominations (mid-2000)	23,000	8,105,000	13,358,340	1.37	252	5	1	1	42	200	3
Total churches, members, and denominations (mid-2025)	26,000	10,375,000	17,100,000	0.99	368	10	1	1	50	300	6

(*6 Megablocs:* O, R, A, P, I, m)

.NOTES ON TABLE ABOVE

NATIONAL COUNCILS (Column 4, 5th letter).

E = Confraternidad Evangelica de Chile (CEC) Evangelical Fellowship of Chile).

I = Unión de Misioners Pentecostales Libres (UMPL) (Union of Free Pentecostal Missions and Churches) (35 member smaller denominations, in 1975; affiliated to UNELAM and CWME/WCC).

N = Pentecostal Council of Chile

K = Confraternidad Cristiana de Iglesias (CCI, Christian Fellowship of Churches in Chile (CFCC).

R = Conferencia Episcopal de Chile (CECH) (Episcopal Conference of Chile).

T = Confederación Fundamentalista de Iglesias Evangélicas de Chile (CFEC or CIEF or DDIEF) (Confederation of Evangelical Fundamentalist Churches of Chile).

Other national councils. Nuevo Concilio Evangélico Nacional (New National Evangelical Council) (Holiness churches; pro-communist in 1972). Also, Concilio Evangélico Independiente (inactive).

OTHER INDIGENOUS PENTECOSTAL CHURCHES. The total of over 100 other distinct denominations begun by Chileans (mostly Mestizos, with some Indians), of which over 70 are legally registered, includes the following: Asociación Ev Metodista Pentecostal, Corporación Ev Pentecostal 'Neuvo Amanecer', Corporación Ev Universal de Cristo, Corporación Iglesia Ev Nacional Belén (1952), Corporación Iglesia Ev Pentecostal (1956), Corporación Iglesia Metodista Pentecostal, Corporación Iglesia Unida Metodista Pentecostal, Ejército Ev Pentecostal, Iglesia Apostólica Cristiana, Iglesia Apostólica Pentecostal (member of UMPL), Iglesia Cristiana, Iglesia Cristiana Ganada con su Sangre (1936), Iglesia Cristiana Pentecostal (1942), Iglesia Cristiana Universal, Iglesia de Dios en Cristo Jesús, Iglesia de Dios Mensajeros de Jesús, Iglesia del Señor Apostólica (1930), Iglesia del Se or de la Fe Apostólica (1953), Iglesia del Señor Jesús, Iglesia de Señor la cual El ganó con su Sangre (1941), Iglesia Embajadores de Cristo (1959), Iglesia Ev de la Nuevo Jerusalem (1957), Iglesia Ev de los Hermanos (1925), Iglesia Ev de los Hermanos Pentecostales, Iglesia Misión Apostólica Universal, Iglesia Misionera Pentecostal, Iglesia Obreros de Cristo, Iglesia Pentecostal de Cristo (member of UMPL), Iglesia Pentecostal el Pesebre Luz del Mundo, Iglesia Pentecostal Ev de Cristo, Iglesia Pentecostal Indus, Iglesia Pentecostal Somos de Cristo, Iglesia Wesleyana Pentecostal, Misión Cristiana Ev Pentecostal (1953), Misión Cristiana Pentecostal (1942), Misión Ev Misionera, Misión Iglesia de Señor, Movimiento Evangélico Nacional (1960), Templo de la Fe Apostólica del 7 Día (1946).

OTHER PROTESTANT DENOMINATIONS. These include: Baptist Bible Fellowship International (1955), Bible Methodist Missions, Ch of Christ (Non-Instrumental), Ch of Scotland, Ev Methodist Ch (1960), Exclusive Brethren (Kelly-Continental), Friends Ch (Oregon), Gospel Fellowship Missions, Hermanos de Dos en Dos (1936), Iglesia de Cristo (Kansas), Maranatha Baptist Mission (1963), World Baptist Fellowship Mission, World-Wide Missions (1970), Worldwide Evangelization Crusade (UK, USA, Germany). In 1975, 2 parishes seceded from the Evangelical Lutheran Ch in Chile and remain independent (2,100 members; Valparaiso, Puerto Montt).

OTHER INDIGENOUS NON-PENTECOSTAL CHURCHES. These include: Alianza Cristiana Nacional (1935), Asamblea Bíblica Bautista, Asamblea Biblica Misión Mundial (1965), Asamblea Cristiana (1950), Corporación Ev El Redentor Cristo, Iglesia Aliancista Nacional (1940), Iglesia Alianza Ev, Iglesia Bautista Libre, Iglesia Bautista Rural, Iglesia de Cristo, Iglesia de Oración Cristiana, Iglesia de Santidad, Iglesia Hebrea Cristiana, Iglesia Libre, Iglesia Presbiteriana Independiente (1962), Misión Comunidad del Señor, Sociedad Ev de Chile, Tabernaculo Bautista, Unión Cristiana Ev.

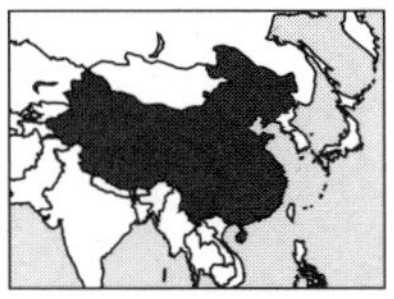

CHINA

SECULAR DATA, AD 2000

STATE
Official name: Zhonghua Renmin Gonghe Guo (The People's Republic of China).
Short name: China. **Adjective of nationality:** Chinese.
Flag: Red field, 5 gold stars.
Area: 9,572,900 sq. km. (3,696,100 sq. mi.).
Government: One-party Communist state, since 1949 (1644 Manchu dynasty, 1912 Republic of China, 1917 Nationalist China).
Legislature: National People's Congress, 2,978 members.
Official language: Chinese (Kuo yu).
Monetary unit: 1 Renminbi (yuan) (Y) = 10 jiao = 100 fen.
US$1= Y 8.28.
Chief cities: Shanghai (Shang-hai) 14,173,000; BEIJING (Pei-Ching, Peking) 12,033,000; Tianjin (Tientsin, T'ien-ching) 10,239,000; Hangzhou (Hangchow, Hang-chou) 6,389,000; Hong Kong (Xianggang) 6,097,000.
Political divisions: 33 provinces.
Armed forces: 2,930,000.

DEMOGRAPHY
Population: 1,262,557,000.
Population density: 131.8/sq. km. (341.5/sq. mi.).
Under 15 years: 313,493,000.
Growth rate p.a.: 0.75% (births 14.60, deaths 6.97).
Mortality: Infant, per 1,000: 36.0; **Maternal per 100,000:** 95.0.
Life expectancy: 71 (male 69, female 74).
Household size: 4.1. **Floor area per person, sq.m:** 10.0.
Major languages: Chinese (Mandarin, Northern, Western, Southern, and numerous other dialects), English, Tibetan, Uighur, Mongolian, Manchu, Korean, Japanese, Russian. In addition there are over 170 other languages.
Urban dwellers: 34.34%. **Urban growth rate p.a.:** 2.9%.
Labor force: 55%.

ETHNOLINGUISTIC PEOPLES
63.6% Han Chinese (Mandarin); 7.5% Han Chinese (Wu); 4.5% Han Chinese (Cantonese); 3.7% Han Chinese (Jinyu); 3.5% Han Chinese (Hunanese).

ECONOMY
National income p.a. per person: US$620; **per family:** US$2,542.

EDUCATION
Adult literacy: 81% (male 89%, female 72%). **Schools:** 953,807.
Universities: 1,065. **School enrolment:** female/male: 81%/91%.

HEALTH
Access to health services: 92%. **Access to safe water:** 90%.
Hospitals: 60,784 (24 beds per 10,000). **Doctors:** 1,832,000.
Blind: 2,000,000. **Deaf:** 75,234,000. **Murder rate:** <1.
Lepers: 3,500,000. **Underweight prevalence under 5:** 16%.

LITERATURE
New book titles p.a.: 116,160 (92 p.a. per million). **Periodicals:** 9,080. **Newspapers:** 38 dailies.

COMMUNICATION (per 1,000 people)
Phones: 34 (15% mobile). **Radios:** 178. **TV sets:** 247.
Daily newspaper circulation: 23. **Computers:** 10.

REFUGEES
Citizen refugees in other countries: 141,000.
Alien refugees from other countries: 294,100.

HUMAN LIFE AND LIBERTY (optimum condition=100.0%)
HDI: 62.6. **HSI:** 39.0. **HFI:** 5.0. **EFL:** 24.0.

Country Table 1. **Religious adherents in China, AD 1900-2025.**

Year	1900		1970		mid-1990		Annual change, 1990-2000				mid-1995		mid-2000		mid-2025	
Name	Adherents	%	Adherents	%	Adherents	%	Natural	Conversion	Total	Rate	Adherents	%	Adherents	%	Adherents	%
Nonreligious	30,000	0.0	391,007,650	47.7	488,036,100	42.8	5,193,618	-740,418	4,453,200	0.88	509,524,300	42.3	532,568,095	42.2	594,163,300	40.6
Chinese folk-religionists	376,293,800	79.7	217,368,000	26.5	325,804,770	28.6	3,467,186	-85,863	3,381,323	0.99	345,426,000	28.7	359,617,996	28.5	418,000,000	28.6
Buddhists	60,000,000	12.7	54,000,000	6.6	94,000,000	8.2	1,000,340	182,514	1,182,854	1.19	99,925,000	8.3	105,828,542	8.4	125,000,000	8.5
Atheists	1,000	0.0	95,000,000	11.6	97,400,000	8.5	1,036,522	-552,725	483,797	0.49	100,685,000	8.4	102,237,969	8.1	110,000,000	7.5
Christians	**1,670,000**	**0.4**	**1,515,000**	**0.2**	**64,864,000**	**5.7**	**690,277**	**1,728,878**	**2,419,155**	**3.22**	**78,500,000**	**6.5**	**89,055,551**	**7.1**	**135,190,000**	**9.2**
PROFESSION																
crypto-Christians	0	0.0	850,000	0.1	62,350,000	5.5	663,523	601,477	1,265,000	1.86	67,000,000	5.6	75,000,000	5.9	117,000,000	8.0
professing Christians	**1,670,000**	**0.4**	**665,000**	**0.1**	**2,514,000**	**0.2**	**26,754**	**1,127,401**	**1,154,155**	**18.78**	**11,500,000**	**1.0**	**14,055,551**	**1.1**	**18,190,000**	**1.2**
AFFILIATION																
unaffiliated Christians	160,000	0.0	28,677	0.0	59,800	0.0	636	3,404	4,040	5.30	69,569	0.0	100,204	0.0	126,000	0.0
affiliated Christians	**1,510,000**	**0.3**	**1,486,323**	**0.2**	**64,804,200**	**5.7**	**689,641**	**1,725,474**	**2,415,115**	**3.22**	**78,430,431**	**6.5**	**88,955,347**	**7.1**	**135,064,000**	**9.2**
Independents	1,000	0.0	848,063	0.1	58,000,000	5.1	617,231	1,653,604	2,270,835	3.36	70,880,016	5.9	80,708,347	6.4	120,000,000	8.2
Roman Catholics	1,100,000	0.2	383,227	0.1	6,200,000	0.5	65,980	64,020	130,000	1.92	6,872,115	0.6	7,500,000	0.6	14,000,000	1.0
Protestants	350,000	0.1	222,165	0.0	520,000	0.1	5,534	6,466	12,000	2.10	587,070	0.1	640,000	0.1	900,000	0.1
Orthodox	29,000	0.0	5,050	0.0	35,000	0.0	372	1,628	2,000	4.62	40,060	0.0	55,000	0.0	90,000	0.0
Marginal Christians	0	0.0	4,418	0.0	26,000	0.0	277	23	300	1.10	27,990	0.0	29,000	0.0	50,000	0.0
Anglicans	30,000	0.0	23,400	0.0	23,200	0.0	247	-267	-20	-0.09	23,180	0.0	23,000	0.0	24,000	0.0
Trans-megabloc groupings																
Evangelicals	270,000	0.1	330,000	0.0	2,050,000	0.2	21,816	25,334	47,150	2.09	2,440,291	0.2	2,521,500	0.2	4,400,000	0.3
Pentecostals/Charismatics	2,000	0.0	150,000	0.0	44,947,000	3.9	478,322	454,478	932,800	1.90	50,427,125	4.2	54,275,000	4.3	90,000,000	6.2
Great Commission Christians	**1,500,000**	**0.3**	**1,230,000**	**0.2**	**68,765,000**	**6.0**	**731,791**	**526,983**	**1,258,774**	**1.70**	**75,000,000**	**6.2**	**81,352,742**	**6.4**	**125,000,000**	**8.5**
Ethnoreligionists	9,924,050	2.1	40,000,000	4.9	53,000,000	4.6	564,021	-448,827	115,194	0.22	53,500,000	4.4	54,151,936	4.3	60,000,000	4.1
Muslims	24,000,000	5.1	21,000,000	2.6	18,200,000	1.6	193,683	-96,785	96,898	0.52	18,118,000	1.5	19,168,976	1.5	21,000,000	1.4
Taoists	75,000	0.0	200,000	0.0	325,000	0.0	3,459	53	3,512	1.03	340,000	0.0	360,122	0.0	500,000	0.0
New-Religionists	0	0.0	80,000	0.0	156,000	0.0	1,660	16,031	17,691	7.87	305,000	0.0	332,910	0.0	225,000	0.0
Hindus	3,000	0.0	12,500	0.0	15,300	0.0	163	-122	41	0.26	15,500	0.0	15,709	0.0	20,000	0.0
Baha'is	100	0.0	500	0.0	4,000	0.0	43	210	253	5.02	5,040	0.0	6,525	0.0	12,000	0.0
Spiritists	500	0.0	1,200	0.0	1,880	0.0	20	-16	4	0.21	1,900	0.0	1,919	0.0	3,000	0.0
Jews	900	0.0	900	0.0	900	0.0	10	-8	2	0.18	900	0.0	916	0.0	1,000	0.0
Sikhs	400	0.0	700	0.0	740	0.0	8	-5	3	0.33	750	0.0	765	0.0	900	0.0
Zoroastrians	200	0.0	500	0.0	550	0.0	6	-4	2	0.30	550	0.0	567	0.0	700	0.0
Confucianists	50	0.0	50	0.0	60	0.0	1	-1	0	0.49	60	0.0	63	0.0	100	0.0
Other religionists	1,000	0.0	8,000	0.0	10,700	0.0	114	-42	72	0.65	11,000	0.0	11,420	0.0	15,000	0.0
doubly-counted religionists	0	0.0	0	0.0	-700,000	-0.1	-7,449	-2,870	-10,319	1.38	-750,000	-0.1	-803,194	-0.1	-1,200,000	-0.1
World A (unevangelized persons)	387,040,000	82.0	656,155,666	80.0	536,326,400	47.0	5,707,519	-14,919,151	-9,211,632	-1.87	518,411,885	43.0	444,420,064	35.2	430,101,714	29.4
World B (evangelized non-Christians)	83,290,000	17.6	162,523,916	19.8	539,929,600	47.3	5,745,886	13,190,273	18,936,159	3.05	608,697,150	50.5	729,081,385	57.7	897,639,286	61.4
World C (Christians)	1,670,000	0.4	1,515,000	0.2	64,864,000	5.7	690,277	1,728,878	2,419,155	3.22	78,500,000	6.5	89,055,551	7.1	135,190,000	9.2
Country's population	**472,000,000**	**100.0**	**820,194,583**	**100.0**	**1,141,120,000**	**100.0**	**12,143,682**	**0**	**12,143,682**	**1.02**	**1,205,609,036**	**100.0**	**1,262,557,000**	**100.0**	**1,462,931,000**	**100.0**

COLUMNS, ROWS.
For meanings and definitions, see Codebook (Part 3). Note that, by definition, total 'Christians' = professing + crypto-Christians, which also = affiliated + unaffiliated Christians, and also = Great Commission Christians + latent Christians. Percentages may not always total exactly, due to rounding.

CENSUSES.
No question on religion has been asked in recent censuses.

NOTES ON RELIGIONS
AFFILIATED CHRISTIANS. From 1900, the membership of all churches rose rapidly. In 1949, churches' statistics of affiliation were: 3,266,000 Roman Catholics, 1,295,000 Protestants (600,000 being communicants) of whom 100,000 were Pentecostals, 440,000 Chinese indigenous (246,000 being communicants), 300,000 Orthodox (90% Russians, with some Chinese converts), and 76,741 baptized Anglicans. Under Communist rule after 1949, numbers were drastically and continuously eroded, although most of the decline had tapered off by 1970.
ANGLICANS. After 1950 the Anglican Church continued to exist only in its own eyes, but not in the eyes of the state for whom it had ceased to exist as a separate entity and operated only through the Three-Self Reform Movement.
ATHEISTS. Chinese Communist Party (CCP) (Chung-kuo Kung Ch'an Tang) (in power since 1949): membership rose from 4.5 million (1949) to 10,750,000 (1956), to 17 million (1961) and to 35 million by 1977. Youth membership: many million Little Red Guards (aged 7-12), several million in the Young Pioneer Corps (Red Scarves; primary schoolchildren), 20 million teenagers aged 14-25 in the Young Communist League (in 1956), and (1967) over 11 million militantly anti-religious Red Guards. More than in other Communist countries, in China atheism, Communism and the cult of Mao have been developed into a secular quasi-religion. By 1968, more than 1,000 million copies of Mao's writings had been distributed. Three decades later all this had collapsed de facto.
BAHA'IS. Operating largely underground, Baha'i is now spreading rapidly in large cities through the use of Baha'i missionaries as tentmakers working in secular jobs.
BUDDHISTS. In 1900, most of the 60 million Buddhists (Mahayana, with 2 million Tibetan Lamaists) also accepted Chinese folk religion to a large extent. Since 1949, large numbers of Buddhists have become nonreligious, although it is thought that at least 40 million conscientious devotees still remain, as well as numerous seasonal or occasional supporters. The one million Buddhists in Tibet (introduced AD 640) follow Lamaism (Tantrayana) and have been more ruthlessly secularized than other Buddhists; by 1976 less than a dozen of Tibet's former 5,000 monasteries were functioning, no new monks were being recruited, and the practice of Buddhism had virtually disappeared. In 1978 there were only 300 practicing monks in Tibet compared to over 100,000 in 1950. Even by 1998 there was little change for the better, but Buddhism and its Tibetan protagonists were clearly if slowly winning this struggle.
CHINESE FOLK-RELIGIONISTS. In 1900, four-fifths of the population adhered to Chinese folk religion, a mixture of Confucian ethics, ancestor veneration, local divinities and deified heroes (some Taoist), popular religious beliefs and practices, and some Buddhist elements; also, about 10% of folk-religionists regarded themselves as Taoists. After 1949, militant communist teaching and action resulted in most village temples being secularized, and vast numbers of rural folk-religionists became nonreligious (estimated above at almost 5 million a year since 1970).
COUNTRY'S POPULATION. During the purges from 1949 to the present day, an estimated 15 million persons were killed and 40 million others imprisoned in labor camps, including a sizeable proportion of all Christians. In 1976, vast numbers were killed in earthquakes, 655,237 alone in the northern city of Tangshan. Overall, these disasters have resulted in today's radically changed situation with regard to the relative fortunes of religions versus militant atheism.
CRYPTO-CHRISTIANS. Although there is no highly-organized underground church, most Christians remain invisible keeping their faith and activities private. Only very occasional glimpses of this activity have been evident. In 1955 authorities discovered 200 physically-underground Catholic churches in the province of Hopei; and 20 years later, mass baptisms of up to 100 youths at a time were being reported from remote areas. Up to 1998, the regime has maintained the fiction of there being only 5 million or so professing Christians in China, which merely leads to the other 75 million being described in the table above as crypto-Christians.
ETHNORELIGIONISTS. A number of hill tribes on the southern borders of China remain mainly animists; these include the Lisu and Yao. The Lolo in southern Yunnan have shamanistic practices; also the Moso or Na-khi (Tibeto-Burmese in southwest China) and the Monguor or T'u-jen of Sining (northwest China). Since 1960 extensive efforts to secularize them all through schools and party structure have been under way. However, the failure of this attempt has permitted vast numbers of former animists and polytheists to practice their former tribal religions again.
INDEPENDENTS. From 1906 onwards a number of new indigenous denominations were begun by Chinese, sometimes as secessions from Western mission churches. In 1949 the 440,000 total community were found in over 30 indigenous denominations. They were subsequently persecuted and suppressed far more than were Western churches; but in 1968 they were observed to be still constituting a more effective Christian witness than the Western-originated denominations. From 1976 these independent movements mushroomed explosively (see details in Country Table 2). The 2 largest traditionally indigenous bodies, Assembly Hall Churches (Little Flock) and the True Jesus Church, each had in 1997 well over a million members in mainland China. They were dwarfed however by the massive house church movements with over 40 million followers and by the 3 Catholic groupings with well over 10 million.
MUSLIMS. Primarily Sunnis (of the Hanafite rite), with some Shias (Tajiks). Mainly-Muslim peoples: Hui (Dungan), Uighurs, Kazakhs, Kirgiz, Uzbeks, Tatars, Tunghsiang, Paoans, Salars. In June 1975, an attempt to suppress Islam among the Hui met with violent resistance and troops arrested 500 Hui.
NOMINAL CHRISTIANS. European expatriates.
NONRELIGIOUS. As a result of a massive anti-religious program of secularization from 1949-1970, something over half of the population became indifferent to religion. However, the initial momen-

Continued overleaf

Country Table 1–concluded

tum slowed considerably by 1970, and resistance on the part of remaining religionists of all kinds increased up to today's revival of religions.
PENTECOSTALS/CHARISMATICS. Virtually all the 50 million in renewal are Independents (Postdenominationalists, Third-Wavers). The Catholic Charismatic Renewal is half in the Vatican-recognized church and half Independent. A 1993 visit from overseas Chinese resulted in thousands of new Charismatics. With the acquisition of Hong Kong in July 1997, 6,000 zealous El Shaddai (CCR) members were added.

Great Commission Instrument Panel: status of China (for explanation see start of Part 4)

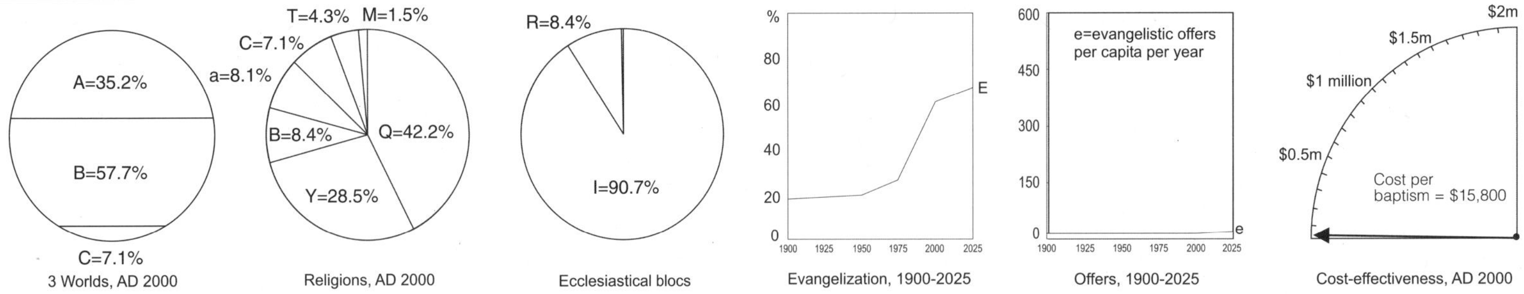

Country status. China is the most populous nation in the world, accounting for one in every 5 human beings. Once known as the Celestial Kingdom, China has evolved a unique culture and society that has had a dominant influence throughout East Asia. Its economy is essentially agricultural making it the world's largest producer of many crops including rice, millet, barley, tea, and potatoes.

HUMAN LIFE AND LIBERTY

Human need and development. In terms of its size and population, China properly ranks among the great nations of the world. Yet, in modern times, it has had a troubled political history and a very mixed economic record. Its enormous population, the first in the world to cross the one billion mark, is both a blessing and a burden.The Chinese are essentially hardworking, conservative, respectful of authority, and frugal. But these qualities have not been mobilized in a meaningful way by China's rulers. Wars and political turmoil have dominated China's 20th century history, so that only haphazard efforts have been directed toward creating a solid economic and industrial base or in improving the quality of life. Nevertheless, significant progress has been achieved under the Communist regime which began shortly after World War II. China has had no famine since World War II except for a brief period in the 1960s. Although living standards are low in comparison with developed countries, desperate poverty and extreme inequalities in the distribution of wealth have been eliminated. Through mass public health and sanitation campaigns, the nation's health has been brought up to par. The average life expectancy has risen to 71 years and the infant mortality rate is among the lowest in Asia at 3.6%. Once among the most illiterate of countries, China has reduced its illiteracy rate to 19%. Through draconian family planning decrees the rate of population growth has been brought down to levels close to those of developed countries. Especially after Deng's economic reforms, a wide range of modern goods and services are available to every Chinese. However, China still lags behind in many respects. There is a wide variance in the living standards between rural areas-where the bulk of China's population is concentrated—and the cities. While basic consumer needs are met, few have anything beyond the basics, and very few can claim any luxury. Despite the construction of millions of new homes, housing is inadequate, and many urban apartments have communal facilities and cramped quarters. Most peasants live in traditional mud houses and, in some regions, in caves or tents. Erratic agricultural policies have resulted in some types of food being more available than others, and all of them are more expensive than they were under the austere Mao regime. Cotton clothing is scarcer than rayon or synthetic clothing. Because families have become smaller than before, and in most cases all members of a family work, the amount of family disposable income has risen, although in most cases savings are spent on the purchase of consumer durables, such as television sets, cameras, washing machines and tape recorders.

Human rights and freedoms. China remains a one-party Communist state with all the negative human rights implications of such a regime. Although party control over the state and the economy has been lessening, there is no tolerance of ideological deviation from Marxism or Maoism. There are no legal or constitutional restraints on the feared security system, composed primarily of the Ministries of State Security and Public Security. The legal system is designed to protect the state rather than the individual citizen. The number of political prisoners is a state secret, but is believed to be in the thousands. Physical abuse, including torture by police and prison officials, continues in politically restive areas, like Tibet. International human rights watchdog groups report a dozen extrajudicial killings in police custody every year. Because the legal system insists on confessions as the basis for convictions, detainees are generally tortured until they submit a confession as required by the police. However, international pressure has forced the Chinese government in recent years to discourage torture as a means of eliciting confessions. Conditions in penal institutions are generally harsh and degrading. Some prisoners are sent to factories and labor camps under the notorious 'reeducation through labor' program. Arbitrary arrest and detention is the rule rather than the exception. Public security officials often circumvent the constitutional proscription of arbitrary arrest, through mechanisms not requiring procuratorial assent, such as 'taking in for shelter and investigation' and 'supervised residence'. According to the Chinese media, more than one million persons are detained annually under these 2 provisions. Sometimes persons are detained as a means of intimidation. In many cases, the family of the detainee is not informed, and the length of the detention is indefinite. The judiciary, subject to party directives, often ignores due process in hearing political cases. The accused are given no opportunity to prepare a defense in the pretrial process, and defense lawyers may be retained only 7 days before the trial. The accused is presumed guilty and trials are essentially sentencing hearings. Conviction rates average 99%. Even those who are released are presumed to have a criminal record. Defense attorneys are generally reluctant to contest a case, their function is confined to requesting clemency. Authorities extensively monitor and regulate personal and family life, especially in the cities, where everything from food, housing, clothing, employment, permission to marry and have more than one child, and passport require government approval. Mail is frequently opened and censored and phone conversations are recorded. Demonstrations are banned by the authorities, who fear a recurrence of Tiananmen. The media remain under government control, although a lively private tabloid sector raises government hackles occasionally. There are no independent human rights organizations. Public criticism of the government's human rights record can be interpreted as counterrevolutionary activity and punished accordingly. There is no official policy of discrimination against women or ethnic minorities; nevertheless, both groups suffer many de facto disabilities.

Human environment. The accelerated economic development of China by Mao's successors has resulted in the rapid deterioration of its natural resources. The large-scale use of coal as the prime source of industrial energy is the prime cause of air pollution. In some regions industrial smog is so bad that visibility is limited to 40 or 50 yards for about half the year. The state-run factories are also major water polluters. About 50% of the population do not have access to safe water, and some regions have permanent water shortage. Deforestation has reduced the area under forest to less than 300 million acres and forced China to import wood. In the late 1970s, China began planting a shelterbelt of trees, known as the Great Green Wall of China. In order to avert an impending environmental disaster, the government passed a comprehensive Environmental Protection Law in 1979 setting aside protected areas. Currently there are 179 protected areas covering 20 million acres.

NON-CHRISTIAN RELIGIONS

Atheism and ***agnosticism*** are now the majority philosophies of modern Chinese. The former Chinese folk religion has been drastically undermined since 1949 as a result of massive anti-religious programs of secularization and indoctrination.

Chinese folk religion is a complex amalgam of 6 elements: ancestor veneration, which is accorded a place in Confucian tradition; Confucian ethics; devotion to local divinities and deified heroes, some of which are Taoist; Chinese universism; some Buddhist elements; and a whole series of practices related to fortune-telling, divination, magic, and sorcery. The government labels this amalgam 'superstition', and a serious effort has been made to rid the masses of their folk rituals. Since the Cultural Revolution from 1966-69, most local shrines have been closed and such traditional worship paraphernalia as joss stocks can no longer be purchased. Attempts have also been made to alter traditional religious practices relating to marriage, burial, and the celebration of national festivals. Folk religion is the most elusive of all China's religions. Although its communal elements have been suppressed, its individual and family aspects continue to hold wide sway over the masses.

Taoism is a system so closely interwoven with folk religion that it is difficult to distinguish one from the other. Some 10% of folk-religionists in the past professed to be also Taoists. Since 1949 they have been accused of being counter-revolutionaries fostering feudalistic and superstitious ideas among the population, but Taoism's lack of centralized organization makes it almost as difficult to suppress as folk religion. In an effort to gain control of the movement, in 1953 the government formed the Chinese Taoist Association. Its purpose was to encourage Taoists 'to continue and develop the beautiful tradition of Taoism so that under the direction of the popular government they might love their nation and actively support the building of socialism in the country'. However, the association has never played an important role, and has not been heard of since 1966. Like other religions, Taoism suffered through the closure of shrines and destruction of religious objects during the Cultural Revolution.

Confucianism is not properly speaking a separate religion but is an ethical system which makes its influence felt on all religion and also on those who claim no religious allegiance. Confucius teachings have been labeled feudalistic by the Party and stated to be contrary to the doctrines of Mao Tse-tung. In 1966, Red Guards initiated a campaign to condemn and burn the writings of Confucius and destroyed a temple built in his honor at his birthplace in Shantung province. An even wider anti-Confucian campaign was launched in August 1973.

Country summary. **Worlds A, B, C by ethnolinguistic peoples, cities, and major civil divisions in China.**

World	PEOPLES Num	Pop 2000	C%	Christians	E%	U%	Unevangelized
A	188	208,982,199	3.13	6,535,568	40	60	124,766,990
B	44	1,052,649,396	7.76	81,670,517	70	30	319,441,340
C	22	925,203	80.98	749,270	100	0	1,759
Total	**254**	**1,262,556,798**	**7.05**	**88,955,355**	**65**	**35**	**444,210,089**

World	CITIES Num	Pop 2000	C%	Christians	E%	U%	Unevangelized
A	21	9,649,949	0.59	56,964	38	62	5,948,201
B	470	319,995,628	6.88	22,011,370	65	35	112,648,125
C	0	0	0.00	0	0	0	0
Total	**491**	**329,645,577**	**6.69**	**22,068,334**	**64**	**36**	**118,596,326**

World	CIVIL DIVISIONS Num	Pop 2000	C%	Christians	E%	U%	Unevangelized
A	2	19,815,955	0.27	54,445	38	62	12,277,024
B	31	1,242,740,832	7.15	88,900,902	65	35	431,933,058
C	0	0	0.00	0	0	0	0
Total	**33**	**1,262,556,787**	**7.05**	**88,955,347**	**65**	**35**	**444,210,082**

Maoism as a quasi-religion. Six members of 11 million militantly anti-religious Red Guards (1966-69 Cultural Revolution) pause near Canton to read from Chairman Mao's *Thoughts* before moving into action against churches and Christians. These 6 are from Mao's birthplace.

Mahayana Buddhism was introduced into China from central Asia in the 1st century AD under the dynasty of Ha. Its principal expansion took place during the Tang Dynasty, from 618-906. Although there were around 60 million Buddhists in 1900, the number had fallen to about 50 million by 1970 through large numbers abandoning religion and religious profession. In Tibet, the form of Buddhism known as Lamaism or Tantrism (Tantrayana) was held by its one million people until Chinese armies occupied Tibet in 1950; therefore, religion was virtually exterminated, over 1,000 monasteries were destroyed, many priests killed and 90% of all lamas were secularized. However, under Communist rule, a Chinese Buddhist Association was started in 1953. Among its honorary presidents originally were the Dalai Lama and the Panchen Lama, and its president was Shirob Jaltso, a Tibetan, who was then vice governor of the province of Tsinghai. All its former leaders have been in disgrace since the beginning of the Cultural Revolution and Red Guard activities. At the end of 1972, the association was revived, although Buddhism as a cultural expression has nearly disappeared. A certain number of monasteries remain active in various parts of China, but many others have been taken over for secular purposes or made into museums. In general, those still functioning seem to be more or less cut off from the people in spite of the attempt by monks to combine their monastic life with productive work outside the monasteries. The existing Buddhists presence in Peking is due at least in part to the desire of the government to create and maintain good contacts with friendly Buddhist nations and foreign delegations visiting the Chinese capital. In 1974, the director of the Buddhist Association of China, Chao Puchu, was invited to an official banquet given in honor of personalities visiting Peking from nearby Buddhist countries, including Japan and Sri Lanka.

Muslims. Most Kazakhs are Hanafi Sunnis, with Sufi influence.

Islam came to China during the Tang dynasty through the silk trade and southeastern ports, but it did not grow extensively until the founding of the Yuan dynasty in 1260. Statistical estimates of adherents range from 48 million, claimed by Muslim sources, to 10 million, as stated by a Chinese Communist source in 1953. A probable figure for 1970 is 20 million. Islam is the predominant religion of 10 ethnic minorities: Hui (3.9 million in 1961), found in all the provinces but dominant in the Nigshia region; Uighurs (3.9 million in 1961), concentrated in the Uighur region of Sinkiang (Chinese Turkestan); Kazakhs (533,000 in 1961), who are located especially northeast of Sinkiang; and seven other groups of less importance (Kirgiz, Tajiks, Uzbeks, Tatars, Tungsiang, Paoans, and Salars). Chinese Muslims are primarily Sunnis, but the Tajiks are Shias. Of all the organized religions, Islam seems to have suffered the least under the Cultural Revolution. It is true that imams and practicing Muslims were imprisoned, most of their centers were closed and a Revolutionary Group for the Abolition of Islam was organized. But of greater significance was the reopening of a mosque to serve diplomats in Peking in January 1967. In 1968, 2 other mosques were opened, in Peking and Shanghai. At the end of 1969, the Hui were again allowed to celebrate Islamic events in several areas. On 17 February 1970, Corban (Eid el Seghir) was solemnly celebrated at the Tan Szu mosque in Peking. The Chinese Islamic Association created in 1953 was revived in 1969, but its former president Burhan Shahidi has not been heard of since 1964. By 1975, mosques had been opened in several other large cities.

Animism is still the predominant belief of the Lisu, Yao and other minority tribal groups inhabiting the mountainous areas of southwest China, despite extensive secularization campaigns among them.

CHRISTIANITY

The first Christian missionary known to have entered China was the Nestorian Alopen from Syria who arrived in Sian the Tang capital in AD 635. A Nestorian monument erected outside Sian in AD 781 was excavated in 1625. However, the so-called Luminous Religion faded and was finally wiped out in 845. Nestorian missionaries returned in the 13th century but with no lasting result.

CATHOLIC CHURCH. The first Franciscan missionary visited Peking in 1294 and later claimed 6,000 converts, but Catholicism did not take root until the arrival of the pioneer missionary Matteo Ricci at the end of the 16th century. When Mao Tse-tung came to power in 1949, the Catholic Church had 3,251,347 baptized faithful and 190,850 catechumens, 144 ecclesiastical jurisdictions (20 archdioceses, 90 dioceses, 33 prefectures and an apostolic exarchate of the Byzantine rite) and a large number of education and medical institutions (1,849 primary schools, 202 secondary schools, 3 universities, 194 hospitals and hostels, 6 leprosariums, 257 orphanages and 864 dispensaries, together with 29 presses and 55 periodicals). There were then 2,542 Chinese and 3,046 foreign priests, 803 major seminarians, 663 Chinese and 414 foreign brothers, 4,717 Chinese and 2,036 foreign religious women. Chinese clergy, 45% of the total, directed 35 ecclesiastical jurisdictions (25% of the total); the rest were confined to 27 European and North American missionary orders. Between 3 November 1949 and 20 September 1955, the Holy See nominated 50 bishops, Chinese and foreign. In 1951, the government closed the Catholic Central Bureau, expelled the nuncio and nationalized all medical and educational institutions with the exception of a school for diplomats' children in Peking run by 14 Franciscan Missionaries of Mary until 1966, when they also were expelled. At the end of 1951, remaining foreign missionaries were arrested or expelled; several Chinese priests also were arrested. The Vatican several times condemned the government-created Three Autonomies corresponding to the Protestant Three-Self Movement (self-support, self-government, self-propagation). By 1952, Taiwan had been recognized by the Holy See and the expelled nuncio designated pro-nuncio in Taipei, and so the rupture between Rome and Peking had become total. In July 1957, the National Patriotic Catholic Association was created on the mainland, directed by the Catholic archbishop of Shenyang (Mukden). Between 1957

Catholic Church in China. Exterior of Catholic Cathedral in Shanghai, with (*top*) interior.

and 1963, a Constitutional Church was developed, followed by the election and consecration of 45 Chinese bishops. These are considered by Rome to be valid but illicit and therefore unacceptable. During the Cultural Revolution, all traces of the visible church, including the Constitutional Church, were obliterated. By 1975, the number of Chinese clergy had been reduced to between 450 and 650, due to emigration, deaths, numerous arrests, sentencing of clergy to forced labor and also the small number of new ordinations. In 1975, however, it was reported that there were still 123 known Jesuit priests in China.

Since 1970, the government has shown signs of a relaxation in its attitude towards the church. In July 1970, it released bishop Walsh, the last foreign bishop still imprisoned in China, and authorized the recommencing of religious services at the Church of the Immaculate Conception (also called Church of the South or Nan Tang) in Peking, a church which has been attended by foreign travelers since November 1971 and which has provided an opportunity for Westerners to meet a handful of priests in Peking. Catholic services in Peking are held only in the Nan Tang Church, where they are led by 4 priests, including bishop Wang Ki-ting (who is not recognized by the Vatican) and the vice president of the Patriotic Committee of the Catholic Church in Peking, Tien Sun. Mass is said in Latin according to the pre-Vatican II liturgy. Those in attendance are for the most part foreigners: diplomats, African students, and visitors. The first public religious marriage, of a French couple, was celebrated in September 1974. By June 1975, no visitors had yet been invited to participate in Catholic services outside Peking. Since November 1971, several interviews with foreign travelers have been given by the bishop of Peking and also by a group consisting of 3 priests. From these interviews, it has been learned that the last ordination in People's China took place in 1963, which confirms the testimony of a Mexican priest as early as 1965 that he had met this new priests. The last 2 major seminaries, Peking and Shanghai, were closed in 1954 and 1955 respectively. These interviews have also revealed that the number of Catholics affiliated to the National Patriotic Catholic Association is estimated by them to be about 2 million. Sources outside China tend to estimate a more drastic erosion by two-thirds since 1949 to 1.2 million by 1970. The number of Chinese Catholics in Peking is likewise stated to be between 5,000 and 6,000, with 20 priests, 30 sisters and 20 seminary students who are following a 15-year training program under the direction of 5 or 6 full-time priests. Younger sisters work in hospitals while older ones have dedicated themselves to prayer in a retirement home. Information has also been obtained that there is a bishop for every region in China, each 'democratically elected', although none has yet been seen by foreigners.

In subsequent years Catholics found they were being given the choice of belonging to 3 rival Catholic Churches (details are given in Country Table 2). Most Catholics responded by attending whatever and wherever it suited them, in any of the three.

The Holy See has no diplomatic relations with China in AD 2000.

PROTESTANT AND ANGLICAN CHURCHES. Protestant missionary work in China began with the arrival of Robert Morrison of the London Missionary Society in 1807. Under difficult, often hostile conditions, his major contribution was in the field of Bible translation. The American Board of Commissioners for Foreign Missions next sent the first medical missionary to China. Over the years, medicine became one of the major areas of service by the churches. Mission work received an impetus following the Opium War, when in 1842 China was forced to open its doors to both opium and foreign residents, including missionaries. Anglican missions began with separate work by 4 English, one Canadian, one American and one Australian, missionary bodies. Shanghai soon became the headquarters of missionary societies from all over the world. Baptist, Methodist, Presbyterian, and Lutheran missions from the USA were at work, in addition to numerous European societies. The China Inland Mission under Hudson Taylor, beginning in 1865, grew to be the largest mission in China (with over 1,000 missionaries in 1914) and became a model for the faith missions approach. Its missionaries adopted Chinese dress and customs, concentrated on small inland cities and towns, constructed 330 mission stations and thousands of out-stations and eventually built up a self-supporting church of 85,000 members.

New missions continued to enter, and by 1907, there were 94 Protestant mission societies with 3,445 missionaries at 632 stations, 166 hospitals, and 389 post-primary schools. Anti-foreigner agitation gradually increased, and the Boxer (League of Righteous Fists) rebellion of 1900, which resulted in the death of 189 Protestant missionaries and their families, was the largest of such demonstrations. During the following decade, more numerical progress was made than in the previous half century. In 1914, there were 543 Protestant high schools, 33 colleges, 265 hospitals, 386 dispensaries, 411 medial doctors, and over 6 million Scriptures were distributed annually. In 1911, the Manchu dynasty fell, and a Christian, Sun Yat-sen, became the leader of the new republic. At the climax of the missionary era (1926), there were 160 Protestant missionary societies in China with over 8,000 missionaries. Pentecostal missions began in China with the entry of British Assemblies of God into Yunnan in 1911. Various marginal Protestant missions also arrived. Jehovah's Witnesses were begun in Shanghai in 1929 by a Japanese, and a branch office was opened in 1932. Although the number of Protestant Christians never rose about 0.2% of the population, in the 1930s, 35% of the Chinese elite had received Christian education, 90% of all nurses were Christians and 70% of all hospitals were mission institutions. The vast amount of mission property and money attracted roaming bandits, and 29 Protestant missionaries were killed and 80 kidnapped between 1924 and 1935.

In 1922, the National Christian Council of China was created, including a home missionary society controlled and supported by Chinese churches. Church union discussions made a certain amount of progress. In 1927, the Church of Christ in China was formed and held its first assembly in Shanghai, uniting 7 denominations.

In the 1930s, Japan was invading China. Many missionaries remained during the Japanese occupation, but after the Japanese attack on Pearl Harbor in 1941, there were imprisoned or fled. After World War II, 4,000 Protestant missionaries returned to China, but they were not to remain long. At the time of the Communist victory in 1949, Protestants numbered 1,295,000 adherents in about 270 denominations, and Anglicans 76,741 in 14 dioceses, with 13 universities and many secondary schools. In 1950, the Christian Manifesto was published, signed by 1,527 church leaders and eventually by 400,000 Christians. It recognized the contributions of missionaries but attacked their association with imperialism. It was announced that Article 88 of China's constitution guaranteeing freedom of religion would not be honored until the church had freed itself of all signs of imperialism. During the next year, almost all missionaries were expelled from China. The Three-Self Reform Movement followed in 1951, led by the YMCA executive Y.T. Wu, which set itself the task of helping churches to rid themselves of imperialism, feudalism, and bourgeois thinking. This was carried out through denunciation meetings, with attacks on both former missionaries and Chinese church leaders and through study sessions concerning Communist doctrine. Many churches succeeded in meeting these requirements and were permitted to continue Sunday morning services.

In the period prior to 1966, Christians were relatively free to worship, but national denominational structures were bypassed and fell into disuse as the Three-Self Reform Movement (or Chinese Christian Three-Self Patriotic Church) and the National Patriotic Catholic Association were organized under the government's Bureau of Religious Affairs. While official government policy tolerated freedom of religious belief, the activities of the churches were increasingly curtailed. The numerous seminaries were consolidated until there was only one, at Nanking, which was itself closed in 1966. Many local churches were closed in a consolidation movement beginning in 1958. In Peking, where there had been 65 Protestant churches the previous year, only 4 remained open by the end of the year. In rural areas, village churches disappeared throughout the land. Members of widely disparate denominations were forced either to worship together or not at all. In 1964, it became illegal to teach religion to children under 18 years of age.

With the outbreak of the Great Proletarian Cultural Revolution in August 1966, a spontaneous attack led by Red Guard youth groups was directed against all visible forms of religion as part of their assault on the 'Four olds' (old habits, old customs, old ideas, old culture). Buddhist temples and Muslim mosques were closed, sacked or converted to secular use. Individual believers lost Bibles and all religious literature. No communications from church leaders were received by the outside world during 1966-69, neither was any official pronouncement made for or against the attack on religion, nor was Article 88 of the constitution revoked.

From 1976 onward virtually all churches grew by leaps and bounds, reaching nearly 80 million by 1995 with the same rapid growth showing no signs of abating.

INDIGENOUS CHURCHES. The first major indigenous quasi-Christian movement was the God Worshippers Society (Pai Shang-ti Hui) begun in 1847 under a visionary, Hung Hsiu-ch'uan, among impoverished peasants in Kwangsi. In 1851, Hung proclaimed a new dynasty, the Heavenly Kingdom of Great Peace (T'ai P'ing T'ien Kuo). Originally religious and nonviolent, it eventually became militant, with one million zealous soldiers. It also became syncretistic, with the addition of Confucian, Buddhist and Taoist elements. Land reforms were included in its program and tens of thousands of peasants joined the march of the Taipings to establish their kingdom. Some 35 million were killed during the 17 years before it was finally suppressed in 1868.

Han Chinese Three-Self Churches. Grace Church in Shanghai is a fabled registered church with huge attendance, vibrant services, and renowned preachers.

Independents. Many house churches, as here, have introduced the ancient practice of foot-washing.

From the 1880s, attempts began to found a Chinese church separate from Western missionary control. The missions gave little ground, and so from 1906 onwards, groups of Chinese Christians began to break off from the Western foreign missions and found indigenous self-supporting churches, developing their own high-successful evangelistic outreach. Their numbers increased rapidly, and by 1949, there were 440,000 adherents in 30 or more denominations, including (in order of size) True Jesus Church (125,000, begun 1917 by separation from the Apostolic Faith Movement), Little Flock or Assembly Hall Churches (70,000, begun 1926 by Watchman Nee), China Jesus Independent church (30,000, begun 1906), China Christian Independent Church (begun 1912), Jesus Family (6,000 adults in 141 communal societies, begun 1921). Although such churches were completely Chinese in leadership and outlook, they were among the first to be persecuted and suppressed after 1949. Watchman Nee himself was sentenced to 15 years in prison where he died in 1972. And at least one body, the Jesus Family, is thought to have been wiped out completely by 1955. Nevertheless, there is evidence that indigenous churches are continuing to exist and even expanding underground.

ORTHODOX CHURCH. Russian Orthodox chaplains accompanied cossacks to Peking in 1686, and an Orthodox mission was set up there in 1715. Large-scale missionary work began about 1900, and by 1914, there were 5,000 Chinese converts, with Chinese priests and a seminary. This activity increased considerably after the Russian revolution of 1917, with many Russian clergy fleeing from Siberia to China. By 1939, there were 200,000 Orthodox in China and Manchuria (mostly Russians) with 5 bishops and an Orthodox university at Harbin. In 1949, the diocese in Manchuria had 100,000 faithful, mainly White Russian refugees, 60 parishes, 200 priests, 2 monasteries and a seminary. The rest of China had 150 parishes and 200,000 parishioners. But with the coming of the Chinese Communists to power, Orthodoxy fared no better than the rest of the churches, and Russian bishops, clergy, and laity were expelled. In 1955, there were only 30 Russians priests left. By 1957, the Orthodox Church had become entirely Chinese, an autonomous church loosely related to the Moscow Patriarchate, with 20,000 faithful and 2 bishops (Shanghai, Peking).

MARGINAL CHURCHES. These have had virtually no impact on China. Jehovah's Witnesses began in 1883 with a former Presbyterian missionary, had their first baptism of 2 Chinese in 1931, had only 13 members in 1939 and were finally completely suppressed in 1958.

Renewal movements. In the 1990s the Pentecostal/Charismatic Renewal continued to spread rapidly across most older churches, and numbered over 54,275,000 adherents (of whom 0% Pentecostals, 1% Charismatics, and 99% Independents).

Indigenous missions. Chinese Christians, unable to leave their homeland, have begun to express their missions commitment by reaching out to less reached ethnic groups in China. Whether this means Lisu evangelists among the peoples of the South or Han businessmen in the Northwest frontier, new mission initiatives are resulting in the penetration of previously unreached peoples.

CHURCH AND STATE

The constitution of 17 January 1975, which contains only 30 articles, stipulates in Article 28 'Citizens . . have the freedom to practice a religion, the freedom to not practice a religion and to propagate atheism'. The earlier constitution of 1954, in Article 88, limited itself to affirming freedom of religious belief: 'Citizens of the People's Republic of China enjoy freedom of religious belief'. The addition of freedom to propagate atheism is a direct consequence of the Cultural Revolution of 1966-69. In fact, the Party always interpreted the 1954 Article 88 to mean also freedom to oppose religion. Article 87 of the 1954 constitution provided for freedom of speech, press, assembly, association, procession and demonstrations. But whereas these freedoms are applied to religious bodies only within church and temple buildings, atheism has the right to propagate its doctrines throughout society's public domain. The government's position is that all religion has its basis in class oppression and fear of natural forces. Socialism will thus automatically undermine its appeal. As if by a natural law of development, freedom of religious belief, combined with education, will result ultimately in the destruction of religion. Religious associations formed under government pressure in the early 1950s are considered 'organizations of the masses' and are regulated by the Bureau of Religious Affairs under the Central Committee of the Party. The government's objective has been to exercise direct Party control over all activities of religious bodies, cutting them off from their corresponding foreign communities and utilizing them for political purposes in both internal and external affairs. The imprisonment of clergy, closure of churches and the like have always been interpreted officially not as anti-religious acts but as political acts against feudalists and counter-revolutionaries. However, the argument loses much of its force in the light of the regime's avowed atheism and especially the attacks suffered by religious groups during the Cultural Revolution. The violently antireligious campaign unleashed through the Red Guards during 1966-69 resulted in the closure of virtually all places of worship and the suspension of religious associations. Since the 19th Party Congress of April 1969, which marked the end of the Cultural Revolution, there has been a more tolerant attitude towards churches and religions. Many church buildings continue to belong to Christian communities, although few are now used for worship services. Such churches, along with Buddhist and Taoist temples and the Three-Self theological school in Nanking, are exempt from property taxes. Nevertheless,the negative attitude of the regime towards religion continues unaltered. Indeed, the anti-Confucian campaign inaugurated in August 1973 manifests traces of the earlier anti-religious and anti-Christian violence. Since the death of Mao Tse-tung in 1976, the Four Modernizations program has resulted in a new openness in China towards the Western world. This has been accompanied by a lifting of repressive restrictions on Christians in China. Some Western mission societies, Catholic as well as Protestant, have entertained the prospect of returning soon to the Mainland. Others, however, have sought to restrain any such premature attempt to reintroduce foreign missions.

To 'handle the problem of religion' correctly, the regime convened 2 major study conferences: the China Atheistic Seminar (Nanking, December 1978) calling for scholarly research on atheism and the National Planning Conference on Religious Studies (Kunning, February 1979) calling for scholarly research on religions from the Marxist standpoint. The China Society for Religious Studies was then founded. On 15 March 1979, the regime promulgated a new policy statement entitled 'Religion and Superstition', reestablishing the pre-1966 religious policy as 'correct'. The Religious Affairs Bureau in Peking formally resumed operation the next day. Open persecution of believers is now expected to decline, but authentic legal toleration remains unlikely. In fact, the widely-heralded state toleration of religion after 1978 is interpreted by many observers as a tactic to allow the church to surface in order to assess its strength.

After 1981, evidence was increasing of very rapid church growth in many areas of China, including among tribal peoples, with large numbers of young people present everywhere. Reports have been received indicating that by 1995 as many as 10 million new believers were pouring into the churches every year.

Word processor with 3,000 Chinese characters for Bible typesetting and production (Amity Press, Nanjing).

BROADCASTING AND MEDIA

Broadcasting is an absolutely vital component of ministry in China. The typical Chinese believer will tune in to any broadcast they can find, and many Chinese Christians have come to faith as a result of radio programs alone. FEBC (Philippines) broadcasts into China in Akha, Zhuang, Amoy, Swatow, Mandarin, English, Lisu, Shan, Tibetan, Uighur, Wa, Cantonese, and Mien. Mandarin language programming comes from FEBC stations in Russia, Korea, and Saipan. A 30-minute daily Tibetan-language shortwave radio programs, started in 1991, is recorded by ethnic Tibetans and broadcast from FEBA (Seychelles), with good response, particularly among university students. These programs are known to be recorded and duplicated for mass distribution. TWR (Guam) has over 140 hours a week in 12 different languages over 4 different shortwave channels (one each for children, Bible teaching for young Christians, education for church leaders, and minority groups); these have had tremendous response. KNLS and VERITAS also have shortwave programs. IBRA-produced programs broadcast from Radio Moscow in Tashkent can be heard.

Although television programming is tightly controlled, some successes have been seen. CBN's animated programs *Superbook* and *Micah's Christmas Treasure* have been aired in some regions of China with a total viewership of over 20 million. Some TBN programs have appeared in China on national television.

Videotapes are greatly underutilized and highly effective. Half the homes in Beijing alone are estimated to own a VCR, and most rural villages have at least one. There are more than 140 film teams showing the 'Jesus' Film in China, and the films are copied and passed around through large unscheduled distribution chains. It is not unusual for several hundred to watch the film in one setting: more than 7 million have seen it—half through videotapes, and half through film team presentations. This has led to more than one million decisions for Christ. CD-ROMs are widespread due to rampant software piracy, but few Christian titles are in distribution. Internet access is controlled and monitored, and many overseas sites are blocked; few Chinese own computers or have Internet access, but this will change rapidly in the next 2 decades, and access to Christian web sites may prove of great value.

INTERDENOMINATIONAL ORGANIZATIONS

Protestant and Anglican denominations as separate entities have disappeared, the only existing national structure being the Three-Self Patriotic Movement. In general, Catholics and Protestants work separately from each other and rarely meet.

FUTURE TRENDS AND PROSPECTS

Indigenous churches, though persecuted by the Communist government, are expected to continue to flourish resulting in Christians representing 9.2% of the population by 2025. In the light of religious resurgence in China the nonreligious are expected to decline from a high of 47.7% in 1970 to 40.6% by 2025.

If Christian growth trends continue into the distant future, it could eventually claim 20% of China's population, perhaps as early as 2050.

BIBLIOGRAPHY

A century of Protestant missions in China (1807–1907): the Centenary Conference historical volume. D. MacGillivray (ed). 1907; reprint, San Francisco: Chinese Materials Center, 1979.

A classified catalogue of Chinese books in The Library of The Institute for Advanced Studies of World Religions. L. L. Yang. Stony Brook, NY: The Institute for Advanced Studies of World Religions, 1981.

A expansão da fé no Extremo Oriente (subsidios para a história colonial). A. L. Farinha. Lisbon: Agência Geral das Colónias, 1946. 3 vols.

A history of Christian missions in China. K. S. Latourette. London: SPCK, 1929.

A history of Hong Kong. F. Welsh. HarperCollins, 1993. 624p.

'A people divided: the tame Nosu of Yunnan and the wild Nosu of Sichuan,' R. R. Covell, chapter 9 in *The liberating gospel in China: the Christian faith among China's minority peoples.* Grand Rapids, MI: Baker, 1995.

A vision betrayed: the Jesuits in Japan and China 1542–1742. A. Ross. Edinburgh: Edinburgh University Press, 1994. 233p.

Against the tide: the story of Watchman Nee. A. I. Kinnear. Eastbourne: Victory Press, 1973.

All under heaven: Chinese tradition and Christian life in the People's Republic of China. A. Hunter & D. Rimmington (eds). Kampen: J.H. Kok, 1992. 142p.

An historical sketch of the Portuguese settlements in China; and of the Roman Catholic Church and missions in China. A. Ljungstedt. Boston: James Munroe, 1836. 323p.

'An historical study of Nestorian Christianity in the T'ang dynasty between A.D. 636–845.' P. C. H. Chiu. Ph.D. dissertation, Southwestern Baptist Theological Seminary, Fort Worth, TX, 1987. 327p.

Buddhism of Tibet. Tenzin Gyatso, Fourteenth Dalai Lama. Trans. and ed., J. Hopkins. Ithaca, NY: Snow Lion, 1987. 219p.

Catalog of Protestant missionary works in Chinese: Harvard-Yenching Library, Harvard University. J. Y. H. Lai. Boston: G. K. Hall & Co., 1980

Catholic politics in China and Korea. E. O. Hanson. *American Society of Missiology series,* no. 2. Maryknoll, NY: Orbis Books, 1980. 160p.

China. P. Cheng. *World bibliographical series,* vol. 35. Oxford, UK: CLIO Press, 1983. 390p. (See especially 'Religion and philosophy,' 89f).

China and the Christian impact: a conflict of cultures. J. Gernet. Trans., J. Lloyd. Cambridge, UK: Cambridge University Press, 1985. 316p.

China and the cross: a survey of missionary history. C. Cary-Elwes OSB. New York: P. J. Kennedy and Sons, 1956. 347p.

China bibliography: a research guide to reference works about China past and present. H. T. Zurndorfer. *Handbuch der Orientalistik,* Vierte Abteilung, China, 1. Leiden and New York: E. J. Brill, 1995. 394p.

China miracle: a voice to the Church in the West. A. Wallis. Eastbourne, UK: Kingsway, 1985.

China: the church's long march. D. H. Adeney. Ventura, CA: Regal/Overseas Missionary Fellowship, 1985.

China, the emerging challenge. P. E. Kauffman. Grand Rapids, MI: Eerdmans, 1982.

China's bloody century: genocide and mass murder since 1900. R. J. Rummel. New Brunswick: Transaction Publishers, 1991. 348p.

China's minority nationalities. M. Yin (ed). Beijing: Foreign Languages Press, 1989. 455p.

'Chinese ancestor practices and Christianity: toward a viable contextualization of Christian ethics in a Hong Kong setting.' H. N. Smith. Ph.D. dissertation, Southwestern Baptist Theological Seminary, Fort Worth, TX, 1987. 374p.

Chinese Christians: élites, middlemen, and the church in Hong Kong. C. T. Smith. Hong Kong: Oxford University Press, 1985. 286p.

Chinese churches handbook. G. Law. Hong Kong: Chinese Coordination Centre of World Evangelism, 1982. 378p.

Chinese creeds and customs. V. R. Burkhardt. Hong Kong: South China Morning Post, 1953–58. 3 vols.

'Chinese geomancy: some observations in Hong Kong,' M. Freedman, in *The study of Chinese society: essays by Maurice Freedman,* p.189–211. G. W. Skinner (ed). Stanford, CA: Stanford University Press, 1979.

Chinese religions. J. Ching. Maryknoll, NY: Orbis Books, 1993.

Chinese women and Christianity, 1860–1927. P. Kwok. *American Academy of Religion academy series,* no. 75. Atlanta: Scholars Press, 1992. 233p.

Christian souls and Chinese spirits: a Hakka community in Hong Kong. N. Constable. Berkeley, CA: University of California Press, 1994. 256p.

Christianity and Chinese religions. H. Küng & J. Ching. New York: Doubleday, 1989. 333p.

Christianity in China: a scholars' guide to resources in the libraries and archives of the United States. A. R. Crouch. Armonk, NY: M.E. Sharpe, 1989. 765p.

Christianity in China: foundations for dialogue. B. Leung & J. D. Young (eds). *Centre of Asian Studies occasional papers and monographs,* no. 108. [Hong Kong]: Centre of Asian Studies, University of Hong Kong, 1993. 329p.

Christianity in China: from the eighteenth century to the present. D. H. Bays (ed). Stanford, CA: Stanford University Press, 1996.

Christianity in Communist China. G. Patterson. Waco, TX: Word Books, 1969. 186p.

Christianity in the People's Republic of China. G. T. Brown. 2d ed. Atlanta: John Knox Press, 1986. 252p.

Church archives in Hong Kong. E. Sinn & L. Ha (eds). Hong Kong: Centre of Asian Studies, University of Hong Kong, 1994.

Continued persecution of Christians in China. Washington, DC: Puebla Institute, 1993. 52p.

Cultural atlas of China. C. Blunden & M. Elvin. New York: Facts on File, 1983.

'Cutting the ancient cords: the Lahu and Wa are liberated from demons,' R. R. Covell, chapter 10 in *The liberating gospel in China: the Christian faith among China's minority peoples.* Grand Rapids, MI: Baker, 1995.

Die Religionen Tibets und der Mongolei. G. Tucci & W. Heissig. *Die Religionen der Menschheit,* Bd. 20. Stuttgart: W. Kohlhammer, [1970]. 455p.

Documents of the Three–Self Movement: source materials for the study of the Protestant church in Communist China. F. P. Jones (ed). New York: National Council of Churches of Christ, USA, 1963. 226p.

Encyclopedia of China today. F. M. Kaplan & J. M. Sobin. 3d rev. ed. New York: Eurasia Press. 448p.

Evangelical awakenings in Eastern Asia. J. E. Orr. Minneapolis, MN: Bethany Fellowship, 1975. (See chapters 5, 9-14 and 18).

'Evangelism on the perpendicular among the Lisu people of Yunnan,' R. R. Covell, chapter 6 in *The liberating gospel in China: the Christian faith among China's minority peoples.* Grand Rapids, MI: Baker, 1995.

Facing 1997, what Hong Kong pastors are saying: a survey report. T. Lawrence (ed). Hong Kong: Chinese Church Research Center, 1987. 112p.

Generation of giants: the first Jesuits in China. G. H. Dunne. London: Burnes and Oates, 1962. 389p.

God reigns in China. L. Lyall. London: Hodder & Stoughton, 1985.

Guide to the Catholic Church in China. J. Charbonnier. Singapore: China Catholic Communication, 1989.

Historiography of the Chinese Catholic Church: nineteenth and twentieth centuries. J. Heyndrickx (ed). *Louvain Chinese studies,* 1. Leuven: Ferdinand Verbiest Foundation, 1994. 511p. (Proceedings of the first International Conference on the Historiography of the Chinese Catholic Church, Leuven, September, 1990).

Hong Kong. I. Scott. *World bibliographical series,* vol. 115. Oxford, UK: CLIO Press, 1990. 258p. (See especially 'Religion,' p.75-9).

Hong Kong 1997: a Christian perspective. Kwok Nai Wang. *URM series,* 2. Kowloon, Hong Kong: Christian Conference of Asia, Urban Rural Mission, 1991. 117p.

Hong Kong Catholic directory and yearbook, 1972. Hong Kong: Catholic Truth Society, 1972.

Hong Kong church directory, 1976. Hong Kong: Chinese Christian Literature Council, 1976.

Households of God on Chinese soil. R. Fung. Geneva: WCC, 1982.

Hsiang–kang chiao hui li shih (Church history of Hong Kong). E. Sinn & L. Ha (eds). Hong Kong: Centre of Asian Studies, University of Hong Kong, 1993.

Igrejas de Macau. M. R. Valente. *Colecção macaense,* 4. Macau: Instituto Cultural de Macau Ao-men wen hua ssu shu, 1993. 155p.

In search of China's minorities. Z. Weiwen & Z. Qingnan. Beijing: New World Press, 1993. 354p.

In the prisons of Mao. D. T. Yee-MIng. : Hong Kong, 1991. (By Catholic archbishop of Canton on his 22 years in Chinese prisons).

Indo–Tibetan Buddhism: Indian Buddhists and their Tibetan successors. D. L. Snellgrove. London: Serindia; Boston: Shambhala, 1987. 2 vols., 640p.

'Inquiry and proposals on key issues in three major areas of pastoral ministry of a Chinese church in Hong Kong.' W. Lam. D.Min. thesis, Trinity Evangelical Divinity School, Deerfield, IL, 1992. 224p.

Islam in China: a critical bibliography. R. Israeli. Westport, CT: Greenwood Press, 1994.

J. Hudson Taylor: a man in Christ. R. Steer. *OMF book.* Wheaton, IL: Harold Shaw, 1993. 372p.

Macau. R. L. Edmonds. *World bibliographical series,* vol. 105. Oxford, UK: CLIO Press, 1989. 157p. (See especially 'Religion,' 44-9).

Macau beyond 1999. St. Louis, MO: Lutheran Church—Missouri Synod, 1992. (23 min. videocassette).

Macau, mãe das missões no Extremo Oriente. E. Arnáiz. Trans., A. A. Neves. Macau: Tipografia Salesiana, 1957. 182p.

Mennonites in China. R. L. Ramseyer & A. P. Ramseyer. Winnipeg, Manitoba: China Educational Exchange, 1988. 116p.

'Ministering beyond 1997: some reflection and suggestion as to how the churches in Hong Kong may carry out their mission faithfully and effectively.' F. Luk. D.Min. thesis, Westminster Theological Seminary, Chestnut Hill, PA, 1991. 380p.

Mission in urban Hong Kong. D. Ngai & K. Lo (eds). Kowloon, Hong Kong: Chinese Coordinating Center of World Evangelism, 1988. (Text in Chinese).

'Missionary enigma: the return of Hong Kong to China and the prospect for Christian mission.' J. Y. Chien. M.A. thesis, Reformed Theological Seminary, 1991. 111p.

Monasteries and culture change in Inner Mongolia. R. J. Miller. *Asiatische Forschungen,* Band 2. Wiesbaden, Germany: Harrassowitz, 1959. 152p.

Muslim Chinese: ethnic nationalism in the People's Republic. D. C. Gladney. *Harvard East Asian Monographs,* 149. Cambridge, MA and London: Council on East Asian Studies at Harvard University, and Harvard University Press, 1991. 499p. (Treats the Chinese government's response to rising ethnic nationalism among the Hui).

'Muslims in China: the people,' J. Lawton, *Aramco world,* 36, 4 (1985), 36–48.

New spring in China: a Christian appraisal. L. Lyall. London: Hodder & Stoughton, 1979.

Nomads of western Tibet: the survival of a way of life. M. C. Goldstein & C. M. Beall. Berkeley, CA: University of California Press, 1990. 191p.

On the threshold of three closed lands: the guild outpost in the Eastern Himalayas. J. A. Graham. Edinburgh: T & T Clark, 1897. 166p. (Church of Scotland work in Tibet, Nepal, and Bhutan).

Peaks of faith: Protestant mission in revolutionary China. J. Tien. *Studies in Christian mission,* vol. 8. Leiden: E. J. Brill, 1993. 161p.

Piecing together the China puzzle. P. E. Kauffman. Hong Kong: Asian Outreach, 1987.

Prayers and thoughts of Chinese Christians. K. Chan & A. Hunter (eds). Boston: Cowley Publications, 1991. 105p.

Protestantism in contemporary China. A. Hunter & K. Chan. *Cambridge studies in ideology and religion.* Cambridge, UK: Cambridge University Press, 1993. 310p.

Religion and modernization in China. D. Kangsheng, Z. Xinying & M. Pye (eds). Cambridge, UK: Roots and Branches, 1995.

Religion in China today: policy and practice. D. E. McInnis. Maryknoll, NY: Orbis Books, 1989.

Religion in postwar China: a critical analysis and annotated bibliography. D. C. Yu. *Bibliographies and Indexes in Religious Studies,* no. 28. Westport, CT, and London: Greenwood Press, 1994.

Religions of China: the world as a living system. D. L. Overmyer. San Francisco: Harper & Row, 1986. 125p.

Religious observances in Tibet: patterns and functions. R. B. Ekvall. Chicago: Chicago University Press, 1964. 313p.

Seeking the common ground: Protestant Christianity, the Three–Self Movement, and China's united front. P. L. Wickeri. Maryknoll, NY: Orbis Books, 1988. 384p.

Select Papers from China Consultation '87. I. Tam (ed). Wheaton, IL: Institute of Chinese Studies, Billy Graham Center, Wheaton College, 1988.

Spring has returned . . . listening to the Church in China. D. Lotz (ed). McLean, VA: Baptist World Alliance, 1986.

Taoist ritual and popular cults of Southeast China. K. Dean. Princeton, NJ: Princeton University Press, 1993. 320p.

Temple rituals & public ceremonies. J. Levy. *Tibetan Buddhist rites from the monasteries of Bhutan,* vol. 3. New York, NY: Lyrichord. (Sound recording on compact disc).

The Catholic Church in China. L. Ladany. New York: Freedom House, 1987.

The Catholic church in modern China: perspectives. E. Tang & J. Wiest. Maryknoll, NY: Orbis Books, 1993. 280p.

The Catholic Church in post–Mao China. A. S. Lazzarotto. Hong Kong: Holy Spirit Study Center, 1982.

'The Catholic Church in the People's Republic of China,' E. Tang, *Pro Mundi Vita* (Leuven), no. 15 (1990), 1–34.

The challenge of Central Asia: a brief survey of Tibet and its borderlands, Mongolia, NW Kansu, Chinese Turkestan and Russian Central Asia. M. Cable et al. London: World Dominion Press, 1932. 141p.

The China mission handbook: a portrait of China and its church. J. Chao (ed). Hong Kong: Chinese Church Research Center, 1989. 272p.

The Christian occupation of China. M. T. Stauffer (ed). Shanghai: China Continuation Committee, 1922. 580p. ('A general survey of the numerical strength and geographical distribution of the Christian forces in China made by the Special Committee on Survey and Occupation, China Continuation Committee, 1918-1921.').

The Church in China: how it survives and prospers under Communism. C. Lawrence. Minneapolis, MN: Bethany House, 1985.

The Church in Communist China. F. P. Jones. Waco, TX: Word Books, 1969.

The church in contemporary China. J. Chao & R. Dunch. Copenhagen: Scandinavia Publishing House, 1988.

'The church in Macau,' M. Teixeira, in *Macau: city of commerce and culture,* p.39–49. R. D. Cremer (ed). Hong Kong: UEA Press, 1987.

The church of St. Paul in Macau. M. Teixeira. Lisbon: Centro de Estudos Históricos Ultramarinos da Junta de Investigações do Ultramar, 1979. 60p.

The churches of China: taking root downward, bearing fruit upward. B. E. Towery Jr. 2d ed. Hong Kong: Long Dragon Books, 1987.

'The despised serfs of southwest China: liberation in Christ of the Miao,' R. R. Covell, chapter 4 in *The liberating gospel in China: the Christian faith among China's minority peoples.* Grand Rapids, MI: Baker, 1995.

'The diakonia function of the Church in Hong Kong.' M. Berndt. Ph.D. dissertation, Concordia Seminary, 1970.

The diocese of Victoria, Hong Kong: a hundred years of church history 1849–1949. G. B. Endacott & D. E. She. Hong Kong: Kelly & Walsh, 1949. 174p.

The dragon and the lamb: the resurgence of Christianity in the PRC. W. Dehoney. Nashville, TN: Broadman Press, 1988.

The enduring church: Christians in China and Hong Kong. G. V. Coulson, C. Herlinger & C. S. Anders. New York: Friendship Press, 1996.

The forgotten Christians of Hangzhou. D. E. Mungello. Honolulu: University of Hawaii Press, 1994. 259p.

The forgotten tribes of China. K. Sinclair. Hong Kong and Missisauga, Ontario: Intercontinental Publishing Corp. Ltd. and Cupress Ltd., 1984. 128p. (A photo essay highlighting some of the fifty five nationalities in China besides the majority Han people.).

The God–Men: an inquiry into Witness Lee and the local church. N. T. Duddy and the Spiritual Counterfeits Project. Downers Grove, IL: InterVarsity Press, 1981.

The history of Buddhism in India and Tibet. Bu-ston. Trans., E. Obermiller. *Bibliotheca Indo-Buddhica*, 26. Delhi: Sri Satguru, 1986. 231p.

The iconography of Chinese Buddhism in traditional China. No. 5 of section 12, *East and Central Asia*, of *Iconography of religions.* H. A. van Oort. Leiden: E. J. Brill, 1986. 2 vols.

The imperial metaphor: popular religion in China. S. Feuchtwang. London: Routledge, 1992. 223p.

The Jesuits, 1594–1994, Macao and China: East meets West. L. S. Cunha (ed). Macau: Instituto Cultural de Macau, 1994. 285p.

The Jesus Family in Communist China. D. V. Rees. Exeter: Paternoster Press, 1959.

The liberating gospel in China: the Christian faith among China's minority peoples. R. R. Covell. Grand Rapids, MI: Baker, 1995. 288p.

The life and theology of Watchman Nee, including a study of the Little Flock Movement. N. H. Cliff. Leiden: Pharos, 1994. 300p.

'The Lutheran Church in Hong Kong, 1949–1980.' J. T. Lindner. M.Div. thesis, Concordia Theological Seminary, Fort Wayne, IN, 1981. 83p.

The minorities of northern China: a survey. H. Schwartz. Bellingham, WA: Western Washington University Press, 1984.

The missionary enterprise in China and America. J. K. Fairbank (ed). *Studies in American—East Asian Relations*, No. 6. Cambridge, MA: Harvard University Press, 1974. 442p.

The monasteries of the Himalayas: Tibet, Bhutan, Ladakh, Sikkim. S. Held. Italy: Edita, 1988. 150p.

'The Muslim face of China,' D. Gladney, *Current history*, (Sept 1993), 275–80.

The people of Tibet. C. Bell. Oxford, UK: Clarendon Press, 1928. 319p.

The Phoenix rises: the phenomenal growth of eight Chinese churches. L. Lyall (ed). *OMF book.* Singapore: Overseas Missionary Fellowship, 1992. 146p.

The pivot of the four quarters: a preliminary inquiry into the origins and character of the ancient Chinese city. P. Wheatley. New York: Aldine-Atherson, 1971. 602p.

The Reformed Church in China, 1842–1951. G. F. De Jong. *Historical series of the Reformed Church in America*, no. 22. Grand Rapids, MI: Eerdmans, 1992. 398p.

The religion of Tibet. C. A. Bell. Oxford, UK: Clarendon Press, 1931. 235p.

The religions of Tibet. G. Tucci. Trans., G. Samuel. London: Routledge & Kegan Paul, 1980. 340p.

The resurrection of the Chinese church. T. Lambert. *OMF book.* Wheaton, IL: Harold Shaw, 1994. 366p.

The story of a hundred years: the Pontifical Institute of Foreign Missions (P.I.M.E.) in Hong Kong, 1858–1958. T. F. Ryan. Hong Kong: Catholic Truth Society, 1959. 258p.

The tenacity of Chinese folk tradition: two studies of Hong Kong Chinese. M. I. Berkowitz. *Occasional paper*, no. 33. Singapore: Institute of Southeast Asian Studies, 1975. 32p.

The treasury of good sayings: a Tibetan history of Bon. S. G. Karmay (ed). *London Oriental series*, vol. 26. London: Oxford University Press, 1972. 365p.

The turning of the tide: religion in China today. J. F. Pas (ed). Hong Kong: Royal Asiatic Society, Hong Kong Branch Oxford University Press, 1989. 389p.

'The Uighurs of Xinjiang,' A. al-Hada (pseudonym), *International journal of frontier missions*, 2, 4 (1985), 373–83.

This is Hong Kong: temples. J. Savidge. Hong Kong: Government Information Services, 1977. 122p.

Tibet. J. Pinfold. *World bibliographical series*, vol. 128. Oxford, UK: CLIO Press, 1991. 285p. (See especially 'Religion,' p.70-86).

Tibet: Bon religion: a death ritual of the Tibetan Bonpos. No. 13 of section 12, *East and Central Asia*, of *Iconography of religions.*H. P. Kvaerne. Leiden: E. J. Brill, 1985. 34p.

'Toward courage and reconciliation: a pastoral response to the crisis of Hong Kong in the face of the sociopolitical changes in 1991.' T. M. Fong. D.Min. thesis, Lutheran Theological Seminary, Philadelphia, 1994. 138p.

Towards a contextual ecclesiology: the Catholic Church in the PRC, its life and theological implications. K. Chan. Hong Kong: Chinese Church Research Center, 1987.

'Towards a new model of community church in Hong Kong.' W. So. D.Min. thesis, Fuller Theological Seminary, Pasadena, CA, 1983. 262p.

Trente ans aux portes du Thibet interdit 1908–1938. F. Gore. Hong Kong: Sociétés des Missions-Étrangères de Paris, Maison de Nazareth, 1939. 388p. (Catholic missions in Tibet).

Turmoil in Hong Kong on the eve of communist rule: the fate of the Territory and its Anglican Church. D. A. Brown. San Francisco: Mellen Research University Press, 1993. 477p.

Unfinished encounter: China and Christianity. B. Whyte. London: Fount Paperbacks, 1988. 537p.

Urban church growth in Hong Kong, 1958–1962. L. E. Noren. Hong Kong: American Baptist Foreign Mission Society, 1962. 60p.

'Western evangelicals and the church in China.' J. H. Stewart. D.Min. thesis, Reformed Theological Seminary, Jackson, MS, 1988. 271p.

Wise as serpents, harmless as doves. J. Chao & R. van Houten. Pasadena, CA: William Carey International University, 1988.

Country Table 2. **Organized churches and denominations in China.**

Official name (bold type = church with over 10% of all affiliated) 1	*Begun* 2	*Type* 3	*Counc* 4	*Congs* 5	*Adults* 6	*Affiliated 1970* 7	*Affiliated 1995* 8	*G%* 9	*Names, notes, and other statistics* (see Codebook, Part 3) 10
MAINLAND CHINA									
Achang Church	c1940	I-eth	.....	40	800	20	2,000	20.23	Yunnan, also Burma. Churches in nearly every Achang village. Bilingual in Chinese and Dai.
Akha Church	c1930	I-Bap	.....	140	3,000	30	7,000	24.37	Southwest Yunnan and Kengtung State; also in Burma, Thailand, Laos, Viet Nam.
Assemblies of God	1907	P-Pe2	ZF...	150	4,000	100	10,000	20.23	Yunnan. M=AoG. 1989 attempt at recognition as separate denomination; failed.
Assembly Hall Churches	1922	I-3nC	.....	4,000	800,000	30,000	1,200,000	15.90	*Chu Hui So. Little Flock.* F=Watchman Nee. 1949: 636 churches, 70,000 members. Jiangxi.
Bai Church	c1890	I-eth	....K	500	20,000	30	62,000	35.71	Strong national church (TSPM/CCC). M=OMF,NTCM,CSI,ELIC,CAPS,MOP,GRI.
Catholic Church in China (Clandestine)	1298	R-Lat	P...R	15,000	4,856,000	100,000	6,600,000	18.24	*Tien Chu Chiao Hui.* Illegal, loyal to pope, but cooperating with state. Strong in Hebei and Fujian.
Catholic Church in China (Underground)	1979	I-Lat	P....	2,000	400,000	–	1,100,000	6.25	More organized, confrontational, aggressive, militant part of pro-Rome loyalists. Gansu, Shanxi.
Chinese Catholic Church (Patriotic)	1957	I-Lat	C	15,500	3,384,000	10,000	4,600,000	27.79	*Open Ch.* Under Ai Guo Hui (Chinese Catholic Patriotic Association, CCPA). Set up by regime.
Dai Churches	c1940	I-eth	.....	240	11,600	50	24,000	28.01	Yunnanese Shan (Chinese Tai). Yunnan, Sichuan. Very rapid growth. M=AIMS,CSI.
Dong Church	c1920	I-Bap	....K	20	1,000	20	2,400	21.11	Southeast Guizhou, western Hunan, Guangxi. M=CSI,SIL,TELL. R=FEBC.
Han charismatic house churches	c1950	I-3cC	.....	198,000	11,200,000	10,000	29,740,000	37.70	In 500 Regional Councils, 5,000 Pastoral Districts. M=Taiwanese/Diaspora short-termers; CCRC
Han Chinese Three-Self Churches	1807	I-Uni	....K	27,000	4,000,000	200,000	10,500,000	17.17	*TSPM.* 1950, all non-RCs forcibly united. 1966-79, all churches closed. Now 40% registered.
Han unregistered house churches	1950	I-Non	.....	62,000	3,800,000	400,000	9,910,000	13.70	Hundreds of small illegal networks, many isolated, mostly noncharismatic. Rural persecutions.
Hani Churches	c1930	I-eth	....K	400	20,000	500	50,000	20.23	Ailao Mountains, South Yunnan; also in Viet Nam, Laos, Myanmar. R=FEBC.
Hidden Buddhist believers in Christ	c1970	I-Bud	.....	10,000	350,000	10,000	693,000	18.48	Buddhists converted to Christ but remaining within Buddhism as a witness.
Hidden nonreligious believers in Christ	c1950	I-Non	.....	5,000	200,000	7,000	250,000	15.38	Agnostics converted to Christ but remaining in agnostic organizations as a witness.
Isolated radio churches	1933	I-3rC	.....	40,000	1,200,000	12,000	2,500,000	23.81	Isolated radio believers, mostly students and youths. R=FEBC,Radio Vatican,et alia.
Jesus Family	1921	I-3nC	x....	300	10,000	500	20,000	15.90	*Ye-su Chia Ting.* F=Jing Tianying. 1950, virtually destroyed; 1990s reactivated.
Kachin Church	c1930	I-Bap	....K	500	25,000	5,000	60,000	10.45	Western Yunnan; also in Burma, India. Strong national church. M=BBC/KBC,SIL.
Korean Churches	c1910	I-3hK	.....	2,000	150,000	10,000	360,000	15.41	Inner Mongolia, Jilin, Liaoning. Most TSPM but vast house networks. M=25 agencies(S Korea).
Lahu Churches	c1930	I-eth	....K	1,000	60,000	2,000	140,000	18.52	Southwest Yunnan, Lanaong Lahu Autonomous County; also in Burma, Thailand, Laos. M=GRI.
Lisu Church	c1890	I-eth	....K	1,800	160,000	40,000	380,000	9.42	Large ethnic church, White and Black Lisu. M=CIM/OMF. Widespread cross-cultural evangelism.
Local Church (Shouters/Yellers)	c1979	I-3nC	.....	2,000	120,000	–	300,000	6.25	*Huhanpai.* Witness Lee's Chs. Slogan-shouting in unison ('Denominationalism is a sin!').
Manchu Churches	c1900	I-3hE	.....	20	700	20	1,600	19.16	In 15 Provinces (Liaoning, Hebei). M=SJ,CSI,PRI,JENSCO,CCRC. Korea churches.
Maonan Church	c1920	I-Bap	....K	30	1,000	200	3,000	11.44	Guangxi Zhuang Autonomous Region. Bilingual in Zhuang and Chinese.
Miao (Meo) Churches	c1900	I-3pE	....K	1,400	120,000	20,000	320,000	11.73	Widespread ethnic church among Black, Flowery, Northern, Red, Western Meo. M=AoG.
Mien (Yao) Churches	c1920	I-eth	....K	130	5,000	100	13,000	21.49	Highland & Lowland Yao. In 5 Provinces, also Viet Nam, Thailand, Laos, USA. M=TELL,HCJB.
Nakhi Churches	c1930	I-3pE	.....	30	1,000	20	2,000	20.23	Yunan, Sichuan, Xizang; Burma. M=SFM(Sweden/1930s),DPMS. House churches, none TSPM.
New Apostolic Church	c1980	I-3aX	x....	50	4,000	–	9,006	6.67	*NAC. Neuapostolische Kirche*, with HQ in Zurich (Switzerland).
New Birth Movement	c1980	I-3cC	.....	10,000	2,943,000	–	4,000,000	6.67	*NBM*, or *Born Again Movement (BAM)* One branch of the whole house church movement.
Northern Zhuang Churches	c1890	I-eth	....K	400	25,000	30	62,000	35.71	Rapid growth from12,000 in 1980. M=CSI,YWAM,CCCI,SIL,FEBC,CMA,&c. Charismatics 15%.
Nung Church	c1895	I-eth	....K	50	2,500	100	6,000	17.79	Along Nu (Salween) river, Yunnan; also in Burma, Thailand. Bilingual in Lisu. M=SIL.
Orthodox Church of China	1686	O-Rus	M...K	800	16,000	5,000	40,000	8.67	*Tung Cheng Hui.* 1953, 280,000 Russians depart; return as engineers, prostitutes. 2 Dioceses.
Parauk (Va) Churches	c1940	I-eth	.....	250	30,000	2,000	70,000	15.28	Awa Mountains, southwest Yunnan Province; majority in Burma. Strong national church.
People's Organization churches	c1995	I-3cC	.....	4,200	1,200,000	–	2,000,000	50.00	Churches begun with full approval of local authorities, because no TSPM or foreign links.
Puyi Church	c1890	I-Lat	C	150	18,000	500	44,000	19.61	*Bouyei Church.* Ex Catholics. Guizhou, Yunnan. M=OMF,CSI,SIL,WEC,TELL. R=FEBC.
Rawang Church	c1990	I-eth	.....	150	3,000	100	7,000	20.00	Southeast Yunnan, Tibet; also in Burma, India. M=North Burma Christian Mission.
Seventh-day Adventist Church	c1920	P-Adv	x...K	500	153,000	5,000	250,000	16.94	*SDA.* Officially under TSPM, but insisting on SDA distinctives (in TSPM churches on Saturdays).
Southern Zhuang Churches	c1980	I-Bap	....K	150	8,000	–	20,000	6.67	Southwest Guangxi. M=SIL,YWAM,CSI. Charismatics 15%. Many church workers. R=FEBC.
Tibetan Churches	c1700	I-Lat	C	400	25,000	200	55,000	25.19	Central Tibet. Survivors of long RC history. M=TCF,LBI,AoG,PI,BMMF,CSI,SIL,&c.
True Jesus Church	1917	I-3oC	x....	3,500	400,000	3,000	1,000,000	26.16	*Chen Ye-su Chiao Hui.* 1949: 1,000 churches. Now with global diaspora. (HQ Taipei, Taiwan).
Tujia Church	c1880	I-eth	....K	200	6,000	20	15,000	30.32	Northwest Hunan, Hubei, Sichuan Provinces. Most speak Southwestern Mandarin. R=TWR.
Tulang Church	c1960	I-eth	.....	50	1,500	20	4,000	23.61	NW Yunnan. No written language. Strong church due to Lisu evangelists visiting every village.
Vietnamese Church	c1900	I-Lat	C	210	12,000	200	29,000	22.03	Around Dongxing on coast; also in Viet Nam, Laos, Cambodia, 8 other countries. M=CMA,CSI.
Wa Churches	c1930	I-Bap	.....	200	10,000	1,000	24,000	13.56	Va, Kawa, Vo. In Awa Mountains, southwest Yunnan; mostly in Burma. Strong national church.
Yi Churches	c1890	I-3pE	....K	1,000	110,000	4,000	270,000	18.35	Central, Eastern, Northern, Southern, Western Yi. M=AoG(USA,HK,Singapore).
Other smaller ethnic churches	c1900	I-eth	....K	1,400	100,000	3,000	250,000	19.35	Small groups in some 200 minority tribes who are active witnessing Christians.
Other Chinese indigenous churches	1873	I-	.....	3,000	250,000	6,000	600,000	20.23	Chinese Ev Ch (1873), Indep Chinese Jesus Ch (1906); 225,000 (1949); now 50 bodies.
Jesus is Lord Fellowship	1985	I-3fF	.....	100	12,000	–	25,000	10.00	*JILF.* Outreach from M=JILF(Philippines),WOM.
Subtotals				**415,960**	**36,232,100**	**887,760**	**77,630,006**		
HONG KONG									
Assembly Hall Churches	c1950	I-3nC	.....	11	8,500	8,000	17,000	3.06	*Chu Hui So. Church Assembly Hall.. Little Flock.* Begun on mainland in 1922.
Assoc of Baptists for World Evangelism	1945	I-Bap	x.T.T	19	1,710	850	5,700	7.91	M=ABWE. Filipino missionaries. 2 schools. 1n,7x,22f,2h,1p,W=32%,20Y,23z.
Association of Vineyard Churches	c1990	I-3cW	.....	3	700	–	1,800	20.00	M=AVC(USA). Charismatic network from USA.
Baptist Convention of Hong Kong	1842	P-Bap	T...w	112	50,150	50,000	62,228	0.88	1842, M=ABFMS; 1949 SBC(USA). 40n,21x,80f,1H,1j,1k,4r,1s,W=45%,730Y.
Bethel Mission of China	1920	I-Hol	.....	5	1,250	600	2,080	5.10	Small Holiness mission.
Canadian Holiness Mission	1954	P-Hol	.....	6	1,000	1,000	1,670	2.07	M=Independent Holiness Ch (Canada). Links with, but not merger with, FMC(USA).
Catholic Church: D Hong Kong	1841	R-Lat	PxF..	90	147,000	256,227	249,182	-0.11	C=11+3+22. (1970) 128n,231x,125m,804w,3378Y,2926y. (1990) 77n, 253x, 332m, 632w,4397Yy.
China Peniel Missionary Society	1909	P-Hol	x....	6	5,000	10,000	10,900	0.35	M=Voice of China & Asia Miss Soc (USA). Cantonese. 5 schools, orphanage. W=23%,151Y.
Chinese Christian Church of Amoy	1938	I-Non	.....	4	500	1,100	1,000	-0.38	Dialect church, part of CCC before 1950 but refused to join it in Hong Kong. W=50%,40Yy.
Chinese Evangelical Zion Church	1950	P-Con	x....	1	400	950	1,330	1.35	*Wang Tau Hom Sion.* M=Swedish Alliance Mission. 2n,1x,5f,W=16%,31Y,16z.
Chinese Evangelistic Crusade	1951	I-Eva	.....	10	1,500	2,000	2,500	0.90	*Chinese Native Evangelistic Crusade.* Churches: HK 1, Kowloon 5, New Territories 1.
Chinese Full Gospel Church	1955	P-Pe2	Z...	7	3,570	5,000	7,140	1.44	*Zion Churches.* M=Swedish Free Mission. HQ Kowloon. 2f,1h,W=27%,60Y.

Continued overleaf

Country Table 2–concluded

Official name (bold type = church with over 10% of affiliated) 1	*Begun* 2	*Type* 3	*Counc* 4	*Congs* 5	*Adults* 6	*Affiliated 1970* 7	*Affiliated 1995* 8	*G%* 9	*Names, notes, and other statistics (see Codebook, Part 3)* 10
Chinese Methodist Church	1880	P-Met	VwE.W	15	9,017	7,200	20,000	4.17	*Hong Kong District, Methodist Ch(UK).* M=MMS. Cantonese. 4n,2x,8f,1h,1r,W=31%,240Yy.
Chinese Rhenish Ch, Hong Kong Synod	1847	P-Lut	L....	14	7,500	7,682	10,200	1.14	M=RM,VEM(Germany). Other 5 Districts were in mainland China. 5f,1h,W=14%,161Yy.
Christian & Missionary Alliance	1933	P-Hol	xF..E	83	20,450	8,000	32,828	5.81	*HK Church Union, Tong Chs.* M=CMA(USA). 11n,6x,18f,1j,3k,1s(70),W=80%,246Y.
Christian Brethren		P-CBr	x....	8	300	400	600	0.05	*Plymouth (Open) Brethren.* M=CMML(UK, USA, NZ, Australia). 4 schools. 13f,1h.
Ch of the United Brethren in Christ	1950	P-Hol	.....	6	589	860	1,180	1.27	M=UBC(USA).
Christian Chs & Chs of Christ		I-Dis	.....	7	1,400	308	2,150	0.05	Mission of large body in USA.
Chr Nationals Evangelism Commission	1950	P-Non	xF..E	13	4,000	3,000	6,670	3.25	*CNEC.* Begun China 1942. HQ Kowloon. 9 schools. 6f,3h,1j,2s,W=61%,107Y.
Church of Christ, Hong Kong Council	1863	P-Uni	WWE.W	35	24,000	30,000	34,300	0.54	*CCC.* Cantonese. 72 schools (47000),22n,7x,61m,32f,1H,10r,1s,184t(3527),W=27%,650Yy.
Church of Christ (Non-Instrumental)	1925	I-Dis	x....	20	1,000	1,000	2,000	2.81	M=CC(Non-Instrumental) (USA). Mostly expatriates and USA naval personnel. 10f.
Church of Christ, Scientist	1905	m-Sci	x....	1	20	50	40	-0.89	*Christian Science.* M=CCS(Boston, USA). No licensed practitioners.
Church of Hong Kong	c1950	I-3pC	.....	2	50	200	100	-2.73	Schism ex CCC led by prophetess, former film star; died 1967. Most back in CCC.
Ch of Jesus Christ of Latter-day Saints	1949	m-LdS	x....	31	11,200	3,598	20,000	7.10	*Southern Far East (Hong Kong-Taiwan) Mission. Mormons.* M=CJCLdS(USA). 80f.
Church of the Nazarene	1974	P-Hol	....E	2	97	–	245	4.76	M=CoN. Nazarenes.
Conference of Mennonite Chs in HK	1985	P-Men	.....	3	59	–	85	10.00	M=GCMC.
Conservative Baptist Association	1963	I-Bap	xF...	7	900	545	1,800	4.90	M=CBFMS/CBI(USA). Cantonese, English. 7 primary schools. 1n,3m,1w,14f,2h,W=95%,57Y.
Cumberland Presbyterian Church	1949	P-Ref	R....	9	810	780	1,800	3.40	*South China Mission.* M=CPC (USA White). 10% refugees. 3 schools. 3n,4m,2f,W=70%,5Y,4y.
Elim Full Gospel Church	c1963	P-Pe2	ZG...	1	250	800	500	-1.86	M=EMA(USA),EFGA(UK). Classical Pentecostals (2-stage). 1f.
Emmanuel Church	1927	I-3pC	.....	5	1,300	750	2,170	4.34	*Ling Kuang Tong.* Pentecostals. 1 school. 1n,1x,2h,1k,W=44%,40Y,9z.
English Methodist Church	1890	P-Met	Vwc.W	3	600	1,000	1,100	0.38	*District, Methodist Ch (UK).* English-speaking. Sailors and Soldiers Home. 1x.
Evangelical Free Church of China	1937	P-Con	KF..E	29	4,445	2,000	8,730	6.07	M=EFCA,China Mission (USA). HQ Kowloon. 4n,2x,20f,1H,1j,1k,1s,W=82%,56Yy.
Evangelical Hakka Church	1846	P-LuR	L...W	17	4,200	7,600	7,000	-0.33	*Tsung Tsin Hui.* From mainland. M=Basel Mission. Hakka. 13n,2x,12f,1,1s,W=50%,325Yy.
Evangelical Lutheran Ch of Hong Kong	1890	P-Lut	L...W	54	9,180	9,819	13,100	1.16	*Hsiang Kang Hsin Yi Hui.* Mandarin, Cantonese, Hakka. 33n,4x,1j,1s(8),W=45%,298Yy.
Evangelize China Fellowship	1949	I-Eva	x....	12	3,960	3,000	6,600	3.20	*HK-Macau Synod.* Begun in China by Chinese. M=ECF(USA). 2 schools. 1j,2s,W=84%,52Y.
Full Gospel Assemblies of God	1907	P-Pe2	ZF..E	21	7,511	10,000	16,680	2.07	3 Districts. M=AoG; 1948, PAoC. 4,840 in schools. 25n,11f,1h,1j,1s(17),W=61%,226Y.
German Evangelical Lutheran Church	1965	P-Lut	....W	2	290	500	400	-0.89	For German-speaking expatriates. In Hong Kong. 1n,W=10%,12Yy,5z.
Grace Evangel Mission		I-Eva	.....	2	400	800	1,000	0.05	M=Grace Evangel Mission. Small independent mission. 2 schools. 1n,1w,1f,2h.
Harbour Mission	1914	I-Eva	.....	1	1,100	2,000	1,800	-0.42	Early independent mission in Hong Kong. In Aplichau, Aberdeen. 185Y.
Heap Gay Churches	1950	I-Eva	.....	6	1,000	2,000	2,200	0.38	*Hip Kei Tong (Conservative Co-operative Christian).* Rooftop school. 1h,1j.
HK & Macao Lutheran Church	1964	P-Lut	x....	13	1,300	1,450	2,600	2.36	*CELC.* Lutheran refugees from China. M=Wisconsin ELS(USA). 5n,6f,1r,1s,156Y.
Hong Kong Evangelical Churches	1954	P-Hol	xF..E	12	2,420	2,000	4,410	3.21	*Yan Poon. Grace Rock.* M=OMS Internat (USA). 8n,3x,7f,1h,W=58%,67Y,72z.
Hong Kong Free Methodist Church	1951	I-Hol	VF...	13	1,081	5,300	2,000	-3.82	*Chung Wah Chun Lei Wui.* M=FMC(USA). 5 schools. 5n,3x,10f,9t(822),W=43%,74Y.
Hong Kong Methodist Church	1952	P-Met	VwE.W	18	3,780	3,500	6,300	2.38	*Wei Li King Hui.* M=UMC(USA). A=1972. Mandarin. 16n,4x,18f,1H,1s,9t,106Yy,369z.
Hong Kong Sheng Kung Hui	1843	A-Eva	AvEAW	29	15,900	23,200	23,000	-0.03	HKSKH Province (1998). *Holy Cath Ch.* M=CMS.39n,21x,1s,W=31%,2Y,506y.
Hong Kong Swatow Christian Church	1909	P-Ref	.....	16	8,000	6,492	13,300	2.91	From mainland China. English Presbyterian background. No missionaries. W=35%,291Y.
Independent Assemblies of God	c1968	I-3pC	.....	16	4,800	2,500	12,000	6.48	A split in USA from original Assemblies of God.
Jehovah's Witnesses	1933	m-Jeh	x....	30	2,153	720	5,800	8.70	1933 under Australian branch. 1970: 678 attend. 9f(Filipinos). (1975) 22Y. (1995) 361Y.
Joyous Word Christian Chs Association	1947	I-Bap	.....	6	1,000	2,000	2,200	0.38	*Lock Tao (Joyous Word) Baptist Mission.* Ex CCC. Swatow. 3 schools. 1h,W=56%,65Y.
Lutheran Church, Hong Kong Synod	1950	P-Lut	e...E	39	5,000	9,021	10,000	0.41	M=LCMS(USA). Refugee Bible camp. 19n,9x,1s(5),W=49%,348Yy.
Mission Covenant Church	c1969	P-Con	.....	9	1,980	733	3,300	6.20	Mission Church from USA.
New Life Temple	1959	I-3pC	.....	1	500	1,000	1,100	0.38	M=Lester Sumrall Evangelistic Association (USA). Church is one floor of skyscraper.
Norwegian Lutheran Mission	1946	P-Lut	.....	2	450	1,375	1,100	-0.89	Refugees from church begun 1891 in Honan, Hupeh, N Manchuria. M=NLM(Norway). 10f.
Oriental Christian Churches Association	1950	P-Bap	.....	6	400	650	600	-0.32	*Tung Fong Kei Tuk Kaau Wooi.* Formerly M=Oriental Boat M. 1x,W=80%,73Y,35z.
Peace Evangelistic Centre	c1969	I-CBr	.....	1	1,800	250	3,000	10.45	Independent mission of Brethren tradition.
Pentecostal Church of God	c1960	P-Pe2	Z....	10	1,000	1,000	2,000	2.81	M=PCG in America (USA). Classical 2-stage Pentecostals. World HQ Joplin, MO (USA).
Pentecostal Holiness Church	1907	P-Pe3	ZF...	20	4,713	6,000	11,000	2.45	*Hong Kong Conference.* M=IPHC(USA). 2 schools. HQ Kowloon. 21nm,11f,1h,W=30%,58Y.
Russian Orthodox Church	c1920	O-Rus	.....	1	40	50	60	0.73	Small congregation of Russians and Russian-speaking Chinese.
Salvation Army	1930	P-Sal	xwE.W	27	2,200	5,345	4,400	-0.78	*Kau Shai Kwan/Chiu Shih Chiin* (Cantonese/Mandarin). 35n,18x,6h,1s,W=65%,143Y.
Seventh-day Adv Ch. HK-Macao Mission	1888	P-Adv	x...W	20	4,300	7,000	9,560	1.25	*SDA.* South China Island UM. 1 boat. 6nx,105mw,15f,2H,3h,4r,20t(3267),W=64%,155Y.
South China Foursquare Gospel Church	1936	P-Pe2	ZF...	7	360	1,500	900	-2.02	*Internat Ch of Foursquare Gospel.* M=ICFG(USA). 6nm,2x,5f,W=58%,14Y,90z.
Spiritual Food Worldwide Ev Mission	1950	I-Eva	x....	15	8,400	9,000	16,800	2.53	*Ling Liang WEM.* Chinese missionaries to 10 nations. HQ Kowloon. 1s,W=29%,220Y.
True Jesus Church	c1930	I-3oC	x....	10	2,000	1,500	3,330	3.24	*TJC, World Conference* (HQ Taiwan). Chinese indigenous church begun 1917 on mainland.
Unification Church		m-HSA	x....	5	1,000	–	2,000	0.05	*HSAUWC. Holy Spirit Assoc of Unification of World Christianity.* F=S.Y. Moon (Korea).
Union Churches	1923	P-com	....W	2	1,200	2,000	2,000	0.00	*Union Ch, Hong Kong; Union Ch, Kowloon.* English-speaking. Expatriates. 2x.
West China Evangelistic Band	1949	I-Eva	.....	1	200	300	500	2.06	*HK Christian Ev Preaching Band.* Begun 1936 in Szechwan. Spiritual Light Centre. 2f,1h.
Other independent charismatic chs	c1980	I-3cC	.....	100	7,000	–	10,000	6.67	Including New Apostolic Church (30 members), JILF (Philippines).
Other indigenous churches		I-	.....	200	15,000	20,000	30,000	0.05	Total about 70 non-pentecostal, including INC and PIC; many single churches.
Other Protestant denominations		P-	.....	70	6,000	7,000	10,000	0.05	Total about 25.
Other indigenous pentecostal churches		I-3pC	.....	150	10,000	5,000	15,000	0.05	Total about 30.
Subtotals				**1,532**	**450,885**	**565,505**	**766,068**		
MACAO									
Aliança Bíblica e Missionária	1978	P-Hol	.....	1	28	–	56	5.88	*Christian and Missionary Alliance.* M=CMA(USA).
Assembleias de Deus	1954	P-Pe2	ZF...	1	30	600	75	-7.98	*Assemblies of God.* M=PAoC(Canada). Radio broadcast to China, aided by FEBC. 1n.
Igreja Adventista do Sétimo Dia	1949	P-Adv	x....	2	400	500	1,000	2.81	*SDA. Seventh-day Adventists,* in Hong Kong-Macao Mission, South China Island UM.
Igr Anglicana: D Hong Kong & Macao	c1940	A-Cen	AweA.	2	90	200	180	-0.42	*Sheng Kung Hui Kong O Kau Kiu, Anglican Ch.* Cantonese. 4 schools. 1n,W=80%,2Y,6y.
Igreja Baptista	1910	P-Bap	T....	7	616	2,000	1,540	-1.04	*Baptist Ch.* M=SBC(USA). 7 schools. Sunday School enrollment 414. 4n,25Y.
Igreja Baptista Bama	1972	P-Bap	T....	1	100	–	167	4.35	*Burmese Baptist Church.*
Igreja Baptista Conservador	1986	I-Bap	.....	3	59	–	80	11.11	Conservative Baptists. M=CBI(USA). 10f.
Igreja Católica: D Macau	1557	R-Lat	BzF..	13	13,000	27,000	22,933	-0.65	C=3+0+13. (1970) 80nx,14m,224w,831Yy. (1990) 31n, 38x, 46m, 176w, 388Yy.
Igreja de Deus Pentecostal	1956	P-Pe2	.....	2	40	63	100	1.87	*Pentecostal Church of God.* M=ICFG,PCG.
Igreja do Cristo e Cina	1906	P-Uni	.....	1	115	280	230	-0.78	*Church of Christ in China.*
Igreja Evangelica Cina	1950	P-Eva	.....	4	420	500	1,050	3.01	*Chinese Evangelical Church.*
Igreja Luterana (Missouri)	1952	P-Lut	x....	2	110	513	150	-4.80	In Hong Kong Mission. M=LCMS(USA). 1 primary school. 13m,2t(222),5Yy.
Igreja Metodista Livre	c1955	I-Hol	VF...	1	25	200	100	-2.73	*Free Methodist Ch.* M=FMC(USA). Small holiness congregation.
Igreja Presbiteriana	1949	P-Ref	.....	1	65	180	180	0.00	*Presbyterian Church.*
Igreja Sion (Zion)	1954	P-Con	x....	3	70	230	233	0.05	*Chinese Ev Zion Ch.* M=SAM(Sweden). 1 orphanage, 50 orphans. 4f,G=0,W=26%,12z.
Igrejas CNEC	1962	P-Non	.....	2	200	42	333	8.63	*CNEC Churches.*
Igrejas radiofónicas isoladas	1950	I-3rC	.....	100	2,000	200	4,000	12.73	Isolated Chinese radio believers, mostly youths, pupils and students aged 12-25.
Testemunhas de Jeová	1961	m-Jeh	x....	2	30	50	150	4.49	*Jehovah's Witnesses. Watch Tower. IBSA.* First activity reported 1961. (1995) 11Y.
Other Protestant denominations		P-	.....	28	1,200	500	1,800	0.05	Total about 8, including ECF, WWM (1965).
Subtotals				**176**	**18,598**	**33,058**	**34,357**		
Totals for all China				**417,668**	**36,701,583**	**1,486,323**	**78,430,431**		

Churches, members, growth, 1900-2025	*Congs*	*Adults*	*Affiliated*	*G%*	*Total denominations*	*6 Megablocs:* O	R	A	P	I	m
Total churches, members, and denominations (mid-1900)	10,000	837,000	1,510,000	-0.02	24	1	3	1	8	11	0
Total churches, members, and denominations (mid-1970)	5,305	823,877	1,486,323	-0.02	368	2	3	2	61	296	4
Total churches, members, and denominations (mid-1990)	300,000	30,325,000	64,804,200	20.77	514	2	3	2	82	420	5
Total churches, members, and denominations (mid-1995)	1,251,120	109,616,668	78,430,431	3.89	534	2	3	2	83	439	5
Total churches, members, and denominations (mid-2000)	520,000	41,627,000	88,955,347	2.55	546	2	3	2	84	450	5
Total churches, members, and denominations (mid-2025)	950,000	63,203,000	135,064,000	1.68	1,032	10	1	1	110	900	10

NOTES ON TABLE ABOVE
NATIONAL COUNCILS (Column 4, 5th letter).
C = National Patriotic Catholic Association.
E = Hong Kong Evangelical Fellowship (HKEF).
K = China Christian Council (formerly Three-Self Reform Movement which replaced the pre-1949 National Christian Council of China).
R = Chinese Catholic Bishops' Conference on the Mainland (CBCM).
T = Hong Kong ICCC-related Council.
W = Hong Kong Christian Council (HKCC).

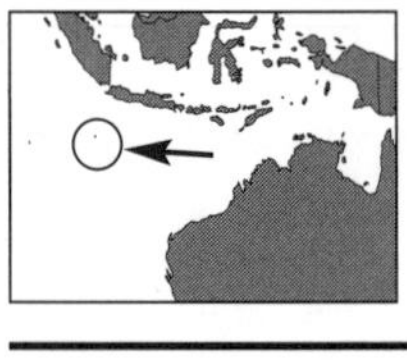

CHRISTMAS ISLAND

SECULAR DATA, AD 2000

STATE
Official name: The Territory of Christmas Island.
Short name: Christmas Island. **Adjective of nationality:** Christmas Islanders.
Flag: Similar to that of Papua New Guinea, though with a different bird and a mpa of Christmas Island in the center.

Area: 135 sq. km. (52 sq. mi.).
Government: External territory (dependency) of Australia, since 1958 (1888 British territory).
Legislature: Shire Council.
Official language: English.
Chief cities: FLYING FISH COVE 1,540.
Political divisions: 1 province.

DEMOGRAPHY
Population: 3,000.
Population density: 25.3/sq. km. (65.8/sq. mi.).
Under 15 years: 1,000.
Growth rate p.a.: 0.91% (births 12.57, deaths 7.65).
Mortality: Infant, per 1,000 5.5; **Maternal per 100,000:** 15.0.
Life expectancy: 79 (male 76, female 82).
Household size: 4.0. **Floor area per person, sq.m:** 20.0.

Major languages: English, Chinese, Malay, Javanese.
Urban dwellers: 75.00%. **Urban growth rate p.a.:** 0.00%.
Labor force: 60%.

ETHNOLINGUISTIC PEOPLES
67.5% Han Chinese (Mandarin); 16.0% Malay (Cocos Islander); 9.9% Anglo-Australian; 2.0% Eurasian; 1.9% Indo-Pakistani.

ECONOMY
National income p.a. per person: US$876; **per family:** US$3,504.

EDUCATION
Adult literacy: 72% **Schools:** 1.
Universities: 0. **School enrolment:** female/male: 75%/75%.

HEALTH
Access to health services: 80%. **Access to safe water:** 90%.
Hospitals: 1 (20 beds per 10,000). **Doctors:** 5.
Blind: 20. **Deaf:** 200. **Murder rate:** 4.
Lepers: 0.

LITERATURE
New book titles p.a.: 1 (250 p.a. per million). **Periodicals:** 0.
Newspapers: 0 dailies.

COMMUNICATION (per 1,000 people)
Phones: 200 (99% mobile). **Radios:** 700. **TV sets:** 200.
Daily newspaper circulation: <1. **Computers:** 500.

HUMAN LIFE AND LIBERTY (optimum condition=100.0%)
HDI: 80.0. **HSI:** 85.0. **HFI:** 80.0. **EFL:** 55.0.

Country Table 1. **Religious adherents in Christmas Island, AD 1900-2025.**

Year	1900		1970		mid-1990		Annual change, 1990-2000				mid-1995		mid-2000		mid-2025	
Name	Adherents	%	Adherents	%	Adherents	%	Natural	Conversion	Total	Rate	Adherents	%	Adherents	%	Adherents	%
Chinese folk-religionists	460	65.7	600	40.0	780	26.0	23	1	24	2.73	980	29.7	1,021	30.0	1,200	30.0
Buddhists	0	0.0	0	0.0	560	18.7	12	1	13	2.15	660	20.0	693	20.4	820	20.5
Nonreligious	0	0.0	250	16.6	470	15.7	10	1	11	2.04	555	16.8	575	16.9	740	18.5
Muslims	210	30.0	250	16.6	450	15.0	9	1	10	1.99	530	16.1	548	16.1	650	16.3
Christians	**30**	**4.3**	**400**	**26.6**	**500**	**16.7**	**4**	**-1**	**3**	**0.53**	**520**	**15.8**	**527**	**15.4**	**600**	**15.0**
PROFESSION																
professing Christians	**30**	**4.3**	**400**	**26.6**	**500**	**16.7**	**4**	**-1**	**3**	**0.53**	**520**	**15.8**	**527**	**15.4**	**600**	**15.0**
AFFILIATION																
unaffiliated Christians	0	0.0	70	4.7	110	3.7	-3	0	-3	-2.55	87	2.6	85	2.5	120	3.0
affiliated Christians	**30**	**4.3**	**330**	**22.0**	**390**	**13.0**	5	0	**5**	**1.26**	**433**	**13.1**	**442**	13.0	**480**	**12.0**
Roman Catholics	20	2.9	150	10.0	210	7.0	4	0	4	1.76	240	7.3	250	7.4	260	6.5
Protestants	0	0.0	100	6.7	110	3.7	1	0	1	0.87	120	3.6	120	3.5	130	3.3
Anglicans	10	1.4	80	5.3	70	2.3	0	0	0	0.28	73	2.2	72	2.1	90	2.3
Trans-megabloc groupings																
Evangelicals	0	0.0	40	2.7	60	2.0	1	0	1	0.80	63	1.9	65	1.9	80	2.0
Pentecostals/Charismatics	0	0.0	30	2.0	75	2.5	3	0	3	2.92	91	2.8	100	2.9	140	3.5
Great Commission Christians	**20**	**2.9**	**200**	**13.3**	**250**	**8.3**	**0**	**0**	**0**	**-0.12**	**250**	**7.6**	**247**	**7.3**	**250**	**6.3**
Hindus	0	0.0	0	0.0	20	0.7	1	0	1	5.14	30	0.9	33	1.0	40	1.0
New-Religionists	0	0.0	0	0.0	20	0.7	1	0	1	2.66	25	0.8	26	0.8	50	1.3
World A (unevangelized persons)	650	92.9	751	50.0	1,329	44.3	-3	-1	-4	-0.30	1,250	37.9	1,053	35.1	1,192	29.8
World B (evangelized non-Christians)	19	2.8	351	23.3	1,171	37.8	63	1	64	1.95	1,529	46.3	1,420	49.5	2,208	55.6
World C (Christians)	30	4.3	400	26.7	500	17.9	3	0	3	0.53	520	15.8	527	15.4	600	14.6
Country's population	**700**	**100.0**	**1,502**	**100.0**	**3,000**	**100.0**	**63**	**0**	**63**	**1.26**	**3,300**	**100.0**	**3,400**	**100.0**	**4,000**	**100.0**

COLUMNS, ROWS.
For meanings and definitions, see Codebook (Part 3). Note that, by definition, total 'Christians' = professing + crypto-Christians, which also = affiliated + unaffiliated Christians, and also = Great Commission Christians + latent Christians. Percentages may not always total exactly, due to rounding.

CENSUSES.
30.VI.1961: 84.6% Chinese folk-religionists and Muslims, 5.9% Roman Catholics, 4.8% Anglicans, 4.3% Protestants, 0.5% nonreligious, 0.4% Orthodox (7 persons only). **30.VI.1966:** 58.1% Chinese folk-religionists and Muslims, 14.0% nonreligious, 12.3% Roman Catholics, 8.2% Anglicans, 7.3% Protestants. **30.VI.1971:** 44.4% Chinese folk-religionists, 21.1% Muslims, 18.9% nonreligious, 6.9% Roman Catholics, 5.4% Protestants, 3.3% Anglicans. **1981:** 40.7% Chinese folk-religionists, 25.4% Muslims, 15.9% nonreligious, 8.2% Roman Catholics, 6.6% Protestants, 3.2% Anglicans. **1986:** 53.9% Chinese folk-religionists, 19.5% nonreligious, 8.4% Protestants, 7.8% Muslims, 6.3% Roman Catholics, 3.2% Anglicans, 0.9% Hindus.

NOTES ON RELIGIONS
MUSLIMS. 91% Malays, 9% Javanese and other Indonesians.
NONRELIGIOUS. Mainly former Buddhist Chinese, mostly young persons who have abandoned family religion.

Great Commission Instrument Panel: status of Christmas Island (for explanation see start of Part 4)

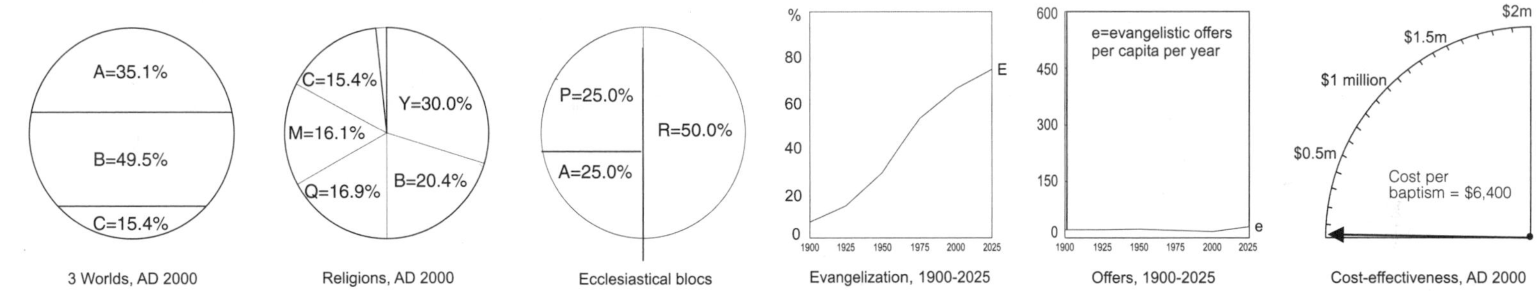

Country summary. **Worlds A, B, C by ethnolinguistic peoples, cities, and major civil divisions in Christmas Island.**

	PEOPLES							CITIES							CIVIL DIVISIONS						
World	Num	Pop 2000	C%	Christians	E%	U%	Unevangelized	Num	Pop 2000	C%	Christians	E%	U%	Unevangelized	Num	Pop 2000	C%	Christians	E%	U%	Unevangelized
A	3	623	0.32	2	35	65	405	0	0	0.00	0	0	0	0	0	0	0.00	0	0	0	0
B	3	2,393	6.94	166	67	33	797	1	1,540	12.99	200	66	34	524	1	3,424	12.91	442	65	35	1,203
C	2	407	67.32	274	100	0	1	0	0	0.00	0	0	0	0	0	0	0.00	0	0	0	0
Total	**8**	**3,423**	**12.91**	**442**	**65**	**35**	**1,203**	**1**	**1,540**	**12.99**	**200**	**66**	**34**	**524**	**1**	**3,424**	**12.91**	**442**	**65**	**35**	**1,203**

Country status. Christmas Island is a territory of Australia in the Indian Ocean south of Java, Indonesia. It contains large deposits of phosphate of lime.

HUMAN LIFE AND LIBERTY

Human rights and freedoms. Australian laws fully protect all human rights.

NON-CHRISTIAN RELIGIONS

Chinese folk religion is predominant in Christmas Island whose population was 50% Chinese in 1970. This is a mixture of Buddhist, Taoist, and Confucian ideas and practices, together with ancestor veneration.

Islam is second in importance, among the Malay population, and those professing to be without religion (mainly Chinese) have increased substantially in the last decade or two.

CATHOLIC CHURCH. The Holy See has no diplomatic relations with Christmas Island in AD 2000.

Indigenous missions. There is virtually no missionary outreach from the Christmas Islands.

CHURCH AND STATE

Christmas Island is administered by an official representative appointed by the Ministry of Territories of the Australian government. Freedom of religion is guaranteed under the Australian constitution.

FUTURE TRENDS AND PROSPECTS

The religious situation on Christmas Island is not likely to change much in the next 30 years.

Unless evangelistic effort becomes a priority among Christians it is likely that Christianity will decline slowly throughout the 21st century, perhaps falling as low as 10% by AD 2050.

BIBLIOGRAPHY

Christmas Island: the early years, 1888 to 1958: historic photographs with many untold tales from the early years of Christmas Island, an isolated island in the Indian Ocean. J. Adams. Chapman, ACT: B. Neale, 1993. 96p.

Country Table 2. **Organized churches and denominations in Christmas Island.**

Official name (bold type = church with over 10% of all affiliated) 1	Begun 2	Type 3	Counc 4	Congs 5	Adults 6	Affiliated 1970 7	Affiliated 1995 8	G% 9	Names, notes, and other statistics (see Codebook, Part 3) 10
Catholic Church (AD Singapore)		R-Lat	p.F..	1	110	150	240	0.05	Part of AD Singapore. Australians; including many Chinese, some Eurasians.
Ch of England in Australia (D Perth)	1888	A-Cen	awe..	1	45	80	73	-0.37	Included in Diocese of Perth. Australians, a few Eurasians and Chinese.
Other Protestant denominations		P-	.....	5	45	100	120	0.05	Informal groups serving Congregationalists, Methodists, Presbyterians.
Totals				**7**	**200**	**330**	**433**		

Churches, members, growth, 1900-2025	*Congs*	*Adults*	*Affiliated*	*G%*	*Total denominations*	*6 Megablocs:* *O*	*R*	*A*	*P*	*I*	*m*
Total churches, members, and denominations (mid-1900)	1	18	30	3.48	1	0	0	1	0	0	0
Total churches, members, and denominations (mid-1970)	5	200	330	3.48	3	0	1	1	1	0	0
Total churches, members, and denominations (mid-1990)	6	180	390	0.84	3	0	1	1	1	0	0
Total churches, members, and denominations (mid-1995)	7	200	433	2.11	3	0	1	1	1	0	0
Total churches, members, and denominations (mid-2000)	7	200	442	0.41	4	0	1	1	2	0	0
Total churches, members, and denominations (mid-2025)	10	220	480	0.33	7	0	1	1	5	0	0

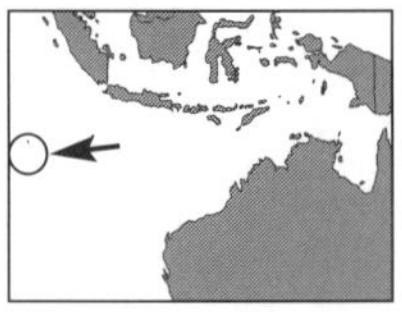

COCOS (KEELING) ISLANDS

SECULAR DATA, AD 2000

STATE
Official name: The Territory of Cocos (Keeling) Islands.
Short name: Cocos (Keeling) Islands. **Adjective of nationality:** Cocos Islanders.
Flag: That of Australia.
Area: 14 sq. km. (5 sq. mi.).
Government: Australian dependency, since 1955 (1857 British colony).
Legislature: Cocos (Keeling) Islands Council.
Official language: English.
Monetary unit: 1 Australian dollar ($A) = 100 cents. **US$1=** $A 1.70.
Chief cities: WEST ISLAND 551.
Political divisions: 1 province.

DEMOGRAPHY
Population: 1,000.
Population density: 51.8/sq. km. (145.2/sq. mi.).
Under 15 years: 200.
Growth rate p.a.: 0.91% (births 12.57, deaths 7.65).
Mortality: Infant, per 1,000: 5.5; **Maternal per 100,000:** 25.0.
Life expectancy: 79 (male 76, female 82).
Household size: 4.0. **Floor area per person, sq.m:** 22.0.
Major languages: Malay, English, Chinese.
Urban dwellers: 80.00%. **Urban growth rate p.a.:** 1.77%.
Labor force: 40%.

ETHNOLINGUISTIC PEOPLES
69.6% Cocos Islander (Malay); 14.0% Anglo-Australian; 14.0% British; 1.0% Han Chinese.

ECONOMY
National income p.a. per person: US$1,377; **per family:** US$5,509.

EDUCATION
Adult literacy: 62% (male 68%, female 56%). **Schools:** 4.
Universities: 0. **School enrolment:** female/male: 65%/65%.

HEALTH
Access to health services: 75%. **Access to safe water:** 80%.
Hospitals: 1 (30 beds per 10,000). **Doctors:** 2.
Blind: 5. **Deaf:** 10. **Murder rate:** 5.
Lepers: 0.

LITERATURE
New book titles p.a.: 1 (200 p.a. per million). **Periodicals:** 0.
Newspapers: 0 dailies.

COMMUNICATION (per 1,000 people)
Phones: 120 (10% mobile). **Radios:** 500. **TV sets:** 150.
Daily newspaper circulation: <1. **Computers:** 50.

HUMAN LIFE AND LIBERTY (optimum condition=100.0%)
HDI: 70.0. **HSI:** 60.0. **HFI:** 80.0. **EFL:** 55.0.

Country Table 1. **Religious adherents in Cocos (Keeling) Islands, AD 1900-2025.**

Year / Name	1900 Adherents	1900 %	1970 Adherents	1970 %	mid-1990 Adherents	mid-1990 %	Annual change 1990-2000 Natural	Conversion	Total	Rate	mid-1995 Adherents	mid-1995 %	mid-2000 Adherents	mid-2000 %	mid-2025 Adherents	mid-2025 %
Muslims	522	87.0	159	45.6	389	63.9	9	1	10	2.21	465	66.4	484	66.7	573	65.6
Christians	**60**	**10.0**	**150**	**43.0**	**160**	**26.3**	**3**	**-2**	**1**	**0.49**	**165**	**23.6**	**168**	**23.1**	**180**	**20.6**
PROFESSION																
professing Christians	**60**	**10.0**	**150**	**43.0**	**160**	**26.3**	**3**	**-2**	**1**	**0.49**	**165**	**23.6**	**168**	**23.1**	**180**	**20.6**
AFFILIATION																
unaffiliated Christians	6	1.0	40	11.5	40	6.6	1	0	1	1.18	45	6.4	45	6.2	50	5.7
affiliated Christians	**54**	**9.0**	**110**	**31.5**	**120**	**19.7**	**2**	**-2**	**0**	**0.25**	**120**	**17.1**	**123**	**16.9**	**130**	**14.9**
Anglicans	48	8.0	70	20.1	80	13.1	2	-2	0	0.37	80	11.4	83	11.4	85	9.7
Roman Catholics	6	1.0	40	11.5	40	6.6	1	-1	0	0.00	40	5.7	40	5.5	45	5.2
Trans-megabloc groupings																
Evangelicals	20	3.3	10	2.9	8	1.3	0	0	0	2.26	8	1.1	10	1.4	20	2.3
Pentecostals/Charismatics	0	0.0	0	0.0	10	1.6	0	1	1	4.14	12	1.7	15	2.1	20	2.3
Great Commission Christians	**50**	**8.3**	**35**	**10.0**	**60**	**9.9**	**1**	**-1**	**0**	**0.49**	**60**	**8.6**	**63**	**8.7**	**65**	**7.5**
Nonreligious	0	0.0	10	2.9	35	5.8	1	0	1	1.34	40	5.7	40	5.5	60	6.9
Baha'is	0	0.0	10	2.9	20	3.3	0	1	1	3.05	25	3.6	27	3.7	50	5.7
Chinese folk-religionists	18	3.0	20	5.7	5	0.8	0	0	0	3.42	5	0.7	7	1.0	10	1.2
World A (unevangelized persons)	480	80.0	150	43.0	339	55.8	9	-6	3	0.74	370	52.9	365	50.4	399	45.8
World B (evangelized non-Christians)	60	10.0	48	14.0	109	17.9	1	8	9	5.81	164	23.5	192	26.5	293	33.6
World C (Christians)	60	10.0	150	43.0	160	26.3	3	-2	1	0.49	165	23.6	168	23.1	180	20.6
Country's population	**600**	**100.0**	**349**	**100.0**	**609**	**100.0**	**13**	**0**	**13**	**1.77**	**700**	**100.0**	**726**	**100.0**	**873**	**100.0**

COLUMNS, ROWS.
For meanings and definitions, see Codebook (Part 3). Note that, by definition, total 'Christians' = professing + crypto-Christians, which also = affiliated + unaffiliated Christians, and also = Great Commission Christians + latent Christians. Percentages may not always total exactly, due to rounding.

CENSUSES.
30.VI.1961: 73.2% Muslims and Chinese folk-religionists, 13.5% Anglicans, 6.8% Protestants, 5.8% Roman Catholics, 0.5% nonreligious. **30.VI.1966:** 71.2% Muslims and Chinese folk-religionists, 16.3% Anglicans, 6.9% Roman Catholics, 5.4% Protestants, 0.2% nonreligious. **1981:** 67.3% Muslims, 10.3% nonreligious, 8.5% Anglicans, 7.2% Protestants, 6.7% Roman Catholics. **1986:** 66.9% Muslims, 12.7% nonreligious, 8.6% Roman Catholics, 6.2% Protestants, 5.6% Anglicans.

NOTES ON RELIGIONS
BAHA'IS. A first spiritual assembly was begun in 1960 on West Island, and is still the sole assembly (1998).
CHRISTIANS. Europeans, Anglo-Australians, and some Chinese.
MUSLIMS. Descendants of Malays, among whom there are still animistic practices.
NONRELIGIOUS. Europeans and Anglo-Australians.

Great Commission Instrument Panel: status of Cocos (Keeling) Islands (for explanation see start of Part 4)

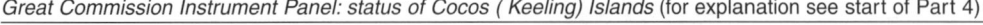

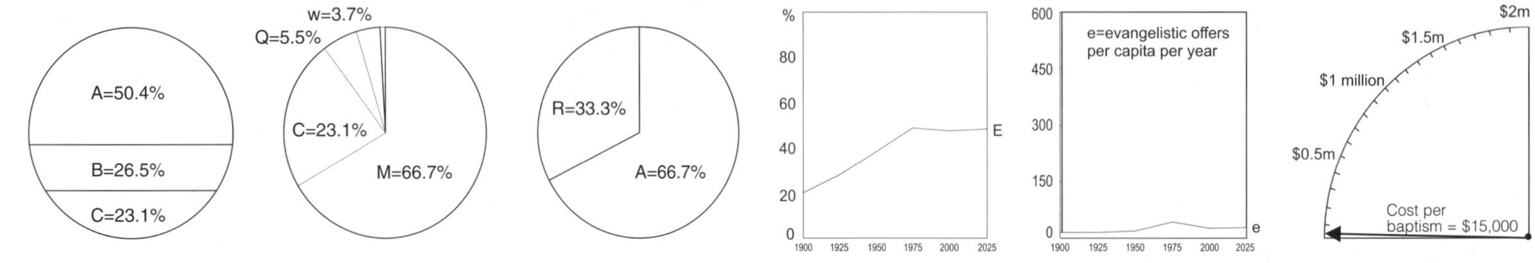

3 Worlds, AD 2000 | Religions, AD 2000 | Ecclesiastical blocs | Evangelization, 1900-2025 | Offers, 1900-2025 | Cost-effectiveness, AD 2000

Country summary. **Worlds A, B, C by ethnolinguistic peoples, cities, and major civil divisions in Cocos (Keeling) Islands.**

	PEOPLES							CITIES							CIVIL DIVISIONS						
World	Num	Pop 2000	C%	Christians	E%	U%	Unevangelized	Num	Pop 2000	C%	Christians	E%	U%	Unevangelized	Num	Pop 2000	C%	Christians	E%	U%	Unevangelized
A	2	515	0.39	2	29	71	364	0	0	0.00	0	0	0	0	1	726	16.94	123	50	50	366
B	2	109	54.13	59	98	2	2	1	551	19.06	105	54	46	255	0	0	0.00	0	0	0	0
C	1	102	59.80	61	100	0	0	0	0	0.00	0	0	0	0	0	0	0.00	0	0	0	0
Total	**5**	**726**	**16.80**	**122**	**50**	**50**	**366**	**1**	**551**	**19.06**	**105**	**54**	**46**	**255**	**1**	**726**	**16.94**	**123**	**50**	**50**	**366**

Country status. Cocos (Keeling) Islands is an Australian territory comprised of a group of 27 islands in the Indian Ocean. The chief product of the economy is copra.

HUMAN LIFE AND LIBERTY

Human rights and freedoms. As a territory of Australia, Australian laws fully protect human rights.

NON-CHRISTIAN RELIGIONS

Islam is the main religion of the Malays who make up 66% of the population. There are also a few Chinese folk-religionists.

CHRISTIANITY

Christians are largely Europeans and Australians, with some Chinese. For Anglicans, the Cocos Islands are part of the Church of England in Australia. For Catholics, the territory is under the archdiocese of Perth. The number of Catholics varies according to the work force on the island. There are no resident religious personnel, but a priest visits the island yearly. Anglicans numbered 20% of the population in 1970, mostly from Australia, but then fell rapidly to 11.4% by 1995.

CATHOLIC CHURCH. The Holy See has no diplomatic relations with Cocos (Keeling Island) in AD 2000.

Indigenous missions. There is no missionary outreach from the Cocos Islands.

CHURCH AND STATE

As a private and commercial property, then later a British and Australian territory, the islands have never made religion a factor of importance. Uninhabited until 1826, the islands were first discovered by William Keeling of the East India Company in 1609. John Clunies-Ross arrived in 1827 and developed extensive coconut plantations, virtually ruling the area as his private possession after 1831. Britain annexed the islands in 1878, but the Clunies-Ross family was left in control until 1955 when they became an Australian Commonwealth territory. The Australian constitution makes provision for free profession and practice of religion in all its territories.

FUTURE TRENDS AND PROSPECTS

The nonreligious have exhibited steady growth and are likely to increase to 7.2% of the population from a 1970 figure of 2%.

Christians, Muslims, and the nonreligious will likely represent the population in an approximate 40:40:10 ratio well into the 21st century.

BIBLIOGRAPHY

Cocos (Keeling) Islands: Cocos Malay culture. P. Bunce. West Island, Cocos (Keeling) Islands: Department of Territories, 1987. 31p.

Cocos Keeling: the islands time forgot. K. Mullen. Sydney: Angus & Robertson, 1974. 121p.

Kings of the Cocos: the story of the settlement on the atoll of Keeling–Cocos in the Indian Ocean. J. S. Hughes. London: Methuen, 1950. 164p.

Country Table 2. **Organized churches and denominations in Cocos (Keeling) Islands.**

Official name (bold type = church with over 10% of all affiliated) 1	Begun 2	Type 3	Counc 4	Congs 5	Adults 6	Affiliated 1970 7	Affiliated 1995 8	G% 9	Names, notes, and other statistics (see Codebook, Part 3) 10
Catholic Church (M Perth)		R-Lat	P....	1	20	40	40	0.05	Expatriate laborers. No resident personnel; annual visit from Perth (Australia).
Ch of England in Australia (D Perth)		A-Cen	awe..	1	30	70	80	0.05	Included in Diocese of Perth. Expatriates; services in English.
Totals				**2**	**50**	**110**	**120**		

Churches, members, growth, 1900-2025	Congs	Adults	Affiliated	G%	Total denominations	6 Megablocs: O	R	A	P	I	m
Total churches, members, and denominations (mid-1900)	1	30	54	1.02	1	0	0	1	0	0	0
Total churches, members, and denominations (mid-1970)	2	60	110	1.02	2	0	1	1	0	0	0
Total churches, members, and denominations (mid-1990)	2	50	120	0.44	2	0	1	1	0	0	0
Total churches, members, and denominations (mid-1995)	2	50	120	0.00	2	0	1	1	0	0	0
Total churches, members, and denominations (mid-2000)	3	51	123	0.50	2	0	1	1	0	0	0
Total churches, members, and denominations (mid-2025)	10	54	130	0.22	9	0	1	1	1	5	1

COLOMBIA

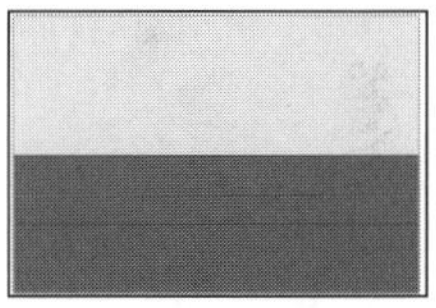

SECULAR DATA, AD 2000

STATE

Official name: La República de Colombia (The Republic of Colombia).
Short name: Colombia. **Adjective of nationality:** Colombian.
Flag: Tricolor with wide yellow stripe atop narrower blue and red stripes.
Area: 1,141,568 sq. km. (440,762 sq. mi.).
Government: Unitary multiparty republic with two legislative houses, since 1990 (1514 Spanish colony, 1819 Independence from Spain as New Granada, 1863 renamed United States of Colombia, 1974 2-party republic).
Legislature: Congress: Senate, 102 members; House of Representatives, 165 members.
Official language: Spanish (Español/Castella).
Monetary unit: 1 peso (Col$) = 100 centavos. **US$1=** Col$1,547.
Chief cities: BOGOTA 6,834,000; Medellin 3,831,000; Cali 2,082,000; Barranquilla 1,246,000; Cartagena 918,000.
Political divisions: 26 provinces.
Armed forces: 146,000.

DEMOGRAPHY

Population: 42,321,000.
Population density: 37.0/sq. km. (96.0/sq. mi.).
Under 15 years: 13,852,000.
Growth rate p.a.: 1.68% (births 22.31, deaths 5.48).
Mortality: Infant, per 1,000: 25.6; **Maternal per 100,000:** 100.0.
Life expectancy: 72 (male 69, female 75).
Household size: 5.4. **Floor area per person, sq.m:** 11.0.
Major languages: Spanish, English, German, Chibcha, Guajiro, and about 90 other tribal languages.
Urban dwellers: 74.94%. **Urban growth rate p.a.:** 2.0%.
Labor force: 34%.

ETHNOLINGUISTIC PEOPLES

47.3% Colombian Mestizo; 23.0% Colombian Mulatto; 20.0% Colombian White; 6.0% Colombian Black; 1.0% Zambo.

ECONOMY

National income p.a. per person: US$1,910; **per family:** US$10,314.

EDUCATION

Adult literacy: 91% (male 91%, female 91%). **Schools:** 44,693. **Universities:** 235. **School enrolment:** female/male: 92%/85%.

HEALTH

Access to health services: 60%. **Access to safe water:** 76%.
Hospitals: 947 (14 beds per 10,000). **Doctors:** 36,551.
Blind: 30,000. **Deaf:** 2,334,300. **Murder rate:** 81.
Lepers: 50,000. **Underweight prevalence under 5:** 8%.

LITERATURE

New book titles p.a.: 6,350 (150 p.a. per million). **Periodicals:** 112.
Newspapers: 46 dailies.

COMMUNICATION (per 1,000 people)

Phones: 100 **(21% mobile). Radios:** 150. **TV sets:** 188.
Daily newspaper circulation: 64. **Computers:** 50.

REFUGEES

Alien refugees from other countries: 400.
Internal displacement: 600,000.

HUMAN LIFE AND LIBERTY (optimum condition=100.0%)

HDI: 84.8. **HSI:** 49.0. **HFI:** 35.0. **EFL:** 40.0.

Country status. Colombia is generally considered to be the third most important South American country after Brazil and Argentina, although it is only the fourth largest in size. It is a heavily urbanized nation and has 4 cities with a population of one million or more. Coffee is the most important product.

HUMAN LIFE AND LIBERTY

Human need and development. Colombia has a substantial underclass, estimated at 75% of the population, whose human needs remain unmet. Because class consciousness is historically strong, these lower class members do not feel themselves bound by a common national identity with the middle and upper classes. Although the lower class includes union laborers, small merchants, some white-collar workers, and the minifundistas, or small landowners, in the mass, they are composed of illiterate and impoverished peasants and workers who live on the margin of subsistence and possess few skills. The vast majority of them are Blacks, Indians and other dark-skinned persons. For the rural poor the only means of changing the vicious cycle of poverty is to migrate to the city, but for the large part such migration does not ameliorate their condition but only helps them to exchange their country dwellings for shantytowns, called barrios, with no running water or electricity. There is also a high rate of unemployment in this migrant population, contributing to the spread of violence and drug trafficking. Criminal attacks and homicide, often called as 'bloody deaths', account for 45% of deaths in persons between 15 and 44 years of age. Although Colombians enjoy significantly better health care and nutrition than previous generations, the benefits of health care are not evenly distributed among the different strata and regions. Life expectancy is much higher in the cities than in the countryside. Infant mortality rates are among the highest in Latin America at close to 26 per 1,000 live births.

Human rights and freedoms. Colombia is a multiparty democracy whose civilian governments have withstood extraordinary levels of violence within the country for over 40 years. The main source of human rights violations is not the government as much

Country Table 1. **Religious adherents in Colombia, AD 1900-2025.**

Year	1900		1970		mid-1990		Annual change, 1990-2000				mid-1995		mid-2000		mid-2025	
Name	*Adherents*	*%*	*Adherents*	*%*	*Adherents*	*%*	*Natural*	*Conversion*	*Total*	*Rate*	*Adherents*	*%*	*Adherents*	*%*	*Adherents*	*%*
Christians	**3,055,000**	**79.9**	**22,040,700**	**97.7**	**33,919,150**	**97.0**	**713,049**	**-10,668**	**702,381**	**1.90**	**37,355,660**	**96.9**	**40,942,956**	**96.7**	**57,713,500**	**96.6**
PROFESSION																
professing Christians	**3,055,000**	**79.9**	**22,040,700**	**97.7**	**33,919,150**	**97.0**	**713,049**	**-10,668**	**702,381**	**1.90**	**37,355,660**	**96.9**	**40,942,956**	**96.7**	**57,713,500**	**96.6**
AFFILIATION																
unaffiliated Christians	0	0.0	5,700	0.0	5,650	0.0	119	23	142	2.26	5,660	0.0	7,068	0.0	13,500	0.0
affiliated Christians	**3,055,000**	**79.9**	**22,035,000**	**97.7**	**33,913,500**	**97.0**	**712,930**	**-10,691**	**702,239**	**1.90**	**37,350,000**	**96.9**	**40,935,888**	**96.7**	**57,700,000**	**96.6**
Roman Catholics	3,058,980	80.0	21,807,580	96.7	33,640,000	96.2	707,142	-4,142	703,000	1.92	37,063,780	96.2	40,670,000	96.1	56,172,000	94.0
Protestants	2,000	0.1	324,927	1.4	740,000	2.1	15,555	20,445	36,000	4.04	940,840	2.4	1,100,000	2.6	2,500,000	4.2
Independents	0	0.0	110,000	0.5	425,000	1.2	8,934	2,066	11,000	2.33	480,473	1.3	535,000	1.3	900,000	1.5
Marginal Christians	20	0.0	23,694	0.1	225,000	0.6	4,730	270	5,000	2.03	251,390	0.7	275,000	0.7	500,000	0.8
Orthodox	0	0.0	4,000	0.0	6,800	0.0	143	-103	40	0.57	7,000	0.0	7,200	0.0	9,000	0.0
Anglicans	0	0.0	2,000	0.0	3,400	0.0	71	-51	20	0.57	3,500	0.0	3,600	0.0	5,000	0.0
doubly-affiliated	-2,000	-0.1	-34,201	-0.2	-716,700	-2.1	-15,066	-30,755	-45,821	5.07	-946,983	-2.5	-1,174,912	-2.8	-1,736,000	-2.9
disaffiliated	-4,000	-0.1	-203,000	-0.9	-410,000	-1.2	-8,619	1,619	-7,000	1.59	-450,000	-1.2	-480,000	-1.1	-650,000	-1.1
Trans-megabloc groupings																
Evangelicals	2,000	0.1	210,000	0.9	420,000	1.2	8,829	8,171	17,000	3.46	498,745	1.3	590,000	1.4	1,200,000	2.0
Pentecostals/Charismatics	0	0.0	565,000	2.5	10,200,000	29.2	214,413	24,087	238,500	2.12	11,362,583	29.5	12,585,000	29.7	19,500,000	32.6
Great Commission Christians	**230,000**	**6.0**	**1,922,000**	**8.5**	**2,203,000**	**6.3**	**46,309**	**759**	**47,068**	**1.96**	**2,428,000**	**6.3**	**2,673,679**	**6.3**	**4,183,000**	**7.0**
Nonreligious	3,000	0.1	99,000	0.4	375,000	1.1	7,883	3,624	11,507	2.71	424,700	1.1	490,070	1.2	900,000	1.5
Spiritists	1,000	0.0	10,000	0.0	305,000	0.9	6,411	3,822	10,233	2.94	354,700	0.9	407,326	1.0	600,000	1.0
Ethnoreligionists	765,000	20.0	280,000	1.2	195,000	0.6	4,099	1,965	6,064	2.74	216,300	0.6	255,635	0.6	250,000	0.4
Atheists	1,000	0.0	44,000	0.2	66,000	0.2	1,387	514	1,901	2.56	71,970	0.2	85,009	0.2	105,000	0.2
Baha'is	0	0.0	24,300	0.1	48,000	0.1	1,009	667	1,676	3.04	54,800	0.1	64,758	0.2	100,000	0.2
Muslims	0	0.0	50,000	0.2	40,000	0.1	841	-4	837	1.92	40,900	0.1	48,373	0.1	60,000	0.1
Jews	0	0.0	10,000	0.0	8,750	0.0	184	-29	155	1.64	9,700	0.0	10,299	0.0	8,000	0.0
Hindus	0	0.0	0	0.0	8,000	0.0	168	57	225	2.51	8,670	0.0	10,248	0.0	12,500	0.0
Chinese folk-religionists	0	0.0	1,000	0.0	1,700	0.0	36	9	45	2.36	1,800	0.0	2,147	0.0	3,000	0.0
Buddhists	0	0.0	1,000	0.0	1,300	0.0	27	12	39	2.64	1,400	0.0	1,687	0.0	2,500	0.0
Other religionists	0	0.0	1,000	0.0	2,100	0.0	44	31	75	3.11	2,400	0.0	2,852	0.0	3,500	0.0
World A (unevangelized persons)	650,250	17.0	225,605	1.0	104,910	0.3	2,039	222	2,261	2.12	115,624	0.3	126,963	0.3	239,032	0.4
World B (evangelized non-Christians)	119,750	3.1	294,230	1.3	945,940	2.7	20,050	10,446	30,496	2.84	1,070,324	2.8	1,251,081	3.0	1,805,468	3.0
World C (Christians)	3,055,000	79.9	22,040,700	97.7	33,919,150	97.0	713,049	-10,668	702,381	1.90	37,355,660	96.9	40,942,956	96.7	57,713,500	96.6
Country's population	**3,825,000**	**100.0**	**22,560,536**	**100.0**	**34,970,000**	**100.0**	**735,138**	**0**	**735,138**	**1.93**	**38,541,609**	**100.0**	**42,321,000**	**100.0**	**59,758,000**	**100.0**

COLUMNS, ROWS.
For meanings and definitions, see Codebook (Part 3). Note that, by definition, total 'Christians' = professing + crypto-Christians, which also = affiliated + unaffiliated Christians, and also = Great Commission Christians + latent Christians. Percentages may not always total exactly, due to rounding.

CENSUSES.
The religion question has not been asked in government censuses.

NOTES ON RELIGIONS
ATHEISTS. 2 parties: Communist Party of Colombia (PCC) (legal; pro-Soviet): and Communist Party of Colombia Marxist-Leninist (pro-Chinese).
BAHA'IS. Very rapid growth from 11 local spiritual assemblies (1964) to 161 (1973), and to 252 (1996). Mass conversions have occurred in the Guajira in the extreme north.
BUDDHISTS. Chinese.
COUNTRY'S POPULATION. During the undeclared civil war La Violencia of 1940-52, over 100,000 persons were killed including many Protestants.
DISAFFILIATED. This term is used here to describe persons who, although baptized Roman Catholics and therefore regarded by the Catholic Church as still affiliated to it (and hence enumerated as such), have recently withdrawn or disaffiliated themselves completely from Christianity and now profess publicly to be either nonreligious (agnostics) or atheists. Because their statistics represent a duplication, they are shown in the table above as a negative quantity (with a minus sign).
DOUBLY-AFFILIATED. The term covers those affiliated to, or claimed by, both the Catholic Church and also a church termed Evangélica by the state (Protestant, Colombian indigenous, marginal Protestant or Anglican), i.e. baptized Catholics who have recently become Evangelicals or others. Because their statistics represent a duplication, they are shown in the table as a negative quantity (with a minus sign).
ETHNORELIGIONISTS. In 1850, Amerindians numbered over a million (almost all then being ethnoreligionists) and made up 50% of the entire nation, falling to 2.5% (390,000) by 1950 and 1.6% by 1970. Of the 360,000 lowland or jungle Amerindians in over 50 tribes left in the interior in 1970, a high proportion were still animists. The largest tribe today, the Guajiro (114,000), remains 80% traditionalist. Others include the Ica (Arhuaco 6,000), Coreguaje, Cuna, Macu, Barasano and Tatuyo.
HINDUS. Converts since 1972 to the Divine Light Mission from India and the USA (led by Guru Maharaj Ji); young people in Cali and other cities. ISKCON (Hare Krishna) also operates a center.
INDEPENDENTS. In over 50 denominations or groupings in 1995 (see Table 2).
JEWS. Greeks, Turks, Germans and other Europeans since 1918; in large cities; 4 synagogues and 3 communities (Ashkenazi, Sefardi, Eastern), declining due to emigration to Israel.
MUSLIMS. Arab immigrants from the Middle East, including numerous Palestinians.
OTHER RELIGIONISTS. Adherents of smaller religions and cults including Rosicrucians (4 AMORC centers).
PENTECOSTALS/CHARISMATICS. Begun in 1967, the Catholic Charismatic Renewal in Colombia has seen vast crowds at its activities, with 10,000 regular weekly prayer groups. In 1989, 80 bishops participated at La Ceja, Colombia, in the 3rd Latin American Bishops Retreat in a Charismatic Context, with the 4th in September 1990. In 1994, the 5th National Leaders Congress, in Bogota, drew 1,300 CCR leaders.

Great Commission Instrument Panel: status of Colombia (for explanation see start of Part 4)

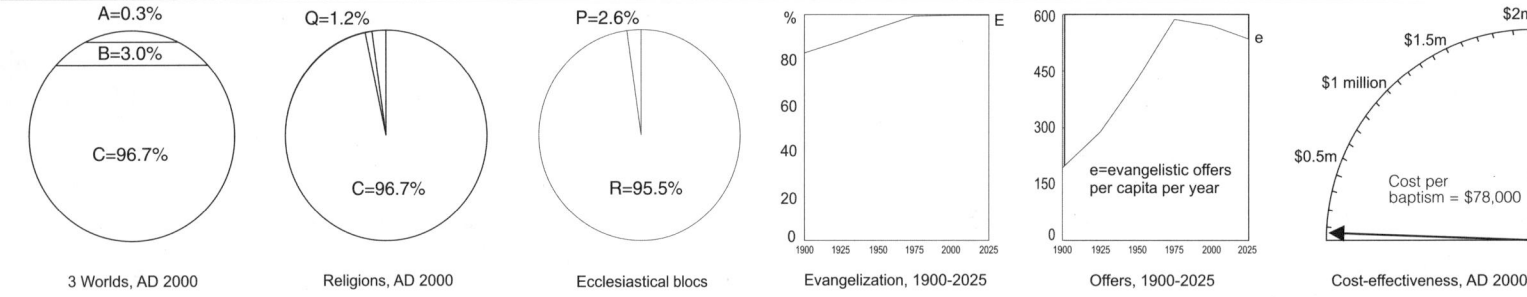

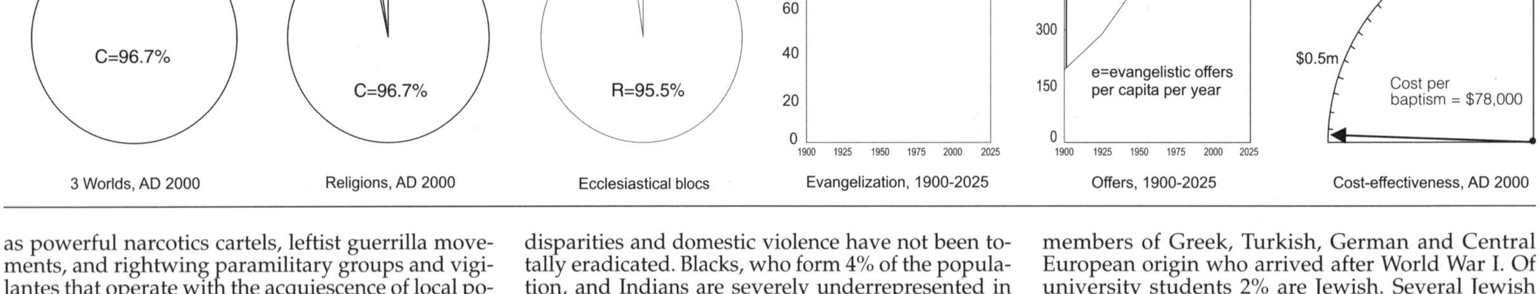

as powerful narcotics cartels, leftist guerrilla movements, and rightwing paramilitary groups and vigilantes that operate with the acquiescence of local police and military officials. Narcotics traffickers and drug lords control multi-billion dollar enterprises and attempt to intimidate the government, the judiciary, and the public through narcoterrorism. The guerrillas, acting with the financial support of the drug cartels kidnap local government officials and provoke reprisals. Antiguerrilla operations by the police and military often result in human rights abuses, including murders, disappearances, and torture. As a result, Colombia has one of the highest murder rates in the world, estimated at several thousands by the Jesuit-run Center for Investigations and Popular Education. The government has taken a number of measures to curb abuses by security and police personnel through its watchdog agency, the Procuraduria. The criminal justice system appears ineffective against the simultaneous threats from the left and right. Most detainees never come to trial but merely serve the minimum sentence applicable to their crimes. Despite guarantees of equality in the Constitution, both women and minorities suffer de facto discrimination. In the case of women, salary disparities and domestic violence have not been totally eradicated. Blacks, who form 4% of the population, and Indians are severely underrepresented in public service as well as parliament.

Human environment. Largescale and indiscriminate logging is the principal environmental problem. Heavy rains in cleared areas often wash the soils away resulting in clogged streams. It also leads to soil degradation and depletion of natural forest resources. The large stock of endemic plant and bird species, particularly in the Choco region, has been disappearing at a fast rate in recent years.

NON-CHRISTIAN RELIGIONS

Amerindian tribal religions are practiced by a number of unevangelized lowland and jungle tribes in the interior, including the Arhuaco, Coreguaje, Cuna, Guajiro, Macu, Barasano, and Tatuyo.

Baha'i has grown very rapidly since 1964, to 161 local spiritual assemblies by 1973. By 1995 adherents had mushroomed to 55,000 in 252 assemblies.

Judaism, with about 10,000 adherents, is present in the larger urban centers of Bogotá, Medellín, Cali and Barranquilla. There are 4 Jewish synagogues and 3 communities (Ashkenazi, Sefardi and Eastern), with members of Greek, Turkish, German and Central European origin who arrived after World War I. Of university students 2% are Jewish. Several Jewish sports and social clubs are active, as well as the organizations B'nai B'rith and WIZO.

Other religions include Islam, Hinduism (the Divine Light Mission since 1972), and spiritism. In 1975 a first World Congress of Sorcery was held in Bogota.

Christians. Stamps honoring (*left*) St. Vincent de Paul, (*right*) Christ and all Martyrs.

Country summary. **Worlds A, B, C by ethnolinguistic peoples, cities, and major civil divisions in Colombia.**

	PEOPLES							*CITIES*							*CIVIL DIVISIONS*						
World	*Num*	*Pop 2000*	*C%*	*Christians*	*E%*	*U%*	*Unevangelized*	*Num*	*Pop 2000*	*C%*	*Christians*	*E%*	*U%*	*Unevangelized*	*Num*	*Pop 2000*	*C%*	*Christians*	*E%*	*U%*	*Unevangelized*
A	8	21,022	3.96	833	43	57	12,034	0	0	0.00	0	0	0	0	0	0	0.00	0	0	0	0
B	22	272,918	23.18	63,267	66	34	93,999	0	0	0.00	0	0	0	0	0	0	0.00	0	0	0	0
C	69	42,027,419	97.25	40,871,792	100	0	13,576	35	21,146,165	96.25	20,352,909	100	0	57,751	26	42,321,359	96.73	40,935,888	100	0	119,611
Total	**99**	**42,321,359**	**96.73**	**40,935,892**	**100**	**0**	**119,609**	**35**	**21,146,165**	**96.25**	**20,352,909**	**100**	**0**	**57,751**	**26**	**42,321,359**	**96.73**	**40,935,888**	**100**	**0**	**119,611**

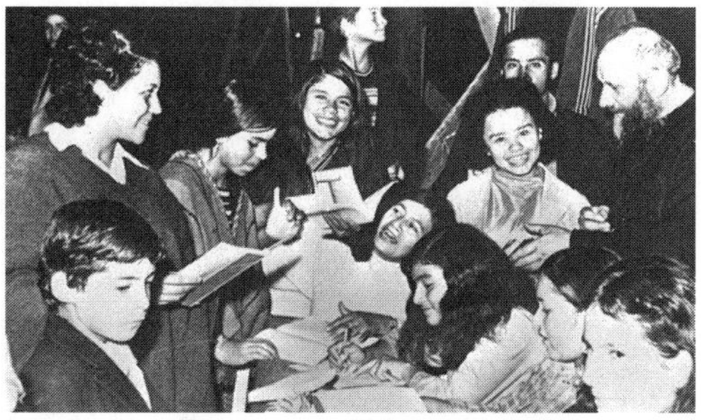

(*Above*) Catholic Charismatics; (*below*) Bible Impact March in Villavicencio, 1995.

CHRISTIANITY

CATHOLIC CHURCH. Spanish explorers touched northwestern South America in 1499, and it became known as New Granada with headquarters at Bogotá·. The first Catholic diocese was established in 1534 and the first seminary in 1582. Encomiendas (commissions) were established and made responsible for organizing the material welfare of the Indians, and peaceful relations with them, but because of their abuses, missionaries often found themselves in conflict with the encomienda system. A severe decline in the number of clergy took place with the declaration of Independence in 1819 and the dissolution of the patronage system with Spain. Six episcopal sees were vacant by 1813. The government's usurpation of the right of patronage was rejected by Rome, and religious persecution increased during the next decades. By 1853 separation of church and state was established and civil marriage and divorce introduced. In 1861, all church property was appropriated by the government and church officials continued to be exiled; and 2 years later a new constitution was promulgated which disregarded the juridical personality of the church. Negotiations were renewed with the Holy See in 1878 and a concordat eventually completed in 1887.

In Columbia, where the church is reputed to be the most uniformly conservative of all Roman Catholic churches in Latin America, the specific action of the church is carried on in good measure by the need to conserve, defend, and extend what is frequently called the Catholic 'fact', that is the existence of a Colombian people who are considered to be almost 100% Catholic. Thus episcopal documents do not speak of the faith as being the free and conscious response of a person but insist on a collective understanding of 'customs', 'traditions', and the 'Christian heritage'. Another criterion of church action is protection of the people's faith against errors and deviations from religious conduct, and the importance given to large meetings and massive concentrations of the faithful, for motives which are detached from the concerns of the People of God themselves.

Several concrete examples of this situation can be given. The first concerns the International Eucharistic Congress of 1965. Shortly beforehand in April 1965, the metropolitan archbishops published a declaration listing alleged evils of the country against which the forthcoming Congress should serve as a protection; this list varied from 'comic programs on the radio' to the advance of Communism identified as 'the most serious peril for religion and the country'. Secondly, in 1958 Marian congresses were organized in every parish in Colombia specifically to combat crime, violence and guerrilla warfare. The same objects had earlier been the case also in the National Marian Congress of 1954, the procession of the statue of the Virgin of Fatima in 1950, and the National Eucharistic Congress of 1949.

On the other hand, it was at Medellín in Colombia that the Second General Conference of CELAM took place in 1968, which made a major impact on the Catholic Church in Latin America and provided the basis for change in its life and attitudes. At Medellín the Latin American bishops affirmed their intention of involving the church in the life of the people and seeking their full liberation. It was decided there that the church's preaching, catechesis, and liturgy should reflect the communal nature of Christianity, and should denounce class conflicts, colonialism, and repression as affronts to the gospel. A few years later, however, the Colombian bishops provided active support for those opposed to a theology of liberation and rejected a catechetical plan patterned after the directives of Medellín. The archbishop of Bogota even prevented Dom Helder Camara, a radical fellow-prelate from Recife in Brazil, from speaking in Colombia. This situation resulted in the creation of several opposition movements within the church, the most renowned being Golconda, founded in Buenaventura in 1968 by about 50 priests, which had drawn in numerous laity also before going out of existence in 1970 to be succeeded by other smaller less-structured bodies. All of these groups have in common a socialist orientation and opposition to privilege in the church and to its pre-conciliar structures.

A majority of the institutions of CELAM are located in Medellín, including its general secretariat, its only pastoral institute and a large number of its departments. The same is true for CLAR, which serves a similar function for religious personnel in Latin America.

With regard to individual faith and practice, a 1970 survey found that 63% of all Catholics claim to attend mass at least once a week, 67% pray to God daily, and 66% pray to the Virgin Mary; only 24% do not pray at all. This is in marked contrast to the situation in 1951 when only 10% of the Colombian people were said to fulfill the minimum requirements of Catholicism. Since then there has been a resurgence of conservative Catholic practice.

Colombia is characterized by a severe scarcity of priests. In 1969, 2,873 diocesan priests (68% of the total) worked in the 9 archdioceses and 29 dioceses which cover 35% of the country and 92% of the population; 1,363 religious priests (32%) were responsible for the remaining 18 mission vicariates and prefectures. This was a density of 220 per million Catholics. By 1992 priests had greatly increased to 4,351 diocesan and 2,071 religions, but since the church had grown enormously over those years, the ratio had in fact fallen to 199 priests per million Catholics.

Most priests and religious are native Colombians, although the first Indian priest, of the Paez people, was not ordained until 1973.

The Holy See has diplomatic relations with Colombia and in AD 2000 is represented to government and the Catholic hierarchy by a nuncio residing in Bogotá.

PROTESTANT CHURCHES. The first Protestant missionary arrived in Colombia in 1825, an agent of the British and Foreign Bible Society, and by the second half of the century the society had published the first New Testament in South America. In 1856 the Presbyterian Church, USA sent its first missionary to Bogota. For many years Presbyterians were the only Protestant workers in Colombia and achieved renown through their well-developed schools and medical centers. However, church membership has remained small compared with more recent arrivals. The Evangelical Alliance Mission (TEAM) opened work in 1906 in both Venezuela and then eastern Colombia, while the Gospel Missionary Union extended its work from neighboring Ecuador to Colombia in 1908, beginning a printing press and a monthly publication. The Christian and Missionary Alliance entered Colombia from Ecuador in 1923. Its bookstore in Cali supplies 80% of all literature sold in Colombia's Evangelical bookshops.

With the exception of Cumberland Presbyterians (1925), Adventists (1921) and Salvation Army (1929), the remaining Protestant churches all appeared after 1930. The United Pentecostal Church had the largest membership until 1970, followed by the International Church of the Foursquare Gospel, which is also Pentecostal, and the Seventh-day Adventists. Protestantism is especially strong among the large Negro population on the islands of San Andres and Providencia, which are located near Nicaragua, 400 miles from Colombia.

With the close alliance at times between the Catholic Church and the Colombia government, Protestantism, as been as suspect as Communism, and Protestant missions consistently met with frequent harassment until recent years. Only when the Liberal party came to power in 1930 did Protestant missions receive government recognition. The influx of Protestant missionaries during the period of the Liberal Party, particularly during World War II, was immediately followed by the undeclared civil war La Violencia during 1948-52, when the Conservative Party returned to power. More than 100,000 persons were killed, including many Protestants, and in addition 270 Protestant schools were closed and 60 churches destroyed including three-quarters of all churches of the Gospel Missionary Union. During this period, however, Protestantism grew rapidly from 7,908 baptized believers in 1948 to 11,958 in 1953 and to 33,156 in 1960. In recent years the atmosphere has improved markedly, and Evangelicals are given increasing freedom to hold open-air meetings, street parades, city-wide campaigns, and radio broadcasts. As one result, Protestant growth today is rapid, with a multiplication of small churches and out-stations by conservative and Pentecostal churches, which are particularly successful in the large shanty areas of urban centers.

INDIGENOUS CHURCHES. A number of independent, mostly pentecostal, churches have been formed in Colombia since World War II, but all remain small except for a massive schism in 1970 of Colombian pentecostals rejecting centralized control from the USA headquarters of the United Pentecostal Church. The new body developed extensive overseas mission work by Colombians. By 1997, independent Charismatic churches were making vast inroads.

Art and architecture. The capital contains hundreds of churches including some of the oldest colonial ones. The cathedral, a blend of Ionic, Doric, and Tuscan styles, has been rebuilt twice. It includes several relics and treasures, including a turquoise sepulcher inlaid with ivory and silver and gold filigree and set with thousands of precious stones. In one of the chapels is buried Gregorio Vasquez Arce y Ceballos, the national painter, many of whose paintings are in the cathedral. Other Bogota churches include the Chapel of Sagrario, La Concepcion, the oldest church built in the 16th century as part a nunnery, the Church of Santa Clara, the Jesuit church of San Ignacio, the Church of San Agustin, Santa Barbara Church, Church of San Juan de Dios, San Francisco Church, Church of La Veracruz, which became the National Pantheon in 1910, La Tercera Orden, and Church of Maria del Carmen. In Cartagena are equally ancient churches, including the Church of San Francisco, where the Inquisitors were lodged in the 17th century, the Jesuit Church of San Pedro Claver, the Church of Santisima Trinidad, the Chapel of San Roque, the Cathedral begun in 1575 and partially destroyed by Sir Francis Drake in 1586, the Church and Monastery of Santo Domingo, the Church and Convent of La Merced, the Monastery of San Agustin, the Church of Santo Torribio de Mongrovejo, and the Church and Monastery of Santa Clara of Assisi. Popayan is dominated by churches of which the most impressive are those of San Agustin and San Francisco. Equally famous are the La Incarnacion Chapel and the Chapel at Belen.

Renewal movements. In the 1990s the Pentecostal/Charismatic Renewal continued to spread rapidly across most older churches, and numbered over 12,585,000 adherents (of whom 4% Pentecostals, 92% Charismatics, and 4% Independents).

Indigenous missions. Though many Catholic Christians serve outside of Colombia, very few Protestants have embraced the missionary vision.

CHURCH AND STATE

Two juridical tests provide the foundation for defining the relationship between church and state in Colombia: the constitution of 1886, frequently revised; and the new concordat signed on 12 July 1973 between the government and the Holy See replacing the concordat of 31 December 1887 and all other conventions later signed by the 2 parties, notably the Convention concerning Missions of 29 January 1953 intended to last for 25 years.

The constitution (Article 53) guarantees freedom of conscience, declares that 'No-one will be disturbed because of his religious opinions nor obliged to profess belief nor to observe practices contrary to his conscience', and ensures also 'freedom of all religions which are not contrary to Christian morals or to the law'.

The new concordat, of 32 articles, continues to accord the Catholic Church a privileged status, although this is formulated in language more adapted to the modern era. Certain former privileges have been removed. Whereas Article 1 of the former concordat stated that 'The Roman Catholic Apostolic Religion is the religion of Colombia', Article 1 of the new concordat expresses it in these terms: 'The State, in view of the traditional Catholic sentiment of the Colombian nation, considers the Roman Catholic Apostolic Religion as an essential element of the common welfare and of the integral development of the national community. The State guarantees to the Catholic Church and to those who belong to it the full enjoyment of their religious rights without prejudice to the just religious liberty of other confessions and their members, as well as those of every citizen'. The most significant change of the new agreement is the ending of the 1953 missions treaty, which gave to religious orders exclusive rights in evangelization and education in mission territories, ignoring the rights of Protestant and other missionaries.

Article 7 recognizes the validity of marriages within the church, although it is understood that these marriages must be recorded also in a civil registry. A more controversial subject is dealt with in Article 9, which provides an opening for legislation making civil marriage possible for Catholics without their having to renounce their faith. Thus Article 9 opens the way to divorce for Colombians who are not married in religious ceremonies. Among other provisions, the Catholic Church is guaranteed 'full freedom and independence' (Article 2); the government is to make available public funds for the support of Catholic educational institutions (Article 11); Catholic instruction is to be offered in all public schools (Article 12); canonical law, although independent of civil law, is to be 'respected by the authorities of the Republic'; the Catholic Church is to be the beneficiary of a juridical personality, as are dioceses, religious communities and other entities permitted such by canon law; and the exemption from taxes on all property, which the Catholic Church previously profited from, is to be removed, except in the case of worship places, diocesan curias, dwellings of bishops and priests, and seminaries.

The signing of the concordat provoked considerable controversy among the public and impassioned debate in parliament, the House of Representatives finally approving it at the end of 1974 by 111 votes to 39. The opponents of the new concordat, especially the Evangelical Confederation of Colombia, were especially critical of the articles concerning marriage and generally all matters that they considered constituted an 'infringement of religious liberty'. Many Catholics are also skeptical concerning the real changes brought by the new text and hold that a concordat is no longer necessary. In January 1975, tax exemption was extended to Protestant churches and Jewish synagogues.

In recent years, an increasing number of Catholic priests and militant laymen, especially trade union members, have clashed with the dominant oligarchy and that part of the Catholic hierarchy closely linked with it. The most celebrated of these figures was Camilo Torres, chaplain of students at the University of Bogotá· in 1958. Trying various non-political movements of social action, he decided to enter the political arena as the only sphere offering possibilities for fundamental social change. Disavowed by cardinal Concha for having founded the United Front, a movement aiming to regroup all forces on the left, including communists, Torres ultimately requested lay status for himself. He was killed in February 1966 by Colombian forces fighting a Castroite guerrilla organization the Army of National Liberation (ELN). He had joined the movement 4 months earlier, convinced that armed revolt was the only hope for social change. Torres was influential in leading other priests and laymen to enter the ranks of the ELN. Several of these have been captured by the Colombian army. Domingo Lain, a Spanish priest expelled from Colombia in 1969 who later returned clandestinely to a position of leadership within the ELN, was killed in February 1974 during a clash between the army and the ELN. In 1975, increasingly frequent accusations were made by progressivist Catholic groups of priests and religious personnel to the effect that certain North American Protestant missions, the Evangelical Confederation of Colombia and various sectors of the Catholic Church, especially the papal nuncio, were linked to the CIA (Central Intelligence Agency, USA). The nunciature was burned to the ground during student demonstrations.

There is no government ministry of religious affairs in Colombia, nor obligation for churches or religions to be registered. In the 1990s the churches still had powerful voice, especially as the government's battle with drug lords heightened.

BROADCASTING AND MEDIA

IBRA-produced radio programs can be received from 14 stations in Bogota and Medellin. Shortwave programs from KNLS, HCJB (Ecuador), TWR (Antilles) and AWR (Costa Rica) can be easily received. Colombia is a member of UNDA. There are 11 local Catholic stations, most operating on AM frequencies.

CBN's *700 Club* and *Flying House* can be seen daily on 7 local channels, and is followed up by 2 counseling centers, soup kitchens, schools, orphanages, medical relief work, literature campaigns, and discipleship programs. This ministry has seen great response, particularly in Bogotá. TBN's programs can be viewed in Cali on channel 53.

Around 8.3 million people (22%) have seen the 'Jesus' Film: mainly through television (6.5 million) and film teams (1.7 million).

INTERDENOMINATIONAL ORGANIZATIONS

Twenty Protestant churches belong to the Evangelical Confederation of Colombia (Confederación Evangélica de Colombia) begun in 1950, with a Presbyterian as secretary. The Ministerial Association of Bogotá·, composed of both Protestant and Catholic clergy, was founded in 1970 for the purpose of dialogue and prayer.

FUTURE TRENDS AND PROSPECTS

Little change in the religious makeup of Colombia up to AD 2025 is envisaged.

The nonreligious could make significant inroads into the Christian community after AD 2025, perhaps growing past 5% before AD 2050. Another factor that could alter the religious situation is unexpected immigration of non-Christians from various world religions.

BIBLIOGRAPHY

'A comparative study of the political and social activism of new religious groups in Colombia.' M. L. Vanden Eykel. Ph.D. dissertation, George Washington University, Washington, DC, 1986. 463p.

'Bogotá, the middle-class, and the Héroes Alliance Church,' R. M. Searing Jr, *Urban mission*, 10 (March 1993), 43–51.

Called to die: the story of American linguist Chet Bitterman, slain by terrorists. S. Estes. Grand Rapids, MI: Zondervan, 1986. 214p.

Camilo Torres. Sondeos, no. 5. Cuernavaca, Mexico): CIDOC, 1966. 377p.

Colombia. R. H. Davis. *World bibliographical series*, vol. 112. Oxford, UK: CLIO Press, 1990. 206p. (See especially 'Religion,' 72-9).

'Colombia: "flashpoint of growth",' R. Niklaus, *Evangelical Missions Quarterly*, 21, 2 (April 1985), 174–176.

'Colombia: the institutional church and the popular,' D. H. Levine, in *Religion and political conflict in Latin America*, p.187–217. D. H. Levine (ed). Chapel Hill, NC: University of North Carolina Press, 1986.

'Continuities in Colombia [Catholic Church],' D. H. Levine, *Journal of Latin American Studies*, 17 (November 1985), 295–317.

Directorio de la Iglesia en Colombia, 1969. Bogota: Departmento de Sociologiá, 1969. (Roman Catholic).

Directorio Evangélico y Calendario de Oración de Colombia, 1975–76. Medellin: Tipografia Unión, 1975. (Annual).

Directorio nacional cristiano. Bogotá: Dinal, 1986. (annual).

Drame d'une minorité religieuse: le martyre de l'église protestante en Colombie: avant le Concile, un interdit à lever. E. Chastand. [Anduze, France]: The Author, [1961]. 37p.

'El Concordato en Colombia,' Cardinal a. López Trujillo (ed), *Revista Javeriana*, , 107 (September 1987), 611–667. (Indexer-assigned title).

'El proceso hacia la ministerialidad a partir de grupos de base en Colombia: una experiencia,' I. Marín López, in *Los ministerios en la Iglesia: perspectivas teológicas y realidades pastorales*, p.261–277. L. Rubio Morán et al. (eds). *Lux Mundi*, 60. Salamanca, Spain: Ediciones Súgueme, 1985. (Conference papers, Mexico City, 1983; Madrid, Spain, 1984.).

Explosion of people evangelism. D. C. Palmer. Wheaton, IL: Moody, 1977. 91p. (Pentecostal growth in Colombia).

For this cross I'll kill you. B. Olson. London: Lakeland, 1977. 191p. (Originally published Carol Stream, IL: Creation House, 1973).

'Goliath meets David: secularization and the rise of Protestantism in Colombia.' A. E. Worthington. M.A. thesis, Vanderbilt University, Nashville, TN, 1995. 100p.

Guia de las Iglesias Evangélicas de Colombia. Medellín: Retiro Nacional de Pastores, 1971.

Historia del Cristianismo Evangélico en Colombia. F. Ordoñez. Medellín: Tipografia Unión, 1956.

Iglesia, pueblo y política: un estudio de conflictos de intereses: Colombia, 1930–1955. A. M. Bidegaín. Bogotá: Pontificia Universidad Javeriana, Facultad de Teología, 1985. 201p.

'La Iglesia Católica y los indígenas del Putumayo,' A. Córdoba, *Revista Javeriana*, 96 (Auguat 1981), 113–123.

La Iglesia en Colombia: estructuras eclesiásticas. G. Pérez & I. Wust. Bogotá: Centro de Investigaciones Sociales, 1961. 194p.

'Las misiones protestantes y la resistencia indígena en el sur de Colombia,' J. Rappaport, *América Indígena*, 44, 1 (January–March 1984), 111–126.

Los evangélicos en Colombia: un analisis critico. [Colombia: CEDEC, 1979]. 268p.

Pentecostalism in Colombia: baptism by fire and spirit. C. B. Flora. Rutherford, NJ: Fairleigh Dickinson University Press, 1976. 288p.

Popular voices in Latin American Catholicism. D. H. Levine. *Studies in church and state.* Princeton, NJ: Princeton University Press, 1992. 425p.

'Protestantism, profile and process: a case study in religious change from Colombia, South America.' W. P. Thornton. Ph.D. dissertation, Southern Methodist University, Dallas, TX, 1981. 297p.

Reconciling heaven and earth: the transcendental enthusiasm and growth of an urban Protestant community, Bogotá, Colombia. K. W. Westmeier. New York: Verlag Peter Lang, 1986.

Religion and politics in Latin America: the Catholic Church in Venezuela and Colombia. D. H. Levine. Princeton, NJ: Princeton University Press, 1981. 342p.

'Resocialization: Roman Catholics becoming Protestants in Colombia, South America,' W. P. Thornton, *Anthropological Quarterly*, 57, 1 (January 1984), 28–37.

'Teaching missiology in the Biblical Seminary of Colombia: a study in Latin American contextualization.' J. W. Voelkel. D.Miss. thesis, Fuller Theological Seminary, Pasadena, CA, 1990. 427p.

'The Catholic church and political development in Colombia.' S. J. Brzezinski. Ph.D. dissertation, University of Illinois, 1973. 241p.

The church and labor in Colombia. K. N. Medhurst. Manchester, UK: Manchester University Press, 1984. 233p.

'The church in Colombia and Venezuela,' R. R. de Roux, in *The church in Latin America, 1492-1992*, p.271–283. E. Dussel (ed). Maryknoll, NY: Orbis Books, 1992. Trans. P. Burns.

The Colombian concordat: in the light of recent trends in Catholic thought concerning church–state relations and religious liberty. G. C. Cardenas. *Sondeos*, no. 22. Cuernavaca, Mexico: CIDOC, 1968. 140p.

'The enthusiastic Protestants of Bogotá, Colombia: reflections on the growth of a movement,' K. W. Westmeier, *International review of mission*, 75 (January 1986), 13–24.

'The growth of the Pentecostal churches in Colombia.' D. C. Palmer. Thesis, Trinity Evangelical Divinity School, Deerfield, IL, 1972. 196p.

'The household basis of evangelical religion and the reformation of machismo in Colombia.' E. E. Brusco. Ph.D. dissertation, City University of New York, 1986. 305p.

The persecution of Protestant Christians in Colombia, 1948–1958, with an investigation of its background and causes. J. E. Goff. *SONDEOS*, no. 23. Cuernavaca, Mexico: Centro Intercultural de Documentación, 1968. 492p.

'The reformation of machismo: asceticism and masculinity among Colombian Evangelicals,' E. Brusco, in *Rethinking Protestantism in Latin America*, p.143–158. V. Garrard-Burnett et al. (eds).

The sacred mountain of Colombia's Kogi Indians. No. 2 of section 9, *South America*, of *Iconography of religions.* G. Reichel-Dolmatoff. Leiden: E. J. Brill, 1990. 38p.

The shaman and the jaguar: a study of narcotic drugs among the Indians of Colombia. G. Reichel-Dolmatoff. Philadelphia: Temple University Press, 1975. 318p.

'Traducciones competivas del evangelio en el Vaupés, Colombia,' J. E. Jackson, *América Indígena*, 44, 1 (January–March 1984), 49–94.

Up from zero: a history of the development of Baptist work in Colombia. C. Ridenour. Cali, Colombia: Historical Commission of the Colombia Baptist Mission, 1989. 252p.

Country Table 2. **Organized churches and denominations in Colombia.**

Official name (bold type = church with over 10% of all affiliated) 1	*Begun* 2	*Type* 3	*Counc* 4	*Congs* 5	*Adults* 6	*Affiliated 1970* 7	*Affiliated 1995* 8	*G%* 9	*Names, notes, and other statistics* (see Codebook, Part 3) 10
Alianza Cristiana y Misionera	1923	P-Hol	xF..C	341	15,765	10,000	23,647	3.50	*ACM.* M=CMA,MC(USA). 1969, pentecostal movement. 23 schools. 2k,34f,2s.
Asambleas de Dios de Colombia	1930	P-Pe2	ZF..C	523	112,294	20,500	139,000	7.96	*Assemblies of God.* M=AoG(USA). Since 1961, 198m,10x,18f,3s(181),500Y,1059z.
Asambleas Locales	c1970	I-3nC	.....	59	2,255	–	5,000	40.59	*Little Flock. Local Churches.* Begun 1922 in China.
Asoc de Iglesias Ev de C del Oriente	1906	P-Eva	xM...	96	3,650	2,400	9,130	5.49	*Association of Chs of Eastern C. Alianza Ev.* 1923, M=TEAM.10n,9x33f,1s(75),157Y.
Asociación de Iglesias Ev del Caribe	1937	P-Eva	xN..C	398	20,000	12,000	35,000	4.37	*Federation of Ev Ministries.* M=LAM(USA). 7n,1x,23f,1p.2s,W=50%,734Y. Uses TEE.
Asoc de Iglesias Ev del Magdalena	1941	P-Eva	xM..C	28	3,700	2,000	5,670	4.26	*Assoc of Chs of Magdalena.* M=EUSA(UK, USA). 4n,2x,30f,1p(10),W=28%,107Y.
Asoc de Iglesias Ev Interamericanas	1943	P-Hol	xF..C	71	31,600	11,215	48,200	6.01	*Assoc of Interamerican Chs.* M=OMS(Interamerican M) (USA). 8n,40f,1s311Y,158z.
Asoc Nacional de Iglesias Cristianas	c1965	I-Non	.....	10	500	300	1,000	4.93	*National Association of Christian Churches.* Small Colombian indigenous grouping.
Bambinos de Dios		I-mar	.....	1	69	–	122	0.05	*Hijos de Dios. Children of God.* Family. Group from USA organization.
Centro Carismatico Mundial		I-3gL	.....	1	2,000	–	5,000	0.05	*World Charismatic Center.*
Centro Misionero Bethesda	1975	I-3gL	.....	6	4,000	–	10,000	5.00	*Bethesda Missionary Center.* Indigenous urban body. In Bogota and 5 other cities.
Congregaciones Luteranas	1949	P-Lut	L....	16	980	1,507	2,800	2.51	*Congregación San Mateo, Bogotá* (Germans, 957); San Martín, Cali(550). 1x,11Yy,85z.
Convención Bautista Colombiana	1941	P-Bap	T...h	111	12,500	10,000	34,700	5.10	*Colombian Baptist Conv.* M=SBC(USA). SS=11,095. 61n,62f,I1H,7h,1s,900Y.
Corporación Pro-Cultural		I-Non	.....	1	100	50	200	0.05	*CPC. Corporation for Culture.* Small independent foreign mission, Bucaramanga. 1k.
Cruzada Hispanoamericana	1937	P-Non	x....	1	200	1,000	500	-2.73	M=Spanish America Inland Mission (USA). Decline since 1966.
Ejército de Salvación	1929	P-Sal	xw...	1	100	100	200	2.81	*Salvation Army.* Work began 1929, later discontinued officially.
Embajadores Cristianos de Colombia	c1950	I-3pL	.....	30	600	500	1,000	2.81	*Christian Ambassadors of Colombia. Asambleas de Jesucristo. Assemblies of JC.* 5m.
Evangelical Community Church	c1970	P-Eva	.....	30	2,400	–	6,000	41.62	Small community church with several congregations.
Hermanos		P-EBr	x....	100	3,000	4,000	5,000	0.05	*Exclusive (Plymouth) Brethren.* Group: Kelly-Continental (links with UK, USA, NZ).
Hermanos en Cristo	c1933	P-CBr	x...C	30	2,000	1,000	3,000	4.49	*Christian Brethren, Plymouth (Open) Brethren.* M=CMML(USA, UK, NZ). HQ Pasto. 43f.
Hermanos Menonitas	1943	P-Men	GF..C	30	1,000	1,500	2,000	1.16	*Conferencia de los HM.* M=Mennonite Brethren Ch (USA). HQ Cali. 10f,1h,1k,1p.
Iglesia Adventista del Séptimo Día	1921	P-Adv	x....	567	83,735	60,000	209,000	5.12	*Seventh-day Adventists, Colombia-Venezuela UM.* 35nx,20f,165mw,6r,427t,2347Y.
Iglesia Anglicana Ortodoxa	1972	I-ReA	xT...	2	200	–	400	4.35	*Anglican Orthodox Church.* Schism ex Episcopal Church. M=AOC(USA). 2n.
Iglesia Apostolica de Jesucristo		I-3oL	.....	15	1,000	–	3,000	0.05	*Apostolic Church of Jesus Christ.* Links with USA bodies of same name.
Iglesia Bautista Independiente	1929	I-Bap	x....	1	100	100	300	4.49	*Independent Baptist Ch.* M=ABWE(USA), In Leticia, Amazones. 2f,1h.
Iglesia Biblica de Colombia	c1990	I-3nL	.....	10	700	–	2,000	20.00	*IBC. Bible Ch of Colombia.* M=BALL World Missions (USA). School, clinic.
Iglesia Católica en Colombia:	1512	R-Lat	B.L.R	3,678	19,612,100	21,807,580	37,063,780	2.14	*Catholic Ch.* C=46+2+128. 5p,38q,15s(1378),W=63%. 4243n 2019x 4250m18196w 775540Yy
M Barranquilla	1932	R-Lat	Bs	99	862,800	780,000	1,631,923	3.00	90% urban, highly industrialized. 1s. 80n 57x 95m 549w 56108Yy
D Riohacha	1952	R-Lat	Bs	24	101,000	80,000	191,000	3.54	Atlantic littoral in northeast. High % Black. P=17%. 22n 5x 5m 69w 8556Yy
D Santa Marta	1534	R-Lat	Bs	51	638,000	515,000	1,207,000	3.47	20% urban, 50% industrialized. Tourism. 52n 10x 11m 123w 21936Yy
D Valledupar	1952	R-Lat	Bs	100	352,000	312,000	666,000	3.08	Very low priest/people ratio. 1:12000.P=14%. 32n 5x 6m 76w 16584Yy
M Bogotá	1562	R-Lat	Bs	282	2,595,000	2,200,000	4,908,000	3.26	Ecclesiastical centre for Latin America. 1s. 410n 774x 1836m 3814w 101031Yy
D Facatativá	1962	R-Lat	Bs	32	215,000	350,000	406,000	0.60	Rural, impoverished, traditional religiosity. 35n 26x 123m 182w 7056Yy
D Girardot	1956	R-Lat	Bs	54	327,000	451,482	618,000	1.26	Rural, poor, Priest/people 1:7000. 68n 14x 35m 322w 9700Yy
D Villavicencio	1903	R-Lat	Bs	52	285,000	256,760	540,000	3.02	Mission zone. Very poor. High % Black. 34n 22x 29m 62w 9990Yy
D Zipaquirá	1951	R-Lat	Bs	119	305,000	348,467	578,000	2.04	Rural, with industrialization beginning. M=CIM. 119n 20x 110m 336w 8646Yy
M Bucaramanga	1952	R-Lat	Bs	114	493,000	579,118	932,925	1.93	20% urban, half industrialized. 1p,1s. 121n 65x 113m 596w 18944Yy
D Barrancabermeja	1928	R-Lat	Bs	37	228,000	327,000	431,000	1.11	20% urban, half industrialized. 34n 10x 13m 116w 9090Yy
D Málaga-Soatá	1987	R-Lat	Bs	31	125,000	–	237,000	12.50	Population is 99% Catholic. 43n 0x 0m 100w 3296Yy
D Socorro & San Gil	1895	R-Lat	Bs	74	218,000	417,356	413,000	-0.04	Mission zone. Extremely impoverished. 1s. 101n 8x 8m 278w 7267Yy
M Cali	1910	R-Lat	Bs	100	974,000	974,385	1,842,637	2.58	90% urban, industrialized, Mass immigration. W=10%. 135n 107x 131m 1045w 46650Yy
D Buga	1966	R-Lat	Bs	76	264,000	650,000	500,000	-1.04	20% urban, half industrialized. M=PSS. 64n 29x 41m 166w 12273Yy
D Cartago	1962	R-Lat	Bs	58	354,000	430,000	669,000	1.78	Rural, poor, traditional religiosity. 61n 3x 4m 127w 8778Yy
D Palmira	1952	R-Lat	Bs	61	380,000	281,000	720,000	3.84	Half industrialized. Adjacent to Cali. 38n 13x 32m 220w 9900Yy
M Cartagena en Colombia	1534	R-Lat	Bs	82	740,000	560,000	1,400,000	3.73	20% urban, half industrialized; touristic center. 66n 48x 62m 271w 22339Yy
D Maganguá	1969	R-Lat	Bs	23	256,000	292,000	485,000	2.05	Mission zone, high % Black. 24n 8x 10m 64w 9110Yy
D Monteria	1954	R-Lat	Bs	84	654,000	657,000	1,237,000	2.56	Mission zone. Many Blacks. M=OFM. 49n 6x 14m 200w 20000Yy
D Sincelejo	1969	R-Lat	Bs	35	300,000	343,000	567,000	2.03	Mission zone, Very poor. High % Black. 1:13000. 26n 6x 11m 131w 15371Yy
PN Alto Sinú	1969	R-Lat	Bs	13	132,000	117,000	250,000	3.08	Mission zone. Poor. High % Black. 1"12000. M=CMP 16n 5x 6m 52w 3837Yy
M Ibagué	1900	R-Lat	Bs	45	217,000	745,000	410,000	-2.36	20% urban, industrial. M=CIM. Priest/people 1:7000. 62n 15x 22m 128w 11282Yy
D Espinal	1957	R-Lat	Bs	48	401,000	400,000	758,000	2.59	Rural, poor, Very traditional religiosity. 66n 0x 0m 63w 12150Yy
D Florencia	1951	R-Lat	Pimc	30	126,000	193,000	238,000	0.84	Amazon. White settlers, bilingual Indians. P=46%. 27n 5x 5m 76w 6595Yy
D Garzón	1900	R-Lat	Bs	47	248,000	486,820	469,000	-0.15	Rural, impoverished. 1s. 55n 16x 20m 135w 8902Yy
D Libano-Honda	1989	R-Lat	Bimc	28	99,000	–	188,000	16.67	M=IMC. 37n 2x 4m 119w 5646Yy
D Neiva	1972	R-Lat	Bs	33	232,000	–	440,120	4.35	Diocese is 97% Catholic. 43n 9x 13m 53w 11460Yy
M Manizales	1900	R-Lat	Bs	74	289,000	545,000	547,000	0.01	20% urban, half industrialized. 1s. 143n 50x 99m 339w 11373Yy
D Armenia	1952	R-Lat	Bs	31	225,000	448,000	425,000	-0.21	20% urban. Small dense diocese. 64n 9x 21m 202w 9096Yy
D La Dorada-Guaduas	1984	R-Lat	Bs	38	209,000	–	395,000	9.09	Population 94% Catholic. 47n 3x 5m 90w 6673Yy
D Pereira	1952	R-Lat	Bs	87	532,000	600,000	1,006,000	2.09	20% urban. Densely populated. 139n 29x 39m 307w 15000Yy
M Medellín	1868	R-Lat	Bs	246	1,242,000	1,607,183	2,350,000	1.53	90% urban. Site of 1968 CELAM 'Vatican II'. 2s. 483n 268x 651m 4188w 45841Yy
D Caldas	1988	R-Lat	Bcm	22	90,000	–	170,200	14.29	M=CM. 33n 0x 0m 89w 3645Yy
D Girardota	1988	R-Lat	Bs	24	107,000	–	203,000	14.29	Population 99% Catholic. 40n 0x 0m 91w 7733Yy
D Jericó	1915	R-Lat	Bs	52	152,000	240,000	287,000	0.72	Rural, poor. Sufficient clergy. 84n 2x 7m 180w 5470Yy
D Sonsón-Rionegro	1957	R-Lat	Bs	49	340,000	398,110	644,000	1.94	Rural. Industry growing. Many charismatics. 179n 18x 57m 533w 14092Yy
M Nueva Pamplona	1835	R-Lat	Bs	27	158,000	159,500	300,000	2.56	Rural, very poor. Traditional religiosity. 1p,1s. 45n 0x 0m 102w 2756Yy
D Arauca	1915	R-Lat	Pmsy	18	88,000	145,000	167,000	0.57	Orinoco. White settlers, bilingual Indians. M=CSsR. 21n 7x 8m 54w 4481Yy
D Cúcuta	1956	R-Lat	Bs	95	325,000	335,000	616,000	2.47	20% urban, half industrialized. 10. 73n 34x 46m 218w 14779Yy
D Ocaña	1962	R-Lat	Bs	44	225,000	274,000	427,000	1.79	Rural, impoverished. Traditional religiosity. 39n 0x 0m 68w 20780Yy
PN Tibú (Bertrania en el Catatumbo)	1951	R-Lat	Bs	40	115,000	96,000	218,000	3.33	Mission zone. Poor. White settlers, Indians. M=OP. 15n 6x 8m 42w 2431Yy
M Popayán	1546	R-Lat	Bs	81	381,000	610,000	721,000	0.67	Rural, poor, very traditional religiosity. 1p,1s. M=PSS. 77n 37x 76m 328w 16928Yy
D Ipiales	1964	R-Lat	Bs	46	219,000	320,000	415,000	1.05	Rural, very poor area, on Ecuador border. 53n 10x 18m 120w 2950Yy
D Pasto	1859	R-Lat	Bs	53	307,000	366,024	581,000	1.87	Rural, impoverished, traditional religiosity. M=OAR. 75n 30x 103m 265w 13553Yy
M Santa Fe de Antioquia	1804	R-Lat	Bs	27	102,000	346,000	193,000	-2.31	Rural, impoverished, traditional religiosity. 60n 5x 5m 85w 5124Yy
D Apartadó	1988	R-Lat	Bs	26	184,000	–	349,000	14.29	Population 87% Catholic. 32n 10x 13m 65w 12131Yy
D Istmina-Tadó	1952	R-Lat	Pmxy	43	166,000	148,500	315,000	3.05	Humid. Pacific coast. High % Black. M=MXY. 59n 3x 3m 133w 6180Yy
D Quibdó	1952	R-Lat	Pcmf	44	89,000	99,500	168,640	2.13	Humid, unhealthy, coastal. High % Black. M=CMF. 17n 7x 9m 34w 3455Yy
D Santa Rosa de Osos	1917	R-Lat	Bs	87	256,000	423,775	484,000	0.53	Rural, impoverished, traditional religiosity. 1s. 157n 12x 74m 268w 17117Yy
M Tunja	1880	R-Lat	Bs	58	226,000	608,000	427,000	-1.40	Rural, poor, traditional religiosity. 1p, 1s. 96n 14x 21m 117w 6410Yy
D Chiquinquirá	1977	R-Lat	Bs	35	156,000	–	295,000	5.56	Population 96% Catholic. 52n 20x 24m 120w 5600Yy
D Duitama-Sogamoso	1955	R-Lat	Bs	51	177,000	420,000	336,000	-0.89	Rural, with beginnings of industrialization. M=SDB. 86n 4x 8m 136w 6148Yy
D Garagoa	1977	R-Lat	Bs	28	136,000	–	257,000	5.56	Population 98% Catholic. 47n 1x 1m 44w 2654Yy
VA Ariari	1964	R-Lat	Psdb	16	120,000	115,000	227,000	2.76	Arid. 8% Protestants. 1,500 spiritists. M=SDB. 11n 16x 19m 38w 3849Yy
VA Buenaventura	1952	R-Lat	Pmxy	22	147,000	140,000	279,000	2.80	Humid, unhealthy, along Pacific. High % Black. 6n 38x 48m 79w 3625Yy
VA Casanare	1893	R-Lat	Poar	19	92,000	98,000	174,242	2.33	Orinoco. White settlers, bilingual Indians. M=OAR. 19n 12x 17m 58w 4046Yy
VA Mitú-Puerto Inírida	1949	R-Lat	Pmxy	56	60,000	35,000	113,500	4.82	Largest diocese (167,785 km2).73% Catholic. 2n 15x 16m 25w 640Yy
VA San José del Guaviare	1989	R-Lat	Bmxy	12	60,800	–	115,000	16.67	M=MXY. 22n 2x 2m 8w 1014Yy
VA San Vicente-Puerto Leguizamo	1985	R-Lat	Bimc	14	117,000	–	222,000	10.00	M=IMC. 4n 16x 22m 22w 2724Yy
VA Sibundoy	1904	R-Lat	Pcssr	19	73,000	78,500	138,978	2.31	Amazon basin. 1969, OFM accused of 'theocracy'. 14n 14x 23m 87w 4468Yy
VA Tumaco	1927	R-Lat	Pocd	17	117,000	199,600	222,000	0.43	Ecuador frontier, coastal. High % Black. 1:10500. 9n 10x 12m 33w 5893Yy
PA Guapí	1954	R-Lat	Pofm	9	31,000	67,000	58,800	-0.52	Humid, unhealthy, Pacific coast. High % Black. 1n 9x 10m 31w 1440Yy
PA Leticia	1951	R-Lat	Pofmc	6	22,700	18,000	43,000	3.54	Virgin forest, Amazon basin. Southeast. P=58%. 13n 4x 7m 48w 819Yy
PA San Andrés & Providencia	1912	R-Lat	Pofmc	14	20,800	14,000	39,400	4.23	Isles. 67% Catholic, 30% Protestant, M=OFMCap. 4n 3x 4m 26w 825Yy
PA Tierradentro	1921	R-Lat	Pcm	11	31,700	44,500	60,000	1.20	Dry region in the interior. P=29%. 2n 13x 15m 50w 1300Yy
PA Vichada	1956	R-Lat	Psmm	12	21,300	12,000	40,415	4.98	Orinoco. White settlers, Indians. 44% RC. P=10%.
OM Colombia	1949	R-Lat	Bs	193	80,000	50,000	100,000	2.81	*Military Ordinariate of Colombia.* 156 ordinaries, 4 auxiliaries.
Iglesia Católica Liberal		I-Lib	x....	2	40	100	100	0.05	*Liberal Catholic Ch.* Split ex Swedenborgians. Province of M=LCC(USA). 1 bishop,2n.
Iglesia Cristana de Cristo		I-Non	.....	13	1,300	–	3,250	0.05	*Christian Church of Christ.*
Iglesia Cristiana Cruzada	1973	P-Pe2	.....	250	30,000	–	75,000	4.55	M=WEC.
Iglesia Cristiana del Norte	c1950	I-3pL	.....	10	2,000	1,000	3,000	4.49	*ICN. Christian Ch. of the North.* Indigenous pentecostals. HQ Bogotá.
Iglesia Cristiana Elim	1964	P-Pe2	Z....	1	200	200	300	1.64	*Elim Christian Ch.* M=EMA(USA). One congregation in Bogotá. 7f.
Iglesia Cristiana Pentecostés	c1965	I-3pL	.....	20	1,000	1,000	2,000	2.81	*Pentecost Christian Ch.* 9 churches in Cundinamarca, Meta, Santanders.
Iglesia Cruzada Evangélica Colombiana	1933	P-Pe2	xF..C	20	3,000	3,600	6,670	2.50	*Pentecosta.* M=WEC,CHC,CoN. 45% Indian. 40n,30x,G=8%pa,1H,1j,1p,1s(40),W=53%,277Y.
Iglesia de Cristo Pentecostal	c1965	I-3pL	x....	15	1,100	700	2,000	4.29	*Pentecostal Ch of Christ.* Indigenous. 9 congregations in Cundinamarca.
Iglesia de Dios de la Profecia	1970	P-Pe3	Z....	9	342	–	1,140	32.52	*Church of God of Prophecy.* M=CGP(USA).
Iglesia de Dios en Colombia	1954	P-Pe3	ZF...	66	3,540	2,500	8,850	5.19	*Ch of God in Colombia.* M=CoG(Cleveland) (USA). 24n,G=17.7%pa,1s(4),W=95%,31Y,50z.
Iglesia de Dios Pentecostal		P-Pe2	Z....	25	2,500	1,000	6,250	0.05	*Pentecostal Ch of God.* M=PCG(Puerto Rico, also USA). Classical Pentecostals.
Iglesia de JC de los Santos de los UD	c1967	m-LdS	x....	129	45,600	3,394	76,000	13.24	*Latter-day Saints. Mormons.* M=CJCLdS(USA). Indians. Rapid growth, 11.8%pa. 50f.
Iglesia de la Roca	1987	I-3gL	.....	1	2,000	–	5,000	12.50	*Church of the Rock.*
Iglesia del Evangelio Cuadrangular	1942	P-Pe2	ZF..C	225	31,500	70,000	95,500	1.25	*Int Ch of the Foursquare Gospel.* M=ICFC(USA). 250nm,7f,9p(239),W=29%,742Y
Iglesia del Nazareno	1975	P-Hol	.....	25	1,320	–	2,269	5.00	*Church of the Nazarene.* M=CON(USA).
Iglesia Episcopal: D Colombia	1963	A-Cen	aw.JC	21	2,100	2,000	3,500	2.26	*Episcopal Ch.* In PECUSA, Province IV. 50% local, 50% USA. 4nx4x,W=36%,25Yy.
Iglesia Ev Cristiana Casa de Oración	c1963	I-3pL	.....	10	500	300	1,000	4.93	*House of Prayer Mission.* Indigenous Colombian pentecostals.
Iglesia Ev Cristiana Independiente		I-Non	.....	10	200	150	400	0.05	*Independent Ev Christian Ch. Assoc of Ev Christian Chs.* HQ Bucaramanga.

Continued overleaf

Country Table 2–concluded

Official name (bold type = church *with over 10% of all affiliated)* 1	*Begun* 2	*Type* 3	*Counc* 4	*Congs* 5	*Adults* 6	*Affiliated 1970* 7	*Affiliated 1995* 8	*G%* 9	*Names, notes, and other statistics* (see Codebook, Part 3) 10
Iglesia Evangélica La Hermosa		I-Non	.....	1	100	100	300	0.05	*The Beautiful Evangelical Church.* Small local indigenous congregation.
Iglesia Ev Luterana, Sinodo de Colombia	1936	P-Lut	L...C	20	1,200	1,055	2,000	2.59	*Lutheran Ch.* 1944, M=ALC(USA). 1948-57 severe persecution. 5n,7x,8f,lu,18Yy.
Iglesia Ev Menonita de Colombia	1943	P-Men	G...C	11	800	850	2,000	3.48	*Mennonite Ch.* M=General Conf MC(USA). 2n,3x,13f,1h,1p(2),W=41%,29Y,20z.
Iglesia Evangélica Nacional Colombiana	c1965	I-3pL	.....	5	700	400	1,100	4.13	*Colombian National Ev Ch.* Indigenous body in Cundinamarca and Caldas.
Iglesia Evangélica Pentecostal		I-3pL	x....	5	1,000	300	2,000	0.05	*Ev Pentecostal Ch.* Related to IEP from Chile. HQ Bogotá. 6f.
Iglesia Fundacion	1982	I-Non	.....	18	1,800	–	4,000	7.69	*Foundation Church.*
Iglesia Metodista en Colombia		P-Met	.....	9	540	–	1,080	0.05	*Methodist Church in Colombia.*
Iglesia Metodista Wesleyana de C	1940	P-Hol	VF..C	21	1,675	2,250	2,534	0.48	M=Wesleyan Ch(USA). Medellín. 6n,2x,7f,1h,1j,1k,1p(11),W=50%,66Yy,125z.
Iglesia Nueva Apostólica		I-3aX	x....	20	2,000	1,000	3,751	0.05	*New Apostolic Ch.* In Canada Bezirk (District). Germans. HQ Zurich (Switzerland).
Iglesia Ortodoxa Griega		O-Gre	Cwo..	1	3,500	4,000	7,000	0.05	In 12th Archdiocesan District, Greek Orthodox AD N&S America. Greeks, Arabs.
Iglesia Panamericana de Colombia	1956	I-3aL	x....	250	82,000	2,000	125,000	17.99	*Panamerican Mission.* Run by Colombians. Rapid growth. Medellin, Bogota.
Iglesia Pentecostal Unida de Colombia	1969	I-3oL	.....	1,006	80,500	95,000	230,000	3.60	95% split ex UPC rejecting USA control. Many Arhuacos. 14 missionaries in Spain.
Iglesia Pentecostal Unida (USA)	1936	P-Pel	.....	48	73,400	55,000	112,000	2.89	M=UPC(Canada, USA). Remnant after 95% split rejecting control from St. Louis (USA).
Iglesia Presbiteriana Cumberland	1925	P-Ref	C	28	3,000	3,000	5,000	2.06	M=Cumberland Presbyterian Ch (USA Whites). 3 schools. HQ Cali. 10f.
Iglesia Presbiteriana de Colombia	1856	P-Ref	R...C	64	16,400	21,200	25,000	0.66	M=UPUSA. 1967, pentecostalism. 18n,3x,29f,6h,87t(3600),1u,W=10%,15Yy.
Iglesia Swedenborgiana		m-Swe	x....	1	100	200	200	0.05	*Swedenborgian Ch. Ch of the New Jerusalem.* Links with USA, UK. 2d.
Iglesia Unión de Bogotá		P-com	.....	1	800	1,000	1,500	0.05	*Union Church of Bogotá.* Interdenominational. English-speaking expatriates.
Iglesias de Cristo	1962	I-Dis	x....	23	575	100	1,150	10.26	*Churches of Christ.* M=CCCC(Instrumental) (USA). In Medellín, Bogotá. 8f.
Iglesias radiofónicas solitarias	c1940	I-3rL	.....	500	9,000	2,000	15,000	8.39	Isolated radio believers in jungles &c. R=18500 (TWR, HCJB, FEBC, Radio Vatican).
Miembros del Cuerpo de Cristo	c1965	I-3gL	.....	10	1,000	1,000	2,000	2.81	*Members of the Body of Christ.* Indigenous pentecostals. In Cundinamarca.
Misión Biblica Cristadelfiana		m-Ade	x....	1	50	50	150	0.05	M=Christadelphian Bible Mission (USA). 1 ecclesia (church). Pacifist. Growing.
Misión Cristiana La Fe	c1962	I-3gL	.....	10	400	300	600	2.81	*Faith Christian Mission.* Indigenous Colombian pentecostals.
Misión Evangélica de Colombia	1946	P-Eva	.....	15	14,800	10,000	22,500	3.30	*MEC, CEM.* M=Colombia Evangelistic Mission (Canada). HQ Sincelejo, Bolivar.
Misión Indigena de Sur América	1934	P-Non	xM..C	15	1,300	500	2,000	5.70	M=South America Indian Mission (SAIM) (USA). In far north, Guajira peninsula. 20f,2h.
Misión Nuevas Tribus de Colombia	1944	P-Fun	x...C	450	8,000	10,000	20,000	2.81	*MNT.* M=New Tribes Mission. In 6 main Indian tribes in eastern region. 30x,59f,1h.
Misiones Mundiales de Colombia	1964	I-Non	x....	5	400	600	800	1.16	Evangelicals from Pasadena, CA (USA). M=World-Wide Missions (USA).
Sociedad de Amigos		P-Qua	Q....	1	50	50	100	0.05	*Religious Society of Friends. Quakers.*
Sociedad de la Ciencia Cristiana		m-Sci	x....	1	20	50	40	0.05	*Ch of Christ, Scientist. Christian Science.* M=CCS(Boston, USA). Bogota Society. 1w.
Testigos de Jehová	c1895	m-Jeh	x....	651	46,793	20,000	175,000	9.06	*Jehovah's Witnesses. Watch Tower.* Active witnessing under way by 1929. 1277Y.
Unión Misionera Evangélica	1908	P-Hol	xM..C	207	10,200	3,500	15,300	6.08	M=Gospel Missionary Union (USA). 63n,15x,21f,1H,1j,3k,1u,W=91%,173Y,225z.
Viña del Señor	1980	I-3gL	.....	20	1,300	–	2,000	6.67	*The Lord's Vineyard.* Work among Achagua, Cuiba, Guahibo, Piapoco, Puinave, Saliba. M=CAM.
Other Protestant denominations		P-	.....	60	5,000	2,000	10,000	0.05	Total about 10 (see list below).
Other independent charismatic chs	c1980	I-3gL	.....	100	15,000	–	30,000	6.67	Also termed grassroots (GR) churches; including Ekklesia Bolivia, Assoc of Vineyard Chs.
Other indigenous pentecostal churches		I-3pL	.....	50	9,800	2,000	15,000	0.05	Total about 20 (see list below), including among West Indian Blacks, also IURD (Brazil).
Other Colombian indigenous churches		I-	.....	20	1,000	1,000	3,000	0.05	A small number of transitory independent congregations (see below).
Doubly-affiliated		2-aff			-500,000	-34,201	-946,983		Evangelicals who also are or were baptized Roman Catholics.
Disaffiliated		X-Aff			-237,000	-203,000	-450,000		Baptized Catholics who have become completely disaffiliated agnostics or atheists.
Totals				**10,657**	**19,701,993**	**22,035,000**	**37,350,000**		

Churches, members, growth, 1900-2025	*Congs*	*Adults*	*Affiliated*	*G%*	*Total denominations*	*6 Megablocs:* O	R	A	P	I	m
Total churches, members, and denominations (mid-1900)	1,000	1,617,000	3,055,000	2.86	3	0	1	0	1	0	1
Total churches, members, and denominations (mid-1970)	5,612	11,666,295	22,035,000	2.86	80	1	1	1	35	37	5
Total churches, members, and denominations (mid-1990)	7,000	17,889,000	33,913,500	2.18	168	1	1	1	45	115	5
Total churches, members, and denominations (mid-1995)	10,657	19,701,993	37,350,000	1.95	172	1	1	1	46	118	5
Total churches, members, and denominations (mid-2000)	9,000	21,594,000	40,935,888	1.85	175	1	1	1	47	120	5
Total churches, members, and denominations (mid-2025)	12,000	30,437,000	57,700,000	1.38	376	4	1	1	60	300	10

NOTES ON TABLE ABOVE

NATIONAL COUNCILS (Column 4, 5th letter).

E = Association of Evangelical Churches of Colombia (AIEC).

F = Confederación Evangélica de Colombia (CEC) (Evangelical Confederation of Colombia).

h = Asociación Pro-Indigenas de Colombia (Association for the Indians of Colombia), which also has as members the Episcopal Ch, Lutheran Ch, Presbyterian Ch, CMA, GMU, and others

R = Conferencia Episcopal de Colombia (CEC, Episcopal Conference of Colombia).

OTHER PROTESTANT DENOMINATIONS. These, mostly missions from the USA, include: Baptist Bible Fellowship International (1972), Brethren in Christ, Chs of Christ, Ev Covenant Ch of America (1968), Ev Methodist Ch (1948), Fellowship of Ev Baptist Chs (Canada: 1969), Fundamental Baptist Mission of Canada (mainly correspondence courses), Missionary Ch, United Ev Chs, World Baptist Fellowship Mission Agency (1967).

OTHER INDIGENOUS PENTECOSTAL CHURCHES. Among these are: independent Pentecostal Ch of Luruaco (31 communicants), Independent Pentecostal Chs of Barranquilla (50), and bodies among West Indian Blacks.

OTHER COLOMBIAN INDIGENOUS CHURCHES. A handful of smaller West Indian Black or Mestizo bodies come into existence as independent congregations and tend shortly thereafter to disappear or merge with other churches. These include: Iglesia Fundamental Trinitaria.

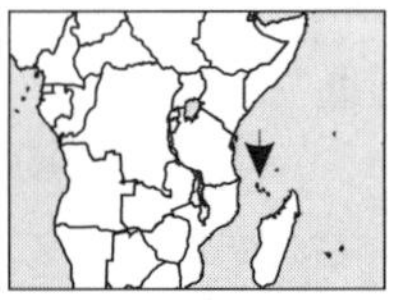

COMOROS

SECULAR DATA, AD 2000

STATE

Official name: Al-Jumhuriyat al-Qumur al-Ittihadiyah al-Islamiyah/La République Fédérale Islamique des Comores (The Federal Islamic Republic of the Comoros).
Short name: Comoros. **Adjective of nationality:** Comorian.
Flag: Red stripe over green stripe; white crescent and 4 white stars.
Area: 1,862 sq. km. (719 sq. mi.).
Government: Republic under revolutionary council, since 1975 coup (1843 French colony, 1947 French overseas territory, 1975 Independence. In 1976 Mayotte voted to secede as a dependency of France).
Legislature: Legislative Council, 42 members; Senate, 5 members.
Official language: Comorian, Arabic, French.
Monetary unit: 1 Comorian franc (CF) = 100 centimes. **US$1=** CF 418.73.
Chief cities: MORONI 31,187.
Political divisions: 3 provinces.
Armed forces: 520.

DEMOGRAPHY

Population: 593,000.
Population density: 318.3/sq. km. (824.4/sq. mi.).
Under 15 years: 249,000.
Growth rate p.a.: 2.64% (births 34.81, deaths 8.41).
Mortality: Infant, per 1,000: 67.0; **Maternal per 100,000:** 950.0.
Life expectancy: 61 (male 59, female 62).
Household size: 5.6. **Floor area per person, sq.m:** 9.0.
Major languages: Comorian, Swahili, French, Kikomozo (Kingazidja), Malagasy, Makua, French Creole, Arabic.
Urban dwellers: 33.23%. **Urban growth rate p.a.:** 4.7%.
Labor force: 44%.

ETHNOLINGUISTIC PEOPLES

48.8% Comorian (Ngazija); 43.7% Comorian (Nzwani); 4.5% Comorian (Mwali); 1.6% Makua (Makhua); 0.4% French.

ECONOMY

National income p.a. per person: US$470; **per family:** US$2,635.

EDUCATION

Adult literacy: 57% (male 64%, female 50%). **Schools:** 275.
Universities: 2. **School enrolment:** female/male: 44%/53%.

HEALTH

Access to health services: 55%. **Access to safe water:** 48%.
Hospitals: 20 (25 beds per 10,000). **Doctors:** 57.
Blind: 500. **Deaf:** 36,700. **Murder rate:** 10.
Lepers: 3,000. **Underweight prevalence under 5:** 19%.

LITERATURE

New book titles p.a.: 30 (50 p.a. per million). **Periodicals:** 0.
Newspapers: 0 dailies.

COMMUNICATION (per 1,000 people)
Phones: 8 (3% mobile). **Radios:** 97. **TV sets:** 5.
Daily newspaper circulation: 100. **Computers:** 2.

HUMAN LIFE AND LIBERTY (optimum condition=100.0%)
HDI: 41.2. **HSI:** 37.0. **HFI:** 15.0. **EFL:** 25.0.

Country status. The Comoros is a group of 3 volcanic islands in the northern entrance of the Mozambique Channel about halfway between Madagascar and the African mainland. The nearby island of Mayotte is geographically part of the group but administratively under France. Comoros is the second-largest producer of vanilla in the world. Other products include copra, cloves, and perfume.

HUMAN LIFE AND LIBERTY

Human need and development. Geographical isolation, poor transportation infrastructure, feudal social structure, rudimentary educational facilities, and falling world prices for the islands' agricultural commodities combine to depress the standards of living on the islands.

Human rights and freedoms. During its brief history The Comoros has had 3 presidents, 2 of whom were assassinated, and 3 coups d'etat. The form of government may be described as autocracy tempered by the threat of coups. Under the first 2 presidents, the country experienced some of the worst human rights abuses. The first democratic elections held in 1991 has brought some stability to the country as well as a relaxation of the political controls instituted earlier. However, the institutionalization of democratic practices and the protection of human rights are hampered by the lack of internal security as well as poor economic conditions. These same factors also militate against any government attempts to renew its repressive programs. Although The Comoros describes itself as an Islamic state, women enjoy a slightly better status than in other countries that go under that label. Women do not wear the veil and they have equal property rights.

Human environment. The Comoros is running out of arable land, and soil erosion on the steep volcanic slopes is exacerbating the problem. However, the islands do not suffer from any form of industrial pollution nor are its coastal waters threatened by spillage from passing ships.

NON-CHRISTIAN RELIGIONS

Islam, the predominant religion of the islands, dates from the settlement of Arabs in the 14th century, and the The Comoros were islamized in the following century. Muslims are Sunnis of the Shafiite rite, with 780 mosques and numerous Quranic schools.

Country Table 1. **Religious adherents in The Comoros, AD 1900-2025.**

Year	1900		1970		mid-1990		Annual change, 1990-2000				mid-1995		mid-2000		mid-2025	
Name	Adherents	%	Adherents	%	Adherents	%	Natural	Conversion	Total	Rate	Adherents	%	Adherents	%	Adherents	%
Muslims	69,900	99.9	229,210	98.5	440,460	98.1	14,101	-14	14,087	2.81	505,660	98.0	581,330	98.0	969,550	97.9
Christians	**100**	**0.1**	**1,490**	**0.6**	**4,800**	**1.1**	**154**	**85**	**239**	**4.13**	**6,150**	**1.2**	**7,192**	**1.2**	**14,850**	**1.5**
PROFESSION																
crypto-Christians	0	0.0	30	0.0	200	0.0	6	14	20	7.18	300	0.1	400	0.1	1,000	0.1
professing Christians	**100**	**0.1**	**1,460**	**0.6**	**4,600**	**1.0**	**148**	**71**	**219**	**3.97**	**5,850**	**1.1**	**6,792**	**1.2**	**13,850**	**1.4**
AFFILIATION																
unaffiliated Christians	0	0.0	39	0.0	105	0.0	3	0	3	2.24	125	0.0	131	0.0	300	0.0
affiliated Christians	**100**	**0.1**	**1,451**	**0.6**	**4,695**	**1.1**	**151**	**86**	**237**	**4.17**	**6,025**	**1.2**	**7,061**	**1.2**	**14,550**	**1.5**
Roman Catholics	100	0.1	1,091	0.5	3,800	0.9	122	73	195	4.23	5,000	1.0	5,751	1.0	11,600	1.2
Protestants	0	0.0	330	0.1	640	0.1	21	5	26	3.47	720	0.1	900	0.2	2,000	0.2
Independents	0	0.0	30	0.0	250	0.1	8	7	15	4.81	300	0.1	400	0.1	900	0.1
Marginal Christians	0	0.0	0	0.0	5	0.0	0	1	1	7.18	5	0.0	10	0.0	50	0.0
Trans-megabloc groupings																
Evangelicals	0	0.0	150	0.1	200	0.0	6	-4	2	0.96	210	0.0	220	0.0	500	0.1
Pentecostals/Charismatics	0	0.0	50	0.0	420	0.1	13	1	14	2.92	470	0.1	560	0.1	1,200	0.1
Great Commission Christians	**95**	**0.1**	**800**	**0.3**	**2,400**	**0.5**	**77**	**39**	**116**	**4.02**	**3,000**	**0.6**	**3,558**	**0.6**	**7,300**	**0.7**
Ethnoreligionists	0	0.0	2,000	0.9	2,900	0.7	93	-88	5	0.16	3,200	0.6	2,947	0.5	4,000	0.4
Nonreligious	0	0.0	0	0.0	400	0.1	13	23	36	6.61	500	0.1	759	0.1	800	0.1
Baha'is	0	0.0	300	0.1	440	0.1	14	-6	8	1.70	490	0.1	521	0.1	800	0.1
World A (unevangelized persons)	69,300	99.0	185,712	79.8	291,850	65.0	9,340	-1,407	7,933	2.43	330,286	64.0	371,811	62.7	550,440	55.6
World B (evangelized non-Christians)	600	0.9	45,520	19.6	152,350	33.9	4,881	1,322	6,203	3.46	179,635	34.8	213,997	36.1	424,710	42.9
World C (Christians)	100	0.1	1,490	0.6	4,800	1.1	154	85	239	4.13	6,150	1.2	7,192	1.2	14,850	1.5
Country's population	**70,000**	**100.0**	**232,723**	**100.0**	**449,000**	**100.0**	**14,375**	**0**	**14,375**	**2.82**	**516,072**	**100.0**	**593,000**	**100.0**	**990,000**	**100.0**

COLUMNS, ROWS.
For meanings and definitions, see Codebook (Part 3). Note that, by definition, total 'Christians' = professing + crypto-Christians, which also = affiliated + unaffiliated Christians, and also = Great Commission Christians + latent Christians. Percentages may not always total exactly, due to rounding.

CENSUSES.
No question on religion has ever been asked.

NOTES ON RELIGIONS
BAHA'IS. In 1973, 2 local spiritual assemblies and 3 other centers, declining to 1 LSA (1996).
CHRISTIANS. All were expatriate French, Réunionais, and Malagasy, until the first 2 Comorian converts in 1975.
COUNTRY'S POPULATION. In 1976, the government agreed to receive back the 60,000 Comorian citizens resident in Madagascar, all of whom were Muslims.
INDEPENDENTS. Isolated radio believers across the islands (see Table 2).
MUSLIMS. Sunnis (of the Shafiite rite). 780 mosques, numerous Quranic schools. The Comoros were islamized in the 15th century. A grand mufti resides in the capital. *Hajj pilgrims to Mecca.* (1976) 131.

Great Commission Instrument Panel: status of The Comoros (for explanation see start of Part 4)

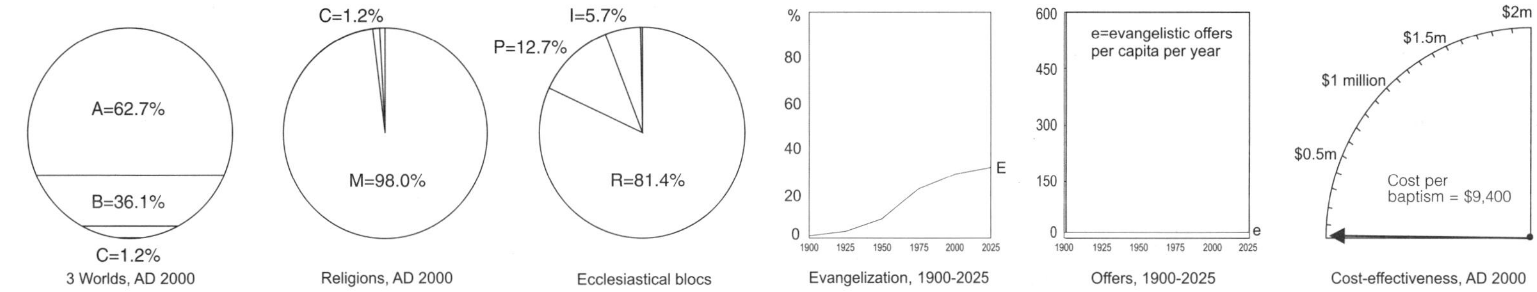

Country summary. **Worlds A, B, C by ethnolinguistic peoples, cities, and major civil divisions in The Comoros.**

	PEOPLES							CITIES							CIVIL DIVISIONS						
World	Num	Pop 2000	C%	Christians	E%	U%	Unevangelized	Num	Pop 2000	C%	Christians	E%	U%	Unevangelized	Num	Pop 2000	C%	Christians	E%	U%	Unevangelized
A	6	577,634	0.02	121	36	64	368,187	1	31,187	1.30	405	39	61	18,881	3	592,750	1.19	7,061	37	63	371,334
B	3	12,151	36.88	4,481	74	26	3,142	0	0	0.00	0	0	0	0	0	0	0.00	0	0	0	0
C	2	2,964	83.00	2,460	100	0	5	0	0	0.00	0	0	0	0	0	0	0.00	0	0	0	0
Total	**11**	**592,749**	**1.19**	**7,062**	**37**	**63**	**371,334**	**1**	**31,187**	**1.30**	**405**	**39**	**61**	**18,881**	**3**	**592,750**	**1.19**	**7,061**	**37**	**63**	**371,334**

CHRISTIANITY

CATHOLIC CHURCH. Catholics are composed mostly of those of mixed race from Reunion, or metropolitan French, and were attached to the diocese of Ambanja in Madagascar until a separate apostolic administration was set up in 1975. There are 4 chapels organized into 2 parishes, one for Grande Comore and MohÈli and the other for Anjouan, also covering Mayotte.

The Holy See has no diplomatic relations with The Comoros in AD 2000.

PROTESTANT CHURCH. There is a loosely-structured community consisting of a small number of Malagasy Protestants of various denominations, some of whom are seasonal workers in the islands. There is also one congregation of Adventists. The African Inland Mission sent several missionaries from 1975 onwards, but in 1978 the 18 Protestant missionaries were expelled.

CHURCH AND STATE

The Portuguese first sighted the islands in 1503, and the French arrived in 1517. The Comoros were placed under a French protectorate in 1886, granted internal autonomy in 1961, and eventually declared independence from France in 1975. Freedom of religion has been guaranteed under the French and subsequently, but special deference is made to Islam in the legal system. Islamic courts are given responsibility for questions of marriage and divorce and other personal matters relating to Muslims; and although basic education is provided for Muslim students in French in the morning, the afternoons are reserved for Quranic schools.

BROADCASTING AND MEDIA

No religious broadcasts are allowed. Reception is possible on SW radio from FEBA.

Eglise de Jésus-Christ aux Comores. Christians of Moroni parish bid farewell to their Malagasy pastor (centre, dark suit) at Moroni airport.

FUTURE TRENDS AND PROSPECTS

Muslims are expected to dominate, maintaining 98% of the population through 2025. No other figures are expected to change significantly before then.

Christians are not likely to reach 2% before AD 2050. Muslims will then continue as the vast majority.

BIBLIOGRAPHY

2000 titres: littératures de l'océan indien: Comores, Madagascar, Maurice, Réunion, Seychelles. Notre Librairie, no. 116. [Paris: CLEF, 1994]. 174p.

Bibliographie des Comores: sciences humaines. M. Girardin et al. Paris: Institut des langues et civilisations orientales, 1992. 49p.

Contes et mythes de Madagascar et des Comores. Paris: Institut des langues et civilisations orientales, 1987. 152p.

Langues, cultures et sociétés de l'océan Indien. Asie du sud-est et monde insulindien, vol. 8, nos. 3-4. Paris: A.S.E.M.I, 1977. 263p.

Les îles de l'Océan indien: Comores, Madagascar, Maurice, Réunion, Seychelles: bibliographie réalisée à partir de la Banque de données IBISCUS, triée par grands domaines. P. Hue. Collection Réseaux documentaires sur le développement, Série Références bibliographiques. Paris: Ministère de la coopération et du développement, [1991]. 285p.

Les Musulmans à Madagascar et aux Iles Comores. G. Ferrand. Algiers Université Faculté des lettres Publications, Ser. 1, t. 9. Paris: E. Leroux, 1891–1902. 3 vols.

L'islam aux Comores. S. H. M. Adihami. Port-Louis, Ile Maurice, Océan Indien: New Print, [1980]. 62p.

Country Table 2. **Organized churches and denominations in The Comoros.**

Official name (bold type = church *with over 10% of all affiliated)* 1	*Begun* 2	*Type* 3	*Counc* 4	*Congs* 5	*Adults* 6	*Affiliated 1970* 7	*Affiliated 1995* 8	*G%* 9	*Names, notes, and other statistics* (see Codebook, Part 3) 10
Eglise Adventiste du Septième Jour		P-Adv	x....	1	20	30	50	0.05	*SDA. Seventh-day Adventists.* In Indian Ocean Union Mission (HQ Tananarive).
Eglise Catholique: AA Comoro Islands	1517	R-Lat	P.S.r	2	2,400	1,091	5,000	6.28	Till 1975 in D Ambanja. French, Reunionese. M=OFMCap. C=1+0+1. 2x,7w,2b,1h,1r,19Yy.
Eglise de Jésus-Christ aux Comores		P-Ref	.....	4	275	300	550	0.05	*EJCC.* Malagasy Protestants (seasonal workers, officials), French military. 1x.
Eglise de l'Africa Inland Mission	1975	P-Non	xMG..	2	84	–	120	5.00	Linked to EJCC. M=AIM(USA, UK; doctors, teachers). 2 converts training as pastors.
Eglises radiophoniques isolées	1970	I-3rA	.....	30	100	30	300	9.65	Isolated radio believers (through FEBA, RVOG), mainly young people aged 12-25.
Témoins de Jéhovah	1989	m-Jeh	x....	1	5	–	5	16.67	*Jehovah's Witnesses. Watch Tower.*
Totals				**40**	**2,884**	**1,451**	**6,025**		

Churches, members, growth, 1900-2025	*Congs*	*Adults*	*Affiliated*	*G%*	*Total denominations*	*6 Megablocs:* *O*	*R*	*A*	*P*	*I*	*m*
Total churches, members, and denominations (mid-1900)	1	53	100	3.90	1	0	1	0	0	0	0
Total churches, members, and denominations (mid-1970)	11	770	1,451	3.90	4	0	1	0	2	1	0
Total churches, members, and denominations (mid-1990)	30	2,200	4,695	6.05	6	0	1	0	3	1	1
Total churches, members, and denominations (mid-1995)	40	2,884	6,025	5.11	6	0	1	0	3	1	1
Total churches, members, and denominations (mid-2000)	50	3,400	7,061	3.22	6	0	1	0	3	1	1
Total churches, members, and denominations (mid-2025)	100	7,000	14,550	2.93	20	0	1	0	6	10	3

NOTES ON TABLE ABOVE
NATIONAL COUNCILS (Column 4, 5th letter).

r = attached to Conférence Episcopale de Madagascar (Episcopal Conference of Madagascar).

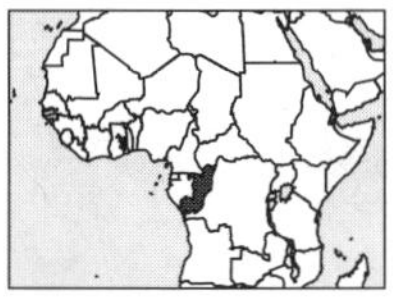

CONGO-BRAZZAVILLE

SECULAR DATA, AD 2000

STATE
Official name: La République du Congo (The Republic of the Congo).
Short name: Congo. **Adjective of nationality:** Congolese.
Flag: Red field with green wreath, yellow star, hammer and hoe.
Area: 342,000 sq. km. (132,047 sq. mi.).
Government: Transitional republic with a Parliament consisting of two legislative chambers, since 1992 (1785 French influence, 1885 French rule, 1910 colony in French Equatorial Africa, 1960 Independence as republic, 1970 one-party Marxist state).
Legislature: Senate, 60 members; National Assembly, 125 members.
Official language: French (Français).
Monetary unit: 1 CFA franc (CFAF) = 100 centimes. **US$1=** CFAF 560.38.
Chief cities: BRAZZAVILLE 1,234,000; Pointe-Noire 480,266; Loubomo (Dolisie) 79,543; Nkayi (formerly Jacob) 50,726.
Political divisions: 15 provinces.
Armed forces: 10,000.

DEMOGRAPHY
Population: 2,943,000.
Population density: 8.6/sq. km. (22.2/sq. mi.).
Under 15 years: 1,364,000.
Growth rate p.a.: 2.71% (births 41.28, deaths 14.24).
Mortality: Infant, per 1,000: 85.3; **Maternal per 100,000:** 890.0.
Life expectancy: 50 (male 48, female 52).
Household size: 4.7. **Floor area per person, sq.m:** 12.6.
Major languages: Kongo (Kikongo), French, Lingala, Munokotoba, Kibougo, Teke, and about 30 other tribal languages.
Urban dwellers: 62.53%. **Urban growth rate p.a.:** 3.7%.
Labor force: 30%.

ETHNOLINGUISTIC PEOPLES
16.8% Kongo (Congo); 11.5% Yombe (Bayombe, Kiombi); 8.0% Kunyi; 5.4% Mbosi (Mbochi, Mboshe); 4.4% Kongo (Monokutuba).

ECONOMY
National income p.a. per person: US$680; **per family:** US$3,196.

EDUCATION
Adult literacy: 74% (male 83%, female 67%). **Schools:** 1,623.
Universities: 124. **School enrolment:** female/male: 40%/40%.

HEALTH
Access to health services: 83%. **Access to safe water:** 60%.
Hospitals: 500 (33 beds per 10,000). **Doctors:** 613.
Blind: 4,000. **Deaf:** 178,900. **Murder rate:** 5.
Lepers: 66,000. **Underweight prevalence under 5:** 24%.

LITERATURE
New book titles p.a.: 440 (150 p.a. per million). **Periodicals:** 4.
Newspapers: 6 dailies.

COMMUNICATION (per 1,000 people)
Phones: 8 (25% mobile). **Radios:** 95. **TV sets:** 17.
Daily newspaper circulation: 8. **Computers:** 1.

REFUGEES
Alien refugees from other countries: 15,000.

HUMAN LIFE AND LIBERTY (optimum condition=100.0%)
HDI: 50.0. **HSI:** 36.0. **HFI:** 20.0. **EFL:** 24.0.

Country Table 1. **Religious adherents in Congo-Brazzaville, AD 1900-2025.**

Year	*1900*		*1970*		*mid-1990*		*Annual change, 1990-2000*				*mid-1995*		*mid-2000*		*mid-2025*	
Name	*Adherents*	*%*	*Adherents*	*%*	*Adherents*	*%*	*Natural*	*Conversion*	*Total*	*Rate*	*Adherents*	*%*	*Adherents*	*%*	*Adherents*	*%*
Christians	**13,500**	**2.5**	**1,161,720**	**92.0**	**2,026,000**	**91.3**	**65,982**	**-322**	**65,660**	**2.85**	**2,333,890**	**91.1**	**2,682,602**	**91.2**	**5,160,000**	**90.7**
PROFESSION																
professing Christians	**13,500**	**2.5**	**1,161,720**	**92.0**	**2,026,000**	**91.3**	**65,982**	**-322**	**65,660**	**2.85**	**2,333,890**	**91.1**	**2,682,602**	**91.2**	**5,160,000**	**90.7**
AFFILIATION																
unaffiliated Christians	5,000	0.9	473,155	37.5	309,500	13.9	10,080	-6,058	4,022	1.23	320,234	12.5	349,724	11.9	285,600	5.0
affiliated Christians	**8,500**	**1.6**	**688,565**	**54.5**	**1,716,500**	**77.3**	**55,902**	**5,736**	**61,638**	**3.12**	**2,013,656**	**78.6**	**2,332,878**	**79.3**	**4,874,400**	**85.7**
Roman Catholics	8,500	1.6	399,165	31.6	1,080,000	48.7	35,173	1,945	37,118	3.00	1,259,230	49.2	1,451,178	49.3	3,000,000	52.7
Protestants	0	0.0	167,100	13.2	363,000	16.4	11,822	1,878	13,700	3.25	427,126	16.7	500,000	17.0	1,050,000	18.5
Independents	0	0.0	119,000	9.4	265,000	11.9	8,630	1,870	10,500	3.39	317,400	12.4	370,000	12.6	800,000	14.1
Marginal Christians	0	0.0	3,000	0.2	8,100	0.4	264	56	320	3.39	9,500	0.4	11,300	0.4	24,000	0.4
Orthodox	0	0.0	300	0.0	400	0.0	13	-13	0	0.00	400	0.0	400	0.0	400	0.0
Trans-megabloc groupings																
Evangelicals	0	0.0	70,000	5.5	142,000	6.4	4,625	675	5,300	3.22	186,982	7.3	195,000	6.6	450,000	7.9
Pentecostals/Charismatics	0	0.0	42,000	3.3	402,000	18.1	13,092	5,608	18,700	3.89	492,893	19.3	589,000	20.0	1,365,000	24.0
Great Commission Christians	**12,960**	**2.4**	**114,000**	**9.0**	**395,000**	**17.8**	**12,864**	**4,410**	**17,274**	**3.69**	**462,000**	**18.0**	**567,743**	**19.3**	**1,092,000**	**19.2**
Ethnoreligionists	526,500	97.5	84,580	6.7	114,068	5.1	3,763	-947	2,816	2.23	125,800	4.9	142,232	4.8	188,500	3.3
Nonreligious	0	0.0	6,400	0.5	40,000	1.8	1,303	568	1,871	3.91	49,500	1.9	58,706	2.0	185,850	3.3
Muslims	0	0.0	5,600	0.4	25,000	1.1	814	393	1,207	4.02	32,000	1.3	37,071	1.3	95,000	1.7
Baha'is	0	0.0	3,100	0.3	9,000	0.4	293	100	393	3.69	11,200	0.4	12,927	0.4	40,000	0.7
New-Religionists	0	0.0	500	0.0	2,500	0.1	81	139	220	6.51	4,100	0.2	4,696	0.2	10,000	0.2
Atheists	0	0.0	500	0.0	1,562	0.1	51	11	62	3.39	1,920	0.1	2,180	0.1	4,000	0.1
Chinese folk-religionists	0	0.0	0	0.0	170	0.0	6	-2	4	1.94	180	0.0	206	0.0	400	0.0
Buddhists	0	0.0	0	0.0	100	0.0	3	0	3	2.42	110	0.0	127	0.0	250	0.0
Other religionists	0	0.0	600	0.1	1,600	0.1	52	60	112	5.44	2,300	0.1	2,718	0.1	5,000	0.1
World A (unevangelized persons)	464,940	86.1	88,389	7.0	26,640	1.2	873	-690	183	0.66	28,167	1.1	29,430	1.0	34,134	0.6
World B (evangelized non-Christians)	61,560	11.4	12,602	1.0	167,360	7.5	5,493	1,012	6,505	3.27	198,613	7.8	230,968	7.9	494,866	8.7
World C (Christians)	13,500	2.5	1,161,720	92.0	2,026,000	91.3	65,982	-322	65,660	2.85	2,333,890	91.1	2,682,602	91.1	5,160,000	90.7
Country's population	**540,000**	**100.0**	**1,262,712**	**100.0**	**2,220,000**	**100.0**	**72,348**	**0**	**72,348**	**2.86**	**2,560,671**	**100.0**	**2,943,000**	**100.0**	**5,689,000**	**100.0**

COLUMNS, ROWS.
For meanings and definitions, see Codebook (Part 3). Note that, by definition, total 'Christians' = professing + crypto-Christians, which also = affiliated + unaffiliated Christians, and also = Great Commission Christians + latent Christians. Percentages may not always total exactly, due to rounding.

CENSUSES.
IX.1960-II.1961 (Africans): 52.8% Roman Catholics, 27.0% Protestants, 11.1% ethnoreligionists, 8.9% African indigenous, 0.3% Muslims.

NOTES ON RELIGIONS
AFRICAN INDIGENOUS. In over 20 denominations in 1995 (see Table 2).
ATHEISTS. The Parti Congolais du Travail (PCT), although Marxist in ideology, has few avowed atheists among its members.
BAHA'IS. Rapid growth to 21 local spiritual assemblies by 1973, then slow climb to 31 (1996).
ETHNORELIGIONISTS. Tribes over 60% traditionalist (animist) in 1995: only the Buraka-Gbanziri (90%). Though professed animists are now few in number, festishism is increasing.
MUSLIMS. Non-Congolese expatriate traders (Sunnis of the Malikite rite) from francophone North and Western African states, living in the cities and towns; and over 20,000 Congolese in Pointe Noire and Brazzaville.
NEW-RELIGIONISTS (followers of new East Asian religions). Tenrikyo, a Shinto sect from Japan, began in Brazzaville in 1966.
NONRELIGIOUS. Including many French expatriates.
OTHER RELIGIONISTS. Including Rosicrucians (5 AMORC centres).
PENTECOSTALS/CHARISMATICS. Rapid growth of the Catholic Renewal caused Brazzaville to be chosen as venue for the 1992 2nd Pan-African Catholic Charismatic Renewal Conference.
ROMAN CATHOLICS. In 1900 there were 4,492 baptized Catholics and about 4,000 catechumens.
UNAFFILIATED CHRISTIANS. The expansion of Christianity in the Congo has been so rapid that there has been a large number of unaffiliated Christians (professing but not affiliated). In 1970 this nominal fringe numbered 34% of the population, or 59% the size of all affiliated Christians. As the expansion of Christianity slowed down after 1970, the nominal fringe began to decrease in proportion to affiliated Christians, indicating that the churches had begun to catch up with the expansion and to initiate and disciple the large number of unaffiliated Christians.

Country status. Congo is located near the equator in Central Africa. Known under French rule as Middle Congo, it was the one of the most important units of the French Equatorial Africa of which Brazzaville was the capital. The country is densely forested and its main exports are oil, timber, coffee, and tobacco.

HUMAN LIFE AND LIBERTY

Human need and development. Congo is one of the many African countries whose economy has suf-

Great Commission Instrument Panel: status of Congo-Brazzaville (for explanation see start of Part 4)

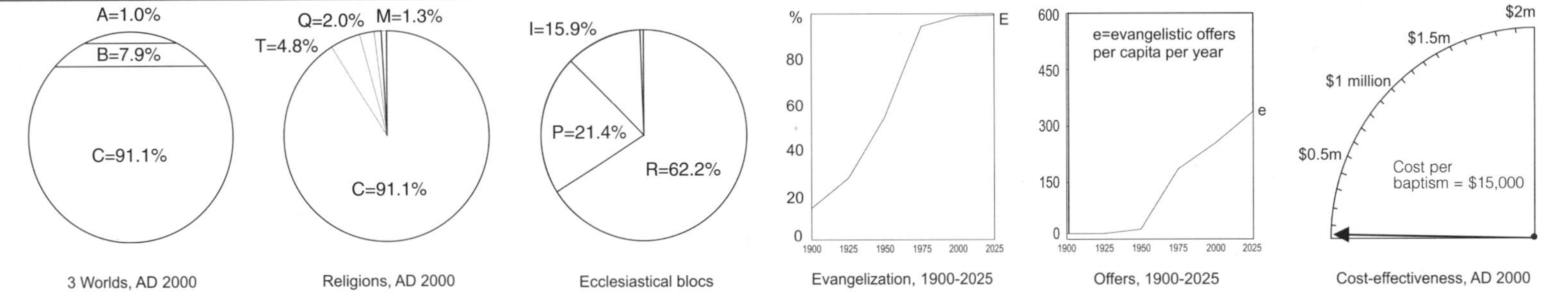

fered and whose resources have been frittered away in the post-independence years as a result of political mismanagement and experiments with Marxism. About 1% of the population may be described as modern and they live in atypical affluence with access to imported luxury goods. The remaining 99% constitute the urban and rural poor and middle class who manage to eke out a bare subsistence. Rapid flow of population from the rural areas into the towns has produced unsettled social and economic conditions as well as serious unemployment and overcrowded shantytowns. The year-round hot and humid climate is a contributory factor in the high incidence of respiratory disorders, which is one of the most widely prevalent diseases in the country. No sewage systems exist and water disposal facilities are primitive. Most wells and streams are heavily polluted and they help to spread contagious diseases. Poorly ventilated one-room huts are used for both sleeping and cooking. Sanitary conditions in the cities are only slightly better. The diet is starchy and lacking in basic nutrients, meat and fish being limited to the rich. The medical facilities have expanded since independence, but fall short of providing basic healthcare for all. There is a shortage of trained medical personnel which is met by traditional witch doctors and medicine men.

Human rights and freedoms. The restoration of democracy in 1991 after years of Marxist rule signaled the most important shift in direction in the history of Congo. The National Conference which shepherded the transition, charted a new political course for the country. It adopted the Fundamental Act, including the Comprehensive Bill of Rights. Formerly the Congolese military was closely tied with the Congolese Workers Party under the one-party regime. The military was responsible for internal security and for suppressing dissident activity. High-ranking military officers held party positions and party officials served in the military. With the fall of the one-party regime, the military has been depoliticized and stripped of its internal security functions. The responsibility for law enforcement and public order has been placed with the civilian police. The potential for human rights abuses has thus been effectively reduced. The state monopoly over the press has been ended and numerous private newspapers operate without hindrance. The new Bill of Rights prohibits discrimination of all kinds. But Pygmies, numbering about 7,000, are virtually isolated in the northern forests and receive very little, if any, government attention. There are also reports of slavery practiced in the interior regions. In the traditional Congolese family, women fill a subservient role and are subject to the legal authority of the husband over all her actions. Divorce is legal for men, but not for women. Polygamy is legal and widely practiced. On the death of the husband, the wives are lumped together with other moveable property and parceled out to the relatives.

Human environment. Congo's lush equatorial forests are being depleted at the rate of 50,000 acres per year. Deforestation poses a threat to the native wildlife and floral biodiversity. In some areas, improper waste disposal and resulting water pollution are the main environmental problems.

NON-CHRISTIAN RELIGIONS

Traditional religions were still followed by 11.1% of the population in 1961 although by 1972 most of these professed to be Christians. Two small tribes (Bakwili and Ngwili) have been more resistant to evangelization and remain 60% traditionalist. Traditional beliefs continue to manifest themselves within Christianity. Most of the country's peoples share a common name for God: Nzambi (among Kongo-Sundi, Dondo, Ndasa), Nzama (Teke) and Nziame (Kuta). Nzambi is the all-powerful creator of the sky, earth, and man. He is conceived of in 2 aspects: Nzambi Watanda (above) who is good and Nzambi Wamutsele (below) who is wicked. The double-sided nature of God thus explains the reality of life itself with its alternating periods of good and bad fortune. Two classes of ancestral spirits widely believed in are the Binyumba who inhabit the kingdom of the dead, and the Bakuyu who have not yet been admitted to the abode of deceased spirits. These latter wander restlessly about and are much feared and propitiated through offerings.

Fetishism, which was widely practiced prior to the prophetic activity of Simon Kimbangu in 1921, is now once again reviving.

Islam has made little impact in Congo-Brazzaville and makes up no more than 1.3% of the population. Most of these are expatriate Muslims from northern Muslim countries.

Tenrikyo, one of the Japanese so-called New Religions, is a Shinto sect founded in Japan in 1838; in 1966 it established a center in Brazzaville. In 1971 the mission consisted of 200 followers, 4 stations, and a dispensary with a doctor and 5 nurses. Tenrikyo doctrine gives special emphasis to health care and healing of the sick.

CHRISTIANITY

CATHOLIC CHURCH. Portuguese explorers discovered the Congo river in 1482 and the first missionary expedition was sent to the Kingdom of the Congo in 1491. The result was a flourishing Christian community during the 16th century under Afonso I, one of the major Christian figures of African history. Afonso's son, Henrique, was the first Catholic bishop of African descent. Ravaged by the slave trade, both the kingdom and its church disintegrated during the 17th and 18th centuries. However, the church was never as influential in the area now in Congo-Brazzaville as it was in Zaire and northern Angola to the south.

A new era for Catholic missions began in 1883 with the arrival of the first Holy Ghost priests at the coast, and a vicariate of the French Congo was begun in 1886. A mission was sent to the upper Congo in 1889, and the following year a second vicariate was erected for that area. The first Congolese priest of modern times was ordained in 1895. Since World War II further progress has been made in the organization of the church. The archdiocese of Brazzaville, with 2 suffragan dioceses, was established in 1955 and a Congolese bishop consecrated in 1961. Catholic growth has been steady since the beginning, climbing to 1,259,000 by 1995.

The Holy See has diplomatic relations with Congo and in AD 2000 is represented to government and the Catholic hierarchy by a nuncio residing in Brazzaville.

PROTESTANT CHURCHES. Protestant work was not begun until 1909 and was the result of the expansion of the Swedish Evangelical Mission (Svenska Missionsforbundet) from neighboring Belgian Congo. The growth of this church has been strongly affected by fluctuating indigenous movements which have come and gone in the area over the past half century. The prophetic activity of Simon Kimbangu in 1921 created a revival in the church, characterized by spirit possession (*ngunza*) and the burning of fetishes. In 1941 there was a movement away from the church and a drop in baptisms due to a widespread belief that the newly-arrived Salvation Army provided protection from sorcery (*kindoki*) and that its flag was efficacious in healing the sick and raising the dead. Similar decreases were noted in 1946 and 1952 when other Ngunzist movements made their appearance. Nevertheless these periods of decline were often followed by renewal, as in the revival of 1947. The Evangelical Church became autonomous in 1961. Today it is by far the largest Protestant church. The majority of its centers are located in the densely-populated southern region.

The Salvation Army entered Brazzaville in 1935 and has also concentrated its attention in the south. With a heavy emphasis on church planting in addition to its traditional concern for social service, the increase in its membership has been significant. The Baptist Church, which is aided by the Swedish Pentecostal-Baptist örebro Mission, has been at work in the sparsely-populated northeast since 1921.

INDIGENOUS CHURCHES. The Kimbanguist Church (Eglise de Jésus-Christ sur la terre par le Prophéte Simon Kimbangu, EJCSK), which is the largest independent church in Africa, has a large following in Congo-Brazzaville, although only a fraction of the parent church in neighboring Zaire. After a long history of persecution as an underground church until 1960, Kimbanguists have now become part of the ecumenical movement, being members of the WCC, AACC and the newly-formed Federation of Christian Churches in the Congo.

Other groups of a more syncretistic nature include the Eglise Matsouaniste, Eglise DieudonnÈ au Congo, and Lassyism or Nzambi ya Bougie (God of the Candle). Begun by the Vili prophet Zepherin Lassy in 1953, the Bougists numbered 8.7% of the population in 1961. Their membership and influence have however subsequently declined.

Mouvement Croix-Koma. The Nailed-to-the-Cross movement was begun in 1964 by a Roman Catholic layman, Ta Malanda, with massive followings. *Above*, Malanda reads Croix-Koma's unique liturgy. *Below*, Malanda and the Cross.

Country summary. **Worlds A, B, C by ethnolinguistic peoples, cities, and major civil divisions in Congo-Brazzaville.**

	PEOPLES							CITIES							CIVIL DIVISIONS						
World	Num	Pop 2000	C%	Christians	E%	U%	Unevangelized	Num	Pop 2000	C%	Christians	E%	U%	Unevangelized	Num	Pop 2000	C%	Christians	E%	U%	Unevangelized
A	2	7,212	1.91	138	46	54	3,864	0	0	0.00	0	0	0	0	0	0	0.00	0	0	0	0
B	11	66,373	40.47	26,861	75	25	16,316	0	0	0.00	0	0	0	0	0	0	0.00	0	0	0	0
C	66	2,869,875	80.35	2,305,881	100	0	8,456	4	1,844,535	74.84	1,380,399	99	1	27,077	15	2,943,464	79.26	2,332,878	99	1	28,634
Total	**79**	**2,943,460**	**79.26**	**2,332,880**	**99**	**1**	**28,636**	**4**	**1,844,535**	**74.84**	**1,380,399**	**99**	**1**	**27,077**	**15**	**2,943,464**	**79.26**	**2,332,878**	**99**	**1**	**28,634**

Another more recent religious movement has been the notable campaign against witchcraft, magic, and sorcery known as the Mouvement Croix-Koma (Nailed to the Cross) begun in 1964 by a Roman Catholic layman of the Lari tribe, Ta (Father) Malanda. By 1966, 30,000 persons a year (50% pagans, 30% Catholics, 20% Protestants) were coming to spend a structured 7-day period at his Kankata headquarters, surrendering their nkisi (fetishes) for public and permanent exhibition. Individuals were allowed to visit Kankata for the ceremonies only once, and the founder always regarded his movement as not a church but as a movement within the Roman Catholic Church. In 1967, the JMNR (Jeunesse du Mouvement National Revolutionnaire) under president Massamba-Débat proposed that Croix-Koma become the Congo's 'église officielle', but Malanda refused. By the end of 1970, a total of 184,789 pilgrims had visited Kankata; by the end of 1971, 20% of the entire population of the Congo had taken part, including virtually the entire Kongo, Lari, and Sundi populace. After Malanda's death in 1971, the movement was carried on by his nephew. In 1976 it was still a highly-influential movement, but had abandoned all links with the Roman Catholic Church and operated as an independent religious movement or institution.

Meanwhile, new charismatic movements proliferated from 1980 on.

Renewal movements. In the 1990s the Pentecostal/Charismatic Renewal continued to spread rapidly across most older churches, and numbered over 589,000 adherents (of whom 9% Pentecostals, 33% Charismatics, and 58% Independents).

Indigenous missions. Only a few Congolese have become missionaries and almost all of these have served in neighboring Zaire.

CHURCH AND STATE

Since Independence the country has had 3 constitutions, namely those of the first republic under abbe Fulbert Youlou, 1960-63; the second republic under Massamba-Débat, 1963-68; and the third republic since December 1968, under commandant Marien Ngouabi. According to the latest constitution of 30 December 1969, 'The Congo is a popular republic, one, indivisible and secular' (Article 1). 'Citizens enjoy freedom of speech, of the press, of association, of processions and demonstrations under conditions determined by the law' (Article 17). 'Freedom of conscience and religion are guaranteed to all citizens'. 'Religious communities are free in all questions relating to their beliefs and their external practices. It is forbidden to misuse religion or the church for political ends. Political organizations based on religion are forbidden' (Article 19).

Since 1964, the government has become progressively more socialist, defining its socialism as first scientific and then Marxist. In 1964 a single national party, trade union, and youth movement were established, resulting in the prohibition of religious trade unions and the de facto suppression of various Christian movements for youth and adults. At the end of 1964 and during 1965, a number of priests and lay missionaries were expelled or imprisoned, and in August 1965 a decree nationalized all Evangelical, Salvation Army and Catholic private schools with the exception of those training 'servants of God' (major and minor seminaries, religious novitiates and theological colleges). At the time of the decree, half of all primary pupils were in Catholic schools.

The third republic, which has subsequently proclaimed itself to be Marxist-Leninist, has not changed the preceding legislation, and the position of the churches remains ambiguous. On the one hand, the government is developing at intermediate levels, including schools, army, and trade unions, an intense program of ideological indoctrination emphasizing the incompatibility of being at the same time a militant revolutionary and a professing Christian; and at the level of political leadership anti-religious propaganda is evident here and there. On the other hand, at the level of government and law the authorities do everything possible to prevent disturbances and they retain courteous relationships with the leaders of the principal Christian denominations, including Catholics, Evangelicals, Salvationists and Kimbanguists. Seminaries for clergy and schools for catechists operate normally.

Medical personnel at the numerous church-related dispensaries (11 Catholic, 14 Evangelical, 7 Salvation Army) are paid by the state, which also itself employs 11 Catholic sisters in state hospitals, as well as 11 other sisters and 2 priests in state schools. The Catholic weekly *La semaine* continues to appear without hindrance, and through prudent self-censorship enjoys a freedom and independence rare in French-speaking Africa.

In March 1977 the Catholic cardinal Biayenda was murdered soon after assassination of the head of state.

In February 1978, the regime banned over 30 Christian and non-Christian religious bodies, including the Assemblies of God, Baha'i, Jehovah's Witnesses, Rosicrucians, Seventh-day Adventists, and all religious youth organizations; and confiscated all their buildings, furniture and other property. Only 7 groups were allowed to continue in legal existence: the Roman Catholic Church, Evangelical Church of the Congo, Salvation Army, Muslim Committee of the Congo, 2 indigenous churches (Kimbanguist Church, and Church of Zepherin Lassy), and Tenrikyo. However, even these 7 were forbidden to teach religion to young people.

The recent history of the churches shows a continuation of this mixture of progress and violence.

BROADCASTING AND MEDIA

French and English programs from AWR (Slovakia) can be received. Congo is a member of UNDA. A Catholic program is aired for 30 minutes each Sunday morning, and for an hour on television each Sunday.

INTERDENOMINATIONAL ORGANIZATIONS

The Federation of Evangelical Churches and Missions of Cameroon and Equatorial Guinea was established in 1943 to serve churches and missions in Cameroon, Rio Muni, Gabon and Congo-Brazzaville, but the organization disintegrated during the 1960s due to new political realities after independence in those countries. In the Congo, a desire for closer contacts at the local level brought together 4 denominations in a new ecumenical venture in September 1970: the Federation of Christian Churches in the Congo (Fédération des Eglises Chrétiennes du Congo-Brazzaville). Member bodies are the Salvation Army, Kimbanguist, Baptist, and Evangelical churches, and much later the Catholic Church also. The Salvation Army, Evangelical Church and Kimbanguist Church are all members both of the AACC and the WCC.

Concerning Catholic-Protestant relations, an interconfessional committee without official title has functioned since 1969. It has been responsible for organizing the Week of Prayer for Christian Unity, mutual invitations to church festivals and other events, and represents a significant step in the direction of wider ecumenical dialogue.

FUTURE TRENDS AND PROSPECTS

Nominalism among Christians will probably decline into the 21st century falling to 5% by 2025. At the same time affiliation is expected to rise to 86% by 2025 (from 55% in 1970).

Christianity as a whole is likely to continue its slow decline into the 21st century passing below the 90% mark for the first time since the mid-20th century. Gains would be made by the nonreligious and Muslims.

BIBLIOGRAPHY

Bwiti: an ethnography of the religious imagination in Africa. J. W. Fernandez. Princeton, NJ: Princeton University Press, 1982. 731p. (Religion of the Fang).

Churches at the grass-roots: a study in Congo–Brazzaville. E. Andersson. London: Lutterworth, 1968. 296p.

Congo. R. Fegley. *World bibliographical series*, vol. 162. Oxford, UK: CLIO Press, 1993. 220p. (See especially 'Religion and philosophy,' 51f).

Congo: 1958–1968: New nation, new church. V. G. Pruitt. , [1970]. 103p.

'Drugs and mysticism: the Bwiti of the Fang,' J. Binet, *Diogènes* (Paris), 86 (Summer 1974), 31–54.

Ethnologie religieuse des Kuta, mythologie et folklore. E. Andersson. Uppsala: Almquist & Wiksell, 1987. 164p.

Introduction à l'ethnographie du Congo. J. Vansina. Kinshasa: Université Lovanium, 1965. 228p.

La Bouenza, 1892–1992: les sources de l'église au Congo. M. de Dreuille. *Eglise aux quatre vents.* Paris: Editions Beauchesne, 1994. 140p.

'La Mission Evangélique Suédoise et la naissance de l'Eglise Evangélique du Congo.' H. N'Kounkou. Thesis, Faculté Libre de Théologie Protestante, Montpellier, France, 1961.

'Le Harrisme et le Bwiti: deux réactions Africaines à l'impact Chrétien,' R. Bureau, *Recherches de Sciences Religieuses*, 63, 1 (1975), 83–100.

Le Matsouanisme. F. Youlou. Brazzaville: Imprimerie Centrale, 1955.

Le messianisme Congolais et ses incidences politiques. M. Sinda. Paris: Payot, 1972. 390p.

'Le mouvement Croix-Koma: une nouvelle forme de lutte contre la sorcellerie en pays Kongo', J. F. Vincent, *Cahiers d'études africaines*, 24 (1966) 527-63.

'Les peuples de la République démocratique du Congo, du Rwanda et du Burundi,' A. Dorsinfang-Smets, in *Ethnologie régionale*, p.566–661, vol. 1. J. Poirier (ed). Paris: Gallimard, 1972.

Mgr. Prosper Augouard et l'implantation du Christianisme au Congo Français (1877–1921). B. Gassongo. Brazzaville: Les Lianes, [1978]. 38p.

Modern Kongo prophets: religion in a plural society. W. MacGaffey. *African systems of thought series.* Bloomington, IN: University of Indiana Press, 1983. 285p.

'Situations et interpellations de l'Eglise aujourd'hui: le cas du Congo,' Archbishop E. Kombo, in *Eglises et démocratisation en Afrique: actes de la Dix-neuviäme Semaine Théologique de Kinshasa du 21 au 27 novembre 1993*, p.17–26. Buetubela Balembo, R. De Haes & E. Kombo. *Semaines théologiques de Kinshasa.* Kinshasa: Facultés Catholiques de Kinshasa, 1994.

'The environment, establishment and development of Protestant missions in French Equatorial Africa.' B. A. Hamilton. Ph.D. dissertation, Grace Theological Seminary, Goshen, IN, 1959. 353p.

Country Table 2. **Organized churches and denominations in Congo-Brazzaville.**

Official name (bold type = church with over 10% of all affiliated) 1	*Begun* 2	*Type* 3	*Counc* 4	*Congs* 5	*Adults* 6	*Affiliated 1970* 7	*Affiliated 1995* 8	*G%* 9	*Names, notes, and other statistics* (see Codebook, Part 3) 10
Armée du Salut	1935	P-Sal	xwA.C	242	22,000	40,000	62,900	1.83	*Salvation Army, Congo Territory. Nkangu a Luvulusu.* 96n,10x,7h,1j,1k,1s,W=50%.
Assemblées de Dieu de Pentecôte	c1990	I-3pA	.....	500	30,000	–	70,000	20.00	*ADP. Assemblies of God of Pentecost.* HQ Brazzaville.
EdeJC sur la Terre par le Prophète SK	1921	I-3pA	xwi.C	200	60,000	30,000	90,000	4.49	*EJCSK. Eglise Kimbanguiste.* M=Kimbanguist Ch (Zaire). Mostly Bakongo.
Eglise Adventiste du Septième Jour	1965	P-Adv	x....	1	148	100	296	4.44	*SDA. Seventh-day Adventists.*
Eglise Apostolique Unie en Afrique	c1970	I-3aA	.v...	20	2,000	3,000	4,000	1.16	*EAUA. United Apostolic Ch (Zaire).* HQ Brazzaville. 1973 applied to WCC. 3n,23m.

Continued opposite

Country Table 2–concluded

Official name (bold type = church with over 10% of affiliated) 1	*Begun* 2	*Type* 3	*Counc* 4	*Congs* 5	*Adults* 6	*Affiliated 1970* 7	*Affiliated 1995* 8	*G%* 9	*Names, notes, and other statistics* (see Codebook, Part 3) 10
Eglise Baptiste du Congo Populaire	1921	P-Pe2	Zvg.C	69	2,500	4,000	8,330	2.98	M=Örebro M (Sweden). 40% Bonguili, 40% Dzem. 7n,4x,1p(7),W=50%,62Y,553z.
Eglise Catholique au Congo:	1883	R-Lat	P.SBV	109	730,300	399,165	1,259,230	4.70	*Catholic Ch in Congo.* C=5+4+16. 3p,1s(19). 112n 90x 176m 285w 43639Yy
M Brazzaville	1890	R-Lat	Ps	31	287,200	165,215	495,157	4.49	Capital, 50% urban. Mainly Balali tribe. 42n 42x 102m 114w 32992Yy
D Kinkala	1987	R-Lat	Bs	21	51,100	–	88,200	12.50	Population is 50% Catholic. 17n 4x 12m 22w 2375Yy
D Nkayi	1983	R-Lat	Bs	20	158,700	–	273,775	8.33	50% baptized Catholics. 23n 21x 26m 59w 3933Yy
D Ouesso	1983	R-Lat	Bs	7	40,000	–	69,000	8.33	48% Catholics. 5n 5x 7m 24w 366Yy
D Owando (Fort Rousset)	1950	R-Lat	Psj	17	49,300	77,400	85,098	0.38	Formerly D Fort-Rousset. Many tribes. M=SJ. 17n 10x 18m 44w 1606Yy
D Pointe-Noire	1886	R-Lat	Ps	13	144,000	156,550	248,000	1.86	Diocese with most Protestants. M=CSSp. 8n 8x 11m 22w 2367Yy
Eglise Charismatique de Brazzaville	c1990	I-3cA	.....	35	15,000	–	30,000	20.00	Large indigenous megachurch in capital city. Many daughter congregations.
Eglises de Dieu du Congo	1961	P-Pe2	Z....	170	20,200	–	35,000	51.97	*EDD, CAPEC (Full Gospel Assemblies).* M=AoG (France; also, USA since 1990).
Fédérationdes Eglises de Réveil	c1985	I-3pA	.....	100	7,000	–	15,000	10.00	*FER, FAR. Federation of Revival Assemblies/Churches.* HQ Pointe Noire
Eglise des Noirs en Afrique Centrale	1941	I-3mA	.....	7	700	2,000	1,500	-1.14	*ENAC. Ch of the Black Race. Kaki Ch.* Founder patriarch Simon Mpadi, Zaire. Ex SA.
Eglise Evangélique de la Likouala	1946	P-Eva	xF...	28	3,500	3,000	10,600	5.18	*Mission d'Impfondo.* M=UWM(USA). Rain-forest along river. Bondjo, Bondongo. 9f,1h.
Eglise Evangélique du Congo	1909	P-Con	xWA.C	221	155,000	120,000	310,000	3.87	*EEC.* M=SMF,MCCN. A=1961. 1947 revival. Kongo. 67n,3988m,14th,12i,1k,1s,W=80%,3190Y.
Eglise Matsouaniste	1930	I-mar	.....	8	400	1,000	800	-0.89	*Amical Balali.* Remnants of politico-messianic movement begun by André Matswa.
Eglise Neo-Apostolique	c1980	I-3aX	x....	90	18,000	–	27,100	6.67	*NAC. New Apostolic Ch.* M=Neuapostolische Kirche (HQ Zurich, Switzerland).
Eglise Orthodoxe: AD Afrique Centrale		O-Gre	Cw...	1	280	300	400	0.05	Under P Alexandria (Egypt). HQ Burundi. Lebanese, Greeks. Parish in Pointe-Noire.
Mission de Dieu du Bougie	1953	I-Sal	.....	70	18,000	50,000	45,000	-0.42	*Ch of God of the Candle.* Vili messiah Zepherin Lassy. Ex SA. Declining.
Mouvement Croix-Koma	1964	I-ReC	.....	50	5,000	30,000	16,000	-2.48	*Dibundu dia Croix-Koma (Nailed to the Cross).* Ex RCC; renouncing witchcraft.
Témoins de Jéhovah	c1945	m-Jeh	x....	80	2,250	3,000	9,500	4.72	*Jehovah's Witnesses.* Active witnessing by 1948. Severe persecution. (1975) 151Y. (1995) 266Y.
Other African indigenous churches		I-3pA	.....	100	10,000	3,000	15,000	0.05	Total about 15, including Eglise Dieudonné au Congo; all banned in 1978.
Other independent charismatic chs	c1990	I-3cA	.....	25	1,500	–	3,000	20.00	Independent charismatic churches.
Totals				**2,126**	**1,103,888**	**688,565**	**2,013,656**		

Churches, members, growth, 1900-2025	*Congs*	*Adults*	*Affiliated*	*G%*	*Total denominations*	*6 Megablocs:* *O*	*R*	*A*	*P*	*I*	*m*
Total churches, members, and denominations (mid-1900)	50	4,600	8,500	6.48	1	0	1	0	0	0	0
Total churches, members, and denominations (mid-1970)	814	372,508	688,565	6.48	21	1	1	0	5	13	1
Total churches, members, and denominations (mid-1990)	1,600	941,000	1,716,500	4.67	34	1	1	0	6	25	1
Total churches, members, and denominations (mid-1995)	2,126	1,103,888	2,013,656	3.24	64	1	1	0	6	55	1
Total churches, members, and denominations (mid-2000)	2,200	1,279,000	2,332,878	2.99	65	1	1	0	6	56	1
Total churches, members, and denominations (mid-2025)	4,000	2,672,000	4,874,400	2.99	85	3	1	0	10	70	1

NOTES ON TABLE ABOVE
NATIONAL COUNCILS (Column 4, 5th letter).
C = Fedération des Eglises Chrétiennes du Congo (FECC) (Federation of Christian Churches in the Congo), or Conseil Oecumenique des Eglises Chretiennes du Congo (COECC), or Conseil Oecuménique du Congo (Ecumenical Council of the Congo).
K = Conseil Oecumenique des Eglises du Congo.
V = Conférence Episcopale du Congo (CEC, Episcopal Conference of the Congo), also member of Ecumenical Council of the Congo.

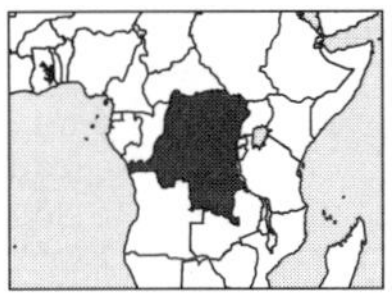

CONGO-ZAIRE

SECULAR DATA, AD 2000

STATE
Official name: La République Démocratique du Congo (The Democratic Republic of the Congo).
Short name: Congo-Zaire. **Adjective of nationality:** Congolese.
Flag: Green field with yellow circle in centre showing arm carrying torch.
Area: 2,345,095 sq. km. (905,446 sq. mi.).
Government: Revolutionary military regime, since 1997 (15th-century kingdom of the Congo, 1885 Congo Free State (absolute monarchy), 1908 Belgian Congo colony, 1960 Independence as republic, 1965 military dictatorship, 1971 parliamentary republic).
Legislature: National Assembly, 420 members.
Official language: French (Français), English.
Monetary unit: Congolese franc (FC). **US$1=** FC 1.4.
Chief cities: KINSHASA (Leopoldville) 5,068,000; Lubumbashi (Elisabethville) 967,000; Mbuji-Mayi (Bakwanga) 810,491; Kolwezi 693,621; Kisangani (Stanleyville) 529,366.
Political divisions: 11 provinces.
Armed forces: 49,000.

DEMOGRAPHY
Population: 51,654,000.
Population density: 22.0/sq. km. (57.0/sq. mi.).
Under 15 years: 24,970,000.
Growth rate p.a.: 2.97% (births 42.91, deaths 12.91).
Mortality: Infant, per 1,000: 76.6; **Maternal per 100,000:** 870.0.
Life expectancy: 53 (male 51, female 54).
Household size: 6.0. **Floor area per person, sq.m:** 11.0.
Major languages: Ngala (Lingala), Kongo (Kikongo), Swahili, French, Luba (Tshiluba), Mongo, Azande, and over 450 other tribal languages.
Urban dwellers: 30.28%. **Urban growth rate p.a.:** 4.5%.
Labor force: 36%.

ETHNOLINGUISTIC PEOPLES
6.4% Kongo Creole (Tuba, Leta); 5.2% Luba-Lulua (Western Luba); 4.1% Luba (Luba-Bambo); 4.0% Lingala; 3.1% Ekonda.

ECONOMY
National income p.a. per person: US$120; **per family:** US$720.

EDUCATION
Adult literacy: 77% (male 86%, female 67%). **Schools:** 12,987.
Universities: 0. **School enrolment:** female/male: 39%/58%.

HEALTH
Access to health services: 26%. **Access to safe water:** 27%.
Hospitals: 400 (21 beds per 10,000). **Doctors:** 2,469.
Blind: 73,000. **Deaf:** 3,105,000. **Murder rate:** 1.
Lepers: 800,000. **Underweight prevalence under 5:** 34%.

LITERATURE
New book titles p.a.: 50 (1 p.a. per million). **Periodicals:** 95.
Newspapers: 9 dailies.

COMMUNICATION (per 1,000 people)
Phones: <1 (29% mobile). **Radios:** 81. **TV sets:** 41.
Daily newspaper circulation: 3. **Computers:** 2.

REFUGEES
Citizen refugees in other countries: 58,600.
Alien refugees from other countries: 1,332,000.
Internal displacement: 225,000.

HUMAN LIFE AND LIBERTY (optimum condition=100.0%)
HDI: 38.1. **HSI:** 12.0. **HFI:** 12.5. **EFL:** 16.0.

Country Table 1. **Religious adherents in Congo-Zaire, AD 1900-2025.**

Year / *Name*	*1900* *Adherents*	*%*	*1970* *Adherents*	*%*	*mid-1990* *Adherents*	*%*	*Annual change, 1990-2000* *Natural*	*Conversion*	*Total*	*Rate*	*mid-1995* *Adherents*	*%*	*mid-2000* *Adherents*	*%*	*mid-2025* *Adherents*	*%*
Christians	**124,650**	**1.4**	**18,569,000**	**91.6**	**35,392,480**	**94.7**	**1,353,781**	**32,561**	**1,386,342**	**3.36**	**43,289,860**	**95.3**	**49,255,901**	**95.4**	**100,935,700**	**96.3**
PROFESSION																
professing Christians	**124,650**	**1.4**	**18,569,000**	**91.6**	**35,392,480**	**94.7**	**1,353,781**	**32,561**	**1,386,342**	**3.36**	**43,289,860**	**95.3**	**49,255,901**	**95.4**	**100,935,700**	**96.3**
AFFILIATION																
unaffiliated Christians	0	0.0	82,000	0.4	1,292,480	3.5	49,436	31,754	81,190	5.00	1,834,860	4.0	2,104,376	4.1	5,053,700	4.8
affiliated Christians	**124,650**	**1.4**	**18,487,000**	**91.2**	**34,100,000**	**91.3**	**1,304,345**	**808**	**1,305,153**	**3.29**	**41,455,000**	**91.3**	**47,151,525**	**91.3**	**95,882,000**	**91.5**
Roman Catholics	74,600	0.8	9,907,949	48.9	18,750,000	50.2	717,170	37,830	755,000	3.44	23,000,950	50.6	26,300,000	50.9	55,000,000	52.5
Independents	0	0.0	4,164,744	20.6	8,620,000	23.1	329,707	13,293	343,000	3.41	10,526,425	23.2	12,050,000	23.3	27,000,000	25.8
Protestants	50,000	0.6	4,644,780	22.9	7,780,000	20.8	297,578	-27,078	270,500	3.03	9,328,718	20.5	10,485,000	20.3	18,862,000	18.0
Anglicans	0	0.0	100,000	0.5	310,000	0.8	11,857	1,143	13,000	3.56	380,000	0.8	440,000	0.9	964,000	0.9
Marginal Christians	0	0.0	30,000	0.2	230,000	0.6	8,797	4,203	13,000	4.58	295,000	0.7	360,000	0.7	1,150,000	1.1
Orthodox	50	0.0	7,000	0.0	7,900	0.0	302	-282	20	0.25	10,000	0.0	8,100	0.0	9,000	0.0
doubly-affiliated	0	0.0	-367,473	-1.8	-1,597,900	-4.3	-61,118	-28,250	-89,368	4.54	-2,086,093	-4.6	-2,491,575	-4.8	-7,103,000	-6.8
Trans-megabloc groupings																
Evangelicals	48,000	0.5	1,419,000	7.0	3,100,000	8.3	118,572	15,428	134,000	3.66	3,831,407	8.4	4,440,000	8.6	10,590,000	10.1
Pentecostals/Charismatics	0	0.0	4,630,000	22.8	12,500,000	33.5	478,113	46,887	525,000	3.57	15,514,150	34.2	17,750,000	34.4	37,800,000	36.1
Great Commission Christians	**118,000**	**1.3**	**1,013,000**	**5.0**	**2,727,000**	**7.3**	**104,305**	**12,819**	**117,124**	**3.64**	**3,361,000**	**7.4**	**3,898,238**	**7.6**	**9,430,000**	**9.0**
Ethnoreligionists	8,865,350	98.1	1,286,000	6.3	1,150,000	3.1	43,986	-32,881	11,105	0.93	1,150,000	2.5	1,261,049	2.4	1,500,000	1.4
Muslims	50,000	0.6	280,000	1.4	435,000	1.2	16,638	-3,272	13,366	2.72	500,000	1.1	568,656	1.1	900,000	0.9
Nonreligious	0	0.0	5,000	0.0	135,000	0.4	5,164	3,949	9,113	5.29	180,000	0.4	226,127	0.4	750,000	0.7
Baha'is	0	0.0	128,000	0.6	170,000	0.5	6,502	-1,042	5,460	2.82	198,000	0.4	224,596	0.4	450,000	0.4
Hindus	0	0.0	1,000	0.0	64,000	0.2	2,448	450	2,898	3.81	81,000	0.2	92,978	0.2	200,000	0.2
Atheists	0	0.0	0	0.0	11,000	0.0	421	115	536	4.05	14,400	0.0	16,363	0.0	35,000	0.0
Buddhists	0	0.0	0	0.0	2,100	0.0	80	45	125	4.77	2,900	0.0	3,346	0.0	7,000	0.0
Jews	0	0.0	500	0.0	420	0.0	16	-12	4	0.98	440	0.0	463	0.0	300	0.0
Other religionists	0	0.0	500	0.0	3,000	0.0	115	87	202	5.28	4,400	0.0	5,018	0.0	10,000	0.0
World A (unevangelized persons)	7,503,200	83.0	1,418,865	7.0	485,719	1.3	19,125	-22,974	-3,849	-0.80	499,633	1.1	464,886	0.9	523,940	0.5
World B (evangelized non-Christians)	1,412,150	15.6	281,635	1.4	1,484,801	4.0	56,245	-9,587	46,658	2.67	1,631,750	3.6	1,933,213	3.7	3,328,360	3.2
World C (Christians)	124,650	1.4	18,569,000	91.6	35,392,480	94.7	1,353,781	32,561	1,386,342	3.36	43,289,860	95.3	49,255,901	95.4	100,935,700	96.3
Country's population	**9,040,000**	**100.0**	**20,269,500**	**100.0**	**37,363,000**	**100.0**	**1,429,151**	**0**	**1,429,151**	**3.29**	**45,421,244**	**100.0**	**51,654,000**	**100.0**	**104,788,000**	**100.0**

Continued overleaf

Country Table 1–concluded

COLUMNS, ROWS.
For meanings and definitions, see Codebook (Part 3). Note that, by definition, total 'Christians' = professing + crypto-Christians, which also = affiliated + unaffiliated Christians, and also = Great Commission Christians + latent Christians. Percentages may not always total exactly, due to rounding.

CENSUSES.
No question on religion has been asked in government censuses. However, before 1960 government statistics were collected of affiliated Roman Catholics including catechumens, as follows, which indicate the extremely rapid expansion of Catholics in those days: 1936, 20.6% Roman Catholics; 1937, 20.9%; 1954, 32.6%, 1955, 33.5%; 1958, 39.0%, 1959, 39.9%.

NOTES ON RELIGIONS
BAHA'IS. In a 1963 mass movement, 20,000 Africans became members; there has been subsequent very rapid growth from 223 local spiritual assemblies (1964) to 858 (1973); but thereafter it plateaued at 907 (1996).
ETHNORELIGIONISTS. Animists, and adherents of witchcraft, eradication cults, and other traditionalist sects. Tribes with over 60% traditionalists in 1995: Mbuti Pygmies (70% animists), Bamassa Pygmy (65%), Bayaka Pygmy (70%), Buraka Pygmy (90%), Gundi Pygmy (80%), and Mbacca Pygmy (80%).
HINDUS. Indian traders.
INDEPENDENTS. In over 500 denominations in 1995 (see Table 2). The totals from 1970 onwards exclude the 13 indigenous churches with 440,500 adherents (in 1970; rising to 38 churches by 1977) which have joined the Eglise du Christ au Zaire, here classified as a Protestant body.
JEWS. One main community, in Lubumbashi, with 1 synagogue; decline from 1,377 Jews in 1961.
MUSLIMS. All African Muslims are Sunnis (Shafiite); there are also Arabs from Oman and Zanzibar who are Sunnis (mainly Shafiite), Pakistanis and Indians, about 1,000 Shia (Indians), and 20,000 West African Senegalese traders in the Qadiriya and Tijaniya orders. Waves of conversion to Islam took place in 1925-27 and 1932-35. A 1957 survey indicated 115,500 Muslims, but allowing for heavy underenumeration in actual figure then was 200,000. Since 1960 there has been substantial immigration of Muslims from East and West Africa. *Missionaries.* There are a number of Egyptian missionaries sent by Al-Azhar University (Cairo). *Hajj pilgrims to Mecca.* (1970) 7 persons; (1976) 158.
NONRELIGIOUS. Mostly European expatriates, with some Zairean intellectuals.
OTHER RELIGIONISTS. Adherents of smaller religions and cults, including Rosicrucians (3 AMORC centres).
PROFESSING CHRISTIANS. The state from 1975 only recognized 4 Christian bodies: Roman Catholic, ECZ (Protestant), EJCSK, and Greek Orthodox. Others were officially illegal and unknown to the state.
PROTESTANTS. The totals of the ECZ from 1970 onwards include not only the 39 Protestant communities but also 13 African indigenous churches (in 1970) with 440,500 adherents and (rising by 1977 to 38 indigenous denominations), also the Anglican church with 100,000 adherents (1970) and 2 dioceses (from 1976) on).
ROMAN CATHOLICS. In the year 1900, there were 30,777 baptized (2,600 being Europeans), and 43,830 catechumens.

Great Commission Instrument Panel: status of Congo-Zaire (for explanation see start of Part 4)

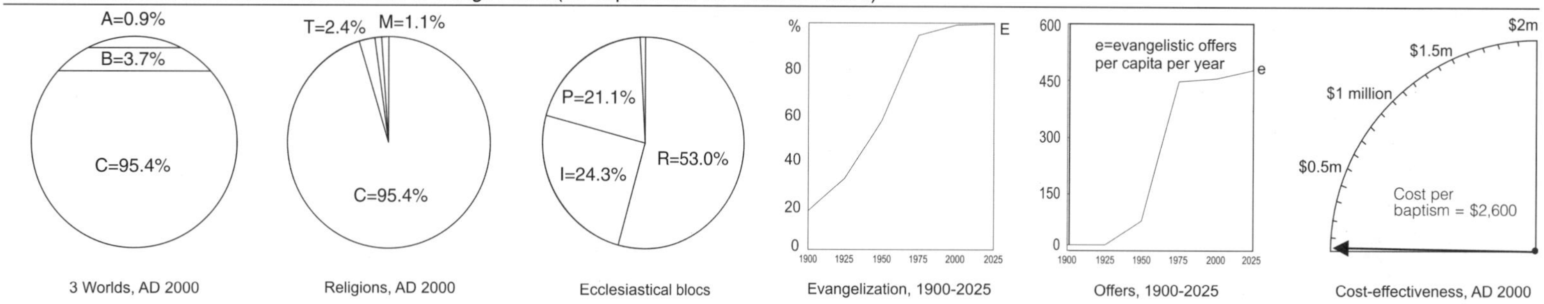

Country status. Congo-Zaire is nearly landlocked in central Africa but has a short shoreline on the Atlantic Ocean. It is one of the world's leading producers of copper.

HUMAN LIFE AND LIBERTY

Human need and development. Congo-Zaire is a rich country with enormous mineral resources, but decades of mismanagement and looting by President Mobutu until his ouster in 1997 have left the country destitute. Most of the national income was diverted into the personal coffers of the president as well as his cronies, with the result that the World Bank does not even report on the country's economic and social situation. About one third of Zaireans are still illiterate and life expectancy has not crept past 53. High inflation has caused numerous devaluations of the Zairean currency which has become quite worthless both within and without the country. In 1993 annual inflation rate rose to 9,000%. A national budget has not been published for many years. Virtually no funds are being spent on social programs, health, education or housing. Many schools are run by parents' cooperatives. There are hundreds of cities and towns without hospitals or medical services. Consequently there are dire unmet needs in the country.

Human rights and freedoms. Congo-Zaire has long undergone the worst human rights crisis in its history. Backed by the army and the security forces (both under the control of his relatives) former president Mobutu became one of the worst dictators on the continent. Like the president, his minions were engaged in systematic looting, extortion, blackmail, and embezzlement. To cow the people, the government used a number of brutal techniques. These included assassination, illegal detention, pillage, and torture. Civilians were shot at indiscriminately in public in order to inspire fear. More than 1,000 persons, including the French ambassador, were killed on one day in 1993. The judicial system ground to a halt. A number of disappearances were reported every month, and unidentified bodies were seen floating in the Zaire River occasionally. These disappearances were attributed to a special antiterrorist unit known as 'hiboux' or 'owls'. Conditions in Zaire's 220 crowded prisons are inhuman and appalling. Inmates have no access to water or sanitation and are often kept on a starvation diet. Security forces enter private homes at will without warrants and engage in robbing, raping, and looting. Freedom of the press and speech, guaranteed in the Constitution, is a dead letter because the government owns radio and television broadcasting and harasses and intimidates the print media. Many ethnic groups continue to suffer discrimination and persecution (and in some cases, expulsion from their home territories). Mobutu's Ngbandi ethnic group was disproportionately represented in security and intelligence services. Women suffer a host of disabilities, some of them traditional and some of them legal.

Human environment. Congo-Zaire suffers from all the environmental problems common to Africa, particularly water pollution, deforestation and loss of wildlife. Most human waste is discharged into the rivers which are also used for drinking, bathing and cleaning. Zaire has the second largest tropical forest in the world (after Brazil), but is losing its tree stands to poor land use practices. Many of Zaire's wildlife species, especially the elephant and the square-lipped rhinoceros, are hunted down by poachers and may soon become extinct.

NON-CHRISTIAN RELIGIONS

Traditional African religions are practiced everywhere, but they are strongest among the Azande, Bira, Budu, Central Twa Pygmies, Hunde, Kela, Mbuti Pygmies, Rega, Shila, Songomeno, and Tabwa. Tribal religions are characterized by magical practices, ancestral veneration and belief in a supreme being who is known under different names: Akongo (among the Ngombe), Arebati (Mbuti), Djakomba (Bachwa and Nkundo), Leza (Baluba), Nceme (Kuba), Njambi (Lole), Nzambi (Bakongo and Lunda), and Shungu (Tetela). Movements for the renewal of traditional religions, with a strong emphasis on witchcraft eradication, have played a significant role, especially among the Bakongo. Some have used Christian elements, but their tendency has been traditionalist. A movement known as Kiyoka (Burning) swept through northern Angola and Lower Zaire in the late 19th century, and more recent sects of similar type are Mvungism, Tonsi, and Dieudonné. Eastern Zaire was also affected by the Mchape (Medicine) movement which began in Nyasaland in 1930 and subsequently spread to neighboring countries.

Islam exists primarily in the Maniema, especially in the area of Kasongo, and in northern Shaba, with a small group in northeastern Zaire. Zairian Muslims are descendants of those converted in the 19th century. They are Sunnis, but their beliefs and practices display the continued influence of traditional religions. Other Muslim groups are composed of Arabs originating from Oman and Zanzibar (mostly Shafiite Sunnis), Pakistanis and Indians (mostly Ismailis), and some West African Blacks mostly belonging to the Qadiriya and Tijaniya brotherhoods.

Baha'i has spread rapidly since 20,000 Africans were converted in a 1963 mass movement. From 128,000 followers in 1970, the total grew to 198,000 by 1995, though this represented a plateauing organizationally.

CHRISTIANITY

Christianity reached Congo-Zaire in 1482 with the arrival of the Portuguese explorer, Diogo Cão. Early contacts were made with the Congo king, and Congolese were taken to Portugal for study. The first missionary party, which arrived in 1491, consisted of Franciscans, Dominicans, Canons of St John the Evangelist, and secular priests; and before long they had baptized the king and built a large stone church at the royal capital (in present-day northern Angola), which they renamed San Salvador. Between 1506 and 1543 one of the most remarkable Christians of African history, Afonso I, ruled the Congo kingdom. His son Henry studied in Portugal and was the first Black African to be appointed a Catholic bishop, in 1518. He returned to Congo in 1521 where he served until his death in 1534. Afonso hoped that Henry would be replaced by another Congolese and that San Salvador would become the episcopal see for all Guinea. However, neither of these wishes were fulfilled. The island of São Tomé was chosen as the see for Guinea, Congo and the south-western coast as far as the Cape of Good Hope, and the Portuguese dean of the royal chapel in Lisbon was named bishop. The growth of the Portuguese slave trade became an increasingly negative factor sapping the vitality of the Christian movement; and after Luanda was established in the latter half of the 16th century, attention was diverted to the area south of San Salvador. A revival of Catholic activity among the Bakongo took place in the 17th century. A prefecture of the Congo was erected in 1640 and placed under the care of Italian Capuchins, although this soon declined. When the modern era dawned, with the arrival of Holy Ghost priests at Boma in 1865, and Baptist missionaries at San Salvador in 1878, there was little left of the church which had flourished there nearly 400 years before.

CATHOLIC CHURCH. The Catholic Church enjoyed a privileged status during the colonial period. From the creation of the Congo Free State in 1885, the Belgian king Leopold II controlled placement of missionaries who in return received large concessions in the form of property, subsidies, the right to fulfill certain state functions and a virtual monopoly over education and medical service. When Belgium assumed control of the colony in 1908, the 'trinity of power' (colonial administration; missions, especially Catholics; and the business world) continued to exercise their respective roles. For political reasons Leopold II had obtained agreement from the Vatican that the evangelization of Congo should be an essentially Belgian affair and that only 'Belgian national missions' (those having their headquarters in Belgium, directed by Belgians and counted a fixed number of Belgians among their missionaries to Congo) should be involved. Protestant missions were placed at a severe disadvantage, and the colonial regime did not hesitate to serve as secular arm for the Catholic Church. A new climate was eventually produced by the concession of land to national missions (due to Protestant criticism), the extension of subsidies to Protestant schools in 1946 and the opening of state schools in 1954. In 1956 through the publication of a

Country summary. Worlds A, B, C by ethnolinguistic peoples, cities, and major civil divisions in Congo-Zaire.

	PEOPLES							CITIES							CIVIL DIVISIONS						
World	*Num*	*Pop 2000*	*C%*	*Christians*	*E%*	*U%*	*Unevangelized*	*Num*	*Pop 2000*	*C%*	*Christians*	*E%*	*U%*	*Unevangelized*	*Num*	*Pop 2000*	*C%*	*Christians*	*E%*	*U%*	*Unevangelized*
A	5	216,123	10.58	22,858	48	52	112,586	0	0	0.00	0	0	0	0	0	0	0.00	0	0	0	0
B	43	1,282,889	35.87	460,139	76	24	306,290	0	0	0.00	0	0	0	0	0	0	0.00	0	0	0	0
C	212	50,155,466	93.05	46,668,519	100	0	42,627	30	12,282,529	90.02	11,057,285	98	2	304,068	11	51,654,494	91.28	47,151,524	99	1	461,511
Total	**260**	**51,654,478**	**91.28**	**47,151,516**	**99**	**1**	**461,503**	**30**	**12,282,529**	**90.02**	**11,057,285**	**98**	**2**	**304,068**	**11**	**51,654,494**	**91.28**	**47,151,524**	**99**	**1**	**461,511**

In city of Mbuji-Mayi, 360,000 people attend one of many services to hear German Pentecostal evangelist R. Bonnke in August 1991.

document entitled 'Declaration of the Bishops of Belgian Congo and Ruanda-Urundi', the Catholic Church took a position in opposition to the status quo by denouncing the injustices of the colonial regime, proclaiming the legitimacy of Congolese political emancipation, criticizing the paternalism and unfair salary scales of commercial enterprises, and urging Christians to join labor unions for redress of their grievances. This political reorientation assisted the church to retain its dominant position after Independence in 1960 as well as during the period of disintegration from 1960-65. Anti-clericalism began to manifest itself among the elite, and 200 national and expatriate priests, brothers, and sisters were killed during the disturbances. Under the Mobutu regime a determined attempt to reduce the church's power was made. Nevertheless, the Catholic Church continues to play a significant role in the country and carries on important educational, medical, philanthropic, and social services.

In 1973 Catholics formed about 50% of the population. Catholics exceed 50% in the dioceses of Boma, Kikwit, Kisantu, and Popokabaka, southwest and southeast of Kinshasa; the dioceses of Lisala and Mbandaka in the northwest; the dioceses of Mahagi, Bunia, Butembo-Beni in the northeast; and the diocese of Sakania in southeastern Shaba. These regions contain only 18% of Zaire's area and 23% of its population, but they contain 35% of the total number of Catholics. In contrast, there are dioceses with Catholics less than 20% of the population, especially the dioceses of Bokungu-Ikala, Uvira, Kongolo, and Kole. These regions cover 39% of the national territory and 31% of the total population but only 20% of all Catholics.

Independents. Part of overflow congregation at a charismatic Church of Praise, Kinshasa, 1996.

The major problem in the eyes of Catholic bishops is the lack of religious depth among the Catholic masses. An attempt at the africanization of Christian life, both older and more original, is the charismatic movement known as Jamaa (Family, in Swahili) begun by Belgian missionary Placide Tempels among workers in Katanga (Shaba) in 1954. Most of its 20,000 members are married laymen between 30 and 40 years of age who are peasants or workers with limited formal education. The movement, now spread throughout Zaire, has brought a renewal of Christian life through emphasis on spiritual conversion, church attendance, the deepening of religious experience, the ideals of Christian marriage, and the practicing of brotherhood and community. Some Jamaa groups have deviated beyond the recognized limits of faith and morals, resulting in episcopal intervention, and a few have become in effect separatist bodies.

The Holy See has diplomatic relations with Zaire and in AD 2000 is represented to government and the Catholic hierarchy by a nuncio residing in Kinshasa.

PROTESTANT CHURCHES. There has been since 1970 only one recognized Protestant church, the Eglise du Christ au Zaire, ECZ (Church of Christ in Zaire), which was formed at the March 1970 assembly of the Congo Protestant Council. The union is unique in that the assembly vote which was not unanimous was taken as definitive without reference back to its member churches. During 1970 and 1971, 8 member churches led by the Methodist Church refused to accept the Council's decision and attempted to withdraw from the united body, and founded in February 1971 a new one known as the Council of Protestant Churches of the Congo (CEPCO, later CEPZA). However, they were unable to obtain government recognition and were forced by government to return to the ECZ.

The ECZ member churches are known officially as Communities (Communautés). In 1974, they numbered 53; in 1977, some 30 new Communities, mostly indigenous prophet-type splits from existing Communities, were admitted as full members. The ECZ has permitted them all to maintain their previous ecclesiastical traditions, structures and fraternal ties with churches outside Congo-Zaire, building its unity principally through national co-ordination. The church thus displays more internal diversity than perhaps any other united church in the world. The principal communities represent Baptist, Disciples, Methodist, Pentecostal and Presbyterian traditions, plus the work of the interdenominational Africa Inland Mission.

British Baptist missionaries were the first Protestants to arrive, in 1878, and built a series of stations following the course of the Zaire river. This work is now combined in the Baptist Community of the River Zaire. The Baptist Community of West Zaire, which includes the Lower Zaire area with an area east of Kinshasa, was begun by American Baptists. The Baptist Communities of Bandundu and the Lower Uele owe their origin to Scandinavian Baptists, the former being Swedish and the latter Norwegian. Baptist Mid-Missions have been active east and north of Kikwit and Conservative Baptists in Goma.

American Southern Presbyterians reached Luebo in 1891 and have concentrated their attention on the Kasai with headquarters at Kananga. The Disciples of Christ, which also arrived prior to the turn of the century, took over American Baptist work at Bolenge near Mbandaka in 1899.

The African Inland Mission opened its first station at Kasengu in 1912 and built up an important work in northeastern Zaire. This church maintains fraternal ties with sister denominations in East Africa.

Methodists of both the northern and southern churches in the USA began work in 1913; and although united in 1939, they continue to exist as 2 communities within the ECZ. Free Methodists from Burundi have opened new stations in the region north of Kalemie since Independence.

Pentecostals have come from the UK, the USA, and Scandinavia. The British Pentecostals of the Congo Evangelistic Mission initiated a strong work in northern Shaba in 1915 which is now known as the Pentecostal Community of Zaire, while the British Assemblies of God have been active at Kalemie since 1918. The Assemblies of God from the USA began work in Isiro, also in 1918, and have since spread to other parts of the country including Kinshasa, the Kinshasa group being an autonomous body. Norwegian and Swedish Pentecostals have been concentrated in the Bukavu area.

Other important communities are those which have sprung from the Christian Brethren in Shaba and the northeast, Christian and Missionary Alliance in Boma, Congo Balolo Mission (RBMU) in Basankusu, Covenant Church in Gemena, Heart of Africa Mission in Isiro, Mennonite groups in Kikwit and Tshikapa, Salvation Army in Kinshasa and the Lower Zaire, Seventh-day Adventists in Shaba, Swedish Covenant Mission in Lower Zaire, and the Unevangelized Fields Mission in Kisangani.

On the national level these various activities are coordinated by the Bureau de l'Enseignement Protestant (BEP) and Entr'aide Protestante. The latter organization provides aid and relief for the needy and operates a central pharmacy.

INDIGENOUS CHURCHES. The largest independent church in Congo-Zaire and indeed in all of Africa is the Church of Jesus Christ on Earth through the Prophet Simon Kimbangu (EJCSK). The EJCSK also has the distinction of being one of the 4 Christian churches recognized by the government of Zaire (the others being the Catholic Church, ECZ and Greek Orthodox Church) and the first African indigenous church to be received into full membership of the WCC (1969). The church was founded by Baptist catechist Simon Kimbangu, from the Bakongo of Lower Zaire. Kimbangu began an extensive preaching and healing ministry in 1921 which attracted immense crowds. This alarmed the Belgian authorities who feared the movement as potentially a political insurrection. Kimbangu was brought to trial and condemned to death, a sentence which was later reduced to life imprisonment. The prophet was exiled to Shaba where he died 30 years later in 1951. The reaction of the mission churches to Kimbanguism was mixed but generally negative. Catholic priests uniformly opposed it while Protestant missionaries varied from outright opposition to seeing it as a genuine spiritual revival. Following the prophet's exile in 1921, the movement suffered severe persecution. Many were exiled, thus inadvertently contributing to the spread of Kimbanguism throughout the country; and the movement in Lower Zaire went underground. Because of the absence of centralized leadership, the movement splintered into a number of factions some of which took on syncretistic elements. In the mid-1950s the 3 sons of the prophet began to openly reorganize the church, and in 1959 the EJCSK was officially recognized by the Belgian authorities. The growth of the denomination has accelerated considerably since Independence in 1960. Some groups which claim to be Kimbanguist remain outside the EJCSK, but the tendency is towards reabsorption, especially since government recognition is confined to the one church. The EJCSK has an extensive educational, medical, and social service program, including an agricultural demonstration farm near Kinshasa; it also has a large seminary in Kinshasa.

By 1970 over 500 other indigenous churches had arisen in Congo-Zaire. In 1971 a large number which had previously held *personnalité civile* were deprived of legal existence when the government restricted its official recognition to only 4 Christian denominations (Greek Orthodox in 1972). Several joined the

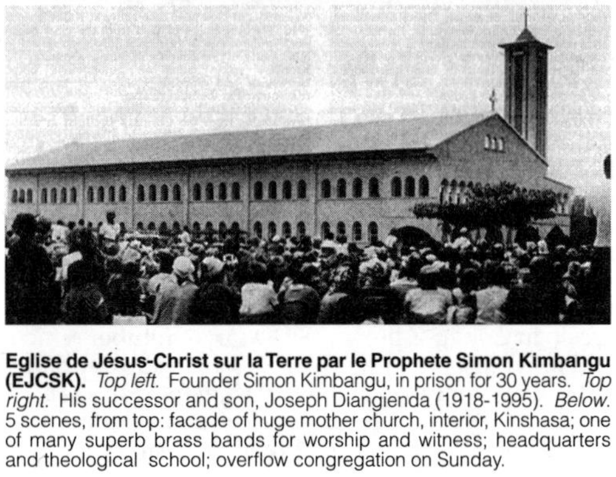

Eglise de Jésus-Christ sur la Terre par le Prophete Simon Kimbangu (EJCSK). *Top left.* Founder Simon Kimbangu, in prison for 30 years. *Top right.* His successor and son, Joseph Diangienda (1918-1995). *Below.* 5 scenes, from top: facade of huge mother church, interior, Kinshasa; one of many superb brass bands for worship and witness; headquarters and theological school; overflow congregation on Sunday.

ECZ to legalize their existence. Of the other bodies, which remain unrecognized but active, the most important are the African Apostolic Church of Johane Maranke, which spread to Congo-Zaire from Rhodesia and is found mostly in Shaba and the Kasai, and the Church of Jesus Christ on Earth through the Holy Spirit, which has its strength in Kananga.

Indigenous missions. Missionaries have been sent out from all of the Christian traditions to surrounding African countries and to farther points around the world.

Renewal movements. In the 1990s the Pentecostal/Charismatic Renewal continued to spread rapidly across most older churches, and numbered over 17,750,000 adherents (of whom 0% Pentecostals, 16% Charismatics, and 84% Independents).

CHURCH AND STATE

The revolutionary constitution of 24 June 1967 began begins by an acknowledgement of God in its Preamble: 'We the Congolese people... conscious of our responsibilities before God, the nation and Africa...' It then stipulated in Article 10: 'Everyone has the right to freedom of thought, conscience and religion. In the Republic, there is no state religion. Everyone has the right to manifest his religion or his convictions, alone or in common, in public or private, by worship, teaching, practice, performance of rites and living a religious life, provided that public order and good morals are not infringed.' The first article of Law 71-012 elaborated that 'teaching' here was understood as the teaching of religion. Further, Article 13 stated: '(Religious education) is provided for the education of youth by the national teaching service'. This 'includes public as well as recognized primary schools which are controlled by public authority and regulated by statutes fixed by law... National teaching establishments, working in collaboration with interested religious authorities, guarantee to minors whose parents request it and to students of age who also request it, an education which corresponds to their religious convictions. Private schools may be opened when they have fulfilled the requirements fixed by the law'. Moreover, according to Articles 3 and 5, any act of racial, ethnic or religious discrimination was prohibited, particularly in relation to educational material and access to public services.

The practice of religion has been regulated by Law 71-012 of 31 December 1971 which stipulates that 'No church or religious sect may be constituted except in the form of a non-profit association with juridical personality. No one may preach any religion publicly unless he is a member of a church or religious sect having juridical personality' (Article 2). Only citizens might found new churches; expatriates only represent their bodies while in Congo- Zaire. No one was permitted to be a 'founder' of a church or religious sect, or a 'representative' of a foreign church or sect, unless he fulfilled the following conditions: to be of sane mind, of irreproachable conduct, of at least 40 years of age, to have had no prison sentence of over 5 months duration, to have a licentiate or doctoral degree in theology or another document attesting that he has completed a 4-year theological course in a local or foreign theological school, and to possess funds held in a Zairian bank account totalling not less than 100,000 zaires. Moreover, any would-be founder, who had to be a citizen, could not previously have exercised the functions of pastor or priest in any other church nor have left another church as a dissident. Any representative of a foreign church had to have already exercised his functions for at least 10 years (Articles 4 and 5). Requests for the granting of juridical personality had to be presented to the Ministry of Justice (Article 7).

Seven religious bodies succeeded in obtaining juridical personality in Congo-Zaire by 1973, thus being the only recognized groups as far as the government was concerned. They were the Catholic Church, Church of Christ in Zaire (ECZ), Kimbanguist Church (EJCSK), Greek Orthodox Church, Islamic Community, Jewish Community, and the Baha'i Assembly. The first 3 were recognized in Article 11 of Law 71-012; Muslims, Jews and Greek Orthodox were added to the list in March 1972, and Baha'i on 9 June 1972. During March 1972 the government banned the Council of the Protestant Churches in Zaire (CEPZA). On 29 April 1972 the Ministry of Justice then published an appendix of Law 71-012 listing 76 Protestant communities recognized as members of the ECZ. The list was, however, disputed by the ECZ, and the number was reduced to 53 by Law 73-013 of 14 February 1973, the 23 excluding churches allegedly being bodies under expatriate control supported with foreign funds.

Until 1975 the teaching of religion or non-confessional ethics was obligatory in all primary and secondary schools of the national-educational system, the choice of courses being left to the discretion of parents or students themselves if of age. In fact, religious education was often confined to the primary level and sometimes ignored completely, depending upon the local headmaster. At the secondary level, this course was given most often by priests, pastors, brothers, sisters or laymen trained in the various institutes of religious sciences. Since only institutes attached to universities are recognized by the state, those trained in non-recognized institutes had to possess another pedagogical diploma. The national Catholic educational system was responsible for the majority of primary and secondary schools, while the Protestant Education Office (BEP) of the ECZ, earlier the Congo Protestant Council, catered for Protestant schools.

When the Mobutu era came to a violent end in 1997, there seemed to be little prospect of less government interference in the practice of the Christian faith. All churches, however, continued to mount formidable pressure for full human rights and religious freedom.

BROADCASTING AND MEDIA

Radios are owned by one out of 12 people. IBRA programming can be heard on Radio Bukavo (Swahili, French); Radio Goma (Swahili); and on private stations (Swahili). Programs in French and Lingala can be received via shortwave radio from TWR (Swaziland), and in French from FEBA (Seychelles). HCJB World Radio has helped to start local stations in Zaire in cooperation with ministries like African Inland Mission, Believer's Express and the Christian & Missionary Alliance. Zaire is a member of UNDA, and Catholics broadcast a 30 minute program over radio, and a 45 minute program over television. There is one Catholic radio station, Radio Lendisa, which broadcasts in Lingala, Ngbaka, and French.

Some 11 million have seen the 'Jesus' Film, chiefly through television broadcasts (5 million) and film team presentations (6.6 million), and one million have responded.

INTERDENOMINATIONAL ORGANIZATIONS

The Congo Protestant Council (Conseil Protestant du Congo, CPC) was formed in 1924, reorganized in 1955, and in March 1970 was replaced by the Church of Christ in Congo, later the ECZ. Although ecumenism has been suspect in many Protestant circles, attempts to found other councils have been vetoed by government. Among councils banned in 1972 were: CEPZA, AEZ (Evangelical Alliance of Zaire/Alliance Evangélique du Zaire), and COSSEUJCA (Supreme Council of Priests for the United Church of Jesus Christ in Africa), an association of independent churches. On the Catholic side, the Episcopal Conference sponsors a Secretariat for Unity which is responsible for ecumenical relations between Catholics and Zaire's other churches.

There are no joint Catholic-Protestant organizations, but there is co-operative work. At Boende, an ecumenical hospital has been opened under joint sponsorship. The Bible Society of Zaire (SBZ), with Catholic participation, is at work on a common translation of the Bible into the Lomongo, Kituba and Lingala languages.

FUTURE TRENDS AND PROSPECTS

Tribal religions will likely decline to 1.4% of the population by 2025 (from 98.1% in 1900) while Christianity will probably grow to over 96% in the same period.

Christianity could plausibly claim over 98% of the population over the next 50 years.

BIBLIOGRAPHY

'A church educational ministry by cassette for oral learners in northeast Zaire.' D. G. Langford. D.Min. thesis, Denver Conservative Baptist Seminary, Denver, CO, 1989. 364p.

'A program for recruiting and training leadership for the Christian churches in Zaire.' R. C. Butler. D.Miss. thesis, Trinity Evangelical Divinity School, Deerfield, IL, 1994. 236p.

Actes de la VIIe assemblée plénière de l'Episcopat du Congo, 1967. Kinshasa: Secrétariat Général de l'Episcopat, 1969.

African Christian theology: the quest for selfhood. K. G. Molyneux. San Francisco: E. Mellen Press, 1993. 422p.

Alliances avec le Christ en Afrique: inculturation des rites religieux au Zaïre. F. Kabasele Lumbala. 2d ed. Paris: Karthala, 1994. 379p.

'Analyse socio–culturelle et spirituelle de l'oeuvre missionnaire de l'église méthodiste unie parmi les Tetela du Zaïre central: la contextualisation de l'évangile pour une inculturation de la foi chrétienne.' L. Djundu. Ph.D. dissertation, Université Laval, 1991. 435p.

Annuaire de l'église du Congo, 1974–1975. Kinshasa: Centre de Recherches Sociologiques, Service des Statistiques, 1975. 600p. (Annual).

Aspects du catholicisme au Zaire. Cahiers des religions africaines, vol. 14, no. 27-28. Kinshasa, Zaire: Faculté de Théologie catholique de Kinshasa, 1981. 316p.

'Authenticity and Christianity in Zaire,' N. Mushete, in *Christianity in independent Africa*, p.228–41. E. Fasholé-Luke et al. (eds). London: Rex Collings, 1978.

Brief history of Methodist missionary work in the Southern Congo during the first fifty years. E. C. Hartzler. Elisabethville: Methodist Church of Southern Congo, 1960. 53p.

'Case study: Kinshasa, Zaire—an African strategy for urban church growth,' M. F. Polding, *Urban mission*, 3, 4 (March 1986), 36–38.

'Church and authenticity in Zaire,' *Pro Mundi Vita*, Special note, 39 (1975), 1–32.

'Congo–Kinshasa 1969,' *Pro Mundi Vita* (Brussels), 32 (1970).

Culte et société: le culte chrétien comme réflexion critique d'une société moderne africaine: cas du chant la Communauté Evangélique du Zaïre. J. Nsumbu. *Studia missionalia upsaliensia*, 62. Uppsala: Uppsala University, 1995. 373p.

'Daily life as worship and gospel communication in the Presbyterian community of Kinshasa.' D. L. Kabambi. M.A. thesis, Fuller Theological Seminary, Pasadena, CA, 1991. 159p.

English–speaking missions in the Congo Independent State. R. M. Slade. Brussels: Duculot, 1959.

'Femmes, possession et christianisme au Zaïre: analyse diachronique des productions et pratiques de la spiritualité chrétienne africaine.' T. K. Biaya. Ph.D. dissertation, Université Laval à Montréal, 1992. 510p.

Histoire du Protestantisme au Congo. E. M. Braekman. Brussels: Eclaireurs Unionistes, 1961. 300p.

'In the body, on the heart: toward an understanding of the Bakongo quest for redemption.' M. A. Perry. M.A. thesis, Catholic Theological Union, Chicago, 1991. 217p.

Introduction à l'ethnographie du Congo. J. Vansina. Kinshasa: Université Lovanium, 1965. 228p.

'Introduction de l'influence de l'Islam au Congo,' P. Ceulemans, in *Islam in tropical Africa*, p.174–92. I. M. Lewis (ed). London: Oxford University Press, 1966.

Kimbangu: an African prophet and his church. M. L. Martin. Oxford, UK: Blackwell, 1975. 198p.

'Kimbanguism, prophetic Christianity in the Congo,' H. W. Fehderau, *Practical anthropology*, 9, 4 (1962), 157–78.

Kitawala: Ursprung, Ausbreitung und Religion der Watch–Tower–Bewegung in Zentralafrika. H. J. Greschat. Marburg, West Germany: Elwert Verlag, 1967.

'La secte "eglise unie du saint esprit du Congo",' J. F. Makaya, *Studia Missionalia*, 41 (1992).

'Le mouvement "Jamaa" au Katanga,' T. Theuws, *Rythmes du Monde*, 8, 1 (1960), 201–12.

'L'Eglise à l'épreuve de la tradition: la Communauté évangélique du Zaïre et le kindoki.' Å. Dalmalm. Doctoral dissertation, Uppsala University, Paris, 1986. 286p. (Summary in English).

L'Eglise du Christ au Zaïre: formation et adaptation d'un protestantisme en situation de dictature. P. B. Kabongo-Mbaya. Paris: Karthala, 1992. 467p.

'Les églises congolaises et la construction nationale,' G. Bernard, in *Sociologie de la 'construction nationale' des les nouveaux états.* Brussels: Institut de Sociologie de l'Université libre de Bruxelles, 1967.

Messianic popular movements in the Lower Congo. E. Andersson. Uppsala: Almquist & Wiksell, 1958. 287p.

Midday in missions: Zaire 1977. D. A. MacGavran & N. G. Riddle.

'Ministerial formation in Africa: implications of the experiential component for training Zairian Alliance Church leadership.' R. J. Downey. Ph.D. dissertation, Fuller Theological Seminary, Pasadena, CA, 1985. 325p.

Modern Kongo prophets: religion in a plural society. W. MacGaffey. *African systems of thought series.* Bloomington, IN: University of Indiana Press, 1983. 285p.

'Nurture and discipleship of new converts: a specialized training program for pastors of the Evangelical Community of the Ubangi–Mongala of Zaire.' D. A. Stockamp. D.Miss. thesis, Western Conservative Baptist Seminary, 1994. 374p.

One hundred years of Christian mission in Angola and Zaire, 1878–1978. London: Baptist Missionary Society, 1978. 50p.

Presbyterian reformers in Central Africa, a documentary account of the American Presbyterian Congo mission and the human rights struggles in the Congo, 1890–1918. R. Benedetto (ed). Kindehook, NY: E. J. Brill, 1996. 580p. (Named one of 15 best new books of 1997 in mission studies by the *International bulletin of missionary research*).

'Prolifération et persistance des sectes dans le milieu urbain de Kinshasa: analyse de quelques cas,' R. de Haes, *Studia Missionalia*, 41 (1992), 1-389.

Protestant missions in Congo, 1878–1969. J. R. Crawford. Kinshasa: Librairie Evangélique du Congo, 1970. 26p.

'Quest for ecclesiological self–understanding of the Church of Christ in Zaire: toward the retrieval of contextual models of the church in an African setting.' K. Molo. Th.D. thesis, Lutheran School of Theology\, Chicago, 1987. 325p.

'Sectes dans l'est du Congo ex–Belge,' in *Devant les sectes non-chrétiennes: rapports et compte rendu. Museum Lessianum. Section missiologique*, no. 42. [Paris]: Desclée, De Brouwer, [1961].

'Teach them unto your children: contextualization of Basanga puberty rites in the United Methodist Church.' D. N. Persons. Ph.D. dissertation, Fuller Theological Seminary, Pasadena, CA, 1990. 344p.

'Teaching theology in the Ubangi.' K. Kuzuli. D.Miss. thesis, Trinity Evangelical Divinity School, Deerfield, IL, 1990. 198p.

The Church of Christ in Zaire: a handbook of Protestant missions, churches and communities, 1878–1978. C. Irvine (ed). Indianapolis, IN: Disciples of Christ, 1978. 161p.

'The curse on Ham's descendants: its missiological impact on Zairian Mbala Mennonite Brethren.' N. U. Lumeya. Ph.D. dissertation, Fuller Theological Seminary, Pasadena, CA, 1988. 238p.

The Jamaa and the Church: a Bantu Catholic movement in Zaire. W. de Craemer. Leiden: E. J. Brill, 1977. 212p.

'The "rite zairois" in the context of liturgical inculturation in middle–belt Africa since the Second Vatican Council.' C. N. Egbulem. S.T.D. thesis, Catholic University of America, Washington, DC, 1989. 410p.

The Sheppards and Lapsley: pioneer Presbyterians in the Congo. W. E. Phipps. Louisville, KY: The Presbyterian Church (USA), 1991. 140p.

'The southern Methodists and the Atetela: the history of the Methodist Episcopal Church, South, in the central Congo, 1912–1960.' Okenge Owandji Kasongo. Ph.D. dissertation, University of Kentucky, Lexington, KY, 1982. 230p.

Un rayon d'espoir: évangélisation dans les Eglises Africaines Indépendantes. Luntadila Ndala Za Fwa (EJCSK). Kinshasa: CEDI, 1975. 82p.

'Witchcraft among the Kasaian people of Zaire: challenge and response.' M. M. Mukundi. Ph.D. dissertation, Fuller Theological Seminary, Pasadena, CA, 1988. 287p.

Witchcraft, oracles and magic among the Azande. E. E. Evans–Pritchard. Oxford, UK: Clarendon, 1937. 558p.

'Zaire's super–church,' R. L. Niklaus, *Christianity today*, 16, 14 (1972), 4–10.

Country Table 2. **Organized churches and denominations in Congo-Zaire.**

Official name (bold type = church with over 10% of all affiliated) 1	*Begun* 2	*Type* 3	*Counc* 4	*Congs* 5	*Adults* 6	*Affiliated 1970* 7	*Affiliated 1995* 8	*G%* 9	*Names, notes, and other statistics* (see Codebook, Part 3) 10
Eglise Apost Africaine de J Maranke	1953	I-3aA	x...I	1,100	160,000	100,000	300,000	4.49	*AACJM. Bapostolo.* M=African Apostolic Ch of Johane Maranke (Zimbabwe). Initially in Kasai.
Eglise Apostolique Unie en Afrique	1971	I-3aA	.v...	500	90,000	80,000	200,000	4.17	*EAUA. United Apost Ch.* Also Brazzaville. 1973 applied to WCC. 42n,475m,2H,42h,2p.
Eglise Catholique au Congo-Zaire:	1482	R-Lat	P.S.R	1,298	13,329,500	9,907,949	23,000,950	3.43	*Catholic Ch.* C=37+23+162. 11p,1q,9x(472). 1829n 1360x 3142m 5653w 498598Yy
M Bukavu (Kivu)	1929	R-Lat	Ps	73	528,700	363,800	911,558	3.74	Catholics 90% Bashi; Bahavu, refugees. M=SJ. 74n 81x 178m 457w 29097Yy
D Butembo-Beni	1934	R-Lat	Ps	28	541,000	601,504	933,093	1.77	Ruwenzori. 90% Nande (Konjo); Bira, Lese. 84n 30x 99m 294w 41895Yy
D Goma	1959	R-Lat	Ps	18	366,000	272,150	630,743	3.42	70% Ruanda, 20% Nande; Hunde. Tourism. 49n 51x 93m 166w 13524Yy
D Kasongo	1952	R-Lat	Ps	16	133,000	124,200	229,420	2.49	Rega, Zimba, Bangu-Bangu. 15% Muslim. M=SJ. 16n 31x 39m 55w 5108Yy
D Kindu	1956	R-Lat	Ps	12	90,000	71,793	155,920	3.15	Tetela, Songola, Langa. Rural medical aid. 17n 8x 19m 38w 6793Yy
D Uvira	1962	R-Lat	Ps	15	147,000	70,482	254,603	5.27	Vira, Fuleru, Bembe, Bwari, Hutu refugees. M=SX. 36n 20x 21m 82w 6661Yy
M Kananga (Luluabourg)	1904	R-Lat	Ps	22	523,000	561,902	902,000	1.91	80% Lulua, 14% Bakwaluntu, 5% Babindi. 85n 33x 80m 259w 11350Yy
D Kabinda	1953	R-Lat	Ps	20	86,000	134,384	149,076	0.42	80% Songe; Tetela, Luba. Lusambo schools. 32n 10x 23m 92w 1887Yy
D Kole	1951	R-Lat	Ps	34	33,600	22,792	58,000	3.81	Kela, Tetela, Songomeno. No sisters. M=CICM. 15n 9x 16m 63w 2200Yy
D Luebo	1959	R-Lat	Ps	21	365,000	295,100	630,000	3.08	55% Luiua, 10% Luba, 9% Pende, 9% Chokwe. 37n 3x 3m 64w 4015Yy
D Luiza	1967	R-Lat	Ps	26	326,000	209,200	562,501	4.04	55% Basalampasu, 30% Mbagani, 15% Ambala. 40n 18x 82m 160w 4294Yy
D Mbuji-Mayi	1966	R-Lat	Ps	62	494,000	403,900	852,000	3.03	85% Luba, refugees from 1960 tribal wars. 75n 16x 59m 166w 19657Yy
D Mweka	1953	R-Lat	Ps	11	95,600	56,947	165,356	4.36	37% Kuba, 30% Luba, 17% Lulua. Art trade. M=SJ. 13n 17x 23m 16w 5000Yy
D Tshumbé	1936	R-Lat	Ps	26	130,000	94,482	225,000	3.53	70% Tetela, Nkutshu, Twa Pygmies. 38n 4x 27m 101w 5080Yy
M Kinshasa (Leopoldville)	1886	R-Lat	Ps	108	1,798,000	722,854	3,100,000	6.00	200 tribes. 65% Kongo, 10% Yaka, M=CICM. 169n 182x 376m 554w 60304Yy
D Boma	1934	R-Lat	Ps	37	539,000	380,510	930,000	3.64	80% Yombe, 15% Kongo, 5% Woyo. 110n 7x 39m 154w 14569Yy
D Idiofa	1937	R-Lat	Ps	38	309,000	209,490	533,000	3.81	45% Dzing, 39% Bunda. 1964 Simba rising. 76n 15x 82m 79w 18598Yy
D Inongo	1953	R-Lat	Ps	14	167,000	134,575	289,000	3.10	Many tribes. 55% Ekonda, 45% Sakata. M=CICM. 25n 14x 17m 85w 7565Yy
D Kenge	1957	R-Lat	Ps	26	191,000	127,918	330,000	3.86	45% Yanzi, 20% Yaka, 12% Mbala, Suku. M=SVD. 45n 17x 34m 71w 6869Yy
D Kikwit (Koango, Kwango)	1903	R-Lat	Ps	52	884,000	620,326	1,524,046	3.66	Suku, Chokwe, Pende, Kwese, Mbala. M=OCSO. 73n 73x 142m 285w 30148Yy
D Kisantu	1931	R-Lat	Ps	22	323,000	239,300	558,000	3.44	90% Kongo (Ntandu, Ndibu, Manianga). 66n 22x 391m 281w 3388Yy
D Matadi	1911	R-Lat	Ps	44	348,000	396,753	600,000	1.67	84% Kongo, 16% Sundi, Angolan refugees. 62n 31x 50m 143w 13235Yy
D Popokabaka	1961	R-Lat	Ps	16	197,000	194,784	340,000	2.25	95% Yaka, 5% Suku, Chokwe. M=OCSO. 29n 25x 38m 74w 5851Yy
M Kisangani (Stanleyville)	1904	R-Lat	Ps	35	322,000	250,200	555,000	3.24	Small tribes: 8% Soko, 8% Kumu, 7% Ndaka. 31n 59x 129m 92w 3989Yy
D Bondo	1926	R-Lat	Ps	11	29,000	92,191	50,010	-2.42	Ancient Zande kingdom. Bandia, Kare. M=CICM. 14n 12x 15m 26w 5600Yy
D Bunia	1922	R-Lat	Ps	12	292,000	342,319	503,623	1.56	45% Lendu, 35% Bahema, 15% Bira, pygmies. 39n 25x 52m 236w 11368Yy
D Buta	1911	R-Lat	Ps	17	109,000	113,303	189,850	2.09	Babwa, Makere, Bati. 1964 Simba massacres. 23n 9x 11m 49w 3764Yy
D Doruma-Dungu	1958	R-Lat	Ps	14	61,000	98,000	105,000	0.28	70% Azande, 30% Abarambo, Amadi. M=OSA. 17n 16x 44m 52w 5265Yy
D Isangi	1951	R-Lat	Ps	8	53,800	45,375	92,819	2.90	47% Ngandu, 30% Topoke, 13% Lokele. M=OMI. 2n 12x 16m 32w 1427Yy
D Isiro-Niangara	1911	R-Lat	Ps	20	301,000	238,350	519,127	3.16	40% Logo, 30% Azande, 20% Mangbetu. 40n 35x 58m 134w 15068Yy
D Mahagi-Nioka	1962	R-Lat	Ps	16	309,000	417,618	533,013	0.98	45% Aiur, 35% Lugbara: Logo, Lendu. 35n 28x 35m 80w 22978Yy
D Wamba	1949	R-Lat	Ps	17	85,800	72,195	147,866	2.91	30% Budu, 30% Lika, 30% Ndaka, 10% Lese. M=AA. 16n 23x 35m 45w 3978Yy
M Lubumbashi (Elizabethville)	1910	R-Lat	Ps	55	315,000	260,426	543,288	2.98	Shaba, 50% Sanga, 10% Lamba, 1,556 Orthodox. 49n 92x 235m 493w 23557Yy
D Kalemie-Kirungu (Baudouinville)	1887	R-Lat	Ps	46	233,000	126,989	402,099	4.72	42% Tabwa, 26% Hemba, 18% Luba-Hemba. 15n 15x 31m 66w 2996Yy
D Kamina	1948	R-Lat	Ps	22	116,000	91,711	201,424	3.20	38% Lunda, 15% Luba, 13% Chokwe, Swahili. 14n 18x 26m 84w 3595Yy
D Kilwa-Kasenga	1948	R-Lat	Ps	77	92,000	31,116	158,909	6.74	60% Shiia, 20% Luba, 20% Zela, Tabwa. M=SDB. 9n 9x 13m 34w 2430Yy
D Kolwezi	1971	R-Lat	Ps	28	201,000	120,000	346,066	4.17	Copper mines, Angola-Zambia border. 21n 27x 178m 79w 9277Yy
D Kongolo	1911	R-Lat	Ps	15	76,000	54,000	131,423	3.62	Tembo, Songe, Buye, 1962 massacre 21 CSSp. 21n 10x 12m 132w 3858Yy
D Manono	1971	R-Lat	Ps	14	88,000	75,004	152,158	4.17	Formed from Kongolo and Kalemie dioceses. 16n 4x 4m 6w 2875Yy
D Sakania-Kipushi	1925	R-Lat	Ps	8	68,000	77,033	118,000	1.72	45% Lamba, 16% Kaonde, 14% Lala, 12% Aushi. 16n 30x 55m 50w 3273Yy
M Mbandaka-Bikoro	1924	R-Lat	Ps	38	165,000	142,305	285,459	2.82	Former D Bikoro. 70% Mongo, 20% Nkundo, Mbole. 39n 35x 59m 135w 8106Yy
D Basankusu	1926	R-Lat	Ps	20	147,000	80,197	254,147	4.72	36% Ngombe, 33% Ngandu, 31% Mongo. M=CICM. 13n 4x 21m 30w 5259Yy
D Bokungu-Ikela	1961	R-Lat	Ps	14	51,000	29,848	88,281	4.43	Rain-forest, Boyela, Lalia, Yasayama. 11n 12x 20m 31w 1844Yy
D Budjala	1964	R-Lat	Ps	16	246,000	186,090	424,304	3.35	25% each Bwaka, Banza, Ngbandi, Ngala. 23n 11x 18m 62w 8155Yy
D Lisala	1919	R-Lat	Ps	23	277,000	283,800	478,197	2.11	40% Ngombe, 35% Budja; Mongo, Ngbandi. 47n 7x 27m 63w 9171Yy
D Lolo	1937	R-Lat	Ps	9	39,000	41,983	67,470	1.92	80% Budja; Babango, Babwa, Ngbaka. 19n 2x 2m 19w 1499Yy
D Molegbe	1911	R-Lat	Ps	22	1,038,000	328,750	1,790,101	7.01	Near CAR, Congo, Ngbaka, BAnda, Mbanza. 33n 32x 66m 49w 22178Yy
Eglise Anglicane du Zaire	1895	A-Eva	AwaVK	614	125,000	100,000	380,000	5.49	*CAZ. Province of Zaire*, 6 Dioceses. M=CMS. HQ Bunia. 35n,3x,W=80%,848Y,255y.
Eglise Chrétienne Ev en Afrique	1959	I-Bap	.T..T	70	20,000	30,000	40,000	1.16	*ECEA, Ev Christian Ch in Africa.* Ex Eglise de la Conscience Chrétienne. 120n.

Continued overleaf

Country Table 2–concluded

Official name (bold type = church with over 10% of all affiliated) 1	*Begun* 2	*Type* 3	*Counc* 4	*Congs* 5	*Adults* 6	*Affiliated 1970* 7	*Affiliated 1995* 8	*G%* 9	*Names, notes, and other statistics* (see Codebook, Part 3) 10
Eglise de Dieu	1966	P-Pe3	ZF...	152	28,460	10,000	51,700	6.79	Former link with M=Church of God (Cleveland) (USA). 27 churches, 2 missions. 19n.
EdeJC sur la Terre par le Prophète SK	1921	I-3nA	xWi.N	12,000	4,000,000	3,500,000	7,500,000	3.10	*EJCSK. Ch of Christ on Earth thru Prophet Simon Kimbangu.* 1H,1s(82),W=44%,36747Y.
EdeJC sur la Terre par le St-Esprit	1951	I-3pA	.v...	140	70,000	110,069	230,000	2.99	*Ch of JC on Earth thru Holy Spirit.* Healings. 85% Luba. 100n,5000m,W=98%,2778Y.
Eglise de la Foi par Messie JC	1954	I-CCa	.v..I	40	2,000	9,000	4,000	-3.19	*EFMJC. Ch of Faith thru Messiah JC.* Ex RCC. Aim: 'Love thy neighbour'. Lulua, Luba.
Eglise des Noirs en Afrique Centrale	1939	I-Sal	I	60	7,000	20,000	10,000	-2.73	*ENAC.* Founder-patriarch Simon Mpadi. Persecuted 21 years. 90% Kongo, 10% Chokwe.
Eglise Dieu-Donné au Zaire	1945	I-mar	.v..I	10	2,600	20,000	5,000	-5.39	Syncretistic body among Teke, also Yaka. HQ Ngaba, Kinshasa. 1971 applied to WCC.
Eglise du Christ au Congo-Zaire:	1924	P-Uni	....K	26,699	4,573,560	4,628,280	9,260,018	2.81	*ECZ. Ch of Christ in Z.* 1924, CPC; 1970, united ch. 2538n,10044m,1710f,180000z.
Autres Communautés		I-	....K	800	100,000	100,000	300,000	0.05	*Other Communities.* Mostly splits ex other Communities, admitted to ECZ, including 30 in 1977.
Co Armée du Salut	1934	P-Sal	xwA.K	595	24,000	31,000	80,000	3.86	*CAS, SA, Z Terr. Basolda na Kobikisa.* 70% Kongo. 150n,25x,8h,12r,1s,W=83%,275Y.
Co Assemblée de Dieu au Zaire-K	1922	P-Pe2	ZFG.a	708	197,660	75,000	282,860	5.45	*CADZ. Assembly of God in Zaire in Kinshasa.* Autonomous body. M=AoG(USA). 62n,10f.
Co Assemblée des Frères Ev au Z	1923	P-CBr	x.G.a	293	22,000	12,000	40,000	4.93	*CAFEZA. Assembly of Brethren.* M=Emmanuel M (CMML, USA). Nyankunde. 52n,31f,1H,1j.
Co Assemblées de Dieu à l Est du Z	1918	P-Pe2	ZG..K	500	18,000	10,780	34,000	4.70	*CADEZA.* M=UPMGBI(AoG)(UK). HQ Kalemie, 59% Bembe, 31% Buye. 29n,2f,W=73%,302Y.
Co Assemblées de Frères au Shaba	1961	I-CBr	xv..K	150	18,500	25,000	35,000	1.35	*CAFS*(formerly AFK). *Christian Brethren.* Ex CFCG. Lamba. 1968, applied to WCC. 57n.
Co Assoc des Egls Ev de la Lulonga	1878	P-Eva	xGG.a	986	70,000	75,000	103,000	1.28	*CADELU. Ev Chs of the Lulonga.* M=Congo Balolo M(RBMU)(UK). HQ Basankusu. 67n,9f,2H.
Co Assoc des Frères en Christ au Z	1931	I-CBr	....K	22	1,900	3,000	3,500	0.62	*CM.* Mambasa. Split ex Emmanuel Mission. HQ Dibaya-Lubwe (Ituri). 5n,1f.
Co Baptiste au Kivu	1928	I-Bap	TPg.a	1,099	93,800	60,000	140,000	3.45	*CBK* (formerly AEBK,EPBK). 1928, UAM; 1946, M=CBFMS. HQ Goma. 100n,3663Y.
Co Bapt Autonome entre Wamba-Bakali	1949	I-Bap	T...K	30	24,400	7,500	36,000	6.48	*CBAWB. Autonomous Baptists in WB.* Ex CEBB(Swedish Baptists). HQ Bandundu. 15n.
Co Baptiste du Bas-Uélé	1918	P-Bap	....K	250	35,000	35,000	70,000	2.81	*CBBU* (formerly EBBU). Lower Uélé. M=Norwegian Baptist Mission. HQ Bondo. 38n,15f.
Co Baptiste du Fleuve Zaire	1878	P-Bap	T.A.K	221	234,000	450,000	442,000	-0.07	*CBFZ.* Merger of 4 regions, M=BMS(UK). 50n,4s,97f,4s,W=73%,2460Y.
Co Baptiste du Zaire-Ouest	1878	P-Bap	T...K	600	252,000	450,000	568,000	0.94	*CBZO* (formerly) EBCO). *Bapt Ch of WZ.* 1884, M=ABFMS,CBOMB. 34n,110f,7H,33h,7369Y.
Co Baptiste Mission du Sud-Kwango	1961	I-Bap	T...K	30	24,000	12,000	30,000	3.73	*CBMSK. Baptist Mission of SKwango.* M=Independent Baptist M (USA). Mainly Yaka. 4n.
Co Centrale du Christ en Afrique	1956	I-Met	.T..K	18	2,000	7,500	5,000	-1.61	*CCCA. Central Comm of Christ in A.* Ex Methodists. HQ Lubumbashi. Lunda, Bemba. 3n.
Co Coopération Evangélique au Zaire	1965	I-3pA	....K	20	6,000	8,000	17,000	3.06	*CCEZ.* Ex CEBB(SBM). M=Coop Ev Mondiale (France). HQ Feshi (Bandundu). 4n,10f.
Co des Assemblées de Dieu au Zaire	1918	P-Pe2	ZFG.a	400	50,000	50,000	130,000	3.90	*CADZ* (formerly EADC). *Assemblies of God.* M=AoG(USA). HQ Isiro. 81n,9f,3h,2s(130).
Co des Disciples du Christ au Zaire	1897	P-Dis	xWA.K	1,217	280,000	650,000	700,000	0.30	*CDCZ*(DCC). *Disciples of Christ.* 1899, M=UCMS. HQ Mbandaka. 65n,22f,5H,I3h,1s.
Co des Eglises Baptistes de Bandundu	1892	P-Bap	....K	75	29,100	50,000	83,000	2.05	*CEBB* or *CBB* (formerly EB du Maindombe). M=SBM(Sweden). HQ Semendwa. 55n,39f.
Co des Eglises Bapt Indépendantes Ev	1932	I-Bap	x...K	300	20,000	25,000	45,000	2.38	*CEBIE* (formerly AEBI). *Independent Baptist Chs.* 1953, M=BMM. HQ Kikwit. 35n,13f.
Co des Egls Chrétiennes en Afrique	1948	I-Dis	x...K	50	4,000	8,000	12,000	1.64	*CECA. Community of Christian Chs in Africa.* M=ACM(CCCC) (USA). HQ Bukavu. 65n,13f.
Co des Eglises de Grace au Zaire	1939	P-Eva	xFg.a	200	15,900	20,000	30,000	1.64	*CEGZ* (formerly MEM). *Chs of Grace in Z.* M=Maniema M(GM) (USA). HQ Bukavu. 69n,15f.
Co des Eglises de Pentecôte	1921	P-Pe2	Z...K	1,000	264,000	200,000	500,000	3.73	*CEP.* M=SFM. HQ Bukavu. 43% Bafulero, 31% Hunde. 194n,3x,49f,2H,1j,1s(47),7001Y.
Co des E des Frères Mennonites au Z	1912	P-Men	GFG.a	228	46,900	16,000	125,000	8.57	*CEFMZ*(AEFMC). Mennonite Brethren. M=AMBM. HQ Kikwit. 50n,4x,43f,2H,2h,W=50%,350Y.
Co des Eglises Libres du Zaire	1922	P-Pe2	Z...K	350	60,000	75,000	200,000	4.00	*CELZA. Free Chs of Z.* M=NPY. Bukavu. 59% Bashi, 30% Rega. 43n,6x,30f,1p,W=85%,3040Y.
Co des Fidèles Protestants	1957	I-Bap	....K	50	3,000	15,000	7,000	-3.00	*CFP. Mission of Protestant Faithful.* Schism ex NBM. HQ Bondo. 80% Azande. 16n.
Co des Frères en Christ Garenganze	1886	P-CBr	x...K	450	20,000	31,000	60,000	2.68	*CFCG. Garenganze Brethren in Christ.* M=GEM(CMML) (UK). HQ Lubumbashi. 155n,15f.
Co du Christ Lumière du St-Esprit	1931	I-3pA	IWA.K	420	58,000	150,000	180,000	0.73	*CL. Community of Light.* Schism ex EJCSK. 95% Luba. 300 schools. 160n.
Co Eglises Luthériennes	1976	P-Lut	.....	123	16,000	–	40,000	5.26	2 groups of Lutherans from USA, Europe.
Co Episcopale Baptiste Africaine	1956	I-3pA	.uA.K	300	110,000	80,000	170,000	3.06	*CEBA* (formerly EPROBA). *African Episcopal Baptist Ch.* Ex CEM. HQ Manono. 57n,1f.
Co Ev au Centre de l'Afrique	1912	P-Eva	xMg.a	1,575	66,100	300,000	176,000	-2.11	*CECA*(CCZO,EVACO). *Central Africa Ch.* M=AIM. HQ Bunia. 210n,115f,5H,19H,4s,4000Y.
Co Evangélique Beréenne au Zaire	1938	P-Eva	.MG.a	100	30,000	60,000	90,000	1.64	*CEBZ* (formerly EEBC). *Berean Ch in Z.* M=BAMS(USA). HQ Shabunda (Kivu). 44n,19f.
Co Evangélique de l'Alliance au Z	1884	P-Hol	xFG.a	526	50,300	60,000	94,258	1.82	*CEAZ* (formerly EEAC). *Ch of Alliance in Z.* M=CMA(USA). HQ Boma. 106n,30f,1H,6h,1s.
Co Ev de Pentecôte au Shaba	c1950	I-3pA	....K	350	60,000	50,000	150,000	4.49	*CEPS. Ch of Pentecost in Shaba.* Related to CEM. HQ Lubumbashi. 152n.
Co Ev des Adventistes du 7e Jour	1919	P-Adv	x...K	970	230,000	70,000	595,000	8.94	*Seventh-day Adv, Zaire U.* 2 planes. 141n,5x,26f,1H,9h,1r,1s,507t(56191),W=77%,3452Y.
Co Ev du Christ au Coeur d'Afrique	1913	P-Eva	xGG.a	1,545	80,000	110,000	230,000	2.99	*CECCA. Heart of Africa Ch.* M=HAM(WEC)(UK). HQ Isiro.157n,28f,1H,12h,1j,2s,690Y.
Co Evangélique du Christ en Ubangi	1922	P-Con	xPG.a	450	42,000	75,000	80,000	0.26	*CECU*(MEU,ECU). *Ch of Christ in U.* M=EFCA(USA). HQ Gemena. 29n,53f,1H,1h,2s.
Co Evangélique du Haut-Zaire	1931	P-Eva	xMG.a	530	53,000	40,000	88,300	3.22	*CEHZ. Ev Ch of Upper Zaire.* M=UFM(UK). HQ Kisangani. 12n,26f,1H,9h,4s.
Co Evangélique du Kwango	1952	P-Eva	....K	210	10,000	20,000	30,000	1.64	*CEK* (formerly EEK). *Ch of Kwango.* M=MEB(Ev M Among the Bayaka) (Switz). 16n,15f.
Co Evangélique du Zaire	1881	P-Con	.WA.K	200	40,000	75,000	115,000	1.72	*CEZ* (formerly EE de Manianga-Manianga-Matadi,EEMM). M=SMF(Sweden).HQ Luozi. 141n,44f
Co Evangélique en Ubandi-Mongala	1937	I-Con	....K	1,157	96,000	70,000	214,000	4.57	*CEUM. Ev Ch in U-M.* Ex CECU(EFCA), supported by M=ECCA(USA). HQ Gemena. 50n,50f.
Co Ev Mennonite du Sud-Kasai	1960	I-Men	....K	145	16,000	9,000	33,600	5.41	*CEMSK.* Split ex Congo Inland Mission, now reconciled. HQ Mbuji-Mayi. 20n.
Co Evangélique Zairoise	1927	P-Bap	....K	182	66,500	12,000	175,000	11.32	*CEZ*(AEBI). M=ZGM/CGM,BIM(USA). Badinga, Mbunda. 43n,1x,3f,2p,1s,W=58%,1601Y.
Co Libre de Maniema-Kivu	1922	I-3aA	X	200	20,000	20,000	40,000	2.81	*CLMK* (formerly ELMK). *Free Ch of the Maniema.* M=ESAM(USA). HQ Shabunda. 59n,25f,3s.
Co Libre Méthodiste au Zaire-Est	1962	I-Hol	VFg.K	540	52,600	30,000	150,000	6.65	*CLMZ*(ELMCE). M=FMC(USA). 91% Bembe, 6% Ruanda. 81n,1x,12m,5f,1h,1s,W=99%,489Y.
Co Méthodiste Unie au Zaire	1885	P-Met	VwA.K	2,432	291,900	250,000	550,000	3.20	*CMUZ. North Shaba & Southern Zaire Confs*, Africa CC, UMC(USA).
Co Mennonite au Zaire	1896	P-Men	GW..K	350	50,000	110,000	112,500	0.09	*CMZ* (formerly EMC). M=Congo Inland Mission(GCMC) (USA). HQ Chikapa. 195n,81f,5H,2s.
Co Pentecôtiste au Zaire	1915	P-Pe2	ZGG.a	2,800	190,000	180,000	543,000	4.52	CPZ(EPCO). *Pentecostal Ch in Zaire.* M=CEM(ZEM)(UK). HQ Kamina. 611n,1j,33f,1p.
Co Presbytérienne au Zaire	1889	P-Ref	RWA.K	740	1,001,000	300,000	1,250,000	5.87	*CPZA* (formerly EPC). *Presbyterian Ch in Z.* M=APCM(PCUS). HQ Kananga. 225n,89f,1s.
Co Presbytérienne de Kinshasa	1955	P-Ref	..A.K	52	12,000	20,000	30,000	1.64	*CPK* (formerly EPK). *Presbyterian Ch in K.* M=APCM(PCUS). 17n,7f.
Co Protestante du Shaba	1954	I-Met	.T..K	20	5,000	8,000	12,000	1.64	*CPS* (formerly EPROKAT). *Prot Ch in Shaba.* Ex Methodist. M=CBMEC(Belgium). Luba. 6n.
Co Région de Sankuru	1897	P-EBr	x...K	100	8,000	20,000	25,000	0.90	*CRS.* M=North Kasai M (Westcott, North Sankuru). Glanton Brethren. HQ Kole. 31n,8f.
Co Union des Egls Baptistes du Kwilu	1953	I-Bap	....K	40	3,000	7,500	8,000	0.26	*CUEBK.* Baptist Churches of Kwilu. Split ex BMM. HQ Kikwit. 35n,8f.
Eglise du Christ Unie de l'Angola	1973	I-Uni	.v...	200	100,000	100,000	200,000	4.55	*ECUA. United Ch of Christ of Angola.* Ex ECZ by Angolans. 85% Kongo, 10% Kimbundu.
Eglise du Zaire Sankuru à Kondji	1936	P-Non	.....	15	1,000	1,500	2,000	1.16	Formerly M=Africa Evangelistic Band (UK, SAfrica). Pilgrims. HQ Kasai-Orientale.
Eglise Evangélique Africaine	1959	I-CBr	.T..T	35	6,000	10,000	11,000	0.38	Schism ex Garenganze. In Zambia, Central Africa Ch (ex CMML). Lamba, Bemba, Yeke.
Eglise Evangélique du Haut-Uélé	1960	I-Eva	..G.G	20	3,000	10,000	5,000	-2.73	Formerly ECC(Gamba). Schism of all Mayogo ex HAM(WEC). 90% Mayogo. 180Y,635z.
Eglise Ev Zairoise au Mayombe	1962	I-Hol	.T..T	10	500	5,000	1,000	-6.23	*APROCO* (Assoc Prot du Congo). Schism of 50% ex M=CMA(USA), mostly returned.
Eglise Kitawala	1923	I-Jeh	I	1,000	120,000	50,000	200,000	5.70	*Ch of the Watchtower.* Ex Jehovah's Witnesses. 1950s, ruthlessly suppressed. In NE.
Eglise Lumpa	1964	I-mar	.....	10	500	10,500	1,000	-8.98	*'Church which itinerates abroad'.* Refugees from church crushed by Zambia military.
Eglise Orthodoxe: AD Afrique Centrale	1958	O-Gre	Cw...	7	5,600	6,800	8,000	0.65	Under P Alexandria. Greeks. 1958, HQ Lubumbashi; 1962, Bujumbura (Burundi). 3x,6f.
Eglise Neo-Apostolique	c1970	I-3aX	x....	700	500,000	–	1,421,425	76.24	*NAC. New Apostolic Church.* M=Neuapostolische Kirche (HQ Zurich, Switzerland).
Eglise Sabbatique du Saint-Esprit	1954	I-3pA	.v...	60	4,000	7,175	12,000	2.08	*ESSE. Sabbatical Church of the Holy Spirit.* 70% Luba, 20% Chokwe. 53n,W=99%,289Y.
Eglise Pentecotiste de Zaire	c1975	I-3oA	.....	30	2,000	–	4,000	5.00	*Pentecostal Church of Zaire.* Oneness body in AWCF. HQ Kinshasa.
Eglise Unie du Saint-Esprit	1965	I-3pA	.v..I	140	50,000	50,000	120,000	3.56	*EUSE. United Holy Spirit Ch.* 6 Ecclesiastical Provinces in Kasai, Shaba. 1974 applied to WCC.
Eglise Union du Septième Jour	1961	I-Adv	I	5	1,000	3,000	2,000	-1.61	*Union 7th-day Ch.* Schism ex SDAs. Members Bemba, Lamba, Lunda.
Groupes du Christ	c1970	I-3hA	x....	193	4,000	–	10,000	44.54	*Christ Groups.* Home churches for isolated converts after nationwide EHC campaign.
Témoins de Jéhovah	c1940	m-Jeh	x....	1,327	67,917	30,000	295,000	9.57	*Jehovah's Witnesses.* 1970, forced into ECZ. 1973, 240 in prison. (1975) 1486Y. (1995) 10526Y.
Other African indigenous churches		I-3pA	.....	1,500	100,000	50,000	250,000	0.05	Total about 800 (see list below), including many small local groupings.
Other Protestant denominations		P-	.....	50	6,000	5,000	15,000	0.05	Total about 30 (see list below).
Other Orthodox churches		O-	.....	20	1,000	200	2,000	0.05	Total 4 bodies, including: Eglise Orth Copte, Eglise Orth Catholique Americaine.
Doubly-affiliated		2-aff			-1,120,000	-367,473	-2,086,093		
Totals				**48,005**	**22,260,637**	**18,487,000**	**41,455,000**		

Churches, members, growth, 1900-2025	*Congs*	*Adults*	*Affiliated*	*G%*	*Total denominations*	*6 Megablocs:* O	R	A	P	I	m
Total churches, members, and denominations (mid-1900)	1,000	67,200	124,650	7.40	2	0	1	1	0	0	0
Total churches, members, and denominations (mid-1970)	31,626	9,972,467	18,487,000	7.40	395	3	1	1	16	373	1
Total churches, members, and denominations (mid-1990)	40,000	18,311,000	34,100,000	3.11	860	5	1	1	33	819	1
Total churches, members, and denominations (mid-1995)	48,005	22,260,637	41,455,000	3.98	861	5	1	1	33	820	1
Total churches, members, and denominations (mid-2000)	49,000	25,319,000	47,151,525	2.61	864	5	1	1	34	822	1
Total churches, members, and denominations (mid-2025)	80,000	51,487,000	95,882,000	2.88	1,271	15	1	1	50	1200	4

NOTES ON TABLE ABOVE

NATIONAL COUNCILS (Column 4, 5th letter).

- a = member of ECZ, also of AEZ.
- E = Alliance Evangélique du Zaïre (AEZ) (Alliance of Zaire), declared illegal 1970.
- I = Conseil Supérieur des Sacrificateurs pour les Eglises-Unies de Jésus-Christ en Afrique (COSSEUJCA) (Supreme Council of Priests for the United Churches of Jesus Christ in Africa); 28 member churches in 1967, 40 in 1969 when applied to join WCC; illegal after 1970; 1977, most joined ECZ.
- K = Eglise du Christ au Zaire (ECZ) (Church of Christ in Zaire), formerly 1924-71 CPC (Conseil Protestant du Congo).
- N = Eglise de Jésus-Christ sur la Terre par le Prophète Simon Kimbangu (affiliated to CWME of WCC).
- R = Conférence Episcopale du Congo-Zaire (CEZ) (Episcopal Conference of Congo-Zaire).
- T = Congo-Zaire Council of ICCC (10 member churches).

Other national councils. (1) Conseil des Eglises Protestantes du Congo/Zaire (CEPCO/CEPZA): this attempt in 1971 to form an evangelical council outside the ECZ supported by various churches including Methodists and Assemblies of God (USA) was banned by government in 1972. (2) Conseil des Eglises Libres du Congo (CONELCO): founded by 16 indigenous churches before 1970 ban. (3) Alliance Réformée du Congo-Kinshasa, 1997 (ARCK, formerly COREZA, 1988).

OTHER AFRICAN INDIGENOUS churches. In 1968, of the total of over 500 distinct African independent churches, about 200 were in process of obtaining government registration or had already obtained it. With the new law of 1970 all were ordered either to be suppressed or to join the Church of Christ in Zaire. In practice, by 1977 only a few had so joined, including 2 separatist movements which rejoined their parent bodies (CEBK, a large Nande schism in 1960 of 9,000 members ex CBFMS; and CEBI, a schism ex BMM with HQ Mangai). A number of other indigenous churches are still trying to join, and due to the impossibilities of communicating and enforcing the law the rest exist as formerly, more or less tolerated or ignored. Among these other unregistered indigenous churches are the 17 shown in the table, and the following smaller bodies: Apostolic Ch of Johane Masowe (Gospel of God, 1972 from Zimbabwe; 1,000 adult followers), Children of God of the Uganda Martyrs (Bena Nzambi wa BaMartyre ya Baganda), Eglise Chrétienne en Afrique (Eglise de la Conscience Chrétienne), Eglise de Dieu de Nos Ancêtres (Nzambi wa Bankambue, Bena Luhemba; 1956), Eglise de Digne (Fwanda, St Immanuel; ex RCC), Eglise de Notre Seigneur Jésus-Christ dans le Monde, Eglise de Pentecôte, Eglise de Pentecôte Zairoise Universelle, Eglise Don de Dieu, Eglise du Christ Roi (ex RCC), Eglise du St-Esprit au Zaire (ESEZA; Eglise Malembe, begun 1942 in Kasai), Eglise Ev Branche Indigène, Eglise Ev Kukebakeba (Church which Seeks People), Eglise Protection et Vérité du Christ (ex RCC), Eglise Ste Sara (1960, ex RCC; 10,000 members), Eglise Universelle (1965; marginal body begun by Eglise Chrétienne Universelle, from Paris, France; messianic healer Georges Roux), Followers of the Archangel Michael (Bena Michel), Katete (super-Jamaa), Maria Legio of Africa (from Kenya), Union Chrétienne de la Charité (1965 philanthropic movement partly within existing churches). There is also in Shaba a small work of the USA Black mission, African Methodist Episcopal Ch, begun in 1957 by Africans from Northern Rhodesia.

OTHER PROTESTANT DENOMINATIONS. Although all Protestant missions are required to operate through the Church of Christ in Zaire, there are also a few other smaller missions with adherents who have only a very loose relation to it. These include: Africa Christian Mission (1964: USA Churches of Christ), Baptist Bible Fellowship International (1957), Christian Nationals' Evangelism Commission 1969), Exclusive Brethren (Booth group; in NE Zaire), Luanza Mission (1884, now counted with CFCG in ECZ), Reformed Episcopal Ch (USA; 1951; works in CECA/AIM), World-Wide Missions (1963).

OTHER ORTHODOX CHURCHES. (1) An Orthodox body related to episcopi vagantes (bishops-at-large) operates a mission field in Zaire: Eglise Orthodoxe Catholique Américaine, a branch of the American Orthodox Catholic Church (a USA Ukrainian schism). (2) The Coptic Orthodox Patriarchate of Alexandria (Egypt) has 25 families in Zaire (1978).

OTHER MARGINAL BODIES. These include: Ch of Jesus Christ of Latter-day Saints (Mormons).

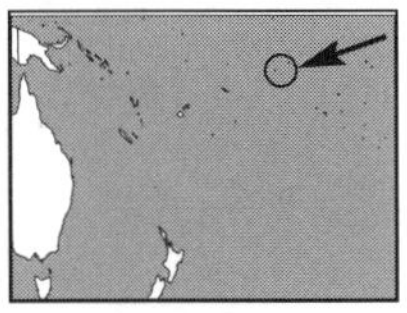

COOK ISLANDS

SECULAR DATA, AD 2000

STATE
Official name: The Territory Overseas of the Cook Islands.
Short name: Cook Islands. **Adjective of nationality:** Cook Islanders.
Flag: That of New Zealand.
Area: 233 sq. km. (90 sq. mi.).
Government: Self-governing territory overseas of New Zealand, since 1965 (1888 British protectorate, 1901 annexed to New Zealand).
Legislature: Parliament, 25 members.
Official language: English.
Monetary unit: Cook Island dollar. **US$1=** 1.48.
Chief cities: AVARUA 11,675.
Political divisions: 1 province.

DEMOGRAPHY
Population: 20,000.
Population density: 83.7/sq. km. (216.9/sq. mi.).
Under 15 years: 7,000.
Growth rate p.a.: 1.85% (births 27.33, deaths 4.64).
Mortality: Infant, per 1,000: 19.3; **Maternal per 100,000:** 30.0.
Life expectancy: 73 (male 71, female 75).
Household size: 5.0. **Floor area per person, sq.m:** 20.0.
Major languages: English, Maori (Rarotongan), Manohiki, Pukapukan, Rakahanga.
Urban dwellers: 63.01%. **Urban growth rate p.a.:** 1.6%.
Labor force: 40%.

ETHNOLINGUISTIC PEOPLES
58.9% Cook Islands Maori (Kuki); 15.4% Euronesian (Park-Maori); 13.9% Rakahanga-Manihiki; 4.5% Bukabukan; 3.3% Penrhyn (Tongareva).

ECONOMY
National income p.a. per person: US$1,997; **per family:** US$9,988.

EDUCATION
Adult literacy: 92% (male 94%, female 90%). **Schools:** 35.
Universities: 0. **School enrolment:** female/male: 90%/90%.

HEALTH
Access to health services: 90%. **Access to safe water:** 90%.
Hospitals: 18 (100 beds per 10,000). **Doctors:** 25.
Blind: 20. **Deaf:** 1,200. **Murder rate:** 3.
Lepers: 700.

LITERATURE
New book titles p.a.: 15 (750 p.a. per million). **Periodicals:** 4.
Newspapers: 0 dailies.

COMMUNICATION (per 1,000 people)
Phones: 200 (15% mobile). **Radios:** 200. **TV sets:** 700.
Daily newspaper circulation: 100. **Computers:** 50.

HUMAN LIFE AND LIBERTY (optimum condition=100.0%)
HDI: 70.5. **HSI:** 85.0. **HFI:** 70.0. **EFL:** 60.0.

Country Table 1. **Religious adherents in the Cook Islands, AD 1900-2025.**

Year	1900		1970		mid-1990		Annual change, 1990-2000				mid-1995		mid-2000		mid-2025	
Name	Adherents	%	Adherents	%	Adherents	%	Natural	Conversion	Total	Rate	Adherents	%	Adherents	%	Adherents	%
Christians	**8,200**	**100.0**	**20,560**	**99.1**	**17,960**	**99.8**	**119**	**-6**	**113**	**0.61**	**18,500**	**97.9**	**19,088**	**95.4**	**22,750**	**94.8**
PROFESSION																
professing Christians	**8,200**	**100.0**	**20,560**	**99.1**	**17,960**	**99.8**	**119**	**-6**	**113**	**0.61**	**18,500**	**97.9**	**19,088**	**95.4**	**22,750**	**94.8**
AFFILIATION																
unaffiliated Christians	160	2.0	584	2.8	560	3.1	6	-2	4	0.62	600	3.2	596	3.0	800	3.3
affiliated Christians	**8,040**	**98.1**	**19,976**	**96.3**	**17,400**	**96.7**	**113**	**-4**	**109**	**0.61**	**17,900**	**94.7**	**18,492**	**92.5**	**21,950**	**91.5**
Protestants	7,990	97.4	16,336	78.8	13,600	75.6	80	-20	60	0.43	13,980	74.0	14,200	71.0	16,200	67.5
Roman Catholics	50	0.6	2,260	10.9	3,200	17.8	36	9	45	1.32	3,423	18.1	3,650	18.3	4,800	20.0
Marginal Christians	0	0.0	1,140	5.5	1,350	7.5	15	15	30	2.03	1,447	7.7	1,650	8.3	2,200	9.2
Anglicans	0	0.0	100	0.5	100	0.6	1	-1	0	0.00	100	0.5	100	0.5	100	0.4
Independents	0	0.0	140	0.7	50	0.3	1	0	1	1.84	50	0.3	60	0.3	100	0.4
doubly-affiliated	0	0.0	0	0.0	-900	-5.0	-10	-17	-27	2.64	-1,100	-5.8	-1,168	-5.8	-1,450	-6.0
Trans-megabloc groupings																
Evangelicals	5,000	61.0	1,450	7.0	1,380	7.7	15	0	15	1.04	1,455	7.7	1,530	7.7	2,000	8.3
Pentecostals/Charismatics	0	0.0	200	1.0	2,750	15.3	31	4	35	1.21	3,127	16.5	3,100	15.5	4,200	17.5
Great Commission Christians	**330**	**4.0**	**1,600**	**7.7**	**2,320**	**12.9**	**26**	**-6**	**20**	**0.83**	**2,420**	**12.8**	**2,521**	**12.6**	**3,300**	**13.8**
Nonreligious	0	0.0	40	0.2	210	1.2	2	4	6	2.66	250	1.3	273	1.4	600	2.5
Baha'is	0	0.0	100	0.5	130	0.7	1	2	3	2.16	150	0.8	161	0.8	350	1.5
World A (unevangelized persons)	0	0.0	20	0.1	18	0.1	0	-1	-1	-3.97	18	0.1	20	0.1	24	0.1
World B (evangelized non-Christians)	0	0.0	161	0.6	22	1.8	3	7	10	44.81	381	2.0	892	2.1	1,226	3.9
World C (Christians)	8,200	100.0	20,560	99.3	17,960	98.1	119	-6	113	0.61	18,500	97.9	19,088	97.8	22,750	96.0
Country's population	**8,200**	**100.0**	**20,742**	**100.0**	**18,000**	**100.0**	**122**	**0**	**122**	**1.06**	**18,900**	**100.0**	**20,000**	**100.0**	**24,000**	**100.0**

COLUMNS, ROWS.
For meanings and definitions, see Codebook (Part 3). Note that, by definition, total 'Christians' = professing + crypto-Christians, which also = affiliated + unaffiliated Christians, and also = Great Commission Christians + latent Christians. Percentages may not always total exactly, due to rounding.

CENSUSES.
25.IX.1945: 89.1% Protestants, 9.8% Roman Catholics, 1.0% other religionists, 0.1% nonreligious. **25.IX.1956:** 99.5% Christians, 0.2% other religionists, 0.1% Baha'is, 0.1% nonreligious. **1.IX.1966:** 82.7% Protestants (76.2% Cook Islands Christian Ch, 6.1% SD Adventists), 12.3% Roman Catholics, 3.3% marginal Protestants, 0.8% Polynesian indigenous (Free Ch), 0.7% Anglicans, 0.2% nonreligious, 0.1% Baha'is.

NOTES ON RELIGIONS
BAHA'IS. Begun about 1950. In 1973, there was 1 local spiritual assembly, and 2 other centers; in 1996, 2 LSAs.
INDEPENDENTS. In 1 small group in 1995 (see Table 2).

Great Commission Instrument Panel: status of the Cook Islands (for explanation see start of Part 4)

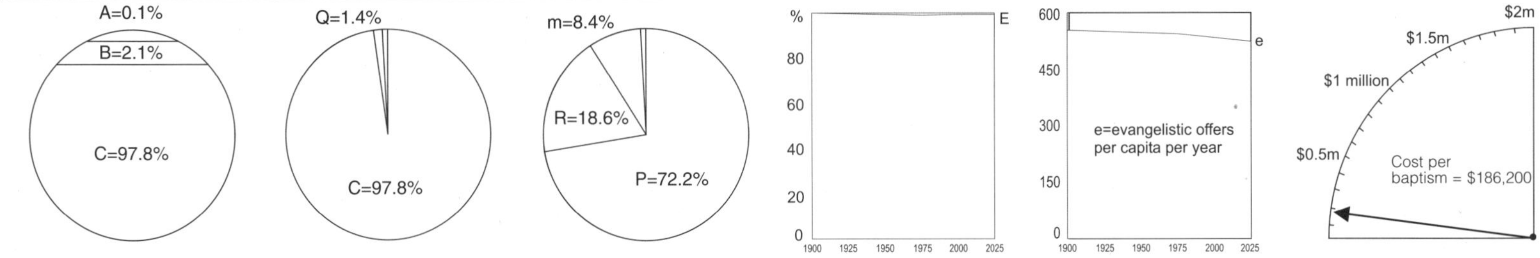

3 Worlds, AD 2000 — Religions, AD 2000 — Ecclesiastical blocs — Evangelization, 1900-2025 — Offers, 1900-2025 — Cost-effectiveness, AD 2000

Country status. The Cook Islands is a group of 15 islands in the South Pacific. It is a self-governing territory in free association with New Zealand. Fruit and copra are its main products.

HUMAN LIFE AND LIBERTY

Human rights and freedoms. As a territory of New Zealand, there are no human rights problems.

NON-CHRISTIAN RELIGIONS

Since almost the entire population was converted to Christianity during the 19th century, traditional religions have long ceased to exist as separate entities although they continue to manifest themselves in indigenous expressions of the Christian faith. A small Baha'i community has been formed.

CHRISTIANITY

PROTESTANT CHURCHES. The principal denominations in the territory is the Cook Islands Christian Church which owes its origin to LMS missionary activity beginning in 1823. The church played a prominent role in the early expansion of Christianity in the Pacific; from 1872-96 it sent 70 of its own missionaries to evangelize Papua. Despite the encroachments of Catholicism, Mormonism, and Seventh-day Adventists in the 20th century, two-thirds of the population are still members of the CICC. In addition, 12,000 other members have emigrated to or are temporarily working in New Zealand, where they come loosely under the care of the Presbyterian Church of New Zealand.

Seventh-day Adventists arrived in 1892 and have built up a sizeable community. The SDA Cook Islands Mission is part of the Central Park Union Mission. A small Assemblies of God work was begun from New Zealand in 1963.

In 1971 there were 112 primary schools operated by Protestants (mainly the CICC), as well as several secondary and technical schools.

CATHOLIC CHURCH. Catholics first reached the islands in 1894, and in 1922 a prefecture was established. The diocese of Rarotonga is now a suffragan of the archdiocese of Suva in Fiji.

The Holy See has no diplomatic relations with Cook Islands in AD 2000, but is represented there by an apostolic delegate for the Pacific Ocean residing in Wellington, New Zealand.

OTHER CHURCHES. Mormons were extremely active in the latter half of the 1960s and are now the second largest church of the islands. Many Maori missionaries from New Zealand have worked here, and growth is rapid, largely at the expense of losses

Country summary. **Worlds A, B, C by ethnolinguistic peoples, cities, and major civil divisions in the Cook Islands.**																					
	PEOPLES							CITIES							CIVIL DIVISIONS						
World	Num	Pop 2000	C%	Christians	E%	U%	Unevangelized	Num	Pop 2000	C%	Christians	E%	U%	Unevangelized	Num	Pop 2000	C%	Christians	E%	U%	Unevangelized
A	0	0	0.00	0	0	0	0	0	0	0.00	0	0	0	0	0	0	0.00	0	0	0	0
B	0	0	0.00	0	0	0	0	0	0	0.00	0	0	0	0	0	0	0.00	0	0	0	0
C	8	19,521	94.72	18,491	100	0	10	1	11,675	94.10	10,986	100	0	6	1	19,522	94.72	18,492	100	0	10
Total	**8**	**19,521**	**94.72**	**18,491**	**100**	**0**	**10**	**1**	**11,675**	**94.10**	**10,986**	**100**	**0**	**6**	**1**	**19,522**	**94.72**	**18,492**	**100**	**0**	**10**

The Islands' postage stamps often carry Christian themes, here The Resurrection of Christ by Raphael.

from CICC.

One small indigenous church is known to exist, the Amuri Free Church, which came into being on Aitutaki island through a schism from the Cook Islands Christian Church at the beginning of World War II.

An Anglican church has been built to serve the expatriate community. The church is administratively part of the diocese of Polynesia, in the Church of the Province of New Zealand.

Indigenous missions. The Cook Islands has a long history of missionary sending. Since 1830 the Cook Islands Christian Church has sent out over 200 foreign missionaries. Today most of the missionaries from all denominations serve in neighboring New Zealand where many of their countrymen have moved for work.

CHURCH AND STATE

There is no established church and no government ministry or department handling religious affairs. The churches receive no direct financial aid from government although they are exempt from certain taxes and their educational and charitable institutions receive some subsidy. Clergy may obtain recognition as officiating ministers for the purpose of conducting weddings.

BROADCASTING AND MEDIA

TBN programming appears in Rarotonga on cable channels. Cook Islands is a member of UNDA.

INTERDENOMINATIONAL ORGANIZATIONS

The Cook Islands Christian Church is a member of the National Council of Churches in New Zealand, founded in 1941.

FUTURE TRENDS AND PROSPECTS

Christianity is expected to decline slightly to 94.8% by AD 2025 because of the rise of the nonreligious.

Church membership should remain above 90% up to AD 2050 but could gradually lose adherents to the nonreligious.

BIBLIOGRAPHY

'A modern Polynesian cargo cult,' R. G. Crocombe, *Man*, 61, 28 (1961), 40–41. (On Atiu Island among LMS Christians in 1947 led by woman healer and prophetess Kapuvai).

Arts and crafts of the Cook Islands. P. H. Buck. 1944; reprint, New York: Kraus Reprint, 1971. 550p.

Cannibals and converts: radical change in the Cook Islands. Maretu. Trans. and ed., M. T. Crocombe. [Suva, Fiji]: Institute of Pacific Studies, University of the South Pacific, 1983. 223p. (Translated from Rarotongan).

Diocesan archives, 1891–1993. Catholic Church Diocese of the Cook Islands and Niue. Canberra, Australia: Pacific Manuscripts Bureau, Australian National University, [1994]. (53 microfilm reels).

'The transformation of the Mangaian religion.' P. Aratangi. M.Th. thesis, Pacific Theological College, Suva, Fiji, 1988. 127p.

Torea Katorika. Catholic Church Diocese of the Cook Islands and Niue, 1982–. (Monthly periodical; published bimonthly before 1982).

'Worship in the culture and church of the Cook Islands, with special reference to the needs of the Cook Islands Christian church to–day.' T. Makirere. B.D. thesis, Pacific Theological College, Suva, Fiji, 1971. 120p.

Country Table 2. **Organized churches and denominations in the Cook Islands.**

Official name (bold type = church with over 10% of all affiliated) 1	*Begun* 2	*Type* 3	*Counc* 4	*Congs* 5	*Adults* 6	*Affiliated 1970* 7	*Affiliated 1995* 8	*G%* 9	*Names, notes, and other statistics* (see Codebook, Part 3) 10
Amuri Free Church	c1940	I-Con	.....	1	20	140	50	-4.03	Schism ex LMS. On Aitutaki island. 50% decline from 296 adherents in 1951.
Anglican Church (D Polynesia)		A-Hig	awpKK	1	50	100	100	0.05	In Diocese of Polynesia, Ch of the Province of New Zealand. Expatriates.
Assemblies of God	1963	P-Pe2	Z....	9	550	100	930	9.33	M=AoG(New Zealand). Classical Pentecostals (2-stage). 56n.
Catholic Church: D Rarotonga	1894	R-Lat	P.PYK	16	1,700	2,260	3,423	1.67	Suffragan, M Suva (Fiji). M=SSCCSM. C=2+0+1. (1970) 13x,7w. (1990) 5n,5x,8m,8w,111Yy.
Ch of Jesus Christ of Latter-day Saints	c1952	m-LdS	x....	6	420	1,100	1,100	0.00	*Mormons.* M=CJCLdS(USA). 20f.
Cook Islands Christian Church	1823	P-Con	.WP.W	94	4,220	14,746	11,220	-1.09	*CICC.* M=LMS(UK). 12,000 other members are emigres in New Zealand. 23n,1x,1s,481Yy.
Jehovah's Witnesses	1961	m-Jeh	x....	3	118	40	347	9.03	Active witnessing reported 1962, lapse, then since 1968 new activity. 13Y.
Seventh-day Adventist Church	1892	P-Adv	x....	14	748	1,300	1,400	0.30	*CI Mission.* Mass emigration to New Zealand. 2n,2x,1s,12t(1228),W=90%,211Y.
United Pentecostal Church	c1980	P-Pel	.....	3	100	–	200	6.67	M=UPC (USA). Oneness (Jesus Only) dogmas.
Other Protestant churches		P-	.....	2	115	190	230	0.05	Including Presbyterian Ch (40).
Doubly-affiliated		2-aff			-470	0	-1,100		Independents who are also members of the 2 largest denominations.
Totals				**149**	**7,571**	**19,976**	**17,900**		

Churches, members, growth, 1900-2025	*Congs*	*Adults*	*Affiliated*	*G%*	*Total denominations*	*6 Megablocs:* O	R	A	P	I	m
Total churches, members, and denominations (mid-1900)	50	4,100	8,040	1.31	3	0	1	0	2	0	0
Total churches, members, and denominations (mid-1970)	132	10,124	19,976	1.31	10	0	1	1	5	1	2
Total churches, members, and denominations (mid-1990)	140	7,400	17,400	-0.69	13	0	1	1	8	1	2
Total churches, members, and denominations (mid-1995)	149	7,571	17,900	0.57	13	0	1	1	8	1	2
Total churches, members, and denominations (mid-2000)	160	7,800	18,492	0.65	13	0	1	1	8	1	2
Total churches, members, and denominations (mid-2025)	200	9,300	21,950	0.69	23	0	1	1	15	1	5

NOTES ON TABLE ABOVE
NATIONAL COUNCILS (Column 4, 5th letter).

K = Religious Advisory Council of the Cook Islands.
w = National Council of Churches in New Zealand (NCCNZ).

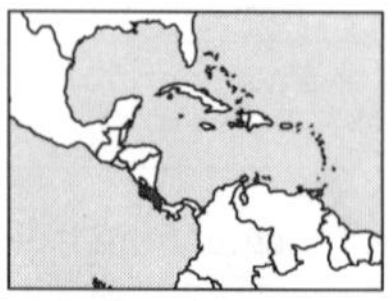

COSTA RICA

SECULAR DATA, AD 2000

STATE

Official name: La República de Costa Rica (The Republic of Costa Rica).
Short name: Costa Rica. **Adjective of nationality:** Costa Rican.
Flag: Stripes top to bottom of blue, white, red, white, blue; national crest in white oval.
Area: 51,100 sq. km. (19,730 sq. mi.).
Government: Parliamentary republic, since 1838 (1502 Spanish colony, 1838 Independence, 3 dictatorships since).
Legislature: Legislative Assembly, 57 members.
Official language: Spanish (Español/Castella).
Monetary unit: 1 Costa Rican colón (C) = 100 céntimos. **US$1=** C263.10.
Chief cities: SAN JOSE 1,063,000; Limon 82,664; Desamparados 64,130.
Political divisions: 7 provinces.
Armed forces: 8,000.

DEMOGRAPHY

Population: 4,023,000.
Population density: 78.7/sq. km. (203.9/sq. mi.).
Under 15 years: 1,302,000.
Growth rate p.a.: 2.03% (births 21.91, deaths 3.98).
Mortality: Infant, per 1,000: 10.9; **Maternal per 100,000:** 55.0.
Life expectancy: 77 (male 75, female 80).
Household size: 4.2. **Floor area per person, sq.m:** 17.0.
Major languages: Spanish, English, Chinese.
Urban dwellers: 51.88%. **Urban growth rate p.a.:** 2.9%.
Labor force: 38%.

ETHNOLINGUISTIC PEOPLES

77.7% Costarican White; 8.6% Mestizo; 8.0% Nicaraguan Mestizo; 1.0% Han Chinese (Cantonese); 1.0% Mulatto.

ECONOMY

National income p.a. per person: US$2,609; **per family:** US$10,961.

EDUCATION

Adult literacy: 94% (male 94%, female 95%). **Schools:** 3,729.
Universities: 6. **School enrolment:** female/male: 82%/81%.

HEALTH

Access to health services: 80%. **Access to safe water:** 92%.
Hospitals: 33 (21 beds per 10,000). **Doctors:** 4,027.
Blind: 2,000. **Deaf:** 227,900. **Murder rate:** 5.
Lepers: 3,000. **Underweight prevalence under 5:** 2%.

LITERATURE

New book titles p.a.: 1,130 (280 p.a. per million). **Periodicals:** 35.
Newspapers: 5 dailies.

COMMUNICATION (per 1,000 people)

Phones: 167 (9% mobile). **Radios:** 224. **TV sets:** 220.
Daily newspaper circulation: 102. **Computers:** 80.

REFUGEES

Alien refugees from other countries: 20,500.

HUMAN LIFE AND LIBERTY (optimum condition=100.0%)

HDI: 88.9. **HSI:** 66.0. **HFI:** 77.5. **EFL:** 44.0.

Country Table 1. **Religious adherents in Costa Rica, AD 1900-2025.**

Year / Name	1900 Adherents	%	1970 Adherents	%	mid-1990 Adherents	%	Annual change, 1990-2000 Natural	Conversion	Total	Rate	mid-1995 Adherents	%	mid-2000 Adherents	%	mid-2025 Adherents	%
Christians	**318,800**	**99.6**	**1,697,600**	**98.1**	**2,944,650**	**96.6**	**94,108**	**-76**	**94,032**	**2.81**	**3,434,270**	**96.6**	**3,884,968**	**96.6**	**5,683,500**	**95.9**
PROFESSION																
professing Christians	**318,800**	**99.6**	**1,697,600**	**98.1**	**2,944,650**	**96.6**	**94,108**	**-76**	**94,032**	**2.81**	**3,434,270**	**96.6**	**3,884,968**	**96.6**	**5,683,500**	**95.9**
AFFILIATION																
unaffiliated Christians	1,000	0.3	3,840	0.2	11,000	0.4	351	30	381	3.02	14,270	0.4	14,807	0.4	16,000	0.3
affiliated Christians	**317,800**	**99.3**	**1,693,760**	**97.9**	**2,933,650**	**96.2**	**93,756**	**-105**	**93,651**	**2.81**	**3,420,000**	**96.2**	**3,870,161**	**96.2**	**5,667,500**	**95.6**
Roman Catholics	316,600	98.9	1,688,471	97.6	2,800,000	91.8	89,446	-3,446	86,000	2.71	3,248,792	91.4	3,660,000	91.0	5,200,000	87.7
Protestants	2,000	0.6	51,422	3.0	240,000	7.9	7,667	1,333	9,000	3.24	286,998	8.1	330,000	8.2	600,000	10.1
Independents	0	0.0	16,888	1.0	83,000	2.7	2,651	-151	2,500	2.67	96,569	2.7	108,000	2.7	220,000	3.7
Marginal Christians	0	0.0	14,524	0.8	56,000	1.8	1,789	111	1,900	2.96	64,900	1.8	75,000	1.9	150,000	2.5
Anglicans	200	0.1	1,864	0.1	1,600	0.1	51	-51	0	0.00	1,600	0.1	1,600	0.0	2,000	0.0
doubly-affiliated	-1,000	-0.3	-79,409	-4.6	-246,950	-8.1	-7,889	2,140	-5,749	2.11	-278,859	-7.9	-304,439	-7.6	-504,500	-8.5
Trans-megabloc groupings																
Evangelicals	2,000	0.6	48,000	2.8	200,000	6.6	6,389	1,611	8,000	3.42	242,757	6.8	280,000	7.0	505,000	8.5
Pentecostals/Charismatics	0	0.0	28,000	1.6	364,000	11.9	11,628	1,372	13,000	3.10	429,421	12.1	494,000	12.3	870,000	14.7
Great Commission Christians	**16,000**	**5.0**	**138,000**	**8.0**	**350,000**	**11.5**	**11,181**	**5,273**	**16,454**	**3.93**	**440,000**	**12.4**	**514,542**	**12.8**	**950,000**	**16.0**
Nonreligious	0	0.0	9,300	0.5	43,220	1.4	1,381	324	1,705	3.38	52,000	1.5	60,265	1.5	150,000	2.5
Chinese folk-religionists	400	0.1	5,000	0.3	35,000	1.2	1,118	8	1,126	2.83	40,400	1.1	46,260	1.2	55,000	0.9
Baha'is	0	0.0	5,600	0.3	9,400	0.3	300	-83	217	2.10	9,800	0.3	11,571	0.3	17,000	0.3
Atheists	0	0.0	5,000	0.3	7,300	0.2	233	-25	208	2.54	7,900	0.2	9,382	0.2	13,000	0.2
Jews	100	0.0	1,500	0.1	3,800	0.1	121	-47	74	1.80	4,000	0.1	4,540	0.1	5,000	0.1
Spiritists	0	0.0	4,000	0.2	2,750	0.1	88	-57	31	1.07	2,600	0.1	3,058	0.1	2,000	0.0
Buddhists	200	0.1	2,000	0.1	2,000	0.1	64	-30	34	1.60	2,100	0.1	2,343	0.1	2,500	0.0
Ethnoreligionists	500	0.2	1,000	0.1	800	0.0	26	-15	11	1.34	830	0.0	914	0.0	500	0.0
Hindus	0	0.0	0	0.0	80	0.0	3	1	4	4.22	100	0.0	121	0.0	500	0.0
World A (unevangelized persons)	320	0.1	1,730	0.1	3,049	0.1	105	20	125	3.27	3,553	0.1	4,023	0.1	11,858	0.2
World B (evangelized non-Christians)	880	0.3	31,435	1.8	101,301	3.3	3,229	56	3,285	2.84	116,057	3.3	134,009	3.3	233,642	3.9
World C (Christians)	318,800	99.6	1,697,600	98.1	2,944,650	96.6	94,108	-76	94,032	2.81	3,434,270	96.6	3,884,968	96.6	5,683,500	95.9
Country's population	**320,000**	**100.0**	**1,730,766**	**100.0**	**3,049,000**	**100.0**	**97,442**	**0**	**97,442**	**2.81**	**3,553,881**	**100.0**	**4,023,000**	**100.0**	**5,929,000**	**100.0**

COLUMNS, ROWS.
For meanings and definitions, see Codebook (Part 3). Note that, by definition, total 'Christians' = professing + crypto-Christians, which also = affiliated + unaffiliated Christians, and also = Great Commission Christians + latent Christians. Percentages may not always total exactly, due to rounding.

CENSUSES.
27.XI.1864: 99.75% Roman Catholics, 0.24% Evangelicals (286 persons), 0.01% Hindus. No subsequent census has included a question on religion, but in 1972 an official estimate was published by the Civil Registry of the Republic, as follows: 90.0% Roman Catholics, 7.0% Protestants (128,912 persons), 2.5% others (46,390 persons) including Jews, Masons, Rosicrucians, Theosophists, Baha'is, Spiritists, Mormons, and Aquarians *(Registro Civil de la Republica, 1972).* After adjusting these categories to fit the definitions in this Encyclopedia, we arrive at the percentages given in the table above for professing Christians and non-Christian religions in 1970.

NOTES ON RELIGIONS
ATHEISTS. Popular Vanguard Party (PVP) (Communist, proscribed; pro-Soviet): best-organized and most sophisticated Communist party in Central America.
BAHA'IS. Growth from 22 local spiritual assemblies (1964) to 56 (1973); then decline to 52 (1996).
DOUBLY-AFFILIATED. The term covers those affiliated to, or claimed by, both the Catholic Church and also an Evangelical church (Protestant, marginal Protestant, Anglican or Non-White indigenous), i.e. baptized Catholics who have recently become Evangelicals. Because their statistics represent a duplication, they are shown in the table as a negative quantity (with a minus sign).
ETHNORELIGIONISTS. Of the 10,000 Amerindians, a proportion are still animists, mainly on the Caribbean side in the southern Talamanca district; tribes include the Bribri, Cabecar, Boruca, Guatuso and Teribe.
INDEPENDENTS. In over 40 denominations in 1995 (see Table 2).
JEWS. Only a small proportion are practicing Jews.
NONRELIGIOUS. Costa Rican Whites, but also many Chinese especially youths rejecting family religion.

Great Commission Instrument Panel: status of Costa Rica (for explanation see start of Part 4)

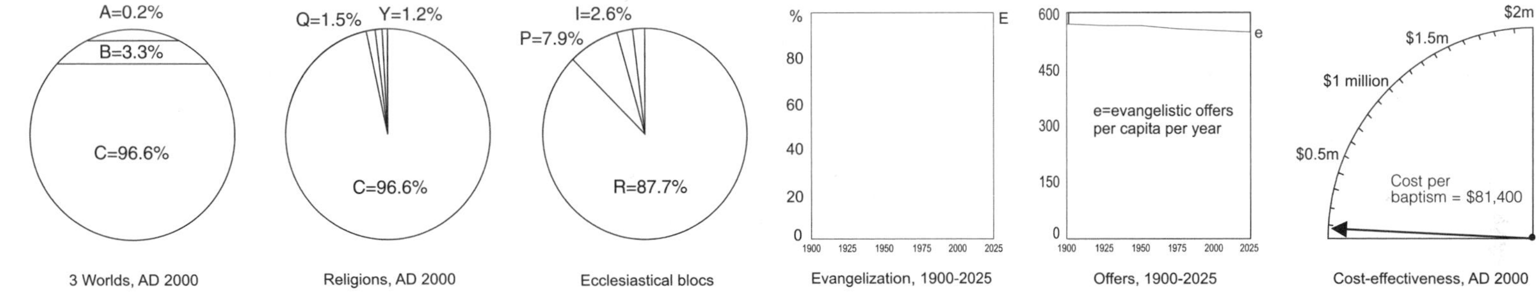

Country status. Costa Rica is the second smallest country in Central America, but it is noted as one of the most stable democracies in the region. It shares the same cultural, religious, and linguistic traditions as its neighbors. The country is largely forested with timber and coffee as its main exports.

HUMAN LIFE AND LIBERTY

Human need and development. Although Costa Rica is prosperous relative to the other countries in the region, it suffers from many of their social and economic problems. About 40% of the rural and 30% of the urban housing are considered substandard. Many rural areas have no piped water or sewage systems. Although the death rates have been steadily falling, infant and maternal mortality rates are quite high. In the Southern areas, the landless peasants sometimes occupy public lands, resulting in violent confrontations with the police.

Human rights and freedoms. As one of the few countries in the world without a national army, Costa Rica is never in danger of a military takeover. A number of other factors also help to preserve constitutional democracy. One is the provision barring a president from standing for reelection and the other is the provision establishing the Supreme Electoral Tribunal as the fourth branch of government. As a result, human rights abuses are rare and are limited to sporadic incidents. Most Indians live in one of 21 reserves but face no legal discrimination. They manage their own affairs through the National Indian Commission.

Human environment. Costa Rica loses about 680 million tons of top soil each year as a result of deforestation, and conversion of forest land to pasture. Costa Rica has developed one of the most ambitious conservation programs in the region, and has established an extensive network of parks and reserves. The country remains rich in biodiversity and is home to 2 endangered species.

NON-CHRISTIAN RELIGIONS

According to an estimate of the Civil Registry of the republic, in 1972 about 2.5% of the population belonged to numerous marginal Protestant and quasi-Christian bodies: Rosicrucians, Theosophists, Spiritists, Mormons, Aquarians, Masons; there were also Jews and followers of Baha'i. During the last century, Freemasonry made some impact in intellectual circles, contributing towards a degree of anticlericalism among government officials.

Judaism is only practiced by a small part of the Jewish population, living mostly in San José and consisting mainly of descendants of immigrant Jews.

Traditional religions have virtually disappeared due to the decline of the indigenous Indian population.

CHRISTIANITY

CATHOLIC CHURCH. Columbus arrived off Costa Rica in 1502, and the first Catholic missionaries disembarked in 1514. Originally a province under the viceroy of Guatemala (1569), the rugged terrain and inadequate labor supply contributed to the development of small farms in contrast to the more common latifundia (landed aristocracy) pattern of most Latin American countries.

This in turn resulted in the growth of an independent, individualistic character among the people. In spite of early mass baptisms among the Chorotega Indians (6,000 being baptized in 1522 with their chief) and Costa Rica's inclusion in the diocese of Leon (Nicaragua) in 1531, little effective pastoral attention was given to the area. In 1711, a visiting bishop noted the spiritual poverty of the people and ordered the building of chapels in all parishes and the fulfillment of church obligations by all families; but nothing came of this. Spain's negative reaction to the Protestant Reformation resulted in Central America being closed to the influence of all other European nations, thus limiting economic as well as religious development. Upon achieving independence from Spain in 1821, Costa Rica invited Europeans and Americans to help develop its resources. Expatriate businessmen in turn contributed to the coffee and banana trade and helped initiate the first Protestant services in a private home in 1848.

Christianity is often represented on postage stamps: here (1975), *left*, The Nativity and the Comet, *right*, Joseph in his workshop, both by Jorge.

Country summary. **Worlds A, B, C by ethnolinguistic peoples, cities, and major civil divisions in Costa Rica.**

	PEOPLES							CITIES							CIVIL DIVISIONS						
World	Num	Pop 2000	C%	Christians	E%	U%	Unevangelized	Num	Pop 2000	C%	Christians	E%	U%	Unevangelized	Num	Pop 2000	C%	Christians	E%	U%	Unevangelized
A	1	5,045	0.10	5	49	51	2,568	0	0	0.00	0	0	0	0	0	0	0.00	0	0	0	0
B	4	73,226	33.63	24,623	99	1	1,042	0	0	0.00	0	0	0	0	0	0	0.00	0	0	0	0
C	17	3,945,150	97.47	3,845,532	100	0	944	2	1,145,664	95.54	1,094,522	100	0	2,374	7	4,023,422	96.19	3,870,161	100	0	4,553
Total	**22**	**4,023,421**	**96.19**	**3,870,160**	**100**	**0**	**4,554**	**2**	**1,145,664**	**95.54**	**1,094,522**	**100**	**0**	**2,374**	**7**	**4,023,422**	**96.19**	**3,870,161**	**100**	**0**	**4,553**

The Catholic Church continued to be the only recognized religious body after Independence, but the constitution was liberalized in 1848, and even greater religious liberty was granted in 1860. A concordat with the Holy See was concluded in 1852. Jesuits entered in 1875 but were suppressed in 1884, and the church was forbidden to interfere in the affairs of the state. Throughout its history, however, Costa Rica has experienced little political turmoil, in part the result of the general absence of a landed aristocracy.

Religious practice among Catholics is largely confined to Sunday observance, about 15% of the faithful participating in Sunday mass in large cities and up to 25% in rural areas. For the majority, religion is individualistic, centered in the veneration of saints and often mixed with superstition.

The Holy See has diplomatic relations with Costa Rica and in AD 2000 is represented to government and the Catholic hierarchy by a nuncio residing in San José.

OTHER CHURCHES. In 1865, when the first nondenominational church was built in San José, there were only 286 Protestants known in the country. The church was served intermittently by Congregationalist and Methodist clergy prior to being taken over by Anglicans in 1896. Negro immigrants from the West Indies began to flood into the country in the latter part of the 19th century, and several West Indies churches sent missionaries to serve them: the Jamaica Baptist Missionary Society in 1887, the Methodist Missionary Society (UK) in 1894, and the Anglican SPG in 1896. The Baptist Convention was later aided by the BMS (UK) and since 1949 by Southern Baptists from the USA. The Methodist Church maintains ties with British Methodism and American Episcopalians have assumed responsibility for the early SPG work.

The first North American missionary society was the Central American Mission, in 1891. This was followed by American Methodists in 1917 and the Latin America Mission in 1921. Pentecostals made their initial appearance in 1930-32, with the arrival of missionaries from the Assemblies of God and the Church of God of Prophecy. These were followed by others from the Church of God (Cleveland) in 1935, and the International Church of the Foursquare Gospel in 1953. The former (AoG) is the largest Protestant denomination in Costa Rica at the present time.

Some 14 other new missions have established themselves in various parts of the country since World War II. However, none has yet achieved a significant following.

Renewal movements. In the 1990s the Pentecostal/Charismatic Renewal continued to spread rapidly across most older churches, and numbered over 494,000 adherents (of whom 45% Pentecostals, 40% Charismatics, and 14% Independents).

Indigenous missions. Costa Rican Christians, particularly Roman Catholics, have been involved in missions for many decades, primarily in surrounding Spanish-speaking countries and in Europe. Today, both Catholics and Protestants are becoming more involved in missions to non-Christian countries with a focus on North Africa. Protestants hope to increase their missionary force from just over 100 to 500 by AD 2000.

CHURCH AND STATE

The constitution of 1949 invokes the 'name of God', in its preamble. Article 76 declares that the Catholic religion 'is that of the State'; the latter therefore contributes to its support while guaranteeing freedom of conscience and practice to all other religions. Article 28 in its last paragraph prohibits priests from engaging in any political propaganda based on religious beliefs or motivations.

The only church marriages which have civil validity are those celebrated in the Catholic Church, to the exclusion of other churches. Priests must register marriages with the state, in addition to providing proper information concerning the civil state of the contracting parties, failure to provide which may lead to legal prosecution. The Catholic religion is taught in the public schools and the Catholic Church is exempt from property taxes. In 1973 a law was proposed in parliament extending these privileges to all churches, but it had not yet been acted upon by 1974. Concerning episcopal appointments, beginning in 1952 the state no longer presents to the apostolic nuncio a list of 3 candidates when a new archbishop is to be chosen, as had formerly been the custom in virtue of the Spanish system of patronage.

Since the expulsion of religious orders at the end of the 19th century, which was repealed in 1942, there have been no serious conflicts between church and state. In 1943 the Catholic Church played an important role in the implementation of a number of major social reforms, including promulgation of a code of employment, creation of a social security fund for medical assistance to workers, and the founding of a national university. At the political level, these endeavors have obliged the church to support publicly a coalition government consisting of reformists and communists.

The Spanish Language Institute, begun in Colombia in 1942 by United Presbyterians (USA) for training their missionary personnel, was transferred to San José in 1950 and serves all Christian groups. By 1967, 3,325 missionary students representing well over 100 different societies had studied at the institute. The average annual enrollment is 320.

The Catholic Church has no official ecumenical organizations, but there are in Costa Rica several small interconfessional movements. The various progressivist youth groups including Movimiento Iglesia Joven, Juventud Obrera Cristiana and Juventud Universitaria Cristiana, although principally composed of Catholics, also have Protestant members. Another progressivist interdenominational group Exodo, founded in 1971 in San José publishes a critical weekly paper entitled *Pueblo*, which is dedicated to the systematic conscientization of the oppressed classes. Exodo is related to ISAL in Uruguay. The Asociaciun Latinoamericana de Escuelas Teologicas (ALET), in San José, sponsors a SODEPAX program for Costa Rica, in cooperation with SODEPAX headquarters in Switzerland.

Christian Community Churches. Several new Independent believers are baptized, 1988.

BROADCASTING AND MEDIA

AWR has a studio and transmitter located in Chavita which covers most of South America with daily 2 hour programs in 7 languages. Its studio produces programs in Spanish and English. TIFC owns and operates a Christian radio station in the country as well. Shortwave radio programs can be received from KNLS, HCJB (Ecuador) and TWR (Antilles). For Catholics, Costa Rica is a member of UNDA, and there are 7 local Catholic radio stations, plus a national Catholic radio broadcast each Sunday and occasional short TV programs. 2.2 million people (59%) have seen the 'Jesus' Film: mainly through television.

CBN's *700 Club*, *Superbook* and *Flying House* can be seen daily on 5 different television channels. CBN maintains a full-time ministry center offering personal counseling services and counselor training, as well as activities for children. In addition, Christian television programs can also be seen via several satellite channels.

INTERDENOMINATIONAL ORGANIZATIONS

The Costa Rican Evangelical Alliance (Alianza Evangélica Costarricense), formed in 1951 to represent the cause of Evangelical Christians before government, has a constituency of 14 member churches. Adventists, Baptists, and Episcopalians are not members. In 1962 the Alliance initiated the Good Will Caravans to provide medical, nutritional, literacy, and agricultural assistance to areas affected by floods, and by 1968, 75 caravans had visited 37 isolated rural communities. The program is now administered separately from the Alliance with Episcopalian co-operation.

The Catholic Church has no official ecumenical organizations, but there are in Costa Rica several small interconfessional movements. The various progressivist youth groups including Movimiento Iglesia Joven, Juventud Obrera Cristiana and Juventud Universitaria Cristiana, although principally composed of Catholics, also have Protestant members. Another progressivist interdenominational group Exodo, founded in 1971 in San José, publishes a critical weekly paper entitled *Pueblo* which is dedicated to the systematic conscientization of the oppressed classes. Exodo is related to ISAL in Uruguay. The Asociación Latinoamericana de Escuelas Teologicas (ALET), in San José, sponsors a SODEPAX program for Costa Rica, in co-operation with SODEPAX headquarters in Switzerland.

FUTURE TRENDS AND PROSPECTS

Roman Catholic affiliation will probably continue to drop off steadily, down to 87.7% by 2025, but the total Christian community will only decline slowly, perhaps to 95.6% by 2025 because of church growth among Pentecostals and Evangelicals.

Due to the anticipated meteoric rise of the nonreligious in the 21st century, Christians are expected to fall below 90% of the population for the first time in nearly 500 years. By AD 2050, Christians might represent less than 85% of Costa Rica's population.

BIBLIOGRAPHY

A history of Protestantism in Costa Rica. W. M. Nelson. Lucknow, India: Lucknow Publishing House, 1963. 268p.

Bibliografía antropológica aborigen de Costa Rica. J. A. Lines, E. M. Shook & M. D. Olien. *Occasional papers*, no. 7. San José: Tropical Science Center, 1967. 196p.

'Bibliografía antropológica de Costa Rica,' M. E. B. de Wille, *Boletín bibliográfico de antroplogía Americana*, 38, 47 (1976), 63–82.

Breve historia de la Iglesia Católica en Costa Rica, 1502–1992. E. Payne, C. Vargas & C. Velazquez. [Costa Rica]: Universidad de Costa Rica, Escuela de Historia y Geografía, Centro de Investigaciones Históricos, 1992. 75p.

Costa Rica. C. L. Stansifer. *World bibliographical series*, vol. 126. Oxford, UK: CLIO Press, 1991. 318p. (See especially 'Religion,' p.87–91).

Die mennonitische Mission in Costa Rica (1960–1978). J. A. Prieto Valladares. *Perspektiven der Weltmission*, Bd. 15. Ammersbek bei Hamburg: Verlag an der Lottbek, 1992. 250p.

El Crecimiento y la deserción en la iglesia evangélica costarricense. J. I. Gómez V. San José: Publicaciones IINDEF, 1996. 153p.

El judío en Costa Rica. J. Schifter, L. Gudmundson & M. S. Castro. *Serie estudios sociopolíticos,* no. 4. San José: Editorial Universidad Estatal a Distancia, 1979. 385p.
El nacimiento y la muerte entre los bribris. M. E. B. Wille. San José: Editorial Universidad de Costa Rica, 1979. 264p.
Estado del Clero de la Provincia de Costa Rica. San Jose: Exodo, 1972.
'Explosive growth of the evangelical church in Costa Rica.' W. S. Bieske. 1989.
Historia eclesiástica de Costa Rica: del descubrimiento a la erección de la diócesis, 1502–1850. R. Blanco Segura. San José: Editorial Costa Rica, 1967. 401p.
Imagen del protestantismo en Costa Rica 1983. A. Molina Saborío. Costa Rica: Publicaciones IINDEF, 1984. 31p.
La Iglesia costarricense entre el pueblo y el estado: de 1949 a nuestros días. M. Picado. [San José]: Guayacán, [1989]. 323p.
La Iglesia de Costa Rica en la historia: desafíos y respuestas: 50 años de la educación religiosa en Costa Rica. Colección D.E.R. [Costa Rica]: Departamento de Educacación Religiosa, 1991. 100p.
Las sectas en Costa Rica: pentecostalismo y conflicto social. J. Valverde. *Colección Sociología de la religión.* San José: Editorial Departamento Ecuménico de Investigaciones, 1990. 95p.
Los 500 años de la Iglesia Catolica de Costa Rica: calendario histórico fundamental. G. A. Soto Valverde. San José: Ediciones CECOR, 1992. 227p.
Obispos, arzobispos y representantes de la santa sede en Costa Rica. R. B. Segura. San José: Editorial Universidad Estatal a Distancia, 1984. 153p.
'Protestant—Catholic relations in Costa Rica,' R. L. Millett, *Journal of Church and State,* 12, 1 (1970), 41–57.
Religión y magia entre los indios de Costa Rica de origen sureño. C. H. A. Piedra. *Publicaciones de la Universidad de Costa Rica, Serie historia y geografía,* no. 6. San José: Universidad de Costa Rica, 1965. 83p.
Reminiscencias de la evangelización en Costa Rica. R. Cruz Aceituno. San José, Costa Rica: Publicaciones IINDEF, 1984. 191p.
Reseña histórica de la iglesia en Costa Rica desde 1502 hasta 1850. V. S. Martínez. San José: Departamento Ecuménico de Investigaciones, 1984. 290p.
Reseña historica de la Iglesia Metodista de Costa Rica 50 aniversario, 1917–1967. , [1967]. 39p.
The Catholic Church and politics in Nicaragua and Costa Rica. P. J. Williams. *Pitt Latin American series.* Pittsburgh: University of Pittsburgh Press, 1989. 244p.

Country Table 2. **Organized churches and denominations in Costa Rica.**

Official name (bold type = church with over 10% of all affiliated) 1	*Begun* 2	*Type* 3	*Counc* 4	*Congs* 5	*Adults* 6	*Affiliated 1970* 7	*Affiliated 1995* 8	*G%* 9	*Names, notes, and other statistics* (see Codebook, Part 3) 10
Arbol de la Vida	c1900	I-3gL	.....	10	500	–	2,000	0.05	*Tree of Life.* Independents, Protestants, Roman Catholics worship together.
Asambleas de Dios	1930	P-Pe2	ZF..C	860	98,631	7,500	120,000	11.73	*Conferencia Ev de la AdD.* M=AoG(USA). 74n,3x,14f,2s(72),W=33%,345Y,1245z.
Asambleas Locales	c1990	I-3nC	.....	4	180	–	500	20.00	*Local Churches. Little Flock.* Begun 1922 in China.
Asociación Asambleas Elim	1966	P-Pe2	.....	9	270	143	643	6.20	M=Elim Assembles (USA).
Asociacion Bautista Misionera Hebron	1980	P-Bap	.....	18	1,200	–	2,610	6.67	M=Hebron Baptist Mission (USA).
Asoc Concilio Iglesias Ev Nacionales	c1960	I-Eva	.....	63	8,000	1,190	11,000	9.30	*National Ev Ch.* Local Costa Rican indigenous body.
Asoc Convención Bautista de Costa Rica	1887	P-Bap	T....	32	1,903	2,419	3,590	1.59	1887, M=JBMS(Jamaica); 1949, SBC(USA). 10% Jamaicans. 26n,8x,16f,1s(6),222Y.
Asoc Cristiana La Nueva Jerusalém		I-3gL	.....	7	1,540	440	3,080	0.05	*Christian Association of the New Jerusalem.*
Asociacion Cristiana Roca del Pedernel		I-3gL	.....	39	2,365	1,580	5,260	0.05	*Christian Association Rock.*
Asoc de Igls Bíblicas Costarricenses	1921	P-Non	xN..C	112	7,200	3,000	12,000	5.70	*Association of CR Bible Chs.* M=LAM(USA). Rural. Radio station. 7n,88f,1H,1j,1k,1s.
Asociación de Iglesias Cristianas		I-Non	.....	24	1,750	2,730	3,980	0.05	*Association of Christian Churches.*
Asociacion de Igls Ev Centroamericanas	1891	P-Eva	xM...	70	3,391	2,000	9,690	6.52	*Assoc of Central American Chs.* M=CAM(USA). 1937, major schism. A=1948. 9n,18m,16f.
Asoc de Igs Pentecostales Bautistas		I-3pL	.....	11	997	222	2,220	0.05	*Association of Pentecostal Baptist Churches.*
Asoc Iglesia Ap de Fe en Cristo Jesus		I-3oL	.....	39	1,200	500	3,080	0.05	M=Apos Ch of Faith in Christ Jesus (USA).
Asoc Igl Congregacional Pentecostes	1966	I-3pL	.....	28	1,639	500	4,100	8.78	M=Congregational Holiness Ch (USA).
Asociación Iglesia de Cristo	1967	I-Dis	x...C	20	1,000	500	2,500	6.65	*Chs of Christ.* M=CC(Non-Instrumental) (USA). San José, Limón, Buffalo, et al. 1p.
Asoc Igls Alianza Cristiana y Misioners	1976	P-Hol	.....	8	463	–	1,010	5.26	M=Christian & Missionary Alliance(USA).
Asociacion Iglesias 'Casa de Banqueté'	c1980	I-3gL	.....	11	1,500	–	3,260	6.67	*Association of House of Feasting Churches.*
Asoc Ig Biblica Bautista Fund de CR	1968	I-Bap	x....	19	5,180	574	10,400	12.29	M=BBFI(USA).
Asociacion Ig Manantias de Vida		I-3cL	.....	7	810	–	1,800	0.05	*Springs of Life Association of Churches.*
Asoc Misiones Transmundiales de CR	1968	P-Non	.....	16	1,970	456	3,640	8.66	M=Trans World Miss (USA).
Communidad Mis Cris Puerto de Fe	c1975	I-3gL	.....	10	870	–	1,740	5.00	*Door of Faith Christian Community.*
Compañerismo Bautista Mundial	1963	I-Bap	xT...	16	2,050	100	4,100	16.01	M=World Baptist Fellowship Mission Agency (USA). Fundamentalists.
Consejo de Igls Luteranas en CA & P	1962	P-Lut	x...C	2	35	52	70	1.20	*Sinodo de Misuri. Lutheran Ch.* M=LC Missouri Synod (USA). HQ San Jos. 1n,1x,5Yy.
Convencion Menonite de CR	1962	P-Men	G...C	17	1,050	200	1,415	8.14	*Ev Mennonite Ch.* M=Conservative Mennonite BMC (USA). Some Amish from USA. 3x,22f.
Costa Rica para Cristo	c1975	I-3gL	.....	17	1,360	–	3,020	5.00	Assisted by M=OBPC(Brazil).
Ejército de Salvación	1907	P-Sal	xwM..	8	190	300	576	2.64	*Salvation Army.* In Caribbean & CA Territory. After 1969 eruption, Mercy Caravan. 2f.
Hermanos Libres	c1968	P-CBr	.....	6	300	222	667	4.50	*Open Brethren.*
Ig Cristiana Pentecostal de CR		I-3pL	.....	39	1,029	1,190	2,450	0.05	*Movimiento Mission Mundial.* M=MMM(Puerto Rico).
Iglesia Adventista del Séptimo Día	1903	P-Adv	x....	63	12,746	5,000	29,000	7.28	*Seventh-day Adventists, CR Mission,* CAmerican UM. Declining. 2nx,2f,1r,35t,194Y.
Iglesia Bautista Immanuel		I-Bap	.....	1	500	727	909	0.05	*Immanuel Baptist Church.*
Iglesia Biblica Bautista Independiente	c1950	I-Bap	.....	6	1,200	50	3,000	17.79	*National Baptist Ch.* Small local indigenous Costa Rican body.
Iglesia Católica en Costa Rica:	1514	R-Lat	B.LDR	855	1,721,100	1,688,471	3,248,792	2.65	*Catholic Ch in CR.* C=8+5+23. (1970) 225n,1p,1q,1s. 404n 175x 321m 872w 78452Yy
M San José de Costa Rica	1850	R-Lat	Bs	173	951,100	767,898	1,794,600	3.45	Urban, suburban, industrial. Spaniards. 211n 114x 234m 623w 48200Yy
D Alajuela	1921	R-Lat	Bs	48	265,000	317,464	500,000	1.83	Rural. Descendants of original Spanish settlers. 81n 38x 46m 90w 12066Yy
D Limón	1921	R-Lat	Pcm	17	138,000	111,109	261,025	3.48	Rural. Bananas. Slave descendants. Jamaica Blacks. 22n 13x 13m 54w 4775Yy
D San Isidro de El General	1954	R-Lat	Bs	586	193,000	180,000	363,717	2.85	Rural. Large banana plantation with expatriate labor. 32n 8x 26m 37w 6473Yy
D Tilarán	1961	R-Lat	Bs	31	174,000	312,000	329,450	0.22	Rural. Mestizos. Vast latifundia (landlordist) estates. 58n 2x 2m 68w 6938Yy
Iglesia de Dios de CR (Anderson)	1935	P-Hol	x...C	8	198	400	566	1.40	M=CoG(Anderson) (USA). San Jos, Siquirres, Limon, Cimarrones. 2x,4f,W=95%.
Iglesia de Dios de CR (Cleveland)	1935	P-Pe3	ZF..C	441	16,087	3,300	28,700	9.04	M=CoG(Cleveland) (USA). 10% English-speaking Blacks. Several splits. 40n,2f,1p.
Iglesia de Dios de la Profecía	1932	P-Pe3	Z....	12	557	500	1,390	4.17	*Ch of God of Prophecy.* M=CGP(USA). Split ex CoG(Cleveland) in USA. HQ San José.
Iglesia de Dios Pentecostal de CR		P-Pe3	.....	55	2,220	1,580	5,840	0.05	M=PCG(USA).
Iglesia de Dios (Universal)	c1962	I-3pL	.....	3	100	80	200	3.73	*Ch of God (Universal).* Schism ex CoG(Cleveland) (USA). 1n.
Iglesia de JC de los Santos de los UD	c1953	m-LdS	x....	51	8,840	2,524	13,000	6.78	*Latter-day Saints. Mormons.* M=CJCLdS(USA). HQ San José. 40f.
Iglesia del Evangelio Cuadrangular	1953	P-Pe2	ZF..C	84	3,750	8,000	12,100	1.67	*International Ch of the Foursquare Gospel.* M=ICFG(USA). 53nm,3f,1s(15),W=63%,212y.
Iglesia del Nazareno	1948	P-Hol	xF..C	32	4,700	300	7,150	13.52	*Ch of the Nazarene.* M=CoN(USA). 1n,15m,5f,1s(32),7t(242),W=71%,12Y,16z.
Iglesia Episcopal: D Costa Rica	1896	A-Hig	aw.R.	18	561	1,864	1,600	-0.61	*Ch of Prov of Central Am Region.* 90% Blacks in banana trade. 9n,2x,1s,11Y,91y.
Iglesia Ev Luterana de Costa Rica	c1946	P-Lut	L....	1	402	750	600	-0.89	*Ev Luth Ch in CR, El Sal, Hond, Nic, Panama.* Germans, Scandinavians. 1x,W=5%,7y,65z.
Iglesia Ev Metodista de Costa Rica	1917	P-Met	Vu..C	48	1,569	2,500	4,000	1.90	*CR Annual Conference, United Methodist Ch* (USA). 1 school (1120). 23n,17f,1k,1s,25t.
Iglesia La Luz del Mundo (Aaronistas)	c1960	I-3oL	x....	24	1,200	100	2,400	13.56	*Light of the World Ch,* from Guadalajara (Mexico). Unitarian pentecostals.
Iglesia Metodista Britanica de las Amer	1894	P-Met	VwV.C	4	372	1,500	791	-2.53	In *MCCA* (HQ Antigua). M=MMS(UK). Declining. Coast Blacks. 1n,3f,11Yy.
Iglesia Pentecostal Unida	1975	P-Pe1	.....	16	1,322	–	2,940	5.00	M=UPC(USA).
Iglesias de Santidad Pentecostal	1930	P-Pe3	ZF...	70	7,000	1,000	16,700	11.92	*International Pentecostal Holiness Ch.* M=IPHC(USA). HQ San José. 3n,1x,7f,1s.
Iglesia Union de San José		P-com	C	1	80	1,000	250	0.05	*Union Ch of San José.* English-speaking, mainly expatriates. 1x.
Mision Bautista de Jamaica y CA		I-Bap	.....	6	520	405	1,240	0.05	M=CBHMS(USA).
Mision Cristiana Mundial Rosa de Saron		I-3gL	.....	25	4,000	1,000	8,000	0.05	*Rose of Sharon World Christian Mission.*
Testigos de Jehová	c1915	m-Jeh	x....	228	14,018	7,000	35,900	6.76	*Jehovah's Witnesses, Watch Tower. IBSA.* Witnessing since 1920s. (1975) 190Y. (1995) 1878Y.
Union Nacional Igs Bautistas de CR	1940	P-Bap	T...C	14	923	300	2,560	8.95	*Costa Rican Baptist Association.* M=American Baptist Association (USA). HQ San Jos.
Other Black indigenous churches		I-	.....	50	5,000	5,000	8,330	0.05	Total about 10, including NBCUSA(1961; USA Blacks).
Other independent charismatic chs	c1985	I-3gL	.....	50	5,000	–	10,000	10.00	GR churches, Rose of Sharon Mission, New Apostolic Ch (245 members), Vineyard (3 chs).
Other marginal Protestant bodies		m-	.....	80	8,000	5,000	16,000	0.05	Several fringe cults, including Christian Spiritists. Total about 8.
Other Protestant denominations		P-	.....	155	7,770	9,000	18,500	0.05	Total about 34.
Doubly-affiliated		2-aff			-149,000	-79,409	-278,859		Evangelicals who also are or were baptized Roman Catholics.
Totals				**3,913**	**1,828,808**	**1,693,760**	**3,420,000**		

Churches, members, growth, 1900-2025	*Congs*	*Adults*	*Affiliated*	*G%*	*Total denominations*	*6 Megablocs:* *O*	*R*	*A*	*P*	*I*	*m*
Total churches, members, and denominations (mid-1900)	300	168,000	317,800	2.42	5	0	1	1	3	0	0
Total churches, members, and denominations (mid-1970)	862	893,408	1,693,760	2.42	67	0	1	1	38	21	6
Total churches, members, and denominations (mid-1990)	3,000	1,569,000	2,933,650	2.78	116	0	1	1	59	45	10
Total churches, members, and denominations (mid-1995)	3,913	1,828,808	3,420,000	3.12	119	0	1	1	60	47	10
Total churches, members, and denominations (mid-2000)	4,500	2,069,000	3,870,161	2.50	122	0	1	1	61	48	11
Total churches, members, and denominations (mid-2025)	6,000	3,030,000	5,667,500	1.54	197	0	1	1	80	100	15

NOTES ON TABLE ABOVE

NATIONAL COUNCILS (Column 4, 5th letter).

E = Alianza Evangélica Costarricense (AEC) (Costa Rican Evangelical Alliance).

R = Conferencia Episcopal de Costa Rica (CECOR) (Episcopal Conference of Costa Rica).

Other national councils. There is also an Alianza Evangélica de Costa Rica, whose constitution forbids it to enter into foreign correspondence.

OTHER PROTESTANT DENOMINATIONS. These smaller bodies, mostly denominations from the USA, include: Baptist Bible Fellowship International (1968). Baptist International Missions (1968), Baptist Missionary Association of America (1961), Bethel Temple World Missionary Assistance Plan, Children of God International (in Guadalupe), Christadelphian Ecclesias, Christian Brethren (Open), Congregational Holiness Ch (1967), Conservative Baptist Home Mission Society (1955; 2 churches), Elim Missionary Assemblies (1964), Ev Lutheran Synod (1972), Pentecostal Ch of God, Religious Society of Friends (1946 immigrant community from USA), World-Wide Missions (1965). There are also a few independent congregations.

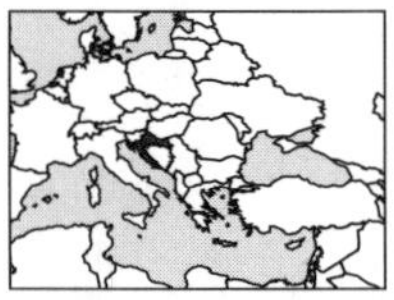

CROATIA

SECULAR DATA, AD 2000

STATE
Official name: Republika Hrvatska (The Republic of Croatia).
Short name: Croatia. **Adjective of nationality:** Croatian.
Flag: Red, white, and blue stripes with red and white checkered shield.
Area: 56,538 sq. km. (21,829 sq. mi.).
Government: Multiparty republic with a two-chambered legislature, since 1990 (1918 Kingdom of Serbs, Croats, and Slovenes, 1929 Yugoslavia).
Legislature: House of Zupanije, 68 members; House of Representatives, 127 members.
Official language: Croatian.
Monetary unit: 1 kuna (plural Kune) = 100 lipa. **US$1=** 6.13 kune.
Chief cities: ZAGREB 1,060,000; Rijeka 196,419; Split 188,329; Osijek 160,156; Cakovec 121,927.
Political divisions: 21 provinces.
Armed forces: 60,000.

DEMOGRAPHY
Population: 4,473,000.
Population density: 79.1/sq. km. (204.8/sq. mi.).
Under 15 years: 763,000.
Growth rate p.a.: -0.14% (births 10.41, deaths 11.84).
Mortality: Infant, per 1,000: 9.7; **Maternal per 100,000:** 35.0.
Life expectancy: 74 (male 70, female 77).
Household size: 3.1. **Floor area per person, sq.m:** 22.1.
Major languages: Serbo-Croatian, Istriot, Romani.
Urban dwellers: 57.72%. **Urban growth rate p.a.:** 0.6%.
Labor force: 45%.

ETHNOLINGUISTIC PEOPLES
82.0% Croat; 5.9% Serb; 3.3% Istro-Romanian (Istriot); 2.0% Vlach Gypsy (Gurbeti); 1.5% German.

ECONOMY
National income p.a. per person: US$3,250; **per family:** US$10,075.

EDUCATION
Adult literacy: 96% (male 98%, female 94%). **Schools:** 2,413.
Universities: 54. **School enrolment:** female/male: 84%/83%.

HEALTH
Access to health services: 75%. **Access to safe water:** 96%.
Hospitals: 98 (61 beds per 10,000). **Doctors:** 9,280.
Blind: 3,700. **Deaf:** 269,100. **Murder rate:** 7.
Lepers: 500.

LITERATURE
New book titles p.a.: 2,680 (600 p.a. per million). **Periodicals:** 493.
Newspapers: 6 dailies.

COMMUNICATION (per 1,000 people)
Phones: 269 (10% mobile). **Radios:** 230. **TV sets:** 230.
Daily newspaper circulation: 575. **Computers:** 70.

REFUGEES
Citizen refugees in other countries: 200,000.
Alien refugees from other countries: 189,500.
Internal displacement: 240,000.

HUMAN LIFE AND LIBERTY (optimum condition=100.0%)
HDI: 76.0. **HSI:** 40.0. **HFI:** 30.0. **EFL:** 26.0.

Country Table 1. **Religious adherents in Croatia, AD 1900-2025.**

Year	1900		1970		mid-1990		Annual change, 1990-2000				mid-1995		mid-2000		mid-2025	
Name	Adherents	%	Adherents	%	Adherents	%	Natural	Conversion	Total	Rate	Adherents	%	Adherents	%	Adherents	%
Christians	**2,700,000**	**96.3**	**3,960,000**	**95.0**	**4,245,000**	**94.0**	**-4,176**	**5,556**	**1,380**	**0.03**	**4,208,000**	**93.7**	**4,258,803**	**95.2**	**4,031,000**	**96.1**
PROFESSION																
crypto-Christians	0	0.0	450,000	10.8	0	0.0	0	0	0	0.00	0	0.0	0	0.0	0	0.0
professing Christians	**2,700,000**	**96.3**	**3,510,000**	**84.2**	**4,245,000**	**94.0**	**-4,176**	**5,556**	**1,380**	**0.03**	**4,208,000**	**93.7**	**4,258,803**	**95.2**	**4,031,000**	**96.1**
AFFILIATION																
unaffiliated Christians	135,000	4.8	7,928	0.2	5,000	0.1	-5	-253	-258	-7.01	21,774	0.5	2,417	0.1	3,000	0.1
affiliated Christians	**2,565,000**	**91.5**	**3,952,072**	**94.8**	**4,240,000**	**93.9**	**-4,171**	**5,810**	**1,639**	**0.04**	**4,186,226**	**93.2**	**4,256,386**	**95.2**	**4,028,000**	**96.1**
Roman Catholics	2,292,000	81.7	3,542,808	85.0	3,850,000	85.2	-3,750	14,750	11,000	0.28	3,872,179	86.2	3,960,000	88.5	3,775,000	90.0
Orthodox	270,000	9.6	370,000	8.9	347,200	7.7	-338	-9,382	-9,720	-3.23	270,000	6.0	250,000	5.6	200,000	4.8
Protestants	3,000	0.1	25,904	0.6	25,800	0.6	-25	45	20	0.08	25,897	0.6	26,000	0.6	26,000	0.6
Independents	0	0.0	10,160	0.2	11,000	0.2	-11	50	39	0.35	11,070	0.3	11,386	0.3	13,000	0.3
Marginal Christians	0	0.0	3,200	0.1	6,000	0.1	-6	306	300	4.14	7,080	0.2	9,000	0.2	14,000	0.3
Trans-megabloc groupings																
Evangelicals	2,000	0.1	4,200	0.1	5,900	0.1	-6	86	80	1.28	6,289	0.1	6,700	0.2	10,000	0.2
Pentecostals/Charismatics	0	0.0	3,500	0.1	117,000	2.6	-114	1,196	1,082	0.89	125,166	2.8	127,820	2.9	161,000	3.8
Great Commission Christians	**112,000**	**4.0**	**250,000**	**6.0**	**252,900**	**5.6**	**-246**	**-1,727**	**-1,973**	**-0.81**	**247,000**	**5.5**	**233,171**	**5.2**	**252,000**	**6.0**
Muslims	0	0.0	70,000	1.7	130,000	2.9	-127	-2,614	-2,741	-2.34	160,000	3.6	102,591	2.3	70,000	1.7
Nonreligious	100,000	3.6	75,000	1.8	100,000	2.2	-97	-1,852	-1,949	-2.14	90,000	2.0	80,511	1.8	75,000	1.8
Atheists	0	0.0	64,000	1.5	40,000	0.9	-39	-1,093	-1,132	-3.27	33,000	0.7	28,683	0.6	15,000	0.4
Jews	4,000	0.1	0	0.0	2,000	0.0	-2	3	1	0.06	2,000	0.0	2,013	0.1	2,000	0.1
World A (unevangelized persons)	28,040	1.0	125,076	3.0	90,340	2.0	-88	-5,545	-5,633	-9.31	58,407	1.3	35,784	0.8	29,351	0.7
World B (evangelized non-Christians)	75,960	2.7	84,143	2.0	181,660	4.0	-177	-11	-188	-0.18	226,498	5.0	178,413	4.0	132,649	3.2
World C (Christians)	2,700,000	96.3	3,960,000	95.0	4,245,000	94.0	-4,176	5,556	1,380	0.03	4,208,000	93.7	4,258,803	95.2	4,031,000	96.1
Country's population	**2,804,000**	**100.0**	**4,169,220**	**100.0**	**4,517,000**	**100.0**	**-4,441**	**0**	**-4,441**	**-0.10**	**4,492,906**	**100.0**	**4,473,000**	**100.0**	**4,193,000**	**100.0**

COLUMNS, ROWS.
For meanings and definitions, see Codebook (Part 3). Note that, by definition, total 'Christians' = professing + crypto-Christians, which also = affiliated + unaffiliated Christians, and also = Great Commission Christians + latent Christians. Percentages may not always total exactly, due to rounding.

NOTES ON RELIGIONS
BAHA'IS. Organized into 5 local spiritual assemblies (1996).
MUSLIMS. Mainly Bosnian Muslims, also Rumelian Turks & Gypsies.
PENTECOSTALS/CHARISMATICS. The Catholic Charismatic Renewal has grown slowly, to some 103,000 by 1990, with 10 prayer groups in the capital, Zagreb (one with 400 members). A rally in Split drew 4,000 attenders.

Great Commission Instrument Panel: status of Croatia (for explanation see start of Part 4)

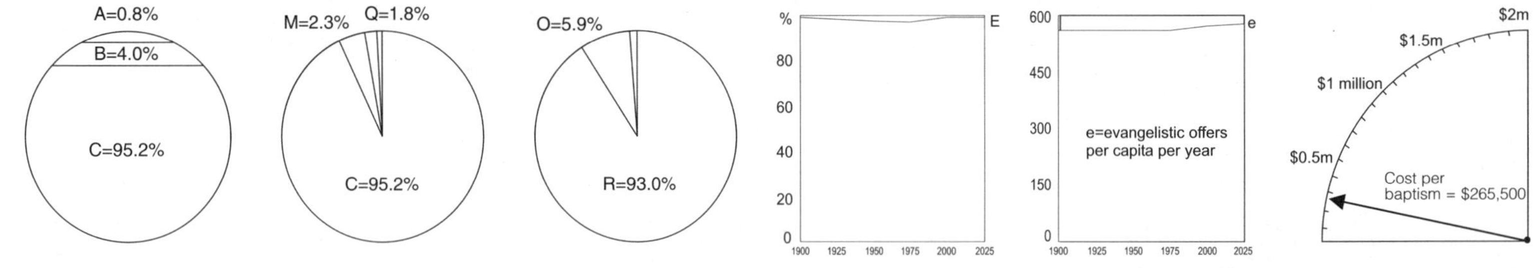

3 Worlds, AD 2000 — Religions, AD 2000 — Ecclesiastical blocs — Evangelization, 1900-2025 — Offers, 1900-2025 — Cost-effectiveness, AD 2000

Country status. Croatia is a crescent-shaped Balkan country comprising the Dalmatian coast of the Adriatic Sea, Istria, and Croatia-Slavonia. The independence of 1991 brought victory to a long-frustrated national ambition. Croatians have perceived themselves as cultured West Europeans bound to the backward Balkans. The country's main products are oil, grain, livestock, and timber.

HUMAN LIFE AND LIBERTY

Human rights and freedoms. Croatia declared its independence from the former Socialist Federal Republic of Yugoslavia in 1991. Following independence, the new republic lost about one-fourth of its national territory to Serb forces of the so-called Republic of Serbian Krajina (RSK). This forms the background to widespread human rights violations by both Croatians and Serbs. On the Croatian side, physical violence against Serbs has continued to escalate in retaliation against Serbian victories in the field. These abuses include illegal detention, murder, harassment, destruction of property, rape, summary eviction from homes, disappearances and beatings. Serbs are denied legal rights to a free trial and generally expelled from Croatian national territory. The government controls all television stations, all national radio stations save one, and 2 out of 4 national dailies. Editors of the few independent journals are subject to physical violence and constant harassment by the government. The International Federation of Journalists has requested delay in Croatia's admission to the Council of Europe because of the lack of press freedom. The Croatian Helsinki Committee has issued a document criticizing state policy on media freedom. It cites government efforts to discourage the development of an independent press as well as favoritism toward state publications. Despite the religious orientation of the ethnic conflict, Croats permit Orthodox, Protestant, Muslim, and Jewish communities to maintain their places of worship and receive the services of their clergy. Although the majority of the Orthodox clergy left at the start of the war, Orthodox churches (including the main cathedral in Zagreb) continue to operate. However, the Orthodox church in Osijek was blown up by unknown persons, and similar incidents continue to occur in disputed areas. Bosnian Muslim refugees are systematically deported, but, nevertheless, some 200,000 Muslims are reported to be in the country as refugees. Peace groups in Zagreb, Rijeka, and Osijek are active in monitoring human rights abuses, but their efforts to correct these abuses are not always successful.

Country summary. **Worlds A, B, C by ethnolinguistic peoples, cities, and major civil divisions in Croatia.**																						
	PEOPLES							***CITIES***							***CIVIL DIVISIONS***							
World	*Num*	*Pop 2000*	*C%*	*Christians*	*E%*	*U%*	*Unevangelized*	*Num*	*Pop 2000*	*C%*	*Christians*	*E%*	*U%*	*Unevangelized*	*Num*	*Pop 2000*	*C%*	*Christians*	*E%*	*U%*	*Unevangelized*
A	2	4,472	0.09	4	46	54	2,410	0	0	0.00	0	0	0	0	0	0	0.00	0	0	0	0
B	6	92,136	17.30	15,935	67	33	30,060	0	0	0.00	0	0	0	0	0	0	0.00	0	0	0	0
C	23	4,375,993	96.90	4,240,446	100	0	1,500	7	1,958,983	92.30	1,808,152	99	1	25,304	21	4,472,600	95.17	4,256,386	99	1	33,972
Total	**31**	**4,472,601**	**95.17**	**4,256,385**	**99**	**1**	**33,970**	**7**	**1,958,983**	**92.30**	**1,808,152**	**99**	**1**	**25,304**	**21**	**4,472,600**	**95.17**	**4,256,386**	**99**	**1**	**33,972**

NON-CHRISTIAN RELIGIONS

Islam was introduced to the area by the Ottomans in the 14th century. Most of the Muslims in Croatia in the mid-1990s were among the 250,000 refugees from the war in neighboring Bosnia-Herzegovina, and were treated as unwelcome. Croatia in the mid-1990s was caring for more refugees per capita than any nation in the world. In 1995 the country was 4.3% Muslim.

Judaism was never as great a presence in Croatia as in other nearby countries, but the Jews that did live in Croatia suffered severely in the Nazi era. A community that numbered 4,000 in 1900 was completely eradicated through emigration, deportation, and the Holocaust. By the early 1990s Judaism had recovered to some degree, with a population of more than 2,000.

Atheism and ***non-religion.*** Under Yugoslavia's distinct brand of Communism relatively few dropped their religious faith, in great contrast to, for example, Russia. Even a large number of Communist party members were allowed to remain Christian or Muslim. A 1960 survey of youth showed the Croats retained the highest percentage of Christian believers among all Yugoslavian nationalities. Still, government-backed programs of modernization, urbanization, industrialization, and anti-religious propaganda resulted in a rise in the number of nonreligious that peaked in the late 1970s, before resurgent nationalism and the end of Yugoslavian Communist rule opened the way for a revival of religion. Many nonreligious and atheist then converted back to the Catholic faith of their ancestors. In the 25 years between 1970 and 1995, the number of atheists in Croatia dropped 50%, from 64,000 to about 33,000, and the number of nonreligious leveled off at about 80,000. Most of that decline came in the late 1980s and early 1990s.

Independents. Two Croatian missionaries from Network of Christian Ministries, serving in Bosnia.

CHRISTIANITY

The first Christians arrived in Dalmatia and Illyricum near the end of the Apostle Paul's ministry, likely converted Jews of the Diaspora. By the middle of the 4th century, organized Christianity came to the area both from Rome and the east. The ancient territorial division between lands controlled by Rome and those controlled by Byzantium cut close to the eastern border of present-day Croatia, setting Croatia's allegiance with Rome and Serbia's with Byzantium. This division is reflected in the dominance of Roman Catholicism in Croatia and the dominance of the Serbian Orthodox Church across the border.

CATHOLIC CHURCH. Though Croatia was under Byzantine rule in the 8th century, that rule was loose enough that Latin culture and influence were strengthened in the coastal cities. The Franks sent missionaries who baptized many in the Latin rite. In 1091 Croatia, then an independent kingdom since 925, united its crown with that of Hungary. This Catholic union lasted, for the most part, until 1918. King László I founded the bishopric of Zagreb which became an important ecclesiastical center, and Hungarian Catholic culture permeated Croatia. With the Counterreformation of the 17th century, Jesuits founded schools and produced books that had wide influence not only in religion but in the language and literature of the nation.

In the Nazi era Croatia was essentially run by the terrorist Ustase, who were Roman Catholic and viciously anti-Serb and anti-Semitic. Their campaign of ethnic 'purification' involved killing hundreds of thousands of Serbs, Jews, Gypsies, and dissidents. Many clergy apparently sympathized with this violent regime. In the post-war Yugoslavian era and in the following civil wars, this dark chapter of history has been evoked repeatedly to mar the reputation of Catholicism and Croatian nationalism. On the other hand, Alcjzije Stepinac, archbishop of Zagreb, is remembered by the church for heroic efforts to protect Serbs and Gypsies from slaughter, and for courageous opposition to later Communist oppression.

Croatian clerics participated in Vatican II, some prominently, and that event has split the Catholic community into progressivist and conservative wings. In the early 1980s many students took pilgrimages to Rome. Authorities were unhappy and applied threats to discourage the trend. Among religious, the Franciscans are the largest order in the country (as in all former Yugoslavian republics), with nearly 10 times as many members as the next largest order, the Salesians. Pope John II's visit in 1994 to Zabreb was the culmination of 20 years' effort by the Vatican to obtain permission for such a visit. Croatia was nearly 86% Roman Catholic in 1900. That dominant position dropped to only about 57% in 1970, but then recovered in the post-independence revival to 77.3%

The Holy See has diplomatic relations with Croatia and in AD 2000 is represented to government and the Catholic hierarchy by a nuncio residing in Zagreb.

Serbian Orthodox Church. Priest (*left*) in Zagreb still shares love of Christ with Croats.

ORTHODOX CHURCH. The Orthodox in Croatia have always been almost entirely ethnic Serbs. The Croatian state ruled by the Ustase during World War II was, at the start, about 50% Serbian Orthodox. The terrorist regime made it their stated policy to obliterate this presence through conversion, deportation, or execution. All Orthodox schools were closed, the Cyrillic alphabet was banned, and all Serbs had to wear colored armbands. Many Serbian Orthodox submitted to forced conversion administered by ultra-nationalist Catholic priests. In 1990, as Croatia was moving toward independence, Serbs felt extremely vulnerable and the hierarchy of the Serbian Orthodox Church in Croatia issued a statement urging their faithful 'to secure for themselves the right to life on their age-old hearths in Croatia by [setting up] armed sentinels [and] barricades'. The war that soon followed left a portion of Croatia under Serbian control (the 'Republic of Serb Krajina'). Serbian forces dynamited 115 Catholic churches to support their claim that only Serbs had ever lived in the area. Through the course of centuries, Catholic-Orthodox/Croat-Serb conflict has obscured and marred the essential Christian message shared by both faiths. Croatia, including the Serb-controlled territory, was 6.0% Orthodox in 1995.

PROTESTANT CHURCHES. Many Croatian and Dalmatian nobles became Protestant in the 16th century and the first Croatian Bible was published in 1562. The Counterreformation came to the country at the start of the 17th century, the most powerful Protestant rulers reverted to Catholicism, and the Sabor (the national legislature) voted in 1609 to allow only the Catholic faith. Protestants were persecuted and their numbers declined to a small minority, as they remain today. In the late 1800s, representatives from the British and Foreign Bible Society distributed Bibles in Croatia. Colporteurs and returning Croats who had lived in the USA or Russia were instrumental in the founding of Baptist and other Protestant churches. Early church-planting efforts often met with Catholic-backed resistance and police interference. Two of the largest Protestant denominations in the country are Lutheran, dating from 1680 and 1750, respectively—the Slovak Evangelical Christian Church and the Evangelical Christian Church and the Evangelical Church of Croatia (Lutheran). The Seventh-day Adventists, who began work in Croatia in 1909, are the second-largest Protestant group in the country with nearly 5,000 affiliated in 1995. Evangelicals and other Protestants have played a significant role in compassionate service to Croatia's many refugees and internally-displaced persons from the civil wars of the 1990s. The Evangelical Theological Seminary in Osijek is a prominent institution, training 80% of the Evangelical Christian workers serving in the former Yugoslavia. In the mid-1990s, after recovering from damage and temporary exile during the civil war, it was the largest residential Evangelical seminary in Eastern Europe. It has served as an important contact point for the many Evangelical and Pentecostal missions that have entered the country since the fall of Communism. Protestants remain a tiny minority, only 0.6% of Croatia's Christians, dwarfed by Roman Catholics.

OTHER CHURCHES. From reaction to the doctrine of papal infallibility in 1870 and from a Roman Catholic reform movement that began in 1919, an Old Catholic Church began in 1923, and then split, resulting in two denominations that together had nearly 8,000 affiliated in 1995. The Croatian Old Catholic Church joined the Utrecht Union of Old Catholic Churches. Jehovah's Witnesses are the fourth largest denomination in the country with about 7,000 affiliated in 1995.

Renewal movements. In the 1990s the Pentecostal/Charismatic Renewal continued to spread rapidly across most older churches, and numbered over 128,000 adherents (of whom 2% Pentecostals, 94% Charismatics, and 4% Independents).

Indigenous missions. The missionary movement from Croatia has been strong, even during the Communist era. Over 120 Catholics served in 40 countries in 1974. This number has remained steady even with the breakup of Yugoslavia.

CHURCH AND STATE

In 1945 a bloody era of persecution began that lasted into the early 1950s. This arose partly as a reaction against the partnership between the Ustase and some Roman Catholic leaders, and partly as an exercise of the establishment of Communist control. Church lands were confiscated. Many clergy were imprisoned, tortured, and executed. As part of the propaganda campaign, Communist media attacked church and clergy, even claiming the Vatican had wanted Nazi victory. Catholic leaders complained that children in school were taught to sing, 'We will fight against God! There is no God!' Religious repression eased when Josip Broz Tito broke with the Soviet Union in 1948 and sought help from the West. When Archbishop Stepinac was released from 5 years of imprisonment in 1952, Rome elevated him to cardinal. In reaction, Marshall Tito severed relations with the Vatican. The protocol signed in 1966 between Belgrade and Rome re-established relations, gave the Church jurisdiction over spiritual and ecclesiastical matters, but also restricted the clergy from political activity. In the early 1970s relations between the state and Croatian Catholics were difficult, due to Croatian nationalism and the Church's continuing loyalty to an outside power, Rome. Expanding church power and influence were quelled by a heavy-handed crackdown in Croatia in 1971. Into the 1980s many openly-practicing Christians were limited to low-paying, low-status work.

The 1974 constitution of Yugoslavia suspended the Religious Law of 1953 and required each republic to set their own policies concerning religion. Croatia was the last to do so, passing its law in 1978 after vigorous debate. Some earlier restrictions were removed, and in other matters compromises were struck, notably concerning the religious instruction of children. Catholic clergy succeeded in 1990 in their quest for the re-establishment of mandatory religious instruction in public schools. This measure passed, over the objections of non-Catholic parents, partly because Roman Catholicism was again becoming recognized as an important symbol of Croatian national identity. Serbs complained that, in their view, the purpose of this instruction was to convert Orthodox children to Catholicism. The party that came to power with Franjo Tudjman in the election of 1990 played to Croatian religion and nationalism with the prominent slogan, 'God is in the Heavens and Tudjman in the Homelands'. Under Tudjman's regime the Catholic Church was allowed not only freedom but a prominent role in the political and social life of the nation.

BROADCASTING AND MEDIA

Shortwave radio programs from HCJB (Ecuador), AWR (Slovakia), TWR (Monaco, Albania) and the Vatican all blanket Croatia with European-language programming. IBRA-produced programs can be heard on local stations in 17 cities. Croatia is a member of UNDA.

In 1990, Roman Catholic and Orthodox Easter services were broadcast on TV for the first time, a significant sign of a new day in the religious life of Yugoslavia. The 'Jesus' Film has been shown to 163,000: about half through film teams and the rest through videocassette copies. Satellite TV and radio programs are received in English, Arabic, German and Italian.

FUTURE TRENDS AND PROSPECTS

Christians are likely to gain back most of the losses from the Communist era but will probably level off just above 96% as the Muslims and nonreligious constitute 3% of the population.

Christians may lose significant numbers through defection to nonreligion in the first half of the 21st century.

BIBLIOGRAPHY

'A history of Baptists in Yugoslavia, 1862–1962.' J. D. Hopper. Ph.D. dissertation, Southwestern Baptist Theological Seminary, Fort Worth, TX, 1977. 180p.

'A history of the Congregational and Methodist Churches in Bulgaria and Yugoslavia.' P. B. Mojzes. Ph.D. dissertation, Boston University, Boston, 1965. 674p.

'Catholicism among Croats and its critique by Marxists,' J. Kristo, in *Religion and nationalism in Eastern Europe & the Soviet Union*, p.77–95. D. J. Dunn (ed). Boulder, CO: Rienner, 1987.

'Changing functions of religion in a socialist society: the case of Catholicism in Yugoslavia,' S. Vrcan, *Social compass*, 28, 1 (1981), 43–61.

Church and state in Yugoslavia since 1945. S. Alexander. Cambridge, UK: Cambridge University Press, 1979. 351p.

'Church–state relations in Yugoslavia since 1967,' S. Alexander, *Religion in Communist lands*, 4, 1 (Spring 1976), 18–27.

'Croatia: the Catholic Church and the clergy, 1919–1945,' S. Alexander, in *Catholics, the state, and the European radical right, 1919-1945*, p.31–66. R. Wolff & J. Hoensch (eds). *Atlantic Studies on Society in Change*, 50. Boulder, CO: Social Science Monographs, 1987.

'Denominational affiliation in Yugoslavia, 1930–1989,' S. Flere, *East European quarterly*, 25 (June 1991), 145–65.

'Factionalism in Church–State interaction: the Croatian Catholic Church in the 1980s,' P. Ramet, *Slavic review*, 44 (Summer 1985), 298–315.

Forced conversions of Croatians to the Serbian faith in history: paper presented to the III World Congress for Soviet and East European Studies, October 30–November 4, 1985, Washington, DC. I. Omrcanin. Washington, DC: Samizdat, 1985. 84p.

In the claws of the red dragon: ten years under Tito's heel. W. Gruber. Toronto: St. Michaelswerk, 1988. 208p.

'Islam in Yugoslavia today,' S. Ramet, *Religion in Communist lands*, 18, 3 (Autumn 1990), 226–35.

Istria religiosa. P. Blasi & P. Zovatto. Trieste: [il Centro], 1989. 290p.

Kirche in einer sozialistischen Gesellschaft: Analyse der gegenwärtigen pastoralen Situation in der Erzdiözese Zagreb (Nordkroatien) unter besonderer Berücksichtigung der distanzierten Kirchlichkeit. J. Baloban. Zurich: Benziger, 1982. 309p.

Krscanstvo na hrvatskom prostoru: pregled religiozne povijesti Hrvata (7–20. st.). F. Sanjek. Zagreb: Krscanska sadasnjost, 1991. 567p.

'La situación religiosa en Yugoslavia,' G. Canders, *Revista de estudios politicos*, 161 (1968), 259–67.

'Marxist critique of religion and Croatian Catholic culture,' J. Kristo, *Journal of ecumenical studies*, 22 (Summer 1985), 474–86.

Medjugorje unfolds in peace and in war. R. Faricy & L. Rooney. 2nd ed. Leominster: Gracewing, 1993. 117p.

Nations and nationalities of Yugoslavia. K. Joncic (ed). Belgrade: Medjunarodna politika, 1974. 549p.

Opci sematizam katolicka crkve u Jugoslaviji, cerkerv Jugoslaviji, 1974 (General survey of the Catholic Church in Yugoslavia). Zagreb: Biskupska konferencija Jugoslavije, 1975. 1,166p. (Parts in Croat, Slovenian, Latin, English, French, German).

'Recent developments in church–state relations in Yugoslavia,' C. Criic, *Religion in Communist lands*, 1, 1 (Spring 1973), 6–8.

'Relations between the State and the Roman Catholic Church in Croatia, Yugoslavia in the 1970's and 1980's,' J. Kristo, *Occasional papers on religion in Eastern Europe*, 1 (June 1982), 22–33.

'Religion and nationality in Yugoslavia,' P. Ramet, in *Religion and nationalism in Soviet and East European politics*, p.299–327. P. Ramet (ed). 2nd ed. Durham, NC: Duke University Press, 1989.

'Religion in Yugoslavia: the background,' J. Broun, *America*, 165 (November 30, 1991), 414–16.

Religions in Yugoslavia: historical survey, legal status, church in socialism, ecumenism, dialogue between Marxists and Christians, etc. Z. Frid (ed). Zagreb: Binoza, 1971. 168p.

Socijalisticko drustvo, crkva i religija. S. Bahtijarevic & B. Bosnjak. Zagreb: Institut za drustvena istrazivanja Sveucilista, 1969. 2 vols.

'Some social expectations of Christians in Yugoslavia with primary emphasis on the Protestant churches,' N. G. Shenk, *Occasional papers on religion in Eastern Europe*, 1 (November 1981), 1–10.

'The "Croatian Christian martyrs",' *East Europe*, 23 (August 1974), 12–15.

'The Gypsy population of Yugoslavia,' T. P. Vukanovic, *Journal of the Gypsy Lore Society*, 42, 1/2 (1963), 10–27.

'The position of believers as second–class citizens in Socialist countries: the case of Yugoslavia,' Z. Roter, *Occasional papers on religion in Eastern Europe*, 9 (June 1989), 1–17.

The position of the Church in Yugoslavia. R. Vidic. Belgrade: Izdavac, 1962.

'The social role of religion in contemporary Yugoslavia.' N. G. Shenk. Ph.D. dissertation, Northwestern University, Evanston, IL, 1987. 264p.

'The teaching ministry of the Church and how it is practiced through the weekday religious instruction in the Seventh-day Adventist Church in the Socialist Republic of Croatia.' J. Mihaljcic. Ph.D. dissertation, Andrews University, Barrien Springs, MI, 1987.

'The Zagreb mosques, a study of non–Muslim sponsorship of Islamic art in the Balkan heart of Christendom.' J. N. Blaskovich. M.A. thesis, University of California at Los Angeles, 1992. 70p.

War damage sustained by Orthodox churches in Serbian areas of Croatia in 1991. D. Davidov, R. Stanic & M. Timotijevic. [Belgrade]: Ministry of Information of the Republic of Serbia, 1992. 88p.

'Yugoslavia,' A. Fiamengo, in *Western religion: a country by country sociological enquiry*, p.587–99. H. Mol (ed). The Hague: Mouton, 1972.

Yugoslavia. J. J. Horton. 2nd ed. *World bibliographical series*, vol. 1. Oxford, UK: CLIO Press, 1990. 304p. (See especially 'Religion,' p.72f, and 'Nationalities,' p.97–103).

Yugoslavia: a comprehensive English–language bibliography. F. Friedman (ed). Wilmington, DE: Scholarly Resources, Inc., 1993. 547p. (Section on 'Religion,' p.453–61).

Yugoslavia inferno: ethnoreligious warfare in the Balkans. P. Mojzes. , 1994.

Yugoslavia: the church and the state. London: Information Office, Embassy of the Federal People's Republic of Yugoslavia, 1953. 92p.

'Yugoslavie aujourd'hui: une église entre l'est et l'ouest,' *Information catholique internationale* (Paris), 400 (January 1972), 7–15.

Country Table 2. Organized churches and denominations in Croatia.

Official name (bold type = church with over 10% of all affiliated) 1	*Begun* 2	*Type* 3	*Counc* 4	*Congs* 5	*Adults* 6	*Affiliated 1970* 7	*Affiliated 1995* 8	*G%* 9	*Names, notes, and other statistics* (see Codebook, Part 3) 10
Baptist Union of Croatia		P-Bap	T....	41	1,000	2,500	2,000	0.05	Baptists with links across Europe. 1442n 712x 999m 3845w 59137Yy
Catholic Church in Croatia:	250	R-Lat	B....	1,538	3,117,000	3,542,808	3,872,179	0.06	750-year-old church, strong traditions. 99n 55x 64m 221w 4150Yy
M Rijeka-Senj (Fiume-Segna)	c350	R-Lat	Bs	153	209,000	430,000	260,000	0.06	Ancient diocese. 47n 23x 24m 88w 611Yy
D Krk (Veglia)	900	R-Lat	Bs	51	26,400	34,000	32,850	0.09	Northwest coastal area. 82n 17x 45m 37w 2264Yy
D Porec i Pula	c250	R-Lat	Bs	133	128,000	149,455	158,726	0.06	On extreme northwest peninsula. 201n 148x 199m 417w 7565Yy
M Split-Makarska (Spalato)	c250	R-Lat	Bs	181	335,000	320,000	416,578	0.06	Southern coast. 60n 31x 35m 257w 1423Yy
D Dubrovnik (Ragusa)	990	R-Lat	Bs	65	58,400	73,000	72,640	0.10	At southern extremity of Croatia. 33n 17x 17m 85w 413Yy
D Hvar (Lesina)	c1150	R-Lat	Bs	46	19,700	33,000	24,543	-1.18	Diocese is 92% Catholic. M=OP. 12n 3x 3m 50w 190Yy
D Kotor	c950	R-Lat	Bs	26	10,200	9,500	12,700	0.10	Diocese: 13% Catholic. 29n 49x 50m 118w 1265Yy
D Sibenik	1298	R-Lat	Btor	74	101,000	140,853	125,873	-0.45	M=TOR. 561n 301x 485m 1929w 30378Yy
M Zagreb	1093	R-Lat	Bs	472	1,621,900	1,900,000	2,014,294	0.23	Capital city. 195n 33x 38m 352w 7807Yy
D Djakovo (Bosna i Srijem)	c350	R-Lat	Bs	173	451,000	420,000	560,000	0.06	Suffragan of Zagreb. 60n 2x 2m 111w 774Yy
D Krizevci *(Byzantine)*	1777	R-Byz	Os	51	39,400	36,700	48,975	1.16	Crisio. Byzantine-rite Catholics. 63n 33x 37m 180w 2297Yy
AD Zadar (Zara)	c350	R-Lat	Bs	113	117,000	108,800	145,000	0.06	On coastline midpoint. 63n 41x 45m 170w 2092Yy
Doubly-counted Catholics		R-Lat		0	0	-112,500	0		Catholics counted in 2 dioceses or jurisdictions when creations of new dioceses are frequent.
Christian Brethren	1905	P-CBr	.....	2	50	105	77	-1.23	Some relations with Plymouth Brethren in Britain.
Church of God		P-Pe3	.....	6	100	154	150	0.05	M=Church of God (Cleveland, USA).
Church of United Brethren	1900	P-LuR	.....	5	390	620	600	-0.13	Joint Lutheran/Reformed denomination.
Croatian National Old Catholic Church	1933	I-OCa	.....	8	1,900	4,000	3,800	-0.20	Many links with Union of Utrecht.
Ev Ch in Croatia & Bosnia-Herzegovina		P-Pe2	.....	18	1,500	1,170	2,500	0.05	M=AoG. Baptistic Pentecostals.
Evangelical Ch in Croatia (Lutheran)	1750	P-Lut	.....	13	2,250	4,600	4,500	-0.09	Lutherans, many German contacts.
Independent charismatic churches	c1985	I-3cW	.....	10	500	–	800	10.00	Recently formed.
Jehovah's Witnesses		m-Jeh	.....	69	3,609	3,200	7,080	0.05	(1995) 419Y. Aggressive witnessing.
Methodist Church	1895	P-Met	.....	1	40	115	100	-0.56	Related to UK, USA.
New Apostolic Church	c1980	I-3aX	x....	10	500	–	1,200	6.67	*NAC.* M=Neuapostolische Kirche (HQ Zurich, Switzerland).
Old Catholic Church	1923	I-OCa	.....	3	1,600	4,700	4,000	-0.64	Altkatholische Kirche.
Serbian Orthodox Church		O-Ser	C....	300	200,000	370,000	270,000	0.05	M Zabreb, D Dalmacija, D Gornji Karlovac, D Slavonija.
Seventh-day Adventist Church	1909	P-Adv	.....	90	3,048	4,750	4,690	-0.05	M=SDA (USA).
Slovak Evangelical Christian Church	1680	P-Lut	.....	13	7,140	10,500	10,200	-0.12	Early Reformation body.
Other pentecostal bodies		I-3pW	.....	5	700	1,460	1,270	0.05	Independent pentecostals.

Continued opposite

Country Table 2–concluded

Official name (bold type = church with over 10% of affiliated) 1	*Begun* 2	*Type* 3	*Counc* 4	*Congs* 5	*Adults* 6	*Affiliated 1970* 7	*Affiliated 1995* 8	*G%* 9	*Names, notes, and other statistics* (see Codebook, Part 3) 10
Other Protestant denominations	c1960	P-	.....	10	700	1,390	1,080	-1.00	Several recent arrivals, Protestant missions from Germany, UK, USA.
Totals				**2,142**	**3,342,027**	**3,952,072**	**4,186,226**		

Churches, members, growth, 1900-2025	*Congs*	*Adults*	*Affiliated*	*G%*	*Total denominations*	*6 Megablocs:* *O*	*R*	*A*	*P*	*I*	*m*
Total churches, members, and denominations (mid-1900)	1,200	1,661,000	2,565,000	0.62	6	1	1	0	4	0	0
Total churches, members, and denominations (mid-1970)	1,858	2,559,267	3,952,072	0.62	24	1	1	0	15	6	1
Total churches, members, and denominations (mid-1990)	2,300	3,385,000	4,240,000	0.35	45	1	1	0	29	13	1
Total churches, members, and denominations (mid-1995)	2,142	3,342,027	4,186,226	-0.25	46	1	1	0	29	14	1
Total churches, members, and denominations (mid-2000)	2,200	3,398,000	4,256,386	0.33	48	1	1	0	30	15	1
Total churches, members, and denominations (mid-2025)	2,000	3,216,000	4,028,000	-0.22	91	4	1	0	40	45	1

NOTES ON TABLE ABOVE
NATIONAL COUNCILS (Column 4, 5th Letter).
E = Protestant Evangelical Council in Croatia (PECC).
R = Hrvatska Biskupska Konferencija (HBK, Croatian Episcopal Conference).

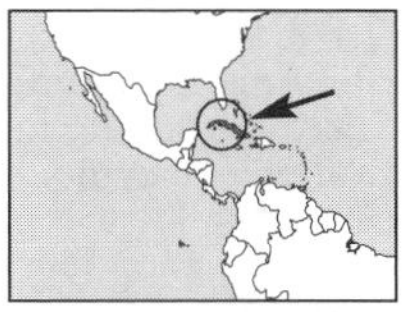

CUBA

SECULAR DATA, AD 2000

STATE
Official name: La República de Cuba (The Republic of Cuba).
Short name: Cuba. **Adjective of nationality:** Cuban.
Flag: Alternate blue and white stripes, red triangle with white star.
Area: 110,861 sq. km. (42,804 sq. mi.).
Government: One-party Communist state, since 1959 (1492 Spanish possession, 1898 Independence).
Legislature: National Assembly of the People's Power, 589 members.
Official language: Spanish (Español/Castella).
Monetary unit: 1 Cuban peso (CUP) = 100 centavos. **US$1=** 23.00 CUP.
Chief cities: LA HABANA (Havana) 2,302,000; Santiago de Cuba 462,628; Camaguey 304,916; Holguin 252,283; Guantanamo 229,816.
Political divisions: 15 provinces.
Armed forces: 106,000.

DEMOGRAPHY
Population: 11,201,000.
Population density: 101.0/sq. km. (261.6/sq. mi.).
Under 15 years: 2,377,000.
Growth rate p.a.: 0.30% (births 11.65, deaths 7.22).
Mortality: Infant, per 1,000: 8.1; **Maternal per 100,000:** 95.0.
Life expectancy: 76 (male 75, female 79).
Household size: 3.7. **Floor area per person, sq.m:** 18.0.
Major languages: Spanish, Russian, Chinese, English.
Urban dwellers: 77.92%. **Urban growth rate p.a.:** 0.8%.
Labor force: 45%.

ETHNOLINGUISTIC PEOPLES
71.6% Cuban White; 15.0% Mulatto; 12.0% Black; 0.3% Han Chinese; 0.3% Indo-Pakistani.

ECONOMY
National income p.a. per person: US$1,300; **per family:** US$4,810.

EDUCATION
Adult literacy: 95% (male 96%, female 95%). **Schools:** 12,233.
Universities: 35. **School enrolment:** female/male: 92%/88%.

HEALTH
Access to health services: 98%. **Access to safe water:** 93%.
Hospitals: 244 (61 beds per 10,000). **Doctors:** 46,860.
Blind: 4,600. **Deaf:** 672,000. **Murder rate:** 5.
Lepers: 11,000.

LITERATURE
New book titles p.a.: 900 (80 p.a. per million). **Periodicals:** 224.
Newspapers: 17 dailies.

COMMUNICATION (per 1,000 people)
Phones: 32 (10% mobile). **Radios:** 326. **TV sets:** 200.
Daily newspaper circulation: 120. **Computers:** 40.

REFUGEES
Alien refugees from other countries: 1,800.

HUMAN LIFE AND LIBERTY (optimum condition=100.0%)
HDI: 72.3. **HSI:** 62.0. **HFI:** 12.5. **EFL:** 15.0.

Country Table 1. **Religious adherents in Cuba, AD 1900-2025.**

Year	*1900*		*1970*		*mid-1990*		*Annual change, 1990-2000*				*mid-1995*		*mid-2000*		*mid-2025*	
Name	*Adherents*	*%*	*Adherents*	*%*	*Adherents*	*%*	*Natural*	*Conversion*	*Total*	*Rate*	*Adherents*	*%*	*Adherents*	*%*	*Adherents*	*%*
Christians	**1,796,000**	**99.1**	**4,012,700**	**47.1**	**4,758,000**	**44.8**	**25,623**	**-3,020**	**22,603**	**0.47**	**4,900,000**	**44.7**	**4,984,033**	**44.5**	**5,600,000**	**47.5**
PROFESSION																
crypto-Christians	0	0.0	497,700	5.8	900,000	8.5	4,823	2,177	7,000	0.75	940,000	8.6	970,000	8.7	1,100,000	9.3
professing Christians	**1,796,000**	**99.1**	**3,515,000**	**41.3**	**3,858,000**	**36.3**	**20,800**	**-5,197**	**15,603**	**0.40**	**3,960,000**	**36.1**	**4,014,033**	**35.8**	**4,500,000**	**38.1**
AFFILIATION																
unaffiliated Christians	148,000	8.2	909	0.0	112,750	1.1	608	4,229	4,837	3.63	165,342	1.5	161,124	1.4	74,500	0.6
affiliated Christians	**1,648,000**	**90.9**	**4,011,791**	**47.1**	**4,645,250**	**43.7**	**25,015**	**-7,249**	**17,766**	**0.38**	**4,734,658**	**43.2**	**4,822,909**	**43.1**	**5,525,500**	**46.8**
Roman Catholics	1,644,000	90.7	3,819,229	44.8	4,250,000	40.0	22,914	-11,123	11,791	0.27	4,313,000	39.3	4,367,909	39.0	4,800,000	40.7
Protestants	3,000	0.2	108,062	1.3	170,000	1.6	917	1,083	2,000	1.12	178,698	1.6	190,000	1.7	250,000	2.1
Independents	0	0.0	60,400	0.7	120,000	1.1	647	853	1,500	1.18	127,700	1.2	135,000	1.2	230,000	2.0
Marginal Christians	0	0.0	10,100	0.1	100,000	0.9	539	1,961	2,500	2.26	110,100	1.0	125,000	1.1	240,000	2.0
Anglicans	1,000	0.1	12,000	0.1	3,800	0.0	20	-40	-20	-0.54	3,710	0.0	3,600	0.0	4,000	0.0
Orthodox	0	0.0	2,000	0.0	1,450	0.0	8	-13	-5	-0.35	1,450	0.0	1,400	0.0	1,500	0.0
Trans-megabloc groupings																
Evangelicals	2,500	0.1	80,000	0.9	122,000	1.2	658	582	1,240	0.97	129,488	1.2	134,400	1.2	177,000	1.5
Pentecostals/Charismatics	0	0.0	80,000	0.9	500,000	4.7	2,696	4,404	7,100	1.34	537,396	4.9	571,000	5.1	767,000	6.5
Great Commission Christians	**109,000**	**6.0**	**770,000**	**9.0**	**2,450,000**	**23.1**	**13,209**	**212**	**13,421**	**0.53**	**2,528,000**	**23.1**	**2,584,208**	**23.1**	**2,850,000**	**24.2**
Nonreligious	2,000	0.1	2,485,000	29.2	3,121,450	29.4	16,829	4,821	21,650	0.67	3,253,000	29.7	3,337,945	29.8	3,158,200	26.8
Spiritists	5,000	0.3	1,516,500	17.8	1,930,000	18.2	10,405	-2,610	7,795	0.40	1,966,390	17.9	2,007,947	17.9	2,100,000	17.8
Atheists	0	0.0	490,000	5.8	761,000	7.2	4,103	623	4,726	0.60	785,000	7.2	808,263	7.2	850,000	7.2
Hindus	0	0.0	3,000	0.0	21,000	0.2	113	106	219	0.99	22,000	0.2	23,185	0.2	35,000	0.3
Chinese folk-religionists	0	0.0	4,000	0.1	20,000	0.2	108	31	139	0.67	20,500	0.2	21,388	0.2	30,000	0.3
Muslims	0	0.0	1,000	0.0	8,000	0.1	43	64	107	1.27	8,500	0.1	9,073	0.1	15,000	0.1
Buddhists	0	0.0	5,000	0.1	6,000	0.1	32	-23	9	0.14	6,000	0.1	6,085	0.1	6,000	0.1
Baha'is	0	0.0	500	0.0	800	0.0	4	30	34	3.60	1,000	0.0	1,139	0.0	2,000	0.0
Jews	9,000	0.5	1,800	0.0	1,000	0.0	5	-23	-18	-1.93	840	0.0	823	0.0	800	0.0
Other religionists	1,000	0.1	500	0.0	750	0.0	4	1	5	0.69	770	0.0	803	0.0	1,000	0.0
World A (unevangelized persons)	3,626	0.2	2,981,890	35.0	244,444	2.3	1,294	-15,231	-13,937	-8.32	142,535	1.3	100,809	0.9	106,182	0.9
World B (evangelized non-Christians)	13,374	0.7	1,525,096	17.9	5,625,556	52.9	30,352	18,251	48,603	0.84	5,921,700	54.0	6,116,158	54.6	6,091,818	51.6
World C (Christians)	1,796,000	99.1	4,012,700	47.1	4,758,000	44.8	25,623	-3,020	22,603	0.47	4,900,000	44.7	4,984,033	44.5	5,600,000	47.5
Country's population	**1,813,000**	**100.0**	**8,519,687**	**100.0**	**10,628,000**	**100.0**	**57,269**	**0**	**57,269**	**0.53**	**10,964,236**	**100.0**	**11,201,000**	**100.0**	**11,798,000**	**100.0**

COLUMNS, ROWS.
For meanings and definitions, see Codebook (Part 3). Note that, by definition, total 'Christians' = professing + crypto-Christians, which also = affiliated + unaffiliated Christians, and also = Great Commission Christians + latent Christians. Percentages may not always total exactly, due to rounding.

NOTES ON RELIGIONS
ANGLICANS. Growth and decline of affiliated Episcopalians: 2,029 (1925), 12,278 (1938), 35,284 (1948), 48,800 (1951), 62,100 (1956), and 74,400 (1960); after this the mass exodus of Cubans and North Americans to the USA reduced the total to 12,000 by 1970, and to only 3,600 by 1995.
ATHEISTS. Communist Party of Cuba (PCC) (in power since 1959; pro-Soviet).
BAHA'IS. In 4 local spiritual assemblies (1964, 1973 increasing despite Communist obstructionism) to 10 LSAs by 1996.
BUDDHISTS. Chinese.
COUNTRY'S POPULATION. After the 1959 revolution, a total of 650,000 Cubans had, by 1974, either fled or been expelled, mostly to the USA, including a large proportion of the business and middle classes, the great majority of all Protestants and Anglicans, and a substantial Catholic minority.
CRYPTO-CHRISTIANS. Christians affiliated to churches but not known as such to the state, of 3 kinds: (1) unorganized individuals in the recognized churches, who remain practicing Catholics or Protestants but keep it private; (2) members of unrecognized, banned, underground or persecuted denominations (Jehovah's Witnesses, Batiblancos, Seventh-day Adventists); and (3) isolated radio believers.
INDEPENDENTS. In about 23 denominations in 1995 (see Table 2).
NONRELIGIOUS. Agnostics, indifferent to religion. In 1957 before the Communist revolution, they already numbered 19% of the population; after 10 years of Communist rule, they numbered 44%. In addition, there are another 8.6% of the population (in 1995) whom the state (through polls and surveys) regards as nonreligious but who are affiliated to churches and so are classified here as crypto-Christians.
OTHER RELIGIONISTS. Including Rosicrucians (AMORC, 4 centers), and adherents of other non-Christian religions or cults.
SPIRITISTS. Negroes and Mulattoes belonging to numerous Afro-Cuban syncretistic cults, including: Santería (Lucumis or Yoruban, based on Yoruba rites), Na and Ganga (Bantu).

Country status. Cuba is historically the most important Caribbean country, and it remains the bellwether of the region, despite its isolation under the Castro regime. Its society and polity reflect some of the best and the worst of the Spanish heritage in the West Indies. Sugar is the most important export.

HUMAN LIFE AND LIBERTY

Human need and development. Under the Marxist regime of Fidel Castro, Cuban economy has made impressive strides. Nevertheless, as the only Communist country in the Western Hemisphere, it has not been able to consolidate its gains. In fact, it has lost ground steadily after the collapse of Communism worldwide and the loss of its powerful patrons in

Great Commission Instrument Panel: status of Cuba (for explanation see start of Part 4)

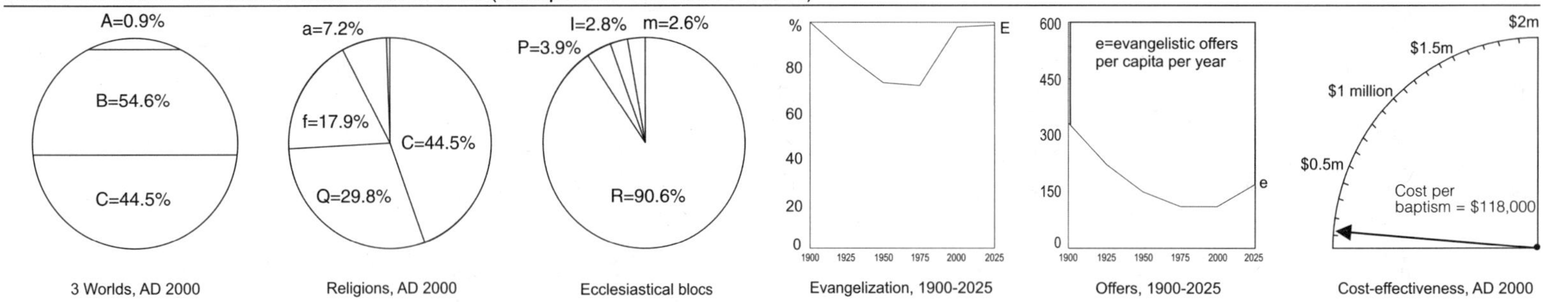

the Kremlin. Political repression has made economic growth appear artificial and forced. In many cases questionable and conflicting statistics make it difficult to assess the standards of living and quality of life in contemporary Cuba. In the early years as a besieged country, the revolutionary planners engaged in largescale redistribution of income and decreed austerity as a planned policy. This austerity has been a constant in Castro's Cuba; everything, including food, is rationed. After the loss of Soviet subsidies, rationing has become a sheer necessity with the amount of the rations decreasing steadily every month. On the positive side, some of the most conspicuous successes of the Revolution have been in the fields of health and welfare. Cuba's healthcare system is regarded as among the best in the Americas. The comprehensive social security system created in 1963 covers all workers and provides generous benefits. Shortages in housing have not entirely been eliminated. Most new houses are multifamily, rather than single family, units reflecting the communal nature of the new society.

Human rights and freedoms. As in most Communist countries, the word freedom does not appear in the official lexicon. For over 3 decades, all vestiges of civil rights and personal freedoms have been consistently erased. The Ministry of Interior is the principal organ of state security and totalitarian control. It operates border and police forces, orchestrates 'spontaneous' public demonstrations, investigates cases of nonconformist behavior, regulates migration, and maintains pervasive vigilance through a series of mass organizations and informants. It is also charged with the suppression of dissent and opposition of all kinds. Dissidents are discredited as mental patients or agents of hostile foreign powers. Numerous instances of extrajudicial killings by government agents and torture and physical abuse of prisoners are reported every year. The Constitution states that all civil liberties may be denied any one who actively opposes the 'decision of the Cuban people to build socialism'. The Penal Code also contains several articles prohibiting counterrevolutionary activities, enemy propaganda, illicit association, contempt for authority, clandestine printing and the general charge of rebellion. An average of 100 people are arrested every month for political crimes. Cuban judges are controlled by the Communist party and have never ruled against the government in any political trial. Defendants rarely receive the benefit of counsel or due process. Privacy of home, family and correspondence is routinely violated as part of an effort to regiment the lives of all citizens. The Ministry of Interior employs a network of block committees and informants for this purpose. In schools teachers ferret out information on the families of their students and encourage children to spy on their parents. Freedoms of press, speech, and association do not exist. The electronic and print media are state property. Foreign broadcasts are banned and unfriendly foreign correspondents are arrested and expelled. Freedom of assembly is not guaranteed by the Constitution. Any unauthorized assembly of more than 3 persons, even in a private home, is punishable by up to 3 months in jail. The Penal Code forbids illegal or unrecognized groups. Suspected counterrevolutionaries are harassed by 'spontaneous' demonstrations in which pro-Castro hooligans throw rocks and shout slogans. Emigration is strictly controlled. Although the Constitution forbids discrimination, blacks tend to occupy low-status jobs at all levels. Nonwhites make up only 15% of the 25 Politburo members and 200 Party Central Committee members, and they occupy only one of the 12 vice presidencies and 6 of the 29 seats on the Council of State.

Human environment. Cuba has the greatest species diversity in the West Indies and the highest degree of endemic species. These include a giant shrew, a rare crocodile, and blind cave fishes. With its expanse of wet lands and mangrove forests, Cuba is host to the most diverse marine life of all the Antillean Islands. However, since 1800 over 100 vertebrate species have become extinct in Cuba. Similarly, whereas over 90% of the land was forested in 1812, only 14% is so in 1992.

NON-CHRISTIAN RELIGIONS

Agnosticism and ***atheism*** have increased markedly in numbers after 1959, but were in gradual decline by 1990.

Afro-Cuban cults, whose followers are principally Negroes and Mulattoes, represented 0.5% of the population in 1957. These sects can be divided into 3 categories: (1) Santería, also called Lucumis or Yoruban after the Yoruba slaves originally brought to Cuba, is a syncretistic movement which borrows images and ceremonies from the cult of Catholic saints, and which usually conducts its services during the celebration of Catholic feasts. (2) Naoiguismo, the society of the Naoigos or the Abakua cult, which originated in Calabar (Nigeria) and was brought to Cuba in 1834-36, is made up of Naguerian secret societies who have kept their African characteristics and continue to include traditional occult practices. (3) Bantu religions have in several cases evolved into magical cults, such as the Mayombe sect embodying the Yoruba and Congolese world-view, and the Ganga sect which organizes funeral rites for its members. Most followers of Afro-Cuban cults call themselves either Catholics, or revolutionaries and communists, but the Cuban government has not assisted them and has taken measures to control their expansion. Sociological and ethnographic studies of them undertaken by the Institute of Ethnology and Folklore have increased considerably since the revolution.

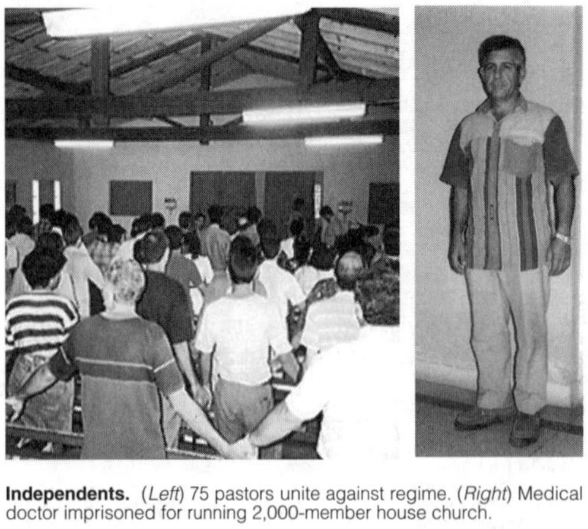

Independents. (*Left*) 75 pastors unite against regime. (*Right*) Medical doctor imprisoned for running 2,000-member house church.

CHRISTIANITY

CATHOLIC CHURCH. Dominican missionaries came to Cuba in 1512 soon after Columbus' arrival in 1492. The first jurisdiction was established in 1517 and Franciscans arrived a few years later. Owing to the absence of gold on the island and the decimation of most of the original population, both church and government remained stagnated for the next 2 and a half centuries. Towards the end of the 18th century more liberal Spanish policies were set in motion, the island began to flourish economically, and a progressive bishop for the first 30 years of the 19th century contributed much to the expansion of church institutions. During the remainder of the century, however, the church again went into decline due to the identification of the hierarchy with the Spanish government and the arrival of conservative Spanish clergy from newly-independent Latin American countries. Strongly anti-clerical feeling arose resulting in the separation of church and state after Cuban independence in 1898. The church took on new life in the 20th century, largely due to the influence of Catholic lay movements from abroad, new institutions for education and social services, and an increase in Cuban clergy including a cardinal, 2 archbishops and 5 bishops. Nevertheless, the continued use of conservative Spanish priests and the close relationship with the Batista government after 1930 left the church unprepared for the radical changes in political and economic policies that followed the 1959 revolution.

Church attendance for Catholics has declined catastrophically since 1959. In 1957 a survey found that 72.5% of the population professed to be Catholics, 65% had at some time made their first communion, and about 27% attended mass every Sunday. A further survey in 1970, organized by the episcopate and carried out by parish priests, reported that only 1% of the population attended Sunday mass in the diocese of Matanzas and 0.73% in Camagey. Attenders in other dioceses ranged from 0.7% to 1.5%. A third survey was made in 1972 in which the laity counted those present at mass in 62 churches throughout the island, yielding an average attendance of about 1.5% of the population. In 1968, 4.8% of all weddings took place in church.

Church-state conflicts since the beginning of Fidel Castro's regime in 1959 have had severe repercussions on religious vocations. At the end of 1958, the Cuban church had 725 diocesan and religious priests, 461 brothers, 2,407 sisters, and 81 seminarians. In July 1962, there remained no more than 231 priests, under 200 sisters and very few brothers. This drastic decrease was due in large part to a massive exodus from the island, at times on the orders of religious superiors. Fear of the new regime was the major factor, but there was as well inability to adapt to other work following the nationalization of Catholic schools. In 1953 the city of Havana, with a population of one million, had 16 parishes with on average 2 priests each, but there were 200 priests working in Catholic secondary schools in the city. Among the priests who emigrated were the bishops of Cienfuegos and Camagey. All seminarians, both diocesan and religious, left Cuba in 1961 on the orders of superiors. In 1961 there were further losses due to expulsion by government of 136 priests, including 46 Cubans and the auxiliary bishop of Havana; at that time however no brothers or sisters were expelled. Of the 136 exiled priests, 18 later returned, including the present archbishop of Havana. From 1962 to 1967, 79 new priests entered Cuba, whereas from 1963 to 1967, 7 more priests were expelled including 2 Cubans. There have been no further expulsions. Early in 1971 there were held the first ordinations in Cuba since 1961, all 15 ordinands having received their complete training in Cuba. All of Cuba's 8 active residential bishops at the present time including, 2 auxiliaries, have been appointed since the revolution without any state interference. The small number of priests (one to every 39,175 Cubans in 1969) and the exclusively religious character of their activities (only one Cuban priest was doing secular work in 1972) have restricted the life of faith entirely to the sacramental level. The situation gradually worsened then until in 1995 the ratio had increased to 49,700 Cubans per priest. In 1997 there was some hope of a change with the possibility of an official visit from pope John Paul II and his request for numerous foreign clergy to serve in Cuba once again.

Country summary. **Worlds A, B, C by ethnolinguistic peoples, cities, and major civil divisions in Cuba.**

	PEOPLES							CITIES							CIVIL DIVISIONS						
World	*Num*	*Pop 2000*	*C%*	*Christians*	*E%*	*U%*	*Unevangelized*	*Num*	*Pop 2000*	*C%*	*Christians*	*E%*	*U%*	*Unevangelized*	*Num*	*Pop 2000*	*C%*	*Christians*	*E%*	*U%*	*Unevangelized*
A	1	1,176	0.09	1	44	56	658	0	0	0.00	0	0	0	0	0	0	0.00	0	0	0	0
B	7	11,149,217	42.93	4,786,361	99	1	99,839	19	5,227,177	40.69	2,127,040	99	1	53,679	15	11,200,683	43.06	4,822,909	99	1	100,632
C	7	50,290	72.67	36,545	100	0	136	0	0	0.00	0	0	0	0	0	0	0.00	0	0	0	0
Total	**15**	**11,200,683**	**43.06**	**4,822,907**	**99**	**1**	**100,633**	**19**	**5,227,177**	**40.69**	**2,127,040**	**99**	**1**	**53,679**	**15**	**11,200,683**	**43.06**	**4,822,909**	**99**	**1**	**100,632**

The Holy See has diplomatic relations with Cuba and in AD 2000 is represented to government and the Catholic hierarchy by a nuncio residing in Havana.

OTHER CHURCHES. In 1957, 6% of the population professed to be Protestants or Anglicans. The largest single tradition is Pentecostalism which owes its origin to the missionary activity of the Assemblies of God from the USA in 1920. Today there are many different pentecostal groups, the largest being the indigenous Iglesia Evangélica Pentecostal. In fact, except for Catholicism this independent church is the largest denomination in Cuba at present.

The first non-Catholic services were held in Cuba in 1741 by British Anglicans, and in 1871 the first permanent pastor was sent by the Episcopal Church of the USA to serve the increasing number of Americans and British in the country. Anglicanism developed most rapidly among Cubans who fled the country for the USA during the revolutionary fervor of the latter part of the 19th century. Several Episcopal laymen returned to Cuba for evangelistic work, but this was halted during the Spanish-American war. The first resident bishop was appointed in 1906 and the first Cuban bishop in 1967, and now all clergy are Cubans. The Anglican Church is strongest in the cities and towns.

In 1873 Southern Methodists began working in Florida among exiles who flooded into the USA prior to Cuban independence in 1898. Ten years later 2 Cubans returned as missionaries to Havana. Following the war of 1898, Methodists built some of the best schools and dispensaries in the country, concentrating on rural areas. Continued work among Cuban exiles in the USA since 1959 has resulted in their membership equalling that in Cuba itself. The Methodist Church in Cuba became autonomous in 1964.

The Baptist Convention of Cuba grew out of the early efforts of a Cuban exile who returned in 1883 as a Bible colporteur, developing a small group of believers who later amalgamated with the USA Southern Baptist Convention. The work of this original group centers in the west and south. North American Baptist missionaries (ABHMS) have been active in eastern Cuba. The Baptist Convention of Cuba unites these 2 groups and is the largest non-Catholic non-Pentecostal denomination in the country. In 1965, 30 Baptist preachers were imprisoned as alleged American spies, but most were subsequently released.

In 1884 a Cuban organized small churches which served as the nucleus for the Presbyterian Church in Cuba, and after 1898 Presbyterian missionaries from the USA made their appearance. When Congregationalists left Cuba in 1909 and Disciples in 1918, their work was passed on to the Presbyterians. The church became independent of the New Jersey Synod in 1967.

The Salvation Army, Friends, Nazarenes, Church of God and many others are active in Cuba. Greek Orthodox also have one congregation in Havana. Following the 1959 revolution all churches experienced leadership losses with the departure of more than 500,000 Cubans to the USA. Compulsory military training further reduced the number of clergy and theological students.

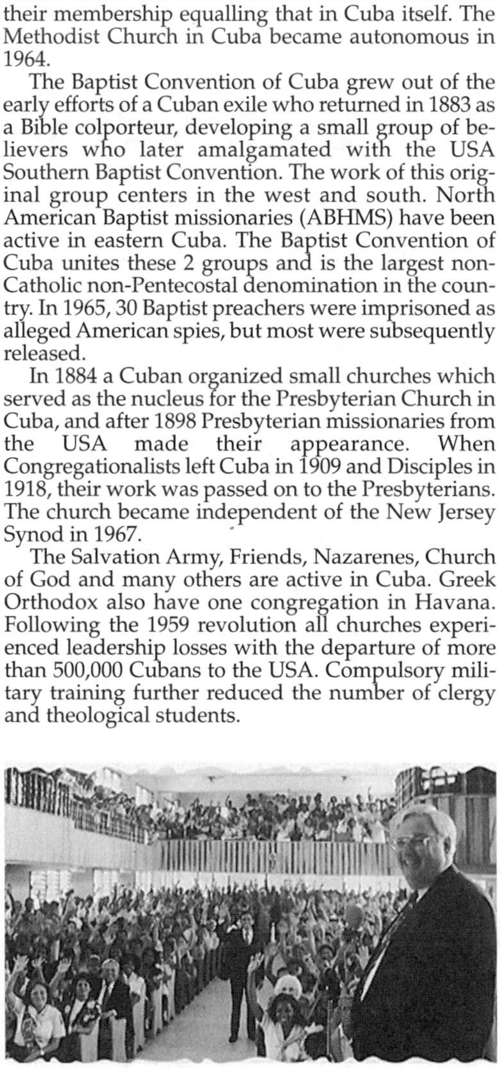

Iglesia Adventista del Séptimo Dia. Enthusiastic SDA congregation in Santiago de Cuba greets SDA world president R.S. Folkenburg.

However, the churches have recuperated markedly and are now stronger than before the revolution. Reports in 1975 indicated that many Protestant church services are full to overflowing every Sunday, with young people prominent.

Renewal movements. In the 1990s the Pentecostal/Charismatic Renewal continued to spread rapidly across most older churches, and numbered over 571,000 adherents (of whom 12% Pentecostals, 64% Charismatics, and 24% Independents).

Indigenous missions. Cuban Christians have been unable to practice foreign missionary outreach due to the strict policies enforced by the Castro regime.

CHURCH AND STATE

After Independence in 1898, the constitution of 1901 declared that church and state were to be absolutely separated and that there was to be freedom of worship. Before the eventual promulgation of the socialist constitution announced in 1965, to be voted on in a national citizens referendum in 1976, the theoretical juridical status of churches and other religious organizations continues to be regulated by Article 35 of the constitution of 1940, as was reaffirmed in the basic laws of the republic of Cuba of 7 February 1959. This article proclaims and guarantees 'free profession of all religions', freedom of worship, separation of church and state, and prohibits the state from granting subsidies to any religious body. The official position of the revolution in regard to religious activities has moreover been clearly stated in a declaration adopted by delegates at the first national congress of education and culture held at Havana in April 1971 (Declaración del Primer Congreso Nacional de Educación y Cultura). This policy rests on 7 basic principles, as follows. (1) Priority is given to the construction of a socialist society, the 'religious phenomenon' being only a subsidiary matter. (2) There is absolute separation between church and state, and between church and education, in all areas. (3) There can be no support nor aid for any kind of religious group; and in return, nothing can be asked of them. (4) There is no official adherence nor support for either religious beliefs or worship. (5) Respect will be given to the religious belief and practice of each individual and no-one is to be persecuted for his beliefs. (6) Freedom is accorded to all independent of their religious or philosophical beliefs to participate in 'the work of transformation of the Revolution'. (7) There must be vigilance against 'obscurantist and counter-revolutionary sects'. The whole declaration also embodies a short analysis of the situation of 3 sects and of the Catholic Church, no other groups being cited by name. Jehovah's Witnesses, Bando Evangelistico Gedeon or Batiblancos, and Seventh-day Adventists are described as 'the major sects in their position of confrontation with regard to the Revolution'. They are particularly reproached as vehicles of counter-revolutionary ideology, and for 'infiltrating the culturally poorest sectors of the population'. Concerning the Catholic Church, it is stated that the situation in Cuba needs to be analyzed in the light of that church's worldwide reform movement, the attitude of the hierarchy to revolutionary process, and the role played today in Latin America by Catholic revolutionary groups relating their activity to the Cuban model. The declaration adds that the separation of socio-economic problems from philosophical problems has opened the door to the individual participation of Catholics in the economic and social construction of the revolution.

To enter the Communist Party, it is necessary to suppress one's religious ideas, if such are held. As far as the churches are concerned, they have complete internal freedom of administration. Religious instruction, prohibited in public schools since 1902, continues to be given in places of worship and adjoining buildings. All private schools and universities were nationalized in 1961. All external religious manifestations, such as processions or public meetings, have been banned since the Catholic processions of 1960-61 which took a counter-revolutionary turn. Because of the Law of Urban Reform of 14 October 1960 abolishing rental property, the churches have lost a large number of their properties. Nevertheless, government provides an indemnity to former owners, which in the case of the Catholic archdiocese of Havana constitutes one of its principal financial resources. The celebration of Christmas and other religious feasts falling during the week is implicitly prohibited by a 1972 law which established the number of legal holidays. Prior to that Christmas vacations were moved to July so as not to interfere with the sugar-cane harvest which is most pressing during December.

The recent history of the Catholic Church in Cuba can be interpreted in terms of its unpreparedness for confronting a revolutionary situation. When in January 1959 Castro declared that 'The Catholics of Cuba have provided decisive collaboration with the cause of freedom', he was referring to priests, chaplains to guerrillas, and militant laymen who took arms against the Batista regime. But both hierarchy and laity were too closely linked to the ideology of preceding regimes to be able to adjust to the progressive socialization of Cuban life and its economy. Relations between the Catholic Church and the new regime rapidly deteriorated during the first years of the revolution. The episcopate protested in 1960 against the establishment of diplomatic relations with the USSR. The policy of nationalization was also criticized as 'excessive state control' in social and economic life. The USA forces invading the Bay of Pigs in April 1961 included a group of Catholics accompanied by 3 Spanish priests who claimed they have come 'in the name of God' to fight 'against atheists'. The holding of politico-religious demonstrations further exacerbated tensions. In September 1961 a procession of several thousand faithful in Havana turned into a protest against the regime as a result of which the government expelled the auxiliary bishop and 135 priests. At the beginning of 1963, the new papal chargéd'affaires, who later in 1974 became nuncio, adopted a conciliatory attitude towards the regime and cultivated good personal relations. The situation however remained strained until 1969 when the Cuban episcopate made a step in the direction of the revolution by publishing 2 collective pastoral letters. The letter of 20 April called on Catholics to reconsider their conception of social morality and to play a role in the development of society. It also condemned the economic blockade against Cuba, without making any pronouncement regarding its origin. The letter of 3 September listed the conditions necessary for Christians to conserve and develop their faith in the context of Cuban society. Symbolic gestures of voluntary agricultural work were made by priests and seminarians in 1968 and 1971, and in 1970 an ecumenical groups of priests and pastors participated in the harvest of sugar cane. In 1973 the general of the Society of Jesus visited Jesuits in Cuba; and between 27 March and 7 April 1974, Msgr Casaroli, secretary of the Council for Public Affairs of the Church, of the Holy See, also visited the Cuban church, carrying on at the same time important discussions with the political authorities. The amelioration of relations is also explained by the ideological flexibility of Fidel Castro. Attacking 'dogmatism' in 1968, he affirmed that Christians should be shown the possibility of their being true revolutionaries. There have also been ideological shifts in the church in Latin America, the death of the guerrilla priest Camilo Torres in Colombia, and the political and social evolution of progressivist sectors of the church on the continent.

Since the 1970s and 1980s the period of open conflict between church and state seems to have ended in Cuba. This does not however mean that the Cuban church has yet fully accepted a new mode of existence within the framework of a socialist society, nor has it yet been clarified what the role of the church will be.

In the subsequent 2 decades, relations tended to mature and stabilize somewhat. By 1997, pope John Paul II, a long time advocate of the lifting of the

USA's trade ban on Cuba, was negotiating for the return of foreign missionaries to assist Cuba's small remnant of clergy. He visited Cuba around the turn of the Third Millennium.

BROADCASTING AND MEDIA

Shortwave programs from KNLS, HCJB (Ecuador), TWR (Antilles) and AWR (Costa Rica) can be easily received. Cuba is a member of UNDA.

Christian television programs can be received via satellite. Some 550,000 have seen the 'Jesus' Film, mainly through film teams.

INTERDENOMINATIONAL ORGANIZATIONS

The Cuban Council of Protestant Churches (Consejo de Iglesias Evangélicas de Cuba) was begun in 1941, and in 1977 was renamed the Ecumenical Council of Cuba. It has 14 member churches, including representatives of the Protestant, Anglican, and Orthodox traditions. It works through 6 commissions: Christian Education, Ecumenical Education, Church and Society, Laity, Promotion of Bible Reading, and Youth. In 1947 a Union Theological Seminary was founded in Matanzas, attended by Presbyterian, Methodist, and Episcopalian seminarians.

The Catholic episcopate sponsors the National Episcopal Commission of Ecumenism (Comisión Episcopal Nacional de Ecumenismo), and the Episcopal Conference has created at the major seminary at Havana a Centre for Ecumenical Studies (Centro de Estudios Ecuménicos, CENDESEC) with a Catholic as president and staff of various confessions. Another similar study center was created by Protestants at Camaguey in collaboration with priests and lay Catholics.

FUTURE TRENDS AND PROSPECTS

Christians are maintaining approximately 46% of the population and are expected to do so at least until 2025.

If greater religious freedom is granted in the 21st century it is likely that Christianity will grow to over 60% of the population by AD 2050. If Communism in Cuba collapses many nonreligious and atheists would likely become church members as has been the case in other countries.

BIBLIOGRAPHY

Christianity and revolution: the lesson of Cuba. L. Dewart. New York: Herder & Herder, 1963.

'Cuba,' J. L. Gonzalez, in *The development of Christianity in the Latin Caribbean*, p.83–98. Grand Rapids, MI: Eerdmans, 1969.

Cuba at the crossroads. I. Batista. *Occasional study pamphlet*, 6. [Geneva]: World Council of Churches' Commission on Churches' Participation in Development, [1991]. 31p.

Cuba: Castro's war on religion. Washington, DC: Puebla Institute, 1991. 45p.

Cuba, church and crisis. L. Dewart. London: Sheed & Ward, 1963.

Cuba: después del derrumbe del comunismo: residuo del pasado, o, gérmen de un futuro nuevo? G. Girardi. Madrid: Nueva Utopía, [1994]. 247p.

'Cuba: la chiesa in una società rivoluzionaria,' L. Muratori, *Humanitas*, 25, 6 (1970), 625–635.

Cuba, testimonio cristiano, vivencia revolucionaria. C. Alvarez. *Colección historia de la Iglesia y de la teología.* San José, Costa Rica: DEI, 1990. 198p.

'Cuban spiritism.' M. Daley. Thesis, Union Theological Seminary, New York, (Based on a strong Efik (Nigeria) culture, revived from 1890 onwards).

Cultos afrocubanos: un estudio etnolingüístico. J. Fuentes Guerra & G. Gómez Gómez. Havana: Editorial de Ciencias Sociales, 1994. 66p.

Das Exil der Götter: Geschichte und Vorstellungswelt einer afrokubanischen Religion. S. Palmié. Frankfurt am Main: P. Lang, 1991. 527p.

Directorio eclesiástico de Cuba, 1971. Havana: Conferencia Episcopal de Cuba, 1971. (Roman Catholic).

Ecué, changó y yemayá: ensayos sobre la sub–religión de los afro–cubanos. J. L. Martin. Havana: Cultural, 1930. 164p. (Essays on Afro-Cuban religion).

El monte: igbo–finda, ewe orisha, vititi nfinda: notas sobre las religiones, la magia, las supersticiones y el folklore de los negros criollos y el pueblo de Cuba. L. Cabrera. 7th ed. Miami: Ediciones Universal, 1992. 589p.

El sistema religioso de los afrocubanos. R. Lachatañeré. Havana: Editorial de Ciencias Sociales, 1992. 450p.

El vodú en Cuba. J. James Figarola, J. Millet & A. Alarcón. Santo Domingo: Ediciones CEDEE Casa del Caribe, 1992. 348p.

Fidel & religion: conversations with Frei Betto. F. Castro & F. Betto. Trans., M. Todd. Melbourne: Ocean Press, 1990. 284p.

Four new world Yoruba rituals. J. Mason. 3d ed. Brooklyn: Yoruba Theological Archministry, 1993. 141p. (In English and Yoruba).

Historia eclesiàstica de Cuba. I. Teste. Burgos, Spain: Editorial El Monte Carmelo, 1969. 527p.

Itutu: la muerte en los mitos y rituales afrocubanos. N. Bolívar Aróstegui & C. Gonzáles Diaz de Villegas. Miami: Editorial Arenas, 1992. 159p.

Law and religion in Marxist Cuba: a human rights inquiry. M. I. Short. Coral Gables, FL: Transactions Publishers for North-South Center, University of Miami, 1993. 216p.

Los llamados cultos sincréticos y el espiritismo: estudio monográfico sobre su significación social en la sociedad cubana contemporánea. A. Arguelles Mederos & I. Hodge Limonta. Havana: Editorial Academia, 1991. 278p.

On freedom's edge: ten years under communism in Cuba. H. Caudill. Atlanta: Home Mission Board of the Southern Baptist Convention, 1975. 122p.

Panteón Yoruba: conversación con un santero. A. Frutos. Holguín, Cuba: Ediciones Holguín, 1992. 144p.

Religion in Cuba. D. A. Abich & J. M. Clark. Miami: Cuba Independiente y Democrática. 34p.

Religion in Cuba today: a new church in a new society. A. L. Hageman & P. E. Wheaton (eds). New York: Association Press, 1971. 317p.

'Ritual systems in Cuban Santería.' J. M. Murphy. Ph.D. dissertation, Temple University, Philadelphia, 1981. 396p.

'Sect and party: religion under revolution in Cuba.' C. Rosado. Ph.D. dissertation, Northwestern University, Evanston, IL, 1985. 384p. (Seventh-day Adventism).

The church and socialism: reflections from a Cuban context. S. Arce Martínez. New York: New York CIRCUS Publications, 1985. 222p. (Speeches on Christianity by F. Castro).

'The focus of Cuban Santeria,' W. R. Bascom, *Southwestern journal of anthropology*, (spring 1950), 64–68.

'The popular piety of the Cuban People.' A. A. Roman. M.A. thesis, Barry University, Miami Shores, FL, 1976. 106p.

'The use of language in Afro–Cuban religion.' I. Castellanos. Ph.D. dissertation, Georgetown University, Washington, DC, 1976. 202p.

Through a long tunnel: a story of survival in Cuba. H. T. Reza. Kansas City, MO: Nazarene Publishing House, 1976. 61p. (Church of the Nazarene).

Walking with the night: the Afro–Cuban world of Santeria. R. Canizares. Rochester, VT: Destiny Books, 1993. 148p.

Country Table 2. **Organized churches and denominations in Cuba.**

Official name (bold type = church with over 10% of all affiliated) 1	*Begun* 2	*Type* 3	*Counc* 4	*Congs* 5	*Adults* 6	*Affiliated 1970* 7	*Affiliated 1995* 8	*G%* 9	*Names, notes, and other statistics* (see Codebook, Part 3) 10
Asambleas de Dios	1920	P-Pe2	ZF...	375	17,000	10,000	50,000	6.65	*Assemblies of God.* M=AoG(USA). Vast campaigns 1950s; decline 1960. 121n,1k,1s.
Asambleas Locales	c1992	I-3nC	.....	2	60	–	200	33.33	*Little Flock. Local Churches.* Begun 1922 in China.
Asociación Evangélica de Cuba	1928	P-Eva	xMu.N	140	14,000	10,000	23,300	3.44	*Evangelical Association.* Formerly, M=West Indies Mission (USA). 2f,2s.
Asoc Conv Bautista de Cuba Occidental	1883	P-Bap	T....	127	7,600	12,000	13,100	0.35	*Baptist Convention of Western Cuba.* M=SBC(USA). 1965, 30 pastors jailed. 1s,319Y.
Convención Bautista de Cuba Oriental	1899	P-Bap	T....	151	9,654	15,000	12,500	-0.73	*Baptist Convention of Eastern Cuba.* Formerly M=ABHMS(USA), left 1961. 1s.
Convención Bautista Libre de Cuba	1941	I-Bap	T.u.N	15	1,480	3,000	4,500	1.64	*Free Baptist Convention of Cuba.* Formerly M=NAFWB(USA). Missions abroad. 8n.
Ejército de Salvación	1918	P-Sal	xwV.N	4	700	2,000	1,400	-1.42	*Salvation Army, Cuba Division*, Caribbean & CAmerica Territory (HQ Jamaica). 1s.
Grupos de Cristo	c1991	I-3hL	x....	52	1,500	–	4,000	25.00	*Christ Groups.* Isolated house churches for converts after nationwide EHC campaign.
Hermanos Libres		P-CBr	x....	19	650	1,000	1,300	0.05	*Open Brethren. Plymouth Brethren.* Decline from 20 congregations in 1959.
Iglesia Adventista del Séptimo Día	1905	P-Adv	x....	114	9,991	20,000	22,200	0.42	*SDA. Seventh-day Adventist Ch in Cuba.* HQ Santiago de las Vegas.
Iglesia Apostólica de Jesucristo		I-3oL	.....	3	1,100	2,000	2,200	0.05	*Apostolic Ch of Jesus Christ.* Related to Mexican indigenous IAFCJ. HQ Havana. Oneness body.
Iglesia Católica en Cuba:	1512	R-Lat	B.L.R	628	2,760,000	3,819,229	4,313,000	0.49	*Catholic Ch.* C=13+1+15. Low practice: W=2%. 121n 92x 127m 396w 70081Yy
M San Cristóbal de la Habana	1787	R-Lat	Bs	77	880,000	1,060,000	1,375,000	1.05	Havana, the capital. 90% urban. 45% Catholic. 1s. 40n 51x 76m 218w 32375Yy
D Holguin	1979	R-Lat	Bs	44	283,000	–	442,000	6.25	Population is 27% Catholic. 13n 5x 6m 27w 2982Yy
D Matanzas	1912	R-Lat	Bs	68	320,000	275,000	500,000	2.42	Half urban industrial. 55% Catholic. W=2%. 5n 7x 7m 26w 6055Yy
D Pinar del Río	1903	R-Lat	Bs	95	277,000	400,000	433,000	0.32	Extreme west of island. 70% rural. 63% Catholic. 11n 2x 2m 19w 7159Yy
M Santiago de Cuba	1522	R-Lat	Bs	75	214,000	949,229	334,000	-4.09	60% rural; sugar, cattle. 25% Catholic. 15n 12x 17m 39w 3966Yy
D Camagüey	1912	R-Lat	Bs	135	338,000	500,000	529,000	0.23	Half urban; sugar, cattle. 59% Catholic. W=-1.5%. 17n 4x 7m 37w 6092Yy
D Cienfuegos-Santa Clara	1903	R-Lat	Bs	134	448,000	635,000	700,000	0.39	60% rural, rapid urbanization. 46% Catholic. 20n 11x 12m 30w 11452Yy
Iglesia Congregacional Pentecostal	1955	I-3pL	x.u.n	12	1,080	5,000	1,800	-4.00	*Congregational Holiness Ch.* Formerly M=CHC(USA). Holiness Pentecostals.
Iglesia Cristiana Pentecostal de Cuba	1956	I-3pL	..u.N	80	8,000	10,000	20,000	2.81	*Christian Pentecostal Ch.* Schism 1956 ex AoG. 1976, M=CC(Disciples) (USA). HQ Camaguey.
Iglesia de Dios	1910	P-Pe3	ZF...	10	890	500	1,140	3.35	*Ch of God.* Formerly M=CoG(Cleveland) (USA). HQ Santiago de Cuba.
Iglesia de Dios de la Profecía		P-Pe3	Z.u.N	4	100	3,000	286	0.05	Formerly M=CoG of Prophecy (USA). Split in USA ex Cleveland. HQ Güines, Havana.
Iglesia de Dios en Cuba		P-Hol	x.u.M	20	1,000	1,000	2,000	0.05	*Ch of God in Cuba.* Formerly M=CoG(Anderson) (USA). Holiness denomination.
Iglesia de Dios Pentecostal		I-3pL	Z....	10	800	1,000	1,600	0.05	*Pentecostal Ch of God.* Formerly mission from Puerto Rico, and USA.
Iglesia de los Amigos	1900	P-Qua	Q.u.N	6	1,000	2,000	1,320	-1.65	*Iglesia de los Cuaqueros (Quakers, Friends).* M=FUM(USA). HQ Banes (Oriente).
Iglesia del Evangelio Cuadrangular		P-Pe2	ZF...	46	1,600	2,000	3,200	0.05	*Internat Ch of the Foursquare Gospel.* M=ICFG(USA), until workers expelled 1960.
Iglesia del Nazareno	1902	P-Hol	xFu.N	16	767	1,450	1,752	0.76	*Ch of the Nazarene.* Formerly M=CoN(USA). HQ Marianao, Havana. 1s.
Iglesia Episcopal de Cuba	1741	A-Hig	AwuRN	25	1,300	12,000	3,710	-4.59	Under a Metropolitan Council. A=1966. Decline from 74,400 (1960). 15n,1u,65Y,910y.
Iglesia Evangélica Pentecostal de Cuba		I-3pL	.....	156	28,000	30,000	56,000	0.05	*Evangelical Pentecostal Ch.* Largest Cuban independent pentecostal church.
Iglesia Luterana de Cuba (Misurí)	1912	P-Lut	x....	10	200	207	500	3.59	*Lutheran Ch.* 1947, M=LC Missouri Synod (USA). HQ Nueva Gerona, Isla de Pinos.
Iglesia Metodista en Cuba	1883	P-Met	Vuu.N	107	8,500	10,000	11,000	0.38	*Methodist Ch in Cuba.* Begun by Cubans. A=1964. Affiliated to UMC(USA). 23n,1u.
Iglesia Orthodoxa Africana	c1920	I-ARo	x....	10	700	1,000	1,200	0.73	*African Orthodox Ch.* M=AOC(USA) Blacks. West Indian Blacks. 1 bishop.
Iglesia Ortodoxa de Cuba		O-Gre	Cwu.n	1	725	2,000	1,450	0.05	*Orthodox Ch.* 12th Archdiocesan District, Greek Orthodox AD N&S America. Havana.
Iglesia Presbiteriana Reformada en C	1884	P-Ref	Ruu.N	63	7,000	8,872	9,050	0.08	*Presbyterian Reformed Ch.* Formerly M=UPUSA. A=1967. Decline since 1960. 21n,23t,1u.
Iglesia Santa Pentecostés	1952	P-Pe3	ZFu.N	18	1,250	1,000	3,050	4.56	*Pentecostal Holiness Church.* Formerly M=PHC(USA). HQ Bayamo (Oriente). 34nm.
Iglesia Biblicas	1937	I-3pL	Z....	11	350	500	700	1.35	*Open Bible Standard Chs.* Until 1960, M=OBSC(USA), a schism in USA ex ICFG. 1p.
Iglesias de la Fe Apostólica		I-3aL	x....	5	200	200	500	0.05	*Churches of the Apostolic Faith.* Formerly M=AFM(Portland, Oregon, USA). HQ Havana.
Iglesiás Elim		P-Pe2	Z....	20	1,000	1,000	1,500	0.05	Formerly M=Elim Missionary Churches (USA). HQ Matanzas.
Iglesias radiofónicas solitarias	1959	I-3rL	.....	500	20,000	6,700	30,000	6.18	Isolated radio believers (students &c). R=480(279 HCJB, 92 FEBC, TWR, Radio Vatican).
Sociedad de la Ciencia Cristiana		m-Sci	x....	1	40	100	100	0.05	*Ch of Christ, Scientist. Christian Science.* M=CCS(USA). First Church, Havana. 1w.
Soc Mis Cubana Hermanos en Cristo	1954	P-Men	.....	2	45	33	100	4.53	M=BICC(USA).
Testigos de Jehová	c1925	m-Jeh	x....	800	28,000	10,000	110,000	10.07	*Jehovah's Witnesses.* Active witnessing under way by 1929. Largely underground. (1995) 7964Y.
Other Protestant denominations		P-	.....	300	10,000	7,000	20,000	0.05	Total about 15 (see list below); also 5,000 USA Protestants at military base.
Other independent pentecostal chs		I-3pL	.....	50	2,000	1,000	5,000	0.05	Total about 12 (see list below), including New Apostolic Church (101 members).
Totals				**3,913**	**2,948,282**	**4,011,791**	**4,734,658**		

Churches, members, growth, 1900-2025	*Congs*	*Adults*	*Affiliated*	*G%*	*Total denominations*	*O*	*R*	*A*	*P*	*I*	*m*
Total churches, members, and denominations (mid-1900)	900	1,045,000	1,648,000	1.28	6	0	1	1	4	0	0
Total churches, members, and denominations (mid-1970)	2,149	2,544,209	4,011,791	1.28	48	1	1	1	28	15	2
Total churches, members, and denominations (mid-1990)	2,000	2,893,000	4,645,250	0.74	67	1	1	1	39	23	2
Total churches, members, and denominations (mid-1995)	3,913	2,948,282	4,734,658	0.38	68	1	1	1	39	24	2
Total churches, members, and denominations (mid-2000)	3,900	3,003,000	4,822,909	0.37	69	1	1	1	39	25	2
Total churches, members, and denominations (mid-2025)	5,000	3,441,000	5,525,500	0.55	159	1	1	1	50	100	6

(6 Megablocs: O R A P I m)

Continued opposite

Country Table 2–concluded

NOTES ON TABLE ABOVE
NATIONAL COUNCILS (Column 4, 5th letter).
N = Consejo de Iglesias de Cuba (CIC, Council of Churches of Cuba), associate of WCC, also affiliated to CWME; formerly Consejo Ecuménico de Cuba (Ecumenical Council of Cuba) (until 1977, Consejo de Iglesias Evangélicas de Cuba/Cuban Council of Protestant Churches).
n = observer member of Ecumenical Council of Cuba.
R = Conferencia de Obispos Catolicos de Cuba (COCC, Bishops' Conference of Cuba).

OTHER PROTESTANT DENOMINATIONS. There were about 15 other Protestant missions, mostly from the USA, at work in 1960; although all foreign personnel were subsequently expelled or left, the work of many bodies still continues, sometimes under different names. These bodies include; Berean Mission (c1950), Brethren in Christ (1953-60), Christian Reformed Ch (c1957), Chs of Christ, International Pentecostal Assemblies, Berean alia among the 5,000 USA Protestants (half Military, half civilian) at Guantánamo US naval base.
OTHER INDIGENOUS PENTECOSTAL CHURCHES. There are a small number of other Black or Cuban smaller indigenous bodies, including: African Methodist Episcopal Ch (USA), Bando Evangelistico Gedeft, the work of many bodies still continues, sometimes under different names. These bodies include; Bereanns), Iglesia Bethel, Iglesia de Cristo, Iglesia de Los Pinos (split ex Presbyterian Ch; rural). There are also remnants of earlier Black churches, including the Episcopal Orthodox Church (Greek Communion) begun in Cuba in 1921.

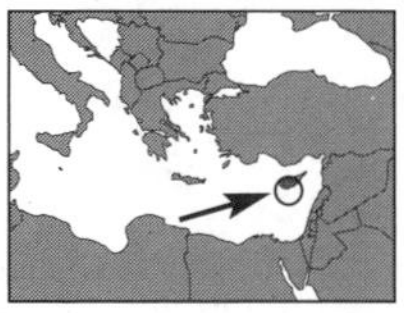

CYPRUS

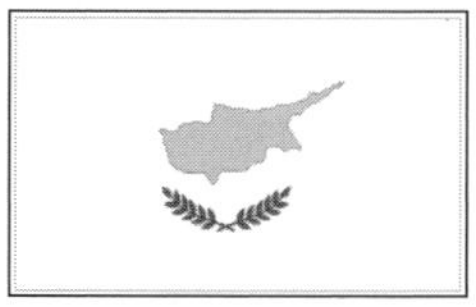

SECULAR DATA, AD 2000

STATE
Official name: Kypriaki Dimokratia/Kibris Çumhuriyeti (The Republic of Cyprus).
Short name: Cyprus. **Adjective of nationality:** Cypriot.
Flag: White field, map of Cyprus in gold, crossed green olive branches.
Area: 5,916 sq. km. (2,284 sq. mi.).
Government: Republic, since 1974 divided into de facto Greek and Turkish states, the latter declared autonomous in 1975 (1925 British crown colony, 1960 Independence).
Legislature: House of Representatives, 80 members.
Official language: Greek (Ellinika) and Turk.
Monetary unit: 1 Cyprus pound = 100 cents. **US$1=** ª1.20.
Chief cities: Lemesos (Limassol) 119,797; Ammokhostos (Famagusta) 62,141; Larnax (Larnaca) 58,865; LEVKOSIA (Nicosia-I) 45,857.
Political divisions: 5 provinces.
Armed forces: 10,000.

DEMOGRAPHY
Population: 601,000.
Population density: 101.5/sq. km. (262.9/sq. mi.).
Under 15 years: 140,000.
Growth rate p.a.: 0.79% (births 13.64, deaths 7.58).
Mortality: Infant, per 1,000: 8.1; **Maternal per 100,000:** 5.0.
Life expectancy: 78 (male 76, female 81).
Household size: 3.5. **Floor area per person, sq.m:** 30.0.
Major languages: Greek, Turkish, English, Armenian, Arabic.
Urban dwellers: 56.77%. **Urban growth rate p.a.:** 1.9%.
Labor force: 46%.

ETHNOLINGUISTIC PEOPLES
91.8% Greek Cypriot; 3.3% Armenian (Ermeni, Hai); 2.5% Lebanese Arab; 1.4% British; 0.4% Cypriot Arab.

ECONOMY
National income p.a. per person: US$13,420; **per family:** US$46,971.

EDUCATION
Adult literacy: 95% (male 97%, female 92%). **Schools:** 501.
Universities: 30. **School enrolment:** female/male: 95%/95%.

HEALTH
Access to health services: 90%. **Access to safe water:** 100%.
Hospitals: 110 (18 beds per 10,000). **Doctors:** 1,441.
Blind: 1,209. **Deaf:** 36,500. **Murder rate:** 1.
Lepers: 700.

LITERATURE
New book titles p.a.: 1,110 (1,850 p.a. per million). **Periodicals:** 67.
Newspapers: 15 dailies.

COMMUNICATION (per 1,000 people)
Phones: 474 (22% mobile). **Radios:** 288. **TV sets:** 143.
Daily newspaper circulation: 110. **Computers:** 80.

REFUGEES
Internal displacement: 265,000.

HUMAN LIFE AND LIBERTY (optimum condition=100.0%)
HDI: 90.7. **HSI:** 50.0. **HFI:** 40.0. **EFL:** 48.0.

Country Table 1. **Religious adherents in Cyprus, AD 1900-2025.**

Year	1900		1970		mid-1990		Annual change, 1990-2000				mid-1995		mid-2000		mid-2025	
Name	*Adherents*	*%*	*Adherents*	*%*	*Adherents*	*%*	*Natural*	*Conversion*	*Total*	*Rate*	*Adherents*	*%*	*Adherents*	*%*	*Adherents*	*%*
Christians	**185,570**	**99.8**	**459,770**	**97.5**	**481,350**	**94.6**	**8,649**	**-224**	**8,425**	**1.63**	**532,200**	**94.4**	**565,600**	**94.1**	**635,800**	**92.4**
PROFESSION																
professing Christians	**185,570**	**99.8**	**459,770**	**97.5**	**481,350**	**94.6**	**8,649**	**-224**	**8,425**	**1.63**	**532,200**	**94.4**	**565,600**	**94.1**	**635,800**	**92.4**
AFFILIATION																
unaffiliated Christians	700	0.4	680	0.1	11,200	2.2	202	79	281	2.26	12,685	2.3	14,006	2.3	15,800	2.3
affiliated Christians	**184,870**	**99.4**	**459,090**	**97.4**	**470,150**	**92.4**	**8,447**	**-303**	**8,144**	**1.61**	**519,515**	**92.1**	**551,594**	**91.8**	**620,000**	**90.1**
Orthodox	182,670	98.2	437,950	92.9	448,000	88.0	8,097	-368	7,729	1.60	495,100	87.8	525,294	87.4	582,500	84.7
Roman Catholics	1,900	1.0	6,400	1.4	8,000	1.6	145	35	180	2.05	9,000	1.6	9,800	1.6	13,000	1.9
Marginal Christians	0	0.0	5,600	1.2	6,700	1.3	121	29	150	2.04	7,500	1.3	8,200	1.4	13,500	2.0
Protestants	100	0.1	3,140	0.7	3,750	0.7	68	17	85	2.06	4,215	0.8	4,600	0.8	7,000	1.0
Anglicans	200	0.1	6,000	1.3	3,600	0.7	65	-95	-30	-0.87	3,500	0.6	3,300	0.6	3,000	0.4
Independents	0	0.0	0	0.0	100	0.0	2	28	30	14.87	200	0.0	400	0.1	1,000	0.2
Trans-megabloc groupings																
Evangelicals	100	0.1	2,350	0.5	2,540	0.5	46	5	51	1.85	2,835	0.5	3,050	0.5	3,750	0.6
Pentecostals/Charismatics	0	0.0	500	0.1	2,240	0.4	40	56	96	3.63	2,801	0.5	3,200	0.5	5,100	0.7
Great Commission Christians	**5,600**	**3.0**	**14,000**	**3.0**	**54,600**	**10.7**	**987**	**169**	**1,156**	**1.94**	**61,000**	**10.8**	**66,156**	**11.0**	**88,400**	**12.9**
Nonreligious	0	0.0	8,500	1.8	17,300	3.4	313	297	610	3.07	20,865	3.7	23,404	3.9	36,000	5.2
Muslims	310	0.2	500	0.1	5,300	1.0	96	-44	52	0.94	5,600	1.0	5,822	1.0	8,500	1.2
Atheists	0	0.0	2,000	0.4	4,200	0.8	76	-27	49	1.11	4,400	0.8	4,690	0.8	6,000	0.9
Baha'is	0	0.0	200	0.0	700	0.1	13	0	13	1.69	780	0.1	828	0.1	1,500	0.2
Jews	120	0.1	30	0.0	150	0.0	3	-2	1	0.77	155	0.0	162	0.0	200	0.0
World A (unevangelized persons)	186	0.1	2,357	0.5	1,018	0.2	18	-9	9	0.83	1,127	0.2	1,202	0.2	1,376	0.2
World B (evangelized non-Christians)	244	0.1	9,283	1.9	26,632	5.2	483	233	716	2.53	30,662	5.4	34,198	5.6	50,824	7.4
World C (Christians)	185,570	99.8	459,770	97.6	481,350	94.6	8,649	-224	8,425	1.63	532,200	94.4	565,600	94.2	635,800	92.4
Country's population	**186,000**	**100.0**	**471,411**	**100.0**	**509,000**	**100.0**	**9,150**	**0**	**9,150**	**1.68**	**563,990**	**100.0**	**601,000**	**100.0**	**688,000**	**100.0**

COLUMNS, ROWS.
For meanings and definitions, see Codebook (Part 3). Note that, by definition, total 'Christians' = professing + crypto-Christians, which also = affiliated + unaffiliated Christians, and also = Great Commission Christians + latent Christians. Percentages may not always total exactly, due to rounding.

CENSUSES.
1881: 73.9% Greek Orthodox, 24.4% Muslims, 1.1% Roman Catholics, 0.1% Armenian Apostolic. **1891:** 75.8% Greek Orthodox, 22.9% Muslims, 1.0% Roman Catholics, 0.1% Armenian Apostolic, 0.1% Anglicans, 0.1% Protestants, 0.1% Jews. **1.IV.1901:** 77.1% Greek Orthodox, 21.6% Muslims, 0.8% Roman Catholics, 0.2% Armenian Apostolic, 0.1% Anglicans, 0.1% Protestants. **2.IV.1911:** 78.2% Greek Orthodox, 20.6% Muslims, 0.7% Roman Catholics, 0.2% Armenian Apostolic, 0.1% Protestants. **1921:** 78.8% Greek Orthodox, 19.8% Muslims, 0.7% Roman Catholics, 0.4% Armenian Apostolic. **1931:** 79.5% Greek Orthodox, 18.5% Muslims, 1.0% Armenian Apostolic, 0.7% Roman Catholics. **10.XI.1946** (excluding 12,422 UK military): 80.2% Greek Orthodox, 17.9% Muslims, 0.8% Armenian Apostolic, 0.7% Roman Catholics, 0.3% Protestants. **11.XII.1960** (excluding 4,049 UK military and tourists): 77.6% Orthodox (77.0% Greek, 0.6% Armenian), 18.3% Muslims, 1.3% Roman Catholics.

NOTES ON RELIGIONS
ANGLICANS. Mostly expatriate UK military, dependents and civilians.
ATHEISTS. Communist Party of Cyprus (Anorthotikon Komma Ergazomenou Laou, AKEL) (legal; pro-Soviet). Communists are all Greek Cypriots (no Turkish), and most are practicing Orthodox Christians.
BAHA'IS. With 5 local spiritual assemblies (1996).
MUSLIMS. All Arabs except for 100 Rumelian Turks; mostly Sunnis (of the Hanafite rite) under the mufti of Cyprus, with some Shias in dervish orders (Ticani, Mevlevi or Whirling Dervishes, Bektasi, Fufai or Howling Dervishes). *Hajj pilgrims to Mecca.* (1976) 1.
ORTHODOX. Among the many groups within Orthodoxy are a small number of crypto-Orthodox known as Linobambakoi (linsey-woolseys), who throughout the Ottoman period concealed their faith by taking Muslim names and keeping Muslim ceremonies externally while practicing the Orthodox faith in secret.

Great Commission Instrument Panel: status of Cyprus (for explanation see start of Part 4)

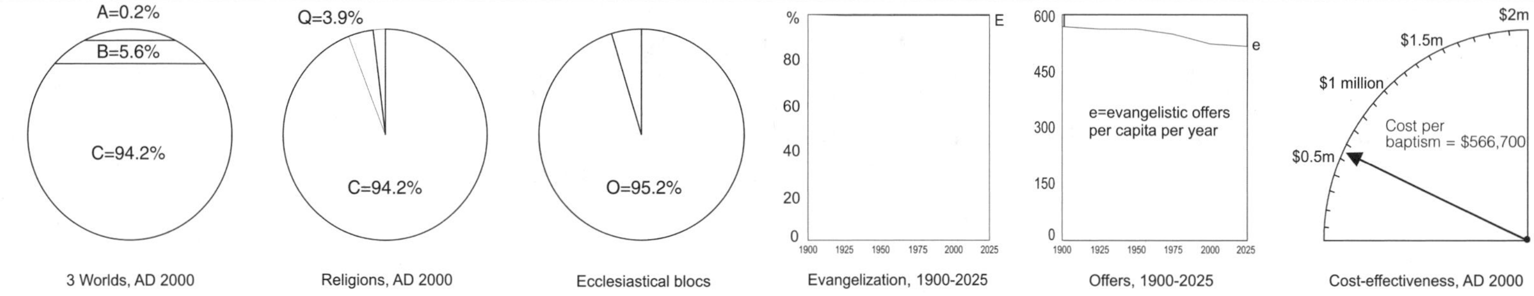

Country summary. **Worlds A, B, C by ethnolinguistic peoples, cities, and major civil divisions in Cyprus.**

	PEOPLES							CITIES							CIVIL DIVISIONS						
World	Num	Pop 2000	C%	Christians	E%	U%	Unevangelized	Num	Pop 2000	C%	Christians	E%	U%	Unevangelized	Num	Pop 2000	C%	Christians	E%	U%	Unevangelized
A	2	288	0.00	0	41	59	171	0	0	0.00	0	0	0	0	0	0	0.00	0	0	0	0
B	2	2,972	31.02	922	85	15	449	0	0	0.00	0	0	0	0	0	0	0.00	0	0	0	0
C	6	597,246	92.20	550,674	100	0	466	4	286,660	91.26	261,612	100	0	659	5	600,506	91.85	551,594	100	0	1,086
Total	**10**	**600,506**	**91.86**	**551,596**	**100**	**0**	**1,086**	**4**	**286,660**	**91.26**	**261,612**	**100**	**0**	**659**	**5**	**600,506**	**91.85**	**551,594**	**100**	**0**	**1,086**

Country status. Cyprus is a truncated island nation in the Mediterranean. Its southern part consists of the legitimate Republic of Cyprus and the northern part, occupied by Turkish troops, consists of the self-styled Turkish Republic of Northern Cyprus, recognized by only Turkey. The partition of the island follows the religious division of the population, the south being almost entirely Christian and the north almost entirely Muslim.

HUMAN LIFE AND LIBERTY

Human need and development. In many respects, the citizens of the Republic of Cyprus enjoy a standard of living comparable to that of their compatriots in Greece. This is in contrast to the Turkish zone where economic conditions have steadily deteriorated since the partition. The contrast is all the more remarkable because the south inherited by far the more sweeping and serious problems. The economy is prosperous in the south and budgets for health and welfare are substantial. Most of the refugees have been integrated into the economy, and there is no shortage of skilled talents. The educational level of the Cypriots is high. Because the illegal Turkish backed government in the northern sector is not recognized by the United Nations, it does not receive any international aid. It has a high unemployment rate and its standards of living are as low as those of Turkey.

Human rights and freedoms. The unilateral partition of Cyprus and the military occupation of the northern one-third of the island constitutes a violation of international law and the civil rights of Cypriots. The Turkish regime still forbids travel by Cypriots within their sector. The electronic media in the Turkish sector are controlled by the government. Greek Cypriots living in the north are not permitted to change their housing and Greek Cypriot schools in the north are not free to use textbooks of their choice. In the South the Constitution guarantees the full array of civil rights and freedoms.

Human environment. The partition of the island had unforeseen negative consequences for the fragile eco-system. Tourists, numbering twice the island's population, add to the environmental strains. Unplanned urban sprawl has depleted available land and water resources and has caused coastal degradation. The famed beaches of Cyprus are threatened by pollution from industrial runoff as well as tourist activities.

NON-CHRISTIAN RELIGIONS

Islam is the religion of 18% of the entire island, virtually the entire Turkish population being Muslim. Most Muslims are Sunnis of the Hanafite rite under the mufti of Cyprus. The few Shias belong for the most part to dervish orders, particularly the Ticani, Mevlevi, and Bektasi. Turkish Cypriots tend to be more conservative than those in mainland Turkey, but they are increasingly influenced by recent reforms instituted by the Turkish government.

CHRISTIANITY

The apostles Paul and Barnabas visited Salamis, Barnabas' birthplace, in AD 46, and Barnabas later became the first bishop of Cyprus. In 441 the third ecumenical council of Ephesus discussed the separation of the Church of Cyprus from the Church of Antioch, and during the reign of the eastern emperor Zeno (474-491) the Cypriot church received autocephalous status along with the patriarchates of Antioch, Jerusalem, Alexandria, and Constantinople. From the 8th to the 10th centuries, Cyprus was subjected to a series of Arab raids, after which a considerable number of monasteries were built. In 1054, the schism between the Eastern and Western churches became a reality. At the invitation of the Latin king Gui de Lusignan, the initial immigration of Maronites from Lebanon to Cyprus occurred during the Crusades at the end of the 12th century. Their number ultimately reached 80,000 divided into 60 villages. The Maronite archdiocese of Cyprus was founded in 1352. From the 12th to the 15th centuries Cyprus was ruled by followers of the Latin rite, the Franks and then the Genoese, who placed a Latin hierarchy over both the Latin and Orthodox churches. When Venice gained control of Cyprus in 1489, it relaxed many of the former restrictions on the Eastern church, but antagonism between the 2 churches continued. Many Gothic churches and cathedrals were built during this period of domination by the Latin church. When the Turks invaded the island in 1572, they restored the Orthodox church to its former position in recognition of its help in the war against Venice. The Latin church was banished. The Maronites were also persecuted because of their alliances with the Lusignan dynasty and later the Venetians. Some returned to Lebanon, including the Maronite bishop, while other converted to the Orthodox Church or Islam. Only a small minority of Maronites remained in Cyprus. Franciscans, who first came to Cyprus in 1226 during the lifetime of Francis of Assisi, were later given permission to reestablish the Latin rite at Nicosia and Larnaca. Through the Muslim policy of using the religious leader of a conquered people as their political leader, the archbishop (ethnarch) of the Orthodox church increased in power, being given responsibility for collecting taxes and maintain law and order. By the beginning of the 19th century both Greeks and Turks were restive under his growing domination, and in 1821 following the Greek war of independence the ethnarch and several of his closest collaborators were executed. In 1878 Cyprus came under British influence, formal annexation following in 1914. Agitation for union with Greece (enosis) gradually increased among the Greeks under British rule, with church leaders playing an active part; and in 1956 the ethnarch, archbishop Makarios, was banished from the island. He was later allowed to return and was elected president in 1959. Formal independence was declared in August 1960.

Orthodox Church of Cyprus. *Lower.* A priest at home, dressed similarly to his portrait of the Apostle Barnabas, by tradition first Bishop of Cyprus. *Upper.* Former President and Archbishop Makarios on 1971 visit to Kenya when he baptized 5,000 Africans.

ORTHODOX CHURCHES. Three-quarters of the population, and 96% of all Christians, are members of the Orthodox Church of Cyprus. The Orthodox constitution of 1909 states that the church is governed by the Holy Synod, consisting of its 3 diocesan bishops under the presidency of the archbishop.

There are 11 major Orthodox monasteries active at present in Cyprus, with most of the remaining 67 disused and in ruins. Income from these islands is an important source of finance for the church. Only a small percentage of the people attend liturgical services regularly, but feast days are widely observed. Traditional fasting is now seldom practiced, but the Great Week leading up to Easter is considered a highly important religious holiday. Orthodox religion in Cyprus centers on the home, each of which has its own honored icon. Church weddings and funerals are also widely observed. Cypriot village priests have little theological training but are adept in the exact performance of Orthodox ritual. They have a close relationship with the people and are proud upholders of the national culture. The Theological Seminary of the Apostle Barnabas became in 1972 a major seminary providing a full training for the priesthood. Cyprus has no university, but some, mostly lay theologians who become teachers, go on for further studies at the University of Athens.

The Armenian Apostolic Church has 18,000 members in Cyprus. Armenians have lived on the island since the 11th century, but a large number of immigrants fled there from Turkey during and after World War I. Cyprus forms a diocese under the Catholicate of Cilicia, located in Lebanon.

CATHOLIC CHURCH. There are 9,000 faithful divided among 4 rites, including 200 Armenian Catholics, 200 Greek Catholics, 1,000 Latin-rite Catholics and 7,000 Maronites, but only the latter 2 have organized communities in Cyprus. The Maronite archdiocese of Cyprus includes both the island of Cyprus and a part of Lebanon. The Cypriot part is the more extensive geographically but less important numerically, with only 7,000 faithful out of a total of 83,000 baptized members in the archdiocese. They live in 4 exclusively Maronite villages, and in a few towns. In all there are 10 parishes served by clergy, with 150 baptisms and 70 marriages annually. On the island, there are 12 Maronite secular priests, 3 monks in the Monastery of the Prophet Elijah and about 40 Maronite sisters enrolled in Latin congregations, mostly Franciscan missionaries. Outside Cyprus these are 7 Cypriot nuns in Lebanon, 10 monks, and 4 seminarians at the Jesuit seminary in Athens. The Maronite community in Cyprus is led by a Cypriot vicar-general.

Latin-rite Catholics are mostly expatriates. Cyprus forms part of the Latin patriarchate of Jerusalem, the present head being a Franciscan patriarchal vicar-general. Ecclesiastical personnel include 10 Franciscan priests, 39 Franciscan Sisters of the Sacred Heart, and 24 St Joseph Sisters.

The Holy See has diplomatic relations with Cyprus and in AD 2000 is represented to government and the Catholic hierarchy by a pro-nuncio in Nicosia.

OTHER CHURCHES. Anglicans are mostly expatriates served by 3 British clergy. There are 10 congregations, the largest being in Nicosia. The island forms a diocese in the Episcopal Church in Jerusalem and the Middle East, formerly called the Jerusalem Archbishopric. Protestants are divided into a number of small groups, the largest of which is the Greek Evangelical Church. The Reformed Presbyterian Church sponsors 2 secondary schools, one for girls in Nicosia and the other for boys in Larnaca, and Seventh-day Adventists administer a physiotherapy clinic and a Bible correspondence course. Jehovah's Witnesses also have an active community in Cyprus.

Indigenous missions. Orthodox priests have long served as foreign missionaries from Cyprus to other countries abroad, totaling some 80 priests in 8 countries.

CHURCH AND STATE

The constitution of 16 August 1960 was the result of a joint effort on the part of Britain, Greece, and Turkey to stabilize a political situation endangering the security of the Western world. The constitution united Greeks and Turks in the same state, while clearly maintaining their separation. With the exception of foreigners, the population was divided into 2 communities, Greek and Turkish, with all citizens having to choose either one or the other. In general, citizens belonging to the Greek Orthodox Church, or those of Greek origin, culture and language, were officially part of the Greek community. The same was true for Muslims, or those of Turkish origin, culture and language who were considered to belong to the Turkish community (Article 2, items 1 and 2). Any Greek or Turkish citizen, however, could individually choose to be part of the other community (Article 2, items 5 and 6). Nationals not belonging to either of the 2 communities still had to choose one or the other. If they belonged to a religious group, the religious body made the choice, but the right of each individual to decide otherwise was guaranteed (Article 2, item 3). There were 1,000 such persons in Cyprus at the time the constitution went into force, at least 500 of whom became citizens of the new republic on that date. Each community had its own communal chamber (Article 86), and each religious group elected representatives to its chamber (Article 109). The communal chambers were given authority to levy taxes and to safeguard the right of members of their community. They were also authorized to handle all religious and cultural questions, and they had full jurisdiction in matrimonial matters (Article 87). The autonomous Greek Orthodox Church of Cyprus was given the sole right of regulating and administering its internal affairs and properties according to its holy canons and its charter (Article 110, item 1). Moreover, the constitution recognized the institution of Waqfs (Muslim religious trusts), all questions concerning them being regulated solely by the Laws or Principles of Waqfs (*ahkamul evkaf*) as well as by the laws and regulations promulgated by the Turkish communal chamber (Article 110, item 2). For other religious groups, the former colonial legislation remained basically unchanged under the republic. If at any time the Greek or Turkish communities determined that the number of teachers or ministers of religion (*din adami*) was sufficient for the operation of their institutions, they could ask the Greek or Turkish government to supply additional personnel, but only that 'strictly necessary to meet their needs' (Article 108, item 2).

In December 1959, the ethnarch of the Church of Cyprus, archbishop Makarios, became president of the republic. He had been a firm supporter of independence from colonial rule, with the ultimate aim of union with Greece (*enosis*). However, he later withdrew his support of enosis and also rejected the demand of the church's Holy Synod in March 1972 that he resign from his secular duties. Opposition on the part of bishops to his dual role increased, and in mid-1973 Makarios, with the support of heads of other Eastern Orthodox churches, deposed the 3 diocesan bishops who had been calling for his resignation.

On 15 July 1974 archbishop Makarios was forcibly evicted from power by a coup d'etat engineered from Athens, which provoked Turkey's armed forces to invade the island 5 days later. Although Makarios returned as president on 7 December 1974, he was unable to heal the de facto division of the island between Turks and Greeks. On 13 February 1975 an autonomous Turkish Cypriot state was proclaimed in the north and a referendum to accept a new constitution for the Turkish zone voted on 8 June 1975. However, Greek Cypriots in the south have refused to accept the validity of these decisions. Makarios died in mid-1977. Subsequently the division has lasted over 20 years with only occasional killings.

BROADCASTING AND MEDIA

TWR has a studio in Cyprus that produces Armenian and Farsi program broadcasts out of Monaco, and uses a transmitter in Cyprus to broadcast 90 minutes of daily programs throughout the Middle East. AWR has a studio in Cyprus as well, producing programs in Arabic and Farsi. Residents can hear IBRA-produced programs can be received via local radio stations, and shortwave radio programs from Voice of Hope (Lebanon), FEBA (Seychelles), AWR (Slovakia) and HCJB (Ecuador) in Arabic and English.

Christian television programming can be received from METV in southern Lebanon. Satellite TV programs are received mainly in Arabic. Orthodox Church of Cyprus has regular broadcasts on TV and radio.

INTERDENOMINATIONAL ORGANIZATIONS

Prior to the coup d'etat in 1974, an informal organization of Cypriot church leaders met monthly in Nicosia including the Armenian Orthodox vicar, Latin-rite vicar, Anglican priest, pastor of the Nicosia Community Church, with the Maronite vicar as secretary, and with occasional participation by Greek Orthodox priests.

FUTURE TRENDS AND PROSPECTS

Christianity will probably experience a slight decline due to the increase of nonreligious (expected to reach 5.2% by AD 2025).

Although Christianity will likely remain strong into the future, the nonreligious could grow to over 10% by AD 2050.

BIBLIOGRAPHY

A history of the Orthodox Church of Cyprus. J. Hackett. New York: Burt Franklin, 1972. 720p.

A report on the archiepiscopal question. S. Araouzos. Nicosia: Kypriakos Syllogos, 1908. 13p.

'A study in Roman Catholic and Greek Orthodox Church relations on the island of Cyprus between the years A.D. 1196 and 1360,' H. J. Magoulias, *Greek Orthodox Theological Review*, 10, 1 (1964), 75–106.

Byzantine churches of Greece and Cyprus. E. Mastrogiannopoulos. Brookline, MA: Holy Cross Orthodox Press, 1984. 134p.

Cypriote shrines. H. C. Luke. London: Faith Press, 1920. 47p.

Cyprus. P. M. Kitromilides & M. L. Evriviades. *World bibliographical series*, vol. 28. Oxford, UK: CLIO Press, 1982. 213p. (See especially 'Religion,' p.101–4).

Griechische Sitten und Gebrauche auf Cypern. M. Ohnefalsch-Richter. Berlin: Dietrich Reimer, 1913. 369p.

Les Maronites de Chypre. Cirilli J. M. Lille, France: Imprimerie de l'Orphelinat de Don Bosco, 1898. 30p.

'Les petites minorités à Chypre (Maronites, Arméniens et "Latins"),' P. Sergy, *Revue française d'etudes politiques mediterranéennes*, nos. 18/19 (1976), 75–82.

'Religion,' in *US Army area handbook for Cyprus*, p.139–65. *Department of Army Pamphlet.* Washington, DC: US Government Printing Office, 1964.

Researches into the traditions of the popular religious feasts of Cyprus. M. Paraskevopoulou. Nicosia: M. Paraskevopoulou, 1982. 184p.

Studies on the history of the church of Cyprus 4th–20th centuries. B. Englezakis. Ed., S. Ioannou & M. Ioannou. Aldershot: Variorum, 1995. 501p.

'The Church of Cyprus during the period of the Arab wars, AD 649–965,' A. I. Dikigoropoulos, *Greek Orthodox Theological Review*, 11, 2 (1965–1966), 237–279.

The churches and saints of Cyprus. C. D. Cobham. London, 1910. 43p.

The Cyprus problem: religious tolerance and all that! F. Plümer. , 1988. 57p.

The inner life of Cyprus. D. Stylianou. Nicosia, 1931. 100p.

The painted churches of Cyprus: treasures of Byzantine art. A. Stylianou & J. Stylianou. London: Trigraph for the A. G. Leventis Foundation, 1985. 518p.

'The Reformed Presbyterian Mission to Cyprus: a history and evaluation.' H. T. Panayiotides-Djaferis. Th.M. thesis, Western Conservative Baptist Seminary, 1995. 101p.

'The religion of ancient Cyprus,' K. Nicolaou, *Stasinos*, 2 (1964–65), 11–21.

Country Table 2. **Organized churches and denominations in Cyprus.**

Official name (bold type = church with over 10% of all affiliated) 1	*Begun* 2	*Type* 3	*Counc* 4	*Congs* 5	*Adults* 6	*Affiliated 1970* 7	*Affiliated 1995* 8	*G%* 9	*Names, notes, and other statistics* (see Codebook, Part 3) 10
Ancient Church of the East	c1950	O-Nes	Y....	1	40	50	100	2.81	Remnant of once-strong Assyrian (Nestorian) church.
Anglican Church: D Cyprus & the Gulf		A-Cen	Aw.N.	7	1,400	6,000	3,500	0.05	In Episcopal Ch in Jerusalem & the ME. 95% UK military and civilians. 3x.
Armenian Apostolic Church: D Cyprus	c1050	O-Arm	Sw.N.	5	9,900	3,500	18,000	6.77	Under jurisdiction of C Sis (Lebanon). Cathedral in Muslim hands. 4 schools. 1r.
Catholic Church in Cyprus:	1099	R-LEr	O....	20	5,600	6,400	9,000	1.37	*Katholici Eklissia.* Maronite, Latin, Armenian, Melkite. Baptisms: 99.3% infant.
P Jerusalem (V Cyprus)	1099	R-Lat	Os	10	1,200	1,400	2,000	1.44	2% of P Jerusalem. Latin-rite, in 6 towns. M=OFM. Also 200 Armenians. 10x,63w.
AD Cyprus *(Maronite)*	1353	R-Mar	Os	10	4,400	5,000	7,000	1.35	95% of AD is in Lebanon. In 4 Greek-speaking villages.12n,3m,40w,2d(3),150Yy.
Christian Brethren		P-CBr	x....	1	60	300	120	0.05	*Plymouth (Open) Brethren.* M=CMML(UK). Mainly English, some Cypriots. 2f.
Church of God of Prophecy	1935	P-Pe3	Z....	3	330	300	660	3.20	*Pentecostal Church.* M=CGP(USA). No schools or institutions. HQ Neapolis, Nicosia.
Church of God Pentecostal	1947	P-Pe3	ZF...	6	300	200	500	3.73	M=CoG(Cleveland) (USA). Holiness Pentecostals (3-stage).
Ch of Jesus Christ of Latter-day Saints		m-LdS	.....	5	2,790	3,600	4,500	0.05	*Mormons.* Pairs of USA youths serve as missionaries.
Greek Evangelical Church		P-Ref	Rwc..	3	280	500	700	0.05	*Hellenike Evangelike Ekkesia.* Greeks. HQ Athens (Greece).
Jehovah's Witnesses	c1925	m-Jeh	x....	14	1,433	2,000	3,000	1.64	*Watch Tower. IBSA.* Active witnessing under way by 1940. 1k(Nicosia). (1975) 63Y. (1995) 42Y.
Nicosia Community Church		P-com	.....	2	100	100	150	0.05	Small English-speaking union church in capital. British, American expatriates.
Orthodox Church of Cyprus:	46	O-Gre	CWCN.	660	260,000	434,400	477,000	0.05	Autocephalous. 67 disused monasteries. 9 bishops. 2s(60).
AD Nicosia (New Justiniana)		O-Gre	Cs	226	98,000	199,400	223,000	0.05	*AD Levkosia.* Kykkos monastery (business, agriculture).
D Paphos (Néa Páfos)		O-Gre	Cm	139	49,000	75,000	78,000	0.05	Western part of island. HQ Néa Páfos.
D Kition		O-Gre	Cm	156	64,000	90,000	98,000	0.05	Larnaca and Limassol. Southern parts. HQ Larnaca.
D Kyrenia (Kirínia)		O-Gre	Cm	139	49,000	70,000	78,000	0.05	Northern coast of island. HQ Kirínia.
Reformed Presbyterian Church	1887	P-Ref	xF...	1	20	40	50	0.90	*Covenanters.* M=RPCNA(USA). Armenians, Cypriots. 2 schools (Nicosia, Larnaca). 14f.
Seventh-day Adventist Church	1932	P-Adv	x....	1	100	100	200	2.81	*Cyprus Station*, East Mediterranean Field. Correspondence courses. Nicosia. 2f,1h.
Union of Armenian Ev Chs in Near East		P-Con	Rw.N.	1	140	300	350	0.05	Armenian refugees from 1915-16 Turkey massacres. Main body in Lebanon, Syria, USA.
Other independent churches	c1980	I-3aX	x....	4	100	–	200	6.67	Including New Apostolic Ch (43 members).
Other Protestant denominations		P-	.....	14	707	1,300	1,485	0.05	About 12: Chs of Christ, Missionary Ch (USA), USA & UK military chaplaincies.
Totals				**748**	**283,300**	**459,090**	**519,515**		

Churches, members, growth, 1900-2025	*Congs*	*Adults*	*Affiliated*	*G%*	*Total denominations*	*6 Megablocs:* *O*	*R*	*A*	*P*	*I*	*m*
Total churches, members, and denominations (mid-1900)	200	112,000	184,870	1.31	6	2	1	1	2	0	0
Total churches, members, and denominations (mid-1970)	638	277,706	459,090	1.31	20	3	1	1	13	0	2
Total churches, members, and denominations (mid-1990)	640	256,000	470,150	0.12	30	3	1	1	20	3	2
Total churches, members, and denominations (mid-1995)	748	283,300	519,515	2.02	30	3	1	1	20	3	2
Total churches, members, and denominations (mid-2000)	750	301,000	551,594	1.21	30	3	1	1	20	3	2
Total churches, members, and denominations (mid-2025)	800	338,000	620,000	0.47	67	10	1	1	30	20	5

NOTES ON TABLE ABOVE

NATIONAL COUNCILS (Column 4, 5th letter).

E = Cyprus Evangelical Alliance (CEA).

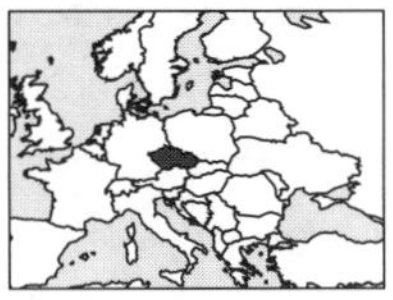

CZECH REPUBLIC

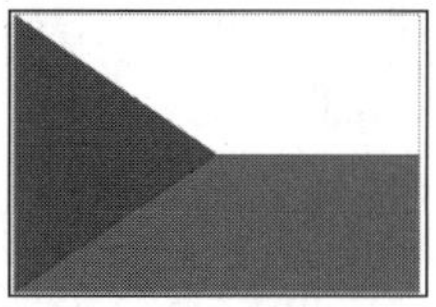

SECULAR DATA, AD 2000

STATE
Official name: Ceská Republika (The Czech Republic).
Short name: Czech Republic. **Adjective of nationality:** Czech.
Flag: White and red stripes with blue triangle on left.
Area: 78,864 sq. km. (30,450 sq. mi.).
Government: Unitary multiparty republic with two legislative houses, since 1992 (1918 republic created, 1946 one-party Communist state).
Legislature: Senate, 81 members; Chamber of Deputies, 200 members.
Official language: Czech.
Monetary unit: 1 koruna (Kc) = 100 halura. **US$1=** 29.97 Kc.
Chief cities: PRAHA (Prague) 1,233,000; Ostrava 763,177; Brno 451,881; Plzen 210,878; Liberec 175,731.
Political divisions: 8 provinces.
Armed forces: 44,000.

DEMOGRAPHY
Population: 10,244,000.
Population density: 129.9/sq. km. (336.4/sq. mi.).
Under 15 years: 1,696,000.
Growth rate p.a.: -0.14% (births 8.91, deaths 10.84).
Mortality: Infant, per 1,000: 6.1; **Maternal per 100,000:** 15.0.
Life expectancy: 75 (male 72, female 79).
Household size: 2.7. **Floor area per person, sq.m:** 25.5.
Major languages: Czech, Slovak, Hungarian, Romany, Russian, German, Polish, Ukrainian.
Urban dwellers: 66.26%. **Urban growth rate p.a.:** 0.2%.
Labor force: 53%.

ETHNOLINGUISTIC PEOPLES
92.7% Czech (Bohemian); 3.0% Slovak; 1.2% German (High German); 1.0% Polish (Pole); 0.3% Russian.

ECONOMY
National income p.a. per person: US$3,870; **per family:** US$10,449.

EDUCATION
Adult literacy: 100% (male 100%, female 100%). **Schools:** 5,344.
Universities: 23. **School enrolment:** female/male: 96%/93%.

HEALTH
Access to health services: 85%. **Access to safe water:** 100%.
Hospitals: 287 (98 beds per 10,000). **Doctors:** 31,897.
Blind: 10,000. **Deaf:** 611,700. **Murder rate:** 2.
Lepers: 500. **Underweight prevalence under 5:** 1%.

LITERATURE
New book titles p.a.: 10,190 (995 p.a. per million). **Periodicals:** 4,057. **Newspapers:** 23 dailies.

COMMUNICATION (per 1,000 people)
Phones: 237 (20% mobile). **Radios:** 884. **TV sets:** 406.
Daily newspaper circulation: 219. **Computers:** 131.

REFUGEES
Alien refugees from other countries: 2,400.

HUMAN LIFE AND LIBERTY (optimum condition=100.0%)
HDI: 88.2. **HSI:** 75.0. **HFI:** 15.0. **EFL:** 60.0.

Country Table 1. **Religious adherents in the Czech Republic, AD 1900-2025.**

Year	1900		1970		mid-1990		Annual change, 1990-2000				mid-1995		mid-2000		mid-2025	
Name	Adherents	%	Adherents	%	Adherents	%	Natural	Conversion	Total	Rate	Adherents	%	Adherents	%	Adherents	%
Christians	**7,848,000**	**96.9**	**7,929,412**	**80.9**	**6,251,000**	**60.7**	**-3,745**	**24,376**	**20,631**	**0.33**	**6,400,000**	**62.0**	**6,457,310**	**63.0**	**7,102,000**	**74.7**
PROFESSION																
crypto-Christians	0	0.0	1,660,400	16.9	0	0.0	0	0	0	0.00	0	0.0	0	0.0	0	0.0
professing Christians	**7,848,000**	**96.9**	**6,269,012**	**63.9**	**6,251,000**	**60.7**	**-3,745**	**24,376**	**20,631**	**0.33**	**6,400,000**	**62.0**	**6,457,310**	**63.0**	**7,102,000**	**74.7**
AFFILIATION																
unaffiliated Christians	408,000	5.0	1,116,758	11.4	1,468,100	14.3	-883	17,890	17,007	1.10	1,658,479	16.1	1,638,174	16.0	1,420,000	14.9
affiliated Christians	**7,440,000**	**91.9**	**6,812,654**	**69.5**	**4,782,900**	**46.4**	**-2,861**	**6,485**	**3,624**	**0.08**	**4,741,521**	**45.9**	**4,819,136**	**47.0**	**5,682,000**	**59.7**
Roman Catholics	6,984,000	86.2	5,743,000	58.6	4,132,000	40.1	-2,486	2,880	394	0.01	4,087,392	39.6	4,135,936	40.4	4,800,000	50.5
Protestants	450,000	5.6	429,654	4.4	320,000	3.1	-193	193	0	0.00	310,730	3.0	320,000	3.1	400,000	4.2
Independents	0	0.0	560,300	5.7	250,000	2.4	-150	2,150	2,000	0.77	261,729	2.5	270,000	2.6	350,000	3.7
Orthodox	6,000	0.1	60,000	0.6	50,000	0.5	-30	1,030	1,000	1.84	50,000	0.5	60,000	0.6	80,000	0.8
Marginal Christians	0	0.0	19,500	0.2	30,000	0.3	-18	218	200	0.65	30,670	0.3	32,000	0.3	50,000	0.5
Anglicans	0	0.0	200	0.0	900	0.0	-1	31	30	2.92	1,000	0.0	1,200	0.0	2,000	0.0
Trans-megabloc groupings																
Evangelicals	100,000	1.2	115,000	1.2	124,000	1.2	-75	375	300	0.24	125,328	1.2	127,000	1.2	192,000	2.0
Pentecostals/Charismatics	0	0.0	10,000	0.1	216,000	2.1	-130	4,130	4,000	1.71	246,881	2.4	256,000	2.5	385,000	4.1
Great Commission Christians	**650,000**	**8.0**	**1,176,000**	**12.0**	**2,475,000**	**24.0**	**-1,489**	**13,121**	**11,632**	**0.46**	**2,530,000**	**24.5**	**2,591,316**	**25.3**	**2,500,000**	**26.3**
Nonreligious	26,000	0.3	1,046,988	10.7	3,396,080	33.0	-2,043	-11,200	-13,243	-0.40	3,391,000	32.8	3,263,653	31.9	2,200,000	23.1
Atheists	8,000	0.1	820,000	8.4	650,000	6.3	-391	-13,225	-13,616	-2.32	525,000	5.1	513,844	5.0	200,000	2.1
Jews	218,000	2.7	8,000	0.1	7,300	0.1	-4	-14	-18	-0.25	7,100	0.1	7,120	0.1	6,000	0.1
Muslims	0	0.0	200	0.0	800	0.0	0	50	50	4.98	1,000	0.0	1,301	0.0	2,000	0.0
Baha'is	0	0.0	400	0.0	820	0.0	0	13	13	1.48	900	0.0	950	0.0	2,000	0.0
World A (unevangelized persons)	24,300	0.3	490,257	5.0	103,060	1.0	-60	-3,992	-4,052	-5.06	72,277	0.7	61,464	0.6	28,536	0.3
World B (evangelized non-Christians)	227,700	2.8	1,385,488	14.1	3,951,940	38.3	-2,378	-20,384	-22,762	-0.59	3,853,029	37.3	3,725,226	36.4	2,381,464	25.0
World C (Christians)	7,848,000	96.9	7,929,412	80.9	6,251,000	60.7	-3,745	24,376	20,631	0.33	6,400,000	62.0	6,457,310	63.0	7,102,000	74.7
Country's population	**8,100,000**	**100.0**	**9,805,158**	**100.0**	**10,306,000**	**100.0**	**-6,183**	**0**	**-6,183**	**-0.06**	**10,325,307**	**100.0**	**10,244,000**	**100.0**	**9,512,000**	**100.0**

COLUMNS, ROWS.
For meanings and definitions, see Codebook (Part 3). Note that, by definition, total 'Christians' = professing + crypto-Christians, which also = affiliated + unaffiliated Christians, and also = Great Commission Christians + latent Christians. Percentages may not always total exactly, due to rounding.

CENSUSES.
31.XII.1910 (adjusted to 1921 boundaries): 90.2% Roman Catholics (4.4% Greek Catholics), 6.8% Protestants (4.3% Lutherans, 2.5% Reformed), 2.7% Jews, 0.3% nonreligious. **1930:** 77.5% Roman Catholics (including 4.0% Greek Catholics), 7.7% Protestants, 5.8% nonreligious, 5.3% Catholics (non-Roman) (Czechoslovak Church), 2.7% Jews, 1.0% Orthodox. **1991:** 47.8% nonreligious, 47.2% Roman Catholics (0.1% Greek Catholics), 4.5% Protestants, 0.2% Orthodox, 0.3% other religionists.

NOTES ON RELIGIONS
ATHEISTS. Czechoslovak Communist Party (in power 1948-1990; pro-Soviet). About 25% of Communist party members are estimated to be committed atheists, the rest being nonreligious with a very few professing Christians.
BAHA'IS. With 5 local spiritual assemblies (1996).
CRYPTO-CHRISTIANS. Before 1990, Christians affiliated to churches but not known as such to the state, were of 3 kinds: (1) unorganized individuals in the legal churches, (2) members of illegal or underground churches, and (3) isolated radio believers. After 1990 this category went out of existence.
JEWS. Decline from 360,000 in 1938 by over 85% as a result of massacres during Nazi holocaust, and subsequent emigration. During the disturbances of 1968, 4,500 Jews escaped the country. They have since been rapidly declining by emigration. Now they remain only in cities (1,200 in Prague with 2 synagogues) and in the sub-Carpathian Ukraine.
NONRELIGIOUS. Agnostics, indifferent to religion, including most Communist party members.

Great Commission Instrument Panel: status of the Czech Republic (for explanation see start of Part 4)

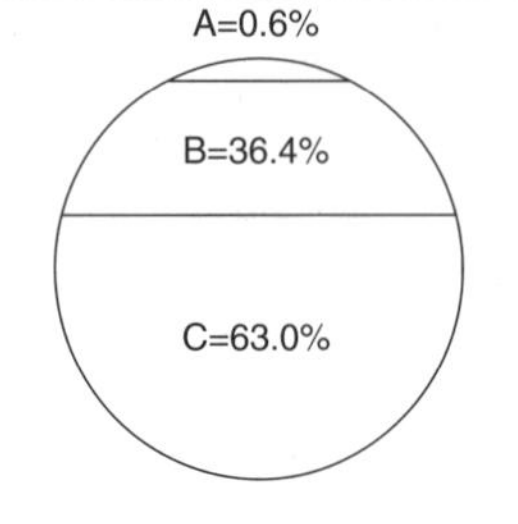

3 Worlds, AD 2000

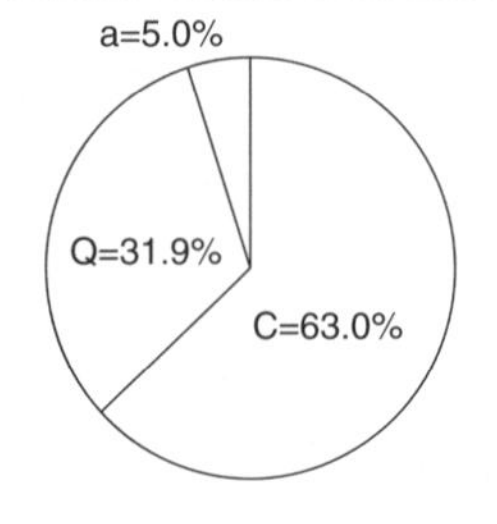

Religions, AD 2000

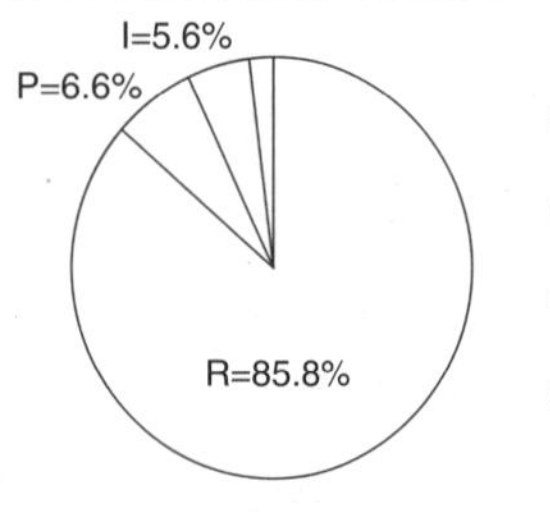

Ecclesiastical blocs

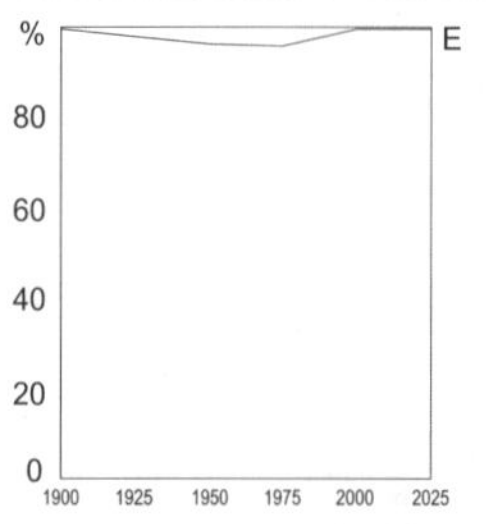

Evangelization, 1900-2025

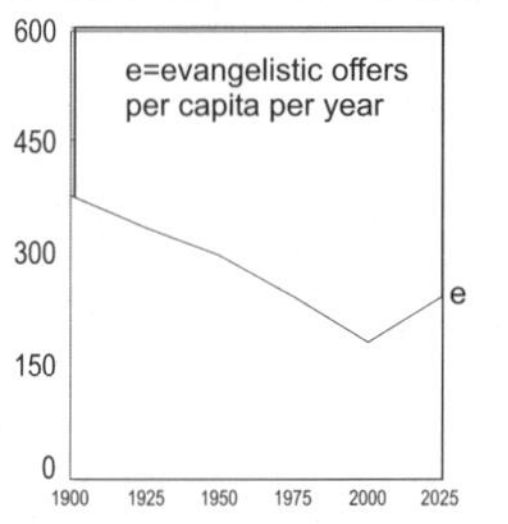

Offers, 1900-2025

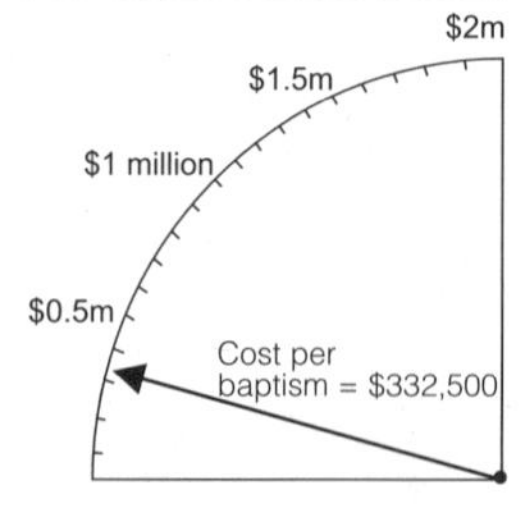

Cost-effectiveness, AD 2000

Country status. The Czech Republic is one of the 2 constituent republics of the erstwhile Czechoslovak Federation. It occupies the heartland of Europe and is the scene of some of the church's most enduring successes and monuments. Its chief agricultural products are wheat, barley, and sugar beets.

HUMAN LIFE AND LIBERTY

Human need and development. The Czech Republic has had a troubled history since it was carved from the territories of the Habsburg Empire at the end of World War II. It was one of the earliest victims of Hitler's aggression, and after World War II became a Soviet satellite and thus missed being part of the economic resurgence of Western Europe. The collapse of Communism in the late 1980s brought further economic and political disruptions. This was followed in 1992 by the dismemberment of the federation with Slovakia. The economic costs of such instability have been high. Although it occupies one of the most productive regions in Europe, Czech standards of living are closer to those of Eastern Europe rather than those of the West. There is no dire poverty; but many people, especially the old and infirm, lead marginal lives. About one-third of the population lives on some kind of state pension. Nevertheless, there are signs of affluence in the major cities comparable to those of the West. Shops are relatively well stocked and car ownership is high.

Human rights and freedoms. The Czech Republic made one of the quickest transitions of any East European country to a democratic system guaranteeing basic rights and liberties to all its citizens. Even after the rupture of the federation, these rights have been incorporated in the constitutions of both republics. Under a screening law, officials of the former

Country summary. **Worlds A, B, C by ethnolinguistic peoples, cities, and major civil divisions in the Czech Republic.**

World	PEOPLES Num	Pop 2000	C%	Christians	E%	U%	Unevangelized	CITIES Num	Pop 2000	C%	Christians	E%	U%	Unevangelized	CIVIL DIVISIONS Num	Pop 2000	C%	Christians	E%	U%	Unevangelized
A	1	1,537	0.07	1	48	52	798	0	0	0.00	0	0	0	0	0	0	0.00	0	0	0	0
B	5	9,539,941	44.78	4,272,323	99	1	55,752	23	4,428,658	46.57	2,062,581	99	1	39,126	8	10,244,176	47.04	4,819,136	99	1	59,479
C	20	702,699	77.82	546,812	100	0	2,932	0	0	0.00	0	0	0	0	0	0	0.00	0	0	0	0
Total	**26**	**10,244,177**	**47.04**	**4,819,136**	**99**	**1**	**59,482**	**23**	**4,428,658**	**46.57**	**2,062,581**	**99**	**1**	**39,126**	**8**	**10,244,176**	**47.04**	**4,819,136**	**99**	**1**	**59,479**

Communist regime are barred from holding public office. Acts of discrimination against minorities and small ethnic groups are punishable under law.

Human environment. Air pollution is a major problem in the Czech Republic. Sulfur dioxide from power generation and carbon dioxide from steel, chemical, and metallurgic plants seriously impair the health of Czechs, especially children. Water pollution also is serious, and many towns have contaminated water supplies.

NON-CHRISTIAN RELIGIONS

Atheism and ***agnosticism*** are significant forces in Czech life, representing as they do the official ideology of the government in power. Communist Party membership has however decreased markedly since 1948, when 20% of the population were members, to 12% in the 1960s and 8% in the 1970s. Membership in fact fell to 1.2 million members in 1971 as contrasted with 1.7 million in 1968, a half million resigning or being purged after the overthrow of the Dubcek regime.

Judaism decreased in number by more than 85% as a result of the Nazi massacres of the 1930s and 1940s. However there still exists an historic community in Prague and in the large cities, as well as a Jewish folk-community in the sub-Carpathian Ukraine. The Jewish Museum of the State of Prague conducts scientific research into the history of the Jewish people, particularly in Czechoslovakia, and published a journal in French and German.

Despite state repression of religion, Christian topics recur on the state's postage stamps. Here, Slovak icons on stamps issued in 1970: (*left*) 'Mandylion' (Icon of Christ) (16th century); (*right*) 'Archangel Michael' (18th century).

CHRISTIANITY

The history of Czechoslovakia has been influenced by its central European position, the country being subject between AD 600 and 1000 to Franco-Teutonic pressures from the north and west, and Magyar and Slavic pressures from the south and east. Early German missionaries originally propagated the Roman faith, while the growing rift between Rome and Constantinople resulted in Slavic-speaking people to the south coming increasingly under the influence of the Byzantine church, particularly because of its acceptance of the vernacular for liturgical purposes. Moravia, the central portion of the present-day Czech Republic, achieved its greatest glory in the 9th and 10th centuries, largely through the missionary efforts of Cyril and Methodius. The kingdom of Bohemia under king Wenceslas also became Catholic in the 10th century. Bohemia flourished during the 14th century with the Holy Roman Emperor who was also king of Bohemia, Charles IV, established Prague as an archdiocese in 1344, and introduced the first university of central Europe there in 1348. Religious congregations grew, monasteries were built, and many priests ordained; but their extravagant living drew condemnation. The influence of John Wycliffe of England was augmented when the English king married Anne of Bohemia; and John Huss, the Bohemian Protestant martyr, emerged as one of the first pre-Reformation figures, combining Bohemian nationalist feelings against the domination of Germans within their population as well as against worldliness of the clergy and the authority of the pope.

A second movement within Czech Protestantism developed when a number of Christians left Prague in 1457 to establish a village of their own based on early Christian principles. These became known as the Unitas Fratrum (Unity of Brethren), later called the Moravian Brethren when they had become dispersed in other lands. A third movement was Lutheranism, which developed more fully the ideas promulgated by Huss; and in 1573 these 3 movements adopted a joint declaration of faith. The Czech Reformation reached its height at this time, with sympathetic Hussite and Calvinist kings in power. However, this came to an end in 1621 when the Austrian Catholic Hapsburgs gained control of Bohemia and Moravia, and Protestantism was suppressed. In 1781 an Edict of Toleration was issued, but only the Lutheran Augsburg Confession and the Calvinist Helvetic Confession were permitted, approximately one-third of the Protestants choosing to affiliate with the former, and two-thirds with the latter. In 1848 another edict permitted the use of local languages, and Protestants were granted equal rights with Catholics.

World War I created a new political entity when Slovakia was removed from the Hungarian empire, necessitating new ecclesiastical alignments; and World War II was followed by the rise of Communism with even more drastic repercussions on the life of the churches.

Czechoslovak Hussite Church. 1920 by secession of 20% of the Roman Catholic Church. *Above.* Divine service on July 6 (Magister John Huss Day) in Rabi castle ruins. *Below.* The Patriarch, Dr Miroslav Novak, presiding.

CATHOLIC CHURCH. Catholicism remains the majority religion of Czech Republic in spite of the impediments imposed on it by the former Communist regime. Of the Latin-rite dioceses, 7 were without residential bishops in 1973. Four of these were in the Czech part of the country and 3 in Slovakia. The archdiocese of Prague was under an apostolic administrator who was also archbishop but only in name. The bishop named by the Holy See to the diocese of Hradek Kralove in 1950 was never allowed to carry out his functions. Three of the residential bishops belonged to or were connected with either the Pacem in Terris Association, an official movement sanctioned and controlled by the Communist Party, or its predecessor, the Priests for Peace Movement, as were the capitular vicars (appointed directly by the government) for the 4 dioceses without residential bishops. The jurisdictions of Trnava and the Tesin zone were both under apostolic administrators equally bound to Pacem in Terris. The jurisdiction of Szatmar had no administrator. The chancellors of several dioceses and jurisdictions also belonged to Pacem in Terris.

Religious orders and congregations were dissolved in 1950 and were able to reconstitute themselves somewhat only in 1968. This included the creation of Czech and Slovak committees of religious congregations. However, since the fall of the Dubcek regime, they were again suppressed. They were not forcibly dissolved, but their activities were closely watched and held in check. According to a confidential report of a meeting of the Communist Party of Slovakia, the situation in that republic in 1970 was as follows. There were 16 male orders and congregations, 2 being Greek Catholic, with 581 members, 372 being priests, and 209 brothers. Of the 372 priests, 170 were active in the pastoral ministry, 129 occupied in other matters', and 73 had reached the age of retirement. Women's congregations were 22 in number, 2 being Greek Catholic, with 3,080 members including those formerly at work in Bohemia but now deported. Among these were 2,124 still at work and 956 in retirement. Some 664 were over 60 years of age, and 591 were aged 55-60. The total number of sisters including those without employment was at least 7,247 for all Czechoslovakia. The Ministry of Culture's 'Plan for limiting the activity of the Churches in Slovakia' severely limited the field of action of religious personnel to pastoral work by brothers, and to social welfare for sisters, that is to the degree that they had not been deprived of all activity. This is in marked contrast to the situation in 1968 when the majority of sisters had become parish assistants. For both, it was now forbidden to admit novices or to erect new communities. It appears, nevertheless, that the policy adopted in the Czech Republic was less rigorous. According to the Austrian Catholic agency Kipa, the Office of Ecclesiastical Affairs in Prague did not give in to the demand of its counterpart in Bratislava to terminate all activities of Slovakian sisters in hospitals and sanitoria in areas under its competence. Even in Slovakia sisters often succeed in asserting their rights to have work contracts conforming to the law, and in asserting that no legal disposition prevents them from exercising their religious vocation.

The Greek Catholic (Uniate) Church (Grecko-Katolicka Cirkev), of the Byzantine rite, was limited to the diocese of Presov in Slovakia. Its future was bound to that of its counterpart in Romania as well as its tenuous relationship with the Orthodox Church. On 28 April 1950 some irregularly-authorized delegates of the Greek Catholic clergy and laity in Czechoslovakia were brought to Presov by the Orthodox metropolitan Eleutheros and there proclaimed the reunion of their church with the Orthodox Church. On the following 27 May a decree of the government in Prague recognized the legitimacy of this transfer and ipso facto endorsed the disappearance of the Greek Catholic Church of Czechoslovakia. The Orthodox Church inherited its parishes, churches and all its pastoral properties. Some 320,000 faithful were thus officially and forcibly reintegrated into Orthodoxy. Of the 311 Greek Catholic priests at the time, 28 accepted the new situation; the rest were imprisoned. The bishop and his auxiliary were both deported. During the liberalization of 1968, a government decree of 13 June (which had among its signatories G. Husak who succeeded Dubcek as chief of government in 1969) authorized the reconstitution of the Greek Catholic Church, recognizing that its liquidation had been a political act of assimilation which had trampled on its rights. A referendum in each parish was then organized, based on a simple majority vote of the faithful. In March 1969, of the 246 Greek Catholic parishes in existence in 1950, 200 voted to rejoin the Roman Catholic Church and only 2 to remain in the Orthodox Church, with 40 others not yet reported; and in addition 69 priests asked to be received by the Roman Catholic Church. At the end of 1973, however, the existence of the Greek Catholic Church was again threatened. In 1974-75 the regime removed from Greek Catholics control over their own worship places and required that they be used jointly with the Orthodox, an action which could provoke conflicts among the 2 churches and bring discredit on Christianity in general.

A new era began after 1989 with the church's freeing from all government and party controls. A new diocese, of Pilsen, was erected in 1993.

The Holy See has diplomatic relations with Czech Republic and in AD 2000 is represented to government and the Catholic hierarchy by a nuncio residing in Copenhagen.

PROTESTANT CHURCHES. Lutheranism is the predominant Protestant tradition in Czech Republic. The largest body was the Slovak Evangelical Church of the Augsburg Confession, established in 1530, which except for 2 congregations in the Czech lands is now confined to Slovakia. The Silesian Evangelical Church of the Augsburg Confession is a Polish-speaking Lutheran denomination found in the Tesin, Karvina and Ostrava border areas of Moravia and Slovakia. The principal administrative organ is the Church Council which is elected by the Synod for a 6-year period, the synod itself meeting every 3 years.

The Evangelical Church of Czech Brethren is the result of a union in 1918 of the former Lutheran and Czech Reformed churches; it traces its origin to the Hussite and Brethren reformation beginning in the 14th century. Today there are 600 congregations in 13 seniorates. The chief legislative body is the Synod, which meets every 3 years, while administration is lodged in the Synodical Council. The Comenius Theological Faculty has had an important influence on the church in large part due to the activities of J.L. Hromodka, who played an important role in trying to initiate Christian-Communist dialogue in Czechoslovakia. The Reformed Christian Church in Slovakia was created in 1918 after Slovakia was severed from the Hungarian empire, and the Hungarian and Slovak languages are accorded equal status in the liturgical and administrative life of the church. The supreme legislative and executive organs are the Synod and the Synodal Presidium.

Other smaller denominations include Moravians, Methodists, Adventists, Baptists, and Pentecostals.

INDEPENDENT CATHOLIC CHURCHES. At the conclusion of World War I, the refusal of Rome to respond to the request of Czech Catholic priests and laymen for the use of the vernacular in the liturgy, married priests, and greater participation of laity in the administration of the church, resulted in Los von Rom, a massive exodus of Catholics who then formed the Czechoslovak Church, which was renamed the Czechoslovak Hussite Church in 1972, and after 1992 the Hussite Church of the Czech Republic. Leaving behind an earlier trend towards unitarianism, the church reintroduced the apostolic succession of bishops in 1935 and has tended towards greater orthodoxy in recent years. While adopting Hussite emphases, it has retained also many Catholic features and considers itself to be a Reformed Catholic rather than a Protestant church. It remains the largest denomination in Czechoslovakia today after the Catholic Church itself.

Other, smaller, secessionist churches from Rome exist.

Orthodox Church in the Czech Republic. *Top.* Metropolitan Dorotheos of Prague & All Czechoslovakia celebrates divine liturgy in Teplice, 1974. *Bottom.* Parish church of St Cyril & St Methodius at Stropkov.

ORTHODOX CHURCH. The first Orthodox communities were established in Prague in 1863. Suppressed during World War I, they were re-established after peace was restored. Over the years the Orthodox Church, which is strongest in eastern Slovakia, has functioned under the jurisdictions of the patriarchs of Serbia, Constantinople and Moscow. Suffering persecution again during World War II, Prague was reconstituted as a metropolitan see under Moscow in 1949. In 1950 the conflict with Catholicism erupted over the status of the Greek Catholic (Uniate) Church. In 1951 the church was declared autocephalous.

Art and architecture. Prague contains many impressive churches. The best known is the Church of St Vitus, one of the largest Gothic structures in Europe. It is entered through the Hradcany Palace. The best example of a baroque church is the Church of St Nicholas.

Renewal movements. In the 1990s the Pentecostal/Charismatic Renewal continued to spread rapidly across most older churches, and numbered over 256,000 adherents (of whom 4% Pentecostals, 61% Charismatics, and 36% Independents).

Indigenous missions. During the Communist era, very few Czechs were sent abroad as missionaries. In the midst of rebuilding after the collapse of Communism, a few new missionaries have been sent out to surrounding countries.

CHURCH AND STATE

The constitutional law of the Czechoslovakian Federation promulgated on 27 October 1968 and put into effect on 1 January 1969 included no reference to religious questions. Article 32 of the 1960 constitution took up the article of the same number in the preceding constitution of 1948, as follows: 'Freedom of religion is guaranteed. One may profess any religion or no religion. Religious practices may be observed inasmuch as they do not transgress the law' (Paragraph 1). 'Religious faith or convictions cannot be used as a pretext for refusing to carry out individual civil responsibilities fixed by law' (Paragraph 2).

The Federal Office of State for Ecclesiastical Affairs within the Ministry of Culture (Ministerstvo Kultury, Urad Predsednictva Vlády, Sekretariát pro Veci Církevní) was authorized to handle all religious questions. Created by Parliament in 1949, it was given the task of 'watching over ecclesiastical and religious life to see that it develops in harmony with the constitution and the principles of the Popular Democratic Regime, assuring thus that each citizen has the freedom of religion guaranteed by the constitution, on the basis of religious tolerance and juridical equality for all denominations'. All churches and religious communities required official recognition. According to a report published in 1972 by the Central Committee of the Czechoslovak Communist Party, the state recognized 18 religious communities. After 1968 the Office was divided into Czech (Církevne Urad v Praze) and Slovak (Církevne Urad v Bratislava) sections, which in turn, were further decentralized into districts. In actuality, it was an organ for control and opened the door for the state to enter into the internal affairs of the churches.

On 27 February 1973, after negotiations since October 1970, the Vatican formally announced the conclusion of a partial settlement with the Czech government, providing for the naming of 4 new bishops who were all members of the Pacem in Terris Czechoslovak Association of Priests, on the condition nevertheless that one of them, Msgr Vrana, named apostolic administrator of the archdiocese of Olomouc, renounced all participation in Pacem in Terris of which he had been federal president. Just before that, Pacem in Terris had chosen a new federal president in the person of another ordinary, Msgr Vesely, apostolic administrator of Tesin. In March 1978, cardinal Frantisek Tomasek was appointed archbishop of Prague after that post had been vacant for 30 years. A new Catholic province of Slovakia was also set up.

With the collapse of Communism, the church was restructured to cover 2 provinces (Olomouc and Prague) with 7 jurisdictions. A vast range of updatings and changes were then implemented.

BROADCASTING AND MEDIA

Shortwave radio programs from KNLS, HCJB (Ecuador), TWR (Albania, Monaco), and AWR (Slovakia) blanket the nation in the major European languages. AWR's Prague studio produces Czech-language programs. The Czech Republic is a member of UNDA.

Some 800,000 have seen the 'Jesus' Film, most through cinematic showings. Satellite TV and radio programs are received in English, Arabic, German and Italian.

INTERDENOMINATIONAL ORGANIZATIONS

Since the beginning of 1971 there were 2 church councils authorized for Czechoslovakia, one for the Slovak Republic and the other for the Czech Socialist Republic. The division was required by government due to the strength of the former Czech Ecumenical Council, which was founded in 1970, building on the Ecumenical Council of Churches in Czechoslovakia in 1956. However, by 1974 there was still no council in Slovakia due to Lutheran/Reformed rivalry and government determination to deal directly with individual denominations.

The Christian Peace Conference (CPC) (Krestansk Mírov Konference) grew out of consultations between the 2 Protestant theological faculties (Slovak Faculty in Bratislava and Comenius Faculty in Prague) in 1957. The first conference sessions were held in 1958 and the first All-Christian Peace Assembly in 1961. Its headquarters were in Prague.

Several Catholic dioceses have commissions for ecumenism, including the diocese of Prague. The Ecumenical Institute (Ekumenicky Institut) of the Comenius Evangelical Faculty of Theology in Prague is undoubtedly the most advanced center for ecumenical studies in Czech Republic. Conferences, dialogue, and research are carried on in co-operation with a wide range of Czech denominations, including the Catholic Church.

The Ecumenical Section of the Huss Theological Faculty (Joannis Hus Facultas Theologica Pragae, Sectio Oecumenica), founded in Prague in 1969, is a university research institute which involves the collaboration of several Protestant, Orthodox, and Old Catholic bodies, in addition to its sponsor, the Hussite Church. Special attention is given to ecclesiology, ecumenical relations, and the Czech Reformation. In addition to a large annual conference for clergy, smaller conferences and special courses are offered periodically at the theological school.

In 1968, on the initiative of the Paulus Gesellschaft from Austria, a Marxist-Christian dialogue was begun in Prague, with the participation of several well-known Western visitors. Nothing further happened in this area since 1969.

Since 1990 a whole new area of cooperation and collaboration between the churches has begun.

FUTURE TRENDS AND PROSPECTS

The collapse of Communism and the breakup of the Republic into ethnic states may result in church growth making the Czech Republic almost 75% Christian by 2025, reversing a decline in effect since 1900.

The nonreligious and atheists are expected to decline throughout the next few decades perhaps stabilizing at 10% of the population. Christians would then make up most of the remaining 90%.

BIBLIOGRAPHY

Bohemia sacra: das Christentum in Böhmen 973–1973. F. Seibt (ed). Düsseldorf: Schwann, 1974. 645p.

Byzantine rite Rusins in Carpatho–Ruthenia and America. W. C. Warzeski. Pittsburgh, PA: Byzantine Seminary Press, 1971. 332p.

'Christianity and national heritage among the Czechs and Slovaks,' P. Ramet, in *Religion and nationalism in Soviet and East European politics*, p.264–285. P. Ramet (ed). 2d ed. Durham, NC: Duke University Press, 1989.

Christianity in Great Moravia. Z. R. Dittrich. Groningen: J. B. Wolters, 1962. 316p.

Christians and churches in Socialist countries: report of a visit by church leaders from South East Asia and Australia. J. S. Udy. Delhi: ISPCK, 1982. 204p.

Church and state in Czechoslovakia: historically, juridically, and theologically documented. L. Nemec. New York: Vantage Press, 1955. 577p.

Church in a Marxist society: a Czechoslovak view. J. M. Lochman. New York: Harper & Row, [1970]. 198p.

Czech ecumenical fellowship. M. Salajka & J. Svoboda (eds). Prague: Ecumenical Council of Churches in the Czech Socialist Republic, 1981. 187p.

'Czechoslovakia,' E. Kadlecovà, in *Western religion: a country by country sociological enquiry*, p.117–134. H. Mol (ed). The Hague: Mouton, 1972.

Czechoslovakia. D. Short. *World bibliographical series*, vol. 68. Oxford, UK: CLIO Press, 1986. 411p. (See especially 'Religion and theology,' p.103–8).

'Czechoslovakia: a church reborn in resistance,' G. Weigel, in *The final revolution: the resistance church and the collapse of Communism*, p.159–90. New York: Oxford University Press, 1992.

Fellowship of service: life and work of Protestant churches in Czechoslovakia. D. Capek (ed). Prague: Ecumenical Council of Churches, 1961. 152p.

Freedom denied: Czechoslovakia after Helsinki. A. Hlinka. Trans., H. E. Oborg. , [1977]. 36p.

Icons in Czechoslovakia. H. Skrobucha. London: Hamlyn, 1971. 155p.

Our Lady of Hostyn: queen of the Marian Garden of the Czech, Moravian, Silesian and Slovak Madonnas. L. Nemec. New York: RCH Press, 1981. 171p.

'Panorama historique du protestantisme tchèque,' A. Molnar, *Christianisme social*, 73 (1965), 229–47.

Politics and religion in Eastern Europe: Catholicism in Hungary, Poland, and Czechoslovakia. P. Michel. Oxford, UK: Polity, 1991. 329p.

Prager Kirchen = Prague's churches. I. Dolezal, J. Dolezal & J. Burian. Prague: Mladá fronta, 1992. 163p. (Text in German and English. Photographic essay of Prague's churches).

Prague winter: restrictions on religious freedom in Czechoslovakia twenty years after the Soviet invasion. Washington, DC: Puebla Institute, 1988. 59p.

Religion in Czechoslovakia. M. Navrat. Prague: Orbis Books, 1984. 108p.

Stimmen aus der Kirche der CSSR: Dokumente und Zeugnisse. B. Ruys & J. Smolik. Munich: Kaiser, 1968. 208p.

The anabaptists and the Czech Brethren in Moravia 1526–1628: a study of origins and contacts. J. K. Zeman. The Hague: Mouton, 1969. 407p.

The first unified church in the heart of Europe: the Evangelical Church of Czech Brethren. J. Otter. 3d ed. Prague: Synodal Council of the ECCB, 1992. 110p. (Presbyterian).

The origins of Christianity in Bohemia: sources and commentary. M. Kantor. Evanston, IL: Northwestern University Press, 1990. 307p.

'The Orthodox Church in Czechoslovakia,' G. Novak, *Orthodoxy*, (1964), 240–52.

'The position of the church in Czechoslovakia,' *Pro Mundi Vita* (Brussels), Special note 28 (1973).

'The re–establishment of the Greek Catholic Church in Czechoslovakia,' M. Lacko, *Slovak studies* (Rome), 11 (1971), 159–89.

'The religious situation in Czechoslovakia,' M. Kalinovska, *Religion in Communist lands*, 5, 3 (Autumn 1977), 148–57.

The witness of Czech Protestantism. J. Otter. Prague: Evangelical Church of Czech Brethren, 1970. 92p.

Thoughts of a Czech pastor. J. L. Hromádka. London: Student Christian Movement Press, 1970. 123p.

Yesterday and today: a survey of Czechoslovak Protestantism. Prague: Preparatory Committee, Ecumenical Council of Churches in Czechoslovakia, 1955. 56p.

Country Table 2. **Organized churches and denominations in the Czech Republic.**

Official name (bold type = church with over 10% of all affiliated) 1	*Begun* 2	*Type* 3	*Counc* 4	*Congs* 5	*Adults* 6	*Affiliated 1970* 7	*Affiliated 1995* 8	*G%* 9	*Names, notes, and other statistics* (see Codebook, Part 3) 10
Anglican Church (D Europe)	c1850	A-plu	awc..	4	500	200	1,000	6.65	*Anglican Ch in Europe, J. Fulham.* Chaplaincies, begun in Prague and Marienbad.
Apostolic Faith	1918	P-Pe3	x....	18	1,200	2,000	1,850	-0.31	*Apostolska Vira.* Linked AFM(Portland, Oregon, USA). Holiness Pentecostals. Formerly banned.
Assemblies of God (Apostolic Ch)	c1985	P-Pe2	Z....	74	2,160	–	3,000	10.00	*Apostolic Church* under communism.M=AoG(USA, UK, France).
Baptist Unity of Brethren	1885	P-Bap	Tv..W	37	4,000	4,000	10,000	3.73	*Ustredi Bratrske-Jednoty-Baptistu.* 50% Slovak. 1948, applied to WCC. 21n,110m.
Catholic Ch in the Czech Republic:	828	R-Lat	B....	3,146	2,983,000	5,743,000	4,087,392	0.09	*Katolicka Cirkev.* 1,621 unstaffed parishes. 332de. 1203n 447x 635m 2291w 39350Yy
M Olomouc	1063	R-Lat	Bs	734	984,000	1,500,000	1,348,000	-0.43	North Moravia. Population traditionally Catholic. 350n 131x 248m 1124w 15005Yy
D Brno	1777	R-Lat	Bs	457	547,000	980,000	750,000	-1.06	*Dieceze Brno.* Moravia capital. Vigorous Catholicism. 309n 90x 106m 393w 9548Yy
M Praha (Prague)	973	R-Lat	Bs	390	438,000	1,500,000	600,000	0.10	*Arcidiecéze Praha.* Province covers Bohemia. 160n 105x 160m 403w 3583Yy
D Ceské Budejovice	1785	R-Lat	Bs	360	290,000	563,000	398,000	-1.38	South Bohemia. Originally Germans. M=CSSR. 111n 36x 36m 168w 3983Yy
D Hradec Králové	1664	R-Lat	Bs	447	343,000	800,000	470,000	-2.11	NE Bohemia (N Sudeten). Till 1945, half Germans. 150n 49x 49m 0w 5100Yy
D Litomerice	1655	R-Lat	Bs	433	204,000	400,000	279,392	-1.43	1972, 3 Silesian deaneries lost to D Gorzow, Poland. 123n 36x 36m 203w 2131Yy
D Plzen (Pilsen)	1993	R-Lat	Bs	325	177,000	–	242,000	50.00	New diocese in extreme west center of country.
Christian Communities (Closed)		P-EBr	.....	11	420	1,000	1,050	0.05	*Exclusive Brethren* (Kelly-Continental). Ex Open Brethren, rejecting state recognition.
Christian Communities (Open)	c1905	P-CBr	x....	43	5,500	5,000	10,000	2.81	*Kretanské Sbory.* Christian Brethren. German Bohemia. Not recognized by state. 2f.
Christian Fellowship of Prague	c1985	I-3cW	.....	60	15,000	–	25,000	10.00	Renewal ex Ev Ch of Czech Brethren. Home cell groups for outreach.
Church of Brethren (Congregational Ch)	1868	P-Con	r...W	222	6,000	10,000	12,000	0.73	*Církev Braská. Formerly Unity of Czech Brethren. Workers, farmers. 56n.*
Czech Apostolic Church	c1930	P-PeA	.....	20	2,000	2,000	3,330	0.05	Links with Apostolic Church across Europe. Severely harassed by Nazis, then Soviets.
Czechoslovak Unitarian Association	1921	m-Unt	.....	6	2,000	4,000	2,670	-1.60	*Religious Society of Unitarians in Czechoslovakia.* Linked UUA(USA). Prague. 3b.
Evangelical Church of Czech Brethren	c1370	P-LuR	RWC.W	600	117,000	295,354	192,000	-1.71	*Ceskobratrská Církev Evangelická* (1918). 70% urban. Slovaks, Poles. 293n.
Evangelical Free Church		I-Eva	.....	7	1,400	1,800	3,500	0.05	Local indigenous body with wider connections.
Hussite Church of the Czech Republic	1920	I-ReC	.WC.W	432	130,000	550,000	185,000	-4.26	*Ceskoslovenská Církev Husitská. Los von Rom* (20% RCC split). 5 Dioceses. 347n,1u(57).
Isolated radio churches	c1950	I-3rW	.....	500	6,000	1,500	10,000	7.88	Isolated radio believers (students, youths). R=2000 (790 TWR,107 HCJB, Radio Vatican, &c).
Jehovah's Witnesses	1912	m-Jeh	x....	219	7,000	15,000	21,000	1.35	1948, suppressed; underground, but rapid growth. Many Gypsies. (1995) 950Y.
Lutheran Ev Ch of the Augsburg Conf	c1990	P-Lut	.....	3	450	–	1,000	20.00	Secession from Silesian Evangelical Church.
New Apostolic Church Community		I-3aX	x....	2	200	1,000	229	0.05	*Bezirk Schweiz.* World HQ Zurich (Switzerland). Leader jailed 1965.
Old Catholic Church	1898	I-OCa	U...W	9	1,500	3,000	2,750	-0.35	*Starokatolicka Církev, D Warnsdorf.* 1945, 50,000; then all Germans deported. 11n.
Orthodox Ch in the Czech Republic:	1863	O-Cze	MWC.W	55	40,000	60,000	50,000	-0.73	*Církev Pravoslavná v Ceskoslovenská.* Mainly Slovaks in east. A=1951. 4 bps,137n,1s.
M Praha (Prague)	1921	O-Cze	Mm	35	27,000	40,000	35,000	-0.53	Seat of Metropolitan. West. Remnants of Czech Orthodox Ch liquidated 1942. 28n.
D Olomouc-Brno	1945	O-Cze	Mb	20	13,000	20,000	15,000	-1.14	Slovaks, Hungarians, some Ukrainians. Gains from Uniates (1946) lost from 1990. 11n.
Pentecostal Movement		I-3pW	ZF...	95	2,200	2,000	3,250	0.05	*Letnicní Hnutí.* Formerly prohibited. Links with M=AoG(USA). 60n.
Reformed Christian Church	1918	P-Ref	RWC.f	2	1,000	4,000	2,000	-2.73	Until 1918 in Reformed Ch of Hungary. 95% Hungarian, 5% Slovak. Mostly farmers. 60n.
Seventh-day Adventist Church	1919	P-Adv	x....	170	8,500	15,000	15,000	0.00	*SDA, Czechoslovakian Union Conference.* HQ Prague. 48nx,42mw,1s,190t(10200),334Y.
Silesian Ev Ch of Augsburg Confession	1528	P-Lut	LWC.W	40	35,300	50,100	49,000	-0.09	*Slezká Církev Evangelická Augsburského Vyznáni y CSSR.* Polish speaking. 26n.
United Methodist Church	1922	P-Met	VwC.W	24	2,000	20,000	3,500	-6.73	*Ev Církev Metodistická.* Autonomous. M=C&S Europe CC, UMC(USA). HQ Prague. 16n,10t.
Unity of Brethren (Unitas Fratrum)	1457	P-Mor	xv..W	18	4,100	20,000	5,000	-5.39	*Jednota Bratrská. Moravian Ch, Czechoslovak Province.* 1949 applied to WCC. 17n.
Other independent charismatic chs	1988	I-3cW	.....	100	20,000	–	30,000	14.29	In largest cities: Chr Miss Soc (all Czechs), Assoc of Vineyard Chs, Manna Ch (Portugal).
Other independent Catholic churches		I-CCa	.....	10	1,000	1,000	2,000	0.05	Including: New Catholic Ch (1925, ex RCC, HQ Roudnice/Elbe).
Other marginal Christian bodies		m-	.....	100	4,000	500	7,000	0.05	Including: Anthroposophical Society, CJCLdS(Mormons, began 1929), New Church.
Other Protestant denominations		P-	.....	53	800	1,200	2,000	0.05	About 3 groups.
Totals				**6,080**	**3,404,230**	**6,812,654**	**4,741,521**		

Churches, members, growth, 1900-2025	*Congs*	*Adults*	*Affiliated*	*G%*	*Total denominations*	*6 Megablocs:* *O*	*R*	*A*	*P*	*I*	*m*
Total churches, members, and denominations (mid-1900)	6,800	5,504,000	7,440,000	-0.13	8	1	1	1	4	1	0
Total churches, members, and denominations (mid-1970)	6,550	5,039,444	6,812,654	-0.13	28	1	1	1	13	7	5
Total churches, members, and denominations (mid-1990)	6,200	3,434,000	4,782,900	-1.75	50	1	1	1	16	23	8
Total churches, members, and denominations (mid-1995)	6,080	3,404,230	4,741,521	-0.17	53	1	1	1	17	25	8
Total churches, members, and denominations (mid-2000)	6,100	3,460,000	4,819,136	0.33	56	1	1	1	18	26	9
Total churches, members, and denominations (mid-2025)	6,200	4,079,000	5,682,000	0.66	91	4	1	1	30	35	20

NOTES ON TABLE ABOVE
NATIONAL COUNCILS (Column 4, 5th letter).
E = Czech Evangelical Alliance (CEA).
f = member of ECCC until withdrew in 1971.
R = Ceska Biskupska Konference (CBK, Czech Bishops' Conference).
W = Ecumenical Council of Churches in the CSR, (ECC-CSR) (Ekumenická Rada Církví v Ceské Republice), 1955.

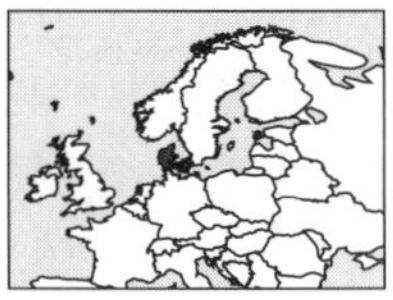

DENMARK

SECULAR DATA, AD 2000

STATE
Official name: Det Kongeriget Danmark (The Kingdom of Denmark).
Short name: Denmark. **Adjective of nationality:** Danish, a Dane.
Flag: White Latin cross on red field.
Area: 43,094 sq. km. (16,639 sq. mi.).
Government: Constitutional monarchy, since 1849 (1660 absolute monarchy).
Legislature: Folketing, 179 members.
Official language: Danish (Dansk).
Monetary unit: 1 Danish krone (Dkr; plural kroner) = 100 Ø. **US$1=** Dkr 6.36.
Chief cities: KOBENHAVN (Copenhagen) 1,326,000; Arhus (Aarhus) 270,518; Odense 181,259; Alborg (Aalborg) 158,160; Frederiksberg 87,225.
Political divisions: 16 provinces.
Armed forces: 33,000.

DEMOGRAPHY
Population: 5,293,000.
Population density: 122.8/sq. km. (318.1/sq. mi.).
Under 15 years: 952,000.
Growth rate p.a.: 0.13% (births 11.28, deaths 11.69).
Mortality: Infant, per 1,000: 6.9; **Maternal per 100,000:** 9.0.
Life expectancy: 76 (male 74, female 79).
Household size: 2.2. **Floor area per person, sq.m:** 51.0.
Major languages: Danish, German, Swedish, English, Norwegian, Polish, Turkish, Faroese, and several others.
Urban dwellers: 85.74%. **Urban growth rate p.a.:** 0.27%.
Labor force: 56%.

ETHNOLINGUISTIC PEOPLES
93.7% Danish (Dane); 1.2% Serbiac (Serb); 1.1% German; 0.5% Turk; 0.5% Dutch.

ECONOMY
National income p.a. per person: US$29,890; **per family:** US$65,758.

EDUCATION
Adult literacy: 100% (male 100%, female 100%). **Schools:** 2,952.
Universities: 235. **School enrolment:** female/male: 109%/106%.

HEALTH
Access to health services: 95%. **Access to safe water:** 100%.
Hospitals: 163 (35 beds per 10,000). **Doctors:** 14,497.
Blind: 8,000. **Deaf:** 316,500. **Murder rate:** 4.
Lepers: 300.

LITERATURE
New book titles p.a.: 12,540 (2,370 p.a. per million). **Periodicals:** 399. **Newspapers:** 51 dailies.

COMMUNICATION (per 1,000 people)
Phones: 612 (30% mobile). **Radios:** 988. **TV sets:** 536.
Daily newspaper circulation: 308. **Computers:** 510.

REFUGEES
Alien refugees from other countries: 9,600.

HUMAN LIFE AND LIBERTY (optimum condition=100.0%)
HDI: 92.7. **HSI:** 99.0. **HFI:** 95.0. **EFL:** 61.0.

Country Table 1. **Religious adherents in Denmark, AD 1900-2025.**

Year	1900		1970		mid-1990		Annual change, 1990-2000				mid-1995		mid-2000		mid-2025	
Name	Adherents	%	Adherents	%	Adherents	%	Natural	Conversion	Total	Rate	Adherents	%	Adherents	%	Adherents	%
Christians	**2,439,980**	**99.6**	**4,763,200**	**96.6**	**4,749,930**	**92.4**	**14,164**	**- 4,463**	**9,701**	**0.20**	**4,803,800**	**91.9**	**4,846,944**	**91.6**	**4,674,000**	**89.2**
PROFESSION																
professing Christians	**2,439,980**	**99.6**	**4,763,200**	**96.6**	**4,749,930**	**92.4**	**14,164**	**-4,463**	**9,701**	**0.20**	**4,803,800**	**91.9**	**4,846,944**	**91.6**	**4,674,000**	**89.2**
AFFILIATION																
unaffiliated Christians	2,500	0.1	24,803	0.5	49,140	1.0	146	4,523	4,669	6.91	88,335	1.7	95,834	1.8	100,000	1.9
affiliated Christians	**2,437,480**	**99.5**	**4,738,397**	**96.1**	**4,700,790**	**91.5**	**14,017**	**-8,986**	**5,032**	**0.11**	**4,715,465**	**90.3**	**4,751,110**	**89.8**	**4,574,000**	**87.3**
Protestants	2,430,280	99.2	4,786,050	97.1	4,680,000	91.1	13,931	-17,960	-4,029	-0.09	4,613,216	88.3	4,639,710	87.7	4,407,200	84.1
Independents	0	0.0	2,970	0.1	30,000	0.6	89	511	600	1.84	32,380	0.6	36,000	0.7	60,000	1.2
Marginal Christians	2,000	0.1	28,093	0.6	29,000	0.6	86	614	700	2.19	32,000	0.6	36,000	0.7	65,000	1.2
Roman Catholics	5,000	0.2	27,254	0.6	30,000	0.6	89	231	320	1.02	31,609	0.6	33,200	0.6	36,000	0.7
Anglicans	200	0.0	6,000	0.1	5,000	0.1	15	-35	-20	-0.41	5,000	0.1	4,800	0.1	4,000	0.1
Orthodox	0	0.0	200	0.0	1,200	0.0	4	16	20	1.55	1,260	0.0	1,400	0.0	1,800	0.0
doubly-affiliated	0	0.0	-112,170	-2.3	-74,410	-1.5	-221	7,662	7,441	-67.43	0	0.0	0	0.0	0	0.0
Trans-megabloc groupings																
Evangelicals	367,000	15.0	345,000	7.0	267,000	5.2	795	-1,095	-300	-0.11	264,162	5.1	264,000	5.0	234,000	4.5
Pentecostals/Charismatics	0	0.0	35,000	0.7	195,000	3.8	580	520	1,100	0.55	199,894	3.8	206,000	3.9	230,000	4.4
Great Commission Christians	**220,000**	**9.0**	**591,000**	**12.0**	**660,000**	**12.8**	**1,965**	**287**	**2,252**	**0.34**	**672,000**	**12.9**	**682,522**	**12.9**	**680,900**	**13.0**
Nonreligious	3,640	0.2	96,500	2.0	250,520	4.9	746	2,909	3,655	1.37	270,000	5.2	287,073	5.4	362,900	6.9
Atheists	2,000	0.1	47,000	1.0	70,000	1.4	208	487	695	0.95	74,000	1.4	76,947	1.5	92,000	1.8
Muslims	0	0.0	12,000	0.2	55,000	1.1	164	991	1,155	1.92	62,000	1.2	66,551	1.3	90,000	1.7
Jews	3,480	0.1	7,000	0.1	6,700	0.1	20	-13	7	0.10	6,720	0.1	6,765	0.1	6,800	0.1
Hindus	0	0.0	0	0.0	3,400	0.1	10	29	39	1.08	3,600	0.1	3,785	0.1	5,000	0.1
Baha'is	0	0.0	1,300	0.0	1,500	0.0	4	25	29	1.75	1,600	0.0	1,785	0.0	2,500	0.1
Buddhists	0	0.0	1,000	0.0	850	0.0	3	3	6	0.67	880	0.0	909	0.0	1,500	0.0
Other religionists	900	0.0	1,000	0.0	2,100	0.0	6	32	38	1.68	2,400	0.1	2,480	0.1	3,300	0.1
World A (unevangelized persons)	0	0.0	4,928	0.1	35,980	0.7	99	674	773	2.10	36,573	0.7	42,344	0.8	68,094	1.3
World B (evangelized non-Christians)	9,520	0.4	160,628	3.3	354,090	6.9	1,062	3,789	4,851	1.32	384,455	7.4	403,712	7.6	495,906	9.5
World C (Christians)	2,439,980	99.6	4,763,200	96.6	4,749,930	92.4	14,164	-4,463	9,701	0.20	4,803,800	91.9	4,846,944	91.6	4,674,000	89.2
Country's population	**2,449,500**	**100.0**	**4,928,757**	**100.0**	**5,140,000**	**100.0**	**15,325**	**0**	**15,325**	**0.29**	**5,224,829**	**100.0**	**5,293,000**	**100.0**	**5,238,000**	**100.0**

COLUMNS, ROWS.
For meanings and definitions, see Codebook (Part 3). Note that, by definition, total 'Christians' = professing + crypto-Christians, which also = affiliated + unaffiliated Christians, and also = Great Commission Christians + latent Christians. Percentages may not always total exactly, due to rounding.

CENSUSES.
1901: 99.3% Protestants (98.7% state church), 0.2% Roman Catholics, 0.2% Catholics (non-Roman) (3,810 Irvingites). **1921:** 97.2% state church. **1966** (estimate): 97.0% Protestants, 2.4% nonreligious and atheists, 0.6% Roman Catholics.

NOTES ON RELIGIONS
ATHEISTS. Danish Communist Party (Danmarks Kommunistiske Parti, DKP) (legal; pro-Soviet).
BAHA'IS. Growth from 5 local spiritual assemblies (1964) to 9 (1973, then declining to 7 (1996).
BUDDHISTS. With headquarters for Scandinavia in Copenhagen; Tibetans, and sympathizers.
DOUBLY-AFFILIATED. A large majority of members of Protestant free churches (including Salvation Army, Evangelical Church of Germany, also marginal Protestant bodies) are also regarded as members of the state church which therefore enumerates them all as such.
JEWS. In Denmark since 1600; mostly in Copenhagen, with 2 synagogues.
MUSLIMS. Mostly migrant laborers from the Balkans and Turkey, with a vigorous Ahmadiya Mission (enumerated here as Muslims although declared non-Muslim by Pakistan).
OTHER RELIGIONISTS. Including members of the Theosophical Society in 15 Lodges, also Rosicrucians (AMORC, 2 centers).

Great Commission Instrument Panel: status of Denmark (for explanation see start of Part 4)

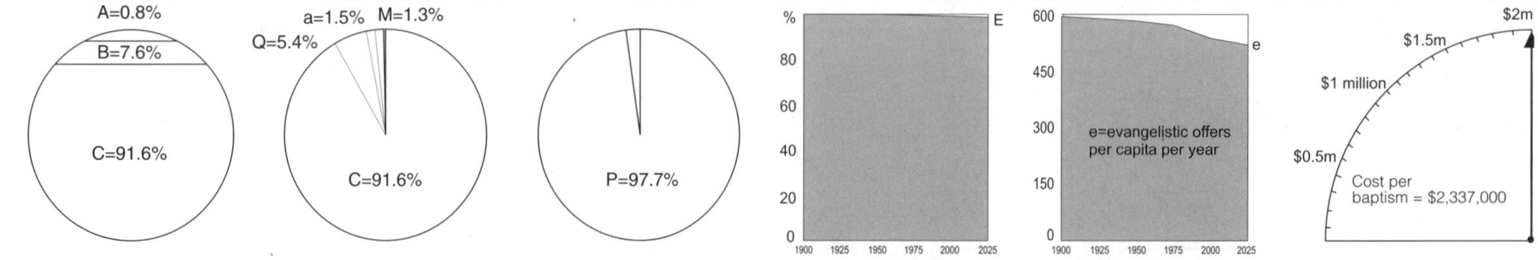

3 Worlds, AD 2000 | Religions, AD 2000 | Ecclesiastical blocs | Evangelization, 1900-2025 | Offers, 1900-2025 | Cost-effectiveness, AD 2000

Country status. Denmark is the most southerly country of Scandinavia, occupying the Jutland Peninsula and over 400 small islands. It is one of the flattest countries in the world and has a temperate, damp climate that makes it ideal for agriculture. State-owned companies predominate in a well-designed and maintained transportation system.

HUMAN LIFE AND LIBERTY

Human need and development. Denmark is a developed country with a strong economy. Under socialist rule for a good part of this century, Denmark has an extensive cradle-to-grave social welfare system which provides Danes with all basic medical, educational, and other amenities.

Human rights and freedoms. As a constitutional monarchy, Denmark is a model democracy where all basic human rights are guaranteed and protected. Anyone may protest to the ombudsman, public defender of human rights, mandated by the Constitution. Although the electronic media are state-owned, its independence is assured by a non-partisan council. An influx of asylum seekers has created some racial disharmony, and incidents of random racially motivated violence have occurred in many towns. Racial and ethnic quotas in housing have been declared illegal.

Country summary. **Worlds A, B, C by ethnolinguistic peoples, cities, and major civil divisions in Denmark.**

	PEOPLES							CITIES							CIVIL DIVISIONS						
World	*Num*	*Pop 2000*	*C%*	*Christians*	*E%*	*U%*	*Unevangelized*	*Num*	*Pop 2000*	*C%*	*Christians*	*E%*	*U%*	*Unevangelized*	*Num*	*Pop 2000*	*C%*	*Christians*	*E%*	*U%*	*Unevangelized*
A	2	19,585	2.35	461	42	58	11,274	0	0	0.00	0	0	0	0	0	0	0.00	0	0	0	0
B	8	65,742	12.70	8,351	62	38	24,996	0	0	0.00	0	0	0	0	0	0	0.00	0	0	0	0
C	19	5,207,912	91.06	4,742,298	100	0	4,859	10	2,294,289	89.21	2,046,649	99	1	19,973	16	5,293,239	89.76	4,751,110	99	1	41,131
Total	**29**	**5,293,239**	**89.76**	**4,751,110**	**99**	**1**	**41,129**	**10**	**2,294,289**	**89.21**	**2,046,649**	**99**	**1**	**19,973**	**16**	**5,293,239**	**89.76**	**4,751,110**	**99**	**1**	**41,131**

Human environment. Like most developed countries Denmark suffers from serious pollution problems. Pollution from the North Sea is increasing, especially nitrogen and phosphorus pollution from rivers in Central and Western Europe. Hazardous waste dumps number over 3,100 and laws governing dumping are very lax. Denmark's many livestock-only farms produce excess animal manures causing increased nitrate concentrations in surface and drinking waters.

NON-CHRISTIAN RELIGIONS

Islam has entered Denmark through the recent immigration of foreign workers; in 1995 those from Muslim countries legally present numbered 62,000 mainly from Turkey, the Balkans, and Pakistan.

Judaism is represented by a small community of about 7,000, centered primarily in Copenhagen. Jews have been in Denmark since the beginning of the 17th century, although they were not legally recognized by the state until 1849.

Buddhism in Scandinavia has its headquarters in Copenhagen, where are located the Centre for Tibetan Buddhism and the Kagyudpa-Karmapa Tibetan School, with extensive facilities for individual and collective meditation. Local centers have also been established in Stockholm, Goteborg, and Oslo.

CHRISTIANITY

Anskar, apostle of the north, visited Denmark as early as AD 826, and the first church was built in 850. Lutheranism was officially adopted by king Christian III in 1536 and all Roman Catholic activity forbidden after 1569. In 1648 Catholics made a new attempt at work through the auspices of the Spanish ambassador, followed by French Huguenots during the latter part of the 17th century and Moravians in the 18th century.

PROTESTANT CHURCHES. The foremost church of Denmark, as has been true since the Reformation, is the Evangelical Lutheran People's Church of Denmark, which includes in its membership over 95% of the total population of the country. Since its final legislative and financial authority is the Danish Parliament, it is sometimes referred to as the State Church, but its leaders prefer the term National Church of Denmark.

The juridical character of the regular assembly of bishops, under the presidency of the bishop of Copenhagen, remains ambiguous. Bishops are appointed by the king, in each case on presentation of a candidate elected by priests and delegates of parish councils (menighedsrad) which are themselves elected by universal suffrage in order to choose the priests for the king's nomination. Clergy are trained at the theological faculties of the Universities of Copenhagen and Aarhus. Numbers of new ordinations have shown a steady decline in recent years: from 1930-39, there were 620; 1940-49, 564;1950-59, 462; and 1960-69, 320. Ordination of laymen lacking full theological education is now beginning, and women are also admitted to the pastoral ministry. There were 35 ordained women in 1970: 90 in 1975.

Theoretically the National Church is limited to the frontiers of the kingdom, which includes Greenland and the Faeroe Islands, but in practice it includes work among Danes in other parts of the world. Danish Church Abroad was founded in 1919 to care for such communities, the largest of which is composed of 52 congregations in south Schleswig, an ancient Danish territory taken over by Germany in 1864. An important work is also carried on among Danish sailors in foreign ports. Missionary activities in Africa and Asia have originated with missionary societies which are independent of the Danish church. The National Church has strongly influenced the total life of the country. The parish minister was until recently invariably the president of the commune's school commission, and the church was largely responsible for the formation of People's Upper Schools. Today, a significant program of social service is carried on by the church's National Church Aid (Folkekirkens Nodhjaelp).

Although the number of convinced and practicing adherents is limited, the Evangelical Lutheran Church remains a national institution which one rarely withdraws from. In Copenhagen and surroundings, official acts of departure or withdrawals from the National Church rose from 2,967 in 1968 to 4,564 in 1969; and names of new-born babies declared to the state by civil action without baptism rose from 12% in 1968 to 23% in 1972. In Denmark, a new-born child is declared simply as boy or girl and must then, within a year, receive a name communicated to the state either after baptism or by a simple declaration.

Free church movements in Denmark have been generally much less successful in winning adherents than their counterparts in other Scandinavian countries. The largest of the free churches is the Baptist Union.

CATHOLIC CHURCH. The modern era of the Catholic Church in Denmark dates from 1849 when a new constitution proclaiming freedom of religion was adopted. In its early years there was a strong foreign element in its congregations, but today most of the faithful are Danes. The Catholic community is largely urban, about 40%, living in or near Copenhagen and forming the greatest density of Catholics in any Nordic country. An exception to this is found in the rural parishes of southern Denmark, especially South Jutland and the southern islands, where Polish immigrants settled during World War I. In 1956 those born in Slavic countries represented 25% of the total Catholic population in the southern islands.

Moreover, the number of new immigrant Catholic workers including Croats from Yugoslavia and Portuguese is constantly growing. Mixed marriages (with a Protestant partner) are common among Catholics; in 1965 the figure was 81%. A study made in 1969 of 9,212 Catholics married for more than 16 years showed that 4,860 were married to Catholics and 4,352 were partners in mixed marriages.

Weekly attendance at mass is 30%, declining gradually. About the same proportion participate in parish elections and donations to the freely-organized church tax. To understand this relatively low percentage, one must consider the large number of baptized Catholics not known to or affiliated with parishes, the number of those not eligible or fit to attend (children and the aged), and the relatively large distances between parishes outside Copenhagen, which are on average 30 kilometers. In Copenhagen itself Sunday attendance in 1969 was nearly 40%, although regular practice has been decreasing since then. The post-conciliar organization of the church in Denmark was established by a Diocesan Synod in 1969 composed of 65 priests, 25 religious personnel and 110 lay persons, three-fourths of whom were chosen by universal suffrage.

Since 1970 the following elected councils have begun to function: parish councils, exercising pastoral responsibilities in all parishes; 6 regional councils, namely 3 for Copenhagen and outskirts, one for North Jutland, one for South Jutland and Fionia, and one for the other islands; pastoral and presbyterial councils; and a council of religious personnel. In 1977 Denmark was transferred from the jurisdiction of Propaganda to that of the Congregation for Bishops.

The Holy See has diplomatic relations with Denmark and in AD 2000 is represented to government and the Catholic hierarchy by a nuncio residing in Copenhagen.

Renewal movements. In the 1990s the Pentecostal/Charismatic Renewal continued to spread rapidly across most older churches, and numbered over 206,000 adherents (of whom 13% Pentecostals, 69% Charismatics, and 18% Independents).

Indigenous missions. Danes have been involved in missionary outreach to surrounding countries since shortly after the establishment of the church in the 9th century. After the Reformation, most of the outreach of the national church has been to Danes in others countries. Evangelical missionaries have been sent out through other societies, though these have been declining steadily since 1970.

National Church of Denmark. (*Lower*) Lutheran pastor Yrsa Ludvigsen. (*Upper*). Clergy in procession in Copenhagen Cathedral.

CHURCH AND STATE

Article 4 of the constitution of 1953 recognizes the Evangelical Lutheran Church as the National Church, or People's Church (Danske Folkekirke), for which the state is responsible. The king must be a member (Article 6), but liberty of worship is guaranteed to all by Articles 67 to 70.

In reality, the term Danske Folkekirke, which is purely descriptive, means that this is the church of almost all the Danish people. Article 66 of the constitution states that the church's status is subject to regulation by law, but no general legislation has ever been developed. The church is under the general control of Parliament and the government's Ministry for the Church (Kirkeministeriet) which exercise their authority with tact and tolerance.

The state's support of the church is evident in its respect for Christian festivals, its provision for religious instruction at all levels in schools (although students who are not members of the National Church are exempt) and its financial support from the general budget. In addition, the state levies directly an ecclesiastical tax (Kirkeskat) on all except those members of recognized confessions who prove that they contribute an equivalent amount to their own religious bodies.

National Church of Denmark. Eucharist in the Lutheran Cathedral, Copenhagen.

No special restrictions are placed on the activities of other churches or religious communities. Many of them have received official recognition, including Anglicans, Baptists, Catholics, Norwegian and Swedish Lutherans, French and German Reformed, and Russian Orthodox, as well as the Jewish community. Among these groups, religious acts such as baptism, marriage and burial, and their corresponding certificates, have legal validity.

In 1975 Parliament passed a law stipulating that henceforth members of all religious confessions could be interred in cemeteries belonging to the National Church, following ceremonies led by their own ministers in their own places of worship.

BROADCASTING AND MEDIA

IBRA programming in Farsi, Turkish, and Arabic can be heard on local radio stations. Radio Stene is a local Catholic radio station that broadcasts 8 hours weekly on the publicly-owned transmitter. KNLS, HCJB (Ecuador), TWR (Albania, Monaco), and AWR (Slovakia) blanket Denmark with shortwave radio programs in the major European languages. Denmark is a member of UNDA. Radio Steno is a Catholic station broadcasting 8 hours weekly on the publicly owned transmitter.

A number of television programs are also available. CBN's *700 Club* and animated specials are available in Copenhagen on various channels at least one day a week. Satellite TV and radio programs are received in English, Arabic, German and Italian.

INTERDENOMINATIONAL ORGANIZATIONS

The Ecumenical Council of Denmark (Okumeniske Faellesrad i Danmark) was founded in 1939 and adopted a new constitution in 1971. Present membership includes the Evangelical Lutheran, Catholic, Baptist, Salvation Army, Mission Covenant, Apostolic, Methodist, Reformed, Anglican, and Russian Orthodox churches. Affiliated organizations include the Ecumenical Institute annexed to the theological faculty of the University of Copenhagen, and the Ecumenical Centre, a private institution created by students of the University of Aarhus which provides facilities for meetings of youth and international students. The Institute of Ecumenical Theology and Missiology, with its library, is attached to the center. In 1973 another Ecumenical Centre (Okumeniske Centre) was founded in Copenhagen, including an ecumenical hostel, to which numerous Catholic organizations are attached.

FUTURE TRENDS AND PROSPECTS

Under the continuing influence of secularism, Christian affiliation is expected to decline slowly into the 21st century to 89% by 2025. Muslims are expected to increase from only 0.2% of the population in 1970 to 1.7% by 2025.

The nonreligious and atheists together could constitute 10% of Denmark's population by AD 2050. Muslims, in the same period, could potentially grow to over 5% of the population. Christians would then experience declines to well below 80%, the first time in many centuries.

BIBLIOGRAPHY

'Communities of faith: sectarianism, identity, and social change on a Danish island.' A. S. Buckser. Ph.D. dissertation, University of California, Berkeley, 1993. 335p.

Danmarks kirkehistorie. M. S. Lausten. 2d ed. [Copenhagen]: Gyldendal, 1987. 351p.

Dansk kristendom og katolsk tradition: i anledning af pavens besøg i Danmark. B. Dalsgaard Larsen. Copenhagen: Katolsk forlag, 1988. 152p.

Denmark. K. E. Miller. *World bibliographical series*, vol. 83. Oxford, UK: CLIO Press, 1988. 218p. (See especially 'Religion,' p.51–61).

'Denmark,' J. Thorgaard, in *Western religion: a country by country sociological enquiry*, p.135–41. H. Mol (ed). The Hague: Mouton, 1972.

Folk og folkekirke: kirkens plads i menneskers hverdagsliv og tankeverden. I. Børgesen. [Copenhagen]: Akademisk Forlag, 1991. 253p.

Freedom of religion in Denmark. H. Fledelius & B. Juul. Denmark: Danish Centre for Human Rights, 1992. 111p.

Fundamentalisme på dansk. S. A. Madsen. [Denmark]: Forlaget Cicero, 1988. 122p.

History of the Church of Denmark: an outline. J. C. Kjaer. Blair, NE: Lutheran Publishing House, 1945. 127p.

Homeward to Zion: the Mormon migration from Scandinavia. W. Mulder. Minneapolis, MN: University of Minnesota Press, 1957. 375p.

Kierkegaard and the Church in Denmark. N. Thulstrup. *Bibliotheca Kierkegaardiana*, vol. 13. Copenhagen: Reitzel, 1984. 276p.

'Kierkegaard, the church and theology of Golden–Age Denmark,' M. P. Plekon, *Journal of ecclesiastical history*, 34 (1983), 245–66.

'Kierkegaard's attack on the church: images of ministry to the church.' V. Sherwood. D.Div. thesis, Vanderbilt University, Nashville, TN, 1972. 181p.

Myth and religion of the North: the religion of ancient Scandinavia. E. O. G. Petre. London: Weidenfeld & Nicolson, 1964. 340p.

Pagan Scandinavia. H. R. E. Davidson. London: Thames & Hudson, 1967. 214p.

Scandinavian churches: a picture of the development and life of the churches of Denmark, Finland, Iceland, Norway and Sweden. L. S. Hunter (ed). London: Faber & Faber, 1965. 200p.

Scandinavian mythology. H. R. E. Davidson. London: Paul Hamlyn, 1975. 141p.

Som om intet var hændt: den danske folkekirke under besættelsen. E. T. Jacobsen. [Odense]: Odense universitetsforlag, 1991. 381p. (Summary in English).

The church beneath the northern lights: Fenno–Scandian historical theology. A. J. Kristoffersen. , [1990]. 105p.

The Danish Church. P. Hartling (ed). Trans., S. Mammen. Copenhagen: Danish Institute, 1965. 161p.

The Reformation in Denmark. E. H. Dunkley. London: SPCK, 1948. 188p.

The religion of ancient Scandinavia. W. A. Craigie. 1906; reprint, Freeport, NY: Books for Libraries Press, 1969. 71p.

The Viking Jews: a history of the Jews in Denmark. I. N. Bamberger. New York: Shengold Publishers, 1983. 159p.

The Viking world. J. Graham-Campbell. New Haven: Ticknor & Fields, 1980. 224p.

Country Table 2. **Organized churches and denominations in Denmark.**

Official name (bold type = church with over 10% of all affiliated) 1	*Begun* 2	*Type* 3	*Counc* 4	*Congs* 5	*Adults* 6	*Affiliated 1970* 7	*Affiliated 1995* 8	*G%* 9	*Names, notes, and other statistics* (see Codebook, Part 3) 10
Apostolic Church in Denmark	1923	P-PeA	Z.D.z	40	2,314	15,000	4,881	-4.39	*Apostolske Kirke i Danmark.* Begun through Apostolic Ch (UK), Elim (UK). 1j,1s.
Apostolic Faith Mission	1943	P-Pe3	x....	3	200	200	400	2.81	*Apostolisk Tro's Mission.* M=AFM(Portland, Oregon, USA). Holiness Pentecostals.
Assemblies of God		P-Pe2	Z....	2	138	–	212	0.05	M=AoG. Mainline Pentecostals.
Baptist Union of Denmark	1839	P-Bap	TWX.z	45	5,929	20,000	10,000	-2.73	*Danske Baptistsamfund.* Begun by Danes. Declining. 43n,1s,55Y,284z.
Catholic Apostolic Church	c1850	I-3aX	x....	1	100	500	167	-4.29	*Katolsk-Apostolske Kirke. Irvingites.* In 1900, 3,812 adherents. No clergy left.
Catholic Church: D Kobenhavn	1648	R-Lat	bxBQW	52	23,000	27,254	31,609	0.59	*Katolske Kirke.* M=SJ,OSB. C=10+0+14. (1970) 40n,84x,543Yy. (1990) 36n, 55x,634Yy.
Children of God		I-mar	.....	4	57	–	138	0.05	Former Jesus People in USA. Strong in USA, Australia.
Christian Brethren		P-CBr	x....	5	280	300	560	0.05	*Plymouth Brethren. Open Brethren.* 3 gospel halls.
Christian Fellowship		P-CBr	.....	4	380	1,000	950	0.05	*Honour Oak Christian Fellowship* (England).
Church of Christ, Scientist		m-Sci	x....	2	50	200	100	0.05	*Christian Science.* M=CCS. 2 churches (Aarhus, Copenhagen), 1 society (Odense). 6w.
Church of England (D Europe)	1887	A-plu	awc.W	1	4,100	6,000	5,000	-0.73	St Alban's, Copenhagen. English chaplaincy. In 1900, 176, 176 Anglicans. 1x.
Church of God		P-Pe3	x....	3	160	100	400	0.05	Holiness (3-stage) Classical Pentecostals, links with USA body. 3n.
Church of God (Anderson)		P-Hol	x....	10	200	300	400	0.05	M=CoG(Anderson) (USA). No longer any missionaries from USA. 4n,W=71%.
Ch of Jesus Christ of Latter-day Saints	1850	m-LdS	x....	22	2,750	4,193	4,300	0.10	*Mormons.* M=CJCLdS(USA). HQ Copenhagen. In 1900, 717 adherents. 190f.
Church of Norway		P-Lut	.....	5	1,700	900	3,000	0.05	Norwegian immigrants and residents.
Church of Sweden		P-Lut	Lwc..	1	6,600	2,500	8,000	0.05	*Svenska Kyrkan.* Swedish immigrants and residents, with own church organization.
Church of the Nazarene	1959	P-Hol	xF...	4	56	50	117	3.46	*Nazaraeerens Kirke.* Holiness denominations. M=CoN(USA). HQ Rodovre. 2n,1x.
Churches of Christ		I-Dis	x....	5	120	200	240	0.05	*Kristi Kirke.* M=CC(Non-Instrumental) (USA). In Copenhagen, Aarhus, Odense.
Congregation of God		P-Lut	C	2	400	1,000	800	0.05	*Guds Menighed.* Danish/Norwegian Old Lutherans; old Bible versions used.
Danish Moravian Church	1727	P-Mor	xwc..	1	275	500	393	-0.96	*Continental Province, Unity of the Brethren.* Danish Moravian Missionary Association.
Dutch Reformed Church		P-Ref	.....	5	2,000	1,000	3,000	0.05	Dutch immigrants and residents from Netherlands.
Elim Church	1918	P-Pe2	Z....	60	6,000	10,000	12,000	0.73	*Elimforsamlingen.* M=AoG(UK). Widespread missions overseas.
Evangelical Lutheran Free Ch of D		P-Lut	e....	10	600	–	1,000	0.05	Persons leaving state church on various protests. M=LCMS(USA).
Free Church Union	1928	m-Unt	.....	3	200	500	300	-2.02	*Fri Kirkesamfund.* Unitarian. M=UUA(USA). Missions abroad. In 1900, 62 adherents.

Continued opposite

Country Table 2–concluded

Official name (bold type = church with over 10% of affiliated) 1	*Begun* 2	*Type* 3	*Counc* 4	*Congs* 5	*Adults* 6	*Affiliated 1970* 7	*Affiliated 1995* 8	*G%* 9	*Names, notes, and other statistics* (see Codebook, Part 3) 10
Free Lutheran Congregations		I-Lut	.....	7	580	1,000	1,160	0.05	Congregations separated from national church, retaining Lutheran tradition.
Jehovah's Witnesses	1891	m-Jeh	x....	227	16,120	23,200	27,300	0.65	*Watch Tower. IBSA.* Active witnessing under way before 1926. HQ Virum. 947Y. (1995) 342Y.
Methodist Church in Denmark	1853	P-Met	Vwx.z	25	1,572	5,000	2,540	-2.67	*Denmark Annual Conf. UMC(USA).* 1900: 3,895 adherents. 22n,1s,W=36%,60Yy.
Mission Covenant Church of Denmark	1888	P-Con	K.D.z	29	1,982	6,000	3,150	-2.54	*Danske Missionsforbund.* 19th-century revival in state church. 18n,W=90%.
National Church of Denmark	826	P-Lut	LWX.a	2,200	3,400,000	4,700,000	4,540,300	0.09	*Evangelisk-lutherske Folkekirke i Danmark.* 10 Dioceses. 99 Deaneries. 1824n,P=40%,2s.
New Apostolic Church		I-3aX	x....	30	300	1,000	375	0.05	*NAC,* in Hamburg Bezirk (District). Germans. World HQ Dortmund (Germany).
Old Catholic Church		I-OCa	U...W	3	180	270	300	0.05	Remnant of an earlier Old Catholic movement.
Pentecostal Movement in Denmark	1907	P-Pe2	..D.x	52	5,180	7,000	9,090	1.05	*Pinsebevaegelsen. Tabor Meningheden.* Smallest Scandinavian Pentecostal movement.
Reformed Church Synod in Denmark	1685	P-Ref	R.D.a	3	390	1,500	534	-4.05	French, German, Dutch, Huguenot refugees from France. 1900: 1,112 adherents. 3n,20Yy.
Religious Society of Friends	1875	P-Qua	Q....	1	20	100	50	-2.73	*Vennernes Samfund (Kvaekerne).* Quakers. In 1900, 66 adherents. Copenhagen.
Romanian Orthodox Church		O-Rum	.....	1	70	–	100	0.05	Romanian refugees from former Communist rule in Romania.
Russian Orthodox Church	1920	O-Rus	....W	1	180	200	360	2.38	Russian refugees from USSR. One congregation in Copenhagen.
Salvation Army	1887	P-Sal	xwx.z	39	3,900	5,000	5,000	0.00	*Frelsens Haer. Denmark Territory. Eastern, Western Divs.* 26 institutions. 210n,1s.
Seamen's Churches		P-Lut	.....	5	300	500	600	0.05	Swedish, Norwegian and Icelandic seamen's congregations.
Serbian Orthodox Ch	1991	O-Ser	C....	1	500	–	800	25.00	Refugees from Yugoslav civil war, 1991 onwards.
Seventh-day Adventist Church	1872	P-Adv	x....	53	1,614	7,000	3,239	-3.04	*Syvende Dags Adventister. E,W Denmark Confs.* 21nx,1H,1j,1r,W=60%,137Y.
United Pentecostal Church	c1960	P-Pel	x....	10	500	100	1,000	9.65	*Jesus Only Church.* M=UPC(USA). Unitarian Pentecostals.
Other Independent charismatic chs	c1985	I-3cW	.....	150	20,000	–	30,000	10.00	Several large congregations in the main cities.
Other Protestant denominations		P-	.....	20		1,000	1,600	0.05	Total about 15 (see list below), including National Ch of Iceland.
Doubly-affiliated		2-aff			0	-112,170	0		Salvation Army and free church members also counted as state church members.
Totals				**3,147**	**3,511,797**	**4,738,397**	**4,715,465**		

Churches, members, growth, 1900-2025	*Congs*	*Adults*	*Affiliated*	*G%*	*Total denominations*	*6 Megablocs:* O	R	A	P	I	m
Total churches, members, and denominations (mid-1900)	1,000	1,802,000	2,437,480	0.95	14	0	1	1	9	1	2
Total churches, members, and denominations (mid-1970)	3,377	3,502,618	4,738,397	0.95	43	1	1	1	31	5	4
Total churches, members, and denominations (mid-1990)	3,000	3,501,000	4,700,790	-0.04	84	3	1	1	40	35	4
Total churches, members, and denominations (mid-1995)	3,147	3,511,797	4,715,465	0.06	86	3	1	1	41	36	4
Total churches, members, and denominations (mid-2000)	3,010	3,538,000	4,751,110	0.15	88	3	1	1	42	37	4
Total churches, members, and denominations (mid-2025)	2,900	3,406,000	4,574,000	-0.15	148	6	1	1	50	80	10

NOTES ON TABLE ABOVE

NATIONAL COUNCILS (Column 4, 5th letter).

- a = member of both ECD and EAD.
- C = Council of Free Churches (CFC) (Evangelisk Frikirkerad).
- E = Evangelical Alliance of Denmark (EAD) (Evangelisk Alliance i Danmark) (members: National Church and 7 free churches).
- W = Ecumenical Council of Denmark (ECD, Okumeniske Faellesrad i Danmark).
- x = member of both CFC and EAD.
- z = member of ECD, CFC and EAD.

OTHER PROTESTANT DENOMINATIONS. There are over 10 other small denominations, including: Ev Ch of Germany (EKD), Lutheran Ch of Greenland, Norwegian Reformed Parishes, Old Reformed Ch (Tysk-Reformerte Kirke), Reformed Ch of France, Seventh-day Adventist Reform Movement (HQ Charlottenlund), Swedish Reformed Parishes.

OTHER MARGINAL BODIES. The General Ch of the New Jerusalem has a Circle in Copenhagen.

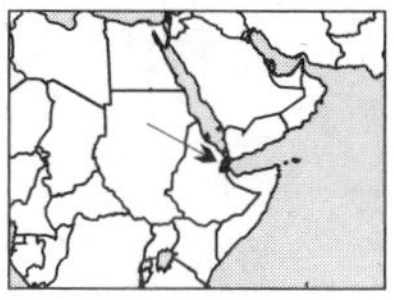

DJIBOUTI

SECULAR DATA, AD 2000

STATE

Official name: Jumhouriya Jibuti/La République de Djibouti (The Republic of Djibouti).
Short name: Djibouti. **Adjective of nationality:** of Djibouti, a Djiboutian.
Flag: Blue and green stripes with red star in White triangle on left.
Area: 23,200 sq. km. (8,950 sq. mi.).
Government: Republic, since 1977 (1862 French protectorate, 1888 French colony, 1958 French overseas territory, 1977 Independence).
Legislature: National Assembly, 65 members.
Official language: French (Français).
Monetary unit: 1 Djibouti franc (DF) = 100 centimes. **US$1=** DF 177.72.
Chief cities: DJIBOUTI (Jibuti) 354,548.
Political divisions: 5 provinces.
Armed forces: 10,000.

DEMOGRAPHY

Population: 638,000.
Population density: 27.4/sq. km. (71.2/sq. mi.).
Under 15 years: 264,000.
Growth rate p.a.: 2.11% (births 34.70, deaths 13.60).
Mortality: Infant, per 1,000: 97.3; **Maternal per 100,000:** 570.0.
Life expectancy: 52 (male 51, female 54).
Household size: 5.6. **Floor area per person, sq.m:** 13.1.
Major languages: French, Somali, Afar, Arabic.
Urban dwellers: 83.30%. **Urban growth rate p.a.:** 2.7%.
Labor force: 62%.

ETHNOLINGUISTIC PEOPLES

46.0% Somali (Issa); 35.4% Danakil (Afar); 11.0% Arab; 3.0% Eurafrican; 1.6% French.

ECONOMY

National income p.a. per person: US$850; **per family:** US$4,760.

EDUCATION

Adult literacy: 46% (male 60%, female 32%). **Schools:** 82.
Universities: 1. **School enrolment:** female/male: 22%/30%.

HEALTH

Access to health services: 40%. **Access to safe water:** 90%.
Hospitals: 8 (27 beds per 10,000). **Doctors:** 97.
Blind: 300. **Deaf:** 41,200. **Murder rate:** 4.
Lepers: 9,000. **Underweight prevalence under 5:** 23%.

LITERATURE

New book titles p.a.: 32 (50 p.a. per million). **Periodicals:** 10.
Newspapers: 1 daily.

COMMUNICATION (per 1,000 people)

Phones: 13 **(2% mobile). Radios:** 61. **TV sets:** 73.
Daily newspaper circulation: 7. **Computers:** 2.

REFUGEES

Alien refugees from other countries: 25,000.

HUMAN LIFE AND LIBERTY (optimum condition=100.0%)

HDI: 31.9. **HSI:** 90.0. **HFI:** 90.0. **EFL:** 5.0.

Country Table 1. **Religious adherents in Djibouti, AD 1900-2025.**

Year	*1900*		*1970*		*mid-1990*		*Annual change, 1990-2000*				*mid-1995*		*mid-2000*		*mid-2025*	
Name	*Adherents*	*%*	*Adherents*	*%*	*Adherents*	*%*	*Natural*	*Conversion*	*Total*	*Rate*	*Adherents*	*%*	*Adherents*	*%*	*Adherents*	*%*
Muslims	19,900	99.5	135,400	91.5	484,500	93.7	11,303	258	11,561	2.16	563,500	93.8	600,110	94.1	965,660	94.1
Christians	**100**	**0.5**	**12,000**	**8.1**	**25,620**	**5.0**	**600**	**-310**	**290**	**1.08**	**29,350**	**4.9**	**28,516**	**4.5**	**42,000**	**4.1**
PROFESSION																
crypto-Christians	0	0.0	1,000	0.7	4,000	0.8	94	56	150	3.24	5,200	0.9	5,500	0.9	11,000	1.1
professing Christians	**100**	**0.5**	**11,000**	**7.4**	**21,620**	**4.2**	**506**	**-366**	**140**	**0.63**	**24,150**	**4.0**	**23,016**	**3.6**	**31,000**	**3.0**
AFFILIATION																
unaffiliated Christians	0	0.0	0	0.0	390	0.1	9	-16	-7	-1.90	388	0.1	322	0.1	500	0.1
affiliated Christians	**100**	**0.5**	**12,000**	**8.1**	**25,230**	**4.9**	**590**	**-294**	**296**	**1.12**	**28,962**	**4.8**	**28,194**	**4.4**	**41,500**	**4.0**
Orthodox	0	0.0	800	0.5	17,000	3.3	398	-208	190	1.07	20,230	3.4	18,900	3.0	28,000	2.7
Roman Catholics	100	0.5	11,000	7.4	8,000	1.6	187	-102	85	1.02	8,475	1.4	8,854	1.4	12,500	1.2
Protestants	0	0.0	200	0.1	150	0.0	4	5	9	4.81	157	0.0	240	0.0	500	0.1
Independents	0	0.0	0	0.0	80	0.0	2	10	12	9.60	100	0.0	200	0.0	500	0.1
Trans-megabloc groupings																
Evangelicals	0	0.0	70	0.1	70	0.0	2	-2	0	0.00	69	0.0	70	0.0	80	0.0
Pentecostals/Charismatics	0	0.0	20	0.0	850	0.2	20	-5	15	1.64	991	0.2	1,000	0.2	2,000	0.2
Great Commission Christians	**100**	**0.5**	**5,000**	**3.4**	**11,500**	**2.2**	**269**	**-219**	**50**	**0.42**	**12,000**	**2.0**	**11,995**	**1.9**	**20,000**	**2.0**
Nonreligious	0	0.0	200	0.1	6,350	1.2	149	49	198	2.75	7,500	1.3	8,329	1.3	17,000	1.7
Baha'is	0	0.0	100	0.1	400	0.1	9	6	15	3.27	520	0.1	552	0.1	1,200	0.1
Hindus	0	0.0	300	0.2	130	0.0	3	-3	0	-0.15	130	0.0	128	0.0	140	0.0
World A (unevangelized persons)	19,000	95.0	96,200	65.0	310,200	60.0	7,219	-3,685	3,534	1.09	342,392	57.0	345,796	54.2	499,662	48.7
World B (evangelized non-Christians)	900	4.5	39,800	26.9	181,180	35.0	4,245	3,995	8,240	3.82	228,945	38.1	263,688	41.3	484,338	47.2
World C (Christians)	100	0.5	12,000	8.1	25,620	5.0	600	-310	290	1.08	29,350	4.9	28,516	4.5	42,000	4.1
Country's population	**20,000**	**100.0**	**148,000**	**100.0**	**517,000**	**100.0**	**12,064**	**0**	**12,064**	**2.13**	**600,688**	**100.0**	**638,000**	**100.0**	**1,026,000**	**100.0**

COLUMNS, ROWS.
For meanings and definitions, see Codebook (Part 3). Note that, by definition, total 'Christians' = professing + crypto-Christians, which also = affiliated + unaffiliated Christians, and also = Great Commission Christians + latent Christians. Percentages may not always total exactly, due to rounding.

NOTES ON RELIGIONS
BAHA'IS. In one local spiritual assembly (1973), begun in 1955. In 1972 extensive missionary activity from Ethiopia began; 1996, still 1 LSA.
CRYPTO-CHRISTIANS. Roman Catholics, almost all Somalis (including Issas), many from former Italian Somaliland; with only one or 2 Afars (Danakils).
HINDUS. Indians.
MUSLIMS. Islam was planted definitively in the 12th century. Muslims are Sunnis (Hanafite and Shafite rites), with a few Shias (Indians). Brotherhoods: Qadiriya, Salihiya, Rifaiya, and Ahmadiya (enumerated here under Muslims, though declared non-Muslim by Pakistan). Hajj pilgrims to Mecca. (1975) 124; (1976) 483.
ROMAN CATHOLICS. In 1947, there were 2,200 European Catholics (1,000 being French) and 300 indigenous.

Great Commission Instrument Panel: status of Djibouti (for explanation see start of Part 4)

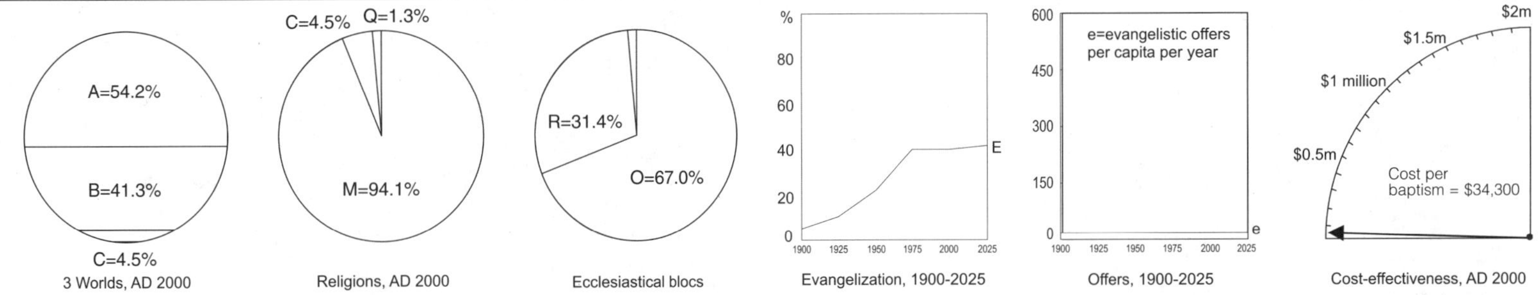

Country summary. **Worlds A, B, C by ethnolinguistic peoples, cities, and major civil divisions in Djibouti.**

	PEOPLES							CITIES							CIVIL DIVISIONS						
World	Num	Pop 2000	C%	Christians	E%	U%	Unevangelized	Num	Pop 2000	C%	Christians	E%	U%	Unevangelized	Num	Pop 2000	C%	Christians	E%	U%	Unevangelized
A	5	601,736	0.60	3,636	43	57	345,224	1	354,548	5.00	17,727	49	51	179,330	5	637,634	4.42	28,194	46	54	345,336
B	1	19,129	55.00	10,521	100	0	86	0	0	0.00	0	0	0	0	0	0	0.00	0	0	0	0
C	4	16,770	83.70	14,037	100	0	27	0	0	0.00	0	0	0	0	0	0	0.00	0	0	0	0
Total	**10**	**637,635**	**4.42**	**28,194**	**46**	**54**	**345,337**	**1**	**354,548**	**5.00**	**17,727**	**49**	**51**	**179,330**	**5**	**637,634**	**4.42**	**28,194**	**46**	**54**	**345,336**

Country status. Djibouti is a small nation on the Red Sea coast of the Horn of Africa. The land is one of the most desolate in Africa, marked by a dry and barren landscape in which the most prominent features are sharp cliffs, deep ravines, burning sands, and thorny shrubs.

HUMAN LIFE AND LIBERTY

Human need and development. There are few countries where human needs are so stark as in Djibouti; Somalia would perhaps be the most comparable country. Basic necessities, like water, are scarce because of recurring drought. The arid soil grows very little food, which consequently has to be imported. Medical and other human services are available only in the city of Djibouti and serve primarily the expatriate community of Arabs, Frenchmen, and Greeks. The national literacy rate is only 46%.

Human rights and freedoms. Djibouti is in a state of civil war because of the insurgency of the Afar tribe, which is numerically the dominant ethnic group, but excluded from power by the current Somali-dominated government. The government security forces (FNS) and the National Army (AND) have carried out a campaign of terror against the Afars, including systematic rape of women and murder of civilians. Security forces abuse and torture civilians suspected of opposing the government. One police interrogation technique includes the 'swing', by which the victims are tied by their wrists and ankles to a horizontal pole and beaten all over the body. Many Afars who held important political positions in former governments, including Ali Aref Bourhan, the ex-prime minister, are in jail, and are subjected to inhuman treatment. 'Offending the president of the republic' is a general charge used to keep political opponents in detention. The judiciary is not independent of the executive, and in most cases simply carries out the dictates of the president. Reprisals against the Afar insurgents include the forced evacuation of towns. Freedoms of speech and press are severely curtailed. Both print and electronic media are state-owned and are not permitted to publish anything critical of the government. Political protests are effectively banned by selective enforcement of public assembly laws. Periodically, the government closes public meeting places, such as cafes, where political discussions are held. The leaders of human rights organizations are routinely jailed. Djibouti hosts over 100,000 refugees, a number equal to a fifth of the country's total population. Most of them are from neighboring strife-torn Somalia. Although the Constitution bars discrimination, de facto discrimination is practiced against the native Afars by the immigrant Somalis who are in power. The Issa, the dominant Somali clan (to which President Hassan Gouled Aptidon belongs) holds all key positions of authority, and the president's subclan, the Mammasan, wields disproportionate power in the highest councils of state. Violence against women is routine and is rarely punished.

Human environment. Djibouti is one of the bleakest places on earth, and has one of its most inhospitable environments. Droughts have reduced most of the country to a wasteland. The current civil war has hastened the process of soil and water degradation. There are virtually no conservation programs.

NON-CHRISTIAN RELIGIONS

Islam was definitively planted in the 12th century and today accounts for about 94% of the population. Most are Sunnis of the Hanafite and Shafiite rites except for a few Indian Shias. The principal religious brotherhoods are Qadiriya, Salihiya, and Rifaiya; Ahmadiya from Pakistan is also present.

Hinduism is the religion of a small community of 100 Indians.

CHRISTIANITY

CATHOLIC CHURCH. The French bought an area on the coast from Danakil chiefs in 1862, extending their protectorate in 1884 and building the port of Djibouti in 1888. Catholic priests from the vicariate of Arabia arrived in 1883. A prefecture was erected in 1914 and attached to the vicariate apostolic of Gallas. In 1955 the diocese of Djibouti was created, directly subject to the Holy See.

The Catholic Church is the most active of the 4 Christian denominations in the country, and is the only church that has made converts from the local population. Of 11,000 members in 1970, 10,400 were metropolitan French on temporary contracts and 600 were native Catholics, mostly middle-class Somalis. By 1995 numbers had only dropped slightly, to 8,500. The church has 6 parishes and is served by Capuchin priests, FSC brothers and 3 congregations of sisters.

The Holy See has no diplomatic relations with Djibouti in AD 2000, but an apostolic delegate residing in Addis Ababa.

ORTHODOX CHURCHES. The Orthodox community is composed of 2 groups: Greek Orthodox (Europeans) and Ethiopians. The latter use or attend the Greek Orthodox church in Djibouti.

PROTESTANT CHURCHES. There is only one Protestant body in the territory, the Protestant Church of Djibouti, which dates from World War II and is related to the Reformed Church of France. Its small membership consists entirely of Europeans, principally French and German nationals.

Indigenous missions. There are very few indigenous Djiboutian believers and no foreign missionary outreach from them.

CHURCH AND STATE

As a French overseas territory until 1976, its legal statutes relating to freedom of religion were the same as in metropolitan France. Catholic schools receive subsidies from the government, and an official convention between the Catholic diocese and the local government allows 9 nursing sisters to work in government hospitals.

BROADCASTING AND MEDIA

About 8% of the population owns a radio. FEBA (Seychelles) broadcasts in Afar.

FUTURE TRENDS AND PROSPECTS

Church membership will likely continue to decline to 4.1% of the population through 2025, which will be made up of primarily Christians from other countries such as France, Ethiopia, and Greece.

Christianity is not expected to grow much in the 21st century. Muslims will probably remain around 94% well after AD 2040.

Muslims. The Afar (Danakil) people, as this warrior outside Tadjoura, have long been completely islamized.

BIBLIOGRAPHY

'Côte Français des Somalis,' *Vivante Afrique* (Belgium), 250 (May–June, 1967).

Dijbouti. P. J. Schraeder. *World bibliographical series*, vol. 118. Oxford, UK: CLIO Press, 1991. 282p. (See especially 'Religion,' p.85–8).

Le ginnili devin, poète et guerrier afar: (Ethiopie et République de Djibouti). D. Morin. *Langues et cultures africaines*, 16. Paris: Peeters, 1991. 146p. (Summaries in English and Afar).

'Les populations de la côte française des Somalis,' R. Muller, in *Mer Rouge Afrique orientale, études sociologiques et linguistiques: préhistoire—explorations—perspectives d'avenir*, p.45–102. M. Albospeyre et al. (ed). *Cahiers de l'Afrique et l'Asie*, no. 5. Paris: J. Peyronnet, 1959.

Peoples of the Horn of Africa: Somali, Afar and Saho. I. M. Lewis. London: International African Institute, 1969.

'Spirit possession and deprivation cults,' I. M. Lewis, *Man*, 1, 3 (1966), 307–329.

The Christian Church and missions in Ethiopia (including Eritrea and the Somalilands). J. S. Trimingham. London: World Dominion Press, 1950. 74p.

'The influence of Islam on the Afar.' K. Shehim. Ph.D. dissertation, University of Washington, Seattle, WA, 1982. 230p.

Country Table 2. **Organized churches and denominations in Djibouti.**

Official name (bold type = church with over 10% of all affiliated) 1	*Begun* 2	*Type* 3	*Counc* 4	*Congs* 5	*Adults* 6	*Affiliated 1970* 7	*Affiliated 1995* 8	*G%* 9	*Names, notes, and other statistics* (see Codebook, Part 3) 10
Eglise Catholique: D Djibouti	1883	R-Lat	p.SLr	6	5,000	11,000	8,475	-1.04	80% French, 10% Somali, 10% Ethiopian. M=OFMCap. C=1+1+3. (1990) 1n,6x,12m,18w,31Yy. ,
Eglise Orthodoxe Ethiopienne		O-Eth	Nwa..	2	11,800	500	20,000	0.05	*Ethiopian Orthodox Ch.* Amharas from Ethiopia working in Djibouti; using Greek church.
Eglise Orthodoxe Grecque		O-Gre	Cw...	1	152	300	230	0.05	*Greek Orthodox Ch.* Europeans (Greeks). 1 church building in Djibouti.
Eglise Protestante de Djibouti	c1940	P-Ref	..A..	1	50	200	100	-2.73	*Protestant Ch of Djibouti.* Related to Reformed Church of France. French, Germans.
Ethiopian Protestant Churches	c1975	I-Lut	.....	2	50	–	100	5.00	Mainly refugees from EECMY,WLEC, other Lutherans, Pentecostals.
Red Sea Mission Team	1975	P-Non	.....	1	40	–	57	5.00	M=RSMT.
Totals				**13**	**17,092**	**12,000**	**28,962**		

Churches, members, growth, 1900-2025	*Congs*	*Adults*	*Affiliated*	*G%*	*Total denominations*	*6 Megablocs:* O	R	A	P	I	m
Total churches, members, and denominations (mid-1900)	1	55	100	7.08	1	0	1	0	0	0	0
Total churches, members, and denominations (mid-1970)	9	6,600	12,000	7.08	4	2	1	0	1	0	0
Total churches, members, and denominations (mid-1990)	10	14,900	25,230	3.79	6	2	1	0	2	1	0
Total churches, members, and denominations (mid-1995)	13	17,092	28,962	2.80	6	2	1	0	2	1	0
Total churches, members, and denominations (mid-2000)	20	16,600	28,194	-0.54	6	2	1	0	2	1	0
Total churches, members, and denominations (mid-2025)	60	24,500	41,500	1.56	14	3	1	0	5	5	0

NOTES ON TABLE ABOVE
NATIONAL COUNCILS (Column 4, 5th letter).

r = consultative member, Conférence Episcopale de France (Episcopal Conference of France).

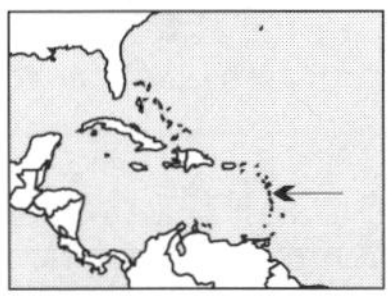

DOMINICA

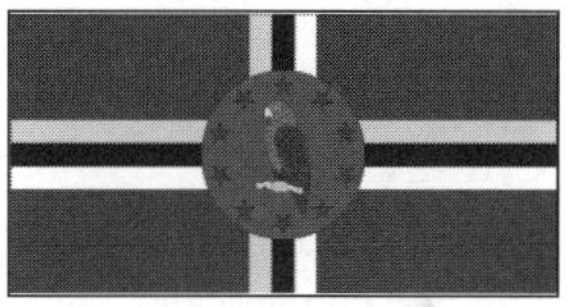

SECULAR DATA, AD 2000

STATE
Official name: The Commonwealth of Dominica.
Short name: Dominica. **Adjective of nationality:** of Dominica.
Flag: Multicolored background with green Sisserou parrot.
Area: 750 sq. km. (290 sq. mi.).
Government: Republic, since 1978, formerly self-governing state in association with the United Kingdom (Britain), since 1967 (c1600 French colony, 1759 British colony, 1978 Independence).
Legislature: House of Assembly, 32 members.
Official language: English.
Monetary unit: 1 East Caribbean dollar (EC$) = 100 cents. **US$1=** EC$2.70.
Chief cities: ROSEAU 9,133.
Political divisions: 10 provinces.
Armed forces: 500.

DEMOGRAPHY
Population: 71,000.
Population density: 94.2/sq. km. (243.8/sq. mi.).
Under 15 years: 17,000.
Growth rate p.a.: 1.19% (births 15.26, deaths 5.77).
Mortality: Infant, per 1,000: 7.8; **Maternal per 100,000:** 50.0.
Life expectancy: 78 (male 75, female 82).
Household size: 4.3. **Floor area per person, sq.m:** 15.0.
Major languages: English, Dominican Creole (French patois), Carib, Hindi.
Urban dwellers: 71.01%. **Urban growth rate p.a.:** 0.7%.
Labor force: 38%.

ETHNOLINGUISTIC PEOPLES
82.0% Black; 7.3% Mulatto; 6.0% West Indian Black; 1.7% Black Carib; 1.0% British.

ECONOMY
National income p.a. per person: US$2,983; **per family:** US$12,830.

EDUCATION
Adult literacy: 90% (male 94%, female 86%). **Schools:** 77.
Universities: 2. **School enrolment:** female/male: 70%/70%.

HEALTH
Access to health services: 70%. **Access to safe water:** 77%.
Hospitals: 53 (25 beds per 10,000). **Doctors:** 38.
Blind: 60. **Deaf:** 4,300. **Murder rate:** 4. **Lepers:** 400.

LITERATURE
New book titles p.a.: 19 (270 p.a. per million). **Periodicals:** 8.
Newspapers: 1 daily.

COMMUNICATION (per 1,000 people)
Phones: 240 (15% mobile). **Radios:** 875. **TV sets:** 141.
Daily newspaper circulation: 60. **Computers:** 15.

HUMAN LIFE AND LIBERTY (optimum condition=100.0%)
HDI: 87.3. **HSI:** 40.0. **HFI:** 45.0. **EFL:** 28.0.

Country Table 1. **Religious adherents in Dominica, AD 1900-2025.**

Year	*1900*		*1970*		*mid-1990*		*Annual change, 1990-2000*				*mid-1995*		*mid-2000*		*mid-2025*	
Name	*Adherents*	*%*	*Adherents*	*%*	*Adherents*	*%*	*Natural*	*Conversion*	*Total*	*Rate*	*Adherents*	*%*	*Adherents*	*%*	*Adherents*	*%*
Christians	**28,800**	**100.0**	**68,880**	**98.5**	**68,075**	**95.9**	**0**	**-102**	**-102**	**-0.15**	**67,370**	**95.0**	**67,052**	**94.8**	**68,070**	**93.3**
PROFESSION																
professing Christians	**28,800**	**100.0**	**68,880**	**98.5**	**68,075**	**95.9**	**0**	**-102**	**-102**	**-0.15**	**67,370**	**95.0**	**67,052**	**94.8**	**68,070**	**93.3**
AFFILIATION																
unaffiliated Christians	590	2.1	658	0.9	429	0.6	0	-13	-13	-3.68	303	0.4	295	0.4	900	1.2
affiliated Christians	**28,210**	**98.0**	**68,222**	**97.5**	**67,646**	**95.3**	**0**	**-89**	**-89**	**-0.13**	**67,067**	**94.6**	**66,757**	**94.4**	**67,170**	**92.0**
Roman Catholics	26,780	93.0	62,500	89.3	57,600	81.1	0	-130	-130	-0.23	57,000	80.4	56,300	79.3	56,800	77.8
Protestants	1,150	4.0	4,200	6.0	10,600	14.9	70	-10	60	0.55	10,934	15.4	11,200	15.8	13,000	17.8
Independents	0	0.0	222	0.3	1,700	2.4	60	-20	40	2.14	1,900	2.7	2,100	3.0	4,000	5.5
Anglicans	280	1.0	1,000	1.4	1,280	1.8	14	-10	4	0.31	1,300	1.8	1,320	1.9	1,520	2.1
Marginal Christians	0	0.0	300	0.4	600	0.9	10	5	15	2.26	658	0.9	750	1.1	1,400	1.9
doubly-affiliated	0	0.0	0	0.0	-4,134	-5.8	-48	-30	-78	1.74	-4,725	-6.7	-4,913	-6.9	-9,550	-13.1
Trans-megabloc groupings																
Evangelicals	900	3.1	2,000	2.9	4,640	6.5	4	2	6	0.13	4,645	6.6	4,700	6.6	6,600	9.0
Pentecostals/Charismatics	0	0.0	500	0.7	4,600	6.5	10	30	40	0.84	4,755	6.7	5,000	7.0	7,000	9.6
Great Commission Christians	**900**	**3.1**	**2,100**	**3.0**	**5,000**	**7.0**	**2**	**4**	**6**	**0.11**	**5,040**	**7.1**	**5,057**	**7.1**	**6,100**	**8.4**
Spiritists	0	0.0	1,070	1.5	1,800	2.5	4	5	9	0.48	1,835	2.6	1,888	2.7	2,200	3.0
Baha'is	0	0.0	50	0.1	1,000	1.4	7	16	23	2.05	1,160	1.6	1,225	1.7	2,000	2.7
Muslims	0	0.0	0	0.0	150	0.2	1	0	1	0.83	160	0.2	163	0.2	300	0.4
Hindus	0	0.0	0	0.0	140	0.2	0	0	0	0.07	140	0.2	141	0.2	170	0.2
Buddhists	0	0.0	0	0.0	90	0.1	0	0	0	0.22	90	0.1	92	0.1	150	0.2
Nonreligious	0	0.0	0	0.0	90	0.1	0	0	0	0.22	90	0.1	92	0.1	400	0.6
Chinese folk-religionists	0	0.0	0	0.0	40	0.1	0	0	0	0.49	40	0.1	42	0.1	70	0.1
New-Religionists	0	0.0	0	0.0	15	0.0	0	0	0	1.84	15	0.0	18	0.0	40	0.1
World A (unevangelized persons)	0	0.0	69	0.1	71	0.1	-1	0	-1	-1.21	70	0.1	71	0.1	73	0.1
World B (evangelized non-Christians)	0	0.0	1,017	1.5	2,854	4.6	-16	50	34	3.11	3,479	4.9	3,877	5.1	4,857	7.2
World C (Christians)	28,800	100.0	68,880	98.4	68,075	95.3	-52	-50	-102	-0.15	67,370	95.0	67,052	94.8	68,070	92.7
Country's population	**28,800**	**100.0**	**69,967**	**100.0**	**71,000**	**100.0**	**-69**	**0**	**-69**	**0.00**	**70,920**	**100.0**	**70,713**	**100.0**	**73,000**	**100.0**

COLUMNS, ROWS.
For meanings and definitions, see Codebook (Part 3). Note that, by definition, total 'Christians' = professing + crypto-Christians, which also = affiliated + unaffiliated Christians, and also = Great Commission Christians + latent Christians. Percentages may not always total exactly, due to rounding.

CENSUSES.
7.IV.1960: 90.0% Roman Catholics, 8.1% Protestants (6.1% Methodists), 1.7% Anglicans, 0.2% marginal Protestants.

NOTES ON RELIGIONS
BAHA'IS. In 10 local spiritual assemblies (1996).

Country status. Dominica is a mountainous island dominated by volcanic peaks in the eastern Caribbean. It is noteworthy as the only island in the region where the pre-Columbian population of Carib Indians survives.

HUMAN LIFE AND LIBERTY

Human need and development. Although not prosperous, Dominica has a stable economy based on agriculture. Because it is mostly volcanic with few beaches, tourism is not a major revenue earner. There are no areas of dire poverty as in some of the larger islands. The major threat to development is weather. The economy was crippled by Hurricane David in 1979, Hurricane Allen in 1980 and Hurricane Hugo in 1989.

Human rights and freedoms. Dominica is a parliamentary democracy on the British model. All constitutionally mandated freedoms are respected in practice and no human rights abuses have been reported in recent years.

Human environment. The absence of a large tourist sector has been a blessing in disguise for the small island, where the environment is easily susceptible to abuse and degradation. However, because of the frequent hurricanes, the island's ecosystem has suffered considerable damage.

Great Commission Instrument Panel: status of Dominica (for explanation see start of Part 4)

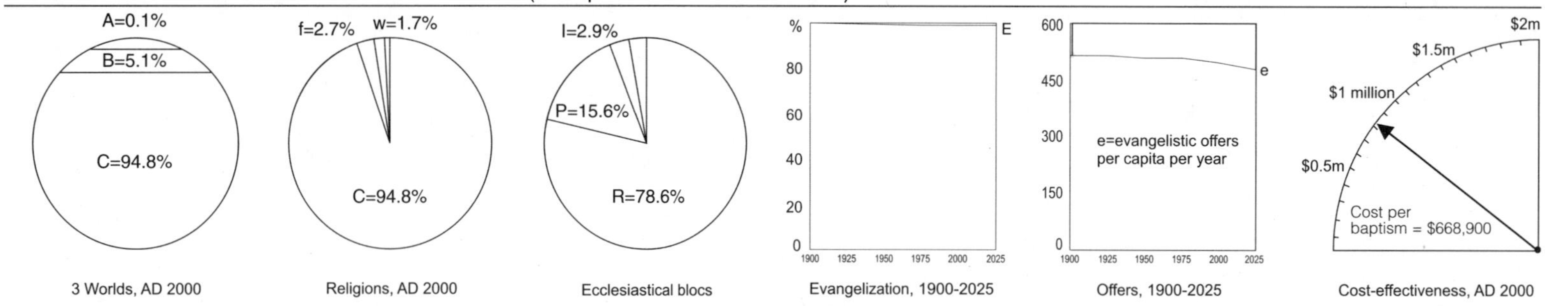

Country summary. **Worlds A, B, C by ethnolinguistic peoples, cities, and major civil divisions in Dominica.**

	PEOPLES							CITIES							CIVIL DIVISIONS						
World	Num	Pop 2000	C%	Christians	E%	U%	Unevangelized	Num	Pop 2000	C%	Christians	E%	U%	Unevangelized	Num	Pop 2000	C%	Christians	E%	U%	Unevangelized
A	0	0	0.00	0	0	0	0	0	0	0.00	0	0	0	0	0	0	0.00	0	0	0	0
B	3	424	38.44	163	93	7	28	0	0	0.00	0	0	0	0	0	0	0.00	0	0	0	0
C	7	70,289	94.74	66,593	100	0	35	1	9,133	94.00	8,585	100	0	8	10	70,714	94.40	66,757	100	0	62
Total	**10**	**70,713**	**94.40**	**66,756**	**100**	**0**	**63**	**1**	**9,133**	**94.00**	**8,585**	**100**	**0**	**8**	**10**	**70,714**	**94.40**	**66,757**	**100**	**0**	**62**

NON-CHRISTIAN RELIGIONS

There are small numbers of Muslims, Hindus, Buddhists, Baha'is, and Spiritists.

CHRISTIANITY

CATHOLIC CHURCH. Dominican priests (OP) began work in 1642, but from 1702 to 1730 there was no priest on the island. French Franciscans arrived in 1747 but were expelled when the British assumed control in 1782. Roseau became a diocese in 1850. Dominica is predominantly Catholic, and the island now makes up the entire diocese of Roseau. In 1974 there were in Dominica 16 parishes, 31 stations, 28 religious and 3 diocesan priests, and 35 Missionary Sisters of the Immaculate Heart of Mary. By 1995 Catholics had dropped slightly to 57,000 in 18 parishes.

The Holy See has diplomatic relations with Dominica and in AD 2000 is represented to government and the Catholic hierarchy by a pro-nuncio residing in Port of Spain.

OTHER CHURCHES. Methodism, which first came to Dominica in 1787, is the principal non-Catholic faith. Adventists are next followed by Anglicans. In the 4 Windward Islands, Anglicans are strong in Grenada and St. Vincent and weak in St. Lucia and Dominica, the latter 2 being more than 90% Catholic. Several other small missionary societies are also active in Dominica. Since 1975, Pentecostals have become increasingly influential.

Indigenous missions. There is virtually no foreign missions outreach from Dominica, with perhaps one or 2 nationals serving in surrounding countries in the Caribbean.

CHURCH AND STATE

In 1967 Dominica became a state in association with Britain, with full responsibility for internal affairs. Catholics, Anglicans, and Protestants had equal status before the law, and freedom of religion, as in other Britain-related territories of the Caribbean. After Independence in 1978 the same situation prevailed.

Christian scenes are often portrayed on postage stamps: here, Virgin and Child.

BROADCASTING AND MEDIA

Shortwave programs from HCJB (Ecuador), TWR (Antilles) and AWR (Costa Rica) can be easily received. Local Christian radio stations: Gospel Broadcasting Corporation (ZGBC, Protestant, which carries *Back to the Bible* programs), Caribbean Voice of Life (which carries WEC programs), and Voice of the Islands (Catholic). There are regular Catholic radio programs each weekend. Dominica is a member of UNDA.

CBN's *International 700 Club* and Christian soap opera *Another Life* can be seen on local television channels. Christian television programs can be received via satellite.

INTERDENOMINATIONAL ORGANIZATIONS

The Anglican, Catholic, and Methodist church cooperate in the Dominica Christian Council.

FUTURE TRENDS AND PROSPECTS

The island is expected to remain predominately Roman Catholic but spiritists are beginning to make an inroad growing to 3.0% of the population by 2025, causing the overall Christian percentage to fall to 93.3% in the same period.

Spiritists are expected to make significant gains in the 21st century, passing 5% of the population after AD 2040. Christianity could decline further after that.

BIBLIOGRAPHY

Black religions in the New World. G. E. Simpson. New York: Columbia University Press, 1978. 429p.

'Carib folk–beliefs and customs from Dominica, B.W.I.,' D. Taylor, *Southwestern Journal of Anthropology*, 1, 4 (1945), 507–530.

Dominica. R. A. Myers. *World bibliographical series*, vol. 82. Oxford, UK: CLIO Press, 1987. 192p. (See especially 'Religion,' p.46–7).

'Religion among the Caribs,' A. Layng, *Caribbean Review*, 8, 2 (1979), 36–41.

'The Carib population of Dominica.' A. Layng. Ph.D. dissertation, Case Western Reserve University, 1976. 242p.

'The Dominican knot: an analysis of folktales and storytelling on a Caribbean island.' G. R. Smith. Ph.D. dissertation, University of Texas, Austin, 1991. 731p.

Country Table 2. **Organized churches and denominations in Dominica.**

Official name (bold type = church with over 10% of affiliated) 1	Begun 2	Type 3	Counc 4	Congs 5	Adults 6	Affiliated 1970 7	Affiliated 1995 8	G% 9	*Names, notes, and other statistics* (see Codebook, Part 3) 10
Anglican Church (D Antigua)		A-ACa	awMRC	3	650	1,000	1,300	0.05	*CPWI.* In Ch of Province of West Indies. M=USPG. 90% West Indian (Black).
Baptist Convention	1975	P-Bap	.....	5	152	–	304	5.00	M=SBC.
Berean Mission	1973	I-Non	.....	3	140	–	400	4.55	M=Berean Mission (USA).
Catholic Church: D Roseau	1642	R-Lat	P.NMC	18	30,000	62,500	57,000	-0.37	500 Whites. M=CSSR. C=2+1+2. (1970) 31nx,7m,37w,2000Yy. (1990) 6n,23x,28m,31w,1180Yy.
Church of God of Prophecy	c1963	P-Pe3	Z....	10	300	200	750	5.43	M=CGP(USA). Split in USA ex CoG(Cleveland). Holiness Pentecostals.
Church of God (Cleveland)	c1963	P-Pe3	ZF..E	3	140	100	350	5.14	M=CoG(Cleveland) (USA). Holiness Pentecostals (3-stage). Large 1975 open-air crusade.
Church of the Nazarene	1974	P-Hol	....E	3	201	–	260	4.76	M=CoN.
Churches of Christ in Christian Union	1943	P-Hol	xF...	16	900	200	1,800	9.19	M=CCCU(USA). Holiness denomination with Wesleyan doctrine. 1 school. 5f,1p.
Jehovah's Witnesses		m-Jeh	x....	6	263	300	658	0.05	*Watch Tower. IBSA.* Rapid growth since 135 adherents in 1960. (1975) 6Y. (1995) 26Y.
Maranatha Baptist Church		I-Bap	.....	3	130	22	289	0.05	Small Independent Baptist community.
Methodist Ch in Caribbean & Americas	1787	P-Met	VwM.C	5	1,250	2,000	2,080	0.16	In *MCCA* (1967 union). Leeward Islands District. M=MMS(UK). Blacks. 4n.
New Apostolic Church	c1985	I-3aX	x....	2	70	–	111	10.00	*NAC.* M=Neuapostolische Kirche (HQ Zurich, Switzerland).
Seventh-day Adventist Church		P-Adv	x....	11	2,200	1,200	3,140	0.05	*SDA, East Caribbean Ccnf, Caribbean Union Conference* (HQ Bridgetown, Barbados).
Other pentecostal bodies	c1960	I-3pU	.....	9	660	200	1,100	7.06	About 5, including various small Black indigenous pentecostal bodies.
Other Protestant denominations		P-	.....	10	900	500	2,250	0.05	About 5, including Christian Brethren, PAoWI, WEC.
Doubly-affiliated		2-aff			-2,500	0	-4,725		Evangelicals who are also baptized Roman Catholics.
Totals				**107**	**35,456**	**68,222**	**67,067**		

Churches, members, growth, 1900-2025	*Congs*	*Adults*	*Affiliated*	*G%*	*Total denominations*	*6 Megablocs:* O	R	A	P	I	m
Total churches, members, and denominations (mid-1900)	30	15,000	28,210	1.27	3	0	1	1	1	0	0
Total churches, members, and denominations (mid-1970)	79	36,223	68,222	1.27	12	0	1	1	7	2	1
Total churches, members, and denominations (mid-1990)	100	35,800	67,646	-0.04	21	0	1	1	11	7	1
Total churches, members, and denominations (mid-1995)	107	35,456	67,067	-0.17	23	0	1	1	12	8	1
Total churches, members, and denominations (mid-2000)	120	35,300	66,757	-0.09	23	0	1	1	12	8	1
Total churches, members, and denominations (mid-2025)	150	35,500	67,170	0.02	53	0	1	1	20	30	1

NOTES ON TABLE ABOVE

NATIONAL COUNCILS (Column 4, 5th letter).
C = Dominica Christian Council.
E = Dominica Association of Evangelical Churches (DAEC).

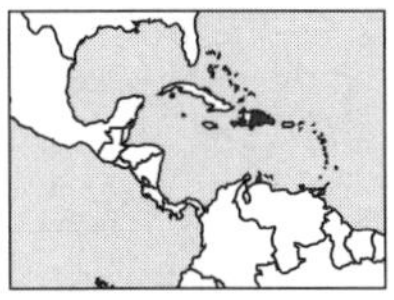

DOMINICAN REPUBLIC

SECULAR DATA, AD 2000

STATE
Official name: La República Dominicana (The Dominican Republic).
Short name: Dominican Republic. **Adjective of nationality:** Dominican.
Flag: Alternating blue and red rectangles with white cross in center.
Area: 48,443 sq. km. (18,704 sq. mi.).
Government: Republic, since 1962 (1492 Spanish colony, 1844 Independence from Spain and Haiti, 1930 military dictatorship).
Legislature: Senate, 30 members; Chamber of Deputies, 120 members.
Official language: Spanish (Español/Castella).
Monetary unit: 1 Dominican peso (RD$) = 100 centavos. **US$1=** RD$15.80.
Chief cities: SANTO DOMINGO 3,601,000; Santiago de los Caballeros 1,540,000; La Vega 229,757; San Francisco de Macoris 197,497; La Romana 176,589.
Political divisions: 30 provinces.
Armed forces: 25,000.

DEMOGRAPHY
Population: 8,495,000.
Population density: 175.3/sq. km. (454.2/sq. mi.).
Under 15 years: 2,808,000.
Growth rate p.a.: 1.43% (births 21.77, deaths 5.18).
Mortality: Infant, per 1,000: 30.0; **Maternal per 100,000:** 110.0.
Life expectancy: 72 (male 70, female 74).
Household size: 5.1. **Floor area per person, sq.m:** 14.0.
Major languages: Spanish, English, French Creole, French.
Urban dwellers: 65.18%. **Urban growth rate p.a.:** 2.3%.
Labor force: 34%.

ETHNOLINGUISTIC PEOPLES
69.5% Dominican Mulatto; 16.1% Dominican White; 9.4% Dominican Black; 2.4% Haitian Black; 0.9% Spaniard.

ECONOMY
National income p.a. per person: US$1,459; **per family:** US$7,445.

EDUCATION
Adult literacy: 82% (male 82%, female 82%). **Schools:** 6,207.
Universities: 7. **School enrolment:** female/male: 86%/81%.

HEALTH
Access to health services: 80%. **Access to safe water:** 71%.
Hospitals: 103 (20 beds per 10,000). **Doctors:** 11,130.
Blind: 2,850. **Deaf:** 509,700. **Murder rate:** 11.
Lepers: 528. **Underweight prevalence under 5:** 10%.

LITERATURE
New book titles p.a.: 590 (70 p.a. per million). **Periodicals:** 388.
Newspapers: 11 dailies.

COMMUNICATION (per 1,000 people)
Phones: 76 (15% mobile). **Radios:** 154. **TV sets:** 87.
Daily newspaper circulation: 35. **Computers:** 10.

REFUGEES
Alien refugees from other countries: 900.

HUMAN LIFE AND LIBERTY (optimum condition=100.0%)
HDI: 71.8. **HSI:** 47.0. **HFI:** 52.5. **EFL:** 31.0.

Country Table 1. **Religious adherents in the Dominican Republic, AD 1900-2025.**

Year	*1900*		*1970*		*mid-1990*		*Annual change, 1990-2000*				*mid-1995*		*mid-2000*		*mid-2025*	
Name	*Adherents*	*%*	*Adherents*	*%*	*Adherents*	*%*	*Natural*	*Conversion*	*Total*	*Rate*	*Adherents*	*%*	*Adherents*	*%*	*Adherents*	*%*
Christians	**588,000**	**98.0**	**4,355,650**	**98.5**	**6,790,000**	**95.5**	**132,300**	**-2,951**	**129,349**	**1.76**	**7,465,225**	**95.4**	**8,083,492**	**95.2**	**10,484,350**	**93.9**
PROFESSION																
professing Christians	**588,000**	**98.0**	**4,355,650**	**98.5**	**6,790,000**	**95.5**	**132,300**	**-2,951**	**129,349**	**1.76**	**7,465,225**	**95.4**	**8,083,492**	**95.2**	**10,484,350**	**93.9**
AFFILIATION																
unaffiliated Christians	30,000	5.0	481,323	10.9	59,200	0.8	1,153	-1,394	-241	-0.42	56,785	0.7	56,787	0.7	10,000	0.1
affiliated Christians	**558,000**	**93.0**	**3,874,327**	**87.6**	**6,730,800**	**94.7**	**131,146**	**-1,555**	**129,591**	**1.78**	**7,408,440**	**94.7**	**8,026,705**	**94.5**	**10,474,350**	**93.8**
Roman Catholics	555,800	92.6	3,730,663	84.4	6,328,000	89.0	123,267	-3,836	119,431	1.74	6,949,066	88.8	7,522,305	88.6	9,643,000	86.4
Protestants	2,000	0.3	89,035	2.0	285,000	4.0	5,552	1,948	7,500	2.36	324,144	4.1	360,000	4.2	570,000	5.1
Independents	100	0.0	41,490	0.9	102,000	1.4	1,987	813	2,800	2.46	118,664	1.5	130,000	1.5	250,000	2.2
Marginal Christians	0	0.0	10,000	0.2	47,000	0.7	916	384	1,300	2.47	53,450	0.7	60,000	0.7	130,000	1.2
Anglicans	100	0.0	3,139	0.1	3,800	0.1	74	-14	60	1.48	4,000	0.1	4,400	0.1	6,000	0.1
disaffiliated	0	0.0	0	0.0	-35,000	-0.5	-682	-818	-1,500	3.63	-40,884	-0.5	-50,000	-0.6	-124,650	-1.1
Trans-megabloc groupings																
Evangelicals	2,000	0.3	78,000	1.8	213,000	3.0	4,149	1,251	5,400	2.29	239,010	3.1	267,000	3.1	558,000	5.0
Pentecostals/Charismatics	0	0.0	63,000	1.4	839,000	11.8	16,343	3,357	19,700	2.13	941,341	12.0	1,036,000	12.2	1,550,000	13.9
Great Commission Christians	**12,000**	**2.0**	**155,000**	**3.5**	**408,000**	**5.7**	**7,948**	**913**	**8,861**	**1.98**	**453,000**	**5.8**	**496,611**	**5.9**	**781,000**	**7.0**
Spiritists	12,000	2.0	43,000	1.0	155,000	2.2	3,019	39	3,058	1.82	171,000	2.2	185,582	2.2	260,000	2.3
Nonreligious	0	0.0	12,000	0.3	118,400	1.7	2,306	2,719	5,025	3.60	135,000	1.7	168,652	2.0	330,000	3.0
Atheists	0	0.0	5,600	0.1	30,000	0.4	584	246	830	2.47	34,000	0.4	38,297	0.5	60,000	0.5
Chinese folk-religionists	0	0.0	0	0.0	5,500	0.1	107	-1	106	1.78	6,000	0.1	6,563	0.1	9,000	0.1
Baha'is	0	0.0	3,900	0.1	5,000	0.1	97	-7	90	1.68	5,400	0.1	5,904	0.1	10,000	0.1
Muslims	0	0.0	0	0.0	1,600	0.0	31	-4	27	1.57	1,720	0.0	1,869	0.0	3,000	0.0
Buddhists	0	0.0	1,500	0.0	1,470	0.0	29	-23	6	0.39	1,480	0.0	1,529	0.0	1,600	0.0
Jews	0	0.0	350	0.0	540	0.0	11	-4	7	1.26	580	0.0	612	0.0	850	0.0
New-Religionists	0	0.0	0	0.0	90	0.0	2	-1	1	1.26	95	0.0	102	0.0	200	0.0
Other religionists	0	0.0	1,000	0.0	2,400	0.0	47	-13	34	1.32	2,500	0.0	2,735	0.0	5,000	0.0
World A (unevangelized persons)	1,200	0.2	4,422	0.1	7,110	0.1	113	-65	48	0.80	7,823	0.1	8,495	0.1	11,164	0.1
World B (evangelized non-Christians)	10,800	1.8	62,673	1.4	312,890	4.4	6,120	3,016	9,136	2.56	350,217	4.5	403,013	4.7	668,486	6.0
World C (Christians)	588,000	98.0	4,355,650	98.5	6,790,000	95.5	132,300	-2,951	129,349	1.76	7,465,225	95.4	8,083,492	95.2	10,484,350	93.9
Country's population	**600,000**	**100.0**	**4,422,746**	**100.0**	**7,110,000**	**100.0**	**138,533**	**0**	**138,533**	**1.80**	**7,823,266**	**100.0**	**8,495,000**	**100.0**	**11,164,000**	**100.0**

COLUMNS, ROWS.
For meanings and definitions, see Codebook (Part 3). Note that, by definition, total 'Christians' = professing + crypto-Christians, which also = affiliated + unaffiliated Christians, and also = Great Commission Christians + latent Christians. Percentages may not always total exactly, due to rounding.

CENSUSES.
6.VIII.1950: 98.3% Roman Catholics, 1.5% Evangelicals (0.1% SD Adventists), 0.1% Anglicans, 0.1% nonreligious, 0.2% other religionists. **7.VIII.1960:** 98.1% Roman Catholics, 1.3% Evangelicals (0.2% SD Adventists), 0.1% Anglicans, 0.1% nonreligious, 0.4% other religionists. Evangelicals (including Adventists and Anglicans) enumerated in these censuses increased slightly in numbers from 33,440 in 1950 to 35,070 in 1960. Excluding the rapid increase in Adventists (from 2,902 to 5,380), the rest decreased from 30,538 to 29,690 during this 10-year period. Subsequent to 1970 Evangelicals were increasing again with the growth of Pentecostal bodies.

NOTES ON RELIGIONS
ATHEISTS. 6 rival Communist factions, illegal since 1947.
BAHA'IS. Growth from 7 local spiritual assemblies (1964) to 26 (1973), and to 56 (1996). In 1972, 1,700 new believers were enrolled in 6 areas, but there have been many defections.
BUDDHISTS. Chinese, and a small Japanese farming community in the Constanza Valley.
INDEPENDENTS. In 40 denominations in 1995 (see Table 2).
JEWS. A small colony of German Jews.
OTHER RELIGIONISTS. Including Rosicrucians (1 AMORC centre).
SPIRITISTS. Usually termed Afro-American spiritists. The term here is restricted to non-Catholic and non-Christian followers of spiritism and Voodoo. Spiritism is strong in the republic; and the many immigrants from Haiti as well as numerous Dominicanos follow Voodoo (Vodoun). In addition, there are many adherents of the Liborismo cult, a syncretistic movement which is a recent revival of a cult begun about 1900 by Liborio. There are also a few Rastafarians (from Jamaica).

Great Commission Instrument Panel: status of Dominican Republic (for explanation see start of Part 4)

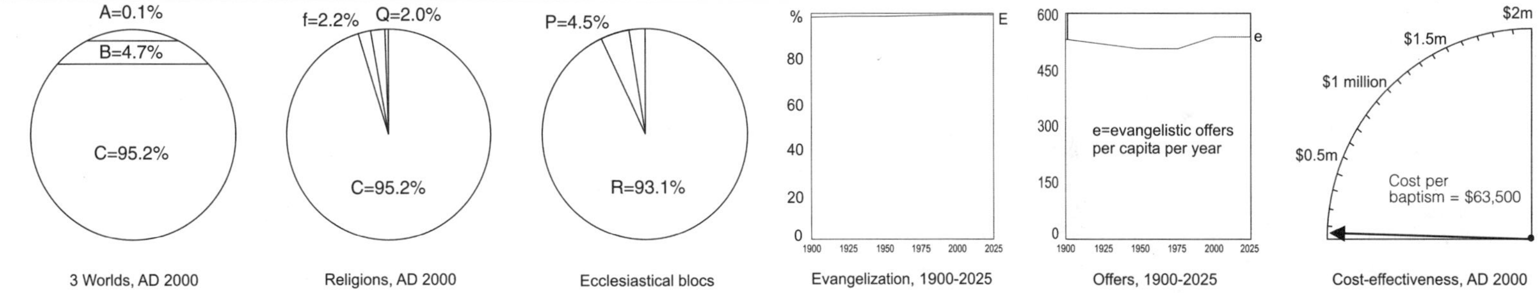

Country status. The Dominican Republic occupies the eastern two thirds of the island of Hispaniola, the second largest island in the Caribbean, discovered by Christopher Columbus in 1492. The island is noteworthy for the fact that its capital, Santo Domingo, is the oldest permanent European settlement in the Western Hemisphere and also the site of the first university and the first cathedral in the Americas.

HUMAN LIFE AND LIBERTY

Human need and development. Although it shares the same island with Haiti, the Dominican Republic has a stronger economy than its neighbor, and its standards of living are less deplorable. Its per capita income is 3 times that of Haiti. Although there are pockets of poverty, it is not as degrading as in Haiti. Further, many Dominicans immigrate to the United States every year and their remittances home constitute a major source of national income. Despite considerable mismanagement by successive governments from the time of Trujillo, economic and social ser-

Country summary. **Worlds A, B, C by ethnolinguistic peoples, cities, and major civil divisions in the Dominican Republic.**

	PEOPLES							CITIES							CIVIL DIVISIONS						
World	*Num*	*Pop 2000*	*C%*	*Christians*	*E%*	*U%*	*Unevangelized*	*Num*	*Pop 2000*	*C%*	*Christians*	*E%*	*U%*	*Unevangelized*	*Num*	*Pop 2000*	*C%*	*Christians*	*E%*	*U%*	*Unevangelized*
A	0	0	0.00	0	0	0	0	0	0	0.00	0	0	0	0	0	0	0.00	0	0	0	0
B	4	14,527	26.06	3,786	89	11	1,583	0	0	0.00	0	0	0	0	0	0	0.00	0	0	0	0
C	10	8,480,811	94.60	8,022,921	100	0	4,696	11	6,515,715	93.12	6,067,616	100	0	8,995	30	8,495,340	94.48	8,026,705	100	0	6,280
Total	**14**	**8,495,338**	**94.48**	**8,026,707**	**100**	**0**	**6,279**	**11**	**6,515,715**	**93.12**	**6,067,616**	**100**	**0**	**8,995**	**30**	**8,495,340**	**94.48**	**8,026,705**	**100**	**0**	**6,280**

vices have not suffered a breakdown and people receive adequate medical care. Official social security programs provide old age, disability, sickness, maternity, survivor, and work accident and occupational disease coverage. The population is notably clean in habits, but environmental sanitation is deficient. The average diet falls below the recommended values in protein and calories, but nevertheless is quite filling.

Human rights and freedoms. In contrast to the Trujillo years, when it was the pariah in interAmerican councils, the Dominican Republic is now one of the freest countries in the region. The nation enjoys a functioning multiparty system, and its elections are generally free of the corrupt practices that plagued the country in the years immediately after the fall of Trujillo. The principal human rights problem is the treatment of Haitian migrants, which often translates into a de facto discrimination against all those with a darker skin. Haitians are denied citizenship and their children may be denied admission to schools. There are credible reports that security personnel habitually beat detainees and prisoners from lower income backgrounds. In an effort to fight crime, police indiscriminately roundup people in poorer neighborhoods.

Human environment. The major environmental problem is deforestation which has caused soil erosion. So large is the volume of topsoil carried by the rivers to the sea that it chokes coral reefs. Deforestation has also aggravated water shortages. The rivers become raging torrents after rains but recede to a trickle afterwards. In the capital, water is sold in sidewalk markets.

Spiritist Catholics Followers of Liborismo cult kneel before movement's shrine, 3 crosses in village of Palma Sola. Pilgrims, mostly Catholics, come from all over the Republic.

NON-CHRISTIAN RELIGIONS

Voodooism (Vodoun), a syncretistic mixture of Catholic practices with traditional African rites, is strong in the republic, particularly through immigrants from neighboring Haiti. In addition, the Liborismo cult, which originally began around 1900 and has recently been revived, has many followers. Although the majority of these are Catholics, a number have no Catholic affiliation or profession.

Catholic pentecostals. Crowd of over 42,000 at charismatic renewal meeting in Pimentel, July 1975, with numerous healings reported.

CHRISTIANITY

CATHOLIC CHURCH. From the nation's origins, the Catholic Church has been intimately bound up with the culture and history of the people. The first bishopric west of the Atlantic was established here in 1511 and St Thomas University in 1538. Recently, there has been a marked decline in its influence on people's lives. There has been a continual decrease in the proportion of church marriages; in 1960, 68% of all marriages were canonical (in church), decreasing to 59% in 1956 and to 54% by 1968. In 1967, weekly attendance at Sunday mass was 11.5% in urban centers across the country. Among sugar-cane cutters, attendance then was 14.5%.

The attention of the church in recent years has centered on 3 developments: (1) a pastoral assembly, at national and diocesan levels, which created the Institute of Pastoral Adaptation with courses for both foreign and local priests and religious personnel; (2) small rural communities with voluntary assembly presidents serving with the approval of the bishop in preaching, distributing communion and presiding at marriages, which provide for closer involvement with the popular culture as well as counter-balancing the shortage of priests; and (3) presbyterial councils, largely consultative in nature, erected in each diocese between 1968 and 1970.

The Holy See has diplomatic relations with Dominican Republic and in AD 2000 is represented to government and the Catholic hierarchy by a nuncio residing in Santo Domingo.

OTHER CHURCHES. Protestantism entered the Dominican Republic during the Haitian occupation when North American Negroes were encouraged to populate the island. Requests for religious leadership resulted in the arrival of the first Methodist pastor from England in 1834, followed by a North American from the African Methodist Episcopal Church.

The Dominican Republic was, however, the last of the Latin American countries to receive sustained Protestant missionary activity. In 1907 the Free Methodist Church (USA) entered the country, building on the foundations laid by an independent missionary in 1889. Further missionary work was initiated through Puerto Rican churches in 1911. Appeals to various mission boards in the USA resulted in the formation of the Board for Christian Work in 1920, with the participation of North American Methodists, Presbyterians and Evangelical United Brethren, joined in later years by Moravians. The resulting church (Iglesia Evangélica Dominicana), became autonomous in 1953. In addition to evangelistic work, medical services, rural reconstruction and education, its bookstore and publishing house have printed and distributed a wide variety of Christian and secular books, many by local authors. The relatively slow growth of this church has been attributed in part to this emphasis on institutional concerns.

In 1941 the Assemblies of God (USA) took over responsibility for several churches which had been established by a Puerto Rican evangelist as early as 1933. Its total community is now the largest non-Catholic body in the republic, followed by Seventh-day Adventists who entered in 1908.

Protestantism has thus made relatively small numerical inroads in the Dominican Republic, though its cultural and social contributions have been significant. For a long time Dominican Protestantism has had the smallest number of national pastors and the lowest membership relative to the total population of any country in the Latin Caribbean.

Renewal movements. In the 1990s the Pentecostal/Charismatic Renewal continued to spread rapidly across most older churches, and numbered over 1,036,000 adherents (of whom 16% Pentecostals, 74% Charismatics, and 9% Independents).

Indigenous missions. Catholic Dominican Christians have served in surrounding Caribbean countries since the beginning of the church. Recently, some Christians, Protestant and Catholic, have began to serve in North Africa and Southern and Central Africa.

Iglesia Catolica. Charismatic leader Fr Emiliano Tardif leads in prayer in Pimentel meeting.

CHURCH AND STATE

Relations between church and state are delineated in the constitution of November 1966, in which Article 8 guarantees 'freedom of conscience and of religion, subject to public order and good morals', and in the concordat of June 1954 negotiated by the Trujillo regime and the apostolic nuncio at that time. The principal dispositions of the latter are as follows: (1) the government recognizes Catholicism as the religion of the Dominican nation and accepts the prerogatives of canon law; (2) Catholic dioceses, institutions and associations are given legal status; (3) government finances diocesan administration and the construction of cathedrals; (4) priests, religious personnel and seminarians are exempt from military service, and clergy and church property are exempt from taxation; (5) civil recognition is given to canonical marriages as well as marriage annulments pronounced by ecclesiastical tribunals; Catholic married couples however may not be divorced; (6) government public schools must orient their teaching to the religious and moral principles of Catholicism and must also offer courses in the Catholic religion, subject to inspection by the ordinary; and (7) provision is made for religious chaplaincies to the armed forces.

The Secretary of State for Education, Fine Arts and Religion is in charge of religious affairs, but there is no special register for churches. Protestant denominations are customarily established juridically as nonprofit civil organizations.

The Catholic Church enjoys wide respect among the middle class and government officials, but not among nonconformists. Since the 1965 civil war 8 priests have identified themselves openly with opposition constitutionalists, who are considered communist by Catholic conservatives; and in 1965 also the nuncio and the bishop of Santiago exerted pressure on the Episcopal Conference to issue a communique dissociating itself from the forces of the right. The nuncio also played a role in preventing the crushing of the constitutionalists. Some clergy have denounced social injustices and the crimes of the Banda, a paramilitary group acting for some sections of the army. Among the population, however, especially among youth and students, disillusionment towards the church grows with each indication of ecclesiastical identification with the established political power. This identification inevitably appears when patriotic and liturgical elements are mixed in cathedral and other functions.

BROADCASTING AND MEDIA

The Dominican Republic is a member of UNDA and there are 5 local Catholic radio stations (one on FM and the rest on AM). UDECA is the national organization of Catholic broadcasters. Shortwave programs from KNLS, HCJB (Ecuador), TWR (Antilles) and AWR (Costa Rica) can be easily received.

Spanish versions of CBN's programs can be seen on 2 local television channels on a daily basis. There are 4 follow-up centers for ministry and discipleship, and counselor training seminars. In 1996 CBN had completed its 'Fisher of Men Operation' with good response; in Santo Domingo there were 23 cell groups involved in discipleship training programs. TBN programs are aired on local channel 36. LeSEA programming is available through the World Harvest Satellite. The 'Jesus' Film has been shown to 4.4 million: 4 million through a TV broadcast, and 39,000 have responded.

INTERDENOMINATIONAL ORGANIZATIONS

There is no national council of churches. Presbyterians, United Methodists, and Moravians work in the united Dominican Evangelical Church, which co-operates also with the Episcopal Church. In 1962 the Social Service of Dominican Churches (Servicio Social de Iglesias Dominicanas) was started, with stimulus and substantial help from Church World Service in the USA. About 20 churches participate, distributing USA surplus food through various organizations and handling a number of agricultural projects. A Centre for Ecumenical Planning and Action (CEPAE) attempted to create a sense of community among the churches.

FUTURE TRENDS AND PROSPECTS

The nonreligious, only 0.3% of the population in 1970, are expected to grow to 3.0% by 2025. Christians would correspondingly decline to 93.9% in the same period.

Though the nonreligious will possibly grow beyond 5% of the population by AD 2050, Christians probably will claim over 90% of the population for the next few decades.

BIBLIOGRAPHY

25th anniversary of the Evangelical Mennonite Church in the land Columbus loved best. M. Zimmerman. Fort Wayne, IN: Commission on Overseas Missions, Evangelical Mennonite Church, 1971. 101p.

500 anos de evangelização e Santo Domingo: antes e depois da IV Conferência do episcopado Latino– Americano. M. Nieves Tapia & C. Donegana. *Coleção vida em comunidade.* São Paulo: Editora Cidade Nova, 1993. 110p.

'Afro–Dominican religious brotherhoods: structure, ritual, and music.' M. E. Davis. Thesis, University of Illinois, Urbana, 1976. 452p.

'Cane harvest: a kingdom multi–ministry strategy for mission: a strategy for the Christian Reformed mission outreach in the Dominican Republic.' R. G. Brinks. Th.M. thesis, Calvin Theological Seminary, Grand Rapids, MI, 1985. 201p.

'Church ministry among marginal peoples: a study project on church ministry and leadership training among the Haitian immigrant sugar cane cutters in the Dominican Republic.' N. Hegeman. D.Min. thesis, Westminster Theological Seminary, Chestnut Hill, PA, 1985. 309p.

Cinco siglos de Iglesia dominicana. J. L. Sáez. Santo Domingo: Editora Amigo del Hogar, 1987. 153p.

Directorio de la Iglesia Católica en República Dominicana, 1972. Santo Domingo: Conferencia del Episcopado Dominicano, 1972.

Dominican Republic. K. Schoenhals. *World bibliographical series*, vol. 111. Oxford, UK: CLIO Press, 1990. 211p. (See especially 'Religion,' p.91–3, and 'Voodoo,' p.94).

'Dominican vodú, historical and contemporary perspectives.' J. G. López. M.A. thesis, University of Florida, Gainesville, FL, 1981. 141p.

El auge pentecostal: certeza, identidad, salvación. M. Villamán P. Mexico City: Centro Antonio de Montesinos, 1993. 174p.

El protestantismo en Dominicana. G. A. Lockward. 2d ed. *Colección CETEC*, vol. 8. Santo Domingo: Editora Educativa Dominicana, 1982. 462p.

'Equipping pastors for church planting in the Dominican Republic.' B. W. Hagewood. D.Min. thesis, Southeastern Baptist Theological Seminary, Wake Forest, NC, 1989. 140p.

Fe popular e identidad cultural. B. Matías. Santo Domingo: CEDEE, 1987. 33p.

'Foundations for a pastoral training program for the Evangelical Mennonite Church in the Dominican Republic.' H. L. Hyde. D.Miss. thesis, Trinity Evangelical Divinity School, Deerfield, IL, 1986. 233p.

Heterodoxia e inquisición en Santo Domingo, 1492–1822. C. E. Deive. Santo Domingo: Taller, 1983. 400p.

Historia de la Iglesia Metodista Libre Dominicana. I. Brito Bruno. Santo Domingo: Editora Educativa Dominicana, [1975]. 225p.

Iglesia católica y oligarquía. E. Rosario. Santiago, 1991. 236p.

La iglesia dominicana entre dos dictaduras. L. García. Santo Domingo: Imprenta Félix, 1972. 61p.

La isla Española: cuna de la evangelización de América. J. A. F. Santana. Santo Domingo: Amigo del Hogar, 1986. 242p.

Los jesuítas en la República Dominicana. J. L. Sáez. Santo Domingo: Museo Nacional de Historia y Geografía Archivo Histórico de las Antillas, 1988–1990. 2 vols.

Miracles are happening in the Dominican Republic. L. Bustle & E. Bustle. *Missionary resource book*, 1978-79. Kansas City, MO: Nazarene Publishing House, 1978. 94p.

'New hope for Santo Domingo: a preliminary church growth survey of the Protestant and Evangelical churches in the Dominican Republic, West Indies.' D. L. Platt. M.A. thesis, Fuller Theological Seminary, Pasadena, CA, 1975. 166p.

Pistas metodologicas para el estudio de las conclusiones de Santa Domingo. E. Peña Vanegas. [San Salvador, El Salvador: Dept. de Educación], 1993. 29p.

'Power, influence and impotence: the church as a socio–political factor in the Dominican Republic.' W. L. Wipfler. Ph.D. dissertation, Union Theological Seminary, New York, 1978. 2 vols.

Qué nuevas nos trae Santo Domingo?: la novedad de Santo Domingo al alcance del pueblo. G. Iriarte & M. Orsini Puente. *Colección 'Evangelio con rostro L.A.'*, 3. Bogotá: Ediciones Paulinas, HSP, 1993. 122p.

Santo Domingo and after: the challenges for the Latin American Church. G. Gutiérrez et al. London: Catholic Institute for International Relations, 1993. 68p.

The Church and the crisis in the Dominican Republic. J. A. Clark. Westminster, MD: Newman Press, 1966. 292p. (Catholic).

The churches of the Dominican Republic in the light of history: a study of the root causes of current problems. W. L. Wipfler. *Centro Intercultural de Documentación*, 11. Cuernavaca, Mexico: Centro Intercultural de Documentación, 1966. 210p.

'The Dominican Republic,' J. L. Gonzalez, in *The development of Christianity in the Latin Caribbean*, p.73–82. Grand Rapids, MI: Eerdmans, 1969.

'The formation of a non–formal education team.' R. G. Brinks. D.Min. thesis, Westminster Theological Seminary, Chestnut Hill, PA, 1989. 432p.

'The missionary church in the Dominican Republic.' D. W. Dyck. M.A. thesis, Fuller Theological Seminary, Pasadena, CA, 1975. 179p.

'Toward the renewal and growth of the Dominican Episcopal Church: a practical and theological case study.' M. I. Short. D.Min. thesis, Fuller Theological Seminary, Pasadena, CA, 1992. 336p.

Trujillo y la Iglesia. J. Rodríguez Grullón. [Santo Domingo]: Editora Panamericana, 1991. 149p.

Voodoo: its origins and practices. H. Gilfond. New York: Franklin Watts, 1976. 114p.

Country Table 2. **Organized churches and denominations in the Dominican Republic.**

Official name (bold type = church with over 10% of all affiliated) 1	*Begun* 2	*Type* 3	*Counc* 4	*Congs* 5	*Adults* 6	*Affiliated 1970* 7	*Affiliated 1995* 8	*G%* 9	*Names, notes, and other statistics* (see Codebook, Part 3) 10
Acción Misionera Iglesia de Dios	1983	I-3gL	.....	3	80	–	222	8.33	*Missionary Action of the Church of God.*
Arca de Salvación	c1960	I-3pL	.....	35	3,500	8,000	10,000	0.90	*Ark of Salvation.*
Asamblea Cristiana Nueva Vida	c1980	I-3gL	.....	1	50	–	76	6.67	*Christian New Life Assembly.*
Asamblea Cristiana Unida	c1960	I-3pL	.....	107	4,800	5,000	7,390	1.58	*United Christian Assembly.*
Asamblea de Iglesias Cristianas	1939	I-3pL	x...k	98	6,000	500	10,000	12.73	*Assembly of Christian Chs.* M=ACC(Puerto Ricans from USA). 1p.
Asambleas de Dios	1933	P-Pe2	ZF..k	1,544	38,185	27,000	72,414	4.03	*Igl Ev AdD. Assemblies of God.* M=AoG(USA). 132n,4x,6f,1s(49),685Y,2472z.
Asambleas Locales	c1990	I-3nC	.....	2	125	–	300	20.00	*Local Churches. Little Flock.* Begun 1922 in China.
Associación Adventista del Séptimo Día	1908	P-Adv	x...k	246	29,000	20,000	72,500	5.29	*Seventh-day Adv, Central Dominican Conf.* 16nx,6f,98mw,1h,1f,208t(23591),1313Y.
Associación de Templos Evangélicos	1938	P-Eva	xM..K	20	1,400	3,545	4,240	0.72	*Association of Ev Churches.* M=West Indies Mission (USA). HQ La Vega. 3n,19f,1p.
Convención Bautista Dominicana	1962	P-Bap	T....	14	1,150	1,000	2,050	2.91	*Dominican Baptist Convention.* M=SBC(USA). 2 schools. 5n,15f,7h,1s,37Y.
Defensores de la Fe	1951	I-3pL	.....	24	10,800	8,330	16,700	2.82	*Defenders of the Faith.*
Hermanos Libres	c1925	P-CBr	x....	100	4,000	1,400	8,000	7.22	*Christian (Plymouth, Open) Brethren. Brethren Assemblies.* M=CMML(USA). 15f.
Ig Bíblica del Señor Jesus Cristo	1978	I-3gL	.....	5	900	–	2,310	5.88	*Bíblical Ch of the Lord Jesus Christ.*
Ig Bautista Mis Haitiana y VEE	1922	I-Bap	.....	35	950	1,550	2,380	1.73	*Haitian Missionary Baptist Church.*
Ig Evang Pent Cruzada Misionera	1968	I-3pL	.....	3	200	50	550	10.07	*Evangelical Pentecostal Church Missionary Crusade.*
Iglesia Africana Metodista Episcopal	c1840	I-Met	VwM.k	13	1,300	1,800	2,600	1.48	*Dominican Rep Annual Conference*, 16th Episcopal District. M=AMEC (USA Blacks).
Igelsia Alianza Cristiana y Misionera	1976	P-Hol	.....	43	1,548	–	3,096	5.26	*Christian & Missionary Alliance Church.* M=CMA(USA).
Iglesia Bautista Bethel		I-Bap	.....	17	600	500	1,500	0.05	*Bethel Baptist Church.*
Iglesia Bautista Fundamental	1969	I-Bap	.....	10	380	150	950	7.66	*Fundamental Baptist Church.* M=BIM(USA).
Iglesia Bautista Haitiana		I-Bap	.....	16	1,300	1,240	2,600	0.05	*Haitian Baptist Ch.*
Iglesia Católica en la Rep Dominicana:	1494	R-Lat	B.L.R	1,528	3,676,100	3,730,663	6,949,066	2.52	*Catholic Ch.* C=19+1+32. 5p,2q,2s(55). 221n 377x 720m 1509w 117487Yy
M Santiago de los Caballeros	1953	R-Lat	Bs	48	415,000	1,041,118	785,000	-1.12	Rural. Most progressive diocesan structure. 1s. 44n 46x 49m 207w 16243Yy
D La Vega	1953	R-Lat	Bs	426	376,500	643,100	712,340	0.41	Rural. Many smallholders. In north center. 32n 38x 123m 155w 17984Yy
D Mao-Monte Cristi	1978	R-Lat	Bs	285	204,000	–	387,392	5.88	In Val verde, 94% Roman Catholic. 8n 11x 14m 51w 8327Yy
D San Francisco de Macoris	1978	R-Lat	Bs	533	282,000	–	534,000	5.88	New diocese, 95% Roman Catholic. 23n 11x 11m 56w 5281Yy
M Santo Domingo	1511	R-Lat	Bs	119	1,433,000	1,237,445	2,711,334	3.19	50% urban. Many Haitian sugar workers. M=SJ,OP. 72n 209x 426m 740w 40856Yy
D Bani	1986	R-Lat	Bs	18	306,000	–	579,000	11.11	New diocese. Heavily Catholic. 11n 27x 53m 103w 5880Yy
D Barahona	1976	R-Lat	Bsdb	18	103,000	–	195,000	5.26	M=SDB. 6n 12x 12m 42w 3041Yy
D NS de la Altagracia en Higüey	1959	R-Lat	Bs	18	276,000	254,000	523,000	2.93	NS=Nuestra Señora. Rural. 1971 Shrine controversy. 16n 12x 18m 86w 7502Yy
D San Juan de la Maguana	1953	R-Lat	Bs	20	264,000	545,000	500,000	-0.34	Rural. Impoverished soil (rain scarcity). M=CSSR. 9n 11x 14m 69w 12373Yy
OM Republica Dominicana	1958	R-Lat	B....	43	16,600	10,000	22,000	3.20	*Dominican Military Ordinariate.* 23 ordinaries.
Iglesia Cristiana Biblica	1949	P-Non	xM...	28	2,800	300	7,000	13.43	*Alianza Biblica Cristiana.* M=UFM(USA). HQ San Pedro de Macorís. 14f,1p.
Iglesia Cristiana Reformada	1976	P-Ref	.....	95	3,500	–	11,300	5.26	M=CRWM(USA).
Iglesia Cristo la Unica Espíritu	1972	I-3gL	.....	34	960	–	2,400	4.35	*One Spirit Church of Christ.*
Iglesia de Cristo		I-Dis	x....	10	500	200	1,000	0.05	*Churches of Christ.* M=CC(Non-Instrumental) (USA). In Santo Domingo.
Iglesia de Dios de la Profecía	1940	P-Pe3	Z...k	172	14,000	3,000	40,000	10.92	*Ch of God of Prophecy.* M=CGP(USA), ex CoG(Cleveland). HQ San Pedro de Macorís.
Iglesia de Dios en Cristo		I-3pB	Z....	35	2,200	500	5,500	0.05	*Church of God in Christ.* M=CoGiC(Black mission from USA). Strong in Haiti.
Iglesia de Dios (Anderson)		P-Hol	x...k	35	2,500	2,000	5,000	0.05	*Ch of God.* M=CoG(Anderson) (USA). Holiness denomination.
Iglesia de Dios (Cleveland)	1939	P-Pe3	ZF..k	227	14,170	6,000	30,000	6.65	*Pentecostal Ch of God.* M=CoG(Cleveland) (USA). 72 churches, 77 missions. 70n,2f,1p.
Iglesia de la Cristianizacion	1982	I-3gL	.....	5	300	–	441	7.69	*Church of Christianization.*
Iglesia de la Nazareno	1974	P-Hol	x....	138	9,902	–	21,614	4.76	M=CoN. Nazarenes.
Iglesia del Principe de Paz	1976	I-3pL	x....	17	1,500	–	3,410	5.26	*Prince of Peace Church.* Strong in Guatemala.
Iglesia Dominicana Fronterizo		I-Non	.....	7	700	1,210	2,120	0.05	*Dominican Border Ch.*
Iglesia del Evangelio Cuadrangular		P-Pe2	ZF...	10	800	100	1,500	0.05	*Internat Ch of the Foursquare Gospel.* M=ICFG(USA). Classical Pentecostals.
Iglesia Episcopal Dominicana	1898	A-Cen	aw.RK	28	1,570	3,139	4,000	0.97	*Episcopal Ch.* Diocese, ECUSA IX. 94% citizens (10% Black). 5n,5x,16Y,136y.
Iglesia Evangélica Dominicana	1834	P-Uni	V.U.K	146	5,400	12,000	15,900	1.13	*Dominican Ev Ch.* 1920 union, M=Board for Christian Work. A=1953. 19n,8h,1j,1k,39t.
Iglesia Evangélica Menonita	1945	P-Men	GF..K	23	1,313	1,500	2,790	2.51	M=Ev Mennonite Ch (Defenseless Mennonite Ch) (USA). 10f,2h,1s.
Iglesia Evangelica Pentecostal	c1980	I-3pL	.....	3	200	–	350	6.67	*Evangelical Pentecostal Church.*
Iglesia Metodista Libre Dominicana	1889	I-Hol	VF..K	102	9,300	10,000	21,100	3.03	1907, M=FMC(USA). North coast. 13n,8f,6h,1k,1r,1s(20),1716z.
Iglesia Misionera	1945	P-Hol	xF...	51	2,000	1,000	3,040	4.55	*Missionary Church.* M=MCA, since 1969 Missionary Ch (USA). 17f.
Iglesia Morave	1898	P-Mor	x....	44	6,600	7,690	16,900	3.20	*Moravian Church.*
Iglesia Nueva Apostolica	c1990	I-3aX	x....	30	3,000	–	4,555	20.00	*NAC. New Apostolic Church.* M=Neuapostolische Kirche (HQ Zurich).
Iglesia Pentecostal Unida	1962	P-Pe1	x....	38	1,900	1,000	3,800	5.49	*United Pentecostal Ch.* M=UPC(USA). Unitarian Pentecostals. 7n.
Iglesia Pentecostal y Misionera	1972	I-3pL	.....	10	600	–	1,500	4.35	*Pentecostal and Missionary Church.*
Iglesias Buenas Nuevas	1976	I-3gL	.....	4	490	–	750	5.26	*Churches of the Good News.*
Iglesias de la Fe Apostólica	1950	I-3aL	x....	40	1,000	100	2,000	12.73	*Chs of the Apostolic Faith.* M=AFM(Portland, Oregon, USA). Holiness Pentecostals.
Misión Bautista Dominicana	1950	I-Bap	x....	7	500	360	1,110	4.61	M=Baptist Mid-Missions (USA). Fundamentalist Baptists. 10f.

Continued overleaf

Country Table 2–concluded

Official name (bold type = church with over 10% of affiliated) 1	*Begun* 2	*Type* 3	*Counc* 4	*Congs* 5	*Adults* 6	*Affiliated 1970* 7	*Affiliated 1995* 8	*G%* 9	*Names, notes, and other statistics (see Codebook, Part 3)* 10
Misión Biblica Evangelica	1987	I-Eva	.....	2	20	–	80	12.50	*Biblical Evangelical Mission.*
Misión Posible	1987	I-3aL	.....	5	150	–	375	12.50	*Mission Possible.*
Misionera Asamblea Cristiana	c1970	I-3gL	.....	30	1,800	–	3,600	38.76	*Christian Missionary Assembly.*
Tabernaculo Evangelistica	1972	I-Non	.....	20	1,800	–	5,460	4.35	*Evangelistic Tabernacle.* M=WT.
Templo de Renacimiento	1981	I-3gL	.....	2	220	–	335	7.14	*Temple of Revival.*
Testigos de Jehová	1945	m-Jeh	x....	230	12,108	9,500	50,700	6.93	*Jehovah's Witnesses. Watch Tower. IBSA.* First missionaries 1945. (1975) 464Y. (1995) 1808Y.
Other Non-White indigenous churches		I-3gU	.....	35	3,000	2,000	5,000	0.05	Total about 10 (see below), mostly from Puerto Rico, Jamaica, Trinidad et alia.
Other Protestant denominations		P-	.....	20	1,000	1,500	3,000	0.05	Total about 10 (see list below).
Other marginal Protestant bodies		m-	.....	11	1,100	500	2,750	0.05	Including: Unity School of Christianity (from USA; 2 ministers).
Disaffiliated		X-Aff			-21,400	0	-40,884		Evangelicals who are also baptized Roman Catholics.
Totals				**5,558**	**3,869,871**	**3,874,327**	**7,408,440**		

Churches, members, growth, 1900-2025	*Congs*	*Adults*	*Affiliated*	*G%*	*Total denominations*	*6 Megablocs:* O	R	A	P	I	m
Total churches, members, and denominations (mid-1900)	400	296,000	558,000	2.81	6	0	1	1	2	2	0
Total churches, members, and denominations (mid-1970)	2,059	2,056,940	3,874,327	2.81	44	0	1	1	19	20	3
Total churches, members, and denominations (mid-1990)	4,000	3,516,000	6,730,800	2.80	75	0	1	1	27	40	6
Total churches, members, and denominations (mid-1995)	5,558	3,869,871	7,408,440	1.94	78	0	1	1	28	42	6
Total churches, members, and denominations (mid-2000)	6,000	4,193,000	8,026,705	1.62	81	0	1	1	29	44	6
Total churches, members, and denominations (mid-2025)	7,000	5,471,000	10,474,350	1.07	132	0	1	1	40	80	10

NOTES ON TABLE ABOVE
NATIONAL COUNCILS (Column 4, 5th letter).
There is no national council of churches, but there is a service organization, SSID.

- E = Dominican Association of Evangelical Churches (DAEC), Dominican Evangelical Fraternity (DEF/FED, Fraternidad Evangélico Dominicano).
- K = Servicio Social de Iglesias Dominicanas (SSID) (Social Organization of the Dominican Churches).
- k = associate member of SSID.
- R = Conferencia del Episcopado Dominicano (CED, Conference of the Dominican Episcopate).

OTHER NON-WHITE INDIGENOUS CHURCHES. These, mostly of pentecostal background from Puerto Rico, Jamaica, Trinidad and elsewhere, include the following: Ch of Our Lord Jesus Christ of the Apostolic Faith (1950) (USA Black pentecostals), Iglesia Bautista Bethel, Iglesia Defensores de la Fe (begun 1947 by Puerto Ricans), Iglesia del Dios Vivo, Iglesia Monte Zión, Iglesia Pentecostal de JC, Primer Concilio Evangélico Pentecostés Dominicano.
OTHER PROTESTANT DENOMINATIONS. Baptist International Missions (1970), Exclusive Brethren (Continuing Tunbridge Wells), International Gospel League (1970), Maranatha Baptist Mission, Moravian Ch (1907), Salvation Army (1971), Union Ch of Santo Domingo, Worldwide Evangelization Crusade (Cruzada Evangelistica Mundial) (1941).

ECUADOR

SECULAR DATA, AD 2000

STATE
Official name: La República del Ecuador (The Republic of Ecuador).
Short name: Ecuador. **Adjective of nationality:** Ecuadorian.
Flag: Yellow, blue, and red stripes, national coat of arms at centre.
Area: 272,045 sq. km. (105,037 sq. mi.).
Government: Unitary multiparty republic with one legislative house, since 1979 (1534 Spanish conquest, 1830 Independence, several dictatorships, 1972 military junta).
Legislature: National Congress, 82 members.
Official language: Spanish (Español/Castella).
Monetary unit: 1 Sucre (S/.) = 100 centavos. **US$1=** S/. 6,310.00.
Chief cities: Guayaquil 2,127,000; QUITO 1,505,000; Cuenca 240,229; Machala 177,660; Portoviejo 163,787.
Political divisions: 21 provinces.
Armed forces: 58,000.

DEMOGRAPHY
Population: 12,646,000.
Population density: 46.4/sq. km. (120.4/sq. mi.).
Under 15 years: 4,278,000.
Growth rate p.a.: 1.74% (births 23.24, deaths 5.81).
Mortality: Infant, per 1,000: 41.5; **Maternal per 100,000:** 150.0.
Life expectancy: 70 (male 68, female 74).
Household size: 4.1. **Floor area per person, sq.m:** 17.0.
Major languages: Spanish, Quechua, English, German, Jivaro, Norwegian, Chinese, and about 15 other languages.
Urban dwellers: 62.41%. **Urban growth rate p.a.:** 2.7%.
Labor force: 35%.

ETHNOLINGUISTIC PEOPLES
41.9% Mestizo; 25.1% Detribalized Quichua; 10.0% Latin American White; 9.4% Chimborazo Highland Quichua; 5.0% Black.

ECONOMY
National income p.a. per person: US$1,390; **per family:** US$5,698.

EDUCATION
Adult literacy: 90% (male 92%, female 88%). **Schools:** 18,353.
Universities: 21. **School enrolment:** female/male: 90%/91%.

HEALTH
Access to health services: 88%. **Access to safe water:** 70%.
Hospitals: 429 (16 beds per 10,000). **Doctors:** 12,853.
Blind: 10,000. **Deaf:** 758,800. **Murder rate:** 10.
Lepers: 6,300. **Underweight prevalence under 5:** 17%.

LITERATURE
New book titles p.a.: 1,010 (80 p.a. per million). **Periodicals:** 70.
Newspapers: 24 dailies.

COMMUNICATION (per 1,000 people)
Phones: 65 (23% mobile). **Radios:** 277. **TV sets:** 148.
Daily newspaper circulation: 72. **Computers:** 70.

REFUGEES
Alien refugees from other countries: 100.

HUMAN LIFE AND LIBERTY (optimum condition=100.0%)
HDI: 77.5. **HSI:** 42.0. **HFI:** 60.0. **EFL:** 37.0.

Country Table 1. **Religious adherents in Ecuador, AD 1900-2025.**

Year / *Name*	*1900* Adherents	%	*1970* Adherents	%	*mid-1990* Adherents	%	*Annual change, 1990-2000* Natural	Conversion	Total	Rate	*mid-1995* Adherents	%	*mid-2000* Adherents	%	*mid-2025* Adherents	%
Christians	**1,430,000**	**87.7**	**5,869,600**	**98.3**	**10,037,500**	**97.8**	**232,951**	**-2,687**	**230,264**	**2.09**	**11,191,440**	**97.7**	**12,340,137**	**97.6**	**17,231,300**	**96.8**
PROFESSION																
professing Christians	**1,430,000**	**87.7**	**5,869,600**	**98.3**	**10,037,500**	**97.8**	**232,951**	**-2,687**	**230,264**	**2.09**	**11,191,440**	**97.7**	**12,340,137**	**97.6**	**17,231,300**	**96.8**
AFFILIATION																
unaffiliated Christians	0	0.0	0	0.0	26,800	0.3	622	-67	555	1.90	28,440	0.3	32,350	0.3	73,300	0.4
affiliated Christians	**1,430,000**	**87.7**	**5,869,600**	**98.3**	**10,010,700**	**97.5**	**232,329**	**-2,620**	**229,709**	**2.09**	**11,163,000**	**97.4**	**12,307,787**	**97.3**	**17,158,000**	**96.4**
Roman Catholics	1,430,000	87.7	5,843,556	97.9	9,740,000	94.9	226,039	-10,039	216,000	2.02	10,803,099	94.3	11,900,000	94.1	16,500,000	92.7
Protestants	100	0.0	82,900	1.4	185,000	1.8	4,293	1,207	5,500	2.64	211,096	1.8	240,000	1.9	430,000	2.4
Independents	0	0.0	82,780	1.4	160,000	1.6	3,713	2,787	6,500	3.47	186,027	1.6	225,000	1.8	500,000	2.8
Marginal Christians	0	0.0	13,668	0.2	140,000	1.4	3,249	1,251	4,500	2.83	160,000	1.4	185,000	1.5	530,000	3.0
Orthodox	0	0.0	1,000	0.0	1,600	0.0	37	-17	20	1.18	1,700	0.0	1,800	0.0	2,500	0.0
Anglicans	0	0.0	510	0.0	1,300	0.0	30	0	30	2.10	1,430	0.0	1,600	0.0	3,000	0.0
doubly-affiliated	-100	0.0	-154,814	-2.6	-217,200	-2.1	-5,041	2,200	-2,841	1.24	-200,352	-1.8	-245,613	-1.9	-807,500	-4.5
Trans-megabloc groupings																
Evangelicals	100	0.0	130,000	2.2	231,000	2.3	5,361	1,039	6,400	2.48	262,272	2.3	295,000	2.3	534,000	3.0
Pentecostals/Charismatics	0	0.0	62,000	1.0	1,125,000	11.0	26,108	2,392	28,500	2.28	1,266,200	11.1	1,410,000	11.2	2,400,000	13.5
Great Commission Christians	**65,000**	**4.0**	**418,000**	**7.0**	**523,000**	**5.1**	**12,137**	**168**	**12,305**	**2.14**	**585,000**	**5.1**	**646,048**	**5.1**	**1,067,000**	**6.0**
Nonreligious	0	0.0	19,000	0.3	114,600	1.1	2,660	3,131	5,791	4.17	146,700	1.3	172,505	1.4	400,000	2.3
Ethnoreligionists	200,000	12.3	50,000	0.8	54,900	0.5	1,274	-141	1,133	1.89	60,500	0.5	66,229	0.5	75,000	0.4
Atheists	0	0.0	6,000	0.1	14,000	0.1	325	45	370	2.38	16,000	0.1	17,704	0.1	29,000	0.2
Baha'is	0	0.0	16,400	0.3	14,400	0.1	334	-214	120	0.80	14,600	0.1	15,599	0.1	15,000	0.1
Buddhists	0	0.0	2,000	0.0	11,200	0.1	260	-53	207	1.71	12,000	0.1	13,266	0.1	17,500	0.1
Chinese folk-religionists	0	0.0	4,000	0.1	10,500	0.1	244	-67	177	1.57	11,100	0.1	12,269	0.1	15,000	0.1
Jews	0	0.0	2,000	0.0	3,400	0.0	79	-35	44	1.21	3,600	0.0	3,836	0.0	4,200	0.0
Muslims	0	0.0	0	0.0	1,200	0.0	28	24	52	3.67	1,560	0.0	1,720	0.0	4,000	0.0
Other religionists	0	0.0	1,000	0.0	2,300	0.0	53	-3	50	2.00	2,500	0.0	2,804	0.0	5,000	0.0
World A (unevangelized persons)	163,000	10.0	41,789	0.7	51,320	0.5	1,184	858	2,042	3.42	57,300	0.5	75,876	0.6	124,572	0.7
World B (evangelized non-Christians)	37,000	2.3	58,519	1.0	175,180	1.7	4,073	1,829	5,902	2.76	211,347	1.8	229,987	1.8	440,128	2.5
World C (Christians)	1,430,000	87.7	5,869,600	98.3	10,037,500	97.8	232,951	-2,687	230,264	2.09	11,191,440	97.7	12,340,137	97.6	17,231,300	96.8
Country's population	**1,630,000**	**100.0**	**5,969,909**	**100.0**	**10,264,000**	**100.0**	**238,208**	**0**	**238,208**	**2.11**	**11,460,088**	**100.0**	**12,646,000**	**100.0**	**17,796,000**	**100.0**

COLUMNS, ROWS.
For meanings and definitions, see Codebook (Part 3). Note that, by definition, total 'Christians' = professing + crypto-Christians, which also = affiliated + unaffiliated Christians, and also = Great Commission Christians + latent Christians. Percentages may not always total exactly, due to rounding.

CENSUSES.
The religion question has not been asked in government censuses.

NOTES ON RELIGIONS
ATHEISTS. 3 rival Communist parties.
BAHA'IS. Very rapid growth from 5 local spiritual assemblies (1964) to 164 (1973); 2 centers on Galapagos Islands. Subsequently LSAs fell to 78 (with one on Galapagos), partly dues to secular boundary revisions. Mainly Indians and Blacks with a school in Esmeraldas (1,000 children). Radio and TV are widely used.
BUDDHISTS. Chinese.
DOUBLY-AFFILIATED. The term covers those affiliated to, or claimed by, both the Catholic Church and also a church termed Evangélica by the state (Protestant, Anglican, Independents mar-

Continued opposite

Country Table 1–concluded

ginal Protestant), i.e. baptized Catholics who have recently become Evangelicals or others. Because their statistics represent a duplication, they are shown in the table as a negative quantity (with a minus sign).
ETHNORELIGIONISTS. Of the 70,000 jungle or lowland or pure tribal Amerindians (Araguro, Auca, Cayapa, Cofán, Colorado, Jivaro, Salasaca, Secoyas, et alii) in 1970, a very high proportion are still animists.
INDEPENDENTS. In about 74 denominations or groupings in 1995 (see Table 2).
OTHER RELIGIONISTS. Including Rosicrucians (2 AMORC centers).
PENTECOSTALS/CHARISMATICS. Begun in 1970, the Catholic Charismatic Renewal has expanded to (1996) 604 regular weekly prayer groups and 26 covenant communities, with 23,000 regular attenders, 30 priests and 7 bishops. The 17th ECCE (Encuentro Carismatico Catolico Ecuatoriano (October 1996) drew 300 leaders and 8,000 attenders.

Great Commission Instrument Panel: status of Ecuador (for explanation see start of Part 4)

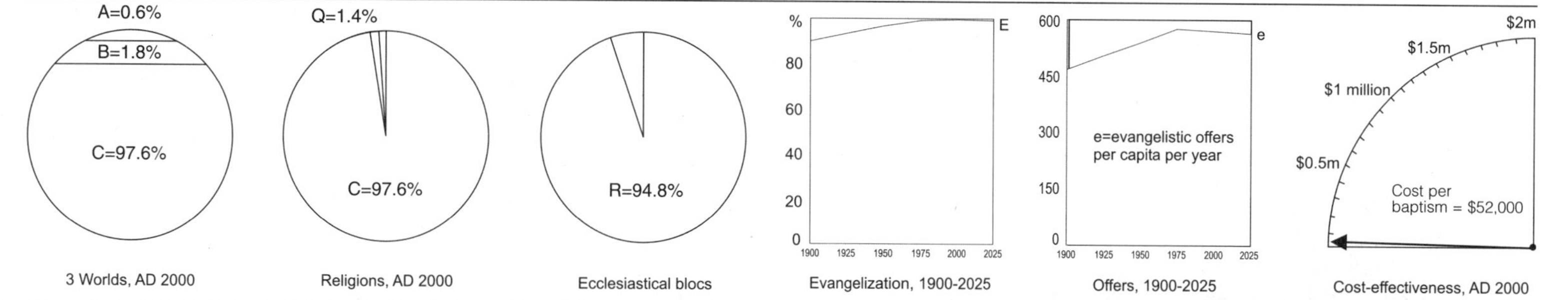

Country status. Ecuador is located on the northwest coast of South America, straddling the Equator from which it derives its name. It is a constitutional republic with a president and a unicameral legislature. The economy is dependent on agriculture with the main exports being coffee, bananas, and fish.

HUMAN LIFE AND LIBERTY

Human need and development. Living conditions in Ecuador have been influenced by a variety of divisive elements. As a consequence of poor communication routes, societies in the Sierra and Costa have developed in relative isolation from one another. Society is stratified economically as well as geographically. Higher classes and higher income people live in the cities and towns while the rural Indians of the Sierra live virtually outside the mainstream of national life. Few Indian communities are found in the Costa, and the faster growth and the greater mobility of the Costa population have led to the development of a more open society in the region. The Sierra, however, remains bound by its conservative and traditional past. Regional and subregional differences affect all patterns of life from holidays, dress, food, to health and welfare institutions. The per capita daily consumption of food is below the recommended minima, and is deficient particularly in fish, beef, and milk, but it is generally adequate. Housing shortages exist in the cities, where only 15% of the houses meet minimum standards and 29% are unacceptable. Small slums are found in all towns and cities, but they are more satisfactory than the Indian villages in the Sierra where a typical unit consists of a single room, and a dirt floor, mud walls, and a thatch roof. There are no windows, and the walls are coated with soot from cooking and heating fires. The single room serves also as a storage place during the rainy season and shelter for domestic animals. Public health programs are concentrated in the urban areas in the Costa. Reported causes of death vary between the urban and rural localities. Three-fourths of the deaths resulting from cardiovascular diseases and two-thirds of those resulting from cancer occur in Costa cities and towns. In the Sierra, the principal cause of death is respiratory ailments. Health attitudes and practices also vary between regions. The lower and working classes rely to a great extent on home treatment and rural folks depend on folk medicine. Water and sewage services are limited and environmental sanitation has made little headway in the countryside. Social welfare is not universal but limited to a portion of the working population.

Human rights and freedoms. Ecuadorians enjoy a wide range of civil and political freedoms, but human rights problems remain. Foremost among these are torture and other mistreatment of prisoners and detainees, the immunity of the military and the police from proper accountability for their illegal actions, violence by paramilitary groups in rural areas, brutal prison conditions, lengthy detention before trial, and a pervasive discrimination against women, blacks, and Indians. Indigenous groups charge that they are the target of violence and lethal reprisals by paramilitary groups. These paramilitary groups are armed bands of security guards hired by private landowners, using military-style uniforms and weapons and trained by police and military officials. Another fundamental concern is over shortcomings in the legal and judicial systems. Persons are subject to arbitrary arrest, and once arrested may have to wait for years before coming to trial. Corruption is endemic in the judicial and police branches of government. The Constitution provides for freedom of speech, but the media are required to give the government free air time or space. Discrimination against Indians is one of historic injustices that have been never been satisfactorily addressed. It exploded in nationwide protest demonstrations in 1990 and again in 1992.

Human environment. According to botanists, Ecuador has the greatest number of plant species of any South American country—more than twice that of the entire continental United States. The Oriente contains 70% of all species found in the Brazilian Amazonia, though it is only one-fifth its size. Norman Myers calls the Costa one of the world's 10 'hot spots', in terms of the pace of extinction and deforestation. The clearing of mangrove forests is reducing biodiversity and degrading coastal ecosystems. In the Costa approximately 95% of the forests have been cut down and the Sierra is almost completely devoid of forest cover. All of the Oriente's forest cover will be gone in 40 years if the present rate of deforestation continues. Deforestation is also the cause of soil degradation and erosion.

NON-CHRISTIAN RELIGIONS

Traditional religions are practiced by several jungle and lowland Indian tribes in the eastern headwaters of the Amazon, among whom are the Araguro, Auca, Cayapa, Cofn, Colorado, Jivaro, Salasaca, and Secoyas.

Baha'i built up a strong following since 1960, but lately has experienced some decline.

Iglesia Catolica en el Ecuador. *Above.* Church School. ***Right.*** Penitent with candles. *Below* Catholic demonstration in Quito, the capitol.

CHRISTIANITY

CATHOLIC CHURCH. By the time the Spanish founded Quito in 1534, the Inca race had gained supremacy over other Indians. Quito then became part of the viceregency of Peru, later of New Grenada (Colombia). The diocese of Quito was established in 1545, the first hospital built in 1565 and the first diocesan synod held in 1594; and the evangelization of the Amazon region was begun in 1599. During the next 200 years an increasing number of schools and colleges were built. By 1780 there were 896 priests and religious personnel in Quito, whose population then was 28,500. Independence from Spain in 1822 resulted in a rapid decline in the number of priests. The 19th century was a period of conflict as liberals and conservatives alternated in their control of government, while Ecuador lost increasing amounts of territory in conflicts with neighboring countries. A concordat with Rome was signed in 1862 but was revoked by the anti-clerical government of 1895. Divorce was legalized in 1906 and church lands appropriated in 1908.

Catholic rituals today are taken most seriously by people living in the Andes, and many travel long distances to observe them. Catholicism in the mountains is of a popular type, cosmological and closely linked to ancestral beliefs; the usual term describing it is christo-paganism. In the coastal regions, where both urban and rural populations are more middle class and have received Catholic secondary school education, religious observance is of a formal and socially conservative nature. Here rates of baptism, confirmation and Sunday mass attendance are the lowest in the country; not more than 25% of marriages are performed in church in contrast to 80% in the mountains.

Country summary. **Worlds A, B, C by ethnolinguistic peoples, cities, and major civil divisions in Ecuador.**

World	PEOPLES Num	Pop 2000	C%	Christians	E%	U%	Unevangelized
A	4	60,333	7.54	4,551	48	52	31,276
B	7	86,622	18.64	16,145	56	44	38,154
C	22	12,499,114	98.30	12,287,095	100	0	1,989
Total	**33**	**12,646,069**	**97.33**	**12,307,791**	**99**	**1**	**71,419**

World	CITIES Num	Pop 2000	C%	Christians	E%	U%	Unevangelized
A	0	0	0.00	0	0	0	0
B	0	0	0.00	0	0	0	0
C	16	5,465,934	96.67	5,283,704	99	1	38,997
Total	**16**	**5,465,934**	**96.67**	**5,283,704**	**99**	**1**	**38,997**

World	CIVIL DIVISIONS Num	Pop 2000	C%	Christians	E%	U%	Unevangelized
A	0	0	0.00	0	0	0	0
B	0	0	0.00	0	0	0	0
C	21	12,646,066	97.33	12,307,787	99	1	71,413
Total	**21**	**12,646,066**	**97.33**	**12,307,787**	**99**	**1**	**71,413**

Iglesia Catolica. Over 100,000 persons, mainly tribal Indians, meet John Paul II at Latacunga in 1985.

There are 4 Catholic archdioceses, 10 dioceses and 9 apostolic vicariates, prefectures, and prelatures.

For several years now attention has been focused on the diocese of Riobamba and its bishop who is an avowed defender of Indian rights and an instigator of profound pastoral reforms. He has been responsible for numerous conscientization movements, especially radiophonic schools for peasants, and an institute for training rural community directors. A group of conservative Catholics linked to the political and social establishment has attempted to divide the bishop from his diocese or to obtain his dismissal, and in 1973 prevailed upon the Holy See to send an apostolic visitor to examine the administrative and pastoral situation in his diocese. The visitor eventually concluded his investigation by reporting strongly in favor of the bishop, without however succeeding in reconciling him with the other Ecuadorian bishops, who have continued to exclude him from meetings of the episcopal conference. The bishop of Riobamba played a key role in the creation of the Latin American Pastoral Institute (IPLA) at Quito in 1968, which of the 4 such institutes of CELAM has been the most involved in conciliar renewal. However, when CELAM decided in 1973 to reorganize its institutes, IPLA along with the other 3 went out of existence, being replaced by a single institute located in Medellín, Colombia.

Further progress in the 1980 and 1990s on these issues has been widely noted.

The Holy See has diplomatic relations with Ecuador and in AD 2000 is represented to government and the Catholic hierarchy by a nuncio residing in Quito.

Fraternal cooperation. Visit by leaders of CLAI (Latin American Council of Churches), to leaders of World Council of Churches, in Geneva, Switzerland (12-13 April 1989).

PROTESTANT CHURCHES. An agent of the British and Foreign Bible Society, who was also the first Protestant missionary to Colombia and Venezuela, entered Ecuador to initiate the sale of Bibles in 1824. However, no permanent mission was established until 1896 when 3 missionaries of the Gospel Missionary Union took up work in the country. Their arrival coincided with the promulgation of the liberal constitution of Eloy Alfae and the repudiation of the concordat signed with the Holy See. The GMU has been active among the Mestizos of the coastal lowlands and Jivaro Indians in the Amazon area, but its strength is among the Quechua in the Andes, among whom a mass movement has been taking place. The Evangelical Missionary Union Church is now the largest Protestant denomination in Ecuador. The Christian and Missionary Alliance, beginning in 1897, also works in the coastal, mountain, and eastern areas. Its large missionary staff is concentrated primarily in the Alliance Academy, which serves 18 missionary societies, and in its numerous Bible school programs. Seventh-day Adventists arrived in 1905 although they have not been as successful among the Indians here as in other nearby countries. In 1945, 4 major USA denominations (Evangelical and Reformed Church, (later part of the USA's UCC), Presbyterian Church US, United Presbyterian Church USA and the Evangelical United Brethren (which later joined the UMC) formed the United Andean Indian Mission to evangelize Andean Indians in Ecuador, Peru, and Bolivia. Thus far Ecuador remains its only field. Although it is engaged in agricultural, educational, medical, and evangelistic programs, its growth has been very small. The second largest Protestant group in Ecuador at the present time, the International Church of the Foursquare Gospel, did not appear on the scene until 1953. In 1962 there were only 2 churches and 70 members; but following widely-publicized miraculous healings during a Roberto Espinoza evangelistic and healing campaign in 1964, 2,300 converts were reported with 15 new churches and 19 meeting places opened.

Missionary work in Ecuador received worldwide attention in 1956 when Auca Indians killed 5 missionaries from 3 different societies. The wife and sister of 2 of those killed later returned, and today most Aucas have been baptized, including the original killers. Numerous other small denominations also exist, the majority having entered Ecuador since World War II.

Art and architecture. There are 86 churches in Quito. The Church of San Francisco, 1534, is the largest. There are some paintings in the aisles by the noted mestizo painter, Miguel de Santiago. Many of the heroes of Ecuador's struggle for independence are buried in the Monastery of San Agustin. The Monastery of San Diego has some unique paintings. The main cathedral is on the Plaza Indepedencia. Inside are the grave of Sucre and a famous Descent from the Cross by the Indian painter Caspicara. The Church and Monastery of San Francisco on Plaza Bolivar is one of the earliest churches in the Western Hemisphere, built in 1535. Close by are the Church of La Compania, the Church and Monastery of La Merced, and the Church and Monastery of Santo Domingo. In Guayaquil is another old church, the Church of Santo Domingo built in 1548. The main cathedral in Guayaquil is the Church of San Francisco. All the 3 major religious museums are in Quito: the Museum of Colonial History and Religious Art, Museum of La Merced Monastery, and Museum of the Monastery of Santo Domingo.

Renewal movements. In the 1990s the Pentecostal/Charismatic Renewal continued to spread rapidly across most older churches, and numbered over 1,410,000 adherents (of whom 9% Pentecostals, 86% Charismatics, and 4% Independents).

Indigenous missions. Both Catholic and Protestant churches have been sending missionaries to surrounding countries. Evangelical Quichua Christians are planning outreach to peoples in Peru and Bolivia.

CHURCH AND STATE

According to the constitution of 1945, which was abolished in 1946 but revived again in 1972 by the military government of Guillerma Rodrigues Lara, 'The State recognizes no official religion, each person being free to profess the religion of his choice' (Article 141, item 11). However, the state regards itself as religious, as is evident from the Preamble to the constitution: 'The people of Ecuador...invoke the protection of God'. The constitution guarantees freedom of opinion, expression, propagation and conscience (Article 141: 10-11). Public education is lay and free at all levels. There is a Ministry of Government and Religions but no obligatory registration of churches.

Relations between the state and the Catholic Church are subject to the modus vivendi signed in July 1937 by the government and the Holy See. It is an agreement consisting of 10 points, which guarantees to the Catholic Church the free exercise of its proper activities (Article 1) and the right to establish and manage schools (Article 2). Other articles provide for missionary work in the eastern Amazon forests (Article 3), prohibition of clergy from taking part in partisan or political activities (Article 4), recognition of the juridical personality of dioceses as well as other Catholic organizations and institutions (Article 5), and the right of government to oppose for political reasons the nomination of bishops (Article 7). An additional convention of 5 articles regulates the church's freedom to preach and publish, as well as the nationalization of church property. This 1937 agreement has been generally respected by both parties over the subsequent years.

In 1965 the Catholic episcopate of Ecuador decided to proceed with agrarian reform for lands owned by the church. At that time the church was considered second only to the state in the size of its holdings. After converting its property into investments, the church now finds itself in a transition stage between latifundism and capitalism in its economic involvement. In the name of the 9 dioceses holding the greatest amounts of land, the Episcopal Conference has asked the Interamerican Bank for Development to furnish it with the funds necessary to carry out major agrarian reform. The dioceses of Quito, Riobamba, Ibarra and Cuenca then began the reform in 1971, entrusting its implementation to the Ecuadorian Centre for Agricultural Services (CESA).

By 1976 these reforms had irritated the right-wing government to the point where the Riobamba cooperative was denounced as subversive; and in August, 17 Catholic bishops from Mexico, Brazil and other Latin American countries who were meeting for a pastoral conference at Riobamba were suddenly arrested and deported.

The situation has tended to calm down and stabilize in the 1980s and 1990s.

BROADCASTING AND MEDIA

HCJB maintains a large transmitter station in Quito, Ecuador. It contains 10 studios, which are used to record programs in 12 languages. Programs in more than 40 languages total are broadcast from 20 transmitters to 140 countries, sparking an average of 6,000 letters of response each month and printing 4 million pieces of Christian literature each year. The station carries programs from other producers as well, and feeds several local Ecuador stations. In addition to this, shortwave programs from KNLS, TWR (Antilles) and AWR (Costa Rica) can also be heard. Ecuador is a member of UNDA, and 15 local Catholic radio stations broadcast daily, most on AM frequencies.

Christian television programming from CBN can be seen across the country on 3 channels on a daily basis; response is followed up from 4 ministry centers (Guayaquil, Quito, Quevedo) with discipleship and counseling. CBN has a film and video evangelism unit in the country, and the Guayaquil center has organized a group of counselors that visit those with extreme needs (e.g. sick, suicidal). TBN's programs are aired in Ambato, Quito, and Guayaquil on local television channels.

Some 5.8 million have seen the 'Jesus' Film: mainly through a TV broadcast (5 million) and film team showings (560,000).

INTERDENOMINATIONAL ORGANIZATIONS

The Inter-Mission Fellowship embracing all Protestant missions was discontinued in 1965 and replaced by the Ecuador Evangelical Fellowship. Churches as well as missions are included in the latter, with churches encouraged to assume the greater leadership. A number of study seminars have been sponsored, but the Fellowship continues to experience tensions between its conservative and ecumenical members. In 1967, in cooperation with Lutherans and Roman Catholics, the Episcopal Church established in Quito an ecumenical library.

FUTURE TRENDS AND PROSPECTS

Roman Catholics are expected to lose members for the next 30 years but these losses are recouped in the total Christian community by growth in non-Catholic traditions.

The nonreligious could reach 5% by AD 2050 but more significant changes are expected within the Christian movement where Protestants and Independents (2.8% in 1970) could grow to over 10% of the population around 2050.

BIBLIOGRAPHY

'A componential analysis of the Ecuadorian Protestant church.' J. F. Reed. Ph.D. dissertation, Fuller Theological Seminary, Pasadena, CA, 1974.

'A historical survey of the Christian and Missionary Alliance in Ecuador.' E. C. Smith. Thesis, Canadian Theological College, 1974. 176p.

'An Ecuadorian impasse.' W. C. Weld. Thesis, Fuller Theological Seminary, Pasadena, CA, 1968.

'Christianity and religion: Evangelical identity and sociocultural organization in urban Ecuador.' K. A. Maynard. Ph.D. dissertation, Indiana University, Bloomington, IN, 1981. 294p.

Echoes of the call: identity and ideology among American missionaries in Ecuador. J. Swanson. New York: Oxford University Press, 1995. 212p.

'Ecuador,' *Pro Mundi Vita* (Brussels), 31 (1970).

Ecuador. D. Corkill. *World bibliographical series*, vol. 101. Oxford, UK: CLIO Press, 1989. 158p. (See especially 'Religion,' 57–9).

Ecuador, open door on the equator: the story of the beginnings of the Church of the Nazarene in Ecuador. R. A. Swain. Kansas City, MO: Nazarene Publishing House, 1974. 78p.

'History of Southern Baptist work in Ecuador, 1950–1977.' W. L. Baker. D.Min. thesis, Vanderbilt University, Nashville, TN, 1979. 154p.

'Images of power and the power of images: identity and place in Ecuadorian shamanism.' M. Rogers. Ph.D. dissertation, University of Chicago, 1995. 334p.

Is Latin America turning Protestant? The politics of evangelical growth. D. Stoll. Berkeley & Los Angeles: University of California Press, 1990. 445p. (Focuses especially on Guatemala, Nicaragua, and Ecuador).

La Iglesia en Venezuela y Ecuador. I. Alonso et al. Fribourg, Switzerland: FERES, 1962.

'Protestant missionary activity and freedom of religion in Ecuador, Peru, and Bolivia.' P. E. Kuhl. Ph.D. dissertation, Southern Illinois University at Carbondale, 1982. 500p.

'Religion in Ecuador: from paganism to Protestantism.' K. Carpenter. Doctoral thesis, Bethany Theological Seminary, Richmond, IN, [1993]. 194p.

'The evangelization of the Quichuas of Ecuador.' D. R. Dilworth. Thesis, Fuller Theological Seminary, Pasadena, CA, 1967. 124p.

'The Protestant movement in Ecuador and Peru: a comparative socio–anthropological study of the establishment and diffusion of Protestantism in two central highland regions.' R. E. Paredes-Alfaro. Ph.D. dissertation, University of California at Los Angeles, 1980. 278p.

The rise of Protestant evangelism in Ecuador, 1895–1990. A. M. Goffin. Gainesville, FL: University Press of Florida, 1994. 213p.

'The separation of church and state: the Ecuadorian case,' L. A. Aguilar-Monsalve, *Thought*, 59 (1984), 205–18.

Through gates of splendor: the martyrdom of 5 missionaries in the Ecuador jungle. E. Elliot. Wheaton, IL: Tyndale House, 1981. 273p. (Among the Auca Indians).

Unfolding destinies: the untold story of Peter Fleming and the Auca mission. O. F. Liefeld. Ed., V. Becker. Grand Rapids, MI: Zondervan Pub. House, 1990. 255p.

Voices in the Andes: the churches' use of radio in Ecuador. A. M. Mitchell. Edinburgh: Centre for Theology and Public Issues, New College, University of Edinburgh, 1993. 78p.

You heard it on HCJB: messages, talks, poems, prose given by missionaries on radio station HCJB, Quito, Ecuador, South America. N. Woolnough. Quito, Ecuador: Vozandes Print Shop, 1975. 79p.

Country Table 2. **Organized churches and denominations in Ecuador.**

Official name (bold type = church with over 10% of all affiliated) 1	*Begun* 2	*Type* 3	*Counc* 4	*Congs* 5	*Adults* 6	*Affiliated 1970* 7	*Affiliated 1995* 8	*G%* 9	*Names, notes, and other statistics* (see Codebook, Part 3) 10
Asamblea del Señor	c1969	I-3pL	.....	2	180	100	360	5.26	*Assembly of the Lord.* An indigenous pentecostal group.
Asambleas de Dios en el Ecuador	1962	P-Pe2	ZF...	300	27,350	5,000	37,500	8.39	*Assemblies of God in E.* M=AoG(USA). 25n,3x,10f,1k,1s(56),W=56%,112Y,125z.
Asambleas Locales	c1980	I-3nC	.....	14	719	–	2,000	6.67	*Local Churches. Little Flock* (from China, begun there in 1922).
Asoc de Iglesias Ev Interamericanas	1952	P-Hol	xF...	33	1,252	2,000	3,580	2.36	*Assoc of Interamerican Ev Chs.* M=OMS(USA). Coast.19n,4x,19f,1h,1s(30),131Y.
Asociación del Iglesias Misioneras	1945	P-Hol	xF...	12	692	1,000	1,540	1.74	*Association of Missionary Chs.* M=Missionary Church (USA). 11n,10f,1h,1k,1s.
Convencion Bautista en el Ecuador	1950	P-Bap	T....	146	13,615	4,000	29,100	8.26	*Baptist Ch.* M=SBC(USA). 3,145 in Sunday schools 40n,32f,1h,2k,2s,269Y.
Hermanos Libres	c1935	P-CBr	x....	17	1,000	800	2,220	4.17	*Brethren Assemblies. Christian Brethren (Open).* M=CMML(USA, UK, NZ). Quito. 20f,1p.
Hijos de Dios	c1975	I-mar	.....	38	89	–	200	5.00	*Children of God.* Former Jesus People from USA.
Iglesia Adventista del Séptimo Dia	1905	P-Adv	x....	32	8,250	10,000	13,747	1.28	*Seventh-day Adventists, Ecuador Mission*, Inca UM. 9nx,8f,63mw,1H,2h,1r,44t(3640),420Y.
Iglesia Alianza Cristiana y Misionera	1897	P-Hol	xF...	179	12,500	8,000	25,000	4.66	*Christian & Missionary Alliance Ch.* M=CMA(USA). 24n,60f,7h,1j,2k,1p,1s.
Iglesia Católica en el Ecuador:	1534	R-Lat	BzL.R	2,245	5,952,500	5,843,556	10,803,099	2.49	*Catholic Ch in E.* C=20+2+37. 744n 736x 1409m 4051w 223041Yy
M Cuenca	1786	R-Lat	Bs	69	360,000	480,685	654,000	1.24	10% Indian. 31% urban, increasing rapidly. M=OCD. 58n 52x 137m 350w 11705Yy
D Azogues	1968	R-Lat	Bs	30	115,000	143,750	209,159	1.51	50% Indian. 7% urban. In southwest. 19n 11x 22m 60w 5305Yy
D Loja	1862	R-Lat	Bs	57	203,000	386,909	370,000	-0.18	10% Indian. 10% urban. South, Peru border. M=OFM. 58n 22x 49m 213w 17810Yy
D Machala	1954	R-Lat	Bs	49	256,000	202,000	466,000	3.40	24% urban. Export industry in bananas. 21n 14x 16m 72w 7030Yy
M Guayaquil	1838	R-Lat	Bs	195	1,602,000	1,210,000	2,913,000	3.58	Urban. Port, commercial center. M=OFM,MCCI. 139n 78x 96m 538w 52415Yy
D Babahoyo (Los Rios)	1948	R-Lat	Bs	20	289,000	345,000	525,000	1.69	80% Mestizo. Banana industry. 6% urban. 22n 7x 9m 16w 14951Yy
M Portovíejo	1870	R-Lat	Bs	315	651,000	600,000	1,183,000	2.75	80% Mestizo. Banana industry. 6% urban. 55n 51x 54m 242w 27484Yy
PN Santo Domingo de los Colorados	1987	R-Lat	Bs	152	283,000	–	515,000	12.50	M=CM. 28n 17x 29m 71w 7246Yy
M Quito	1546	R-Lat	Bs	359	822,000	715,000	1,494,041	2.99	Mainly urban (Quito 565,000). Rural areas Indian. 1s. 151n 298x 759m 1546w 34445Yy
D Ambato	1948	R-Lat	Bs	45	210,000	321,090	381,000	0.69	40% Indian. 30% urban: industrialization growing. 39n 29x 48m 191w 7256Yy
D Guaranda	1957	R-Lat	Bs	23	77,000	187,000	140,000	-1.15	5% Indian. 7% urban. Very small area. M=SDB. 19n 7x 7m 60w 2672Yy
D Ibarra	1862	R-Lat	Bs	283	167,000	205,000	304,500	1.60	30% Indian, 5% Black. 17% urban. North. M=OFM. 61n 29x 64m 224w 7695Yy
D Latacunga	1963	R-Lat	Bs	37	186,000	235,844	338,000	1.45	35% Indian. 7% urban. Industrialization beginning. 29n 17x 23m 86w 7560Yy
D Riobamba (Bolivar)	1862	R-Lat	Bs	46	184,000	370,000	334,000	-0.41	55% Indian. 14% urban. Major diocesan reforms. 39n 17x 24m 200w 7758Yy
D Tulcán	1965	R-Lat	Bs	280	80,700	121,500	146,854	0.76	Very few Indians. High literacy. 17% urban. 25n 4x 11m 99w 3885Yy
VA Aguarico	1953	R-Lat	Pofmc	12	43,200	11,745	78,500	7.89	Amazon. 70% Indian, rest Mestizo; 18 expatriates. 4n 16x 27m 40w 1573Yy
VA Esmeraldas	1945	R-Lat	Pmcci	18	184,000	173,933	335,100	2.66	80% Black; some Cayapas. 30% urban. Bananas. 15n 34x 48m 111w 9456Yy
VA Méndez	1893	R-Lat	Psdb	48	56,600	41,000	103,000	3.75	Amazon forest. Southeast. On Peru border. M=SDB. 4n 34x 46m 77w 2322Yy
VA Napo	1871	R-Lat	Pcsj	17	40,400	35,000	73,541	3.01	Amazon. 76% Indian, 34% Mestizo. M=CSJ. P=41%. 3n 24x 30m 75w 2632Yy
VA Puyo (Candos)	1886	R-Lat	Pop	15	25,700	15,500	46,800	4.52	Amazon (selva oriental; total 200,000 Indians). 2n 5x 11m 44w 414Yy
VA San Miguel de Sucumbíos	1924	R-Lat	Pocd	52	40,700	15,400	74,104	6.49	Amazon forest. 69% Indian tribes, 26% Mestizo. 3n 11x 18m 25w 1104Yy
VA Zamora	1893	R-Lat	Pofm	14	31,000	22,700	57,000	3.75	Amazon. Extreme south. 94% settlers. M=OFM. 7n 8x 12m 55w 1847Yy
PA Galapagos	1950	R-Lat	Pofm	5	5,200	4,500	9,500	3.03	Population 5,000 on 13 islands 600 miles west. 1n 3x 6m 6w 181Yy
OM Ecuador	1983	R-Lat	Bs	104	40,000	–	52,000	8.33	*Military Ordinariate of Ecuador.* 70 ordinaries, 4 auxiliaries. M=OdeM. 60mw,422Yy.
Iglesia de Cristo Jesús, Mision Ev	1960	I-3pL	.....	8	200	380	606	1.88	*Ch of Christ Jesus, Ev Mission.* HQ Guayaquil. 4n,1p(7),W=58%,24Y,16z.
Iglesia de Dios	1969	P-Pe3	.....	88	12,434	750	31,100	16.07	*Church of God.* M=CoG(Cleveland).
Iglesia de Dios de la Profecía	1982	P-Pe3	Z....	7	735	–	1,230	7.69	*Church of God of Prophecy.* M=CGP.
Iglesia de JC de los Santos de los UD	1966	m-LdS	x....	103	43,400	1,668	70,000	16.12	*Ch of JC of Latter-day Saints. Mormons.* M=CJCLdS(USA). 30f.
Iglesia del Espíritu Santo	1967	I-3pL	.....	12	1,200	1,000	2,670	4.01	*Church of the Holy Spirit.* Small grouping of indigenous pentecostals.
Iglesia del Evangelio Cuadrangular	1953	P-Pe2	ZF...	97	7,000	20,000	23,300	0.61	*Int Ch of the Foursquare Gospel.* M=ICFG(USA). 116nm,4f,1s(90),W=33%,1800Y.
Iglesia del Pacto Ev en el Ecuador	1947	P-Con	K...C	40	2,970	1,500	6,750	6.20	*Ev Covenant Ch.* M=SMCC(Sweden),ECCA(USA). Quito. 6n,2x,27f,W=30%,78Yy,50z.
Iglesia Episcopal: D Ecuador	1963	A-ACa	aw,JC	17	1,000	510	1,430	4.21	*Episcopal Ch.* 1966, missionary diocese, PECUSA, Province IX. 1n,3xW=60%,3Y,10y.
Iglesia Evangélica Bereana	1958	I-Eva	xM...	7	103	400	278	-1.44	*Berean Ev Ch.* M=Berean Mission (USA). Only in Guaranda. Quechuas, 2n,6x,4f,1p,15Y.
Iglesia Evangélica Cristo Rey	1958	I-3pL	.....	6	2,600	5,000	4,100	-0.79	*Evangelical Ch of Christ the King.* West of Quito. 55Y,30z.
Iglesia Evangélica del Nazareno	1969	P-Hol	xF...	70	3,125	400	4,409	10.08	*Ch of the Nazarene.* M=CoN(USA). Holiness denomination. 2f.
Iglesia Evangélica Luterana	1953	P-Lut	L...C	11	900	2,000	1,500	-1.14	*Ev Lutheran Ch.* Germans, Norwegians, in Quito, Guayaquil, Cuenca. 1x,12f,1p,5Yy.
Iglesia Evangélica Menonita del E	1983	P-Men	.....	3	140	–	320	8.33	*Evangelical Mennonite Church of Ecuador.* M=Menn.
Iglesia Evangélica Unida del Ecuador	1945	P-Uni	..U..	18	600	2,000	1,500	-1.14	1965 union UPUSA,PCUS,EUB,UCC,CoB. Indians. 3n,3x,24f,1p(4),1s,105Yy,500z.
Iglesia Independiente Nacional		I-Non	.....	178	16,000	6,000	35,600	0.05	*National Independent Churches.* Loose grouping of many indigenous congregations.
Igl Independiente Universal de Cristo	1968	I-3pL	.....	12	1,200	1,500	4,000	4.00	*Universal Independent Church of Christ.* Large group of indigenous pentecostals.
Iglesia La Voz de Jesucristo		I-3pL	.....	2	100	100	300	0.05	*Voice of Jesus Christ Church.* One indigenous pentecostal congregation.
Iglesia Metodista Libre	1982	I-Hol	.....	7	184	–	368	7.69	*Free Methodist Church.* M=FMC(USA).
Iglesia Nueva Apostolica	c1980	I-3aX	x....	30	2,500	–	3,354	6.67	*NAC, NAK. New Apostolic Church.* M=Neuapostolische Kirche (HQ Zurich).
Iglesia Ortodoxa		O-Ara	Cwo..	1	850	1,000	1,700	0.05	Under Antiochian Orthodox Ch (USA) and Greek P Antioch. Arab Lebanese and Syrians.
Iglesia Pentecostal Unida del Ecuador	1959	P-Pel	x....	50	11,500	20,000	20,500	0.10	*United Pentecostal Ch. Jesús Solo.* M=UPC(Colombia, USA). 1 school. 25n,4f,1p(35).
Iglesia Unión Misionera Ev en el E	1896	I-Hol	xM...	474	61,165	56,000	105,141	2.55	M=GMU(USA). Mass movement, 98% Quechua. In Chimburazo. 6n,76f,2h,1k,1p.
Iglesias de Cristo	1959	I-Dis	x....	122	1,220	2,000	3,050	1.70	*Chs of Christ.* 1966, M=CC(Non-Instrumental) (USA). Quito, Guayaquil. 2n,15f,45Y,20z.

Continued overleaf

Country Table 2–concluded

Official name (bold type = church with over 10% of affiliated) 1	*Begun* 2	*Type* 3	*Counc* 4	*Congs* 5	*Adults* 6	*Affiliated 1970* 7	*Affiliated 1995* 8	*G%* 9	*Names, notes, and other statistics* (see Codebook, Part 3) 10
Iglesias radiofónicas solitarias	1931	I-3rL	.....	100	3,000	2,300	6,000	3.91	Isolated radio believers (jungle &c). R=25600(25332 HCJB,Radio Vatican, &c),S=355(ICI).
Iglesias WRMF/HCJB	1931	P-Non	.M...	25	1,000	2,000	2,000	0.00	Radio/TV, Voice of the Andes. M=World Radio Missionary Fellowship (USA, UK). 168f,2H,1h,2r.
Misión Evangélica Luterana	1951	P-Lut	l....	6	200	200	300	1.64	*Ev Lutheran Mission.* M=WMPL(USA). Andean Indians. 1n,1x,1s(5),W=40%,10Yy,14z.
Misión Lut Sudamericana de Noruega	1968	P-Lut	.....	10	200	250	500	2.81	*Lut=Luterana.* M=Norwegian Lutheran South American Mission. 3x,W=36%,4Y.
Testigos de Jehová	c1930	m-Jeh	x....	345	22,763	12,000	90,000	8.39	*Jehovah's Witnesses.* Missionaries began 1947. 124m,39f. (1975) 671Y. (1995) 3417Y.
Voz de Aclamación	c1969	I-3oL	x....	4	1,000	1,000	2,000	2.81	*Branhamites.* M=William Branham Evangelistic Assoc (USA). Jesus-Only Unitarians.
Other independent indigenous chs		I-	.....	90	2,600	4,000	6,000	0.05	Total about 30, mostly independent single congregations (non-Pentecostal).
Other indigenous pentecostal chs		I-3pL	.....	120	4,500	3,000	10,000	0.05	Total about 30 (see list below), including many single congregations.
Other Protestant denominations		P-	.....	80	2,000	3,000	5,000	0.05	Total about 20 (see list below), including SIM churches.
Doubly-affiliated		2-aff			-110,000	-154,814	-200,352		Evangelicals who also are or were baptized Roman Catholics.
Totals				**5,161**	**6,116,536**	**5,869,600**	**11,163,000**		

Churches, members, growth, 1900-2025	*Congs*	*Adults*	*Affiliated*	*G%*	*Total denominations*	*6 Megablocs:* O	R	A	P	I	m
Total churches, members, and denominations (mid-1900)	300	783,000	1,430,000	2.04	3	0	1	0	1	1	0
Total churches, members, and denominations (mid-1970)	1,728	3,214,547	5,869,600	2.04	69	1	1	1	26	38	2
Total churches, members, and denominations (mid-1990)	4,200	5,485,000	10,010,700	2.71	118	1	1	1	38	75	2
Total churches, members, and denominations (mid-1995)	5,161	6,116,536	11,163,000	2.20	120	1	1	1	39	76	2
Total churches, members, and denominations (mid-2000)	6,200	6,744,000	12,307,787	1.97	122	1	1	1	40	77	2
Total churches, members, and denominations (mid-2025)	10,000	9,402,000	17,158,000	1.34	190	3	1	1	50	130	5

NOTES ON TABLE ABOVE

NATIONAL COUNCILS (Column 4, 5th letter).

E = Confraternidad Evangélica Ecuatoriana (CEE) (Ecuador Evangelical Fellowship), 1980

R = Conferencia Episcopal Ecuatoriana (Ecuador Episcopal Conference).

Other national councils. Consejo Evangélico Luterano del Ecuador (CELE), in 1974 renamed Federación de Iglesias Evangélicas Luteranas del Ecuador (FIEL).

OTHER INDIGENOUS PENTECOSTAL CHURCHES. In addition to numerous independent pentecostal single congregations, these include: Iglesia Apostólica del Nombre de Jesús, Iglesia de Dios Pentecostal Trinitaria.

OTHER PROTESTANT DENOMINATIONS. These smaller bodies with congregations include: Alas de Socorro (Missionary Aviation Fellowship), Asambleas de Dios (M=AdD, Brazil), Bethesda Missions, Ch of the Brethren (1942, Elim Missionary Assemblies (1966), English Fellowship, Ev Methodist Ch (1962), Fellowship of Independent Missions (1967), Free Will Baptist Mission, Iglesia Ev Luterana (Misúri), Mennonite Brethren Ch of NAmerica (1953). Mennonite Ch (1969), Pentecostal Ch of God of America, Slavic Gospel Association (1942), World Baptist Fellowship Mission Agency (1972).

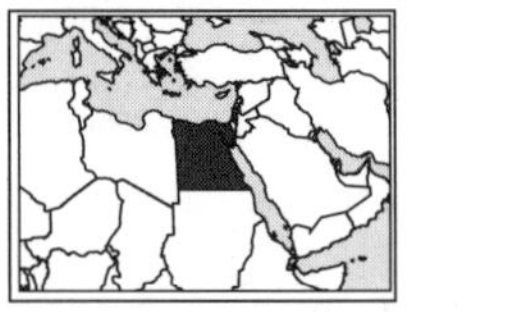

EGYPT

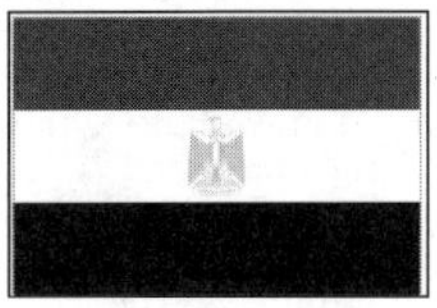

SECULAR DATA, AD 2000

STATE
Official name: Al-Jumhuriyah Misr al-Arabiyah (The Arab Republic of Egypt).
Short name: Egypt. **Adjective of nationality:** Egyptian.
Flag: Red, white, and black stripes, with gold hawk emblem.
Area: 997,739 sq. km. (385,229 sq. mi.).
Government: One-party socialist state, since 1953 (c1200 Turkish rule, 1914 British protectorate, 1922 Independence as constitutional monarchy, 1953 republic, 1958 United Arab Republic, United Arab States).
Legislature: People's Assembly, 454 members.
Official language: Arabic.
Monetary unit: 1 Egyptian pound (£E) = 100 piastres. **US$1=** £E 3.41.
Chief cities: AL-QAHIRAH-AL-JIZAH (Cairo) 10,772,000; Al-Iskandariyah (Alexandria) 3,995,000; Al-Jizah (Giza) 2,534,403; Shubra al-Khaymah 963,074; Bur Said (Port Said) 541,690.
Political divisions: 27 provinces.
Armed forces: 450,000.

DEMOGRAPHY
Population: 68,470,000.
Population density: 68.6/sq. km. (177.7/sq. mi.).
Under 15 years: 24,197,000.
Growth rate p.a.: 1.70% (births 23.52, deaths 6.13).
Mortality: Infant, per 1,000: 40.0; **Maternal per 100,000:** 170.0.
Life expectancy: 68 (male 67, female 70).
Household size: 4.9. **Floor area per person, sq.m:** 12.0.
Major languages: Arabic, English, French, Greek, Russian, Armenian, Nile Nubian (Fiadija, Kenuzi), Siwa and several others.
Urban dwellers: 45.94%. **Urban growth rate p.a.:** 2.6%.
Labor force: 29%.

ETHNOLINGUISTIC PEOPLES
84.1% Egyptian Arab; 5.5% Sudanese Arab; 2.0% Arabized Berber; 2.0% Bedouin; 1.6% Halebi Gypsy (Nawari).

ECONOMY
National income p.a. per person: US$790; **per family:** US$3,871.

EDUCATION
Adult literacy: 51% (male 63%, female 38%). **Schools:** 19,150.
Universities: 12. **School enrolment:** female/male: 81%/93%.

HEALTH
Access to health services: 99%. **Access to safe water:** 64%.
Hospitals: 6,418 (20 beds per 10,000). **Doctors:** 101,500.
Blind: 75,000. **Deaf:** 4,087,100. **Murder rate:** 1.
Lepers: 115,000. **Underweight prevalence under 5:** 17%.

LITERATURE
New book titles p.a.: 6,160 (90 p.a. per million). **Periodicals:** 372.
Newspapers: 17 dailies.

COMMUNICATION (per 1,000 people)
Phones: 46 **(2% mobile). Radios:** 265. **TV sets:** 126.
Daily newspaper circulation: 64. **Computers:** 20.

REFUGEES
Alien refugees from other countries: 10,400.

HUMAN LIFE AND LIBERTY (optimum condition=100.0%)
HDI: 61.4. **HSI:** 41.0. **HFI:** 27.5. **EFL:** 31.0.

Country Table 1. **Religious adherents in Egypt, AD 1900-2025.**

Name	*1900 Adherents*	*%*	*1970 Adherents*	*%*	*mid-1990 Adherents*	*%*	*Annual change, 1990-2000 Natural*	*Conversion*	*Total*	*Rate*	*mid-1995 Adherents*	*%*	*mid-2000 Adherents*	*%*	*mid-2025 Adherents*	*%*
Muslims	8,514,900	81.1	28,806,825	81.6	47,353,200	84.1	1,020,229	22,432	1,042,661	2.01	52,418,810	84.2	57,779,805	84.4	81,169,500	84.9
Christians	**1,954,000**	**18.6**	**6,346,375**	**18.0**	**8,743,000**	**15.5**	**188,340**	**-28,061**	**160,279**	**1.70**	**9,571,000**	**15.4**	**10,345,789**	**15.1**	**13,710,000**	**14.3**
PROFESSION																
crypto-Christians	1,169,000	11.1	4,250,628	12.1	5,650,000	10.0	121,730	8,270	130,000	2.09	6,300,000	10.1	6,950,000	10.2	9,900,000	10.4
professing Christians	**785,000**	**7.5**	**2,095,747**	**5.9**	**3,093,000**	**5.5**	**66,639**	**-36,360**	**30,279**	**0.94**	**3,271,000**	**5.3**	**3,395,789**	**5.0**	**3,810,000**	**4.0**
AFFILIATION																
unaffiliated Christians	0	0.0	0	0.0	20,000	0.0	431	101	532	2.39	16,244	0.0	25,323	0.0	35,000	0.0
affiliated Christians	**1,954,000**	**18.6**	**6,346,375**	**18.0**	**8,723,000**	**15.5**	**187,938**	**-28,191**	**159,747**	**1.70**	**9,554,756**	**15.3**	**10,320,466**	**15.1**	**13,675,000**	**14.3**
Orthodox	1,800,000	17.1	6,001,400	17.0	7,950,000	14.1	171,284	-34,577	136,707	1.60	8,693,763	14.0	9,317,066	13.6	12,000,000	12.6
Protestants	40,000	0.4	136,747	0.4	400,000	0.7	8,618	6,382	15,000	3.24	451,820	0.7	550,000	0.8	780,000	0.8
Roman Catholics	100,000	1.0	139,328	0.4	200,000	0.4	4,309	-1,809	2,500	1.18	214,042	0.3	225,000	0.3	380,000	0.4
Independents	2,000	0.0	67,550	0.2	170,000	0.3	3,663	1,837	5,500	2.84	191,941	0.3	225,000	0.3	509,000	0.5
Anglicans	12,000	0.1	1,000	0.0	2,300	0.0	50	-30	20	0.84	2,400	0.0	2,500	0.0	3,000	0.0
Marginal Christians	0	0.0	350	0.0	700	0.0	15	5	20	2.54	790	0.0	900	0.0	3,000	0.0
Trans-megabloc groupings																
Evangelicals	35,000	0.3	120,000	0.3	315,000	0.6	6,787	2,513	9,300	2.62	358,818	0.6	408,000	0.6	766,000	0.8
Pentecostals/Charismatics	0	0.0	60,000	0.2	563,000	1.0	12,130	6,870	19,000	2.95	655,372	1.1	753,000	1.1	1,200,000	1.3
Great Commission Christians	**735,000**	**7.0**	**2,822,000**	**8.0**	**6,680,000**	**11.9**	**143,921**	**7,728**	**151,649**	**2.07**	**7,400,000**	**11.9**	**8,196,488**	**12.0**	**12,000,000**	**12.6**
Nonreligious	1,000	0.0	100,000	0.3	220,000	0.4	4,740	5,711	10,451	3.96	275,000	0.4	324,509	0.5	700,000	0.7
Atheists	0	0.0	30,000	0.1	52,000	0.1	1,120	44	1,164	2.04	57,000	0.1	63,637	0.1	100,000	0.1
Baha'is	100	0.0	1,100	0.0	5,000	0.0	108	-32	76	1.43	5,300	0.0	5,760	0.0	8,000	0.0
Jews	30,000	0.3	700	0.0	1,200	0.0	26	-10	16	1.23	1,260	0.0	1,356	0.0	1,500	0.0
Hindus	0	0.0	0	0.0	600	0.0	13	-5	8	1.29	630	0.0	682	0.0	1,000	0.0
doubly-counted religionists	0	0.0	0	0.0	-42,000	-0.1	-905	-79	-984	2.13	-47,000	-0.1	-51,843	-0.1	-75,000	-0.1
World A (unevangelized persons)	6,930,000	66.0	18,348,200	52.0	15,209,910	27.0	327,485	-317,103	10,382	0.07	15,508,128	24.9	15,337,280	22.4	17,975,620	18.8
World B (evangelized non-Christians)	1,616,000	15.4	10,590,425	30.0	32,380,090	57.5	697,846	345,164	1,043,010	2.83	37,202,513	59.7	42,786,931	62.5	63,929,380	66.9
World C (Christians)	1,954,000	18.6	6,346,375	18.0	8,743,000	15.5	188,340	-28,061	160,279	1.70	9,571,000	15.4	10,345,789	15.1	13,710,000	14.3
Country's population	**10,500,000**	**100.0**	**35,285,000**	**100.0**	**56,333,000**	**100.0**	**1,213,671**	**0**	**1,213,671**	**1.97**	**62,281,642**	**100.0**	**68,470,000**	**100.0**	**95,615,000**	**100.0**

COLUMNS, ROWS.
For meanings and definitions, see Codebook (Part 3). Note that, by definition, total 'Christians' = professing + crypto-Christians, which also = affiliated + unaffiliated Christians, and also = Great Commission Christians + latent Christians. Percentages may not always total exactly, due to rounding.

CENSUSES.
1.VI.1897: 92.2% Muslims, 6.09% Coptic Orthodox, 0.6% Roman Catholics (0.05% Coptic), 0.5% other Orthodox (Greek, Oriental), 0.26% Jews, 0.25% Protestants (0.13% Coptic). **29.IV.1907:** 91.8% Muslims, 5.96% Coptic Orthodox, 0.69% Greek Orthodox, 0.65% Roman Catholics (0.13% Coptic), 0.35% Jews, 0.33% Protestants (0.22% Coptic), 0.25% Oriental Orthodox. **1.III.1917:** 91.4% Muslims, 6.74% Orthodox (Coptic, Greek, Oriental), 0.8% Roman Catholics, 0.5% Jews, 0.4% Protestants, 0.1% other Christians. **18.II.1927:** 91.2% Muslims, 6.1% Coptic Orthodox, 0.9% other Orthodox (Greek, Oriental), 0.8% Roman Catholics (0.2% Coptic), 0.5% Protestants, 0.4% Jews. **26.III.1937:** 91.4% Muslims, 8.2% Christians (6.2% Coptic Orthodox, 0.8% Roman Catholics (0.2% Coptic), 0.7% other Orthodox (Greek, Oriental), 0.5% Protestants), 0.4% Jews. **26.III.1947:** 91.7% Muslims, 7.9% Christians (7.1% Coptic Orthodox), 0.3% Jews. **20.IX.1960:** 92.6% Muslims, 7.4% Christians, 0.0% Jews. **31.V.1966:** 93.3% Muslims, 6.7% Christians, 0.0% Jews. **22.XI.1976:** 93.7% Muslims, 6.3% Christians. **1986:** 94.2% Muslims, 5.8% Christians.

NOTES ON RELIGIONS
AFFILIATED CHRISTIANS. The column Natural' includes some 21,000 Christian emigrants a year during 1990-2000. The column

Continued opposite

Country Table 1–concluded

'Conversion' shows losses to Islam; in the Nile Delta, around 750 baptized Coptic Orthodox are converted to Islam every month.
ANGLICANS. In 1900, almost entirely expatriate British; in 1995, 95% Egyptian Arabs.
ATHEISTS. No legal or organized communist party, but numerous intellectuals are atheists, as well as expatriates.
BAHA'IS. Reached Egypt before 1892. Banned by decree 1960, severe persecution; in 1964, only 13 local spiritual assemblies.
CRYPTO-CHRISTIANS. Affiliated Christians claimed by the churches have always been over twice the size of Christians as enumerated in government censuses. The reason advanced in this survey is that due to Muslim pressure on the Christian minority many Christians are recorded, or record themselves, in censuses as Muslims; in this survey we term them crypto-Christians.
INDEPENDENTS. This term describes churches begun by Arabs within the last hundred years, including since 1950 isolated radio believers in radio churches; in 18 denominations in 1995 (see Table 2).
JEWS. Rapid emigration since 1957 has almost completely removed the Jewish community, which in 1950 numbered 75,000 (of whom 5,000 were Egyptian citizens, 30,000 aliens from France, Italy, UK or Germany, and 40,000 stateless).
MUSLIMS. The numbers in the table above are lower than those in the censuses; the difference is due to crypto-Christians, namely persons considered as Muslims by the state but who are at the same time affiliated to churches. Muslims in Egypt are all Sunnis (of the Shafiite and Malikite rites in Upper Egypt, or the Hanafite rite in Lower Egypt). There are also about 2,000 Asians (Indo-Pakistanis and others), and a very small persecuted Ahmadiya minority based in Cairo. *Hajj pilgrims to Mecca.* (1968) 7,134; (1969) 10,875; (1970) 11,490; (1971) 29,171; (1972) 39,606; (1973) 36,452; (1974) 89,617; (1975) 51,230; (1976) 28,045.
NONRELIGIOUS. In 1900, all expatriate Europeans; in 1995, French, British and other European expatriates.
ORTHODOX. From a few thousand in 1900, Greek Orthodox increased rapidly in 2 waves of immigration to 100,000 by 1915, almost all retaining Greek nationality. After 1955, tens of thousands of Orthodox of Lebanese or Syrian origin emigrated to Lebanon; Greek Orthodox were reduced from 150,000 in 1930 to 80,000 in 195, to 30,000 in 1970, and to 14,300 by 1990.
PROFESSING CHRISTIANS. In AD 640, Christianity was the religion of Egypt, and Coptic Christians were estimated at about 3 million in 100 dioceses in Egypt, with 200,000 Chalcedonians (Greek Orthodox). After the rise of Islam these numbers were continuously eroded to 10% of the population by 1400, until professing Christians numbered only 160,000 in 1800, and 100,000 in 1820. Thereafter, as active persecution receded, the numbers of professing Christians increased rapidly to 785,000 in 1900.

Great Commission Instrument Panel: status of Egypt (for explanation see start of Part 4)

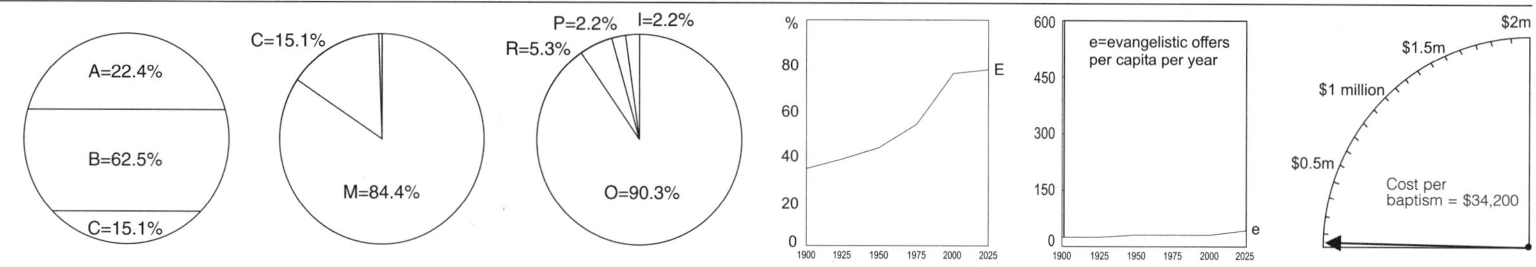

3 Worlds, AD 2000 | Religions, AD 2000 | Ecclesiastical blocs | Evangelization, 1900-2025 | Offers, 1900-2025 | Cost-effectiveness, AD 2000

Country status. Egypt is one of the oldest centers of human civilization, located in northeast Africa where it is joined to Asia. It is remarkable for the unusual concentration of population along the thin ribbon of land on both sides of the River Nile, leaving about 90% of the country a barren desert. The main product of the economy is cotton. Tourism is also a major industry.

The City of the Dead in Cairo where over 350,000 live in cemetery-mosques.

HUMAN LIFE AND LIBERTY

Human need and development. Uncontrolled demographic growth has made Egypt a classic case of a country locked into a vicious cycle of poverty. However, the lot of the average Egyptian is far from bleak. The national diet is adequate. Despite the prevalence of some endemic diseases, the health picture is relatively bright. The people enjoy a good medical care system. Despite serious housing shortages, especially in Cairo, modern facilities such as electricity and piped water are widely available. Nevertheless, in absolute terms, the average Egyptian has to struggle hard each day to maintain his standard of living, let alone improve it. In the opinion of most observers, the urban poor—most of them unskilled migrants from villages—are a miserable group, living precariously in cramped, unsanitary slums. Cairo has become the Calcutta of the Arab world with its infrastructure, designed for one-tenth of its present population, nearing total collapse. Housing shortages are critical not only in Cairo but in all major cities where an entire family of nine persons or more may live in one room. Overcrowding has led to a breakdown in major public services as transportation and sanitation. One-half of Cairo's raw sewage, for example, is carried in open sewers to the sea. Even where piped water is available, generally in communal taps, its poor quality makes it unfit for human consumption. Health care is one bright spot in the picture. Over the years, the authorities have set in place an extensive medical care program accessible to all the people without cost. Health units are found even in the smallest villages. There is no shortage of physicians. Unlike in many conservative Islamic countries, there is no prejudice against women serving as nurses. Welfare activities are conducted under both state and wakf auspices. Private philanthropy is extensive, as the duty to give a portion—generally 2%—of one's wealth as alms or zakat is one of the 5 pillars of Islam.

Human rights and freedoms. The principal threat to human rights in Egypt comes not so much from the government but from hardline Muslim fundamentalists who have in recent years unleashed a reign of terror. More than 80 persons were killed in civil disturbances in 1992, the highest recorded level since 1981. The dead included 27 Copts and 9 police officers. Seeking revenge for the killing of a Muslim in a land dispute, a group of Islamic extremists entered a predominantly Christian village in May 1992 in Assiyut Governorate and shot to death 13 Copts. In October 6 Copts were killed in Sohag Governorate during 2 days of anti-Christian rioting. In November Muslims opened fire on a tourist bus carrying 55 Coptic pilgrims. Islamic extremists also have assassinated secular Muslims, such as Farag Foda. Such violence has provoked the government to use lethal force to quell Islamic extremist outbreaks. There are reports that the government uses torture during interrogation of suspects. Under the Emergency Law passed immediately after the assassination of Anwar Sadat, the police may detain persons without warrant or indictment for up to 90 days. Serious national security cases are heard by the Emergency State Security Court from which there is no appeal. Under the Emergency Law all constitutional provisions regarding the right to privacy have been curtailed. The freedoms of speech and press have survived the emergency in tact, although with some restrictions. Criticism of the president or a foreign head of state is punishable. Most major dailies are state-owned and follow the government line. Thee government also influences the press through its Higher Press Council which has the power to approve new publications or suspend issues under the Penal Code. Radio and television are entirely state-owned. Books and works of art may be banned by decrees of various ministries without a court order. The Islamic Research Association of Al-Azhar University has legal authority to censor and confiscate publications and films dealing with Islam in any manner. Using this right it banned a documentary on the Bible as contrary to the Koran. Al Azhar clerics also have removed books critical of Islam from the Cairo Book Fair. The Ministry of Social Affairs has the right to license or dissolve any private organization it finds distasteful. In 1991, the government dissolved the Arab Women's Solidarity Association headed by secularist author Nawal al-Saadawi because it opposed certain tenets of Islam describing women as chattels. Although Egypt has not adopted the Sharia as its legal system, laws on the statute book weigh almost as severely on non Muslims and women. Women need the permission of their husband or father to travel abroad. Social pressures against working women are strong and the resurgence of Islamic fundamentalism has tended to erode the small gains they had made earlier.

Human environment. The 3 main environmental problems are water pollution, soil damage and loss, and oil pollution. Water pollution is the result of industrial effluents and sewage. Soil damage is caused by salinized drainage water from irrigated areas. About 28% of irrigated soils suffer from some degree of salination. Along the Mediterranean coast, oil pollution plagues beaches and poses a significant threat to coral reefs, fisheries, and mangroves.

Muslims. Public prayers as huge crowd kneels in direction of Mecca.

NON-CHRISTIAN RELIGIONS

Islam was established in Egypt in the 7th century. Egyptian Muslims are Sunnis of the Shafiite, Hanafite, and Malikite rites. Since the revolution of 1952, successive Egyptian governments have contributed significantly to the renewal of Islam both internally and internationally, making Egypt the major world center for modern Islam. Several important Islamic institutions have been created or reformed, among them the following. (1) The Supreme Council for Islamic Affairs (Al-Majlisal-Ala li al Sh'un al-Islamiya) was founded in 1960, with the purpose of extending Islamic culture in Egypt and overseas. Between 1960 and 1970, the council has edited and distributed, of-

Country summary. **Worlds A, B, C by ethnolinguistic peoples, cities, and major civil divisions in Egypt.**

World	PEOPLES Num	Pop 2000	C%	Christians	E%	U%	Unevangelized
A	21	6,260,321	0.18	11,535	30	70	4,398,641
B	7	61,714,679	16.04	9,896,786	82	18	10,904,352
C	10	494,695	83.31	412,149	100	0	826
Total	**38**	**68,469,695**	**15.07**	**10,320,470**	**78**	**22**	**15,303,819**

World	CITIES Num	Pop 2000	C%	Christians	E%	U%	Unevangelized
A	0	0	0.00	0	0	0	0
B	60	24,173,668	18.28	4,417,854	83	17	4,111,082
C	0	0	0.00	0	0	0	0
Total	**60**	**24,173,668**	**18.28**	**4,417,854**	**83**	**17**	**4,111,082**

World	CIVIL DIVISIONS Num	Pop 2000	C%	Christians	E%	U%	Unevangelized
A	0	0	0.00	0	0	0	0
B	27	68,469,694	15.07	10,320,465	78	22	15,303,819
C	0	0	0.00	0	0	0	0
Total	**27**	**68,469,694**	**15.07**	**10,320,465**	**78**	**22**	**15,303,819**

ten gratuitously, 8 million copies of works on Islamic culture in 14 languages, mostly African and Asian. It also edits a journal and a large number of pamphlets dealing with the Quran and the call to prayer. It makes financial grants for the construction of mosques and Islamic institutes throughout the world as well as scholarships for foreign students studying in Egypt. (2) The Council for Islamic Studies, founded in 1961, aims 'to re-activate Islamic culture, to purify it of all sectarian or political fanaticism, and to offer advice and counsel regarding religious and social problems in conformity with Islamic doctrine'. (3) The University of Al-Azhar was founded in AD 973, and, after a complete reorganization by the government in 1961, has become a vast complex consisting of: (a) the Supreme Court of Azhar; (b) the Academy for Islamic Research (Majm· al-Buhuth al-Islamiya), administered jointly with the Council for Islamic Studies; (c) a Department of Culture and Islamic Missions; (d) a number of other Azharian institutes; and (e) the university itself. In addition to its traditional faculties and a faculty for Muslim young women. Azhar also administers a large complex dedicated to Muslim missions (Madinat al-Buhuth al-Islamiya), consisting of facilities for training 5,000 foreign students and from which numerous missionaries are sent to various countries of Africa, Asia and, more recently, Latin America. (4) Other institutions include Quran House (Dar al-Qur'an) which distributes the Quran; Radio Cairo, which broadcasts daily Muslim religious programs to listeners in many foreign countries; the Halabi Press which publishes the Quran and other religious books in Arabic, French, English, and several African languages; and such international journals as Liwa al-Islam (Islamic Standard) and Minbar al-Islam (Islamic Tribune), the Muslim cultural journal published by the Supreme Council for Islamic Affairs; and, finally, the Egyptian Institute of Islamic Studies in Madrid, Spain, which is supported financially by the Egyptian government.

Baha'i has had a long history in Egypt going back to 1892, but has been subject to both governmental ban and severe popular persecution.

Judaism has been reduced to less than 700 persons, since the exodus of 75,000 Jews from 1950 onwards.

New-Age religionists. Followers of New Age Movement head for ceremonies at Great Pyramid of Giza.

CHRISTIANITY

Christianity came to Egypt during the 1st century AD, when tradition states that St Mark was the founder of the church of Alexandria. In the following centuries many important Christian movements were begun there: the catechetical school of Pantaenus and Origen (2nd and 3rd centuries), monasticism under the anchorite Anthony (4th century), the Arian-Athanasian controversy (4th century), Cyril's opposition to Nestorianism (5th century) and the controversy over the nature of Christ which came to a head at the Council of Chalcedon in 451. Monophysitism grew in strength in Egypt, with the term Melkite being given to those Christians who accepted the dogmatic decisions of Chalcedon. By 639 the overwhelming majority of Christians had accepted the Monophysite position, and this remains the official stance of the Coptic Orthodox Church. Massive conversions to Islam took place during the following 5 centuries, in part the result of opposition to the Byzantine administration. During the 17th century Capuchins and Jesuits opened Catholic work in Egypt, followed later by the formation of several Uniate Catholic churches. The first Protestant missionaries, Presbyterians from the USA, began work in 1854.

Coptic Orthodox Church. *Left.* Bishops, priests, nuns, laity and guests at 1965 foundation stone ceremony for new St. Mark's cathedral in Cairo. *Centre.* St. Mark's Cathedral, Cairo after completion, with (right) the Parish Church of SS Peter and Paul. *Top,* inset. Bishop Yohannes of Al Gharbiyah-Tanta (rear centre) leaves Cairo cathedral after service, preceded (foreground) by priests (in black) and deacons (in white).

The Christian churches today are faced with 2 major problems: conversions to Islam, and emigration. The conversion of Christians to Islam is most evident among Coptic Orthodox, who lose 7,000 professing members every year. The principal reasons for these conversions are the difficulties encountered by non-Muslims in finding employment, the desire to obtain posts in the administration, problems associated with mixed marriages (a Muslim woman is not allowed to marry a non-Muslim man), and the possibility of obtaining a divorce in cases where the churches will not give permission. The second problem is emigration, which has until recently affected mostly the other churches but is now a major factor for Coptic Orthodox also, as evidenced by the formation of new Coptic Orthodox parishes in Lebanon, Canada, the USA, and Australia. Some Christian communities have lost more than half their members and some, such as the Greek Orthodox, Armenian Catholics, Chaldeans and Syrians are rapidly disappearing. Among Catholics, information supplied by bishops lists the following estimated losses: Syrians, 3,000 in 7 years (1963-70); Armenians, more than 2,000 in 10 years (1960-70); Copts, 2,000 in the last years of the 1960s, largely through emigration to Canada; Latins, 4,780 (mostly Europeans) in the diocese of Heliopolis alone between 1960 and 1970. All Catholic parishes in the region of the Suez Canal were abandoned following the Arab-Israeli war of 1967, although by 1974 these had been re-occupied. The Christian community of Egypt remains by far the most important numerically in the entire Arab world. Egyptian Christians emphasize the fact that they are the purest descendants of the Egyptians of Pharaonic times, the term Copt being an Arabic deformation of the Greek world for Egyptian.

Although coexistence between Christians and Muslims in terms of domicile and work seems to function reasonably well in the cities, in villages the 2 groups live in separate residential quarters and have few contacts with one another. Christians display considerable fear of being absorbed by the Muslim masses.

ORTHODOX CHURCHES. The Coptic Orthodox Church is numerically the most important national church in the Near East. According to tradition the church was founded through the preaching of St Mark in AD 42. The Copts have always contested government statistics of their membership, which were listed as only 2.3 million in 1976, the last year that official statistics were published. Coptic Orthodox estimates for 1975, based on carefully-kept membership lists, were about 6.6 million. As Table 1 indicates, this implies a large crypto-Christian community to over 4 million. Although this continual erosion of members persists, by 1995 demographic increase due to births had swelled the church to 9.3 million members—a startling turn of events.

The Coptic Orthodox Church is characterized by a strong monastic trait. All its bishops are former monks, and its laity are also influenced by monasticism. Cases of Coptic university students losing their faith are rare. The church has experienced a marked renaissance over the past few years, due principally to lay initiatives. Evidences of renewal are as follows. (1) Church schools have arisen offering courses in the catechism on Fridays (the Egyptian day of rest) to pre-school children and those frequenting government schools deficient in religious instruction. (2) Large numbers of new monastic vocations to the desert monasteries have occurred among young people; these have been especially numerous for Wadi El-Natroun (Nitrie Valley). Monastic life has also been re-established for the first time in 1,300 years in Wadi El-Bayyan, 40 kilometers from Fayyum. (3) There has been a marked flowering of religious literature, dealing especially with spirituality. Of particular significance, and illustrative of these various tendencies, is the existence in Cairo of the House of Consecration for the Service of Preaching of St Mark (Bait al-Takris li Khidmat al-Kiraza al-Marqusiya), where laymen, some dedicated to celibacy, live in common and engage in the work of the apostolate, at the same time supporting themselves. It is also a center for religious literature. This initiative and many others are due largely to Matta El-Meskin, a lay monk who has exercised a profound influence on Coptic youth. Parish clergy are for the most part married and are recruited according to local needs. Priests are often deficient in educational background, but the Holy Synod decided in 1959 that in future only seminary graduates would be ordained. Coptic seminaries train both priests and preachers, the latter either retaining their lay status or becoming deacons. During recent years, a number of university graduates have become priests. In August 1970, a professor of Cairo University faculty of sciences was ordained, which provoked unfavorable comment in the Egyptian press and forced him to offer his resignation. This the university refused to accept, and thus for the first time in its history Cairo University had on its teaching staff a Coptic Orthodox priest.

The Greek Orthodox Church has never been a properly indigenous movement, and the Greek population has declined markedly in recent years. Nevertheless, the Alexandrian Patriarchate enjoys a prestige in the world-wide Byzantine community second only to that of the Ecumenical Patriarchate. Armenian Orthodox are administratively related to the Catholicate of Echmiadzin (in Soviet Armenia) and not to that of Sis (Antelias in Lebanon). There were at one time 3 times as many Armenians in Egypt as now, but their numbers have been drastically reduced by emigration in recent years. Syrian Orthodox once composed a flourishing community in Egypt with a bishop in Cairo until recently, but they also have been reduced by emigration to 50 families most of whom reside in Cairo.

Coptic Orthodox Church. Pope Shenouda III and bishops read newspaper (*top*), then vest in their robes for the Liturgy (*below*).

CATHOLIC CHURCH. Catholicism in Egypt is the most liturgically diverse of any country in the world; it is divided into 7 communities, each of which worships according to its own rite and serves its own ethnic group, as follow. (1) Coptic Catholics are native Egyptians and form the largest community. United with Rome since the 18th century, their principal centers are the Faggalah quarter of Cairo, the suburbs of Heliopolis and the cities of Minia, Tahta, and Luzor in Upper Egypt. They also operate a number of schools in the south and in Cairo, as well as seminaries in Maadi and Giza. They are the only Egyptian Catholic community which is expanding numerically at the present time. (2) Greek Catholic Melkites are a small community whose original background was Syrian, Lebanese or Palestinian. There are several schools and colleges in Cairo, Heliopolis, and Alexandria. (3) Maronites are from a background in Lebanon, where the Maronite patriarch now resides. Churches are found in Shubra, Daher, and Heliopolis, and schools in the 2 latter cities. (4) Syrian Catholics have churches and schools in Daher and Heliopolis. (5) Armenian rite Catholics are of Armenian extraction, the remnants of a once sizeable community. (6) Chaldeans form the smallest Catholic community and are centered in Heliopolis. They are of distant Iraqi origin. (7) Latin-rite Catholics are mostly foreign, especially Italians. They have very few parishes but their missionary service through education, study, research, and medical and social services is noteworthy, some of it dating back more than a century. The existence of these 7 communities makes Egypt the only country in the world where most major Catholic rites and sub-rites coexist. A large number of these Catholics are Egyptians by birth or nationality which nevertheless does not prevent the Catholic Church from being considered a foreign body. The church has 260 worship places, of which over 70 are in Cairo spread in 26 different quarters of which Shubra and Heliopolis have the most dense population. Half are Coptic centers in 98 cities and villages in Upper Egypt.

The Holy See has diplomatic relations with Egypt and in AD 2000 is represented to government and the Catholic hierarchy by a nuncio residing in Cairo.

OTHER CHURCHES. Moravians from Europe undertook a mission to Copts in the 18th century but later withdrew. The Church Missionary Society arrived in 1818, also attempting to work with the Coptic Orthodox Church, but had little success. Anglicans have been a separate denomination since 1882, part of the former Jerusalem Archbishopric.

The strongest Protestant Church in the Middle East is the Coptic Evangelical Church, which was begun by 3 American Presbyterian missionaries in 1854. Drawing its membership mostly from nominally Orthodox Copts, the church has grown rapidly. By 1899 there were 4 presbyteries, and 7 by 1972. Originally part of the United Presbyterian Church of North America, the church has been autonomous since 1957. It continues to carry on extensive medical and educational programs.

The Christian Brethren are a large independent body which split from the Coptic Evangelical Church in 1869 and since that time have been entirely under Egyptian leadership. Several Holiness missions entered Egypt before the turn of the century and are responsible for the establishment of 2 churches, Faith Church and the larger Free Methodist Church. Adventist and Pentecostal communities also owe their origin to this period. Small Greek and Armenian Protestant denominations exist as well but are declining rapidly due to emigration.

Renewal movements. In the 1990s the Pentecostal/Charismatic Renewal continued to spread rapidly across most older churches, and numbered over 753,000 adherents (of whom 22% Pentecostals, 56% Charismatics, and 22% Independents).

Indigenous missions. Egyptian Christians were some of the earliest sent out by the church. In the early Christian centuries Egypt was a stronghold of missionary outreach. Since the advent of Islam in the 7th century missions have been more difficult, but the two oldest traditions, Catholic and Orthodox, have continued to send out missionaries. Protestant Evangelicals carried on that tradition. Today Egyptian Christian missionaries are some of the most strategically placed in the world—working among many hard-to-reach peoples in the Middle East and North Africa.

CHURCH AND STATE

The constitution of the Arab Republic of Egypt promulgated in September 1971 displays a more pronounced religious and Islamic character than the constitution of 1956. Numerous references to religion are made in the 'Act of Proclamation of the Constitution' (preamble). Article 2 of the new constitution declares that 'Islam is the religion of the State and Arabic its official language; the principles of Islamic law constitute a major source for legislation', Article 46 stipulates that 'The State guarantees freedom of belief and religious practice'. Moreover, religion is, along with ethics and patriotism, one of the foundations of the family (Article 9). Society 'should assure the maintenance of a high level of religious education' (Article 12), this latter being a 'principal element in programs of general education' (Article 19).

Coptic Orthodox Church. Parish church in Munira Ghab neighborhood, Cairo, attacked by Muslim extremists throwing incendiary bombs.

Although the constitution declares that 'All citizens are equal before the law...without distinction of race, origin, language, religion or belief' (Article 40), it is the case that Egyptian Christians are victims of non-official discrimination in numerous sectors of social and political life. Hardly any high government functionaries are Christians; in the army, Coptic officers never go beyond the grade of captain or commandant and are often retired prematurely. This situation is not so much due to government policy as to the Muslim mentality, which without being hostile to non-Muslims is unable to place them on the same level of equality with Muslims. It is strictly forbidden to all churches to proselytize among Muslims, but under certain conditions it is possible for Muslims to become Christians as well as for Christians to become Muslims. Concerning worship itself, freedom is in general assured, although Copts have sometimes encountered difficulties in obtaining the necessary permission from the president of the republic for the construction of churches.

Between 1971 and the end of 1972, a number of incidents of conflict occurred between Copts and Muslims. On 13 November 1972, the day following the burning of the Coptic Orthodox Church of Khanka (a suburb of Cairo), president Sadat appointed a parliamentary commission of investigation composed of 3 Muslims and 3 Copts. In its official report of 28 November, the commission, without placing the responsibility for the incident on one or the other party, mentioned among the various causes of unrest the 1934 law dealing with the construction of churches, which it considered unconstitutional. This law imposed 10 conditions for obtaining permission to construct a Christian church, one of which required that no mosque exist in the neighborhood. The result is that advantage is often taken of administrative delays and a mosque is rapidly constructed near the terrain chosen for the construction of a church, which in turn encourages Copts to open worship centers without prior authorization.

The policy of president Sadat which systematically favored elements of traditional and religious law tended to encourage rightist forces which were difficult to control. Among the principal beneficiaries of this political reorientation were the Muslim Brotherhood who were kept in check by the Nasser regime but have since reorganized themselves in semi-clandestine groups for the purpose of combatting leftist forces, notably those in university circles. However, since 1973 the Coptic Orthodox Church has had an agreement with the government on the procedure for opening new churches. The church prepares each year a list of up to 50 new church buildings needed and presents it to the minister of the interior, who then approves. By 1975, 50 a year were in fact being opened.

Religious teaching, Muslim or Christian, is provided for in all government and private schools. Between the 4th year of primary and the 2nd year of secondary education, students must obtain a grade of 55% in this subject. In government schools, the Christian religion is often taught by teachers who lack competence and, although nominally Christian, are indifferent to religion. In public and private schools, beginning with the 5th year of primary education, all teachers of Arabic must be Muslims.

There exists at the Ministry of Waqfs (religious trusts) a section which is responsible for religious and ecclesiastical affairs. Church representatives related to this ministry are: for the Oriental churches (Catholic and Orthodox) their respective patriarchs, for Latin Catholics the apostolic pro-nuncio, for Egyptian Protestants the community council (Majlis Milli). Churches are required to register with government, which sometimes refuses such requests, as has been the case with Jehovah's Witnesses. Churches do not pay taxes; neither do priests or nuns, whether nationals or expatriates, for although religious workers require work permits they are not classed as salaried workers.

From 1993 onwards there occurred a nation-wide buildup of anti-Coptic incidents, attacks on priests, stonings of bishops, and numerous murders of Coptic villagers, at least some of which appear to have been organized with the knowledge of Al Azhar University. The situation worsened with the government's determination, under pressure from militant Islamic nations, to introduce harsh Islamic law including amputation of hands for theft and the death penalty for apostasy from Islam.

BROADCASTING AND MEDIA

Shortwave programs from FEBC (Seychelles), AWR (Slovakia) and HCJB (Ecuador) cover Egypt. Voice of Hope (Lebanon) has extensive Arabic programs which have proved very fruitful.

Television programs aired from METV can be seen. These include the *700 Club* and other programs, most in English but subtitled in Arabic. Satellite TV programs are received mainly in Arabic. Christian television programs can be received via satellite eg SAT-7. They are complimented by an extensive video and literature distribution campaign.

Some 8.6 million (13%) have seen the 'Jesus' Film: through television (2.1 million), radio (3 million), film teams (2.4 million), videocassettes (467,000) and mission agencies (500,000). 249,000 have responded.

INTERDENOMINATIONAL ORGANIZATIONS

Ecumenical relationships in Egypt are complex and are promoted by a number of diverse organizations. Before the 1956 Suez war, almost all Protestant missions co-operated through the Egypt Inter-Mission Council, but with the expulsion of many missionaries this ceased to function. There is no national council of churches, but there is a de facto council for practical co-operation, the Ecumenical Advisory Council for Church Service in Egypt (EACCSE), with representation from Orthodox, Catholic, and Protestant churches. The council deals primarily with the distribution of inter-church aid and scholarships. It works in close co-operation with government through the Joint Committee for the Co-ordination of Services and Aid to Displaced Persons and Victims of Aggression, with 5 government members and 5 representatives from the churches; and the Commission on Christian Religious Tourism which handles the visits of Christians to the republic and furnishes information to visitors regarding Christian worship services. Protestants and Anglicans, and Coptic, Greek and Syrian Orthodox co-operate in the Middle East Council of Churches which was founded in 1927 as the NECC and renamed MECC in 1974; it has its headquarters in Beirut, Lebanon. It carries on a variety of services, with an especially fine film library and audio-visual programs which are widely used by all the churches including Catholics. A more conservative Protestant organization is the Evangelical Fellowship of Egypt which was formed in 1966 and now has 7 members, some very small in size. The Association for Theological Education in the Near East (ATENE) has since 1967 attempted to provide opportunities for contacts between the various theological faculties of the region. In Cairo the Coptic Orthodox, Coptic Evangelical, and Coptic and Franciscan Catholic seminaries are members. Although the Upper Egypt Christian Association for Schools and Social Services was founded by Catholics in 1941, 4 Coptic Orthodox were added to its administrative council in 1972; and this is now a fully interdenominational organization. There are also local inter-confessional pastoral committees (such as the Council of Churches in Alexandria) which sponsor the Week of Prayer for Christian Unity annually in January.

FUTURE TRENDS AND PROSPECTS

Christian affiliation is expected to decline to 14.3% by 2025 due to conversion losses of Coptic Orthodox to Islam. Muslims account for 85% of religious adherents in 2025.

Unless more Christian outreach is focused on non-Christians, Christianity will probably remain below 15% of the population well into the 21st century.

BIBLIOGRAPHY

A history of Eastern Christianity. A. S. Atiya. 1968; reprint, Millwood, NY: Kraus Reprint, 1980. 492p. (Extensive treatment of Coptic Church).

A lonely minority: the modern story of Egypt's Copts. E. Wakin. New York: William Morrow, 1963. 178p.

'A resource manual for church development for the Church of God in Egypt.' J. A. Albrecht. D.Miss. thesis, Trinity Evangelical Divinity School, Deerfield, IL, 1990. 261p.

An analytical guide to the bibliographies on modern Egypt and the Sudan. C. L. Geddes. *Bibliographic series*, no. 2. Denver, CO: American Institute of Islamic Studies, 1972. 78p. (Deals with Muslim peoples in Egypt and Sudan).

Annuaire Catholique d'Egypte. Cairo: Nonciature Apostolique, 1973.

Atlas of Christian sites in Egypt. O. Meinardus. Cairo: Société d'Archéologie Copte, 1962. 7p.

Cairo, the Coptic museums & old churches. G. Gabra & A. Alcock. Cairo: Egyptian International, 1993. 143p.

Christian Egypt: ancient and modern. O. F. A. Meinardus. 2d ed. Cairo: American University in Cairo Press, 1977. 761p.

Christian Egypt: faith and life. O. F. A. Meinardus. Cairo: American University in Cairo Press, 1970. 525p.

Christianity in Egypt: a cultural history to 1171 AD. C. C. Walters. London: E. J. Brill, 1978.

Christians in Egypt: Church under siege. J. Eibner (ed). Zurich: Institute for Religious Minorities in the Islamic World, 1993. 40p.

Contemporary Coptic nuns. P. van Doorn-Harder. Columbia, SC: University of South Carolina Press, 1995. 266p.

Coptic Egypt: history and guide. J. Kamil. Cairo: American University in Cairo Press, 1987. 149p.

Copts and Muslims in Egypt: a study on harmony and hostility. S. M. Solihin. Markfield, Leicester, UK: Islamic Foundation, 1991. 120p.

Early Egyptian Christianity: from its origins to 451 C.E. C. W. Griggs. 3d ed. *Coptic studies*, vol. 2. Leiden: E. J. Brill, 1993. 283p.

Egypt. R. N. Makar. *World bibliographical series*, vol. 186. Oxford, UK: CLIO Press, 1988. 338p. (See especially 'Religion,' p.84–95).

Egypt and the crisis of Islam. Z. R. Dajani. *American university studies, Series IX: History*, vol. 56. New York: P. Lang, 1990. 264p.

Egypt, Islam and social change: al–Azhar in conflict and accommodation. A. C. Eccel. *Islamkundliche Untersuchungen*, vol. 81. Berlin: Klaus Schwarz Verlag, 1984. 611p.

'Egypt's Coptic Christians: contested creations of place in the struggle for survival.' M. H. Purcell. M.A. thesis, University of California at Los Angeles, 1995. 150p.

Footprints in the sand: religious interests of Egyptian Arab youth: survey report. G. Henning. , 1980. 56p.

'God's heart is in Egypt.' S. Z. Ouida. D.Min. thesis, Western Conservative Baptist Seminary, 1987. 2 vols.

Histoire de l'Eglise Copte. M. Moncaglia. Beirut: Dar Al-Kalima, 1966–. 6 vols.

Islam in Egypt today: social and political aspects of popular religion. M. Berger. New York: Cambridge University Press, 1970. 131p.

Islam, nationalism and radicalism in Egypt and the Sudan. G. R. Warburg & U. M. Kupferschmidt (eds). New York: Praeger, 1983. 383p.

Islamic movements in Egypt, Pakistan, and Iran: an annotated bibliography. A. Hussain. London: Mansell, 1983. 168p.

Martyrs and martyrdom in the Coptic church. Los Angeles: Saint Shenouda the Archimandrite Coptic Society, [1984]. 229p.

Monks and monasteries of the Egyptian deserts. O. F. A. Meinardus. Cairo: American University in Cairo Press, 1961. 436p.

'Music in the Coptic Church of Egypt and Ethiopia.' J. P. Bennett. M.A. thesis, University of Washington, Seattle, WA, 1945. 88p.

Pagan and Christian Egypt: Egyptian art from the first to the tenth century AD: exhibited at the Brooklyn Museum by the Department of Ancient Art, January 23–March 9, 1941. Brooklyn Museum. 1941; reprint, New York: Arno, 1974. 193p.

'Presbyterian missionaries in the Middle East.' D. Dawson. S.T.M. thesis, Yale Divinity School, New Haven, CT, 1987. 109p.

Prisoner of conscience: Christian patriarch: human rights and Egypt's Christians. J. Watson. Deal: Medan, [1984]. 15p.

'Religious community and social control in a lower–class area of Cairo.' A. B. Rugh. Thesis, American University, Washington, DC, 1978. 401p.

Religious strife in Egypt: crisis and ideological conflict in the seventies. N. R. Farah. New York: Gordon & Breach, 1986. 135p.

Saint and Sufi in modern Egypt: an essay in the sociology of religion. M. Gilsenan. New York: Oxford University Press, 1973. 241p.

St. Mark and the Coptic Church. Cairo: Coptic Orthodox Patriarchate, 1968. 164p.

'The Coptic Church and social change in Egypt,' M. M. Assad, *International review of mission*, 61, 242 (1972), 117–29.

The Coptic encyclopedia. A. S. Atiya (ed). New York: Macmillan, 1991. 8 vols.

'The Copts and Muslims of Egypt,' M. Samaan & S. Sukkary, in *Muslim–Christian conflicts: economic, political and social origins*, p.129–55. S. Joseph & B. L. K. Pillsbury (eds). Boulder, CO: Westview Press and Folkestone, UK: Dawson, 1978.

The Copts in Egyptian politics. B. L. Carter. London: Croom Helm, 1986. 328p.

'The Copts in modern Egypt,' J. D. Pennington, *Middle Eastern studies*, 18, 2 (1982), 158–79.

The Copts through the ages. Bishop Athanasius of Beni-Suef and Bahnasa. 3d ed. Cairo: State Information Service, 1973.

'The course of secularization in modern Egypt,' D. Crecelius, in *Islam and development: religion and sociopolitical change*, p.49–70. J. L. Esposito (ed). Syracuse, NY: Syracuse University Press, 1980.

The Eastern Christian churches: a brief survey. R. G. Roberson. 3rd ed. Rome: Pontificum Studiorum Orientalium, 1990. 129p.

'The Mobile Church Movement: a strategy for establishing believing communities among highly hostile environments.' B. F. Gergis. D.Min. thesis, Reformed Theological Seminary, 1995. 218p. (On Cairo).

The Prophet and the Pharoah: Muslim extremism in Egypt. G. Kepel. Trans., J. Rothschild. London: Al Saqi, 1985. 251p. (Translated from the French, *Le prophète et Pharaon.* Paris: La Découverte, 1984.).

The roots of Egyptian Christianity. B. A. Pearson & J. E. Goehring. Philadelphia: Fortress Press, 1986. 319p.

The rumbling volcano: Islamic fundamentalism in Egypt. N. Jabbour. Pasadena, CA: Mandate Press, 1993. 311p.

The story of the Coptic Church of Egypt, established by St. Mark. I. H. el-Masry. Cairo: Coptic Orthodox Patriarchate, 1978. 400p. (Translation from 4-volume Arabic version. History, up to 1970).

The Word in the desert: scripture and the quest for holiness in early Christian monasticism. D. Burton-Christie. New York: Oxford University Press, 1993. 345p.

'The world turned inside out: forms of Islam in Egypt,' M. Gilsenan, in *Recognizing Islam: an anthropologist's introduction*, p.215–50. London: Crrom Helm, 1982.

'Towards an indigenous understanding of principles of Christian ethics for Egyptian Christians.' F. Fares. D.Min. thesis, San Francisco Theological Seminary, San Anselmo, CA, 1981. 171p.

Country Table 2. **Organized churches and denominations in Egypt.**

Official name (bold type = church with over 10% of all affiliated) 1	*Begun* 2	*Type* 3	*Counc* 4	*Congs* 5	*Adults* 6	*Affiliated 1970* 7	*Affiliated 1995* 8	*G%* 9	*Names, notes, and other statistics* (see Codebook, Part 3) 10
Armenian Apostolic Church: AD Cairo	553	O-Arm	Ew..K	4	8,450	20,000	13,000	0.07	Begun 1250 with 70,000 Armenian slaves at Sohag. Rapid emigration. 1j.
Armenian Evangelical Church	1896	P-Con	.T...	3	110	500	275	-2.36	Congregation in Alexandria. Split ex Union of AEC. Armenians.
Assemblies of God in Egypt	1907	P-Pe2	ZF..C	170	103,000	20,000	130,000	7.77	1910, Asyut work; 1,100 orphans. M=AoG(USA). 90% former Copts. 65n,5f,1h,1s(20).
Baptist International Church	1982	I-Bap	.....	10	308	–	616	7.69	M=BIM(USA).
Catholic Church in Egypt:	1219	R-LEr	O.S.S	266	124,370	139,328	214,042	1.73	*Al-Kanissa al-Katholikia.* C=10+1+31. 196n 169x 264m 490w 2775Yy

Continued opposite

Country Table 2–concluded

Official name (bold type = church with over 10% of affiliated) 1	*Begun* 2	*Type* 3	*Counc* 4	*Congs* 5	*Adults* 6	*Affiliated 1970* 7	*Affiliated 1995* 8	*G%* 9	*Names, notes, and other statistics* (see Codebook, Part 3) 10
P Al Iskandariya (Alexandria)	1895	R-Cop	Os	47	49,400	40,000	85,000	3.06	Egyptians, Coptic rite. Patriarch lives in Cairo. M=CM. 57n 38x 66m 230w 462Yy
D Al Minya (Ermopoli Maggiore)	1895	R-Cop	Os	56	20,800	18,000	35,816	2.79	Egyptians (Copts). 19 schools, 7 institutes. 33n 1x 2m 13w 1046Yy
D Asyut (Lycopolis)	1947	R-Cop	Os	41	19,700	27,000	33,970	0.92	Coptic dioceses are expanding. 37n 5x 22m 52w 766Yy
D Isma'iliya	1982	R-Cop	Os	9	2,900	–	5,000	7.69	Northern coastal diocese in east. 5n 0x 0m 57w 18Yy
D Sohag	1981	R-Cop	Oofm	23	7,200	–	12,476	7.14	M=OFM. 17n 0x 0m 28w 253Yy
D Thebes (Luxor) (Tahta)	1895	R-Cop	Os	26	10,500	22,000	18,000	-0.80	Egyptians (Copts). 30 schools (6,905). 5H,13h. 9n 9x 11m 75w 120Yy
P Al Iskandariya (Alexandria)	1772	R-Mel	Os	15	4,300	8,200	7,400	-0.41	Melkites under VP Egypt & Sudan. M=MSSP. 18n 1x 1m 16w 63Yy
D Al Iskandariya	1885	R-Arm	Os	3	1,080	1,750	1,800	0.11	Armenians in P Cilicia (Lebanon). Rapid emigration. . 2n 1x 1m 8w 12Yy
D Al Qahirah (Cairo)	1946	R-Mar	Os	8	3,200	8,000	5,500	-1.49	Egyptian Lebanese Maronites (P Antioch). M=OMM. 2n 4x 4m 0w 22Yy
D Al Qahirah (Cairo)	1970	R-Cha	Os	2	290	525	500	-0.19	Egyptian Chaldean-rite Iraqis under P Babylon. Bishop. 1n 0x 0m 8w 1Yy
D Al Qahirah (Egypt & Sudan)	1965	R-Syr	Os	3	1,200	2,700	2,080	-1.04	Egyptians of Syrian rite. Under P Antioch (Lebanon). 8n 0x 0m 3w 12Yy
VA Al Iskandariya of Egypt (*Latin*)	1839	R-Lat	Oofm	33	3,800	11,153	6,500	-2.14	Mostly Italians. 1987, merged VA Port Said, VA Heliopolis. 7n 110x 157m 946w 33107Yy
Christian Brethren (Exclusive)	1869	I-EBr	x....	143	8,600	20,000	17,200	-0.60	Schism ex American M (Coptic Ev Ch), now large Egyptian-run denominations.
Christian Brethren (Open)	1878	P-CBr	x....	36	1,450	2,500	2,420	-0.13	*Open Brethren. Plymouth Brethren.* M=CMML(UK). 20 assemblies in Upper Egypt. 5m.
Church of Christ, Scientist		m-Sci	x....	1	20	50	40	0.05	*Christian Science.* M=CCS(Boston, USA). In Cairo.
Church of God	1907	P-Hol	x...d	8	250	800	625	-0.98	In Asyut; Cairo, Alexandria. Linked with Faith Ch. M=CoG(Anderson) (USA). 7n,W=99%.
Church of God of Prophecy	1935	P-Pe3	.....	13	650	2,200	1,630	-1.19	M=CoGP. Pentecostal mission from USA.
Church of the Nazarene	1986	P-Hol	.....	15	100	–	200	11.11	M=CoN. Nazarenes.
Church of Sinai: AD Mount Sinai	c 200	O-Ara	Cw...	1	240	900	800	-0.47	*St Catherine's Monastery*, begun 537. Autonomous, under Greek P Jerusalem. 28 monks.
Coptic Orthodox Church:	33	O-Cop	NWANK	2,213	5,029,000	5,950,000	8,669,600	0.05	*Al-Kanisah al-Kebtiah al-Orthodoxiah.* 42 Dioceses worldwide, 77 bps,5e(200),1500n,5s(200).
P Al Iskandariya (Alexandria)	42	O-Cop	Np	170	424,000	500,000	730,600	0.05	Traditional base of pope/patriarch of Alexandria, though HQ in Cairo. 27 churches.
D Al Qahirah (Cairo)	356	O-Cop	Np	310	763,000	900,000	1,315,000	0.06	Under patriarch as bishop. Many Coptic institutions. 2e,P=82%,4s(Cairo),W=10%.
D Abu Tig, Tima & Tahta	c 330	O-Cop	Nb	30	101,000	120,000	175,000	1.52	*Iparshia Abu Tij. Upper Egypt. Bishop lives in Abu Tig, 10 km south of Asyut.*
D Akhmim & Saqulta	c350	O-Cop	Nb	4	13,000	16,000	23,000	0.06	*Iparshia Akhmim wa Saqulta. Smallest diocese, also one of poorest financially.*
D Al Balyana	c 850	O-Cop	Nb	5	17,000	20,000	29,000	1.50	Bishop in Al Balyana, Upper Egypt; small diocese, south of Girga.
D Al Fayyum (Fayoum)	c 320	O-Cop	Nb	30	101,000	120,000	175,000	1.52	Upper Egypt. Noted for ancient pilgrimage church, Al Azab. Rich diocese.
D Al Gharbiyah	c 270	O-Cop	Nb	15	50,000	60,000	87,000	1.50	Bishop in Tanta, between 2 branches of Nile. Extensive textile industries.
D Al Jizah (Giza)	c 350	O-Cop	Nb	160	508,000	600,000	876,000	1.53	Area of Pyramids, Sphinx. 15 new parish churches built since 1960. Rich diocese.
D Al Minufiyah (Menoufia)	1150	O-Cop	Nb	30	101,000	120,000	175,000	1.52	Bishop in Shibinel-Kom. Province of Al Manufiyah, north of Cairo between Nile.
D Al Minya & Ashmunayn	c 850	O-Cop	Nb	240	594,000	700,000	1,023,000	1.53	Upper Egypt. Largest diocese in area, many Coptic activities. 1976, divided into 3.
D Al Uqsur (Luxor), Isna, Aswan	c 350	O-Cop	Nb	30	105,000	124,000	181,000	1.52	Upper Egypt: pharaohs' tombs, Aswan high dam, steel industry. 1975, divided into 2.
D Asyut (Assyout)	c 230	O-Cop	Nb	140	424,000	500,000	730,000	1.53	Upper Egypt. Youth work in University of Asyut. Many Protestant activities.
D Bani Suwayf & Bahnasa	c 340	O-Cop	Nb	115	339,000	400,000	584,000	1.53	Bani Suwayf, in Upper Egypt. Youth work, home industries. 2 retreat houses. Rich.
D Buhayrah (Behera, The Lake)	c 270	O-Cop	Nb	40	93,000	110,000	161,000	1.54	Includes Mudiriyat Al-Tahrir (Liberation Province reclaimed from desert), and North Africa.
D Dairut & Sanabu	c 350	O-Cop	Nb	20	68,000	80,000	117,000	1.53	Upper Egypt. Small diocese north of Manfalut. One small monastery.
D Daqahliya (Dakahlia)	1925	O-Cop	Nb	30	101,000	120,000	175,000	1.52	Bishop in Mensurah, on Nile near sea. Noted healing pilgrimage centre Meitdemsis.
D Dumyat (Damietta) & Kafr El S	c 450	O-Cop	Nb	4	17,000	20,000	29,000	1.50	Damietta & Kafr El Sheikh. 4 parishes only; Christians very small minority.
D Girga	c1650	O-Cop	Nb	20	68,000	80,000	117,000	1.53	Relatively poor diocese, south of Sohag. Girga, Naga Hamadi & Bahgourah.
D Hulwan (Helwan)	1967	O-Cop	Nb	30	85,000	100,000	146,000	1.53	Area for new heavy industry and military base, 20km south of Cairo on east bank.
D Manfalut & Abnub	c1450	O-Cop	Nb	20	68,000	80,000	117,000	1.53	Upper Egypt. Small diocese between Asyut to the south and Al Minya to north.
D Qalyub (Kalyubia)	1965	O-Cop	Nb	30	127,000	150,000	219,000	1.53	HQ Benha, north of Cairo. Districts of Quweisna, Qalyub, Shibin al-Qanatir, Benha.
D Qena (Kena) & Qus	969	O-Cop	Nb	120	237,000	280,000	409,000	0.10	Upper Egypt: area of tombs of pharaohs, immediately north of Luxor.
D Sharqiyah & Mohafazat	1925	O-Cop	Nb	20	85,000	100,000	146,000	1.53	In Delta. 1976-7, 3 new Dioceses divided off: Zagazig; Port Said; Suez & Ismailia.
D Sohag (Sawhaj)	c1952	O-Cop	Nb	150	424,000	500,000	730,000	1.53	Sohag & Menshah. Upper Egypt, boundary of Southern Desert province. Monastery.
18 other (newer) dioceses	c1980	O-Cop	Nb...	450	116,000	150,000	200,000	6.67	New dioceses for recent housing estates, industrial, and university populations.
Egyptian Baptist Convention	1980	P-Bap	T....	12	1,000	427	2,070	6.67	M=SBC-IMB(USA). 10f.
Episcopal Ch in Jerus & ME: D Egypt	1847	A-Cen	Aw.UK	20	1,200	1,000	2,400	3.56	*Al Kanisa el Usqufiya.* ME=Middle East. M=MCS,JEM,CMJ. 95% Egyptians. 5n,2x,6f,1h.
Ev Ch of Egypt, Synod of the Nile	1854	P-Ref	RWANK	320	185,000	100,000	300,000	4.49	*Coptic Ev Ch.* 7 Presbyteries. M=UPUSA. 95% former Orthodox. 200n,98m,19f,2H,10r,1s.
Faith Church	1895	I-Hol	xF..C	19	480	1,500	1,600	0.26	*Kenisa el Eeman.* 1905, M=EFM(USA),CHM(Canada). 13n,6m,2f,1s,W=90%,72Y,26y,43z.
Free Methodist Church	1895	I-Hol	VF..C	120	24,800	15,250	40,200	3.95	*Holiness Ch.* M=Peniel Missionary Soc, FMC(USA). Many new converts and churches. 6f,1s.
Gospel Preaching Churches	1960	I-3pS	x....	12	3,600	4,000	7,200	2.38	M=World-Wide Missions (USA). 1993, pentecostalized, merged with M=PHC.
Greek Evangelical Church	1920	P-Ref	Rwc..	1	40	500	100	-6.23	Greek Protestants. Remnant among rapidly-emigrating Greek community.
Greek Orth Patriarchate of Alexandria:	33	O-Ara	CW.NK	30	4,000	30,000	10,000	0.05	Broke with Copts at Chalcedon, AD 451. Rapid emigration. 19 bps,4d,495y.
P Alexandria		O-Ara	Cp	17	2,000	15,000	5,000	0.05	Alexandria, Cairo. 13,000 Greeks plus many Arab Orthodox (since 1832). 16nx.
D Hermopolis (Tanta)		O-Ara	Cm	4	1,000	5,000	2,000	0.05	HQ Tanta. Remnants of once large Greek community. 2 priests only left.
D Leontopolis (Isma'iliya)		O-Ara	Cm	5	700	7,000	2,000	0.05	Az-Zaqaziq and Al Isma'iliyah. Greeks. HQ Ismailia. 4nx.
D Pelusium (Bur Sa'id & Kantara)		O-Ara	Cm	4	300	3,000	1,000	0.05	Port Said area. HQ Port Said. Only handful of Greeks left, with 3 priests.
Hidden Muslim believers in Christ	c1970	I-Mus	.....	300	25,000	–	42,000	53.08	Individuals and small groups accepting Christ but staying within Islam.
Isolated radio churches	c1950	I-3rS	.....	2,000	40,000	19,700	70,000	5.20	Isolated radio believers; youths. R=3800 (TWR,ELWA,RV),T=72000 (ICI,GMU,RSB).
Jehovah's Witnesses	c1925	m-Jeh	x....	18	300	300	750	3.73	*Watch Tower. IBSA.* Underground. 1970: severe persecution, many deportations.
Pentecost Faith Mission		I-3pS	.....	20	3,000	4,000	6,000	0.05	Mission from Indiana, USA. Classical Pentecostals.
Pentecostal Church of God	1910	P-Pe3	ZF...	27	1,300	5,000	3,250	-1.71	*Apostolic Church of God.* M=COG(Cleveland) (USA). 18 churches, 6 missions. 13n,5m.
Pentecostal Holiness Church	c1975	P-Pe3	.....	10	1,065	–	1,780	5.00	M=IPHC(USA). 1993, merges with Gospel Preaching Churches.
Russian Orthodox Church		O-Rus	Mw...	1	30	100	50	0.05	*Russkaya Pravoslavnaya Tserkov.* Under P Moscow. Russian officials, technicians.
Russian Orthodox Ch Outside Russia		I-Rus	x....	1	50	100	125	0.05	M=ROCOR(HQ New York, USA). Conservative Russians in exile.
Seventh-day Adventist Church	1879	P-Adv	x....	14	1,337	3,000	2,230	-1.18	*SDA, Egypt Field,* Middle East Union. HQ Heliopolis. 5nx,39mw,1f,1r,25t(1674),155Y.
Syrian Orthodox Church (P Antioch)	c 600	O-Syr	Dw.NK	1	250	400	313	-0.98	*Jacobites.* Long History; bishop still in Cairo, only 50 families left.
Union of Armenian Ev Chs in Near East	1896	P-Con	Rw.N.	2	15	200	60	-4.70	Armenian Protestants. Declining. Losses to Armenian Spiritual Brethren. HQ Cairo.
United Pentecostal Church	1960	P-Pe1	.....	3	90	120	180	1.64	M=UPC(USA). Oneness Pentecostals.
Other Egyptian indigenous churches	1948	I-3cS	.....	40	3,000	3,000	6,000	2.81	Total about 10 (see list below).
Other independent churches	c1980	I-3aX	.....	15	500	–	1,000	6.67	Including New Apostolic Church (113 members).
Other Protestant denominations		P-	.....	25	4,000	1,500	7,000	0.05	Total about 20 (see list below).
Totals				**5,894**	**5,576,605**	**6,346,375**	**9,554,756**		

Churches, members, growth, 1900-2025	*Congs*	*Adults*	*Affiliated*	*G%*	*Total denominations*	*6 Megablocs:* *O*	*R*	*A*	*P*	*I*	*m*
Total churches, members, and denominations (mid-1900)	1,000	1,128,000	1,954,000	1.70	15	5	1	1	5	3	0
Total churches, members, and denominations (mid-1970)	4,134	3,663,215	6,346,375	1.70	43	6	1	1	21	12	2
Total churches, members, and denominations (mid-1990)	4,800	5,091,000	8,723,000	1.60	66	6	1	1	33	23	2
Total churches, members, and denominations (mid-1995)	5,894	5,576,605	9,554,756	1.84	68	6	1	1	34	24	2
Total churches, members, and denominations (mid-2000)	6,500	6,024,000	10,320,466	1.55	68	6	1	1	34	24	2
Total churches, members, and denominations (mid-2025)	8,100	7,981,000	13,675,000	1.13	142	10	1	1	50	70	10

NOTES ON TABLE ABOVE

NATIONAL COUNCILS (Column 4, 5th letter).

C = Fellowship of Evangelicals in Egypt (FEE).
d = member of FEE and also associate member of EACCSE.
K = Ecumenical Advisory Council for Church Service in Egypt (EACCSE).
S = Bishops' Assembly of Egypt (for all rites), also member of EACCSE.

OTHER EGYPTIAN INDIGENOUS CHURCHES. These smaller bodies begun by Egyptians include: Baptist Ev Ch (1955), Baptist Evangelistic Mission (1932), Ch of Christ (1948), Ch of Grace (1940), First Baptist Biblical Ch (1961), Holiness Ev Coptic Ch. A USA Black pentecostal mission is also at work: Pentecostal Assemblies of the World.

OTHER PROTESTANT DENOMINATIONS. These smaller bodies include: Armenian Brotherhood, Armenian Ev Spiritual Brethren, Baptist Chs, Children of God International (USA), Ch of Christ (Non-Instrumental), Ch of God of Prophecy (1950), Ch of God (General Conference) (1972), Day of Pentecost Ch, Eglise de Langue Française (Cario), Middle East General Mission (previously Egypt Mission Band, then Egypt General Mission), Egypt Salaam Mission, German Ev Mission, Ma'adi Community Ch, Missionary Ch, North Africa Mission, Pentecostal Grace Ch, Salvation Army (1936), Unevangelized Field Mission (1964), World Gospel Mission (1949).

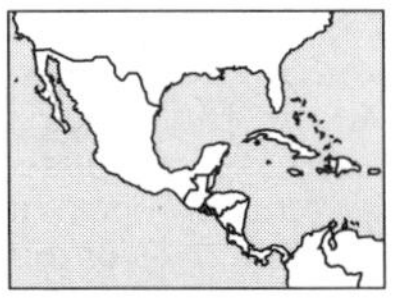

EL SALVADOR

SECULAR DATA, AD 2000

STATE

Official name: La República de El Salvador (The Republic of El Salvador).
Short name: El Salvador. **Adjective of nationality:** Salvadoran.
Flag: Blue, white, and blue stripes.
Area: 21,041 sq. km. (8,124 sq. mi.).
Government: Republic with one legislative house, since 1983 (1525 Spanish rule, 1841 Independence from Spain, many dictatorships).
Legislature: Legislative Assembly, 84 members.
Official language: Spanish (Español/Castella).
Monetary unit: 1 colón = (C) 100 centavos. **US$1=** C8.76.
Chief cities: SAN SALVADOR 1,415,000; Santa Ana 186,953; Mejicanos 124,019; San Miguel 120,026; Delgado 91,774.
Political divisions: 14 provinces.
Armed forces: 31,000.

DEMOGRAPHY

Population: 6,276,000.
Population density: 298.2/sq. km. (772.5/sq. mi.).
Under 15 years: 2,234,000.
Growth rate p.a.: 1.82% (births 25.31, deaths 5.94).
Mortality: Infant, per 1,000: 26.4; **Maternal per 100,000:** 300.0.
Life expectancy: 70 (male 68, female 74).
Household size: 4.9. **Floor area per person, sq.m:** 11.0.
Major languages: Spanish, English, Pipil, Lenca.
Urban dwellers: 46.63%. **Urban growth rate p.a.:** 2.8%.
Labor force: 35%.

ETHNOLINGUISTIC PEOPLES

88.3% Mestizo; 4.4% Part-Indian; 4.0% Pipil; 1.6% Salvadorian White; 0.7% Lenca.

ECONOMY

National income p.a. per person: US$1,609; **per family:** US$7,888.

EDUCATION
Adult literacy: 74% (male 77%, female 71%). **Schools:** 3,806. **Universities:** 6. **School enrolment:** female/male: 68%/67%.

HEALTH
Access to health services: 40%. **Access to safe water:** 55%. **Hospitals:** 78 (17 beds per 10,000). **Doctors:** 4,525. **Blind:** 3,961. **Deaf:** 379,200. **Murder rate:** 25. **Lepers:** 600. **Underweight prevalence under 5:** 11%.

LITERATURE
New book titles p.a.: 310 (50 p.a. per million). **Periodicals:** 28. **Newspapers:** 6 dailies.

COMMUNICATION (per 1,000 people)
Phones: 53 (18% mobile). **Radios:** 373. **TV sets:** 241. **Daily newspaper circulation:** 53. **Computers:** 50.

REFUGEES
Citizen refugees in other countries: 12,400. **Alien refugees from other countries:** 150.

HUMAN LIFE AND LIBERTY (optimum condition=100.0%)
HDI: 59.2. **HSI:** 36.0. **HFI:** 50.0. **EFL:** 51.0.

Country Table 1. **Religious adherents in El Salvador, AD 1900-2025.**

Year	*1900*		*1970*		*mid-1990*		*Annual change, 1990-2000*				*mid-1995*		*mid-2000*		*mid-2025*	
Name	*Adherents*	*%*	*Adherents*	*%*	*Adherents*	*%*	*Natural*	*Conversion*	*Total*	*Rate*	*Adherents*	*%*	*Adherents*	*%*	*Adherents*	*%*
Christians	**1,029,000**	**98.0**	**3,579,000**	**99.5**	**4,995,010**	**97.8**	**113,979**	**-1,283**	**112,696**	**2.06**	**5,535,000**	**97.6**	**6,121,971**	**97.6**	**8,755,150**	**96.6**
PROFESSION																
professing Christians	**1,029,000**	**98.0**	**3,579,000**	**99.5**	**4,995,010**	**97.8**	**113,979**	**-1,283**	**112,696**	**2.06**	**5,535,000**	**97.6**	**6,121,971**	**97.6**	**8,755,150**	**96.6**
AFFILIATION																
unaffiliated Christians	31,500	3.0	30,927	0.9	30,010	0.6	685	-1,291	-606	-2.23	29,000	0.5	23,949	0.4	20,150	0.2
affiliated Christians	**997,500**	**95.0**	**3,548,073**	**98.6**	**4,965,000**	**97.2**	**113,294**	**8**	**113,302**	**2.08**	**5,506,000**	**97.1**	**6,098,022**	**97.2**	**8,735,000**	**96.4**
Roman Catholics	997,400	95.0	3,313,086	92.1	4,665,000	91.3	106,446	-646	105,800	2.07	5,170,000	91.2	5,723,000	91.2	8,000,000	88.3
Independents	0	0.0	68,574	1.9	550,000	10.8	12,550	3,450	16,000	2.59	623,933	11.0	710,000	11.3	1,200,000	13.2
Protestants	100	0.0	149,197	4.2	418,000	8.2	9,538	1,662	11,200	2.40	471,831	8.3	530,000	8.4	940,000	10.4
Marginal Christians	0	0.0	17,061	0.5	80,000	1.6	1,825	1,175	3,000	3.24	93,500	1.7	110,000	1.8	250,000	2.8
Anglicans	0	0.0	155	0.0	340	0.0	8	-2	6	1.64	360	0.0	400	0.0	600	0.0
doubly-affiliated	0	0.0	0	0.0	-748,340	-14.6	-17,076	-5,628	-22,704	2.69	-853,624	-15.1	-975,378	-15.5	-1,655,600	-18.3
Trans-megabloc groupings																
Evangelicals	100	0.0	127,000	3.5	327,000	6.4	7,461	2,139	9,600	2.61	374,016	6.6	423,000	6.7	737,000	8.1
Pentecostals/Charismatics	0	0.0	185,000	5.1	1,185,000	23.2	27,039	2,461	29,500	2.25	1,327,418	23.4	1,480,000	23.6	2,270,000	25.1
Great Commission Christians	**21,000**	**2.0**	**108,000**	**3.0**	**382,000**	**7.5**	**8,716**	**4,176**	**12,892**	**2.95**	**442,000**	**7.8**	**510,916**	**8.1**	**875,000**	**9.7**
Nonreligious	0	0.0	2,400	0.1	70,000	1.4	1,597	778	2,375	2.96	80,060	1.4	93,752	1.5	200,000	2.2
Baha'is	0	0.0	5,100	0.1	20,000	0.4	456	315	771	3.32	24,500	0.4	27,712	0.4	60,000	0.7
Ethnoreligionists	21,000	2.0	9,500	0.3	16,000	0.3	365	223	588	3.18	19,700	0.4	21,884	0.4	30,000	0.3
Atheists	0	0.0	600	0.0	4,200	0.1	96	-8	88	1.92	4,600	0.1	5,081	0.1	8,500	0.1
Muslims	0	0.0	0	0.0	1,550	0.0	35	-14	21	1.30	1,600	0.0	1,763	0.0	2,500	0.0
Chinese folk-religionists	0	0.0	300	0.0	700	0.0	16	-8	8	1.13	740	0.0	783	0.0	900	0.0
Buddhists	0	0.0	300	0.0	540	0.0	12	-6	6	1.09	570	0.0	602	0.0	750	0.0
Jews	0	0.0	300	0.0	500	0.0	11	-4	7	1.23	530	0.0	565	0.0	700	0.0
Other religionists	0	0.0	500	0.0	1,500	0.0	34	7	41	2.44	1,700	0.0	1,909	0.0	3,500	0.0
World A (unevangelized persons)	5,250	0.5	7,196	0.2	5,110	0.1	119	-7	112	1.97	5,668	0.1	6,276	0.1	9,062	0.1
World B (evangelized non-Christians)	15,750	1.5	12,034	0.3	109,880	2.1	2,503	1,290	3,793	3.01	127,926	2.3	147,753	2.3	297,788	3.3
World C (Christians)	1,029,000	98.0	3,579,000	99.5	4,995,010	97.8	113,979	-1,283	112,696	2.06	5,535,000	97.6	6,121,971	97.6	8,755,150	96.6
Country's population	**1,050,000**	**100.0**	**3,598,231**	**100.0**	**5,110,000**	**100.0**	**116,601**	**0**	**116,601**	**2.08**	**5,668,595**	**100.0**	**6,276,000**	**100.0**	**9,062,000**	**100.0**

COLUMNS, ROWS.
For meanings and definitions, see Codebook (Part 3). Note that, by definition, total 'Christians' = professing + crypto-Christians, which also = affiliated + unaffiliated Christians, and also = Great Commission Christians + latent Christians. Percentages may not always total exactly, due to rounding.

CENSUSES.
The religion question has not been asked in government censuses.

NOTES ON RELIGIONS
ATHEISTS. Communist Party of El Salvador (PCES) (illegal).
BAHA'IS. Rapid growth from 3 local spiritual assemblies (1964) to 54 (1973), and to 103 LSAs (1996). Mass literature distributions take place as well as radio programs.
BUDDHISTS. Chinese.
DOUBLY-AFFILIATED. The term covers those affiliated to, or claimed by, both the Catholic Church and also a church termed Evangélica by the state (Protestant, marginal Protestant, Anglican or Independents), i.e. baptized Catholics who have recently become Evangelicals or others. Because their statistics represent a duplication, they are shown in the table as a negative quantity (with a minus sign).
ETHNORELIGIONISTS. Of the 300,000 Amerindians in 1995, a proportion remain animists among the Pipil, Lenca and others.
INDEPENDENTS. In about 33 denominations in 1995 (see Table 2).
OTHER RELIGIONISTS. Including Rosicrucians (1 AMORC centre) and a few Muslims (Palestinian Arabs).

Great Commission Instrument Panel: status of El Salvador (for explanation see start of Part 4)

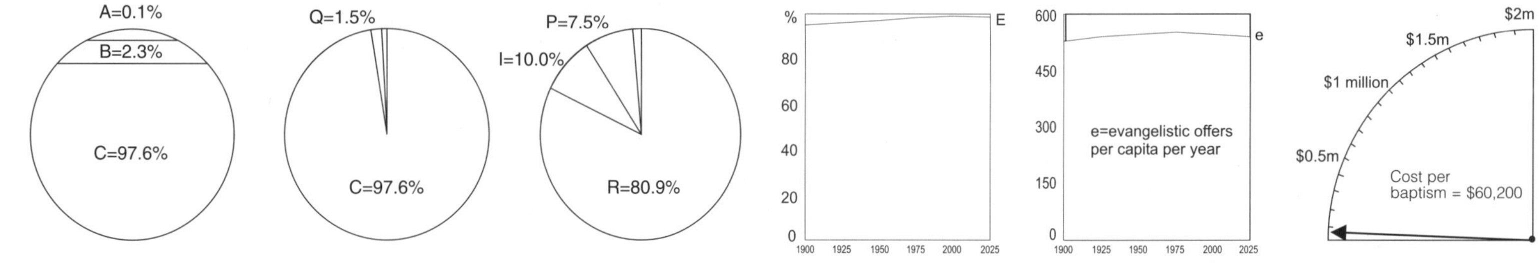

3 Worlds, AD 2000 | Religions, AD 2000 | Ecclesiastical blocs | Evangelization, 1900-2025 | Offers, 1900-2025 | Cost-effectiveness, AD 2000

Country status. El Salvador is the smallest mainland nation in the Western Hemisphere and is located on the western coast of Central America. Volcanic mountain ranges run from east to west. Most economic activity is agricultural—the main crops are coffee, cotton, and sugar cane.

HUMAN LIFE AND LIBERTY

Human need and development. Living conditions have not changed basically since the turn of the century, and are characterized by extremes of poverty and wealth. The middle class is small, but growing. Social and economic progress is halting, interrupted by periodical outbreaks of civil violence. The major quality of life indicators have lagged behind many of El Salvador's neighbors. Environmental sanitation is rudimentary in rural areas and poor water supply and sewage have been contributory causes in depressing health standards. Medical services are inadequate except in the capital. Social security programs have been increasing but the coverage is not complete. The diet is adequate and varied but not rich and is generally the same at all socioeconomic levels. Because of earthquakes which have destroyed most of the old colonial structures, buildings are generally limited to one or 2 stories. There are rundown buildings and shantytowns in all urban areas. In the rural areas most of the single-family houses are of adobe or wattle construction. Government housing is available only to a small percentage of the population.

Human rights and freedoms. The end of the civil war has brought some respite to the war-weary people and some improvement to the human rights situation which had been deteriorating for years. But both government forces and the opposition FMLN (Frente Farabundo Marti para la Liberacion Nacional) forces continue to assassinate their opponents. There was some progress in resolving long-outstanding incidents of human rights-abuse from earlier years. The assassins of the 6 Jesuit priests killed in 1989 remain in prison The investigation of the 1981 El Mozote massacre in which over 700 men, women and children were killed was completed and forensic experts exhuming the mass grave confirmed that government forces were responsible for the atrocity. Although torture, arbitrary arrest and unlawful detention are illegal under the Constitution, they are generally practiced by government security forces. Many detainees have been incarcerated for 4 or more years without being allowed to see a lawyer. Compounding the problem is the inefficiency of the legal system, insufficient criminal investigation capabilities, limited number of legal aid lawyers, weaknesses in the Criminal Procedure Code, and poor court administration. Although nominally independent, the judiciary is weakened by political pressures, although this may change as a result of the setting up of the new National Council of the Judiciary. According to the Supreme Court the government has released all political prisoners, but this is disputed by human rights groups. Freedom of speech and of the press is guaranteed by the Constitution but is inhibited by threats of violence as well as actual violence. Reporters and editors frequently receive death threats and newspapers offices are bombed, set on fire or vandalized in an effort to curb investigative reporting. Women suffer economic and social discrimination, as usual in times of civil unrest. Further, they are also subject to violence. Over 60 rapes are reported in San Salvador alone in an average month.

Human environment. Because El Salvador is a small country, population pressures have a direct and adverse effect on the environment. The principal environmental problems are soil degradation, caused by the fragility of the soils, steep terrain, improper cultivation methods, river water pollution, loss of biodiversity and buildup of toxic chemicals in the soil.

NON-CHRISTIAN RELIGIONS.

Traditional religions exist among the Pipil and Lenca Indians, although the majority are baptized Catholics.

Baha'i has grown rapidly from 3 local spiritual assemblies in 1964 to 54 by 1973; by 1995 its adherents had mushroomed fivefold to near 25,000.

Country summary. **Worlds A, B, C by ethnolinguistic peoples, cities, and major civil divisions in El Salvador.**

	PEOPLES							CITIES							CIVIL DIVISIONS						
World	Num	Pop 2000	C%	Christians	E%	U%	Unevangelized	Num	Pop 2000	C%	Christians	E%	U%	Unevangelized	Num	Pop 2000	C%	Christians	E%	U%	Unevangelized
A	2	1,256	0.64	8	46	54	676	0	0	0.00	0	0	0	0	0	0	0.00	0	0	0	0
B	3	11,673	32.54	3,798	67	33	3,859	0	0	0.00	0	0	0	0	0	0	0.00	0	0	0	0
C	10	6,263,095	97.30	6,094,216	100	0	1,783	4	1,794,775	95.68	1,717,208	100	0	1,077	14	6,276,020	97.16	6,098,023	100	0	6,316
Total	**15**	**6,276,024**	**97.16**	**6,098,022**	**100**	**0**	**6,318**	**4**	**1,794,775**	**95.68**	**1,717,208**	**100**	**0**	**1,077**	**14**	**6,276,020**	**97.16**	**6,098,023**	**100**	**0**	**6,316**

CHRISTIANITY

Spanish Catholic priests first came to El Salvador in 1525 when it was conquered by Spain, but Spanish indifference to the territory because of its lack of precious metals resulted in a slower rate of christianization than in surrounding countries. When Central America separated from Spain in 1821, it claimed to inherit the right of patronage and established the diocese of San Salvador, but this was not officially recognized by Rome until 1842. El Salvador in the meantime (1838) had gained its independence from Guatemala. During the next 40 years, successive governments alternated in accepting and rejecting Catholicism as the official religion. In 1886, the 8th constitution established freedom of religion and secular education, in addition to prohibiting religious orders; but the systematic religious persecution of the early years gradually abated with passage of time.

CATHOLIC CHURCH. The number of Catholic baptisms decreased considerably in urban districts between 1965-69. Infant baptisms in relation to births in the city of San Salvador fell from 90% in 1965 to 85% in 1969. This has been a result of the development, after 1950, of Pentecostal churches and other bodies from North America.

Religious behavior among the Catholic population can be classified according to a 3-fold typology born in the colonial period: (1) bourgeois Catholicism, representing about 4% of the total population, is composed of the upper classes largely of Spanish descent who send their children to Catholic schools and help in social work; (2) popular Catholicism, about 30%, is held by those who have little religious education but who participate in popular religious festivals; and (3) mayanized Catholicism, a mixture of Catholicism and traditional Mayan Indian beliefs and customs, is accepted by 60% of the population although pure-blooded Indians practicing christo-paganism number under 4%. A number of Catholics, principally in the archdiocese of San Salvador, are involved in Catholic action under the influence of the 1968 Medellín conference in Colombia. The tensions in the Salvadorian church can be seen in the fact that the conclusions of a National Pastoral Week in June 1970 calling for a 'revolutionary attitude with regard to the problem of sin and oppression' were condemned by the Episcopal Conference, although 2 of its members defended these views. However, even if the conclusions of the Week have not led to institutional change, the pastoral action of the church has taken on an orientation which favors concrete proposals for change.

The Holy See has diplomatic relations with El Salvador and in AD 2000 is represented to government and the Catholic hierarchy by a nuncio residing in San Salvador.

PROTESTANT CHURCHES. Protestant work began in El Salvador in 1896 with the arrival of the Central American Mission, followed by the Church of God (Cleveland), Seventh-day Adventists and American Baptists before World War I. All of these churches have made progress, but the most spectacular gains have come in recent years among the Assemblies of God, who have built up a large following since their arrival in 1922. Pentecostalism represents the principal alternative to Catholic dominance in El Salvador at the present time.

Renewal movements. In the 1990s the Pentecostal/Charismatic Renewal continued to spread rapidly across most older churches, and numbered over 1,480,000 adherents (of whom 26% Pentecostals, 27% Charismatics, and 47% Independents).

Indigenous missions. In the early and middle part of the 20th century missions from El Salvador were mainly Catholics involved in parish renewal and evangelism in surrounding Latin American countries. In recent years many Protestants have been sent out, also mainly to surrounding countries. Today, mission vision is on the rise and though the vast majority still serve in neighboring countries, some Salvadorians are serving in North Africa and the Middle East.

Iglesia Catolica en El Salvador. Many martyrs: 1980 at archbishop Romero's funeral (*above*), violence breaks out (*left*). 1984, 4 nuns murdered (*top*), 1989 6 Jesuits.

CHURCH AND STATE

The constitution of January 1962 states in its Preamble: 'The Constituent Assembly in the name of the Salvadorian people, with trust in God and the high destiny of the country...'. It guarantees the free exercise of religion and forbids clergy from engaging in 'all forms of political propaganda calling on religious motivations'. It also forbids criticism of laws of the state and government during religious acts in Protestant churches (Article 157). The Catholic Church, which is the official state religion, has a juridical personality and other churches may obtain it in accordance with the law (Article 161). Protestant churches and their dependencies are exempt from land tax (Article 119).

Church and state maintain an attitude of mutual recognition and try to avoid conflict. Government does not allow itself to be pressured by the Catholic Church, and the Catholic hierarchy shows concern for the wishes of government. However, the archbishop of San Salvador is widely known for his courageous stand on social issues and his statements sometimes provoke strong reactions in economic, political, and military circles.

In the election of 1972, the Christian Democratic Party joined with the Socialist Party to form a unified front (UNO); but although results by provinces were never published, the conservative party was declared the winner.

In 1977 serious trouble erupted between leftist terrorists and rightist landowners. Conflict had been building up for some time between the Catholic Church and the regime of A. Molina, primarily on the issue of land reform as a result of the Church's calls for a more equitable distribution of wealth. A number of priests, especially Jesuits, encouraged peasants to take over unused lands belonging to large landowners. From January 1977 over 15 priests, mainly Jesuits, were expelled; in May the country's foreign minister was assassinated by the Popular Forces of Liberation, and in June the clandestine rightist White Warriors Union threatened to kill 50 Jesuit priests unless they left the country. A vast number of murders did in fact take place. From 1977-89, some 70,000 killings, massacres, and crucifixions took place. In 1980 archbishop Oscar Romero was murdered while leading the eucharist; followed by in 1984 4 American nuns, 1988 4 Lutheran workers, 1989 6 Jesuit priests.

During the 1990s the situation stabilized somewhat.

BROADCASTING AND MEDIA

La Voz Panamericana is a local Catholic radio station. Shortwave programs from KNLS, HCJB (Ecuador), TWR (Antilles) and AWR (Costa Rica) can be easily received. El Salvador is a member of UNDA.

Spanish versions of CBN's programs can be seen on 2 local television channels on a daily basis. Three ministry centers follow-up respondents with discipleship training and personal counseling, as well as film and video evangelism. LeSEA'S programs can be viewed on the World Harvest Satellite Network.

Sme 6.3 million (98%) have seen the 'Jesus' film, chiefly through TV (2.9 million) and film team presentations (3.1 million). A total of 342,000 have responded with a decision.

INTERDENOMINATIONAL ORGANIZATIONS

El Salvador has no council of churches. The Baptist Association is an affiliate member of UNELAM founded in 1965 at Campinas, Brazil. The Catholic Episcopal Conference sponsors a Commission for Ecumenism and Non-believers (Comisión de Ecumenismo y No Creyentes).

FUTURE TRENDS AND PROSPECTS

Christians are expected to decline slightly to about 96.6% by 2025 with the nonreligious increasing from only 0.1% of the population in 1970 to 2.2% by 2025.

Increasing secularization, immigration, and other factors will probably lower the Christian percentage to under 95% before AD 2050. The nonreligious could reach 4% then and Baha'is could pass 1% around the same time.

BIBLIOGRAPHY

A question of conscience: the murder of the Jesuit priests in El Salvador. L. Brown & I. Ziv. : First Run Features, 1990. (48 min. videocassette focusing on the November 16, 1989 murder of six Jesuit priests in El Salvador by uniformed soldiers. In English and Spanish with English subtitles).

Anuario eclesiástico de El Salvador, 1970. San Salvador: Secretariado Social Interdiocesano, 1970.

Archbishop Romero: memories and reflections. J. Sobrino. Maryknoll, NY: Orbis Books, 1990. 223p.

Companions of Jesus: the Jesuit martyrs of El Salvador. J. Sobrino et al. Maryknoll, NY: Orbis Books, 1990. 208p.

El Salvador. R. L. Woodward Jr. *World bibliographical series,* vol. 98. Oxford, UK: CLIO Press, 1988. 214p. (See especially 'Religion,' p.65–9).

El Salvador in revival. T. W. Drost. Hazelwood, MO: Word Aflame Press, 1983. 141p.

Faith of a people: the story of a Christian community in El Salvador, 1970–1980. P. Galdámez. Maryknoll, NY: Orbis Books, 1986. 109p.

Fire against fire: Christian ministry face–to–face with persecution. M. E. Gómez. Minneapolis, MN: Augsburg Press, 1990. 94p.

'From death we are reborn: martyrdom and resistance in El Salvador.' A. L. Peterson. Ph.D. dissertation, University of Chicago Divinity School, 1991. 343p.

'Is the evangelical church in El Salvador presenting an alternative to the solution of Liberation Theology in the area of social ministry?' P. J. Reid. Th.M. thesis, Dallas Theological Seminary, Dallas, TX, 1985. 41p.

La Lucha: the struggle of the church in Central America. B. Dale. [Cincinnati, OH]: Friendship Press, 1990. (28 min. videocassette).

Martyrdom and the politics of religion: progressive Catholicism in El Salvador's civil war. A. L. Peterson. Albany, NY: State University of New York Pres, 1997. 235p.

Martyrdom in El Salvador: the murders at the Central American University, San Salvador, 16 November 1989. Trans., D. Livingston. *Church in the world,* 27. Sydney: Australian Catholic Relief, [1990]. 8p. (Funeral sermons by Jesuits on martyrdom in El Salvador).

Promised land: death and life in El Salvador. S. Wright. Maryknoll, NY: Orbis Books, 1994. 269p.

'Sanguine saints: Pentecostalism in El Salvador,' E. A. Wilson, *Church history,* 52 (June 1983), 186–98.

Steadfastness of the saints: a journal of peace and war in Central and North America. D. Berrigan. Maryknoll, NY: Orbis Books, 1985. 142p.

'The Church in El Salvador,' *Pro Mundi Vita* (Brussels), (1982), 1–27.

'The church in the Salvadoran revolution,' T. S. Montgomery, *Latin American perspectives,* 10, 1 (1983), 62–87.

The harvest of justice: the church of El Salvador ten years after Romero. D. Santiago. New York: Paulist Press, 1993. 199p.

'The politics of Salvadoran refugee popular religion.' H. J. Recinos. Ph.D. dissertation, American University, Washington, DC, 1993. 327p.

The religious roots of rebellion: Christians in Central American revolutions. P. Berryman. Maryknoll, NY: Orbis Books, 1984. 464p.

Voices of many crying. J. S. Munday. Ocean City, MD: Skipjack Press, 1992. 123p.

Country Table 2. **Organized churches and denominations in El Salvador.**

Official name (bold type = church *with over 10% of all affiliated)* 1	*Begun* 2	*Type* 3	*Counc* 4	*Congs* 5	*Adults* 6	*Affiliated 1970* 7	*Affiliated 1995* 8	*G%* 9	*Names, notes, and other statistics* (see Codebook, Part 3) 10
Asambleas de Dios	1922	P-Pe2	ZF..E	3,032	172,064	100,000	238,900	3.54	*Assemblies of God.* M=AoG(USA). 12,100 baptized. Radio LARE. 408n,7f,1k,1s(95).
Asambleas Locales	c1990	I-3nC	.....	4	100	–	300	20.00	*Local Churches. Little Flock.* Begun 1922 in China.
Asociación Bautista de El Salvador	1911	P-Bap	TvU..	58	7,229	6,000	14,500	3.59	*Baptist Association of ES.* M=ABCIM(USA). 1966, applied to join WCC. 4f.
Concilio Latinoamericano		I-3pL	.....	161	9,000	1,240	20,000	0.05	*Latin American Council.* Grassroots pentecostals.
Consejo de Igls Luteranas en CA & P	1947	P-Lut	e....	76	7,600	476	10,000	12.95	*Lutheran Ch (Missouri Synod).* 1952, M=LCMS(USA). German-speaking. 9t,W=29%,5Yy,7z.
Convención Bautista Nacional	1965	I-3cD	T....	53	8,000	1,500	17,800	10.40	*National Baptist Convention.* M=NBCUSA(USA Black missionaries).
Fraternidad Cristiana de ES	c1985	I-3pL	x....	3	2,000	–	3,000	10.00	*Christian Brotherhood of ES.* Large central church. M=FC Guatemala.
Hermanos Libres		P-CBr	x....	20	700	400	1,400	0.05	*Christian Brethren. Plymouth (Open) Brethren.* M=CMML(USA,NZ). 4f.
Igl Apostólica de la Fe en Cristo Jesus	1950	I-3oL	x....	33	1,300	2,000	4,060	2.87	*Apostolic Ch of the Faith in CJ.* Mexicans; with UPC(USA). Mestizos. 38nx,160z.
Iglesia Adventista del Séptimo Día	1915	P-Adv	x....	160	23,000	15,000	38,396	3.83	*SDA. Seventh-day Adventists, ES Mission, CAmerican UM.* 12n,2x,W=60%,724Y.
Iglesia Adventista Reformada		I-Adv	x....	10	1,000	875	2,500	0.05	*Reformed Adventist Church.*
Iglesia Apostolica Aposento		I-3aL	x....	32	4,800	1,500	12,000	0.05	*Apostolic Ch of the Upper Room.*
Iglesia Apostolica de Dios en Cristo		I-3pL	.....	9	1,800	500	4,500	0.05	*Apostolic Church of God in Christ.*
Iglesia Após de los Apóstoles y Profetas		I-3pL	.....	300	45,000	5,940	100,000	0.05	*Apostolic Ch of the Apostles and Prophets.*
Iglesia Apostolica de Neuva Jerusalem		I-3pL	.....	4	700	–	1,750	0.05	*Apostolic Ch of the New Jerusalem.*
Iglesia Batista Independiente San Miguel		I-Bap	.....	9	4,500	625	11,300	0.05	*San Miguel Indep Baptist Ch.*
Iglesia Católica en El Salvador:	1525	R-Lat	B.LDR	308	2,837,000	3,313,086	5,170,000	1.80	*Catholic Ch.* C=18+1+29. 1s(122) (closed in 1973). 290n 182x 360m 1277w 92196Yy
M San Salvador	1842	R-Lat	Bs	110	1,526,000	1,115,603	2,783,000	3.72	50% urban. 50% rural. 104n 133x 289m 875w 30944Yy
D Chalatenango	1987	R-Lat	Bs	16	89,000	–	162,400	12.50	Population is 80% Catholic. 14n 6x 6m 20w 3138Yy
D San Miguel	1913	R-Lat	Bs	26	401,000	551,433	732,000	1.14	Main zone for cotton production. East. M=CM. 27n 6x 13m 33w 15810Yy
D Santa Ana	1913	R-Lat	Bs	37	294,000	705,000	536,000	-1.09	Main zone for coffee production. Extreme west. 40n 18x 30m 105w 14522Yy
D Santiago de Maria	1954	R-Lat	Bs	25	343,000	489,250	625,000	0.98	Coffee, cotton, grain. Strip adjourning D San Miguel. 31n 7x 8m 62w 7704Yy
D San Vicente	1943	R-Lat	Bs	28	208,000	441,800	380,000	-0.60	Agricultural area; from coast to Honduras border. 39n 3x 4m 96w 8112Yy
D Sonsonate	1986	R-Lat	Bs	16	234,000	–	428,000	11.11	Population 92% Catholic. 19n 3x 3m 60w 7700Yy
D Zacatecoluca	1987	R-Lat	Bs	19	162,000	–	296,000	12.50	M=OFM. 16n 6x 7m 26w 4266Yy
OM El Salvador	1968	R-Lat	Bs	31	20,000	10,000	29,000	4.35	*Military Ordinariate of El Salvador.* 2 ordinaries, 29 auxiliaries. 66Yy.
Doubly-counted Catholics		R-Lat		0	-440,000	–	-801,400		Persons counted in an older diocese and also in a newly formed diocese.
Igl de JC de los Santos de los UD	c1952	m-LdS	x....	77	22,400	12,061	32,000	3.98	*Ch of JC of Latter-day Saints. Mormons.* M=CJCLdS(USA). 200f.
Iglesia Centroamericana	1896	P-Non	xM...	250	13,222	6,500	29,400	6.22	*Central American Church.* M=CAM(USA). Interdenominational in emphasis. 13f,1k.
Iglesia Cristiana Reformada	1978	P-Ref	x...E	2	80	–	160	5.88	*Christian Reformed Ch.* M=CRWM.
Iglesia de Dios (Anderson)		P-Hol	x...E	20	2,000	1,000	5,000	0.05	*Ch of God.* M=CoG(Anderson) (USA). Holiness denomination. 10n.
Iglesia de Dios (Cleveland)	1904	P-Pe3	ZF...	312	17,808	13,000	44,500	5.05	M=CoG(Cleveland) (USA). 140 churches, 203 missions. 1 brickery, 1 dairy, 140n,1p.
Iglesia de Dios de la Profecía Universal	1954	P-Pe3	Z....	101	5,475	600	13,700	13.33	*Ch of God of Prophecy.* M=CGP(USA). Split in USA ex CoG(Cleveland). 2f.
Iglesia de Dios de la Profetie Zion		I-3pL	.....	80	5,800	13,300	19,300	0.05	*Holy Zion CoGP.* M=CoGP.
Iglesia de los Amigos	1915	P-Qua	Q....	20	400	186	800	6.01	*Central America Yearly Meeting of Ev Friends Ch. Quakers.*W=51%,10Y.
Iglesia del Evangelio Cuadrangular	1973	P-Pe2	Z....	7	305	–	763	4.55	*International Ch of Foursquare Gospel.* M=ICFG(USA).
Iglesia del Nazareno	1964	P-Hol	xF...	25	2,560	800	3,887	6.53	M=Ch of the Nazarene (USA). Holiness body. 1n,3x,10m,6f,15t(712),W=85%,74Y,80z.
Iglesia del Principe de Paz	c1945	I-3pL	x....	556	50,000	5,000	125,000	13.74	*Ch of the Prince of Peace.* Indigenous pentecostals from Guatemala.
Iglesia Dios Manantiales Vida Eterna		I-3gL	.....	153	6,600	3,780	14,700	0.05	*Springs of Eternal Life Church of God.*
Iglesia Episcopal: D El Salvador		A-Cen	aw.R.	2	180	155	360	0.05	*Episcopal Ch.* 1968, missionary diocese, PECUSA, Province IX. 1x,W=55%,3y.
Iglesia Evangelica de la Profetia		I-3gL	.....	13	2,000	500	5,000	0.05	*Evang Ch of Prophecy.*
Iglesia Evangelica Menonita	1968	P-Men	.....	3	125	75	170	3.33	*Evang Mennonite Ch.* M=Evangelical Mennonite Ch (USA).
Iglesia Evangélica Profética Peniel	1979	I-3pL	.....	11	1,100	–	2,440	6.25	*Peniel Prophetic Evangelical Ch.*
Iglesia Ev Luterana de CR,ES,H,N,P	1954	P-Lut	l....	81	6,450	390	10,755	14.19	*ELC in Costa Rica, ES, Hond, Nic, Panama.* Germans, Scandinavians. 1x,W=10%,6Yy.
Iglesia Pentecostal de Dios		P-Pe2	.....	20	3,000	2,670	10,000	0.05	*Pentecostal Ch of God.* M=PCG(New York, USA).
Iglesia Pentecostal Unida	1975	P-Pe1	.....	487	19,500	–	39,000	5.00	*United Pentecostal Church. M=UPC(USA).*
Iglesias de Cristo		I-Dis	x....	167	4,000	1,000	10,000	0.05	*Churches of Christ.* M=CC(Non-Instrumental) (USA). Radio work. 2f.
Misión Bautista Internacional	1955	I-Bap	.....	4	1,000	600	2,000	4.93	*Baptist International Missions.* M=BIM(USA).
Misión Cristiana Elim	c1965	I-3kL	.....	71	72,000	500	175,000	26.40	*Elim Christian Mission.* Massive evangelism and church growth. 116,000 in 600 weekly calls.
Misión Esandarte de la Biblia Abierta	1975	I-3pL	.....	9	293	–	733	5.00	M=OBSC(USA).
Mision Evangelica do Voz de Dios		I-3gL	.....	35	3,500	1,500	8,750	0.05	*Evang Miss of Voice of God.*
Misión La Luz del Mundo	1960	I-3oL	.....	38	3,800	1,500	9,500	7.66	*Light of the World Church. Aaronistas.* Based in Mexico.
Misíon Mundo Unida		P-Hol	.....	10	1,000	1,100	2,500	0.05	*United World Mission.* M=UWM.
Misión sin Fronteras		I-3gL	.....	15	1,500	2,000	3,750	0.05	*Mission without Frontiers.*
Mov Ev Interden El Tabernaculo de Fe	1978	I-3gL	.....	100	1,300	–	2,890	5.88	*Tabernacle of Faith Interdenominational Gospel Movement.*
Movimiento del Iglesia de Israel		I-3gL	.....	47	2,800	1,670	9,330	0.05	*Church of Israel Movement.*
Profecía del Sinai		I-3gL	.....	44	1,500	44	3,330	0.05	*Prophecy from Mount Sinai.*
Testigos de Jehová	c1930	m-Jeh	x....	326	18,445	5,000	61,500	10.56	*Jehovah's Witnesses. IBSA.* Witnessing under way by 1932. (1975) 329Y. (1995) 2087Y.
Other independent charismatic chs		I-3gL	.....	100	10,000	3,000	15,000	0.05	Normally termed grassroots (GR) churches; also New Apostolic Church (292 members).
Other indigenous pentecostal churches		I-3pL	.....	300	20,000	20,000	40,000	0.05	Total about 10, including: Asamblea Espiritual Nacional, Iglesia Santa Sion.
Other Protestant denominations		P-	.....	40	5,000	1,000	8,000	0.05	Total about 10 (see list below).
Doubly-affiliated		2-aff			-461,000	0	-853,624		Evangelicals who also are or were baptized Roman Catholics.
Totals				**7,798**	**2,969,936**	**3,548,073**	**5,506,000**		

Churches, members, growth, 1900-2025	*Congs*	*Adults*	*Affiliated*	*G%*	*Total denominations*	*6 Megablocs:* *O*	*R*	*A*	*P*	*I*	*m*
Total churches, members, and denominations (mid-1900)	600	554,000	997,500	1.83	2	0	1	0	1	0	0
Total churches, members, and denominations (mid-1970)	1,713	1,970,989	3,548,073	1.83	55	0	1	1	19	32	2
Total churches, members, and denominations (mid-1990)	6,000	2,679,000	4,965,000	1.69	84	0	1	1	27	53	2
Total churches, members, and denominations (mid-1995)	7,798	2,969,936	5,506,000	2.09	86	0	1	1	28	54	2
Total churches, members, and denominations (mid-2000)	9,500	3,290,000	6,098,022	2.06	87	0	1	1	28	55	2
Total churches, members, and denominations (mid-2025)	10,500	4,712,000	8,735,000	1.45	177	0	1	1	40	130	5

NOTES ON TABLE ABOVE

NATIONAL COUNCILS (Column 4, 5th letter).

E = Confraternidad Evangelica Salvadorena (CES).

R = Conferencia Episcopal de El Salvador (CEDES) (Episcopal Conference of El Salvador).

OTHER PROTESTANT DENOMINATIONS. These smaller bodies include: Evangelistic Faith Missions (1963), Iglesia Menonita (48 adherents), union congregations (in cities), World-Wide Missions (1955).

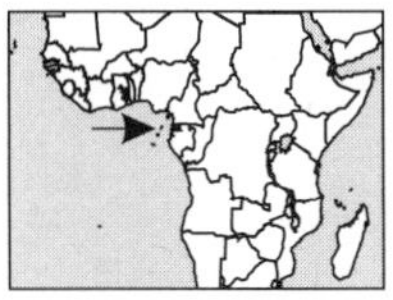

EQUATORIAL GUINEA

SECULAR DATA, AD 2000

STATE
Official name: La República de Guinea Ecuatorial (The Republic of Equatorial Guinea).
Short name: Equatorial Guinea. **Adjective of nationality:** of Equatorial Guinea.
Flag: Green, white, and red stripes, blue triangle at hoist: centered coat of arms.
Area: 28,051 sq. km. (10,831 sq. mi.).
Government: Republic with one legislative house, since 1982 (1471 Portuguese possession, 1778 ceded to Spain, 1968 Independence as republic, 1969 dictatorship).
Legislature: Chamber of People's Representatives, 80 members.
Official language: Spanish (Español).
Monetary unit: 1 CFA franc (CFAF) = 100 centimes. **US$1=** CFAF 560.38.
Chief cities: MALABO (Santa Isabel) 132,037.
Political divisions: 7 provinces.
Armed forces: 1,300.

DEMOGRAPHY
Population: 453,000.
Population density: 16.1/sq. km. (41.7/sq. mi.).
Under 15 years: 196,000.
Growth rate p.a.: 2.42% (births 38.84, deaths 14.63).
Mortality: Infant, per 1,000: 98.8; **Maternal per 100,000:** 820.0.
Life expectancy: 52 (male 50, female 54).
Household size: 4.5. **Floor area per person, sq.m:** 8.0.
Major languages: Spanish, Bulu Fang, Yoruba, French, Bubi, Pidgin English, Portuguese patois, and 10 others.
Urban dwellers: 48.21%. **Urban growth rate p.a.:** 4.5%.
Labor force: 39%.

ETHNOLINGUISTIC PEOPLES
56.6% Fang (Ntumu, Okak, Pahouin); 10.0% Bube (Fernandian, Ediya); 8.0% Yoruba; 4.0% Igbo (Ibo); 2.9% Seke (Seki, Sheke).

ECONOMY
National income p.a. per person: US$379; **per family:** US$1,709.

EDUCATION
Adult literacy: 78% (male 89%, female 68%). **Schools:** 713.
Universities: 4. **School enrolment:** female/male: 40%/40%.

HEALTH
Access to health services: 35%. **Access to safe water:** 95%.
Hospitals: 15 (29 beds per 10,000). **Doctors:** 99.
Blind: 800. **Deaf:** 27,100. **Murder rate:** 12.
Lepers: 16,000.

LITERATURE
New book titles p.a.: 45 (100 p.a. per million). **Periodicals:** 8.
Newspapers: 0 dailies.

COMMUNICATION (per 1,000 people)
Phones: 6 (8% mobile). **Radios:** 488. **TV sets:** 92.
Daily newspaper circulation: 2. **Computers:** 15.

HUMAN LIFE AND LIBERTY (optimum condition=100.0%)
HDI: 46.2. **HSI:** 40.0. **HFI:** 40.0. **EFL:** 22.0.

Country Table 1. **Religious adherents in Equatorial Guinea, AD 1900-2025.**

Year	1900		1970		mid-1990		Annual change, 1990-2000				mid-1995		mid-2000		mid-2025	
Name	Adherents	%	Adherents	%	Adherents	%	Natural	Conversion	Total	Rate	Adherents	%	Adherents	%	Adherents	%
Christians	**6,500**	**5.4**	**256,887**	**88.2**	**310,450**	**88.2**	**8,875**	**112**	**8,987**	**2.58**	**352,400**	**88.2**	**400,320**	**88.4**	**708,600**	**89.1**
PROFESSION																
crypto-Christians	0	0.0	33,987	11.7	41,450	11.8	1,189	6	1,195	2.57	47,200	11.8	53,400	11.8	95,000	12.0
professing Christians	**6,500**	**5.4**	**222,900**	**76.5**	**269,000**	**76.4**	**7,685**	**107**	**7,792**	**2.58**	**305,200**	**76.4**	**346,920**	**76.6**	**613,600**	**77.2**
AFFILIATION																
unaffiliated Christians	0	0.0	4,900	1.7	5,400	1.5	155	-133	22	0.40	5,000	1.3	5,622	1.2	8,600	1.1
affiliated Christians	**6,500**	**5.4**	**251,987**	**86.5**	**305,050**	**86.7**	**8,753**	**212**	**8,965**	**2.61**	**347,400**	**87.0**	**394,698**	**87.1**	**700,000**	**88.1**
Roman Catholics	6,000	5.0	230,712	79.2	303,500	86.2	8,708	42	8,750	2.57	344,500	86.2	391,000	86.3	675,000	84.9
Independents	0	0.0	5,875	2.0	13,100	3.7	376	114	490	3.23	15,110	3.8	18,000	4.0	40,000	5.0
Protestants	500	0.4	14,900	5.1	15,100	4.3	433	-423	10	0.07	15,708	3.9	15,200	3.4	22,000	2.8
Marginal Christians	0	0.0	500	0.2	850	0.2	24	11	35	3.51	1,000	0.3	1,200	0.3	6,000	0.8
doubly-affiliated	0	0.0	0	0.0	-27,500	-7.8	-789	469	-320	1.11	-28,918	-7.2	-30,702	-6.8	-43,000	-5.4
Trans-megabloc groupings																
Evangelicals	500	0.4	5,800	2.0	8,500	2.4	244	26	270	2.80	9,991	2.5	11,200	2.5	20,000	2.5
Pentecostals/Charismatics	0	0.0	500	0.2	18,500	5.3	531	109	640	3.02	21,394	5.4	24,900	5.5	56,100	7.1
Great Commission Christians	**5,400**	**4.5**	**29,000**	**10.0**	**45,700**	**13.0**	**1,311**	**456**	**1,767**	**3.32**	**53,800**	**13.5**	**63,372**	**14.0**	**135,150**	**17.0**
Muslims	0	0.0	1,300	0.5	14,000	4.0	402	30	432	2.73	16,100	4.0	18,324	4.1	32,000	4.0
Nonreligious	0	0.0	10,000	3.4	11,000	3.1	316	-35	281	2.30	12,200	3.1	13,807	3.1	25,000	3.1
Ethnoreligionists	113,500	94.6	19,313	6.6	9,000	2.6	258	-199	59	0.64	9,100	2.3	9,590	2.1	8,000	1.0
Atheists	0	0.0	2,800	1.0	6,000	1.7	172	36	208	3.02	7,000	1.8	8,078	1.8	16,000	2.0
Baha'is	0	0.0	700	0.2	1,400	0.4	40	52	92	5.17	2,000	0.5	2,317	0.5	4,800	0.6
Hindus	0	0.0	0	0.0	150	0.0	4	4	8	4.18	200	0.1	226	0.1	600	0.1
World A (unevangelized persons)	99,960	83.3	11,655	4.0	5,984	1.7	172	-126	46	0.74	6,391	1.6	6,342	1.4	8,745	1.1
World B (evangelized non-Christians)	13,540	11.3	22,837	7.7	35,566	10.1	1,020	14	1,034	2.68	40,694	10.1	46,338	10.2	77,655	9.8
World C (Christians)	6,500	5.4	256,887	88.3	310,450	88.2	8,875	112	8,987	2.58	352,400	88.3	400,320	88.4	708,600	89.1
Country's population	**120,000**	**100.0**	**291,380**	**100.0**	**352,000**	**100.0**	**10,067**	**0**	**10,067**	**2.55**	**399,486**	**100.0**	**453,000**	**100.0**	**795,000**	**100.0**

COLUMNS, ROWS.
For meanings and definitions, see Codebook (Part 3). Note that, by definition, total 'Christians' = professing + crypto-Christians, which also = affiliated + unaffiliated Christians, and also = Great Commission Christians + latent Christians. Percentages may not always total exactly, due to rounding.

CENSUSES.
The religion question has not been asked.

NOTES ON RELIGIONS
ATHEISTS. Party militants, mostly Fang.
BAHA'IS. Growth from nothing in 1964 to 5 local spiritual assemblies (4 on Fernando Poo) in 1973, then a plateau at 4 LSA BY 1996.
COUNTRY'S POPULATION. Since Independence in 1968 and the subsequent reign of full-scale terror, tens of thousands have been murdered and about 95,000 including Nigerians and other expatriates have fled as refugees to Cameroon, Gabon, Europe or their own countries. In 1978, a further 50,000 were reported murdered. Subsequent decades have been similar except for smaller totals.
ETHNORELIGIONISTS. Mostly among Fang sub-tribes (Okak, Ntumu, Bulu), with some Nigerians also.
INDEPENDENTS. In 8 groupings in 1995 (see Table 2).
MUSLIMS. Sunnis of the Malikite rite, mainly Hausa expatriate traders and laborers from Nigeria, with some Indo-Pakistani traders.

Great Commission Instrument Panel: status of Equatorial Guinea (for explanation see start of Part 4)

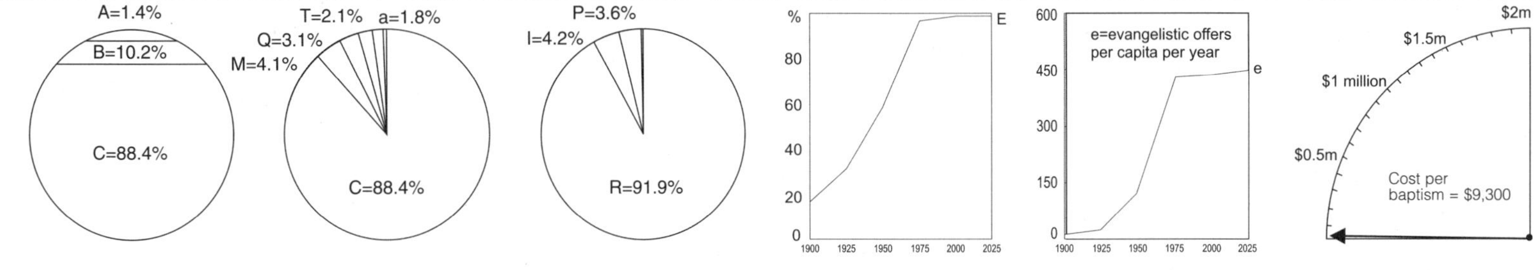

3 Worlds, AD 2000 — Religions, AD 2000 — Ecclesiastical blocs — Evangelization, 1900-2025 — Offers, 1900-2025 — Cost-effectiveness, AD 2000

Country status. Equatorial Guinea lies on the western coast of West Central Africa and consists of a mainland province and 5 islands of which Bioko and Pagalu are the largest. Once a Spanish colony, its recent history has been marked by a brutal dictatorship that has left scars on the political and economic condition of the people. The main exports are coffee, cocoa, and timber.

HUMAN LIFE AND LIBERTY

Human need and development. Equatorial Guinea is the classic example cited by African observers of a country where political independence turned into a nightmare. Under the 11-year rule of Macias Nguema Biyogo from 1968 to 1979, the country, relatively prosperous under the Spanish, was pillaged by his supporters and turned into a basketcase. After his overthrow, the economy had to be rebuilt with help from Spain and international aid organizations. Nevertheless, the annual per capita income remains below $400. The birth rate is a high 4.3%. There is virtually no manufacturing or mining, and the transportation infrastructure is very primitive. Of the 2,000 miles of roads only 12% is paved, and even they are impassable during the rainy season. Three out of 4 Equatorial Guineans are illiterate. There are only 100 doctors and 1,300 hospital beds for the entire country and there are no dentists. The life expectancy is 50 for males and 54 for females. There is no organized public welfare or social security system.

Human rights and freedoms. Although a benevolent ruler compared to his uncle Macias Biyogo whom he overthrew in 1979, President Obiang Nguema Mbasogo is a dictator who rules under a Constitution that he devised in 1991 giving him lifetime power and immunity. The Constitution also was a step backwards for individual liberties because it does not provide for protection against arbitrary arrest and torture. Obiang is head of the military and the sole effective

Country summary. **Worlds A, B, C by ethnolinguistic peoples, cities, and major civil divisions in Equatorial Guinea.**

World	PEOPLES Num	Pop 2000	C%	Christians	E%	U%	Unevangelized
A	2	9,506	0.09	9	48	52	4,980
B	1	3,169	37.99	1,204	68	32	1,014
C	20	439,986	89.43	393,486	100	0	469
Total	**23**	**452,661**	**87.20**	**394,699**	**99**	**1**	**6,463**

World	CITIES Num	Pop 2000	C%	Christians	E%	U%	Unevangelized
A	0	0	0.00	0	0	0	0
B	0	0	0.00	0	0	0	0
C	1	132,037	85.00	112,231	97	3	3,473
Total	**1**	**132,037**	**85.00**	**112,231**	**97**	**3**	**3,473**

World	CIVIL DIVISIONS Num	Pop 2000	C%	Christians	E%	U%	Unevangelized
A	0	0	0.00	0	0	0	0
B	0	0	0.00	0	0	0	0
C	7	452,662	87.19	394,698	99	1	6,463
Total	**7**	**452,662**	**87.19**	**394,698**	**99**	**1**	**6,463**

political party, the Democratic Party of Equatorial Guinea. But the actual source of his power is the Moroccan Guard, a presidential guard of some 600 Moroccan mercenaries, which, together with the security forces, commit most of the human rights abuses. Opposition leaders are routinely arrested and beaten up. Torture of detainees and prisoners is so elaborately contrived that it goes under various names, such as Ethiopian Torture or Chinese Water Torture, depending on the instruments used. Torture victims receive as many as 500 or 600 strokes with rubber truncheons or whips during the course of one night. The main prison is located in the presidential compound and prisoners are often beaten in the presence of the president or his advisers. The authorities make arrests without judicial order and deny detainees their constitutional rights of bail and legal counsel. Many detainees are held incommunicado. Civilians are detained in military camps and also sentenced to internal exile, or banishment to home villages. There is no separation between the executive and the judiciary; justices as well as the country's 30 lawyers are poorly trained and depend on the government for their survival. All opposition party members are under constant surveillance and have their phones as well as mail routinely monitored. The government has absolute control over the media, but no newspapers were published in the country for many years. Foreign newspapers and magazines are not available on sale. Even mild criticism of the president is deemed as a criminal offense. No public meetings may be held without government sanctions, which are generally denied. There are numerous restrictions on travel abroad as well as internal travel. Police extort payments for passage through traffic checkpoints on major roads. Ethnic discrimination is openly practiced against persons who are not members of the Fang group to which the president belongs. While all ethnic groups are represented in the cabinet, the president and a small group of his relatives dominate public life.

Human environment. Lack of development, ironically, is a major factor in preserving the natural forests and environment of Equatorial Guinea. However, poor agricultural practices have led to soil degradation.

NON-CHRISTIAN RELIGIONS

Traditional religions are followed by under 5% of the population, mostly among the interior sub-tribes of the Fang: Okak, Ntumu and Bulu. The Fang word for God is Nzame, while the ancestral spirits are known as Bekon and the medicine man as uganga or ngang. The principal secret society is Bwiti which entered from neighboring Gabon after 1927. It is dedicated to the remembrance of the great Fang ancestors and includes as initiates both men and women. A certain part of this society has been sufficiently christianized to be regarded as an indigenous church (Iglesia de los Banzie).

Atheism has spread as a result of the regime's militantly atheistic policies since 1968.

Islam has not taken root in Equatorial Guinea due largely to Catholicism's strong influence on society. Muslims were less than 1% of the population in 1970; nevertheless, they had grown by 1995 to 4%.

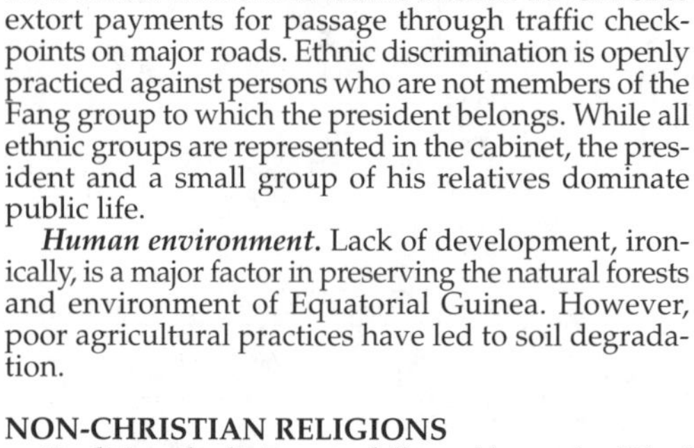

Numerous postage stamps have had Christian themes. *Left.* Baptism of an African convert (1955). *Right.* The Risen Christ by the Lakeside, by K. Witz (1973).

CHRISTIANITY

CATHOLIC CHURCH. Equatorial Guinea has had a long association with Catholicism dating from the 15th century, and it existed for lengthy periods under Portuguese, Spanish, and French colonial administrations prior to Independence in 1968. A prefecture was erected at Fernando Poo in 1855 which was elevated to a vicariate in 1904. In 1965 a second vicariate was formed for work in Río Muni. At present the diocese of Bata is responsible for the mainland and the diocese of Malabo (Santa Isabel) for the islands. Both dioceses are under the supervision of Spanish CMF priests.

Equatorial Guinea has a higher proportion of baptized Catholics (86%) than any other country of continental Africa. Because of the political situation, most Spanish priests were expelled a few months prior to Independence. The Spanish bishop of Malabo was expelled in 1970, and the Guinean bishop of Bata has been unable to return from Rome due to illness. Both bishops resigned their posts in 1974. In their place the Holy See appointed 2 Guinean apostolic administrators, although the one assigned to Bata and his secretary are now under house arrest. In 1973 the government expelled numerous Spanish sisters, Oblates of Mary Immaculate, who had refused to enroll their pupils in the notorious 'Forward with Macias' Youth Movement. Many Guinean priests have been imprisoned and only about 20 priests were actively in service in 1973. Nevertheless, the country's first major seminary was opened in October 1973 at Niefang, in the diocese of Bata.

Throughout the 1980s and 1990s the church maintained a witness to Christ, without however provoking a massive crackdown by the regimes in power.

The Holy See has diplomatic relations with Equatorial Guinea and in AD 2000 is represented to government and the Catholic hierarchy by a pronuncio residing in Yaoundé.

PROTESTANT CHURCHES. Baptist missionaries from the West Indies arrived in Fernando Poo as early as 1841 but were expelled by the Spanish authorities in 1858. In 1870 an appeal from the local Protestant community via a ship's captain was received favorably by the Primitive Methodist Church in England, and missionaries were sent to the island. Methodism is still the major Protestant body on Fernando Poo. The Evangelical Church, which is autonomous but receives support from the United Presbyterian Church in the USA and since 1970 the Worldwide Evangelization Crusade (WEC) of UK, is the principal denomination in Río Muni. Beginning in 1850 on the island of Corisco, the Presbyterian mission reached the mainland in 1865. The first African pastor was ordained in 1870, and within 10 years an African missionary had been sent to open work at Batanga in Cameroon. Although evangelistic activity was impeded by the Spanish government, progress has been made. The church's strongest congregations today are found inland on the borders with Cameroon and Gabon. The WEC entered Río Muni in 1933, during a period of religious freedom, and has had some success among the Okak people. In 1970 it merged its work with that of the Presbyterians to form the Evangelical Church.

INDIGENOUS CHURCHES. The Bwiti movement, also called the Church of the Initiates (Iglesia de los Banzie), originated among the Fang in Gabon at the turn of the century and spread from there into Equatorial Guinea. Highly syncretistic in its early years, Bwiti has become progressively more Christian with increasing emphasis on Jesus as divine Saviour. A more orthodox denomination is the Assembly of Brethren (Asamblea de los Hermanos) which split from the Kombe Presbyterians in 1937.

OTHER CHURCHES. The most recent group to establish itself in the nation is the Free Protestant Episcopal Church, which is a Catholic (non-Roman) body from the UK and USA under African leadership and based in Liberia and Nigeria. In Equatorial Guinea it is composed mostly of expatriate English-speaking Africans from Nigeria and Sierra Leone.

Indigenous missions. There has been virtually no missionary sending from Equatorial Guinea with the possible exception of a number of priests working among Guinean refugees in Spain since the 1970s.

CHURCH AND STATE

Portugal ceded Fernando Poo to Spain in 1778, but Río Muni did not become a Spanish territory until after the Berlin conference of 1885. Except for a brief period following the founding of the Spanish Republic (1932-36), Protestant activity under Spanish rule was severely restricted. Baptists had been expelled in 1858 and Methodists were only allowed to remain in 1870 through the intervention of the British consul. In Río Muni, the Catholic Church was declared the 'only' and 'official' church, and Presbyterians were not recognized until 1906. Protestant missionaries were withdrawn between 1924 and 1932 due to government opposition. The Spanish constitution of 1948 stated that 'No one will be molested because of his religious belief'; but the 1853 concordat with the Holy See, which identified Catholicism as the state religion and provided for its legal protection from 'competing' faiths, seemed to take precedence. All Protestant chapels were closed in 1952, but those established prior to Franco's assumption of power in 1939 were later allowed to re-open. The close relationship between the Catholic Church and the Spanish state also had its influence on the educational system, instruction being founded on the 'principles of dogma and Catholic morals'. Protestant schools were not permitted during the period of Spanish rule.

With the granting of internal self-government in 1963 and full independence in 1968, numerous difficulties arose between the government and Catholic clergy. The constitution of 1968 provided for the full exercise of religious liberty, and the constitution of 1973 prohibits, in Article 24, all discrimination based on race, ethnic origin, religion, sex or social condition. Article 35 stipulates: 'The exercise of any religion is free provided that it respects the law and public order. It is illegal and punishable to place faith and religious belief in opposition to the principles and purpose of the state'.

However, since its accession to power at Independence, the regime of president Macias Nguema subjected the country to despotic rule and an unprecedented reign of terror. The constitutions of 1968 and 1973 were completely ignored, and anti-Christian propaganda was openly encouraged and promoted by the regime, whose de facto philosophy became one of militant atheism. At Malabo, Protestant buildings were confiscated; one Catholic church building was converted into an arms depot and the Catholic cathedral of Bata closed. By 1975, almost all foreign missionaries had been expelled, and local clergy suffered increasing pressures, including imprisonment and torture. Thousands of Guineans in all walks of life were victims of political assassination. In June 1974, 150 prisoners were killed in Bata prison, the official explanation being that they had formed a religious group called Christ Liberation Crusade but committed collective suicide when discovered. Guineans studying abroad were unable to return, and church leaders were refused permission to leave the country. In the attempt to suppress political intrigue all meetings of more than 10 persons were banned, which limited the activity of the church to personal contacts and officially recognized worship services. Group activity was no longer possible, and religious education was also prohibited. In 1974 a presidential decree was announced requiring priests and pastors to read at each worship service a message of praise to president Macias, as follows: 'Never without Macias, all for Macias. Down with colonialism and those who are ambitious'.

Harsher measures began in 1975. In July, the 3 seminaries were closed. In October, the pastoral vicar and acting bishop of Bata was executed with 22 others after torture. New anti-religious laws in February 1976 prohibited religious meetings, funerals, giving money to churches, baptism without government supervision, and the giving of Christian names to children by parents.

In 1978 anti-church measures instigated by the president included live burials in jails, torture, a mock Way of the Cross in Bata jail, and at least 2 public crucifixions of political prisoners.

In 1979, Macias was overthrown and executed. In the 1980s and 1990s, regrettably, similar dictatorship including by Macias relatives continued the oppression of the country.

BROADCASTING AND MEDIA

One out of 4 people own a radio, so broadcasting is an effective way of reaching the population. Equatorial Guinea is represented in UNDA.

The Spanish version of CBN's *700 Club* can be seen daily in the evenings throughout the country. Mission agencies have shown the 'Jesus' Film to 4,400 (1%).

INTERDENOMINATIONAL ORGANIZATIONS

There is no national council of churches. From 1943-70 the Evangelical Church was a member of the Federation of Evangelical Churches of Cameroon and Equatorial Africa based at YaoundÈ, Cameroon. It is now a member of the All Africa Council of Churches.

FUTURE TRENDS AND PROSPECTS

Church membership is expected to climb gradually over the 35 years from 1990-2025 from 87.0% to 88.1%. Muslims and the nonreligious together will likely account for 7% of the population by AD 2025.

Christianity could lose adherents to secular influences throughout the 21st century. By AD 2050, nonreligious and atheists could rise to over 7% of the population with Christians declining to less than 85% in the same period.

BIBLIOGRAPHY

Actuación de los misioneros españoles en la cuestión del Muny. M. de Zarco. Madrid: Instituto de Estudios Africanos, 1950. 57p.

Bwiti: an ethnography of the religious imagination in Africa. J. W. Fernandez. Princeton, NJ: Princeton University Press, 1982. 731p. (Religion of the Fang).

'Cameroons and Fernando Po.' J. J. Fuller. Unpublished manuscript, Baptist Missionary Society, London, 1887. 22p. (History of Baptists in Cameroon and Fernando Po).

Cien años de evangelización en Guinea Ecuatorial (1883–1983). Misioneros Claretianos. Barcelona: Editorial Claret, [1983]. 59p.

Corisco days: the first thirty years of the West African Mission. R. H. Nassau. Philadelphia: Allen, Lane and Scott, 1910.

'Drugs and mysticism: the Bwiti of the Fang,' J. Binet, *Diogènes* (Paris), 86 (Summer 1974), 31–54.

Du Mvett: essai sur la dynastie Ekang Nna. D. A. Ndoutombe. Paris: L'Harmattan, 1986. 184p. (Deals with religion of the Fang).

'El Mbueti y sus doctrinas,' G. de Pablo, *Cuadernos de estudios africanos* (Madrid), 2 (1946), 69–92.

Equatorial Guinea. R. Fegley. *World bibliographical series*, vol. 136. Oxford, UK: CLIO Press, 1991. 180p. (See especially 'Religion,' p.42–6).

Equatorial Guinea, Macias country: the forgotten refugees. R. A. Klintenberg. Geneva: International University Exchange Fund, 1978. 87p.

Fetishism in West Africa: forty years' observations of native customs and superstitions. R. H. Nassau. 1904; reprint, New York: Negro Universities Press, 1969. 389p.

La Iglesia en la Guinea Ecuatorial. T. L. Pujadas. Madrid: Iris de Paz, 1968. 528p. (Catholic Church).

La secta del Bwiti en la Guinea Española. A. de V. Vilaldach. Madrid: Instituto de Estudios Africanos, 1958. 63p.

Misiones y misioneros en la Guinea Española. C. Fernàndez. Madrid: Editorial Co. SA, 1962. 817p.

'Persécutions religieuses en Guinée Equatoriale,' *Parole et Sociéte*, 87, 3 (1979), 184–89.

'Terror grips Equatorial Guinea,' *One world* (Geneva), 1 (November, 1974), 7–9.

The beginnings of Christian evangelism and African responses: American Presbyterians in Equatorial Guinea and Gabon: papers presented at the 19th Annual Meeting of the African Studies Association (Boston), 3–6 Nov. 1976. P. Campbell. *Paper no. 15.* 27p.

The Gabon and Corisco missions. R. H. Nassau. New York: Presbyterian Board of Foreign Missions, 1873.

Country Table 2. **Organized churches and denominations in Equatorial Guinea.**

Official name (bold type = church with over 10% of all affiliated) 1	*Begun* 2	*Type* 3	*Counc* 4	*Congs* 5	*Adults* 6	*Affiliated 1970* 7	*Affiliated 1995* 8	*G%* 9	*Names, notes, and other statistics* (see Codebook, Part 3) 10
Asamblea de los Hermanos	1937	I-EBr	.....	2	150	300	455	1.68	*Assembly of Brethren.* Schism ex Kombe Presbyterians. M=Swiss Brethren(closed).
Asambleas de Jéhova	1985	P-Pe2	.....	16	2,165	–	2,740	10.00	*Assemblies of God.* M=AoG. 9f.
Iglesia Vida Profunda	c1985	I-3cA	x....	2	35	–	58	10.00	*Deeper Life Bible Ch.* Mainly expatriates of Nigerian origin. M=DLBC(Lagos, Nigeria).
Iglesia Adventista del Séptimo Día	1961	P-Adv	x....	4	155	300	258	-0.60	*SDA. Seventh-day Adventists, EG Mission District.* On Fernando Poo. 1nx,2mw,30Y.
Iglesia Bautista	1981	P-Bap	C	5	78	–	210	7.14	*Baptist Convention.* M=SBC.
Iglesia Betania	1990	I-3cA	.....	1	50	–	100	20.00	*Bethany Church.*
Igl Católica en la Guinea Ecuatorial:	1484	R-Lat	P.S.R	56	230,900	230,712	344,500	1.62	*Catholic Ch in EG.* M=CMF. C=2+0+2. 44n 41x 86m 206w 8769Yy
M Malabo (Santa Isabel)	1904	R-Lat	Ps	29	51,600	58,512	77,000	1.10	Fernando Poo and Annóbon. (1970) 2,300 Whites. 7n 12x 23m 71w 2222Yy
D Bata (Rio Muni)	1965	R-Lat	Ps	16	90,600	172,200	135,241	-0.96	Rio Muni, Corisco, Elobeys. 90% Fang. 2,700 Whites. 18n 20x 51m 79w 5139Yy
D Ebebiyin	1982	R-Lat	Pcmf	11	102,000	–	152,170	7.69	M=CMF. 19n 9x 12m 56w 1408Yy
Doubly-counted Catholics		R-Lat		0	-13,300	–	-19,911		*Catholics counted in older diocese and also in a newly-formed diocese.*
Iglesia de los Banzie (Bwiti)	c1910	I-mar	.....	50	1,000	2,700	2,700	0.00	*Ch of the Initiates.* Mbueti. Religion d'Eboga (a drug). Fang syncretistic body.
Iglesia del Evangelizacion Mundial	1986	I-3cA	.....	4	110	–	300	11.11	*World Evangelization Church.*
Iglesia Evangélica Cruzada	1937	P-Non	C	20	440	600	1,100	2.45	*Gospel Crusade Church.* M=WEC.
Iglesia Evangélica en la Guinea E	1850	P-Ref	RuA.C	130	4,000	12,000	10,000	-0.73	*Ev Ch in EG.* M=UPUSA,WEC(UK). A=1960. 90% Fang, 6% Kombe. 5n,2f,60Y,150y.
Iglesia Evangelica Episcopal Libre	1968	I-ARo	xv...	210	1,000	2,575	3,000	0.61	*Free Protestant Episcopal Ch*, D West Africa. Nigerians. 4n,6x,2p,2r,W=71%,500Y,275y.
Iglesia Metodista	1870	P-Met	Vwa..	4	300	2,000	800	-3.60	1870, Primitive Methodists (UK) on Fernando Poo. Circuit of Methodist Ch, Nigeria.
Iglesia Nueva Apostólica	c1980	I-3aX	x....	6	3,700	–	6,497	6.67	*NAK. New Apostolic Church.* World HQ Dortmund (Germany).
Iglesias radiofónicas solitarias	c1968	I-3rA	.....	70	1,000	300	2,000	7.88	Isolated radio believers; scattered. R=250 (ELWA, RVOG, Radio Vatican, et alia).
Testigos de Jehová	c1945	m-Jeh	x....	4	193	500	1,000	2.81	*Jehovah's Witnesses.* First witnessing reported 1949 Fernando Poo, 1964 Rio Muni. 89Y.
Other Protestant churches	c1980	P-	.....	20	300	–	600	6.67	About 10 additional bodies.
Doubly-affiliated		2-aff			-18,900	0	-28,918		Evangelicals who are also baptized Roman Catholics.
Totals				**604**	**226,676**	**251,987**	**347,400**		

Churches, members, growth, 1900-2025	*Congs*	*Adults*	*Affiliated*	*G%*	*Total denominations*	*6 Megablocs:* O	R	A	P	I	m
Total churches, members, and denominations (mid-1900)	20	4,200	6,500	5.36	3	0	1	0	2	0	0
Total churches, members, and denominations (mid-1970)	456	161,943	251,987	5.36	10	0	1	0	4	4	1
Total churches, members, and denominations (mid-1990)	540	199,000	305,050	0.96	15	0	1	0	6	7	1
Total churches, members, and denominations (mid-1995)	604	226,676	347,400	2.63	17	0	1	0	7	8	1
Total churches, members, and denominations (mid-2000)	620	258,000	394,698	2.59	16	0	1	0	6	8	1
Total churches, members, and denominations (mid-2025)	950	457,000	700,000	2.32	59	0	1	0	15	40	3

NOTES ON TABLE ABOVE

NATIONAL COUNCILS (Column 4, 5th letter).

C = Council of Evangelical Churches in Equatorial Guinea (CIEGE, 1996; formerly IRGE).

R = Conferencia Episcopal de Guinea Ecuatorial (CEGE, Episcopal Conference of Equatorial Guinea).

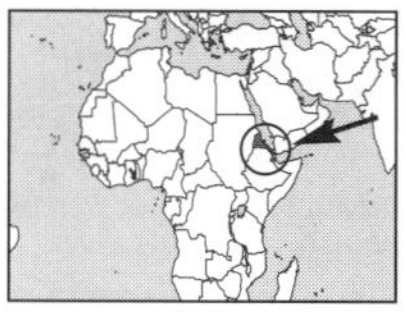

ERITREA

SECULAR DATA, AD 2000

STATE

Official name: The State of Eritrea.
Short name: Eritrea. **Adjective of nationality:** Eritrean.
Flag: Green and blue stripes bisected by red triangle on left with coat of arms in center.
Area: 117,400 sq. km. (45,300 sq. mi.).
Government: Transitional regime with one interim legislative body, since 1993 (3rd century empire, absolute monarchy, 1936-41 Italian rule, 1966-75 constitutional monarchy, 1975 Socialist military junta).
Legislature: Constituent Assembly, 150 members.
Official language: Arabic, Tigrinya.
Monetary unit: Nafka = 100 cents. **US$1=** Br 7.28.
Chief cities: ASMERA (Asmara) 440,272; Assab (Aseb) 53,102.
Political divisions: 6 provinces.
Armed forces: 46,000.

DEMOGRAPHY

Population: 3,850,000.
Population density: 32.8/sq. km. (85.0/sq. mi.).
Under 15 years: 1,699,000.
Growth rate p.a.: 2.49% (births 38.17, deaths 13.29).
Mortality: Infant, per 1,000: 81.9; **Maternal per 100,000:** 1,400.0.
Life expectancy: 52 (male 51, female 53).
Household size: 4.0. **Floor area per person, sq.m:** 9.0.
Major languages: Tigray, Tigre, Afar, Bilin, Arabic.
Urban dwellers: 18.74%. **Urban growth rate p.a.:** 4.4%.
Labor force: 30%.

ETHNOLINGUISTIC PEOPLES

51.8% Tigrai; 17.9% Tigre (Khasa); 8.1% Danakil (Afar, Adali); 4.3% Saho (Sao, Minifere, Irob); 4.1% Kunama (Cunama, Diila).

ECONOMY

National income p.a. per person: US$570; **per family:** US$2,280.

EDUCATION

Adult literacy: 20% (male 30%, female 10%). **Schools:** 581.
Universities: 1. **School enrolment:** female/male: 28%/37%.

HEALTH

Access to health services: 30%. **Access to safe water:** 25%.
Hospitals: 7 (9 beds per 10,000). **Doctors:** 68.
Blind: 3,200. **Deaf:** 228,500. **Murder rate:** 20.
Lepers: 25,000. **Underweight prevalence under 5:** 41%.

LITERATURE

New book titles p.a.: 130 (35 p.a. per million). **Periodicals:** 0.
Newspapers: 1 daily.

COMMUNICATION (per 1,000 people)
Phones: 4 (8% mobile). **Radios:** 80. **TV sets:** 6.
Daily newspaper circulation: 5. **Computers:** 25.

REFUGEES
Citizen refugees in other countries: 342,500.

HUMAN LIFE AND LIBERTY (optimum condition=100.0%)
HDI: 26.9. **HSI:** 45.0. **HFI:** 30.0. **EFL:** 20.0.

Country Table 1. Religious adherents in Eritrea, AD 1900-2025.

Year	1900		1970		mid-1990		Annual change, 1990-2000				mid-1995		mid-2000		mid-2025	
Name	Adherents	%	Adherents	%	Adherents	%	Natural	Conversion	Total	Rate	Adherents	%	Adherents	%	Adherents	%
Christians	**70,000**	**15.9**	**950,000**	**51.9**	**1,460,000**	**50.5**	**48,605**	**-253**	**48,352**	**2.90**	**1,610,000**	**50.5**	**1,943,516**	**50.5**	**3,400,000**	**50.9**
PROFESSION																
professing Christians	**70,000**	**15.9**	**950,000**	**51.9**	**1,460,000**	**50.5**	**48,605**	**-253**	**48,352**	**2.90**	**1,610,000**	**50.5**	**1,943,516**	**50.5**	**3,400,000**	**50.9**
AFFILIATION																
unaffiliated Christians	5,000	1.1	13,964	0.8	10,300	0.4	343	-457	-114	-1.17	9,538	0.3	9,158	0.2	13,000	0.2
affiliated Christians	**65,000**	**14.8**	**936,036**	**51.1**	**1,449,700**	**50.2**	**48,262**	**204**	**48,466**	**2.93**	**1,600,462**	**50.2**	**1,934,358**	**50.2**	**3,387,000**	**50.7**
Orthodox	44,900	10.2	832,200	45.5	1,328,000	46.0	44,175	481	44,656	2.94	1,470,100	46.1	1,774,558	46.1	3,075,000	46.0
Roman Catholics	20,000	4.6	91,000	5.0	100,000	3.5	3,326	-326	3,000	2.66	105,962	3.3	130,000	3.4	250,000	3.7
Protestants	100	0.0	9,736	0.5	16,000	0.6	532	68	600	3.24	17,900	0.6	22,000	0.6	46,000	0.7
Independents	0	0.0	3,100	0.2	5,700	0.2	190	20	210	3.19	6,500	0.2	7,800	0.2	16,000	0.2
Trans-megabloc groupings																
Evangelicals	100	0.0	17,900	1.0	10,370	0.4	345	-12	333	2.82	11,300	0.4	13,700	0.4	26,000	0.4
Pentecostals/Charismatics	0	0.0	200	0.0	24,900	0.9	828	462	1,290	4.26	29,978	0.9	37,800	1.0	93,000	1.4
Great Commission Christians	**44,000**	**10.0**	**146,480**	**8.0**	**217,000**	**7.5**	**7,218**	**-286**	**6,932**	**2.81**	**238,000**	**7.5**	**286,321**	**7.4**	**535,000**	**8.0**
Muslims	220,000	50.0	840,000	45.9	1,304,300	45.2	43,386	-1,647	41,739	2.82	1,435,430	45.0	1,721,691	44.7	2,955,300	44.2
Nonreligious	0	0.0	0	0.0	105,000	3.6	3,493	1,921	5,414	4.25	120,000	3.8	159,139	4.1	300,000	4.5
Ethnoreligionists	150,000	34.1	40,000	2.2	18,000	0.6	599	-16	583	2.84	19,700	0.6	23,827	0.6	22,000	0.3
Baha'is	0	0.0	500	0.0	900	0.0	30	0	30	2.90	1,000	0.0	1,198	0.0	2,000	0.0
Hindus	0	0.0	500	0.0	600	0.0	20	-3	17	2.46	670	0.0	765	0.0	1,200	0.0
Atheists	0	0.0	0	0.0	200	0.0	7	-2	5	2.34	200	0.0	252	0.0	500	0.0
World A (unevangelized persons)	286,000	65.0	585,888	32.0	858,033	29.7	28,541	-12,586	15,955	1.72	898,672	28.2	1,016,400	26.4	1,503,225	22.5
World B (evangelized non-Christians)	84,000	19.1	295,012	16.1	570,967	19.8	18,994	12,839	31,833	4.54	678,108	21.3	890,084	23.1	1,777,775	26.6
World C (Christians)	70,000	15.9	950,000	51.9	1,460,000	50.5	48,605	-253	48,352	2.90	1,610,000	50.5	1,943,516	50.5	3,400,000	50.9
Country's population	**440,000**	**100.0**	**1,830,900**	**100.0**	**2,889,000**	**100.0**	**96,140**	**0**	**96,140**	**2.91**	**3,186,781**	**100.0**	**3,850,000**	**100.0**	**6,681,000**	**100.0**

COLUMNS, ROWS.
For meanings and definitions, see Codebook (Part 3). Note that, by definition, total 'Christians' = professing + crypto-Christians, which also = affiliated + unaffiliated Christians, and also = Great Commission Christians + latent Christians. Percentages may not always total exactly, due to rounding.

NOTES ON RELIGIONS
BAHA'IS. Organized under 5 local spiritual assemblies (1996).
ETHNORELIGIONISTS. Only among the Nara and the Saho.

Great Commission Instrument Panel: status of Eritrea (for explanation see start of Part 4)

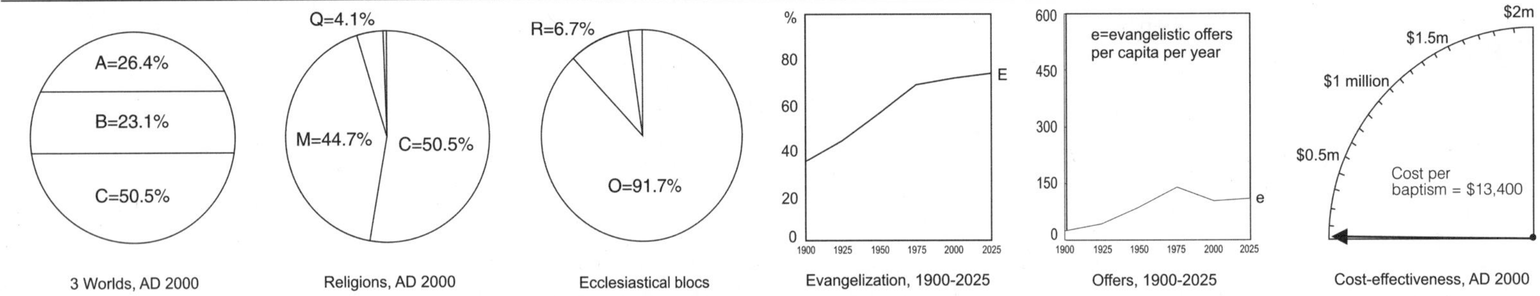

Country status. Eritrea, until 1993 a northern province of Ethiopia, is an independent state on the Red Sea. Though most of the economy is agricultural, the country has reserves of iron, potassium, copper, and gold.

HUMAN LIFE AND LIBERTY

Human rights and freedoms. Eritrea is one of the world's youngest republics, having achieved independence on 24 May 1993 after a long and bloody war against Ethiopian forces. The government is still dominated by a single party led by the leaders of the Eritrean People's Liberation Front. Human rights are generally respected and the first referendum held in April 1993 was free and fair. Later during the year the regime released many of the Ethiopian nationals and sympathizers detained during the civil war. The government is carefully balanced to reflect the even division of the population between Christians and Muslims. Muslim fundamentalists as well as communists associated with the former Mengistu regime are subject to detention. There are no official restrictions on free speech, but a daily press does not exist in the country. Freedom of religion is extended to all religious groups, including Jehovah's Witnesses who were banned under the Mengistu regime. There are plans to hold multiparty elections within 4 years. There is one local human rights organization, the Regional Committee for Human Rights Development.

NON-CHRISTIAN RELIGIONS

Islam is at present 44.7% of the population.

Baha'i and ***Hinduism*** have a small number of adherents each.

Tribal religion is still strong with many adherents.

CHRISTIANITY

ORTHODOX CHURCH. The diocese of Eritrea has long been a strong part of the Ethiopian Orthodox Church, with nearly a million members. It played a significant role in the struggle for independence.

Catholic Church of Eritrea. School of Evangelization under way in Asmara.

CATHOLIC CHURCH. As the second largest church in Eritrea, this body's history goes back to the 19th century. Today it has 2 jurisdictions, an Ethiopian-rite diocese and a Latin-rite vicariate.

The Holy See has no diplomatic relations with Eritrea in AD 2000.

PROTESTANT CHURCHES. There are some 27 organized Protestant denominations. All have a history of involvement or areas of abstention in the independence struggle. However there is little resentment of the past and a widespread determination to work only for the present and future.

Indigenous missions. The Ethiopian Orthodox Church has been sending a limited number of missionaries outside of Eritrea (primarily to surrounding countries) for many centuries. Recently, Protestant and Catholic groups have also begun sending missionaries.

CHURCH AND STATE

With its determination to avoid strife between religions, Islam and Christianity in particular, the government has harnessed the goodwill and creative energies of both communities.

BROADCASTING AND MEDIA

Shortwave programs in Somali from FEBC (Seychelles) and and in Tigrinya from TWR (South Africa) can be received. The Lutheran World Federation has a studio that produces Tigrinya-language programs. IBRA-produced programs can be heard on local radio stations.

Board of newly established Bible Society in Eritrea.

INTERDENOMINATIONAL ORGANIZATIONS

The most energetic and future-looking cooperative body is the Bible Society of Eritrea, whose scripture ministry demonstrates both reconciliation for the past and enthusiasm for the future.

FUTURE TRENDS AND PROSPECTS

Christians are expected to maintain about 51% of the population through 2025. Muslims could decline slightly in the same period to 44.2%.

Country summary. **Worlds A, B, C by ethnolinguistic peoples, cities, and major civil divisions in Eritrea.**																					
	PEOPLES							*CITIES*							*CIVIL DIVISIONS*						
World	*Num*	*Pop 2000*	*C%*	*Christians*	*E%*	*U%*	*Unevangelized*	*Num*	*Pop 2000*	*C%*	*Christians*	*E%*	*U%*	*Unevangelized*	*Num*	*Pop 2000*	*C%*	*Christians*	*E%*	*U%*	*Unevangelized*
A	7	801,622	1.59	12,754	29	71	565,152	0	0	0.00	0	0	0	0	0	0	0.00	0	0	0	0
B	5	981,450	6.19	60,715	54	46	450,427	2	493,374	46.00	226,965	73	27	131,569	6	3,850,388	50.24	1,934,358	74	26	1,017,551
C	4	2,067,316	90.01	1,860,889	100	0	1,972	0	0	0.00	0	0	0	0	0	0	0.00	0	0	0	0
Total	**16**	**3,850,388**	**50.24**	**1,934,358**	**74**	**26**	**1,017,551**	**2**	**493,374**	**46.00**	**226,965**	**73**	**27**	**131,569**	**6**	**3,850,388**	**50.24**	**1,934,358**	**74**	**26**	**1,017,551**

Throughout the next five decades, Christians and Muslims are likely to share Eritrea's population evenly at about 50% each. However, if Christians become more evangelistic, Christianity may have a slight edge resulting in a 60/40 ratio over Islam in the future.

BIBLIOGRAPHY

Annual report. Evangelical Church of Eritrea. Asmara: LWF/WS-Eritrea: Evangelical Church of Eritrea, 1992. (Annual.).

'Complicated peace,' C. F. Nielsen, *One World*, 194 (April 1994), 4–5.

Eritrea & neighbors in the 'New world order': geopolitics, democracy, and 'Islamic fundamentalism'. T. Medhanie. *Bremer Afrika-Studien*, Bd. 15. Münster: LIT, [1994]. 132p.

The Christian Church and missions in Ethiopia (including Eritrea and the Somalilands). J. S. Trimingham. London: World Dominion Press, 1950. 74p.

'The influence of Islam on the Afar.' K. Shehim. Ph.D. dissertation, University of Washington, Seattle, WA, 1982. 230p.

The roots of the Eritrean disagreements and how to solve them. O. S. Sabbe. , [1978]. 62p.

'They not only survive, but build something new,' A. Goytom, *Engage/Social Action*, 13, 3 (March 1985), 2–6.

Usanze islamiche hanafite di Massaua e dintorni. I. Capomazza. Macerata [Italy]: Giorgetti, 1910. 86p.

'Women soldier artists,' B. LaDuke, *Witness*, 78 (June 1995), 28–29.

Country Table 2. **Organized churches and denominations in Eritrea.**

Official name (bold type = church with over 10% of all affiliated) 1	*Begun* 2	*Type* 3	*Counc* 4	*Congs* 5	*Adults* 6	*Affiliated 1970* 7	*Affiliated 1995* 8	*G%* 9	*Names, notes, and other statistics* (see Codebook, Part 3) 10
Catholic Church in Eritrea:		R-LEr	O.SES	145	62,500	91,000	105,962	0.05	Recovered and reorganized after civil war. 69n 221x 371m 339w 2467Yy
D Asmara (Asmara)	1930	R-Eth	Os	118	43,600	50,000	73,962	1.58	*Katholikawi Membre Pepesenna.* Tigrai, Mensa. 69n 181x 291m 293w 2153Yy
VA Asmara of the Latins	1894	R-Lat	Oofmc	27	18,900	41,000	32,000	-0.99	80% Kunama, 20% Italians, Europeans. M=OFMCap. 0n 40x 80m 46w 314Yy
Christian Brethren	1952	P-CBr	x....	2	50	30	100	4.93	*Open Brethren.* M=CMML(UK). Among Danakil Muslims.
Evangelical Church Mekane Yesus	c1930	P-Lut	LWA.K	10	2,000	600	3,000	6.65	*ECMY. Dwelling of Jesus.* Amharas.
Evangelical Church of Eritrea	1866	P-Lut	L....	100	4,000	7,138	12,000	2.10	*Wangelawit Bete Kristian Ertra.* M=EFS. 82% Tigrinya, 12% Mensa. 7n,8x,5h,13Y,148y.
Faith Church of Christ	1950	I-Hol	xF...	40	2,800	3,000	5,000	2.06	Western Eritrea. M=Evangelistic Faith Missions (USA). 19n,10x,5m,8f,1s,73Y,484z.
Full Gospel Church of Eritrea	1961	I-3fA	.....	20	750	100	1,500	11.44	M=FFFM (Finland). Begun via Ethiopian evangelists.
Greek Orth P Alexandria (D Aksum)	c1920	O-Ara	Cw...	1	50	500	100	-6.23	Greeks and Arabs in church under Patriarchate of Alexandria.
Lutheran Church of Eritrea	1911	P-Lut	l....	25	600	1,168	1,300	0.43	1911 split from EFS. M=SLM(BVM, Bible True Friends) (Sweden). HQ Asmara. 14f,li.
Middle East General Mission	c1957	P-Non	.G...	5	100	100	300	4.49	Formerly Egypt General Mission. Aids EC of Eritrea; Kunama, Barea. 50m,49f,1H,1h,7i.
Orthodox Church of Eritrea	1955	O-Eth	Na	800	500,000	831,700	1,470,000	2.30	Related to Ethiopian OC. 9 Dioceses and bps. 9% urban. Tigre and others.
Orthodox Presbyterian Church	1944	P-Ref	Jt...	10	100	100	200	2.81	M=OPC(USA). HQ Mekele (Tigre). 12f,1H.
Other Protestant churches		P-	.....	20	500	600	1,000	0.05	Total 20, including SDA,WLEC,FGC,RSMTI.
Totals				**1,178**	**573,450**	**936,036**	**1,600,462**		

Churches, members, growth, 1900-2025	*Congs*	*Adults*	*Affiliated*	*G%*	*Total denominations*	*6 Megablocs:* O	R	A	P	I	m
Total churches, members, and denominations (mid-1900)	50	38,200	65,000	3.88	2	0	1	0	1	0	0
Total churches, members, and denominations (mid-1970)	943	550,196	936,036	3.88	20	2	1	0	15	2	0
Total churches, members, and denominations (mid-1990)	1,000	519,000	1,449,700	2.21	31	2	1	0	26	2	0
Total churches, members, and denominations (mid-1995)	1,178	573,450	1,600,462	2.00	31	2	1	0	26	2	0
Total churches, members, and denominations (mid-2000)	1,200	693,000	1,934,358	3.86	32	2	1	0	27	2	0
Total churches, members, and denominations (mid-2025)	2,100	1,214,000	3,387,000	2.27	66	5	1	0	40	20	0

NOTES ON TABLE ABOVE
NATIONAL COUNCILS (Column 4, 5th letter).
E = Evangelical Fellowship of Eritrea (EFE).

ESTONIA

SECULAR DATA, AD 2000

STATE
Official name: Eesti Vabariik (The Republic of Estonia).
Short name: Estonia. **Adjective of nationality:** Estonian.
Flag: Blue, navy, and white stripes.
Area: 45,227 sq. km. (17,462 sq. mi.).
Government: Unitary multiparty republic with a single legislative body, since 1991 (1721 Russian empire, 1939 Soviet rule).
Legislature: Riigikogu, 101 members.
Official language: Estonian.
Monetary unit: 1 kroon (EEK) = 100 sents. **US$1=** EEK 13.36.
Chief cities: TALLINN (Revel) 457,950; Tartu (Dorpat) 109,660; Narva 78,940; Kohtla-Jarve 71,046; Parnu 51,549.
Political divisions: 15 provinces.
Armed forces: 3,500.

DEMOGRAPHY
Population: 1,396,000.
Population density: 30.8/sq. km. (79.9/sq. mi.).
Under 15 years: 244,000.
Growth rate p.a.: -1.02% (births 9.12, deaths 13.46).
Mortality: Infant, per 1,000: 14.5; **Maternal per 100,000:** 41.0.
Life expectancy: 70 (male 65, female 76).
Household size: 3.1. **Floor area per person, sq.m:** 21.3.
Major languages: Estonian, Russian, Finnish, Ukrainian.
Urban dwellers: 74.30%. **Urban growth rate p.a.:** -0.3%.
Labor force: 55%.

ETHNOLINGUISTIC PEOPLES
46.9% Northern Estonian; 28.9% Russian; 7.3% Southern Estonian; 6.3% Finnish (Finn); 3.6% Estonian (Estlased).

ECONOMY
National income p.a. per person: US$2,859; **per family:** US$8,865.

EDUCATION
Adult literacy: 99% (male 99%, female 99%). **Schools:** 825.
Universities: 22. **School enrolment:** female/male: 95%/97%.

HEALTH
Access to health services: 85%. **Access to safe water:** 90%.
Hospitals: 115 (84 beds per 10,000). **Doctors:** 4,680.
Blind: 1,200. **Deaf:** 85,100. **Murder rate:** 24. **Lepers:** 200.

LITERATURE
New book titles p.a.: 2,230 (1,600 p.a. per million). **Periodicals:** 350.
Newspapers: 4 dailies.

COMMUNICATION (per 1,000 people)
Phones: 277 (33% mobile). **Radios:** 400. **TV sets:** 411.
Daily newspaper circulation: 242. **Computers:** 40.

HUMAN LIFE AND LIBERTY (optimum condition=100.0%)
HDI: 77.6. **HSI:** 50.0. **HFI:** 35.0. **EFL:** 53.0.

Country status. Estonia is a parliamentary democracy on the Baltic Sea that regained independence in 1991 after more than 50 years of Soviet occupation. It is a major producer of oil shale and also has significant shipbuilding and fishing industries.

HUMAN LIFE AND LIBERTY

Human rights and freedoms. The major human rights problem is the treatment of the large Russian ethnic minority. Russians constitute about 38% of the population, but are considered aliens under the Alien Registration Law. Russia has accused Estonia of ethnic cleansing. Under prodding from the Council of Europe and the High Commissioner on National Minorities of the Conference on Security and Cooperation in Europe, a number of measures have been passed to extend basic civic rights to the Russian minority, but many problems remain. For example, ethnic Russians may not run for local government offices. Another human rights concern is the excessive use of force by the police and the harsh treatment of prisoners, both legacies of the Soviet rule. A Helsinki Watch report has criticized Estonia for inhuman conditions in its prisons. A judicial reform law went into effect in 1993 and an interim criminal code in 1992 decriminalizing many economic and political crimes in the old Soviet system. Constitutional guarantees of freedom of the press are generally respected. The media, however, are restrained because of harsh and punitive libel laws that put the burden of proof on the press. The churches enjoy complete religious freedom.The law on churches and religious organizations requires all religious groups to have at least 12 members and register with the Interior Ministry and the Board of Religion. Heads of religious organizations are required to be Estonian nationals.

NON-CHRISTIAN RELIGIONS

Nonreligion formed 27% of the population in 1995, and ***atheism*** another 11%. Both these totals have been falling rapidly.

Begun in 1869, the Estonia Song Festival draws many church choirs; here, choir of 35,000 voices.

Country Table 1. **Religious adherents in Estonia, AD 1900-2025.**

Year / Name	1900 Adherents	1900 %	1970 Adherents	1970 %	mid-1990 Adherents	mid-1990 %	Annual change, 1990-2000 Natural	Conversion	Total	Rate	mid-1995 Adherents	mid-1995 %	mid-2000 Adherents	mid-2000 %	mid-2025 Adherents	mid-2025 %
Christians	**637,000**	**98.5**	**618,300**	**45.3**	**936,000**	**59.6**	**-10,411**	**5,466**	**-4,945**	**-0.54**	**916,700**	**61.7**	**886,553**	**63.5**	**800,300**	**70.8**
PROFESSION																
crypto-Christians	0	0.0	203,000	14.9	0	0.0	0	0	0	0.00	0	0.0	0	0.0	0	0.0
professing Christians	**637,000**	**98.5**	**415,300**	**30.4**	**936,000**	**59.6**	**-10,411**	**5,466**	**-4,945**	**-0.54**	**916,700**	**61.7**	**886,553**	**63.5**	**800,300**	**70.8**
AFFILIATION																
unaffiliated Christians	6,800	1.1	7,787	0.6	420,200	26.8	-4,681	-1,671	-6,352	-1.63	444,126	29.9	356,678	25.6	192,300	17.0
affiliated Christians	**630,200**	**97.4**	**610,513**	**44.7**	**515,800**	**32.8**	**-5,731**	**7,139**	**1,408**	**0.27**	**472,574**	**31.8**	**529,875**	**38.0**	**608,000**	**53.8**
Protestants	350,000	54.1	327,313	24.0	240,000	15.3	-2,673	2,673	0	0.00	214,830	14.5	240,000	17.2	235,000	20.8
Orthodox	275,200	42.5	280,000	20.5	245,000	15.6	-2,729	1,229	-1,500	-0.63	211,000	14.2	230,000	16.5	280,000	24.8
Independents	0	0.0	200	0.0	20,000	1.3	-223	2,823	2,600	8.69	35,094	2.4	46,000	3.3	70,000	6.2
Marginal Christians	0	0.0	500	0.0	6,000	0.4	-67	267	200	2.92	6,550	0.4	8,000	0.6	15,000	1.3
Roman Catholics	5,000	0.8	2,500	0.2	4,800	0.3	-53	161	108	2.04	5,100	0.3	5,875	0.4	8,000	0.7
Trans-megabloc groupings																
Evangelicals	195,000	30.1	157,000	11.5	78,000	5.0	-869	269	-600	-0.80	65,415	4.4	72,000	5.2	75,000	6.6
Pentecostals/Charismatics	0	0.0	1,800	0.1	36,000	2.3	-401	2,801	2,400	5.24	48,053	3.2	60,000	4.3	85,000	7.5
Great Commission Christians	**39,000**	**6.0**	**150,000**	**11.0**	**345,000**	**22.0**	**-3,843**	**-1,432**	**-5,275**	**-1.65**	**340,000**	**22.9**	**292,255**	**20.9**	**300,000**	**26.5**
Nonreligious	1,000	0.2	410,000	30.0	426,050	27.1	-4,746	-2,878	-7,624	-1.95	398,950	26.9	349,814	25.1	241,000	21.3
Atheists	500	0.1	318,500	23.3	200,000	12.7	-2,228	-2,518	-4,746	-2.67	162,500	10.9	152,543	10.9	80,000	7.1
Muslims	500	0.1	10,000	0.7	5,000	0.3	-56	30	-26	-0.54	5,000	0.3	4,737	0.3	7,000	0.6
Jews	8,000	1.2	8,000	0.6	3,500	0.2	-39	-106	-145	-5.20	2,400	0.2	2,052	0.2	2,000	0.2
Baha'is	0	0.0	200	0.0	450	0.0	-5	6	1	0.20	450	0.0	459	0.0	700	0.1
World A (unevangelized persons)	1,294	0.2	136,500	10.0	100,544	6.4	-1,114	-6,194	-7,308	-12.30	57,941	3.9	26,524	1.9	15,834	1.4
World B (evangelized non-Christians)	8,706	1.3	610,200	44.7	534,456	34.0	-5,960	728	-5,232	-1.01	511,033	34.4	482,923	34.6	314,866	27.8
World C (Christians)	637,000	98.5	618,300	45.3	936,000	59.6	-10,411	5,466	-4,945	-0.54	916,700	61.7	886,553	63.5	800,300	70.8
Country's population	**647,000**	**100.0**	**1,365,000**	**100.0**	**1,571,000**	**100.0**	**-17,485**	**0**	**-17,485**	**-1.17**	**1,485,675**	**100.0**	**1,396,000**	**100.0**	**1,131,000**	**100.0**

COLUMNS, ROWS.
For meanings and definitions, see Codebook (Part 3). Note that, by definition, total 'Christians' = professing + crypto-Christians, which also = affiliated + unaffiliated Christians, and also = Great Commission Christians + latent Christians. Percentages may not always total exactly, due to rounding.

NOTES ON RELIGIONS
BAHA'IS. Organized under 3 local spiritual assemblies (1996).
JEWS. Declining due to emigration.
MUSLIMS. Found primarily among Azerbaijanis, Chuvash, Tatars, and Uzbeks.

Great Commission Instrument Panel: status of Estonia (for explanation see start of Part 4)

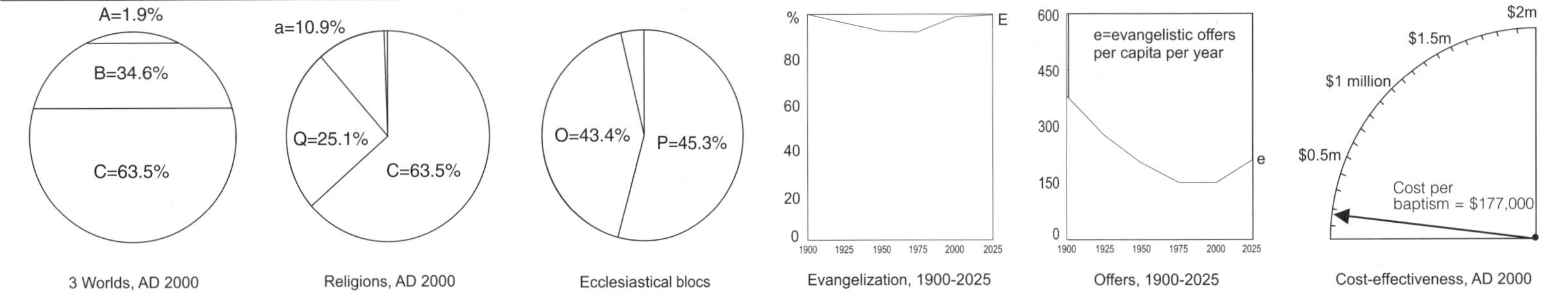

Country summary. **Worlds A, B, C by ethnolinguistic peoples, cities, and major civil divisions in Estonia.**

World	PEOPLES Num	Pop 2000	C%	Christians	E%	U%	Unevangelized	CITIES Num	Pop 2000	C%	Christians	E%	U%	Unevangelized	CIVIL DIVISIONS Num	Pop 2000	C%	Christians	E%	U%	Unevangelized
A	4	8,056	0.65	52	43	57	4,616	0	0	0.00	0	0	0	0	0	0	0.00	0	0	0	0
B	6	1,164,982	32.83	382,465	98	2	21,545	7	769,145	41.29	317,575	98	2	15,637	15	1,396,158	37.95	529,875	98	2	26,919
C	14	223,122	66.05	147,361	100	0	758	0	0	0.00	0	0	0	0	0	0	0.00	0	0	0	0
Total	**24**	**1,396,160**	**37.95**	**529,878**	**98**	**2**	**26,919**	**7**	**769,145**	**41.29**	**317,575**	**98**	**2**	**15,637**	**15**	**1,396,158**	**37.95**	**529,875**	**98**	**2**	**26,919**

Islam has a small community of 5,000 Muslims, and ***Judaism*** has 2,000 Jews.

CHRISTIANITY

ORTHODOX CHURCH. The largest denomination is the Estonian Apostolic Orthodox Church. It is under the authority and care of the Ecumenical Patriarchate of Constantinople, but the Russian Orthodox Church claims it as its own diocese of Tallinin & Estonia as indeed it was in the days of Soviet rule in the USSR.

PROTESTANT CHURCHES. Almost as large is the Evangelical Lutheran Church of Estonia, although it has lost sizable membership since 1970. There are also large Baptist, Methodist, Pentecostal, and Adventist churches.

CATHOLIC CHURCH. There exists one jurisdiction under Rome, the Apostolic Administration of Estonia which dates back to its formation in 1924, with 5,900 Catholics.

The Holy See has diplomatic relations with Estonia and in AD 2000 is represented to government and the Catholic hierarchy by a nuncio residing in Vilnius, Lithuania.

Indigenous missions. After decades of oppression, the Estonian church is beginning to respond to the missionary call of Christ. A handful of Estonians are serving among ethnic minorities in Russia.

CHURCH AND STATE

The state has attempted to keep out of the dispute which in 1996 caused mutual excommunications between the ecumenical patriarch in Turkey and the Russian Orthodox patriarch in Moscow.

'Fat Margaret' tower, with the Lutheran church.

BROADCASTING AND MEDIA

Christian programs in Estonian produced by IBRA and Back to the Bible can be heard on local radio stations such as KPR, TPR and Radio 7. TBN programming appears on Cable and channel B4. Shortwave programs in the major European languages can be received from KNLS, HCJB (Ecuador), AWR (Slovakia), and TWR (Monaco, Albania). HCJB is planting a local radio ministry in Estonia in partnership with Estonia Christian Ministries.

Satellite TV programs are received mainly in Arabic. CBN's programs can be seen on local television channels, and response is followed up from ministry centers in Russia and the Ukraine. Over 519,000 have seen the 'Jesus' Film on television.

FUTURE TRENDS AND PROSPECTS

Christians will probably continue the dramatic rise in the post-Communist era rising from only 45% in 1970 to 70.8% in 2025.

Atheists and the nonreligious will most likely gradually decline throughout the 21st century. By AD 2050, Christians could represent over 80% of the population, with atheists and nonreligious together less than 20%.

BIBLIOGRAPHY

A bibliography of English–language sources on Estonia: periodicals, bibliographies, pamphlets, and books. M. R. Parming & T. Parming. New York: Estonian Learned Society, 1974. 72p.

A message to the churches from the Estonian Evangelical Lutheran Church. Stockholm: Estonian Evangelical Lutheran Church (in Exile), [1975]. 16p.

'Atheism vs religion in contemporary Soviet society: with special reference to predominantly Lutheran Estonia,' K. Laantee, *Lutheran scholar*, 25 (April 1968), 36–53.

'Baltic Protestantism,' W. Kahle, *Religion in Communist lands*, 7, 4 (Winter 1979), 220–25. (Deals with Estonia, Latvia, and Lithuania).

Called to freedom and charity: the state of the Estonian nation and the church. Stockholm: Estonian Evangelical Lutheran Church, 1983. 36p.

Catalogue of books and periodicals on Estonia in the British Library Reference Division. S. Pruuden. Trans., D. B. Chrástek & C. G. Thomas. *Garland Reference Library of Social Science*, no. 71. London: British Library, 1981. 309p.

Church in bondage: Estonian Evangelical Lutheran Church. Stockholm: The Church, 1979. 49p.

Estonia and the Estonians. T. U. Raun. 2d ed. Stanford, CA: Hoover Institution Press, 1991. 355p.

Estonia Christiania: eximio domino Johanni Köpp. U. S. P. Eesti (ed). Holmiae: Estonian Theological Society in Exile, 1965. 334p.

Germanische und Baltische Religion. A. V. Strom & H. Biezais. *Die Religionen der Menschheit.* Stuttgart: Verlag W. Kohlhammer, 1975. 391p.

Lutherans in Latvia and Estonia. D. Krueger. Lansing, IL: D. Krueger, 1984. 36p.

'Methodism in the Soviet Union since World War II,' M. Elliott, *Asbury theological journal,* 46 (Spring 1991), 5–47. (Focuses on Estonia).

Religious life and the church in Estonia. J. Aunver. Stockholm: Consistory of Estonian Evangelical Lutheran Church, 1961. 21p.

Studies in the history of the Estonian people: with reference to aspects of social conditions, in particular, the religious and spiritual life and the educational pursuit. A. Vööbus. *Papers of the Estonian Theological Society in Exile,* nos. 18-19, 26, 30, 32-33, 35, 37-38, 40. Stockholm: Estonian Theological Society in Exile, 1969–84.

The Baltic States: Estonia, Latvia, Lithuania. I. A. Smith & M. V. Grunts. *World bibliographical series,* vol. 161. Oxford, UK: CLIO Press, 1993.

'The beginning of the Reformation in Estonia,' K. Laantee, *Church history,* 22 (December 1953), 269–78.

The Estonian Evangelical Lutheran Church today. E. Hark. Tallinn: Perioodika, 1982. 70p.

The Evangelical Lutheran Church of Estonia in exile. Stockholm: Consistory of Estonian Church, 1963. 17p.

The martyrs of Estonia: the suffering, ordeal, and annihilation of the churches under the Russian occupation. A. Vööbus. *Papers of the Estonian Theological Society in Exile,* vol. 34. Stockholm: Estonian Theological Society in Exile, 1984. 158p.

The old Estonian folk religion. I. Paulson. *Indiana University publications: Uralic and Altaic series,* no. 108. Bloomington, IN: Indiana University, 1971. 237p.

'The role of the Lutheran Church in Estonian nationalism,' A. R. Hart, *Religion in Eastern Europe,* 13 (June 1993), 6–12.

Country Table 2. **Organized churches and denominations in Estonia.**

Official name (bold type = church with over 10% of all affiliated) 1	*Begun* 2	*Type* 3	*Counc* 4	*Congs* 5	*Adults* 6	*Affiliated 1970* 7	*Affiliated 1995* 8	*G%* 9	*Names, notes, and other statistics* (see Codebook, Part 3) 10
Assembly Hall Churches	c1992	I-3nC	.....	1	5	–	50	33.33	*Local Churches. Little Flock.* Begun 1922 in China.
Catholic Church: AA Estonia	1924	R-Lat	b....	7	3,000	2,500	5,100	2.89	Small remnant often Nazi and Communist repression. C=3. 3 clergy.
Ch of Jesus C of Latter-day Saints	c1970	m-LdS	x....	3	210	–	350	26.40	*Mormons.* M=CJCLdS(Utah, USA).
Estonia Charismatic Episcopal Ch	1996	I-3cW	x....	22	2,000	–	3,000	50.00	*International Communion (ICCEC).* 1997, some UECCE join CEC.
Estonian Apostolic Orthodox Ch	1842	O-Est	C....	52	124,000	270,000	200,000	-1.19	Formerly Russian OC (D-Tallinn & Estonia); 1996, placed under EP Constantinople. 11n.
Estonian Ev Moravian Brethren	1729	P-Mor	x....	1	200	–	500	28.22	*EEMB.* Unity of Brethren. Small Moravian community.
Estonian Christian Pentecostal Church	c1909	P-Pe2	....E	36	1,500	1,700	5,000	4.41	Formerly known as Estonian Christian Church. 56n.
Evangelical Christian Baptist Union	c1920	P-Bap	T...E	83	6,511	20,000	20,000	0.00	*ECBU. Eesti Evangeeliumi Kristlaste ja Baptistide.*
Ev Lutheran Church of Estonia	c1250	P-Lut	LWC.	168	75,431	300,000	172,000	-2.20	*ELCE, EELC. Estonian Ev Lutheran Ch.* Long history of persecution. 143n.
Ev Lutheran Church of Finland	c1970	P-Lut	LWC..	12	4,000	–	9,000	43.94	Finns from state church of Finland.
Faith Free Church	c1985	I-3cW	....E	14	2,800	–	4,300	10.00	Led by charismatic missionaries from Norway, Canada, and Australia.
Jehovah's Witnesses	c1935	m-Jeh	x....	20	1,260	500	6,200	10.60	*JWs. IBSA. Watch Tower.* (1995) 567Y.
Methodist Church in Estonia	1907	P-Met	Vv..E	22	2,000	4,700	3,330	-1.37	In 1940, 16 churches, 1,600 members; in 1995, 22 churches, 2,000 members. 22n.
New Apostolic Church	c1980	I-3aX	x....	20	2,000	–	3,744	6.67	*NAC.* M=Neuapostolische Kirche (HQ Zurich, Switzerland).
Old Ritualist Church	c1700	I-OBe	x....	11	4,500	200	11,000	17.39	*Union of Estonian OB Congs. Old Believers* dating from the earliest days of the movement. 5n
Seventh-day Adventist Church	c1950	P-Adv	x...E	18	1,640	913	2,000	3.19	*Union of Seventh-day Adventists. 13n.*
Union of Estonian Chr Free Congs	1990	I-3wW	.....	5	1,000	–	2,000	20.00	*UECFC. Word of Life Congregations.* 18n.
Union of Estonian Full Gospel Congs	c1990	I-3fW	.....	5	1,000	–	3,000	20.00	*UEFGC.*
Union of Ev Charismatic Chs of E	c1990	I-3cW	.....	27	2,000	–	3,000	20.00	*UECCE.* Ex ELCE. *New Life Congs.* Finland, Switzerland. 1997, joins M=ICCEC (USA). 18n.
Other independent charismatic chs	1980	I-3cW	.....	34	2,500	–	5,000	6.67	Most begun independently without outside aid.
Other Orthodox churches	c1950	O-	.....	7	7,150	10,000	11,000	0.38	Russian Orthodox Ch claims buildings, members; also other churches.
Other Protestant bodies	c1985	P-	.....	15	1,200	–	3,000	10.00	About 3.
Totals				**583**	**245,907**	**610,513**	**472,574**		

Churches, members, growth, 1900-2025	*Congs*	*Adults*	*Affiliated*	*G%*	*Total denominations*	*6 Megablocs:* *O*	*R*	*A*	*P*	*I*	*m*
Total churches, members, and denominations (mid-1900)	200	295,000	630,200	-0.05	4	1	0	0	2	1	0
Total churches, members, and denominations (mid-1970)	276	286,120	610,513	-0.05	10	2	1	0	5	1	1
Total churches, members, and denominations (mid-1990)	400	268,000	515,800	-0.84	24	4	1	0	9	8	2
Total churches, members, and denominations (mid-1995)	583	245,907	472,574	-1.74	26	4	1	0	10	9	2
Total churches, members, and denominations (mid-2000)	580	276,000	529,875	2.32	26	4	1	0	10	9	2
Total churches, members, and denominations (mid-2025)	600	316,000	608,000	0.55	87	10	1	0	20	50	6

NOTES ON TABLE ABOVE

NATIONAL COUNCILS (Column 4, 5th letter).

E = Estonian Evangelical Alliance (EEA).

K Estonian Council of Churches.

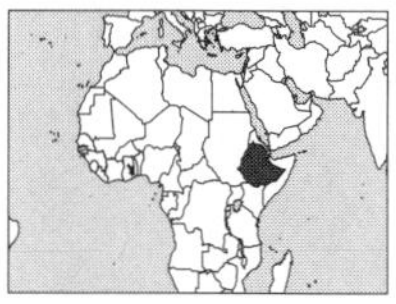

ETHIOPIA

SECULAR DATA, AD 2000

STATE

Official name: The Federal Democratic Republic of Ethiopia (Ethiopia).
Short name: Ethiopia. **Adjective of nationality:** Ethiopian.
Flag: Green, yellow, and red stripes.
Area: 1,133,882 sq. km. (437,794 sq. mi.).
Government: Federal republic with two legislative houses, since 1991 (3rd century empire (absolute monarchy), 1936-41 Italian rule, 1966-75 constitutional monarchy, 1975 Socialist military junta).
Legislature: Federal Council, 117 members; Council of People's Representatives, 548 members.
Official language: Amharic (Amharinya).
Monetary unit: 1 birr (Br) = 100 cents. **US$1=** Br 6.99.
Chief cities: ADIS ABEBA (Addis Ababa) 3,112,000; Dire Dawa 161,480; Gonder (Gondar) 132,806; Nazret (Nazareth) 125,260; Dese (Dessye, Dessie) 116,205.
Political divisions: 10 provinces.
Armed forces: 100,000.

DEMOGRAPHY

Population: 62,565,000.
Population density: 55.1/sq. km. (142.9/sq. mi.).
Under 15 years: 28,874,000.
Growth rate p.a.: 2.38% (births 43.05, deaths 18.80).
Mortality: Infant, per 1,000: 103.4; **Maternal per 100,000:** 1,400.0.
Life expectancy: 44 (male 43, female 45).
Household size: 4.5. **Floor area per person, sq.m:** 11.0.
Major languages: Amharic, Gallinya, Tigrinya, Tigre, Arabic, Somali, Afar, Italian, English, French, Sidamo, Nilotic, and about 90 other smaller languages.
Urban dwellers: 17.65%. **Urban growth rate p.a.:** 5.7%.
Labor force: 41%.

ETHNOLINGUISTIC PEOPLES

31.5% Amhara; 7.5% Tulama (Shoa Galla); 5.6% Wallega (Western Galla); 5.4% Macha (Central Galla); 5.3% Tigrai.

ECONOMY

National income p.a. per person: US$99; **per family:** US$449.

EDUCATION

Adult literacy: 35% (male 45%, female 25%). **Schools:** 8,120.
Universities: 11. **School enrolment:** female/male: 16%/24%.

HEALTH

Access to health services: 46%. **Access to safe water:** 27%.
Hospitals: 86 (3 beds per 10,000). **Doctors:** 1,466.
Blind: 90,000. **Deaf:** 3,970,500. **Murder rate:** 16.
Lepers: 400,000. **Underweight prevalence under 5:** 48%.

LITERATURE

New book titles p.a.: 310 (5 p.a. per million). **Periodicals:** 4.
Newspapers: 4 dailies.

COMMUNICATION (per 1,000 people)

Phones: 2 (**5% mobile). Radios:** 167. **TV sets:** 4.
Daily newspaper circulation: 10. **Computers:** 25.

REFUGEES

Citizen refugees in other countries: 110,700.
Alien refugees from other countries: 308,000.

HUMAN LIFE AND LIBERTY (optimum condition=100.0%)

HDI: 24.4. **HSI:** 15.0. **HFI:** 5.0. **EFL:** 26.0.

Country status. Ethiopia is the most important country in the Horn of Africa, and it is also one of the world's oldest independent nations, dating back to Solomonic times. The country consists of a high plateau with mountain ranges and lakes and semiarid desert. Its chief export is coffee.

HUMAN LIFE AND LIBERTY

Human need and development. Few countries in the world have been plagued so often and so harshly by famine as Ethiopia. In the largely bleak and barren land agriculture is a gamble at best and the vagaries of weather often wipe out even the meager produce that the peasant may wrest from the earth. Periodic crop failures and losses of livestock followed by widespread flooding spell hunger and starvation for thousands. Because adverse ecological conditions are prevalent in all areas of the country, even migration is not a possibility. The pastoral nomads who move seasonally to take advantage of the rains are themselves trapped by the general tendency of their cattle to overgraze. Although this is the normal pattern of life in the country, it reached crisis proportions in the 1970s and 1980s as a result of the military conflict in the Ogaden and Eritrea creating a flood of refugees. The net result was that in these 2 decades the death toll from starvation reached over half a million, with Tigray and Welo being the hardest hit regions. The Marxist regime also proved costly in human terms, disrupting the traditional lifestyles of the peasants and diverting national resources into military misadventures. As a result Ethiopia may be said to have missed at least 2 decades of development and its infrastructure, medical and educational facilities, and social welfare systems are among the least developed in Africa. Its maternal mortality rate is the highest in the world, its under-5 infant mortality rate is 10%, and its life expectancy rates are 43 for males and 45 for females. Its urbanization rate has advanced only 5% from 1965 to 1990 from 8 to 13%. In education its record is even more abysmal with only 45% males and 25% females attending primary schools, 15% males and 12% females attending secondary schools and 4% males and 1% females attending colleges. The daily calorie supply has declined between 1965 and 1990 from 1853 to 1667. Similarly the physician ratio has declined from 1 per 70,190 to 1 per 78,780. Its per capita GNP of $99 per year is higher than only

Country Table 1. **Religious adherents in Ethiopia, AD 1900-2025.**

Year	1900		1970		mid-1990		Annual change, 1990-2000				mid-1995		mid-2000		mid-2025	
Name	Adherents	%	Adherents	%	Adherents	%	Natural	Conversion	Total	Rate	Adherents	%	Adherents	%	Adherents	%
Christians	**2,871,000**	**38.0**	**15,433,000**	**53.6**	**27,520,000**	**57.2**	**828,111**	**30,693**	**858,804**	**2.75**	**31,850,000**	**57.5**	**36,108,040**	**57.7**	**68,488,000**	**59.4**
PROFESSION																
professing Christians	**2,871,000**	**38.0**	**15,433,000**	**53.6**	**27,520,000**	**57.2**	**828,111**	**30,693**	**858,804**	**2.75**	**31,850,000**	**57.5**	**36,108,040**	**57.7**	**68,488,000**	**59.4**
AFFILIATION																
unaffiliated Christians	95,000	1.3	3,416,266	11.9	3,927,200	8.2	118,176	-16,208	101,968	2.34	4,444,692	8.0	4,946,881	7.9	6,161,000	5.3
affiliated Christians	**2,776,000**	**36.7**	**12,016,734**	**41.7**	**23,592,800**	**49.1**	**709,934**	**46,902**	**756,836**	**2.82**	**27,405,308**	**49.5**	**31,161,159**	**49.8**	**62,327,000**	**54.0**
Orthodox	2,751,600	36.4	11,072,100	38.5	17,600,000	36.6	529,614	-5,828	523,786	2.64	20,251,550	36.6	22,837,859	36.5	42,500,000	36.8
Protestants	900	0.0	745,975	2.6	6,230,000	13.0	187,471	40,529	228,000	3.17	7,411,171	13.4	8,510,000	13.6	17,500,000	15.2
Independents	0	0.0	132,060	0.5	600,000	1.3	18,055	7,945	26,000	3.67	727,384	1.3	860,000	1.4	2,400,000	2.1
Roman Catholics	23,500	0.3	62,549	0.2	280,000	0.6	8,426	8,574	17,000	4.86	346,188	0.6	450,000	0.7	1,400,000	1.2
Marginal Christians	0	0.0	1,050	0.0	12,000	0.0	361	-311	50	0.41	12,203	0.0	12,500	0.0	26,000	0.0
Anglicans	0	0.0	3,000	0.0	800	0.0	24	-24	0	0.00	800	0.0	800	0.0	1,000	0.0
doubly-affiliated	0	0.0	0	0.0	-1,130,000	-2.4	-34,004	-3,996	-38,000	2.94	-1,343,988	-2.4	-1,510,000	-2.4	-1,500,000	-1.3
Trans-megabloc groupings																
Evangelicals	900	0.0	702,000	2.4	4,568,000	9.5	137,459	62,641	200,100	3.70	5,558,791	10.0	6,569,000	10.5	14,500,000	12.6
Pentecostals/Charismatics	0	0.0	130,000	0.5	2,880,000	6.0	86,664	31,936	118,600	3.51	3,485,413	6.3	4,066,000	6.5	9,230,000	8.0
Great Commission Christians	**605,000**	**8.0**	**3,742,000**	**13.0**	**7,358,000**	**15.3**	**221,415**	**17,349**	**238,764**	**2.85**	**8,524,000**	**15.4**	**9,745,644**	**15.6**	**20,500,000**	**17.8**
Muslims	1,860,000	24.6	8,628,000	30.0	14,448,400	30.0	434,777	19,656	454,433	2.77	16,802,600	30.4	18,992,727	30.4	35,500,000	30.8
Ethnoreligionists	2,819,000	37.3	4,695,000	16.3	6,023,000	12.5	181,242	-52,311	128,931	1.96	6,570,000	11.9	7,312,311	11.7	11,000,000	9.5
Nonreligious	0	0.0	0	0.0	65,000	0.1	1,956	2,165	4,121	5.03	90,000	0.2	106,205	0.2	300,000	0.3
Baha'is	0	0.0	7,000	0.0	17,000	0.0	512	-53	459	2.42	19,500	0.0	21,592	0.0	50,000	0.0
Jews	10,000	0.1	28,000	0.1	10,000	0.0	301	-109	192	1.77	11,000	0.0	11,919	0.0	14,000	0.0
Atheists	0	0.0	0	0.0	6,000	0.0	181	-39	142	2.15	6,700	0.0	7,422	0.0	20,000	0.0
Hindus	0	0.0	0	0.0	3,600	0.0	108	-2	106	2.61	4,200	0.0	4,660	0.0	10,000	0.0
World A (unevangelized persons)	3,704,400	49.0	6,909,912	24.0	9,089,577	18.9	273,834	-213,132	60,702	0.65	9,410,130	17.0	9,697,575	15.5	11,999,728	10.4
World B (evangelized non-Christians)	984,600	13.0	6,448,388	22.4	11,483,423	23.9	345,243	182,439	527,682	3.85	14,093,580	25.5	16,759,385	26.8	34,894,272	30.2
World C (Christians)	2,871,000	38.0	15,433,000	53.6	27,520,000	57.2	828,111	30,693	858,804	2.75	31,850,000	57.5	36,108,040	57.7	68,488,000	59.4
Country's population	**7,560,000**	**100.0**	**28,791,300**	**100.0**	**48,093,000**	**100.0**	**1,447,188**	**0**	**1,447,188**	**2.67**	**55,353,711**	**100.0**	**62,565,000**	**100.0**	**115,382,000**	**100.0**

COLUMNS, ROWS.
For meanings and definitions, see Codebook (Part 3). Note that, by definition, total 'Christians' = professing + crypto-Christians, which also = affiliated + unaffiliated Christians, and also = Great Commission Christians + latent Christians. Percentages may not always total exactly, due to rounding.

CENSUSES.
No censuses of population have been taken for the whole of Ethiopia. A city census of Addis Ababa dated **10-11.IX**.1961 gave: 86.9% Ethiopian Orthodox, 9.8% Muslims, 2.5% other Christians, 0.9% other religionists. The 1990 figures above of religious profession for the whole nation are based on a number of estimates over the years.

NOTES ON RELIGIONS
ATHEISTS. The first Communist activity began in 1975 and within a year 2 clandestine Marxist-Leninist parties were operating underground: the Ethiopian Communist Party, and the People's Ethiopian Revolutionary Party.
BAHA'IS. Growth from 3 local spiritual assemblies in 1964 (2 in Eritrea) to 51 in 1973 and to 152 by 1996. In 1970, over 1,000 converts were enrolled but little mass movement in the subsequent 2 decades.
COUNTRY'S POPULATION. In the 1973 famine at least 150,000 died.
ETHNORELIGIONISTS. Tribes over 60% traditionalist (animist) in 1995 numbered 61 with the largest being: Gideo, 726,700 (69% animist); Konso, 163,000 (80%); Mocha, 95,000 (60%); Eastern Nuer, 93,700 (95%); and Gimira, 87,000 (70%).
INDEPENDENTS. These groups of former Orthodox and crypto-Orthodox, who have seceded to form pentecostal bodies, have had to operate largely underground since their formation and have been subjected to severe police harassment, persecution and imprisonments. In 1995 they formed 12 separate groups including bodies from Black Africa (see Table 2).
JEWS. Archaic Judaism is practiced by the Falashas (Felashas) or Black Jews; (language Amharic), who accept the Old Testament but not the Talmud. Since 1860, about 120 Falashas each year have been baptized by the Anglican CMJ and the Theiopian Orthodox Church. There are also 500 foreign (expatriate) Jews in the country.
MUSLIMS. Mainly Sunnis (of the Shafiite rite). There are also 2,500 Asian Muslims. Among pagan tribes, the Shangalla are gradually being islamized. *Hajj pilgrims to Mecca.* (1970) 2,955; (1974) 3,473; (1975) 1,889; (1976) 2,246. *Pilgrimages in Ethiopia.* The most renowned among a number of centers are Sheikh Hussein north of Goba in the Galla province of Bale, where 100,000 pilgrims gather twice a year; Abred, in Gurage land, where 10,000 pilgrims gather on festivals; and Ja'a between Begi and Asosa near the Sudan border, also with 10,000. *Quranic schools.* There are over 10,000 local schools, 100 advanced, and a small number of higher schools. *Missionaries.* A large number of Egyptian missionaries sent by Al-Azhar University (Cairo) have begun work in the recent past, especially Eritrea.
ORTHODOX. Conversions to the Ethiopian Orthodox Church came from pagan tribes in the south and west, and come via 2 agencies: (1) the 2 Orthodox home mission societies, and (2) Protestant missions permitted to evangelize in certain areas on the understanding that converts are passed to the Orthodox Church for baptism.
PROTESTANTS. Although most conversions are from tribal religion, Muslims are becoming Protestants in some areas. In 1970 among the Kambatta, 100 Muslims became Lutherans and were baptized.
ROMAN CATHOLICS. In 1900, 41,089 indigenous baptized Catholics (including 14,000 in Eritrea), 2,072 catechumens, and a few Europeans.

Great Commission Instrument Panel: status of Ethiopia (for explanation see start of Part 4)

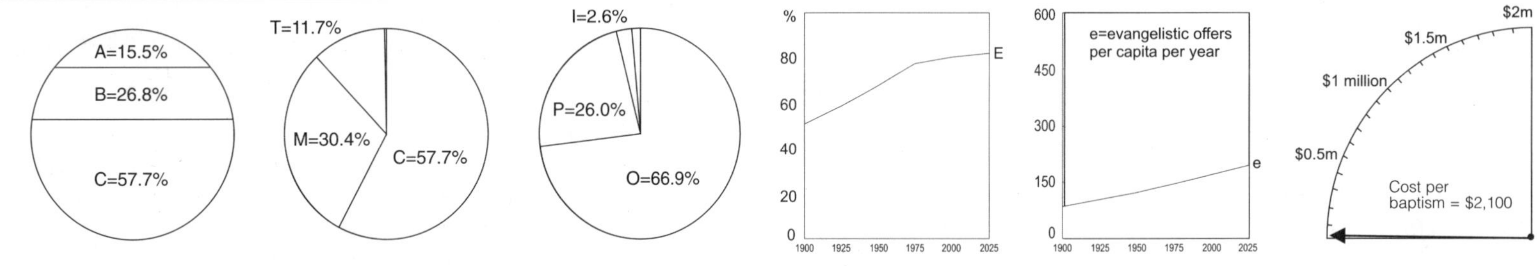

3 Worlds, AD 2000 | Religions, AD 2000 | Ecclesiastical blocs | Evangelization, 1900-2025 | Offers, 1900-2025 | Cost-effectiveness, AD 2000

Mozambique and has actually declined by 0.2% between 1965 and 1990. Meanwhile, its population is growing by 2.7% annually.

Human rights and freedoms. The Transitional Government that took over from Mengistu in 1991 committed to establish a multiparty democracy by 1994. While considerable progress has been made in extending and promoting human rights, a number of problems, mostly legacies of the Marxist regime, remain, such as extrajudicial and politically motivated killings. Over 2,000 former regime officials languish in prison without trial and members of the former Workers' Party remain disenfranchised. In many areas the Transitional Government does not exercise effective judicial or police control, and virtual anarchy prevails in them. There is still no criminal code and steps to develop a professional police force were initiated only in 1992. Respect for freedoms of speech and press have been restored by the Transitional Government through a new press law, but authorities may still prosecute journalists for threats to vaguely defined national security reasons. The 1991 National Charter also endorses freedom of association and assembly and the right to engage in unrestricted political activity. However, the first regional elections held in 1992 in 10 of the 14 new regions were marked by serious irregularities and allegations of fraud and official intimidation. The Transitional Government is also making efforts to mitigate historic discrimination practices against minorities, such as the Oromo. Minority languages are now taught in schools. A national committee has been established to review the status of women and to campaign against traditional social practices discriminating against them. These practices include genital mutilation, tattooing, and child marriage.

Human environment. The environmental devastation caused by the droughts of the 1970s and 1980s are still felt in the country. The droughts themselves are caused by the destruction of vegetation and forests as a result of overgrazing and improper land usage practices. Many areas once rich with vegetation are now bare and rocky. More than 2 million acres of forests are lost each year as a result of the burning of trees for firewood. Only 3% of the Ethiopian Plateau is forested compared to 30% some 50 years. In some areas villagers walk 10 miles for firewood.

NON-CHRISTIAN RELIGIONS

Islam has an ancient history in Ethiopia, Muhammed having sent a group of his followers there prior to the Hegira in AD 662. The islands of the Dahlak archipelago, off Massawa, were occupied by Muslims in 705 as a bridgehead for contacts with East Africa, and this was followed by trade and conversions to Islam, especially in the coastal region. In 1506 Ahmed Granj of Harar succeeded in establishing Islam in the Amhara highlands, although he was later defeated by the Orthodox Christians with the help of the Portuguese. Nevertheless, Islam continues to play an important role in the country and is strongest in the east and southeast of the country (principally among the Danakil, Somali and Harari peoples) and on the northwestern border with Sudan. Muslims in Ethiopia are mostly Sunnis of the Shafiite rite. The principal centers of learning are located in rural areas: at Dana on the western edge of the Danakil desert, Abred southwest of Addis Ababa, and Kolito near Sodo in southern Ethiopia. The principal shrine is that of Sheikh Hussein near Ginir to the east of Goba, where up to 100,000 pilgrims gather on Muslim feast days; another shrine is found at Ja'a near Asosa on the Sudan border.

Traditional religions retain the allegiance of a number of ethnic groups in the southwestern part of the country. The largest tribes, each with traditionalists over 60%, are the Darasa, Ometo, and Wallega Galla. Smaller tribes (all with over 90%) include the Anuak, Bako, Gimira, Mesongo, Nuer, Reshiat and Suri. The idea of a supreme being is prevalent under various names, the principal ones being Waka, Tosa and Tuma, or their derivatives: Waka or Wakaio (among the Boran, Wallega Galla, Mesongo), Wak (Guleb), Wa'a (Hadya); Tosa (Kullo, Tishena,

Country summary. **Worlds A, B, C by ethnolinguistic peoples, cities, and major civil divisions in Ethiopia.**

World	PEOPLES Num	Pop 2000	C%	Christians	E%	U%	Unevangelized
A	64	5,795,083	3.26	189,122	37	63	3,652,453
B	63	31,603,138	31.11	9,832,908	81	19	6,012,727
C	18	25,166,652	84.00	21,139,132	100	0	41,851
Total	**145**	**62,564,873**	**49.81**	**31,161,162**	**84**	**16**	**9,707,031**

World	CITIES Num	Pop 2000	C%	Christians	E%	U%	Unevangelized
A	1	125,260	20.00	25,052	45	55	69,306
B	7	756,085	34.55	261,234	65	35	264,513
C	2	3,244,806	69.59	2,258,084	98	2	64,029
Total	**10**	**4,126,151**	**61.66**	**2,544,370**	**90**	**10**	**397,848**

World	CIVIL DIVISIONS Num	Pop 2000	C%	Christians	E%	U%	Unevangelized
A	0	0	0.00	0	0	0	0
B	8	41,466,623	32.36	13,420,208	77	23	9,551,405
C	2	21,098,253	84.09	17,740,951	99	1	155,620
Total	**10**	**62,564,876**	**49.81**	**31,161,159**	**84**	**16**	**9,707,025**

Walamo), Tsosa (Zala), Tsuossa (Gofa), Tosso (Kuca); Tuma (Mekan, Suri-Surma, Tishena), Tummu (Murle). Other names are Tel (Ingessana), Yaro (Kafa), Sosi (Male), Yere (Mao), Magano (Sidamo) and Arumgimis (Udhuk). Among the Wallega Galla the obda tree is the center of village worship, prayers of thanksgiving and offerings being made to the spirit which resides in the tree. The kolo rites performed by men at the obda tree involve the offering of sacrifices to placate the spirits of mountains and springs. Two female spirit-possession cults are Atete and Maram, both for aid in child-bearing.

Judaism has existed for many centuries in an archaic form among some 28,000 Falasha (Black Jews) in the region of Gondar, north of Lake Tana, as well as in isolated communities near Addis Ababa. In the 1990s however a large majority were finally admitted into the state of Israel, including a last-minute mass airlift. There is no unanimity of opinion regarding the origin of the Falasha although it has been well established that they date back some 20 centuries and were probably converted to Judaism by the large number of Jews who emigrated to Ethiopia between the 1st and 7th centuries AD. They resisted assimilation in a remarkable way and scrupulously observe the sabbath and the Mosaic rituals. Their liturgical language is Ge'ez, but they also use many Hebrew words in their prayers. Prior to the creation of the state of Israel, the Jews of Palestine built dispensaries for them and 13 primary schools, training their headmasters in Palestine. Nevertheless, it was not until 1972 that the 2 chief rabbis of Israel recognized them officially as Jews and descendants of the tribe of Dan. At the same time it was suggested that they needed to be 'converted' since they did not observe all the rites of present-day Judaism. The state of Israel did not extend to the Falasha the benefits of its Law of Return in the same way as it did to other Jews throughout the world, and from 1967 until 1994 only about 250 Falasha succeeded in emigrating to Israel. Their perseverance led to their final entrance into Israel.

In addition to the remnants of the Falasha, there are also about 500 foreign Jews in Ethiopia.

of Alexandria later appointed Frumentius bishop. The Ethiopian Orthodox Church dates its foundation to AD 332. In spite of constant pressure from Islam after the 7th century, Ethiopia remained officially Orthodox. A new Muslim threat in the early part of the 16th century was met with the aid of Portugal, and this was followed in 1555 by the arrival of the first Jesuit missionary. Although well received initially their attempt to propagate Roman Catholicism provoked lasting resentment and produced few fruits. The first Protestants, Swedish Lutherans, arrived in 1866, but neither Protestants nor Catholics made much impact on the scene prior to the present century

Emperor Haile Selassie, murdered 1977, and Patriarch Tewoffles (Theofilas) killed 1980.

ORTHODOX CHURCHES. The Ethiopian Orthodox Church is both the largest denomination in Ethiopia and also the largest non-Chalcedonian Orthodox church in the world. It continues to be the established church although its relationship to the new revolutionary government since 1974 has been increasingly tenuous. From earliest times the abuna (archbishop) had always been an Egyptian appointed by the Coptic patriarch of Alexandria, but in 1959 agreement was reached between the patriarch and the emperor Haile Selassie providing that the abuna should in future be an Ethiopian national bearing the title of patriarch-catholicos. The abuna has ecclesiastical precedence over all Coptic bishops except the Alexandrian patriarch. The church's strength is found almost entirely among the Amhara and Tigrai rural population, but its quasi-feudal conservative attachment to the past and its lack of trained priests have contributed to a weakening of its position in the cities and among youth. Reforms regarding the training of a more adequate priesthood have resulted from the establishment of Holy Trinity Seminary, a secondary school, and Holy Trinity Theological College (a faculty of Haile Selassie University), as well as the Lake Zwai Training Centre aided by the World Council of Churches. A total of 1,463 traditional schools are under the direct supervision of the church. Two Anglican societies (Church's Ministry among the Jews (CMJ) since 1855, and Bible Churchmen's Missionary Society (BCMS) from 1933 withdrawing in 1975) have worked within the Orthodox Church, teaching in convents and seminaries and helping in literature production

Holy Trinity Society (Mahbere Sellassie), Dissemination of Light (Fenote Berhan) Society, and Fruit of the Faith (Fere Haimanot) Society.

Two other Orthodox churches have communities in Ethiopia. The Armenian Apostolic Church has a priest in Addis Ababa, and the Greek Orthodox Patriarchate of Alexandria has an archbishop and 2 priests in the Greek diocese of Aksum (Axum).

PROTESTANT CHURCHES. With a Christian community of about half a million, the Word of Life Evangelical Church related to the Sudan Interior Mission is the largest Protestant denomination. It supports 433 schools, 6 hospitals and leprosaria, 25 clinics, several orphanages, a literature publication center and its own national missionary society. The church is active in 35 different areas and is strongest among the Wallamo (Ometo).

Lutheran bodies include the Evangelical Church Mekane Years (Dwelling-place of Jesus, in Amharic), second in size to the Word of Life Church, and the Evangelical Church of Eritrea. The Mekane Yesus Church has its strength in the western part of the country, but there is also an important nucleus in Addis Ababa and some congregations in the north. It is supported by Lutheran missions from the USA, Germany, Norway, Sweden, Denmark, and Iceland. The church's extensive social service program includes 9 secondary schools, 3 teacher-training colleges, 4 hospitals and 24 dispensaries. The Evangelical Church of Eritrea was founded in 1866 by the Swedish Lutheran EFS mission and has a large secondary school at Asmara.

Other Protestant bodies are Seventh-day Adventists (1907) in southern and western areas, the Meserete Kristos Church which receives help from American Mennonites, 3 Baptist denominations and several small Pentecostal groups.

CATHOLIC CHURCH. Although there are no uniate churches, Ethiopic-rite and Latin-rite congregations exist together within an ecclesiastically unified church. A vicar apostolic in Asmara has primary responsibility for Latin-rite Catholics, and an eparch in Addis Ababa for those of the Ethiopicrite. More than half of Ethiopia's Catholic membership is found in Eritrea province because of the long Italian influence there. The church has suffered extensively as a result of mistakes made by its missionaries in the 16th century and more recently by its identification with the Italian occupation during 1936-41. Nevertheless, the Catholic Church has made substantial contributions to the development of education and social service.

The Holy See has diplomatic relations with Ethiopia and in AD 2000 is represented to government and the Catholic hierarchy by a pro-nuncio residing in Addis Ababa.

INDIGENOUS CHURCHES. Ethiopia's largest indigenous denomination is the Full Gospel Church which has sprung from an extensive pentecostal revival since the beginning of the 1960s, mainly among nominally Orthodox populations, with assistance from Swedish and Finnish Pentecostal missionaries. The church has undergone severe persecution since 1972 and for a long time was forced to operate underground. Another indigenous body, the Kambatta Evangelical Church, split in 1955 from the Word of Life Church opposing SIM control. In 1965 it applied to join the Lutheran Mekane Yesus Church, and after lengthy preparation was admitted as a synod of that church. Another pentecostal body beginning in 1966 has been the God's All Times Association (also called Yesemaye Berhan, Light of Heaven), formed by a group of young Orthodox and Protestant students after participation in revival meetings held at several colleges and the university in Addis Ababa beginning

Ethiopian Orthodox Church. (*Top*) Archbishop Bartolomeos in Awassa seminary. (*Middle*) clergy courses in Gondar. (*Bottom*) Clergy-musicians predominate.

of a rectangle with battlements and a bell tower and surrounded by an inner enclosure before which is David's Throne. A small chapel within the cathedral is believed to have contained the lost Ark of the Covenant. Another famous church is Dabra Damo situated on a flat-topped mountain and accessible only by means of a rope. The smaller Imruhanna Kerestos is a church built in a cave in Lasta. Another cave church is Jammadu Mariam, built of red stone in the form of a cross. In the south the more popular form is the round or octogonal church, of which the most typical are the Enda Medhane Alem and Enda Selassie at Adawa. The celebrated monolithic churches in Lalibela in Lasta were built during the time of the Zagwe Dynasty. Hewn out of rock, they are believed to have been built by Coptic workmen. The interiors are hollowed out, decoratively carved and provided with varieties of vaulted roofs and complex arches. Beautiful columns appear to support the roof. Some of the churches are in the shape of a cross while others are rectangular.

Renewal movements. In the 1990s the Pentecostal/Charismatic Renewal continued to spread rapidly across most older churches, and numbered over 4,066,000 adherents (of whom 27% Pentecostals, 55% Charismatics, and 18% Independents).

Indigenous missions. The Ethiopian Orthodox Church has been sending a limited number of missionaries outside of Ethiopia (primarily to surrounding countries) for many centuries. Recently, Protestant and Catholic groups have begun sending missionaries.

CHURCH AND STATE

According to Article 126 of the revised constitution of 4 November 1955, the Ethiopian Orthodox church, which bases itself on the teaching of St Mark of Alexandria, was recognized as the established church of the empire and as such was supported by the state. Article 127 stated that the organization and secular administration of the established church was to be governed by law. The archbishop and bishops were elected by the Ecclesiastical Electoral College composed of representatives of clergy and laity. These elections were approved by the emperor, who also had the right to promulgate decrees, edicts and public regulations concerning the church, except on matters concerning monastic life and spiritual ministrations. In addition to these 2 articles, the constitution contained references to the emperor as 'elected by God', to the archbishop and his membership in the Council of Regency and the Crown Council (Articles 10 and 70) and to the 'Ethiopian Orthodox Faith' to which all members of the imperial family had to belong (Article 16). The terms Coptic (Egyptian) and Monophysite did not appear in the constitution, and indeed the latter word is repudiated by the Orthodox Church. Finally, Article 40 introduced into Ethiopia for the first time the constitutional principle of religious toleration, with the free exercise of rites of any religion or creed provided that such religious practices were not utilized for political purposes. In Ethiopian usage, the appellation 'established church' meant that the church was spiritually independent, did not owe its origin to the state, yet was nevertheless supported and protected by the state. The government later withdrew certain privileges previously enjoyed by the Orthodox Church, including exemption from taxation, and affirmed its jurisdiction over temporal matters. The emperor took particular interest in pressing the established church to evolve and adapt to the modern world. A governmental office, the General Administration of the Ethiopian Orthodox Church (ye-Biete Kehnet wanna Sera askeaje), handled relations between church and state.

With regard to foreign missionary societies, under Decree 3 of 1944 'Regulations governing the activities of missions', the emperor established a Committee of Missions under the presidency of the Ministers of Education, the Interior and Foreign Affairs, with the Ministry of Education bearing primary responsibility for the execution of its decisions. The committee considered applications of non-Orthodox groups and assigned them areas where they could operate. Such areas were inhabited predominantly by non-Christians and were know as 'open areas', as contrasted with 'Ethiopian Church areas' where the majority of the population were Orthodox. Permission was also on occasion granted to non-Orthodox missions to establish hospitals and non-denominational schools in closed areas provided that no proselytizing was carried on. The capital city itself was declared to be an open area.

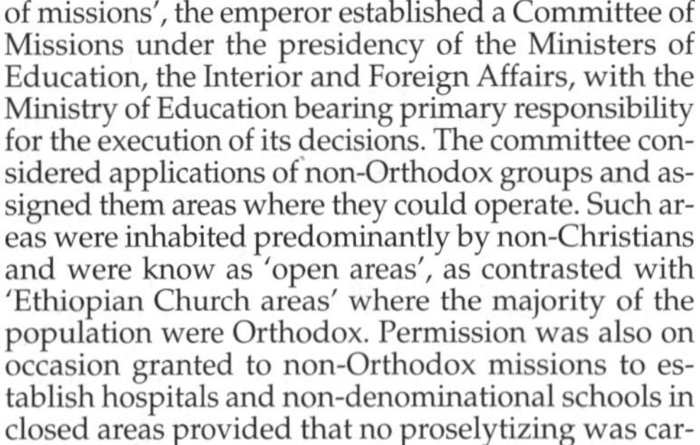

Full Gospel Believers Church. Members were severely persecuted 1972-1975 and went underground.

In the late 1930s, the Italian dictator Mussolini expelled all non-Italian missionaries from Ethiopia, but at the end of World War II Italian missionaries suffered the same fate. In 1971, the newly inaugurated Ethiopian patriarch, Abuna Thewophlos, publicly stated that he would 'exert all my energy against every teaching and movement that may battle against the Ethiopian Church', a fact which has led some observers to blame the Orthodox Church for the recent persecution of indigenous pentecostals in the country. In mid-1972 nearly 300 members of the Full Gospel Church were imprisoned on charges of treason and immorality.

In the early months of 1974 the army began progressively to take control of the country. In March a petition was circulated among Orthodox lower clergy, protesting against the general social and economic situation and particularly the wealth and mode of life of the Orthodox hierarchy. On 20 April a demonstration was organized by Muslims in Addis Ababa advocating an equality with Coptic Orthodox Christians, and a mammoth Coptic counter-demonstration took place 2 days later. On 22 August the national synod of the Orthodox Church published a memorandum proclaiming its hostility to the proposed constitution, which would involve an alleged disestablishment of their church. According to this memorandum, clergy should continue to sit in parliament and the patriarch preside at the coronation ceremonies of emperors. However, on 11 September 1974 the patriarch affirmed that 'God blessed the great revolutionary movement directed by the armed forces with the support of the people'. This action appeared to be due to pressure exercised by the military on the Orthodox hierarchy, the latter being criticized for indifference concerning the famine in Wallo and Tigre and threatened with the loss of church wealth and imprisonment. The following day the military co-ordination committee (DEURG) deposed and later murdered emperor Haile Selassie, who had been in power since 1928 and whose titles included the following: Conquering Lion of Judah, Elect of God, 225th Descendant of the Queen of Sheba and King Solomon, and Emperor of Ethiopia.

Ethiopia was now moving in the direction of a multi-confessional secular state. The proposed constitution prepared by the army stipulated that 'Religion is an individual matter' and that no religious differences might exist in the country. In December 1974 to gain the support of Muslims, the DEURG proclaimed Id El Adeha (Aid el Kabir) a national holiday, which had the effect of equalizing even more the religious factor, although the Orthodox Church by 1976 had still not been disestablished.

In Eritrea, the guerrilla war begun in 1960 by Muslims of the Front for the Liberation of Eritrea (FLE), was reinforced in May 1971 by a new group called the Popular Liberation Force (PLF). The PLF was composed of leftist Christians who were much more radical ideologically than the leaders of the FLE. In the beginning the PLF formed a united front with the more progressive wing of the FLE, but the front collapsed in April 1972 with religious divisions playing a major role.

On 4 March 1975 the provisional military council proclaimed an agrarian reform throughout the country. All land was nationalized and became the collective property of the Ethiopian people, the state promising nevertheless to redistribute 10-hectare lots to peasants. Because of its extensive properties the Ethiopian Orthodox Church was bound to be seriously affected. The same decree also abolished the rights of spiritual and customary chiefs. Also during 1975, the Orthodox bishop of Hosanna was murdered and his successor detained by the military, who then gave the entire Orthodox Church one year to put their financial and personnel affairs in order. Finally, in 1976 the regime arrested patriarch Thewopholos and declared him deposed for corrupt practices, and later announced the election as patriarch (with the title Abuna Tikle Haimanot) of Malaku Wolde Mikael, an evangelistic monk credited with converting 300,000 animists and building over 100 churches and schools in Wallo province since 1934. However, the Coptic Orthodox pope in Cairo refused to recognize the deposition and prevailed on all other WCC member churches, and also the Church of Rome, to boycott the enthronement of the new patriarch on 29 August.

In February 1977 a further military coup brought to power a regime more Marxist-Leninist than its predecessor, which the following month seized the radio station RVOG and announced its nationalization under the new name 'Radio Voice of the Revolution'. In 1978 a wave of local persecution of Protestant churches was reported; and the regime forcibly retired 8 Orthodox bishops and attempted to force its own candidates to replace them.

Ethiopian Christianity's traditional confrontation with Islam has created political problems with such neighboring Muslim countries as Somalia, Sudan, Egypt and Libya. In 1991, regional uprisings together with severe droughts and famines caused the collapse of the Marxist regime. Multiparty elections followed, then the ending of the guerrilla war with Eritrea which then became independent. With a new Ethiopian Orthodox patriarch appointed, all parties had the chance to forge new understandings and new beginnings.

Mural in traditional Ethiopic style depicting coming of the gospel to islands.

BROADCASTING AND MEDIA

About 17% of the general populace owns a radio. Shortwave programs in Afar, Amharic, Guragena and Somali from FEBA (Seychelles) and in Tigrinya, Amharic and Oromo from TWR (South Africa) are received in Ethiopia. The Lutheran World Federation has a studio that produces programs in Oromigna and Amharic.

The 'Jesus' Film has been viewed by 3.4 million (5%), mostly as a result of teams showing the 16mm version.

INTERDENOMINATIONAL ORGANIZATIONS

The Ethiopian Inter-Mission Council, founded in 1943 with 15 member bodies, was the only ecumenical council in the country until 1978, although not officially recognized. Regarding the Orthodox Church, Anglican BCMS and CMJ missions have worked within it; and there have been signs recently of co-operation in specific projects between Orthodox and Protestant groups, most notably with Presbyterians. The Ethiopian Orthodox Church is a member of both the AACC and the WCC. At Sabbata near Addis Ababa is located a Christian community composed of 2 Ethiopian Orthodox, 2 English Protestants and 2 Catholic Combonian of Verona sisters. The sisters live together and jointly operate a dispensary. Capuchins have also founded an ecumenical center at Adi Ugri, called the St Frumentius Ecumenical Centre. In 1973 an ecumenical committee for development aid, the Christian Relief and Development Association, was formed by Catholics and other churches and voluntary agencies.

In 1978, 9 of the largest churches in Ethiopia, after some years' discussions, founded the Council for Co-operation of Churches in Ethiopia (CCCE), to co-operate in developmental and welfare work.

FUTURE TRENDS AND PROSPECTS

Christians will continue to experience gains at the expense of ethnoreligionists who will probably fall from 16.3% in 1970 to 9.5% by 2025. Christians should make significant gains in the non-Muslim segments of Oromo (now at 3% Christian).

By 2050, Christians and Muslims could share the country's population in a 65/35 ratio. Both of these could then suffer losses to the nonreligious increasingly.

BIBLIOGRAPHY

African ark: people and ancient cultures of Ethiopia and the horn of Africa. A. Fisher. New York: H. N. Abrams, 1990. 328p.

Against great odds. D. M. Hostetler. Worcester, PA: Gateway Films/Vision Video, 1992. (29 min. videocassette).

'An analysis of the Amhara, Tigrean, and Oromo traditional socio–cultural system and their relationship to Christianity.' K. T. Belihu. M.A.B.S. thesis, Dallas Theological Seminary, Dallas, TX, 1981. 200p.

'An annotated and classical bibliography of English literature pertaining to the Ethiopian Orthodox Church.' J. J. Bonk. Thesis, Trinity Evangelical Divinity School, Deerfield, IL, 1972. 177p. (466 items, covering AD 33—1959).

'An ethnohistory of Ethiopia: a study of the factors which affect the planting and growth of the church.' E. J. Elliston. M.A. thesis, Fuller Theological Seminary, Pasadena, CA, 1968. 177p.

Born at midnight. P. Cotterell. Addis Ababa: SIM, 1972. (On the SIM revival).

Catholic directory of Ethiopia, 1968. Addis Ababa: Conference of Catholic Bishops, 1968.

'Christian ministry: patterns and functions within the Ethiopian Evangelical Church Mekane Yesus.' J. Bakke. Doctoral thesis, Uppsala University, 1986. 321p.

Church and state in Ethiopia, 1270–1527. Taddesse Tamrat. *Oxford studies in African affairs.* Oxford, UK: Clarendon Press, 1972. 348p.

Die Kirche Athiopiens. F. Heyer. Berlin: Walter de Gruyter, 1971. 360p.

Die Kirche in Däbrä Tabor. F. Heyer. *Oikonomia*, Bd. 13. Erlangen, 1981. 173p.

Distribution and foundation of churches in Ethiopia. V. Stitz. 36p.

Ethiopia Tikdem—Ethiopia First: the shades of things past and the shape of things to come for Roman Catholic Christianity in Southern Ethiopia. M. Singleton. Brussels: Pro Mundi Vita, 1977. 232p.

Ethiopia: where Lutheran is spelled 'Mekane Yesus'. W. Bockelman & E. Bockelman. Minneapolis, MN: Augsburg, [1972]. 112p.

Evangelical pioneers in Ethiopia: origins of the Evangelical church Mekane Yesus. G. Arén. Stockholm, 1978.

General survey concerning Christian literature in Ethiopia. J. R. H. Conacher. Addis Ababa: Bible Churchmen's Missionary Society, 1970. 384p.

God's higher ways: the birth of a church. C. W. Duff. Nutley, NJ: Presbyterian and Reformed, 1977. 338p.

In the wake of martyrs: a modern saga in ancient Ethiopia. A. E. Brant. Langley, British Columbia: Omega Publications, 1992. 300p.

Islam in Ethiopia. J. S. Trimingham. London: Oxford University Press, 1952. 299p.

Koptisches Christentum: die orthodoxen Kirchen Ägyptens und Äthiopiens. P. Verghese. *Kirchen der Welt*, Bd. 12. Stuttgart: Evangelisches Verlagswerk, 1973. 284p.

Land beyond the Nile. M. Forsberg. New York: Harper & Brothers, 1958. 232p. (Missionary account).

Le ginnili devin, poète et guerrier afar: (Ethiopie et République de Djibouti). D. Morin. *Langues et cultures africaines*, 16. Paris: Peeters, 1991. 146p. (Summaries in English and Afar).

Les Ethiopiens. K. Stoffregen-Pedersen. *Fils d'Abraham.* [Turnhout]: Brepols, 1990. 195p.

Miracle in Ethiopia: a partnership response to famine. R. W. Solberg. New York: Friendship Press, 1991. 222p.

'Missionaries in an indigenous church: a comparison of national and expatriate perceptions of social development within the Ethiopian Evangelical Church Mekane Yesus (EECMY).' I. H. Rydland. M.A. thesis, Wheaton College, Wheaton, IL, 1991. 184p.

Molo Wongel: a documentary report on the life and history of the independent Pentecostal movement in Ethiopa, 1960–1975. T. Engelsviken. Oslo: Free Faculty of Theology, 1975. 223p.

'Music in the Coptic Church of Egypt and Ethiopia.' J. P. Bennett. M.A. thesis, University of Washington, Seattle, WA, 1945. 88p.

'Myths and rituals of the Ethiopian Bertha,' A. Triulzi, in *Peoples and cultures of Ethio–Sudan borderlands.* M. L. Bender (ed). *Committee on Northeast African Studies*, no. 10. East Lansing, MI: African Studies Center, Michigan State University Press, 1981. 214p.

On church–mission relations in Ethiopia 1944–1969: with special reference to the Evangelical Church Mekane Yesus and the Lutheran missions. O. Sæverås. *Studia missionalia Upsaliensia*, vol. 27. Lunde: Lunde Forlag og Bokhandel, 1974. 215p.

'Oral theology and dynamic Christianity: Eastern Macha Christians theologizing in rural Ethiopia.' E. Erickson. D.Miss. thesis, Fuller Theological Seminary, Pasadena, CA, 1985. 340p.

Peoples and cultures of Ethio–Sudan borderlands. M. L. Bender (ed). *Committee on Northeast African Studies*, no. 10. East Lansing, MI: African Studies Center, Michigan State University Press, 1981. 214p.

Rediscovering Christianity where it began: a survey of contemporary churches in the Middle East and Ethiopia. N. A. Horner. Beirut: Near East Council of Churches, 1974. 110p.

Religious practices of the Guji Oromo. J. Van de Loo. Addis Ababa, 1991. 153p.

'The challenge of Marxism to evangelical Christianity with special reference to Ethiopia.' S. Väisänen. D.Miss. thesis, Fuller Theological Seminary, Pasadena, CA, 1981. 291p.

The Christian Church and missions in Ethiopia (including Eritrea and the Somalilands). J. S. Trimingham. London: World Dominion Press, 1950. 74p.

The church of Ethiopia: a panorama of history and spiritual life. Addis Ababa: The Ethiopian Orthodox Church, 1970. 101p.

'The development of the Ethiopian Orthodox Church and its relationship with the Ethiopian Government from 1930 to 1970.' C. E. Shenk. Ph.D. dissertation, New York University, 1972. 447p.

The Eastern Christian churches: a brief survey. R. G. Roberson. 3rd ed. Rome: Pontificum Studiorum Orientalium, 1990. 129p.

The hand of God in Ethiopia: and other subjects. W. Curtwright. New York: Vantage Press, 1974. 84p.

The lost empire: the story of the Jesuits in Ethiopia, 1555–1634. P. Caraman. : Sidgwick and Jackson, 1985. 176p. (Also in French).

The monastic holy man and the Christianization of early Solomonic Ethiopia. S. Kaplan. Wiesbaden: F. Steiner, 1984. 162p.

'The paradigm of servant leadership and the implications for the Ethiopian Evangelical Church Mekane Yesus (EECMY).' B. Ofgaa. S.T.M. thesis, Trinity Lutheran Seminary, Columbus, OH, 1992. 294p.

The word of God in Ethiopian tongues: rhetorical features in the preaching of the Ethiopian Evangelical Church Mekane Yesus. E. Forslund. *Studia missionalia Upsaliensia*, 58. Uppsala: The Swedish Institute for Missionary Research, 1993. 274p.

Country Table 2. **Organized churches and denominations in Ethiopia.**

Official name (bold type = church *with over 10% of all affiliated)* 1	*Begun* 2	*Type* 3	*Counc* 4	*Congs* 5	*Adults* 6	*Affiliated 1970* 7	*Affiliated 1995* 8	*G%* 9	*Names, notes, and other statistics* (see Codebook, Part 3) 10
Anglican Church (D Egypt)	1926	A-Cen	aw.U.	1	430	3,000	800	-5.15	M=USPG(UK). Expatriates. Other Anglican work (1855 CMJ, 1934 BCMS) is within EOC.
Apostolic Church	c1965	I-3aA	.....	11	2,500	1,000	7,250	8.25	Small African indigenous church, mainly rural.
Armenian Apostolic Ch: V Addis Abeba	1887	O-Arm	Ewc..	1	170	1,200	300	-5.39	Armenian residents. 1 priest, 1 primary school (Addis Ababa). Under C. Echmiadzin.
Broadsheet Readers' Clubs	c1980	I-3nA	....	17	500	–	1,000	6.67	Readers of Gospel Broadsheets, produced by M=WEC(UK).
Catholic Church in Ethiopia:	1555	R-LEr	O.SES	170	204,200	62,549	346,188	7.08	*Katolikawit Bete-Cristian.* C=10+1+20. 118n 209x 374m 344w 16231Yy
M Addis Abeba (Addis Ababa)	1951	R-Eth	Os	39	29,500	28,700	50,000	2.25	Includes 10,000 Latins (foreigners) in Addis. 1H,1s. 26n 82x 183m 183w 8Yy
D Adigrat	1937	R-Eth	Os	35	9,800	8,639	16,546	2.63	*Bete-Papas Katolikawi.* 60% Irob, 40% Tigrina. 1s. 60n 11x 34m 62w 591Yy
VA Awasa (Neghelli) *(Latin)*	1937	R-Lat	Pmcci	14	60,500	1,780	102,601	17.61	*Mision Katolic.* Desert. 70 expatriates. M=MCCI. 7n 39x 45m 76w 5921Yy
VA Harar *(Latin)*	1846	R-Lat	Pofmc	16	11,100	9,030	18,908	3.00	48% Kambatta, 32% Galla, 20% Wallamo. P=64%. 3n 13x 22m 55w 327Yy
VA Meki	1991	R-Lat	Ps	10	9,800	–	16,596	25.00	M=IMC. Mainly rural. 9n 12x 16m 49w 698Yy
VA Nekemte	1982	R-Lat	Pcm	36	13,000	–	22,050	7.69	M=CM. Rural and part urban. 6n 14x 31m 44w 1679Yy
VA Soddo-Hosanna *(Latin)*	1940	R-Lat	Pofmc	15	63,100	14,400	107,007	8.35	Fast-expanding church in responsive Hosanna tribe. 5n 36x 38m 45w 6615Yy
PA Jimma-Bonga	1994	R-Lat	Pcm	5	7,400	–	12,480	100.00	Galla, Kaffa. M=CM. 2n 2x 5m 13w 400Yy
Chrischona Mission in Ethiopia	1854	P-Non	x...E	3	100	100	200	2.81	M=Chrischona Mission (Switzerland). Falashas, also SW of Addis. HQ Addis Ababa. 8f,2i,1r.
Christ Foundation Church	1948	P-Men	G.A.E	583	104,000	2,000	150,000	18.85	*Meserete Kristos Ch.* Cell-based churches. M=EMBMC. 60% Galla, 30% Amhara.
Christian Brethren	1952	P-CBr	x....	10	430	210	800	5.50	*Open Brethren.* M=CMML(UK). Among Galla and Danakil Muslims. 50% Galla, 50% Amhara.
Christian Missionary Fellowship	1965	I-3cW	....E	55	5,000	5,560	16,600	4.47	M=Lion and Lamb Fellowship (USA).
Ch of Jesus Christ of Latter-day Saints		m-LdS	x....	1	20	50	33	0.05	*Mormons.* M=CJCLdS(Utah, USA). Mainly USA expatriates.

Continued overleaf

Country Table 2–concluded

Official name (bold type = church with over 10% of affiliated) 1	*Begun* 2	*Type* 3	*Counc* 4	*Congs* 5	*Adults* 6	*Affiliated 1970* 7	*Affiliated 1995* 8	*G%* 9	*Names, notes, and other statistics* (see Codebook, Part 3) 10
Churches of Christ	1963	I-Dis	x...E	437	45,990	15,000	73,000	6.53	M=CMF,CCC(Instrumental) (USA). Southwest. 1n,3x,26f,W=80%,200Y,300z.
Emmanuel Baptist Church	1960	I-Bap	x...E	12	10,000	3,000	25,000	8.85	M=BBFI(USA). Mainly in east (Bale, Harar). HQ Addis Ababa. 36f,1s.
Ethiopia Gospel Deliverance Church	c1990	I-3vA	.....	30	5,000	–	14,000	20.00	In Addis Ababa. Full Gospel theology.
Ethiopian Orthodox Church:	332	O-Eth	NWA.K	12,185	10,025,800	11,065,900	20,250,000	0.06	*EOC. Ethiopia Tewahido Bete-Cristian.* 20 Dioceses. 53 bps, 250000n. 200,000 Charismatics.
P Shewa (Shoa, Addis Ababa)	332	O-Eth	Np	2,400	2,034,000	2,244,500	4,118,000	0.06	Capital. 18% urban. 55% Orthodox, 45% Muslim. 317r,1s.
D Arusi	1955	O-Eth	Na	300	537,000	592,500	1,090,000	2.47	97% rural. 50% Orthodox, 40% Muslim, 10% pagan. 20r.
D Bale	1960	O-Eth	Na	70	15,000	17,000	31,000	2.43	12% urban. 60% Muslim, 30% pagan, 10% Orthodox. 18r.
D Begemdir	1928	O-Eth	Na	2,100	1,238,000	1,366,500	2,500,000	2.45	96% rural. 95% Orthodox (Amhara), 5% pagan. 148r.
D Gemu Gefa	1955	O-Eth	Na	110	81,000	90,000	164,000	2.43	97% rural. 80% pagan, 10% Orthodox, 10% Muslim. 7r.
D Gojam (Gojjam)	1928	O-Eth	Na	2,600	1,447,000	1,597,100	2,920,000	2.44	95% rural. 95% Orthodox, 3% pagan, 2% Muslim. 322r.
D Harer (Harar, Harage)	1955	O-Eth	Na	115	647,000	714,100	1,305,000	2.44	95% rural. 80% Muslim, 20% Orthodox. 34r.
D Ilubabor	1955	O-Eth	Na	150	63,000	70,000	127,000	2.41	96% rural. 60% pagan, 30% Muslim, 10% Orthodox. 11r.
D Kefa (Kaffa)	1955	O-Eth	Na	200	165,000	182,100	333,000	2.44	7% urban. 70% Muslim, 25% Orthodox, 5% pagan. 31r.
D Sidamo	1955	O-Eth	Na	190	74,000	82,000	150,000	2.45	95% rural. 85% pagan, 5% Orthodox, 5% Muslim. 31r.
D Tigre	1928	O-Eth	Na	2,000	2,119,000	2,338,000	4,273,000	2.44	96% rural. 95% Orthodox (Tigrai, Amhara), 5% Muslim. 253r.
D Welega (Wallega)	c1935	O-Eth	Na	450	550,000	607,400	1,110,000	2.44	97% rural. 40% Orthodox (Galla), 25% Muslim, 25% pagan. 19r.
D Welo (Wallo)	c1935	O-Eth	Na	1,500	1,055,800	1,164,700	2,129,000	2.44	97% rural. 65% Muslim, 35% Orthodox (Amhara). 252r.
Evangelical Church Mekane Yesus	c1880	P-Lut	LWA.E	6,626	1,200,000	177,000	2,091,851	10.38	*ECMY. Dwelling of Jesus.* A=1958. (1970) 675n,61x,558m,239f,4H,2s,2872Y,5871y. (1990) 450n.
Full Gospel Believers Church	c1960	I-3fA	....E	1,200	150,000	100,000	300,000	4.49	Indigenous; Swedish & Finnish aid. 1972-75 severe persecution, 300 imprisoned. 200n.
God's All Times Association	1966	I-3cA	....E	240	60,000	4,000	200,000	16.94	*Mulu Wangel (Full Gospel), Yesemaye Berhan (Light of Heaven).* Students; banned 1968.
Greek Orth P Alexandria: D Aksum	c1900	O-Ara	Cw...	1	500	5,000	1,250	-5.39	Mostly Greeks and Arabs; 3,000 in Addis Ababa. Archbishop, 2 expatriate priests.
Internat Ch of the Foursquare Gospel	1980	P-Pe2	....E	2	500	–	970	6.67	M=ICFG(USA). Overseas aid.
International Evangelical Church	c1965	P-Uni	....E	1	1,200	615	1,850	4.50	Assisted by M=SIM as a union congregation.
Jehovah's Witnesses	c1950	m-Jeh	x....	76	1,300	1,000	12,170	10.51	*Watch Tower. IBSA.* Witnessing under way by 1951. Underground. (1975) 50Y. (1995) 581Y.
Light of the Gospel Church	1950	P-Bap	TF..E	75	15,000	2,000	45,500	13.31	*Birhane Wengel Church.* M=BGC(USA). 80% Shoa Galla, 20% Amhara. 2 schools. 36f,3H,3h,1s.
Light of Life Church	1959	P-Pe2	Z...E	979	365,000	8,000	630,000	19.08	*Heywet Birhane.* M=Philadelphia Ch (SFM, Sweden),AoG. South. Darasa. 34x,27f,8i,3p,470Y.
Lutheran Ch of Bible True Friends in E	1921	P-Lut	l...E	50	3,000	3,500	5,000	1.44	M=SLM(BVM, Bible True Friends) (Sweden). Low-church Lutherans. HQ Addis Ababa.
New Apostolic Church	c1990	I-3aX	x....	10	400	–	534	20.00	*NAC.* M=Neuapostolische Kirche (HQ Zurich, Switzerland).
New Covenant Church	1967	P-Bap	T...E	83	2,000	50	5,000	20.23	M=SBC(USA). Home meetings. Rural development in Amhara closed (EOC) area. 22f,9h.
Place of Paradise Ch	1956	I-3pA	.....	211	38,000	2,500	75,000	14.57	*Sefer Genet.* M=Free Pentecostal Mission/FFFM (Finland).
Seventh-day Adventist Church	1907	P-Adv	x....	163	57,000	45,000	190,000	5.93	*Ethiopia UM.* 39% Galla, 20% Wallamo, 15% Amhara. 4n,20x,81f,4H,3h,3r,226t(39888),3124Y.
United Pentecostal Church of Ethiopia	1967	P-Pe1	x....	1,600	91,000	6,000	280,000	16.62	*Jesus Only Church.* M=UPC(USA). Unitarian Pentecostals. Very rapid growth. 6n,3p(24).
Word of Life Evangelical Church	1927	P-Bap	xM..E	3,950	2,000,000	500,000	4,000,000	8.67	*WLEC.* M=SIM. 1438n,100x,600m,332f,6H,25h,50p,2s(25),W=85%,10000Y,40000z.
Other Protestant denominations		P-	.....	40	4,000	1,500	10,000	0.05	Total about 17 (see below).
Other African indigenous churches		I-3pA	.....	20	6,000	1,000	15,000	0.05	Total 5: including Apostolic Ch of Johane Masowe (Zimbabwe), Holy Ghost Fire Ch (Nigeria).
Doubly-affiliated		2-aff			-673,000	0	-1,343,988		Evangelicals who are also baptized Orthodox.
Totals				**28,843**	**13,726,040**	**12,016,734**	**27,405,308**		

Churches, members, growth, 1900-2025	*Congs*	*Adults*	*Affiliated*	*G%*	*Total denominations*	*6 Megablocs:* O	R	A	P	I	m
Total churches, members, and denominations (mid-1900)	2,000	1,604,000	2,776,000	2.12	6	3	1	0	2	0	0
Total churches, members, and denominations (mid-1970)	15,869	6,943,305	12,016,734	2.12	36	3	1	1	20	9	2
Total churches, members, and denominations (mid-1990)	21,000	11,816,000	23,592,800	3.43	51	3	1	1	30	14	2
Total churches, members, and denominations (mid-1995)	28,843	13,726,040	27,405,308	3.04	52	3	1	1	30	15	2
Total churches, members, and denominations (mid-2000)	30,000	15,607,000	31,161,159	2.60	52	3	1	1	30	15	2
Total churches, members, and denominations (mid-2025)	61,000	31,216,000	62,327,000	2.81	122	10	1	1	45	60	5

NOTES ON TABLE ABOVE

NATIONAL COUNCILS (Column 4, 5th letter).

E = Evangelical Churches Fellowship of Ethiopia (ECFE), 1976.
K = Council for Co-operation of Churches in Ethiopia (CCCE).
S = Ethiopian Episcopal Conference (EEC), also full member of CCCE.

Other national councils. Ethiopian Inter-Mission Council (Protestant missions).

OTHER PROTESTANT DENOMINATIONS. These smaller bodies include: Christian Union (1951), Eglise Francophone d'Addis Ababa, Elim Fellowship (1956), German-speaking Ev Lutheran Ch in Ethiopia (1952), International Pentecostal Holiness Church, Mennonite Brethren Chs, Red Sea Mission Team (1951, 16 missionaries among the Afar). M=FFFM; member of CCCE), Southern Methodist Ch, World-Wide Missions (1966); also USA military chaplaincies until 1974.

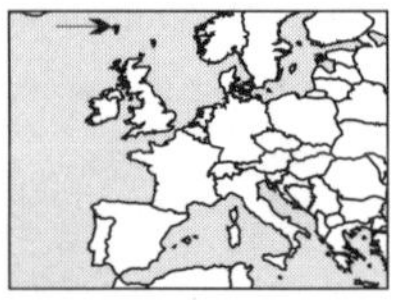

FAEROE ISLANDS

SECULAR DATA, AD 2000

STATE
Official name: Føroyar/Færøerne (The Faeroe Islands).
Short name: Faeroe Islands. **Adjective of nationality:** Faeroe Islanders.
Flag: White with red blue-edged Scandinavian cross.
Area: 1,399 sq. km. (540 sq. mi.).
Government: Self-governing overseas area of the Kingdom of Denmark, since 1948 (1380 Danish crown possession, 1948 home rule granted).
Legislature: Lagting (Parliament), 32 members.
Official language: Faeroese.
Monetary unit: Faeroese krona. **US$1=** Fkr5.70.
Chief cities: THORSHAVN (Torshavn) 15,125.
Political divisions: 1 province.

DEMOGRAPHY
Population: 43,000.
Population density: 30.5/sq. km. (79.1/sq. mi.).
Under 15 years: 8,000.
Growth rate p.a.: 0.13% (births 11.28, deaths 11.69).
Mortality: Infant, per 1,000: 6.9; **Maternal per 100,000:** 12.0.
Life expectancy: 76 (male 74, female 79).
Household size: 3.0. **Floor area per person, sq.m:** 30.0.
Major languages: Faeroese, Danish.
Urban dwellers: 34.73%. **Urban growth rate p.a.:** 2.0%.
Labor force: 42%.

ETHNOLINGUISTIC PEOPLES
97.0% Faeroe Islander; 2.5% Danish (Dane); 0.2% Norwegian; 0.2% Swedish (Swede); .

ECONOMY
National income p.a. per person: US$14,994; **per family:** US$44,983.

EDUCATION
Adult literacy: 99% (male 99%, female 99%). **Schools:** 77.
Universities: 1. **School enrolment:** female/male: 95%/95%.

HEALTH
Access to health services: 95%. **Access to safe water:** 90%.
Hospitals: 3 (57 beds per 10,000). **Doctors:** 81.
Blind: 20. **Deaf:** 2,900. **Murder rate:** 2. **Lepers:** 0.

LITERATURE
New book titles p.a.: 34 (800 p.a. per million). **Periodicals:** 8.
Newspapers: 2 dailies.

COMMUNICATION (per 1,000 people)
Phones: 400 (16% mobile). **Radios:** 447. **TV sets:** 286.
Daily newspaper circulation: 100. **Computers:** 200.

HUMAN LIFE AND LIBERTY (optimum condition=100.0%)
HDI: 92.4. **HSI:** 90.0. **HFI:** 80.0. **EFL:** 50.0.

Country status. The Faeroe Islands is a group of 18 islands in the North Atlantic Ocean near Iceland. It is part of the Danish realm and a self-governing overseas administrative division of Denmark. Fishing, textiles, and tourism are the main economic activities.

HUMAN LIFE AND LIBERTY

Human rights and freedoms. Residents of this territory enjoy the same civil and political rights as their fellow Danes on the mainland.

CHRISTIANITY

PROTESTANT CHURCHES. The principal denomination in the islands, as in Denmark itself, is the Evangelical Lutheran Church, often referred to as the Danish National Church. In the Faeroes, the church is dependent on the Lutheran bishop of Copenhagen, but the dean of Tórshavn has been elevated to the rank of assistant bishop and enjoys considerable autonomy. The country is divided into 11 clerical districts with 57 churches. Most of the priests are native Faeroese, trained in Danish universities. Because of difficulties of travel between the islands, a priest can hold services in only one church within his district on any Sunday. In his absence in his other churches, lay parish-clerks conduct worship services. The Old and New Testaments and the Danish hymnal are in use, translated into Faeroese, which is the church-language of the people. In the Faeroes the Lutheran Church generally receives rather more enthusiastic support than in Denmark.

Other Protestant denominations include the Christian Brethren who began work in 1865 and have developed a significant following in the northern islands; in percentage terms, Brethren are stronger in the Faeroes than in any other country in the world. There are also small Adventist and Salvation Army, Pentecostal, and house church movements.

Lutheran Church. Ruins of unfinished Magnus Cathedral at Kirkebo (7 miles from Torshavn), oldest cultural centre in islands. At left, ancient bishop's residence, of logs with thatched roof.

Country Table 1. **Religious adherents in the Faeroe Islands, AD 1900-2025.**

Year	1900		1970		mid-1990		Annual change, 1990-2000				mid-1995		mid-2000		mid-2025	
Name	Adherents	%	Adherents	%	Adherents	%	Natural	Conversion	Total	Rate	Adherents	%	Adherents	%	Adherents	%
Christians	**15,000**	**100.0**	**38,760**	**100.0**	**46,055**	**98.0**	**-398**	**-12**	**-410**	**-0.93**	**43,830**	**98.2**	**41,953**	**98.1**	**35,400**	**95.7**
PROFESSION																
professing Christians	**15,000**	**100.0**	**38,760**	**100.0**	**46,055**	**98.0**	**-398**	**-12**	**-410**	**-0.93**	**43,830**	**98.2**	**41,953**	**98.1**	**35,400**	**95.7**
AFFILIATION																
unaffiliated Christians	0	0.0	200	0.5	2,265	4.8	-19	29	10	0.42	2,376	5.3	2,363	5.5	2,000	5.4
affiliated Christians	**15,000**	**100.0**	**38,560**	**99.5**	**43,790**	**93.2**	**-379**	**-41**	**-420**	**-1.00**	**41,454**	**92.9**	**39,590**	**92.6**	**33,400**	**90.3**
Protestants	15,000	100.0	38,350	98.9	43,300	92.1	-369	-75	-444	-1.08	40,890	91.6	38,860	90.9	32,000	86.5
Independents	0	0.0	60	0.2	250	0.5	-2	17	15	4.81	300	0.7	400	0.9	820	2.2
Marginal Christians	0	0.0	100	0.3	150	0.3	-1	6	5	2.92	164	0.4	200	0.5	400	1.1
Roman Catholics	0	0.0	50	0.1	90	0.2	-1	5	4	3.75	100	0.2	130	0.3	180	0.5
Trans-megabloc groupings																
Evangelicals	7,500	50.0	10,000	25.8	8,500	18.1	-72	-28	-100	-1.24	7,992	17.9	7,500	17.5	6,000	16.2
Pentecostals/Charismatics	0	0.0	300	0.8	2,900	6.2	-25	33	8	0.27	2,853	6.4	2,980	6.9	3,400	9.2
Great Commission Christians	**300**	**2.0**	**1,940**	**5.0**	**12,500**	**26.6**	**-106**	**35**	**-71**	**-0.58**	**12,000**	**26.9**	**11,794**	**27.6**	**10,500**	**28.4**
Nonreligious	0	0.0	0	0.0	650	1.4	-6	8	2	0.32	670	1.5	671	1.6	1,000	2.7
Baha'is	0	0.0	40	0.1	95	0.2	-1	4	3	2.70	100	0.2	124	0.3	200	0.5
World A (unevangelized persons)	0	0.0	0	0.0	47	0.1	0	1	1	1.84	44	0.1	43	0.1	37	0.1
World B (evangelized non-Christians)	0	0.0	9	0.1	898	1.5	-7	11	4	1.12	746	1.6	1,004	1.8	1,563	3.2
World C (Christians)	15,000	100.0	38,760	99.9	46,055	98.4	-398	-12	-410	-0.93	43,830	98.3	41,953	98.1	35,400	96.7
Country's population	**15,000**	**100.0**	**38,769**	**100.0**	**47,000**	**100.0**	**-405**	**0**	**-405**	**-0.89**	**44,621**	**100.0**	**42,750**	**100.0**	**37,000**	**100.0**

COLUMNS, ROWS.
For meanings and definitions, see Codebook (Part 3). Note that, by definition, total 'Christians' = professing + crypto-Christians, which also = affiliated + unaffiliated Christians, and also = Great Commission Christians + latent Christians. Percentages may not always total exactly, due to rounding.

CENSUSES.
The religion question has not been asked.

NOTES ON RELIGIONS
BAHA'IS. In 1 isolated group.

Great Commission Instrument Panel: status of the Faeroe Islands (for explanation see start of Part 4)

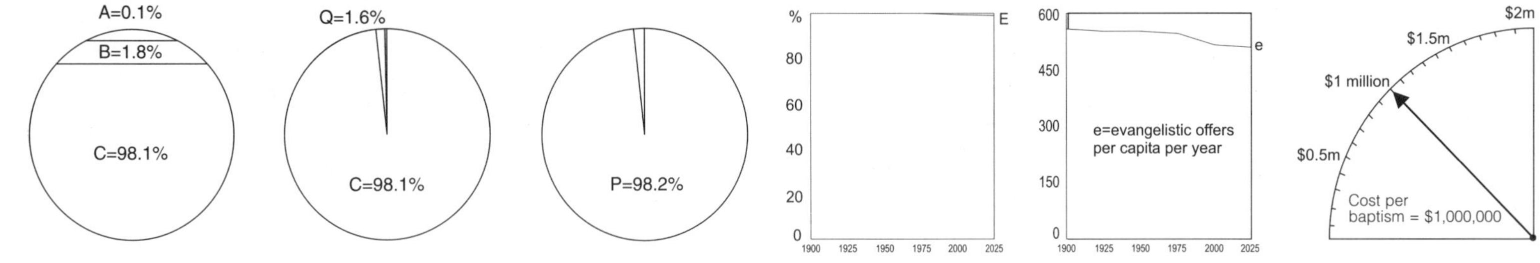

3 Worlds, AD 2000 — Religions, AD 2000 — Ecclesiastical blocs — Evangelization, 1900-2025 — Offers, 1900-2025 — Cost-effectiveness, AD 2000

Country summary. **Worlds A, B, C by ethnolinguistic peoples, cities, and major civil divisions in the Faeroe Islands.**

	PEOPLES							CITIES							CIVIL DIVISIONS						
World	Num	Pop 2000	C%	Christians	E%	U%	Unevangelized	Num	Pop 2000	C%	Christians	E%	U%	Unevangelized	Num	Pop 2000	C%	Christians	E%	U%	Unevangelized
A	0	0	0.00	0	0	0	0	0	0	0.00	0	0	0	0	0	0	0.00	0	0	0	0
B	0	0	0.00	0	0	0	0	0	0	0.00	0	0	0	0	0	0	0.00	0	0	0	0
C	5	42,749	92.61	39,590	100	0	30	1	15,125	93.00	14,066	100	0	12	1	42,749	92.61	39,590	100	0	30
Total	**5**	**42,749**	**92.61**	**39,590**	**100**	**0**	**30**	**1**	**15,125**	**93.00**	**14,066**	**100**	**0**	**12**	**1**	**42,749**	**92.61**	**39,590**	**100**	**0**	**30**

CATHOLIC CHURCH. Roman Catholic worship, suppressed after the 16th-century Reformation, began again in 1931 with the arrival of 2 priests and 5 sisters. The territory is under the jurisdiction of the parish at Tórshavn with 50 members, most of whom are natives of the isles and reside in the capital. A parish council was created in 1970. Personnel include members of the Franciscan Missionaries of Mary.

The Holy See has no diplomatic relations with Faeroe Islands in AD 2000.

Indigenous missions. In the 1970s a handful of Faeroese served as missionaries, mostly in Greenland and Iceland. By 1990 over 50 served in 14 countries with many more in preparation to become missionaries.

CHURCH AND STATE

Legal statutes and relationships between church and state are the same as in Denmark.

INTERDENOMINATIONAL ORGANIZATIONS

Relations between Lutherans and Catholics are good. During the Week of Prayer for Christian Unity (each January), joint worship services are held in Tórshavn.

FUTURE TRENDS AND PROSPECTS

Christians should experience a slight decline to 95.7% in 2025 due to the rise of the nonreligious (virtually none in 1970 rising to 2.7% by 2025).

If the nonreligious continue to grow after 2025, the Faeroe Islands will be less than 90% Christian before AD 2050. If this trend then continues, Christians could fall below 85% within a few years.

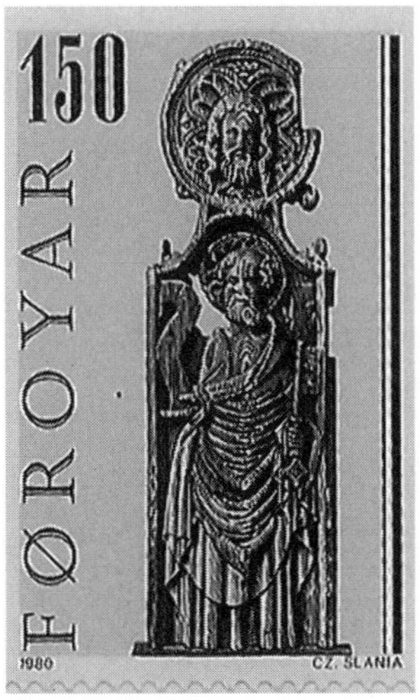

Christ's head on 15th-century Kirkjabour pew gables.

BIBLIOGRAPHY

Faroe: the emergence of a nation. J. F. West. London: C. Hurst, [1972]. 320p.

Färöer: Bibliographie des deutschsprachigen Schrifttums. N. B. Vogt. *Schriftenreihe des Deutsch-Färöischen Freundeskreises e.V. Düsseldorf*, Bd. 2. Leverkusen: Literaturverlag Norden, 1991. 96p.

Faroese folk–tales & legends. J. F. West. Ill., B. Jákupsson. Lerwick, UK: Shetland Pub. Co., 1980. 188p.

Føroya biskupa, prósta og prestatal. J. Øssursson. Tórshavn: Mentunargrunnur Føroya løgtings, 1962. 72p.

Från väckelse till samfund: Svensk pingstmission på öarna i Nordatlanten. P. Pétursson. *Bibliotheca historico-ecclesiastica Lundensis*, 22. Lund, Sweden: Lund University Press, 1990. 296p. (English summary).

Kirkjubøarstólarir og Kirkjubøur: brot úr søgu føroyska biskupssætisins. K. J. Krogh. Tórshavn: E. Thomsen, 1988. 133p. (Treats the history and art of the church on the Faeroe Islands).

Tættir úr Føroya kirjusøgu. P. M. Rasmussen. Tórshavn: Føroya skúlabókagrunnur, 1978. 165p.

The Atlantic Islands: a study of the Faeroe life and scene. K. Williamson & E. Kallsberg. London: Routledge & K. Paul, 1970. 410p.

The Faroe Islands. L. K. Schei & G. Moberg. London: John Murray, 1991. 264p.

The Faroe Islands: interpretations of history. J. Wylie. Lexington, KY: University Press of Kentucky, 1987. 278p.

The Faroes: the faraway islands. A. Jackson. London: Robert Hale, 1991. 239p.

The Faroese Reformation and its consequences. J. S. Wylie. *Papers on European and Mediterranean societies*, no. 10. [Amsterdam]: Anthropologisch-Sociologisch Centrum, Universiteit van Amsterdam, 1978. 84p.

The ring of dancers: images of Faroese culture. J. Wylie & D. Margolin. *Symbol and culture.* Philadelphia: University of Pennsylvania Press, 1981. 204p.

Vækkelsesbevægelsernes møde med færingernes enhedskultur: en analyse, ca. 1850–1918. G. Hansen. *Annales Societatis Scientiarum Faeroensis, Supplementum*, 10. Tórshavn: Føroya, 1984. 275p.

Country Table 2. **Organized churches and denominations in the Faeroe Islands.**

Official name (bold type = church with over 10% of all affiliated) 1	*Begun* 2	*Type* 3	*Counc* 4	*Congs* 5	*Adults* 6	*Affiliated 1970* 7	*Affiliated 1995* 8	*G%* 9	*Names, notes, and other statistics* (see Codebook, Part 3) 10
Catholic Church (D Kobenhavn)	1931	R-Lat	bxBQ.	1	50	50	100	2.81	In Bispedomment Kobenhavn, Katolske Kirke. Closed from Reformation to 1931. 1x,20w.
Christian Brethren	1865	P-CBr	x....	27	3,200	8,000	5,000	-1.86	*Plymouth (Open) Brethren.* M=CMML(UK). Begun by Scots. Strongest in northern isles.
House churches	1965	I-3hW	.....	6	180	60	300	6.65	Small groupings of independent house churches.
Jehovah's Witnesses	c1950	m-Jeh	x....	4	115	100	164	2.00	*Watch Tower. IBSA.* First activity reported 1954. (1975) 8Y. (1995) 3Y.
Lutheran Ch of Denmark: D Faeroe Is	c 750	P-Lut	Lwc..	57	24,400	30,000	35,050	0.62	In Evangelisk-lutherske Folkekirke i Danmark. 11 Districts. Active laity. 16n,1x.
Pentecostal Church		P-Pe2	.....	5	390	150	600	0.05	Mainly Pentecostals.
Salvation Army	1924	P-Sal	xwc..	1	75	100	150	1.64	*Frelsunarherurin* (in Faeroese). *Iceland & Faeroes Div.* Norway & Iceland Territory.
Seventh-day Adventist Church		P-Adv	x....	1	63	100	90	0.05	*Syvende Dags Adventist. SDAs, East Denmark Conference.*
Totals				**102**	**28,473**	**38,560**	**41,454**		

Churches, members, growth, 1900-2025	*Congs*	*Adults*	*Affiliated*	*G%*	*Total denominations*	*6 Megablocs:* *O*	*R*	*A*	*P*	*I*	*m*
Total churches, members, and denominations (mid-1900)	40	9,300	15,000	1.36	2	0	0	0	2	0	0
Total churches, members, and denominations (mid-1970)	91	23,825	38,560	1.36	8	0	1	0	5	1	1
Total churches, members, and denominations (mid-1990)	110	30,100	43,790	0.64	8	0	1	0	5	1	1
Total churches, members, and denominations (mid-1995)	102	28,473	41,454	-1.09	8	0	1	0	5	1	1
Total churches, members, and denominations (mid-2000)	90	27,200	39,590	-0.92	8	0	1	0	5	1	1
Total churches, members, and denominations (mid-2025)	80	22,900	33,400	-0.68	22	0	1	0	10	10	1

FALKLAND ISLANDS

SECULAR DATA, AD 2000

STATE
Official name: The Crown Colony of the Falkland Islands and Dependencies.
Short name: Falkland Islands. **Adjective of nationality:** Falkland Islanders.
Flag: British Blue Ensign with arms of the Colony on white disc in the fly.
Area: 12,173 sq. km. (4,700 sq. mi.).
Government: Crown colony of the United Kingdom (1765 British settlement).
Legislature: Legislative Council, 11 members.
Official language: English.
Monetary unit: Falkland Island pound (£). **US$1=** £ 0.59.
Chief cities: STANLEY (Port Stanley) 1,302.
Political divisions: 1 province.

DEMOGRAPHY
Population: 2,000.
Population density: 0.1/sq. km. (0.4/sq. mi.).
Under 15 years: 0.
Growth rate p.a.: 0.11% (births 11.09, deaths 10.70).
Mortality: Infant, per 1,000: 6.6; **Maternal per 100,000:** 40.0.
Life expectancy: 78 (male 75, female 81).
Household size: 3.0. **Floor area per person, sq.m:** 24.0.
Major languages: English, Spanish.
Urban dwellers: 89.63%. **Urban growth rate p.a.:** 1.4%.
Labor force: 40%.

ETHNOLINGUISTIC PEOPLES
92.7% British; 3.5% Latin American White; 1.0% Japanese; 0.5% Mestizo; 0.3% Norwegian.

ECONOMY
National income p.a. per person: US$7,095; **per family:** US$21,286.

EDUCATION
Adult literacy: 98% (male 98%, female 98%). **Schools:** 2.
Universities: 0. **School enrolment:** female/male: 90%/90%.

HEALTH
Access to health services: 70%. **Access to safe water:** 90%.
Hospitals: 1 (40 beds per 10,000). **Doctors:** 10.
Blind: 10. **Deaf:** 100. **Murder rate:** 3. **Lepers:** 0.

LITERATURE
New book titles p.a.: 1 (400 p.a. per million). **Periodicals:** 0.
Newspapers: 0 dailies.

COMMUNICATION (per 1,000 people)
Phones: 200 (30% mobile). **Radios:** 900. **TV sets:** 200.
Daily newspaper circulation: <1. **Computers:** 500.

HUMAN LIFE AND LIBERTY (optimum condition=100.0%)
HDI: 80.0. **HSI:** 80.0. **HFI:** 75.0. **EFL:** 45.0.

Country Table 1. **Religious adherents in the Falkland Islands, AD 1900-2025.**

Year	*1900*		*1970*		*mid-1990*		*Annual change, 1990-2000*				*mid-1995*		*mid-2000*		*mid-2025*	
Name	*Adherents*	*%*	*Adherents*	*%*	*Adherents*	*%*	*Natural*	*Conversion*	*Total*	*Rate*	*Adherents*	*%*	*Adherents*	*%*	*Adherents*	*%*
Christians	**2,255**	**100.2**	**1,960**	**95.1**	**1,850**	**88.1**	**8**	**0**	**8**	**0.43**	**1,895**	**86.3**	**1,931**	**85.6**	**2,000**	**80.0**
PROFESSION																
professing Christians	**2,255**	**100.2**	**1,960**	**95.1**	**1,850**	**88.1**	**8**	**0**	**8**	**0.43**	**1,895**	**86.3**	**1,931**	**85.6**	**2,000**	**80.0**
AFFILIATION																
unaffiliated Christians	155	6.9	240	11.6	145	6.9	0	0	0	0.20	149	6.8	148	6.6	100	5.0
affiliated Christians	**2,100**	**93.3**	**1,720**	**83.5**	**1,705**	**81.2**	**8**	**0**	**8**	**0.45**	**1,746**	**79.5**	**1,783**	**79.1**	**1,900**	**76.0**
Anglicans	1,460	64.9	1,000	48.5	860	41.0	-4	0	-4	-0.44	850	38.7	823	36.5	800	32.0
Protestants	290	12.9	500	24.3	600	28.6	6	0	6	0.96	631	28.8	660	29.3	800	32.0
Roman Catholics	350	15.6	210	10.2	230	11.0	4	0	4	1.62	250	11.4	270	12.0	350	14.0
Marginal Christians	0	0.0	10	0.5	15	0.7	2	0	2	7.18	15	0.7	30	1.3	50	2.0
Trans-megabloc groupings																
Evangelicals	800	35.6	500	24.3	325	15.5	2	0	2	0.45	337	15.4	340	15.1	400	16.0
Pentecostals/Charismatics	0	0.0	100	4.9	270	12.9	3	0	3	1.06	285	13.0	300	13.3	400	16.0
Great Commission Christians	**180**	**8.0**	**290**	**14.1**	**670**	**31.9**	**8**	**1**	**9**	**1.23**	**725**	**33.0**	**757**	**33.6**	**875**	**33.0**
Nonreligious	0	0.0	60	2.9	150	7.1	3	1	4	2.50	180	8.2	192	8.5	250	10.0
Baha'is	0	0.0	40	1.9	50	2.4	2	0	2	2.97	60	2.7	67	3.0	130	5.2
Atheists	0	0.0	10	0.5	20	1.0	0	0	0	0.96	20	0.9	22	1.0	40	1.6
Buddhists	0	0.0	0	0.0	0	0.0	0	0	0	17.46	5	0.2	5	0.3	10	0.5
New-Religionists	0	0.0	0	0.0	0	0.0	0	0	0	14.87	5	0.2	4	0.2	10	0.5
Other religionists	45	2.0	30	1.5	30	1.4	1	0	1	1.84	30	1.6	36	1.6	60	2.4
World A (unevangelized persons)	4	0.2	4	0.2	6	0.3	0	0	0	-3.31	6	0.3	4	0.2	12	0.6
World B (evangelized non-Christians)	-9	1.8	96	6.5	244	11.6	6	1	7	-7.65	299	13.6	315	14.2	488	19.4
World C (Christians)	2,255	98.0	1,960	93.3	1,850	88.1	9	-1	8	0.43	1,895	86.1	1,931	85.6	2,000	80.0
Country's population	**2,250**	**100.0**	**2,061**	**100.0**	**2,100**	**100.0**	**15**	**0**	**15**	**0.00**	**2,200**	**100.0**	**2,250**	**100.0**	**2,500**	**100.0**

COLUMNS, ROWS.
For meanings and definitions, see Codebook (Part 3). Note that, by definition, total 'Christians' = professing + crypto-Christians, which also = affiliated + unaffiliated Christians, and also = Great Commission Christians + latent Christians. Percentages may not always total exactly, due to rounding.

CENSUSES.
1901 census of the British Empire (as in 1900 column above, adjusted). **28.III.1953:** 86.1% Anglicans and Protestants, 10.6% Roman Catholics, 3.4% other religionists. **18.III.1962:** 64.7% Anglicans, 24.2% Protestants, 10.9% Roman Catholics, 0.2% marginal Protestants. **3.XII.1972:** 54.2% Anglicans, 27.6% Protestants, 11.0% Roman Catholics, 4.8% nonreligious, 1.9% other religionists, 0.5% marginal Protestants.

NOTES ON RELIGIONS
BAHA'IS. In 1 local spiritual assembly, unchanged from 1973 to 1996.

Country status. The Falkland Islands are 2 main islands and over 100 smaller ones in the South Atlantic Ocean off the coast of Argentina. It is a colony of the United Kingdom and its residents enjoy all civil and political rights. A major source of income is the granting of fishing licenses for a large maritime region it controls.

HUMAN LIFE AND LIBERTY

Human rights have the same significance as in Britain.

CHRISTIANITY

The population is almost entirely Christian and is primarily Anglican in denomination. The first colonial chaplain was J. L. Moody who arrived in Stanley in 1845, but the great builder of the Anglican Church was L. E. Brandon during 1877-1907. Missionaries of the South American Missionary Society established their first station in the Falklands in 1854. Smaller Catholic and free church communities also exist in the islands. The first Catholic church was built in 1857 and the first Presbyterian minister settled at Darwin in 1872.

In 1869 the Anglican diocese of the Falkland Islands was founded, with its cathedral in Port Stanley, serving the islands and also British expatriates throughout all South American except British Guiana. In 1910 the diocese of Argentina and Eastern South America was separated off, and the diocese of the Falkland Islands became particularly responsible for Anglicans in Chile, Bolivia and Peru. In 1946 the 2 dioceses were reunited in a single diocese of Argentina, Eastern South America & the Falkland Islands; in 1964 the diocese of Paraguay was separated off, and in 1965 the diocese of Northern Argentina separated off.

In 1977 the Falkland Islands were detached from the diocese of Argentina and from the autonomous Anglican province (CASA), and were returned once more to the metropolitical jurisdiction of the archbishop of Canterbury.

Great Commission Instrument Panel: status of the Falkland Islands (for explanation see start of Part 4)

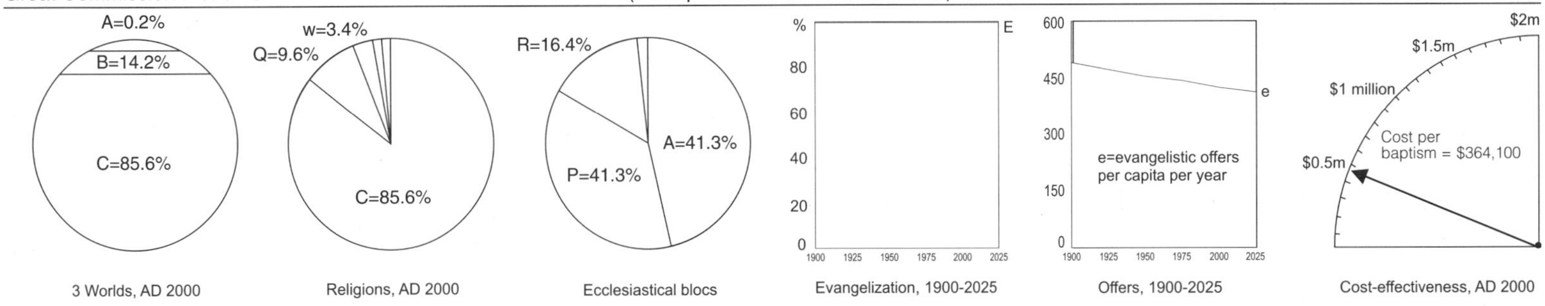

Country summary. **Worlds A, B, C by ethnolinguistic peoples, cities, and major civil divisions in the Falkland Islands.**

	PEOPLES							*CITIES*							*CIVIL DIVISIONS*						
World	*Num*	*Pop 2000*	*C%*	*Christians*	*E%*	*U%*	*Unevangelized*	*Num*	*Pop 2000*	*C%*	*Christians*	*E%*	*U%*	*Unevangelized*	*Num*	*Pop 2000*	*C%*	*Christians*	*E%*	*U%*	*Unevangelized*
A	0	0	0.00	0	0	0	0	0	0	0.00	0	0	0	0	0	0	0.00	0	0	0	0
B	0	0	0.00	0	0	0	0	0	0	0.00	0	0	0	0	0	0	0.00	0	0	0	0
C	6	2,255	79.11	1,784	100	0	4	1	1,302	79.03	1,029	100	0	3	1	2,255	79.07	1,783	100	0	5
Total	**6**	**2,255**	**79.11**	**1,784**	**100**	**0**	**4**	**1**	**1,302**	**79.03**	**1,029**	**100**	**0**	**3**	**1**	**2,255**	**79.07**	**1,783**	**100**	**0**	**5**

Church of England in the Falkland Islands. Anglican cathedral in Port Stanley, with in foreground whalebone monument commemorating British occupancy.

CATHOLIC CHURCH. The Holy See has no diplomatic relations with Falkland Islands in AD 2000.

Indigenous missions. Since the 1982 war of the South Atlantic, a larger population of British military personnel have lived in the Falklands, most of them Anglican or nonreligious.

CHURCH AND STATE

Since the Falkland Islands are a British crown colony, freedom of religion is guaranteed. There is no established church.

BROADCASTING AND MEDIA

Shortwave programs from HCJB (Ecuador), TWR (Antilles) and AWR (Costa Rica) can be easily received.

Christian television programs can be received via satellite.

INTERDENOMINATIONAL ORGANIZATIONS

Ecumenical relations between the churches are informal but cordial; no formal organization exists.

FUTURE TRENDS AND PROSPECTS

Due to the meteoric rise of the nonreligious (2.9% in 1970 to 10% by 2025) Christians could decline from 95.1% in 1970 to 80% by 2025.

By AD 2050, secularism will potentially have eroded Christianity to below 70%. This trend could continue indefinitely.

Postage stamp set commemorating centenary of Bishop Stirling's 1869 consecration (1969).

BIBLIOGRAPHY

After the Falklands: a Christian perspective on war. A. Litherland. New Malden, UK: Fellowship of Reconciliation, [1983]. 17p.

Christ Church Cathedral, The Falkland Islands: its life and times 1892 to 1992. G. Murphy. Stanley: Lance Bidwell on behalf of Christ Church Cathedral Council, 1991. 32p.

Churches of the South Atlantic Islands, 1502–1991. E. Cannan. Oswestry, UK: Anthony Nelson, 1992. 315p.

Conflict in the South Atlantic: documents on the Falklands/Malvinas crisis. Geneva: Commission of the Churches on International Affairs, World Council of Churches, 1983. 68p.

La patria y el orden temporal: el simbolismo de las Malvians. A. Caturelli. Buenos Aires: Ediciones Gladius, 1993. 353p.

'Patagonian Missionary Society—Keppel Island 1855–1911,' S. Miller, *Falkland Islands Journal*, 9 (1975), 8–13.

Primeras capillas y templos de las Islas Sansón y Patos (Malvinas) sus capellanes y parrocos. L. R. Altamira. *Universidad Nacional de Córdoba Instituto de Estudios Americanistas*, 12. Córdoba, Argentina: Imprenta de la Universidad, 1947. 51p.

'The Catholic Church on the Falkland Islands,' A. Agreiter, *Falkland Islands Journal*, 6, 1 (1992), 6–9. (Brief historical sketch of the Catholic Church on the Falkland Islands, by Msgr. Agreiter).

The Falkland Islands and their natural history. I. J. Strange. Newton Abbot, UK: David & Charles, 1987. 160p. (Chapter 6 contains description of peoples and settlements).

The Falkland Islands, South Georgia and The South Sandwich Islands. A. Day. *World bibliographical series*, vol. 184. Oxford, UK: CLIO Press, 1996. (See especially 'Religion,' p.103–6).

'The history of the Non–Conformist Church in the Falkland Islands,' J. F. Gerry-Hoppé, *Falkland Islands Journal*, 6, 1 (1992), 17–25.

The South Sandwich Islands: 1. General description. M. W. Holdgate & P. E. Baker. *BAS scientific reports*, 91. Cambridge, UK: BAS, 1979. 76p.

Country Table 2. **Organized churches and denominations in the Falkland Islands.**

Official name (bold type = church with over 10% of all affiliated) 1	*Begun* 2	*Type* 3	*Counc* 4	*Congs* 5	*Adults* 6	*Affiliated 1970* 7	*Affiliated 1995* 8	*G%* 9	*Names, notes, and other statistics* (see Codebook, Part 3) 10
Catholic Church: PA Falkland Islands	1857	R-Lat	P....	1	200	210	250	0.70	*PA Malvinas.* Not in CELAM. 39% expatriates. M=MHM. C=1+0+0. 3x, 3m, 10Yy.
Church of England in the Falkland Is	1765	A-Eva	aw...	17	690	1,000	850	-0.65	Until 1977, in D Argentina (CASA). 1854, M=SAMS(UK). 99% British. 1n,W=27%.
Jehovah's Witnesses	c1960	m-Jeh	x....	1	9	10	15	1.64	*Watch Tower. IBSA.* Very little growth since 1962 total of 5 adherents.
United Free Ch of the Falkland Is	1872	P-Ref	.....	5	450	500	560	0.45	Includes Lutherans and some Baptists. M=Ch of Scotland Overseas Council (UK). 1f.
Other Protestant churches	c1980	P-	.....	3	50	–	71	6.67	In 2 recent denominations.
Totals				**27**	**1,399**	**1,720**	**1,746**		

Churches, members, growth, 1900-2025	*Congs*	*Adults*	*Affiliated*	*G%*	*Total denominations*	*6 Megablocs: O*	*R*	*A*	*P*	*I*	*m*
Total churches, members, and denominations (mid-1900)	20	1,400	2,100	-0.28	3	0	1	1	1	0	0
Total churches, members, and denominations (mid-1970)	18	1,126	1,720	-0.28	4	0	1	1	1	0	1
Total churches, members, and denominations (mid-1990)	20	1,400	1,705	-0.04	5	0	1	1	2	0	1
Total churches, members, and denominations (mid-1995)	27	1,399	1,746	0.48	6	0	1	1	3	0	1
Total churches, members, and denominations (mid-2000)	30	1,400	1,783	0.42	6	0	1	1	3	0	1
Total churches, members, and denominations (mid-2025)	50	1,500	1,900	0.25	15	0	1	1	6	4	3

FIJI

SECULAR DATA, AD 2000

STATE
Official name: The Sovereign Democratic Republic of the Fiji Islands.
Short name: Fiji. **Adjective of nationality:** Fijian.
Flag: Similar to British Blue Ensign with coat of arms in light blue fly.
Area: 18,272 sq. km. (7,055 sq. mi.).
Government: Republic with two legislative houses, since 1987 (c1800 chiefdoms, 1874 British crown colony, 1970 Independence).
Legislature: Senate, 34 members; House of Representatives, 70 members.
Official language: English.
Monetary unit: 1 Fiji dollar (F$) = 100 cents. **US$1=** F$2.06.
Chief cities: SUVA 168,965; Lautoka 46,713.
Political divisions: 15 provinces.
Armed forces: 4,000.

DEMOGRAPHY
Population: 817,000.
Population density: 44.7/sq. km. (115.7/sq. mi.).
Under 15 years: 256,000.
Growth rate p.a.: 1.40% (births 20.99, deaths 4.67).
Mortality: Infant, per 1,000: 17.2; **Maternal per 100,000:** 90.0.
Life expectancy: 74 (male 72, female 76).
Household size: 6.0. **Floor area per person, sq.m:** 18.0.
Major languages: English, Fijian, Hindustani, Tongan, Tamil, Bihari, Telugu, Chinese, Rotuman, Kadavu, Lauan, Nadroga, and several others.
Urban dwellers: 42.33%. **Urban growth rate p.a.:** 2.6%.
Labor force: 34%.

ETHNOLINGUISTIC PEOPLES
29.5% Fijian (Bauan, Mbau); 27.0% Fijian Hindi; 8.6% Tamil; 6.5% Western Fijian (Nadroga); 3.7% Bihari.

ECONOMY
National income p.a. per person: US$2,439; **per family:** US$14,638.

EDUCATION
Adult literacy: 91% (male 93%, female 89%). **Schools:** 693.
Universities: 5. **School enrolment:** female/male: 97%/97%.

HEALTH
Access to health services: 75%. **Access to safe water:** 100%.
Hospitals: 25 (22 beds per 10,000). **Doctors:** 426.
Blind: 4,000. **Deaf:** 50,900. **Murder rate:** 11.
Lepers: 8,000. **Underweight prevalence under 5:** 8%.

LITERATURE
New book titles p.a.: 430 (530 p.a. per million). **Periodicals:** 21.
Newspapers: 1 daily.

COMMUNICATION (per 1,000 people)
Phones: 83 (6% mobile). **Radios:** 574. **TV sets:** 89.
Daily newspaper circulation: 45. **Computers:** 80.

HUMAN LIFE AND LIBERTY (optimum condition=100.0%)
HDI: 86.3. **HSI:** 60.0. **HFI:** 40.0. **EFL:** 38.0.

Country Table 1. **Religious adherents in Fiji, AD 1900-2025.**

Year	1900		1970		mid-1990		Annual change, 1990-2000				mid-1995		mid-2000		mid-2025	
Name	Adherents	%	Adherents	%	Adherents	%	Natural	Conversion	Total	Rate	Adherents	%	Adherents	%	Adherents	%
Christians	**103,800**	**86.5**	**262,540**	**50.5**	**410,000**	**56.5**	**5,130**	**234**	**5,364**	**1.24**	**433,500**	**56.5**	**463,635**	**56.8**	**621,000**	**56.3**
PROFESSION																
professing Christians	**103,800**	**86.5**	**262,540**	**50.5**	**410,000**	**56.5**	**5,130**	**234**	**5,364**	**1.24**	**433,500**	**56.5**	**463,635**	**56.8**	**621,000**	**56.3**
AFFILIATION																
unaffiliated Christians	12,000	10.0	18,469	3.6	5,000	0.7	63	-174	-111	-2.48	3,800	0.5	3,890	0.5	3,000	0.3
affiliated Christians	**91,800**	**76.5**	**244,071**	**46.9**	**405,000**	**55.8**	**5,067**	**408**	**5,475**	**1.28**	**429,700**	**56.0**	**459,745**	**56.3**	**618,000**	**56.0**
Protestants	86,800	72.3	188,662	36.3	326,000	44.9	4,086	814	4,900	1.41	347,657	45.3	375,000	45.9	500,000	45.3
Independents	0	0.0	2,920	0.6	68,000	9.4	852	948	1,800	2.38	78,457	10.2	86,000	10.5	130,000	11.8
Roman Catholics	4,800	4.0	43,515	8.4	72,000	9.9	902	398	1,300	1.67	78,683	10.3	85,000	10.4	120,000	10.9
Marginal Christians	0	0.0	2,474	0.5	11,000	1.5	138	262	400	3.15	13,027	1.7	15,000	1.8	24,000	2.2
Anglicans	200	0.2	6,500	1.3	8,100	1.1	102	-82	20	0.24	8,200	1.1	8,300	1.0	8,500	0.8
doubly-affiliated	0	0.0	0	0.0	-80,100	-11.0	-1,004	-1,942	-2,946	3.18	-96,324	-12.6	-109,555	-13.4	-164,500	-14.9
Trans-megabloc groupings																
Evangelicals	72,000	60.0	105,000	20.2	101,640	14.0	1,274	-818	456	0.44	102,453	13.4	106,200	13.0	132,480	12.0
Pentecostals/Charismatics	0	0.0	20,000	3.8	148,200	20.4	1,858	1,822	3,680	2.24	166,603	21.7	185,000	22.6	298,000	27.0
Great Commission Christians	**8,400**	**7.0**	**83,200**	**16.0**	**90,000**	**12.4**	**1,128**	**384**	**1,512**	**1.57**	**97,000**	**12.6**	**105,120**	**12.9**	**154,500**	**14.0**
Hindus	13,400	11.2	209,900	40.3	243,930	33.6	3,058	-248	2,810	1.10	256,755	33.4	272,031	33.3	365,670	33.1
Muslims	2,600	2.2	40,500	7.8	50,600	7.0	634	-95	539	1.02	54,000	7.0	55,993	6.9	75,000	6.8
Nonreligious	0	0.0	2,560	0.5	9,000	1.2	113	65	178	1.82	10,000	1.3	10,783	1.3	20,000	1.8
Baha'is	0	0.0	1,000	0.2	4,800	0.7	60	27	87	1.69	5,400	0.7	5,674	0.7	8,700	0.8
Sikhs	200	0.2	3,200	0.6	4,500	0.6	56	26	82	1.68	5,000	0.7	5,318	0.7	8,500	0.8
Chinese folk-religionists	0	0.0	200	0.0	2,800	0.4	35	-9	26	0.90	2,950	0.4	3,063	0.4	4,600	0.4
Ethnoreligionists	0	0.0	100	0.0	270	0.0	3	0	3	1.03	290	0.0	299	0.0	400	0.0
Jews	0	0.0	0	0.0	100	0.0	1	0	1	0.87	105	0.0	109	0.0	130	0.0
World A (unevangelized persons)	6,000	5.0	130,076	25.0	113,256	15.6	1,416	-3,554	-2,138	-2.08	106,711	13.9	91,504	11.2	100,464	9.1
World B (evangelized non-Christians)	10,200	8.5	127,690	24.5	202,744	27.9	2,544	3,320	5,864	2.59	227,499	29.6	261,861	32.0	382,536	34.6
World C (Christians)	103,800	86.5	262,540	50.5	410,000	56.5	5,130	234	5,364	1.24	433,500	56.5	463,635	56.8	621,000	56.3
Country's population	**120,000**	**100.0**	**520,307**	**100.0**	**726,000**	**100.0**	**9,090**	**0**	**9,090**	**1.19**	**767,711**	**100.0**	**817,000**	**100.0**	**1,104,000**	**100.0**

COLUMNS, ROWS.
For meanings and definitions, see Codebook (Part 3). Note that, by definition, total 'Christians' = professing + crypto-Christians, which also = affiliated + unaffiliated Christians, and also = Great Commission Christians + latent Christians. Percentages may not always total exactly, due to rounding.

CENSUSES.
21.X.1946: 46.5% Protestants and Anglicans, 38.8% Hindus, 7.4% Roman Catholics, 6.6% Muslims, 0.4% Sikhs, 0.1% Chinese folk-religionists, 0.1% nonreligious. **27.IX.1956:** 42.2% Protestants (40.1% Methodists), 39.8% Hindus, 8.0% Roman Catholics, 7.4% Muslims, 1.5% Anglicans, 0.5% Sikhs, 0.5% nonreligious, 0.1% Chinese folk-religionists. **12.IX.1966:** 41.1% Protestants (38.3% Methodists), 40.3% Hindus, 8.4% Roman Catholics, 7.8% Muslims, 1.4% Anglicans, 0.6% Sikhs, 0.3% nonreligious.

NOTES ON RELIGIONS
BAHA'IS. Growth of local spiritual assemblies: 1964, none; 1973, 17, rising steadily to 43 LSAs by 1996.
COUNTRY'S POPULATION. Indians came as indentured laborers from 1879-1916; of the 60,000 who came to Fiji, only 60 were Christians. In the 1901 census, of the 120,124 population, 94,937 were Fijians and 17,105 (14.2%) Indians.
HINDUS. South Indians originally from Kerala and Madras. Among Hindu sects, ISKCON (Hare Krishna) has 1 centre, the Ramakrishna Mission others.
INDEPENDENTS. In 6 bodies in 1995 (see Table 2).
MUSLIMS. Sunnis. There is also an Ahmadiya Mission (enumerated here under Muslims though declared non-Muslim by Pakistan). *Hajj pilgrims to Mecca.* (1976) 36.
NONRELIGIOUS. Europeans, and young Chinese who are abandoning family folk religion.
PROTESTANTS. All Fijians had become Christians, at least nominally, by 1885. By 1900 there were no traditional religionists left. In 1900 a large number of Methodists were children in Methodist schools; in 1909, there were 1,019 Methodist schools in Fiji and 22 in Rotuma.
SIKHS. Indians (Punjabis).

Great Commission Instrument Panel: status of Fiji (for explanation see start of Part 4)

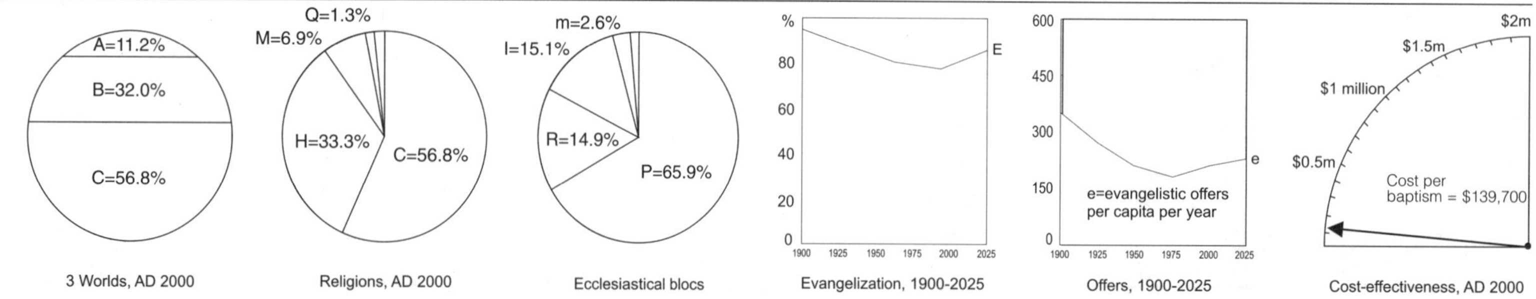

Country status. Fiji comprises a group of some 330 volcanic islands in the South Pacific. Originally a British territory, Fiji's population bears the impress of its colonial history. The British imported over 60,000 indentured Indian laborers between 1879 and 1916 to work in the sugarcane fields. The descendants of these laborers constitute a numerical majority on the islands, while the native Fijians constitute a minority. The main exports are sugar, rice, copra, and ginger.

HUMAN LIFE AND LIBERTY

Human need and development. A sugar-based economy, Fiji has been fairly prosperous both under the British and as an independent nation. Much of the local economy is controlled by Indians, who are also well represented in the middle levels of public service. There are no signs of dire want on the islands where human needs are few and easily met. Fiji has also made considerable advances in education, agriculture, health, and nutrition. Fiji has a high literacy rate of 91% and its medical indicators are uniformly high.

Human rights and freedoms. Fiji has been singled out by Amnesty International as a country with an unblemished record in human rights. This record is remarkable because Fiji has been riven by ethnic conflicts since the military-led coups of 1987. The four-year military regime that followed these coups did not result in violence or suppression of rights. The judiciary remains independent of the executive and rights of due process are strictly observed in all cases. The occasional instances of police brutality have grown fewer over the years. Freedom of speech and

Country summary. **Worlds A, B, C by ethnolinguistic peoples, cities, and major civil divisions in Fiji.**

	PEOPLES							CITIES							CIVIL DIVISIONS						
World	Num	Pop 2000	C%	Christians	E%	U%	Unevangelized	Num	Pop 2000	C%	Christians	E%	U%	Unevangelized	Num	Pop 2000	C%	Christians	E%	U%	Unevangelized
A	1	114	0.00	0	43	57	65	0	0	0.00	0	0	0	0	0	0	0.00	0	0	0	0
B	9	407,659	17.39	70,884	78	22	91,360	2	215,678	55.01	118,653	88	12	25,240	13	591,182	53.90	318,651	86	14	80,352
C	20	409,131	95.05	388,864	100	0	195	0	0	0.00	0	0	0	0	2	225,724	62.51	141,094	95	5	11,270
Total	**30**	**816,904**	**56.28**	**459,748**	**89**	**11**	**91,620**	**2**	**215,678**	**55.01**	**118,653**	**88**	**12**	**25,240**	**15**	**816,906**	**56.28**	**459,745**	**89**	**11**	**91,622**

press, restricted for a few years after the coups, have been fully restored, but the government retains discretionary powers to discipline erring journalists. Elections are free but the Constitution guarantees ethnic Fijian dominance of the government by mandating that 37 of the 74 parliamentary seats must be held by ethnic Fijians. The prime minister and president are also required to be ethnic Fijians. Inheritance and citizenship laws discriminate against non-ethnic Fijians. Control of land is also secured in ethnic Fijian hands through legislation enacted under the British. About 84% of the land is held communally by ethnic Fijians under laws that prohibit their transfer or sale to non-ethnic Fijians. Women suffer less discrimination than in most Asian countries. Some Fijian women hold high positions in the traditional chiefly system.

Human environment. Fiji has a rich ecosystem. Habitats include savannas, rainforests, marshes, reefs, and lagoons. Although the number of mammalian species is small, the variety of plant life is great. However, indiscriminate logging between 1969 and 1988 has led to a 30% reduction in the forest resources. Because of the rough terrain of the interior, farming practices are not land-friendly, and have encouraged soil erosion on steep terraces. In addition, the marine environment is also threatened by sewage and waste disposal.

Postage stamp set (1973) illustrating festivals of major religions: Chinese folk religion (New Year), Islam (Id-ul-Fitar), Hinduism (Diwali), and Christianity (Christmas).

NON-CHRISTIAN RELIGIONS

Hinduism is the largest religion of the island after Christianity, 40% of the population being Hindus in 1966 and 33.4% in 1995. Indians, who are 80% Hindu, first came to Fiji mostly from Kerala and Madras as plantation workers after 1879; many of their descendants are now successful farmers. They make up the largest single ethnic group in the country. Since the political strife of 1987 a large number of Indians have emigrated. Still, the Indian community of Fiji constitutes the largest non-Christian population in the Pacific.

Islam is also confined to the Indian population. In 1995, 7.0% of the population were Muslims.

Sikhism was represented by more than 5,000 persons (0.7%) in 1995. Sikhs are all of Indian background.

Chinese folk religion still plays a part in Chinese life, although the proportion of Chinese who state that they have no religion is higher than for any other group; most are young persons who are in process of abandoning their family religion.

Traditional religion has virtually disappeared as a distinct religious category, and almost all ethnic Fijians today profess to be Christians. Nevertheless, the heritage of traditional religion continues to manifest itself both in indigenous expressions of Christianity and also in periodic movements such as the Tuka cult founded by the prophet Ndungumoi in 1885, which was an anti-Christian revival of ritual cannibalism. Witchcraft remains widespread; most practicing witchdoctors now are Christians.

Inter-religious conflict has increased in Fiji since the race-based constitutional crisis of 1987. Hindu temples and Muslim mosques were destroyed.

Methodist Church in Fiji. *Above.* Sunday service at local church in Ba. *Below.* Church in Lautoka.

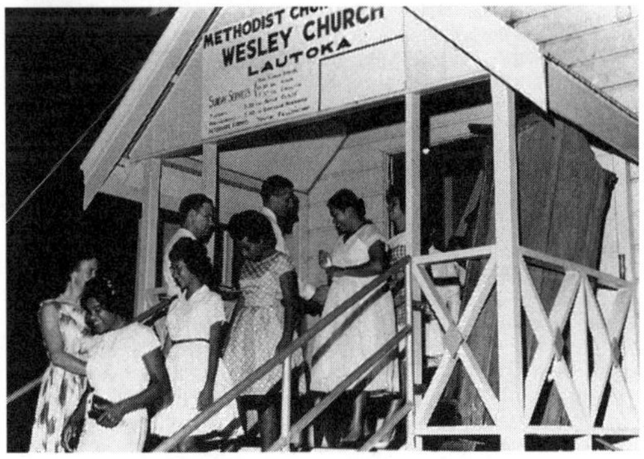

CHRISTIANITY

PROTESTANT CHURCHES. Two Tahitian teachers of the LMS arrived in 1830. Later through comity agreements the islands were assigned to Methodists who sent 2 missionaries and a team of Tongan teachers to Fiji in 1835. Little progress was made prior to the baptism of the principal chief, Thakombau, in 1854. Fijians have since become missionaries to many other parts of the South Pacific. The Methodist church continues to be the principal denomination. It has its strength among the ethnic Fijian population, 83% of whom claim to be Methodists, as well as among the Rotumans (62%), part-Europeans (39%) and other Pacific islanders (38%). Work among Indians began in 1897 and a separate Indian synod had developed by 1945. The Methodist Church has also been heavily involved in education, more than one thousand village schools being established by 1876.

The Assemblies of God came to Fiji in 1926 but made little impact prior to 1965. They have since grown from less than 3,000 in 1966 to 31,000 by 1990. Seventh-day Adventists have been active since 1889. There are also small groups of Brethren, Congregationalists and Presbyterians, the latter being almost entirely Europeans. In the early 1990s, a number of Bible schools and theological colleges served not only Fiji but also the south Pacific region. These included Ambassadors for Christ Bible School, the Assemblies of God Bible School, the Baptist Christian Leadership College, the Methodist Theological College, and South Pacific Missionary Village Training Centre. The latter is a Korean Protestant ministry which also teaches practical trades.

CATHOLIC CHURCH. The first Catholic missionaries arrived in 1844. The islands became a vicariate apostolic in 1887, and the first Fijian priest was ordained in 1955. Catholicism is strongest among the part-Europeans, Rotumans, and other Pacific islanders. From the early 1970s the Catholic Church put out special effort to reach the Indians, which was somewhat fruitful. Attention has been given to language study and the development of contacts through the bishops of India, and on the invitation of the government a group of Gabriel Brothers arrived from India in 1973 to set up a boys' town in Fiji. A strong charismatic movement has been active in Fiji. By 1992 there were 7 Catholic charismatic centers in Suva. The movement spreads through the work of laypersons who conduct 'Life in the Spirit' seminars from church to church.

The Holy See has diplomatic relations with Fiji and in AD 2000 is represented to government and the Catholic hierarchy by a pro-nuncio residing in Wellington, New Zealand.

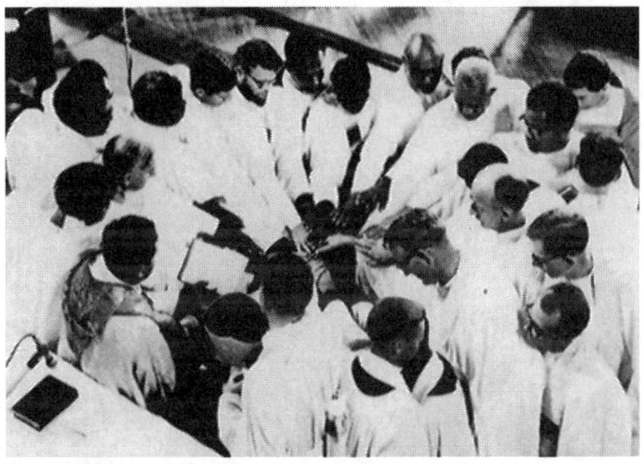

Anglican Church, Diocese of Polynesia. Ordination of a priest by laying on of hands, Holy Trinity Cathedral, Suva, in 1968.

ANGLICAN CHURCH. Anglicans are mostly Europeans. Fiji belongs to the diocese of Polynesia and is part of the Church of the Province of New Zealand. Anglicans sponsor a number of primary and secondary schools.

INDIGENOUS CHURCHES. In 1942 a prophet named Kelevi Nawai, who was termed the Vessel of Christ, established himself at Kadavu-Levu. His emphasis on magical healing, communication with the dead and the raising of dead persons, and immortality, had a strong appeal among Methodists prior to the suppression of the the movement by government.

Another schism from Methodism, begun by Ratu Emosi after World War II and still active, is the Church of Time, which lays great stress on the right use of time by members. Still a third split is the Messiah Club of Sairusi Nabogibogi who has modeled his services on those of the Methodists and whose members are still encouraged to attend the Methodist Church. A cargo-cult emphasis is given to the higher standard of living which the messiah is expected to bring about in the future. Also stressed are the Ten Commandments and exposition of the Bible.

Renewal movements. In the 1990s the Pentecostal/Charismatic Renewal continued to spread rapidly across most older churches, and numbered over 185,000 adherents (of whom 35% Pentecostals, 19% Charismatics, and 45% Independents).

Indigenous missions. Fijians have been sending out missionaries for over 150 years-mainly to other islands. Today, nearly 100 Fijians serve overseas.

CHURCH AND STATE

Early Methodist opposition to Catholicism had government backing and sanction. Catholic conversions were actually forbidden by the governor in 1888; but freedom of religion was restored in 1897.

All denominational schools must also be registered and church medical institutions receive government subsidies. The Methodist Church is involved in a government-sponsored adult rural education program, and Catholic sisters work in the government's anti-leprosy campaign.

The phrases 'dedication to God' and 'reverence for God' appear in the Preamble to the constitution of 1970, with the words: 'Whereas all the peoples of Fiji have...acknowledged...their reverence for God ...' Freedom of religion is guaranteed in Article II. Sections 2-4 give religious communities the right to open schools and teach religious education, provided that no person is forced to participate against his will; while section 5 prohibits the use of oaths which are contrary to a person's religion or belief. All of these freedoms are assured provided that they do not conflict with the rights of others or the interests of public safety, order, morality, health, and defense (Article II, section 6). Following the 2 military coups of 1987 that prevented power from going to a part-Indian regime, government policy has tended to give a preferred place to certain Christian observances, notably Sunday Regulations.

Seminarians in library of Pacific Theological College, Suva.

BROADCASTING AND MEDIA

Shortwave radio programs from KNLS have generated response. A third of the populace have viewed the 'Jesus' Film; 89,700 (31%) have responded with decisions for Christ. Programs by WEC's Radio Worldwide are aired on Radio Fiji. Fiji is a member of UNDA. Catholics air a 'Morning Devotion' daily and the Mass once a month.

INTERDENOMINATIONAL ORGANIZATIONS

The Fiji Council of Churches was founded in 1964 with 4 members: the Methodist, Anglican, Congregational, and Presbyterian churches. The Catholic Church joined in 1968. Activities include the Week of Prayer for Christian Unity, Bible Week, a chaplaincy program (hospital, prison and university) and joint service projects such as HART (Housing and Relief Trust) and a low-cost housing scheme in Suva.

The Pacific Conference of Churches, founded in 1969, has its headquarters in Suva, Fiji. It began originally as a regional Protestant body, but the Catholic Episcopal Conference of the Pacific (CEPAC) joined as a full member in January 1976 after applying for membership a few years earlier.

Evangelicals are served by 2 organizations, the Evangelical Fellowship of Fiji and the younger Evangelical Alliance of Fiji.

FUTURE TRENDS AND PROSPECTS

Christians will likely grow from 50.5% in 1970 to 56.3% by AD 2025 with a corresponding drop in Hindus (40.3% to 33.1% in the same period).

Hindus could decline to less than 30% before AD 2050 with further decline possible later. Christians, conversely, would rise to 60% and beyond in the same period. Islam is likely to stay close to 6% throughout the near future.

BIBLIOGRAPHY

A bibliography of bibliographies of the South Pacific. I. Leeson. London: Oxford University Press, 1954. 61p.
A hundred years in Fiji. J. W. Burton & W. Deane. London: Epworth Press, 1936. 144p. (On Methodism).
'A new religious cult in Fiji,' A. C. Cato, *Oceania*, 18 (1947), 145–56.
'A search for soil for the mustard seed: the impact of ecumenical social thought in Fiji and the Pacific,' S. Siwatibau & W. Flannery, *Ecumenical review*, 40, 2 (1988), 233–40.
'Christianity, people of the land, and chiefs in Fiji,' M. Kaplan, in *Christianity in Oceania: ethnographic perspectives*, p.127–47. J. Barker (ed). *Association for Social Anthropology in Oceania monographs*, no. 12. Lanham, MD: University Press of America, 1990.
Churches and church workers in Fiji. C. S. Ross. Geelong, Victoria: H. Thacker, 1909. 108p.
Directory, Archdiocese of Suva, Fiji, 1973. Suva: Catholic Supply Store, 1973.
Disease, religion and society in the Fiji islands. D. M. Spencer. *Monographs of the American Ethnological Society*, no. 2. New York: J. J. Augustin, 1941. 82p.
'Disintegration, syncretization and change in Fijian religion,' A. C. Cato, *Mankind*, 5, 3 (1956), 101–106.
Fiji. G. E. Gorman & J. J. Mills. *World bibliographical series*, vol. 173. Oxford, UK: CLIO Press, 1994. 240p. (See especially 'Religion,' p65-74).
Fiji and the Fijians. T. Williams & J. Calvert. 1884; reprint, New York: AMS Press, 1977. 592p. (Contains 2 classic works on Fiji).
Fiji revisited: a Columban father's memories of twenty-eight years in the islands. E. Fischer. New York: Crossroad, 1981. 158p.
'Fijian Methodism, 1874–1945: the emergence of a national church.' A. W. Thornley. Thesis, Australian National University, Canberra, Australia, 1979. 348p.
'Fijian mutilatory practices I: earlobe splitting and distortion,' F. Clunie & W. Ligairi, *Domodomo: Fiji Museum quarterly*, 1 (1983), 22–44. (Fijian death rituals).
Footsteps in the sea: Christianity in Oceania to World War II. J. Garrett. Suva, Fiji: University of the South Pacific, Institute of Pacific Studies in association with the World Council of Churches, 1992. 514p. (Two chapters on Fiji).
Fulton's footprints in Fiji. E. B. Hare. *The best of Eric B. Hare stories.* Washington, DC: Review and Herald Publishing Association, 1969. 252p. (On Seventh-day Adventism).
Histoire religieuse de l'Archipel fidjien. J. Blanc. Toulon: Impr. Sainte-Jeanne d'Arc, 1926. 2 vols.
'History of the Methodist Church in its Rotuman setting,' J. Langi, in *Island churches: challenge and change*, p.1–73. C. W. Foreman (ed). Suva, Fiji: University of the South Pacific, Institute of Pacific Studies, 1992.
'I remember: personal memories of a New Zealand missionary in Fiji,' I. Hames, *Wesley Historical Society (New Zealand) proceedings*, 27, 5 (1972), 1–90.
'Institutions religieuses et messianismes modernes à Fiji,' J. Guiart, *Archives de sociologie des religions*, 4 (1957), 3–30.
La croix dans l'archipel Fidji (de 1844 à nos jours). R. P. Destable & J. M. Sédès. Paris: Éditions Spes, [1944]. 222p.
'Lessons from our Methodist Pacific story: past trends and present issues.' S. Loatoukefu. Paper presented to the World Methodist Historical Society Conference, 1991. 32p.
Messengers of grace: evangelical missionaries in the South Seas 1779–1860. N. Gunson. Melbourne: Oxford University Press, 1978. 437p.
Methodist Church in Fiji, 1835–1985: 150th anniversary celebration. Suva: Lotu Pasifika Production, 1985. 70p.
'Methodist missionary influence on native education in Tonga, Fiji and Papua–New Guinea with special reference to government–mission relationships since 1942.' R. C. Wilkinson. M.Ed. thesis, University of Sydney, Sydney, Australia, 1959. 372p.
Oral tradition and ethnohistory: the transmission of information and social values in early Christian Fiji, 1835–1905. A. R. Tippett. Canberra: St. Mark's Library, 1980. 70p.
Overseas missions of the Australian Methodist Church. A. H. Wood. Melbourne: Aldersgate Press, 1978. 3 vols. (Vols. 2 and 3 treat Fiji).
'Religion and reconciliation in the multi–ethnic states of the Third World: Fiji, Trinidad, and Guyana.' R. R. Premdas. Ph.D. dissertation, McGill University, Montreal, Canada, 1991. 290p.
'Religion and symbolism in Fiji,' W. C. Mann, *Journal of general psychology*, 23 (1940), 169–84.
'Text and context in Fijian Hinduism: uses of religion,' J. Wilson, *Religion*, 5 (1975), 53–68.
The Congregation of the Poor. P. Rokotuiviwa. Suva, Fiji: South Pacific Social Sciences Association, 1975. 62p.
The dynamics of church–planting in Fiji (Ono, Viwa, Bau, Kadavu, Vanua Levu & the hill tribes of Viti Levu). A. R. Tippett. [Eugene, OR: Fuller Theological Seminary], 1962. 220p.
The Fiji Indian community and its church. A. R. Tippett. [Eugene, OR]: Fuller Theological Seminary], 1962. 102p.
The growth of an indigenous church: a collection of essays on the emergence of the Methodist Church in Fiji. A. R. Tippett. Pasadena, CA: Fuller Theological Seminary, 1967. 129p.
The growth of the Indian church in Fiji. A. H. Blackett. South Australia: privately printed, 1960.
The Marist Brothers in New Zealand, Fiji and Samoa, 1876–1976. P. O. Gallagher. Tuakau, NZ: New Zealand Marist Brother Trust Fund, 1976. 210p.
'The role of the laity in the church and its implications for the life of the Methodist Church in Fiji.' I. J. Meo. B.D. thesis, Pacific Theological College, Suva, Fiji, 1973. 153p.
'Thinking theology aloud in Fiji,' S. Tuwere, in *The gospel is not Western: black theologies from the Southwest Pacific*, p.148–54. G. W. Trompf (ed). Maryknoll, NY: Orbis Books, 1987.
To live among the stars: Christian origins in Oceania. J. Garrett. Geneva: World Council of Churches in association with the University of the South Pacific, Institute of Pacific Studies, 1982. 412p. (Two chapters on Fiji, p102-115, 279-88).
Yesterday and today: with the Indians in the Church in Fiji. E. H. Smith. [Suva]: Lotu Pasifika Productions, 1979. 80p.

Country Table 2. **Organized churches and denominations in Fiji.**

Official name (bold type = church with over 10% of all affiliated) 1	*Begun* 2	*Type* 3	*Counc* 4	*Congs* 5	*Adults* 6	*Affiliated 1970* 7	*Affiliated 1995* 8	*G%* 9	*Names, notes, and other statistics* (see Codebook, Part 3) 10
Anglican Church: D Polynesia	1860	A-Hig	awPKK	51	3,840	6,500	8,200	0.93	*Lotu Jiaji.* CPNZ. 34% Indian, 26% Solomoni, 19% White. 16n,13x,1u,W=27%,97Y,217y.
Anglican Orthodox Church	1969	I-ReA	.....	3	650	500	1,050	3.01	Dissident body ex Anglican Communion in USA.
Apostles Gospel Outreach Fellowship Int	1988	I-3aP	.....	16	3,500	–	5,000	14.29	*AGOFI.* Indigenous body with apostolic government. Ex AoG, but now 80% ex-Methodists.
Assemblies of God of Fiji	1926	P-Pe2	ZF..E	36	27,610	20,000	56,349	4.23	Rapid growth since 1957. M=AoG(USA). 65% Fijian, 35% Indian. 1287n,4f,1s(56),W=75%.
Baptist Churches	c1969	I-Bap	.....	2	720	120	1,100	9.27	Independent Baptists.
Baptist Convention of Fiji	1983	P-Bap	T...E	12	600	–	900	8.33	M=SBC. Mainline Baptists.
Catholic Church: M Suva	1844	R-Lat	PxPYK	37	39,000	43,515	78,683	2.40	9.1% Indian, 3.8% Chinese. M=SM. C=5+4+5. (1990) 28n,73x,143m,195w,2022Yy.
Christ Groups	c1980	I-3hP	x....	512	20,000	–	50,000	6.67	Isolated home churches for converts after nationwide EHC campaign.
Christian Outreach Centre	1987	I-3cP	.....	9	500	–	1,100	12.50	*COC.* Services in English. 14 pastors.
Christian Mission Fellowship	1990	I-3cP	....E	60	5,000	–	12,000	20.00	*CMF,* new church established to assist M=Every Home for Christ. 21n.
Church of Christ	1968	I-Dis	x....	8	720	1,000	1,440	1.47	M=CC(Non-Instrumental) (USA). Churches in Suva. Rapid growth.
Church of God (Cleveland)	c1980	P-Pe3	Z...E	20	500	–	1,151	6.67	M=CoG(Cleveland, USA).
Ch of Jesus Christ of Latter-day Saints	1954	m-LdS	x....	19	3,750	1,424	8,297	7.30	*Mormons.* M=CJCLdS(USA). Rapid growth. 50% Fijian, 50% Indian. 1x,10f,W=30%,200Yy.
Church of Time (Daku Community)	c1945	I-Met	.....	1	150	300	455	1.68	*Lotu ni Gauna.* Founder red-robed Ratu Emosi, ex Methodist. Stress on use of time.
Congregational Christian Church	c1950	P-Con	Rwp.K	1	650	1,000	1,300	1.05	*LMS Church in Fiji.* M=London Missionary Society (UK). Expatriate Samoans. 1u.
Fiji Gospel Churches	1934	P-CBr	x...E	23	1,400	427	2,000	6.37	*Samabula Gospel Chapel.* Open Brethren. M=CMML(NZ). 2n,1x,16f,W=80%,6Y,8z.
Jehovah's Witnesses	1930	m-Jeh	x....	41	1,542	1,000	4,000	5.70	*Watch Tower. IBSA.* First limited witnessing began in 1930. (1975) 88Y. (1995) 81Y.
Messiah Club	c1965	I-Met	.....	20	600	1,000	900	-0.42	Ex Methodists, young messiah Sairusi. HQ Ra. Only Fijians and Solomonis may join.
Methodist Church in Fiji	1835	P-Met	VWP.K	2,192	168,000	157,635	259,000	2.01	M=MCA(Austr). 94% Fijian, 4% Indian. 205n,7x,1H,9p,1s,1u,W=50%,73Y,4687y.
New Apostolic Church	c1980	I-3aX	x....	10	500	–	1,212	6.67	*NAC, NAK.* M=Neuapostolische Kirche (HQ Zurich, Switzerland).
Presbyterian Church	1876	P-Ref	....K	5	350	1,000	700	-1.42	*St Andrew's Ch.* All Whites (Australian, NZ, British), from scattered areas. W=8%.
Reorganized Ch of JC of LdS		m-LdS	x....	2	200	–	350	0.05	M=RCJCLdS(USA).
Rewa Wesleyan Mission	c1980	I-Hol	.....	20	1,000	–	2,000	6.67	*Christian Mission Fellowship.*

Continued opposite

Country Table 2–concluded

Official name (bold type = church with over 10% of affiliated) 1	*Begun* 2	*Type* 3	*Counc* 4	*Congs* 5	*Adults* 6	*Affiliated 1970* 7	*Affiliated 1995* 8	*G%* 9	*Names, notes, and other statistics* (see Codebook, Part 3) 10
Salvation Army	1973	P-Sal	x....	4	690	–	1,057	4.55	World headquarters in London, England. Social services strongly emphasized.
Seventh-day Adventist Church in Fiji	1889	P-Adv	x....	92	8,020	8,000	20,000	3.73	In CPacific UM. Fijians, 150 Indians. 16n,2x,1r,1s(8),80t(7041),W=90%,502Y.
South Pacific Evangelical Fellowship	c1975	P-Eva	.....	4	650	–	1,000	5.00	M=WEC.
United Pentecostal Church	1972	P-Pel	x....	33	1,100	–	2,200	4.35	*Oneness Pentecostals*: M=UPC(USA). 66 ministers. 5f.
Other independent churches		I-3cP	.....	12	1,000	–	2,200	0.05	Including: Revival Centre International (300).
Other Protestant denominations	c1960	P-	.....	20	1,000	600	2,000	4.93	Total 6 (see list below), including Covenant Evangelical Ch (300).
Other marginal Protestant bodies		m-	.....	4	190	50	380	0.05	Including: Church of Christ, Scientist.
Doubly-affiliated		2-aff			-53,700	0	-96,324		Evangelicals also belonging to Catholic Church.
Totals				**3,269**	**239,732**	**244,071**	**429,700**		

Churches, members, growth, 1900-2025	*Congs*	*Adults*	*Affiliated*	*G%*	*Total denominations*	*6 Megablocs:* O	R	A	P	I	m
Total churches, members, and denominations (mid-1900)	1,000	51,100	91,800	1.41	5	0	1	1	3	0	0
Total churches, members, and denominations (mid-1970)	2,377	135,827	244,071	1.41	19	0	1	1	8	5	4
Total churches, members, and denominations (mid-1990)	3,000	226,000	405,000	2.56	41	0	1	1	16	15	8
Total churches, members, and denominations (mid-1995)	3,269	239,732	429,700	1.19	43	0	1	1	17	16	8
Total churches, members, and denominations (mid-2000)	4,000	256,000	459,745	1.36	45	0	1	1	18	17	8
Total churches, members, and denominations (mid-2025)	6,000	345,000	618,000	1.19	94	0	1	1	30	50	12

NOTES ON TABLE ABOVE
NATIONAL COUNCILS (Column 4, 5th letter).
E = Evangelical Fellowship of Fiji (EFF).
K = Fiji Council of Churches (FCC).

OTHER PROTESTANT DENOMINATIONS. These include: Christadelphian Ecclesias, Lutheran Ch in America, Pentecostal (Vakapenitiko) Ch, World-Wide Missions (1968). In Fijian, Protestant = Porotesitedi.

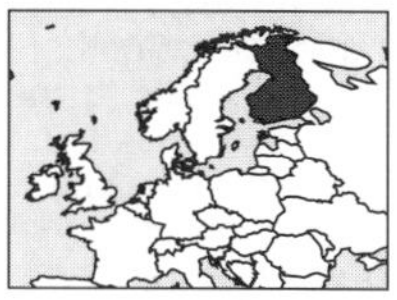

FINLAND

SECULAR DATA, AD 2000

STATE
Official name: Suomen Tasavalta/Republiken Finland (The Republic of Finland).
Short name: Finland. **Adjective of nationality:** Finnish, a Finn.
Flag: Light blue cross on a white field.
Area: 338,145 sq. km. (130,559 sq. mi.).
Government: Parliamentary republic, since 1917 (1809 Russian grand duchy, 1917 Independence declared).
Legislature: Parliament, 200 members.
Official language: Finnish (Suomi) and Swedish.
Monetary unit: 1 markka (Fmk) = 100 penniä. **US$1=** Fmk 5.09.
Chief cities: HELSINKI (Helsingfors) 1,163,000; Tampere (Tammerfors) 249,063; Turku (Åbo) 235,628; Espoo (Esbo) 181,547; Vaanta (Vanda) 162,536.
Political divisions: 12 provinces.
Armed forces: 31,000.

DEMOGRAPHY
Population: 5,176,000.
Population density: 15.3/sq. km. (39.6/sq. mi.).
Under 15 years: 936,000.
Growth rate p.a.: 0.16% (births 10.79, deaths 9.93).
Mortality: Infant, per 1,000: 5.5; **Maternal per 100,000:** 11.0.
Life expectancy: 78 (male 74, female 81).
Household size: 2.3. **Floor area per person, sq.m:** 45.0.
Major languages: Finnish, Swedish, Russian, Lapp, Romany.
Urban dwellers: 65.00%. **Urban growth rate p.a.:** 0.7%.
Labor force: 50%.

ETHNOLINGUISTIC PEOPLES
91.9% Finnish (Finn); 5.9% Swedish (Swede); 0.8% Karelian; 0.2% Russian; 0.1% Estonian.

ECONOMY
National income p.a. per person: US$20,580; **per family:** US$47,334.

EDUCATION
Adult literacy: 100% (male 100%, female 100%). **Schools:** 5,490.
Universities: 20. **School enrolment:** female/male: 115%/105%.

HEALTH
Access to health services: 95%. **Access to safe water:** 100%.
Hospitals: 317 (90 beds per 10,000). **Doctors:** 13,344.
Blind: 3,345. **Deaf:** 310,700. **Murder rate:** <1.
Lepers: 300.

LITERATURE
New book titles p.a.: 13,350 (2,580 p.a. per million). **Periodicals:** 7,995. **Newspapers:** 56 dailies.

COMMUNICATION (per 1,000 people)
Phones: 547 (51% mobile). **Radios:** 966. **TV sets:** 519.
Daily newspaper circulation: 464. **Computers:** 505.

REFUGEES
Alien refugees from other countries: 750.

HUMAN LIFE AND LIBERTY (optimum condition=100.0%)
HDI: 94.0. **HSI:** 92.0. **HFI:** 90.0. **EFL:** 54.0.

Country Table 1. **Religious adherents in Finland, AD 1900-2025.**

Year	*1900*		*1970*		*mid-1990*		*Annual change, 1990-2000*				*mid-1995*		*mid-2000*		*mid-2025*	
Name	*Adherents*	*%*	*Adherents*	*%*	*Adherents*	*%*	*Natural*	*Conversion*	*Total*	*Rate*	*Adherents*	*%*	*Adherents*	*%*	*Adherents*	*%*
Christians	**2,713,000**	**100.0**	**4,439,320**	**96.4**	**4,648,250**	**93.2**	**17,687**	**-2,155**	**15,532**	**0.33**	**4,750,000**	**93.0**	**4,803,568**	**92.8**	**4,780,600**	**91.0**
PROFESSION																
professing Christians	**2,713,000**	**100.0**	**4,439,320**	**96.4**	**4,648,250**	**93.2**	**17,687**	**-2,155**	**15,532**	**0.33**	**4,750,000**	**93.0**	**4,803,568**	**92.8**	**4,780,600**	**91.0**
AFFILIATION																
unaffiliated Christians	35,500	1.3	12,864	0.3	201,630	4.0	768	1,481	2,249	1.06	221,000	4.3	224,117	4.3	230,600	4.4
affiliated Christians	**2,677,500**	**98.7**	**4,426,456**	**96.1**	**4,446,620**	**89.2**	**16,919**	**-3,636**	**13,283**	**0.29**	**4,529,000**	**88.7**	**4,579,451**	**88.5**	**4,550,000**	**86.6**
Protestants	2,635,600	97.2	4,473,407	97.1	4,500,000	90.3	17,148	-3,648	13,500	0.30	4,588,220	89.8	4,635,000	89.6	4,650,000	88.5
Independents	0	0.0	14,919	0.3	63,500	1.3	242	1,178	1,420	2.04	69,074	1.4	77,700	1.5	105,000	2.0
Orthodox	45,000	1.7	56,774	1.2	56,000	1.1	213	-223	-10	-0.02	59,950	1.2	55,900	1.1	55,000	1.1
Marginal Christians	100	0.0	18,219	0.4	32,500	0.7	124	426	550	1.58	34,425	0.7	38,000	0.7	75,000	1.4
Roman Catholics	800	0.0	2,868	0.1	5,700	0.1	22	48	70	1.17	5,838	0.1	6,400	0.1	8,000	0.2
Anglicans	0	0.0	269	0.0	170	0.0	1	-1	0	0.00	169	0.0	170	0.0	200	0.0
doubly-affiliated	-4,000	-0.2	-140,000	-3.0	-211,250	-4.2	-805	-1,442	-2,247	1.02	-228,676	-4.5	-233,719	-4.5	-343,200	-6.5
Trans-megabloc groupings																
Evangelicals	550,000	20.3	736,960	16.0	727,956	14.6	2,774	-1,511	1,263	0.17	737,957	14.5	740,585	14.3	714,690	13.6
Pentecostals/Charismatics	0	0.0	66,000	1.4	620,000	12.4	2,363	2,337	4,700	0.73	646,969	12.7	667,000	12.9	745,000	14.2
Great Commission Christians	**163,000**	**6.0**	**460,000**	**10.0**	**977,000**	**19.6**	**3,723**	**1,954**	**5,677**	**0.57**	**1,010,000**	**19.8**	**1,033,772**	**20.0**	**1,100,000**	**20.9**
Nonreligious	0	0.0	112,800	2.5	252,000	5.1	960	1,897	2,857	1.08	268,710	5.3	280,573	5.4	350,000	6.7
Atheists	0	0.0	49,000	1.1	70,000	1.4	267	63	330	0.46	72,000	1.4	73,299	1.4	95,000	1.8
Muslims	0	0.0	920	0.0	7,800	0.2	30	108	138	1.64	8,700	0.2	9,176	0.2	15,000	0.3
Buddhists	0	0.0	0	0.0	2,000	0.0	8	47	55	2.44	2,300	0.1	2,546	0.1	4,500	0.1
Baha'is	0	0.0	1,500	0.0	1,500	0.0	6	12	18	1.12	1,600	0.0	1,676	0.0	2,000	0.0
Chinese folk-religionists	0	0.0	0	0.0	1,100	0.0	4	11	15	1.29	1,200	0.0	1,251	0.0	1,800	0.0
Jews	0	0.0	1,460	0.0	1,250	0.0	5	-7	-2	-0.14	1,240	0.0	1,232	0.0	1,300	0.0
New-Religionists	0	0.0	0	0.0	400	0.0	2	10	12	2.62	450	0.0	518	0.0	800	0.0
Other religionists	0	0.0	1,000	0.0	1,700	0.0	6	14	20	1.13	1,800	0.0	1,903	0.0	3,000	0.1
World A (unevangelized persons)	0	0.0	4,606	0.1	9,972	0.2	46	252	298	2.24	15,323	0.3	15,528	0.3	26,270	0.5
World B (evangelized non-Christians)	0	0.0	162,074	3.5	327,778	6.6	1,242	1,903	3,145	0.85	342,478	6.7	356,904	6.9	447,130	8.5
World C (Christians)	2,713,000	100.0	4,439,320	96.4	4,648,250	93.2	17,687	-2,155	15,532	0.33	4,750,000	93.0	4,803,568	92.8	4,780,600	91.0
Country's population	**2,713,000**	**100.0**	**4,606,000**	**100.0**	**4,986,000**	**100.0**	**18,975**	**0**	**18,975**	**0.37**	**5,107,802**	**100.0**	**5,176,000**	**100.0**	**5,254,000**	**100.0**

COLUMNS, ROWS.
For meanings and definitions, see Codebook (Part 3). Note that, by definition, total 'Christians' = professing + crypto-Christians, which also = affiliated + unaffiliated Christians, and also = Great Commission Christians + latent Christians. Percentages may not always total exactly, due to rounding.

CENSUSES.
1860: 97.7% Lutherans, 2.3% Greek Orthodox. **1880:** 98.0% Lutherans, 1.9% Greek Orthodox, 0.1% Roman Catholics. **1900:** 98.1% Lutherans, 1.7% Greek Orthodox, 1.0% Baptists, 0.03% Roman Catholics. Since 1917 there has been in censuses a civil register for those not wishing to belong to any recognized religion or denomination. Those on it are mostly men, mostly urban, workers and intellectuals, former Christians now withdrawn from the Lutheran church, atheists, and communists; but there is also a sizable proportion in unrecognized new denominations (Pentecostals and others). **1920:** 99.9% registered Christians, 0.0% civil register. **1940:** 98.0% registered Christians, 1.9% civil register. **31.XII.1950:** 95.0% registered Protestants, 3.0% civil register, 1.8% Orthodox. **31.XII.1960** (de jure): 92.8% registered Protestants (not on civil register) (92.5% Lutherans), 5.5% civil register (nonreligious, and unregistered Protestants), 1.4% Orthodox, 0.2% non-Christians, 0.05% Roman Catholics. **31.XII.1970** (including returns from church bodies): 92.7% registered Protestants (not on civil register) (92.4% Lutherans), 5.2% civil register (3.3% nonreligious and atheists, 1.9% unregistered Protestants), 1.3% Orthodox, 0.4% marginal Protestants, 0.1% Catholics.

NOTES ON RELIGIONS
ATHEISTS. Finnish Communist Party (Suomen Kommunistinen Puolue, SKP) (legal): Although most communists are atheists, many others belong to the Lutheran church; and the SKP has as members several theological students and clergy in Helsinki.
BAHA'IS. Finnish Baha'i Association (Suomen Baha'iyhdyskunta). Growth from 4 local spiritual assemblies (1964) to 9 (1973), and to 12 LSAs (1996). Converts include Gypsies and Lapps.
DOUBLY-AFFILIATED. The term describes the large number of individuals who are members of Free churches (including Salvation

Continued overleaf

Country Table 1–concluded

Army and also marginal cults) who are also still regarded as members of the state Lutheran Church which therefore enumerates them all as such.
JEWS. Mostly in Helsinki, with synagogues in Helsinki and Turku.
MUSLIMS. Including Kurdish and Turkish laborers.
NONRELIGIOUS. Mostly persons on the civil register in censuses, who register their protest by withdrawal from the state Lutheran Church. These are mainly urban male workers and intellectuals.
The size of the civil register is 4 times as large in the cities as in rural areas.
OTHER RELIGIONISTS. Adherents of smaller religions and cults, including Rosicrucians (1 AMORC centre).

Great Commission Instrument Panel: status of Finland (for explanation see start of Part 4)

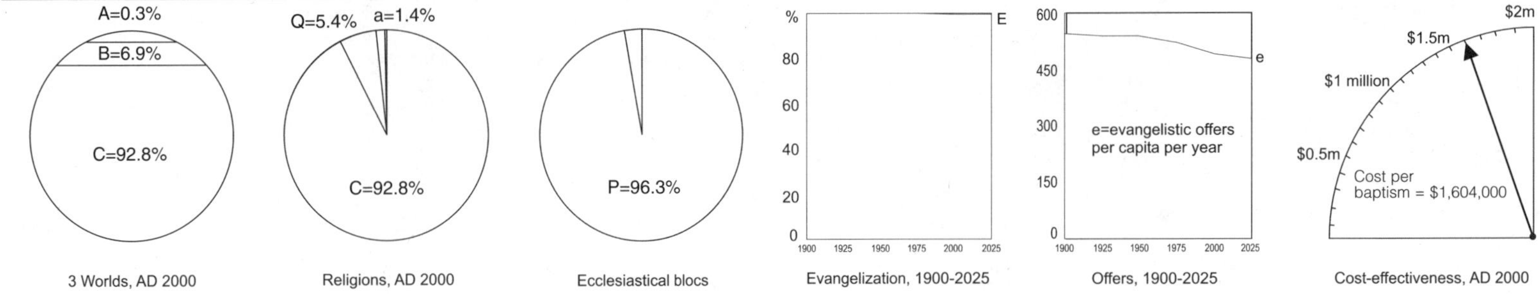

Country status. Finland is a North European country on the Baltic Sea within both the Russian and Scandinavian cultural zones. Its history has been a centuries-long effort to establish its independence from its powerful neighbors, an effort that bore fruit ultimately only after World War II. The greater part of the country is covered with forests and lakes and the major export is timber.

HUMAN LIFE AND LIBERTY

Human need and development. Finland is one of the most developed countries in Europe with few of its developmental needs unmet. Although not rich in resources, the Finns are hardworking and ingenious in making the best of what is available. They are served by advanced educational institutions and medical facilities.

Human rights and freedoms. Finland is a full fledged democracy where historic traditions of individual freedom are jealously preserved. Freedom from arbitrary arrest as well as cruel and inhuman punishment is provided for in law. Infractions of this law are reviewed and corrected by the Parliamentary Ombudsman. Under a 1992 law police have access to telephone records and wiretapping is permitted under controlled conditions. The influx of asylees since 1990 has placed strains on the rigorous laws against discrimination. The Sami, or Lapps, receive special constitutional protection and also financial assistance to maintain their traditional lifestyles. The Council for Equality coordinates and sponsors legislation to combat discrimination against women.

Human environment. Finland has an unusual settlement pattern. About 68% of the population lives in the large coastal cities, especially Helsinki. Although this helps to minimize ecological damage in the interior, Finland's forest industries cause many environmental problems. The country's distinctive bedrock and climate make it especially vulnerable. Lakes are shallow and highly susceptible to acid rain. Wastes from paper mills add to the water pollution in the Baltic Sea. Since 1950 some 22% of the wetlands have reportedly been destroyed. About 1,011 species of Finland's 40,000 known species of plants and animals are considered endangered.

NON-CHRISTIAN RELIGIONS

Small communities of Jews (about 1,200 in synagogues in Turku and Helsinki, mostly the latter), Muslims (over 9,000) and Baha'i exist in Finland. The fastest-growing non-Christian community is the Muslims, due largely to immigration. Finland has welcomed hundreds of refugees from Somalia and other troubled nations.

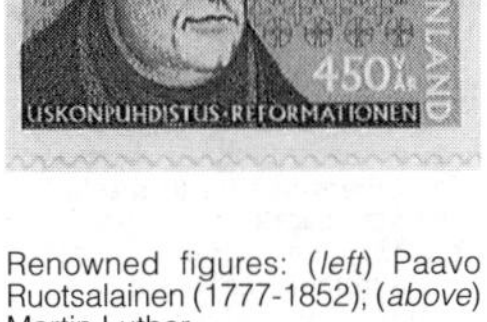

Renowned figures: (*left*) Paavo Ruotsalainen (1777-1852); (*above*) Martin Luther.

CHRISTIANITY

In spite of some penetration through seamen and merchants touching its ports, Finland remained largely pagan prior to the crusade launched by Eric IX of Sweden in AD 1155. A Catholic bishop, Henry of Uppsala, accompanied the Swedish forces and was later martyred; he is now looked on as the founder of Christianity in Finland. Orthodoxy was introduced into eastern Finland from neighboring Russia in the middle of the 12th century. Dominicans entered in 1249 and an important step forward was taken in 1291 when a Finn, Magnus, was appointed bishop of Abo. Finland was attached to Sweden at the time of the 16th-century Reformation and gradually followed king Gustavus Adolphus into accepting Lutheranism, particularly through the efforts of a Finn, Michael Agricola. Catholicism did not return until the middle of the 19th century, a period which also saw the introduction of Free churches into the country.

PROTESTANT CHURCHES. Although there are 2 national churches in Finland, Lutheran and Orthodox, the Evangelical Lutheran Church is by far the largest and most influential body. This church has numerical strength in all parts of the country and all strata of society, although in recent decades it has suffered a gradual decline in membership.

Regular Sunday attendance is low, averaging about 4% of the population above 15 years of age, with the figure in parishes varying from 1% to 15%. Nevertheless, participation in evening prayers and religious radio and TV programs is more common, and the proportion being confirmed remains high (94%). Two-thirds of the national population attend church at least annually.

The Lutheran Church is composed of 8 dioceses, one of which (Porvoo/Borga) unites the Swedish-speaking congregations of the west and south. The highest administrative and legislative organ of the church is the Church Assembly which meets every 5 years. Interim matters are handled by the Enlarged Bishops' Meeting (with lay, ministerial, and episcopal members) and the Administrative Board. The archbishop of Finland is chairman of all these bodies. As a result of revival movements in the 1960s and following, there is a strong evangelical character to the Lutheran Church. It has also long been a missionary-minded church, with 6 official missionary societies. From the mid-1970s to the mid-1990s, support for foreign missionary work more than doubled, and offerings for compassionate foreign aid increased many times over. Only 10% of the church's employees are parish ministers. Most are involved in children's work, the maintenance of cemeteries, and other tasks.

The Free church movement came to Finland from Sweden after the middle of the last century. The first was a Baptist congregation formed among Swedish-speakers in Foglo in 1856, and by 1870 Baptist work had also begun among Finnish-speaking peoples. Today these are separate churches. Methodism, which was brought to Finland by a sailor in the 1860s and which organized its first congregation in 1881, also has Finnish-speaking and Swedish-speaking conferences. A similar pattern is evident in churches of the congregationalist tradition, which came from Sweden in 1878 and are represented in Finnish-speaking Free Church of Finland and the Swedish-speaking Free Mission Covenant Church. Other free churches established at the end of the 1880s include the Salvation Army and Seventh-day Adventists, and a number of Pentecostal groups during the present century. The Pentecostal movement expanded rapidly until 1965 when it began to decline numerically. More recently, growth has returned. Unlike Catholicism, Jehovah's Witness and Mormons, all of which are growing, most non-Pentecostal Protestant denominations are declining in numbers today. From the 1970s to the 1990s, Pentecostal/Charismatic renewal has been widespread in Finland, resulting not only in the emergence of healthy Pentecostal denominations, but also flavoring congregational life and worship in all denominations.

ORTHODOX CHURCH. Members of the Orthodox Church of Finland, originally in large part farmers from the eastern region, have now spread throughout the country, this dispersion having arisen from the USSR's annexation of Karelia after World War II. Their number is slowly diminishing because of mixed marriages with Lutherans. Although autonomous, the church is under the authority of the ecumenical patriarch of Constantinople.

CATHOLIC CHURCH. Now largely Finnish in leadership, the Catholic Church is growing faster than the general population, with births and conversions outnumbering deaths and defections. The diocese of Helsinki, with the smallest membership of any Catholic diocese in Europe, consists of 5 parishes, 2 in Helsinki and one each in Turku, Tampere and Jyvaskyla. Although there are influential Catholics among both intellectuals and workers, most of the faithful belong to the middle class. In 1977 Finland was transferred from the jurisdiction of Propaganda to that of the Congregation for Bishops.

The Holy See has diplomatic relations with Finland and in AD 2000 is represented to government and the Catholic hierarchy by a nuncio residing in Copenhagen.

Procession in Helsinki protesting against persecution of Christians in Soviet Union's underground churches, 1970.

Art and architecture. Early Finnish churches were modest and sturdy, generally built of granite with low walls and steeply raked roofs. Many of them, such as those at Hattula and Lohja, have murals. The Gothic tradition did not strike roots in Finland, and even the great cathedral at Turku, built in the 13th century, has simple lines. Later, wooden churches became common, but many were ravaged by fire. Among the oldest surviving churches are the church of Sipoo, the church of Hattula, near Hameenlinna,

Country summary. **Worlds A, B, C by ethnolinguistic peoples, cities, and major civil divisions in Finland.**

	PEOPLES							CITIES							CIVIL DIVISIONS						
World	Num	Pop 2000	C%	Christians	E%	U%	Unevangelized	Num	Pop 2000	C%	Christians	E%	U%	Unevangelized	Num	Pop 2000	C%	Christians	E%	U%	Unevangelized
A	7	11,283	2.63	297	35	65	7,281	0	0	0.00	0	0	0	0	0	0	0.00	0	0	0	0
B	3	4,037	7.73	312	53	47	1,885	0	0	0.00	0	0	0	0	0	0	0.00	0	0	0	0
C	21	5,160,424	88.73	4,578,841	100	0	5,815	12	2,372,618	86.05	2,041,578	100	0	6,907	12	5,175,742	88.48	4,579,451	100	0	14,981
Total	**31**	**5,175,744**	**88.48**	**4,579,450**	**100**	**0**	**14,981**	**12**	**2,372,618**	**86.05**	**2,041,578**	**100**	**0**	**6,907**	**12**	**5,175,742**	**88.48**	**4,579,451**	**100**	**0**	**14,981**

and the 18th century churches at Keuruu and Petajavesi in central Finland. The Sipoo church has a detached bell tower, 3 aisles, heavy, unbroken walls with small windows, and decorated arches. In contrast to the older churches, the 20th century churches are of modern architectural styles using glass and wood to good effect. The cube-shaped Institute of Technology chapel at Otaniemi, near Helsinki, was built in the late 1950s by architects Kaija and Heikki Siren. Its altar wall is a single large window looking into a forest. Other strikingly modernistic churches include the chapel near Turku by Erik Bryggman, Vuoksenniska church at Imatra by Alvar Aalto and church in Hyvinkaa by Aarno Ruusuvuori.

Renewal movements. In the 1990s the Pentecostal/Charismatic Renewal continued to spread rapidly across most older churches, and numbered over 667,000 adherents (of whom 11% Pentecostals, 77% Charismatics, and 12% Independents).

Indigenous missions. Finns have been active in foreign missions since the introduction of Christianity. Recently there has been renewed interest with many young people in all of the traditions volunteering for missionary service.

Evangelical Lutheran Church of Finland. Finnish Primate, Archbishop Simojoki of Turku (*left*), receives 1974 award for promoting freedom of press.

CHURCH AND STATE

Article 8 of the constitution of 1919 guarantees freedom of conscience and worship, and this is further clarified by the earlier Law of the Church (Kirkkelaki, 1869) and the Religious Liberty Law of 1922. The parish registers of the 2 national churches, Lutheran and Orthodox, replace civil state registers, and marriages celebrated by them are valid as civil marriages. Religious instruction is given in all state and private schools. As for the Lutheran Church, the principal state church, the Law of the Church stipulates that 'Its supreme government in the whole of the country is the concern of the Finnish government' (paragraph 14). The fact is that the church makes its laws freely but must submit them to Parliament which may approve or reject but not modify them. The state imposes on the faithful and on church societies a church tax which is then administered by the church without external constraint. The state also provides funds for various subsidies and salaries. The Orthodox Church of Finland receives similar treatment.

Other churches and religious groups may either obtain legal recognition at their own request, under certain conditions, or allow themselves to come under the general laws covering societies and groups. Their marriages receive civil recognition, and they are given permission to tax their own members. Since 1971, the official register kept by each of these churches has been replaced by a central register. Citizens belonging to no religious confession have been registered since 1917 in a special civil register. The ministry of Public Education (Opetusministerio) is charged with religious questions which must be submitted to Parliament or to the head of state. Jews and Muslims are also officially recognized.

In September 1971, the main political party of the country, the Social Democrats, presented a detailed program for the eventual separation of church and state. A new Ecclesiastical Order and Church Election Order, which came into effect in 1994, increased the decision-making authority of the Lutheran Church and was a significant step toward greater separation of church and state.

BROADCASTING AND MEDIA

Shortwave programs from KNLS, HCJB (Ecuador), TWR (Monaco, Albania) and AWR (Slovakia) can be easily received. Finland is a member of UNDA.

Christian television programs can be received via satellite.

INTERDENOMINATIONAL ORGANIZATIONS

Ecumenical work in Finland is co-ordinated through the Ecumenical Council of Finland. (Suomen Ekumeeninen Neuvosto), founded in 1950, in which the Catholic Church is a member. Several ecumenical institutes are active, connected with the University of Helsinki and the University of Turku. The country also has several centers for dialogue and inter-confessional cooperation. Ten major churches were full members of the Ecumenical Council of Finland in 1987, including Lutheran, Orthodox, Catholic, Baptist, Methodist, and Salvation Army churches. Many other denominations and organizations held observer status.

FUTURE TRENDS AND PROSPECTS

Secularization and disenchantment with the institutional churches will probably cause a steep decline in church membership through 2025 to an all time low of 86.6% (98.7% in 1900).

The nonreligious could rise above 10% by AD 2040 and continue to climb. Christianity could fall to lower than 90% by mid-century.

BIBLIOGRAPHY

'800 years of Orthodox faith in Finland,' L. Venkula-Vauraste, *Look at Finland*, no. 5 (1977), 42–47.

An open or a closed community: leadership in the parish. H. Palmu. *Publication of the Research Institute of the Lutheran Church in Finland*, no. 41. Tampere, Finland: Research Institute of the Lutheran Church in Finland, 1991. 58p.

Changes in religiosity from the Finnish viewpoint. H. Heino. *Publication of the Research Institute of the Lutheran Church in Finland*, no. 37. Tampere, Finland: Research Institute of the Lutheran Church in Finland, 1988. 40p.

Church in Finland: the history, present state and outlook for the future of the Evangelical Lutheran Church of Finland. Helsinki: Church Council for Foreign Affairs Ecclesiastical Board, 1989. 58p.

Churchgoing and churchgoers in Finland. H. Heino. Pieksämäki: Sisälähetysseuran kirjapaino Raamattutalo, 1991. 35p.

Dialogues: with the Evangelical Free Church of Finland and the Finnish Pentecostal Movement. Documents of the Evangelical Lutheran Church of Finland, 2. Helsinki: Church Council for Foreign Affairs Ecclesiastical Board, 1990. 63p.

Die Kirche Finnlands. G. Sentzke. 3d ed. Helsinki: Pohjois-Karjalan Kirjapaino Oy, 1968. 283p.

Ecclesiastical trends in Finland in the late Sixties. P. Niemelä. Tampere, Finland: Research Institute of the Lutheran Church, 1977.

Expansion and change of Christian social activity in the Church of Finland during the years 1962–1973. P. Niemelä & J. Laurinkari. [Helsinki]: University of Helsinki, Department of Social Policy, [1979]. 48p.

Finland. J. E. O. Screen. *World bibliographical series*, vol. 31. Oxford, UK: CLIO Press, 1981. 212p. (See especially 'Religion,' p49–50).

'Finland,' P. Seppänen, in *Western religion: a country by country sociological enquiry*, p.143–73. H. Mol (ed). The Hague: Mouton, 1972.

Finland: its church and its people. G. Sentzke. Helsinki: [Printed by Kirjapaino Oy Lause], 1963. 212p. (Also in German).

Missions growth: a case study on Finnish Free Foreign Mission. L. Ahonen. Pasadena, CA: William Carey Library, 1984. 83p.

Orthodoxy in Finland: past and present. V. Purmonen (ed). 2d rev. and enlarged ed. Kuopio, Finland: Orthodox Clergy Association, 1984. 110p.

Religiousness in Finland. J. Sihvo. Tampere, Finland: Kirjapaino Hermes Oy, 1979. 25p.

Scandinavian churches: a picture of the development and life of the churches of Denmark, Finland, Iceland, Norway and Sweden. L. S. Hunter (ed). London: Faber & Faber, 1965. 200p.

Some aspects of the religiousness of the Finns, 1951 and 1982. L. Lotti. Helsinki: Suomen Gallup, 1983. 18p.

Suomen evankelis–luterilainen kirkko, vuosina 1972–1975. M. Lindqvist et al. Tampere, Finland: Kirkon tutkimuslaitos, 1977. 339p.

Suomen uskonnolliset liikkeet (Religious movements in Finland). A. Haavio. Helsinki: WSOY, 1955.

The challenge for Evangelical missions to Europe: a Scandinavian case study. H. Mäläskä. South Pasadena, CA: William Carey Library, 1970. 178p.

The church in Finland. M. Sinnemäki. Helsinki: Otava, 1973. 64p.

The church of Finland = (Die Kirche Finnlands). M. Juva. Ed., M. Ojala. [Pieksämäki]: Inner Mission Society of the Church of Finland = Innermissionsges-ellschaft der Kirche Finnlands, [1963]. 48p. (English and German in parallel).

The Church of the Finns. M. Paananen. Trans., G. Coogan. Helsinki: Department of Communications of the Evangelical Lutheran Church, 1991. 21p.

The Churches in Finland. [Helsinki]: Evangelical Lutheran Church of Finland, 1992. 42p.

The English missionaries in Sweden and Finland. C. J. A. Opperman. London: Society for Promoting Christian Knowledge, 1937. 221p.

The Evangelical Lutheran Church in Finland, 1988–1991. H. Heino, J. Kauppinen & R. Ahonen. Tampere, Finland: Research Institute of the Lutheran Church in Finland, 1993. 61p.

The Evangelical Lutheran Church in Finnish society. P. Työrinoja. *Documents of the Evangelical Lutheran Church of Finland*, 6. Helsinki: Church Council for Foreign Affairs, Church Council, 1994. 91p.

The Faith of the Finns: historical perspectives on the Finnish Lutheran church in America. R. J. Jalkanen (ed). East Lansing, MI: Michigan State University Press, 1972. 376p.

The history of Finnish theology, 1828–1918. E. Murtorinne. *History of learning and science in Finland, 1828-1918.* Helsinki: Societas Scientiarum Fennica, 1988. 251p.

'The Orthodox Church in Finland,' E. Piiroinen, *International review of mission*, 62, 245 (1973), 51–56.

The question of religious freedom in Finland. M. Reijonen. Tampere, Finland: Research Institute of the Lutheran Church in Finland, 1977. 13p.

The religious communities in Finland. H. Heino. Tampere, Finland: Research Institute of the Lutheran Church in Finland, 1985. 30p.

Country Table 2. **Organized churches and denominations in Finland.**

Official name (bold type = church with over 10% of all affiliated) 1	Begun 2	Type 3	Counc 4	Congs 5	Adults 6	Affiliated 1970 7	Affiliated 1995 8	G% 9	Names, notes, and other statistics (see Codebook, Part 3) 10
Baptist Union of Finland	1854	P-Bap	T...C	10	832	3,000	1,190	-3.63	*Suomen Baptistiyhadyskunta.* Finnish-speaking, 70% Finns. 15n,2s,W=50%,20Y.
Bible Speaks Church	1975	I-3pW	.....	8	280	–	467	5.00	*Raamathu Puhvu.* Small independent pentecostal body.
Catholic Ch in Finland: D Helsinki	1860	R-Lat	bzBQW	11	0	2,868	5,838	2.88	*Katolinen Kirkko Suomessa.* M=SCJ. (1970) 1n,21x,4m,36w. (1990) 4n, 17x, 18m, 38w, 137Yy.
Church of Christ, Scientist		m-Sci	x....	1	10	50	25	0.05	*Christian Science.* M=CCS(Boston, USA). *Helsinki Society.*
Church of England (D Europe)	c1850	A-plu	awc.W	4	120	269	169	-1.84	*Englantilainen Kirkkokunta.* English chaplaincy. Cathedral chapel. Senaatintori. 1x.
Church of God of Prophecy	1981	P-Pe3	.....	1	50	–	71	7.14	M=CoGP. Holiness Pentecostals from USA.
Ch of Jesus Christ of Latter-day Saints	c1880	m-LdS	x....	30	2,650	3,169	4,200	1.13	*Myöhempien Aikojen Pyhien Jeesuksen Kristuksen Kirkjko/Mormoonit.* Mormons.100f.

Continued overleaf

Country Table 2–concluded

Official name (bold type = church with over 10% of affiliated) 1	*Begun* 2	*Type* 3	*Counc* 4	*Congs* 5	*Adults* 6	*Affiliated 1970* 7	*Affiliated 1995* 8	*G%* 9	*Names, notes, and other statistics* (see Codebook, Part 3) 10
Church of Sweden		P-Lut	Lwc.W	3	1,240	2,188	1,800	0.05	*Olaus Petri. Ruotsinmaalainen Seurakunta.* Parish of Sweden state church.
Churches of Christ		I-Dis	x....	2	50	100	100	0.05	*Kristuksen Seurakunta.* M=CC(Non-Instrumental) (USA). In Helsinki, Tampere.
Confessional Lutheran Ch of Finland	1929	P-Lut	e....	22	248	431	370	-0.61	*Suomen Tunnustuksellinen Lutherilainen Kirkko.* Pure Lutheran. M=LCMS. 4n,7Yy.
Evangelical Free Church of Finland	1878	P-Con	Kv..C	96	13,600	8,100	17,600	3.15	*Suomen Vapaakirkko.* 1879 revival. Finnish-speaking. 49n,1s,W=60%,95Yy.
Evangelical Lutheran Ch of Finland	c1100	P-Lut	LWC.W	598	3,300,000	4,360,588	4,472,500	0.10	*Suomen Evankelis-Luterilainen Kirkko.* 8 Dioceses. 1300n,17p,2s(1400),71575Yy.
Filadelfia Assemblies		P-Pe2	Z...C	50	600	1,000	1,000	0.05	*Filadelfiaforsamlingen.* Swedish-speaking, linked to Swedish Filadelfia. M=SFM.
Finnish Mission Church		I-3pW	.....	2	200	500	500	0.05	*Suomen Lähetysseurakunta.* Small independent Finnish-speaking Pentecostal body.
Free Assoc of Ev Luth Congregations		P-Lut	.....	9	371	1,100	618	0.05	*Suomen Vapaat Evankelis-Luterilainen Seurakuntalüto.* Decline. M=LCMS. HQ Lahti.
Free Catholic Church of Finland		I-Lib	x....	1	50	119	75	0.05	*Suomen Vapaa Katolinen Kirkko.* Small conservative Liberal Catholic group. Declining.
Free Mission Covenant Church	1921	P-Con	K...W	25	890	2,500	1,590	-1.79	*Fria Missionsförbundet. Assoc of Free Ev Congs.* Swedish-speaking, ex FCF. 30n.
Free Pentecostal Revival of Finland		I-3pW	.....	36	2,500	4,000	5,000	0.05	*Suomen Vapaa-Helluntailähetys.* Free Pentecostals (renewal). HQ Helsinki.
Greater Helsinki Church	c1985	I-3cW	.....	20	20,000	–	40,000	10.00	Finnish charismatics. M=Bible Temple (Oregon, USA). 30000 at special meetings.
International Evangelical Church		I-Eva	.....	1	220	200	338	0.05	Small independent Protestant group of believers.
Jehovah's Witnesses	1909	m-Jeh	x....	274	17,531	15,000	30,200	2.84	*Jehovan Todistajat.* Active witnessing under way by 1926. (1975) 771Y. (1995) 686Y.
Local Church		I-3nC	.....	10	500	–	714	0.05	*Assembly Hall Churches. Little Flock* Chinese, in China-based body.
Maranatha Pentecostal Church	1959	I-3pW	x....	24	2,400	5,000	6,000	0.73	*Maranata Helluntailaiset.* Schism in Sweden ex Filadelfia Churches.
Methodist Church in Finland	1866	P-Met	Vwc.d	35	1,200	3,000	2,000	-1.61	*Metodistikirkko.* 2 Confs(Swedish, Finnish), NEurope CConf,UMC(USA). 28n.
Orthodox Church of Finland:	c1150	O-Fin	CwC.W	25	41,000	54,000	59,000	0.35	*Suomen Ortodoksinen Kirkko.* 3 Dioceses. Autonomous 1923. Karelians. 5 bps,64n,20 deacons.
D Helsinki	1925	O-Fin	Cb	10	20,000	25,000	28,000	0.45	40% in capital; urban influx. 93% intermarriage losses to Lutherans. 28n,W=4%.
D Karelia (Kuopio)	1925	O-Fin	Ca	15	21,000	29,000	31,000	0.27	Heavy losses in World War II. Diaspora farmers. Liturgy in Finnish only. 24n,1s.
Pentecostal Friends	1923	I-3pW	.....	24	3,800	5,000	5,280	0.22	Schism ex Pentecostal Revival, opposing organization. 10n,W=85%.
Pentecostal Revival of Finland	1911	P-Pe2	Z...C	206	48,000	50,000	68,600	1.27	*Helluntal-Ystävät.* Finnish- and Swedish-speaking congregations. 1j,1s.
Private Greek Catholic Church		O-Rus	Mwc..	1	178	1,412	250	0.05	*Yksityinen Kreikkalaiskatolienn Kirkkolinen Yhdyskunta.* Russians under D Leningrad.
Russian Orthodox Church		O-Rus	Mwc..	1	560	1,362	700	0.05	*Private Russian Orthodox Congregations.* Under jurisdiction of P Moscow.
Salvation Army, Finland Territory	1889	P-Sal	xwc.W	56	7,880	30,000	10,500	-4.11	*Pelastursameija* (Finnish). *Frälsningsarmén* (Swedish). 234n1s.
Seventh-day Adventist Ch of Finland	1892	P-Adv	xv..w	68	4,640	7,500	6,181	-0.77	*Suomen Adventtikirkko.* Finl UC; Swedish C. 25n,1x,2H,1h,1j,1r,W=59%,303Y.
Siloam Pentecostal Church		I-3pW	.....	1	2,800	–	7,000	0.05	A recent attempt at a new pentecostal network.
Swedish Baptist Church of Finland	1856	P-Bap	T...C	21	1,761	3,000	2,200	-1.23	*Finlands Svenska Baptistmission.* Swedish-speaking. 20n,W=50%,35Y.
Other independent charismatic chs	c1985	I-3cW	.....	30	2,000	–	3,000	10.00	Including 25 churches in Helsinki.
Other independent churches	c1980	I-3cW	.....	6	300	–	600	6.67	Ethnic churches: Iranian (2), Chinese (1), Spanish (1), Lingala Congolese (1); New Apostolic Ch.
Other Protestant denominations		P-	.....	20	1,000	1,000	2,000	0.05	Total over 5 (see list below), including UPCI,BMM.
Doubly-affiliated		2-aff			-167,000	-140,000	-228,676		Free church members (Salvation Army, &c) who retain membership in state Lutheran church.
Totals				**1,732**	**3,317,243**	**4,426,456**	**4,529,000**		

Churches, members, growth, 1900-2025	*Congs*	*Adults*	*Affiliated*	*G%*	*Total denominations*	*6 Megablocs:* *O*	*R*	*A*	*P*	*I*	*m*
Total churches, members, and denominations (mid-1900)	800	1,789,000	2,677,500	0.72	12	1	1	1	8	0	1
Total churches, members, and denominations (mid-1970)	1,787	2,957,159	4,426,456	0.72	31	3	1	1	16	7	3
Total churches, members, and denominations (mid-1990)	1,750	3,256,000	4,446,620	0.02	55	3	1	1	21	26	3
Total churches, members, and denominations (mid-1995)	1,732	3,317,243	4,529,000	0.37	56	3	1	1	21	27	3
Total churches, members, and denominations (mid-2000)	1,740	3,354,000	4,579,451	0.22	56	3	1	1	21	27	3
Total churches, members, and denominations (mid-2025)	1,900	3,332,000	4,550,000	-0.03	104	6	1	1	30	60	6

NOTES ON TABLE ABOVE

NATIONAL COUNCILS (Column 4, 5th letter).

C = Council of Free Christians and Churches in Finland (CFCCF) (Suomen Vapaitten Kristittyjen ja Kirkkokuntien Neuvosto) (2 branches: Finnish- and Swedish-speaking).

d = member of both ECF and CFCCF.

W = Finnish Ecumenical Council (FEC, Suomen Ekumeeninen Neuvosto; in Swedish, Ekumeniska Radet i Finland).

w = observer member of ECF.

OTHER PROTESTANT DENOMINATIONS. These include: American Advent Mission Society (1967), Friends of Truth (Totuuden Ystävät), Gypsy Evangelical Movement (France, Switzerland).

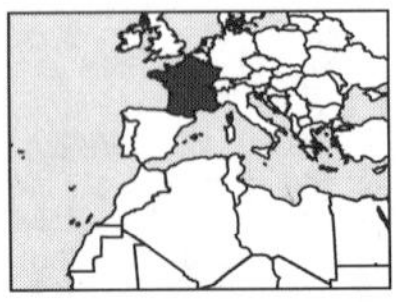

FRANCE

SECULAR DATA, AD 2000

STATE

Official name: La République Française (The French Republic).
Short name: France. **Adjective of nationality:** French; a Frenchman, the French.
Flag: Tricolor of blue, white, and red bars.
Area: 543,965 sq. km. (210,026 sq. mi.).
Government: Parliamentary republic, since 1871 (c1500 kingdom and empire, 1789 revolutionary republic, 1799 military dictatorship, 1821 monarchy, 1848 Second Republic).
Legislature: Parliament: Senate, 321 members; National Assembly, 577 members.
Official language: French (Français).
Monetary unit: 1 franc (F) = 100 centimes. **US$1=** F=5.60.
Chief cities: PARIS 9,638,000; Paris 2,314,901; Lyon (Lyons) 1,359,000; Marseille (Marseilles) 1,243,000; Lille 991,000.
Political divisions: 96 provinces.
Armed forces: 410,000.

DEMOGRAPHY

Population: 59,080,000.
Population density: 108.6/sq. km. (281.3/sq. mi.).
Under 15 years: 11,048,000.
Growth rate p.a.: 0.28% (births 11.85, deaths 9.51).
Mortality: Infant, per 1,000: 5.9; **Maternal per 100,000:** 15.0.
Life expectancy: 79 (male 75, female 83).
Household size: 2.6. **Floor area per person, sq.m:** 50.0.
Major languages: French, Occitan (Provençal, Languedoc), Yiddish, Flemish, English, German, Armenian, Russian, Polish, Romany, Arabic, Portuguese, Spanish, Italian, Vietnamese, Breton, Catalan, Basque, In addition there are over 20 other languages.
Urban dwellers: 75.57%. **Urban growth rate p.a.:** 0.5%.
Labor force: 45%.

ETHNOLINGUISTIC PEOPLES

45.4% French; 11.0% North Gallo-Romance; 4.6% Provencal; 4.0% Languedocian; 4.0% Provencal (South French).

ECONOMY

National income p.a. per person: US$24,990; **per family:** US$64,974.

EDUCATION

Adult literacy: 98% (male 98%, female 98%). **Schools:** 52,981.
Universities: 1,062. **School enrolment:** female/male: 106%/105%.

HEALTH

Access to health services: 90%. **Access to safe water:** 100%.
Hospitals: 3,834 (120 beds per 10,000). **Doctors:** 155,896.
Blind: 43,000. **Deaf:** 3,543,600. **Murder rate:** 4.
Lepers: 400.

LITERATURE

New book titles p.a.: 45,490 (770 p.a. per million). **Periodicals:** 3,741. **Newspapers:** 118 dailies.

COMMUNICATION (per 1,000 people)

Phones: 558 (24% mobile). **Radios:** 862. **TV sets:** 579.
Daily newspaper circulation: 237. **Computers:** 368.

REFUGEES

Alien refugees from other countries: 30,000.

HUMAN LIFE AND LIBERTY (optimum condition=100.0%)

HDI: 94.6. **HSI:** 93.0. **HFI:** 87.5. **EFL:** 54.0.

Country status. France is the largest country in Europe and one of the 2 European countries bordering on both the Atlantic and the Mediterranean. It is considered one of the world's superpowers and its culture and language have dominated Europe for centuries. Although France is an industrialized country, agriculture is still important with many regions known for their fine wines.

HUMAN LIFE AND LIBERTY

Human need and development. Although a highly developed country with high levels of education, housing and medical care, France has been, since the 1950s, the destination of over 5 million immigrants, mostly from its former colonies in Africa. These immigrants live in substandard conditions in virtual ghettoes that resemble shantytowns of Third World countries. Political policy makers have met with considerable resistance in trying to devise a humane policy of meeting the real social needs of these immigrants. Most of the immigrants are engaged in low-paying menial work, and since few of them have been enfranchised they have very little political power to change their conditions. Further, through their sheer numbers, they provoke the hostility of right-wing nationalists and sometimes suffer physical violence at the latter's hands. Although the national physical quality of life index is 98, it masks the much lower standards for immigrants and those at the bottom of the social ladder. Like many other large cities, the homeless are a familiar feature in Paris, Marseilles and other large towns.

Human rights and freedoms. France has been called the Cradle of Liberties, and the French are proud that the range of personal liberties they enjoy is equalled only in Anglo Saxon and Scandinavian countries. Nevertheless, the presence of over 3 million African-born immigrants has placed a great strain on these rights. Blacks and persons from the Maghreb are generally suspected of being connected with the drug traffic and subjected to arbitrary identity checks. The rise of the nationalist right has brought to the fore latent racism and anti-semitism among a small minority of Frenchmen. In 1992, 200 Jewish graves were vandalized at a cemetery in Herrilsheim in eastern France. Women's rights are strongly protected both under the Penal Code and under special regulations against sexual harassment and violence. Despite France's long history as a haven for refugees, restrictions have been placed on asylees designating special waiting zones for them at ports and airports.

Human environment. France has highly diversified flora and fauna representing 40% of those found in Europe. It also has abundant water resources. Nevertheless, it lags behind other Western European countries in waste water treatment. Like all industrialized countries it also suffers from widespread air pollution. Damage to forests is slight because acid rain has been moderate.

NON-CHRISTIAN RELIGIONS

Islam forms the second largest religious community in France, after the Catholic Church, France hav-

Country Table 1. **Religious adherents in France, AD 1900-2025.**

Year	1900		1970		mid-1990		Annual change, 1990-2000				mid-1995		mid-2000		mid-2025	
Name	Adherents	%	Adherents	%	Adherents	%	Natural	Conversion	Total	Rate	Adherents	%	Adherents	%	Adherents	%
Christians	**40,731,100**	**99.3**	**42,557,500**	**83.8**	**40,626,950**	**71.6**	**169,159**	**-53,260**	**115,899**	**0.28**	**41,300,000**	**71.2**	**41,785,935**	**70.7**	**41,807,000**	**67.8**
PROFESSION																
professing Christians	**40,731,100**	**99.3**	**42,557,500**	**83.8**	**40,626,950**	**71.6**	**169,159**	**-53,260**	**115,899**	**0.28**	**41,300,000**	**71.2**	**41,785,935**	**70.7**	**41,807,000**	**67.8**
AFFILIATION																
unaffiliated Christians	0	0.0	0	0.0	630,000	1.1	2,624	1,274	3,898	0.60	644,000	1.1	668,976	1.1	857,000	1.4
affiliated Christians	**40,731,100**	**99.3**	**42,557,500**	**83.8**	**39,996,950**	**70.5**	**166,536**	**-54,535**	**112,001**	**0.28**	**40,656,000**	**70.1**	**41,116,959**	**69.6**	**40,950,000**	**66.4**
Roman Catholics	40,344,000	98.4	44,578,898	87.8	47,200,000	83.2	196,563	-56,563	140,000	0.29	48,064,066	82.8	48,600,000	82.3	49,000,000	79.5
Independents	0	0.0	299,884	0.6	1,250,000	2.2	5,206	2,294	7,500	0.58	1,296,997	2.2	1,325,000	2.2	1,500,000	2.4
Protestants	902,000	2.2	860,166	1.7	890,000	1.6	3,706	-1,706	2,000	0.22	901,723	1.6	910,000	1.5	900,000	1.5
Orthodox	10,000	0.0	363,000	0.7	620,000	1.1	2,582	1,418	4,000	0.63	629,500	1.1	660,000	1.1	810,000	1.3
Marginal Christians	1,000	0.0	153,390	0.3	295,000	0.5	1,229	2,271	3,500	1.13	310,600	0.5	330,000	0.6	430,000	0.7
Anglicans	500	0.0	15,000	0.0	13,400	0.0	56	-76	-20	-0.15	13,300	0.0	13,200	0.0	12,400	0.0
doubly-affiliated	-397,000	-1.0	-955,300	-1.9	-3,271,450	-5.8	-13,624	8,645	-4,979	0.15	-3,310,186	-5.7	-3,321,241	-5.6	-3,602,400	-5.8
disaffiliated	-129,400	-0.3	-2,757,538	-5.4	-7,000,000	-12.3	-29,151	-10,849	-40,000	0.56	-7,250,000	-12.5	-7,400,000	-12.5	-8,100,000	-13.1
Trans-megabloc groupings																
Evangelicals	120,000	0.3	259,000	0.5	227,000	0.4	945	-45	900	0.39	234,226	0.4	236,000	0.4	302,000	0.5
Pentecostals/Charismatics	0	0.0	150,000	0.3	1,241,000	2.2	5,168	17,432	22,600	1.69	1,364,088	2.4	1,467,000	2.5	2,450,000	4.0
Great Commission Christians	**3,690,000**	**9.0**	**12,693,000**	**25.0**	**22,970,000**	**40.5**	**95,658**	**61,310**	**156,968**	**0.66**	**23,788,000**	**41.0**	**24,539,680**	**41.5**	**25,898,000**	**42.0**
Nonreligious	92,000	0.2	4,575,000	9.0	8,650,000	15.3	36,023	21,839	57,862	0.65	8,926,360	15.4	9,228,617	15.6	10,269,000	16.7
Muslims	50,000	0.1	1,353,000	2.7	3,850,000	6.8	16,033	16,650	32,683	0.82	4,040,000	7.0	4,176,833	7.1	4,800,000	7.8
Atheists	30,000	0.1	1,524,000	3.0	2,200,000	3.9	9,162	8,960	18,122	0.79	2,300,000	4.0	2,381,223	4.0	3,000,000	4.9
Jews	86,900	0.2	550,000	1.1	575,000	1.0	2,395	-815	1,580	0.27	585,000	1.0	590,797	1.0	600,000	1.0
Buddhists	0	0.0	27,000	0.1	400,000	0.7	1,666	3,168	4,834	1.15	420,000	0.7	448,340	0.8	600,000	1.0
Chinese folk-religionists	0	0.0	30,000	0.1	120,000	0.2	500	987	1,487	1.17	128,000	0.2	134,867	0.2	180,000	0.3
Ethnoreligionists	0	0.0	50,000	0.1	85,000	0.2	354	1,539	1,893	2.03	100,000	0.2	103,931	0.2	110,000	0.2
New-Religionists	0	0.0	30,000	0.1	60,000	0.1	250	249	499	0.80	62,000	0.1	64,988	0.1	80,000	0.1
Hindus	0	0.0	20,000	0.0	40,000	0.1	167	294	461	1.10	42,000	0.1	44,605	0.1	60,000	0.1
Spiritists	0	0.0	12,000	0.0	21,500	0.0	90	123	213	0.95	22,500	0.0	23,632	0.0	30,000	0.1
Baha'is	0	0.0	3,100	0.0	4,000	0.0	17	-3	14	0.33	4,060	0.0	4,136	0.0	5,200	0.0
Zoroastrians	0	0.0	400	0.0	550	0.0	2	2	4	0.72	580	0.0	591	0.0	800	0.0
Other religionists	10,000	0.0	40,000	0.1	85,000	0.2	354	267	621	0.71	89,500	0.2	91,214	0.2	120,000	0.2
World A (unevangelized persons)	41,000	0.1	1,015,444	2.0	2,041,848	3.6	8,504	6,135	14,639	0.69	2,146,738	3.7	2,185,960	3.7	3,021,438	4.9
World B (evangelized non-Christians)	227,900	0.6	7,199,256	14.2	14,049,202	24.8	58,509	47,125	105,634	0.73	14,573,231	25.1	15,108,105	25.6	16,833,562	27.3
World C (Christians)	40,731,100	99.3	42,557,500	83.8	40,626,950	71.6	169,159	-53,260	115,899	0.28	41,300,000	71.2	41,785,935	70.7	41,807,000	67.8
Country's population	**41,000,000**	**100.0**	**50,772,200**	**100.0**	**56,718,000**	**100.0**	**236,172**	**0**	**236,172**	**0.41**	**58,019,970**	**100.0**	**59,080,000**	**100.0**	**61,662,000**	**100.0**

COLUMNS, ROWS.
For meanings and definitions, see Codebook (Part 3). Note that, by definition, total 'Christians' = professing + crypto-Christians, which also = affiliated + unaffiliated Christians, and also = Great Commission Christians + latent Christians. Percentages may not always total exactly, due to rounding.

CENSUSES.
The religion question has not been asked in government censuses, except for Alsace-Lorraine as follows. **1954:** 77.5% Roman Catholics, 21.7% Protestants, 0.6% Jews, 0.2% Muslims: and **1962:** 78.0% Roman Catholics, 20.7% Protestants, 0.7% Jews, 0.6% Muslims.

NOTES ON RELIGIONS
ATHEISTS. Parti Communiste Français (PCF) (legal; neutral re Sino-Soviet split). In France there is no Christian or Catholic socialist party, hence many Christians vote Communist.
BAHA'IS. Entered before 1921. Growth from 8 local spiritual assemblies (1964) to 16 (1973), and to 38 LSAs (1996).
BUDDHISTS. Mahayana, Vietnamese, Laotian, Cambodian, and Chinese immigrants since 1950, and 12,000 French Buddhists. From 1980-1995 further waves arrived from Asia.
DISAFFILIATED. This term is used here to describe dechristianized persons who, although baptized Roman Catholics and therefore regarded by the Catholic Church as still affiliated to it (and hence enumerated in Table 2 as such), have recently withdrawn or disaffiliated themselves completely from Christianity and now profess to be either nonreligious (agnostics) or atheists. Because their statistics represent a duplication, they are shown in the table above as a negative quantity (with a minus sign). The vast majority of these dechristianized persons are in the Paris region.
DOUBLY-AFFILIATED. The term covers those affiliated to, or claimed by, both the Catholic Church and also a church termed Evangélique by state or society (Protestant, Anglican, marginal Protestant) or other church, i.e. baptized Catholics who have recently become Evangelicals or others. Because their statistics represent a duplication, they are shown in the table as a negative quantity (with a minus sign).
INDEPENDENTS. In about 120 denominations in 1995 (see Table 2).
JEWS. Increasing due to immigration from North Africa (100,000 from Egypt); now throughout France. Since 1960, Sefardis outnumber Ashkenazis for the first time in France. City populations: Paris 300,000, Marseilles 80,000, Nice 30,000, Lyons 16,000, Strasbourg 15,000.
MUSLIMS. There has been a rapid increase in numbers from 0.7% of the population (350,000) in 1966. Almost all are Sunnis. *Hajj pilgrims to Mecca.* (1970) 372; (1974) 556; (1975) 795; (1976) 563. *Immigration.* The column 'Natural change' above includes 9,000 annual immigrants as well as about 7,000 biological increase. *Conversions.* Each year a number of former Muslims who had lapsed are won back to Islam.
NEW-RELIGIONISTS. Mainly Cao Daists among the 500,000 Vietnamese in France; and a Soka Gakkai mission headquarters for Europe in Paris.
NONRELIGIOUS. Of these persons, about 90% were once baptized Catholics; 72% once made their first communion (at 12 years old) but then ceased all church attendance, 19% at one time belonged to a Christian youth movement, 4% have parents who were practicing Christians.
OTHER RELIGIONISTS. Including adherents of numerous esoteric religions including Rosicrucians (98 AMORC Lodges and centers; also Lectorium Rosicrucianum). There are also in France some 10,000 Freemasons, often considered a quasi-religion.
PENTECOSTALS/CHARISMATICS. Begun in 1972, the Catholic Charismatic Renewal has 1,694 regular weekly prayer groups, with 25,900 regular adult attenders, 411 involved priests and 16 bishops. Rallies have had up to 10,000 attenders each time. France is noted for having more and more-developed covenant communities than any other. One, the Community of the Beatitudes (formerly Lion of Judah) is now established in 25 French dioceses and in 17 foreign countries.

Great Commission Instrument Panel: status of France (for explanation see start of Part 4)

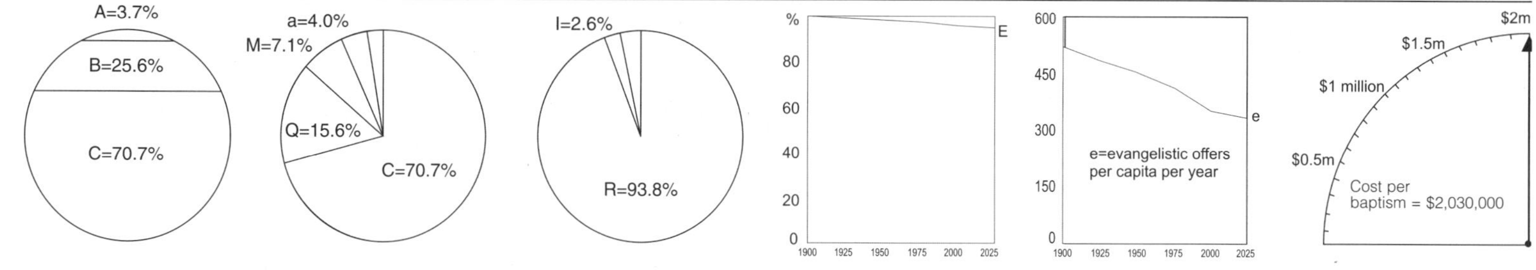

3 Worlds, AD 2000 | Religions, AD 2000 | Ecclesiastical blocs | Evangelization, 1900-2025 | Offers, 1900-2025 | Cost-effectiveness, AD 2000

ing more Muslims than any other West European country. Muslim immigration began in the early part of the present century, with the arrival of Algerian male workers, followed later by a broad spectrum of North African workers with their families. During the early 1960s other Muslims entered from Yugoslavia, Turkey, and former French Black Africa; and by 1973, over 1.3 million persons from Muslim countries or regions had settled legally in France. The largest communities of legal immigrants by 1973 were those from Algeria (798,690), Morocco (226,496), Tunisia (133,315), Turkey (25,066) and such Black African countries as Senegal, Mali and Mauritania (more than 150,000). These figures do not include clandestine immigration, which is significant among Algerians, Tunisians and Black Africans and which is only partially compensated by the number of registered aliens leaving the country after the expiration of their residence permits.

Although Muslim immigrants are dispersed throughout France, they are especially numerous in the southeast (Provence; Cote d' Azur) and in the regions of Paris and Lyons. Their living conditions are often difficult, and French policy and attitudes toward non-white immigrants has been a fiery national issue. The Grand Mosque of Paris was built in 1922 and has served since then as the center of Muslim life for the nation. It has been the home of important organizations such as the Muslim Institute of Paris and the International Muslim Union. In the early 1970s the muezzin ceased chanting the call to prayer, to avoid attracting hostility from non-Muslim neighbors. In 1990 the French Interior Ministry set up a Committee on Reflection on Islam (Corif), and that body was soon involved in a controversy with Algeria over control of certain aspects of the mosque's leadership and operation.

Judaism is widespread and extensive, the Jewish community of France being the largest in Europe (with the exception of Russia) and the fourth largest in the world, after the USA, Russia and Israel. In 1995 there were 585,000 Jews in France of which about half were from North Africa. Of the 270,000 French Jews at the beginning of World War II, 120,000 were deported during the Nazi occupation. The rapid increase in the Jewish population after the war has been due for the most part to immigration: first displaced persons from other parts of Western Europe; then Jews from Poland, Romania and Hungary; 100,000 from Egypt between 1954 and 1961; others from Morocco and Tunisia after their independence in 1956 (a movement which continues to this day); and 120,000 from Algeria after 1962.

The massive immigration from North Africa has introduced important changes in Jewish life. For the first time in French history Sefardis (who originate in the eastern Mediterranean and North Africa) outnumber Ashkenazis (from central Europe), a fact which has created material, cultural and religious problems of adjustment as well as causing considerable strains on existing Jewish organizations. The extensive multiplication of Jewish communities, from 128 in 1957 to 600 in 1970, has also created new problems of adjustment relating to the integration of Judaism into French society as a whole. Many cities now have Jewish communities for the first time.

Country summary. **Worlds A, B, C by ethnolinguistic peoples, cities, and major civil divisions in France.**

World	PEOPLES Num	Pop 2000	C%	Christians	E%	U%	Unevangelized	CITIES Num	Pop 2000	C%	Christians	E%	U%	Unevangelized	CIVIL DIVISIONS Num	Pop 2000	C%	Christians	E%	U%	Unevangelized
A	12	644,311	0.32	2,067	39	61	390,108	0	0	0.00	0	0	0	0	0	0	0.00	0	0	0	0
B	32	5,792,509	11.28	653,434	71	29	1,671,035	0	0	0.00	0	0	0	0	1	1,831,896	58.49	1,071,476	93	7	124,752
C	53	52,642,893	76.86	40,461,457	100	0	127,248	119	30,248,985	66.79	20,203,063	95	5	1,391,844	95	57,247,813	69.95	40,045,483	96	4	2,063,641
Total	**97**	**59,079,713**	**69.60**	**41,116,958**	**96**	**4**	**2,188,391**	**119**	**30,248,985**	**66.79**	**20,203,063**	**95**	**5**	**1,391,844**	**96**	**59,079,709**	**69.60**	**41,116,959**	**96**	**4**	**2,188,393**

Communities of Orthodox Judaism, Liberal or Reformed Judaism, and Consistorial Judaism (the later being similar to conservative Judaism in the USA), are also found in France, although most Jews are not attached to any of these traditions. The Orthodox have only a few hundred adherents and Liberal Judaism not more than 3,000 while even the third group, the largest, counts no more than 70 consistorial rabbis in the whole of France.

An international Jewish organization based in France is the Universal Israelite Alliance, founded in Paris in 1860. The principal national organizations are: (1) Consistoire Israelite de France, founded in the 19th century, which is concerned primarily with worship and administers the Israelite Seminary of France in Paris, (2) Consel Representatif des Israelites de France (CRIF), founded in Paris in 1944, which is dedicated to the defense of Jewish interests; and (3) Fonds Social Juif Unifie (FSJU) founded in Paris after World War II.

Buddhism exists both among aliens from southeast Asia (from Viet-Nam, Cambodia and Laos) and native French citizens. Vietnamese are found in relatively large numbers and have built a Buddhist temple at Frejus (Var). Their principal associates are: Federation des Bouddhistes Vietnamiens d'Outre-Mer and Eglise Unifiee du Vietnam. Buddhist monasteries are found at Gretz (Mahayana Zen), Fort-les-Bancs (Lamaism) and Mougins (Zen Soto).

Other religions, including Vietnamese New-Religionists (Cao Daist Missionary Church), Confucianism, and Baha'i, have small communities. In addition about 20% of the population is without religion.

Baptism of Judas, bishop of Jerusalem, AD 350; in 13th-century Sainte-Chapelle, Paris.

CHRISTIANITY

The first Christians entered France at an early date from Italy, and a strong Christian community had been established in Lyons by AD 150. There were 10 bishops by AD 250, and the first general council of the West was held at Arles in France in 314. The mass baptism of the Frank king, Clovis, with his warriors in 496 was a major milestone in the development of French Christianity. The Middle Ages were characterized by the missionary activity of Columban and Boniface from Ireland and Britain, the theological studies of Thomas Aquinas in Paris, the Crusades, and the monastic reform of Benedict of Cluny and Bernard of Clairvaux, followed by the 14th-century schism which produced rival popes at Avignon and Rome. France was also affected by the Reformation. The influence of Luther and Zwingli was strongest in Alsace while Calvinism gained many followers in other parts of the country. Calvin's Huguenots established 2,000 churches prior to holding their first National synod of Reformed Churches in 1559. The Counter-Reformation resulted in serious religious conflict and persecution of Protestants; and it was not until the proclamation of the Edict of Nantes in 1598 that a degree of religious freedom was restored. The revocation of that edict by Louis XIV in 1585 resulted in a new wave of persecution which drove thousands into exile. Protestants were to remain a persecuted minority until the French Revolution of 1794. Napoleon negotiated a concordat with Rome in 1801 recognizing Catholicism as the religion of the majority, and in the following year the Lutheran and Reformed churches were also officially recognized. A number of new Protestant bodies entered France during the 19th century and this influx has increased during the present century. During this century also, French Catholics became predominate in the Catholic missionary world.

Eglise Catholique de France. Basilica of the National Vow to the Sacred Heart (Sacre Coeur), in Montmartre, Paris, built in 1876-1919.

CATHOLIC CHURCH. The period since World War II had been marked by profound structural and pastoral changes in the French Church. In 1964, the old Plenary Assembly of Cardinals and Archbishops gave place to the French Episcopal Conference which, according to the new statutes adopted in 1973, includes a permanent council of 13 members and a Bureau of Doctrinal Studies. The conciliar period has witnessed an acceleration of this transformation of structures while at the same time the lay organization Catholic Action has developed and been reorganized. It has had a great influence on pastoral life and on ecclesiastical appointments, including those of bishops. The orientation of the Church of France towards the working classes is perhaps its most marked characteristic. The worker-priest movement began in France in 1943-45, but there were confrontations and arrests involving priests in 1954 and 1959 which resulted in the demise of the movement. Official sanction to begin again was given in 1966, after an unanimous decision by the plenary assembly of the French episcopate, with papal agreement, during the last session of Vatican II. However, more difficulties appeared, and in 1969 the administrative council of the Mission de France was dismissed.

Concerning membership, a census of baptized Catholics took place in 1958, showing that 91.5% of the French population had been baptized in the Catholic Church. By 1971 the figure had dropped to 88.7%. This national figure however showed important regional variations: 27% of Paris' population were not baptized Catholics, and 21% of that of Marseilles. In urban areas, about 80% of marriages and virtually all funerals are religious.

Concerning religious practice, it is estimated that 13% of the total population attend Sunday mass at least once a month. Rural practice is by no means always higher than urban practice. In districts where church attendance by the rural population is strong, in the local towns it is relatively weak; whereas in areas where the level of practice is weak, it is higher in the towns than in the countryside. The main factor affecting town practice is the general level of practice in any given socio-cultural region, and not (as is often widely thought) the percentage of working-class persons in the population. In some regions 50% of all young persons abandon church attendance immediately following their first communion.

Vocations have progressively decreased since 1948 when there 779 ordinations to the priesthood, to 284 in 1970, and only 99 in 1977. Less than 100 were ordained in 1990. Moreover, departures from the priesthood increased to 150 in 1969. Brothers occupy an important place in Catholic education at all levels, and in pastoral work they play a significant role in liturgical, scriptural, and theological renewal.

With regard to the laity, over the past 50 years specialized Catholic Action programs for youth and adults have been developed to serve the 3 major categories of French society: workers, independents (middle, bourgeois, and aristocratic classes), and rural inhabitants. Education and childhood are also influenced by Catholic Action with the most noticeable effects taking place among school populations. Catholic Action also influences almost all parishes, enlisting in its programs about 8% of all practicing Catholics. Other movements are active and well-developed, but the episcopate give priority to Catholic Action Movements of dissent, traditionalist, and progressivist, have also developed considerably since 1968.

The Holy See has diplomatic relations with France and in AD 2000 is represented to government and the Catholic hierarchy by a nuncio residing in Paris.

PROTESTANT CHURCHES. Among the Protestants of France since World War II, attention has been centered on rebuilding churches, liturgical renewal (especially that relating to the Holy Communion), exploring the possibilities of a more complete regional community life, and evangelization of industrial areas.

The 2 principal Lutheran groups are the Church of the Augsburg Confession of Alsace and Lorraine, which is the main Protestant church of Alsace, and the Evangelical Lutheran Church of France, which is divided into 2 sections (inspections): one for Paris and the other for Montbeliard. The Lutheran Interior Mission of Paris and worker-pastors are active in urban areas where Christian influence is marginal. Lutherans have also been involved in liturgical renewal.

Enfants de Dieu. Children of God witness along Rue Saint Severin, Paris.

The Assemblies of God have built up a strong following since their arrival in 1929 and, with its autonomous Gypsy counterpart (Eglises Tziganes), it is now the largest Protestant denomination in France. Other Pentecostal and Charismatic groups exist, some of which showed notable growth into the 1990s.

Smaller churches begun during the 19th century include the Federation of Evangelical Baptist Churches in 1832, Darbyites (Plymouth Brethren) in 1844 and Seventh-day Adventists in 1874. The former is a member of the Protestant Federation of France and has a special relationship with the Southern Baptist Convention in the USA, although numerically there are less than 6,000 adult Baptists (1995).

Although Protestants are found in all parts of the country, their strength varies considerably from one area to another. They are most numerous in Alsace and the Rhone valley. The following 8 departments, each report relatively large numbers of Protestants: Bas-Rhin, Gard, Doubs, Ardeche, Haut-Rhin, Drome, Lozere, and Deux-Sevres.

ORTHODOX CHURCHES. Greeks, Armenians, and Russians form the bulk of Orthodoxy in France, the latter 2 owing their numbers principally to emigres and refugees since the 1917 revolution in the USSR. The Russians are divided ecclesiastically into

3 groups: The Russian Orthodox Church belonging to the Exarchate for Western Europe (with headquarters in Germany) under the Moscow Patriarchate; the Russian Orthodox Church Outside of Russia with it headquarters in New York, which is opposed to Moscow; and, by far the largest, the Orthodox Church, Archdiocese of France and Western Europe, since 1971 under the jurisdiction of the Ecumenical Patriarchate in Constantinople. The Armenian Apostolic Church is under the Catholicate of Echmiadzin in Armenia (with a small faction under Sis in Lebanon). Paris is an important center for diaspora Armenians. The last king of Armenia is buried there and the city is host to the Armenian Cathedral of St John the Baptist, a school for girls, and an important research library, the Biblioteque Nubarian in Place Alboni, with more than 10,000 volumes in several languages. The Greek Orthodox Church of France, which is in the Greek tradition, is under the Ecumenical Patriarchate through the archbishop of London. Smaller groups of Romanian, Serbian, Ukrainian, and Georgian Orthodox are also found in France.

MARGINAL CHURCHES. A number of marginal Protestant bodies have been active in France since the last century. The first to arrive were American Mormons, who continue to maintain hundreds of missionaries in France although their work has been singularly unsuccessful, numerically. A major schism around 1900 from Jehovah's Witnesses produced the Aurore (Dawn) Association of the Students of the Bible which moved its headquarters from Lille to Nice in 1953. Shortly after the turn of the century, the Lay Interior Missionary Movement (Mouvenment Missionnaire Interieur Laique), a schism from Aurore and Jehovah's Witnesses in the USA, set up headquarters in Denain. However, they have lost membership to the Witnesses since World War II. Their name was changed in 1959 to the French Association of Free Students of the Bible. Jehovah's Witnesses themselves entered France also around 1900, but they were not officially installed in Paris until 1930. Since then they have grown rapidly and now rank fourth in size among non-Catholics.

Tragic and mysterious murder-suicide rituals in the 1990s connected with the Order of the Solar Temple resulted in more than 70 deaths in France, Switzerland, and Canada. The government responded with measures that set suspicion upon a wide range of newer denominations and religious movements, Christian, marginal Christian, and non-Christian. One official report identified 173 'cult groups' and another 800 'smaller sects'. The prime minister promised more careful and extensive surveillance of minority religious groups.

CATHOLIC INDEPENDENT CHURCHES. At least 75 distinct bodies have split from the Church of Rome in the last hundred years, usually over faith-healing, ecclesiastical authority, gallicanism, or insistence on Latin or Celtic rites. Most remain small and localized in influence. The largest are the Antoinistes (Religious Association of Antoine) begun by a Belgian Catholic healer, and the Old Roman Catholic Church which has grown rapidly since 1960.

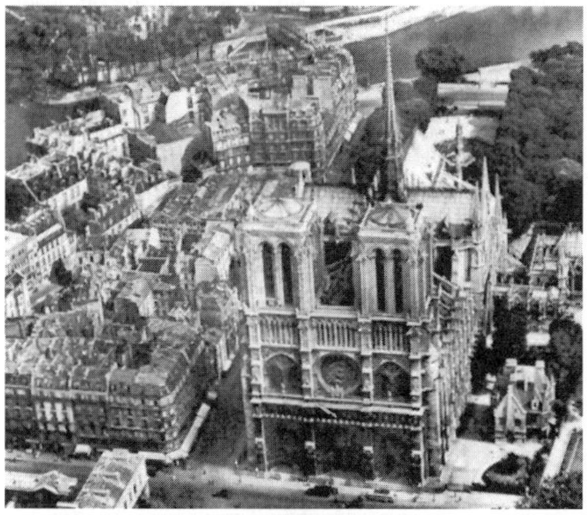

Eglise Catholique de France, Archdiocèse de Paris. Gothic Cathedral of Notre-Dame de Paris, on Ile Saint-Louis, built AD 1163-1240.

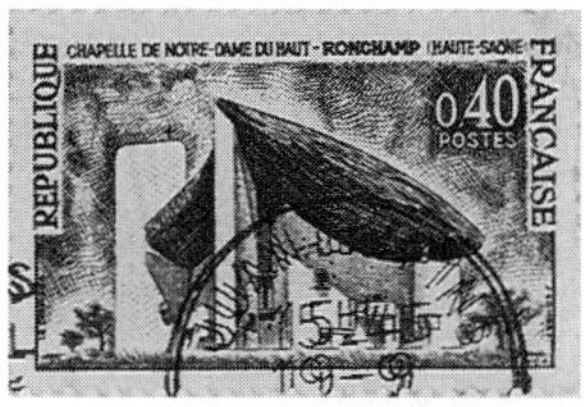

Eglise Catholique de France. Le Corbusier's typical but cavernous pilgrimage Chapel of Notre Dame du haut, Ronchamp (France, 1955) sets new trend.

Art and architecture. France is home to some of the grandest cathedrals in Europe and they stand as silent sentinels to the devotion of the French to the Christian faith. The queen of these cathedrals is that of Notre Dame in Paris which dominates the center of Paris. Even bereft of much its original color and ornament, it is unsurpassed in its grandeur. Closeby is La Sainte Chapel, hidden away in one of the courtyards of the Palais de Justice, with its overpowering ensemble of stained glass. Saint-Severin in the Left Bank is an ancient church and a center of liturgical experimentation. It is close to the oldest church in Paris, Saint-Germain-des-Pres, and also Saint Sulpice Church, marked (or marred, according to one's taste) by highly ornate and baroque decorations. Although architecturally undistinguished, the Rue de Bac Church is the center of the Vincentian Order. In Montmartre is the Basilica of the Sacred Heart. The enormous Byzantine sanctuary is considered as the place where Ignatius Loyola and his followers first pledged themselves to Christ on August 15, 1534, although the exact location is down the hill, in the chapel of Saint-Denis. Also in Montmartre is the ancient church of Saint-Pierre. Just outside Paris, in the suburb of Saint-Denis, is the famous abbey where the kings of France were traditionally crowned, and where most of them are buried. Most historians consider it the mother church of Gothic. France's most famous place of pilgrimage is the Grotto of Lourdes. Among the cathedrals outside Paris the most famous is that of Chartres, one of the earliest shrines to be devoted to Mary. Chartres has been the subject of numerous books, including Henry Adams' classic Mont-Saint-Michel and Chartres. Interestingly, the twin spires of the cathedral belong to different epochs, the left one, called the North Tower, dating much later than the right one. The grandeur of Chartres is difficult to define. Part of it comes from its perfect architectural proportions, part of it from the 186 stained glass windows and some 1800 carved figures. In the Isle de France are many other ancient Gothic cathedrals, the chief being Amiens and Rheims. Both were built a bit later, but are more soaring than Chartres. Amiens, considered the Gothic Church par excellence, is more transparently built than Chartres with a verticality that is matched only at Beauvais. Rheims has been called the Queen of French cathedrals, and is more graceful and more ornamental than its peers. It also was used for the crowning of the French monarchs. Between Amiens and Rheims is the Cathedral of Laon. Other notable cathedrals include Bourges, Le Mans, Sens, and Rouen. Not all of the great great religious buildings are cathedrals. There are a number of churches that rival the cathedrals in their beauty: Saint-Ouen and Saint Maclou, for example. Nor are all the fine churches Gothic. Many of them are in the Romanesque style In Burgundy, not far from Dijon, is the Shrine of St Mary Magdalene, where St Bernard preached his crusade. The Church of Saint-Lazare in Autun is noted for its statuary, created almost entirely by Gislebertus, a 12th century sculptor whose fame has survived into the 20th century. The region of Dijon and Grenoble was the heartland of French religious life in the Middle Ages. Four of the greatest monasteries of France were located here: Cluny, Citeaux, Clairveaux, and La Grande Chartreuse. Paray-le-Mondial, to the south, is celebrated for the apparitions of Our Lord to St Margaret Mary in the 17th century. One of the rarest examples of the French Romanesque is the exquisitely proportioned Abbey Church of Saint-Benoit-sur-Loire. Nearby is Germigny-des-Pres, with its ancient Byzantine mosaics. Although it is now a museum, Mont Saint-Michel in northwestern France is undoubtedly the most unforgettable of abbeys built in France in the Middle Ages. Called the 'Marvel of the West', it embodies a number of styles, from early Romanesque to late Gothic spanning a number of centuries, but, nevertheless, achieves a mysterious harmony. Another shrine dedicated to St Michael is that at Le Puy built on a volcanic rock rising from a valley. Normandy has many abbeys and cathedrals, those at Caen, Coutances, and Bayeux, being the largest. In Western France, the Cathedral of Angers is associated with a 17-tower castle, housing priceless tapestries. Near Angers is Solesmus Abbey, and the Cathedral and Shrine of St Martin in Tours, the capital city of the Loire Valley. Between Tours and Poitiers is the battleground where, in 732, Charles Martel beat back the Arab hordes and saved Christian Europe. Poitiers, Angouleme, Perigueux, and Bordeaux all have impressive cathedrals. In Provence is Albi with its brooding cathedral, and to its south lies the fortified town of Carcassonne. At Vence is the lovely chapel built by Matisse in the 20th century. Arles, better known for its Roman theater and arena, contains the superb church of Saint-Trophime. To the north is Avignon, where the popes lived from 1308 to 1377 during the so-called Avignon Captivity. There are equally stately cathedrals in the eastern cities of Strasbourg and Metz. Domremy is the place associated with Joan of Arc. The church at Colmar contains Gruenewald's masterpiece, the Altarpiece of Isenheim. Lyons and Vienne are important in church history—being the site of 3 Ecumenical Councils, the 13th, 14th, and 15th- and contain churches considered as mother churches.

Renewal movements. In the 1990s the Pentecostal/Charismatic Renewal continued to spread rapidly across most older churches, and numbered over 1,467,000 adherents (of whom 11% Pentecostals, 76% Charismatics, and 13% Independents).

Indigenous missions. From the earliest times of Christian influence in France, missionaries have been sent out in response to the command of Christ. After the mass baptism of Franks by Clovis shortly before AD 500, the French sent out large numbers of missionaries to surrounding countries in Europe. After the advent of the Franciscans, the Dominicans, and later, the Jesuits, French Catholic missionaries served all over the world. In the 19th century France became a leading missionary-sending nation and has remained so throughout the 20th century. French Protestants have an equally impressive missionary-sending record, though their numbers are much smaller.

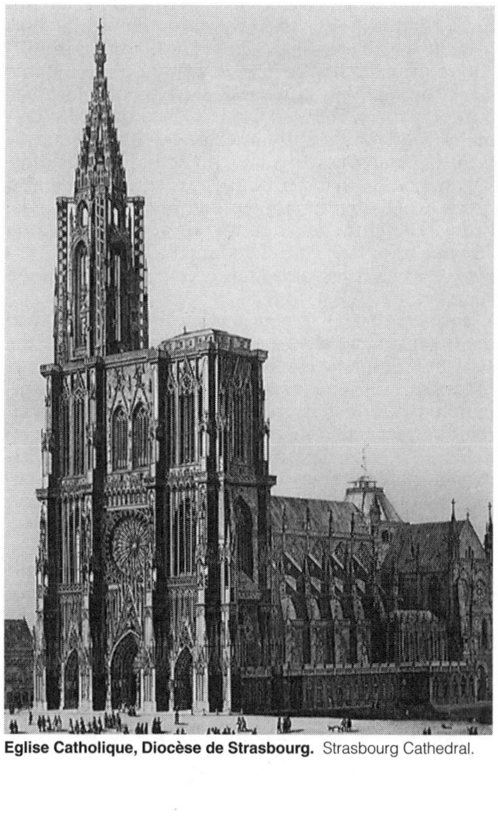

Eglise Catholique, Diocèse de Strasbourg. Strasbourg Cathedral.

CHURCH AND STATE

For centuries the established church, the Catholic Church was finally separated from the state in 1905.

The juridical status of the churches in France at present is governed by the principle that the state is secular, as promulgated by the law of 9 December 1905. 'The separation of the churches and state' (Article 1 and 2), and repeated in the constitutions of 1946 (4th Republic) and 1958 (5th Republic: Article 2). The result is that the state gives no preference to any religion and refuses to intervene in religious and spiritual matters. Public services and public education must be completely secular in character, including their locations, programs and personnel. Clergy may not teach in primary schools in virtue of the law of 30 October 1886, Article 17, nor in secondary schools since the decision of the council of state of 10 May 1912. The secular nature of the state excludes subsidies to denominations for specifically religious work, although this does not extend to secular activities of religious inspiration such as cultural, welfare and social work. An exception regarding clergy is made for chaplains of such public institutions as schools, prisons, hospitals, hostels, and the army, which then pay clergy delegated to them, although in actuality not all receive remuneration from government sources. Primary schools are required to set aside a day each week for the religious instruction of those children whose parents request it.

Church property must receive a juridical basis conforming to law, the churches having the status of 'moral personalities'. Diocesan associations, created in 1924, have handled this problem for the Catholic Church, while Protestants and Jews have organized themselves since 1905 into 'religious associations' as defined by the law of that year.

Private denominational instruction may be freely conducted, with only a few somewhat liberal juridical conditions. Subsidies from public funds for this are subject to different regulations depending on the educational level: forbidden at the primary level, permitted under certain conditions in secondary schools, largely authorized for technical instruction, and free for higher education.

The principle of secularity imposes on the state the need to respect the religious freedom of its citizens and the right to manifest both individually and collectively their convictions, including private and public worship, except where public order is endangered. Certain special dispositions, however, govern the separation of church and state. The Holy See is obliged to consult with the government before the appointment of bishops. Clergy may not officiate at marriages or funerals before first completing the required formalities. Moreover, clergy, seminarians and religious novices are subject to military conscription.

There is one striking exception to this separation of church and state. Alsace and Lorraine, consisting of the 3 departments of Haut-rhin, Bas-Rhin, and Moselle which were annexed by the Germans in 1870 and returned to France in 1918, enjoy a unique status since the 1905 law of church-state separation does not apply there. The Napoleonic Concordat of 1801 remains valid for the Catholic Church with the state officially naming new bishops (in actuality only after negotiations with the Vatican); state agreement is also necessary before the appointment of parish priests. Protestant churches operate under the Organic Articles of 1801-2, completed in 1852. All clergy are ranked as civil servants and receive salary from the state.

In recent years, 3 new factors have emerged to modify relations between the Catholic Church and the state in France: the rise of political issues on the part of Catholic movements, a desire on the part of the hierarchy to retreat from its traditional semi-official role alongside state authorities and certain protests by the church on issues such as nuclear weapons. This change of climate, seen by some observers as the beginning of a 'second separation' of church and state.

BROADCASTING AND MEDIA

Virtually everyone in France has a radio set, and nearly half own televisions. France is a member of UNDA, and there are 41 local Catholic radio stations. Though they are not specifically targeted at the nation, shortwave programs from KNLS, HCJB (Ecuador), TWR (Monaco, Albania) and AWR (Slovakia) can be easily received.

Satellite TV and radio programs are received in English, Arabic, German and Italian. Catholics produce and broadcast about 3 hours of weekly television programming. Institut Catholique de Lyon and CREC-AVEX are both Catholic educational institutions with courses in media.

Eglise Catholique de France. Basilica of St. Nicholas de Porte (Meurthe-et-Moselle Department), a major tourist attraction.

INTERDENOMINATIONAL ORGANIZATIONS

The major Protestant co-ordinating body is the Protestant Federation of France (Federation Protestante de France, FPF), founded in 1913. In 1983 its membership included the Church of the Augsburg Confession of Alsace and Lorraine, Evangelical Lutheran Church of France, Reformed Church of Alsace and Lorraine, Reformed Church of France, Federation of Evangelical Baptist Churches, Evangelical Gypsy Mission, National Union of Independent Evangelical Reformed Churches, People's Mission, and Apostolic Church. Catholic ecumenical questions are handled by the French Secretariat for the Unity of Christians (Secretariat Francais pour l'Unite des Chretiens), founded in 1967 as an organ of the Catholic Episcopal Committee for Unity.

Certain joint commissions exist. The Comite Mixte Catholique-Protestant was formed in 1968 by the FPF and the Catholic Episcopal Committee for Unity. It is a technical committee which engages in theological study, prepares theological and pastoral documents and make joint declarations.; The Groupe Mixte Anglican-Catholique romain was formed in 1969 by the Catholic Episcopal Committee and the Anglican bishops having jurisdiction in France. Its interests are theological and pastoral and it provides support for the isolated Anglican community in France.

Several international ecumenical bodies have their base in France. These include Entraide Missionnaire Internationale (EMI) which was founded in Geneva in 1965 by Catholic religious personnel and Protestant pastors but now has its headquarters at Levallois, near Paris. It provides economic and social assistance to religious institutes, dioceses, associations and movements with special emphasis on the needs of Christian groups in the Third World. Secondly, the Conference Mondiale des Chretiens pour la Palestine (CMCP), founded in Paris in 1969, united Anglicans, Catholics, Orthodox, and Protestants of 57 countries in informing Christians concerning the Palestinian question, building bridges between Arab Christians on one side and Western and African Christians on the other and affirming solidarity with the Palestinian victims of the partition of Palestine in 1947. There are numerous ecumenical institutes and centers.

Among interchurch aid agencies is CIMADE (Comite Inter-Mouvements aupres des Evacues), established by the Reformed churches during World War II to provide aid to refugees and migrants as well as other disadvantaged persons in French society. The Orthodox later joined CIMADE and more recently but unofficially the Catholics. It works in close co-operation with the Protestant Federation of France and the WCC. For Protestant foreign missionary agencies, there is the French Federation of Evangelical Missions with 13 active member organizations in 1991, as well as 6 associate member missions and several others relating to it in more informal ways.

Ecumenical information centers include the Centre d'Information sur le Developpement (CIDEV), founded in Paris in 1970, which attempts to inform the public concerning the Third World, the causes of underdevelopment and the questions that his poses for developed countries. There is also BIPSNOP in Paris, which is jointly sponsored by the Catholic National Secretariat of Public Opinion and the Protestant Information Bureau. Stasbourg was the site of a major ecumenical and charismatic gathering in recent European history, Pentecost 82, attended by 20,000 from 24 countries in Eastern and Western Europe. The event was organized by a joint Catholic-Lutheran-Reformed committee with representatives from 9 nations. Catholics comprised 13,000 of the participants.

FUTURE TRENDS AND PROSPECTS.

Nearly 100% Christian in AD 1900, France has gradually become secularized over the 20th century and into the 21st. The nonreligious (9% in 1970) could rise to near 17% by 2025 leaving church membership at 66.4%.

By AD 2050 it is probable that less than 60% of France's population will be Christian. If immigration patterns continue into the distant future, Muslims may even reach 10% by AD 2050.

BIBLIOGRAPHY

A history of Protestantism. E. G. Leonard. Trans., M. H. Joyce. London: Nelson, 1965. 3 vols. (Major work on Protestantism in France).

A new look at Protestant churches in France. H. Foreman. *MARC monograph*, no. 9. Bromley, UK: MARC Europe, 1987. 118p.

A religious history of modern France. A. Dansette. Freiburg: Herder, 1961. 2 vols.

American evangelical missionaries in France, 1945–1975. A. V. Koop. Lanham, MD: University Press of America, 1986. 219p.

Annuaire catholique de France 1973. Paris: Publicat, 1973.

Annuaire des Eglises, associations et institutions orthodoxes. Paris: CIMADE, 1966.

Annuaire évangélique, 1970. Grenoble, France: DEFI, 1970.

Catholiques en politique: un siècle de Ralliement. B. Dumons. *Petite encyclopédie moderne du Christianisme.* Paris: Desclée de Brouwer, 1993. 140p.

'De forêts en banlieues: la transplantation du bouddhisme lao en France,' C. Choron-Baix, *Archives de Sciences Sociales des Religions*, 36, 73 (January–March 1991), 17–34.

Destin du Catholicisme français. A. Dansette. Paris: Flammarion, 1967.

Eglises et évêques catholiques non romains. I. D. de la Thibauderie. Paris: Dervy-Livres, 1962. 134p.

Fête populaire et tradition religieuse en pays niçois. P. Canestrier. Nice, France: Serre, 1978. 208p.

France. F. Chambers. 2nd ed. *World bibliographical series*, vol. 13. Oxford, UK: CLIO Press, 1990. 308p. (See especially 'Religion,' p40–f).

French prophets of yesterday: a study of religious thought under the Second Empire. A. L. Guerard. London: T. F. Unwin, 1913. 288p.

'Gott in Frankreich: zur Glaubenspraxis basiskirchlicher Lebensgemeinschaften.' M. Gmelch. Echter thesis, Universität Würzburg, Würzburg, 1988. 298p.

Guide juif de France. J. Berg, C. Chémouny & F. Didi (eds). 2d ed. Paris: Editions Migdal, 1971. 507p.

Guide religieux de la France. L. Chaigne et al. (eds). Paris: Hachette, 1967. 1235p.

Histoire religieuse de la France contemporaine. G. Cholvy & Y. M. Hilaire. Toulouse: Privat, 1985–88. 3 vols.

La Christianisation de la France (IIe–VIIIe s.). P. Pierrard. *Petite encyclopédie moderne du christianisme.* Paris: Desclée de Brouwer, 1994. 166p.

La France protestante, Annuaire 1974. Paris: Fédération Protestante de France, 1974. 504p.

La liberté de choisir: pluralisme religieux et pluralisme politique dans le catholicisme français contemporain. J. M. Donegani. Paris: Presses de la Fondation nationale des sciences politiques, 1993. 485p.

La religion en France de la fin du XVIIIe à nos jours. G. Cholvy. *Carré histoire.* Paris: Hachette, 1991. 219p.

Le droit des religions en France. A. Boyer. *Politique d'aujourd'hui.* Paris: Presses Universitaires de France, 1993. 260p.

Le monde spirituel des sectaires. K. Hutten. Neuchâtel, France: Delachaux et Niestlé, 1965. 110p.

Le renouveau de la religion populaire: sources et racines de la religion populaire, sources et étapes du renouveau conciliaire. J. Vinatier. *Croire aujourd'hui.* [Paris]: Desclée De Brouwer, 1981. 156p.

L'église catholique dans la France contemporaine. J. Imbert. *Mieux connaître.* Paris: Economica, 1990. 174p.

L'Église catholique en France: approches sociologiques. J. Potel. *Petite encyclopédie moderne du christianisme.* Paris: Desclée de Brouwer, 1994. 222p.

L'Eglise en France: 30 ans de bouleversements, les grand débats du catholicisme, le renouveau théologique. Paris: Compagnie Européenne d'Editions et Publications Périodiques, 1981. 246p.

L'Eglise et les ouvriers en France: 1940–1990. P. Pierrard. [Paris]: Hachette littérature, 1991. 444p.

Les Chrétiens en France. R. Solé. *Dossier thémis*, no. 43. Paris: Presses Universitaires de France, 1972. 95p.

Les finances de l'Église de France. R. Gaucher. Paris: A. Michel, 1981. 288p.

Les forces religieuses dans la société française. A. Coutrot et al. Paris: Beauchesne et fils, 1956.

Les protestants en France de 1800 à nos jours: histoire d'une réintégration. A. Encrevé. Paris: Stock, 1985. 281p.

Les sectes protestantes dans la France contemporaine. J. Séguy. Paris: Beauchesne et fils, 1956.

L'islam en France: les musulmans dans la communauté nationale. F. Lamand. *Présence de l'islam.* Paris: A. Michel, 1986. 159p.

Lourdes: city of the sick. C. T. Watling. Slough: St. Pauls, 1993. 131p.

Medieval France: an encyclopedia. W. W. Kibler & G. A. Zinn (eds). New York and London: Garland Publishing, 1995.

Paris et ses religions au XXième siècle. M. Meslin. *Cahiers d'anthropologie religieuse,* 2. Sorbonne: Université de Paris-Sorbonne, 1993. 151p.

Petites églises de France. G. Dagon. Anneville: Armand, 1971.

Petites églises et grandes sectes. G. Dagon. Paris: S.C.E., 1951, 1963. 128p.

Profession, pasteur: sociologie de la condition du clerc à la fin du XXe siècle. J. Willaime. *Histoire et société,* no. 11. Geneva: Labor et Fides, 1986. 422p.

'Reaching Muslims in French cities,' J. F. Haines, *Urban mission,* 2 (September 1984), 20–32.

Religion, politics, and preferment in France since 1890: la Belle Epoque and its legacy. M. Larkin. Cambridge, UK: Cambridge University Press, 1995. 263p.

Renouveau charismatique chez les Catholiques: essai bibliographique de langue française. M. Lambert. Brussels: Bureau de Documentation Pastorale, 1975. 32p. (327 items).

'The church, the sect, and the poor in France, 1880–1965.' M. T. Moser. Ph.D. dissertation, Graduate Theological Union, San Francisco, 1983. 238p.

Traité de sociologie du Protestantisme. R. Mehl. Neuchâtel, France: Editions Delachaux et Niestlé, 1965.

Visage du Protestantisme français. P. Lestringant. Tournai, Belgium: Les Cahiers de Réveil, 1959. 214p.

Country Table 2. **Organized churches and denominations in France.**

Official name (bold type = church with over 10% of all affiliated) 1	*Begun* 2	*Type* 3	*Counc* 4	*Congs* 5	*Adults* 6	*Affiliated 1970* 7	*Affiliated 1995* 8	*G%* 9	*Names, notes, and other statistics* (see Codebook, Part 3) 10
Action Biblique	1906	P-Non	.....	15	330	1,000	825	-0.77	*Maisons de la Bible (Bible Houses). Alexandrists* (after founder H. E. Alexander).
Alliance Baptiste Ev de Paris E et N	1962	P-Bap	xF...	9	500	225	1,390	7.56	*EBC.* Evangelical Baptist Alliance of East & North Paris. M=CBI(USA). 7x,19f,W=13%,13Y.
Alliance des Eglises Chrétiennes Miss	1962	P-Hol	xf..C	26	705	250	1,340	6.95	*ACM.* M=Christian & Missionary Alliance (USA). Many Vietnamese. 2n,2x,W=60%,15Y.
Alliance des Egls Ev Indépendantes	1953	I-Eva	C	25	671	1,000	1,340	1.18	*AEEI. Alliance of Independent Ev Chs.* M=TEAM(USA). HQ Orsay (Seine-et-Oise). 7n.
Alliance Spirituelle et Fraternelle		I-3pW	.....	40	1,500	2,000	3,000	0.05	*ASF. Spiritual & Fraternal Alliance.* Widespread Pentecostal grouping.
Amis de l'Homme (Freytag)	1934	m-Jeh	x....	50	4,200	5,000	5,600	0.45	*Friends of Man.* Split by A. Freytag ex Jehovah's Witnesses. Many in Switzerland.
Amis de l'Homme (Sayerce)	1947	m-Jeh	x....	100	10,000	15,000	15,400	0.11	*Friends of Man.* Schism by former Catholic B. Sayerce ex Freytag. Philanthropic.
Amis du Charpentier		I-Non	.....	1	70	–	117	0.05	*Friends of the Carpenter.*
Armée du Salut	1881	P-Sal	xwx.E	40	3,180	6,000	4,890	-0.81	*Salvation Army, France Territory.* 5 million free meals yearly. HQ Paris. 208n,1s.
Assemblée des Béguins	1789	I-CCa	.....	5	300	400	500	0.90	*Assembly of Hooded Brotherhood.* Rigid morality, closed services. In Loire area.
Assemblées de Dieu en France	1929	P-Pe2	ZF...	687	90,500	60,000	133,000	3.24	*Assemblies of God.* 90% former RCs. Mainly Normandy. 252n,7f,1s(29).
Assemblées des Frères Alexandre		P-Non	.....	5	200	500	400	0.05	*Assemblies of the Brothers Alexandre.* In Lille, Dunkerque, HQ St-Michel (Aisne).
Assemblées des Frères (Darbystes)	1844	P-EBr	x....	101	11,600	20,000	23,200	0.60	*Frères Etroits* (Closed). *Momiers* (Bigots). Raven-Taylor, Kelly-Continental.
Association Culturelle Antoiniste	1910	I-mar	x....	133	44,300	50,000	55,000	0.38	*Religious Assoc of Antoine* (a Belgian Catholic faith-healer). HQ Paris. In 15 nations.
Assoc des Etudiants de la Bible Aurore	c1900	m-Jeh	.....	60	7,500	10,000	12,500	0.90	*Dawn Association of Bible Students.* Schism ex Jehovah's Witnesses. In north.
Assoc des Eglises Ev Mennonites de F	1953	P-Men	G....	28	2,000	3,000	3,000	0.00	*Association des EEMF. Ev Mennonite Chs.* German-speaking; Alsace-Lorraine.
Assoc Evangélique des Egls Baptistes	1850	P-Bap	TT...	20	1,100	2,000	1,720	-0.60	*AEEB. French Bapt Chs. French Bible Mission.* Ex FEEBF. 12n,1x,1s,W=35%,23Y.
AF des Libres Etudiants de la Bible	c1905	m-Jeh	.....	30	1,500	2,000	3,000	1.64	*AF=Assoc Française. French Assoc of Free Bible Students.* Schism ex-Association Aurore.
Aumônerie Générale Indép Mixte		I-Epi	.v...	2	40	100	50	0.05	*Orient-Occident, Abbaye Missionnaire de Behéme.* 1968, applied to WCC, rejected.
Communauté des Chrétiens	c1925	P-Non	.....	2	400	300	615	2.91	*Community of Christians.* Centered on eucharistic worship. Across Europe. HQ Paris.
Communautés et Assemblées Ev de F	1857	P-CBr	x....	110	4,300	10,000	7,170	-1.32	*Brethren Assemblies. Open Brethren.* 1857 broke with Darbyites. HQ Lyons.
Communautés Ev Nazaréennes	1845	P-Hol	x....	5	270	400	450	0.47	*Nazarene Ev Communities.* Alsace-Lorraine. M=ACC(N)(USA). HQ Strasbourgh-Neudorf.
Communautés Judéo-Chrétiennes	c1960	I-3mJ	.....	5	500	1,000	1,000	0.00	*Jewish-Christian Communities.* Jewish converts unwilling to join public churches.
Congregations Messianiques	c1970	I-3mJ	.....	20	1,000	–	2,000	35.53	*Messianic Jewish Congregations.* Mainly among Paris' 350,000 Jews. M=JFJ.
Eglise Adventiste du Septième Jour	1874	P-Adv	x....	123	10,100	10,000	15,500	1.77	*SDA. Seventh-day Adventists, N&S French Confs.* 35n,1j,1s(25),W=80%,245Y.
Eglise Adv du SJ Mouv de Réforme		I-Adv	x....	10	200	200	500	0.05	*Seventh-day Adventist Ch, Movement of Reform.* HQ Colmar. World HQ Denmark.
Eglise Anglicane (D Europe)	c1580	A-plu	awc..	10	10,700	15,000	13,300	-0.48	*Church of England.* M=CCCS(UK). English chaplaincies, several seasonal. 12x.
Eglise Apostolique	1924	P-PeA	ZG...	24	1,200	3,000	3,640	0.78	*Apostolic Ch.* Linked with Apostolic Ch (UK). HQ Sanvic. Mainly in Normandy. 2f.
Egl Apostolique Arménienne: D France	1956	O-Arm	Sw.N.	30	19,800	33,000	30,000	-0.38	*Gregorians.* Under C Cilicia (Sis) (Lebanon). 1956 schism ex C Echmiadzin (USSRO.
Egl Apost Arménienne: D WEurope	1917	O-Arm	Ewc..	108	186,000	150,000	315,000	3.01	*Gregorians.* Under C Echmiadzin (USSR); 1917 Armenian refugees from Turkey.
Eglise Baptiste Libre		I-Bap	.....	4	170	–	262	0.05	*Free Baptist Church.*
Eglise Catholique Apostolique	c1840	I-3aX	x....	2	50	200	100	-2.73	*Irvingites.* Adventist schism ex ConfS (UK). No clergy left; dying out.
Egl Catholique Apostolique Gallicane	1935	I-CCa	.v...	30	15,000	40,000	30,000	-1.14	*Cath Apostolic Gallican Ch.* Schism ex Rome. 1975, large synod held in Bordeaux.
Egl Cath Apost Primitive d'Antioche	1956	I-CCa	.v...	1	300	1,000	500	-2.73	*Eglise Catholique Ancienne.* Syrian (Jacobite) succession. In 19 nations.
Eglise Catholique de France:	c 80	R-LEr	B.B.R	35,781	35,258,600	44,578,898	48,064,066	0.30	*Catholic Ch in F.* C=71+9+397. 4p,11q,39s. 22812n 6099x10838m58898w 431139Yy
M Aix	c 90	R-Lat	Bs	132	467,000	393,417	637,000	1.95	Aix. Arles & Embrun. HQ Aix. D=PC. 174n 60x 90m 504w 5858Yy
D Ajaccio	c 250	R-Lat	Bs	410	169,000	179,000	231,000	1.03	Covers Corsica. Population 275,600. 45% urban. 85n 29x 42m 68w 1700Yy
D Digne	c 370	R-Lat	Bs	198	77,000	100,000	105,000	0.20	Population 103,900. 51% urban. 65n 19x 24m 196w 1131Yy
M Fréjus & Toulon	374	R-Lat	Bs	203	502,000	500,000	684,652	0.06	Southern coast. HQ Fréjus. 70% urban. 217n 141x 178m 520w 6034Yy
D Gap	517	R-Lat	Bs	213	70,000	82,000	96,000	0.07	Population 92,000. 51% urban. 84n 11x 11m 163w 975Yy
D Nice	c 250	R-Lat	Bs	248	645,000	650,000	880,000	1.22	Population 722,070. 93% urban. 250n 87x 102m 552w 4229Yy
M Albi	c 250	R-Lat	Bs	519	221,000	300,000	301,000	0.01	Population 332,000. 62% urban. 186n 8x 30m 786w 2136Yy
D Cahors	c 250	R-Lat	Bs	403	103,000	136,078	140,900	0.14	Population 151,000. 30%. 30% urban. 101n 11x 12m 137w 1339Yy
D Mende	314	R-Lat	Bs	132	47,000	64,000	65,000	0.06	30% urban. Towns under 50,000. 181n 1x 18m 306w 626Yy
D Perpignan-Elne	571	R-Lat	Bs	254	215,000	268,797	293,000	0.07	Population 281980. 69% urban. M=OFM. 96n 32x 48m 143w 2553Yy
D Rodez	c 450	R-Lat	Bs	475	194,000	279,793	265,000	-0.22	Population 281,600. 39% urban. 393n 15x 61m 1187w 2279Yy
M Auch	c 450	R-Lat	Bs	501	112,000	180,000	153,900	-0.62	Population 181580. 32% urban. 126n 4x 12m 240w 1334Yy
D Aire	506	R-Lat	Bs	354	199,000	245,000	271,500	0.07	HQ Dax. Population 277,380. 42% urban. D=PC. 1s 217n 36x 55m 291w 2582Yy
D Bayonne	c 350	R-Lat	Bs	523	403,000	505,000	550,000	0.34	Population 508,700. 65%. 65% urban. 1s. 484n 143x 226m 1271w 5011Yy
D Tarbes & Lourdes	c 350	R-Lat	Bs	522	147,000	170,000	200,000	0.65	Lourdes shrine: 3 million pilgrims a year. 150n 59x 102m 738w 1573Yy
M Avignon	c 350	R-Lat	Bs	168	258,000	340,000	352,000	0.14	Population 354,000. 70% urban. 1s. 134n 48x 98m 351w 3843Yy
D Montpellier	c 250	R-Lat	Bs	393	395,000	500,000	538,000	0.29	Population 591,400. 73% urban. 1s. 284n 123x 190m 651w 5739Yy
D Nîmes	396	R-Lat	Bs	303	249,000	380,000	340,000	0.06	Protestants strong. Population 478,500. 71% urban. 194n 42x 78m 211w 4010Yy
D Valence	374	R-Lat	Bs	244	279,000	310,000	380,000	0.06	Population 341,950. 64% urban. 169n 85x 157m 415w 2980Yy
D Viviers	c 250	R-Lat	Bs	395	180,000	228,000	246,000	0.30	Population 257,900. 47% urban. M=SMA. 212n 47x 109m 919w 3145Yy
M Besançon	c150	R-Lat	Bs	770	376,000	740,000	513,000	-1.45	Haute-Saône, Doubs, Belfort. About 70% urban. 1s. 385n 22x 75m 877w 5172Yy
D Belfort-Montbéliard	1979	R-Lat	Bs	167	191,000	–	261,000	6.25	Recent diocese. 83% Catholic. 133n 10x 15m 99w 2379Yy
D Nancy	1777	R-Lat	Bs	641	481,000	671,600	656,000	-0.09	Population 723,600. 78% urban. 1s. 422n 41x 65m 713w 6652Yy
D Saint-Claude	1742	R-Lat	Bs	396	148,000	220,000	202,000	-0.34	Population 233,550. 45% urban. 1s. 218n 15x 43m 335w 2305Yy
D Saint-Dié	1777	R-Lat	Bs	462	267,000	380,000	392,000	0.12	Population 388,200. 64% urban 274n 11x 43m 620w 3831Yy
D Verdun	c 350	R-Lat	Bs	578	122,000	203,000	167,000	-0.78	Population 201,000. 92% Catholic. 132n 7x 12m 148w 1912Yy
M Bordeaux	c 260	R-Lat	Bs	168	682,000	800,000	929,000	0.60	Population 1,009,400. 70% urban. D=PC. 2s. 297n 92x 124m 695w 7903Yy
D Agen	357	R-Lat	Bs	439	180,000	269,755	246,000	0.06	Population 289,800. 51% urban. D=PC. 129n 47x 56m 137w 1930Yy
D Angoulême	c 250	R-Lat	Bs	363	240,000	328,050	328,050	0.00	Population 331,000. 45% urban. 123n 31x 38m 323w 2930Yy
D La Rochelle	1648	R-Lat	Bs	474	368,000	440,000	502,000	0.53	Population 496,340. 50% urban. D=PC. 148n 42x 106m 336w 3719Yy
D Luçon	1317	R-Lat	Bs	316	354,000	400,000	483,000	0.76	Population 421,250. 39% urban. 1s. 462n 71x 186m 1533w 5386Yy
D Périgueux	c 270	R-Lat	Bs	538	277,000	360,000	378,400	0.20	Population 374,070. 39% urban. D=PC. 135n 21x 60m 323w 3245Yy
D Poitiers	c 300	R-Lat	Bs	604	510,000	632,000	695,000	0.38	Vienne (43% urban), Deux-Sèvres (34% urban). 1s. 285n 54x 94m 821w 5807Yy
M Bourges	c 250	R-Lat	Bs	556	369,000	500,000	503,000	0.02	Cher 53% urban, Indre 56% rural. Pop 563,500 160n 90x 170m 397w 4312Yy
D Blois	1697	R-Lat	Bs	295	187,000	265,000	255,000	-0.15	Population 273,500. 46% urban. Growth 1.1%pa. 105n 8x 12m 143w 2452Yy
D Chartres	c 250	R-Lat	Bs	102	259,000	269,000	353,000	1.09	56% urban, 44% rural. Annual students' pilgrimage. 121n 8x 8m 433w 3803Yy
D Clermont	c 250	R-Lat	Bs	520	369,000	525,000	503,000	-0.17	Clermont-Ferrand. 60% urban. 1s. 233n 5x 30m 500w 4314Yy
D Le Puy-en-Velay	c 250	R-Lat	Bs	288	145,000	200,480	198,000	-0.05	Population 208,300. 41% urban. 1s. 256n 5x 97m 819w 2048Yy
D Limoges	c 90	R-Lat	Bs	116	307,000	420,000	419,000	-0.01	Haute-Vienne; Creuse (81% rural, declining-0.7%pa). 158n 35x 41m 345w 3378Yy
D Orléans	346	R-Lat	Bs	295	346,000	395,500	472,000	0.06	Population 430,500. 64% urban. 1s 178n 37x 70m 290w 4746Yy
D Saint-Flour	1317	R-Lat	Bs	302	110,000	165,000	151,500	-0.34	Population 168,800. 2% urban. D=PC. 147n 11x 12m 247w 1388Yy
D Tulle	1317	R-Lat	Bs	296	160,000	225,000	218,000	-0.13	Pop 237,900. 41% urban. Towns all under 50,000. 104n 15x 15m 105w 1667Yy
M Cambrai	c 550	R-Lat	Bs	452	681,000	1,017,986	928,000	-0.37	Département du Nord. 89% urban. 356n 17x 30m 498w 10902Yy
D Arras	c 550	R-Lat	Bs	1,043	879,000	1,100,000	1,198,000	0.34	Population 1,397,200. 86% urban. 511n 66x 76m 710w 14650Yy
D Lille	1913	R-Lat	Bs	343	886,000	1,265,000	1,208,000	-0.18	City of Lille: 1,410,674 people. 90% urban. 1p,2s. 701n 162x 333m 1049w 16653Yy
M Chambéry, St-Jean	1779	R-Lat	Bs	359	245,000	256,973	335,000	1.07	Includes old D Tarentaise, D St-Jean-de-Maurienne. 224n 55x 96m 522w 2850Yy
D Annecy	1822	R-Lat	Bs	320	369,000	365,620	503,000	1.28	Savoie, Haute Savoie. 65% urban. 303n 75x 101m 320w 2580Yy
M Lyon	c 150	R-Lat	Bs	521	891,000	1,170,000	1,214,000	0.15	Rhône, 1,325,600. 90% urban. 1p,2s. 611n 383x 708m 2464w 10650Yy
D Autun	c 200	R-Lat	Bs	545	405,000	520,000	552,000	0.24	Population 562,000. 55% urban. M=CIM. 308n 13x 60m 633w 4856Yy
D Belley-Ars	c 450	R-Lat	Bs	355	258,000	290,000	352,000	0.78	Pop 366,400. 51% urban. Ars pilgrimage centre. 218n 42x 90m 415w 4289Yy
D Dijon	1731	R-Lat	Bs	527	298,000	430,290	406,214	-0.23	Population 432,300. 62% urban. 1s. 205n 67x 115m 455w 4086Yy
D Grenoble	c 350	R-Lat	Bs	611	645,000	700,000	880,000	0.92	Population 849,700. 76% urban. 308n 93x 130m 927w 8868Yy
D Langres	c 250	R-Lat	Bs	545	138,000	205,000	188,000	-0.35	Population 214,300. 46% urban. 93n 12x 21m 132w 2023Yy
D Saint-Etienne	1969	R-Lat	Bs	265	384,000	540,000	524,000	-0.12	Loire, 722,880. 79% urban. 218n 41x 138m 349w 4242Yy
M Paris	c 250	R-Lat	Bs	172	1,250,000	2,316,388	1,703,000	-1.22	Urban diocese, growing at 1.5% per year. 1p,3s. 732n 863x 1205m 2808w 7785Yy
D Créteil	1966	R-Lat	Bs	115	546,000	737,892	744,000	0.03	95% urban. Pan-diocesan services. M=PSS. 187n 189x 254m 845w 5064Yy
D Evry-Corbeil-Essonnes	1966	R-Lat	Bs	206	675,000	770,000	921,000	0.72	Corbeil-Essonnes. About 95% urban. 121n 74x 141m 699w 5774Yy
D Meaux	c 250	R-Lat	Bs	195	558,000	525,000	761,000	1.50	95% urban. Ecclesiastical, civil boundaries same. 160n 50x 59m 518w 7014Yy
D Nanterre	1966	R-Lat	Bs	118	854,000	1,300,000	1,165,000	-0.44	96% urban. Central metropolitan area. 192n 122x 222m 711w 3119Yy
D Pontoise	1966	R-Lat	Bs	194	620,000	500,000	845,000	2.12	Northwest of Paris area. 95% urban. 115n 92x 114m 360w 6096Yy
D Saint-Denis	1966	R-Lat	Bs	114	919,000	876,400	1,253,000	1.44	96% urban. Many services common to all dioceses. 122n 39x 64m 253w 5652Yy

Continued overleaf

Country Table 2–continued

Official name (bold type = church with over 10% of all affiliated) 1	*Begun* 2	*Type* 3	*Counc* 4	*Congs* 5	*Adults* 6	*Affiliated 1970* 7	*Affiliated 1995* 8	*G%* 9	*Names, notes, and other statistics* (see Codebook, Part 3) 10
D Versailles	1801	R-Lat	Bs	269	738,000	600,000	1,006,000	2.09	Area southwest of Paris. 96% urban. 236n 72x 76m 605w 8516Yy
M Reims	c 150	R-Lat	Bs	695	432,000	537,598	589,000	0.37	Ardennes and Reims (550,000). 1s. 204n 20x 59m 357w 5712Yy
D Amiens	c 250	R-Lat	Bs	835	364,000	475,000	496,000	0.17	Population 512,113. 54% urban. Growing 0.8%pa. 159n 32x 46m 311w 5608Yy
D Beauvais	c 250	R-Lat	Bs	706	440,000	486,900	600,000	0.84	Population 541,000. 58% urban. 179n 46x 72m 339w 7560Yy
D Châlons	c 300	R-Lat	Bs	92	177,000	240,000	241,000	0.02	HQ Châlons-sur-Marne. Population 250,600. 118n 2x 4m 152w 2548Yy
D Soissons	c 250	R-Lat	Bs	864	339,000	473,711	462,000	-0.10	Population 526,300. 54% urban. 176n 8x 8m 243w 5410Yy
M Rennes	c 250	R-Lat	Bs	402	552,000	650,000	752,000	0.58	Population 652,700. 52% urban.2s. 599n 18x 140m 1793w 6679Yy
D Quimper	c 450	R-Lat	Bs	337	546,000	763,500	744,000	-0.10	Population 768,900. 59% urban. 535n 69x 279m 1224w 7273Yy
D Saint-Brieuc	c 450	R-Lat	Bs	416	386,000	500,000	528,000	0.22	Population 506,100. 37% urban. D=PC 376n 60x 103m 1522w 4585Yy
D Vannes	c 450	R-Lat	Bs	300	449,000	535,069	612,000	0.54	Population 540,470. 43% urban. 483n 105x 396m 1981w 6378Yy
M Rouen	c 150	R-Lat	Bs	637	550,000	1,050,000	750,000	-1.34	Population 1114000. 69% urban. D=PC. 199n 85x 118m 443w 6733Yy
D Bayeux	c 150	R-Lat	Bs	728	374,000	490,000	510,000	0.16	Pilgrimage centre, Ste Thérèse de Lisieux. 2s. 270n 78x 127m 899w 6062Yy
D Coutances	c 450	R-Lat	Bs	670	317,000	448,000	432,000	-0.15	Population 451,900. 41% urban. 332n 18x 32m 620w 5528Yy
D Evreux	c 250	R-Lat	Bs	583	268,000	330,000	365,000	0.40	Population 383,400. 47% urban. 142n 17x 18m 342w 4194Yy
D Le Havre	1974	R-Lat	Bs	175	194,000	–	265,000	4.76	Port in north. Population 403,000. 82% Catholic. 96n 5x 6m 143w 3007Yy
D Sées	c 250	R-Lat	Bs	514	206,000	270,000	281,600	0.17	Population 280,550. 40% urban. 220n 41x 70m 418w 2335Yy
M Sens	c 90	R-Lat	Bs	110	177,000	214,526	241,000	0.47	HQ Auxerre. 60% rural, 40% urban. D=PC. 112n 58x 95m 206w 2606Yy
D Moulins	1817	R-Lat	Bs	86	216,000	375,000	295,000	-0.96	Population 386,530. 56% urban. 122n 50x 100m 298w 2514Yy
D Nevers	c 400	R-Lat	Bs	63	166,000	240,000	227,000	-0.22	Population 247,700. 48% urban. M=PSS. 95n 6x 10m 194w 1581Yy
D Troyes	313	R-Lat	Bs	423	152,000	200,000	207,000	0.06	Population 270,300. 57% urban. 104n 24x 48m 308w 2304Yy
PN Mission de France o Pontigny	1954	R-Lat	Bs	1	600	774	850	0.38	43 priest-teams in 30 dioceses: 11 in 10 dioceses overseas. 400 priests.
M Toulouse	c 250	R-Lat	Bs	634	671,000	600,000	915,000	1.70	Population 690,700. 74% urban. 3s. 258n 137x 273m 802w 5989Yy
D Carcassonne	589	R-Lat	Bs	339	154,000	210,000	211,000	0.07	48% urban, with towns all under 50,000. 143n 24x 24m 380w 1698Yy
D Montauban	1317	R-Lat	Bs	297	143,000	177,000	195,000	0.39	Population 183,600. 46% urban. 121n 11x 15m 244w 1612Yy
D Pamiers	1295	R-Lat	Bs	304	73,000	130,000	100,500	-1.02	Population 138,500. 48% urban. 78n 5x 9m 84w 986Yy
M Tours	c 250	R-Lat	Bs	102	340,000	350,000	464,000	1.13	Population 437,870. 61% urban. 1s. 164n 46x 58m 600w 3950Yy
D Angers	c 350	R-Lat	Bs	420	446,000	500,000	608,000	0.79	Population 584,700. 53% urban. 3s. 521n 62x 165m 2179w 7026Yy
D Laval	1855	R-Lat	Bs	277	201,000	227,485	275,000	0.76	Population 252,800. 33% urban. 278n 36x 84m 690w 3047Yy
D Le Mans	453	R-Lat	Bs	153	315,000	423,117	430,000	0.06	Population 461,800. 52% urban. 219n 100x 140m 684w 4784Yy
D Nantes	c 350	R-Lat	Bs	293	624,000	800,000	850,000	0.24	59% in urban areas of over 50,000. M=PSS. 642n 102x 397m 1683w 8374Yy
M Marseille	c 90	R-Lat	bs	128	480,000	900,000	654,000	-1.27	Port, 950,000 people. 94% urban. 1p,2s. 217n 165x 236m 1038w 5428Yy
D Strasbourg	346	R-Lat	bs	767	959,000	1,170,199	1,307,000	0.06	Bas & Haut-Rhin, 1,412,400. 70% urban. D=PC. 2x. 788n 330x 467m 2358w 13623Yy
D Metz	c 250	R-Lat	bs	684	604,000	865,000	824,000	-0.19	Moselle, 994,100. 74% urban. M=OP. 1s. 480n 116x 174m 1117w 9867Yy
D Ste-Croix de Paris (*Armenian*)	1960	R-Arm	os	6	22,000	15,000	30,000	2.81	Suffragan ad instar of M Paris, Armenian emigres. 2n 6x 6m 5w 41Yy
EA France (*Ukrainian*)	1960	R-Ukr	Os	12	12,000	17,000	16,000	-0.24	Suffragan ad instar of M Paris, Refugees. M=CSSR. 12n 0x 0m 10w 12Yy
O France (*Oriental rites*)	1954	R-Ori	Os	13	30,000	7,000	45,000	7.73	For all Oriental-rite Catholics without a bishop. 40n 11x 11m 70w 60Yy
OM France	1952	R-Lat	Bs	170	260,000	200,000	300,000	1.64	*Military Ordinariate of France (Evêché aux Armées).* M=CIM. 113 ordinaries, 90 auxiliaries.
Eglise Catholique des Mariavites	1906	I-CCa	Uv...	20	500	200	1,000	6.65	*Mariavite Catholic Ch. Imitators of Mary.* Founded in Poland by nun. 1 bishop,4n.
Eglise Catholique Française	1883	I-CCa	.....	12	600	1,000	900	-0.42	*Eglise Gallicane.* 1907, restored by Vilatte. Gnostic, occult, faith-healing, magic.
Egl Catholique Gallicane Autocéphale	1959	I-Lib	.v...	5	800	2,000	1,500	-1.14	*D Normandie, Egl Vieille-Cath Libérale. Succession Apostolique Oecuménique.* 4 bishops.
Eglise Catholique Libérale	1923	I-Lib	x....	5	300	600	500	-0.73	*Liberal Catholic Ch.* Branches UK, USA, Netherlands. Theosophical. 16n,W=50%,3Yy.
Eglise Cath Orthodoxe Ev de France	1924	I-Lib	C....	30	3,000	4,000	5,000	0.90	Ex LCC(UK), joined P Moscow, later ROCOR, then P Bucharest. 15n,1s(St Denys).
Eglise Catholique Traditionalle	1976	I-CCa	x....	500	400,000	–	900,000	5.26	Schism under abp M. Lefebvre (died 1991). In Germany, Switzerland, UK, USA, 250n.
Eglise Charismatique Indep de Paris	c1980	I-3cW	.....	3	2,000	–	4,000	6.67	Large independent church in Paris.
Eglise Chrétienne Universelle	1950	I-Lib	.....	6	2,000	5,000	3,000	-2.02	*Universal Chr Ch. Témoins du Christ Revenu (Witnesses).* Messiah Georges Roux.
Eglise Christique Primitive	1938	I-ReC	.....	10	300	1,000	800	-0.89	*Primitive Christian Ch.* Begun by Catholic faith-healer. Also Germany, Switzerland.
Eglise de Dieu en France	1960	P-Pe3	ZF...	15	393	250	1,300	6.82	*Church of God in France.* M=CoG(Cleveland) (USA). 7n,1x,W=48%,17Y.
Eglise de J-C des Saints des DJ	1850	m-LdS	x....	120	13,000	8,190	21,000	3.84	*Ch of JC of Latter-day Saints.* Mormons. 600 USA missionaries. HQ Paris. G=3.3%pa.
Eglise de la CA d'Alsace et de Lorraine	1521	P-Lut	LWC.K	250	177,000	233,366	220,000	-0.24	*ECAAL.* CA=Augsburg Confession. 7 Inspectorates (districts). 245n,2x,1x,1s(60),3552Yy.
Eglise de Pentecôte Primitive		I-3pW	.....	9	550	500	1,100	0.05	*Primitive Pentecostal Church.*
Eglise du Christ-Roi Rénovée	1951	I-CCa	.....	2	1,000	4,000	2,000	-2.73	*Holy Cath Ap & Roman Renewed Ch.* Ex RC D Nancy. Papal claimant Clement XV, died 1974.
Eglise du Christ, Scientiste	c1890	m-Sci	x....	10	300	1,000	600	-2.02	*Ch of Christ, Scientist. Christian Science.* M=CCS(Boston, USA). HQ Paris. 5m,18w.
Eglise Evangélique des Frères		P-Bap	.....	6	220	–	338	0.05	M=General Baptist For Miss Soc.
Eglise Evangélique Hinschiste	1831	P-Non	.....	1	100	300	200	-1.61	Founded by Coraly Hinsch. In Nîmes. Bible studies, no sacraments. One girls' home.
Egl Evangélique Luthérienne de France	1871	P-Lut	LWC.K	41	32,200	60,000	40,000	-1.61	*EELF.* Ev Lutheran Ch. ECAAL. 2 Inspectorates: Paris. Montbéliard. 59n,55b,2s(6).
Eglise Evangélique Luthérienne Libre	1921	P-Lut	e....	11	840	3,100	1,400	-3.13	*Synode de France et Belgique. Free Ev Luth Ch.* Ex ECAAL. M=LCMS(USA). 13n,W=56%,32Yy.
Eglise Evangélique de Réveil		I-3pW	.....	10	620	83	1,030	0.05	*Evangelical Revival Church.*
Eglise Gnostique Apostolique	1953	m-Lib	.....	154	22,000	2,000	31,400	11.64	*Apostolic Gnostic Ch.* Closed group protecting Gospel from world. Belgium, Brazil, Italy.
Eglise Néo-Apostolique	1900	I-3aX	x....	120	9,000	20,000	13,796	-1.47	*New Apostolic Ch* (HQ Zurich). Almost all in Alsace-Lorraine. HQ Vanves (Seine).
Eglise Orthodoxe Copte (P Alexandria)	c1970	O-Cop	NwaN.	5	1,000	1,000	2,000	2.81	Led by 2 bishops formerly French Catholic bishops. In Paris, Toulon, Marseilles.
Eglise Orthodoxe Grecque en France	1963	O-Gre	Cwc.O	21	48,000	40,000	64,000	1.90	*D France,* and E Spain. Under EP Constantinople. Greeks, Cypriots, Levantines. 1d.
Eglise Orth Roumaine en Europe Occ	1948	I-Rum	x...	5	2,500	7,000	7,500	0.28	*Romanian OC.* Under ROCOR (New York). 1973, split over rejoining P Bucharest. 15x.
Eglise Orth Russe Hors-Frontières	1920	I-Rus	x....	40	11,500	9,000	20,000	3.25	*D Western Europe, ROC Outside of Russia.* HQ New York. Russian influx 1920-30.
Egl Orth Russe (PE Europe Occidentale)	1922	O-Rus	Mwc.O	20	23,000	15,000	32,500	3.14	*Russian Orthodox Ch.* In Patriarchal Exarchate of Moscow (HQ London). Russians. 3d.
Eglise Orthodoxe Serbe		O-Ser	Cwc.O	15	20,000	15,000	25,000	0.05	*Serbian Orthodox Ch.* Under P Belgrade. Migrant workers. Paris, L'Hôpital/Moselle.
Eglise Orthodoxe Syrienne		O-Syr	Dw.N.	2	500	500	1,000	0.05	*Syrian Orthodox Ch. P Antioch.* 100 Syrian families in Marseilles, Lyons, Paris.
Eglise Orth: AD France & Europe Occ	1922	O-Rus	Cwc.O	100	100,000	100,000	140,000	1.35	Under EP Constantinople 1931-65 and since 1971. 90% Russians. Romanians. 1s.
Eglise Primitive Cath et Apostolique	1937	I-CCa	.v...	10	100	300	200	-1.61	*Eglise Catholique Primitive.* Ex LCC(UK). Based on first Antioch Christian rites. HQ Paris.
Eglise Protestante Evangélique	1945	I-3pW	.....	22	4,400	3,000	5,500	2.45	*Ev Protestant Ch.* Pentecostals around Lyons. Begun by faith-healer Soeur Gaillard.
Eglise Réformée de France	1520	P-Ref	RWC.K	379	182,005	328,700	320,000	-0.11	*ERF. Reformed Ch of F.* 1938 union (Congr, Meth, 2 Reformed chs). 563n,3x(119).
Egl Réformée d'Alsace et de Lorraine	1528	P-Ref	RWC.K	78	25,800	50,368	32,000	-1.80	*ERAL. Reformed Ch of A-L.* French, German. 68n,1x,1s(12),W=80%,705Yy.
Eglise Ukrainienne Orth Autocéphale		I-Ukr	X....	10	6,000	5,000	10,000	0.05	*Ukrainian Orthodox Autocephalic Ch.* Linked to UOC of USA. 1 parish in Paris.
Eglise Vieille-Catholique de France	1870	I-OCa	Uv...	2	390	700	900	1.01	*Old Catholic Church of France.* Uses borrowed buildings. 3n,W=10%,4Yy,10z.
Eglise Vieille-Catholique Romaine en F	1960	I-CCa	.....	5	26,000	30,000	39,000	1.05	*Old Roman Catholic Ch.* Rapid expansion claimed since 1960. 7n,1p,1s(5),W=12%,280Yy.
Eglise Vieille-Cath (Branche Française)		I-OCa	.v...	1	300	500	600	0.05	Part of American Orthodox Catholic Ch (USA). Russians. Work in Nigeria, Zaire.
Eglises Baptistes Indépendantes	1948	I-Bap	x....	13	700	100	1,080	9.99	*Independent Baptist Churches.* M=Baptist Mid-Missions (USA). HQ Paris. 13f.
Eglise Cath Apost Orth d'Occident	c1940	I-Epi	.v...	1	40	100	90	-0.42	*Cath Apostolic Orth Chs of the West.* HQ Alouette-Pessac (Gironde). 1947, rejected by WCC.
Eglises du Christ	c1910	I-Dis	x....	14	900	1,000	1,500	1.64	*Chs of Christ.* M=CC(Non-Instrumental) (USA). Paris, Lille, Reims. USA civilians.
Eglises ethniques		I-eth	.....	58	5,200	3,570	7,430	0.05	*Ethnic churches.*
Eglises Ev Méthodistes de France	1852	P-Met	.....	2	350	1,000	1,060	0.23	Methodists refusing 1938 ERF merger. Paris, SE France. 8n,1H,W=60%,10Yy.
Eglises Luthériennes Ethniques		P-Lut	.....	7	680	900	971	0.05	*Ethnic Lutheran churches.*
Egls Mennonites de Langue Francaise		P-Men	G....	12	600	1,000	1,200	0.05	*French-speaking Mennonite Churches.* HQ Montbéliard (Doubs).
Egls Réformées Ev Indépendantes de F	1872	I-Ref	Jt..K	70	10,500	20,000	13,000	-1.71	*EREI. National Union of Indep Ev Ref Chs.* Rejected 1938 ERF merger. 35n,1s(4).
Enfants de Dieu	c1968	I-mar	xv...	12	2,000	2,000	3,000	1.64	*Children of God International.* Jesus People. Communes. HQ Montgeron, Paris.
Fédération Ev Libre de Pentecôte de F		I-3pW	.....	32	8,000	5,000	13,300	0.05	*Federation of Assemblies of Revival.* Schism ex Assemblies of God. HQ in Rouen.
Fédération des Egls Ev Baptistes de F	1832	P-Bap	T...K	101	6,400	5,000	13,400	4.02	*FEEBF. French Baptist Federation.* 1960, M=SBC(USA). HQ Paris. 53n,4f,1p(7),114Y.
Fédération Parole Vivante		I-3cW	.....	4	224	–	373	0.05	*Federation of the Living Word.*
Féd des E et C Bap Charismatiques		I-3cW	.....	20	2,000	–	3,330	0.05	*E et C Bap=Eglises et Communautés Baptistes.*
France-Mission		P-Non	.....	20	400	600	800	0.05	A Protestant attempt to evangelize France.
France pour Christ		I-Non	.....	10	250	167	417	0.05	*France for Christ.*
Frères Larges Pentecôtisants		I-3pW	....	10	500	500	1,000	0.05	*Pentecostal Christian Brethren.* Grouping of former Plymouth Brethren.
La Porte Ouverte et Associés	c1958	I-3pW	.....	70	1,000	300	2,000	7.88	*The Open Door.* HQ Châlon-sur-Saône. Foreign missions in Chad, CARepublic, et alia.
La Première Pentecôte	1949	I-3pW	.....	10	600	500	900	2.38	*The First Pentecost.* Begun by Ceylon Pentecostal Mission. HQ Dieppe.
Ligue Biblique Française		I-Non	.....	2	275	–	458	0.05	*Bible League of France.* M=GEM.
Mission Baptiste Internationale	1970	I-Bap	.....	4	115	–	288	25.42	*Baptist International Mission.* M=BIM(USA).
Mission Chrétienne Européenne		I-Non	.....	1	220	154	338	0.05	*European Christian Mission.* M=ECM.
Mission de l'Evangile		I-3pW	.....	30	600	500	900	0.05	*Mission of the Gospel.* Pentecostals. From Basel, Switzerland. Mainly Alasce.
Mission Evangélique des Tziganes	1950	I-3pE	x...K	68	11,500	40,000	38,300	-0.17	*Gypsy Ev Movement.* Nomadic caravan churches. M=GGMS,AoG(USA). 200m,1p.
Mission Evangélique Baptiste	1956	P-Bap	.....	10	410	100	631	7.65	*Evangelical Baptist Mission.* M=EBM(USA).
Mission Ev des Alpes Françaises	c1910	P-Non	xM...	1	500	200	781	5.60	*French Alps/Mission Ev de Thonon.* 1962, M=UFM(UK, USA). 1n,4x,25f,W=60%,1Y.
Mission Foi-Evangile		I-Non	.....	8	184	100	368	0.05	*Gospel Faith Mission.*
Mission Populaire Ev de France	1872	P-Ref	....K	3	300	3,000	909	-4.66	*French Protestant Industrial Mission (McAll M).* 20 settlements. Immigrants. 27nm.
Mission Suisse de Pentecôte		P-Pe2	Z....	20	600	1,000	2,000	0.05	*SPM. Schweizerische Pfingstmission. Swiss Pentecostal Mission.* Classical.
Nouvelle Eglise (Swedenborgiens)		m-Swe	x....	5	50	200	100	0.05	*New Church, Swedenborgian Ch.* French HQ in Paris.
Pentecôtistes des Eaux Vives		I-3pW	.....	12	500	600	1,000	0.05	*The Living Waters.* Schism ex Assemblies of God. Based in Marseilles.
Petite Eglise (Vendéenne)	1801	I-CCa	.....	10	1,000	5,000	2,000	-3.60	*Little Ch.* Schism of 38 bishops ex RCC rejecting 1801 concordat. Dying; no clergy.
Rassemblement Frat (Ravinistes)		P-EBr	.....	15	240	500	600	0.05	*Closed Brethren.* Schism ex Taylor Brethren (Exclusive).
Sainte Eglise Apostolique	1955	I-Lib	.....	3	300	1,500	1,000	-1.61	*Holy Apostolic Ch.* Uniate Armenian succession. Gallican. Healing, exorcism. HQ Colombes.
Ste Egl Ap Orth Celtique en Brétagne	1956	I-CCa	.....	10	600	1,500	1,100	-1.23	*Celtic Apostolic Orthodox Ch in Brittany.* 300 Celtic-rite Breton families. 10 bishops, 20n.
Société Religieuse des Amis	1785	P-Qua	Q....	6	200	300	400	1.16	*Religious Society of Friends. Quakers.* M=FSC(UK). HQ Paris. No sacraments. 4f.
Témoins de Jéhovah	1900	m-Jeh	x....	1,428	114,308	100,000	191,000	2.62	*Jehovah's Witnesses. Watch Tower.* HQ Boulogne-Billancourt. (1975) 4977Y. (1995) 4866Y.
Union de l'Eglise Evangélique		I-Ref	.....	40	600	1,100	1,200	0.05	*Union of the Ev Ch.* Pietist schism ex ERAL in Alsace-Lorraine, through USA influence.
Union des Chrétiens Apostoliques	1954	I-3aX	x....	12	900	2,000	1,900	-0.20	*Union of Apostolic Christians.* Schism ex New Apostolic Ch. 60,000 in world.
Union des Egls Chrétiennes Bibliques	1946	I-Non	.M..C	3	480	640	1,020	1.88	*Union of Bible Christian Chs.* HQ Courbevoie (Seine). 5n,9x,W=47%,18Y,17z.
Union des Eglises Ev Chrischona		P-Eva	.....	18	910	667	1,520	0.05	*Union of Chrischona Evangelical Churches.*
Union des Eglises Ev Libres de France	1849	I-Ref	K...C	96	1,900	3,000	2,710	-0.41	*Union of Free Ev Chs of France.* Calvinist origin. Mainly Marseilles. 9n. 1987: merger FEEBF.
Union des Eglises Nazarenes	1977	P-Hol	.....	2	63	–	113	5.56	*Union of Churches of the Nazarene.* M=CoN. 4f.
Union des Sociétés Evangéliques	1840	P-Eva	x....	60	600	1,000	1,300	1.05	*St-Chrischona* (near Basel). *Union of Ev Socs.* Europe, Ethiopia. HQ Colmar. 12n.
Union d'Eglise Ev Méthodiste	1868	P-Met	Vwc.K	18	1,800	250	2,570	9.77	*United Methodist Ch*(USA). 60% French-speaking, 40% German. 2n,1x,W=40%,5Yy.
Union Nat des Eg Ev Arméniennes	c1930	P-Con	Rw...	18	490	1,890	1,090	-2.18	*Armenian Evangelical Union of Churches of France.* HQ Beirut. 1918 refugees.
Union pour le Réveil		I-3pW	.....	5	300	1,000	600	0.05	*Union for Revival.* Founded by George Jeffreys (Elim Church). Pentecostals.
Vrai Eglise Catholique	1964	I-3cW	.....	1	200	1,000	500	-2.73	*True Catholic Ch.* In Lorraine and Belgium, begun by excommunicated RC priest.
Other independent charismatic chs	c1975	I-3cW	.....	400	30,000	–	40,000	5.00	Including Jesus is Lord Fellowship (Philippines), Manna Church (Portugal).

Continued opposite

Country Table 2–concluded

Official name (bold type = church with over 10% of all affiliated) 1	*Begun* 2	*Type* 3	*Counc* 4	*Congs* 5	*Adults* 6	*Affiliated 1970* 7	*Affiliated 1995* 8	*G%* 9	*Names, notes, and other statistics* (see Codebook, Part 3) 10
Other independent congregations	c1930	I-	.....	199	10,900	6,670	18,200	4.10	Independent single congregations, in about 35 very loose geographical networks.
Other Protestant denominations		P-	.....	400	30,000	50,000	60,000	0.05	Total over 100 (see list below). Includes many independent single congregations.
Other independent Catholic churches		I-CCa	.....	150	7,000	10,100	15,000	0.05	Total about 50, including over 30 led by bishops-at-large; also Polish OC Mariavite Ch.
Other marginal Protestant bodies		m-	.....	200	15,000	10,000	30,000	0.05	Many small groups and cults (see list below), including HSAUWC.
Other Orthodox churches		O-	.....	50	10,000	8,500	20,000	0.05	Several bodies including Eglise Orthodoxe Géorgienne (refugees from USSR).
Other Third-World indigenous chs		I-3pA	.....	200	6,000	2,000	10,000	0.05	Total about 7 bodies (see below), including EJCSK, IURD (Brazil).
Doubly-affiliated		2-aff			-2,398,000	-955,300	-3,310,186		Evangelicals who also are or were baptized Roman Catholics.
Disaffiliated		X-Aff			-5,251,000	-2,757,538	-7,250,000		Baptized Catholics who have become completely disaffiliated agnostics or atheists.
Totals				**43,671**	**29,447,393**	**42,557,500**	**40,656,000**		

Churches, members, growth, 1900-2025	*Congs*	*Adults*	*Affiliated*	*G%*	*Total denominations*	*6 Megablocs:* *O*	*R*	*A*	*P*	*I*	*m*
Total churches, members, and denominations (mid-1900)	30,000	29,947,000	40,731,100	0.06	63	3	1	1	35	16	7
Total churches, members, and denominations (mid-1970)	44,612	31,290,447	42,557,500	0.06	236	15	1	1	89	103	27
Total churches, members, and denominations (mid-1990)	44,000	28,970,000	39,996,950	-0.31	413	23	1	1	154	185	49
Total churches, members, and denominations (mid-1995)	43,671	29,447,393	40,656,000	0.33	422	23	1	1	158	190	49
Total churches, members, and denominations (mid-2000)	43,000	29,781,000	41,116,959	0.23	429	23	1	1	160	195	49
Total churches, members, and denominations (mid-2025)	42,000	29,660,000	40,950,000	-0.02	587	35	1	1	190	300	60

.NOTES ON TABLE ABOVE

NATIONAL COUNCILS (Column 4, 5th letter).

C = Fédération Evangélique de France (Evangelical Federation of France) (a few denominations, and over 25 single congregations); formerly Union des Eglises et Associations Evangéliques Françaises, founded 1967.

E = Alliance Evangélique Française (AEF, French Evangelical Alliance) (members: Salvation Army; one college; and individuals).

K = Fédération Protestante de France (FPF) (Protestant Federation of France).

O = Comité Interépiscopal Orthodoxe de France (Orthodox Interepiscopal Liaison Committee of France).

R = Conférence des Evêques de France (CEF) (Episcopal Conference of France).

Other national councils. National Alliance of the Lutheran Churches of France. Council of Christian Churches in France.

OTHER PROTESTANT DENOMINATIONS. The total is over 100, many of which are small independent groups, large single congregations, or chaplaincies of a number of large national churches in other countries throughout the world. These include (with names in French or English according to which is better known): American Baptist Association, American Ch (Paris), Association Ev de Générargues, Baptistes Pentecôtisants, Christian Ch of North America, Ch of Scotland, Eglise Allemande Luthérienne, Eglise Danoise de Paris, Eglise de Pentecôte 'Latter Rain', Eglise Elim, Eglise Espagnole, Eglise Ev des Frères, Eglise Ev Russe, Eglise Ev Vietnamienne (CMA/ACM), Eglise Protestante Malgache de France, Eglise Réformée Hongroise en France, Eglise Réformée Néerlandaise, Eglise Roumaine Ev Baptiste, Eglise Suédoise Luthérienne, Eglise Suisse-Allemande, Eglises Baptiste de la Mission Ev de France, Eglises Vaudoises d'Italie en France (Waldensians), Emmanuel Baptist Ch, European Christian Mission (17 missionaries), Gospel Missionary Union (1960), Greater Europe Mission (1949), Mission Alpine, Mission Chrétienne Française, Mission de Réveil, Mission du Tabernacle, Mission Ev Baptiste, Mission Ev de France, Mission Ev en Brétagne, Mission Foi Evangile, Mission Internationale aux Mineurs, Mission Libre Suédoise (SFM), Mission Norvégienne des Marins, Mouvement Ev Russe, National Association of Free Will Baptist (1966), National Fellowship of Brethren Chs, North Africa Mission (1963, 43 missionaries), Pentecôtistes Libres, Reformed Baptists (USA), Slavic Gospel Association, Strict Baptist Mission, Union Chrétienne Baptiste, Union Chrétienne Ev de Pentecôte, Union Missionnaire d'Auvergne, Worldwide Evangelization Crusade (11 missionaries).

OTHER MARGINAL PROTESTANT BODIES. Among the many bodies are: Eglise Réformée du Foyer de l'Ame (Unitarians), Eglise Rosicrucienne Apostolique, Order of the Cross, Reorganized Ch of Jesus Christ of Latter-day Saints (USA), Unitarian Universalist Association (3 churches), Unité Métaphysique Chrétienne (Unité Universelle) (from USA), United Ch of Religious Science (from USA; 1 church).

OTHER THIRD-WORLD INDIGENOUS CHURCHES. These include small groups from francophone Africa (EJCSK from Zaire, in Paris; &c), Hong Kong, also the Unification Ch of France (from Korea; 1,000 members by 1976), also the Father Divine Peace Mission Movement (USA Blacks).

FRENCH GUIANA

SECULAR DATA, AD 2000

STATE

Official name: Le Departement du Guyana Française (The Department of French Guiana).
Short name: French Guiana. **Adjective of nationality:** French Guianan.
Flag: That of France.
Area: 86,504 sq. km. (33,399 sq. mi.).
Government: Overseas department of France, since 1946 (1677 French possession).
Legislature: Council-General, 19 members.
Official language: French (Français).
Monetary unit: 1 franc (F) = 100 centimes. **US$1=** F=5.60.
Chief cities: CAYENNE 89,608.
Political divisions: 2 provinces.

DEMOGRAPHY

Population: 181,000.
Population density: 2.1/sq. km. (5.4/sq. mi.).
Under 15 years: 54,000.
Growth rate p.a.: 0.64% (births 18.82, deaths 6.91).
Mortality: Infant, per 1,000: 51.5; **Maternal per 100,000:** 70.0.
Life expectancy: 66 (male 63, female 69).
Household size: 3.4. **Floor area per person, sq.m:** 15.0.
Major languages: French, French Creole, Arawak, Portuguese, English, Chinese, Javanese.
Urban dwellers: 78.13%. **Urban growth rate p.a.:** 3.7%.
Labor force: 43%.

ETHNOLINGUISTIC PEOPLES

37.9% Guianese Mulatto; 8.0% French; 8.0% Haitian Black; 7.0% Guianese White; 6.0% Surinamese Creole.

ECONOMY

National income p.a. per person: US$10,578; **per family:** US$35,966.

EDUCATION

Adult literacy: 83% (male 83%, female 82%). **Schools:** 110.
Universities: 1. **School enrolment:** female/male: 60%/60%.

HEALTH

Access to health services: 75%. **Access to safe water:** 60%.
Hospitals: 6 (66 beds per 10,000). **Doctors:** 200.
Blind: 150. **Deaf:** 10,700. **Murder rate:** 27.
Lepers: 8,500.

LITERATURE

New book titles p.a.: 18 (100 p.a. per million). **Periodicals:** 3.
Newspapers: 1 daily.

COMMUNICATION (per 1,000 people)

Phones: 288 (7% mobile). **Radios:** 486. **TV sets:** 170.
Daily newspaper circulation: 11. **Computers:** 30.

HUMAN LIFE AND LIBERTY (optimum condition=100.0%)

HDI: 76.5. **HSI:** 60.0. **HFI:** 30.0. **EFL:** 24.0.

Country Table 1. **Religious adherents in French Guiana, AD 1900-2025.**

Year	*1900*		*1970*		*mid-1990*		*Annual change, 1990-2000*				*mid-1995*		*mid-2000*		*mid-2025*	
Name	*Adherents*	*%*	*Adherents*	*%*	*Adherents*	*%*	*Natural*	*Conversion*	*Total*	*Rate*	*Adherents*	*%*	*Adherents*	*%*	*Adherents*	*%*
Christians	**19,500**	**92.9**	**45,030**	**91.6**	**100,000**	**85.5**	**5,502**	**-166**	**5,336**	**4.37**	**124,900**	**85.1**	**153,362**	**84.6**	**346,480**	**83.3**
PROFESSION																
professing Christians	**19,500**	**92.9**	**45,030**	**91.6**	**100,000**	**85.5**	**5,502**	**-166**	**5,336**	**4.37**	**124,900**	**85.1**	**153,362**	**84.6**	**346,480**	**83.3**
AFFILIATION																
unaffiliated Christians	0	0.0	1,030	2.1	400	0.3	22	1	23	4.58	400	0.3	626	0.4	3,480	0.8
affiliated Christians	**19,500**	**92.9**	**44,000**	**89.5**	**99,600**	**85.1**	**5,480**	**-166**	**5,314**	**4.37**	**124,500**	**84.8**	**152,736**	**84.3**	**343,000**	**82.5**
Roman Catholics	19,500	92.9	42,500	86.4	96,500	82.5	5,279	-429	4,850	4.16	120,000	81.8	145,000	80.0	320,000	76.9
Protestants	0	0.0	2,800	5.7	5,200	4.4	284	-104	180	3.02	6,036	4.1	7,000	3.9	12,500	3.0
Marginal Christians	0	0.0	300	0.6	3,400	2.9	186	24	210	4.93	4,320	2.9	5,500	3.0	12,000	2.9
Independents	0	0.0	200	0.4	1,050	0.9	57	8	65	4.94	1,342	0.9	1,700	0.9	4,000	1.0
Anglicans	0	0.0	50	0.1	80	0.1	4	-3	1	1.18	83	0.1	90	0.1	150	0.0
doubly-affiliated	0	0.0	-1,850	-3.8	-6,630	-5.7	-363	371	8	-0.12	-7,281	-5.0	-6,554	-3.6	-5,650	-1.4
Trans-megabloc groupings																
Evangelicals	0	0.0	1,000	2.0	2,400	2.1	131	-11	120	4.14	2,984	2.0	3,600	2.0	8,000	1.9
Pentecostals/Charismatics	0	0.0	700	1.4	6,200	5.3	339	81	420	5.31	8,084	5.5	10,400	5.8	27,500	6.6
Great Commission Christians	**600**	**2.9**	**3,400**	**6.9**	**14,900**	**12.7**	**815**	**70**	**885**	**4.77**	**18,800**	**12.8**	**23,745**	**13.1**	**58,200**	**14.0**
Chinese folk-religionists	0	0.0	670	1.4	4,000	3.4	219	28	247	4.93	5,100	3.5	6,473	3.6	16,000	3.9
Spiritists	400	1.9	960	2.0	3,600	3.1	197	84	281	5.94	5,000	3.4	6,411	3.5	15,000	3.6
Nonreligious	0	0.0	480	1.0	2,365	2.0	129	94	223	6.87	3,580	2.4	4,594	2.5	15,000	3.6
Ethnoreligionists	1,000	4.8	1,210	2.5	2,500	2.1	137	-39	98	3.36	2,900	2.0	3,479	1.9	7,500	1.8
Hindus	0	0.0	0	0.0	1,760	1.5	96	18	114	5.12	2,200	1.5	2,901	1.6	7,000	1.7
Muslims	100	0.5	480	1.0	1,000	0.9	55	2	57	4.64	1,250	0.9	1,574	0.9	3,600	0.9
Atheists	0	0.0	0	0.0	520	0.4	28	6	34	5.17	680	0.5	861	0.5	1,800	0.4
Baha'is	0	0.0	300	0.6	550	0.5	30	-12	18	2.80	600	0.4	725	0.4	1,600	0.4
New-Religionists	0	0.0	0	0.0	550	0.5	30	-12	18	2.80	620	0.4	725	0.4	1,500	0.4
Jews	0	0.0	20	0.0	75	0.1	4	-2	2	2.71	80	0.1	98	0.1	220	0.1
Other religionists	0	0.0	50	0.1	80	0.1	4	-1	3	3.24	90	0.1	110	0.1	300	0.1
World A (unevangelized persons)	609	2.9	1,229	2.5	2,106	1.8	115	-101	14	0.65	2,201	1.5	2,172	1.2	4,160	1.0
World B (evangelized non-Christians)	891	4.2	2,905	6.0	14,894	12.7	814	267	1,081	5.51	19,656	13.5	25,466	14.2	65,360	15.7
World C (Christians)	19,500	92.9	45,030	91.5	100,000	85.5	5,502	-166	5,336	4.37	124,900	85.0	153,362	84.6	346,480	83.3
Country's population	**21,000**	**100.0**	**49,165**	**100.0**	**117,000**	**100.0**	**6,431**	**0**	**6,431**	**4.46**	**146,758**	**100.0**	**181,000**	**100.0**	**416,000**	**100.0**

Continued overleaf

Country Table 1–concluded

COLUMNS, ROWS.
For meanings and definitions, see Codebook (Part 3). Note that, by definition, total 'Christians' = professing + crypto-Christians, which also = affiliated + unaffiliated Christians, and also = Great Commission Christians + latent Christians. Percentages may not always total exactly, due to rounding.

NOTES ON RELIGIONS
BAHA'IS. In 2 local spiritual assemblies (1973), rising to 11 (1996).
COUNTRY'S POPULATION. In 1976 the government of France began a massive immigration and colonization scheme designed to bring in at least 30,000 new French colonists from France (farmers, forestry workers, investors et alii).
ETHNORELIGIONISTS. Of the 7,000 lowland or jungle Amerindians in the interior, a large proportion are animists, especially among the Emerillon (90%), Oyampi (80%), and Wayana (90%).
MUSLIMS. Javanese and Lebanese Arabs.
NONRELIGIOUS. French.
OTHER RELIGIONISTS. Including Rosicrucians (1 AMORC centre).
SPIRITISTS. Termed Afro-American spiritists, these are Black and Mulatto followers of Vodoun, Obeah, Boni, and Bush Negro syncretistic cults, including Brazilians. Since around the year 1800 there have been isolated Negro spirit-possession cults in the interior.

Great Commission Instrument Panel: status of French Guiana (for explanation see start of Part 4)

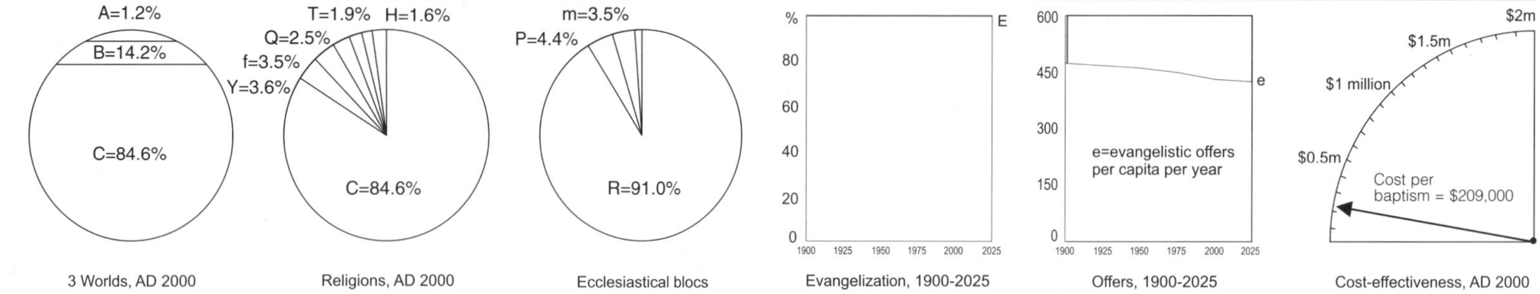

Country summary. **Worlds A, B, C by ethnolinguistic peoples, cities, and major civil divisions in French Guiana.**

	PEOPLES							CITIES							CIVIL DIVISIONS						
World	*Num*	*Pop 2000*	*C%*	*Christians*	*E%*	*U%*	*Unevangelized*	*Num*	*Pop 2000*	*C%*	*Christians*	*E%*	*U%*	*Unevangelized*	*Num*	*Pop 2000*	*C%*	*Christians*	*E%*	*U%*	*Unevangelized*
A	3	880	8.41	74	43	57	500	0	0	0.00	0	0	0	0	0	0	0.00	0	0	0	0
B	7	24,297	39.42	9,577	93	7	1,603	0	0	0.00	0	0	0	0	0	0	0.00	0	0	0	0
C	14	156,139	91.64	143,090	100	0	136	1	89,608	0.85	76,167	100	0	341	2	181,313	84.24	152,736	99	1	2,240
Total	**24**	**181,316**	**84.24**	**152,741**	**99**	**1**	**2,239**	**1**	**89,608**	**0.85**	**76,167**	**100**	**0**	**341**	**2**	**181,313**	**84.24**	**152,736**	**99**	**1**	**2,240**

Country status. French Guiana is a department of France in South America north of Brazil. Once a penal colony, it is still one of the most backward regions in Latin America. The population is highly mixed, consisting of Haitians, Surinamese, Brazilian, Chinese, Hmong, Javanese, and Bush Negro. Underdevelopment, rather than human rights, is the main problem in the department.

HUMAN LIFE AND LIBERTY

Human need and development. The situation is similar to that in France itself.

NON-CHRISTIAN RELIGIONS

Although the population of French Guiana is overwhelmingly Catholic, there is a residue of adherents to traditional religions among the Oyampi, Carib, and Emerillon Indians, in addition to a few small communities from other world religions.

CHRISTIANITY

CATHOLIC CHURCH. France began to colonize Guiana in 1635, and the Catholic Church gained an early foothold which it has never relinquished. The great majority of Catholics are either people born in Guiana (Whites, Mulattoes, and Amer-indians), or immigrant technicians and laborers from France, the Antilles, and Brazil, primarily for work at the space base of Kourou. There are 24 parishes served by Holy Ghost priests and 3 congregations of sisters.

The Holy See has no diplomatic relations with French Guiana in AD 2000.

OTHER CHURCHES. Protestant work has never been strong in Guiana. The Protestant Church (Eglise Evangélique) consists of chaplaincies to the military and civilian French communities. Adventists have a similar constituency, followed by the Assemblies of God and Brethren, the latter concentrating its attention on radio and literature distribution. A Hmong church in 1991 voted to join the Christian and Missionary Alliance.

Indigenous missions. The first indigenous priest was not ordained until 1971. Since then a few French Guianan Roman Catholics have studied abroad and now serve overseas as missionaries, with some in surrounding countries.

BROADCASTING AND MEDIA

Shortwave programs from HCJB (Ecuador), TWR (Antilles) and AWR (Costa Rica) can be easily received. Christian television programs can be received via satellite.

FUTURE TRENDS AND PROSPECTS

Christians will probably continue to decline to 83% by 2025 (from over 90% in 1970) due to increasing secularization.

Though the nonreligious are expected to reach 8% around mid-century, Christians should remain above 70% into the future.

Eglise Catholique, Diocèse de Cayenne. Cathedral in Cayenne, with Chinese shops to left.

BIBLIOGRAPHY

'Developing cross–cultural fellowship within a multiethnic group of Christians in Cayenne, French Guiana.' V. Suttles. D.Min. thesis, Southwestern Baptist Theological Seminary, Fort Worth, TX, 1994.

'From the Creole God to the God of Jesus: an essay on the concept of God in French Guiana,' P. Chanson & M. Méranville, *Exchange*, 22 (April 1993), 18–45.

Histoire spirituelle des Antilles et de la Guyane. E. Antébi (ed). *Arawak Univers des Antilles et de la Guyane.* [Paris]: Tchou, 1979. 317p.

The good news on the wild coast: highlights of the early efforts of the Catholic Church in Guiana, 1650's to 1850's. J. Bridges. Arima, Trinidad: St. Dominic Press, 84p.

Country Table 2. **Organized churches and denominations in French Guiana.**

Official name (bold type = church with over 10% of all affiliated) 1	*Begun* 2	*Type* 3	*Counc* 4	*Congs* 5	*Adults* 6	*Affiliated 1970* 7	*Affiliated 1995* 8	*G%* 9	*Names, notes, and other statistics* (see Codebook, Part 3) 10
Armée de Salut		P-Sal	x....	1	160	–	267	0.05	*Salvation Army.*
Assemblées de Dieu	1968	P-Pe2	ZF...	2	800	500	1,600	4.76	*Assemblies of God.* M=AoG(USA) 5n,2f. 48% Haitian, 36% Brazilian, 16% mixed.
Courants de Puissance		I-3pW	x....	2	260	200	520	0.05	*Currents of Power.* Led by Dutch missionaries. HQ Saint-Laurent-du-Maroni.
Croisade Evangélique	c1985	I-3cW	.....	1	70	–	117	10.00	*Evangelical Crusade.*
Eglise Adventiste du Septième Jour	1940	P-Adv	x....	4	803	1,000	1,750	2.26	*SDA. Seventh-day Adventists, FG Mission.* 1n,13mw,8t(477),W=80%,33Y,20z.
Eglise Anglicane (D Guyana)		A-ACa	awMR.	1	50	50	83	0.05	In Ch of the Province of the West Indies. Europeans, some Blacks.
Eglise Baptiste	1982	P-Bap	T....	2	460	–	685	7.69	*Baptist Convention.* M=SBC(USA).
Eglise Baptiste Evangélique	1985	P-Bap	x....	1	6	–	10	10.00	*Evangelical Baptist Church.* M=EBM(USA).
Eglise Catholique: D Cayenne	1604	R-Lat	PzNMr	27	50,000	42,500	120,000	4.24	18% White. M=CSSp. C=1+0+3. (1970) 1n,29x,1m,89w. (1990) 7n,23x,25m,101w,1738Yy.
Eglise de Dieu		P-Pe3	Z....	1	26	–	43	0.05	*Church of God.* M=CoG(Cleveland) (USA).
Eglise du Nazarene	1988	P-Hol	x....	1	190	–	290	14.29	*Church of the Nazarene.* M=CoN(USA).
Eglise Evangélique		P-Ref	.....	4	350	1,000	700	0.05	French military and civilian chaplaincies, especially to Kourou space base. 1x.
Eglise Neo-Apostolique	c1980	I-3aX	x....	10	300	–	705	6.67	*New Apostolic Ch. NAC/NAK.* M=Neuapostolische Kirche (HQ Zurich).
Frères Larges Mission Evangélique	c1905	P-CBr	x....	10	380	300	691	3.39	*Open Brethren.* Begun by a Barbadian. M=CMML(UK, USA, Switzerland). Haitian, Hmong.
Témoins de Jéhovah	c1945	m-Jeh	x....	12	660	300	4,320	11.26	*Jehovah's Witnesses.* Active witnessing under way by 1947. (1975) 24Y. (1995) 129Y.
Doubly-affiliated		2-aff			-3,000	-1,850	-7,281		Evangelists who are also baptized Roman Catholics.
Totals				**79**	**51,515**	**44,000**	**124,500**		

Churches, members, growth, 1900-2025	*Congs*	*Adults*	*Affiliated*	*G%*	*Total denominations*	*O*	*R*	*A*	*P*	*I*	*m*
Total churches, members, and denominations (mid-1900)	20	10,300	19,500	1.17	1	0	1	0	0	0	0
Total churches, members, and denominations (mid-1970)	53	23,163	44,000	1.17	8	0	1	1	4	1	1
Total churches, members, and denominations (mid-1990)	70	41,200	99,600	4.17	13	0	1	1	8	2	1
Total churches, members, and denominations (mid-1995)	79	51,515	124,500	4.56	15	0	1	1	9	3	1
Total churches, members, and denominations (mid-2000)	100	63,200	152,736	4.17	15	0	1	1	9	3	1
Total churches, members, and denominations (mid-2025)	200	142,000	343,000	3.29	51	0	1	1	20	26	3

(Columns O, R, A, P, I, m are headed "6 Megablocs:".)

Continued opposite

Country Table 2–concluded

NOTES ON TABLE ABOVE
NATIONAL COUNCILS (Column 4, 5th letter).
r = member, Conférence Episcopale de France (Episcopal Conference of France).

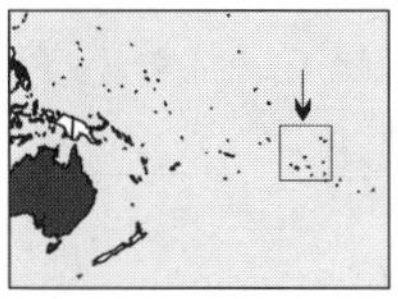

FRENCH POLYNESIA

SECULAR DATA, AD 2000

STATE
Official name: La Territoire de la Polynésie Française (The Overseas Territory of French Polynesia).
Short name: French Polynesia. **Adjective of nationality:** French Polynesian.
Flag: That of France.
Area: 4,000 sq. km. (1,544 sq. mi.).
Government: Overseas territory of France, since 1946 (1842 French protectorate, 1880 French colony).
Legislature: Government Council, 5 members; Territorial Assembly, 41 members.
Official language: French (Français).
Monetary unit: 1 franc (F) = 100 centimes. **US$1=** F=5.60.
Chief cities: PAPEETE 102,992.
Political divisions: 5 provinces.

DEMOGRAPHY
Population: 235,000.
Population density: 58.7/sq. km. (152.2/sq. mi.).
Under 15 years: 78,000.
Growth rate p.a.: 1.56% (births 21.09, deaths 4.65).
Mortality: Infant, per 1,000: 10.0; **Maternal per 100,000:** 20.0.
Life expectancy: 73 (male 71, female 76).
Household size: 4.7. **Floor area per person, sq.m:** 18.0.
Major languages: Tahitian, French, Chinese.
Urban dwellers: 56.94%. **Urban growth rate p.a.:** 2.1%.
Labor force: 40%.

ETHNOLINGUISTIC PEOPLES
41.0% Tahitian; 17.0% Euronesian; 11.3% Han Chinese (Hakka); 11.0% French; 8.4% Tuamotuan (Paumotu).

ECONOMY
National income p.a. per person: US$16,940; **per family:** US$79,619.

EDUCATION
Adult literacy: 95% (male 94%, female 95%). **Schools:** 316.
Universities: 4. **School enrolment:** female/male: 103%/94%.

HEALTH
Access to health services: 80%. **Access to safe water:** 70%.
Hospitals: 34 (58 beds per 10,000). **Doctors:** 323.
Blind: 96. **Deaf:** 14,400. **Murder rate:** <1. **Lepers:** 2,200.

LITERATURE
New book titles p.a.: 35 (150 p.a. per million). **Periodicals:** 14.
Newspapers: 4 dailies.

COMMUNICATION (per 1,000 people)
Phones: 219 (17% mobile). **Radios:** 488. **TV sets:** 177.
Daily newspaper circulation: 112. **Computers:** 60.

HUMAN LIFE AND LIBERTY (optimum condition=100.0%)
HDI: 86.6. **HSI:** 65.0. **HFI:** 70.0. **EFL:** 30.0.

Country Table 1. **Religious adherents in French Polynesia, AD 1900-2025.**

Year	1900		1970		mid-1990		Annual change, 1990-2000				mid-1995		mid-2000		mid-2025	
Name	Adherents	%	Adherents	%	Adherents	%	Natural	Conversion	Total	Rate	Adherents	%	Adherents	%	Adherents	%
Christians	**36,700**	**99.2**	**105,100**	**94.8**	**174,100**	**88.8**	**3,472**	**-199**	**3,273**	**1.74**	**189,710**	**88.2**	**206,832**	**88.0**	**279,200**	**86.2**
PROFESSION																
professing Christians	**36,700**	**99.2**	**105,100**	**94.8**	**174,100**	**88.8**	**3,472**	**-199**	**3,273**	**1.74**	**189,710**	**88.2**	**206,832**	**88.0**	**279,200**	**86.2**
AFFILIATION																
unaffiliated Christians	2,200	6.0	12,256	11.1	9,900	5.1	197	-376	-179	-1.98	7,410	3.4	8,107	3.5	9,200	2.8
affiliated Christians	**34,500**	**93.2**	**92,844**	**83.7**	**164,200**	**83.8**	**3,275**	**178**	**3,453**	**1.93**	**182,300**	**84.7**	**198,725**	**84.6**	**270,000**	**83.3**
Protestants	26,650	72.0	47,000	42.4	89,000	45.4	1,771	329	2,100	2.14	99,475	46.2	110,000	46.8	150,000	46.3
Roman Catholics	7,000	18.9	36,058	32.5	79,500	40.6	1,582	468	2,050	2.32	89,186	41.4	100,000	42.6	140,000	43.2
Marginal Christians	850	2.3	7,936	7.2	20,000	10.2	398	102	500	2.26	22,350	10.4	25,000	10.6	35,000	10.8
Independents	0	0.0	1,850	1.7	3,900	2.0	78	12	90	2.10	4,368	2.0	4,800	2.0	7,000	2.2
doubly-affiliated	0	0.0	0	0.0	-28,200	-14.4	-561	-727	-1,288	3.83	-33,079	-15.4	-41,075	-17.5	-62,000	-19.1
Trans-megabloc groupings																
Evangelicals	23,000	62.2	4,400	4.0	5,300	2.7	105	-22	83	1.47	5,745	2.7	6,130	2.6	8,000	2.5
Pentecostals/Charismatics	0	0.0	1,200	1.1	19,400	9.9	386	154	540	2.49	21,927	10.2	24,800	10.6	42,500	13.1
Great Commission Christians	**2,200**	**6.0**	**13,300**	**12.0**	**26,500**	**13.5**	**527**	**58**	**585**	**2.01**	**29,300**	**13.6**	**32,345**	**13.8**	**48,500**	**15.0**
Chinese folk-religionists	200	0.5	2,800	2.5	14,800	7.6	294	63	357	2.18	17,000	7.9	18,366	7.8	26,000	8.0
Nonreligious	0	0.0	2,400	2.2	5,900	3.0	117	126	243	3.51	6,900	3.2	8,332	3.6	16,000	4.9
Baha'is	0	0.0	200	0.2	500	0.3	10	10	20	3.35	620	0.3	695	0.3	1,500	0.5
Buddhists	100	0.3	300	0.3	300	0.2	6	-1	5	1.41	320	0.2	345	0.2	500	0.2
Ethnoreligionists	0	0.0	100	0.1	200	0.1	4	-2	2	1.00	210	0.1	221	0.1	300	0.1
Other religionists	0	0.0	100	0.1	200	0.1	4	3	7	3.05	240	0.1	270	0.1	500	0.2
World A (unevangelized persons)	37	0.1	2,217	2.0	2,940	1.5	58	-29	29	0.96	3,012	1.4	3,290	1.4	3,888	1.2
World B (evangelized non-Christians)	263	0.7	3,555	3.3	18,960	9.7	377	228	605	2.75	22,490	10.4	24,878	10.6	40,912	12.6
World C (Christians)	36,700	99.2	105,100	94.7	174,100	88.8	3,472	-199	3,273	1.74	189,710	88.2	206,832	88.0	279,200	86.2
Country's population	**37,000**	**100.0**	**110,873**	**100.0**	**196,000**	**100.0**	**3,907**	**0**	**3,907**	**1.83**	**215,213**	**100.0**	**235,000**	**100.0**	**324,000**	**100.0**

COLUMNS, ROWS.
For meanings and definitions, see Codebook (Part 3). Note that, by definition, total 'Christians' = professing + crypto-Christians, which also = affiliated + unaffiliated Christians, and also = Great Commission Christians + latent Christians. Percentages may not always total exactly, due to rounding.

CENSUSES.
10.VI.1946: 57.7% Protestants, 24.0% Roman Catholics, 12.4% Chinese nonreligious and folk-religionists, 5.3% marginal Protestants, 0.6% Buddhists. **17.IX.1951:** 55.9% Protestants, 24.2% Roman Catholics, 14.1% Chinese nonreligious, folk-religionists and Buddhists, 5.1% marginal Protestants, 0.5% other religionists. **9.XI.1962:** 56.5% Protestants, 29.7% Roman Catholics, 6.3% nonreligious, 6.3% marginal Protestants, 0.6% Polynesian/Chinese indigenous, 0.3% Chinese folk-religionists, 0.3% Buddhists. **8.II.1971:** 52.9% Protestants, 34.6% Roman Catholics, 6.6% marginal Protestants (3.2% Mormons, 2.9% Sanitos, 0.4% Jehovah's Witnesses), 4.6% nonreligious, 0.7% Chinese folk-religionists and Buddhists, 0.6% Polynesian/Chinese indigenous.

NOTES ON RELIGIONS
BAHA'IS. Begun in 1955. In 2 local spiritual assemblies (1973), declining to 1 (1996).
BUDDHISTS. Chinese. The first Chinese workers arrived in 1865. Most are Hakkas from southern China.
INDEPENDENTS. In 3 denominations in 1995 (see Table 2).
NONRELIGIOUS. Mainly Chinese youth who have abandoned their family religion, also French.
OTHER RELIGIONISTS. Including Rosicrucians (1 AMORC center on Tahiti).

Great Commission Instrument Panel: status of French Polynesia (for explanation see start of Part 4)

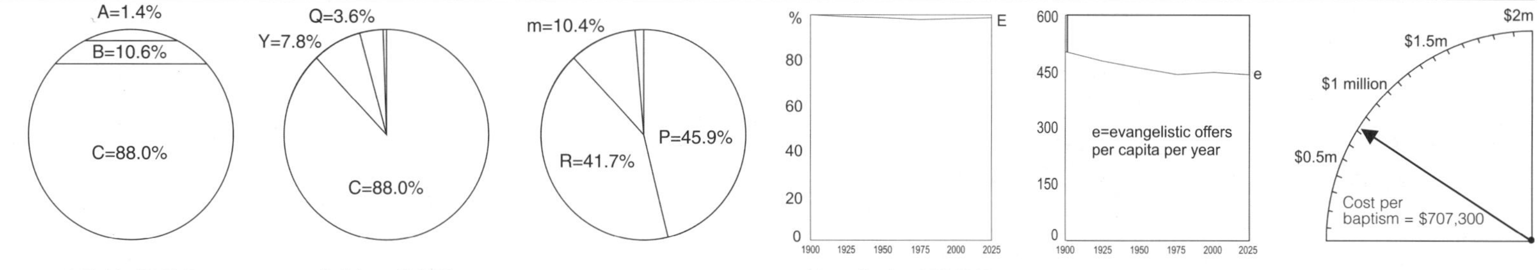

3 Worlds, AD 2000 | Religions, AD 2000 | Ecclesiastical blocs | Evangelization, 1900-2025 | Offers, 1900-2025 | Cost-effectiveness, AD 2000

Country status. French Polynesia is a territory of France in the South Pacific. Several groups of islands constitute the country: the Marquesas Islands, the Tuamotu Archipelago, the Society Islands, and the Austral Islands (Tubuai Islands). Tourism is the main industry.

HUMAN LIFE AND LIBERTY

Human need and development. The situation is as in France.

NON-CHRISTIAN RELIGIONS

Tribal religion, now virtually without followers, includes belief in a supreme being, Ta'aroa, who is recognized as creator, and an extensive pantheon of divinities (Oro, Tane, Ro'o, Tu) who preside over local cults, occupational pursuits, and such natural phenomena as the sea, thunder, and wind. The most important of these is Oro, who is the divinity of war and patron of the Ariori society, a religious cult group noted for its erotic dances and songs. Other elements include ancestral veneration, divination, spirit possession, and belief in the evil activity of sorcerers.

Country summary. **Worlds A, B, C by ethnolinguistic peoples, cities, and major civil divisions in French Polynesia.**

	PEOPLES							CITIES							CIVIL DIVISIONS						
World	Num	Pop 2000	C%	Christians	E%	U%	Unevangelized	Num	Pop 2000	C%	Christians	E%	U%	Unevangelized	Num	Pop 2000	C%	Christians	E%	U%	Unevangelized
A	0	0	0.00	0	0	0	0	0	0	0.00	0	0	0	0	0	0	0.00	0	0	0	0
B	2	26,797	24.82	6,652	91	9	2,498	0	0	0.00	0	0	0	0	0	0	0.00	0	0	0	0
C	13	208,264	92.23	192,072	100	0	166	1	102,992	82.00	84,453	98	2	1,957	5	235,061	84.54	198,725	99	1	3,191
Total	**15**	**235,061**	**84.54**	**198,724**	**99**	**1**	**2,664**	**1**	**102,992**	**82.00**	**84,453**	**98**	**2**	**1,957**	**5**	**235,061**	**84.54**	**198,725**	**99**	**1**	**3,191**

Ethnoreligionists. 18th-century wooden representation of Tahitian deity Tangaroa, in act of creating other gods and man. Traditional religion now has no organization or followers, but its influence remains.

Traditional religion has largely disappeared as a separate entity although traditional concepts continue to influence the Polynesian expression of Christianity.

Chinese folk religion, including Buddhism and Confucianism, exists among the Chinese inhabiting Papeete. A growing number of Chinese youth however have abandoned their family religion.

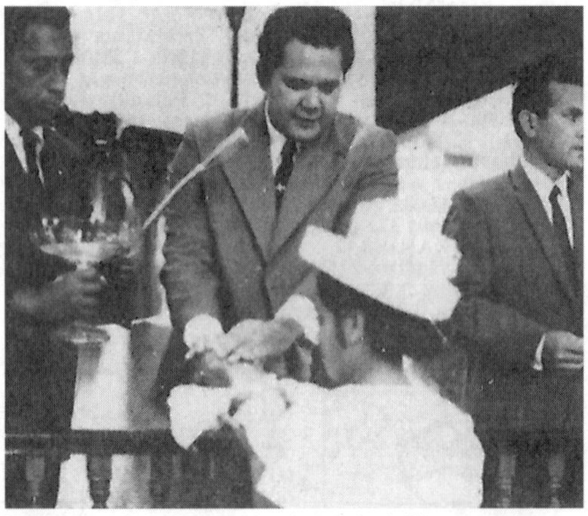

Protestants. Christmas 1974 baptism service in Siloama parish.

CHRISTIANITY

Originally discovered by the British and Spanish, these islands alternated under their control during the 17th and 18th centuries, finally coming under French rule during the 19th century. Protestant and Catholic dominance shifted accordingly with the colonial power.

PROTESTANT CHURCHES. The Evangelical Church of Polynesia owes its origin to the missionary activity of 3 societies (London Mission, Basel Mission, Paris Mission) from as early as 1797, and became autonomous in 1963. It is still the largest denomination, though Roman Catholicism is a close second. Following a schism in 1968, the Chinese community within the Evangelical Church was reduced to about 200. Theological training has been provided for students at both Montpelier, France, and Yaoundé, Cameroon, in Africa.

Protestantism is strongest in the Society and Austral Islands. In 1971, 2,000 pupils were enrolled in Protestant schools.

CATHOLIC CHURCH. The first Catholic efforts to evangelize the islands began during 1659-1667. An attempt was made in 1772 by Franciscans from Peru, followed by French priests in the Gambier Islands in 1831, the Marquesas in 1838, Tahiti in 1842, and Tuamotu in 1849.

Catholicism has grown rapidly in recent years, having its greatest strength in the Gambier and Marquesas Islands. The Rotatoria Movement (Living Rosary) of Pauline Jaricot is very strong having enlisted the majority of the Catholic population in its membership.

The Holy See has no diplomatic relations with French Polynesia in AD 2000, but is represented there by an apostolic delegate for the Pacific Ocean residing in Wellington, New Zealand.

MARGINAL CHURCHES. The Mormon church is increasing rapidly, having grown from 2,330 professing adherents in the 1962 census to 4,800 affiliated in 1970, to 11,000 in 1990. During the same period Jehovah's Witnesses expanded their membership from 152 (1962) to 1,500 (1990). A large schism from the Mormons is the Reorganized Church of Jesus Christ of Latter-day Saints, known as Kanito or Sanito (Saints); beginning in the Tuamotu archipelago in 1884, it later spread throughout the territory. It has nativistic tendencies, giving prominence to the magical powers of its priests and the evocation of the dead.

INDIGENOUS CHURCHES. There has been a history of independent movements. From 1823-35 the Mamaia sect flourished, begun by an LMS deacon (elder) who announced he was Jesus Christ or his immediate representative, come to evict all Whites. Three groups have split from the Evangelical Church since World War II: Keretitiano in 1950, the Autonomous Church in 1954 and the Polynesian Pentecostal Churches in 1968. The latter group is entirely Chinese.

Indigenous missions. In the 19th century, Tahitians were sent as missionaries all over the Pacific. This movement has been in decline for the past 40 years and shows little sign of reviving.

CHURCH AND STATE

Relations between church and state in French Polynesia are similar to those in metropolitan France. However, the separation of church and state does not prevent government from providing funds for specific projects, including a financial grant towards the building of a girls' hostel belonging to the Evangelical Church in Papeete.

INTERDENOMINATIONAL ORGANIZATIONS

There is no Christian council, but the Evangelical Church is represented on the continuation committee of the Pacific Conference of Churches as well as being a member of the WCC. Relations between the Evangelical and Catholic churches are healthy as evidenced by their joint participation in ceremonies related to the Week of Prayer for Christian Unity.

FUTURE TRENDS AND PROSPECTS

Chinese folk-religionists and the nonreligious together could represent 13% of the population in AD 2025. In that scenario, Christians would fall to 86.2% in 2025 from 94.8% in 1970.

The impact of secularization will probably be felt long into the future with the nonreligious reaching 10% before AD 2050. Christianity, however, will likely hold on to at least 70% of the country's population well into the future.

Eglise Evangelique. Parish church of Pueu, oldest church in French Polynesia (1888).

BIBLIOGRAPHY

A statement shewing the present position of the missionaries of the London Missionary Society in Tahiti. [Papeete, Tahiti: 1852]. 28p.

Au vent des cyclones: missions protestantes et Eglise évangélique à Tahiti et en Polynésie française = Puai noa mai te vero. H. Vernier. [Papeete, Tahiti: Eglise évangélique de Polynésie française, 1986]. 465p.

Cent ans au service de la jeunesse tahitienne: les Frères de l'Instruction Chrétienne en Polynésie française 1860–1960. Papeete, Tahiti: Ecolé des Frères, 1960. 95p.

Documents concernant la situation de l'église protestante nationale de Tahiti en l'année 1875. [Papeete, Tahiti: 1875]. 43p.

'Essai historique sur l'introduction du Christianisme dans l'île de Tahiti.' S. Lombard. Th.B. thesis, Faculté de Théologie protestante de Paris, 1892. 105p.

La belle histoire de Pierre Nédellec: récit. R. Piacentini. Paris: Imprimerie des Orphelins-apprentis, 1929. 177p.

'L'Enseignement protestant en Polynésie française: histoire, analyse, perspectives d'avenir.' E. Male. Thesis (licentiate), Université de Strasbourg, 1974, 1974. 130p.

L'histoire de l'Église mormone en Polynésie française de 1844 à 1982. Y. R. Perrin. Papeete, Tahiti: Imprimerie CES-STP, 1982. 49p.

Mémoires pour servir à l'histoire de Mangareva ère chrétienne, 1834–1871. H. Laval. Ed., C. W. Newbury & P. O'Reilly. Paris: Musée de l'homme, 1968. 817p.

Missionnaires au quotidien a Tahiti: les Picpuciens en Polynésie au XIXe siècle. P. Toullelan. *Studies in Christian mission*, vol. 13. Leiden: E. J. Brill, 1995. 354p.

Naissance d'une tradition: changement culturel et syncrétisme religieux aux iles Australes (Polynésie française). A. Babadzan. *Travaux et documents de l'ORSTOM*, no. 154. Paris: ORSTOM, 1982. 313p.

People movements in Southern Polynesia: studies in the dynamics of church–planting and growth in Tahiti, New Zealand, Tonga, and Samoa. A. R. Tippett. Chicago: Moody Press, 1971. 288p.

Protestant church at Tahiti. D. Mauer. Paris: Nouvelles Editions Latines, 1970. 35p.

Seasons of faith and courage: the Church of Jesus Christ of Latter–day Saints in French Polynesia, a sesquicentennial history, 1843–1993. S. G. Ellsworth & K. C. Perrin. Sandy, UT: Yves R. Perrin, 1994. 407p.

Tahiti, où vas–tu? D. Mouly. Montgeron: Lectures missionnaires, [1965]. 162p. (Catholic).

Tahitian Catholic church. P. O'Reilly. Paris: Société des Océanistes, 1969. 30p. (Also in French).

The gospel graced by a people. A. D. Tyree. Independence, MO: Herald, 1993. 111p. (Mormon).

Country Table 2. Organized churches and denominations in French Polynesia.

Official name (bold type = church with over 10% of all affiliated) 1	*Begun* 2	*Type* 3	*Counc* 4	*Congs* 5	*Adults* 6	*Affiliated 1970* 7	*Affiliated 1995* 8	*G%* 9	*Names, notes, and other statistics* (see Codebook, Part 3) 10
Assemblées de Dieu	1978	P-Pe2	Z....	6	600	–	1,000	5.88	*Assemblies of God.* M=AoG(France).
Assemblées de Dieu (USA)	1977	P-Pe2	Z....	1	75	–	125	5.56	*Assemblies of God.* M=AoG(USA).
Christianisme	1950	I-Ref	.....	1	75	300	227	-1.11	*Keretitiano. Christianity.* Schism of EEPF pastor and his parish. Declining.
Confédération des Egls Reformées	1982	I-3nP	.....	10	500	–	1,100	7.69	*Confederation of Reformed Churches of FP.* Split ex EEPF. 4n.
Eglise Adventiste du Septième Jour	1892	P-Adv	x....	22	6,300	2,000	9,600	6.48	*SDA. Seventh-day Adventists,* FP Mission, Central Pacific UM. (1970) 7nx,29t(1616)92Y.
Eglise Alleluia	1967	I-3pP	.....	1	45	50	100	2.81	*Hallelujah Church.* Chinese (Cantonese), ex EEPF.
Eglise Autonome	1954	I-Ref	.....	5	500	500	1,100	3.20	*Autonomous Church.* Founded by pastor expelled from EEPF. Now very active.
Eglise Catholique de Polynésie Fr:	1659	R-Lat	P.PY.	85	43,300	36,058	89,186	3.69	On Gambier, Marquesas. 10% Chinese. C=1+1+3. 13n 19x 76m 69w 1666Yy
M Papeete	1848	R-Lat	Ps	82	40,000	31,000	82,000	3.97	Excludes Marquesas. 2,000 Catholics are Chinese. 12n 15x 66m 63w 1500Yy
D Taiohae (Tefenuaenata)	1848	R-Lat	Psscc	3	3,300	5,058	7,186	1.41	Covers Marquesas Islands in north. 90% Catholic. 1n 4x 10m 6w 166Yy
E de JC des Saints des Derniers Jours	1844	m-LdS	x....	45	6,820	4,836	12,000	3.70	*Latter-day Saints. Mormons.* M=CJCLdS(USA). Only in Papeete. 70f.
Eglise Evangélique de Polynésie Fr	1797	P-Ref	.WP..	80	45,100	45,000	88,750	2.75	*EEPF.* M=LMS, Basel M,PEMS(CEVAA)(France). A=1963. 200 Chinese. 50n,5x,20f.ls.
Eglise Libre de Polynésie	c1980	I-Ref	.....	5	200	–	300	6.67	*Free Church of Polynesia.* Split from EEPF.
Eglise Neo-Apostolique	c1990	I-3aX	x....	1	30	–	41	20.00	*New Apostolic Church. NAC/NAK.* M=Neuapostolische Kirche (HQ Zurich).
Eglise Sanito (Saints)	1884	m-LdS	x....	22	4,200	2,800	7,000	3.73	*Sanitos, Kanitos (Saints).* M=Reorganized Ch of JC of LdS(USA). On Tuamotu.
Eglises Pentecostales Polynésiennes	1968	I-3pP	.....	5	900	1,000	1,500	1.64	*Polynesian Pentecostal Chs.* Schism of all EEPF Tahitians of Chinese descent; Alleluia Pente Ch
Témoins de Jéhovah	1932	m-Jeh	x....	19	1,173	300	3,350	10.13	*Jehovah's Witnesses. Watch Tower.* 1970, international assembly held. (1975) 17Y. (1995) 134Y.
Doubly-affiliated		2-aff			-16,900	0	-33,079		Evangelicals who are also baptized Roman Catholics.
Totals				**308**	**92,918**	**92,844**	**182,300**		

Churches, members, growth, 1900-2025	*Congs*	*Adults*	*Affiliated*	*G%*	*Total denominations*	*6 Megablocs:* *O*	*R*	*A*	*P*	*I*	*m*
Total churches, members, and denominations (mid-1900)	50	18,000	34,500	1.42	5	0	1	0	2	0	2
Total churches, members, and denominations (mid-1970)	207	48,445	92,844	1.42	10	0	1	0	2	4	3
Total churches, members, and denominations (mid-1990)	250	83,700	164,200	2.89	15	0	1	0	4	7	3
Total churches, members, and denominations (mid-1995)	308	92,918	182,300	2.11	15	0	1	0	4	7	3
Total churches, members, and denominations (mid-2000)	320	101,000	198,725	1.74	15	0	1	0	4	7	3
Total churches, members, and denominations (mid-2025)	500	138,000	270,000	1.23	37	0	1	0	10	20	6

NOTES ON TABLE ABOVE
NATIONAL COUNCILS (Column 4, 5th letter).
C = Confederation of Reformed Churches of French Polynesia.

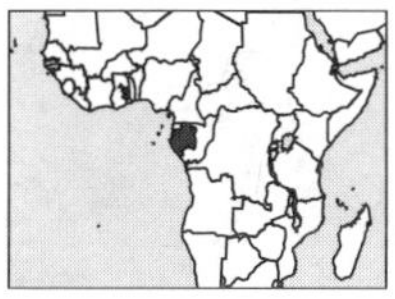

GABON

SECULAR DATA, AD 2000

STATE

Official name: La République Gabonaise (The Gabonese Republic).
Short name: Gabon. **Adjective of nationality:** Gabonese.
Flag: Stripes of green (top), yellow, and blue (bottom).
Area: 267,667 sq. km. (103,347 sq. mi.).
Government: Unitary multiparty republic with two legislative houses since, 1991 (1850 French colony, 1910 in French Equatorial Africa, 1960 Independence as republic, 1968 one-party state).
Legislature: National Assembly, 120 members; Senate, 91 members.
Official language: French (Français).
Monetary unit: 1 CFA franc (CFAF) = 100 centimes. **US$1=** CFAF 560.38.
Chief cities: LIBREVILLE 362,899; Port Gentil 191,534; Franceville 90,532; Lambarene 76,213.
Political divisions: 9 provinces.
Armed forces: 5,000.

DEMOGRAPHY

Population: 1,226,000.
Population density: 4.5/sq. km. (11.8/sq. mi.).
Under 15 years: 493,000.
Growth rate p.a.: 2.17% (births 34.81, deaths 15.47).
Mortality: Infant, per 1,000: 81.0; **Maternal per 100,000:** 500.0.
Life expectancy: 52 (male 51, female 53).
Household size: 4.0. **Floor area per person, sq.m:** 9.0.
Major languages: Bulu Fang, French, Eshira, Bandjabi, Kota, and over 40 tribal languages.
Urban dwellers: 55.19%. **Urban growth rate p.a.:** 4.0%.
Labor force: 44%.

ETHNOLINGUISTIC PEOPLES

23.6% Fang (Ogowe); 10.2% Punu (Puno); 8.8% Nzebi (Ndjabi, Bandzabi); 6.6% French; 5.0% Fang (Pahouin, Pangwe).

ECONOMY

National income p.a. per person: US$3,489; **per family:** US$13,959.

EDUCATION

Adult literacy: 63% (male 73%, female 53%). **Schools:** 1,024.
Universities: 1. **School enrolment:** female/male: 40%/40%.

HEALTH

Access to health services: 90%. **Access to safe water:** 67%.
Hospitals: 27 (51 beds per 10,000). **Doctors:** 448.
Blind: 1,300. **Deaf:** 74,100. **Murder rate:** 1.
Lepers: 40,000.

LITERATURE

New book titles p.a.: 370 (300 p.a. per million). **Periodicals:** 6.
Newspapers: 1 daily.

COMMUNICATION (per 1,000 people)

Phones: 24 (20% mobile). **Radios:** 119. **TV sets:** 76.
Daily newspaper circulation: 16. **Computers:** 20.

REFUGEES

Alien refugees from other countries: 1,000.

HUMAN LIFE AND LIBERTY (optimum condition=100.0%)

HDI: 56.2. **HSI:** 45.0. **HFI:** 25.0. **EFL:** 38.8.

Country Table 1. Religious adherents in Gabon, AD 1900-2025.

Year	*1900*		*1970*		*mid-1990*		*Annual change, 1990-2000*				*mid-1995*		*mid-2000*		*mid-2025*	
Name	*Adherents*	*%*	*Adherents*	*%*	*Adherents*	*%*	*Natural*	*Conversion*	*Total*	*Rate*	*Adherents*	*%*	*Adherents*	*%*	*Adherents*	*%*
Christians	**20,900**	**7.5**	**482,500**	**95.7**	**850,600**	**91.0**	**26,486**	**-457**	**26,029**	**2.71**	**978,000**	**90.8**	**1,110,893**	**90.6**	**1,775,900**	**89.7**
PROFESSION																
professing Christians	**20,900**	**7.5**	**482,500**	**95.7**	**850,600**	**91.0**	**26,486**	**-457**	**26,029**	**2.71**	**978,000**	**90.8**	**1,110,893**	**90.6**	**1,775,900**	**89.7**
AFFILIATION																
unaffiliated Christians	2,650	1.0	6,387	1.3	18,600	2.0	579	75	654	3.06	23,000	2.1	25,137	2.1	25,900	1.3
affiliated Christians	**18,250**	**6.5**	**476,113**	**94.5**	**832,000**	**89.0**	**25,906**	**-531**	**25,376**	**2.70**	**955,000**	**88.7**	**1,085,756**	**88.6**	**1,750,000**	**88.3**
Roman Catholics	12,500	4.5	321,113	63.7	575,000	61.5	17,896	-896	17,000	2.62	655,175	60.8	745,000	60.8	1,180,000	59.6
Protestants	2,950	1.1	92,000	18.3	175,500	18.8	5,462	288	5,750	2.87	202,398	18.8	233,000	19.0	400,000	20.2
Independents	2,800	1.0	62,500	12.4	132,000	14.1	4,108	692	4,800	3.15	154,318	14.3	180,000	14.7	320,000	16.2
Marginal Christians	0	0.0	500	0.1	4,900	0.5	153	107	260	4.35	6,000	0.6	7,500	0.6	15,000	0.8
doubly-affiliated	0	0.0	0	0.0	-55,400	-5.9	-1,724	-710	-2,434	3.71	-62,891	-5.8	-79,744	-6.5	-165,000	-8.3
Trans-megabloc groupings																
Evangelicals	2,500	0.9	21,000	4.2	42,500	4.6	1,323	177	1,500	3.07	49,252	4.6	57,500	4.7	120,000	6.1
Pentecostals/Charismatics	0	0.0	4,000	0.8	63,500	6.8	1,976	624	2,600	3.49	75,947	7.1	89,500	7.3	185,000	9.3
Great Commission Christians	**9,800**	**3.5**	**30,000**	**6.0**	**74,800**	**8.0**	**2,328**	**455**	**2,783**	**3.21**	**88,300**	**8.2**	**102,629**	**8.4**	**188,200**	**9.5**
Muslims	0	0.0	4,000	0.8	40,000	4.3	1,245	425	1,670	3.55	49,200	4.6	56,699	4.6	110,000	5.6
Ethnoreligionists	259,100	92.5	17,000	3.4	31,000	3.3	965	-294	671	1.98	33,500	3.1	37,707	3.1	50,000	2.5
Nonreligious	0	0.0	0	0.0	7,000	0.8	218	378	596	6.35	9,260	0.9	12,958	1.1	30,000	1.5
New-Religionists	0	0.0	0	0.0	4,800	0.5	149	-33	116	2.19	5,300	0.5	5,960	0.5	11,000	0.6
Atheists	0	0.0	0	0.0	600	0.1	19	-1	18	2.68	690	0.1	782	0.1	1,500	0.1
Baha'is	0	0.0	200	0.0	400	0.0	12	-11	1	0.12	400	0.0	405	0.0	1,000	0.1
Other religionists	0	0.0	300	0.1	600	0.1	19	-7	12	1.90	650	0.1	724	0.1	1,600	0.1
World A (unevangelized persons)	215,600	77.0	15,120	3.0	20,570	2.2	641	-353	288	1.32	22,622	2.1	23,294	1.9	29,715	1.5
World B (evangelized non-Christians)	43,500	15.5	6,380	1.3	63,830	6.8	1,986	810	2,796	3.70	76,652	7.1	91,813	7.5	175,385	8.8
World C (Christians)	20,900	7.5	482,500	95.7	850,600	91.0	26,486	-457	26,029	2.71	978,000	90.8	1,110,893	90.6	1,775,900	89.7
Country's population	**280,000**	**100.0**	**504,000**	**100.0**	**935,000**	**100.0**	**29,113**	**0**	**29,113**	**2.75**	**1,077,275**	**100.0**	**1,226,000**	**100.0**	**1,981,000**	**100.0**

COLUMNS, ROWS.
For meanings and definitions, see Codebook (Part 3). Note that, by definition, total 'Christians' = professing + crypto-Christians, which also = affiliated + unaffiliated Christians, and also = Great Commission Christians + latent Christians. Percentages may not always total exactly, due to rounding.

NOTES ON RELIGIONS
BAHA'IS. In 8 isolated groups (1973), increasing to 22 local spiritual assemblies (1996).
ETHNORELIGIONISTS. Fetishism remains very powerful among

Continued overleaf

Country Table 1–concluded

the Kota and others.
INDEPENDENTS. In about 11 denominations in 1995 (see Table 2).
MUSLIMS. Mainly Fulani, Hausa, and Wolof traders in the north (Sunnis of the Malikite rite). *Hajj pilgrims to Mecca.* (1976) 21.
OTHER RELIGIONISTS. Including Rosicrucians (3 AMORC centers).
PROTESTANTS. In 1902, the Paris Mission reported 900 members and 2,200 catechumens in 4 stations with 40 annexes, 58 African evangelists and 13 French missionaries.

Great Commission Instrument Panel: status of Gabon (for explanation see start of Part 4)

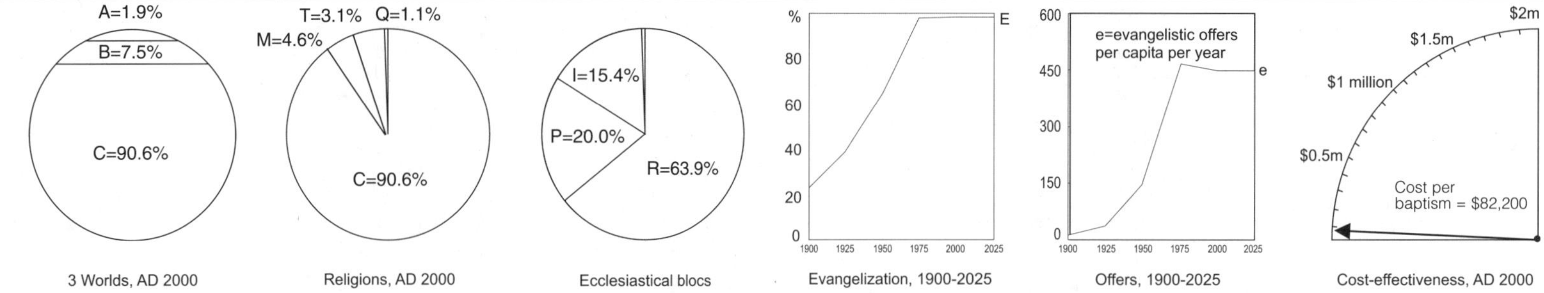

Country status. Straddling the equator in Western Africa, Gabon lies partly in the Northern and partly in the Southern Hemisphere. Gabon is covered in dense tropical rainforest with high temperatures and high humidity. Although it is physically a small country with a small population, it stands out because of its oil wealth.

Postage stamps commemorating (*below*) Protestant pioneer Albert Schweitzer, and (*above*) Roman Catholic pioneer Msgr J. R. Bessieux.

HUMAN LIFE AND LIBERTY

Human need and development. Because of its oil revenues, Gabon is a relatively affluent country. Its per capita GNP is the highest in sub-Saharan Africa and it is one of the few African countries with a trade surplus. Nevertheless, the mass of its people remain poor and only a small portion of the national wealth is being devoted to development. Most of the food and manufactured goods have to be imported, and half the population living in villages do not have any access to modern amenities. The plunge in oil prices in the mid-1980s hit Gabon's economy hard, leading to spending cuts and violent protests. But Gabon is unlikely to experience the kind of economic crises that have brought its neighbors to the brink of disaster. Gabon has been especially favored by French investors and there is a large expatriate community that serves as an anchor for the economy.

Human rights and freedoms. Gabon is one of the oldest dictatorships in Africa, with president Omar Bongo in power uninterruptedly since 1967. But external and internal pressures forced the aging president in 1990 to acquiesce in token political reforms. The one-party political system was abandoned. A new constitution, passed in 1991, restored some of the original powers of the National Assembly, scheduled a new presidential election in 1993, and limited President Bongo to only 5 more years in office. However, these political gains have been marred by violent strikes and demonstrations by groups clamoring for more radical reforms. Security forces have been accused of using excessive force to deal with protesters and strikers. All political prisoners held in jail for their opposition to Bongo have been released and those in exile have been allowed to return except for Pierre Mamboundou. With the establishment of a multiparty system, most restrictions on freedom of speech and press have been eliminated. In 1992 a constitutionally mandated National Communications Council was established and charged with ensuring freedom of speech, equal access to the media, and equitable treatment in the press for all political parties and associations. The Constitution bars discrimination based on race, sex or religion, but 2 groups have complained of bias and mistreatment: the Pygmies who live in the southeastern section of the country and immigrants from Nigeria, Equatorial Guinea or Cameroon who are sometimes subjected to inhumane treatment.

Human environment. Gabon is over 75% virgin forest. Gabon's flora and fauna are among the richest in all of Africa. Gabon has a large elephant population as well as 20 species of primates. The forests are being threatened by heavy logging which is surpassed only by oil as a revenue earner. As oil revenues decreased in the late 1980s, pressure on forest reserves has increased.

NON-CHRISTIAN RELIGIONS

Traditional religions have reduced in influence to a following of only about 3% of the population, although traditional ideas continue to influence the African expression of Christianity. All of Gabon's peoples have a belief in God, who is called Anambye (among the Omyene), Ndjambe (Seke), Nyambi (Eshira), Manambi (Okande), Nzambye (Bakele), Nzame (Fang), and Nzambe (Bakota). The veneration of ancestral spirits (Malumbi among Eshira, Mabambe among Bakele, Bekon among Fang) is also widely practiced. Three important secret societies with elaborate ceremonies are Bwiti, a male group dedicated to the remembrance of the great ancestors; Mwiri, a male group concerned for the protection of nature and maintenance of public places as well as the punishment of those who desecrate them; and Njembe, a female society. Among the Fang, Bwiti initiates women as well as men and includes anti-Catholic elements. Although part of the Bwiti movement remains predominantly traditionalist, another part has developed sufficiently in a Christian direction to be listed as an indigenous church.

Islam has grown significantly in Gabon since 1973, when the president announced his conversion. In 1970 there were only a few thousand Muslims in the north, including Hausa and Senegalese traders, who represented less than 1% of the population. Many new mosques were planned for the 1980s, but only a few were actually built. One new mosque, at Port Gentil, was burned in the riots of 1990. By 1995 there were 49,000 Muslims in Gabon and 30 mosques.

CHRISTIANITY

CATHOLIC CHURCH. Italian Capuchins began work in Gabon in the 17th century but were expelled by the Portuguese in 1777. The Congregation of the Sacred Heart of Mary came in 1841 and was later strengthened by its amalgamation with the Holy Ghost (CSSp) mission in 1848. The vicariate apostolic of Senegambia and the Two Guineas was established soon after, with the vicar residing in Gabon. This was a large area comprising the western half of Africa between the Senegal prefecture and the Orange river with no clear boundaries in the interior. By 1863 the area was divided and separate vicariates came into existence. In 1958 the diocese of Mouila and archdiocese of Libreville were formed. Growth in the number of Catholics has been steady since the end of the last century: 1,100 in 1850, 16,000 in 1910, 120,300 (including catechumens) in 1940, over 300,000 in 1972, and 655,000 by 1995.

The Holy See has diplomatic relations with Gabon and in AD 2000 is represented to government and the Catholic hierarchy by a pro-nuncio residing in Yaounde, Cameroon.

Eglise Evangélique du Gabon. Open-air service outside church. Members are Fang, and 80% are women.

PROTESTANT CHURCHES. There are 4 Protestant churches, the largest being the Evangelical Church of Gabon. Begun by the American Board (ABCFM) in the lower region of the Gabon river in 1842, the mission was turned over to American Presbyterians in 1870. The latter left in 1892 when French was made a requirement in mission schools, and the work was then transferred to the Paris Mission (PFMS). After a slow beginning, the church grew rapidly and became autonomous in 1961. Gabon's best-known missionary was Albert Schweitzer who worked at Lambarene until his death in 1965.

In 1934 the Christian and Missionary Alliance in Congo was asked by the Paris Mission to undertake evangelistic activity in the southern part of the country. The result was the formation of the Alliance Christian Church of Gabon in 1956. A revival in 1968 increased the membership of this church by 20% in a single year.

A third much smaller group is the Evangelical Church of Pentecost, which was formed in 1936 by a dissident PEMS missionary.

Eglise des Banzie (Bwiti). Church of the Initiates, a syncretistic body.

INDIGENOUS CHURCHES. The Church of the Initiates (Eglise des Banzie), also known as the Religion d'Eboga (after the drug eboga it employs) or the Bwiti movement, began originally at the end of the last century as a secret society with syncretistic ele-

Country summary. **Worlds A, B, C by ethnolinguistic peoples, cities, and major civil divisions in Gabon.**

PEOPLES

World	Num	Pop 2000	C%	Christians	E%	U%	Unevangelized
A	2	8,252	5.21	430	42	58	4,792
B	5	102,995	43.85	45,159	83	17	17,942
C	44	1,114,879	93.30	1,040,164	100	0	745
Total	**51**	**1,226,126**	**88.55**	**1,085,753**	**98**	**2**	**23,479**

CITIES

World	Num	Pop 2000	C%	Christians	E%	U%	Unevangelized
A	0	0	0.00	0	0	0	0
B	0	0	0.00	0	0	0	0
C	4	721,178	90.43	652,129	99	1	9,784
Total	**4**	**721,178**	**90.43**	**652,129**	**99**	**1**	**9,784**

CIVIL DIVISIONS

World	Num	Pop 2000	C%	Christians	E%	U%	Unevangelized
A	0	0	0.00	0	0	0	0
B	0	0	0.00	0	0	0	0
C	9	1,226,127	88.55	1,085,756	98	2	23,478
Total	**9**	**1,226,127**	**88.55**	**1,085,756**	**98**	**2**	**23,478**

ments, attempting to express in more relevant terms the traditional concerns of the Fang ancestral cult in the face of challenges from Christianity and the Western secular world. With the passage of time, however, some Bwiti groups have become increasingly Christian, with a significant new impulse towards the adoption of Christian symbolism after 1945. The present emphasis on Jesus as divine Saviour has changed the movement into a more specifically Christian one, although ambiguities remain. Bwiti is not a separatist church since no schism from an existing church or mission body has been involved. Following Independence became increasingly active, virile and aggressive, and aspired to be the national church of Gabon. There is no ecclesiastical organization and no hierarchy, and initiation with eboga replaces baptism.

Indigenous missions. Since the 1960s Roman Catholic missionaries have been sent out from Gabon to surrounding countries, but by 1995 this only amounted to a dozen or so individuals. Two Protestant missionaries were sent out in the early 1990s.

Renewal movements. In the 1990s the Pentecostal/Charismatic Renewal continued to spread rapidly across most older churches, and numbered over 89,500 adherents (of whom: 14% Pentecostals, 47% Charismatics, and 40% Independents).

CHURCH AND STATE

The constitution of 21 February 1961, revised in 1967, begins in its Preamble: 'The Gabonese people, conscious of their responsibility before God. . . .' It then recognizes 'the freedom of conscience, the free practice of religion' (Article 1, paragraph 1) as well as the right 'to form religious communities' (Article 1, paragraph 8). The republic of Gabon 'respects all beliefs' (Article 2). Public education is organized on the basis of 'religious neutrality' and religious instruction is provided to students at the request of their parents (Article 1, paragraph 12).

In 1972, numerous government ministers and officials were Protestants; but in 1973, the president of the republic, A. Bongo, who had never been baptized as a Christian, converted to Islam, and the following year Gabon became a member of the Islamic Conference (centered in Saudi Arabia) although Muslims were, and are, a small minority. The religious climate of the country was affected when all government leaders were forced to join indigenous secret societies and freemasonry. On 15 January 1974 an official communique reaffirming the freedom of religion was published following a meeting of the council of ministers, which was given over especially to 'a broad exchange of views on confessional questions'.

In the 1980s, the government took action against several churches, starting in 1983 when it banned the Jehovah's Witnesses and the Salvation Army. In the following year, 3 small indigenous churches were banned (Christianisme Celeste, Church of the Cherubim & Seraphim, and Order of the Temple of Jerusalem) along with 2 small, international new religious movements. Bethany Church and the Full Gospel were banned in 1989. But these bans were not enforced and nearly all groups continued to function. With the restoration of multi-party democracy in 1991 came a lifting of restrictions on religion.

BROADCASTING AND MEDIA

Nearly a quarter of the populace own a radio. Gabon is a member of UNDA, and there are several Catholic broadcasts. A 30 minute Bible study is broadcast each Sunday, and a 30 minute religious program each Tuesday in 3 different areas of the country. 'Dimanche chretien' is aired each Sunday afternoon for 45 minutes.

Over 750,000 have seen the 'Jesus' Film, mostly through television.

INTERDENOMINATIONAL ORGANIZATIONS

The Evangelical Church of Gabon is a member of the All Africa Conference of Churches and also of the World Council of Churches.

FUTURE TRENDS AND PROSPECTS

Muslims, 0.8% of the population in 1970, are expected to increase to 5.6% by AD 2025. Christians are expected to decline from 95.7% to 89.7% in the same period.

Muslims could grow to over 10% of the population by as early as AD 2050, rising steadily. Christianity, in this scenario, would fall below 80% around mid-century.

BIBLIOGRAPHY

Bwiti: an ethnography of the religious imagination in Africa. J. W. Fernandez. Princeton, NJ: Princeton University Press, 1982. 731p. (Religion of the Fang).

'Christian acculturation and Fang witchcraft,' J. W. Fernandez & P. Bekale, *Cahiers d'études africaines*, 2, 6 (1961), 224–70.

'Drugs and mysticism: the Bwiti of the Fang,' J. Binet, *Diogènes* (Paris), 86 (Summer 1974), 31–54.

Ethnologie religieuse des Kuta, mythologie et folklore. E. Andersson. Uppsala: Almquist & Wiksell, 1987. 164p.

Fetishism in West Africa: forty years' observations of native customs and superstitions. R. H. Nassau. 1904; reprint, New York: Negro Universities Press, 1969. 389p.

Gabon. D. E. Gardinier. *World bibliographical series*, vol. 149. Oxford, UK: CLIO Press, 1993. 218p. (See especially 'Religion & missions,' p62–77).

Gabon, un réveil religieux, 1935–37. A. Perrier. Paris: Harmattan, 1988. 240p.

Histoire de la religion bouiti. S. Swiderski. *Forschungen zur Anthropologie und Religionsgeschichte*, Bd. 5. Saarbrücken: Homo et Religio, 1978. 138p. (Summary in English and German).

'La harpe sacrée dans les cultes syncrétiques au Gabon,' S. Swiderski, *Anthropos*, 65, 5-6 (1970), 833–57.

La naissance à l'envers: essai sur le rituel du Bwiti Fang au Gabon. A. Mary. Paris: L'Harmattan, 1983. 384p.

La poésie populaire et les chants religieux du Gabon. S. Swiderski and M.–L. Girou–Swiderski. Ottawa: Editions de l'Université d'Ottawa, 1981. 290p. (Summary in English, French, German, Italian, Polish, and Spanish).

La religion Bouiti. S. Swiderski. *Série culture du Gabon.* Ottawa: Legas, 1989–. In progress to 5 vols. (Summaries in English, Italian, German, Spanish, and Polish).

Le Christ au Gabon. Sister Marie-Germaine. *Museum Lessianum*, no. 15. Louvain: Museum Lessianum, 1931. 199p.

'Le Gabon,' E. Kruger, in *Histoire des missions protestantes françaises*, p.157–69. R. Blanc, J. Blocher & E. Kruger (eds). Flavion, Belgium: Editions Le Phare, 1970.

'Le Harrisme et le Bwiti: deux réactions Africaines à l'impact Chrétien,' R. Bureau, *Recherches de Sciences Religieuses*, 63, 1 (1975), 83–100.

'Le mouvement oecuménique dans la religion Bouiti au Gabon,' S. Swiderski, *Journal of religion in Africa*, 18, 2 (1988), 125–40.

L'Eglise Evangélique du Gabon, 1842–1961. P. Stoecklin et al. Alençon, France: Imprimerie Corbière et Jugain, 1962. 52p.

Letters, 1905–1965. A. Schweitzer. Ed., H. W. Bähr. New York: Macmillan, 1992. 443p.

'Muslims in Gabon, West Africa,' O. H. Kasule, *Journal of the Institute of Muslim Minority Affairs*, 6, 1 (1985), 192–206.

Rites et croyances des peuples du Gabon: essai sur les pratiques religieuses d'autrefois et d'aujord'hui. A. Raponda-Walker & R. Sillans. Paris: Présence Africaine, 1962. 377p.

'Robert Hamill Nassau, 1835–1921: Presbyterian pioneer missionary to equatorial West Africa.' R. W. Teeuwissen. M.Th. thesis, Louisville Presbyterian Theological Seminary, Louisville, KY, 1973. 212p.

The beginnings of Christian evangelism and African responses: American Presbyterians in Equatorial Guinea and Gabon: papers presented at the 19th Annual Meeting of the African Studies Association (Boston), 3–6 Nov. 1976. P. Campbell. *Paper no. 15.* 27p.

'The beginnings of French Catholic evangelization in Gabon and African responses, 1844–1883,' D. E. Gardinier, *French colonial studies*, 2 (1978), 49–74.

'The environment, establishment and development of Protestant missions in French Equatorial Africa.' B. A. Hamilton. Ph.D. dissertation, Grace Theological Seminary, Goshen, IN, 1959. 353p.

The Gabon and Corisco missions. R. H. Nassau. New York: Presbyterian Board of Foreign Missions, 1873.

'The idea and symbol of the Saviour in a Gabon syncretistic cult: basic factors in the mythology of messianism,' J. W. Fernandez, *International review of missions*, 53, 211 (1964), 281–89.

We went to Gabon. C. M. Klein. Harrisburg, PA: Christian Publications, 1974. 184p.

Country Table 2. **Organized churches and denominations in Gabon.**

Official name (bold type = church with over 10% of all affiliated) 1	*Begun* 2	*Type* 3	*Counc* 4	*Congs* 5	*Adults* 6	*Affiliated 1970* 7	*Affiliated 1995* 8	*G%* 9	*Names, notes, and other statistics* (see Codebook, Part 3) 10
Eglise Bethany	1983	I-3cA	.....	7	1,500	–	5,000	8.33	Begun as a youth camp.
Eglise Adventiste du Septième Jour	c1980	P-Adv	x....	2	109	–	273	6.67	*SDA. Seventh-day Adventists, FG Mission.*
Eglise Catholique au Gabon:	1673	R-Lat	P.S.R	70	431,000	321,113	655,175	2.89	*Catholic Ch in Gabon.* C=2+3+12. 27n 63x 122m 163w 8762Yy
M Libreville	1863	R-Lat	Ps	31	265,000	137,261	402,000	4.39	Capital. 4,500 expatriates. 40% Fang. 11n 37x 85m 92w 4590Yy
D Franceville	1974	R-Lat	Ps	11	51,000	–	78,025	4.76	M=CMF. 2n 12x 14m 27w 1527Yy
D Mouila	1958	R-Lat	Pcssp	14	31,000	103,000	48,150	-3.00	42% Bandjabi, 32% Bapounou. M=CSSp,SDB. 7n 6x 9m 25w 825Yy
D Oyem	1969	R-Lat	Psdb	14	84,000	80,852	127,000	1.82	Formed out of M Libreville. Iron mining. M=SDB. 7n 8x 14m 19w 1820Yy
Eglise des Banzie (Bwiti)	c1890	I-mar	.....	1,200	76,900	60,000	125,000	2.98	*Ch of the Initiates. Religion d'Eboga* (a drug). Eglise du Gabon. Fang syncretism.
Eglise Evangélique de Pentecôte	1936	P-Pe2	.....	20	6,200	1,000	10,000	9.65	*Ev Ch of Pentecost.* Begun by PEMS missionary. M=MFSP,AdD(French, Swiss).
Eglise Evangélique du Gabon	1842	P-Ref	.WA..	500	92,300	75,000	150,000	2.81	*EEG. Ev Ch of Gabon.* M=PEMS(France). 96% Fang (80% women). 22n,5x,195m,18f,2p.
Eglise de l'Alliance Chrétienne du G	1934	P-Hol	xF...	213	13,975	15,000	40,125	4.01	South. A=1956. M=CMA(USA). 1968 revivals. 17n,9x,55mw,31f,3h,2p,W=73%,264Y.
Eglise Kimbanguiste	c1955	I-3pA	xwi..	50	1,000	500	2,000	5.70	*Ch of Christ on Earth through Prophet Simon Kimbangu.* M=EJCSK(Zaire). In Libreville.
Eglise Neo-Apostolique	c1980	I-3aX	x....	20	1,000	–	2,318	6.67	*New Apostolic Church. NAC/NAK.* M=Neuapostolische Kirche (HQ Zurich).
Témoins de Jéhovah	c1945	m-Jeh	x....	15	1,253	500	6,000	10.45	*Jehovah's Witnesses.* 1970, suppressed. Canada missionaries. (1975) 35Y. (1995) 225Y.
Other indigenous churches	c1960	I-3pA	.....	160	8,000	2,000	20,000	9.65	About 8 African independent churches.
Other Protestant denominations		P-	.....	30	1,000	1,000	2,000	0.05	Total 5, served by M=UFM et alia.
Doubly-affiliated		2-aff			-39,200	0	-62,891		Evangelicals who are also baptized Roman Catholics.
Totals				**2,287**	**595,037**	**476,113**	**955,000**		

Churches, members, growth, 1900-2025	*Congs*	*Adults*	*Affiliated*	*G%*	*Total denominations*	*6 Megablocs:* O	R	A	P	I	m
Total churches, members, and denominations (mid-1900)	50	12,000	18,250	4.77	3	0	1	0	1	1	0
Total churches, members, and denominations (mid-1970)	1,468	312,685	476,113	4.77	11	0	1	0	5	4	1
Total churches, members, and denominations (mid-1990)	2,000	518,000	832,000	2.83	22	0	1	0	9	11	1
Total churches, members, and denominations (mid-1995)	2,287	595,037	955,000	2.80	23	0	1	0	9	12	1
Total churches, members, and denominations (mid-2000)	3,000	677,000	1,085,756	2.60	23	0	1	0	9	12	1
Total churches, members, and denominations (mid-2025)	4,000	1,090,000	1,750,000	1.93	49	0	1	0	15	30	3

Continued overleaf

Country Table 2–concluded

NOTES ON TABLE ABOVE
NATIONAL COUNCILS (Column 4, 5th letter).
R = Conférence Episcopale du Gabon (CEG) (Episcopal Conference of Gabon).

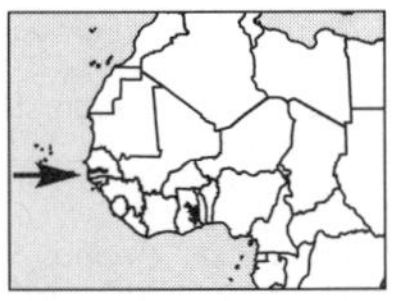

GAMBIA

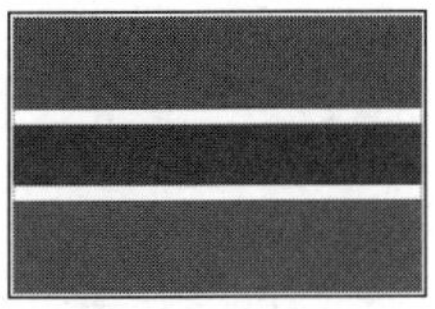

SECULAR DATA, AD 2000

STATE
Official name: The Republic of the Gambia.
Short name: Gambia. **Adjective of nationality:** Gambian.
Flag: Red (top), white, blue, white, and green stripes.
Area: 10,689 sq. km. (4,127 sq. mi.).
Government: Parliamentary republic, since 1970 (1843 British crown colony, 1965 Independence, 1994 military junta, 1997 new constitution).
Legislature: House of Representatives, 49 members.
Official language: English.
Monetary unit: 1 dalasi (D) = 100 butut. **US$1=** D= 10.22.
Chief cities: BANJUL (Bathurst) 296,398.
Political divisions: 7 provinces.
Armed forces: 1,000.

DEMOGRAPHY
Population: 1,305,000.
Population density: 122.1/sq. km. (316.3/sq. mi.).
Under 15 years: 526,000.
Growth rate p.a.: 2.52% (births 37.39, deaths 15.84).
Mortality: Infant, per 1,000: 112.4; **Maternal per 100,000:** 1,100.0.
Life expectancy: 49 (male 47, female 51).
Household size: 8.3. **Floor area per person, sq.m:** 7.0.
Major languages: Mandingo, Fulani, English, Wolof, Diola, Soninke, and about 8 other languages.
Urban dwellers: 32.46%. **Urban growth rate p.a.:** 4.08%.
Labor force: 47%.

ETHNOLINGUISTIC PEOPLES
36.9% Mandinka (Sose); 14.4% Gambian Wolof; 13.5% Fulakunda; 7.3% Soninke (Sarakole); 6.6% Tukulor (Takarir).

ECONOMY
National income p.a. per person: US$320; **per family:** US$2,657.

EDUCATION
Adult literacy: 38% (male 52%, female 24%). **Schools:** 277.
Universities: 9. **School enrolment:** female/male: 35%/53%.

HEALTH
Access to health services: 93%. **Access to safe water:** 76%.
Hospitals: 13 (7 beds per 10,000). **Doctors:** 61.
Blind: 2,700. **Deaf:** 74,600. **Murder rate:** <1.
Lepers: 33,000.

LITERATURE
New book titles p.a.: 160 (120 p.a. per million). **Periodicals:** 14.
Newspapers: 2 dailies.

COMMUNICATION (per 1,000 people)
Phones: 17 (16% mobile). **Radios:** 125. **TV sets:** 5.
Daily newspaper circulation: 2. **Computers:** 15.

REFUGEES
Alien refugees from other countries: 5,000.

HUMAN LIFE AND LIBERTY (optimum condition=100.0%)
HDI: 28.1. **HSI:** 36.0. **HFI:** 20.0. **EFL:** 20.0.

Country Table 1. **Religious adherents in the Gambia, AD 1900-2025.**

Year	1900		1970		mid-1990		Annual change, 1990-2000				mid-1995		mid-2000		mid-2025	
Name	Adherents	%	Adherents	%	Adherents	%	Natural	Conversion	Total	Rate	Adherents	%	Adherents	%	Adherents	%
Muslims	72,120	81.0	389,700	84.0	790,760	86.0	33,128	1,160	34,288	3.67	963,000	86.7	1,133,639	86.9	1,916,100	89.1
Ethnoreligionists	13,100	14.7	55,600	12.0	81,500	8.9	3,411	-1,342	2,069	2.29	88,120	7.9	102,191	7.8	120,000	5.6
Christians	**3,700**	**4.2**	**14,500**	**3.1**	**36,500**	**4.0**	**1,527**	**-130**	**1,397**	**3.29**	**44,000**	**4.0**	**50,467**	**3.9**	**82,000**	**3.8**
PROFESSION																
crypto-Christians	100	0.1	856	0.2	7,460	0.8	312	12	324	3.67	9,100	0.8	10,700	0.8	18,000	0.8
professing Christians	**3,600**	**4.0**	**13,644**	**2.9**	**29,040**	**3.2**	**1,215**	**-142**	**1,073**	**3.19**	**34,900**	**3.1**	**39,767**	**3.1**	**64,000**	**3.0**
AFFILIATION																
unaffiliated Christians	0	0.0	674	0.2	2,180	0.2	91	18	109	4.13	2,797	0.3	3,269	0.3	4,000	0.2
affiliated Christians	**3,700**	**4.2**	**13,826**	**3.0**	**34,320**	**3.7**	**1,436**	**-148**	**1,288**	**3.24**	**41,203**	**3.7**	**47,198**	**3.6**	**78,000**	**3.6**
Roman Catholics	1,800	2.0	9,328	2.0	22,400	2.4	937	-53	884	3.38	27,200	2.5	31,238	2.4	50,000	2.3
Independents	0	0.0	800	0.2	6,200	0.7	259	16	275	3.74	7,710	0.7	8,950	0.7	18,000	0.8
Protestants	900	1.0	1,578	0.3	2,700	0.3	113	-16	97	3.12	3,115	0.3	3,670	0.3	5,000	0.2
Anglicans	1,000	1.1	2,000	0.4	2,600	0.3	109	-89	20	0.74	2,700	0.2	2,800	0.2	4,000	0.2
Orthodox	0	0.0	100	0.0	350	0.0	15	-5	10	2.54	400	0.0	450	0.0	800	0.0
Marginal Christians	0	0.0	20	0.0	70	0.0	3	-1	2	2.54	78	0.0	90	0.0	200	0.0
Trans-megabloc groupings																
Evangelicals	900	1.0	1,900	0.4	1,200	0.1	50	-50	0	0.00	1,188	0.1	1,200	0.1	1,800	0.1
Pentecostals/Charismatics	0	0.0	500	0.1	7,500	0.8	314	36	350	3.90	9,246	0.8	11,000	0.8	24,000	1.1
Great Commission Christians	**3,000**	**3.4**	**9,300**	**2.0**	**20,000**	**2.2**	**837**	**224**	**1,061**	**4.35**	**24,400**	**2.2**	**30,607**	**2.4**	**50,000**	**2.3**
Baha'is	0	0.0	4,100	0.9	5,800	0.6	243	256	499	6.40	9,000	0.8	10,790	0.8	17,000	0.8
Nonreligious	0	0.0	0	0.0	5,300	0.6	222	55	277	4.29	6,700	0.6	8,066	0.6	15,500	0.7
Hindus	80	0.1	100	0.0	140	0.0	6	1	7	4.19	180	0.0	211	0.0	400	0.0
World A (unevangelized persons)	73,870	83.0	347,856	75.0	560,280	60.9	23,435	-6,425	17,010	2.69	639,722	57.6	729,495	55.9	1,000,215	46.5
World B (evangelized non-Christians)	11,430	12.8	101,452	21.9	323,220	35.1	13,576	6,555	20,130	4.97	426,907	38.4	525,038	40.2	1,068,785	49.7
World C (Christians)	3,700	4.2	14,500	3.1	36,500	4.0	1,527	-130	1,397	3.29	44,000	4.0	50,467	3.9	82,000	3.8
Country's population	**89,000**	**100.0**	**463,808**	**100.0**	**920,000**	**100.0**	**38,537**	**0**	**38,537**	**3.56**	**1,110,630**	**100.0**	**1,305,000**	**100.0**	**2,151,000**	**100.0**

COLUMNS, ROWS.
For meanings and definitions, see Codebook (Part 3). Note that, by definition, total 'Christians' = professing + crypto-Christians, which also = affiliated + unaffiliated Christians, and also = Great Commission Christians + latent Christians. Percentages may not always total exactly, due to rounding.

CENSUSES.
1901 Census of the British Empire: (Colony only): 57.3% Muslims, 26.3% Christians, 16.4% tribal religionists. In this 1901 census, 3,540 Christians were recorded in the Colony (including 200 Whites mostly British, 910 Aku, 350 Ibos, 145 Popos and 20 Goans); also 81 Hindus. **1911** (Colony): 51.4% Muslims, 42.7% Christians, 5.9% tribal religionists. **1911** (Protectorate): 84.6% Muslims, 14.8% tribal religionists, 0.6% Christians. **1911** (Colony and Protectorate): 82.9% Muslims, 14.3% tribal religionists, 2.8% Christians. **1921:** 78.2% Muslims, 18.9% tribal religionists, 2.9% Christians. **1931:** 84.5% Muslims, 12.7% tribal religionists, 2.7% Christians (1.2% Roman Catholics, 0.9% Protestants, 0.6% Anglicans). **1945:** 82.8% Muslims, 14.3% tribal religionists, 2.9% Christians; (Colony: Bathurst and Kombo St Mary): 57.5% Muslims, 32.5% Christians, 10.0% tribal religionists; (Protectorate): 85.1% Muslims, 14.7% tribal religionists, 0.2% Christians.

NOTES ON RELIGIONS
BAHA'IS. Growth from 7 local spiritual assemblies (1964) to 27 (1973), then decline to 22 (1996). Most Baha'is are Diola (Jola), and expansion among them is continuing.
CRYPTO-CHRISTIANS. Since the expansion of Christian ministries among Muslims, and in particular the growth of Bible correspondence courses and radiophonic evangelism for Muslims, the number of secret believers (non-professing Christians) rose markedly during the 1990s.
ETHNORELIGIONISTS. Mainly Serer, Diola (Jola), Pacari, Bassari, Animists among the Fulbe (Fulani) and Wolof, and some professional castes (including the Mangsuanka palmwine tappers), are still untouched by Islam.
MUSLIMS. Sunnis (of the Malikite rite). Mainly among the Mandingo, Fula (Fulani), Wolof and Sarakole. Several professional castes (drummers, tanners, praise-singers) have been partially islamized. Orders include Tariqiya and Muridiya from Senegal. There is also a small Ahmadiya mission (Qadianis; enumerated here as Muslims though declared non-Muslim by Pakistan). *Hajj pilgrims to Mecca.* (1969) 250; (1970) 347; (1974) 597; (1975) 590 (1976) 667.

Great Commission Instrument Panel: status of the Gambia (for explanation see start of Part 4)

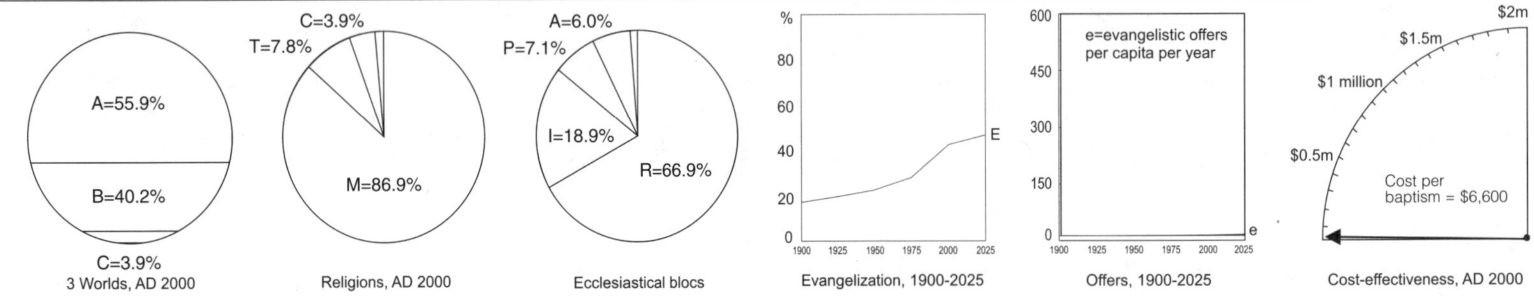

Country status. The Gambia, on the western coast of Africa, straddling the Gambia River, is virtually an enclave within Senegal, with which it has a formal political association. Tourism and the export of fish and peanuts are the main economic activities.

Country summary. **Worlds A, B, C by ethnolinguistic peoples, cities, and major civil divisions in the Gambia.**

	PEOPLES							CITIES							CIVIL DIVISIONS						
World	*Num*	*Pop 2000*	*C%*	*Christians*	*E%*	*U%*	*Unevangelized*	*Num*	*Pop 2000*	*C%*	*Christians*	*E%*	*U%*	*Unevangelized*	*Num*	*Pop 2000*	*C%*	*Christians*	*E%*	*U%*	*Unevangelized*
A	19	1,200,974	1.56	18,679	42	58	697,144	0	0	0.00	0	0	0	0	6	1,221,501	3.41	41,663	44	56	689,051
B	6	73,935	12.63	9,341	56	44	32,845	1	296,398	5.60	16,598	51	49	145,087	1	83,861	6.60	5,535	51	49	41,050
C	7	30,454	62.97	19,178	100	0	113	0	0	0.00	0	0	0	0	0	0	0.00	0	0	0	0
Total	**32**	**1,305,363**	**3.62**	**47,198**	**44**	**56**	**730,102**	**1**	**296,398**	**5.60**	**16,598**	**51**	**49**	**145,087**	**7**	**1,305,362**	**3.62**	**47,198**	**44**	**56**	**730,101**

HUMAN LIFE AND LIBERTY

Human need and development. The Gambia River winds through the country, providing water, the most important natural resource. Yet, The Gambia is one of the poorest countries in Africa. Peanut farming accounts for the livelihood of most of the adult Gambians, but yields just to sustain life in the growing seasons. For the rest of the year, Gambians undergo what is called sordure, or the famine that results when the food stocks run out. Located on the periphery of the Sahel, The Gambia is subject to periodic droughts, the most severe of which may wipe out entire cattle stocks. In the summer, the dry harmattan winds tend to scorch both man and beast alike. Floods are common in the rainy season. Because the Gambia River is tidal, irrigation is possible only along the nonsaline tributaries. Droughts decrease the waterflow and push the saline water further upriver. There is hardly any development work either to harness the Gambia River or to reduce the intensity of the drought. Both the Mandingo and the Fulani who constitute the major tribes have learned to adapt themselves to the hardships of the environment.

Human rights and freedoms. The Gambia is a political democracy, and it has had a stable government since independence, marred only by a coup attempt in 1981. Although virtually a one-party state, opposition parties are tolerated and some even flourish. Some police abuses are uncovered periodically, but there are no systematic violations of human rights, and erring police officials are generally brought to justice. No person may be detained for more than 21 days before trial, although, because of the overcrowded court schedules, this detention period may be much longer in practice. The Gambia has 3 types of legal systems: general, customary and Sharia, but the first, based on English law, governs most legal transactions. Appeals to the Privy Council in London are allowed. There are few restrictions on freedoms of speech and press. However, The Gambia has no television and only 3 radio stations, and the print media have historically exercised a high degree of self-censorship. The Constitution specifically bans all forms of discrimination. As in other traditional Islamic societies, women suffer many social and economic disadvantages with no access to remedies. Additionally, young boys, known as Almudos, given by their parents to Islamic scholars to learn the Koran, are treated as slaves and suffer many indignities. They are forced to go hungry and often beaten if they do not bring home enough money from begging. UNICEF is conducting a study of the plight of the Almudos.

Human environment. Once The Gambia was heavily forested, but 90% of the forest land has been lost through fuel cutting. The Gambia River is a very unhealthy one, and is a breeding ground for a number of water-borne diseases, such as schistosomiasis and onchocerciasis. Government plans to build a dam on the Gambia River are likely to reduce the extent of the mangrove swamps and also disrupt fish population depending on the river's salinity.

NON-CHRISTIAN RELIGIONS

Islam has its strongest concentration among the Mandingo, Fula (Fulani, Peul), Wolof and Sarakole peoples. The Gambia is largely a Muslim country (nearly 87%) with mosques found in the majority of its towns and villages. Three sufi brotherhoods are widespread and influential.

African traditional religions are strongest among the Serer, Diola (Jola), and Bassari peoples. The total population is still nearly 8% traditionalist. The Serer know God as Rog (Creator). Prayers are not common, but appeal is made to Rog when the Serer are threatened with war. Close contact is maintained with departed ancestral spirits, especially in the period following a funeral when they are believed to hover temporarily about the homes of the living. The Serer also believe in the transmigration of souls, the living dead taking abode in both animate and inanimate objects.

Methodist Church in the Gambia. Gambia postage stamps commemorating 150th Anniversary.

CHRISTIANITY

Although Catholicism touched The Gambia through Portuguese mariners and merchants as early as 1445, the first permanent Catholic mission was not founded until 1849. An Anglican chaplain arrived in 1816 and was followed later by missionaries of the SPG, while the first British Methodist entered in 1821. The Worldwide Evangelization Crusade has had missionaries since 1966. None of these, nor those that have followed, have been particularly successful in attracting members. Christianity is now the professed religion of only about 3% of the people, being strongest in urban areas among the detribalized Aku Creoles who are descendants of freed slaves. Among the indigenous peoples, some Mandingo and recently larger numbers of Wolof tribesmen have come into the churches. All the denominations are active in Banjul; in addition Catholics work in the Kombo region, Anglicans in Fatoto and Methodists in Mausa Konko, Georgetown and south of Brikams. The churches are also engaged in educational, medical and agricultural ministries. Catholic missionary work is run by Irish Holy Ghost priests, assisted by Gambian and expatriate sisters and a large number of local catechists. A shrine at Kunkujang dedicated in 1987 to Mary, Queen of Peace has become an important pilgrimage and retreat site for Catholics and also other Christians. The Anglican and Methodist churches have both indigenous and expatriate clergy.

The Holy See has diplomatic relations with The Gambia and in AD 2000 is represented to the government and the Catholic hierarchy by a pro-nuncio residing in Freetown.

Indigenous missions. Very few Gambian Christians have gone abroad for missionary work.

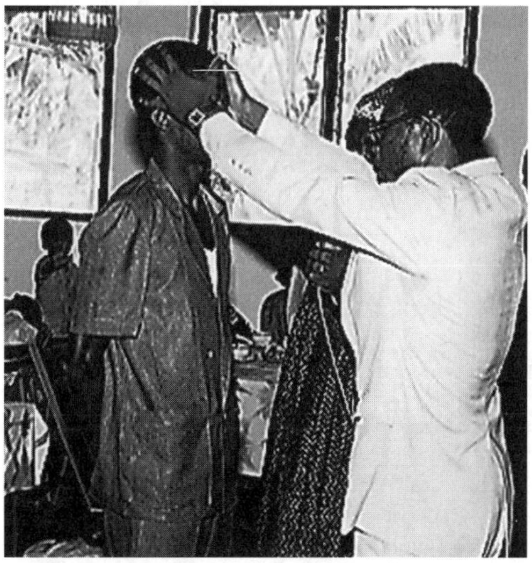

Christian Missionary Fellowship. Healing by laying on of hands, practiced by many Independents.

CHURCH AND STATE

The constitution of 24 April 1970 guarantees freedom of conscience for all, including freedom of thought and religion and their public manifestation and propagation (Article 21, paragraph 1). 'Every religious community shall be entitled, at its own expense, to establish and maintain places of education and to manage any place of education which it wholly maintains' (Article 21, paragraph 3). There is no ministry for religious affairs.

BROADCASTING AND MEDIA

Most families own a radio. Local station FM1 broadcasts a 30 minute program of reflections, prayers and hymns twice on Sunday. Gambia is represented in UNDA. Catholics broadcast nearly 3 hours of programming each Sunday featuring prayers, liturgies, Scriptures and sermons, and hymns.

Some 282,000 have seen the 'Jesus' Film, mainly through film team presentations.

INTERDENOMINATIONAL ORGANIZATIONS

The Gambia Christian Council was established in 1963 and includes Catholics, Anglicans, and Methodists in its membership. These 3 churches also co-operate in the production and distribution of scriptures and other Christian literature as well as joint services of worship and witness. Representatives from a small group of denominations and mission organizations came together in 1976 to form the Evangelistic Outreach Committee of the Gambia, to encourage and coordinate cooperative evangelistic work. They helped with the visit of the Operation Mobilization ship *Doulos* in 1986. By 1990 the Methodists, Anglicans, WEC, Evangelical Church of the Gambia, Baptists, Church of Pentecost, Scripture Union, YFC, CEF, Campus Crusade for Christ, SIL, and Abiding Word Ministries were represented on the committee. All denominations, including the Catholics, came together in the early 1990s for a New Life for All program of evangelism.

FUTURE TRENDS AND PROSPECTS

Ethnoreligionists will likely drop off steadily into the 21st century (from 12% in 1970 to 5.6% by 2025) with conversions mainly to Islam. Muslims, in this scenario, would grow to 89.1% by AD 2025.

By mid-century, animism will likely virtually disappear leaving Gambians divided between 3 religions: Islam, over 90%; Christianity, 4-6%; and Baha'i, 1%. These percentages could remain stable well into the future.

BIBLIOGRAPHY

'A contribution to the study of Islam in Gambia,' S. S. Nyang, *Journal of the Pakistan Historical Society*, 25, 2 (1977), 125–138.

'Developing and facilitating lay ministries: a case study in the Methodist Church, The Gambia (West Africa).' R. V. Wilson. D.Min. thesis, Boston University, Boston, 1980. 157p.

'Diola masking traditions and the history of the Casamance (Senegal),' P. Mark, *Paideuma*, 29 (1983), 3–22.

Four mitres: reminiscences of an irrepressible bishop. J. Daly. , [1983].

Gambia: country, people, and church in the diocese of Gambia and the Rio Pongas. J. R. C. Laughton. 2d ed. London: S. P. G., [1938]. 48p.

Island base: a history of the Methodist Church in the Gambia, 1821–1969. B. Prickett. Bo, Sierra Leone: Bunumbu Press, 1969. 246p.

Kambi Bolongo: the land of roots. O. Naylor. Bognor Regis: Anchor Publications, 1985. 169p.

Mandingo kingdoms of the Senegambia: traditionalism, Islam, and European expansion. C. A. Quinn. Evanston, IL: Northwestern University Press, 1972. 211p.

Peace is everything: world view of Muslims in the Senegambia. D. E. Maranz. Dallas: Summer Institute of Linguistics, 1993. 316p.

Pope John Paul II greets The Gambia: the complete and official text of the Holy Father's speeches to us in the Gambia in February, 1992. John Paul II. Banjul, The Gambia: Gambia Pastoral Institute, [1992]. 16p.

Reaping a rich harvest: a history of the Catholic Church in the Gambia. W. Cleary. , [1990]. 87p.

Reminiscences of the founding of a Christian mission on the Gambia. J. Morgan. London: Wesleyan Mission House, 1864. 124p.

The Gambia. D. P. Gamble. *World bibliographical series*, vol.

91. Oxford, UK: CLIO Press, 1988. 135p. (See especially 'Religion,' p51f).

The Jakhanke: the history of an Islamic clerical people of the Senegambia. L. O. Sanneh. London: International African Institute, 1979. 276p.

Country Table 2. **Organized churches and denominations in the Gambia.**

Official name (bold type = church *with over 10% of all affiliated)* 1	*Begun* 2	*Type* 3	*Counc* 4	*Congs* 5	*Adults* 6	*Affiliated 1970* 7	*Affiliated 1995* 8	*G%* 9	*Names, notes, and other statistics* (see Codebook, Part 3) 10
Anglican Ch: D Gambia & Rio Pongas	1816	A-ACa	AwAVK	6	1,600	2,000	2,700	1.21	Begun for British troops. 1935, D in CPWA. Bishop from Haiti. 4n,2x,W=60%.
Baptist Convention	1982	P-Bap	.....	4	94	–	188	7.69	M=FMB-SBC.
Catholic Church: D Banjul (Bathurst)	1849	R-Lat	pxSGQ	13	13,000	9,328	27,200	4.37	M=CSSp. 54% Wolof, 16% Serer, 15% Diola. C=1+0+2. (1990) 8n,17x,31m,51w,1171Yy.
Christian Missionary Fellowship	1990	I-3cA	x....	2	50	–	100	20.00	*CMF.* Peoples: Fulacunda, Mandjak, Mandinka. M=CAM.
Church of Pentecost	1988	P-PeA	.....	7	105	–	162	14.29	M=Ch of Pentecost (Ghana).
Churches of Christ	c1968	I-Dis	x....	5	50	300	71	-5.60	M=Churches of Christ(Non-Instrumental) (USA). Gambia Bible Seminar, Banjul. 4f.
Evangelical Church of the Gambia	1966	P-Eva	xFg..	8	70	50	200	5.70	ECG. M=WEC(UK),WEK(Germany). Formerly within Methodist Church, now separate. 12f.
Greek Orthodox P Alexandria	c1950	O-Gre	Cw...	1	200	100	400	5.70	In Diocese of Accra (HQ Yaounde). Mostly Greeks and Arabs, mainly traders.
Jehovah's Witnesses	1968	m-Jeh	.....	1	31	20	78	5.59	*Jehovah's Christian Witnesses. Watch Tower. IBSA.* 2Y
Methodist Church in the Gambia	1821	P-Met	VwA.K	6	1,230	1,528	2,234	1.53	*Gambia District.* M=MMS. 88% Aku, 6% Manjak. 1n,2x,3w,4f,3h,W=75%,33Yy.
New Apostolic Church	c1970	I-3aX	x....	100	3,000	–	5,624	41.25	*NAC/NAK.* M=Neuapostolische Kirche. HQ Zurich (Switzerland).
New Covenant Worship Centre	1988	I-3cA	.....	1	60	–	86	14.29	One of several new charismatic nations.
Seventh-day Adventist Church	c1970	P-Adv	.....	2	136	–	248	24.67	*SDA.* Strong denomination across West Africa.
West African Mission Church	1987	I-Non	.....	1	20	–	29	12.50	No-church body.
Yoruba independent churches	c1950	I-3sA	x....	30	900	500	1,800	5.26	Churches of immigrant laborers and traders from Nigeria, including CAC,CLA,C&S,DLBC,et alia.
Other Protestant churches	c1975	P-	.....	5	50	–	83	5.00	About 20, including ABWE,AoG,CMF(Nigeria),Korean Presbyterian Mission,Lutherans,et alia.
Totals				**192**	**20,596**	**13,826**	**41,203**		

Churches, members, growth, 1900-2025	*Congs*	*Adults*	*Affiliated*	*G%*	*Total denominations*	*6 Megablocs:* O	R	A	P	I	m
Total churches, members, and denominations (mid-1900)	20	2,100	3,700	1.90	3	0	1	1	1	0	0
Total churches, members, and denominations (mid-1970)	42	7,873	13,826	1.90	8	1	1	1	2	2	1
Total churches, members, and denominations (mid-1990)	150	17,200	34,320	4.65	33	1	1	1	24	5	1
Total churches, members, and denominations (mid-1995)	192	20,596	41,203	3.72	35	1	1	1	25	6	1
Total churches, members, and denominations (mid-2000)	200	23,600	47,198	2.75	37	1	1	1	26	7	1
Total churches, members, and denominations (mid-2025)	300	39,000	78,000	2.03	65	3	1	1	35	20	5

NOTES ON TABLE ABOVE

NATIONAL COUNCILS (Column 4, 5th letter).

E = Evangelical Fellowship of the Gambia (EFG).
Q = Inter-Territorial Catholic Bishops' Conference of the Gambia, Liberia & Sierra Leone (ITCABIC), also member of GCC.
W = Gambia Christian Council (GCC).

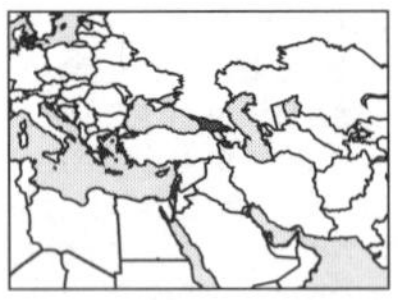

GEORGIA

SECULAR DATA, AD 2000

STATE
Official name: Sakartvelos Respublika (The Republic of Georgia).
Short name: Georgia. **Adjective of nationality:** Georgian.
Flag: Red field with black and white stripes in upper left-hand corner.
Area: 69,700 sq. km. (26,900 sq. mi.).
Government: Unitary multiparty republic with a single legislative body, since 1990 (1918 Independence, 1936 Soviet rule).
Legislature: Parliament, 335 members.
Official language: Georgian.
Monetary unit: 1 Georgian lari = 100 tetri. **US$1=** 1.36 lari.
Chief cities: TBILISI (Tiflis) 1,389,000; Kutaisi 242,321; Rustavi 164,701; Batumi 139,878; Suchumi (Sukhumi) 122,076.
Political divisions: 13 provinces.
Armed forces: 20,000.

DEMOGRAPHY
Population: 4,968,000.
Population density: 71.2/sq. km. (184.6/sq. mi.).
Under 15 years: 1,099,000.
Growth rate p.a.: 0.01% (births 13.75, deaths 9.67).
Mortality: Infant, per 1,000: 18.1; **Maternal per 100,000:** 33.0.
Life expectancy: 74 (male 70, female 78).
Household size: 4.1. **Floor area per person, sq.m:** 18.2.
Major languages: Georgian, Azerbaijani, Armenian, Russian.
Urban dwellers: 60.70%. **Urban growth rate p.a.:** 0.8%.
Labor force: 46%.

ETHNOLINGUISTIC PEOPLES
57.8% Georgian (Gruzin, Adzhar); 9.0% Mingrelian; 8.1% Armenian; 6.3% Russian; 5.6% Azerbaijani (Azeri Turk).

ECONOMY
National income p.a. per person: US$440; **per family:** US$1,804.

EDUCATION
Adult literacy: 100% (male 100%, female 99%). **Schools:** 3,808.
Universities: 19. **School enrolment:** female/male: 75%/75%.

HEALTH
Access to health services: 80%. **Access to safe water:** 90%.
Hospitals: 422 (105 beds per 10,000). **Doctors:** 30,000.
Blind: 4,500. **Deaf:** 325,100. **Murder rate:** 10.
Lepers: 500.

LITERATURE
New book titles p.a.: 320 (65 p.a. per million). **Periodicals:** 105.
Newspapers: 2 dailies.

COMMUNICATION (per 1,000 people)
Phones: 103 (4% mobile). **Radios:** 400. **TV sets:** 220.
Daily newspaper circulation: 703. **Computers:** 30.

REFUGEES
Citizen refugees in other countries: 105,000.
Internal displacement: 280,000.

HUMAN LIFE AND LIBERTY (optimum condition=100.0%)
HDI: 63.7. **HSI:** 45.0. **HFI:** 40.0. **EFL:** 23.0.

Country Table 1. **Religious adherents in Georgia, AD 1900-2025.**

Year / *Name*	*1900* Adherents	%	*1970* Adherents	%	*mid-1990* Adherents	%	*Annual change, 1990-2000* Natural	Conversion	Total	Rate	*mid-1995* Adherents	%	*mid-2000* Adherents	%	*mid-2025* Adherents	%
Christians	**2,030,000**	**92.0**	**1,350,000**	**28.7**	**3,218,100**	**58.9**	**-29,042**	**16,280**	**-12,762**	**-0.40**	**3,164,000**	**60.3**	**3,090,480**	**62.2**	**3,471,000**	**67.0**
PROFESSION																
crypto-Christians	0	0.0	600,000	12.8	0	0.0	0	0	0	0.00	0	0.0	0	0.0	0	0.0
professing Christians	**2,030,000**	**92.0**	**750,000**	**15.9**	**3,218,100**	**58.9**	**-29,042**	**16,280**	**-12,762**	**-0.40**	**3,164,000**	**60.3**	**3,090,480**	**62.2**	**3,471,000**	**67.0**
AFFILIATION																
unaffiliated Christians	135,000	6.1	29,400	0.6	181,200	3.3	-1,633	-8,320	-9,953	-7.66	44,835	0.9	81,666	1.6	71,000	1.4
affiliated Christians	**1,895,000**	**85.9**	**1,320,600**	**28.1**	**3,036,900**	**55.6**	**-27,409**	**24,600**	**-2,809**	**-0.09**	**3,119,165**	**59.4**	**3,008,814**	**60.6**	**3,400,000**	**65.7**
Orthodox	1,875,000	85.0	1,304,500	27.7	2,950,000	54.0	-26,582	20,263	-6,319	-0.22	3,011,600	57.4	2,886,814	58.1	3,231,000	62.4
Roman Catholics	15,000	0.7	3,000	0.1	34,000	0.6	-306	2,406	2,100	4.93	50,020	1.0	55,000	1.1	70,000	1.4
Independents	0	0.0	3,000	0.1	34,000	0.6	-306	1,106	800	2.14	36,875	0.7	42,000	0.9	55,000	1.1
Protestants	5,000	0.2	10,000	0.2	18,500	0.3	-167	717	550	2.64	20,170	0.4	24,000	0.5	40,000	0.8
Marginal Christians	0	0.0	100	0.0	400	0.0	-4	64	60	9.60	500	0.0	1,000	0.0	4,000	0.1
Trans-megabloc groupings																
Evangelicals	4,500	0.2	4,000	0.1	8,200	0.2	-74	174	100	1.16	8,942	0.2	9,200	0.2	14,000	0.3
Pentecostals/Charismatics	0	0.0	1,000	0.0	19,000	0.4	-171	1,271	1,100	4.67	24,114	0.5	30,000	0.6	45,000	0.9
Great Commission Christians	**155,000**	**7.0**	**518,000**	**11.0**	**797,000**	**14.6**	**-7,182**	**1,716**	**-5,466**	**-0.71**	**777,000**	**14.8**	**742,337**	**14.9**	**932,000**	**18.0**
Muslims	150,500	6.8	850,000	18.1	1,040,000	19.1	-9,371	1,218	-8,153	-0.81	1,000,000	19.1	958,475	19.3	1,000,000	19.3
Nonreligious	0	0.0	1,707,000	36.3	937,400	17.2	-8,447	-9,287	-17,734	-2.08	870,000	16.6	760,065	15.3	600,000	11.6
Atheists	500	0.0	775,500	16.5	238,000	4.4	-2,145	-8,181	-10,326	-5.53	190,000	3.6	134,738	2.7	80,000	1.6
Jews	25,000	1.1	25,000	0.5	25,000	0.5	-225	-67	-292	-1.24	24,300	0.5	22,078	0.4	22,000	0.4
Baha'is	0	0.0	500	0.0	1,500	0.0	-14	37	23	1.41	1,700	0.0	1,725	0.0	5,000	0.1
World A (unevangelized persons)	90,446	4.1	1,647,625	35.0	660,660	12.1	-5,947	-3,472	-9,419	-1.53	619,476	11.8	566,352	11.4	460,842	8.9
World B (evangelized non-Christians)	85,554	3.9	1,709,875	36.3	1,581,240	29.0	-14,255	-12,808	-27,063	-1.86	1,466,328	27.9	1,311,168	26.4	1,246,158	24.1
World C (Christians)	2,030,000	92.0	1,350,000	28.7	3,218,100	58.9	-29,042	16,280	-12,762	-0.40	3,164,000	60.3	3,090,480	62.2	3,471,000	67.0
Country's population	**2,206,000**	**100.0**	**4,707,500**	**100.0**	**5,460,000**	**100.0**	**-49,244**	**0**	**-49,244**	**-0.94**	**5,249,805**	**100.0**	**4,968,000**	**100.0**	**5,178,000**	**100.0**

COLUMNS, ROWS.
For meanings and definitions, see Codebook (Part 3). Note that, by definition, total 'Christians' = professing + crypto-Christians, which also = affiliated + unaffiliated Christians, and also = Great Commission Christians + latent Christians. Percentages may not always total exactly, due to rounding.

NOTES ON RELIGIONS
ATHEISTS. Rapid decline after 1989 and collapse of the USSR.
BAHA'IS. In 2 local spiritual assemblies (1994).
MUSLIMS. Mainly Azerbaijanis, Mingrelians, Kurds, Ossetians, and Georgians (5% Muslim).

Great Commission Instrument Panel: status of Georgia (for explanation see start of Part 4)

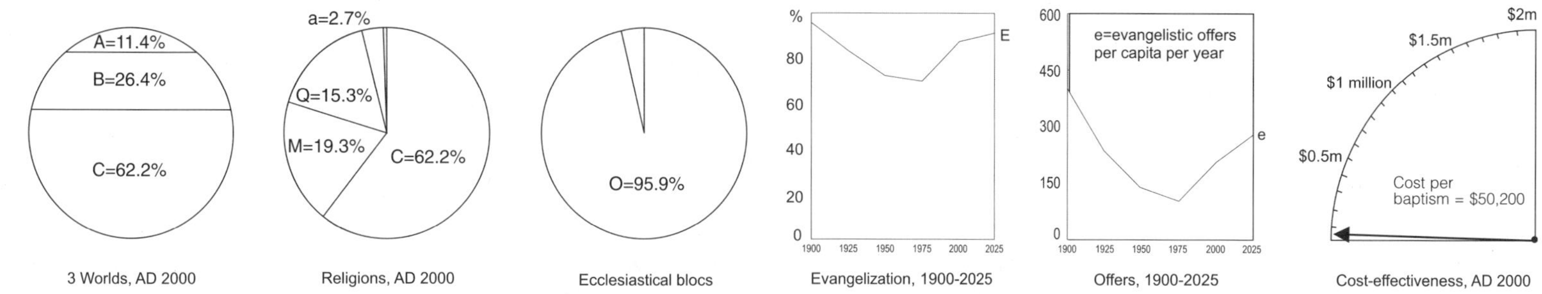

Country status. Georgia, a former republic of the Soviet Union, is a largely mountainous nation bordering on the Black Sea, between Russia and Turkey. Tobacco, tea, and grapes are the most important products.

HUMAN LIFE AND LIBERTY

Human rights and freedoms. Georgia declared its independence from the Soviet Union in 1991, but since then has continued to struggle against severe political instability, internal armed conflict, economic ruin, and runaway crime. For a period of time, the country was racked by total anarchy, fueled by the armed conflict in the breakaway region of Abkhazia. The separatists who captured the Abkhazian capital of Sukhumi are reported to have committed widespread atrocities against the Georgian civilian population. Armed Zviadists, supporters of the former president, Zviad Gamsakhurdia, have turned to banditry, and the unsuccessful civil war they unleashed in 1993 has ravaged the countryside. Paramilitary forces, including pro-government ones like the Mkhedrioni, commit human rights abuses intermittently and intimidate civilians with impunity.

The internal security service, modeled on the old KGB, thrives in this chaotic situation. Many people are arrested without warrants, detained, and physically abused. Soviet-era legislation regarding arrest and incarceration still remain on the statute books and such legal protection for the people as exists is largely ignored. Law enforcement officials, paramilitary groups and the military all misuse their powers to intimidate citizens and extort money from them. Military posts are used as prisons and military 'kommandants' have wide law enforcement powers.

The law permits detention without warrant for several kinds of violations, including breach of curfew. Administrative detention laws are used extensively against Zviadists. The judiciary is vulnerable to political and other forms of influence, particularly at the local level. Certain supervisory rights exercised by the procuracy further limit judicial independence. One Soviet legacy that continues is the right of the procuracy to 'ask' judges to review their decisions. This practice is known as 'telephone justice'. Some judges are openly corrupt and demand bribes before announcing their decisions. Freedoms of association and speech are severely curtailed, and the state of emergency is a cover for denying these freedoms even without legitimate reasons. All Zviadist newspapers have been closed and only official newspapers are being published without interruption. Anti-government demonstrations are prohibited and authorities use force to prevent unauthorized demonstrations. Jewish Georgians have been permitted to emigrate to Israel. The old Soviet restrictions on freedom of movement remain in force. People need to register their place of residence with the authorities, and unauthorized residents are sometimes expelled. The civil war has reduced the effectiveness of the Georgian parliament as the watchdog of human right and also made it subservient to the presidency. There are frequent conflicts between the parliament and the president in which the latter generally tends to win decisively. Minorities and women play only a nominal role in Georgian politics and the interests of both groups have suffered as a result of the civil war.

NON-CHRISTIAN RELIGIONS

Islam has, at 19%, a sizeable share of Georgia's population. These are mainly Azeris, Kurds, Mingrelians, Ossetians, and 5% of ethnic Georgians.

Nonreligion or atheism retains a substantial hold, 18% in AD 2000.

CHRISTIANITY

ORTHODOX CHURCHES. The Georgian Orthodox Church stands among the most ancient churches of Christendom. Missionary activity began in Georgia in the era of Constantine, although one tradition links the church with the apostle Andrew. Another tradition emphasizes the evangelizing role of the holy captive woman, St Nino. In the first several centuries of the Georgian church, its members suffered in the cross-fire of the conflict between Byzantium and Persia. Few Georgians ever converted to Islam despite Muslim rule in various eras, including that following the year 654, when an Arab caliph established an emirate in T'bilisi. Timur brought ruin to the country and its church between 1386 and 1403, and the Turks invaded and sacked major cities in 1510, starting a long period of Turkish and Persian domination. Through many difficult centuries the Georgian church was the main force for preserving Georgian identity and culture. From the 1917 figures of 2,455 parishes in 15 dioceses, there were in 1970 only 80 officially-recognized churches. The 1970s witnessed a revival of church-going. Churches were crowded with young people. In the early 1990s, patriarch Ilya II encouraged a revival of devotion by writing a prayer book, by urging Christians to pray throughout the day, and by appealing to the faithful to do charitable work each Saturday. He declared, 'The world needs to know that we are a Christian nation, and that we are returning to our Christian roots'. In 1992 Georgian president Eduard Shevardnadze, formerly a top Soviet Communist and professed atheist, was baptized in the Orthodox cathedral of T'bilisi. At the same time, many other Georgians were returning to their ancient faith.

Georgian Orthodox Church. (*Above*) Sveti-Tshoveli Church, Metekhi, Tiflis. *Top.* At a Muslim conference on 'Islam and Modern Life', invited guest Christian archbishop Kalistrat of Kutaisi & Gainat talks with Muslim participants.

The Armenian Orthodox Church has been present in Georgia since ancient times, and included more than 340,000 affiliated in 1995, nearly all ethnic Armenians. Other Orthodox churches with a substantial presence include the Russian, Ukrainian, and Assyrian churches.

Georgian Orthodox Church, Catholicate of Mtskheta. Ilya II, catholicos from 1977.

CATHOLIC CHURCH. The Holy See has diplomatic relations with Georgia and in AD 2000 is represented to government and the Catholic hierarchy by a nuncio residing in Tiflis. Catholicism was suppressed in 1917 but finally revived in 1990. It is now part of the Caucasus jurisdiction, with 30 parishes.

OTHER CHURCHES. Franciscan missionaries began work among the remaining pagans of Georgia about 1230, and the Dominicans entered soon after. The church never grew very large, and in the early 16th century Catholic missions ended. In 1920 it was estimated that there were 32,000 Latin-rite Catholics in Georgia and 8,000 Armenian-rite. Due to persecution and emigration, this population diminished to 12,000 in 1970, recovering to about 50,000 by 1995.

Baptist presence in Georgia began in 1872, and they remain the largest Protestant church. Baptists complained in 1992 that they were not allowed to obtain property or publish literature, and that, due to the influence of hostile Orthodox priests, they were threatened with attack. The patriarch spoke against Protestant proselytization, but also affirmed Georgia's long history of religious toleration.

Indigenous missions. Georgian Orthodox missionaries are beginning to be sent to surrounding countries, though often to minister only in Georgian ethnic enclaves.

CHURCH AND STATE

This ancient nation in 1921 became the Georgian Soviet Socialist Republic. When in the following year it joined the USSR, it exposed itself to the typical elements of Soviet oppression, persecution, restriction,

Country summary. **Worlds A, B, C by ethnolinguistic peoples, cities, and major civil divisions in Georgia.**

	PEOPLES							CITIES							CIVIL DIVISIONS						
World	*Num*	*Pop 2000*	*C%*	*Christians*	*E%*	*U%*	*Unevangelized*	*Num*	*Pop 2000*	*C%*	*Christians*	*E%*	*U%*	*Unevangelized*	*Num*	*Pop 2000*	*C%*	*Christians*	*E%*	*U%*	*Unevangelized*
A	17	824,901	0.66	5,405	33	67	549,851	0	0	0.00	0	0	0	0	0	0	0.00	0	0	0	0
B	3	554,634	51.27	284,380	99	1	7,036	7	2,072,357	56.02	1,160,988	87	13	266,421	4	719,024	59.02	424,344	87	13	93,029
C	15	3,588,026	75.78	2,719,026	100	0	8,919	0	0	0.00	0	0	0	0	9	4,248,538	60.83	2,584,470	89	11	472,778
Total	**35**	**4,967,561**	**60.57**	**3,008,811**	**89**	**11**	**565,806**	**7**	**2,072,357**	**56.02**	**1,160,988**	**87**	**13**	**266,421**	**13**	**4,967,562**	**60.57**	**3,008,814**	**89**	**11**	**565,807**

and condemnation of religion. The years of Stalin's rule (1928-53), a Georgian himself, were particularly severe and bloody. In the 1970s a religious revival amongst the younger generation of Georgians, with packed churches at Eastertide, provoked a major Soviet government attack on the church and a massive attempt to subvert and discredit the hierarchy, infiltrate its leadership with KGB agents, and stimulate substantial ecclesiastical corruption implicating the patriarch David V and another bishop. With Georgia's declaration of sovereignty in 1989 and independence in 1991, a new era of freedom, even encouragement of religion began. The short-lived regime of Gamsakhurdia, in line with its fierce nationalism, favored the Georgian Orthodox Church. The government and the Orthodox Church together launched a tough media campaign against non-Orthodox Christians. Since that time the government has acted in a more fair manner, but the Catholic Church has not succeeded in recovering churches lost earlier, and non-Orthodox have suffered from opposition sometimes backed by local officials.

BROADCASTING AND MEDIA

Shortwave programs from HCJB (Ecuador), TWR (Monaco, Albania) and AWR (Slovakia) can be easily received. HCJB launched its first gospel broadcasts in the Georgian language in February 1991 after translating the English program *Words of Hope* into the language at a portable studio installed in Georgia the previous year. HCJB is planting a local radio ministry in Georgia in partnership with Union Baptist.

Some 1.9 million watched the 'Jesus' Film on television, and 240,000 have seen it in cinematic showings. Satellite TV programs are received mainly in Arabic.

Baptist Union of Georgia. Congregations in Tiflis are large and vibrant.

FUTURE TRENDS AND PROSPECTS

In the post-Communist era, the Christian community is expected to grow to 67% by AD 2025 (from only 29% in 1970). Muslims are also expected to grow from 18% in 1970 to over 19% by 2025.

Christianity could grow beyond 70% soon after. Islam is likely to remain under 20%. The nonreligious and atheists plausibly will decline to 5% and 1% respectively by AD 2050.

BIBLIOGRAPHY

A short history of the Georgian church. S. C. Malan (ed.). Trans., P. Ioseliani. London: Saunders, Otley, 1866. 227p.

'Georgien und der christliche Orient,' C. D. G. Müller, *Ostkirchlichen studien*, 35, 2-3 (1986), 168–75.

'L'autocéphalie de l'Eglise de Géorgie,' B. Dupuy, *Istina*, 35 (July–September 1990), 277–87.

Le Système religieux de la Géorgie païenne analyse structurale d'une civilisation. G. Charachidzé. Paris: F. Maspero, 1968. 739p.

'Notes sur l'hagiographie et l'hymnographie géorgiennes,' E. Mélia, in *Liturgie de l'église particulière et liturgie de l'eglise universelle: conférences Saint-Serge, XXIIe semaine d'études liturgiques, Paris, 30 juin-3 juillet 1975*, p.231–44. A. Pistoia (ed). Rome: Edizioni liturgiche, 1976.

'Religion and nationalism in Soviet Georgia and Armenia,' S. F. Jones, in *Religion and nationalism in Soviet and East European politics*, p.171–195. P. Ramet (ed). 2nd ed. Durham, NC: Duke University Press, 1989.

Seeking God: the recovery of religious identity in Orthodox Russia, Ukraine, and Georgia. S. K. Batalden (ed). DeKalb, IL: Northern Illinois University Press, 1993. 299p.

'The Georgian Orthodox Church,' E. Mélia, in *Aspects of religion in the Soviet Union, 1917-1967*, p.223–37. R. H. Marshall (ed). Chicago: University of Chicago Press, 1971.

The origins of Caucasian civilization: the Christian component. R. W. Thomson. Washington, DC: The Wilson Center, Kennan Institute for Advanced Russian Studies, [1980]. 28p.

Country Table 2. **Organized churches and denominations in Georgia.**

Official name (bold type = church *with over 10% of all affiliated)* 1	*Begun* 2	*Type* 3	*Counc* 4	*Congs* 5	*Adults* 6	*Affiliated 1970* 7	*Affiliated 1995* 8	*G%* 9	*Names, notes, and other statistics* (see Codebook, Part 3) 10
Ancient Ch of the East (P Tehran)	c 500	O-Nes	YW...	4	3,000	500	5,000	9.65	*Assyrian Apostolic Ch of the East.* Eastern-Syriac-speaking Assyrians.
Armenian Apostolic Church	c 500	O-Arm	E....	50	238,000	50,000	340,000	7.97	*Gregorians.*
Baptist Union of Georgia	1872	P-Bap	T....	28	12,200	8,000	16,000	2.81	Formerly in AUCECB. M=CSI-IMB.
Catholic Church (AA Caucasus)	c1920	R-Lat	B....	30	22,100	3,000	50,020	11.91	Suppressed 1917-1990. 53% Latin-rite, 47% Oriental-rite, including 5,000 Ukrainians.
Evangelical Lutheran Ch of Georgia	c1960	P-Lut	.....	2	1,000	2,000	2,000	0.00	Ethnic Germans, Estonians (ELCE).
Georgian Orthodox Ch: C Mtskheta	c150	O-Geo	MW..u	500	1,100,000	1,200,000	2,500,000	2.98	*Catholicate of Mtskheta & Tiflis.* 15 Dioceses, 26 bishops.
Independent Pentecostal Churches	c1980	I-3pW	.....	30	2,500	–	5,000	6.67	Independent pentecostals with large crowds.
Jehovah's Witnesses	c1950	m-Jeh	x....	10	150	100	500	6.65	Small despite aggressive evangelism for decades.
Old Ritualist Churches	c1900	I-OBe	x....	5	2,000	1,000	5,000	6.65	*Old Believers.* Byelorussians, Russians.
Pentecostal Church of Georgia	c1975	I-3pW	.....	2	950	–	1,250	5.00	Indigenous body, run by Georgians.
Russian Orthodox Church	c1700	O-Rus	.....	200	112,000	50,000	160,000	4.76	Russians, Byelorussians.
Salvation Army in Georgia	1990	P-Sal	x....	5	1,000	–	2,000	20.00	Based in London (UK). Full range of social and evangelistic ministries.
Seventh-day Adventist Church	c1970	P-Adv	x....	1	100	–	170	22.81	*SDA.* Support from Europe and USA.
Syrian Orthodox Church		O-Syr	D....	50	3,360	4,000	5,600	0.05	Under Patriarchate of Damascus/Antioch.
Ukrainian Orthodox Church	c1850	I-Ukr	MWC.u	20	15,000	2,000	25,000	10.63	Ukrainian Orthodox rejecting ROC (P Moscow) and Russian control.
Other Orthodox churches	c1985	O-	M....	10	500	–	1,000	10.00	Total 10 including Bulgarian Orthodox Ch, Moldavian Orthodox Ch, et alia.
Other pentecostal/charismatic chs	c1980	I-3pW	.....	5	250	–	625	6.67	Including New Apostolic Church.
Totals				**952**	**1,514,110**	**1,320,600**	**3,119,165**		

Churches, members, growth, 1900-2025	*Congs*	*Adults*	*Affiliated*	*G%*	*Total denominations*	*6 Megablocs:* O	*R*	*A*	*P*	*I*	*m*
Total churches, members, and denominations (mid-1900)	70	818,000	1,895,000	-0.51	8	5	0	0	1	2	0
Total churches, members, and denominations (mid-1970)	139	570,150	1,320,600	-0.51	11	5	1	0	2	2	1
Total churches, members, and denominations (mid-1990)	450	1,474,000	3,036,900	4.25	28	14	1	0	3	9	1
Total churches, members, and denominations (mid-1995)	952	1,514,110	3,119,165	0.54	31	15	1	0	4	10	1
Total churches, members, and denominations (mid-2000)	990	1,461,000	3,008,814	-0.72	31	15	1	0	4	10	1
Total churches, members, and denominations (mid-2025)	1,200	1,650,000	3,400,000	0.49	52	20	1	0	10	20	1

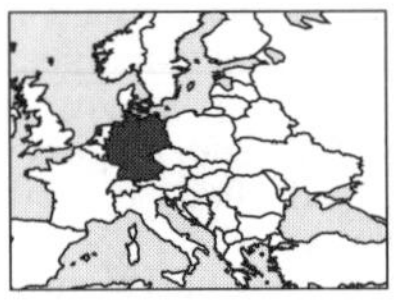

GERMANY

SECULAR DATA, AD 2000

STATE

Official name: Die Bundesrepublik Deutschland (The Federal Republic of Germany).
Short name: Germany. **Adjective of nationality:** German.
Flag: Black, red, and yellow stripes.
Area: 356,974 sq. km. (137,828 sq. mi.).
Government: Federal multiparty republic with two legislative houses, since 1990 (1871 unified constitutional empire, 1919 Weimar republic, 1933 Nazi dictatorship, 1948 West, federal republic, 1949, East, one party Communist rule).
Legislature: Federal Council, 68 members; Federal Diet, 672 members.
Official language: German.
Monetary unit: 1 Deutsche Mark (DM) = 100 Pfennige. **US$1=** DM 1.67.
Chief cities: Rhein-Ruhr (Ruhrgebiet) 6,559,000; Essen 6,559,000; Frankfurt am Main 3,700,000; Berlin 3,337,000; Dusseldorf 3,251,000.
Political divisions: 16 provinces.
Armed forces: 367,000.

DEMOGRAPHY

Population: 82,220,000.
Population density: 230.3/sq. km. (596.5/sq. mi.).
Under 15 years: 12,752,000.
Growth rate p.a.: 0.04% (births 8.42, deaths 10.98).
Mortality: Infant, per 1,000: 4.9; **Maternal per 100,000:** 22.0.
Life expectancy: 78 (male 75, female 81).
Household size: 2.3. **Floor area per person, sq.m:** 36.2.

Major languages: German, Russian, Sorabian, German, Turkish, Serbo-Croatian, Italian, Greek, Spanish, English, Arabic, French, Frisian, Danish.
Urban dwellers: 87.54%. **Urban growth rate p.a.:** 0.2%.
Labor force: 50%.

ETHNOLINGUISTIC PEOPLES
68.9% German (High German); 11.3% Low German (Saxon); 6.0% Franconian; 2.7% Turk; 1.0% Italian.

ECONOMY
National income p.a. per person: US$27,510; **per family:** US$63,273.

EDUCATION
Adult literacy: 100% (male 100%, female 100%). **Schools:** 18,867. **Universities:** 314. **School enrolment:** female/male: 99%/100%.

HEALTH
Access to health services: 95%. **Access to safe water:** 100%. **Hospitals:** 2,381 (80 beds per 10,000). **Doctors:** 259,981. **Blind:** 15,000. **Deaf:** 4,961,300. **Murder rate:** 4. **Lepers:** 1,000.

LITERATURE
New book titles p.a.: 72,350 (880 p.a. per million). **Periodicals:** 10,963. **Newspapers:** 411 dailies.

COMMUNICATION (per 1,000 people)
Phones: 494 (23% mobile). **Radios:** 1,875. **TV sets:** 550. **Daily newspaper circulation:** 317. **Computers:** 361.

REFUGEES
Alien refugees from other countries: 442,700.

HUMAN LIFE AND LIBERTY (optimum condition=100.0%)
HDI: 92.4. **HSI:** 94.0. **HFI:** 87.5. **EFL:** 58.0.

Country Table 1. **Religious adherents in Germany, AD 1900-2025.**

Year	*1900*		*1970*		*mid-1990*		*Annual change, 1990-2000*				*mid-1995*		*mid-2000*		*mid-2025*	
Name	*Adherents*	*%*	*Adherents*	*%*	*Adherents*	*%*	*Natural*	*Conversion*	*Total*	*Rate*	*Adherents*	*%*	*Adherents*	*%*	*Adherents*	*%*
Christians	**41,533,000**	**98.6**	**69,666,107**	**89.7**	**61,157,600**	**77.1**	**220,053**	**-103,197**	**116,856**	**0.19**	**62,317,000**	**76.3**	**62,326,161**	**75.8**	**59,150,000**	**73.7**
PROFESSION																
crypto-Christians	0	0.0	1,799,907	2.3	0	0.0	0	0	0	0.00	0	0.0	0	0.0	0	0.0
professing Christians	**41,533,000**	**98.6**	**67,866,200**	**87.3**	**61,157,600**	**77.1**	**220,053**	**-103,197**	**116,856**	**0.19**	**62,317,000**	**76.3**	**62,326,161**	**75.8**	**59,150,000**	**73.7**
AFFILIATION																
unaffiliated Christians	740,000	1.8	5,410,665	7.0	3,547,600	4.5	12,762	-13,228	-466	-0.01	3,577,000	4.4	3,542,939	4.3	3,200,000	4.0
affiliated Christians	**40,793,000**	**96.8**	**64,255,442**	**82.7**	**57,610,000**	**72.6**	**207,292**	**-89,970**	**117,322**	**0.20**	**58,740,000**	**71.9**	**58,783,222**	**71.5**	**55,950,000**	**69.7**
Protestants	25,734,000	61.1	34,467,110	44.4	30,440,000	38.4	109,502	-111,502	-2,000	-0.01	30,393,186	37.2	30,420,000	37.0	29,500,000	36.8
Roman Catholics	15,050,000	35.7	27,956,540	36.0	28,200,000	35.5	101,444	-51,444	50,000	0.18	28,478,332	34.9	28,700,000	34.9	27,800,000	34.7
Independents	0	0.0	850,692	1.1	730,000	0.9	2,626	-2,826	-200	-0.03	763,221	0.9	728,000	0.9	700,000	0.9
Orthodox	4,000	0.0	565,300	0.7	645,000	0.8	2,320	1,180	3,500	0.53	662,700	0.8	680,000	0.8	750,000	0.9
Marginal Christians	4,000	0.0	395,800	0.5	500,000	0.6	1,799	2,201	4,000	0.77	525,390	0.6	540,000	0.7	620,000	0.8
Anglicans	1,000	0.0	20,000	0.0	25,000	0.0	90	110	200	0.77	26,000	0.0	27,000	0.0	27,500	0.0
doubly-affiliated	0	0.0	0	0.0	-2,930,000	-3.7	-10,540	72,362	61,822	-2.34	-2,108,829	-2.6	-2,311,778	-2.8	-3,447,500	-4.3
Trans-megabloc groupings																
Evangelicals	3,864,000	9.2	2,331,000	3.0	1,428,000	1.8	5,137	-15,637	-10,500	-0.76	1,369,243	1.7	1,323,000	1.6	1,150,000	1.4
Pentecostals/Charismatics	20,000	0.0	800,000	1.0	2,380,000	3.0	8,562	13,438	22,000	0.89	2,505,799	3.1	2,600,000	3.2	3,235,000	4.0
Great Commission Christians	**3,792,000**	**9.0**	**11,656,000**	**15.0**	**24,600,000**	**31.0**	**88,494**	**66,157**	**154,651**	**0.61**	**25,800,000**	**31.6**	**26,146,513**	**31.8**	**27,280,000**	**34.0**
Nonreligious	80,000	0.2	5,551,693	7.1	13,360,000	16.8	48,060	29,053	77,113	0.56	14,000,000	17.1	14,131,127	17.2	14,151,200	17.6
Muslims	0	0.0	450,000	0.6	2,850,000	3.6	10,252	70,085	80,337	2.51	3,257,300	4.0	3,653,365	4.4	4,950,000	6.2
Atheists	40,000	0.1	1,927,900	2.5	1,750,000	2.2	6,295	-1,949	4,346	0.25	1,790,000	2.2	1,793,457	2.2	1,500,000	1.9
Jews	480,000	1.1	32,900	0.0	47,000	0.1	169	4,733	4,902	7.41	80,000	0.1	96,017	0.1	150,000	0.2
Buddhists	0	0.0	5,000	0.0	75,000	0.1	270	691	961	1.21	83,000	0.1	84,605	0.1	130,000	0.2
Hindus	0	0.0	0	0.0	45,000	0.1	162	454	616	1.29	50,000	0.1	51,159	0.1	85,000	0.1
New-Religionists	0	0.0	0	0.0	17,500	0.0	63	74	137	0.76	18,500	0.0	18,870	0.0	30,000	0.0
Baha'is	0	0.0	9,400	0.0	12,000	0.0	43	-4	39	0.32	12,300	0.0	12,391	0.0	20,000	0.0
Chinese folk-religionists	0	0.0	0	0.0	5,000	0.0	18	5	23	0.45	5,150	0.0	5,229	0.0	8,000	0.0
Sikhs	0	0.0	0	0.0	3,000	0.0	11	18	29	0.92	3,200	0.0	3,289	0.0	5,300	0.0
Ethnoreligionists	0	0.0	0	0.0	3,000	0.0	11	1	12	0.41	3,100	0.0	3,124	0.0	4,500	0.0
Confucianists	0	0.0	0	0.0	1,900	0.0	7	6	13	0.67	1,950	0.0	2,031	0.0	4,000	0.0
Other religionists	5,000	0.0	66,000	0.1	38,000	0.1	137	30	167	0.43	39,500	0.1	39,665	0.1	50,000	0.1
World A (unevangelized persons)	126,414	0.3	3,108,352	4.0	2,222,220	2.8	7,993	-35,901	-27,908	-1.33	2,204,846	2.7	1,973,280	2.4	2,246,664	2.8
World B (evangelized non-Christians)	478,586	1.1	4,934,341	6.3	15,985,180	20.1	57,505	139,098	196,603	1.15	17,139,118	21.0	17,920,559	21.8	18,841,336	23.5
World C (Christians)	41,533,000	98.6	69,666,107	89.7	61,157,600	77.1	220,053	-103,197	116,856	0.19	62,317,000	76.3	62,326,161	75.8	59,150,000	73.7
Country's population	**42,138,000**	**100.0**	**77,708,800**	**100.0**	**79,365,000**	**100.0**	**285,551**	**0**	**285,551**	**0.35**	**81,660,965**	**100.0**	**82,220,000**	**100.0**	**80,238,000**	**100.0**

COLUMNS, ROWS.
For meanings and definitions, see Codebook (Part 3). Note that, by definition, total 'Christians' = professing + crypto-Christians, which also = affiliated + unaffiliated Christians, and also = Great Commission Christians + latent Christians. Percentages may not always total exactly, due to rounding.

CENSUSES.
(a) *Undivided German empire in 1900:* 62.5% Protestants, 36.1% Roman Catholics, 1.0% Jews, 0.4% other Christians. (b) *Area covered by FRG (BRD) in 1970.* **1871:** 51.1% Protestants, 47.5% Roman Catholics. **1890:** 51.7% Protestants, 46.9% Roman Catholics. **1910:** 51.4% Protestants, 46.9% Roman Catholics. **1925:** 50.8% Protestants, 46.6% Roman Catholics. **1933:** 50.0% Protestants, 46.4% Roman Catholics. **1939:** 48.6% Protestants, 46.4% Roman Catholics. (c) *Federal Republic of Germany* (1970 territory, including West Berlin). **29.X.1946** (including 931,971 refugees, internees, prisoners of war): 49.7% Protestants, 45.9% Roman Catholics, 3.0% nonreligious, 1.1% other religionists, 0.3% Jews. **13.IX.1950** (de jure): 51.2% Protestants (50.2% Ev Ch of Germany), 45.4% Roman Catholics, 3.2% nonreligious, 0.1% Orthodox, 0.1% Catholics (non-Roman). **6.VI.1961** (de jure): 52.3% Protestants (50.8% Ev Ch of Germany), 44.4% Roman Catholics, 3.0% nonreligious, 0.1% Orthodox, 0.1% other religionists (Muslims, Jews, Buddhists, Hindus). **27.V.1970:** 48.5% Protestants (47.0% Ev Ch of Germany), 44.6% Roman Catholics, 3.9% nonreligious and atheists, 1.0% Orthodox, 0.7% other Christians, 0.7% Muslims, 0.5% marginal Protestants, 0.1% Jews. (b) *GDR* (1970 territory). **29.X.1946** (de jure, including 133,327 refugees, internees, prisoners of war): 82.2% Protestants, 12.2% Roman Catholics, 5.5% nonreligious, 0.1% other religionists. **31.VIII.1950** (de jure): 82.1% Protestants, 11.1% Roman Catholics, 6.8% nonreligious. **31.XII.1964:** 68.0% Christians (59.4% Protestants, 8.1% Roman Catholics), 31.9% nonreligious and atheists.

NOTES ON RELIGIONS
ATHEISTS. Deutsche Kommunistische Partei, DKP (formerly KPD, banned 1956; split on Sino-Soviet dispute) and rival factions: membership (1930: all Germany) 124,000, Communist voters (election of 1949) 1,362,000 (5.75% of all votes), (19.XI.1972) 113,891 (0.3% of all votes). West Berlin: Sozialistische Einheitspartei Westberlins (SEW) (legal; pro-Soviet) and Socialist Unity Party (pro-Soviet).
BAHA'IS. Entered before 1921. Recent growth from 31 local spiritual assemblies (1964) to 59 (1973), with 392 other isolated centers or groups, and to 106 LSAs (1996). One of the 7 Baha'i temples in the world is at Langenhain/Hofheim, Frankfurt.
BUDDHISTS. Mostly Theraveda, from the intellectual classes in Germany, served by the German Buddhist Union (1958); also about 1,500 Chinese.
DOUBLY-AFFILIATED. This term describes Free Church members, Jehovah's Witnesses, New Apostolic Church members, aliens (including refugees and members of USA and UK military chaplaincies) and members of other churches who are also enumerated as affiliated by either the EKD or the Catholic Church.
EVANGELICALS. The English term as used here is equivalent to Conservative Evangelicals (in German, Evangelikale, as distinct from Evangelische which is usually translated as 'Protestant'), and refers to (1) all persons affiliated to Protestant denominations which are Conservative Evangelical in theology and emphasis, and (2) individual Evangelicals within the non-Evangelical or conciliar Protestant churches affiliated to the Ecumenical Movement.
INDEPENDENTS. In over 60 denominations in 1995 (see Table 2), with several others entering or attempting to enter.
JEWS. 564,000 (1.4% of population) in 1925, declining to 27,000 by 1945 due to Nazi pogroms.
MUSLIMS. The total increased very rapidly from 1970 to 1995 due to massive labor immigration. In 1995 Muslims had risen to over 3 million composed of 2.1 million laborers from Turkey (including 500,000 Kurds), 285,000 Bosnians, 46,000 Moroccan Arabs, 80,000 Black Africans, and 98,000 Persians. *Hajj pilgrims to Mecca.* (1976) 7.
ORTHODOX. The large natural increase around and after 1970 was due to heavy immigration of Greek and Serbian Orthodox foreign workers.
OTHER RELIGIONISTS. There is a large variety of followers or smaller bodies, including Theosophists and Rosicrucians (19 AMORC Lodges and centers). Although the number of committed occultists is only a few thousand, it is estimated that 3 million West Germans subscribe to some form of the occult, and perhaps 7 million more sympathize with the occult sciences. There are also many Freemasons, members of a worldwide quasi-religious secret brotherhood, some of whom practice it as a non-Christian religion although in Germany most are either Protestants or nonreligious.
PENTECOSTALS/CHARISMATICS. Long-standing hostility against Pentecostalism has resulted in the slow growth of all 3 waves of the Renewal. The Catholic Charismatic Renewal, begun in 1972, has 1,000 regular weekly prayer groups with 8,000 weekly adult attenders, 123 priests, 6 bishops, and 10 covenant communities. The Catholic Church in Germany has over 1,100,000 charismatics.

Great Commission Instrument Panel: status of Germany (for explanation see start of Part 4)

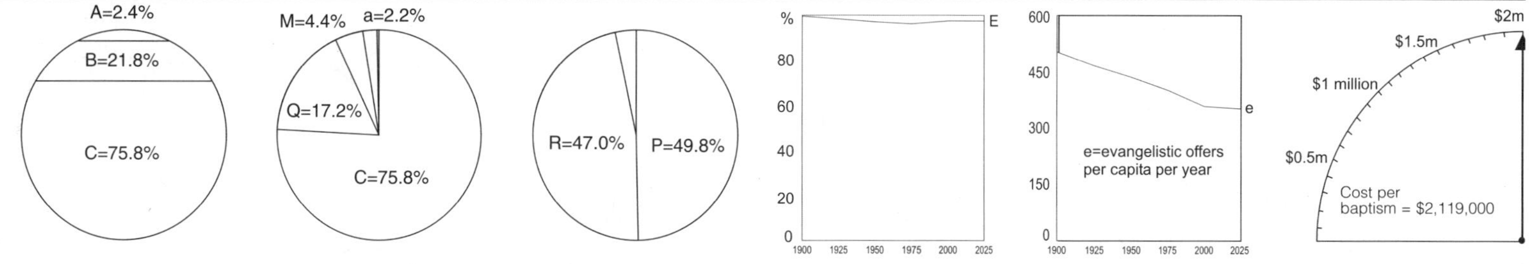

3 Worlds, AD 2000 — Religions, AD 2000 — Ecclesiastical blocs — Evangelization, 1900-2025 — Offers, 1900-2025 — Cost-effectiveness, AD 2000

Country status. The Republic of Germany was reunited in 1990 after being divided since the end of World War II, thus enhancing its large and central position in Europe geographically, politically, and economically. It is a major exporter of chemicals, motor vehicles, and other manufactured goods.

HUMAN LIFE AND LIBERTY

Human need and development. Germany is a highly developed nation where the material needs of its citizens are almost fully met. Yet, the reunification of the country has not yet been economically consummated, although it is a political reality. Parts of the former East German Republic still show scars of the 45 years of Communist misrule. Eastern Germans have a lower standard of living than Western Germans because of lower industrial development and a crumbling infrastructure. The disparity, however, may not last beyond the end of the century. The

Country summary. **Worlds A, B, C by ethnolinguistic peoples, cities, and major civil divisions in Germany.**																					
	PEOPLES							*CITIES*							*CIVIL DIVISIONS*						
World	*Num*	*Pop 2000*	*C%*	*Christians*	*E%*	*U%*	*Unevangelized*	*Num*	*Pop 2000*	*C%*	*Christians*	*E%*	*U%*	*Unevangelized*	*Num*	*Pop 2000*	*C%*	*Christians*	*E%*	*U%*	*Unevangelized*
A	4	632,867	0.20	1,247	39	61	388,039	0	0	0.00	0	0	0	0	0	0	0.00	0	0	0	0
B	24	3,527,430	5.65	199,373	62	38	1,353,236	3	1,880,582	55.00	1,034,320	94	6	110,476	0	0	0.00	0	0	0	0
C	51	78,060,187	75.05	58,582,603	100	0	201,646	145	50,459,954	70.38	35,514,002	97	3	1,321,452	16	82,220,488	71.49	58,783,223	98	2	1,942,920
Total	**79**	**82,220,484**	**71.49**	**58,783,223**	**98**	**2**	**1,942,921**	**148**	**52,340,536**	**69.83**	**36,548,322**	**97**	**3**	**1,431,928**	**16**	**82,220,488**	**71.49**	**58,783,223**	**98**	**2**	**1,942,920**

other developmental anomaly is the position of the large immigrant population, estimated at 10% and growing. Many of these immigrants live in substandard homes in ghettoized sectors and have lower incomes.

Human rights and freedoms. After many decades of an unblemished human rights record, Germany was faced in the early 1990s with serious threats to the constitutional guarantees of protection against racial and ethnic intolerance. In 1990 alone there were over 2,000 incidents of violence directed against non-European foreigners, particularly Turks. Arson attacks accounted for almost one-third of the crimes. Individual foreigners, including diplomats, suffered verbal and physical abuse. Jewish cemeteries and memorials also were increasingly the targets of vandalism. Most of these attacks were perpetrated by rightwing extremists, known as skinheads, and a small core of neo-Nazis. Discrimination against Gypsies increased in 1992. On the positive side, terrorism by the Red Army faction, which had troubled the country for many decades, ceased in 1992. Pro-human rights groups, including many associated with Protestant and Catholic churches, took to the streets in a series of demonstrations against right-wing violence. These demonstrations, along with a firm official response, have helped to curb the spread of racist violence.

Human environment. Under the Communist regime, East Germany was not subject to the kind of environmental regulations that were in force in West Germany and as a result is environmentally backward. On a per capita basis, emissions of sulfur dioxide are 15 times greater in the eastern region than in the west. Similarly East German rivers need to be cleaned up from the toxic wastes and raw sewage that were allowed to be dumped in them for many decades. The Baltic Sea into which these rivers flowed is also heavily polluted. Forests have been significantly damaged from pollution in both regions.

NON-CHRISTIAN RELIGIONS

Islam has in recent years become significant in Germany. According to the Federal Office of Statistics in Wiesbaden and the Federal Bureau for Work in Nuremberg, there were resident in the FRG and West Berlin in 1973 about 1.2 million Muslims (1,189,000 Sunnis, 10,000 Shias, 990 Ahmadis). These included diplomats from 29 Muslim states (a few hundred persons), merchants mostly Shia Iranians in Hamburg and Frankfurt (10,000), students (8,000), trainees (6,000), Germans converted to Islam (300), and workers in various industrial centers (Berlin, the Ruhr, Cologne, Bielefeld, Hannover, Frankfurt, Stuttgart, Munich) from Turkey (1 million), Yugoslavia (65,000), Morocco (15,000), Tunisia (11,000), and other countries (12,000). To these figures must be added a fluctuating but important number of illegal immigrants (between 75,000 and 250,000), as well as 3,500 Muslims from Turkestan and the Soviet Caucasus who took refuge around Munich and Bamberg after World War II. By 1995 the number of Muslims in reunited Germany was more than 3 million, growing from 0.6% of the national population to 4.0%. Most of this growth came from legal and illegal immigration. The Muslim population of East Germany was very small.

In addition to meeting places and other facilities made available to Muslims by Christian institutions, factories, railways and universities (Munster, Cologne, Bonn, Gressen, Heidelberg (Union of Islamic Students), Stuttgart (Association of Islamic Students) and Munich, Sunnis have maintained the following mosques and centers: an Islamic center and mosque at Aix-la-Chapelle (Aachen); mosques for workers at Allendorf, Hamm and Bielefeld; a mosque and center belonging to the Muslim Community of South Germany in Munich; small communities of converted Germans at Bremen, Hamburg, Mannheim and Berlin, the latter having close relations with the Pakistani Ahmadiya community which built a mosque in Berlin as early as 1926. Ahmadis are also found in Hamburg, Frankfurt, Hannover, and Nuremberg. In addition Shias have a mosque and center in Hamburg. In the 1980s and 1990s, mistreatment of non-German minorities, usually Muslims, has arisen as a significant national social problem. These actions have many times crossed the line to violence and even killing. This has been perpetrated by a small criminal minority, mostly young people, and has persisted despite police and government efforts to protect people of all races and faiths.

Judaism continues to decrease in numbers and significance. In 1925, the Jewish population of Germany was 564,379. Between 1933 and 1939 some 295,000 Jews emigrated. Of those remaining 30,000 died natural deaths, 25,000 escaped during World War II (mostly through Russia and Japan or through Portugal) and 160,000 were murdered in Nazi concentration camps. At the end of the war, 8,000 Jews returned from exile to join 19,000 who had survived illegally through marriage to non-Jews. In addition, a few thousand displaced persons, while in transit across the FRG after the war, decided to remain there. At the beginning of the 1960s, some 6,000 more German Jews returned and 2,000 others took up residence in Germany, making a total Jewish population of about 40,000 (30,000 affiliated to communities and 10,000 others). However their numbers have decreased since then because of the unfavorable age pyramid, deaths exceeding both births and new immigrants. At the end of 1973, Jewish members of communities numbered only 26,906. Most of these communities were small, with no more than 100 to 200 members. Only 6 had more than 1,000 members: West Berlin (5,277 in 1973 as contrasted with 5,965 in 1966), Frankfurt (4,168 in 1966), Munich (3,345 in 1966), Dusseldorf (1,579 in 1966), Hamburg (1,500 in 1966), and Cologne (1,304 in 1966). The future of Judaism in Germany is linked to the more important communities. In spite of these unfavorable circumstances, Jewish life in Germany has undergone a certain development. The federal law of 1965 concerning damaged property made possible the restoration of many synagogues. Moreover, a Jewish school was reopened in Frankfurt and an academy in Heidelberg. In East Germany before reunification, the state subsidized for the most part the financial expenses as well as all costs involved in the construction, reconstruction and upkeep of the 9 synagogues and Jewish cemeteries in the country. Between 1970 and 1995 the Jewish community in all of Germany grew from nearly 33,000 to almost 80,000, thanks both to natural increase and immigration.

Non-religion. The number of atheists in Germany has shown a slight decline since the fall of Communism in the east, but the number of nonreligious continues to grow at a fairly rapid pace. Atheists and nonreligious together constituted 9.6% of the population in 1970, and 19.3% in 1995. These figures exclude all those who retain affiliation with a church but who are non-practicing Christians—an additional 24.3% of the national population in 1990, growing to 34.5% in 1995.

Baha'is. First Baha'i House of Worship (Temple) on European continent, and one of only 7 in the world, in Langenhain/Hofheim west of Frankfurt.

Baha'i entered before 1921, and has subsequently spread across Germany. One of the 7 Baha'i temples in the world is at Langerhain/Hofheim, Frankfurt.

CHRISTIANITY

Three Catholic episcopal sees were erected in Germany during the 3rd century, but Christianity did not become dominant until after the conversion of the Frankish king, Clovis, in 496. Scottish-Irish missionary monks, including Columba, were active during the 6th century, and Charles Martel protected the efforts of Boniface, who became archbishop without a fixed see in 722 and gave himself to the conversion of the German people. Charlemagne enforced christianization with the sword during the 9th century, arousing the enmity of Saxons; but his son Louis the Pious encouraged the peaceful means of Anskar, who carried the Christian faith to Scandinavia. Power conflicts between papacy and German emperors over the mutual responsibilities of church and state were largely resolved by the Concordat of Worms in 1122. By the end of the 12th century, Saxony, the last independent duchy, was subdued; and through the military campaigns of the Order of Teutonic Knights, Christianity was extended to the northeast. In 1415,

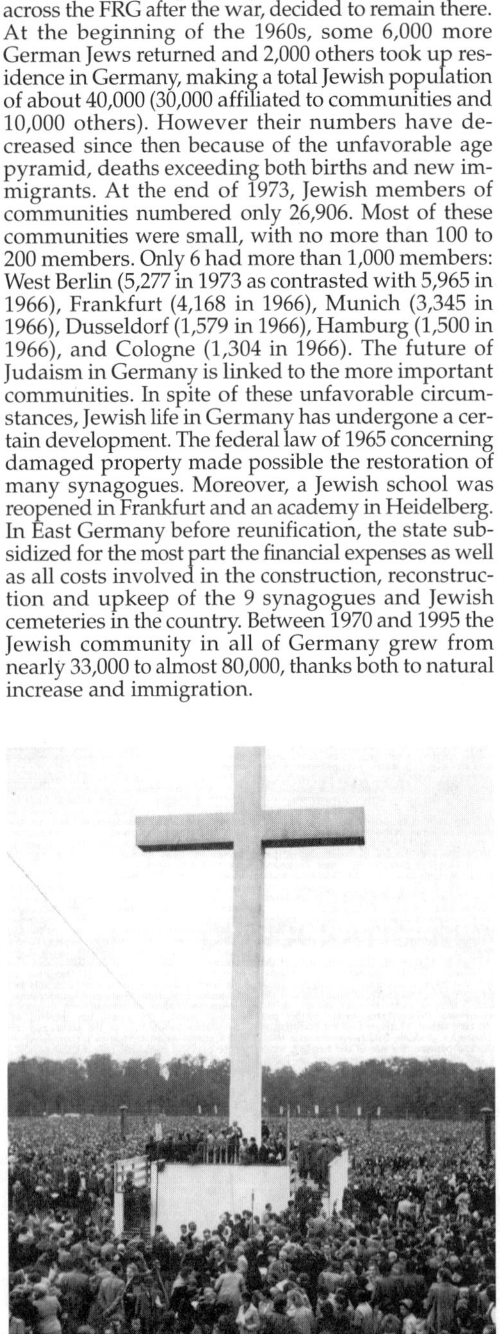

Kirchentagen (church days). Huge mass rallies every 2 years, have played a vital role in confronting; (*left*) atheism in East Germany (Leipzig 1954) and (*right*) secularism in West Germany (Frankfurt 1956); (*top*) Dusseldorf 1973.

John Huss was burned at the stake because of his critical attitude towards the abuses of the clergy; and a century later, in 1517, Martin Luther issued his 95 theses at Wittenberg, signalling the start of the Protestant Reformation. The Schmalkaldic League was formed in 1531 primarily among northern princes following the Lutheran position; and intermittent fighting took place with the emperor Charles V and Catholic princes to the south. Sparked in part by the presence of Turks at Vienna, the Peace of Augsburg of 1555 provided for agreement that the faith of a principality would be either Lutheran or Catholic as determined by its leader. The Council of Trent (1545-1563) consolidated the position of the Catholic Church and brought on the Counter-Reformation, led by Jesuits, Benedictines, and Capuchins. Another direct though delayed result was the Thirty Years' War (1618-1648) between Catholic and Protestant princes. Germany was devastated, its population being reduced from 16 to 6 million; and its commerce and intellectual life was destroyed. The Protestant cause was ultimately saved by the military genius of Gustavus Adolphus, king of Sweden. The Peace of Westphalia (1648) again accorded the princes the right to determine the religion of their subjects, with the Reformed tradition of Calvin and Zwingli also added as an accepted religion. The religious unity of the German territorial states remained largely unaltered until the time of Napoleon, when numerous small states were amalgamated into larger political units characterized by greater religious heterogeneity. Following World War I and the fall of the monarchy, the Protestant territorial churches lost their political supremacy although they continued to count as their membership a majority of the population. At the time of the Third Reich an attempt was made to create a united Protestant church under government control, but the move was unsuccessful.

Protestants. *Right.* Martin Luther *Left.* Lutherhaus in Wittenberg.

PROTESTANT CHURCHES. The population of Germany was just over 50% Protestant in 1970, dropping to 37.5% Protestant by 1995. Most of these are found in 28 territorial people's churches (Landeskirchen). All are members of the Evangelical Church in Germany (Evangelische Kirche in Deutschland, EKD) formed after World War II with the object of creating a strong Protestant church out of the confused divisions resulting from the groupings and regroupings of the preceding 400 years. This hope has not been realized, and the EKD remains much more a federation of autonomous churches than a single church.

The EKD originally included the 8 regional churches of East Germany (GDR); but under pressure from the East German regime in 1968, these churches were forced to drop their EKD affiliation. Following reunification in 1990, these 8 rejoined. In terms of tradition, of the present member churches, 14 are Lutheran: Bavaria, Braunschweig, Eutin, Hamburg, Hannover, Lübeck, Mecklenberg, Nordelbein, Oldenburg, Saxony (Ev. Luth. Ch. of Saxony), Schaumburg-Lippe, Schleswig-Holstein, Thuringia, and Württemberg; 12 are United Lutheran and Reformed: Anhalt, Baden, Berlin-Brandenburg, Bremen, Görlitz (Silesia), Pomerania, Hessen and Nassau, Saxony (Ev. Ch. of Province of Saxony), Kurhessen-Waldeck, Palatinate (Pfalz), Rhineland, and Westfalia; and 2 are Reformed: Lippe and Northwest Germany. While retaining their membership in the EKD, 5 of the 7 Lutheran territorial churches have also formed their own church federation, called the United Evangelical Lutheran Church of Germany (Vereinigte Evangelisch-Lutherischen Kirche in Deutschland, VELKD). Another federation, the Evangelical Church of the Union (Evangelische Kirche der Union, EKU), groups together 3 of the united churches (Berlin-Brandenburg, Rhineland, Westphalia). The evangelical churches of West Germany did experience the large loss in membership which characterized the situation in East Germany and a number of other Western countries, although the 10% church tax deducted automatically by the government for all registered church members has provoked an increase in the withdrawal rate since 1970. Polls in the early 1970s indicated that 27% of the total population claimed to go regularly to church (which German Protestants define as monthly attendance), while 20% said that they never attended. Baptisms and church funerals are still observed for nearly all members, while church weddings account for about 85% of all marriages.

The territorial churches of the EKD are heavily involved in development and social service. Although most schools in Germany are now under direct state control, some secondary schools sponsored by churches (Gymnasien) have been in existence since the time of the Reformation.

Medical and social service is coordinated by the Diaconal work of the Evangelical Church in Germany (Diakonisches Werk der EKD), founded in 1957, which carries on the responsibilities of Evangelical Relief (Evangelisches Hilfswerk) begun in 1945 and the Inner Mission (1948). Diakonisches Werk coordinates the activities of more than 300 medical institutions (hospitals, clinics, dispensaries) and thousands of other institutions (homes for orphans, youth, aged, alcoholics, ex-convicts, et alia). In order to provide for joint collaboration in the various activities of the churches in development aid, the Joint Committee for Church Development Service (Arbeitsgemeinschaft Kirchlicher Entwicklungsdienst, KED) was founded in 1969. Participating agencies are: (1) several church development committees and boards of the EKD (Ausschuss Kirchliche Mittel fur Entwick-lungsdienst, Kammer fur Entwicklungsdienst, Kirchliches Aussenamt, et alia); (2) Bread for the World (Brot fur die Welt), which makes appeal to both the EKD and free churches; (3) Joint Committee for Overseas Service (Arbeitsgemein-schaft Dienste in Ubersee), which has since 1960 sent 421 specialists to 34 countries, plus 129 other persons in short-term emergency programs; (4) Evangelical Joint Committee for World Mission (Evangelische Arbeitsgemeinschaft fur Weltmis-sion), which was formed in 1963 for the purpose of integrating church and mission in Germany and supports, through its annual budget of 10 million DM, ecumenical missionary ventures abroad; and (5) Protestant Central Agency for Development Aid (Evangelische Zentralstelle fur Entwicklungshilfe) which provides for health assistance projects in developing countries. Within the EKD a pietist, Evangelical movement has a substantial presence. Called the Gnadau Union, it included 340,000 Christians and over 63 agencies and institutions in the early 1990s.

Apart from the territorial churches, a number of other Lutheran and Reformed denominations are also active. The largest is the Independent Evangelical Lutheran Church which was created in 1972 by the merger of the Evangelical Lutheran Free Church with the Old Lutherans, the latter tracing their history back to 1830. There is also a separate Evangelical Lutheran Church in Baden and a small Confessional Evangelical Lutheran Church related to Missouri and Wisconsin Synod Lutherans in the USA. Several other Lutheran churches have also been established to cater to refugees from Eastern Europe, namely the Estonian, Hungarian, Latvian, and Lithuanian Evangelical Lutheran Churches in Exile. The Church of Denmark and the Church of Sweden minister to the needs of Scandinavian Lutherans living in the FRG. Two small Reformed churches serving refugees and expatriates are the Reformed Church of Hungary and the Reformed Church of the Netherlands, while the Old Reformed churches continue their work in the northwest.

Mennonites trace their history to the 16th century and Moravians to the 18th century, while several other Protestant traditions have been represented in Germany since the early part of the 19th century. The Moravian Brethren had only a small presence in East Germany before reunification, but their center at Herrnhut (founded by count Zinzendorf in 1722) continued to serve as the Moravian world headquarters. At present, the Baptists (1834) are strongest and work in cooperation with Southern Baptists from the USA. The Evangelical Methodist Church (1830) was greatly strengthened by the merger in 1968 of the former Methodist and Evangelical United Brethren churches both in the USA and Germany, and this church retains its status as a central conference affiliated to the United Methodist Church with headquarters in the USA. Since 1968, the Methodists of Germany have had their own separate central conference. Other important groups originating in the last century are the Plymouth Brethren (1847), Congregationalists (1854) and Salvation Army (1886). Other earlier groups include Seventh-day Adventists (1875), Assemblies of God (1907, and the Association of Christian Assemblies (1909); and many other small Pentecostal denominations have been formed. In 1971 a spontaneous charismatic youth movement began in the GDR independently of the Protestant churches. By 1976 it was still spreading, though still unrelated to the structures and officials of the churches. In the early 1990s hundreds of independent 3rd-wave church fellowships arose across Germany. They ranged in size from house meetings with only a handful of participants to worship services attended by thousands. These independent churches positioned themselves as an alternative to the EKD and other older denominations, and were often very critical of the established churches. They emphasized vigorous worship, biblical preaching, evangelism programs, and appeal to young people.

Charismatics. In the mainline churches there are 1.1 million Catholic and 0.8 million Protestant Charismatics.

CATHOLIC CHURCH. The situation of the Catholic Church in Germany can be explained only in terms of the profound disorders that followed World War II. The creation of the 2 states of East and West Germany brought about not only differing developments in Catholicism within each state but it also imposed political boundaries that no longer coincided with ecclesiastical jurisdictions. The vast migration of over 15,000,000 refugees following 1945 from (then) East Germany and Eastern Europe brought about 2 fundamental and permanent changes in the churches of West Germany, particularly for the Catholic Church. These include: (1) the loss of the minority character of the latter, and this for the first time since 1871 (First Reich); by 1970, 44.6% of the total population declared themselves to be Catholic; and (2) a reduced denominational homogeneity in the regions, present since the Reformation and Counter-Reformation, each having been formerly dominated by a single church. Following the influx of refugees, the Catholic proportion rapidly increased in all regions of the north. Catholicism generally declined numerically in the south and west. In 2 southern provinces, however, Catholics increased: Baden-Wurttemberg and the Saar.

Katholikentagen (Catholic Days). The 79th, held in Hanover in 1962 on theme 'Faith, Thanksgiving, Service'.

One of the consequences of the decline of denominational homogeneity in these regions was the growth of contacts between Protestants and Catholics, changing the image each community had of the other. Other factors were the diminution of internal cohesiveness within Catholicism coinciding with the end of the minority character of this church, the betterment of the economic situation of Catholics ending earlier feelings of inferiority, and the new political constellation which took place after 1945 when the 3 Western allies assigned to the Catholic and Protestant churches a definite role in the reorganization of the new Germany. One result was the establishment of the Christian Democrats (CDU/CSU), an accomplishment of both Catholics and Protestants. This party played an important role in the political development of the FRG and governed the country without interruption until 1969. Catholics formed 75% of its party membership, as well as the majority of its electorate. This link with the government party also reinforced the institutional and juridical position of the church, notably in the areas of education, family, youth, public health, social security, property, and social participation. Moreover, the revenue from ecclesiastical tax, plus government grants for public institutions operated by the church assured for the church both economic prosperity and freedom of action.

As external political threats ceased to trouble the church, internal problems became more grave. In the FRG, church membership was to a large extent taken for granted. In 1970, only 3.9% of the population belonged to no religious community, and the annual exodus of Catholics from the church, while increasing from 23,089 in 1962 to 53,772 in 1972, did not constitute a significant change. Almost all children of Catholics are baptized and most marriages are celebrated in church. Despite this large and relatively constant increase in membership, however, other factors have declined, including weekly attendance at Sunday mass, the number of secular priests, the advancing average age of priests, the number of theological students in religious orders, annual ordinations, and the number of religious brothers and sisters.

In contrast, one notes a definite increase in the number of lay theologians. Moreover, there has been a significant increase in the involvement of the laity in ecclesiastical service. This indicates clearly that what is happening is that willingness to tie oneself to the church is being called into question. Identification with the church binding one to irreversible decisions seems to receive less and less acceptance. This is underlined by the fact that 6% of all priests abandoned their ministry during the first 4 years of service. It is also within this context that one must understand the debates on divorce and remarriage. The creation of inflexible norms of behavior, linked to the requirement of obedience, seems to leave too little space for individual initiative and thus have become increasingly unacceptable. One notes rather a desire for norms permitting action more adaptable to situations and alternative behavior. Creativity and spontaneity have become in actuality central values in society, and this cannot fail to have repercussions on the church.

These changes in relations between the Catholic and Protestant churches, one evidence of which is the increasing number of mixed marriages, have resulted in sharp confrontations within the church. The post-conciliar age has seen a decrease in uniformity and a diversifying of opinions within Catholicism. Communities of work and action among priests and laity have developed which openly defend their opinions in partial opposition to the ecclesiastical hierarchy. The church has tried to recuperate structurally from this differentiation by an enlargement of its bureaucracy, always important in Germany, as well as by the revitalization of its synodal structures. This extension of bureaucratization has only been possible because of the vast revenue available from ecclesiastical taxes. On the other hand, in establishing councils at diocesan and parish levels, as well as sanctioning the Joint Synod of the dioceses of the FRG (Gemeinsame Synode, GD) during 1971-75, the hierarchy tried to overcome the contradiction emphasized by a section of the laity and minor clergy concerning the relative importance of laity and priests and their ability to influence ecclesiastical decisions. These attempts at reorganization, however, have not developed without friction. The powers of the new councils have not been clearly defined, and their relationships with other existing institutions have not been sufficiently clarified.

The interdiocesan Joint Synod was requested in the beginning by the Critical Catholicism (Kritischer Katholizismus) group at the time of the Katholikentag in Essen in 1968; it was convoked by the Episcopal Conference in 1969 and was approved the following year by the Holy See. Synod sessions were preceded by a mammoth survey of almost 21 million German Catholics 16 years of age and over. It constitutes an important event in the Catholic life of the FRG because it provided for the opening of dialogues within the body of a church which was strongly hierarchical and highly structured. For all that, it was very different from the Netherlands Pastoral Council as far as the composition of its assembly and its powers are concerned. The caution exhibited at the time of the establishment of the commissions, as well as that exercised in the choice of themes for discussion, with subjects considered too controversial being put aside, did not prevent the Synod from adopting a moderate line of openness and renewal. This was manifest by the adoption during the third session (January 1973) of a report concerning the 'participation of the laity in the homily of the mass'. The decisions taken on this occasion created serious tensions with the Congregation for the Clergy in Rome, which maintained that they were in opposition to the conclusions of the interpretative commission of Vatican II. The firm position of the German episcopate, however, made possible a softening of the Roman decision to invalidate this schema.

Beyond strictly intra-ecclesial concerns, the problems of foreign workers in Germany and also in the Third World have preoccupied the Catholic Church; and pastoral assistance to Catholics of foreign cultures, who numbered between 1.3 and 1.8 million in 1973, has been the object of considerable concern. In 1973, the third session of the Joint Synod adopted a vigorous report on the 'social and ecclesial situation of the foreign worker' which included passages strongly critical of governmental policy in the matter as well as of the attitude of German Catholics. As for the problems of the Third World, this has held the attention of the Catholic Church since the end of the 1950s. Already existing aid organizations have been enlarged, and others have been created. These are either organizations of interchurch aid or those oriented to socioeconomic development. Considerable financial resources have thus been disbursed.

In 1990, 90,000 Catholics had their names removed from membership while only 22% attended mass weekly in the areas of former West Germany.

The Holy See has diplomatic relations with Germany and in AD 2000 is represented to government and the Catholic hierarchy by a nuncio in Bonn and Berlin.

ORTHODOX CHURCHES. More than 9 Orthodox bodies are present in West Germany, the largest being Greek Orthodox who are part of the diocese of Germany and East Middle Europe under the Ecumenical Patriarchate. Russian Orthodox are divided into 2 groups, a small community under the Patriarchate of Moscow with headquarters in East Berlin, and a much larger exile body, Orthodox Church Outside of Russia, with headquarters in New York. Other communities of refugees in exile from Russian and Eastern Europe include the Armenian, Romanian, Serbian, and Ukrainian Orthodox churches.

Roman Catholics. *Left.* Cologne Cathedral. *Right.* Parish church, Bad Waldsee, packed every Sunday.

INDEPENDENT CHURCHES. A large number of bodies exist intermediate between Protestantism and Roman Catholicism. The Old Catholic Church, the result of a split from the Catholic Church following the promulgation of the dogma of papal infallibility at Vatican I, was formed in 1874. A quite different body is the Catholic Apostolic Church, which began in England in 1830 and made its first German converts in 1840. In 1863, a dispute over leadership produced a schism resulting in the creation of the New Apostolic Church, a sacramentalist and hierarchical body stressing the Catholic concepts of the unified church, ritual, liturgy and authority. It is governed by a college of 48 living apostles in a successional apostolate with at its head a Chief Apostle with quasi-papal powers regarded as the successor of the Apostle Peter and visible representative or incarnation of Christ on earth. The NAC has expanded widely outside Germany, has over a million members worldwide and maintains its world headquarters in Dortmund. Displaying an extraordinary vitality, this is now Germany's largest Christian community outside the Roman Catholic and territorial churches. A number of splits from the New Apostolic Church have taken place including the Small Apostolic Community in 1921; but there has also been an attempt to unite these schisms. In 1954, the Union of Apostolic Christians was formed in Switzerland for this purpose, and its work was extended two years later to Germany with the formation of the Apostolic Fellowship.

In addition, there are numerous independent Charismatic churches throughout the country.

MARGINAL CHURCHES. Jehovah's Witnesses first came to Germany at the end of the last century and continue to expand. Over the years, schisms from the Witnesses have produced the Kingdom of God Church and the Free Bible Congregation. The Witnesses were banned in East Germany from 1949, but still had a zealous underground following. Mormons have been on the scene since the 1840s, as have the Unitarians. Other marginal Protestant groups include Christian Science (1907), Anthroposophical society (1922), Nature Philosophy Union (1927), Evangelical Church of the Revelation for St John the Divine (1926), and Free Christian People's Church (1945).

Benedictine Abbey, Otto-beuren: founded AD 764, rebuilt 1744; 1964 postage stamp on 1,200-year anniversary.

Art and architecture. Germany is the cradle of Christian architecture in Europe and contains some of its most representative masterpieces. It ranges from the great cathedral at Koln to magnificent contemporary churches, such as St Anna at Dueren, Christ Church at Leverkusen-Buerig, St Albert at Saarbruecken, and Trinity Church at Mannheim. In between are the historic shrines that mark various stages of the evolution of German Christianity. At Fulda, in Central Germany, is the grave of the Apostle of Germany, an Englishman named St Boniface, whose monastery became the focal point for the conversion of Germans. Chronologically, the next important cathedral is at Aachen, known in French as Aix-la-Chapelle, where Charlemagne was buried and some 32 Holy Roman Emperors were crowned. The octagonal dome of the Aachen Cathedral is modeled on that of St Vitale in Ravenna. South of Aachen, where the 3 rivers, Moselle, Saar, and Ruwer meet, is the ancient Roman city of Trier which contains the Church of Our Lady and the the baroque St Paulinus' Church. North of Trier is Koln, or Cologne, whose cathedral, 500 ft high with towers that rise even higher, is one of the highest in the world. It was one of the few buildings that survived vicious Allied bombing in World War II. Also in Koln are other famous churches, among them the Basilica of St Pantaleon, the Church of St Gereon with its 10-sided nave, and the rebuilt churches of St Peter and St Cecilia. Koln also is the birthplace of St Bruno, founder of the Carthusian Order. To the south lies Bonn, whose basilica, with its 308-ft high octagonal tower, is a fine example of Rhineland Romanesque.

Coblenz is particularly rich in Romanesque churches. Near the city is the Maria Laach Monastery, founded 1,000 years ago in 1093, which has a played an important role in the development of the church. Speyer's Cathedral of St Mary and St Stephen is the largest Romanesque church in Germany. Mainz is noted as the city where St Boniface was archbishop, and its St Martin's Cathedral, begun in 975, is a remarkable example of Romanesque architecture. The Gothic Cathedral at Ulm has the tallest tower in Germany, 528 ft high. To the south, in the Black Forest is Freiburg-im-Breisgau, whose 380-ft high cathedral is set against gracious squares and picturesque valleys. The Archabbey of Beuron, midway between Freiburg and Ulm, was founded in 1077, suppressed during the Napoleonic era, but reestablished by monks from St Paul's outside-the-Walls in Rome. It is noted for its Beuron chant and Beuron art. Lake Constance, where the Sixteenth Ecumenical Council was held, is notable for the Benedictine Abbey at Reichenau Island and 3 other Romanesque churches. The Cathedral of Augsburg claims the oldest stained glass window in the world. Nearby is Wurzburg with its Cathedral of St Kilian and the 11th century church of St Burkard. Nuremburg and Regensburg are both centers of German Gothic, represented by the St.Sebald Church and the Cathedral of St Peter whose twin towers rival those of Koln. The Frauen-Kirche Cathedral at Munich, with its onion domes, offers an unusual use of brick in Gothic. There are half a dozen other baroque and rococo churches, such as St John Nepomuk. Other notable churches include Marien-Kirche in Lubeck and St Peter and St Paul in Munster. There are hundreds of religious museums including the Luther House in Eisenach, Luther's Birthplace at Eisleben, Monastery of Our Lady at Magdeburg, Monastery Church at Bayern, St Xavier Mission Church at Bad Dreiburg, Collection of Medieval Art in Cistercian Abbey at Baden-Wurttemberg, Benedictine Abbey of St Walburg, Cathedral Treasury at Eichstatt, Aachen, Fritzlar, Essen, Limburg, Freising, Sackingen, Paderborn and Salem, Cathedral Museum at Freiburg im Breisgau, Mainz, Munster, Reichenau, Trier and Wurzburg, Church Museum at Gengenbach, Nikolai Church at Kalkar, Archdiocesan Museum and Schnutgen Museum at Koln, John Hus Museum at Konstanz, St Catherine's Church at Lubeck, Lune Monastery at Lune, Benedictine Abbey at Munsterschwarzach and Niederalteich, St John's Church Treasury at Osnabruck, Icon Museum at Recklinghausen, Museum at the Old Church at Reken, Diocesan Museum at Rottenburg Am Neckar and Speyer, Bible Museum in Stuttgart, and Monastery Museum at Wienhausen.

Renewal movements. In the 1990s the Pentecostal/Charismatic Renewal continued to spread rapidly across most older churches, and numbered over 2,600,000 adherents (of whom 6% Pentecostals, 73% Charismatics, and 21% Independents).

Pentecostals. Enthusiastic response to address by mega-evangelist Reinhard Bonnke.

Indigenous missions. Germany has sent out missionaries from the very beginnings of the Christian faith there. Lutheran missionaries, though slow in getting started, made significant contributions in the 19th and 20th centuries. A new trend is the sending of missionaries directly from independent churches, most of these charismatic or third wave.

CHURCH AND STATE

The experiences of the churches in the 2 Germanies of 1945 to 1990 were different from each other. The churches in West Germany enjoyed a generous array of privileges and freedoms, while those in East Germany suffered under a sometimes repressive, anti-religious communist regime that was still, in other ways, helpful to the churches. But subtle pressures were great, the churches were closely watched, restrictions hindered, and church leadership was infiltrated by secret police. In the GDR all religious matters came under the State Secretariat for Religious Questions (Staatssekretariat für Kirchenfragen). East Germany did not, like West Germany, recognize the validity of the concordat of 1933 with the Holy See and so had no diplomatic relations with the Vatican. Though they were not recognized legally, Evangelical and Catholic churches received regular state subsidies which were used mostly for their charitable institutions. The state also provided materials for the reconstruction of old churches destroyed during the War and more rarely for the construction of new ones. The universities of Berlin, Leipzig, Halle, Jena, Rostock, and Griefswald each retained a faculty of Protestant theology. Pastoral work, liturgy and religious instruction were unobstructed, but all church activities organized outside ecclesiastical edifices required prior authorization from the local authorities. The churches of the GDR showed substantial vitality in some ways—notably the large, open-air prayer meetings and rallies, which was partly fueled by the desire to protest the restrictions of the socialist state.

Since the return of freedom, some of these manifestations of religious vigor have waned. A survey in 1992 commissioned by *Der spiegel* showed that 62% of the former East German population thought of themselves as belonging to no church, and only 17% claimed belief in Jesus Christ. Among younger East Germans, 21% of those aged 19-29 belonged to a church, and only 13% of those aged 15-17 years. This contrasts with the survey findings from West Germany, where 91% considered themselves to be church members and 61% believed in the existence of God.

The churches in East Germany fought against the restrictions placed upon them. The Catholic bishops disseminated in all their churches on 17 November 1974 a pastoral letter opposing monopolization of education by the state. Similarly, in May 1975, the synod of the Evangelical Church of Berlin-Brandenburg requested the competent authorities to terminate their 'discrimination against practicing Christian youth' in schools and professional training. It needs to be stressed that, in its totality, the Evangelical Church in the GDR was less reluctant than the Catholic Church to participate in the building of a new socialist society. For the former the situation became even clearer when, in 1969, it broke its last institutional links with the West German EKD. From 1958-78 only 10 new Protestant church buildings had been permitted, but an agreement in 1978 allowed 55 more to be built over the following 2 years. The same agreement pledged an end to discrimination against Christian children and youths, and allowed for church congresses (Kirchentagen) to convene once again. Still, the 1970s also saw the government institute a new wave of ideological repression meant to stifle dissent. A number of artists, authors, and intellectuals were imprisoned or banned, including many Christians. This hindered the churches and made it more difficult once again for them to work, proclaim, and worship. By the late 1980s, a clandestine ecological movement and an underground, independent peace movement were functioning, growing, and agitating—while enjoying sanctuary and aid from Protestant churches.

The Christian Democratic Union (Christlich Demokratische Union, CDU), which before reunification had nothing to do with the West German party of the same name (though both included Protestants and Catholics), was one of 5 legal political parties in the GDR. As with all parties in the country, it supported the socialist policy of the government. It was represented in parliament (50 delegates out of 500 in 1973, including some ecclesiastics and theologians) and in the government (one minister in 1973), but had only a secondary influence over the population because its position among the workers was very weak. Still, it played a crucial role in 1990. Following the opening of the Berlin wall, ever-larger demonstrations demanded a voice in government for the people, and the ruling socialists were forced to call free, multiparty elections. The socialists suffered a huge defeat, and the largest and leading party in the new government was the CDU, which had campaigned on a pledge of speedy reunification. Negotiations began immediately with the FRG. When reunification was ratified later the same year, churches and Christians of the east immediately enjoyed the freedoms, rights, and privileges of the more positive church-state situation in the west.

The Preamble to the Basic Law (Grundgesetz) of Germany of 8 May 1949, as amended to 1 January 1966, reads: 'The German People . . . conscious of their responsibility before God and men . . ..' The constitution then guarantees a 'free church in a free State'. While retaining effectively the freedom of religion both from an individual and the collective standpoints, allowances are made for cooperative arrangements between the state and the religious communities, especially the 2 largest, the Evangelical Church in Germany (EKD) and the Catholic Church.

In regard to constitutional law, the fundamental norms regulating the relationship between church and state in Germany are found in the Basic Law. These norms include the fundamental right to religious liberty (Article 4), the institutional guarantee concerning the teaching of religion (Article 7, paragraph 3), as well as Article 140 on the church which reproduces the principal dispositions concerning ecclesiastical law of the Weimar constitution of 1919. According to that constitution (Article 137, paragraph 1), no state church exists, there being neither an ecclesiastical state regime nor an ecclesiastical jurisdiction with special official status; but on the other hand, separation between church and state is not total. This situation is manifest in the involvement of the churches in education, social service and military chaplaincies to the armed forces.

Article 137, paragraph 3, of the Weimar constitution guarantees to all religious and philosophical communities the right to regulate and administer their affairs without interference and within the limits of general legislation valid for all. Each religious community assumes responsibility for itself, without the intervention of the state or public authorities.

Article 137, paragraph 5, of the same constitution is concerned with the status of religious communities. They remain entities in public law in the same way that they have always been. The same rights will be accorded to other religious societies on their request if, because of their constitution and membership, they show signs of permanence. Their organic status however is only 'formal'; it does not signify any integration with the state but merely the capacity to retain certain rights and legal dispositions by virtue of Article 141, and to the extent that there is a need to provide for worship and a pastoral ministry in the army, hospitals, penal institutions and other public establishments, religious communities are free to exercise their religious functions.

Other regulations concerning ecclesiastical questions in the cultural realm are left to the competence of the provinces. The provincial constitutions contain numerous dispositions relative to these questions. Further, Article 137, paragraph 8, of the Weimar constitution adds to the list of religious communities 'associations which have the purpose of serving in common a specified conception of the universe'.

There have been several concordats and treaties involving the churches. Between World Wars I and II, concordats were signed between the Roman Catholic Church and the provinces of Bavaria (1924), Prussia (1929), and Baden (1932). These concordats remained valid until after 1945. In addition, the concordat concluded on 20 July 1933, between the Holy See and the Third Reich was declared valid by a decision of the Constitutional Court on 26 March 1957.

The concordat of the Reich includes conventions concerning the juridical rights of ecclesial communities, bishoprics and their establishments, the right of the Roman Catholic Church to administer its own affairs, exchange of ambassadors, the guarantee of independence for the church by the state, authorization for Catholic theological faculties and the possibility of creating confessional schools. Regarding schools, however, since the provinces retain sovereignty in cultural matters, they are not legally obligated to follow federal treaty agreements in educational matters. Moreover, the concordat of the Reich determines the special content of state legislation relative to civil marriage as well as the suppression of ecclesiastical jurisdiction over temporal affairs.

On 22 February 1957, the Federal Republic concluded a convention with the Evangelical Church in Germany (EKD) concerning organization of the Protestant chaplaincy to the armed forces. There are also ecclesiastical conventions between the EKD and the following provinces: Baden (9 December 1932), Hesse, Lower Saxony, Palatinate Rhineland and Schleswig-Holstein.

Five special issues are important for an understanding of church-state relations in Germany. The first is the religious education of children. According to the law of the Reich of 15 July 1921, it is the free agreement of parents which prevails in this domain. After the age of 12, no child's confession can be changed without his consent, and after 14, each individual is free to decide which confession he belongs to.

Second, with regard to religious instruction, private schools, and theological faculties, Article 7, paragraph 3, of the Basic Law clarifies that religious instruction is a regular part of the curriculum of public schools, with the exception of nonconfessional schools. Article 141 permits the solution adopted by the province of Bremen, namely that religious instruction is assured by the church outside school. Although the state retains the right of supervision, religious instruction is offered in agreement with the principles of the religious communities. The right to establish private schools is guaranteed by Article 7, paragraph 4, of the Basic Law. Private schools which replace public schools must have state approval and must conform to the laws of the province. Theological faculties are state institutions and are in part under the constitutional protection of the provinces (as in Hesse and in Palatinate Rhineland).

A third special issue relates to the military chaplaincy. The juridical base of the Protestant military chaplaincy is the convention of 1957 between the FRG and the EKD. The legal dispositions are also analogous for Catholic military chaplains although the juridical basis for the Catholic chaplaincy rests on Article 27 of the concordat of the Reich (1933). The ecclesiastical direction of these 2 chaplaincies rests with a bishop appointed by each church (by the Vatican for the Catholic Church) after consultation with the federal government. The central administrative tasks are assured by 2 ecclesiastical offices for the federal army, one directed by a Protestant military general dean and the other by a Catholic general vicar, who depend directly on the Ministry of Defense.

Fourth, concerning ecclesiastical taxes (Kirchensteuer) and direct financial contributions by the state, as entities in public law the churches have the right to collect taxes according to the official lists of each province. To this effect, they utilize the provinces' administrative channel for finances, and it is the task of the provinces to arrange the details by appropriate laws. In 1975, the church tax represented 8 to 9% of all revenue in the provinces. All persons are subject to this tax except those whose income is not taxable (their number varies between 30% and 40% depending on the province) and those who expressly request to be excluded from their religious community and so are exempt. A growing number of persons are formally declaring before the state that they belong to no church in order to obtain exemption from paying. In addition to the ecclesiastical tax, state and church are linked by numerous other dispositions, some involving financial obligations including paying salaries of Protestant church authorities, Catholic bishops, and cathedral deans. The federal authorities pay the expenses of the military chaplaincy and the cost of the federal border police chaplaincy. The provinces assume responsibility for the police chaplaincy, the salaries of teachers of religion and catechists, and they also subsidize the salaries of pastors.

Fifth, there also exists close cooperation between church and state in the domain of social assistance. From the public budget, contributions are made for specific aid projects and are administered by a 'working group of central associations for private aid in Germany'. Six private organizations are members, of which 3 are confessional (Protestant, Catholic, Jewish). Government assistance to Catholic development projects reached 44 million DM by 1974. In addition, the churches are represented on governing boards of radio and TV stations and similarly in other areas.

There is no federal ministry for ecclesiastical affairs. Questions concerning the churches are mostly handled by provincial ministries of religion as responsible for cultural matters. Problems arising at the federal level are handled by the Ministries of the Interior and Foreign Affairs. The Evangelical Church is represented to the legislative organs of the federal government and other federal agencies by a member of the council of the EKD. The corresponding Catholic organ is the Commissariat of the German Bishops (Katholisches Buro).

In general, all churches are well satisfied with their relations with the state. Nevertheless, the Protestant churches find themselves in a more difficult situation in church-state relations than the Catholic Church, because of both their doctrine concerning the state and their unique historical experience. This does not, however, impede them from participating in political life even at the level of parliament and active participation in all parties. This is not true of the Catholic Church, which continues to retain its special allegiance to the Christian Democrats. Catholics have abandoned their original aim of keeping equidistant from all parties and now justify their position by various theories. Only sporadically do reform groups engage in self-criticism of the Catholic political stance. On the other hand, the political forces of youth, liberalism, humanism and socialism are pressing inexorably towards a clear separation between the state and the churches.

BROADCASTING AND MEDIA.

AWR's World Radio Europe headquarters is located in Germany; its studio in Darmstadt produces German-language programs, and its transmitter in Julit covers Africa (French, Dyula, English) and Europe (Bulgarian, Hungarian, Italian, and Romanian). ERF (TWR's European affiliate, based in Germany) broadcasts programs on several local FM and AM stations. Germany is a member of UNDA. Shortwave programs from KNLS, HCJB (Ecuador), TWR (Monaco, Albania) and AWR (Slovakia) can be easily received.

Satellite TV and radio programs are received in English, Arabic, German and Italian.

INTERDENOMINATIONAL ORGANIZATIONS

Ecumenical activity and structure was largely separated while Germany was divided into 2 countries from 1945-1990. In the GDR, the expectation that greater unity might result from the churches' situation in an anti-religious state was not realized. Rather the opposite occurred, with new divisions based on intellectual and ideological concerns coming to the fore. Despite that climate, the Council of Christian Churches in the GDR (Arbeitsgemeinschaft Christlicher Kirchen in der DDR) was founded in 1970 with, as members, the 8 territorial Protestant churches, plus the Baptists, Reformed, Mennonites, Methodists, Moravians, Congregationalists, Old Catholics, and Old Lutherans. It was an associate council of the WCC. Following reunification it merged into the Council of Christian Churches in Germany founded in 1948 with headquarters in Frankfurt. Members include the EKD with its territorial churches, Roman Catholics, Greek Orthodox, Baptists, Mennonites, Methodists, Moravians, Old Catholics, Old Reformed and Salvation Army. Several others are observers including Congregationalists, Quakers and Mulheim-Ruhr Pentecostals. Conceived as a platform for dialogue leading to mutual understanding and joint action, the council promotes theological study, research, and ecumenical cooperation on the local, national, and international level and is an associate council of the WCC.

The Commission for Ecumenical Questions of the Conference of German Catholic Bishops (Komission für Okumenische Fragen der Konferenz der Katholischen Bischofe Deutschlands) coordinates ecumenical affairs through 4 sections dealing with the Reformed (including Lutheran), Orthodox, Anglican, and Old Catholic churches.

Two joint commissions involving direct ecumenical dialogue are those dealing with relations between the Catholic Church and the EKD (Germeinsame Kommission des Rates der EKD und der Konferenz der Katholishen Bischofe Deutschlands) and between Catholics and Old Catholics (Germeinsame Kommission der Konferenz der Katholischen Bischofe Deutschlands und der Alt-Katholischen Kirche in Deutschland). There are numerous other cooperative agencies coordinating Catholic and EKD work at all levels.

The main interconfessional body dealing with foreign missions is the German Missionary Council (Deutscher Evangelischer Missions-Rat), founded in 1934, building on the foundations laid by the Standing Committee of German Protestant Missions (Ausschuss der Deutschen Evangelischen Missionsgesellschaften) in 1885 and the German Protestant Missionary Alliance (Deutsche Evangelische Missionsbund) in 1922. At the present time, the council has 36 regular and 15 special member bodies and is affiliated with the CWME/WCC. Some of the more Evangelical missionary societies belong to this council but others belong either to Deutscher Evangelischer Missions-Tag (DEMT), or to Arbeitsgemeinschaft Evangelikaler Missionen or to both.

Renewal. By AD 2000 many leaders in the mainline churches in Germany were worshiping together as Charismatics linked by denominational renewal services.

International interconfessional associations and societies active in the FRG include: (1) International Society for Liturgical Study and Renewal (Societas Liturgica), founded at Driebergen in the Netherlands in 1967, with German headquarters at Trier, which unites teachers, researchers and those responsible for liturgical renewal; (2) Ecumenical Association of Directors of Academies and Laity Training Centers in Europe (EDA) (Okumenischer Leiterkreis der Akademien und Laieninstitute in Europa), founded in 1958 in Bad Boll uber Goppingen, an independent association uniting groups involved in social and international justice and changes of lifestyle; (3) International Association for Religious Freedom (Weltbund fur Religiose Freiheit), founded in Frankfurt in 1900, with member churches and groups in 20 countries on 5 continents (1973), which is dedicated to the promotion of liberal elements in the churches and religious freedom; and (4) European Contact Groups on Church and Industry in Mainz.

Germany is home to dozens of significant institutes of an ecumenical nature, which study historical, doctrinal, organizational, and practical matters related to the Catholic Church, Lutheranism, Anglicanism, patristics, and the Byzantine churches.

The Evangelical Alliance unites the Evangelicals of Germany (about 1.5 million in 1990), and provides an avenue for joint ministries in social action, national weeks of prayer, evangelism, and missionary information and outreach. Closely related is the Association of Evangelical Missions with 51 members (1990).

An organization dedicated to the improvement of Jewish, Christian, and Muslim relations is the Standige Konferenz Europaischer Juden, Christen und Muslims, which is a local branch of the Permanent Conference of Jews, Christians and Muslims in Europe, with headquarters in the UK.

There are also in the country a number of significant organizations working in the area of Christian-Jewish dialogue. One is related to the International Council of Christians and Jews. Others work specifically in the areas of Jewish-Catholic dialogue, shared spirituality, the organizing of specific retreats and events, proclaiming the Christian gospel to Jews, research, and reconciliation with the Jews as the principal victims of Nazism.

A number of nonconfessional associations and institutes of religious studies are active. The International Association for the Psychology of Religion (Internationale Gesellschaft fur Religionpsychologie), founded in Nuremberg in 1914 and now located in Munich, is an international organization of specialists in religious psychology from several different countries with its headquarters in Germany. Three national associations are: Gesellschaft fur Geistesgeschichte, founded in Erlangen in 1958, a society dedicated to the study of the history of ideas; Jahrbuch fur Religions- und Wissens-Soziologie, in Freiburg, concerned with religious sociology; and Germania Judaica, founded in Cologne in 1958, which maintains a library on the history of the Jews in Germany. Nonconfessional institutes of religious studies are for the most part joined to theological faculties. These and their institutes are largely governmental bodies and are not linked institutionally to any church. Nevertheless, they often present a denominational character from the fact that they are either Protestant or Catholic in background. The more important are located at the following universities: (1) for the history of religions, Erlangen-Nuremberg, Freiburg, Gottingen, Heidelberg, Mainz and Marburg; (2) for general questions related to Christianity, Frankfurt, Freiburg and Marburg; (3) for religious sociology, Freiburg, Marburg, Munich, Munster, Tübingen and Wurzburg; and (4) for religious sciences, Berlin, Bonn, Mainz, Marburg, Munich, and Munster.

FUTURE TRENDS AND PROSPECTS

After unification of the two German states (1990), the Communist-fueled decline of church membership in the former East Germany has taken a turn in the opposite direction while atheists and the nonreligious continue to grow in the former West Germany. The net effect of these trends is for Christianity to fall from 77.1% in 1990 to 73.7% by AD 2025.

Christianity could potentially decline to below 70% of the country's population around mid-century. The nonreligious may subsequently climb to over 20% and Muslims close to 10%.

BIBLIOGRAPHY

Adressbuch für das katholische Deutschland. Bonn: Zentralkomitee der Deutschen Katholiken, 1972.

Berlin. I. Wallace. *World bibliographical series*, vol. 155. Oxford, UK: CLIO Press, 1993. 182p.

Christ in der DDR. J. Hamel. Berlin: Käthe Vogt, 1957. 51p.

Church and culture: German Catholic theology, 1860–1914. T. F. O'Meara. Notre Dame, IN: University of Notre Dame Press, 1991. 270p.

'Church and state in East Germany,' C. Ward, *Religion in Communist lands*, 6, 2 (Summer 1978), 89–96.

'Detente and conservatizing liberalization: the state and the evangelical churches in the German Democratic Republic, 1968–1974.' R. F. Goeckel. Ph.D. dissertation, Harvard University, Cambridge, MA, 1982. 2 vols.

Die evangelischen Kirchen in der DDR: Beiträge zu einer Bestandsaufnahme. R. Henkys. Munich: Chr. Kaiser Verlag, 1982. 462p.

Die Evangelischen Kirchen in der DDR: ein Uberblick. I. Roitsch. *Informationsdienst des Katholischen Arbeitskreises für Zitgeschichtliche Fragen*, no. 83. Bonn, 1977.

Die Rolle der Kirchen in der DDR: eine erste Bilanz. H. Dähn. *Geschichte und Staat*, Bd. 291. Munich: Olzog Verlag Vertrieb, 1993. 242p.

'East Germany: the federation of Protestant churches,' R. Williamson, *Religion in Communist lands*, 9, 1 (Spring 1981), 6–17.

East Germany: The German Democratic Republic. I. Wallace. *World bibliographical series*, vol. 77. Oxford, UK: CLIO Press, 1987. 294p. (See especially 'Religion,' p55–60).

For the soul of the people: Protestant protest against Hitler. V. Barnett. New York: Oxford University Press, 1992. 366p.

Freikirchen in Deutschland: Geschichte, Lehre, Ordnung. W. Bartz. Trier, West Germany: Spee-Buchverlag, 1973. 180p.

German and Scandinavian Protestantism, 1700–1918. N. Hope. *Oxford history of the Christian Church.* Oxford, UK: Clarendon Press, 1995. 712p.

'German Democratic Republic,' B. Wilhelm, in *Western religion: a country by country sociological enquiry*, p.213–28. H. Mol (ed). The Hague: Mouton, 1972.

Germanische und Baltische Religion. A. V. Strom & H. Biezais. *Die Religionen der Menschheit.* Stuttgart: Verlag W. Kohlhammer, 1975. 391p.

Geschichte des Christentums in Deutschland: Religion, Politik und Gesellschaft vom Ende der Aufklärung bis zur Mitte des 20. Jahrhunderts. K. Nowak. Munich: C.H. Beck, 1995. 389p.

God and Caesar in East Germany: the conflicts of Church and state in East Germany since 1945. R. W. Solberg. New York: Macmillan, 1961. 294p.

Golgotha and Götterdämmerung: German religious paradigm shifts and the proclamation of the Gospel. S. P. Scheibler. *American University studies, Series VII: Theology and religion*, vol. 175. New York: P. Lang, 1996.

Handbuch zu Freikirchen und Sekten. Hannover, West Germany: Lutherischer Kirchenamt, 1966. 2 vols.

'Katholische Kirche in der DDR,' K. Richter, *Jahrbuch für christliche Sozialwissenschaften*, 13 (1972), 215–45.

Katholische Kirche in der DDR: Gemeinden in der Bewährung 1945–1980. W. Knauft. Mainz: Matthias-Grünewald-Verlag, 1980. 240p.

Kirche und Katholiken in der Bundesrepublik: Daten und Analysen. E. Golomb. *Der Christ in der Welt.* Aschaffenburg: Paul Pattloch Verlag, 1974. 142p.

Kirchliches Handbuch: Amtliches statistisches Jahrbuch der katholischen Kirche Deutschlands, 1968. Cologne: Amtlichen Zentralstelle für kirchliche statistik des katholischen Deutschlands, 1968.

Konfrontation oder Kooperation? Das Verhältnis von Staat und Kirche in der SBZ/DDR 1945–1980. H. Dähn. *Studien zur Sozialwissenschaft*, Band 52. Opladen, West Germany: Westdeutscher Verlag, 1982. 295p.

Neue Erde ohne Himmel: der Kampf des Atheismus gegen das Christentum in der DDR: Modell einer Weltweiten Auseinandersetzung. H. G. Koch. Stuttgart: Quell-Verlag, 1963. 591p.

New move forward in Europe: growth patterns of German speaking Baptists in Europe. W. L. Wagner. South Pasadena, CA: William Carey Library, 1978. 362p.

Seher Grübler Enthusiasten: Sekten und Religiöse Sondergemeinschaften der Gegenwart. K. Hutten. Stuttgart: Quell-Verlag, 1958. 751p.

'Sonderdruck aus Kirchliches Jahrbuch für die Evangelische Kirche in Deutschland,' , p.425–85. Gütersloh: Verlagshaus Gerd Mohn, 1972. (Part of a regularly-updated statistical documentation).

Stimmen aus der Kirche in der DDR (B/CD). B. Ruys. Zurich: EVZ-Verlag, 1965. 210p.

Taschenbuch der Evangelischen Kirchen in Deutschland, 1974. Stuttgart: Evangelisches Verlagswerk, 1974. 924p.

'The Church in the German Democratic Republic,' R. Smith, in *Honecker's Germany*, p.66–81. D. Childs (ed). London: Allen & Unwin, 1985.

'The church struggle and the Baptist community.' R. A. Loomis. Th.M. thesis, Fuller Theological Seminary, Pasadena, CA, 1992. 73p.

The churches and politics in Germany. F. Spotts. Middletown, CT: Wesleyan University Press, 1977. 431p.

The Nazi state and the new religions: five case studies in non–conformity. C. E. King. New York: E. Mellen Press, 1982. 326p.

The Reformation in Germany and Switzerland. P. Johnston & R. W. Scribner. Cambridge, UK: Cambridge University Press, 1993. 160p.

'The status of religion in the German Democratic Republic,' G. H. Brand, in *Religion and atheism in the U.S.S.R. and Eastern Europe.* B. R. Bociurkiw & J. W. Strong (eds). London: Basingstoke, 1975. 412p.

Twisted cross: the German Christian movement in the Third Reich. D. L. Bergen. Chapel Hill, NC: University of North Carolina Press, 1996.

West Germany. D. Detwiler & I. Detwiler. *World bibliographical series*, vol. 72. Oxford, UK: CLIO Press, 1988. 372p.

Wie Stabil ist die Kirche? H. Hild. Berlin: Burckhardthaus-Verlag, 1974.

Zwischen Gestern und Morgen: Evangelische Gemeinden in der DDR. L. Borgmann. Berlin: Evangelische Verlagsanstalt, 1969.

Country Table 2. **Organized churches and denominations in Germany.**

Official name (bold type = church with over 10% of all affiliated) 1	*Begun* 2	*Type* 3	*Counc* 4	*Congs* 5	*Adults* 6	*Affiliated 1970* 7	*Affiliated 1995* 8	*G%* 9	*Names, notes, and other statistics* (see Codebook, Part 3) 10
Aethiopische Orthodoxe Kirche	c1970	O-Eth	N....	3	3,000	–	5,000	40.59	*Ethiopian Orthodox Ch.* Amhara migrant labor.
Altreformierte Kirchen in Deutschland	1834	P-Ref	....W	73	18,200	8,000	24,000	4.49	*Old Reformed/Christian Reformed Chs in WGermany.* Northwest. 12n,W=50%.
Alt-Katholische Kirche in Deutschland	1874	I-OCa	UWC.W	311	21,800	22,000	29,000	1.11	*Old Catholic Ch, D Bonn.* Schism ex Ch of Rome over papal infallibility. 62n,1s.
Anglikanische Kirche (D Europe)	1630	A-plu	awc..	100	13,000	20,000	26,000	1.05	*Ch of England.* English-speaking chaplaincies, some seasonal, some military. 10x.
Apostelamt Jesu Christi	1923	I-3aX	.....	100	2,000	10,000	6,000	-2.02	*Apostolate of Jesus Christ.* Ex Apostelamt Juda. Churches across to Oder.
Apostelamt Juda	1902	I-3aX	.....	10	1,000	5,000	3,000	-2.02	*Apostolate of Judah. Gemeinschaft des Gottlichen Sozialismus.* Ex NAK. HQ Berlin.
Apostolische Gemeinschaft	1956	I-3aX	x....	56	9,000	15,000	13,600	-0.39	Belongs to VAC (Switzerland). Union of splits ex New Apostolic Ch. In 6 nations.
Apostolische Kirche in Deutschland	1946	P-PeA	Z....	7	800	1,000	1,600	1.90	*Urchristliche Mission. Apostolic Ch in G.* Begun by UK & Danish churches. 1j.
Arb Mennonitischer Brüdergemeinden D	1966	P-Men	G....	7	1,044	656	1,700	3.88	*Arb=Arbeitsgemeinschaft. Fellowship of Mennonite Brethren Congregations.* M=MBC(USA).
A Unterstütz in Mennonitengemeinden	1978	P-Men	G....	12	3,850	–	5,920	5.88	*Arb zur G=Arbeitsgemeinschaft zur Geistliche. Mennonite Spiritual Support Fellowship.* M=EMC.
Armenische Apostolische Kirche		O-Arm	Ewc..	3	9,000	20,000	18,000	0.05	*Armenian Apostolic Ch,* C Echmiadzin *Gregorian.* Refugees from USSR and Turkey.
Bund der Kämpfer für Glaube & Wahrheit	1918	m-Spi	x....	10	2,000	5,000	4,000	-0.89	*W=Wahrheit Warriors for Faith & Truth Horpenites.* In Saxony, FRG, Spain, USA, SW Africa.
Bund Ev-Freikirchlicher Gemeinden in D	1834	P-Bap	T.C.W	930	310,000	350,000	370,000	0.22	*Baptist Union.* Until 1990 included Elim and underground Pentecostals. 125n,1s(16).
Bund Freier Ev Gemeinden in D	1854	P-Con	KF..w	321	26,600	49,048	60,500	0.84	*Fed of Free Ev Congs in G. Congregational Union.* 130n,1p(2),W=50%,750Y.
Bund Freikirchlichen Pfingstgemeinden	1907	P-Pe2	ZF...	632	40,200	40,000	60,000	1.64	*Assemblies of God.* 1953 union M=AoG(USA, UK). Some Korean chs. 233n,11f,1s(80). BFP.
Bund Freireligiöser Gem Deutschlands	c1845	m-Unt	.....	35	700	3,000	2,120	-1.38	*Gem=Gemeinden.* Free Religious Congregations. *Unitarians. 7 groups. HQ Hannover.*
Bund Taufgesinnter Gemeinden	1989	P-Men	G....	7	2,500	–	6,000	16.67	*Fellowship of Anabaptist Congs.* Links with Mennonite Brethren Ch.
Christadelphianer		m-Ade	x....	8	8,000	15,300	13,300	0.05	*Christadelphian Bible Mission (CBM).* 10 ecclesias (churches). Pacifist, adventist.
Christengemeinschaft	1922	m-Gno	x....	150	54,600	30,000	65,200	3.15	*Sonnenwesen/Being Anthroposophical Society.* 7 sacraments. HQ Stuttgart. 150n.
Christliche Gemeinschaft Hirt & Herde	1894	P-Hol	.....	20	4,000	10,000	8,000	-0.89	*Christian Society of Shepherd & Flock.* Holiness doctrines. Legal recognition 1951.
Christliche Missionsunternehmen	c1945	P-Pe2	.....	26	1,300	3,000	3,940	1.10	*Freie Volkmission Free People's Mission.* Classical Pentecostals (2-stage).
Christliche Wissenschaft	1907	m-Sci	x....	69	3,300	10,000	5,500	-2.36	*Ch of Christ, Scientist. Christian Science.* M=CCS(Boston, USA). Declining. 13m,75w.
Chr Gem der D Pfingstbewegung	1907	P-Pe2	Zv..w	122	11,000	40,000	31,400	-0.96	*Mülheim-Ruhr Bewegung. Assoc of Chr Assemblies.* Declining. 1967 applied to WCC. 1j.
Deutschen Spätregen Gemeinden	c1930	I-3pW	x....	20	1,000	2,000	2,500	0.90	*Latter Rain Mission.* Pentecostal renewal. Missionaries from and to South Africa.
Evangelische Brüder-Unität	1722	P-Mor	xWC.W	35	8,000	13,600	21,455	1.84	*Unity of Brethren.* District Herrnhut. European Continental Province.
Evangelische Kirche in Deutschland:	1946	P-Uni	1WC.W	18,122	22,741,000	33,417,077	29,205,000	-0.54	*EKD.* 20 Landeskirchen, 8 other denominations. 300p,39s,P=26%,W=6%.
Anhalt: Ev Landeskirche Anhalts	1534	P-LuR	.wC.x	196	93,000	275,000	120,000	-3.26	*Evangelical Ch of Anhalt.* Parts of Halle and Magdeburg districts. 100n.
Baden, Evangelische Landeskirche in	1520	P-LuR	.wc..	548	1,071,000	1,372,000	1,375,000	0.01	*Ev Ch in Baden.* Territorial ch. HQ Karlsruhe. 1s.
Bayern, Ev-Lutherische Kirche in	1530	P-Lut	LWc.d	1,522	2,091,000	2,555,000	2,685,000	0.20	Bavaria. Disestablished 1919. Conservative. Munich, 1s.
Berlin-Brandenburg, Ev Kirche in	1528	P-LuR	.wc.x	1,769	1,373,000	1,421,000	1,763,000	0.87	Covers West Berlin. HQ Berlin.
Braunschweig, Ev-l Landeskirche in	1528	P-Lut	LWc.d	390	387,000	622,000	497,000	-0.89	*ELC Brunswick.* Kirchentags. HQ Wolfenbüttel. 1s.
Bremen: Bremische Ev Kirche	1522	P-LuR	.wc..	69	240,000	487,000	308,000	-1.82	*Ev Ch of Bremen.* FRG's second largest port.
Görlitz: EK Görlitzer Kirchengebietes	1815	P-LuR	xwC.x	72	62,000	180,000	80,000	-3.19	*Ev Ch of Görlitz Region* (until 1968, Silesia). Parts of Dresden, Cottbus. 80n.
Greifswald, Ev Landeskirche	1534	P-LuR	LwC.x	356	156,000	550,000	200,000	-3.97	*Ev Ch of Greifswald* (Pomerania). Part Rostock, Neubrandenburg. 190n,Is(55),2790Yy.
Hannover, Ev-luth Landeskirche	1533	P-Lut	LWc.d	1,562	2,624,000	3,905,000	3,369,000	-0.59	Organized 1866, disestablished 1918. 1s,W=5%.
Hessen und Nassau, Ev Kirche in	1523	P-LuR	.wc..	1,201	1,586,000	2,289,000	2,037,000	-0.47	*EC in Hessen & Nassau.* HQ Darmstadt. 2s(380),W=5%.
Kirchenprovinz Sachsen, Ev K der	1517	P-LuR	.wC.x	2,209	464,000	2,400,000	596,000	-5.42	*Ev Ch of Province of Saxony.* Halle, Magdeburg Erfurt. 930n,3s(80+90+30).
Kurhessen-Waldeck, Ev Kirche von	1934	P-LuR	.wc..	966	818,000	1,106,000	1,051,000	-0.20	*United Ch of K-W.* HQ Kassel-Wilhelmshöhe. 1s.
Lippe: Lippische Landeskirche	1605	P-Ref	Rwc.h	70	173,000	249,000	223,000	-0.44	82% Reformed, 18% Lutheran; 6 classes. HQ Detmold.
Mecklenberg, Ev-Luth Landeskirche	1523	P-Lut	LwC.d	393	251,000	850,000	323,000	-3.80	*Ev Luth Ch of Mecklenberg.* Schwerin, Rostock, Mecklenberg. 340n,1s(40).
Nordelbien: Nordelbische Ev-L Kirche	1977	P-Lut	LWeid	679	1,988,000	–	2,553,000	5.56	*North Elbian ELC.* Merger of 4 Landeskirchen: Eutin, Hamburg, Lübeck, Schlesing-Holstein.
Nordwestdeutschlands, Ev-ref K in	1882	P-Ref	Rwc.h	138	156,000	202,000	200,000	-0.04	*Ev Reformed Ch in Germany.* HQ Leer. 1s,W=8%.
Oldenburg, Ev-Lutherische Kirche in	1523	P-Lut	Lwc..	124	384,000	539,000	494,000	-0.35	*Ev Lutheran Ch in Oldenburg.* 1919 disestablished.
Pfalz, Vereinigte Prot-Ev-Chr K der	1530	P-LuR	.wc..	429	522,000	724,000	671,000	-0.30	*United Prot Ev Chr Ch of Palatinate.* HQ Speyer.

continued overleaf

Country Table 2–continued

Official name (bold type = church with over 10% of all affiliated) 1	*Begun* 2	*Type* 3	*Counc* 4	*Congs* 5	*Adults* 6	*Affiliated 1970* 7	*Affiliated 1995* 8	*G%* 9	*Names, notes, and other statistics* (see Codebook, Part 3) 10
Rheinland, Ev Kirche im	1520	P-LuR	.wc.x	833	2,525,000	3,756,000	3,242,000	-0.59	*EC in Rhineland.* HQ Dusseldorf. 4p,1s(540), W=6%.
Sachsen: Ev-L Landeskirche Sachsens	1517	P-Lut	LwC.d	1,136	996,000	2,741,077	1,279,000	-3.00	*Ev Luth Ch of Saxony.* Dredsden, Leipzig, Karl-Marx-Stadt. 1100n,2s(110+150).
Schaumburg-Lippe, E-L Landeskirche	1559	P-Lut	LWc.d	23	50,000	75,000	64,000	-0.63	Synodical structure under council of 7. W=9%.
Thuringen, Ev-Lutherische Kirche in	1527	P-Lut	LwC.d	1,365	529,000	1,200,000	679,000	-2.25	*Ev Luth Ch in Thuringia.* Reformation heartland: Erfurt, Gera, Suhl 620n,1s(95).
Westfalen, Ev Kirche von	1817	P-LuR	.wc.x	654	2,275,000	3,392,000	2,922,000	-0.59	*EC of Westphalia.* HQ Bielefeld. 3p,1s(585),W=10%.
Württemberg, Ev Landeskirche in	1534	P-Lut	Lwc..	1,418	1,927,000	2,527,000	2,474,000	-0.08	1918 disestablished. Swabians. 1s,W=10%.
Evangelisch-Johannische Kirche	1926	m-Spi	x....	80	9,000	14,000	16,000	0.54	*Ev Ch of Revelation of St John the Divine.* HQ Dusseldorf. Mainly in GDR. Growing.
Ev-Luth (Altlutherische) Kirche	1830	P-Lut	e.C.W	35	7,000	9,864	8,000	-0.83	*Ev Lutheran (Old Lutheran) Ch in the GDR* (formerly Prussia). HQ Berlin. M=LCMS. 25n.
Ev-lutherische Bekenntniskirche		P-Lut	e....	33	4,880	1,500	6,500	0.05	*Confessional ELC.* Pure Lutheranism. M=Missouri, Wisconsin Synods (USA). HQ Bremen.
Ev-Lutherische Kirche Estlands in Exil	1940	I-Lut	LwC..	100	20,000	2,500	30,000	10.45	*Estonian Ev Lutheran Ch in Exile.* Refugees from Estonia (USSR). HQ Stockholm.
Ev-lutherische Kirche in Baden		P-Lut	Lw...	6	3,500	4,886	4,100	0.05	*Ev Lutheran Ch in Baden.* Lutheran minority in United church area.
Ev-luth Kirche Lettlands in Exil	1940	I-Lut	LwC..	18	1,840	11,400	4,000	-4.10	*Latvian ELC in Exile.* Refugees from USSR, HQ Esslingen. 9n,W=35%,28Yy.
Ev-Lutherische Kirche von Dänemark	1864	P-Lut	Lwc..	100	20,000	3,000	31,000	9.79	*Church of Denmark.* Parishes of state church of Denmark, in south Schleswig. Danes. 20nx.
Evangelisch-methodistische Kirche in D	1830	P-Met	VwC.W	1,250	66,000	140,000	104,000	-1.18	1968 merger with Ev Gemeinschaft D/EUB in UMC(USA). 398n. 14H,1s,W=65%,654Yy.
Freie Bibelgemeinde	1931	m-Jeh	.....	20	3,000	4,000	6,000	1.64	*Free Bible Congregation.* Schism ex Jehovah's Witnesses. HQ Bunde (Westphalia).
Freie Christliche Volkskirche in D	1945	m-Unt	.....	70	6,000	20,000	17,000	-0.65	*Free Christian People's Church.* HQ Stuttgart. Expanding. Liberal theology.
Freier Brüderkreis	1847	P-CBr	x....	173	26,000	82,000	59,100	-1.30	*Free Brethren Plymouth-Bruder.* 3 Open groups. Unions with Baptists. HQ Betzdorf.
Freier Evangelische Gemeinden		I-Eva	.....	140	26,000	20,000	43,300	0.05	*Free Evangelical congregations.*
Gemeinde Christi	1947	I-Dis	x....	30	2,500	5,000	4,500	-0.42	*Chs of Christ.* M=CC(Non-Instrumental) (USA). 70% USA military personnel. 29f.
Gemeinde Christi	1956	I-Dis	x....	25	1,500	4,000	3,500	-0.53	*Christian Chs/Chs of Christ.* M=CCCC(Instrumental). USA military personnel. 21f.
Gemeinde der Christen Ecclesia	1944	P-Pe2	.....	140	5,000	15,000	12,000	-0.89	*Community of Christians Ch.* Begun by industrialist. Healing ministry. Declining.
Gemeinde Gottes (Anderson)	1901	P-Hol	x....	33	2,600	6,000	4,000	-1.61	M=Ch of God(Anderson) (USA). HQ Essen. Mainly in rural areas. 40n,1s.
Gemeinde Gottes (Cleveland)	1936	P-Pe3	ZF...	50	1,699	7,000	3,780	-2.43	M=Ch of God(Cleveland) (USA). HQ near Stuttgart. Some Black members. 57n,2f,2s.
Gemeinde Gottes der Prophezeiung		P-Pe3	Z....	3	1,800	880	3,600	0.05	*Church of God of Prophecy.* Mainly USA expatriates.
Gemeinde Jesu Christi in Deutschland	1943	I-3pW	.....	10	400	1,000	900	-0.42	Small Pentecostal body founded in Stammheim by a German-American. 1p.
Gemeinde Lokale	c1990	I-3nC	.....	4	60	–	200	20.00	*Assembly Hall Churches. Little Flock. Local Churches.* Begun in China 1922.
Gemeinschaft Entschiedener Christen		P-Pe2	.....	5	500	1,000	1,500	0.05	*Society of Definite Christians.* In Karlsruhe (HQ), Lörrach, Scharzwald.
Gesellschaft zur Vereinigung des WC	c1965	m-HSA	x....	5	1,000	1,000	2,000	2.81	*WC=Weltchristentums. Unification Ch of Germany.* M=HSAUWC(Korea). 6,000 by 1976.
Gralsbewegung	1927	m-The	x....	46	1,610	2,000	2,300	0.56	*Nature Philosophy Union.* Theocratic, messianic. HQ Vomperberg/Tyrol. In 8 nations.
Griechisch-Orth Metropolie von D		O-Gre	Cwc.W	60	352,000	368,000	460,000	0.05	*Greek Orthodox Diocese,* & E Middle Europe, under EP Constantinople. Greek labourers.
Isolated radio churches	1939	I-rad	.....	1,500	30,000	17,600	50,000	4.26	Isolated radio believers. R=5200 (Radio Vatican since 1939; TWR,HCJB,RVOG,&c).
Heilsarmee	1886	P-Sal	xwc.W	57	6,200	15,000	7,400	-2.79	*Salvation Army, Germany Territory.* 3 Divisions. 33 institutions. Officers. 162,1s.
Katholische Apostolische Kirche	c1840	I-3aX	xv...	10	10,000	20,000	22,200	0.42	*Urkirche. Catholic Apostolic Ch (Original Ch).* Declining. 1948, applied to WCC.
Katholische Kirche Deutschlands:	c 90	R-LEr	B.B.S	14,322	22,171,000	27,956,540	28,478,332	0.07	*Catholic Ch in G.* C=44=15=302. 10q,20s(1895). 16363n 4908x 7529m44504w 284540Yy
M Bamberg	1007	R-Lat	Bs	364	624,000	801,000	801,896	0.00	*Erzbistum Bamberg.* Northern Bavaria. 447n 116x 174m 1050w 8358Yy
D Eichstätt	745	R-Lat	Bs	285	352,000	396,000	452,789	0.08	*Bistum Eichstätt.* Central Bavaria. 338n 77x 125m 827w 5121Yy
D Speyer	c 350	R-Lat	Bs	358	517,000	688,000	664,483	-0.14	South of Rhineland Palatinate and east Saar. 438n 65x 76m 1184w 6594Yy
D Würzburg	741	R-Lat	Bs	625	712,000	898,000	914,621	0.08	NW Bavaria. Small part in GDR (EC Meiningen). 601n 213x 384m 2039w 10732Yy
M Berlin	1930	R-Lat	Bs	231	315,000	243,000	405,567	2.07	*Bistum Berlin.* East Berlin (D also covers W Berlin). 292n 129x 171m 813w 2214Yy
D Dresden-Meissen	968	R-Lat	Bs	167	133,000	307,540	171,500	0.10	Saxonia. Only diocese with a priests' council. 205n 47x 52m 248w 863Yy
D Görlitz	1972	R-Lat	Bs	88	37,000	–	48,035	4.35	In southeast. In east there are Slav Catholics. 67n 2x 3m 175w 201Yy
M Freiburg im Breisgau	1821	R-Lat	Bs	1,085	1,702,000	2,220,000	2,186,803	-0.06	Northwest and west Baden-Württemberg. 1233n 261x 411m 3453w 22783Yy
D Mainz	c 350	R-Lat	Bs	344	670,000	881,000	861,025	-0.09	Part Baden-Württemberg/Hesse/Rhineland-Palatinate. 518n 127x 151m 704w 7645Yy
D Rottenburg-Stuttgart	1821	R-Lat	Bs	1,052	1,638,000	1,973,000	2,103,973	0.26	Center and east of Baden-Württemberg. 1031n 290x 388m 3119w 21916Yy
M Hamburg	1994	R-Lat	Bs	180	318,000	–	409,642	50.00	Population is 7.2% Catholic. 223n 52x 62m 482w 2636Yy
D Hildesheim	800	R-Lat	Bs	526	579,000	703,000	744,160	0.08	Lower Saxony. 13% RC. 4 parishes of 7,000 in GDR. 433n 107x 123m 449w 5784Yy
D Osnabrück	772	R-Lat	Bs	471	705,000	820,000	905,635	0.08	13% RC. Part in GDR (EC Schwerin); 2 parts in FRG. 501n 134x 185m 1517w 9200Yy
M Köln (Cologne)	c 150	R-Lat	Bs	811	1,856,000	2,696,000	2,384,866	-0.49	North Rhineland-Westphalia, including Bonn. 1175n 547x 862m 3259w 23051Yy
D Aachen	1801	R-Lat	Bs	561	1,004,000	1,427,000	1,290,443	-0.40	N Rhineland-Westphalia (Belgian/Dutch frontiers). 662n 198x 269m 1578w 13620Yy
D Essen	1957	R-Lat	Bs	353	879,000	1,290,000	1,129,316	-0.53	Centre of North Rhineland-Westphalia. 610n 161x 184m 818w 9622Yy
D Limburg	1821	R-Lat	Bs	445	593,000	880,000	762,838	-0.57	Western Hesse, eastern Rhineland-Palatinate. 373n 204x 324m 1186w 6163Yy
D Münster	800	R-Lat	Bs	709	1,643,000	2,074,000	2,110,000	0.08	2 areas apart: Lower Saxony, Rhineland-Munster. 1131n 343x 583m 4184w 25187Yy
D Trier	c 90	R-Lat	Bs	978	1,330,000	1,810,000	1,708,200	-0.23	Rhineland-Palatinate, most of Saar. 75% RC. 916n 424x 743m 2988w 17532Yy
M München (Munich) & Freising	739	R-Lat	Bs	755	1,602,000	2,215,000	2,057,000	0.08	Southeast Bavaria. HQ Munich. 79% RC. 1023n 421x 604m 3939w 19944Yy
D Augsburg	c 550	R-Lat	Bs	1,029	1,198,000	1,462,000	1,539,789	0.21	M=OSB. Also called D Augusta. Bavaria. 79% RC. 889n 272x 591m 2909w 17683Yy
D Passau	737	R-Lat	Bs	309	421,000	493,000	541,090	0.08	Also called D Passavia. Eastern Bavaria. 93% RC. 338n 150x 194m 1176w 6470Yy
D Regensburg (Ratisbon)	739	R-Lat	Bs	771	1,038,000	1,264,000	1,333,179	0.08	Ratisbon. Northeastern Bavaria. 86% RC. 961n 203x 362m 2381w 15539Yy
M Paderborn	805	R-Lat	Bs	973	1,444,000	1,904,000	1,854,095	0.08	33% RC Rhineland. Part in GDR (EC Magdeburg). 1213n 228x 321m 2997w 19217Yy
D Erfurt	1973	R-Lat	Bs	201	165,000	–	212,970	4.55	Episcopal Commissariat until 1994. Part of D Fulda. . 182n 33x 35m 300w 1252Yy
D Fulda	1752	R-Lat	Bs	241	358,000	429,000	460,107	0.28	Half in GDR (EC Erfurt). In FRG, in Hesse. 350n 81x 122m 505w 4591Yy
D Magdeburg	1973	R-Lat	Bs	212	140,000	–	180,000	4.55	Episcopal Commissariat until 1994. In M Paderborn. 187n 19x 26m 210w 600Yy
EA Deutschland (Ukrainian)	1959	R-Ukr	Os	23	18,000	32,000	24,310	-1.09	For Ukrainians of Byzantine rite. HQ Munich. 26n 4x 4m 14w 22Yy
OM Deutschland	1933	R-Lat	Bs	175	180,000	50,000	220,000	6.11	*Military Ordinariate.* 94 ordinaries, 72 auxiliaries. 270Yy.
Kinder Gottes	c1970	I-mar	x....	2	135	–	342	26.29	*Children of God.*
Kirche des Nazareners	1958	P-Hol	xF...	19	1,335	1,000	3,611	5.27	*Ch of the Nazarene.* Holiness body. M=CoN(USA). HQ Frankfurt. Expanding. 15n,1s.
Kirche des Reiches Gott	1950	m-Jeh	x....	10	2,000	50,000	6,670	-7.74	*Menschenfreunde. Kingdom of God/Friends of Man* (Sayerce). Ex J. In 12 nations.
Kirche Gottes in Christus		I-3pB	Z....	20	2,500	2,000	5,000	0.05	M=CoG in Christ (Memphis, TN, USA). Blacks in US armed forces. Non-combatants.
Kirche JC der Heiligen der Letzten Tage	1845	m-LdS	x....	450	23,000	31,000	45,000	1.50	*KJC=Kirche Jesus Christi, Ch of JC of Latter-Day Saints, Mormons.* 950f.
Kirchenbund Ev-reformierter Gem	1949	P-Ref	R...W	15	3,500	8,100	6,000	-1.19	*G=Gemeinden. Conference of Reformed Congregations in the GDR.* 5 Districts, 3 parishes. 20n.
Kirche Schwedens	c1950	P-Lut	Lwc..	1	500	350	800	3.36	*Church of Sweden, Svenska Kyrkan.* Chaplaincy of state church. Swedes. 1x.
Koptische-Orthodoxe Kirche		O-Cop	NWA..	8	1,300	800	2,000	0.05	*Coptic Orthodox Church.*
Litauische Ev-Lutherische Kirche	1945	P-Lut	LvC..	3	6,750	12,000	9,000	-1.14	*Lietuviu Evangeliku Liuteronu Baznycia. Lithuanian ELC.* Began from USSR refugees.
Missions-Allianz Kirche		P-Hol	.....	3	79	20	110	0.05	*Christian and Missionary Alliance.* M=CMA(USA).
Mennonitenbrüder-Gemeinden		P-Men	G....	13	2,168	1,200	3,100	0.05	*Mennonite Brethren* (Independent). Includes former DDR Mennonitengemeinden. M=MBC(USA).
Mennonitische Heimatmission	1969	P-Men	G....	13	310	242	500	2.95	*Mennonite Home Mission.*
Neuapostolische Kirche	1863	I-3aX	x....	3,050	350,000	610,000	401,179	-1.66	*New Apostolic Ch.* Ex Catholic Apostolic Ch. World HQ Zurich. 16 Apostles, 1j.
Neue Kirche in Deutschland	1824	m-Swe	xv...	2	200	500	300	-2.02	*New Church in Germany.* Swedenborgian. HQ Essen-Werden. 1968, applied to join WCC.
Orthodoxe Kirche von Rumänien		O-Rum	Cwc..	9	6,300	7,500	9,000	0.05	*Biserica Ortodoxa Romana din Baden-Baden, Romanian Orthodox Ch.* Under P Bucharest.
Philadelphia-Verein	1946	P-Pe2	.....	50	6,000	7,000	8,570	0.81	*Philadelphia Community.* In Württemberg. School of prophets, unction, visions. 1j.
Pilgermission St Chrischona	1877	P-Non	.....	53	3,600	5,000	6,000	0.73	M=P StC(Switzerland).
Reformierte Kirche von Niederlande		P-Ref	Rwc..	25	6,000	4,937	10,000	0.05	*Netherlands Reformed Church.* Congregations of Dutch residents.
Reformiert-Apostolische Gemeindebund	1921	I-3aX	x....	3	1,000	1,000	2,000	2.81	*Reformed Apostolic Community.* Schism ex New Apostolic Church. HQ Dresden (GDR).
Religiose Gesellschaft der Freunde	1830	P-Qua	Q...w	30	500	1,050	900	-0.61	*Quäker. Religious Society of Friends (Quakers).* Links with Quakers in UK, USA.
Russisch-Orth K ausserhalb Russlands	1920	I-Rus	x....	46	18,500	30,000	28,000	-0.28	*D Germany, ROC Outside of Russia* (HQ New York). Conservative. 3 bishops. 33b.
Russisch-Orth Kirche (PE Mitteleuropa)		O-Rus	Mwc..	23	7,000	5,000	8,700	0.05	*Russian Orth Ch.* Patriarchal Exarchate of Moscow.
Selbständige Ev-Lutherische Kirche	1830	I-Lut	..C.w	179	25,900	48,192	37,000	-1.05	*Indep ELC.* 1972 merged with Altluth K (1830), EL Freikirche. 105n,1s,W=35%,500Yy.
Serbische Orthodoxe Kirche		O-Ser	Cwc..	11	75,000	160,000	150,000	0.05	*D Western Europe, Serbian Orthodox Ch.* Under P Belgrade. Serbian migrant workers.
Siebenten-Tags-Adventisten in D	1875	P-Adv	x....	610	33,000	70,000	63,000	-0.42	*Seventh-day Adventists, S&W German UCs.* 10 Confs. 201n,1H,1j,1r,886t(30599),650Y.
Syrisch-Orthodoxe Kirche (P Antioch)		O-Syr	Dw.N.	2	3,000	2,000	5,000	0.05	*Syrian Orthodox Ch. P Antioch.* By 1975, 600 immigrant families. Arabs.
Ukrainische Autokephale Orth Kirche		I-Ukr	X....	35	12,000	15,000	20,000	0.05	*Ukrainian Autocephalic Orthodox Ch in Exile.* Links with UOC of USA. 19nx.
Ukrainische Ev-Baptistische Kirche		P-Bap	.v...	4	800	1,000	1,500	0.05	*Ukrainian Ev Baptist Chs in Germany.* HQ Augsburg. 1948, applied to join WCC.
Ungarisch-Lutherische Exilkirche	c1945	P-Lut	.....	10	600	1,000	900	-0.42	*Hungarian Lutheran Ch in Exile.* Refugees from Hungary, especially since 1956.
Ungarisch-Reformierte Kirche	c1945	P-Ref	.....	5	1,800	3,500	3,000	-0.61	*Reformed Church of Hungary.* Refugees, especially since 1956 uprising in Hungary.
Verband B-W-B Mennonitengemeinden	1854	P-Men	G....	22	1,400	3,000	1,700	-2.25	*B-W-B=Badisch-Wurttembergisch-Bayrischer. Union of Mennonite Congs.* Declining.
Vereinigte Pfingstkirche	c1950	P-Pe1	.....	5	400	200	1,000	6.65	*United Pentecostal Ch. Jesus Only Church.* M=UPC(USA). 1 school. 5f.
Vereinigung der D Mennonitengemeinden	1525	P-Men	GWC.W	34	7,034	14,000	20,000	1.44	*Assoc of German Mennonite Congs* (1886). Saar, Rhineland, 15n.
Volksmission Entschiedener Christen	1934	P-Pe2	.....	180	4,500	10,000	9,000	-0.42	*People's Mission of Definite Christians.* HQ Stuttgart. Overseas missions, 1j.
Zeugen Jehovas	1897	m-Jeh	x....	1,990	154,108	160,000	240,000	1.64	*Jehovah's Witnesses.* 150,313 at 1973 Memorial. 1j,(1975)5438Y. (1995)6193Y.
Zigeunerische Kirche	c1950	I-3pE	.....	100	20,000	2,000	30,000	11.44	*GEM. Gypsy Evangelical Movement.* M=GGMS(Switzerland).
Other Protestant denominations		P-	.....	600	100,000	105,000	200,000	0.05	Total over 115 (see list below), including USA military chaplaincies.
Other marginal Protestant bodies		m-	.....	50	40,000	50,000	100,000	0.05	Total over 20 (see list below).
Other independent Catholic churches		I-CCa	.....	30	2,000	5,000	3,000	0.05	Total 39: Antoinists, Apostelamt Juda, Liberal Cath Ch, Mariavite Ch, 20 episcopi vagantes, &c.
Other Orthodox churches		O-	.....	30	3,000	2,000	5,000	0.05	Total over 5: Byelorussian, Estonian Orthodox.
Other independent charismatic chs	c1968	I-3cW	.....	160	12,000	2,000	24,000	10.45	In Berlin, Hamburg, Munich, Stuttgart. Manna Ch (Portugal), Vineyard Chs (4). M=YWAM.
Doubly-affiliated		2-aff			-1,629,000	0	-2,108,829		Free Protestants and others enumerated also by EKD or Roman Catholic dioceses.
Totals				**47,419**	**45,388,202**	**64,255,442**	**58,740,000**		

Churches, members, growth, 1900-2025	*Congs*	*Adults*	*Affiliated*	*G%*	*Total denominations*	*6 Megablocs:* *O*	*R*	*A*	*P*	*I*	*m*
Total churches, members, and denominations (mid-1900)	30,000	31,579,000	40,793,000	0.65	30	1	1	1	16	6	5
Total churches, members, and denominations (mid-1970)	47,137	49,741,838	64,255,442	0.65	180	11	1	1	100	40	27
Total churches, members, and denominations (mid-1990)	47,000	44,515,000	57,610,000	-0.54	336	17	1	1	173	100	44
Total churches, members, and denominations (mid-1995)	47,419	45,388,202	58,740,000	0.39	338	17	1	1	174	101	44
Total churches, members, and denominations (mid-2000)	47,500	45,421,000	58,783,222	0.01	342	17	1	1	175	102	46
Total churches, members, and denominations (mid-2025)	45,000	43,232,000	55,950,000	-0.20	548	21	1	1	220	250	55

NOTES ON TABLE ABOVE

NATIONAL COUNCILS (Column 4, 5th letter).

d = Vereinigte Evangelisch-Lutherische Kirche Deutschlands (VELKD) (United Evangelical Lutheran Church in Germany), a 1948 federation of Lutheran Landeskirchen (members also belong to the CCCG).

E = Deutsche Evangelische Allianz (DEA).

h = Reformierte Bund (Federation of Reformed Churches), representing the over 1,000 Reformed congregations and churches in Germany, with 2 million members and 1,000 ministers, mostly in Lutheran-Reformed United churches.

R = Deutsche Bischofskonferenz, also a member of ACKD (CCCG).

W = Arbeitsgemeinschaft Christlicher Kirchen in Deutschland (ACKD (Council of Christian Churches in Germany, CCCG).

w = associate (guest) member of ACKD (CCCG).

x = Evangelische Kirche der Union (EKU) (Evangelical Church of the Union) (a confederation of United churches); mem-

Continued opposite

Country Table 2–concluded

bers also belong to the CCCG.

Other national councils. Deutsche Evangelische Allianz (DEA) (German Evangelical Alliance) (members individuals, not denominations; affiliated to EEA and WEF). Arbeitsgemeinschaft der Christengemeinden (Working Fellowship of Christian Churches), a Pentecostal council. Vereinigung Evangelischer Freikirchen in Deutschland (Association of Free Churches in Germany): members = Bund Ev-Freikirchlicher Gemeinden in D, Bund Freier Ev Gemeinden in D, and Evmethodistische Kirche in D. Konferenz Bekennender Gemeinschaften in den Evangelischen Kirchen Deutschlands (anti-ecumenical). *Local councils.* 10 subregional councils and 150 local councils, affiliated with ACKD.

OTHER PROTESTANT DENOMINATIONS. The over 100 more smaller bodies include (with names given in the language they are best known in): American Baptist Association (1957; 2 churches; Korean pastor), Apostolic Christian Ch (Nazarean) (31 churches), Apostolische Glaubensgemeinde, Baptist Mid-Missions (1949), Bible Christian Union (20 missionaries), Biblische Glaubensgemeinde, Brüderhand, Brüderschaft 'Der König kommt!', Children of God (from USA), Chrischona Mission, Christengemeinden Elim, Christian Ch of North America, Communauté des Chrétiens, Conservative Mennonite Conference, Cooneyites (Ireland), Exclusive Brethren (Raven-Taylor, and Kelly-Continental), Freie Ev Lukasgemeinde Guissen, Freie Innere Mission, Glaubenshaus Bethanien, Glaubenshaus in Warngau, Gospel Missionary Union (1961), Greater Europe Mission, Greek Evangelical Ch (3 congregations, HQ Darmstadt), Gypsy Evangelical Movement (France), Hungarian Free Protestant Ch in Western Europe, International Ch of the Foursquare Gospel, Jugendhilfswerk Brüderliebe, Mennonite Brethren Ch, Mission zum Dienst am Vollem Evangelium, National Fellowship of Brethren Chs, Remonstrantse Broederschap, Seventh-day Adventist Reform Movement (with world HQ), Seventh Day Baptist Churches in Germany, Slavic Gospel Association, Tabernakelbewegung, The Way International (USA), Urgemeinde Gottes, Verband Christlicher Glaubensgemeinschaften, Worldwide Evangelization Crusade (1969), World-Wide Missions (1960). In addition, there are large numbers in USA and UK military chaplaincies not already listed in the table above.

OTHER MARGINAL PROTESTANT BODIES. These include: Arbeitsgemeinschaft Freier Religion (Offenbach-aM), Branhamites (End Time Believers; HQ Jeffersonville, IN, USA); Jesus-Only (Unitarians), Deutscher Bund für Freies Christentum (Frankfurt), Eglise Chrétienne Universelle (Témoins du Christ Revenu), Reichs-Israel-Gemeinde, Reorganized Ch of Jesus Christ of Latter-day Saints (1,200), Tempelgesellschaft (begun 1861; 800 adherents, most near Stuttgart; Unitarian), Unity School of Christianity. Other Unitarian groups, with over 40,000 members, include: Free Religious Community, German Unitarian Religious Community, German Unitarian Union, Union of Free Communities, Unitarian Religious Community (Free Protestant).

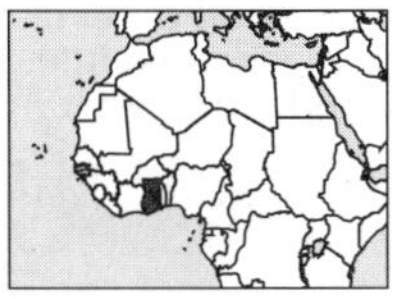

GHANA

SECULAR DATA, AD 2000

STATE
Official name: The Republic of Ghana.
Short name: Ghana. **Adjective of nationality:** Ghanaian.
Flag: Red, gold, and green stripes with centered black star.
Area: 238,533 sq. km. (92,098 sq. mi.).
Government: Unitary multiparty republic with one legislative house, since 1992 (1874 Gold Coast colony (British), 1957 Independence, 1960 republic, 1972 military junta).
Legislature: House of Parliament, 200 members.
Official language: English.
Monetary unit: 1 cedi (C) = 100 pesewas. **US$1=** C2,325.
Chief cities: ACCRA (Accra-Tema) 2,010,000; Kumasi 992,273; Sekondi-Takoradi 392,945; Sekondi 290,891; Tamale 279,280.
Political divisions: 10 provinces.
Armed forces: 7,000.

DEMOGRAPHY
Population: 20,212,000.
Population density: 84.7/sq. km. (219.4/sq. mi.).
Under 15 years: 8,724,000.
Growth rate p.a.: 2.70% (births 35.46, deaths 8.46).
Mortality: Infant, per 1,000: 58.2; **Maternal per 100,000:** 740.0.
Life expectancy: 62 (male 60, female 64).
Household size: 4.9. **Floor area per person, sq.m:** 5.5.
Major languages: Twi (Akan), Ewe, Ga, English, Hausa, Mole. There are over 100 other tribal languages.
Urban dwellers: 38.36%. **Urban growth rate p.a.:** 4.2%.
Labor force: 45%.

ETHNOLINGUISTIC PEOPLES
13.7% Ashanti (Akan); 11.3% Fante; 10.0% Ewe (Ebwe, Eve, Krepi); 3.9% Brong; 3.3% Gurenne (Frafra).

ECONOMY
National income p.a. per person: US$390; **per family:** US$1,911.

EDUCATION
Adult literacy: 64% (male 75%, female 53%). **Schools:** 16,653.
Universities: 16. **School enrolment:** female/male: 50%/65%.

HEALTH
Access to health services: 60%. **Access to safe water:** 56%.
Hospitals: 121 (13 beds per 10,000). **Doctors:** 628.
Blind: 65,000. **Deaf:** 1,195,700. **Murder rate:** 2.
Lepers: 120,000. **Underweight prevalence under 5:** 27%.

LITERATURE
New book titles p.a.: 4,040 (200 p.a. per million). **Periodicals:** 169.
Newspapers: 4 dailies.

COMMUNICATION (per 1,000 people)
Phones: 3 (17% mobile). **Radios:** 76. **TV sets:** 16.
Daily newspaper circulation: 18. **Computers:** 25.

REFUGEES
Alien refugees from other countries: 85,000.
Internal displacement: 150,000.

HUMAN LIFE AND LIBERTY (optimum condition=100.0%)
HDI: 46.8. **HSI:** 19.0. **HFI:** 27.5. **EFL:** 36.0.

Country Table 1. **Religious adherents in Ghana, AD 1900-2025.**

Year	1900		1970		mid-1990		Annual change, 1990-2000				mid-1995		mid-2000		mid-2025	
Name	Adherents	%	Adherents	%	Adherents	%	Natural	Conversion	Total	Rate	Adherents	%	Adherents	%	Adherents	%
Christians	**103,000**	**4.7**	**4,534,900**	**52.7**	**8,280,300**	**54.7**	**278,324**	**13,156**	**291,480**	**3.06**	**9,696,000**	**54.9**	**11,195,095**	**55.4**	**22,097,200**	**59.9**
PROFESSION																
professing Christians	**103,000**	**4.7**	**4,534,900**	**52.7**	**8,280,300**	**54.7**	**278,324**	**13,156**	**291,480**	**3.06**	**9,696,000**	**54.9**	**11,195,095**	**55.4**	**22,097,200**	**59.9**
AFFILIATION																
unaffiliated Christians	23,000	1.1	1,306,423	15.2	1,943,900	12.9	65,328	-6,906	58,422	2.66	2,206,120	12.5	2,528,119	12.5	4,644,700	12.6
affiliated Christians	**80,000**	**3.6**	**3,228,477**	**37.5**	**6,336,400**	**41.9**	**212,996**	**20,061**	**233,058**	**3.18**	**7,489,880**	**42.4**	**8,666,976**	**42.9**	**17,452,500**	**47.3**
Protestants	70,000	3.2	944,227	11.0	2,400,000	15.9	80,656	15,344	96,000	3.42	2,870,406	16.3	3,360,000	16.6	7,000,000	19.0
Independents	500	0.0	958,427	11.1	2,150,000	14.2	72,254	4,784	77,038	3.11	2,536,576	14.4	2,920,376	14.5	6,150,000	16.7
Roman Catholics	7,500	0.3	1,167,312	13.6	1,500,000	9.9	50,410	-7,910	42,500	2.53	1,705,498	9.7	1,925,000	9.5	3,200,000	8.7
Anglicans	2,000	0.1	100,000	1.2	150,000	1.0	5,041	4,959	10,000	5.24	210,000	1.2	250,000	1.2	500,000	1.4
Marginal Christians	0	0.0	57,511	0.7	135,000	0.9	4,537	2,963	7,500	4.52	165,900	0.9	210,000	1.0	600,000	1.6
Orthodox	0	0.0	1,000	0.0	1,400	0.0	47	-27	20	1.34	1,500	0.0	1,600	0.0	2,500	0.0
Trans-megabloc groupings																
Evangelicals	55,000	2.5	404,000	4.7	1,080,000	7.1	36,295	4,705	41,000	3.27	1,279,854	7.3	1,490,000	7.4	3,270,000	8.9
Pentecostals/Charismatics	0	0.0	1,050,000	12.2	3,160,000	20.9	106,197	25,803	132,000	3.55	3,820,488	21.7	4,480,000	22.2	9,000,000	24.4
Great Commission Christians	**99,000**	**4.5**	**1,033,000**	**12.0**	**2,723,000**	**18.0**	**91,511**	**28,695**	**120,206**	**3.72**	**3,265,000**	**18.5**	**3,925,064**	**19.4**	**8,485,000**	**23.0**
Ethnoreligionists	1,987,000	90.3	2,863,000	33.2	3,837,460	25.4	128,964	-18,983	109,981	2.55	4,422,000	25.1	4,937,270	24.4	6,367,000	17.3
Muslims	110,000	5.0	1,196,000	13.9	2,930,000	19.4	98,467	5,954	104,421	3.10	3,440,000	19.5	3,974,212	19.7	8,200,000	22.2
Nonreligious	0	0.0	9,000	0.1	48,000	0.3	1,613	-30	1,583	2.89	54,700	0.3	63,829	0.3	150,000	0.4
New-Religionists	0	0.0	200	0.0	13,000	0.1	437	41	478	3.18	15,300	0.1	17,780	0.1	22,000	0.1
Baha'is	0	0.0	6,600	0.1	9,800	0.1	329	-94	235	2.17	10,500	0.1	12,146	0.1	18,000	0.1
Hindus	0	0.0	1,000	0.0	3,200	0.0	108	-24	84	2.36	3,500	0.0	4,042	0.0	7,000	0.0
Atheists	0	0.0	0	0.0	2,500	0.0	84	-12	72	2.55	2,700	0.0	3,216	0.0	6,000	0.0
Chinese folk-religionists	0	0.0	0	0.0	500	0.0	17	-8	9	1.60	540	0.0	586	0.0	800	0.0
Buddhists	0	0.0	300	0.0	340	0.0	11	-5	6	1.74	360	0.0	404	0.0	1,000	0.0
Other religionists	0	0.0	1,000	0.0	2,900	0.0	97	5	102	3.05	3,400	0.0	3,915	0.0	7,000	0.0
World A (unevangelized persons)	1,694,000	77.0	2,583,590	30.0	2,632,272	17.4	88,452	-41,052	47,400	1.67	2,929,771	16.6	3,112,648	15.4	4,019,484	10.9
World B (evangelized non-Christians)	403,000	18.3	1,493,478	17.3	4,215,428	27.9	141,675	27,896	169,571	3.43	5,023,453	28.5	5,904,257	29.2	10,759,316	29.2
World C (Christians)	103,000	4.7	4,534,900	52.7	8,280,300	54.7	278,324	13,156	291,480	3.06	9,696,000	54.9	11,195,095	55.4	22,097,200	59.9
Country's population	**2,200,000**	**100.0**	**8,611,969**	**100.0**	**15,128,000**	**100.0**	**508,451**	**0**	**508,451**	**2.94**	**17,649,225**	**100.0**	**20,212,000**	**100.0**	**36,876,000**	**100.0**

COLUMNS, ROWS.
For meanings and definitions, see Codebook (Part 3). Note that, by definition, total 'Christians' = professing + crypto-Christians, which also = affiliated + unaffiliated Christians, and also = Great Commission Christians + latent Christians. Percentages may not always total exactly, due to rounding.

CENSUSES.
Before 1960, all censuses (especially 1891, 1901, 1931 and 1948) collected religion data supplied direct from the churches, hence reported affiliated members only, and that incompletely, as follows. **1891:** 25,000 total Christians. **1901:** 40,305. **1911:** 100,000 total Christians, 63,491 total Muslims. **1931:** 89.5% ethnoreligionists, 8.6% Christians, 1.8% Ahmadis. **1.II.1948** (Gold Coast, including Togoland): 84.1% ethnoreligionists, 15.9% Christians (7.7% Roman Catholics, 7.2% Protestants, 0.9% Anglicans), 0.6% Ahmadis. **20.III.1960** (national sample, adults aged 15 and over): 45.2% ethnoreligionists, 42.8% Christians (13.4% Roman Catholics, 10.3% Methodists, 9.9% Presbyterians, 5.0% African indigenous, 2.6% Anglicans, 1.6% other Christians), 12.0% Muslims (6.8% Malikites, 4.7% Ahmadis, 0.5% Shafites and others). **1.III.1970** (national sample, over 15 years old): 52.7% Christians (15.8% Roman Catholics, 12.0% Presbyterians, 11.4% Methodists, 10.2% African indigenous, 2.3% Anglicans, 0.6% marginal Protestants, 0.4% other Christians), 33.3% ethnoreligionists, 13.9% Muslims (6.4% Malikites, 6.3% Ahmadis, 1.2% Shafiites and others), 0.1% Baha'is.

NOTES ON RELIGIONS
BAHA'IS. Growth from 10 local spiritual assemblies (1964) to 39 (1973) and to 58 LSAs (1996).
BUDDHISTS. Chinese.
COUNTRY'S POPULATION. In 1969-70 the government deported 2 million alien African (1 million Nigerians, 196,000 Togolese, 186,000 Upper Voltans, et alii).
ETHNORELIGIONISTS. Mainly in the north, among the Gurensi (81% traditionalist in 1995), Dagari (LoDagaa) (46%), and (all over 60% traditionalist) Builsa, Chakossi, Konkomba, Mamprus.
HINDUS. Until the 1970s, only a handful of Indian traders. In 1975, an Indian missionary (the Black Monk of Africa) established in Accra the first Hindu monastery in Africa, headed by a Ghanaian, with 24 other African Monks (sanyasis). They are opening branches in other parts of Ghana and of West Africa, with emphasis on clinics and social welfare organizations. A Hindu sect also at work is Ananda Marga.
INDEPENDENTS. In over 430 denominations in 1995 (see Table 2).
MUSLIMS. The first Muslims date from about 1380. In 1900, 1% of the South were Muslims, and far more in the North. Muslims are mostly Sunnis of the Malikite rite, and Shafite rite; also Ahmadiya enumerated here under Muslims, though declared non-Muslim by Pakistan). Islam is strongest in the north, among the Wala (50%), Dagomba (60%), Mamprusi (15%), Chakossi (18%), among all of whom conversions of pagans are still taking place. There are also about 4,000 Asian Muslims. In 1969 the Aliens Act resulted in the expulsion of some 200,000 immigrant Muslims and the closure of many small Quranic schools. As a result, the conservative alien-dominated Ghana Muslim Community gave way to the rival and progressivist southern-dominated Ghana Muslim Mission. *Missionaries.* A number of Egyptian missionaries sent by Al-Azhar University (Cairo) are at work. *Hajj pilgrims to Mecca.* (1970) 402; (1974) 1,105; (1975) 2,703; (1976) 3,107.
NEW-RELIGIONISTS. By 1995, 13,000 converts to the Japanese movement Nichiren Shoshu (Soka Gakkai).
OTHER RELIGIONISTS. Adherents of smaller religions and cults, including Rosicrucians (5 AMORC centers), and the Church Universal & Triumphant (Summit; from USA).
PENTECOSTALS/CHARISMATICS. The largest single component is the Catholic Charismatic Renewal, begun in 1970, and in 1997 with 800 regular weekly prayer groups with 50,000 adult weekly attenders (20,000 young people ages 15-25), with 100 involved priests and 2 bishops.
ROMAN CATHOLICS. In 1900, 7,000 indigenous baptized Catholics and 500 catechumens.
UNAFFILIATED CHRISTIANS. In 1995, these were mainly nominal Protestants (Methodists and Presbyterians) and nominal Anglicans, and can be seen from the table to be slightly greater in number than those actually affiliated to these churches. It is from this huge nominal fringe around the older denominations that a majority of new converts to the African indigenous (spiritual) churches were coming in the period 1970-1990.

Great Commission Instrument Panel: status of Ghana (for explanation see start of Part 4)

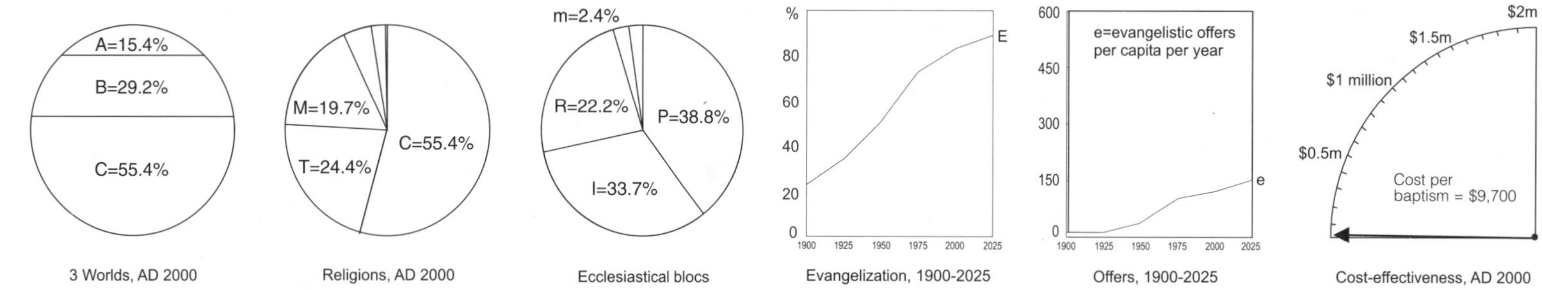

Country status. Known formerly as the Gold Coast, Ghana is one of the more important English-speaking countries in Africa. It is located on the Gulf of Guinea in West Africa, wedged between 3 French-speaking countries: Ivory Coast and Togo on either side and Burkina Faso to the north. The country is traditionally divided into north and south, the former mostly Gur-speaking and Muslim and the latter mostly Kwa-speaking and Christian. Cocoa, coffee, and coconuts are the main exports.

HUMAN LIFE AND LIBERTY

Human need and development. Ghana was one of the earliest among African countries to become free from its colonial masters, and at the time of independence was considered as the model for others. However, its political and economic history reflects fundamental developmental weaknesses in African countries. Ethnic rivalries and political instability dissipated the initial momentum of growth and the country became mired in corruption. Several revolving door military and civilian governments, following in close succession, have failed to reverse the decline or provide the necessary leadership. The result is that standards of living have not notably improved in the 3 decades of independence and human needs in many areas remain unmet. These needs are most severe in health, housing, education and transportation. Perhaps half the population are living at subsistence level. In many of the rural areas, housing is substandard, mostly huts built of mud and wattle or adobe. Running water and electricity are limited to the larger towns. In many small towns, sewage is carried in open ditches. Hard-surfaced streets are few and usually limited to commercial sections of the larger towns. Although the country as a whole has adequate supply of food, there are local and seasonal shortages, particularly in the northern areas. Nutritional deficiencies are the cause of much of the poor health. The life expectancy rate remains in the 50s for both men and women, and many of the killer diseases still take a heavy toll.

Human rights and freedoms. Ghanaians have enjoyed political freedoms only intermittently since independence. Under the periodic military rule, such as the current one under President Jerry Rawlings, human rights are heavily curtailed in favor of state security. The Criminal Code provides little protection against arbitrary arrest and detention. Any person may be detained without warrants and held incommunicado for extended periods of time without any legal recourse. The judiciary is not independent, and judges may be summarily dismissed at the government's pleasure. Citizens engaged in any activity objectionable to the government are subject to surveillance, including monitoring of telephones and mail. With the repeal of the Newspaper Licensing Law, some measure of freedom of speech and press has been restored. Although the government owns the radio and television stations and 2 principal daily newspapers, there are scores of opposition papers as well and criticism of the government and even of the president is fairly common in print. Freedom of assembly is restricted by the use of official permits for public meetings and demonstrations. Ethnic differences are downplayed by the government, but political leadership is dominated by the Ewe group from eastern Ghana to which president Rawlings belongs. Discrimination against women is no more prevalent in Ghana than in neighboring countries, but the present government has promulgated a number of laws that overturned traditional or colonial laws that discriminated against women.

Human environment. Ghana's major environmental problems are soil damage resulting from overgrazing and slash-and-burn agriculture, loss of forest cover from 34% in 1977 to 5% in 1992 and consequent depletion of wildlife, and water pollution as a result of open sewage ditches.

Ethnoreligionists. Gurensi, Dagari and other northerners venerate tribal ancestors (the 'living dead'), their guests and fetish objects.

NON-CHRISTIAN RELIGIONS.

Traditional religions were followed by 90% of the population in 1900, but then this has been rapidly shrinking through the 20th century due to conversions to Christianity. In 1960, 45% of the population followed traditional religions, 33.2% in 1970, and 25.1% in 1995. The heaviest concentration of traditionalists is among the northern peoples. Tribes with more than 75% traditionalist include the Achode (Atyoti), Adele (Bedere), Bondoukou Kulango (Nkurang), Bulsa (Builsa, Kanjaga), Chakali, Chakosi (Anufo), Eastern Kusasi, Gurenne (Frafra), Gurunsi (Nankani), Hanga, Kasena (Awuna), Konkomba (Bikpakpam), Lobi (Lobiri), Mamprusi (Mannelle), Talensi, Tamprusi (Tampele), and the Tumulung Sisala. Names for God include Nyame and Nyankopon (among the Akan, Ashanti, Fanti), Onyankopon (Twi), We (Birifor, Grunshi, Tallensi), Mawu (Ewe), Dzemawon (Ga), Omborr (Konkomba) and Na'angmin (LoDagaa). Among the Ashanti, prior to 1930, altars (called Nyame Dua, God's tree) for daily offerings to God were found in most compounds, but they are now rare. In addition to the worship of God, there is a belief in Asase Yaa, old mother earth; an elaborate pantheon of divinities (Abosom) who are remembered in annual festivals, the most important being the river spirits Tani, Bea and Bosomtwe; a continuing relationship between the living and their ancestral spirits (Ntoro) involving food offerings and libations; and dynamistic practices which express themselves positively in the forms of charms or amulets (suman) or negatively through the work of witches (abayifo).

Islam has its strength in northern Ghana although Muslim penetration is not as extensive as is commonly thought. Most northern tribes are about 30% Muslim. Islam is stronger among the Dagomba (60%). In the south, Islam has been confined largely to Hausa immigrants from Nigeria and Cameroon. However, the Aliens' Compliance Order of December 1969 resulted in the expulsion from Ghana of nearly two-thirds of all Hausas during 1970. Muslims are mostly of the Malikite rite (6.4 % of the population in 1970) or Ahmadis (6.3%). Only 1.2% belong to the Shafiite rite or other Muslim sects. Ghana experienced inter-religious strife and violence in the mid-1990s between Christians and Muslims. The troubles began in the coastal town of Sekondi-Takoradi and soon moved to the city of Kumasi. In November of 1995, at least 2 churches were damaged. One month later about 3,000 Muslim youths, mobilized by the group Jihad Preachers, stormed the police station in Kumasi and demanded the release of some who had been arrested earlier.

CHRISTIANITY

PROTESTANT CHURCHES. The 4 largest Protestant denominations in Ghana are the Methodist, Presbyterian, Seventh-day Adventist, and Evangelical Presbyterian churches. The Presbyterian Church was the first Protestant denomination in the Gold Coast resulting from the activity of the Swiss Basel Mission. Beginning at Christiansborg in 1828, the work was greatly strengthened by Moravian Christians from Jamaica after 1843. During World War I, the Basel Mission had to withdraw and the church became autonomous, but aid was later provided by the United Free Church of Scotland and the Netherlands Reformed Church. The first missionary from the British Wesleyan Methodist Church came to Cape Coast in 1835, followed 3 years later by a missionary pioneer of mixed race, Thomas Birch Freeman, who remained for 52 years during which time the Methodist mission expanded greatly. The formation of an African clergy has always been a major concern, and in 1961 the church became autonomous. The Evangelical Presbyterian Church grew out of the Bremen Mission from northern Germany. The mission opened work among the Ewe tribe of Togoland beginning at Peki in 1847. This area, formerly a German colony and later the Trusteeship Territory of British Togoland, is now the Volta region of Ghana. When the mission was expelled in 1914, the church gained its autonomy. These churches have sponsored hundreds of primary schools, secondary schools, teacher-training colleges, hospitals, dispensaries, and mobile clinics. They have also been involved in agricultural and community development projects. Baptists, Salvation Army and several Pentecostal missionary bodies are also present.

Catholic Church in Ghana. Mass is celebrated during papal visit in presence of an enormous open-air crowd.

CATHOLIC CHURCH. The first Catholics to reach the Gold Coast were Portuguese in 1471, who built a fort at Mina off the coast in 1482. Although occasional preaching forays were made into the interior, extensive missionary work was not begun until the arrival of Lyons missionaries in 1880, aided by White Fathers after World War I. Following the establish-

Country summary. **Worlds A, B, C by ethnolinguistic peoples, cities, and major civil divisions in Ghana.**

World	PEOPLES Num	Pop 2000	C%	Christians	E%	U%	Unevangelized
A	24	1,757,228	3.79	66,545	43	57	995,958
B	39	12,648,692	35.98	4,551,030	84	16	2,086,666
C	45	5,806,574	69.74	4,049,401	100	0	23,383
Total	**108**	**20,212,494**	**42.88**	**8,666,976**	**85**	**15**	**3,106,007**

World	CITIES Num	Pop 2000	C%	Christians	E%	U%	Unevangelized
A	1	279,280	10.00	27,928	42	58	162,681
B	4	1,574,447	47.54	748,437	91	9	149,555
C	2	2,153,153	64.67	1,392,392	98	2	51,309
Total	**7**	**4,006,880**	**54.13**	**2,168,757**	**91**	**9**	**363,545**

World	CIVIL DIVISIONS Num	Pop 2000	C%	Christians	E%	U%	Unevangelized
A	1	719,925	9.00	64,793	47	53	383,360
B	9	19,492,573	44.13	8,602,182	86	14	2,722,647
C	0	0	0.00	0	0	0	0
Total	**10**	**20,212,498**	**42.88**	**8,666,975**	**85**	**15**	**3,106,007**

ment of the hierarchy in 1950, the first Ghanaian bishop was consecrated in 1957 and became archbishop in 1960. The number of affiliated Catholics grew from 8,716 in 1906 to 51,842 in 1924 to over a million by 1970 and over 1.7 million by 1995. In 1995, 9.7% of the population professed to be Catholics.

The Holy See has diplomatic relations with Ghana and in AD 2000 is represented to the government and the Catholic hierarchy by a a nuncio resident in Accra.

Catholic Church in Ghana, Diocese of Wa. 'Rejoice in the Lord.' Sunday mass at Nandom in extreme northwest, among Dagari and Grunshi traditionalists.

INDIGENOUS CHURCHES. The first independent church in the Gold Coast was the short-lived Methodist Society, a Fante schism from the Wesleyan Methodists in Cape Coast in 1862. In 1896, the AME Zion Church was begun by a Fante named Pinanko, supported later by American Black missionaries. Two other similar Methodist denominations owing their origin to American Black missionary influence are the AME and CME churches. Prior to World War I, the Church of the Twelve Apostles arose as the first of Ghana's many spiritual churches; it was formed through the preaching of John Nackabah, a disciple of prophet William Wade Harris. Other early churches include the Army of the Cross of Christ Church in 1922 and Prophet Wovenu's Apostles Revelation Society in 1939. Nigerian independent churches have also spread to Ghana in recent years, the most important being Christ Apostolic Church. The Eden Revival Church, with a Christian community of 45,000 (1990) was the first of the locally founded indigenous churches to be accepted into membership in the Christian Council of Ghana. The growth of the spiritual churches in Ghana has been phenomenal. By 1970, over 420 indigenous denominations were active, and many more have started since. By 1995, indigenous Christians made up 34% of the entire affiliated Christian community in Ghana.

ANGLICAN CHURCH. Anglican missionaries arrived as early as 1752, but work was for many years confined to Cape Coast. The Society for the Propagation of the Gospel (UK) has been active; and by 1960, 2.6% of the population claimed to be Anglicans, falling to 2.3% by 1970 and 1% by 1995. The diocese of Accra, formed in 1909, is part of the Church of the Province of West Africa.

Renewal movements. In the 1990s the Pentecostal/Charismatic Renewal continued to spread rapidly across most older churches, and numbered over 4,480,000 adherents (of whom 19% Pentecostals, 20% Charismatics, and 61% Independents).

Indigenous missions. Since the rise of the African independent churches, several hundred Ghanaians have served as foreign missionaries—primarily in other African countries. A new emphasis has been on training Ghanaians as cross-cultural missionaries to non-Christian peoples in the northern parts of Ghana.

CHURCH AND STATE

In the preamble to the constitution of the Second Republic dated 22 August 1969, later suspended by the National Redemption Council in 1972, the following phrase was found: 'In the name of Almighty God, from whom all authority is derived and to whom all actions of both men and states should be referred'. One of the purposes of the constitution was stated to be that of guaranteeing 'freedom of thought, expression and religion'. (Preamble). Article 21 also speaks of 'freedom of conscience'. No new constitution has since been promulgated, and this religious emphasis has not been revoked.

Denominational schools have not been nationalized except in the Volta region during 1959-60 under the Nkrumah regime. An incident occurred there which led to a takeover by the government of Protestant schools, followed a short time later by Catholic schools. However, in the course of 1960, the matter was resolved and the schools were returned to their respective owners. In 1974, Ghana's director of Pedagogical Service declared that the government envisaged the nationalization of some 80 private schools. Since Nkrumah's overthrow in 1966, some members of the military regimes that followed were hostile to Christianity. A greater stability came with the multi-party elections in 1992. The Mormons and Jehovah's Witnesses were banned in 1989 and all expatriate workers expelled. After negotiations, the government reversed this action. At the same time, the Nyame Sompa Church and the Jesus Christ of Dzowuly Church were disbanded by the government. The secretary for internal affairs charged that such churches in their doctrines and practices 'abominate basic moral principles and violate religious decency', adding that some leaders were 'known freaks, frauds, and fakes whose activities cannot be said to be honorable or venerable'. A controversial Religious Bodies (Registration) Law was introduced in 1989 by the ruling Provisional National Defense Council, that required all religious groups to register, and that established a regime of close governmental scrutiny of organized religion. About 19,000 registration forms were distributed, 1,700 applications were submitted, and 960 were recommended for legal registration. Some groups had difficulty being accepted because of their policy of discouraging or forbidding members to seek medical care when ill. Several large mainline churches (Catholics, Methodists, Anglicans, and Presbyterians) resisted the law to the end. The military government repealed the law just days before it relinquished power to civilian rule at the start of 1993. Expatriate missionary visas were difficult to obtain and a quota system was in effect in the 1990s.

Large numbers of buses and trucks carry exuberant religious mottos.

BROADCASTING AND MEDIA

Ghana is a member of UNDA, and nearly every family owns a radio. Shortwave radio programs from KNLS have been received. CABS TV is an initiative by Ghanaian churches to produce and air Christian radio and TV programs.

Some 7 million (35%) have seen the 'Jesus' Film: through TV (2.3 million), film teams (3 million) and mission agencies (1.7 million). There have been 880,000 responses.

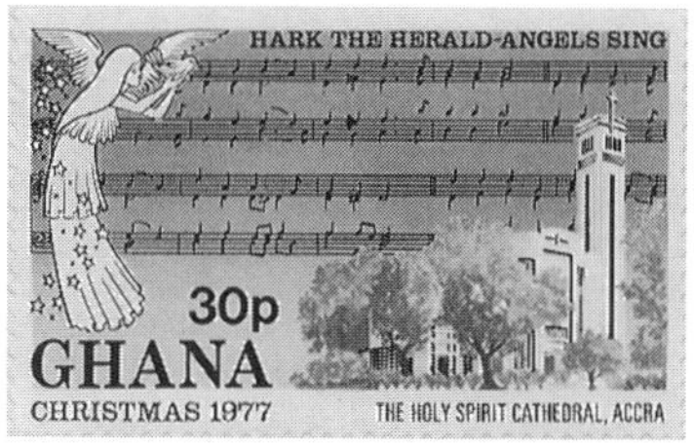

Worship at Holy Spirit Cathedral, Accra.

INTERDENOMINATIONAL ORGANIZATIONS

The Christian Council of the Gold Coast was founded in 1929 and changed its name in 1957 to Christian Council of Ghana. By 1994 it had 14 church members, including Protestants, Independents, Catholics, Orthodox and Anglicans. It provides member churches with an opportunity to participate in a united ministry of service and outreach. Areas of common action include literature production, family planning clinics, preparation of religious education material, united theological education, and a Christian Service Committee conducting relief, agricultural, and development programs. Seven member denominations of the council have been engaged in negotiations towards church union, with 3 others as observers. Local Christian councils have been formed in Accra, Akwatia, Cape Coast, Ho, Koforidua, Kumasi, Northern Region, Sekondi, Tema, and Winneba. A dozen organizations joined together in 1977 to form the National Association of Evangelicals of Ghana, which was registered in 1979. A meeting of 40 Evangelical leaders in 1991 revived interest in the association. Ecumenical relations between the Catholic Church and the Christian Council

African indigenous churches. The National Council of Spiritual Churches of Ghana, shown in procession in 1973, is one of 4 nationwide councils uniting Ghana's 420 indigenous denominations.

of Ghana have improved greatly since Vatican II. In 1966, a Committee of Cooperation was established to coordinate the activities of the Christian Council and the National Catholic Secretariat. Other organizations include the Joint Committee on Christian Marriage and Family Life, Christian Medical Workers Fellowship (CMWF) and Christian Hospital Association of Ghana (CHAG). The Ghana Evangelism Committee and the New Life For All programs were significant ecumenical projects in the 1980s. The former conducted a national church survey (1985-89) culminating in a conference of denominational leaders showing the way forward in church growth and evangelization. Most every major denomination, mission, and para-church agency in the country was represented at the conference. Hundreds of Christian leaders came together again in June 1993 for a similar event.

Ghana has seen several nationwide councils form seeking to unite the many indigenous churches. Prominent among them is the Council of Independent Churches of Ghana (CIC) which includes about 500 spiritual churches. The older Pentecostal churches have joined together under the Ghana Pentecostal Council which had 66 member churches in 1993. The 4 oldest and largest Pentecostal denominations created and continue to lead this council, namely the Church of Pentecost, Assemblies of God, Apostolic Church, and the Christ Apostolic Church. A more informal group is the Charismatic Ministers Network founded in 1984, based on individual participation of key leaders.

FUTURE TRENDS AND PROSPECTS

Careful plans for countrywide evangelization in the 1990s will likely increase the Christian community to over the 55% by AD 2000 and on to 60% by 2025.

By AD 2050 ethnoreligionists will probably have all but disappeared and Ghana will be 70% Christian, 25% Muslim, and 5% nonreligious. These percentages could remain stable for a very long time.

BIBLIOGRAPHY

150 years of North German mission, 1836–1986. E. Schöck-Quinteros & D. Lenz (eds). Bremen, 1989. 83p. (Deals with work of North German missions in Togo, Ghana, and Japan).
A history of Christianity in Ghana. H. W. Debrunner. Accra: Waterville Publishing House, 1967. 375p.
A short history of the Catholic Church in Ghana. H. M. Pfann. 2d ed. Cape Coast, Ghana: Catholic Mission Press, 1970. 116p.
Akan religion and the Christian faith: a comparative study of the impact of two religions. S. G. Williamson. Accra: Ghana University Press, 1965. 186p.
'Asante Catholicism: ritual communication of the Catholic faith among the Akan of Ghana.' J. P. Obeng. Ph.D. dissertation, Boston University, Boston, 1991. 327p.
'Aspects of religion'. C. G. Baëta. Chapter VII in W. Birmingham et al, A study of contemporary Ghana. Vol II, Some aspects of social structure (Evanston, IL: Northwestern University Press, 1967), p. 240-250.
Bibliography of the Ewes. R. Arkaifie. Cape Coast, Ghana: University of Cape Coast, 1976. 81p. (Large section on Christianity).
'Church and state in Ghana, 1949–1966,' J. S. Pobee, in *Religion in a pluralistic society: essays presented to Professor C. G. Baëta.* J. S. Pobee (ed). Leiden: E. J. Brill, 1976.
'De–westernizing Christianity among the Krobo of Ghana.' D. K. Tei-Kwabla. D.Miss. thesis, Fuller Theological Seminary, Pasadena, CA, 1983. 460p.
Eden Revival: spiritual churches in Ghana. D. M. Beckmann. St. Louis, MO: Concordia Publishing House, 1975.
Five hundred churches: a brief survey of Christianity in Ghana. P. Barker (ed). Accra: Christian Council of Ghana, 1978. 210p.
Ghana. R. A. Myers. *World bibliographical series*, vol. 124. Oxford, UK: CLIO Press, 1991. 466p. (See especially 'Religion,' p.151–5).
Ghana Catholic diary, 1970. Accra: Catholic Press, 1970. (Annual).
Ghana in retrospect: some aspects of Ghanaian culture. P. Sarpong. Tema, Ghana: Ghana Publishing Corporation, 1974. 134p. (Deals with numerous religious topics).
God: ancestor or creator? Aspects of traditional beliefs in Ghana, Nigeria and Sierra Leone. H. Sawyerr. London: Longman, 1970. 118p.
Honey from the lion: an African journey. W. L. Belcher. Toronto: Fitzhenry & Whiteside, 1988. 188p. (Story of a Bible translator).
Kpele lala: Ga religious songs and symbols. M. Kilson. Cambridge, MA: Harvard University, 1971. 313p.
Le système religieux des Evhé. A. de Surgy. Paris: L'Harmattan, 1988. 343p.
Les Senufo et le christianisme. R. Deniel. Korhogo–Abidjan: Inades, 1979. 67p.
Mustard seed: the growth of the church in Kroboland. E. M. L. Odjidja. Accra: Waterville Pub. House, [1973]. 162p.
National church survey, 1993 update: facing the unfinished task of the church in Ghana. Accra North: Ghana Evangelism Committee, 1993. 112p.
'One hundred and fifty years of Christianity in a Ghanaian town,' J. Middleton, *Africa*, 53, 3 (1983), 2–19. (Treats Presbyterian Church of Ghana in Akuopon, Ghana).
'Opening a new door to dialogue between Christians and Muslims in Ghana.' J. P. Dretke. D.Miss. thesis, Fuller Theological Seminary, Pasadena, CA, 1974. 349p.
Prophetism in Ghana: a study of some 'spiritual' churches. C. G. Bäeta. London: SCM Press, 1962.
'Radical nationalists and Protestant Christian churches in Ghana, 1949–1966.' F. K. Kokuma. Ph.D. dissertation, Northwestern University, Evanston, IL, 1982. 469p.
'Rededication and prophetism in Ghana,' J. W. Fernandez, *Cahiers d'études africaines*, 10 (1970), 228–305.
Religion and art in Ashanti. R. S. Rattray. 1927; reprint, New York: AMS Press, 1979. 414p.
Religion and politics in Ghana. J. S. Pobee. *Studia missionalia Upsaliensia*, 48. Accra: Asempa Publishers, 1991. 150p.
'Religion in a Fante town of Southern Ghana.' H. D. Hornsey. Ph.D. dissertation, University of London, 1979. 354p.
Religion, morality and the person: essays on Tallensi religion. M. Fortes. *Cambridge paperback library. Essays in social anthropology.* Cambridge, UK: Cambridge University Press, 1987. 347p.
'Religious change and social stratification in Labadi, Ghana: the Church of the Messiah,' L. Mullings, in *African Christianity: patterns of religious continuity*, p.65–88. G. Bond, W. Johnson & S. S. Walker (eds). *Studies in anthropology.* New York: Academic Press, 1979.
Saturday God and Adventism in Ghana. K. Owusu-Mensa. Frankfurt: P. Lang, 1993. 108p.
'Split–level Christianity in Africa: a study of the persistence of traditional religious beliefs and practices among the Akan Methodists of Ghana.' M. K. Forson. D.Miss. thesis, Asbury Theological Seminary, Wilmore, KY, 1993. 337p.
'Sunsum edwuma, the spiritual work: forms of symbolic action and communication in a Ghanaian healing movement.' P. S. Breidenbach. Thesis, Northwestern University, Evanston, IL, 1973. 440p.
The Akan doctrine of God: a fragment of Gold Coast ethics and religion. J. B. Danquah. 2nd ed. *Cass library of African studies, Africana modern library*, no. 2. 1944; reprint, London: Frank Cass, 1968. 206p.
'The Bible and the crown: Thomas Birch Freeman's synthesis of Christianity and social reform in Ghana (1838–1890).' S. A. Aryee. Ph.D. dissertation, Drew University, Madison, NJ, 1993. 344p.
The Christian chronicle (Accra). , 1988–. (Periodical).
'The church in Ghana: towards a redemptive African ecclesiology.' R. B. Otchere. D.Min. thesis, Wesley Theological Seminary, Washington, DC, 1990. 157p.
The churches and Ghana society, 1918–55. R. T. Parsons. Leiden: E. J. Brill, 1963.
The culture of Ghana: a bibliography. E. Y. Amedekey. Accra: Ghana Universities Press for the University of Ghana, 1970. 215p. (1,670 items with sections on religion).
'The Evangelical Presbyterian Church (Ghana and Togo), 1914–1946: a study in European mission relations affecting the beginning of an indigenous church.' E. E. Grau. Ph.D. dissertation, Hartford Seminary Foundation, Hartford, CT, 1964. 262p.
The Ewe–speaking peoples of the Slave Coast of West Africa, their religion, manners, customs, laws, languages, &c. A. B. Ellis. London: Chapman & Hall, 1890. 331p.
The Ghanaian's image of the missionary: an analysis of the published critiques of Christian missionaries by Ghanaians, 1897–1965. H. W. Mobley. *Studies on religion in Africa*, 1. Leiden: E. J. Brill, 1970. 180p.
'The interaction between Christianity and Ashanti religion.' P. Nkrumah. Ph.D. dissertation, Drew University, Madison, NJ, 1992. 2 vols.
The Mennonite Church in Ghana 1957–1964. S. J. Hostetler. Elkhart, IN: Mennonite Board of Missions, [1979]. 53p.
The natives of the Northern Territories of the Gold Coast: their customs, religion and folklore. A. W. Cardinall. London: G. Routledge, 1925. 158p.
'The perception of the people in Accra (Ghana) as to the interrelation of Christianity and culture.' S. Y. Nortey. Doctoral thesis, Howard University, Washington, DC, 1988. 137p.
'The presence of Islam among the Akan of Ghana: a bibliographic essay,' R. A. Silverman & D. Owusu–Ansah, *History in Africa*, 16 (1989), 325–39.
The prophet Harris: a study of an African prophet and his mass–movement in the Ivory Coast and the Gold Coast, 1913–1915. G. M. Haliburton. London: Longmans, 1971. 250p.
The rise of independent churches in Ghana. Accra: Asempa Publishers, 1990. 92p.
The rise of the charismatic movement in the mainline churches in Ghana. A. O. Atiemo. Accra, Ghana: Asempa Publishers, Christian Council of Ghana, 1993. 84p.
The roots of Ghana Methodism. F. L. Bartels. Cambridge, UK: Cambridge University Press in association with the Ghana Methodist Book Depot, 1965. 368p.
The social control of religious zeal: a study of organizational contradictions. J. Miller. *The Arnold and Caroline Rose monograph series of the American Sociological Association.* New Brunswick, NJ: Rutgers University Press, 1994. 254p. (Deals with Swiss and German missions in Ghana).
The spirit–seekers: new religious movements in southern Ghana. R. W. Wyllie. *American Academy of Religion. Studies in religion*, no. 21. Missoula, MT: Scholars Press, 1980. 139p.
The Tshi–speaking peoples of the Gold Coast of West Africa: their religion, manners, customs, laws, language, etc. A. B. Ellis. 1887; reprint, Chicago: Benin Press, 1964. 343p.
Together we sow and reap: the Christian Council of Ghana, 1929–1979. J. Anquandah. Accra: Asempa Publishers, 1979. 144p.
Witchcraft in Ghana: a study on the belief in destructive witches and its effect on the Akan tribes. H. Debrunner. 2d ed. Accra: Presbyterian Book Depot, 1961. 213p.

Country Table 2. **Organized churches and denominations in Ghana.**

Official name (bold type = church with over 10% of all affiliated) 1	*Begun* 2	*Type* 3	*Counc* 4	*Congs* 5	*Adults* 6	*Affiliated 1970* 7	*Affiliated 1995* 8	*G%* 9	*Names, notes, and other statistics* (see Codebook, Part 3) 10
African Faith Tabernacle Church	1919	I-3oA	I	860	92,900	50,000	116,000	3.42	*AFTC.* Link with Faith Tabernacle Ch (USA). Medicine allowed. Missions in 3 nations. 500n.
African Methodist Episcopal Church	1933	I-Met	Vw..W	39	1,800	12,400	3,000	-5.52	M=AMEC(USA). Ex AMECZ. 65% Ashanti, 25% Fante, 8% Akim. 27n,W=58%,1500Y,500y.
African Methodist Episcopal Zion Ch	1896	I-Met	Vw..W	138	24,800	36,296	51,800	1.43	M=AMEZC(USA). 60% Fante, 29% Ewe. 118 schools. 51n,15m,5w,2H,2h,5r,1s,475Y,838y.
African Orthodox Church	1931	I-ARo	x....	10	1,000	2,000	2,000	0.00	*Diocese of Accra.* Link with M=AOC(USA Blacks). Akwapim and Kwahu tribes. 3n,1x.
Anglican Church of Ghana	1752	A-ACa	AwAVW	432	100,000	100,000	210,000	3.01	In *CPWA.* 6 Dioceses. 1904, M=USPG. 69n,1x,500m,100w,23f,1H,5r,1u,4795Y,8156y.
Apostles Revelation Society	1939	I-3aA	x...I	256	42,800	60,000	85,500	1.43	*ARS. Apostolowo be Dedefia Habobo.* Founder prophet CKN Wovenu. 90% Ewe. 101n,1s.
Apostolic Church, Ghana	1936	P-PeA	ZG..C	827	37,500	50,000	104,000	2.97	M=ACMM(UK). 1953, missionary founder splits, forms Ch of Pentecost. 50n,2x,4f.
Apostolic Divine Church of Ghana	1957	I-3sA	I	73	22,000	15,000	31,400	3.00	Schism ex Methodists. Indigenous pentecostals. HQ Accra. 7n.
Apostolic Reformed Church of Ghana	1958	I-3sA	.....	37	3,160	1,601	5,270	4.88	Schism ex Presbyterian Ch of Ghana. Indigenous pentecostals. 2n.
Army of the Cross of Christ Church	1922	I-3sA	.v..I	1,094	68,900	55,542	125,000	3.30	*MDCC. Musama Disco Christo Ch.* Fante. 1958, applied to WCC. 60n,1s,2208Y,4417y.
Assemblies of God in Ghana	1916	P-Pe2	ZF..C	528	95,600	30,000	120,000	5.70	M=AoG(USA). 44% Ashanti, 15% Kusasi, 8% Ga, 8% Dagomba. 25n,45f,2h,1j,2s(46).
Assembly Hall Churches	c1985	I-3nC	.....	40	800	–	2,000	10.00	*Little Flock. Local Churches.* Begun 1922 in China.
Baptist International Missions		I-Bap	.....	6	450	250	1,500	0.05	M=BIM(USA).
Baptist Mid-Missions	1946	I-Fun	xT...	40	2,000	238	3,330	11.13	M=BMM(USA). Work in northwest among Dagati and Sissala. HQ Tumu. 11n,17m,24f,1s.
Bethany Church Mission	1962	I-3sA	I	20	2,000	2,000	4,000	2.81	*Bethany Chapel.* Split ex Holy Trinity Healing Ch, by founder's son. 85% women. Ashanti.
Bethel Church of Christ	1967	I-3sA	I	10	1,000	1,350	2,500	2.50	*Bible Ch of Christ.* Ex CLA. 56% Akan, 33% Ga, 11% Ewe. 3n,13m,10w,W=81%,100Y.
Bethesda Church Mission	1965	I-3sA	.....	68	30,000	11,000	42,900	5.59	Ex Divine Healer's Ch. Kumasi. 66% Ashanti, 27% Ga, 5% Fante, 2% Ewe. 8n,W=70%.
Bethlehem Revival Church	1951	I-3sA	.....	10	4,000	5,000	7,000	1.35	Ex Apostolic Ch. 27% Ga, 26% Akan, 21% Ewe, 14% Frafra, 11% Hausa. 6n,5m,1w,500Y.
Bible Missionary Church	1985	I-Non	.....	3	150	–	250	10.00	M=BMC(USA).
Broadsheet Readers' Clubs	c1980	I-3nA	.....	195	2,500	–	6,000	6.67	Readers of Gospel Broadsheets produced by M=WEC(UK).
Buem-Krachi Presbyterian Church	1954	I-Ref	.....	10	200	1,000	500	-2.73	Schism ex EPC over polygamy; 1964, part rejoined EPC. Buem and Krachi tribes. 2n.
Calvary Church of the Coastlands	1991	I-3cA	.....	7	300	–	500	25.00	Fante. Most are former animists. M=YWAM.
Calvary Pentecostal Church	c1983	I-3pA	.....	4	700	–	2,000	8.33	Fante. Link with Ch of God Mission International (Benin City, Nigeria).
Catholic Church in Ghana:	1481	R-Lat	P.SGR	237	901,000	1,167,312	1,705,498	1.53	C=4+7+20. (1970)113n,237x. 558n 166x 377m 706w 50391Yy

Continued opposite

Country Table 2–concluded

Official name (bold type = church with over 10% of all affiliated) 1	*Begun* 2	*Type* 3	*Counc* 4	*Congs* 5	*Adults* 6	*Affiliated 1970* 7	*Affiliated 1995* 8	*G%* 9	*Names, notes, and other statistics* (see Codebook, Part 3) 10
M Accra	1943	R-Lat	Ps	27	60,000	146,041	114,000	-0.99	35% Twi, 30% Ewe, 20% Krobo, 12% Ga. M=SVD. 34n 27x 38m 49w 3009Yy
D Keta-Ho	1923	R-Lat	Ps	34	89,000	245,200	169,220	-1.47	82% Ewe, 10% Buem, 8% Akyem. 5% Muslim. 82n 9x 11m 73w 7538Yy
D Koforidna	1992	R-Lat	Ps	16	112,000	–	212,000	33.33	24n 25x 35m 75w 4120Yy
M Cape Coast	1879	R-Lat	Ps	18	130,000	163,000	245,390	1.65	Central Region. 10% Protestant, 1.5% Muslim. 80n 11x 30m 82w 9708Yy
D Kumasi	1932	R-Lat	Ps	43	106,000	304,712	200,000	-1.67	Area 24% Muslim. 90% Ashanti, 10% Fante. 78n 27x 63m 96w 9171Yy
D Sekondi-Takoradi	1969	R-Lat	Ps	27	178,000	184,000	335,400	2.43	Western Region. 11% Protestant. 1.5% Muslim. 67n 8x 40m 26w 6032Yy
D Sunyani	1973	R-Lat	Ps	28	102,000	–	193,540	4.55	50n 19x 25m 77w 5588Yy
M Tamale	1926	R-Lat	Ps	17	7,000	15,862	12,940	-0.81	7% Dagomba, 3% Chakossi; rest from south. M=WF. 29n 29x 72m 49w 959Yy
D Navrongo-Bolgatanga	1956	R-Lat	Ps	11	35,000	19,467	67,585	5.10	Kasena, Frafra, Talensi, Kusasi, Bulsa. M=WF. 25n 7x 16m 32w 1850Yy
D Wa	1959	R-Lat	Ps	16	82,000	89,030	155,423	2.25	99% Dagari, 1% Sissala (neglected by RCs). 89n 4x 47m 147w 2416Yy
Celestial Church of Christ	c1960	I-3aA	x....	16	5,000	500	10,000	12.73	Large Nigerian indigenous church, mainly of Yoruba elites. Now in 11 countries, expanding.
Christ Apostolic Church	1921	I-3aA	x.I.C	579	34,000	100,000	40,000	-3.60	M=CAC(Nigeria). 9 Regional Apostles in Ghana. 32% ex Methodist. Schisms.150n,19x,1s,3000Y
Christ Revival Church	1960	I-3aA	.v..I	10	900	2,000	1,500	-1.14	Ex Apostolic Ch. Healing ministry. Twi-speaking. 1971 applied to join WCC. 3n,4m.
Christian Action Faith Ministries	1978	I-3fA	x....	20	15,000	–	20,000	5.88	*CAFM.* In Accra. Ex Full Gospel. F=N. Duncan-Williams. Also: London,Paris, USA, Togo.
Christian Assembly	1947	I-mar	I	30	2,000	6,318	4,000	-1.81	Use of occult. Mechanized farm, commercial school, carpet firm. 20n,15m,4w,1500Y.
Christian Divine Church	1960	I-3sA	I	100	5,000	6,000	7,000	0.62	Ex Methodists. Healings of incurables, mental cases. 20n,28m,1p,1p,W=80%,200Y.
Christian Hope Ministry	1984	I-3wA	.....	20	3,000	–	5,000	9.09	Small independent ministry.
Christian Methodist Episcopal Church	c1950	I-Met	Vw..W	10	1,540	2,200	2,800	0.97	*Ghana-Togoland Conference.* Ex AMEC. 1959, invited in M=CMEC(USA Blacks). 5n,1r.
Christian Outreach Missions	1989	I-3cA	.....	4	800	–	1,500	16.67	Krobo area. Begun by a Krobo. Southwest tip of Lake Volta. M=YWAM.
Church of Christ (Spiritual Movement)	1958	I-3oA	.....	119	34,000	20,000	42,500	3.06	Split ex Ghana Apostolic Ch. 50% Ashanti, 30% Ga, 8% Fante, 3% Ewe. 30n,W=70%.
Church of Gethsemane	1969	I-3sA	I	20	1,000	1,354	2,000	1.57	Team of 12 evangelists and bandsmen. Converts join any pentecostal church. 3n,12m.
Church of God	1963	P-Pe3	ZF...	92	4,109	4,000	13,300	4.92	1966, M=CoG(Cleveland) (USA). Holiness Pentecostals. 12n,2x,12m,1s,W=76%,29Y.
Church of God of Prophecy	c1980	P-Pe3	.....	7	420	–	700	6.67	M=CoGP. *Church of God of Prophecy (USA).*
Church of Grace	1949	I-3sA	I	20	2,500	3,500	4,000	0.54	Begun by healing prophetess evicted ex Methodists. 57% Ashanti. 13n,W=90%,100Y.
Ch of Jesus Christ of Latter-day Saints		m-LdS	.....	39	5,340	685	15,900	0.05	*Mormons.* M=CJCLdS(USA). Temple in Accra.
Church of Messiah	1965	I-3sA	I	5	1,000	2,000	1,500	-1.14	Begun by prophetess. HQ Kumasi. Healings. Mostly Twi. 9n,3m,W=78%,250Y.
Church of Pentecost	1937	P-PeA	ZG..C	3,871	240,000	100,000	429,000	6.00	1953, ex Apostolic Ch. M=EMS(UK). 60% Akan,15% Ewe, 12% Ga. 118n,3x,4f,6998Y,4864y.
Church of the Lord (Aladura)	1953	I-3sA	xwI.I	313	56,000	60,000	70,000	0.62	*Aladura=Praying.* M=CLA(Nigeria). Healings, oils, incense. 40n,8x,W=50%,1000Y.
Church of the Lord (Ghana)	1953	I-3sA	..I.I	50	6,000	7,000	10,000	1.44	Ex CLA(Nigeria); 1971, 10 more CLA churches joined. 60% Akan, 16% Ga. 46n,5m,4w.
Church of the Messiah	1967	I-3sA	I	10	2,000	4,000	5,000	0.90	Split ex Ransomed Ch. HQ Accra. 78% Ga, 15% Akan, 7% Ewe. 3n,12m,13w,W=65%,400Y.
Church of the Twelve Apostles	1914	I-3sA	I	1,150	8,000	14,030	12,000	-0.62	Founder Prophet Harris' disciple John Nackabah; now under John Nackabah III. HQ Kormantse.
Churches of Christ	1961	I-Dis	x....	483	31,200	4,200	51,100	10.51	M=CCCC(Instrumental) (USA). 90% Ashanti, 10% Kwahu. 40n,4x,254m,9f,2p,W=85%,750Y.
Deeper Life Bible Church	c1975	I-3cA	.....	274	20,800	–	40,000	5.00	*DLBC.* Yoruba and other Nigerian immigrants. M=DLBC(Nigerian,HQ Lagos).
Divine Fellowship	1962	I-3sA	I	15	4,000	5,500	7,000	0.97	*Twer Nyame Ch.* Ex CLA. Healings, oils, incense. 98% Akan, 2% Ga. 15n,12m,3w,120Y.
Divine Healer's Church	1954	I-3pA	I.I..	170	120,700	150,000	200,000	1.16	*The Lord is There Temple*, Accra. Brother GA Lawson. Strong % Ga. 76n,W=40%,2400Y.
Divine Healing Church of Christ	1950	I-3sA	I	20	1,000	2,517	2,000	-0.92	Founded by prophetess. Indigenous pentecostals. Midnight vigils. 10n,8m,4w,80Y.
Eden Revival Church	1963	I-3sA	xvI.W	18	27,000	50,000	45,000	-0.42	*F'Eden Church.* Akan, Ga. 1971 applied to WCC, blocked. HQ Accra. 31n,40m,4r,1s.
Faith Gospel Ministry	c1980	I-3pA	I...I	2,000	150,000	–	300,000	6.67	*FGM.* Active in OAIC events.
Emissaries of Divine Light	1954	I-3pA	I	10	2,000	5,000	4,000	-0.89	Link with Emissaries Ch (USA). Ashanti, Ga, Akwapim. HQ Sekondi. 19n,W=12%,200Y.
Epis Holy Temple & Tabernacle Mission	1920	I-3nA	.T..I	5	1,000	2,000	2,000	0.00	1920, National Ch of Christ; name changed 1953. Ashanti. 6n,1p,1s,W=60%,50Y.
Evangelical Church of Ghana	1940	P-Eva	xF..C	83	2,500	2,600	4,520	2.24	M=WEC(UK). North. 56% Konkomba, 32% Birifor, 12% Bassari. 7n,22x,3h,2p,W=90%,12Y.
Evangelical Lutheran Church of Ghana	c1950	P-Lut	e...W	160	3,000	422	10,000	13.50	M=LCMS(USA). Fante, Ashanti, Kusasi. Nigerian Efiks deported 1969. 1n,5x,9t,W=90%.
Evangelical Presbyterian Church	1847	P-Ref	RWA.W	710	102,000	122,292	308,000	3.76	*EPC.* Formerly Ewe Presb Ch. M=BrM,CSM,CSM,UCBWM. 55% Ewe. 76n,3x,1s,2060Y,10300y.
Evangelical Presbyterian Ch of Ghana	1993	I-Ref	.....	100	10,000	–	30,000	50.00	Split ex EPC insisting that only Ewes can be members.
Evangelical Presbyterian Reformed Ch	1964	I-Ref	.....	20	2,000	3,000	3,500	0.62	HQ Accra New Town. Mainly Ewe, also Ga, Akan. One school. 4n,9m,2w,W=17%,40Y.
Evangelistic Tabernacle of Jesus	c1980	I-3oA	.....	30	3,000	–	7,000	6.67	Oneness body. F=bp Sammy Kweku. HQ Accra.
First Miracle Healing Church	1959	I-3pA	.....	10	2,000	5,000	3,000	-2.02	Healing by oil, water, incense, handkerchiefs. 80% Ga. Declining. 4n,18m,3w,325Y.
Free Prot Episcopal Ch: D West Africa	c1960	I-ARo	xv...	2	150	300	300	0.00	*Ecumenical Church Foundation.* M=FPEC(UK,USA). HQ Monrovia (Liberia).
Full Gospel Church in Ghana		I-3fA	.....	5	1,500	–	3,000	0.05	Assisted by mission from Canada.
Gateway Worship Centers	1992	I-3fA	.....	2	1,000	–	2,000	33.33	Ashaiman. Ex Full Gospel. Twi speakers, also many Ewe. M=YWAM.
Ghana Baptist Convention	1920	P-Bap	T...W	450	45,500	2,000	80,800	15.95	M=NBC(Nigeria); 1947, SBC(USA). Yorubas. Now radically charismatic. 23n,8x,51f,1H,104Y.
Ghana Mennonite Church	1956	P-Men	G...W	17	1,200	700	1,800	3.85	Begun by a Ghanaian. M=MCNA. In south. HQ Accra. 45% Ga. 1x,11m,12f,W=70%,25Y.
Good News Churches	1956	P-Non	xM...	60	2,885	300	8,740	14.44	M=ECWA(Nigeria); 1956, SIM(USA), in schools and literature. 14f,1s.
Greek Orth P Alexandria: D Accra		O-Gre	Cw...	2	1,000	1,000	1,500	0.05	Under P Alexandria (Egypt). HQ Yaounde, Cameroon. Covers all West Africa. Bishop in Greece.
Harrist Church	c1940	I-Met	.vI..	70	2,000	3,770	5,000	1.14	Harrists from Ivory Coast, 1913. Organized in Ghana 1964. Many chs around Kumasi. 40n.
Holy Trinity Healing Church	1954	I-3jA	I	15	2,000	2,419	3,000	0.86	Ex RCs. HQ Kumasi. 1962. founder's son broke off, formed Bethany Church Mission.
Inner Temple of Christ	1964	I-3pA	I...I	9	2,000	7,000	4,000	-2.21	Ex Divine Healer's Ch. 40% decline since 1966. 50% Ashanti, 30% Ga. 7N,W=70%,600Y.
International Central Gospel Ch	1982	I-3cA	x....	50	14,000	–	28,000	7.69	In Accra (7,000 members), many branches. F=Mensah Otabil (ex SU). Branches in Nigeria, UK.
Internat Ch of the Foursquare Gospel	1965	P-Pe2	.....	3	557	100	1,110	10.11	M=ICFG.
International Pentecostal Holiness Ch	c1990	P-Pe3	Z....	100	8,000	–	15,000	20.00	*IPHC.* M=IPHC(USA). Mainly former charismatics in AICs especially Christian Action.
Jehovah's Witnesses	1924	m-Jeh	x....	680	37,376	55,826	140,000	3.75	*Watch Tower.* First Lectures 1924. HQ Accra. 898mw,1j (1975) 1700Y. (1995) 3619Y.
Jesus Divine Healing Church	1952	I-3jA	.....	10	1,500	1,600	2,000	0.90	Ex RCC. Epileptics healed with crucifix, oils. Akan, Ewe, Ga. 2n,3m,1w,120Y.
Liberal Catholic Church in Ghana		I-Lib	x....	1	40	100	90	0.05	Split in UK ex Old Roman Catholic Ch. Theosophical. M=LCC(UK, USA) HQ Accra.
Live Ministries Africa	1984	I-3cA	.....	12	1,692	–	5,000	9.09	*LMA.* Peoples: Ga, Frafra, Wolof, Nzema, Aowin. M=CAM.
Methodist Church, Ghana	1835	P-Met	VWA.W	2,467	193,058	257,649	490,000	2.60	40% Akan, 35% Ga-Adangbe, 12% Nzima, 10% Ewe. 133n,7x,21f,1H,5r,1s,1u,3250Y,12796y.
Miracle Life Gospel Centers	1987	I-3cA	.....	30	2,000	–	5,000	12.50	*MLGC.* Begun in Tema. Ex AoG. Mother tongue Twi. M=MLM. 11 pastors, 1 school
Nazarene Healing Church	1939	I-3jA	.....	10	8,000	14,000	15,000	0.28	Ex Methodists. Healing herbs, shea-butter, soap. Akan, Ga, Ewe. 9n,3m,600Y.
New Apostolic Church	c1980	I-3aX	x....	700	200,000	–	434,666	6.67	*NAC. Neuapostolische Kirche* (HQ Zurich, Switzerland).
New Covenant Apostolic Ch	c1980	I-3aA	.....	74	4,500	–	9,000	6.67	An Apostolic indigenous church.
Nigritian Episcopal Church	1907	I-3pA	I	60	4,000	7,924	8,000	0.04	Ex Methodists. 46% Fante, 28% Ga, 22% Ashante. 31n,19m,25w,1p,1s,W=95%,200Y,100y.
Open Bible Standard Churches	c1970	I-3pA	.....	12	887	148	1,770	10.44	M=OBSC. An open pentecostal body.
Pentecostal Holy Church of Ghana	1954	I-3pA	.....	20	600	2,000	1,500	-1.14	Ex AoG. M=CGC(USA). Ashanti. Declining; schism in 1970. 6n,W=80%,20Y,20z.
Presbyterian Church of Ghana	1818	P-Ref	RWA.W	1,791	449,000	279,104	814,000	4.37	M=BM,UFCSM. 48% Akyem, 20% Ashanti, 17% Adangbe. 116n,5x,3H,3h,2s,1u,2426Y,20444y.
Religious Society of Friends	1927	P-Qua	Q...W	1	18	60	36	-2.02	Begun by expatriate British at Achimota. Decline since 1961. M=FSC(UK). 2f.
Sacred Action Church	c1980	I-3cA	.....	83	2,700	–	6,000	6.67	Catholic founder and members. Until 1995 fully within Catholic Ch. Exorcisms.
Sacred Cherubim & Seraphim Ch of G	1952	I-3aA	I.I.I	169	4,900	4,000	12,300	4.60	M=C&S(Nigeria). Members Akan, Ewe, Ga; Nigerians deported 1969. 25n,100m,150w.
Sacred Order of the Silent Brotherhood	1961	I-3pA	.....	10	1,200	2,500	2,000	-0.89	*Divine Healing Crusade.* HQ Ho. 3 Temples, 8 rented halls. W=83%,194Y.
Salvation Army	1922	P-Sal	xwA.W	140	12,200	15,000	20,300	1.22	*Nkwagye Don No* (in Twi). SA, Ghana Command. 75% Akan.
Savior Church of Ghana	1924	I-Met	.....	257	13,100	10,000	18,700	2.54	*SCG. Memeneda Gyidifo. Saturday Believers.* 14 Districts. Ex Methodist. Akyem/Twi. 500Y.
Seventh-day Adventist Church	1894	P-Adv	x....	1,296	130,000	50,000	383,000	8.48	*Ghana Conf.* 53% Ashanti, 29% Akyem, 9% Dagomba. 25n,3x,43f,1H,1j,4r,W=93%,1615Y.
Supreme Healing Home	1963	I-3jA	.....	2	1,600	2,000	3,000	1.64	One of many healing homes; Accra. 23% Akan, 23% Guan, 23% Fanti, 19% Ga, 12% Ewe.
True Church of Christ (New Bethlehem)	1957	I-3aA	I	40	7,000	6,000	9,000	1.64	Founder Lucy Kudjo. Incurables healed; power handkerchiefs. Ashanti. 25n,600Y.
True Faith Church	1921	I-3pA	.....	183	22,000	15,000	28,600	2.62	One of earliest indigenous pentecostal bodies, ex Methodists. 6 Districts. 45n.
United Christians Church	1940	I-3pA	.....	10	500	2,000	1,500	-1.14	Begun by 85-yrs-old prophetess Salome Mamle Odum; 1963, evicted ex Presb Ch. Krobos.
United Christian Chs Brotherhood	1975	I-Con	.....	52	2,120	–	3,300	5.00	Moderate indigenous churches.
United Pentecostal Church of Ghana	1968	P-Pe1	x....	144	13,000	20,000	36,100	2.39	*Jesus Only Ch.* Unitarian Pentecostals. M=UPC(USA). 40n,3x,5f,1p(30),W=70%,1000Y.
Universal Prayer Group	1932	I-3pA	.....	50	3,500	12,500	9,000	-1.31	Ex Presbyterians; led by prophetesses since 1932. Akan, Ewe, Ga. 150n,1500Y.
White Cross Society	1941	I-3pA	.....	20	3,000	5,370	5,000	-0.29	*Atitso Gaxie Habobo. EP Healing Group*, expelled by EPC. 76% Ewe, 15% Kabre. 123Y.
World-Wide Missions of Ghana	1961	I-Non	x....	500	70,000	90,000	95,000	0.22	M=World-Wide Missions (USA). Evangelicals based in Pasadena, CA (USA).
Other African indigenous churches	c1900	I-3sA	.....	4,000	150,000	60,000	300,000	6.65	Total over 370, including CFC, GRM, NCC, CTC, FGC, SRC.
Other indep charismatic networks	c1970	I-3cA	.....	1,200	20,000	–	40,000	52.79	Including World Miracle Bible Ch (21 chs).
Other independent Oneness bodies	c1970	I-3oA	.....	250	20,000	–	50,000	54.16	25, incl African Outreach, Christ Ambassadors Ch of G, Power Incarnation Ch.
Other marginal Protestant bodies		m-	.....	50	6,000	1,000	10,000	0.05	Total over 10 Western spiritist and other bodies.
Other Protestant denominations		P-	.....	90	15,000	10,000	30,000	0.05	Total about 20.
Totals				**30,736**	**3,827,652**	**3,228,477**	**7,489,880**		

Churches, members, growth, 1900-2025	*Congs*	*Adults*	*Affiliated*	*G%*	*Total denominations*	*6 Megablocs:* *O*	*R*	*A*	*P*	*I*	*m*
Total churches, members, and denominations (mid-1900)	80	42,400	80,000	5.42	8	0	1	1	5	1	0
Total churches, members, and denominations (mid-1970)	11,458	1,710,516	3,228,477	5.42	382	1	1	1	26	345	8
Total churches, members, and denominations (mid-1990)	20,000	3,238,000	6,336,400	3.43	535	1	1	1	37	480	15
Total churches, members, and denominations (mid-1995)	30,736	3,827,652	7,489,880	3.40	581	1	1	1	39	524	15
Total churches, members, and denominations (mid-2000)	40,500	4,429,000	8,666,976	2.96	598	1	1	1	40	540	15
Total churches, members, and denominations (mid-2025)	70,000	8,919,000	17,452,500	2.84	2,147	5	1	1	60	2000	80

NOTES ON TABLE ABOVE

NATIONAL COUNCILS (Column 4, 5th letter).

C = Ghana Council of United Churches (GCUC).
E = National Association of Evangelicals of Ghana (NAEG).
H = Ghana Pentecostal Council (GPC).
I = Supreme Council for Ghana Pentecostal Churches (formerly National Council of Spiritual Churches, or Ghana Council for Liberal Churches).
J = Pentecostal Association of Ghana (PAG), with 89 member Spiritual churches.
R = Ghana Bishops' Conference (GBC).
W = Christian Council of Ghana (CCG).

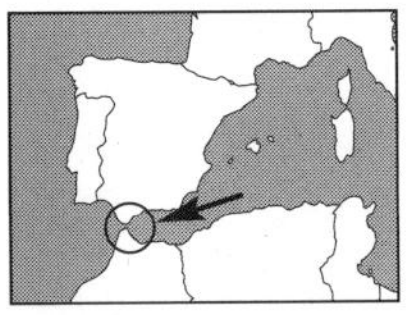

GIBRALTAR

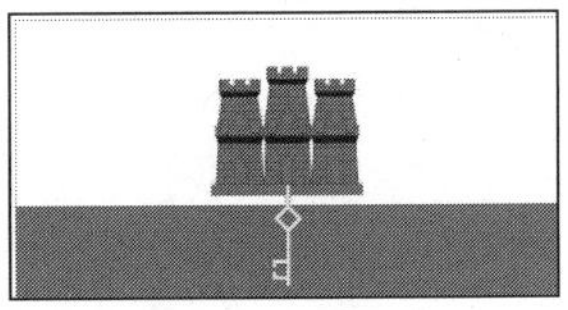

SECULAR DATA, AD 2000

STATE
Official name: The Colony of Gibraltar.
Short name: Gibraltar. **Adjective of nationality:** Gibraltarian.
Flag: White with red stripe along bottom, red triple-towered castle with gold key depending from gateway.
Area: 6 sq. km. (2 sq. mi.).
Government: Self-governing British colony (1704 British possession).
Legislature: Gibraltar House of Assembly, 18 members.
Official language: English.
Monetary unit: 1 pound sterling (£) = 100 new pence. **US$1=** £ 0.59.
Chief cities: GIBRALTAR 25,082.
Political divisions: 1 province.

DEMOGRAPHY
Population: 25,000.
Population density: 4,180.3/sq. km. (12,541.0/sq. mi.).
Under 15 years: 5,000.
Growth rate p.a.: 0.11% (births 11.09, deaths 10.70).
Mortality: Infant, per 1,000: 6.6; **Maternal per 100,000:** 12.0.
Life expectancy: 78 (male 75, female 81).
Household size: 3.2. **Floor area per person, sq.m:** 28.0.
Major languages: English, Spanish, Italian, Maltese, Arabic, Yiddish.
Urban dwellers: 100.00%. **Urban growth rate p.a.:** .0.%.
Labor force: 54%.

ETHNOLINGUISTIC PEOPLES
67.7% Gibraltarian; 10.0% British; 10.0% Spaniard; 9.0% Moroccan Arab; 2.0% Jewish.

ECONOMY
National income p.a. per person: US$6,618; **per family:** US$21,178.

EDUCATION
Adult literacy: 99% (male 99%, female 99%). **Schools:** 22.
Universities: 1. **School enrolment:** female/male: 95%/95%.

HEALTH
Access to health services: 90%. **Access to safe water:** 90%.
Hospitals: 2 (86 beds per 10,000). **Doctors:** 29.
Blind: 140. **Deaf:** 1,700. **Murder rate:** 3.
Lepers: 20.

LITERATURE
New book titles p.a.: 15 (600 p.a. per million). **Periodicals:** 21.
Newspapers: 2 dailies.

COMMUNICATION (per 1,000 people)
Phones: 696 (30% mobile). **Radios:** 573. **TV sets:** 275.
Daily newspaper circulation: 214. **Computers:** 100.

HUMAN LIFE AND LIBERTY (optimum condition=100.0%)
HDI: 92.9. **HSI:** 80.0. **HFI:** 80.0. **EFL:** 40.0.

Country Table 1. **Religious adherents in Gibraltar, AD 1900-2025.**

Year	1900		1970		mid-1990		Annual change, 1990-2000				mid-1995		mid-2000		mid-2025	
Name	Adherents	%	Adherents	%	Adherents	%	Natural	Conversion	Total	Rate	Adherents	%	Adherents	%	Adherents	%
Christians	**19,480**	**96.4**	**23,670**	**88.8**	**23,400**	**87.0**	**-156**	**-22**	**-178**	**-0.79**	**22,440**	**86.4**	**21,618**	**86.2**	**17,730**	**82.9**
PROFESSION																
professing Christians	**19,480**	**96.4**	**23,670**	**88.8**	**23,400**	**87.0**	**-156**	**-22**	**-178**	**-0.79**	**22,440**	**86.4**	**21,618**	**86.2**	**17,730**	**82.9**
AFFILIATION																
unaffiliated Christians	600	3.0	2,180	8.2	260	1.0	-2	1	-1	-0.39	240	0.9	250	1.0	230	1.1
affiliated Christians	**18,880**	**93.5**	**21,490**	**80.6**	**23,140**	**86.0**	**-154**	**-23**	**-177**	**-0.79**	**22,200**	**85.4**	**21,368**	**85.2**	**17,500**	**81.8**
Roman Catholics	17,780	88.0	19,130	71.7	22,700	84.4	-168	18	-150	-0.68	22,000	84.7	21,200	84.5	17,000	79.4
Anglicans	1,000	5.0	1,900	7.1	2,000	7.4	-15	5	-10	-0.51	2,000	7.7	1,900	7.5	1,600	7.5
Protestants	100	0.5	360	1.4	360	1.3	-3	5	2	0.54	368	1.4	380	1.5	420	2.0
Marginal Christians	0	0.0	100	0.4	150	0.6	-1	10	9	4.81	162	0.6	240	1.0	360	1.7
doubly-affiliated	0	0.0	0	0.0	-2,070	-7.7	15	-43	-28	1.29	-2,330	-9.0	-2,352	-9.4	-1,880	-8.8
Trans-megabloc groupings																
Evangelicals	100	0.5	270	1.0	310	1.2	-2	5	3	0.93	319	1.2	340	1.4	430	2.1
Pentecostals/Charismatics	0	0.0	100	0.4	3,800	14.1	-28	38	10	0.26	3,871	14.9	3,900	15.5	4,300	20.1
Great Commission Christians	**1,200**	**5.9**	**2,400**	**9.0**	**2,420**	**9.0**	**-18**	**4**	**-14**	**-0.57**	**2,350**	**9.0**	**2,285**	**9.1**	**2,000**	**9.3**
Muslims	0	0.0	2,120	8.0	2,190	8.1	-16	12	-4	-0.18	2,200	8.5	2,150	8.5	2,200	10.3
Nonreligious	0	0.0	30	0.1	400	1.5	-3	12	9	2.13	460	1.8	494	2.0	600	2.9
Jews	700	3.5	590	2.2	540	2.0	-4	-2	-6	-1.23	520	2.0	477	1.9	400	1.9
Hindus	20	0.1	260	1.0	300	1.1	-2	-1	-3	-1.01	300	1.2	271	1.1	350	1.7
Baha'is	0	0.0	30	0.1	70	0.3	-1	1	0	0.42	80	0.3	73	0.3	120	0.6
World A (unevangelized persons)	20	0.1	1,600	6.0	1,458	5.4	-11	1	-10	-0.71	1,403	5.4	1,350	5.4	1,176	5.5
World B (evangelized non-Christians)	699	3.5	1,397	5.2	2,042	7.6	-15	21	6	-0.53	2,139	8.2	2,032	8.4	2,494	11.7
World C (Christians)	19,480	96.4	23,670	88.8	23,400	87.0	-156	-22	-178	-0.79	22,440	86.4	21,618	86.2	17,730	82.9
Country's population	**20,200**	**100.0**	**26,668**	**100.0**	**26,900**	**100.0**	**-182**	**0**	**-182**	**-0.77**	**25,983**	**100.0**	**25,100**	**100.0**	**21,400**	**100.0**

COLUMNS, ROWS.
For meanings and definitions, see Codebook (Part 3). Note that, by definition, total 'Christians' = professing + crypto-Christians, which also = affiliated + unaffiliated Christians, and also = Great Commission Christians + latent Christians. Percentages may not always total exactly, due to rounding.

CENSUSES.
3.VII.1951: 87.9% Roman Catholics, 8.3% Anglicans & Protestants, 3.0% Jews, 0.5% Hindus, 0.2% other religionists, 0.1% nonreligious. **3.X.1961** (excluding 2,717 military and shipping personnel): 87.5% Roman Catholics, 7.5% Anglicans, 3.0% Jews, 1.2% Protestants, 0.6% Hindus, 0.2% marginal Protestants, 0.1% nonreligious. **6.X.1970** (excluding families of servicemen): 78.6% Roman Catholics, 8.2% Muslims, 8.0% Anglicans, 2.3% Jews, 1.5% Protestants, 1.0% Hindus, 0.3% marginal Protestants, 0.1% nonreligious. **1991:** 76.9% Roman Catholics, 6.9% Anglicans, 6.9% Muslims, 3.0% other Christians, 2.4% Jews, 2.1% Hindus, 1.8% nonreligious.

NOTES ON RELIGIONS
ANGLICANS. Including a number of expatriate British military, dependents and civilians.
BAHA'IS. In 1 isolated center in 1970; 1 local spiritual assembly in 1996.
HINDUS. Indians.
JEWS. With 4 synagogues.
MUSLIMS. Almost all Moroccans, immigrants since 1961.
PENTECOSTALS/CHARISMATICS. Begun in 1975, the Catholic Charismatic Renewal had (in 1997) 11 regular weekly prayer groups with 400 regular adult attenders, 4 priests, and attendances of 500 at annual rallies; members have recently visited 9,000 households, virtually every home.

Great Commission Instrument Panel: status of Gibraltar (for explanation see start of Part 4)

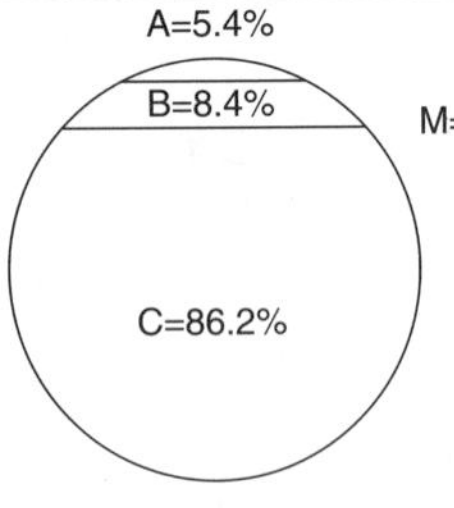

3 Worlds, AD 2000

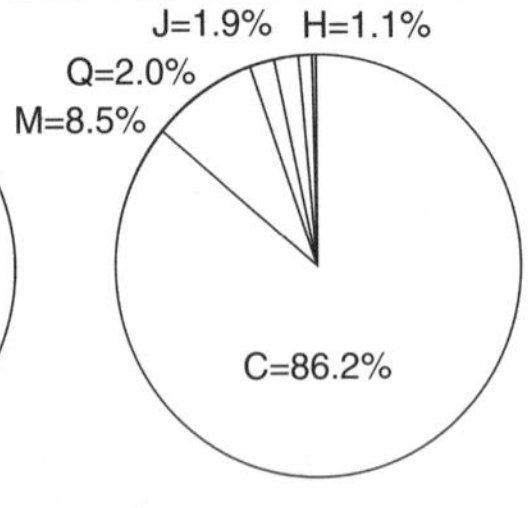

Religions, AD 2000

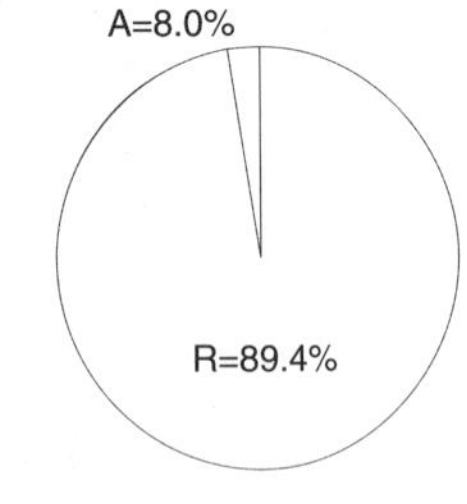

Ecclesiastical blocs

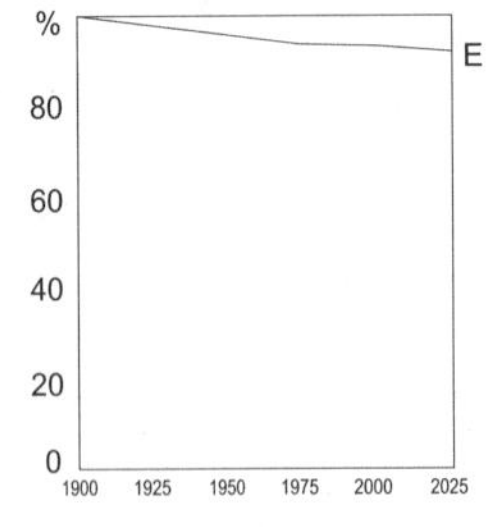

Evangelization, 1900-2025

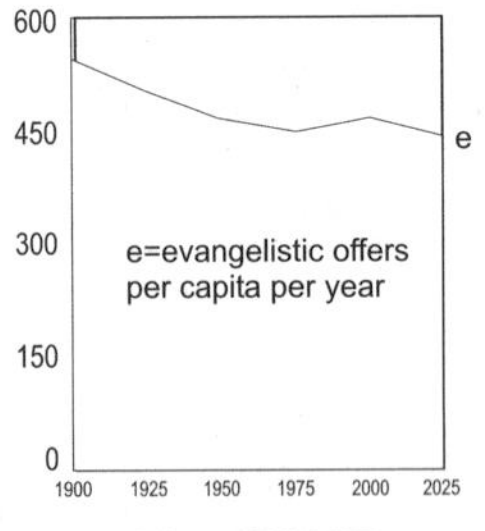

Offers, 1900-2025

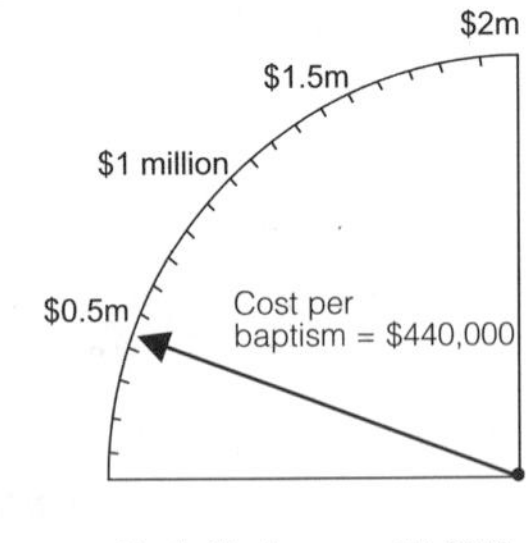

Cost-effectiveness, AD 2000

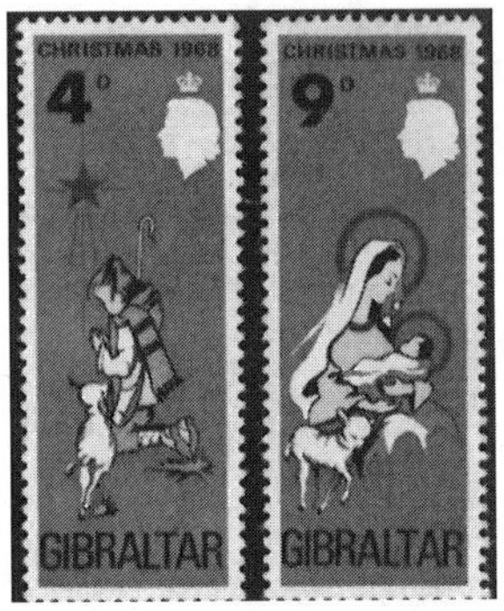

Many postage stamps portray the Nativity of Christ.

Country status. Gibraltar is a British colony since 1704, comprising a small rocky peninsula guarding the Atlantic entrance of the Mediterranean Sea. It is a popular tourist destination.

HUMAN LIFE AND LIBERTY

Human rights and freedoms. Gibraltar is a crown dependency of the United Kingdom. Basic rights are protected by the colonial administration and the Constitution. There are no major human rights problems.

NON-CHRISTIAN RELIGIONS

In 1970 Gibraltar was 2.3% Jewish, 1.0% Hindu, and 0.1% professed no religion. This status changed little to 1995. There are 4 synagogues in the colony. Islam has entered since 1961 in the persons of over 2,000 immigrant Moroccan Arabs.

CHRISTIANITY

CATHOLIC CHURCH. Catholics were active in Gibraltar in 1492, but the church was suppressed by the British when they took possession in 1704. In 1806 a Catholic priest was appointed for Italian immigrants. Gibraltar became a vicariate apostolic in 1817 and a diocese in 1910, now under Propaganda in Rome and immediately subject to the Holy See. Most of the civilian population is Catholic (87.5% in

Country summary. **Worlds A, B, C by ethnolinguistic peoples, cities, and major civil divisions in Gibraltar.**

	PEOPLES							CITIES							CIVIL DIVISIONS						
World	Num	Pop 2000	C%	Christians	E%	U%	Unevangelized	Num	Pop 2000	C%	Christians	E%	U%	Unevangelized	Num	Pop 2000	C%	Christians	E%	U%	Unevangelized
A	0	0	0.00	0	0	0	0	0	0	0.00	0	0	0	0	0	0	0.00	0	0	0	0
B	3	3,060	4.58	140	56	44	1,351	0	0	0.00	0	0	0	0	0	0	0.00	0	0	0	0
C	4	22,022	96.39	21,227	100	0	8	1	25,082	85.19	21,367	95	5	1,359	1	25,082	85.19	21,368	95	5	1,359
Total	**7**	**25,082**	**85.19**	**21,367**	**95**	**5**	**1,359**	**1**	**25,082**	**85.19**	**21,367**	**95**	**5**	**1,359**	**1**	**25,082**	**85.19**	**21,368**	**95**	**5**	**1,359**

1961, 84.7% by 1995), the principal ethnic groups being of Italian (Genoese), Maltese, Portuguese, and Spanish descent.

The Holy See has no diplomatic relations with Gibraltar in AD 2000.

Catholic Church, Diocese of Gibraltar. Church of Our Lady of Dolours, in Catalan Bay (La Caleta), where first settlers arrived from Genoa in 17th century.

OTHER CHURCHES. Anglicans are the principal non-Catholic denomination. Their proportion has fluctuated from 8.8% in 1921, to 7.5% in 1961, and to 7.7% in 1995. The diocese of Gibraltar was established in 1842 and co-ordinates the activities of Anglican chaplaincies throughout southern and eastern Europe including Turkey. It is a missionary diocese of the Church of England under the jurisdiction of the archbishop of Canterbury, and forms part of the Anglican Church in Europe.

The services of the Scottish Presbyterian church are attended by a wide variety of Christians, the majority being Presbyterians and Methodists; and there is also a small Adventist community. Protestants formed 1.4% of the population in 1995.

Indigenous missions. Only a handful of Roman Catholic missionaries have been sent out, mainly to Spain or other European countries.

CHURCH AND STATE

There is no established church or state religion, and freedom of religion is guaranteed to all. Each communion (Catholic, Anglican, Presbyterian) receives an annual subsidy of 500 pounds from the government.

BROADCASTING AND MEDIA

Satellite TV and radio programs are received in English, Arabic, German and Italian.

FUTURE TRENDS AND PROSPECTS.

Both immigrant Muslims and the nonreligious are expected to increase gradually through 2025 raising their combined percentages from 8.0% in 1970 to 13.4% by 2025.

Christians could remain above 70% well into the 21st century. Muslims should stabilize at 15% with Hindus and the nonreligious comprising the majority of the final 15%.

BIBLIOGRAPHY

A church was built. J. E. Lewington. Gibraltar: J. E. L. Lewington, 1955. 29p. (On St. Andrew's Church).

A Gibraltar bibliography. M. M. Green. London: University of London Institute of Commonwealth Studies, 1980. 108p. (See section on religion).

A story in stone, being a history of the King's Chapel, Gibraltar. R. Yale. Portsmouth, UK: W. H. Barrell, 1948. 41p.

El catolicismo en Gibraltar durante el siglo XVIII. A. Béthencourt Massieu. [Valladolid, 1967]. 89p.

Gibraltar. G. J. Shields. *World bibliographical series*, vol. 87. Oxford, UK: CLIO Press, 1987. 138p. (See especially 'Religion,' p.31–2).

'Holy Trinity Cathedral Gibraltar: a history and description.' D. H. Simpson. Unpublished typescript, 1948. 138p. (Available from Royal Commonwealth Society Library, London).

Padre Brown of Gibraltar: a memoir. E. R. Taylor. London: Epworth Press, 1955. 60p.

St. Joseph's Parish Church centenary 1885–1986. Gibraltar: Trico, 1985. 38p.

The diocese of Gibraltar: a sketch of its history, work and tasks. H. J. C. Knight. London: SPCK, 1917. 217p.

Upon this Rock, 1769–1969: a short history of Methodism in Gibraltar. Gibraltar, 1969. 71p.

Country Table 2. **Organized churches and denominations in Gibraltar.**

Official name (bold type = church with over 10% of all affiliated) 1	*Begun* 2	*Type* 3	*Counc* 4	*Congs* 5	*Adults* 6	*Affiliated 1970* 7	*Affiliated 1995* 8	*G%* 9	*Names, notes, and other statistics* (see Codebook, Part 3) 10
Catholic Church: D Gibraltar	1492	R-Lat	p.B..	8	15,000	19,130	22,000	0.56	Nationals (Genoese, Portuguese, Maltese, Spanish). (1990) 10n,1x,1m,5w,344Yy. ,
Church of England (D Europe)	1704	A-plu	awc..	3	900	1,900	2,000	0.21	Missionary diocese under D Canterbury, for SE Europe to Turkey. 70% aliens. 5x.
Jehovah's Witnesses	c1955	m-Jeh	x....	2	131	100	162	1.95	*Watch Tower, IBSA.* Active witnessing under way by 1959. 7Y.
Methodist Church		P-Met	Vwc..	1	36	100	90	0.05	Related to Methodist Ch of Great Britain. Mainly English-speaking expatriates.
Presbyterian Church		P-Ref	Rw...	1	56	140	80	0.05	Scottish and other Presbyterians. M=Church of Scotland (UK). 1f.
Seventh-day Adventist Church		P-Adv	x....	1	40	60	60	0.05	SDA, part of Spanish Church (Iglesia Española), Southern European Union Mission.
Other Protestant bodies		P-	.....	3	90	60	138	0.05	In 2 recent denominations.
Doubly-affiliated		2-aff			-1,500	0	-2,330		Roman Catholics who are also members of Evangelical bodies.
Totals				**19**	**14,753**	**21,490**	**22,200**		

Churches, members, growth, 1900-2025	*Congs*	*Adults*	*Affiliated*	*G%*	*Total denominations*	*6 Megablocs:* O	R	A	P	I	m
Total churches, members, and denominations (mid-1900)	10	11,000	18,880	0.19	2	0	1	1	0	0	0
Total churches, members, and denominations (mid-1970)	15	13,273	21,490	0.19	7	0	1	1	4	0	1
Total churches, members, and denominations (mid-1990)	20	17,000	23,140	0.37	8	0	1	1	5	0	1
Total churches, members, and denominations (mid-1995)	19	14,753	22,200	-0.83	8	0	1	1	5	0	1
Total churches, members, and denominations (mid-2000)	20	15,000	21,368	-0.76	8	0	1	1	5	0	1
Total churches, members, and denominations (mid-2025)	40	10,000	17,500	-0.80	32	1	1	1	15	10	4

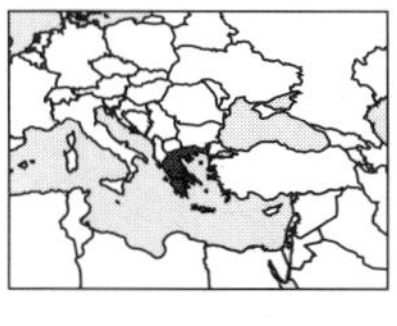

GREECE

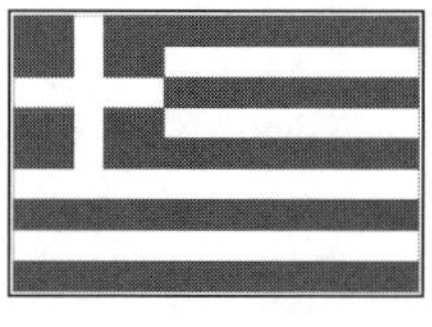

SECULAR DATA, AD 2000

STATE

Official name: Elliniki Dimokratia (The Hellenic Republic).
Short name: Greece. **Adjective of nationality:** Greek.
Flag: Blue field with large white cross.
Area: 131,957 sq. km. (50,949 sq. mi.).
Government: Parliamentary republic, since 1974 (1830-1973 monarchy, 1967 military junta).
Legislature: Greek Chamber of Deputies, 300 members.
Official language: Greek (Ellinika).
Monetary unit: 1 drachma (Dr) = 100 lepta. **US$1=** DR 290.03.
Chief cities: ATHINAI (Greater Athens) 3,103,000; Thessaloniki (Salonica) 1,083,000; Piraieus (Piraeus) 174,300; Patrai (Patras) 168,066; Peristerion 149,877.
Political divisions: 13 provinces.
Armed forces: 162,000.

DEMOGRAPHY

Population: 10,645,000.
Population density: 80.6/sq. km. (208.9/sq. mi.).
Under 15 years: 1,592,000.
Growth rate p.a.: 0.01% (births 8.79, deaths 10.32).
Mortality: Infant, per 1,000: 7.6; **Maternal per 100,000:** 10.0.
Life expectancy: 79 (male 76, female 81).
Household size: 3.3. **Floor area per person, sq.m:** 26.0.
Major languages: Greek, Turkish, Albanian, Macedonian, English, Bulgarian, Armenian, Romany, Ladino.
Urban dwellers: 60.10%. **Urban growth rate p.a.:** 0.51%.
Labor force: 41%.

ETHNOLINGUISTIC PEOPLES

88.4% Greek (Hellenic, Dimotiki); 1.9% Pontic; 1.8% Macedonian; 1.5% Arvanite (Albanian); 1.4% Rumelian Turk.

ECONOMY

National income p.a. per person: US$8,209; **per family:** US$27,092.

EDUCATION

Adult literacy: 95% (male 97%, female 93%). **Schools:** 11,317.
Universities: 17. **School enrolment:** female/male: 95%/97%.

HEALTH

Access to health services: 95%. **Access to safe water:** 99%.
Hospitals: 372 (50 beds per 10,000). **Doctors:** 40,116.
Blind: 13,000. **Deaf:** 635,800. **Murder rate:** 2. **Lepers:** 5,000.

LITERATURE

New book titles p.a.: 4,260 (400 p.a. per million). **Periodicals:** 433.
Newspapers: 168 dailies.

COMMUNICATION (per 1,000 people)

Phones: 493 (14% mobile). **Radios:** 400. **TV sets:** 442.
Daily newspaper circulation: 156. **Computers:** 124.

REFUGEES

Alien refugees from other countries: 1,300.

HUMAN LIFE AND LIBERTY (optimum condition=100.0%)

HDI: 92.3. **HSI:** 81.0. **HFI:** 77.5. **EFL:** 44.0.

Country status. Greece is a cultural and geographical bridge between Europe and Asia. As a crucible of democracy, it was the first European nation to fashion a civilization of its own. There is hardly any field of human endeavor, be it architecture, military science, philosophy, literature, or the sciences, on

Country Table 1. **Religious adherents in Greece, AD 1900-2025.**

Name	1900 Adherents	1900 %	1970 Adherents	1970 %	mid-1990 Adherents	mid-1990 %	Annual change, 1990-2000 Natural	Conversion	Total	Rate	mid-1995 Adherents	mid-1995 %	mid-2000 Adherents	mid-2000 %	mid-2025 Adherents	mid-2025 %
Christians	**2,599,000**	**85.2**	**8,643,000**	**98.3**	**9,724,180**	**95.2**	**40,413**	**-4,534**	**35,879**	**0.36**	**9,947,900**	**94.8**	**10,082,974**	**94.7**	**9,251,900**	**93.8**
PROFESSION																
professing Christians	**2,599,000**	**85.2**	**8,643,000**	**98.3**	**9,724,180**	**95.2**	**40,413**	**-4,534**	**35,879**	**0.36**	**9,947,900**	**94.8**	**10,082,974**	**94.7**	**9,251,900**	**93.8**
AFFILIATION																
unaffiliated Christians	10,000	0.3	53,482	0.6	21,000	0.2	87	8	95	0.45	21,900	0.2	21,954	0.2	21,900	0.2
affiliated Christians	**2,589,000**	**84.9**	**8,589,518**	**97.7**	**9,703,180**	**94.9**	**40,326**	**-4,542**	**35,784**	**0.36**	**9,926,000**	**94.6**	**10,061,020**	**94.5**	**9,230,000**	**93.6**
Orthodox	2,573,800	84.4	8,316,519	94.6	9,520,000	93.2	39,589	-1,589	38,000	0.39	9,762,600	93.1	9,900,000	93.0	9,100,000	92.3
Independents	0	0.0	207,400	2.4	223,000	2.2	927	-427	500	0.22	226,210	2.2	228,000	2.1	200,000	2.0
Roman Catholics	60,000	2.0	45,723	0.5	59,000	0.6	245	55	300	0.50	60,591	0.6	62,000	0.6	75,000	0.8
Marginal Christians	0	0.0	50,226	0.6	42,000	0.4	175	-375	-200	-0.49	41,000	0.4	40,000	0.4	45,000	0.5
Protestants	5,000	0.2	26,771	0.3	21,800	0.2	91	-131	-40	-0.19	21,661	0.2	21,400	0.2	20,000	0.2
Anglicans	200	0.0	3,000	0.0	3,450	0.0	14	1	15	0.43	3,500	0.0	3,600	0.0	4,500	0.1
doubly-affiliated	-50,000	-1.6	-60,121	-0.7	-166,070	-1.6	-691	-2,100	-2,791	1.57	-189,562	-1.8	-193,980	-1.8	-214,500	-2.2
Trans-megabloc groupings																
Evangelicals	4,000	0.1	10,000	0.1	11,200	0.1	47	63	110	0.94	11,797	0.1	12,300	0.1	14,000	0.1
Pentecostals/Charismatics	0	0.0	7,500	0.1	112,000	1.1	466	534	1,000	0.86	117,645	1.1	122,000	1.2	128,000	1.3
Great Commission Christians	**183,000**	**6.0**	**351,000**	**4.0**	**250,000**	**2.5**	**1,040**	**178**	**1,218**	**0.48**	**257,000**	**2.5**	**262,176**	**2.5**	**246,000**	**2.5**
Muslims	390,000	12.8	130,000	1.5	311,000	3.0	1,293	2,959	4,252	1.29	344,690	3.3	353,517	3.3	400,000	4.1
Nonreligious	1,000	0.0	10,000	0.1	160,000	1.6	665	1,372	2,037	1.21	170,000	1.6	180,373	1.7	180,000	1.8
Atheists	0	0.0	5,000	0.1	15,000	0.2	62	386	448	2.65	18,000	0.2	19,480	0.2	22,000	0.2
Jews	60,000	2.0	3,800	0.0	6,600	0.1	27	-191	-164	-2.81	5,100	0.1	4,963	0.1	4,000	0.0
Spiritists	0	0.0	0	0.0	900	0.0	4	0	4	0.46	920	0.0	942	0.0	1,500	0.0
Baha'is	0	0.0	200	0.0	520	0.0	2	7	9	1.63	560	0.0	611	0.0	1,100	0.0
Other religionists	0	0.0	1,000	0.0	1,800	0.0	7	1	8	0.46	1,830	0.0	1,884	0.0	2,500	0.0
World A (unevangelized persons)	201,300	6.6	87,930	1.0	153,300	1.5	638	607	1,245	0.78	157,338	1.5	170,320	1.6	197,260	2.0
World B (evangelized non-Christians)	249,700	8.2	62,070	0.7	342,520	3.3	1,422	3,927	5,349	1.35	383,964	3.7	391,706	3.7	413,840	4.2
World C (Christians)	2,599,000	85.2	8,643,000	98.3	9,724,180	95.2	40,413	-4,534	35,879	0.36	9,947,900	94.8	10,082,974	94.7	9,251,900	93.8
Country's population	**3,050,000**	**100.0**	**8,793,000**	**100.0**	**10,220,000**	**100.0**	**42,473**	**0**	**42,473**	**0.41**	**10,489,203**	**100.0**	**10,645,000**	**100.0**	**9,863,000**	**100.0**

COLUMNS, ROWS.
For meanings and definitions, see Codebook (Part 3). Note that, by definition, total 'Christians' = professing + crypto-Christians, which also = affiliated + unaffiliated Christians, and also = Great Commission Christians + latent Christians. Percentages may not always total exactly, due to rounding.

CENSUSES.
The first census was taken in 1828 (giving a population of 938,765) and thereafter at least once a decade. From 1870 to 1947, however, new territories were being annexed every 2 decades, hence the censuses cannot be compared without considerable adjustment, as has been done in the 1900 column above. **1928:** 96.1% Orthodox, 2.0% Muslims, 1.2% Jews, 0.6% Roman Catholics, 0.1% Protestants. **1940:** 96.7% Orthodox, 1.9% Muslims, 0.9% Jews, 0.4% Roman Catholics, 0.1% Protestants. **7.IV.1951** (excluding foreign military personnel, but including Greek military overseas): 97.9% Greek Orthodox, 1.5% Muslims, 0.4% Roman Catholics, 0.1% Protestants, 0.1% other Christians, 0.1% Jews. **1961:** 97.8% Greek Orthodox, 1.3% Muslims, 0.4% Roman Catholics, 0.2% Protestants, 0.1% marginal Protestants, 0.1% Jews.

NOTES ON RELIGIONS
ATHEISTS. Greek Communist Party (Kommonistikon Komma Elladas, KKE) (proscribed 1947, illegal 1967-74, pro-Soviet). A large number of party members regard themselves as Orthodox Christians and many still attend church on festivals.
BAHA'IS. In 1 local spiritual assembly and 4 other centers, (1970, increasing to 6 local spiritual assemblies (1996).
COUNTRY'S POPULATION. In 1923, 1,500,000 Greek Orthodox resident in Turkey, including the 50,000 Karamanlis (Turkish-language Orthodox) were forcibly repatriated to Greece in exchange for 400,000 Muslim Turks resident in Greece.
DOUBLY-AFFILIATED. The term covers those affiliated to or claimed both by minority churches (Protestant, Roman Catholic, marginal Protestant, Catholic (non-Roman), Anglican) and also by the state church; this includes baptized members of the Church of Greece who have recently become Protestants or Jehovah's Witnesses but are still enumerated as Orthodox by the Church of Greece and its dioceses.
JEWS. Decrease from 75,000 in 1943 due to Nazi massacres. Now mostly in Thessalonika, and mostly Ladino-speaking.
MUSLIMS. In 1923, 400,000 Muslims (Turks) in Greece were forcibly repatriated to Turkey in exchange for 1,500,000 Greeks from Turkey. Muslims today are Sunnis (of the Hanafite rite) in eastern Thrace, with 300 mosques. They are Turkish, Pomak (Bulgarian-speaking Muslims), Arabs, Gypsies, with a small number of Chamurians (Albanians) adjacent to Albania. Almost all Pomaks are Muslims, but about 100,000 Turkish-speakers are Orthodox. *Hajj pilgrims to Mecca.* (1970) 223; (1974) 175; (1975) 487; (1976) 144.
NONRELIGIOUS. Many expatriates from France, Germany, UK, USA, et alia.
OTHER RELIGIONISTS. Including the Spiritual Association of Athens (denied legal registration in 1970), and the Theosophical Society.
PROTESTANTS. Including many expatriates (USA civilian, USA military, et alii).

Great Commission Instrument Panel: status of Greece (for explanation see start of Part 4)

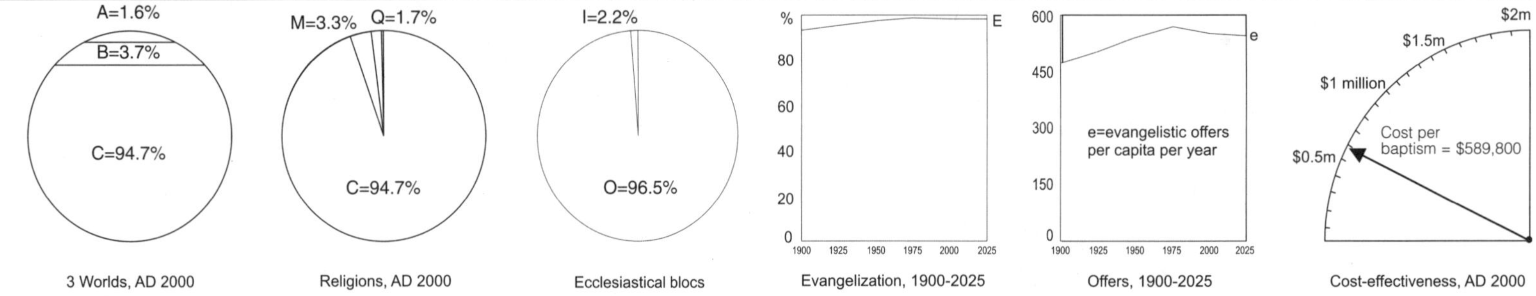

which the Greeks have not left their impress. The economy is equally divided between agriculture and industry. Its major products are olive oil, wine, textiles, and pharmaceuticals.

HUMAN LIFE AND LIBERTY

Human need and development. Greece is part of the European Community, where it trails almost every other member country in its standards of living and economy. The reasons for its relative backwardness are to be found in its largely mountainous terrain, lack of natural resources, and the flight of the more resourceful Greeks to other countries in the 20th century. In fact, the Greek Diaspora is believed to be equal in number to the national population. Moreover, since the 1920s, the country has suffered from depression, dictatorship, wars, foreign occupation, civil wars, and constant bullying from the Turks. A reasonably prosperous economy was built up in the 1980s, reinforced by help from the European Community. Although Greece ranks low on some indicators, like literacy, relative to other European countries, it does better on others, like health. With large remittances from abroad, its GNP per capita is higher than that of Portugal. Continued infusion of capital from EC may help Greece to reach European standards of living within the next decade.

Human rights and freedoms. Greece is the cradle of democracy where the lexicon of freedom first took shape. After the fall of the last dictatorship in the 1970s, Greece renewed its commitment to democratic institutions and has successfully weathered constitutional storms without resorting to authoritarianism. Terrorist violence from many quarters plague the country. As a result, there are harsh laws on the statute books, which are often implemented even more harshly by law enforcement officials and prison guards. Although the press is diverse and robust, there are a number of restrictions on freedom of expression. The Constitution allows for seizure, although not prior restraint, of publications that insult the president, offend religious beliefs, contain obscene materials, advocate violent overthrow of the political system or disclose defense information. Greek law also prohibits publications that place Greece's relations with friendly foreign powers in jeopardy by spreading rumors or false information. Private radio and television stations flourish in the absence of regulatory media. They, like the print media, are often threatened by the state prosecutor for 'insulting authority', but no charges are ever filed. Probably the most serious threat to human rights is Article 19 of the Citizenship Code, which gives many privileges to ethnic Greeks vis a vis non-ethnics. This makes Albanian-Greeks, Turkish-Greeks, and Macedonian-Greeks second class citizens and deprives them of constitutional guarantees of certain human rights. The status of the 'Muslim Minority', the only minority officially recognized by Greece under the Treaty of Lausanne of 1923, has always been precarious and frequently degenerates into open discrimination. Muslims are estimated at 120,000 in Thrace, in addition to Pomaks. Discriminatory practices against Turks are probably fewer than those practiced in Turkey against Christians. Further, many former complaints, such as impediments in buying lands; in opening, improving, and expanding mosques; and in obtaining driving, trading, hunting, and tractor licenses; and building construction and maintenance permits, have not been heard since 1992. There are few Muslims in public service, but the government cites the lack of fluency of many Turks in Greek. The use of the noun 'Tourkos' is generally prohibited in public use because it connotes loyalties to Turkey rather than to Greece. However, the adjective 'Turkoyennis' (people of Turkish ethnic descent) is permitted. The Treaty of Lausanne grants the Turkish minority the right to education in the Turkish language with a reciprocal right for the Greek minority in Istanbul. There are Koranic and secular Turkish-Language schools in Thrace, but many of them do not have adequate teaching materials because of disputes with Turkey. Most elementary school pupils in Turkish language schools go to Turkey for secondary and post-secondary education. Other minorities facing less serious discriminatory practices include Gypsies and speakers of a Slavic dialect who identify themselves as Macedonians. Many municipalities do not allow Gypsies to vote or register as citizens.

Country summary. **Worlds A, B, C by ethnolinguistic peoples, cities, and major civil divisions in Greece.**

	PEOPLES							CITIES							CIVIL DIVISIONS						
World	*Num*	*Pop 2000*	*C%*	*Christians*	*E%*	*U%*	*Unevangelized*	*Num*	*Pop 2000*	*C%*	*Christians*	*E%*	*U%*	*Unevangelized*	*Num*	*Pop 2000*	*C%*	*Christians*	*E%*	*U%*	*Unevangelized*
A	4	258,987	0.08	212	42	58	149,741	0	0	0.00	0	0	0	0	0	0	0.00	0	0	0	0
B	4	41,621	17.69	7,363	68	32	13,313	0	0	0.00	0	0	0	0	0	0	0.00	0	0	0	0
C	23	10,344,135	97.19	10,053,445	100	0	2,696	17	5,344,445	93.04	4,972,311	98	2	109,942	13	10,644,743	94.52	10,061,020	98	2	165,749
Total	**31**	**10,644,743**	**94.52**	**10,061,020**	**98**	**2**	**165,750**	**17**	**5,344,445**	**93.04**	**4,972,311**	**98**	**2**	**109,942**	**13**	**10,644,743**	**94.52**	**10,061,020**	**98**	**2**	**165,749**

Human environment. Air pollution, called nephos in Greek, is the bane of Greek cities. Combined with the environmental problems associated with tourism, nephos damage discolors the priceless outdoor monuments and treasures. Water pollution is severe in Saronikos where 50% of the industrial plants are located. Saronikos also collects the wastewater and untreated sewage from Athens and the bilge from ships.

NON-CHRISTIAN RELIGIONS

Islam is the religion of 3.3% of the population (AD 2000; up from 1.5% in 1970), most being Turks in eastern Thrace, the area of Greece adjoining the small part of Turkish territory in Europe. According to Law 2345 concerning minorities, the Great Mufti of Greece is the recognized head of the Muslim community. Muslims in Greece have about 300 mosques and several Quranic schools.

Judaism has greatly decreased in influence since World War II. The AD 2000 total of about 5,000 Jews contrasts vividly with the 75,000 living there in 1943 before the Nazi deportations and massacres. The Central Board of the Jewish Communities in Greece, founded in Athens in 1945, is their officially recognized governing body.

CHRISTIANITY

The Apostle Paul brought the gospel to Greece in the first century, and in spite of periods of persecution Christianity found fertile soil in the Greco-Roman world. In 312 Constantine became the first Roman emperor to embrace the Christian faith; and in 330 he built a new capital at Byzantium, which he renamed Constantinople. After his death, the Roman empire was divided, the western capital being at Rome while the east continued to have its center in Constantinople. Barbarian invasions from the north radically altered the situation in the western part of the empire, producing further estrangement between east and west. The crowning of Charlemagne as emperor of the Holy Roman Empire by the pope in 800 was interpreted by the Byzantine emperor as an act of schism.

These political events were accompanied also by theological controversy, the main issues being the growth of papal claims and the filioque conflict over the procession of the Holy Spirit in the Nicene creed. Matters came to a head when in 1054 the Catholic cardinal Humbert placed a bull for excommunication on the altar of Santa Sophia cathedral in Constantinople, an event which is generally recognized as the beginning of the Great Schism. In subsequent centuries various attempts were made to heal the wounds of division between the Catholic and Orthodox churches, but without success.

Church of Greece. Parish church (*right*) in residential section of Githion, Peloponnese.

ORTHODOX CHURCHES. The proclamation of the Greek war of independence against the Turks in 1821 resulted in the immediate rupture of relations between the Church of Greece and the Ecumenical Patriarchate in Constantinople, with the administration of the church placed in the hands of regional committees for eastern and western Greece and for the Peloponnese. The demand for self-determination was welcomed by most Greeks and was expressed by the government of the time in the following manner: 'Greece is autonomous and independent, and her Church is autocephalous'. In 1833 bishops and government published jointly the first constitutional charter of the Church of the Kingdom, by which the church proclaimed itself to be the Autocephalous Church of Greece. This charter was submitted to the patriarch of Constantinople for his approval: and after much discussion and many objections, autocephality was finally recognized in 1850.

Originally the church was called simply the 'Greek Church' to correspond to the political appellation 'Greek State', and its jurisdiction covered the regions of the Hellenic kingdom, continental Greece and the Peloponnese. In 1864 the Ionian islands were added and in 1881 Thessalia. Together these are known today as the Ancient Regions (*Palaiai Chorai*) with 37 dioceses.

Following the liberation from the Turks in 1912-13 of Macedonia, Epirus and the islands of the Aegean Sea, these also were annexed by the Church of Greece, although this was not recognized by the ecumenical patriarch until 1928. These are now known as the New Regions (*Neai Chorai*) with 33 dioceses.

Monastic Republic of Mount Athos. 20 monasteries and 1,200 monks.

The Monastic Republic of Mount Athos, the Church of the Dodecanese, the Patriarchal Exarchate of Patmos and the Church of Crete have all subsequently developed independently of the state church. The Church of Crete with 8 dioceses is semiautonomous but is still dependent upon the patriarch of Constantinople. Its supreme administration is the Holy Synod at Iraklion, consisting of the bishops of the island together with, as president, the archbishop of Crete. The Church of the Dodecanese with 4 dioceses, by contrast, is under the direct jurisdiction of the ecumenical patriarch. Mount Athos and the patriarchal exarchate of Patmos are also directly dependent on Constantinople, although their regions do not constitute dioceses. Mount Athos is a sovereign self-administering region of the Greek state, governed by a Holy Community consisting of a representative from each of its 20 monasteries (11 conservative, 9 liberal). These representatives are in turn divided into 4 groups of 5, each group serving as the region's Holy Administration (*Iera Epistasia*) for a year. Recent years have witnessed a radical decline in the number of monks serving on Mount Athos; from 40,000 in earlier days the total fell to 7,970 by 1913, to 3,000 by 1954, to 1,350 in 1969 and to 1,145 in 1971. A further problem is that whereas this was a center for theological scholarship in Byzantine times, most of its monks now come from peasant families, with little education.

Greece remains the only country in the world which is officially Eastern Orthodox and in which the state church is Orthodox, in spite of the periodic shifts in governmental structure of the Greek nation in recent times. The church's dioceses remain very small and in consequence Greek bishops are able to maintain close contact with their people, delegating less responsibility to parish priests than is the case in the Western churches. Married parish priests usually do not preach sermons, which is due in part to their having received relatively little education. Being natives of the villages where they serve, after ordination they frequently return to their previous trades, such as carpentry. The universities at Athens and Salonika maintain schools of theology in which the majority of the teaching staff are laymen, many of whom have studied in Western Europe, Germany in particular. Greek theology today is thus characterized more by this Western academic influence than by the mysticism that once characterized Greek theology when its center was on Mount Athos. Male monastic communities throughout Greece have been declining in membership, whereas the number of nuns has been increasing, many belonging to communities founded in the 20th century.

The major recent innovation within the Greek church has been the home missionary movements concerned with evangelistic and educational work. Apostolic Service, the church's official organization for home missions, was created in 1930. Parallel privately-begun movements include Zoe (Life), Sotir (Savior) and the Orthodox Christian Unions, with at least 30 related organizations for men, women, youth, publishing, and other activities. The oldest, largest and most controversial is Zoe which was begun in 1907. Semi-monastic, its members remain unmarried but take no formal vows and are free to leave at any time. One-fourth of the Zoe membership of 50 (a decline from 135 in 1959) consists of monks, although they do not live regularly in community; the rest are laymen. The home missionary movements stress Bible study and frequent communion, and publish numerous periodicals and books.

Thousands of catechetical schools now exist, and a wide program of youth work has been established.

In addition to these Greek churches in communion with Greek Orthodoxy, a number of other Orthodox bodies have small communities: the Ancient Church of the East, Armenian Apostolic Church, Bulgarian Orthodox Church, Russian Orthodox Church, and the Authentic Old Calendar Orthodox Church. The latter, also called Paleohemerologites (Old Calendar Orthodox), consists of a large number of laity, clergy, and bishops who split from the state church in 1924 rejecting the church's change in that year from the Old (Julian) Calendar to the New (Gregorian) Calendar. They still have a widespread structure of parishes and dioceses with a hierarchy, 250 priests, 81 monasteries and convents, and nearly a quarter of a million faithful.

Church of Crete, Diocese of Kissamos & Selinos. 'Christ is risen!'. In 1972, bishop Ireneos (an active protagonist of lay renewal) with 6 priests celebrates Easter liturgy in small monastery outside Orthodox academy.

MARGINAL CHURCHES. Jehovah's Witnesses have made extraordinary progress since their entry in 1900. They are strong in Athens but also found in many of Greece's smaller towns and villages. At present there are over 300 congregations with a total Christian community greater than that of any other non-Orthodox body including the Catholic Church.

CATHOLIC CHURCH. Roman Catholicism is represented in Greece by 3 rites (Latin, Byzantine, and Armenian), of which the Latin is the most important. There are 9 Latin ecclesiastical divisions and one each for the Byzantine and Armenian rites. There have been Latin Catholics in Greek territories since the time of the Crusades, especially on the Ionian Islands and the islands of the Aegean Sea where Genoan and Venetian merchants lived. Under Turkish occupation in the years following the Crusades, ancient Catholic episcopal sees fell into disuse. After the 19th-century Greek struggle for independence, the Catholic archdiocese of Athens was restored in 1875. The vicariate of Salonica (Thessaloniki) was created in 1926 following the annexation of Turkish territories in eastern Thrace, and today a majority of Latin Catholics are again scattered among the islands.

The establishment of Catholic parishes and the apostolic exarchate of the Byzantine rite dates from the arrival in Greece of Greeks formerly living in Turkey, particularly in that part of Europe in dispute during the Greco-Turkish war of 1922. The total number of refugee Greeks was 1.5 million among whom Catholics of the Byzantine rite constituted only a small minority of 2,000, including a few priests and a bishop. In 1972 its 2 parishes and one quasi-parish (2 in Athens, and one at Yannitsa in Macedonia) were responsible for serving members widely dispersed throughout the whole country. Nine chapels are in use, most of which are located in the houses of Pammakaristos sisters and Little Sisters of Jesus under the jurisdiction of the Greek Catholic exarch. The exarchate has played an important role in moving Latin Catholics in the direction of ecumenism. It has also developed a network of institutions for philanthropic works, publications and news services out of all proportion to its very modest membership of lay and religious personnel.

Armenian-rite Catholics also came to live in Greece after the Greco-Turkish war of 1922. The 2 Armenian parishes are located in Athens but serve dispersed families across the entire country.

Of the 60,500 Catholics living in Greece (1995), about 80% belong to the worker and peasant classes. Little by little the number of Catholic students, intellectuals, and businessman is increasing, which presents the church with a novel challenge.

The Holy See has diplomatic relations with Greece and in AD 2000 is represented to government and the Catholic hierarchy by a pro-nuncio residing in Athens.

PROTESTANT CHURCHES. The 2 main Protestant denominations are the Greek Evangelical Church and the Free Evangelical Churches of Greece, founded respectively in 1858 and 1908. The former is Presbyterian in structure while the latter is more congregational in polity. A number of smaller evangelical bodies exist, some being of Greek origin while others are of foreign background. Greek-Americans have also had an impact on the development of Protestantism. The Armenian Evangelical Church entered Greece following the Greco-Turkish war of 1922 and is now divided into 3 parishes. Six different Greek and foreign Pentecostal bodies, the first being the Church of God of Prophecy in 1927, make up a Pentecostal community of slightly over 4,000. Seventh-day Adventists were the first foreign missionaries to work in Greece, but as with most Protestant groups, their progress has been slow. Rules regarding proselytism are very strict in Greece, and Protestants have been imprisoned for attempting to share their faith with Greek Orthodox. Protestant clergy, both foreign and Greek, are permitted to minister only to their own faithful.

Art and architecture. Most Greek churches are of comparatively recent origin because of the Turkish hiatus in Greek history. But the monasteries, especially those of Athos, are a different story, and represent a link between the early centuries and modern times. Many famous monasteries are also found elsewhere, including Panagia Xenia at Almyros, Panagia Tourliani at Ano Mera, St John the Divine at Antissa, Agios Nikolaos Apoikia, Monastery of the Taxiarchs at Aigion, Chozoviotissa at Amorgos, Zoodochos Pigi Or Agia at Batsi, St John the Divine at Chora, Agia Triada and Olympiotissa at Elasson, St George of Ilia at Eretria, Panachrantos at Falika, Nea Moni at Chios, St George Epanosifis at Iraklion, St Panteleimon at Ioannina, Agia Lavra and Mega Spileon ay Kalavryta, St Ignatios at Kallonia, Koroni and Rendia at Karditsa, Proussou and Tatarna at Karpenission, Odigitria at Kolymvari, Agion Panton, Agios Stephanos and Metamorphosis Sotiros at Meteora, Timios Stavros at Mavradzei, St John at Patmos, Agios Andreas at Peratata, Profitis Ilias and Koimissis Tis Theotokou Kechrovouni at Pyrgos, Arkadi and Agios Ioannis Prevelis at Rethymnon, Evangelismos Tis Theotoku at Skiathos, Evangelistria at Skopelos, Agii Saranda at Sparta, Ossios Loukas at Steiri, Archangel Michael Panormitis at Symi, Agios Vissarion at Trikala, Agothonos at Ypati, Ossios Nikanor at Zavorda and Thekoimissis This Theotokou at Zerbitsa. Among the ancient churches the most historic are the Church of St George at Thessaloniki, Panagia Evangelistria at Tinos, Panagia at Samarina, Holy Apostles at Parga, St Nicholas at Naoussa, Koimissis Tis Theotokou, St Dimitrios at Mystras, Agia Marina at Kissos, Evangelistria at Kastron Agiou Georgiou, The Pantocrator in Korfu, and Panagia at Agiassos.

Indigenous missions. Since the time of the Apostle Paul, Greek Christians have been sent out as missionaries. In recent times most missionaries have been Greek Orthodox bishops and priests with a rising number of Protestants serving in surrounding countries.

Church-State controversy, 1962. *Left.* Primate Iakovos is sacked under government pressure. *Right.* 82-year-old Chrysostomos is elected by 57 metropolitans.

CHURCH AND STATE

The national constitution of 1 January 1952 began: 'In the name of the Holy, Consubstantial and Indivisible Trinity. . . . The established religion in Greece is that of the Eastern Orthodox Church of Christ. . . 'That of 15 November 1968, amended by the constitutional Act of 1 June 1973 which installed the presidential Republic, stipulates that 'The dominant religion is that of the Eastern Orthodox Church of Christ' (Article 1, paragraph 1) and that this church 'is indissolubly united, as to dogma, to the Great Church of Christ at Constantinople and to every other *homodoxe* (of the same faith) Church of Christ. She observes immutably, as do they, the sacred apostolic and synodal canons concerning dogma and worship as well as the holy traditions. She is autocephalous, exercises her sovereign rights independently of every other Church and is administered by a Holy Synod of Bishops' (Article 1, paragraph 2).

The constitutional guarantee of the administrative independence of the Orthodox Church contains an essential recognition of its sanctifying spiritual acts, in which any state intervention would be inadmissible. The constitutional recognition of the Eastern Orthodox Church as 'dominant' does not signify the sovereignty of this church over other confessions or religions, but rather the fact that this is the religion of the majority of Greece's citizens. Nevertheless, this 'dominant' character of the Orthodox Church gives it a special significance, implying on the one hand obligatory stipulations concerning the person of the head of state and on the other the granting by the state to the Orthodox Church a series of privileges guaranteed by the constitution and by legislation promulgated later in the same vein.

The president and vice-president of the Greek republic must profess the religion of the Orthodox Church (Article 33), and their own oaths are taken according to the rites of this church (Article 36, paragraphs 2-3). Moreover, the calendar of state holidays and their official ceremonies are fixed to correspond with the feast days of this same church.

In the chapter dealing with the privileges granted to the Orthodox Church are mentioned the following: (1) the prohibition of proselytism and anything else detrimental to the official religion (Article 1, paragraph 1) which implies a certain right of surveillance over the activities of other confessions; (2) the unchanging conservation of the Greek text of the Holy Scriptures (Article 1, paragraph 4); (3) the recognition of the Orthodox Church of Greece as autocephalous (Article 1, paragraph 2); and (4) the requirement that the permanent Holy Synod be consulted regarding any proposed law concerning the organizations or administration of the church (Article 1, paragraph 5). This last stipulation was introduced for the first time in the constitution of 1968.

Beyond these special privileges, the Greek government provides the Orthodox Church with other forms of aid: direct material assistance to parish clergy, tax exemptions for the church, the requirement that religious education be obligatory in elementary and middle schools, and support of faculties of theology in the universities of Athens and Salonica, as well as of schools and seminaries for the training of clergy and candidates for the priesthood.

The recognition of the autocephalous nature of the Church of Greece signifies the proclamation by the state of the ecclesiastical and administrative independence of the Church of Greece relative to other Orthodox churches and especially to the Phanar, the ecumenical patriarchate of Constantinople. Nevertheless, it is necessary to note that, both by right and practice, this autonomy is not complete. The ecumenical patriarch's Tomos of 1850 recognized the detachment from his jurisdiction of the church of southern Greece whose autonomy had been proclaimed in 1833. The patriarchal Act of 4 September 1928 proclaimed the temporary transfer 'by procuration' (*epitropikôs*) of the dioceses of northern Greece to the Church of Greece. The Holy Mountain of Athos is governed by a charter approved by the Greek government in 1926 and is dependent from a civil point of view on the Greek Ministry of Foreign Affairs. More recently the archbishop of Athens and all Greece, with support from the Greek government, has attempted to become even more independent of the Phanar, as have other autocephalous churches.

In March 1969 the then head of state, G. Papadopoulos, placed before archbishop Hieronymos and the hierarchical synod in Athens a constitutional charter of the Church of Greece (Law 126 of 1969). The government had earlier expressed the desire that the church's hierarchy should accept a more pyramidical structure similar to that of the government and the army. The charter, described as very democratic by the archbishop, placed the responsibility for the administration of the church in the hands of both clergy and laymen. For the first time in the history of the Church of Greece, this charter conferred on the hierarchy and on the permanent Holy Synod the power to legislate: 'Within the limits of law and according to the authority attributed to it by its holy canons, the hierarchical synod shall publish decrees and decisions of validity for the entire Church of Greece concerning questions of faith, divine worship, ecclesiastical discipline, organization and the internal government of the Church' (Articles 6, paragraph D; 10, paragraph 2 and 51, paragraph 3). Because of this, the archbishop and Holy Synod were in possession of the state seal which allowed them to promulgate and publish in the state gazette. The charter was rescinded in September 1975.

Beyond the constitutional privileges of the Orthodox Church the state exercises ultimate supervision over it through the Ministry of Foreign Affairs for that which concerns the Ecumenical Patriarchate, Mount Athos, and Greek clergy in foreign lands: and especially through the Ministry of National Instruction and Religions (*Hypourgeion Ethnikis Paideias kai Thriskevmaton*). This latter consists of an Office for Religions (*Geniki Dievthynsis Thriskevmaton*), with 3 sub-offices and 3 councils: (1) Office of Ecclesiastical Government, with one section for the Church of Greece and another for the Churches of Crete and the Dodecanese; (2) Office for Ecclesiastical Instruction and Religious Education, with a section corresponding to each of its domains; (3) Office for Non-Orthodox Religions (*Heterothriskon*) with sections for Christians and for other religions; (4) Legal Council (*Nomimophro Synis*); (5) Council of Personnel for Ecclesiastical Instruction; and (6) Council for Control of Ecclesiastical Instruction.

The Minister of National Instruction and Religions represents the state during the election of an archbishop of Athens. He publishes the presidential decree by which one of the 3 candidates proposed by the Holy Synod is chosen as metropolitan of any vacant see. By virtue of Article II of the constitutional charter of the Church of Greece, he may participate (either personally or through the Director General for Religions), but without the right of vote, at the regular and special meetings of the hierarchical Synod and the Permanent Holy Synod. He must be invited in writing, with a list of the questions to be discussed; but the omission of the prior invitation does not make null and void the decisions taken at these meetings. Between 1972 and 1974 this minister required all bishops to ordain only priests holding a 'certificate of civics' given by the Ministry of Public Order after a security check.

Church of Greece, Diocese of Zakinthos (Zante). Paralyzed woman is carried by relatives to bishop in search of miraculous healing. Every 24 August the well-preserved body of patron saint Dyonisios, a 17th century abbot, is paraded on the island, and sick and crippled persons come from all over Greece to lie in the streets. Many cures are attested; but in 1979 a major scandal erupted across Greece involving alleged commercialism.

Other churches and confessions may seek recognition from the Office for Non-Orthodox Religions, and their clergy act as officers of the civil state. Article 1, paragraph 1, which forbids proselytism, gives the Church of Greece the right of surveillance over other confessions in the following areas: a permit from the local Orthodox bishop must be obtained before construction of any non-Orthodox church; under pain of nullity, mixed marriages must be celebrated before an Orthodox priest; and special permission must be obtained from the Orthodox bishop, as well as from the Ministry of National Instruction and Religions, for the residence in Greece of foreign priests and their appointments. The Catholic Church benefits from a special situation due to the fact that the Western powers in 1821 imposed on Greece the recognition of existing Catholic dioceses. The bishops of these dioceses remain official personages and enjoy certain privileges, such as the right to hold processions of the sacraments, which are not shared by Catholic dioceses created after 1821. From the mid-1980s the atmosphere has been somewhat freer for non-Orthodox Christians seeking to evangelize in Greece. Pentecostals, Mormons, and Jehovah's Witnesses have especially felt harassed. Visas for foreign Christian workers are difficult. An Evangelical leader, Costas Macris, and 2 YWAM missionaries were arrested in 1982 for the crime of proselytism. They were convicted in a lower court and faced several years in jail and stiff fines, but their conviction was overturned on appeal in 1986.

In daily life the question of church-state relations is extremely complex due both to the Byzantine heritage and also to the development of Hellenic nationalism over the past century and a half. The intervention of the state in the affairs of the Orthodox Church is continual and considered natural even when not desired. These interventions are especially evidenced during church crises and are frequently accompanied by appeals from clergy and laity, especially those involved in government. At times the internal conflicts have been so severe that solutions are possible only by resort to the politicization of the issue and the passage of government laws.

Ultimately, therefore, the Greek state proclaims itself the guardian of the Orthodox Faith and traditions. Bishops and theologians occasionally call for the separation of church and state, but such a divorce would be extremely difficult to affect. The church meanwhile continues to experience the difficulty of trying to retain its Byzantine heritage in a modern state.

In 1993 the Greek parliament passed a new law requiring religious preference to be stated on all identity cards and passports. Jewish, Catholic, and other non-Orthodox religious groups in Greece, and the european Parliament outside, both protested loudly. The former feared discrimination. Greece is the only country in the European Community with such a provision.

BROADCASTING AND MEDIA

IBRA-produced programs can be heard on local radio stations, and received from transmitters in Portugal. Programs in Armenian can be received from Voice of Hope (Lebanon), and in Macedonian from TWR (Macedonia). Shortwave programs from WORHAR (USA), KNLS, HCJB (Ecuador), TWR (Monaco, Albania) and AWR (Slovakia) can be easily received.

CBN's news programs and drama series are available on a weekly basis over several local television channels. Satellite TV programs are received mainly in Arabic. TBN programs appear in Athens and Macedonia on channel 62, and in Corinth on channel 54.

INTERDENOMINATIONAL ORGANIZATIONS

Relations between the Church of Greece and the Church of Rome, bad during the days of Catholic proselytism, have remained frigid since Vatican II, with periodic denunciations of Roman Catholicism by Orthodox bishops and officials. No official ecumenical organizations exist; but an Orthodox-Catholic discussion group, consisting of priests and laymen from both sides, has been meeting in Athens since 1964. The Byzantine Institute in Athens also engages in ecumenical projects of a cooperative nature. The Catholic episcopal conference does not have a special commission for ecumenism. Since 1972 all Catholics in Greece celebrate Easter on the same day as the Orthodox. Several Protestant groups came together in 1977 to form the Pan Hellenic Evangelical Alliance.

FUTURE TRENDS AND PROSPECTS

Christians are likely to decline from 98.3% in 1970 to 93.8% by 2025. Muslims and the nonreligious are expected to rise jointly from 1.6% in 1970 to 5.9% by 2025.

Christians will probably fall below 90% before AD 2050. Muslims and the nonreligious could then comprise well over 10% of the population.

BIBLIOGRAPHY

Anatomy of a church: Greek Orthodoxy today. M. Rinvolucri. London: Burns & Oates, 1966. 192p.

Anchored in God: an account of life, art, and thought on the Holy Mountain of Athos. C. Cavarnos. Athens: Astir, 1959. 230p.

'Between partnership and separation: relations between church and state in Greece under the constitution of June 1975,' A. Basdekis, *Ecumenical review* (Geneva), 29, 1 (1977), 52–61.

Byzantine churches of Greece and Cyprus. E. Mastrogiannopoulos. Brookline, MA: Holy Cross Orthodox Press, 1984. 134p.

Contemporary ascetics of Mount Athos. C. Karambelas. Platina, CA: St. Herman of Alaska Brotherhood Press, 1991. 2 vols.

Experiencing the feast days of the Festal Menaion in Greece. M. Winterer-Papatassos. Minneapolis, MN: Light and Life, 1987. 69p.

Firewalking and religious healing: the Anastenaria of Greece and the American firewalking movement. L. M. Danforth. *Princeton modern Greek studies.* Princeton, NJ: Princeton University Press, 1989. 348p.

Greece. M. J. Clogg & R. Clogg. *World bibliographical series,* vol. 17. Oxford, UK: CLIO Press, 1980. (See especially 'Religion,' p.71–6).

Greece and Babylon: a comparative sketch of Mesopotamian, Anatolian and Hellenic religions. L. R. Farnell. Edinburgh: T. & T. Clark, 1911.

Hemerologion tes Ekklesias tes Hellados (Yearbook of the Church of Greece). Athens: Apostolic Service, 1977. 540p. (Annual).

Mount Athos: the garden of the Panaghia. E. A. de Mendieta. *Berliner Byzantinistische Arbeiten,* vol. 41. Berlin: Akademie Verlag, with Adolf M. Hakkert, Amsterdam, 1972. 360p.

'Rapports des recherches sur la sociologie religieuse en Grèce.' Athens: EKKE, 1971. (5 papers).

'Religious brotherhoods: a sociological view,' B. Jioultsis, *Social Compass,* 22, 1 (1975), 67–83.

'Sociology of Greek Orthodoxy,' *Social compass,* 22, 1 (1975), 1–147. (7 articles).

'The beginning of Protestant mission to the Greek Orthodox in Asia Minor and Pontos.' S. L. Burch. M.A. thesis, Fuller Theological Seminary, Pasadena, CA, 1977. 183p.

The Eastern Orthodox Church: a bibliography. D. T. Andrew. 2d ed. Brookline, MA: Greek Archdiocese of North and South America, Holy Cross Orthodox Theological School, 1957. 79p.

The festivals of Greek Easter. C. Papoutsis. [Greece: C. Papoutsis], 1982. 79p.

The Old Calendar Orthodox Church of Greece. Bishop Chrysostomos, Bishop Auxentios, and Archimandrite Ambrosios. 3d ed. Etna, CA: Center for Traditionalist Orthodox Studies, 1991. 99p.

'The Orthodox Church of Greece: the last fifteen years,' C. A. Frazee, *Indiana Social Studies Quarterly,* 32, 1 (1979), 89–110.

'The political influence of the Orthodox Church of Greece.' G. D. Kent. Ph.D. dissertation, University of Colorado, 1971. 473p.

The religious minorities of Chios: Jews and Roman Catholics. P. P. Argenti. Cambridge, UK: Cambridge University Press, 1970. 590p.

Thriskeutiki kai ithiki egyklopaidia (Religious and ethical encyclopedia). Athens: A. Martinos, 1962–68. 12 vols. (Articles on dioceses and church history).

Thriskeutiki kai ithiki egyklopaidia (Religious and ethical encyclopedia). Athens: A. Martinos, 1962–68. 12 vols. (articles on all Greek dioceses, church events, festivals, bishops, theologians, movements).

Time, religion, and social experience in rural Greece. L. K. Hart. Lanham, MD: Rowman & Littlefield, 1992. 310p.

Tradition in Greek religion. B. C. Dietrich. Berlin: de Gruyter, 1986. 229p.

Country Table 2. **Organized churches and denominations in Greece.**

Official name (bold type = church with over 10% of all affiliated) 1	*Begun* 2	*Type* 3	*Counc* 4	*Congs* 5	*Adults* 6	*Affiliated 1970* 7	*Affiliated 1995* 8	*G%* 9	*Names, notes, and other statistics* (see Codebook, Part 3) 10
Ancient Church of the East	1850	O-Nes	Yw...	1	50	100	100	0.00	*Nestorians.* Assyrian refugees from massacres in Middle East since 1850.
Armenian Apostolic Church: D Athínai	1922	O-Arm	Sw.N.	9	4,050	11,000	9,000	-0.80	*Gregorians.* Under C Cilicia (Lebanon). 1956 schism ex C Echmiadzin. 6n,W=30%,41y.
Assemblies of God	1931	P-Pe2	ZF...	11	1,300	2,000	1,585	-0.93	*Ekklesia tes Pentecostes.* Greek origin. M=AoG(USA). Katerini, Athens. 20n,5f,1s.
Authentic Old Calendar Orthodox Ch	1924	I-OCd	c....	180	106,000	200,000	212,000	0.23	*Paleohemerologites. Old Calendar Greek OC.* Ex Ch of G. In USA, Canada. 250n,81de,1100w.
Baptist Churches	c1969	P-Bap	T....	3	184	83	341	5.81	M=FMB-SBC. Assisted mainly by Southern Baptist Convention (USA).
Bulgarian Orthodox Church		O-Bul	Mwc..	2	2,000	5,000	5,000	0.05	*Balgarskata Pravoslavna Crkva.* Under P Sofia. Bulgarian residents.
Catholic Church in Greece:	c 300	R-LEr	OzB.R	98	44,060	45,723	60,591	1.13	*Katholiki Eklissia.* Declining. C=4+2+12. 49n 50x 87m 134w 664Yy
M Corfú, Zante & Cefalonia	1212	R-Lat	Oaa	6	2,200	2,700	3,000	0.42	Kérkira/Zákinthos/Kefallinía. United 1919. Ionians. 4n 4x 4m 9w 22Yy
M Náxos, Andros, Tinos & Mykonos	c 850	R-Lat	Os	25	1,900	3,135	2,597	-0.75	Tinos, c850. 3 dioceses united 1919. Cyclades. 7% RC. 7n 2x 4m 7w 36Yy
D Candia (Iráklion)	1213	R-Lat	Os	3	360	420	500	0.70	Crete. Suffragan diocese of M Naxos. M=OFMCap. 0n 4x 4m 0w –
D Chíos (Khios)(Diikissiş)	c1250	R-Lat	Os	3	60	47	80	2.15	On Tinos island. Northern Cyclades next to Turkey. – – – – –
D Santorini (Thera, Thira)	1204	R-Lat	Os	1	70	140	84	-2.02	Southern Cyclades. HQ Syros. M=OFMCap,SJ. 1n 1x 1m 11w 2Yy
D Syros & Mílos (Syra & Milo)	c1250	R-Lat	Os	24	5,100	7,235	6,980	-0.14	Covers western Cyclades. HQ Syros. M=OFMCap,SJ. 9n 3x 9m 8w 42Yy
AD Athínai (Athens)	1205	R-Lat	os	15	29,000	26,000	40,000	1.74	Central Greece, Euboea and isles. Restored 1875. 15n 25x 47m 74w 509Yy
AD Ródhos (Rhodes)	c 350	R-Lat	os	5	1,000	421	1,400	4.92	Archdiocese under Malta from 1797-1928. M=OFM. 0n 4x 5m 0w 9Yy
VA Salonica (Thessaloniki)	1926	R-Lat	Os	8	2,200	2,000	3,000	1.64	Northern Greece. HQ Thessaloniki. M=AA,SJ. 0n 6x 12m 8w 11Yy
EA Greece (Hellas)(*Greek*)	1923	R-Gre	Os	6	1,700	3,000	2,300	-1.06	Byzantine-rite Catholics. HQ Athens. 10n 0x 0m 17w 33Yy

continued overleaf

Country Table 2–continued

Official name (bold type = church with over 10% of all affiliated) 1	*Begun* 2	*Type* 3	*Counc* 4	*Congs* 5	*Adults* 6	*Affiliated 1970* 7	*Affiliated 1995* 8	*G%* 9	*Names, notes, and other statistics (see Codebook, Part 3)* 10
O Greece (Hellas)(*Armenian*)	1925	R-Arm	Os	2	470	625	650	0.16	Armenian-rite Catholics. HQ Athens. 3n 1x 1m 0w 3Yy
Christ's Church of Pentecost	c1975	P-Pe2	.....	1	30	–	50	5.00	M=Elim Pentecostal Ch(UK).
Church of Christ in Greece	1962	I-Dis	x....	3	100	200	300	1.64	*Ekklesia tou Kristou.* M=CC(Non-Instrumental) (USA). USA civilians, military. 5x.
Church of Christ, Scientist		m-Sci	x....	1	40	100	100	0.05	*Christian Science.* M=CCS(Boston, USA). First Church, Athens. 1w.
Church of Crete:	c 50	O-Gre	Cwc..	3,897	363,000	456,246	497,000	0.34	Under EP Constantinople. A=1967. 1s(278).
AD Kríti (Archiepiscopi Kristis)	1967	O-Gre	Ca	776	112,000	140,000	153,000	0.36	Covers north central Crete. HQ Iráklion.
D Gortuni & Arcadia	1962	O-Gre	Cm	617	47,000	60,000	65,000	0.32	South central Crete. HQ Mirai.
D Ierápetra & Sitía	1962	O-Gre	Cm	483	32,000	40,000	44,000	0.38	Eastern extremity of Crete. HQ Ierápetra.
D Kissamos & Selinos	1962	O-Gre	Cm	669	24,000	30,000	33,000	0.38	Numerous social projects. HQ Kastelli.
D Kydonia & Apocoronos	1962	O-Gre	Cm	556	72,000	90,000	98,000	0.34	HQ Chania (Khaniá). Lay academy.
D Labi & Sfekíon	1962	O-Gre	Cm	182	14,000	17,666	19,000	0.29	West south central area. HQ Spilion.
D Petra (Petras)	1962	O-Gre	Cm	320	26,000	33,024	36,000	0.35	East central Crete. HQ Neapolis.
D Réthimnon & Avlopotamos	1962	O-Gre	Cm	294	36,000	45,556	49,000	0.29	North west centre of island. HQ Réthimnon.
Church of England (D Europe)	1804	A-plu	awc..	3	2,900	3,000	3,500	0.62	Chaplaincies 1836 at Athens (St Paul), 1816 Corfu (seasonal), Patras (St Andrews). 1x.
Church of God of Pentecost	1952	P-Pe3	ZF...	6	299	300	544	2.41	*Ekklesia tou Theou tou Plerous Evangelion.* M=CoG(Cleveland). 2n,W=99%,5Y,8z.
Church of God of Prophecy	1927	P-Pe3	Z....	6	130	300	300	0.00	*Ekklesia Theou Pentecostes.* M=CGP(USA). Holiness Pentecostals (3-stage). 3n.
Church of God (Anderson)	1947	P-Hol	x....	6	180	300	545	2.42	*Ekklesia tou Theou.* M=CoG(Anderson, USA). No missionaries now. 1n,W=25%.
Church of Greece:	50	O-Gre	CWC..	28,893	6,618,200	7,719,723	9,098,000	0.05	*Ekklesia tes Hellados.* 95 bps,7530n,7184b,144d(891m),163e(1709w).
Old regions (Palaiai Chorai):	1881	O-Gre	C	–	–	–			Regions annexed to Greek state and church from Turks over period 1833-1881.
AD Athínai (Athens)	50	O-Gre	Ca	301	1,509,000	1,750,000	2,069,000	0.05	*Archiepiscopi Athnon.* HQ Athens. 2s,1v.
D Aitolia & Acarnania	1922	O-Gre	Cm	910	173,000	201,313	237,000	0.65	Bishop's residence (HQ) Messologion.
D Argolis (Argolidos)	1189	O-Gre	Cm	523	65,000	76,823	89,000	0.59	Northeast Peloponnese. HQ Nafplion.
D Arta (Artis)	1922	O-Gre	Cm	233	48,000	56,885	66,000	0.60	West centre of Greece. HQ Arta.
D Attica & Megaridos (Attikis)	1936	O-Gre	Cm	750	174,000	201,460	238,000	0.67	Area all around Athens city. HQ Kifissia.
D Dimitriados (Demetrias)	1922	O-Gre	Cm	404	138,000	160,000	189,000	0.67	Southeastern part of Thessaly. HQ Volos.
D Gortynos & Megalópolis	1922	O-Gre	Cm	166	51,000	60,000	71,000	0.68	Central Peloponnese. HQ Megalópolis.
D Idhra, Spetson & Egines	1936	O-Gre	Cm	914	30,000	35,000	41,000	0.63	Extreme east Peloponnese. HQ Idhra (Hydra).
D Ilia (Ilias)	1899	O-Gre	Cm	347	141,000	164,860	194,000	0.65	Northwest Peloponnese. HQ Pyrgos.
D Kalávrita & Egialia	1923	O-Gre	Cm	651	69,000	80,000	95,000	0.69	In northern Peloponnese. HQ Egion.
D Káristos & Skiros	1923	O-Gre	Cm	232	41,000	47,995	56,000	0.62	Eastern Evvoia and Skiros island. HQ Kymi.
D Kafallinia (Kefallinías)	1790	O-Gre	Cm	214	31,000	36,657	43,000	0.64	Extreme western island. HQ Argostalion.
D Kérkira (Corfu) & Paxoi	1824	O-Gre	Cm	668	79,000	92,300	109,000	0.67	Extreme northwestern island. HQ Kerkyra.
D Khalkís (Khalkidos)	1922	O-Gre	Cm	746	108,000	126,769	149,000	0.65	Seminary in Khalkís monastery. HQ Khalkís.
D Kíthira (Kithiron)	1922	O-Gre	Cm	265	3,200	4,083	5,000	0.81	Smallest diocese (one island). HQ Chora.
D Kórinthos (Kórinthias)	c 350	O-Gre	Cm	930	95,000	111,000	131,000	0.66	NE Peloponnese. HQ Kórinthos (Corinth). 1s.
D Láris & Platamonos	c 650	O-Gre	Cm	272	115,000	134,520	158,000	0.65	In central Thessaly. HQ Lárisa.
D Levkás & Itháki	1922	O-Gre	Cm	122	20,000	24,559	28,000	0.53	Ithaca and western islands. HQ Levkás.
D Mantinia & Kynouria	1924	O-Gre	Cm	667	59,000	69,397	81,000	0.62	Centre west of Peloponnese. HQ Tripolis.
D Messíni (Messinias)	1922	O-Gre	Cm	681	103,000	119,876	142,000	0.68	South of Peloponnese. HQ Kalamata.
D Monemvasía & Spárti	1920	O-Gre	Cm	1,038	51,000	60,000	71,000	0.68	Southeastern part of Peloponnese. HQ Spárti.
D Návpaktos & Evrytania	1933	O-Gre	Cm	780	48,000	57,813	67,000	0.59	In centre of country. HQ Návpaktos.
D Neas Pelagonias & ED	1968	O-Gre	Cm	145	293,000	340,276	402,000	0.67	HQ Nikaia (western suburb of Athens).
D Páronaxia (Páronaxias)	1083	O-Gre	Cm	623	20,000	23,000	27,000	0.64	2 islands. 14 vacant monasteries. HQ Naxos.
D Pátrai (Pátron)	c750	O-Gre	Cm	306	129,000	150,000	177,000	0.08	In north of Peloponnese. HQ Pátrai.
D Phokidos	1923	O-Gre	Cm	229	35,000	41,310	48,000	0.60	North of Gulf of Corinth. HQ Amphissa.
D Phthiotidos	1922	O-Gre	Cm	897	132,000	154,720	182,000	0.65	In southern Thessaly. HQ Lamia.
D Piraiéus (Pireos)	1962	O-Gre	Cm	42	188,000	218,270	258,000	0.67	New diocese. HQ Piraiéus (port of Athens).
D Síros, Tínos, Andros & Kéa	1922	O-Gre	Cm	1,954	43,000	50,000	59,000	0.66	HQ Ermoupolis. Population 30% Catholics.
D Thessaliotis & Phanariophersala	1921	O-Gre	Cm	484	112,000	131,756	155,000	0.65	In southern Thessaly. HQ Kardista.
D Thíra, Amorgós & Nissa	1814	O-Gre	Cm	525	17,000	20,000	24,000	0.73	Many scattered islands. HQ Thíra.
D Thívai (Thebes) & Levádheia	1922	O-Gre	Cm	374	95,000	110,000	130,000	0.67	In north of Attica. HQ Levadia.
D Trika & Stagon	1910	O-Gre	Cm	610	108,000	125,300	148,000	0.67	In west centre of country. HQ Tricala.
D Triphylia & Olympia	1922	O-Gre	Cm	1,135	86,000	100,000	118,000	0.66	In west Peloponnese. HQ Kyparissia.
D Yítheion & Itylos	1922	O-Gre	Cm	696	17,000	20,251	24,000	0.68	Extreme southern promontory. HQ Gythion.
D Zákinthos (Zákinthou, Zante)	1824	O-Gre	Cm	192	25,000	30,156	35,000	0.60	One of Ionian islands in west. HQ Zákinthos.
New regions (Neai Chorai):	1928	O-Gre	C	–	–				Assigned 1928 to Ch of Greece by EP Constantinople after Macedonia liberated.
D Alexandroúpolis	1885	O-Gre	Cm	80	47,000	55,366	65,000	0.64	Thrace, also Samothrace. Many Muslims.
D Dhidhimóteikhon & OrestiEas	1387	O-Gre	Cm	130	69,000	80,800	95,000	0.65	Extreme northeast. HQ Dhidhimóteikhon.
D Dráma (Drámas)	1359	O-Gre	Cm	144	78,000	91,015	108,000	0.69	In northeast along Bulgaria border. HQ Dráma.
D Dryinopolis, Pogonianí, K	1834	O-Gre	Cm	519	16,000	19,140	22,000	0.56	*K=Kónitsa. Extreme NW. HQ Deirniakion.*
D Edhessa. Pélla & Almopia	1922	O-Gre	Cm	398	108,000	126,201	149,000	0.67	Edge of Macedonia. HQ Edhessa.
D Elasson (Elassonos)	1814	O-Gre	Cm	154	42,000	49,528	58,000	0.63	In northern Thessaly. HQ Elasson.
D Elevtheroupolis	1889	O-Gre	Cm	87	30,000	35,000	41,000	0.63	East of Salonica. HQ Elevtheroupolis.
D Flórina, Prespa & Eordea	1925	O-Gre	Cm	164	73,000	85,253	100,000	0.64	In 1967, 200 Muslims baptized. HQ Flórina.
D Grevená (Grevenon)	c1450	O-Gre	Cm	314	30,000	35,385	41,000	0.59	On southern edge of Macedonia. HQ Grevená.
D Ierissós, Agion Oros, & A	1932	O-Gre	Cm	138	32,000	37,756	44,000	0.61	*A=Ardamerios.* Mount Athos. HQ Arnea.
D Ioánnina (Ioánninon)	1319	O-Gre	Cm	284	115,000	134,356	158,000	0.65	Greece's richest diocese. HQ Ioánnina.
D Kassándra (Kassándrias)	1932	O-Gre	Cm	329	56,000	65,112	77,000	0.67	Covers Khalkidhiki. HQ Polygyros.
D Kastoría (Kastorías)	1384	O-Gre	Cm	293	46,000	54,075	64,000	0.68	Edge of Macedonia. HQ Kastoría.
D Kateríni (Kitrous)	1924	O-Gre	Cm	200	86,000	100,000	118,000	0.66	HQ Kateríni. Many Greek Evangelicals in area.
D Khíos (Chios), Psará & I	1571	O-Gre	Cm	874	46,000	53,929	63,000	0.62	*I=Inoussos.* 14 vacant monasteries. HQ Chios.
D Langadhás	1967	O-Gre	Cm	64	43,000	50,100	59,000	0.66	Orthodox fire-walking sect, Anasternarides.
D Límnos & Agios Evstrátios	1450	O-Gre	Cm	437	20,000	23,000	27,000	0.64	North Aegean Sea. HQ Myrina, Limnos.
D Maronia (Maronias)	1365	O-Gre	Cm	156	52,000	60,000	71,000	0.68	Thrace, Thasos. HQ Komotini. Many Muslims.
D Mithimna (Mithimnis)	c1250	O-Gre	Cm	125	22,000	25,996	31,000	0.71	Northern half island of Lesbos. HQ Kalloni.
D Mitilíni, Eresós & Plomárion	c 950	O-Gre	Cm	812	60,000	70,189	83,000	0.67	Southern half of Lesbos. HQ Mytilene.
D Nicopolis & Préveza	1881	O-Gre	Cm	338	74,000	86,616	102,000	0.66	Mid-western coast of Greece. HQ Préveza.
D Paramithiá, Philiaton & Gir	1895	O-Gre	Cm	594	43,000	51,284	60,000	0.63	In Ipeiros, in northwest. HQ Paramithiá.
D Philippi, Neapolis & Thásos	1924	O-Gre	Cm	116	104,000	121,491	143,000	0.65	Also called D Kavalla. HQ Kavalla.
D Poliana & Kilkis	1924	O-Gre	Cm	181	80,000	93,500	110,000	0.65	In Macedonia. HQ Kilkís.
D Sámos & Ikaría	1841	O-Gre	Cm	460	35,000	41,687	48,000	0.57	Off Turkey mainland. 11 vacant monasteries.
D Sérrai & Nigríta	c1050	O-Gre	Cm	163	174,000	202,771	239,000	0.66	In north near Bulgaria border. HQ Sérrai.
D Sérvia & Kozáni	1882	O-Gre	Cm	157	60,000	70,000	83,000	0.68	In northern Thessaly. HQ Kozáni.
D Sidhirókastron (Sidirokastrou)	1913	O-Gre	Cm	131	43,000	51,000	60,000	0.65	Along Bulgaria border. HQ Sidhirókastron.
D Sissanios & Siátista	1855	O-Gre	Cm	453	43,000	50,000	59,000	0.66	Northwest, near Albania border. HQ Siátista.
D Thessaloniki (Thessalonikis)	796	O-Gre	Cm	111	258,000	300,000	354,000	0.08	Major city. Strong seminary and university.
D Véroia & Náousa	c1350	O-Gre	Cm	245	107,000	125,000	147,000	0.65	Area west of Salonica. HQ Véroia.
D Zánthi & Peritheorios	1284	O-Gre	Cm	131	37,000	43,824	51,000	0.61	Thrace. Many Muslims in area. HQ Xáanthi. 1s.
D Zichnon & Nevrokopis	1924	O-Gre	Cm	85	38,000	44,000	52,000	0.67	Northeast, near Bulgaria. HQ Nea Zichni.
Ch of Jesus Christ of Latter-day Saints		m-LdS	x....	3	210	126	300	0.05	*Mormons. M=CJCLdS(USA). Mostly USA expatriates and military personnel.*
Church of the Dodecanese:	c 60	O-Gre	Cwc..	913	103,800	117,517	143,000	0.79	Under EP Constantinople. Off Turkey mainland. 159n,138b,4d(9m),6e(80w),1s(12).
D Kárpathos & Kásos	1948	O-Gre	Cm	56	6,500	8,000	9,000	0.47	3 islands SW of Rhodes. 2 disused monasteries.
D Kos (Cos)	1838	O-Gre	Cm	164	14,600	16,561	20,000	0.76	Single island 5 km from Turkey. HQ Kos.
D Léros, Kálimnos & Astipalea	1888	O-Gre	Cm	116	19,700	22,000	27,000	0.82	HQ (winter) Leros. (Summer) Kálimnos.
D Ródhos (Rhodes)	c 450	O-Gre	Cm	577	63,000	70,956	87,000	0.82	22 monasteries (20 disused). Many Muslims.
Free Apostolic Church of Pentecost	1965	I-3aW	.....	10	2,000	1,500	2,410	1.91	*Eleuthera Apostolike Ekklesia Pentecostes.* Greek origin. 1n (Athens).
Free Evangelical Churches of Greece	1908	I-CBr	K....	50	1,380	3,000	2,500	-0.73	*Eleuthera Evangelike Ekklesia. Brethren.* Members mostly ex state church. 10n,2f,1p,40Y.
German Evangelical Church	1837	P-LuR	.....	7	500	700	1,000	1.44	Serving German-speaking community, mostly expatriates. 1x,W=12%,34Yy,20z.
Greek Bible Centre	1964	I-Non	.....	3	300	200	500	3.73	*Hellenikon Kentron Biblou.* Greek origin, few expatriate links. 2n (Athens).
Greek Evangelical Church	1858	P-Ref	RWC..	35	2,000	9,000	4,000	-3.19	*Hellenike Evangelike Ekklesia.* HQ Athens. 18n,1p(Katerini),W=80%,50Yy,250z.
Gypsy Evangelical Movement		I-3pE	x....	50	5,000	1,500	8,000	0.05	Nomadic caravan communities. Large meetings round Thessalonica. M=GGMS(Switzerland).
Internat Ch of the Foursquare Gospel	1946	P-Pe2	ZF...	4	267	500	668	1.17	M=ICFG(USA). Classical Pentecostals (2-stage). 11 national workers, 2f,W=41%,8Y.
Jehovah's Witnesses	1900	m-Jeh	x....	332	24,348	50,000	40,600	-0.83	Many in Athens; throughout country. State hostility: banned till 1972. (1975) 545Y. (1995) 957Y.
Monastic Republic of Mount Athos	c 350	O-Gre	Cwc..	23	1,200	2,687	2,500	-0.29	*Agion Oros.* Under Ecumenical Partriarchate. 20d (1,233 monks; once 40,000).
New Apostolic Church		I-3aX	x....	7	420	1,000	500	0.05	*NAC.* In Wiesbaden Bezirk (District); world HQ Zurich (Switzerland). Germans.
OMS Churches		P-Hol	.....	1	45	38	75	0.05	*Oriental Missionary Society Churches.* M=OMS(USA).
Oriental Apostolic Church	1947	P-Hol	xF...	6	60	50	100	2.81	*Anatolike Apostolike Ekklesia.* Foreign origin. M=Oriental MS(USA). 5n.
Patriarchal Exarchate of Pátmos	1088	O-Gre	Cwc..	72	2,000	3,246	3,000	-0.31	Under EP Constantinople. 11n,7b,1d(St John the Divine: 28m),3e(64w),1s(10).
Seventh-day Advent Ch, Greek Mission	1903	P-Adv	x....	9	303	500	433	-0.57	*Adventistai tes Evdomes Hemeras.* 5n,1x,1j,1p,16t(314),W=80%,18Y.
Union of Armenian Ev Chs in Near East	1923	P-Con	Rw.N.	3	335	1,000	1,020	0.08	*Armenike Evangelike Ekklesia.* Armenian residents. 1n (in Piraeus). 2 schools.
Other Protestant denominations		P-	.....	15	5,000	12,000	11,000	0.05	Total about 20 (see list below), including USA military chaplaincies.
Other Orthodox churches		O-	.....	20	2,500	1,000	5,000	0.05	Russian O C (16 monks on Mount Athos); Bulgarian, Albanian , Serbian, Macedonian, OCs.
Doubly-affiliated		2-aff			–137,000	-60,121	-189,562		Minority church members still enumerated as baptized Orthodox in state church.
Totals				**34,683**	**7,157,191**	**8,649,639**	**9,926,000**		

Churches, members, growth, 1900-2025	*Congs*	*Adults*	*Affiliated*	*G%*	*Total denominations*	*6 Megablocs: O*	*R*	*A*	*P*	*I*	*m*
Total churches, members, and denominations (mid-1900)	15,000	1,100,000	2,589,000	1.73	14	8	1	1	3	0	1
Total churches, members, and denominations (mid-1970)	30,003	6,226,636	8,589,518	1.73	45	12	1	1	21	7	3
Total churches, members, and denominations (mid-1990)	32,000	5,000,000	9,703,180	0.61	63	18	1	1	33	7	3
Total churches, members, and denominations (mid-1995)	34,683	7,157,191	9,926,000	0.46	63	18	1	1	33	7	3
Total churches, members, and denominations (mid-2000)	35,000	5,010,000	10,061,020	0.27	64	19	1	1	33	7	3
Total churches, members, and denominations (mid-2025)	34,000	4,900,000	9,230,000	-0.34	119	30	1	1	50	30	7

Continued opposite

Country Table 2–concluded

NOTES ON TABLE ABOVE
NATIONAL COUNCILS (Column 4, 5th letter).
E = Panhellenic (Greek) Evangelical Alliance (PEA).
R = Conferentia Episcopolis Graeciae, formerly Catholic Episcopal Conference of Greece (Synodos Katholikis Ierarchias Ellados).
OTHER PROTESTANT DENOMINATIONS. There are a large number of bodies catering for USA civilians, also USA military chaplaincies. Foreign chaplaincies include Christus Kirche, Kifissia Protestant Chapel, St Andrew's American Ch. Other groups with some Greek membership include: American Mission to Greeks (1942), Bible Christian Union, Children of God International (discotheque in Athens), Christadelphian Ecclesias, Ch of the Brethren (1951), Corfu Evangelistic Association, Exclusive Brethren (Kelly-Continental), Gospel Missionary Union (1959), Greek Ev Mission (1920)/Greater Europe Mission (Greek Bible Institute/Society of Biblical Studies), Independent Pentecostal Ch, Southern Baptist Convention (1972), Swedish Free Mission, Trinity Baptist Ch, United Pentecostal Ch (1975).

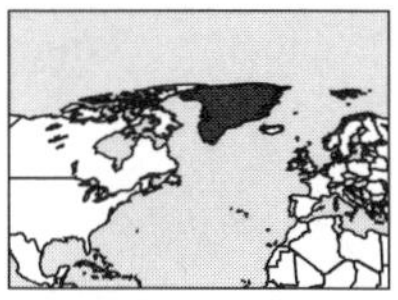

GREENLAND

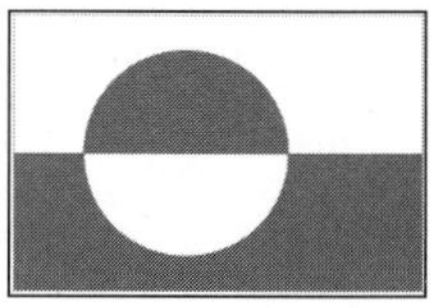

SECULAR DATA, AD 2000

STATE
Official name: Grønland/Kalaallit Nunaat (Greenland).
Short name: Greenland. **Adjective of nationality:** Greenlander.
Flag: That of Denmark.
Area: 2,175,600 sq. km. (840,000 sq. mi.).
Government: Self-governing overseas area of the Kingdom of Denmark, since 1953 (1979 home rule).
Legislature: Home Rule Parliament, 31 members.
Official language: Greenlandic, Danish (Dansk).
Monetary unit: 1 Danish krone (Dkr; plural kroner) = 100 Ø. **US$1=** Dkr 6.36.
Chief cities: GODTHAB (Nuuk) 13,047.
Political divisions: 6 provinces.

DEMOGRAPHY
Population: 56,000.
Population density: <0.1/sq. km. (<0.1/sq. mi.).
Under 15 years: 10,000.
Growth rate p.a.: 0.13% (births 11.28, deaths 11.69).
Mortality: Infant, per 1,000: 6.9; **Maternal per 100,000:** 25.0.
Life expectancy: 76 (male 74, female 79).
Household size: 1.8. **Floor area per person, sq.m:** 15.0.
Major languages: Greenlandic, Danish, English.
Urban dwellers: 82.37%. **Urban growth rate p.a.:** 0.91%.
Labor force: 43%.

ETHNOLINGUISTIC PEOPLES
79.1% Greenland Eskimo; 13.6% Danish (Dane); 6.0% USA White; 0.6% USA Black.

ECONOMY
National income p.a. per person: US$15,492; **per family:** US$27,886.

EDUCATION
Adult literacy: 100% (male 100%, female 100%). **Schools:** 88.
Universities: 2. **School enrolment:** female/male: 60%/60%.

HEALTH
Access to health services: 80%. **Access to safe water:** 90%.
Hospitals: 16 (75 beds per 10,000). **Doctors:** 78.
Blind: 50. **Deaf:** 3,600. Murder **rate:** 18. **Lepers:** 0.

LITERATURE
New book titles p.a.: 28 (500 p.a. per million). **Periodicals:** 3.
Newspapers: 1 daily.

COMMUNICATION (per 1,000 people)
Phones: 305 (21% mobile). Radios: 374. **TV sets:** 380.
Daily newspaper circulation: 150. **Computers:** 100.

HUMAN LIFE AND LIBERTY (optimum condition=100.0%)
HDI: 85.6. **HSI:** 75.0. **HFI:** 75.0. **EFL:** 40.0.

Country Table 1. **Religious adherents in Greenland, AD 1900-2025.**

Year	1900		1970		mid-1990		Annual change, 1990-2000				mid-1995		mid-2000		mid-2025	
Name	Adherents	%	Adherents	%	Adherents	%	Natural	Conversion	Total	Rate	Adherents	%	Adherents	%	Adherents	%
Christians	**10,530**	**90.0**	**45,600**	**98.2**	**53,680**	**96.7**	**40**	**4**	**44**	**0.08**	**53,890**	**96.6**	**54,123**	**96.4**	**56,700**	**95.1**
PROFESSION																
professing Christians	**10,530**	**90.0**	**45,600**	**98.2**	**53,680**	**96.7**	**40**	**4**	**44**	**0.08**	**53,890**	**96.6**	**54,123**	**96.4**	**56,700**	**95.1**
AFFILIATION																
unaffiliated Christians	1,170	10.0	10,470	22.6	14,520	26.2	23	2	25	0.17	14,603	26.2	14,773	26.3	15,480	26.0
affiliated Christians	**9,360**	**80.0**	**35,130**	**75.7**	**39,160**	**70.6**	**17**	**2**	**19**	**0.05**	**39,287**	**70.4**	**39,350**	**70.1**	**41,220**	**69.2**
Protestants	9,360	80.0	34,980	75.3	38,800	69.9	8	0	8	0.02	38,877	69.7	38,880	69.2	40,000	67.1
Marginal Christians	0	0.0	100	0.2	180	0.3	4	2	6	2.92	210	0.4	240	0.4	600	1.0
Independents	0	0.0	0	0.0	90	0.2	2	1	3	2.92	100	0.2	120	0.2	220	0.4
Roman Catholics	0	0.0	50	0.1	90	0.2	1	1	2	2.03	100	0.2	110	0.2	400	0.7
Trans-megabloc groupings																
Evangelicals	4,700	40.2	4,000	8.6	2,300	4.1	-15	-5	-20	-0.91	2,200	3.9	2,100	3.8	2,000	3.3
Pentecostals/Charismatics	0	0.0	700	1.5	5,000	8.9	20	40	60	1.14	5,391	9.7	5,600	10.0	7,500	12.5
Great Commission Christians	**470**	**4.0**	**4,600**	**9.9**	**12,100**	**21.8**	**25**	**9**	**34**	**0.28**	**12,270**	**22.0**	**12,438**	**22.1**	**13,700**	**23.0**
Nonreligious	0	0.0	100	0.2	1,060	1.9	14	3	17	1.52	1,100	2.0	1,233	2.2	2,000	3.3
Ethnoreligionists	1,170	10.0	500	1.1	460	0.8	-2	0	-2	-0.35	470	0.8	444	0.8	300	0.5
Baha'is	0	0.0	200	0.4	300	0.5	5	1	6	1.70	340	0.6	355	0.6	600	1.0
World A (unevangelized persons)	304	2.6	92	0.2	168	0.3	2	0	2	1.02	167	0.3	168	0.3	240	0.4
World B (evangelized non-Christians)	865	7.4	739	1.5	1,652	3.0	23	-4	19	-2.28	1,740	3.1	1,709	3.3	3,060	4.5
World C (Christians)	10,530	90.0	45,600	98.2	53,680	96.7	40	4	44	0.08	53,890	96.6	54,123	96.4	56,700	95.1
Country's population	**11,700**	**100.0**	**46,432**	**100.0**	**55,500**	**100.0**	**65**	**0**	**65**	**0.00**	**55,798**	**100.0**	**56,150**	**100.0**	**59,600**	**100.0**

COLUMNS, ROWS.
For meanings and definitions, see Codebook (Part 3). Note that, by definition, total 'Christians' = professing + crypto-Christians, which also = affiliated + unaffiliated Christians, and also = Great Commission Christians + latent Christians. Percentages may not always total exactly, due to rounding.

CENSUSES.
The religion question has not been asked.

NOTES ON RELIGIONS
BAHA'IS. In 3 local spiritual assemblies (1996).
CHRISTIANS. Virtually all Greenlanders are baptized Christians, the last known adult baptism of a heathen Eskimo having taken place in Thule in 1934. Only a small residue of traditional religion remains in the remote north.
COUNTRY'S POPULATION. The totals, being of de facto population, include 3,000 USA troops from 1970 onwards.
ETHNORELIGIONISTS. Non-Christian Eskimos still following traditional Eskimo religion are few in number, mainly in the remote north.
NONRELIGIOUS. Danish and North Americans.
PROTESTANTS. Including a number of expatriate USA military and civilians.

Great Commission Instrument Panel: status of Greenland (for explanation see start of Part 4)

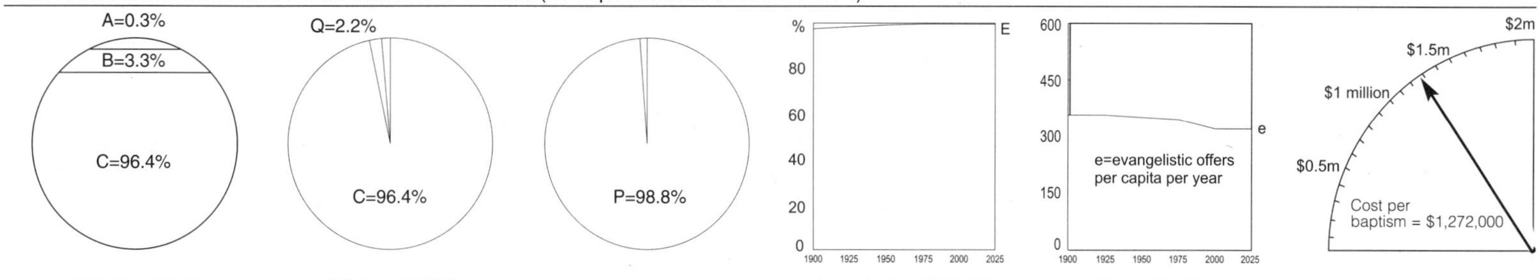

3 Worlds, AD 2000 | Religions, AD 2000 | Ecclesiastical blocs | Evangelization, 1900-2025 | Offers, 1900-2025 | Cost-effectiveness, AD 2000

Country Status. Greenland, the world's largest island, blocks the northern edge of the Atlantic Ocean. Glacial ice covers 85% of the country. The economy is almost entirely based on the fishing industry.

HUMAN LIFE AND LIBERTY

Human rights and freedoms. Greenland is a self-governing administrative division of Denmark and is a part of the Danish realm. Greenlanders enjoy all human rights as Danes do on the mainland.

NON-CHRISTIAN RELIGIONS

Although most native Greenlanders have become Christians, a residue of traditional Eskimo religion remains. This includes a vague belief in a supreme being, Tornarsuk (the Great Tornak). However, the principal place in popular devotion is held by a female divinity, the Old Woman of the Sea, variously called Nerrivik or Sedna.

CHRISTIANITY

PROTESTANT CHURCHES. The first Christians came with the Norse leader Lief Ericson around AD 990. The Lutheran Church of Greenland, organized in

Country summary. **Worlds A, B, C by ethnolinguistic peoples, cities, and major civil divisions in Greenland.**

World	PEOPLES Num	Pop 2000	C%	Christians	E%	U%	Unevangelized	CITIES Num	Pop 2000	C%	Christians	E%	U%	Unevangelized	CIVIL DIVISIONS Num	Pop 2000	C%	Christians	E%	U%	Unevangelized
A	0	0	0.00	0	0	0	0	0	0	0.00	0	0	0	0	0	0	0.00	0	0	0	0
B	0	0	0.00	0	0	0	0	0	0	0.00	0	0	0	0	0	0	0.00	0	0	0	0
C	5	56,155	70.07	39,350	100	0	166	1	13,047	70.00	9,133	100	0	46	6	56,156	70.07	39,350	100	0	166
Total	**5**	**56,155**	**70.07**	**39,350**	**100**	**0**	**166**	**1**	**13,047**	**70.00**	**9,133**	**100**	**0**	**46**	**6**	**56,156**	**70.07**	**39,350**	**100**	**0**	**166**

1721, is an integral part of the Evangelical Lutheran Church of Denmark and retains the allegiance and fidelity of the majority of the population. Church services are popular and festive occasions, and enjoy considerable community support. Because of the difficulties of travel, catechists assume important clerical responsibility. The administrative head of the church is the dean of Greenland who lives at Godthab and works under the bishop of Copenhagen. In view of the special conditions of the country, the dean's authority is great and corresponds to that of a bishop. Regular synods consisting of all pastors make recommendations which carry considerable weight. Committees of lay representatives have consultative voice in dealing with their local pastors and with the dean. Secularization is growing with the increase in higher education in Danish, but at present it has much less influence than in Denmark.

Pentecostals, Adventists, Brethren and other have begun work in Greenland, but their influence remains small.

Pentecostal Churches. *Top.* Zionsborg, a mission station at Holsteinsborg built by Swedish missionaries in 1965. *Bottom.* On steps, a 70-year-old woman Greenlander converted in 1965, and now a mission administrator.

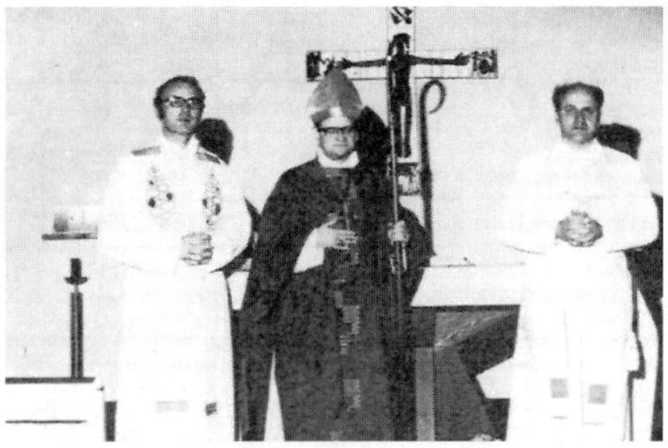

Catholic Church. Blessing of parish church of Greenland in 1972 by Catholic bishop of Copenhagen, a Danish Jesuit.

CATHOLIC CHURCH. Roman Catholicism came to Greenland in 1960. Its work consists of a single parish (the largest in the world in area, with one of the smallest memberships), confided to the Oblates of Mary Immaculate, forming part of the diocese of Copenhagen. There is one church at Godthab with a total membership of 130 Catholics in 1995 (60 in 1975) of whom half are at Godthab and the others widely dispersed. Most are Danish, plus a few foreigners. The Catholic clergy cooperate in existing cultural and social activities following the traditions of the Protestant pastors of Greenland. The first mass in the Greenlandic language was celebrated in May 1973.

The Holy See has no diplomatic relations with Greenland in AD 2000.

Indigenous missions. Cultural and geographic isolation have made missionary sending difficult until modern times. Today, a handful of Protestant missionaries from Greenland serve in other countries.

CHURCH AND STATE

With the exception of the activity of Moravian missionaries between 1732 and 1900, the Lutheran Church had a monopoly on Christian work during the colonial period. With the promulgation of the Danish constitution in 1953, Greenland obtained the freedom of religion prevailing in the rest of the Danish kingdom. Nevertheless, certain special regulations indicate a continuing close relation between the Lutheran Church and the state, in Greenland, although there are no taxes and thus no church tax. The church's final legislative and financial authority is parliament and its highest administrative authority is thus a political minister. The advent of home rule in 1979 changed some of the *de jure* administrative apparatus of church-state relations, but caused no notable effect for the life of the churches.

INTERDENOMINATIONAL ORGANIZATIONS

There are no ecumenical organizations in Greenland, but the good relations between Catholics and Lutherans in Denmark (both being members of the Ecumenical Council of Denmark) have had an important influence on the ecumenical climate in Greenland.

FUTURE TRENDS AND PROSPECTS.

Christianity is expected to experience only slight decline in the next thirty years.

The nonreligious could climb above 5% of the population by AD 2050. Christians potentially will dominate well into this future period.

BIBLIOGRAPHY

A history of the missions in Greenland and Labrador. J. Carne. New York: Lane & Tippett, 1848. 218p.

Amid Greenland snows, or the early history of Arctic missions. J. Page. 2d ed. New York: Revell. 160p.

'Bibliography of bibliographies on the Inuit,' I. Kleivan, in *Artica 1978: 7th Northern Libraries Colloquy, 19–23 September 1978*, p.39–41. S. Devers (ed). Paris: Éditions du Centre National de la Recherche Scientifique, 1982.

Die Herrnhuter Brüdergemeine in Grönland: Missionsarbeit von 1733 bis 1900. W. Driesen. Leverkusen: Philatelia, 1986. 39p.

Die religionen Nordeurasiens und der amerikanischen Arktis. I. Paulson, Å. Hultkrantz & K. Jettmar. *Die Religionen der Menschheit*, vol. 3. Stuttgart: W. Kohlhammer, 1962. 425p.

Eskimos: Greenland and Canada. No. 2 of section 8: *Arctic peoples*, of *Iconography of religions.* I. Kleivan & B. Sonne. Leiden: E. J. Brill, 1985. 52p.

Från väckelse till samfund: Svensk pingstmission på öarna i Nordatlanten. P. Pétursson. *Bibliotheca historico-ecclesiastica Lundensis*, 22. Lund, Sweden: Lund University Press, 1990. 296p. (English summary).

Greenland. K. E. Miller. Oxford, UK: Clio Press, 1991. (Brief section on religion).

Greenland. M. Vahl, G. C. Andrup & L. J. ,. Bobé (eds). Copenhagen: C. A. Reitzel, 1928–29. 3 vols. (Volume 3, information on Church of Greenland and missionaries to Greenland).

Greenland since 1979: an annotated, cross–referenced bibliography. F. Benoit (ed). Ottawa: Cirumpolar and Scientific Affairs Directorate, Department of Indian Affairs and Northern Development, 1989. 292p.

Grønlands kirker (Nunatsinni oqaluffiit). O. Sandgreen. [Copenhagen]: O. Sandgreenip atuakkiorfi, 1992. 304p. (In Danish and Eskimo).

Hans Egede: colonizer and missionary of Greenland. L. Bobé. Copenhagen: Rosenkilde and Bagger, 1952. 207p.

'Hans Egede: missionary and colonizer of Greenland,' M. Lidegaard, *Scandinavian review*, 59, 3 (1971), 229–44.

Kirken under polarstjernen: Fra den grønlandske kirke. W. Larsen. Copenhagen: Lohse, 1972. 127p.

'La chrétienté du Grœnland au moyen age,' E. Beauvois, *Revue des questions historiques*, 71 (1902), 538–82.

'Profetens roll i religionsmötet: iakttagelser från religionsmötets Västgrönland.' S. Söderberg. Thesis, Lunds Universitet, Lund, Sweden, 1974. 154p.

Religions of the circumpolar north. R. Minion. *BINS bibliographic series*, no. 15. Edmonton, Alberta: University of Alberta, Boreal Institute for Northern Studies, 1985. 92p.

'The first Christian Northmen in America,' R. H. Clarke, *American Catholic quarterly review*, 14 (1889), 598–615.

The history of Greenland, including an account of the mission carried on by the United Brethren in that country . . . with an continuation to the present time; illustrative notes; and an appendix, containing a sketch of the Brethren in Labrador. D. Crantz. 2d ed. London: Longman, 1820. (First edition, 1767).

The Moravians in Greenland. 3rd ed. Edinburgh: William Oliphant, 1839. 360p.

'The prime mover and fear in Inuit religion: a discussion of "native views",' J. G. Oosten, in *Continuity and identity in native America: essays in honor of Benedikt Hartmann*, p.69≠83. M. Jansen et al. (eds). Leiden: E. J. Brill, 1988.

'The revival at Pisugfik in 1768: an ethnohistorical approach,' H. C. Gulløv, *Arctic anthropology*, 23, 1-2 (1986), 151–75.

'The twelfth century Christian mission to Greenland,' A. G. Hahn, *Iliff Review*, 30 (Winter 1973), 15–32.

Country Table 2. **Organized churches and denominations in Greenland.**

Official name (bold type = church with over 10% of all affiliated) 1	*Begun* 2	*Type* 3	*Counc* 4	*Congs* 5	*Adults* 6	*Affiliated 1970* 7	*Affiliated 1995* 8	*G%* 9	*Names, notes, and other statistics* (see Codebook, Part 3) 10
Assemblies of God	c1980	P-Pe2	Z....	10	600	–	970	6.67	Assisted by AoG (USA, Europe).
Catholic Church (D Kobenhavn)	1960	R-Lat	b.BQ.	1	50	50	100	2.81	*Katolske Kirke*, Godthab. Part of Bispedommet Kobenhavn. M=OMI. Danish. 1n,2x.
Christian Brethren	1969	P-CBr	x....	2	40	50	100	2.81	Small Open Brethren grouping.
Jehovah's Witnesses	c1950	m-Jeh	x....	7	126	100	210	3.01	*Watch Tower.* International Bible Students Association. First witnessing 1955. 6Y.
Lutheran Church of Greenland	1721	P-Lut	Lwc..	91	26,900	34,000	36,400	0.27	*Ilagit Kaladlit Luterkussut D Greenland.* Formerly in D Kobenhavn. Eskimos. 26n,174m,1485Yy.
Pentecostal Churches	c1952	P-Pe2	Z....	5	500	500	1,000	2.81	*Zionmenigheden.* M=Elim(Denmark),SFM(Sweden),NPY(Norway). HQ Julianehab.
Seventh-day Adventist Church	1953	P-Adv	x....	1	30	30	50	2.06	*SDA. Greenland Mission, West Nordic Union Conference.* HQ Godthab. 1m,1h,W=99%,2Y,8z.
Other independent churches		I-	.....	3	50	–	100	0.05	Including New Apostolic Church (48 members).
Other Protestant denominations		P-	.....	3	250	400	357	0.05	Total 3; including Apostolic Ch, USA military chaplaincy, New Tribes Mission.
Totals				**123**	**28,546**	**35,130**	**39,287**		

Churches, members, growth, 1900-2025	*Congs*	*Adults*	*Affiliated*	*G%*	*Total denominations*	*6 Megablocs:* O	R	A	P	I	m
Total churches, members, and denominations (mid-1900)	30	6,900	9,360	1.91	1	0	0	0	1	0	0
Total churches, members, and denominations (mid-1970)	102	25,720	35,130	1.91	7	0	1	0	5	0	1
Total churches, members, and denominations (mid-1990)	110	28,500	39,160	0.54	10	0	1	0	8	0	1
Total churches, members, and denominations (mid-1995)	123	28,546	39,287	0.06	13	0	1	0	8	3	1
Total churches, members, and denominations (mid-2000)	130	28,600	39,350	0.03	13	0	1	0	8	3	1
Total churches, members, and denominations (mid-2025)	150	30,000	41,220	0.19	26	0	1	0	14	10	1

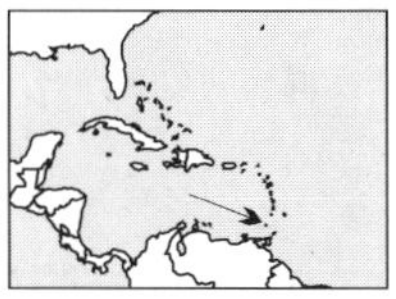

GRENADA

SECULAR DATA, AD 2000

STATE
Official name: The Dominion of Grenada.
Short name: Grenada. **Adjective of nationality:** Grenadian.
Flag: Red border with yellow stars above and below green and yellow triangles; red circle with yellow star in centre; nutmeg on green triangle.
Area: 344 sq. km. (133 sq. mi.).
Government: Parliamentary state (constitutional monarchy), since 1974 (1815 British colony, 1967 self-governing state in association with the UK, 1974 Independence).
Legislature: House of Representatives, 15 members; Senate, 13 members.
Official language: English.
Monetary unit: 1 East Caribbean dollar (EC$) = 100 cents. **US$1=** EC$2.70.
Chief cities: ST GEORGE'S 25,851.
Political divisions: 9 provinces.
Armed forces: 100.

DEMOGRAPHY
Population: 94,000.
Population density: 272.4/sq. km. (704.6/sq. mi.).
Under 15 years: 23,000.
Growth rate p.a.: 0.53% (births 13.72, deaths 6.01).
Mortality: Infant, per 1,000: 12.8; **Maternal per 100,000:** 30.0.
Life expectancy: 75 (male 73, female 77).
Household size: 3.7. **Floor area per person, sq.m:** 16.0.
Major languages: English, French patois.
Urban dwellers: 37.91%. **Urban growth rate p.a.:** 1.91%.
Labor force: 40%.

ETHNOLINGUISTIC PEOPLES
51.7% Black; 40.4% Mulatto; 4.0% Indo-Pakistani; 2.0% Creole; 0.8% British.

ECONOMY
National income p.a. per person: US$2,977; **per family:** US$11,015.

EDUCATION
Adult literacy: 85% (male 89%, female 81%). **Schools:** 76.
Universities: 1. **School enrolment:** female/male: 95%/95%.

HEALTH
Access to health services: 75%. **Access to safe water:** 85%.
Hospitals: 3 (38 beds per 10,000). **Doctors:** 47.
Blind: 90. **Deaf:** 5,600. Murder **rate:** 7.
Lepers: 50.

LITERATURE
New book titles p.a.: 9 (100 p.a. per million). **Periodicals:** 17.
Newspapers: 1 daily.

COMMUNICATION (per 1,000 people)
Phones: 255 (4% mobile). Radios: 489. **TV sets:** 158.
Daily newspaper circulation: 45. **Computers:** 80.

HUMAN LIFE AND LIBERTY (optimum condition=100.0%)
HDI: 84.3. **HSI:** 70.0. **HFI:** 60.0. **EFL:** 35.0.

Country Table 1. **Religious adherents in Grenada, AD 1900-2025.**

Year	1900		1970		mid-1990		Annual change, 1990-2000				mid-1995		mid-2000		mid-2025	
Name	Adherents	%	Adherents	%	Adherents	%	Natural	Conversion	Total	Rate	Adherents	%	Adherents	%	Adherents	%
Christians	**63,150**	**99.5**	**93,460**	**99.0**	**88,385**	**97.1**	**295**	**-40**	**255**	**0.28**	**89,500**	**97.1**	**90,935**	**97.0**	**100,490**	**95.7**
PROFESSION																
professing Christians	**63,150**	**99.5**	**93,460**	**99.0**	**88,385**	**97.1**	**295**	**-40**	**255**	**0.28**	**89,500**	**97.1**	**90,935**	**97.0**	**100,490**	**95.7**
AFFILIATION																
unaffiliated Christians	590	0.9	1,960	2.1	185	0.2	1	0	1	0.27	190	0.2	190	0.2	490	0.5
affiliated Christians	**62,560**	**98.6**	**91,500**	**96.9**	**88,200**	**96.9**	**295**	**-40**	**255**	**0.28**	**89,310**	**96.9**	**90,745**	**96.8**	**100,000**	**95.2**
Roman Catholics	36,240	57.1	60,000	63.6	53,000	58.2	179	-209	-30	-0.06	52,868	57.4	52,700	56.3	56,000	53.3
Protestants	4,120	6.5	9,800	10.4	17,800	19.6	59	71	130	0.71	18,316	19.9	19,100	20.4	24,000	22.9
Anglicans	22,200	35.0	20,000	21.2	14,600	16.0	48	-68	-20	-0.14	14,500	15.7	14,400	15.4	14,000	13.3
Independents	0	0.0	1,200	1.3	3,300	3.6	11	29	40	1.15	3,482	3.8	3,700	4.0	5,500	5.2
Marginal Christians	0	0.0	500	0.5	1,200	1.3	4	16	20	1.55	1,300	1.4	1,400	1.5	2,500	2.4
doubly-affiliated	0	0.0	0	0.0	-1,700	-1.9	-6	121	115	-10.59	-1,156	-1.3	-555	-0.6	-2,000	-1.9
Trans-megabloc groupings																
Evangelicals	2,500	3.9	4,000	4.2	9,450	10.4	31	34	65	0.67	9,730	10.6	10,100	10.8	14,000	13.3
Pentecostals/Charismatics	0	0.0	1,500	1.6	13,200	14.5	44	56	100	0.73	13,654	14.8	14,200	15.2	19,000	18.1
Great Commission Christians	**1,000**	**1.6**	**4,000**	**4.2**	**6,200**	**6.8**	**20**	**6**	**26**	**0.41**	**6,330**	**6.9**	**6,456**	**7.0**	**8,000**	**7.6**
Spiritists	120	0.2	400	0.4	1,000	1.1	3	12	15	1.42	1,100	1.2	1,151	1.2	1,800	1.7
Hindus	90	0.1	50	0.1	550	0.6	2	7	9	1.48	620	0.7	637	0.7	1,000	1.0
Nonreligious	0	0.0	100	0.1	300	0.3	1	19	20	5.14	400	0.4	495	0.5	1,000	1.0
Muslims	40	0.1	220	0.2	280	0.3	1	1	2	0.83	290	0.3	304	0.3	500	0.5
Baha'is	0	0.0	120	0.1	135	0.2	0	1	1	0.72	140	0.2	145	0.2	160	0.2
Other religionists	0	0.0	50	0.1	50	0.1	0	0	0	-0.41	50	0.1	48	0.1	50	0.1
World A (unevangelized persons)	63	0.1	94	0.1	0	0.0	0	0	0	-0.69	0	0.0	0	0.0	0	0.0
World B (evangelized non-Christians)	226	0.3	846	0.9	2,615	2.9	7	40	47	1.60	2,635	2.9	2,765	3.0	4,510	4.3
World C (Christians)	63,150	99.6	93,460	99.0	88,385	97.1	295	-40	255	0.28	89,500	97.1	90,935	97.0	100,490	95.7
Country's population	**63,440**	**100.0**	**94,401**	**100.0**	**91,000**	**100.0**	**302**	**0**	**302**	**0.32**	**92,135**	**100.0**	**93,700**	**100.0**	**105,000**	**100.0**

COLUMNS, ROWS.
For meanings and definitions, see Codebook (Part 3). Note that, by definition, total 'Christians' = professing + crypto-Christians, which also = affiliated + unaffiliated Christians, and also = Great Commission Christians + latent Christians. Percentages may not always total exactly, due to rounding.

CENSUSES.
1901: Census of the British Empire (as in 1900 column above). **7.IV.1960:** 63.1% Roman Catholics, 24.7% Anglicans, 11.6% Protestants (4.0% Methodists, 3.0% SDAs, 1.7% Presbyterians, 0.9% Pentecostals), 0.4% marginal Protestants (Jehovah's Witnesses), 0.2% nonreligious and other religionists. **1981:** 60.3% Roman Catholics, 17.6% Anglicans, 17.8% Protestants (5.7% SDAs, 3.9% Pentecostals, 2.8% Methodists), 3.7% nonreligious and other religionists, 0.6% marginal Christians (Jehovah's Witnesses). **1991:** 54.1% Roman Catholics, 24.2% Protestants (8.6% SDAs, 7.2% Pentecostals, 2.7% Baptists), 13.9% Anglicans, 5.3% other religionists, 1.5% nonreligious, 1.1% marginal Christians (Jehovah's Witnesses).

NOTES ON RELIGIONS
BAHA'IS. Growth from 1 local spiritual assembly (1964) to 6 (1973) and to 11 (1996).
INDEPENDENTS. In about 7 denominations in 1995 (see Table 2).
MUSLIMS. Of whom about 200 are Ahmadis, begun around 1955, in 1 community (world HQ Rabwah, Pakistan). Though proclaimed non-Muslim and heretical by Pakistan, Ahmadis are enumerated in this survey as Muslims and are included in totals of Muslims.
OTHER RELIGIONISTS. Including Rosicrucians (1 AMORC centre).
SPIRITISTS. There are numerous centers of Shango (Yoruba syncretism). Unlike in Trinidad, women predominate in its leadership. There are also a few Rastafarians (from Jamaica), Big Drum, et alia.

Great Commission Instrument Panel: status of Grenada (for explanation see start of Part 4)

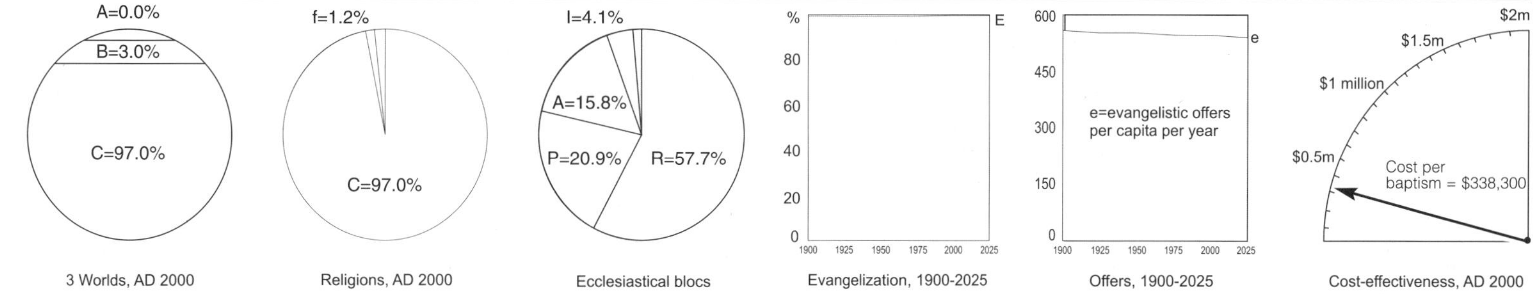

Country status. Grenada is the smallest of the Caribbean countries in the West Indies. It consists of Grenada, the most southerly of the Windward Islands, the islands of Carriacou and Petit Martinique, and a number of smaller islets of the Grenadines. Grenada exports cocoa, spices, and bananas.

HUMAN LIFE AND LIBERTY

Human rights and freedoms. Human rights are similar to those in Britain.

NON-CHRISTIAN RELIGIONS

Afro-American spiritism is widespread, with numerous centers of Shango (Yoruba syncretism), in whose leadership women play the major role.

CHRISTIANITY

CATHOLIC CHURCH. As the island of Grenada was settled in the mid-17th century by the French before being finally ceded to Britain in 1783, the majority of the people are Catholics. All 20 parishes are situated on Grenada island except for one parish and 4 stations in Carriacou and a station in Petit Martinique served from Carriacou. In 1956 the diocese of St George's in Grenada was erected as a suffragan of the archdiocese of Port-of-Spain (Trinidad); in 1974, it became a suffragan of Castries (St Lucia).

The Holy See has diplomatic relations with Grenada and in AD 2000 is represented to government and the Catholic hierarchy by a pro-nuncio residing in Port of Spain.

Country summary. **Worlds A, B, C by ethnolinguistic peoples, cities, and major civil divisions in Grenada.**																					
	PEOPLES							***CITIES***							***CIVIL DIVISIONS***						
World	*Num*	*Pop 2000*	*C%*	*Christians*	*E%*	*U%*	*Unevangelized*	*Num*	*Pop 2000*	*C%*	*Christians*	*E%*	*U%*	*Unevangelized*	*Num*	*Pop 2000*	*C%*	*Christians*	*E%*	*U%*	*Unevangelized*
A	0	0	0.00	0	0	0	0	0	0	0.00	0	0	0	0	0	0	0.00	0	0	0	0
B	0	0	0.00	0	0	0	0	0	0	0.00	0	0	0	0	0	0	0.00	0	0	0	0
C	10	93,718	96.83	90,746	100	0	29	1	25,851	96.50	24,946	100	0	16	9	93,716	96.83	90,745	100	0	27
Total	**10**	**93,718**	**96.83**	**90,746**	**100**	**0**	**29**	**1**	**25,851**	**96.50**	**24,946**	**100**	**0**	**16**	**9**	**93,716**	**96.83**	**90,745**	**100**	**0**	**27**

ANGLICAN CHURCH. The Church of England began work in 1784 shortly after the island came under British control. The diocese of the Windward Islands was formed in 1878 and is part of the Church of the Province of the West Indies. During the 20th century, Anglicans have declined gradually as a proportion of the population, from 35% in 1900 to 15% by AD 2000.

PROTESTANT CHURCHES. Two of the principal Protestant bodies are Methodists and Seventh-day Adventists. The Methodist Church, historically related to British Methodism, opened work in Grenada in 1789, and Adventists arrived in 1903, later initiating the South Caribbean Conference of which Grenada is a part. The 3 Pentecostal churches together account for a community of about 5,000 faithful. The largest is the New Testament Church of God, begun in 1958 by missionaries from Trinidad. Small groups of Baptists, Presbyterians, and Salvation Army have also established congregations in Grenada. Two additional American societies have been active since 1957, the West Indies Mission and the Berean Mission.

Indigenous missions. Christians in Grenada have had difficulty in sending out missionaries. A handful have been sent but mainly to heavily-Christian countries like Britain or the USA.

The capital, St George's, showing cathedral and some of the other 130 churches.

CHURCH AND STATE

Discovered by Columbus, the Windward Islands were first under Spanish rule and Catholic influence, passing later to the French and then to the British. Grenada was granted home rule by Britain in 1967 and became independent in 1974 as a state with acknowledged religious foundations.

The constitution of 7 February 1974 declares (Schedule 3): 'Whereas the people of Grenada have affirmed that their nation is founded upon principles that acknowledge the fatherhood and supremacy of God and man's duties toward his fellow man. . .' and that they 'firmly believe that all men are endowed by the Creator with equal right'. In Article 1 of chapter 1, among the fundamental rights and freedoms enjoyed by every person in Grenada is listed 'freedom of conscience, of expression and of assembly and association'. The constitutional protection of freedom of conscience is further explained in Article 9, which allows for complete freedom of religious belief and practice and prohibits any hindrance thereof, entitles religious communities to establish and maintain schools at their own expense, and to provide for religious instruction in such schools while also exempting those who do not wish to participate and prohibits the administration of oaths contrary to a person's religious convictions. In practice, all private schools are grant-aided by the state. The situation could have changed notably had the Marxist coup of 1983 not been overturned by the USA invasion and restoration of democratic government.

BROADCASTING AND MEDIA

The Harbor Light of the Windwards is a local radio station with daily programs on medium wave. Shortwave programs from HCJB (Ecuador), TWR (Antilles) and AWR (Costa Rica) can be easily received. Grenada is a member of UNDA.

Christian television programs can be viewed on local channels and via satellite. CBN's programming and dramas can be seen every weekday in the early evenings.

INTERDENOMINATIONAL ORGANIZATIONS

The Grenada Inter-Church Council for Social Welfare includes in its membership 9 churches including Anglican and Catholic. In 1974 the formation began of a Grenada Christian Council.

FUTURE TRENDS AND PROSPECTS

Christianity is likely to experience a slight decline in the next 30 years.

Although Christianity is almost sure to predominate into the distant future, the nonreligious could grow beyond 5% in that same period.

BIBLIOGRAPHY

A church in the sun. J. A. Parker. London: Cargate, 1959. 109p. (Mainly, Methodist Church of Grenada).

'A strategy for Christian service in a Marxist society for use by the Evangelical Church of the West Indies (Grenada).' A. A. Horsford. M.A. thesis, Columbia Graduate School of Bible and Missions, Columbia SC, 1983. 50p.

Bibliography of Grenada. B. A. Steele. St. George's: University of the West Indies, Department of Extra Mural Studies, 1983. 119p.

Black religions in the New World. G. E. Simpson. New York: Columbia University Press, 1978. 429p. (Various chapters deal with Grenada).

Conception Island or the troubled story of the Catholic church in Grenada, B.W.I. R. Devas. London: Sands & Sons, 1932. 430p.

'East Indian indenture and the work of the Presbyterian Church among the Indians in Grenada,' B. Steele, *Caribbean quarterly*, 22, 1 (1976), 28–37.

'Faith healing and medical practice in the southern Caribbean,' F. Mischel, *Southwestern journal of anthropology*, 15, 4 (1959), 407–417.

Grenada. K. Schoenhals. *World bibliographical series*, vol. 119. Oxford, UK: CLIO Press, 1990. 182p. (See especially 'Religion,' p.93–5).

'Historic events in Grenada, 1950–1983, and the response of the church.' J. Hepburn. M.A. thesis, Drew University, Madison, NJ, 1987. 151p.

In bloody terms: the betrayal of the church in Marxist Grenada. A. J. Zwerneman. South Bend, IN: Greenlawn, 1986. 113p.

Obeah: witchcraft in the West Indies. H. H. J. Bell. Westport, CT: Negro University Press, 1970. 200p. (Focuses on Grenada).

'Shango–Cult und Shouter–Kirche auf Trinidad und Grenada,' A. Pollak-Eltz, *Anthropos*, 65, 5-6 (1970), 814–32.

'Wrestling with the Bible in the Caribbean basin: a case study on Grenada in light of Romans 13:1–7,' N. S. Murrell, *Caribbean journal of religious studies*, 8 (April 1987), 12–23.

The life of Christ is often portrayed on Grenada's postage stamps: here, The Adoration of the Shepherds (Roberti), Christ crowned with Thorns (Van Dyck), and the Risen Christ (Bellini).

Country Table 2. **Organized churches and denominations in Grenada.**									
Official name (bold type = church *with over 10% of all affiliated*) *1*	*Begun* *2*	*Type* *3*	*Counc* *4*	*Congs* *5*	*Adults* *6*	*Affiliated 1970* *7*	*Affiliated 1995* *8*	*G%* *9*	*Names, notes, and other statistics* (see Codebook, Part 3) *10*
Anglican Church (D Windward Isles)	1784	A-ACa	awMRC	25	5,080	20,000	14,500	-1.28	In CPWI, based on St Vincent. 95% West Indians (90% Black). HQ St George's. W=20%.
Assembly Hall Churches	c1980	I-3nC	.....	1	50	–	100	6.67	*Little Flock. Local Churches.* Begun in China 1922.
Baptist Convention	1975	P-Bap	.....	4	205	–	410	5.00	M=FMB-SBC.
Berean Bible Church	1957	I-Non	xM...	18	530	500	883	2.30	M=BM(USA). 9 Districts Mass campaigns in Queen's Park. 8f,1k (St George's).
Catholic Ch: D St George's in G	c1650	R-Lat	PxNMC	20	28,000	60,000	52,868	-0.50	1974, suffragan of M Castries (St Lucia). C=2+1+5. 7n,16x,20m,35w,951Yy.
Christian Brethren	c1960	P-CBr	x...C	8	380	700	1,230	2.28	*Gospel Hall. Plymouth Brethren, Open Brethren.* M=CMML(USA). HQ St George's. 2f.
Church of the Nazarene	1977	P-Hol	.....	1	34	–	70	5.56	M=CoN.
Evangelical Church of the West Indies	1957	P-Eva	xM...	7	330	500	688	1.28	M=WT(USA). Evangelical faith mission. 3f.
Internat Ch of the Foursquare Gospel	c1975	P-Pe2	.....	4	450	–	668	5.00	M=ICFG.
Jehovah's Witnesses	1931	m-Jeh	x....	7	409	450	1,200	4.00	*Watch Tower.* Including on Carriacou Island. Witnessing since 1932. (1975)17Y. (1995)30Y.
Methodist Ch in Caribbean & Americas	1789	P-Met	VwM.C	10	1,000	2,000	1,500	-1.14	*MCCA.* S Caribbean District. M=MMS(UK). Decline from 3,600 in 1900. 2n,19m,70y.
New Apostolic Church	c1980	I-3aX	x....	3	100	–	132	6.67	*NAC/NAK.* M=Neuapostolische Kirche (HQ Zurich).
New Testament Church of God	1958	P-Pe3	ZF..C	10	793	300	1,930	7.73	Founded from Trinidad. M=CoG(Cleveland) (USA). 4 churches, 2 missions. 4n.
Open Bible Standard Church	c1980	I-3pU	.....	3	400	–	667	6.67	M=OBSC. Mission from USA.
Pentecostal Assemblies of the W Indies	c1960	P-Pe2	ZF..C	20	1,481	800	2,470	4.61	M=PAoC(Canada). Many emigrants to UK, forming Shilo Pentecostal Fellowship there.
Presbyterian Ch in Trinidad & Grenada	1800	P-Ref	RWM.C	5	550	1,000	1,150	0.56	Black; many East Indians. In 1900, 580 adherents. HQ St George's. 1n,
Salvation Army	c1960	P-Sal	xwM.C	10	300	500	600	0.73	In Caribbean & C America Territory (HQ Jamaica). HQ St George's.
Seventh-day Adventist Church	1903	P-Adv	x...C	28	2,800	3,000	5,600	2.53	*SDA. South Caribbean Conference. Caribbean Union Conference.* HQ St George's. 1r.
Spiritual Baptist Churches	c1900	I-3sU	.....	5	300	400	700	2.26	*Shouters, Shakers.* White robes, vestments, birettas, RC ritual, Obeah practised.
Other Protestant denominations		P-	.....	10	1,000	1,000	2,000	0.05	Total about 8 (see list below).
Other Black indigenous churches		I-	.....	10	900	300	1,000	0.05	Including: AMEC(USA), Ch of God Fellowship, New Testament Assembly, PAoW(USA).
Other marginal Protestant bodies		m-	.....	2	50	50	100	0.05	Including: Unity School of Christianity (from USA; 2 churches).

Continued opposite

Country Table 2–concluded

Official name (bold type = church with over 10% of affiliated) 1	*Begun* 2	*Type* 3	*Counc* 4	*Congs* 5	*Adults* 6	*Affiliated 1970* 7	*Affiliated 1995* 8	*G%* 9	*Names, notes, and other statistics* (see Codebook, Part 3) 10
Doubly-affiliated		2-aff			-580	0	-1,156		Evangelicals who also are or were baptized Roman Catholics.
Totals				**211**	**44,562**	**91,500**	**89,310**		

Churches, members, growth, 1900-2025	*Congs*	*Adults*	*Affiliated*	*G%*	*Total denominations*	*6 Megablocs:* O	R	A	P	I	m
Total churches, members, and denominations (mid-1900)	70	30,500	62,560	0.54	5	0	1	1	2	1	0
Total churches, members, and denominations (mid-1970)	129	44,578	91,500	0.54	22	0	1	1	12	6	2
Total churches, members, and denominations (mid-1990)	160	44,000	88,200	-0.18	38	0	1	1	18	14	4
Total churches, members, and denominations (mid-1995)	211	44,562	89,310	0.25	40	0	1	1	19	15	4
Total churches, members, and denominations (mid-2000)	220	45,300	90,745	0.32	41	0	1	1	20	15	4
Total churches, members, and denominations (mid-2025)	270	49,900	100,000	0.39	70	1	1	1	30	30	7

NOTES ON TABLE ABOVE
NATIONAL COUNCILS (Column 4, 5th letter).
C = Grenada Inter-Church Council for Social Welfare.

Other national councils. Grenada Christian Council (in formation). Conference of Churches in Grenada, 1950.
OTHER PROTESTANT DENOMINATIONS. These include: Bethany Fellowship Missions (1968), Ch of Christ (Non-Instrumental), Ch of God (Anderson), Ch of Scotland, Holiness Ch, Southern Baptist Convention (1972).

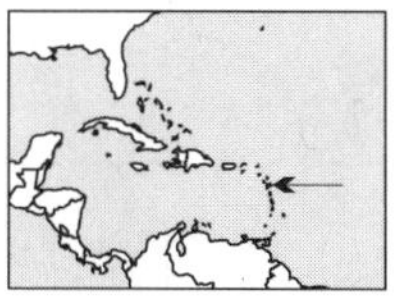

GUADELOUPE

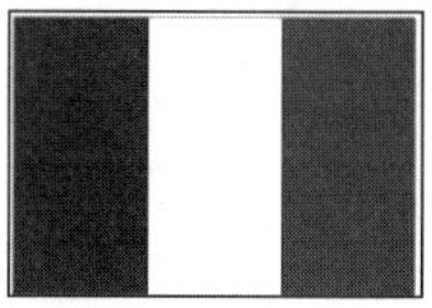

SECULAR DATA, AD 2000

STATE
Official name: Le Département de la Guadeloupe et Dépendances (The Department of Guadeloupe and Dependencies).
Short name: Guadeloupe. **Adjective of nationality:** of Guadeloupe.
Flag: That of France.
Area: 1,780 sq. km. (687 sq. mi.).
Government: Overseas department of France, since 1946 (1635 French colony).
Legislature: General Council, 43 members; Regional Council, 41 members.
Official language: French (Français).
Monetary unit: 1 French franc (F) = 100 centimes. **US$1=** F 5.60.
Chief cities: Pointe-a-Pitre 114,548; Les Abymes 77,513; BASSE-TERRE 36,710.
Political divisions: 3 provinces.
Armed forces: 500.

DEMOGRAPHY
Population: 456,000.
Population density: 256.0/sq. km. (663.3/sq. mi.).
Under 15 years: 109,000.
Growth rate p.a.: 1.19% (births 15.26, deaths 5.77).
Mortality: Infant, per 1,000: 7.8; **Maternal per 100,000:** 20.0.
Life expectancy: 78 (male 75, female 82).
Household size: 3.4. **Floor area per person, sq.m:** 14.0.
Major languages: French, French Creole, Tamil.
Urban dwellers: 99.73%. **Urban growth rate p.a.:** 1.25%.
Labor force: 45%.

ETHNOLINGUISTIC PEOPLES
76.7% French Creole (Mulatto); 10.0% Guadeloupian Black; 10.0% Guadeloupian Mestizo; 2.0% French (White); 1.0% East Indian (Tamil).

ECONOMY
National income p.a. per person: US$9,199; **per family:** US$31,277.

EDUCATION
Adult literacy: 90% (male 89%, female 90%). **Schools:** 418.
Universities: 1. **School enrolment:** female/male: 90%/90%.

HEALTH
Access to health services: 70%. **Access to safe water:** 80%.
Hospitals: 30 (80 beds per 10,000). **Doctors:** 590.
Blind: 90. **Deaf:** 27,400. Murder **rate:** 13.
Lepers: 2,500.

LITERATURE
New book titles p.a.: 110 (250 p.a. per million). **Periodicals:** 14.
Newspapers: 1 daily.

COMMUNICATION (per 1,000 people)
Phones: 378 **(6% mobile).** Radios: 208. **TV sets:** 262.
Daily newspaper circulation: 83. **Computers:** 70.

HUMAN LIFE AND LIBERTY (optimum condition=100.0%)
HDI: 87.2. **HSI:** 70.0. **HFI:** 60.0. **EFL:** 40.0.

Country Table 1. **Religious adherents in Guadeloupe, AD 1900-2025.**

Year / *Name*	*1900* Adherents	%	*1970* Adherents	%	*mid-1990* Adherents	%	*Annual change, 1990-2000* Natural	Conversion	Total	Rate	*mid-1995* Adherents	%	*mid-2000* Adherents	%	*mid-2025* Adherents	%
Christians	**180,000**	**98.9**	**311,500**	**97.3**	**373,640**	**95.6**	**6,179**	**-116**	**6,063**	**1.52**	**404,530**	**95.4**	**434,273**	**95.3**	**535,360**	**94.1**
PROFESSION																
professing Christians	**180,000**	**98.9**	**311,500**	**97.3**	**373,640**	**95.6**	**6,179**	**-116**	**6,063**	**1.52**	**404,530**	**95.4**	**434,273**	**95.3**	**535,360**	**94.1**
AFFILIATION																
unaffiliated Christians	900	0.5	1,500	0.5	1,300	0.3	22	-19	3	0.19	1,300	0.3	1,325	0.3	3,200	0.6
affiliated Christians	**179,100**	**98.4**	**310,000**	**96.9**	**372,340**	**95.2**	**6,158**	**-197**	**6,061**	**1.52**	**403,230**	**95.0**	**432,948**	**95.0**	**532,160**	**93.5**
Roman Catholics	179,100	98.4	307,000	95.9	373,000	95.4	6,169	-169	6,000	1.50	404,000	95.2	433,000	95.1	530,000	93.2
Protestants	0	0.0	11,090	3.5	18,000	4.6	299	151	450	2.26	20,018	4.7	22,500	4.9	38,000	6.7
Marginal Christians	0	0.0	5,000	1.6	16,500	4.2	274	46	320	1.79	18,000	4.2	19,700	4.3	40,000	7.0
Independents	0	0.0	500	0.2	80	0.0	1	103	104	30.20	1,091	0.3	1,120	0.3	180	0.0
doubly-affiliated	0	0.0	-13,590	-4.3	-35,240	-9.0	-586	-227	-813	2.10	-39,879	-9.4	-43,372	-9.5	-76,020	-13.4
Trans-megabloc groupings																
Evangelicals	0	0.0	4,650	1.5	10,950	2.8	182	88	270	2.23	12,174	2.9	13,650	3.0	25,000	4.4
Pentecostals/Charismatics	0	0.0	1,000	0.3	18,780	4.8	312	91	403	1.96	20,827	4.9	22,810	5.0	34,730	6.1
Great Commission Christians	**9,100**	**5.0**	**28,800**	**9.0**	**52,800**	**13.5**	**878**	**417**	**1,295**	**2.22**	**59,750**	**14.1**	**65,752**	**14.4**	**91,680**	**16.1**
Nonreligious	0	0.0	2,900	0.9	6,670	1.7	111	142	253	3.27	8,000	1.9	9,202	2.0	16,000	2.8
Atheists	0	0.0	2,000	0.6	4,200	1.1	70	12	82	1.80	4,650	1.1	5,021	1.1	7,000	1.2
Hindus	0	0.0	0	0.0	1,950	0.5	32	1	33	1.57	2,100	0.5	2,278	0.5	4,000	0.7
Muslims	2,000	1.1	3,000	0.9	1,800	0.5	30	-41	-11	-0.60	1,750	0.4	1,695	0.4	1,500	0.3
Baha'is	0	0.0	500	0.2	1,380	0.4	23	-1	22	1.46	1,480	0.4	1,595	0.4	3,000	0.5
Spiritists	0	0.0	0	0.0	1,200	0.3	20	1	21	1.65	1,300	0.3	1,413	0.3	1,800	0.3
Other religionists	0	0.0	100	0.0	160	0.0	3	2	5	2.76	190	0.0	210	0.1	340	0.1
World A (unevangelized persons)	364	0.2	640	0.2	391	0.1	6	2	8	2.17	424	0.1	456	0.1	569	0.1
World B (evangelized non-Christians)	1,636	0.9	7,860	2.5	16,969	4.3	283	114	397	2.29	19,308	4.5	21,271	4.6	33,071	5.8
World C (Christians)	180,000	98.9	311,500	97.3	373,640	95.6	6,179	-116	6,063	1.52	404,530	95.4	434,273	95.3	535,360	94.1
Country's population	**182,000**	**100.0**	**320,000**	**100.0**	**391,000**	**100.0**	**6,468**	**0**	**6,468**	**1.55**	**424,263**	**100.0**	**456,000**	**100.0**	**569,000**	**100.0**

COLUMNS, ROWS.
For meanings and definitions, see Codebook (Part 3). Note that, by definition, total 'Christians' = professing + crypto-Christians, which also = affiliated + unaffiliated Christians, and also = Great Commission Christians + latent Christians. Percentages may not always total exactly, due to rounding.

CENSUSES.
The religion question has not been asked.

NOTES ON RELIGIONS
ATHEISTS. Communist Party of Guadeloupe (legal; pro-Soviet). Many party members are also practicing or professing Catholics.
BAHA'IS. In 5 local spiritual assemblies (1973), rising to 12 (1996). Missionaries from Haiti are at work.
DOUBLY-AFFILIATED. The term covers those affiliated to, or claimed by, both the Catholic Church and also a Protestant or marginal Protestant church, i.e. baptized Catholics who have recently joined other churches. Because their statistics represent a duplication, they are shown in the table as a negative quantity (with a minus sign).
MUSLIMS. Immigrants from other islands, and Syrians.
NONRELIGIOUS. Largely metropolitan French and French Creoles.
OTHER RELIGIONISTS. Including Rosicrucians (1 AMORC centre).

Country status. Guadeloupe, a French colony in the Caribbean since 1635 and overseas department since 1946, consists of one larger island and 5 smaller dependencies all in the Lesser Antilles: Marie Galante, Iles des Saintes, La Désirade, St Martin, and St Barthélemy. Tourism is the major industry.

HUMAN LIFE AND LIBERTY

Human rights and freedoms. Guadeloupe is an overseas department of France to which French laws apply. Guadeloupians enjoy all the freedoms guaranteed in the French Constitution.

Eglise Catholique. Concelebration of liturgy in Basilica on Centenary (center, bishop Oualli of Guadeloupe).

CHRISTIANITY

CATHOLIC CHURCH. Colombus discovered Guadeloupe in 1493, opening the way for Catholic penetration of the island. In 1523 the first missionaries were killed by Carib Indians but their place was taken by Dominicans, Capuchins, Jesuits, and Carmelites during the 17th century. A prefecture apostolic for Guadeloupe and Martinique was formed in 1816, and in 1850 the island became a suffragan diocese of Bordeaux in France. Almost the whole of the population are baptized Catholics, but magical and superstitious practices continue. Anti-clericalism and

Great Commission Instrument Panel: status of Guadeloupe (for explanation see start of Part 4)

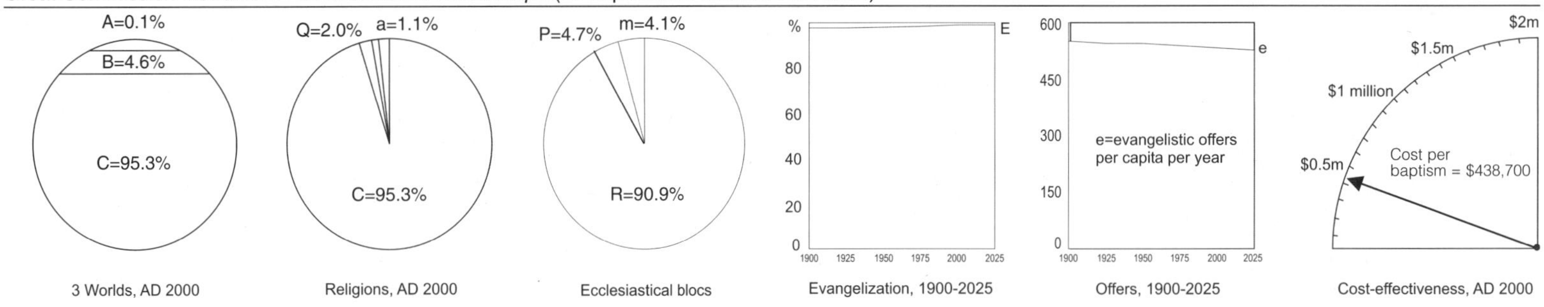

Country summary. **Worlds A, B, C by ethnolinguistic peoples, cities, and major civil divisions in Guadeloupe.**

	PEOPLES							CITIES							CIVIL DIVISIONS						
World	*Num*	*Pop 2000*	*C%*	*Christians*	*E%*	*U%*	*Unevangelized*	*Num*	*Pop 2000*	*C%*	*Christians*	*E%*	*U%*	*Unevangelized*	*Num*	*Pop 2000*	*C%*	*Christians*	*E%*	*U%*	*Unevangelized*
A	0	0	0.00	0	0	0	0	0	0	0.00	0	0	0	0	0	0	0.00	0	0	0	0
B	2	5,468	49.84	2,725	96	4	202	0	0	0.00	0	0	0	0	0	0	0.00	0	0	0	0
C	5	450,220	95.56	430,225	100	0	233	3	228,771	95.06	217,471	100	0	244	3	455,687	95.01	432,948	100	0	434
Total	**7**	**455,688**	**95.01**	**432,950**	**100**	**0**	**435**	**3**	**228,771**	**95.06**	**217,471**	**100**	**0**	**244**	**3**	**455,687**	**95.01**	**432,948**	**100**	**0**	**434**

atheism have spread, especially among youth, intellectuals, and in the liberal professions.

The first indigenous priests were ordained in 1925 and now include several serving outside Guadeloupe. There are also nearly 200 local sisters, of whom almost half work in other countries: Martinique, France, French Guiana, Algeria, Haiti, and Ecuador.

The Holy See has no diplomatic relations with Guadeloupe in AD 2000.

PROTESTANT CHURCHES. The oldest Protestant Church in Guadeloupe is that of the Moravians who began Protestant missionary work in the Antilles. Since World War II a number of new North American-based missionary societies have entered, including the Church of God (Cleveland), Pentecostal Assemblies of Canada, Seventh-day Adventists and West Indies Mission. Of these the most successful have been the latter two.

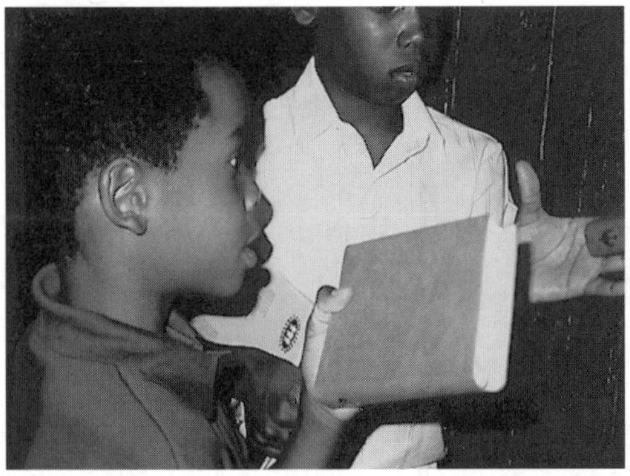

Guadeloupian youngsters receiving new Bibles from French Bible Society.

Indigenous missions. Guadeloupean Christians were sent out as missionaries to other Caribbean islands in the 16th and 17th centuries. Today the majority of the missionaries are Roman Catholics, most sent to France and nearby Martinique.

CHURCH AND STATE

The official laws of Guadeloupe relating to church and state are the same as those of metropolitan France. In the context of its general policy of departmentalization and to deal with the demand for autonomy which is very strong in Guadeloupe, the French government has long insisted on the maintenance of a Catholic hierarchy of French metropolitan origin. However, since August 1970 the diocese has been under an indigenous bishop who made notable public statements of a liberal nature at the time of the strike of agricultural workers in 1971. The Presbyteral Council also intervened in similar fashion, thus reflecting the development of a more independent attitude on the part of the Catholic Church with regard to state patronage.

BROADCASTING AND MEDIA

Guadeloupe is a member of UNDA; there are 2 local Catholic FM radio stations, including Radio Voix Chretiennes de St Martin. Shortwave programs from HCJB (Ecuador), TWR (Antilles), and AWR (Costa Rica) can be easily received.

There is a regular Catholic television program. Christian television programs can also be received via satellite.

FUTURE TRENDS AND PROSPECTS

The nonreligious and atheists, 1.5% of the population in 1970, are expected to grow steadily to 4.0% by 2025 with corresponding declines in the Christian percentage.

Guadeloupe will probably remain predominantly Christian but the nonreligious could reach 5% before AD 2040 and perhaps even 10% midway into the 21st century.

BIBLIOGRAPHY

Dans le sillage des caravelles: annales de l'Église en Guadeloupe, 1635–1970. C. Fabre. [Basse-Terre]: C. Fabre, 1976. 420p.
Guadeloupe: mission field in the West Indies. R. E. Brady. Brookhaven, MS: The Author, 1966. 78p.
'Le double fonctionnement des sectes aux Antilles: le cas du Mahikari en Guadeloupe,' L. Hurbon, *Archives de sciences sociales des religions*, 25 (July–September 1980), 59–75.
Leonora: the buried story of Guadeloupe. D. Bébel-Gisler. *CARAF books.* Charlottesville, VA: University of Virginia, 1994. 284p.
Les étapes de la Guadeloupe religieuse. Guilbaud. Basse-Terre: Imprimerie Catholique, [1936]. 244p.
Lettres du R.P. Jean Mongin: l'évangélisation des esclaves au XVIIe siècle. J. Mongin & M. Chatillon. , [1984]. 136p.
'Philosophy of Christian education and a general outworking for the churches in Guadeloupe, FWI.' J. L. Johnson. M.A. thesis, Wheaton College, Wheaton, IL, 1967. 106p.
Présence protestante en Guadeloupe au XVIIe siècle. G. Lafleur. Pointe-à-Pitre: Centre départemental de documentation pédagogique de la Guadeloupe, [1980]. 48p.
'The church and the socio–economic situation in Guadeloupe,' S. Plaucoste, in *New mission for a new people: voices from the Caribbean*, p.35–38. D. I. Mitchell (ed). New York: Friendship Press, 1977.
'The French presence and the church in Martinique and Guadeloupe,' O. La Croix, in *New mission for a new people: voices from the Caribbean*, p.30–34. D. I. Mitchell (ed). New York: Friendship Press, 1977.

Country Table 2. **Organized churches and denominations in Guadeloupe.**

Official name (bold type = church with over 10% of all affiliated) 1	*Begun* 2	*Type* 3	*Counc* 4	*Congs* 5	*Adults* 6	*Affiliated 1970* 7	*Affiliated 1995* 8	*G%* 9	*Names, notes, and other statistics* (see Codebook, Part 3) 10
Assemblées de Dieu	1957	P-Pe2	ZF...	10	1,000	500	2,500	6.65	M=PAoC(Canada), Assemblées de Dieu (France). Radio work. 2f(1x).
Association des Egls de la Guadeloupe	1947	P-Non	xM...	29	3,120	3,000	7,000	3.45	*Association of Churches in Guadeloupe.* M=WT(USA). 14f,1s.
Convention Baptiste	1964	P-Bap	.....	8	443	190	738	5.58	*Baptist Convention.* M=SBC(USA).
Eglise Adventiste du Septième Jour	1965	P-Adv	x....	44	4,140	5,000	6,900	1.30	*Seventh-day Adventists.* In Franco-Haitian UM. 6nx,43mw,1r,42t(4444),182Y.
Eglise Catholique: D Basse-Terre	1635	R-Lat	PxNMr	103	230,000	307,000	404,000	1.10	*Catholic Ch.* Suffragan of M Fort-de-France. C=1+1+10. 46n,19x,21m,198w,5252Yy.
Eglise de Dieu	1946	P-Pe3	ZF...	8	666	200	1,110	7.10	M=Ch of God (Cleveland) (USA). Guadeloupe: 2 congs; St Martin: 3 congs. 4n.
Eglise du Nazarène	1980	P-Hol	.....	1	15	–	70	6.67	*Church of the Nazarene.* M=CoN.
Eglise Evangélique de la Guadeloupe		P-Ref	C	7	800	2,000	1,400	0.05	*Protestant Ch.* French missionaries and military chaplains to French personnel. 12nx,9m.
Eglise Morave		P-Mor	xwM..	1	200	200	300	0.05	*Moravian Ch.* Immigrants from other Moravian areas in Caribbean.
Eglise Neo-Apostolique	c1980	I-3aX	x....	2	50	–	91	6.67	*New Apostolic Church.* M=NAC/NAK(HQ Zurich, Switzerland).
Témoins de Jéhovah	c1935	m-Jeh	x....	71	6,288	5,000	18,000	5.26	*Jehovah's Witnesses, Watch Tower. IBSA.* Witnessing by 1940. (1975) 210Y. (1995) 412Y.
Other independent denominations		I-	.....	10	500	500	1,000	0.05	Including: Streams of Power.
Doubly-affiliated		2-aff			-22,200	-13,590	-39,879		Evangelicals who also are or were baptized Roman Catholics.
Totals				**294**	**225,022**	**310,000**	**403,230**		

Churches, members, growth, 1900-2025	*Congs*	*Adults*	*Affiliated*	*G%*	*Total denominations*	*6 Megablocs:* O	R	A	P	I	m
Total churches, members, and denominations (mid-1900)	60	103,000	179,100	0.79	1	0	1	0	0	0	0
Total churches, members, and denominations (mid-1970)	160	178,098	310,000	0.79	10	0	1	0	7	1	1
Total churches, members, and denominations (mid-1990)	180	208,000	372,340	0.92	14	0	1	0	8	4	1
Total churches, members, and denominations (mid-1995)	294	225,022	403,230	1.61	14	0	1	0	8	4	1
Total churches, members, and denominations (mid-2000)	310	242,000	432,948	1.43	14	0	1	0	8	4	1
Total churches, members, and denominations (mid-2025)	400	297,000	532,160	0.83	30	1	1	0	12	15	1

NOTES ON TABLE ABOVE
NATIONAL COUNCILS (Column 4, 5th letter).
C = member of Fédération Evangélique de France (Evangelical Federation of France).
r = member of Conférence Episcopale de France (Episcopal Conference of France).

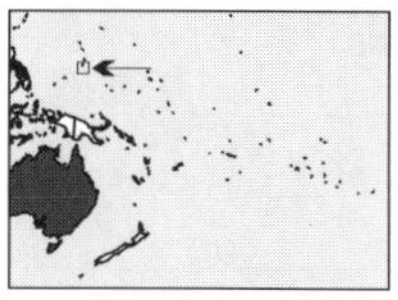

GUAM

SECULAR DATA, AD 2000

STATE
Official name: The United States Territory of Guam.
Short name: Guam. **Adjective of nationality:** Guamanian.
Flag: Territorial seal on blue field bordered in red.
Area: 1,478 sq. km. (571 sq. mi.).
Government: Self-governing unincorporated territory of the USA, since 1950 (1668 Spanish colony, 1898 US colony).
Legislature: Unicameral, 21 seats.
Official language: English.
Monetary unit: 1 dollar (U.S.$) = 100 cents. **US$1=** 1.00.
Chief cities: AGANA 61,259.
Political divisions: 1 province.

DEMOGRAPHY
Population: 168,000.
Population density: 113.3/sq. km. (293.4/sq. mi.).
Under 15 years: 55,000.
Growth rate p.a.: 1.60% (births 20.74, deaths 4.71).
Mortality: Infant, per 1,000: 9.3; **Maternal per 100,000:** 15.0.
Life expectancy: 76 (male 73, female 78).
Household size: 4.0. **Floor area per person, sq.m:** 20.0.
Major languages: English, Chamorro, Filipino, Korean.
Urban dwellers: 39.23%. **Urban growth rate p.a.:** 2.30%.
Labor force: 50%.

ETHNOLINGUISTIC PEOPLES
44.2% Guamanian; 17.8% Filipino; 13.0% Ilocano; 12.6% USA White; 3.5% Korean.

ECONOMY
National income p.a. per person: US$20,297; **per family:** US$81,190.

EDUCATION
Adult literacy: 99% (male 99%, female 99%). **Schools:** 63.
Universities: 1. **School enrolment:** female/male: 95%/95%.

HEALTH
Access to health services: 85%. **Access to safe water:** 90%.
Hospitals: 1 (6 beds per 10,000). **Doctors:** 147.
Blind: 150. **Deaf:** 9,900. Murder **rate:** 7.
Lepers: 800.

LITERATURE
New book titles p.a.: 50 (300 p.a. per million). **Periodicals:** 13.
Newspapers: 1 daily.

COMMUNICATION (per 1,000 people)
Phones: 461 (7% mobile). Radios: 1,827. **TV sets:** 648.
Daily newspaper circulation: 170. **Computers:** 120.

HUMAN LIFE AND LIBERTY (optimum condition=100.0%)
HDI: 90.2. **HSI:** 80.0. **HFI:** 80.0. **EFL:** 50.0.

Country Table 1. **Religious adherents in Guam, AD 1900-2025.**

Year / Name	1900 Adherents	1900 %	1970 Adherents	1970 %	mid-1990 Adherents	mid-1990 %	Annual change, 1990-2000 Natural	Conversion	Total	Rate	mid-1995 Adherents	mid-1995 %	mid-2000 Adherents	mid-2000 %	mid-2025 Adherents	mid-2025 %
Christians	**9,580**	**99.5**	**82,300**	**96.3**	**127,500**	**95.2**	**3,190**	**-168**	**3,022**	**2.15**	**142,840**	**94.5**	**157,723**	**94.1**	**213,250**	**93.5**
PROFESSION																
professing Christians	**9,580**	**99.5**	**82,300**	**96.3**	**127,500**	**95.2**	**3,190**	**-168**	**3,022**	**2.15**	**142,840**	**94.5**	**157,723**	**94.1**	**213,250**	**93.5**
AFFILIATION																
unaffiliated Christians	0	0.0	757	0.9	950	0.7	24	-12	12	1.17	1,000	0.7	1,067	0.6	1,250	0.6
affiliated Christians	**9,580**	**99.5**	**81,543**	**95.4**	**126,550**	**94.4**	**3,166**	**-155**	**3,011**	**2.16**	**141,840**	**93.9**	**156,656**	**93.5**	**212,000**	**93.0**
Roman Catholics	9,580	99.5	70,000	81.9	113,200	84.5	2,827	-207	2,620	2.10	127,000	84.1	139,400	83.2	185,000	81.1
Protestants	0	0.0	12,634	14.8	15,500	11.6	393	-193	200	1.22	16,741	11.1	17,500	10.4	24,000	10.5
Marginal Christians	0	0.0	743	0.9	3,100	2.3	79	41	120	3.33	3,640	2.4	4,300	2.6	9,000	4.0
Independents	0	0.0	1,000	1.2	2,100	1.6	53	27	80	3.28	2,429	1.6	2,900	1.7	6,000	2.6
Anglicans	0	0.0	500	0.6	750	0.6	19	-4	15	1.84	830	0.6	900	0.5	1,200	0.5
doubly-affiliated	0	0.0	-3,334	-3.9	-8,100	-6.0	-206	182	-24	0.30	-8,800	-5.8	-8,344	-5.0	-13,200	-5.8
Trans-megabloc groupings																
Evangelicals	0	0.0	5,400	6.3	7,000	5.2	178	-28	150	1.96	7,708	5.1	8,500	5.1	12,000	5.3
Pentecostals/Charismatics	0	0.0	1,300	1.5	7,770	5.8	197	16	213	2.45	8,797	5.8	9,900	5.9	16,000	7.0
Great Commission Christians	**300**	**3.1**	**7,300**	**8.5**	**13,000**	**9.7**	**330**	**63**	**393**	**2.68**	**14,800**	**9.8**	**16,931**	**10.1**	**26,000**	**11.4**
Nonreligious	0	0.0	700	0.8	1,600	1.2	41	84	125	5.94	2,100	1.4	2,849	1.7	4,000	1.8
Buddhists	0	0.0	200	0.2	1,250	0.9	32	58	90	5.59	1,850	1.2	2,154	1.3	3,600	1.6
Baha'is	0	0.0	500	0.6	1,300	1.0	33	23	56	3.66	1,500	1.0	1,863	1.1	3,400	1.5
Chinese folk-religionists	0	0.0	650	0.8	1,050	0.8	27	-1	26	2.21	1,170	0.8	1,307	0.8	1,700	0.8
New-Religionists	0	0.0	0	0.0	500	0.4	13	21	34	5.31	750	0.5	839	0.5	1,200	0.5
Ethnoreligionists	20	0.2	1,000	1.2	600	0.5	15	-16	-1	-0.24	580	0.4	586	0.4	550	0.2
Confucianists	0	0.0	150	0.2	200	0.2	5	-1	4	1.63	210	0.1	235	0.1	300	0.1
World A (unevangelized persons)	9	0.1	341	0.4	1,072	0.8	28	33	61	4.50	1,510	1.0	1,680	1.0	3,192	1.4
World B (evangelized non-Christians)	40	0.1	2,819	3.3	5,428	4.0	138	135	273	4.71	6,744	4.4	8,597	4.9	11,558	5.1
World C (Christians)	9,580	99.8	82,300	96.3	127,500	95.2	3,190	-168	3,022	2.15	142,840	94.6	157,723	94.1	213,250	93.5
Country's population	**9,630**	**100.0**	**85,461**	**100.0**	**134,000**	**100.0**	**3,356**	**0**	**3,356**	**2.29**	**151,095**	**100.0**	**167,600**	**100.0**	**228,000**	**100.0**

COLUMNS, ROWS.
For meanings and definitions, see Codebook (Part 3). Note that, by definition, total 'Christians' = professing + crypto-Christians, which also = affiliated + unaffiliated Christians, and also = Great Commission Christians + latent Christians. Percentages may not always total exactly, due to rounding.

NOTES ON RELIGIONS
BAHA'IS. Growth of local spiritual assemblies: 1964, none; 1973, 6; 1996, 11 LSAs.
BUDDHISTS. Mainly Koreans.
INDEPENDENTS In about 4 groupings in 1995, one denomination from the Philippines (see Table 2).
NONRELIGIOUS. North Americans.

Great Commission Instrument Panel: status of Guam (for explanation see start of Part 4)

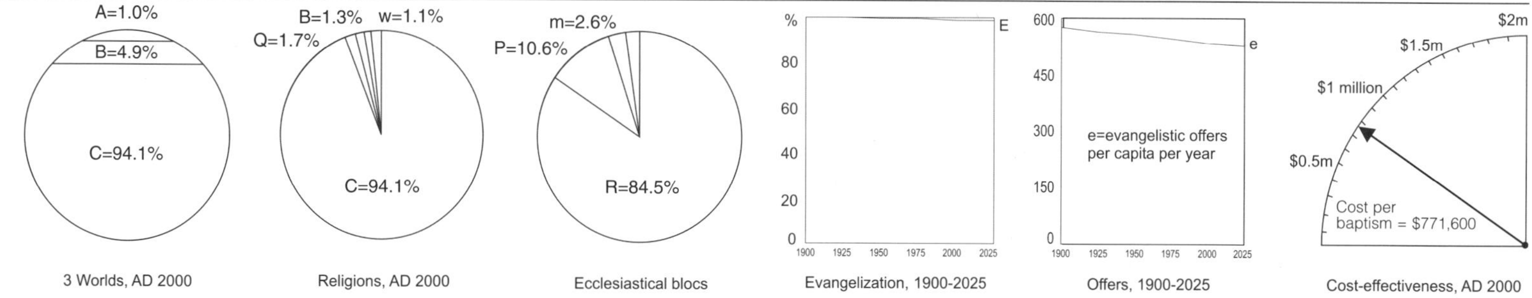

Country status. Guam is the largest and most southerly island of the Northern Marianas Archipelago, to the west of the Philippines in the eastern Pacific Ocean. It is administered as an unincorporated territory of the United States and the economy is based on financial services and the military installations.

HUMAN LIFE AND LIBERTY

Human need and development. Guam is an unincorporated territory of the United States of America, to which all freedoms guaranteed in the US Constitution are applicable.

NON-CHRISTIAN RELIGIONS

Traditional religions have disappeared among the Guamanian indigenous population, but shamanism has been introduced through the large community of Korean immigrant workers.

Buddhism, Confucianism and the ***Asian New Religions*** have followers among the Korean and Chinese population. ***Baha'i*** has a small following with 6 local spiritual assemblies.

CHRISTIANITY

CATHOLIC CHURCH. The first Spanish priests arrived in 1668, and today the large majority of Guamanians are Catholics. The diocese of Agaña is a suffragan of the archdiocese of San Francisco (USA). The church's attention has been turned to the growing Chinese community, many of whom have immigrated from the Ryukyu Islands since these were returned to Japan in 1972.

The Holy See has no diplomatic relations with Guam in AD 2000, but is represented there by an apostolic delegate for the Pacific Ocean residing in Wellington, New Zealand.

OTHER CHURCHES. Although General Baptists have been at work in Guam since 1911, no other Protestant groups entered until after World War II. The largest Protestant denominations today are Seventh-day Adventists and Southern Baptists. Two American Pentecostal groups are active, Assemblies of God and the Church of God (Cleveland), in addition to a number of small conservative and holiness groups. The Anglican mission is part of the diocese of Hawaii of the Episcopal Church in the USA. In the mid-1990s Guam had 4 Korean Presbyterian congregations, a Chinese church, and several churches serving various Micronesian immigrant peoples.

Indigenous missions. Guam, for centuries only receiving missionaries, is beginning to send missionaries to other countries. Guam also hosts a powerful transmitter for reaching south and east Asia.

Country summary. **Worlds A, B, C by ethnolinguistic peoples, cities, and major civil divisions in Guam.**

	PEOPLES							CITIES							CIVIL DIVISIONS						
World	Num	Pop 2000	C%	Christians	E%	U%	Unevangelized	Num	Pop 2000	C%	Christians	E%	U%	Unevangelized	Num	Pop 2000	C%	Christians	E%	U%	Unevangelized
A	1	2,798	2.00	56	42	58	1,623	0	0	0.00	0	0	0	0	0	0	0.00	0	0	0	0
B	2	2,179	39.97	871	99	1	13	0	0	0.00	0	0	0	0	0	0	0.00	0	0	0	0
C	10	162,580	95.79	155,731	100	0	72	1	61,259	93.00	56,971	98	2	925	1	167,556	93.49	156,656	99	1	1,708
Total	**13**	**167,557**	**93.50**	**156,658**	**99**	**1**	**1,708**	**1**	**61,259**	**93.00**	**56,971**	**98**	**2**	**925**	**1**	**167,556**	**93.49**	**156,656**	**99**	**1**	**1,708**

Catholic Church, Diocese of Agaña. Faithful enter cathedral in Agaña for Sunday mass.

CHURCH AND STATE

Guam was first discovered by Magellan in 1521, and Spain took possession of the island in 1565. Early Catholic work was closely associated with Spanish colonial conquest. Following the Spanish-American War in 1898, Guam was ceded to the USA and became a US naval base. As in all its possessions, American policy has attempted to maintain a clear line of separation between church and state. However, Protestant and Catholic chaplains serving with the armed forces are recruited and paid by government.

BROADCASTING AND MEDIA

TWR has a strategic transmitter on Guam that covers China, the CIS, and most of eastern Asia, broadcasting in 24 mainly Asian languages daily. This station has also been important in reaching out to some refugee groups, particularly Iraqi Kurds. Shortwave programs from FEBC and KNLS can also be received. Local stations carry Christian programs, including some produced by IBRA and *Back to the Bible*. Likewise, AWR has a strategic transmitter which covers Asia with daily programs in 33 languages.

Guam is a member of UNDA: Catholics have a recording studio on the island.

FUTURE TRENDS AND PROSPECTS

Christianity is expected to experience only slight decline in the next thirty years.

Although Christianity will potentially experience a steady decline in the next few decades, it should remain above 90% through AD 2050.

BIBLIOGRAPHY

'Patron saints and pagan ghosts: the pairing of opposites,' R. E. Mitchell, *Asian folklore studies*, 45, 1 (1986), 101–23. (Deals with Agana, Guam).

'Praying and feasting: modern Guamanian fiestas,' N. R. Crumrine, *Anthropos*, 77, 1–2 (1982), 89–112.

'The Church of God on Guam: a brief history.' G. M. Diaz. Thesis, Anderson School of Theology, Anderson, IN, 1979. 122p.

The historical visit to Guam of Pope John Paul II: a documentary photo–essay. A. P. DiMalanta. , [1981]. 64p.

The phoenix rises: a mission history of Guam. J. Sullivan. New York: Seraphic Mass Association, 1957. 231p.

Country Table 2. **Organized churches and denominations in Guam.**

Official name (bold type = church with over 10% of all affiliated) 1	*Begun* 2	*Type* 3	*Counc* 4	*Congs* 5	*Adults* 6	*Affiliated 1970* 7	*Affiliated 1995* 8	*G%* 9	*Names, notes, and other statistics* (see Codebook, Part 3) 10
Assemblies of God	1960	P-Pe2	ZF...	6	1,250	1,000	1,640	2.00	M=AoG(USA). Classical Pentecostals (2-stage). HQ Agaña 2f.
Baptist Church		P-Bap	.....	2	400	167	667	0.05	M=GARB. General Baptists.
Baptist Convention	1961	P-Bap	T....	3	358	2,000	1,190	-2.06	M=FMB-SBC(USA). Sunday School enrollment 560. 10f,41Y.
Catholic Church: D Agaña	1668	R-Lat	P....	26	60,000	70,000	127,000	2.41	Suffragan of M San Francisco. 13% White. C=2+0+5. 55nx,6m,153w,1h,P=68%,1s 2736Yy.
Christian Reformed Church	1962	P-Ref	JF...	3	200	200	400	2.81	M=CRC(USA). Small mission run by body from Grand Rapids MI (USA). 6f.
Church of Christ	1969	I-	x....	2	300	300	429	1.44	M=Iglesia ni Cristo (Manalista). HQ Quezon (Philippines). Filipinos. 2f.
Church of Christ, Scientist		m-Sci	x....	1	20	50	40	0.05	*Christian Science.* M=CCS(Boston, USA). Agaña Heights Society. 1w.
Church of God (Anderson)		P-Hol	x....	4	200	300	400	0.05	M=CoG(Anderson) (USA). Begun by USA government teachers. Holiness body. 1t(100).
Church of God (Cleveland)	1956	P-Pe3	ZF...	10	300	200	500	3.73	M=CoG(Cleveland) (USA). Members mostly Filipino-Americans; Holiness Pentecostals.
Ch of Jesus Christ of Latter-day Saints	c1932	m-LdS	x....	3	1,320	493	2,200	6.17	*Mormons.* M=CJCLdS(Utah, USA). USA personnel and military. 20f.
Church of the Nazarene	1970	P-Hol	.....	1	75	–	210	23.85	M=CoN. Nazarenes based in USA.
Churches of Christ		I-Dis	x....	4	400	500	600	0.05	M=CC(Non-Instrumental) (USA). In Agaña. USA servicemen and personnel.
Conservative Baptist Churches	1956	I-Bap	xF...	2	200	200	400	2.81	M=Conservative Baptist Home Mission Society (USA). 4f,22Y.
Episcopal Church in the USA	1960	A-Cen	aw...	3	500	500	830	2.05	Part of Diocese of Hawaii, PECUSA. Many USA expatriates, military. W=80%.
General Baptist Mission	1911	P-Bap	TF...	4	300	1,000	667	-1.61	M=GBFMS(General Association of Genera l Baptists, USA). 6n,4f.
Jehovah's Witnesses	c1950	m-Jeh	x....	7	379	200	1,400	8.09	*Watch Tower. IBSA.* First witnessing 1952. (1975) 14Y. (1995) 44Y.
Korean Presbyterian Churches	c1975	I-Ref	.....	4	600	–	1,000	5.00	Part of Korea's worldwide missionary expansion.
Lutheran Church	c1980	P-Lut	.....	1	100	–	154	6.67	Lutheran mission and ministries.
Methodist Church		P-Met	.....	2	200	167	333	0.05	Methodist evangelistic outreach.
Pacific Ocean Mission	1956	P-Hol	.....	6	100	100	150	1.64	Mission from USA. Members expatriate Americans, Filipinos, Koreans. 1n,W=80%,2Y.
Seventh-day Adventist Church	1930	P-Adv	x....	18	1,700	2,000	2,430	0.78	*Far Eastern Island Mission*, Far Eastern Div. 7n,2h,1r,8t(950) W=80%,89Y.
Other Protestant denominations		P-	.....	26	3,200	5,500	8,000	0.05	Total about 26, including USA military chaplaincies.
Doubly-affiliated		2-aff			-4,200	-3,334	-8,800		Evangelicals who are or were also baptized Roman Catholics.
Totals				**138**	**67,902**	**81,543**	**141,840**		

Churches, members, growth, 1900-2025	*Congs*	*Adults*	*Affiliated*	*G%*	*Total denominations*	*6 Megablocs:* O	R	A	P	I	m
Total churches, members, and denominations (mid-1900)	10	5,300	9,580	3.11	1	0	1	0	0	0	0
Total churches, members, and denominations (mid-1970)	88	44,726	81,543	3.11	30	0	1	1	22	3	3
Total churches, members, and denominations (mid-1990)	100	60,600	126,550	2.22	46	0	1	1	37	4	3
Total churches, members, and denominations (mid-1995)	138	67,902	141,840	2.31	47	0	1	1	38	4	3
Total churches, members, and denominations (mid-2000)	150	75,000	156,656	2.01	47	0	1	1	38	4	3
Total churches, members, and denominations (mid-2025)	210	101,000	212,000	1.22	79	0	1	1	50	20	7

NOTES ON TABLE ABOVE

OTHER PROTESTANT DENOMINATIONS. Including Baptist Bible Fellowship International (1975), Guam National Ch (Liebenzell Mission), and USA military chaplaincies.

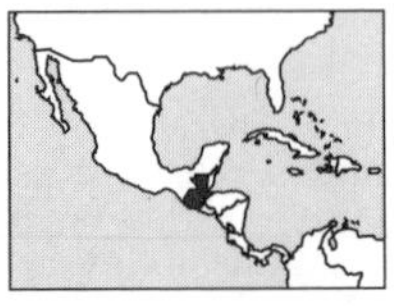

GUATEMALA

SECULAR DATA, AD 2000

STATE

Official name: La República de Guatemala (The Republic of Guatemala).
Short name: Guatemala. **Adjective of nationality:** Guatemalan.
Flag: Blue, white, and blue bars, national coat of arms in centre.
Area: 108,889 sq. km. (42,042 sq. mi.).
Government: Republic, since 1944 (1524 Spanish possession, 1821 Independence, many military dictatorships, 1984 new constitution).
Legislature: National Congress, 80 members.
Official language: Spanish (Español/Castella).
Monetary unit: 1 quetzal (Q) = 100 centavos. **US$1=** Q 6.51.
Chief cities: GUATEMALA (Guatemala City) 2,697,000; Quezaltenango (Quetzaltenango) 121,420; Escuintla 82,989.
Political divisions: 22 provinces.
Armed forces: 44,000.

DEMOGRAPHY

Population: 11,385,000.
Population density: 104.5/sq. km. (270.8/sq. mi.).
Under 15 years: 4,965,000.
Growth rate p.a.: 2.58% (births 34.16, deaths 6.77).
Mortality: Infant, per 1,000: 41.2; **Maternal per 100,000:** 200.0.
Life expectancy: 66 (male 63, female 69).
Household size: 5.4. **Floor area per person, sq.m:** 15.0.
Major languages: Spanish, Quiché, Cakchiquel, Mam, Kekchi, English, and 40 smaller languages.
Urban dwellers: 40.35%. **Urban growth rate p.a.:** 3.68%.
Labor force: 34%.

ETHNOLINGUISTIC PEOPLES

63.7% Ladino (Mestizo); 4.8% Southwestern Quiche; 3.6% Kekchi (Quecchi); 2.4% West Central Quiche; 2.2% Central Quiche.

ECONOMY

National income p.a. per person: US$1,339; **per family:** US$7,235.

EDUCATION

Adult literacy: 55% (male 62%, female 48%). **Schools:** 12,670.
Universities: 5. **School enrolment:** female/male: 53%/60%.

HEALTH

Access to health services: 34%. **Access to safe water:** 64%.
Hospitals: 160 (16 beds per 10,000). **Doctors:** 7,601.
Blind: 6,000. **Deaf:** 733,300. Murder **rate:** 27.

Lepers: 1,200. **Underweight prevalence under 5:** 27%.

LITERATURE
New book titles p.a.: 3,420 (300 p.a. per million). **Periodicals:** 56. **Newspapers:** 5 dailies.

COMMUNICATION (per 1,000 people)
Phones: 27 (13% mobile). Radios: 52. **TV sets:** 122. **Daily newspaper circulation:** 23. **Computers:** 60.

REFUGEES
Citizen refugees in other countries: 34,150.

Alien refugees from other countries: 2,500.
Internal displacement: 200,000.

HUMAN LIFE AND LIBERTY (optimum condition=100.0%)
HDI: 57.2. **HSI:** 31.0. **HFI:** 50.0. **EFL:** 43.0.

Country Table 1. **Religious adherents in Guatemala, AD 1900-2025.**

Year	1900		1970		mid-1990		Annual change, 1990-2000				mid-1995		mid-2000		mid-2025	
Name	Adherents	%	Adherents	%	Adherents	%	Natural	Conversion	Total	Rate	Adherents	%	Adherents	%	Adherents	%
Christians	**1,689,700**	**99.4**	**5,207,600**	**99.3**	**8,583,750**	**98.1**	**258,621**	**-4,629**	**253,992**	**2.63**	**9,766,060**	**97.9**	**11,123,666**	**97.7**	**19,203,500**	**96.9**
PROFESSION																
professing Christians	**1,689,700**	**99.4**	**5,207,600**	**99.3**	**8,583,750**	**98.1**	**258,621**	**-4,629**	**253,992**	**2.63**	**9,766,060**	**97.9**	**11,123,666**	**97.7**	**19,203,500**	**96.9**
AFFILIATION																
unaffiliated Christians	128,800	7.6	574,376	11.0	343,750	3.9	10,357	-781	9,576	2.49	386,060	3.9	439,513	3.9	703,500	3.6
affiliated Christians	**1,560,900**	**91.8**	**4,633,224**	**88.4**	**8,240,000**	**94.2**	**248,264**	**-3,849**	**244,415**	**2.63**	**9,380,000**	**94.0**	**10,684,153**	**93.8**	**18,500,000**	**93.4**
Roman Catholics	1,560,000	91.8	4,346,449	82.9	7,350,000	84.0	221,449	3,551	225,000	2.71	8,401,071	84.2	9,600,000	84.3	16,400,000	82.8
Protestants	800	0.1	269,594	5.1	1,060,000	12.1	31,937	7,063	39,000	3.18	1,241,194	12.4	1,450,000	12.7	3,000,000	15.1
Independents	0	0.0	90,480	1.7	730,000	8.3	21,994	8,006	30,000	3.50	867,153	8.7	1,030,000	9.1	2,100,000	10.6
Marginal Christians	0	0.0	20,821	0.4	110,000	1.3	3,314	1,686	5,000	3.82	132,700	1.3	160,000	1.4	500,000	2.5
Anglicans	100	0.0	750	0.0	1,300	0.0	39	11	50	3.31	1,520	0.0	1,800	0.0	3,000	0.0
doubly-affiliated	0	0.0	-94,870	-1.8	-1,011,300	-11.6	-30,470	-24,165	-54,635	4.41	-1,263,638	-12.7	-1,557,647	-13.7	-3,503,000	-17.7
Trans-megabloc groupings																
Evangelicals	800	0.1	205,000	3.9	825,000	9.4	24,857	10,643	35,500	3.64	994,626	10.0	1,180,000	10.4	2,500,000	12.6
Pentecostals/Charismatics	0	0.0	175,000	3.3	1,875,000	21.4	56,492	5,008	61,500	2.88	2,163,948	21.7	2,490,000	21.9	4,800,000	24.2
Great Commission Christians	**57,800**	**3.4**	**367,000**	**7.0**	**735,000**	**8.4**	**22,145**	**1,810**	**23,955**	**2.86**	**848,000**	**8.5**	**974,549**	**8.6**	**3,250,000**	**16.4**
Nonreligious	0	0.0	9,000	0.2	78,000	0.9	2,379	4,747	7,126	6.71	109,500	1.1	149,264	1.3	400,000	2.0
Atheists	0	0.0	3,000	0.1	40,000	0.5	1,205	386	1,591	3.40	48,000	0.5	55,908	0.5	110,000	0.6
Spiritists	1,700	0.1	10,000	0.2	20,000	0.2	603	-219	384	1.77	22,200	0.2	23,835	0.2	40,000	0.2
Baha'is	0	0.0	4,400	0.1	16,000	0.2	482	-75	407	2.29	18,000	0.2	20,073	0.2	45,000	0.2
Chinese folk-religionists	0	0.0	1,000	0.0	3,100	0.0	93	-35	58	1.74	3,500	0.0	3,684	0.0	5,800	0.0
Ethnoreligionists	8,500	0.5	5,000	0.1	3,150	0.0	95	-119	-24	-0.79	3,140	0.0	2,910	0.0	2,000	0.0
Buddhists	0	0.0	1,000	0.0	1,600	0.0	48	-10	38	2.16	1,850	0.0	1,981	0.0	3,600	0.0
Jews	100	0.0	1,000	0.0	950	0.0	29	-23	6	0.65	1,000	0.0	1,014	0.0	900	0.0
Muslims	0	0.0	0	0.0	800	0.0	24	-13	11	1.31	850	0.0	911	0.0	1,200	0.0
Other religionists	0	0.0	1,000	0.0	1,650	0.0	50	-10	40	2.19	1,900	0.0	2,049	0.0	4,000	0.0
World A (unevangelized persons)	1,700	0.1	5,243	0.1	8,749	0.1	265	-352	-87	-1.04	9,975	0.1	11,385	0.1	0	0.0
World B (evangelized non-Christians)	8,600	0.5	30,571	0.6	156,501	1.8	4,743	4,981	9,724	4.79	199,859	2.0	249,949	2.2	612,500	3.1
World C (Christians)	1,689,700	99.4	5,207,600	99.3	8,583,750	98.1	258,621	-4,629	253,992	2.63	9,766,060	97.9	11,123,666	97.7	19,203,500	96.9
Country's population	**1,700,000**	**100.0**	**5,243,415**	**100.0**	**8,749,000**	**100.0**	**263,629**	**0**	**263,629**	**2.67**	**9,975,895**	**100.0**	**11,385,000**	**100.0**	**19,816,000**	**100.0**

COLUMNS, ROWS.
For meanings and definitions, see Codebook (Part 3). Note that, by definition, total 'Christians' = professing + crypto-Christians, which also = affiliated + unaffiliated Christians, and also = Great Commission Christians + latent Christians. Percentages may not always total exactly, due to rounding.

CENSUSES.
1940: 98.1% Roman Catholics, 1.5% Evangelicals. **18.IV.1950:** 96.9% Roman Catholics, 2.8% Evangelicals, 0.3% other religionists. In this census, Evangelicals were 29% Indians, 71% Ladinos.

NOTES ON RELIGIONS
ATHEISTS. Guatemalan Labor Party (PGT) (proscribed since 1954; pro-Soviet). There have also long been communist guerrillas in remote parts of the country.
BAHA'IS. Growth from 8 local spiritual assemblies (1964) to 29 (1973 to 36 (1996), mainly among Indian areas in the west, with from 1971 many coastal Blacks.
BUDDHISTS. Chinese.
ETHNORELIGIONISTS. A small number of monolingual Amerindians have resisted both Catholicism, christo-paganism and also Protestant missions.
INDEPENDENTS. In about 30 denominations in 1995 (see Table 2).
MUSLIMS. Palestinian Arabs.
OTHER RELIGIONISTS. Including Rosicrucians (2 AMORC centers).
PROTESTANTS. Growth of Protestants among the various Maya peoples, was marked, from 1969 onwards, among these Maya peoples: Quiché, Cakchiqual, Kekchi, Tzutuhil, Chuj, Mam, Kanjobal, Aguacatec, Chorti, Jacaltec, Achi.
SPIRITISTS. Non-Christian adherents of Afro-Caribbean spirit-possession cults syncretizing Christianity with African religion; mostly Jamaicans and other Blacks.

Great Commission Instrument Panel: status of Guatemala (for explanation see start of Part 4)

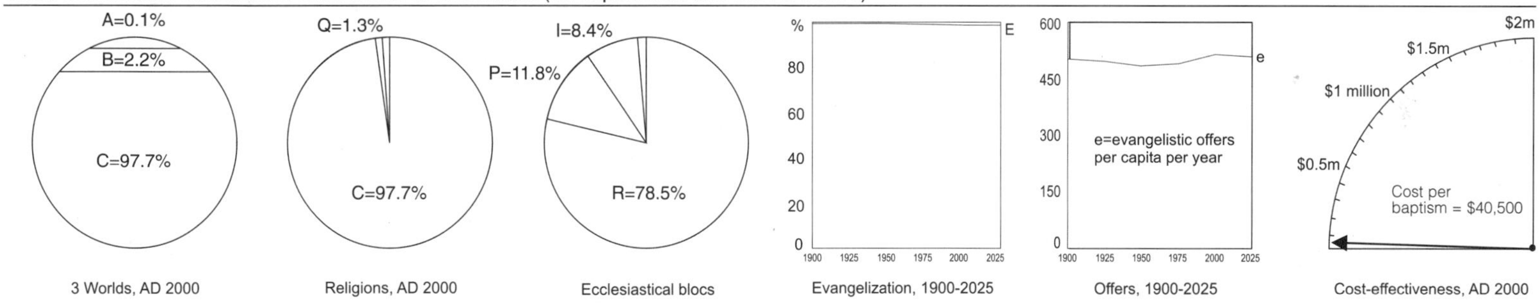

Country status. Guatemala is the most populous of all Central American nations, containing a third of the population of the entire region. It is also one of the most politically troubled, with only brief intervals of peace in otherwise continual civil strife during the past quarter of a century. The great variety of its climate and landforms is matched only by its ethnic and cultural diversity. Guatemala is one of the most Mayan of Central American republics with more than half of its population belonging to pure Mayan stock.

HUMAN LIFE AND LIBERTY

Human need and development. Living conditions in the country are among the lowest in the region. The majority of the Indians live in highland villages, and their way of life has changed little over the centuries. Many live on the subsistence level, and on basic indicators, such as longevity and infant mortality, they fare worse than the Ladinos, who are of Spanish descent. The Ladinos live mostly in the lowlands and in the cities, and their houses are generally better built than those of the Indians. Indians tend to live on the outskirts of town or in the rural areas of the municipio in one-room, windowless dwellings, sharing their quarters with their domestic animals. The floors are packed dirt and the roofs are thatched with grass or palm leaves. Most of the rural dwellings do not have access to piped water, sanitation or electricity. Although the diet is deficient in many nutrients, the vast majority of the people have enough to eat and the daily caloric intake is judged to be adequate. Since the presidency of Juan Jose Arevalo (1945-51) a strong public health program has been established along with a social security system. The national life expectancy is 66 but that of the Indians is considerably less. Most of the major diseases have been brought under control.

Human rights and freedoms. There has been considerable progress in human rights in recent years. Statistics prepared by the official Human Rights Ombudsman as well the Archbishop's Human Rights Office showed a substantial drop in 1992 in reported human rights violations. Some progress was made in investigating past and present human rights abuses, but the overall record was poor. Guerrillas also commit many serious human rights violations, including murders and kidnappings, providing a pretext for government to retaliate. According to the ombudsman there were 228 confirmed and 203 unconfirmed extrajudicial killings in 1991 of which over one-half was attributed to state security forces. In addition, there were 65 complaints of disappearances during the first 6 months of 1992. There are credible reports of torture and mistreatment by security forces. Corpses buried in clandestine rural cemeteries bear signs of severe disfigurement and mutilation. Police abuse of street children had become less common as the result of the work of Caza Alianza, a human rights group. Constitutional safeguards notwithstanding, persons may be illegally detained. The judicial system is ineffective. Judges are susceptible to intimidation and corruption and suffer low pay, low morale, and bad working conditions. Some judges are deterred by death threats from hearing cases involving opposition figures. Freedom of the press and speech is guaranteed by the Constitution and is not subject to official curtailment. However, leftwing journalists are occasionally subject to death threats from rightwing vigilante groups. The media brave government displeasure to report all major human rights stories as well as investigative reports on official corruption Although the indigenous people suffer no constitutional disabilities, they are virtually excluded from all areas of public life. They also suffer the most serious human rights abuses and have the least ability to obtain redress. Most of them are illiterate and many do not speak Spanish. Thus they are unable to defend their interests against the incursions of the ruling Ladinos.

Human environment. The highland and forest areas of the country are inhabited by Indians, who are unschooled in conservation practices. Their agricultural systems as well as their need of fuelwood have led to an alarming rate of deforestation. Such deforestation also causes a steep reduction in the biodiversity of animal and plant species.

Country summary. **Worlds A, B, C by ethnolinguistic peoples, cities, and major civil divisions in Guatemala.**

World	PEOPLES Num	Pop 2000	C%	Christians	E%	U%	Unevangelized
A	1	1,025	0.10	1	46	54	552
B	1	1,139	18.96	216	80	20	228
C	63	11,383,131	93.86	10,683,935	100	0	7,150
Total	**65**	**11,385,295**	**93.84**	**10,684,152**	**100**	**0**	**7,930**

World	CITIES Num	Pop 2000	C%	Christians	E%	U%	Unevangelized
A	0	0	0.00	0	0	0	0
B	0	0	0.00	0	0	0	0
C	3	2,901,409	88.99	2,581,870	100	0	5,523
Total	**3**	**2,901,409**	**88.99**	**2,581,870**	**100**	**0**	**5,523**

World	CIVIL DIVISIONS Num	Pop 2000	C%	Christians	E%	U%	Unevangelized
A	0	0	0.00	0	0	0	0
B	0	0	0.00	0	0	0	0
C	22	11,385,294	93.84	10,684,153	100	0	7,928
Total	**22**	**11,385,294**	**93.84**	**10,684,153**	**100**	**0**	**7,928**

NON-CHRISTIAN RELIGIONS

Although Guatemalans are nearly all professing Christians, many Mayan Indians, especially the Quiché, continue to accommodate their traditional rites and beliefs to those of Catholicism. The resulting christo-paganism of 26% of the population is most notable at Chichicastenango and at many similar Indian centers. An overt revival of the pre-Christian Mayan religion attracted some attention in the early 1990s, but not a large number of followers. More influential have been the older *confradias*, or syncretic religious brotherhoods, with practices based on a mix of ancient Mayan religion and 16th-century saint veneration. Village confradia priests or shamans would settle disputes, do divination with coral seeds and crystals, cure illnesses, cast spells, prescribe herbs, and lead dances, chants, and feasts. In this century, both Catholic and Protestant missionaries have preached against this syncretic movement and it has suffered sharp decline. Less than 1% of the population denies any association with Christianity. This includes a small Jewish community of about 1,000, resident for the most part in the capital. The principal Jewish organization is the Consejo Central de la Comunidad Israelita de Guatemala. There were less than 1,000 Muslims in Guatemala in 1995. Among their number was a Pakistani Ahmadiyya missionary doctor serving in a clinic with an accompanying mosque.

Iglesia Catolica en Guatemala. *Top.* Christopagan shamans offer incense on steps of (*lower*) St Thomas, Chichicastenango,

CHRISTIANITY

CATHOLIC CHURCH. In their 16th-century conquest of Guatemala, the Spanish found in the Quiché-speaking Maya Indians a deeply religious people, whose worship included the recognition of a supreme being named Qabovil, with Tikal in the north being their great cultural center. The socio-religious organization of these people did not survive Spanish colonization. Regrouped into Spanish-type villages, Indians were forced to study Catholic doctrine in the churches, which they then accommodated to their own religious ethos. Four centuries later popular Catholicism still strongly manifests this mixture, in some areas revealing many Indian and Spanish cultural elements existing side-by-side without blending, with little or no religious acculturation. From 1524 to 1821 Guatemala was the center of the Spanish government in Central America with which the Catholic Church was closely associated. Little change took place after Guatemala's independence. In 1871 the church was separated from the state and its property confiscated; and in 1874 the religious orders were dissolved. Free to operate without impediment since 1954, the church in Guatemala continues to suffer from a shortage of priests, in large measure due to the absence of any interest in the priesthood on the part of the over 2 million Indians, since baptism is in fact the only sacrament widely accepted by them.

The vast gulf that exists between on the one hand the clergy and bishops, who are almost all foreigners with close ties to the Ladinos (Mestizos), and on the other hand the Indian population, has generated considerable tension between local and foreign clergy and poses serious problems in the area of pastoral action. In addition, a large number of foreign religious personnel are absorbed in functions not directly pastoral. Thus in Guatemala City many are involved in administration or teaching in schools for children of the middle classes. There do exist, however, especially in dioceses outside Guatemala City, a number of important institutions for social development, although their relations with the hierarchy are frequently tenuous.

The Holy See has diplomatic relations with Guatemala and in AD 2000 is represented to government and the Catholic hierarchy by a nuncio residing in Guatemala City.

PROTESTANT CHURCHES. Protestantism has grown steadily since 1940 at the expense of Catholicism, as the following figures of professing Christians indicate: 1940, 98.5% Catholics, 1.5% Evangelicals (Protestants); 1950, 96.9% Catholics, 2.8% Evangelicals; 1970, 95% Catholics, 4.3% Evangelicals. The size of the Protestant population varies among the states, from around 15% in the northwest state of Huehuetenango (next to the strongly Protestant Mexican state of Chiapas) to 2% in the north central state of Alta Verapaz. The religio-ethnic composition also varies from state to state, Indians forming over 90% of Protestants in Huehuetenango, and Ladinos over 90% in El Progreso.

The Protestant population includes many converts and evidences a somewhat higher education than the general population. Among the Maya Indians, the Evangelical community grew rapidly from 68,800 in 1969 to 99,100 in 1974. A government poll taken prior to the 1990 elections showed 45% of the population considered themselves Evangelicals (which figure included a very large number also counted as affiliated Catholics).

American Presbyterians entered Guatemala in 1882 upon the invitation of president Barrios who believed Protestants could make a contribution to the progress and development of the country. The National Presbyterian Church of Guatemala became fully autonomous in 1962, and is today the third largest of the non-Pentecostal Protestant churches. Presbyterians developed a new method of theological education in which men and women study at home, as well as in regional centers which receive weekly visits from seminary teachers. This church in fact originated the method of the theological education by extension (TEE) which quickly became a worldwide movement. The Quiché Bible Institute in San Cristobal, established especially to serve the needs of the Quiché Indians, is conducted jointly with the Primitive Methodists, the latter being a denomination from the USA with foreign missionaries only in Guatemala. The Central American Church, autonomous since 1927, owes its origin to the pioneer work of the Central American Mission in 1899. Its Robinson Bible Institute has been preparing pastors for work among Indians since 1923, and another Bible institute in Guatemala City trains leaders for all Central American countries. Other early arrivals who have made considerable progress are the Friends who came in 1902, Nazarenes in 1904, Adventists in 1908, and Brethren in 1925. Of groups coming after World War II, Baptists have recorded the most significant growth.

As is true of most Latin American countries, Pentecostals, who first entered in 1916, have made a significant impact on Guatemala. Guatemala's largest single Protestant denomination is the Assemblies of God which began in 1937, and another important Pentecostal group is the Full Gospel Church of God.

As with Catholics, Protestants have been heavily involved in education and social service. The Presbyterian Church sponsors secondary schools, clinics, a cultural and recreational center and an agricultural extension program. In addition, Protestants maintain their own university, Universidad Mariano Galvez, the first of its kind to be established in Latin American (1966).

Indigenous churches. Street preacher extending outreach of some 104 denominations.

INDIGENOUS CHURCHES. The formation of independent churches in Guatemala is a recent phenomenon dating from the end of World War II. The majority are Pentecostal, the largest being the Church of the Prince of Peace. It is also just one of more than 10 third-wave independent groups, more than half of which began in the mid-1980s. Together they account for nearly 1 million Christians or about 9% of the national population.

Renewal movements. In the 1990s the Pentecostal/Charismatic Renewal continued to spread rapidly across most older churches, and numbered over 2,490,000 adherents (of whom 28% Pentecostals, 37% Charismatics, and 35% Independents).

Indigenous missions. While a substantial number of Roman Catholics have served as missionaries in surrounding countries, only recently are Protestants sending missionaries; some to North Africa and Western Asia.

CHURCH AND STATE

Although church and state were legally separated in 1871, the latest constitution (15 September 1965) still states: 'The Catholic Apostolic Roman religion is that of the State which contributes to its maintenance without preventing the free exercise of other faiths'. After invoking 'the protection of God' in its preamble, the constitution, which became law on 6 may 1966, stipulates in Article 66: 'Freedom of religion is guaranteed. Everyone has the right to practise his religion or belief, both publicly and privately, through education, worship and observance, with no limitations except that public order, morals and peace be observed and respect given to national symbols. Religious associations or groups may not intervene in party political activity nor may clergy engage in political action within such parties.' Article 67 states: 'The Catholic Church and other denominations are recognized as juridical personalities. They can acquire and dispose of property to be used for religious purposes, for social service or education. Such property is exempt from taxation'. Religious manifestations taking place outside of church buildings are permitted and regulated by law (Article 63). Religious education is declared to be of 'national interest' with the same rights as civil and moral education; it is optional in state schools and may be included in the ordinary curriculum in all schools in the country (Article 92).

In September 1971 a declaration was signed in common by representatives of the different churches in the country requesting an end to the state of emergency that had been in effect since November 1970 and to the wave of terror which resulted from it. In response to this ecumenical document without precedent in Guatemala, the government immediately deported all foreigners who had signed it, including Catholic priests, Protestant clergy, and the Episcopalian bishop.

During the presidential election of 8 March 1974, the organizations of the democratic Left regrouped themselves around the Christian Democratic Party in an unsuccessful attempt to defeat the candidate of the extreme Right. Several of its leaders were assassinated following the election. By 1977 a serious feud had developed between the Catholic Church and the officialist political party, previously its staunchest ally. The Bishops' Conference had released a document calling for greater social justice. In reply, the country's vice-president claimed that the Church was becoming a vehicle for Communism by its actions in the name of renewal. The 1970s and 1980s were a bloody era for Guatemala, both from guerilla insurgents and unofficial army death squads, and many Christians and churches were caught in the crossfire. There was not, however, any actual government-sanctioned persecution of Christians. Some positive change came with the more democratic constitution of 1986. The elections of 1990 saw Evangelicals installed as president and vice-president.

BROADCASTING AND MEDIA

Local stations carry Christian programming produced by such groups as IBRA and *Back to the Bible*. AWR maintains a transmitter in Guatemala that blankets most of South America with 8 hours of daily programming in concert with a sister station in Costa Rica. Its studio produces Spanish-language programs. Guatemala is a member of UNDA, and there are 11 Catholic local radio stations operating on shortwave and mediumwave. Shortwave radio programs from other broadcasters (including KNLS, HCJB and TWR) can also be received.

CBN's *700 Club* can be seen on a daily basis on 10 different channels, and heard on UHF stations and radio 4 times a week. Response is followed-up from 3 full-time and 5 volunteer ministry centers. Extensive counselor training, weekly discipleship meetings and Bible studies and neighborhood video/film showings are offered. Other Christian television programs can be received via satellite.

Some 6 million (51%) have seen the 'Jesus' Film. 2 million watched it on a television broadcast, 2.1 million have seen a film team presentation, and 1.8 million were reached by mission agencies using the video, with 275,500 responding.

INTERDENOMINATIONAL ORGANIZATIONS

Although there is no national council of churches, the Evangelical Alliance of Guatemala (Alianza Evangelica de Guatemala, AEG), founded in 1953, provides a united forum for its 17 member churches. A non-official Association of Evangelical Ministers of Guatemala (Associación de Pastors Evangelicos de Guatemala) meets periodically in Guatemala City to discuss co-operative ventures. In 1976, Central America's worst earthquake devastated many areas of Guatemala, killing 24,000, injuring 77,000, leaving 1.2 million homeless and destroying 254,000 homes and over 500 Protestant churches alone. Amongst other Christian responses, the AEG-sponsored CEPA (Comité Evangélica Permanente Ayuda), begun in 1974 representing 45% of all Protestants, administered massive relief aid. In 1977 it was reorganized as CEDI (Evangelical Committee for Integral Development).

The Evangelical Committee for Social and Cultural Service (Junta Evangélica de Servicio Social y Cultural, JESSYC) was formed in 1963 and is responsible for an extensive program of health care, literacy, and leadership training in co-operation with Church World Service. Other important joint projects of Evangelicals included the 1992 Luis Palau evangelistic campaign (with attendance of 700,000 at one meeting), and the DAWN (Discipling A Whole Nation, also known in Guatemala as *Amanacer*) evangelization strategy conference of 1984. There are no Catholic ecumenical organizations.

Guatemala CIty Crusade, December 1977, led by Argentinian evangelist Luis Palau: here in Santiago Atitlan, 1,000 decisions for Christ were recorded.

FUTURE TRENDS AND PROSPECTS

Though the total Christian community will likely remain at 98% for some time, this masks a cauldron of internal changes in which Protestants and Independents are expected to grow from only 7% of the population in 1970 to over 25% by AD 2025. Losses in the Roman Catholic church are minor and the difference is made up through a dramatic rise in double affiliation.

The nonreligious are the only category expected to take large numbers of adherents from Christianity. Even so, this is not expected to exceed 5% before AD 2050.

BIBLIOGRAPHY

'A history of Protestantism in Guatemala.' V. C. Garrard. Ph.D. dissertation, Tulane University, New Orleans, 1987. 332p.

'An historical and critical review of the Full Gospel Church of God of Guatemala.' R. E. Waldrop. D.Miss. thesis, Fuller Theological Seminary, Pasadena, CA, 1993. 215p.

'"And be ye transformed": the socio-economic consequences of the 'evangelical explosion' in Guatemala.' A. L. Sherman. Ph.D. dissertation, University of Virginia, Charlottesville, VA, 1994. 518p.

Caminos de Cristo en Centroamérica. Heredia, Costa Rica: Editorialpec, [1991]. 103p.

Catholic colonialism: a parish history of Guatemala, 1524–1821. A. C. van Oss. *Cambridge Latin American studies*, 57. Cambridge, UK: Cambridge University Press, 1986. 268p.

Chichicastenango: a Guatemalan village. R. Bunzel. Seattle, WA: University of Washington Press, 1952. (Christo-paganism: Quiché syncretism with Catholicism).

Christians in Guatemala's struggle. P. Berryman. London: Catholic Institute for International Relations, 1984. 82p.

Church identity between repression and liberation: the Presbyterian Church in Guatemala. H. Schäfer. Trans., C. Koslofsky. Geneva: World Alliance of Reformed Churches, 1991. 178p.

De indios y cristianos en Guatemala. R. Mondragón. *Claves latinoamericanas.* Mexico City: COPEC/CECOPE, 1983. 239p.

Death and resurrection in Guatemala. F. Bermúdez. Maryknoll, NY: Orbis Books, 1986. 93p.

Directorio de la Arquidiócesis de Guatemala, 1971. Guatemala City: Palacio Arzobispal, 1972.

Disciplina social para la sociedad Guatemalteca desde tres ópticas pentecostales. Mexico City: Ciencia y Tecnología para Guatemala, [1990]. 77p.

Estadistica de la obra religioso–cristiana en Guatemala. L. E. Stahlke. Guatemala City: Iglesia Luterana, 1966. 235p.

'Evangelical Christianity in Guatemala, 1824–1974.' C. S. Cadwallader. Th.D. thesis, Mid-America Baptist Theological Seminary, Memphis, TN, 1975. 153p.

Façades and festivals of Antigua: a guide to church fronts and celebrations. D. L. Jickling & E. Elliott. Antigua, Guatemala: Casa del Sol, 1989. 75p.

God's hour for Guatemala. J. H. Montgomery. San Jose, CA: [DAWN Ministries], 1986.

Guatemala. R. L. Woodward Jr. 2nd ed. *World bibliographical series*, vol. 9. Oxford, UK: CLIO Press, 1992. 290p. (Complements first edition, focusing upon material since 1980).

Historia de la Iglesia de Guatemala. L. Díez de Arriba. , 1988–. (Multivolume work in progress).

Historia de la Iglesia Evangélica en Guatemala. V. Zapata. Guatemala City: Genesis Publicidad, S.A., 1982.

Influencia de la religión en la actitud política de un grupo protestante. M. I. Mendieta Benítez. Guatemala: Facultad de Humanidades, Universidad de San Carlos de Guatemala, 1970. 77p.

Is Latin America turning Protestant? The politics of evangelical growth. D. Stoll. Berkeley & Los Angeles: University of California Press, 1990. 445p. (Focuses especially on Guatemala, Nicaragua, and Ecuador).

Las iglesias evangélicas de Guatemala. L. Corral Prieto. Guatemala: Instituto Teológico Salesiano, 1980. 199p.

'Le culte de Zié: éléments de la religion Kono (Haute Guinée Française),' B. Holas, *Mémoires de l'IFAN* (Dakar), 39 (1954), 217–21. (Study of a river cult).

Los cristianos y los derechos humanos en Guatemala. M. T. Ruiz. San José, Costa Rica: DEI, 1994. 119p.

Los protestantes en Guatemala. J. M. Sarasa. , [1991]. 118p.

Martires de Guatemala. [Guatemala, 1988]. 231p.

Maya history and religion. J. E. S. Thompson. Norman, OK: University of Oklahoma Press, 1970. 415p.

'Maya paganism and Christianity: a history of the fusion of two religions,' D. E. Thompson, in *Nativism and syncretism*, p.1–35. M. S. Edmonson et al. *Publication 19, Middle American Research Institute.* New Orleans: Tulane University, 1960.

'Maya peasant evangelism.' H. Weerstra. Thesis, Fuller Theological Seminary, Pasadena, CA, 1972. 393p.

'Mountain spirits and maize: Catholic conversion and renovation of traditions among the Q'eqchi' of Guatemala.' R. Wilson. Ph.D. dissertation, University of London, 1990. 382p.

Nativism and syncretism. M. S. Edmonson et al. *Publication 19, Middle American Research Institute.* New Orleans: Tulane University, 1960. 203p.

'Piety, power, and politics: the role of religion in the formation of the Guatemalan nation–state, 1839–1871.' D. C. Sullivan-Gonzalez. Ph.D. dissertation, University of Texas at Austin, 1994. 379p.

'Planning for Baptist church growth in Guatemala by a joint task force of the Convention of Baptist Churches of Guatemala and the Guatemala Baptist Mission.' F. E. Johnson. D.Min. thesis, Southwestern Baptist Theological Seminary, Fort Worth, TX, 1993. 157p.

'Protestant and Catholic churches in Guatemala: history of social action and the birth of a popular christian wisdom.' N. F. Colmenares. M.A. thesis, University of Florida, Gainesville, FL, 1992. 154p.

Protestantism in Guatemala: its influence on the bicultural situation, with reference to the Roman Catholic background. G. M. Emery. *Sondeos No. 65.* Cuernavaca, Mexico: CIDOC, 1970. 242p.

'Religion and world–view in a Guatemalan village.' E. M. Mendelson. Microfilm Collection of Manuscripts on Middle American Cultural Anthropology, no. 52, University of Chicago Libraries, 1957.

'Religious conversion in Guatemala.' T. E. Evans. Ph.D. dissertation, University of Pittsburgh, 1990.

Santa Eulalia: the religion of a Cuchumatán Indian town. O. La Farge. Chicago: Chicago University Press, 1947.

'The Catholic church in Guatemala, 1944–1982,' T. P. Melville, *Cultural survival quarterly*, 7 (Spring 1983), 23–7.

'The Evangelical awakening in Guatemala: Fundamentalist impact on education and media,' S. Rose & Q. J. Schultze, in *Fundamentalisms and society: reclaiming the sciences, the family, and education*, p.415–51. M. E. Marty & R. S. Appleby (eds). Chicago: University of Chicago Press, 1993.

'The king, the traitor and the Cross: an interpretation of a highland Maya religious conflict,' E. M. Mendelson, *Diogenes*, 21 (Spring 1958), 1–10. (Mayan Judas-Iscariot worship).

'The Maya evangelical church in Guatemala.' A. J. Lloret. Th.D. thesis, Dallas Theological Seminary, Dallas, TX, 1976. 357p.

'The process and the implications of change in the Guatemalan Catholic Church.' J. L. Chea. Ph.D. dissertation, University of Texas at Austin, 1988. 710p.

'The roots of fundamentalism in liberal Guatemala: missionary ideologies and local response, 1882–1944.' T. E. Bogenschild. Ph.D. dissertation, University of California, Berkeley, CA, 1992. 307p.

The santos of Guatemala. T. Pasinski. Guatemala City: DIDACSA, 1990. 2 vols.

The social and religious life of a Guatemalan village. C. Wagley. *Memoirs of the American Anthropological Association, no. 71.* Menasha, WI: American Anthropological Association, 1949. 150p.

The two crosses of Todos Santos: survivals of Mayan religious ritual. M. Oakes. *Bollingen series 27.* New York: Pantheon, 1951. (Mam shamans).

Unidos en la esperanza: presencia de la Iglesia en la reconstrucción de Guatemala. Episcopado de Guatemala. Guatemala: Libreria Loyala, 1976. 58p.

'What kind of church?: integral church growth: research and analysis of the qualitative nature of the Evangelical Church in Guatemala.' S. L. Herod. Ed.D. thesis, School of Intercultural Studies, Biola University, La Mirada, CA, 1991. 316p.

What prize awaits us: letters from Guatemala. B. Kita. Maryknoll, NY: Orbis Books, 1988. 254p.

Country Table 2. Organized churches and denominations in Guatemala.

Official name (bold type = church with over 10% of all affiliated) 1	*Begun* 2	*Type* 3	*Counc* 4	*Congs* 5	*Adults* 6	*Affiliated 1970* 7	*Affiliated 1995* 8	*G%* 9	*Names, notes, and other statistics* (see Codebook, Part 3) 10
Asambleas de Dios en Guatemala	1937	P-Pe2	ZF...	3,659	148,529	60,000	224,751	5.42	*Assemblies of God.* M=AoG(USA). 501n,14x,1i,1k,2s(148), W=77%,1373Y,1096z.
Asambleas de Hermanos	1925	P-CBr	x....	750	30,000	8,000	75,000	9.37	*Assemblies of Brethren. Open Brethren.* M=CMML(USA, UK, NZ). South coast. 11f.
Asambleas de Igls Cristianas	1963	I-3gL	.....	33	3,000	1,270	6,670	6.86	*Assemblies of Christian Churches.*
Asambleas Locales	c1990	I-3nC	.....	2	100	–	300	20.00	*Little Flock. Local Churches.* Chinese.
Asoc de Igls Ev Hispanoamericanas	1947	P-Eva	x...C	100	7,000	10,000	15,000	1.64	*Assoc of Spanish American Chs. Cruzada Hispanoamericana.* M=SAIM(USA). W=80%.
Asociacón Ev Verbo de Dios	1976	I-3gL	.....	274	26,000	–	65,000	5.26	AEVD. *Word of God Ev Assoc.* Prosperity gospel. M=Gospel Outreach (USA).
Asoc Monte Basan de Igs Evangélicas		I-Eva	.....	106	8,500	6,250	21,300	0.05	*Mt Basan Association of Evangelical Churches..*
Asociación Emanual (Guatemala)	1937	P-Hol	.....	20	2,000	2,000	3,000	1.64	Linked with M=Emmanuel Association (USA), 2 schools. 7f,1p(10),W=80%.
Bambinos de Dios	c1985	I-mar	.....	1	14	–	33	10.00	*Children of God.* Mission from USA.
Consejo Nacional de Iglesias Luteranas	c1935	P-Lut	e...C	32	1,298	2,583	4,132	1.90	*CNIL. National Council of Lutheran Chs.* 1947, M=LCMS. Germans. 1n,5x,2h,W=30%,78Yy.
Convención Bautista de Guatemala	1946	P-Bap	T...C	152	16,500	16,000	55,000	5.06	*CBG. Baptist Convention of G.* 1948, M=FMB-SBC(USA). 32n,7x,26f,4p,2s(26). W=70%,386Y.
Fraternidad Cristiana de Guatemala	1979	I-3pL	x....	20	5,000	–	10,000	6.25	*Christian Brotherhood of G.* Clinics, choirs, lyceum, radio, cable TV, many cell groups.
Iglesia Adventista del Séptimo Día	1908	P-Adv	x....	158	40,000	25,000	114,000	6.26	*Seventh-day Adventists, Guatemala Mission,* CAmerican UM. 6nx,12f,1h,1r,148t,758Y.
Igl Apostólica de la Fe en Cristo Jesus		I-3oL	x....	80	8,000	1,000	22,900	0.05	*IAFCJ Apostolic Ch of the Faith in CJ.* Mexican. Mestizos. 14m,2f,1s,47z.
Iglesia Católica en Guatemala:	1524	R-Lat	B.LDR	1,217	4,539,900	4,346,449	8,401,071	2.67	*Catholic Ch in Guatemala.* C=14+2+27. 255n 539x 1488m 1542w 267343Yy
M Guatemala	1534	R-Lat	Bs	131	1,261,000	886,972	2,333,000	3.94	*Arquidiócesis de Guatemala.* City south. M=CM. 82n 382x 1274m 785w 135500Yy
D Escuintla	1969	R-Lat	Bs	219	330,000	200,000	610,000	4.56	Until 1994 *Prelatura Nullius de Escuintla.* South. 0n 1x 1m 32w 4822Yy
D Huehuetenango	1961	R-Lat	Bs	30	248,000	320,000	459,000	1.45	In west. Extensive social action program. 16n 4x 11m 56w 11541Yy
D Jalapa en Guatemala	1951	R-Lat	Bs	630	313,000	420,527	580,891	1.30	*Diocesis de Jalapa.* Near El Salvador. M=CM. 20n 6x 8m 60w 13084Yy
D Quetzaltenango (Los Altos)	1921	R-Lat	Bs	31	508,000	585,000	940,000	1.92	In southwest. Strong Mayan christo-paganism. M=SJ. 34n 25x 33m 146w 18248Yy
D San Marcos	1951	R-Lat	Bs	29	438,000	315,000	810,000	3.85	In extreme southwest, bordering on Mexico. 18n 7x 9m 39w 9504Yy
D Santa Cruz del Quiché	1967	R-Lat	Bs	19	210,000	240,000	388,000	1.94	Maya christo-pagan stronghold at Chichicastenango. 12n 7x 12m 75w 9055Yy
D Sololá	1951	R-Lat	Bs	37	428,000	510,128	792,000	1.78	Christo-paganism widespread. M=OFM. 36n 9x 11m 80w 25200Yy
D Vera Paz (Coban)	1921	R-Lat	Bs	29	367,000	323,400	679,000	3.01	Tropical rain-forest in north of diocese. 14n 58x 69m 147w 14100Yy
D Zacapa	1951	R-Lat	Bs	23	191,000	233,500	354,000	1.68	East centre, bordering Honduras. M=OFM. 12n 10x 16m 45w 7273Yy
PN Santo Cristo de Esquipulas	1956	R-Lat	Bs	6	17,300	21,922	32,180	1.55	Famed pilgrimage centre (Black Christ). M=OSB. 0n 10x 18m 10w 755Yy
VA El Petén	1951	R-Lat	P cm	15	94,600	110,000	175,000	1.87	Tropical rain-forest. M=OP,CM,IEME. Charismatics. 4n 8x 10m 24w 5390Yy
VA Izabal	1968	R-Lat	Pop	18	134,000	180,000	248,000	1.29	Tropical rain-forest, bordering on sea. Many Blacks. 7n 12x 16m 43w 12871Yy
Iglesia Católica Nacional Guatemalteca	1978	I-ReC	.....	20	3,900	–	7,000	5.88	*Guatemalan National Catholic Ch.* Split ex RCC by ultraliberal RC priest Padre Chemita. 8n.
Iglesia de Cristo	1959	I-Dis	x....	225	9,000	2,000	22,500	10.17	*Chs of Christ.* M=CC(Non-Instrumental) (USA). Has a colony in Petén. 10m,12f,1h.
Iglesia de Dios de la Profecía	1923	P-Pe3	Z....	187	9,000	5,000	22,500	6.20	*CoG of Prophecy.* Schism by Guatemalans, who then align with M=CGP(USA).
Igl de Dios de la Profecía Universal	c1950	I-3pL	.....	120	5,000	1,000	7,000	8.09	Indigenous Guatemalan denomination.
Iglesia de Dios del Evangelio Completo	1916	P-Pe3	ZF...	1,512	70,872	30,000	187,000	7.59	*IDEC. Full Gospel CoG. IdD Pentecostal.* Largely Mayans. M=CoG(Cleveland). 391n,8f,1s(44).
Iglesia de Dios Galilea	1954	I-Hol	.....	217	13,000	2,500	43,300	12.08	*Ch of God (Galilee).* Indigenous holiness body. 12n,165Y,90z.
Iglesia de Dios Independiente	c1970	I-3pL	.....	30	1,000	1,200	2,000	2.06	Locally-initiated pentecostal body begun by Guatemalans. HQ Tontonicapan.
Iglesia de Dios Misionera	1954	I-3pL	.....	183	11,000	3,000	33,300	10.11	Schism ex CGP. Link with M=Missionary Ch of God (Houston, USA), Escuintla. 114nm.
Iglesia de Dios Nueva Jerusalém	c1984	I-3pL	.....	119	11,900	–	29,800	9.09	*New Jerusalem Ch of God.* In Santa Maria Chiquimula, Tontonicapan. Ethnic church.
Iglesia de Dios Pentecostal	1965	P-Pe2	.....	125	6,250	4,240	17,900	5.93	*Pentecostal Ch of God.* M=PCG(USA).
Iglesia de Dios (Anderson)	c1950	P-Hol	x...C	136	9,500	3,000	19,000	7.66	*Ch of God.* M=CoG(Anderson) (USA). Some work in Cakchiquel. No missionaries. 8n,1s.
Iglesia de Dios (Bethesda)		I-3pL	.....	40	4,000	2,500	10,000	0.05	*Church of God (Bethesda). Grassroots pentecostals.*
Iglesia de JC de los Santos de los UD	c1952	m-LdS	x....	288	53,500	15,721	99,000	7.64	*Latter-Day Saints. Mormons.* M=CJCLdS(USA). Maya Indians. 290f.
Iglesia Defensores de la Fe	1956	I-3pL	.....	30	3,000	2,000	5,000	3.73	*IDF. Defenders of the Faith Ch.* Loose affiliation with Mexico and DFM(USA) 9n.
Iglesia del Biblia Abierto	1976	I-3pL	.....	11	474	–	1,190	5.26	*Open Bible Standard Church.* M=OBSC.
Iglesia del Evangelio Cuadrangular	1945	P-Pe2	ZF...	22	4,370	5,000	6,239	0.89	*International Ch of the Foursquare Gospel.* M=ICFG(USA). 23nm,2f,1p(8),W=43%,97Y.
Iglesia Ev Cristiana Calvario	1942	I-3pL	.....	462	60,000	28,100	167,000	7.39	*Calvary Christian Ministries. ICC.* Begun by M=SAM, Became neopentecostal in 1963.
Iglesia Emanuel (Jalapa)	1945	I-Hol	xF...	53	1,600	1,000	4,000	5.70	*Emmanuel Mission, Jalapa.* 1960, M=Evangelistic Faith Missions. 16n,8f,1k,1n(25).
Iglesia Episcopal: D Guatemala	c1870	A-Hig	aw.R.	25	1,000	750	1,520	2.87	In *ECUSA Province IX.* 80% Ladino, 10% UK/USA White, 7% Black, 3% Kekchi. 3n,4x,1s,15y.
Iglesia Ev Centroamericana en G	1899	P-Eva	xM..C	1,167	67,700	30,000	169,000	7.16	*IECG,ICG.* M=CAM(USA). A=1927. West Indians: Cakchiquel, Conob, Chuj. 70n,93f,1h,1k,3p,1s.
Iglesia Evangélica del Príncipe de Paz	1945	I-3pL	x....	900	72,000	20,000	180,000	9.19	*IPP,PDP. Ch of the Prince of Peace.* Ex AoG. 10 Indian peoples. Peten. Exorcism, healing.
Iglesia Evangelica Menonita	1968	P-Men	G...C	54	3,500	82	5,000	17.87	*Ev Mennonite Ch.* M=EMBMC(USA). Non-German origin. HQ Chimaltenango. 10f,1h.
Iglesia Evangélica Betania	1972	P-Ref	.....	111	10,000	2,860	28,600	4.35	*Bethany Evangelical Church.* Begun as neopentecostal movement within Presbyterian chs.
Iglesia Ev del Nazareno de Guatemala	1904	P-Hol	xF..C	181	24,014	8,260	38,341	6.33	*Nazarenes.* M=CoN(USA). 25n,2x,48m,6f,4h,2p,2s(108),98t(9697),W=39%,469Y.
Iglesia Gethsemane	1928	I-Eva	.T..C	44	4,000	2,000	8,000	5.70	Misión Ev Independiente. Long history of litigation, schisms, 8n,2x,W=42%,21Y
Iglesia Metodista Primitiva	1921	P-Hol	VF..C	56	3,500	2,100	5,500	3.93	*IMP.* Main foreign field of M=Primitive Methodist Ch (USA). 95% Quiche. 15n,14f,1H,4h,1u.
Iglesia Menonita de Guatemala	1977	P-Men	.....	7	500	–	750	5.56	*Mennonite Ch of G.* M=EMC.
Iglesia Misíonero Alianza	1969	P-Hol	.....	46	2,496	4,830	4,981	0.12	*Christian and Missionary Alliance Church.* M=CMA(USA).
Iglesia Monte Sinaí		I-Eva	.....	50	3,000	400	10,000	0.05	*Mount Sinai Church.* Indigenous body in capital and El Progreso department.
Iglesia Nacional Presbiteriana de G	1882	P-Ref	R...C	178	23,000	25,000	50,000	2.81	*INPG,NPC. National Presbyterian Ch.* M=UPUSA. A=1962. Many Quiché, Mam. 45n,18f,5h,6r,1s
Iglesia Presbiteriana Biblica de G	1962	I-Ref	.TT..	136	9,500	1,350	23,800	12.16	*Presbiterio Biblico Fundamentalista.* 1964, M=IBPFM. 9n,1s,W=70%,104Yy.
Iglesias Ev Amigos de Centroamérica	1902	P-Qua	QF..C	327	9,810	7,489	24,500	4.86	*CAYM of Friends.* M=California YM. Northeast. 29n,6x,11f,1p,1s,W=56%,175Y.
Iglesias radiofónicas solitarias	c1950	I-3rL	.....	100	4,000	700	6,000	8.97	Isolated radio believers. R=4400 (TGNA,HCJB,FEBC, Radio Vatican), T=1150 (ICI).
Manatial de Vida Eterna	c1985	I-3gL	.....	79	7,500	1,710	21,400	10.00	*Springs of Eternal Life Ev Ch.*
Misión Bautista Internacional	1971	I-Bap	.....	8	2,000	–	4,000	4.17	*Baptist International Mission.* M=BIM(USA).
Mision Cristiana Elim	1965	P-Pe2	.....	714	50,000	4,440	139,000	14.77	*Elim Christian Mission.* MCE.
Misión Evangélica del Espíritu Santo	c1985	I-3gL	.....	333	30,000	–	93,800	10.00	*Evangelical Mission of the Holy Spirit.*
Misión Evangélica Interdenominacional	1938	I-Non	.T...	50	1,500	1,500	4,410	4.41	*Ev Interdenominational Mission.* Split by missionary ex CAM(USA). In capital.
Misión Evangélica Puerto del Cielo	c1985	I-3gL	.....	55	5,500	–	15,700	10.00	*Door to Heaven Evangelical Mission.*
Misión Mundo Unido	1947	P-Hol	xF..C	20	700	1,710	2,000	0.63	*United World Mission.* 1953, M=UWM(USA). HQ Guatemala City. 6n,1m,6f,1s.
Misiones Mundiales de Guatemala	1962	I-Non	x....	39	3,500	3,000	8,750	4.37	M=World-Wide Missions (USA). Linked with Evangelicals from Pasadena, CA (USA).
Templo Espiritualista		m-Spi	....	2	100	100	200	0.05	*Spiritualist Temple.* One congregation in Guatemala City.
Testigos de Jehová	1920	m-Jeh	x....	184	12,230	5,000	33,500	7.91	*JWs..* First English-speaking convert 1920, Spanish 1923. (1975) 283Y. (1995) 1368Y.
Unificación Evangélica de Pentecostés		I-3pL	C	30	1,500	1,000	3,000	0.05	*Ev Pentecostal Union.* Loose federation in Escuintla and Guatemala City. 3n.
Other Protestant denominations		P-	.....	200	16,500	12,000	30,000	0.05	Total about 30 (see list below).
Other charismatic networks	c1985	I-3gL	.....	100	10,000	–	20,000	10.00	Grassroots churches; also New Apostolic Church (375 members).
Other indigenous churches		I-	.....	50	5,000	7,000	10,000	0.05	Total about 40 (see list below).
Doubly-affiliated		2-aff			-653,000	-94,870	-1,263,638		Evangelicals who also are or were baptized Roman Catholics.
Totals				**15,630**	**4,844,257**	**4,633,224**	**9,380,000**		

Churches, members, growth, 1900-2025	*Congs*	*Adults*	*Affiliated*	*G%*	*Total denominations*	*6 Megablocs:* *O*	*R*	*A*	*P*	*I*	*m*
Total churches, members, and denominations (mid-1900)	1,000	835,000	1,560,900	1.57	4	0	1	1	2	0	0
Total churches, members, and denominations (mid-1970)	3,954	2,477,123	4,633,224	1.57	79	0	1	1	35	39	3
Total churches, members, and denominations (mid-1990)	8,000	4,256,000	8,240,000	2.92	156	0	1	1	53	98	3
Total churches, members, and denominations (mid-1995)	15,630	4,844,257	9,380,000	2.63	159	0	1	1	53	101	3
Total churches, members, and denominations (mid-2000)	17,000	5,518,000	10,684,153	2.64	162	0	1	1	53	104	3
Total churches, members, and denominations (mid-2025)	26,000	9,555,000	18,500,000	2.22	280	1	1	1	70	200	7

NOTES ON TABLE ABOVE

NATIONAL COUNCILS (Column 4, 5th letter).

- E = Alianza Evangélica de Guatemala (AEG) (Evangelical Alliance of Guatemala).
- F = Council of Evangelical Churches of Guatemala (CIEDEG).
- R = Conferencia Episcopal de Guatemala (CEG) (Episcopal Conference of Guatemala).

OTHER PROTESTANT DENOMINATIONS. These include: Apostolic Ch of Pentecost (Canada, 2 missionaries), Apostolic Lutheran Ch of America (Laestadians), Baptist International Missions (1969), Baptist Missionary Association of America (1964), Children of God International, Christian and Missionary Alliance (1970), Christian Nationals Evangelism Commission (1963), Conservative Mennonite Fellowship (1964), Iglesia Bautista Libre, Pentecostal Ch of God of America, Salvation Army, Union Church (Guatemala City), United Evangelical Churches, World Baptist Fellowship Mission Agency (1967).

OTHER INDIGENOUS CHURCHES. These include: Assembly of Christian Churches (1962) from Puerto Rico, Iglesia Cinco Calles Misionera Primitiva, Iglesia de Dios del Séptimo Día, Iglesia Fuenta de Vida (Fountain of Life Ch), Iglesia La Luz del Mundo (Aaronistas), Iglesias del Aposento Alto (Churches of the Upper Room), and churches among the West Indian Black population. A USA Black mission, National Baptist Convention USA, also began work in 1964.

OTHER MARGINAL PROTESTANT BODIES. Church of Christ, Scientist (Guatemala Society).

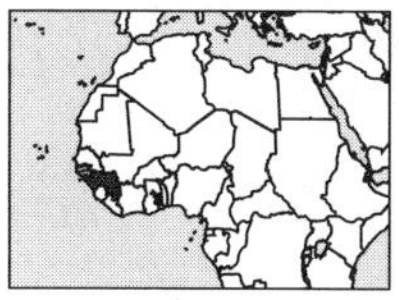

GUINEA

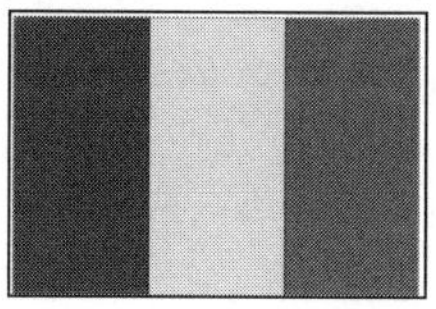

SECULAR DATA, AD 2000

STATE
Official name: La République de Guinée (The Republic of Guinea).
Short name: Guinea. **Adjective of nationality:** Guinean.
Flag: Red, yellow, and green bars.
Area: 245,857 sq. km. (94,926 sq. mi.).
Government: Unitary multiparty republic with one legislative house, since 1993 (12th century in empire of Ghana, 1849 French protectorate, 1958 Independence as republic, 1958 one-party Socialist state).
Legislature: National Assembly, 114 members.
Official language: French (Français).
Monetary unit: 1 Guinean franc (GF) = 100 cauris. **US$1=** GF 1,243.
Chief cities: CONAKRY (Konakry) 1,896,000; Labe 166,609; Kankan 151,462; Kindia 121,170; Nzerekore 90,477.
Political divisions: 33 provinces.
Armed forces: 10,000.

DEMOGRAPHY
Population: 7,430,000.
Population density: 30.2/sq. km. (78.2/sq. mi.).
Under 15 years: 3,269,000.
Growth rate p.a.: 2.42% (births 40.37, deaths 15.96).
Mortality: Infant, per 1,000: 114.4; **Maternal per 100,000:** 1,600.0.
Life expectancy: 49 (male 48, female 49).
Household size: 4.7. **Floor area per person, sq.m:** 10.0.
Major languages: Fulani, Mandingo, French, Susu, Kpelle, Loma, Kissi, and about 15 smaller languages.
Urban dwellers: 32.78%. **Urban growth rate p.a.:** 4.89%.
Labor force: 39%.

ETHNOLINGUISTIC PEOPLES
37.0% Fula Jalon (Futa Dyalon); 25.6% Southern Maninka; 12.1% Susu (Soso); 5.1% Guerze (Kpelle, Pessy); 4.8% Kissi (Northern Kisi).

ECONOMY
National income p.a. per person: US$550; **per family:** US$2,585.

EDUCATION
Adult literacy: 35% (male 49%, female 21%). **Schools:** 2,849.
Universities: 10. **School enrolment:** female/male: 19%/41%.

HEALTH
Access to health services: 80%. **Access to safe water:** 62%.
Hospitals: 38 (6 beds per 10,000). **Doctors:** 773.
Blind: 45,000. **Deaf:** 471,700. **Murder rate:** <1.
Lepers: 250,000. **Underweight prevalence under 5:** 26%.

LITERATURE
New book titles p.a.: 370 (50 p.a. per million). **Periodicals:** 4.
Newspapers: 1 daily.

COMMUNICATION (per 1,000 people)
Phones: 1 (37% mobile). **Radios:** 35. **TV sets:** 9.
Daily newspaper circulation: 2. **Computers:** 3.

REFUGEES
Alien refugees from other countries: 640,000.

HUMAN LIFE AND LIBERTY (optimum condition=100.0%)
HDI: 27.1. **HSI:** 14.0. **HFI:** 15.0. **EFL:** 33.0.

Country Table 1. **Religious adherents in Guinea, AD 1900-2025.**

Year	1900		1970		mid-1990		Annual change, 1990-2000				mid-1995		mid-2000		mid-2025	
Name	Adherents	%	Adherents	%	Adherents	%	Natural	Conversion	Total	Rate	Adherents	%	Adherents	%	Adherents	%
Muslims	574,200	58.0	2,651,280	68.0	3,847,000	66.9	111,967	3,215	115,182	2.65	4,798,220	67.1	4,998,824	67.3	8,866,400	71.0
Ethnoreligionists	414,015	41.8	1,188,364	30.5	1,676,760	29.1	48,802	-4,507	44,295	2.37	2,060,000	28.8	2,119,710	28.5	3,000,000	24.0
Christians	**1,785**	**0.2**	**55,256**	**1.4**	**220,000**	**3.8**	**6,438**	**1,085**	**7,523**	**2.98**	**280,000**	**3.9**	**295,229**	**4.0**	**580,000**	**4.6**
PROFESSION																
crypto-Christians	285	0.0	5,756	0.2	0	0.0	0	0	0	0.00	0	0.0	0	0.0	0	0.0
professing Christians	**1,500**	**0.2**	**49,500**	**1.3**	**220,000**	**3.8**	**6,438**	**1,085**	**7,523**	**2.98**	**280,000**	**3.9**	**295,229**	**4.0**	**580,000**	**4.6**
AFFILIATION																
unaffiliated Christians	0	0.0	0	0.0	55,820	1.0	1,625	-816	809	1.36	68,262	1.0	63,907	0.9	27,300	0.2
affiliated Christians	**1,785**	**0.2**	**55,256**	**1.4**	**164,180**	**2.9**	**4,813**	**1,901**	**6,714**	**3.49**	**211,738**	**3.0**	**231,322**	**3.1**	**552,700**	**4.4**
Roman Catholics	1,785	0.2	48,356	1.2	85,000	1.5	2,474	726	3,200	3.25	109,297	1.5	117,000	1.6	300,000	2.4
Protestants	0	0.0	3,100	0.1	47,000	0.8	1,368	850	2,218	3.94	61,250	0.9	69,182	0.9	130,000	1.0
Independents	0	0.0	1,300	0.0	30,000	0.5	873	427	1,300	3.67	38,996	0.6	43,000	0.6	120,000	1.0
Anglicans	0	0.0	2,000	0.1	1,500	0.0	44	-54	-10	-0.69	1,500	0.0	1,400	0.0	1,500	0.0
Marginal Christians	0	0.0	500	0.0	680	0.0	20	-14	6	0.85	695	0.0	740	0.0	1,200	0.0
Trans-megabloc groupings																
Evangelicals	0	0.0	3,500	0.1	40,300	0.7	1,173	207	1,380	2.99	51,785	0.7	54,100	0.7	96,500	0.8
Pentecostals/Charismatics	0	0.0	1,300	0.0	46,000	0.8	1,339	301	1,640	3.10	58,320	0.8	62,400	0.8	125,000	1.0
Great Commission Christians	**1,700**	**0.2**	**43,000**	**1.1**	**104,000**	**1.8**	**3,027**	**3,551**	**6,578**	**5.02**	**130,180**	**1.8**	**169,775**	**2.3**	**370,000**	**3.0**
Nonreligious	0	0.0	4,000	0.1	8,000	0.1	233	215	448	4.55	10,800	0.2	12,481	0.2	40,000	0.3
Atheists	0	0.0	1,000	0.0	3,000	0.1	87	-6	81	2.43	3,700	0.1	3,814	0.1	10,000	0.1
Baha'is	0	0.0	100	0.0	240	0.0	7	-2	5	1.84	280	0.0	288	0.0	600	0.0
World A (unevangelized persons)	924,660	93.4	3,432,299	88.0	3,700,465	64.3	107,689	-43,988	63,701	1.60	4,398,852	61.5	4,339,120	58.4	6,798,368	54.4
World B (evangelized non-Christians)	63,555	6.4	412,784	10.6	1,834,535	31.9	53,407	42,903	96,310	4.30	2,473,752	34.6	2,795,651	37.6	5,118,632	41.0
World C (Christians)	1,785	0.2	55,256	1.4	220,000	3.8	6,438	1,085	7,523	2.98	280,000	3.9	295,229	4.0	580,000	4.6
Country's population	**990,000**	**100.0**	**3,900,340**	**100.0**	**5,755,000**	**100.0**	**167,534**	**0**	**167,534**	**2.59**	**7,152,605**	**100.0**	**7,430,000**	**100.0**	**12,497,000**	**100.0**

COLUMNS, ROWS.
For meanings and definitions, see Codebook (Part 3). Note that, by definition, total 'Christians' = professing + crypto-Christians, which also = affiliated + unaffiliated Christians, and also = Great Commission Christians + latent Christians. Percentages may not always total exactly, due to rounding.

CENSUSES.
1958 (estimated): 62.0% Muslims, 36.5% ethnoreligionists, 1.5% Christians. **1983:** 86.9% Muslims, 4.6% animists, 4.3% Christians, 4.2% other religionists.

NOTES ON RELIGIONS
ATHEISTS. Intellectuals, a few communists.
BAHA'IS. In 1 local spiritual assembly (1973), rising to 12 (1996).
COUNTRY'S POPULATION. Since the 1970s, several hundred thousand had fled as refugees to neighboring countries.
CRYPTO-CHRISTIANS. Christians affiliated to churches but unknown as such to state or society; unorganized individuals in the recognized churches, members of clandestine churches, and a few isolated radio believers.
ETHNORELIONISTS. Tribes over 50% traditionalist (animist) in 1995: Kissi (72%), Loma (58%), Gbande (75%), Koranko (70%, and 30% Muslim), Malinke (50%), Yalunka (99%). The Konyanke are about 60% Muslim and 40% traditionalist.
INDEPENDENTS. In about 5 groupings in 1995, including isolated radio believers (see Table 2).
MUSLIMS. Sunnis (of the Malikite rite). Islamized tribes: Dialonke, Sarakole, Susu (85%). Most Muslims belong to the Tijaniya brotherhood; there are also some Ahmadis, Qadianis linked with Pakistani missionaries (enumerated here under Muslims although declared non-Muslim by Pakistan). *Conversion of Islam.* These are taking place among ethnoreligionists, although the forest tribes, Guerze, Loma (Toma) and Kissi form a resistant barrier. The Kissi remain only 8% islamized, the Coniagui-Bassari 3%. A number of Christians also defect to Islam each year, mostly through marriage to Muslims. *Hajj pilgrims to Mecca.* (1970 2,631; (1974) 988; (1975) 986; (1976) 1,334.

Great Commission Instrument Panel: status of Guinea (for explanation see start of Part 4)

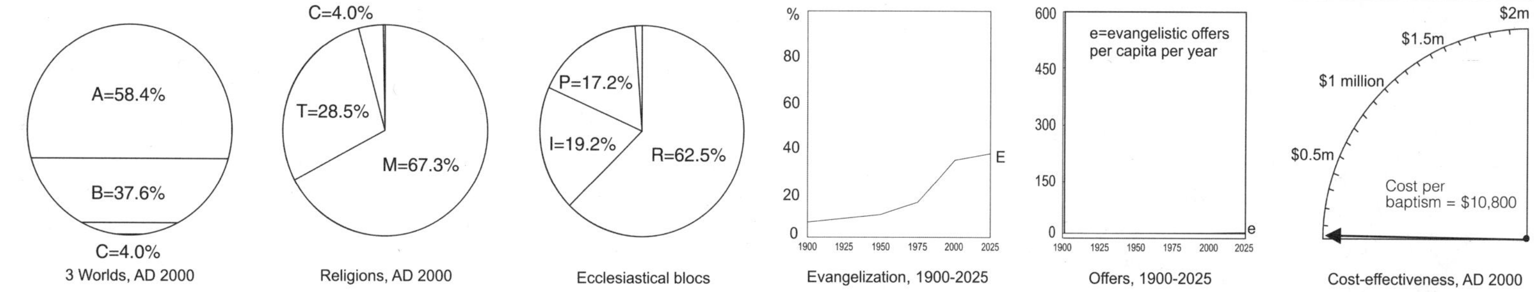

Country status. Guinea is located on the southwestern edge of the great bulge of West Africa. It is part of francophone Africa, and is notable as representing the fusion of Peul, Soussou, and Malinke cultures. Bauxite and aluminum deposits make up 90% of Guinea's foreign exchange.

HUMAN LIFE AND LIBERTY

Human need and development. Although one of the earliest francophone countries to achieve independence, Guinea has been moving downhill since then. Almost all the social and economic ills to which contemporary Africa is heir, exists in Guinea: Food shortages, rapid inflation, unemployment, black market, smuggling, political corruption, ethnic conflicts, racial discrimination, human rights abuses, police brutality, to name only the most serious. The economy was virtually destroyed under the 26-year rule of president Sekou Toure. By the time Toure died in 1984, the standard of living in the country, once among the more prosperous French colonies, had sunk to the bottom among African countries. Housing is primitive, consisting generally of round, windowless dwellings made of wattle and daub or mud bricks, with a floor of packed earth and a conical roof of thatch. Severe health problems range from malnutrition to lack of adequate sanitation and poor health services. A host of communicable diseases still ravage the countryside. Among the chief endemic diseases are malaria, venereal diseases, and tuberculosis. Malaria is prevalent in the swampy coastal areas. Venereal diseases are prevalent as are bilharziasis, sleeping sickness, and parasitic worm infections. Rural folks resort to folk medicine more than modern medicine, attributing ailments to witchcraft or malevolent spirits. A formal system of social security or

Country summary. **Worlds A, B, C by ethnolinguistic peoples, cities, and major civil divisions in Guinea.**

	PEOPLES							CITIES							CIVIL DIVISIONS						
World	Num	Pop 2000	C%	Christians	E%	U%	Unevangelized	Num	Pop 2000	C%	Christians	E%	U%	Unevangelized	Num	Pop 2000	C%	Christians	E%	U%	Unevangelized
A	33	6,583,846	0.58	38,114	39	61	4,044,144	5	2,425,718	3.32	80,532	45	55	1,325,850	32	6,523,849	2.33	151,917	40	60	3,897,762
B	5	835,206	22.11	184,663	65	35	292,846	0	0	0.00	0	0	0	0	1	906,498	8.76	79,405	52	48	439,253
C	6	11,294	75.64	8,543	100	0	26	0	0	0.00	0	0	0	0	0	0	0.00	0	0	0	0
Total	**44**	**7,430,346**	**3.11**	**231,320**	**42**	**58**	**4,337,016**	**5**	**2,425,718**	**3.32**	**80,532**	**45**	**55**	**1,325,850**	**33**	**7,430,347**	**3.11**	**231,322**	**42**	**58**	**4,337,015**

welfare exists only for the few people who are gainfully employed in the public or private sector.

Human rights and freedoms. Guinea has not known human rights since independence, either under the dictator Sekou Toure or under his successor Lansana Conte. However, under president Conte, the dictatorship has become more benign and less paranoid than it was under Toure. The principal human rights abuses include unlawful violence and killings by poorly trained security forces, use of arbitrary arrest and detention to harass opponents of the government, restrictions on the rights of free speech and assembly, and discrimination against women. Ineffective administrative controls and limited resources make the legal system vulnerable to abuses. In politically sensitive cases, judges obtain the advice of the government on how they should decide. Suspected criminals are often lynched with police approval. A new press law, while proclaiming freedom of the press, is narrow and restrictive. It prohibits insulting the president, chanting seditious cries in public, as well as incitement to violence. Publishers, authors, printers and vendors are subject to severe penalties if they run afoul of the law. Public gatherings may take place only with prior notification to the government. Ethnic identification is strong in Guinea and many of the laws are directed against manifestations of ethnic hatred. Although all major ethnic groups are represented in the cabinet, a disproportionate number belong to the Soussou from which president Conte hails. Wifebeating is a major cause of domestic violence to which the law does not provide a remedy. Female genital mutilation is practiced by about 60% of Guineans irrespective of religion.

Human environment. The coastal swamplands are breeding grounds of many kinds of disease-carrying vectors, such as those that cause river blindness and sleeping sickness. Mismanagement of land has resulted in widespread contamination, depletion and erosion of soil, the loss of vegetative cover, desertification, and groundwater pollution. Guinea's first national park and biosphere reserves were set up in the 1980s to protect the dense tropical forests in the southern mountains.

Ethnoreligionists. Masked traditional dancers at Nzérékoré among Guerze (Kpelle), who are still 60% pagans.

NON-CHRISTIAN RELIGIONS

Islam was introduced into Guinea by the Fulani during the 18th century in a jihad from 1725 on, and is now the majority religion of the country. The Dialonke, Sarakole, and Susu peoples are highly islamized. Most Guinean Muslims belong to the Tijaniva brotherhood.

Traditional religions are followed by nearly 30% of the population. Tribes that have resisted both Christianity and Islam, and that remain 80% traditionalist or more include the Bande (Bandi, Gbandi), Bassari, Kissi, Konyagi (Coniagui, Tenda), Limba (Yimbe), Loko (Landogo), Mano (Ngere, Mawe), and the Papel (Pepel). As in other parts of Africa, magical practices, ancestral veneration, and a belief in God are characteristic of these religions. The supreme being is called Hala by the Kissi, and Hounounga (Unknown) by the Tenda. The Malinke have 3 names for God: Gala, Guele, and Jalang.

Muslims. Fulah boy reads Quranic tablet at Gaoual, northwest of Fouta Djallon.

CHRISTIANITY

Guinea was part of the large medieval empires of Ghana (prior to the 13th century) and of Malinke which began to decline 2 centuries later. During the 15th century, Portuguese ships penetrated further south along the West African coast, passing Guinea by 1462. An attempt was made to introduce Christianity when the Portuguese tried to establish trading posts along the Atlantic coast, but these Christian overtures diminished as Portugal declined in power. A Muslim holy war was proclaimed in 1725 which initiated the process of islamization among the indigenous peoples. French rights to the Guinea coast were affirmed at the Treaty of Paris in 1814, and in 1849 the area was declared a French protectorate. By 1882 France had begun to occupy the interior, and in 1891 Guinea became a colony. Catholic missionaries entered in 1877 and Protestants in 1918, but by 1995 Christians still constituted only about 2% of the population.

CATHOLIC CHURCH. Holy Ghost priests opened a mission at Boff in 1877 and a second one near Conakry in 1890, with White Fathers beginning work in the southeast in 1896. In 1897 Guinea became a prefecture. By 1900 there were 1,800 Catholics, rising to 6,000 (including catechumens) in 1920, 20,000 in 1949 and 26,500 in 1965. The first Guinean priest was ordained in 1940, and by 1949 another priest and 13 African sisters had been added. In 1955 an archdiocese was established at Conakry, with the first African appointed archbishop in 1962.

Up to 1967, the archdiocese of Conakry in the west and the apostolic prefecture of Kankan in the center were entrusted to the Holy Ghost mission and the diocese of N'Zekekore to White Fathers. In 1967 all foreign missionaries were expelled (including 73 priests, 10 brothers, 55 sisters and 16 women lay missionaries), and only 8 Guinean priests were left to carry the entire work, which created a serious pastoral crisis. However, by 1976 there were 15 African priests, including one from Mali, and 24 sisters, 4 being from Upper Volta. In addition there were 18 major seminarians, and 60 minor seminarians at Kindia in the archdiocese of Conakry.

The Holy See has diplomatic relations with Guinea and in AD 2000 is represented to government and the Catholic hierarchy by a pro-nuncio residing in Freetown.

OTHER CHURCHES. The Christian and Missionary Alliance from the USA began work in 1918 at Baro in the Niger valley, and since then has built a number of other stations throughout the country. Although its weekly radio broadcasts from Radio ELWA in Liberia have covered large Muslim areas, its converts have come primarily from traditionalist peoples. The CMA distributes scripture portions in 8 languages, and the New Testament is now available in Fulani. When foreign missionaries were ordered to leave Guinea in 1967, an arrangement was made for 26 CMA missionaries to remain, although their activity was restricted. The church is said to have grown in strength through the increased responsibility assumed by its 80 national workers. Foreign missionaries belonging to the Open Bible Standard Mission were also expelled, which began work among Muslims and traditionalists in both rural and urban areas in 1952; the Paris Evangelical Missionary Society; and the Anglican Church which is still part of the Diocese of Gambia and the Rio Pongas, in the Church of the Province of West Africa. Following the change of government in 1984 many Evangelical missions entered or re-entered the country: the Christian Reformed Church of North America, Assemblies of God of France and Ivory Coast, WEC (to work among the Sousou), Calvary Ministries of Nigeria, SIM (especially among the Malinke), Open Bible Standard Mission, NTM, Southern Baptists, Canadian Pentecostal Assemblies, and CCCI. Other than isolated radio believers there are only 2 small African indigenous churches in Guinea.

Indigenous missions. Missionaries from Guinea were recently sent out to surrounding countries.

CHURCH AND STATE

According to the constitution of 10 November 1958, Guinea is a secular state (Article 1) which assures to all citizens equal rights without distinction of religion (Article 39). In 1961 all denominational schools (Quranic, Catholic and Protestant) were nationalized, and the Catholic archbishop of Conakry, a Frenchman, was deported. The national political office of the Democratic Party of Guinea, the country's only political party, declared in June that 'no foreign persons, not even priests, will be tolerated in Guinea without the prior consent of the government'. African priests already present were confined to the city of Conakry prior to their subsequent repatriation. Following an attempted invasion with Portuguese backing in 1970, archbishop Tchidimbo was arrested on Christmas Eve, 1970; and although widely known as a militant anti-colonialist, he was sentenced on 24 January 1971 to life imprisonment with hard labor for 'collaboration with the enemy'. He was finally released from prison in 1978.

The brutal Marxist regime of Sékou Touré ended with a military coup in 1984, and a transition process to civilian rule was set in motion in the 1990s. This has brought a new era of religious freedom in sharp contrast to the difficult years of the prior anti-Christian, pro-Islamic, brutal regime.

BROADCASTING AND MEDIA

Guinea is a member of UNDA. There is a 30-minute Catholic religious program aired weekly.

Catholics broadcast 2 hours of television programming each month. The 'Jesus' Film has been shown to 2.8 million (31%) , most on television (1.7 million) or through film team presentations (870,000).

INTERDENOMINATIONAL ORGANIZATIONS

Most Protestant Evangelical ministries are members of the Association of Evangelical Churches and Missions in Guinea (Association des Eglises et Missions Evangélique en Guinée). This association organized a Reinhard Bonnke evangelistic and healing crusade in Conakry (1992) with attendance each night of some 20,000.

FUTURE TRENDS AND PROSPECTS

Losses among ethnoreligionists will likely be offset by gains among Christians and Muslims. Christians are expected to grow to 4.6% by AD 2025 while ethnoreligionists drop from a 1970 level of 30% to 24% by 2025.

Christians and Muslims are expected to continue converting ethnoreligionists. By AD 2050 it is possible that about 90% of Guineans will be Muslims and about 10% Christians.

BIBLIOGRAPHY

'Attitudes et role des glises l'gard des regimes totalaires en Afrique [Guinea],' Abp. R. Sarah, in *Eglises et democratisation en Afrique*, p.37–62. B. Balembo et al.

'Cosmology and symbolism on the central Guinea coast,' M. C. Jedrej, *Anthropos*, 81, 4–6 (1986), 497–515.

Gambia: country, people, and church in the diocese of Gambia and the Rio Pongas. J. R. C. Laughton. 2d ed. London: S. P. G., [1938]. 48p.

'Pedagogical principles for training pastors in West Africa.' P. R. Keidel. D.Min. thesis, Trinity Evangelical Divinity School, Deerfield, IL, 1994. 213p. (Studies pedagogical principles used at Telekoro Bible Institute, Guinea).

Sous le signe du la¨icat: documentation pour l'histoire de l'Eglise catholique en Guin'ee. G. Vieira. Dakar: Presses de l'Imprimeria Saint–Paul, 1992–. 1 vol. to date.

'The Church in Guinea,' *International Fides Service* (Rome), no. 2695 (January 7, 1976), NE 6–9.

'Touba in Guinea: holy places of Islam,' J. Suret–Canale, in *African perspectives*, p.53–81. C. Allen (ed).

Country Table 2. **Organized churches and denominations in Guinea.**

Official name (bold type = church with over 10% of all affiliated) 1	*Begun* 2	*Type* 3	*Counc* 4	*Congs* 5	*Adults* 6	*Affiliated 1970* 7	*Affiliated 1995* 8	*G%* 9	*Names, notes, and other statistics* (see Codebook, Part 3) 10
Assemblées de Dieu e Guinée	1985	P-Pe2	Z...E	29	3,000	–	5,000	10.00	*Assemblies of God.* M=AdG (France), SFM. On Liberia border.
Convention Baptiste	c1990	P-Bap	T...E	4	67	–	100	20.00	*Baptist Convention.* M=FMB-SBC,NBCUSA.
Egl Anglicane (D Gambia & Rio Pongas)	1935	A-ACa	awaV.	8	555	2,000	1,500	-1.14	*Anglican Ch.* In CPWA Declining; many reverting to Islam. 2n,1x,W=45%,5Y,25y.
Eglise Catholique au Guinée:	1877	R-Lat	P.SFR	33	61,250	48,356	109,297	3.32	*Catholic Ch in G.* C=0+0+4. (1970) 13n, 26w,935Yy. 45n 16x 31m 73w 2082Yy
M Conakry (Konakry)	1897	R-Lat	Ps	12	16.850	18,200	30,090	2.03	Area 1% Catholic. 1971, archbishop jailed. M=CSSp. 14n 11x 22m 46w 1103Yy
D Kankan	1949	R-Lat	Ps	13	28,200	15,048	50,290	4.94	Rapid growth. 2% Catholic. Kissi, some Kpelle. 9n 5x 8m 6w 265Yy
D N'Zérekoré	1937	R-Lat	Ps	8	16,200	15,108	28,917	2.63	55% Kpelle, 27% Toma, 13% Kono. 1.1% baptized. 22n 0x 1m 21w 714Yy
Eglise de la Bible Ouverte	1952	I-3pW	Z...E	2	65	100	150	1.64	*Open Bible Standard Churches.* Formerly based at Kindia, with M=OBSC(USA).
Eglise Evangélique Protestante	1918	P-Hol	xF..E	212	27,200	3,000	50,000	11.91	*Ev Protestant Ch.* M=CMA(USA), SAM/AME. Toma (Loma), Kissi, a few Malinke. 80m,17f,1h,1p.
Eglise Evangélique Shekina	1991	I-3jA	.....	20	3,000	–	6,000	25.00	*Shekinah Ch.* F=Apostle Williams (Liberia).
Eglise l'Amour de Dieu	1992	I-3jA	.....	5	1,000	–	2,000	33.33	*Eglise Chemin de Fer.* (Railway Ch).
Eglise Libre Pentecôtiste	c1960	I-3pA	Z....	5	1,000	1,000	2,000	2.81	Formerly M=SFM(Sweden). Begun by mass-movement Liberians (Kissi, Loma, Gbande).
Eglise Neo-Apostolique	c1970	I-3aX	x....	70	10,000	–	20,746	48.83	*New Apostolic Church.* M=NAK(HQ Zurich, Switzerland).
Eglise Pentecôtiste Alleluia	1985	P-Pe2	Z...E	20	2,000	–	3,000	10.00	*Pentecostal Hallelujah Church.* M=PAOC (Canada).
Eglise Réformée		P-Ref	....E	1	100	100	150	0.05	*Reformed Ch.* Former chaplaincy work to Frenchmen by Eglise Réformée de France.
Eglise radiophoniques isolées	c1965	I-3rA	.....	100	2,000	200	5,000	13.74	Isolated radio believers, mostly youths. R=10 (ELWA, Radio Vatican, &c).
Ministères de Calvaire	1982	I-3cA	.....	2	30	–	100	7.69	*Calvary Ministries.* M=CM(Nigeria). Work among Susu.
Témoins de Jéhovah	c1955	m-Jeh	x....	10	278	500	695	1.33	*Jehovah's Witnesses.* Active witnessing by 1959. 626 at 1973 Memorial. (1975) 27Y. (1995) 75Y.
Other African independent churches	c1980	I-3pA	.....	50	2,000	–	3,000	6.67	Charismatics from Liberia (Kru), Nigeria, Ghana, Ivory Coast, as labor migrants in Guinea.
Other Protestant bodies	c1985	P-	.....	30	1,500	–	3,000	10.00	Chs of Christ,CRC,LCMS,UMC,NTM,SDA, Shekina, SIM,WEC,WPMC, MCA, MERN, PAOC.
Totals				**601**	**115,045**	**55,256**	**211,738**		

Churches, members, growth, 1900-2025	*Congs*	*Adults*	*Affiliated*	*G%*	*Total denominations*	*6 Megablocs:* O	*R*	*A*	*P*	*I*	*m*
Total churches, members, and denominations (mid-1900)	5	1,000	1,785	5.03	1	0	1	0	0	0	0
Total churches, members, and denominations (mid-1970)	273	31,217	55,256	5.03	8	0	1	1	2	3	1
Total churches, members, and denominations (mid-1990)	400	89,200	164,180	5.60	48	0	1	1	5	40	1
Total churches, members, and denominations (mid-1995)	601	115,045	211,738	5.22	51	0	1	1	6	42	1
Total churches, members, and denominations (mid-2000)	700	126,000	231,322	1.78	51	0	1	1	6	42	1
Total churches, members, and denominations (mid-2025)	1,300	300,000	552,700	3.55	78	0	1	1	15	60	1

NOTES ON TABLE ABOVE
NATIONAL COUNCILS (Column 4, 5th letter).
E = Association des Eglises et Missions Evangéliques de Guiné.
R = Conférence Episcopal de la Guinée (CEG).
OTHER AFRICAN INDIGENOUS CHURCHES. Eglise l'Amour de Dieu No. 2 Mission, Vie Profonde, Rhema Church (1995), Baptiste Oeuvre Mission (from Ivory Coast), Eglise Pentecôtiste du Réveil (from CAR), Ch of Pentecost of Ghana, Eglise Bethel, Eglise Mission Alpha (3 chs; 1987).

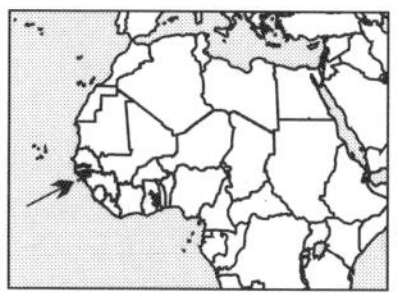

GUINEA-BISSAU

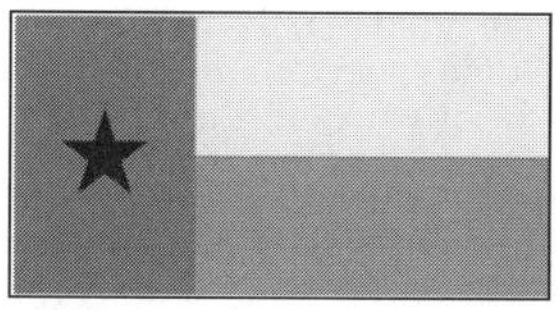

SECULAR DATA, AD 2000

STATE
Official name: La República da Guiné-Bissau (The Republic of Guinea-Bissau).
Short name: Guinea-Bissau. **Adjective of nationality:** of Guinea-Bissau.
Flag: Yellow and green stripes with red bar on left with black star.
Area: 36,125 sq. km. (13,948 sq. mi.).
Government: Multiparty republic with one legislative house, since 1984 (1446 Portuguese possession, 1879 colony, 1952 overseas province, 1973 Independence, 1980 military coup).
Legislature: National People's Assembly, 100 members.
Official language: Portuguese.
Monetary unit: 1 CFA franc (CFAF) = 100 centimes. **US$1=** CFAF 560.38.
Chief cities: BISSAU 161,201.
Political divisions: 9 provinces.
Armed forces: 7,000.

DEMOGRAPHY
Population: 1,213,000.
Population density: 33.5/sq. km. (86.9/sq. mi.).
Under 15 years: 516,000.
Growth rate p.a.: 2.08% (births 40.26, deaths 19.52).
Mortality: Infant, per 1,000: 122.0; **Maternal per 100,000:** 910.0.
Life expectancy: 45 (male 43, female 46).
Household size: 4.1. **Floor area per person, sq.m:** 9.0.
Major languages: Fulani, Mandingo, Portuguese, Portuguese Creole, Felup, Papel (Pepel), Balante, Manjaco, and 15 other tribal languages.
Urban dwellers: 23.73%. **Urban growth rate p.a.:** 3.9%.
Labor force: 46%.

ETHNOLINGUISTIC PEOPLES
25.0% Balanta (Bulanda, Belante); 17.1% Fulakunda (Fula Cunda); 12.0% Mandyak (Manjaco, Caio); 9.9% Mandinka; 9.1% Guinean Mestico.

ECONOMY
National income p.a. per person: US$249; **per family:** US$1,024.

EDUCATION
Adult literacy: 54% (male 68%, female 42%). **Schools:** 648.
Universities: 4. **School enrolment:** female/male: 27%/49%.

HEALTH
Access to health services: 40%. **Access to safe water:** 53%.
Hospitals: 16 (13 beds per 10,000). **Doctors:** 274.
Blind: 5,000. **Deaf:** 70,800. Murder rate: <1.
Lepers: 35,000. **Underweight prevalence under 5:** 23%.

LITERATURE
New book titles p.a.: 120 (100 p.a. per million). **Periodicals:** 4.
Newspapers: 1 daily.

COMMUNICATION (per 1,000 people)
Phones: 8 **(0% mobile).** Radios: 36. **TV sets:** 10.
Daily newspaper circulation: 6. **Computers:** 4.

REFUGEES
Alien refugees from other countries: 15,000.

HUMAN LIFE AND LIBERTY (optimum condition=100.0%)
HDI: 29.1. **HSI:** 18.0. **HFI:** 20.0. **EFL:** 20.0.

Country status. Guinea-Bissau is a small enclave on the west coast of Africa, bounded by Senegal and Guinea. It represents a remnant of a once-powerful Portuguese presence in West Africa. It is one of the least-developed countries in the world and is dependent on fishing and agriculture.

HUMAN LIFE AND LIBERTY

Human need and development. Guinea-Bissau is one of the poorest countries in a poor region that has few natural resources and few sources of external help. The small economy was battered by a long civil war and still retains its scars. Most of the one million inhabitants are engaged in what is known as subsistence agriculture, an euphemism for desperate poverty. Although the post-Marxist government of general Joao Bernardo Vieira began liberalizing the economy in 1986, living conditions have steadily deteriorated because of inflation. Sanitation is poor even in the capital city of Bissau. Tap water is not potable. The 2 hospitals are not adequately staffed, and medicines often are in short supply. Malaria, gastrointestinal infections, bilharzia, and tuberculosis are endemic. Infant mortality rate is 12.2% and life expectancy 45 years.

Human rights and freedoms. Although some progress has been made in moving toward a more democratic society, human rights remain circumscribed. Arbitrary detention and physical mistreatment of political opponents are still practiced. The Constitutional

Year	1900		1970		mid-1990		Annual change, 1990-2000				mid-1995		mid-2000		mid-2025	
Name	Adherents	%	Adherents	%	Adherents	%	Natural	Conversion	Total	Rate	Adherents	%	Adherents	%	Adherents	%
Ethnoreligionists	97,200	81.0	273,900	52.2	460,180	47.3	11,351	-2,532	8,819	1.77	500,000	46.0	548,367	45.2	730,000	37.5
Muslims	18,000	15.0	183,750	35.0	371,000	38.1	9,151	2,180	11,331	2.70	425,960	39.2	484,307	39.9	877,000	45.1
Christians	**4,800**	**4.0**	**66,800**	**12.7**	**127,000**	**13.1**	**3,145**	**148**	**3,293**	**2.33**	**142,400**	**13.1**	**159,930**	**13.2**	**295,000**	**15.2**
PROFESSION																
professing Christians	**4,800**	**4.0**	**66,800**	**12.7**	**127,000**	**13.1**	**3,145**	**148**	**3,293**	**2.33**	**142,400**	**13.1**	**159,930**	**13.2**	**295,000**	**15.2**
AFFILIATION																
unaffiliated Christians	0	0.0	4,434	0.8	4,000	0.4	99	-70	29	0.69	4,400	0.4	4,285	0.4	5,000	0.3
affiliated Christians	**4,800**	**4.0**	**62,366**	**11.9**	**123,000**	**12.6**	**3,046**	**219**	**3,265**	**2.38**	**138,000**	**12.7**	**155,645**	**12.8**	**290,000**	**14.9**
Roman Catholics	4,800	4.0	59,626	11.4	112,000	11.5	2,763	137	2,900	2.33	125,637	11.6	141,000	11.6	240,000	12.3
Independents	0	0.0	0	0.0	20,000	2.1	493	607	1,100	4.48	25,106	2.3	31,000	2.6	70,000	3.6
Protestants	0	0.0	2,540	0.5	7,000	0.7	173	77	250	3.10	8,384	0.8	9,500	0.8	24,000	1.2
Anglicans	0	0.0	200	0.0	250	0.0	6	-3	3	1.14	250	0.0	280	0.0	500	0.0
Marginal Christians	0	0.0	0	0.0	50	0.0	1	1	2	3.42	50	0.0	70	0.0	150	0.0
doubly-affiliated	0	0.0	0	0.0	-16,300	-1.7	-402	-589	-991	4.86	-21,427	-2.0	-26,205	-2.2	-44,650	-2.3
Trans-megabloc groupings																
Evangelicals	0	0.0	2,500	0.5	7,300	0.8	180	30	210	2.56	8,329	0.8	9,400	0.8	21,000	1.1
Pentecostals/Charismatics	0	0.0	200	0.0	26,000	2.7	641	189	830	2.81	29,980	2.8	34,300	2.8	69,000	3.6
Great Commission Christians	**4,560**	**3.8**	**36,800**	**7.0**	**75,000**	**7.7**	**1,850**	**440**	**2,290**	**2.70**	**85,000**	**7.8**	**97,900**	**8.1**	**200,000**	**10.3**
Nonreligious	0	0.0	500	0.1	13,600	1.4	335	156	491	3.13	16,000	1.5	18,507	1.5	40,000	2.1
Atheists	0	0.0	0	0.0	1,000	0.1	25	42	67	5.24	1,400	0.1	1,667	0.1	3,500	0.2
Baha'is	0	0.0	50	0.0	220	0.0	5	6	11	4.23	240	0.0	333	0.0	500	0.0
World A (unevangelized persons)	111,000	92.5	368,066	70.1	535,150	55.0	13,196	-3,826	9,370	1.63	579,943	53.4	628,334	51.8	930,188	47.8
World B (evangelized non-Christians)	4,200	3.5	90,192	17.2	310,850	31.9	7,671	3,678	11,349	3.17	363,693	33.5	424,736	35.0	720,812	37.0
World C (Christians)	4,800	4.0	66,800	12.7	127,000	13.1	3,145	148	3,293	2.33	142,400	13.1	159,930	13.2	295,000	15.2
Country's population	**120,000**	**100.0**	**525,059**	**100.0**	**973,000**	**100.0**	**24,012**	**0**	**24,012**	**2.23**	**1,086,037**	**100.0**	**1,213,000**	**100.0**	**1,946,000**	**100.0**

COLUMNS, ROWS.
For meanings and definitions, see Codebook (Part 3). Note that, by definition, total 'Christians' = professing + crypto-Christians, which also = affiliated + unaffiliated Christians, and also = Great Commission Christians + latent Christians. Percentages may not always total exactly, due to rounding.

CENSUSES.
1950: 62.5% ethnoreligionists, 35.0% Muslims, 2.4% Roman Catholics (1.5% civilized, 0.9% non-civilized), 0.04% Protestants (185 civilized, 43 non-civilized), 0.02% Druzes (85 persons, Lebanese).

NOTES ON RELIGIONS
BAHA'IS. Response has mushroomed notably since 1970, to 57 local spiritual assemblies by 1996.
COUNTRY'S POPULATION. From 1959-74 a large Portuguese military presence was in Portuguese Guinea, averaging 20,000 and as high as 35,000 at one period. After Independence in 1973, the 20,000 troops with some civilians (almost all Roman Catholics), who made up about 4.1% of the 1974 population, departed for Portugal. The table therefore includes them for the year 1970, excludes them for 1990-2025.
ETHNORELIGIONISTS. Strongest in the west. Tribes over 60% traditionalist in 1995: Banyun (85%). Bijago (80%), Manjaco-Papel (80%), Balante (83%), Bassari (90%).
MUSLIMS. Predominant in the east and south; Sunnis (of the Malikite rite). Islamized tribes: Soninke, Fula, Susa. Others: Diola (60% Muslim), Biafada (70%), Balante (12%), Manjaco (14%). The total includes Druzes from Lebanon (85 in 1950). *Hajj pilgrims to Mecca.* (1976) 1.

Great Commission Instrument Panel: status of Guinea-Bissau (for explanation see start of Part 4)

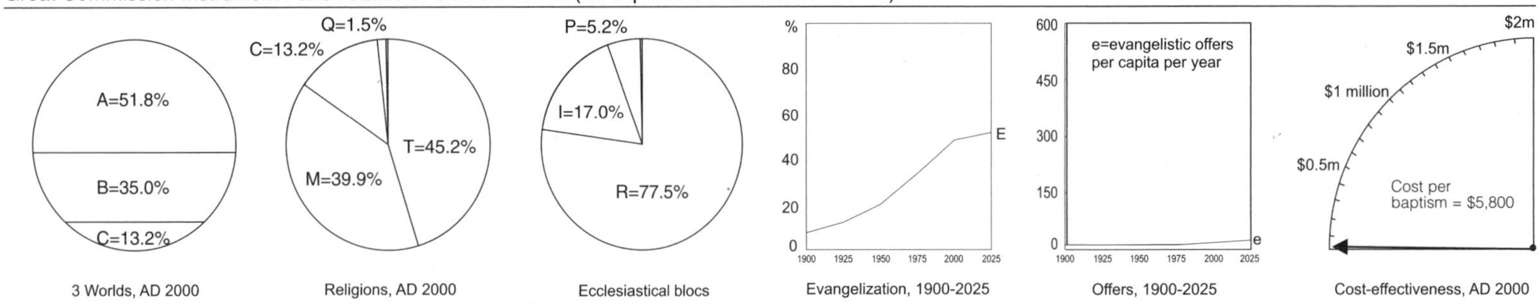

provision against cruel and inhuman punishment is rarely enforced. Persons suspected of anti-state activities are held without charge or trial, sometimes for extended periods of time, and often incommunicado. Some suspects are detained without the required judicial warrant, through the device of house arrest. Freedom of the press was enhanced in 1992 with the emergence of 2 private newspapers and increased access to television and radio air time. Nevertheless, restrictions remain on certain types of public comments and criticisms. As in all tribal societies, women suffer from historical discrimination as well as brutal customs and practices, such as female genital mutilation. Most domestic violence leads to wife beating for which women have no legal recourse.

Human environment. Guinea-Bissau is protected from growing Sahelian desertification by a number of rivers, which have incised a small coastal plain pierced by inlets. However, the dry season brings the threat of brushfires, particularly in areas denuded of their natural cover or forests through slash-and-burn cultivation. In addition to drought, the main cause of soil degradation is overgrazing, which results in much of the topsoil being lost.

NON-CHRISTIAN RELIGIONS

Traditional religions are strongest among the western tribes. Tribes that are more than 80% animist include the Balanta, Banyum, Bayot, Ganja (Bandal), Kasanga (Haal), Kobiana, and the Mandyak (Manjaco, Caio). Three of these are noted for an especially strong ancestor cult: the Balanta, Banyum, and the Mandyak. The proportion of traditionalists is declining rapidly due to conversions to Christianity and Islam. The idea of a supreme being is universal, God being identified as Emit among the Diola and Orrebuco-Ocoto among the Bijago. The ancestral cult, called Choro by the Banyum, is also highly developed. The use of wooden images (*iras*) to represent the ancestral presence is common with the Papel, Balanta, and Mandyak.

Ethnoreligionists. Bassaris (from extreme northeast of country) playing traditional religio-musical instruments.

Islam, which has the allegiance of 40% of the population (up from 35% in 1970), is predominant among the eastern and southern peoples. The Soninke of the northeast are almost entirely Muslim, and the southeastern Fulakunda and southern Susu are strongly influenced by Islam. Islam has also made inroads in the west, with the Diola about 62% Muslim, the Biafada 70%, the Balanta 10%, and the Mandyak 10% Muslim. Muslim missionaries have been active since the late 1970s, and many tribes are becoming more and more Muslim in religious allegiance.

CHRISTIANITY

CATHOLIC CHURCH. The first Catholic missionaries (OFM) arrived in 1462. When the diocese of St James of Cape Verde (Santiago do Cabo Verde) was erected in 1532, it was given responsibility for the mission on the mainland. Although Jesuits later joined the Franciscans, the work progressed slowly. In 1694 there were only 2,000 Catholics, nor were significant gains achieved later. Indeed in 1929 only one priest remained in the territory. When the concordat was signed between Portugal and the Holy See in 1940, Guinea became a mission sui juris independent of the diocese of Cape Verde; and in 1955 the mission was raised to the status of prefecture apostolic, and in 1977 to diocese. The diocese is now composed of 3 ecclesiastical districts: Bissau, Bafata, and Cumura. After the outbreak of armed insurrection under the PAICG in 1962, missions retreated from the interior area held by nationalists to regrouped villages and cities along the western coast.

The Holy See has diplomatic relations with Guinea-Bissau and in AD 2000 is represented to government and the Catholic hierarchy by a nuncio residing in Dakar.

Country summary. **Worlds A, B, C by ethnolinguistic peoples, cities, and major civil divisions in Guinea-Bissau.**

	PEOPLES							CITIES							CIVIL DIVISIONS						
World	Num	Pop 2000	C%	Christians	E%	U%	Unevangelized	Num	Pop 2000	C%	Christians	E%	U%	Unevangelized	Num	Pop 2000	C%	Christians	E%	U%	Unevangelized
A	23	930,988	4.61	42,903	39	61	569,960	0	0	0.00	0	0	0	0	4	508,063	8.25	41,933	39	61	308,396
B	6	265,628	37.78	100,353	78	22	58,702	1	161,201	15.00	24,180	55	45	71,992	5	705,050	16.13	113,712	55	45	320,308
C	3	16,498	75.08	12,387	100	0	41	0	0	0.00	0	0	0	0	0	0	0.00	0	0	0	0
Total	**32**	**1,213,114**	**12.83**	**155,643**	**48**	**52**	**628,703**	**1**	**161,201**	**15.00**	**24,180**	**55**	**45**	**71,992**	**9**	**1,213,113**	**12.83**	**155,645**	**48**	**52**	**628,704**

Igreja Evangélica da Guiné. Congregation at Binar outside thatch church, with WEC missionary.

OTHER CHURCHES. Protestantism was not introduced until 1939, when missionaries of the Worldwide Evangelization Crusade arrived in Bissau. They were the only Protestant mission permitted until 1990. Others began to enter at that time. The Igreja Evangélica da Guiné is the product of this effort and is the only large Protestant church in the country. Ten mission posts have been erected, 3 on the Arquipelago dos Bijagos. All are concentrated in western Guinea. In 1950 there were 228 Protestants, 43 being indigenous Africans. By 1995 the church had a community of 8,000. The Church has no schools but carries on general medical and maternity work among the Papel of Biombo. An extensive leprosy control program among the Balante at Bissora was abandoned due to guerrilla activity. On the Bijagos Islands, a rural development scheme provides training in improved agricultural methods and better care of livestock. Literacy work is carried on among the Bijago, Papel and Balante. There is also a small Anglican community which is part of the diocese of Gambia and the Rio Pongas.

Indigenous missions. Apart from a handful of Roman Catholics working in Portugal, only recently have missionaries been sent out to surrounding countries.

CHURCH AND STATE

The concordat of 1940 between Portugal and the Holy See provided for the special status of the Catholic Church in all Portuguese territories. Protestants were tolerated but looked upon with suspicion. The civil war which began in the territory in 1962 adversely affected the ability of the churches to carry on evangelistic activity in the interior, and they tended to concentrate their attention in the western part of the country. However, with the proclamation of independence by the African Party for the Independence of Guinea Bissau and Cape Verde (PAIGC) in 1973, a new situation was created. The constitution passed by the PAIGC in 1973 stipulates in Article 13 that all citizens are equal before the law, without regard to their ethnic origin, social class, philosophy or religion. Article 17 guarantees the 'freedom to practice a religion'; the name 'God' however does not appear. Since Independence was recognized by Portugal in September 1974, this became the constitution of Guinea-Bissau. Visas for Western missionaries were difficult until a more relaxed policy came in 1990.

Several of the country's postage stamps have had Christian themes: here, the 1951 Exposition of Missionary Art.

BROADCASTING AND MEDIA

Guinea is a member of UNDA. Shortwave radio programs can be received.

FUTURE TRENDS AND PROSPECTS

Christianity will see some growth from 2000-2025, but most ethnoreligionists are expected to convert to Islam. Muslims could claim 45.1% of the population by AD 2025.

Ethnoreligionists are then expected to continue their decline, dropping from over 80% in 1900 to less than 25% by AD 2050. Muslims and Christians will likely both benefit, reaching 75% and 20% respectively over the same period.

BIBLIOGRAPHY

'Arte Nalu,' A. Augusto da Silva, *Boletim Cultural da Guiné Portuguesa*, 11, 44 (1956), 27–47. (Art and religion).

As viagens do Bispo D. Frei Vitoriano Portuense a Guiné e a cristianização dos reis de Bissau. A. Teixeria da Mota. Lisbon: Junta de Investigações Científicas do Ultramar, 1989. 192p.

Atlas missionário português, 1964. A. da Silva Rego & E. dos Santos (eds). 2nd ed. Lisbon: Junta de Investigações do Ultramar e Centro de Estudos Históricos Ultramarinos, 1964. 206p.

Caminhos africanos, (1979–). (Catholic periodical).

'Colonisation et religion, depuis la première évangélisation jusqu'à la colonisation des peuples de Guinée–Bissau,' V. Cabral, *Mondes en Développement*, 17, 65 (1989), 233–37.

'Contracts with the spirits: religion, asylum, and ethnic identity in the Cacheu Region of Guinea–Bissau.' E. L. Crowley. Ph.D. dissertation, Yale University, New Haven, CT, 1990. 2 vols.

Gambia: country, people, and church in the diocese of Gambia and the Rio Pongas. J. R. C. Laughton. 2d ed. London: S. P. G., [1938]. 48p.

Going for God. E. Julian. Gerrards Cross: Worldwide Evangelization Crusade, [1979]. 33p.

Guinea–Bissau. R. E. Galli. *World bibliographical series*, vol. 121. Oxford, UK: CLIO Press, 1991. 206p. (See especially 'Religion,' p.62–5).

Guinea–Bissau and Cape Verde Islands. J. M. McCarthy. *Garland Reference Library of Social Science*, no. 27. New York: Garland, 1977. 196p. (2,547 entries).

História das missões católicas da Guiné. H. P. Rema. Braga, Portugal: Editorial Franciscana, 1982. 950p.

In terra d'Africa. S. Munno. Milan: Pontificio Istituto Missioni Estere, [1958]. 156p.

Manding: focus on an African civilization. International Conference on Manding Studies. London: School of Oriental and African Studies, University of London, 1972. 5 vols.

'Mito, religion y pensamiento filosófico de Guinea–Bissau,' C. Cardoso, *Enfoques*, 15 (1989), 1–77.

'No segredo das crenças: das instituições religiosas na Guiné Portuguesa,' F. R. R. Quintino, *Boletim Cultural da Guiné Portuguesa*, 4, 15 (1949), 419–88.

O islamismo na Guiné Portuguesa. J. J. Gonçalves. Lisbon: Agência-Geral do Ultramar, 1961. 215p.

'O totemismo na Guiné Portuguesa,' F. R. R. Quintino, *Boletim Cultural da Guiné Portuguesa*, 19, 74 (1964), 117–28.

'The land as body: an essay on the interpretation of ritual among the Manjaks of Guinea–Bissau,' W. V. Binsbergen, *Medical anthropology quarterly*, 2, 4 (1988), 386–401. (Treats religious rituals).

The light shines in the darkness: the story of the Evangelical Church of Guinea–Bissau, 1940–1974. H. Willis. Balstrade, U.K.: WEC 1996. 96p.

'The observance of All Souls' Day in the Guinea–Bissau region: a Christian holy day, an African harvest festival, an African New Year's celebration, or all of the above?,' G. E. Brooks, *History in Africa*, 11 (1984), 1–34.

Country Table 2. **Organized churches and denominations in Guinea-Bissau.**

Official name (bold type = church with over 10% of all affiliated) 1	*Begun* 2	*Type* 3	*Counc* 4	*Congs* 5	*Adults* 6	*Affiliated 1970* 7	*Affiliated 1995* 8	*G%* 9	*Names, notes, and other statistics* (see Codebook, Part 3) 10
Assembleias de Deus	1974	P-Pe2	ZF..E	4	234	–	300	4.76	*Assemblies of God.* M=Assembleias de Deus (Brazil). Classical Pentecostals. 2f.
Igreja Adventista	1965	P-Adv	x....	1	42	40	84	3.01	*SDA. União Portuguesa dos Adventistas do Sétimo Dia.* In Portuguese Union Mission.
Igr Anglicana (D Gambia & Rio Pongas)		A-ACa	awaV.	1	150	200	250	0.05	*Anglican Ch.* In Ch of the Province of West Africa. HQ Banjul (Gambia).
Igreja Católica: D Bissau	1462	R-Lat	P.S.P	32	80,000	59,626	125,637	3.03	Included military until 1974 peace. C=2+0+3. M=OFM. 7n,51x,68m,133w,550Yy.
Igreja Evangélica da Guiné	1939	P-Eva	xF..E	60	4,500	2,500	8,000	4.76	*IEPG. Evangelical Church of Guinea Bissau.* M=MEGP(WEC, UK). 9m,14f,1h,1k,W=90%.
Igreja Nova Apostólica	c1970	I-3aX	x....	72	10,100	–	25,106	49.97	*NAC. New Apostolic Church.* Phenomenal church growth over last 2 decades.
Testemunhas de Jeová	1980	m-Jeh	x....	1	10	–	50	6.67	*Jehovah's Witnesses.* (1995)11Y.
Other Protestant bodies		P-	....E	0	0	–	0	0.05	Including: SBC,WEC.
Doubly-affiliated		2-aff			-12,800	0	-21,427		Evangelicals who are also baptized Roman Catholics.
Totals				**171**	**82,236**	**62,366**	**138,000**		

Churches, members, growth, 1900-2025	*Congs*	*Adults*	*Affiliated*	*G%*	*Total denominations*	*O*	*R*	*A*	*P*	*I*	*m*
Total churches, members, and denominations (mid-1900)	10	3,200	4,800	3.73	1	0	1	0	0	0	0
Total churches, members, and denominations (mid-1970)	40	41,372	62,366	3.73	4	0	1	1	2	0	0
Total churches, members, and denominations (mid-1990)	110	73,300	123,000	3.45	7	0	1	1	3	1	1
Total churches, members, and denominations (mid-1995)	171	82,236	138,000	2.33	7	0	1	1	3	1	1
Total churches, members, and denominations (mid-2000)	190	92,800	155,645	2.44	7	0	1	1	3	1	1
Total churches, members, and denominations (mid-2025)	300	173,000	290,000	2.52	25	0	1	1	10	10	3

(6 Megablocs: O, R, A, P, I, m)

NOTES ON TABLE ABOVE
NATIONAL COUNCILS (Column 4, 5th letter).
E = Igrejas Evangélicas da Guinea-Bissau.
P = Conférence des Evêques du Sénégal, de la Mauritanie, du Cap-Vert, et de Guinée-Bissau (Episcopal Conference of S, M, C-V, & G-B).

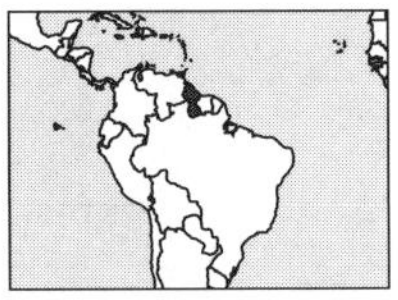

GUYANA

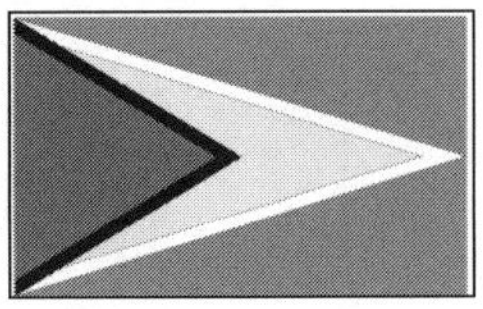

SECULAR DATA, AD 2000

STATE
Official name: The Co-operative Republic of Guyana.
Short name: Guyana. **Adjective of nationality:** Guyanese.
Flag: Green field with black-edged red triangle superimposed on white-edged yellow triangle.
Area: 215,083 sq. km. (83,044 sq. mi.).
Government: Parliamentary republic, since 1970 (1620 Dutch colony, 1831 British Guiana, 1966 Independence).
Legislature: National Assembly, 65 members.
Official language: English.
Monetary unit: 1 Guyana dollar (G$) = 100 cents. **US$1=** G$147.30.
Chief cities: GEORGETOWN 212,882.
Political divisions: 10 provinces.
Armed forces: 2,000.

DEMOGRAPHY
Population: 861,000.
Population density: 4.0/sq. km. (10.3/sq. mi.).
Under 15 years: 257,000.
Growth rate p.a.: 0.64% (births 18.82, deaths 6.91).
Mortality: Infant, per 1,000: 51.5; **Maternal per 100,000:** 500.0.
Life expectancy: 66 (male 63, female 69).
Household size: 5.1. **Floor area per person, sq.m:** 13.0.
Major languages: English, Guyanese Creole, Hindi, Urdu, Arawak, Portuguese, Chinese, and about 8 other languages.
Urban dwellers: 38.18%. **Urban growth rate p.a.:** 2.7%.
Labor force: 36%.

ETHNOLINGUISTIC PEOPLES
41.4% Hindi (Hindustani); 32.3% Guyanese Black (Creolese); 11.4% Guyanese Mulatto; 4.0% Hindi (Hindustani); 1.8% Arawak.

ECONOMY
National income p.a. per person: US$589; **per family:** US$3,007.

EDUCATION
Adult literacy: 98% (male 98%, female 97%). **Schools:** 524.
Universities: 1. **School enrolment:** female/male: 82%/82%.

HEALTH
Access to health services: 50%. **Access to safe water:** 61%.
Hospitals: 30 (33 beds per 10,000). **Doctors:** 138.
Blind: 1,300. **Deaf:** 52,400. Murder **rate:** 4.
Lepers: 4,400. **Underweight prevalence under 5:** 18%.

LITERATURE
New book titles p.a.: 34 (40 p.a. per million). **Periodicals:** 28.
Newspapers: 2 dailies.

COMMUNICATION (per 1,000 people)
Phones: 63 (2% mobile). Radios: 454. **TV sets:** 42.
Daily newspaper circulation: 63. **Computers:** 18.

HUMAN LIFE AND LIBERTY (optimum condition=100.0%)
HDI: 64.9. **HSI:** 39.0. **HFI:** 55.0. **EFL:** 32.0.

Country Table 1. **Religious adherents in Guyana, AD 1900-2025.**

Year	1900		1970		mid-1990		Annual change, 1990-2000				mid-1995		mid-2000		mid-2025	
Name	Adherents	%	Adherents	%	Adherents	%	Natural	Conversion	Total	Rate	Adherents	%	Adherents	%	Adherents	%
Christians	**167,300**	**58.7**	**382,900**	**54.0**	**412,000**	**51.8**	**3,455**	**-737**	**2,718**	**0.64**	**425,000**	**51.2**	**439,180**	**51.0**	**506,800**	**48.5**
PROFESSION																
professing Christians	**167,300**	**58.7**	**382,900**	**54.0**	**412,000**	**51.8**	**3,455**	**-737**	**2,718**	**0.64**	**425,000**	**51.2**	**439,180**	**51.0**	**506,800**	**48.5**
AFFILIATION																
unaffiliated Christians	22,000	7.7	48,067	6.8	59,100	7.4	491	113	604	0.98	63,989	7.7	65,144	7.6	42,800	4.1
affiliated Christians	**145,300**	**51.0**	**334,833**	**47.2**	**352,900**	**44.4**	**2,965**	**-851**	**2,114**	**0.58**	**361,011**	**43.5**	**374,036**	**43.4**	**464,000**	**44.4**
Protestants	59,900	21.0	96,033	13.5	148,000	18.6	1,229	835	2,064	1.31	156,964	18.9	168,636	19.6	250,000	23.9
Roman Catholics	21,700	7.6	110,000	15.5	88,000	11.1	731	-881	-150	-0.17	87,000	10.5	86,500	10.1	83,000	7.9
Anglicans	62,700	22.0	100,000	14.1	80,000	10.1	664	-964	-300	-0.38	78,000	9.4	77,000	8.9	70,000	6.7
Independents	1,000	0.4	20,100	2.8	24,100	3.0	200	90	290	1.14	25,297	3.1	27,000	3.1	42,000	4.0
Orthodox	0	0.0	6,000	0.9	7,800	1.0	65	35	100	1.21	8,180	1.0	8,800	1.0	15,000	1.4
Marginal Christians	0	0.0	2,700	0.4	5,000	0.6	42	68	110	2.01	5,570	0.7	6,100	0.7	16,000	1.5
Trans-megabloc groupings																
Evangelicals	43,000	15.1	35,900	5.1	89,000	11.2	739	861	1,600	1.67	96,087	11.6	105,000	12.2	160,000	15.3
Pentecostals/Charismatics	0	0.0	22,000	3.1	112,600	14.2	935	405	1,340	1.13	119,417	14.4	126,000	14.6	170,000	16.3
Great Commission Christians	**20,000**	**7.0**	**70,000**	**9.9**	**93,800**	**11.8**	**779**	**306**	**1,085**	**1.10**	**99,600**	**12.0**	**104,650**	**12.2**	**150,000**	**14.4**
Hindus	71,200	25.0	226,550	31.9	254,680	32.0	2,114	411	2,525	0.95	269,000	32.4	279,934	32.5	355,020	34.0
Muslims	18,000	6.3	63,800	9.0	64,400	8.1	535	36	571	0.85	67,000	8.1	70,113	8.1	86,000	8.2
Ethnoreligionists	22,800	8.0	20,000	2.8	19,000	2.4	158	-129	29	0.15	18,700	2.3	19,290	2.2	15,000	1.4
Spiritists	5,700	2.0	7,000	1.0	14,400	1.8	120	178	298	1.90	16,000	1.9	17,380	2.0	22,000	2.1
Baha'is	0	0.0	1,700	0.2	13,000	1.6	108	50	158	1.16	14,340	1.7	14,584	1.7	27,000	2.6
Nonreligious	0	0.0	3,000	0.4	10,000	1.3	83	97	180	1.67	11,400	1.4	11,796	1.4	18,000	1.7
Atheists	0	0.0	1,000	0.1	4,000	0.5	33	24	57	1.33	4,400	0.5	4,565	0.5	7,500	0.7
Chinese folk-religionists	0	0.0	1,000	0.1	1,960	0.3	16	24	40	1.87	2,200	0.3	2,360	0.3	3,600	0.3
Buddhists	0	0.0	2,000	0.3	1,500	0.2	12	45	57	3.26	1,900	0.2	2,067	0.2	4,000	0.4
Jews	0	0.0	50	0.0	60	0.0	0	1	1	0.80	60	0.0	65	0.0	80	0.0
World A (unevangelized persons)	109,155	38.3	177,345	25.0	190,005	23.9	1,577	-4,424	-2,847	-1.61	175,098	21.1	161,868	18.8	150,480	14.4
World B (evangelized non-Christians)	8,545	3.0	149,137	21.0	192,995	24.3	1,602	5,161	6,763	3.02	229,753	27.7	259,952	30.2	387,720	37.1
World C (Christians)	167,300	58.7	382,900	54.0	412,000	51.8	3,455	-737	2,718	0.64	425,000	51.2	439,180	51.0	506,800	48.5
Country's population	**285,000**	**100.0**	**709,383**	**100.0**	**795,000**	**100.0**	**6,634**	**0**	**6,634**	**0.80**	**829,852**	**100.0**	**861,000**	**100.0**	**1,045,000**	**100.0**

COLUMNS, ROWS.
For meanings and definitions, see Codebook (Part 3). Note that, by definition, total 'Christians' = professing + crypto-Christians, which also = affiliated + unaffiliated Christians, and also = Great Commission Christians + latent Christians. Percentages may not always total exactly, due to rounding.

CENSUSES.
9.IV.1946 (adjusted to include 6,023 Amerindians in remote districts): 46.4% Protestants & Anglicans, 31.5% Hindus (0.7% Arya Samajists), 11.6% Roman Catholics, 7.8% Muslims, 2.6% ethnoreligionists, 0.1% other religionists. **7.IV.1960:** 33.4% Hindus, 22.1% Protestants, 19.6% Anglicans, 14.9% Roman Catholics, 8.8% Muslims, 1.0% ethnoreligionists, 0.2% marginal Protestants. **7.IV.1970** (incomplete): 37.3% Hindus, 17.4% Anglicans, 13.8% Protestants, 13.5% Roman Catholics, 17.9% all others (Muslims, ethnoreligionists, other religionists, also other Protestants and Christians, and a large number of unknown religion).

NOTES ON RELIGIONS
ATHEISTS. People's Progressive Party (PPP) (legal; pro-Soviet).
BAHA'IS. Rapid growth from 1 local spiritual assembly (1964) to 17 (1973), then to 68 LSAs by 1996.
BUDDHISTS. Chinese.
ETHNORELIGIONISTS. Of the over 33,000 pure tribal jungle or lowland Amerindians in the interior, a large proportion are still animists, including among the Arekuna and Macushi.
INDEPENDENTS. In 15 denominations in 1995, among Blacks and Amerindians (see Table 2). The first began around 1870 among Amerindians.
HINDUS. Hindi-speaking: 70% of the Indian population, with a few Blacks. About 2% of all Hindus are Arya Samajists, who gain a number of Black converts each year.
MUSLIMS. Urdu-speaking; 18% of all Indians, with a few Black converts each year; mostly rural; Sunnis, some adherents of Ahmadiya (enumerated here under Muslims, though declared non-Muslim by Pakistan). There is also a political party, the Guyana United Muslim Party (GUMP).
SPIRITISTS. Vodoun (Voodoo) is widely practiced. Bush Negroes have cults derived from Ashanti religion (from Ghana). There are also a few Rastafarians (from Jamaica).

Great Commission Instrument Panel: status of Guyana (for explanation see start of Part 4)

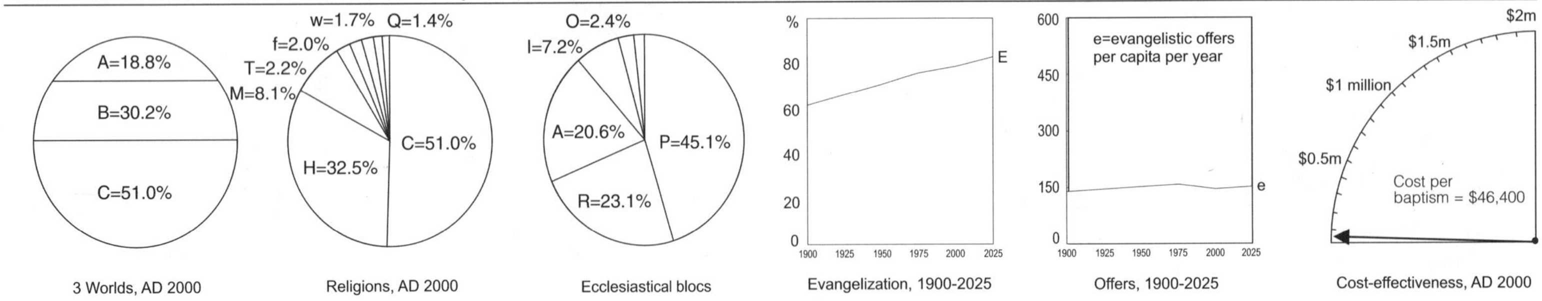

Country status. Guyana is a tropical country on the northeast coast of South America. Called the 'Land of the Six Peoples', it is remarkable for the racial diversity of its population which includes East Indians, Afro-Guyanese, Amerindians, Portuguese, Chinese, and British. Although formerly a British colony, British influences have been waning in recent years. Sugar and rice are the most important crops.

HUMAN LIFE AND LIBERTY

Human need and development. The present Guyanese society is essentially the successor to a slave society; the blacks were brought in as slaves, and the East Indians, and Portuguese as indentured laborers. As a result, society is extremely egalitarian, and the social divisions found in other societies on the continent are not found here. Living conditions also are uniform. Although for many years the country was considered unfit to live, it is now one of the healthiest, with very low rate of infant mortality and high rate of life expectancy. The major problems are

Country summary. **Worlds A, B, C by ethnolinguistic peoples, cities, and major civil divisions in Guyana.**

	PEOPLES							CITIES							CIVIL DIVISIONS						
World	Num	Pop 2000	C%	Christians	E%	U%	Unevangelized	Num	Pop 2000	C%	Christians	E%	U%	Unevangelized	Num	Pop 2000	C%	Christians	E%	U%	Unevangelized
A	1	69	0.00	0	41	59	41	0	0	0.00	0	0	0	0	0	0	0.00	0	0	0	0
B	10	429,719	9.38	40,322	63	37	160,510	1	212,882	40.00	85,153	80	20	42,960	10	861,334	43.43	374,036	81	19	161,535
C	13	431,545	77.33	333,713	100	0	982	0	0	0.00	0	0	0	0	0	0	0.00	0	0	0	0
Total	**24**	**861,333**	**43.43**	**374,035**	**81**	**19**	**161,533**	**1**	**212,882**	**40.00**	**85,153**	**80**	**20**	**42,960**	**10**	**861,334**	**43.43**	**374,036**	**81**	**19**	**161,535**

protein malnutrition and inadequate housing. The spread of many infectious water-borne diseases is facilitated by extensive irrigation networks in the coastlands. In rural areas sewage treatment is not available. Health services are rudimentary and are often supplemented by witch doctors or Obeah. Although Obeah is an African term, it is practiced mostly by East Indians. Housing is uniformly dismal. Most houses are crowded and privacy is rare. Generally Black houses are poorly maintained in contrast to East Indian dwellings which are brightly painted. The difference between Blacks and East Indians is even more striking in their consumption patterns. The former tend to spend all that they earn in living well, while East Indians tend to be thrifty, although they tend to be lavish in celebrating weddings and in their numerous religious ceremonies.

Human rights and freedoms. Guyana is a parliamentary democracy in principle, but ethnic polarization has introduced some unusual elements into its actual working. Government is the arena where one or the other ethnic group tries to gain dominance and thereby curtail the influence of the other. The People's National Congress, led by the Blacks and Portuguese, in power since 1964, was ousted in 1992 by the People's Progressive Party controlled by the East Indians. As usual in many developing democracies, the spoils of office include the right to exercise certain prerogatives to the detriment of the opposition. This does not, however, entail the abridgment of liberties or abuse of human rights. Occasionally there are reports of torture and ill treatment in police custody. Prisons are overcrowded as a result of mandatory prison sentences for narcotics offenses. Delays in judicial proceedings are common, and the inefficiency of the judicial system is so great as to undermine due process. In both Black and East Indian societies, women suffer numerous disabilities, for which there are no legal remedies. In 1990 Parliament passed legislation granting women equal property and inheritance rights.

Human environment. Most of Guyana's wilderness is without regulatory protection. Urban sewage systems are nonexistent and there are no pollution controls on industry or mining. The water-intensive cultivation practices are not environment friendly and also place heavy strains on the fragile soil systems. Water is drawn mostly from artesian wells and overuse of these wells has caused a drop in the water table.

NON-CHRISTIAN RELIGIONS

Hinduism is followed by 32% of the population of Guyana (1995) and by more than 70% of the East Indian population. Various organizations are active including the American Aryan League, which represents the reformed wing of Hinduism, and the traditionalist Hindu Orthodox Guyana Sanathan Dharma Maha Sabba whose influence extends beyond the borders of the country.

Islam, with 8% of the population and 18% of all East Indians, has its main strength among rural Asians. Organizationally Muslims are divided into orthodox Sunni and heterodox Ahmadiya sects.

Traditional Amerindian religions are still practiced by a majority of the members of the following tribes: the Arekuna (Pemong), Macushi, and the Warrau, and also are strong among the detribalized Amerindian population.

Vodoun (Voodoo) beliefs and practices are observed by non-Christians of African descent (Afro-American spiritists), and also by many nominal Christians. A small number of other Blacks also have been converted to Hinduism and Islam.

CHRISTIANITY

Christians make up about 51% of the population (in 1995). They include a majority of the Black and Mulatto populations and are most frequently found in urban areas. A considerable number of East Indians, around 35,000, have been converted to Christianity. Other ethnic groups are largely Christian.

CATHOLIC CHURCH. Although Guyana was evangelized initially during the 16th century, Catholicism was virtually erased during the long Dutch occupation after 1620. The first Catholic priest of the modern era arrived in 1826, and in 1837 a vicariate was erected. In spite of the fact that Catholicism has been active in Guyana for the past century and a half, only 15 of its 78 priests in 1971 were natives. A Jesuit survey in 1967 reported that approximately 60% of nominal Catholics were of African and mixed descent, 20% were Amerindians and 6% Portuguese. The remaining 14% were East Indians, Chinese and Europeans. The number of nominal Catholics is decreasing slowly in relation to population growth. One factor is the emigration of a high percentage of the Portuguese, who at one time formed the bulk of the Catholic population. With the exception of the Amerindians, a high proportion of Catholics live in the greater Georgetown area, with relatively few in the rural areas of Berbice and Essequibo.

The Holy See has no diplomatic relations with Guyana in AD 2000.

Anglican Church, Diocese of Guyana. 'And he entered into a boat...' Emulating practice of Jesus beside Galilee, a priest of USPG preaches to small crowd from boat.

ANGLICAN CHURCH. The London Missionary Society began work in Guyana in 1807, sponsored by several churches including Anglicans. In 1810 the Anglican Church itself was established in Georgetown, later the archepiscopal see of the West Indies. The Anglican Church was in 1995 the second largest denomination in Guyana. It is strongly Anglo-Catholic in churchmanship and maintains close ties with the Guyana Catholic Church.

PROTESTANT CHURCHES. Guyana has a long history of missionary endeavor and displays a proliferation of churches and mission agencies, both long-established denominations and more recent arrivals especially in the urban areas. The racially mixed population is reflected in its church membership. Of the 15 churches belonging to the Council of Churches, 5 have a mixed population, 7 are predominantly Black and 2 are mostly East Indian.

Guyana was a colony of the Netherlands until the early 19th century when it passed into British hands. The first Protestant Church was founded in 1743 by Dutch Lutherans to cater for the settler community. From 1766 planters from Scotland began what is now the Presbytery of Guyana, which remained part of the Church of Scotland until its autonomy in 1967. During 1837-1945 it was supported by state subsidies. The first Methodists were freed slaves who emigrated from Nevis in 1802 and were followed later by British Methodists.

The Guyana Presbyterian Church began in 1885 with missionaries from Canada, but its growth remains slow. Seventh-day Adventists on the other hand have established a large community since their arrival in 1887. Of the many new denominations coming after World War II the most significant growth rates have been experienced by the Assemblies of God and the Southern Baptists. The Unevangelized Fields Mission works with several Indian tribes in the interior near the Brazilian border.

INDIGENOUS CHURCHES. A number of indigenous bodies have arisen, including the Jordanites of the 1920s and the Hallelujah Church. The latter began over a hundred years ago and extends into Venezuela; it remains an Amerindian prophet movement syncretizing traditional religion with Christianity. The recent entrance of missionaries into the area where it originated has resulted in its revival after a period of decline. Several Black denominations from the USA have also been active, including the AME and the AME Zion churches both of which are members of the Guyana Council of Churches.

Renewal movements. In the 1990s the Pentecostal/Charismatic Renewal continued to spread rapidly across most older churches, and numbered over 126,000 adherents (of whom 61% Pentecostals, 23% Charismatics, and 17% Independents).

Indigenous missions. Only a handful of Guyanese Christians have served as missionaries outside of the country, with most of these going to Western countries.

CHURCH AND STATE

The constitution, promulgated 26 May 1966, begins in its Preamble: 'Whereas the people of Guyana acknowledge that reverence for the Deity (is) the foundation of freedom, justice and peace in society...'. It then goes on to guarantee freedom of religion in its Chapter II. The government gives a grant to those churches concerned with social work among Amerindians. Churches are exempt from a number of taxes.

Expatriate ministers of religion need a permit to enter and work in Guyana. Since Independence in 1966, most denominations, especially those dependent on manpower and finance from abroad, have been engaged in a process of reassessing their role in a strongly nationalistic society.

Religious matters are dealt with by the Ministry of Home Affairs. Church buildings must be registered insofar as this is necessary for the calling of marriage bans, and ministers of religion must be appointed as marriage officers in order to officiate at weddings.

In September 1976 the government nationalized all private schools, in the face of vocal Catholic and Anglican opposition.

In November 1978, Peoples Temple, a Protestant cult with 90% USA Black membership, which had had close illegal dealings with the ruling political party, organized a mass suicide-murder at Jonestown in the northwestern jungle, killing 912 persons.

Atheism was promoted by a series of Marxist governments that ruled until the multi-party elections of 1992. Before 1985 the country experienced much conflict between the main churches and the government, but greater religious freedom was introduced at that time.

BROADCASTING AND MEDIA

Shortwave programs from KNLS, HCJB (Ecuador), TWR (Antilles) and AWR (Costa Rica) can be easily received. Guyana is a member of UNDA.

CBN's *700 Club* and animated children's programs can be seen during the week, and other Christian television programs can be received via satellite. TBN can be received in Georgetown on channel 2.

Well over 81,000 (10%) have seen the 'Jesus' Film, mainly through film teams, with 3,100 responding. TWR (Antilles) and AWR (Costa Rica) can be easily received.

INTERDENOMINATIONAL ORGANIZATIONS

In 1937, through the efforts of an Anglican layman, a Christian Social Council was established, to which both Catholics and Protestants belonged. In 1967 it merged with an Evangelical Council, formed in 1960, to become the present Guyana Council of Churches. The council now numbers 15 churches and includes 4 autonomous regional councils. It sponsors the David

Rose Centre, a self-help community project in the poorest sections of Georgetown, providing medical and social services and self-employment training in collaboration with several governmental agencies. There is also a diocesan Catholic Ecumenical Commission. The March for Jesus in June of 1993 was an important, visible ecumenical effort.

FUTURE TRENDS AND PROSPECTS

Christians may well continue a slow decline from 54% in 1970 to 48.5% in 2025.

Hindus are expected to grow to around 40% by the middle of the 21st century. Christianity may go below 45% but is not likely to fall beyond this without major conversions to Hinduism or Islam.

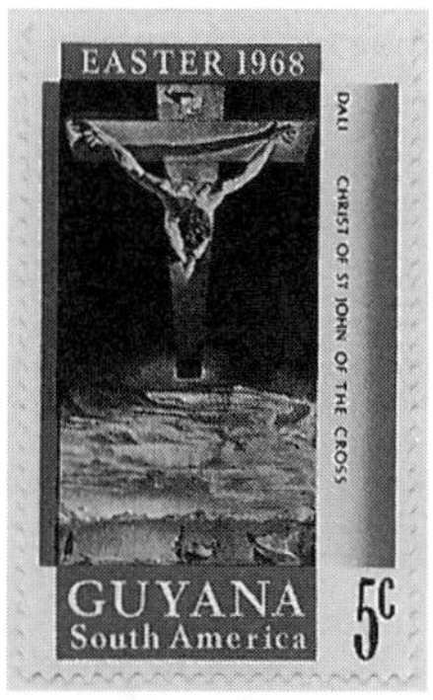

Guyana's postage stamps include many Christian themes; (*left*), Christ of St John, and (*bottom, far left*), The Last Supper (both after Salvador Dali).

BIBLIOGRAPHY

A history of the Lutheran Church in Guyana. P. Beatty. South Pasadena, CA: William Carey Library, 1972. 245p.

A month for the entertainment of spirits: African–Guyanese spiritualist ceremonies. K. Gibson. Berkeley, CA: University of California Extension, Center for Media and Independent Learning, 1991. (29 min. videocassette).

A short history of the Guyana Presbyterian Church. D. A. Bisnauth. Georgetown, Guyana: Printed by Labor Advocate Printery, 1970. 91p.

An inquiry into the animism and folk–lore of the Guiana Indians. W. E. Roth. 1915; reprint, New York: Johnson Reprint Corp., [1970]. 453p.

Guyana. F. Chambers. *World bibliographical series*, vol. 96. Oxford, UK: CLIO Press, 1989. 208p. (See especially 'Religion,' p.71f).

Journal of the proceedings of the Annual Synod, Diocese of Guyana, 1969–1970. Georgetown, Guyana: Diocesan Office, 1970.

New religious movements, mass suicide, and Peoples Temple: scholarly perspectives on a tragedy. R. Moore & F. M. McGehee (eds). *Studies in American religion*, vol. 37. Lewiston, NY: E. Mellen Press, 1989. 251p.

Notes on the history of the church in Guiana. T. Farrar (ed). British Guiana: Wm. Macdonald, [1892]. 226p.

Out of the depths: papers presented at four missiology conferences held in Antigua, Guyana, Jamaica and Trinidad, 1975. I. Hamid (ed.). San Fernando, Trinidad: St. Andrew's Theological College, 1977. 261pp.

'Religion and reconciliation in the multi–ethnic states of the Third World: Fiji, Trinidad, and Guyana.' R. R. Premdas. Ph.D. dissertation, McGill University, Montreal, Canada, 1991. 290p.

'Religious belief and social change: aspects of the development of Hinduism in British Guiana,' C. Jayawardena, *Comparative Studies in Society and History: an International Quarterly*, 8, 2 (1966), 211–40.

'The birth of a religion: the origins of Hallelujah, the semi–Christian religion of the Carib–speaking people of the borderlands of British Guiana, Venezuela and Brazil,' A. J. Butt, *Timehii*, 38 (September, 1959), 37–48.

'The Canadian Mission in British Guiana: the pioneer years, 1885–1927.' C. A. Dunn. Thesis, Queen's University, 1971. 236p.

The good news on the wild coast: highlights of the early efforts of the Catholic Church in Guiana, 1650's to 1850's. J. Bridges. Arima, Trinidad: St. Dominic Press. 84p.

'The people and church in Guyana.' D. A. D. Gossai. M.Div. thesis, Concordia Theological Seminary, Fort Wayne, IN, 1977. 59p.

'The white–robed army: cultural nationalism and a religious movement in Guyana.' J. Roback. Thesis, McGill University, Montreal, Canada, 1973. 316p.

Country Table 2. Organized churches and denominations in Guyana.

Official name (bold type = church with over 10% of all affiliated) 1	*Begun* 2	*Type* 3	*Counc* 4	*Congs* 5	*Adults* 6	*Affiliated 1970* 7	*Affiliated 1995* 8	*G%* 9	*Names, notes, and other statistics* (see Codebook, Part 3) 10
African Methodist Episcopal Church		I-Met	VwM.K	11	648	1,000	1,730	0.05	*Guyana-Surinam Annual Conference.* 16th Episcopal District. M=AMEC(USA Blacks).
African Methodist Episcopal Zion Ch	1911	I-Met	Vw..K	13	1,300	3,000	2,170	-1.29	M=AMEZC(USA Blacks). 2 schools. Many emigrants to UK. HQ Lacytown. 13n,1r.
Anglican Church: D Guyana	1810	A-ACa	AWMRK	150	52,700	100,000	78,000	-0.99	1842, Diocese in Ch of Province of West Indies. M=USPG(UK). 33n,18x,68Y,2946y.
Assemblies of God in Guyana	1952	P-Pe2	ZFA.L	194	38,000	6,000	56,285	9.37	M=AoG(USA). 53% Black, 42% East Indians. 79n,1x,2f,1s(125),W=90%,250Y,200z.
Baptist Co-operative Convention	1962	P-Bap	T...K	14	1,071	3,609	1,960	-2.41	M=SBC,NBCUSA. Mostly along coast. Rapid growth. 8n,6x,14f,42h,2s(29), W=60%,244Y.
Baptist Mid-Missions	1958	I-Bap	x....	7	200	200	400	2.81	*Regular Baptists.* M=BMM(USA). Fundamentalists from North America. 2f.
Bible Missionary Church	1957	P-Hol	x.H.L	3	300	300	500	2.06	M=Bible Missionary Church (USA). Holiness denomination. 2n,2x,1p,1s,22Y,10z.
Bible Protestant Congregational Chs		I-Fun	.TT.T	2	800	2,000	1,450	0.05	Fundamentalist schism ex Congregational Union, with USA support. HQ Georgetown.
Catholic Church: D Georgetown	1548	R-Lat	PxNMK	30	45,000	110,000	87,000	-0.93	Under M Port-of-Spain. 60% Black M=SJ. C=2+0+3. , 6n, 28x, 31m, 50w, 1738Yy
Christadelphian Ecclesias		m-Ade	x....	4	50	100	100	0.05	*Christadelphian Bible Mission.* 4 ecclesias in New Amsterdam. M=Birmingham (UK).
Christian Brethren Assemblies	c1835	P-CBr	x.H.L	50	2,700	2,000	4,150	2.96	*Plymouth (Open) Brethren. M=CMML(UK,USA). No HQ, but mainly Georgetown. 4f.*
Christian Catholic Church	1948	I-Con	x.H.L	5	50	200	150	-1.14	M=CCC(Zion, Illinois, USA). Healing emphases. Small group in Bel Air Park.
Church of Christ, Scientist		m-Sci	x....	1	35	100	50	0.05	*Christian Science.* M=CCS (Boston, USA). First Church, Georgetown.
Church of God of Prophecy	1956	P-Pe3	Z....	7	220	200	579	4.34	M=CGP(USA). Holiness Pentecostals. Split in USA ex CoG (Cleveland). HQ Albouystown.
Church of God (Anderson)	1914	P-Hol	x...K	52	3,550	2,000	5,920	4.44	*General Assembly of CoG (Guyana).* M=CoG (Anderson) (USA). All races. 6n,2f,1j,28t.
Church of the Nazarene	1945	P-Hol	xF..K	45	2,184	4,000	3,899	-0.10	M=CoN Urban Blacks, rural East Indians. 7n,2x,2f,52t(3233) W=54%,150Y,239z.
Elim Pentecostal Churches		P-Pe2	ZGH.L	21	4,700	1,000	7,000	0.05	M=EFGA(UK). Classical Pentecostals (2-stage). HQ Georgetown. 4f.
Episcopal Orth Ch (Greek Communion)	c1940	I-Lib	x....	1	150	300	250	-0.73	Black. Ex AOC(USA). Begun 1920 in Trinidad. HQ in Bridgetown (Barbados).
Ethiopian Orthodox Church		O-Eth	Nwa..	30	5,400	6,000	8,180	0.05	*EOC.* Under P Addis Ababa (Ethiopia). Blacks. M=EOC(Jamaica, Trinidad). 2x.
Evangelical Methodist Ch in Guyana	1960	I-Hol	xTT.T	4	200	200	300	1.64	*Bible Methodists.* M=EMC(USA). Fundamentalists from Holidaysburg, PA (USA). 4f.
Guyana Congregational Union	1807	P-Con	R.M.K	44	3,100	17,000	8,000	-2.97	M=LMS(UK), now CWM. HQ New Amsterdam. Black. 3n,3x,W=60%,768Yy,253z.
Hallelujah Church	c1870	I-3pR	.....	12	2,400	10,000	4,800	-2.89	Begun by prophet Abel. Macushi and tribes for 200 miles near Brazil and Venezuela.
Isolated radio churches	c1965	I-3rL	.....	200	3,000	200	5,000	13.74	Isolated radio believers, in the southern forests, mostly youths and pupils.
Jehovah's Witnesses	1900	m-Jeh	x....	30	1,651	2,000	4,720	3.49	*Watch Tower. IBSA.* Active witnessing by 1926. HQ Georgetown. (1975) 89Y. (1995) 135Y.
Jordanites	c1920	I-3pU	.....	3	590	1,000	1,180	0.66	*WEMP Church.* Blacks, in Georgetown. Earliest indigenous pentecostal church.
Lutheran Church in Guyana	1683	P-Lut	LvM.K	52	5,210	13,058	13,026	-0.01	Dutch origins. M=LCA(USA). A=1943. East Indians. HQ New Amsterdam. 5f.
Methodist Ch in Caribbean & Americas	1802	P-Met	VwM.K	46	3,658	10,000	9,000	-0.42	*MCCA*(1967 union) *Guyana District.* M=MMS(UK). Black. 7n,5x,5Y,570y.
Moravian Church	1878	P-Mor	xwM.K	8	513	2,500	1,282	-2.64	First attempt 1735-38. *Guyana Province, UoB.* M=Moravian Ch (USA). Black. 3x,43y.
New Apostolic Church	c1965	I-3aX	x....	10	1,000	–	1,367	33.48	*NAC/NAK.* M=Neuapostolische Kirche (HQ Zurich).
New Testament Church of God	1956	P-Pe3	ZFH.a	37	1,900	600	3,500	7.31	M=CoG(Cleveland) (USA). 15 churches, 1 mission 16n,4f,1p.
Pioneers		I-Non	.....	6	240	–	500	0.05	M=Pioneers (USA).
Presbyterian Church of Guyana	1885	P-Ref	R.M.K	44	2,033	6,000	3,000	-2.73	M=PCC(Canada). A=1945. All East Indians till 1945. HQ Queenstown. 15n,1s.
Presbytery of Guyana	1766	P-Ref	R.M.K	40	3,360	5,600	5,800	0.14	Begun by Scots planters. In Ch of Scotland till 1967 autonomy. Black. 9n,1x.
Salvation Army	1895	P-Sal	xwM.K	13	1,200	3,000	1,600	-2.48	*SA, Guyana Division*, Caribbean & CAmerica Territory. All races HQ Georgetown.
Seventh day Baptist Church	1920	P-Bap	Tw...	9	220	300	458	1.71	*Guyana Conference.* Sabbatarian Baptists. M=SDBC(USA). HQ Kitty. 2f.
Seventh-day Adventist Church	1887	P-Adv	x....	85	13,900	12,000	23,105	2.66	*SDA, Guyana Mission* Caribbean Union Conf. 8nx,142mw,6f,1H,1r,78t(6500),1053Y.
Unevangelized Fields Mission	1949	P-Non	xM...	1	700	1,000	1,400	1.35	M=UFM(UK, USA). In jungle, Brazil border. Indians: Wai-Wai, Wapishana, Macushi. 5f.
Wesleyan Church in Guyana	1909	P-Hol	VFH.L	37	1,627	3,866	2,500	-1.73	Formerly Pilgrim Holiness Ch until 1968 merger. 10n,1x,3f,W=22%,482Y.
Other Protestant denominations		P-	.....	40	0	2,000	4,000	0.05	Total about 20 (see list below).
Other Black indigenous churches		I-3pU	.....	50	3,000	2,000	6,000	0.05	Including African Apostolic Ch, FDPMM, Good Shepherd Universal Ch of Christ, House of Israel.
Other marginal Protestant bodies		m-	.....	15	300	500	700	0.05	Total over 5, including: Christian Mystic Faith, New Jerusalem Ch, Unitarian Ch.
Totals				**1,426**	**211,666**	**334,833**	**361,011**		

Churches, members, growth, 1900-2025	*Congs*	*Adults*	*Affiliated*	*G%*	*Total denominations*	*6 Megablocs:* O	R	A	P	I	m
Total churches, members, and denominations (mid-1900)	300	75,000	145,300	1.20	14	0	1	1	10	1	1
Total churches, members, and denominations (mid-1970)	958	172,870	334,833	1.20	52	1	1	1	29	13	7
Total churches, members, and denominations (mid-1990)	1,300	207,000	352,900	0.26	72	1	1	1	40	18	11
Total churches, members, and denominations (mid-1995)	1,426	211,666	361,011	0.46	73	1	1	1	40	19	11
Total churches, members, and denominations (mid-2000)	1,500	219,000	374,036	0.71	76	1	1	1	42	20	11
Total churches, members, and denominations (mid-2025)	3,000	272,000	464,000	0.87	140	3	1	1	55	65	15

NOTES ON TABLE ABOVE

NATIONAL COUNCILS (Column 4, 5th letter).

a = member of both GCC and GEF.
E = Guyana Evangelical Fellowship (GEF).
K = Guyana Council of Churches (GCC) (1967 merger of Christian Social Council, and Council of Evangelical Churches).
T = Guyana Council of the ICCC.

Local councils. 4 regional councils, related to GCC.

OTHER PROTESTANT DENOMINATIONS. These include: Association of Baptists for World Evangelism, Christian Mission Chs (member of GEF), Chs of Christ (Instrumental) (1959), Chs of Christ, Exclusive Brethren (Kelly-Continental), Full Gospel Fellowship (member of GEF), Guyana Mennonite Mission (35 adherents), Guyana Missionary Baptist Ch (member of GCC), Independent Assemblies of God, Missionary Aviation Fellowship (1958: a few congregations in areas without other missions), Open Bible Standard Chs, Peoples Temple (1974 exodus from USA to Jonestown in jungle; 1,200 followers, 90% USA Blacks; November 1978, mass suicide-murder of 912), Streams of Power Movement (Stromen van Kracht, Netherlands), Worldwide Evangelization Crusade, World-Wide Missions (1967).

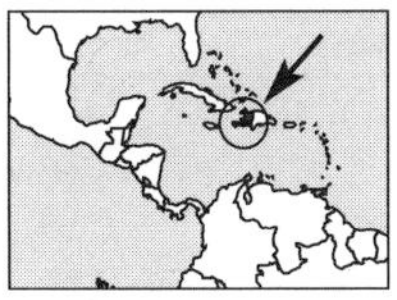

HAITI

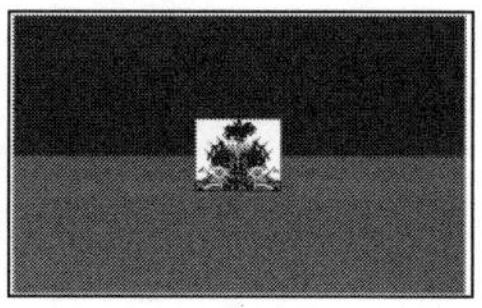

SECULAR DATA, AD 2000

STATE
Official name: Repiblik Dayti/La République d'Haïti (The Republic of Haiti).
Short name: Haiti. **Adjective of nationality:** Haitian.
Flag: Black and red bars; centered white rectangle with emblems of war around palm tree.
Area: 27,700 sq. km. (10,695 sq. mi.).
Government: Multiparty republic with two legislative houses, since 1987 (1492 Spanish possession, 1697 French colony, 1804 Independence as empire, 1915-34 USA rule, 1957 dictatorship, 1971 dictatorship).
Legislature: Senate, 27 members; Chamber of Deputies, 83 members.
Official language: French (Français).
Monetary unit: 1 gourde (G) = 100 centimes. **US$1=** G 16.72.
Chief cities: PORT-AU-PRINCE 1,791,000; Cap-Haitien (Le Cap) 94,124; Gonaives 48,306.
Political divisions: 9 provinces.
Armed forces: 3,000.

DEMOGRAPHY
Population: 8,222,000.
Population density: 296.8/sq. km. (768.7/sq. mi.).
Under 15 years: 3,347,000.
Growth rate p.a.: 1.64% (births 30.55, deaths 11.74).
Mortality: Infant, per 1,000: 61.1; **Maternal per 100,000:** 1,000.0.
Life expectancy: 55 (male 52, female 57).
Household size: 4.4. **Floor area per person, sq.m:** 10.0.
Major languages: French, French Creole (Haitian Creole), Spanish, Arabic.
Urban dwellers: 34.89%. **Urban growth rate p.a.:** 3.6%.
Labor force: 41%.

ETHNOLINGUISTIC PEOPLES
94.2% Haitian Black; 5.0% Haitian Mulatto; 0.4% Dominican Mulatto; 0.1% USA White; 0.0% Levantine Arab.

ECONOMY
National income p.a. per person: US$250; **per family:** US$1,100.

EDUCATION
Adult literacy: 45% (male 48%, female 42%). **Schools:** 6,741. **Universities:** 2. **School enrolment,** female/male: 39%/41%.

HEALTH
Access to health services: 50%. **Access to safe water:** 28%. **Hospitals:** 87 (8 beds per 10,000). **Doctors:** 564. **Blind:** 9,000. **Deaf:** 469,000. Murder **rate:** 18. **Lepers:** 1,500. **Underweight prevalence under 5:** 28%.

LITERATURE
New book titles p.a.: 250 (30 p.a. per million). **Periodicals:** 56. **Newspapers:** 4 dailies.

COMMUNICATION (per 1,000 people)
Phones: 8 **(3% mobile).** Radios: 41. **TV sets:** 5. **Daily newspaper circulation:** 7. **Computers:** 15.

HUMAN LIFE AND LIBERTY (optimum condition=100.0%)
HDI: 33.8. **HSI:** 11.0. **HFI:** 22.5. **EFL:** 16.0.

Country Table 1. **Religious adherents in Haiti, AD 1900-2025.**

Year	1900		1970		mid-1990		Annual change, 1990-2000				mid-1995		mid-2000		mid-2025	
Name	Adherents	%	Adherents	%	Adherents	%	Natural	Conversion	Total	Rate	Adherents	%	Adherents	%	Adherents	%
Christians	**1,499,100**	**99.9**	**4,362,200**	**96.5**	**6,659,300**	**96.3**	**125,757**	**-4,220**	**121,537**	**1.69**	**7,270,000**	**96.2**	**7,874,670**	**95.8**	**11,373,200**	**94.9**
PROFESSION																
professing Christians	**1,499,100**	**99.9**	**4,362,200**	**96.5**	**6,659,300**	**96.3**	**125,757**	**-4,220**	**121,537**	**1.69**	**7,270,000**	**96.2**	**7,874,670**	**95.8**	**11,373,200**	**94.9**
AFFILIATION																
unaffiliated Christians	218,100	14.5	61,945	1.4	172,000	2.5	3,248	3,077	6,325	3.18	200,000	2.7	235,246	2.9	323,200	2.7
affiliated Christians	**1,281,000**	**85.4**	**4,300,255**	**95.1**	**6,487,300**	**93.8**	**122,509**	**-7,297**	**115,212**	**1.65**	**7,070,000**	**93.5**	**7,639,424**	**92.9**	**11,050,000**	**92.2**
Roman Catholics	1,270,000	84.7	3,797,400	84.0	5,520,000	79.8	104,238	-4,238	100,000	1.68	6,012,028	79.5	6,520,000	79.3	9,200,000	76.7
Protestants	60,000	4.0	400,073	8.9	1,130,000	16.3	21,339	9,661	31,000	2.45	1,278,299	16.9	1,440,000	17.5	2,300,000	19.2
Independents	2,000	0.1	139,330	3.1	332,042	4.8	6,270	3,526	9,796	2.62	332,042	4.4	430,000	5.2	850,000	7.1
Anglicans	1,000	0.1	38,452	0.9	84,000	1.2	1,586	514	2,100	2.26	103,000	1.4	105,000	1.3	200,000	1.7
Marginal Christians	0	0.0	5,000	0.1	37,000	0.5	699	601	1,300	3.06	42,200	0.6	50,000	0.6	100,000	0.8
doubly-affiliated	-52,000	-3.5	-80,000	-1.8	-615,742	-8.9	-11,628	-17,355	-28,983	3.93	-697,569	-9.2	-905,576	-11.0	-1,600,000	-13.4
Trans-megabloc groupings																
Evangelicals	30,000	2.0	350,000	7.7	920,000	13.3	17,373	7,627	25,000	2.43	1,088,068	14.4	1,170,000	14.2	1,900,000	15.9
Pentecostals/Charismatics	0	0.0	180,000	4.0	1,231,000	17.8	23,246	3,254	26,500	1.97	1,357,935	18.0	1,496,000	18.2	2,400,000	20.0
Great Commission Christians	**45,000**	**3.0**	**316,000**	**7.0**	**449,500**	**6.5**	**8,488**	**93**	**8,581**	**1.76**	**491,500**	**6.5**	**535,309**	**6.5**	**779,000**	**6.5**
Spiritists	500	0.0	100,000	2.2	160,000	2.3	3,021	1,687	4,708	2.61	178,000	2.4	207,084	2.5	320,000	2.7
Nonreligious	0	0.0	44,000	1.0	77,100	1.1	1,456	2,390	3,846	4.13	91,000	1.2	115,558	1.4	250,000	2.1
Baha'is	0	0.0	10,700	0.2	14,000	0.2	264	42	306	1.99	14,700	0.2	17,055	0.2	33,000	0.3
Atheists	0	0.0	500	0.0	1,300	0.0	25	80	105	6.09	1,740	0.0	2,349	0.0	4,000	0.0
Muslims	400	0.0	1,500	0.0	1,660	0.0	31	-3	28	1.57	1,700	0.0	1,940	0.0	2,700	0.0
Chinese folk-religionists	0	0.0	0	0.0	180	0.0	3	0	3	1.65	190	0.0	212	0.0	300	0.0
Jews	0	0.0	100	0.0	160	0.0	3	1	4	2.05	170	0.0	196	0.0	300	0.0
Other religionists	0	0.0	1,000	0.0	2,300	0.0	43	23	66	2.55	2,500	0.0	2,960	0.0	4,500	0.0
World A (unevangelized persons)	0	0.0	4,520	0.1	6,916	0.1	85	58	143	2.80	7,560	0.1	8,222	0.1	11,988	0.1
World B (evangelized non-Christians)	900	0.1	153,699	3.4	249,784	3.6	4,761	4,162	8,923	3.10	282,805	3.7	339,108	4.1	602,812	5.0
World C (Christians)	1,499,100	99.9	4,362,200	96.5	6,659,300	96.3	125,757	-4,220	121,537	1.69	7,270,000	96.2	7,874,670	95.8	11,373,200	94.9
Country's population	**1,500,000**	**100.0**	**4,520,420**	**100.0**	**6,916,000**	**100.0**	**130,603**	**0**	**130,603**	**1.74**	**7,560,366**	**100.0**	**8,222,000**	**100.0**	**11,988,000**	**100.0**

COLUMNS, ROWS.
For meanings and definitions, see Codebook (Part 3). Note that, by definition, total 'Christians' = professing + crypto-Christians, which also = affiliated + unaffiliated Christians, and also = Great Commission Christians + latent Christians. Percentages may not always total exactly, due to rounding.

CENSUSES.
31.VIII.1971: 84.3% Roman Catholics, 14.2% Protestants, 1.0% nonreligious, 0.6% other Christians and other religionists.

NOTES ON RELIGIONS
ATHEISTS. There are small numbers, of 2 varieties: (1) Unified Party of Haitian Communists (PUCH) (proscribed under penalty of death); and (2) de facto atheists among Tontons Macoutes and other secret police thugs.
BAHA'IS. Rapid growth from 12 local spiritual assemblies (1964) to 65 (1973), then plateauing at 59 (1996). Missionary pioneers from Haiti have settled in Benin (Dahomey), the Central African Republic, and Guadeloupe.
BLACK INDIGENOUS. In about 40 denominations in 1995 (see Table 2).
DOUBLY-AFFILIATED. The term covers those affiliated to, or claimed by, both the Catholic Church and also an Evangelical church (Protestant, Anglican, marginal Protestant, Black indigenous), i.e. baptized Catholics who have recently become Evangelicals. Because their statistics represent a duplication, they are shown in the table as a negative quantity (with a minus sign).
MUSLIMS. Immigrant Syrian and Lebanese Arab traders since 1880, also East Indians and others.
OTHER RELIGIONISTS. Adherents of smaller religions and cults, including Rosicrucians (5 AMORC centers).
PENTECOSTALS/CHARISMATICS. Begun in 1973, the Catholic Charismatic Renewal has 150 regular weekly prayer groups with 18,200 regular adult attenders (10,000 aged 15-25), including 50 involved priests and 11 bishops, with one covenant community. Up to 30,000 attend the annual Congrès National.
PROTESTANTS. Conversions to Protestantism come primarily from active participants of Vodoun (Voodoo); often whole families are converted at the same time.
ROMAN CATHOLICS (affiliated). 1872: 927,000. 1880: 970,000. 1890: 1,000,000. 1900: 1,270,000. 1937: 2,663,000. 1940: 2,666,300. 1942: 2,688,000. Some 90% of all Catholics, mainly the rural peasantry but not the upper and middle urban classes, regularly practice a form of spiritist christo-paganism termed Vodoun (Voodooism, or The Gods, of Fon (Dahomean) origin), including Arada (Rada) and many other cults.
SPIRITISTS. Non-Christian (mostly immigrant) adherents of Afro-Caribbean non-Christian spirit-possession cults syncretizing African religion with elements of Christianity. There are also a few Rastafarians (from Jamaica).

Great Commission Instrument Panel: status of Haiti (for explanation see start of Part 4)

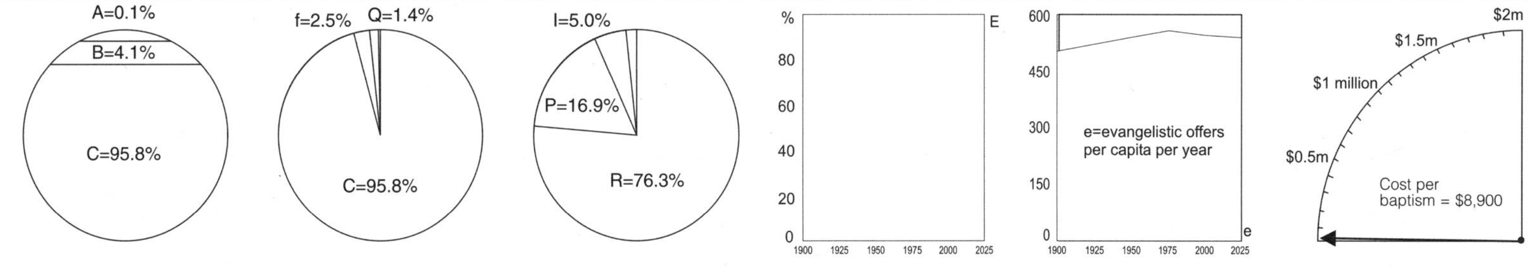

3 Worlds, AD 2000 | Religions, AD 2000 | Ecclesiastical blocs | Evangelization, 1900-2025 | Offers, 1900-2025 | Cost-effectiveness, AD 2000

Country status. Haiti occupies the western third of the island of Hispaniola in the Caribbean Sea. It has the dubious distinction of being the poorest country in the Western Hemisphere. It is also the largest French-speaking country in the Americas with a history as colorful as its landscape. It is also the world's first Black republic. Its chief exports are coffee and bananas.

HUMAN LIFE AND LIBERTY

Human need and development. Haiti has become over the last century a byword for poverty and misery, the home of the Wretched of the Earth, in Frantz Fanon's classic phrase. In almost every social and economic indicator, it ranks the lowest in the Hemisphere and among the lowest in the world. It has the highest density of population of any country in the Hemisphere. Its national literacy rate is officially

Country summary. **Worlds A, B, C by ethnolinguistic peoples, cities, and major civil divisions in Haiti.**

	PEOPLES							CITIES							CIVIL DIVISIONS						
World	*Num*	*Pop 2000*	*C%*	*Christians*	*E%*	*U%*	*Unevangelized*	*Num*	*Pop 2000*	*C%*	*Christians*	*E%*	*U%*	*Unevangelized*	*Num*	*Pop 2000*	*C%*	*Christians*	*E%*	*U%*	*Unevangelized*
A	1	197	1.02	2	50	50	99	0	0	0.00	0	0	0	0	0	0	0.00	0	0	0	0
B	2	4,235	44.58	1,888	99	1	23	0	0	0.00	0	0	0	0	0	0	0.00	0	0	0	0
C	6	8,217,593	92.94	7,637,534	100	0	5,813	3	1,933,430	92.20	1,782,546	100	0	3,386	9	8,222,024	92.91	7,639,424	100	0	5,933
Total	**9**	**8,222,025**	**92.91**	**7,639,424**	**100**	**0**	**5,935**	**3**	**1,933,430**	**92.20**	**1,782,546**	**100**	**0**	**3,386**	**9**	**8,222,024**	**92.91**	**7,639,424**	**100**	**0**	**5,933**

45% but is closer in fact to 20%, the life expectancy is 55 years, and per capita GNP is $250. Only 19% of its students reach secondary school. Its infant mortality rate is 95 per 1,000. Political repression for many decades under the Duvaliers pushed it even deeper into the mire of poverty, from which only occasional handouts from the United States provided some relief. The gulf between the rich and the poor is probably greater here than in any other country in the region. There is only a small middle class, and the standard of life for the urban poor is not much better than that of the subsistence farmer in the countryside and, in many respects, is much worse. Emigration to the United States provided an escape valve until it was closed by the Bush and Clinton Administrations. Most of the educated Haitians as well as professionals have fled abroad during and after the Duvalier era, with the result that there is a dearth of skilled service personnel in all areas. As a result of the embargo placed by the international community in retaliation for the military's ouster of the popularly elected president Jean-Bertrand Aristide in 1991, the economy has been hard hit and many essential commodities are in short supply. Although considerable advance was made in public health programs under the elder Duvalier (himself a doctor), lack of doctors and medical facilities has depressed the medical sector to primitive levels. The high incidence of diseases creates a climate in which the national religion of voodoo flourishes. Many of Haiti's problems may be attributable to the persistent hold of this religion on all aspects of national life.

Human rights and freedoms. Haiti's economic problems pale in comparison with its political problems. It is one of the few nations in the world under continuous dictatorship from the 1930s to the present day. Following the military coup that ousted president Aristide, human rights violations became more numerous and severe, including killings by security forces, beatings, arbitrary arrests, and mistreatment of prisoners. Many of these violations are carried out by commando-style government groups armed with rifles and sub machine guns. Arrests and harassment of journalists form part of an overall post-coup crackdown against the media. Since the days of the Duvaliers, the judiciary has been a puppet of the government. The government shows its contempt for the judiciary by dismissing judges at will and ordering them to carry out official instructions in deciding cases. The clergy, because of their pro-Aristide sympathies, are the frequent targets of official wrath, and churches are ransacked in police raids. Freedoms of assembly and association are severely restricted and the government is engaged in a systematic effort to wipe out all forms of civic associations, including health, education, and literacy organizations. Freedom of the press and speech is often abridged by violence and intimidation, and a number of journalists have left the country. Because of the inhuman conditions within the country, Haitians have been fleeing the country in droves, even though they find themselves unwelcome in other countries, including the United States. Haitian law makes no distinctions based on race, and blacks as well as nonblacks receive equal treatment. However, historic animosities persist between the French-speaking elite and the Creole-speaking masses. Officially, there is no discrimination against women, and many women have attained prominent positions in recent years.

Human environment. The quite chaotic social and political environment is paralleled by the physical environment which has been undergoing an irreversible process of degradation in recent years. Only 2% of the country remains forested, accelerating the process of soil erosion. Because sewage treatment and sewage systems are nonexistent outside Port-au-Prince, water pollution is severe, causing the spread of water-borne diseases.

NON-CHRISTIAN RELIGIONS

Vodoun (Vodun, Voodooism) first appeared in the 17th century, a syncretism of African rites mainly from Benin with Catholic practices, resulting in a form of spiritism often termed christo-paganism in other countries. Vodoun priests and priestesses (*hounganor*) have great prestige and power among their followers, their word being taken as law in many regions. Under their leadership Vodoun worship revolves around offerings, bloody and bloodless, to the spirits (*loa*) who control nature and daily human life. It includes ritual dances accompanied by a heady rhythm and heavy drinking and often involves spirit-possession. Black and white magic and divining the future are also important features. While ancient African spirits have often been identified with Christian saints, Vodoun has been subject to attack by the Catholic Church, such as the anti-superstition campaign of 1941-42. It was placed under the penal code, but this was revoked in 1946 by president Estimé. It is widely practiced by the peasantry and urban proletariat and by a majority of Catholics. The government has officially recognized Vodoun and registered the National Association of Voodoo Practitioners. The religion has been accepted as a significant and distinctive element of national life and culture.

Baha'i has recently experienced rapid growth, from 12 local spiritual assemblies in 1964 to 65 by 1973, and has sent missionaries to West and Central Africa. By 1995 Baha'i had nearly 15,000 followers.

CHRISTIANITY

The island of which Haiti forms part was the first land colonized by the Spanish, and within a century the indigenous Indian population had disappeared. Catholic missionaries arrived in 1493, and the first Franciscan college was established in 1503. Dominicans entered in 1511, including the renowned Bartolomeu de las Casas, and St Thomas University was opened in 1538. The west became more heavily occupied after 1630 by buccaneers, with African slaves and indentured Frenchmen working the land. Jesuits came in 1704, and in 1777 the island was divided between Spain and France, the latter receiving Haiti. Plantations were developed at the expense of the Negroes who finally revolted in 1791 and seized their own independence in 1804. Three years later Protestant missionary activity was begun. Political control of the island shifted frequently during the 19th century with different European governments, the Dominican republic, Colombia, and Haiti itself alternating in power. During 1915-34 the island was occupied by military forces of the USA.

CATHOLIC CHURCH. The modern era of the Catholic Church in Haiti dates from the signing of a concordat with the Holy See in 1860. The following year 5 episcopal sees were erected, including the archdiocese of Port-au-Prince. As a result of the concordat, the Catholic Church was organized on a parochial basis instead of a missionary basis. For many years most of its missionaries were French, especially from Brittany, although this began to change in 1942 with the arrival of Canadian missionaries from Quebec. An important effort has also been put into the creation of an indigenous clergy by the opening of the Seminary of Haiti in 1872 and the St James Seminary in 1894, and later through the creation of a major seminary by Jesuits in 1948. The continued control of the church by the political regime remains one of the major problems of Catholicism in the country and has greatly hampered its pastoral work.

The Holy See has diplomatic relations with Haiti and in AD 2000 is represented to government and the Catholic hierarchy by a nuncio residing in Port-au-Prince.

PROTESTANT CHURCHES. Haiti has the largest number of Protestants in the Latin Caribbean. Most denominations are experiencing rapid growth, particularly among the lower classes. The conversion of whole families from Voodooism is common although individual conversions also take place among migrants to the cities. In addition there are large numbers of unbaptized adherents. Protestant expansion was initially aided by the USA military occupation between 1915 and 1934. Pastors are scarce, but most are nationals. The level of theological training is low. Because of this, missionaries tend to remain in leadership positions, with missions rather than national church organizations often being recognized by government. Most pastors and churches continue to rely heavily on financial subsidies from North America.

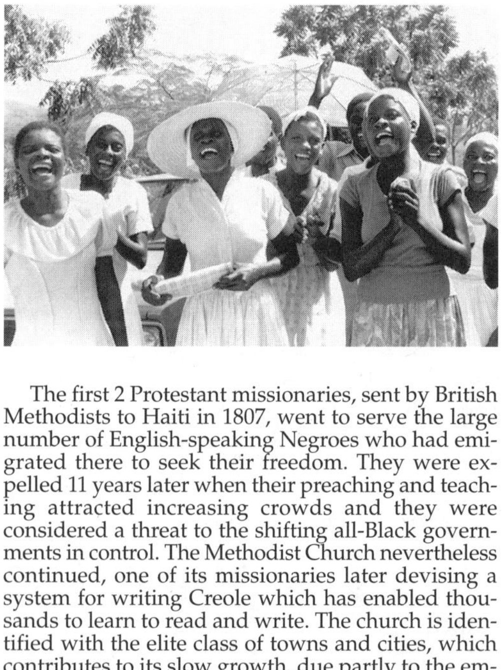

Eglise Méthodiste d'Haïti. *Above.* Crowd enter church at Oliviers, Petit-Goâve. *Below.* Zealous believers after church.

The first 2 Protestant missionaries, sent by British Methodists to Haiti in 1807, went to serve the large number of English-speaking Negroes who had emigrated there to seek their freedom. They were expelled 11 years later when their preaching and teaching attracted increasing crowds and they were considered a threat to the shifting all-Black governments in control. The Methodist Church nevertheless continued, one of its missionaries later devising a system for writing Creole which has enabled thousands to learn to read and write. The church is identified with the elite class of towns and cities, which contributes to its slow growth, due partly to the emigration of many of these elite to Europe and North America for political and other reasons. Since 1823 different British and American Baptist missions have attempted to start churches. Little success was achieved until the entrance of the American Baptists in 1923 while the country was under USA occupancy. Other conservative Baptist societies followed, the rapidity of increase of Baptist churches since then constituting almost a mass conversion. By 1990 they were the second largest Protestant tradition and are active in all parts of the country. The pastoral training given Haitian Baptist pastors is said to provide the highest educational standards of any Protestant church. Seventh-day Adventists, with heaviest membership in the north, form the largest Haitian Protestant church, their greatest strength residing in their effective use of lay workers. The Church of God of Prophecy and the Church of God (Cleveland) are next in size, indicating the rapid development of Pentecostal churches in Haiti. Other North American groups, many of which have entered Haiti since World War II, are characterized by a regional orientation.

INDIGENOUS CHURCHES. Over 150,000 persons are found in indigenous Black churches (1990). Some were begun by USA Black churches, the earliest being the AMEC in 1823. But over 25 others have been begun by Haitians independent of any outside aid.

Mission Evangélique Baptiste du Sud-Haïti. Adult (believer's) baptism near Les Cayes, 1970.

ANGLICAN CHURCH. The Episcopal Church dates back to 1861 when 110 American Blacks settled there and, with proselytes from Roman Catholicism, began the Eglise Orthodoxe Apostolique Haïtienne. In 1911 the Haitian clergy requested that their church become a missionary district of the Protestant Episcopal Church of the USA, due to inadequacies in local leadership, and this took place in 1913. Members today are mostly of the elite class, this church suffering also from the migration of much of its leadership to Europe and the USA.

Renewal movements. In the 1990s the Pentecostal/Charismatic Renewal continued to spread rapidly across most older churches, and numbered over 1,496,000 adherents (of whom 22% Pentecostals, 65% Charismatics, and 13% Independents).

Indigenous missions. Though missionaries were sent out from Haiti from the earliest period of Christian expansion, more recently missionary activity has become coordinated. Catholic and Protestant missionaries are beginning to branch out beyond the Caribbean to a few African countries.

Armée du Christ, one of 63 Haitian independent denominations.

CHURCH AND STATE

Freedom of religion is guaranteed, on paper, by the constitution of 1964 (Article 27). Catholicism enjoys a unique status as a result of the concordat of 1860 when it was considered the religion of the majority of Haitians. According to this concordat, the Catholic Church and its ministers are especially protected (Article 1). The bishops are paid by the state (Article 3), nominated by the president of the republic, subject to the approval of the Holy See (Article 4), and are obliged, as are other members of the clergy and directors of religious institutions, to take an oath the text of which is provided in Article 5. The president must approve the nomination of vicars-general and parish clergy as well as any modifications within the ecclesiastical jurisdictions (Article 11). Homage must be made to him through special prayers at the end of each mass (Article 15). Churches are obliged to register with the Department of Foreign Affairs and Religions.

The regime established by president Francois Duvalier exercised progressive control over the Catholic Church through intimidation and violence, in particular through: the expulsion of many clergy, including the archbishop of Port-au-Prince, the arrest of several priests, and the closure of the seminary, the Christian trade union, and Catholic periodicals. In 1966 Rome signed a common protocol that provided for a number of high church positions to be filled with Haitians, and for re-establishment of diplomatic relations. This agreement permitted president Duvalier to present himself as the champion of the indigenization of the church. He was assured at the same time of the unconditional fidelity of the newly-nominated hierarchy. Nevertheless, under the pretext of subversive activities, arrests and expulsions of priests continued. The Episcopalian bishop, a USA citizen, was also expelled in 1964. In that same year, the Vatican announced that the Haitian ruler would no longer have a role in the naming of bishops. When pope John Paul II visited the country in 1984 he greeted his hosts by saying, 'There must be changes here', and the crowd of 100,000 that was present erupted into cheers and applause while the president ignored the scene.

In August 1974 the journal *World evangelism* published on its cover a photograph of a naked and undernourished child with the caption 'Hunger in Haiti'. In reaction the Ministry of the Interior let it be known that president Jean-Claude Duvalier, who succeeded his father after his death in April 1971, 'could not but criticize the methods used by certain missions to obtain assistance' and that authorization accorded to guilty missions would simply be withdrawn.

The Duvalier regime, globally famous for violation of human rights, ended in 1986. Former Catholic priest Jean-Bertrand Aristide came to the presidency by the nation's first democratic elections, was ousted by the military in 1991, and was later returned to power with the help of USA military presence. The official national policy has continued to be one of religious freedom, and the church has not suffered widespread overt oppression since the mid-1980s, though many supporters of Aristide and other Christians were killed in the 1980s and early 1990s, often by local police or military personnel.

BROADCASTING AND MEDIA

Shortwave programs from HCJB (Ecuador), TWR (Antilles) and AWR (Costa Rica) can be easily received. Radio Lumiere is a network of 5 AM and one FM broadcast stations which reach nearly 6 million people. It is owned by a network of 280 Haitian churches working in partnership with Worldteam, and is supported financially in part by Haitians. It provides news, evangelism, health education, and Haitian Gospel music. Radio Soleil is a Catholic station that provides religious programming. Other Catholic stations are Radio La Voix de l'Ave Maria and Radio Min Contre. Haiti is a member of UNDA.

TBN programs are aired in Port-au-Prince on channel 16. LeSEA's programming is available via the World Harvest Satellite.

Some 2.9 million (37%) have seen the 'Jesus' Film, mainly through film teams; 54,000 have responded.

Eglise Catholique au Haïti. *Above.* Cathedral in Port-au-Prince. *Left.* Christ's Ascension.

INTERDENOMINATIONAL ORGANIZATIONS

Although there is no national ecumenical Christian council, 11 of Haiti's conservative denominations joined together to form the Council of Evangelical Churches of Haiti. The Ecumenical Research Group, founded in January 1968, has representatives from Catholic, Episcopal, Methodist, and African Methodist Episcopal churches, as well as the Salvation Army. It includes also some Baptist pastors as individuals. In addition to a library and common religious activities, it sponsors joint social action projects. In 1971 its activities were limited to Port-au-Prince. The Haitian Commission of the Churches for Development (Commission Haitienne des Eglises pour le Developpment, CHED), founded at Port-au-Prince in 1974, brings together delegates from some 30 churches (including the Catholic Church) and interconfessional organizations to encourage co-operation between churches, co-ordinate their efforts in development and integrate their initiatives into the national plan for the country as a whole. The national Protestant Federation formed in 1986.

FUTURE TRENDS AND PROSPECTS

A steady rise in the nonreligious and spiritists in Haiti through 2025 will probably cause the total Christian community to fall from 96.5% in 1970 to 94.9% in 2025.

The only significant religious change expected in the distant future is the steady rise in the percentage of the nonreligious—possibly reaching 10% by AD 2050.

BIBLIOGRAPHY

'A history of the Baptist work in Haiti.' I. T. Heneise. D.Min. thesis, Colgate Rochester Divinity School, Rochester, NY, 1974. 293p.

Annuaire de l'Eglise d'Haïti (Numéro Spécial 1972). Port-au-Prince: Archevêché de Port-au-Prince, 1973. (Catholic).

Annuaire Protestant 1971–1972. Port-au-Prince: Centre d'Information et de Statistiques Evangéliques, 1972.

Black religions in the New World. G. E. Simpson. New York: Columbia University Press, 1978. 429p.

Dieux en diaspora: les loa haitiens et les vaudou du Royaume d'Allada (Bénin). G. Montilus. *Cultures africaines.* Niamey: CELHTO, 1988. 143p.

Haiti. F. Chambers. 2d ed. *World bibliographical series*, vol. 39. Oxford, UK: CLIO Press, 1994. 272p.

Haiti, history, and the gods. J. Dayan. Berkeley, CA: University of California Press, 1995. 262p.

History of Methodism in Haiti. L. Griffiths. Port-au-Prince: Imprimerie Méthodiste, 1991. 406p.

La coexistence de types religieux différents dans l'Haïtien contemporain. L. Petit-Monsieur. Immensee: Neue Zeitschrift für Missionswissenschaft, 1992. 427p.

Le Christianisme en Haiti. E. A. Jeanty. Port-au-Prince: La Librairie de la Presse Evangélique, 1990. 130p.

Le protestantisme dans la société haïtienne: contribution à l'étude sociologique d'une religion. C. Romain. Port-au-Prince: Impr. H. Deschamps, [1986]. 380p.

Le protestantisme Haïtien. Catts Pressoir. Port-au-Prince: Imprimerie de la Société Biblique et des Livres Religieux d'Haïti, 1945. vol. 1; Port-au-Prince: Imprimerie du Séminaire Adventiste, 1977. vol. 2.

'Le role du Vaudou dans l'indépendance d'Haïti,' A. M. Rigaud, *Présence africaine* (Paris), (February—March, 1958), 43–67.

'Life in Haiti: Voodoo and the Church,' J. Breda [pseud], *Commonweal*, 78, 9 (1963), 241–44.

'Médicine et Vodou en Haïti,' A. Metraux, *Acta tropica*, Separatum Vol. 10, 1 (1953), 28–68.

'Pentecostalism in the context of Haitian religion and health practice.' F. J. Conway. Ph.D. dissertation, American University, Washington, DC, 1978. 291p.

Pour une église authentiquement haïtienne: essai d'introduction à une théologie chrétienne haïtienne. J. Casséus. Limbé, Cap Haitien: Séminaire théologique baptiste d'Haïti, 1987. 110p.

'Réactions psychologiques à la christianisation de la Valée de Marbial (Haïti),' A. Metraux, *Revue de psychologie des peuples*, 8 (1953), 250–67. (Official government attempt to destroy Voodoo in Haiti, and its failure).

Religion and politics in Haiti. H. Courlander & R. Bastien. Washington, DC: Institute for Cross-Cultural Research, 1966. 81p.

Religion in the art of Haiti. L. Chalom. [New York]: Maple Press, 1968.

Religions et politique en Haïti (1804–1990). M. M. Nérestant. Paris: Karthala, 1994. 285p.

Religious cults of the Caribbean: Trinidad, Jamaica and Haiti. G. E. Simpson. 3rd ed. *Caribbean Monograph Series*, No. 15. Río Piedras, Puerto Rico: Institute of Caribbean Studies, University of Puerto Rico, 1980. 347p.

Spirits of the night: the vaudun gods of Haiti. S. Rodman & C. Cleaver. Dallas: Spring Publications, 1992. 160p.

'Spiritual conflict resolution in a Haitian context.' D. W. Taylor. D. Miss. thesis, Trinity Evangelical Divinity School, Deerfield, IL, 1993. 183p.

'Survivance des cultes africains et syncrétisme en Haiti,' J. M. Salgado, in *Devant les sectes non-chrétiennes: rapports et compte renu*, p.225–52. Paris: Desclée de Brouwer, 1961.

'The belief system of Haitian Vodun,' G. E. Simpson, *American anthropologist*, (January, 1945), 35–59.

'The Catholic Church and rural social change: priests, peasant organizations. and politics in Haiti.' M. McClure. Ph.D. dissertation, Harvard University, Cambridge, MA, 1986.

The Catholic church in Haiti: political and social change. A. Greene. East Lansing, MI: Michigan State University Press, 1993. 312p.

The faces of the gods: vodou and Roman Catholicism in Haiti. L. G. Desmangles. Chapel Hill, N.C.: The University of North Carolina Press, 1992. 231p.

The growing church in Haiti. H. A. Johnson. Coral Gables, FL: West Indies Mission, 1970. 88p.

'The politicizing of religious groups and elites in the Latin America–Caribbean region: Haiti, 1980–1986.' G. K. Freeland. Ph.D. dissertation, University of California, Santa Barbara, 1990. 326p.

'The scourged Christ of Haiti: politics, economics and the church in the Island Republic.' F. D. Wood. D.Min. thesis, Wesley Theological Seminary, Washington, DC, 1985.

'The transformation of the Catholic Church in Haiti.' S. M. Mathieu. Ph.D. dissertation, Indiana University, Bloomington, IN, 1991. 228p.

'The Vodun service in northern Haiti,' G. E. Simpson, *American anthropologist*, (April 1940), 236–54.

Voodoo and the church in Haiti. B. Richards. Berkeley, CA: University of California, Extension Media Center, 1988. (60 min. videocassette).

Voodoo in Haiti. A. Metraux. New York: Oxford University Press, 1959; reprint, New York: Schocken Books, 1972.

Voodoos and obeahs: phases of West Indian witchcraft. J. J. Williams. 1932; reprint, New York: AMS, 1970. 257p. (Focuses on Haiti and Jamaica).

Country Table 2. **Organized churches and denominations in Haiti.**

Official name (bold type = church with over 10% of all affiliated) 1	*Begun* 2	*Type* 3	*Counc* 4	*Congs* 5	*Adults* 6	*Affiliated 1970* 7	*Affiliated 1995* 8	*G%* 9	*Names, notes, and other statistics* (see Codebook, Part 3) 10
Armée du Christ		I-3oU	.....	10	1,000	–	2,000	0.05	*Christ's Army.* An indigenous Haitian denomination.
Armée du Salut	1950	P-Sal	xwM..	30	1,000	1,000	2,000	2.81	*Salvation Army, Haiti Division*, Caribbean & CAmerica Territory (HQ Jamaica). 1h.
Assemblées de Dieu	1945	P-Pe2	ZF...	203	65,735	20,000	96,478	6.50	M=Assemblies of God (USA). Splits. 5 schools. HQ Port-au-Prince. 89n,6f,1s(14).
Convention Baptiste d'Haïti	1823	P-Bap	T.H.E	89	125,000	60,000	220,000	5.33	*Baptist Convention.* 1923, M=ABHMS(USA). 65n,2x,11f,5p,1s,W=85%,2920Y,10840z.
Eglise Adventiste du Septième Jour	1879	P-Adv	x....	262	148,800	60,000	298,000	6.62	*Seventh-day Adventists, N&S Haiti Missions.* 25nx,10f,1h,1j,1r,1s,320t(47707) 3330Y.
Eglise Apostolique de Déliverance		I-3oU	.....	25	1,500	–	3,000	0.05	*Deliverance Evangelistic Ch of Apostolic Faith.*
Eglise Catholique au Haïti:	1493	R-Lat	B.L.R	1,156	3,483,000	3,797,400	6,012,028	1.85	*Catholic Ch in Haiti.* C=8+3+21. (1970) 150n. (1990). 294n 204x 502m 1025w 203144Y
M Cap-Haïtien	1861	R-Lat	Bs	121	436,000	743,800	752,830	0.05	Northeast. Rural. 27 priests are Haitians. 1p. 42n 28x 36m 127w 13869Yy
D Fort-Liberté	1991	R-Lat	Bs	21	182,000	–	315,000	25.00	M=OMI. 9n 20x 42m 32w 5951Yy
D Hinche	1972	R-Lat	Bs	114	156,000	–	270,000	4.35	Rapid expansion (migrants, refugees). 18n 7x 56m 69w 10630Yy
D Les Gonaïves	1861	R-Lat	Bs	257	417,000	555,600	720,000	1.04	Rural. 7 priests are Haitians. 600 catechumens. 20n 23x 34m 61w 6412Yy
D Port-de-Paix	1861	R-Lat	Bs	15	190,000	220,000	327,000	1.60	Extreme northwest. Rural Voodoo strong. M=SMM. 10n 19x 49m 40w 8061Yy
M Port-au-Prince	1861	R-Lat	Bs	53	1,160,000	1,348,000	2,000,000	1.59	Capital urban. Extreme impoverishment in slums. 1s. 104n 59x 184m 428w 121321Yy
D Jacmel	1988	R-Lat	Bs	124	186,000	–	322,198	14.29	Population 75% Catholic. 16n 7x 13m 48w 8500Yy
D Jérémie	1972	R-Lat	Bs	23	214,000	–	370,000	4.35	70% Catholic. 29n 11x 35m 75w 5704Yy
D Les Cayes	1861	R-Lat	Bs	428	542,000	930,000	935,000	0.02	Extreme southwest peninsula. Rural. Voodoo strong. 46n 30x 53m 145w 22696Yy
Eglise de Dieu (Anderson)		P-Hol	.....	50	3,000	3,190	6,380	0.05	M=Church of God(Anderson) (USA).
Eglise de Dieu (Cleveland)	1934	P-Pe3	ZFH.E	289	38,569	40,000	117,000	4.39	M=Ch of God(Cleveland) (USA). 15 Districts. HQ Port-au-Prince. 173n,5f,1p(30).
Eglise de Dieu de Prophétie	1931	P-Pe3	Z.H.E	206	15,700	34,000	39,100	0.56	*Ch of God of Prophecy.* M=CGP(USA), split in USA from Ch of God (Cleveland).
Eglise de Dieu en Christ		I-3pB	Z....	127	14,000	15,000	35,000	0.05	*Ch of God in Christ.* M=CoGiC(Black mission from USA). HQ Port-au-Prince.
Eglise de Dieu Pentecôtiste	1952	P-Pe2	Z....	100	9,000	18,889	18,000	-0.19	*Pentecostal Ch of God.* M=PCG(Puerto Rico). HQ Port-au-Prince. 153n,2f,1s.
Egl Déliverance de Foi Apostolique	c1980	I-3oU	.....	20	2,000	–	4,000	6.67	*Deliverance Evangelistic Church of Apostolic Faith.* Oneness. HQ Port-au-Prince.
Eglise du Nazarène	1946	P-Hol	xFH.E	287	57,474	30,000	140,566	6.37	M=CoN. 40 schools. 10n,5x,154m,11f,1h,1j,1r,1s(33),159t,W=72%,975Y,13427z.
Eglise Episcopale d'Haïti	1861	A-Hig	aw.R.	324	58,500	38,452	103,000	4.02	Begun by US Blacks. Since 1913 in ECUSA, Province 2. 26n,1x,1s,W=40%,36Y,921y.
Eglise Episcopale Méthodiste Chrétienne		I-Met	.....	100	13,000	3,330	21,700	0.05	*Christian Methodist Episcopal Ch.*
Eglise Evangelique d'Haïti	1946	P-Hol	xFH.E	120	18,000	2,915	60,000	12.86	*Ev Ch of H.* Begun by M=EWIBM; 1958 M=OMS(USA). Radio station 4VEH. 4n,39f,1h,24Y.
Eglise Internationale Quadrangular	1981	P-Pe2	Z....	1	19	–	48	7.14	*International Ch of the Foursquare Gospel.* M=ICFG(USA).
Eglise Luthérienne d'Haiti		P-Lut	.....	5	525	–	1,050	0.05	*Lutheran Church of Haiti.*
Eglise Mennonite	1966	P-Men	G....	18	354	190	1,010	6.91	*Mennonite Ch.* M=Ch of God in Christ (Mennonite) (USA). 2 schools. 13f.
Eglise Méthodiste d'Haïti	1807	P-Met	VwM..	270	6,739	22,500	20,000	-0.47	*MCCA, Haiti District.* M=MMS(UK). Urban. 30 schools. 4n,5x,11f,1h,3r,341Yy,2182z.
Eglise Méthodiste Episcopale Africaine	1823	I-Met	VwM..	8	1,700	15,000	3,000	-6.23	In 16th Episcopal District, AMEC(USA). Begun by 500 USA Negroes invited in.
Eglise Méthodiste Libre	1949	I-Hol	VFH.E	49	18,800	2,000	33,100	11.88	*Free Methodist Ch.* Begun 1949 by Haiti Inland Mission; 1964 joined M=FMC(USA). 5f,1h,1s.
Eglise Missionnaire	1900	P-Hol	xFH.E	74	19,300	3,000	34,000	10.20	1951, M=MCA, now MC(USA). Central Plateau. Strong Vodun area. 14 schools, 11f,1h,1p.
Eglise Neo-Apostolique	c1970	I-3aX	x....	20	2,000	–	3,152	38.02	*New Apostolic Church. NAC/NAK.* World HQ Zurich (Switzerland).
Eglise Pentecostale d'Sainteté	1973	P-Pe3	.....	42	3,600	–	9,000	4.55	*Pentecostal Holiness Church.* M=IPHC(USA).
Eglise Pentecôtiste Unie	1962	P-Pe1	x....	140	5,600	10,000	13,000	1.05	*United Pentecostal Ch/Jesus Only.* M=UPC(USA). Unitarian Pentecostals. 60n,1p(28).
Eglise Reformée Chrétienne	1985	P-Ref	.....	3	180	–	360	10.00	*Christian Reformed Church.* M=CRWM.
Eglise Réorganisée de J-C des SDJ		m-LdS	x....	3	1,000	766	1,500	0.05	M=Reorganized Ch of Jesus Christ of Latter-Day Saints (USA). Schism in USA ex Mormons.
Eglise Wesleyenne d'Haïti	1946	P-Hol	VFH.E	113	5,440	8,000	9,890	0.85	*Wesleyan Ch.* M=WC(USA). 32 schools. 6n,3x,13f,2H,3h,W=62%,344Y,210z.
Eglises Baptistes Indépendantes	1982	I-Bap	.T...	10	1,000	1,000	2,000	7.69	*Independent Baptist Churches of Cap Haitien.* HQ Port-au-Prince. Fundamentalists.
Eglises Ebenezer	1960	I-Bap	..M..	75	6,000	8,000	12,000	1.64	*Ebenezer Mission.* Rejected 1960 formation of Baptist Convention. Jacmel area.
Jesus Nom Temple Apostolique	c1980	I-3oU	.....	12	1,500	–	3,800	6.67	*Jesus Name Apostolic Temple.* Oneness. HQ Gonaives. 11n.
Mission Baptiste	1934	I-Bap	x....	5	600	1,000	1,090	0.35	*Baptist Mid-Missions. M=BMM(USA). Fundamentalist Baptists. 6f.*
Mission Baptiste Conservatrice	1946	I-Bap	TFH.E	345	38,800	24,000	68,200	4.27	*Conservative Baptist Haiti Mission.* M=CBFMS(USA). Many splits. 93 schools. 13n,1H.
Mission Ev Baptiste du Sud-Haïti	1936	P-Bap	xMH.E	275	35,000	35,000	100,000	4.29	*Baptist Mission of South Haiti.* M=WT(USA). 38 Districts, 117n,40f,1h,1r,1s(57).
Mission Evangélique Baptiste d'Haïti	1928	P-Bap	xMH.E	345	13,325	35,389	28,417	-0.87	*Baptist Mission of Haiti.* 1943, M=UFM(USA). 20n,9x,45f,1H,2h,1p(4)W=57%,858Y,1238z.
Mission Foi et Sainteté	1962	P-Hol	.....	235	25,000	6,000	44,000	8.30	*Faith Holiness Mission.* M=WGM.
Missions Mondiales	1961	I-Non	x....	278	25,000	30,000	50,000	2.06	M=World-Wide Missions (USA). Evangelicals based in Pasadena, CA (USA).
Témoins de Jéhovah	1944	m-Jeh	x....	170	6,427	4,234	40,700	9.47	*Jehovah's Witnesses. Watch Tower.* 1944, Brooklyn responsible. (1975) 197Y. (1995) 1072Y.
Other Black indigenous churches		I-3pU	.....	60	40,000	40,000	80,000	0.05	Total about 30 (see below), mainly splits from Baptist and other denominations.
Other independent Oneness bodies		I-3oU	.....	100	5,000	–	10,000	0.05	About 20 different smaller bodies.
Other Protestant denominations		P-	.....	20	10,000	10,000	20,000	0.05	Total over 130 (see list below).
Doubly-affiliated		2-aff			-389,000	-80,000	-697,569		Evangelicals who also are or were baptized Roman Catholics.
Totals				**6,074**	**3,939,187**	**4,300,255**	**7,070,000**		

Churches, members, growth, 1900-2025	*Congs*	*Adults*	*Affiliated*	*G%*	*Total denominations*	*6 Megablocs:* *O*	*R*	*A*	*P*	*I*	*m*
Total churches, members, and denominations (mid-1900)	1,000	737,000	1,281,000	1.75	7	0	1	1	3	2	0
Total churches, members, and denominations (mid-1970)	3,909	2,474,561	4,300,255	1.75	106	0	1	1	80	22	2
Total churches, members, and denominations (mid-1990)	5,500	3,615,000	6,487,300	2.08	225	0	1	1	160	61	2
Total churches, members, and denominations (mid-1995)	6,074	3,939,187	7,070,000	1.74	230	0	1	1	162	64	2
Total churches, members, and denominations (mid-2000)	6,500	4,257,000	7,639,424	1.56	234	0	1	1	164	66	2
Total churches, members, and denominations (mid-2025)	14,000	6,157,000	11,050,000	1.49	400	2	1	1	190	200	6

NOTES ON TABLE ABOVE

NATIONAL COUNCILS (Column 4, 5th letter).

C = Protestant Federation of Haiti (FPH, 1986).

E = Concile des Eglises Evangéliques d'Haïti (CEEH) (Council of Evangelical Churches of Haiti, CECH), 1964.

R = Conférence Episcopale de Haïti (CEH) (Episcopal Conference of Haiti).

OTHER BLACK INDIGENOUS CHURCHES. These are largely a vast number of independent congregations, either unorganized, or in groupings or organized ephemerally in associations. Among the latter are: African-Negro Mission (under a bishop), Foi Apostolique Nationale, Mission Patriotique Chrétienne. Also there are various USA Black missions at work, including: AME Zion Ch, National Baptist Convention of America, Pentecostal Assemblies of the World, Progressive National Baptist Convention (1965).

OTHER PROTESTANT DENOMINATIONS. These number over 130, mostly smaller bodies from the USA, and include the following: Ch of God Holiness (1966), Ch of the Faith (Faith Holiness Mission/World Gospel Mission, 1965), Chs of God in North America (1967), Elim Missionary Assemblies (1968), Ev Bible Mission (1963), Ev Methodist Ch (1962), Haiti Mountain Mission, Maranatha Baptist Mission (1968, Strict Baptist Mission, Worldwide Evangelization Crusade.

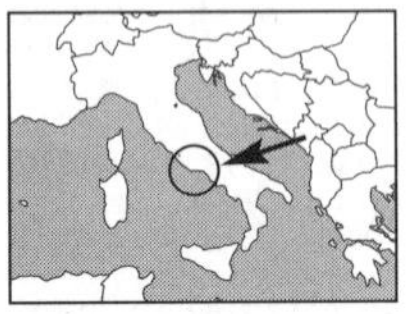

HOLY SEE

SECULAR DATA, AD 2000

STATE
Official name: Santa Sede/Stato della Città del Vaticano (The Holy See).
Short name: Holy See. **Adjective of nationality:** of the Holy See.
Flag: Yellow and white bars; crossed keys of St Peter under papal tiara on white bar.
Area: 1 sq. km. (0.4 sq. mi.).
Government: Ecclesiastical sovereign state, since 1929 (in papal lands before 1850, 1870 part of Italian kingdom, 1929 sovereign state).
Legislature: Commission (appointed by the Pope).
Official language: Latin.
Monetary unit: 1 lira (Lit, plural lire) = 100 centesimi. **US$1=** Lit 1,652.
Chief cities: CITTA DEL VATICANO (Vatican City) 1,000.
Political divisions: 1 province.

DEMOGRAPHY
Population: 1,000.
Population density: 1,000.0/sq. km. (2,600/sq. mi.).
Under 15 years: 200.
Growth rate p.a.: -0.18% (births 8.48, deaths 10.90).
Mortality: Infant, per 1,000: 6.6; **Maternal per 100,000:** 10.0.
Life expectancy: 79 (male 76, female 82).
Household size: 2.0. **Floor area per person, sq.m:** 50.0.
Major languages: Latin, Italian, English, French, Spanish, Portuguese, German.
Urban dwellers: 100.00%. **Urban growth rate p.a.:** 0.0%.
Labor force: 90%.

ETHNOLINGUISTIC PEOPLES
62.0% Italian.

ECONOMY
National income p.a. per person: US$20,000; **per family:** US$40,000.

EDUCATION
Adult literacy: 100% (male 100%, female 100%). **Schools:** 1.
Universities: 1. **School enrolment:** female/male: 100%/100%.

HEALTH
Access to health services: 95%. **Access to safe water:** 100%.
Hospitals: 1 (40 beds per 10,000). **Doctors:** 20.
Blind: 20. **Deaf:** 100. Murder **rate:** 1.
Lepers: 0.

LITERATURE
New book titles p.a.: 400. **Periodicals:** 140. **Newspapers:** 1 daily.

COMMUNICATION (per 1,000 people)
Phones: 500 (25% mobile). Radios: 1,200. **TV sets:** 700.
Daily newspaper circulation: 1. **Computers:** 1,000.

HUMAN LIFE AND LIBERTY (optimum condition=100.0%)
HDI: 95.0. **HSI:** 95.0. **HFI:** 90.0. **EFL:** 60.0.

Country Table 1. Religious adherents in the Holy See, AD 1900-2025.

Year	1900		1970		mid-1990		Annual change, 1990-2000				mid-1995		mid-2000		mid-2025	
Name	Adherents	%	Adherents	%	Adherents	%	Natural	Conversion	Total	Rate	Adherents	%	Adherents	%	Adherents	%
Christians	**1,000**	**100.0**	**1,000**	**100.0**	**1,000**	**100.0**	**0**	**0**	**0**	**0.00**	**1,000**	**100.0**	**1,000**	**100.0**	**1,000**	**100.0**
PROFESSION																
professing Christians	**1,000**	**100.0**	**1,000**	**100.0**	**1,000**	**100.0**	**0**	**0**	**0**	**0.00**	**1,000**	**100.0**	**1,000**	**100.0**	**1,000**	**100.0**
AFFILIATION																
unaffiliated Christians	0	0.0	20	2.0	20	2.0	0	0	0	0.00	20	2.0	20	2.0	20	2.0
affiliated Christians	**1,000**	**100.0**	**980**	**98.0**	**980**	**98.0**	**0**	**0**	**0**	**0.00**	**980**	**98.0**	**980**	**98.0**	**980**	**98.0**
Roman Catholics	1,000	100.0	980	98.0	980	98.0	0	0	0	0.00	980	98.0	980	98.0	980	98.0
Trans-megabloc groupings																
Evangelicals	0	0.0	0	0.0	20	2.0	0	0	0	0.00	20	2.0	20	2.0	40	4.0
Pentecostals/Charismatics	0	0.0	80	8.0	115	11.5	0	1	1	0.43	118	11.8	120	12.0	150	15.0
Great Commission Christians	**400**	**40.0**	**300**	**30.0**	**450**	**45.0**	**0**	**1**	**1**	**0.24**	**450**	**45.0**	**461**	**46.1**	**480**	**48.0**
World A (unevangelized persons)	0	0.0	0	0.0	0	0.0	0	0	0	0.00	0	0.0	0	0.0	0	0.0
World B (evangelized non-Christians)	0	0.0	0	0.0	0	0.0	0	0	0	0.00	0	0.0	0	0.0	0	0.0
World C (Christians)	1,000	200.0	1,000	100.0	1,000	100.0	0	0	0	0.00	1,000	100.0	1,000	100.0	1,000	100.0
Country's population	**1,000**	**100.0**	**1,000**	**100.0**	**1,000**	**100.0**	**0**	**0**	**0**	**0.00**	**1,000**	**100.0**	**1,000**	**100.0**	**1,000**	**100.0**

COLUMNS, ROWS.
For meanings and definitions, see Codebook (Part 3). Note that, by definition, total 'Christians' = professing + crypto-Christians, which also = affiliated + unaffiliated Christians, and also = Great Commission Christians + latent Christians. Percentages may not always total exactly, due to rounding.

NOTES ON RELIGION
COUNTRY'S POPULATION. In 1853 the Pontifical States in Italy had a population of 3,134,188 (99.7% Roman Catholics, 0.3% Jews); in 1870 they became part of the Italian state. The territory that is now the Vatican state was part of Italy until its creation as a sovereign state in 1929. In 1975 it consisted of Vatican City property, together with a number of extra-territorial buildings (churches and offices) in Rome. The population figures above refer to the de facto population in these territories and properties.
ROMAN CATHOLICS. Vast numbers of Catholics attend services in St Peter's basilica regularly. *Pilgrims.* The first Holy Year in Rome in AD 1300 attracted 200,000 pilgrims. In the 1950 Holy Year the total was 2.5 million; and in the 1975 Holy Year, 8,370,000 pilgrims.

Great Commission Instrument Panel: status of the Holy See (for explanation see start of Part 4)

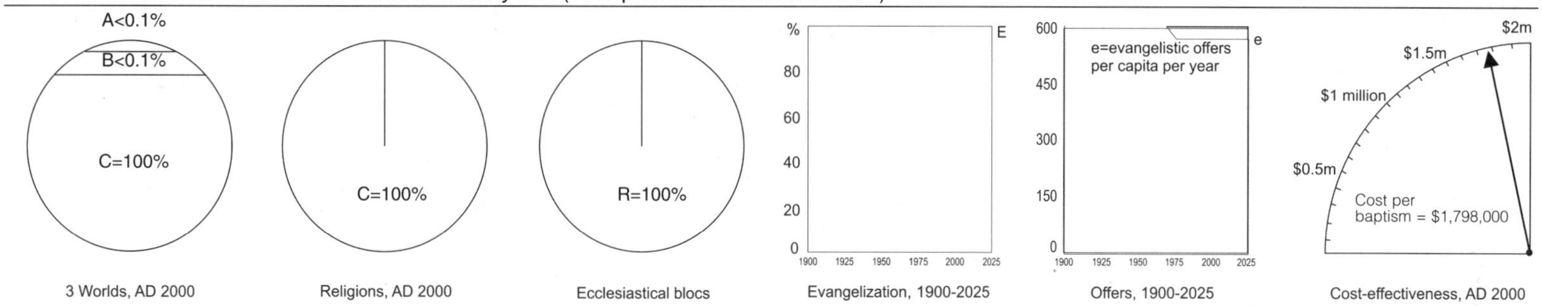

Country status. The Holy See (officially known as the State of the Vatican City) is the world's smallest sovereign territorial unit and also the world's only sacerdotal government. The vast majority of the inhabitants of the Vatican City are officials of the Roman Catholic Church, governed by the Apostolic Constitution of 1967.

HUMAN LIFE AND LIBERTY

Human rights and freedoms. A large part of the concerns and work of Vatican officials and staff relates to monitoring human rights situations worldwide and upholding Christian values and standards for the world's populations of any religion or none.

The Vatican has the world's largest output of postage stamps with Christian themes. *Above left.* Christ's Resurrection. *Right.* Pentecost. *Left.* Pius XI in 1929 year of Lateran Agreements.

CHRISTIANITY

CATHOLIC CHURCH. **The Holy See** is the supreme organ of the Roman Catholic Church and is, at the same time, a widely-international juridical entity. The existence of the City of the Vatican and of the state dates from the signing of the Lateran Agreements with Italy in November 1929, as a result of which the Holy See possesses full ownership of the Vatican territory, with exclusive power and sovereign jurisdiction. The creation of this state had as its purpose the assurance of a territorial base essential to the exercise of international sovereignty. Prior to this, in the intervening period after 1870 when the last papal states were annexed by the kingdom of Italy, the papacy had nevertheless continued to exercise its traditional state prerogatives, particularly those concerned with the sending and receiving of diplomatic personnel and the conclusion of treaties and concordats. These prerogatives were validated through an Italian law according a series of privileges to the Holy See because of its spiritual role but refusing it all territorial sovereignty. The Holy See had never ceased protesting against this dispossession. A new agreement was signed on February 18, 1984, with a comprehensive text in Italian.

In international public law, the state character of the Vatican has not been unanimously accepted. Some authorities hold that since the demographic element essential to statehood is lacking, Vatican citizenship is not a permanent tie between citizen and state but as purely functional qualification in which the individual retains the nationality of his country of origin. Vatican citizenship does in fact have only a provisional character and ceases when the function ceases for which it has been accorded. The question has therefore been raised whether the sovereign pontiff can exercise any real political power in the absence of any real population base.

The terminology of the Lateran Agreements involves certain ambiguities, particularly in relation to the term 'state', which is used sometimes with reference to the Holy See and sometimes with reference to Vatican City. Nevertheless, the latter regards itself as a true sovereign state and is a member of several international organizations including the Universal Postal Union, International Telecommunications Union, International Wheat Council, International Union for the Protection of Literary and Artistic Works and the International Union for the Protection of Industrial Property.

Vatican City. With an area of 44 hectares (0.44 square kilometers), Vatican City (Stato della Citta del Vaticano) is the smallest country in the world. It includes St Peter's square and basilica, the apostolic palace, and the papal gardens. Twelve other buildings in the vicinity of Rome but outside the City have extra-territorial rights, including exemption from expropriation and taxes: the Lateran basilica and palace, the basilicas of St Mary Major and St Paul Outside-the-Walls, the papal summer residence at Castelgandolfo 25 kms south of Rome, as well as the palaces of the Dataria, Chancellery, Propagation of the Faith, St Calixtus of Trastevere, Congregation for the Eastern Churches, Holy Office, ancient vicariate of Rome at the Villa della Pigna, and College of the Propaganda. Since 1951, the area holding the transmitting antennas of Radio Vatican at Santa Maria di Galeria 20 kms out of Rome has also been extra-territorialized; the recording studios themselves are lodged in an old tower in the center of the papal gardens. In 1994, Vatican City had as its population the pope, 462 citizens (33 cardinals, 200 representatives of the Holy See serving abroad, 34 secular and 4 religious priests, 66 members of the Swiss Guard and 68 laymen), and also 307 juridically-defined 'residents', all of whom retain in addition their nationality of origin. Furthermore, some 5,000 people were residing in buildings belonging to the Holy See but located on Italian territory. The Vatican issues its own currency and postage stamps, and has its own flag, police force, radio station, museums, art galleries, printing press, daily newspaper and its own railway station.

After his 1978 election pope John Paul I addresses 2 million faithful from balcony of St Peter's Basilica.

Secular administration. According to the founding Law of the Vatican City (7 June 1929), the pope has full legislative, executive, and judicial powers. Diplomatic relations with foreign countries and treaty-making are also his prerogatives but are carried out through an intermediary, the cardinal secretary of state. The pope today delegates his legislative and executive powers to the Pontifical Commission for the State of Vatican City (Pontificia Commissione per lo

Country summary. Worlds A, B, C by ethnolinguistic peoples, cities, and major civil divisions in the Holy See.

	PEOPLES							CITIES							CIVIL DIVISIONS						
World	Num	Pop 2000	C%	Christians	E%	U%	Unevangelized	Num	Pop 2000	C%	Christians	E%	U%	Unevangelized	Num	Pop 2000	C%	Christians	E%	U%	Unevangelized
A	0	0	0.00	0	0	0	0	0	0	0.00	0	0	0	0	0	0	0.00	0	0	0	0
B	0	0	0.00	0	0	0	0	0	0	0.00	0	0	0	0	0	0	0.00	0	0	0	0
C	4	1,000	98.00	980	100	0	0	1	1,000	98.00	980	100	0	0	1	1,000	98.00	980	100	0	0
Total	**4**	**1,000**	**98.00**	**980**	**100**	**0**	**0**	**1**	**1,000**	**98.00**	**980**	**100**	**0**	**0**	**1**	**1,000**	**98.00**	**980**	**100**	**0**	**0**

Stato della Citta del Vaticano), composed of cardinals named by him for 5-year terms, assisted by a special delegate also appointed by the pope and on whom executive powers are conferred except in those areas where the commission decides otherwise. This commission has been aided since 1968 by a consultative council of 24 laymen residing in Rome (Consulta dello Stato). The pope's judicial powers are exercised by 3 courts: Apostolic Penitentiary, Rota, and Apostolic Signature. The judicial system is based on canon law where applicable; in other cases, the laws of the city of Rome are used.

Religious administration. Vatican City is an integral part of the Diocese of Rome; nevertheless it has its own religious administration, the Vicariate of Vatican City (Vicariato della Citta del Vaticano), under the direction of a vicar-general whose jurisdiction extends over the whole of the Vatican City with the exception of St Peter's Basilica and its sacristy, the Lateran palace and the papal villa of Castelgandolfo. St Anne's Church is the parish church of Vatican City and the Basilica of St John Lateran, which dates back to AD 324, is the pope's personal patriarchal basilica. The Basilica of St Peter, built between 1506 and 1626, is the largest Catholic church building in the world and is where most papal ceremonies take place.

The papacy. At the summit of the ecclesiastical hierarchy of the Catholic Church is the bishop of Rome, also called pope, sovereign pontiff, holy father, and head of the universal church. Catholic dogma considers the papal primacy as being of divine origin, the pope receiving this primacy as the successor to the apostle Peter appointed by Jesus as head of the college of apostles. According to Vatican Council I (1870), in virtue of his charge as vicar of Christ and pastor of the whole church, the pope has direct authority over the entire body of the faithful and bishops, and over each one in particular, a power greater than the usual authority of a bishop. As patriarch of the West, also, he exercises a special authority over Western Christendom, over Italy and over the ecclesiastical province of Rome. Lastly, he is temporal sovereign of the Vatican state. The sum of his titles, therefore, is as follows: bishop of Rome, vicar of Jesus Christ, successor of the prince of the apostles, supreme pontiff of the universal church, patriarch of the West primate of Italy, archbishop and metropolitan of the Roman province, and sovereign of Vatican City.

The scope of papal powers has not been the same at all periods of history. In particular, the relation between the authority of the pope and that of bishops has not always followed the pattern of centralization which was at its peak between Vatican Council I (1869-70) and Vatican II (1962-65). In the Dogmatic Constitution on the Church ('Lumen gentium') of November 1964, Vatican II returned to an honored position the doctrine of collegiality in which the whole body of bishops, in union with the pope, exercises the supreme teaching and pastoral authority over the entire church, in addition to the authority which they have in their own dioceses. Lumen Gentium affirms that this collegiality of bishops with the pope is exercised in a solemn way through an ecumenical council, and can also be effected in other ways, 'provided that the head of the college calls them to collegiate action, or at least so approves or freely accepts the united action of the dispersed bishops, that it is made a true collegiate act' (paragraph 22). All ecumenical councils must be convoked, presided over and confirmed, or at least accepted, by the pope himself. This doctrine is based on the fact that 'by the institution of the Lord', 'St Peter and the other apostles constituted one apostolic college' (paragraph 22). In this spirit, Paul VI created in 1965 the Synod of Bishops to make permanent the exercise of collegiate authority. In practice, however the doctrine of collegiality is still nascent and is difficult to reconcile with the prerogatives of papal primacy.

Prior to the visit of John XXIII to Assisi and Loreto in 1963, no official papal visits had been made outside the Vatican since 1857, and until Paul VI no pope had left Italy since Pius VII was forced out by

Historic meeting in Vatican of Soviet president Mikhail Gorbachev, a Communist and an atheist, with pope John Paul II.

Napoleon between 1809 and 1814. In January 1964, Paul VI began his international journeys with a pilgrimage to the Holy Land where he met Athenagoras of Constantinople, the first meeting of a pope with an ecumenical patriarch in 900 years. Thereafter he visited Bombay, India for a eucharistic congress in November 1964; New York and the UN in October 1965; Fatima, Portugal in May 1967; Constantinople and Ephesus, Turkey in July 1967; Bogota, Colombia in August 1968; Geneva, Switzerland for visits to the World Council of Churches and the International Labour Organization in June 1969; Kampala, Uganda in July 1969; and the Far East in November-December 1970 for visits to Manila, Pago Pago (American Samoa), Sydney, Jakarta, Hong Kong, and Colombo.

From 1978 this tradition was taken further by John Paul II's extensive visits abroad, of which the most notable were to Mexico, Poland, Ireland, and the USA. By 1997 he had undertaken 75 such apostolic travels, traversing the entire globe a number of times.

A major watershed of historic significance took place when in 1988 the pope was visited in the Vatican by the president of the USSR, Mikhail Gorbachev.

College of Cardinals. Formed by the whole body of cardinals, the Sacred College or Council of the Pope has the crucial role of meeting in conclave to elect a new pope when the seat of Peter falls vacant. Individually, cardinals counsel the pope and many serve in the Curia.

The College of Cardinals received its definitive form in 1150. In 1586, their number was fixed at 70, which is still the norm established by canon law (Canon 231 of 1917). In 1959 John XXIII deviated for the first time from this principle in raising the number to 79, in order to assure greater international representation within the college. After several fluctuations, the number was finally brought to 145 by Paul VI at the time of the consistory or general meeting of cardinals in March 1973. Meanwhile, by motto proprio 'Ingravescentem aetatem' of 21 November 1970, the pope established 80 years as the maximum age for cardinals to continue in office, both within the Roman Curia and as papal electors. Thus only 117 of the 145 cardinals at the 1973 consistory were eligible as electors. By March 1973, the number of cardinals in each continent (with electors in brackets) was: Africa 9 (9), North America (Canada and USA) 15 (13), Latin America 21 (18), Asia 11 (11), Europe 84 (61), and Oceania 5 (5). Countries with the largest number of cardinals were: Italy 40 (30), USA 11 (10), France 11(8), Spain 7 (5), West Germany 6 (4), and Brazil 6 (5). Altogether, 51 countries were represented in the college, 34 of which had a single cardinal, several of whom in addition were over 80 years of age.

Twenty-three years later in 1996, the number of cardinals had risen to 165.

Below. 1975 Synod of Bishops in Sistine Chapel, on 'Evangelization'.

Synod of Bishops. Since 1965 the Synod of Bishops (Synodus Episcoporum) has been a permanent, central ecclesiastical institution with the function of counseling and assisting the pope in the government of the universal church. Its constitutive charter (motu proprio 'Apostolica sollictudo'), promulgated by Paul VI on 15 September 1965 during the last session of Vatican II, presents as the purposes of the Synod of Bishops 'to encourage close union and valued assistance between the Sovereign Pontiff and the bishops of the entire world; to ensure that direct and real information is provided on questions and situations touching upon the internal action of the Church and its necessary activity in the world today; to facilitate agreement on essential points of doctrine and on methods of procedure in the life of the Church'. The Synod is under the direct and immediate authority of the pope, who alone fixes dates of sessions, sets the agenda, confers deliberative power on its members when judged useful, presides over the sessions personally or by delegation and ratifies decisions taken. The Synod has a permanent or general secretary with several assistants, while the assemblies have a special secretary, all secretaries being nominated by the pope. Three types of assembly (general, extraordinary, and special) are provided for (1) A general assembly is made up of patriarchs, leading archbishops and metropolitans of Eastern-rite churches and not under patriarchs, elected bishops from national episcopal conferences (regional conferences such as CELAM and FABC, Federation of Asian Bishops' Conferences not being represented as such), 10 male religious personnel elected by the Union of General Superiors, the cardinals in charge of the dicasteries of the Roman Curia, together with other bishops, priests, and religious appointed directly by the pope up to 15% of the total membership. (2) A special assembly may be convoked at the regional level, and is made up of those members of the general assembly who belong to the region. Lastly (3) an extraordinary assembly has the same membership as the general assembly except that only presidents of episcopal conferences and 3 delegates from the Union of Male General Superiors may be members. The extraordinary assembly of 1969 decided that general assemblies should be convened every 2 years, but this was extended to 3 years in 1971 to permit better preparation. The 1969 assembly also fixed the organization of the permanent secretariat and requested that bishops be consulted before the agenda of any succeeding assembly was determined. The pope ratified this proposition and created in 1970 the Council of the General Secretariat of the Synod of Bishops to assist the secretary-general in maintaining liaison with episcopal conferences and in determining agendas. This council, composed of 15 members (12 elected by the assembly and 3 named by the pope), continues its work between assembly sessions.

By 1997, 12 assemblies had been held: the general assembly of October 1967, which had as its objective 'to preserve and reinforce the Catholic faith, its integrity, its strength, its development, its doctrinal and historical cohesiveness'; the extraordinary assembly of October 1969 which defined the principles of episcopal collegiality; the general assembly of October 1971 on justice in the world and the priestly ministry; the general assembly of October 1974 on evangelization in the modern world; 1977 on 'Catechetics in Our Time', 1980 the Christian family; 1983 on reconciliation and penance in the church; 1985, Extraordinary Synod on commemoration, evaluation, and promotion of Vatican Council II; 1987 on vocation and mission of laity in the church; 1990 on training of priests; 1993 on the consecrated life (religious personnel).

Roman Curia. The Curia is the church's highest-level centralized administrative and judicial body in Rome whose function is to assist the pope to govern. It consists of the Office of Secretary of State (the private secretariat of the pope), the Council for the Public Affairs of the Church, 10 congregations, 3 tribunals, 3 secretariats, as well as a large number of commissions, councils and offices. The Roman Curia has developed progressively over a lengthy period. It was reorganized in March 1968 by Paul VI who internationalized both its top executive posts, until then held exclusively by Italians, and also its entire personnel; whereas in 1961 its staff including consultants consisted of 749 Italians (57%) and 573 non-Italians (43%), by 1970 Italians were 854 (38%) and non-Italians 1,400 (62%). In 1970, Italians headed 11 of the 28 principal dicasteries of the Curia. The Office of Secretary of State has staff who are almost 80% Italian. The number of laymen has also increased, from 40 in 1961 to 200 in 1970 to several hundreds by 1997.

In the organization and functioning of the Curia, several procedures are commonly followed. Joint councils are constituted among the various congregations for dealing with common issues and problems. Seven diocesan bishops are appointed as members of each congregation, with full rights in annual plenary assemblies. The heads of dicasteries are now appointed for 5 years only and their posts automatically become vacant on the death of the pope. The new pope has 3 months to reconfirm them in their functions. Each congregation is directed by a cardinal prefect, assisted by a secretary and an under-secretary, all 3 appointed by the pope. Both prefect and secretary are appointed for 5 years and require similar reconfirmation. Laymen may be named as consultants of the Curia's departments, all appointed for 5 years which is renewable. Lastly, each congregation has its own direct liaison with episcopal conferences and communicates to the bishops decisions which concern them before they are promulgated.

Office of Secretary of State. Until recently this was simply one of several offices on the Holy See, ranking lower than the Curia's congregations and courts. However, in 1967 Paul VI elevated it to its present position of pre-eminence in the Curia. Its head, the cardinal secretary of state, is the principal adviser to the pope, is received regularly by him and accompanies him on all travels of note. His position corresponds to that of prime minister and minister of foreign affairs for the pontiff. The responsibilities of the secretary of state extend to any matters referred to him by the pope, in addition to his role as co-ordinator of the Curia's activities. The Secretariat of State has 2 sections: general affairs, and relations with states. He exercises authority over heads of dicasteries and can convene them whenever he requires. He supervises the Council of Cardinals and Bishops and serves as president of the Cor Unum Council, commissions for the Vatican State, Administration of Property of the Holy See, and Special Administration of the Holy See. He is also a member of 4 congregations (Doctrine of the Faith, Bishops, Evangelization of Peoples, Cause of the Saints) and of the commissions for the revision of Canon Law and Eastern Canon Law. He controls the diplomatic service of the Holy See, the Commission for Social Communications, and also General Services which is responsible for 2 important publications: *Annuario Pontificio*, and *Acta Apostolica Sedis*, the official journal of the Holy See (begun 1908) which publishes definitive texts of all official acts. Legal texts have the force of law 3 months after their publication in the *Acta*. Because of the sporadic publication of the *Acta, L'Osservatore Romano*, the official daily newspaper of the Holy See, gives temporary authority for such documents. The editing of *AP* is carried on in collaboration with the Central Office of Statistics of the church, now also under the secretary of state.

A former organization, the Council for the Public Affairs of the Church, was begun in 1814 under the title Congregation of Extraordinary Ecclesiastical Affairs. In 1967 the council changed its name. It has recently again been changed to Secretariat for Relations with States, being the second of the 2 sections under the Secretariat of State. It is charged with diplomatic and all other relations with foreign governments, and functions through nunciatures, apostolic delegations and other representatives of the Holy See. The Pontifical Commission for Russia was formerly under this council. It was also the congregation responsible for ecclesiastical affairs in Portugal and in Portuguese overseas territories; however, the latter have now been transferred to the jurisdiction of Propaganda.

Papal representatives. There are 3 types of pontifical representative: nuncios (for nations with a Catholic majority) and pro-nuncios (for nations with a Catholic minority) are accredited to countries which have diplomatic relations with the Holy See; permanent observers or delegates are appointed to certain international organizations; and apostolic delegates, with no diplomatic status, represent the Holy See to bishops in countries which have no diplomatic relations with the Holy See. A nuncio, according to customary law, is dean of the diplomatic corps in the country to which he is appointed, as stated in the Treaty of Vienna of 1815 and confirmed by the convention on diplomatic relations of Vienna in 1961. The development of diplomatic relations with non-Catholic countries led Paul VI in 1965 to adopt the term pro-nuncio to describe a representative with the powers of a nuncio but not given the honor by a country of being dean of its diplomatic corps.

In June 1974, the Holy See was represented throughout the world by 37 nunciatures with a nuncio (3 in Africa, 19 in America, 3 in Asia, and 12 in Europe including one for the European Community); 42 nunciatures headed by a pro-nuncio (22 in Africa, one in America, 12 in Asia, 5 in Europe including Turkey and 2 in Oceania); and 26 apostolic delegations (15 in Africa (including the Red Sea), 2 in America, 4 in Asia, 2 in Europe and 3 in Oceania). By 1997 this sit-

Huge crowds attend appearances and addresses of (*left*) John Paul II in Vatican Audience Hall and (*right*) John Paul I.

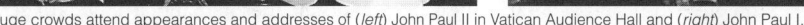

John Paul II and enthusiastic church workers at audience.

uation had been considerably extended to cover virtually all states and even mini-states (see this Encyclopedia's texts on individual countries for the Holy See's exact AD 2000 diplomatic status).

Recent years have witnessed a significant increase in the number of nunciatures and apostolic delegations in Third-World countries, especially Africa and the Middle East. Under Paul VI, in fact, diplomatic ties had been established with 5 more Arab countries than in 1963: Algeria, Iraq, Kuwait, Sudan, and Tunisia.

Nine permanent representatives of the Holy See to international governmental organizations include: permanent observes at the UN in New York; WHO, ILO and UN in Geneva; FAO in Rome; UNESCO in Paris; one to the Council of Europe in Strasbourg; delegates in Vienna to the International Agency for Atomic Energy and the UN Organization for Industrial Development, one to the Council for Cultural Co-operation of the Council of Europe, International Committee of Military Medicine and Pharmacy, and Union of Official Organizations for Tourism; the Holy See is also represented at the International Geographical Union.

Six permanent representatives of the Holy See are appointed to non-governmental international organizations including permanent observers or delegates to international committees concerned with the historical sciences, paleography, history of art, anthropology, and of medicine, as well as the International Study Centre for the Conservation and Restoration of Culture. Long considered an Italian domain, papal representation has recently been broadened to include a number of high-level representatives of other European countries; and in 1970 the Holy See began the recruitment of priests from the Third World for diplomatic work. There are now Korean, Japanese, Kenyan, and Zairean representatives in the diplomatic service, among many others. After having completed their studies of canon law, candidates study diplomacy at the Pontifical Ecclesiastical Academy in Rome, which was founded in 1701 and is now located outside Vatican City.

Congregations. The 9 congregations are primarily executive offices, each charged with a specific area in the government of the universal church and placed under the supervision of the cardinal secretary of state.

(1) The ***Congregation for the Doctrine of the Faith*** was created in 1542 under the title Congregation of the Universal Inquisition; it became the Congregation of the Holy Office in 1908 and received its present name in 1965. Vatican II called for re-organization and reform in the methods of the Holy Office, and Paul VI undertook this, suppressing inter alia the Index of prohibited books. The congregation is responsible for all questions of faith and morals. It examines new doctrines; promotes study and general meetings; criticizes doctrines judged contrary to the faith, after consultation with interested bishops; examines and condemns books, after having alerted the ordinary and having given the author a hearing and the right to defend himself and his work; it also administers the 'privilege of faith' (or Pauline privilege), which is the right to dissolve a legitimate marriage between a Catholic and a so-called infidel if the faith of the believing spouse is considered to be in danger. The congregation is served by 2 commissions, the Theological Commission and the Pontifical Biblical Commission.

(2) The ***Congregation for Bishops*** was erected in 1588 under the title Consistorial Congregation and reorganized under its present name in 1967. It is responsible for all matters concerning bishops and dioceses with the exception of the Eastern churches and the church's foreign missions under Propaganda. It includes in its jurisdiction the Pontifical Commission for Latin America, and the Pontifical Commission for Migration and Tourism.

(3) The ***Congregation for the Oriental Churches*** was created in 1862, united with Propaganda, then finally became autonomous in 1917 under the name Congregation for the Eastern Church. The last word in the title was changed from the singular to the plural in 1967 to show more respect for the distinctive character of the churches of the Eastern rite. This was also manifest in the appointment by John XXIII of 5 Eastern-rite patriarchs as members of the congregation, as well as Eastern-rite consultants by Paul VI. The responsibility of the congregation extends to all affairs concerning dioceses, personnel (bishops, clergy, religious and laity), and discipline in churches of the Eastern rite. Similar matters are handled for the Church of the Latin rite by the congregations for Bishops, Sacraments and Divine Worship, Clergy, Religious Personnel, and Catholic Education. The congregation exercises exclusive authority over all jurisdictions independent of rite in the following countries; Afghanistan, southern Albania, Bulgaria, Cyprus, Egypt, Eritrea and northern Ethiopia, Greece, Iran, Iraq, Jordan, Lebanon, Palestine (Gaza, Israel, West Bank), Syria, and Turkey. It includes the Special Commission for the Liturgy and issues an information service bulletin in Italian, French and English.

(4) The ***Congregation for Divine Worship and the Sacraments*** was formed in July 1975 by joining together the former Congregation for the Discipline of the Sacraments (created in 1908) and the Congregation for Divine Worship (created in 1969), the latter having taken over some of the responsibilities of the former Congregation of Rites. The new congregation is responsible for all matters relating to the discipline of the 7 sacraments, with the exception of those which fall under the competence of the Congregation for the Doctrine of the Faith, the courts of the Rota and Apostolic Signature; it is also responsible for the liturgical and extra-liturgical worship and life of the Latin church. Its jurisdiction extends over all territories of the Latin church and includes countries under Propaganda.

(5) The ***Congregation for the Clergy*** was established in 1564 under the name Congregation of the Council, its first task being to interpret the decrees of the Council of Trend. Its responsibility was later extended to cover general discipline of clergy and laity, but it was reorganized in 1967 to fulfill a more pastoral function. Its province now includes all that concerns the persons, pastoral work and ministry of clergy exercising their apostolate in dioceses, that is diocesan priests, deacons, and religious personnel engaged in normal pastoral work in a diocese. It operates through 3 offices, dealing with the training and spiritual growth of clergy, the preaching of the Word of God and the material needs of clergy and church properties.

(6) The ***Congregation for Institutes of Consecrated Life*** was created in 1586. After a variety of changes, it became in 1908 the Congregation for Religious Personnel and was reorganized and renamed in 1967. Being concerned with personnel in a non-territorial manner its jurisdiction extends to all male and female religious personnel, secular institutes and third orders of the Latin church. It consists of 2 sections: one for institutes and societies of male and female religious personnel; and the other for secular institutes, that is institutes of laymen who have professed the evangelical counsels and wish to implement them in the world. It sponsors a council for relations between the congregation and the international unions of general superiors.

(7) The ***Congregation for the Evangelization of Peoples*** was formed in 1622 as the Congregation of Propaganda Fide (Spreading the Faith), and received its present name in 1967. It is responsible for all foreign mission territories, with the exception of Portuguese territories and Goa, which came under the Council for the Public Affairs of the Church until 1975. Its territories are independent of those included under the Congregation for the Eastern Churches and include almost all of Africa, Asia and Oceania, several areas in the 2 Americas, and several countries and regions of Europe (Denmark, Norway, Finland, Sweden, Gibraltar, northern Albania and 5 ecclesiastical districts in former Yugoslavia). Its authority is final within these territories, except in matters which are in the competence of the congregations for the Doctrine of the Faith, Causes of Saints, and Divine Worship and Sacraments, including such matters as non-consummated marriages. Its authority also extends over the efforts of mission-sending countries in aid of mission-receiving countries. It sponsors a supreme council for administration of papal missionary works (in 51 countries, to promote missionary co-operation), which in turn is responsible for the Missionary Union of Clergy (in 53 countries), Society for the Propagation of the Faith, Society of St Peter the Apostle (for training clergy of mission countries, operating 85 major seminaries) and Society of the Holy Childhood (in 36 countries), in addition to 4 commissions including those for catechesis and catechists. The congregation also sponsors the Agenzia Internazionale Fides (AIF) which produces bulletins in Italian, French, English, Spanish, and German.

(8) The ***Congregation for the Causes of Saints*** was erected in 1969 with some of the responsibilities of the former Congregation of Rites, first established in 1588. It is concerned with beatifications, canonizations and the conservation of relics.

(9) The ***Congregation for Catholic Education*** was created in 1915 under the title Congregation of Seminaries, Universities and Studies, and was reorganized under its present name in 1967. It supervises the work and institutions of Catholic education, with the exception of those in territories under the congregations for the Oriental Churches and Evangelization of Peoples. It has 3 offices, dealing with seminaries, higher education (church-related universities and faculties) and lower schools of all types. In addition it sponsors the pontifical work for priestly vocations.

Courts. The Holy See's courts are colleges of cardinals and prelates handling judicial cases relating to internal questions of conscience and external matters. They consist of 3 distinct entities.

(1) The ***Apostolic Penitentiary*** originated in the 13th century, with its most recent reorganization in 1935. As a court, it is concerned with questions of conscience, both of a sacramental and extra-sacramental nature, and rules on the usage and concession of indulgences, absolutions, and dispensations.

(2) The ***Rota***, dating back to 1331, is the court of appeal of the Holy See and is particularly well known for its decisions concerning requests for nullifying marriages.

(3) The ***Apostolic Signature*** was established in the 13th century and reorganized by Paul VI. It is the supreme court of the church, composed of cardinals chosen by the pope, and is divided into 2 sections; one corresponding to a court of appeals which judges the competence of other courts as well as the observance of laws and rights at the highest level, and the second serving as a council of state which pronounces on controversies concerning acts of ecclesiastical administration, appeals against decisions of the Roman dicasteries and conflicts over areas of competence among the dicasteries. Decisions of the Rota may also be appealed to this body.

Pontifical Councils. Eleven Pontifical Councils, created or reorganized after Vatican II, are related to new concerns of the conciliar church.

(1) The ***Pontifical Council for the Promotion of Christian Unity*** was established by John XXIII in 1960 in preparation for Vatican II, received the rank of conciliar commission in 1962 and was definitively confirmed by Paul VI in 1966. Its general aim is to promote unity among Christians, to which end it creates relations with other ecclesiastical communities, sends Catholic observers to their meetings and invites them to send representatives to Catholic functions, co-ordinates at both the national and international levels efforts to promote unity, enters into dialogue on ecumenical questions, engages in activities with other churches, interprets and watches over the execution of the principles of ecumenism and conciliar decrees touching ecumenical questions and supports Catholic ecumenical groups. Each staff member is a specialist either concerning a particular Christian denomination or tradition, or concerning the World Council of Churches or theological questions, and there are also regional desks. The Office for Catholic-Jewish Relations was added to its responsibilities in 1967, and in 1974 the Commission for Religious Relations with Judaism was formed. The statues of the latter define it as a distinct body attached to the secretariat.

(2) The ***Pontifical Council for Inter-religious Dialogue*** was formed by Paul VI in 1964. It is concerned with promoting dialogue and studies to develop mutual understanding and respect between Catholics and all persons professing religions other than Christianity and to prepare manuals on dialogue with other religions. Its sub-sections include Asia, Hinduism, Buddhism, and Africa; and in October 1974 a new Commission for Religious Relations with Islam was created as a distinct body but attached to the secretariat. In 1970 the Islamic Council of Cairo and the Holy See agreed on a mutual exchange of appointed representatives.

(3) The ***Pontifical Council for Culture*** combines the former Pontifical Council for Dialogue with Non-Believers, and was created in 1965 by Paul VI to study the bases of theoretical and situational atheism, the latter being concerned with atheism not supported by philosophical or theoretical conceptualizations; and

One-month reign of Pope John Paul I, 1978. *Above.* Immediately after election in conclave of cardinals: first words 'We wish to remind the entire Church that its first duty is that of evangelization'. *Below left.* Public audience. *Below right.* At his funeral.

to open up and pursue dialogue with non-believers, and in particular to develop national commissions and secretariats, without itself becoming a substitute for the Pontifical Council for Culture set up in 1982 by John Paul II to cover the gospel and its relevance to today's culture.

(4) The ***Pontifical Council of the Laity*** (Consilium pro Laicis) was established in 1967 by Paul VI to implement the conciliar decree 'Apostolicam actuositatem' as a service to the whole church, to be a means of communication and dialogue and a sign of the co-responsibility of all the faithful. Its aim is to promote the development of the apostolate of the laity by co-ordinating apostolic work; establish bonds between laity and hierarchy; carry out doctrinal and practical studies, with special emphasis on opening the way for more lay participation in the church's pastoral program; as well as to serve as a documentation center. It publishes a journal.

(5) The ***Pontifical Council on Justice and Peace*** (Justitia et Pax) was created by Paul VI to implement Vatican II's pastoral constitution 'Gaudium et Spes'. Its purposes are to promote social justice at the international level, stimulate development in poor countries, and examine means of furthering peace in the world. National commissions for justice and peace had been established in 63 countries by June 1972, but their role and influence varies. Some have been very effective in bringing about a change of mentality and influencing action at the level of the local church. Nevertheless, the statutes of the pontifical commission are ambiguous and tensions have arisen with the office of the secretary of state because of the political nature of the problems with which the commission is confronted.

(6) The ***Pontifical Council for Interpretation of Legislative Texts*** was instituted by John XXIII in 1963 to prepare, in the light of the conciliar decrees of Vatican II, a revision of the 1917 Code of Canon Law. Its scope was revised and enlarged in 1967 and 1988.

(7) The ***Pontifical Council for Social Communications*** was established in 1948, acquired a permanent character in 1959 and received its present name in 1964. Its purpose is to put into affect the norms of the 1964 conciliar decree 'Inter mirifica' on social communications. Placed under the supervision of the secretary of state, it controls the press office of the Holy See, which was created in 1966, and administers the Vatican film library formed in 1959 to assemble and preserve films and TV programs dealing with the life of the church.

(8) The ***Pontifical Council for Migrants and Itinerants*** was formed in 1970 by Paul VI to offer pastoral assistance to migrants and travelers. It falls under the supervision of the Congregation for Bishops and includes 5 specialized sectors: Emigrants and Refugees, co-ordinating the work of 26 national directors (1971) without encroaching on the work of the International Catholic Commission on Migration (CICM) located in Geneva; Apostolatus Maris (Apostolate of the Sea), founded in 1922 with 29 national administrations and 2 regional organizations (Latin America and French West Africa), whose activities cover the maritime world; Apostolatus Aeris (Apostolate of the Air), which in 1971 co-ordinated the work of 19 airport chaplains; Apostolatus Nomadum (Apostolate for Nomads), which included 22 episcopal promoters and national directors in 1971; and the general pastoralia of tourism.

(9) The ***Cor Unum Pontifical Council***, created by Paul VI in 1971 and placed under the direct authority of the cardinal secretary of state, is neither an operational agency nor a regrouping of agencies. Rather it is a body dedicated to furthering the harmonization and co-ordination of aid by various Catholic organizations to the church in developing countries and as such is concerned with the integration of efforts with the directives of the hierarchy, especially the pope. The particular purpose of the council is to enable those representing the receiving or mission churches to have a stronger voice. It is composed of some 30 members, representing sending agencies, dicasteries of the Roman Curia, national churches, and laity.

(10) The ***Pontifical Council for the Family*** was established by Paul VI in 1973 on a 3-year experimental basis, and finally instituted by John Paul II in 1981. Its purpose is pastoral study and research, with an emphasis on promoting and safeguarding the spiritual, moral, and social realities of the family. It is part of the Council of the Laity, without however being dependent upon it. In addition to a co-ordinating group of 7 persons, it is composed of 18 members and 9 consultants, all appointed by the pope.

(11) The ***Pontifical Council for Health-Care Workers*** was begun as a commission in 1985 and in 1988 was raised to council status.

Commissions. A small number of commissions handle a variety of concerns, including the following:

(a)The ***Pontifical Commission for Latin America*** (CAL) was instituted in 1958 by Pius XII and placed under the supervision of the Congregation for Bishops in 1969. Its principal aim is to follow the activities of the Latin American Episcopal Council (CELAM) and national episcopal organizations in order to provide personnel and funds in aid of the Latin American church. Attached to it is the General Council for Latin America (COGECAL), formed in 1963 by Paul VI to integrate CAL; CELAM; presidents of the national episcopal organizations for Latin America found in Europe, USA and Canada; and presidents of the Union of Male General Superiors, International Union of Female General Superiors and Latin America Confederation of Religious Personnel. Its purpose is to study topics contributing to better co-operation in service to Latin America.

(b) The ***Study Commission on the Role of Woman in Society and Church***, composed of 15 women and 10 men (7 priests and 3 laymen), was established by Paul VI in 1973 following the recommendation of the 1971 Synod of Bishops.

(c) The ***Theological Commission*** is an international body instituted by Paul VI in 1969 on the recommendation of the first Synod of Bishops in 1967 to assist, on a consultative basis, the Congregation for the Doctrine of the Faith. The commission is under the prefect of this congregation and includes not more than 30 specialists representing different schools of thought. The latter are appointed by the pope after nomination by the prefect.

(d) The ***International Council for Catechesis*** was founded in 1975 by Paul VI to respond to the wish expressed by the Second International Catechetical Congress. It serves as a consultative organ to the Congregation for Clergy.

(e) The ***Pontifical Biblical Commission*** was created in 1902 and restructured in 1971 by Paul VI who placed it under the Congregation for the Doctrine of the Faith. It is a study commission to prepare instructions and decrees which are then promulgated by the congregation with the approval of the pope. The commission must be consulted on all proposals for new biblical norms.

(f) The ***Abbey of St Jerome for the Revision and Correction of the Vulgate*** was instituted by Pius XI in 1933 with the aim of improving the original text of St Jerome's 4th-century Latin translation of the Bible and also to prepare a scholarly edition as well. Its work has been replaced by the ***Pontifical Commission for the New Vulgate***, established in 1965 in order to amend the Vulgate's text to bring it into conformity with the original Hebrew and Greek texts of the Bible. The complete text appeared in 1979, and the second edition in 1986. This is the official text for the liturgy and documents of the Latin church.

(g) The ***Pontifical Commission for Sacred Archeology*** was created in 1852 for the preservation of the catacombs and other ancient buildings and Christian cemeteries in Rome and vicinity. Its authority has been extended by the Lateran Agreements to all other catacombs in Italy.

(h) The ***Pontifical Commission for Historical Sciences*** was formed in 1954 to represent the Holy See before the International Committee of Historical Sciences.

(i) ***Other commissions*** of lesser importance include: Pontifical Commission for Ecclesiastical Archives of Italy (founded in 1955); Central Pontifical Commission for Sacred Art in Italy (1924); Cardinal Commission for the Pontifical Sanctuaries of Pompei and Loreto (19th century); Pontifical Commission for Russia (1930; at present placed under the supervision of the Council for the Public Affairs of the Church, treating matters relating to clergy and faithful of the Latin rite in Russia); Commission for the Protection of Historical and Artistic Monuments of the Holy See (1923, reorganized in 1963); Pontifical Work for the Preservation of the Faith and for the Erection of New Churches in Rome (1930); Cardinal Commission of the Institute for the Work of Religion (1942, which administers funds for religious work); and the Pontifical Commission for the State and City of the Vatican.

Seen from the top of St Peter's: right, the Bernini colonnade, and left, the Apostolic Palace.

Offices. Vatican offices of particular significance include: (1) Prefecture of Economic Affairs, created in 1967 to supervise all financial agencies of the Holy See; (2) Apostolic Chamber, formed in 1934 to administer property and temporal rights during a vacancy in the Holy See; (3) Administration of the Patrimony of the Apostolic See, established in 1878 and reorganized in 1967; (4) Prefecture of the Pontifical House, instituted in 1967 under the name Prefecture of the Apostolic Palace and renamed in 1968, which caters for audiences and non-liturgical pontifical ceremonies and, in collaboration with the secretary of state, arranges for papal voyages and the reception of foreign heads of state; (5) Service of the Assistance of St Peter, formed in the 13th century as a charitable agency and reorganized in 1968, which distributes alms and assistance to persons in need and supervises and administers charitable institutions under the auspices of the Holy See; (6) ***Archives of Vatican Council II***; (7) Office for Relations with the Personnel of the Holy See, created in 1971; (8) ***Central Office of Statistics of the Church***, created in 1967, and under the direct supervision of the secretary of state, which analyzes data on the state of the church and its pastoral ministry; (9) Palatine Administrations, maintaining the various apostolic palaces; (10) Works of St Peter, to administer the Basilica of St Peter; (11) ***Vatican Apostolic Library*** founded in the 15th century with some 60,000 manuscripts, 7,000 incunabula and 900,000 other volumes, which includes a Christian museum (founded 1745), a secular museum (1767), a Numismatic Cabinet (1738) and a School of Librarianship (1934); (12) ***Secret Archives of the Vatican***, created in 1611, which were open for research until 1878 but are now inaccessible except on the authorization of the secretary of state; (13) Vatican School of Paleography and Diplomacy, founded in 1884, which is annexed to the administration of the secret archives and offers an advanced 2-year course; (14) ***Vatican Polyglot Printing Press*** (founded 1587) and Vatican Publishing House (1926), under the supervision of Salesians; and (15) ***L'Osservatore Romano***, founded in 1861, the official newspaper of the Holy See published daily in Italian with weekly editions in French, English, Italian, Portuguese, Spanish, and German.

Pontifical academies. The most important of these is the ***Pontifical Academy of Sciences***, founded in 1603, which is a unique scientific body composed of 70 pontifical academicians who are scholars of the world repute in the applied sciences. It is the only academy actually located within Vatican City. Others in Rome include the Roman Academy of St Thomas Aquinas and the Catholic Religion (1879), Pontifical Academy of Roman Theology (1718), Pontifical Academy of the Immaculate Conception (1835), International Marian Pontifical Academy (1946), Academy of the Liturgy (1740), Academy of the Virtuous of the Pantheon (1542), Roman Pontifical Academy of Archeology (1740), and College of the Cults of the Martyrs (1879).

Indigenous missions. The Holy See has been the focal point for Roman Catholic missions since the earliest days. Each of the various Roman Catholic missionary orders has representatives in the Vatican.

BROADCASTING AND MEDIA.

The official voice of the Vatican state is ***Radio Vaticana***, inaugurated in 1931 by Pius XI in the gardens of Vatican City. Subsequently it has become a powerful international station broadcasting to 157 countries of the world in 32 languages for 16 hours a day. It has 2 centers of transmission, one within the Vatican and since 1957 another in Santa Maria di Galeria 20 km outside Rome; it has no other foreign or overseas studio or transmitters. Of note are the programs directed to countries in 15 languages of Eastern Europe and the former USSR. There are also regular programs in Spanish for Latin America, in Portuguese for Angola and Mozambique, and for Japan and China. Recording studios are in the Vatican, and Vatican Radio also has a regular service of producing programs in Spanish, French, Portuguese, and English for transmission over Western radio chains and stations in Latin America and Africa. The Holy See is a member of UNDA.

The Holy See's activities are well covered by Catholic radio stations. Regular transmissions on TV go out worldwide by satellite each day.

INTERDENOMINATIONAL ORGANIZATIONS

A number of joint international commissions have been formed between the Roman Catholic Church (through its Pontifical Council for Christian Unity) and other Christian denominations.

(1) The ***Joint Working Group of the Roman Catholic Church and the World Council of Churches*** was created in 1966 and reorganized in 1969, and has since had numerous plenary meetings.

(2) The ***Roman Catholic/Anglican International Commission*** (ARCIC) was officially established in 1968 but owes its origin to a meeting of the pope and the archbishop of Canterbury in Rome in 1966.

(3) The ***Joint Roman Catholic/Lutheran International Commission*** goes back to 1966 when a working group appointed by LWF and the Secretariat for Christian Unity began preparation for its formation. A joint Catholic/Lutheran commission for study of 'The Gospel and the Church' was established in 1967.

(4) The ***Methodist/Roman Catholic Joint Commission*** was created in 1966 and reorganized in 1972. The first commission considered theological questions and ecclesiastical problems at annual meetings held between 1967 and 1970: Ariccia (Rome, 1967); London (1968); Malta (1969); and Lake Junaluska (USA, 1970). Its final product was published in 1990.

(5) The ***Roman Catholic/Reformed Study Commission*** on 'The presence of Christ in the Church and in the world' was formed in 1969 on the basis of preparations begun in June 1968 by WARC and the Secretariat for Christian Unity. Meetings have been held frequently.

6) ***The Joint Roman Catholic/Lutheran/Reformed Study Commission*** on 'The theology of marriage and the problems of mixed marriages' was formed in 1970 following a consultation of the 3 churches in 1969 dealing with the same theme.

(7) The ***Joint Catholic/Coptic Orthodox Commission*** was initiated by the heads of the 2 churches at the time of their meeting in Rome in May 1973.

(8) Without taking on the formal substance of commissions, non-official conversations have been carried on between representatives of the Roman Catholic Church, through its Secretariat for Christian Unity, and representatives of the Russian Orthodox Church. Conversations have also occurred with Pentecostal churches and charismatic movements within various Protestant, Anglican, and Orthodox churches. Joint Russian Orthodox/Catholic meetings have been held in Leningrad (December 1967), Bari (Italy, December 1970), and Zagorsk (USSR, June 1973), and subsequently. Joint Catholic/Pentecostal meetings, including representatives of churches and movements have been held in Zurich-Horgen (Switzerland, June 1972), and Rome (June 1973) on the role of the Holy Spirit and gifts of the Spirit in mystical tradition, particularly in the mystical tradition of the East. Many other meetings have taken place.

(9) The ***International Catholic/Jewish Liaison Committee*** was formed in 1971. Meetings have been frequent.

FUTURE TRENDS AND PROSPECTS

No religious changes are foreseen for the next thirty years in the Holy See as the community is expected to remain 100% Roman Catholic.

Given its design and purpose, the Holy See is likely to remain 100% Christian well into the future.

BIBLIOGRAPHY

Annuario Pontificio per l'anno 1998. Vatican City: Segreteria di Stato, 1998. 1,960p. (Annual).

Annuario statistico della Chiesa. Annuarium statisticum Ecclesiae. Vatican City: Segreteria di Stato. (Bi–annual; tables for all countries).

Breve compendium informationum de Conferentiis Episcoporum, MCMLXXI. Vatican City: Cura Secretariae Generalis Synodi Episcoporum, 1971. 183p.

Connaissance du Vatican. P. Poupard. Paris: Beauchesne, 1st ed. 1968, 230p.; 2nd ed. 1974, 205p.

Guida delle missioni cattoliche. Vatican City: SC Propaganda, 1975. 1,628p. (Earlier editions 1934, 1946, 1950, 1970).

In the Vatican. P. Hebblethwaite. Oxford, UK: Oxford University Press, 1987. 240p.

'Inside the Vatican' (CD–ROM). Jasmine Multimedia Publishing.

Inside the Vatican. B. McDowell & J. L. Stanfield. Washington, DC: National Geographic Society, 1991. 232p. (A photographic essay on Vatican City).

La Diocesi di Roma, 1972–73. Rome: Editoriale Italiana, 1972.

Oriente cattolico. Cenni storici e statistiche. Vatican City: SC per le Chiese Orientali, 1974. 857p. (Earlier editions 1929, 1932, 1962).

Richerche per la Storia Religiosa di Roma. Rome: Edizioni di Storia e Letteratura.

The Sistine Chapel. F. Papava (ed). Vatican City: Monumenti, 1992.

The Vatican empire. N. Lo Bello. New York: Trident Press, 1968. 186p. (Unfavorable but well-documented account of Vatican finances).

Vatican City State. M. J. Walsh. *World bibliographical series,* vol. 41. Oxford, UK: CLIO Press, 1983. 142p.

Vatican, fortress of Christianity. J. Madvo (prod). *Countries and peoples.* 1977; reissue, Princeton, NJ: Films for the Humanities & Sciences, 1992. (29 min. videocassette).

Vatican Radio: propagation by the airwaves. M. J. Matelski. *Media and society series.* Westport, CT: Praeger, 1995. 219p.

Country Table 2. **Organized churches and denominations in the Holy See.**

Official name (bold type = church with over 10% of all affiliated) 1	*Begun* 2	*Type* 3	*Counc* 4	*Congs* 5	*Adults* 6	*Affiliated 1970* 7	*Affiliated 1995* 8	*G%* 9	*Names, notes, and other statistics* (see Codebook, Part 3) 10
Chiesa Cattolica: V Città del Vaticano	c40	R-LEr	b.B..	70	900	980	980	0.05	*Vicariato della Città del Vaticano.* Part of D Rome under pastoral care of pope.
Totals				**70**	**900**	**980**	**980**		

Churches, members, growth, 1900-2025	*Congs*	*Adults*	*Affiliated*	*G%*	*Total denominations*	*6 Megablocs:* *O*	*R*	*A*	*P*	*I*	*m*
Total churches, members, and denominations (mid-1900)	30	1,800	2,000	-1.01	1	0	1	0	0	0	0
Total churches, members, and denominations (mid-1970)	60	900	980	-1.01	1	0	1	0	0	0	0
Total churches, members, and denominations (mid-1990)	70	900	980	0.00	1	0	1	0	0	0	0
Total churches, members, and denominations (mid-1995)	70	900	980	0.00	1	0	1	0	0	0	0
Total churches, members, and denominations (mid-2000)	70	900	980	0.00	1	0	1	0	0	0	0
Total churches, members, and denominations (mid-2025)	100	900	980	0.00	11	0	1	0	0	10	0

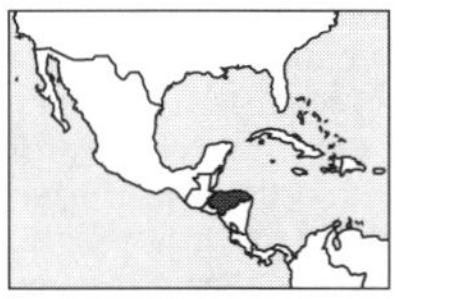

HONDURAS

SECULAR DATA, AD 2000

STATE
Official name: La República de Honduras (The Republic of Honduras).
Short name: Honduras. **Adjective of nationality:** Honduran.
Flag: Stripes of blue, white, and blue, with 5 blue stars in centre.
Area: 112,492 sq. km. (43,433 sq. mi.).
Government: Multiparty republic, since 1982 (1524 Spanish possession, 1838 Independence, several military regimes).
Legislature: National Assembly, 128 members.
Official language: Spanish (Español/Castella).
Monetary unit: 1 Honduran lempira (L) = 100 centavos. **US$1=** L 13.62.
Chief cities: TEGUCIGALPA 1,241,000; San Pedro Sula 394,554; La Ceiba 96,449; El Progreso 78,419; Choluteca 75,984.
Political divisions: 18 provinces.
Armed forces: 19,000.

DEMOGRAPHY
Population: 6,485,000.
Population density: 57.6/sq. km. (149.3/sq. mi.).
Under 15 years: 2,701,000.
Growth rate p.a.: 2.49% (births 29.98, deaths 5.08).
Mortality: Infant, per 1,000: 31.2; **Maternal per 100,000:** 220.0.
Life expectancy: 71 (male 69, female 73).
Household size: 5.7. **Floor area per person, sq.m:** 14.0.
Major languages: Spanish, English, Miskito, Pipil, Lenca, Chinese, Arabic.
Urban dwellers: 46.91%. **Urban growth rate p.a.:** 3.8%.
Labor force: 35%.

ETHNOLINGUISTIC PEOPLES
83.7% Mestizo; 4.1% Detribalized Amerindian; 3.0% Nicaraguan Mestizo; 2.0% Honduran Black; 2.0% Honduran White.

ECONOMY
National income p.a. per person: US$599; **per family:** US$3,419.

EDUCATION
Adult literacy: 72% (male 72%, female 72%). **Schools:** 8,838.
Universities: 10. **School enrolment:** female/male: 80%/74%.

HEALTH
Access to health services: 64%. **Access to safe water:** 65%.
Hospitals: 86 (12 beds per 10,000). **Doctors:** 3,803.
Blind: 1,000. **Deaf:** 389,100. Murder **rate:** 9.
Lepers: 1,300. **Underweight prevalence under 5:** 18%.

LITERATURE
New book titles p.a.: 50 (8 p.a. per million). **Periodicals:** 28.
Newspapers: 5 dailies.

COMMUNICATION (per 1,000 people)
Phones: 29 **(5% mobile).** Radios: 354. **TV sets:** 80.
Daily newspaper circulation: 44. **Computers:** 30.

REFUGEES
Alien refugees from other countries: 50.

HUMAN LIFE AND LIBERTY (optimum condition=100.0%)
HDI: 57.5. **HSI:** 38.0. **HFI:** 45.0. **EFL:** 37.0.

Country Table 1. **Religious adherents in Honduras, AD 1900-2025.**

Year	1900		1970		mid-1990		Annual change, 1990-2000				mid-1995		mid-2000		mid-2025	
Name	Adherents	%	Adherents	%	Adherents	%	Natural	Conversion	Total	Rate	Adherents	%	Adherents	%	Adherents	%
Christians	**524,000**	**97.0**	**2,559,250**	**98.7**	**4,746,610**	**97.3**	**156,290**	**-1,774**	**154,516**	**2.86**	**5,492,300**	**97.2**	**6,291,766**	**97.0**	**10,270,000**	**96.4**
PROFESSION																
professing Christians	**524,000**	**97.0**	**2,559,250**	**98.7**	**4,746,610**	**97.3**	**156,290**	**-1,774**	**154,516**	**2.86**	**5,492,300**	**97.2**	**6,291,766**	**97.0**	**10,270,000**	**96.4**
AFFILIATION																
unaffiliated Christians	2,700	0.5	79,250	3.1	166,610	3.4	5,484	1,272	6,756	3.46	192,300	3.4	234,166	3.6	770,000	7.2
affiliated Christians	**521,300**	**96.5**	**2,480,000**	**95.7**	**4,580,000**	**93.9**	**150,806**	**-3,006**	**147,760**	**2.84**	**5,300,000**	**93.8**	**6,057,600**	**93.4**	**9,500,000**	**89.2**
Roman Catholics	520,800	96.4	2,412,601	93.1	4,250,000	87.1	139,943	-5,943	134,000	2.78	4,883,708	86.4	5,590,000	86.2	8,950,000	84.0
Protestants	500	0.1	61,889	2.4	300,000	6.2	9,875	2,625	12,500	3.54	357,182	6.3	425,000	6.6	1,000,000	9.4
Independents	0	0.0	30,930	1.2	122,000	2.5	4,016	1,784	5,800	3.97	158,346	2.8	180,000	2.8	450,000	4.2
Marginal Christians	0	0.0	6,405	0.3	42,000	0.9	1,382	1,418	2,800	5.24	55,000	1.0	70,000	1.1	200,000	1.9
Orthodox	0	0.0	5,200	0.2	6,500	0.1	214	-144	70	1.03	6,860	0.1	7,200	0.1	10,000	0.1
Anglicans	0	0.0	210	0.0	4,000	0.1	132	68	200	4.14	4,800	0.1	6,000	0.1	8,000	0.1
doubly-affiliated	0	0.0	-37,235	-1.4	-144,500	-3.0	-4,756	-2,854	-7,610	4.32	-165,896	-2.9	-220,600	-3.4	-1,118,000	-10.5
Trans-megabloc groupings																
Evangelicals	500	0.1	48,000	1.9	210,000	4.3	6,912	3,088	10,000	3.97	259,022	4.6	310,000	4.8	750,000	7.0
Pentecostals/Charismatics	0	0.0	34,000	1.3	620,000	12.7	20,408	3,592	24,000	3.33	735,516	13.0	860,000	13.3	1,600,000	15.0
Great Commission Christians	**10,800**	**2.0**	**130,000**	**5.0**	**310,800**	**6.4**	**10,230**	**119**	**10,349**	**2.92**	**361,000**	**6.4**	**414,293**	**6.4**	**703,000**	**6.6**
Spiritists	1,000	0.2	12,000	0.5	51,000	1.1	1,679	187	1,866	3.17	60,000	1.1	69,658	1.1	120,000	1.1
Nonreligious	0	0.0	2,500	0.1	35,000	0.7	1,152	953	2,105	4.82	46,000	0.8	56,045	0.9	155,750	1.5
Baha'is	0	0.0	8,000	0.3	20,000	0.4	658	606	1,264	5.02	25,000	0.4	32,635	0.5	56,000	0.5
Atheists	0	0.0	1,000	0.0	9,400	0.2	309	108	417	3.74	11,500	0.2	13,571	0.2	23,000	0.2
Muslims	0	0.0	1,600	0.1	6,000	0.1	197	23	220	3.18	7,000	0.1	8,203	0.1	15,000	0.1
Ethnoreligionists	15,000	2.8	5,000	0.2	6,100	0.1	201	-107	94	1.44	6,600	0.1	7,039	0.1	6,000	0.1
Buddhists	0	0.0	1,000	0.0	2,500	0.1	82	34	116	3.88	3,100	0.1	3,658	0.1	6,300	0.1
Chinese folk-religionists	0	0.0	500	0.0	400	0.0	13	-7	6	1.34	400	0.0	457	0.0	500	0.0
Jews	0	0.0	150	0.0	290	0.0	10	-5	5	1.57	300	0.0	339	0.0	450	0.0
Other religionists	0	0.0	1,000	0.0	1,700	0.0	56	-18	38	2.01	1,800	0.0	2,075	0.0	3,000	0.0
World A (unevangelized persons)	5,400	1.0	2,592	0.1	4,879	0.1	161	-9	152	2.74	5,653	0.1	6,485	0.1	10,656	0.1
World B (evangelized non-Christians)	10,600	2.0	30,334	1.2	127,511	2.6	4,196	1,783	5,979	3.89	155,551	2.8	186,749	2.9	375,344	3.5
World C (Christians)	524,000	97.0	2,559,250	98.7	4,746,610	97.3	156,290	-1,774	154,516	2.86	5,492,300	97.1	6,291,766	97.0	10,270,000	96.4
Country's population	**540,000**	**100.0**	**2,592,177**	**100.0**	**4,879,000**	**100.0**	**160,647**	**0**	**160,647**	**2.89**	**5,653,505**	**100.0**	**6,485,000**	**100.0**	**10,656,000**	**100.0**

COLUMNS, ROWS.
For meanings and definitions, see Codebook (Part 3). Note that, by definition, total 'Christians' = professing + crypto-Christians, which also = affiliated + unaffiliated Christians, and also = Great Commission Christians + latent Christians. Percentages may not always total exactly, due to rounding.

CENSUSES.
24.VI.1945: 97.8% Roman Catholics, 1.9% Evangelicals, 0.3% other religionists. The religion question has subsequently not been asked.

NOTES ON RELIGIONS
ATHEISTS. Communist Party of Honduras (PCH) (proscribed since 1957; pro-Soviet) and rival faction: membership (1970) 300.
BAHA'IS. Rapid growth from 15 local spiritual assemblies (1964) to 60 (1973), then to 117 LSAs (1994).
BUDDHISTS. Chinese.
ETHNORELIGIONISTS. Of the 100,000 Amerindians in 1995, a small proportion were still animists, including among the Miskito, Suma, Torrupan (Jicaque) and Lenca.
EVANGELICAL CATHOLICS. This term is used here to describe persons who are affiliated to churches termed by the state Evangélica (Protestant, marginal Protestant, Anglican or Non-White indigenous churches), but who are regarded by state and society as, or who profess to be, Roman Catholics.
MUSLIMS. Palestinian Arab immigrants from 1910 onwards, with some Syro-Lebanese traders, mainly around San Pedro Sula.
ORTHODOX. Palestinian Arab settlers with some Syrians and Lebanese, immigrating from Jordan from 1910 onwards, most of whom have been and are Christians. Living mainly in San Pedro Sula, they form the backbone of the nation's industrial and commercial classes.
OTHER RELIGIONISTS. Including Rosicrucians (2 AMORC centers).
PENTECOSTALS/CHARISMATICS. The Catholic Charismatic Renewal, begun in 1971, has in 1997, 1,057 regular weekly prayer groups with 12,983 regular adult attenders, 7 involved priests and 5 bishops, and annual rallies with 20,000 participants.
ROMAN CATHOLICS. Many Roman Catholics are actively and regularly involved in the practice of high or low spiritism, mainly Afro-American low spiritism.
SPIRITISTS. There are 2 varieties: (1) Non-Christian adherents of Afro-Caribbean spirit-possession cults (low spiritism) syncretizing Christianity with African religion; mostly Jamaicans and other Blacks. (2) Non-Christian adherents of high spiritism. The rapid growth of spiritism comes mostly from the ranks of nominal Catholics. In 1930 a large new spiritist movement began among the Miskito and Suma Indians.

Great Commission Instrument Panel: status of honduras (for explanation see start of Part 4)

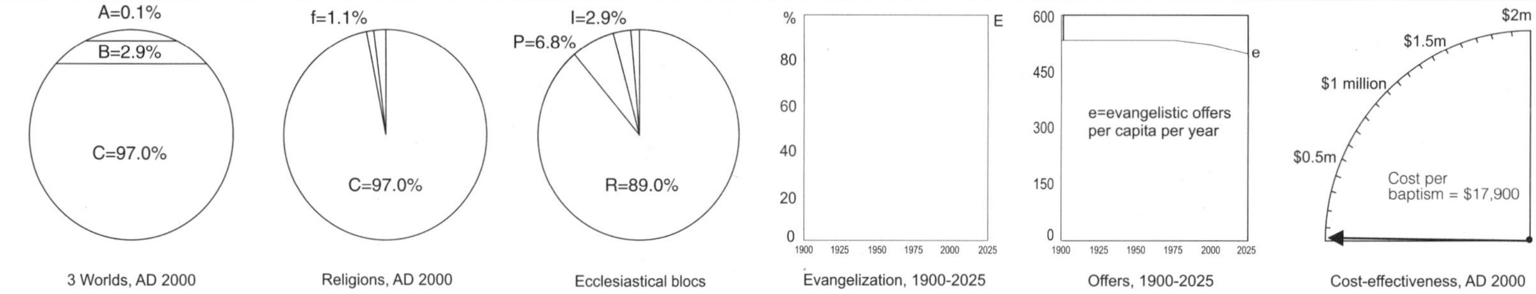

Country status. Located in the Central American isthmus, Honduras is the second largest country in Central America and it is also the most mountainous. Bananas, sugar, and coffee are the chief exports but Honduras also has significant timber and marine resources.

HUMAN LIFE AND LIBERTY

Human need and development. Honduras has not suffered to the same extent the political troubles that have long plagued its neighbors, Guatemala, Nicaragua, and El Salvador. Nevertheless, living conditions in many parts of the country have deteriorated as a result of reverberations from the troubles in neighboring countries. Rural houses are primitively built and are frequently one-room shacks, called ranchos, with earthen floors and palm leaf roofs without proper sanitation facilities. In rural areas dietary and nutritional diseases are prevalent. Lack of potable water and unsanitary conditions cause many of the diseases from which Hondurans suffer, such as enteritis. In terms of basic quality of life indicators Honduras belongs to the same league as Indonesia, Egypt, and Lesotho. Its adult literacy rate is 72%, its life expectancy 71 years and annual per capita income $599. The daily calorie supply is 2,247, less than that of Ghana and Niger. Nearly 74% of Hondurans live in poverty. Unemployment and underemployment runs as high as 45%.

Human rights and freedoms. Although Honduras has been a constitutional democracy since 1982, the military operate with considerable legal and institutional autonomy and commit many human rights abuses with impunity. The principal violations are extrajudicial killings, arbitrary and incommunicado detentions, torture and abuse of detainees, legal immunity of armed forces personnel from investigation, and the weakness of the judicial system in rendering impartial justice. The same immunity from prosecution and punishment enjoyed by military personnel is enjoyed by other elite groups. Despite the rise in politically motivated killings, virtually no arrests or convictions are ever made in such cases. Torture of detainees is common, including such innovative methods as helicopter torture (where prisoners are tied and suspended in air) and the capucha, a hood dusted on the inside with lime. The legal system is ineffective, because the rich and politically influential are almost never brought to trial, much less convicted and jailed. Those few who are incarcerated buy their way out and 'escape.' The civilian judiciary is underfunded, weak, politicized, inefficient, and corrupt. Detention without sentencing averages 14 months. A number of defendants serve the maximum possible sentence even before their trials begin. About 75% of the prison population have not been sentenced. Freedom of speech and press is generally respected but the media themselves are highly politicized and corrupt. The indigenous people have little or no influence on national affairs or even on issues affecting their welfare. Because tribal lands are poorly defined and are not safeguarded by legal titles, usurpation by nontribal farmers and cattle growers is common. The courts generally favor nonindigenous persons of wealth and influence. Failure to obtain legal redress prompts indigenous groups to attempt to regain lands through land invasions and other tactics which are then forcibly suppressed by the government. Women suffer many disabilities. Rape of women over 21, for example, is prosecuted by the state only in a limited number of cases and the penalties are relatively light. There are no shelters for battered women, and the law offers few legal remedies for them.

Human environment. The principal environment problems are deforestation and the resultant degradation of land. Because Honduras has one of the highest birth rates in the region, the pressures on land are severe. The mountainous nature of the terrain encourages farming on steep slopes causing loss of top soil and water runoff. On hillsides many farmers practice a primitive form of slash-and-burn cultivation.

NON-CHRISTIAN RELIGIONS

Traditional religions are still practiced by a small proportion of these Amerindian tribes: the Miskito, Sumo, Jicaque (Torrupan), Charti, Paya (Secon, Tawka), Pipil, and the Lenca; many others follow traditional practices but also profess at the same time to be Catholics.

Country summary. **Worlds A, B, C by ethnolinguistic peoples, cities, and major civil divisions in Honduras.**

	PEOPLES							CITIES							CIVIL DIVISIONS						
World	*Num*	*Pop 2000*	*C%*	*Christians*	*E%*	*U%*	*Unevangelized*	*Num*	*Pop 2000*	*C%*	*Christians*	*E%*	*U%*	*Unevangelized*	*Num*	*Pop 2000*	*C%*	*Christians*	*E%*	*U%*	*Unevangelized*
A	2	1,673	0.24	4	44	56	934	0	0	0.00	0	0	0	0	0	0	0.00	0	0	0	0
B	3	5,208	13.50	703	75	25	1,306	0	0	0.00	0	0	0	0	0	0	0.00	0	0	0	0
C	22	6,478,563	93.49	6,056,893	100	0	4,184	5	1,886,406	92.32	1,741,519	100	0	4,414	18	6,485,445	93.40	6,057,600	100	0	6,422
Total	**27**	**6,485,444**	**93.40**	**6,057,600**	**100**	**0**	**6,424**	**5**	**1,886,406**	**92.32**	**1,741,519**	**100**	**0**	**4,414**	**18**	**6,485,445**	**93.40**	**6,057,600**	**100**	**0**	**6,422**

Spiritism has grown in recent decades, taking its converts from the nominal fringe of Catholicism.

CHRISTIANITY

CATHOLIC CHURCH. Honduras was a major center of the ancient Mayan culture before the 10th century. It was the first sighted by Columbus in 1502. In 1524 Cortes entered from Mexico, attracted by tales of gold. The territory became part of Spanish-controlled Guatemala in 1538, but evangelization did not get under way until the arrival of Spanish Franciscans about 1550. By 1807 there were 145 churches. Honduras became independent in 1838, and church and state were legally separated in 1880.

The great majority of the population has been baptized in the Catholic Church, although the proportion of Catholics relative to the population as a whole is slowly diminishing due to conversions to Protestantism and spiritism. Catholic concern and activity in the realms of society, laity, and evangelization are recent phenomena dating only from the 1960s. This has taken such forms as the creation of new movements of the lay apostolate, concern for social and human development, integration of mass into wider parish structures, and an attempt to achieve a global understanding of the pastoral function. A first national meeting of diocesan pastoral teams took place in August 1970.

Although expatriate priests have continued to increase in number, from 45 in 1955 to 188 in 1970, the number of national priests has not grown in proportion, falling from 55 in 1955 to 48 in 1970.

The Holy See has diplomatic relations with Honduras and in AD 2000 is represented to government and the Catholic hierarchy by a nuncio residing in Tegucigalpa.

PROTESTANT CHURCHES. Although the origins of Methodism in Honduras go back to 1860, the first major organized Protestant activity in Honduras began in 1896 with the arrival of the Central American Mission. Other early pioneers include the Friends in 1902, Adventists in 1891, Evangelical and Reformed Church (ERC) in 1920, and Moravians in 1930. Pentecostalism made its initial appearance in 1937 when the first Assemblies of God missionaries entered from nearby El Salvador; and such other USA-based Pentecostal denominations as the Church of God (Cleveland), International Church of the Foursquare Gospel, and Church of God of Prophecy followed after World War II. Many other small missions have also appeared since. Although Assemblies of God Brethren, and Church of God (Cleveland) have the largest Protestant constituencies, no single church or tradition stands out as predominant.

Protestants have through the years shown a keen interest in educational and medical work. The Central American Mission built an important hospital at Siguatepegue in 1960 and operates a nursing school there as well. The United Church of Christ, formerly the ERC, is noted for its educational and medical program, and other Protestant bodies have also devoted considerable resources to social work.

INDEPENDENT CHURCHES. The fifth largest church in the country is the Church of the Prince of Peace, begun in 1960 by missionaries from the church begun in Guatemala in 1945. There are numerous other bodies at work also.

Renewal movements. In the 1990s the Pentecostal/Charismatic Renewal continued to spread rapidly across most older churches, and numbered over 860,000 adherents (of whom 23% Pentecostals, 62% Charismatics, and 15% Independents).

Indigenous missions. Hondurans have been involved in foreign missions since the earliest days but only recently have sent missionaries outside of Latin America. Today, both Honduran Protestants and Roman Catholics can be found in the Middle East, North Africa, and Asia.

CHURCH AND STATE

Since the separation of church and state in 1880, in advocating the freedom of religion and worship, the various constitutions of Honduras have borne the stamp of the masonic influence of the age; instruction was lay and clergy had no right of vote. These characteristics were not retained in the constitution of 1965, which invokes in its Preamble the 'protection of God' and from whose text on educational instruction the term 'lay' has been removed. The state has therefore not renounced its original religious character. A supplementary decree of February 1967 allowed for the establishment of a course on religion in state schools, if requested by parents and teachers. In addition, the constitution does not deprive clergy of their right to vote. Article 187 'assures the free exercise of all religions and all worship without any preeminence', prohibits ministers of the various religious bodies from holding public office and from carrying on 'in any fashion political propaganda by invoking religious motives or by making use of the religious beliefs of the people for this purpose'. A constitutional decree published in September 1969, 2 months after the short war between Honduras and El Salvador, placed the armed forces of Honduras under the protection of the Virgin of Suyapa and compelled the entire military corps to render her public homage. Although the Catholic Church is not recognized as the state church, it nevertheless still figures prominently in state and government activities.

The hierarchy and clergy of the Catholic Church in general use the constitutional guarantees of freedom of expression to address themselves to the country's social problems, as evidenced by numerous episcopal and clerical declarations. Indeed, the involvement of clergy in social affairs has caused a certain uneasiness on the part of governmental authorities. The Catholic clergy are opposed by the ruling class through which the mass media threatens foreign priests with expulsion and accuses the church's centers for social training of being responsible for the occupation of lands by the poor in the southern part of the country. Because of these difficulties, the clergy of Honduras in their June 1971 meeting underlined the necessity of adopting a unified position and passed a resolution calling for solidarity in the face of any attacks which might arise.

There is no ministry nor ministerial department responsible for religious affairs nor registration of churches as such by government. Nevertheless, every secular or religious group desiring to obtain or sell property must, according to the law, first obtain a juridical personality.

BROADCASTING AND MEDIA

There are 6 local Catholic stations on medium-wave frequencies. Shortwave programs from HCJB (Ecuador), TWR (Antilles) and AWR (Costa Rica) can be easily received. Honduras is a member of UNDA.

CBN's *700 Club* and other programs can be seen on 9 local channels and 10 cable channels, covering the entire nation on a daily basis. Two full-time ministry centers offer follow-up counselor training, Bible studies, and film evangelism. Counseling seminars in cooperation with 40 local churches have been held, and medical brigades have distributed dental kits to poor communities in coordination with medical ministries. Other Christian television programs can be received via satellite.

INTERDENOMINATIONAL ORGANIZATIONS

The Honduras Evangelical Alliance (Alianza Evangélica Hondureña), founded in 1945, met annually but otherwise had limited activities, and suffered from internal troubles that led to the withdrawal of several members in the early 1970s. A National Evangelical Fraternity (Confraternidad Evangélica de Honduras) was organized in 1990 as a renewed attempt to promote fellowship and cooperation among Evangelical Protestants. The growth of Honduran missions vision, and the desire to mobilize more Honduran Evangelicals to cross-cultural missions, led to the formation of the interdenominational Evangelical Missions Federation of Honduras in 1991 (Federación Misionera Evangélica de Honduras, FEMEH). It began with 11 member churches or organizations.

CONCORDE is an agency for the co-ordination of the work of private institutions, both confessional and non-confessional, in social development. A pioneer in central America, CONCORDE is also engaged in applied research and long-range planning.

FUTURE TRENDS AND PROSPECTS

Roman Catholic losses (93.1% in 1970 to 84.0% in 2025) are expected to be mainly offset by Protestant and Independent gains (3.6% in 1970 to 13.6% by 2025) so that Christians decline only slightly to 96.4% by 2025 (from 98.7% in 1970).

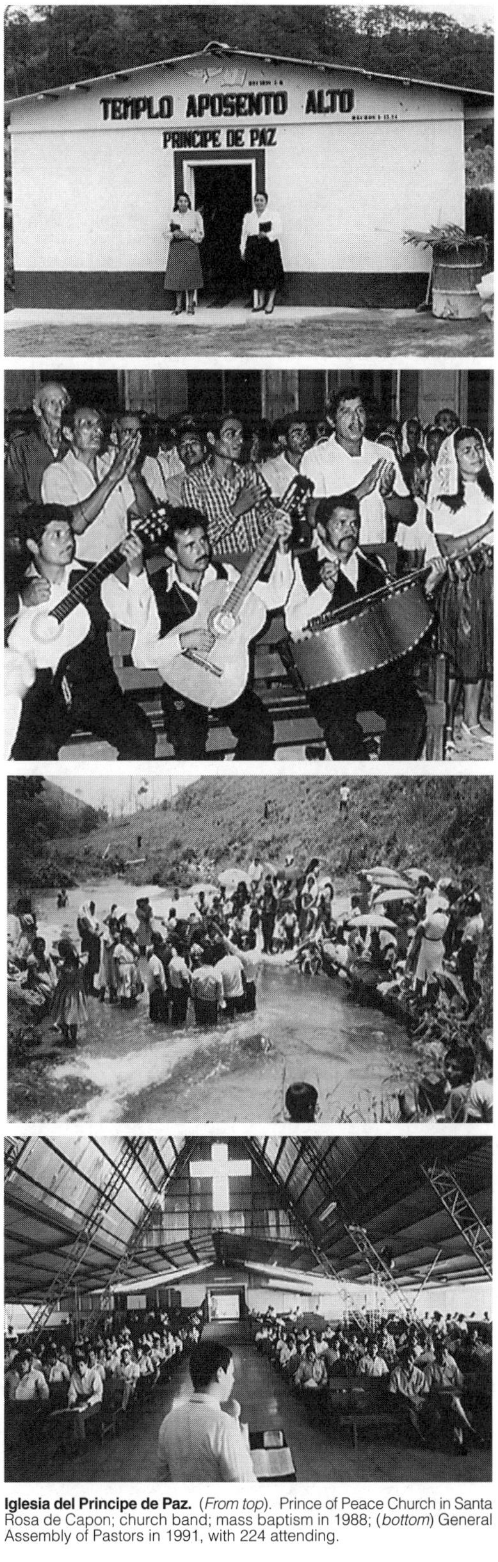

Iglesia del Principe de Paz. (*From top*). Prince of Peace Church in Santa Rosa de Capon; church band; mass baptism in 1988; (*bottom*) General Assembly of Pastors in 1991, with 224 attending.

Though Christianity is expected to remain strong well into the 21st century, the nonreligious and spiritists could claim as much as 10% of the population by AD 2050. Within the Christian tradition, Protestants and Independents are likely to make gains throughout this period.

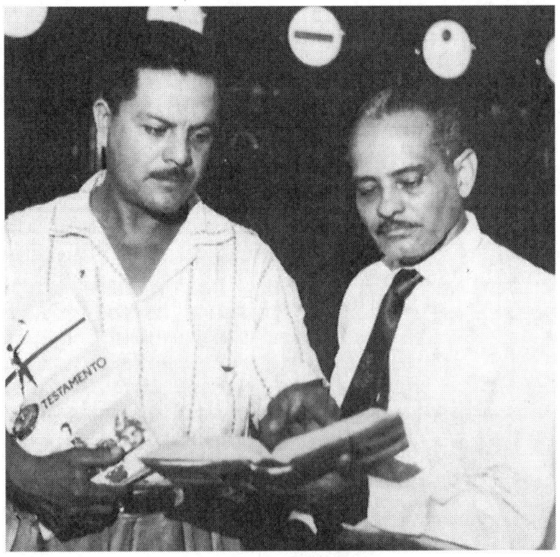

Factory worker (*left*) purchases New Testament from Bible colporteur (*right*).

BIBLIOGRAPHY

'A strategy for achieving cooperation among the evangelical bodies of Honduras.' M. Alvarez. D.Min. thesis, Ashland Theological Seminary, Ashland, OH, 1992. 134p.

Anuario de la Iglesia Católica de Honduras. Tegucigalpa: Secretaría de la Conferencia Episcopal de Honduras, 1989. (Annual).

Ethnographical survey of the Miskito and Sumu Indians of Honduras and Nicaragua. E. Conzemius. Washington, DC: Bureau of American Ethnology, 1932. Bulletin no. 106. 191p.

Fuentes y bibliografía: para el estudio de la historia de la Iglesia de Honduras. R. Sierra Fonseca. *Colección Padre Manuel Subirana*, 9. Obispado, Honduras: Centro de Publicaciones, [1993]. 106p.

Historia de la Iglesia en Honduras. J. M. Tojeira. La Ceiba, Honduras: Talleres 'Claret', 1987. 159p.

Historia y misión del protestantismo hondureño. M. R. López. [San José, Costa Rica: Oficina Regional para América Latina y el Caribe de Visión Mundial Internacional, 1993]. 209p.

Honduras. P. F. Howard-Reguindin. *World bibliographical series*, vol. 139. Oxford, UK: CLIO Press, 1992. 260p.

Honduras: iglesia y cambio social. G. Blanco & J. Valverde. *Colección Sociología de la religión.* San José, Costa Rica: Departamento Ecuménico de Investigaciones, 1987. 228p.

Honduras: religiosidad popular, raíz de la identidad. I. L. de Oyuela. Obispado de Choluteca, Honduras: Centro de Publicaciones, 1995. 264p.

Iglesia e historia en Honduras: una introducción a la historiografía eclesiástica hondureña. R. Sierra Fonseca. *Colección Padre Manuel Subirana*, 5. Tegucigalpa, Honduras: Centro de Publicaciones Obispado Choluteca, 1993. 80p.

La Iglesia Católica en Honduras, 1492–1975. M. Carías. *Colección Códices.* Tegucigalpa, Honduras: Editorial Guaymuras, 1991. 150p.

Los nuevos movimientos religiosos en Honduras al servicio de quién?: 1980–1989. Tegucigalpa, Honduras: Iglesia Cristiana Luterana de Honduras, 1993. 77p.

Memorias de un sacerdote en Honduras. J. G. Carney. 1983; reprint, Tegucigalpa, Honduras: Ediciones CODEH, 1990. 207p.

'Observations on a Lenca ceremony, Honduras,' W. W. Plowden, *El Palacio* (Santa Fe), 66 (December 6, 1959), 203–5.

'Planting the church in Honduras: the development of a culturally relevant witness.' E. F. Mathews. M.A. thesis, Fuller Theological Seminary, Pasadena, CA, 1970. 268p.

The Honduras Holiness Church. B. W. Harrell. *Fuller Theological Seminary School of World Mission projects*, 1983. Pasadena, CA: Fuller Theological Seminary, 1983. 165p.

Country Table 2. **Organized churches and denominations in Honduras.**

Official name (bold type = church with over 10% of all affiliated) 1	*Begun* 2	*Type* 3	*Counc* 4	*Congs* 5	*Adults* 6	*Affiliated 1970* 7	*Affiliated 1995* 8	*G%* 9	*Names, notes, and other statistics* (see Codebook, Part 3) 10
Asambleas de Dios	1937	P-Pe2	Zf...	825	35,395	8,000	53,000	7.86	*Assemblies of God.* M=AoG(USA). 2 fields, begun from El Salvador. 97n,8f,1s(50).
Asambleas Locales	c1980	I-3nC	.....	4	292	–	600	6.67	*Little Flock. Local Churches.* Begun 1922 in China.
Asociación Bautista de Mosquito	1967	I-Bap	.....	64	6,000	2,170	10,700	6.59	*Baptist Assoc of Mosquito.*
Asociacion Bautista Islas Bay	1846	I-Bap	.....	56	7,900	6,000	14,000	3.45	*Bay Islands Baptist Assoc.*
Centro de Formación Cristiana	1973	I-3gL	.....	10	3,500	–	10,000	4.55	*Center for Christian Formation. Brigadas de Amor.*
Consejo de Igls Luteranas en CA & P	1964	P-Lut	e....	11	105	200	175	-0.53	*Council of Lutheran Chs in CAmerica & Panama (Misuri).* M=LCMS(USA). 1m,1t(142).
Convención Nac Bautista Hondureña	1954	P-Bap	T...C	109	8,500	2,000	19,000	9.42	*HBC,CBH. Honduras Baptist Convention.* M=FMB-SBC(USA). 20n,21f,1h,1s,209Y.
Gran Comisíon	1979	I-3pL	.....	9	4,000	–	11,400	6.25	*Great Commission Church.*
Hermanos en Cristo	1989	P-Men	.....	16	500	–	1,110	16.67	*Brethren in Christ.*
Hermanos Libres	1898	P-CBr	x....	225	20,500	1,500	62,100	16.06	*Christian Brethren. Plymouth (Open) Brethren.* M=CMML(UK, USA). 12f.1i.
Iglesia Adventista del Séptimo Día	1891	P-Adv	x...	75	15,100	8,000	25,172	4.69	*Seventh-day Adventists, Honduras Mission,* CAmerican UM. 8nx,8f,1r,48t(4581),355Y.
Iglesias Biblio Bautista	1970	I-Bap	.....	35	4,000	2,500	10,000	5.70	*Bible Baptist Churches.* M=BIM(USA).
Iglesia Católica en Honduras:	1550	R-Lat	B.LDR	835	2,534,000	2,412,601	4,883,708	2.86	*Catholic Ch in Honduras.* C=11+1+23. 2p,1s(19). 113n 185x 224m 504w 58689Yy
M Tegucigalpa	1561	R-Lat	Bs	50	776,000	624,013	1,495,000	3.56	Shortage of priests in rural areas. M=SDB,PIME. 32n 86x 98m 249w 14268Yy
D Choluteca	1964	R-Lat	Bs	576	220,000	290,000	423,000	1.52	1,000s of impoverished squatters. Charismatics. M=PME. 10n 12x 12m 57w 10020Yy
D Comayagua	1963	R-Lat	Bs	25	194,000	227,000	375,655	2.04	M=OFM. 23n 8x 13m 42w 5203Yy
D Juticalpa (Olancho)	1949	R-Lat	Bs	10	175,000	144,718	337,192	3.44	Until 1987, PN Concepcion de la BVM en Olancho. 6n 9x 11m 28w 6172Yy
D San Pedro Sula	1916	R-Lat	Ps	133	626,000	451,620	1,205,000	4.00	Coast. 2 Mission Zones, among Aborigines. M=CM,CMF. 10n 34x 48m 56w 7785Yy
D Santa Rosa de Copán	1916	R-Lat	Bs	33	438,000	675,250	844,861	0.90	West of Honduras. Population 80% rural. M=SDB. 31n 21x 25m 46w 11779Yy
D Trujillo	1987	R-Lat	Bs	8	105,000	–	203,000	12.50	Population is 86% Catholic. 1n 15x 17m 26w 3462Yy
Iglesia Centroamericana	1896	P-Non	xM..C	251	14,800	4,868	26,400	7.00	*Central American Ch.* M=CAM(USA). 1 school. HQ Choluteca. 38f,1H,2k,1r.1s.
Iglesia Congregationalista de Santidad	1967	I-3pL	.....	105	2,100	1,710	6,000	5.15	M=Congregational Holiness Church World Mission.
Iglesia Cristiana Reformada	1970	P-Ref	.....	33	500	–	1,250	33.01	*Christian Reformed Church.* M=CRWM(USA).
Iglesia de Cristo		I-Dis	x....	29	700	1,000	1,750	0.05	*Church of Christ (Non-instrumental).* M=CC(Non-instrumental).
Iglesia de Dios de la Profecia	1952	P-Pe3	Z....	136	4,400	500	13,300	14.02	M=Ch of God of Prophecy (USA). Holiness Pentecostals. Split in USA ex CoG(Cleveland).
Iglesia de Dios (Anderson)		P-Hol	x....	15	900	3,000	2,730	0.05	M=Ch of God (Anderson) (USA). Holiness denomination. 1 primary school.
Iglesia de Dios (Cleveland)	1944	P-Pe3	ZF...	463	14,564	6,675	44,100	7.84	M=CoG(Cleveland) (USA). Congs: 17 English-speaking (Blacks), 36 Spanish. 77n,4f.
Iglesia de Dios Pentecostal	1978	P-Pe2	.....	105	2,510	–	7,610	5.88	*Pentecostal Church of God.* M=PCG(USA).
Iglesia de JC de los Santos de los UD	1952	m-LdS	x....	84	17,400	3,314	29,000	9.06	*Latter-day Saints. Mormons.* M=CJCLdS(USA). Many USA personnel. 70f.
Igl de los Hermanos Unidos en Cristo	1944	P-Hol	xF..C	43	1,775	1,000	4,440	6.14	*United Brethren in Christ Ch.* M=UBC(USA). HQ La Ceiba. 2f.
Iglesia del Evangelio Cuadrangular	1952	P-Pe2	ZF..C	77	5,000	6,000	15,000	3.73	*International Ch of the Foursquare Gospel.* M=ICFG(USA). 33nm,5f,2p(35),W=45%,141Y.
Iglesia del Nazareno	1969	P-Hol	xF...	23	1,101	2,083	2,399	0.57	*Ch of the Nazarene.* M=CoN(USA). Holiness denomination. 2f.
Iglesia del Principe de Paz	1960	I-3pL	.....	157	20,600	5,330	36,700	8.02	*Prince of Peace Church.*
Iglesia Episcopal Hondureña	c1900	A-ACa	aw.R.	41	2,880	210	4,800	13.33	*Episcopal Ch.* 1969, missionary diocese, ECUSA, Province IX. 90% Black. 3x,W=82%.
Ig Evangelica Bautista Independiente		I-Bap	.....	34	2,600	1,000	4,670	0.05	*Independent Evangelical Baptist Church.*
Iglesia Ev Luterana de CR,ES,H,N,P	1954	P-Lut	l....	4	100	116	200	2.20	*ELC of Costa Rica, El Salvador, H, Nic, Panama.* Germans. Scandinavians. 1n,1x,3Yy.
Iglesia Evangélica Menonita	1950	P-Men	G...C	85	3,000	1,000	3,500	5.14	*Honduras Mennonite Ch.* M=EMBMC(USA). NCoast, Aguan, Agalta, central. 36f,1h,1s.
Iglesia Evangelista Bautista	1955	I-Fun	x....	16	350	150	875	7.31	M=Baptist Mid-Missions (USA). Fundamentalist Baptists. 10f.
Iglesia Filadelfia	1967	P-Pe2	Z....	84	4,200	500	14,000	14.26	*Philadelphia Ch.* M=SFM(Sweden). Classical Pentecostals (2-stage). 6n,10x,49Y,6z.
Iglesia Independiente		I-Non	.....	2	600	300	1,000	0.05	*Independent Church.* Small indigenous Honduran body.
Iglesia Maranatha	1984	I-3pL	.....	1	40	–	133	9.09	*Maranatha Church.*
Ig Menonita Balvarte de la Verdad	1986	I-Men	.....	2	100	–	300	11.11	Mennonite Church of the Truth.
Iglesia Menonita	1982	I-Men	.....	3	40	–	100	7.69	*Mennonite Church.*
Iglesia Metodista	1860	P-Met	VwM..	14	600	1,500	1,500	0.00	In Belize District, MCCA. Bay Islands. M=MMS(UK). Blacks. 1n,1x,5f,110Yy.
Iglesia Morava: Provincia de Honduras	1930	P-Mor	xw..C	118	4,180	5,000	8,368	2.08	*Moravians. Unity of Brethren.* M=MC(USA). Miskito Indians. 3n,2x,7f,1H,3h,44Y,99y.
Iglesia Nueva Apostolica	c1985	I-3aX	x....	10	400	–	884	10.00	*New Apostolic Church. NAC/NAK.* World HQ Zurich (Switzerland).
Iglesia Ortodoxa (P Jerusalem)	c1910	O-Ara	Cwo..	3	1,650	4,400	5,500	0.90	Under Greek Orthodox Patriarchate of Jerusalem. Palestinian Arabs. HQ San Pedro Sula.
Iglesia Ortodoxa Siriana		O-Syr	D....	2	950	800	1,360	0.05	*Syrian Orthodox Ch (P Antioch).* From Syria and Holy Land (Palestinian Arab immigrants).
Iglesia Pentecostal Unida	1977	P-Pe1	.....	95	5,700	–	17,300	5.56	*United Pentecostal Church.*
Iglesia Puerta al Clelo	1986	I-3gL	.....	1	1,200	–	3,000	11.11	*Door to Heaven.*
Iglesia Reorganizada de JC de los SUD		m-LdS	x....	1	50	91	100	0.05	M=Reorganized Ch of Jesus Christ of Latter-day Saints (USA). Schism ex Mormons.
Iglesia Unida de Cristo	1920	P-Ref	C	68	1,700	2,000	3,400	2.15	*United Ch of Christ.* Formerly M=ERC, now UCBWM(USA). Northeast. Schools. 3f,1s.
Iglesia Wesleyana	1957	P-Hol	VF..C	2	34	2,000	113	-10.86	M=WC(USA). English-speaking Blacks on north coast. 1n,1x,2f,1h,1k,W=33%,37Y.
Iglesias de Cristo (Discípulos)		P-Dis	x....	6	134	–	335	0.05	*Churches of Christ (Disciples).*
Iglesias Ev Amigo de Centroamerica	1902	P-Qua	QF..C	45	2,700	1,947	8,180	5.91	*Junta Anual. YM of Friends.* M=California YM(USA). 10n,5x,2p,W=29%,48Y.
Misión Bautista Conservador	1951	I-Bap	xF..C	130	2,600	2,000	7,880	5.64	*Conservative Baptist Mission.* M=CBHMS(USA). Radio HRVC: T=10000, v=1000. 16f,1s,275Y.
Misión Biblica Pioneira	1949	I-Non	x....	5	200	300	500	2.06	M=Pioneer Bible Mission (1967, United Missionary Fellowship, USA). Medical, dental. 4f,2h.
Misión Cristiana Elim de Guatemala		I-3pL	.....	37	2,800	2,420	8,490	0.05	*Elim Christian Mission of Guatemala.*
Misión Evangelico Mundial	1943	P-Hol	xF..C	90	7,000	2,000	12,500	7.61	*World Gospel Holiness Ch.* M=World Gospel Mission (USA). 2 schools. 27f,1s.
Org Cristiana El Amor Viviente	1976	I-3xL	.....	26	14,880	–	18,834	5.26	*Living Love Christian Organization.* Cell-based, with 1,000 house cells.
Sinodo Evangelico y Reformada	1934	I-Ref	.v..C	73	1,100	4,850	3,330	-1.49	*Evangelical and Reformed Synod.* HQ San Pedro Sula. 1973, membership enquiry to WCC.
Testigos de Jehova	1930	m-Jeh	x....	105	5,983	3,000	25,900	9.01	*Jehovah's Witnesses.* Missionary visit 1930; work restarted 1945. (1975) 194Y. (1995) 817Y.
Union de los Hermanos		I-Mor	.....	1	100	200	200	0.05	*Unity of the Brethren.* Small indigenous split ex Moravian Church.
Other Protestant denominations		P-	.....	40	5,000	2,000	10,000	0.05	Total about 20 (see list below).
Other Black indigenous churches		I-3pU	.....	30	4,000	1,000	7,000	0.05	Mostly begun by, and spread among, Jamaicans and other West Indian Blacks.
Doubly-affiliated		2-aff			-85,100	-37,235	-165,896		Evangelicals who also are or were baptized Roman Catholics.
Totals				**4,969**	**2,717,913**	**2,480,000**	**5,300,000**		

Churches, members, growth, 1900-2025	*Congs*	*Adults*	*Affiliated*	*G%*	*Total denominations*	*6 Megablocs:* *O*	*R*	*A*	*P*	*I*	*m*
Total churches, members, and denominations (mid-1900)	200	270,000	521,300	2.25	10	0	1	1	5	3	0
Total churches, members, and denominations (mid-1970)	1,230	1,282,947	2,480,000	2.25	61	2	1	1	30	24	3
Total churches, members, and denominations (mid-1990)	4,500	2,349,000	4,580,000	3.11	96	2	1	1	45	44	3
Total churches, members, and denominations (mid-1995)	4,969	2,717,913	5,300,000	2.96	98	2	1	1	46	45	3
Total churches, members, and denominations (mid-2000)	5,200	3,106,000	6,057,600	2.71	100	2	1	1	47	46	3
Total churches, members, and denominations (mid-2025)	9,000	4,872,000	9,500,000	1.82	280	6	1	1	65	200	7

Continued opposite

Country Table 2–concluded

NOTES ON TABLE ABOVE
NATIONAL COUNCILS (Column 4, 5th letter).
C = Confraternidad Evangélica de Honduras (CEH), formerly Alianza Evangélica Hondureña (AEH) (Honduras Evangelical Alliance).
R = Conferencia Episcopal de Honduras (CEH) (Episcopal Conference of Honduras).
OTHER PROTESTANT DENOMINATIONS. These include: Associated Brotherhood of Christians (Jesus Only Pentecostals), Baptist Faith Missions (1972), Christian Reformed Ch (1971), Churches of Christ in Christian Union, Congregational Holiness Ch (1968), Congregational Methodist Ch, Ev Methodist Ch (1964), Evangelistic Faith Missions (1970), World Baptist Fellowship (1967), World-Wide Missions.

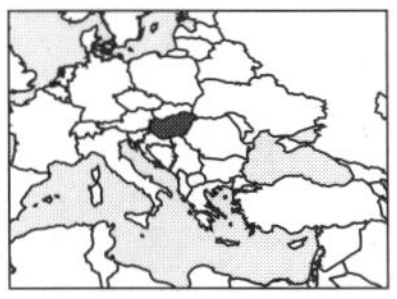

HUNGARY

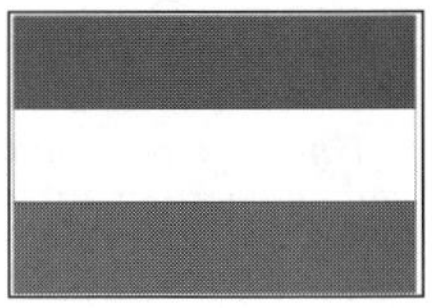

SECULAR DATA, AD 2000

STATE
Official name: Magyar Köztársaság (The Republic of Hungary).
Short name: Hungary. **Adjective of nationality:** Hungarian.
Flag: Red, white, and green tricolor.
Area: 93,033 sq. km. (35,920 sq. mi.).
Government: Unitary multiparty republic with one legislative house, since 1989 (1001 independent kingdom, 1919 independent republic, 1949 one-party Communist state).
Legislature: National Assembly, 386 members.
Official language: Hungarian (Magyar).
Monetary unit: 1 forint (Ft) = 100 filler. **US$1=** Ft 218.38.
Chief cities: BUDAPEST 2,017,000; Debrecen 206,155; Miskolc 186,983; Szeged 169,736; Pecs 163,846.
Political divisions: 20 provinces.
Armed forces: 49,000.

DEMOGRAPHY
Population: 10,036,000.
Population density: 107.8/sq. km. (279.3/sq. mi.).
Under 15 years: 1,706,000.
Growth rate p.a.: -0.40% (births 9.34, deaths 13.32).
Mortality: Infant, per 1,000: 9.6; **Maternal per 100,000:** 30.0.
Life expectancy: 72 (male 68, female 76).
Household size: 2.9. **Floor area per person, sq.m:** 29.4.
Major languages: Hungarian, Romany, German, Russian Slovak, Serbo-Croatian, Romanian.
Urban dwellers: 66.95%. **Urban growth rate p.a.:** 0.1%.
Labor force: 49%.

ETHNOLINGUISTIC PEOPLES
84.4% Hungarian (Magyar); 5.2% Hungarian Gypsy; 2.9% Ruthenian (Rusin); 2.3% German; 0.9% Romanian.

ECONOMY
National income p.a. per person: US$4,120; **per family:** US$11,948.

EDUCATION
Adult literacy: 98% (male 99%, female 98%). **Schools:** 5,094.
Universities: 91. **School enrolment:** female/male: 91%/90%.

HEALTH
Access to health services: 70%. **Access to safe water:** 94%.
Hospitals: 148 (98 beds per 10,000). **Doctors:** 36,643.
Blind: 10,000. **Deaf:** 588,700. Murder **rate:** 4.
Lepers: 1,000. **Underweight prevalence under 5:** 2%.

LITERATURE
New book titles p.a.: 8,530 (850 p.a. per million). **Periodicals:** 1,684.
Newspapers: 27 dailies.

COMMUNICATION (per 1,000 people)
Phones: 185 **(18% mobile).** Radios: 590. **TV sets:** 444.
Daily newspaper circulation: 228. **Computers:** 153.

REFUGEES
Alien refugees from other countries: 9,100.

HUMAN LIFE AND LIBERTY (optimum condition=100.0%)
HDI: 85.7. **HSI:** 68.0. **HFI:** 17.5. **EFL:** 42.0.

Country Table 1. **Religious adherents in Hungary, AD 1900-2025.**

Year	1900		1970		mid-1990		Annual change, 1990-2000				mid-1995		mid-2000		mid-2025	
Name	Adherents	%	Adherents	%	Adherents	%	Natural	Conversion	Total	Rate	Adherents	%	Adherents	%	Adherents	%
Christians	**6,411,000**	**93.5**	**8,783,928**	**85.0**	**8,954,450**	**86.4**	**-28,466**	**9,388**	**-19,078**	**-0.22**	**8,881,000**	**86.8**	**8,763,672**	**87.3**	**8,078,200**	**90.8**
PROFESSION																
crypto-Christians	0	0.0	725,928	7.0	0	0.0	0	0	0	0.00	0	0.0	0	0.0	0	0.0
professing Christians	**6,411,000**	**93.5**	**8,058,000**	**78.0**	**8,954,450**	**86.4**	**-28,466**	**9,388**	**-19,078**	**-0.22**	**8,881,000**	**86.8**	**8,763,672**	**87.3**	**8,078,200**	**90.8**
AFFILIATION																
unaffiliated Christians	340,000	5.0	80,800	0.8	19,450	0.2	-62	-489	-551	-3.28	15,000	0.2	13,940	0.1	10,200	0.1
affiliated Christians	**6,071,000**	**88.6**	**8,703,128**	**84.2**	**8,935,000**	**86.2**	**-28,404**	**9,877**	**-18,527**	**-0.21**	**8,866,000**	**86.7**	**8,749,732**	**87.2**	**8,068,000**	**90.7**
Roman Catholics	4,153,000	60.6	6,125,328	59.3	6,400,000	61.8	-20,358	13,358	-7,000	-0.11	6,363,075	62.2	6,330,000	63.1	5,800,000	65.2
Protestants	1,850,000	27.0	2,486,500	24.1	2,550,000	24.6	-8,094	9,094	1,000	0.04	2,558,740	25.0	2,560,000	25.5	2,400,000	27.0
Independents	0	0.0	21,600	0.2	140,000	1.4	-444	2,944	2,500	1.66	153,786	1.5	165,000	1.6	200,000	2.3
Orthodox	65,000	1.0	66,100	0.6	85,500	0.8	-271	721	450	0.51	87,000	0.9	90,000	0.9	90,000	1.0
Marginal Christians	3,000	0.0	3,600	0.0	35,000	0.3	-111	611	500	1.34	37,000	0.4	40,000	0.4	60,000	0.7
doubly-affiliated	0	0.0	0	0.0	-275,500	-2.7	874	-16,851	-15,977	4.68	-333,601	-3.3	-435,268	-4.3	-482,000	-5.4
Trans-megabloc groupings																
Evangelicals	190,000	2.8	450,000	4.4	445,000	4.3	-1,412	2,412	1,000	0.22	448,896	4.4	455,000	4.5	450,000	5.1
Pentecostals/Charismatics	0	0.0	27,000	0.3	660,000	6.4	-2,095	5,095	3,000	0.45	686,147	6.7	690,000	6.9	730,000	8.2
Great Commission Christians	**343,000**	**5.0**	**724,000**	**7.0**	**1,088,000**	**10.5**	**-3,453**	**1,331**	**-2,122**	**-0.20**	**1,084,000**	**10.6**	**1,066,779**	**10.6**	**1,068,000**	**12.0**
Nonreligious	23,000	0.3	891,672	8.6	822,000	7.9	-2,609	-5,260	-7,869	-1.00	789,210	7.7	743,314	7.4	500,000	5.6
Atheists	10,000	0.2	570,000	5.5	479,400	4.6	-1,522	-3,885	-5,407	-1.19	450,000	4.4	425,327	4.2	220,000	2.5
Muslims	0	0.0	2,000	0.0	48,000	0.5	-152	993	841	1.63	52,000	0.5	56,405	0.6	65,000	0.7
Jews	410,000	6.0	90,000	0.9	60,000	0.6	-190	-1,319	-1,509	-2.86	53,300	0.5	44,909	0.5	35,000	0.4
Buddhists	0	0.0	300	0.0	1,000	0.0	-3	73	70	5.42	1,300	0.0	1,695	0.0	1,400	0.0
Baha'is	0	0.0	100	0.0	150	0.0	0	10	10	5.07	190	0.0	246	0.0	400	0.0
World A (unevangelized persons)	13,708	0.2	620,274	6.0	82,920	0.8	-263	-1,483	-1,746	-2.33	81,814	0.8	70,252	0.7	53,400	0.6
World B (evangelized non-Christians)	429,292	6.3	933,707	9.0	1,327,630	12.8	-4,213	-7,905	-12,118	-0.99	1,264,041	12.4	1,202,076	12.0	768,400	8.6
World C (Christians)	6,411,000	93.5	8,783,928	85.0	8,954,450	86.4	-28,466	9,388	-19,078	-0.22	8,881,000	86.8	8,763,672	87.3	8,078,200	90.8
Country's population	**6,854,000**	**100.0**	**10,337,910**	**100.0**	**10,365,000**	**100.0**	**-32,942**	**0**	**-32,942**	**-0.32**	**10,226,856**	**100.0**	**10,036,000**	**100.0**	**8,900,000**	**100.0**

COLUMNS, ROWS.
For meanings and definitions, see Codebook (Part 3). Note that, by definition, total 'Christians' = professing + crypto-Christians, which also = affiliated + unaffiliated Christians, and also = Great Commission Christians + latent Christians. Percentages may not always total exactly, due to rounding.

CENSUSES.
Note: before 1920 boundaries referred to Hungary proper, but differed from present ones. **1857:** 57.9% Roman Catholics (10.1% Greek Catholics), 20.8% Protestants, 17.9% Greek Orthodox, 3.0% Jews, 0.4% marginal Protestants (Unitarians). **1870:** 58.9% Roman Catholics (10.2% Greek Catholics), 20.3% Protestants, 16.8% Greek Orthodox, 3.6% Jews, 0.4% Unitarians. **1900** (Hungary proper): 59.6% Roman Catholics (10.9% Greek Catholics), 21.9% Protestants, 13.1% Greek Orthodox, 4.9% Jews, 0.4% Unitarians. **1910** (Hungary proper, old boundaries): 60.3% Roman Catholics (11.0% Greek Catholics), 21.4% Protestants, 12.8% Greek Orthodox, 5.0% Jews, 0.4% Unitarians. **1920** (new boundaries): 66.1% Roman Catholics (2.2% Greek Catholics), 27.2% Protestants (21.0% Reformed, 6.2% Lutherans), 5.9% Jews, 0.6% Greek Orthodox, 0.1% Unitarians. **1930:** 67.1% Roman Catholics (2.3% Greek Catholics), 27.1% Protestants (20.9% Reformed, 6.1% Lutherans), 5.1% Jews, 0.5% Greek Orthodox. **1992:** (Population age 14 years and over), 67.8% Roman Catholic, 20.9% Calvinist, 4.2% Lutheran, 4.8% Independents, 2.3% no religion.

NOTES ON RELIGIONS
ATHEISTS. Hungarian Socialist Workers' Party (pro-Soviet).
BAHA'IS. In 1 center (1970), growing to 8 local spiritual assemblies (1996).
BUDDHISTS. Centered on a Buddhist mission in Budapest.
CRYPTO-CHRISTIANS. Only before 1990. Christians affiliated to churches but not known as such to the state, being (1) unorganized individuals in the legal churches, (2) members of illegal or underground churches, and (3) a few isolated radio believers.
JEWS. Before 1939, they numbered 800,000, but 600,000 perished in the Nazi massacres. Of the present total, 80% live in Budapest with 32 synagogues, a seminary, and a library of 60,000 volumes. Declining due to emigration to Israel.
MUSLIMS. A small minority including a community in Budapest.
NONRELIGIOUS. Agnostics, indifferent to religion, including most Communist party members.
PENTECOSTALS/CHARISMATICS. The Catholic Charismatic Renewal, begun in 1976, in 1997 had 300 regular weekly prayer groups, with 3,000 regular adult attenders (1,500 being youths aged 15-25), 7 covenant communities, 65 involved priests and 4 bishops, with annual conferences of 10,000 participants.

Country status. Hungary lies in the heart of the Danube Basin in east-central Europe. Once part of the Austro-Hungarian empire, Hungary is historically a link between Germany and the eastern Balkan republics. Along with the rest of Eastern Europe, it experienced the rigors of a brutal communist regime until 1990, and since then has successfully rebuilt its democratic institutions.

HUMAN LIFE AND LIBERTY

Human need and development. The communist years from 1945 to 1990 were traumatic for Hungary. Although marked by progress in many areas, such as health and social insurance, they depressed the national standard of living, and cut Hungary off from the mainstream of European economy. Housing, for example, is one of the worst affected areas. Middle class housing is substandard in most parts of the country. Hungary has a negative population growth which means that its population is aging. Certain trends in the general health of the population are matters of national concern. Life expectancy at birth is the lowest among 33 developed countries and the infant mortality rate is highest among industrialized countries at 19 per 1,000 live births. Another historic peculiarity of the Hungarian health system is the high suicide rate. In the mid-1980s, its suicide rate of 44 per 100,000 was the highest in the world. Another problem is the growing incidence of alcoholism and substance abuse. After the collapse of communism, Hungary was one of the countries to move ahead forcefully into free market economy. However, liberalization programs were accompanied by declining standards of living, with a fourth of the population living at or below the poverty line. Unemployment reached 11% by the end of 1992.

Great Commission Instrument Panel: status of Hungary (for explanation see start of Part 4)

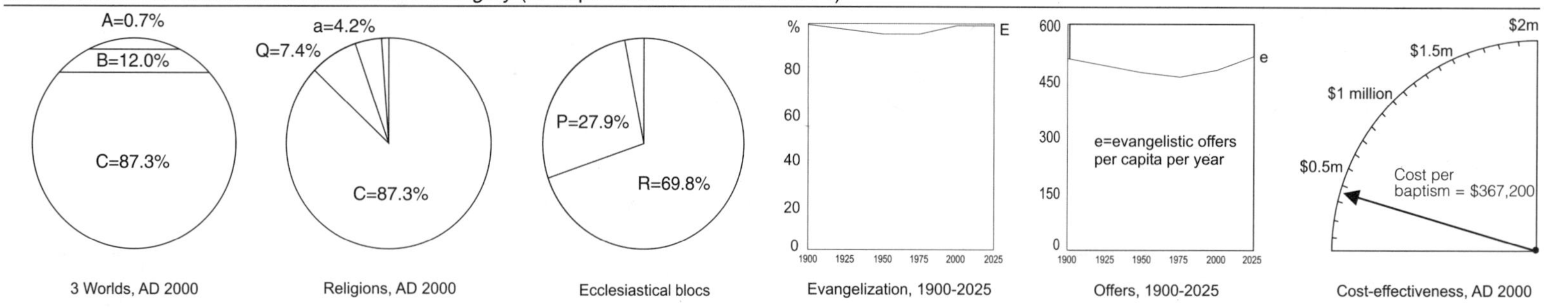

Human rights and freedoms. Hungary is a full-fledged parliamentary democracy and all human rights are guaranteed by the Constitution and respected in practice. The judicial system, in particular, has been cleansed of the authoritarian features it acquired under the communists. The rights of defendants for a fair public trial and access to counsel are recognized. The Constitutional Court is charged with reviewing the constitutionality of laws and statutes. The laws relating to freedom of speech and expression are comparable to those in Western Europe. There are occasional incidents when the government tries to clamp down on particular newspapers for publishing stories that it deems libelous, but these are few and far between. Efforts to expand private radio and television broadcasting have been stymied by inter-party conflicts in Parliament. Discrimination against minorities has not entirely disappeared from the country. Antisemitism finds a home among the rightwing political parties and media but is disavowed by the government. Gypsies form the largest minority group, estimated at between 400,000 and 600,000. The press regularly carries reports of police abuse against Gypsies and anti-Gypsy graffiti are found in many places. Neo-Nazi skinheads target Gypsy homes for fire bomb attacks. Conditions of life within the Gypsy community are significantly poorer than among the general population. They are less educated, have lower than average income and life expectancy, and higher unemployment and crime rates.

Human environment. Air pollution, although substantially less than experienced by neighboring countries, is severe enough to reduce national life expectancy. Nearly 41% of the population is exposed to high levels of sulfur and nitrogen oxides. Some 25% of urban settlements do not have safe water supplies, 80% do not have proper waste water treatment, and 54% do not have adequate sewerage facilities. Water pollution posed a major threat to Lake Balaton, one of the largest fresh-water lakes in Central Europe.

Throughout the Communist period, Christian themes appeared on postage stamps. *Left.* Apostolic king Stephen I, AD 1001. *Above.* Summer Drama Festival, Szeged Cathedral.

NON-CHRISTIAN RELIGIONS

Atheism and ***agnosticism*** were professed by most members of the Communist party and their circles, amounting to around 15% of the population in 1970. The fall of communism brought rapid change. By 1995 the population was 4.4% atheist and a further 7.7% nonreligious.

Judaism had about 53,000 adherents in 1995, 80% of whom live in Budapest. Before World War II they numbered more than 800,000, but 600,000 died in the Nazi holocaust. Judaism's principal organization is the Central Board of Hungarian Jews in Budapest. Also found in Budapest are 32 synagogues, a Jewish secondary school for boys and girls, and a rabbinic seminary with a Jewish library of 60,000 volumes; this has been the only seminary for rabbis in eastern Europe. In those exceptional cases when the USSR government allowed it, rabbis from the USSR were trained here.

Islam has a small minority of followers including a community in Budapest. Due mainly to immigration, the number of Muslims in Hungary grew from 2,000 in 1970 to 52,000 in 1995.

Buddhism is represented by a Buddhist mission in the capital.

Buddhists. East European Buddhist Center, Budapest, with director.

CHRISTIANITY

Christians in Hungary trace their history back to the 3rd century. Christianity having entered the northern Pannonian and Dacian provinces of the Roman empire at that period. Arian, Roman, and Orthodox missionaries were also active among the Goths, Huns, Avars, Franks, and Slavs, who played significant roles at various periods of Hungarian history. The greatest missionaries were Cyril and Methodius, Catholics who worked in Moravia, introduced the Greek rite and translated the liturgy and Bible into the Slavic language. Moravian converts were later dispersed, spreading the Byzantine rite throughout Bulgaria and Russia, and the Roman rite in Hungary. The Magyars (Hungarians), who invaded from the east, although having had strong ties with the Byzantine church, finally opted for the Latin church under prince Geza and his son, Stephen I. The latter was given by the pope the title apostolic king. Aided by Italian, German and Bohemian missionaries, Stephen established Catholicism in AD 1001; and he and his son were later canonized by the Catholic Church. In the 13th century, Hungarian missionaries set out for the Urals to christianize kinsmen left behind centuries before. There they were met by Mongolians who captured the entire Magyar kingdom in 1241, with great loss of life and property. After their withdrawal, the task of reconstruction was begun. Two centuries later the expanding power of the Ottoman empire reached the country's southern borders. Although the Hungarian army resisted the Turks for 100 years, they were finally defeated in 1526; and for the next 150 years the central part of the country was occupied by Turkey. During the Reformation period, Hungary was divided into 3 regions: the west (the kingdom of Hungary) under the control of the Austrian Hapsburgs, the central plains under the Turks, and the principality of Transylvania in the east, which remained independent.

The Lutheran Reformation entered in 1518 under the influence of the writings of Luther and the return of Hungarian reformers from Wittenberg. The Augsburg Confession was adopted in 1545 and the Lutheran catechism in 1550. During the latter part of the 16th century, the Swiss Reformation gained more ground, and the emerging Reformed church adopted the Second Helvetic Confession at Debrecen in 1567. Later the Heidelberg Catechism was adopted and became influential in the church. In Transylvania, the law of the land granted freedom of worship to the Catholic, Lutheran, Reformed and Unitarian churches in 1568; and by the end of the 16th century the majority of Hungarians were Protestants, mostly of the Reformed faith. A century later the Hapsburgs had expelled the Turks and the country was reunited under Vienna, whereupon Counter-Reformation activities, until then limited to the kingdom in the West, were extended to the whole country and launched with new vigor. The war of liberation of Ferenc Rakoczi II in 1703-11, attempting to wrest political and religious freedom from Austria, was ultimately lost and was followed by an even more vigorous oppression, as well as the arrival of Catholic settlers in the regions left desolate by Turks and wars. At the close of the 18th century the number of Protestants had been reduced to one-third of the population. Legal guarantees of religious freedom were given by the royal decree of 1780, the Edict of Toleration of Joseph II, and were reaffirmed at the Diet of 1791. In that year Lutheran and Reformed churches were reorganized with the laity assuming greater control. Further steps towards religious equality were taken progressively before the unsuccessful political uprising of 1848-49, and also in 1867 when the Austro-Hungarian dual monarchy came into being. Hungary achieved independence from the Hapsburgs following World War I but suffered a great loss of territory and population. The Lutheran Church, formerly with over a million adherents, lost more than half its membership, a large number being dispersed to areas with no Lutheran churches. In 1881 the Reformed Church adopted its book of church law affirming a synodal-presbyterian form of government, but with bishops. It also faced new difficulties after World War I, not only because of loss of membership through the reduction of Hungarian territory, but also through rationalism and theological liberalism. However, a theological renewal inspired by dialectical theology and a popular revival movement, particularly during the years following World War II, gave the church new strength and identity.

During all these years when Protestantism was repressed, the Catholic Church had grown in influence, and it experienced a new awakening towards the end of the 19th century. Religious vocations increased, parishes were reorganized, lay and missionary movements developed and publications increased. As a result, the Catholic Church remains the dominant spiritual influence in the country up to the present day.

Country summary. **Worlds A, B, C by ethnolinguistic peoples, cities, and major civil divisions in Hungary.**

	PEOPLES							CITIES							CIVIL DIVISIONS						
World	Num	Pop 2000	C%	Christians	E%	U%	Unevangelized	Num	Pop 2000	C%	Christians	E%	U%	Unevangelized	Num	Pop 2000	C%	Christians	E%	U%	Unevangelized
A	2	57,203	0.01	3	49	51	29,221	0	0	0.00	0	0	0	0	0	0	0.00	0	0	0	0
B	2	87,069	23.78	20,709	72	28	24,699	0	0	0.00	0	0	0	0	0	0	0.00	0	0	0	0
C	19	9,891,297	88.25	8,729,022	100	0	11,624	23	4,027,962	84.83	3,417,040	99	1	24,453	20	10,035,570	87.19	8,749,732	99	1	65,547
Total	**23**	**10,035,569**	**87.19**	**8,749,734**	**99**	**1**	**65,544**	**23**	**4,027,962**	**84.83**	**3,417,040**	**99**	**1**	**24,453**	**20**	**10,035,570**	**87.19**	**8,749,732**	**99**	**1**	**65,547**

CATHOLIC CHURCH. Catholics live mostly in western Transdanubia, in the area between the Danube and Tisza rivers and in the mountains of the north. They form the majority in 70% of the towns and are especially strong among the ethnic minorities: Croats, Germans, Slovaks, and Gypsies. Catholics of the Byzantine rite live in Budapest and in the rural communities of the northern Great Plains.

The Catholic Church had to face the double problem of secularization accompanied by official atheistic propaganda. Nevertheless, institutional religious life in Hungary remained active and influential, especially in rural areas and among intellectuals. Christmas midnight mass, Easter offices and places of pilgrimage continue to hold a strong attraction. These external manifestations of religiosity were not concealed, nor engaged in merely as open opposition to the former communist regime. In part they were an expression of popular folk religion, but in part also of genuine spiritual needs. In both rural and urban communities, the 3 major events of life (birth, marriage, death) are usually accompanied by religious ceremonies. Marriages and burials are carried out as solemn occasions with massive participation.

The Holy See has diplomatic relations with Hungary and in AD 2000 is represented to government and the Catholic hierarchy by a nuncio residing in Budapest.

PROTESTANT CHURCHES. Protestant churches consider that discrimination against them in favor of Rome finally ended following World War II, when the new Communist government made individual agreements with each body and the Roman Catholic Church was no longer given special preference. Moreover, the government subsidized the reconstruction of churches extensively damaged during the war, and continues to finance religious education with teachers provided by the churches. The Reformed Church of Hungary, with about 20% of the population (in 1995), has more than 1,000 autonomous parishes in 4 church districts or dioceses. Organized on the synodal-presbyterian principle, it has a dual chairmanship, with ministerial and lay chairmen. There are 2 theological academies. The Church also administers several institutions of higher learning and 20 charitable organizations. It is attempting to move from its earlier status as a folk church with automatic membership based on birth, to a gathered church with membership voluntarily chosen through a decision based on faith. The Evangelical Lutheran Church with 4% of the population, is divided into 2 districts with 341 parishes forming 16 seniorates. It has one theological academy and operates 18 social service institutions. The largest of the smaller denominations is the Baptist Church begun in 1846. It has 400 congregations and maintains a theological seminary and 3 institutions for social service. Methodists entered Hungary in 1900 and have 73 congregations and one charitable institution (in 1995). Seventh-day Adventists and Evangelical-Christian Pentecostals each have several thousand members. Other bodies are the Apostolic Church, Church of God, Nazarenes and several groups of Brethren. Sunday church attendance for Protestants averages 14% of the entire population weekly, rising to 20% at Easter and festivals.

ORTHODOX CHURCH. The Orthodox Church in Hungary has 10 parishes consisting mostly of Serbian and Romanian ethnic minorities in Szentendre and Budapest. Hungarian Orthodoxy is under the authority of the Moscow Patriarchate. The Bulgarian, Romanian, Russian, and Serbian Orthodox churches also have their own jurisdictions.

INDEPENDENT CHURCHES. A large number of new independent charismatic churches have been begun in recent years, especially since the collapse of Communism.

Art and architecture. The crown jewels of Christian art and architecture are the St Stephen's Basilica and the Mathias or Coronation Church, the Hungarian Westminster Abbey, where the kings of Hungary were crowned between 1309 and 1916. In Esztergom, the treasury of the cathedral contains priceless gold and silver work and vestments. The Museum of Christianity, also in Esztergom, includes 13th to 16th century paintings. Serb religious art is found in Szentendre.

Renewal movements. In the 1990s the Pentecostal/Charismatic Renewal continued to spread rapidly across most older churches, and numbered over 690,000 adherents (of whom 2% Pentecostals, 75% Charismatics, and 24% Independents).

Indigenous missions. Hungarian missionaries were active in surrounding countries from the third century to the thirteenth. During the thirteenth century missionaries were sent to Russia to reach their kinsmen who did not migrate in the earlier centuries. By the end of the nineteenth century Roman Catholicism was dominant and had a vigorous missionary-sending character, which has once again revived after the collapse of Communist restrictions.

CHURCH AND STATE

Hungary, a religious state in the year 1900, became an atheistic state in 1949. The constitution of 1972 guaranteed freedom of conscience, the free exercise of worship (paragraph 67, item 1) and proclaimed the separation of church and state in the interests of freedom of conscience (paragraph 63, item 2).

The communist government of Hungary enacted sweeping legislation affecting the churches. Half of all ecclesiastical estates, forest and pasture land, passed into the hands of the state, and the other half was distributed among peasants. All church schools were nationalized, though a few were returned in 1950. In 1950, 53 religious orders and congregations were banned. Provision was made for state funding of the churches, according to their numerical importance. In 1964 Hungary concluded an agreement with the Vatican, the first of its kind between the Holy See and a communist country, that granted new rights and freedoms to the church. Involvement in clerical appointments by the state did not begin with the communists and their State Office for Ecclesiastical Affairs (Allami Egyhazugyi Hitaval); under the former monarchy there was a State Secretariat for Ecclesiastical Affairs, although its ideological orientation was very different.

The Protestant churches succeeded better in accommodating themselves to the People's Republic than the Catholic Church. The latter was bound to the old regime politically, as the official church under the Austro-Hungarian empire and later the Horthy regency, and also economically, as exemplified by the feudal character of its hierarchy. Reformers before 1939 were aware of the dangers facing the church but were unsuccessful in changing existing structures. The struggle of the Catholic Church against the new regime began in 1945 and was characterized by public manifestations of strength, including pilgrimages, public novenas, meetings, the celebration of the marian year 1948, and open hostility to nationalization. This campaign was conducted personally under the direction of cardinal Mindszenty, who was finally arrested on 25 December 1948, and sentenced the following February to life imprisonment. In 1971 the Catholic Church in Hungary celebrated its millennium with the government permitting the organization of local pilgrimages, authorizing for the first time the publication of a children's catechism and ignoring its right to review such lower ecclesiastical appointments as vicars and parish priests. After October 1971, priests accused of collaborating with the regime were no longer excommunicated by the hierarchy, and the number of imprisoned priests began to diminish.

The Mindszenty affair was resolved when, on 28 September 1971, through papal pressure he agreed to leave the American Embassy in Budapest where he had lived since 1956. In 1978, diplomatic relations with the Holy See were finally established. In 1990 Hungary became the first Iron Curtain country to break free from Marxism to multi-party democracy.

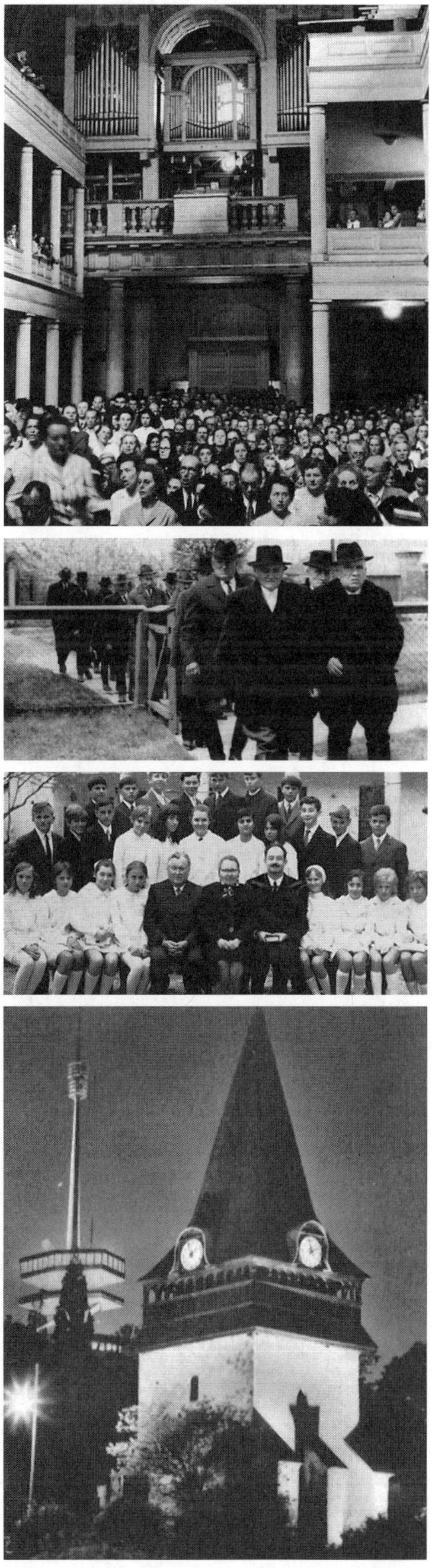

Reformed Church of Hungary. (*From top*). Interior, Calvin Square Church; elders in Sunday dress; confirmands with pastors in village near River Tisza; Miskolc Church (16th century), with state television tower.

Since then the churches have enjoyed complete religious freedom. As in other post-communist countries, the churches face the difficult task of dealing with church leaders who compromised with the Communist repression.

BROADCASTING AND MEDIA

Shortwave programs from KNLS, HCJB (Ecuador), TWR (Monaco, Albania) and AWR (Slovakia) can be easily received. AWR's Budapest studio develops programs in Hungarian. TWR is locally registered in Hungary as Hungarian Evangelical Radio, and it has local facilities to produce Hungarian radio programs. Hungary is a member of UNDA.

Some 912,000 have seen the 'Jesus' Film: over 500,000 watched it on national television. Satellite TV and radio programs are received in English, Arabic, German and Italian. During Billy Graham's most recent campaign, a large press corps recorded the event and broadcast a 90-minute prime-time special the following week.

INTERDENOMINATIONAL ORGANIZATIONS

A Union of Free Churches, which brought together most of the leaders of the smaller churches of Hungary, was formed prior to World War II, becoming in 1948 the Council of Free Churches. In 1943 an Ecumenical Committee composed of Reformed and Lutheran representatives was established to prepare the ground for the formation in 1948 of the Ecumenical Council of Churches (Magyarorszagi Eghazak Okumenikus Tanasca). Members include the Reformed, Lutheran, Baptist, Methodist and Orthodox churches as well as the Council of Free Churches as a corporate member. The Ecumenical Council has from the beginning been active in the international Faith and Order movement as well as at all World Council of Churches assemblies. Faculty and student exchanges take place among the various denominational theological academies.

FUTURE TRENDS AND PROSPECTS

With the collapse of Communism, downward trends in church membership will probably rebound with significant losses to the nonreligious and atheist adherents. Christians are expected to grow from 85% in 1970 to 90.8% by 2025.

Christianity may eventually reach its 1900 mark of 93.5% but by the middle of the 21st century a reversal in the post-cold war decline of the nonreligious may limit growth beyond that point.

BIBLIOGRAPHY

1000 years of Hungarian Christianity. [Toronto]: Hungarian Christianity Millennium Committee, 1973. 44p.

'A model for evangelism in the Reformed Church in Hungary.' A. Lovas. Th.M. thesis, Columbia Theological Seminary, Decatur, GA, 1993. 112p.

A protestáns teológia Magyarországon, 1945–1985. J. Poór. [Budapest]: Kossuth, 1986. 184p.

Beiträge zur Lage der Katholischen Kirche im Ungarn in Jahre 1961. Vienna: Ungarisches Katholische Institut für Kirchliche Sozialforschung, 1962.

Bilanz des ungarischen Katholizismus: Kirche and Gesellschaft in Dokumenten, Zahlen und Analysen. I. Andras & J. Mrel. Munich: Heimatwerk Verlag, 1969. 255p.

Billy Graham in Budapest. E. E. Plowman, J. N. Akers & R. Busby. : World Wide Publications, 1989. 110p.

Calvinist churches in Hungary. B. Dercsényi et al. Budapest: Hegyi, 1992. 186p.

Christianity and the holocaust of Hungarian Jewry. M. Y. Hertsel. New York: New York University Press, 1993. 308p.

Christians and churches in Socialist countries: report of a visit by church leaders from South East Asia and Australia. J. S. Udy. Delhi: ISPCK, 1982. 204p.

Church in transition: Hungary's Catholic Church from 1945 to 1982: collected studies of the Hungarian Institute for Sociology of Religion. Vienna: The Institute, 1983. 434p.

Churches, denominations, and congregations in Hungary, 1991. Budapest: Ministry of Foreign Affairs, [1991]. 62p.

De l'oppression à la liberté: l'Eglise en Hongrie, 1945–1992: chronique des événements ordinaires et extraordinaires, témoins et témoignages. P. G. Bozsoky & L. Lukács. Paris: Beauchesne, 1993. 385p.

Der Protestantismus in Ungarn, 1521–1977: Ungarns Reformations–Kirche in Gechichte und Gegenwart. M. Bucsay. Leiden: E. J. Brill, 1978. 320p.

Die Lage der Katholischen Kirche in Ungarn im Jahre 1960. Vienna: Ungarisches Katholische Institut für Kirchliche Sozialforschung, 1960.

Five years of Hungarian Protestantism, 1945–1950. I. Kadar (ed). Budapest: Hungarian Church Press, 1950. 129p.

God moves in a mysterious way: the Hungarian Protestant Foreign Mission Movement, 1756–1951. A. M. Kool. Zoetermeer: Uitgeverij Boekencentrum, [1993]. 1043p. (Summary in Dutch and Hungarian).

God moves in a mysterious way: the Hungarian Protestant foreign mission movement (1756–1951). A. M. Kool. Zoetermeer, Netherlands: Boekencentrum, 1993. 1,025p.

Handbuch des ungarischen Katholizismus. Vienna: UKI, 1975. 208p.

History of the Orthodox church in Hungary. M. G. Dampier. London: Rivingtons, for the Eastern Church Association, 1905. 78p.

History of the Protestant church in Hungary: from the beginning of the Reformation to 1850; with reference also to Transylvania. J. Craig. London: James Nisbet & Co., 1864. 464p.

Hope preserved: the past and present of Hungarian Lutheranism. T. Fabiny. Budapest: Nyomda, 1984. 119p.

Hungarian Catholicism: a handbook. E. András & J. Morel. Vienna: Hungarian Institute for Sociology of Religion, 1983. 191p.

Hungarian Protestantism, its past and present. Budapest: Ecumenical Council of Churches, 1956.

Hungary. T. Kabdebo. *World bibliographical series,* vol. 15. Oxford, UK: CLIO Press, 1980. 337p. (See especially 'Religion,' p.63–7).

'Hungary,' I. Varga, in *Western religion: a country by country sociological enquiry,* p.277–94. H. Mol (ed). The Hague: Mouton, 1972.

'L'Eglise de Hongrie sous le Régime Communiste,' *Informations catholiques internationales,* 36 (1956).

Lutheran churches in Hungary. B. Dercsényi et al. Budapest: Hegyi & Co, 1992. 198p.

Pilgrimaging in Hungary. J. F. Bango. Vienna: UKI, 1979. 169p.

Pogány magyarság keresztény magyarság. J. Deér. Budapest: Holnap Kiado, 1993. 271p. (Study of medieval Hungary's impact upon Christianity and the culture of Europe).

Politics and religion in Eastern Europe: Catholicism in Hungary, Poland, and Czechoslovakia. P. Michel. Oxford, UK: Polity, 1991. 329p.

'Religion and nationality in Hungary,' L. László, in *Religion and nationalism in Soviet and East European politics,* p.286–97. P. Ramet (ed). 2nd ed. Durham, NC: Duke University Press, 1989.

Religion und Kirche in Ungarn: Ergebnisse religionssoziologischer Forschung, 1969–1988. M. Tomka. Vienna: Ungarischen Kirchensoziologischen Institut, 1990. 588p.

'Renewal in the American Hungarian Reformed Church.' A. B. Fuleki. D.Min. thesis, Ashland Theological Seminary, Ashland, OH, 1990. 152p.

Studies on shamanism. A. L. Siikala and M. Hoppál. *Ethnologica uralica,* 2. Helsinki: Finnish Anthropological Society, 1992. 230p.

'The church in Hungary,' I. András, *Pro Mundi Vita,* (1984), 1–32.

The church in the storm of time. I. Kadar. Budapest: Bibliotheca, 1957. 175p. (History of the Hungarian Reformed Church).

'The habitation of thy house, Lord, I have loved well ...': Reformed ecclesiastical art in Hungary. J. Hapák & B. Takács. Budapest: Officina Nova, 1991. 79p.

The Hungarian Protestant Reformation in the sixteenth century under the Ottoman impact. A. S. Unghváry. Lewiston, NY: E. Mellen Press, 1989. 419p.

The Hungarian Reformed Church. London: Cambrensis Production, 1993. (30 min. videocassette).

Country Table 2. **Organized churches and denominations in Hungary.**

Official name (bold type = church with over 10% of all affiliated) 1	*Begun* 2	*Type* 3	*Counc* 4	*Congs* 5	*Adults* 6	*Affiliated 1970* 7	*Affiliated 1995* 8	*G%* 9	*Names, notes, and other statistics* (see Codebook, Part 3) 10
Apostolic Christian Church (Nazarean)		P-Hol	x....	71	2,500	4,000	2,940	0.05	Holiness Christians of Swiss origin, related to Mennonites. In 17 nations.
Apostolic Ch (Primitive Chr Brethren)	1930	P-PeA	Z...C	130	3,000	5,000	10,000	2.81	*Öskeresztyén Felekezet.* Centrally organized: 4 apostles, 6 prophets, 14 preachers.
Baptist Union of Hungary	1846	P-Bap	TW..d	400	10,994	40,000	25,000	-1.86	*Magyarországi Baptista Egyház. Hungarian Baptist Union.* 2 homes for the aged. 92n, 2s(23).
Bulgarian Orthodox Church		O-Bul	Mwc..	5	600	100	1,000	0.05	*Balgarskata Pravoslavna Crkva.* Under jurisdiction of P Sofia. Bulgarian residents and refugees.
Catholic Church in Hungary:	c 250	R-LEr	B.B.R	2,633	4,775,000	6,125,328	6,363,075	0.15	*Római Katolikus Egyház.* C=3+0+1. 2188n 282x 407m 615w 68363Y
M Eger	c 950	R-Lat	Bs	307	450,000	862,257	600,000	-1.44	*Egri Föegyhàzmegye.* 60% urban. M=OCist. 1s. 205n 17x 17m 55w 10071Yy
D Debrecen-Nyiregyhaza	1993	R-Lat	Bs	113	240,000	–	320,000	50.00	New diocese. Population is 29% Roman Catholic. 82n 0x 0m 54w 3181Yy
D Vác	c1050	R-Lat	Bs	223	517,000	1,300,000	690,000	-2.50	*Vàci egyhàazmegye.*Many Protestants. M=OCist.1s. 279n 36x 62m 193w 8207Yy
M Esztergom-Budapest	c 950	R-Lat	Bs	219	943,000	760,000	1,258,000	2.04	*Esztergomi Föegyhàzmegye.* Primatial see. M=OFM. 299n 97x 97m 0w 9250Yy
D Györ	c1050	R-Lat	Bs	203	352,000	415,000	470,000	0.50	*Györi egyhàzmegye.* Pilgrimage centres. 1s. 179n 19x 25m 31w 4640Yy
D Hajdudorog *(Hungarian)*	1912	R-Hun	Os	135	190,000	245,000	253,000	0.13	Hungarian-speaking. Ruthenian parishes. 1s. 191n 5x 6m 15w 3248Yy
D Székesfehérvár	1777	R-Lat	Bs	159	336,000	385,425	448,744	0.61	Rural. First royal capital. M=OCD. 139n 14x 14m 58w 4404Yy
M Kalocsa-Kecskemet	1000	R-Lat	Bs	119	327,000	218,529	435,681	2.80	*Kalocsai Föegyhàzmegye.* Rural villages. 129n 10x 10m 36w 4628Yy
D Pécs	1009	R-Lat	Bs	197	330,000	444,000	440,500	-0.03	'Five Churches'. Rural. German minority. 150n 13x 14m 63w 3780Yy
D Szeged-Csanád	1035	R-Lat	Bs	100	329,000	371,700	440,000	0.68	*Csanadi egyhàzmegye.* Mixed Catholics/Protestants. 121n 17x 79m 6w 4300Yy
M Veszprém	1009	R-Lat	Bs	179	225,000	753,538	299,670	-3.62	*Veszprémi eghàzmegye.* Tourism (Lake Balaton). 138n 18x 22m 25w 4266Yy
D Kaposvar	1993	R-Lat	Bs	157	241,000	–	321,140	50.00	New diocese. 70% Roman Catholic. 110n 0x 0m 2w 3870Yy
D Szombathely	1777	R-Lat	Bs	176	223,000	319,279	297,000	-0.29	*Szombathelyi egyhàzmegye.* Developed. M=OCist. 136n 25x 34m 59w 3996Yy
EA Miskolc *(Hungarian)*	1924	R-Hun	Os	31	20,800	24,100	27,750	0.57	Magyarized Ruthenians living outside D Hajdudorog. 30n 0x 0m 0w 367Yy
AN Pannonhalma	997	R-Lat	bosb	15	16,200	26,500	21,590	0.10	Long tradition of Catholic education. M=OSB. 0n 11x 27m 18w 155Yy
OM Hungary	1994	R-Lat	Bs	300	35,000	–	40,000	50.00	*Military Ordinariate of Hungary.* 11 ordinaries.
Christian Advent Fellowship		I-Adv	.....	35	1,267	–	3,000	0.05	*Kereszteny Advent Kozosseg.*
Christian Brethren	c1910	P-CBr	x...C	27	2,000	3,000	3,000	0.00	*Keresztyén Testvérgyülekezetek. Open Brethren.* Many intellectuals are members.
Church of God	1907	I-3pW	.....	5	200	500	500	0.00	*Isten Egyhaza.* M=Church of God (Cleveland, USA).
Community of Evangelical Brethren	1974	I-Met	.....	25	2,300	–	5,000	4.76	Schism ex Hungarian Methodist Ch. Slowly growing.
Congregation of God	c1965	I-3cW	.....	23	2,750	1,000	5,500	7.06	Indigenous charismatics.
Congregation of the Living God	1960	I-3pW	ZF..C	19	2,700	3,700	3,250	-0.52	*Isten Egyhàza. Church of the Living God.* Link with M=CoG(Cleveland) (USA). 1n.
Congregation of the Nazarenes	1830	P-Hol	.....	110	3,000	16,000	6,000	-3.85	Rapid decline over many years.
Evangelical Lutheran Ch in Hungary	1518	P-Lut	LWC.W	341	368,000	450,000	450,000	0.00	*Magyarorszàgi Evangélikus Egyház. Diaspora church. Dioceses: North, South. 400n,1s(55).*
Faith Christian Fellowship	1978	I-3cW	.....	152	35,000	–	53,000	5.88	*Hit Gyulekezete.* (Word of Faith Church). 100,000 conversions, 20 Gypsy churches.
Fellowship of Evangelical Pentecostals	1926	I-3pW	ZF..C	215	7,755	13,000	14,000	0.30	*Evangéliumi Keresztyének-Pünkösdiek. Punkosdi Egyház.* Links M=AoG(USA). 22n,1s(13).
Hungarian Free Christian Church	1924	I-3cW	C	25	2,000	1,000	3,000	4.49	*Szabad Keresztyének Gyülekezete.* Many professionals, doctors et alii.
Hungarian Latter Rain Church	1981	I-3pW	.....	15	200	–	400	7.14	*Magyarorszagi Kesoi Eso Gyulekezat.*
Hungarian Methodist Church	1895	P-Met	VvC.d	73	3,000	6,000	5,000	-0.73	Autonomous, but links with Central & Southern Europe Central Conference. UMC(USA).13n.
Hungarian Orthodox Greek Catholic Ch	1933	I-Hun	.....	1	200	400	500	0.90	*Greek Oriental HOC.* Split begun by Serbian P Belgrade. Jacobite succession. Also in USA.
Isolated radio churches	c1950	I-3rW	.....	200	3,000	500	5,000	9.65	Isolated radio believers, mostly youths aged 12-25. R=1000 (TWR, Radio Vatican, &c).
Jehovah's Witnesses	c1910	m-Jeh	x....	200	10,697	2,000	30,200	11.47	First missionaries arrived c1910. Legally proscribed; very active but declining .2054Y
New Apostolic Church	1872	I-3aX	x....	10	150	1,000	286	-4.88	In Bezirk Schweiz (Switzerland District). Germans. World HQ Dortmund (Germany).
Old Catholic Church of Hungary	1945	I-OCa	.....	1	140	500	350	-1.42	Schism ex Rome. Close links with and succession from, Mariavite Ch (Poland).
Orthodox Church in Hungary	c1200	O-Hun	Mwc.W	40	30,000	40,000	50,000	0.90	Autonomous, under P Moscow. Greek/Serbian/Romanian. Many refugees since 1989. 8n.
Paulician Church (Bogomils)	c 250	m-Pau	x....	10	700	1,500	2,000	1.16	Regarded as heretical in 3rd century. (dualist, anti-OT). A few communities speaking Palityan.
Reformed Church of Hungary	1530	P-Ref	RWC.W	1,133	1,600,000	1,950,000	2,040,000	0.18	*Magyarországi Reformàtus Egyház.* 4 Districts & bishops. 85% farmers. 1650n,1j,2s.
Romanian Orthodox Church	c1200	O-Rum	Cwc..	18	10,900	15,000	19,000	0.95	*Biserica Ortodoxa Romana.* Parishes under jurisdiction of P Bucharest.
Russian Orthodox Church	c1920	O-Rus	Mwc..	5	1,000	1,000	2,000	2.81	*Russkaya Pravoslavnaya Cerkov.* Under jurisdiction of P Moscow. Many refugees since 1988.
Serbian Orthodox Church: D Budim	1552	O-Ser	Cwc..	400	10,000	10,000	15,000	1.64	Under jurisdiction of P Belgrade. Many Serb refugees since 1991 war. 11n,35b,1d,W=90%.
Seventh-day Adventist Church	1890	P-Adv	x...C	111	5,599	10,000	11,200	0.45	*SDA, Hungarian UC (Duna & Tisza Confs).* (1970) 32n,1s(20),142t(5585),132Y.
Unitarian Church in Hungary	1568	m-Unt	.v...	8	2,880	100	4,800	16.75	*Unitárius Egyház.* Links with UUA,(USA). Transylvanians. Refugees from Romania et alia.
United Pentecostal Church	1926	P-Pel	x....	46	200	500	600	0.73	*Nemzetkozi Egyesult Punkosdista Egyhaz.* M=UPC(USA).
Other independent charismatic chs	1985	I-3cW	.....	300	40,000	–	60,000	10.00	Many smaller churches among former Catholic Charismatics; Assoc of Vineyard Chs.
Other Protestant denominations		P-	.....	50	3,000	2,000	5,000	0.05	Ch of God (Anderson) (6 chs), CoG(Cleveland), CON, World-Wide Mission, Salvation Army.

Continued opposite

Country Table 2–concluded

Official name (bold type = church with over 10% of affiliated) 1	*Begun* 2	*Type* 3	*Counc* 4	*Congs* 5	*Adults* 6	*Affiliated 1970* 7	*Affiliated 1995* 8	*G%* 9	*Names, notes, and other statistics* (see Codebook, Part 3) 10
Doubly-affiliated		2-aff			-252,000	0	-333,601		Charismatics and Evangelicals who are also baptized Roman Catholics.
Totals				**6,837**	**6,688,732**	**8,703,128**	**8,866,000**		

Churches, members, growth, 1900-2025	*Congs*	*Adults*	*Affiliated*	*G%*	*Total denominations*	*6 Megablocs:* O	R	A	P	I	m
Total churches, members, and denominations (mid-1900)	2,000	4,593,000	6,071,000	0.52	13	3	1	0	6	1	2
Total churches, members, and denominations (mid-1970)	6,968	6,584,877	8,703,128	0.52	37	5	1	0	19	9	3
Total churches, members, and denominations (mid-1990)	6,900	6,741,000	8,935,000	0.13	69	5	1	0	30	30	3
Total churches, members, and denominations (mid-1995)	6,837	6,688,732	8,866,000	-0.15	71	5	1	0	30	32	3
Total churches, members, and denominations (mid-2000)	6,800	6,601,000	8,749,732	-0.26	72	5	1	0	30	33	3
Total churches, members, and denominations (mid-2025)	7,100	6,087,000	8,068,000	-0.32	181	10	1	0	40	120	10

NOTES ON TABLE ABOVE
NATIONAL COUNCILS (Column 4, 5th letter).
C = Council of Free Churches in Hungary (CFCH) (Magyarországi Szabadegyházak Tanácsa) (before 1948, Union of Free Churches; since 1965, member of ECHC).
d = member of both CFCH and ECHC.
E = Magyar Evangeliumi Alliansz (MEA) (Hungarian Evangelical Alliance).
R = Assembly of Catholic Bishops of Hungary, or Hungarian Episcopal Council (HEC) (Magyar Püspöki Kar Konferenciaja).
W = Ecumenical Council of Hungarian Churches (ECHC) (Magyarországi Egyházak Ökumenikus Tanácsa).
w = observer member of ECHC.

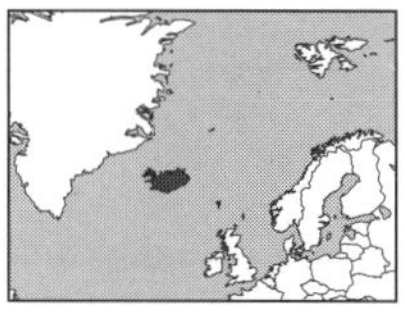

ICELAND

SECULAR DATA, AD 2000

STATE
Official name: Lydhveldidh Island (The Republic of Iceland).
Short name: Iceland. **Adjective of nationality:** Icelandic, an Icelander.
Flag: White-bordered red cross on blue field.
Area: 102,819 sq. km. (39,699 sq. mi.).
Government: Parliamentary republic, since 1944 (1262 Norwegian possession, 1874 home rule, 1918 sovereign state under Danish crown, 1944 Independence as republic).
Legislature: Parliament (Althing): Upper House, 21 members; Lower House, 42 members.
Official language: Icelandic (Islenzka).
Monetary unit: 1 króna (ISK) = 100 aurar. **US$1=** ISK 69.06.
Chief cities: REYKJAVIK 163,799.
Political divisions: 7 provinces.

DEMOGRAPHY
Population: 281,000.
Population density: 2.7/sq. km. (7.0/sq. mi.).
Under 15 years: 66,000.
Growth rate p.a.: 0.83% (births 15.11, deaths 6.84).
Mortality: Infant, per 1,000: 5.1; **Maternal per 100,000:** 10.0.
Life expectancy: 80 (male 77, female 82).
Household size: 2.9. **Floor area per person, sq.m:** 38.0.
Major languages: Icelandic, Danish, Norwegian.
Urban dwellers: 92.31%. **Urban growth rate p.a.:** 1.0%.
Labor force: 55%.

ETHNOLINGUISTIC PEOPLES
95.0% Icelander; 2.0% French-Icelandic Creole; 0.8% Danish (Dane); 0.5% USA White; 0.4% Swedish (Swede).

ECONOMY
National income p.a. per person: US$24,949; **per family:** US$72,353.

EDUCATION
Adult literacy: 100% (male 100%, female 100%). **Schools:** 80.
Universities: 5. **School enrolment:** female/male: 101%/103%.

HEALTH
Access to health services: 95%. **Access to safe water:** 100%.
Hospitals: 26 (111 beds per 10,000). **Doctors:** 726.
Blind: 434. **Deaf:** 16,900. Murder **rate:** <1. **Lepers:** 0.

LITERATURE
New book titles p.a.: 1,490 (5,300 p.a. per million). **Periodicals:** 837.
Newspapers: 5 dailies.

COMMUNICATION (per 1,000 people)
Phones: 556 (28% mobile). Radios: 733. **TV sets:** 447.
Daily newspaper circulation: 515. **Computers:** 300.

HUMAN LIFE AND LIBERTY (optimum condition=100.0%)
HDI: 94.2. **HSI:** 93.0. **HFI:** 85.0. **EFL:** 55.0.

Country Table 1. **Religious adherents in Iceland, AD 1900-2025.**

Year	*1900*		*1970*		*mid-1990*		*Annual change, 1990-2000*				*mid-1995*		*mid-2000*		*mid-2025*	
Name	*Adherents*	*%*	*Adherents*	*%*	*Adherents*	*%*	*Natural*	*Conversion*	*Total*	*Rate*	*Adherents*	*%*	*Adherents*	*%*	*Adherents*	*%*
Christians	**77,900**	**99.9**	**199,940**	**98.0**	**249,130**	**97.7**	**2,537**	**-141**	**2,396**	**0.92**	**261,000**	**97.2**	**273,089**	**97.2**	**314,850**	**96.0**
PROFESSION																
professing Christians	**77,900**	**99.9**	**199,940**	**98.0**	**249,130**	**97.7**	**2,537**	**-141**	**2,396**	**0.92**	**261,000**	**97.2**	**273,089**	**97.2**	**314,850**	**96.0**
AFFILIATION																
unaffiliated Christians	300	0.4	1,726	0.9	4,960	2.0	51	236	287	4.67	6,167	2.3	7,830	2.8	10,850	3.3
affiliated Christians	**77,600**	**99.5**	**198,214**	**97.1**	**244,170**	**95.8**	**2,487**	**-378**	**2,109**	**0.83**	**254,833**	**95.0**	**265,259**	**94.4**	**304,000**	**92.7**
Protestants	77,580	99.5	184,900	90.6	230,000	90.2	2,345	-299	2,046	0.86	240,451	89.6	250,459	89.1	286,200	87.3
Independents	0	0.0	12,046	5.9	11,100	4.4	113	-123	-10	-0.09	11,051	4.1	11,000	3.9	12,000	3.7
Roman Catholics	20	0.0	1,018	0.5	2,350	0.9	24	31	55	2.13	2,553	1.0	2,900	1.0	4,000	1.2
Marginal Christians	0	0.0	250	0.1	720	0.3	7	11	18	2.26	778	0.3	900	0.3	1,800	0.6
Trans-megabloc groupings																
Evangelicals	23,000	29.5	5,800	2.8	6,200	2.4	63	-33	30	0.47	6,343	2.4	6,500	2.3	7,500	2.3
Pentecostals/Charismatics	0	0.0	2,000	1.0	19,900	7.8	203	107	310	1.46	21,484	8.0	23,000	8.2	30,000	9.2
Great Commission Christians	**4,700**	**6.0**	**18,400**	**9.0**	**27,000**	**10.6**	**275**	**72**	**347**	**1.22**	**28,700**	**10.7**	**30,470**	**10.8**	**39,400**	**12.0**
Nonreligious	100	0.1	1,900	0.9	2,550	1.0	26	110	136	4.38	3,335	1.2	3,914	1.4	8,000	2.4
Spiritists	0	0.0	600	0.3	1,200	0.5	12	2	14	1.07	1,260	0.5	1,335	0.5	2,000	0.6
Atheists	0	0.0	1,000	0.5	960	0.4	10	1	11	1.10	1,020	0.4	1,071	0.4	1,300	0.4
Baha'is	0	0.0	300	0.2	550	0.2	6	19	25	3.83	700	0.3	801	0.3	800	0.2
Ethnoreligionists	0	0.0	100	0.1	230	0.1	2	2	4	1.50	250	0.1	267	0.1	400	0.1
Hindus	0	0.0	60	0.0	150	0.1	2	0	2	1.20	160	0.1	169	0.1	250	0.1
Muslims	0	0.0	0	0.0	50	0.0	1	0	1	1.14	55	0.0	56	0.0	100	0.0
Other religionists	0	0.0	100	0.1	180	0.1	2	7	9	4.02	220	0.1	267	0.1	300	0.1
World A (unevangelized persons)	0	0.0	204	0.1	255	0.1	1	0	1	0.96	268	0.1	281	0.1	328	0.1
World B (evangelized non-Christians)	100	0.1	3,959	1.9	5,615	2.2	60	141	201	3.11	7,129	2.7	7,630	2.7	12,822	3.9
World C (Christians)	77,900	99.9	199,940	98.0	249,130	97.7	2,537	-141	2,396	0.92	261,000	97.2	273,089	97.2	314,850	96.0
Country's population	**78,000**	**100.0**	**204,104**	**100.0**	**255,000**	**100.0**	**2,598**	**0**	**2,598**	**0.98**	**268,398**	**100.0**	**281,000**	**100.0**	**328,000**	**100.0**

COLUMNS, ROWS.
For meanings and definitions, see Codebook (Part 3). Note that, by definition, total 'Christians' = professing + crypto-Christians, which also = affiliated + unaffiliated Christians, and also = Great Commission Christians + latent Christians. Percentages may not always total exactly, due to rounding.

CENSUSES.
1920: 99.7% Protestants (91.9% state church, 7.6% other Lutherans, 0.2% SD Adventists), 0.2% nonreligious, 0.1% Roman Catholics. **1930:** 99.1% Protestants (90.8% state church, 7.8% other Lutherans, 0.4% SD Adventists), 0.7% nonreligious, 0.2% Roman Catholics. **1940:** 98.2% Protestants (90.7% state church, 6.9% other Lutherans, 0.4% SD Adventists, 0.1% Pentecostals), 1.5% nonreligious, 0.3% Roman Catholics. **1950:** 98.1% Protestants (90.6% state church, 6.8% other Lutherans, 0.3% SD Adventists, 0.2% Pentecostals), 1.6% nonreligious, 0.3% Roman Catholics. **1.XII.1960:** 98.3% Protestants (91.6% state church, 6.1% other Lutherans, 0.3% SD Adventists, 0.3% Pentecostals), 1.1% nonreligious and atheists, 0.5% Roman Catholics, 0.1% other Christians.

NOTES ON RELIGIONS
ATHEISTS. People's Alliance (Altydubandalagid, AB) (pro-Soviet).
BAHA'IS. Growth of local spiritual assemblies: 1964, none; 1973, 5, by 1996 9 LSAs. Mostly youths.
ETHNORELIGIONISTS. Begun about 1962, the Fellowship of Norse-god Believers (Asa, or Asatruarmenn, Believers in the Great Gods) is a heathen revival of pre-Christian Icelandic religion. In 1974 there were 100 adherents, 10 priests and a high priests. The movement aimed to dechristianize Iceland by the year 2000.
HINDUS. Adherents of a new Hindu sect, the Bengali Sri Chinmoy Centre (HQ New York, USA).
NONRELIGIOUS. Mainly in the southwest, with a few in the south.
OTHER RELIGIONISTS. Including Rosicrucians (1 AMORC centre).
SPIRITISTS. Arising out of liberalism around 1900, interest in Spiritism, occultism, and Theosophy has grown considerably. Though supported by numerous state church clergy and exercising considerable influence, the movement has been hostile to the state church and critical of it.

Country status. Iceland is the westernmost country of Europe, an island in the North Atlantic Ocean just below the Arctic Circle. Culturally it is considered a Scandinavian country and it has historic ties with Denmark and Norway. It has a remarkably homogeneous population and very insular institutions and traditions.

HUMAN LIFE AND LIBERTY

Human need and development. Iceland is a developed country with an excellent track record of social and human development. It leads the industrialized world in many key indicators, such as book and newspaper readership. It has a perfect literacy rate and high life expectancy rates for men and women, an extensive social welfare program, and one of the lowest crime rates in Europe. Iceland also has one of the highest per capita GNP in the Western world. The small population as well as isolation from the rest of the world help rather than hinder the high levels of social development.

Great Commission Instrument Panel: status of Iceland (for explanation see start of Part 4)

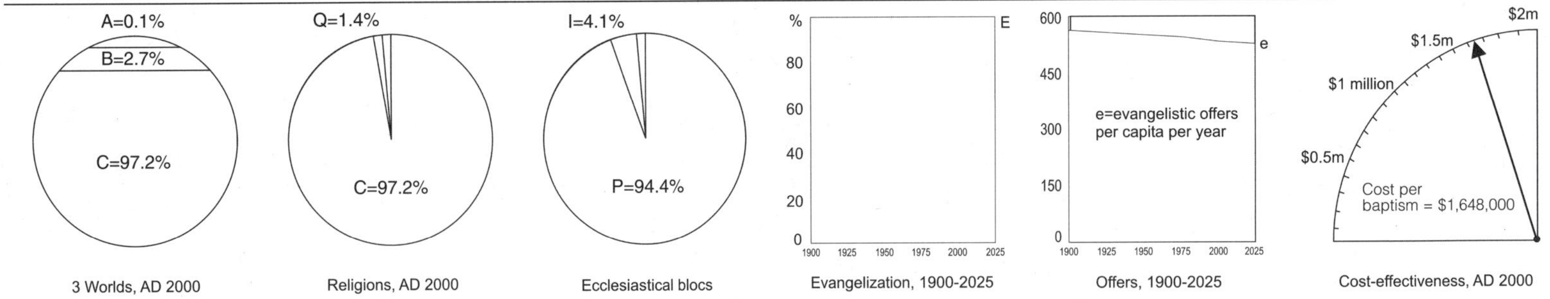

Human rights and freedoms. As a multiparty constitutional democracy, Iceland is a model republic in guaranteeing all human rights for its citizens. As befits an open society, it has no national military forces nor political security apparatus. Icelanders are fiercely egalitarian and opposed to discrimination of all kinds. The judiciary is vigorous in defending the rights of individuals as well as its own independence.

Human environment. In greenhouse gas emissions Iceland ranks among the lowest among all nations. It is also one of the countries actively involved in the development of nonpolluting geothermal resources and one of the signatories of the 1991 8-nation treaty to monitor arctic air pollution. The major environmental problems relate to fishing, Iceland's main economic occupation. Overfishing and overwhaling has brought only dubious benefits to the country, but have helped to deplete fishing stocks in the North Atlantic.

NON-CHRISTIAN RELIGIONS

Norse pagan religion has recently been reintroduced in Iceland. The Fellowship of Norse-god Believers or Asatruarmenn, meaning believers in the Aesir or 'greatest gods' and commonly known in Icelandic as Asa, is a pagan revival begun during the early 1960s and officially recognized as a religion and subsidized by the state from 1973 on. Founded by an Icelandic farmer, a former Lutheran, who has served as the high priest of the sect, Asa is a revival of traditional Norse pre-Christian religion. The principal deities worshiped include Odin, king of the gods; Erica, Odin's wife; Thor, Odin's son and god of thunder, whose symbol is a hammer; Frey, god of farming and fertility, who is known for his magic sword and is identified with a red plastic graven image with a large phallus; Freyja sister of Frey and goddess of love; Idun, a king of northern Atlanta; Loge, god of fire; Ull, god of archery and skiing; and a large pantheon of lesser deities. Plans to revive ancient animal sacrifices (Iceland's renowned small ponies) and the brewing of mead, the potent Norse drink formerly used in religious ceremonies, have thus far been thwarted by Icelandic law. The Asa community, which in the mid-1990s consisted of less than 300 adherents (many Danish) have had hopes to dechristianize Iceland by AD 2000, the one thousandth anniversary of the christianization of the country.

CHRISTIANITY

The first missionaries to Iceland were monks from Ireland around AD 740. Norwegians established themselves in Iceland in 874, and a parliament was formed in 930. Christianity became the state religion shortly afterwards, and by 1005 there were 2 dioceses and many monasteries and abbeys. Iceland was ruled by Norway after 1262, with Danish influence exercised following the creation of the Danish-Norwegian state in 1381. Iceland followed Denmark in becoming Lutheran at the time of the Reformation and Catholicism was proscribed from 1544 to 1874. Free Protestant denominations and Catholics then began work at the end of the 19th century.

PROTESTANT CHURCHES. Lutheranism became the state religion of Iceland in 1550, following the Reformation in 1544, and remains so today. The overwhelming majority of the population (89.6% in 1995) belong to the National Church of Iceland, also called the Evangelical Lutheran Church and the People's Church. The church has one seminary for the training of Lutheran ministers. Only 12% of the church's membership attend weekly services.

Apart from the state church, the most influential grouping is known as the Lutheran Free Churches of Iceland, organized in 1899. Two denominations which entered Iceland earlier but have been less successful in attracting members are the Salvation Army (1895) and the Seventh-day Adventists (1879). After the turn of the century came Plymouth Brethren (1911) and Swedish Pentecostals (1920), the latter now having the largest constituency outside the Lutheran tradition, and also the largest church building in the country. Charismatic renewal grew in the mid-1980s, both within some of the Lutheran churches and in new, independent fellowships.

National Church of Iceland. *Above.* Consecration in 1963 of new church at Skalholt by Lutheran bishop. *Top.* Congregation in another newly-opened church.

CATHOLIC CHURCH. In 1896 the Roman Catholic Church opened work again, concentrated in the Reykjavik area. It is small but continues to grow slowly. In 1977 Iceland was transferred from the jurisdiction of Propaganda to that of the Congregation for Bishops.

The Holy See has diplomatic relations with Iceland and in AD 2000 is represented to government and the Catholic hierarchy by a nuncio residing in Copenhagen, Denmark.

Indigenous missions. Only 2 dozen missionaries serve outside of Iceland but several missionary organization are actively mobilizing Icelanders for missions.

CHURCH AND STATE

The only legal religion was the Lutheran state church until religious liberty, or freedom for all religions to enter, was proclaimed in 1874. The constitution of 1917, promulgated in 1917, assures freedom of conscience and worship, as well as freedom to found religious associations (Article 63). The Evangelical Lutheran Church, or National Church of Iceland (Thjodkirkja Islands), is still recognized as the official state church (Article 62) and receives complete subsidies which pay the salaries of ministers, as well as the cost of building and maintaining churches and schools; however, other churches and religions are now recognized and receive state subsidies, including the Norse religion Asa. Acts of baptism, marriage and burial, and their corresponding certificates, are also legally valid for other communities, including the Catholic Church since 1896, Christian Brethren (1911), Seventh-day Adventists (1912), the Sjonarhaed Community (1926) and Asatruarmenn (1973). The state imposes a church tax, but citizens who are not members of the National Church may give the corresponding sum instead to the University of Iceland or one of the foundations which support it. In the same way, gifts given to religious associations whose heads are recognized by the Ministry of Finance may be deducted from one's tax. All religious associations are exempt from the land tax on buildings. Religious matters are dealt with by the Ministry of Justice and Ecclesiastical Affairs (Doms-og Kirkjumalara-dueneytid).

BROADCASTING AND MEDIA

Local ministry Alpha & Omega broadcasts 4 hours of daily Christian programming in English, German, Danish, Norwegian, and Swedish via shortwave radio transmitters out of Rikisurvarpid.

CBN's *700 Club* and *Studio 7* are both available on a daily basis in Reykjavik. Satellite TV programs are received mainly in Arabic. TBN programs appear on Omega TV in Reykjavik.

National Church of Iceland. *Top.* Hallgrims Memorial Church (Hallgrimskirkju). Reykjavik, consecrated 1974. *Bottom.* Sermon in Hallgrims Church.

Country summary. **Worlds A, B, C by ethnolinguistic peoples, cities, and major civil divisions in Iceland.**

	PEOPLES							CITIES							CIVIL DIVISIONS						
World	Num	Pop 2000	C%	Christians	E%	U%	Unevangelized	Num	Pop 2000	C%	Christians	E%	U%	Unevangelized	Num	Pop 2000	C%	Christians	E%	U%	Unevangelized
A	0	0	0.00	0	0	0	0	0	0	0.00	0	0	0	0	0	0	0.00	0	0	0	0
B	0	0	0.00	0	0	0	0	0	0	0.00	0	0	0	0	0	0	0.00	0	0	0	0
C	10	280,969	94.41	265,260	100	0	154	1	163,799	94.40	154,626	100	0	66	7	280,969	94.41	265,259	100	0	154
Total	**10**	**280,969**	**94.41**	**265,260**	**100**	**0**	**154**	**1**	**163,799**	**94.40**	**154,626**	**100**	**0**	**66**	**7**	**280,969**	**94.41**	**265,259**	**100**	**0**	**154**

INTERDENOMINATIONAL ORGANIZATIONS

The Ecumenical Centre (Centrum for Kontakt og Ekumenisme) is a Catholic diocesan organization charged with ecumenical relations. There are no national councils of churches.

FUTURE TRENDS AND PROSPECTS

Secularization will potentially continue to slowly take its toll on church affiliation which could fall to 96.0% by 2025 (down from nearly 100% one hundred years earlier).

Christianity is expected to continue its slow decline into the 21st century. By AD 2050 the nonreligious may grow to 5-10% of the country's population.

BIBLIOGRAPHY

'A bibliography for ethnographic research on Iceland,' F. E. Bredahl-Petersen, *Behavior science research*, 14, 1 (1979), 1–35.

'A study of factors related to the numerical growth of the Seventh–day Adventist Church in Iceland from 1950 to 1980.' S. Thordarson. D.Min. thesis, Andrews University, Seventh-day Adventist Theological Seminary, Barrien Springs, MI, 1985. 269p.

'Christianity in Iceland,' G. Arnason, *Sixty-five degrees*, 2, 3 (1968), 11–13.

'Church and religion,' in *Iceland 1946*. P. Thorsteinsson (ed). Reykjavik: 1946.

'Church and social change: a study of the secularization process in Iceland, 1830–1930.' P. Pétursson. Plus Ultra thesis, Lunds Universitet, Lund, Sweden, 1983. 199p.

Churches of Iceland. Gunnar Kristjánsson. Reykjavík: Iceland Review, 1988. 112p.

Från väckelse till samfund: Svensk pingstmission på öarna i Nordatlanten. P. Pétursson. *Bibliotheca historico-ecclesiastica Lundensis*, 22. Lund, Sweden: Lund University Press, 1990. 296p. (English summary).

Iceland. J. J. Horton. Oxford, UK: CLIO Press, 1983. (See especially 'Religion,' p. 105–11).

Icelandic church saga. J. C. F. Hood. 1946; reprint, Westport, CT: Greenwood Press, 1981. 242p.

Icelandic feasts and holidays: celebrations past and present. A. Björnsson. Trans., M. Hallmundsson & H. Hallmundsson. Reykjavík: Iceland Review, 1980. 104p.

Scandinavian churches: a picture of the development and life of the churches of Denmark, Finland, Iceland, Norway and Sweden. L. S. Hunter (ed). London: Faber & Faber, 1965. 200p.

'State and church in Iceland: past history and present problems,' P. Wilson-Kastner, *Lutheran quarterly*, 28, 2 (1976), 125–39.

The Catholic Church returns to Iceland (mid 19th century). R. Bradshaw. : The Author, 1991. 72p.

'The Church in Iceland,' S. Einarsson, *Iceland review*, 5, 5 (1967).

The conversion of Iceland: a survey. D. Strömbäck. Trans., P. G. Foote. [London]: Viking Society for Northern Research, University College, 1975. 121p.

'The most treasured Nordic Bible,' J. Gíslason, *Atlantica and Iceland review*, 17, 4 (1977), 24–29. (Deals with the first Icelandic Bible).

Under the cloak: the acceptance of Christianity in Iceland, with particular reference to the religious attitudes prevailing at the time. J. H. Adalsteinsson. *Studia ethnologica Upsaliensa*, 4. Uppsala: University of Uppsala, 1978. 151p.

Country Table 2. **Organized churches and denominations in Iceland.**

Official name (bold type = church *with over 10% of all affiliated)* 1	*Begun* 2	*Type* 3	*Counc* 4	*Congs* 5	*Adults* 6	*Affiliated 1970* 7	*Affiliated 1995* 8	*G%* 9	*Names, notes, and other statistics* (see Codebook, Part 3) 10
Baptist Mission	1963	P-Bap	T....	1	40	100	100	0.00	M=FMB-SBC(USA). Missionary 1963 as pastor of Keflavik English-language church. 1x,2f.
Catholic Church; D Reykjavik	1056	R-Lat	bxBQ.	5	1,400	1,018	2,553	3.75	*Rómversk Kathólska Kirkjan, Reykjavik Bispedomme.* C=1+0+3. 6n,5x,5m,43w,62Yy.
Charismatic Church	1990	I-3cW	.....	1	184	–	297	20.00	*Vegurinn.* Recent independent charismatic body.
Christian Brethren	1911	P-CBr	x....	1	37	200	50	-5.39	*Open Brethren.* Originated from Faeroe Islands. One congregation in Akureyri. 4f.
Church of Christ		I-Dis	x....	1	100	200	300	0.05	M=CC(Non-Instrumental) (USA). Meeting on USA naval base. Largely USA military.
Ch of Jesus Christ of Latter-day Saints		m-LdS	.....	3	106	–	161	0.05	*Kirkja Jesú Krists L.s.d.h. Mormons.* M=CJCLdS(USA).
Ev Lutheran Free Churches of Iceland	1899	I-Lut	.....	6	5,545	10,000	7,159	-1.33	Free local churches. Schism from state church. 2 in Reykjavik, 1 Hafnarfjörur.
Independent Lutheran Churches	c1930	I-Lut	.....	4	848	1,846	1,053	-2.22	Secessions from state church stressing complete liberty of thought and action.
Jehovah's Witnesses	1932	m-Jeh	x....	5	246	200	517	3.87	*Watch Tower. IBSA.* Work began via Scandinavia. Widespread activity. (1975) 15Y. (1995) 18Y.
National Church of Iceland	931	P-Lut	LWC..	310	173,817	180,000	236,959	0.09	*Thjódkirkja Islands.* State church since 1550. 114n,1s,W=12%,3600Yy.
Pentecostal Fellowship	1985	I-3pW	.....	1	173	–	242	10.00	*Krossinn.* Recent pentecostal body.
Pentecostal Movement in Iceland	1920	P-Pe2	Z....	12	815	2,000	1,050	-2.54	*Hvitasunnusofnourinn a Islandi.* Largest building. M=SFM(Sweden). 15n,37Y.
Salvation Army	1895	P-Sal	xwc..	1	90	300	273	-0.38	*Hjälpraedisherinn, Iceland & the Faroes Division. Norway & Iceland Territory.* 16n.
Seventh-day Adventist Church	1897	P-Adv	x....	7	567	1,000	769	-1.05	*Sjounda-Dags Adventistar. Iceland Conference.* 4n,1j,1r,9t(576),W=75%,20Y.
Unitarian Church		m-Unt	.....	1	60	50	100	0.05	Small, but has 20 congregations in Canada (United Conference of Icelandic Chs in America).
Worldwide European Fellowship	c1960	P-Non	.M...	2	110	200	250	0.90	M=WEF(Canada, USA); 1972 merger with Harvesters International Mission. Broadcasting. 7f.
Other independent charismatic chs	c1980	I-3cW	.....	20	1,000	–	2,000	6.67	Including New Apostolic Ch (13 members).
Other Protestant denominations		P-	.....	20	600	1,100	1,000	0.05	Including: European Missionary Fellowship, and USA military chaplaincies.
Totals				**401**	**185,738**	**198,214**	**254,833**		

Churches, members, growth, 1900-2025	*Congs*	*Adults*	*Affiliated*	*G%*	*Total denominations*	*6 Megablocs:* O	R	A	P	I	m
Total churches, members, and denominations (mid-1900)	40	49,900	77,600	1.35	5	0	1	0	3	1	0
Total churches, members, and denominations (mid-1970)	364	127,517	198,214	1.35	16	0	1	0	10	3	2
Total churches, members, and denominations (mid-1990)	390	178,000	244,170	1.05	28	0	1	0	14	10	3
Total churches, members, and denominations (mid-1995)	401	185,738	254,833	0.86	29	0	1	0	14	11	3
Total churches, members, and denominations (mid-2000)	410	193,000	265,259	0.81	30	0	1	0	14	12	3
Total churches, members, and denominations (mid-2025)	600	222,000	304,000	0.55	72	0	1	0	25	40	6

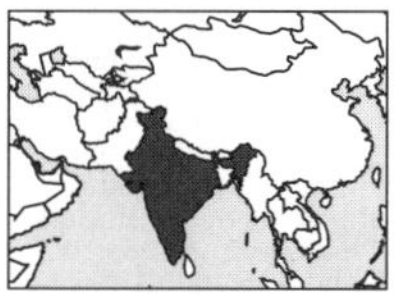

INDIA

SECULAR DATA, AD 2000

STATE

Official name: Bharat (The Republic of India).
Short name: India. **Adjective of nationality:** Indian.
Flag: Deep saffron, white, and green stripes, with centered 24-spoke Wheel of Asoka in blue.
Area: 3,165,596 sq. km. (1,222,243 sq. mi.).
Government: Parliamentary federal republic or union of states, since 1950 (19th century under Britain, 1947 Independence, 1950 republic).
Legislature: Parliament: Rajya Sabha (Council of States), 245 members; Lok Sabha (House of the People), 545 members.
Official language: Hindi (Devanagari script), English.
Monetary unit: 1 Indian rupee (Re, plural Rs) = 100 paise. **US$1=** Rs 42.51.
Chief cities: Mumbai (Bombay) 18,042,000; Calcutta 12,900,000; Delhi 11,680,000; Hyderabad 6,833,000; Chennai (Madras) 6,639,000.
Political divisions: 32 provinces.
Armed forces: 1,265,000.

DEMOGRAPHY

Population: 1,013,662,000.
Population density: 320.2/sq. km. (829.3/sq. mi.).
Under 15 years: 337,651,000.
Growth rate p.a.: 1.41% (births 22.56, deaths 8.38).
Mortality: Infant, per 1,000: 64.6; **Maternal per 100,000:** 570.0.
Life expectancy: 64 (male 63, female 65).
Household size: 5.6. **Floor area per person, sq.m:** 12.0.
Major languages: Hindi (Devanagari script) and English, Fourteen others are official in one or more states: Assamese, Bengali, Gujarati, Kannada, Kashmiri, Malayalam, Marathi, Oriya, Punjabi, Sanskrit, Sindhi, Tamil, Telugu, Urdu and 1,650 other mother tongues.
Urban dwellers: 28.44%. **Urban growth rate p.a.:** 2.9%.
Labor force: 38%.

ETHNOLINGUISTIC PEOPLES

7.4% Maratha (Maharathi); 7.3% Bengali; 7.2% Telugu (Andhra, Tolangan); 6.3% Tamil (Madrasi, Tamalsan); 6.2% Hindi (High Hindi).

ECONOMY

National income p.a. per person: US$340; **per family:** US$1,904.

EDUCATION

Adult literacy: 52% (male 65%, female 37%). **Schools:** 812,975.
Universities: 7,958. **School enrolment:** female/male: 62%/83%.

HEALTH

Access to health services: 85%. **Access to safe water:** 81%.
Hospitals: 15,067 (8 beds per 10,000). **Doctors:** 405,253.
Blind: 9,000,000. **Deaf:** 60,406,200. Murder **rate:** 4.
Lepers: 5,500,000. **Underweight prevalence under 5:** 53%.

LITERATURE

New book titles p.a.: 15,200 (15 p.a. per million). **Periodicals:** 910.
Newspapers: 520 dailies.

COMMUNICATION (per 1,000 people)

Phones: 13 **(4% mobile).** Radios: 121. **TV sets:** 61.
Daily newspaper circulation: 21. **Computers:** 6.

REFUGEES

Alien refugees from other countries: 319,200.
Internal displacement: 250,000.

HUMAN LIFE AND LIBERTY (optimum condition=100.0%)

HDI: 44.6. **HSI:** 37.0. **HFI:** 35.0. **EFL:** 25.0.

Country Table 1. **Religious adherents in India, AD 1900-2025.**

Year	*1900*		*1970*		*mid-1990*		*Annual change, 1990-2000*				*mid-1995*		*mid-2000*		*mid-2025*	
Name	*Adherents*	*%*	*Adherents*	*%*	*Adherents*	*%*	*Natural*	*Conversion*	*Total*	*Rate*	*Adherents*	*%*	*Adherents*	*%*	*Adherents*	*%*
Hindus	184,022,700	80.0	433,214,000	78.1	639,696,000	75.2	12,246,522	-702,614	11,543,908	1.67	700,513,000	75.0	755,135,081	74.5	969,491,800	72.9
Muslims	31,552,000	13.7	62,877,000	11.3	101,000,000	11.9	1,933,576	223,428	2,157,004	1.95	111,000,000	11.9	122,570,042	12.1	162,500,000	12.2
Christians	**3,820,200**	**1.7**	**23,353,000**	**4.2**	**48,100,000**	**5.7**	**920,842**	**503,259**	**1,424,101**	**2.63**	**54,500,000**	**5.8**	**62,341,006**	**6.2**	**98,200,000**	**7.4**
PROFESSION																
crypto-Christians	1,150,200	0.5	9,110,528	1.6	17,500,000	2.1	335,026	64,974	400,000	2.08	19,588,901	2.1	21,500,000	2.1	30,000,000	2.3
professing Christians	**2,670,000**	**1.2**	**14,242,472**	**2.6**	**30,600,000**	**3.6**	**585,816**	**438,285**	**1,024,101**	**2.93**	**34,911,099**	**3.7**	**40,841,006**	**4.0**	**68,200,000**	**5.1**
AFFILIATION																
unaffiliated Christians	0	0.0	123,000	0.0	100,000	0.0	1,914	-2,168	-254	-0.26	100,000	0.0	97,460	0.0	100,000	0.0
affiliated Christians	**3,820,200**	**1.7**	**23,230,000**	**4.2**	**48,000,000**	**5.6**	**918,927**	**505,428**	**1,424,355**	**2.63**	**54,400,000**	**5.8**	**62,243,546**	**6.1**	**98,100,000**	**7.4**
Independents	90,000	0.0	6,944,080	1.3	22,700,000	2.7	434,576	715,424	1,150,000	4.18	28,232,240	3.0	34,200,000	3.4	65,500,000	4.9
Protestants	650,000	0.3	8,136,595	1.5	13,600,000	1.6	260,363	62,237	322,600	2.15	15,311,398	1.6	16,826,000	1.7	22,900,000	1.7
Roman Catholics	1,920,000	0.8	8,432,713	1.5	13,050,000	1.5	249,833	-4,833	245,000	1.74	14,285,857	1.5	15,500,000	1.5	20,700,000	1.6
Orthodox	610,000	0.3	1,425,100	0.3	2,615,500	0.3	50,072	-1,622	48,450	1.71	2,922,500	0.3	3,100,000	0.3	4,400,000	0.3
Marginal Christians	200	0.0	15,552	0.0	40,000	0.0	766	234	1,000	2.26	42,900	0.0	50,000	0.0	85,000	0.0
Anglicans	550,000	0.2	0	0.0	0	0.0	0	0	0	0.00	0	0.0	0	0.0	0	0.0
doubly-affiliated	0	0.0	-1,724,040	-0.3	-4,005,500	-0.5	-76,683	-266,012	-342,695	6.38	-6,394,895	-0.7	-7,432,454	-0.7	-15,485,000	-1.2
Trans-megabloc groupings																
Evangelicals	500,000	0.2	3,020,000	0.5	7,100,000	0.8	135,925	84,075	220,000	2.74	8,095,899	0.9	9,300,000	0.9	16,302,000	1.2
Pentecostals/Charismatics	1,800	0.0	2,050,000	0.4	26,400,000	3.1	505,410	207,590	713,000	2.42	29,927,828	3.2	33,530,000	3.3	56,000,000	4.2
Great Commission Christians	**3,450,000**	**1.5**	**16,300,000**	**2.9**	**37,700,000**	**4.4**	**721,741**	**544,686**	**1,266,427**	**2.94**	**42,900,000**	**4.6**	**50,364,266**	**5.0**	**75,000,000**	**5.6**
Ethnoreligionists	6,670,000	2.9	19,230,000	3.5	29,800,000	3.5	570,501	-74,383	496,118	1.55	32,500,000	3.5	34,761,177	3.4	40,000,000	3.0
Sikhs	2,180,000	1.0	10,287,000	1.9	18,450,000	2.2	353,213	20,040	373,253	1.86	20,250,000	2.2	22,182,528	2.2	29,800,000	2.2
Nonreligious	10,000	0.0	2,000,000	0.4	10,000,000	1.2	191,443	93,418	284,861	2.54	11,400,000	1.2	12,848,612	1.3	25,248,000	1.9
Buddhists	200,000	0.1	3,779,000	0.7	5,950,000	0.7	113,909	16,029	129,938	1.99	6,458,000	0.7	7,249,384	0.7	9,600,000	0.7
Jains	1,320,000	0.6	2,582,000	0.5	3,800,000	0.5	72,748	-39,043	33,705	0.85	3,820,000	0.4	4,137,052	0.4	6,000,000	0.5
Baha'is	100	0.0	730,000	0.1	1,400,000	0.2	26,802	4,813	31,615	2.06	1,440,000	0.2	1,716,148	0.2	2,500,000	0.2
Atheists	5,000	0.0	700,000	0.1	1,400,000	0.2	26,802	-265	26,537	1.75	1,525,000	0.2	1,665,367	0.2	2,500,000	0.2
Zoroastrians	93,000	0.0	90,000	0.0	170,000	0.0	3,255	1,011	4,266	2.26	195,000	0.0	212,661	0.0	350,000	0.0
Chinese folk-religionists	10,000	0.0	60,000	0.0	110,000	0.0	2,106	186	2,292	1.91	120,000	0.0	132,917	0.0	250,000	0.0
Jews	17,000	0.0	9,000	0.0	9,000	0.0	172	-160	12	0.13	9,000	0.0	9,118	0.0	9,200	0.0
doubly-counted religionists	0	0.0	-4,000,000	-0.7	-9,100,000	-1.1	-174,213	-45,719	-219,932	2.19	-10,065,000	-1.1	-11,299,316	-1.1	-16,000,000	-1.2
World A (unevangelized persons)	195,415,000	85.0	360,137,174	64.9	399,868,950	47.0	7,655,216	-6,429,966	1,225,250	0.30	405,210,663	43.4	412,560,434	40.7	449,691,762	33.8
World B (evangelized non-Christians)	30,664,800	13.3	171,420,725	30.9	402,816,050	47.3	7,711,620	5,926,707	13,638,327	2.95	473,954,459	50.8	538,760,560	53.1	782,557,238	58.8
World C (Christians)	3,820,200	1.7	23,353,000	4.2	48,100,000	5.7	920,842	503,259	1,424,101	2.63	54,500,000	5.8	62,341,006	6.2	98,200,000	7.4
Country's population	**229,900,000**	**100.0**	**554,910,900**	**100.0**	**850,785,000**	**100.0**	**16,287,678**	**0**	**16,287,678**	**1.77**	**933,665,123**	**100.0**	**1,013,662,000**	**100.0**	**1,330,449,000**	**100.0**

COLUMNS, ROWS.

For meanings and definitions, see Codebook (Part 3). Note that, by definition, total 'Christians' = professing + crypto-Christians, which also = affiliated + unaffiliated Christians, and also = Great Commission Christians + latent Christians. Percentages may not always total exactly, due to rounding.

CENSUSES.

The following censuses for 1881, 1891, 1901 and 1911 refer to the area of the present India, Pakistan, Bangladesh and Burma. The figures for 1900 in the table above have therefore been adjusted to cover the 1975 boundaries of India only. **1881:** 74.3% Hindus, 19.7% Muslims, 2.6% ethnoreligionists, 1.4% Buddhists, 0.7% Christians, 0.7% Sikhs, 0.5% Jains. **1891:** 72.3% Hindus, 20.0% Muslims, 3.2% ethnoreligionists, 2.5% Buddhists, 0.8% Christians, 0.7% Sikhs, 0.5% Jains. **1.III.1901:** 70.4% Hindus, 21.2% Muslims, 3.2% Buddhists, 2.9% ethnoreligionists, 1.0% Christians (1,524,755 Roman Catholics, 453,462 Anglicans, 250,450 Orthodox, 221,040 Baptists, 155,455 Lutherans, et alii), 0.7% Sikhs, 0.4% Jains. **1911:** 69.4% Hindus, 21.2% Muslims, 3.4% Buddhists, 3.3% ethnoreligionists, 1.2% Christians (1,904,005 Roman Catholics, 492,752 Anglicans, 337,226 Baptists, 240,789 Orthodox, 218,500 Lutherans, et alii), 1.0% Sikhs, 0.4% Jains. **1921** (India only): 84.4% Hindus, 9.6% Muslims, 3.3% ethnoreligionists, 1.8% Christians, 0.5% Jains, 0.4% Sikhs. **26.II.1931** (India excluding Assam, West Bengal, and Punjab): 84.3% Hindus, 9.9% Muslims, 2.7% ethnoreligionists, 2.1% Christians, 0.5% Jains, 0.5% Sikhs. **1941** (with race/caste/tribe definition of religion): 63.3% Hindus (1.4% scheduled castes), 12.6% Muslims, 7.9% ethnoreligionists, 1.8% Christians, 1.3% Sikhs, 0.5% Jains. **1.III.1951** (de jure; excluding Kashmir-Jammu and Assam tribal areas): 85.0% Hindus, 9.9% Muslims, 2.3% Christians, 1.7% Sikhs, 0.5% Jains, 0.5% ethnoreligionists, 0.1% Buddhists. **1.III.1961:** 83.5% Hindus, 10.7% Muslims, 2.4% Christians, 1.8% Sikhs, 0.7% Buddhists, 0.5% Jains, 0.3% ethnoreligionists. **1.IV.1971:** 82.7% Hindus (including Hindu crypto-Christians and many tribal animists), 11.2% Muslims, 2.6% Christians, 1.9% Sikhs, 0.7% Buddhists, 0.5% Jains, 0.4% ethnoreligionists. **1981:** 82.6% Hindus, 11.4% Muslims, 2.4% Christians, 2.0% Sikhs, 0.7% Buddhists, 0.5% Jains, 0.4% other religionists. **1991:** 82.4% Hindus, 11.7% Muslims, 2.3% Christians, 2.0% Sikhs, 0.8% Buddhists, 0.4% Jains, 0.4% other religionists. *Notes.* (1) The definition of 'ethnoreligionists' has varied considerably from census to census, often covering only a part of the animistic population. (2) All figures for Hindus in these censuses include the persons this survey is calling crypto-Christians, and also many tribals who are in fact still animists.

NOTES ON RELIGIONS

ANGLICANS. In the year 1900, Anglicans were 67% Indians, 25% Europeans, 8% Eurasians (Anglo-Indians). The Anglican Church (CIPBC) remained a major denomination until its merger in the CSI in South India (1947) and in the CNI in North India (1970), united churches here classified as Protestant. Thereafter there were no specifically Anglican churches in India except for the miniscule Reformed Episcopal Church.

ATHEISTS. Three rival parties since 1964 split: Communist Party of India (CPI) (pro-Soviet), Communist Party of India/Marxist (CPM) (pro-Chinese), Communist Party of India/Marxist-Leninist (Naxalites): Most party members are atheists, though anti-religious persons opposed to all religion are not numerous. Communist voters are mainly in Kerala and Bengal, with little or no atheistic connotation. In Kerala, the Communist vote is related to 2 Malayalam-speaking castes, Pulayas and Ezhavas, both regarded as outcaste by Hindus.

BAHA'IS. Origins in India began around 1860. Until 1960 most Baha'is in India were Persians. In 1961, when there were only 850 Baha'is, mass conversions began; by 1963, there were 65,355 Baha'is with 10,000 adult converts a month. Very rapid growth then took place from 1,064 local spiritual assemblies (1964) to 4,869 (1973), with 17,034 other isolated centers or groups (1973). From 1964-73, 157,000 converts were enrolled. Then growth peaked and reorganization resulted in 3,286 LSAs by 1996. Radio, TV, press and correspondence courses are widely used.

BUDDHISTS. After flourishing in India from the 6th century BC to the 6th century AD, Buddhism declined in India and was eventually finally extinguished by Islam in the 12th century. In 1956, the neo-Buddhist movement began, leading to the conversion to Buddhism of over 3 million Mahars and other Harijans (scheduled-caste Hindus) over 5 years. Subsequently, large numbers have been converted back to Hinduism by the Arya Samaj. The Maha Bodhi Society of Ceylon has developed centers throughout India to spread the Buddhist religion. In 1995 also there were about 100,000 Tibetans and 125,000 Chinese Buddhists (Mahayana), also Burmese.

COUNTRY'S POPULATION. Immediately after Partition in 1947, about 7 million Muslims fled from homes in India to Pakistan, with a further 2 million following over the 2 subsequent decades: and about the same number of non-Muslims fled from Pakistan to India. Some 7% (1.1 million) were massacred or starved to death en route. This was the greatest population transfer in history.

CRYPTO-CHRISTIANS. At every government census since before 1900 the number of Christians enumerated (here termed professing Christians) has been considerably less than the aggregate of Christians reported then by the churches (here termed affiliated Christians). These affiliated Christians unknown to the state (here termed crypto-Christians) are of 4 distinct kinds: the first consists of known church members in recognized churches, but the last 3 are here termed Independents.

(1) The best-known category has been, and continues to be, Christians who are scheduled-caste persons (formerly, outcastes) regarded as Hindus by society and state. If such backward-class persons declare themselves to be Christians, they lose their scheduled-caste status and privileges (education, employment, quotas in government, university places, etc). They continue, therefore, as secret church members known only to the major church bodies. (2) Since 1952, a completely new type of crypto-Christian has arisen all over India, namely isolated radio believers unrelated to existing denominations (see Table 2, and methodology in Part 3).(3) One of the oldest categories consists of separate high-caste or low-caste Hindus, mostly unorganized individuals unknown to the recognized Christian churches. Since 1887 and the formation of the Calcutta Christo Samaj, there have been a number of organized movements of believers in Christ as Lord or Messiah who regard themselves, corporately as well as individually, as still Hindus. Of those Hindu-Christian movements, the largest is the Subba Rao movement which rejects Christian baptism (see Table 2). Regarding Jesus as God's Messiah and exercising many charismatic gifts, these believers are here termed Messianic Neocharismatics (see listing in Country Table 2). (4) The last group is the most difficult to detect—committed converts to Jesus as Lord who then decide they are called by God to remain as Hindus within the Hindu religion (or Muslims within Islam) and to live and witness for him there. These isolated non-Christian believers in Christ live among virtually all of India's 3,000 Hindu castes. Evidence for their existence and commitment to Christ is very extensive, including the known witness of some 4 million Hindus who read the Bible daily, participate in Bible correspondence courses, and even openly attend Christian events. Thus 20% of all 10,000 persons on each of the 50 weekly retreats conducted each year at the world's biggest Charismatic retreat center (Divine Retreat Center, CCR, Murinoor, Kerala) are Hindus, Jains, Sikhs, or Muslims.

ETHNORELIGIONISTS. This term refers to animists among the Aboriginal and tribal peoples including hill tribes. The total tribal population of India was 22,615,708 (6.7%) in 1931, rising in 1941 to 25,441,489 (7.9%), of whom 8,775,000 (2.26% of the total population) were animists, in 1961 to (scheduled tribes) 29,883,470 (6.8%), and by 1970 to about 38 million (7.0%). The proportion of animists (ethnoreligionists) to total population increased slightly from 2.6% in 1881, to 2.9% in 1901, and to 3.2% in 1911; and has since declined slowly from 3.0% in 1921 to 2.7% (7,630,000) in 1931. Before 1941, government census reports termed these persons animists; in 1941 the category was dropped and all tribals (7.9% of the population) were classed as tribals irrespective of religion. From 1951 large numbers of these animists were henceforth for political reasons enumerated as Hindus. Various analysts from Kingsley Davis (1951) onwards have shown however that tribal religion has persisted remarkably, numerically, over the decades, despite consistent and widespread underenumeration, and hence this category can be estimated to have declined only slightly to 1.7% of the population by 1970. In the 1971 census, the category 'Other religions and persuasions' (2,184,556 persons) covered only a quarter of these animists, namely those who refused to allow themselves to be classified as Hindus. These formed 63.5% of the entire population in Arunachel Pradesh, 31.5% of Meghalaya, 20.9% of Nagaland, 7.8% of Manipur, and 1.8% of Bihar. Among the larger tribes in India either predominantly-animist, or with large numbers of animists, are the Gond (3 million), Santal (20% animist), Bhil, Oraon (20% animist), Kond (900,000), Munda (20% animist), Ho (still 70% animist), Korku (250,000), and Kaipeng-Koloi (200,000). Conversions. There is in 1979 a steady number of animists each year who are either hinduized, i.e. assimilated into Hinduism (the more numerous), or converted to Christianity (less numerous). Conversions to Islam are almost non-existent. Several tribes have been completely christianized during the 20th century: thus the Mizo (Lushai), numbering 300,000 now, were all animists when the first missionary arrived in 1891; in the 1901 census, only 45 Mizo were Christians, but by 1975 all were Christians with not a single known Mizo animist remaining.

HINDUS. (1961) 82.4% high-caste and other caste (totalling over 26,000 castes in the 4 categories of Vedic theory: Brahman (1,886 castes), Ksatriya (warriors), Vaisya (merchants), Sudra (servants)), 17.6% Scheduled Caste (formerly, Outcastes, Untouchables, or (Gandhi's term) Harijans (Children of God); Scheduled Castes can only be Hindus or Sikhs (clause 3 of constitution (Scheduled Castes) Order, 1950); in 1961 they were 98.6% Hindus, 1.4% Sikhs. There are hundreds of Hindu sects, of 3 main types. (A) 0.5% of all Hindus belong to intellectual reform movements opposed to polytheism and idol-worship: Arya Samaj (92,419 in 1901, 243-445 in 1911), which rejects belief in incarnations of gods, Shankar Acharya (Vedanta Hinduism), and the Ramakrishna Mission, all of whom claim to be converting large numbers of non-Hindus back to Hinduism. The Ramakrishna Mission has 150 centers in over 12 countries (126 in India). (B) 98% of all Hindus, popularly called idol-worshippers or Sanatanists (Sanskrit: Old Ways), believe in incarnations of gods and are either (a) Shaivites (followers of Siva), predominant in south India (AP, Kerala, Tamil Nadu, also West Bengal), or (b) Vaishnavites (followers of Vishnu), predominant in all other states, especially in western, northern, eastern India and Assam, or (c) Saktas, worshippers of the divine mother, Sakti, female aspect of the deity. As well as organized priesthoods with 9 million priests, these 3 groupings have also produced around 15 million sadhus (holy beggars) at the present time. (C) Lastly, there are many newer sects and neo-Hindu movements. Among the largest are (1) the Divine Light Mission, a Vedantist movement first spread in north India in the 1920s, organized and founded in 1960, and now of Europeanized type centered on devotion to the internationally-known Guru Maharaj Ji (born 1958); 5 million followers in India are claimed; (2) Ananda Marga (Path of Bliss), a violent politico-religious Bengali sect with 2.5 million converts in India and a network of branches in 30 countries; (3) 50,000 followers of Sri Aurobindo (died 1950) and the divine mother (died 1973) at the international city-state of Auroville (Pondicherry) with 1,800 devotees in India's largest ashram and hundreds of action centers throughout India, with centers in 23 other countries also; (4) the Theosophical Society, a neo-Hindu movement with marked Hindu influences, begun in 1875 in New York (USA), moved to India, and in 1912 a Hindu youth Krishnamurti proclaimed Supreme World Teacher, and headquarters in Adyar, Madras; (5) the Self-Realization Fellowship (in India known as the Yogoda Satsang) begun in the USA in 1920 and now with 150 centers on 4 continents; finally (6) there are millions of Hindus who are committed followers of Jesus Christ as Lord (elaborated here in note under 'Crypto-Christians'. *Conversions.* Many Hindu women marry non-Hindus and take their spouses' religion. A number of conversions to Baha'i, Sikhism, Buddhism and Christianity take place every year; the Arya Samaj claims to be winning back to Hinduism large numbers of such converts. *Fertility.* The major reason for the gradual proportionate decline of the Hindu community over the last 100 years is markedly lower fertility due to the prohibition of widow remarriage. *Pilgrims.* Pilgrimages to shrines (in Sanskrit, *tirthayatra*) play a major role in Hindu practice, and increasing millions of pilgrims visit the 7 holy cities of Varanasi (Benares), Ayodhya (UP), Mathura (UP), Dvaraka (Gujarat), Kanchipuram (Tamil Nadu), Hardwar (UP), and Ujjain (MP); the sources or confluences of the 7 sacred rivers; and the 4 great abodes of the gods, Badrinath in the north, Dvaraka in the west, Rameswaram in the south, and Puri in the east. The largest religious mass festival in the world is the 43-day bathing festival Kumbh Mela, held every 12 years at the confluence of the Ganges and the Jumna near Allahabad, with over 10 million pilgrims.

INDEPENDENTS. In about 150 denominations in 1995 (see Table 2).

JAINS. In 3 sects: Digambaras, Svetambaras, Sthanakyasis. Largely in Gujarat and Rajasthan. Since 1880 Jains have declined proportionately due to low fertility, itself due to the taboo on widow remarriage.

JEWS. 2,000 Cochin Jews from Kerala: and Bney Israel in Bombay province (5,500 in 1850), who are Marathi-speaking.

MUSLIMS. About 65% Sunnis (of the Hanafite and Shafite rites), and 35% Shias mostly in Uttar Pradesh (Ithna-Asharis, Ismailis (Bombay), Bohoras); also 300,000 Ahmadis (enumerated here under Muslims though declared non-Muslim by Pakistan). The dis-

Continued opposite

Country Table 1–concluded

puted territory of Kashmir is 78% Muslim. *Proportional increase.* Since 1881 the Muslim community has increased faster than the total population increase, due to higher Muslim than Hindu fertility, itself due to greater Muslim tolerance of widow remarriage. *Hajj pilgrims to Mecca.* (1968) 15,826; (1969) 16,057; (1970) 16,470; (1971) 16,657; (1972) 18,306; (1973) 19,879; (1974) 21,874; (1975) 18,863; (1976) 17,510.
PENTECOSTALS/CHARISMATICS. The Third Wave of the Renewal accounts for some 90% of all members of this Renewal. Among Second Wavers in mainline churches, the largest grouping is the Catholic Charismatic Renewal, which in 1997 had 10,400 regular weekly prayer groups with 150,000 regular adult attenders (40,000 aged 15-25), with 3 covenant communities, 200 involved priests and 10 bishops; and vast annual conferences/conventions/rallies—40,000 at 1990 8th National Convention in Cochin, 20,000 at 1993 9th National Convention in Madras; 25,000 at 1997 10th National Convention in Bombay.
PROFESSING CHRISTIANS. In the year 1900, Christians were 91% Indians, 6% Europeans, and 3% Anglo-Indians.
ROMAN CATHOLICS. Pilgrims. Among the large number of Catholic pilgrimage centers is the 16th-century shrine at Velankanni ('The Lourdes of India'), 270 miles south of Madras which attracts pilgrims all the year round and 500,000 (many being non-Christians) during the Feast of the Nativity of Our Lady (28 August-8 September). Another center is Old Goa, where 600,000 venerated the body of St Francis Xavier from 23 November 1974 for 6 weeks.
SIKHS. Sects: Akali, Nanapanthi, Udasi, Khalsa, Nirmali, Sewapanthi. The Namdharis and Nirankaris are groups worshipping living Gurus. At Partition in 1947, the 2.5 million Sikhs living in Pakistan were either compelled to flee to India or all massacred. *Conversions.* Although up to the early part of the 20th century converts from Hinduism were still numerous due to the Akali proselytizing movement among depressed classes, by the 1970s the rate of lapsing back to Hinduism had become appreciable. However, numbers of Hindu women in the Punjab (which is 60% Sikh) were still becoming Sikhs through marriage, and in addition a number of full-time Sikh missionaries were active including some posted to international airports at New Delhi and elsewhere. *Fertility.* A major reason for the rapid proportionate growth of the Sikh community since 1880 is that Sikhs, being the most rural of the major religions, and tolerating widow remarriage, have a higher fertility than Hindus and also a lower mortality.
ZOROASTRIANS. Parsis, Gujarati-speaking; originally refugees from Persia in the 8th century AD; mainly in Bombay. Since 1900 they have been declining proportionately to the total population, due to their very low marital fertility.

Great Commission Instrument Panel: status of India (for explanation see start of Part 4)

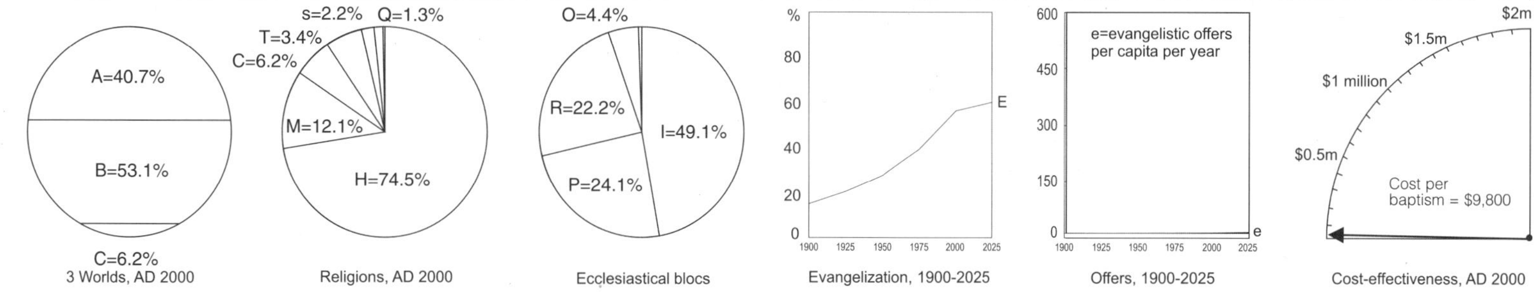

Country status. India is the second most populous nation in the world and it is likely that by 2050 it will become the most populous. Occupying the fertile Indo-Gangetic plain and the Deccan Plateau, it covers most of the Indian subcontinent. Few nations can match India in the infinite variety of its races, tongues, religions, and cultures. It is home to 14 major languages and hundreds of minor ones, five major religions and thousands of minor ones, and two major races, and thousands of ethnic and tribal groups. The political unity of India was a creation of the British who ruled India for over a century. Although India is ostensibly a secular state, Hinduism, practiced by 75% of the people, dominates the national culture.

Hindus. Largest mass gathering in world: 10 million pilgrims at 12-yearly 43-day Kumbh Mela ritual bathing festival seeking salvation at confluence of Ganges and Jumna, Allahabad, in January 1977.

HUMAN LIFE AND LIBERTY

Human need and development. India's huge and growing population magnifies every human need and problem into Himalaya-like proportions. With a growth rate of 1.8% annually, the people added to the country every year equal the population of Australia. India's carrying capacity has been estimated at no more than 300 million, so that, in effect, over 600 million are not being properly fed, clothed or housed. A further debilitating factor is the gulf between the rich and the poor which is wider in India than in any but the least developed countries of the world. Disparities in wealth and living conditions are reinforced by disparities in literacy, health, food, and nutrition, and other basic social indicators. Illiteracy is estimated at 48% nationally, but in certain areas and among certain disadvantaged groups it is as high as 87%. Life expectancy is 64 years but a variety of diseases ravage the impoverished villagers, cutting their productive years to no more than 40. Per capita income is $240 but there are hordes of unemployed in the cities who eke out their daily lives on less than 10 cents a day. The daily calorie supply is 2,229, but the average diet is so deficient in vital nutrients and proteins that it can be described as only little better than fasting. Good housing is limited to parts of cities. In the villages, most people still live in one-room hovels, which in many instances, also house the cattle, and in the cities, millions live in slums in shacks built of cardboard or tin. Sanitation facilities are nonexistent in villages and small towns beyond open latrines serviced by the untouchable class of scavengers. Most of the villages have only dirt roads, with open ditches at the sides to carry off water. Bullock carts may be still seen along these roads along with occasional cars and trucks, many of them several decades old. Much of the industry is low-tech. In construction sites, labor-intensive methods predominate and hundreds of men and women may be seen carrying on their heads loads that could be more efficiently carried in wheelbarrows. Although electricity is available in most cities, firewood and dried cowdung are the most common means of cooking in the villages. Nearly 41% of the urban population and 51% of the rural population live below the poverty level. This means that the majority of Indians live in unrelieved misery all their lives. At the same time, India has a reasonably good infrastructure, most of it built under the British, a flourishing industrial base, considered the 10th largest in the world in output, and one of the best systems of higher education in the world. The stark contrast between these sectors and the bare subsistence life of more than three fourths of Indians who live in rural areas is the most dramatic proof of India's underdevelopment.

Human rights and freedoms. India is the largest parliamentary democracy in the world, an astonishing fact considering the disparate races and peoples that make up the country and the chronic violence that has marred its political history in modern times. It is one of the few Third World countries where there has never been even a threat of military takeover since independence. Its elections, held regularly, although chaotic, have been relatively fair and its legal and judicial system is considered one of the finest in the world. The country's constitution, one of the world's longest, guarantees all basic liberties, and these guarantees have been upheld and respected even in the worst of times. In terms of human rights violations per capita, India ranks lowest in the world, a record that is applauded even by Amnesty International. While this record is not entirely unblemished, excesses and abuses are mainly related to India's political troubles, particularly, the violent ethnic, religious, caste, communal and secessionist activities and the need to contain these troubles by force. Army and police excesses against civilians occur almost entirely in the hot spots, such as Kashmir, Punjab, and Assam in response to attacks by militant insurgents. Widespread arrests of dissidents are generally followed by their incommunicado detention for prolonged periods Police, army, and paramilitary forces have wide discretion in the use of lethal force.There are also credible reports that police engage in 'faked encounter' killings. Press reports indicate that in 1992 alone 1,106 civilians and 982 combatants died in Kashmir and 4,049 people (including 2,036 civilians and 1,787 militants), died in Punjab. Although torture and cruel treatment are prohibited by law, they are commonly used to extract confessions from detainees. According to human rights groups, police brutality is most frequent during interrogation and may include beatings, rape, burning with cigarettes, suspension by the feet, crushing of limbs with heavy rollers and electric shocks. Army and police personnel guilty of such mistreatment of prisoners receive only mild punishment, such as suspension or transfer. Amnesty International's 1992 report detailed 400 documented cases of torture, rape and deaths in custody. Sexual abuse of women and children in jails have been reported by the press. Despite Constitutional guarantees against arbitrary arrest and detention, there are a number of preventive detention laws on the statute books designed to preserve national security and public order. These include the National Security Act of 1980 and the Terrorist and Disruptive Acts (Prevention) Act (TADA) Act of 1985. Civil liberties groups claim that over 37,000 persons are being detained under TADA, most of them in Punjab. TADA trials are held in secret to protect witnesses, and defendants are presumed guilty and required to prove their innocence. Use of excessive military force in response to insurgent attacks is common in Punjab and Kashmir. Freedom of speech and press is protected by the Constitution and fostered by a vigorous press. However, the government may prohibit publication of sensitive security stories, but this is sometimes interpreted quite broadly to suppress criticism of government policies. The national television and radio services are government monopolies and are frequently accused of manipulating the news to the benefit of the government. Discrimination of various kinds are built into Indian society, and while the government is pledged to reduce or eliminate them, social pressures have continued to sustain them. Gender discrimination is the most flagrant. In both Hindu and Muslim societies, women suffer legal disabilities for which no redress is available. Women do not have equal property or inheritance rights and are discouraged from participating in equal measure in public life. Female bondage, forced prostitution, dowry deaths (killing of young brides by the husband or his family because they do not bring enough money as dowry), and child marriage remain common in many parts of India. Child prostitution is rampant in the large urban areas. In Bombay alone there are over 100,000 prostitutes, most of them minors. Female infanticide is so widely practiced that India has one of the most skewed sex ratios in the world at 929 females for 1,000 males. Although violence against women has increased since 1980, few rape trials end in conviction. The second group subject to severe discrimination is that of Scheduled Castes (also called Untouchables or Dalits) and

Country summary. **Worlds A, B, C by ethnolinguistic peoples, cities, and major civil divisions in India.**

World	PEOPLES Num	Pop 2000	C%	Christians	E%	U%	Unevangelized
A	308	288,679,216	1.47	4,240,634	37	63	181,041,410
B	67	721,436,567	7.65	55,185,123	68	32	231,073,649
C	64	3,545,987	79.83	2,830,758	100	0	7,432
Total	**439**	**1,013,661,770**	**6.14**	**62,256,515**	**59**	**41**	**412,122,491**

World	CITIES Num	Pop 2000	C%	Christians	E%	U%	Unevangelized
A	418	91,963,424	0.71	655,746	40	60	54,968,009
B	222	113,898,014	7.92	9,020,295	63	37	42,072,314
C	2	244,424	88.72	216,852	99	1	1,643
Total	**642**	**206,105,862**	**4.80**	**9,892,893**	**53**	**47**	**97,041,966**

World	CIVIL DIVISIONS Num	Pop 2000	C%	Christians	E%	U%	Unevangelized
A	4	35,055,466	1.17	410,403	49	51	17,748,327
B	25	974,209,453	6.01	58,530,577	60	40	394,346,268
C	3	4,396,860	75.11	3,302,566	99	1	27,902
Total	**32**	**1,013,661,779**	**6.14**	**62,243,546**	**59**	**41**	**412,122,497**

Scheduled Tribes. Despite Constitutional safeguards, both these groups remain disadvantaged, economically and socially, and they suffer from acts of harassment and violence from the general population and the police.

Human environment. Generally, underdeveloped countries do not suffer from air pollution, but India is an exception. Almost all major cities have intolerable levels of sulfur dioxide and particulates. India has abundant water resources overall, although certain regions are dry. In 1993, the city of Madras had to be shut down for a week because of lack of water. All rivers and streams are highly polluted because they also carry much of the sewage and industrial waste. Of the 3,119 towns and cities, only 209 have partial sewage treatment and only 8 have complete treatment. Waterborne illnesses account for two-thirds of all illnesses. Soils are being degraded at a fast rate because of the growing pressures of population and the ineffectiveness of soil conservation measures.

Hindus. Festival of god Subrahmanya (with, behind his statue, his 2 wives, Lord Shiva, and his sacred bull Nandi) in Saidapet district, Madras.

NON-CHRISTIAN RELIGIONS

Hinduism is the principal religion of India, having developed over the past 5 millennia through a series of definite periods each with its own distinctive emphases: Vedic, Brahmanic, Philosophic, Devotional, and Reformed Hinduism. Strongly influenced by both Islam and Christianity, the principal reform movements have been the Brahmo Samaj (1828), Arya Samaj (Assembly of Noble Men, 1875), Ramakrishna Mission (1886), and Servants of India. Unifying factors are esteem for the Vedas; the ideas of Karma, reincarnation and non-violence (ahimsa); respect for the holy man (sanyasi); and the acceptance of caste as the socio-religious framework of society. The Hindu proportion of the population has decreased gradually over the last century by on average 1% every 10 years, due to the influx and growth of immigrant religions and also to Muslim fertility being higher than that of the Hindu population.

Hinduism is divided into hundreds of sects centering on various deities (totalling 3 million in number), which can be classified under 3 heads. (1) About 0.5% of Hindus belong to the more intellectual reform movements opposed to polytheism and idol worship which reject belief in incarnations of gods; these include Arya Samaj, Shankar Acharya (Vedanta Hinduism), and the Ramakrishna Mission (and also Sikhism). (2) The vast majority, 98%, popularly called Sanatanists or idol-worshippers, believe in incarnations of gods and are either Shaivites (followers of Siva, the goddess Kali and other deities), or, by far the larger number, Vaishnavites (followers of Vishnu, Ram, Krishna and other deities). There are also Saktas, worshippers of the divine mother Sakti, female aspect of the deity. Shaivites predominate in South India, whereas Vaishnavites predominate in western and northern India, the east (Bihar, Orissa) and Assam. (3) Lastly, there are many newer sects several of which have spread abroad to the Western world. These include the Divine Light Mission, a Vedantist movement first spread in north India in the 1920s, the movement centered on devotion to the internationally-known Guru Maharaj Ji (born 1958); Ananda Marga (Path of Bliss), a violent politico-religious Bengali sect; followers of Sri Aurobindo, Sri Chinmoy, Sai Baba, et alii.

Although traditionally Hinduism has not been a missionary religion, the reform movements and newer sects have been active in proselytism and conversion. In South India, Shankar Acharya followers have succeeded in converting thousands of Christians back to Hinduism at Rameshwaram Madras; and they have other conversion centers at Ujjain (MP), Jaganath Puri, Kedarnadh (UP), Badrinath (Kashmir), and Shringeri (Kerala). The Arya Samaj also claims many reconversions of Christians in Assam, Orissa and central India, and to have won back a large number of outcaste Hindus who converted to neo-Buddhism in 1956 under their leader Ambedkar. The Divine Light Mission claims 5 million followers in India including many former nominal Indian Christians and also European and American youth; Auroville and other neo-Hindu centers also have many Western converts; and Ananda Marga claims 2.5 million converts in India and a network of branches in 30 countries abroad.

Among the principal orthodox Hindu organizations in India are: (1) Bharat Sevak Samaj, founded by Pandit Nehru in New Delhi in 1952, which works in the social field (famine relief, housing reconstruction, schools) irrespective of caste and community, acts as liaison between the needs of people and governmental agencies, and fosters interreligious co-operation; (2) Bharatiya Vidya Bhavan, in Bombay, whose aims are cultural and religious; (3) Ramakrishna Institute of Culture, in Calcutta, which works in the field of religion and culture; (4) Gandhi Smarak Sangrahalaya, in Ahmedabad and New Delhi, which promotes the Gandhi heritage; the World Hindu Council (Vishwa Hindu Parishad, VHP), which seeks to unify the many Hindu sects, runs orphanages, trains missionaries, teaches Sanskrit, and is related to the militant, and infamous, National Volunteer Corps (Rashtriya Swayamsevak Sangh, RSS); and (6) Banaras Hindu University, in Varanasi (Banaras), which has a faculty of oriental learning and theology.

The Bhratiya Janta Party (BJP) grew in power and influence in the late 1980s and early 1990s, capturing many state governments. As a Hindu party with a declared intent to turn India into a Hindu state, its growing strength was a matter of deep concern to the minority religious communities. BJP militancy was expressed in such slogans as, 'None of our gods is unarmed'. When the BJP came to power in Madhya Pradesh in 1991 it passed laws limiting conversions to Christianity, and launched 'Operation Homecoming', which sought to reconvert Christians to Hinduism, especially targeting tribal Christians in remote areas. Similar actions were taken in other BJP states, including Orissa and Rajasthan. When Hindu mobs destroyed the Babri Mosque in Ayodhya, Uttar Pradesh, in 1992, the central government reacted swiftly, dissolving several BJP state governments and arresting key BJP leaders. The event, the most serious inter-communal conflict in decades, was followed by violent rioting (1,150 killed) in many cities. It served both as a sign of rising Hindu militancy and as a warning of the dangers in such a movement.

Islam is the second largest religion and has been active in India since the 8th century AD. Virtually the whole gamut of Muslim sects are found on the sub-continent. The principal Sunni law schools are the Hanafite and Shafite; and Shias are represented in their Ithna-Ashari, Ismaili Khoja and Bohora branches, the Dawoodi Boharas having their headquarters in Bombay. The Ahmadiya Movement of Islam, which began in Lahore in 1890 and is considered heretical by other Muslims, is also numerous. India has been noted for its reform movements going back to the Moghul emperor Akbar in the 16th century. Among the early reformers were Shakykh Ahmad Sirhindi Shah Wali Allah of Delhi, Sayyid Ahmad, and Hajji Shariat Allah; while more recent influential thinkers have been Jamal al-Din al-Afghani, Muhammed Abduh, Sayyid Ahmad Khan, Sayyid Amir Ali, and Muhammad Iqbal.

At Partition in 1947, the proportion of Muslims in India fell drastically due to the violent exchange of population with Pakistan; it has since increased gradually, from 9.9% in 1951 to 10.7% in 1961 and to 11.2% in 1971. After the serious rioting and massacres between Hindus and Muslims at Partition, communal riots against Muslims have erupted periodically especially in northwestern cities. Conversions both to and from Hinduism have taken place; the Arya Samaj claims converts from Islam, and Ahmadiya attempts conversions to Islam.

The principal Muslim organizations in India are: (1) Muslim Community of India (Jamaate Islami-Al-Hind), in Delhi, which is the most important co-ordinating body for Indian Islam; (2) Islam and Modern Age Society, in New Delhi, whose aim is to reinterpret Islam in the light of modern needs; (3) Indian Institute of Islamic Studies, in New Delhi, which has a large library and engages in research; (4) Darul-Musannifin, in Azamgarh, UP, which is a research center dealing mostly with Arabic and Persian sources; (5) Islamic Research Association founded in Bombay in 1933, which publishes research on Islam; and (6) Aligarh Muslim University, which has a faculty of theology and also sponsors the Islamic Research Circle.

Sikhism owes its origin to Guru (teacher) Nanak (AD 1469-1538) who was a follower of the poet Kabri. Although a Hindu by birth, Nanak was influenced by the Islam of his native Lahore. He repudiated caste, found little help in the Hindu scriptures, refused to accept the Brahman priesthood, and emphasized the oneness of God. On the other hand be continued the Hindu belief in Karma and reincarnation and taught release through bhakti, the way of faith or devotion. Arjun, the fifth Guru, was responsible for the compilation of the Granth, the Sikh scriptures, which consist of the songs of Nanak, Kabri and others; and the tenth Guru declared that thereafter the Granth should be their Guru. Sikhism, which is therefore a reform movement out of Hinduism, has its center in Amritsar where the Golden Temple has been built. Sikhs grew from 4,335,771 in 1931 to 7,845,915 (1.79%) in 1961, 10,378,797 (1.9%) in 1971, and 20,448,395 in 1995.

Sikhs. Golden Temple (Harimandir, or Darbar Sahib), Amritsar, chief gurdwara (house of worship) of Sikhs and their most important pilgrimage center. Built in 1604, it stands in amrit-sar ('pool of nectar') tank of water approached on west by marble causeway. *Right.* Militant Sikh fights police.

Traditional religions, collectively described as animism, continue to exist among India's multitudinous tribal peoples, and are particularly strong among hill tribesmen especially in Assam. Ethnoreligionists have been consistently underenumerated in recent government censuses, but the fact is that numerically they have persisted remarkably since 1880 despite the inroads of Hindu proselytism and the constant pressure towards detribalization and acculturation with rural and urban Hindu society. From being 2.6% of the total population in 1881, animists increased slightly to 2.7% in 1931; then increased gradually to 3.5% by 1970. Their total in absolute numbers increased meanwhile, from 6.7 million in 1900 to 19.2 million in 1970 to a staggering 32.5 million by 1995; this huge increase being due to millions of tribals who were formerly enumerated as Hindus now asserting their own ethnoreligions.

Tribal religions are particularly widely followed by a number of tribes of Aboriginal peoples: the Naga people of western India, who have an elaborate ancestral cult using megalithic monuments and elaborate ceremonies for their 5 rites of passage; the Kandyans of Bengal, who formerly made human sacrifice to Tari Pennu, old mother Earth, at the planting season; and the pastoral Toda of Nilgris whose religions are centered in their cattle and sacred milk houses. Among the Birhors of Chota Nagpur, both ancestral spirits (Haprom) and clan divinities (Buru-Bongas or Ora-Bongas) are venerated, and the mother goddesses Devi Mai and Bushi Mai are appealed to in times of severe illness, barrenness or famine. Also recognized is the existence of a supreme being, Singabonga, who is creator but takes little interest in men. Although virtually devoid of witchcraft beliefs, the Birhors place great reliance on the powers of the diviner-medicine man (mati) who is adept at offering sacrifices and exorcising evil spirits. Other traditionalist Indian peoples include the Bhils, Garo, Ho, Kaipeng-Koloi, Khasi, Kolam, Kond, Korku and Santal. Most are rapidly becoming hinduized.

Buddhists. Statutes of Christ and Buddha side by side in temple.

Buddhism began in India where its founder, Gautama Buddha (BC 560-480), lived out his life; and enjoyed great prestige for a thousand years thereafter under outstanding emperors including Asoka, Kanishka, Chandragupta II and Harsha. Between the 3rd and 1st centuries BC, Mahayana Buddhism took form in northwestern India, from which it later spread to China and Japan. By the 7th century AD Indian Buddhism began to decline, sparked by internal rivalries, the resurgence of Hinduism and the later arrival of Islam. The virtual eclipse of Buddhism in India continued until 1956 when the neo-Buddhist movement, led by the untouchables' leader B. R. Ambedkar, swept across the country resulting in the conversion of over 3 million scheduled-caste Hindus to Buddhism in Maharashtra, and spread from UP to Mysore and Madras states, where it rejuvenated a 1909 Buddhist movement. The major tribes affected were the Mahars, Jatavs or Chamars, and leather workers in UP, Punjab, Jammu, and Kashmir. This dramatic growth in the 1950s is evident in the census figures, rising from 180,828 Buddhists (0.05% of the population) in 1951 to 3,250,227 (0.74% of the population) in 1961. However, momentum was not maintained, and in the 1971 census the proportion of Buddhists dropped slightly to 0.70% (3,812,325 persons). In several areas large numbers were reconverted back to Hinduism by the Arya Samaj, and in Kolhapur (southeast of Bombay) 12,000 neo-Buddhists asked the Church of North India for Christian baptism in 1971. The number of Buddhists grew to 6.5 million by 1995, remaining at 0.70% of the population.

Bodh Gaya is the place in central Bihar where the Buddha found enlightenment. In the 1980s and 1990s a major global Buddhist center began to develop there. An 80-foot statue of Buddha was erected and monasteries multiplied, representing groups from Sri Lanka, Burma, Tibet, China, Thailand, Japan, Bhutan, Vietnam, Nepal, Bangladesh, and Korea. Some of the monasteries are showpieces of Asian architecture, representing distinctive national culture, theology, and worship.

Jains. Worshipers during Jain service in temple in Mumbai.

Jainism is a Hindu reform movement dating back to the 6th century BC. Its founder, Mahavira (BC 599-527), better known as the Great Hero, was the last of the 24 Tirthankaras, those who obtained salvation (*moksha*) through self-abnegation. Jains emphasize asceticism, the Three Jewels (knowledge, faith, and right conduct), non-violence (*ahimsa*) and a modified view of transmigration from that prevalent among Hindus. Jains have some of India's most beautiful temples. The Jain community declined numerically from 1,378,596 in 1891 to 1,178,596 in 1921, then increased to 1,252,105 in 1931, 0.45% in 1951, 0.46% in 1961, and 2,604,646 (0.50%) in 1971. By 1995 the number of Jains grew to nearly 3.9 million, but their strength relative to the national population declined to 0.40%.

Baha'i has had in India its most spectacular successes in any country, numerically. Baha'i was introduced into India from Persia around 1860, and until 1960 most Baha'is in India (850 in 1961) were Persians. In that year, however, mass conversion of Indian Hindus began. By 1963, 10,000 adult converts a month were being claimed. There has subsequently been very rapid expansion from 1,064 local spiritual assemblies in 1964 to 4,869 assemblies with 17,034 other isolated centers and groups by 1973, the largest Baha'i community of any country in the world. By 1995, nearly 1.5 million Indians were followers of the Baha'i faith.

Other religions are numerous, including Parsiism (about 195,000 in 1995) descended from the ancient Zoroastrianism of Persia and found mainly in Bombay, and a number of smaller new syncretistic religions mostly of Hindu background. There are also about 9,000 Jews (Cochin Jews, and Bney Israel in Bombay) and a large, growing number of atheists and nonreligious persons. The Cochin Jewish community began with refugees from the Roman destruction of Jerusalem in 70 AD, and has survived through all the centuries since.

CHRISTIANITY

According to Malabar tradition, Christianity was introduced into India by the apostle Thomas in AD 52. By 200, the Orthodox tradition is considered to have been established in south. A bishop is known to have been sent from Jerusalem to India in AD 345, and a traveller in 530 reported Christian communities in the southwest and in Ceylon. The Franciscan, John of Monte Corvino, spent a year in Malabar prior to going on to China in 1924, and in 1498 Vasco da Gama claimed India for the Portuguese monarchy.

In 1514 pope Leo X accorded to the kings of Portugal the right of patronage, the development of missions in Asia; and the diocese of Goa was established in 1533. Francis Xavier arrived in India in 1542, and in subsequent years the Jesuits worked for the conversion to Catholicism of both non-Christians and the Orthodox. Although the Thomas Christians at one point affirmed their allegiance to Rome, in 1653 a sizeable number declared their autonomy.

During the first half of the 17th century, the Jesuit Robert de Nobili developed the missionary method of 'adaptation' to Indian life as a way of winning high-caste Brahmins to Catholicism, but the rites controversy which this provoked proved to be a serious blow to Catholic outreach in subsequent years.

From 1612 onwards, Anglican clergy served in India as chaplains under the East India Company. Although occasional converts were made in the early days, the policy of the company was opposed to missionary activities.

Protestant missions began in 1706 with the arrival of the Danish-Halle Lutherans, B. Ziegenbalg and H. Plutschau, at Tranquebar on the coast of Coromandel, which at that time was under Danish control; and by 1800 a Christian community of 20,000 had been formed. In 1793 the BMS missionary William Carey arrived at Serampore and the modern era of Protestant missions began. He was soon followed by other British missionaries, those of the LMS in 1798, CMS in 1813, Methodist in 1819 and Scottish Presbyterians in 1823. American missionaries were also active during this period: Congregationalists (American Board) in 1810, Presbyterians in 1834, Baptists in 1836, Lutherans in the 1840s and Methodists in 1856. The German Gossner Mission sent missionaries to India as early as 1839, and the first Scandinavian Lutherans arrived in 1867.

The numerical growth of professing Christians over the last century has been remarkable: from 1,506,098 in British India in 1881 to 8,392,038 (2.35%) in 1951, 10,728,086 (2.44%) in 1961, 14,223,382 (2.60%) in 1971, and about 35 million (3.7%) in 1995.

Christianity is the second largest religious minority, after Islam, but the geographical spread of Christians is very uneven. The faithful are concentrated mostly in the extreme south, where Christianity was first established, and the east, where important minority groups have been converted. The states of Kerala, Tamil Nadu and Andhra Pradesh together account for more than 60% of India's Christians. The following states and territories had in 1971 the highest proportion of Christians in comparison to total population: Nagaland (66.8%); Meghalaya (47.0%); Goa, Daman and Diu (31.8%); Andaman and Nicobar Islands (26.35%); Manpuri (26.03%) and Kerala (21.05%). Kerala has the largest number of denominations in India; but outside Kerala, Christianity is strongest in states and territories with relatively small populations. On the other hand, Christians are extremely scattered in the west (except in the Bombay area) and in the center and north of the country including the Ganges Valley, areas of high population density. Indian Christianity has been firmly in the hands of nationals since the government began in the 1950s to discourage the arrival of new foreign missionaries. According to official statistics published in New Delhi in 1971, the number of professional foreign missionaries known to the government of India diminished by one third between 1968 and 1970 (from 6,420 in 1968 to 4,903 in 1970); in addition, there were in 1973 over a thousand others. All of these, however, amounted to less than 6% of the total of all Indian church workers.

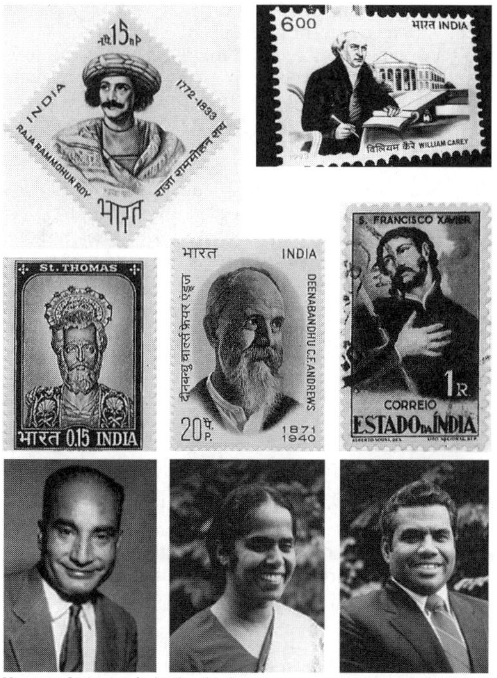

Names of renown in India. (*Left to right, top to bottom*). Ram Mohan Rei, William Carey, Apostle Thomas, C.F. Andrews, Francis Xavier, Bakht Singh, Mary Matthews, Thomas Matthews.

One of the most remarkable examples of the indianization of the church has been in the growth of Christian ashrams. Following the ideal of ancient and modern Hindu ashrams, these aim primarily at being centers for prayer where people may experience union with God in an atmosphere conducive to silence and meditation. Study, research, and social work may be carried on but these are subordinate to the main objectives. The role of Christian ashrams in India is to bear witness to the importance of contemplation in the life of the church which is usually associated in the minds of non-Christians with institutions only; to provide a place where all who wish, irrespective of race, caste, religion or nationality, may find a spiritual oasis for meeting God in prayer; to give an example of a wholly Indian life-style, simple and austere, but always welcoming to guests, thus showing non-Christians that Christianity is not necessarily Western; and where possible, to use Indian forms of liturgical worship.

Catholic Church in India. Syro-Malabarese worshipers at new cathedral in Ernakulam.

CATHOLIC CHURCH. The ecclesiastical hierarchy was established in 1558, with the formation of the metropolitan archdiocese of Goa, and was re-established for the whole of India in 1878. The total Catholic population was nearly 16 million in 1995 compared to 1.9 million in 1900, 2,606,000 in 1921 and 6,282,000 in 1961. Most Catholics are of the Latin rite, but the Syro-Malabar rite is also strong, and a not insignificant number belong to the Syro-Malankara rite.

Following Vatican II, the Indian Catholic Church has shown a remarkable dynamism, although the traditional folk-religiosity of the majority of Catholics and the clerical authoritarianism of many priests are still strong realities. Nevertheless, the meeting of the All India Seminar at Bangalore in May 1969, as well as its various extensions, marked a major turning point in Indian Catholic life and its post-conciliar renewal. Seen from the standpoint of work accomplished and conclusions adopted, the seminar proved to be a highly important medium for the expression of new ideas concerning the church in India. Among the tendencies which came increasingly to the fore may be mentioned the desire to further the indianization of the liturgy (for the first time, a mass was celebrated officially according to a ritual using certain symbolic gestures with the imprint of Hindu culture), the participation of laity in the organs of the church, a less intransigent attitude concerning birth control, a clearer position regarding social justice, a more open training for clergy and religious personnel, and a greater concern for ecumenism. An important agreement was reached concerning rites guaranteeing unity of jurisdiction and plurality of rites in North India. Moreover, a permanent committee was elected to prepare a constitution for a national pastoral council.

Several important meetings followed the All India Seminar. The first was the All India Christian Consultation on Development, which met in an ecumenical atmosphere in New Delhi in February 1970, with its focus on the idea that integral development necessarily includes institutional and structural changes in society. The idea of distributive justice is central, the church having an essential role in education and an important contribution to make to the urban and rural development of the country. A second meeting was the National Consultation on Evangelization, at Patna in October 1973.

The recent development of Indian Catholicism has been accompanied by an important ecumenical rapprochement and new contacts between the religions. In this latter domain, the way had already been prepared by the various Catholic ashrams beginning in 1950. The Charismatic movement has been a definite presence in the Indian Catholic church since the late 1960s. The 9th Charismatic National Convention was held at Layola College, Madras in 1992, with 25,000 Catholic Charismatics attending.

The Holy See has diplomatic relations with India and in AD 2000 is represented to government and the Catholic hierarchy by a pro-nuncio residing in New Delhi.

Catholic Church in India. 'Inasmuch as you did it unto the least of these my brethren, you did it unto Me'. Mother Teresa at her Home for Dying Destitutes, Calcutta.

PROTESTANT CHURCHES. India's principal united churches are the Church of North India and the Church of South India. In 1901, 2 Reformed bodies joined together in the South India United Church, followed by the amalgamation of 2 Congregational groups in the Congregational General Union of South India in 1905. In 1908 these 2 united churches in turn merged to form the United Church of South India, and in 1947 a further union with Anglicans and Methodists created the Church of South India. The church in 1973 consisted of 16 dioceses, with a Christian community exceeding 1.5 million.

Church union first came to North Indian in 1924 with the merger of the Presbyterian and Congregational churches. By 1929, 11 different denominations had joined while negotiations continued with other bodies. In 1970 the Anglican, Baptist, Brethren Disciples, Methodist (British and Australian conferences), and United churches came together to form the Church of North India.

Although many Baptist went into the Church of North India in 1970, a larger number remained outside. The Council of Baptist Churches in North East India was (in 1995) the second largest Protestant community in the country; it consists of 4 conventions. Another important Baptist group which refused to enter the CNI in 1970 was the Baptist Church of Mizo District. The Nagaland Baptist Church Council was very influential in the early 1990s, with a strong presence on local radio and a powerful influence on election campaigns. Baptists in Southern India are found principally in the Convention of Telugu Baptist Churches and the Convention of Baptist Churches in the Northern Circars.

Nine autonomous Lutheran bodies owing their origin to German, Scandinavian, and American missionary outreach as early as 1706, came together to form in 1975 the United Evangelical Lutheran Churches in India (UELCI).

The Salvation Army has made extraordinary progress in India since its arrival from the UK in 1882. Organized into 5 territories, they had in 1970 more than 4,000 congregations and a Christian community of half a million. They suffered a marked decline in the following decades, however, and by 1990 had only about 270,000 affiliated.

As with the Baptists, not all Presbyterians entered into the CNI in 1970. The large Presbyterian Church in North East India, with a Christian community of nearly 325,000, continues to maintain its identity as a separate denomination. Consisting of 3 synods, the church maintains its historic links with Welsh Presbyterianism. Negotiations for organic union in a Church of North East India have been made with the Council of Baptist Churches in North East India and remaining elements of the Church of North India.

The largest Pentecostal group in India is the United Pentecostal Church, related to the church of the same name in the USA. Two Assemblies of God groups related to the USA and UK denominations are active, as are the Swedish Free Mission, Norwegian Free Mission, Church of God (Full Gospel), and the Church of God of Prophecy.

Other important groups include the Plymouth Brethren, Seventh-day Adventists, Mennonites, Evangelical Congregationalists and Church of God (Anderson). In addition there are nearly 200 smaller Protestant denominations.

Protestants have been heavily involved in education and social service. Protestant churches related to the National Christian Council of India continue to sponsor hundreds of secondary schools and degree-granting colleges, while Protestant, Orthodox, and Mar Thoma Christians are responsible for hundreds of hospitals and dispensaries. Two renowned Christian medical colleges, Vellore and Ludhiana, have produced thousands of medical graduates. Since the 1920s the churches have also been engaged in rural reconstruction and community development, including road-building, improving agriculture, distributing improved seed and fertilizer, well-drilling, irrigation schemes, and education in nutrition. Urban industrial mission is carried on through programs in Calcutta, Durgapur, Nagpur, Madras, Bangalore, Coimbatore, and Alwaye.

Theological colleges of the member churches of the NCCI number over 15, of which the better known are Bishop's College (Calcutta), Leonard Theological College (Jabalpur), Serampore College (Serampore), Tamilnad Theological College (Tirumaraiyur), and the United Theological College at Bangalore. In addition there are 50 other Protestant seminaries and hundreds of Bible Schools.

ORTHODOX CHURCHES. The Orthodox Syrian Church of the East traces its history to the Apostle Thomas and originally maintained spiritual ties with the Nestorians of Mesopotamia. When the Portuguese Catholics arrived in the 16th century, they attempted to convert the Syrians forcibly to Catholicism and actually succeeded in doing so at the Synod of Diamper in 1599. However, in 1653 a group met at Koonen Cross in the Mattasncheri churchyard which proclaimed its autonomy and consecrated its own bishop, Mar Thoma I. Although the Church of Rome later recovered nearly two-thirds of these Syriac Malankara-rite Christians, the autonomous Orthodox body succeeded in maintaining its independence. In 1665 Mar Gregorios, an Eastern bishop long sought by the Thomas Christians, arrived in Kerala to take charge of the work. Ironically he was a Monophysite from Diarbekir rather than a Nestorian from Mesopotamia, which accounts for the present christological stance of the church. A major schism from the Syrian Orthodox occurred in the 19th century when the Mar Thoma Syrian Church of Malabar broke off. In spite of the divisions which the church has suffered through the years, largely due to foreign ecclesiastical intervention, the Orthodox Syrian Church of the East has continued to grow numerically though only by natural population increase.

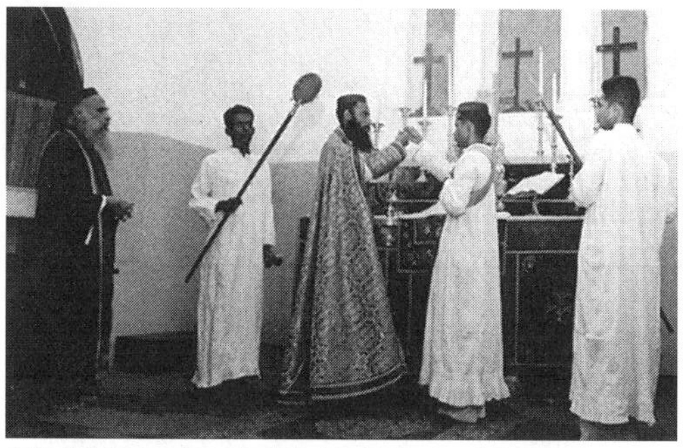

Orthodox Syrian Church of the East, Diocese of Quilon. Blessing of censer during liturgy by vicar and assistant vicar, in Trivandrum Church.

Other small Orthodox communities include the Chaldean Syrian Church (Nestorian), Armenian Apostolic Church (Gregorian) and Greek Orthodox Church under Constantinople.

INDIGENOUS CHURCHES A large number of independent indigenous churches begun by Indians have been formed in India, the most important being the Mar Thoma Syrian Church of Malabar. In 1816 the Anglican CMS sent 4 missionaries to assist the Orthodox Syrian Church of the East in the training of its priests. They began a theological school at Kottayam, translated the Bible into Malayalam and became the centered of a reform movement which led to conflict within the church by 1829. At the Mavelikkara Synod in 1836, the missionaries were severed from the church, although they continued to carry on their educational work. The vision of reform affected a significant element within the Orthodox Church, led by a teacher of Syriac at the Kottayam seminary, Abraham Malpan, leading to conflict and ultimately schism. The Mar Thoma Church maintains many Orthodox elements including priestly vestments, ecclesiastical structures and liturgical emphases.

Mar Thoma Syrian Church of Malabar. Bishop of Outside Kerala baptizes an infant.

From 1858 began the first of many indigenous attempts to form a Hindu-Christian church affirming faith in Jesus Christ but rejecting Western missionary control and retaining Hindu culture and Indian nationalism. The first bodies to be formed were: 1858, Hindu Church of the Lord Jesus (Tinnevelly); 1868, the proposal for a National Church of Bengal; 1870, Chet Ramis (Punjab); 1880, Church of the New Dispensation (Nava Vidhana, Calcutta): 1886, National Church of Madras; 1887, Calcutta Christo Samaj; and 1893, the proposal for an all-embracing National Church in India. Others followed in 1920, 1921, 1933 (Fellowship of the Followers of Jesus, begun by Kandiswamy Chetti in Madras), and in 1942 the largest still existing in 1975, the Subba Rao movement. Begun among the Telugu in Andhra Pradesh, the latter is strongly opposed to all churches, stresses elements of Hindu culture as well as study of the Bible, is virtually unorganized, and holds massive healing crusades.

Subba Rao Movement. Prayer meeting: note garlanded crucifix with bloodstained body of Jesus, always present on special table, perpetuating founder's 1942 vision. Movement is anti-churches and anti-baptism, and is a high-caste Hindu revival featuring massive healing crusades.

Altogether, from 1858 to 1975 there were over 150 such indigenous Hindu-Christian movements or churches, and many since. Many other modern movements in Hinduism and Neo-Hinduism group together devotees of Jesus who explicitly acknowledge Jesus as their central source of inspiration and message.

Other indigenous movements have been more strictly Christian. The Assemblies (Jehova Shammah) of Brother Bakht Singh, with headquarters in Hyderabad, form one of India's faster-growing denominations. Noted for its large open-air Bible conferences, this completely self-supporting group of churches has spread beyond the borders of India to Africa and the Middle East.

Several splits have occurred within the Church of South India, the first being the London Mission Church composed of LMS Christians who opposed the union scheme in 1947 and kept litigation going for 17 years. In 1966 a schism of Pulaya outcastes from the CSI produced the large CMS Anglican Church of India, and in 1970 dissident Methodists formed the Wesleyan Methodist Church of India.

Among important indigenous Pentecostal bodies may be mentioned the Indian Pentecostal Church of God begun among the Telugu in 1924, the Pentecostal Church of God of Andhra Pradesh, the Ceylon Pentecostal Mission, and the Nagaland Christian Revival Church.

Huge numbers of Hindu believers in Christ must also be recognized at this point as Independents in the same sense. (For elaboration see footnote 'Crypto-Christians under Country Table 1, and the listings in Country Table 2).

Renewal movements. In the 1990s the Pentecostal/Charismatic Renewal as a whole continued to spread rapidly across most older churches, and numbered over 33,530,000 adherents (of whom 4% were Pentecostals, 15% Charismatics, and 81% Independents).

True Jesus Church of India. Baptism in 1974 of first Indian convert to this large Chinese indigenous church.

Indigenous missions. Indian Christians serve in many other countries in Asia and around the world. Still the vast majority of Indian missionaries are home missionaries, serving among the thousands of peoples and castes in their own country. In particular, many South Indians have taken on the task of reaching the largely non-Christian North India.

CHURCH AND STATE

India is a multi-religious state in which 'secularism' means equal protection for all religions and non-interference by the state in purely religious concerns. Some of the provisions of Indian law concerning religion include: that the state may not discriminate against any citizen on the basis of law alone; that all have the right freely to profess, practice and propagate religion; no taxes may be levied to assist a particular religion or religious denomination; religious instruction is forbidden in schools or colleges wholly maintained out of state funds; and no pupils may be compelled to attend religious instruction in any institutions receiving funds from the state.

There is no ministry of religious affairs, nor other government department dealing specifically with religion on the national level.

Persons promoting feelings of enmity between classes or religious groups are liable to detention. It is a criminal offense to promote enmity between different groups on the grounds of religion or to prejudice the maintenance of harmony between religious groups or to damage or defile a place of worship or any object held sacred to outrage religious feelings or insult religion; to disturb religious ceremonies; or to wound religious feelings by sounds or gestures.

Foreign missionaries who have not previously entered India are generally refused visas, and those already admitted find the reissue of visas facilitated by a 'No objection to return' endorsement made on their passports before leaving India. Those foreign missionaries involved in medical or educational work obtain them more readily than those engaged in other forms of service or witness. As the economy of India moved from severe protectionism to a more internationalist and open posture in the late 1980s and early 1990s, visas in general were more freely granted. Some mission agencies found it easier to obtain new visas than before.

Many churches serve members of the scheduled castes or the recognized tribes, some of these tribes living in areas under emergency legislation. The status of the church is indirectly affected by the rule that for purposes of serving as representatives in state or union legislatures, no non-Hindu or non-Sikh may be deemed to be a member of a scheduled caste (Scheduled Castes and Scheduled Tribes Orders Amendment Act, No 63 of 1956, Sch. I (1); for the various orders themselves see H. M. Seervai, Constitutional law of India, 1967, P. A-96, concerning Article 341). This discrimination has been challenged. The novel concept of dual religious affiliation (a person being both a Christian and a Hindu) has arisen in social terms and also beginning in law. Several forces including the growth of secularism are contributing to the elimination of legal discrimination on the ground of religion.

An attempt by the legislature of Orissa and Madhya Pradesh to make it a punishable offense to attempt to convert any person from one religious faith to another by offering him any 'inducement' has been struck down by the High Court as a violation of the right conferred by the constitution (Article 25, item 1) guaranteeing to 'Christians the right to propagate their faith' (Yulitha Hyde vs State of Orissa, AIR 1973, Or. 116). On the other hand, in the Subansiri District of Arunachel Pradesh in northeast India, Christians have experienced severe harassment at the hands of anti-Christian elements since 1971, including the burning of churches and dwellings. A team of OM missionaries were attacked by Hindu militants in Orissa in 1992; 6 workers were severely beaten. With many such incidents, Christians have often felt that police and governmental protection has been inadequate if not discriminatory.

BROADCASTING AND MEDIA

Although only 5% of the population owns a radio receiver, this still represents an audience of over 50 million people, making it a considerable tool. FEBA (Seychelles) broadcasts in 24 major Indian languages, and FEBC (Philippines) broadcasts in 6 languages. These programs reach tens of thousands of villages throughout the country. TWR beams programs into India from transmitters in Sri Lanka, Guam, and eastern Russia, reaching all of India as well as Bhutan, Nepal, and Tibet and sparking over 50,000 letters per month. Follow-up is accomplished from TWR's office in India, where over 400 Indian nationals respond with handwritten letters and most respondents are contacted in person, resulting in the planting of more than 250 churches since 1990. AWR operates a studio in Pune which develops programs in Tamil, Telegu, Marathi, Malayalam, Hindi, and Punjabi; its transmitter broadcasts programs to Africa and Europe. Programs from Veritas (Philippines), KNLS and TWR (Guam) can also be received. India is represented in UNDA: Catholics broadcast several daily programs over Radio Veritas and SLBC (Sri Lanka). Among these programs are more than 200 annual radio plays and special Christmas programs. Communication courses are offered at 18 training centers. Unfortunately, despite the large number of languages broadcasted, more actual air time is given to programming in English than indigenous languages. If more air time were given to national languages the results could be far greater.

There are an estimated 20 million television sets in India, and television has been an effective evangelistic tool. CBN airs programs nationally and partners with Indian ministries for follow-up. The 'Flying House' was aired in 1995 and 1996, and CBN has begun producing locally-created programs, the first of these being the 'Innkeeper'. In 1997 CBN and Dayspring Intl launched an initiative to produce a 52-episode series on the life of Christ. Another ministry's television serial, 'Stories from the Bible', was discontinued following protests by Muslim radicals; it had a popular appeal and many people responded requesting Bibles in the Hindi language. Christian television programs can be received via satellite television.

At the famed Tambaram 1938 meeting of the International Missionary Council.

INTERDENOMINATIONAL ORGANIZATIONS

The National Christian Council of India (NCCI) was founded in 1953, building on the foundations laid by the Missionary Council of 1912, the National Christian Council of India, Burma, and Ceylon in 1921, and the National Christian Council of India and Pakistan in 1947. The NCCI is an associate council of the WCC and affiliated to CWME, as well as being a member council of the Christian Conference of Asia. Eighteen of its member churches are also members of CCA. Fourteen regional Christian councils are part of the NCCI, namely those of Andhra Pradesh, Bengal, Bihar, Gujurat, Karnataka, Kerala, Madhya Pradesh, Maharashtra, North East India, North West India, Santal, Tamilnad, Uttar Pradesh, and Uktal.

In 1950 the Evangelical Fellowship of India (EFI) came into being; by 1973 it had 94 member denominations, organizations, and local congregations; by 1990, 100. The Fellowship sponsors its own Indian missionaries and in 1965 was responsible for the creation of the indigenous Indian Evangelical Mission. The India Missions Association serves 50 Evangelical organizations that send and support thousands of Indian missionaries, most of whom work cross-culturally within India. The autonomous Union of Evangelical Students of India (UESI) is also active. A more recent council formed after 20 year's endeavor is the Federation of Evangelical Churches of India (FECI); although it co-operates with the EFI, it limits membership to non-conciliar Evangelical bodies, numbering 30 denominations by 1978.

A Commission for Ecumenism of the Catholic Bishops' Conference of India (CBCI) has been formed, and ecumenical interest among Catholics has increased significantly since the All India Seminar of 1969.

The Joint Faith and Order Study Project was formed in August 1972 at the Nasrapur Consultation near Poona, bringing together for the first time Indian representatives of the Protestant, Syrian Orthodox, and Catholic churches. Subjects studied were the structure of visible unity, priesthood, ministry and ordination, scripture, tradition, authority, and mariology. The committee asked officials of their respective churches to continue to sponsor, and support with funds and personnel, a continuation committee of the conference at the national level.

At the national level, other inter-church bodies include the following. Action for Food Production (AFPRO), founded in New Delhi in 1966, is a non-profit joint service agency co-ordinating food production projects of church-related and voluntary agencies without regard for race, caste, community or creed. This secular agency of Christian inspiration brings together the resources of voluntary agencies in a single program. Accomplishments up to 1972 include water development, groundwater investigation, small credit schemes, poultry, livestock, and technical information services. The Co-ordinating Agency for Health Planning (CAHP), founded in New Delhi in 1970, is a small group endeavoring to develop the ecumenical aspect of Catholic and Protestant medical work in India, working through some 5 national seminars a year. In 1971 the CAHP described a new secular concept, the voluntary health association (VHA), open to all medical institutions in the voluntary non-profit class. The Christian Medical Association includes 430 institutions. Other ecumenical organizations serving the Christian medical community include the Emmanuel Hospitals Association, the Evangelical Medical Fellowship of India, and the Evangelical Nurses Fellowship. The All India Association for Christian Higher Education provides for ecumenical contacts between the 171 Catholic, Protestant, and Orthodox institutions associated with India's official universities.

At the regional level, several inter-church bodies have come into existence in Kerala. Two are working at the city-wide level in Trivandrum. The United Christmas Celebration Committee, founded in 1957, is a permanent body consisting of leaders of all the Christian churches in Trivandrum (Catholic, Jacobite, Mar Thoma, and the Church of South India) which organizes in the city every year a joint Christmas celebration and other festivals of common interest, including St Thomas Day. A related body is the United Christian Housing Committee, set up in 1971 to engage in social welfare in the slums of Trivandrum. On the state level in Kerala, the Kerala Social Action Council is an ecumenical committee founded in 1972 in Christhavashram (Kottayam), which is involved in conscientization concerning social justice and stimulates social action aimed at improving the living conditions of the poor.

Organizations at the regional level in Bihar include: (1) the Bihar Association of Voluntary Agencies (BAVA), a permanent registered body founded after the Bihar famine; and (2) Vikas Maitri, founded in Ranchi in 1968, which is an ecumenical association for agricultural, socioeconomic, and health projects in the Chota Nagpur region of Bihar and contiguous districts of neighboring states. The Catholic, Lutheran, Anglican, Mennonite, and Mar Thoma churches participate in this association.

Several institutes and research centers carry on their work in an ecumenical context. The Christian Institute for the Study of Religion and Society (CISRS), founded in Bangalore in 1953, is an interdenominational study and research institute with emphasis on dialogue with non-Christian religions. The Ecumenical Christian Centre, founded in Whitefield, Bangalore in 1963, is sponsored by 20 national churches (Catholic, CNI, SCI, Lutheran, Methodist, Mar Thoma, Baptist et alia) and such ecumenical national Christian organizations as the YMCA and YWCA. This is a study, research, and inspirational center open to Christians and non-Christians, which offers schools of politics, economics and other subjects. The Christian Retreat and Study Centre, founded at Dehra Dun (Rajpur, UP) in 1954, is an ecumenical action center affiliated to and sponsored by all of the major Protestant denominations working in North India.

A number of world interreligious organizations, which include to varying degrees co-operation with Christian churches, have their headquarters in India. (1) The Theosophical Society was founded in New York in 1875 and its world headquarters was transferred to Adyar, Madras in 1882. It considers itself as a religion or school of thought providing a synthesis of all religions. In 1973 it had 32,000 members belonging to 1,223 lodges in 62 countries. (2) The World Fellowship of Religions was founded in New Delhi in 1957, its principal aim being to foster religious tolerance and co-operation. (3) The World Union, founded in Pondicherry in 1958, is a body dedicated to the search for the unity of mankind and the world built on spiritual values. The union sponsors seminars, conferences and a world parliament of youth with affiliated centers found in various countries.

Among India's non-denominational institutes of religious studies, a major one is the Department of Religious Studies (Guru Gobind Singh Bhayan) affiliated to the Faculty of Humanities and Religious Studies of the Punjab University in Patiala. Founded in 1967, the department sponsors studies and research in 5 major religious traditions: Hinduism, Buddhism, Christianity, Islam, and Sikhism. Other centers and institutes for the study of world religions and dialogue are: (1) Henry Martyn Institute of Islamic Studies (HMI), founded in Lahore in 1930 and now located at Hyderabad, AP; (2) Christian Institute of Sikh Studies, founded at Patiala, Punjab in 1966; (3) Aikya Alayam, founded at Madras by Jesuits in 1966, a Tamil culture and inter-faith research and dialogue center; (4) Centre for the CMI in 1971; (5) Institute of Indian Culture, founded in Bombay by the SVD; and (6) Chavara Library and Cultural Centre, founded in Cochin by the CMI, which maintains a library and sponsors discussions involving Christians, Hindus, Muslims and Marxists.

Argentinian evangelist Luis Palau with 41,000 attenders in Cuttack, 1988.

FUTURE TRENDS AND PROSPECTS

Christians and Muslims will probably both find room to grow in the mosaic of India's peoples so that by 2025 Christians account for 7.4% and Muslims 12.2% while Hindus decline to under 73% (down from 80% in 1900).

With sustained growth over the next few decades Christianity could grow to near 10% of India's population by AD 2050. The nonreligious could also grow to over 100 million in the same period. Hindus will potentially decline as a percentage of India's population as other religions continue to win adherents over the next few decades.

BIBLIOGRAPHY

A bibliography. K. Baago. *Library of Christian theology*. Madras: The Christian Literature Society, 1969. 110p. (A bibliography of theological works by Indian authors.).

A century for Christ in India and Pakistan, 1855–1955. Lahore, Pakistan: United Presbyterian Church, 1958.

A concise dictionary of Indian philosophy. J. Grimes. Rev. ed. Albany, NY: State University of New York (SUNY) Press, 1996. 500p.

A concise history of ancient India. A. K. Majumdar. New Delhi: Munshiram Manoharlal, 1980. 3 vols. (Vol. 3 deals with religion).

A glossary of the tribes and castes of the Punjab and North–West Frontier Province. D. Ibbetson, E. Maclagan & H. A. Rose. Reprint, New Delhi: Rima, 1985. 3 vols.

A history of Christianity in India. S. C. Neill. Cambridge, UK: Cambridge University Press, 1984–85. 2 vols.

A history of Christianity in India from early times to St. Francis Xavier, AD 52–1542. G. M. Moraes. Bombay: Manaktalas, 1964. 320p.

A history of Sufism in India. S. A. A. Rizvi. Delhi, India: Munshiram Manoharlal, 1978–83. 2 vols.

A history of the Dalit Christians in India. J. C. B. Webster. San Francisco: Mellen Research University Press, 1992. 247p.

A select bibliography of periodical literature on India and Pakistan, 1947–70. P. I. Cheema. Islamabad, Pakistan: National Commission on Historical and Cultural Research, 1976–84. 3 vols. (Over 5,000 titles).

'A study of the Adventist church and the Dalit movement in India.' R. S. Rajarathinam. Ph.D. dissertation, Howard University, Washington, DC, 1993. 64p.

A time to remember: a history of the Redemptorists in India and Sri Lanka, 1938–1972. J. C. Morgan. Bangalore, India: Redemptorist Publications, India, 1992. 287p.

A united church: faith and order in the North India/Pakistan unity plan: a theological assessment. W. J. Marshall. Delhi: I.S.P.C.K, 1987. 159p.

'An Indian view of Christ,' A. Basu, in *Religion in the Pacific Era*, p.179–87. F. K. Flinn & T. Hendricks (eds). *Studies in the Pacific Era series.* New York: Paragon House, 1985.

An intellectual history of Islam in India. A. Ahmad. *Islamic Surveys*, no. 7. Edinburgh: Edinburgh University Press, 1969. 226p.

An introduction to Indian church history. C. B. Firth. Madras: Christian Literature Society, 1961. 263p.

Atlas of South Asia. A. K. Dutt & M. M. Geib. Boulder, CO, and London: Westview Press, 1987. 255p.

Baptism in the Malankara church: a study on the baptismal ritual of the Malankara church. M. Elenjikal. *Dharmaram College studies*, 14. Bangalore, India: Dharmaram Publications, 1974. 218p.

Baptist missions in Nagaland. J. Puthenpurakal. Calcutta: Firma KLM, 1984. 300p.

Bengal divided: Hindu communalism and partition, 1932–1947. J. Chatterji. New York: Cambridge University Press, 1994. 323p.

Bibliography of original Christian writings in India in Tamil. J. G. Muthuraj (comp). Ed., Mabry/H. P. & H. S. Wilson. [Serampore: Research Committee of the Board of Theological Education of the Senate of Serampore College, 1980]. 159p. (1,953 entries).

Bihar: church and people groups. S. V. Albert (ed). Madras: Church Growth Association of India, 1992. 168p.

'Bridegroom price in urban India: class, caste and 'dowry evil' among Christians in Madras,' L. Caplan, *Man*, n.s. no. 19 (1984), 216–33.

Buddhist monks and monasteries of India: their history and their contribution to Indian culture. S. Dutt. London: George Allen and Unwin, 1962. 397p.

Caste and Christianity. D. B. Forrester. London: Curzon/Humanities, 1979.

Catholic directory of India, 1972. New Delhi: St Paul International Book Centre, 1973. (In 1969 edition, 826p. Biennial or triennial).

Christian art in India. J. F. Butler. Madras: Christian Literature Society, 1986. 199p.

Christian ashrams: a new religious movement in contemporary India. H. Ralston. Lewiston, NY: Edwin Mellen Press, [1987]. 157p.

'Christian conversion movements among the hills tribes of North East India in the nineteenth and twentieth centuries,' F. S. Downs, in *Religion in South Asia: religious conversion and revival movements in South Asia in medieval and modern times*, p.155–74. G. A. Oddie (ed). 2nd ed. Columbia, MO: South Asia Publications, 1991.

Christian handbook of India, 1970. Nagpur: National Christian Council of India, 1971. 74p. (Previous edition 1959).

Christian mass movements in India: a study with recommendations. J. W. Pickett. New York: Abingdon Press, 1933.

Christian missions in North India 1813–1913: a case study of Meerut Division and Dehra Dun District. R. B. Sharma. Delhi: Mittal Publications, 1988.

Christianity and social change in northeast India: a study of the role of Christianity in social change among the Khasi–Jaintia Hill tribes of Meghalaya. O. L. Snaitang. Shillong: Vendrame Institute, 1993. 230p.

Christianity in India. South Asia ephemera collection India. New Delhi: Library of Congress Office, 1993–94. (3 parts with total of 69 microfiches; collections of pamphlets published during 1986-92, 1977-93, 1914-94 respectively).

Christianity in India and a brief history of the Mar Thoma Syrian Church. J. M. Thoma. Madras: K. M. Cherian, 1968. 50p.

Christianity in India: unique and universal mission. C. Turaicoami. Madras: Christian Literature Society, 1986. 296p.

Christianity in Indian dance forms. F. P. Barboza. Delhi: Sri Satguru Publications, 1990. 249p.

Christianity in the north eastern hills of South Asia: social impact and political implications. F. A. Quarishi. Dhaka, Bangladesh: University Press, 1987. 86p.

Churchless Christianity. Herbert E. Hoefer. Madras: Gurukul Lutheran Theological College and Research Institute, 1991.

Class and culture in urban India: fundamentalism in a Christian community. L. Caplan. Oxford, UK: Clarendon Press, 1987.

Conversion to Islam: Untouchables' strategy for protest in India. A. M. Mujahid. Chambersburg, PA: Anima Books, 1989. 167p.

Development of religion in south India. K. A. N. Sastri. Bombay: Orient Longman, 1963. 148p.

Encyclopaedia of caste, customs, rites and superstitions of the races of northern India. H. M. Elliot. Columbia, MO: South Asia Books, 1985. 2 vols.

Encyclopaedia of Puranic beliefs and practices. S. A. Dange. New Delhi: Narraing, 1986–90. 5 vols.

Encyclopedia India. J. S. Sharma. 2nd rev. ed. : Asia Book Corp., 1981. 2 vols.

Essays on Christianity in North–East India. F. S. Downs. *NEHU history series*, no. 4. New Delhi: Indus, 1994. 270p.

Festivals of India. B. N. Sharma. New Delhi: Abhinav, 1978. 156p.

Focus on North East Indian Christianity. O. M. Rao. Delhi: ISPCK, 1994. 94p.

Guide to Hindu religion. D. J. Dell et al. Boston: G. K. Hall, 1981. 461p.

Hindu and Christian in South–East India. G. A. Oddie. *London studies on South Asia*, no. 6. London: Curzon Press, 1991. 290p.

Hindu religion, customs, and manners. P. Thomas. 6th ed. Bombay: Taraporevala, 1975. 144p.

Hua–yen Buddhism: the jewel net of India. F. H. Cook. University Park, PA: Pennsylvania State University Press, 1969. 141p.

Iconographic dictionary of the Indian religions. G. Liebert. Leiden: E. J. Brill, 1976. 377p. (Hindu iconographic terminology).

India. B. K. Gupta & D. S. Kharbas. *World bibliographical series*, vol. 26. Oxford, UK: CLIO Press, 1984. 274p. (See especially 'Religion,' p.46–61).

India Christian handbook. M. Philip et al. , 1992–98. (Unpublished research project).

Indian Buddhism. A. K. Warder. 2nd ed. Delhi: Motilal Banarsidass, 1980. 627p.

Indian Christian directory. M. Aprem. Bangalore: Bangalore Parish, Church of the East, 1984. 264p.

Indian Christians: search for identity and struggle for autonomy. A. M. Mundadan. *Placid lecture series*, 4. Bangalore: Dharmaram Publications, 1984. 233p.

'Indian church growth dynamics.' K. C. Daniel. Thesis, Fuller Theological Seminary, Pasadena, CA, 1971. 161p.

'Indigenization of worship: a concern among South Indian Christians,' B. S. Hansen, in *South Asian religion and society*, p.245–62. A. Parpola & B. S. Hansen (eds). *Studies on Asian topics*, no. 11. London: Curzon Press, 1986.

Indo–Tibetan Buddhism: Indian Buddhists and their Tibetan successors. D. L. Snellgrove. London: Serindia; Boston: Shambhala, 1987. 2 vols., 640p.

Integral mission dynamics: an interdisciplinary study of the Catholic Church in India. A. Kanjamala (ed). New Dehli: Intercultural Publications, 1995. 688p.

Islam in India and Pakistan. No. 9 in section 22, *Islam*, in *Iconography of religions.* A. Schimmel. Leiden: E. J. Brill, 1982. 34p.

Islam in India and Pakistan: a religious history in India and Pakistan. M. T. Titus. *Christian students' library*, no. 20. Madras: Christian Literature Society, 1959. 328p.

Islam in the Indian subcontinent. A. Schimmel. *Handbuch der Orientalistik*, Abteilung 2, Band 4, Abschnitt 3. Leiden: The Netherlands, 1980. 303p.

Islamic modernism in India and Pakistan 1857–1964. A. Ahmad. London: Oxford University Press, 1967. 294p.

Kerala Christian directory, 1969. Ernakulam: Women Welfare Services, 1969. 747p. (All denominations).

Lands of the thunderbolt: Sikkim, Chumbi & Bhutan. L. J. L. Zetland. 1923; reprint, Berkeley, CA: Snow Lion Graphics, 1987. 316p.

Let the Indian church be Indian. S. Clarke. 2nd ed. Madras: Christian Literature Society, 1985. 155p.

Library of Indian Christian theology: a bibliography. K. Baago. Madras: Christian Literature Society for The Department of Research and Postgraduate Studies, United Theological College, Bangalore, 1969. 110p.

Living religions of the Indian people. N. MacNicol. New Delhi: YMCA, 1964.

Missionaries in India: continuities, changes, dilemmas. A. Shourie. New Delhi: ASA Publications, 1994. 317p.

Modern religious movements in India. J. N. Farquhar. 1914; New York: Garland, 1980. 471p.

Muslims and missionaries in pre–Mutiny India. A. A. Powell. *London studies on South Asia*, 7. Richmond, UK: Curzon Press, 1993. 349p.

Muslims in India: a bibliography of their religious, socio–economic and political literature. Satyaprakash. Haryana, India: Indian Documentation Service, 1985. 299p.

Muslims of India: their literature on education, politics, religion, socio–economic and communal problems. M. Haroon. Delhi: Indian Bibliographies Bureau, 1991.

'Nagaland church growth.' N. Y. Sema. Thesis, Bethel Theological Seminary, San Diego, CA, 1972. 127p. (Baptist expansion).

Origins of Muslim consciousness in India: a world–system perspective. S. N. Ahmad. *Contributions to the study of world history*, no. 29. New York: Greenwood Press, 1991. 326p.

Pioneers of indigenous Christianity. K. Baago. Madras: Christian Literature Society, 1969.

Quakers in India. M. Sykes. London: George Allen & Unwin, 1980. 190p.

Quest for an Indian church: an exploration of the possibilities opened up by Vatican II. K. Kunnumpuram & L. Fernando (eds). Anand, Gujarat, India: Gujarat Sahitya Prakash, 1993. 226p.

Readings in Indian Christian theology. R. S. Sugirtharajah & C. Hargreaves (eds). London: SPCK. 271p.

Rebellious prophets: a study of messianic movements in Indian religions. S. Fuchs. New York: Asia Publishing House, 1965. (77 movements described).

Religion in modern India. R. D. Baird (ed). 2nd rev. ed. New Dehli: Manohar Publications, 1989. 515p.

'Religion: numerical aspects,' in *The population of India and Pakistan*, p.177–94. K. Davis. New York: Russel & Russel, 1951. (Analysis of decennial censuses).

Religious festivals in South India and Sri Lanka. G. R. Welbon & G. E. Yocum (eds). *Studies on religion in South India and Sri Lanka*, vol. 1. New Delhi: Manohar Publications, 1982. 357p.

Rights of religious minorities in India. M. Subhash. New Delhi: National Book Organisation, 1988. 309

Ritual and religion among Muslims in India. I. Ahmad (ed). New Delhi: Manohar, 1981, 1984. 262p.

Saints, goddesses, and kings: Muslims and Christians in South Indian Society, 1700–1900. S. Bayly. *Cambridge South Asian studies*, 43. Cambridge, UK: Cambridge University Press, 1989. 519p.

Social and religious reform movements in the nineteenth and twentieth centuries. S. P. Sen (ed). Calcutta: Institute of Historical Studies, 1979. 536p.

The Buddha and his dharma. B. R. Ambedkar. 2nd ed. Bombay: Siddharth, 1974. 430p.

The camphor flame: popular Hinduism and society in India. C. J. Fuller. Princeton, NJ: Princeton University Press, 1992. 328p.

The Catholic community in India. K. N. Subramanyam. Madras: Macmillan, 1970. 148p.

The Chaitanya movement: a study of Vaishnavism in Bengal. M. T. Kennedy. *The religious life of India.* 1925; reprint, 1993. 280p.

The Christ of the Indian road. E. S. Jones. 1925; reprint, 1996. 187p.

The Christian community and change in nineteenth century North India. J. C. B. Webster. Delhi: Macmillan, 1976. 293p.

'The Christian minority in India, 1947–1980.' A. K. Mondal. Th.D. thesis, Graduate Theological Union, San Francisco, 1984. 329p.

The Christians of Kerala: history, belief, and ritual among the Yakoba. S. Visvanathan. Madras: Oxford University Press, 1993. 302p.

The churchman's handbook 1989. Madras: The Christian Literature Society, [1988]. 323p.

The crown of Hinduism. J. N. Farquhar. 1913; reprint, 1971. 458p.

The encyclopedias of India. H. Scholberg. New Delhi: Promilla and Co.; Columbia, MO: South Asia Books, 1986. 119p.

'The first independence movement among Indian Christians,' K. Baago, *Indian church history review*, 1, 1 (1967), 65–78.

'The growth of Pentecostal churches in South India.' T. C. George. Thesis, Fuller Theological Seminary, Pasadena, CA, 1975.

The history of Buddhism in India and Tibet. Bu-ston. Trans., E. Obermiller. *Bibliotheca Indo-Buddhica*, 26. Delhi: Sri Satguru, 1986. 231p.

The impact of Christianity on the tribes of Northeast India. S. Karotemprel. Shillong, India: Sacred Heart Theological College, 1994. 63p.

The Indian church: identity and fulfilment. M. Zachariah. Madras: Christian Literature Society, 1971. 220p.

The movement around Subba Rao: a study of the Hindu–Christian movement around K. Subba Rao in Andhra Pradesh. K. Baago. Madras: Christian Literature Society, 1968. 32p.

The population of India and Pakistan. K. Davis. Princeton, NJ: Princeton University Press, 1951. 279p.

The religion of India: the sociology of Hinduism and Buddhism. M. Weber. New York: Free Press, 1958. 392p.

The religions of India. A. Barth. Trans., J. Wood. 1882; reprint, Delhi: Low Price Publications, 1990. 333p.

The religious culture of India: power, love, and wisdom. F. Hardy. New York: Cambridge University Press, 1993. 627p.

The rise of Islam and the Bengal frontier, 1204–1760. R. M. Eaton. *Comparative studies on Muslim societies*, 17. Berkeley, CA: University of California Press, 1993. 386p.

'The role of Christian education in the evangelization of India.' G. V. Mathai. Thesis, Talbot Theological Seminary, La Mirada, CA, 1970.

The role of the Christian community in a secular state: India as a case study. A. V. Thomas. Ann Arbor, MI: University Microfilms, 1970. 536p. (Dissertation).

The Sikh diaspora: migration and the experience beyond Punjab. N. G. Barrier & V. A. Dusenbery (eds). Delhi: Chanakya Publications, 1989. 362p.

The SPCK in India, 1710–1985: an account of the work of the Society for Promoting Christian Knowledge, London, and the Indian SPCK. V. Koilpillai. Delhi: I.S.P.C.K, 1985. 80p.

The St. Thomas Christian encyclopaedia of India. G. Menachery (ed). Trichur, India: St. Thomas Christian Encyclopaedia, 1973–76. 2 vols.

The story of the Christian Church in India and Pakistan. S. C. Neill. Grand Rapids, MI: Eerdmans, 1970. 183p.

The Syrian Christians of Kerala. S. G. Pothan. Bombay: Asian Publishing House, 1963.

The village gods of South India. H. Whitehead. *The religious life of India.* 1921; reprint, 1988. 176p.

Women and religion in India: an annotated bibliography of sources in English, 1975–92. N. A. Falk. Kalamazoo, MI: New Issues Press, College of Arts and Sciences, Western Michigan University, 1994. 241p.

Country Table 2. **Organized churches and denominations in India.**

Official name (bold type = church with over 10% of all affiliated) 1	*Begun* 2	*Type* 3	*Counc* 4	*Congs* 5	*Adults* 6	*Affiliated 1970* 7	*Affiliated 1995* 8	*G%* 9	*Names, notes, and other statistics* (see Codebook, Part 3) 10
Advent Christian Conference	1882	P-Adv	xF..E	63	3,700	5,000	6,730	1.20	M=AAM(USA). 89% Tamil, 8% Telugu. 17 schools. 13n,5x,6f,1h,1p,W=75%,175Y.
Anglican Church of India	c1960	I-Ang	.....	114	150,000	160,000	225,000	1.37	Schism of Outcastes ex Ch of South India. Almost all in Kerala. 141n.
Apatani Christian Fellowship		I-Bap	.....	127	3,000	–	4,000	0.05	In Arunachal Pradesh. Independent Baptists.
Apostolic Christian Assembly	1948	I-3aI	.....	144	25,000	3,500	44,851	10.74	*ACA.* Strong appeal to Hindus; HQ Madras (12,000 in mother church).
Apostolic Church (GB)	1929	P-PeA	ZG..E	5	3,000	2,000	4,000	2.81	M=Apostolic Church Missionary Movement (UK). HQ Bangalore Madras. 2f.
Apostolic Church of Pentecost in India	1946	P-Pe1	x....	140	11,250	5,000	19,000	5.49	M=ACP(Canada). Malayalam-speaking, all in Kerala state. HQ Kottayam. 176n.
Apostolic Fellowship Tabernacle (Ind)		I-3aI	.TT.T	20	2,000	3,000	4,000	0.05	*Ind=Independent.* Madras area. Workers' training centre, 2 orphanages. 18n,12m.
Apostolic Pentecostal Church, India		I-3oI	.....	200	20,000	5,000	30,000	0.05	Oneness body. Mainly Malayalis. HQ Perunkodavia, Trivandrum (Kerala).
Armenian Apostolic Church: D India	1704	O-Arm	Ewc..	10	7,000	10,000	12,000	0.73	*D India & Far East.* Gregorians. Based on Calcutta. Under C Echmiadzin (USSR). 2r.
Asia Evangelistic Fellowship	1984	I-Non	.....	3	100	–	250	9.09	M=AEF. No-church movement.
Assam Baptist Convention	1927	P-Bap	Tv...	266	24,597	7,752	30,000	5.56	M=ABMS(Australia). 1962 applied to WCC. Garo Boro.
Assemblies of Christ Church		I-3oI	.....	20	1,000	–	2,000	0.05	Member of Apostolic World Christian Fellowship. HQ Mandapeta.
Assemblies of God	1933	P-Pe2	ZG..H	140	6,300	5,000	14,000	4.20	1933, M=AoG(Australia), HQ Poona; 1936, AoG(UK), around Madras, Bombay. 4f.
Assemblies of God (North & South India)	1906	P-Pe2	ZF..Z	2,795	259,427	40,000	410,000	9.76	*AGNI*(NIndia), *SIAG*(SIndia), M=AoG(USA). 70% in south. 290n,41f,6h,6s(214).
Assemblies of Jesus Christ		I-Fun	.TT.T	10	1,000	1,000	2,000	0.05	Local independent congregations, in Kakinada (Andhra Pradesh). Telugu-speaking.
Assemblies (Jehova Shammah)	1941	I-CBr	x....	1,350	140,000	120,000	216,000	2.38	F=Brother Bakht Singh. Chaubra/Sikh converts. Strong in AP; also abroad. M=WEC. 30f.
Assembly Ch of JC Full Gospel	1930	I-3fI	.....	300	20,000	6,000	40,000	7.88	*ACJCFG.* In Megalaya, HQ Shillong. Schism ex PCNEI. 1966, pentecostalized. Khasis, Garos.
Assembly Hall Churches	c1985	I-3nC	.....	8	192	–	500	10.00	*Little Flock. Local Churches.* Movement begun 1922 in China.
Association of Oriya Baptist Churches	1910	P-Bap	....W	550	13,800	8,442	45,800	7.00	*Ganjama Mala OB Mandali.* M=CBOMB. 90% Madiga Harijan. 11n,4s,W=50%,205Y.
Assoc of Regular Indep Chs of India	1935	I-Bap	xTT.T	70	3,000	4,000	6,000	1.64	*Fellowship of Baptist Chs. NT Bapt Ch Assoc.* M=BMM. Assam. 3n,3x,19f,2H,W=85%,140Y.
Association of Vineyard Chs	c1986	I-3cI	.....	2	400	–	1,000	11.11	Churches linked with M=AVC(USA).
Baptist Bible Believers Assembly	1968	I-Bap	.TT.T	6	300	500	800	1.90	Begun for Koya Aborigines (Hill Tribes) in Hyderabad area, AP. 2n.
Baptist Christian Association	1945	I-Bap	xF..E	145	2,762	2,500	6,910	4.15	*Ev Baptist Assoc.* M=CIBM(CBI). Took over KCIHM(UK). 44n,3x,24f,2h,1s,120Y.
Baptist Church of Mizoram	1902	P-Bap	T....	394	91,912	50,411	137,000	4.08	*Zoram Baptist Kohhran.* 1970 refused to join CNI. M=BMS. 20n,5x,1p,1p,W=30%,2261Y.
Baptist International Missions	1978	I-Bap	.....	26	4,000	–	10,000	5.88	M=BIM(USA). Foreign mission from USA.
Baptist Union of North India	1947	P-Bap	.....	137	18,300	25,000	30,000	0.73	Scattered congregations across the north. Formed at Partition. 45n.
Believers' Churches in India	c1960	I-3nI	x....	3,000	120,000	20,000	200,000	9.65	Based on indigenous ministry M=Gospel for Asia (GFA). F=K.P. Yohanan. 8,500 Indian workers.
Bengal Baptist Fellowship		P-Bap	T....	44	1,225	–	2,000	0.05	Mainline Baptists.
Bengal-Orissa-Bihar Baptist Convention	1836	P-Bap	TuE.W	170	9,500	8,000	19,700	3.67	M=ABFMS. 37% Santal, 25% Orlya, 12% Bengali, 12% Hindi, 15n,W=75%,183Y.
Bethel Assemblies	1963	I-3cI	.....	25	2,000	200	4,500	13.26	Village churches. Street evangelizing, literature distribution. M=CAM.
Bethel Pentecostal Church	1917	P-Pe2	.....	60	3,000	2,500	6,000	3.56	M=Bethel Pentecostal Temple (Seattle, USA). In Bihar, UP. 55n,2x,W=52%,537Y.
Bharat Evangelical Fellowship	1952	I-3cI	.....	29	1,500	200	3,000	11.44	*BEF.* Work among Madigas, Malas, tribals. 30 Indian missionaries. M=CAM.
Bharatiya General Conf Mennonite Chs	1900	P-Men	G...x	131	16,000	6,394	22,000	5.07	M=GCMC(USA). 95% Harijan Gara. Raipur. 49n,7x29f,3H,1s,W=35%,165Y,100z.
Bharatiya Jukta Christa PM	1958	I-Men	.....	30	2,500	3,110	6,250	2.83	PM=*Prachar Mandhi.*
Bible Believing Churches in India		I-Fun	.TT.T	5	700	1,000	1,400	0.05	Baptist schism in Hubli (Mysore) and Salem district, South India. 1n,2m.
Bible Brethren Fellowship	1973	I-3cI	.....	52	5,000	–	10,000	4.55	*BBF.* 52 full-time Indian workers. M=CAM.
Bible Christian Mission		I-3nI	.....	1,812	20,000	–	30,000	0.05	*BCM.* Massive church-planting across North India.
Bible Crusade Missionary Society	1934	I-Non	.....	20	2,300	2,800	3,500	0.90	Formerly Victory Prayer Crusade. Madras. Tract work. 10n,1h,W=45%,36Y,42z.
Bible Mission	1938	I-Lut	.....	110	11,000	15,000	18,000	0.73	Guntur district, AP. Telugu-speaking. HQ Railpet. 40n,W=70%,150Y.
Bible Pattern Church		I-3pI	.....	6	500	1,000	1,500	0.05	Mission from UK, split ex Elim Foursquare Gospel Alliance. British-Israelite.
Bible Presbyterian Church of India	1936	I-Ref	.TT.T	3	50	200	100	-2.73	*BPCI.* M=IBPFM(USA). HQ Kanpur, UP. Declining in numbers; defections to RPCES.
Bihar Mennonite Mandli	1940	P-Men	G...w	16	700	1,000	1,270	0.96	M=MCNA(Bihar MM). Tribal; 85% Oraon, 15% Munda. 9n,3x,6f,1H,1k,1p,1s,W=60%,19Y.
Blessing Youth Mission	1971	I-3cI	.....	95	5,000	–	10,000	4.17	*BYM.* HQ Sitteri Hills, Tamil Nadu. 185n. M=CAM.
Brethren in Christ Church in India	1904	P-Men	GF..x	42	1,920	1,800	5,490	4.56	In Bihar state. M=BiCC(USA). HQ Barjora. 4n,3x,15f,1H,1p,W=39%,65Y,20z.
Brethren in Christ-Orissa	1981	P-Men	.....	14	1,300	–	2,000	7.14	M=BiCC(USA).
Broadsheet Readers' Clubs	c1980	I-3nI	.....	80	1,000	–	3,000	6.67	Readers of Gospel Broadsheets produced by M=WEC(UK).
Cachar Hill Tribes Presb Synod		P-Ref	.....	234	21,000	–	28,561	0.05	In Assam. 42n.
Catholic Church in India:	1319	R-LEr	PxF.R	8,592	8,414,260	8,432,713	14,285,857	2.13	C=35+15+122. 8892n 6632x 14787m 70332w 329916Yy
P Goa/East Indies (AD Goa, Damao)	1533	R-Lat	Ps	163	265,000	249,037	450,360	2.40	Goa, DNH. Konkani. 1s. 382n 257x 482m 869w 5567Yy
M Agra	1886	R-Lat	Ps	6	5,200	5,458	8,897	1.97	UP, Rajasthan. Hindi, Urdu. M=OFMCap. 39n 5x 11m 180w 134Yy
D Ajmer & Jaipur	1913	R-Lat	Ps	56	6,500	20,390	10,959	-2.45	Rajasthan, MP. Hindi, Bhil Boli. 41n 22x 30m 524w 240Yy
D Allahabad	1886	R-Lat	Ps	33	5,400	8,604	9,222	0.28	UP. Hindi, Urdu, Bengali. 1s. 62n 12x 45m 312w 170Yy
D Bareilly	1989	R-Lat	Ps	36	2,900	–	4,919	16.67	0.05% Roman Catholic. 28n 11x 17m 157w 119Yy
D Bijnor *(Syro-Malabarese)*	1972	R-SyM	Ocmi	37	600	–	1,036	4.35	UP. Hindi. Detached D Meerut. 3n 32x 66m 160w 121Yy
D Gorakhpur	1984	R-SyM	Os	42	1,000	–	1,673	9.09	Catholics 0.01% of population. 1n 24x 30m 157w 46Yy
D Jhansi	1940	R-Lat	Ps	23	3,300	2,472	5,574	3.31	UP. Hindi. 45n 7x 20m 207w 130Yy
D Lucknow	1940	R-Lat	Ps	24	4,200	5,872	7,090	0.76	UP. Formerly M=OFMCap. Hindi. 50n 9x 21m 263w 112Yy
D Meerut	1956	R-Lat	Ps	49	13,600	13,481	23,049	2.17	UP. Hindi, Urdu. M=OFMCap. 54n 27x 59m 433w 438Yy
D Udaipur	1984	R-Lat	Ps	52	16,300	–	27,596	9.09	Catholics 0.4% of population. 40n 11x 13m 188w 670Yy
D Varanasi (Benares)	1946	R-Lat	Ps	32	8,000	9,034	13,725	1.69	UP. Hindi, Bhodjpuri. 58n 38x 100m 382w 373Yy
M Bangalore	1940	R-Lat	Ps	93	149,000	129,758	252,460	2.70	Karnataka. Kannada, Tamil. 1s. 104n 425x 2137m 4895w 9180Yy
D Bellary	1928	R-Lat	Ps	34	13,000	11,520	22,100	2.64	Karnataka, Kannada, Tamil. M=OFM. 49n 4x 4m 185w 680Yy
D Chikmagalur	1963	R-Lat	Ps	30	22,000	36,578	37,741	0.13	Karnataka. Kannada, Konkani. 40n 13x 17m 221w 598Yy
D Karwar	1976	R-Lat	Ps	64	29,000	–	49,800	5.26	Catholics 3%. 68n 6x 8m 209w 820Yy
D Mangalore	1886	R-Lat	Ps	167	194,500	219,282	329,707	1.64	Karnataka. Kannada, Konkani. 1s. 240n 87x 114m 1422w 4197Yy
D Mysore	1886	R-Lat	Ps	53	47,000	42,401	79,791	2.56	Karnataka. Kannada, Konkani. 80n 38x 203m 605w 1908Yy
D Shimoga	1988	R-Lat	Ps	18	13,800	–	23,360	14.29	Catholics 0.6%. 24n 2x 2m 130w 438Yy
M Bhopal	1963	R-Lat	Pmsfs	23	5,600	3,818	9,500	3.71	MP. Hindi, some Urdu. M=MSF,SJ. 38n 34x 92m 307w 290Yy
D Ambikapur	1977	R-Lat	Ps	34	35,000	–	59,464	5.56	Catholics 3%. 44n 26x 46m 227w 1688Yy
D Indore	1935	R-Lat	Psvd	26	14,700	31,232	24,983	-0.89	MP. Hindi, Bhili, Korku, Malvi. 38n 52x 414m 320w 1019Yy
D Jabalpur	1932	R-Lat	Ps	48	15,500	16,762	26,300	1.82	MP. Hindi. 28 expatriates. M=O Praem. 52n 21x 45m 209w 552Yy
D Jagdalpur *(Syro-Malabarese)*	1972	R-SyM	Ocmi	28	2,300	–	3,922	4.35	Detached from PA Raipur. 4n 41x 64m 148w 99Yy
D Khandwa	1977	R-Lat	Ps	27	16,200	–	27,475	5.56	Catholics 1%. 34n 17x 22m 211w 450Yy
D Raigarh	1951	R-Lat	Ps	45	131,500	180,329	222,942	0.85	MP. Hindi. 106n 52x 63m 339w 4431Yy
D Raipur	1964	R-Lat	Ps	59	25,000	29,500	42,450	1.47	MP. Hindi, 7 others. Fast growth. M=SAC. 75n 28x 34m 334w 725Yy
D Sagar *(Syro-Malabarese)*	1968	R-SyM	Ocmi	36	2,100	1,612	3,512	3.16	MP. Hindi. Under M Bhopal. 3n 30x 38m 290w 45Yy
D Satna *(Syro-Malabarese)*	1968	R-SyM	Ocv	9	1,200	685	2,174	4.73	M. Hindi. Under M Bhopal. M=CV. 15n 20x 37m 120w 71Yy
D Ujjain *(Syro-Malabarese)*	1968	R-SyM	Osmst	35	1,760	440	3,019	8.01	MP. Hindi. Under M Bhopal. M=SMST. 6n 54x 153m 202w 99Yy
M Bombay	1886	R-Lat	Ps	131	323,000	435,995	548,665	0.92	Maharashtra. Marathi. 1s. 329n 288x 440m 1611w 7580Yy
D Ahmedabad	1949	R-Lat	Psj	42	44,000	48,876	74,575	1.70	Gujarat. Gujarati, Konkani. M=SJ. 54n 110x 147m 335w 1332Yy
D Baroda	1966	R-Lat	Ps	63	33,000	11,269	56,750	6.68	Gujarat. Gujarati, Adivasi. M=SJ. 25n 79x 96m 270w 2442Yy
D Belgaum	1953	R-Lat	Ps	26	18,000	55,759	31,000	-2.32	Karnataka. Konkani, Kannada. 46n 44x 90m 222w 460Yy
D Kalyan *(Syro-Malabarese)*	1988	R-Lat	Ps	155	59,000	–	100,000	14.29	M=MCBS. 21n 48x 63m 109w 425Yy
D Nashik	1987	R-Lat	Ps	26	45,000	–	76,500	12.50	Catholics 0.6%. 14n 78x 137m 224w 1554Yy
D Poona (Pune)	1886	R-Lat	Ps	152	50,700	122,950	85,984	-1.42	Maharashtra. Marathi. 1p,1s. 71n 144x 658m 477w 1319Yy
D Rajkot *(Syro-Malabarese)*	1977	R-SyM	Ocmi	39	5,000	–	8,400	5.56	M=CMI. 0n 38x 99m 251w 104Yy
M Calcutta	1886	R-Lat	Ps	64	73,600	82,389	124,708	1.67	West Bengal. Bengali, Hindi. 1s. 76n 150x 272m 920w 2692Yy
D Baruipur	1977	R-Lat	Ps	13	26,000	–	44,350	5.56	M=SJ. 20n 13x 38m 70w 823Yy
D Darjeeling	1929	R-Lat	Ps	48	37,000	26,694	63,020	3.50	WB, Sikkim. Nepali, Tibetan. 62n 55x 141m 326w 2242Yy
D Jalpaiguri	1952	R-Lat	Ps	20	51,000	47,571	86,665	2.43	WBengal. Oraon, Munda, Sadri. 32n 11x 29m 146w 3152Yy
D Krishnagar	1886	R-Lat	Psdb	12	27,000	14,665	46,346	4.71	West Bengal. Bengali, Santali. 10n 39x 52m 231w 3977Yy
D Raiganj	1978	R-Lat	Ps	19	31,000	–	53,646	5.88	M=SJ. 28n 17x 31m 110w 2810Yy
M Changanacherry *(Syro-Malabarese)*	1887	R-SyM	Os	271	208,000	387,870	353,000	-0.38	Kerala. Malayalam, Tamil. 1s. 261n 400x 477m 2360w 10214Yy
D Kanjirapally *(Syro-Malabarese)*	1977	R-SyM	Os	140	94,000	–	159,920	5.56	Population is 15% Roman Catholic. 144n 46x 63m 1298w 2550Yy
D Kottayam *(Syro-Malabares)*	1911	R-SyM	Os	130	78,000	84,342	132,465	1.82	Malayalam. For Southists. 130n 25x 72m 1091w 2208Yy
D Palia *(Syro-Malabarese)*	1950	R-SyM	Os	188	195,000	266,560	331,456	0.88	Kerala. Malayalam. 354n 106x 119m 3982w 4670Yy
M Cuttack-Bhubaneswar	1937	R-Lat	Ps	25	24,000	47,088	41,478	-0.51	Orissa. Oriya, Kui, Savara. M=SFD. 36n 28x 41m 143w 1717Yy
D Balasore	1968	R-Lat	Pcm	40	8,900	2,956	15,104	6.74	Orissa. Oriya, Santali, Hindi. M=CM. 23n 17x 25m 121w 1309Yy
D Berhampur	1974	R-Lat	Ps	26	34,000	–	58,702	4.76	New diocese, 0.8% Roman Catholic. 16n 51x 82m 166w 822Yy
D Rourkela	1979	R-Lat	Ps	31	107,000	–	182,382	6.25	M=SVD. 31n 59x 92m 272w 5576Yy
D Sambalpur	1951	R-Lat	Psvd	21	18,000	126,267	31,212	-5.44	Orissa. Oriya, Kharia, Kisani. M=SVD. 15n 45x 49m 122w 718Yy
M Delhi	1910	R-Lat	Ps	107	34,000	24,855	58,000	3.45	UTC. Hindi, Punjabi, Urdu. 1s. 66n 93x 247m 472w 1487Yy
D Jammu-Srinagar	1952	R-Lat	Pmhm	17	5,300	3,619	9,000	3.71	J & K. Kashmiri, Urdu, Dogri. M=MHM,OFMCap. 11n 16x 24m 120w 1000Yy
D Jullundur	1952	R-Lat	Pofmc	73	35,000	21,983	59,974	4.10	Punjab, Chandigarh, Hariyana,HP. 37n 40x 54m 438w 2712Yy
D Simla & Chandigarh	1959	R-Lat	Ps	29	6,500	6,866	11,280	2.01	In 4 states. Punjabi. M=SDR. 21n 40x 57m 191w 435Yy
MM Ernakulam-Angamaly *(Syro-Malab)*	1896	R-SyM	Os	320	236,000	302,000	401,830	1.15	Kerala. One of only 2 Major ADs (also MM Lviv) 294n 250x 520m 3771w 8748Yy
D Irinjalakuda *(Syro-Malabarese)*	1978	R-SyM	Os	142	144,000	–	244,566	5.88	New diocese, Catholics 22%. 133n 45x 53m 1559w 4443Yy
D Kothamangalam *(Syro-Malab)*	1956	R-SyM	Os	224	227,000	206,129	385,500	2.54	Kerala. Malayalam, Tamil. 267n 77x 106m 2930w 6060Yy
D Mananthavady *(Syro-Malab)*	1973	R-SyM	Os	154	90,000	–	153,131	4.55	Recent diocese. Population 1.8% Catholic. 110n 50x 223m 863w 7509Yy
D Polghat *(Syro-Malabarese)*	1974	R-SyM	Os	76	34,000	–	57,908	4.76	Recently established. 54n 71x 110m 1143w 981Yy
D Tellicherry *(Syro-Malabarese)*	1953	R-SyM	Os	204	156,000	312,711	265,486	-0.65	Kerala. Malayalam. 168n 40x 49m 1090w 4519Yy
D Thamarasserry *(Syro-Malab)*	1986	R-SyM	Os	114	66,000	–	112,280	11.11	One of 4 new Syro-Malabarese dioceses. 80n 54x 58m 682w 1832Yy
D Trichur *(Syro-Malabarese)*	1887	R-SyM	Os	251	241,000	445,101	409,875	-0.33	Kerala, Malayalam. 1s. 199n 10x 283m 3412w 7336Yy
M Hyderabad	1886	R-Lat	Ps	56	48,000	37,070	82,536	3.25	AP. Telugu, Kannada. 1s. 81n 80x 127m 721w 1393Yy
D Cuddapah	1976	R-Lat	Ps	47	38,000	–	65,000	5.26	New diocese, 3.2% Roman Catholic. 74n 12x 24m 225w 2600Yy
D Eluru	1976	R-Lat	Ps	65	97,000	–	165,016	5.26	New diocese, 1.4% Roman Catholic. 78n 46x 184m 382w 14640Yy
D Guntur	1940	R-Lat	Ps	52	81,000	75,815	137,307	2.40	AP. Telugu. 10 expatriate RCs. 57n 42x 62m 448w 6138Yy
D Khammam	1988	R-Lat	Ps	34	52,000	–	88,824	14.29	New diocese, 4% Catholic. 23n 26x 40m 132w 3291Yy
D Kurnool	1967	R-Lat	Ps	38	31,600	38,523	53,680	1.34	AP. Telugu, Urdu, Kannada, Tamil. M=PIME. 39n 15x 17m 232w 1420Yy
D Nalgonda	1976	R-Lat	Ps	35	33,000	–	56,000	5.26	New diocese, 1.1% Catholic. 55n 17x 26m 257w 651Yy
D Nellore	1928	R-Lat	Ps	51	31,600	50,000	53,631	0.28	AP. Telugu. Formerly M=MHM. 65n 8x 9m 192w 1202Yy

Continued opposite

Country Table 2–continued

Official name (bold type = church with over 10% of all affiliated) 1	*Begun* 2	*Type* 3	*Counc* 4	*Congs* 5	*Adults* 6	*Affiliated 1970* 7	*Affiliated 1995* 8	*G%* 9	*Names, notes, and other statistics* (see Codebook, Part 3) 10
D Srikakulam	1993	R-Lat	Ps	17	22,000	–	37,585	50.00	Very recent diocese, 1.6% Catholic. 9n 14x 22m 68w 1358Yy
D Vijayawada	1933	R-Lat	Ps	66	122,000	171,785	188,474	0.37	AP. Telugu. Formerly M=PIME. 1p. 66n 59x 106m 570w 4816Yy
D Visakhapatnam	1886	R-Lat	Pmsfs	42	54,000	89,377	91,629	0.10	AP, Orissa. Telugu, Oriya. M=MSFS. 41n 44x 54m 406w 6212Yy
D Warangal	1952	R-Lat	Ps	36	26,000	72,156	44,401	-1.92	AP. Telugu, Urdu. M=PIME. 39n 23x 31m 278w 1435Yy
M Madras & Mylapore	1606	R-Lat	Ps	124	216,000	164,558	367,217	3.26	TN. Tamil, Telugu. 1p,1s. 136n 219x 464m 1602w 6862Yy
D Coimbatore	1886	R-Lat	Ps	62	105,000	92,640	178,632	2.66	TN. Tamil, Malayalam. 92n 10x 50m 818w 1760Yy
D Ootacamund	1955	R-Lat	Ps	56	46,000	52,450	79,000	1.65	TN. Tamil, Kanarese. 1s. 85n 23x 68m 530w 1588Yy
D Vellore	1952	R-Lat	Ps	60	69,000	81,284	117,782	1.49	TN. Tamil, Telugu. M=SDB. 93n 46x 137m 566w 2392Yy
M Madurai	1938	R-Lat	Ps	53	160,000	256,876	271,000	0.21	TN. Tamil, Malayalam. M=SJ. 1s. 80n 99x 209m 1050w 2640Yy
D Kottar	1930	R-Lat	Ps	104	236,000	274,156	399,526	1.52	TN. Tamil. No expatriates. 145n 32x 44m 530w 8473Yy
D Palayamkottai	1973	R-Lat	Ps	31	55,000	–	94,000	4.55	TN. Tamil. Recently begun. 35n 29x 112m 275w 2238Yy
D Sivagangai	1987	R-Lat	Ps	54	105,000	–	178,982	12.50	TN. Tamil. New diocese. 65n 31x 53m 310w 2750Yy
D Tiruchchirappalli	1846	R-Lat	Ps	109	222,000	174,351	376,642	3.13	TN. Tamil. Trichinopoly. 1s. 104n 87x 238m 1000w 7147Yy
D Tuticorin	1923	R-Lat	Ps	77	177,000	165,325	300,090	2.41	TN. Tamil. No expatriates. 144n 8x 49m 684w 5590Yy
M Nagpur	1887	R-Lat	Ps	27	11,000	11,383	18,700	2.01	Maharashtra, MP. Marathi. 1s. 50n 40x 301m 252w 310Yy
D Amravati	1955	R-Lat	Pmsfs	22	4,200	19,951	7,230	-3.98	M. Marathi, Korku Gondi, Urdu. M=MSFS. 19n 5x 5m 177w 136Yy
D Aurangabad	1977	R-Lat	Ps	19	9,600	–	16,301	5.56	Recent jurisdiction. 25n 19x 21m 100w 140Yy
D Chanda *(Syro-Malabarese)*	1968	R-SyM	Ocmi	158	13,900	9,235	23,682	3.84	Maharashtra, AP. Marathi, Telugu. M=CMI. 8n 52x 94m 243w 735Yy
M Pondicherry & Cuddalore	1886	R-Lat	Ps	74	152,000	167,555	258,290	1.75	Pondicherry. Tamil, French. 1p. 117n 13x 26m 895w 4346Yy
D Kumbakonam	1899	R-Lat	Ps	70	113,000	143,627	192,954	1.19	Tamil Nadu. tamil. 17 expatriates. 94n 23x 61m 487w 3849Yy
D Salem	1930	R-Lat	Ps	56	64,000	62,195	108,850	2.26	Tamil Nadu. Tamil, Telugu. 103n 18x 130m 549w 2077Yy
D Tanjore (Thanjavur)	1952	R-Lat	Ps	69	123,000	130,045	209,000	1.92	Tamil Nadu. Tamil, Telugu. 124n 17x 27m 475w 3789Yy
M Ranchi	1927	R-Lat	Ps	43	91,800	318,665	155,591	-2.83	Bihar, ANI. Santali. M=SJ. 1p,1s. 53n 204x 325m 635w 3234Yy
D Bhagalpur	1956	R-Lat	Ptor	40	30,600	24,093	52,000	3.13	Bihar. Santali, Hindi, Malto. M=TOR. 61n 22x 77m 245w 1400Yy
D Daltonganj	1971	R-Lat	Psj	30	44,000	–	75,336	4.17	Bihar. Santali, Hindi. M=SJ. 55n 67x 141m 481w 1751Yy
D Dumka	1952	R-Lat	Ps	28	40,000	46,198	67,865	1.55	Bihar. Santali, Hindi, Mundari. M=SJ. 45n 47x 93m 231w 2668Yy
D Gumla	1993	R-Lat	Ps	34	78,000	–	133,331	50.00	Very recent diocese. 67n 21x 29m 186w 2530Yy
D Jamshedpur	1962	R-Lat	Psj	29	28,000	20,794	48,000	3.40	Bihar, WB. Santali, Ho, Mundari. M=SJ. 43n 56x 112m 444w 1240Yy
D Muzaffarpur	1980	R-Lat	Ps	21	5,600	–	9,500	6.67	M=SJ. 19n 34x 56m 238w 223Yy
D Patna	1919	R-Lat	Psj	43	36,000	45,917	60,975	1.14	Bihar. Hindi, Nepali, Tibetan. M=SJ. 47n 80x 153m 447w 685Yy
D Port Blair	1984	R-Lat	Ps	9	18,000	–	30,807	9.09	Recently begun. 1n 21x 22m 66w 627Yy
D Simdega	1993	R-Lat	Ps	24	92,000	–	156,059	50.00	New diocese. 46n 16x 21m 136w 3986Yy
M Shillong	1934	R-Lat	Psdb	29	157,000	136,352	265,628	2.70	Meghalaya. Assamese, tribals. 1s. M=SDB. 50n 127x 291m 384w 13684Yy
D Dibrugarh	1951	R-Lat	Psdb	36	56,000	77,523	96,450	0.88	Nagaland, ARP. Assam, tribals. M=SDB. 49n 36x 42m 200w 4070Yy
D Diphu	1983	R-Lat	Ps	15	20,500	–	34,874	8.33	Recent diocese. 11n 12x 23m 68w 1782Yy
D Guwahati (Gauhati)	1992	R-Lat	Ps	20	39,000	–	66,689	33.33	M=SDB. 15n 41x 49m 153w 3000Yy
D Imphal	1980	R-Lat	Ps	40	36,000	–	62,248	6.67	In NorthEast India. 37n 42x 58m 153w 1650Yy
D Kohima	1980	R-Lat	Ps	30	21,600	–	36,736	6.67	Northeast. New diocese. 31n 51x 124m 204w 2043Yy
D Silchar (Haflong)	1952	R-Lat	Ps	23	17,000	9,856	29,332	4.46	Tripura, Mizoram. Nizo, Khasi. 19n 27x 44m 125w 1704Yy
D Tezpur	1964	R-Lat	Ps	25	86,000	72,448	145,600	2.83	Assam, ARP. Assamese, tribals. M=SDB. 34n 16x 18m 155w 5383Yy
D Tura	1973	R-Lat	Ps	25	83,000	–	141,606	4.55	New diocese. 26n 26x 39m 109w 6747Yy
M Trivandrum *(Syro-Malankarese)*	1932	R-Mal	Os	614	139,000	165,016	236,200	1.44	Kerala. Malayalam, Tamil. 1p. 183n 43x 103m 765w 3450Yy
D Battery *(Syro-Malankarese)*	1978	R-Mal	Ooic	98	12,100	–	20,550	5.88	M=OIC. 52n 8x 8m 167w 237Yy
D Tiruvalla *(Syro-Malankarese)*	1932	R-Mal	Os	173	31,700	36,573	53,750	1.55	Kerala, TN, Karnataka. Malayalam. 107n 38x 49m 232w 641Yy
M Verapoly	1886	R-Lat	Ps	136	139,000	224,779	236,253	0.20	Kerala. Malayalam. 1s. 118n 85x 237m 799w 3735Yy
D Alleppey	1952	R-Lat	Ps	30	80,000	89,306	135,000	1.67	Kerala. Malayalam. No aliens. 57n 9x 12m 263w 2031Yy
D Calicut (Kozikhode)	1923	R-Lat	Psj	66	32,800	30,571	55,610	2.42	Kerala. Malayalam. 28 expatriates. 66n 71x 103m 1134w 958Yy
D Cochin	1558	R-Lat	Ps	62	97,000	131,955	164,234	0.88	Kerala. Mother Latin diocese. 65n 28x 38m 183w 3269Yy
D Kottapuram	1987	R-Lat	Ps	41	43,000	–	72,963	12.50	New diocese. 43n 12x 13m 113w 1274Yy
D Punalur	1985	R-Lat	Ps	34	20,500	–	34,801	10.00	Recent diocese. 21n 13x 15m 181w 1015Yy
D Quilon	1886	R-Lat	Ps	79	118,000	163,569	199,645	0.80	Kerala. Diocese first in 1349. 60n 23x 28m 766w 1833Yy
D Trivandrum of the Latins	1937	R-Lat	Ps	109	236,000	327,748	400,000	0.80	Kerala, TN. Malayalam, Tamil. M=OFMCap. 127n 79x 134m 510w 7250Yy
D Vijayapuram	1930	R-Lat	Ps	67	51,000	68,213	86,305	0.95	Kerala. Malayalam, Tamil. M=OCD. 77n 38x 55m 371w 2063Yy
Chaldean Syrian Church: D Trichur	1814	O-Nes	Yw..W	5	6,300	2,000	12,600	7.64	*Chaldia Suriyani Sabha. Ancient Ch of the East.* 1874 ex Rome. 13n,W=50%,250y.
Chaldean Syrian Church: P Baghdad	1969	I-Nes	y....	35	20,000	13,000	45,000	5.09	Schism ex Shimun XXIII (USA) supporting rival patriarch Addai (Iraq). 27n.
Children of God	c1980	I-mar	.....	20	327	–	415	6.67	M=ChG. Small group from USA.
Christ Church the Full Gospel Church	1966	I-3fI	.v...	34	2,000	2,000	3,000	1.64	Churches in southern Orissa. 1969 applied to join WCC, rejected. 4n,1p(7),W=80%,86Y,50z.
Christ Groups	c1970	I-3hI	x....	9,364	80,000	–	233,000	63.94	M=EHC. Literature distribution campaigns, visiting 4.6 million homes across India every year.
Christian & Missionary Alliance of India	1887	P-Hol	xF..x	101	7,210	25,000	12,000	-2.89	M=CMA(USA). Central eastern India. HQ Bombay. 21n,34f,2s(12),W=90%,285Y.
Christian Assemblies	1973	I-3cI	.....	145	5,000	–	10,000	4.55	Telugu-speaking ministries. M=CAM.
Christian Assemblies in India	1829	P-CBr	x....	1,200	172,000	100,000	267,000	4.01	*Plymouth Brethren. Open Brethren.* M=CMML(UK, Australia, NZ, USA). E Godavari. 99f,4p.
Christian Community Ch, Bhilai Nagar	1957	P-com	C	10	3,900	5,000	6,000	0.73	Begun for all Protestants in major new steel city Bhilai (MP). Steel, mines. 3n.
Christian Evangelistic Assemblies of India		I-3pI	.....	57	1,670	2,000	3,000	0.05	Orissa et al. 47n.
Christian Fellowship Centre	1984	I-3cI	.....	58	5,050	–	10,000	9.09	Indian charismatics. Strong among Kachari, Karbi (in Assam).
Christian Mission	1918	I-3pI	x....	7	500	500	1,000	2.81	1923, M=International Pentecostal Assemblies/IPCC(USA). Hamirpur (UP), Kerala. 2f.
Christian Revival Movement	1875	I-3mH	.....	2	100	500	300	-2.02	*Yuomayam.* Hindu-Christian messianic movement in Kerala caused by new Malayalam Bible.
Church of Christ, Scientist		m-Sci	x....	2	100	300	200	0.05	*Christian Science.* M=CCS(Boston, USA). Bombay, Bangalore, Calcutta, Delhi. 5w.
Church of God (Anderson)	1904	P-Hol	x....	800	40,000	50,000	60,000	0.73	M=Ch of God(Anderson) (USA). In Assam, WBengal, Orissa, SIndia. 95n,6f,1s.
Church of God (Full Gospel) in India	1913	P-Pe3	ZF..Z	879	59,022	30,000	148,000	6.59	M=Ch of God(Cleveland) (USA). HQ Chengannur, Kerala. 331 churches. 274n,6f,3p.
Church of God in Christ in India		I-3pI	x....	85	3,500	2,000	6,280	0.05	Begun by Indians, no aid until 1991. M=CoGiC(USA). In Kerala and 14 more Indian states. 65n.
Church of God of Prophecy	1957	P-Pe3	Z....	260	15,600	10,000	52,000	6.82	M=CGP(USA). Holiness Pentecostals (3-stage). 33n,1p,W=58%,280Y,100z.
Church of God (Seventh-day)	1936	P-Adv	.....	51	2,810	4,130	7,010	2.14	M=Ch of God(Seventh-day) (USA).
Ch of Jesus C of Latter-day Saints		m-LdS	x....	10	500	252	1,000	0.05	*Mormons.* M=CJCLdS(Utah, USA). Mainly expatriate North Americans.
Church of North India	1612	P-Uni	RWE.W	4,050	600,000	579,554	1,300,000	3.28	*CNI.* 1970 union. 24 Dioceses. 60% Harijan (Chamar, Sweepers). 4s,1u.
Church of South India	1640	P-Uni	.WE.W	10,000	1,471,000	1,589,658	2,955,000	2.51	*CSI.* 70% former Harijans. 21 Dioceses. M=CWMCMS. 56x,1s,3u(142).
Church of the Apostolic Faith	1955	P-Pe3	.....	3	900	1,000	2,000	2.81	M=CAF(USA). Holiness Pentecostals (3-stage). 2n,W=50%,15Y,30z.
Church of the Nazarene of Bharat	1902	P-Hol	xF..x	454	52,299	2,260	71,988	14.85	M=CoN(USA). HQ Buldana. 200n,55mw,15f,1H,4h,1s(16),63t,W=90%,140Y,266z.
Church of Revealed Salvation	1992	I-3mH	.....	5	1,300	4,000	2,000	33.33	*Pratyaska Raksha Sabha.* Begun among Outcastes in Travancore. Declined.
Churches of Christ	c1892	I-Dis	x....	11	600	1,129	1,200	0.24	*MKPK. Mandivon ki Pratinidhi Kaunsil.* M=CC(GB & Ireland). HQ Bhandaria. 6f.
Churches of Christ in Western India	1905	I-Dis	x...x	14	1,200	2,000	2,200	0.38	*Conference of CCWI.* M=CC(Australia). Institutions closed, declining. 7n,W=60%.
Churches of Christ (Instrumental)	1928	I-Dis	x....	610	11,000	20,000	23,000	0.56	M=CCCC(Instrumental) (USA). Across entire nation, including Assam. 37f.
Churches of Christ (Non-Instrumental)	1963	I-Dis	x....	110	2,100	3,000	4,000	1.16	M=CC(Non-Instrumental) (USA). Main cities of North India, also Madras. 31f.
Churches of God	1908	P-Ref	x...E	10	700	1,000	1,200	0.73	*India Eldership.* M=Chs of God in NA, General Eldership (USA). Howrah, WBengal. 4f.
CMS Anglican Church of India	1966	I-Ang	.TT.T	310	90,000	107,000	120,000	0.46	*D Travancore & Cochin.* Pulaya outcaste schism ex CSI(M Kerala). 24n,W=83%,7500Yy.
Conv of Baptist Chs of Maharashtra		P-Bap	T....	37	7,420	8,000	15,000	0.05	Mainline Baptists in Maharashtra state.
Conv of Bapt Chs of Northern Circars	1874	P-Bap	T...W	250	125,000	80,000	250,000	4.66	*CBCNC.* M=CBOMB. 90% Madigas (Telugu,Oriya). 160n,5H,1p,W=77%,300Y.
Conv of Krishna-Godvari Baptist Chs		P-Bap	T....	60	40,000	25,000	50,000	0.05	Mainline Baptists formerly with foreign missionaries.
Council of Baptist Chs in Northern India	1801	P-Bap	T....	470	60,000	75,000	120,000	1.90	*CBCNI.* M=BMS(UK). Bengal, Orissa, Mizo.
Council of Baptist Chs in NE India	1836	P-Bap	T.E.W	3,969	1,053,000	1,064,990	1,630,000	1.72	*CBCNEI.* M=ABFMS(USA). Doubled 1950-70. 97n,1x,5704m,54w,9f,6H,12p,1s(110),16363Y.
Crusaders for Christ of India	1968	I-3cI	.....	10	1,000	30	1,600	17.24	*CCI.* Multimedia evangelism in Delhi, Punjab, UP, Rajasthan. M=CAM.
Delhi Gospel Outreach	1981	I-3cI	.....	32	1,600	–	3,000	7.14	*DGO.* Work among unreached areas, with 42 Indian missionaries. M=CAM.
Dhulia Nandurbar Church	1900	P-Con	x...W	9	1,000	2,000	1,900	-0.20	*Dhule/Nandurbar:* NE of Bombay. M=SAM(Sweden). 90% Bhil. 6n,3x,16f,W=61%,27Y,45y.
Dipti Mission	1925	I-Non	....E	1	130	150	200	1.16	*Mission of Light.* Begun by Bengali woman. 2 schools in Sahibgunj, Bihar. 2f,1k.
Disciples of Christ, India Ch Council	1882	P-Dis	x...C	20	1,400	3,000	3,000	0.00	*ICCDC. Continuing Chr Chs in India.* Formerly M=UCMS; 1970 refused to join CNI. 12n,1H.
Dohnavur Fellowship	1901	P-Non	.....	3	500	1,000	1,100	0.38	Boys and girls nurseries, Tirunelveli. Tamil. Medical and evangelistic work. 11f.
Elim Church		P-Pe2	Z....	3	100	100	300	0.05	M=NZ Full Gospel Mission (New Zealand). HQ Karmala, Scholapur district, Bombay.
Elim Churches of India	1929	P-Pe2	ZG...	6	1,000	1,000	2,000	2.81	M=Elim Foursquare Gospel Alliance (UK). HQ Mirzapur district, UP. 6f.
El Shaddai		I-	.....	60	7,080	–	15,000	0.05	In West Bengal and Sikkim. 62n.
Eternal Light Ministries		I-3cI	.....	37	2,480	–	4,000	0.05	In Punjab and Tamil Nadu. 17n.
Evangelical Alliance of Churches	1892	P-Eva	xM..C	119	21,100	7,000	32,700	6.36	M=TEAM(USA), Swedish Alliance M. Bhils. 6n,5x,64f,G=3.7%pa,2H,3h,1p,W=80%,193Y.
Evangelical Christian Church of India	1941	P-Hol	xF..E	1,350	173,670	2,465	300,000	21.17	*ECCI.* M=OMS(USA,Korea). Rapidly growing in Madras area. 60n,9f,3s(38),207Y,274z.
Evangelical Congregational Church	1910	P-Eva	....E	520	27,600	49,599	72,500	1.53	M=NEIGM(IBPM, now BFTW) (USA). Manipur. Paite, Thado, Hmar. 50n,1r,1s,W=62%,596Y.
Evangelical Free Church of India	1973	I-Eva	....E	263	37,000	–	59,000	4.55	*EFCI.* Manipuris. HQ Sielmat, Churachandpur, Manipur. M=BFTW(USA). 86n,180m.
Evangelised Friends Church	1896	P-Qua	QF..x	4	300	500	600	0.73	Former *Bundelkhand* (town in MP) *Masihi Mitra Samaj.* M=EFC(USA). 2n,4f,1H,1s,W=57%.
Ev Missionary Society in Mayurbhanj	1895	P-Eva	.....	20	870	314	1,400	6.16	All churches in Orissa state. Oriya. M=EMSM(Australia). 20n,4f,2h,1j,W=74%,1Y.
Fell of Ev Churches in North Bihar	1899	P-Eva	xM..C	12	400	1,000	1,100	0.38	M=RBMU(UK). Conservative Evangelical. Located in north Bihar. 10f,W=62%,4Y,3z.
Fell of Free Baptist Chs in North India	1908	P-Pe2	Z...Z	60	1,500	2,430	3,000	0.85	M=Örebro M (Sweden). A=1967. HQ Deoria (UP). 8n,1H,4h,12t(1083),W=70%,59Y.
Fellowship of Evangelical Friends	1960	I-3cI	.....	3	60	40	100	3.73	*FEF.* Mission to Kankkars and other tribals. 29n. M=CAM.
Fellowship of Full Gospel Churches	c1980	I-3fI	.....	75	12,900	–	20,000	6.67	HQ Hyderabad; very strong in Andhra Pradesh.
Fellowship of Gospel Churches	1981	I-3cI	.....	48	3,000	–	6,000	7.14	*FGC.* Eastern India hill areas. 60n. M=CAM.
Fellowship of Indigenous Gospel Chs	1954	I-Non	.....	200	12,000	15,000	19,000	0.95	Members mostly Telugu, 20% converts from Hinduism. 70n,W=99%,384Y.
Fell of Pentecostal Chs of God, India	1962	I-3pI	Z....	415	32,000	2,000	43,000	13.06	HQ Itarsi, MP. Schism ex India Pentecostal CoG. 360n1p(25),W=75%,150Y,250z.
Filadelphia Fellowship		I-3nI	.....	550	15,000	–	30,000	0.05	Vast church-planting activity across North India.
Free Methodist Church of India	1881	I-Hol	VF..x	33	4,153	2,000	13,800	8.03	M=FMC(USA). HQ Yeotmal, also Chikalda (Maharashtra). 45n,1H,1p.
Free Will Baptist Conference of India	1935	P-Bap	xF..x	47	15,106	2,000	23,000	10.26	Members Tamil. M=NAFWB(USA). HQ Nilgiris; also in Bihar. 2n,4x,4f,42Y,50z.
Friends Missionary Prayer Band	1967	I-Non	.....	1,950	90,500	11,900	175,500	11.37	*FMPB.* Indian national missionaries. M=CAM. Work among Kukna, Malto. (70% Christians)
Full Gospel Church Fellowship of India	1911	I-3fI	.....	20	2,600	2,000	4,000	2.81	*FGCF.* M=Bharosa Ghar Mission (USA). HQ Jabalpur. A=1952. 34n,W=80%,25Y,30z.
Garo Baptist Convention	1835	P-Bap	T....	1,483	161,964	150,000	250,000	2.06	Strong in Meghalaya. M=ABFMS(USA),BMS(UK).
God's Church of Visible Salvation	1921	I-3mH	.....	10	1,300	5,000	2,000	-3.60	Outcastes ex Mar Thoma SCEA. Led by founder's wife. Hindu Christian revival.
Golgotha Prayer Team	1978	I-3cI	.....	100	5,000	–	10,000	5.88	*GPT.* Work among Tamils. 150 Indian missionaries. M=CAM.
Gospel Association of India	c1945	I-Bap	.....	70	6,000	10,000	13,000	1.05	*GAI.* Schism ex CBOMB. Healing. Telugu, 50% former Kamma (Sudra) high-caste Hindus.
Gospel Echoing Missionary Society	1972	I-3cI	.....	83	8,000	–	15,000	4.35	*GEMS.* Bihar. 370 full-time home missionaries. M=CAM.
Gospel Outreach Ministries	c1970	I-3nI	.....	600	25,000	–	35,000	51.97	Among 14 tribes in Andhra Pradesh and Orissa: 303 cross-cultural workers. F=S. Gokanakonda.

Continued overleaf

Country Table 2–continued

Official name (bold type = church with over 10% of all affiliated) 1	*Begun* 2	*Type* 3	*Counc* 4	*Congs* 5	*Adults* 6	*Affiliated 1970* 7	*Affiliated 1995* 8	*G%* 9	*Names, notes, and other statistics* (see Codebook, Part 3) 10
Greek Orthodox Ch (D New Zealand)		O-Gre	Cwc..	2	500	1,000	900	0.05	Part of D New Zealand, under jurisdiction of EP Constantinople. Greeks.
Gypsy Evangelical Movement		I-3pE	x....	300	10,000	2,000	15,000	0.05	Nomadic caravan communities among 300,000 Gypsies. M=GGMS(Switzerland, France). 8m.
Hebron Missionary Fellowship	1968	I-3cI	.....	350	43,000	30	70,000	36.37	*HMF.* Work among lower castes. 31 Indian missionaries. M=CAM.
Hidden Muslim believers in Christ	c1970	I-Mus	.....	200	40,000	–	65,000	55.78	Isolated Muslim believers in Christ who choose to witness in Muslim society.
High-caste Hindu believers in Christ	c1800	I-Hin	.....	3,000	1,800,000	1,000,000	2,500,000	3.73	Isolated Brahmin believers in Christ as Lord who choose to remain in Hindu society and families.
Himalaya Crusade	1970	I-3cI	.....	100	10,000	–	20,000	48.61	Ganges Valley and Himalaya region. 138 Indian workers. M=CAM. 97n.
Himalaya Evangelical Mission	1963	I-3nI	.....	0	0	–	0	0.00	Began as Kashmir Evangelical Fellowship. F=P.M. Thomas, 120n.
Himalayan Free Church	1892	I-3pE	.....	49	4,055	425	6,500	11.53	HQ Ghoom, Darjeeling, Sikkim. Lepchas, Nepalis. 98n,W=31%,36Y,20z.
Hindustani Covenant Church	1940	P-Con	....W	16	1,658	760	3,500	6.30	M=Swedish Mission Covenant Ch. HQ Bombay. Ministry to Muslims. 16n,W=24%,44Y,12z.
House of Prayer Fellowship		I-3pI	.....	17	6,000	–	8,000	0.05	In Andhra Pradesh. 15n.
Immanuel Bible College	c1970	I-3nI	x....	1,700	50,000	–	100,000	58.49	Movement aiming to plant a church in every village in Maharashtra.
Independent Assemblies of God Int	c1922	I-3pI	.....	250	70,000	50,000	100,000	2.81	Kerala, Andhra Pradesh. Large split from AoG in USA. 250n.
Indep Chr Bible Believers Gospel Fell	1966	I-Non	.TT.T	450	13,000	20,000	21,000	0.20	Telugu members. In Northern Circars. HQ Ramachandrapuram, AP. 20n,W=75%,823Y.
Independent Churches of India	1910	I-Non	....E	150	30,000	45,000	55,000	0.81	Ex IBPM, now aided by them. Manipur. Hmars, Karbi, Toipuri. 42n,226m,5p,W=39%,520Y.
Independent Full Gospel Chs of India	1953	I-3fI	.....	39	5,200	5,000	8,000	1.90	Oneness body in Coimbatore and E Godavari, AP. Telugu. 34n,84Y.
Independent Local Churches of Kerala	1969	I-Non	.TT.T	10	500	400	1,000	3.73	In Cochin district, Kerala state. Malayalam-speaking. 6n,1s.
India Association of General Baptists		P-Bap	T....	81	9,400	4,000	15,000	0.05	M=GAGB(USA).
India Bible Church Fellowship	1952	I-Non	.....	47	2,000	1,200	2,500	2.98	Agricultural work. Ahmednagar, Maharashtra. 19n,1x,1p,W=40%,75Y,100z.
India Bible Mission Church		I-Non	.....	100	2,000	3,200	3,000	0.05	Revival movement in E Godavari, AP; HQ Rajahmundry. Split ex Baptist mission.
India for Christ Ministries	1988	I-3cI	.....	10	1,100	–	2,000	14.29	*ICM.* 49 Indian missionaries. M=CAM.
India Christian Assemblies	1938	P-Pe2	Z...H	20	4,000	5,000	7,000	1.35	*ICA.* M=Finnish Free Foreign Mission (Finland). Mainly in Krishna district, AP.
India Christian Mission	1897	I-Non	....E	80	7,000	9,593	12,000	0.90	Eluru, AP. Formerly USA aid. Healing revivals among Hindus. 6n,W=71%,534Y,681z.
India Evangelistic Association	1983	I-3cI	.....	50	5,500	–	10,500	8.33	*IEA.* Orissa. M=CAM.
India Gospel Fellowship Mission		I-Non	.....	2	200	200	300	0.05	Independent body in Nilgiris: indigenous Indian origin.
India Gospel League	1906	P-Bap	.....	50	2,000	2,000	3,000	1.64	M=IGL(USA). Medical work around Salem (Tamil Nadu). 8n,4f,1H,25h,1p,W=85%,31Y,40z.
India Mission	1933	P-Non	xM...	100	7,000	7,000	10,000	1.44	M=International Mission (USA). Good News Literature Centre, AP. 30n,27f,4h,2s,W=70%,150Y.
India Pentecostal Assemblies	1979	I-3fI	.....	353	6,579	–	15,000	6.25	In Tamil Nadu. Work among Mudakas.
India United Evangelical Mission	1924	P-Eva	.....	10	1,000	1,345	2,000	1.60	M=IUEM(USA). Independent mission, now indigenous workers only. HQ Bangalore. 1h.
Indian Church of the Only Saviour	1857	I-Hin	.....	10	1,000	2,000	2,000	0.00	1857,*Hindu Ch of the Lord Jesus*, or *Hindu Christian Community*, of 6,000 ex SPG at Nazareth
Indian Evangelical Team	1972	I-3cI	.....	740	28,000	–	35,000	4.35	*IET.* Begun in Punjab; now also in MP, Orissa, Maharashtra. 720n (Indians). M=CAM.
Indian National Church	1955	I-ARo	.....	20	700	1,000	1,200	0.73	Schism ex D Bombay, CIPBC(Anglican). Bishops in Vilatte succession. HQ Delhi.
Indian Nat Full Gospel Chs Fed of I		I-3fI	.....	97	10,000	2,000	16,000	0.05	In Gujarat, Maharashtra. 97n.
Indian Orthodox Church: P India	1956	I-CCa	.v...	20	1,000	2,000	2,000	0.00	*Eastern Orthodox Catholic P India.* Ex RCC. 5 Dioceses, no buildings; services in homes.
Indian Pentecostal Assemblies		I-3pI	.....	122	7,370	2,200	11,000	0.05	In Tamil Nadu, 122n.
Indian Pentecostal Church of God	1924	I-3pI	Z....	9,950	581,000	500,000	900,000	2.38	*IPC.* Ex CPM, AoG. 80% Malayali, but congregations throughout India. Abroad: in 10 countries.
International Christian Fellowship	1893	P-Non	xM..x	73	4,500	500	8,040	11.75	M=SIM (former Church, HQ Poona. 4n,2x,41f,1H,2h.
Internat Ch of the Foursquare Gospel	c1970	P-Pe2	.....	27	613	–	1,362	33.46	M=ICFG(USA).
Isolated radio churches	1952	I-3rI	.....	100,000	6,000,000	650,000	9,000,000	11.08	Radio believers (youths &c). (1970) R=75000 (FEBA,RVOG),T=2810000 (ICI,TEAM,EHC,&c).
Itarsi Native Missionary Outreach	1945	I-3cI	.....	400	35,000	2,000	70,000	15.28	*INMO* Madhya Pradesh. Across northern India. 470 Indian missionaries. M=CAM.
Jehovah Jireh Churches	1958	I-3cI	.....	30	2,000	100	5,000	16.94	*JJC.* In Andhra Pradesh. M=CAM.
Jehovah's Witnesses	1905	m-Jeh	x....	360	10,272	10,000	35,700	5.22	*Watch Tower.* 25% ex RCs. HQ Santa Cruz, Bombay. (1975) 328Y. (1995) 1542Y.
Karbi-Anglong Baptist Convention		I-3nI	T....	186	15,613	–	30,000	0.05	Local indigenous grouping 4 Baptists.
Karnataka Baptist Convention		P-Bap	T....	105	13,000	4,000	25,000	0.05	Major Baptist body among Karnataka's denominations.
Kashmir Evangelical Fellowship	1954	I-3cI	.....	37	1,397	200	2,000	9.65	*KEF.* 96 Indian workers. M=CAM. Work strongest in Punjab, Dogri.
Kuki Christian Church		I-Bap	.....	359	62,000	20,000	80,000	0.05	In Manipur, Assam, Nagaland. 470n.
Lakher Independent Evangelical Church	1907	I-Eva	.....	100	12,000	19,991	22,000	0.38	Church includes 95% of whole Lakher headhunting tribe (Assam & Burma). M=LPM(UK). 13n,3f.
Laymen's Evangelical Union/Fellowship	1935	I-Bap	.....	410	36,000	10,000	73,000	8.28	*LEF.* Founder Brother N. Daniel, ex CBOMB. Telugu, now also Tamil. 2 factions.Strong in Madras
Local Churches of India	1974	I-3cI	.....	320	10,000	–	20,000	4.76	*LCI.* Work in interior rural areas. M=CAM.
London Mission Church	1947	I-Con	.TT.T	90	19,400	40,000	30,000	-1.14	Schism ex LMS opposing 1947 CSI union (D Kannyiakumari). Litigation from 1947-64.
Low-caste Hindu believers in Christ	c1800	I-Hin	.....	10,000	5,000,000	3,000,000	7,500,000	3.73	Numerous movements but mostly isolated believers and families witnessing within Hinduism.
Madras Pentecostal Assembly Church	1920	I-3pI	.....	50	2,000	1,238	3,000	3.60	Rapid growth. Healing, exorcism. HQ Royapettah. 4n,1p,W=85%,128Y,40z.
Malabar Basel German Mission Church	c1970	I-LuR	.TT.T	5	900	2,000	1,500	-1.14	Fundamentalist split ex CSI, D North Kerala (United Basel Mission Ch). HQ Calicut.
Malabar Independent Syrian Church	1771	I-ReO	.....	20	6,600	3,780	10,200	4.05	*Malabar Swathanthra Suriani Sabha.* D Thozhiyur. Orthodox split. 8n, 1 H,1s,W=50%,52y.
Manipur Baptist Convention		P-Bap	T....	1,243	118,737	150,000	250,000	0.05	Composed of over 20 separate tribal Baptist Associations, all autonomous.
Manna Full Gospel Chs & Ministries	c1968	I-3fI	.....	5,000	140,000	4,000	275,000	18.44	Indigenous chs in Andhra Pradesh. Telugus. Welsh missionary aid. M=Mana Igreja(Portugal).
Mar Thoma Syrian Church of Malabar	1843	I-ReO	xWE.W	1,000	550,000	350,017	875,000	3.73	Reform ex Orthodox Syrian Ch. Syrians. 6 Dioceses. 272n,6H,1j,1k,P=95%,30r,2s,575t,W=37%.
Mara Independent Evangelical Church	1907	I-Con	.....	100	16,000	30,000	33,000	0.38	Member of NEIndia Christian Council. Manipuris. 17n,500Y,100z.
Maranatha Full Gospel Churches	c1980	I-3fI	x....	380	10,775	–	20,000	6.67	Charismatic churches begun by Indians with some help from M=MM(USA). Tamil Nadu.
Mennonite Church in India	1899	P-Men	G...z	15	2,060	3,000	2,980	-0.03	M=Mennonite Ch NA(USA). HQ Dhamtari, MP. 11n,2x,13f,2H,2r,1u,W=60%,76Y.
Mennonite Sarodara Sangam	1899	P-Men	GF..x	810	155,000	120,000	240,000	2.81	M=Mennonite Brethren Ch of NAmerica. 99% Telugu. 175n,14f,3H,3h,9p,100Y.
Methodist Church in India	1856	P-Met	VwE.W	3,000	473,125	901,306	1,100,000	0.80	*SAsia CC, UMC*(USA). 11 Annual Conferences. 80% Harijan (Madiga). 20H,4s,735n.
Metropolitan Church Association	1904	P-Hol	x...E	20	6,000	7,000	8,000	0.54	Southern India; some camp work in north India. M=MCA(USA). HQ Siqait, UP. 2n,2x.
Mid-India Yearly Meeting of Friends	1866	P-Qua	Q....	19	570	1,000	950	-0.20	*Quakers.* M=Religious Society of Friends (UK). A=1953. HQ Itarsi, MP.
Mizoram Bible Fellowship	1965	I-3cE	.....	10	500	30	1,000	15.06	*MBF.* In an impoverished area of Mizoram. M=CAM.
Moravian Church	c1975	P-Mor	x....	4	140	–	400	5.00	Recent mission of ancient Protestant confession from Europe.
Nagaland Baptist Ch Council	1835	P-Bap	T....	1,275	283,191	320,000	450,000	1.37	Collaboration of 15 separate Naga Baptist tribal Associations.M=ABFMS(USA).
Nagaland Christian Revival Churches	1952	I-3pE	.....	855	185,000	40,000	260,000	7.77	*NCRC.* Pentecostal split ex Nagaland Baptists. Nagas. M=DNR(USA). (1970) 65n. (1990) 1020n.
Nagaland for Jesus	1990	I-3cI	.....	10	800	–	1,500	20.00	*NFJ.* 41 Indian missionaries working among 60 language groups. M=CAM.
National Missionary Society of India	1905	I-Non	.....	20	1,000	1,000	1,500	1.64	*NMS. Bharat Christya Sevak Samaj.* Aids CSI & ELC, but has own churches. 40n,300nw.
Native Church (Protestant)		I-Non	.....	40	3,000	8,000	6,000	0.05	Independent separatist body, of indigenous Indian origin. 12n,10m,1p.
Native Missionary Movement	1963	I-3cI	.....	263	18,000	30	35,000	32.64	*NMM.* 285 workers. Bible school. M=CAM. Work among Bhil, Gamit, Vasavi.
Navajeeva Ashram	1984	I-Eva	.....	50	3,680	–	8,000	9.09	In Karnataka. Kanarese. M=CAM.
New Apostolic Church	1969	I-3aX	x....	3,400	530,000	20,000	1,448,209	18.68	*Canada Bezirk.* HQ Zurich. Rapid growth. 1973 mission in Kenya, Africa.
New Life Churches	1978	I-3cI	.....	22	2,000	–	4,000	5.88	*Neva Jeeva Ashram*, Bangalore. Kannada language. 45 home missionaries. M=CAM.
New Life Crusaders	1975	I-3cI	.....	27	450	–	1,000	5.00	*NLC.* 27 Indian home missionaries. M=CAM.
New Life Fellowship	1968	I-3pI	.....	2,050	240,000	5,000	480,000	20.03	HQ Bombay, Calcutta. Members ex CNI,RCC. In 1995, 11,000 Hindus baptized.
New Life Fellowship (Rajasthan)	c1975	I-3nI	x....	1,500	30,000	–	60,000	5.00	Movement in Rajasthan with 10 Bible colleges, supervising 1,700 churches.
New Life Outreach	1974	I-3nI	.....	184	34,870	–	70,000	4.76	Work among: Vasavi, Kukna, Chodhari, Korava, Malto.
New Testament Church of India	c1970	I-3pI	x...C	250	10,000	–	20,000	48.61	In Pentecostal Fellowship of India. M=COTR(USA). 520 full-time workers. Youth ministry, schools
North Bank Baptist Christian Assoc	c1930	P-Bap	TF..E	607	46,522	25,500	60,900	3.54	*Uttor Par Bapt Christian Sanmilan.* M=BGC. Assam. 41n,2H,5h,2p,W=55%,650Y.
Norwegian Free Evangelical Church	1910	P-Pe2	Z...Z	350	30,000	43,018	70,000	1.97	M=NPY(Norway),SFM(Sweden),FFFM(Finland),Elim(Denmark). NIndia. HQ Banda, UP. 1H.
Omega Full Gospel Assembly	c1960	I-3fI	.....	50	180,000	10,000	230,000	13.36	In Karnataka. One of many expanding Full Gospel networks.
Open Bible Church of God		I-3pI	.TT.T	15	500	500	1,000	0.05	Independents in Nilgiris & Coimbatore districts. Village evangelism. HQ Tatabad.
Orissa Baptist Evangelical Crusade		I-3nI	.....	307	28,390	–	50,000	0.05	In Orissa state. 100 pastors, 730 baptisms p.a.
Orissa Follow-up Churches	1982	I-3cE	.....	90	1,200	–	3,000	7.69	Work begun first among Ho tribe. 70 Indian home missionaries. M=CAM.
Orissa Missionary Movement	1974	I-3cI	.....	60	2,000	–	5,000	4.76	*OMM.* Use of crusades, films, seminars, personal evangelism. M=CAM.
Orthodox Syrian Church of the East:	c 52	O-SyM	DWE..	1,458	1,307,000	1,412,100	2,197,000	1.78	*Malankara OSC, Catholicate of the East.* Syrians. 22 bps,942n,1s(85),W=55%,7820Yy.
D Angamaly (Ankamaly)	1886	O-SyM	Dm	150	133,000	144,700	225,000	1.78	HQ Trikkunnathu Seminary. alwaye. Orthodox Youth League. 50 units. 130n,12r,123t.
D Bahya Keralam (Outside Kerala)	1959	O-SyM	Dm	60	57,000	61,800	96,000	1.78	Across India. 5 further parishes abroad. HQ Devalokam, Kottayam.
D Chingavanom (Knanaya)	1910	O-SyM	Dm	67	60,000	64,800	101,000	1.79	Knanaya Syrian Christians date from AD 350 in unbroken line. 35n,1e.1H,4r,1s.
D Cochin	1876	O-SyM	Dm	125	121,000	120,600	188,000	1.79	HQ Zion Seminary, Kuratty, via Alwaye. Strong Sunday schools, youth work.
D Kandanad	1876	O-SyM	Dm	114	101,000	110,000	171,000	1.78	HQ Muvattupuzha. Scattered churches to east of Cochin. 5 bishops since 1876.
D Kottayam	1876	O-SyM	Dp	199	177,000	192,900	300,000	1.78	Diocese of Catholicos of the East, but with own bishop. 1s (Kottayam).
D Malabar	1953	O-SyM	Dm	131	116,000	126,600	197,000	1.78	22,000 converts through Servants of the Cross mission. HQ Calicut. 3r.
D Niranam	1876	O-SyM	Dm	117	104,000	113,000	176,000	1.79	Site of one of St Thomas' 7 churches. HQ Pathanapuram. 2H,6r,1s.
D Quilon	1876	O-SyM	Dm	290	255,000	278,800	433,000	1.78	HQ Cross Junction, Quilon. Medical missions, many schools. 2d,2e,11r.
D Thumpamon (Thumpaman)	1876	O-SyM	Dm	205	183,000	198,900	310,000	1.79	HQ Pathanamthitta. Active Orthodox youth movement. 9 bishops since 1876.
Pentecostal Assemblies of God	1983	P-Pe2	.....	1	15	–	25	8.33	M=PAoC(Canada). Mainline Trinitarian Classical Pentecostals.
Pente Ch of God of Andhra Pradesh		I-3pI	.....	800	30,000	30,000	50,000	0.05	Large indigenous pentecostal body. M=PCG(Jamaican Blacks from UK).
Pentecostal Free Will Baptist Church	c1960	P-Pe3	.....	12	700	500	1,000	2.81	M=PFWBC(USA), schism in USA ex Free Will Baptists. 80 workers. 1p.
Pentecostal Holiness Church	1920	P-Pe3	ZF..H	127	24,201	3,000	63,700	13.00	M=IPHC(USA). In Bihar. HQ Jha Jha. Member, All India Pentecostal Fellowship. 62nm,8f.
Pentecostal Mission	1927	I-3pI	Z....	1,071	75,000	40,000	125,000	4.66	1927 ex AoG. Former Ceylon Pentecostal Mission. Strong in Madras, Kerala.
Pioneers International of India	1982	I-Non	.....	85	4,250	–	10,625	7.69	M=Pioneers (USA). No-church movement.
Presbyterian Ch of India	1812	P-Ref	.....	3,543	389,385	324,091	797,732	3.67	3 Synods, Bangladesh, Burma. M=PCW.60% Mizo, 30% Khasi. 165n,3H,2j,2s,W=70%,13709Yy.
Prince of Peace Church		I-3cI	.....	92	12,000	–	16,000	0.05	In Tamil Nadu and Andhra Pradesh. 46n.
Pure Church	1925	I-Ang	.....	1	200	1,500	500	-4.30	*Suttangam Sabhi. Alvaneri's Ch.* Split of 7,000 ex CMS (D Tinnevelly). Declining.
Rabha Baptist Church Union	1959	I-Bap	.....	5	200	500	400	-0.89	In Goalpara district, Assam. HQ Debitala. 1n,4p,1s,W=20%,45Y.
Ramabai Mukti Mission	1905	I-Hol	.M..E	2	500	800	900	0.47	Begun by woman, Pandita Ramabai, at Mukti. 2,000 widows and orphans. 32f,1H,3h.
Reaching Indians Ministries	1993	I-3nI	.....	25	500	–	1,000	50.00	Based in USA, with 70 Indian missionaries (12 cross-cultural). F=S. Lukos.
Rajasthan Bible Institute		I-3nI	.....	650	12,000	–	20,000	0.05	Independent Bible School with string of new congregations across Rajasthan.
Reformed Episcopal Church	1890	I-ReA	x...E	2	150	250	300	0.73	*Calvary Church.* M=REC(USA), Anglican schism. HQ Lalitpur, Jhansi, UP. 2f,1H,1h.
Reformed Presbyterian Ch, Ev Synod	1860	I-Ref	x....	10	300	337	450	1.16	M=RPCES(USA),WPM(USA). HQ Roorkee, UP. 6n,4x,10f,1s,W=61%,12Yy.
St Thomas Evangelical Church of India	1961	I-ReO	.TT.C	675	54,000	25,000	90,000	5.26	*Pathiopadesa Samiti.* Split ex Mar Thoma Syrian Ch. In Kerala. 91n,2p,1r,W=75%,254Yy.
Salvation Army	1882	P-Sal	xwE.W	3,573	162,000	500,000	270,000	-2.43	*Muktifauj.* 5 Territories: Madras & AP, NE, SE, SW, Western. 1952nx,34f,9H,3s.
Samavesam of Telugu Baptist Churches	1836	P-Bap	TWE.a	1,625	856,389	500,000	1,180,000	3.49	*Samavesam of TBC.* M=ABFMS. 99% Mala,Madiga. 418n,2s(120),W=40%,4091Y.
Saora Association of Baptist Churches	c1900	P-Bap	.....	250	16,200	18,000	25,000	1.32	Orissa and AP. M=CBOMB(Canada). 90% Harijan (Madiga, Saora). Rapid growth.
Separate Baptists in Christ	1917	I-Bap	.....	3	1,000	4,000	3,000	-1.14	*India Mission.* Covers 70 villages in Ahmednagar district. HQ Vambori. HQ Vambori. 7n,W=75%.
Seventh Day Baptist Church	c1900	P-Bap	Tw...	320	19,200	25,000	27,400	0.37	M=SDBC(USA). Sabbatarian Baptists with USA and UK links.
Seventh-day Adventist Church	1895	P-Adv	x....	829	160,635	80,000	247,000	4.61	*SDA,C,N,SIndia Unions.* 164n,44x,95f,6H,1j,2p,11r,1s(60),882t(55721),W=94%,5784Y.
Sharon Pentecostal Fellowship Church	c1960	I-3pI	.....	355	48,814	25,000	60,000	3.56	In Kerala.+schism ex PCG Unusual manifestations. 339n.
Siloam Baptist Brethren Fellowship	1975	I-Bap	.....	26	3,930	–	8,000	5.00	In Andhra Pradesh. Work among Madiga, Pattapu. M=CAM.
Subba Rao Movement	1942	I-3mH	.....	500	50,000	100,000	150,000	1.64	High-caste Hindus. Anti-churches, anti-baptism. Massive healing crusades. Telugu.
Swedish Free Mission Churches		P-Pe2	Z...H	250	55,000	50,000	100,000	0.05	M=Svenska Fria Missionen (Sweden). In UP. Member, All India Pentecostal Fellowship.

Continued opposite

Country Table 2–concluded

Official name (bold type = church with over 10% of all affiliated) 1	*Begun* 2	*Type* 3	*Counc* 4	*Congs* 5	*Adults* 6	*Affiliated 1970* 7	*Affiliated 1995* 8	*G%* 9	*Names, notes, and other statistics* (see Codebook, Part 3) 10
Syrian Orth Patriarchate of Antioch	c1975	O-Syr	DW.N.	300	300,000	–	700,000	5.00	Reassertion by P-Antioch of original authority over OSC; now under 14 new SOC bps
Tamil Baptist Churches	1861	P-Bap	.....	100	2,000	3,000	4,000	1.16	M=Strict Baptist Mission(UK). Around Tiruchi. Tamils. HQ Kovilpatti. 7n,9f,30Y.
Tamil Christian Fellowship	1957	I-3cI	.....	115	9,000	1,000	16,000	11.73	*TCF.* Mission to tribals and lepers. 290n,2p. M=CAM.
Telugu Baptist Churches	1968	I-Bap	.TT.T	30	1,500	2,000	2,500	0.90	Schism ex Convention of Telugu Baptist Chs. Many years' lawsuits against ABFMS.
Theistic Church of India	1795	m-Unt	.....	60	3,000	5,000	6,000	0.73	*Brahmo Samaj. Unitarian Union.* 1795 Madras; Assam (Khasi), Calcutta. M=UUA(Canada).
Tribal Gospel Mission	1979	I-3cI	.....	149	83,000	–	152,000	6.25	*TGM.* Work among mainly the Ao Naga, also Sora, Uraon, and other tribals. M=CAM.
Tripura Baptist Christian Union	1938	P-Bap	Tv...	360	27,500	12,000	47,000	5.61	M=NZBMS(New Zealand). 1962, applied to join WCC. 16n,2x,1p,W=67%,262Y.
True Jesus Church of India	1969	I-3oC	x....	50	1,000	300	2,000	7.88	*TJC, World Conference* (HQ Taiwan). Chinese. Indian pastors in South India.
Undenominational Ch of the Lord in India	1958	I-Hol	.....	150	13,600	15,000	21,000	1.35	Mission from USA. Members Telugu, tribals. 15n,250Y,500z.
United Basel Mission Church	1834	P-Ref	.....	39	20,000	22,000	28,000	0.97	Begun in Karnataka and Bombay. Malayali, Kanerese. Slow growth. 34n.
United Evangelical Lutheran Chs in India	1706	P-Lut	LWE.W	10,000	850,000	790,440	1,500,000	2.60	*UELCI.* Formed 1975. 9 ELCs. Large % Harijan. Missions to Malaysia, Burma, Tanzania
United Missionary Church of India	1908	P-Hol	xF..E	15	1,500	2,000	2,500	0.90	Mennonite. West Bengal. M=UMS(USA). 1969 Missionary Church. HQ Calcutta. 1 school. 3f.
United Pentecostal Church in India	1949	P-Pel	x....	770	84,700	100,000	223,000	3.26	M=UPC. Fields: NE(Assam) 123 congs, S(Kerala)41. 145n,3x,2p(74),W=80%,1600Y.
Wesleyan Church of India	1910	P-Hol	VF..E	18	794	836	2,560	4.58	*India Conference.* M=WC(USA). HQ Surat, Bombay. 7n,1x,2f,2H,3h,1p,W=66%,42Yy.
Wesleyan Methodist Ch of India	1970	I-Met	.TT.C	135	27,000	30,000	32,500	0.32	Schism ex Diocese of Medak, Church of South India, opposing new bishop. Telugu.
World Missions	1965	P-Non	x....	15	4,000	5,000	6,000	0.73	M=World Missions (USA). North American Evangelicals based on Long Beach, CA (USA).
World-Wide Missions of India	1960	I-Non	x....	100	20,000	30,000	35,000	0.62	M=World-Wide Missions (USA). Evangelicals linked with Pasadena, CA (USA).
Zeme Baptist Church Council		P-Bap	.....	24	25,000	29,000	35,000	0.05	In Assam and Manipur. 27n.
Other Protestant denominations		P-	.....	1,000	30,000	35,000	70,000	0.05	Total about 100 (see list below).
Other Indian indigenous churches		I-3pI	.....	400	50,000	20,000	100,000	0.05	Total about 40 (see list below).
Other independent charismatic chs	c1980	I-3cI	.....	2,500	100,000	–	200,000	6.67	Including SIWA (450 chs), HBI (816 chs).
Other independent single congregations	1920	I-sin	.....	7,000	280,000	200,000	400,000	2.81	Most of these are large city congregations: 500 in Madras.
Other independent Oneness bodies		I-3oI	.....	20	100,000	–	200,000	0.05	Total 40 bodies, with many USA connections.
Doubly-affiliated		2-aff			-3,837,000	-1,724,040	-6,394,895		Baptized Catholics or Protestants who are also members of Renewal bodies.
Totals				**257,052**	**32,643,646**	**23,230,000**	**54,400,000**		

Churches, members, growth, 1900-2025	*Congs*	*Adults*	*Affiliated*	*G%*	*Total denominations*	*6 Megablocs:* O	R	A	P	I	m
Total churches, members, and denominations (mid-1900)	9,000	2,040,000	3,820,200	2.61	56	2	1	1	36	15	1
Total churches, members, and denominations (mid-1970)	78,889	12,402,863	23,230,000	2.61	585	4	1	0	124	452	4
Total churches, members, and denominations (mid-1990)	230,000	28,803,000	48,000,000	3.70	1,225	5	1	0	185	1030	4
Total churches, members, and denominations (mid-1995)	257,052	32,643,646	54,400,000	2.53	1,278	5	1	0	186	1,082	4
Total churches, members, and denominations (mid-2000)	280,000	37,350,000	62,243,546	2.73	1,327	5	1	0	187	1130	4
Total churches, members, and denominations (mid-2025)	460,000	58,866,000	98,100,000	1.84	3,251	10	1	0	230	3000	10

NOTES ON TABLE ABOVE

NATIONAL COUNCILS (Column 4, 5th letter).

- a = member of both NCCI and EFI.
- C = Federation of Evangelical Churches of India (FECI) (non-conciliar Evangelicals only).
- E = Evangelical Fellowship of India (EFI) (conciliar and non-conciliar Evangelicals).
- H = All-India Pentecostal Fellowship (AIPF) (Northern and Southern Regions; formed 1957).
- R = Catholic Bishops' Conference of India (CBCI).
- T = Council of Christian Churches in India (formerly India Bible Christian Council IBCC).
- W = National Council of Churches in India (NCCI: 1921, 1947, 1979).
- x = Member of both EFI and FECI.
- Z = member of AIPF, FECI and/or EFI.
- z = member of both NCCI, EFI and FECI.

Other national councils. (1) All-India Ecumenical Coordinating Body (AECB) (leading eventually to a National Council of Churches of India, including the Catholic Church). (2) Two councils link a number of indigenous churches, and aim to create an independent indigenous national church of India: All India Federation of National Churches, and Fellowship of Christ in India (Bharat Khrist Sangh). (3) Various Western bodies belong to the Christian Holiness Association, Mennonite Christian Fellowship of India, and other bodies. (4) A Joint Council, formed 1978, links the CSI, CNI and Mar Thoma Syrian Church of Malabar.

Other councils. Many bodies not in national councils belong to local Christian councils; there are 14 regional councils affiliated to the NCCI.

OTHER PROTESTANT DENOMINATIONS. In addition to those listed, there is a large number of over 90 small Protestant denominations. These include (with year begun and/or total affiliated in parentheses where known): Amazing Grace Missions, American Baptist Association, Apostolic Faith, Assembly of Yahvah, Baptist Bible Fellowship International (1955), Behat Village Mission, Bible Holiness Mission (Canada), Bible Missionary Ch, Brethren Ch (Ashland) (1971), Calvary Pentecostal Ch, Central Asian Mission, Children of God International (many communes; work with hippies and drug addicts), Chowpatta Agricultural & Industrial Mission, Christian Ch of North America, Christian Churches (Direct-support Mission), Christian Nationals Evangelism Commission (1967), Ch of Christ (Bailey Mission), Ch of God (General Conference) (1964), Ch of God (Queen's Village), Chs of God in the British Isles & Overseas, Exclusive Brethren (Kelly-Continental), Free Ch of Finland Mission (1909, Darjeeling), Free Ch of Scotland Mission (85), Free Gospel Church Mission (begun 1928; 300), Glad Tidings Missionary Society (1965), Grace Mission (1969), Moravian Ch (Tibetan Unity Undertaking), National Revival Crusade, Nepal Evangelistic Band, New Tribes Mission (1945), Peniel Chs of VOCA (1950), Pilgrims Mission (1908, Pentecostal), South India Ch of Christ Mission, United World Mission (begun 1958; 65), World Gospel Mission (begun 1937; 100), Worldwide Evangelization Crusade (1926).

OTHER INDIAN INDIGENOUS CHURCHES. Since the early movements in 1843, 1858, 1880, 1886, 1887, 1921 and 1925 (see above, and text under Indigenous Churches) there have been numerous Christian and Hindu-Christian indigenous churches formed. In addition to those given in the table above, others still existing in 1970 include: Anglican Episcopal Ch of India (HQ Dehra Dun, UP), Apostolic Pentecostal Faith, Baptist Christian Chs (member of ICCC), Bharat Ev Mission, Bible Brethren Assemblies (member of ICCC), Bible Standard Ch (member of ICCC), Church of the Country (Nattusabai), Delhi Bible Fellowship, Elim Bible Fellowship (member of ICCC), Independent Assembly, Independent Ch of South India (South Kerala Diocese) (member of ICCC), India Independent Ch of God, Indian Orthodox Catholic Apostolic Ch (bishop consecrated 1967 in New York, USA), Madras Bethesda Mission (member of ICCC), Masihi Mandali (Pentecostal Church), Nagaland Suffering Ch, National Ch of India, New Testament Baptist Christian Association (member of ICCC), Revival Centre, South India United Mission, Voice of Full Gospel Assembly, Zion Assembly (Siyon Sangham). In addition, certain USA Black missions are assisting, including: Apostolic Overcoming Holy Ch of God, Lott Carey Baptist Foreign Mission Convention, NBCUSA. There are also indigenous bodies from other races, including the Spiritual Food Worldwide Evangelistic Mission (Chinese from Hong Kong).

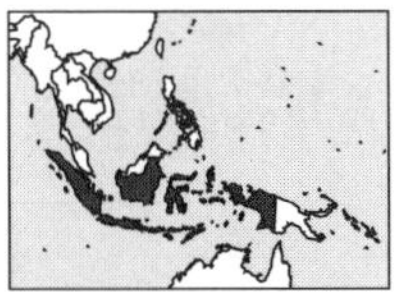

INDONESIA

SECULAR DATA, AD 2000

STATE

Official name: Republik Indonesia (The Republic of Indonesia).
Short name: Indonesia. **Adjective of nationality:** Indonesian.
Flag: Red stripe above white stripe.
Area: 1,919,317 sq. km. (741,052 sq. mi.).
Government: Republic, since 1971 (1800 Dutch possession (East Indies), 1945 Independence, 1957 dictatorship, 1967 military junta).
Legislature: House of Representatives, 500 members; People's Consultative Congress, 1,000 members.
Official language: Indonesian (Bahasa Indonesia).
Monetary unit: 1 Indonesian rupiah (Rp) = 100 sen. **US$1=** Rp 10,850.
Chief cities: JAKARTA (Batavia) 9,815,000; Bandung (Bandoeng) 3,420,000; Surabaja (Surabaya) 2,507,000; Medan 1,910,000; Palembang 1,429,000.
Political divisions: 26 provinces.
Armed forces: 284,000.

DEMOGRAPHY

Population: 212,107,000.
Population density: 110.5/sq. km. (286.2/sq. mi.).
Under 15 years: 64,926,000.
Growth rate p.a.: 1.22% (births 20.09, deaths 7.04).
Mortality: Infant, per 1,000: 39.5; **Maternal per 100,000:** 650.0.
Life expectancy: 67 (male 65, female 69).
Household size: 4.5. **Floor area per person, sq.m:** 14.4.
Major languages: Indonesian, English, Javanese, Sundanese, Madurese, Chinese, Balinese, Batak, Bugi, and about 840 other local ones. Some 13 are used by over 1 million speakers each.
Urban dwellers: 40.20%. **Urban growth rate p.a.:** 3.40%.
Labor force: 43%.

ETHNOLINGUISTIC PEOPLES

25.6% Javanese (Orang Jawa); 10.7% Javanese Indonesian; 10.6% Sundanese (Urang Sunda); 5.7% Madurese; 3.1% Sundanese Indonesian.

ECONOMY

National income p.a. per person: US$980; **per family:** US$4,410.

EDUCATION

Adult literacy: 83% (male 89%, female 78%). **Schools:** 180,604.
Universities: 1,000. **School enrolment:** female/male: 77%/83%.

HEALTH

Access to health services: 80%. **Access to safe water:** 62%.
Hospitals: 971 (6 beds per 10,000). **Doctors:** 25,135.
Blind: 1,000,000. **Deaf:** 12,753,900. Murder **rate:** <1.
Lepers: 200,000. **Underweight prevalence under 5:** 35%.

LITERATURE

New book titles p.a.: 3,820 (18 p.a. per million). **Periodicals:** 164.
Newspapers: 56 dailies.

COMMUNICATION (per 1,000 people)

Phones: 17 **(16% mobile).** Radios: 132. **TV sets:** 147.
Daily newspaper circulation: 20. **Computers:** 15.

HUMAN LIFE AND LIBERTY (optimum condition=100.0%)

HDI: 66.8. **HSI:** 36.0. **HFI:** 12.5. **EFL:** 43.0.

Country Table 1. **Religious adherents in Indonesia, AD 1900-2025.**

Year	1900		1970		mid-1990		Annual change, 1990-2000				mid-1995		mid-2000		mid-2025	
Name	Adherents	%	Adherents	%	Adherents	%	Natural	Conversion	Total	Rate	Adherents	%	Adherents	%	Adherents	%
Muslims	15,520,000	40.0	50,822,080	42.3	100,014,850	54.7	1,602,704	6,342	1,609,046	1.50	108,031,640	54.7	116,105,310	54.7	145,246,700	53.1
New-Religionists	3,880,000	10.0	45,000,120	37.4	41,060,000	22.5	657,973	-140,502	517,471	1.19	43,554,000	22.1	46,234,714	21.8	53,000,000	19.4
Christians	**536,050**	**1.4**	**12,330,000**	**10.3**	**23,450,000**	**12.8**	**375,818**	**59,594**	**435,412**	**1.72**	**25,550,000**	**12.9**	**27,804,116**	**13.1**	**43,000,000**	**15.7**
PROFESSION																
crypto-Christians	51,050	0.1	2,477,280	2.1	5,340,000	2.9	85,572	60,428	146,000	2.45	6,000,000	3.0	6,800,000	3.2	12,000,000	4.4
professing Christians	**485,000**	**1.3**	**9,852,720**	**8.2**	**18,110,000**	**9.9**	**290,247**	**-835**	**289,412**	**1.49**	**19,550,000**	**9.9**	**21,004,116**	**9.9**	**31,000,000**	**11.3**
AFFILIATION																
unaffiliated Christians	0	0.0	13,458	0.0	1,174,810	0.6	18,826	7,619	26,445	2.05	1,211,552	0.6	1,439,258	0.7	1,504,800	0.6
affiliated Christians	**536,050**	**1.4**	**12,316,542**	**10.2**	**22,275,190**	**12.2**	**356,992**	**51,975**	**408,967**	**1.70**	**24,338,448**	**12.3**	**26,364,858**	**12.4**	**41,495,200**	**15.2**
Protestants	473,400	1.2	6,278,696	5.2	10,340,000	5.7	165,695	12,805	178,500	1.61	11,244,690	5.7	12,125,000	5.7	18,400,000	6.7
Independents	3,000	0.0	3,404,026	2.8	7,000,000	3.8	112,173	31,427	143,600	1.88	7,711,880	3.9	8,436,000	4.0	14,500,000	5.3
Roman Catholics	55,650	0.1	2,620,140	2.2	4,900,000	2.7	78,521	6,715	85,236	1.62	5,340,588	2.7	5,752,358	2.7	8,500,000	3.1
Marginal Christians	0	0.0	11,580	0.0	32,000	0.0	513	1,087	1,600	4.14	38,000	0.0	48,000	0.0	90,000	0.0
Anglicans	0	0.0	2,000	0.0	3,100	0.0	50	-20	30	0.93	3,200	0.0	3,400	0.0	5,000	0.0
Orthodox	4,000	0.0	100	0.0	90	0.0	1	0	1	1.06	90	0.0	100	0.0	200	0.0
Trans-megabloc groupings																
Evangelicals	210,000	0.5	1,885,000	1.6	3,350,000	1.8	53,683	14,317	68,000	1.87	3,687,094	1.9	4,030,000	1.9	5,980,000	2.2
Pentecostals/Charismatics	0	0.0	3,590,000	3.0	7,860,000	4.3	125,954	33,046	159,000	1.86	8,687,592	4.4	9,450,000	4.5	14,500,000	5.3
Great Commission Christians	**465,000**	**1.2**	**6,200,000**	**5.2**	**11,750,000**	**6.4**	**188,290**	**96,632**	**284,922**	**2.19**	**12,920,000**	**6.5**	**14,599,219**	**6.9**	**25,070,000**	**9.2**
Hindus	776,000	2.0	2,318,000	1.9	5,800,000	3.2	92,943	52,926	145,869	2.27	6,600,000	3.3	7,258,687	3.4	10,300,000	3.8
Ethnoreligionists	17,692,950	45.6	6,570,000	5.5	5,200,000	2.8	83,328	-69,888	13,440	0.26	5,270,000	2.7	5,334,395	2.5	5,000,000	1.8
Nonreligious	0	0.0	950,000	0.8	3,100,000	1.7	49,676	51,018	100,694	2.85	3,650,000	1.9	4,106,941	1.9	9,000,000	3.3
Chinese folk-religionists	195,000	0.5	980,000	0.8	2,350,000	1.3	37,658	31,261	68,919	2.61	2,800,000	1.4	3,039,190	1.4	5,000,000	1.8
Buddhists	200,000	0.5	1,099,000	0.9	1,630,000	0.9	26,120	4,664	30,784	1.74	1,751,000	0.9	1,937,836	0.9	2,450,000	0.9
Atheists	0	0.0	200,000	0.2	400,000	0.2	6,410	3,977	10,387	2.34	460,000	0.2	503,873	0.2	750,000	0.3
Baha'is	0	0.0	10,700	0.0	22,000	0.0	353	101	454	1.89	24,700	0.0	26,537	0.0	45,000	0.0
Jews	0	0.0	100	0.0	150	0.0	2	0	2	1.14	160	0.0	168	0.0	300	0.0
doubly-counted religionists	0	0.0	0	0.0	-215,000	-0.1	-3,445	507	-2,938	1.29	-227,500	-0.1	-244,382	-0.1	-350,000	-0.1
World A (unevangelized persons)	29,488,000	76.0	60,140,050	50.0	79,523,220	43.5	1,274,329	-1,346,041	-71,712	-0.09	80,368,048	40.7	78,903,804	37.2	85,040,462	31.1
World B (evangelized non-Christians)	8,775,950	22.6	47,810,050	39.7	79,838,780	43.7	1,279,393	1,286,447	2,565,840	2.82	91,546,444	46.4	105,399,080	49.7	145,401,538	53.2
World C (Christians)	536,050	1.4	12,330,000	10.3	23,450,000	12.8	375,818	59,594	435,412	1.72	25,550,000	12.9	27,804,116	13.1	43,000,000	15.7
Country's population	**38,800,000**	**100.0**	**120,280,100**	**100.0**	**182,812,000**	**100.0**	**2,929,540**	**0**	**2,929,540**	**1.50**	**197,464,493**	**100.0**	**212,107,000**	**100.0**	**273,442,000**	**100.0**

COLUMNS, ROWS.
For meanings and definitions, see Codebook (Part 3). Note that, by definition, total 'Christians' = professing + crypto-Christians, which also = affiliated + unaffiliated Christians, and also = Great Commission Christians + latent Christians. Percentages may not always total exactly, due to rounding.

CENSUSES.
In 1930 a partial census produced these figures for the whole country: 48.7% Muslims, 47.2% animists, 1.9% Hindus and Buddhist. 1.6% Protestants, 0.6% Roman Catholics. The *Statistical pocketbook of Indonesia* has for many years published annual religion statistics provided by the government Department of Religion, compiled in each region by local government officials using in the main information direct from the churches. The only census claiming complete enumeration for religion is as follows. **24.IX.1971:** 87.50% Muslims (Quranic and syncretistic), 7.38% Christians (4.35% Protestants, 2.27% Roman Catholics, 0.76% other Christians), 1.94% Hindus, 0.92% Buddhists, 0.82% Confucians (Chinese folk-religionists), 1.42% others. **1990:** 87.2% Muslims, 9.6% Christians (3.6% Roman Catholics), 1.8% Hindus, 1.0% Buddhists, 0.4% other religionists.

NOTES ON RELIGIONS
ATHEISTS. The Communist Party of Indonesia (PKI) was suppressed in 1966 after an abortive coup, with over 250,000 massacred, and was driven underground with 90,000 imprisoned, and only a few thousand remained in 1973. However, something over 100,000 members and sympathizers are believed still to exist, making a total atheistic community of around 500,000, with at least 4 million more nonreligious.
BAHA'IS. Local spiritual assemblies: 62 (1964), increasing slightly to 71 (1973), and very gradually in the following 25 years.
BUDDHISTS. Prevalent among urban Chinese, and Javanese military and government officials. There are 30 Buddhist monasteries, and 355 temples (*rumah ibadat*). Since 1965 a large movement of nominal Muslims into Buddhism and Hinduism has taken place in East and Central Java. The resurgence of Buddhism has taken a neo-Theravada form.
CHRISTIANS. Over 95% have come into Christianity from an animistic background, particularly the Batak church and those of Nias, Timor, and Minahasa; the Java churches have arisen out of a Muslim background; and the Bali church has 11,000 converts from Hinduism. The large numbers of annual converts during 1965-1980 (over 2.5 million Protestant and Catholic converts) are mainly former nominal Muslim, animists, Hindus, and Chinese.
CRYPTO-CHRISTIANS. Protestants and indigenous Christians affiliated to churches but in areas of strong Muslim hostility, and therefore not known to state or society as professing Christians nor recorded as such in censuses; including organized and unorganized isolated radio believers, and numbers of illegal or underground churches.
ETHNORELIGIONISTS. Two groupings: (a) partially-islamized folk-religionists and animists, and (b) predominantly or completely animistic peoples. Animists are numerically significant among Bataks, Dayaks, Torajas, Halmaherans, Irianese, and in Nias, Mentawei, Aru, Seram, Buru, and Nusatenggara. In West Irian, many of the 350 tribes are still predominantly animist, and for some decades nativistic and messianic or cargo-cult movements have been frequent among them. On Kalimantan, about one million follow the primal religion Kaharingan. HINDUS. Predominant among the Balinese, also in some mountainous areas of Java, and among the Tenggarese (550,000). In addition, though not enumerated here as Hindus, 50% of the national population mostly in Java are strongly hinduized; they are enumerated here as New-Religionists. Since 1965 many hundreds of thousands of nominal Muslims have become Hindus, mostly in East and Central Java. ISKCON (Hare Krishna) operates 1 center.
INDEPENDENTS. In over 140 denominations in 1995 (see Table 2).
MUSLIMS. This line in the table enumerates only Quranic Muslims properly so called. Indonesian Islam has been characterized as malleable, tentative, syncretistic, and multi-voiced. The government Department of Religion in its annual enumerations classifies 87.5% of the population as Muslims (the term *Islam statistik*, i.e nominal or 'statistical Muslims', is used), by extending the term to include all peoples who are islamized or who are under Muslim influence, covering the 4 distinct groups shown as separate categories in the table above: (1) 43% who are Quranic Muslims, or strict Muslims, or Muslims properly so called; these are Sunnis (of the Shafiite rite), mostly coastal peoples including Sumatra Malays, Achinese, Buginese, Makassarese, with Wahhabi reform movement centers in north Sumatra and southwest Celebes, in 2 groups of similar size: (a) reformist favoring arabization, and (b) traditionalist; and also Ahmadiya (enumerated here under Muslims although declared non-Muslim by Pakistan);Ahmadiya has 57 mosques and numerous foreign missionaries (Pakistanis), scattered across the nation. Both Ahmadi factions, Qadianis and Lahoris, are present. Islam is most strictly practiced in Atieh (west Sumatra), west Java, southeast Kalimantan, and some of the Lesser Sunda islands; (2) 29.4% belonging to islamized and hinduized new religions and mystical sects syncretizing Islam, Hinduism, Buddhism and animism (here termed New-Religionists); (3) 12.6% who are animistic ethnoreligionists either partially islamized or completely non-islamized; and (4) 2% who, while labeled 'statistical Muslims' are in fact (unknown to the state) either atheists, or nonreligious, or Chinese folk-religionists, or crypto-Christians. Peoples strongly Muslim include the Achinese, Minangkabau, Sundanese, Madurese, Banjarese, Buginese and Javanese. *Mosques.* The total of mosques (*Mesdjid*) was 58,059 in 1958, 62,976 in 1962, rising to 83,914 in 1970, and houses of worship (*langgar, surau*) 198,832 (1958), 219,745 (1962) and 240,520 (1970). *Mosque attendance.* About 3% of the population attend mosques regularly or occasionally. Total capacity of all mosques is about 7% of the population. *Hajj pilgrims to Mecca.* (1963) 8,637; (1968) 17,565; (1969) 10,615; (1970) 14,633; (1971) 22,753; (1972) 22,659; (1973) 40,668; (1974) 68,872; (1975) 55,617; (1976) 25,624. From the early days of Islam in Indonesia (9th century), pilgrims to Mecca have been a main means of communication, especially for Muslim reform movements.
NEW-RELIGIONISTS. These fall into 2 categories, the first indigenous to Indonesia and found there only, the second international movements introduced from outside. (1) By far the larger group are followers of new Muslim or islamized and hinduized syncretistic religions (syncretizing Islam, Hinduism, Buddhism, and animism). The origins of these religions go back several centuries, when the traditional animistic element was predominant. Since 1800 this element has receded in importance as Muslim, Hindu, and Christian elements have come to the fore. In this survey, they are classified among the so-called New Religions of Asia because of this recent syncretistic development, and also because they have become especially widespread since 1950. They include: Javanese religion (Agama Jawa), Java-Sundanese religion (Agama Jawa-Sunda), Javanese and other mystical sects (Golongan-golongan Kebatinan: including Budi Setia, Sumarah, Kawruh Bedja, Ilmu Sejati), and similar syncretistic religions outside Java. A representative movement is Pangestu, a syncretistic religion with 100,000 adherents (mainly intellectuals) on Java, teaching 'one Divine Being' derived from Islam, Christianity, Buddhism, and Hinduism. A number of these new religions have been banned for alleged subversion but continue to operate underground. The total of all such sects is probably over 300, less than half of which are registered with government. A handful have followings outside Indonesia, such as the experiential cult Subud begun by Bapak on Java in 1933 and since 1956 spread abroad, with centers in over 70 USA cities alone. (2) There are also a few followers of Japanese and Chinese New Religions, including 4,000 in Soka Gakkai (Nichiren Shoshu).
NONRELIGIOUS. Three separate groupings: (1) those related to the underground communist movement, (2) former Chinese folk-religionists who have abandoned religion, and (3) intellectuals and other humanists.
ORTHODOX. Armenians rapidly emigrating since the year 1900.
PENTECOSTALS/CHARISMATICS. The Catholic Charismatic Renewal began in 1975, and by 1997 had 397 regular weekly prayer groups with 20,000 regular advent attenders (6,000 aged 15-25), 75 involved priests and one bishop, 3 covenant communities.
PROTESTANTS. Conversions have been very numerous since 1965. On Kalimantan alone, there were 300,000 persons baptized from 1965-74.
ROMAN CATHOLICS. In the year 1900, there were 54,909 baptized (29,009 indigenous, including 1,461 in West Irian, and 25,900 Europeans) and 729 catechumens.

Great Commission Instrument Panel: status of Indonesia (for explanation see start of Part 4)

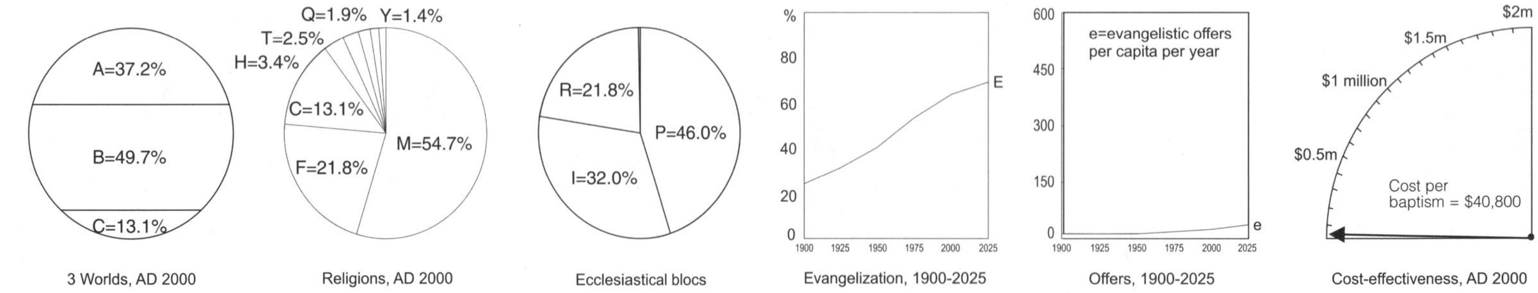

Country summary. **Worlds A, B, C by ethnolinguistic peoples, cities, and major civil divisions in Indonesia.**

	PEOPLES							CITIES							CIVIL DIVISIONS						
World	*Num*	*Pop 2000*	*C%*	*Christians*	*E%*	*U%*	*Unevangelized*	*Num*	*Pop 2000*	*C%*	*Christians*	*E%*	*U%*	*Unevangelized*	*Num*	*Pop 2000*	*C%*	*Christians*	*E%*	*U%*	*Unevangelized*
A	285	64,205,522	0.75	483,553	35	65	41,622,689	54	14,524,532	2.90	421,403	38	62	8,991,231	0	0	0.00	0	0	0	0
B	151	135,686,068	11.90	16,143,783	73	27	37,131,052	36	24,081,316	17.07	4,109,583	74	26	6,205,596	23	203,367,500	9.61	19,541,502	61	39	78,644,794
C	308	12,215,786	79.71	9,737,533	100	0	52,135	4	651,060	89.34	581,677	98	2	13,829	3	8,739,885	78.07	6,823,357	98	2	161,083
Total	**744**	**212,107,376**	**12.43**	**26,364,869**	**63**	**37**	**78,805,876**	**94**	**39,256,908**	**13.02**	**5,112,663**	**61**	**39**	**15,210,656**	**26**	**212,107,385**	**12.43**	**26,364,859**	**63**	**37**	**78,805,877**

Country status. Located astride the equator, Indonesia is an archipelago of 13,667 islands of which only 1,000 are inhabited. Five of these islands—Java, Sumatra, Sulawesi, Kalimantan, and Irian Jaya—comprise 90% of the land area. Indonesia is the third largest Muslim nation in the world, accounting for over 10% of the world's Muslims. Rice is the major crop and Indonesia exports rubber and palm oil.

HUMAN LIFE AND LIBERTY

Human need and development. Because of its enormous natural resources, Indonesia is considered one of the more developed of the developing nations, but in terms of the standards of life, it fares only slightly better than other low-income economies. Its per capita income of $980 is less than that of Morocco and Philippines, but higher than that of India, Pakistan or Moldavia. Its national literacy rate of 83% and a life expectancy of 67, show that it has been able to make impressive progress in key quality of life sectors. It has been able to do this despite a rapidly growing population that has passed 200 million. However, for the majority of the people life remains austere and difficult, particularly in overcrowded islands, such as Java. Food scarcities are not unknown, and about a third of the population is malnourished according to FAO standards. Shortage of housing is a chronic problem in the cities where thousands of makeshift huts are jammed in a labyrinth of unpaved streets and byways that become quagmires during the heavy rains. Sewage systems and central water systems exist only in Djakarta and other major cities. In other areas all waste is dumped in open sewage canals and open wells and surface water sources are used for bathing and washing as well as for cooking. Traditional attitudes toward personal hygiene contribute to the spread of disease. Most rural folk depend on folk healers and sorcerers known as dukun rather than doctors to cure their illnesses. There is no comprehensive or universal system of social welfare or social insurance. Generally civic and religious organizations perform a variety of welfare functions, such as caring for the destitute and handicapped.

Human rights and freedoms. Indonesia has an authoritarian regime which restricts basic human rights, but human rights abuses occur primarily in connection with the secessionist movements in Irian Jaya, East Timor and Aceh. In these areas, government troops have been accused of conducting a campaign of terror against the population and engaging in atrocities against innocent people. Police use excessive lethal force in efforts to apprehend suspected criminals and to force confession after arrest. Although the Indonesian Criminal Procedures Code contains a number of safeguards against inhuman and degrading punishments as well as arbitrary arrests and detention, none of these safeguards are observed in practice. Bail is rarely granted and authorities frequently interfere with access to defense counsel. Suspects may be held without trial for years. The use of forced confessions and limits on the presentation of defense evidence are common during trials. Defendants do not have the right to remain silent. The judiciary is not independent, and is subject to considerable pressure from the military and the government. In addition, most judges are corrupt and openly seek bribes before conviction and sentencing. Since 1980 nearly 270 judges have been prosecuted for corruption and dismissed from the bench. The 1963 Anti-Subversion Law is used to prosecute opponents of the government under a broad rubric that includes acts that 'distort state ideology or disseminate feelings of hostility or anxiety among the population'. Significant restrictions on press freedom remain. Although the media, including 273 daily newspapers, are largely free, the government exercised strong supervision over them by controlling publishing permits, the number of pages and the amount of advertising. Occasionally, domestic and foreign publications are censored and officials have been known to telephone editors and ask them to suppress stories. Under the 1985 Social Organizations Law all groups, including religious bodies, are required to adhere to the national ideology known as Pancasila, or Five Tenets. Indonesians generally are very tolerant, but the most important exception is the informal discrimination against ethnic Chinese. The use of Chinese language is prohibited in schools and in business, and ethnic Chinese are denied the right to run businesses in rural areas or form exclusive cultural groups or trade associations. However, these laws are observed more in the breach, and many Chinese conduct successful businesses and Chinese societies and associations flourish. Women occupy a distinctly subordinate position in society, and reports of violence against women appear in the daily press.

Human environment. Indonesia contains one of the largest remaining tropical rain forests in the world, estimated to cover half of the country's land area. The national development plans call for the sustained exploitation of these rain forests at the rate of 2 million acres of virgin forest annually. The resulting erosion is expected to destroy the natural ecological systems of the area which includes both sides of the Wallace Line. Large areas of watershed lands also are threatened. The rivers have been polluted for years by industrial waste and sewage and now pose a serious threat to the health of the inhabitants.

Muslims. Worshippers outside Mesjid Agung Mosque in Jakarta during 1964 Idul Adha (Feast of Sacrifice): after prayers the faithful will sacrifice cattle.

NON-CHRISTIAN RELIGIONS

Islam was introduced into northern Sumatra in 1272. In general, western Indonesia is more islamized than the east where Muslims are confined largely to coastal areas. The principal ethnic groups accepting Islam include the following: Achinese, a small part of the Bataks, Sumatra Coastal Malays, Minangkabaus, Palembangese, Jambirese, Rejong-Lebongers and Lampongers of Sumatra; Sundanese, Madurese and a portion of the Javanese in Java and Madura; Banjarese and Kutanese of Kalimantan; Gorontalese, Makassarese, Buginese, Butungese of Sulawesi; Ternatenese, Tidorese of Maluku; Sasaks of Lombok; Bimans, and Sumbawans. The percentage of adherents attributed to Islam varies considerably according to how Muslims are defined. The government Department of Religion uses the figure of 89% of the population in 1965 rising to 91% in 1970, based on the principle that whoever is not Catholic, Protestant, Hindu or Buddhist must be married in a Muslim ceremony and is therefore counted as Muslim (the term 'statistical Muslims' is used). On the other hand, many sociologists and observers estimate that only 43% of the population are Quranic Muslims (Muslims in the strict or correct sense of the term), a figure which is based on the percentage of votes obtained by the 5 Islamic political parties in 1955, since during the electoral campaign this vote was considered a minimal requirement for being called a Muslim, and also on the voting percentage in 1959 on the proposition to transform Indonesia into an Islamic state.

Muslims on Java are slightly less urbanized than Christians or Buddhists, whereas on the other islands the reverse is true. Most Muslims are peasants, but in coastal areas there are many who are merchants and seafarers. Particularly in Central and East Java, one finds relatively more convinced Muslims in the middle class and among the wealthier portion of the peasant class than among the very poor. Quranic Muslims are Sunnis of the Shafiite rite. They are divided into 2 groups: (1) a reformist branch which favors the arabization of Indonesian Islam, purifying it of pre-Islamic customs, and seeking to prepare Muslims for their encounter with modernity; and (2) a traditionalist branch which does not favor secular education and wishes to maintain the present mixture of Islamic and Indonesian customs. At the first general elections held in 1955, the reformist party obtained 20.9% of the votes and the traditionalist party 18.4%. Since the accession to power of general Suharto as acting president in 1967, the position and influence of Muslims in national affairs was noticeably reduced. That situation changed as the parliamentary elections of 1992 and the presidential elections of 1993 approached. Several government actions that were extremely friendly to Islam were widely interpreted as motivated by the desire to gain more votes from the Muslim community.

New Religions syncretizing traditional animism with, firstly, Hinduism and Buddhism and later Islam, have arisen over the centuries mainly on Java. They are of the same generic, synthetic kind as the other new Asian syncretistic religions of Japan, China, Korea, Viet Nam, et alia, except that in Indonesia today the main background religion is Islam. The following 3 distinct religions are in this category; from one point of view they may be described as islamized new religions.

Javanese religion (Agama Jawa), composed of animistic, Hindu, Buddhist, and Muslim elements, is the religion of a large number of Javanese of the urbanized upper classes among whom Hindu elements predominate, as well as being found among poor peasants of the Central and East Javanese plains, among whom animistic elements are more significant. Originally these were all considered animists, as in the census of 1930 which listed Indonesia as 47.2% animist and 48.4% Muslim. The Department of Religion today classes the adherents of Agama Jawa as Muslims; but many, reacting against the campaign of islamization, are turning towards Hinduism, Buddhism, and Christianity.

Java-Sundanese religion (Agama Jawa-Sunda) was not widely recognized as a distinct religion until 1964 when Muslims tried forcibly to islamize its adherents. The religious head, followed by some of his faithful, sought refuge in the Catholic Church. The exact number of members is not known, but it appears to be found only among the Sundanese in the interior of west Java. This religion categorically rejects practices permitted by Muslims such as polygamy, divorce, and child marriage.

Mystical sects (Golongan-golongan Kebatinan) are also important in Indonesia. There has never been any lack of mystical movements in Indonesia, but their number has grown considerably since 1950 mainly as a result of the general social disorder. Mystical movements are most common in Java and are found among members of all social classes. Representing a great diversity of beliefs from pantheism to monotheism, most of them evidence belief in spirits and the use of magical practices. In varying degrees they engage in occultism, theosophy, and metaphysical phenomena. A number have been banned by the government for alleged subversion but continue to operate underground. Their attraction lies in the emphasis they give to certain indigenous religious values and concerns which are ignored by Indonesia's others religions. In general they manifest uneasiness and even animosity towards the established religions, especially to legalistic Islam. Nevertheless, one occasionally finds Javanese Christians among their members. One Javanese movement that has existed for centuries is Aliran Kepercayaan (flow of faith), which grew greatly in numbers and influence in the 1980s. Its followers believe in one supreme God, but have little dogma, and no scripture of clergy. Its most important practices are meditation, fasting, and chanting. In 1980 Kepercayaan was granted half an hour per week of television time, the same as for other religions. Its leaders have lobbied for its marriage ceremony to be legally recognized and for it to be taught in the schools. The Association of Believers in One Supreme God is an umbrella organization for 20 Aliran Kepercayaan groups; 267 such groups have registered with the government.

Tribal religionists. Head of Batak sorcerer's carved staff, Sumatra.

Traditional tribal religion, commonly called animism, still exists among the Bataks of northern Sumatra; the inhabitants of Nias and Mentawai; the Dayaks of Kalimantan; the Torajas of Sulawesi; the inhabitants of the archipelago of Aru; the peoples of Seram and Buru, and Halmaherans in Maluku; the Irianese of West Irian; as well as on the islands of Nusatenggara. These peoples are for the most part the inhabitants of small islands or isolated regions of the interior. Some, such as several of the Papuan tribes, follow stone age culture. Most tribal religions are complex, with numerous names for God; among the Toba Bataks the supreme being is called Mula Dyadi, while Batara Guru (Sanskrit: Bhattara Guru) is the name more commonly used by the Dairi and Karo Bataks. Their adherents can be classified into 2 groups: partially islamized folk-religionists, and predominantly or completely animistic peoples. Islam is making an effort to reach them, but most are more attracted to Christianity. In West Irian by 1973 a total of over 21 distinct cargo cults of animistic origin had arisen, mainly in Geelvink Bay and in the highlands.

Hindus. Balinese song-and-dance drama in Hindu village on Bali.

Hinduism and ***Buddhism*** are the most ancient of Indonesia's immigrant religions. Both have shown a new flowering since Independence in 1945. Hinduism is the predominant religion among the Balinese who mix with it pre-Hindu and Hindu-Javanese elements. Denpasar, the capital of Bali, has a university for training Hindu teachers. Hinduism also exits in some of the mountainous areas of Java where the Parisada Hindu Dharma Society has been actively engaged in literature distribution and establishment of Hindu schools. Buddhism in Indonesia dates at least from the 10th century, when the famous temple at Borobudur in Java was built. Buddhism is especially prevalent among the Chinese who are largely city-dwellers, and also among Javanese army officers and government officials. In 1970 there were 30 Buddhist monasteries and 355 temples in Indonesia. There are in addition large numbers of 'statistical Muslims' among whom Hindu elements predominate, and who account for much of the estimated half a million conversions from nominal Islam to Hinduism since 1965.

Buddhists. World's largest Buddhist monument in Borobudur, Central Java, AD 800.

CHRISTIANITY

A Catholic community established itself on the island of Sumatra as early as the 7th century, and in 1323 Franciscans had some contacts with Sumatra, Java and Borneo. Portuguese colonial expansion was extended to the Moluccas and the Celebes in 1522 and the evangelization of Timor began in 1530. The first Portuguese missionary to the Moluccas arrived in 1534. Francis Xavier spent nearly a year there in 1546, and was followed by other Jesuits and Dominicans in 1562. By the end of the 16th century, there were 18 Catholic mission posts and 25,000 Christians. With the defeat of Portugal by the Dutch in 1605, Catholic missionaries were expelled and replaced by Dutch Reformed chaplains supported by the Dutch East India Company. The Dutch Reformed Church was virtually the only Christian influence in the islands for the next 300 years. The beginning of the 19th century saw a change in both the political and religious climates. France conquered Holland in 1799 and disbanded the Dutch East India Company, and England began to exert its colonial influence in the area in 1811. This was accompanied by the Protestant awakening epitomized by William Carey's missionary journey to India. In 1827 the Netherlands Missionary Society began work in the Celebes and the Rhenish Mission among the Dayaks of Borneo. These beginnings were followed by many others, including the notable work of German Lutherans among the Bataks of Sumatra beginning in 1861. Catholic missionaries also returned to Indonesia during the 19th century. In 1807 the prefecture apostolic of Batavia was erected, which was eventually in 1961 renamed as the archdiocese of Jakarta. Dutch Jesuits appeared on the scene in 1859 and Catholic evangelization of all the major islands began. The 20th century has witnessed the influx of many new Protestant missionary groups, as well as the continued growth of Catholicism and of large regional Reformed and Lutheran churches.

Since 1966 Protestants and Catholics have experienced massive growth in membership. During July-August 1966 the East Java Christian Church (then with 63,000 followers) baptized nearly 10,000 persons. The Karo Batak Protestant Church (30,000 in 1965) baptized over 26,000 persons in 1966-67. Prolonged revival movements broke out, notably on Timor where the Evangelical Christian Church in Timor grew by over 100,000 members in 4 years. In the 8 months before March 1967, 250,000 joined member churches of the Christian Council of Indonesia alone. Altogether, Protestants and Catholics received well over 2.5 million converts from nominal Islam (former 'statistical Muslims') since 1965. The largest numbers came from the following areas (in order of magnitude): central Java, east (but not west) Java, north Sumatra, Alor, Timor (eastern part). Lampung, Sulawesi (among the Torajas), and the interiors of Kalimantan and West Irian.

Karo Batak Protestant Church. Mass conversion and mass baptism of Karo Bataks, Sumatra 1968.

Part of this widespread increase is explained by the violence of anti-communist repression following the abortive coup d'etat of 1965, and also by the requirement, subsequently enforced on all citizens, that everyone belong to one of the 4 recognized religions. In the Catholic Church this phenomenon has manifested itself since 1966 by a sudden rise in the number of catechumens and since 1967 by a marked increase in adult baptisms. Not uncommonly the vigorous campaign aimed at islamizing animists and 'atheists' (communist sympathizers being automatically considered as atheists) has paradoxically resulted in pushing many towards Christianity, Hinduism, and Buddhism rather than towards Islam. This sudden growth is more evident in areas with a relatively large proportion of animists, Chinese or 'statistical Muslims', the latter being the animists and Javanese religionists listed as Muslims by the Department of Religion. There has been virtually no additional growth in strongly Muslim areas or where Christians already form a large part of the population. Irian Barat is an exception in that the events of 1965-66 had little influence; and Muslims, who in any case are few in number and largely confined to the coast, show little interest in the Irianese peoples.

Protestants. North Sumatran choir sing at DGI ecumenical worship service in football stadium at Pematang Siantar, 1971.

PROTESTANT CHURCHES. Of the 24.3 million affiliated Christians in Indonesia (1995), 11.2 million (46%) are Protestants. Protestant strength by regions may be listed in order as follows: West Irian 65% (Protestants as % of total population), Moluccas 57%, Sulawesi 18%, northern Sumatra 15%, southeast Indonesia and Bali 10%, Kalimantan 6%, Java 2%. Indonesia has several very large Protestant churches, the largest and most extensive being the Protestant Church in Indonesia; totaling nearly 2.66 million members in 1995, it serves as the General Synod for 8 component churches. Among them is the Moluccan Protestant Church, founded in 1536, which holds the distinction of being Asia's oldest Protestant denomination. Initials based on the Indonesian names of churches and organizations are widely used to identify them. The most significant churches in Sumatra are the Batak Christian Protestant Church (HKBP), the Nias Christian Protestant Church (BNKP), and the Simalungun Protestant Christian Church (GKPS). Sulawesi churches of particular importance include the Christian Evangelical Church in Minahasa (GMIM), Evangelical Christian Church in Sangihe-Talaud (GMIST), the Toraja Christian Church, and the Christian Church in Central Sulawesi (GKST). Among the Java churches may be mentioned the East Java Christian Church (GKJW) and the Christian Churches of Java (GKJ). On Irian Barat, the Evangelical Christian Church in West Irian and the Evangelical Church in Kalimantan are the largest Protestant churches. In addition to these large churches, most of which represent the fruit of early European missionary work, there are numerous smaller bodies, most representing recent missionary activity by conservative missions from North America. Of these the largest is the Gospel Tabernacle Christian Church (KINGMI), a product of the missionary activity of the Christian and Missionary Alliance. The Pentecostal movement has expanded rapidly both in numbers of denominations and in membership since the arrival of the first Pentecostal missionaries in the late 1920s. Altogether, there were in 1973 over 1,150 Western Protestant missionaries, 750 in 64 societies being from the USA. The number of expatriate missionaries declined dramatically in the 1990s as the government tightened considerably on the granting of entry visas, visa renewals, and residence permits.

Protestant churches are heavily involved in education, and medical and social services. They sponsor thousands of elementary schools and hundreds of kindergartens, secondary schools, trade schools, and vocational schools. Also there are 17 Christian universities and institutes of higher education. These include 4 well-established universities whose degrees are fully certified by government (Christian University of Indonesia in Jakarta, Nommensen University in North Sumatra, Satya Wacana Christian University in Central Java, Petra Christian University in East Java), and a school of social work at the undergraduate level. Protestant churches operate hundreds of hospitals, clinics, dispensaries, maternity hospitals, health centers, family planning clinics, and leprosaria. They are involved in numerous agricultural and technical schools, and development projects. In various parts of Indonesia, churches are engaged in lumbering, irrigation, upgrading cattle, poultry and fisheries, planting and improving rice, maize, vegetables, coconut and coffee groves, and road and bridge building. One of the Christian universities has an agricultural faculty.

Catholic Church in Indonesia. Pope Paul VI gives homily at mass in Jakarta during December 1970 visit.

CATHOLIC CHURCH. In 1949, 90,000 of the 791,000 Catholics were Europeans, mostly Dutch. Following Independence, and especially the nationalization of foreign-owned installations in 1958, Dutch citizens returned en masse to Europe, the only exception being priests and religious personnel. By 1969 there were only 2,000 Europeans out of a total of 2.2 million Catholics (rising to 2,538,000 baptized Catholics in 1972). In 1969 Chinese, both Indonesian and foreign, made up 7.1% of the total Catholic population. The ecclesiastical province with the greatest number of Catholics (Ende: 1,073,911 out of 2,220,428 in 1969) is also the one which has the smallest percentage of Chinese; and the smallest number of Chinese are in the province of Merauke. On the island of Flores which has 1% of the nation's population, 73% are Catholic, which figure is 36% of all Indonesian Catholics. On Java live 63.8% of the total population, but only 19% of all Catholics. In 8 dioceses (5 of them on Java) less than 0.5% of the population is Catholic, whereas in 5 other dioceses (3 of them on Flores) more than half are Catholics. This inequality in geographical distribution was even more evident 20 years ago, due in part to the Dutch colonial policy of prohibiting certain territories to Catholic work. Java was never closed to Catholics, but Bali was until 1935. The Torajas of Sulawesi and the inhabitants of Nias became accessible only in 1939. Ambon and the northern part of Western Irian were opened after 1925; but the Bataks and the inhabitants of Sumba were closed until 1929. The geographical inequality is now being modified because since Independence many Catholics from outlying islands have joined in the widespread migration to Java and particularly to Jakarta.

The Holy See has diplomatic relations with Indonesia and in AD 2000 is represented to government and the Catholic hierarchy by a pro-nuncio residing in Jakarta.

Church of Christ. 1974 Christmas Eve candlelight service held by Gereja Kristus, a Chinese pentecostal church in West Java, one of 140 indigenous denominations in Indonesia.

INDIGENOUS CHURCHES. Since 1891 there have been numerous secessions led by Indonesians from the major Protestant missions, and numbers of other churches independent of Western missions have been begun by Indonesians and Chinese since 1866. In 1970 there were around 150 such indigenous denominations, of which over 100 were known to, and listed by, the government Department of Religion. With an estimated 7.7 million affiliated adherents in 1995, they represent a powerful factor in the evolution of an indigenous Christianity. At least half of these are adherents of around 50 indigenous Pentecostal denominations. Most of these are clearly-defined denominations; but the largest of these, the Pentecostal Church of Indonesia (GPI), is in reality less an organized denomination than a vast unstructured agglomeration of relatively independent congregations.

Renewal movements. In the 1990s the Pentecostal/Charismatic Renewal continued to spread rapidly across most older churches, and numbered over 9,450,000 adherents (of whom 15% Pentecostals, 10% Charismatics, and 75% Independents).

Indigenous missions. The vast majority of Indonesian missionaries have been home missionaries working in the mosaic of peoples represented in their own country. An increasing number of these have been cross-cultural as opposed to evangelistic work among their own people. There is also a growing movement of foreign missionaries working primarily in other Asian countries.

CHURCH AND STATE

The constitution of 1945 stipulates: 'The State is based on the recognition of one all-powerful God' (Chapter XI, paragraph 29, Article 1), and 'The State guarantees to each citizen the freedom to embrace the religion of his choice and to fulfill the religious obligations which conform to his faith' (Article 2). Liberty to propagate religion is guaranteed 'on condition that it does not disturb religious peace'. The Indonesian state is based on 5 principles, called *pancasila*: faith in one all-powerful God, humanity, national consciousness, sovereignty of the people, and social justice. In reality, since January 1965 freedom of religion has been legally confined to free choice between 4 recognized religions: Islam, Protestantism, Catholicism and 'Hindu-Buddhism', the latter 2 being grouped together as one religion. Every good citizen is expected to adhere formally to one of these. Belief in one God (monotheism) makes formal adherence to any other than the 4 recognized religions practically impossible, and to deride any of the monotheistic religions is punishable with 5 years imprisonment. This situation was modified in 1973 when the New Religions (Kebatinan), of which president Suharto himself was a member, were finally granted official recognition and equal status.

The government Department of Religion (Departemen Agama Republik Indonesia), created in January 1946, has final jurisdiction over religious questions. This ministry has the responsibility for proposing all religious legislation to parliament, which however can only be adopted by unanimous vote. Religious questions are regulated by various principles. Recognized religions are free to erect places of worship 'wherever there are numerous adherents. They are free to build and direct schools, hospitals, orphanages and so on, and also to create political and social movements. The state does not concern itself with the internal affairs of the religions, and it confers certain advantages on religious leaders and exempts them from taxes. Finally, under pain of prison or fine, it is prohibited to offend or insult, orally or in written form, any of the recognized religions or religious groups. It is also worthy of note that the Christian New Year, Good Friday, Ascension Day, and Christmas are considered national holidays.

Nevertheless, in practice the government Department of Religion, which is in the hands of conservative Muslims, favors Islam over the 3 other recognized religions. The major portion of the budget, reputedly as much as 95%, is given to Muslims who according to the department compose around 90% of the population. Large subsidies are provided for the construction of mosques and Quranic schools, the printing and diffusion of Muslim literature, and the like. The entire nation down to the smallest village is divided into a network of 'offices for religious affairs' whose personnel, paid by the state, are almost exclusively Muslim.

The constitutional liberty to propagate religion suffers from the numerous ways such terms can be defined and the many ways of claiming that religious peace has been 'disturbed'. In the same way, the phrase 'wherever there are numerous adherents' is also interpreted differently depending on whether the projected place of worship is Muslim or non-Muslim. Locally, Muslim pressure sometimes turns to violence resulting in the destruction of churches or Christian schools. The treatment received by churches depends on the administrative level concerned, distance from the capital, and personal relations with local officials of the Department of Religion. However, private schools conforming to established norms receive subsidies, as do orphanages and some Christian hospitals. Churches and ministers are exempted from certain taxes. The churches' proposals for social and economic development projects receive authorization from the central government. In spite of Muslim opposition, visas are accorded to new foreign missionaries and their residence permits are regularly renewed. Muslim religious fanaticism is exercised principally against alleged communists and atheists, of whom hundreds of thousands were massacred in 1965-66 after the abortive coup d'etat. By 1973, most of the 95,000 political prisoners and communist suspects had been released, leaving 15,000 in prisons and detention camps.

Christian political parties have had a certain history. The Partai Katolik (Roman Catholic) and PARKINDO (Protestant) had considerable influence; but in 1972 they were fused with 3 other national parties into the secular Democracy party of Indonesia (Partai Demokrasi Indonesia).

In July 1978, the appointment of a new head of the Department of Religion resulted in government edicts banning all proselytism, conversions and house churches, and calling for the expulsion of all foreign missionaries within 2 years (Decrees Nos. 70 and 77). These were however later toned down considerably.

BROADCASTING AND MEDIA

Indonesia is a major target of several shortwave radio broadcasters. Increasing the number of tribal languages being covered by broadcasting has long been a felt need. FEBC began broadcasting in the Sundanese language for the first time in March 1981; and in 1992 Studio Sentosa committed to develop programs in several Indonesian tribal languages for broadcast via TWR (Guam). The first of these programs was in Madurese, and this was achieved in 1992. As of 1996, FEBC (Philippines) is broadcasting in 6 major languages, including Acehenese and Sundanese (begun in March 1981), both World A megapeoples. FEBC (Saipan) has programs in 7 languages, and TWR (Guam) in 4. AWR operates 2 studios (Jakarta and Manado) which develop programs in Indonesian.

For Catholics, Indonesia is a member of UNDA. Over radio, there are 2 hours of daily programs and 2 hours 45 minutes of weekly programs, which feature local programs containing meditations, liturgies and sermons. In addition, there are 15 Catholic radio stations. Over television, Catholics broadcast more than 2 hours of monthly programs. Media training is offered at 6 different centers.

The 'Jesus' Film has been shown to 34 million people through national television and film teams. Response has been low: 2 million recorded decisions for Christ have been made as a result of the effort.

INTERDENOMINATIONAL ORGANIZATIONS

The major Protestant body is the Council of Churches of Indonesia begun in 1950 with 27 members, and by 1973 greatly enlarged in size and activities with 44 autonomous member churches (49 by 1978). A number of indigenous pentecostal and non-pentecostal churches are members; the first pentecostal body being the Church of Jesus the Messiah which joined in 1960. In 1984 its name was changed to the Association of Churches of Indonesia. Including Reformed, Pentecostal, Mennonite, and Lutheran bodies, it then had 20 regional councils spread across the country. There are also 2 smaller Christian councils. Christian Laymen's Evangelical Fellowship (1969), and the Association of Evangelical Churches of Indonesia (Dewan Gereja-Gereja Injil di Indonesia) (1970). Ecumenical relations between Protestants and Catholics improved considerably following Vatican II, with such activities as joint celebrations of Christian feast days in several regions.

FUTURE TRENDS AND PROSPECTS

Java will probably continue to be a hot spot for Muslim conversions to Christianity with up to 30% of the Javanese Christian by 2025. Christians of all kinds among all peoples could claim near 16% of the population by 2025 with corresponding losses among Muslims, ethnoreligionists, and new-religionists.

By the middle of the twenty-first century, Muslims and Christian may reach a symbiotic relationship in an approximately 50/25 percent relationship. New religionists would then level off at about 15%. Significant conversions from the major religious traditions would then be required for any tradition to grow.

BIBLIOGRAPHY

'A balanced growth model for local church ministry in the urban context of Jakarta.' K. G. Hamakonda. D. Miss. thesis, Fuller Theological Seminary, Pasadena, CA, 1986. 244p.

'A christological model for Indonesia.' R. J. Wattimury. Ph.D. dissertation, Baylor University, Waco, TX, 1991. 230p.

A dictionary of Indonesian Islam. H. M. Federspiel. *Monographs in international studies Southeast Asia series*, no. 94. Athens, OH: Ohio University, Center for International Studies, 1995. 327p.

A pattern of peoples: a journey among the tribes of Indonesia's outer islands. R. Hanbury-Tenison. New York: Charles Scribner, 1975. 214p.

'A strategy for planting churches in Java through the Sangkakala Mission: with special emphasis on the Javanese and Chinese people.' A. Sutanto. Ph.D. dissertation, Fuller Theological Seminary, Pasadena, CA, 1986. 211p.

Adat, Islam and Christianity in a Batak homeland. S. R. Siregar. *Papers in international studies, Southeast Asian series*, no. 57. Athens, OH: Ohio University Center for International Studies, Southeast Asia Program, 1981. 108p.

'An Indonesian church in the midst of social change: the Batak Protestant Christian Church, 1942–1957.' E. O. V. Nyhus. Ph.D. dissertation, University of Wisconsin, 1987. 2 vols.

Annotated bibliography of bibliographies on Indonesia. H. C. Kemp. *Bibliographical series*, no. 17. Leiden: Koninklijk Instituut voor Taal-, Land- en Volenkunde, 1990. 433p.

Anthropology in Indonesia, a bibliographical review. R. M. Koentjaraningrat. *Koninklijk Instituut voor Taal-, Land- en Volenkunde, Bibliographical series*, no. 8. The Hague: Martinus Nijhoff, 1975. 343p.

Balinese temple festival. C. Hooykaas. *Bibliotheca Indonesica*, no. 15. The Hague: Martinus Nijhoff, 1977. 109p.

Batak blood and Protestant soul: the development of national Batak churches in North Sumatra. P. B. Pedersen. Grand Rapids, MI: Eerdmans, 1970. 212p.

Bibliografi Ilmu Agama dan Theologia Kristen Dalam Bahasa Indonesia (Bibliography of the scientific study of religions and Christian theology in the Indonesian language). J. A. B. Jongeneel. Jakarta: Unit Pemasaran BPK, 1975–76. 2 vols.

Bibliography of Indonesian peoples and cultures. R. Kennedy. 3rd ed. *Yale anthropological series*, no. 4. New Haven, CT: Yale University Press, 1974. 207p.

Buku Petunjuk Gereja Katolik Indonesia, 1974 (Directory of the Catholic Church in Indonesia). Jakarta: Kantor Waligereja Indonesia, 1974.

Cannibal valley. R. T. Hitt. London: Hodder & Stoughton, 1962. 253p.

'Christianity in the Batak culture: the making of an indigenous church.' G. P. Harahap. M.S.T. thesis, Trinity Lutheran Seminary, Columbus, OH, 1982. 196p.

'Christians and Muslims in Indonesia: the impact of history.' A. F. Walker. M.A. thesis, Hartford Seminary, Hartford, CT, 1991. 105p.

Church growth in the central highlands of West New Guinea. J. Sunda. Lucknow: Lucknow Publishing House, 1963. 51p.

'Cultural contact and culture change in Western New Guinea,' J. M. van der Kroef, *Anthropological quarterly*, 32 (1959), 134–60.

'Das Christentum in Indonesien,' T. Müller-Krüger, in *Indonesien, Malaysia und die Philippinen.* H. Kähler (ed). Leiden: E. J. Brill, 1975.

Der Protestantismus in Indonesien. T. Müller-Krüger. Stuttgart: Evangelisches Verlagswerk, 1968.

Entwicklung in Paradies: Socialer Fortschrift und die Kirchen in Indonesien. U. Beyer. Frankfurt: Lembeck, 1974.

'Explaining the crucifixion to Muslims: with special reference to Indonesia and Malaysia.' K. Tan. Ph.D. dissertation, Fuller Theological Seminary, Pasadena, CA, 1993. 293p.

God's invasion: the story of fifty years of Christian and Missionary Alliance missionary work in Irian Jaya. R. S. Wick. Camp Hill, PA: Buena Book Services, 1990. 247p.

God's miracles: Indonesian church growth. E. C. Smith. South Pasadena, CA: William Carey Library, 1970. 217p.

Headhunters about themselves: an ethnographic report from Irian Jaya, Indonesia. J. H. M. Boelaars. *Koninklijk Instituut voor Taal– Land– en Volkenkunde, Verhandelingen*, no. 92. The Hague: Martinus Nijhoff, 1981. 296p. (Study of Jaqaj tribe by missionary).

'Indonesia,' *Pro Mundi Vita bulletin*, 64 (January–February, 1977), 1–32.

Indonesia. G. H. Krausse & S. C. E. Krausse. *World bibliographical series*, vol. 170. Oxford, UK: CLIO Press, 1994. 453p. (See especially 'Religion,' p. 157–68).

Indonesia: a bibliography of bibliographies. J. N. B. Tairas. New York: Oleander Press, 1975. 123p.

Indonesia: an anthropological perspective. J. L. Peacock. *Goodyear regional anthropology series.* Pacific Palisades, CA: Goodyear Publishing, 1973. 168p.

Indonesia: church and society. F. L. Cooley. New York: Friendship Press, 1968. 128p.

Indonesia in the wake of Islam, 1965–1985. N. Tamara. Kuala Lumpur: Institute of Strategic and International Studies Malaysia, 1986. 35p.

Indonesian Christians and their political parties, 1923–1966: the role of Partai Kristen Indonesia and Partai Katolik. R. A. F. Webb. *Southeast Asian monograph series*, no. 2. Townsville, Australia: James Cook University, 1978. 105p.

Indonesian religions in transition. R. S. Kipp & S. Rodgers. Tuscon, AZ: University of Arizona Press, 1987. 304p.

Indonesian revival: why two million came to Christ. A. T. Willis Jr. South Pasadena, CA: William Carey Library, 1978. 288p.

'Islam and Adat among South Tapanuli migrants in three Indonesian cities,' B. H. Harahap, in *Indonesian religion in transition.* R. S. Kipp & S. Rodgers (Ed). Tucson, AZ: University of Arizona Press, 1987.

Islam observed: religious development in Morocco and Indonesia. C. Geertz. New Haven, CT: Yale University Press, 1968. 136p.

'Messianic movements in the Celebes, Sumatra and Borneo,' J. M. van der Kroef, in *Millennial dreams in action*, p.80–121. S. Thrupp (ed). The Hague: Mouton, 1962.

'Messianic movements in Western New Guinea,' F. U. Kamma, *International review of missions*, 41, 162 (1952), 148–60.

'Missiological dimensions in interreligious marriages between Christians and Muslims in Indonesia.' R. A. Waney. Th.M. thesis, Fuller Theological Seminary, Pasadena, CA, 1991. 139p.

Mission schools in Batakland (Indonesia), 1861–1940. J. S. Aritonang. *Studies in Christian mission*, vol. 10. Leiden: E. J. Brill, 1994. 391p.

'Modernization and religious purification: Islam in Indonesia,' J. B. Tamney, *Review of religious research*, 22 (December 1980), 207–218.

Muslims through discourse: religion and ritual in Gayo society. J. R. Bowen. Princeton, NJ: Princeton University Press, 1993. 370p.

Partner in nation building: the Catholic Church in Indonesia. M. P. M. Muskens. Aachen, Germany: Missio Aktuell Verlag, 1979. 339p.

'Pentecostalism among the Bandjalang,' M. Calley, in *Aborigines now: new perspective in the study of aboriginal communities*, p.44–58. M. Reay (ed). Sydney: Angus and Robertson, 1964.

Protestantse zendingsperiodieken uit de negentiende en twintigste eeuw in Nederland, Nederlands–indie, Suriname en de Nederlandse Antillen: een bibliografische catalogus met inleiding (Protestant missionary periodicals from the nineteenth and twentieth century in the Netherlands, the Dutch East Indies and the Dutch West Indies: a bibliographical catalogue with introduction). J. A. B. Jongeneel. Leiden: Interuniversitair Instituut voor Missiologie en Oecumenica, 1990. 145p.

Religion and nationalism in Southeast Asia: Burma, Indonesia, the Philippines. F. R. Von der Mehden. Madison, WI: University of Wisconsin Press, 1963. 253p.

Religion in Bali. No. 10 of section 13, *Indian Religions*, of *Iconography of religions.* C. Hooykaas. Leiden: E. J. Brill, 1973. 30p.

Religious texts of the oral tradition from Western New Guinea. F. C. Kamma (ed). *Part A: The origin and sources of life. Part B: The threat to life and its defence against natural and supernatural phenomena.* Leiden: E. J. Brill, 1975–78. 2 vols. (Papuan tribal religions).

Religious texts of the oral tradition from western New Guinea (Irian Jaya). F. C. Kamm (trans). *NISABA religious texts translation series*, vol. 8. Leiden: E. J. Brill, 1978. 196p.

Religious tolerance and the Christian faith: a study concerning the concept of divine omnipotence in the Indonesian Constitution in the light of Islam and Christianity. W. B. Sidjabat. 2nd ed. Jakarta: Gunung Mulia, 1982. 284p.

Rural development and tradition: the churches in Bali and Flores. P. Webb. Clayton, Victoria, Australia: Centre of Southeast Asian Studies, Monash University, 1990. 23p.

Sejarah Gereja Katolik Indonesia (History of the Catholic Church in Indonesia). M. P. M. Muskens (ed). Ende, Indonesia: Arnoldus Press (SVD), 1974. 4 vols; 2,800p. (In Bahasa Indonesia language. English version 1977, Melbourne University Press).

Sri and Christ: a study of the indigenous church in east Java. P. van Akkeren. *World studies of churches in mission.* London: Butterworth Press, 1970. 229p.

Survey of the Christian Evangelical Church of Timor. F. L. Cooley (ed). Jakarta: DGI, 1976. 413p.

The Catholic Church in Indonesia. 2nd ed. Jakarta: Documentation-Information Department, Office of Bishops' Conference, 1975. 113p.

The character and theological struggle of the church in Halmahera, Indonesia, 1941–1979. J. Haire. Frankfurt am Main: Lang, 1981. 393p.

The Dani of Irian Jaya before and after conversion. D. J. Hayward. Sentani, Irian Jaya, Indonesia: Regions Press, 1980. 233p.

The early years of a Dutch colonial mission: the Karo field. R. S. Kipp. Ann Arbor, MI: University of Michigan Press, 1990. 272p.

The Gospel facing Islam in Indonesia. Asian perspective, 29. [Taichung, Taiwan: Asia Theological Association, 1981]. 15p.

The growing seed: the Christian Church in Indonesia. F. L. Cooley. Jakarta: Christian Publishing House, 1981. 371p.

'The introduction and expression of Islam and Christianity in the cultural context of north central Java (Indonesia).' L. M. Yoder. Ph.D. dissertation, Fuller Theological Seminary, Pasadena, CA, 1987. 563p.

The Kalimantan Kenyah: a study of tribal conversion in terms of dynamic cultural themes. W. Conley. Nutley, NJ: Presbyterian & Reformed Publishing Co., 1975. 476p.

The mango tree church: the story of the Protestant Christian Church in Bali. D. G. McKenzie & I. W. Mastra. Brisbane: JBCE, 1988. 87p.

The media and development: an exploratory survey in Indonesia and Zambia: with special reference to the role of the churches. K. E. Eapen. Leicester, UK: University of Leicester for the World Association for Christian Communication, 1973. 83p.

The people time forgot. A. Gibbons. Chicago: Moody Press, 1981. 355p.

The religion of Java. C. Geertz. Glencoe, IL: Free Press, 1958.

The religious imagination in New Guinea. G. Herdt & M. Stephen. New Brunswick, NJ: Rutgers University Press, 1989. 262p.

'The renewal of the life and mission of the Church of Christ the Lord in Malang, Indonesia.' D. I. Santoso. Ph.D. dissertation, Fuller Theological Seminary, Pasadena, CA, 1987. 194p.

The revival in Indonesia. K. Koch. Grand Rapids, MI: Kregel Publications, 1972. 310p.

The struggle of Islam in modern Indonesia. B. J. Boland. The Hague: H. H. L. Smits, 1970.

Urban ministry in Indonesia. Jakarta: World Vision International, Indonesia Office, 1990. (Pamphlet).

'Words and blessings: Batak Catholic discourses in North Sumatra.' B. Sutanto. Ph.D. dissertation, Cornell University, Ithaca, NY, 1989. 369p.

Country Table 2. **Organized churches and denominations in Indonesia.**

Official name (bold type = church with over 10% of all affiliated) 1	Begun 2	Type 3	Counc 4	Congs 5	Adults 6	Affiliated 1970 7	Affiliated 1995 8	G% 9	*Names, notes, and other statistics* (see Codebook, Part 3) 10
Anglican Ch (D Papua & New Guinea)		A-Hig	awpK.	8	1,280	2,000	3,200	0.05	Papuans from PNG working in West Irian; British expatriates in Jakarta, Surabaya, Sumatra.
Armenian Apostolic Church		O-Arm	Ew...	1	40	100	90	0.05	*Gereja Armenia.* In 1904, 4,000 Armenians, in prelature of Batavia; rapid emigration.
Assemblies of God	c1930	P-Pe2	ZF..I	927	98,823	40,000	130,426	4.84	*Sidang Jumat Allah.* Java, Sumatra, Ambon, Sulawesi. M=AoG(USA). 267n,32f,4s(91).
Assembly Hall Churches	c1970	I-3nC	.....	40	6,025	–	12,000	45.60	*Local Churches. Little Flock.* Chinese. Begun in China 1922.
Association of Christian Foundations		I-3nG	.....	824	140,000	70,000	326,000	0.05	*Persekutuan Jajasan Kristen.* Unregistered Javanese autonomous congregations.
Australian Baptist Missionary Society	1955	P-Bap	.H...	244	22,000	20,000	62,900	4.69	In West Irian. 1955 began among Dani tribe. Works with M=CMA,UFM,RBMU. 15f,1H.
Bali Christian Protestant Church	1932	P-Ref	Ru..W	48	3,720	11,000	6,759	-1.93	*GKPB.* Ex Hindus. HQ Denpasar. 1975: intense persecution. 25n,40Yy.
Baptist Gospel Association of Indonesia	1961	I-Bap	xF...	16	11,100	5,893	16,500	4.20	*Perhimpunan Injil Baptis I.* West Kalimantan. M=CBFMS/CBI(USA). 3m,2x,25f,1H,82Y,35z.
Baptist International Missions	1969	I-Bap	.....	8	500	155	1,250	8.71	M=BIM(USA). Fundamentalist Baptists with USA links.
Batak Christian Church	1927	I-Lut	.TT.T	52	5,160	7,000	12,000	2.18	*Huria Kristen Batak.* Split ex HKBP, rejecting all Western influences. 10n.
Batak Christian Community Church	1927	I-Lut	LuE.W	40	11,800	10,000	19,585	2.73	*PKB. Punguan Kristen Batak.* HQ Jakarta. Branches in N & S Sumatra. 16n,W=75%.
Batak Christian Protestant Church	1861	P-Lut	LWE.W	2,393	1,250,000	1,044,382	2,500,000	3.55	*HKBP. Huria Kristen Batak Protestan.* Toba Bataks. 298n,25x,1v,W=45%,1657Y,40928y.
Bethel Church in Indonesia	1946	P-Pe3	ZF...	1,086	430,000	400,000	729,000	2.43	*GBI. G Bethel Indonesia (G=Gereja).* 50% Chinese. M=CoG(Cleveland) (USA). 4f,1p.
Bethel Full Gospel Church	1970	I-3fG	Z...b	1,200	360,000	51,279	600,000	10.34	*GBIS. GB Injil Sepenuh.* 50% Chinese. Ex GBI(Gbis) retaining name. 450n,1p.
Bethel Tabernacle Church	1957	I-3pG	I	500	75,000	80,000	188,000	3.48	*GBT. G Bethel Tabernakel.* Work throughout nation. HQ Jakarta. 102n.
Calvary Pentecostal Mission Church	1948	I-3pG	.....	400	30,000	5,000	50,000	9.65	*G Calvari Pantekosta Missi.* Based on Ternate. 15n,1s,W=60%,1000Y.
Catholic Church in Indonesia:	c 650	R-Lat	P.F.R	1,115	2,978,700	2,620,140	5,340,588	2.89	*Gereja Katolik I.* C=19+9+70. 675n 1551x 3784m 5719w 168014Yy
M Ende (Endeh)	1913	R-Lat	Psvd	77	350,000	434,065	624,631	1.47	Central Flores. Rural. Florinese. M=SVD. 2s. 95n 203x 376m 323w 15624Yy
D Atambua	1936	R-Lat	Psvd	38	216,000	239,777	387,533	1.94	Timorese on west central Timor. Rural. M=SVD. 59n 42x 108m 102w 9705Yy
D Denpasar	1950	R-Lat	Psvd	18	12,500	8,281	22,394	4.06	Bali, Lombok. Balinese, urban Chinese. M=SVD. 8n 22x 42m 8w 407Yy
M Kupang	1967	R-Lat	Psvd	61	64,000	33,569	114,741	5.04	Timorese, SW Timor. Rural. 20n 40x 113m 76w 4319Yy
D Larantuka	1951	R-Lat	Psvd	31	124,000	177,809	222,727	0.91	Flores, islands. Florinese. 8H, 15h. 37n 32x 44m 185w 4723Yy
D Ruteng	1951	R-Lat	Psvd	72	284,000	272,570	508,643	2.53	Flores. Rural Florinese. Many schools. 1p. 30n 61x 115m 91w 21509Yy
D Weetebula	1959	R-Lat	Ps	14	46,000	25,054	83,166	4.92	Sumba, Sumbawa. Rural migrants. M=SVD,CSSR. 5n 29x 35m 48w 3897Yy
M Jakarta	1807	R-Lat	Psj	50	188,000	81,702	335,835	5.82	*Keuskupan Agung Jakarta.* 38% Chinese. 34n 163x 317m 471w 13498Yy
D Bandung	1932	R-Lat	Posc	86	40,000	35,639	73,186	2.92	*Keuskupan Bandung.* 30% urban Chinese. 8n 54x 192m 139w 2725Yy
D Bogor	1948	R-Lat	Pofm	13	25,000	10,338	44,909	6.05	39% urban Chinese. 21n 15x 26m 100w 1628Yy
M Medan	1911	R-Lat	Pofmc	42	228,000	218,344	408,302	2.54	NSumatra. Rural. Bataks. 4% Chinese. 2s. 11n 104x 224m 529w 13754Yy
D Padang	1952	R-Lat	Psx	20	30,700	21,309	54,943	3.86	Mentawei. 56% Chinese; Javanese. M=SX,OFMCap. 9n 30x 34m 49w 2215Yy
D Palembang	1923	R-Lat	Pscj	30	38,000	28,585	68,393	3.55	SE Sumatra. 33% Chinese, migrant Javanese. 9n 37x 60m 198w 2394Yy
D Pangkal Pinang	1923	R-Lat	Psscc	8	14,500	13,101	25,936	2.77	Bangka, Riau. 61% Chinese; Batak. M=SVD,SSCC. 10n 12x 20m 41w 983Yy
D Tanjungkarang	1952	R-Lat	Pscj	14	46,000	46,040	82,526	2.36	S Sumatra. Mostly Javanese migrants. M=SCJ,MEP. 14n 20x 39m 166w 2758Yy
D Sibolga	1959	R-Lat	Pofmc	27	92,000	67,491	165,445	3.65	NW Sumatra, Nias, Batu. Rural. Bataks. 5h. 3n 30x 64m 148w 9714Yy
M Merauke	1950	R-Lat	Pmsc	25	68,000	80,005	122,470	1.72	Southern W Irian. Rural. Irianese/Papuans. 3n 27x 32m 31w 3722Yy
D Agats	1969	R-Lat	Posc	11	22,500	22,354	40,251	2.38	Formerly northwest M Merauke. Irianese. 6n 11x 14m 13w 1805Yy
D Jayapura	1949	R-Lat	Pofm	42	57,000	34,960	102,126	4.38	Until 1966, Sukarnapura. Irianese. 1s. 9n 36x 75m 51w 4122Yy
D Manokwari-Sorong	1959	R-Lat	Posa	15	21,000	9,798	37,924	5.56	Islands, west of W Irian. Irianese. M=OSA,OCarm. 4n 13x 23m 32w 1169Yy
M Pontianak	1905	R-Lat	Pofmc	17	93,000	77,540	167,123	3.12	W Kalimantan. Dayaks, urban Chinese. 6H,9h. 3n 31x 59m 184w 7922Yy
D Banjarmasin	1938	R-Lat	Pmsf	7	7,500	11,113	13,540	0.79	SE Kalimantan. Dayaks. Javanese, Chinese. 0n 9x 11m 46w 320Yy
D Ketapang	1954	R-Lat	Pcp	16	37,000	9,449	66,803	8.14	W Kalimantan. Rural. Mostly Dayaks. 1H,2h. 22n 10x 36m 95w 1429Yy
D Samarinda	1955	R-Lat	Pmsf	53	47,000	20,494	84,754	5.84	E Kalimantan. Rural. Dayaks. 9n 34x 46m 43w 2971Yy
D Sintang	1948	R-Lat	Ps	37	55,000	24,177	98,143	5.76	W Kalimantan. Rural. Dayaks. M=SMM,OMI. 6n 24x 29m 36w 5174Yy
D Sanggau (Sekadau)	1968	R-Lat	Pcp	14	113,000	21,533	201,655	9.36	W Kalimantan. Rural. Dayaks. 4n 25x 40m 47w 10027Yy
M Semarang	1940	R-Lat	Psj	90	264,000	243,975	472,599	2.68	Central Java. Javanese & urban Chinese. M=SJ. 1s. 104n 190x 620m 1062w 11766Yy
D Malang	1927	R-Lat	Pocar	16	43,000	48,942	76,811	1.82	D Java, Madura. Javanese; 43% Chinese. 1s. 15n 76x 414m 458w 2497Yy
D Purwokerto	1932	R-Lat	Pmsc	15	37,000	25,770	66,845	3.89	C Java. Javanese, urban Chinese. 7H,8h. 10n 25x 90m 231w 1776Yy
D Surabaya	1928	R-Lat	Ps	38	95,000	75,141	170,425	3.33	E Java. Javanese; 38% Chinese. M=CM. 12H,32h,1s. 27n 57x 90m 273w 5590Yy
M Ujung Pandang (Makassar)	1937	R-Lat	Pcicm	47	86,000	64,159	154,942	3.59	S,SE sulawesi. Torajas, Chinese. 6H,7h. 50n 13x 68m 106w 5675Yy
D Amboina	1902	R-Lat	Pmsc	32	62,000	67,541	111,549	2.03	Naluku. Rural. Mainly Kayese, Tanimbarese. 5n 40x 61m 204w 2809Yy
D Manado	1919	R-Lat	Pmsc	39	72,000	69,515	129,318	2.51	N,C Sulawesi. Mainly rural Minahasans. 1s. 25n 36x 267m 133w 2012Yy
Christ Groups	c1970	I-3hG	x....	283	9,000	–	20,000	48.61	Home churches for isolated converts after nationwide EHC campaign.
Christian Bible Circle	1946	I-Lut	.....	50	1,000	1,000	2,000	2.81	*KPB. Kristen Panangkosi Bibelkring.* HKBP background. Bataks. No ministers.
Christian Ch in Central Sulawesi	1893	P-Ref	.WE.W	328	62,800	125,000	157,000	0.92	*GKST. G Kristen Sulawesi Tengh.* M=NZG. 1909 mass influx. Poso Torajas. 68n,1x.
Christian Church in Luwuk Banggai	1966	P-Ref	.v..W	214	28,100	52,500	70,190	1.17	*GKLB. GK di Luwuk Banggai.* Formerly in GKST. 1972 applied to WCC. Loinangs. 21n,1u.
Christian Church in South Sulawesi	1933	P-Ref	R...W	24	4,300	5,500	6,376	0.59	*GKSS. GK Sulawesi Selatan.* NZG attempts failed 1851, 1895. Makassarese. 14n.
Christian Ch of North Central Java	1891	I-Ref	....W	53	7,980	7,896	21,000	3.99	*GKJTU. GK Jawa Tengh Utara. Salatiga Mission.* HQ Semarang. Javanese. 14n,2x.
Christian Church of Sumba	1870	P-Ref	F...W	306	61,200	43,121	173,000	5.71	*GKS. G Kristen Sumba.* Begun by Sawu immigrants; 1881 M=NCRMS. A=1947. 50n,117m.
Christian Churches & Chs of Christ	1968	I-Dis	x....	20	500	500	1,000	2.81	*SJK. Sidang Jumat Kristus.* M=CCCC(Instrumental) (USA). 13f.
Christian Churches of Java	1858	P-Ref	FWE.W	1,202	156,000	121,500	259,871	3.09	*GKJ. G2 Kristen Jawa.* M=NCRMS. 99% Javanese. 1949 merger. 136n,11x,1u,W=70%.
Christian Fellowship Assemblies	1949	P-Non	xF...	50	11,400	8,000	17,000	3.06	*G Persekutuan Sidang Kristis.* M=WEC. In West Borneo; 6,000 Dayaks in 2 years.
Christian Missionary Fellowship	1970	I-Dis	.....	65	2,871	–	3,500	38.60	M=CMF(USA).
Christian Reformed Chs of Indonesia	1925	P-Ref	.....	15	3,000	5,000	7,000	1.35	*G Gereformeerd Indonesia.* A=1969. Javanese living in Sumatra. HQ Medan. 3n,2x.
Christian Synod	c1985	P-Men	.....	45	2,500	–	4,000	10.00	*Sinode Jemaat Kristen.*
Church of Christ	1905	I-3pC	....W	30	20,000	20,000	40,000	2.81	*G Kristus.* Chinese pentecostal church in West Java. HQ Jakarta. 12n,W=70%.
Church of Christ, Scientist		m-Sci	x....	4	200	1,000	600	0.05	*G Kesatu Kristus Ahli Ilmu.* M=CCS(Boston, USA). In 5 cities. Many Indonesians. 6w.
Church of God of Prophecy	1969	P-Pe3	.....	150	12,000	1,140	26,700	13.44	M=CoGP. Holiness Pentecostals.
Church of the Nazarene	1973	P-Hol	.....	18	1,560	–	2,980	4.55	M=CoN. Holiness denomination with USA support.
Ch of Jesus Christ of Latter-day Saints		m-LdS	x....	18	2,870	580	4,100	0.05	*Mormons.* M=CJCLdS(Utah, USA). Mainly USA personnel, few indigenous.
Church of Jesus Christ (the Messiah)	1945	I-3pC	Z.E.b	78	22,900	20,000	38,189	2.62	*G Isa Almasih/Sing Ling Kauw Hui.* Java Chinese. 15n,1s(35),W=67%,1000Y.
Church of the Lord Jesus Christ	1956	I-Ref	....W	22	4,740	9,834	11,850	0.75	*GKT. G Kristus Tuhan.* Chinese. HQ Malang. 8n,W=60%.
Churches of Christ	1967	I-Dis	x....	20	500	500	1,000	2.81	M=CC(Non-Instrumental) (USA). Loosely affiliated churches. 10f.
Conv of Indonesian Baptist Chs	c1960	P-Bap	T....	82	6,935	5,000	15,000	4.49	Mainline Baptists.
East Java Christian Church	1815	P-Ref	RWE.W	113	48,000	126,000	150,000	0.70	*GKJW. GK Jawi Waten.* 1848, M=NZG. 99% Javanese. HQ Malang. 74n,1x,5H,16h.
Ecumenical Prot Ch of Tanjung Enim	c1975	P-Ref	.....	30	1,500	–	3,000	5.00	*G Protestan TE.*
Evangelical Alliance Mission	1952	P-Eva	xM...	289	24,288	11,000	60,700	7.07	M=TEAM(USA). Churches in West Irian and Java. 1 school. 49f,1H,8h,3x.
Ev Christian Ch in Bolaang-Mongondow	1904	P-Ref	R...W	146	56,000	41,250	80,000	2.68	*GMIBM. G Masehi Injili Bolaang-Mongondow.* Sulawesi. M-NZG. A=1950. 14n,1x,5r,W=60%.
Ev Christian Church in Halmahera	1866	P-Ref	....W	340	68,000	82,000	170,000	2.96	*GMIH.* 1546, first converts. 1866, M=UMS. 30n,4p,1s,W=60%,1045Yy.
Evang Christian Church of Indonesia	1929	P-Hol	xF..E	1,753	155,459	150,000	323,288	3.12	*GKII. G Kristen Injili I. Former Kemah Injil G Masehi I.* M=CMA. 135n,21x,128f,23h,3p,6s(370).
Ev Christian Church in Java	1851	P-Men	G...W	60	47,000	38,000	67,332	2.31	*GITJ. G Injili di Tanah Jawa.* M=European Mennonites (also USA). 32n,2x,1u,W=75%.
Evangelical Christian Ch of Indonesia	c1980	P-Eva	.....	25	1,500	–	3,000	6.67	*G Kristen Injili I.* M=WEC,IMF.
Ev Christian Church in Irian Jaya	1862	P-Ref	RWE.W	1,869	230,000	360,000	650,000	2.39	*GKI Ir-Jay. Irian Jawa/Barat.* M=UM,RM,VEM. A=1956. 200 tribes. 77n,8x,1p,1s,W=40%.
Evangelical Church in Kalimantan	1836	P-Ref	RWE.W	908	73,600	90,000	219,145	3.62	*GKE. G Kalimantan Evangelis* (former Dayak Ev Ch). M=RM,BM. 88n,1x,15f,1s(53),W=60%.
Ev Christian Ch in Sanghir-Talaud	1568	P-Ref	RWE.W	355	88,100	183,344	220,308	0.74	*GMIST. GMI Sanghir-Talaud.* 1856, M=NRMB. A=1947. 90n,189m,1H,8h,4r,1s(50),W=50%.
Evangelical Church in Indonesia	1969	P-Hol	.....	20	4,000	1,810	13,300	8.30	*G Injili di I.*
Evangelical Church of Indonesia	1952	P-Eva	xM...	400	168,000	40,000	250,000	7.61	M=UFM(USA). West Irian among Dani tribe. 4 schools. 36f,1H,3h,2s.
Evangelical Church of South Sumatra	1964	P-Eva	.....	10	3,000	4,000	5,000	0.90	*GEKISUS. GK Sumatera Selatan.* M=IMF. 50% Serawai (Rejang-Lebong) ex Muslims.
Fellowship of Baptist Chs of Irian Jaya	c1960	P-Bap	.....	129	24,500	22,200	54,400	3.65	Papuans with missionaries from Europe, USA, et alia
Fellowship of Preaching Gosp of Christ	1947	P-Non	xM...	150	4,800	50,000	16,000	-4.46	*PPIK* (Borneo), Chinese, Dayaks; *GGIK* (WIrian), Dani. Severe persecution. M=RBMU. 23n,57f.
Free Methodist Church of Indonesia	1964	I-Met	.....	10	1,171	1,500	2,200	1.54	*GMMI. G Methodis Merdeka Indonesia.* Schism ex GMI by indigenous Indonesians. 4n.
Go Ye Fellowship	1938	I-Non	.....	20	3,000	3,000	10,000	4.93	M=Go-Ye Fellowship (USA).
Hidden Hindu believers in Christ	c1970	I-Hin	.....	700	60,000	–	135,000	60.40	Converted Hindus who remain in Hindu society as witnesses for Christ.
Hidden Muslim believers in Christ	c1970	I-Mus	.....	300	40,000	–	80,000	57.08	Converted Muslims who stay within Islamic structures as witnesses to Christ.
Holy Spirit Church of Indonesia		I-3pG	.....	125	25,000	20,000	50,000	0.05	*GSRKI. G Sidang Rohul Kudus Indonesia.* Indigenous pentecostals. HQ Medan.
Holy Word Christian Church	1951	I-Non	x....	30	3,000	7,000	10,000	1.44	*GKKK. GK Kalam Kudus.* HQ Malang. M=Evangelize China Fellowship.200m,5f,8r(5000),1s(100)
Indigenous cargo cult churches		I-mar	.....	15	1,500	3,000	2,500	0.05	Several of the over 21 cargo cults in West Irian have had christianized features.
Indonesia Pentecostal Church		I-3pG	I	247	49,400	40,000	130,000	0.05	*G Pantekosta di Indonesia.* Indigenous Batak and other pentecostals on Sumatra.
Indonesia Protestant Christian Church	1963	I-Lut	LW..W	797	192,000	128,424	497,054	5.56	*GKPI. GK Protestan I.* N Sumatra. Ex HKBP. Batak. 79n,1x,1s,W=55%,7634Yy.
Indonesian Baptist Gospel Fellowship	1961	I-Bap	.....	150	20,000	30,000	40,000	1.16	*Persekutuan Injil Baptis I.* M=CBI(USA). Western Kalimantan, some churches in Java. 1H.
Indonesian Christian Ch in Central Java	1866	I-Ref	FWE.W	99	22,800	31,044	60,120	2.68	*GKI Ja-Teng. Jawa Tengah.* Chinese. HQ Semarang. 37n,2x,1p,2s(50),W=70%,837Yy.
Indonesian Christian Ch in East Java	1898	I-Ref	RwE.W	19	15,250	10,005	19,380	2.68	*GKI Ja-Tim. Jawa Timur.* Chinese, begun by Chinese. HQ Surabaya. 13n,2x.
Indonesian Christian Ch of West Java	1867	I-Ref	RvE.W	61	15,600	23,361	45,240	2.68	*GKI Ja-Bar. Jawa Barat.* Chinese origin and members. HQ Jakarta. 32n,W=70%.
Indonesian Christian Church (HKI)	1927	I-Lut	LWE.W	590	230,000	242,500	342,300	1.39	*Huria Kristen Indonesia.* Ex HKBP. Bataks. 71n,1x,560m,4p,W=50%,3923Yy.
Indonesian Christian Lutheran Church	1965	I-Lut	.....	29	5,490	15,560	14,434	-0.30	*Huria Kristen Batak Protestan Luther.* Schism ex HKBP. 6n,W=65%,435Yy.
Indonesian Ev Christian Church		I-Eva	.....	10	1,100	2,075	2,500	0.05	*GMEI. G Masehi Evangelis Indonesia.* Indigenous grouping based on Makassar, Sulawesi.
Indonesia Missionary Church	1984	I-Non	.....	40	10,100	–	16,790	9.09	M=IMF(Indonesia). Nondenominational movement.
Internat Ch of the Foursquare Gospel	1984	P-Pe2	.....	51	2,710	–	5,420	9.09	M=ICFG(USA). Related to ICFG in Los Angeles, USA.
International Pentecostal Holiness Ch	1962	P-Pe3	.....	9	700	100	1,400	11.13	M=IPHC(USA). Holiness Pentecostals with USA missionary support.
Isolated radio churches	1952	I-3rG	.....	15,000	300,000	66,300	500,000	8.42	Isolated radio believers (youths &c). (1970) R=15000 (FEBC,&c), T=55000 (ICI,FEBC,&c).(1990)
Jehovah's Witnesses	1933	m-Jeh	x....	333	10,000	10,000	33,300	4.93	*Perkumpulan Siswa Alkitab.* 1933 under Australia branch. 1937 Celebes, Borneo. 452Y.
Jesus Christ Church	1952	I-Lut	.....	6	700	1,000	1,200	0.73	*Huria Hatopan ni Kristus Jesus.* N Sumatra. Schism ex HKBP. HQ Hutadipar. 2n,5m.
Karo Batak Protestant Church	1890	P-Ref	RWE.W	571	82,000	72,492	250,000	5.08	*GBKP. G Batak Karo Protestan.* M=NZG,RM,VEM. 1965, mass conversions. 30n,5x,W=60%.
Light of Indonesia	1964	I-3pG	.....	27	1,908	200	4,000	12.73	Work among Javanese.
Mentawei Protestant Christian Church	1901	P-Lut	.....	112	10,600	35,000	21,274	-1.97	*PKPM. Paamian Kristen Protestan Mentawei.* M=HKBP,RM,VEM on Mentawei 1s. 11n,3x,9f.
Methodist Church in Indonesia	1903	P-Met	VvE.W	218	37,000	70,000	70,874	0.05	*GMI. G Methodis I.* M=UMC(USA),A=1964. Chinese, Batak. 45n,19f,1p,148t,W=93%,1506Yy.
Minahasa Protestant Ch Association		I-Ref	.....	130	12,000	25,000	30,000	0.05	*KGPM. Kerapatan Gereja Protestan Minahasa.* Schism ex GMIM. HQ Jakarta.
Muria Christian Church in Indonesia	1925	P-Men	G...W	52	16,160	7,000	35,839	6.75	*GKMI. G Kristen Muria Indonesia* (formerly United Muria Christian Ch of 1). Chinese. 11n,1u.
New Apostolic Church	1881	I-3aX	x....	100	9,000	10,000	15,500	1.77	Begun on Java. M=NAC(Germany). Chief Apostle and world HQ in Zurich (Switzerland).
New Tribes Mission	c1980	P-Fun	x....	35	5,500	–	8,170	6.67	M=NTM. Fundamentalists linked to USA mission
Nias Christian Protestant Church	1865	P-Lut	.WE.W	578	141,000	220,000	312,848	1.42	*BNKP. Banua Niha Keriso Protestan.* Since 1865, M=RM,VEM. A=1940. 53n,2x,14f,1s.
Nias Christian Protestant Organization	1952	I-Lut	.....	60	17,300	32,000	57,613	2.38	*ONKP. Orahua Niha Keriso Protestan.* Indigenous schism ex BNKP. 15n.
Nias Indonesian Christian Association	1940	I-Lut	.....	60	10,200	60,000	20,322	-4.24	*AMIN. Angawuloa Masehi Indonesia Nias.* Large indigenous schism ex BNKP. 6n.

continued overleaf

Country Table 2–continued

Official name (bold type = church with over 10% of all affiliated) 1	*Begun* 2	*Type* 3	*Counc* 4	*Congs* 5	*Adults* 6	*Affiliated 1970* 7	*Affiliated 1995* 8	*G%* 9	*Names, notes, and other statistics* (see Codebook, Part 3) 10
Nusantara Evangelical Church	c1970	P-Hol	.....	38	4,631	657	13,200	12.75	M=OMS. Holiness body with USA origins and support.
Pasundan Christian Church	1861	P-Ref	RWE.W	51	18,800	18,890	28,000	1.59	*GKP. G Kristen Pasundan.* West Java. 1863, M=NZG. 30% Chinese; few Sundanese now. 21n.
Pentecostal Assemblies of God	1982	P-Pe2	.....	186	12,500	–	25,000	7.69	M=PAoC(Canada): Mainline Pentecostals.
Pentecostal Church in Sorong	1948	I-3pG	.....	20	7,000	13,000	20,000	1.74	*GPS. G Pantekosta Sorong.* Salawati and Irianese. 5n,W=40%,75Y,125z.
Pentecostal Church of God	1950	P-Pe2	Z....	160	120,000	100,000	267,000	4.01	M=PCG(USA). Classical Pentecostals. HQ Calvary Mission. Ternate. 1 school. 4f.
Pentecostal Church of Indonesia	1920	I-3oG	Z...I	1,540	770,000	1,000,000	1,280,000	0.99	*GPI,GPdI. G Pantekosta di Indonesia.* 25% Chinese. Many splits, including GBIS. 1500n,3s.
Pentecostal Church (Sihombing)		I-3pG	.....	400	60,000	100,000	200,000	0.05	*G Pantekosta (Sihombing)* (=name of present leader). HQ Pematang Siantar, Sumatra.
Pentecostal Missionary Church	1935	I-3pG	.....	266	58,500	20,000	130,000	7.77	*GUP. G Utusan Pantekosta.* Indigenous pentecostals (2-stage). 19n,11m.
Pentecostal Movement Church	1923	I-3pG	....b	104	16,500	30,000	35,000	0.62	*G Gerakan Pantekosta.* In several regions; HQ Jakarta. 1975: 12,261 adult members.
Protestant Church in Indonesia:	1615	P-Ref	RW..W	4,688	1,578,340	1,958,710	2,661,884	1.23	*GPI. Gereja Protestan Indonesia.* Former state-controlled Church of the Indies. 770n.
Christian Ev Church in Minahasa	1568	P-Ref	RWE.W	624	312,000	556,432	780,000	1.36	*GMIM. G Masehi Injili Minahasa.* 1822 M=NZG. A=1934. 174n,5x,1s(130),W=60%.
Ev Christian Church in Timor	1612	P-Ref	RWE.W	2,890	700,000	517,779	850,000	2.00	*GMIT. G Masehi Injili Timor.* First Dutch pastor 1612; 1821 M=NZG. 106n,9x,1s,W=48%.
Indonesian Prot Church in Donggala	1964	P-Ref	....W	110	9,370	15,340	23,420	1.71	*GPID. G Protestan Indonesia Donggala.* HQ Maesa-Palu (Central Sulawesi). Palus. 11n,W=65%.
Indonesian Prot Church in Gorontalo	1964	P-Ref	....W	56	5,270	7,000	13,185	2.57	*GPIG. G Protestan Indonesia di Gorontalo.* HQ Gorontalo. 5n,W=50%.
Moluccan Protestant Church	1534	P-Ref	RWE.W	796	371,000	505,000	529,845	0.19	*GPM. GP Maluku.* Oldest Protestant church in Asia. 462n,3x,1s(30),W=60%,2183Yy.
Protestant Ch in Western Indonesia	1620	P-Ref	R.E.W	185	171,000	350,000	451,000	1.02	*GPIB. GP Indonesia Bagian Barat.* HQ Jakarta. Ambonese, Timorese, Minahasans. 54n,2x.
Protestant Ch of I in Buol-Toli-toli	1964	P-Ref	.....	27	9,700	7,159	14,434	2.84	*GPI Buol-Toli 2.* Sulawesi. Gorontalo, Tomini, Buginese, Orang-Laut (Sea Gypsies).
Protestant Ch in South East Sulawesi	1915	P-Ref	....W	75	7,370	9,000	19,401	3.12	*GEPSULTRA. G Protestan Sulawesi Tenggara.* M=NZG. First baptism 1929. 14n,1x,W=75%.
Protestant Ch of West Kalimantan	1963	P-Ref	.....	16	6,635	6,000	13,300	3.24	*GPKB. Extensive work in Borneo.*
Ray of the Gospel Christian Church	1960	I-Lut	....W	60	20,000	30,000	45,000	1.64	*GKPI. GK Pemancar Injil.* NE Kalimantan. Very rapid growth. 15n,9x,1s,W=90%.
Salvation Army	1894	P-Sal	xwE.w	203	26,600	200,000	70,000	-4.11	*Bala Keselamatan. Indonesia Territory.* 253n,24x,5H,1p,1s(30),W=79%,627Y.
Seventh-day Adventist Church	1900	P-Adv	x....	1,000	130,000	70,677	217,000	4.59	*GMAHKT.* 137n,9x,29f,2H,23h,1j,9r,2s(92),662t(58746),W=80%,3220Y.
Simalungun Protestant Christian Ch	1903	P-Lut	LW..W	450	73,400	109,500	180,851	2.03	*GKPS. GK Protestan Simalungun.* M=RM,VEM. In HKBP till 1962. 33n,1x,3f,1p(27),W=60%.
Spiritual Food Church of Indonesia		I-Non	xTT.T	25	3,000	6,000	9,000	0.05	*GSRI. G Santopan Rohani Indonesia.* M=LLWEM(Hong Kong). Linked ICCC. HQ Singkawang.
Surabaya Pentecostal Church	1959	I-3pG	Z...b	500	70,000	100,000	200,000	2.81	*GPPS. G Pantekosta Pusat Surabaya.* East Java. Largely Chinese. 250n.
Toraja Christian Church	1913	P-Ref	RWE.W	591	123,000	175,000	300,000	2.18	*G Toraja/Makale-Rantepao.* Doubled 1947-54. 64n,5x,1H,1p,1s(110),W=30%,7317Yy.
Toraja Church in Mamasa	1929	P-Ref	JTT.W	591	51,000	53,923	75,054	1.33	*GTM. G Toraja/Mamasa.* M=NCRMA. HQ Mamasa. 30n,2x,W=60%,1500Yy.
True Jesus Church	1939	I-3oC	x....	20	3,000	2,000	5,000	3.73	*GJJS. G Jesus Jang Sejati.* Chinese indigenous church. 4n,W=70%,140Y.
Union of Indonesian Baptist Churches	1951	P-Bap	T...E	260	35,700	20,000	54,500	4.09	*GGBI. G2 Baptis I.* M=SBC(USA). Urban. 6 schools. 62n,42x,121f,1H,2h,1s,W=70%,1715Y.
United Pentecostal Church	1938	P-Pe1	x....	250	45,000	40,000	100,000	3.73	*GPS. G Pantekosta Serikat.* M=UPC(USA). HQ Semarang. 1970, schism. 73n,4f,1p(29).
West Kalimantan Christian Church	1938	I-Non	.....	15	3,930	5,000	7,853	1.82	*GKKB. G Kristen Kalimantan Barat.* 60% Chinese. 3n,1x,W=75%,140Y.
World-Wide Missions of Indonesia	1963	I-Non	x....	30	5,000	7,000	10,000	1.44	M=World-Wide Missions (USA). Links with Evangelicals from Pasadena, CA (USA).
Other Indonesian indigenous chs		I-3pG	.....	8,000	850,000	1,050,000	2,320,000	0.05	Total over 100 (see list below).
Other Protestant denominations		P-	.....	100	30,000	30,000	60,000	0.05	Total about 30 (see list below).
Totals				**58,799**	**12,326,346**	**12,316,542**	**24,338,448**		

Churches, members, growth, 1900-2025	*Congs*	*Adults*	*Affiliated*	*G%*	*Total denominations*	*6 Megablocs:* *O*	*R*	*A*	*P*	*I*	*m*
Total churches, members, and denominations (mid-1900)	2,000	265,000	536,050	4.58	25	0	1	0	18	6	0
Total churches, members, and denominations (mid-1970)	24,280	6,088,514	12,316,542	4.58	171	1	1	1	60	105	3
Total churches, members, and denominations (mid-1990)	54,000	11,281,000	22,275,190	3.01	270	1	1	1	82	182	3
Total churches, members, and denominations (mid-1995)	58,799	12,326,346	24,338,448	1.79	273	1	1	1	84	183	3
Total churches, members, and denominations (mid-2000)	63,000	13,353,000	26,364,858	1.61	276	1	1	1	86	184	3
Total churches, members, and denominations (mid-2025)	95,000	21,015,000	41,495,200	1.83	422	10	1	1	100	300	10

NOTES ON TABLE ABOVE

ABBREVIATIONS ABOVE (columns 1 & 8). G=Gereja (Church); G2=Gereja-Gereja (Churches). GK=Gereja Kristen (Christian Church). I=Indonesia. Note that English names of many Protestant churches are in use in 2 forms: (1) as shown in column 1, and (2) with the last part of the name first.

NATIONAL COUNCILS (Column 4, 5th letter).
- b = member of both DGI and UPFGCI.
- E = Persekutuan Imjili Indonesia (PII, Association of Evangelical Churches of Indonesia), formerly Dewan Gereja-Gereja Injil di Indonesia (Evangelical Fellowship of Indonesia, Indonesian Evangelical Fellowship) (80 associations and denominations), 1973.
- I = United Pentecostal Full Gospel Churches of Indonesia (UPFGCI) (Alamat Jemaat-Jemaat Dari Gereja-Gereja Injil Penuh) (23 members; inoperative by 1974).
- R = Konperensi Waligereja Indonesia (KWI), formerly Bishops Conference of Indonesia (Majelis Agung Para Waligereja Indonesia, MAWI).
- T = Indonesian Council of Christian Churches.
- W = Communion of Churches in Indonesia (CCI, ICC) (Dewan Gereja-Gereja di Indonesia, DGI/PGI), 1984.
- w = associate (extraordinary) member of DGI.

Other national councils. The Council of Chinese Christian Churches in Indonesia (Dewan Gereja-Gereja Kristen Tionghoa di Indonesia), formed in 1949, has now merged in the DGI. Indonesian Baptist Alliances.

Local councils. 14 regional councils are affiliated to the DGI.

OTHER INDONESIAN INDIGENOUS CHURCHES. Most of these 100 are registered with the government's Department of Religion, and were begun for either Indonesians or Chinese. They include: Ch of the New Apostolate, Holy Ghost Guided Christian Assembly, Voice of Salvation Ch.

OTHER PROTESTANT DENOMINATIONS. Most are recent missions with only small followings. These include: Apostolic Christian Ch of I, Baptist Mid-Missions, Bethany Fellowship Missions (1971), Bethel Pentecostal Temple (Seattle, USA), Christadelphian Ecclesias, Christian Faith Missionary Union, Christian Nationals' Evangelism Commission (1971), First Baptist Ch, Grace Christian Ch, Oriental Missionary Society (1970), Overseas Missionary Fellowship (1954; 39 missionaries), United Evangelical Chs, West Java United Baptist Chs, West Kalimantan Pioneer Mission (member of ICCC), Wisconsin Evangelical Lutheran Synod (1969), World Baptist Fellowship Mission Agency (1969), World Gospel Mission (1968).

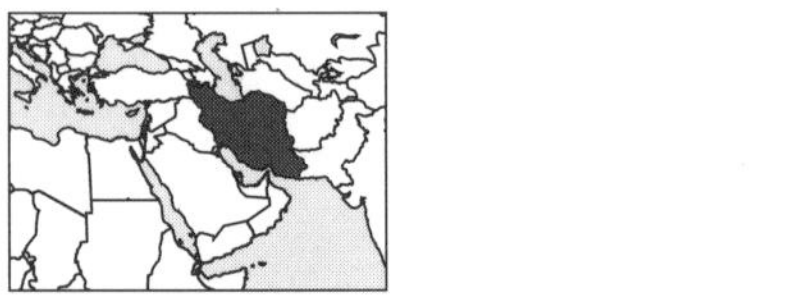

IRAN

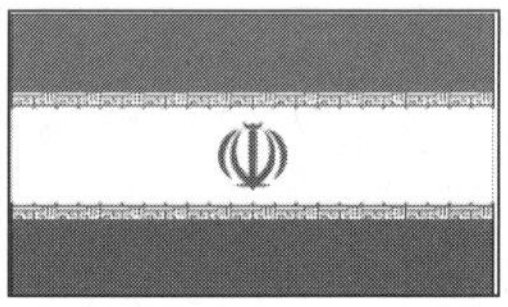

SECULAR DATA, AD 2000

STATE
Official name: Jomhoori-e-Islami-e-Iran (The Islamic Republic of Iran).
Short name: Iran. **Adjective of nationality:** Iranian.
Flag: Green, white, and red stripes; Monograph of Allah in centre.
Area: 1,638,057 sq. km. (632,457 sq. mi.).
Government: One-party Islamic revolutionary republic, since 1979 (1921 military dictatorship, 1953 absolute monarchy, 1979 revolution).
Legislature: Islamic Consultative Assembly, 270 members.
Official language: Persian (Farsi).
Monetary unit: 1 rial (Rls). **US$1=** Rls 3,000.
Chief cities: TEHRAN (Teheran) 7,380,000; Esfahan (Isfahan, New Julfa) 2,644,000; Mashhad (Meshed) 2,378,000; Tabriz 1,624,000; Shiraz 1,113,000.
Political divisions: 27 provinces.
Armed forces: 518,000.

DEMOGRAPHY
Population: 67,702,000.
Population density: 41.3/sq. km. (107.0/sq. mi.).
Under 15 years: 24,522,000.
Growth rate p.a.: 0.99% (births 21.15, deaths 5.19).
Mortality: Infant, per 1,000: 29.6; **Maternal per 100,000:** 120.0.
Life expectancy: 71 (male 70, female 72).
Household size: 5.1. **Floor area per person, sq.m:** 15.0.
Major languages: Persian, Azerbaijani, Kurdish, Arabic, Turkish, Armenian, English, French, Baluchi, Brahui, and about 30 other languages.
Urban dwellers: 61.61%. **Urban growth rate p.a.:** 3.36%.
Labor force: 26%.

ETHNOLINGUISTIC PEOPLES
34.9% Persian (Irani); 15.9% Azerbaijani (Turk); 7.1% Luri (Lori, Feyli); 6.0% Iranian Kurd; 5.0% Gilaki.

ECONOMY
National income p.a. per person: US$4,700; **per family:** US$23,969.

EDUCATION
Adult literacy: 72% (male 78%, female 65%). **Schools:** 81,134.
Universities: 0. **School enrolment:** female/male: 78%/89%.

HEALTH
Access to health services: 80%. **Access to safe water:** 83%.
Hospitals: 609 (15 beds per 10,000). **Doctors:** 37,000.
Blind: 200,000. **Deaf:** 4,585,700. **Murder rate:** <1.
Lepers: 30,000. **Underweight prevalence under 5:** 16%.

LITERATURE
New book titles p.a.: 19,630 (290 p.a. per million). **Periodicals:** 445.
Newspapers: 12 dailies.

COMMUNICATION (per 1,000 people)
Phones: 85 (3% mobile). **Radios:** 213. **TV sets:** 134.
Daily newspaper circulation: 20. **Computers:** 40.

REFUGEES
Citizen refugees in other countries: 49,500.
Alien refugees from other countries: 2,075,500.

HUMAN LIFE AND LIBERTY (optimum condition=100.0%)
HDI: 78.0. **HSI:** 44.0. **HFI:** 10.0. **EFL:** 6.0.

Country status. Iran is located in southwestern Asia between Turkey and Pakistan between the Persian Gulf and the Caspian Sea. It is the largest Shia Muslim country in the world, and it is also uniquely a theocracy run by mullahs. Oil is the main source of revenue.

HUMAN LIFE AND LIBERTY

Human need and development. Iran's oil wealth has not brought prosperity to the country. During the 1970s much of the wealth was looted by the shah and his cronies. In the 1980s the war with Iraq drained the treasury and actually increased national indebtedness. As a result, despite its paper wealth, living conditions of the Iranians have declined since the 1960s. The per capita GNP at $4,700 is only slightly higher than Chile and the annual growth rate of 0.1% is one of the lowest among oil producers. The national illiteracy rate of 28% is not surprising because of the low priority placed on education by the mullahs. Although consumption patterns do not reveal any shortage of essential commodities, income is unevenly divided. About 10% of the population lives at the apex of the scale with 40% of consumption funds. The 40% at the bottom consumes only 8%. The ruling mullahs have little interest in raising the standards of living for the masses because they are afraid of the political consequences of a stronger middle class. Inflation runs at 30% to 40% annually, about 30% of the work force is unemployed and black market and corruption are rampant. Housing is superior to that found in other countries in the Middle East although a few shanty towns exist on the outskirts of Tehran, Abadan, and other cities. Social welfare is in the hands of the mullahs who dispense the zakat, or alms collected from the believers, to the indigent. Medical services are constrained by lack of proper facilities and villagers turn to folk healers in times of illness. There is a high incidence of parasitic and gastrointestinal diseases caused by polluted water supply.

Country Table 1. **Religious adherents in Iran, AD 1900-2025.**

Year	*1900*		*1970*		*mid-1990*		*Annual change, 1990-2000*				*mid-1995*		*mid-2000*		*mid-2025*	
Name	*Adherents*	*%*	*Adherents*	*%*	*Adherents*	*%*	*Natural*	*Conversion*	*Total*	*Rate*	*Adherents*	*%*	*Adherents*	*%*	*Adherents*	*%*
Muslims	9,518,800	98.1	27,764,072	97.7	53,869,700	95.7	1,089,963	-6,256	1,083,707	1.85	59,622,200	95.7	64,706,769	95.6	89,268,000	94.5
Zoroastrians	10,000	0.1	22,500	0.1	1,500,000	2.7	30,350	9,968	40,318	2.41	1,700,000	2.7	1,903,182	2.8	3,200,000	3.4
Baha'is	5,000	0.1	250,000	0.9	410,000	0.7	8,296	-2,981	5,315	1.23	436,000	0.7	463,151	0.7	800,000	0.9
Christians	**116,200**	**1.2**	**275,528**	**1.0**	**310,000**	**0.6**	**6,272**	**-967**	**5,305**	**1.59**	**325,000**	**0.5**	**363,054**	**0.5**	**620,000**	**0.7**
PROFESSION																
crypto-Christians	35,200	0.4	105,000	0.4	254,000	0.5	5,139	-139	5,000	1.81	287,000	0.5	304,000	0.5	465,000	0.5
professing Christians	**81,000**	**0.8**	**170,528**	**0.6**	**56,000**	**0.1**	**1,133**	**-828**	**305**	**0.53**	**38,000**	**0.1**	**59,054**	**0.1**	**155,000**	**0.2**
AFFILIATION																
unaffiliated Christians	0	0.0	0	0.0	43,790	0.1	886	-359	527	1.14	49,142	0.1	49,064	0.1	47,000	0.1
affiliated Christians	**116,200**	**1.2**	**275,528**	**1.0**	**266,210**	**0.5**	**5,386**	**-608**	**4,778**	**1.66**	**275,858**	**0.4**	**313,990**	**0.5**	**573,000**	**0.6**
Orthodox	90,000	0.9	222,600	0.8	190,000	0.3	3,844	-2,615	1,229	0.63	188,400	0.3	202,290	0.3	300,000	0.3
Independents	0	0.0	10,350	0.0	44,000	0.1	890	2,710	3,600	6.16	55,468	0.1	80,000	0.1	240,000	0.3
Roman Catholics	22,900	0.2	23,978	0.1	16,800	0.0	340	-380	-40	-0.24	16,600	0.0	16,400	0.0	17,000	0.0
Protestants	3,000	0.0	15,650	0.1	13,900	0.0	281	-291	-10	-0.07	13,883	0.0	13,800	0.0	14,000	0.0
Anglicans	300	0.0	2,600	0.0	1,200	0.0	24	-24	0	0.00	1,200	0.0	1,200	0.0	1,500	0.0
Marginal Christians	0	0.0	350	0.0	310	0.0	6	-7	-1	-0.33	307	0.0	300	0.0	500	0.0
Trans-megabloc groupings																
Evangelicals	2,800	0.0	13,800	0.1	17,700	0.0	358	-128	230	1.23	18,750	0.0	20,000	0.0	40,000	0.0
Pentecostals/Charismatics	0	0.0	14,000	0.1	47,300	0.1	957	1,913	2,870	4.86	58,108	0.1	76,000	0.1	190,000	0.2
Great Commission Christians	**78,000**	**0.8**	**113,000**	**0.4**	**100,000**	**0.2**	**2,023**	**914**	**2,937**	**2.61**	**112,000**	**0.2**	**129,374**	**0.2**	**250,000**	**0.3**
Nonreligious	0	0.0	10,000	0.0	160,000	0.3	3,237	1,304	4,541	2.53	180,000	0.3	205,413	0.3	500,000	0.5
Hindus	1,000	0.0	8,000	0.0	25,000	0.0	506	95	601	2.18	31,300	0.1	31,008	0.1	50,000	0.1
Jews	44,000	0.5	88,900	0.3	30,000	0.1	607	-1,154	-547	-1.99	24,700	0.0	24,529	0.0	25,000	0.0
Mandeans	5,000	0.1	5,000	0.0	7,600	0.0	154	-78	76	0.96	8,000	0.0	8,361	0.0	12,000	0.0
Sikhs	0	0.0	3,000	0.0	7,000	0.0	142	-30	112	1.50	7,700	0.0	8,124	0.0	11,000	0.0
Atheists	0	0.0	2,000	0.0	7,400	0.0	150	-107	43	0.57	7,600	0.0	7,830	0.0	12,000	0.0
Ethnoreligionists	0	0.0	0	0.0	3,800	0.0	77	-51	26	0.67	3,900	0.0	4,062	0.0	6,000	0.0
New-Religionists	0	0.0	0	0.0	2,500	0.0	51	-30	21	0.80	2,600	0.0	2,708	0.0	4,000	0.0
doubly-counted religionists	0	0.0	0	0.0	-24,000	0.0	-486	287	-199	0.80	-25,000	0.0	-25,993	0.0	-45,000	-0.1
World A (unevangelized persons)	8,439,000	87.0	21,321,750	75.0	38,515,356	68.4	778,988	-378,259	400,729	1.00	40,822,449	65.5	42,516,856	62.8	52,521,428	55.6
World B (evangelized non-Christians)	1,144,800	11.8	6,831,722	24.0	17,483,644	31.0	354,059	379,226	733,285	3.57	21,176,900	34.0	24,822,090	36.7	41,321,572	43.7
World C (Christians)	116,200	1.2	275,528	1.0	310,000	0.6	6,272	-967	5,305	1.59	325,000	0.5	363,054	0.5	620,000	0.7
Country's population	**9,700,000**	**100.0**	**28,429,000**	**100.0**	**56,309,000**	**100.0**	**1,139,319**	**0**	**1,139,319**	**1.86**	**62,324,350**	**100.0**	**67,702,000**	**100.0**	**94,463,000**	**100.0**

COLUMNS, ROWS.
For meanings and definitions, see Codebook (Part 3). Note that, by definition, total 'Christians' = professing + crypto-Christians, which also = affiliated + unaffiliated Christians, and also = Great Commission Christians + latent Christians. Percentages may not always total exactly, due to rounding.

CENSUSES.
1-15.XI.1956: 98.7% Muslims (including Baha'is), 0.6% Christians (114,528 persons), 0.3% Jews (65,232 persons), 0.3% other religionists, 0.1% Parsis (15,723 persons). **1-29.XI.1966:** 98.8% Muslims (including Baha'is), 0.6% Christians (0.5% Orthodox, 0.1% Roman Catholics) (149,427), 0.3% other religionists, 0.2% Jews (60,683 persons), 0.1% Parsis (19,816 persons). **1976:** 99.0% Muslims, 0.5% Christians, 0.18% Jews, 0.06% Zoroastrians, 0.26% other religionists. **1986:** 99.6% Muslims, 0.2% Christians, 0.08% other religionists, 0.07% Zoroastrians, 0.05% Jews. In censuses, Baha'is are recorded as Muslims.

NOTES ON RELIGIONS
ATHEISTS. Communist Party of Iran (Tudeh/Masses) (proscribed; pro-Soviet). A growing number of Iranian intellectuals are atheists.
BAHA'IS. Iran has been the original homeland since 1844 of the Baha'i World Faith. There have been sporadic persecutions and confiscations from 1850 up to the present day, especially 1955, at which time there were 200,000 Baha'is in Iran (40,000 in Tehran alone); many then were forced underground. There has since been rapid growth from 530 local spiritual assemblies (1964) to 949 (1973), with 2,037 other isolated centers or groups. In 1970 there were about 20,000 active adult Baha'is in Tehran in 300 groups, and a similar number in the provinces, making a total of about 40,000 active adults, a total adult community of 80,000, and a total Baha'i community including children, infants and adherents of about 250,000. A large number of Persian Baha'is work abroad as missionaries, and many others resident abroad form the nucleus of the Baha'i communities in Pakistan, India, and elsewhere. From 1964-73, 3,500 Persian pioneers and 5,000 traveling teachers were active. Over 184 books and periodicals have been published (mimeographed due to the prohibition on printing). From the Islamic Revolution of 1979 onwards, Baha'is have been severely harassed and persecuted, including expulsions and executions. Several thousands emigrated. *Schisms.* About 5,000 unorganized and underground Babis (Azalis) still exist, followers of the Bab (Baha'i forerunner) of 1850 and of a schism out of Baha'i since 1868. Statistics of this group, and of other very small schisms, are included in the total for Baha'is given in the table.
CRYPTO-CHRISTIANS. Iranian Christians affiliated to churches (mostly Orthodox) but recorded as Muslims in government censuses.
HINDUS. Indians. ISKCON (Hare Krishna) operates 1 center.
INDEPENDENTS. In about 5 groupings in 1995 including isolated radio and Bible correspondence course believers (see Table 2).
MANDAEANS. Descendants of the Jewish-Christian Gnostic religion of the 2nd century AD, the Mandaeans call themselves Gnostics and are also called Christians of St John, Followers of John the Baptist, Dippers, Sabaeans (the name used by Arabs) or (the priestly caste) Nasoreans. They are found in Khuzistan in the southwest. The only other organized Mandaean community abroad is in Iraq. The cult is centered on fertility worship.
MUSLIMS. 90% Shia Imamites (Ithna-Asharis (Twelvers), also Ismailis (Seveners) in the west), 8% Sunnis (mainly Shafiite Kurds, Hanafite Afghanis, Turkmen); also some Yazidis. The Shias include 500,000 Ahl-i-Haqq (Men of God), Kurds accepting 7 incarnational manifestations of God. *Priests* (mullahs, imams). Total 60,000. *Hajj pilgrims to Mecca.* (1968) 22,903; (1969) 15,132; (1970) 48,367; (1971) 30,299; (1972) 45,298; (1973) 57,230; (1974) 57,314; (1975) 74,095; (1976) 39,296.
NONRELIGIOUS. Expatriate Europeans, also Iranian intellectuals.
PROTESTANTS. Including a number of expatriates.
SIKHS. Indians, first arriving in 1920.
ZOROASTRIANS. Descendants of Zoroastrians, now concentrated in Yazd in central Iran, Kerman to the south, and Tehran. Counted as Muslims before 1975, now experiencing a renaissance. Also called Guebers or Parsis.

Great Commission Instrument Panel: status of Iran (for explanation see start of Part 4)

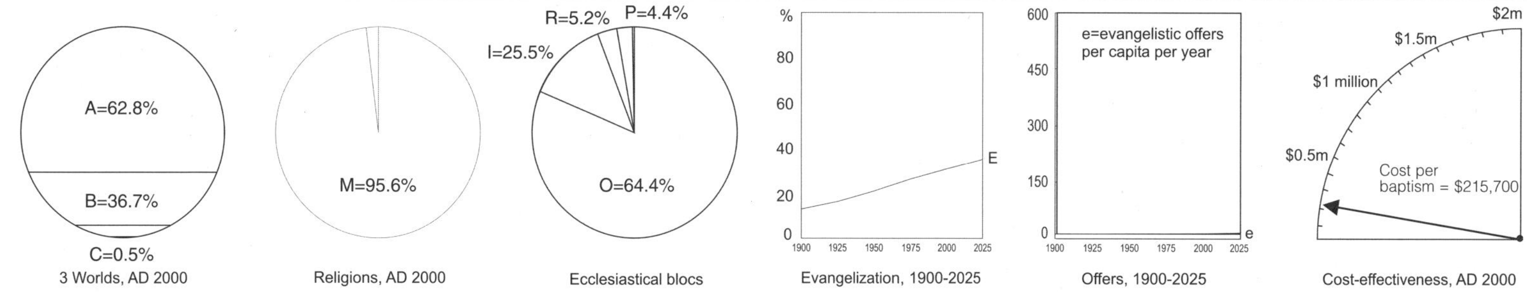

Human rights and freedoms. Iran is one of the major abusers of human rights and one that encourages such abuse in other countries as well. These abuses include summary executions of political and religious opponents, widespread torture, repression of the freedoms of press, speech, assembly and association, persecution of the Baha'is, and severe restriction of the rights of women and workers. The state power is backed up by an extensive internal security system and largescale arrests are made by the Revolutionary Guards. Even mild opposition to the Islamic regime is equated with terrorism. In addition the government continues to carry out political assassinations of its opponents residing abroad, including former prime minister Shahpour Bakhtiar and his assistant in Paris and 4 Iranian Kurdish dissidents in Berlin. Detainees are assaulted in detention and brutalization of prisoners is common. Methods of torture include suspension for long periods in contorted positions, burning with cigarettes, and most frequently, severe and repeated beatings with cables or other instruments on the back and on the soles of feet. Arbitrary arrest and detention on trumped-up criminal charges is a favorite device, especially used against Baha'is. No judicial determination of the legality of detention exists in Iranian law, neither is there a time limit on incommunicado detention. There are 2 different court systems: Civil courts dealing with criminal offenses, and Revolutionary Courts, established in 1979 to try political and narcotics offenses and 'crimes against God'. Trials in Revolutionary Courts are neither fair nor public. If the trial is staged publicly, it is generally because the prisoner has already been forced to confess to a crime. The accused enjoy virtually no procedural or substantive safeguards and the foregone verdict is summary execution. Some trials last less than 5 minutes. Accused do not have access to a lawyer and are unable to call witnesses on their behalf or to appeal the verdicts. Revolutionary courts may take over cases formally being heard by the civil and criminal courts and also overturn decisions of the civilian courts. Even civilian courts are not independent of the government and are manned by theologically and politically correct judges appointed by the mullahs. The severity of the system is mitigated only by the fact that many of the judges are corrupt and verdicts are often on sale. Because Islam rejects the distinction between private and public spheres, authorities may enter homes and check domestic conduct and personal activities. Women whose clothing does not completely cover the hair and all of the body except hands and face, or who wear makeup, are subject to arrest, and so are men who wear immodest dress, such as short sleeves. Periodic crackdowns on dress code and moral violations are conducted by the Head Office for Combating Unlawful Acts. The media are required to conform to Islamic principles, and violators run the risk of confiscation of publications and equipment as well as arrest and summary punishment. All books must be submitted to the Ministry of Islamic Guidance for review before publication. The right to censorship on religious grounds includes the issuance of deadly fatwas, as was done in the case of the British Indian author Salman Rushdie's *Satanic Verses*. Newspapers are prohibited from criticizing Islam or from promoting ethnic rights. Foreign publications may be imported only after they have been reviewed by the Ministry of Islamic Guidance. The only public meetings allowed are those

Country summary. **Worlds A, B, C by ethnolinguistic peoples, cities, and major civil divisions in Iran.**

	PEOPLES							*CITIES*							*CIVIL DIVISIONS*						
World	*Num*	*Pop 2000*	*C%*	*Christians*	*E%*	*U%*	*Unevangelized*	*Num*	*Pop 2000*	*C%*	*Christians*	*E%*	*U%*	*Unevangelized*	*Num*	*Pop 2000*	*C%*	*Christians*	*E%*	*U%*	*Unevangelized*
A	65	43,045,864	0.08	34,135	26	74	31,780,169	78	28,026,403	0.40	110,969	38	62	17,448,190	27	67,702,198	0.46	313,989	37	63	42,507,291
B	5	24,391,619	0.23	56,675	56	44	10,726,706	2	3,084,329	3.43	105,740	54	46	1,404,465	0	0	0.00	0	0	0	0
C	8	264,714	84.31	223,179	100	0	414	0	0	0.00	0	0	0	0	0	0	0.00	0	0	0	0
Total	**78**	**67,702,197**	**0.46**	**313,989**	**37**	**63**	**42,507,289**	**80**	**31,110,732**	**0.70**	**216,709**	**39**	**61**	**18,852,655**	**27**	**67,702,198**	**0.46**	**313,989**	**37**	**63**	**42,507,291**

sponsored by the government, such as Friday prayers and parades and demonstrations on official occasions portraying the United States as 'satan'. The right of emigration is denied to Iranians who are suspect politically (such as those who were associated with the former regime) and professionals whose skills are in short supply. Normally permission is not granted for all members of a family to travel abroad at the same time. The position of women in society has deteriorated since the 1979 revolution. Self-appointed guardians of public morality hound them if they appear in dress deemed not sufficiently modest.

Human environment. Iran's arid climate and fragile soil, combined with the neglect of natural resources and the devastation of the Iran-Iraq war have created an environmental crisis. The heavily forested Caspian region is now denuded and the forests of the western mountains have been reduced to scattered stands. Acid rain from the burning oil wells in Kuwait has destroyed forests along the Persian Gulf. The Persian Gulf has become one of the most polluted bodies of water in the world as a result of massive oil spills. Much of the marine ecology of the region has become irreversibly damaged. The interior of Iran is one of the driest areas in the Middle East and has experienced severe drought for the past 2 decades. The drought, together with inefficient use of water resources, has created shortages of drinking water.

Muslims. Friday Prayer Meeting, Tehran University, 1980.

NON-CHRISTIAN RELIGIONS

Islam is the professed religion of 97% of the population, of which the majority are Shia Imamites, also called Ithna-Asharis or Twelvers. Indeed, Iran is in many ways the major center of Shiite Islam in the world. Muslim forces finally defeated the last Sassanid Zoroastrian king, Yazdegerd III, in the Battle of Nahavand in 642. Prominent in Iranian emotional and spiritual memory is the martyrdom in AD 680 of Shiite leader al-Husayn ibn Ali and his followers in Karbala, Iraq by the Umayyads. This is commemorated annually at the beginning of each lunar year with *ta'ziya* (passion plays), the wearing of bloody shrouds, and self-flagellation with chains, scimitars, and bare hands. The former Shah tried to re-shape the grim character of the commemoration by encouraging musicians and craftsmen, and by holding national festivals of the arts, but his efforts failed. So an attitude of suffering, martyrdom, and severe discipline hangs over both the majority religion and the national character of Iran. The tragedy of Karbala is referred to constantly in public events of all kinds. There are also over 2.6 million Sunnis, mainly Kurds of the Shafiite rite and Afghanis of the Hanafite rite. The power of the Shiite religious leadership was limited by the government of the Shah, until the 1979 revolution. The veneration of Muslim saints is widely practiced, and the shrines of popular saints are extensively endowed. Iran's most important pilgrimage centers are the cities of Qom and Meshed. The holy city of Qom, with 14 seminaries, is the world center of Shiite Muslim activism. The 18,000 students include about 6,000 from Iraq, Bahrain, Kuwait, Nigeria, Tunisia, Lebanon, Pakistan, Afghanistan, and many other countries, all on full scholarships.

By the early 1990s there were signs that the earlier, revolutionary religious zeal was waning. Mosque attendance appeared to be declining. More women began defying the traditional dress standards. Many complained of official corruption, and observers recognized a general disillusionment with the revolution's long-term effects.

Baha'i owes its origin to a Persian, Sayyid Ali Muhammed, who in 1844 added his name as Bab al-Din (Gate of the Faith) to the list of the Twelve Imams of Shiite Islam. His followers were called Babis. His successor was Baha'u'llah (Glory of God), from whose name comes the term Baha'i. Accused of complicity in a plot to assassinate the Persian shah in 1852, Baha'is fled from Iran en masse. The persecutions and confiscations of 1955 drove them underground for a time, but by the mid-1970s they were no longer molested, despite still being officially banned, and were active in commerce and the professions. From 1979 Baha'is encountered severe harassment, expulsions and executions. The censuses continued to counted them as Muslims. As a missionary religion the Baha'i World Faith in Iran doubled the number of its organized centers from 1960-75, has sent abroad large numbers of missions, and has Persian Baha'is forming the nuclei of Baha'i communities in Pakistan, India and elsewhere. A separate group also exists in Iran named Babis, being 5,000 followers of those who accepted the Bab but refused to recognize Baha'u'llah.

Judaism is still represented by an influential community, in spite of the large numbers of Jews who have emigrated to Israel. The majority reside in Tehran. They operate synagogues, schools, recreation centers, and a hospital.

Zoroastrianism, known elsewhere as Parsiism, began in the 6th century BC as Zoroastrianism, with the preaching of Zarathustra who succeeded in eliminating all deities of the Iranian pantheon except Ahura Mazda, the One True God. During the period of Sassanid rule in Persia, from the 7th to 3rd centuries BC, Zoroastrianism became the symbol of national and cultural identity as well as the state religion, although later it was unable to withstand the Muslim onslaught which began in the 7th century AD. The largest Parsi communities are in Tehran, Tazd, Kerman, and Isfahan.

Mandaeanism is an ancient Jewish-Christian Gnostic syncretistic religion begun in the 2nd century AD, centered on Fertility worship, whose followers call themselves Mandaiia (Gnostics) and who are also variously called Mandaeans, Sabaeans (so termed by Arabs), Nasoreans, Followers of John the Baptist, Dippers, or Christians of St John. They are found in Khuzistan (southwest Iran) and in Iraq.

Sikhism, a reform movement out of Hinduism with a strong monotheistic emphasis, entered Iran about 1920. Sikhs remain for the most part expatriate Indians.

Episcopal Church of Iran. Blind evangelist reads Bible in Braille to group at Fawzia hospital.

CHRISTIANITY

About 98% of all Christians in Iran belong to non-Persian ethnic minorities. Only a few converts from Islam have become members of the Anglican and Evangelical (Presbyterian) churches.

ORTHODOX CHURCHES. The Armenian Apostolic Church is by far the largest church in Iran. It terms itself Apostolic because it traces it origin to the work of the 1st-century apostles Thaddeus and Bartholomew in Armenia and northwest Persia. Until 1946, its 3 dioceses in Iran were under the Catholicate of Echmiadzin in the USSR, and the bishops were Soviet Armenians. In 1959 the communal councils of the dioceses asked to be placed instead under the jurisdiction of then rival Armenian Catholicate of Cilicia (Sis) based on Antelias, Lebanon. The Armenian community in Iran operates numerous schools and publishes books in its own language. Thousands of Armenians make an annual pilgrimage in July to the 14th century church of St Thaddeus in Turkey, on the south side of Mt Ararat.

The Assyrian or Ancient Church of the East has traditionally been termed Nestorian, a name which is however rejected by the church itself on the grounds that it existed before the Greek patriarch Nestorius and reached its theological position independently of him. Membership in Iran consists largely of refugees from persecution in Turkey and Iraq. Concentrated in the northern part of the country at an earlier period, the Assyrian population has gradually moved to the Tehran area. The church sponsors one school.

The Russian Orthodox Church was established in Tehran in 1863 and is directly related to the synod of bishops of the Russian Orthodox Church Outside of Russia whose primate lives in New York, USA. Activities in Tehran include a school, a library, and a club. Greeks came to Iran largely by way of Russia between 1917 and 1936, and in the early years they worshiped with the Russian Orthodox. A separate Greek Orthodox Church was established in Tehran in 1943, whose leader, an archimandrite, serves under the Patriarchate of Antioch through the archbishop of Baghdad. A small school is attached to the church in Tehran.

CATHOLIC CHURCH. Roman Catholicism is represented by 3 rites. (1) The Chaldean Catholic Church is the largest with about two-thirds of the total Catholic population (15,000). It has roots identical with the Assyrian Church of the East and consists of converts to Rome from the year 1552 on. (2) The Latin Church has 7,000 members, more than half being expatriates. Latin missionaries came to Iran in the 13th and in the 17th centuries, but each time their work was destroyed. Another mission entered in 1840 and several new ones since World War II. (3) The Armenian Catholic Church, a uniate church created through Dominican activity, dates its founding to 1605, although the establishment of its own patriarchate came later. Armenian Catholics suffered under the Afghan persecutions of the 18th century and now number only 2,000.

The Holy See has diplomatic relations with Iran and in AD 2000 is represented to government and the Catholic hierarchy by a nuncio residing in Tehran.

PROTESTANT CHURCHES. The pioneer Protestant mission was the American Board (ABCFM) in 1832. Its Presbyterian and Congregationalist missionaries did not intend to organize a separate church but called themselves the Mission to the Nestorians, which was organized in 1834. The Nestorian Church, however, resisted reforms, and instead the mission found itself converting numbers of Assyrians. As a result, the Evangelical Church, which is Presbyterian in polity, came into existence in 1855. Until recent years it was the largest Protestant church in the country and has had an influence out of all proportion to its size. Its membership is 55% Assyrian, 21% Armenian and 24% of other ethnic origins. The church maintains 19 schools and is related through its Christian Service Board to the Nurbakhsh School for Practical Nurses.

Persians who became Pentecostals while living in Chicago (USA) brought Pentecostalism to their homeland in 1909; but during World War I many of them were killed or scattered and their work came to a halt. Missionaries from the Assemblies of God, USA were active during 1924-38 and returned again in 1966. An Armenian group of Pentecostals, Filadelfia, which began in Iran in 1958, has also received support from the Assemblies of God since 1965. By the early 1990s they became the largest Protestant church in the country.

Seventh-day Adventists arrived in 1911 and the first Brethren work began in 1920, but both of these groups have remained small, two-thirds of the Adventist community having emigrated to the USA. There are now numerous small American missions in Iran, the majority having arrived since 1955. Many have only expatriate membership. Protestants have mainly grown at the expense of the Orthodox churches, Armenian and Assyrian, with very few Persian converts.

ANGLICAN CHURCH. The first Anglican to enter Iran (1811) was Henry Martyn, a chaplain of the East India Company, who displayed extraordinary gifts in the translation of the scriptures into the Persian language. In 1844 the London Society for the Propagation of Christianity among the Jews sent missionaries to the Jewish community of Tehran. The Church Missionary Society made its appearance in 1869 and the diocese of Persia was formed in 1912. In contrast to the Protestant churches, however, it has not won converts from Orthodoxy but is, rather, a church of converts from Judaism, Islam and Parsiism. The church operates 2 hospitals, 2 schools and a school for the blind.

Renewal movements. In the 1990s the Pentecostal/Charismatic Renewal continued to spread rapidly across most older churches, and numbered over 76,000 adherents (of whom 7% Pentecostals, 5% Charismatics, and 88% Independents).

Indigenous missions. Christians from the boundaries of present-day Iran have been active in mission since the first century when apostles Thaddeus and Bartholomew were working in Armenia and northwest Persia. A couple of centuries later the Church of the East was actively sending missionaries further east. This continued until the church was virtually wiped out under Tamerlane. In more recent times, Iranian Christians have been active in the diaspora and in surrounding countries.

CHURCH AND STATE

The revolution of 1978-79, led by ayatollah Khomeini, brought in a new theocratic constitution. Massive public demonstrations showed the overwhelming popular reaction against Western presence and influence, perceived to be anti-religious and anti-Muslim. Iran is an Islamic republic with a system of government based on Muslim law. Final authority in all executive, legislative, and legal matters rests with the *faqih*, a supreme spiritual leader whose most important qualification is knowledge of Islamic law and theology. Islamic law allows for the toleration of certain religious minorities—notably Jews and Christians—so persecution is not at all inherent, and in fact these groups are accorded certain privileges. Both communities are represented in the national, unicameral legislature, the Islamic Consultative Assembly. In practice, the mullahs hold the preeminent power in the country, both through direct participation in government and through their influence over popular thought and action. As soon as Khomeini came to power revolutionary committees began to circulate throughout the country, checking for compliance with Muslim codes of dress and behavior. Many Christian properties were confiscated, including hospitals in Isfahan and Shiraz, the Christoffel Blind Mission, and many churches. Christian education has been dramatically affected, as mixed-sex schools were banned, all schools and universities were required to reflect Islamic thought, and university admission became partially based on the student's belief in Islam. In 1984 all Armenian (and other Christian) schools were given Muslim headmasters and actions were taken against the teaching of the Armenian language. In 1983 the Ministry of Education published a new textbook on the catechism that reflected the Koran's teachings about Jesus.

Muslim converts to Christianity, and those that converted or baptized them, have generally been martyred. In a typical incident, 3 converts were imprisoned in 1990. Two of them then allegedly returned to Islam and were released. After their release they told of how their confessions were extracted by torture, and they continued as believers in Jesus Christ. Despite many appeals to government officials, the Bible Society was closed in 1990, following years of extremely high Bible sales in Iran. All Christian bookshops were closed at the same time. Many churches have gone underground, with believers meeting clandestinely in different homes week by week. Other churches have police guards at their gates and informants infiltrating their meetings. In 1991 the Supreme Revolutionary Cultural Council ordered a new campaign against Protestant Evangelical churches, carried out by the Ministry of Islamic Guidance for Minorities. Many churches across the country were closed.

BROADCASTING AND MEDIA

FEBA (Seychelles) has shortwave radio programs in Arabic, Azeri and Farsi. Programs from KNLS have generated response.

Some 2.6 million have seen the 'Jesus' Film: through videocassettes (1.1 million), radio broadcasts (1 million) and film teams (525,000), with 56,500 responding. Satellite TV programs are received mainly in Arabic.

Former Shah of Iran in audience with Anglican, Catholic, and Protestant leaders including secretary of Iran Council of Churches.

INTERDENOMINATIONAL ORGANIZATIONS

The Iran Council of Churches was formed in 1951 to 'strengthen Christian Churches in their internal life; to encourage evangelistic outreach; (and) to work toward a united Church'. There have been 3 members (Anglican, Presbyterian and Tehran Community churches), with unofficial cooperation also with the Catholic Church. Projects have included literature development, youth activity, correspondence courses and preparation of programs in Farsi for Radio Voice of the Gospel in Addis Ababa (until 1977). In Teheran a number of church leaders gather together on a regular, informal basis for mutual encouragement and fellowship, and to support those under persecution.

FUTURE TRENDS AND PROSPECTS

The unexpected conversions to Christianity from Islam that commenced in the late 1980s could continue into the 21st century with Muslims declining slightly from 98% in 1900 to less than 95% by 2025 while Christians remain at less than 1% through 2025.

Christians could grow to over 1 million before AD 2050. Muslims should remain above 90% for the next few decades.

BIBLIOGRAPHY

A century of mission work in Iran (Persia) 1834–1934: a record of one hundred years of the work of the Iran (Persia) Mission of the Board of Foreign Missions of the Presbyterian Church in the U.S.A. Beirut, Lebanon: Presbyterian Church in the U.S.A. Iran Mission, 1936. 171p.

A chronicle of the Carmelites in Persia and the papal mission of the XVIIth and XVIIIth centuries. H. Chick (ed, trans). London: Eyre & Spottiswoode, 1939. 2 vols.

'A handbook on the Christian communities in Iran.' N. A. Horner. [Tehran: United Presbyterian Commission in Iran], 1970. 22p.

'A study of the Protestant Evangelical Church in Iran: with implications for ministry and missions in the 70's and 80's.' S. Little. D.Min. thesis, San Francisco Theological Seminary, San Anselmo, CA, [1977]. 296p.

'American missionaries in Iran, 1834–1934.' A. Mansoori. Ph.D. dissertation, Ball State University, Muncie, IN, 1986. 188p.

Christians in Persia: Assyrians, Armenians, Roman Catholics and Protestants. R. E. Waterfield. London: Allen & Unwin, 1973. 176p.

Design of my world. H. B. Dehqani-Tafti. London: Lutterworth, 1960. (Autobiography of Anglican bishop).

Encyclopaedia Iranica. E. Yar-Shater (ed). London: Routledge & Kegan Paul, 1982–.

Folk religion of the Kurds. A. Rahman. Altadena, CA: Friends of the Kurds, Zwemer Institute, 1988. 60p.

Imam Khomeini, Pope, and Christianity. Tehran: Islamic Propagation Organization, 1984. 44p. (Chiefly messages exchanged between Ruhollah Khomeini and Pope John Paul II, 1978-1980).

Iran. R. Navabpour. *World bibliographical series*, vol. 81. Oxford, UK: CLIO Press, 1988. 328p. (See especially 'Religion,' p.81–91).

Iran: from religious dispute to revolution. M. M. J. Fischer. *Harvard studies in cultural anthropology*, 3. Cambridge, MA: Harvard University Press, 1980. 328p.

'Iran: implementation of an Islamic state,' S. Akhavi, in *Islam in Asia: religion, politics, & society*, p.27–52. J. L. Esposito (ed). New York: Oxford University Press, 1987.

Iranian cities: formation and development. M. Kheirabadi. Austin: University of Texas Press, 1991. 146p.

Islam and the post–revolutionary state in Iran. H. Omid. New York: St. Martin's Press, 1994. 273p.

'Islam et babysme,' R. Leniir, *Revue de synthèse*, 78, 8 (1957), 471–77.

Islam in practice: religious beliefs in a Persian village. R. Loeffler. Albany, NY: State University of New York Press, 1988. 312p.

Islamic movements in Egypt, Pakistan, and Iran: an annotated bibliography. A. Hussain. London: Mansell, 1983. 168p.

La chiesa in Iran. A. Bugnini. Rome: Edizione Vincenziane, 1981. 487p.

L'Eglise et les Chrétiens aujourd'hui, en Iran. J. Basset. Teheran: Centre d'Etudes et d'Informations, 1978. 41p.

My Persian pilgrimage. W. M. Miller. Rev. ed. Pasadena, CA: William Carey Library, 1989. 403p.

Nomad: a year in the life of a Qashqa'i tribesman in Iran. L. Beck. Berkeley, CA: University of California Press, 1991. 503p.

Religion and politics in contemporary Iran: clergy–state relations in the Pahlavi period. S. Akhavi. Leiden: E. J. Brill, 1980.

Religion and politics in Iran: Shiism from quietism to revolution. N. R. Keddie (ed). London: Yale University Press, 1984. 288p.

Religion and state in Iran 1785–1906. H. Algar. Leiden: E. J. Brill, 1970. 304p.

Resurrection and renewal: the making of the Babi Movement in Iran, 1844–1850. A. Amanat. Ithaca, NY and London: Cornell University Press, 1989. 479p.

'Shia movements in Lebanon: their formation, ideology, social basis, and links with Iran and Syria,' M. Deeb, *Third world quarterly*, 10, 2 (1988), 683–98.

Something new in Iran. J. N. Hoare. London: Church Missionary Society, 1937. 77p.

'The Armenian Apostolic Church in Iran,' J. Hananian, *Al-Mushir* (Rawalpindi, Pakistan), 12, 7-8 (1970), 1–10.

The Cambridge history of Iran. Vol. 3: *The Seleucid, Parthian and Sasanian periods.* E. Yar-Shater (ed.). Cambridge, UK: Cambridge University Press, 1983. (See especially 'Christians in Iran,' p.924–48).

The Iranians: Persia, Islam and the soul of a nation. S. Mackey. New York: Dutton, 1996. 448p.

The mantle of the Prophet: religion and politics in Iran. R. Mottahedeh. New York: Simon & Schuster, 1985. 416p.

The Presbyterian Church in Iran. J. Elder. New York: United Presbyterian Church.

'The Qashqa'i,' R. Weekes, in *Muslim peoples*, p.631–37, vol. 2. Westport, CT: Greenwood Press, 1984. (Lists 25 books and articles on the Qashqa'i).

The Qashqa'i nomads of Fars. P. Oberling. The Hague: Mouton, 1974. 277p.

The Qashqa'i of Iran. L. Beck. New Haven, CT: Yale University Press, 1986. 400p.

'The resilience of religious institutions and the making of protest movements: a comparative study of Tunisia and Iran.' K. Ghozzi. Ph.D. dissertation, University of Pennsylvania, Philadelphia, 1994. 265p.

The shadow of God and the hidden imam: religion, political order, and societal change in Shi'ite Iran from the beginning to 1890. S. A. Arjomand. *Publications of the Center for Middle Eastern Studies*, no. 17. Chicago: University of Chicago Press, 1984. 368p.

The structure of Christian–Muslim relations in contemporary Iran. R. M. Schwartz. *Occasional papers in anthropology*, no. 13. [Halifax, Nova Scotia: Department of Anthropology, Saint Mary's University, 1985]. 133p.

Zoroastrians: their religious beliefs and practices. M. Boyce. London and Boston: Routledge & Kegan Paul, 1979. 374p.

Country Table 2. Organized churches and denominations in Iran.

Official name (bold type = church with over 10% of all affiliated) 1	Begun 2	Type 3	Counc 4	Congs 5	Adults 6	Affiliated 1970 7	Affiliated 1995 8	G% 9	Names, notes, and other statistics (see Codebook, Part 3) 10
Ancient Church of the East: P Tehran	c 50	O-Nes	Yw...	9	9,100	20,000	18,000	-0.42	*D Urmia/Rezayeh.* Assyrians. 2,700 families. No dissidents as in Iraq. Patriarch, 6n,1s.
Armenian Apostolic Church:	c 64	O-Arm	Sw.N.	100	100,000	202,000	170,000	-0.69	*Gregorians.* Under jurisdiction of C Sis (Lebanon). Armenians. 73,000 in 1908.
D Julfa-Isfahan	c1600	O-Arm	Sa	30	13,000	40,000	30,000	-1.14	Armenians in eastern Iran, transferred en masse in c1600 from Julfa. 17n,1H.
D Tabriz (Azerbaijan)	c 64	O-Arm	Sa	40	7,000	12,000	10,000	-0.73	Azerbaidzhan province of Iran. Until c1820, named D Artaz. 3n,2d.
D Tehran	1944	O-Arm	Sb	30	80,000	150,000	130,000	-0.57	Irak province. Archbishop, 16n,1h,3r (and 14 primary schools). Many youth clubs.
Armenian Closed Brethren	1945	I-EBr	.....	1	30	100	86	-0.60	Exclusive separation from Armenian Ev Spiritual Brethren in 1945. Armenians.
Armenian Ev Spiritual Brethren	c1920	I-CBr	x....	1	50	150	132	-0.51	*Holiness Brethren.* Schism ex various Armenian churches. Tehran. No ministers.
Assemblies of God (Assyrian)	1909	I-3pS	ZF...	11	550	1,000	1,000	0.00	Assyrians, in Azerbaijan Province. M=AoG(USA) since 1924. 55% of members in Tehran.
Assemblies of God (Filadelfia)	1958	P-Pe2	Z....	19	1,600	3,000	4,000	1.16	Armenians. Origin USSR. M=AoG(USA). Correspondence courses (8000). 15n,4f,1s(9).
Catholic Church in Iran:	1552	R-LEr	O...R	30	8,900	23,978	16,600	-1.46	*Kelisa-ye-Katolik.* Ex Nestorians. C=3+1+5. 9n 7x 7m 31w 120Yy
M Urmya (Rezayeh) *(Chaldean)*	c250	R-Cha	Os	11	1,700	4,000	3,300	0.06	Chaldeans (Kaldani), united with Rome 1552. 1n 1x 1m 1w 30Yy
D Salmas (Shahpur) *(Chaldean)*	1709	R-Cha	Os	2	500	700	700	0.00	For some time counted as part of M Urmya. 0n 0x 0m 1w 3Yy
M Tehran *(Chaldean)*	1853	R-Cha	Os	5	2,500	9,500	4,500	-2.94	In capital. Until 1971, M Sehna. Many ex-Nestorians. 8n 0x 0m 13w 46Yy
AD Ahwaz *(Chaldean)*	1966	R-Cha	Os	4	300	778	400	-2.63	Suffragan diocese of P Babilonia (Iraq). Declining. 0n 1x 1m 0w 8Yy
AD Ispahan *(Latin)*	1629	R-Lat	os	6	2,600	7,000	5,000	-1.34	*Kelisa-ye-Latini-e-Katolik.* 60% expatriates. M=SDB. 0n 4x 4m 12w 26Yy
D Ispahan (Esfaan) *(Armenian)*	1605	R-Arm	Os	2	1,300	2,000	2,700	1.21	340 Armenian families, mostly in Tehran. HQ Tehran. 0n 1x 1m 4w 7Yy
Church of Christ, Scientist	1960	m-Sci	x....	1	20	50	40	-0.89	*Christian Science.* M=CCS(Boston, USA). In Tehran.
Ch of Jesus Christ of Latter-day Saints	1965	m-LdS	x....	3	100	200	200	0.00	Under Swiss Mission, LdS. Mainly Americans, Europeans, Tehran, Bandar Abbas, Ahwaz.
Episcopal Church of Iran	1811	A-Eva	Aw.MK	4	480	2,600	1,200	-3.05	*D Iran*, in *ECJME.* M=CMS,CMJ,CB. 10% expatriates. 6n,5x,39f,2k,2H,3r,W=61%,7Y,18y.
Evangelical Church of Iran	1832	P-Ref	RW.MK	10	1,650	6,000	3,000	-2.73	1835, M=UPUSA. A=1934. North. 55%, Assyrian, 21% Armenian. 19 schools. 12n,37f,1r,1s.
French Evangelical Church	1967	P-Ref	.....	1	20	50	50	0.00	*Eglise Evangélique Française.* French-speaking congregation in Tehran.
German Evangelical Church in Iran	c1930	P-Lut	.....	1	300	400	500	0.90	*Deutsche Evangelische Kirche.* Serving large German community in Tehran. 1x,1k.
Greek Orth P Antioch (D Baghdad)	1917	O-Gre	Cw.N.	2	264	600	400	-1.61	Greeks, Arabs, also former Nestorians; in Tehran, Abadan. 1x.
Hidden Muslim believers in Christ	c1970	I-Mus	.....	200	14,000	–	24,000	49.70	Converted Muslims who remain within Islamic structures as witnesses for Christ.
International Missions	1955	P-Non	xM...	3	50	100	150	1.64	M=IM(USA). Faraman Church (rural), Good Shepherd Church (Tehran). 25f.
Isolated radio churches	1960	I-3rS	.....	500	15,000	8,400	30,000	5.22	Isolated radio believers (youths etc). R=900 (RVOG,TWR),T=53500 (1M,ICI,VOP).
Jehovah's Witnesses	1926	m-Jeh	x....	1	40	100	67	-1.59	*Watch Tower. IBSA.* 1926, missionaries' arrival; 1954, active witnessing under way.
Khuzestan Church Council	c1970	P-Uni	.....	5	100	300	200	-1.61	Joint project of Episcopal Ch/Evangelical Ch/ICC Abadan and Ahwaz. 1n,2x.
Russian Orthodox Church	1863	I-Rus	x....	1	99	600	150	-5.39	Related to ROC Outside of Russia (New York, USA). Tehran, 15,000-volume library.
Seventh-day Adventist Church	1911	P-Adv	x....	3	80	300	133	-3.20	*Iran Field.* 60% emigrated to USA. 5n,4x,17mw,14f,1h,1r,5t(176),W=83%,8Y.
Tehran Bible Church	1964	I-Non	.M...	1	50	100	100	0.00	English-speaking. Linked with International Missions. 1x.
Tehran Community Church	c1930	P-com	....K	2	100	500	300	-2.02	English-speaking congregation in Tehran. Mostly expatriates.
Tehran Lutheran Church	1970	P-Lut	.....	1	50	100	100	0.00	English-speaking congregation in Tehran. Mostly expatriates. 1x.
Union of Armenian Ev Chs in Near East		P-Con	Rw.N.	2	100	300	250	0.05	*Armenian Protestants.* HQ Beirut. 2 congregations and 1 school in Tehran.
United Pentecostal Church	1930	P-Pel	x....	4	120	100	200	2.81	*Jesus Only Church.* M=UPC(USA). Early work not followed up until much later. 2m,2f.
Other Protestant denominations		P-	.....	70	3,000	4,500	5,000	0.05	Total about 10 (see list below), including Korean Presbyterians, some charismatic groups.
Totals				**986**	**155,853**	**275,528**	**275,858**		

Churches, members, growth, 1900-2025	*Congs*	*Adults*	*Affiliated*	*G%*	*Total denominations*	*6 Megablocs:* *O*	*R*	*A*	*P*	*I*	*m*
Total churches, members, and denominations (mid-1900)	200	74,600	116,200	1.24	6	2	1	1	1	1	0
Total churches, members, and denominations (mid-1970)	539	176,960	275,528	1.24	29	3	1	1	15	6	3
Total churches, members, and denominations (mid-1990)	1,000	150,000	266,210	-0.17	36	3	1	1	21	7	3
Total churches, members, and denominations (mid-1995)	986	155,853	275,858	0.71	36	3	1	1	21	7	3
Total churches, members, and denominations (mid-2000)	990	177,000	313,990	2.62	36	3	1	1	21	7	3
Total churches, members, and denominations (mid-2025)	1,700	324,000	573,000	2.44	67	8	1	1	30	20	7

NOTES ON TABLE ABOVE
NATIONAL COUNCILS (Column 4, 5th letter).
K = Iran Council of Churches (ICC) (Shovraye Kelissye Iran).
R = Iranian Episcopal Conference (formerly Inter-Rite Episcopal Conference), begun 1977.

OTHER PROTESTANT DENOMINATIONS. These include: Baptist Bible Fellowship International (1966), Ch of Christ (Non-Instrumental), International Christian Fellowship (1969), Lutheran Orient Mission Society (1911), Southern Baptist Convention (1968), United Evangelical Chs, World-wide Evangelization Crusade (1963); also USA military chaplaincies.

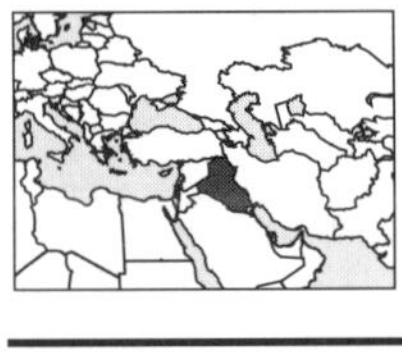

IRAQ

SECULAR DATA, AD 2000

STATE
Official name: Al-Jumhouriya al-`Iraqia (The Republic of Iraq).
Short name: Iraq. **Adjective of nationality:** Iraqi.
Flag: Red, white, and black stripes, with 3 green stars.
Area: 435,052 sq. km. (167,975 sq. mi.).
Government: One-party socialist-military state, since 1963 (1920 monarchy, 1958 military junta).
Legislature: National Assembly, 220 members.
Official language: Arabic.
Monetary unit: 1 Iraqi dinar (ID) = 20 dirhams = 1,000 fils. **US$1=** 1,500 ID.
Chief cities: BAGHDAD 4,796,000; Irbil (Arbil) 2,368,000; Al-Mawsil (Mosul) 1,034,000; Al Basrah (Basra) 956,389; Kirkuk 527,821.
Political divisions: 18 provinces.
Armed forces: 388,000.

DEMOGRAPHY
Population: 23,115,000.
Population density: 53.1/sq. km. (137.6/sq. mi.).
Under 15 years: 9,556,000.
Growth rate p.a.: 2.85% (births 33.75, deaths 5.35).
Mortality: Infant, per 1,000: 39.4; **Maternal per 100,000:** 310.0.
Life expectancy: 69 (male 68, female 71).
Household size: 8.9. **Floor area per person, sq.m:** 13.0.
Major languages: Arabic, Kurdish, Chaldean (Aramaic-Syriac), Persian, Turkish, Turkoman, Armenian, English, French, Circassian, and several others.
Urban dwellers: 76.82%. **Urban growth rate p.a.:** 3.4%.
Labor force: 25%.

ETHNOLINGUISTIC PEOPLES
57.5% Iraqi Arab; 8.5% Southern Kurd (Sorani); 6.5% Northern Kurd (Kermanji); 6.0% Iraqi Kurd; 5.6% Azerbaijani (Azeri Turk).

ECONOMY
National income p.a. per person: US$2,000; **per family:** US$17,800.

EDUCATION
Adult literacy: 58% (male 70%, female 45%). **Schools:** 11,045.
Universities: 20. **School enrolment:** female/male: 61%/77%.

HEALTH
Access to health services: 93%. **Access to safe water:** 44%.
Hospitals: 177 (18 beds per 10,000). **Doctors:** 9,366.
Blind: 75,000. **Deaf:** 1,386,500. **Murder rate:** 7.
Lepers: 7,000. **Underweight prevalence under 5:** 12%.

LITERATURE
New book titles p.a.: 690 (30 p.a. per million). **Periodicals:** 21.
Newspapers: 4 dailies.

COMMUNICATION (per 1,000 people)
Phones: 33 (15% mobile). **Radios:** 630. **TV sets:** 74.
Daily newspaper circulation: 27. **Computers:** 20.

REFUGEES
Citizen refugees in other countries: 622,900.
Alien refugees from other countries: 115,200.
Internal displacement: 1,000,000.

HUMAN LIFE AND LIBERTY (optimum condition=100.0%)
HDI: 53.1. **HSI:** 35.0. **HFI:** 0.0. **EFL:** 2.0.

Country status. Iraq, known also as Mesopotamia until the end of World War II, is an almost landlocked Arab nation in Western Asia. Nearly 75% of the population lives on the fertile plain that drains into the reedy marshes of the southeast. Much of the southwest is desert or wasteland. The country is the site of a flourishing ancient civilization.

HUMAN LIFE AND LIBERTY

Human need and development. The Gulf War of 1991-92 wrought much destruction in the towns and cities of Iraq and, in the words of one observer, reduced the country to stone age living conditions. Until then Iraq was considered one of the more prosperous in the Middle East, helped by vast revenues from its oil. However, the long war with Iran, followed on its heels by the Gulf War, drained the national treasury, and the UN-imposed embargo led to the scarcity of all types of goods, other than in the flourishing black market. Heavy US air bombing destroyed the fragile infrastructure and left many buildings in ruins. The actual extent of the damage will never be known, because Iraq remains a pariah in the international community, isolated from normal media scrutiny. Reports from the country indicate that life continues in the major cities much like before, and there are few visible signs of deprivation or starvation. In Baghdad, even luxuries are openly available, although at a price. Medical facilities and other amenities are disproportionately concentrated in the capital. Poor sanitation and polluted water sources remain the principal factors in the spread of disease in rural areas. Some of the rivers, notably, the Shatt al Arab, are breeding grounds for mosquitoes and parasites that spread waterborne diseases.

Human rights and freedoms. Under Saddam Hussein, Iraq has an abysmal record in human rights. His dictatorship rests on intimidation and terror, and his systematic abuse of power has few parallels in the modern world. Political killings of the regime's opponents, barbarous attacks against Kurds in the north and Shiite dissidents in the Southern marshes, the use of chemical weapons against civilians, torture of prisoners, including mutilation and gouging out of eyes, systematic rape of women and arbitrary arrests and detentions are some of the hallmarks of the Hussein regime. Freedom of the press and speech do not exist, and political dissent is not tolerated. The government owns all print and electronic media and periodically attempts to jam radio broadcasts from outside. The regime practices open discrimination against ethnic and religious minorities, such as Kurds, Assyrians, and Turcomans. Mass forced relocations have rendered thousands of Kurds homeless. Power is wielded almost entirely by the Sunni Arabs, who constitute a small minority of 12%, while the Shias, who make up 60%, are the targets of official hostility.

Country Table 1. **Religious adherents in Iraq, AD 1900-2025.**

Year / Name	1900 Adherents	1900 %	1970 Adherents	1970 %	mid-1990 Adherents	mid-1990 %	Annual change, 1990-2000 Natural	Conversion	Total	Rate	mid-1995 Adherents	mid-1995 %	mid-2000 Adherents	mid-2000 %	mid-2025 Adherents	mid-2025 %
Muslims	2,012,790	89.5	8,911,286	95.3	17,318,920	95.8	482,540	5,090	487,630	2.51	19,266,670	95.9	22,195,217	96.0	39,385,850	96.0
Christians	**144,110**	**6.4**	**385,014**	**4.1**	**631,000**	**3.5**	**17,581**	**-6,603**	**10,978**	**1.62**	**671,500**	**3.3**	**740,778**	**3.2**	**1,270,500**	**3.1**
PROFESSION																
crypto-Christians	62,110	2.8	127,382	1.4	310,000	1.7	8,637	422	9,059	2.60	345,000	1.7	400,589	1.7	790,000	1.9
professing Christians	**82,000**	**3.6**	**257,632**	**2.8**	**321,000**	**1.8**	**8,944**	**-7,025**	**1,919**	**0.58**	**326,500**	**1.6**	**340,189**	**1.5**	**480,500**	**1.2**
AFFILIATION																
unaffiliated Christians	0	0.0	0	0.0	12,325	0.1	343	36	379	2.72	14,870	0.1	16,116	0.1	24,700	0.1
affiliated Christians	**144,110**	**6.4**	**385,014**	**4.1**	**618,675**	**3.4**	**17,238**	**-6,639**	**10,599**	**1.59**	**656,630**	**3.3**	**724,662**	**3.1**	**1,245,800**	**3.0**
Independents	0	0.0	36,100	0.4	220,000	1.2	6,130	3,425	9,555	3.67	252,100	1.3	315,547	1.4	740,000	1.8
Roman Catholics	44,000	2.0	278,953	3.0	272,000	1.5	7,579	-7,979	-400	-0.15	270,909	1.4	268,000	1.2	300,000	0.7
Orthodox	100,000	4.4	68,450	0.7	125,000	0.7	3,483	-2,034	1,449	1.10	132,150	0.7	139,485	0.6	200,000	0.5
Protestants	60	0.0	979	0.0	1,150	0.0	32	-7	25	1.99	1,247	0.0	1,400	0.0	5,000	0.0
Anglicans	50	0.0	500	0.0	200	0.0	6	-6	0	0.00	200	0.0	200	0.0	500	0.0
Marginal Christians	0	0.0	32	0.0	25	0.0	1	0	1	1.84	24	0.0	30	0.0	300	0.0
doubly-affiliated	0	0.0	0	0.0	300	0.0	8	-38	-30	-43.47	0	0.0	0	0.0	0	0.0
Trans-megabloc groupings																
Evangelicals	50	0.0	6,300	0.1	54,000	0.3	1,505	-5	1,500	2.48	62,240	0.3	69,000	0.3	125,000	0.3
Pentecostals/Charismatics	0	0.0	18,000	0.2	200,000	1.1	5,573	927	6,500	2.85	227,924	1.1	265,000	1.2	500,000	1.2
Great Commission Christians	**102,000**	**4.5**	**125,000**	**1.3**	**167,000**	**0.9**	**4,653**	**-1,658**	**2,995**	**1.66**	**178,000**	**0.9**	**196,953**	**0.9**	**315,000**	**0.8**
Nonreligious	0	0.0	30,000	0.3	85,000	0.5	2,368	1,282	3,650	3.64	106,000	0.5	121,503	0.5	250,000	0.6
Atheists	0	0.0	10,000	0.1	25,000	0.1	697	402	1,099	3.71	31,000	0.2	35,987	0.2	75,000	0.2
Mandeans	3,000	0.1	18,000	0.2	24,000	0.1	669	-7	662	2.46	27,000	0.1	30,616	0.1	46,000	0.1
Baha'is	100	0.0	500	0.0	2,000	0.0	56	5	61	2.69	2,300	0.0	2,607	0.0	4,000	0.0
Buddhists	0	0.0	500	0.0	900	0.0	25	17	42	3.89	1,150	0.0	1,318	0.0	2,500	0.0
Jews	90,000	4.0	700	0.0	180	0.0	5	-6	-1	-0.51	180	0.0	171	0.0	150	0.0
doubly-counted religionists	0	0.0	0	0.0	-9,000	-0.1	-251	-180	-431	3.99	-10,800	-0.1	-13,311	-0.1	-20,000	-0.1
World A (unevangelized persons)	1,755,000	78.0	6,549,200	70.0	10,394,850	57.5	289,761	-138,065	151,696	1.37	11,052,058	55.0	11,927,340	51.6	18,005,146	43.9
World B (evangelized non-Christians)	350,890	15.6	2,421,786	25.9	7,052,150	39.0	196,348	144,668	341,016	4.01	8,371,093	41.7	10,446,882	45.2	21,738,354	53.0
World C (Christians)	144,110	6.4	385,014	4.1	631,000	3.5	17,581	-6,603	10,978	1.62	671,500	3.3	740,778	3.2	1,270,500	3.1
Country's population	**2,250,000**	**100.0**	**9,356,000**	**100.0**	**18,078,000**	**100.0**	**503,690**	**0**	**503,690**	**2.49**	**20,094,652**	**100.0**	**23,115,000**	**100.0**	**41,014,000**	**100.0**

COLUMNS, ROWS.
For meanings and definitions, see Codebook (Part 3). Note that, by definition, total 'Christians' = professing + crypto-Christians, which also = affiliated + unaffiliated Christians, and also = Great Commission Christians + latent Christians. Percentages may not always total exactly, due to rounding.

CENSUSES.
19.X.1947: 93.6% Muslims, 3.1% Christians, 2.4% Jews, 0.7% Yazidis, 0.1% Mandaeans. **12.X.1957** (including 49,984 nationals abroad): 95.6% Muslims, 3.3% Christians (206,206 persons), 0.9% Yazidis, 09.2% Mandaeans (Followers of St John), 0.1% Jews. **14.X.1965:** 96.0% Muslims, 2.9% Christians (232,406 persons), 0.9% Yazidis, 0.2% Mandaeans, 0.0% Jews (3,187 persons).

NOTES ON RELIGIONS
ANGLICANS. Expatriates, largely Whites.
ATHEISTS. Communist Party of Iraq (CPI) (proscribed; internal factions). Also Russian military advisers.
BAHA'IS. Begun in Iraq from Persia about 1850. In 1964, 6 local spiritual assemblies; 1970, banned by decree and property confiscated; 1973, only 19 isolated centers or groups. Little progress since.
BUDDHISTS. Chinese. Buddhism was first introduced into Iraq around AD 550.
CRYPTO-CHRISTIANS. Iraqi Christians affiliated to churches but recorded in government censuses as Muslims.
INDEPENDENTS. In about 7 groupings in 1995 including isolated Arab radio and Bible correspondence course believers, also 3 Nestorian schisms (see Table 2).
JEWS. Rapid decline from 250,000 in 1945 by massive emigration to Israel from 1950 onwards, to 4,906 in 1957 and 3,187 in 1965.
MANDAEANS. Calling themselves Mandaiia (Gnostics), and descendants of the Jewish-Christian Gnostic religion of the 2nd century AD, the Mandaeans are also called Christians of St John, Followers of John the Baptist, Dippers, Sabaeans (the name used by Arabs) or (the priestly caste) Nasoreans. The only other organized Mandaean community abroad is in Iran.
MUSLIMS. 62% Shias (Ithna-Asharis (Twelvers), and Ismailis (Seveners) in the southeast), 38% Sunnis (of the Hanafite rite, and Shafiite rite including the Kurds). Shias are all Arabs; Sunnis are Arabs, Turkmen, Turkish and Kurdish. The figures for Muslims here include Yazidis. A 12th-century Muslim syncretistic religion; enumerated here under Muslims. Yazidis speak a Kurdish dialect and are thought to be descendants of the original Iraqi population. *Hajj pilgrims to Mecca.* (1968) 19,475; (1969) 24,902; (1970) 19,482; (1971) 17,628; (1972) 24,681; (1973) 35,567; (1974) 58,983; (1975) 10,368; (1976) 49,703.

Great Commission Instrument Panel: status of Iraq (for explanation see start of Part 4)

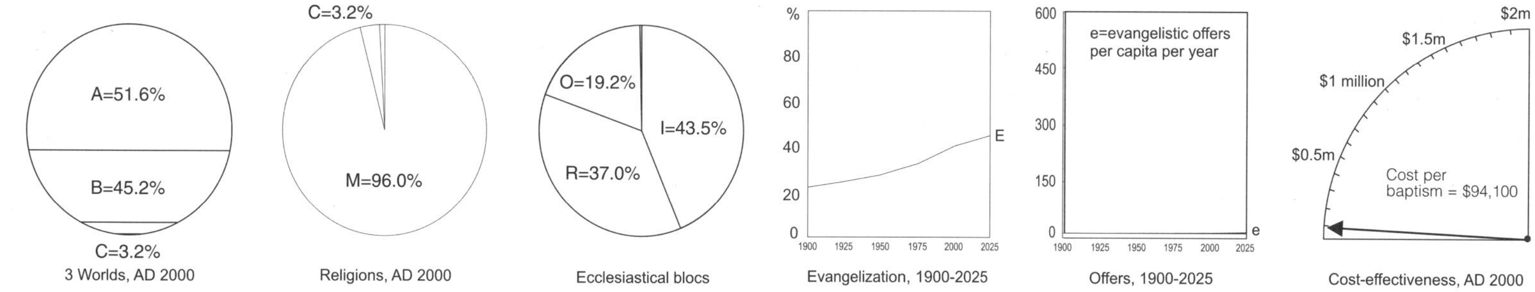

Human environment. The Gulf War accelerated the deterioration of the environment both on water and on land. Movements of tanks and troops caused extensive soil damage in a region already threatened with desertification. Official acts of vandalism such as the deliberate dumping of oil into the Persian Gulf and the burning of Kuwaiti oil wells have taken a heavy toll on the environment that may take decades to reverse.

Muslims. The secular regime puts a Muslim face on this Baghdad monument to troops killed in combat.

NON-CHRISTIAN RELIGIONS

Islam was established in Iraq in the 7th century. Shias form a majority of the population (62% of the 96% who are Muslims), but the influence exercised by Sunnis of both the Hanafite and Shafiite rites is preponderant. Sunnis in fact form the urban middle class and are predominant among government officials. The important Kurdish community follows basically the Shafiite rite, but there are also Kurds who are Christians and also Yazidis. Iraq is noted for its Shia sanctuaries, Karbala and An Najaf west of the Euphrates as well as Samarra and Al Khadimain (a suburb of Baghdad) bordering the Tigris. There is an Institute of Islamic Studies at Baghdad.

Yazidi religion is a syncretistic mixture of traditional, Manichaean, Zoroastrian, Jewish, Nestorian, and Muslim elements of which the latter are predominant. Yazidis are often called devil worshippers because of the prominence given to the fallen angle Malak Ta'us who manifested himself in Shaikh Adi, the founder of the religion in the 12th century. They have 2 sacred books, the Black Book and the Book of Revelation. Yazidis live mostly in the Jebel Sinjar west of Mosul; but they are also found in other parts, notably northeast of Mosul where their religious and civil leaders live and where the principal sanctuary dedicated to Shaikh Adi is located.

Mandaeanism began in the 2nd century AD as Gnosticism, a syncretistic religion with Mesopotamian, Iranian, Jewish, and Christian elements. Its followers today call themselves Mandaiia (Gnostics), and are also variously called Mandaeans, Christians of St John, Followers of John the Baptist, Dippers, Sabaeans (so termed by Arabs) and (the priestly caste) Nasoreans. The religion is centered on fertility worship. The principal sacred books are the Kinza or Treasure, which is a collection of hymns, with cosmological and doctrinal tests; the Book of John, a late popular account of the life of John the Baptist; and the Qolasta, a book of hymns. Mandaeans live in lower Mesopotamia, centered at Basra, Kut and Suq al-Shuyukh; the only other community is in Khuzistan (southwest Iran). They have a hierarchical clergy and rudimentary temples and worship on Sundays.

Judaism is practiced by a very small remnant community in Baghdad. Until recent times, Jews were relatively numerous; at the end of World War II, Iraqi Jews numbered 250,000. After 1950, they began to emigrate massively to the new state of Israel. Due to the prolonged Israeli-Arab conflict, their situation has become increasingly precarious, and in 1972 only 600 remained, decreasing to 170 by AD 2000.

Baha'i has a history of over 120 years in Iraq, but due to severe repression and confiscations and banning by decree in 1970, by AD 2000 only 2,600 remain.

CHRISTIANITY

In the first century of the Christian era, Jewish colonies were evangelized, an activity traditionally ascribed to the Apostle Thomas. Church structures developed under the patriarch of Antioch in the 4th century, but a century later the church in Mesopotamia declared its independence from Antioch and subsequently became almost entirely

Country summary. **Worlds A, B, C by ethnolinguistic peoples, cities, and major civil divisions in Iraq.**

World	PEOPLES Num	Pop 2000	C%	Christians	E%	U%	Unevangelized	CITIES Num	Pop 2000	C%	Christians	E%	U%	Unevangelized	CIVIL DIVISIONS Num	Pop 2000	C%	Christians	E%	U%	Unevangelized
A	22	8,575,725	0.06	4,907	32	68	5,844,933	10	2,194,808	0.43	9,392	35	65	1,422,881	12	11,034,023	0.30	33,326	33	67	7,373,547
B	5	13,947,101	1.23	171,775	56	44	6,071,589	6	10,115,545	4.52	457,527	56	44	4,468,743	6	12,080,863	5.72	691,336	62	38	4,543,417
C	9	592,057	92.56	547,980	100	0	441	0	0	0.00	0	0	0	0	0	0	0.00	0	0	0	0
Total	**36**	**23,114,883**	**3.14**	**724,662**	**48**	**52**	**11,916,963**	**16**	**12,310,353**	**3.79**	**466,919**	**52**	**48**	**5,891,624**	**18**	**23,114,886**	**3.14**	**724,662**	**48**	**52**	**11,916,964**

Nestorian. Up until the 10th century, the Nestorians exercised an energetic missionary activity towards the east; but Islam, which entered the country in the 7th century, became increasingly more important. From the 13th century onwards, Latin missionaries made strenuous efforts towards obtaining Nestorian reunion with Rome, which resulted in the establishment of the uniate Chaldean Catholics in Baghdad in 1553. A Latin diocese was formed in 1632, but no resident Latin bishop was permitted until 1820. Protestantism also made its appearance during the 19th century.

Christians who today use a Syriac liturgy are divided into Chaldeans, Nestorians (Assyrian Church of the East), Syrian Catholics, and Syrian Orthodox, the latter also called Jacobites. These churches are of Mesopotamian origin, and in certain villages Syriac is still the spoken as well as the liturgical language. After the dismemberment of the Ottoman empire in 1917, Armenian Orthodox (Gregorians) and Armenian Catholics fled from Turkish massacres and established themselves in Iraq. Greek Orthodox and greek Catholics are small communities composed largely of immigrants from Syria, Lebanon, and Palestine. Latin Catholics are mostly foreigners and their clergy (OP, OCD, CSSR) are occupied with schools, youth, medical and seminary work, along with parish and inter-rite activities.

Religious instruction in Christianity is given to all Christian children in state schools having a Christian majority. Christian students in state schools with a Christian minority receive no religious instruction, except that provided irregularly by churches during holiday periods and in preparation for first communion. Of Catholic students of all rites, 44% receive catechetical instruction during primary schooling, 22% being students in private schools and 22% in state schools. In the latter case, however, the teacher is often a Christian layman with no special qualifications. The remaining 56% receive instruction only sporadically or not at all. At the secondary level, the corresponding proportions are respectively 13.6% and 23.7% with 62.7% receiving no instruction.

CATHOLIC CHURCH. Most Catholics belong to the Chaldean Church which was organized in union with Rome under its own patriarchate in 1553 following dissension within the Assyrian (Nestorian) community. Chaldean Catholics now number 242,000 divided into 10 dioceses served by 10 bishops and 102 priests. The patriarch of Babylon lives in Baghdad. Chaldean and Syrian Catholics jointly sponsor the Pontifical Seminary at Mosul, Iraq's main major seminary; and a number of minor seminaries exist in various parts of the country. In 1972, there were 10 married Catholics priests in Iraq, all Chaldeans. They were for the most part aged and some no longer exercise their ministry. There has been no ordination of married priests since 1948. However, in 1970, a group of innovative Chaldean priests founded the Chaldean Sacerdotal Alliance (Al-Rabita al-Kahnutiya al-Kaldaniya) with 31 members in 1971, to renew missionary zeal and to implement the decisions of Vatican II.

Syrian Catholics number 50,000 in 2 dioceses, the first established in 1790, with 2 bishops and 32 priests. Five Syrian and Chaldean priests, 3 of whom are teachers in the Pontifical Seminary, have formed a semi-monastic community in Mosul dedicated to the advancement of lay education and church renewal.

The 2,150 Armenian Catholics belong to the archdiocese of Baghdad created in 1954, with an archbishop and 4 priests. The Greek Catholic community of 350 members is served by a priest residing in Baghdad. Latin Catholics also have a small membership (3,200) composed mostly of expatriates with only a handful of native Iraqis. The apostolic administrator in 1973 was a French Carmelite missionary. There were 14 Dominican, 8 Carmelite and 5 Redemptorist priests engaged in parish and school work, the Christian Student Center in Baghdad, the Pontifical Seminary in Mosul and also in scholarly research. About 200 Dominican and Presentation sisters, mostly Iraqis, are involved in education and medical work, and a number of other Iraqi sisters serve abroad.

The Holy See has diplomatic relations with Iraq and in AD 2000 is represented to government and the Catholic hierarchy by a nuncio residing in Baghdad.

Ancient Church of the East. *(From left).* Mar Youkhanan (Iraq), Mar Timotheous (India), Mar Claudio (Sicily), Patriarch-Catholicos Mar Dinkha IV (Iran), Mar Narsay (Lebanon), Mar Aprim (USA), Mar Bascio (Italy).

ORTHODOX CHURCHES. The Ancient Church of the East, or the Assyrian Church, is the oldest Christian church in Iraq. It became regarded as Nestorian in tradition because its theology was similar to that of the Orthodox patriarch of Constantinople, Nestorius and for this reason also can be regarded as a branch of Orthodoxy. The Nestorian center, Seleucia-Ctesiphon near Baghdad, was at one time the most important patriarchate beyond the borders of the Roman empire and was largely responsible for the early extension of the Christian faith to other parts of the Middle East and Asia. Several schisms have split the church down the ages, and several such bodies have followers in present-day Iraq. The major split is between the faction of Mar Addai, claimed to have been recognized as patriarch by the state since 1972 and the larger grouping under Mar Dinkha IV, who is recognized as patriarch of the East by the Vatican, WCC, Anglican Communion, et alia. Since 1976, his headquarters has been based in Tehran.

Syrian Orthodox entered Iraq in the 6th century; and although later in time than the Nestorians, they still consider themselves the true Iraqis among the various Orthodox groups in the country. The oldest Christian monastery in Iraq is Mar Matta near Mosul with 6 resident monks. Its historical importance to Syrian Orthodoxy equals that of the monasteries of Tur Abdin in Turkey. Three bishops and 18 priests serve a community of 30,000.

The Armenian Apostolic Church, Diocese of Baghdad, is related to the Catholicate of Echmiadzin in Armenia, as contrasted with dioceses in Iran which are attached to the Catholicate of Cilicia (Sis) in Antelias, Lebanon. Primary schools exist in the 5 cities where there are congregations and resident priests, and a large high school is maintained in Baghdad. School enrollment is entirely Armenian, and the Armenian tongue is taught as an auxiliary language.

Greek Orthodox have one congregation in Baghdad under the jurisdiction of the Patriarchate of Antioch. The titular archbishop of Baghdad resides, however, in Kuwait.

OTHER CHURCHES. The first British missionary contact in Iraq was made by the London Jews Society in 1820 followed by the opening of an American Board (ABCFM) station in Mosul shortly after 1850. The Church Missionary Society arrived in Baghdad in 1882 where it was active until World War I. The Arabian Mission of the Reformed Church in America entered Basra in 1889, initiating work which during the 1920s received support from 2 other American denominations, the Evangelical and Reformed Church and the United Presbyterian Church in the USA. The United Mission, as it was later called, was joined in 1957 by yet a fourth body, the Presbyterian Church in the USA Strongly involved in education work, the United Mission had little success in the evangelistic sphere. No present-day Iraqi church resulted directly from this activity, but undoubtedly converts were made, mostly from the Nestorian and Orthodox milieu, who now participate in the life of a handful of autonomous Arab, Assyrian, and Armenian evangelical churches. Other influences at work on the formation of these churches were Presbyterian and American Board activities in neighboring Turkey and Iran. The Arab Evangelical churches are composed of 10 congregations in Baghdad, Kirkuk, and Basra, all served by Egyptian pastors. There are 2 Assyrian Evangelical churches in Baghdad and Mosul which are independent of each other. The Armenian Evangelical Church is related to the international Union of Armenian Evangelical Churches and consists of one small congregation in Baghdad.

The Episcopal Church is part of the diocese of Cyprus and the Gulf in the Episcopal Church in Jerusalem and the Middle East, formerly the Jerusalem Archbishopric. Membership is almost entirely expatriate Arab and British.

The Lutheran Orient Mission entered in 1911, but in spite of many years of work among the Kurds, few converts have been made. Other small Protestant bodies include the Assemblies of God, Basra Assembly, Evangelical Alliance Mission and Seventh-day Adventists. In 1969, all USA missionaries were expelled from the country and their schools nationalized or closed. However, most of their churches continue to function, under national leadership.

Renewal movements. In the 1990s the Pentecostal/Charismatic Renewal continued to spread rapidly across most older churches, and numbered over 265,000 adherents (of whom <1% were Pentecostals, 3% were Charismatics, and 96% Independents).

Indigenous missions. The Church of the East was involved in vigorous missionary activity from the fifth to tenth centuries. After this Islam, and then the conquest of Tamerlane, effectively stopped missions. Today there is virtually no missionary sending from Iraq.

CHURCH AND STATE

According to the provisional constitution of July 16, 1970, 'Islam is the State religion' (Article 4), but all citizens are equal before the law without distinction of religion (Article 19a). Freedom of religion, belief, and worship are equally guaranteed (Article 25).

The cultural rights of Syriac-speaking Iraqi Christians were recognized by Decree 251 promulgated by the Revolutionary Council on April 22,1972. According to the terms of the decree, which concerns 'Assyrians, Chaldeans and Syrians', the use of Syriac is authorized in primary and secondary schools where this is the mother tongue of a majority of the pupils, although the teaching of Arabic is also obligatory. Moreover, provision is made for the study of Syriac, as an ancient language, in the University of Baghdad. The decree equally makes provision for radio and television broadcasts in Syriac and encourages the publication of books and journals, the formation of theatrical and artistic groups, as well as the participation of Syriac writers in the cultural life of the country. In Decree 110 of October 1972, the Revolutionary Council also recognized the existence of 3 religious holidays for Christians (25 December and 2 days at Easter) and 5 for Jews.

The General Bureau of Waqf in Baghdad is the official Muslim service agency of the administration responsible for religious trusts and finances. It oversees maintenance and construction of mosques and religious schools, training and payment of religious personnel, and the like. Religious judges (qadi) regulate the individual affairs and rights of Muslims. For non-Muslims, there is no governmental bureau of religious affairs, and everything pertaining to the administration of church property or individual rights is regulated by civil courts. In each such court, one judge is especially charged with the affairs of non-Muslims. He renders his verdict, taking into consideration the particular customs with its leader. The 2 basic laws governing the organization of courts for Christian and Jewish communities and the personal status of non-Muslims are Law 32 of 1947, which was modified for Catholics by several decrees in 1948, and Law 188 of 1959. Customary law regulates a number of other matters, such as the recognition by the state of leaders of dioceses and religious communities. The appointment of a new diocesan head is not valid until his name appears in the official governmental journal, after an inquiry has been made by the responsible judge concerning his reliability as a candidate and the legal status of the community, and after this has been confirmed by the head of state.

Muslims. Interior of Cheik Abd el-Qadir el-Galiani Mosque in Baghdad.

BROADCASTING AND MEDIA

FEBA (Seychelles) has shortwave radio programs in Arabic, Azeri and Farsi.

Some 7.2 million has seen the 'Jesus' Film: through TV broadcasts (6.9 million) and videocassettes (210,000). Response has been low: less than 1,000 have made recorded decisions. Satellite TV programs are received mainly in Arabic.

INTERDENOMINATIONAL ORGANIZATIONS

There are no formal nationwide ecumenical councils or bodies. In Mosul, a committee composed of members of the various Christian confessions and rites has recently been formed to decide what measures should be taken when Christians are requested to participate in organizations or programs of the state. Resulting joint actions include publication of a common catechism for use in schools having a Christian majority in Mosul province, and the preparation of television broadcasts at Christmas.

FUTURE TRENDS AND PROSPECTS

Muslims will probably maintain over 95% of the population through 2025 while growth among the nonreligious (0.3% in 1970 to 0.6% by 2025) keeps Christianity at around 3.0% into the 21st century.

Apart from significant numbers of Muslim converts, Christianity will probably decline during the 21st century. Islam would then maintain 95% or more of the population throughout the period.

BIBLIOGRAPHY

A history of Eastern Christianity. A. S. Atiya. 1968. Reprint, Millwood, NY: Kraus Reprint, 1980. 492p.

Babylonian & Assyrian religion. S. H. Hooke. London: Hutchinson's University Library, 1953. 128p.

Bedouin tribes of the Euphrates. L. A. Blunt. Ed., W. S. Blunt. 1879; reprint, London: Cass, 1968. 2 vols.

Christian Arabic of Baghdad. F. Abu-Haidar. *Semitica viva*, Bd. 7. Wiesbaden: Harrassowitz, 1991. 212p.

'Die nestorianische Kirche', B. Spuler, in *Handbuch der Orientalistik*, Abt 1, Bd 8, p.120–69. Leiden: Köln, 1961.

Grace in the gulf: the autobiography of Jeanette Boersma, missionary nurse in Iraq and the Sultanate of Oman. J. Boersma & D. De Groot. *Historical series of the Reformed Church in America*, no. 20. Grand Rapids, MI: Eerdmans, 1991. 315p.

Greece and Babylon: a comparative sketch of Mesopotamian, Anatolian and Hellenic religions. L. R. Farnell. Edinburgh: T. & T. Clark, 1911.

Iraq. A. J. Abdulrahman. *World bibliographical series*, vol. 42. Oxford, UK: CLIO Press, 1984. 182p. (See especially ,Religion,' p.70).

Jalons pour une histoire de l'église en Iraq. J. M. Fiey. Louvain: Secrétariat du Corpus SCO, 1970. 166p.

'Mesopotamia: 7000 years and 4000 gods,' I. Lissner, in *The living past: the great civilizations of mankind*, p.27–46. London: Cape, 1957. Trans. J. M. Brownjohn.

'Religion in Kurdistan,' M. van Bruinessen, *Kurdish times*, 4 (Summer–Fall, 1991), 5–27.

The Arabs of central Iraq, their history, ethnology, and physical characters. H. Field. *Memoirs, Department of Anthropology, Chicago Natural History Museum*, vol. 4. Chicago, 1935.

The history and doctrine of this most ancient Church of Christ. Shimun XXIII (Patriarch). Trichur, India: Church of the East, 1961. 27p.

The Islamic movement of Iraq: 1958–1980. R. Soeterik. Amsterdam: MERA, [1991]. 28p.

The Islamic movement of Iraqi Shi'as. J. N. Wiley. Boulder, CO: Lynne Rienner Publishers, 1992. 202p.

The Jews of Iraq: 3000 years of history and culture. N. Rejwan. Boulder, CO: Westview Press, 1985. 283p.

The Kurds: a concise history and fact book. M. Izady. Washington, DC: Crane Russak, 1991. 285p.

The Kurds of Iraq: tragedy and hope. M. M. Gunter. New York: St. Martin's Press, 1992. 185p.

The Mandaeans of Iraq and Iran: their cults, customs, magic, legends, and folklore. E. S. Drower (Stevens). Oxford, UK: Clarendon Press, 1973. 436p.

The Nestorians and their Muslim neighbors: a study of Western influence on their relations. J. Joseph. Princeton, NJ: Princeton University Press, 1961. 281p.

The old social classes and the revolutionary movements of Iraq. H. Batatu. Princeton, NJ: Princeton University Press, 1978.

The republic of fear: the politics of modern Iraq. S. al-Khalil. Berkeley and Los Angeles: University of California Press, 1989.

The Shi'is of Iraq. Y. Nakash. Princeton, NJ: Princeton University Press, 1994. 328p.

The treasures of darkness: a history of Mesopotamian religion. T. P. R. Jacobsen. London: Yale University Press, 1976. 273p.

Country Table 2. **Organized churches and denominations in Iraq.**

Official name (bold type = church *with over 10% of all affiliated)* 1	*Begun* 2	*Type* 3	*Counc* 4	*Congs* 5	*Adults* 6	*Affiliated 1970* 7	*Affiliated 1995* 8	*G%* 9	*Names, notes, and other statistics* (see Codebook, Part 3) 10
Ancient Church of the East: P Tehran	c 50	O-Nes	YW...	60	31,000	30,000	58,000	2.67	*Assyrian Ch. Nestorians.* 3 Dioceses. Patriarch Mar Dinkha IV lives in USA. 26n.
Ancient Ch of the East: P Baghdad	1967	I-Nes	y....	30	14,000	12,000	23,000	2.64	1972 split under rival state-recognized patriarch Mar Addai. Old Calendar. 7 bishops.
Arab Evangelical Churches	c1855	I-Ref	.....	10	1,580	1,100	3,500	4.74	Formerly M=ABCFM,UPUSA,RCA. Baghdad, Kirkuk, Basra, all with Egyptian pastors.
Armenian Apostolic Ch: D Baghdad	c 300	O-Arm	Ewc..	12	11,400	13,000	20,000	1.74	*Gregorians.* Under C Echmiadzin (USSR). 1917 Turkish refugees. 6 schools. 7n.
Armenian Ev Spiritual Brethren	c1930	I-CBr	x....	1	25	100	50	-2.73	*Holiness Brethren.* Ex Armenian churches. Origins M=ABCFM(USA) in Turkey. Baghdad.
Assemblies of God	c1965	P-Pe2	ZF...	2	100	100	303	4.53	M=AoG(USA). Church built up by 1972 visit by students from Lebanon.
Assyrian Evangelical Churches	c1855	I-Ref	.....	1	25	200	50	-5.39	Formerly M=ABCFM,UPUSA,RCA. Baghdad, Mosul without pastors in 1973.
Catholic Church in Iraq:	c250	R-LEr	O...R	98	146,270	278,953	270,909	0.06	Al-Kanissa al-Kathoulikiah. C=4+0+5. 110n 23x 32m 42W 4592Yy
P Babilonia (Baghdad) *(Chaldean)*	c250	R-Cha	Os	30	81,300	174,800	150,500	0.06	Patriarchate,1553. Rapid Catholic influx from north. 32n 6x 10m 42W 2108Yy
D Alquoch (Alqos) *(Chaldean)*	1960	R-Cha	Os	7	8,000	12,300	14,900	0.77	*Al-Kaldan al-Kathoulik (Chaldeans). Rapid decline.* 14n 1x 3m 13w 394Yy
D Al-Amadiyah *(Chaldean)*	1785	R-Cha	Os	6	1,200	2,000	2,200	0.38	Turkish-Syrian frontier. Rapid Catholic emigration. 5n 0x 0m 26w 25Yy
D Aqrah (Akra) *(Chaldean)*	1850	R-Cha	Os	1	100	180	192	0.26	In north. Arab/Kurdish fighting; Catholic emigration. 2n 1x 1m 0w 3Yy
D As-Sulaymaniyah *(Chaldean)*	1968	R-Cha	Os	1	270	565	500	-0.49	Patriarchal vicariate. On Iran border. 1n 0x 0m 0w 8Yy
D Zakhu (Zakho) *(Chaldean)*	1850	R-Cha	Os	8	3,500	12,292	6,500	-2.52	On Turkish frontier. Catholic migration to Baghdad. 7n 0x 0m 0w 80Yy
M Kerkuk *(Chaldean)*	c350	R-Cha	Os	3	2,800	6,000	5,197	0.06	Founded ADc350. Northeast. Petroleum area. 4n 0x 0m 2w 110Yy
AD Al-Basrah (Basra) *(Chaldean)*	c450	R-Cha	Os	6	1,400	7,646	2,600	0.06	Founded as M Perat of Maishan around AD 450. 1n 1x 1m 3w 62Yy
AD Al-Mawsil (Mosul) *(Chaldean)*	1789	R-Cha	Os	11	10,200	18,000	18,920	0.20	Second city. Patriarchal seat until 1947. 12n 4x 7m 69w 391Yy
AD Irbil (Arbil) *(Chaldean)*	1968	R-Cha	Os	6	6,700	8,370	12,500	1.62	Kurdistan. Catholic emigration from villages in north. 5n 1x 1m 5w 228Yy
AD Al-Mawsil (Mosul) *(Syrian)*	1790	R-Syr	Os	6	15,000	14,750	27,800	2.57	*Al-Sourian al-Kathoulik (Syrian Catholics).* 18n 0x 0m 19w 817Yy
AD Baghdad *(Syrian)*	1862	R-Syr	Os	4	13,000	15,550	23,900	1.73	Syrian-rite, dependent on P Antioch (Lebanon). 8n 0x 0m 0w 325Yy
AD Baghdad *(Latin)*	1632	R-Lat	Os	6	1,600	3,500	3,000	-0.61	Includes Mission Sui Juris in south (1896). M=OCD. 0n 9x 9m 141w 15Yy
AD Baghdad *(Armenian)*	1954	R-Arm	Os	3	1,200	3,000	2,200	-1.23	Under Armenian Catholic P Cilicia (Lebanon). 1n 0x 0m 3w 26Yy
Christian Brethren		P-CBr	x....	1	20	50	40	0.05	*Basra Assembly. Open Brethren.* Begun by British; mainly expatriates.
Church of the East	c1962	I-Nes	.v...	5	2,900	5,000	5,000	0.00	Assyrian schism ex Patriarchate (P Baghdad). 3 Dioceses, 3 bishops. 11 n.
Ch of the Virgin Mary & Mar Gaura		I-Nes	.....	2	100	200	200	0.05	Assyrian (Nestorian) Schism in dispute over ecclesiastical authority. 2 priests.
Coptic Orthodox Ch (P Alexandria)	c1970	O-Cop	NwaN.	1	150	300	450	1.64	Egyptian doctors, lecturers: 60 families by 1977, church in Baghdad. 1 priest monk.
Episcopal Ch in Jerus & the MEast	1882	A-Cen	aw...	1	120	500	200	-3.60	In D Cyprus & the Gulf. Formerly in Jerusalem Archbishopric. 70% Whites, 30% Arabs.
Evangelical Church in Baghdad	c1980	I-3nS	.....	5	5,000	–	10,000	6.67	1,000 attenders a week; public baptisms; wide scripture distribution.
Greek Orthodox P Antioch: D Baghdad		O-Ara	Cw.N.	1	370	450	700	0.05	Arabs, Greeks, and former Nestorians. Archbishop of Baghdad lives in Kuwait. 1n.
Hidden Muslim believers in Christ	c1970	I-Mus	.....	200	5,000	–	10,000	44.54	Converted Muslims who remain within Islam to witness for Christ there.
Isolated radio churches	c1950	I-3rS	.....	4,000	120,000	17,300	200,000	10.29	Isolated Arab radio believers (students &c). Vast increase after 1985.
Jehovah's Witnesses	1962	m-Jeh	x....	1	12	32	24	-1.14	*Watch Tower. IBSA.* Regular attempts at witnessing suppressed.
Lutheran Orient Mission	1911	P-Lut	.....	1	20	29	40	1.29	Kurdistan. 1958, USA missionaries expelled, now run by nationals. HQ Arbil.
Orthodox Syrian Church of the East	c1960	O-SyM	DWE..	4	4,700	5,000	8,000	1.90	Indians, mainly Malayalam-speaking.
Seventh-day Adventist Church	1923	P-Adv	x....	4	132	300	264	-0.51	*SDA, Iraq Field.* Middle East Union. HQ Baghdad. 2n,26mw,2f,1r,5t(132),5Y.
Syrian Orthodox Church (P Antioch)	550	O-Syr	Dw.N.	36	18,000	19,700	45,000	0.07	*Jacobites.* 3 Dioceses: Baghdad, Mar Matta (Sheikh-Matti), Mosul. 18n,1d(6).
World-Wide Missions	1967	I-Non	x....	1	200	200	300	1.64	M=World-Wide Missions (USA). Evangelicals with links in Pasadena, CA (USA).
Other Protestant denominations		P-	.....	10	300	500	600	0.05	Including Ev Alliance Mission, Union of Armenian Ev Chs (1 group in Baghdad), SBC/CSI.
Totals				**4,487**	**361,424**	**385,014**	**656,630**		

Churches, members, growth, 1900-2025	*Congs*	*Adults*	*Affiliated*	*G%*	*Total denominations*	*6 Megablocs:* *O*	*R*	*A*	*P*	*I*	*m*
Total churches, members, and denominations (mid-1900)	250	78,100	144,110	1.41	7	3	1	1	0	2	0
Total churches, members, and denominations (mid-1970)	663	208,598	385,014	1.41	25	6	1	1	8	8	1
Total churches, members, and denominations (mid-1990)	4,000	341,000	618,675	2.40	32	6	1	1	14	9	1
Total churches, members, and denominations (mid-1995)	4,487	361,424	656,630	1.20	33	6	1	1	14	10	1
Total churches, members, and denominations (mid-2000)	5,000	399,000	724,662	1.99	34	6	1	1	14	11	1
Total churches, members, and denominations (mid-2025)	10,000	686,000	1,245,800	2.19	78	10	1	1	30	35	1

NOTES ON TABLE ABOVE
NATIONAL COUNCILS (Column 4, 5th letter).
R = Inter-Rite Bishops' Meeting in Iraq.

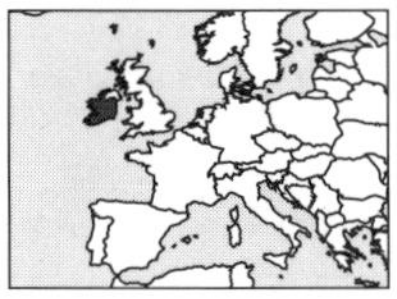

IRELAND

SECULAR DATA, AD 2000

STATE
Official name: Eire/Poblacht na hâireann (The Republic of Ireland).
Short name: Ireland. **Adjective of nationality:** Irish, an Irishman, the Irish.
Flag: Green, white, and orange bars.
Area: 70,285 sq. km. (27,137 sq. mi.).
Government: Parliamentary republic, since 1949 (1800 part of UK, 1922 Independence as Irish Free State, 1949 republic).
Legislature: National Parliament (Oireachtas): Seanad Eireann (Senate), 60 members; Dál Eireann (House), 166 members.
Official language: Irish (Gaelic) and English.
Monetary unit: 1 Irish pound (£Ir) = 100 new pence. **US$1=** $1.49.
Chief cities: DUBLIN (Baile Atha Cliath) 913,000; Cork (Corcaigh) 176,779; Limerick 77,917; Dun Laoghaire 55,687; Galway (Gaillimh) 47,940.
Political divisions: 4 provinces.
Armed forces: 13,000.

DEMOGRAPHY
Population: 3,730,000.
Population density: 53.0/sq. km. (137.4/sq. mi.).
Under 15 years: 792,000.
Growth rate p.a.: 0.72% (births 14.51, deaths 8.07).
Mortality: Infant, per 1,000: 6.6; **Maternal per 100,000:** 10.0.
Life expectancy: 77 (male 75, female 80).
Household size: 3.9. **Floor area per person, sq.m:** 48.0.
Major languages: Irish (Gaelic) (spoken by 20%, used by 5%), English.
Urban dwellers: 58.53%. **Urban growth rate p.a.:** 0.7%.
Labor force: 38%.

ETHNOLINGUISTIC PEOPLES
68.3% Irish; 26.7% Irish Gaelic; 1.4% British (English); 1.0% Ulster Irish; 0.8% USA White.

ECONOMY
National income p.a. per person: US$14,710; **per family:** US$57,369.

EDUCATION
Adult literacy: 100% (male 100%, female 100%). **Schools:** 4,103.
Universities: 26. **School enrolment:** female/male: 109%/107%.

HEALTH
Access to health services: 95%. **Access to safe water:** 100%.
Hospitals: 63 (34 beds per 10,000). **Doctors:** 6,036.
Blind: 7,000. **Deaf:** 214,500. **Murder rate:** 1.

LITERATURE
New book titles p.a.: 4,480 (1,200 p.a. per million). **Periodicals:** 360.
Newspapers: 8 dailies.

COMMUNICATION (per 1,000 people)
Phones: 365 (26% mobile). **Radios:** 610. **TV sets:** 382.
Daily newspaper circulation: 170. **Computers:** 404.

REFUGEES
Alien refugees from other countries: 250.

HUMAN LIFE AND LIBERTY (optimum condition=100.0%)
HDI: 92.9. **HSI:** 89.0. **HFI:** 67.5. **EFL:** 56.0.

Country Table 1. **Religious adherents in Ireland, AD 1900-2025.**

Year	1900		1970		mid-1990		Annual change, 1990-2000				mid-1995		mid-2000		mid-2025	
Name	Adherents	%	Adherents	%	Adherents	%	Natural	Conversion	Total	Rate	Adherents	%	Adherents	%	Adherents	%
Christians	**3,227,000**	**99.9**	**2,942,000**	**99.6**	**3,419,770**	**97.6**	**22,185**	**-1,785**	**20,400**	**0.58**	**3,513,000**	**97.3**	**3,623,767**	**97.2**	**4,227,400**	**96.0**
PROFESSION																
professing Christians	**3,227,000**	**99.9**	**2,942,000**	**99.6**	**3,419,770**	**97.6**	**22,185**	**-1,785**	**20,400**	**0.58**	**3,513,000**	**97.3**	**3,623,767**	**97.2**	**4,227,400**	**96.0**
AFFILIATION																
unaffiliated Christians	30,000	0.9	26,788	0.9	234,250	6.7	1,518	1,889	3,407	1.37	249,703	6.9	268,321	7.2	327,400	7.4
affiliated Christians	**3,197,000**	**99.0**	**2,915,212**	**98.7**	**3,185,520**	**90.9**	**20,677**	**-3,674**	**16,993**	**0.52**	**3,263,297**	**90.4**	**3,355,446**	**90.0**	**3,900,000**	**88.6**
Roman Catholics	2,866,000	88.7	2,682,342	90.8	3,000,000	85.6	19,464	-3,474	15,990	0.52	3,073,114	85.2	3,159,896	84.7	3,658,200	83.1
Anglicans	264,000	8.2	197,520	6.7	126,000	3.6	817	-17	800	0.62	130,000	3.6	134,000	3.6	170,000	3.9
Protestants	66,500	2.1	26,350	' 0.9	31,000	0.9	201	-151	50	0.16	30,923	0.9	31,500	0.8	32,000	0.7
Independents	0	0.0	1,900	0.1	18,000	0.5	117	-17	100	0.54	18,500	0.5	19,000	0.5	25,000	0.6
Marginal Christians	500	0.0	5,800	0.2	9,100	0.3	59	-19	40	0.43	9,280	0.3	9,500	0.3	13,000	0.3
Orthodox	0	0.0	1,300	0.0	1,420	0.0	9	4	13	0.88	1,480	0.0	1,550	0.0	1,800	0.0
Trans-megabloc groupings																
Evangelicals	254,000	7.9	105,000	3.6	122,000	3.5	791	-591	200	0.16	123,273	3.4	124,000	3.3	129,200	2.9
Pentecostals/Charismatics	0	0.0	15,000	0.5	450,000	12.9	2,916	1,084	4,000	0.86	468,875	13.0	490,000	13.1	650,000	14.8
Great Commission Christians	**1,325,000**	**41.0**	**1,181,000**	**40.0**	**1,680,000**	**48.0**	**10,887**	**1,690**	**12,577**	**0.72**	**1,740,000**	**48.2**	**1,805,772**	**48.4**	**2,202,000**	**50.0**
Nonreligious	0	0.0	6,200	0.2	68,600	2.0	445	1,660	2,105	2.71	80,200	2.2	89,647	2.4	150,000	3.4
Muslims	0	0.0	0	0.0	7,000	0.2	45	99	144	1.89	7,900	0.2	8,438	0.2	15,000	0.3
Atheists	0	0.0	1,200	0.0	4,500	0.1	29	36	65	1.36	4,800	0.1	5,150	0.1	7,500	0.2
Jews	3,000	0.1	4,000	0.1	1,800	0.1	12	-22	-10	-0.56	1,660	0.1	1,701	0.1	1,200	0.0
Baha'is	0	0.0	600	0.0	1,100	0.0	7	10	17	1.48	1,200	0.0	1,274	0.0	2,500	0.1
Chinese folk-religionists	0	0.0	0	0.0	230	0.0	1	2	3	1.27	240	0.0	261	0.0	400	0.0
World A (unevangelized persons)	0	0.0	5,907	0.2	7,006	0.2	50	208	258	2.93	10,827	0.3	11,190	0.3	13,212	0.3
World B (evangelized non-Christians)	3,000	0.1	5,792	0.2	76,224	2.2	489	1,577	2,066	2.23	85,336	2.4	95,043	2.5	163,388	3.7
World C (Christians)	3,227,000	99.9	2,942,000	99.6	3,419,770	97.6	22,185	-1,785	20,400	0.58	3,513,000	97.3	3,623,767	97.2	4,227,400	96.0
Country's population	**3,230,000**	**100.0**	**2,953,700**	**100.0**	**3,503,000**	**100.0**	**22,724**	**0**	**22,724**	**0.63**	**3,609,164**	**100.0**	**3,730,000**	**100.0**	**4,404,000**	**100.0**

COLUMNS, ROWS.
For meanings and definitions, see Codebook (Part 3). Note that, by definition, total 'Christians' = professing + crypto-Christians, which also = affiliated + unaffiliated Christians, and also = Great Commission Christians + latent Christians. Percentages may not always total exactly, due to rounding.

CENSUSES.
1861: 89.6% Roman Catholics, 8.5% Anglicans, 1.9% Protestants. **1901:** 89.6% Roman Catholics, 8.2% Anglicans, 2.1% Protestants, 0.1% Jews. **1926:** 92.6% Roman Catholics, 5.5% Anglicans, 1.7% Protestants, 0.1% Jews. **1936:** 93.7% Roman Catholics, 4.9% Anglicans, 1.3% Protestants, 0.1% Jews. **12.V.1946:** 94.5% Roman Catholics, 4.2% Anglicans, 1.1% Protestants, 0.1% Jews. **9.IV.1961:** 95.0% Roman Catholics, 3.7% Anglicans, 1.1% Protestants, 0.1% Jews. **18.IV.1971:** 95.1% Roman Catholics, 3.3% Anglicans, 1.0% Protestants, 0.3% nonreligious and atheists, 0.2% marginal Protestants, 0.1% Jews. **1981:** 95.1% Roman Catholics, 2.8% Anglicans, 0.6% Protestants, 0.3% other religions, 0.1% Jews, 1.1% nonreligious. **1991.** 93.9% Roman Catholics, 2.5% Anglicans, 0.5% Protestants, 1.1% other religions, 0.1% Jews, 1.9% nonreligious.

NOTES ON RELIGIONS
ATHEISTS. Communist Party of Ireland (CPI) (legal; pro-Soviet).
BAHA'IS. Growth from 1 local spiritual assembly (1964) to 4 (1973), to 21 LSAS (1996).
PENTECOSTALS/CHARISMATICS The Catholic Charismatic Renewal has had a long history. Totals (January 1974): 2,500 involved priests, monks, nuns and lay adults (over 15 years old) in 60 prayer groups; total charismatic community including children, 5,000. The movement began before 1970, became noticeable in Dublin about 1972, and then spread outwards; by 1975 most towns and large villages in the republic had prayer groups. In October 1975, a Dublin charismatic conference drew 3,500 adults from all the churches; a year later, 6,000, of whom over 30% were nuns. During the year 1976 prayer groups throughout Ireland (North and South) more than doubled to 220 by the year's end, with 20,000 people active, mostly Catholics, rising by mid-1978 to 300 groups with 35,000 members. The June 1978 International Conference on the Charismatic Renewal in the Catholic Church was held in Dublin with 15,000 participants. By 1980, active charismatics numbered 250,000, including 21% of all Irish nuns and clergy.
From 1992 to 1997, regular prayer groups increased from 400 to 501, but with fewer regular attenders (15,000). There were also 10 covenant communities, 200 involved priests and 3 bishops, with a total of all Charismatics around 450,000.
PRACTICING CHRISTIANS. *Weekly mass attendance.* Average 91% of population. University College, Dublin: 83.5%. Rural areas: 95-100% of eligible Catholics. Urban areas: 80% for young men, 95% young women.

Great Commission Instrument Panel: status of Ireland (for explanation see start of Part 4)

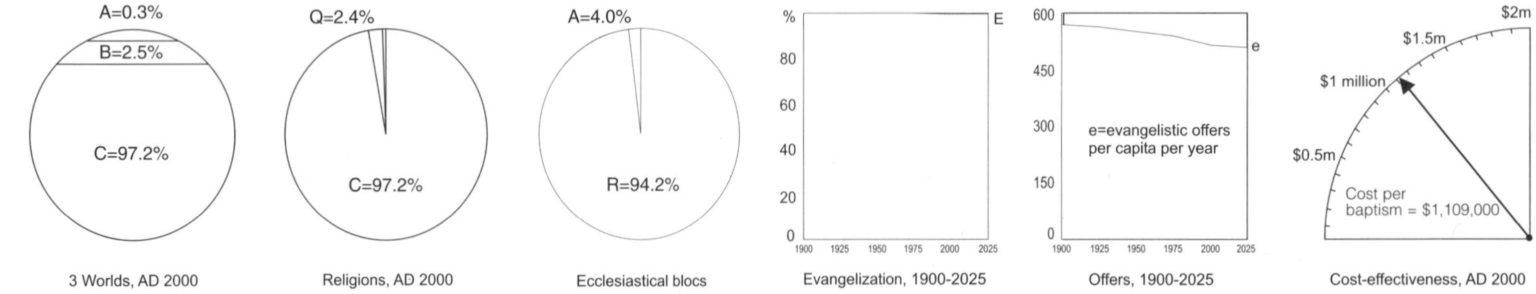

Country status. Ireland, or Eire, occupies the major part of the second largest island in the British Isles. Historically, it shares much of its heritage with England and Scotland, but has developed a separate religious and linguistic identity. The economy is largely based on beef and dairy farming.

HUMAN LIFE AND LIBERTY

Human need and development. Ireland is a developed country, but less developed than the United Kingdom and in many respects more backward than many of the member countries of the European Community. Its economic progress has been slowed by lack of natural resources, and the pressures of massive emigration for the past several centuries. Since the 1970s, Ireland has made considerable strides in industrialization in all sectors. Its annual per capita GNP of $14,710 places it among the most advanced countries in the world, and its annual growth rate of 3.3% is higher than that of all European countries. Although modernization started late in Ireland, the

Country summary. **Worlds A, B, C by ethnolinguistic peoples, cities, and major civil divisions in Ireland.**

World	PEOPLES Num	Pop 2000	C%	Christians	E%	U%	Unevangelized
A	1	9,027	25.00	2,257	47	53	4,784
B	3	4,029	1.89	76	55	45	1,806
C	17	3,717,182	90.21	3,353,113	100	0	3,688
Total	**21**	**3,730,238**	**89.95**	**3,355,446**	**100**	**0**	**10,278**

World	CITIES Num	Pop 2000	C%	Christians	E%	U%	Unevangelized
A	0	0	0.00	0	0	0	0
B	0	0	0.00	0	0	0	0
C	5	1,257,419	88.03	1,106,860	100	0	6,191
Total	**5**	**1,257,419**	**88.03**	**1,106,860**	**100**	**0**	**6,191**

World	CIVIL DIVISIONS Num	Pop 2000	C%	Christians	E%	U%	Unevangelized
A	0	0	0.00	0	0	0	0
B	0	0	0.00	0	0	0	0
C	4	3,730,240	89.95	3,355,445	100	0	10,278
Total	**4**	**3,730,240**	**89.95**	**3,355,445**	**100**	**0**	**10,278**

country has caught up with its neighbors in education, health, housing and other social indicators. Ireland is still heavily rural. About 40% of the population reside within 60 miles of Dublin.

Human rights and freedoms. Ireland is a free country in which all basic freedoms are guaranteed and protected by the Constitution. Trials are fair and public and no one is deprived of liberty except in accordance with the law. The Constitution provides for the creation of special courts to deal with extraordinary offenses against the state. The Constitution prohibits the enactment of any law permitting divorce. Also prohibited is the publication of 'blasphemous, seditious and indecent matter'. Both these prohibitions reflect the strength and influence of Irish Catholicism.

Human environment. Urbanization is altering the traditional landscape and creating landuse problems. The broadleaf forests have been virtually wiped out and now constitute less than 1% of the land area. The exploitation of turf bogs for production of electricity has adverse effects on the environment.

NON-CHRISTIAN RELIGIONS

Judaism with its followers increased in numbers, largely through immigration, during the last quarter of the 19th century. Since World War II, however, a moderate exodus has taken place, and Jew numbered about 1,700 in AD 2000.

CHRISTIANITY

Missionary work in Ireland was begun by Palladius in AD 431 and Patrick in 432, and Ireland soon became a center for the evangelization of several other countries. A century later, Columba founded a monastery at Iona, off the west coast of Scotland, in 563, whose influence spread south to England and east to continental Europe. Charlemagne also appealed to Ireland for missionaries when he became Roman emperor in 800. Government from England became the rule after 1200. In 1537, the English king was declared head of the church of Ireland and submission to Roman authority was forbidden.

Following this establishment of the Church of England as the official church, the Irish suffered persecution in their insistence on identifying Roman Catholicism with patriotism. Baptists and Presbyterians entered Ireland during the Reformation era, followed by Methodists a century later after many notable preaching tours in Ireland by John Wesley.

CATHOLIC CHURCH. The importance of Irish Catholic religious life extends far beyond the borders of Ireland, in part as a result of the large Irish emigration of the 19th century. Ireland has produced several missionary organizations peculiar to the Anglo-Saxon world and today still contributes in large measure to their work. Since the Middle Ages in fact, the country has played a remarkable missionary role. In 1990 approximately 4,100 foreign missionaries were supported by the Irish Catholic Church, although this was a marked decrease from the 7,085 missionaries of 1965. Irish Catholicism has supplied significant numbers of priests to Anglo-Saxon countries. Thus, between 1790 and 1936, of the 260 Catholic bishops then serving in the USA, 103 were from Ireland, with many others being of Irish descent.

Whereas Catholics constituted 90% of the population of the Irish nation in 1861, the proportion rose to 95% after 1946. Meanwhile, however, the actual number of Catholics decreased considerably during that period as a result of the constant emigration of Irish to other lands.

Catholic religious practice is extremely high. A survey in 1991 indicated that Sunday mass attendance in the country was as high as 82% of the population every week.

Irish Catholicism is still profoundly marked by its historic past: the imposition of Anglicanism as the state religion in the 16th century, persecutions, massacres and deportations. It was not until 1829 that Roman Catholics were formally emancipated in Great Britain and Ireland; and in 1867 the Anglican Church ceased to be the state religion in Ireland. The long period of British occupation, until 1921, has resulted in the firm identification of Catholicism with Irish nationalism. This explains the present notable cohesion of Irish Catholicism, its popularity (with its clergy always drawn from all ranks of the people and remaining close to the people) and its all-pervasive influence in all sectors of social life. Strongly attached to tradition, the church has been and remains little prepared to accept Vatican II with all that is implied there in questioning Ireland's commonly held system of values. This is perhaps less conservatism than national independence, for it should be noted that the Irish bishops were also reserved in accepting the full implications of Vatican I in 1870.

The Holy See has diplomatic relations with Ireland and in AD 2000 is represented to government and the Catholic hierarchy by a nuncio residing in DUBLIN.

Catholic Church in Ireland. *Above.* Catholics on barefoot pilgrimage up Cruach Phadraig. *Below.* Cardinal L.-J. Suenens celebrates charismatic mass (Dublin 1975). In 1978 he concelebrated on Irish TV with 17 bishops, 1,500 priests, and 20,000 Catholic charismatics present.

ANGLICAN CHURCH. The Church of Ireland, disestablished in 1867, is the largest non-Catholic denomination in the country. It also claims its origin in Patrick in the 5th century, and its dioceses trace their origins to those early centuries. Although 76% of their membership live in Northern Ireland, Anglicans have played a significant role in the south as well.

Their numbers however have fallen drastically, largely by emigration, falling continually from 8.5 % of the population in 1861 to 2.7% by 1971. By 1975, 5 dioceses had less than 2,000 communicants each. In 1976-77, several small dioceses were regrouped with larger ones.

PROTESTANT CHURCHES. Over the same period since 1861, Protestants have likewise fallen from 2.0% of the total population to 0.9% by 1990. They are even fewer today. This decrease again has been largely due to the great emigration from Ireland, which began with the Potato Famine of the last century and continues to the present time. Of the total population decrease of more than one million people between 1881 and 1961, a disproportionate number were Protestants who left during this period. In Northern Ireland 350 years ago, Presbyterians arrived from Scotland, later spreading to the south. Theologically conservative, the church is a founder member of the World Alliance of Reformed Churches and the World Council of Churches. Methodism was brought to Ireland by John Wesley in the mid-18th century. Today, 93% of its members live in Northern Ireland, with the remaining 7% located in the south. Methodist membership in the south again fell by 50% from 1861 to 1971. A number of other small Protestant churches are also active.

Art and architecture. Ireland's 3 greatest cathedrals are in Dublin. Christ Church Cathedral, the ancient priory church of the Holy Trinity, dates back to 1038, but has been rebuilt many times since. St Patrick's Cathedral was built over the Well of St Patrick, where the saint is said to have been baptized. Jonathan Swift was dean here, and his tomb may be seen not far from the entrance. Both these cathedrals are Anglican. The major Catholic cathedral is the Metropolitan Pro-Cathedral on Marlborough Street. Outside of Dublin the legacy of St Patrick is visible everywhere. The shrine of Lough Derg in Donegal was a rallying point for Irish Catholics after England became Protestant, and it remains a place of pilgrimage. Croagh Patrick is the holy mountain where St Patrick spent Lent in 441 in prayer and fasting. People still climb the mountain in prayer, often barefoot. Not far from Croagh Patrick is the the parish church of Knock where there was an apparition of the Blessed Virgin Mary in 1879, and which is now a place of pilgrimage. The remains of Glendalough near Dublin are noted for their round tower and Celtic crosses. More remote is the craggy Skellig Michael off the coast of Kerry. Bleak as a spike, 700 feet above the ocean, it was a monastery as far back as the seventh century. Its beehive cells are enclosed by heavy masonry. Also in ruins are Cashel in Tipperary and Clonmacnoise, on the River Shannon. Cashel was once the residence of the kings of Munster, but was given to the church in 1101 by king Mortaugh who moved the capital to Limerick. Armagh, the primatial see of Ireland, where St Patrick worked, is almost completely in ruins.

Renewal movements. In the 1990s the Pentecostal/Charismatic Renewal continued to spread rapidly across most older churches, and numbered over 490,000 adherents (of whom 1% were Pentecostals, 95% Charismatics, and 4% Independents).

Indigenous missions. Ireland began to send missionaries into the rest of Europe shortly after the death of Patrick. The Celtic peregrini in the sixth, seventh and eighth centuries represented one of the most vibrant Christian missionary movements in history. Irish missionaries continue to make an impact today as the highest per capita missionary sending country in the world.

CHURCH AND STATE

Ireland has always been a specifically Christian state. Article 44 of the 1937 constitution of the republic of Ireland included the following stipulations regarding religion: (i) The State acknowledges that homage of public worship is due to Almighty God. It shall hold His Name in reverence and shall respect and honor religion; (ii) the State recognizes the special position of the Holy Catholic Apostolic and Roman Church as the guardian of the Faith professed by the great majority of the citizens; (iii) the State also recognizes the Church of Ireland, the Presbyterian Church in Ireland, the Methodist Church in Ireland, the Religious Society of Friends in Ireland, as well as the Jewish Congregations and other religious denominations existing in Ireland at the date of the coming into operation of this constitution. Article 41 of the 1937 constitution, which has been challenged but which nevertheless remains valid, states that the institution of marriage is especially protected and that 'No law shall be enacted providing for the grant of a dissolution of marriage'. Although recognized, the churches have no juridical personality, and parishes and bishoprics are not considered to be persons in civil law. Thus, church properties are generally held through trustees.

There is in fact no official legal relationship between any church and the state. The states does not subsidize the churches, nor does it give the churches the right to levy taxes. No assistance or salary is paid by the state to minister of religion. There is no ministry or government department in charge of religious affairs or responsible for relations with church authorities.

Two legal types of marriage are possible in Ireland, civil and religious. Each is sufficient of itself before the law. For historical reasons, the marriages of Protestants, and only Protestants, come within the field of civil law. In mixed marriages, spouses are bound before the law by prenuptial written promises even though they be given before a priest (decision of the supreme Court, 1951).

The churches on their part do not intervene directly in the functioning of the state. This represents a change in church involvement, since prior to Independence in 1921 it was not unusual for priests to be actively and openly involved in politics. Unofficially, however, there have been recent cases where church influence has been brought to bear on national and local government decisions. When discovered by the public, this has been resented.State authorities have also given opinions in a private capacity on the election of bishops.

In 1967, a committee was set up by all political parties to reconsider and possibly to repeal Articles 41 and 44 of the constitution, which were considered to be an impediment to the reunification of the republic (with its majority of Catholics) and Northern Ireland (with its majority of Protestants). A national referendum held during 1972 resulted in the abolition of Article 44 with its giving to the Catholic Church a 'special position' within the republic.

In December 1973, the Supreme Court judged unconstitutional a part of the law concerning contraceptives. Because of this the minister of justice submitted to parliament a proposed law making possible the importation and sale of contraceptives to married couples by pharmacists. This proposal was rejected by the House of Representatives by a vote of 75 to 61, with 7 government ministers including the prime minister voting with the majority.

In this largely Catholic state, Anglicans and Protestants play a more important role than their numbers would suggest. In 1973, an Anglican, E. Childers, was elected president of the republic.

BROADCASTING AND MEDIA

Radio Telefis Eireann (RTE), the national network, makes available time to religious programs. Catholics produce a weekly radio program on current religious affairs and filmed documentaries on RTE TV.

Masses are also broadcast. In Dublin there is a Catholic communication center founded in 1969 by the Catholic hierarchy, with radio and TV studios. Satellite TV and radio programs are received in English, Arabic, German and Italian. Ireland is a member of UNDA.

Salvation Army. Officers with band in street evangelism.

INTERDENOMINATIONAL ORGANIZATIONS

The Irish Council of Churches, established in Belfast in 1922, serves both the republic and Northern Ireland. In the republic it includes the Anglican and 6 Protestant churches. It has 10 local councils. However, the British Council of Churches based in London is more active and influential. The Irish School of Ecumenics, founded in 1970, is sponsored by Anglican, Methodist, Presbyterian and Catholic churches.

Interdenominational and international in its teaching staff and students, it offers a systematically organized program of postgraduate courses relating to movement for Christian unity. Other interdenominational groups in the republic include the Irish Commission on Justice and Peace, in Dublin, a Catholic group with some Anglican and Protestant members, which serves as an official Catholic commission as well as the recognized Sodepax committee in Ireland. Ecumenical groups based in Northern Ireland but with activities in the south include the Corrymeela Ecumenical Community near Belfast, the Industrial Council in Belfast and Londonderry, and Protestant and Catholic Encounter (PACE), founded in Belfast in 1968, which is an ICC/RCC working group dealing with social problems. Established with the aim of providing an alternative to violence through dialogue, PACE functions through some 30 local groups and a central council. In 1970, a Young PACE Association was formed to reach youth 14 to 25 years of age. Lastly, a significant ecumenical impact is being made by the charismatic movement in Ireland, with several thousand Catholics and Protestants involved.

FUTURE TRENDS AND PROSPECTS

Christians are expected to decline from 99.6% in 1970 to 96% by 2025. This is due almost entirely to the meteoric rise of the nonreligious, only 0.2% in 1970 but likely to grow to over 3% by 2025.

Though Christianity should remain strong for the near future, the nonreligious could grow from 3% in 2025 to over 6% around AD 2050. Immigration of non-Christians may also have an impact on the Christian percentage.

BIBLIOGRAPHY

A guide to Irish bibliographic material: a bibliography of Irish bibliographies and sources of information. A. R. Eager. 2nd ed. Westport, CT: Greenwood, 1980. 502p. (Entries under 'Religion' heading).

A history of Irish Catholicism. P. J. Corish (ed). Dublin: Gill & Macmillan, 1967–69. 6 vols.

A true and lively faith: evangelical revival in the Church of Ireland. A. R. Acheson. Church of Ireland Evangelical Fellowship, 1992. 40p.

Ancestral voices: religion and nationalism in Ireland. C. C. O'Brien. Chicago: University of Chicago Press, 1995.

Being Protestant in Ireland. J. McLoone (ed). Belfast: Cooperation North, 1985. 97p.

Church and state in modern Ireland, 1923–79. J. H. Whyte. 2nd ed. Dublin: Gill & Macmillan, 1980. 480p.

Church of Ireland directory, 1971. Dublin: Irish Church Publications, 1971. 258p.

Early Christian Ireland. M. de Paor & L. de Paor. 2nd ed. *Ancient peoples and places*, no. 8. London: Thames & Hudson, 1960. 264p.

Ecclesiastical history of Ireland. W. D. Killen. London: Macmillan, 1875. 2 vols.

God and greater Britain: religion and national life in Britain and Ireland, 1843–1945. J. Wolffe. London: Routledge, 1994. 336p.

History of the Church of Ireland from the earliest time to the present day. W. A. Phillips (ed). London: Oxford University Press, 1933–34. 3 vols.

History of the Presbyterian Church in Ireland. J. S. Reid. Ed., W. D. Killen. Belfast: W. Mullan, 1867. 3 vols.

'Ireland,' C. K. Ward, in *Western religion: a country by country sociological enquiry*, p.295–303. H. Mol (ed). The Hague: Mouton, 1972.

Ireland: Christianity discredited or pilgrim's progress? R. H. S. Boyd. *Risk book series*, no. 37. Geneva: WCC Publications, 1988. 135p.

Irish Anglicanism, 1869–1969. M. Hurley (ed). Dublin: A. Figgis, 1970. 247p.

Irish Catholics, tradition and transition. J. J. O. Riordáin. Dublin: Veritas, 1980. 98p.

Irish Christian handbook = Lámhleabhar Chríostaí na hEireann, 1995/96. Eltham, London: Christian Research, 1994. 208p.

Irish Methodism. F. Jeffery. London: Epworth House, 1964.

Irish Republic. M. O. Shannon. *World bibliographical series*, vol. 69. Oxford, UK: CLIO Press, 1986. 430p. (Se especially 'Religion,' p.127–34).

Irish spirituality. M. Maher (ed). Dublin: Veritas, 1980. 98p.

Is Irish Catholicism dying? P. Kirby. Dublin: Mercier, 1984. 93p.

Moral monopoly: the Catholic Church in modern Irish society. T. Inglis. Dublin: Gill and Macmillan, 1987. 251p.

Religion, culture, and values: a cross-cultural analysis of motivational factors in native Irish and American Irish Catholicism. B. F. Biever. *The Irish–Americans.* New York: Arno Press, 1976. 869p.

'Religion in Ireland: preliminary analysis,' M. N. G. Phadraig, *Social studies*, 5, 2 (1976).

The Celtic Churches: a history, AD 200–1200. J. T. McNeill. Chicago: University of Chicago, 1974. 290p.

The changing face of Catholic Ireland. D. Fennell. London: Geoffrey Chapman, 1968. 223p.

The Church in contemporary Ireland. J. Blanchard. Dublin: Clonmore & Reynolds, 1963.

The Church of Ireland. K. Milne. Dublin: APCK, 1966. 72p.

The Church of Ireland, 1869–1969. R. B. McDowell. *Studies in Irish history*, 2nd series, no. 10. London: Routledge, 1975. 157p.

The Irish Catholic directory, 1971. Dublin: James Duffy, 1971. 878p.

'The Irish conflict and the Christian conscience,' *Pro Mundi Vita* (Brussels), Special note 30 (1973).

The Jews of Ireland. L. Hyman. Shannon, Ireland: Irish University Press, 1972. 403p.

The Oxford dictionary of saints. D. H. Farmer. 3rd ed. Oxford, UK and New York: Oxford University Press, 1992. 558p.

The Roman Catholic Church and the Home Rule movement in Ireland, 1870–1874. E. J. Larkin. Chapel Hill, NC: University of North Carolina Press, 1990. 437p.

The saints of Ireland, a chronological account of the lives and works of Ireland's saints and missionaries at home and abroad. M. R. D'Arcy. St. Paul, MN: Irish American Cultural Institute, 1974. 241p.

Country Table 2. **Organized churches and denominations in Ireland.**

Official name (bold type = church with over 10% of all affiliated) 1	*Begun* 2	*Type* 3	*Counc* 4	*Congs* 5	*Adults* 6	*Affiliated 1970* 7	*Affiliated 1995* 8	*G%* 9	*Names, notes, and other statistics* (see Codebook, Part 3) 10
Assemblies of God in GB & Ireland	c1915	P-Pe2	ZG...	36	928	300	2,400	8.67	M=AoG(GB). Originally Pentecostal Missionary Union, until 1924. 2f.
Baptist Union of Ireland	1642	P-Bap	.....	12	430	400	1,000	3.73	Not in BUGBI. 92% of Union (75 churches) is in Northern Ireland.
Catholic Church in Ireland:	c 350	R-Lat	B.B.P	1,155	2,107,300	2,682,342	3,073,114	0.55	*Eaglais Chaitliceach Rómhánach.* C=34+11+104. 2928n 1801x 3051m 9071w 46067Yy
M Cashel & Emly	c 350	R-Lat	Bs	46	54,400	81,064	78,921	-0.11	South. Mainly rural. HQ (residence) Thurles. 1s. 127n 56x 104m 264w 1125Yy
D Cloyne	580	R-Lat	Bs	46	82,900	107,881	120,201	0.07	In south, with coastal strip. Mainly rural. M=SPS. 161n 6x 34m 291w 1575Yy
D Cork & Ross	570	R-Lat	Bs	68	159,000	195,097	231,600	0.07	South. 50% urban. Growing industrialization in Cork. 169n 140x 200m 735w 4263Yy
D Kerry	c 570	R-Lat	Bs	55	98,000	125,500	143,000	0.52	Southwest. Rural, depopulation. Gaelic survivals. 146n 16x 37m 397w 1817Yy
D Killaloe	c 450	R-Lat	Bs	59	74,000	100,872	108,848	0.30	In west centre. Rural, depopulation. HQ Ennis. 139n 29x 63m 289w 1661Yy
D Limerick	c 650	R-Lat	Bs	60	104,000	116,200	152,000	1.08	50% urban. Growing industries in Limerick. M=SPS. 135n 91x 134m 428w 2145Yy
D Waterford & Lismore	659	R-Lat	Bs	45	90,000	101,165	131,661	0.07	50% urban. Waterford being industrialized. 1s. 111n 90x 170m 531w 1798Yy
M Dublin	633	R-Lat	Bs	228	628,000	867,000	911,454	0.07	Capital, east coast. Urban, industrialized. 1s. 588n 1003x 1659m 3129w 15996Yy
D Ferns	600	R-Lat	Bs	49	67,000	80,000	98,000	0.07	In southeast. All rural, HQ Wexford. M=SSCC. 1s. 139n 14x 30m 245w 1337Yy
D Kildare & Leighlin	519	R-Lat	Bs	56	118,000	131,600	172,369	0.07	Southwest of Dublin. All rural. HQ Carlow. 1s. 138n 81x 173m 389w 2632Yy
D Ossory	549	R-Lat	Bs	42	50,000	63,152	73,875	0.07	Rural, HQ Kilkenny. 1s. 110n 21x 62m 274w 380Yy
M Tuam	550	R-Lat	Bs	58	82,000	113,199	119,476	0.07	West. Rural, depopulation. Marked Gaelic survivals. 141n 25x 63m 362w 1642Yy
D Achonry	560	R-Lat	Bs	23	25,000	40,000	36,685	0.07	All rural. 99% Catholic. HQ Ballaghaderreen. 56n 4x 7m 83w 408Yy
D Clonfert	550	R-Lat	Bs	24	22,000	33,755	32,200	0.07	In west centre of country. All rural. HQ Loughrea. 62n 33x 36m 176w 466Yy
D Elphin	450	R-Lat	Bs	37	46,000	77,731	68,000	0.06	Almost all rural. HQ Sligo. 88n 6x 12m 220w 800Yy
D Galway, Kilmacduagh, Kilfenore	c 650	R-Lat	Bs	39	57,000	61,379	83,928	1.26	50% urban. Industrializing. Gaelic areas. 84n 2x 21m 251w 1249Yy
D Killala	c 550	R-Lat	Bs	23	26,000	37,847	37,412	-0.05	Northwest extreme. Rural depopulation. HQ Ballina. 54n 1x 5m 90w 503Yy
D Ardagh (Province of Armagh)	c 450	R-Lat	Bs	41	49,000	65,323	71,806	0.38	Next 5 Dioceses are under M Armagh (in Ulster/NI). 94n 14x 22m 323w 921Yy
D Clogher	454	R-Lat	Bs	20	58,000	40,000	84,286	0.06	50% in Eire, 50% in NI. HQ Monaghan. 50n 7x 10m 80w 600Yy
D Kilmore	c 450	R-Lat	Bs	36	37,000	52,000	55,430	0.26	Rural, depopulation. HQ Cavan. 10% of diocese in NI. 103n 12x 12m 79w 850Yy

Continued opposite

Country Table 2–concluded

Official name (bold type = church with over 10% of affiliated) 1	*Begun* 2	*Type* 3	*Counc* 4	*Congs* 5	*Adults* 6	*Affiliated 1970* 7	*Affiliated 1995* 8	*G%* 9	*Names, notes, and other statistics* (see Codebook, Part 3) 10
D Meath	552	R-Lat	Bs	69	125,000	130,000	182,000	0.07	Southern part of province. Rural. HQ Mullingar. 1s. 144n 133x 174m 349w 2783Yy
D Raphoe	c 450	R-Lat	Bs	31	55,000	61,577	79,962	1.05	Extreme north. Rural depopulation. Gaelic areas. 89n 17x 23m 86w 1116Yy
Children of God	c1985	I-mar	.....	1	20	–	50	10.00	Former Jesus Movement members; mainly USA, Australia.
Christian Brethren	1827	P-CBr	x....	20	950	2,000	1,360	-1.53	*Open.* 1827, JN Darby left Anglican ministry, began Brethren in Dublin. 21f (UK, USA).
Christian Brethren (Exclusive)	1849	P-EBr	.....	20	800	1,000	2,000	2.81	*Darbyites.* Kelly-Continental, Glanton, Raven-Taylor, Continuing Tunbridge Wells.
Church of Christ	1988	I-Dis	x....	1	100	100	150	14.29	M=CC(Non-Instrumental) (USA). Independents from USA. One congregation in Dublin.
Church of Christ, Scientist		m-Sci	x....	3	100	300	200	0.05	*Christian Science.* M=CCS(Boston, USA). Dublin, Cork. 1m,3w.
Church of God (Anderson)		P-Hol	x....	1	100	100	150	0.05	M=CoG(Anderson) (USA). Holiness denomination. 1n,W=50%.
Church of Ireland	c 350	A-Low	AWc.K	1,100	70,000	197,520	130,000	-1.66	*Eaglais na hEireann.* 2 Provinces. Declining. M=ICM(London). 12f,1s,W=60%,364n,1406Y.
Ch of Jesus Christ of Latter-day Saints	c1880	m-LdS	x....	9	1,990	3,500	2,800	-0.89	*Ireland Mission. Mormons.* M=CJCLdS(USA). Growing. 140f,W=16%,365Yy,325z.
Church of the Nazarene	c1970	P-Hol	xF...	2	70	100	98	-0.08	M=CoN(USA). Small Holiness denomination with links in UK and USA.
Churches of God in Ireland	c1980	I-3oU	.....	20	700	–	1,200	6.67	Oneness Apostolic Black churches from the Caribbean.
City Gates International Fellowship	c1985	I-Bap	.....	2	500	–	1,000	10.00	Large congregation in Dublin (M=Greater Europe Mission).
Cooneyites (Tramp Preachers)	1894	I-Fun	x....	10	400	1,000	900	-0.42	*Go-Preachers.* Communal itinerants; founder Edward Cooney. Also NI,USA,Canada.
Elim Foursquare Gospel Alliance	1910	P-Pe2	Z....	2	150	200	200	0.00	Movement begun in Monaghan by Welsh evangelist George Jeffreys. Few converts.
Evangelical Presbyterian Church	1927	P-Ref	J...h	14	555	950	1,110	0.62	*Irish Ev Ch.* Split ex PCI over heresy trial. HQ Belfast. 6n,W=49%,4Yy.
Greek Orthodox Church (AD Thyateira)		O-Gre	Cwc..	1	590	1,000	1,180	0.05	Under EP Constantinople. HQ London (UK). One parish of Greek Cypriots.
House church movement	c1960	I-3cW	.....	100	1,550	600	4,000	7.88	Similar to Britain's New Churches; often close links.
Independent charismatic churches	c1985	I-3cW	.....	50	6,000	–	10,000	10.00	Direct parallels with Postdenominations in UK New Churches.
Irish Mennonite Movement	1978	P-Men	.....	1	10	–	30	5.88	M=EMC. Strong links with Mennonites in USA.
Jehovah's Witnesses	1891	m-Jeh	x....	93	3,451	2,000	6,280	4.68	Missionary attempt at entry 1926, by 1948 witnessing under way. (1975) 79Y. (1995) 204Y.
Lutheran Church in Ireland	1952	P-Lut	L...K	3	500	400	800	2.81	Begun due to influx of refugees after World War II. In Dublin, Cork, Killarney.
Methodist Church in Ireland	1747	P-Met	Vwc.K	26	4,700	5,000	5,800	0.60	Also 70,000 adherents in N Ireland. Linked to British Methodist Conference. W=76%.
Non-Subscribing Presbyterian Church	1649	P-Ref	....K	2	100	300	200	-1.61	Unitarian. Bulk of church in Northern Ireland (UK). Churches: Dublin, Cork. 2n.
Presbyterian Church in Ireland	1642	P-Ref	Rw..K	108	9,150	14,000	14,300	0.08	3 Presbyteries: Dublin, Donegal, Monaghan. Decline from 56,498 in 1881. W=60%.
Religious Society of Friends		P-Qua	Qv..K	6	300	600	400	0.05	*Dublin Yearly Meeting. Quakers.* Rapid decline. HQ Dublin.
Russian Orth Ch Outside of Russia		I-Rus	x....	1	100	200	200	0.05	M=ROCOR (New York, USA). Church of emigre Russians in exile.
Russian Orth Ch (PE Western Europe)		O-Rus	Mwc..	1	100	300	300	0.05	Under P Moscow. One parish (Russian emigres) under bishop in London (UK).
Salvation Army	1880	P-Sal	xwc.K	3	200	500	450	-0.42	*SA, Ireland Division.* 3 Corps (2 in Dublin and Cork) 4 officers.
Unevangelized Fields Mission	c1980	P-Non	.....	2	10	–	25	6.67	M=UFM. Nondenominational mission.
Other independent churches	c1975	I-	.....	15	600	–	1,000	5.00	Including New Apostolic Ch (43 members), Assembly Hall Churches (Chinese).
Other Protestant denominations		P-	.....	10	300	500	600	0.05	Total about 10 (see list below).
Totals				**2,830**	**2,212,754**	**2,915,212**	**3,263,297**		

Churches, members, growth, 1900-2025	*Congs*	*Adults*	*Affiliated*	*G%*	*Total denominations*	*6 Megablocs:* O	R	A	P	I	m
Total churches, members, and denominations (mid-1900)	2,500	2,163,000	3,197,000	-0.13	15	0	1	1	10	1	2
Total churches, members, and denominations (mid-1970)	3,088	1,972,269	2,915,212	-0.13	29	2	1	1	18	4	3
Total churches, members, and denominations (mid-1990)	2,900	2,160,000	3,185,520	0.44	58	2	1	1	25	26	3
Total churches, members, and denominations (mid-1995)	2,830	2,212,754	3,263,297	0.48	61	2	1	1	26	28	3
Total churches, members, and denominations (mid-2000)	2,850	2,275,000	3,355,446	0.56	64	2	1	1	27	30	3
Total churches, members, and denominations (mid-2025)	3,200	2,644,000	3,900,000	0.60	159	7	1	1	40	100	10

NOTES ON TABLE ABOVE

NATIONAL COUNCILS (Column 4, 5th letter).

h = British Evangelical Council (BEC).
K = Irish Council of Churches (ICC).
P = Episcopal Conference of Ireland, or Irish Episcopal Conference.

Other national councils. Evangelical Fellowship of Ireland (EFI) (members not churches but individuals; not affiliated to WEF or EEA).

Local councils. 2 affiliated to BCC and ICC.

OTHER PROTESTANT DENOMINATIONS. There are several other groups with very small memberships, mostly well under 100 adults, including: Apostolic Ch of Pentecost of Canada, Barreiro Bible Ch (European Evangelistic Crusade, 1954; 72 members), Children of God International (Dublin), Congregational Union of Ireland, Gospel Halls (independent congregations), Irish Missionary Fellowship, Moravian Ch, Reformed Presbyterian Ch of Ireland (1811), Seventh-day Adventist Ch (Irish Mission).

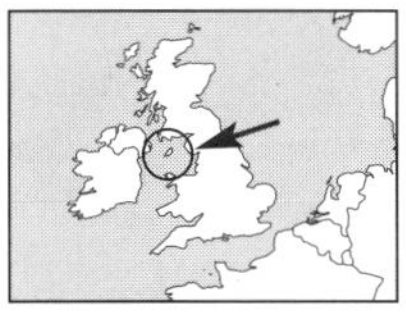

ISLE OF MAN

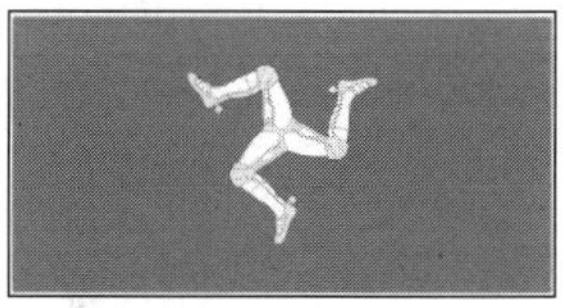

SECULAR DATA, AD 2000

STATE

Official name: The Crown Dependency of the Isle of Man.
Short name: Isle of Man. **Adjective of nationality:** of Isle of Man.
Flag: Red, with 3 steel-colored legs armored and spurred (knees and spurs, yellow) in the centre.
Area: 572 sq. km. (221 sq. mi.).
Government: Self-governing British crown possession, since 1765 and 1828.
Legislature: Court of Tynwald, 11 members; House of Keys, 24 members. Executive Council, 7 members.
Official language: English.
Monetary unit: 1 pound sterling (£) = 100 new pence. **US$1=** £ 0.59.
Chief cities: DOUGLAS 33,957.
Political divisions: 1 province.

DEMOGRAPHY

Population: 79,000.
Population density: 138.4/sq. km. (358.2/sq. mi.).
Under 15 years: 15,000.
Growth rate p.a.: 0.11% (births 11.09, deaths 10.70).
Mortality: Infant, per 1,000: 6.6; **Maternal per 100,000:** 10.0.
Life expectancy: 78 (male 75, female 81).
Household size: 2.0. **Floor area per person, sq.m:** 42.0.
Major languages: English, Irish, Manx (Celtic).
Urban dwellers: 76.57%. **Urban growth rate p.a.:** 1.6%.
Labor force: 48%.

ETHNOLINGUISTIC PEOPLES

87.6% British; 10.0% Irish; 0.2% Manx.

ECONOMY

National income p.a. per person: US$10,800; **per family:** US$21,600.

EDUCATION

Adult literacy: 96% (male 97%, female 95%). **Schools:** 40.
Universities: 1. **School enrolment:** female/male: 95%/95%.

HEALTH

Access to health services: 95%. **Access to safe water:** 100%.
Hospitals: 3 (50 beds per 10,000). **Doctors:** 86.
Blind: 60. **Deaf:** 4,700. **Murder rate:** <1.
Lepers: 0.

LITERATURE

New book titles p.a.: 120 (1,500 p.a. per million). **Periodicals:** 21.
Newspapers: 0 dailies.

COMMUNICATION (per 1,000 people)

Phones: 700 (30% mobile). **Radios:** 900. **TV sets:** 500.
Daily newspaper circulation: 300. **Computers:** 150.

HUMAN LIFE AND LIBERTY (optimum condition=100.0%)

HDI: 91.7. **HSI:** 85.0. **HFI:** 80.0. **EFL:** 58.0.

Country Table 1. **Religious adherents in the Isle of Man, AD 1900-2025.**

Year	*1900*		*1970*		*mid-1990*		*Annual change, 1990-2000*				*mid-1995*		*mid-2000*		*mid-2025*	
Name	*Adherents*	*%*	*Adherents*	*%*	*Adherents*	*%*	*Natural*	*Conversion*	*Total*	*Rate*	*Adherents*	*%*	*Adherents*	*%*	*Adherents*	*%*
Christians	**37,600**	**99.0**	**51,480**	**93.1**	**62,150**	**90.1**	**928**	**-105**	**823**	**1.25**	**66,500**	**89.8**	**70,380**	**88.9**	**86,420**	**85.6**
PROFESSION																
professing Christians	**37,600**	**99.0**	**51,480**	**93.1**	**62,150**	**90.1**	**928**	**-105**	**823**	**1.25**	**66,500**	**89.8**	**70,380**	**88.9**	**86,420**	**85.6**
AFFILIATION																
unaffiliated Christians	1,120	3.0	7,180	13.0	13,510	19.6	196	247	443	2.88	16,209	21.9	17,942	22.7	23,920	23.7
affiliated Christians	**36,480**	**96.0**	**44,300**	**80.1**	**48,640**	**70.5**	**732**	**-352**	**380**	**0.75**	**50,291**	**67.9**	**52,438**	**66.3**	**62,500**	**61.9**
Anglicans	25,080	66.0	28,000	50.7	30,800	44.6	446	-167	279	0.87	32,000	43.2	33,588	42.5	40,000	39.6
Protestants	9,880	26.0	10,800	19.5	11,050	16.0	160	-145	15	0.13	11,120	15.0	11,200	14.2	13,000	12.9
Roman Catholics	1,520	4.0	5,000	9.0	6,150	8.9	89	-24	65	1.01	6,500	8.8	6,800	8.6	8,000	7.9
Marginal Christians	0	0.0	400	0.7	480	0.7	7	9	16	2.92	501	0.7	640	0.8	1,200	1.2
Independents	0	0.0	100	0.2	160	0.2	2	3	5	2.76	170	0.2	210	0.3	300	0.3
Trans-megabloc groupings																
Evangelicals	32,000	84.2	14,700	26.6	16,000	23.2	232	-62	170	1.01	16,746	22.6	17,700	22.4	21,000	20.8
Pentecostals/Charismatics	0	0.0	300	0.5	5,100	7.4	74	16	90	1.64	5,550	7.5	6,000	7.6	9,000	8.9
Great Commission Christians	**7,000**	**18.4**	**17,700**	**32.0**	**22,250**	**32.3**	**322**	**16**	**338**	**1.43**	**23,950**	**32.3**	**25,633**	**32.5**	**33,330**	**33.0**
Nonreligious	380	1.0	3,770	6.8	5,900	8.6	86	58	144	2.21	6,545	8.8	7,342	9.3	12,000	11.9
Atheists	0	0.0	0	0.0	800	1.2	12	47	59	5.66	1,000	1.4	1,387	1.8	2,500	2.5
Jews	20	0.1	50	0.1	50	0.1	1	0	1	1.32	55	0.1	57	0.1	80	0.1
World A (unevangelized persons)	38	0.1	55	0.1	207	0.3	3	6	9	3.86	222	0.3	316	0.4	505	0.5
World B (evangelized non-Christians)	362	0.9	3,748	6.8	6,643	9.6	96	99	195	2.26	7,350	9.9	8,304	10.7	14,075	13.9
World C (Christians)	37,600	99.0	51,480	93.1	62,150	90.1	928	-105	823	1.25	66,500	89.8	70,380	88.9	86,420	85.6
Country's population	**38,000**	**100.0**	**55,284**	**100.0**	**69,000**	**100.0**	**1,027**	**0**	**1,027**	**1.36**	**74,073**	**100.0**	**79,000**	**100.0**	**101,000**	**100.0**

Continued overleaf

Country Table 1–concluded

COLUMNS, ROWS.
For meanings and definitions, see Codebook (Part 3). Note that, by definition, total 'Christians' = professing + crypto-Christians, which also = affiliated + unaffiliated Christians, and also = Great Commission Christians + latent Christians. Percentages may not always total exactly, due to rounding.

CENSUSES.
The religion question has not been asked.

NOTES ON RELIGIONS
JEWS. One congregation of 30 members.

Great Commission Instrument Panel: status of the Isle of Man (for explanation see start of Part 4)

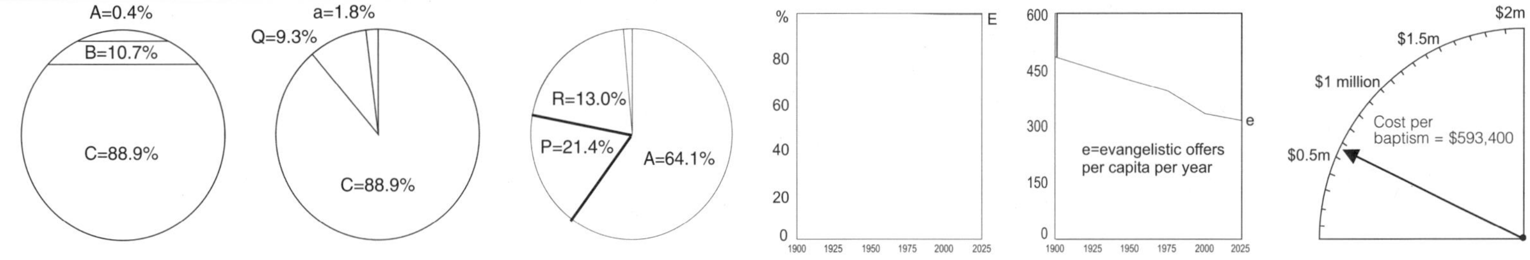

3 Worlds, AD 2000 | Religions, AD 2000 | Ecclesiastical blocs | Evangelization, 1900-2025 | Offers, 1900-2025 | Cost-effectiveness, AD 2000

Country summary. **Worlds A, B, C by ethnolinguistic peoples, cities, and major civil divisions in Isle of Man.**

	PEOPLES							CITIES							CIVIL DIVISIONS						
World	Num	Pop 2000	C%	Christians	E%	U%	Unevangelized	Num	Pop 2000	C%	Christians	E%	U%	Unevangelized	Num	Pop 2000	C%	Christians	E%	U%	Unevangelized
A	0	0	0.00	0	0	0	0	0	0	0.00	0	0	0	0	0	0	0.00	0	0	0	0
B	1	63	1.59	1	59	41	26	0	0	0.00	0	0	0	0	0	0	0.00	0	0	0	0
C	4	79,102	66.29	52,437	100	0	266	1	33,957	65.00	22,072	100	0	156	1	79,166	66.24	52,438	100	0	292
Total	**5**	**79,165**	**66.24**	**52,438**	**100**	**0**	**292**	**1**	**33,957**	**65.00**	**22,072**	**100**	**0**	**156**	**1**	**79,166**	**66.24**	**52,438**	**100**	**0**	**292**

Country status. Isle of Man is a British crown dependency in the Irish Sea. Tourism is an important source of revenue.

HUMAN LIFE AND LIBERTY

Human rights and freedoms. Its inhabitants enjoy all basic rights and freedoms under the Isle of Man Constitution Act of 1961.

NON-CHRISTIAN RELIGIONS

Unlike neighboring Britain the island has not been subject to massive immigration of adherents of non-Christian religions. There are only a few Jews, with no synagogue. Those claiming to be without religion have grown from 1% of the population in 1900 to 11.1% in AD 2000.

Christian topics proliferate on the Isle's postage stamps: *top*, Bi-Centenary of the Manx Bible (1775): *bottom*, John Wesley preaching outside Bradden Church, 1777.

CHRISTIANITY

The island was converted to Christianity prior to AD 600, probably through the outreach of missionaries from Iona. Vikings first visited the island around AD 800, but it was primarily during the second Scandinavian period (1079-1266) that the church was organized. Prior to 1266 the diocese of Sodor and Man was formed, with a metropolitan in Trondheim, Norway, and its cathedral of St German in Man. It was also during this period that in 1134 Cistercian monks from Furness, Lancashire, built the Rushen abbey which played a significant role in the later religious life of the island. Other early institutions include a convent near Douglas and Kirk Arbory founded by Franciscans in 1373.

At the time of the 16th-century English Reformation, Christianity in Man became a part of the Church of England; and this has continued to the present day, the diocese of Sodor and Man being part of its Province of York. Each year the diocese receives from the Church Commissioners for England (in London) a larger subsidy per Anglican than most English dioceses. Nevertheless, there are certain distinctive aspects to the administration of the diocese which give it a national character, including retention of its own canon law, its own convocation and a special relationship with the state. The island's Anglican diocese is Evangelical in churchmanship, and with 44 parishes and one primary school it remains the principal denomination.

The main Protestant community is the Methodist Church which traces its history to successful visits to Man by John Wesley in the 18th century from 1777. The Methodist Isle of Man District is divided into 4 circuits (Douglas, Castletown, Peel and Ramsey), with 28 congregations served by 19 ministers. Other bodies each with a congregation in Douglas include the United Reformed Church, begun as a Congregationalist church in 1808, the Baptist Union begun in 1893, and a more recent independent Pentecostal Revival Church. The Assemblies of God in Great Britain and Ireland have a congregation at Port St Mary.

Catholics in the Isle of Man are part of the diocese of Liverpool in the Catholic Church in England and Wales. There are 10 parishes and one chapel served by 8 priests and 6 Sisters of Mercy, the primary responsibility of the latter being educational work.

The Holy See has no diplomatic relations with Isle of Man in AD 2000.

Indigenous missions. Only a handful of Isle of Man Christians have served as foreign missionaries, with most of these in surrounding Christian countries.

CHURCH AND STATE

Since the English Reformation, there has been a close relationship between the Anglican diocese and the state. The chief secular administrative officer is the lieutenant governor, appointed as lord by the British monarch, while the island's legislative council consisting of 2 houses is called the Tynwald court. The Anglican bishop and archdeacon are chosen by the lord, while the Tynwald retains control over the church's marriage laws as well as the appointment of its vicar of Sodor and Man is himself a member of the Tynwald council. The Church of England is the established church, but measures from the Church Assembly (now General Synod) of the Church of England and of Parliament in London have to be approved by the Tynwald before they become law. Measures passed in this way specifically related to the Isle of Man include the Isle of Man Purchase Act, 1765; and others still in force as legislation there including the Ecclesiastical Commissioners (Sodor and Man) Measure, 1930; and Episcopal Pensions (Sodor and Man) Measure, 1931. No moves towards disestablishment are under way.

BROADCASTING AND MEDIA

Satellite TV and radio programs are received in English, Arabic, German and Italian.

INTERDENOMINATIONAL ORGANIZATIONS

The Isle of Man Council of Churches is an associate member of the British Council of Churches and is in working relationship with the WCC. It has a Douglas Regional Committee in the capital.

FUTURE TRENDS AND PROSPECTS

Secularization is certain to continue into the 21st century with the nonreligious and atheists growing to over 14% of the population by 2025. Christians would therefore decline to under 86% in the same period.

Nonreligious persons could grow to 20% or more by AD 2050. Christians might well be less than 75% of the population in the future.

BIBLIOGRAPHY

Centenaire du methodisme dans les Iles de la Manche 1784–1884: compte–rendu de la célébration du 24 août au 16 septembre 1884. M. Galliene. Jersey: Ahier frères, 1884. 50p.

Christian tradition in Mannin. M. Douglas. *Times longbooks.* Douglas: Times Press, 1965. 102p.

'Isle of Man,' R. Wheatley, *Methodist review*, 69 (July 1887), 550–72.

Saints & sites in Mann: some celebrated saints and ancient places in the Isle of Man. H. C. McNeil. London: S.P.C.K, [1928]. 32p.

Sodor and Man. A. W. Moore. London: SPCK, 1893. 276p.

The Church in the Isle of Man. A. Ashley. *St. Anthony's Hall publications*, 13. London: St. Anthony's Press, 1958. 28p.

The contribution of Methodism to the culture of the isle of Man. R. Kissack. [Port Erin, Isle of Man: Manx Methodist Historical Society]. 18p.

'The early church in West Britain and Ireland,' A. M. Cubbon, in *The early church in West Britain and Ireland: studies presented to C. A. Ralegh Radford*, p.257–82. S. M. Pearce (ed). *Biblical archaeology review, British series*, 102. Oxford, UK: British Archaeological Reports, 1982.

The history of Wesleyan Methodism in the Isle of Man with some account of the island, and of the life and labours of Bishop Wilson; in a series of letters addressed to the Rev. George Marsden. J. Rosser. Douglas, Isle of Man: Rosser, 1849. 214p.

The old church plate of the isle of Man. E. A. Jones. London: Bemrose, 1907. 65p.

The story of the Catholic Church in the Isle of Man. W. S. Dempsey. Billinge, UK: Birchley Hall Press, 1958. 186p.

Women in Manx Methodism. T. Wilson. [Port Erin, Isle of Man: Manx Methodist Historical Society]. 9p.

Country Table 2. **Organized churches and denominations in the Isle of Man.**

Official name (bold type = church with over 10% of all affiliated) 1	*Begun* 2	*Type* 3	*Counc* 4	*Congs* 5	*Adults* 6	*Affiliated 1970* 7	*Affiliated 1995* 8	*G%* 9	*Names, notes, and other statistics* (see Codebook, Part 3) 10
Assemblies of God in GB & Ireland		P-Pe2	ZG...	1	80	100	160	0.05	HQ Nottingham (UK). One church in Port St Mary. Classical Pentecostals.
Baptist Union of GB & Ireland	1893	P-Bap	Twc.K	1	130	200	260	1.05	*General and Particular Baptists.* One church in Douglas.
Catholic Ch in E & W (D Liverpool)	1814	R-Lat	B.B.s	10	4,000	5,000	6,500	1.05	*E&W=England & Wales.* Mostly Irish. 3 schools. C=0+0+1. (1970) 8nx,6w (Sisters of Mercy).
Church of Christ, Scientist		m-Sci	x....	1	35	50	58	0.05	*Christian Science.* M=CCS(Boston, USA). Small group linked to UK body.
Church of England: D Sodor & Man	447	A-Eva	awc.K	44	18,600	28,000	32,000	0.06	Includes 400 Manx (Celts). Tourism. HQ Peel. 1 school. 43n,P=23%,W=17%,16Y,392y.
Greater World Christian Spiritualist Ch		m-Spi	x....	1	55	150	183	0.05	Greater World Sanctuary. Christian spiritualists. Church in Douglas.
Jehovah's Witnesses		m-Jeh	x....	3	130	200	260	0.05	IBSA. *Watch Tower.* Active branches related to Witnesses in England.
Methodist Church of Great Britain	1750	P-Met	Vwc.K	28	2,350	8,000	7,830	-0.09	*Isle of Man District.* 4 Circuits: Douglas, Castletown, Peel, Ramsey. 19nx.
Pentecostal Revival Church		I-3pW	.....	1	85	100	170	0.05	Independent congregation in Douglas. Radical Pentecostals.
Salvation Army	1870	P-Sal	x...K	3	115	200	230	0.56	*SA.* Branches in Douglas, Peel, Port Erin. Linked to SA in UK (HQ London).
United Reformed Church	1808	P-Ref	Rwc.K	2	170	300	340	0.50	*URC.* Formerly Presbyterians, till 1970 URC union. One church in Douglas.
Other Protestant denominations		P-	.....	23	1,150	2,000	2,300	0.05	Total about 10, including Christian Brethren (Open), Religious Society of Friends.
Totals				**118**	**26,900**	**44,300**	**50,291**		

Churches, members, growth, 1900-2025	*Congs*	*Adults*	*Affiliated*	*G%*	*Total denominations*	*6 Megablocs:* O	R	A	P	I	m
Total churches, members, and denominations (mid-1900)	80	21,400	36,480	0.28	9	0	1	1	7	0	0
Total churches, members, and denominations (mid-1970)	114	25,978	44,300	0.28	15	0	1	1	9	1	3
Total churches, members, and denominations (mid-1990)	117	26,000	48,640	0.47	21	0	1	1	15	1	3
Total churches, members, and denominations (mid-1995)	118	26,900	50,291	0.67	21	0	1	1	15	1	3
Total churches, members, and denominations (mid-2000)	119	28,000	52,438	0.84	21	0	1	1	15	1	3
Total churches, members, and denominations (mid-2025)	160	33,400	62,500	0.70	60	1	1	1	30	20	7

NOTES ON TABLE ABOVE
NATIONAL COUNCILS (Column 4, 5th letter).
C = Churches Together in Man.
K = Isle of Man Council of Churches (IOMCC) (associated council of the Council of Churches for Britain & Ireland (CCBI); in working relationship with WCC).
s = represented on Catholic Bishops' Conference of England and Wales, also associate member of IOMCC.
Local councils. Douglas Regional Committee of IOMCC.

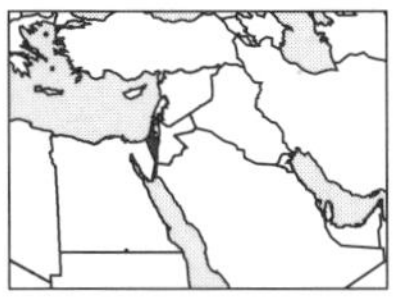

ISRAEL

SECULAR DATA, AD 2000

STATE
Official name: Medinat Israel (The State of Israel).
Short name: Israel. **Adjective of nationality:** Israeli.
Flag: White field bearing blue Star of David between 2 blue stripes.
Area: 20,400 sq. km. (7,876 sq. mi.).
Government: Parliamentary republic, since 1948 (1917 British mandated territory, 1948 Independence proclaimed)
Legislature: Parliament (Knesset), 120 members.
Official language: Hebrew (Ivrit) and Arabic.
Monetary unit: 1 New (Israeli) sheqel (NIS) = 100 agorot. **US$1=** NIS 3.85.
Chief cities: Tel Aviv-Yafo (Jaffa) 2,170,000; Yerushalayim (Jerusalem, Al-Quds) 711,563; Hefa (Haifa) 571,792; Holon 199,110; Petah Tiqwa (Petach Tikva) 182,973.
Political divisions: 6 provinces.
Armed forces: 175,000.

DEMOGRAPHY
Population: 5,122,000.
Population density: 251.0/sq. km. (650.2/sq. mi.)
Under 15 years: 1,420,000.
Growth rate p.a.: 1.66% (births 18.19, deaths 6.23).
Mortality: Infant, per 1000 7.9, ; **Maternal per 100,000:** 7.0.
Life expectancy: 78 (male 76, female 81).
Household size: 3.7. **Floor area per person, sq.m:** 28.0
Major languages: Hebrew, Yiddish, Ladino, Arabic, English, French, German, Aramaic, Circassian, and numerous others.
Urban dwellers: 91.17%. **Urban growth rate p.a.:** 1.7%.
Labor force: 37%.

ETHNOLINGUISTIC PEOPLES
26.3% Israeli Jewish (Sabra); 14.7% Palestinian Arab; 8.9% Russian Jew; 5.8% Romanian Jew; 5.7% Polish Jew.

ECONOMY
National income p.a. per person: US$15,919; **per family:** US$58,903.

EDUCATION
Adult literacy: 96% (male 97%, female 93%). **Schools:** 3,065.
Universities: 7. **School enrolment,** female/male: 93%/91%.

HEALTH
Access to health services: 80%. **Access to safe water:** 99%.
Hospitals: 244 (63.00 beds). **Doctors:** 24,344.
Blind: 5,285. **Deaf:** 298,900. **Murder rate:** 2.
Lepers: 500.

LITERATURE
New book titles p.a.: 5,480 (1,070 p.a. per million). **Periodicals:** 1,130. **Newspapers:** 34 dailies.

COMMUNICATION (per 1,000 people)
Phones: 418 (38% mobile). **Radios:** 481. **TV sets:** 303.
Daily newspaper circulation: 281. **Computers:** 320.

HUMAN LIFE AND LIBERTY (optimum condition=100.0%)
HDI: 91.30. **HSI:** 79.0. **HFI:** 47.5. **EFL:** 42.0.

Country Table 1. **Religious adherents in Israel, AD 1900-2025.**

Year / *Name*	*1900* Adherents	%	*1970* Adherents	%	*mid-1990* Adherents	%	*Annual change, 1990-2000* Natural	Conversion	Total	Rate	*mid-1995* Adherents	%	*mid-2000* Adherents	%	*mid-2025* Adherents	%
Jews	32,000	8.7	2,141,150	85.4	2,906,400	77.2	104,512	-102	104,410	3.12	3,483,430	77.1	3,950,501	77.1	5,109,500	73.8
Muslims	308,200	83.3	265,500	10.6	464,700	12.3	16,715	-1,901	14,814	2.81	550,000	12.2	612,842	12.0	800,000	11.6
Christians	**29,700**	**8.0**	**79,000**	**3.2**	**214,100**	**5.7**	**7,701**	**604**	**8,305**	**3.33**	**259,000**	**5.7**	**297,146**	**5.8**	**480,000**	**6.9**
PROFESSION																
crypto-Christians	5,100	1.4	14,350	0.6	70,000	1.9	2,518	-18	2,500	3.10	84,000	1.9	95,000	1.9	130,000	1.9
professing Christians	**24,600**	**6.7**	**64,650**	**2.6**	**144,100**	**3.8**	**5,183**	**622**	**5,805**	**3.44**	**175,000**	**3.9**	**202,146**	**4.0**	**350,000**	**5.1**
AFFILIATION																
unaffiliated Christians	0	0.0	840	0.0	2,500	0.1	90	-33	57	2.07	2,781	0.1	3,068	0.1	5,000	0.1
affiliated Christians	**29,700**	**8.0**	**78,160**	**3.1**	**211,600**	**5.6**	**7,611**	**637**	**8,248**	**3.35**	**256,219**	**5.7**	**294,078**	**5.7**	**475,000**	**6.9**
Roman Catholics	9,000	2.4	47,110	1.9	102,000	2.7	3,669	131	3,800	3.22	122,525	2.7	140,000	2.7	200,000	2.9
Independents	0	0.0	2,900	0.1	60,000	1.6	2,158	342	2,500	3.54	73,524	1.6	85,000	1.7	140,000	2.0
Orthodox	20,000	5.4	18,400	0.7	33,200	0.9	1,194	174	1,368	3.51	40,640	0.9	46,878	0.9	95,000	1.4
Protestants	200	0.1	8,350	0.3	14,100	0.4	507	-17	490	3.03	16,830	0.4	19,000	0.4	34,000	0.5
Anglicans	500	0.1	900	0.0	1,500	0.0	54	16	70	3.90	1,900	0.0	2,200	0.0	4,000	0.1
Marginal Christians	0	0.0	500	0.0	800	0.0	29	-9	20	2.26	800	0.0	1,000	0.0	2,000	0.0
Trans-megabloc groupings																
Evangelicals	200	0.1	5,500	0.2	20,500	0.5	737	273	1,010	4.09	25,839	0.6	30,600	0.6	50,000	0.7
Pentecostals/Charismatics	0	0.0	2,000	0.1	71,000	1.9	2,554	846	3,400	3.99	87,833	1.9	105,000	2.1	180,000	2.6
Great Commission Christians	**24,000**	**6.5**	**60,000**	**2.4**	**129,000**	**3.4**	**4,640**	**1,703**	**6,343**	**4.08**	**165,000**	**3.7**	**192,425**	**3.8**	**280,000**	**4.0**
Nonreligious	0	0.0	20,000	0.8	145,000	3.9	5,216	1,219	6,435	3.74	179,000	4.0	209,347	4.1	450,000	6.5
Atheists	0	0.0	1,000	0.0	26,000	0.7	935	108	1,043	3.43	31,500	0.7	36,431	0.7	60,000	0.9
Baha'is	100	0.0	400	0.0	9,500	0.3	342	81	423	3.75	11,600	0.3	13,734	0.3	25,000	0.4
Other religionists	0	0.0	950	0.0	1,300	0.0	47	-9	38	2.62	1,470	0.0	1,683	0.0	2,500	0.0
World A (unevangelized persons)	281,940	76.2	1,504,545	60.0	1,800,626	47.8	64,714	-19,441	45,273	2.27	2,050,360	45.4	2,253,680	44.0	2,202,786	31.8
World B (evangelized non-Christians)	58,360	15.8	924,030	36.8	1,752,274	46.5	63,053	18,837	81,890	3.91	2,206,851	48.9	2,571,174	50.2	4,244,214	61.3
World C (Christians)	29,700	8.0	79,000	3.2	214,100	5.7	7,701	604	8,305	3.33	259,000	5.7	297,146	5.8	480,000	6.9
Country's population	**370,000**	**100.0**	**2,507,575**	**100.0**	**3,767,000**	**100.0**	**135,468**	**0**	**135,468**	**3.12**	**4,516,212**	**100.0**	**5,122,000**	**100.0**	**6,927,000**	**100.0**

COLUMNS, ROWS.
For meanings and definitions, see Codebook (Part 3). Note that, by definition, total 'Christians' = professing + crypto-Christians, which also = affiliated + unaffiliated Christians, and also = Great Commission Christians + latent Christians. Percentages may not always total exactly, due to rounding.

CENSUSES.
1919 (Holy Land): 81.7% Muslims, 9.4% Jews, 8.9% Christians. **23.X.1922** (Holy Land): 78.0% Muslims, 11.1% Jews, 9.6% Christians (73,024). **18.XI.1931** (Holy Land): 73.3% Muslims, 16.9% Jews, 8.9% Christians (91,938). **1934:** 67.6% Muslims, 23.1% Jews, 8.2% Christians (99,500). **1939:** 59.5% Muslims, 33.1% Jews, 7.4% Christians (100,000). **22.V.1961** (Israel: de jure, excluding aliens): 88.7% Jews, 7.8% Muslims, 2.3% Christians (50,543), 1.1% Druzes, 0.1% nonreligious. **19-20.V.1972:** 85.4% Jews, 11.2% Muslims, 2.3% Christians (72,131: 0.8% Orthodox, 0.7% Roman Catholics), 1.2% Druzes. **1983:** 79.2% Jews, 11.1% Muslims, 1.9% Christians (1.0% Roman Catholic, 0.5% Orthodox), 1.6% Druzes, 6.2% other religionists and nonreligious. Comparing these censuses is extremely complex because of varying definitions and territories included or excluded; our Tables 1 for Israel, Jordan and Palestine attempt to include and reconcile all the available data.

NOTES ON RELIGIONS
ANGLICANS. In the year 1900 there was a strong Anglican Arab community with numerous Anglican schools around Nazareth.
ATHEISTS. 2 parties since 1965: Israel Communist Party (MAKI), (mainly Ashkenazi Jews), and New Communist (RAKAH), (70% Arabs). Many Communist party members are Muslims or Christians, often practicing.
BAHA'IS. Reached Palestine before 1892. World headquarters now on Mount Carmel, Haifa. Good relations are maintained with the Israeli state, and a vast world Baha'i center is being constructed in Haifa housing the Shrine of the Bab, and all central administrative functions.

Continued overleaf

Country Table 1–concluded

CHRISTIANS. 80% Arabic-speaking, and mostly urban or in Galilee and the Central Plain (Yafo, Lod, Jerusalem). The total excludes 11,000 Christians in East Jerusalem, a disputed area claimed by Israel since 1967 to be part of the state of Israel, but before 1967 part of Jordan (and hence included in this survey under Palestine).
COUNTRY'S POPULATION. This table refers to the territory of Israel proper, i.e. that before June 1967, excluding the administered territories (West Bank, Northern Sinai, Gaza Strip, Golan Heights) and excluding also East Jerusalem; the latter is excluded because the reunification of Jerusalem by Israel has not been internationally accepted. In 1948 the population was 758,700 Jewish, and 120,300 Arabs. From 1948-70, about 1,300,000 Jewish immigrants entered and 200,000 left. In 1970 Arabs numbered 490,000 including refugees. In the column 'Natural change' above are included both biological increase and also the average 1990-2000 immigration rate of around 40,000 Jews a year. Since the establishment of the state, more than 2.6 million people have immigrated to Israel: about 59% from Europe, 18% from Africa, 15% from Asia, and 8% from the Western Hemisphere and Oceania. From 1948-1998, the 3 largest sources have been the former Soviet Union (900,000), Poland (340,000) and Morocco (270,000).
CRYPTO-CHRISTIANS. Secret believers, Israeli Arabs and Israeli Jewish, in all churches and also a number of isolated radio churches amongst Arab and Jewish communities.
INDEPENDENTS. In about 16 groupings in 1995 including isolated radio believers among the Israeli population (see Table 2); mostly Arab, with some Jewish.
JEWS. The Jewish population of Palestine (including present Israel) rose gradually from 10,000 in 1800 to 25,000 in 1880 to 40,000 in 1900, mostly residing in the 4 holy towns (Jerusalem, Hebron, Tiberias, Safad), Jaffa and Haifa. *Immigration.* After 1920 immigration became massive, 35,000 entering in 1925 and 65,000 in 1935. Jewish immigrants from 1919-32: 84,093. 1933-39: 218,099. 1940-47: 92,563. 1948-51: 702,779. 1952-61: 334,000. 1962-69: 299,424. 1970: 36,928. 1971: 42,000. 1972: 55,888. *Origin.* In 1951, Jews were 25% Sabras (born in Israel), 47% born in Europe or USA (Ashkenazis), 28% born in Africa or Asia (Sefardi-Orientals). By 1970, the composition had changed to: 46% Sabras, 28% Ashkenazis, 26% Sefardi-Orientals. In addition to Orthodox and Reformed Jews, there are other parties: Neturei Karta, Agudat Israel, Mizrachis. *Synagogues.* The great majority are Orthodox, with a few Reformed and Conservative. *Practice.* 15% observe all commandments, 15% most, 46% some traditions, 24% none. Karaites. (Readers of the Scriptures). An 8th-century AD Jewish sect similar to the Sadducees, rejecting Jewish Talmudic oral tradition. Now around Ramla, with 9 synagogues, each with its own minister-reader.
MUSLIMS. Mainly Palestinians, with 37,000 Bedouin, and a few Circassians in Galilee; mostly Sunnis (of Shafiite, Hanafite and Hanbalite rites); Shahiliya Sufis (HQ Acre); also Ahmadis and Druzes. An 11th-century Muslim Shia Ismaili schism with Christian and Jewish elements. In 18 Galilean villages and on Mount Carmel. Arabic-speaking, both here enumerated under Muslims. *Hajj pilgrims to Mecca.* (1970) 838 Palestinians from Israel and Jordan.
NONRELIGIOUS. An increasing number of Jews each year regard themselves as having abandoned religion, as the column 'Conversion' above shows.
ORTHODOX. Tens of thousands of Orthodox were displaced, in the 1947-48 fighting, out of Israel of Lebanon, Jordan, Syria, and overseas.
OTHER RELIGIONISTS. Adherents of other non-Christian religions, including Theosophists and Rosicrucians (AMORC, 2 centers).
PROTESTANTS. Arabs or European or USA expatriates (the latter including in over 1,000 young USA Jews converted through the Jews for Jesus movement, and USA non-Jewish persons who convert to Judaism without giving up belief in Christ and then move to Israel as missionaries).
SAMARITANS. A Jewish sect dating from the 8th century BC, accepting only the Pentateuch and Book of Joshua. Now in Holon, near Tel-Aviv (with 250 more in Nablus, West Bank).

Great Commission Instrument Panel: status of Israel (for explanation see start of Part 4)

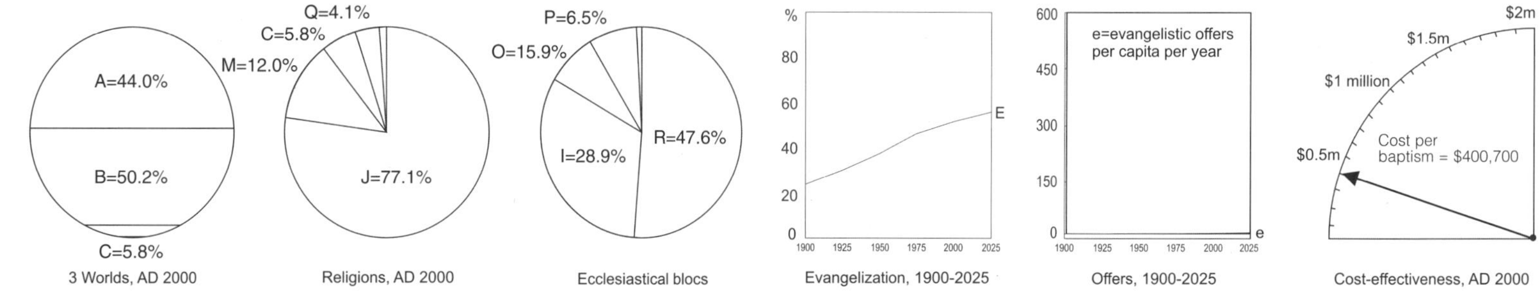

Country status. Israel is on the eastern end of the Mediterranean Sea and comprises much of the area known in Biblical times as Palestine. The boundaries of the state, known as Eretz Israel, have shifted since its founding in 1948 as a result of 3 wars with Arabs, in all of which the Israelis were victors. Israel has few natural resources but through the use of skilled labor produces electronic equipment, chemicals, and oil-based products. Tourism is a major industry.

HUMAN LIFE AND LIBERTY

Human needs and development. Israel has been an embattled country since its founding, and national security has taken precedence over development. Surrounded by enemies and with few natural resources, the country had to depend for survival on the generosity of Jews in other countries and also aid from the United States. For the past 4 decades, the country had the highest per capita military expenditures in the world, and military enlistment took a heavy toll on national manpower needs. Despite such burdens, Israel has a higher standard of living than all of its neighbors. Zionism historically had a socialist bent, and health care and social security were among its earliest goals. The Ministry of Social Welfare began its work soon after independence, and within the next decade authorized a broad range of welfare programs. The Histadrut, an arm of the Labor Party, was also active in providing pensions and insurance for all its Jewish members. Despite such egalitarian and socialist ideals, Israel has become a three-tier society in which there is wide variance in the quality of life of the various groups. At the top are the European Jews, both Ashkenazim and Sephardim, who enjoy standards of life comparable to those of Europe. At the middle level are the Oriental Jews, including Jews from North Africa, Ethiopia, Yemen, India and other places, for whom there are fewer opportunities for advancement and whose lifestyles are correspondingly jejune and meager. At the bottom are the Arabs who live typically Third World lives of constant deprivation, and whose political voicelessness makes them a defiant underclass. Health and social indicators of the Israeli Arabs are little better than those of their brethren across the borders. Most of them are huddled in camps or in slums. They receive little schooling and eke out their livelihood by doing menial jobs.

Human rights and freedoms. Ostensibly a democracy, Israel grants its Jewish citizens all basic human rights. The rights of the non-Jewish citizens are subject to the exigencies of the Arab-Israeli struggle. Arabs are considered as threats to the security of Israel, and are thus treated as a hostile minority. Terrorism and counter-terrorism, violence and retaliation govern the relations between Jews and Arabs, but the balance of advantage has always remained with the Israelis. Under the numerous laws directed against terrorism, the human rights of the Arab minority are violated. Such violations relate to detention of prisoners, deportation of undesirable aliens, arbitrary interference with privacy, family, home and correspondence, censorship of pro-Arab publications, and restrictions on freedom of movement. Torture of Arab prisoners is fairly common and so also are beatings and physical abuse, inhuman and degrading treatment, and extrajudicial killings of unarmed civilians. The Shin Bet, or the Israeli Security Forces, have a carte blanche to use whatever force is considered necessary to browbeat potential opponents. Curfews are routinely used to restrict meetings and demonstrations in Arab areas, and civilian homes are demolished to prevent them from being used as hideouts by suspected terrorists. Commercial policies are designed to discourage Arab participation in the economic life of the country and special passes and permits are used to restrict movement into and out of Arab towns. Thousands are detained without formal charge or trial. Forced confessions are recorded in Hebrew which most Arabs do not read. Trials are deliberately delayed when the attorneys and witnesses do not appear and the files are 'lost', in order to bring psychological pressure on the defendants. Israeli settlers in occupied territories convicted of crimes against Palestinians generally receive lighter sentences than Palestinians accused of comparable crimes against Israelis. The use of excessive force by the security forces has led to the deaths not only of suspects, but also innocent bystanders and children. On a number of occasions, suspects receiving medical treatment have been dragged by security forces from hospitals. The authorities impose a variety of restrictions on freedom of speech, including display of flags and the writing of graffiti. The Arabic press is tightly controlled, and permit is required for import of publications into the occupied territories. Secondary and elementary schools are closed periodically. Palestinians who are abroad are denied the right to return to the country. Internal movement is controlled through the issuance of 'Green Cards', and other devices that discourage all forms of travel by Arabs. Economic discrimination against Arabs include high taxes, exclusion from public service, and policies designed to protect Jewish trade and commerce at the expense of the Palestinians.

Human environment. As a small country, Israel has been subject to environmental pressures resulting from development. Water supply is the main threat, and the quality of water has been deteriorating as a result of heavy pollution from industrial and domestic wastes. Coastal areas are threatened by marine pollution and the degradation of beaches.

NON-CHRISTIAN RELIGIONS

Judaism is the principal religion of Israel, and today Israel is the only nation in the world where Jews are in the majority. In 1995, the composition of the Jewish population in Israel included 53% Sabras (Jews born in Israel); 42% Jews originally from Europe or America, the great majority being Ashkenazis (Jews of the western tradition who speak or whose ancestors spoke Yiddish or Judeo-German); and 5% Jews originally from Africa or Asia, almost all Sefardis (whose traditional language was Latin or Judeo-Spanish) or Orientals (coming from Arab countries). In 1951, these percentages were respectively 25%, 47% and 28%. Tension exists between Ashkenazis and Sefardi-Orientals, due to the former holding leading positions in government and the economy, leaving the latter who were later immigrants in subordinate positions in the social and professional spheres.

Jewish worship is well organized. There are over 6,000 synagogues and 400 rabbis paid by the state officiating in 175 local communities. The synagogues of Sefardi and Ashkenazi rites usually each have a congregation from one particular overseas country and maintain their foreign traditions. Some 178 religious councils and almost 320 religious committees in the villages care for the religious needs of the population. These are under the administrative control of the Ministry of Religion but are also accountable to the Chief rabbinate of Israel for religious questions. The rabbinate consists of the 2 chief rabbis, one Ashkenazi and the other Sefardi, and the Supreme Rabbinical Council; the latter constitutes the highest religious authority, interpreting the law and supervising the rabbinical courts.

Israeli life is deeply permeated by the Bible and by Jewish traditions and festivals; and also by the Sabbath (Saturday) during which public transport does not operate. Each morning the national radio station Qol Israel begins its days with a religious chant and the reading of a psalm. There are also Biblical and Talmudic commentaries on radio and television. Bible study has an important place in the elementary and secondary schools, and a Bible is solemnly given to soldiers at the end of their period of instruction. Jewish food regulations are observed in the army and in all other official institutions.

The Orthodox branch of Judaism plays a far more important role in Israel than the 2 other worldwide Jewish branches, the Reformed (liberal or progressive) and the Conservative which takes an intermediate po-

Country summary. **Worlds A, B, C by ethnolinguistic peoples, cities, and major civil divisions in Israel.**

	PEOPLES							*CITIES*							*CIVIL DIVISIONS*						
World	*Num*	*Pop 2000*	*C%*	*Christians*	*E%*	*U%*	*Unevangelized*	*Num*	*Pop 2000*	*C%*	*Christians*	*E%*	*U%*	*Unevangelized*	*Num*	*Pop 2000*	*C%*	*Christians*	*E%*	*U%*	*Unevangelized*
A	29	1,971,799	0.28	5,581	38	62	1,230,558	5	460,608	0.83	3,831	47	53	242,101	1	618,607	3.20	19,795	46	54	331,078
B	16	3,137,852	8.86	277,976	67	33	1,022,150	4	3,551,195	6.67	236,942	60	40	1,430,829	5	4,503,077	6.09	274,283	57	43	1,921,649
C	8	12,037	87.41	10,521	100	0	16	0	0	0.00	0	0	0	0	0	0	0.00	0	0	0	0
Total	**53**	**5,121,688**	**5.74**	**294,078**	**56**	**44**	**2,252,724**	**9**	**4,011,803**	**6.00**	**240,773**	**58**	**42**	**1,672,930**	**6**	**5,121,684**	**5.74**	**294,078**	**56**	**44**	**2,252,727**

sition. According to law and in actuality, the Orthodox enjoy a complete monopoly over synagogues, marriages, courts, rabbis paid or recognized by the state, military rabbis, religious political parties, as well as 3 government ministries which have been in the hands of these parties for many years (Interior, Social Affairs, and Religious Affairs). A few non-Orthodox rabbis and institutions are fighting to obtain legal status. In the face of this kind of institutionalized orthodoxy and its theocratic designs, there is often manifest in Israel the irritation of believers towards the rigidity of organizations, compromised as well by political and financial matters. Orthodox Judaism does not seem able to free itself from the defense mentality which has made possible the survival of the Jewish people during the long centuries of their exile. In Israel, the original widespread aspirations for a completely renewed Judaism have not come to fruition in any observable fashion.

International Jewish organizations with their headquarters in Israel include the Agudas Israel World Organizations (AIWO), founded in 1912 in Katowice, Upper Silesia, and now located in Jerusalem, which seeks to find a solution for the problems of Jewish people, both in Israel and the diaspora, in the traditional spirit of Judaism.

Karaism emerged out of Judaism in Babylon in the 8th century A.D. The Karaites (Readers of the Scriptures) only recognize the books of the Bible and reject Jewish oral tradition as found in the Talmud. Spiritual descendants of the Sadducees, they had a flourishing period during the Middle Ages. In Israel they now number about 16,000, the majority located in the vicinity of Ramla.

Samaritans. A Samaritan (Shameerim) priest based on Holon, near Tel Aviv, with ancient manuscript of Torah. This Jewish sect dates from the 8th century BC.

Samaritan religion is followed by descendants of Jews who intermarried with colonists placed in Samaria by Assyrian kings during the 8th century BC Samaritans accept only the Pentateuch and the Book of Joshua. They number about 500, of whom 250 are Palestine (West Bank) at Nablus near Mount Gerizim where the ruins of their ancient temple are located and 250 in Israel at Holon, a suburb of Tel-Aviv.

Islam has decreased radically both in numbers and percentage of the population during the present century, from 83% in 1900 to 12.8% by AD 2000. Religious councils direct Muslim affairs and administer their religious foundations (waqfs). The highest dignitaries are the kadis of the 4 religious courts (sharia) and the Court of Appeal in Jerusalem. There are about 200 imams paid by the state and 150 mosques of which the most important are those of Omar and al-Aqsa in East Jerusalem, al-Jazzar a Acre, and the new Mosque of Peace at Nazareth.

Druze religion is a sect which emerged from Islam in the 11th century. The Druze's faith today includes Muslim, Jewish, and Christian elements. They are found in Galilean villages and at Mount Carmel.

Baha'is. *Top.* Headquarters of Baha'i World Faith on Mount Carmel, Haifa. *Lower.* Proposed Centre for the Study of Texts.

Baha'i arose in Persia in the 19th century, claiming to synthesize all religions. Its world center and Universal House of Justice are in Haifa, Israel, where its founder, Baha'u'llah (Glory of God) is buried. The 13,700 Baha'is in Israel live in both Haifa and Acre. Members globally are expected to make at least one pilgrimage to Haifa.

CHRISTIANITY

The Jewish state in Palestine with its capital Jerusalem was destroyed by the Romans in AD 70 and again in AD 132, resulting in the dispersal of the Jews, and also of Jewish Christians, throughout the Mediterranean world and the Near East. Subsequently, Palestine came under the rule of Byzantines (324), Arabs (636), Crusaders (1099), Mamluks (1291), Ottoman Turks (1517), British (1917), finally leading to the founding of the new state of Israel in 1948.

After the conversion of the emperor Constantine in the 4th century, Jerusalem became a place of pilgrimage for Christians. In 451, it was acknowledged as one of the 4 major patriarchates. The Crusades were initially encouraged by pope Hildebrand to heal the growing separation between the Western and Eastern churches but in fact contributed to the Great Schism of 1054. Rome then established a separate Latin patriarchate in Jerusalem in 1099. This was suppressed in 1291 by the Mamluks and not restored until 1847, when Latin clergy were once more allowed to return to Palestine. In 1333, an exception was made for Franciscans who were permitted to return as caretakers of the Christian holy places. During Turkish rule from the 16th to the 19th centuries, the patriarch of Constantinople was given official jurisdiction over all Christians in areas under Turkish control. Only the Greek Melkites in Palestine were able to maintain any relationship with Rome.

In 1882, Zionist agitation began calling for Palestine to become a Jewish state. Following the increasing Jewish immigration to Israel, Britain in 1917 issued the Balfour Declaration, recognizing Palestine as the national homeland of the Jews. This marked the beginning of Jewish-Arab hostility.

The great majority of all Christians living in Israel are Palestinian Arabs. About 85% of them live in Galilee, 61% being city dwellers and 39% rural peasants living in some 25 villages. Christians thus tend to be more urbanized than Muslims. However, the emigration of Christians which began in the Turkish period and has been intensified since 1948, and especially since 1967, may eventually result in the complete evacuation of Christian Arabs from the region, for political, social, psychological and religious reasons. Many Palestinian Christians, especially those with better education, live in the diaspora, in Lebanon, Jordan, Kuwait, as well as in Canada, USA, Brazil, Argentina, and Australia.

Non-Arab Christians are mostly married to Jews or are the children of mixed marriages. Their exact number is unknown because many baptized immigrants are identified as Jews on their official papers, and they often have no relations with local churches. There is also a small group of persons known as Jewish Christians, coming from mixed marriages where the father or mother is ethnically Jewish. Some Catholic priests and laymen have formed a group called the work of St James the Apostle, consisting of from 200 to 300 members, which attempts to develop a community speaking Hebrew and using it in its liturgy. The presence of a minority of Christians among a Jewish majority constitutes a situation unique in the world and without precedent in history, at least since the first Christian communities of the early church.

A special problem for religions in Israel concerns the holy places. Within a radius of one kilometer in Jerusalem are the sacred sites of 3 great monotheistic religions: the Wailing Wall from 1st-century Judaism, 2 mosques from the 7th and 8th centuries which make Jerusalem the third holy city of Islam after Mecca and Medina, and the Christian holy places. The most important of the latter are the Holy Sepulchre built by Constantine and often renovated,the Cenacle on the site of the Last Supper, the Tomb of the Virgin and the Chapel of the Ascension in Jerusalem, as well as the basilica and the Grotto of the Nativity at Bethlehem. The status of these holy places, especially the Christian ones, has always been the subject of controversy involving not uncommonly the great political powers, such as Tsarist Russia and France in the 19th century and Italy and Greece in the 20th. As a result of the rights and prerogatives established in 1757 by the Ottoman empires and which contribute to the lack of Christian unity in the Holy Land, rival and privileged communities share the possession, disposition and exploitation of the holy places, to the exclusion of all other Christian groups. Thus, the Holy Sepulchre is in the possession of Armenian Apostolic, Greek Orthodox and Latin Catholics and the basilica in Bethlehem belongs to Greeks, Armenians, Copts, and Syrians. In this way the holy places continue to present and project the spectacle of a divided Christianity.

CATHOLIC CHURCH. Catholics form the majority of the Christian population of Israel, and 3 different Catholic rites exist in the country. (1) Melkites are the most important group. The Greek Melkite patriarch of Antioch resides in Damascus, Syria and is represented by a patriarchal vicar in Jerusalem who has responsibility for East Jerusalem and the West Bank as well as a parish at Jaffa. The archdiocese of Acre serves the faithful in Galilee. (2) Latin Catholics are under the jurisdiction of the Latin Patriarchate of

Jerusalem, which includes Israel, Jordan, and Cyprus as well as the Catholic parish of Gaza. The patriarch lives in East Jerusalem. He is represented by 3 patriarchal vicars: at Nazareth for Israel, at Amman for Jordan and at Nicosia for Cyprus. (3) Maronites are under the archbishopric of Tyre in Lebanon, represented at Jaffa by a vicar-general who with 4 priests supervises 5 'Palestinian' parishes (Jaffa, Haifa, Nazareth, Jish, and Acre). On the other hand, West Bank Catholics in Jerusalem, Bethlehem, and Ramallah are dependent on the Maronite patriarch of Lebanon. The patriarch is represented by a patriarchal vicar at Jerusalem whose jurisdiction extends also to Jordan.

The Holy See has diplomatic relations with Israel and in AD 2000 is represented to government and the Catholic hierarchy by a nuncio residing in Tel Aviv.

ORTHODOX CHURCHES. The Greek Orthodox are the second largest Christian denomination in Israel. Nevertheless, their strength has steadily decreased since the early 19th century when their members made up nearly 80% of the entire Christian population of the Holy Land. Factors which have contributed to their decline are a shortage of priests, inadequate finances, conversions to other denominations, emigration and a conflict between the hierarchy who are mostly Greeks and the priests and laity who are Palestinian Arabs. The church continues to claim precedence among Christian communities in the Holy Land as the direct successor to the first church in Jerusalem under James the Apostle. The patriarch is assisted by 14 titular archbishops.

Prior to 1917, the Russian Orthodox Church built numerous churches, convents, schools and hostels to cater for pilgrims from Russia to the Holy Land. At the present time, there is an ecclesiastical mission under the jurisdiction of the patriarch of Moscow.

Four Oriental Orthodox or Monophysite churches have followings in Israel: Armenian, Coptic, Syrian, and Ethiopian Orthodox. The largest used to be the Armenian Apostolic Church, led by a patriarch, but the majority have emigrated now. The Copts and Syrians have archbishops and the Ethiopians a bishop.

PROTESTANT CHURCHES. Of active Protestant groups, the one with the oldest history is the Church of Scotland, which dates back to 1839 and continues to sponsor a school and 2 hostels. The Christian and Missionary Alliance opened 3 centers in 1890 and a fourth in 1911. At present it has a book shop in Beersheba and serves an international congregation in Jerusalem.

The largest Protestant denomination in Israel today is the Baptist Convention which owes its origin to the arrival of Southern Baptist missionaries in 1911 but which undertook its greatest expansion in evangelism, education and social service after 1948. With a staff of 50 missionaries, this is the largest Southern Baptist mission in Europe and the Near East. Although 7 congregations are directly related to the Baptist Convention, 9 other Arab Baptist groups joined together in 1965 to form the Association of Baptist Churches in Israel. There are several other denominations also. Most are recent arrivals with very small followings. Jewish newspapers have as a result recently expressed concern about the proselytizing efforts of these bodies.

ANGLICAN CHURCH. In 1820, the London Church's Ministry among the Jews (CMJ), arrived in Jerusalem, where it continues work today with a few centers for worship, education, social relations, and a book store. In 1851, the Church Missionary Society took up work among Arabs and built several hospitals and an orphanage. The Jerusalem and the East Mission began in 1888. The Anglican community developed considerably during the British mandate with the presence of large numbers of British personnel. However, Anglican membership was reduced by three-fourths following the exodus of Christians, mostly Arabs, in 1948. The Jerusalem Archbishopric was enlarged in 1957 to include 8 Near East and North African countries and in 1975 became the Episcopal Church in Jerusalem and the Middle East.

Art and architecture. Israel has a number of Christian shrines, many of them dating back to Roman and Crusader times. The Church of the Holy Sepulchre, shared by all the major denominations, is one of the largest. There are smaller churches in smaller cities, such as Bethlehem, and also many monasteries, predominantly Orthodox, some of them serving as museums. Among them the most notable are the Museum of the Studium Biblicum Franciscanum in the Convent of the Flagellation in Jerusalem, St Anne's Museum in the Monastery of the White Fathers, Alexander Monastery Museum in the Russian Orthodox Mission in Jerusalem, Collection of the Pontifical Biblical Institute, and the Carmelite Monastery Museum in Stella Maris. The Mardigian Museum of Armenian Art and History specializes in Armenian antiquities.

Renewal movements. In the 1990s the Pentecostal/Charismatic Renewal continued to spread rapidly across most older churches, and numbered over 105,000 adherents (of whom 3% Pentecostals, 16% Charismatics, and 81% Independents).

Indigenous missions. Christians in Israel have been sending out missionaries since the first century. However, in more recent times, few missionaries have been sent out and Israel has been primarily the recipient of mission work.

Jewish President Shazar greets church dignitaries (Coptic, Armenian, Greek, Syrian, Roman Catholic, Protestant) on New Year's Eve, 1968.

CHURCH AND STATE

While a constitution originally expected to be promulgated on Oct. 1, 1948, was being prepared, the Provisional National Council which was acting as Provisional State Assembly declared in its proclamation of independence of May 14, 1948, that the State of Israel 'shall be founded on the principles of liberty, justice and peace as taught by the Prophets of Israel; it shall assures complete equality of social and political rights to all its citizens without distinction of belief, race or sex; it shall guarantee full freedom of conscience, worship, education and culture; it shall assures the protection and inviolability of the holy places and sanctuaries of all religions and respect the principles of the charter of the United Nations'.

The constitution has in fact still not been completed, but several fundamental laws dealing with religion have been adopted by the parliament, the Knesset. Among these is the Law of Return of 1950 which accords to all Jews anywhere the right to establish themselves in Israel and become naturalized Israelis. In May 1971, a new law permitted the granting of Israeli nationality to all Jews in other nations who express a desire to emigrate to Israel. There was also a law in 1952 giving to non-Jews Israeli nationality under conditions similar to immigration policy in other countries. In the 1950 law, the term 'Jew' was not defined, and this remained the case until in 1970 the Knesset adopted the following definition: 'A Jew is one who was born of a Jewish mother and has not been converted to any other religion, or one who, not being Jewish, is converted to Judaism'. In this way, a Jew who becomes a Christian is refused the status of Jew but not the convinced atheist. The Supreme Court has made several pronouncements on the definition of this term, notably in 1962 when it dismissed a suit against the Minister of the Interior by a Catholic priest, father Daniel (Oswald Ruffeissen), who was originally Jewish, but to whom the minister had refused to grant citizenship. In January 1970, a month before the passage of the law defining the term, the Supreme Court rendered a liberal verdict granting the status of Jews (always in the ethnic sense of the term) to the children of a marine officer who had been originally a Jew by religion, was now married to a Christian, and who both now declared themselves to be atheists. Israel's religious parties desire that conversions to Judaism be refused recognition unless they are conducted by an Orthodox rabbi according to a long and complex procedure, which would have the effect of excluding from the benefit of the Law of Return those who for the most part are of Jewish background but do not have Jewish mothers and who were converted by liberal or 'conservative' (in the sense of American Judaism) rabbis, these latter, (especially American rabbis) being considered too lenient. Nevertheless, neither the Knesset nor the government has shown any interest in following these traditionalist circles.

Another case involved a couple, Gary and Shirley Berresford, who petitioned the High Court of Justice to allow them to obtain immigrant visas under the Law of Return'. The couple were born as Jews in South Africa but had become Christians and were members of Jews for Jesus. In December 1989 the Supreme Court handed down a decision which states that 'any Jew who proclaims that Jesus is the Messiah is no longer a Jew as concerning the Law of Return'.

Before the establishment of the State of Israel the law defined the personal status of citizens primarily in Islamic terms, and this law is still partially in effect. This follows basically the Ottoman millet system, in that each person is regarded as under the authority of his religious community in matters concerning marriage, divorce, and funerals. The recognized religious authority reports marriages to the Ministry of the Interior who then registers them. There is thus no civil marriage in Israel, and agnostic or atheist citizens must submit to religious laws. Moreover, mixed marriages exist neither in rabbinical law nor in Muslim law, and conversion of one party is required if a mixed marriage is to take place involving these religions. The millet system also involves the recognition of legal status for religious communities. Those religions which were recognized under the Turks have kept this status in the State of Israel. In addition to Orthodox, Judaism, and Islam, these include the following Christian communities: Greek Orthodox, Melkite, Latin, Maronite, Armenian, and Coptic. Since the proclamation of the State of Israel in 1948, 3 others have been recognized: Druzes (1957), Anglicans (1970), and Baha'i (1971). Protestant churches have no legal status which means, as one example, that church weddings are not recognized by the state. The United Christian Council in Israel is serving as an intermediary in negotiations concerning this. The legal situation as it existed under the Ottoman regime and the British mandate prevails also in the domain of the activities, properties and legal rights of religious communities, and the State of Israel continues to support it.

Within the government, religious questions are the responsibility of the Ministry of Religions (Misrad Hadatoth). One of its tasks is to inform religious communities as to how many of their members are converted to other religions. A law forbids changes of religion for young people under 18 years of age unless both parents consent to it. The ministry has a Department of Muslim Affairs and a Department of Christian Affairs. Within the same ministry is also the Keren Yaldenou, a body whose aim is to prevent Jewish children from being influenced by Christian institutions.

The internal policies of Israel primarily revolve around 3 questions with important religious implications: (1) the relationship between religious leaders and lay persons, which will undoubtedly have a growing importance in the years to come and which will probably result in a formula somewhere between the 2 extremes of a theocracy and complete separation of religion and state; (2) the economic tension between socialism and liberalism, which overlays to a great extent the conflict between Sefardi Orientals and Ashkenazis; and (3) relations between Jews and Arabs, which is affected both by the government's policies and by the external situation. Concerning these last 2 questions, a significant role has been played by the World Conference of Christians for Palestine, with headquarters in Parish. This conference was created to help explain the situation of Palestinian Christians, and it has in fact sensitized Christians across the world to the problem involved.

It is also necessary to stress the importance of the function performed by the Greek Catholic Church in defense of the rights of the Palestinian people, which has manifested itself in 2 different ways. First has been the activity of msgr. Joseph Raya, archbishop of Haifa (Acre) from 1968 to 1974, who is well know for his public interventions in favor of Palestinians forced out of their villages. In 1974, he felt obliged to withdraw from his position as archbishop due to pressures from the patriarchate and the Vatican because he accepted, in spite of everything, the reality of the Jewish state and especially because of his declaration that Jerusalem should remain under Israeli control. A second important person has been msgr. Capucci, of Syrian origin and patriarchal vicar of Jerusalem,who has supported the Palestinian resistance and who was arrested on 18 August 1974, and sentenced to 15 years in prison. The prelate denied the Israeli accusation that, at the moment of his arrest, he was transporting arms in his vehicle; but he also refused to answer questions at his trial because he rejected the competence of the court calling it an 'occupation court'.

In subsequent years up to 1988 these situations have continued to smolder, aggravated by the definitive rise of Messianic Jews and the growth of flourishing independent charismatic churches, especially in Tel Aviv.

BROADCASTING AND MEDIA

FEBA (Seychelles) has shortwave radio programs in Arabic, Azeri and Farsi. Other shortwave programs from Voice of Hope, HCJB (Ecuador), AWR (Slovakia), and TWR (Monaco) can be heard.

TBN programs appear in Jericho and Gaza on channels 21 and 23. The 'Jesus' Film has been shown to 260,000: 166,000 watched it on local television broadcasts, and 90,000 have seen it through a film team presentation. Christian television programming can be received from the METV station in Lebanon. Satellite TV programs are received mainly in Arabic.

INTERDENOMINATIONAL ORGANIZATIONS

The United Christian Council in Israel was founded in 1957 and through its 14 subcommittees carries out studies on Christian problems in Israel, has a literature program with emphasis on the use of Hebrew in Bible studies, works on liturgy and music, maintains an educational program, updates Christian tourist information, and prepares contingency plans for emergencies in any area affecting the Christian minority. On the Catholic side, the Latin patriarchate of Jerusalem has an ecumenical commission.

There are 3 cooperative ecumenical centers dedicated to contacts between the churches. (1) The Ecumenical Institute for Advanced Theological Studies (EIATS), located at Tantur between Jerusalem and Bethlehem, was begun in 1971 in accordance with a wish expressed by pope Paul VI on his trip to the Holy Land in 1964. The first director is a Catholic but those who follow will be successively Protestant then Orthodox. The institute is devoted especially to a study of the 'mystery of salvation' in all its aspects. (2) The Ecumenical Theological Research Fraternity in Israel was founded in Jerusalem in 1967. It brings together specialists of different Christian confessions to jointly study aspects of Judeo-Christian relations. (3) The Near East Christian Center, begun by the White Fathers in 1951, is a research center dedicated to the renewal of the churches of the Near East and the furthering of ecumenical contacts among them. It has a library of 30,000 volumes. Also of importance is the ecumenical role played by the first Catholic university in the Holy Land, Bethlehem Regional University, described in this survey under Palestine.

Five further groups are dedicated to interreligious dialogue. (1) The Israeli Committee for Religious Understanding (or, Interface) (Ha'vad lehavana beindatith) was begun in Jerusalem in 1960 and provides a meeting around for representatives of Judaism, Islam and Christianity. (2) The House of Isaiah (Beit Yeshayaou) in Jerusalem is a center for Jewish studies run by Dominicans, with links at the Hebrew University of Jerusalem. (3) The Rainbow, an English-speaking group with 20 members founded in Jerusalem in 1965, brings together Jews and Christians of diverse tendencies. (4) The Tel-Aviv Inter-religious Group (Ha'houg bein dati) is a Hebrew-speaking body consisting of about 100 members who engage in Jewish-Christian dialogue. (5) The Oasis of Peach (Neveshalom), a community of Jews, Christians and Muslims who engage in dialogue and prayer, was founded in Jerusalem in 1972. Also of note is the fact that the 5th annual meeting of the International Catholic-Jewish Committee was held in Jerusalem in March 1976, previous meetings having taken place in Paris, Marseilles, Antwerp and Rome.

FUTURE TRENDS AND PROSPECTS

By 2025 Christians and Muslims are expected to claim about 18% of Israel's population. Judaism will continue to dominate through 2025 but is expected to drop from 85.4% in 1970 to 73.8% by AD 2025.

The long-term future of Christianity in Israel is uncertain. If the Messianic Jewish community makes significant gains Christianity could grow to 8% or more by AD 2050. Otherwise it is expected to remain between 5% and 7% for the near and further future. At the same time, the Muslim community is expected to stay at 12%. Nonreligious persons, nearly nonexistent in AD 1900, will probably exceed 10% by AD 2050.

BIBLIOGRAPHY

A history of the Christian presence in the Holy Land. S. P. Colbi. Lanham, MD: University Press of America, 1988. 343p.

'Annuaire de l'Eglise catholique en Terre sainte,' *Annuaire de l'Eglise Catholique en Terre Sainte, 1972.* Jerusalem: Franciscan Printing Press, 1972.

Asian and African Jews in the Middle East, 1860–1971: Annotated bibliography. H. J. Cohen & Z. Yehuda (eds). Leiden: E. J. Brill, 1976. 453p.

Beyond the basilica: Christians and Muslims in Nazareth. C. F. Emmett. Chicago: University of Chicago Press, 1995. 322p.

Christian communities in Jerusalem and the West Bank since 1948: an historical, social, and political study. D. Tsimhoni. Westport, CT: Praeger, 1993.

Christianity in the Holy Land, past and present. S. P. Colbi. Tel Aviv: Am Hassefer, 1969. 272p.

Civil religion in Israel: traditional Judaism and political culture in the Jewish State. C. S. Liebman & E. Don-Yehiya. Berkeley, CA: University of California Press, 1983. 276p.

Das reformatorische Erbe unter den Palästinensern: zur Entstehung der Evangelisch–Lutherischen Kirche in Jordanien. M. Raheb. *Die Lutherische Kirche, Geschichte und Gestalten*, Bd. 11. Gütersloh: Gütersloher Verlagshaus G. Mohn, 1990. 317p.

Despair and deliverance: private salvation in contemporary Israel. B. Beit-Hallahmi. *SUNY series in Israeli studies.* Albany, NY: State University of New York, 1992. 194p.

Faith and the Intifada: Palestinian Christian voices. N. S. Ateek, M. H. Ellis & R. Radford Ruether (eds). Maryknoll, NY: Orbis Books, 1992. 204p.

For the land and the Lord: Jewish fundamentalism in Israel. I. S. Lustick. New York: Council on Foreign Relations, 1988. 227p.

Hasidism and the State of Israel. H. Rabinowicz. Rutherford, NJ: Fairleigh Dickinson, 1982. 346p.

Israel. E. M. Snyder & E. Kreiner. *World bibliographical series*, vol. 58. Oxford, UK: CLIO Press, 1985. 290p.

Israel and the West Bank and Gaza Strip. C. H. Bleaney. 2nd ed. *World bibliographical series*, vol. 58. Oxford, UK: CLIO Press, 1994. 390p. (Complements 1st edition, focusing upon materials since 1984).

Jerusalem blessed, Jerusalem cursed: Jews, Christians, and Muslims in the Holy City from David's time to our own. T. A. Idinopulos. Chicago: Ivan R. Dee, 1991. 343p.

Jerusalem, the Holy City: a bibliography. J. D. Purvis. *ATLA bibliography series*, no. 20. : American Theological Library Association, 1988–91. 2 vols.

'Judaism,' Part 1 in *Religion in the Middle East: three religions concord & conflict*, p.3–235. A. J. Arberry (ed). Cambridge, UK: Cambridge University Press, 1969. 1

'Les forces religieuses d'Israël,' A. Chouraqui, *Evidences*, (1957), 44–47.

Les minorités chrétiennes de Palestine à travers les siècles: étude historico–juridique et développement moderne international. A. O. Issa. Jerusalem: Franciscan Printing Press, 1978. 363p.

Muslim fundamentalism in Israel. R. Israeli. London: Brassey's, 1993.

New encyclopedia of Zionism and Israel. G. Wigoder (ed). 2nd ed. London and Toronto: Associated University Presses, 1994.

'Panorama religieux d'Israël,' S. Z. Klausner, *Revue Nouvelle*, 19, 1 (1963), 74–83.

Perpetual dilemma: Jewish religion in the Jewish state. S. Z. Abramov. Cranbury, NJ: Associated University Presses, 1976. 432p.

Religious life and communities. Jerusalem: Keter Books, 1974. 214p. (Compiled from material originally in Encyclopaedia Judaica).

Renaissance des Eglises locales: Israël. R. Laurentin. Paris: Seuil, 1973. 172p.

Return to Judaism: religious renewal in Israel. J. Aviad. Chicago: University of Chicago Press, 1983. 208p.

The Arab Christian: a history in the Middle East. K. Cragg. London: Mowbray, 1992. 303p. (See 'Arab Christians in Israel,' p.233–56).

'The Bahá'is in Israel,' B. J. Barrett, *Ariel*, 64 (1986), 37–56.

The forgotten faithful: the Christians of the Holy Land. S. Aburish. London: Quartet, 1993.

The new Jewish encyclopedia. D. Bridger & S. Wolk (eds). New York: Behrman, 1976. 541p.

The origins of the Druze people and religion, with extracts from their sacred writings. P. K. Hitti. New York: AMS Press, 1969. 80p.

The religions of modern Syria and Palestine. F. J. Bliss. New York: Scribner, 1912. 368p.

The Samaritan problem: studies in the relationships of Samaritanism, Judaism and early Christianity. J. Bowman. Trans., A. M. Johnson. Pittsburgh: Pickwick, 1975. 169p.

The Samaritans. A. D. Crown (ed). Tübingen, Germany: Mohr, 1989. 813p.

Tradition, innovation, conflict: Jewishness and Judaism in contemporary Israel. Z. Sobel & B. Beit-Hallahmi (eds). *SUNY series in Israeli studies.* Albany, NY: State University of New York Press, 1991. 304p.

Two worlds of Judaism: the Israeli and American experiences. C. S. Liebman & S. M. Cohen. New Haven, CT: Yale University Press, 1990. 183p.

We belong to the land: the story of a Palestinian Israeli who lives for peace and reconciliation. E. Chacour. San Francisco: HarperSanFrancisco, 1990. 205p. (By a Melkite priest).

Country Table 2. **Organized churches and denominations in Israel.**

Official name (bold type = church with over 10% of all affiliated) 1	*Begun* 2	*Type* 3	*Counc* 4	*Congs* 5	*Adults* 6	*Affiliated 1970* 7	*Affiliated 1995* 8	*G%* 9	*Names, notes, and other statistics* (see Codebook, Part 3) 10
Armenian Apostolic P of Jerusalem	c 500	O-Arm	Ew.N.	3	50	600	100	-6.92	*Gregorians.* 2 Vicariates; Haifa, Jaffa. 1950-73: 90% emigrated.
Assemblies of God	1908	P-Pe2	Z....	12	925	100	1,500	11.44	M=AoG(USA,UK,France,many other countries).
Assyrian Church of the East	c 50	O-Nes	YW...	5	500	200	800	5.70	*Nestorians.* Palestinian Arabic speakers. Remnants of presence in earlier centuries.
Association of Baptist Chs in Israel	1965	I-Bap	T...K	12	711	700	1,100	1.82	Scattered Arab congs, loose link with Baptist Conv. 2n,1p,W=40%,16Y,10z.
Baptist Convention in Israel	1911	P-Bap	T...K	16	803	1,000	2,600	3.90	*BCI.* M=FMB-SBC(USA). 5n,50f,1j,2k,1r,1s (Central Training Centre). 23Y. 1 art gallery.
Bible Evangelistic Mission	1927	P-Pe2	....K	2	100	100	200	2.81	*BEM.* Linked with Pentecostal Jewish Mission (UK). 1k (Bakaa, Jerusalem).
Brethren Assemblies		P-CBr	x....	6	300	500	600	0.05	*Christian Brethren. Plymouth (Open) Brethren.* M=CMML(UK). 4f.
Catholic Church in Israel:	1099	R-LEr	O...P	115	68,550	47,110	122,525	3.90	*Hakenessia Haratholit.* 2,800 Maronites. C=17+2+32. 109n 254x 600m 1239w 1325Yy
P Jerusalem *(Latin)*	1099	R-Lat	Os	65	36,000	11,000	70,000	7.68	Patriarchate restored 1847. 75% Arabs, Jordan. 82n 250x 596m 1196w 1325Yy
EP (*Armenian* C Cilicia)	1742	R-Arm	Os	1	150	110	250	3.34	*Exarchate Patriarchal*, Armenian C Cilicia.
EP Jerusalem (*Chaldean* P Babylon)	c250	R-Cha	Os	1	200	100	300	0.06	*Exarchate Patriarchal*, Chaldean P Babylon.
EP Jerusalem (*Maronite* P Antioch)	1848	R-Mar	Os	2	100	200	175	-0.53	*Exarchate Patriarchal*, Maronite P Antioch.
EP Jerusalem (*Melkite* P Antioch)	1932	R-Mel	Os	5	1,000	3,000	3,100	0.13	*Patriarchal Vicariate*, Melkite P Antioch.
AD Akka (Acre) *(Melkite)*	c250	R-Mel	Os	31	29,000	30,900	45,000	0.06	Arab laity, alien hierarchy. (1970) 28n,1024Yy. (1995) 27n 4x 4m 43w 0Yy
EP Jerusalem (*Syrian* P Antioch)	c1660	R-Syr	Os	2	600	800	700	-0.53	*Exarchate Patriarchal*, Syrian P Antioch.
Catholics affiliated abroad		R-Lat	Bs	8	1,500	1,000	3,000	0.05	Roman Catholic residents affiliated abroad, but not locally in Israel.
Christian & Missionary Alliance of I	1890	P-Hol	xF..K	1	30	100	45	-3.14	M=CMA(USA). Beersheba; also International Evangelical Ch (Jerusalem). 8f,1k,1Y.
Church of God of Prophecy	1965	P-Pe3	Z....	5	400	300	600	2.81	M=CGP(USA). Memorial built on Horns of Hittin.
Church of Scotland in Israel	1839	P-Ref	Rwc.K	3	100	300	200	-1.61	Educational work, formerly hospital also. 1 school (205), 2 hospices. 11f.
Church of the Nazarene	1921	P-Hol	xF..K	2	40	100	100	0.00	M=CoN(USA). Nazareth, Haifa. Arab congregations. 2m,4f,1t(92),W=70%.
Churches of Christ		I-Dis	x....	4	300	500	600	0.05	M=CC(Non-Instrumental) (USA). West Jerusalem, Nazareth, Bat Yam. 1r (Galilee).
Coptic Orthodox Church: D Jerusalem	c 850	O-Cop	NwaN.	2	150	300	300	0.00	Egyptians. Jaffa, Nazareth (church built 1950). Under bishop in Jerusalem. 2n,2d.
Episcopal Ch in Jerus & the M East	1820	A-plu	Aw.NK	5	1,600	900	1,900	3.03	*D Jerusalem.* Formerly Jerusalem Archbishopric. 86% Arabs. M=CMS,CMJ,JEM. 8n,5x,27f,1s.

Continued overleaf

Country Table 2–concluded

Official name (bold type = church with over 10% of affiliated) 1	*Begun* 2	*Type* 3	*Counc* 4	*Congs* 5	*Adults* 6	*Affiliated 1970* 7	*Affiliated 1995* 8	*G%* 9	*Names, notes, and other statistics* (see Codebook, Part 3) 10
Ethiopian Orthodox Ch: D Jerusalem	c1172	O-Eth	Nwa..	1	60	50	80	1.90	Under P Addis Ababa. Church and monastery in West Jerusalem. 12 monks.
Greek Orth Patriarchate of Jerusalem	30	O-Ara	Cw.N.	40	21,000	17,000	39,000	0.05	99% Arab (laity and priests), 1% Greek (bishops and monks). P=60%,W=10%.
Isolated radio churches	c1950	I-3rS	.....	1,000	30,000	1,100	40,000	15.46	Isolated radio believers (Arabs, Jewish). R=300 (TWR, Radio Vatican), T=10000(ICI).
Jehovah's Witnesses	c1920	m-Jeh	x....	10	400	500	800	1.90	Active witnessing under way in Palestine by 1926, in Israel from 1951. (1975) 10Y. (1995) 58Y.
Messianic Assembly in Israel	1948	I-Bap	.....	1	50	100	150	1.64	M=American Messianic Fellowship (formerly Chicago Hebrew Mission). Jerusalem. 1f.
Messianic Congregations & Synagogues	1971	I-3mJ	.....	60	6,000	–	9,000	4.17	*Messianic Jews.* 1995, split by Toronto Blessing. Largest church in Tel Aviv. M=JFJ.
New Apostolic Church	c1985	I-3aX	x....	10	300	–	674	10.00	*NAC/NAK.* M=Neuapostolische Kirche (HQ Zurich).
Norwegian Lutheran Mission	1949	P-Lut	x	5	100	200	200	0.00	*Hakuesia Haluteranit.* M=NLM,LWF. Jewish Christians from Romania, Hungary. 2x,9f.
Russian Orthodox Church	1848	O-Rus	Mwc..	6	200	200	300	1.64	Ecclesiastical mission under P Moscow. Churches in Jaffa. Mt Carmel, Galilee.
Scandinavian Seamen's Church	1949	P-Lut	.....	3	200	500	600	0.73	For sailors in ports of Haifa, Ashdod. Visited by 6,000 seamen a year.
Seventh-day Adventist Church	1932	P-Adv	x....	4	74	150	185	0.84	*SDA, Israel Mission*, Southern European Union Mission. 2x,3mw,5t(102),W=93%,1Y.
Syrian Orth P of Antioch: D Jerusalem	33	O-Syr	Dw.N.	1	50	50	60	0.05	*Jacobites.* Small community of Israeli adherents. HQ Damascus (Syria).
Other independent charismatic chs	1974	I-3cS	.....	200	10,000	–	20,000	4.76	In around 20 very loose geographical networks or associations.
Other Protestant denominations		P-	.....	100	5,000	5,000	10,000	0.05	Total about 50 (see list below), mainly USA and European expatriates.
Other independent Orthodox chs	c1950	I-Ort	.....	15	1,000	500	2,000	5.70	About 10, including FROC (formerly ROCOR), UAOC.
Totals				**1,649**	**148,993**	**78,160**	**256,219**		

Churches, members, growth, 1900-2025	*Congs*	*Adults*	*Affiliated*	*G%*	*Total denominations*	*6 Megablocs:* *O*	*R*	*A*	*P*	*I*	*m*
Total churches, members, and denominations (mid-1900)	110	17,400	29,700	1.39	13	7	1	1	4	0	0
Total churches, members, and denominations (mid-1970)	267	45,869	78,160	1.39	51	7	1	1	33	8	1
Total churches, members, and denominations (mid-1990)	1,600	123,000	211,600	5.11	106	7	1	1	61	35	1
Total churches, members, and denominations (mid-1995)	1,649	148,993	256,219	3.90	107	7	1	1	61	36	1
Total churches, members, and denominations (mid-2000)	1,700	171,000	294,078	2.79	109	7	1	1	62	37	1
Total churches, members, and denominations (mid-2025)	2,800	276,000	475,000	1.94	292	20	1	1	100	150	20

NOTES ON TABLE ABOVE

NATIONAL COUNCILS (Column 4, 5th letter).

C = International Christian Committee in Israel.

K = United Christian Council in Israel (UCCI), which is a member of WEF as well as in working relationship with WCC.

OTHER PROTESTANT DENOMINATIONS. A certain number of USA and European bodies cater mainly for USA and European expatriate civilians. A number of other bodies, especially USA missions and denominations, have small local followings and church services, and so may be considered as denominations or para-denominations: American Association for Jewish Evangelism in Israel, American Baptist Association (1967; 1 Arab church), Assemblies of God, Children of God International, Christian Catholic Ch (USA; 1948), Ch of God (Seventh-day), Ev Missions to the Muslims (1964), Exclusive Brethren (Kelly-Continental), Finnish Missionary Society (1924), Independent Assemblies of God, Jews for Jesus movement (1,500 converts by 1973: 50% Jewish Christians from USA, registered as Jews in rabbinical courts, who work in Israel as evangelists; the other 50% are Israeli Jewish converts baptized in the Dead Sea or Lake Galilee), Mennonite Association in Israel (1953), Norwegian Pentecostal Mission, Slavic Gospel Association (1959), Swedish Free Mission, Swiss Pentecostal Mission, United Evangelical Chs, United Fundamentalist Ch (USA; 1952), World-Wide Missions (1961).

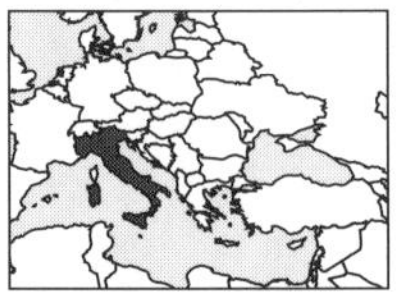

ITALY

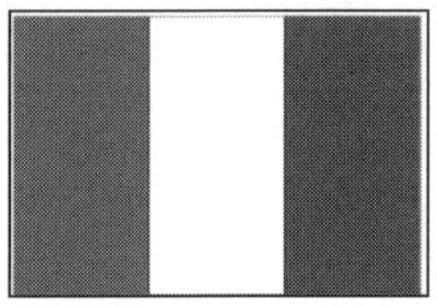

SECULAR DATA, AD 2000

STATE

Official name: Repubblica Italiana (The Italian Republic).
Short name: Italy. **Adjective of nationality:** Italian.
Flag: Green, white, and red bars.
Area: 301,309 sq. km. (116,336 sq. mi.).
Government: Parliamentary republic, since 1946 (1861 Kingdom of Italy proclaimed, 1923 fascist dictatorship, 1946 republic).
Legislature: Parliament: Senate, 325 members; Chamber of Deputies, 630 members.
Official language: Italian (Italiano).
Monetary unit: 1 lira (Lit, plural lire) = 100 centesimi. **US$1=** Lit 1,652.
Chief cities: Milano (Milan) 4,251,000; Napoli (Naples) 3,012,000; ROMA (Rome) 2,688,000; Torino (Turin) 1,294,000; Genova (Genoa) 890,000.
Political divisions: 20 provinces.
Armed forces: 325,000.

DEMOGRAPHY

Population: 57,298,000.
Population density: 190.1/sq. km. (492.5/sq. mi.).
Under 15 years: 8,165,000.
Growth rate p.a.: -0.18% (births 8.48, deaths 10.90).
Mortality: Infant, per 1,000: 6.6; **Maternal per 100,000:** 12.0.
Life expectancy: 79 (male 76, female 82).
Household size: 2.8. **Floor area per person, sq.m:** 50.0.
Major languages: Italian, German, French, Slovenian, Romansh, English, Albanian, Sardinian, Latin.
Urban dwellers: 67.00%. **Urban growth rate p.a.:** 0.1%.
Labor force: 43%.

ETHNOLINGUISTIC PEOPLES

41.4% Italian; 15.3% Lombard; 12.6% Neapolitan-Calabrian; 8.4% Sicilian; 5.3% Piedmontese.

ECONOMY

National income p.a. per person: US$19,020; **per family:** US$53,256.

EDUCATION

Adult literacy: 97% (male 97%, female 96%). **Schools:** 38,459. **Universities:** 50. **School enrolment:** female/male: 87%/87%.

HEALTH

Access to health services: 40%. **Access to safe water:** 100%.
Hospitals: 1,926 (68 beds per 10,000). **Doctors:** 296,385.
Blind: 110,000. **Deaf:** 3,431,700. **Murder rate:** 4.
Lepers: 1,000.

LITERATURE

New book titles p.a.: 36,100 (630 p.a. per million). **Periodicals:** 14,090. **Newspapers:** 74 dailies.

COMMUNICATION (per 1,000 people)

Phones: 433 (44% mobile). **Radios:** 801. **TV sets:** 436.
Daily newspaper circulation: 105. **Computers:** 296.

REFUGEES

Alien refugees from other countries: 60,700.

HUMAN LIFE AND LIBERTY (optimum condition=100.0%)

HDI: 92.1. **HSI:** 88.0. **HFI:** 72.5. **EFL:** 46.0.

Country Table 1. **Religious adherents in Italy, AD 1900-2025.**

Year / *Name*	*1900* Adherents	%	*1970* Adherents	%	*mid-1990* Adherents	%	*Annual change, 1990-2000* Natural	Conversion	Total	Rate	*mid-1995* Adherents	%	*mid-2000* Adherents	%	*mid-2025* Adherents	%
Christians	**32,903,000**	**99.7**	**47,596,800**	**88.4**	**47,437,600**	**83.2**	**22,866**	**-65,583**	**-42,717**	**-0.09**	**47,294,000**	**82.5**	**47,010,426**	**82.1**	**40,959,000**	**79.9**
PROFESSION																
professing Christians	**32,903,000**	**99.7**	**47,596,800**	**88.4**	**47,437,600**	**83.2**	**22,866**	**-65,583**	**-42,717**	**-0.09**	**47,294,000**	**82.5**	**47,010,426**	**82.1**	**40,959,000**	**79.9**
AFFILIATION																
unaffiliated Christians	0	0.0	96,800	0.2	69,600	0.1	34	1,835	1,869	2.41	77,000	0.1	88,286	0.2	110,000	0.2
affiliated Christians	**32,903,000**	**99.7**	**47,500,000**	**88.3**	**47,368,000**	**83.1**	**22,833**	**-67,419**	**-44,586**	**-0.09**	**47,217,000**	**82.4**	**46,922,140**	**81.9**	**40,849,000**	**79.7**
Roman Catholics	32,953,000	99.9	50,697,128	94.2	55,450,000	97.2	26,741	-3,741	23,000	0.04	55,750,000	97.2	55,680,000	97.2	49,500,000	96.6
Protestants	60,000	0.2	405,143	0.8	430,200	0.8	207	1,373	1,580	0.36	440,528	0.8	446,000	0.8	450,000	0.9
Marginal Christians	800	0.0	85,307	0.2	375,000	0.7	181	4,319	4,500	1.14	396,700	0.7	420,000	0.7	600,000	1.2
Independents	0	0.0	62,963	0.1	390,000	0.7	188	2,312	2,500	0.62	404,286	0.7	415,000	0.7	500,000	1.0
Orthodox	200	0.0	28,000	0.1	82,000	0.1	40	860	900	1.05	83,300	0.2	91,000	0.2	110,000	0.2
Anglicans	100	0.0	10,000	0.0	10,400	0.0	5	15	20	0.19	10,500	0.0	10,600	0.0	13,000	0.0
doubly-affiliated	-61,100	-0.2	-243,541	-0.5	-359,966	-0.6	-174	-6,045	-6,219	1.61	-407,544	-0.7	-422,160	-0.7	-324,000	-0.6
disaffiliated	-50,000	-0.2	-3,545,000	-6.6	-9,009,634	-15.8	-4,345	-66,522	-70,867	0.76	-9,460,770	-16.5	-9,718,300	-17.0	-10,000,000	-19.5
Trans-megabloc groupings																
Evangelicals	20,000	0.1	345,000	0.6	335,000	0.6	162	338	500	0.15	340,316	0.6	340,000	0.6	360,000	0.7
Pentecostals/Charismatics	0	0.0	377,000	0.7	3,900,000	6.8	1,881	26,119	28,000	0.70	4,061,138	7.1	4,180,000	7.3	4,614,300	9.0
Great Commission Christians	**6,600,000**	**20.0**	**16,146,000**	**30.0**	**23,920,000**	**42.0**	**11,536**	**18,539**	**30,075**	**0.13**	**24,082,000**	**42.0**	**24,220,748**	**42.3**	**22,046,000**	**43.0**
Nonreligious	50,000	0.2	4,950,000	9.2	7,050,000	12.4	3,400	45,119	48,519	0.67	7,402,800	12.9	7,535,191	13.2	7,300,000	14.2
Atheists	10,000	0.0	1,179,000	2.2	1,820,000	3.2	878	13,628	14,506	0.77	1,900,000	3.3	1,965,060	3.4	1,960,000	3.8
Muslims	1,000	0.0	43,000	0.1	600,000	1.1	289	7,088	7,377	1.17	630,000	1.1	673,771	1.2	900,000	1.8
Chinese folk-religionists	0	0.0	0	0.0	41,000	0.1	20	263	283	0.67	42,800	0.1	43,833	0.1	70,000	0.1
Jews	35,000	0.1	37,000	0.1	41,000	0.1	20	-756	-736	-1.96	33,800	0.1	33,640	0.1	30,000	0.1
New-Religionists	0	0.0	0	0.0	11,500	0.0	6	48	54	0.46	11,800	0.0	12,041	0.0	16,000	0.0
Baha'is	0	0.0	4,200	0.0	5,000	0.0	2	66	68	1.29	5,300	0.0	5,681	0.0	8,000	0.0
Buddhists	0	0.0	2,000	0.0	4,100	0.0	2	20	22	0.52	4,200	0.0	4,320	0.0	6,000	0.0
Hindus	0	0.0	0	0.0	2,000	0.0	1	42	43	1.96	2,200	0.0	2,429	0.0	5,000	0.0
Ethnoreligionists	0	0.0	0	0.0	1,800	0.0	1	20	21	1.08	1,900	0.0	2,005	0.0	4,000	0.0
Other religionists	1,000	0.0	10,000	0.0	9,000	0.0	4	45	49	0.53	9,200	0.0	9,488	0.0	12,000	0.0
World A (unevangelized persons)	33,000	0.1	269,109	0.5	399,161	0.7	192	3,607	3,799	0.91	458,702	0.8	458,384	0.8	666,510	1.3
World B (evangelized non-Christians)	64,000	0.2	5,955,940	11.1	9,186,239	16.1	4,431	61,976	66,407	0.68	9,585,140	16.7	9,829,190	17.1	9,644,490	18.8
World C (Christians)	32,903,000	99.7	47,596,800	88.4	47,437,600	83.2	22,866	-65,583	-42,717	-0.09	47,294,000	82.5	47,010,426	82.1	40,959,000	79.9
Country's population	**33,000,000**	**100.0**	**53,821,850**	**100.0**	**57,023,000**	**100.0**	**27,489**	**0**	**27,489**	**0.05**	**57,337,843**	**100.0**	**57,298,000**	**100.0**	**51,270,000**	**100.0**

Continued opposite

Country Table 1–concluded

COLUMNS, ROWS.
For meanings and definitions, see Codebook (Part 3). Note that, by definition, total 'Christians' = professing + crypto-Christians, which also = affiliated + unaffiliated Christians, and also = Great Commission Christians + latent Christians. Percentages may not always total exactly, due to rounding.

CENSUSES.
1931: 99.6% Roman Catholics. The religion question has generally not been asked in government censuses.

POLLS.
A number of public-opinion polls and sample surveys since 1940 have included religion. *Religious preference.* February 1970: 90% Roman Catholics, 9% nonreligious and atheists, 1% Protestants. Some results for practice are given below.

NOTES ON RELIGIONS
AFFILIATED. By adding up diocesan totals in *Annuario Pontificio* (as is done in Table 2 below), it may been seen that (as is shown in the table above) the Roman Catholic Church in 1995 claimed 97.7% of the total population as affiliated members, on the grounds that those numbers were, or had once been, baptized Catholics and were still on the church's rolls. However, as elaborated below, in 1995 over 400,000 were also Protestants or other Christians and so were doubly-affiliated, and over 9 million regarded themselves as having disaffiliated completely from Christianity and were now nonreligious (agnostics) and atheists. Subtracting these 2 groups from the aggregate totals claimed by the churches produces the figures on the line 'affiliated' i.e. 47.2 million distinct individuals in 1995.
ATHEISTS. Partito Comunista Italiano (PCI) legal; split on Sino-Soviet issue. Of Communist party members, 20% are estimated to be professing atheists, 40% nonreligious, and 40% professing Catholics (including a number of priests and nuns), this latter despite clear statements in 1975 by the pope and the Italian Episcopal Conference that 'One cannot be simultaneously Marxist and Christian' (CEI, 15 December 1975). Of Communist voters, 30% are agnostics, 70% Catholics. The highest % Communist vote is in the former papal states, due to their long anti-clerical history. The south with its depressed rural areas also has a high % Communist vote but this is found together with the highest traditional religious practice (processions, etc).
BAHA'IS. La Fede Baha'i. Entered before 1921. Local spiritual assemblies: 1964, 16; 1973, 28, including centers in 15 cities; increasing by 1996 to 51 LSAs.
BUDDHISTS. In 5 centers. As well as the Associazione Buddista Italiana (HQ Florence), there are Tantric centers and a Centro di Illuminazione Lamaista (in Rome).
DISAFFILIATED. This term is used here to describe dechristianized persons who, although baptized Roman Catholics and therefore regarded by the Catholic Church as still affiliated to it (and hence enumerated in Table 2 as such), have recently withdrawn or disaffiliated themselves completely from Christianity and now profess to be either nonreligious (agnostics) or atheists. Because their statistics represent a duplication, they are shown in the table above as a negative quantity (with a minus sign). The vast majority of these 8.6 million or so persons in 1995 are in and around the so-called 'Red region' in the northeast, the heavily-communist regions of Emilia-Romagna, Lombardia, Veneto, Marche, Umbria, and part of Tuscany, where polls show that at least 4% of the population are militant atheists and about 20% profess to be nonreligious or have no religion. Despite this, Catholic dioceses claim virtually the whole population. The table above incorporates all of these data and interpretations.
DOUBLY-AFFILIATED. The term covers those affiliated to, or claimed by, both the Catholic Church and also a church termed Evangelica by state or society (Protestant, Anglican, marginal Protestant) or a Catholic (non-Roman) or Orthodox church, i.e. baptized Catholics who have recently become Evangelicals or others. Because their statistics represent a duplication, they are shown in the table as a negative quantity (with a minus sign).
JEWS. In 22 communities, mainly in Rome, Milan, Florence and Trieste. Ashkenazis in the north, Sefardis in central Italy.
MUSLIMS. Mainly North African Arab immigrants, also including 25,000 refugees after World War II from Albania, Bulgaria, Hungary, Yugoslavia, 15,000 university students of various nationalities, diplomats, and technical personnel.
OTHER RELIGIONISTS. Small numbers adhering to a large number of groups, including Theosophy, Rosicrucianism (Rosacroce, with 4 AMORC centers), Alaya, Yogasangha and others. Freemasons in Italy are, largely, openly hostile to Christianity and operate as a quasi-religion. ISKCON (Hare Krishna) operates 1 centre and a farm; and Ananda Marga has several centers.
PENTECOSTALS/CHARISMATICS. The charismatic renewal began in Rome in 1971 among foreigners, and by 1977 had involved numerous Italian bishops, clergy and nuns. Totals (January 1974): 450 involved adults (over 15 years old) in 7 prayer groups; total charismatic community including children, 1,000. On Pentecost Sunday 1975, the pope addressed and celebrated mass with 20,000 persons (50% charismatics from 58 countries) in St Peter's Basilica in Rome. In January 1976 there were numerous groups in Rome, Turin (200 in 1 group), and over 15 other cities. Regional groups and conferences then began to proliferate; in October 1977, over 2,000 gathered for a regional charismatic conference in Salerno cathedral with widespread radio/TV coverage.
A decade later the CCR was experiencing very large increases. Annual conventions in 1987, 1988, 1989, 1990 all averaged 55,000 attenders (30% aged under 30) and 1,000 priests. In 1993, the 13th National Convention of Renewal in the Spirit, in Rimini, had 35,000 participants. In Rimini 1997 attenders were 45,000. Largest single conference attendances was 200,000. By 1997 there were 1,500 regular prayer groups (young people attending exceed 35,000), with 850 involved priests and 50 bishops and cardinals; also 22 covenant communities.
THIRD-WORLD INDIGENOUS. In about 50 denominations by 1995 (see Table 2).

Great Commission Instrument Panel: status of Italy (for explanation see start of Part 4)

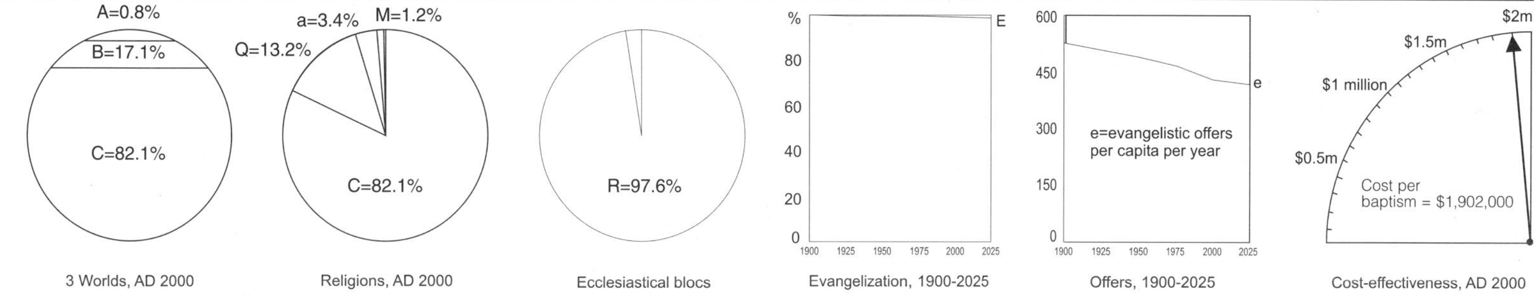

Country status. Next to Greece, Italy has the oldest culture and society in Europe and has played a remarkable role in Western civilization. Its artistic treasures are unparalleled in the Western world. It has a very homogeneous population racially and linguistically. Italy's principal exports include textiles, wine, and fruit.

HUMAN LIFE AND LIBERTY

Human need and development. Italy is a highly developed country, although there are significant differences in the standard of living between the north and south. Economically, northern Italy has more in common with France and Germany than with Italy south of Naples, known as Mezzogiorno. Historically, lack of economic opportunities in the south has been one of the contributory causes for large scale emigration to the United States and South America. Efforts by post-World War II governments to promote the economic development of the south have not been entirely successful. With its entry into the European Union, Italy has lost many of the peculiarities that marked its economy in the 19th and early 20th centuries.

Human rights and freedom. Italian Constitution guarantees respect for all human rights and for the integrity of the person. Police procedures are carefully controlled by law and judicial oversight. A revised Code of Criminal Procedure which entered into force in 1989 provides for a more adversarial system designed to promote speedier trials. There is no censorship, and although laws against obscenity and defamation exist on the statute books, they are rarely invoked. In fact, Italian media publish pornographic materials with impunity. There is no legal discrimination against any minority. However, the rise in immigration of North Africans has led to racial incidents in which skinheads rough up foreigners. Gypsies also suffer periodically from violent attacks. There are sporadic incidents of anti-Semitism. Women's rights are protected by the prime minister's Office on the Status of Women.

Human environment. Lax enforcement of environmental laws has led to deterioration of both air and water. Sulfur dioxide emissions are a threat to Italy's historic monuments. Coastal waters and inland rivers, such as the Po, Adige, and Reno, are heavily polluted.

NON-CHRISTIAN RELIGIONS

Spiritism continues to exist in Italy, especially among southern peasants. It is a remnant of the old religion (la vecchia religione) with its emphasis on magic and spirit communication, as well as a strong belief in fate (destino) believed to be controllable by magical practices. The most renowned medium in Italian history was Eusapie Polladino who plied her art in Naples at the turn of the century, but other lesser-known figures exist in many Italian villages. Today the practices of traditional and pagan religion are so intertwined with Catholicism, especially its religious festivals and veneration of saints, that it is impossible to separate the two. Indeed virtually all spiritists claim also to be Catholics.

Islam is the professed religion of some 675,000 Muslims (AD 2000), the majority of whom are immigrant workers from North Africa. The construction of a mosque in Rome, long opposed by the Vatican in its concern to maintain the 'special character' of the city as the world enter of Catholicism in accordance with the concordat of 1929, was finally sanctioned by the Holy See in 1974, with the proviso that specific conditions concerning its location and external dimensions be observed. A mosque flanked by a Muslim cultural center was built on the edge of the city in the mid 1980s. A restored Roman Catholic church was given to Muslims for a mosque in Palermo in 1990. Rome already has 3 Islamic organizations: the Islamic Cultural Center of Italy (Centro Islamico Culturale d'Italia), the Islamic Union in the West (Unione Islamica in Occidente) and the Center for Islamic Publications and Studies (Centro Editoriale Studi Islamici, CESI). The first 2 provide social services to Muslims, while the latter is an independent body begun in 1972 with the aim of making Islam better known and providing opportunities for dialogue with Christianity, in order to further understanding, justice, and peace. It produces a bulletin entitled CESI: Agenzia d'Informazione Islamic.

Judaism is represented in 22 communities with a total of 33,000 members in AD 2000. The number declined during the fascist period from 47,485 Jews in 1931 to 35,146 in 1939. Jews were forced out of public employment and those who had entered the country after 1919 were forced to leave. In 1943, Jews of the north and center, where the Germans had gained control, were systematically seized, and more than 1,000 were exterminated at Auschwitz. At the end of the war, there were only 29,117 left in the country. Of some 26,300 Jewish refugees from central and eastern Europe who passed through Italy, only a few remained permanently. The civil rights of Jews were restored after the war, and they received support as immigrants from Libya, Egypt and other countries of the Middle East as well as from certain European countries, particularly Hungary.

The principal Jewish communities are located in Rome (with 20,000), Milan (8,000), Florence (1,400), and Trieste (1,200), with very few found in southern Italy. There is also in Rome a very small community of Jews of the Italian rite dating back to pre-Christian times, whose influence is evident in the liturgy of the Sefardic synagogues of Rome. All Italian synagogues are traditional and the 2 principal rabbinical schools are in Rome and Turin. The Jewish educational system is recognized by the state and follows the official program in addition to accenting Jewish concerns. The principal coordinating organization is the Union of Italian Israelite Communities (Unione delle Communita Israelitiche Italiane) in Rome which organizes cultural activities and represents Jewish interests before government. Religious matters are under the jurisdiction of the Italian Rabbinical Council. In Milan is located the Center for Contemporary Hebrew Documentation (Centro di Documentazione Ebraica Contemporanea) which undertakes research concerning anti-Semitic persecutions and Jewish participation in the war-time Resistance.

Buddhism is also present. Although still sporadic, the Communita Buddista Italiana is in the process of formation. The following groups and study centers are active: Zendo Rinzai in Rome; Zen Soto in Milan; Center for Zen Buddhist Studies on the island of Murano near Venice; Ljanna Tibetan Buddhist Center in Rome; and Association for Buddhist Studies in Turin.

Country summary. Worlds A, B, C by ethnolinguistic peoples, cities, and major civil divisions in Italy.

	PEOPLES							CITIES							CIVIL DIVISIONS						
World	Num	Pop 2000	C%	Christians	E%	U%	Unevangelized	Num	Pop 2000	C%	Christians	E%	U%	Unevangelized	Num	Pop 2000	C%	Christians	E%	U%	Unevangelized
A	4	67,961	0.49	330	37	63	42,613	0	0	0.00	0	0	0	0	0	0	0.00	0	0	0	0
B	7	718,471	6.71	48,232	59	41	296,859	0	0	0.00	0	0	0	0	0	0	0.00	0	0	0	0
C	49	56,511,458	82.95	46,873,584	100	0	97,514	115	26,293,551	80.22	21,092,152	99	1	270,402	20	57,297,886	81.89	46,922,140	99	1	436,987
Total	**60**	**57,297,890**	**81.89**	**46,922,146**	**99**	**1**	**436,986**	**115**	**26,293,551**	**80.22**	**21,092,152**	**99**	**1**	**270,402**	**20**	**57,297,886**	**81.89**	**46,922,140**	**99**	**1**	**436,987**

Buddhist Dalai Lama greets pope Paul VI in Rome.

CHRISTIANITY

Christianity came to Rome prior to the first visits of either the apostles Peter or Paul. During the first 2 centuries, periodic persecutions against Christians took place, as internal conflicts and barbarian invasions increased. In 324, the emperor Constantine officially recognized Christianity as the state religion and moved his capital to Constantinople, the division between the eastern and western Roman empire being completed by 395. As Lombards and Goths continued to push from the north, Rome was sacked and the emperor deposed in 476. Theological disputes, exemplified by Arianism and Manicheism, further weakened the structure of Christianity, while such northern bishops as Ambrose of Milan (374) contributed to the strengthening of the western church and Benedict of Nursia (c500) initiated monasticism in the west. In 752, the Roman pope appealed to Pepin of France for protection, and in 800 Charlemagne was crowned Holy Roman emperor. Sicily and southern Italy fell to the Muslims, while Hungarians began pressing from the northeast. Otto I of Germany reestablished the Holy Roman empire in 962, and from then until the Napoleonic invasion of 1796, Italy was the scene of constant power conflicts between the papacy and the growing political powers to the north: Germans and Normans during the 11th and 12th centuries, French during the 13th and 14th centuries, Spanish during the 15th and 16th centuries, followed by the Austrian Hapsburgs. Such city-states as Venice, Bologna and Florence, which became flourishing centers of trade and the arts largely as a result of the Crusades, also entered into the power struggle.

The beginning of the second millennium AD saw the final separation of Greek and Roman Christianity (1054) and the rise of such western pre-Reformation movements as that of Peter Waldo (1173) and his Waldenses in southeastern France and northern Italy. With France's reascendency, the papacy was taken to Avignon in 1309, and this was followed by the schism of rival popes during 1378-1417. The success of Luther and Calvin in the 16th century contributed to the growth of the Waldenses in northern Italy during the 16th century, but this was quickly extinguished by the Counter-Reformation following the Council of Trent (1545-1563) and new reforming bodies, the Capuchins (1525) and Jesuits (1540).

Following the Napoleonic conquest (1796-1814), the Austrian Hapsburgs again attempted to reestablish the power of Italy's former ruling families, but the Risorgimento movement continued to grow throughout the century, resulting in the eventual unification of Italy under Victor Emmanuel I in 1870 and the emergence of the Holy See as a state separate from Italy. The first Protestant missionaries began to enter Italy during the 1860s.

CATHOLIC CHURCH. In Italy, 99% of the population are baptized Roman Catholics, 95% of all children receive first communion, 82% receive confirmation and 99.5% are married in the church, though this latter figure is beginning to decrease. Italy is thus a country with a fundamentally Catholic culture, insofar as this religion historically and psychologically forms the foundation for the life of the people. While these figures demonstrate fidelity to many traditional religious rites, other statistics raise questions regarding the degree of Catholic practice. Only 6% take communion every Sunday, 50% of the children are given no catechetical instruction, and 30% of the population do not receive the sacrament of extreme unction before death. Of those attending Sunday mass, 41% are under 17 years of age and 31% are over 65, with the majority of the 28% in between being women. For the most part, those attending Sunday mass are farmers, artisans, technicians, and clerks. The almost total absence of manual workers and the high proportion of middle-income participants suggest a certain identification of Catholicism with the bourgeois classes.

In a survey of the subcultures within Italian Catholicism, S. Burgalassi distinguishes 5 strata of society: (1) the indifferent subculture, representing a major and growing portion of the population (55-60%), mostly men (77%) and adults (75%) of higher income and education (55%), found primarily in cities (72%) in the center of the country (64%) and the north (11%), which is more agnostic than opposed to religion and pays virtually no attention to the church or what it says; (2) of mostly rural people (93%), of advanced years (60% over 50 years of age), with modest cultural attainment (58%) and generally reduced income, who are characterized by high weekly mass attendance (70-75%), attachment to private devotions, utilitarian attitudes, fatalism (especially in the south), conservatism and an absence of social involvement; in addition to a large number of priests (44%) who are extremely traditional and legalistic in attitude; (3) the official subculture, including 15% of the population and 46% of all priests, who are realistically oriented to the present, obedient to pope and bishops, who adjust to change in social and religious life and advocate reforms in church life and organization; (4) the atheistic subculture, consisting of 5% of all Italians and about 20% of university students (27% of the Catholic University of Milan), who are predominantly male (92%), adult (78%), urban (78%), upper class (64%) with higher income (60%), located in the center (54%) and north (31%) of Italy, whose individual and social involvement is commendable but whose religious practice, if any, is sporadic; and (5) the prophetic subculture, including about 5% of the population and 10% of all clergy, consisting mostly of students and workers who are mainly young idealists (70%), oriented to the future and actively engaged in work for others (86%) against misery and social injustice for the sake of the gospel.

There has also been a breaking up of the monolithic nature of the church in Italy, in part due to Vatican II which permitted existing divergent forces to come to the surface and in part the result of deep socio-political changes which took place in Italian society during the 1960s. Different controversial currents have thus developed during the past decade, including the Italian Catholic University Federation (FUCI) at universities and the Christian Association of Italian Workers (ACLI) among workers. They bear witness to the pressure for greater latitude within the church for such movements and more freedom of choice in temporal matters. The 11th Congress of ACLI, held at Turin in 1969, marked for Italian Catholics an open manifestation of a new concern for social problems. An example of change in political attitudes was the emergence of a block of 'Catholics for No' opposing the repeal of the law permitting divorce, in contrast to other Catholic groups and the official church which urged its repeal. In the past, the Italian Catholic Church exercised great political power due to its role in the Christian Democratic party, its function in education and public assistance programs, its privileged legal position as defined in the concordat and the presence in Italy of the Holy See with its diplomatic pomp and international prestige. However, the unexpected size of the 'No' vote in the 1974 anti-divorce referendum demonstrated the new limits which Catholic laity intend to exercise in reference to the political influence of the episcopate and the Christian Democratic party. The latter is no longer able to lay claim to being the sole party of Catholics.

It is difficult to define precisely the control exercised by the Holy See over Italian Catholic life, since authority is often used in ways scarcely perceptible outwardly. Nevertheless, it is clear that the Holy See exerts its influence on at least 3 levels: through its geographic proximity, which permits permanent surveillance and immediate interventions; through the concordat, which created several power zones administered more or less directly by the Holy See; and especially through the Italian Episcopal Conference whose president is named by the pope as primate of the Italian church.

A final characteristic of Italian Catholicism is the exceptionally high number of dioceses (283) as well as the presence in Italy of the most prestigious diocese of them all, that of Rome. In the teeth of local and conservative opposition, efforts have been under way since Vatican II to reduce the number of dioceses by the pope's refusal to nominate new bishops for the smaller ones. By 1974, 22 had already been eliminated and another 20 were about to be removed, but there still remained 48 dioceses with less than 50,000 residents, found mostly in the center and in the south, and 69 with from 50,000 to 100,000, all well below the Catholic world average size of 200,000 for a diocese. Of the large dioceses, 88 had from 100,000 to 200,000, and only 25 dioceses had more than 400,000 residents, of which 4 exceeded one million (Milan, Naples, Rome and Turin). In contrast, some parishes in the suburbs of Rome, had up to 80,000 residents. Twenty years later, the total of dioceses in Italy was still as high as 227, which illustrates how tradition, history, and lay intransigence can defeat even papal and curial pressures for reform.

Chiesa Cattolica in Italia. Cathedral of Archdiocese of Pisa with (*left*) baptistery and (*right*) campanite (the Leaning Tower).

The diocese of Rome itself has a particular status. The pope as bishop of the diocese is responsible for its administration and spiritual direction. In reality, the pope, engrossed as he is in other responsibilities, delegates his powers to a cardinal-vicar who is responsible for the administration of the diocese. The offices of the vicariate are in the city of Rome, not in the Vatican, which is itself an integral part of the diocese. The power and influence of the Catholic Church is at its most visible in the diocese of Rome, with its 17 pontifical universities, institutes and faculties of theology; its 89 ecclesiastical institutes of education and instruction for secular ore religious seminarians; and its 10 pontifical academies. According to the directory of the diocese of Rome, 5,127 clergy (cardinals, archbishops, bishops, diocesan, and regular priests, approximately one-third being of foreign nationality) lived and worked in Rome in 1972. Of this number, 1,173 priests were destined for the parish ministry, though only 463 were locally incardinated and dependent directly on the vicariate. There were relatively few religious vocations from Rome itself, 241 of the 463 incardinated priests having come from other localities. The number of parishes has now been raised to 249, 53% being under religious priests. Their population varies from 2,000 to 82,000 residents, with 65 suburban parishes having more than 20,000 inhabitants. The reorganization of the diocese of Rome began some time ago and should ultimately resolve many of its pastoral problems, including the reallocation of its clergy. A socio-religious study in 1971 indicated that Rome had one of the highest proportions of Sunday mass attenders in European cities, averaging between 35% and 40% every Sunday. It also revealed, however, that actual participation was weak, with only 10-25% of those attenders receiving communion.

The Holy See has diplomatic relations with Italy and in AD 2000 is represented to government and the Catholic hierarchy by a nuncio residing in Rome.

PROTESTANT CHURCHES. The Evangelical Waldensian Church is the oldest Protestant denomination in Italy and still the largest of the non-Pentecostal bodies. Originating in southern France during the 12th century through the preaching of Peter Waldi, the so-called Poor Men of Lyons spread across the border and established themselves as a people's church with local autonomy in the valleys of Turin in northwestern Italy. By the middle of the 16th century, the church had grown to more than 100,000 members, but severe persecution under the Counter-Reformation during the next hundred years reduced the Waldenses to less than 5,000. By 1900, they had built up their community again to over 20,000. A further period of decline during the early part of this century has been reversed.

Chiesa Evangelica Valdese. Open-air Waldensian service. Founded in 1173, Waldensians are Italy's oldest Protestants.

Lutheranism, which dates back to the Reformation, grew among Germans in the north during the 18th century, but only in recent years have efforts been made by Lutherans to evangelize Italians. The Christian Church of the Brethren is an indigenous body which traces its origin back to small groups of converts meeting together in Florence in 1833. Working under the guidance of lay elders without ordained clergy, their strength remains in northwest Piemonte, where they have recently begun tent campaigns to develop new assemblies.

The 1860s saw the arrival of Protestant missionaries from England: Methodists in 1859, Baptists in 1863, the first Adventists in 1864 and later the Salvation Army in 1886. These were followed during the next decade by their counterparts from America. British Baptists turned their churches over to American Southern Baptists in 1920, and in 1956 the Italian Baptist Union was formed. The majority of its pastors are nationals, but few churches are as yet self-supporting. Following an initial evangelistic ministry, Methodists began directing their efforts to developing institutions. The British and American Methodist missions worked in close cooperation prior to their merger in 1946, and the Evangelical Methodist Church of Italy became autonomous in 1962. Social and ecumenical concerns are carried on at present, but with little increase in membership.

Seventh-day Adventist work was begun by a converted Polish Roman Catholic priest, and Adventists established their first organized mission in 1877. By 1909, 44 converts had been made and the church has continued to grow slowly during the present century. Its publishing house quadrupled its output between 1950 and 1968, and its Bible correspondence courses and radio programs are widely known.

The Assemblies of God were introduced in 1908 with the return of an American immigrant. With the aid of other returned immigrants, membership increased rapidly throughout the south, numbering about 5,000 in 1934, at the time the fascist regime imposed its severest persecutions, prohibiting services, and imprisoning pastors. When work was reopened in 1944, there were 120 churches, 129 having been lost. However, by 1955, they had increased again to over 350 with an adult membership of 50,000, expanding to 600 churches with 100,000 members by 1961. Expansion continued at the same pace through the next decade. The Assemblies of God are by far the most important Protestant church in Italy at the present time. In 1957, another Pentecostal body, the International Evangelical Church, was formed. Becoming a member of the WCC, this denomination has grown rapidly, more by drawing into its membership small unaffiliated Pentecostal groups than by making new converts.

Independents. Pentecostal pastor Mrs. R. Vagnavelli leads in worship.

Protestant groups entering Italy since World War II include the Churches of Christ (1947), Church of the Nazarene (1948), and Mennonites (1949). The most successful has been the Churches of Christ, which reached a membership of 2,000 in 15 years. In spite of severe persecution in the early years, rapid growth has resulted from its policy of church planting and its use of Italian evangelists.

OTHER CHURCHES. Anglicans, under the Anglican Church in Europe and in the diocese of Gibraltar of the Church of England, have maintained chaplaincy services in Italy since 1559; and the New Apostolic Church has built up a large German-speaking constituency since its arrival after World War II. Several Orthodox communities are also present: Armenian, Greek, Russian, and Serbian. The largest is the Greek Orthodox Church which is part of the Ecumenical Patriarchate of Constantinople, under the archbishop of London. Marginal churches include Christian Scientists, Mormons, and Jehovah's Witnesses, the largest being the latter.

Pentecostals/Charismatics. *Top.* Catholics in Renewal exceed 3,300,000 in Italy. *Lower.* Protestants in Renewal exceed 350,000.

Renewal movements. In the 1990s the Pentecostal/Charismatic Renewal continued to spread rapidly across most older churches, and numbered over 4,180,000 adherents (of whom 8% were Pentecostals, 82% Charismatics, and 11% Independents).

Art and architecture. There are few countries in the world that can match Italy for the wealth of its architectural and artistic heritage, and the vast majority of these buildings and art are of Christian origin. Beginning in the north, the most famous churches are the Cathedral of San Lorenzo in Genoa, one of the the city's 400 churches and the Cathedral of San Giovanni which contains the Holy Shroud in Turin. Milan is noted as the place where the Edict of Milan was issued in 313, and where Bishop St Ambrose baptized St Augustine. It contains 3 great churches: San Lorenzo, the fourth century church with the Aquilino Chapel, Sant' Ambrogio, a perfect example of Italian Romanesque, and the gigantic Duomo (cathedral), Christendom's fourth largest church with 135 marble spires and 2,245 marble statues. In the crypt of the Duomo is the crypt of St Charles Borromeo. In Verona are the Church of Sant' Anastasia, a model of Italian Gothic, and San Zeno Maggiore, a fine Romanesque-Lombard, with its graceful campanile. In its crypt is the tomb of St Zeno and on the high altar one of Mantegna's masterpiece triptychs. Padua is celebrated as the home of St Anthony of Padua, a saint revered around the world. His basilica-tomb is venerated as a shrine. Also in the city is the Scrovegni Chapel (also called Arena Chapel) with the incomparable frescoes of Giotto on the walls. Venice, once the Wall Street of Europe, was once more powerful than even Rome. The heart of Venice is San Marco, opening on a piazza that bears its name, considered the most beautiful in the world. Built in 829-832, to enshrine the body of St Mark which had been carried hither from Alexandria in Egypt, its was rebuilt in the 11th century and plundered in the 13th. Many of the Venetian churches contain priceless masterpieces by one or more of the city's famous native artists. For example, the church of the Frari contains 2 of Titian's masterpieces and the Scuolo San Rocco contains 56 Tintorettos. Across the Grand Canal from San Marco are 2 other great churches. San Giorgio Maggiore is a masterpiece of the Palladium style which contains 2 of Tintoretto's most famous works, the Last Supper and the Gathering of Manna. Santa Maria della Salute (St Mary of Salvation) is an octagonal baroque structure. The island of Torcello contains the fine octagonal church of Santa Fosca and a seventh-century Byzantine cathedral. Murano contains the Byzantine Santi Maria e Donato and the Renaissance San Pietro Martire. In Ravenna, which was the capital of the Western Empire under Honorius, is the San Vitale, built under Emperor Justinian, with its vast octagonal dome and panels of Justinian and his wife Theodora. Within the church is the tomb of empress Galla Placidia, sister of Honorius. The Cathedral of Ravenna contains 2 baptisteries, one Byzantine and the other built by the Arian Theodoric. The church of San Francesco has the sarcophagus of St Liberius with 22 columns of Greek marble serving as the altar. The church adjoins the grave of Dante, who died here in 1321 in exile from his native Florence. There are 2 churches dedicated to Ravenna's martyr, St Apollinaris. Within the city is Sant' Apollinare Nuovo, with its resplendent mosaics and the other, built near the former port of Classis, with its apse mosaic portraying Christ surrounded by the symbols of the 4 evangelists. In Bologna, the major shrines are St Dominic, and a composite of 8 churches known as San Stefano. Among them the church of Calvary contains the tomb of St Petronius, begun in 1390. Florence, the capital of Tuscany, is the greatest center of Renaissance art. Its cathedral is the Santa Maria dei Fiore (Saint Mary of the Flowers), begun in 1296 and completed when Brunelleschi's dome crowned it in 1434. It contains the most renowned group of statuary in the world, Michelangelo's last sculpture, The Descent from the Cross, in which the sculptor portrays himself as Joseph of Arimathea. Alongside the cathedral is Giotto's immense campanile and across the piazza is the baptistery, of whose 3 doors, 2 —the north and east —were done by Ghiberti, and one —the south —was done by Pisano. Michelangelo is believed to have said that the east door was 'worthy to be the gates of Paradise'. Florence has countless other churches, all of them masterpieces of one kind or another. Santa Croce, the Franciscan church, contains the burial places of Michelangelo, Rossini, Galileo, Machiavelli, and others, as well as paintings by Giotto. Adjoining the church is the Pazzi Chapel by Brunelleschi. The Monastery of San Marco, the former Dominican friary where Savonarola and St Antoninus lived, contains many of Fra Angelico's work, including the Annunciation. The Church of San Lorenzo contains 2 magnificent sacristies: one by Brunelleschi, Donatello, Lippo Lippi, and Verrocchio, and the other by Michelangelo with his statues Day, Night, Dawn and Twilight, and also Madonna and Child. Santa Maria Novella contains paintings by Masaccio, Ghirlandaio, and Uccello. High above Florence is the Romanesque church of San Miniato al Monte, one of the gems of the Middle Ages. In Fiesole, on the other side, is the church of San Domenico with its classic paintings by Fra Angelico. In nearby Pisa and Lucca are dazzling white cathedrals. Siena is the second most important town in Tuscany after Florence. Its Gothic cathedral is lavish in its ornate details. Its pulpit was created by Nicola Pisano, the father of Renaissance sculpture. In the church of San Domenico are the relics of St Catherine, who persuaded Pope Gregory XI to return to Rome from Avignon. Near Siena is the Benedictine monastery of Monte Oliveto. In Umbria, between Florence and Rome are the cathedrals and churches of Perugia and Orvieto. Also in Umbria is Assisi, renowned for the shrine to its most famous son, St Francis. His basilica, with its superimposed churches, bears the marks of the artistic genius of Giotto. Below the town is the place where St Francis died, Santa Maria degli Angeli, with its Porziuncula chapel, as well as Eremo degli Carceri (Hermitage of the Prisons) where he loved to pray. There are 2 other Franciscan sites: the oratory of San Damiano, where the crucified Lord spoke to St Francis and the church of Santa Chiara (St Clare) where she is buried. Rome is the 'first of cities', as John Cardinal Newman described it, and it is to an even greater extent, the first of all Catholic cities. It is a city of domes, the largest being the great dome of St Peter towering over the city. The Piazza San Pietro is a vast ovoid atrium built by Bernini with 284 enormous columns in triple rows, 2 fountains and a central cross-crowned obleisk. The piazza is so vast that it will hold 500,000 people, and the facade, added by Moderno is so large that it hides the dome from the piazza. Within Vatican proper is the Sistine Chapel with its superb paintings by Perugino, Botticelli and others, and dominated by Michelangelo's Last Judgment behind the altar and the colossal ceiling frescoes. In nearby apartments are many of Raphael's paintings, such as the Disputa, the School of Athens, the Transfiguration, and the Coronation of the Blessed Virgin. In the Pio-Clementino Museum are 2 famous statues, the Laocoon and Apollo Belvedere. In the Vatican Library are a hoard of priceless manuscripts, including the Codex Vaticanus. Rome's second most famous church is the tomb and basilica of St Paul, St-Paul's-Outside-the-Walls, which was rebuilt following a disastrous fire and reconsecrated by Pius IX in 1854. St Ignatius Loyola took his final vows in one of its chapels. There are 2 other basilicas: St John Lateran, officially the pope's cathedral, and Santa Maria Maggiore. The latter contains the finest mosaics and frescoes in Rome and its ceiling is adorned with the first gold brought back by Columbus from America. The church of San Pietro in Vincoli (St Peter-in-Chains) is best known for Michelangelo's statue of Moses. Another ancient church is Santa Maria in Cosmedin. The basilica of San Clemente is fascinating for its triple level, the first being the house of St Clement, one of the earliest popes, the second a church built in the time of Constantine, and the third constructed in the 11th and 12th centuries. Another church built over a house is that of the fifth-century SS John and Paul, which also contains the remains of St Paul of the Cross, founder of the Passionists. The most ancient complete building in Rome is the Pantheon, used as a church since Pope Boniface IV consecrated it in 1609 to Our Lady and All the Martyrs. Built by Agrippa in 27 B C it was given its present facade by Hadrian about 130. As venerable as the churches are the Catacombs which are several miles long. The most celebrated of these catacombs are those of St Callixtus, St Cecilia, St Domitilla, and St Sebastian. The Mamertine Prison is found at the entrance of San Giuseppe dei Falegnami (St Joseph of the Carpenters). The churches of St Pudentiana and St Praxedes also date from apostolic times although the present structures were built some 4 or 5 centuries later. The latter is believed to be the site of the house where St Peter received hospitality. The church of Madonna dei Monti (Madonna of the Mountains) on Via dei Serpenti, is a haven for the homeless where St Benedict Joseph Labre is buried. The church of Santa Croce was built to house the relic which St Helena, mother of Constantine, brought back from the Holy Land. Rebuilt a number of times, it comes alive on Good Friday when the relic is exposed for the veneration of the faithful. There are 3 churches associated with the Jesuit Order: The Gesu, built by Vignola, houses the Society's principal shrines, the image of Our Lady of the Wayside, the altar above the grave of St Ignatius Loyola, and the tomb of St Andrew Bobola. The church of St Ignatius contains a gigantic fresco in the dome showing St Ignatius entering heaven. It also encloses the remains of SS Robert Bellarmine, Aloysius Gonzaga, and John Berchmans. St Stanislaus Kostka is buried in a small church built by Bernini. On Via Aurelia is the mother house of the Brothers of the Christian Schools, where the remains of its founder St John Baptist de la Salle, are buried under a side altar. It was from the Camaldolese monastery in San Gregorio that St Gregory sent St Augustine to convert England. The venerable Byzantine abbey of Grottaferrata in Rocca di Pappa was built by St Nilus in 1004. The pope's summer residence is in Castel Gandolfo. The nearby town of Ostia is immortalized in St Augustine's Confessions. Not far from Tivoli is Subiaco, the birthplace of Western monasticism and of St Benedict. Later he moved to Monte Cassino, midway between Rome and Naples, where he built a monastery that was heavily bombed during World War II but survived. Naples is replete with churches of which the most famous is the cathedral, named after St Januarius, San Gennaro in Italian. It is noted for the strange miracle which takes place twice a year when the saint's blood, kept in a vial, liquifies on the saint's feast day, September 19 and on the first Saturday in May. At Amalfi, on the island of Capri, is the cathedral where the body of Apostle Andrew is reputed to be buried. In Sicily, there are great cathedrals, such as Monreale with its rich mosaics and Cefalu with its Norman cathedral. Throughout Italy there are over a thousand religious museums, one in virtually every town and city, and many with priceless artistic treasures.

Indigenous missions. Italy has been one of the great mission sending countries throughout all of Christian history. In the Roman empire era, Christians were sent all over Europe and North Africa. In the Middle Ages, both Franciscans and Dominicans were sent out in large numbers as foreign missionaries. Today mission sending continues, even from minority Protestant churches.

CHURCH AND STATE

In church-state relations in Italy, it is well to distinguish between the realm of law and that of practice. As far as the law is concerned, relations between the 2 powers are regulated by the Lateran Agreements (Patti Lateranensi) between pope Pius XI and Mussolini on 2 November, 1929 and confirmed by Article 7 of the Republican constitution of 1 January 1948: 'The State and the Catholic Church have each their own independent and sovereign order. Their relations are regulated by the Lateran Agreements. Modifications of the Agreements, when accepted by both parties, do not require a constitutional revision'. Concerning other religions, Article 8 of the constitution stipulates that they 'have the right to organize themselves according to their own statutes, insofar as they are not contrary to Italian law'.

The Lateran Agreements consist of 2 protocols, a treaty and a concordat. The treaty concerns the 'Roman question', the conflict which developed in the 19th century between the new kingdom of Italy and the papacy. At the time, the struggle for unity and independence which culminated in the capture of Rome by Italian troops in 1870 and the royal decree of 1871 making Rome the capital of the kingdom, were seen as placing in jeopardy the Catholic Church, which considered its temporal sovereignty indispensable for the exercise of its divine mission. The Roman question was resolved by the formation of a new pontifical state, small but sovereign, Vatican City, while the problem of reparations was covered by a joint financial convention in the same treaty. The first article of the treaty states: 'Italy recognizes and affirms the principle that the Roman, Apostolic, and Catholic religion is the only religion of the state'. Annex II of the treaty lists the properties of the Holy See in Italy which have the privilege of extraterritoriality with exemption from expropriation and taxes. Annex III lists other properties such as the Gregorian University and the Biblical Institute which without benefit of extraterritoriality, are also exempt from expropriation and taxes.

The purpose of the concordat is 'to regulate the conditions of religion and the Church in Italy'. Its principal stipulations are as follows: (1) the state recognizes Catholic jurisdiction over ecclesiastics and grants its protection (*difesa*) to them when necessary for carrying out their ministerial responsibilities (Article 1, paragraph 1); (2) the state agrees to protect the city of Rome from all that would contradict its sacred character, insofar as it is the seat of the papacy, the center of the Catholic world, and a place of pilgrimage (Article 1, paragraph 2). It was in the application of this second paragraph that the government in 1965 refused to permit the presentation in Rome of the play 'The Vicar' by R. Hochhuth, and that it consulted with the pope in 1973-74 concerning the construction of a mosque in the Eternal City; (3) clergy in charge of souls are excused from military service, even in the case of general mobilization (Article 3); (4) all clergy desiring employment with the state must obtain permission from their diocesan ordinary; if anyone has been suspended, he may not teach nor receive employment which would place him in direct contact with the public (Article 5); (5) clergy accused of common law misdemeanors receive privileged treatment (Article 8); (6) the appointment of military chaplains is subject to the prior consent of the Italian government, which may oppose particular cases and make other appointments (Articles 13 and 15); (7) the state may oppose appointments of particular diocesan bishops and parish priests (Articles 19 and 21); (8) newly appointed bishops must take the oath of fidelity to the head of state (Article 20); (9) clergy benefit from a wage supplement, paid since 1887, to cover deficiencies in ecclesiastical allowances (Article 30).

In Article 34 of the concordat, the state gives civil recognition to marriages performed under canon law, justifying this on the basis of returning to the institution of marriage its 'dignity in conformity with the Catholic traditions' of the Italian people. It renounces all rights to the judicial nullification of marriages, these rights being reserved to ecclesiastical courts. The Holy See, in turn, agrees that civil courts have jurisdiction in cases of separation. Called into question already because of the introduction of divorce in Italy in the Fortuna-Baslini Law of January 1970, Article 34 was for all practical purposes annulled by the results of the referendum on divorce of May 1974, which went against the expressed wishes of Catholic political and ecclesiastical leaders. Only a few bishops invoked freedom of conscience for the faithful; all others as well as the Episcopal Conference campaigned for a 'Yes' vote. The large resulting 'No' vote averaging 59% in each of the 20 civil regions of the country (being largest in the north and center and in the major cities and including these regions considered most Catholic, namely Venice and the south), gives strong support to existing divorce laws in Italy. Prior to the passage of the Fortuna-Baslini Law, non-Catholics were unable to secure annulment of marriage, since such authority lay exclusively with ecclesiastical courts. Article 34 of the concordat was also the basis for the law of June 1929 requiring that non-Catholic clergy wishing to secure civil recognition for marriages performed by them should in each and every case request through their church president such authority from the state, the choice of celebrant being left to the discretion of the civil officer. Thus, Protestant pastors were deemed not competent to judge the validity of marriages they themselves celebrated. Despite declarations of its unconstitutionality, this law of 1929 has remained in effect. In August 1972, the first united synod of Waldenesians and Methodists strongly urged its formal abrogation.

Article 36 of the concordat declares that Italy considers as 'fundamental to public education the teaching of Christian doctrine in the form received through the Catholic tradition'. Accordingly, the teaching of the Catholic religion has been made obligatory in the state educational system. The latter pays, in conformity to the law of 5 May 1930, all teachers of religion, to whom are accorded the same rights and duties as other teachers, except that their employment is submitted each year to their bishop for his approval. A law of 28 February 1930, allows for the possibility of other religions offering religious education courses in local schools, provided that parents request them, that there are a sufficient number of pupils and that 'for well-founded reasons' the school chapel is not used for this purpose.

The pre-eminence of the Catholic religion as the 'religion of the State' affects also the Italian penal code, as reflected in a number of decisions of the Court of Appeals. The court affirmed on 29 December 1949, and again on 16 January 1950, that the first article of the Lateran treaty forms the foundation of the penal code. In the same manner, the Constitutional Court declared on 17 December 1958, that the Catholic religion, professed by 'almost all the citizens', 'merits a particular penal protection'. Thus, remaining in effect are Articles 402 and 406 of the Penal Code, which concern the crime of 'offense' (vilipendio) against the religion of the state. These articles stipulate that there is an aggravating circumstance if the offense is directed against a Catholic clergyman, and extenuating circumstance if directed against a non-Catholic sect or one of its ministers. There is also Article 724 which punishes blasphemy.

In practice, although the concordat of 1929 functioned during the whole period of the fascist dictatorship (with some conflicts between the 2 parties, notably on the subject of Catholic Action and the suppression of Catholic youth organizations) and is still in effect, serious differences of opinion concerning church-state relations remain. Article 7 of the constitution , earlier described, was adopted by the Constituent Assembly in March 1947 by a majority of the 2 principal parties, the Christian Democrats and Communists, plus liberals and neo-fascists, against the socialists, republicans, and a few minor parties. The article itself envisaged the possibility of future modifications to the concordat, and this question was taken up for serious discussion at the end of Vatican II. In the course of the debate which quickly became violently polemical, positions crystallized around 2 poles: (1) those who were partisans of revision (Christians, Democrats, Communists, and Neo-Fascists) and who invoked the importance of maintaining the 'religious peace' of Italy, not wishing to go beyond the stage of a bilateral modification of a few clauses as envisaged in the concordat itself; and (2) those who, convinced of the inadequacies of the concordat, were in favor of its complete abolition. Following a favorable vote in the chamber on 5 October 1967, the government appointed (in October 1968) a commission to make a preparatory study. The Holy See gave its approval for the negotiations, and meetings were begun. However, all discussion was interrupted between 1970 and February 1975 because of the introduction of divorce in Italy despite the Holy See's strenuous opposition. In the spring of 1972, several socialist deputies presented to the Chamber of Representatives a proposed law modifying certain articles of the constitution in such a way as to make the concordat unconstitutional.

By 1976, a draft revised concordat had been drawn up and seemed likely to be ratified within a year or two. Although stopping short of full separation of church and state, it removes the original provision recognizing Catholicism as the official state religion, removes the status of Rome as a 'sacred city', and gives parents or students over the age of 16 the option of retaining or eliminating religious education. By thus lessening the chances of conflict between church and state in a secularized Italy, the new concordat is recognized as an acceptable compromise by the Holy See and the Catholic Church.

Relations between the Catholic world and the political world of the Italian parties are extremely complex, today more so than previously. A complicating factor is the socio-political situation of the country, characterized by class conflicts and regional disequilibrium. The situation is also confused by the contradictions and divergent attitudes held within the Catholic world, both at the top and bottom. The ties between the Catholic Church and the Christian Democrats, strong in the past, are less in evidence today. The ability of the Holy See thus to intervene in Italian life remains, through the party is not nearly so significant as previously. While maintaining its identification as Catholic, the party, in pursuing the interests of the middle classes, has created an infrastructure of power which is to an extent autonomous vis-a-vis the church. The Catholic world remains the major support of the party, but it is not alone in this. Efforts to disassociate themselves from the party continue among Catholics, and the hierarchy intervenes with much greater prudence than in the past. The Italian Communist Party (PCI), the second strongest political force in the country and the foremost Communist party in Western Europe, has always given great attention to the Catholic world, seeking to establish ties with it. If in the past the response of the Catholic hierarchy was for the most part negative, culminating in the celebrated excommunication of 1948, today there are less differences between them. The ideological impasse remains, but its practical importance has decreased. Thus, the Episcopal Conference of Emilia has recently sought agreements with leftist civil regional authorities. With the small traditional 'lay' parties, which in the past have been mostly anticlerical, present relations are ambiguous. On the one hand, these parties retain an appearance of anticlericalism, while in practice they support the Catholic Church and the Christian Democrats, which are considered to be a sure and necessary protection against Communism. On the other hand, the church easily accepts these contacts which enable it to maintain its power. In yet another direction, certain sectors of the hierarchy and the Catholic world have contact with the Italian Social Movement (MSI), which has clearly fascist tendencies.

Catechists, nuns with guitars, lay persons, and Protestants lead in worship at Plenary Assembly, SC Propaganda Fide, Rome.

BROADCASTING AND MEDIA

The largest broadcaster is Vatican Radio (described under the Holy See). There are 437 Roman Catholic radio stations with daily programming. In addition, there are numerous local radio stations which carry Protestant radio programs, including programs produced by IBRA, ERF, and *Back to the Bible*. AWR maintains a shortwave radio transmitter in the country which covers much of Europe. Its Rome studio produces Italian-language programs. Shortwave radio programs can also be received from KNLS, TWR (Monaco, Albania), and HCJB (Ecuador).

TBN programs appear throughout Italy in 36 cities (TBNE, Erreuno, Teletevere). There are 37 local Catholic stations. Satellite TV and radio programs are received in English, Arbic, German and Italian.

INTERDENOMINATIONAL ORGANIZATIONS

Protestant interdenominational activities are centered in the Federation of Evangelical Church in Italy (Federazione delle Chiese Evangeliche in Italia), while the principal agency for coordination within the Catholic Church is the Commission for Ecumenism (Commissione per l'Ecumenismo) of the Italian Episcopal Conference. A number of ecumenical centers and organizations are active, of which 17 may be mentioned. (1) International Documentation on the Contemporary Church (IDOC), founded in Rome in 1962, is an independent center, which through research, publications, and symposia seeks to inform the churches concerning international and interconfessional matters of ecumenical interest. (2) Sezione Ecumenico, Patristica Greco-Bizantina S Nicola, founded in Bari in 1969 as a department of the theological faculty of St Thomas Aquinas Pontifical University in Rome, with Catholic and Orthodox students and faculty, has special interest in stimulating Orthodox and Catholic dialogue in the field of patristics and the recovery of an ecclesiology of communion. (3) Centro Pro Unione, founded in Rome in 1968 by Friars of the Atonement (USA), provides opportunities for ecumenical encounter through conferences, study and information. (4) Associazione Cattolica Italiana per l'Oriente Cristiano, founded in Palermo, promotes unity between Catholic and Orthodox churches. (5) Centro Ecumenico Ut Unun Sint, founded in Rome in 1935 by the Catholic religious congregation Pia Societa San Paolo and since 1973 related to the Vatican's Sacred Congregation for the Clergy, is concerned especially for spiritual, doctrinal and pastoral ecumenism and offers biblical and theological correspondence courses for laymen in conjunction with the Lateran Pontifical University. (6) Associazione Internazionale Unitas, founded in Rome in 1945, is a Catholic center for ecumenical spirituality responsible for the creation of a Eucharistic Prayer Center for Christian Unity at the basilica of Santa Maria in Via Lata; it is linked to Unidad Cristiana (Madrid) and Unite Chretienne (Lyons). (7) The Anglican Center (Centro Anglicano) is the representative in Rome of the faith and practice of the Anglican Communion, working for the reconciliation of the Catholic and Anglican communions. (8) Agape Centro Comunitario, founded in Prali in 1943, is an international ecumenical center founded by Waldensian youth with support from the WCC. (9) Comunita Ecumenica di Bose, founded in Magnano in 1968, is an interconfessional Catholic/Protestant community of men and women living the gospel together in common and celibate life while remaining in communion with their own churches. A similar group was formed in Switzerland in 1972. (10) Comunita Evangelical Ecumenica di Ispra-Varese unites members of different Protestant denominations and nationalities who remain faithful to their own confessions. (11) Centro Internazionale della Pace (Studi Ecumenici) was founded in Turin in 1967. (12) Segretariato Attivita Ecumeniche, founded in Rome in 1963, is an association for ecumenical lay training, especially university students. (13) Centro UNO per l'Unita dei Cristiani, founded in Rome in 1960, is a center for ecumenical spirituality, especially for Focolarini. (14) Piccoli Operai Missionari Ecumenici, founded at Riano in 1947, is a pious society of religious and lay personnel of both sexes and all ages and social classes dedicated to union of Christians. Affiliated with the dioceses of Porto and Santa Rufino, it has founded ecumenical communities in Italy, Spain, USA, Chile, and Malta, as well as other prayer and study centers throughout the world. It publishes periodicals and organizes pilgrimages and international conferences. (15) Centro di Studi Ecumenici Giovanni XXIII in Sotto il Monte, Berg, is a Catholic ecumenical study center. (16) Studi Ecumenici is a Catholic institution involved in ecumenical research in Turin. (17) Other Catholic ecumenical centers mostly of local interest which aid visitors of other denominations are: Foyer & Casa Unitas (Bethany Sisters); Centro Ecumenico Santa Rita (Daughters of the Divine Providence of Don Orioni), founded in 1968 in Rome; Centro Ecumenico Nordico (Nordisk Ekumenisk Centrum), for Scandinavians, founded in 1966; Centro Francescano d'Azione Ecumenica (OFM), founded in 1969; Hospitium Oecumenicum di S Damiano (OFM), founded in 1965, in Assisi; Centro Ecumenico Pastorale, for Catholics of the Italo-Albanian rite, founded in 1967 in Lungro, Consenza; and Centro Ecumenico e Universitario San Martion (for university students) at Perugia.

Italy's first ecumenical sanctuary, the St Gregory the Great chapel, which is open to all member churches of the WCC, was dedicated at Assisi in November 1972.

Several agencies are dedicated to improving relations between the Catholic Church and other religions. (1) The Pontifical Institute of Arab Studies (IPEA) was founded in Tunisia in 1960 and transferred to Rome under its present title in 1964. It is directed by White Fathers and offers linguistic studies and training in Islamics for those wishing to specialize, from a missionary of view, in Muslim-Christian dialogue. Classes are in French and Arabic. (2) The International Information Service for Jewish-Christian Relations, founded in Rome in 1965 by a group of bishops and Vatican II experts and at present supervised by the Congregation of Notre-Dame de Sion, has for its purpose the development of mutual understanding and esteem among Christians and Jews. It has a specialized international library in 5 languages, offers a documentation service, publishes Sidic, a review aimed at aiding the development of Judeo-Christian relations throughout the world, sponsors receptions, courses, study sessions and conferences and conducts visits and trips. (3) The Judeo-Christian Fellowship of Florence (Amicizia Ebraico-Cristiana di Firenze) founded in 1851, has members in other Italian cities, conducts conferences and meetings, produces a liaison bulletin and is affiliated with the International Council of Christians and Jews in London. (4) The Institute for Religious Science (Istituto per le Scienze Religiose), founded in Bologna, is an independent center for socio-religious, historical, and theological research. The institute is under the direction of the Association for the Development of Religious Science, founded in 1952, and has its international headquarters in Italy.

FUTURE TRENDS AND PROSPECTS

Secularism and the burgeoning nonreligious movement will likely continue to sap the strength of Roman Catholicism in Italy as Christian affiliation is expected to fall precipitously from near 100% in 1900 to under 80% by 2025. The nonreligious are expected to grow to near 15% of the population in the same period.

The church is likely to continue its decline well into the 21st century, primarily due to increasing secularization. The nonreligious could rise as high as 20% before AD 2050. The immigration of non-Christians is sure also to become significant in the near future.

BIBLIOGRAPHY

'A handbook for church growth in Italy.' A. P. Nucciarone. D.Min. Thesis, Westminster Theological Seminary, Chestnut Hill, PA, 1988. 358p.

Annuario cattolico d'Italia, 1972–1973. Rome: CNEC, 1973.

Annuario evangelico 1972–73: indirizzi e orari di tutte le chiese ed opere evangeliche in Italia. Torino: Editrice Claudiana, 1972. 346p.

Church and state in Italy, 1850–1950. A. C. Jemelo. Oxford, UK: Blackwell, 1960. 340p.

Comrades and Christians: religion and political struggle in Communist Italy. D. I. Kertzer. Prospect Heights, IL: Waveland Press, 1980. 336p.

Cristianesimo Evangelico, 1967–1968. Torino: Editrice Claudiana, 1968. 219p.

Dati statistici delle diocesi italiane. Rome: Conferenza Episcopale Italiana, 1967. 319p.

Elementi per uno studio della practica religiosa in Italia. C. D. Michelis. Rome: Gregorian Pontifical University, 1965. (Mimeographed).

Il comportamento religioso degli Italiani. S. Burgalassi. Firenze: Vallecchi, 1967.

'Italy,' S. Acquaviva, in *Western religion: a country by country sociological enquiry*, p.305–24. H. Mol (ed). The Hague: Mouton, 1972.

Italy. D. Zancani & L. Sponza. *World bibliographical series*, vol. 30. Oxford, UK: CLIO Press, 1994. 350p.

La Chiesa e la organizzazioni cattoliche in Italia, 1945–1955. C. Falconi. Torino: Einaudi, 1956.

'La Chiesa italiana: tensioni e problemi,' *Humanitas*, 31 (1976), 603–754. (28 articles).

'La religiosità in Italia,' G. D. Rosa, *Civiltà Cattolica*, 2960 (Oct, 1973), 168–73.

L'altra Chiesa in Italia: Gli Evangelici. G. Bouchard & R. Turinetto. Torino: Editrice Claudiana, 1976.

Madonnas that maim: popular Catholicism in Italy since the fifteenth Century. M. P. Carroll. Baltimore, MD: Johns Hopkins University Press, 1992. 214p.

Minoranze religiose in Italia. A. Santini et al. Rome: Edizioni Religioni Oggi, 1969. 390p.

'Politics and religion in Italy,' *Social compass*, 23, 2-3 (1976), 97–278. (11 articles and a bibliography).

'Sicilian pentecostalism: an interpretive study in cultural discontinuity.' S. J. Cucchiari. Ph.D. dissertation, University of Michigan, Ann Arbor, MI, 1985. 588p.

'Sociologie religieuse et sociologie des religions en Italie,' S. Acquaviva, *Archives de sociologie des religions*, 12 (1961).

The Catholic–Communist dialogue in Italy: 1944 to the present. R. M. Giammanco. New York: Praeger, 1989. 184p.

'The Church in Italy,' M. Castelli, *Pro Mundi Vita bulletin*, 66 (May–June, 1977), 1–29.

'The Conservative Baptist Mission in Italy: past achievements, future opportunities.' M. F. Martin. D.Miss. thesis, Trinity Evangelical Divinity School, Deerfield, IL, 1994. 279p.

The Protestant movement in Italy: its progress, problems and prospects. R. E. Hedlund. South Pasadena, CA: William Carey Library, 1970. 257p.

Up and down Catholic Italy. M. F. Ingoldsby. New York: Vantage Press, 1985. 165p.

Country Table 2. **Organized churches and denominations in Italy.**

Official name (bold type = church with over 10% of affiliated) 1	*Begun* 2	*Type* 3	*Counc* 4	*Congs* 5	*Adults* 6	*Affiliated 1970* 7	*Affiliated 1995* 8	*G%* 9	*Names, notes, and other statistics* (see Codebook, Part 3) 10
Assemblea Evangelica Battista	1947	I-Bap	xF...	6	507	593	810	1.26	M=Associazione Missionaria Battista Italiana. M=CBFMS(USA). 10x,5m,27f, W=55%,34Y,60,60z
Assemblee di Dio in Italia	1908	P-Pe2	ZF..k	1,101	163,089	300,000	275,000	-0.35	*CCEP (see below). Assemblies of God.* M=AoG(USA). 1934-58 persecution. 363n,15f,1s(17).
Associazione Missionaria Ev Italiana	1866	P-Bap	.G..K	25	750	1,500	1,500	0.00	*AMEI. Italian Ev Missionary Association.* M=Spezia Mission, also WEC(UK) in Sardinia. 3f.
Azione Biblica	1932	P-Pe2	.....	5	220	1,000	440	-3.23	*Bible Action.* M=Action Biblique (Switzerland).
Bambini di Dio	c1985	I-mar	.....	10	164	–	374	10.00	*Children of God.*
Chiesa Anglicana (D Europe)	1559	A-plu	awc..	7	8,900	10,000	10,500	0.20	*Ch of England*, also M=PECUSA. Chaplaincies: 2 Rome, 2 Sicily, 2 seasonal. 9x.
Chiesa Apostolica Armena: V Milano		O-Arm	Ewc..	1	450	1,000	1,300	0.05	*Armenian Apostolic Ch. Vicariate of Milan. Gregorians.* Armenian refugees from USSR.
Chiesa Apostolica in Italia	1926	P-PeA	ZG..E	154	4,700	5,000	10,400	2.97	*Apostolic Ch.* M=ACMM(UK). HQ Grosseto. Large % are students. 56n,2f,1j,90Y. In 5 countries.
Chiesa Battista Biblica	1979	I-Bap	.....	3	100	–	200	6.25	*Bible Baptist Churches.* M=BIM(USA).
Chiesa Cattolica in Italia:	c 40	R-LEr	B.B.R	30,197	47,387,550	50,697,128	55,750,000	0.33	*Catholic Church in Italy.* 37294n 20010x 27058m 117812w 482246Yy
P Roma (Rome): D Roma	c 40	R-Lat	Bs	1,047	2,200,650	2,486,000	2,589,000	0.16	3840n 4324x 6025m 20992w 18595Yy
M Campobasso-Boiano	c1050	R-Lat	Bs	70	104,700	96,000	123,180	1.00	68n 41x 93m 101w 1161Yy
D Isernia-Venafro	c 450	R-Lat	Bs	48	51,850	48,490	61,000	0.92	54n 6x 14m 39w 503Yy
D Termoli-Larino	c 950	R-Lat	Bs	51	89,080	56,000	104,800	2.54	66n 14x 16m 160w 542Yy
D Trivento	c 950	R-Lat	bs	58	48,600	83,750	57,150	-1.52	56n 4x 4m 69w 360Yy
M Chieti-Vasto	c 450	R-Lat	Bs	188	272,340	297,200	320,400	0.30	162n 93x 117m 377w 3205Yy
AD Lanciano-Ortona	c 450	R-Lat	Bs	41	75,600	79,200	88,934	0.46	40n 30x 46m 93w 653Yy
M L'Aquila	1257	R-Lat	Bs	152	78,200	96,959	92,000	-0.21	91n 53x 80m 280w 803Yy
D Avezzano (Marsi)	c 850	R-Lat	Bs	104	98,700	129,800	116,100	-0.45	84n 27x 32m 195w 1270Yy
D Sulmona-Valva	c 450	R-Lat	Bs	76	71,000	110,725	83,508	-1.12	54n 32x 34m 117w 885Yy
M Pescara-Penne	c 450	R-Lat	bs	144	249,050	270,000	293,000	0.33	136n 68x 80m 396w 2217Yy
D Teramo-Atri	c 450	R-Lat	bs	187	204,000	211,000	240,000	0.52	121n 57x 61m 168w 5039Yy
M Potenza-Muro Lucano	c 350	R-Lat	Bs	59	138,800	110,000	163,300	1.59	72n 42x 42m 193w 1445Yy
AD Acerenza	c 350	R-Lat	Bs	22	51,400	60,100	60,500	0.03	36n 5x 5m 61w 488Yy
AD Matera-Irsina	c 850	R-Lat	Bs	51	116,450	135,000	137,000	0.06	63n 22x 24m 81w 1365Yy
D Melfi-Rapolla-Venosa	c1050	R-Lat	bs	32	74,400	49,000	87,500	2.35	46n 10x 11m 89w 850Yy
D Tricarico	c1050	R-Lat	Bs	32	43,180	66,506	50,800	-1.07	36n 2x 2m 63w 410Yy
D Tursi-Lagonegro	968	R-Lat	Bs	67	112,000	115,300	131,761	0.10	68n 21x 21m 125w 500Yy
AD Catanzaro-Squillace	1121	R-Lat	bs	119	208,700	140,000	245,500	2.27	119n 49x 69m 238w 1207Yy
AD Cosenza-Bisignano	c 650	R-Lat	bs	131	300,400	293,608	353,460	0.74	141n 97x 132m 486w 3010Yy
D Lungro per gli Italo-Albanesi	1919	R-IAb	os	34	28,050	33,900	33,000	-0.11	26n 1x 2m 40w 350Yy
D San Marco Argentano-Scalea	c 950	R-Lat	bs	60	89,700	140,000	105,500	-1.13	81n 9x 9m 102w 905Yy
M Reggio Calabria-Bova	c 90	R-Lat	Bs	250	231,200	231,000	272,000	0.66	112n 52x 59m 605w 3889Yy
D Cassano all'Jonio	c 450	R-Lat	Bs	47	88,400	130,600	104,000	-0.91	54n 9x 34m 86w 961Yy
AD Crotone-Santa Severina	c 550	R-Lat	Bs	80	171,800	61,000	202,075	4.91	83n 30x 33m 170w 2910Yy
D Lamezia Terme (Nicastro)	c 550	R-Lat	Bs	55	118,400	136,000	139,350	0.10	52n 9x 25m 115w 1450Yy
D Locri-Gerace	c 450	R-Lat	Bs	73	111,500	130,000	131,215	0.04	48n 20x 21m 133w 840Yy
D Mileto-Nicotera-Tropea	c 550	R-Lat	Bs	130	137,870	35,302	162,200	6.29	103n 28x 30m 129w 1786Yy
D Oppido Mamertina-Palmi	c1250	R-Lat	Bs	64	149,600	25,872	176,000	7.97	92n 16x 22m 244w 1451Yy
AD Rossano-Cariati	c 650	R-Lat	bs	51	114,300	112,400	134,500	0.72	60n 18x 22m 106w 1614Yy
M Benevento	c 90	R-Lat	Bs	122	228,200	307,741	268,500	-0.54	124n 125x 206m 310w 3035Yy
D Ariano Irpino-Lacedonia	c1050	R-Lat	Bs	40	52,600	65,200	61,940	-0.20	36n 11x 13m 70w 598Yy
D Avellino	c 150	R-Lat	Bs	50	119,600	125,000	140,700	0.47	63n 25x 26m 172w 1262Yy
D Cerreto Sannita-Telese-SAgata	c 450	R-Lat	Bs	60	74,100	49,158	87,133	2.32	55n 28x 32m 113w 1005Yy
AD Sant' Angelo dei Lombardi	c 750	R-Lat	Bs	41	77,700	80,000	91,445	0.54	39n 24x 28m 84w 816Yy
AN Monte Vergine	c1150	R-Lat	bs	8	12,200	9,985	14,300	1.45	9n 0x 10m 39w 164Yy
M Napoli (Naples)	c 90	R-Lat	Bs	285	1,317,500	1,600,000	1,550,000	-0.13	473n 534x 751m 2400w 17110Yy
D Acerra	c1050	R-Lat	Bs	25	39,300	70,242	46,231	-1.66	30n 21x 37m 61w 1309Yy
D Alife-Caiazzo	c 450	R-Lat	Bs	61	58,650	40,690	69,000	2.13	46n 15x 17m 75w 800Yy
D Aversa	c1050	R-Lat	bs	94	425,000	339,650	500,000	1.56	185n 40x 80m 547w 8129Yy
AD Capua	c 150	R-Lat	Bs	89	152,400	129,800	179,300	1.30	78n 11x 11m 285w 1540Yy
D Caserta	c1150	R-Lat	Bs	67	170,850	132,100	201,000	1.69	65n 40x 42m 175w 2000Yy
D Ischia	c1150	R-Lat	Bs	25	38,250	38,348	45,000	0.64	37n 9x 9m 45w 800Yy
D Nola	c 150	R-Lat	Bs	115	400,350	370,000	471,000	0.97	147n 92x 117m 521w 6770Yy
D Pozzuoli	c 90	R-Lat	Bs	82	419,730	421,050	493,800	0.64	64n 51x 61m 240w 6251Yy
D Sessa Aurunca	c 450	R-Lat	Bs	42	101,150	84,450	119,000	1.38	40n 13x 15m 113w 731Yy
AD Sorrento-Castellammare di Stabia	c 450	R-Lat	Bs	86	190,400	81,090	224,000	4.15	131n 70x 84m 596w 3225Yy
D Teano-Calvi	c 450	R-Lat	Bs	70	69,300	86,000	81,500	-0.21	61n 23x 26m 100w 1000Yy
PN Pompei	1926	R-Lat	bs	13	19,100	16,430	22,500	1.27	35n 10x 25m 158w 288Yy
M Salerno-Campagna-Acerno	c 550	R-Lat	Bs	173	397,970	380,051	468,200	0.84	207n 130x 161m 470w 3522Yy
AD Amalfi-Cava de' Tirreni	c 550	R-Lat	bs	76	83,300	43,850	98,019	3.27	70n 42x 52m 130w 1120Yy
D Nocera Inferiore-Sarno	c 650	R-Lat	Bs	54	182,750	141,053	215,000	1.70	72n 55x 74m 244w 2324Yy
D Teggiano-Policastro (Diano)	1850	R-Lat	Bs	81	116,450	90,904	137,000	1.65	75n 7x 8m 140w 1335Yy
D Vallo della Lucania	c1150	R-Lat	Bs	139	134,300	160,950	158,000	-0.07	85n 25x 26m 135w 1298Yy
AN S Trinita di Cava de' Tirreni	1394	R-Lat	bs	8	4,250	35,000	5,000	-7.49	2n 13x 19m 50w 160Yy
M Bologna	c 250	R-Lat	Bs	417	780,500	913,127	918,239	0.02	457n 299x 417m 1287w 5245Yy
D Faenza-Modigliana	c 250	R-Lat	Bs	90	99,100	130,000	116,537	-0.44	158n 27x 34m 230w 594Yy
AD Ferrara-Comacchio	c 550	R-Lat	Bs	170	236,900	65,600	278,700	5.96	148n 56x 62m 342w 876Yy
D Imola	c 350	R-Lat	Bs	114	119,000	145,200	140,000	-0.15	128n 15x 16m 316w 308Yy
M Modena-Nonantola	c 250	R-Lat	Bs	246	377,800	381,093	444,500	0.62	242n 76x 88m 564w 2825Yy
D Carpi	1779	R-Lat	Bs	44	96,050	105,600	113,000	0.27	51n 3x 4m 97w 696Yy
D Fidenza	1601	R-Lat	bs	61	53,720	63,500	63,200	-0.02	61n 14x 15m 54w 155Yy
D Parma	c 350	R-Lat	bs	311	258,900	305,000	304,613	-0.01	218n 121x 183m 674w 2042Yy
D Piacenza-Bobbio	c 350	R-Lat	bs	428	244,800	301,500	288,000	-0.18	367n 62x 97m 489w 808Yy
D Reggio Emilia-Guastalla	c 90	R-Lat	Bs	348	388,800	353,300	457,389	1.04	349n 48x 66m 475w 3223Yy
M Ravenna-Cervia	c 90	R-Lat	Bs	89	170,000	194,000	200,000	0.12	97n 37x 44m 317w 1097Yy
D Cesena-Sarsina	c 90	R-Lat	Bs	138	129,600	128,136	152,500	0.70	152n 40x 49m 132w 1010Yy
D Forli-Bertinoro	c 150	R-Lat	Bs	128	143,100	129,150	168,411	1.07	146n 28x 38m 257w 1053Yy
D Rimini	c 250	R-Lat	Bs	135	243,600	240,000	286,609	0.71	211n 45x 57m 515w 2144Yy
D San Marino-Montefeltro	c 850	R-Lat	Bs	60	34,000	40,000	40,000	0.00	40n 20x 30m 60w 400Yy

Dioceses are arranged below in the current order found in *Annuario Pontificio*. The table on the right gives comparative statistical data for all dioceses. There is a small amount of overlapping due to Catholics counted in newly-formed dioceses still being counted in their parent dioceses. This is corrected at the end of the list of dioceses by means of a line termed 'Doubly-counted Catholics'.

For description of which secular provinces contain which dioceses, consult listing in *Annuario Pontificio* 1997, pages 1138-1141.

Concerning how diocesan statistics add up to give accurate country totals, see technical note on page 1:820.

Continued opposite

Country Table 2–continued

Official name (bold type = church with over 10% of all affiliated) 1	Begun 2	Type 3	Counc 4	Congs 5	Adults 6	Affiliated 1970 7	Affiliated 1995 8	G% 9	Names, notes, and other statistics (see Codebook, Part 3) 10
D Albano	c 350	R-Lat	bs	73	312,800	247,170	368,000	1.60	109n 164x 206m 1117w 3330Yy
D Frascati	c 250	R-Lat	bs	65	97,750	74,950	115,000	1.73	78n 124x 228m 517w 864Yy
D Ostia	c 250	R-Lat	bs	1	1,700	3,920	2,000	-2.66	2n 0x 0m 10w 20Yy
D Palestrina	c 350	R-Lat	bs	39	68,600	57,800	80,750	1.35	48n 31x 34m 230w 1053Yy
D Porto-Santa Rufina	c 250	R-Lat	bs	58	165,750	116,700	195,000	2.07	74n 74x 165m 989w 1694Yy
D Sabina-Poggio Mirteto	c 450	R-Lat	bs	82	122,100	102,158	143,636	1.37	98n 29x 35m 220w 1220Yy
D Velletri-Segni	c 450	R-Lat	bs	50	96,900	52,700	114,000	3.13	49n 40x 61m 160w 1015Yy
AD Gaeta	c 750	R-Lat	bs	57	127,500	126,123	150,000	0.70	57n 36x 39m 218w 1598Yy
D Anagni-Alatri	c 450	R-Lat	bs	66	69,700	40,683	82,000	2.84	47n 33x 40m 277w 557Yy
D Civita Castellana	c 650	R-Lat	bs	76	166,120	80,825	195,435	3.59	99n 60x 89m 412w 1641Yy
D Civitavecchia-Tarquinia	c 350	R-Lat	bs	25	114,750	74,000	135,000	2.43	42n 23x 23m 192w 715Yy
D Frosinone-Veroli-Ferentino	c 750	R-Lat	bs	77	148,750	112,038	175,000	1.80	75n 70x 82m 205w 1806Yy
D Latina-Terracina-Sezze-Priverno	c 90	R-Lat	bs	117	233,750	222,459	275,000	0.85	86n 67x 71m 217w 2247Yy
D Rieti	c 450	R-Lat	bs	94	79,730	111,415	93,800	-0.69	83n 24x 24m 243w 520Yy
D Sora-Aquino-Pontecorvo	c 250	R-Lat	bs	126	129,900	150,251	152,810	0.07	101n 37x 40m 210w 1130Yy
D Tivoli	c 150	R-Lat	bs	69	212,500	131,800	250,000	2.59	68n 45x 73m 195w 850Yy
D Viterbo	c 250	R-Lat	bs	96	141,950	75,000	167,000	3.25	117n 85x 128m 518w 1274Yy
AN Montecassino	c 550	R-Lat	bs	53	51,000	110,000	60,000	-2.40	27n 24x 35m 82w 675Yy
AN Santa Maria di Grottaferrata	1937	R-IAb	os	1	80	88	97	0.39	0n 18x 36m 5w 10Yy
AN Subiaco	c1050	R-Lat	bs	22	22,300	25,959	26,178	0.03	26n 30x 45m 40w 261Yy
M Genova (Genoa)	c 250	R-Lat	Bs	408	738,430	934,000	868,741	-0.29	442n 402x 564m 1940w 4425Yy
D Albenga-Imperia	c 450	R-Lat	Bs	163	134,700	154,450	158,457	0.10	127n 63x 79m 566w 790Yy
D Chiavari	1892	R-Lat	Bs	141	120,870	142,000	142,200	0.01	140n 44x 49m 401w 757Yy
D La Spezia-Sarzana-Brugnato	c 450	R-Lat	Bs	188	190,300	245,009	223,845	-0.36	138n 50x 53m 244w 859Yy
D Savona-Noli	c 950	R-Lat	Bs	74	122,700	169,000	144,374	-0.63	109n 68x 72m 535w 757Yy
D Tortona	c 150	R-Lat	Bs	314	232,900	306,615	274,000	-0.45	225n 71x 80m 471w 1900Yy
D Ventimiglia-San Remo	c 650	R-Lat	Bs	99	127,500	177,500	150,000	-0.67	87n 51x 54m 460w 942Yy
M Milano (Milan)	c 90	R-Lat	Bs	1,631	4,008,000	4,010,000	4,715,285	0.65	2279n 1000x 1406m 8800w 35813Yy
D Bergamo	c 350	R-Lat	Bs	389	711,450	695,200	837,000	0.75	828n 252x 338m 3192w 7161Yy
D Brescia	c 90	R-Lat	Bs	497	849,700	850,000	999,614	0.65	889n 227x 377m 2451w 6576Yy
D Como	c 350	R-Lat	Bs	341	424,150	458,000	499,000	0.34	459n 192x 238m 1250w 4306Yy
D Crema	1579	R-Lat	Bs	62	76,600	74,967	90,087	0.74	123n 3x 3m 130w 690Yy
D Cremona	c 350	R-Lat	Bs	224	283,050	360,178	333,000	-0.31	358n 41x 88m 875w 2293Yy
D Lodi	c 350	R-Lat	Bs	127	200,400	205,212	235,723	0.56	227n 25x 35m 389w 1768Yy
D Mantova	804	R-Lat	Bs	168	287,300	321,180	338,000	0.08	256n 37x 45m 419w 2131Yy
D Pavia	c 90	R-Lat	Bs	99	123,900	154,735	145,749	-0.24	143n 37x 71m 314w 903Yy
D Vigevano	1529	R-Lat	Bs	107	145,350	184,100	171,000	-0.29	117n 15x 16m 245w 1026Yy
D Ascoli Piceno	c 350	R-Lat	bs	95	90,400	102,000	106,340	0.17	105n 36x 39m 162w 930Yy
D Fabriano-Matelica	c 450	R-Lat	bs	58	44,500	37,261	52,350	1.37	55n 39x 48m 108w 283Yy
PN Loreto	1965	R-Lat	bs	8	9,500	10,895	11,158	0.10	2n 44x 51m 236w 180Yy
M Ancona-Osimo	c 250	R-Lat	Bs	73	176,100	154,000	207,151	1.19	109n 85x 128m 214w 1390Yy
D Jesi	c 550	R-Lat	Bs	45	63,750	75,000	75,000	0.00	47n 27x 59m 84w 495Yy
M Fermo	c 250	R-Lat	Bs	123	221,600	220,000	260,665	0.68	203n 80x 98m 427w 2098Yy
AD Camerino-San Severino Marche	c 250	R-Lat	bs	95	49,300	51,471	58,000	0.48	114n 38x 61m 205w 350Yy
D Macerata-Tolentino-Recanati	c 450	R-Lat	Bs	67	112,130	68,697	131,918	2.64	124n 102x 120m 220w 980Yy
D San Benedetto del Tronto	1571	R-Lat	Bs	53	99,200	85,800	116,672	1.24	70n 38x 42m 174w 1134Yy
M Urbino-Urbania-Sant' Angelo	c 550	R-Lat	Bs	53	44,200	38,500	52,000	1.21	77n 11x 11m 132w 281Yy
D Fano-Fossombrone-Cagli	c 90	R-Lat	Bs	75	112,200	75,000	132,000	2.29	134n 54x 54m 212w 817Yy
D Pesaro	c 250	R-Lat	Bs	59	94,010	101,500	110,600	0.34	68n 43x 46m 108w 850Yy
D Senigallia	c 550	R-Lat	Bs	128	98,000	114,378	115,300	0.03	85n 31x 33m 173w 833Yy
M Torino (Turin)	c 450	R-Lat	Bs	586	1,768,000	1,820,000	2,080,000	0.54	719n 906x 1435m 4400w 13091Yy
D Acqui	c 350	R-Lat	Bs	123	123,300	163,000	145,115	-0.46	137n 28x 30m 285w 882Yy
D Alba	c 350	R-Lat	Bs	126	101,900	120,236	119,900	-0.01	155n 40x 86m 416w 981Yy
D Aosta	c 350	R-Lat	Bs	93	99,450	108,300	117,000	0.31	114n 39x 48m 115w 857Yy
D Asti	c 250	R-Lat	Bs	128	127,200	150,000	149,700	-0.01	135n 31x 38m 292w 1110Yy
D Cuneo	1817	R-Lat	Bs	117	90,000	104,000	105,920	0.07	141n 24x 29m 445w 870Yy
D Fossano	1592	R-Lat	Bs	43	33,320	35,420	39,200	0.41	50n 19x 24m 40w 335Yy
D Ivrea	c 450	R-Lat	Bs	148	174,300	198,040	205,016	0.14	160n 42x 68m 475w 1427Yy
D Mondovi	1388	R-Lat	Bs	192	101,600	132,660	119,500	-0.42	187n 6x 10m 275w 720Yy
D Pinerolo	1748	R-Lat	Bs	62	60,350	76,250	71,000	-0.28	105n 20x 26m 470w 396Yy
D Saluzzo	1511	R-Lat	Bs	91	74,800	99,950	88,000	-0.51	126n 0x 3m 148w 834Yy
D Susa	1772	R-Lat	Bs	62	51,000	58,000	60,000	0.14	72n 10x 22m 139w 488Yy
M Vercelli	c 250	R-Lat	Bs	197	152,150	196,251	179,000	-0.37	135n 22x 36m 514w 842Yy
D Alessandria	1175	R-Lat	Bs	75	110,500	153,000	130,000	-0.65	106n 34x 38m 230w 839Yy
D Biella	1772	R-Lat	Bs	114	160,650	201,327	189,000	-0.25	141n 37x 59m 393w 890Yy
D Casale Monferrato	1474	R-Lat	Bs	148	87,100	125,743	102,500	-0.81	119n 35x 42m 173w 657Yy
D Novara	c 350	R-Lat	Bs	346	440,300	529,000	518,000	-0.08	432n 138x 188m 1248w 3825Yy
M Bari-Bitonto	c 350	R-Lat	Bs	170	558,450	625,500	657,000	0.20	220n 175x 303m 868w 5123Yy
D Altamura-Gravina-Acquaviva	1248	R-Lat	bs	53	131,700	61,602	154,950	3.76	72n 25x 30m 276w 2935Yy
D Andria	c1050	R-Lat	Bs	37	110,500	123,018	130,000	0.22	70n 31x 32m 123w 1755Yy
D Conversano-Monopoli	c 450	R-Lat	Bs	57	206,550	105,500	243,000	3.39	101n 64x 73m 221w 2545Yy
D Molfetta-Ruvo-Giovinazzo	c1050	R-Lat	Bs	37	117,500	103,261	138,180	1.17	81n 16x 20m 140w 1537Yy
AD Trani-Barletta-Bisceglie	c 550	R-Lat	Bs	124	225,250	242,840	265,000	0.35	102n 44x 46m 174w 3433Yy
M Foggia-Bovino	c 450	R-Lat	bs	76	183,600	162,000	216,000	1.16	96n 84x 96m 237w 1922Yy
D Cerignola-Ascoli Satriano	c1050	R-Lat	Bs	36	85,000	83,876	100,000	0.71	41n 17x 18m 95w 1210Yy
D Lucera-Troia	c 350	R-Lat	Bs	33	62,500	97,000	73,500	-1.10	69n 23x 27m 86w 766Yy
AD Manfredonia-Vieste	c 250	R-Lat	Bs	46	130,220	139,505	153,200	0.38	75n 67x 74m 203w 2213Yy
D San Severo	c1050	R-Lat	Bs	36	109,200	91,382	128,500	1.37	51n 14x 16m 113w 1190Yy
M Lecce	1057	R-Lat	bs	76	227,900	226,780	268,119	0.67	144n 64x 77m 390w 2541Yy
AD Brindisi-Ostuni	c 350	R-Lat	Bs	61	238,850	248,615	281,000	0.49	122n 31x 32m 265w 2832Yy
D Nardo-Gallipoli	1413	R-Lat	Bs	161	177,650	157,630	209,000	1.13	123n 21x 24m 143w 2355Yy
AD Otranto	c 650	R-Lat	Bs	155	170,000	189,450	200,000	0.22	119n 26x 34m 215w 2111Yy
D Ugento-Santa Maria di Leuca	c1250	R-Lat	Bs	62	105,000	110,000	123,500	0.46	64n 14x 16m 108w 1572Yy
M Taranto	c 550	R-Lat	Bs	90	341,100	358,900	401,236	0.45	133n 84x 90m 416w 4278Yy
D Castellaneta	c1050	R-Lat	Bs	40	102,500	68,972	120,630	2.26	44n 11x 23m 72w 1625Yy
D Oria	1591	R-Lat	Bs	79	147,900	153,440	174,000	0.50	57n 52x 65m 270w 2106Yy
M Cagliari	c 350	R-Lat	Bs	133	463,700	400,000	545,500	1.25	183n 128x 165m 884w 4825Yy
D Iglesias	1763	R-Lat	Bs	72	119,300	142,300	140,300	-0.06	79n 13x 13m 98w 1050Yy
D Lanusei (Ogliastra)	1824	R-Lat	Bs	35	60,400	72,962	71,109	-0.10	40n 10x 12m 48w 678Yy
D Nuoro	c1150	R-Lat	Bs	49	110,500	122,162	130,000	0.25	81n 13x 17m 115w 2052Yy
M Oristano	c1050	R-Lat	Bs	87	128,000	140,000	150,618	0.29	118n 34x 42m 364w 1234Yy
D Ales-Terralba	c 650	R-Lat	Bs	58	87,200	104,310	102,626	-0.07	73n 4x 5m 119w 873Yy
M Sassari	c 450	R-Lat	Bs	85	185,720	180,000	218,494	0.78	100n 68x 85m 255w 2031Yy
D Alghero-Bosa	c1150	R-Lat	Bs	61	93,100	80,720	109,500	1.23	79n 19x 20m 230w 784Yy
D Ozieri	c1250	R-Lat	Bs	30	47,600	57,819	56,000	-0.13	56n 4x 4m 48w 557Yy
D Tempio-Ampurias	c 350	R-Lat	Bs	48	116,900	102,712	137,492	1.17	68n 10x 12m 121w 1108Yy
AD Catania	c 90	R-Lat	bs	150	593,300	614,547	698,000	0.51	256n 250x 303m 875w 8476Yy
D Acireale	1844	R-Lat	bs	111	186,150	176,550	219,000	0.87	150n 37x 60m 362w 2769Yy
D Piana degli Albanesi	1937	R-IAb	os	15	24,200	33,600	28,500	-0.66	25n 3x 3m 44w 273Yy
M Messina-Lipari-SLucia del Mela	c 450	R-Lat	Bs	241	427,550	487,000	503,000	0.13	256n 180x 249m 750w 6600Yy
D Nicosia	1817	R-Lat	Bs	79	72,250	110,200	85,000	-1.03	63n 7x 15m 69w 982Yy
D Patti	c1150	R-Lat	Bs	91	136,000	200,000	160,000	-0.89	132n 10x 21m 115w 2730Yy
M Monreale	1176	R-Lat	Bs	113	157,250	198,000	185,000	-0.27	103n 33x 46m 271w 2934Yy
D Agrigento	c 90	R-Lat	Bs	194	395,000	470,000	464,700	-0.05	238n 48x 48m 522w 6780Yy
D Caltanissetta	1844	R-Lat	Bs	61	132,000	159,000	155,345	-0.09	119n 27x 30m 316w 2120Yy
M Palermo	c 90	R-Lat	Bs	268	803,250	814,000	945,000	0.60	221n 304x 418m 1447w 12929Yy
D Cefalu	1131	R-Lat	Bs	53	96,900	111,703	114,000	0.08	77n 25x 33m 150w 924Yy
D Mazara del Vallo	1093	R-Lat	Bs	78	190,100	226,183	223,632	-0.05	68n 24x 35m 230w 1709Yy
D Trapani	1844	R-Lat	Bs	94	138,100	206,533	162,500	-0.95	88n 44x 48m 243w 1429Yy
M Siracusa	c 150	R-Lat	Bs	76	276,250	268,000	325,000	0.77	119n 44x 48m 357w 3051Yy
D Caltagirone	1818	R-Lat	Bs	137	128,900	160,500	151,615	-0.23	82n 16x 25m 174w 1851Yy
D Noto	1844	R-Lat	Bs	163	176,100	188,950	207,157	0.37	83n 30x 42m 242w 1874Yy
D Piazza Armerina	1817	R-Lat	Bs	149	187,000	240,000	220,000	-0.35	107n 34x 41m 215w 2802Yy
D Ragusa	1950	R-Lat	Bs	71	133,450	163,115	157,000	-0.15	93n 9x 15m 245w 1011Yy
AD Lucca	c 90	R-Lat	bs	362	257,200	264,359	302,533	0.54	292n 63x 79m 594w 1545Yy
AN Monte Oliveto Maggiore	1319	R-Lat	bs	4	390	687	459	-1.60	1n 15x 26m 9w 5Yy
M Firenze (Florence)	c 90	R-Lat	Bs	514	707,200	790,000	831,949	0.21	412n 275x 321m 1695w 4483Yy
D Arezzo-Cortona-Sansepolcro	c 250	R-Lat	bs	269	226,200	194,000	266,156	1.27	261n 88x 112m 506w 1061Yy
D Fiesole	c 90	R-Lat	Bs	218	110,500	135,193	130,000	-0.16	144n 98x 98m 420w 930Yy
D Pistoia	c 250	R-Lat	Bs	164	182,750	210,919	215,000	0.08	137n 35x 37m 273w 1435Yy
D Prato	1653	R-Lat	Bs	101	156,400	150,650	184,000	0.80	98n 37x 39m 217w 1108Yy
D San Miniato	1622	R-Lat	Bs	90	126,000	138,311	148,255	0.28	74n 12x 14m 185w 1292Yy
M Pisa	c 350	R-Lat	Bs	166	257,000	306,500	302,380	-0.05	187n 76x 92m 478w 1939Yy

Continued overleaf

Country Table 2–concluded

Official name (bold type = church with over 10% of all affiliated) 1	*Begun* 2	*Type* 3	*Counc* 4	*Congs* 5	*Adults* 6	*Affiliated 1970* 7	*Affiliated 1995* 8	*G%* 9	*Names, notes, and other statistics (see Codebook, Part 3)* 10
D Livorno	1806	R-Lat	Bs	54	150,200	205,000	176,700	-0.59	61n 46x 52m 449w 750Yy
D Massa Carrara-Pontremoli	1797	R-Lat	Bs	251	171,100	39,980	201,339	6.68	169n 33x 41m 292w 1495Yy
D Pescia	1726	R-Lat	Bs	41	89,250	92,239	105,000	0.52	44n 30x 31m 120w 704Yy
D Volterra	c 450	R-Lat	Bs	92	68,400	86,158	80,520	-0.27	68n 13x 15m 106w 320Yy
M Siena-Colle di Val d'Elsa-Mont	c 350	R-Lat	Bs	205	150,400	99,950	176,900	2.31	136n 64x 71m 398w 445Yy
D Grosseto	1138	R-Lat	Bs	82	93,500	129,576	110,000	-0.65	47n 29x 29m 63w 579Yy
D Massa Marittima-Piombino	c 450	R-Lat	Bs	55	106,250	132,200	125,000	-0.22	56n 11x 11m 80w 784Yy
D Montepulciano-Chiusi-Pienza	1561	R-Lat	bs	46	55,300	14,597	65,114	6.16	55n 12x 12m 122w 446Yy
D Pitigliano-Sovana-Orbetello	c 650	R-Lat	Bs	71	61,600	68,830	72,455	0.21	69n 12x 12m 62w 217Yy
M Gorizia	1751	R-Lat	Bs	91	154,020	178,000	181,200	0.07	122n 41x 49m 427w 1055Yy
D Trieste	c 550	R-Lat	Bs	60	192,700	290,000	226,700	-0.98	125n 68x 80m 244w 1129Yy
M Trento	c 150	R-Lat	Bs	494	390,690	426,000	459,635	0.30	561n 295x 406m 840w 4107Yy
D Bolzano-Bressanone	c 550	R-Lat	Bs	282	378,250	413,637	445,000	0.29	396n 240x 318m 878w 5150Yy
M Udine	1751	R-Lat	bs	373	402,900	491,049	474,000	-0.14	435n 100x 126m 827w 2535Yy
P Venezia (Venice)	1170	R-Lat	Bs	195	324,700	400,000	382,000	-0.18	228n 214x 299m 1063w 2351Yy
D Adria-Rovigo	c 650	R-Lat	Bs	116	172,600	202,568	203,005	0.01	165n 28x 44m 345w 1142Yy
D Belluno-Feltre	c 150	R-Lat	Bs	278	156,700	204,630	184,370	-0.42	215n 44x 49m 277w 1400Yy
D Chioggia	c 650	R-Lat	Bs	99	105,060	123,750	123,600	0.00	96n 32x 62m 174w 784Yy
D Concordia-Pordenone	c 350	R-Lat	Bs	188	282,600	296,246	332,488	0.46	281n 57x 68m 335w 2371Yy
D Padova	c 90	R-Lat	Bs	469	854,400	860,000	1,005,132	0.63	840n 364x 610m 2577w 7905Yy
D Treviso	c 350	R-Lat	Bs	265	634,100	575,000	745,980	1.05	496n 218x 320m 1192w 6369Yy
D Verona	c 250	R-Lat	Bs	413	654,400	700,000	769,920	0.38	732n 412x 714m 3054w 6087Yy
D Vicenza	c 150	R-Lat	Bs	360	629,900	620,879	741,117	0.71	633n 229x 324m 2292w 6490Yy
D Vittorio Veneto	c 550	R-Lat	Bs	180	253,300	277,896	298,000	0.28	284n 86x 110m 815w 2153Yy
AD Spoleto-Norcia	c 90	R-Lat	bs	257	78,200	86,350	92,020	0.25	104n 46x 58m 369w 577Yy
D Orvieto-Todi	c 550	R-Lat	bs	141	76,500	53,000	89,980	2.14	84n 37x 41m 277w 546Yy
D Terni-Narni-Amelia	c 150	R-Lat	bs	81	138,800	139,000	163,349	0.65	79n 37x 40m 132w 726Yy
M Perugia-Città della Pieve	c 150	R-Lat	Bs	165	194,650	186,280	229,000	0.83	172n 82x 108m 524w 1822Yy
D Assisi-Nocera Umbra-Gualdo	c 250	R-Lat	Bs	61	65,000	45,000	76,415	2.14	68n 154x 81m 600w 620Yy
D Città di Castello	c 650	R-Lat	Bs	60	49,600	58,013	58,348	0.02	58n 10x 10m 165w 686Yy
D Foligno	c 90	R-Lat	Bs	41	56,400	59,020	66,375	0.47	48n 36x 48m 154w 446Yy
D Gubbio	c 450	R-Lat	Bs	40	40,970	43,000	48,200	0.46	38n 20x 20m 110w 330Yy
OM Italia	1925	R-Lat	Bs	402	255,000	200,000	300,000	1.64	Military Ordinariate for Armed Services. 198n 54x 54m 175w 468Yy
Doubly-counted Catholics		R-Lat		0	-1,424,000	–	-1,675,282	0.05	Catholics counted in newly-formed dioceses and also in parent diocese.
Chiesa Cattolica Riformata d'Italia	1881	I-ReC	.....	5	180	500	450	-0.42	Schism ex RCC by 12 priests, 6 churches. Support from Swiss Old Catholics. Milan.
Ch Cristiana Avventista del 7 Giorno	1864	P-Adv	x...k	88	5,025	7,000	15,000	3.10	*SDAs. Seventh-day Adventists. Italian Mission.* 30nx,76mw,1j,1p(30),1s,62t,201Y.
Chiesa Cristiana Cattolica		I-OCa	U....	1	60	100	150	0.05	*Old Catholic Ch.* In Scandiano (Reggio Emilia). Links with Union of Utrecht. 1n.
Chiesa Cristiana Ev dei Fratelli in I	1833	P-CBr	x...k	230	14,000	20,000	25,000	0.90	*Christian Ch of the Brethren. Plymouth (Open) Brethren.* Piedmont, Puglie. 25f.
Chiesa di Dio	1963	P-Pe3	ZF...	18	2,635	1,000	4,590	6.29	*Ch of God.* M=CoG(Cleveland) (USA). Calabria and southern Italy. 8n,2f,W=50%,5Y,20z.
Chiese Elim in Italia	1993	P-Pe2	Z....	50	4,000	–	6,000	50.00	*CEI. Italian Elim Churches.* M=Ch (UK). 25 chs of Ghanaians. 11n.
Chiesa di Gesù Cristo dei Santi dUG	1850	m-LdS	x....	89	8,400	2,307	14,000	7.48	*dUG=degli Ultimi Giorni, Ch of JC of Latter-day Saints. Mormons.* HQ USA, 50f.
Chiesa Evangelica del Nazareno	1948	P-Hol	xF...	9	462	2,000	879	-3.23	*Ch of the Nazarene.* M=CoN(USA). 7n,1x,6m,2f,1p,10t,10t(287),W=43%,37Y.
Chiesa Evangelica Internazionale	1957	I-3pW	ZW...	350	25,600	15,000	30,000	2.81	*International Ev Ch.* Ex AoG. Rapidly-growing merger of independents. 70n,1p.
Chiesa Evangelica Luterana in Italia	1648	P-Lut	L.C.K	48	5,000	7,000	7,000	0.00	Germans. Member of VELKD. 1948 union of 9 congregations (Venice, 1648). 2n,8x,400z.
Chiesa Evangelica Mennonita	1949	P-Men	G....	5	129	200	270	1.21	*Ev Mennonite Ch.* M=Mennonite Ch of N America. HQ Florence. 7f.
Chiesa Evangelica Riformata Svizzera		P-Ref	Rwc..	10	600	500	1,000	0.05	*Swiss Evangelical Reformed Ch.* Swiss immigrants. Florence, Genoa, Milan, Naples.
Chiesa Evangelica Valdese e Metodiste	1173	P-Wal	RWC.K	200	21,620	29,413	29,359	-0.01	*Waldensians and Methodists.* 75n,8x,1p,1s(6),W=40%,320Yy,4135z.
Chiesa Neo-Apostolica	c1950	I-3aX	x....	30	1,000	20,000	1,852	-9.08	*New Apostolic Ch.* In Bezirk Schweiz. Germans. World HQ Zurich (Switzerland).
Chiesa Ortodossa Greca (D Austria)		O-Gre	Cwc..	9	40,000	25,000	80,000	0.05	*Greek Orthodox Ch.* Under Ecumenical Patriarchate of Constantinople. Greeks. 5x.
Chiesa Ortodossa Russa	1823	O-Rus	Mwc..	8	1,600	2,000	2,000	0.00	*Russian Orthodox Ch.* 1929, state recognition. Rome, Florence, Bari, Merano. 4x.
Chiesa Ortodossa Russa (ROCOR)		I-Rus	x....	1	300	1,000	500	0.05	*Russian Orthodox Ch Outside of Russia.* M=ROCOR(USA). HQ New York. Conservative.
Chiesa Pentecostal Santita	1986	P-Pe3	.....	2	75	–	150	11.11	Pentecostal Holiness Ch. M=IPHC(USA).
Chiesa Pentecostal Unite	1972	P-Pe1	x....	17	1,190	300	1,980	4.35	*United Pentecostal Ch. Jesus Only Church.* M=UPC(USA). Palermo area. 2n,2f.
Chiesa Presbiteriana Scozzese	1862	P-Ref	Rwc..	15	300	160	1,000	7.61	M=Ch of Scotland (UK). English-speaking congregations: Rome, Genoa, Milan. 2f.
Chiesa Universale Giuris-Davidica	1878	I-mar	.....	2	500	1,800	1,000	-2.32	*Universal Ch of Law revealed to David* (=Catholic heretic, shot 1878). 20n,24Yy.
Chiese Cinese	c1970	I-ind	.....	11	330	–	550	28.71	Chinese Churches.
Chiese di Cristo in Italia	1947	I-Dis	x....	54	2,000	3,000	4,000	1.16	*Churches of Christ.* M=CCCC(Instrumental) (USA). Rapid growth. 42n,15f,1j,1p,230Y.
Chiese Ev Cristiana Independente	c1970	I-3pW	....	10	400	–	800	30.65	*Independent Evangelical Christian Chs.* In Frosinone Province. F=evangelist Abel Aureli.
Chiese Pentecostali Autonome		I-3pW	.....	350	70,000	6,400	140,000	0.05	*Independent Pentecostal Churches.* Several autonomous networks, including Naples.
Communione delle Ch Cris Libere	1969	I-Bap	.....	9	1,400	1,800	2,800	1.78	*Communion of Free Evangelical Churches.*
Comunità Catt dei SS Andrea Ap e di C		I-ReC	.v...	2	600	500	1,000	0.05	*C=Caffa. Comunità Ecclesiale Ecumenica, Roma.* 1972 applied to join WCC.
Comunità Religiosa Serbo-Ortodossa	1782	I-Ser	Cwc..	3	1,500	1,000	2,800	4.20	*Serbian Orthodox Ch.* In Trieste. 1944, rejected P Belgrade; under USA bishop.
Congregazioni Cristiane Pentecostal	1927	P-Pe2	.....	57	10,000	10,000	20,000	48.61	*CCP. Pentecostal Christian Congregations.* Autonomous churches.
Esercito della Salvezza	1886	P-Sal	xwc.k	40	2,000	4,000	3,000	-1.14	*Salvation Army, Italy Territory.* 8 institutions. 43n,6x,W=80%,15Y,30z.
Missione Alleanza Evangelica	1981	P-Eva	.....	2	140	–	400	7.14	Evangelical Alliance Mission. M=TEAM.
Missione Italiana per le Vangelo	1969	P-Non	.....	92	3,640	1,170	6,070	6.81	*MIE. Italian Gospel Mission.*
Mov Evangelico Int Fiumi di Potenza	1957	I-3pW	.....	13	1,400	1,070	1,670	1.80	*Streams of Power Internat Evangelistic Movement.* M=SOP(Netherlands).
Società della Scienza Cristiana		m-Sci	x....	8	600	1,000	700	0.05	*Ch of Christ, Scientist. Christian Science.* M=CCS(Boston, USA). 2m,7w.
Testimoni di Geova	1891	m-Jeh	x....	2,419	180,960	80,000	377,000	6.40	*Jehovah's Witnesses.* 1903 first magazines printed. (1975) 2873Y. (1995) 9813Y.
Unevangelized Fields Mission	1974	P-Non	.....	16	595	–	1,190	4.76	M=UFM.
Unione Cristiana Ev Battista d'Italia	1863	P-Bap	TuC.K	98	4,550	10,100	10,300	0.08	*UCEBI.* 1956 *Baptist Union of I.* M=SBC(USA). 55n,3x,25f,1s,W=75%,174Y,80z.
Other pentecostal/charismatic chs	c1970	I-3pW	.....	1,000	125,000	–	200,000	62.95	50 bodies including: Association of Vineyard Chs, Ch of God in Christ, JILF, CER.
Other Protestant denominations		P-	.....	400	10,000	14,800	20,000	0.05	Total over 120 smaller groups (see list below).
Other independent Catholic chs		I-CCa	.....	42	5,000	10,000	8,330	0.05	Total over 30 small bodies (see list below), 15 being under bishops-at-large.
Other marginal Protestant bodies		m-	.....	45	2,000	2,000	5,000	0.05	Total over 30 (see list below).
Other Third-World indigenous chs		I-3pA	.....	60	5,000	200	7,000	0.05	Rapidly-growing immigrant bodies, totaling 5 by 1976 (see below).
Doubly-affiliated		2-aff			-344,000	-243,541	-407,544		Evangelicals and other minorities who also are or were baptized Roman Catholics.
Disaffiliated		X-Aff			-7,976,000	-3,545,000	-9,460,770		Baptized Catholics who have become completely disaffiliated agnostics or atheists.
Totals				**37,427**	**39,806,221**	**47,500,000**	**47,217,000**		

Churches, members, growth, 1900-2025	*Congs*	*Adults*	*Affiliated*	*G%*	*Total denominations*	*6 Megablocs:* O	R	A	P	I	m
Total churches, members, and denominations (mid-1900)	20,000	24,598,000	32,903,000	0.53	21	1	1	1	10	5	3
Total churches, members, and denominations (mid-1970)	28,356	35,511,624	47,500,000	0.53	137	3	1	1	75	38	19
Total churches, members, and denominations (mid-1990)	33,000	39,934,000	47,368,000	-0.01	303	3	1	1	150	110	38
Total churches, members, and denominations (mid-1995)	37,427	39,806,221	47,217,000	-0.06	319	3	1	1	152	124	38
Total churches, members, and denominations (mid-2000)	38,000	39,558,000	46,922,140	-0.13	337	3	1	1	154	140	38
Total churches, members, and denominations (mid-2025)	21,000	34,438,000	40,849,000	-0.55	512	10	1	1	180	270	50

NOTES ON TABLE ABOVE

NATIONAL COUNCILS (Column 4, 5th letter).

E = Aleanza Evangelica Italiana (AEI, Italian Evangelical Alliance, IEA).
H = Fellowship of Evangelical Pentecostal Churches in Italy (FECI).
K = Federazione delle Chiese Evangeliche in Italia (FCEI) (Federation of Protestant Churches in Italy) (up to 1967, Consiglio Federale).
k = affiliated member of FCEI (Salvation Army), or member of Legal Advisory Board (all other churches).
R = Conferenza Episcopale Italiana (CEI) (Italian Episcopal Conference).

Local councils. 5 regional councils affiliated to FCEI.

OTHER PROTESTANT DENOMINATIONS. There are a large number of smaller denominations. Names are given here in Italian unless more commonly known by English or French names. They include: Action Biblique, Avventisti del 7 Giorno Movimenti di Reforma, Baptist Mid-Missions (1951: 8 missionaries), Baptist Missionary Association of America, Chiesa Battista Autonoma, Chiesa Cristiana Biblica (Bible Christian Union) (1950; 15 missionaries), Chiesa Cristiana Evangelica, Chiesa Cristiana Ev dei Fratelli Stretti (Darbisti) (Strict Brethren, Darbyites; Raven-Taylor group), Chiesa Cristiana Protestante, Chiesa di Cristo, Chiesa Presbiteriana Autonoma di Milano, Children of God International (Rome), Christian Ch of North America, Ch of God (Anderson), Communion of Free Churches, Comunità Cristiana Evangelica, Comunità Evangelica Ecumenica di Ispra-Varese, Congregazione Olandese-Alemanna, Crusaders for Christ, Gospel Missionary Union (1950), Greater Europe Mission (1954), Gypsy Ev Movement (France, Switzerland), Independent Faith Mission, International Pentecostal Assemblies, L'Abri Fellowship, Missionary & Soul-Winning Fellowship, Missione Cristiana Europea (European Christian Mission), Missione di Beatenberg, Missione Norvegese per Marittimi (10,000 visitors a year to Seamen's Mission, Genoa), SDA Movement of Reform, Slavic Gospel Association, Società Religiosa degli Amici (Quaccheri), Unione delle Chiese Libere, US Armed Forces chaplaincies (for 10,000 Protestants), West Indies Mission (1972), World Baptist Fellowship Mission Agency (1970), Worldwide European Fellowship, World-Wide Missions (1963).

OTHER CATHOLIC (NON-ROMAN) CHURCHES. These bodies, mostly schisms from the Roman Catholic Church, are very small, and include: Antoinists (Belgium), Chiesa Cattolica Apostolica Ortodossa, Chiesa Cattolica Liberale, Chiesa Vetero-Cattolica, and about 15 miniscule bodies with few lay followers under episcopi vagantes (bishops-at-large). One larger dissident body follows the papal claimant Clement XV (Michel Collin, died 1974) and his Renewed Church of Christ the King (HQ Dijon, France).

OTHER THIRD-WORLD INDIGENOUS CHURCHES. A large Korean movement has opened centers in Rome and Milan: Associazione dello Spirito Santo per l'Unificazione del Cristianesimo nel Mondo (Holy Spirit Association for the Unification of World Christianity). In 1976, Nigerian students in Rome had formed a small congregation of the Christ Apostolic Church from Ibadan (Nigeria). There is also a church of the Father Divine Peace Mission Movement (USA Blacks).

OTHER MARGINAL PROTESTANT BODIES. These include: Amis de l'Homme, Associazione Universale Alaya (1953), Chiesa del Regno di Dio (Amis de l'Homme/Freytag; begun in Italy 1946; HQ Turin), Ch of Our Lord Jesus Christ (Bickertonites), Missione degli Apostoli della Fede (begun 1936), Missione di Fede (begun 1944), New Ch, Reorganized Ch of Jesus Christ of Latter-day Saints (USA).

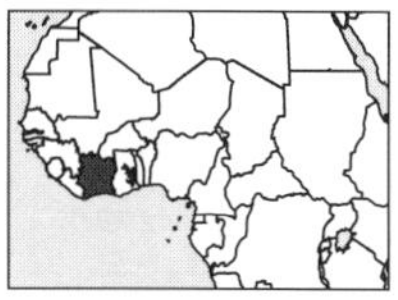

IVORY COAST

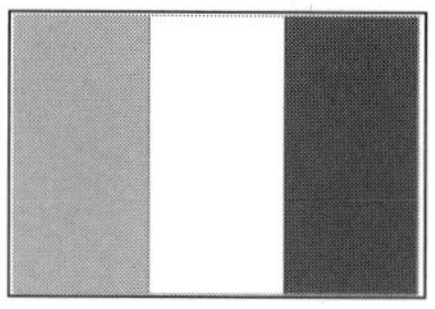

SECULAR DATA, AD 2000

STATE
Official name: La République de Côte d'Ivoire (The Republic of the Ivory Coast).
Short name: Ivory Coast. **Adjective of nationality:** Ivoirien.
Flag: Tricolor of orange, white, and green bars.
Area: 322,463 sq. km. (124,504 sq. mi.).
Government: Multiparty republic with one legislative house, since 1990 (1842 French protectorate, 1893 colony, 1958 autonomous state, 1960 Independence, 1960 one-party republic).
Legislature: National Assembly, 175 members.
Official language: French (Français).
Monetary unit: 1 CFA franc (CFAF) = 100 centimes.
US$1= CFAF 560.38.
Chief cities: ABIDJAN 3,359,000; Bouake 501,010; Korhogo 227,732; Daloa 194,910; Gagnoa 178,073.
Political divisions: 50 provinces.
Armed forces: 8,400.

DEMOGRAPHY
Population: 14,786,000.
Population density: 45.8/sq. km. (118.7/sq. mi.).
Under 15 years: 6,421,000.
Growth rate p.a.: 2.11% (births 35.95, deaths 15.30).
Mortality: Infant, per 1000 79.7; **Maternal per 100,000:** 810.0.
Life expectancy: 48 (male 47, female 48).
Household size: 5.4. **Floor area per person, sq.m:** 10.0.
Major languages: Mandingo, French, Baule, Kru, Dioula, Mande, Senufo, Lagoon, and about 60 other languages.
Urban dwellers: 46.53%. **Urban growth rate p.a.:** 3.6%.
Labor force: 39%.

ETHNOLINGUISTIC PEOPLES
12.1% Baule (Bawule); 11.4% Mossi; 9.0% Ivorian Malinke; 6.4% Southern Senufo (Minianka); 6.0% Dan (Yakuba, Diabula).

ECONOMY
National income p.a. per person: US$660; **per family:** US$3,564.

EDUCATION
Adult literacy: 40% (male 49%, female 30%). **Schools:** 7,249.
Universities: 1. **School enrolment:** female/male: 39%/58%.

HEALTH
Access to health services: 30%. **Access to safe water:** 72%.
Hospitals: 100 (8 beds per 10,000). **Doctors:** 2,020.
Blind: 50,000. **Deaf:** 908,600. **Murder rate:** 2.
Lepers: 250,000. **Underweight prevalence under 5:** 24%.

LITERATURE
New book titles p.a.: 1,480 (100 p.a. per million). **Periodicals:** 25.
Newspapers: 1 daily.

COMMUNICATION (per 1,000 people)
Phones: 8 (34% mobile). **Radios:** 110. **TV sets:** 59.
Daily newspaper circulation: 7. **Computers:** 15.

REFUGEES
Alien refugees from other countries: 290,000.

HUMAN LIFE AND LIBERTY (optimum condition=100.0%)
HDI: 36.8. **HSI:** 26.0. **HFI:** 35.0. **EFL:** 35.0.

Country Table 1. **Religious adherents in the Ivory Coast, AD 1900-2025.**

Year	1900		1970		mid-1990		Annual change, 1990-2000				mid-1995		mid-2000		mid-2025	
Name	Adherents	%	Adherents	%	Adherents	%	Natural	Conversion	Total	Rate	Adherents	%	Adherents	%	Adherents	%
Ethnoreligionists	949,300	94.9	2,705,000	49.1	4,500,400	38.7	121,864	-16,446	105,418	2.13	5,139,000	38.0	5,554,576	37.6	7,300,000	31.3
Christians	**700**	**0.1**	**1,546,800**	**28.1**	**3,645,000**	**31.3**	**98,714**	**6,971**	**105,685**	**2.58**	**4,270,600**	**31.6**	**4,701,854**	**31.8**	**8,076,000**	**34.6**
PROFESSION																
professing Christians	**700**	**0.1**	**1,546,800**	**28.1**	**3,645,000**	**31.3**	**98,714**	**6,971**	**105,685**	**2.58**	**4,270,600**	**31.6**	**4,701,854**	**31.8**	**8,076,000**	**34.6**
AFFILIATION																
unaffiliated Christians	150	0.0	456,022	8.3	305,000	2.6	8,260	-3,963	4,297	1.33	320,448	2.4	347,972	2.4	354,000	1.5
affiliated Christians	**550**	**0.1**	**1,090,778**	**19.8**	**3,340,000**	**28.7**	**90,454**	**10,934**	**101,388**	**2.69**	**3,950,152**	**29.2**	**4,353,882**	**29.5**	**7,722,000**	**33.1**
Roman Catholics	550	0.1	626,855	11.4	1,693,000	14.6	45,850	3,138	48,988	2.57	1,988,862	14.7	2,182,882	14.8	3,750,000	16.1
Independents	0	0.0	308,300	5.6	1,040,000	8.9	28,165	5,135	33,300	2.82	1,239,351	9.2	1,373,000	9.3	2,500,000	10.7
Protestants	0	0.0	151,623	2.8	580,000	5.0	15,708	2,292	18,000	2.74	688,573	5.1	760,000	5.1	1,400,000	6.0
Orthodox	0	0.0	3,000	0.1	15,000	0.1	406	94	500	2.92	18,000	0.1	20,000	0.1	32,000	0.1
Marginal Christians	0	0.0	1,000	0.0	12,000	0.1	325	275	600	4.14	15,366	0.1	18,000	0.1	40,000	0.2
Trans-megabloc groupings																
Evangelicals	0	0.0	60,000	1.1	425,000	3.7	11,510	12,490	24,000	4.58	575,701	4.3	665,000	4.5	1,300,000	5.6
Pentecostals/Charismatics	0	0.0	58,000	1.1	900,000	7.7	24,374	7,126	31,500	3.05	1,087,029	8.0	1,215,000	8.2	2,400,000	10.3
Great Commission Christians	**1,000**	**0.1**	**551,000**	**10.0**	**1,500,000**	**12.9**	**40,623**	**12,931**	**53,554**	**3.10**	**1,800,000**	**13.3**	**2,035,544**	**13.8**	**3,600,000**	**15.4**
Muslims	50,000	5.0	1,255,700	22.8	3,429,000	29.5	92,864	8,695	101,559	2.63	4,042,000	29.9	4,444,589	30.1	7,773,000	33.3
Nonreligious	0	0.0	2,000	0.0	35,000	0.3	948	627	1,575	3.79	45,000	0.3	50,753	0.3	120,000	0.5
Baha'is	0	0.0	4,000	0.1	16,000	0.1	433	196	629	3.37	20,600	0.2	22,289	0.2	50,000	0.2
Hindus	0	0.0	500	0.0	6,600	0.1	179	-11	168	2.29	7,600	0.1	8,280	0.1	18,000	0.1
Other religionists	0	0.0	1,000	0.0	3,000	0.0	81	-32	49	1.53	3,200	0.0	3,491	0.0	8,000	0.0
World A (unevangelized persons)	950,000	95.0	2,757,666	50.0	3,851,185	33.1	104,250	-86,289	17,961	0.46	4,153,203	30.7	4,036,578	27.3	4,995,830	21.4
World B (evangelized non-Christians)	49,300	4.9	1,210,866	21.9	4,138,815	35.6	112,119	79,318	191,437	3.87	5,104,546	37.7	6,047,568	40.9	10,273,170	44.0
World C (Christians)	700	0.1	1,546,800	28.1	3,645,000	31.3	98,714	6,971	105,685	2.58	4,270,600	31.6	4,701,854	31.8	8,076,000	34.6
Country's population	**1,000,000**	**100.0**	**5,515,332**	**100.0**	**11,635,000**	**100.0**	**315,083**	**0**	**315,083**	**2.43**	**13,528,350**	**100.0**	**14,786,000**	**100.0**	**23,345,000**	**100.0**

COLUMNS, ROWS.
For meanings and definitions, see Codebook (Part 3). Note that, by definition, total 'Christians' = professing + crypto-Christians, which also = affiliated + unaffiliated Christians, and also = Great Commission Christians + latent Christians. Percentages may not always total exactly, due to rounding.

CENSUSES.
1957-58 (sample survey, CHEAM): 64.3% ethnoreligionists, 22.4% Muslims, 9.4% Roman Catholics, 1.7% Protestants, 1.4% Harrists. **1975:** 33.3% Muslims, 30.0% ethnoreligionists, 22.0% Roman Catholics, 6.1% nonreligious, 5.7% Protestants, 1.9% Harrists, 2.0% other religionists. **1988:** 38.7% Muslims, 20.8% Roman Catholics, 17.0% ethnoreligionists, 13.4% nonreligious, 5.3% Protestants, 3.4% other religionists, 1.4% Harrists.

NOTES ON RELIGIONS
BAHA'IS. Growth from 1 local spiritual assembly (1964) to 27 (1973), and to 62 LSAs (1996).
ETHNORELIGIONISTS. Tribes over 60% traditionalist (animist) in 1995: Gagu Pygmies (90%), Lobi (97%), Kulango (90%), Ngere (75%), Wobe (71%), Guro (75%), Dan (Yakuba) (62%), Bete (60%). Many peoples remain resistant to Islam.
INDEPENDENTS. In about 45 denominations in 1995 (see Table 2). Strongly Harrist tribes include: Ajukru, Assini, Attie, Dida, Ebrie.
MUSLIMS. Sunnis (of the Malikite rite): strongest among the Malinke (70%), Bambara (70%), Senufo (30%), Minianka (30%). Islam is growing numerically in 4 different ways, in addition to natural increase: (1) conversions to Islam among ethnoreligionists, especially among the Bete and Dida; (2) conversions to Islam in the cities among foreign migrant laborers. (3) conversions of Christians to Islam, especially among the Baule; and (4) the growing influx of foreign Muslims from Mali, Niger, and Burkina Faso, mostly itinerant businessmen. There is also an Ahmadiya Mission Begun 1961: Qadianis in Abidjan (Yorubas from Nigeria), also in northeast from around Wa in Ghana (enumerated here under Muslims although declared non-Muslim by Pakistan). Muslims in Abidjan: (1955) 37%, (1963) 38.4%, (1965) 40%, (1970) 45%. Hajj pilgrims to Mecca. (1970) 567; (1974) 1,165; (1976) 916.
NONRELIGIOUS. French and, after 1970, African intellectuals and others.
OTHER RELIGIONISTS. Adherents of smaller religions and cults, including Rosicrucians (21 AMORC centers).

Great Commission Instrument Panel: status of the Ivory Coast (for explanation see start of Part 4)

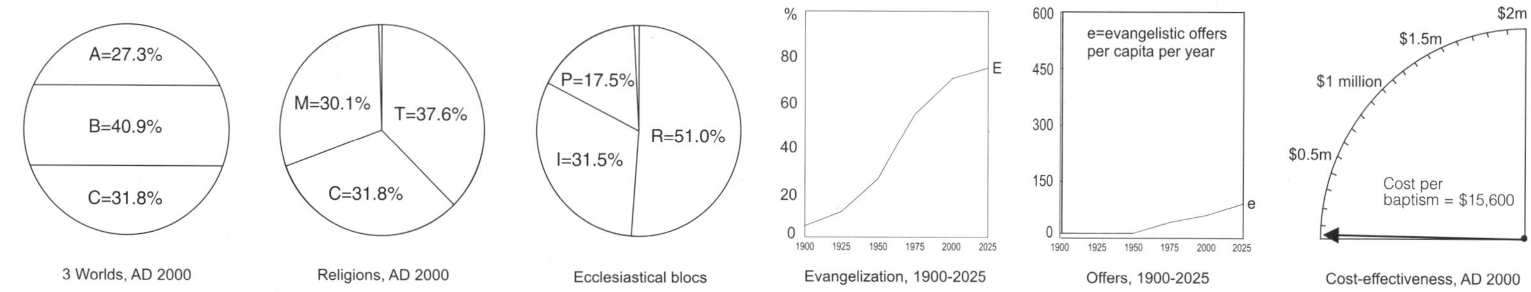

Country status. Ivory Coast, one of the most francophone West African countries, has been described as quite different from the rest of Africa. It is an oasis of political stability and steady economic growth—described as the Ivorian miracle — and it is also one of the most authoritarian states in the region. Ivory Coast is a leading exporter of tropical timber as well as exporting coffee, cacao, and bananas.

HUMAN LIFE AND LIBERTY

Human need and development. As in many other African countries, the standard of living is characterized by extremes of poverty on one hand and relative Western-style affluence on the other. Because opportunities for material advancement are limited to a small segment of the urban population, there is a constant drain of population from the countryside to the cities. This migration in turn aggravates problems such as juvenile delinquency, prostitution, unemployment, and overcrowding. Sanitation is poor throughout the country. Water polluted with human and animal waste is used indiscriminately for bathing, drinking, and laundering. Food is stored and sold in the open, exposed to dirt and flies. Disease is rampant, and medical facilities are limited. In rural areas, the witch doctor is an ever present source of help to the villagers. Nevertheless, the population is more upwardly mobile than in neighboring African countries. Western goods and services are available even

Country summary. **Worlds A, B, C by ethnolinguistic peoples, cities, and major civil divisions in the Ivory Coast.**

World	PEOPLES Num	Pop 2000	C%	Christians	E%	U%	Unevangelized
A	40	2,754,665	1.72	47,507	38	62	1,696,526
B	36	10,299,448	28.06	2,889,705	77	23	2,329,174
C	27	1,731,722	81.81	1,416,667	100	0	3,910
Total	**103**	**14,785,835**	**29.45**	**4,353,879**	**73**	**27**	**4,029,610**

World	CITIES Num	Pop 2000	C%	Christians	E%	U%	Unevangelized
A	4	696,546	3.53	24,594	39	61	426,071
B	3	4,005,758	30.99	1,241,353	80	20	783,349
C	0	0	0.00	0	0	0	0
Total	**7**	**4,702,304**	**26.92**	**1,265,947**	**74**	**26**	**1,209,420**

World	CIVIL DIVISIONS Num	Pop 2000	C%	Christians	E%	U%	Unevangelized
A	8	1,863,796	5.34	99,439	44	56	1,051,274
B	42	12,922,031	32.92	4,254,442	77	23	2,978,329
C	0	0	0.00	0	0	0	0
Total	**50**	**14,785,827**	**29.45**	**4,353,881**	**73**	**27**	**4,029,603**

in remote rural areas. The consumption of these goods and services is causing most families to live beyond their incomes. Another drain on the average family's resources is the traditional practice of allowing all members of an extended family to claim hospitality for indefinite periods from their more fortunate brethren. In rural areas mud huts are the norm, but apartment houses have become popular in the cities.

Human rights and freedoms. As in any authoritarian state, human rights have been always circumscribed in Ivory Coast; nevertheless, it is a benevolent authoritarianism that shuns flagrant abuses. Occasional episodes of brutality are the exceptions rather than the rule. Security forces sometimes carry out extrajudicial killings or arrests of political opponents. Abidjan has one of the highest levels of crime in the world, as a result of which the police use force frequently against armed criminals. There is only a tenuous distinction between the executive and the judicial branches of government, and the judges rarely ignore government interests in their judgments. Freedom of expression is guaranteed by the Constitution, but was significantly limited in practice until 1992. Criticism of the president and defamation of national or foreign state dignitaries are punishable crimes. Abuses of human rights are investigated by an internal, independent human rights organization, the Ivorian League of Human Rights. In traditional society, Ivorian women enjoy considerable political and economic clout. Nevertheless, they occupy a distinctly subordinate position in public and suffer from widespread incidence of domestic violence.

Human environment. Ivory Coast has one of the highest deforestation rates in the world. Uncontrolled birth rates and immigration from neighboring countries have contributed to the encroachment of built up areas into forest lands. Deforestation is accompanied by soil degradation and water pollution. Many endangered species have become extinct in recent years.

NON-CHRISTIAN RELIGIONS

African traditional religions remain very influential. The Kulango, Lobi, Ngere and Gagu are still more than 90% traditionalist; the Anyi, Dan, Baule, Guro and Wobe more than 70%; the Bete, Brong and Senufo more than 60%; and the population as a whole 46% in 1975. Names for God include Nyam (among

Ethnoreligionists. Mask used in traditional religious ceremonies among the Dan (Yacouba) tribes of whom 60% are ethnoreligionists.

the Ajukru), Nyangka (ebrie) and Zra (Dan): Zra is the creator and all other spirits owe their origin to him. All these spirits are good except Kogbin-dy who incites men to practice witchcraft, which is considered to be man's greatest crime and the only one judged by Zra after death. God is the witchcraft eradicator par excellence, but the good spirit Zole-dy is also active in enlisting living men in the service of witchcraft eradication. The rites of several secret societies of eradicators, of which the most important is Yuomi, have as their aim the transformation of their initiates into animals to better observe the activities of witches.

Eglise Déimatiste. *Top.* Church in Seria among Bete tribe. Note crosses in relief, also 2 entrance doors (men's on right, women's on left). *Center.* Procession before church service. The banner reads: 'Pope Lalou rules in Seria'. *Lower.* Officiants vested for the liturgy, with chief prophet (center).

Islam is growing in numbers largely because of the influx of foreign ethnic groups from Mali, Niger and the Upper Volta. The principal agents of its propagation are itinerant traders and small businessmen. Its strength is in the northwest, the Malinke and Bambara being 70% Muslim and the Senufo and Minianka 30%. The capital Abidjan is around 47% Muslim.

Eglise Catholique, Archdiocese de Korhogo. Cathedral, in heavily islamized north.

CHRISTIANITY

CATHOLIC CHURCH. French missionaries worked briefly in the Ivory Coast in 1637, but the difficult coastline discouraged the opening of European ports. France established a protectorate over the area in 1842 which stimulated a renewal of Catholic interest. A prefecture was created in 1895 with responsibility for evangelization given to the African Missions of Lyons (SMA), and missionaries of the Sisters of Our Lady of the Apostles arrived in 1898. The prefecture of Korhogo was erected to serve the north in 1911; it is now an archdiocese.

The first indigenous priests were ordained in 1934 and the first local archbishop was consecrated in 1960. The hierarchy was established with its metropolitan see at Abidjan in 1955. A diocesan synod was organized in Abidjan between March 1969 and November 1971, one session being held each year during the 3-year period. These assemblies brought together all active priests, lay persons chosen by their parishes and movements and delegates elected by sisters, novices, and seminarians. After the second session, lay delegates became more numerous than priests.

Catholicism is localized largely in the south where evangelization was begun in 1895. The church is especially strong in the cities. Surveys undertaken by the Ministry of Planning indicate that more than 50% of the population of Abidjan is Catholic. A desire to rise socially is undoubtedly one of the reasons for becoming Christians; but one notes also among the baptized elite, especially in the capital, a certain dechristianization which is linked to the process of urbanization.

The Holy See has diplomatic relations with Ivory Coast and in AD 2000 is represented to government and the Catholic hierarchy by a nuncio residing in Abidjan.

Eglise Catholique. Yamousoukro Basilica built by former President Houphouet-Boigny, seating 7,000 plus 11,000 standing.

INDIGENOUS CHURCHES. The Harris Church arose through the preaching of the Liberian Grebo prophet William Wade Harris during 1913-15, through whose ministry 120,000 adults were converted and baptized. About 20,000 later became

Catholics and 25,000 Methodists, but the majority organized themselves as an independent church. Though they have a central committee, Harrists are divided into various branches, the principal one being that among the Ebrie at Petit Bassam, near Abidjan. Others are located at Toukouzou and Grand Lahou on the Atlantic coast. Harrism is still strong in rural areas, especially among the Ebrie and Attie of the southeast; but adherents are decreasing in the cities. Other indigenous churches include a large schism in 1922 from Catholicism, the Glise Deimatiste and 2 schisms from Methodism, the Eglise Adaiste (1932) mainly among the Dida and the Eglise Protestante Libre in 1968. Approximately 30 other small independent churches are also active, some of which have entered the Ivory Coast from Ghana and Nigeria. Schisms from Harrism have been especially numerous.

PROTESTANT CHURCH. Protestantism did not enter the Ivory Coast until after World War I, the first British Methodist missionary arriving in 1924. Other missions followed soon afterwards, the Mission Biblique (France) in 1927, CMA (USA) in 1930 and WEC in 1934. Protestant work is characterized by comity agreements which tend to give to the principal churches a regional orientation. Methodists, active among the Alagya, Attie, Ari, Avikam, and Dida in the southeastern part of the country, are the strongest Protestant denomination. Other groups include the Evangelical Protestant Church (related to CMA) and the Protestant Church (WEC) among the Baule, Guro, and Gagu pygmies of central Ivory Coast; the Union of Evangelical Churches (Mission Biblique, UFM) among the Dan, Bete, Wobe, and Ngere of the southwest; Freewill Baptists (1957) among the Lobi, Kulango, and Diula of the northeast; and Conservative Baptists (1947) among the Senufo of the northwest. Seventh-day Adventists are also at work on the southwest coast and Assemblies of God in Abidjan, and there has been a Yoruba community of the Nigerian Baptist Convention in the Ivory Coast since 1930.

Renewal movements. In the 1990s the Pentecostal/Charismatic Renewal continued to spread rapidly across most older churches, and numbered over 1,215,000 adherents (of whom 18% Pentecostals, 16% Charismatics, and 66% Independents).

Eglise Harriste. Temple Biblique Harriste in Abidjan, showing highly original architecture characteristic of this largest of over 34 Ivorian indigenous churches.

Indigenous missions. Missionaries from Ivory Coast have been sent out for the past 4 decades, primarily to surrounding Francophone countries. Recently, some missionaries have been trained specifically for outreach to Muslims.

CHURCH AND STATE

According to the constitution of November 1960, which was further modified in January 1963, the Ivory Coast is a secular republic (Article 2), and 'The Republic . . . shall respect all religious beliefs' (Article 6).

Religious education in public schools is conducted outside class hours, and chaplains are supplied for Catholic and Protestant instruction when at least 10 students make the request. Private confessional education must obey laws common to all private schools.

The president of the republic participates personally in important religious ceremonies. In 1966, without prior consultation with the religious authorities, the government established a special and progressive tax intended to finance the construction of Catholic, Protestant, Harrist, and Muslim cathedrals 'worthy of the urbanism' of Abidjan. At the same time, president Houphouet-Boigny has repeatedly urged the population to cease being animists or traditionalists and to be converted to one of the 3 major religions.

Although at present authorizations for the opening of new classes are suspended, the development of Catholic schools during the colonial period resulted in the presence of a high percentage of Catholics in the upperclasses and in the new national bourgeoisie. Because of this fact, the influence of the Catholic Church in the country, and above all in Abidjan, is greater than its numerical size would indicate.

In 1974, a convention was concluded between the state and Catholic education authorities, guaranteeing a financial contribution towards the salaries of personnel teaching in Catholic schools, at the rate of 66% to 80% of equivalent salaries in the public educational sector. The convention also renewed the guarantee of freedom regarding the exercise of Catholic instruction and allocated to the state the duties of inspection, control of programs and financial oversight of Catholic schools.

BROADCASTING AND MEDIA

Nearly one out of 6 own a radio. Ivory Coast is a member of UNDA, and there are 3 Catholic FM radio stations: Radio Espoir, Radio Sanwi, and Radio Man. Shortwave radio broadcasts from KNLS have generated response. AWR maintains its Africa headquarters in Abidjan; from this studio it develops French and English programs.

Some 7.6 million (41%) have seen the 'Jesus' Film, chiefly through TV (5 million) and film teams (2.3 million). Videotape copies are also widespread, and mission agencies have found it to be a useful tool.

INTERDENOMINATIONAL ORGANIZATIONS

There is no national ecumenical Christian council, but most Protestant bodies belong to the Evangelical Federation of the Ivory Coast, composed of churches and missions related to the CMA, WEC, UFM, Conservative and Freewill Baptists, and the Mission Biblique. The Taizé Community from France attempts to promote dialogue between Protestants and Catholics.

FUTURE TRENDS AND PROSPECTS

Tribal religions are expected to continue a steady decline (94.9% in 1900 to 31.3% by 2025) while Christians could grow from 0.1% in 1900 to 35% by 2025. Muslims also benefit from the demise of ethnoreligionists growing from 5% in 1900 to over 33% by AD 2025.

By mid-century, Christians and Muslims could share the country's population 50%/50%. This situation may continue for a long time.

BIBLIOGRAPHY

'Ahmadiyya and urbanization: easing the integration of rural women in Abidjan,' M. M. Yacoob, *Asian and African studies*, 20, 1 (1986), 125–140.

Ahmadiyya and urbanization: migrant women in Abidjan. M. M. Yacoob. Boston: African Studies Center, Boston University, 1983. (A pamphlet).

Annuaire du clergé, des religieux et religieuses de Côte d'Ivoire, 1971. Abidjan, Ivory Coast: Secrétariat de l'Episcopat, 1971.

Avec Christ à l'oeuvre en Côte d'Ivoire aujourd'hui. S. A. Nandjui et al. Abidjan, Ivory Coast: Eglise Mèthodiste, 1969.

Beyond the stream: Islam and society in a West African town. R. Launay. *Comparative studies on Muslim societies*, 15. Berkeley, CA and Los Angeles: University of California Press, 1992. 275p.

'Carte des religions de l'Afrique de l'Ouest: République de la Côte d'Ivoire.' Paris: Université de Paris, n.d. (c1960). (Maps).

'Christianity African style: the Harrist Church of the Ivory Coast.' S. S. Walker. Ph.D. dissertation, University of Chicago, 1976. 392p.

Croyants dans la ville propos. R. Deniel. *Chemins de chrétiens africains*, 7. Abidjan, Ivory Coast: INADES, 1982. 36p.

Die Toura: zwischen Geisterglaube und Evangelium. I. Bearth-Braun. *Telos-Taschenbucher*, Nr. 7615. Neuheusen-Stuttgart: Hänssler, 1993. 99p.

Eglise et société Africaine: paroisse Saint–Pierre de Jacqueville, un siècle d'apostolat. H. Diabaté. Abidjan, Ivory Coast: Nouvelles éditions africaines, 1988. 203p.

Expression africaine de la foi recherche: rencontre du clergé ivoirien, Katiola, 1973. , [1973]. 52p.

La vie religieuse en Afrique: recherche en Côte d'Ivoire. 3rd ed. Abidjan, Ivory Coast: INADES, 1983. 112p.

'Le Harrisme et le Bwiti: deux réactions Africaines à l'impact Chrétien,' R. Bureau, *Recherches de Sciences Religieuses*, 63, 1 (1975), 83–100.

Le séparatisme religieux en Afrique noire: l'exemple de la Côte d'Ivoire. B. Holas. Paris: Presses Universitaires de France, 1965. 410p.

'L'Eglise Harriste.' R. Bureau. Bregbo, Ivory Coast, 1968. 79p. (Manuscript).

Les sectes et l'esprit sectaire. V. Bissett. 4th ed. Abidjan, Ivory Coast: Coopération et documentation missionnaires, 1992. 28p.

Lumière chrétienne sur le Mahikari. Catholic Church Conférence épiscopale de la Côte d'Ivoire. Ivory Coast, [1987]. 38p.

Religions dans la ville: croyances et changements sociaux à Abidjan. R. Deniel. Abidjan, Ivory Coast: Inades, 1975. 208p.

Sorciers, féticheurs et guérisseurs de la Côte d'Ivoire—Haute Volta. J. Kerharo & A. Bouquet. Paris: Vigot, 1950. 144p.

'Symbolic generalization: religion, health and modernization among the Ebrié of the Ivory Coast.' G. H. Stanton. Ph.D. dissertation, University of Chicago, 1986. 2 vols.

The prophet Harris: a study of an African prophet and his mass–movement in the Ivory Coast and the Gold Coast, 1913–1915. G. M. Haliburton. London: Longmans, 1971.

'The urban challenge of Cote d'Ivoire: toward an effective C&MA strategy of evangelizing Ivorian cities.' D. P. Harvey. D.Min. thesis, Columbia Biblical Seminary and Graduate School of Missions, Columbia, SC, 1994. 189p.

'The urban Muslims of Ivory Coast,' D. Schreiber, *Urban mission*, 3, 3 (January 1986), 39–43.

'Une guérisseur de la Basse Côte d'Ivoire: Josué Edjro,' H. Memel-Foté, *Cahiers d'études africaines*, 7 (1967), 547–605. (On the founder of the Eglise Protestante Libre).

'Une religion syncrétique en Côte d'Ivoire,' D. Paulme, *Cahiers d'études africaines*, 3, 1 (1963), 5–90. (Déima among the Dida).

Country Table 2. **Organized churches and denominations in the Ivory Coast.**

Official name (bold type = church with over 10% of all affiliated) 1	*Begun* 2	*Type* 3	*Counc* 4	*Congs* 5	*Adults* 6	*Affiliated 1970* 7	*Affiliated 1995* 8	*G%* 9	*Names, notes, and other statistics* (see Codebook, Part 3) 10
Alliance des Eglises Evangéliques	1934	P-Eva	xFG.G	175	16,100	5,000	26,800	6.95	M=MEAO(WEC,WEK). 57% Guro, 29% Baule, Animistic area. 8n,10f,W=75%,40Y.
Assemblée Chrétienne Missionnaire	c1970	I-3cA	.....	9	440	–	1,100	32.33	*Christian Missionary Fellowship.* Work among 19 African tribes.
Assemblées de Dieu	1927	P-Pe2	ZF...	760	135,400	5,000	189,000	15.64	*Assemblies of God.* M=AdD(France),AoG(USA). Abidjan area. 2 schools. 24n,16f,2s.
Assoc des Eglises Baptistes du Nord	1947	I-Bap	xFG.G	215	4,360	2,300	10,900	6.42	*ABN. Northern Baptist Chs.* M=CBFMS. Senufo, Diula. 4n,83m,90f,1H,2h,2s,84Y.
Convention Baptiste	1930	P-Bap	T....	116	4,400	2,000	8,000	5.70	M=NBC(Nigeria), 1966 FMB-SBC(USA). Begun by traders. 95% Yoruba. 2x,8f,W=80%,8Y,20z.
Eglise Adaïste	1932	I-mar	.....	90	4,500	5,000	11,300	3.32	Schism ex MMS under prophet Boto Adaï (died 1963). Dida. Major womens' roles.
Eglise Adventiste du Septième Jour	1946	P-Adv	x....	18	2,082	3,672	5,210	1.41	*Seventh-day Adventists, IC Mission,* W Africa UM. 38% Dida, 35% Bete. 5nx,16f,1s,W=80%,66Y.
Eglise Baptiste Libre	1957	P-Bap	xFg.G	42	714	1,000	1,786	2.35	*Free Will Baptist Ch.* M=NAFWB(USA). Northeast. Lobi, Kulango, Diula. 2n,24f,1H,1h.
Eglise Catholique en Côte d'Ivoire:	1637	R-Lat	P.SFR	275	1,150,300	626,855	1,988,862	4.73	C=15+2+17. (1970) 60n,320x,19821Yy. (1990). 300n 278x 496m 653w 44762Yy
M Abidjan	1895	R-Lat	Ps	31	277,000	329,000	478,000	1.51	20% urban. Catholic HQ of West Africa. 1p,1s. 67n 60x 189m 135w 8308Yy
D Grand-Bassam	1982	R-Lat	Ps	12	76,000	–	132,090	7.69	Coastal diocese. 21n 28x 43m 68w 4219Yy
D Yopougon	1982	R-Lat	Ps	22	221,000	–	381,000	7.69	New diocese. Very rapid growth. 10% Catholic. 47n 20x 20m 58w 7467Yy
M Bouaké	1951	R-Lat	Psma	13	37,000	73,943	63,800	-0.59	Strongly animist. 70% Baule, 15% Agni. 13n 25x 42m 66w 2709Yy
D Abengourou	1963	R-Lat	Ps	13	58,000	92,708	100,600	0.33	90% Agni, Brong, Attie. Only South evangelized. 14n 9x 13m 26w 3500Yy
D Bondoukou	1987	R-Lat	Ps	11	26,000	–	45,428	12.50	New diocese. 6n 23x 23m 29w 2240Yy
D Yamoussoukro	1992	R-Lat	Ps	13	45,000	–	78,293	33.33	Very recent diocese, 12.7% Catholic. 13n 16x 19m 35w 2824Yy

Continued overleaf

Country Table 2–concluded

Official name (bold type = church with over 10% of affiliated) 1	*Begun* 2	*Type* 3	*Counc* 4	*Congs* 5	*Adults* 6	*Affiliated 1970* 7	*Affiliated 1995* 8	*G%* 9	*Names, notes, and other statistics* (see Codebook, Part 3) 10
M Gagnoa	1956	R-Lat	Ps	19	69,000	74,543	118,800	1.88	27% Bete, 21% Avikam, 20% Dida, Bakwe. M=SMA. 45n 8x 24m 50w 3102Yy
D Daloa (Sassandra)	1940	R-Lat	Psma	15	19,000	10,685	33,500	4.68	18% Yakuba, 16% Wobe, 14% Bete, 14% Guro. 10n 23x 28m 50w 3000Yy
D Man	1968	R-Lat	Ps	19	249,000	15,976	429,985	14.08	High % animist, but open to evangelism. 1p. 23n 16x 34m 16w 1923Yy
D San Pedro-en-Côte d'I	1989	R-Lat	Ps	70	31,000	–	53,500	16.67	M=SMA. 8n 10x 10m 10w 2870Yy
M Korhogo	1970	R-Lat	Ps	18	9,000	10,000	16,200	1.95	Peoples highly islamized Senufo, Malinke. 12n 17x 25m 72w 1002Yy
D Katiola	1911	R-Lat	Ps	15	28,000	20,000	48,416	3.60	51% Tagwana, 15% Niarafolo, Tiembara. M=SMA. 6n 19x 22m 27w 1398Yy
D Odienné	1994	R-Lat	Ps	4	5,300	–	9,250	50.00	Population is 1.9% Catholic. 15n 4x 4m 11w 200Yy
Eglise de Dieu de Prophétie	1978	P-Pe3	.....	17	680	–	1,700	5.88	*Church of God of Prophecy.* M=CGP.
Eglise de J-C des Saints des DJ	c1985	m-LdS	.....	3	100	–	200	10.00	*Church of JC of Latter-day Saints. Mormons.*
Eglise Déimatiste	1922	I-mar	.....	840	84,000	90,000	140,000	1.78	*Ch of Ashes of Purification.* Schism ex-Catholics, led by female pope Lalou. Bete.
Eglise des Douze Apôtres	1920	I-Met	x....	27	2,700	3,000	7,000	3.45	*Church of the Twelve Apostles* (Ghana). 13 congregations in Abidjan.
Eglise des Oeuvres et Missions	c1980	I-3cA	.....	50	35,000	–	45,000	6.67	*Eglise Prot Baptiste.* Huge cell-based church in Abidjan, in other cities, also USA.
Eglise du Christianisme Céleste	c1970	I-3kA	Iv...	140	15,000	–	45,000	53.51	*Celestial Ch of Christ.* Large Nigerian indigenous church. Yoruba elites. In 11 countries.
Eglise du Nazarène	1986	P-Hol	.....	1	150	–	275	11.11	*Church of the Nazarene.* M=CoN.
Egl Episcopale Prot Libre (D W Africa)	1970	I-ARo	x....	1	1,000	1,000	1,670	2.07	*Free Protestant Episcopal Ch.* HQ Monrovia (Liberia). M=FPEC(UK,USA). Abidjan.
Eglise Ev Baptiste en CI	1971	I-Bap	.....	57	1,539	–	3,000	4.17	*Evangelical Baptist Church in Ivory Coast.* M=EBM(USA). 12f.
Eglise Evangelique du Reveill	1974	I-3pA	.....	300	30,000	–	75,000	4.76	*Revival Churches.* Schism ex Union des Egl Ev du Sud Oest. M=Charismatic chs in Israel, USA.
Eglise Harriste	1913	I-Met	IvI..	290	158,100	150,000	376,000	3.74	*Temples Bibliques Harristes.* Ebrie, Attie, Ajukru, Dida, 20 other tribes. 1968 applied to join WCC
Eglise Neo-Apostolique	c1970	I-3aX	x....	100	8,000	–	17,041	47.66	*New Apostolic Church. NAC.* M=Neuapostolische Kirche (HQ Zurich).
Eglise Orthodoxe		O-Ara	.....	80	10,800	3,000	18,000	0.05	*Orthodox Church.*
Eglise Presbyterienne	1986	P-Ref	.....	1	48	–	80	11.11	*Presbyterian Church.* M=MTW(USA).
Eglise Protestante Ev du Centre	1930	P-Hol	xFG.G	1,550	137,000	20,583	250,000	10.50	*EPEC. Prot Ch of Central IC.* M=CMA(USA). 90% Baule, 4% Agni. 65n,25f,1h,1s.
Eglise Protestante Libre	1968	I-Met	.....	10	3,000	5,000	5,000	0.00	*Free Protestant Ch.* 1965 mass movement under Ajukru Methodist healer Edjro; 1968 schism.
Eglise Protestante Méthodiste en CI	1924	P-Met	VwA.f	750	72,400	99,068	131,600	1.14	*Prot Methodist Ch.* M=MMS(UK). 25n,8x,73m,27f,1H,1h,2r,237t(12581),692Y,4054y,3189z.
Eglise Quadrangular	1975	P-Pe2	.....	2	27	–	45	5.00	*International Church of the Foursquare Gospel.* M=ICFG.
Eglises du Christ	1975	I-Dis	.....	26	536	–	750	5.00	*Churches of Christ.* M=CC(USA).
Eglises Fondamentals Baptistes	1970	I-Fun	.....	18	1,470	–	3,684	38.88	*Indep Fundamentalist Baptist Churches.* M= Macedonian Bap Mission,BIM,BMM,BBFI.
Eglises Independentes Ghanaiennes	c1965	I-3sA	x....	100	9,600	2,000	24,000	10.45	*Ghanaian indigenous churches*: over 80 congregations (in 37 denominations) in Abidjan.
Fraternité Chrétienne	1977	I-3pA	.....	8	800	–	1,330	5.56	*Christian Brotherhood.*
Mission Apostolique du Pentecote	1975	I-3aA	.....	31	2,500	–	6,250	5.00	*Apostolic Pentecost Mission.* M= Church of Pentecost (Ghana).
Mission Baptiste International	1971	I-Bap	.....	22	913	–	1,826	4.17	*Baptist International Mission.* M=BIM(USA).
Mission Lutherienne du Norvège	1984	P-Lut	.....	1	25	–	50	9.09	*Norwegian Lutheran Mission.*
Mission Tribus Nouveaux	1982	P-Fun	x....	1	20	–	50	7.69	*New Tribes Mission.* M=NTM.
Oeuvre Missionnaire	1980	I-3pA	.....	54	15,000	–	30,000	6.67	*Missionary Work.* A pentecostal split ex FMB-SBC and NBC.
Tabernacle Evangélistique de Jésus		I-3oA	.....	10	1,500	–	3,500	0.05	*Evangelistic Tabernacle of Jesus.*
Témoins de Jéhovah	c1945	m-Jeh	x....	137	9,760	1,000	15,166	11.49	*Jehovah's Witnesses..* Active witnessing under way by 1950. (1975) 92Y. (1995) 657Y.
Union des Egls Ev du Côte d'Ivoire	1979	P-Eva	.....	43	150	–	227	6.25	*Evangelical Chs of the Ivory Coast.* M=SIM.
Union des Egls Ev du Sud Ouest de CI	1927	P-Bap	.MG.G	225	21,060	15,000	70,000	6.36	*Chs of Southwest Ivory Coast.* M=MB,UFM. 56% Yakuba, 35% Wobe. 48n,8x,200Y.
Other African indigenous churches		I-3pA	.....	600	172,000	50,000	430,000	0.05	Total about 30.
Other Protestant denominations		P-	.....	30	1,500	300	3,750	0.05	Total about 8.
Totals				**7,225**	**2,114,674**	**1,090,778**	**3,950,152**		

Churches, members, growth, 1900-2025	*Congs*	*Adults*	*Affiliated*	*G%*	*Total denominations*	*6 Megablocs:* O	R	A	P	I	m
Total churches, members, and denominations (mid-1900)	10	280	550	11.46	1	0	1	0	0	0	0
Total churches, members, and denominations (mid-1970)	2,551	563,998	1,090,778	11.46	36	1	1	0	12	21	1
Total churches, members, and denominations (mid-1990)	6,000	1,788,000	3,340,000	5.75	76	1	1	0	22	50	2
Total churches, members, and denominations (mid-1995)	7,225	2,114,674	3,950,152	3.41	78	1	1	0	23	51	2
Total churches, members, and denominations (mid-2000)	8,500	2,331,000	4,353,882	1.97	80	1	1	0	24	52	2
Total churches, members, and denominations (mid-2025)	15,000	4,134,000	7,722,000	2.32	246	1	1	0	36	200	8

NOTES ON TABLE ABOVE

NATIONAL COUNCILS (Column 4, 5th letter).

G = Fédération Evangélique de la Côte d'Ivoire (FECI) (Evangelical Federation of the Ivory Coast).

f = formerly in FECI, from 1960-63.

R = Conférence Episcopale de la Côte d'Ivoire (CECI) (Episcopal Conference of the Ivory Coast).

OTHER AFRICAN INDIGENOUS CHURCHES. There are numerous Ghanaian spiritual churches in the southeast of the country, especially around Port Bouet, also Nigerian bodies, as well as about 20 others indigenous to the Ivory Coast including a large number of unorganized Harrist schisms and groupings. Among the total are: African Faith Tabernacle Ch, Chérubin et Séraphin (Nigeria), Christ Apostolic Ch (1968; from Nigeria), Eglise Akéiste (Harrisme Libéral) (1926), Eglise Aladura (Ch of the Lord (Aladura) from Nigeria), Eglise de Papa Nouveau (1954, Bete), Eglise du Christ (Krastchotche) (c1935, Dida), Eglise du Christ (Mission Harris), Eglise du Christianisme Céleste du Dahomey (Abidjan; HQ Porto Novo), Eglise Protestante de Jésus-Christ, Episcopal Foursquare Gospel Ch. Indigenous bodies from outside Africa include the Unification Church, from Korea.

OTHER PROTESTANT DENOMINATIONS. These smaller missions include: Christian Ch of North America, Churches of Christ (USA), Eglise Ev Chrétienne de l'Ouest Africa (EECOA) (Sudan Interior Mission, ECWA; 1968), United Pentecostal Ch (1975), World-Wide Missions (1967).

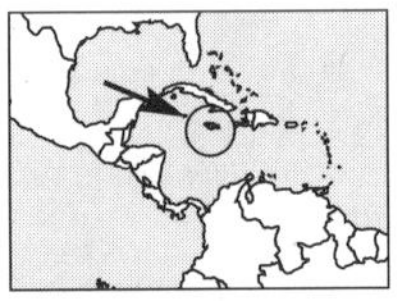

JAMAICA

SECULAR DATA, AD 2000

STATE
Official name: The Dominion of Jamaica.
Short name: Jamaica. **Adjective of nationality:** Jamaican.
Flag: Gold cross with green field in top and bottom quarters, black to left and right.
Area: 10,991 sq. km. (4,244 sq. mi.).
Government: Parliamentary state (constitutional monarchy), since 1962 (1509 Spanish possession, 1866 British crown colony, 1953 internal autonomy, 1958 in Federation of the West Indies, 1962 Independence).
Legislature: Parliament: Senate, 21 members; House of Representatives, 60 members.
Official language: English.
Monetary unit: 1 Jamaica dollar (J$) = 100 cents. **US$1=** J$35.80.
Chief cities: KINGSTON-St Andrew 881,562; Spanish Town 385,522; Montego Bay 167,389; Portmore 84,618.
Political divisions: 13 provinces.
Armed forces: 3,300.

DEMOGRAPHY
Population: 2,583,000.
Population density: 234.9/sq. km. (608.5/sq. mi.).
Under 15 years: 802,000.
Growth rate p.a.: 0.87% (births 19.95, deaths 5.62).
Mortality: Infant, per 1,000: 19.8; **Maternal per 100,000:** 120.0.
Life expectancy: 76 (male 74, female 78).
Household size: 4.2. **Floor area per person, sq.m:** 18.0.
Major languages: English, Jamaican Creole (Bongo Talk, Quashie Talk), Hindi, Chinese, Spanish.
Urban dwellers: 56.09%. **Urban growth rate p.a.:** 1.8%.
Labor force: 44%.

ETHNOLINGUISTIC PEOPLES
77.0% Jamaican Black; 14.6% Jamaican Mulatto; 2.0% Haitian; 1.7% East Indian; 1.6% Afro-East-Indian.

ECONOMY
National income p.a. per person: US$1,510; **per family:** US$6,342.

EDUCATION
Adult literacy: 85% (male 80%, female 89%). **Schools:** 932.
Universities: 15. **School enrolment:** female/male: 88%/83%.

HEALTH
Access to health services: 90%. **Access to safe water:** 70%.
Hospitals: 30 (22 beds per 10,000). **Doctors:** 1,589.
Blind: 3,100. **Deaf:** 155,200. **Murder rate:** 27.
Lepers: 2,500. **Underweight prevalence under 5:** 10%.

LITERATURE
New book titles p.a.: 770 (300 p.a. per million). **Periodicals:** 56.
Newspapers: 3 dailies.

COMMUNICATION (per 1,000 people)
Phones: 116 (12% mobile). **Radios:** 747. **TV sets:** 306.
Daily newspaper circulation: 66. **Computers:** 50.

HUMAN LIFE AND LIBERTY (optimum condition=100.0%)
HDI: 73.6. **HSI:** 56.0. **HFI:** 62.5. **EFL:** 46.0.

Country status. Jamaica is the third largest island in the Caribbean and is dominated by mountain ranges. Three-fourths of the population is black. Major exports include sugar, bananas, citrus, cocoa, aluminum, and bauxite.

HUMAN LIFE AND LIBERTY

Human need and development. The island has an easy tempo of life, due partly to its tropical environment and partly to the prevailing African mode of life. Heavy migration to the United States and Canada, increasing urbanization, and the revenues from bauxite mining, have helped Jamaicans to avoid the kind of stark poverty found in Haiti. Health conditions are generally good. The mortality rate is low, the rates of incidence of most diseases are declining, and hospital facilities are well distributed. However, mental illness is a serious problem and the Bellevue Mental Hospital contains over a quarter of all hospital beds. The average diet is fairly adequate in terms of calories and proteins. There is a housing shortage, particularly in urban localities, and many of the existing units are old and substandard. There are shantytowns on the western flank of Kingston and on the hills overlooking Montego Bay. A Social Security program established in 1966 covers most of the country's workers. There is no national health coverage, but Social Security provides some grants for healthcare.

Human rights and freedoms. The principal human rights problems are extrajudicial killings of suspects and people in police custody, illtreatment of prisoners in overcrowded jails, and an inefficient and overburdened judiciary which is unable to correct police abuses. The Constabulary sometimes engages in summary execution of suspects under the guise of shootouts. Vigilantism, involving spontaneous mob executions occurs with some frequency and is often condoned by the police. The use of excessive force by the police is evidenced by the fact that the government has paid for the past few years $265,000 annually as damages to the victims of such brutality. Prison conditions remain dismal with sanitation and food intake below acceptable standards. At the general penitentiary in Kingston 6 men are held in 7-by-10 foot cells in near-total darkness. Many prisoners are forced

Country Table 1. Religious adherents in Jamaica, AD 1900-2025.

Year / Name	1900 Adherents	%	1970 Adherents	%	mid-1990 Adherents	%	Annual change, 1990-2000 Natural	Conversion	Total	Rate	mid-1995 Adherents	%	mid-2000 Adherents	%	mid-2025 Adherents	%
Christians	**679,700**	**94.4**	**1,707,700**	**91.4**	**2,013,000**	**85.0**	**18,141**	**-2,390**	**15,753**	**0.76**	**2,087,000**	**84.4**	**2,170,527**	**84.0**	**2,630,000**	**81.1**
PROFESSION																
professing Christians	**679,700**	**94.4**	**1,707,700**	**91.4**	**2,013,000**	**85.0**	**18,141**	**-2,390**	**15,753**	**0.76**	**2,087,000**	**84.4**	**2,170,527**	**84.0**	**2,630,000**	**81.1**
AFFILIATION																
unaffiliated Christians	115,000	16.0	756,429	40.5	960,640	40.6	8,678	139	8,817	0.88	1,004,217	40.6	1,048,814	40.6	1,321,900	40.7
affiliated Christians	**564,700**	**78.4**	**951,271**	**50.9**	**1,052,360**	**44.4**	**9,465**	**-2,530**	**6,935**	**0.64**	**1,082,783**	**43.8**	**1,121,713**	**43.4**	**1,308,100**	**40.3**
Protestants	250,700	34.8	502,798	26.9	594,000	25.1	5,366	-425	4,941	0.80	616,630	24.9	643,413	24.9	750,000	23.1
Independents	20,000	2.8	171,700	9.2	215,000	9.1	1,942	-242	1,700	0.76	222,988	9.0	232,000	9.0	270,000	8.3
Roman Catholics	13,000	1.8	160,873	8.6	114,000	4.8	1,030	-1,430	-400	-0.36	111,385	4.5	110,000	4.3	115,000	3.5
Anglicans	281,000	39.0	100,000	5.4	103,000	4.4	930	-930	0	0.00	103,000	4.2	103,000	4.0	110,000	3.4
Marginal Christians	0	0.0	10,900	0.6	23,000	1.0	208	492	700	2.69	25,450	1.0	30,000	1.2	60,000	1.9
Orthodox	0	0.0	5,000	0.3	3,360	0.1	30	-36	-6	-0.18	3,330	0.1	3,300	0.1	3,100	0.1
Trans-megabloc groupings																
Evangelicals	230,000	31.9	210,000	11.2	275,000	11.6	2,484	416	2,900	1.01	288,312	11.7	304,000	11.8	350,000	10.8
Pentecostals/Charismatics	0	0.0	250,000	13.4	347,000	14.7	3,135	665	3,800	1.04	366,531	14.8	385,000	14.9	520,000	16.0
Great Commission Christians	**65,000**	**9.0**	**299,000**	**16.0**	**553,000**	**23.3**	**4,995**	**3,287**	**8,282**	**1.41**	**580,000**	**23.5**	**635,819**	**24.6**	**800,000**	**24.7**
Spiritists	36,000	5.0	128,500	6.9	230,000	9.7	2,078	888	2,966	1.22	245,000	9.9	259,656	10.1	360,000	11.1
Nonreligious	0	0.0	17,000	0.9	79,700	3.4	720	1,289	2,009	2.27	91,300	3.7	99,789	3.9	180,000	5.6
Hindus	1,900	0.3	5,600	0.3	27,100	1.1	245	118	363	1.27	29,000	1.2	30,733	1.2	44,000	1.4
Baha'is	0	0.0	3,100	0.2	6,400	0.3	58	48	106	1.54	7,100	0.3	7,456	0.3	12,000	0.4
Chinese folk-religionists	100	0.0	1,000	0.1	6,200	0.3	56	31	87	1.33	6,600	0.3	7,073	0.3	9,000	0.3
Muslims	2,000	0.3	3,000	0.2	3,000	0.1	27	-11	16	0.51	3,050	0.1	3,156	0.1	3,500	0.1
Atheists	0	0.0	0	0.0	650	0.0	6	7	13	1.77	700	0.0	775	0.0	1,300	0.0
Jews	300	0.0	1,800	0.1	600	0.0	5	-14	-9	-1.59	540	0.0	511	0.0	400	0.0
Buddhists	0	0.0	300	0.0	300	0.0	3	-1	2	0.52	310	0.0	316	0.0	300	0.0
Other religionists	0	0.0	1,000	0.1	2,050	0.1	19	35	54	2.35	2,400	0.1	2,585	0.1	4,500	0.1
World A (unevangelized persons)	720	0.1	37,380	2.0	30,797	1.3	278	-599	-321	-1.09	29,675	1.2	28,413	1.1	32,450	1.0
World B (evangelized non-Christians)	39,580	5.5	123,920	6.6	325,203	13.7	2,939	2,989	5,928	1.68	356,251	14.4	384,060	14.8	582,550	17.9
World C (Christians)	679,700	94.4	1,707,700	91.4	2,013,000	85.0	18,143	-2,390	15,753	0.76	2,087,000	84.4	2,170,527	84.1	2,630,000	81.1
Country's population	**720,000**	**100.0**	**1,869,000**	**100.0**	**2,369,000**	**100.0**	**21,360**	**0**	**21,360**	**0.87**	**2,472,927**	**100.0**	**2,583,000**	**100.0**	**3,245,000**	**100.0**

COLUMNS, ROWS.
For meanings and definitions, see Codebook (Part 3). Note that, by definition, total 'Christians' = professing + crypto-Christians, which also = affiliated + unaffiliated Christians, and also = Great Commission Christians + latent Christians. Percentages may not always total exactly, due to rounding.

CENSUSES.
1943: 61.0% Protestants (25.8% Baptists, 8.9% Methodists, 7.5% Presbyterians, 4.1% Moravians, 3.5% Ch of God, 2.2% SD Adventists, 1.7% Congregationalists, 1.1% Salvation Army), 28.4% Anglicans, 5.7% Roman Catholics, 4.0% Afro-American spiritists (Pocomania, etc) and Black indigenous Christians and nonreligious, 0.3% Hindus, 0.1% Jews. **1953:** 61.7% Protestants (22.7% Baptists, 7.7% Methodists, 6.2% Ch of God, 5.6% Presbyterians, 4.0% SD Adventists, 3.6% Moravians, 1.3% Congregationalists, 1.3% Salvation Army), 23.5% Anglicans, 7.9% Afro-American spiritists (Pocomania, etc), Black indigenous Christians and nonreligious, 6.9% Roman Catholics. **7.IV.1960** (de jure): 59.2% Protestants (20.1% Baptists, 12.6% Ch of God, 7.1% Methodists), 21.0% Anglicans, 12.1% Afro-American spiritists (Pocomania, etc), and Black indigenous Christians and nonreligious, 7.6% Roman Catholics, 0.1% Hindus. **7.IV.1970:** 64.3% Protestants (including Black indigenous), 18.0% Anglicans, 8.6% Roman Catholics, 8.0% other religionists.

NOTES ON RELIGIONS
BAHA'IS. Rapid growth from 6 local spiritual assemblies (1964) to 21 (1973). Mainly East Indians. In 1971 a mass teaching project enrolled 1,000 new believers. (1996) LSAs have now increased to 57.
COUNTRY'S POPULATION. Annual emigration has averaged 30,000 a year since 1960, mainly to the UK at first, then to the USA and Canada.
HINDUS. East Indians. Among Hindu sects, Ananda Marga has a following.
INDEPENDENTS. In over 60 denominations in 1995 (see Table 2). Three groups: (1) Black pentecostals from the USA, Methodists (AMEC) and others founded with aid from USA Black churches; (2) indigenous Jamaican bodies (e.g. New Testament Church of Christ the Redeemer); and (3) Revival Zionists, Shouters, Shakers, Spiritual Baptists and other indigenous Jamaican Afro-Christian cults syncretizing Christianity, spiritism and African religions.
JEWS. United Congregation of Israelites, with synagogues in Kingston; Sefardic.
MUSLIMS. East Indians, Syrians; with one mosque.
NONRELIGIOUS. Chinese and Europeans; with Blacks who either have abandoned religion or have no interest in it.
OTHER RELIGIONISTS. Adherents of smaller religions and cults, including Rosicrucians (1 AMORC centre).
SPIRITISTS. There are 2 distinct types of movement in this category. (1) There are numerous Afro-Caribbean spirit-possession cults syncretizing Christianity with African religion, which are usually referred to as the Revival Zion-Pocomania-Obeah complex, or Afro-Christian cults. In this survey we classify Revival Zion as more Christian than non-Christian and so include it under Independent churches; we classify Pocomania, however, as more non-Christian than Christian, hence include it under our category of non-Christian Afro-American spiritism. Other, related, non-Christian cults include the Black Israelites, a cult band invoking Satan and fallen angels, begun in 1900. Convince and Cumina cults, Obeah, and Myalismo (now almost extinct). Members of these cults wear turbans, use the colors black, white, red and blue, sing Sankey Hymns, take the sacrament of communion (bread and wine) frequently, and perform counter-clockwise dancing-trumping to induce possession; Pocomania in addition uses strong liquor and marijuana. Numerically, censuses have not clearly enumerated these cults, because the name Pocomania is regarded unfavorably and most adherents call themselves Baptists or Revivalists, though usually recorded in the censuses under 'No religion'. (2) A different type of cult is the Ras Tafari movement begun in 1930, with 50,000 followers and over 30,000 sympathizers. Some of its offshoots and branches (e.g. in UK) are specifically Christian. Of all Rastafarians 80% are aged 17-35 years, predominantly male, and most were formerly members of Christian churches.
UNAFFILIATED CHRISTIANS. There are vast numbers of unaffiliated. Methodists, Anglicans and Presbyterians, many of whom participate in Afro-American spiritist cults whilst continuing to regard themselves as Protestants or Anglicans.

Great Commission Instrument Panel: status of Jamaica (for explanation see start of Part 4)

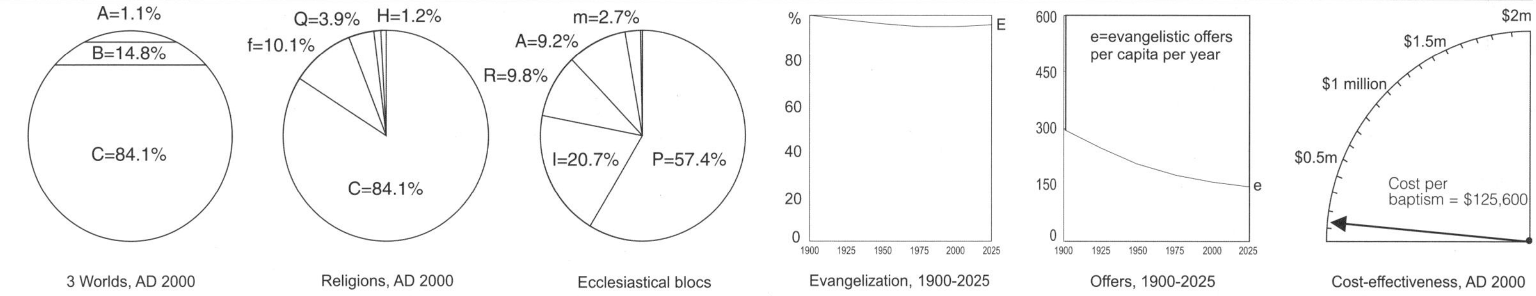

to go hungry while food supplies are diverted for private sale by the staff. The law permits police to make arrests and conduct searches without warrants. In other respects, Jamaicans enjoy considerable freedom, and there are no constraints on free speech, peaceful assembly or free movement. There are small racial minorities, called the Maroons, some of them descended from the Arawak Indians. They suffer no discrimination and are accorded some autonomy.

Human environment. Although a small country, Jamaica is home to animal and plant species found nowhere else: 27 of the 256 birds, 20 of the 24 lizards, 82 of the 579 ferns, and 784 of the 3,000 flowering plants are endemic. These species are threatened by soil erosion (estimated at 80 million tons annually) and the loss of forest cover. Groundwater is contaminated by the discharge of sewage and industrial effluents. Bauxite mining has scarred the landscape irreversibly in many areas.

NON-CHRISTIAN RELIGIONS

Afro-Caribbean syncretistic religions, a mixture of spiritism, Christianity and traditional African rites, abound in Jamaica. The first Afro-Christian movement was the Native Baptist cult begun by an ex-slave in 1783 and which played a significant role in the political disturbances at Port Morant in 1865. During 1861, the Great Awakening came to prominence featuring wild dancing, trances, sexual orgies and public confession. Another marginal Christian group was Bedwardism began in 1920 by Alexander Bedward, who considered himself to be Christ and who predicted his own ascension into heaven and second coming. One of the largest of contemporary sects is the Ras Tafari movement, which built on the back-to-Africa ideas of Marcus Garvey, became a significant politico-religious force in the 1930s, attracted masses of poverty-stricken slum-dwellers, attempted to prepare for repatriation to Ethiopia in the 1960s and numbered in 1990 some 70,000 members with tens of thousands more supports and sympathizers. More recent nativistic cults are the Black Israelites, Pocomania, Convince, and Cumina cults and other revivalist groups.

Other religions include Baha'i (0.3% of the population), Hinduism (1.2%), Chinese folk religion, and a small Sefardic Jewish community.

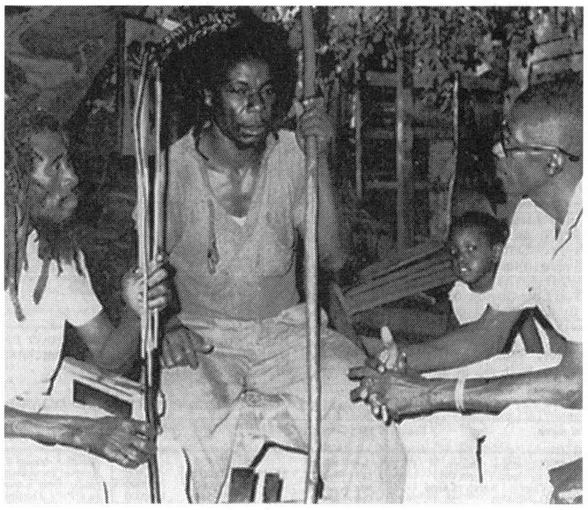

Afro-American spiritists. Two of the 50,000 Rastafarians (*left*) talk with a Methodist minister (*right*).

Country summary. **Worlds A, B, C by ethnolinguistic peoples, cities, and major civil divisions in Jamaica.**

PEOPLES

World	Num	Pop 2000	C%	Christians	E%	U%	Unevangelized
A	1	517	0.00	0	47	53	274
B	6	2,460,524	41.36	1,017,664	99	1	27,144
C	7	121,536	85.61	104,047	100	0	175
Total	**14**	**2,582,577**	**43.43**	**1,121,711**	**99**	**1**	**27,593**

CITIES

World	Num	Pop 2000	C%	Christians	E%	U%	Unevangelized
A	0	0	0.00	0	0	0	0
B	2	1,048,951	44.48	466,560	100	0	4,910
C	0	0	0.00	0	0	0	0
Total	**2**	**1,048,951**	**44.48**	**466,560**	**100**	**0**	**4,910**

CIVIL DIVISIONS

World	Num	Pop 2000	C%	Christians	E%	U%	Unevangelized
A	0	0	0.00	0	0	0	0
B	13	2,582,578	43.43	1,121,713	99	1	27,593
C	0	0	0.00	0	0	0	0
Total	**13**	**2,582,578**	**43.43**	**1,121,713**	**99**	**1**	**27,593**

CHRISTIANITY

PROTESTANT CHURCHES. Protestant work in Jamaica was pioneered by the Friends (Quakers) in 1671, followed by Moravians and Methodists during the 18th century and many other groups since then. The first Baptist missionary to the West Indies was George Lisle, a freed slave from Virginia who arrived in Kingston in 1783. His first Baptist congregation later evolved into both the Native Baptist cult and also the Jamaica Baptist Union. British Baptists were invited in after 1813, but the local church has been entirely independent since 1842. Indeed, the indigenous Jamaica Baptist Missionary Society sent its own missionaries to Fernando Poo off the coast of equatorial Africa as early as 1884. The total community of the Jamaica Baptist Union, numbering 114,000, is now equal in size to the Anglican and Seventh-day Adventists churches, the latter having been at work in Jamaica since 1893. In the present century, a number of Baptist missionary societies from the USA have begun work in the country. Baptist International Missions, Baptist Mid-Missions, General Baptists, National Baptists, Seventh-day Baptists, and Southern Baptists.

The Methodist Church, related to British Methodism, has built up a Christian community of 50,000 since its inception in 1789; and the United Church of Jamaica and Grand Cayman, a merger of Presbyterians and Congregationalists in 1965, has a similar constituency. Another early arrival, the Moravian Church (1754), is half as large.

The predominant Protestant tradition in terms of total membership is now Pentecostalism. The first Pentecostal mission was the Church of God (Cleveland) from the USA in 1917; and its affiliated daughter church, the New Testament Church of God, remains Jamaica's largest Pentecostal denomination. Of some 12 other Pentecostal groups, the next largest is the Church of God of Prophecy (1923).

The Brethren, Church of God (Anderson), Disciples, Friends, Salvation Army, and a host of small independent missions from the USA are also at work.

CATHOLIC CHURCH. Jamaica was discovered by Columbus in 1494, and within 14 years the first sugar cane plantations had been established.

Early Catholic missionary efforts produced limited results due to lack of clergy, but by 1655 when England attacked Spanish possessions in the Caribbean and took over Jamaica, most of the population was Catholic. Catholicism was prohibited thereafter and was not begun again until the arrival of Jesuits in 1837. However, its growth has been rapid since then, and at the present time the Catholic Church has more members than any other denomination in Jamaica.

A significant proportion of Catholics is found among the poorer classes of the population. Of all Jamaica's ethnic groups, the Chinese have the highest proportion of Catholics.

The Holy See has diplomatic relations with Jamaica and in AD 2000 is represented to government and the Catholic hierarchy by a pro-nuncio residing in Port of Spain.

INDIGENOUS CHURCHES. The earliest specifically Christian indigenous movement was Revival Zion, which began in 1783 as the Native Baptist Church and which spread rapidly during the Great Christian Revival of 1861-1862 and subsequently. Despite numerous syncretistic features, it remains today as basically a charismatic Christian movement.

Black denominations from the USA including the AME Church (1912) have been at work in Jamaica since before World War I, but the majority of Jamaica's many indigenous churches were formed after World War II. Most are small, some consisting of only a single congregation, although the New Testament Church of Christ the Redeemer has 55,600 adherents. Jamaica's 60 or so independent churches generally display pentecostal-type features in their mode of worship. As a result of mass emigration to Britain since 1960, many of them now have extensive missionary work in that country.

Revival Zion. A charismatic Black church begun in 1783. *Upper.* 'Table' (combined religious service and feast) at new church's dedication. *Lower.* Leader with staff.

ANGLICAN CHURCH. The Anglican Church is one of Jamaica's oldest and largest denominations, dating back to chaplaincy work in the 17th century. The first Anglican bishoprics in the Caribbean were established in Jamaica and Barbados in 1824, and the diocese of Jamaica has since 1883 been part of the autonomous Church of the Province of the West Indies.

Anglican Church, Diocese of Jamaica. Ancient Cathedral of St James, Spanish Town, built 1523 and 1712.

Renewal movements. In the 1990s the Pentecostal/Charismatic Renewal continued to spread rapidly across most older churches, and numbered over 385,000 adherents (of whom 44% Pentecostals, 17% Charismatics, and 39% Independents).

Indigenous missions. In the latter part of the nineteenth century, Baptist churches made a startling contribution to the evangelization of West Africa. In the 20th century most of the missionaries sent out went to the UK and the USA where they worked among expatriate Jamaicans. Unfortunately, today, though predominantly Christian, Jamaica receives far more missionaries than it sends.

CHURCH AND STATE

There is freedom of conscience and worship in Jamaica. The state neither favors nor supports any church or religion, but financial aid is provided for private schools, and the churches are exempt from taxation. Provision is made for religious instruction in the lower grades of the public school system (junior secondary, primary, infant schools), by means of an ecumenical syllabus prepared through the cooperation of the Protestant and Catholic churches. A similar syllabus is also being prepared for secondary schools. Churches and their properties are registered with government, but there is no ministry or government office dealing specifically with religious affairs.

BROADCASTING AND MEDIA

Local stations JBC-1, RJR, and LOVE-FM carry Christian radio programs. Shortwave programs from KNLS, HCJB (Ecuador), TWR (Antilles) and AWR (Costa Rica) can be easily received. Jamaica is a member of UNDA.

TBN programs are aired in Mandeville on Desalt Cable. LeSEA programming can be seen via the World Harvest Satellite.

Some 2.3 million have seen the 'Jesus' Film: through TV broadcasts (1.9 million) and cinematic showings (372,000), with 14,100 responding.

INTERDENOMINATIONAL ORGANIZATIONS

The Jamaica Council of Churches was established in 1939 as a Protestant organization, but since November 1971 it has included in its membership the Anglican and Catholic churches as well. The council is affiliated to the World Council of Churches and the CWME. The Catholic archdiocese of Kingston has a Commission on Ecumenism. There is also a fundamentalist council, the Jamaica Association of Evangelical Churches.

FUTURE TRENDS AND PROSPECTS

Spiritists and the nonreligious are expected to grow to over 15% of the population by AD 2025. Christians will likely continue to decline to 81.1% by 2025 (from 91.4% in 1970).

Rastafarians, other spiritists, and the nonreligious could together represent 25% of the population by AD 2050. Christianity would then continue its decline to under 75% in the same period.

BIBLIOGRAPHY

'A comparative study of acculturation in Morant Bay and West Kingston, Jamaica', J. G. Moore & G. E. Simpson, *Zaire*, 11 (November-December, 1957), 979-1020, and 12 (January 1958), 65-88.

'A critical examination of the mission of the church in Jamaica.' D. A. Stitt. Paper, Graduate Seminary of Phillips University, Enid, OK, 1983. 53p.

A history of the Diocese of Jamaica. E. L. Evans. 173p.

'Anglican, Methodist and Baptist churches in Jamaica: 1823–1865.' W. A. Lawson. Ph.D. dissertation, University of the West Indies, 1992. 412p.

Black religions in the New World. G. E. Simpson. New York: Columbia University Press, 1978. 429p.

'Born again...and again and again: communitas and social change among Jamaican Pentecostalists,' D. J. Austin, *Journal of anthropological research*, 37, 3 (1981), 226–426.

Caribbean Catholic directory, 1971. Kingston, Jamaica: Antilles Episcopal Conference Executive Secretariat, 1971.

Church growth in Jamaica. D. A. McGavran. Lucknow, India: Lucknow Publishing House, 1962.

Foundations and anticipations: the Jamaica Baptist story: 1783–1892. H. O. Russell. Columbus, GA: Brentwood Christian Press, 1993. 151p.
God Almighty, make me free: Christianity in preemancipation Jamaica. S. C. Gordon. *Blacks in the diaspora.* Bloomington, IN: Indiana Unviersity Press, 1996. 176p.
History of Bedwardism: or the Jamaica Native Baptist Free Church. A. A. Brooks. Kingston, Jamaica, 1917.
History of the Catholic Church in Jamaica. F. J. Osborne. Aylesbury, UK: Caribbean Universities Press, 1977. 210p.
Jamaica. K. E. Ingram. *World bibliographical series*, vol. 45. Oxford, UK: CLIO Press, 1984. 354p. (See especially 'Religion,' p.74–81).
'Jamaican revivalist cults,' G. E. Simpson, *Social and economic studies*, 5, 4 (1956), 231–442.
'Jesuits in Jamaica: re–making a mission.' J. B. Nickoloff. Thesis, Jesuit School of Theology at Berkeley, 1984. 144p.
'New churches, old ideology: the role of fundamentalism in Jamaican politics, 1980–1988.' J. C. Soares. Ph.D. dissertation, Queen's University, Kingston, 1992. 340p.
Obeah, Christ, and Rastaman: Jamaica and its religion. I. Morrish. Cambridge, UK: J. Clarke, 1982. 122p.
Out of the depths: papers presented at four missiology conferences held in Antigua, Guyana, Jamaica and Trinidad, 1975. I. Hamid (ed.). San Fernando, Trinidad: St. Andrew's Theological College, 1977. 261pp.
Pentecostalism in Jamaica: a challenge to the established churches and society. A. A. Smith. Kingston: Literature Committee, Methodist Church, 1975. 20p.
'Protest and mysticism: the Ras Tafari cult of Jamaica,' S. Kitzinger, *Journal for the scientific study of religion*, 8, 2 (1969), 240–262.
'Religion and politics in nineteenth and twentieth century Jamaica with special reference to the Church of Jamaica and its leaders: a critical perspective.' J. C. Soares. M.S. thesis, University of the West Indies, 1984. 235p.
Religion and society in post–emancipation Jamaica. R. J. Stewart. Knoxville, TN: University of Tennessee Press, 1992. 275p.
'Religion of Jamaican Negroes: a study of Afro–Jamaican acculturation.' J. G. Moore. Ph.D. dissertation, Northwestern University, Evanston, IL, 1954.
'Religious broadcasting in Jamaica: an analysis of the history, program content, audience description and viewing motives.' C. A. M. Dawkins. Ph.D. dissertation, Howard University, Washington, DC, 1991. 229p.
Religious cults of the Caribbean: Trinidad, Jamaica and Haiti. G. E. Simpson. 3rd ed. *Caribbean Monograph Series*, No. 15. Río Piedras, Puerto Rico: Institute of Caribbean Studies, University of Puerto Rico, 1980. 347p.
'Religious syncretism in Jamaica,' J. G. Moore, *Practical anthropology*, 12, 2 (1965), 63–70.
Seedtime and harvest: a brief history of the Moravian Church in Jamaica, 1754–1979. S. U. Hastings & B. L. MacLeavy. Kingston: Moravian Church Corporation, 1979. 264p.
Slaves and missionaries: the disintegration of Jamaican slave society, 1787–1834. M. Turner. *Blacks in the New World.* Urbana, IL: University of Illinois Press, 1982. 223p.
The 150th anniversary of the diocese of Jamaica, yesterday, today and tomorrow, 1824–1974. Bishop L. Evans et al. Kingston: Church of England in Jamaica, [1974]. 44p.
The Baptists of Jamaica: 1793–1965. I. K. Sibley. Kingston: Jamaica Baptist Union, 1965. 91p.
The Church in the new Jamaica. J. M. Davis. New York: International Missionary Council, 1942.
'The Convince Cult in Jamaica,' D. Hogg, in *Papers in Caribbean anthropology*, p.21–28. S. Mintz (ed). New Haven, CT: Yale University, 1960.
The folk culture of the slaves of Jamaica. E. K. Brathwaite. 2nd ed. London: New Beacon Books, 1981. 56p.
'The Ras Tafari movement in Jamaica: a study of race and class conflict,' G. E. Simpson, *Social forces*, 34 (December, 1955), 167–171.
'The Rastafarian brethren of Jamaica,' S. Kitzinger, *Comparative studies in society and history*, 9, 1 (1966), 33–39.
Voodoos and obeahs: phases of West Indian witchcraft. J. J. Williams. 1932; reprint, New York: AMS, 1970. 257p. (Focuses on Haiti and Jamaica).

Country Table 2. **Organized churches and denominations in Jamaica.**

Official name (bold type = church with over 10% of all affiliated) 1	*Begun* 2	*Type* 3	*Councr* 4	*Congs* 5	*Adults* 6	*Affiliated 1970* 7	*Affiliated 1995* 8	*G%* 9	*Names, notes, and other statistics* (see Codebook, Part 3) 10
African Methodist Episcopal Church	1912	I-Met	VwM.N	6	823	1,500	2,350	1.81	*Jamaica Annual Conference*, 16th Episcopal District. M=AMEC(USA Blacks).
African Methodist Episcopal Zion Ch	1965	I-Met	Vw...	266	10,900	24,500	26,000	0.24	Revival movement, later invited in M=AMEZC(USA Blacks). Very rapid growth now halted. 65n.
African Reformed Coptic Church of God	1959	I-mar	.....	10	900	4,000	3,000	-1.14	*God's Army Camp. Back to Africa.* 1960-70 jailings; 1970, New Creation Peacemakers.
Anglican Church: D Jamaica	1655	A-Cen	AwMRN	274	51,500	100,000	103,000	0.12	In *CPWI.* Declining 3%pa. 3 Episcopal regions. 90% Black. 71n,22x,1u,4851Yy.
Apostolic Church		P-PeA	Z....	22	5,400	5,000	16,400	0.05	M=Apostolic Church Missionary Movement (UK). Based in Walderston.
Apostolic Ch of God in Christ	c1970	I-3oU	.....	10	2,300	–	3,500	38.60	Mission from Britain.
Apostolic Church of Pentecost		P-Pe1	x....	5	500	500	1,000	0.05	M=Apostolic Ch of Pentecost (Canada). HQ Cambridge. Unitarian Pentecostals. 1f.
Assemblies of God	1937	P-Pe2	ZF...	119	12,500	11,000	17,000	1.76	M=AoG(USA). Classical Pentecostals. HQ Kingston. 71n,3f,1p,1s(118).
Assemblies of the First-Born	c1950	I-3pU	.....	30	3,000	3,000	5,000	2.06	Related to Church of the First-Born, but now pentecostal. HQ Kingston.
Associated Gospel Assemblies	1925	P-CBr	x.Y.1	167	8,000	7,000	16,000	3.36	*Association of Ev Chs. Open Brethren.* M=CMML(UK, USA). 6n,1x,8f,2H,200Y.
Baptist International Missions	1971	I-Bap	....E	10	900	–	1,800	4.17	M=BIM.
Baptist Mid-Missions	1939	I-Fun	xTY.E	10	2,000	3,000	4,000	1.16	M=BMM(USA). Regular Baptists; fundamentalists. 19f,1s.
Catholic Church in Jamaica:	1509	R-Lat	P.NMN	79	64,700	160,873	111,385	-1.46	12% Chinese. C=5+0+9. 42n 69x 89m 177w 1613Y
M Kingston in Jamaica	1837	R-Lat	Ps	35	55,600	139,870	95,712	-1.51	Eastern Jamaica. M=SJ. D=pc,PC. 11r,1s. 35n 49x 59m 139w 1363Yy
D Montego Bay	1967	R-Lat	Ps	26	5,000	21,003	8,500	-3.55	Western part of Jamaica. M=CP. 4r. 2n 11x 11m 13w 171Yy
VA Mandeville	1991	R-Lat	Pcp	18	4,100	–	7,173	25.00	M=CP. 5n 9x 19m 25w 79Yy
Christadelphian Ecclesias		m-Ade	x....	5	100	300	200	0.05	*Christadelphia Bible Mission (CBM).* 7 ecclesias (churches). Pacifist, adventist.
Christian Churches & Chs of Christ	1885	I-Dis	x....	39	1,560	4,000	3,120	-0.99	M=CCCC(Instrumental) (USA). Independent congregations, mainly split ex UCMS. 21f.
Church of Christ, Scientist		m-Sci	x....	1	100	400	200	0.05	*Christian Science.* First Church, Kingston. M=CCS(Boston, USA). 3w.
Church of God Holiness	1933	P-Hol	x....	30	600	1,000	900	-0.42	M=CoG Holiness (Overland Park, Kansas, USA). 1 school. Emigration to UK. 2f,1s.
Church of God in Christ		I-3pB	Z....	25	600	800	1,200	0.05	M=CoGiC(Black pentecostals from USA). Emigration to UK. HQ Kingston.
Church of God in Jamaica	1907	P-Hol	x...N	133	10,700	11,000	16,000	1.51	*General Assembly of CoG (Jamaica).* M=CoG(Anderson) (USA). SS=6,000. 24n,6f,1k,1r,1s.
Church of God of Prophecy	1923	P-Pe3	Z....	290	16,000	25,000	40,000	1.90	M=CGP(USA). Theocratic government. Many emigrants to UK to form church there.
Church of God (Seventh-day)	1931	P-Adv	.....	36	1,440	2,000	2,400	0.73	Mission from USA, 69 years in Jamaica.
Church of the First-Born	c1950	I-3pU	x....	20	1,000	2,000	2,100	0.20	Strict ethics. Branches by emigration in UK, Canada, USA, Barbados. Losses to schisms.
Ch of Jesus Christ of Jamaica	c1970	I-3oU	.....	10	1,000	–	3,000	37.75	Oneness pentecostals, in AWCF. HQ Montego Bay.
Ch of Jesus Christ of Latter-day Saints	1970	m-LdS	.....	13	1,260	–	2,100	35.80	*Mormons* M=CJCLdS.
Church of the Nazarene	1966	P-Hol	xF..E	24	1,638	1,000	3,515	5.16	M=CoN(USA). Small holiness denomination. 3m,7f,6t(715).
Churches of Christ (Non-Instrumental)	1965	I-Dis	x....	16	900	2,000	1,900	-0.20	M=CC(Non-Instrumental) (USA). Many split ex UCMS. In Kingston. 20f.
Disciples of Christ in Jamaica	1858	P-Dis	x.M.N	70	7,000	12,000	15,600	1.05	Rejected 1968 United Ch merger. M=UCMS(USA). 16n,2x,3f,1p,1u,W=66%,510Y.
Ethiopian Orthodox Ch (D Trinidad)	1959	O-Eth	Nwa.N	4	2,000	5,000	3,330	-1.61	*EOC.* Under P Addis Ababa, Ethiopia. Blacks, formerly in Ras Tafari cult. W=10%,1000z.
Evangelical Church of the West Indies	1945	P-Eva	xM...	15	2,000	2,000	4,000	2.81	M=West Indies Mission (USA). Interdenominational mission. 15f,1s.
Faith Temple Pentecostal Assemblies	1980	I-3oU	.....	10	1,000	–	2,500	6.67	Oneness pentecostals.
General Baptist Mission	1966	P-Bap	TF..E	10	900	1,000	2,050	2.91	*General Association of General Baptists.* M=GBFMS(USA). 2f.
Independent Jamaica Baptist Mission	c1947	I-Bap	.TY.1	2	150	400	400	0.00	Fundamentalist Baptists with USA connections. HQ Glenrock, Ramble.
Internat Ch of the Foursquare Gospel	1947	P-Pe2	ZF...	26	3,900	3,000	5,907	2.75	M=ICFG(USA). Classical Pentecostals. HQ Hagley Park. 23nm,2f,1p(35),W=49%,26Y.
International City Mission	c1950	I-3pU	.....	20	900	2,000	2,000	0.00	Healing, schools, orphanages. HQ Kingston. Work in UK, USA, Belize. Women bishops.
Jamaica Baptist Union	1783	P-Bap	T.M.N	281	39,991	100,000	114,000	0.53	1814. M=BMS(UK), 1963 FMB-SBC. 92% Black, 3% Indian. 91n,4f,1u,W=50%,1794Y.
Jamaica Pentecostal Union (Apostolic)	c1970	I-3oU	.....	10	1,000	–	3,000	37.75	Oneness body, member of AWCF. HQ Kingston 10.
Jehovah's Witnesses	1898	m-Jeh	x....	171	9,166	9,000	20,800	3.41	*Watch Tower. IBSA.* Active witnessing under way 1926. HQ Kingston. (1975) 296Y. (1995) 554Y.
Mennonite Church	1955	P-Men	G....	11	422	785	600	-1.07	*Jamaica Mennonite Mission.* M=MCC,Virginia Mennonite Conference (USA). 40f.
Methodist Church in Jamaica	1789	P-Met	VwM.N	180	18,193	50,000	44,500	-0.47	*MCCA, Jamaica District.* M=MMS(UK). 42n,16x,27f,6r,1u,21Y,1608y,1272z.
Missionary Church	1949	P-Hol	xF...	108	7,000	5,000	14,000	4.20	Before 1969 merger, M=Missionary Church Association (USA); now MC(USA). 6f,1s.
Moravian Church in Jamaica	1754	P-Mor	xWM.N	58	7,400	23,298	11,037	-2.94	*Jamaica Province, UoB.* A=1966. Rural. 50 schools. 13n,6x,1r,1u,W=40%,739Yy,260z.
New Apostolic Church		I-3aX	x....	15	1,000	1,000	1,718	0.05	*NAC.* In Canada Bezirk (District). Ex Irvingites. World HQ Zurich (Switzerland).
New Testament Ch of Christ the R		I-Non	.....	125	25,000	40,000	55,600	0.05	*R=Redeemer.* Founded in Kingston, churches across island. 14,000 in Sunday schools.
New Testament Church of God	1917	P-Pe3	ZF...	307	35,104	50,000	58,500	0.63	M=CoG(Cleveland) (USA). Members 70% women; large emigration to UK. 232n,4f,4r,1s.
Open Bible Standard Churches of J	1948	I-3pU	ZFY.1	33	1,980	3,000	6,000	2.81	M=OBSC(USA). Black. Classical Pentecostals. HQ Kingston. 12n,2x,3f,4H,1s,12Y.
Pentecostal Assemblies of Jamaica		I-3oU	.....	10	500	500	1,000	0.05	M=PAoW(Blacks from USA). HQ Duncans. Also Barbados. Branches in UK through emigration.
Pentecostal Church of God	1954	P-Pe2	Z....	42	2,500	2,000	7,140	5.22	*PCG of America Branch.* M=PCG. 1 school. 18n,3x,4f,1p,1s(10),W=99%,213Y.
Pentecostal Holiness Church		P-Pe3	ZF...	1	120	2,000	171	0.05	M=IPHC(USA). Holiness Pentecostals (3-stage). 2f.
Religious Society of Friends	1671	P-Qua	Q...N	8	420	1,300	700	-2.45	*Jamaica Yearly Meeting.* M=FUM(USA). 10 schools. 2n,2x,5f,1r,W=50%,50z.
Revival Zion	1783	I-3zU	.....	382	21,000	35,000	36,800	0.20	1861-62, Great Christian Revival. Charismatics similar to Shouters, Shakers.
Salvation Army	1887	P-Sal	xwM.N	64	7,000	11,000	9,590	-0.55	*SA*, Caribbean & C America Territory (HQ for 12 nations is in Kingston). 1s.
Seventh Day Baptist Church	1927	P-Bap	Tw..E	28	1,700	2,000	3,400	2.15	*SDB, Jamaica Conference.* M=SDBC(USA). 1 school. 1966, Black mission to UK begun. 2f.
Seventh-day Adventist Church	1893	P-Adv	x....	479	67,500	100,000	135,000	1.21	*SDA. Central, E, W Jamaica Conferences.* 55nx,323mw,1H,1h,6r,1s,397t,(73750),5423Y.
Unitarian Universalist Church		m-Unt	.....	1	100	200	150	0.05	M=Unitarian Universalist Service Committee. HQ Mandeville.
United Brethren in Christ	1945	P-Hol	xF...	25	850	300	1,420	6.42	M=UBC(USA). Small holiness denomination.
United Ch in Jamaica & the Cayman Is	1800	P-Uni	RWM.N	148	16,700	47,000	44,000	-0.26	1965 union: Congr Union of J, Presb Ch of J, 1968 Disciples of Christ. 50n,6r,1u.
United Pentecostal Church	1933	P-Pe1	x....	86	8,170	10,000	13,600	1.24	*Jesus Only Church.* M=UPC(USA). Mission to UK through emigration. 35n,4f,1p(12).
Wesleyan Holiness Church	1911	P-Hol	VF...	100	3,000	4,015	7,500	2.53	M=WMM(USA), Pilgrim Holiness, Missionary Bands. 26n,3x,5f,1p,W=46%,411Y.
World Missions	1966	P-Non	x....	1	300	600	700	0.62	M=World Missions (USA). North American Evangelicals based on Long Beach, CA. 1f.
World-Wide Missions of Jamaica	1961	I-Non	x....	10	8,000	20,000	15,000	-1.14	M=World-Wide Missions (USA). Evangelicals with links in Pasadena, CA (USA).
Other Black indigenous churches		I-3pU	.....	250	17,000	25,000	30,000	0.05	Total over 50 bodies, with many single congregations (see list below).
Other independent Oneness bodies	c1970	I-3oU	.....	50	5,000	–	12,000	45.60	Covers a variety of smaller Oneness missions and churches.
Other Protestant denominations		P-	.....	90	5,000	12,000	10,000	0.05	Total about 20 (see list below).
Other marginal Protestant bodies		m-	.....	20	1,000	1,000	2,000	0.05	Including: Divine Science Fed International (1 church), Unity School of Christianity (2 churches).
Totals				**4,901**	**515,667**	**951,271**	**1,082,783**		

Churches, members, growth, 1900-2025	*Congs*	*Adults*	*Affiliated*	*G%*	*Total denominations*	*O*	*R*	*A*	*P*	*I*	*m*
Total churches, members, and denominations (mid-1900)	1,800	240,000	564,700	0.75	13	0	1	1	8	2	1
Total churches, members, and denominations (mid-1970)	4,062	474,572	951,271	0.75	95	1	1	1	39	44	9
Total churches, members, and denominations (mid-1990)	4,800	501,000	1,052,360	0.51	171	1	1	1	50	101	17
Total churches, members, and denominations (mid-1995)	4,901	515,667	1,082,783	0.57	172	1	1	1	50	102	17
Total churches, members, and denominations (mid-2000)	5,000	550,000	1,121,713	0.71	173	1	1	1	50	103	17
Total churches, members, and denominations (mid-2025)	6,400	670,000	1,308,100	0.62	269	2	1	1	70	170	25

(6 Megablocs: O R A P I m)

NOTES ON TABLE ABOVE

NATIONAL COUNCILS (Column 4, 5th letter).

E = Jamaica Association of Evangelical Churches (or National Council of Fundamentalist Churches in Jamaica) (affiliated to WEF, Evangelical Association of the Caribbean (EAC), and ICCC).

N = Jamaica Council of Churches (JCC).

OTHER BLACK INDIGENOUS CHURCHES. These, mostly pentecostal, include: Apostolic Churches (several Jesus-Only independent pentecostal congregations; including Apostolic Ch of God in Christ), Assembly of Yahweh, Bethel Apostolic (Shilo) Ch, Blood-Bought Ch of God, Ch of God Fellowship (split ex NTCoG), Ch of God Pentecostal, Ch of Jesus (Watt Town, St Ann), Ch of the Lord (Aladura) from Nigeria, Emanuel Apostolic United Ch of Christ, First Glorious Temple Ch of God Apostolic, Jamaica Native Baptist Free Ch (Bedwardites; 1891-1921 enormous following throughout Jamaica), Model Ch of God, Ras Tafari Melchizedek Orthodox Ch, Remnant Chs of God, Sanctified Ch of God, Shakers, Shouters, Spiritual Baptists, Universal Ch of the Master. There are also several other USA Black missions at work including: Bible Way Chs of Our Lord Jesus Christ World Wide (1958).

OTHER PROTESTANT DENOMINATIONS. Other smaller denominations totals about 20, including: Baptist Bible Fellowship International (1972), Children of God International (Mona, Kingston), Christian Catholic Ch, Elim Fellowship (1966), Evangelical Methodist Ch (1960), Exclusive Brethren (groups: Raven-Taylor and Kelly-Continental), Independent Assemblies of God, Lutheran Ch in America, Methodist Protestant Ch, United Ev Chs, United World Mission.

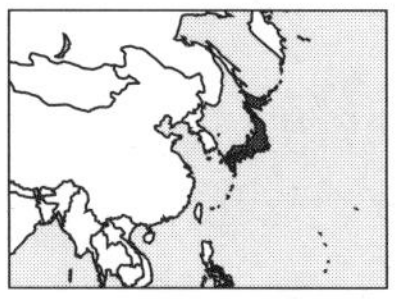

JAPAN

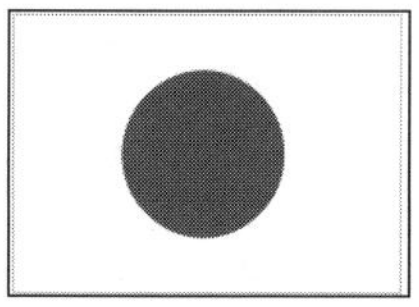

SECULAR DATA, AD 2000

STATE
Official name: Nippon Koku (Land of the Rising Sun).
Short name: Japan. **Adjective of nationality:** Japanese.
Flag: Red sun on white field.
Area: 377,835 sq. km. (145,883 sq. mi.).
Government: Constitutional monarchy, since 1946 (1601 unified empire, 1889 constitutional monarchy with bicameral parliament, 1932 military-ruled empire).
Legislature: Diet: House of Councillors, 252 members; House of Representatives, 500 members.
Official language: Japanese (Nihongo).
Monetary unit: 1 yen (¥) = 100 sen. **US$1=** ¥135.37.
Chief cities: TOKYO-Yokohama 28,025,000; Osaka 17,301,509; Osaka-Kobe 10,609,000; Tokyo 8,722,386; Nagoya 3,377,000.
Political divisions: 47 provinces.
Armed forces: 238,000.

DEMOGRAPHY
Population: 126,714,000.
Population density: 335.3/sq. km. (868.6/sq. mi.).
Under 15 years: 18,766,000.
Growth rate p.a.: 0.12% (births 10.13, deaths 8.97).
Mortality: Infant, per 1,000: 4.3; **Maternal per 100,000:** 18.0.
Life expectancy: 80 (male 77, female 83).
Household size: 3.0. **Floor area per person, sq.m:** 38.0.
Major languages: Japanese, Ryukyuan (Amami), English, Korean, Chinese, Okinawan (Luchu), Sakishima, and others.
Urban dwellers: 78.88%. **Urban growth rate p.a.:** 0.4%.
Labor force: 53%.

ETHNOLINGUISTIC PEOPLES
95.7% Japanese; 2.0% Eta; 0.7% Central Ryukyuan; 0.5% Korean; 0.1% Eurasian.

ECONOMY
National income p.a. per person: US$39,640; **per family:** US$118,920.

EDUCATION
Adult literacy: 100% (male 100%, female 100%). **Schools:** 48,002.
Universities: 1,207. **School enrolment:** female/male: 101%/100%.

HEALTH
Access to health services: 95%. **Access to safe water:** 95%.
Hospitals: 9,963 (136 beds per 10,000). **Doctors:** 219,704.
Blind: 256,455. **Deaf:** 7,585,700. **Murder rate:** 1.
Lepers: 15,000.

LITERATURE
New book titles p.a.: 58,290 (460 p.a. per million). **Periodicals:** 5,485. **Newspapers:** 121 dailies.

COMMUNICATION (per 1,000 people)
Phones: 488 (43% mobile). **Radios:** 801. **TV sets:** 619.
Daily newspaper circulation: 576. **Computers:** 367.

REFUGEES
Alien refugees from other countries: 9,900.

HUMAN LIFE AND LIBERTY (optimum condition=100.0%)
HDI: 94.0. **HSI:** 93.0. **HFI:** 80.0. **EFL:** 59.0.

Country Table 1. Religious adherents in Japan, AD 1900-2025.

Year / Name	1900 Adherents	%	1970 Adherents	%	mid-1990 Adherents	%	Annual change, 1990-2000 Natural	Conversion	Total	Rate	mid-1995 Adherents	%	mid-2000 Adherents	%	mid-2025 Adherents	%
Buddhists	35,666,000	79.6	64,685,000	62.0	68,605,740	55.5	176,456	-43,885	132,571	0.19	69,510,900	55.4	69,931,454	55.2	61,993,500	51.2
New-Religionists	2,000,000	4.5	21,300,000	20.4	31,600,000	25.6	81,266	41,498	122,764	0.38	32,400,000	25.8	32,827,640	25.9	32,500,000	26.8
Nonreligious	0	0.0	9,737,200	9.3	12,400,000	10.0	31,889	18,706	50,595	0.40	12,700,000	10.1	12,905,945	10.2	14,000,000	11.6
Christians	**430,000**	**1.0**	**3,100,000**	**3.0**	**4,375,000**	**3.5**	**11,251**	**7,206**	**18,457**	**0.41**	**4,450,000**	**3.6**	**4,559,573**	**3.6**	**5,000,000**	**4.1**
PROFESSION																
crypto-Christians	30,000	0.1	520,000	0.5	800,000	0.7	2,057	7,943	10,000	1.18	850,000	0.7	900,000	0.7	1,050,000	0.9
professing Christians	**400,000**	**0.9**	**2,580,000**	**2.5**	**3,575,000**	**2.9**	**9,194**	**-737**	**8,457**	**0.23**	**3,600,000**	**2.9**	**3,659,573**	**2.9**	**3,950,000**	**3.3**
AFFILIATION																
unaffiliated Christians	252,910	0.6	1,598,459	1.5	1,126,000	0.9	2,896	-3,227	-331	-0.03	1,112,907	0.9	1,122,692	0.9	1,145,000	1.0
affiliated Christians	**177,090**	**0.4**	**1,501,541**	**1.4**	**3,249,000**	**2.6**	**8,355**	**10,433**	**18,788**	**0.56**	**3,337,093**	**2.7**	**3,436,881**	**2.7**	**3,855,000**	**3.2**
Independents	10,000	0.0	460,479	0.4	1,510,000	1.2	3,883	5,117	9,000	0.58	1,552,452	1.2	1,600,000	1.3	1,800,000	1.5
Marginal Christians	0	0.0	170,722	0.2	680,000	0.6	1,749	2,251	4,000	0.57	697,561	0.6	720,000	0.6	850,000	0.7
Protestants	75,000	0.2	436,059	0.4	540,000	0.4	1,389	1,699	3,088	0.56	553,598	0.4	570,881	0.5	600,000	0.5
Roman Catholics	55,090	0.1	360,679	0.4	439,000	0.4	1,129	971	2,100	0.47	447,482	0.4	460,000	0.4	500,000	0.4
Anglicans	11,000	0.0	49,100	0.1	56,000	0.1	144	256	400	0.69	62,000	0.1	60,000	0.1	75,000	0.1
Orthodox	26,000	0.1	24,502	0.0	24,000	0.0	62	138	200	0.80	24,000	0.0	26,000	0.0	30,000	0.0
Trans-megabloc groupings																
Evangelicals	73,000	0.2	256,000	0.3	405,000	0.3	1,042	3,972	5,014	1.17	445,452	0.4	455,140	0.4	490,000	0.4
Pentecostals/Charismatics	0	0.0	330,000	0.3	1,235,000	1.0	3,176	49,324	52,500	3.61	1,508,974	1.2	1,760,000	1.4	2,060,000	1.7
Great Commission Christians	**150,000**	**0.3**	**1,345,000**	**1.3**	**2,925,000**	**2.4**	**7,522**	**11,632**	**19,154**	**0.64**	**3,000,000**	**2.4**	**3,116,536**	**2.5**	**3,470,000**	**2.9**
Atheists	0	0.0	1,280,000	1.2	3,400,000	2.8	8,744	15,493	24,237	0.69	3,500,000	2.8	3,642,371	2.9	5,500,000	4.5
Shintoists	6,720,000	15.0	4,173,000	4.0	2,999,510	2.4	7,714	-40,748	-33,034	-1.16	2,750,000	2.2	2,669,167	2.1	2,000,000	1.7
Muslims	0	0.0	0	0.0	160,000	0.1	411	1,432	1,843	1.10	168,000	0.1	178,434	0.1	220,000	0.2
Chinese folk-religionists	5,000	0.0	40,000	0.0	140,000	0.1	360	580	940	0.65	145,000	0.1	149,400	0.1	75,000	0.1
Confucianists	0	0.0	0	0.0	130,000	0.1	334	527	861	0.64	134,000	0.1	138,610	0.1	160,000	0.1
Hindus	4,000	0.0	5,000	0.0	21,000	0.0	54	269	323	1.44	23,000	0.0	24,228	0.0	40,000	0.0
Baha'is	0	0.0	9,800	0.0	14,400	0.0	37	81	118	0.79	15,000	0.0	15,579	0.0	25,000	0.0
Ethnoreligionists	0	0.0	0	0.0	9,000	0.0	23	65	88	0.94	9,400	0.0	9,884	0.0	15,000	0.0
Jews	0	0.0	1,000	0.0	2,350	0.0	6	-76	-70	-3.50	1,700	0.0	1,646	0.0	1,500	0.0
doubly-counted religionists	0	0.0	0	0.0	-320,000	-0.3	-823	-1,148	-1,971	0.60	-335,000	-0.3	-339,712	-0.3	-380,000	-0.3
World A (unevangelized persons)	35,860,000	80.0	62,598,600	60.0	46,944,060	38.0	120,749	-626,067	-505,318	-1.13	43,915,200	35.0	41,942,334	33.1	30,045,200	24.8
World B (evangelized non-Christians)	8,535,000	19.0	38,632,400	37.0	72,217,940	58.5	185,722	618,861	804,583	1.06	77,106,800	61.4	80,212,093	63.3	86,104,800	71.1
World C (Christians)	430,000	1.0	3,100,000	3.0	4,375,000	3.5	11,251	7,206	18,457	0.41	4,450,000	3.6	4,559,573	3.6	5,000,000	4.1
Country's population	**44,825,000**	**100.0**	**104,331,000**	**100.0**	**123,537,000**	**100.0**	**317,722**	**0**	**317,722**	**0.25**	**125,472,001**	**100.0**	**126,714,000**	**100.0**	**121,150,000**	**100.0**

COLUMNS, ROWS.
For meanings and definitions, see Codebook (Part 3). Note that, by definition, total 'Christians' = professing + crypto-Christians, which also = affiliated + unaffiliated Christians, and also = Great Commission Christians + latent Christians. Percentages may not always total exactly, due to rounding.

RELIGIOSITY IN JAPAN
It is important to note that contemporary Japanese usually interpret the word 'religion' (and the question 'What is your religion?') to mean 'personal religion' as opposed to 'family religion'. This leads to 2 apparently contradictory sets of statistics. (a) In nation-wide polls and surveys, only 33-35% profess to have a personal religion, and 65-70% (mostly young people who have abandoned the traditional religions) profess no religion. (b) Government statistics of religion, however, are based on family religion, and show that around 85% have a family religion. In our table above both sets of data are combined and reconciled.

CENSUSES.
The religion question is not asked in national population censuses, but the Ministry of Education (and earlier, the Ministry of Home Affairs) has for many years published annual statistics of affiliated members returned by headquarters of the various religions (*Religion year book*). Although methods of counting have varied, and sects not recognized by the state are usually ignored, the series does provide an idea of chronological progression, as follows. **1919:** 81.3% Buddhists (in 56 sects), 15% Sect Shintoists (including 5.0% in Shinto New Religions), 0.42% Christians. **1943** (sects recognized by state only): 62.0% Buddhists (in 28 sects), 14.3% Sect Shintoists, 0.45% Christians. **1959** (sects recognized by state only): 64.8% Buddhists (in 167 sects), 10.9% Sect Shintoists (in 129 sects), 0.75% Christians. **1966** (all sects, including those not recognized by state, and with Shrine Shinto claiming most Buddhists also): 80.8% Buddhists (in 165 sects; about 27% in Buddhist New Religions), 80.2% Shintoists (in 143 sects; including about 12.5% Sect Shintoists in 127 sects), 9.75% Christians. Total of all sects known to the state: 376. **1970:** 81.2% Buddhists (including in New Religions), 79.6% Shintoists (including in New Religions), 0.77% Christians, 9.4% other religionists (including non-Buddhist non-Shintoist New Religions). **1990:** 50.2% Shintoists, 44.3% Buddhists, 0.7% Christians, 4.8% other religionists. A large number of public-opinion polls on religion have been taken for many years.

NOTES ON RELIGIONS
AFFILIATED CHRISTIANS. The totals are over twice as large as government statistics in the *Religion year book* because the latter omits or does not know of many indigenous and Protestant bodies.
ATHEISTS. Japan Communist Party (JCP) (legal; independent of USSR and China). Persons who openly and outspokenly oppose religion and religious structures are well under 5% of the population.
BAHA'IS. Entered in 1914. Recent rapid growth from 13 local spiritual assemblies (1964) to 64 (1973), declining to 40 (1996) after reorganization. Converts include a number of Ainus.
BUDDHISTS. This category here excludes those New Religions which are radical sects of or schisms from Buddhism. Buddhists are of the Mahayana school, including Zen, Amida (Pure Land), and hundreds of other sects. There are 70,000 temples.
CHRISTIANS. Since the Meiji period (1868-1912), the number of those who call themselves Christians but are not baptized nor enrolled in any Christian church has been consistently higher than those known to churches. In addition to affiliated Christians, there has long been a large number of unaffiliated persons who, influenced particularly by the Christian scriptures (found in 50% of all Japanese homes), regard themselves as Christians, sometimes as anonymous or latent Christians. An example is a Buddhist leader at a Catholic conference who said: 'Whether I shall ever be baptized is not for me to say, but one thing is certain: in my own mind I am already an anonymous Christian' (quoted in Spae 1968: 23). Another example is the high degree of interest evident from polls: one survey found that of all Japanese university students, 53.5% of the men and 73.1% of the women professed interest in Christianity. Often there is personal belief in Christ accompanied by disinterest in or rejection of organized Christianity on the grounds that the churches have adulterated the Christian faith by institutionalizing it. Estimates in 1959, 1965, 1971 and 1990 have all put the total of all persons regarding themselves as Christians at 3.0% or more of the population (Spae, et alia). From the public's point of view, this 3.5% consists of around 2.9% who openly profess in polls, leaving 0.5% as crypto-Christians. From the churches' point of view, this 3.5% consists of 2.2% affiliated to churches (as shown in Table 2), which leaves 1.3% unaffiliated Christians; this is the very large number of unchurched persons, youths in particular, who either have had contact with Christianity through its educational institutions, or who grew up in Christian families or environments and know no other religious background, and who answer the question 'What is the religion of your home or family?' with the reply 'Christian'.
CRYPTO-CHRISTIANS. The oldest community is that of the 30,000 Kakure Kirishitan (Hidden Christians, former Catholics) who existed underground (at the same time acting externally as Buddhists) from 1638-1859, after which because of their refusal to return to the Church of Rome they were termed Hanare Kirishitan (Separated Christians). To this day they do not appear in the government's annual census of known religious bodies. The wider term Sempuku Kirishitan (Hidden Christians) is also used, to denote all Christians who maintained their faith throughout the 2 centuries of isolation. In addition, there are a large number of unorganized individuals who are committed Christians affiliated or known to churches but who either do not publicly profess their faith or do not attend church; together with a large number of isolated radio believers.
INDEPENDENTS. In over 100 denominations in 1995 (see Table 2), in 3 groupings: (1) most are in Japanese indigenous churches, the oldest being the Hidden Christians of the South Japan islands; (2) there are also some Chinese indigenous and Korean indigenous Christians, and chaplaincy work among USA armed forces on Okinawa by USA Black churches including the Church of God in Christ; and (3) there are large numbers of isolated radio believers who listen regularly to Christian broadcasts but are not, or not yet, in touch with organized denominations.
MARGINAL CHRISTIANS. Totals were growing rapidly in the 1990s; Mormons (Latter-day Saints) in 1995 were claiming 1,500 Japanese converts a year, and Jehovah's Witnesses 2,000 adult baptisms in 1995.
NEW-RELIGIONISTS. This term describes adherents of the so-called New Religions (Shinko Shukyo), more correctly termed New Religious Movements, or crisis religions, which are mostly post-1945 sects of, or schisms from, Buddhism and Shinto, but which also include new religions syncretizing the major world religions. In 1962, the Union of New Religious Organizations in Japan (Nihon Shin Shukyo Dantai Rengo Kai) had 86 member denominations with 5,442,240 adherents. In 1966, the government's *Religion year book* listed over 150 New Religions, 8 of which had over 500,000 adherents each and totalled 26,691,259. It is widely held by analysts that the actual total of active adult adherents is less than half of this figure (especially Soka Gakkai, which then claimed 15,234,136 adherents although observers estimated it at 6,500,000 adults, and at 8 million by 1972). By 1970, all adherents including children and fringe members totalled around 21 million, with the 7 largest bodies as follows: (1) Nichiren Shoshu, or Soka

Continued opposite

Country Table 1–concluded

Gakkai (Value Creation Society; in 1969, it claimed 6,876,000 families as members), (2) Reiyukaikyodan (Association of Friends of the Spirit; Buddhist, 4,079,000 in 1962, 4,719,988 in 1970), (3) Tenrikyo (Religion of Divine Wisdom; a Shinto sect, founded in 1838; 2,459,000 in 1962, 2,342,131 in 1970), (4) Izumo-taishokyo (begun 1873; 2,261,382), (5) Rissho-koseikai (Society for the Establishment of Righteousness and Friendly Intercourse; 2,205,728 in 1970, rising by (1978 to 4,600,000), (6) Seicho no Ie (House of Growth; neither Buddhist nor Shintoist; founded 1929; 1,457,778 rising to 3 million worldwide by 1974), and (7) PL Kyodan (Perfect Liberty Church, begun 1946; 1,265,422, growing to 2.5 million worldwide by 1975). Growth, backed by detailed statistics, has been most spectacular for Soka Gakkai, as follows: (1937) 60 members, (1940) 350, (1941) 3,000, (1953) 20,000 (families; also all following figures), (1956) 194,000, (1959) 1,050,000, (1964) 3,950,000, (1966) 5,000,000, (1968) 6,720,000, (1969) 6,876,000. Along with other New Religions it has large followings abroad among the Japanese diaspora in Asia and the Americas, and has mission work in (1975) 88 countries.

By 1998 most of these totals had increased, producing a grand total of over 32 million adherents.

NONRELIGIOUS. The term covers those having neither family religion nor personal religion, i.e. agnostics, freethinkers and (the vast majority) those indifferent to religion. Among young men aged 20-40 years, one survey found that 82% have no religious beliefs at all. The rapid growth of this category in the 20th century is due to abandonment of religion by Japanese youth who are highly critical of the major traditional religions. Converts to Christianity come mainly from this group.

ORTHODOX. In the year 1900, there were about 20,000 Russians who were Orthodox.

SHINTOISTS. There are 2 categories of Shintoists: Shrine Shintoists (before 1945 a state politico-religious organization, disestablished 1945) who form the majority of Shintoists, and Sect Shintoists (whose numbers have declined slightly from 15.0% in 1919 to 12.5% in 1966). Shrine Shintoists are usually Buddhists simultaneously, and so are termed Buddhists in this table; Sect Shinto (Kyoha Shinto) with its 13 sects is usually considered as a part of the New Religions, and is treated as such in our table. Shrine Shintoists were never enumerated before 1945, and government statistics since have claimed around 65% for them. However, a private study in 1952-53 by Odaka and Nishira, with residents of the 6 most important cities, showed that Shinto was a family religion for only 3.4% and a personal religion for 2.4%. In polls in the 1960s, around 4% claimed to be Shintoists and only 1.5% professed active Shinto affiliation. Our definition of the category Shintoist in the table also follows this usage, namely persons who profess, or still profess, Shinto as their first or major religion.

UNAFFILIATED CHRISTIANS. As described in the note above on CHRISTIANS, nominal Christians consist of a very large number of unchurched or unaffiliated persons, youths in particular, who either have had contact with Christianity through its schools and colleges, or who grew up in Christian circles and know no other religious background, and who answer the question 'What is the religion of your home or family?' with the reply 'Christian'.

Great Commission Instrument Panel: status of Japan (for explanation see start of Part 4)

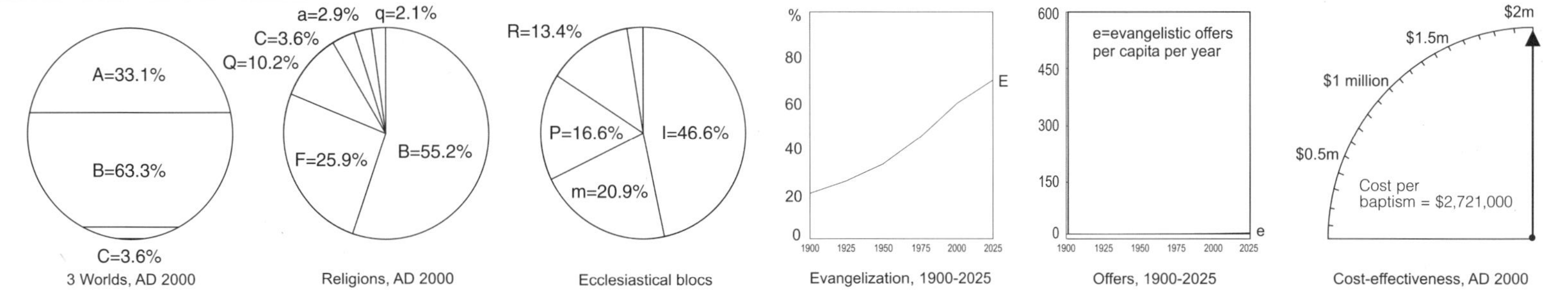

Country status. Japan is the most prosperous non-Christian and non-Western nation in the world. Japan has developed a unique culture and society similar to those of its Asian neighbors, yet strikingly different. In this century, it also has managed to become considerably Westernized without giving up its own traditions. Four-fifths of the islands are mountainous and subject to frequent earthquakes. Japan is a major exporter of motor vehicles and electronic equipment.

HUMAN LIFE AND LIBERTY

Human need and development. Materially, Japan is one of the most affluent nations in the world, and its per capita GNP has already overtaken those of advanced Western countries, including the United States. The so-called Japanese miracle which, beginning in the 1960s, took only about 25 years, has transformed the country into an economic superpower. Its technological prowess is such that observers feel that it has moved beyond the modern age into the postmodern. At the same time, it is subject to the problematique, the complex of problems, including environmental and social decline, that is challenging all advanced nations. Given its small land area and the lack of natural resources, Japan is dependent on foreign trade for its continued prosperity. Many of the large cities are overcrowded, and their living costs are higher than those of U S or West European cities. Japanese workers have to work harder and longer to maintain their lifestyles, and pay a high cost in terms of physical and mental stress.

Human rights and freedoms. Japan is one of the most democratic nations of the modern world, and affords its citizens all basic human rights. Freedom from arbitrary arrest or imprisonment is provided for in the Constitution. Under the Criminal Procedure Code, a suspect may be held in police custody for up to 72 hours without representation by defense counsel. A judge may extend this period for up to 25 days. In some cases the preindictment detention may be extended even further by using a procedure known as bekken taiho, or arrest on a separate charge. Another potential for abuse stems from the practice of substitute detention in a police cell rather than in a house of detention. The Constitution prohibits discrimination based on race, creed, sex, social status or family origin. Women occupy a subordinate role in society, although their position has significantly improved since World War II. Domestic violence against women generally goes unreported to avoid loss of face. Because of the exclusivity of Japanese society, minorities are accorded an inferior status. Discrimination is most severe against Koreans and the 'unclean' class of Burrakumin. Immigrants reportedly face harassment in obtaining housing, jobs, and healthcare.

Human environment. Japan has a rich variety of habitats ranging from subarctic in the northernmost areas of Hokkaido to subtropical in Kyushu and the southern island chains. Because of traditional concern for nature and stringent regulations the environment has escaped serious damage or deterioration. Yet, the air quality is below acceptable levels in urban areas. Acid rain is a serious problem affecting lakes and reservoirs. The coastal waters also are heavily polluted.

Buddhists. In the first 3 days of the 1976 New Year, a record 64.8 million Japanese visited and prayed in Buddhist temples and shrines across Japan. *Above.* Worshipers at Tokyo temple of Akusa Kannon (Bodhisattva or 'Buddha-to-be', also regarded as female goddess of mercy.

NON-CHRISTIAN RELIGIONS

Buddhism was introduced into Japan during the 6th century and since the 7th century has been Japan's principal religion. Its spread among the lower classes began in the 9th century, after having settled on the Mahayana school accompanied by the rapid development of 2 esoteric schools based on severe asceticism: Tendai-shu and Shingon-shu. Although at one point Tendai-shu completely dominated Japanese Buddhism, it was later reduced to a secondary although still important position. In 1975, it had 2.9 million faithful and 4,383 temples with its mother temple and pilgrimage center at Mount Niei near Kyoto. Tendai-shu has recently again become very demanding in its training of monks. As for Shingon-shu, it has now taken the lead in the study and application of Tantric Mahayanist doctrine and numbers 11.9 million faithful and 12,328 temples. Its center at Koya-San consists of a small city with a university of Buddhism (Koya-San Daigaku), which possesses one of the finest specialized libraries in the world. The Rinzai, Soto and Obaku sects of Zen Buddhism arrived from China in respectively the 12th, 13th, and 17th centuries and represent a further development of the Ch'an school of meditation. All have had a profound effect on Japanese culture (arts, flowers, gardens, tea, et alia). The popularity of Zen today, with 13 million followers and 20,494 temples, is due primarily to its techniques of meditation: Zazen and Sanzen of Rinzai and Zazen of Soto. Its expansion in the Western world is well known, and of note is the Zen temple of the Jesuit father Lassalle which uses the techniques of Zen meditation while removing it from Buddhist doctrine.

Zen Buddhists. *Left.* 1,800 Japanese schoolgirls exactly in line in temple. *Right.* Masked monks in Zen Revival.

Nevertheless, the Japanese masses have been most attracted to the 2 pietist schools, Amita Jodo (Pure Land School) and Nichiren-shu. Jodo-shu and its reformed wing, Jodoshin-shu, have the largest number of followers, about 17.7 million with 29,876 temples. An important Jodoshin-shu university, Bukkyo Daigaku, is found at Kyoto and, from its major temple, Nishi-Honganju, Jodoshin-shu is making an effort to expand its influence among non-Japanese in Europe and America.

Founded in the 13th century by the monk Nichiren, whose principal concerns were religious austerity and social justice, Nichiren-shu has gained a popular following among the lower classes and at present has 13 million members with 5,782 temples.

A number of organizations have emerged in recent years to help Buddhism deal with the problems and challenges of the modern era. One of the largest is the Japan Buddhist Federation (Zen-Nihon Buddyo-kai), which includes in its membership 60 Buddhists sects, 37 regional associations, and 19 other groups.

Shinto is the ancestral religion of Japan. It came under the influence of Confucianism towards the end of the 5th century, when was eclipsed by Buddhism from the 7th to the 9th centuries before its revival during the Meiji era. This religion, after having lost its dogmatic hold little by little, ended by being a na-

Country summary. **Worlds A, B, C by ethnolinguistic peoples, cities, and major civil divisions in Japan.**

	PEOPLES							CITIES							CIVIL DIVISIONS						
World	Num	Pop 2000	C%	Christians	E%	U%	Unevangelized	Num	Pop 2000	C%	Christians	E%	U%	Unevangelized	Num	Pop 2000	C%	Christians	E%	U%	Unevangelized
A	18	4,177,095	1.33	55,659	45	55	2,304,198	0	0	0.00	0	0	0	0	0	0	0.00	0	0	0	0
B	11	122,330,579	2.62	3,200,606	68	32	39,586,364	221	83,476,410	2.65	2,212,497	71	29	24,229,172	47	126,714,218	2.71	3,436,881	67	33	41,890,819
C	5	206,544	87.45	180,618	100	0	259	0	0	0.00	0	0	0	0	0	0	0.00	0	0	0	0
Total	**34**	**126,714,218**	**2.71**	**3,436,883**	**67**	**33**	**41,890,821**	**221**	**83,476,410**	**2.65**	**2,212,497**	**71**	**29**	**24,229,172**	**47**	**126,714,218**	**2.71**	**3,436,881**	**67**	**33**	**41,890,819**

tional cult to which all citizens had to submit. The suppression of state Shinto in 1945 on the one hand swept away the institution of shrine Sinto (Jinja Shinto) whose basic unity was a territorial community grouped about a shrine, and on the other hand gave rise to a large number of new heterogeneous sects of Shinto inspiration. Most Shinto shrines are now legally incorporated within the Association of Shinto Shrines (Jinja-honcho) and are concerned more with administrative than doctrinal questions.

As a whole, Shinto includes all groups which revere the Japanese gods, the Kami. A collective religion more than an individual one, the influence of Shinto is especially marked at the family level. Recent sociological studies, however, show a certain evolution towards the formation of bonds with the shrines, bonds that are more spiritual than familial or geographical and which result thus in a process of delocalization. In addition to Jinja-honcho, which includes 90% of all Shinto shrines, there exist other Shinto organizations including the Federation of Sectarian Shinto (Kyoha Shinto Rengokai). The latter includes the 11 traditional sects although the total number of Shinto sects is much higher. There are two Shinto universities, Kokugakuin Daigaku in Tokyo and Kogakukan at Ise, the latter having been reopened in 1962.

New-Religionists (2). Rissho-koseikai (Society for Establishment of Righteousness). *Upper.* Its Great Sacred Hall, Tokyo. *Lower.* Great Sacred Hall's radio/TV studio, with 100 closed circuit TV sets for internal viewing.

New religions or, more correctly, New Religious Movements (Shinko Shukyo), a term in use since 1930, are recently begun religions or sects as contrasted with the older, established ones of orthodox Shinto, Buddhism, and Christianity. Many of them are not, strictly speaking, distinct new religions but are only renewals or new religious movements or sects within either Shinto or Buddhism, although at the same time being radical breaks, with new and distinct religious systems and other innovations. However, a number are quite new in the sense that they syncretize in a new form elements of Shinto, Buddhism, and Christianity, And because they almost all attempt to adapt religion to the modern age, it is best to follow the popular usage of regarding them together forming a new grouping, termed for convenience Shinko Shukyo.

The first of these New Religions were formed in the 19th century at the close of the feudal era and the beginning of the Meiji restoration; Tenrikyo was begun about 1838 and Konkokyo in 1859. The New Religions have had 3 periods of marked development: the first around 1920, the second about 1935 and the third during the decade 1945-55, corresponding respectively to the 3 periods of most rapid social change in Japan: World War I, the rise of fascism and the Sino-Japanese war, and the defeat of 1945. The religious characteristics of these religions can be summarized as follows: the promise of salvation, miracles and the practice of magic, belief in the existence of a divine spirit, shamanism and authoritarianism, syncretism in doctrinal sources and community morale. More than 10 New Religions have branches in North and South America, as well as in Southeast Asia. Although several New Religions are very large, many others are small local groups with barely a few hundred members. Eighty-six of the religions belong to the Union of New Religious Organizations in Japan, which includes many of the major religions with the exception of Soka Gakkai, Reiyukai, Seicho no Ie (House of Growth) and Sekai Kyusei-kyo (Church of World Messianity).

Seven of the so-called New Religions each have over 2 million adherents in 1998. In order of size, the largest are as follows. (1) Soka Gakkai (Value Creation Society) or Nichiren Shoshu, which stems from Nichiren Buddhism, has an active adult membership of around 8 million, though 15,234,136 faithful were officially claimed in 1966 and for 20 years or so thereafter. With its central organization in Tokyo, it was founded in 1930 but has developed extensively only since 1951. It has its strength among persons excluded from the evident economic prosperity of Japan, including small businessmen, the independently employed, and poorly paid workers in the large cities. Soka Gakkai is based on the fundamental unity of religion and politics, conducts intensive propaganda and has created a political party Komei-to which has fascist tendencies and which gives political expression to the middle classes. Soka Gakkai did not develop until after most of the otheı New Religions and is distinguished from them by its political ambitions and its religious intolerance. However, its practice of forced conversion (shakubuku) and the more virulent of its anti-Christian aspects have become less prominent since 1990. (2) Reiyukai (Association of Friends of the Spirit) was founded in Tokyo in 1923 and in 1970 had a following of 4,719,988, with considerable increase by 1995. It follows the lay Buddhist tradition, with a doctrine combining emphasis on temporal concerns with the ancestral cult and patriarchal morals. (3) Tenrikyo (Religion of Divine Wisdom) founded in 1838 with its central organization at Tenri, Nara, had 2,342,131 adherents in 1970 and over 3 million by 1995. It is a popular religion characteristic of the Meiji period which expanded on a national scale during the 1880s. Originally, it developed as a subversive religious movement within the feudal order preceding the Meiji regime, but it then placed itself at the service of the imperial government and became, under government pressure, a sect of National Shinto (Kokka-shinto) in 1890. (4) Izumotaishakyo began in 1873 and is based on Shinto. The headquarters for its 2,261,382 adherents is in Taisha, Shimane prefecture. (5) Rissho-Koseikai (Society for the Establishment of Righteousness), with 2,042,590 adherents, is based on Buddhism and has its central organization in Tokyo. It separated from Reiyukai in 1938, but its doctrine is still centered in the Reiyukai emphasis on personal perfection of the individual realized through faith in Hokke Buddhism. Around 1948, its influence spread rapidly in Tokyo and in the eastern part of the country.

Two other religions had under 2 million adherents in 1970 but, by 1998, had grown to over 3 million each worldwide: Seicho no Ie and PL Kyodan (Perfect Liberty Church).

New-Religionists (1). Soka Gakkai (Value Creation Society), largest of Japan's 150 New Religions. *Above.* Opening service in new temple by Mount Fuji, 1964. *Inset.* New earthquake-proof Sho-Hondo/Grand Main Temple/ High Sanctuary ('largest temple on earth', opened 1972) for 60,000 worshipers at headquarters on lower slopes of Mount Fuji, with shrine for Nichiren's sacred tablet Dai-Gohonson.

Interreligious organizations. A number of bodies are at present active in promoting interreligious understanding and dialogue between all religions. (1) The Japan Religions League (Nihon Shukyo Remmei) is a nationwide interreligious organization established in 1945 to promote religious cooperation and to ensure religious liberty. Each prefecture in the country has its own related religions league. Official members are: the Japan Buddhist Federation (Zen-Nihon Bukkyo-kai), the Association of Shinto Shrines (Jinja-honcho), the Federation of sectarian Shinto (Kyoha Shinto Rengokai), the Japan Christian Federation (Nihon Kirisutokyo Rengokai) and the Union of New Religious Organizations in Japan (Shinshu-remmei). (2) The NCC Center for the Study of Japanese Religions was founded in Kyoto in 1962 and is affiliated to the National Christian Council of Japan. This study center provides both national clergy and others interested in Japanese religions with detailed information about the thought and activities of contemporary religions in Japan. It collaborates with the Oriens Institute, maintains liaison with Buddhists and Shintoists and publishes an English quarterly *Japanese Religions* and a Japanese quarterly *Deai.* (3) The Oriens Institute for Religious Research, established in Tokyo in 1961, is a Catholic research center sponsored by the Scheut Fathers and engaged in the study of present-day religious trends in Japan. There are numerous publications and emphasis is placed on social questions and subsequent action on an ecumenical basis. (4) The International Institute for the Study of Religions (Kokusai Shukyo Kenkyu Sho) is an interreligious organization with headquarters in Sophia University (Catholic) in Tokyo. The institute studies present-day Japanese religions and publishes a journal, *Contemporary religions in Japan.*

A World Conference on Religion and Peace was held in Kyoto in October 1970 bringing together 1,600 delegates and observers from 22 world religions. This conference was the culmination of several smaller interreligious conferences and consultations held in New York in 1965, Washington in 1966, New Delhi in 1968, and Kyoto in 1968. The conference then established a permanent interreligious body called the World Conference of Religion for Peace, with headquarters in New York.

Traditional tribal religions are practiced by the hunting and fishing Ainus who inhabit Sakhalin, Hokkaido, and the southern part of the Kurile Islands. An unusual feature of their cult is the ceremonial sacrifice of a bear each year in October. While the bear is eaten by the community, its spirit serves as intermediary taking messages from the living to their first ancestor, the Mountain Spirit. Demons, nature divinities, and family ancestral spirits have a place in their belief system as well as the idea of a supreme being and a conception of an after-life with rewards and punishments.

CHRISTIANITY

PROTESTANT CHURCHES. Several unsuccessful attempts were made by Protestants to reach Japan in the first half of the 19th century, and it was not until the Townsend Harris treaty of 1858, 4 years after the appearance of admiral Mathew Perry, that they were permitted entry. The first to arrive in 1859 were USA missionaries of the Protestant Episcopal Church, the Presbyterian Board and the Dutch Reformed Church, a number of whom had formerly served in China. Faced with Japanese hostility towards all things Western as the result of the period of exclusion from 1606-1854, they were initially confined to Yokohama and Nagasaki. The first Protestant baptism did not take place until 1864. During these early difficult years, they prepared dictionaries and grammars, translated the Bible and assisted government in building a new system of education. They also developed hospitals and private schools and educated some of the most influential men in Japan's later political development.

American Baptists began their first permanent mission in Yokohama in 1872, the same year a revival took place as a result of work by Reformed missionaries, and converts established the first Japanese Protestant church in Yokohama. The first missionary conference was also held in Yokohama in 1872 with representatives from the Presbyterian, Reformed, and Congregational missions. As a result of their concern for nondenominational emphases, the first converts called their group the Church of Christ. They also joined forces in establishing the Union Theological Seminary in Tokyo in 1877, and in the same year, 5 Presbyterian and 4 Church of Christ denominations united to form the United Church of Christ in Japan.

In 1878, all anti-Christian restrictions were removed, and the number of foreign missionaries doubled from 29 to 58, including newly arrived Methodists and Anglicans. Work spread to Osaka, Kobe, Kyoto, and the northern island of Hokkaido. Revivals again broke out in 1883 in Yokohama and spread throughout central Japan in the next few years largely due to the zeal of converts in bringing others to Christ. Foreign missionaries increased from 145 to 383 and congregations grew from 83 to 448. In a 7-year period, the number of ordained pastors tripled and the number of evangelists quadrupled. The century closed with missionaries from several newly organized interdenominational faith missions beginning to arrive, including the Evangelical Alliance Mission and Christian and Missionary Alliance in 1891 and the Oriental Missionary Society in 1901.

Nationalism increased in fervor under the Meiji regime, and a reaction against Western Christianity set in once again. Although the government in 1884 declared Buddhism and Shinto no longer state religions, in 1890, the Imperial Rescript on Education rejected Christian theology and morality and ordered all Japanese to publicly revere the ancestral gods of Shinto. Missionaries and Japanese Christians at first refused to comply but later made an effort to demonstrate their loyalty during the Chinese and Russian wars.

During the 15-year period following the overthrow of the Meiji regime in 1912, Christianity again gained ground through evangelistic campaigns and literature distribution. Church membership increased from 79,000 to 110,000, with numerous high officials becoming Christians. At the same time there was also a revival of Buddhism, which adopted such traditionally Christian activities as the establishment of schools and hospitals. Militarism also grew as Japan gained territory in Manchuria during the 1930s. Moreover, the government increasingly relied on subservience to Shinto to unite all Japanese in order to further imperialist expansion. Christianity in turn was severely restricted and Japanese Christians were divided as to where to place their loyalty. A special problem was to what extent Christians might acquiesce in the Shinto requirements which the government defined as political rather than religious, although they involved public acknowledgement of the divine ancestry of the emperor.

In 1940, to gain further control, the government ordered the formation of the Kyodan, which was intended to include all Protestant churches in a single United Church of Christ. Denominations which refused to join, including the Salvation Army, Anglican, Adventist and Holiness churches, all ceased to exist officially. The Kyodan survived the war and in 1948 included a majority of all Protestant churches and members.

Following the war, the American general MacArthur called for '1,000 missionaries' from the USA to Japan. Foreign missionaries poured in, totalling over 2,500 Protestants by 1973. Many of these were new to the Orient, the majority being from conservative groups in the USA. The result has been a vast proliferation of almost 200 different churches and missions working in the country. In 1963, 2 Lutheran churches and 6 missions joined to form the Japan Evangelical Lutheran Church, but 7 other Lutheran missions remain independent. More than 20 Baptist denominations work in Japan, and 7 Presbyterian groups remain outside the Kyodan.

The largest Protestant church continues to be the United Church of Christ in Japan, consisting of those churches which remained part of the Kyodan. It has 1,610 ordained pastors assisted by 305 foreign missionaries and, in 1975, sponsored 47 of its own Japanese missionaries serving in 12 overseas countries.

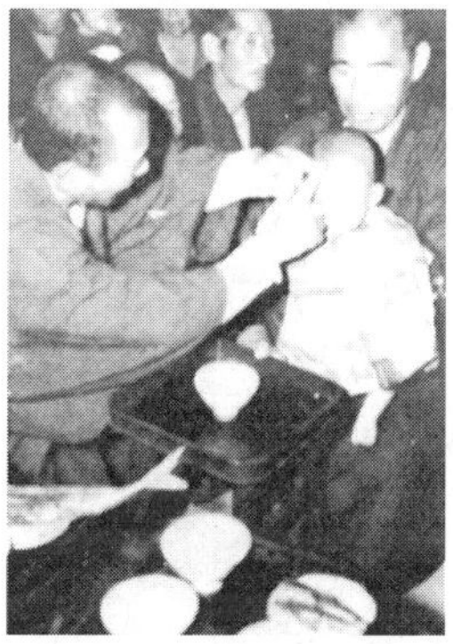

Hidden Christians (Kakure Kirishitan). Begun 1549, forced underground. Child is baptized with Christian, Buddhist, and Shinto elements.

INDIGENOUS CHURCHES. The oldest indigenous group of Christians are 40,000 former Roman Catholics who survived the persecutions of 1606-1859, but who have since 1865 consistently refused to rejoin the Catholic Church. Known as Hidden Christians (Kakure Kirishitan), or Separated Christians (Hanare) by the Catholics, they inhabit islands in Southern Japan and have their own ceremonies and rites embodying Buddhist and Shinto elements.

An early reaction to the proliferation of Protestant foreign missions after the 1860s was the forming by Japanese nationals of antimissionary indigenous movements. One of the earliest was Mukyokai or the No-Church Movement began by a former Methodist, Kanzo Uchimura, based on small Bible study groups. Later, a large number of independent churches were begun by Japanese, often as schisms from Western denominations. By 1995, there were over 100 Japanese indigenous denominations and groups in Japan. The largest is the Spirit of Jesus Church which split from the Assemblies of God in 1937 and how has its own Japanese missionaries in the USA and Brazil. Another important denomination is the Original Gospel (Tabernacle) Movement, a Pentecostal schism from the No-Church Movement. Another body is the Unification Church, from Korea (Holy Spirit Association for the Unification of World Christianity), which has a large student following.

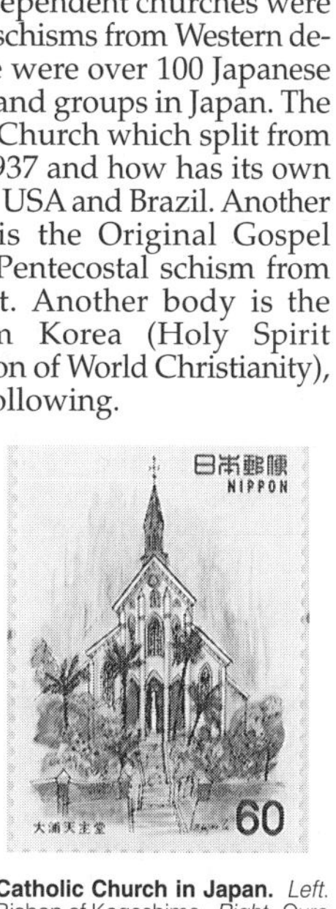

Catholic Church in Japan. *Left.* Bishop of Kagoshima. *Right.* Oura Cathedral on 1980 stamp.

CATHOLIC CHURCH. The first Christian mission to Japan began with the visit of Francis Xavier to Kagoshima in 1549. Catholics expanded rapidly, and there were 300,000 baptized by 1593, many in the Nagasaki region. In 1613, Christianity was prohibited and severe persecution followed. Foreign missionaries were not able to return until 1859, when the present era of missions began.

By 1990, there was a total of 439,000 baptized, or 0.4% of the total population. The archdiocese of Nagasaki has the greatest number and concentration of Catholics in the country; its 70,300 baptized are 4.5% of the local population and 16% of all Catholics in Japan. None of the other 15 dioceses has a local proportion of Catholics above 0.5%, and the Tokyo archdiocese has 0.4%. The only exceptions are a few small islands off South Kyushu, populated by fishermen and farmers; Catholics number 16% on the island of Goto in the archdiocese of Nagasaki and 5% on the island of Amami-Oshima in the diocese of Kagashima.

So far as social distribution is concerned, in the archdiocese of Nagasaki Catholics constitute sociologically a closed milieu, with hardly any adult conversions taking place but with numerous infant baptisms and marriages among Catholics, especially in the countryside. A large proportion of the Catholics in this region are descendants of the Old Christians (Kirishitan) who survived the persecutions of the 16th and 17th centuries and who were rediscovered by missionaries in 1865; all but 33,000 of these have now rejoined the Catholic Church. On the islands of Honshu, Hokkaido, and Shikoku, most Catholics are young adult converts with the same social characteristics as Protestants. The vast majority of Catholics live in urban areas. On Honshu, 45% of Catholics are high school graduates, 60% are women, 50% are unmarried, over 75% are adult converts and over 80% belong to the middle class. The importance of women among Japanese Catholics is the result, in large part, of the disproportionately large number of girls educated in Catholic schools. Equally to be noted is the large number of Japanese sisters, who numbered 5,348 in 1971 in contrast to 950 foreign sisters. This is a remarkably high number in comparison with the total Catholic population, being one sister for every 57 Catholics.

One important Catholic immigrant group is the Koreans, and pastoral work for them is well organized, with centers in Tokyo, Osaka, and Kyoto where a priest and Korean sister are assigned to this task.

Catholics also form a large minority among Japanese emigrants, especially those who have moved to Brazil and other parts of Latin America; and special efforts have been made to minister to them. In 1971, there were 68 priests, 53 sisters, and 24 catechists working with these emigrants in overseas countries. The total number of emigrant Catholics is in fact higher than the number residing in Japan.

There are 2 major characteristics of recent Catholic demography in Japan. In the first place, there has been a marked decrease in the annual rate of Catholic population growth, in contrast to the rapid increases that took place after World War II. From a total of 108,324 baptized Catholics in 1946, the number increased to 357,478 in 1971, an average annual increase of 5%. From 1971 to 1990 the number increased to 438,834, an average annual increase of only 1%. The number of annual adult baptisms in Japan, including the Ryukyu Islands, reached a peak of 10,669 in 1953 but, since then, has decreased annually to 5,269 in 1971, almost back to the level of the 1946 figure of 4,242. The number of infant baptisms reached a peak of 7,521 in 1964 and then began to decrease, to 6,413 in 1971. Most of the converts during the post-war years were young adults; therefore, there should have been a substantial increase in the number of baptized infants, but this has not been the case. One explanation of this is that many Catholics lose touch with the church as a result of widespread internal migration; another is that the Catholic annual birth rate fell from 4.4% per year in 1946 to 1.9% in 1968, to 1.1% by 1995 though it continues to remain slightly higher than the national birth rate, which fell from 3.3% per year in 1946 to 1.85% in 1968, to 1.05 in 1995.

A second factor in recent Catholic demography is the increasing Catholic migration from rural dioceses in the south to dioceses in the highly urbanized and industrialized center of the country: Tokyo, Nagoya, Yokohama, and Osaka. Thus, 4 of the 5 dioceses on Kyushu and Shikoku (Takamatsu, Fukuoka, Nagasaki and Kagoshima) experienced a decline in membership from 1970. The diocese most affected by this exodus is that of Nagasaki. In 1903, Nagasaki had 77% of all Catholics in Japan; this proportion declined to 45% in 1951, 19% by 1971, and 14% by AD 2000. The exodus is due to population mobility caused by urbanization but also to the frequent shifting of public officials and employees of private businesses, social categories in which many Catholics are to be found.

The Holy See has diplomatic relations with Japan and in AD 2000 is represented to government and the Catholic hierarchy by a pro-nuncio residing in Tokyo.

ANGLICAN CHURCH. Two USA Episcopal missionaries from China were the first to arrive in Japan following the 1858 treaty. The CMS from Britain sent missionaries in 1869 and the Woman's Union Missionary Society opened a girl's school in Yokohama in 1871. In 1887, the CMS, SPG and the Protestant Episcopal Church of the USA organized the Japan Holy Catholic Church (NSKK). Its first Japanese bishops were consecrated in 1923. During World War II, the church remained underground rather than comply with government decrees. It is the seventh largest church in Japan after the Catholic church, Unification Church, Jehovah's Witnesses, Kyodan, Spirit of Jesus Church, and the Mormons.

ORTHODOX CHURCH. The Holy Orthodox Church of Japan was begun in 1861 and now consists of 80 congregations with a total Christian community stagnant at 24,000 in 3 dioceses. It has ties with the Russian Orthodox Church, Patriarchate of Moscow.

Renewal movements. In the 1990s the Pentecostal/Charismatic Renewal continued to spread across most older churches, and numbered over 1,760,000 adherents (of whom 3% Pentecostals, 9% Charismatics, and 88% Independents).

Indigenous missions. Japanese Christians, though a small percentage of the national population, have consistently shown a strong commitment to foreign missions. Over 500 Japanese are currently serving in countries on all 6 continents.

CHURCH AND STATE

The constitution of 1946 states in Article 20: 'Freedom of religion is guaranteed to all. No religious organization may receive any privileges whatsoever from the State, nor may it exercise any political authority. No one may be forced to take part in a religious act, service, rite or ceremony. The State and its agencies shall refrain from religious education and all other religious activities'. Article 89 states: 'No public funds or property of the State may be used for the profit or maintenance of a religious institution or association, of whatever kind, nor for any charitable, educational or benevolent enterprise not under the control of public authorities'.

The Meiji constitution of 1889 had made Shinto the state religion, a state of affairs not ended until the separation of Shinto from the state became effective in December 1945 by order of the supreme commander for the Allied Powers. An imperial rescript of 1 January 1946, clearly repudiates the divine character of the emperor, and Imperial Ordinance 719 of 1945, revised in 1946 as Imperial Ordinance 70, suppressed all ancient laws, ordinances, and regulations protecting Shinto or limiting the liberty of other religions. This legislation permits all religious corporations, including the Great Shinto Shrine of Ise, to possess a 'religious juridical personality' (Shukyo-hojin). Today, religious corporations wishing to benefit from this statute must register with an ad hoc department (Shukyo-hojin Bunga-cho) within the Ministry of Public Instruction (Mombusho). Registered groups, churches, dioceses, parishes, and religious communities enjoy certain privileges, notably exemption from taxes on purchase of land and construction of buildings for church use. In return, they must comply with other legal requirements: submission of annual reports, inspection of their worship buildings and the like.

Christian schools have the same rights and obligations as other private schools. In addition to the secular syllabus applied in all schools by the Ministry of Public Instruction, religious education courses are authorized both within and outside the schools.

In 1979, for the first time, a professing Christian, M. Ohira, became premier.

BROADCASTING AND MEDIA

Nearly everyone has a radio receiver and a television. Programs from TWR (Guam), FEBC (Philippines), VERITAS, and other international broadcasters cover Japan along with most of eastern Asia. IBRA-produced programs can be heard over Radio Nippon in Japanese. AWR's studio in Yakohama produces Japanese programs as well.

Several broadcasters have used facilities within Japan to create Christian programs. Japan is a member of UNDA. Most of the 2.5 million who have seen the 'Jesus' Film, viewed it as a film team presentation.

INTERDENOMINATIONAL ORGANIZATIONS

The National Christian Council of Japan (NCCJ) was founded in 1923, building on earlier ecumenical efforts which began with the first National Christian Conference in Tokyo in 1878. The Conference was part of the World Evangelical Alliance between 1884 and 1906 after which it went out of existence. The Christian Church Federation was formed in 1911, taking the name NCCJ in 1923. The Federation of Christian Missions turned over its work to the Council in 1936 and became simply a Fellowship of Christian Missionaries which continues to exist.

The Japan Evangelical Association was formed in 1968, merging the Japan Evangelical Fellowship, Japan Evangelical Missionary Association and Japan Protestant Council. There is also a Japan Church Growth Research Association, formed in 1968, which coordinates research into the factors which foster or inhibit church growth.

Relations between Protestants and Catholics have improved considerably since Vatican II. The Catholic Episcopal Commission for Ecumenism is active as are such other groups as the Sodepax Committee, which was set up in Tokyo in 1970.

The Japan Ecumenical Association (JEA) is an interdenominational organization, founded in 1969, with the following aims: to promote contact, dialogue, study and mutual help between its members, who are the major Protestant churches and the Catholic Church; to study from the ecumenical point of view all problems which the churches face in their proclamation of the gospel to Japan and to promote contact, dialogue and cooperation with the other religions of Japan and with the leaders of Japanese society. In particular, the JEA promotes ecumenism at the grass-roots level through joint social action. One such instance is the Friendship Volunteers, inaugurated in 1970 by the Oriens Institute and which brings together Protestants and Catholics in helping poor people in Tokyo.

Another ecumenical project is the telephone counseling services in Japanese and English. The former of these is Inochi no Denwa (Live-saving Telephone) begun in 1971. This Christian service was the first of its kind in Japan and has had great success. More than 30,000 calls from persons lonely or in distress were received during its first 5 months of operation. A volunteer staff of 185 counselors and 26 supervisors from the principal churches, Protestant and Catholic, operate this service from headquarters located in the Lutheran Center in Tokyo. A similar service in the English language was inaugurated in 1973, known as the Tokyo English Life Line (TELL).

Other joint activities have included the Christian Pavilion at the 1970 World Exposition in Osaka and, during the same year, a mass distribution of ecumenical posters inviting non-Christians to participate in Christmas midnight services in any denomination.

FUTURE TRENDS AND PROSPECTS

Buddhists are sure to continue to lose adherents, falling below 50% of the population after 2025, the first time since Buddhism was introduced to Japan. Christians will probably grow from 3% in 1970 to over 4% by 2025.

If Christian churches in Japan continue to grow, they could claim 5% of the population as early as AD 2050. The other fast-growing segment of the Japanese population is the nonreligious, expected to reach 15% by that time.

BIBLIOGRAPHY

150 years of North German mission, 1836–1986. E. Schöck-Quinteros & D. Lenz (eds). Bremen, 1989. 83p. (Deals with work of North German missions in Togo, Ghana, and Japan).

A bibliography of Christianity in Japan: Protestantism in English sources (1859–1959). F. Ikado & J. R. McGovern. Tokyo: Committee on Asian Cultural Studies, International Christian University, 1966. 125p.

A biographical dictionary of Methodist missionaries to Japan, 1873–1993. J. W. Krummel (ed). [Tokyo]: Kyo Bun Kwan, 1996. 350p.

A century of Protestant Christianity in Japan. C. W. Iglehart. 1959; Rutland, Vt. and Tokyo: Charles E. Tuttle, 1965. 384p.

A history of Christianity in Japan. R. H. Drummond. Grand Rapids, MI: Eerdmans, 1971. 398p.

A history of Christianity in Japan: Roman Catholic, Greek Orthodox, and Protestant missions. O. Cary. 1909; Rutland, Vt. and Tokyo: Charles E. Tuttle, 1982. 2 vols in one; 798p.

A Japanese New Religion: Rissho Kosei–kai in a mountain hamlet. S. Guthrie. Ann Arbor, MI: Center for Japanese Studies, University of Michigan, 1988. 245p.

'A study of the Shamanistic elements in selected new religions of Japan with a suggested evangelical response.' R. T. Dominey. D.Min. thesis, Columbia Biblical Seminary and Graduate School of Missions, Columbia, SC, 1993. 333p.

A vision betrayed: the Jesuits in Japan and China 1542–1742. A. Ross. Edinburgh: Edinburgh University Press, 1994. 233p.

'An evaluation of the non–church movement in Japan: its distinctives, strategy and significance today.' H. Iwabuchi. D. Miss. thesis, Fuller Theological Seminary, Pasadena, CA, 1976. 93p.

Ansätze modernen Denkens in den Religionen Japans. H. Nakamura. *Zeitschrift für Religions- und Geistesgeschichte, Beihefte*, 23. Leiden: E. J. Brill, 1982. 183p.

Buddhism and Christianity in Japan: from conflict to dialogue, 1854–1899. N. R. Thelle. Honolulu, HI: University of Hawaii Press, 1987. 367p.

Catholicism encounters Japan. J. J. Spae. Tokyo: Oriens Institute for Religious Research, 1968. 285p.

Catholicism in Japan. J. J. Spae. Tokyo: ISR Press, 1963. 85p.

Christian presence in Japan: essays in honor of William J. Danker. W. J. Kang & M. Mori (eds). Tokyo: Seibusha, 1981. 265p.

'Christian shrines for Japan?' M. Fukuda. Th.M. thesis, Fuller Theological Seminary, Pasadena, CA, 1991. 170p.

Christianity and Japan: meeting, conflict, hope. S. D. B. Picken. Tokyo: Kodansha International, 1983. 80p.

Christianity in Japan, 1971–1990. K. Yoshinobu & D. C. Swain (eds). Tokyo: Kyo Bun Kwan (Christian Literature Society of Japan), 1991. 369p. (Successor to *The Japan Christian Yearbook* (1932-1970) and its predecessors since 1903).

Christianity, the Japanese way. C. Caldarola. *Monographs and theoretical studies in sociology and anthropology in honour of Nels Anderson*, no. 15. Leiden: E. J. Brill, 1979. 242p.

Christians in Japan = (Niho ni ikiru kirisuto sha tachi). C. Francis & J. M. Nakajima. New York: Friendship Press, 1991. 168p.

Church growth in Japan. T. Yamamori. South Pasadena, CA: William Carey Library, 1974. 196p. (Dissertation, Duke University, 1970, covering 8 denominations, 1859–1939).

'Communicating the Gospel in Japanese cultural terms: practical experiments in the Shintoku Kyodan Church.' T. D. Boyle. D.Min. thesis, Fuller Theological Seminary, Pasadena, CA, 1985. 125p.

Deus destroyed: the image of Christianity in early modern Japan. G. Elison. *Harvard East Asian monographs*, 141. Cambridge, MA: Council on East Asian Studies, Harvard University, 1973. 556p.

'Developing a contextualized church as a bridge to Christianity in Japan.' M. Fukuda. D.Miss. thesis, Fuller Theological Seminary, Pasadena, CA, 1992. 280p.

Directory of Methodist missionaries to Japan, 1873–1990. Biographical dictionary of Methodist missionaries to Japan project report series, Interim report no. B-1. Tokyo: Christianity and Culture Research Center, 1991. 55p.

Flowing traces: Buddhism in the literary and visual arts of Japan. J. H. Sanford, W. R. LaFleur & M. Nagatomi (eds). Princeton, NJ: Princeton University Press, 1992. 296.

Folk religion in Japan: continuity and change. I. Hori. Chicago: University of Chicago, 1968. 278p.

From the rising of the sun: Christians and society in contemporary Japan. J. M. Phillips. *American Society of Missiology Series*, 3. Maryknoll, NY: Orbis Books, 1981. 307p.

Grave and gospel. J.-M. Berentsen. *Beihefte der Zeitschrift für Religions- und Geistesgeschichte*, 30. Leiden: E. J. Brill, 1985. 316p.

Habataku Nihon no Fukuinha. A. Izuta. : Japan Evangelical Alliance, 1978.

Japan. F. J. Shulman. *World bibliographical series*, vol. 103. Oxford, UK: CLIO Press, 1990. 896p. (See especially 'Religion,' p.186–211).

Japan and Christianity: impacts and responses. J. Breen & M. Williams (eds). New York: St. Martin's Press, 1995.

'Japan apartment house evangelism: case study,' S. Barthold & M. Barthold, *Urban mission*, 2 (September 1984), 44–46.

Japan Catholic directory, 1972. Tokyo: National Catholic Committee of Japan, 1972.

Japanese Buddhism. C. Eliot. London: Arnold, 1935; reprint, London: Routledge and Kegan Paul, 1969. 449p.

Japanese religion: unity and diversity. H. B. Earhart. 3rd ed. *The religious life of man series.* Belmont, CA: Wadsworth, 1982. 272p.

Japanese religions: past and present. I. Reader with E. Andreason and F. Stefasson. Honolulu, HI: University of Hawaii Press, 1993.

Japanese religiosity. J. J. Spae. Tokyo: Oriens Institute for Religious Research, 1971. 313p.

Japanese religious attitudes. F. M. Basabe. New York: Orbis, 1972.

Japan's encounter with Christianity: the Catholic mission in pre–modern Japan. N. S. Fujita. New York: Paulist Press, 1991. 302p.

Japan's hidden Christians. A. Harrington. Chicago: Loyola University Press, 1993. 223p.

Japan's new Buddhism: an objective account of Soka Gakkai. K. Murata. Tokyo: Walker/Weatherhill, 1969. 194p.

Kirisutokyo Nenkan (Christian year book). Kirisuto

Shinbunsha, 1992.
Kodansha encyclopedia of Japan. G. Itasaka (ed). Tokyo: Kodansha, 1983. 9 vols. (See also 1986 59p. supplement).
Meiji Protestantism in history and historiography: a comparative study of Japanese and Western interpretation of early Protestantism in Japan. A. Lande. Frankfurt am Main: Peter Lang, 1989. 182p.
New wine: the cultural shaping of Japanese Christianity. D. Reid. *Nanzan studies in Asian religions*, 2. Berkeley, CA: Asian Humanities Press, 1991. 208p.
Nihon no Fukuinha. A. Izuta. : Japan Evangelical Alliance, 1989.
'Non–church Christianity in Japan: Western Christianity and Japan's cultural identity.' C. Caldarola. Ph.D. dissertation, University of California, Berkeley, CA, 1971. 467p.
Of heretics and martyrs in Meiji Japan: Buddhism and its persecution. J. E. Ketelaar. Princeton, NJ: Princeton University Press, 1993. 299.
Perspectives on Christianity in Korea and Japan: the Gospel and culture in East Asia. M. Mullins & R. F. Young (eds). Lewiston, NY: E. Mellen Press, 1995. 253p.
'Planting house churches in Japan through household evangelism and household conversion.' K. Takagi. Thesis, Dallas Theological Seminary, Dallas, TX, 1970. 104p.
Protestant theories in modern Japan. C. Germany. New York: Friendship Press, 1967.
Religion and society in modern Japan: continuity and change. E. Norbeck. Houston: Tourmaline Press, 1970.
Religion in changing Japanese society. K. Morioka. Tokyo: University of Tokyo Press, 1976.
Religion in contemporary Japan. I. Reader. New York: Macmillan, 1991.
Religion in Japan: arrows to heaven and earth. P. F. Kornicki & McMullen (eds). New York: Cambridge University Press, 1995. 341p.
Religions in Japan. W. K. Bunce (ed). Rutland, VT: Tuttle, 1967. 194p.
Religions of Japan: many traditions within one sacred way. H. B. Earhart. *Religious Traditions of the World.* San Francisco: Harper and Row, 1984. 142p.
'Small groups and lay leadership training for church growth in Japan.' M. B. Ogata. D.Miss. thesis, Fuller Theological Seminary, Pasadena, CA, 1985. 383p.
'Sociology of religion in Japan,' *Social compass*, 17, 1 (1970), 1–208. (9 articles, bibliography of 420 items).
The Cambridge encyclopedia of Japan. R. Bowring & P. Kornicki (eds). Cambridge, UK and New York: Cambridge University Press, 1993. 410p.
The Catholic Church in Japan since 1859. J. L. Van Hecken. Tokyo: Herder, 1963.
'The Holiness Movement in Japan, 1890–1939.' T. T. Yajima. Th.M. thesis, Fuller Theological Seminary, Pasadena, CA, 1987. 210p.
The image of Christianity in Japan: a survey. J. P. Colligan (ed). Tokyo: Joochi Daigaku Institute of Christian Culture, Sophia University, 1980. 152p.
The Japan Christian yearbook 1969–1970. Tokyo: Christian Literature Society of Japan, 1969. 429p. (Early editions mainly annual).
'The Japanese church and the Tenno System: a study in encounter.' M. Kurasawa. D.Miss. thesis, Fuller Theological Seminary, Pasadena, CA, 1989. 354p.
The New Religions of Japan: a bibliography of Western language materials. H. B. Earhart. *Monumenta Nipponica Monograph.* Tokyo: Sophia University, 1970. (810 items on 50 New Religions).
The new religions of Japan: a spotlight on the most significant development in postwar Japan. H. Thomsen. Rutland, VT and Tokyo: Tuttle, 1963. 269p.
The rush hour of the Gods: a study of new religious movements in Japan. H. N. McFarland. New York: Macmillan, 1967. 267p.
'The secularization of Japanese religion: measuring the myth and the reality,' W. Davis, in *Transitions and transformations*, p.261–85. F. E. Reynolds (ed). Leiden: E. J. Brill, 1980.
The way of faithfulness: study guide to Christians in Japan. P. J. Patterson. New York: Friendship Press, 1991. 44p.
'Urban church planting in Japan: a study to identify strategic contextual and spiritual factors.' R. B. Pease. D.Miss. thesis, Fuller Theological Seminary, Pasadena, CA, 1994. 275p.

Country Table 2. **Organized churches and denominations in Japan.**

Official name (bold type = church with over 10% of all affiliated) 1	*Begun* 2	*Type* 3	*Counc* 4	*Congs* 5	*Adults* 6	*Affiliated 1970* 7	*Affiliated 1995* 8	*G%* 9	*Names, notes, and other statistics* (see Codebook, Part 3) 10
Advent Christian Conference of Japan	1898	P-Adv	xF...	18	894	778	1,075	1.30	*Nippon Adobento Kirisuto Kyodan.* 1948, M=American Advent MS. 4n,10f,1p,W=78%,25Y.
Assembly Hall Churches	c1970	I-3nC	.....	70	2,198	–	4,000	39.34	*Little Flock. Local Churches.* Originally begun 1922 in China.
Assoc of Baptists for World Evangelism	1953	I-Bap	x....	18	362	500	905	2.40	*Bankoku Baputesuto Fukuin Dendo Kyokai.* M=ABWE(USA). HQ Kobe. 16f,W=73%.
Association of Evangelical Churches	1952	P-Eva	.M...	18	495	340	660	2.69	*Fukuin Kiristokyokai Kyogikai.*M=OMF(CIM). Hokkaido, Aomori. 5n,33f,1s,W=99%,10Y.
Baptist Bible Fellowship of Japan	1949	I-Bap	x....	68	2,042	2,910	2,920	0.01	*Nippon Baputesuto Baiburi Ferouship.* M=BBFI(USA). 17n,26f,1s,150Y.
Baptist International Mission	1962	I-Bap	.....	40	2,500	439	3,570	8.74	M=BIM(USA).
Baptist Mid-Missions in Japan	1949	I-Fun	x.T.T	11	199	300	398	1.14	*Zen Nippon Baputesuto Mid-Mission Senkyodan.* M=BMM(USA). HQ Fukushima. 1n,19f.
Bethany Christian Assemblies	1950	I-3pQ	.....	6	227	200	400	2.81	Small indigenous pentecostal body.
Bible Study Circle	1951	I-Non	.....	11	260	331	300	-0.39	*Seisho Kenkyu Kai.* Japanese founder. HQ Ukyo (Kyoto). 2n,W=99%,35Y.
Biblical Church	1953	I-Ref	.....	28	830	500	1,000	2.81	*Seisho Kirisuto Kyokai.* Many preaching points.
Brethren in Christ Church	1953	P-Men	GF...	10	148	250	247	-0.05	*Nippon Kirisutokyo Keiteinda.* M=BiCC(USA). HQ Koganei, Tokyo. 3x,8f,1p,W=58%,12Y.
Calvary United Church of Christ	1976	I-3cQ	.....	3	571	–	1,000	5.26	*Karubari Kirisuto Kyodan.* Centered in Kobe.
Catholic Church in Japan:	1549	R-Lat	P.F.R	931	312,800	360,679	447,482	0.87	*Nippon Katorikku Kyokai.* C=37+4+86. 487n 1233x 1654m 6804w 10354Yy
M Nagasaki	1891	R-Lat	Ps	71	49,000	69,379	70,011	0.04	SW Kyushu. Many RCs in 16th century. 86n 50x 82m 855w 1174Yy
D Fukuoka	1927	R-Lat	Ps	70	21,400	24,918	30,609	0.83	W Kyushu. D=priests' council begun 1970. M=PSS. 43n 54x 65m 465w 610Yy
D Kagoshima	1927	R-Lat	Ps	30	6,400	8,993	9,134	0.06	SW Kyushu. D=PC(1968),pc(1971). 19n 23x 29m 232w 171Yy
D Naha	1972	R-Lat	Ps	13	4,300	–	6,203	4.35	Ryukyu Isles. Chinese exodus to Guam. M=OFMCap. 4n 13x 16m 73w 133Yy
D Oita (Miyazaki)	1928	R-Lat	Ps	28	4,000	6,211	5,726	-0.32	N Kyushu. D=pc(1970). 10n 46x 65m 228w 105Yy
M Osaka	1891	R-Lat	Ps	93	38,200	53,355	54,642	0.10	S Honshu. D=pc(1967),PC(1967). 50n 153x 186m 768w 1138Yy
D Hiroshima	1923	R-Lat	Ps	48	14,100	18,151	20,246	0.44	SW Honshu. D=PC(1970),pc(1971). 18n 71x 81m 273w 405Yy
D Kyoto	1937	R-Lat	Ps	79	14,800	18,797	21,220	0.49	C Honshu. D==pc(1966),PC(1972). 18n 59x 70m 258w 381Yy
D Nagoya	1922	R-Lat	Ps	60	17,000	16,421	24,280	1.58	C Honshu. 20n 123x 143m 215w 773Yy
D Takamatsu	1904	R-Lat	Ps	29	4,100	5,381	5,870	0.35	On Shikoku. D=pc(1968),PC(1970). 12n 40x 41m 101w 141Yy
M Tokyo	1891	R-Lat	Ps	84	61,900	58,272	88,372	1.68	D=pc(1966),PC(1968),Synod. 81n 335x 532m 1719w 2634Yy
D Niigata	1912	R-Lat	Ps	38	5,300	7,013	7,559	0.30	NW Honshu. D=pc(1967),PC(1967). 13n 21x 21m 116w 184Yy
D Sapporo	1915	R-Lat	Ps	71	12,300	17,830	17,593	-0.05	Hokkaido. Includes PA Karafuto (established 1932). 33n 53x 92m 380w 361Yy
D Sendai (Hakodate)	1891	R-Lat	Ps	62	8,400	12,297	12,040	-0.08	NE Honshu. D=pc(1969). Charismatics. M=OP. 29n 41x 45m 323w 253Yy
D Urawa	1939	R-Lat	Ps	68	16,600	11,341	23,725	3.00	C Honshu. D=pc(1971). 15n 47x 58m 171w 488Yy
D Yokohama	1937	R-Lat	Ps	87	35,000	32,320	50,252	1.78	EC Honshu. D=pc(1966),PC(1968). 36n 104x 128m 627w 1403Yy
Central Japan Pioneer Mission	1925	P-Non	.....	59	1,368	1,000	3,000	4.49	*Fukuin Dendo Kyodan(FDK).* M=CJPM(UK). A=1962. HQ Fukushima. 1p.
Children of God	c1980	I-mar	x....	5	218	–	478	6.67	M=Ch G. Former Jesus Movement people from USA.
Christ Evangelistic Band	c1920	P-Hol	.....	3	389	200	500	3.73	*Kirisuto Dentotai.* West Japan.
Christian Brethren Assemblies	c1925	P-CBr	x....	163	5,550	5,000	9,241	2.49	*Burezaren Kei. Open Brethren.* Growing fast. M=CMML(USA, UK, NZ, Germany). 64f,W=99%.
Christian Brotherhood Church	1946	I-Hol	.....	78	2,500	2,586	3,564	1.29	*Kirisuto Kyodai Dan.* Throughout Japan. HQ Tokyo. 39n,1s(15),W=90%,140Y.
Christian Canaan Church	1948	I-3pQ	.....	13	1,720	2,797	2,459	-0.51	*Kirisutokyo Kanan Kyodan.* Indigenous pentecostals. HQ Sakai (Osaka). 9n,W=22%.
Christian Catholic Church	1950	P-Con	x...w	3	600	1,000	2,000	2.81	*Kirisuto Kodo Kyokai.* M=CCC(Zion, Illinois, USA). Holiness emphasis. HQ Osaka. 5f.
Christian Ch of the Glorious Gospel	1936	I-Hol	.....	15	2,460	3,680	4,100	0.43	*Eiko no Fukuin Kyokai.* Ex Holiness Missions. 12n (5 women). HQ Kumamoto.
Christian Churches & Chs of Christ	1883	I-Dis	x....	80	5,000	15,000	12,000	-0.89	*Kirisuto no Kyokai.* M=CCCC(Instrumental) (USA). USA military bases. 30n,55f,W=33%.
Christian Evangelistic Church	1951	I-3pQ	.....	4	230	165	400	3.61	*Kirisuto Dendo-dan.* In Kyushu. Founded on Early Church lines (tongues, &c). 3n,W=77%,6Y.
Christian Fellowship of Japan	1970	I-3cQ	.....	6	390	–	500	28.22	In Greater Tokyo area. 2 overseas churches in Philippines.
Christian Gospel of Glory		I-3cQ	.....	15	3,000	–	3,987	0.05	*Eiko no Fukuin Kirisuto Kyodan.*
Christian Holy Convention	1958	I-Hol	.....	43	1,530	3,000	2,550	-0.65	*Kirisuto Seikyodan.* Merger with Japan Holiness Church (Arahara-ha). 10n,1p,59Y.
Christian Oriental Salvation Church		I-Non	.....	3	100	100	120	0.05	*Kirisutokyo Toyo Kyureidan.* Small independent group. HQ Nada (Kobe). 1n,W=99%.
Christian Spiritual Church	1927	I-Non	.....	27	1,135	1,193	2,000	2.09	*Kirisuto Shinsu Kyodan. Christ Heart Church.* Completely indigenous life. 4n.
Christians in Action	1956	P-Non	.....	5	240	200	300	1.64	On Okinawa. M=Christians in Action (California, USA).
Church of Christ in Japan (Presb & Ref)	1951	I-Ref	R....	143	6,040	15,772	13,719	-0.56	*Nippon Kirisuto Kyokai.* 1945 schism ex Kyodan (UCCJ). HQ Tokyo. 110n,W=28%,328Yy.
Church of Christ, Scientist	1920	m-Sci	x....	2	50	200	100	-2.73	*Kirisutokyo Kagaku Daiichi Kyokai.* M=CCS(Boston, USA). Tokyo, Kyoto, Okinawa. 4w.
Ch of God in Christ in Japan: D Japan	1969	I-3pB	Z....	5	1,000	1,500	2,000	1.16	M=CoGiC(USA Blacks). HQ Urasoe City, Okinawa; also Tokyo. USA military.
Church of God (Cleveland)	1952	P-Pe3	ZF...	8	517	438	748	2.16	*Kami no Kyokai.* M=CoG(Cleveland) (USA). 5 churches, 6 missions. 5n,2x,2f,1p,37Y.
Church of God (Independent Holiness)	1951	I-3cQ	.....	14	655	500	1,000	2.81	*Independent Holiness People* (USA). HQ Kawasaki. 5n,W=73%,17Y.
Ch of Jesus Christ of Latter-day Saints	1901	m-LdS	x....	264	72,800	19,902	100,411	6.69	*Matsujitsu Seito Iesu Kirisuto Kyokai.* M=CJCLdS(USA). 620nx,940f,1500Y.
Church of Jesus the Victor	1949	P-Non	.....	4	100	300	200	-1.61	*Shorisha Iesu Kyodan. Bible Institute Mission.* M=Life M(USA). 6f,1j,1k,1p,W=33%.
Church of the Eternal Way	1907	I-mar	.....	2	1,164	200	2,000	9.65	Independent body with heterodox theology.
Church of the Resurrected Christ	c1960	I-Non	.....	8	362	1,000	700	-1.42	*Fukkatsu no Kirisuto Kyodan.* Indigenous body. HQ Nagano. 13n,W=56%,6Y.
Church of the Way		I-Non	.....	27	2,000	4,000	4,100	0.05	*Do Kai.* Indigenous Japanese grouping of congregations. 34n.
Churches of Christ (Non-Instrumental)	1890	I-Dis	x....	144	4,592	6,100	5,846	-0.17	M=CC(Non-Instrumental) (USA). Ex Disciples of Christ (UCMS). 2 schools. 20f,2s.
Conservative Baptist Assoc of Chs	1947	I-Bap	xF...	67	1,900	848	2,603	4.59	*Hoshu Baputesuto Domei.* M=CBFMS(USA). HQ Yamagata. 1n,16m,7w,47f,1s,W=82%,101Y.
Cumberland Presbyterian Church	1950	I-Ref	....w	8	1,390	700	1,642	3.47	*Kanbarando Choro Kyokai.* M=CPC(USA) from 1906-45.HQ Kanagawa. 3 schools. 6nx,2f,41Yy.
Evangelical Alliance Mission	1891	P-Eva	xM..C	160	6,430	4,238	8,694	2.92	*NDKK. Nippon Domei Kirisuto Kyodan.* M=TEAM,SAM. Tokyo. 74n,50x,142f,1s,267Y.
Evangelical Ch Association in Hokkaido	1951	P-Eva	.....	27	1,491	500	3,000	7.43	*Hokkaido Fukuin Kyokai Kyogikai.* M=OMF,TEAM.
Evangelical Covenant Church of Japan	1949	P-Con	K....	19	734	1,000	1,390	1.33	*Nippon Seikei Kirisuto Kyodan.* M=ECCA(USA). HQ Meguro. 4n,3x,12f,1s(5),W=64%,38Y.
Evangelical Fellowship Deaconry Ch	1951	P-Lut	.....	13	411	200	548	4.11	*Feroshippu Dikonrii Fukuin Senkyodan.* Begun by Germans expelled from China.
Evangelical Free Church of Japan	1949	P-Con	KF..C	66	3,788	1,622	4,720	4.37	*Nippon Fukuin Jiyu Kyokai.* M=EFCA(USA). HQ Urawa. Rapid growth. (1970) 16n,19f,105Y.
Evangelical Missionary Church		I-Eva	.....	58	1,322	1,000	1,700	0.05	*Fukuin Dendo Kyodan. Gospel Evangelistic Ch.* HQ Maebashi (Gumma). 20n,W=95%,67Y.
Evangelical Orient Mission	1951	P-Eva	.....	11	184	220	460	2.99	*Toyo Fukuin Senkyokai.* M=NEOM(Norway). HQ Fukushima. 6n,W=91%,15Y.
Evangelical Presbyterian Ch in Japan	1979	I-3cQ	.....	9	542	–	800	6.25	*Nihon Fukuin Choro Kyokai* (Yokohama). 1993 joins Presbyterian Ch in Japan.
Family of God Christian Church	1975	I-3cQ	.....	8	450	–	700	5.00	*Kami no Kazoku Kirisuto Kyokai.* Nagoya. M=USA charismatics.
Fellowship of Ev Baptist Churches	1964	P-Bap	.....	12	364	250	455	2.42	*Nippon Fukuin Baputesuto Senkyo Dan.* M=FEBC(Canada). HQ Takaoka. 9f.
Fellowship of Independent Christian Chs	1964	I-Non	.....	63	4,350	400	6,000	11.44	*Tanritsu Kirisuto Kyokai Renmei.* Now affiliated to JECA.
Free Methodist Church of Japan	1895	I-Hol	VF..C	31	2,000	4,246	2,614	-1.92	*Nippon Jiyu Mesojisuto Kyodan.* M=FMC(USA). HQ Osaka. 1 school. 20n,8f,1s,W=68%.
Full Gospel Church in Japan	1974	I-3fK	x....	34	2,350	–	6,700	4.76	*Jun Fukuin Kyokai.* Related to M=Full Gospel Ch (Seoul, Korea). 70% Koreans.
German Alliance Mission	1955	P-Non	.....	27	960	430	1,600	5.40	*Domei Fukuin Kirisuto Kyokai.* M=AMB. Nagoya-Gifu area. 6n,5x,9f,W=99%,30Y.
Gospel Flock of Jesus Christ	1962	I-3cQ	.....	11	460	200	600	4.49	*Iesu Kirisuto no Fukuin no Mure.* Aims to send evangelists to every province of Japan.
Gospel of Jesus Church	1947	I-Non	.....	34	1,130	1,018	1,613	1.86	*Iesu Fukuin Kyodan.* Tokyo, Honshu. Work in Brazil. 11n,W=70%,23Y,200z.
Grain of Wheat	c1980	I-Non	.....	4	353	–	504	6.67	*Ichibaku.*
Hidden Buddhist believers in Christ	c1970	I-Bud	.....	2,000	200,000	–	320,000	66.04	Converted Buddhists who choose to stay in Buddhist structures as a witness.
Hidden Christians	1549	I-CCa	.....	30	20,000	33,000	40,000	0.77	*Kakure Kirishitan.* Catholic survivors of persecution 1606-1859. South (Hanare) Japan islands.
Holiness Church	1946	I-Hol	.....	78	3,526	700	5,000	8.18	*Kirisuto Kyodaidan.* 1946, ex Kyodan and OMS.
Holy Ecclesia of Jesus	1946	I-3cQ	.....	104	6,525	3,767	9,284	3.67	*Sei Iesu Kai.*
Holy Jesus Church	1958	I-3pQ	.....	4	1,000	500	2,432	6.53	*Sei IesuKyokai.* HQ Shinjuju Ku, Tokyo. No foreign mission. 27n,W=84%,224Y.
Holy Orthodox Church of Japan	1861	O-Rus	MW...	80	10,000	24,502	24,000	-0.08	*Nippon Harisutosu Seikyo Kei.* Dioceses: Tokyo, Kyoto, Sendai. 3 bps. 70n,1x,19m,1s.
Holy Spring Church	1969	I-3cQ	.....	10	1,156	200	2,000	9.65	*Nihon Seisan Kirisuto Kyokai Rengo.* Schism ex IGM.
Immanuel General Mission of Japan	1919	I-Hol	.F..C	118	7,090	8,129	12,436	1.72	*Imanuero Sogo Dendo Dan.* M=WC(USA). HQ Chiyoda. 19n,2f,1H,1j,1s,W=40%,339Y.
Independent Pentecostal Churches	c1970	I-3pK	.....	46	4,000	–	5,000	40.59	*Pentekosute Kei.* Mainly Koreans, smaller numbers of Japanese.
Independent Pentecostal Chs Fellowship	1949	I-3pQ	.....	71	2,900	600	4,000	7.88	*Tanritsu Pentekosute Kyokai Feroshippu.* M=Scandinavian missions.
International Chapel Ministries	1981	P-Non	.....	4	200	–	400	7.14	Small Nondenominational body.
International Christian Body		I-Met	.....	3	250	200	300	0.05	*Kokusai Kirisuto Kyodan.* Tokyo area. Roots in original Korean Methodism.
International Christian University Ch	1949	P-Non	....w	2	300	500	600	0.73	*Kokusai Kirisuto Daigaku Kyokai (ICU Kyokai).* M=Japan ICU Foundation. 27f.

Continued overleaf

Country Table 2–continued

Official name (bold type = church with over 10% of all affiliated) 1	*Begun* 2	*Type* 3	*Counc* 4	*Congs* 5	*Adults* 6	*Affiliated 1970* 7	*Affiliated 1995* 8	*G%* 9	*Names, notes, and other statistics* (see Codebook, Part 3) 10
Internat Ch of the Foursquare Gospel	1951	P-Pe2	ZF...	15	982	437	1,640	5.43	*Kokusai Foosukuea Fukuin Kyodan.* M=ICFG(USA). HQ Saitama. 12nm,2f,1p(2),W=50%,48Y.
Isolated radio churches	1952	I-3rQ	.....	8,000	300,000	165,000	500,000	4.53	Isolated radio believers; mostly students and youths. R=164400,T=850000.
Japan Alliance Church	1891	P-Hol	xF...	39	3,303	4,086	9,387	3.38	*Nippon Araiansu Kyodan.* M=CMA(USA). A=1935. 26n,11f,1s,W=50%,88Y.
Japan Apostolic Mission	1917	P-Pe1	.....	15	2,000	3,000	4,000	1.16	*Nippon Shilo Kyodan.* M=Far East Apostolic Mission (USA). HQ Ikoma (Nara).
Japan Assemblies of God	1913	P-Pe2	ZF..C	200	16,634	14,700	26,056	2.32	*Nippon Assenburi Kyodan.* M=AoG(USA, UK). 9 schools. 211n,27f,1s(39),W=70%,311Y.
Japan Baptist Association	1952	I-Bap	x....	11	288	400	720	2.38	*Nippon Baputesuto Rengo.* M=American Baptist Assoc (USA). HQ Kashiwa. 6n,3f,18Y.
Japan Baptist Christian Association	1948	P-Bap	TF...	43	1,360	1,326	2,094	1.84	*Nippon Kirisuto Baputesuto Rengo Senkyodan.* M=BGC(USA). 3n,2x,17f,1u,W=38%,91Y.
Japan Baptist Church Association	1965	P-Bap	.....	51	2,168	400	4,000	9.65	*Nihon Baputesuto Kyokai Rengo.* M=BGC(USA).
Japan Baptist Conference	1951	P-Bap	TF...	8	469	400	1,405	5.15	*Nippon Baputesuto Senkyodan.* M=NABGMS(USA). Linked with USA German Baptists. 4n,18f.
Japan Baptist Convention	1889	P-Bap	T...W	309	31,088	21,260	40,609	2.62	*Nippon Baputesuto Renmei.* M=SBC(USA). 142n,53x,142f,1H,2s(21),W=46%,906Y.
Japan Baptist Union	1872	P-Bap	T...W	73	4,080	4,478	4,884	0.35	*Nippon Baputesuto Domei.* M=ABFMS(USA),SBM(Sweden). 3 schools. 84n,26f,60Y.
Japan Bible Evangelical Church	1951	I-Eva	.....	12	411	200	600	4.49	M=SEMS(Sweden),OEM.
Japan Christ Society	c1937	I-Ref	.....	10	250	300	400	1.16	*Nippon Kirisuto Kai.* Presbyterian schism. Uses Buddhist, Shinto terms. 9n,24Yy.
Japan Christian Church	1923	I-Non	.....	7	400	150	600	5.70	*Nihon Senkyo Kai.* Begun by Japanese pastor.
Japan Christian Ecclesia	1940	I-3pQ	.....	11	530	200	700	5.14	*Nihon Kirisuto Shodan.* Later split ex Original Gospel Movement.
Japan Church of God	1908	P-Hol	x....	18	384	700	591	-0.67	*Nippon Kami no Kyokai Renmei.* M=CoG(Anderson) (USA). S Japan. 13n,4x,7f,W=72%,15Y.
Japan Church of Jesus Christ	1903	P-Non	.G...	110	9,293	8,181	12,242	1.63	*Nippon Iesu Kirisuto Kyodan.* M=JEB(UK). HQ Kobe. 186n,135m,21f,1s(60),W=40%,237Y.
Japan Church of the Nazarene	1905	P-Hol	xF..C	73	7,187	5,431	10,334	2.61	*Nippon Nazaren Kyodan.* M=CoN(USA). 50n,216m,18f,1s(5),73t(4561),W=61%,208Y.
Japan Covenant Christian Church	1949	P-Con	.....	19	741	300	1,000	4.93	*Nihon Seikei Kirisuto Kyodan.* M=CCC(Sweden, 1878).
Japan Evangelical Christian Church	1918	I-Eva	.....	2	200	500	400	-0.89	*Nippon Fukuin Kirisuto Kyodan.* Indigenous group. HQ Chofu (Tokyo). 5n,W=34%,5Y.
Japan Evangelical Church	1951	I-Hol	.TT.T	34	1,623	2,000	2,107	0.21	*Nippon Fukuin Kirisuto Kyodan.* Links with USA Fundamentalist bodies. 87n.
Japan Evangelical Church Association	1992	P-Eva	.....	148	5,000	–	7,818	33.33	*Nihon Fukuin Kirisuto Kyokai Rengo. JECA.*
Japan Evangelical Church of Christ	1950	P-Pe2	x....	14	532	200	700	5.14	*Nihon Kirisuto Senkyodan.* M=Swedish Holiness Mission.
Japan Evangelical Church (Orebro)	1949	P-Pe2	Z....	33	1,757	1,000	3,000	4.49	*Nihon Fukuin Kyokai.* M=Orebro Mission (Sweden). (1970) 12n,13x,1s.
Japan Evangelical Church Union	1971	I-3cQ	.....	20	1,049	–	1,400	4.17	*Nihon Fukuin Kyokai Rengo.* Split ex Japan Gospel Church. Holiness.
Japan Evangelical Lutheran Church	1892	P-Lut	LvE.W	155	7,230	17,225	21,909	0.97	*Nippon Fukuin Ruteru Kyokai. JELC.* M=LCA(USA),ALC,et alia. 126nx,105f,W=61%,515Yy.
Japan Evangelical Mission	1949	P-Bap	.M...	21	558	2,177	1,200	-2.35	*Nippon Dendo Fukuin Kyodan.* M=JEM(Canada). HQ Niigata. 4n,54f,1s(18),W=99%.
Japan Evangelistic Band	1903	P-Hol	.....	13	367	200	500	3.73	*Nihon Dendotai.* Declining. M=JEB, with missionaries now only 10.
Japan Free Religious Association	1948	m-Unt	.....	3	320	3,000	500	-6.92	*Nippon Jiyu Shukyo Renmei.* Unitarians. HQ Minato (Tokyo). 3n.
Japan Free Will Baptist Church	1954	P-Bap	xF...	10	193	300	241	-0.87	*Fukuin Baputesuto Kyodan.* M=NAFWB(USA). HQ Tsukisappu (Sapporo). 4n,10f,W=95%.
Japan Gospel Church	1930	I-Hol	.T..C	32	2,117	1,143	2,500	3.18	*Nippon Fukuin Kyodan.* Japan Bible Seminary. 34n, W=50%,68Y.
Japan Gospel Fellowship	1947	I-Non	.....	21	441	300	1,103	5.35	*Nippon Fukuin Koyukai.* M=Gospel Fellowship Missions (USA). HQ Sakai, Osaka, Kobe. 8n,6f.
Japan Gospel League Church of Christ	1945	P-Non	.....	5	200	500	600	0.73	*Japan Gosuperu Rigu Kirisuto Kyokai.* M=International Gospel League (USA). 4n,2f.
Japan Gospel Mission	1956	I-3cQ	.....	7	830	–	1,100	32.33	*Nihon Fukuin Senkyokai.* Begun in Matsuyama.
Japan Gospel Pentecostal Church	1951	P-Pe1	x....	18	630	380	1,144	4.51	*Nippon Pentekosute Kyodan.* M=ACP(Canada). Unitarian. HQ Nagoya. 7n,4f,W=22%.
Japan Holiness Church	1901	P-Hol	xF...	161	8,130	5,435	11,471	3.03	*Toyo Senkyokai.* M=OMS(USA). Severe persecution 1939-45. Schisms. (1970) 60n,20f,1s,351Y.
Japan Holy Catholic Church	1846	A-plu	AWE.W	350	31,000	49,100	62,000	0.94	*NSKK. Nippon Sei Ko Kai.* 11 Dioceses. M=CMS,USPG,ECUSA. (1970) 27f,4s. (1990) 300n.
Japan Inland Mission	1949	P-Pe2	.....	12	250	500	600	0.73	*Nippon Kaitaku Dendo Kyokai.* Mission from UK. Kyoto, Hyogo, Shiga. 3f,5m.
Japan Jesus Christ Church		I-3pQ	.....	35	0	10,000	10,500	0.05	*Nippon Iesu Kirisuto Kyokai.* HQ Akashi Shi. Indigenous Japanese pentecostals.
Japan Jesus Christ Society		I-Non	.....	10	700	1,000	2,000	0.05	*Nippon Iesu Kirisuto Kai.* Indigenous grouping of congregations.
Japan Lutheran Brethren Church	1949	P-Lut	x....	25	918	346	1,162	4.97	*Nippon Ruteru Doho Kyodan.* M=CLB(USA) begun from China. HQ Akita. 7n,6f,W=90%.
Japan Lutheran Ch (Missouri Synod)	1948	P-Lut	e....	37	2,540	2,987	3,254	0.34	*Nippon Ruteru Kyodan.* M=LCMS. Kanto Hokkaido,Okinawa. (1970) 23n,27x,28f,117Yy. (1990)2f
Japan Mennonite Brethren Conference	1950	P-Men	GF...	25	1,824	2,000	3,440	2.19	*Nippon Menonaito Burezaren Kyodan.* M=Mennonite Brethren Ch of NA. 14n,13f,1s.
Japan Mennonite Christian Ch Conf	1949	P-Men	G....	19	467	1,000	934	-0.27	*Nippon Menonaito Kirisuto Kyokai Kyogikai.* M=Mennonite CNA. 6n,3x,24f,1p,W=63%,4Y.
Japan New Testament Church	1947	P-Bap	xM...	25	1,700	1,500	2,000	1.16	*Nippon Shinyaku Kyodan.* M=Far Eastern GC(USA). 13n,16x,78f,W=90%,31Y.
Japan Open Bible Church	1950	I-3pW	ZF...	12	324	450	600	1.16	*Nippon Opun Baiburu Kyodan.* M=OBSC(USA). HQ Nishinomiya (Hyogo). 3n,7f,W=50%.
Japan Orthodox Church	1967	I-Rus	M....	3	1,700	2,000	2,000	0.00	*Nippon Christos Sei Kyo Kai.* Schism aided by Orthodox P Moscow. 10n.
Japan Regular Baptist Church		I-Bap	.....	5	250	500	600	0.05	*Japan Regyura Baputesuto Mission.* M=Regular Baptist Churches (USA).
Japan Union Mission of SD Adventists	1896	P-Adv	x....	153	12,500	20,000	17,900	-0.44	*Nippon Rengo Dendo Bukai.* 72n,40f,G=3.6%pa,3H,2h,1j,1r,1s(100),111t,W=95%,287Y.
Japan United Pentecostal Church	1947	P-Pe1	x....	22	709	1,000	1,468	1.55	*Nippon Unaito Pentekosute Kyodan.* M=UPC(USA). HQ Kita (Kyoto). 26n,1f,1p(25),75Y.
Jehovah's Witnesses	1911	m-Jeh	x....	3,003	147,622	30,000	246,000	8.78	*Monomi no Toh Seisho Sasshi Kyokai.* Colporteurs 1913. (1975) 2160Y. (1995) 11421Y.
Jesus Christ Presbyterian Ch in Japan	1986	I-Ref	.....	7	200	–	430	11.11	Independent split in Reformed tradition.
Jesus Gospel Church	1952	I-Hol	.....	32	1,676	300	2,000	7.88	M=FEGC.
Kinki Evangelical Lutheran Church	1950	P-Lut	lv...	31	1,180	1,315	2,357	2.36	*Kinki Fukuin Ruteru Kyokai.* M=NMS,Free Ch of Norway. Osaka-Nagoya. (1970) 15nx,15f,71Yy.
Korean Christian Church in Japan	1907	P-Ref	RuE.W	73	4,197	3,000	10,500	5.14	*Zainichi Daikan Kirisuto Kyokai.* M=PCC(Canada). Korean residents in Japan. 30n,8f.
Kyushu Mennonite Christian Church	1951	P-Men	G....	20	200	421	500	0.69	*Kyushu Menonaito Kirisuto Kyokai Kaigi.* HQ Miyazaki. 1n,6f,W=79%.
Liebenzell Mission, Japan	1927	P-Non	xM...	38	1,304	1,000	2,040	2.89	*Riibenzera Nippon Dendokai.* M=LM(BAD Liebenzell, Germany). 18n,32f,W=99%,50Y.
Living Waters Christian Fellowship	1930	I-3pQ	.....	12	1,500	2,199	1,880	-0.62	*Kassui Kirisuto Kyodan.* Ex Japan Evangelistic Band. HQ Odawara. 7n,W=36%,32Y.
Local Church		I-3cQ	x....	70	1,000	500	1,500	0.05	*Jimoto Kyokai.*
Lutheran Ev Christian Ch of Japan	1952	P-Lut	x....	12	191	171	273	1.89	*Ruteru Fukuin Kirisuto Kyokai.* M=Wisconsin EL Synod (USA). HQ Mito (Ibaraki). 3n,4x.
Mino Mission	1918	P-Non	.....	4	183	1,000	300	-4.70	Work in Mino district (Gifu) also Mie & Aichi Prefectures. HQ Yokkaichi. 5n,2f.
Mission Covenant Church in Japan	c1949	P-Con	.....	21	774	1,500	2,000	1.16	*Nippon Seiyaku Kirisuto Kyodan.* Links with Swedish mission SMF. 4n,6f,36Y.
Missions to Japan	1950	P-Non	.....	9	239	150	400	4.00	*Nihon Fukuin Senkyodan.* Inland Sea area. USA missionaries.
New Apostolic Church	c1970	I-3aX	x....	4	100	–	300	25.63	*Shin Shito Kyokai.* M=Neuapostolische Kirche. HQ Zurich (Switzerland).
New Christ Union Church		I-Non	.....	130	5,500	11,370	13,000	0.05	*Union Kirisuto Kyokai.* Independent Japanese grouping of congregations. 50n.
New Testament Church Association	1948	P-Non	.....	34	946	488	1,350	4.15	*Nippon Shinyaku Kyodan.* M=SEND.
Next Towns Crusade in Japan	1957	I-3pQ	.....	21	1,948	1,000	2,780	4.17	*Nippon NTC.* M=Revival Temple, San Antonio, TX (USA). HQ Higashi (Osaka). 10n,8f.
No-Church Movement	1900	I-NoC	.....	90	1,510	2,380	2,383	0.01	*Mukyokai.* Small Bible study groups. No buildings, no clergy, unorganized.
Okinawa Baptist Convention	1953	P-Bap	T...W	37	2,796	2,673	3,386	0.95	*Okinawa Baptist Renmei.* M=SBC(USA). After 1972, in Japan Baptist Conv. 17n,4f,248z.
Okinawa Christian Association		I-Non	.v...	8	300	500	700	0.05	Small independent group on Okinawa island. 1948, applied to join WCC.
Oriental Boat Mission	1966	P-Non	xM...	6	200	500	600	0.73	*Toyo Boat Mission.* M=International Missions (USA).
Oriental Chr Ch for Ev of the Deaf	1952	P-Eva	.....	49	504	1,000	1,007	0.03	*Ev=Evangelization. Toyo Rowa Kirisuto Dendo Kyokai.* HQ Iruma (Saitama). 7n.
Original Gospel (Tabernacle) Movement	1948	I-3pQ	.....	77	10,500	46,000	30,000	-1.70	*Genshi Fukuin. Primitive Gospel Ch. Makuya.* Split ex Mukyokai. 160n,W=34%,1000Y.
Pentecostal Church of God in Japan	1953	P-Pe2	Z....	13	500	1,200	1,000	-0.73	*Nippon Pentekosute Kami no Kyokai Kyodan.* M=PCG(USA). HQ Kita. 3n,4f,W=45%.
Pioneers	1988	I-Non	.....	1	25	–	30	14.29	M=Pioneers (USA).
Praising Church	1951	I-3pQ	.....	2	150	200	300	1.64	*Sanbi Kyodan.* Small Japanese indigenous grouping, ex AoG. HQ Hiroshima. 2n,W=57%.
Presbyterian Church of Japan		P-Ref	R....	40	1,420	541	2,371	0.05	*Nippon Kirisuto Choro Kyokai.* HQ Suginami (Tokyo). 10nx,W=99%,33Yy.
Reformed Church in Japan	1946	P-Ref	JF...	125	4,860	6,000	9,001	1.64	*Nippon Kirisuto Kaikakuha Kyokai.* M=CRC,OPC. 1 school. 81nx,32f,W=66%,199Yy.
Reformed Presbyterian Christian Ch	1950	I-Ref	.....	6	203	80	300	5.43	*Nippon Kirisuto Kaikaku Choro Kyokai.* Missionary split. No hymns. 1n,5f,W=94%.
Religious Society of Friends	1884	P-Qua	Q...w	9	254	500	339	-1.54	*Kirisuto Tomo no Kai Nenkai. Japan Yearly Meeting* (1917). *Quakers.* HQ Tokyo. W=19%.
Reorganized Ch of JC of Latter-D Saints		m-LdS	x....	3	72	100	150	0.05	*Fukugen Iesu Kirisuto Kyokai.* Schism ex Mormons (USA). On Okinawa. 4n,1f,W=69%,2Y.
Salvation Army in Japan	1895	P-Sal	xwE..	70	4,304	20,000	6,940	-4.15	*Kyusei Gun Nippon Honei. Japan Territory.* 178n,12f,2H,1s(10),W=24%,1203z.
Spirit of Jesus Church	1937	I-3oQ	x....	470	353,000	62,726	420,000	7.90	*Iesu no Mitama Kyokai Kyodan.* Ex AoG. Missions to USA. Brazil. 185n (94 women).
Swedish Alliance Mission in Japan	1950	P-Non	x....	12	400	600	1,000	2.06	*Nippon Domei Kirisuto Kyodan.* M=SAM(Sweden). Zainichi Sweden Kirisutokyo DSD. 14f.
Swedish Evangelical Mission in Japan	1951	P-Eva	.....	20	200	300	300	0.00	*Zainichi Sweden FS.* M=Svenska Mongol-och Japanmissionen. 1n,7x,W=80%,7Y,12z.
Swedish Evangelical Orient Mission	1950	P-Lut	.....	5	100	200	210	0.20	*Sweden Toyo Fukuin Dendodan.* HQ Numazu (Shizuoka). 2n,6f,W=40%,4Y,10z.
Swedish Free Mission	1950	P-Pe2	Z....	30	3,000	5,000	7,000	1.35	*Sweden Jiyu Dendodan.* M=SFM(Sweden),NPY(Norway),Elim(Denmark,FFFM(Finland).
Tokyo Mennonite Church	1964	P-Men	.....	5	73	45	164	5.31	*Tokyo Chiku Menonaito Kyokai Rengo.* M=GCMC.
Total Christian Church	1957	I-Non	.....	14	320	200	500	3.73	*TCC.* Begun in Kyushu, now in Tokyo and Hokkaido.
True Jesus Church in Japan	1941	I-3oC	x....	3	193	700	400	-2.21	*Shin Iesu Kyokai Nippon Sokai.* Chinese; begun mainland 1917. HQ Osaka. 6n,W=28%.
Unification Church	1956	m-HSA	x....	250	280,000	117,020	350,000	4.48	*Holy Spirit Association for Unification of World Christianity.* Koreans; many Japanese students.
United Baptist Church		P-Bap	.....	31	600	737	900	0.05	*Nippon Baputesuto Kyokai Rengo.* Japan Baptist Church Assoc. 14n,9f,W=81%,64Y.
United Church of Christ in Japan	1859	P-Uni	RWE.W	1,707	128,017	205,051	204,293	-0.01	*Nippon Kirisuto Kyodan.* (1970) 59x,282f,8s,1434t. (1990) 3000 Yy, W=30%.
United Universalist Church	c1912	m-Unt	.....	5	190	500	400	-0.89	*Kirisutokyo Dojin Shadan.* M=Unitarian Univ Assoc (USA). HQ Bunkyo (Tokyo). 2n.
Uniting Ch of Christ in Japan	1970	I-Uni	.....	8	551	–	800	30.65	*Nihon Kirisuto Godo Kyokai.* Split ex UCCJ. In Kanto area.
Universal Evangelical Church	1948	I-Eva	.....	20	1,200	2,000	2,100	0.20	*Bankoku Fukuin Kyodan.* Ex Japan Evangelistic Band. HQ Matsumoto (Nagano). 20n.
Wesleyan Holiness Church	1919	P-Hol	.....	19	984	1,000	1,405	1.37	*Tanritsu (Wesurean Hoorinesu Kei).* M=WC(USA).
West Japan Evangelical Lutheran Ch	1949	P-Lut	l....	50	2,646	1,500	2,834	2.58	*Nishi Nippon Fukuin Ruteru Kyokai.* N=NLM(Norway). 8nx,12f,1s,W=48%,65Yy.
World Mission Fellowship	c1970	P-Non	.....	5	250	–	400	27.08	In Nagasaki area.
Worldwide Evangelization Crusade	1950	P-Non	xF...	19	343	552	527	-0.19	*Sekai Fukuin Dendodan.* M=WEK(Germany). HQ Kanzaki. 10n,20x,3f,W=80%,9Y.
Yamato (Zama) Christian Church	1953	I-3cQ	.....	5	800	100	1,200	10.45	M=Gospel Crusades.
Zion Christian Church	1934	I-Eva	.....	7	1,050	1,000	1,755	2.28	*Shion Kirisuto Kyokai.* Independent Japanese grouping of congregations. 9n,W=60%.
Other independent Oneness bodies	c1970	I-3oQ	.....	100	5,000	–	10,000	44.54	Total about 10.
Other Protestant denominations		P-	.....	400	22,000	38,700	50,000	0.05	Total about 40 (see list below).
Other Japanese indigenous churches		I-	.....	450	15,000	27,000	30,600	0.05	Total about 20 (see list below).
Other charismatic churches	c1960	I-3cQ	.....	30	1,200	800	3,000	5.43	Including Association of Vineyard Chs (3 chs), JILF.
Totals				**23,763**	**2,216,839**	**1,501,541**	**3,337,093**		

Churches, members, growth, 1900-2025	*Congs*	*Adults*	*Affiliated*	*G%*	*Total denominations*	*6 Megablocs:* O	R	A	P	I	m
Total churches, members, and denominations (mid-1900)	900	106,000	177,090	3.10	17	1	1	1	10	4	0
Total churches, members, and denominations (mid-1970)	12,584	898,320	1,501,541	3.10	186	1	1	1	95	81	7
Total churches, members, and denominations (mid-1990)	22,000	2,158,000	3,249,000	3.93	258	1	1	1	119	129	7
Total churches, members, and denominations (mid-1995)	23,763	2,216,839	3,337,093	0.54	261	1	1	1	120	131	7
Total churches, members, and denominations (mid-2000)	25,000	2,283,000	3,436,881	0.59	262	1	1	1	121	131	7
Total churches, members, and denominations (mid-2025)	31,000	2,561,000	3,855,000	0.46	368	1	1	1	150	200	15

NOTES ON TABLE ABOVE

NATIONAL COUNCILS (Column 4, 5th letter).

C = Japan Evangelical Association (JEA), composed of Japan Evangelical Fellowship (JEF) (Nippon Fukuin Renmei), Japan Protestant Council (JPC), Japan Evangelical Missionary Association (JEMA).

R = Catholic Bishops' Conference of Japan (CBCJ).

T = Japan Bible Christian Council (Nippon Seisho Kirisutokyo Kyogikai), or Japan Evangelical Council, or Bible Council of Japan.

W = National Christian Council in Japan (NCCJ) (Nippon Kirisutokyo Kyogikai).

w = associate member of NCCJ.

Other national councils. Okinawa Christian Council (separate from Japan until 1972).

Local councils. About 40, loosely affiliated to NCCJ.

OTHER PROTESTANT DENOMINATIONS. These smaller groups include: Apostolic Faith Mission, Baptist International Missions

(1966; 23 missionaries), Baptist Missionary Association of America, Bethel Pentecostal Temple (Seattle, USA), Bible Protestant Ch (1953), Children of God International (Tokyo), Ch of the Lutheran Confession (USA) (1 church in Tokyo), Community Baptist Ch Mission, Ev Congregational Ch (1963), Ev Methodist Ch (1968), Exclusive Brethren (Continuing Tunbridge Wells), Free Christian Mission, Grace Mission (1969), International Missions (1950), International Pentecostal Assemblies, Japan Rural Mission, Kobe Union Ch, Maranatha Baptist Mission, Missionary Ch, North American Baptist General Conference (1951), Orthodox Presbyterian Ch, Philadelphia Ch Mission, Reformed Presbyterian Ch of NAmerica (1950), Swedish Holiness Mission (1950), Tokyo Union Ch, World Baptist Fellowship Mission Agency (1966), World Gospel Mission (1952), World-Wide Missions (1964). In addition to these bodies with Japanese membership, there were in 1970 about 20,000 Protestants in USA military chaplaincies (65% in the Ryuku Islands).

OTHER JAPANESE INDIGENOUS CHURCHES. These smaller groups include: Amen Church, International Evangelical Convention; and a number of marginal bodies including. The few bodies from abroad include the Spiritual Food Worldwide Evangelistic Mission (from Hong Kong).

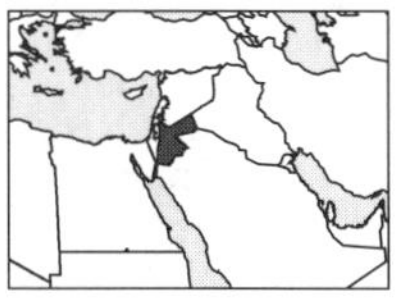

JORDAN

SECULAR DATA, AD 2000

STATE
Official name: Al-Mamlaka al-Urduniya al-Hashemiyah (The Hashemite Kingdom of Jordan).
Short name: Jordan. **Adjective of nationality:** Jordanian.
Flag: Black, white, and green stripes, with 7-pointed white star in red triangle on left.
Area: 89,246 sq. km. (34,458 sq. mi.).
Government: Constitutional monarchy, since 1991 (in Ottoman empire, 1920 British mandated territory of Transjordan, 1946 Independence, 1946 absolute monarchy).
Legislature: Parliament: Senate, 40 members; House of Representatives, 60 members.
Official language: Arabic.
Monetary unit: 1 Jordan dinar (JD) = 1,000 fils. **US$1=** $1.41.
Chief cities: AMMAN 1,449,000; Az-Zarqa (Zarka) 492,988; Irbid 260,068; Ar-Rusayfah 112,499; Al-Baq'ah 99,177.
Political divisions: 12 provinces.
Armed forces: 130,000.

DEMOGRAPHY
Population: 6,669,000.
Population density: 74.7/sq. km. (193.5/sq. mi.).
Under 15 years: 2,798,000.
Growth rate p.a.: 2.89% (births 32.97, deaths 4.12).
Mortality: Infant, per 1,000: 21.9; **Maternal per 100,000:** 150.0.
Life expectancy: 72 (male 70, female 73).
Household size: 6.0. **Floor area per person, sq.m:** 25.0.
Major languages: Arabic, Circassian, Armenian, Kurdish, English.
Urban dwellers: 74.19%. **Urban growth rate p.a.:** 3.7%.
Labor force: 23%.

ETHNOLINGUISTIC PEOPLES
32.4% Jordanian Arab; 32.1% Palestinian Arab; 14.0% Iraqi Arab; 12.8% Bedouin Arab; 5.0% Syrian Arab.

ECONOMY
National income p.a. per person: US$1,510; **per family:** US$9,060.

EDUCATION
Adult literacy: 86% (male 93%, female 79%). **Schools:** 3,277.
Universities: 55. **School enrolment:** female/male: 93%/91%.

HEALTH
Access to health services: 97%. **Access to safe water:** 89%.
Hospitals: 53 (11 beds per 10,000). **Doctors:** 6,395.
Blind: 9,000. **Deaf:** 379,800. **Murder rate:** 2.
Lepers: 600. **Underweight prevalence under 5:** 9%.

LITERATURE
New book titles p.a.: 590 (89 p.a. per million). **Periodicals:** 43.
Newspapers: 4 dailies.

COMMUNICATION (per 1,000 people)
Phones: 73 (14% mobile). **Radios:** 234. **TV sets:** 175.
Daily newspaper circulation: 48. **Computers:** 60.

REFUGEES
Alien refugees from other countries: 1,294,800.

HUMAN LIFE AND LIBERTY (optimum condition=100.0%)
HDI: 73.0. **HSI:** 59.0. **HFI:** 20.0. **EFL:** 44.0.

Country Table 1. **Religious adherents in Jordan, AD 1900-2025.**

Year	1900		1970		mid-1990		Annual change, 1990-2000				mid-1995		mid-2000		mid-2025	
Name	Adherents	%	Adherents	%	Adherents	%	Natural	Conversion	Total	Rate	Adherents	%	Adherents	%	Adherents	%
Muslims	235,400	94.2	2,189,400	95.2	4,343,700	94.0	192,679	-3,246	189,433	3.69	5,382,100	93.9	6,238,033	93.5	11,039,000	91.5
Christians	**14,600**	**5.8**	**83,400**	**3.6**	**181,300**	**3.9**	**8,041**	**1,218**	**9,259**	**4.21**	**227,000**	**4.0**	**273,889**	**4.1**	**640,000**	**5.3**
PROFESSION																
crypto-Christians	4,600	1.8	19,010	0.8	80,000	1.7	3,548	952	4,500	4.56	103,000	1.8	125,000	1.9	275,000	2.3
professing Christians	**10,000**	**4.0**	**64,390**	**2.8**	**101,300**	**2.2**	**4,493**	**266**	**4,759**	**3.93**	**124,000**	**2.2**	**148,889**	**2.2**	**365,000**	**3.0**
AFFILIATION																
unaffiliated Christians	0	0.0	20	0.0	300	0.0	13	-6	7	2.04	335	0.0	367	0.0	600	0.0
affiliated Christians	**14,600**	**5.8**	**83,380**	**3.6**	**181,000**	**3.9**	**8,027**	**1,225**	**9,252**	**4.22**	**226,665**	**4.0**	**273,522**	**4.1**	**639,400**	**5.3**
Orthodox	10,000	4.0	38,600	1.7	83,000	1.8	3,681	1,152	4,833	4.70	106,500	1.9	131,330	2.0	340,000	2.8
Independents	0	0.0	4,900	0.2	48,000	1.0	2,129	771	2,900	4.84	62,108	1.1	77,000	1.2	200,000	1.7
Roman Catholics	4,000	1.6	30,400	1.3	34,850	0.8	1,546	-231	1,315	3.25	42,000	0.7	48,000	0.7	75,000	0.6
Protestants	200	0.1	5,880	0.3	9,000	0.2	399	-317	82	0.88	9,400	0.2	9,822	0.2	15,000	0.1
Anglicans	400	0.2	3,500	0.2	6,000	0.1	266	-146	120	1.84	6,500	0.1	7,200	0.1	9,000	0.1
Marginal Christians	0	0.0	100	0.0	150	0.0	7	-5	2	1.26	157	0.0	170	0.0	400	0.0
Trans-megabloc groupings																
Evangelicals	400	0.2	6,000	0.3	19,000	0.4	843	237	1,080	4.60	24,852	0.4	29,800	0.5	65,000	0.5
Pentecostals/Charismatics	0	0.0	5,000	0.2	51,000	1.1	2,262	1,438	3,700	5.61	70,359	1.2	88,000	1.3	214,000	1.8
Great Commission Christians	**9,500**	**3.8**	**71,000**	**3.1**	**145,000**	**3.1**	**6,431**	**1,885**	**8,316**	**4.64**	**185,000**	**3.2**	**228,157**	**3.4**	**500,000**	**4.1**
Nonreligious	0	0.0	22,000	1.0	70,000	1.5	3,105	1,743	4,848	5.40	93,600	1.6	118,480	1.8	300,000	2.5
Atheists	0	0.0	3,500	0.2	14,000	0.3	621	151	772	4.49	17,500	0.3	21,718	0.3	44,000	0.4
Baha'is	0	0.0	700	0.0	11,000	0.2	488	134	622	4.58	13,800	0.2	17,221	0.3	40,000	0.3
World A (unevangelized persons)	210,000	84.0	1,494,350	65.0	2,402,400	52.0	106,475	-41,347	65,128	2.43	2,798,077	48.8	3,054,402	45.8	4,402,995	36.5
World B (evangelized non-Christians)	25,400	10.2	721,250	31.4	2,036,300	44.1	90,418	40,129	130,547	5.08	2,708,687	47.2	3,340,709	50.1	7,020,005	58.2
World C (Christians)	14,600	5.8	83,400	3.6	181,300	3.9	8,041	1,218	9,259	4.21	227,000	4.0	273,889	4.1	640,000	5.3
Country's population	**250,000**	**100.0**	**2,299,000**	**100.0**	**4,620,000**	**100.0**	**204,934**	**0**	**204,934**	**3.74**	**5,733,765**	**100.0**	**6,669,000**	**100.0**	**12,063,000**	**100.0**

COLUMNS, ROWS.
For meanings and definitions, see Codebook (Part 3). Note that, by definition, total 'Christians' = professing + crypto-Christians, which also = affiliated + unaffiliated Christians, and also = Great Commission Christians + latent Christians. Percentages may not always total exactly, due to rounding.

CENSUSES.
18.XI.1961 (including West Bank and Jerusalem, and including 933 nationals abroad): 93.6% Muslims, 6.4% Christians (109,000). **18XI.1961** (Transjordan only): 6.9% Christians (63,000). **18.XI.1961** (West Bank and East Jerusalem, termed in this survey Palestine): 5.7% Christians (46,000).

NOTES ON RELIGIONS
ATHEISTS. Communist Party of Jordan (CPJ) (illegal; split over Sino-Soviet dispute).
BAHA'IS. Growth from 2 local spiritual assemblies (1964) to 7 (1973) and to 11 LSAs (1996). Strong around Al-Adasiyah, in Jordan valley.
COUNTRY'S POPULATION. The table refers to Jordan's de facto territory and population in 1970-79, i.e. to Transjordan only, excluding West Bank and East Jerusalem (shown in this survey under Palestine) which have been occupied by Israel since 1967, but including the 305,000 Palestinian refugees who entered between 1947 and 5 June 1967 and also the 433,866 refugees who entered after the 1967 war. In 1970, Jordan had a population of 2,317,000 (including West Bank, East Jerusalem, and 818,000 Palestinian refugees) and 2,739,000 in 1975 (UN estimate and projection). West Bank and East Jerusalem in 1970 had a population of 680,000, almost all Palestinian Arabs.
CRYPTO-CHRISTIANS. Secret believers, i.e. Christians affiliated to churches but not known as such to the state nor recorded in censuses as Christians.
INDEPENDENTS. Isolated radio believers in scattered areas, and a couple of small denominations (see Table 2).
MUSLIMS. Mostly Sunnis (of the Shafiite rite), including Circassians (Cherkess), Kurds and Turkmen, also about 1,000 Chechen (Shishan) Shias; also Druzes, An 11th-century Muslim Shia Ismaili schism with Christian and Jewish elements. On border with Syria, and in and around Amman, here enumerated under Muslims; and 3,000 Alawites. *Hajj pilgrims to Mecca.* (1969) 6,376: (1970) 10,909; (1971) 15,933; (1972) 25,819; (1973) 12,851; (1974) 19,391; (1975) 17,331; (1976) 23,427.

Great Commission Instrument Panel: status of Jordan (for explanation see start of Part 4)

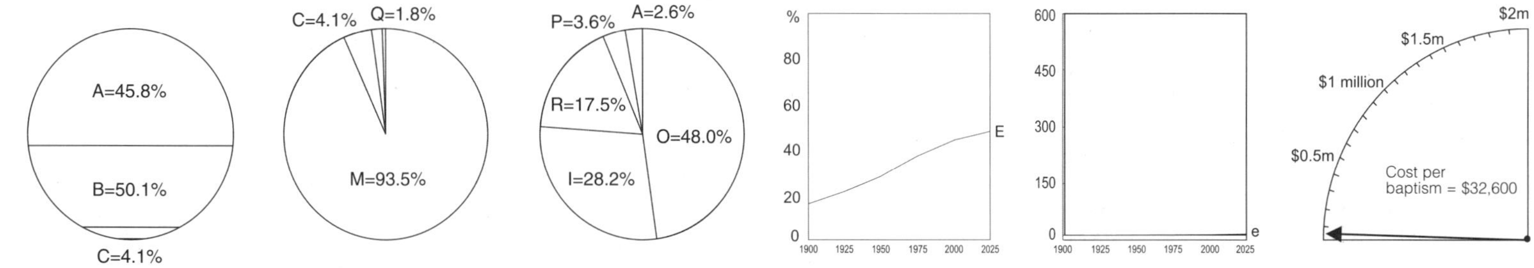

3 Worlds, AD 2000 | Religions, AD 2000 | Ecclesiastical blocs | Evangelization, 1900-2025 | Offers, 1900-2025 | Cost-effectiveness, AD 2000

Country summary. **Worlds A, B, C by ethnolinguistic peoples, cities, and major civil divisions in Jordan.**

	PEOPLES							CITIES							CIVIL DIVISIONS						
World	Num	Pop 2000	C%	Christians	E%	U%	Unevangelized	Num	Pop 2000	C%	Christians	E%	U%	Unevangelized	Num	Pop 2000	C%	Christians	E%	U%	Unevangelized
A	9	1,958,451	0.02	351	28	72	1,402,324	0	0	0.00	0	0	0	0	5	983,909	1.96	19,262	49	51	504,490
B	6	4,681,543	5.27	246,779	65	35	1,648,929	4	2,275,813	5.07	115,405	59	41	928,056	7	5,685,434	4.47	254,260	55	45	2,546,794
C	5	29,345	89.93	26,390	100	0	30	0	0	0.00	0	0	0	0	0	0	0.00	0	0	0	0
Total	**20**	**6,669,339**	**4.10**	**273,520**	**54**	**46**	**3,051,283**	**4**	**2,275,813**	**5.07**	**115,405**	**59**	**41**	**928,056**	**12**	**6,669,343**	**4.10**	**273,522**	**54**	**46**	**3,051,284**

Country status. Jordan is an Arab country east of the Jordan River that occupies a strategic position in the Middle East. It is an artificial creation of the British rulers of Transjordan dating back only to the period following World War I. The land is 90% desert, unfit for cultivation. The most important industries are phosphate mining and tourism.

Bedouins, hardy desert nomads, now mostly live indoors in tent-style housing.

HUMAN LIFE AND LIBERTY

Human need and development. Jordan shares the culture and economy of all Arab countries, but the lack of oil resources has made it dependent on the generosity of richer Arab states as well as the United States. Except in Amman, Jordanians live the typical life of Bedouins, in very primitive conditions, yet not in abject poverty. Among the upper classes, signs of affluence are not lacking, and educational and health facilities are adequate. About as many as one-third of the people have limited or no access to medical care. Most diseases are related to poor sanitation and harsh climatic conditions. There is a severe and chronic shortage of water, and per capita consumption of water is among the lowest in the world. People outside of Amman and the other urban centers regularly use contaminated water supplies and use wells and rivers for conflicting purposes, such as drinking, waste disposal, and irrigation.

Human rights and freedoms. Jordan is a moderate Arab country, and while there are general restrictions based on state security and the need to conform to Islamic regulations in public life, there are few oppressive laws and few abuses of human rights. The principal concern of the state security apparatus is with the Islamic fundamentalists, many of whom are periodically charged with antiregime sermons in mosques, violent intimidation of non-Muslims and secular Muslims, and the distribution of inflammatory leaflets. Legal proceedings do not frequently meet international standards for fair trial. Religious courts have jurisdiction over such family matters as inheritance, marriage, and divorce, but inheritance matters are generally handled on the basis of the sharia. The Constitution provides for freedoms of speech and press, but they are meaningless because the print and electronic media are owned, partly or wholly, by the government. Insults to the royal family as well as heads of Arab or Muslim states are prohibited. Overt discrimination exists only against the Baha'is, but Palestinians, Christians, and women all experience discrimination to varying degrees.

Human environment. Jordan is mostly desert. There are virtually no forests. Nevertheless, the country is home to over 200 species of birds and many species of animals, including the oryx and the Persian fallow deer. Because of desert conditions and little rainfall, there is a shortage of usable water, and 90% of what is available is used for agriculture. Desertification and erosion are serious threats to the land where the cultivable area has been steadily decreasing in the past half a century.

NON-CHRISTIAN RELIGIONS

Islam is the religion of 93.5% of the population. Most Muslims are Sunnis of the Shafite rite. The Chechens, a small group of Caucasian extraction, are Shias. Most well-established families living in urban and village areas observe orthodox Muslim customs and practices, but the nomadic Bedouin give first place to the *urf*, their pre-Islamic tribal law.

Baha'i is practiced by small communities at Adasiya in the northern part of the Jordan valley.

Druze religion is a schism from the Muslim Ismaili sect, whose principal belief is that Hakim (the divine sixth Fatimid caliph) is alive and in hiding. Druzes are found mostly on the Jordanian border with Syria.

CHRISTIANITY

Christians are descended from the ancient Palestinian and Transjordanian inhabitants of the Apostolic era, who have become progressively more arabized in the course of time. They are nevertheless proud of their origin and deeply attached to their ethnic and religious traditions. The survival of Christianity in a world which has become Muslim is explained religiously by the extraordinary zeal of the Orthodox clergy and sociologically by existing tribal structures which have conditioned and stabilized the various religious allegiances. It is in fact in the villages among the farmers (*fellahin*) that Christianity is best preserved. Because of their historic antecedents, one finds Christians today in all strata and classes of society, except among the nomads who make up 6% of the population and, with rare exceptions, among those residing in Palestinian refugee camps. The absence of Christians in these strata is due to their social success. Christians tend to be involved increasingly in rapid urbanization and are now found principally in the merchant and office-worker middle classes and the professions. The inauspicious conditions of life in Jordan, especially due to the economic crises created by 3 Palestinian wars, cause Christians to emigrate in large numbers which is thus the principal problem facing the churches.

Greek Orthodox Patriarchate. Church with newly-built mosque alongside (right).

ORTHODOX CHURCHES. The largest Christian denomination in Jordan is the Greek Orthodox Church, with 89,000 members on the East Bank. The Orthodox theological seminary in Jerusalem has a smaller student body from Jordan due to the difficulties of travel between the 2 areas. Parish priests and laity are for the most part Palestinian Arabs; whereas the patriarch, bishops, and monks are Greeks. The patriarchate sponsors 34 schools of which 2 offer full secondary training for 4,700 students, one orphanage and one home for the aged.

The Armenian Apostolic Church has 7,000 members on the East Bank in Amman. Until recently, they were much more numerous, but Armenians have suffered more from emigration than any other church. The church operates one parish school and a program of charitable relief service. The Syrian Orthodox Church is composed of 15,000 East Bank adherents grouped in one parish served by an Arab priest. The church is also responsible for one school. Russian, Coptic, and Ethiopian Orthodox, which all have small congregations on the West Bank in Jerusalem, have no presence east of the Jordan.

CATHOLIC CHURCH. Catholicism is divided into several communities, the 2 largest groups being Latin-rite and Greek (Melkite) Catholics. The reason for the success of Latin-rite Catholicism in Jordan, as contrasted with other countries of the Middle East, is the extraordinary missionary effort of the Franciscans after the medieval Crusades and the restoration of Jerusalem's Latin patriarchate in 1847. Parish clergy are 90% Palestinian Arabs.

Greek Catholics number 21,000 on the East Bank, which is the archbishopric of Petra and Filadelfia. The Catholic Melkite hierarchy is more indigenous and progressive than its Greek Orthodox counterpart.

Armenian Catholics are found on both sides of the Jordan, about 400 living on the East Bank; whereas, Maronites and Syrian Catholics are confined to the West Bank. The Armenian patriarch resides in Jerusalem.

The Holy See has diplomatic relations with Jordan and in AD 2000 is represented to government and the Catholic hierarchy by a nuncio residing in Baghdad.

OTHER CHURCHES. Anglicans, who entered Jordan in 1860, have a strong work with 6,500 adherents on the East Bank. Arab congregations are found in the northern part of Jordan as well as in Amman and Zerqa. The Episcopal church has 3 schools, of which 2 provide a complete secondary program (1,100 students), one school for the deaf, dumb, and blind and one home for the aged.

The Evangelical Church of the CMA is an autonomous body resulting from the missionary activity of the Christian and Missionary Alliance following World War I. Another denomination which established itself in Jordan during the 1920s, was the Assemblies of God, followed by the church of the Nazarene in 1948. The latter group is found mostly in Salt and Amman where a secondary school has been built. The Assemblies of God have a clinic in Amman. Lutherans are strongest on the West Bank, with 5 congregations of 1,600 total in Amman. East Bank activities, mostly of a welfare and development nature supported by the Lutheran World Federation, include the Schneller School of Agricultural and Manual Training in addition to a secondary school of an orphanage. Two American Baptist denominations exist, one related to the Southern Baptist Convention and the other to Conservative Baptists. The former group has its center at Er Rumman north of Amman and at Ajlun where a hospital and nursing school have been built. They also have a secondary school. The Seventh-day Adventists have 6 congregations east of the Jordan, 2 being in Amman, and a secondary school. The Free Evangelical Church and German Alliance Mission are also present on the East Bank.

Renewal movements. In the 1990s the Pentecostal/Charismatic Renewal continued to spread rapidly across most older churches, and numbered over 88,000 adherents (of whom 3% Pentecostals, 10% Charismatics, and 87% Independents).

Indigenous missions. Jordanian Christians send out very few missionaries but more Christian laymen are consciously accepting the responsibility to witness in the secular jobs they hold in other countries in the Middle East.

CHURCH AND STATE

The constitution of 1952, subsequently amended several times, establishes Islam as the state religion (Article 2), prohibits all religious discrimination (Article 6) and guarantees the free exercise of religion and belief (Article 14).

There is no government ministry or department dealing with religious affairs. To be recognized and to receive state protection, minority religious groups must be registered with the Ministry of the Interior. Official recognition may be of 2 types: either basic recognition, including the right to conduct worship services, teach, open churches and schools (which has been granted to the Armenian Orthodox, Armenian Catholics, Syrian Orthodox, Anglican and a few other communities); or a more complex recognition granting the right to have communal ecclesiastical courts and to pass sentences for the civil authorities (which has been granted only to the Greek Orthodox and the Greek and Latin Catholic churches). The state sometimes refuses to recognize a community, as it did when Jehovah's Witnesses were declared a prohibited society because of alleged subversive activities.

The states does not provide financial aid to churches except for such minor assistance as occasional gifts to Christian work of national significance, gratuitous offers by municipalities of water and electricity to churches and schools at two-thirds the normal cost, or a minimal charge for the upkeep of cemeteries. Nevertheless, churches and private schools are exempt from land taxes. Christian communities possess real autonomy, and their leaders have authority over their members in the personal domain, including questions of marriage, separation, divorce, inheritance, the training of youth, and the like.

The status of private schools, both Christian and Muslim, was established by Rule 16 of the Ministry of Education (May 26, 1964) and additional ministerial instructions issued since then. No school can be opened without the Ministry's permission; this may then have permanent validity, although this is difficult to obtain, or it may be renewable on an annual basis. From a practical standpoint, the Ministry of Education, which is somewhat under the influence of the Muslim Brotherhood, tends more to frustrate than to facilitate the functioning of Christian schools.

In official schools, Muslim religious instruction is obligatory for Muslim students and constitutes a subject for examination. Christian students are exempt, but many frequent the courses in order to improve their knowledge of literary Arabic, of which the Quran is the classic example. The absence of a course in the Christian religion in public schools, such as that used in Syria and which the Jordanian Ministry of Education would like to initiate, may be traced to the small number of Christian students, their division into many churches and the inability of the churches to agree on a common basic syllabus.

With some reservations in view of the power of social pressure, one can say that Christians enjoy a considerable number of advantages in Jordan. They are well represented in government ministries and administrative circles, and in cases of conflict between Christians and Muslims, the Hashemite monarchy has often played a conciliatory role. Paradoxically, the Muslim state has occasionally served as arbiter between rival Christian groups. In the conflict over Palestine, the 3 Christian bishops of Jordan (Greek Orthodox and Greek Catholic archbishops, and the Latin patriarchal vicar) have several times taken clear positions against the policies of Israel. In so doing, they have also on each occasion been careful not to say or do anything to offend the Hashemite monarchy, a policy which is also followed in internal social and political questions. After 1969, the continued support of some Orthodox and Catholic priests for Palestinian resistance organizations placed them in opposition to the government. In 1970, 2 Catholic priests and 2 nuns, who had created workers' wards in the Arab sector of Nazareth in Israel, at Bethlehem and at Brit-Saheur in Jordan, were expelled from the country by the Jordanian authorities for their association with a group of fedayeen Marxists (FDPLP). They had created in the same year, at Hosn, near Irbid, a farm and workshops in aid of refugees. Among the mass of Christian lay men, all political positions are found, from monarchists to revolutionaries. One notes also the presence of many Christians among militant communists, in the Baathist party and in all Palestinian resistance organizations. Many are in fact initiators and leaders of these movements.

BROADCASTING AND MEDIA

FEBA (Seychelles) has shortwave radio programs in Arabic, Azeri, and Farsi. Other shortwave programs from HCJB (Ecuador), AWR (Slovakia), and TWR (Monaco) can be heard. Christian television programming can be received from CBN's ME TV station in Lebanon. Satellite TV programs are received mainly in Arabic.

At least 2.3 million have seen the 'Jesus' film: through videocassette (1.4 million), radio (391,000), RTV (326,000) and film team presentations (113,000), with 10,800 have responding.

INTERDENOMINATIONAL ORGANIZATIONS

Although the Ecumenical Youth Committee in Amman, created by SOJEMO in Lebanon, is the only formal interdenominational organization in Jordan, since 1971 informal but regular meetings of leaders of the different Christian communities, in addition to the 3 Catholic and Orthodox bishops, have been held in Amman. The Greek Orthodox, Episcopal, Armenian Apostolic, Syrian Orthodox and Lutheran churches are all members of the Middle East Council of Churches with its seat in Beirut, Lebanon.

FUTURE TRENDS AND PROSPECTS

Muslims may very likely decline as the nonreligious grow to 2.5% by 2025. Christians will remain near 5% through 2025.

Christianity is not expected to grow past 6% before AD 2050. Effective evangelistic ministry could make a difference but emigration of existing Christians will continue to be a problem. The nonreligious could pass 5% before AD 2050.

BIBLIOGRAPHY

'A case of honor: Arab Christians in a Jordanian town.' N. E. Allison. Ph.D. dissertation, University of Georgia, Athens, GA, 1977. 251p.

'A culturally compatible model for church growth in the Middle East.' N. N. Abbassi. Th.M. thesis, Dallas Theological Seminary, Dallas, TX, 1993. 76p.

'Annuaire de l'Eglise catholique en Terre sainte,'

Das reformatorische Erbe unter den Palästinensern: zur Entstehung der Evangelisch–Lutherischen Kirche in Jordanien. M. Raheb. *Die Lutherische Kirche, Geschichte und Gestalten*, Bd. 11. Gütersloh: Gütersloher Verlagshaus G. Mohn, 1990. 317p.

Jordan. I. J. Seccombe. *World bibliographical series*, vol. 55. Oxford, UK: CLIO Press, 1984. 324p. (See especially 'Religion,' p.97–9).

L'église d'Arabie: essai historique et juridique dès l'origine jusqu'à l'avènement de l'Islam: la conversion des arabes de la province romaine d'Arabie, Transjordanie et Syrie, de Petra à Damas. J. Hijazin. Rome: Pontificia Universitas Lateranensis, 1979. 78p.

Les minorités chrétiennes de Palestine à travers les siècles: étude historico–juridique et développement moderne international. A. O. Issa. Jerusalem: Franciscan Printing Press, 1978. 363p.

'Religion,' in *Area handbook for the Hashemite Kingdom of Jordan*, p.131–39. Washington, DC: US Government Printing Office, 1969.

A fair number of Jordan's postage stamps have carried Christian themes. *Above.* Christ's passion: Stations of the Cross (1966).

Country Table 2. **Organized churches and denominations in Jordan.**

Official name (bold type = church with over 10% of all affiliated) 1	*Begun* 2	*Type* 3	*Counc* 4	*Congs* 5	*Adults* 6	*Affiliated 1970* 7	*Affiliated 1995* 8	*G%* 9	*Names, notes, and other statistics* (see Codebook, Part 3) 10
Armenian Apostolic Church: V Amman	c1800	O-Arm	Ew.N.	10	4,000	1,500	7,000	6.36	*Gregorians.* Under Armenian Patriarchate of Jerusalem. Massive emigration. 1n.
Assemblies of God	1929	P-Pe2	ZF...	16	1,500	600	1,990	4.91	M=AoG(USA). In Amman area. 1972, revival. Classical Pentecostals. 5n,2f,1h.
Bible Preaching Church	1963	I-Eva	x....	1	75	300	150	-2.73	M=World-Wide Missions (USA). Evangelicals based in Pasadena, CA (USA).
Catholic Church in Jordan:	c50	R-LEr	O....	65	21,000	30,400	42,000	0.05	*Al-Kanissa al-Kathoulikiah.* Melkites,Latins, Armenians. 17n 31w 302Yy
P Jerusalem (V Amman) *(Latin)*	1099	R-Lat	Os	30	7,000	15,000	12,000	-0.89	*Al-Latinn.* Member of CELRA. Palestinians. Priests 90% Palestinian Arabs.
AD Petra & Filadelfia (Amman)	c350	R-Mel	Os	35	14,000	15,400	30,000	0.06	In Melkite Patriarchal Synod. Including 400 Armenians (1n). M=BC. (1970) 24n,1x,33w,237Yy.
Christian Brethren		P-CBr	x....	1	20	1,000	33	0.05	Plymouth (Open) Brethren/Baptist type. All indigenous Arab congregations.
Church of God (Cleveland)	c1965	P-Pe3	ZF...	1	100	100	200	2.81	M=CoG(Cleveland) (USA). Holiness Pentecostals (3-stage).
Church of the Nazarene	1948	P-Hol	xF...	7	430	1,000	550	-2.36	M=CoN(USA). Arabs and some Armenians. 4n,1x,28m,2f,1r,11t(825),W=68%,4Y.
Coptic Orthodox Ch (D Jerusalem)	c50	O-Cop	N....	2	300	100	500	0.05	Under P Alexandria. Egyptian residents and workers.
Epis Ch in Jerus & ME: D Jerusalem	1860	A-Low	Aw.N.	20	3,900	3,500	6,500	2.51	ECJME. HQ Jerusalem. M=CMS. 30% rural. 87% Arab, 13% White. 9n,1x,4f,3r,W=40%,84y.
Evangelical Church of the CMA	1921	P-Hol	xF...	6	219	1,000	567	-2.24	M=CMA(USA). Autonomous church, related to similar body in Lebanon et alia.
Evangelical Lutheran Church in Jordan	1860	P-Lut	l..N.	5	960	100	1,600	11.73	1,254 members on West Bank, in Israel since 1967 war. Amman only. Arabs. 1r.
Free Evangelical Church	1956	I-Bap	.....	9	275	300	458	1.71	M=CBI (USA). Small conservative Baptist mission.
German Alliance Mission		P-Non	.....	10	100	430	200	0.05	Small independent Evangelical mission. 6n,5x,W=81%,30Y,25z.
Greek Orth Patr of Jerus: D Amman	33	O-Ara	Cw.N.	32	47,000	36,000	84,000	0.05	99% Palestinian Arabs (laity, priests); bishops, monks are Greeks. 35n,1x,2r.
Isolated radio churches	c1950	I-3rS	.....	800	40,000	4,100	60,000	11.33	Isolated radio believers (students, pupils). R=510 (TWR,&c), T=11000 (ICI,GMU).
Jehovah's Witnesses	1918	m-Jeh	x....	2	55	100	157	1.82	*Watch Tower. IBSA.* Active witnessing under way by 1945. No recent baptisms. Banned.
Jordan Baptist Convention	c1943	P-Bap	T....	13	900	750	1,660	3.23	1952, M=FMB-SBC(USA). Strongest north of Amman. 5 schools. 8n,14f,1H(Ajlun),2h,1r,13Y.
Religious Society of Friends	1869	P-Qua	Q....	1	30	100	50	-2.73	In Near East Yearly Meeting. Quakers. M=FUM(USA). 2 schools. 2f.
Seventh-day Adventist Church	1932	P-Adv	x....	10	330	500	550	0.38	*SDA, Jordan Station.* East Mediterranean Field, Middle East Union. In Amman. 2f,1r.
Syrian Orth P Antioch (D Jerusalem)	33	O-Syr	Dw.N.	20	9,600	1,000	15,000	0.05	SOC.*Jacobites.* 2,500 West Bank members now in Israel since 1967. 1 school, 1n.
Other Protestant denominations		P-	.....	10	1,000	300	2,000	0.05	Total about 3, including: BMM (1970), RPCES,CEC.
Other Arab indigenous churches		I-	.....	15	900	200	1,500	0.05	Including: Essene Church in the Hashemite Kingdom of Jordan (Gnostic).
Totals				**1,056**	**132,694**	**83,380**	**226,665**		

Churches, members, growth, 1900-2025	*Congs*	*Adults*	*Affiliated*	*G%*	*Total denominations*	*6 Megablocs:* O	R	A	P	I	m
Total churches, members, and denominations (mid-1900)	40	8,000	14,600	2.52	9	4	1	1	3	0	0
Total churches, members, and denominations (mid-1970)	293	45,582	83,380	2.52	25	4	1	1	11	7	1
Total churches, members, and denominations (mid-1990)	800	106,000	181,000	3.95	33	4	1	1	13	13	1
Total churches, members, and denominations (mid-1995)	1,056	132,694	226,665	4.60	33	4	1	1	13	13	1
Total churches, members, and denominations (mid-2000)	1,200	160,000	273,522	3.83	33	4	1	1	13	13	1
Total churches, members, and denominations (mid-2025)	2,000	374,000	639,400	3.45	78	10	1	1	25	40	1

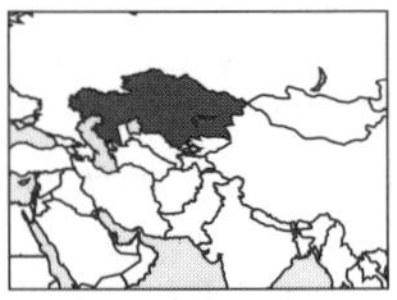

KAZAKHSTAN

SECULAR DATA, AD 2000

STATE

Official name: Qazaqstan Respublikasy (The Republic of Kazakhstan).
Short name: Kazakhstan. **Adjective of nationality:** Kazakh.
Flag: Blue field with sun in center and yellow pattern on left.
Area: 2,717,300 sq. km. (1,049,200 sq. mi.).
Government: Unitary republic with a parliament consisting of two chambers since, 1991 (1920 Russian republic, 1936 Soviet rule).
Legislature: Senate, 47 members; Assembly, 67 members.
Official language: Kazak.
Monetary unit: 1 tenge (T) = 100 tiyn. **US$1=** 80.48 tenge.
Chief cities: Almaty (Alma-ata, Vyermyi) 1,309,000; Karaganda 641,529; Cimkent (Chimkent) 462,542; Semipalatinsk 363,350; Pavlodar 361,031.
Political divisions: 16 provinces.
Armed forces: 35,000.

DEMOGRAPHY

Population: 16,223,000.
Population density: 5.9/sq. km. (15.4/sq. mi.).
Under 15 years: 4,471,000.
Growth rate p.a.: -0.10% (births 17.18, deaths 8.30).
Mortality: Infant, per 1,000: 30.5; **Maternal per 100,000:** 80.0.
Life expectancy: 69 (male 65, female 73).
Household size: 4.0. **Floor area per person, sq.m:** 18.0.
Major languages: Kazakh, Russian, Tartar, Ukrainian, German, Belorussian.
Urban dwellers: 61.69%. **Urban growth rate p.a.:** 1.2%.
Labor force: 44%.

ETHNOLINGUISTIC PEOPLES

53.4% Kazakh; 28.2% Russian; 3.0% Ukrainian; 2.5% German (Volga German); 2.3% Uzbek.

ECONOMY

National income p.a. per person: US$1,330; **per family:** US$5,320.

EDUCATION

Adult literacy: 97% (male 99%, female 96%). **Schools:** 11,956.
Universities: 61. **School enrolment:** female/male: 89%/88%.

HEALTH

Access to health services: 80%. **Access to safe water:** 70%.
Hospitals: 1,805 (134 beds per 10,000). **Doctors:** 66,000.
Blind: 15,000. **Deaf:** 1,015,700. **Murder rate:** 12.
Lepers: 2,000.

LITERATURE

New book titles p.a.: 1,220 (75 p.a. per million). **Periodicals:** 123.
Newspapers: 2 dailies.

COMMUNICATION (per 1,000 people)

Phones: 118 (0% mobile). **Radios:** 150. **TV sets:** 275.
Daily newspaper circulation: 400. **Computers:** 30.

HUMAN LIFE AND LIBERTY (optimum condition=100.0%)

HDI: 70.9. **HSI:** 35.0. **HFI:** 40.0. **EFL:** 20.0.

Country Table 1. **Religious adherents in Kazakhstan, AD 1900-2025.**

Year / *Name*	*1900* Adherents	%	*1970* Adherents	%	*mid-1990* Adherents	%	*Annual change, 1990-2000* Natural	Conversion	Total	Rate	*mid-1995* Adherents	%	*mid-2000* Adherents	%	*mid-2025* Adherents	%
Muslims	2,192,500	93.9	3,520,000	26.9	5,920,900	35.4	-18,396	118,378	99,982	1.57	6,091,600	36.9	6,920,715	42.7	8,850,000	50.0
Nonreligious	1,000	0.0	4,118,000	31.4	5,410,000	32.3	-16,771	-48,365	-65,136	-1.27	5,142,000	31.2	4,758,637	29.3	4,595,000	26.0
Christians	**115,000**	**4.9**	**2,450,000**	**18.7**	**3,350,000**	**20.0**	**-10,385**	**-53,617**	**-64,002**	**-2.10**	**3,260,000**	**19.8**	**2,709,980**	**16.7**	**2,750,000**	**15.5**
PROFESSION																
crypto-Christians	0	0.0	765,000	5.8	200,000	1.2	-620	-5,380	-6,000	-3.50	150,000	0.9	140,000	0.9	125,000	0.7
professing Christians	**115,000**	**4.9**	**1,685,000**	**12.9**	**3,150,000**	**18.8**	**-9,765**	**-48,237**	**-58,002**	**-2.01**	**3,110,000**	**18.8**	**2,569,980**	**15.8**	**2,625,000**	**14.8**
AFFILIATION																
unaffiliated Christians	4,000	0.2	66,470	0.5	227,000	1.4	-704	-10,178	-10,882	-6.32	152,687	0.9	118,177	0.7	92,000	0.5
affiliated Christians	**111,000**	**4.8**	**2,383,530**	**18.2**	**3,123,000**	**18.7**	**-9,681**	**-43,439**	**-53,120**	**-1.85**	**3,107,313**	**18.8**	**2,591,803**	**16.0**	**2,658,000**	**15.0**
Orthodox	71,000	3.0	1,986,700	15.2	2,160,000	12.9	-6,696	-69,124	-75,820	-4.23	1,949,500	11.8	1,401,803	8.6	1,200,000	6.8
Independents	0	0.0	97,500	0.7	480,000	2.9	-1,488	18,488	17,000	3.08	587,483	3.6	650,000	4.0	820,000	4.6
Roman Catholics	20,000	0.9	20,000	0.2	400,000	2.4	-1,240	12,240	11,000	2.46	500,000	3.0	510,000	3.1	600,000	3.4
Protestants	20,000	0.9	278,330	2.1	80,000	0.5	-248	-5,252	-5,500	-10.98	66,830	0.4	25,000	0.2	30,000	0.2
Marginal Christians	0	0.0	1,000	0.0	3,000	0.0	-9	209	200	5.24	3,500	0.0	5,000	0.0	8,000	0.1
Trans-megabloc groupings																
Evangelicals	18,000	0.8	46,000	0.4	15,000	0.1	-46	-454	-500	-3.97	13,496	0.1	10,000	0.1	13,000	0.1
Pentecostals/Charismatics	0	0.0	5,000	0.0	67,000	0.4	-208	1,708	1,500	2.04	74,044	0.5	82,000	0.5	150,000	0.9
Great Commission Christians	**94,000**	**4.0**	**1,180,000**	**9.0**	**1,660,000**	**9.9**	**-5,146**	**-16,507**	**-21,653**	**-1.39**	**1,700,000**	**10.3**	**1,443,467**	**8.9**	**1,595,000**	**9.0**
Atheists	500	0.0	3,000,000	22.9	2,000,000	12.0	-6,200	-16,678	-22,878	-1.21	1,950,000	11.8	1,771,219	10.9	1,400,000	7.9
Ethnoreligionists	20,000	0.9	0	0.0	27,000	0.2	-84	165	81	0.30	28,800	0.2	27,808	0.2	50,000	0.3
Buddhists	1,000	0.0	10,000	0.1	17,000	0.1	-53	55	2	0.01	17,200	0.1	17,021	0.1	32,000	0.2
Jews	4,000	0.2	12,000	0.1	14,300	0.1	-44	8	-36	-0.26	14,400	0.1	13,939	0.1	16,000	0.1
Zoroastrians	0	0.0	0	0.0	2,800	0.0	-9	54	45	1.49	3,000	0.0	3,245	0.0	5,000	0.0
World A (unevangelized persons)	2,000,238	85.7	7,866,000	60.0	6,864,220	41.0	-21,319	-85,160	-106,479	-1.67	6,437,789	39.0	5,807,834	35.8	5,504,078	31.1
World B (evangelized non-Christians)	218,762	9.4	2,794,000	21.3	6,527,780	39.0	-20,238	138,777	118,539	1.67	6,809,362	41.2	7,705,186	47.5	9,443,922	53.4
World C (Christians)	115,000	4.9	2,450,000	18.7	3,350,000	20.0	-10,385	-53,617	-64,002	-2.10	3,260,000	19.8	2,709,980	16.7	2,750,000	15.5
Country's population	**2,334,000**	**100.0**	**13,110,000**	**100.0**	**16,742,000**	**100.0**	**-51,942**	**0**	**-51,942**	**-0.31**	**16,507,152**	**100.0**	**16,223,000**	**100.0**	**17,698,000**	**100.0**

COLUMNS, ROWS.
For meanings and definitions, see Codebook (Part 3). Note that, by definition, total 'Christians' = professing + crypto-Christians, which also = affiliated + unaffiliated Christians, and also = Great Commission Christians + latent Christians. Percentages may not always total exactly, due to rounding.

NOTES ON RELIGIONS
ATHEISTS. Declining rapidly after 1989; most ethnic Kazakhs have been reaffirming their Muslim beliefs.
BAHA'IS. Rapid growth after collapse of Communism in 1991, to 28 local spiritual assemblies by 1996. Baha'i literature is now published in the Kazakh language in both Cyrillic and Latin scripts.
JEWS. Mainly Russian-speaking Jews with a small group of Central Asian Jews.
MUSLIMS. Mainly Sunnis, but with a strong Sufi movement, particularly in rural areas.
ORTHODOX. Almost all ethnic Russians and Ukrainians, with smaller numbers of Greeks and Armenians.

Great Commission Instrument Panel: status of Kazakhstan (for explanation see start of Part 4)

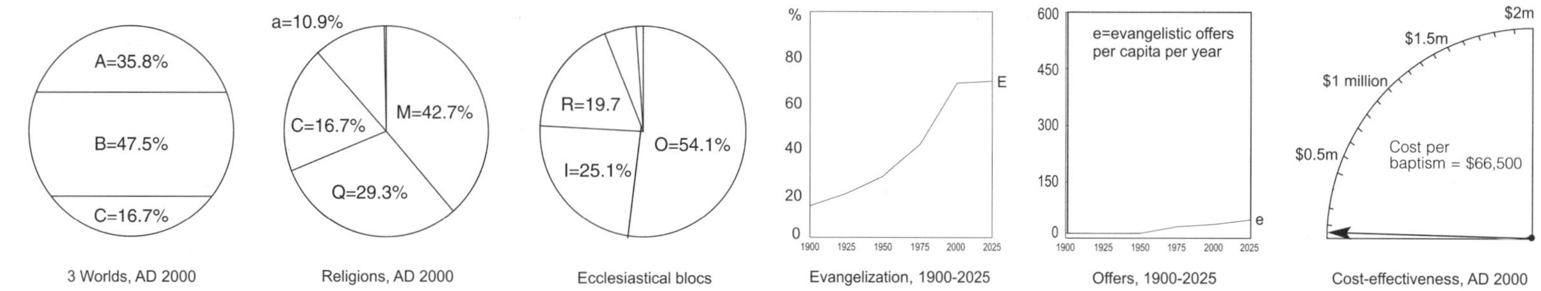

Country status. Kazakhstan, a former republic of the Soviet Union, is an independent state south of Russia in Central Asia. Its agriculture has made a gradual transition from nomadic herding to cash crops such as cotton and tobacco. Kazakhstan is also rich in natural resources.

HUMAN LIFE AND LIBERTY

Human rights and freedoms. Within 2 years of its independence from the Soviet Union in 1991, Kazakhstan passed a new Constitution reinforcing legal guarantees for basic personal and political freedoms and removing the legacies of Soviet rule. However, the Constitution establishes a presidential form of government with only few legislative checks on executive power. The new Committee for National Security is a clone of the old KGB and it has the authority to deny the citizens certain rights, such as that of free travel. Criminal police continue occasionally to arrest people and search their homes without warrants. A huge bureaucracy has successfully stifled the growth of economic freedoms while state ownership of printing facilities has the same dampening effect on press freedoms. All religious freedoms are guaranteed. Muslim fundamentalists have not made headway into this largely secular society. A number of human rights organizations are active in the country.

NON-CHRISTIAN RELIGIONS

Islam was first brought to Kazakhstan by Arabs and Samanids soon after 700 AD. Pre-Islamic Zoroastrianism soon died out, but not the local shamanistic ethnoreligion which is still present today. By the 9th century, only the national leaders and those settled in towns were Muslims, while most people, nomads, remained shamanists. Despite that, Islam has shaped national culture and identity since the early Middle Ages. As in the other Central Asian countries, most Muslim are Hanafi Sunni.

In the 19th century, Russian tsars, hoping to bring greater order to and control over the unruly Kazaks, encouraged them to become Muslim—which is ironic considering the tight link between the Russian throne and the Russian church. The Russian authorities sent zealous Tatars to convert the nomads, they built mosques, and they provided an imam for every tribal unit. The plan succeeded; nearly all Kazakhs became Muslims. Tatar became an official and commonly-used language between tribes and clans. But then official policy was reversed in mid-century. The Russians suddenly made it difficult or impossible to build new mosques and set harsh restrictions on the number of imams allowed. This time they sent Christian missionaries to Kazakhstan, but these gleaned little fruit from a people who by that time were uninterested in changing their religion once again.

In the Soviet era, heavy-handed efforts to control or eradicate Islam met with little real success. Atheist education did not attract Kazakh youth. Though most mosques were closed and the number of officially-registered mullahs was decimated, they were quickly replaced by a large number of itinerant, unofficial, self-ordained mullahs who taught the faith and led religious ceremonies in cemeteries. Sufi groups, influential in the religious life of Kazakhstan for centuries, were considered a particularly dangerous threat to communism and Soviet control, were branded as criminals, and were severely persecuted. The Sufi tariqa were small, well-disciplined, closed societies; anti-Marxist alternative pockets of communalism. Their members engaged in extensive and unrelenting pro-Islam, anti-Russian, and anti-communist activism. Sufis rebuilt and maintained the tombs of Muslims saints, important centers for devotion. From the 18th century through the 20th, Islam profited from its identification with resistance against Russian, and Soviet, domination. Toward the end of the Soviet era, as the communist state power grew more dim, overt Islamic activity quickly grew more bright. In 1986-1987, 20 mosques were opened.

But Communism certainly left its mark. At independence in 1991 the country included a large number of younger adults and youth who were Kazakh in ethnic identity but Russian in language, Russian in education, and nonreligious or atheist in religion. Their newly-reborn ethnic allegiance attracted them more to Islam than to any alternative. A common proverb states, 'To be Kazakh is to be Muslim'. The Muslim Religious Board of Central Asia of the Soviet era has been replaced with a national Islamic Board that serves to foster the peaceful relationship between mosque and state. There have been loud, radical demonstrations, and Iran has screened TV programs celebrating their Islamic republic, but for the most part the Muslims of Kazakhstan have projected little political force.

Former capital, Almaty (Alma Ata).

With independence has come a dramatic revival of Islam. Certain nearly-forgotten festivals, holidays, and practices returned. The Islamic Center in Almaty reported in 1996 that there were 4,000 mosques in the country—hundreds, maybe thousands of them built since independence. Other Muslim countries are contributing to this renaissance. Many Kazakhs made the hajj to Mecca in 1992, thanks to the generosity of the king of Saudi Arabia. They were the first known to make the pilgrimage since 1926. New Islamic colleges were founded, staffed by professors from Turkey. Other expatriates began teaching Arabic to boys. In many towns Turkish clergy trained their Kazakh counterparts. Saudi Arabia sent a million copies of the Koran into Kazakhstan, accompanied by teachers to explain it. United Arab Emirates launched an ambitious scheme to insure that every city and village, in every oblast (province), had a mosque. It included providing $25,000 to each city, and establishing an Islamic school in every oblast seat to train mullahs. Mullahs have also been trained elsewhere. In 1995 alone, 120 mullahs who graduated from schools in Turkey, Pakistan, and Egypt came to Kazakhstan to found new mosques in places without them.

The Muslims of Kazakhstan are generally considered less religious than those in other Central Asian republics. One estimate has it that only 20-40% of Kazakhstan's Muslims pray daily, and even the estimated 50% who keep the fast of Ramadan do so for only 3 days. Muslims in the southern and western regions of the country tend to be more orthodox and diligent in their observance, and keeping the full fast, for example, is more common there, as are religious weddings and burials. The Islam of the ordinary Kazakh, and of other Central Asian peoples in the country, tends to be mixed with many elements of folk religion. People fear the evil eye and wear protective charms, they fear Satan's thwarting power if they speak their hopes aloud, they serve the spirits of their ancestors by offering special bread to them, and they look to their ancestors for good fortune. Though the nation was 94% Muslim at the start of this century, by 1995 there was no majority faith in Kazakhstan, with Islam accounting for only about 37% of the population. This change was primarily due to immigration and secondarily due to the secularizing influences of communism and modernity.

Other religions. An ancient and distinctive strain of shamanism persists especially in the rural areas. People trust in a shaman's influence over good and evil spirits, and with a shaman's help seek the help of auraks, or ancestral spirits, in times of dire trouble. Active and visible missionary work by the Unification Church, the Hare Krishnas, and other new groups has borne some fruit in the newly-independent nation. Eighteen religious groups, including Hare Krishnas, Zoroastrians from India, and Great White Brotherhood adherents from Russia, participated in a high-profile Congress of Spiritual Concord in Almaty in 1992. The religious climate of the country is affected by the many healers, astrologers, and New Religionists appearing often on radio and TV. In 1995 there were about 14,000 Jews in Kazakhstan and about 17,000 Buddhists, the latter largely among peoples of East Asian origin.

Russian Orthodox Church. Russian and Ukrainian believers in Almaty.

CHRISTIANITY

Due to the missionary work of Nestorians along the Great Silk Road, many Central Asians were Christian in the 4th century AD, but this early Christian presence disappeared under the pressure of Sufi Muslim progress in the 6th and 7th centuries.

ORTHODOXY. Kazakh rulers sought protection from the Russian tsar against threatening Kalmyks in 1730. By 1860 Kazakhstan was completely under Russian rule. A thin line of immigrants, nearly all Orthodox, soon widened to a great flow, and the nomadic Kazakh way of life was threatened as Russians seized land for farms. Eventually the numbers were large enough for a special diocese of the Russian Orthodox Church, based in Almaty, to be established.

Country summary. **Worlds A, B, C by ethnolinguistic peoples, cities, and major civil divisions in Kazakhstan.**

World	PEOPLES Num	Pop 2000	C%	Christians	E%	U%	Unevangelized
A	25	10,047,790	0.08	7,692	43	57	5,710,654
B	10	4,955,385	36.62	1,814,492	98	2	84,061
C	14	1,219,389	63.12	769,621	100	0	4,498
Total	**49**	**16,222,564**	**15.98**	**2,591,805**	**64**	**36**	**5,799,213**

World	CITIES Num	Pop 2000	C%	Christians	E%	U%	Unevangelized
A	12	945,633	1.08	10,225	45	55	523,398
B	22	6,504,681	19.22	1,250,509	68	32	2,062,002
C	0	0	0.00	0	0	0	0
Total	**34**	**7,450,314**	**16.92**	**1,260,734**	**65**	**35**	**2,585,400**

World	CIVIL DIVISIONS Num	Pop 2000	C%	Christians	E%	U%	Unevangelized
A	2	2,380,402	5.00	119,020	44	56	1,327,928
B	14	13,842,161	17.86	2,472,783	68	32	4,471,284
C	0	0	0.00	0	0	0	0
Total	**16**	**16,222,563**	**15.98**	**2,591,803**	**64**	**36**	**5,799,212**

Because of Stalin's suspicions, tens of thousands of Ukrainians and other Orthodox, as well as Catholics and German Lutherans, were deported to Kazakhstan around the time of World War II. Another large wave of Russian immigration, planting both farms and factories, followed that war, until ethnic Kazakhs became a minority in the nation.

The tide has turned somewhat since 1991. Emigration of non-ethnic-Kazakhs, and thus of Orthodox, has been vast, though the Orthodox Churches have also received many new members who have converted from atheism or non-religion. In the early 1990s the large Orthodox cathedral building in Almaty was returned to the church after serving as a museum for decades, and renovations were begun to restore it for religious purposes. In 1990 the Russian Orthodox Church was more than twice the size of any other Orthodox body in the country. The 2 Ukrainian churches, together with nearly 500,000 affiliated, comprised the second largest group. Greek, Armenian, Bulgarian, Georgian, Old Ritualist, and other Orthodox churches also suffered losses from emigration, especially since independence.

CATHOLIC CHURCH. Polish Catholics had built churches in the southeast of Kazakhstan before 1800, and Germans from Odessa had established Catholic villages before 1900. Soviet authorities tended to be more severe against Catholics in Kazakhstan than in the other Central Asian republics. Every church was destroyed. In 1981 there were only 15 priests in the country, almost all of them elderly and with prison and labor camp experience. Within 10 years that entire group had died or emigrated. By 1996 there were 33 priests, from America, Canada, South Korea, Poland, the Czech Republic, and Germany. In 1991 the Vatican appointed an apostolic administrator of Kazakhstan, with responsibility also over Catholics in Kyrgyzstan, Tajikistan, Turkmenistan, and Uzbekistan. In 1995 he oversaw a flock in Kazakhstan of about 500,000.

The Holy See has diplomatic relations with Kazakhstan and in AD 2000 is represented to government and the Catholic hierarchy by a nuncio residing in Almaty.

PROTESTANTISM. Probably the first Protestant missionary to the Kazaks was George Hunter of the CIM, who evangelized them in Sinkiang. As with Catholics, unregistered Baptists and certain other Protestants suffered more severe persecution than in neighboring republics. Boldness grew during Glasnost. In 1988 Baptists in Karaganda ventured onto the streets for open evangelism and several ethnic Kazakhs were converted. During the Millennium celebrations of that same year, local authorities allowed numerous open baptisms at a lake in a city park.

In the 1990s a new Protestant presence entered the country, as a number of Christians from the West came to assist national development in medicine, education, and business. Early in this movement, 4 of the 10 expatriate groups involved were Korean. The government formally welcomed this assistance through its cooperation with, and participation in, the 'Kazakh-American Festival' of 1991, which brought in 300 American Christian professionals to hold seminars and lead events in the fields of business, education, medicine, media, sports, performing arts, TV, crafts, and construction. Many expatriate Evangelicals live in Kazakhstan and serve under the Kazakh-American Joint Venture (SENIM), a humanitarian organization that includes workers from the Navigators, CCC, OM, YWAM, SBC-IMB, FI, PCA, and others. Another prominent venture is the Small Business Training Center with hundreds of students, most studying English.

Some new, independent, Evangelical and Charismatic churches have arisen in the 1990s, some experiencing rapid growth. One, Grace Church, was founded by a Korean missionary in 1990. Within 6 years it had grown to an ethnically diverse congregation of 4,000, was sponsoring regular large-scale evangelistic events, and was performing a variety of social ministries. Another church, led by a 20-year-old pastor, began with 12 members and in 3 years had 800 members, 200 enrolled in its Bible School, and 7 daughter churches recently planted. Most of this growth has been among Russian, other Slavic peoples, and Koreans. The greatest factor affecting the Protestant presence in Kazakhstan since independence, however, has been the massive emigration of Germans, a large percentage of whom have been Lutheran. About 65% of the German population left the country in the early 1990s. Emigration of Russians, Ukrainians, and other non-Central-Asian peoples is also strong. The Evangelical Lutheran Church was easily the largest Protestant denomination in 1970, and by 1995 it was still larger than the Baptists (AUCECB).

Evangelical Lutheran Church. Lutherans in Almaty. From 1990, 150,000 German farmers emigrated to Germany.

Renewal movements. In the 1990s the Pentecostal/Charismatic Renewal continued to spread rapidly across most older churches, and numbered over 82,000 adherents (of whom <1% Pentecostals, 54% Charismatics, and 46% Independents).

Indigenous missions. Missionary outreach from Kazakhstan has been almost non-existent. Some Russian, German, and Korean Christians have recently gained a missions vision and are involved in outreach to Muslims in Kazakhstan.

Independents. Students at Agape Bible School, Almaty.

CHURCH AND STATE

All religions were suppressed in the Soviet era. When the constitution of the country was under revision in 1992, the Kazakh Ulama Council did not seek for an Islamic state but only that government and political parties would not interfere in matters of religion. They did, however, propose amendments that would protect ethnic Kazakhs' traditional preference for Islam and hinder activities promoting conversion. Despite the traditional connection of the Kazakh people with Islam, the fact that neither Muslims nor ethnic Kazakhs constitute a majority in the country is likely to foster official religious toleration. Religious freedom is constitutionally guaranteed. Kazakhstan does not issue missionary visas to Christian workers, but national and expatriate Christians have been unhindered in expressing and propagating their faith. In the mid-1990s some village Christians were attacked and beaten. Local authorities placidly witnessed these events and added threats of their own. Such isolated incidents apparently do not reflect any formal or informal national policy. Some newer Evangelical groups with ethnic Kazakh convert members were under government surveillance in the mid-1990s.

BROADCASTING AND MEDIA

Despite the many restrictions on ministry in Kazakhstan, much evangelism has been accomplished especially by broadcasting. Shortwave radio programs in central Asian languages (Kazakh, Tajik, Uzbek, Kyrgyz, Uighur) can be received from TWR (Guam), FEBC (Saipan) and HCJB (Ecuador). IBRA-produced programs in Turkish, Arabic, Azeri, and Farsi can be picked up from powerful Radio Moscow stations in Krasnodar, St Petersburg and Samara. Turkish-language programs can be received from TWR (Monaco) and TWR (Albania).

CBN's *700 Club*, animated specials and *Answers* program are available via television in a weekly basis in virtually every viewing region. The 'Jesus' Film has been shown to 6.2 million, most through television broadcasts. Other Christian programs are available via satellite.

Sick Kazakh children from Aral Sea disaster receive scriptures from the Bible Society of Kazakhstan.

INTERDENOMINATIONAL ORGANIZATIONS

Many expatriate Christians, Christian development ventures, and newer churches communicate with each other and plan joint activities through the somewhat informal Kazakh Partnership. At a meeting in 1995, representatives of 32 organizations and churches signed a document of cooperation. One initial joint project has been to prepare a list of Christian resources in the Kazakh language. The Bible Society of Kazakstan was established in 1994 as an ecumenical project with participation by the Orthodox, Baptists, Seventh-day Adventists, Pentecostals, and others.

FUTURE TRENDS AND PROSPECTS

Though Christians are expected to make a slight rebound in the post-Communist period, a decline is expected after AD 2000 due to the emigration of Russian Orthodox Christians. Islam, 26.9% of the population in 1970 will probably grow to 50% by 2025.

Islam could grow rapidly after 2025 with possibly up to 75% of the population professing to be Muslims by AD 2050. Christianity, if confined to Russians and Koreans, will not likely grow beyond 20% in that period.

BIBLIOGRAPHY

Kazak social structure. A. E. Hudson. New Haven, CT: Department of Anthropology, Yale University Press, 1938.

Liki baptizma: pulitsisticheskie etiudy o baptistakh v Kazakhstane. A. Sulatskov. Alma-Ata: Kazakhstan, 1982. 359p.

'Obraz zhizni, religiia, ateizm: obshchee i osobennoe v obraze zhizni i religioznykh verovaniiakh kazakhov i voprosy ateisticheskogo vospitaniia,' K. S. Shulembaev, Alma-Ata: Kazakhstan, 1983. 172p.

'Popular Islam in Central Asia and Kazakhstan,' V. N. Basilov, *Journal of the Institute of Muslim Minority Affairs*, 8 (January 1987), 7–17.

'Predstavleniia, kulty, obriady u kazakhov: v kontekste bytovogo islama v iuzhnom Kazakhstane v kontse XIX–XX vv.,' R. M. Mustafina, Alma-Ata: Qazaq universiteti, 1992. 172p.

'Sovremennaia khristianskaia propoved: sushchnost i tendentsii: na materialakh khristianskogo sektantstva v Kazakhstane,' I. Trofimov, Alma-Ata: Kazakhstan, 1986. 100p.

The Kazakhs. M. B. Olcott. Stanford, CA: Hoover Institution Press, 1987.

'The survival of Islam in the Soviet Union: the forgotten Muslims of Central Asia and Kazakhstan,' J. Thrower, *Scottish journal of religious studies*, 8 (Autumn 1987), 109–20.

'Unofficial Islam: a Muslim minority in the USSR,' J. Soper, *Religion in Communist lands*, 7, 4 (Winter 1979), 226–31. (Deals with Kazakhstan).

Country Table 2. Organized churches and denominations in Kazakhstan.

Official name (bold type = church with over 10% of affiliated) 1	*Begun* 2	*Type* 3	*Counc* 4	*Congs* 5	*Adults* 6	*Affiliated 1970* 7	*Affiliated 1995* 8	*G%* 9	*Names, notes, and other statistics* (see Codebook, Part 3) 10
Armenian Apostolic Church		O-Arm	E....	7	7,000	22,000	11,000	0.05	Armenians. M=AAC(Echmiadzin, Armenia).
Bulgarian Orthodox Ch		O-Bul	M....	3	3,000	1,000	5,000	0.05	Bulgarians, under P Sofia.
Catholic Church: AA Kazakhstan	1965	R-LEr	Bs	36	200,000	20,000	500,000	13.74	40% Ukrainians (Uniates), 15% Polish, 9% Byelorussians. 10n, 22x, 23m, 30w, 3317Yy.
Christ Groups	c1990	I-3hZ	x....	25	600	–	2,000	20.00	Home churches for isolated converts after nationwide EHC campaign.
Christians of Apostolic Faith	1987	I-3cZ	.....	60	1,300	–	2,000	12.50	Kazakh converts through consortium of agencies: M=IBT,CCCI,PI,FI,WEC,CSI.
Church of God	1935	P-Pe3	Z....	5	200	5,000	500	-8.80	Mainly Germans. Much emigration.
Council of Chs of Ev Christians-Baptists		I-Bap	.....	30	10,100	14,000	14,400	0.05	Unregistered and harassed under Communism.
Evangelical Lutheran Ch of Kazakstan		P-Lut	.....	20	30,000	195,000	50,000	0.05	*GELC.* Nearly all Germans. Vast emigration to Germany. M=LCMS.
Georgian Orthodox Church		O-Geo	M....	4	2,280	3,700	3,500	0.05	Migrant Georgians from Georgia.
Greek Orthodox Church		O-Gre	C....	6	15,000	10,000	30,000	0.05	Greeks who still organize their own churches.
Jehovah's Witnesses		m-Jeh	x....	20	1,050	1,000	3,500	0.05	Witnessing door to door.
Korean Baptist Church		I-Bap	.....	3	450	200	1,130	0.05	Church among ethnic Koreans.
Korea Methodist Ch	1937	I-Met	.....	10	4,000	1,000	7,000	8.09	1937: 1,500 ethnic Koreans with Methodist roots forcibly transplanted from Korea.
Korean Presbyterian Church		I-Ref	.....	4	800	300	2,000	0.05	Ethnic Koreans in Reformed churches.
Mennonite Church		P-Men	.....	20	1,000	6,330	3,330	0.05	Mainly Germans. Much emigration. M=MBMS(USA).
New Apostolic Church	c1985	I-3aX	x....	35	2,500	–	4,823	10.00	*NAC/NAK.* M=Neuapostolische Kirche(HQ Zurich).
Old Ritualist Church		I-OBe	x....	25	17,500	30,000	25,000	0.05	*Old Believers.* Many Russians.
Russian Orthodox Ch: D Almaty & K		O-Rus	M....	45	1,200,000	1,950,000	1,900,000	0.05	Russians, Ukrainians, Byelorussians, Chuvash, Mordvinians. Mass emigration from 1991.
Seventh-day Adventist Church	1975	P-Adv	.....	3	1,000	–	2,000	5.00	Many Russians from ex-Soviet days.
Ukrainian Orthodox Church	c1980	I-Ukr	.....	10	20,000	–	40,000	6.67	Schismatic body.
Ukrainian Orthodox P Kiev	c1900	I-Ukr	.....	50	300,000	50,000	450,000	9.19	Since 1990, the majority church of Ukraine, a schism from ROC (P-Moscow).
Union of Ev Christians-Baptists of K		P-Bap	T....	56	2,792	72,000	8,000	0.05	*AUCECB.* Largely Russians, Ukrainians, other Europeans, but emigrating en masse.
Other independent Orthodox bodies	c1968	I-Ort	.....	30	20,000	2,000	36,000	12.26	Total about 6, including: ROCOR, UAOC, Byelorussian AOC.
Other pentecostal/charismatic chs	c1971	I-3pZ	.....	53	1,250	–	3,130	4.17	Including Pentecostal Union, Association of Vineyard Chs (1 church).
Other Protestant churches	c1990	P-	.....	50	1,500	–	3,000	20.00	Total 40, including ELCE,MCE,ELCL,RCL,CWE,IPKh,PCA.
Totals				**610**	**1,843,322**	**2,383,530**	**3,107,313**		

Churches, members, growth, 1900-2025	*Congs*	*Adults*	*Affiliated*	*G%*	*Total denominations*	*6 Megablocs:* O	R	A	P	I	m
Total churches, members, and denominations (mid-1900)	50	75,000	111,000	4.48	1	1	0	0	0	0	0
Total churches, members, and denominations (mid-1970)	418	1,609,910	2,383,530	4.48	18	5	1	0	4	7	1
Total churches, members, and denominations (mid-1990)	500	1,853,000	3,123,000	1.36	73	5	1	0	44	22	1
Total churches, members, and denominations (mid-1995)	610	1,843,322	3,107,313	-0.10	75	5	1	0	45	23	1
Total churches, members, and denominations (mid-2000)	650	1,538,000	2,591,803	-3.56	77	5	1	0	46	24	1
Total churches, members, and denominations (mid-2025)	600	1,577,000	2,658,000	0.10	139	7	1	0	60	70	1

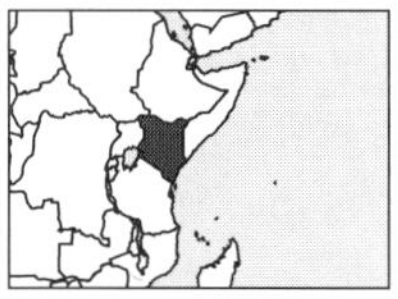

KENYA

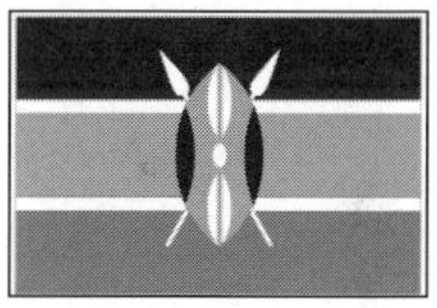

SECULAR DATA, AD 2000

STATE
Official name: Jamhuri ya Kenya/The Republic of Kenya.
Short name: Kenya. **Adjective of nationality:** Kenyan.
Flag: Black, red, and green bands separated by white stripes; red, black, and white shield over crossed white spears in centre.
Area: 582,646 sq. km. (224,961 sq. mi.).
Government: Multiparty republic, since 1991 (1887 British possession, 1920 British crown colony with coastal protectorate, 1963 Independence (Uhuru) as parliamentary republic, 1969 one-party republic).
Legislature: National Assembly, 202 members.
Official language: English.
Monetary unit: 1 Kenya shilling (K Sh) = 100 cents. **US$1=** K Sh 60.23.
Chief cities: NAIROBI 2,320,000; Mombasa 740,871; Kisumu 283,517; Nakuru 172,553; Machakos 162,204.
Political divisions: 8 provinces.
Armed forces: 24,000.

DEMOGRAPHY
Population: 30,080,000.
Population density: 51.6/sq. km. (133.7/sq. mi.).
Under 15 years: 12,944,000.
Growth rate p.a.: 1.63% (births 31.96, deaths 14.06).
Mortality: Infant, per 1,000: 63.5; **Maternal per 100,000:** 650.0.
Life expectancy: 48 (male 48, female 49).
Household size: 6.2. **Floor area per person, sq.m:** 10.0.
Major languages: Swahili, English, Kikuyu, Luo, Luhya, Kamba, Kalenjin, Gusli, Somali, Turkana, Maasai, Hindi, Gujarati, Punjabi, Taita, and about 50 smaller languages.
Urban dwellers: 33.10%. **Urban growth rate p.a.:** 5.0%.
Labor force: 39%.

ETHNOLINGUISTIC PEOPLES
19.0% Kikuyu; 13.2% Luo; 10.7% Kamba; 7.7% Central Luhya; 6.2% Kisii (Gusii).

ECONOMY
National income p.a. per person: US$280; **per family:** US$1,736.

EDUCATION
Adult literacy: 78% (male 86%, female 70%). **Schools:** 18,506.
Universities: 14. **School enrolment:** female/male: 71%/73%.

HEALTH
Access to health services: 77%. **Access to safe water:** 53%.
Hospitals: 877 (14 beds per 10,000). **Doctors:** 3,794.
Blind: 65,000. **Deaf:** 1,820,400. **Murder rate:** 6.
Lepers: 120,000. **Underweight prevalence under 5:** 23%.

LITERATURE
New book titles p.a.: 4,510 (150 p.a. per million). **Periodicals:** 168.
Newspapers: 5 dailies.

COMMUNICATION (per 1,000 people)
Phones: 9 **(1% mobile). Radios:** 103. **TV sets:** 18.
Daily newspaper circulation: 13. **Computers:** 25.

REFUGEES
Alien refugees from other countries: 225,000.
Internal displacement: 210,000.

HUMAN LIFE AND LIBERTY (optimum condition=100.0%)
HDI: 46.3. **HSI:** 25.0. **HFI:** 20.0. **EFL:** 39.0.

Country status. Kenya lies astride the equator in eastern Africa between the Indian Ocean and Lake Victoria, part of which lies within its borders. Once a British colony, Kenya emerged as an independent nation in 1963 as a relatively prosperous and stable nation, although its recent history has been more turbulent. The mainstay of agricultural production are the coffee and tea crops. Tourism also plays a leading role in the economy.

HUMAN LIFE AND LIBERTY

Human need and development. About 90% of Kenyans are rural, and most of them are relatively well off by comparison with rural folks in other African countries. However, over half of the farming families live close to subsistence. There is also a smaller class of landless rural poor. A wide range of living conditions also exist among urban people. At one end of the spectrum the elite have lifestyles nearly comparable to those in the West, while the urban poor are worse off than their rural counterparts. In rural societies, women work as hard as men, although certain jobs are performed only by men and others only by women. Life in the countryside is governed by the seasons. Generally, the wet season is the time for social gatherings, ceremonies, and the dry season for hardship. Urban life is alien to the traditional and tribal ways of life. Kenyans who move to urban areas find that things like food, shelter, transportation and clothing, that were once inexpensive or free, become prohibitively costly in relation to their exiguous incomes. Because city living is precarious, men tend to come without their families or to send them back home when they become too great a financial burden. Traditional obligations are not totally rejected. Many people send money back home and also afford hospitality to kith and kin from the country seeking work in the cities. The small elite lead lives of conspicuous consumption. The penchant of the wealthiest for luxury cars, such as Mercedes-Benz, have earned them the nickname of wabenzi, in contrast to the wanachi, or common people. In urban areas about 70% of the people live in substandard housing or shanties. Generally the food supply is adequate, although poor distribution causes periodic shortages and high prices in some localities. Kenya has the second highest birth rate in the world at 3.2%. Life expectancy, at 48, is the second highest in Africa. Medical facilities compare favorably with neighboring countries. However, population per physician has increased to 10,130 in 1990 compared to 8,000 in 1970.

Country Table 1. **Religious adherents in Kenya, AD 1900-2025.**

Year	1900		1970		mid-1990		Annual change, 1990-2000				mid-1995		mid-2000		mid-2025	
Name	*Adherents*	*%*	*Adherents*	*%*	*Adherents*	*%*	*Natural*	*Conversion*	*Total*	*Rate*	*Adherents*	*%*	*Adherents*	*%*	*Adherents*	*%*
Christians	**5,000**	**0.2**	**7,299,800**	**63.5**	**18,427,000**	**78.2**	**510,787**	**32,497**	**543,284**	**2.62**	**21,426,000**	**78.7**	**23,859,839**	**79.3**	**34,222,400**	**82.0**
PROFESSION																
professing Christians	**5,000**	**0.2**	**7,299,800**	**63.5**	**18,427,000**	**78.2**	**510,787**	**32,497**	**543,284**	**2.62**	**21,426,000**	**78.7**	**23,859,839**	**79.3**	**34,222,400**	**82.0**
AFFILIATION																
unaffiliated Christians	0	0.0	1,217,016	10.6	1,281,000	5.4	35,506	-25,359	10,147	0.77	1,380,462	5.1	1,382,474	4.6	1,222,400	2.9
affiliated Christians	**5,000**	**0.2**	**6,082,784**	**52.9**	**17,146,000**	**72.8**	**475,281**	**57,856**	**533,137**	**2.74**	**20,045,538**	**73.7**	**22,477,365**	**74.7**	**33,000,000**	**79.0**
Roman Catholics	2,700	0.1	1,935,811	16.8	5,250,000	22.3	145,516	29,484	175,000	2.92	6,146,496	22.6	7,000,000	23.3	10,700,000	25.6
Independents	0	0.0	1,645,895	14.3	4,980,000	21.1	138,033	24,667	162,700	2.87	5,919,206	21.8	6,607,000	22.0	10,000,000	24.0
Protestants	300	0.0	1,666,228	14.5	4,575,000	19.4	126,807	53,193	180,000	3.37	5,542,816	20.4	6,375,000	21.2	10,250,000	24.6
Anglicans	2,000	0.1	582,600	5.1	2,300,000	9.8	63,750	6,250	70,000	2.69	2,700,000	9.9	3,000,000	10.0	4,500,000	10.8
Orthodox	0	0.0	248,000	2.2	560,000	2.4	15,522	2,478	18,000	2.83	655,000	2.4	740,000	2.5	1,300,000	3.1
Marginal Christians	0	0.0	4,250	0.0	21,000	0.1	582	318	900	3.63	25,100	0.1	30,000	0.1	60,000	0.1
doubly-affiliated	0	0.0	0	0.0	-540,000	-2.3	-14,967	-58,497	-73,464	8.97	-943,080	-3.5	-1,274,635	-4.2	-3,810,000	-9.1
Trans-megabloc groupings																
Evangelicals	2,300	0.1	1,700,000	14.8	4,945,000	21.0	137,063	43,437	180,500	3.16	5,978,541	22.0	6,750,000	22.4	10,500,000	25.2
Pentecostals/Charismatics	0	0.0	1,025,000	8.9	6,263,000	26.6	173,594	35,106	208,700	2.92	7,406,102	27.2	8,350,000	27.8	12,526,800	30.0
Great Commission Christians	**4,600**	**0.2**	**1,149,800**	**10.0**	**2,826,000**	**12.0**	**78,329**	**8,442**	**86,771**	**2.71**	**3,300,000**	**12.1**	**3,693,709**	**12.3**	**5,845,000**	**14.0**
Ethnoreligionists	2,779,700	95.9	3,228,430	28.1	2,989,900	12.7	82,872	-35,699	47,173	1.48	3,304,910	12.1	3,461,629	11.5	3,500,000	8.4
Muslims	100,000	3.5	735,800	6.4	1,680,000	7.1	46,565	4,135	50,700	2.67	1,965,000	7.2	2,187,002	7.3	3,100,000	7.4
Baha'is	0	0.0	124,000	1.1	240,000	1.0	6,652	177	6,829	2.54	278,000	1.0	308,292	1.0	550,000	1.3
Hindus	10,000	0.3	63,000	0.6	120,000	0.5	3,326	-727	2,599	1.98	135,000	0.5	145,988	0.5	200,000	0.5
Jains	3,000	0.1	31,000	0.3	48,000	0.2	1,330	-598	732	1.43	51,000	0.2	55,317	0.2	70,000	0.2
Nonreligious	0	0.0	2,000	0.0	21,000	0.1	582	518	1,100	4.30	28,000	0.1	32,003	0.1	60,000	0.1
Sikhs	2,000	0.1	13,000	0.1	23,700	0.1	657	-275	382	1.50	25,500	0.1	27,518	0.1	49,000	0.1
Jews	100	0.0	700	0.0	1,600	0.0	44	-25	19	1.11	1,700	0.0	1,786	0.0	2,500	0.0
Zoroastrians	200	0.0	270	0.0	600	0.0	17	-4	13	1.95	650	0.0	728	0.0	1,500	0.0
Buddhists	0	0.0	0	0.0	200	0.0	6	1	7	3.08	240	0.0	271	0.0	600	0.0
World A (unevangelized persons)	2,699,900	93.1	1,724,709	15.0	1,648,640	7.0	45,457	-35,248	10,209	0.61	1,741,794	6.4	1,744,640	5.8	1,586,728	3.8
World B (evangelized non-Christians)	195,100	6.7	2,473,552	21.5	3,476,360	14.8	96,594	2,751	99,345	2.56	4,047,738	14.9	4,475,521	14.9	5,946,872	14.2
World C (Christians)	5,000	0.2	7,299,800	63.5	18,427,000	78.2	510,787	32,497	543,284	2.62	21,426,000	78.7	23,859,839	79.3	34,222,400	82.0
Country's population	**2,900,000**	**100.0**	**11,498,062**	**100.0**	**23,552,000**	**100.0**	**652,838**	**0**	**652,838**	**2.48**	**27,215,533**	**100.0**	**30,080,000**	**100.0**	**41,756,000**	**100.0**

COLUMNS, ROWS.
For meanings and definitions, see Codebook (Part 3). Note that, by definition, total 'Christians' = professing + crypto-Christians, which also = affiliated + unaffiliated Christians, and also = Great Commission Christians + latent Christians. Percentages may not always total exactly, due to rounding.

CENSUSES.
Before 1948, censuses enumerated non-Africans only. **1921** (non-Africans): 20,986 Muslims, 12,284 Christians (5,701 Anglicans, 3,609 Roman Catholics, 1,037 Dutch Reformed Ch), 9,308 Hindus, 1,619 Sikhs, 688 Jains, 215 Jews, 155 Parsis, 153 nonreligious or atheists. **1926** (non-Africans): 22,615 Muslims, 15,418 Christians, 10,859 Hindus, 2,089 Sikhs, 1,405 Jains, 256 Jews, 179 Parsis. **1931** (non-Africans only; total 73,947): 36.8% Muslims, 28.9% Christians (13.2% Anglicans, 8.5% Roman Catholics, 2.8% Presbyterians), 24.9% Hindus, 6.0% Sikhs, 1.8% Jains, 0.3% Parsis. **II-VIII.1948** (including Northern Frontier District): 59.9% ethnoreligionists, 11.2% Protestants, 10.4% Anglicans, 8.6% Muslims, 8.1% Roman Catholics, 0.8% Hindus, 0.7% African indigenous, 0.2% Sikhs, 0.1% Jains, **15.VIII.1962:** 36.8% ethnoreligionists, 33.6% Protestants, Anglicans and African indigenous, 20.3% Roman Catholics, 7.9% Muslims, 1.1% Hindus and Jains, 0.3% Sikhs. The religion question was not asked after 1962.

NOTES ON RELIGIONS
BAHA'IS. Rapid growth from 166 local spiritual assemblies (1964) to 805 (1973), but then after reorganization of boundaries the total fell to 454 LSAs by 1995. Most new converts are Bantu (especially Luhya), including many former Muslims and Christians, but there are also a number of Asians, previously Hindus.

COUNTRY'S POPULATION. In 1900, 32,000 coolies imported from India were at work building the Uganda railway. After its completion in 1901, only 6,700 stayed on permanently in Kenya. In the 1911 census there were 11,886 Asians (of whom 5,939 were Muslims, 3,205 Hindus, and 97 Parsis). The table above shows the 1900 situation.

ETHNORELIGIONISTS. Animists. Tribes over 60% traditionalist in 1995: Dorobo (93% animist), El Molo (97%), Samburu (86%), Turkana (80%), Pokot (Suk) (84%), Mbere (66%), Tharaka (61%).

HINDUS. Asians (Indians), with about 2,500 Black African converts. There are over 50 different Hindu organizations in Kenya (speaking Gujarati, Hindi, Bengali, Punjabi), most cooperating in the Hindu Council of Kenya. The Arya Samaj reform movement has around 9,000 members (1,000 being Africans). ISKCON (Hare Krishna movement) began in 1971 and has about 500 African converts. These gains are offset by considerable emigration and also losses by conversion to Baha'i.

INDEPENDENTS. In about 650 denominations in 1995 (see Table 2), growing rapidly in number.

JAINS. First immigrants from India were in 1886. In 1970, 80% Svetambara sect, 20% Digambara; 50 centers in Kenya. Recently there have been numerical losses due to emigration, with some conversions to Baha'i.

MUSLIMS. In 1970, all were Africans who were Shafiite Sunnis, except for 30,800 Arabs (Shafiites), 32,000 Asian Sunnis (22,000 Shafiites, 10,000 Hanafiites), and 18,000 Asian Shias (13,000 Ismailis, 3,000 Ithna-Asharis, 2,000 Bohoras). There were also 2,000 Ahmadis (begun 1934: Qadiani Ahmadiya from Pakistan); since 1963 most Asian followers have emigrated or been expelled, leaving mainly African followers (enumerated here under Muslims although declared non-Muslims by Pakistan). *Conversions.* Although small numbers of pagans are being converted to Islam in the north, the proportion of Muslims in Kenya has declined markedly since 1948 due to (1) emigration of Somalis and other non-Kenyan Muslims: and (2) several coastal peoples formerly labelled nominal Muslims when subject to the Mombasa sultanate are now reclassifying themselves as traditional religionists (animists). A few hundred Muslims a year also are becoming Christians, almost all through church-related evangelism, and about half that number of Christians become Muslims (usually when marrying Muslim husbands). *Organized missions.* Active proselytism is under way through the Ahmadiya Muslim Mission, and also through the Bilal Muslim Mission operated by the Shia Ithna-Asharis based in Mombasa. *Hajj pilgrims to Mecca.* (1970) under 30; (1974) 531; (1975) 598; (1976) 791.

NONRELIGIOUS. Europeans and a small but growing number of African intellectuals.

PENTECOSTALS/CHARISMATICS. The Catholic Charismatic Renewal began in 1975. By 1995, there were over 60 weekly prayer groups with 3,000 attenders (47% being 15-25 years old), 31 involved priests and 3 bishops, and 1 covenant community.

PROFESSING CHRISTIANS. Persons publicly professing to be Christians. Amongst other Christian and quasi-Christian groupings, this category includes 3,400 Freemasons, a quasi-religious male secret brotherhood begun in Nairobi in 1905 and now with 36 lodges; mostly British members, but with some Hindu, Ismaili, nonreligious and other non-Christian members.

SIKHS. From 21,169 in 1962, there was a decline by emigration to 13,000 in 1970. In 1995 there was a large temple in Nairobi and 21 gurdwaras (centers) throughout Kenya. There are several hundred Africans interested in Sikhism, but full acceptance into the Khalsa is not encouraged.

Great Commission Instrument Panel: status of Kenya (for explanation see start of Part 4)

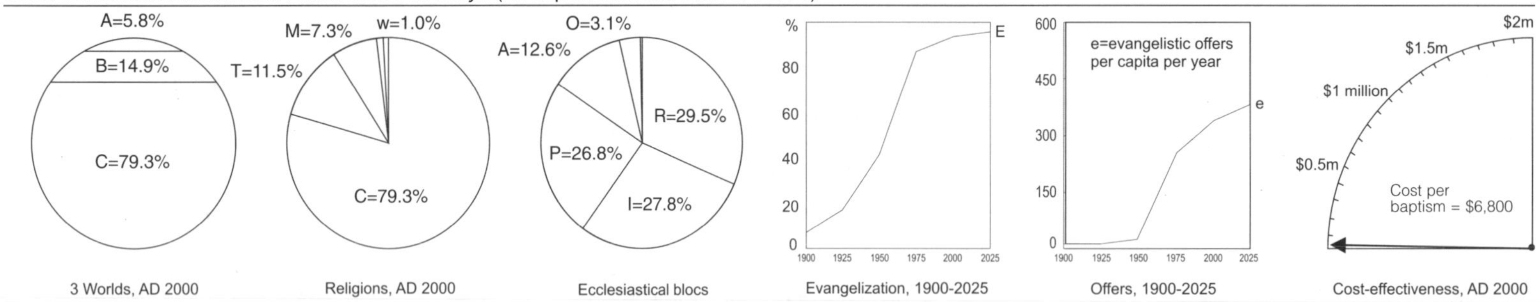

Human rights and freedoms. Although basic human rights are more widely exercised in Kenya following the reintroduction of multiparty elections in 1991, there are serious abridgments under the auspices of a centralized presidency and a puppet legislature and judiciary. Ethnic clashes, in some cases instigated by the government, have become frequent. Kikuyus, Luos and Luhyas are targets of ethnic terrorism, and their homes and farms are burned to make them flee. An increasing number of public executions are carried out by mobs. Conditions in prisons are harsh and sexual abuse is common, and rarely punished. Suspects are often held incommunicado for 2 to 3 weeks before being brought to trial. Persons may be detained indefinitely without charges or trial for the 'preservation of public security'. The judiciary is effectively an arm of the executive, and in 1989 the High Court ruled that the courts have no power to enforce the Bill of Rights. The president has extensive powers over the judiciary, and appoints and dismisses the chief justice, judges and attorney general. Defendants are occasionally denied the right to employ legal counsel of their own choice. Security forces reportedly employ a variety of surveillance techniques and a network of informers, and are empowered to conduct searches without warrants. The constitution provides for freedom of speech and press but there are numerous de jure and de facto restrictions on the exercise of those freedoms. Government harasses and intimidates the press through threats of physical violence, arbitrary arrests, impoundment of printed materials, and pressure on those making editorial decisions. A new libel law mandates crippling minimum penalties on any one convicted of defamation. Rumormongering also is a crime brought against political opponents in order to stifle criticism. The government controls and owns the single radio station and its affiliate television station. A second television station adheres to self-imposed guidelines under threat of state sanctions. Freedom of assembly is seriously limited by the Public Order and Police Act which gives authorities power to control public gatherings, and deny official permission to opposition rallies. As an ethnically diverse country, Kenya does not officially countenance discrimination based on religion, race or sex. The dominant indigenous ethnic group is the Kikuyu and Asians are the richest foreign group, but neither exercises any disproportionate political power.

Human environment. Kenya encompasses a variety of climates and habitats and has some of the best known game preserves in the world. However, it is subject to the triple threats of soil degradation, deforestation, and pollution Wildlife is a major revenue earner, but at the same time, the tourism that it generates affects the ecosystems negatively.

Country summary. **Worlds A, B, C by ethnolinguistic peoples, cities, and major civil divisions in Kenya.**

	PEOPLES							CITIES							CIVIL DIVISIONS						
World	Num	Pop 2000	C%	Christians	E%	U%	Unevangelized	Num	Pop 2000	C%	Christians	E%	U%	Unevangelized	Num	Pop 2000	C%	Christians	E%	U%	Unevangelized
A	45	1,596,415	0.80	12,793	41	59	934,023	0	0	0.00	0	0	0	0	0	0	0.00	0	0	0	0
B	42	4,104,050	30.62	1,256,677	81	19	776,316	1	740,871	50.00	370,436	72	28	203,814	1	2,596,237	55.00	1,427,930	74	26	662,300
C	37	24,379,903	86.99	21,207,897	100	0	31,746	6	3,187,496	75.42	2,403,903	97	3	105,731	7	27,484,135	76.59	21,049,435	96	4	1,079,785
Total	**124**	**30,080,368**	**74.72**	**22,477,367**	**94**	**6**	**1,742,085**	**7**	**3,928,367**	**70.62**	**2,774,339**	**92**	**8**	**309,545**	**8**	**30,080,372**	**74.72**	**22,477,365**	**94**	**6**	**1,742,085**

Traditional stilt dancers greet Pope John Paul II on his official visit to Kenya, 1980.

NON-CHRISTIAN RELIGIONS

Ethnoreligions or Traditional religions, adhered to by over 95% of the population in the year 1900, had declined to 60% in 1948, to 37% in 1962 to about 27% in 1972 and to 12.3% in 1995. The peoples most resistant to conversion are the Samburu (still 97% traditionalists), Turkana (96%), Pokot or Suk (90%), Giriama (82%) and Maasai (78%). Other peoples with traditionalists over 50% include the Mbere, Tugen, Elgeyo, and Meru. As in other parts of Africa, beliefs relating to mystical power (uganga in Kiswahili), medicine men (ombila in Luhya), diviners (chebsageyot among the Kipsigis), taboo (kwer in Luo) and witchcraft (murogi in Kikuyu) continue to exert their influence. The ancestral cult is less prevalent than formerly, whereas God receives more emphasis. All of Kenya's peoples have a traditional belief in a supreme being who is known by different names: Akuj (Turkana), Asis (Dorobo, Elgeyo, Kipsigis, Marakwet, Nandi), Engai (Maasai), Erioba (Gusii), Mlungu (Taita), Mulungu (Digo, Kamba, Rabai), Mungu (Swahili), Murungu (Meru), Muungu (Pokomo), Ngai (Embu, Kikuyu, Mbere), Nyasaye (Luhya, Luo), Tororut (Pokot), Wah (Rendille), Waqa (Boran, Galla) and Wele (Luhya). Some Kenyan peoples associate God with the phenomena of nature. The Suk speak of the moon as God's firstborn son. Engai in Maasai means sky and rain as well as god, while Asis (Nandi) and Erioba (Kuria) refer to both God and the sun. Several attempts have been made to renew traditional religions over the last 3 decades. In 1944, the Religion of the Ancestral Spirits (Dini ya Msambwa) arose in western Kenya, followed by witchcraft eradication movements from the coast led by Kabwere and Kajiwe in the mid-1960s. In 1971, the Medicine Men's Society (Waganga wa Miti Shamba) was organized and registered with government, with 110 medicine men as members, most Kamba.

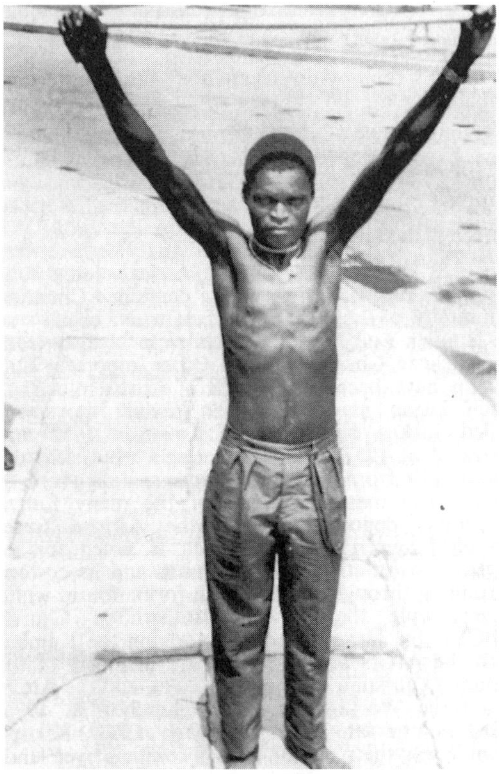

Ethnoreligionists. Kajiwe Washe, a traditional religious practitioner of witchcraft eradication, in action as a witchfinder at the Kenya coast.

Islam is strongest at the coast and in northeast Kenya, with its main strength among the Somalis (100% Muslim), Digo (91%), Boran (90%), Pokomo (85%) and Duruma (25%). Islam has had little or no success among the large and rapidly growing peoples of the interior, resulting in its declining in percentage relative to the population since 1945. Since Independence in 1963, large numbers of Coastal peoples formerly classified as Muslims when subject to the Mombasa sultanate have reclassified themselves as traditional religionists, and numbers of Muslim Somalis have returned to Somalia. In 1995, Muslims were estimated to make up 7% of the total population. Muslims of Arab (30,800) and African (637,000) origin are mostly Sunnis and Shafiites, while Asian Muslims (50,000) are divided into Shafiite (22,000), Hanafite (10,000), and Shia (18,000) communities. Shias are further subdivided as Ismaili Khojas (13,000), Ithna-Asharis (3,000), and Dawoodi Bohoras (2,000). In addition, there are 2,000 Africans who have become Ahmadis.

Hindus. Three Africans, who have become Hindus, in Arya Samaj temple, Nairobi. About 2,500 Black Kenyans have become converts to Arya Samaj or Hare Krishna.

Hinduism, Jainism, and ***Sikhism*** are confined almost entirely to the Asian population. There are no African Jains or Sikhs and not more than 2,500 African Hindus, most of whom are converts to the Arya Samaj plus a few to the Hare Krishna movement. In 1995, Kenya had 135,000 Hindus, 51,000 Jains and 26,000 Sikhs.

Other religions are Baha'i (278,000), Judaism (1,700), and Zoroastrianism (650); only Baha'i has an African constituency, most of its members being Luhya Bantu.

CHRISTIANITY

The Christian faith first came to Kenya in 1498, when Vasco da Gama set anchor off Malindi bay. Contacts were made with the local population, followed later by evangelistic work at various points along the coast. By the end of the 16th century there were missionary priests at Lamu and Augustinian friars in Mombasa with 600 African converts. This mission later collapsed and Catholic work lapsed until started again by Holy Ghost Fathers in 1889. Anglican activity began in Mombasa with the arrival of CMS missionary J. L. Krapf in 1844, and in 1862, British Methodists appeared on the scene. Scottish Presbyterians entered in 1891, followed by the Africa Inland Mission in 1895; and the opening of the railway to Kisumu in 1902 resulted in a Protestant influx into western Kenya. The first of Kenya's many independent indigenous churches, the Nomiya Luo Mission, was begun in Nyanza in 1914.

African response to Christianity was instantaneous and immense from the earliest days of this mass influx of missions, the number of converts doubling or even tripling every year for the first 10 years after 1900. By 1916, a mass movement into all the churches, Protestant, Anglican and Catholic, had begun, and by 1948, 30% of the population professed to be Christians, this figure rising to 54% in 1962 to over 63% in 1970 and to nearly 80% by AD 2000. By 1995, 800 distinct denominations had begun, of which 710 were independent indigenous churches. In 1995, about 20,045,000 persons (73.7% of the total population) were affiliated to churches of which 6,147,000 were Roman Catholics, 5,543,000 Protestants, 5,919,000 Independents, 2,700,000 Anglicans, and 655,000 Orthodox.

As to ethnic compositions, Christianity has now become the majority religion of Kenya's largest peoples, each with over one million in population: the Bantu-speaking Luhya (94% Christian in 1972), Gusii (82%), Kikuyu (77%) and Kamba (61%); as well as the Nilotic Luo (89%).

CATHOLIC CHURCH. Following the recommencement of its mission in 1889, Catholicism grew rapidly under the Holy Ghost priests at the coast and among the Kamba; Consolata priests in Kikuyu country; and Mill Hill priests in western Kenya, in addition to many institutes of brothers and sisters. Growth became even more rapid after World War II. In 1948, 8.1% of the populations professed to be Catholics, rising to 20.3% in 1962 and to about 22.6% in 1995. However, a major problem for the Catholic Church has been its slow progress in the development of indigenous vocations. Although the first African priests were ordained in 1927, in AD 2000 less than half of the country's 1,600 priests were Africans, keeping the Catholic Church still heavily dependent on foreign missionaries and village catechists. On the other hand, the church has been much more successful in challenging Kenyan women and girls to enter the sisterhood. African priests have no indigenous religious congregations of their own and, except for 5 in monasteries, all Kenyan priests are secular. In contrast, 5 indigenous congregations of brothers and 11 of sisters have been founded in Kenya. Sisters led the way founding a sodality in 1918 called the Immaculate Heart of Mary Sisters, which became a religious congregation in 1927. The first African mother superior was elected in 1946.

In 1953, the Catholic ecclesiastical province of Kenya was created, with one archdiocese (Nairobi) and 3 dioceses: Kisumu, Meru, and Nyeri. By 1979, the work had expanded to 14 dioceses and prefectures. The first Kenyan bishop was consecrated in 1957, and in 1974, there were 7 African bishops, including the cardinal archbishop of Nairobi. In 1980 a major event took place with the official state visit of pope John Paul II.

The Holy See has diplomatic relations with Kenya and in AD 2000 is represented to government and the Catholic hierarchy by a pro-nuncio residing in Nairobi.

PROTESTANT CHURCHES. The largest Protestant body is the Africa Inland Church (AIC) which owes its origin to the activity of the interdenominational Africa Inland Mission from 1895 and which became autonomous in 1971. The AIC consists of 4,325 congregations divided into 10 regions and 67 districts. Theological education is provided at Scott Theological College in Machakos, in addition to 7 Bible schools, functioning in various parts of the country. The church also sponsors 667 primary schools and is responsible for 30 harambee (self-help) schools. Other activities include Kenya's largest religious broadcasting studio, a press and a number of medical institutions.

The most important Protestant churches of Central Province are the Presbyterian Church of East Africa (PCEA) among the Kikuyu and the Methodist Church in Kenya (MCK) among the Meru; the latter also maintains work at the coast and in the lower Tana river area. The PCEA was established as an independent body in 1943, while the MCK became an autonomous Methodist conference in 1967. Both churches are heavily involved in education and social service. The PCEA sponsors 275 primary schools, a number of harambee secondary schools and 3 hospitals, the Methodists in turn having 166 primary schools, 10 harambee secondary schools and 2 hospitals.

Western Kenya also has been the scene of extensive Christian activity, the principal denominations being the friends (FAM, later EAYM) in 1902, church of God in 1905, and the Seventh-day Adventists (SDA) in 1906. The first 2 have established large Christian communities and extensive educational and medical institutions among the Luhya, while SDAs have been active among the Luo of Nyanza. Primary schools founded by the 3 churches number 400 for the SDA, 354 for EAYM, and 96 by the CoG. Theological education is provided by Kima Theological School (CoG) and several Bible schools belonging to the various denominations.

Pentecostalism also is strong in western Kenya as well as in other parts of the country. The 2 most important communities are the Pentecostal Assemblies of God (PAG) and the Pentecostal Evangelistic Fellowship of Africa (PEFA). The former, begun among the Luhya in 1910 but now widely spread throughout Kenya, is related to the Pentecostal Assemblies of Canada and has as many members in Kenya as in Canada. PEFA on the other hand was formed in 1962 by bringing together 2 societies, the International Pentecostal Assemblies (1938) and the Elim Missionary Assemblies (1942). Other Pentecostal bodies are the Full Gospel Churches of Kenya, founded by Finnish missionaries in 1949 and the small Norwegian Pentecostal Mission since 1955.

Another large church with extensive evangelistic, educational, medical, and social service interests is the Salvation Army which entered Kenya in 1921. It has its main strength among the Kamba and Luhya, but it also maintains work in Elgon, Eldoret, Embu, Kisumu, Mombasa, and Thika.

Among Kenya's smaller Protestant denominations may be mentioned the Africa Gospel Church, Baptist Churches of Kenya, Gospel Furthering Bible Church, Lutheran Church in Kenya, and the Reformed Church of East Africa.

INDIGENOUS CHURCHES. In 1995, there were over distinct independent African indigenous denominations in Kenya, with a combined Christian community of 5,919,000. The first to be begun was the Nomiya Luo Mission, a schism in Nyanza from the Anglican Church in 1914. Other important Luo schisms have been the Church of Christ in Africa, which began as an Anglican revival movement (called Johera or People of Love) in 1952 and separated in 1957; and Mario Legio of Africa, the largest split from Roman Catholicism anywhere in Africa. The most important of the many Luhya indigenous denominations is the African Israel Church Nineveh (AICN), which is noted for its lengthy charismatic worship services and its custom of running through the streets in formation in white robes; while the African Brotherhood Church (ABC) is the largest such body among the Kamba. Both the AICN and the ABC are members of the National Christian Council of Kenya, and the AICN joined the World Council of Churches in 1975.

During the late 1920s and early 1930s, Kikuyu country was the scene of serious conflicts over land, schools, and female circumcision, which resulted in the formation of some of Kenya's most important independent churches: the African Independent Pentecostal Church (AIPC) and the African Orthodox Church (AOC). The former is today Kenya's largest indigenous Christian community, while in 1946 the AOC was accepted into Greek Orthodoxy and is now in the diocese of Eirenopolis under the patriarchate of Alexandria. Other Kikuyu pentecostal independents tracing their origin to the same period are known collectively as Wakorino, although they are divided into many separate denominations: African Mission of Holy Ghost Church, Chosen Church of the Holy Spirit, Christian Holy Ghost Church of East Africa, Holy Ghost Church of East Africa, Holy Spirit Church of Zayn and Kenya Foundation of the Prophets Church. The Wakorino are noted for the white turbans worn by their members.

African Independent Churches. In Kenya, there are over 740 indigenous denominations, with 6.6 million adherents. As elsewhere in Africa, these churches can be described by one or more of 3 adjectives illustrated here: (1) (*Top left*). African (dress, drums, and other traditional African features); shown here in African Israel Church Nineveh); (2) (*Bottom left*) Charismatic (glossolalic, prophetic, Spirit-possessed; shown here, local Churches of Kenya); (3) (*Right*). Liturgical (rich robes, written liturgies, crosses, beads, and other symbols; shown here, Maria Legio of Africa).

ANGLICAN CHURCH. Anglicanism is second only to Catholicism both in date of arrival and size of its present Christian community. Two missions playing an important role in evangelism and the early formation of the church have been the Church Missionary Society, beginning in 1844 and the Bible Churchmen's Missionary Society from 1931.

The first African ordinations to the Anglican ministry took place in 1885, and the first 2 African bishops we appointed in 1955. In 1960, the church obtained its autonomy from Canterbury as the Church of the Province of East Africa, which included the Anglican churches of Kenya, Tanganyika and Zanzibar. The 2 latter were separated off in 1970 and the Church of the Province of Kenya (CPK) was formed. As with Catholicism, the CPK is found in all parts of the country although it is strongest among the Kikuyu, Luo, and Luhya. The church is organized with a metropolitan diocese in Nairobi and 5 other dioceses (with a sixth added in 1975) with responsibility for property and finance handled by the Church Commissioners for Kenya. Ministerial training is provided at St Paul's United Theological College and at several diocesan Bible schools. Interest in education is maintained through its continued sponsorship of 775 primary schools and 60 harambee secondary schools, and the CPK is still indirectly responsible for 2 hospitals.

Renewal movements. In the 1990s the Pentecostal/Charismatic Renewal continued to spread rapidly across most older churches, and numbered over 8,350,000 adherents (of whom 25% Pentecostals, 21% Charismatics, and 54% Independents).

Indigenous missions. Kenyan Christians have served as foreign missionaries in surrounding countries in Africa since the early 1900s. More recently missionary vision has increased among the churches of all traditions with more missionaries sent out every year. The vast majority of these, however, work in more heavily-Christian countries in East Africa.

CHURCH AND STATE

In affirming freedom of religion, the 1969 constitution of Kenya follows the United Nations' 1948 Universal Declaration of Human Rights. Chapter V, paragraph 78 states: 'No person shall be hindered in the enjoyment of his freedom of conscience . . . freedom of thought and of religion, freedom to change his religion or belief, and freedom to manifest and propagate his religion or belief in worship, teaching, practice and observance'; 'Every religious community shall be entitled, at its own expense, to establish and maintain places of education . . .; and no such community shall be prevented from providing religious instruction for persons of that community'; 'No person attending any place of education shall be required to receive religious instruction or to take part in or attend any religious ceremony or observance'; and 'No person shall be compelled to take any oath which is contrary to his religion or belief'.

The churches continue to participate in education, although in 1968 the government took over the management of all mission-founded primary schools, nearly 5,000 in all. The policy of 'participation' as defined in the Education Act of 1968 seeks to avoid the extremes of a secular school system on the one hand and the use of schools to further religious objectives on the other. It allows for religious sponsorship of primary schools and grants representation to the churches on the governing boards of their former secondary schools and teacher-training colleges. The Education Act also makes provision for religious education in government-maintained schools while stipulating that such courses are purely voluntary. The Kenya government and the churches (Protestant, Anglican, and Catholic) cooperate through the Joint East African Religious Education Committee in the development of syllabuses and text books, and the government assumes responsibility for training religious education teachers at the University of Nairobi and Kenyatta University College.

Government cooperation and aid is also provided to other church-sponsored projects including hospitals, dispensaries, village polytechnic schools, and socio-economic development programs.

Leaders representing all religious traditions are given prominent roles at major government functions, such as the opening of parliament; and the churches are permitted chaplaincy services in the prisons and armed forces.

Major Muslim and Christian holidays are also respected.

Officially a secular state, Kenya makes no attempt to regulate religious observance unless such practices are deemed subversive. The only cases of recent government intervention in religion have been the proscribing in 1968 of the Religion of the Ancestral Spirits and the banning of Jehovah's Witnesses with the deportation of its 34 European missionaries for 7 months in 1973 before the ban was lifted.

BROADCASTING AND MEDIA

Nearly every family owns a radio, and there are several programs to choose from. Kenya is a member of UNDA, and Catholics broadcast a weekly service featuring prayers, reflections, and devotions in Kikamba, Kiswahili, and Kikuyu. About 4 hours of IBRA programming can be heard on local radio station KBC in 9 different languages. FEBA (Seychelles) broadcasts shortwave radio programs in Swahili. AWR has a studio in Nairobi that produces English-language programs.

Several Christian television programs can be received in the country. Catholics air a short program featuring Scripture reading and prayer each week. CBN's *International 700 Club*, animated programs, and talk shows can be seen on Sundays and Mondays.

Christian organizations have produced several short videos focusing on special issues; these have proven very successful. So far 7.6 million have seen the 'Jesus' Film: on television (730,000), through film team showings (4.7 million) and through mission agency use (2 million). A total of 715,000 have responded with decisions.

East African United Churches (EAUC), led by AICN head Kivuli (at desk, white mitre) meet in 1964.

INTERDENOMINATIONAL ORGANIZATIONS

Two Africa-wide interdenominational councils of churches have their headquarters in Kenya. The All Africa Conference of Churches (AACC), formed in 1963 and based in Nairobi, has 100 member churches and councils throughout the continent and represents the conciliar wing of Protestant, Anglican, and Orthodox ecumenism in Africa. Secondly, the Association of Evangelicals of Africa and Madagascar (AEAM), founded in Nairobi in 1966 and united with the Africa Evangelical Office in 1971, has member national associations in 10 countries and provides for cooperation and fellowship among Conservative Evangelical Christians.

Nairobi is also the center for 2 international organizations: the United Bible Societies (UBS) (Africa Regional Center), which serves as a consultative and coordinating body for Africa's 24 national Bible societies; and the World Students Christian Federation (WSCF) (Africa Region). Several national bodies of an interdenominational nature are active. The National Christian Council of Kenya (NCCK) was founded in 1943 as the Christian Council of Kenya, building on the Alliance of Protestant Missions of 1918 and the Kenya Missionary Council of 1924 and received its present name in 1966. The council has 25 member denominations and carries on its work through 8 regional branches and 6 departments: Biblical Study and Research; Christian Communication; Christian Education and Training; Christian Service, Home and Family Life; Relief, Rehabilitation and Rural Development; and Youth. With 120 full-time employees, it is one of the largest such national councils in the world. Over 100 social service projects (including rural training centers and village polytechnics) are directly under NCCK sponsorship, with assistance provided for 50 others belonging to its member churches.

Medical Missionary Sister of Mary, an expert pilot, serves outlying missions.

The Christian Churches Educational Association (CCEA) was founded in 1957 to coordinate the work of Protestant and Anglican churches in education. Membership consists of 15 churches, 6 teacher-training colleges and 59 secondary schools. In 1971, the CCEA sponsored 2,613 primary schools and 149 secondary schools. The Protestant Churches Medical Association (PCMA) was established in 1962 to promote Protestant medical services and, in 1970, coordinated the work of 15 hospitals and 19 dispensaries. Training for the ministry is provided at St Paul's United Theological College, Limuru, which came into existence in 1955 as a joint venture of the Anglican, Presbyterian, and Methodist churches, with the Reformed Church joining later. In addition to these, there were about 300 other Christian organizations of significance at the national level.

Indigenous churches in Kenya have over the years made 14 different attempts to form national councils of independent churches. Most have foundered due to lack of funds and personnel, and several have been refused registration by government. A pioneer was the Kenya Independent Churches Fellowship formed in 1960, and in 1973, the most important were the East African Christian Alliance begun in 1965 and affiliated to the International Council of Christian Churches and the United Orthodox Independent Churches of East Africa begun in 1971.

Kenya Army drumhead service with Catholic cardinal, Anglican archbishop, and Muslim chief Kadhi (right).

FUTURE TRENDS AND PROSPECTS

Ethnoreligionists will probably continue to suffer a massive decline falling to 8.4% by 2025 (from 95.9% in 1900). Christians could grow to 82% by 2025.

Kenya is poised to become 90% Christian around AD 2050. Islam most probably will be the only significant minority with near 10% by that time.

BIBLIOGRAPHY

A history of the Quaker movement in Africa. A. M. B. Rasmussen. London: British Academic Press, 1995. 193p.

A vision of Christian mission: reflections on the Great Commission in Kenya, 1943–1993. M. Crouch (ed). Nairobi: National Council of Churches of Kenya, 1993. 282p.

'Barriers and gateways to church planting among the immigrants in Nairobi.' K. S. Munyiri. D.Min. thesis, Trinity Evangelical Divinity School, Deerfield, IL, 1992. 144p.

Baseline country profiles for Open Doors: country report: Kenya. Nairobi: Daystar Communications, [1984]. 89p.

Catholic directory of Eastern Africa, 1977–79. Tabora, Tanzania: TMP Book Department, 1977. 258p. (Earlier editions: 1959, 1965, 1968, 1971, 1974–76, then irregularly to the present).

'Catholic missions in Kenya: the case of the Spiritans and the Consolata, 1870–1970.' L. Njoroge. Ph.D. dissertation, University of Notre Dame, South Bend, IN, 1991. 250p.

Christentum und sozioökonomische Entwicklung: eine empirische Untersuchung im ruralen Kenia. J. Bergmann. Aachen: Herodot, 1993. 326p. (Originally the author's 1992 doctoral dissertation at University of Göttingen; summary in English).

Christian response to change in East African traditional societies. G. G. Brown. *Woodbrooke occasional papers*, 4. London: Friends Home Service Committee for Woodbrooke College, 1973. 55p.

'Christianity and culture in Kenya: an encounter between the African Inland Mission and the Marakwet belief systems and culture.' S. K. Elolia. Ph.D. dissertation, Toronto School of Theology, Toronto, 1992. 2 vols.

Christianity in contemporary Africa: Kenya old and new. W. B. Anderson. *Makerere University. Department of Religious Studies and Philosophy. Occasional research papers*, vol. 10. Kampala: Department of Religious Studies and Philosophy, Makerere University, 1973. 189p.

'Church growth in Nairobi, Kenya,' L. L. Niemeyer, *Urban mission*, 8, 1 (September 1990), 45–54.

'Contact between the Kipsigis traditional religion and world view and Christianity.' C. C. Cheruiyot. S.T.M. thesis, Drew University, Madison, NJ, 1985. 118p.

Defeating Mau Mau. L. S. B. Leakey. London: Methuen, 1954. 152p.

Doing theology with the Maasai. D. Priest Jr. Pasadena, CA: William Carey Library, 1990. 248p.

Einhundert Jahre Neukirchener Mission am Tana: 1887–1987. F. Gissel et al. Saarbrücken: Homo et Religio, 1991. 240p.

From mission to church: a handbook of Christianity in East Africa. Z. J. Nthamburi (ed). Nairobi, Kenya: Uzima Press, 1991. 150p. (See especially 'The beginning and development of Christianity in Kenya').

'Growth of the Church of God through Ushirika groups among the Luhya in Nairobi, Kenya.' R. E. Edwards. D.Miss. thesis, Fuller Theological Seminary, Pasadena, CA, 1989. 377p.

History of Christianity in Kenya, 1844–1977: a select bibliography. J. K. Gakobo. [Nairobi]: Kenyatta University College Library, 1979. 136p.

Kenya. R. L. Collison. *World bibliographical series*, vol. 25. Oxford, UK: CLIO Press, 1982. (See especially 'Religion,' p.55–7).

Kenya churches handbook: the development of Kenyan Christianity, 1498–1973. D. B. Barrett, G. K. Mambo, J. MacLaughlin & M. J. McVeigh (eds). Kisumu, Kenya: Evangel Press, 1973. 349p. (Includes 'Bibliography of Christianity and religion in Kenya,' p.315-30).

'Kenyan church leaders: perceptions of appropriate leadership behaviors.' K. R. Harder. Ph.D. dissertation, Michigan State University, East Lansing, MI, 1984. 197p.

La Chiesa cattolica in Kenya: una storia centenaria. J. Baur. Bologna, Italy: EMI, 1991. 239p.

Luo religion and folklore. H. E. Hauge. London: E. J. Brill, 1976. 154p.

New Testament eschatology in an African background; a study of the encounter between New Testament theology and African traditional concepts. J. S. Mbiti. London: Oxford University Press, 1971. (A study of the Kamba people).

'Patterns of church growth in Nairobi.' F. V. Tate. M.A. thesis, Fuller Theological Seminary, Pasadena, CA, 1970. 225p.

Peoples and cultures of Kenya. A. Fedders. Nairobi: Transafrica, 1979.

Rabai to Mumias: a short history of the Church of the Province of Kenya, 1844–1994. Nairobi: Uzima, 1994. 203p.

Raising funds in Kenya: a survey of middle to upper income Nairobi churchgoers: a research project. D. R. Downes. Nairobi: Daystar University College, 1991. 100p.

Religion and social change: a sociological study of Seventh–day Adventism in Kenya. N. M. Nyaundi. *Studia theologica Lundensia*, 47. Lund, Sweden: Lund University Press, 1993. 278p.

'Shalom our country: a vision for the Presbyterian Church of East Africa.' E. J. Mbaabu. D.Min. thesis, School of Theology at Claremont, Claremont, CA, 280p.

Status of Christianity country profile: Kenya. Lausanne: ICOWE, 1974. 8p.

'Stewardship practices in Kenya with proposed solutions.' A. N. Birai. D.Min. thesis, Andrews University, Seventh–day Adventist Theological Seminary, Barrien Springs, MI, 1994. 266p.

The freedom of the Spirit: African indigenous churches in Kenya. F. K. Githieya. Atlanta: Scholars Press, 1997. 304p.

'The influence of Western Christianity on the African culture: the Abaluyia of Western Kenya.' L. N. Shamalla. M.T.S. thesis, Emory University, Atlanta, 1995. 99p.

'The Khoja Shia Ithna–Asheriya community in East Africa, 1840–1967,' S. S. A. Rizvi & N. Q. King, *Muslim World*, 64, 3 (1974), 194–204.

'The Kikuyu, Christianity and the Africa Inland Mission.' D. P. Sandgren. Ph.D. dissertation, University of Wisconsin, Madison, WI, 1976. 427p.

'The Maria Legio: the dynamics of a breakaway church among the Luo of East Africa.' P. J. Dirven. Ph.D. dissertation, Pontificia Universitas Gregoriana, Rome, 1970. 343p.

The missionary factor in East Africa. R. Oliver. 2nd ed. London: Longman, 1965. 302p.

'The new people of God: the Christian community in the African Orthodox Church (Karing'a) and the Arathi (Agikuyu spirit churches).' F. K. Githieya. Ph.D. dissertation, Emory University, Atlanta, 1992. 405p.

The Presbyterian Church in Kenya: an account of the origin and growth of the PCEA. R. Macpherson. Nairobi: PCEA, 1970. 151p.

'The social structure of the Pokot and its implications for church planting: a new paradigm for strategic African missions.' R. G. Lewis. D. Miss. thesis, Biola University, La

Mirada, CA, 1991. 260p.

'The urban Presbyterian ministry in Nairobi, Kenya.' L. P. Mbagara. D.Min. thesis, Columbia Theological Seminary, Decatur, GA, 1992. 177p.

Toward an African Christianity: inculturation applied. E. Hillman. New York: Paulist Press, 1993. 106p.

'Understanding church leadership: an analysis and assessment of Africa Inland Church—Kenya.' P. K. Mutinda. D.Min. thesis, Biola University, La Mirada, CA, 1991. 124p.

Unity in diversity: a linguistic survey of the Abaluyia of Western Kenya. R. Angogo Kanyoro. *Veröffentlichungen der Institute für Afrikaistik und Ägyptologie der Universität Wien*, 28. Vienna: Beiträge zur Afrikanistik, 1983.

Unreached peoples of Kenya project. K. Shingledecker et al. Nairobi: Daystar Communications, 1982. 13 vols.

We felt like grasshoppers: the story of Africa Inland Mission. D. Anderson. Nottingham, UK: Crossway Books, 1994. 348p.

'Witchcraft among the Akamba and Africa Inland Church, Kenya.' J. M. Mbuva. M.A. thesis, Fuller Theological Seminary, Pasadena, CA, 1992. 177p.

Women of fire and spirit: history, faith and gender in Roho religion in Nyanza. C. H. Hoehler–Fatton. New York: Oxford University Press, 1995.

Country Table 2. **Organized churches and denominations in Kenya.**

Official name (bold type = church with over 10% of all affiliated) 1	*Begun* 2	*Type* 3	*Counc* 4	*Congs* 5	*Adults* 6	*Affiliated 1970* 7	*Affiliated 1995* 8	*G%* 9	*Names, notes, and other statistics* (see Codebook, Part 3) 10
Africa Gospel Church	1935	P-Hol	xFG.a	557	51,426	15,000	114,000	8.45	*AGC.* 5 Dioceses. M=WGM(USA). A=1961. 95% Kipsigis. 20n,33f,1H,2h,1s,W=84%,266Y.
Africa Gospel Unity Church	1964	I-Hol	.T..T	25	1,100	1,500	2,000	1.16	*AGUC.* Split ex AGC when moderator deposed. Kipsigis. HQ Silibwet. 10n,W=85%,250Y.
Africa Inland Church	1895	P-Non	xMG.a	4,325	1,000,000	300,000	1,500,000	6.65	M=AIM. 33% Kamba, 27% Kalenjin, 20% Kikuyu. 80n,50x,226f,4H,30h,5p,1s,W=65%,2000Y.
African Brotherhood Church	1945	I-Non	xvA.K	765	76,500	64,030	170,000	3.98	*ABC.* Ex AIM, Salvation Army. Kamba. HQ Mitaboni. M=CBOMB. 100n,1s,W=68%,1010Y.
African Christian Church & Schools	1947	I-Bap	IWA.K	74	18,600	30,500	62,000	2.88	*ACC&S.* Split ex AIM. 1967, invited in M=CBOMB(Canada). 99% Kikuyu. 7n,2x,8f,1500Y.
African Church	1961	I-Bap	.T..T	25	20,000	30,000	40,000	1.16	*AC.* Kamba split ex AIM, first known as Kenya African Ch. HQ Machokos. 6n,W=19%.
African Church Mission	1941	I-Ang	I....	20	2,500	3,000	4,000	1.16	*ACM.* Ex Nomiya Luo Mission, permitting post-baptismal polygamy. 3n,W=35%,90Y,80y.
African Ch of Jesus Christ in Kenya	1970	I-Ang	.....	5	350	1,000	1,100	0.38	Kikuyu split ex Anglican D Mount Kenya, linked with CCA. 1n,W=50%,15Y,6y.
African Church of the Holy Spirit	1927	I-3pA	Iu..K	70	4,000	5,455	7,000	1.00	*ACHS. Dini ya Msalaba (Religion of the Cross)*, ex Quakers. 29n,W=75%,460Y,271y.
African Divine Church	1949	I-3pA	I...I	100	2,500	3,850	5,000	1.05	*ADC.* Maragoli schism ex PAoC over desire to wear uniforms. 21n,W=95%,186Y,106y.
African Evangelical Presbyterian Ch	1962	P-Ref	.T..T	50	1,100	800	2,000	3.73	*AEPC.* M=WPM(USA). 88% Kamba, rest Mbere and Imbu. HQ Mwingi. 8n,5f,W=67%,30Y,20y.
African Holy Zionist Church	1959	I-Sal	I...I	5	1,500	3,000	4,000	1.16	Luhya schism formerly called Africa Zion Church. HQ Kegomori, Maragoli. 20n,W=90%.
African Independent Church of Kenya	1943	I-Ang	.....	4	400	1,000	800	-0.89	Kamba schism ex Anglican Church, declining since 1960. HQ Machakos.
African Indep Pentecostal Ch of Africa	1925	I-Ref	IvA.K	408	400,000	496,000	1,200,000	3.60	*AIPC.* 4 Dioceses. Persecution 1939-57; 1964, massive rural growth. Kikuyu. 136n,1p,6000Y.
African Interior Church	1943	I-Hol	I...K	40	15,000	30,000	40,000	1.16	*AIC.* Luhya split ex Church of God (Anderson) mission. 5n,W=68%,160Y,200y.
African Israel Church Nineveh	1942	I-3pA	IW..K	500	108,000	76,200	200,000	3.94	*AICN.* HQ holy city Nineveh. Ex PAoC. 51% Luhya, 49th Luo. 91n,W=80%,160Y,83y.
African Mission of Holy Ghost Church	1930	I-3pA	.....	15	2,500	7,000	7,500	0.28	*AMHGC.* Early Kikuyu Spirit church, formed from Watu wa Mungu. 14n,W=99%,120Y,50y.
African Orthodox Church of Kenya	1928	O-Gre	CwA.k	266	220,000	248,000	650,000	3.93	*D Eirenopolis*, in P Alexandria. 80% Kikuyu, 15% Luhya. 33n,3x,1s,10000Y,15000y.
Anglican Church of Kenya	1844	A-Eva	AWAVK	2,400	1,200,000	582,600	2,700,000	6.33	*ICK/CPK. Kanisa la Jimbo la Kenya.* 26 Dioceses. M=CMS,BCMS. Big losses to ICCEC, NAC.
Apostolic Faith of Africa	1959	I-3pA	.....	60	5,000	7,000	8,000	0.54	Kikuyu split ex PCEA; spread west through Pokot into Uganda. HQ Thogoto. 5n,W=98%.
Apostolic Fellowship Association	c1970	I-3oA	.....	200	15,000	–	30,000	51.04	Oneness body in Apostolic World Christian Fellowship. Mainly Luos. HQ Kisumu.
Apostolic Hierarchy Church	1940	I-CCa	.....	6	500	1,500	1,000	-1.61	Kikuyu. Ex RCC, formerly African God Worshippers Fellowship Church Society.
Assembly Hall Churches	c1985	I-3nC	.....	8	267	–	700	10.00	*Little Flock. Local Churches.* Begun 1922 in mainland China.
Associated Christian Ch of Kenya	c1986	I-Non	.....	20	2,000	–	4,000	11.11	In West Pokot. Controversy with Africa Inland Ch, and Anglican D Eldoret.
Baptist Convention of Kenya	1956	P-Bap	T...K	2,000	193,000	25,000	358,000	11.23	*BCK.* M=BMEA(SBC,USA). 25% Kikuyu, rest Coast, Nyanza. 35n,18x,89f,11h,W=50%,1200Y.
Bible Fellowship Church	c1940	I-Bap	....K	2	300	500	1,000	2.81	Independent group in Thika begun by former GMS woman missionary, ex GMS.
Broadsheet Readers Clubs	c1980	I-3nA	.....	651	8,000	–	20,000	6.67	Readers of Gospel Broadsheets provided by M=WEC(UK).
Catholic Church in Kenya:	1498	R-Lat	P...R	588	3,089,900	1,935,811	6,146,496	4.73	Kanisa Katholiki. C=9+11+40. 607n 830x 1911m 3184w 207626Yy
M Kisumu	1925	R-Lat	Ps	24	184,000	502,374	335,180	-1.61	Capital of Luo country. 26n 16x 35m 151w 10608Yy
D Bungoma	1987	R-Lat	Ps	20	208,000	–	433,753	12.50	In west. Among Luyia. 29n 7x 38m 90w 14705Yy
D Eldoret	1953	R-Lat	Ps	48	250,000	60,050	488,000	8.74	In northwest 50n 39x 50m 190w 21136Yy
D Homa Bay	1993	R-Lat	Ps	19	158,000	–	327,272	50.00	Luo speakers. 19n 16x 43m 271w 9479Yy
D Kakamega	1978	R-Lat	Ps	26	115,000	–	241,001	5.88	Luyia. 28n 22x 36m 268w 16993Yy
D Kisii	1960	R-Lat	Ps	15	156,000	279,950	312,000	0.43	Speakers of Ekogusii. 14n 3x 12m 78w 9005Yy
D Lodwar	1968	R-Lat	Psps	13	7,000	1,550	20,000	10.77	In north. 10n 21x 31m 35w 1925Yy
M Mombasa	1955	R-Lat	Ps	41	86,000	71,206	171,169	3.57	On coast: Swahili capitol. 28n 31x 35m 221w 6325Yy
D Garissa	1976	R-Lat	Pofmc	16	10,500	–	22,256	5.26	M=OFMCap. 2n 16x 22m 22w 715Yy
M Nairobi	1860	R-Lat	Ps	70	459,000	228,274	980,000	6.00	Capital city. 74n 433x 1213m 884w 19211Yy
D Kitui	1956	R-Lat	Ps	19	47,000	21,205	106,990	6.69	Language: Kamba. 19n 14x 19m 47w 4851Yy
D Machakos	1969	R-Lat	Ps	35	210,000	102,596	427,365	5.87	Language: Kamba. 48n 31x 61m 73w 14954Yy
D Nakuru	1968	R-Lat	Ps	64	170,000	109,726	288,932	3.95	In Rift Valley. 66n 39x 97m 138w 18781Yy
D Ngong	1959	R-Lat	Pmhm	20	41,000	12,490	70,862	7.19	Maasai area. 16n 34x 39m 124w 3853Yy
M Nyeri	1905	R-Lat	Ps	29	307,000	355,000	595,250	2.09	Kikuyu stronghold. 64n 13x 48m 150w 18000Yy
D Embu	1986	R-Lat	Ps	14	71,000	–	133,975	11.11	Embu speakers. 22n 11x 13m 58w 5372Yy
D Marsabit	1964	R-Lat	Ps	20	17,800	4,347	42,659	9.57	North. 19n 33x 42m 67w 2386Yy
D Meru	1926	R-Lat	Ps	41	298,000	186,043	568,505	4.57	Meru speakers. 35n 35x 47m 189w 11947Yy
D Muranga	1983	R-Lat	Ps	25	292,000	–	576,327	8.33	Kikuyu center. 38n 16x 30m 128w 17380Yy
OM Kenya	1964	R-Lat	P	29	2,600	1,000	5,000	6.65	Military Ordinariate of Kenya. 5 ordinaries, 11 auxiliaries. 672Yy.
Children of God Regeneration Church	1947	I-Non	.....	110	1,200	3,542	4,000	0.49	*Ayie Remb Yesu (I accept the Blood of Jesus).* 95% Luo, 5% Bantu. 42n,124Y,52y.
Chosen Ch of the Holy Spirit in Kenya	1930	I-3pA	.....	20	1,000	2,500	2,000	-0.89	Early Kikuyu movement out of Watu wa Mungu (People of God). 3n,W=95%,78Y,64y.
Christadelphian Bible Mission (Kenya)	c1970	m-Ade	x....	5	100	150	200	1.16	*CMBK.* M=CBM(UK). Small ecclesias (churches) across Kenya. Pacifist, adventist.
Christian Brethren	c1950	P-CBr	x....	11	330	240	660	4.13	
Christian Brotherhood Church	1952	I-Ang	I....	140	4,000	9,000	10,000	0.42	*CBC.* Schism ex Anglicans. 45% Luhya, 30% Luo, 18% Gusii, 6% Ganda. 8n,30Y,36y.
Christian Church (Disciples of Christ)	1983	P-Dis	x....	550	18,000	–	30,000	8.33	M=Christian Ch (Disciples of Christ). 81 missionaries.
Christian Churches & Chs of Christ	c1960	I-Dis	x....	47	6,400	800	12,800	11.73	
Christian Evangelical Church	1948	I-Ang	.....	50	2,000	4,000	5,000	0.90	*CEC.* First Balokole (Revival) schism ex Anglicans among Luo. 11n,W=94%,65Y.
Christian Holy Ghost Ch of EAfrica	1934	I-3pA	.....	20	1,000	1,500	2,000	1.16	*CHGC.* Conservative wing of the Aroti (Dreamers, Seers). All Kikuyu. 9n,W=95%,60Y.
Christian Missionary Fellowship	1982	I-Dis	.....	87	2,885	–	5,000	7.69	M=CMF(USA).
Christian Science Ch of East Africa	1925	m-Sci	x....	2	100	100	200	2.81	*Church of Christ, Scientist.* M=CCS(Boston, USA). 70% Africans. 1w,W=90%.
Christian Theocratic Holy Ch of God	1958	I-Non	.....	80	3,500	3,870	5,000	1.03	Kikuyu movement. Finally registered 1971. HQ Kawangware Village. 70n,W=75%.
Church of Christ in Africa	1957	I-Ang	IT.TT	879	150,000	120,000	350,000	4.37	*CCA.* Schism of 40% D Maseno. 8 Dioceses. 81% Luo, 10% Luhya. 81n,1p,2400Y,8640y.
Church of God in East Africa	1905	P-Hol	x.G.a	556	89,000	260,000	178,000	-1.50	*CGEA.* M=CoG(Anderson) (USA). 78% Luhya, 20% Gusii. 375n,26f,2H,4h,1800Y.
Church of God of Prophecy	1978	P-Pe3	Z....	110	3,070	–	7,680	5.88	
Church of Saviour, Diocese of Nyakoko	1968	I-Ang	.....	35	2,000	3,293	4,000	0.78	Schism of clergy ex HTCA (itself a schism ex CCA). All Luo. 7n,W=50%,39Y,65y.
Church of the Kenya Family	1948	I-Non	.....	10	1,000	4,000	3,000	-1.14	Embu movement; healing, rejection of word `Amen' after prayers. W=75%,54Y,96y.
Church of the Nazarene	1984	P-Hol	x....	16	1,249	–	1,987	9.09	M=CoN.
Conservative Baptist Fellowship of K	1972	I-Bap	x....	4	131	–	275	4.35	M=CBI(USA).
Cornerstone Evangelistic Ministry	1976	I-3cA	.....	40	2,000	–	4,000	5.26	Work among Kikuyu, Meru, Boran, Samburu, Kipsigis, Turkana, Rendille.
Cross Church of East Africa	c1940	I-Ang	.....	70	5,000	15,000	16,000	0.26	*Roho Musalaba (Spirit Cross Church).* Luo schism ex MHGC. HQ Kabondo. 10n.
Deliverance Church	1969	I-3pA	x....	10	2,000	3,000	6,000	2.81	*YCAF. Young Christian Ambassadors Fellowship.* Youths; healing, shouting for victory. 2n.
East Africa Pentecostal Churches	1953	I-3pA	.....	100	20,000	20,000	50,000	3.73	*EAPC.* M=Kenya Faith Mission (Norway), ex SFM. 80% Meru. 117n,2x,2p,W=80%,7000Y.
East Africa Yearly Meeting of Friends	1902	P-Qua	Q.A.K	1,667	50,000	100,000	111,000	0.42	*EAYM.* M=FUM. Largest Quaker church after USA. 99% Luhya. 130n,2x,16f,3H,1s,W=50%.
Episcopal Church of Africa	1968	I-3cA	....K	440	102,000	5,000	206,000	16.04	*ECA. Diocese of Kenya.* Schism ex CCA. 99% Luo. 1997, huge influx due to M=ICCEC
Elim Church International	1949	P-Pe2	Z....	21	1,200	200	2,000	9.65	Elim Pentecostal Church of Kenya. M=EFGA (UK).
Evangelical Lutheran Ch in Tanzania	1967	P-Lut	Lwa.K	87	21,700	3,284	36,208	10.08	*Kenya Synod.* M=ELCT(Tanzania). Tanzanians. Merger talks with LCK. 73Y,322y.
Free Pentecostal Fellowship in Kenya	1960	P-Pe2	Z....	160	50,000	8,000	120,000	11.44	*FPFK.* M=NPY, SFM. 57% Kikuyu, 34% Luhya, 5% Turkana, 4% Maasai. 60n,8x,850Y.
Friends of the Holy Spirit	1946	I-3pA	.....	12	1,200	2,000	3,000	1.64	*Arata a Roho Mutheru* (=FHS). Unorganized Kikuyu, Kamba Anglican revivalists. 10n.
Full Gospel Churches of Kenya	1949	P-Pe2	Z...K	2,150	150,000	60,000	220,000	5.33	*FGCK.* M=FFFM(Finland). 39% Luo, 33% Kikuyu, 14% Kalenjin. 182n,6x,W=95%,1604Y.
God of the Universe Church	1962	I-3pA	.....	20	1,000	1,274	2,000	1.82	*GUC.* Luo schism ex PAG. Successful evangelism directed by prophecy. 7n,W=75%,80Y.
Good News Church of Africa	1958	I-Bap	.T..T	130	15,000	30,000	40,000	1.16	*GNCA.* Schism of 70% ex GFF over polygamy. 50% Kamba, 25% Kikuyu, Coastal. 60n.
Gospel Assemblies of Kenya	1960	I-3pA	.....	120	8,100	6,000	15,000	3.73	*Local Chs of Kenya.* 35% Luo, 25% Luhya, 25% Kikuyu, 15% Teso. 52n,1x,500Y,50y.
Gospel Furthering Bible Church	1936	I-Bap	.M...	160	9,600	10,000	19,200	2.64	*GFBC.* M=GFF(USA), 1936 schism ex AIM. Kamba. 1958 massive schism, GNCA. 18f,1s.
Gospel of God Church	1967	I-3aA	x....	60	2,000	1,800	4,000	3.25	*Vapostori (Apostles)* of Johane Masowe. M=ACJM(Shona from Rhodesia). 20n,W=95%.
Gospel Tabernacle Church	c1943	I-Bap	I....	16	3,000	8,000	10,000	0.90	Kamba schism ex GFF led by missionary; now autonomous, with M=GFF(USA). 15n,1x.
Holy Ch of Evangelistic Apostles Faith	1958	I-3pA	..I..	32	5,000	11,000	14,000	0.97	Ex AFM(SAfrica) over polygamy. 80% Kikuyu, 7% Luo, 5% Maasai. 19n,W=85%,200Y.
Holy Ghost Church of East Africa	1934	I-3pA	.....	33	7,000	10,000	12,000	0.73	*HGCEA.* Liberal wing of Aroti, modern views. Kikuyu. 31n,W=90%,100Y,100y.
Holy Ghost Coptic Church of Africa	1964	I-CCa	.....	10	5,400	5,000	10,000	2.81	Ex RCC, with Catholic terminology. Holy Father, basilica. mass. Luo. 8n,W=55%.
Holy Spirit Church of East Africa	1927	I-3pA	I....	20	2,500	3,000	4,600	1.72	*Dini ya Roho.* Luhya revival ex Quakers. White robes, turbans. 8n,W=65%,52Y,187y.
Holy Spirit Church of Zayun	c1962	I-3pA	.....	10	600	1,500	2,000	1.16	Known as `*M'Aroti* (red M on robes, red or blue turbans, green forbidden). Kikuyu.
Holy Trinity Church in Africa	1960	I-Ang	.....	180	22,000	50,000	60,000	0.73	*HTCA.* Ex CCA over leadership. 75% Luo, 10% Luhya, 5% Kikuyu. 15n,W=55%,600Y,1000y.
Independent Baptist Churches of EA	1964	I-Bap	.T..T	30	1,000	2,400	3,000	0.90	*IBCEA.* Kamba churches aided by M=Grace Independent Baptist Mission (USA). 7n,2x.
Independent Lutheran Church of Africa	1961	I-Lut	.T..T	22	700	1,000	1,500	1.64	*ILC. Loyalist Religion.* No Lutheran connections. Luhya. 1n,W=80%,31Y,25y.
Independent Presbyterian Church of EA	1946	I-Ref	.T..T	12	2,000	3,000	5,000	2.06	*IPCEA.* Kamba, north of Kitui. M=IBPFM(USA). 1957 split by WPM(now AEPC). 3x.
Intern Ch of the Foursquare Gospel	c1970	P-Pe2	Z....	73	2,260	–	3,770	39.01	M=ICFG.
International Fellowship for Christ	1969	I-3pA	.....	140	2,100	3,000	5,500	2.45	*IFFC.* Indigenous pentecostals, with links with USA and Canada bodies. 8n.
International Pentecostal Holiness Church	1972	P-Pe2	.....	178	8,000	–	13,300	4.35	M=IPHC(USA).
Jehovah's Witnesses	1931	m-Jeh	x....	132	5,600	3,000	18,700	7.59	Missionaries 1956 (1973, 34f expelled). Whites; first Africans 1962. (1975) 164Y. (1995) 1412Y.
Jerusalem Seventh-day Church of God	1959	I-3pA	.....	30	2,400	3,000	4,500	1.64	Kikuyu. 17 Kenyans ordained in 1970 by M=Ch of God Seventh-day (USA).15n,30Y.
Judah Israel Mission	1961	I-Ang	.....	2	1,100	3,009	2,000	-1.62	Bukusu split ex DYM. Temple in Kimilili, sacrifices. 10n,W=95%,70Y,80y.
Kenya Assemblies of God	1968	P-Pe2	.....	1,040	350,000	12,000	560,000	16.62	*KAG.* Split ex IPA by 2 missionaries as Kenya Pentecostal Fellowship. 4n,4x,W=50%,876Y.
Kenya Church of Christ	1965	I-Dis	x....	35	2,000	2,000	5,000	3.73	M=CC(Non-Instrumental) (USA). Nairobi, Kakamega. 50% Kikuyu. 12x,340Y.
Kenya Ev Lutheran Church	1948	P-Lut	L...K	90	5,000	8,694	15,000	2.21	*LCK. Kanisa la Kilutheri.* M=SLM(Sweden). 85% Gusii, 15% Luo. 8n,2x,W=50%,250Y.
Kenya Foundation of the Prophets Ch	1927	I-3pA	.....	7	10,000	41,325	20,000	-2.86	*KFPC.* Kikuyu. Led by 92-year-old founder. Prayer facing Mt. Kenya. W=20%,220Y,405y.
Last Ministry Church	c1965	I-3pA	.....	20	2,000	4,000	5,000	0.90	Coast. Taita body stressing ministry in last days before Second Coming of Christ.
Lavington Church, Nairobi	1960	P-Uni	.aw.k	5	970	1,500	1,800	0.73	First united parish (Angl, Meth, Presb); no other subsequently. 1x,W=50%,20Y,30y.
Lost Israelites of Kenya	1960	I-Non	.....	5	9,000	20,000	15,000	-1.14	*Israel with 10 Commandments.* Flags, uniforms, marching. HQ Kitale. 12n,W=95%,1000Y.
Luo Spirit Church	1968	I-Ang	.....	22	1,500	3,744	4,000	0.26	*Luo Roho Church.* Split ex NLC to assert glossolalia, exorcism. 36n,W=95%,41Y,82y.
Maranatha Church	1967	I-3pA	x....	60	2,000	1,922	3,000	1.80	M=Swedish Maranatha (Aramaic for 'Our Lord, come') Mission. Luo. 42n,1x7Y.

Continued opposite

Country Table 2–concluded

Official name (bold type = church with over 10% of all affiliated) 1	*Begun* 2	*Type* 3	*Counc* 4	*Congs* 5	*Adults* 6	*Affiliated 1970* 7	*Affiliated 1995* 8	*G%* 9	*Names, notes, and other statistics* (see Codebook, Part 3) 10
Maria Legio of Africa	1962	I-3sA	x....	962	130,000	150,000	385,000	3.84	Largest RCC schism in Africa. 90% Luo. 9 Dioceses, 7 cardinals, pope. Charismatics. 500n
Mennonite Church of Kenya	1965	P-Men	G...K	66	4,900	2,000	8,100	5.75	M=EMBMC(MCNA,USA). Luo immigrants from Tanzania in SNyanza. 2n,22f,1h,W=20%,50Y.
Methodist Church in Kenya	1862	P-Met	VWA.K	3,500	140,000	100,000	180,000	2.38	*MCK.* M=MMS(UK). A=1967. 3 Districts. 30n,10x,40f.2H,1u,W=75%,2258Y,1989y.
Miracle Revival Fellowship Pente Ch	c1948	I-3pA	.....	50	2,700	2,000	5,000	3.73	*Weni Mwanguvu/People of Power.* Taita split ex Anglicans after T L Osborn crusades.
Musanda Holy Ghost Church of EA	1934	I-3pA	.....	70	3,800	5,073	7,000	1.30	*MHGC.* First Luo Roho (Spirit) movement. Ex CMS. HQ Musanda. 13n,W=64%,80Y,111y.
National Independent Church of Africa	1929	I-Ang	I....	60	6,000	6,928	8,000	0.58	*NICA.* Embu and Meru ex-Anglicans formerly in AIPC. 41n,W=75%,80Y,165y.
New Apostolic Church	1973	I-3aX	x....	3,000	403,000	–	1,011,531	4.55	M=NAC(World HQ Zurich). Begun from Bombay, India. Phenomenal growth.
New East African Church	c1970	I-Non	.....	30	4,000	10,000	12,000	0.73	*NEAC.* Kamba schism at Mitaboni. HQ Kwakivanyu, Mitaboni, Machakos.
New Testament Church of God	1977	P-Pe3	Z....	23	1,440	–	3,600	5.56	M=CoG, World Mission (Cleveland).
Nomiya Luo Church	1914	I-Ang	I....	600	90,000	120,000	290,000	3.59	*NLC.* Nomiya=The Word of God was given to me. Ex CMS. 3 Dioceses. 31n,2076Y,3504y.
Nomiya Luo Sabbath	c1957	I-Ang	I....	180	7,000	10,680	11,000	0.12	*NLS.* Schism ex NLC. Muslim features stressed. HQ Nairobi. 23n,W=68%,340Y,860y.
Norwegian Pentecostal Mission in K	1955	P-Pe2	Z...K	90	10,000	15,000	30,000	2.81	*NPMK.* M=NPY(Norway). 48% Luo, 38% Kipsigis, 10% Gusii. HQ Ukwala. 60n,924Y.
Open Bible Standard Churches	c1970	I-3pW	.....	70	5,110	–	10,200	44.66	M=OBSC.
Pentecostal Assemblies of God	1910	P-Pe2	ZFG.a	5,000	225,000	192,000	500,000	3.90	*PAG.* M=PAoC. 73% Luhya, 10%, 10% Luo, 10% Gusii. 314n,11x,53f,1j,1s(71),W=65%,15000Y.
Pentecostal Evangelistic Fell of Africa	1938	P-Pe2	ZG..K	2,130	120,000	150,000	310,000	2.95	*PEFA.* 1962 union of IPA(USA) & Elim(USA). 526n,9x,40f,5000Y.
Power of Jesus Around the World Ch	1955	I-3pA	.....	220	11,000	20,000	23,000	0.56	Luo schism ex Voice of Salvation & Healing Ch after TLOsborn crusade in Uganda.
Presbyterian Church of East Africa	1891	P-Ref	RWA.K	1,400	350,000	100,000	600,000	7.43	*PCEA.* M=CSM(UK). 60% Kikuyu, 30% Meru. 71n,6x,14f,3H,9h,1p,18r,1u,W=80%,2450Y,5000y.
Redeemed Gospel Church	c1980	I-3pA	.....	100	10,000	–	26,000	6.67	*RGC.* F=bishop Arthur Gitonga. Cell principle.
Reformed Church of East Africa	1909	P-Ref	Rv..K	104	85,000	6,487	110,000	11.99	*RCEA.* M=DRC(SA), now NHK(Holland). A=1963. 50% Nandi.4n,3x,9f,1u,W=45%,508Y,478y.
Religion of the Ancestral Spirits	1944	I-mar	....	10	10,800	50,000	20,000	-3.60	*Dini ya Msambwa (DYM). Israel Anglican Ch.* Schism ex Quakers. Banned 1948, 1968. Mt Elgon.
Ruwe Holy Ghost Ch of East Africa	1939	I-3pA	I....	90	2,000	5,000	4,000	-0.89	Schism ex MHGC over uniforms, setting up rival HQ at Ruwe. Luo. 5n,W=95%,16Y,86y.
Salvation Army	1921	P-Sal	xwa.K	1,360	100,000	110,000	150,000	1.25	*Jeshi la Wokovu.* 8 Divisions, East Africa Territory. 70% Luhya. 447n,23x,1s,W=75%.
Seventh-day Adventist Church	1906	P-Adv	x...k	1,084	158,000	171,023	263,211	1.74	*East African Union.* 45% Luo, 45% Gusii. 105n,16x,37f,1H,11h,1j,1r,906t(159570),W=64%,8601Y
Sinai Church of East Africa	1965	I-3pA	.T..T	4	540	1,200	1,000	-0.73	*SCEA.* Luhya schism ex AICN, growing very slowly. HQ North Maragoli. 3n,W=50%.
Spirit Church of God of Israel	1960	I-3pA	.v...	5	5,000	40,000	10,000	-5.39	*Roho CGI.* Schism ex AICN as World Spiritual Israel Ch. 60% Luo, 30% Luhya. 36n.
United Pentecostal Church	1971	P-Pe1	.....	214	19,500	–	32,500	4.17	*Jesus Only Church.* M=UPC(USA). Unitarian Pentecostals. HQ Nairobi. 30n,2f,1p.
Voice of Prophecy Church	c1960	I-Adv	.....	8	500	2,000	1,000	-2.73	Luo sabbatarian church led by blind charismatic prophetess Susanna Nyabulwa.
Voice of Salvation & Healing Church	1954	I-3pA	.....	950	52,000	12,000	80,000	7.88	Early Luo schism ex AIM over charismata. Also in Uganda (10 chs), Tanzania (40 chs). M=CAM.
Wokofu (Salvation) African Church	1966	I-Sal	.T.TT	130	6,000	15,000	20,000	1.16	*WAC.* Ex Salvation Army; yellow uniforms, symbol 'W'. 60% Luhya, 30% Kamba. 35n,160Y.
World Christian Soldiers Church	c1966	I-Sal	.....	10	1,000	1,000	2,000	2.81	Luo movement requiring all members to use musical instruments in worship.
Other African indigenous churches	1940	I-3pA	.....	5,000	580,000	30,000	1,200,000	15.90	A very large number of new AICs, charismatic, unregistered, including EJCSK. Total about 600.
Other Protestant denominations		P-	.....	200	20,000	5,000	30,000	0.05	Total about 70 (see list below), including Presbyterian Evangelical Ch of Africa (1995).
Other Orthodox churches	1973	O-	.....	10	2,000	–	5,000	4.55	Ethiopian Orthodox Ch, and Apostolic Ch of St Mark (see below).
Other marginal Protestant bodies		m-	.....	40	3,000	1,000	6,000	0.05	Bodies mainly from USA (see below), including Branhamites, Worldwide Ch of God.
Other independent charismatic chs	c1985	I-3cA	.....	500	50,000	–	80,000	10.00	In around 50 very loose geographical/linguistic networks or fellowships.
Doubly-affiliated		2-aff			-460,000	0	-943,080		Evangelicals and pentecostals who are also baptized Roman Catholics.
Totals				**50,642**	**9,779,628**	**6,082,784**	**20,045,538**		

Churches, members, growth, 1900-2025	*Congs*	*Adults*	*Affiliated*	*G%*	*Total denominations*	*6 Megablocs:*	*O*	*R*	*A*	*P*	*I*	*m*
Total churches, members, and denominations (mid-1900)	10	2,300	5,000	10.68	5	....	0	1	1	3	0	0
Total churches, members, and denominations (mid-1970)	17,699	2,856,178	6,082,784	10.68	446	....	1	1	1	33	398	12
Total churches, members, and denominations (mid-1990)	42,000	8,365,000	17,146,000	5.32	795	....	1	1	1	49	720	23
Total churches, members, and denominations (mid-1995)	50,642	9,779,628	20,045,538	3.17	814	....	7	1	1	51	731	23
Total churches, members, and denominations (mid-2000)	55,000	10,966,000	22,477,365	2.32	825	....	7	1	1	53	740	23
Total churches, members, and denominations (mid-2025)	95,000	16,100,000	33,000,000	1.55	874	....	12	1	1	80	750	30

NOTES ON TABLE ABOVE

NATIONAL COUNCILS (Column 4, 5th letter).

- C = Associated Christian Churches of Kenya (ACCK).
- a = member of both NCCK and EFK.
- b = member of both OAICK and NCCK.
- E = Evangelical Fellowship of Kenya (EFK).
- I = Organization of African Independent/Instituted Churches of Kenya (OAICK).
- J = International Spiritual and United Indigenous African Churches (formerly Int Holy Spirit & United Independent Chs).
- K = National Council of Churches of Kenya (NCCK) (Jumuiya ya Wakristo wa Kenya).
- k = consultative associate member of NCCK.
- R = Kenya Episcopal Conference (KEC).
- T = East Africa Christian Alliance (EACA) (all members are Kenyan churches).

Other national councils. These number at least 11, all being attempts to unite African indigenous churches: African Independent Communion Churches, Council of East African Evangelist Societies of God (1970), East African United Churches and Orthodox Coptic Communion (1962), Ethiopian Orthodox Holy Spirit & United Churches of East Africa (1970), Indigenous African Christian Churches (IACC) (1974), Kenya African United Christian Churches (1961), Kenya Independent Churches Fellowship (1960), National United Churches Association of East Africa (1969), United Churches of Africa (1969), United Churches of East Africa (1969), United Independent Churches of East Africa (1969), United Orthodox Independent Churches of East Africa (1971), United Orthodox Independent Zion Churches of Kenya (1971).

Local councils. 6 local branches of the NCCK.

OTHER AFRICAN INDIGENOUS CHURCHES. In 1973 there were about 90 other smaller bodies, mostly pentecostal, and mostly with well under 1,000 adult members each; about 80 of these were registered with government as lawful societies. The larger of these bodies include the following (with, in brackets, year of founding, and present total of adult members): African Holy Ghost Christian Ch (1968; 600), African Sinai Ch (1965; 350), Apostles Christian Ch of Africa (1968; 542), Christ Evangelistic Association (c1959; 10,000 claimed), Christian Association (1,100), Christian Chs (Chs of Christ) (1968), Ch of Holy Communion of God (1969; 550), Ch of Messiah (1948; 5,000), Ch of Spirit in Grace and Truth in Africa (c1967; 600), Ch of the Living God (c1964; 429), Communion Ch of Africa (c1970; 400), Disciples of Christ in Africa (1970; 700), Divine Christian Ch of East Africa (1962; 3,500), Full Gospel Fellowship Mission of Africa (c1964: 829), Independent African Orthodox Ch (c1965; 968), Israel Holy Ghost Ch of Kenya (1971; 936), Kimbanguist Ch (EJCSK, from Zaire), Miracles and Wonders Ch (1975 application WCC), Muolo Roho Israel Ch (1950; 600), Pentecostal Christian Universal Ch (1968; 970), Sabina Church of the Ark (700), Seventh-day Missionary Ch (1936; 500), Truth of the Apostles (c1966; 300). By 1975 indigenous bodies from other continents were beginning to enter, including the Unification Ch (Moon Ch) from Korea (HSAUWC).

OTHER PROTESTANT DENOMINATIONS. These smaller bodies include: Children of God International (from USA, UK), Christian Faith Mission of Kenya (85), Dutch Reformed Ch (20), East African Mission (1970; 231), Kenya Revival Centre (c1960; 400), Nairobi Baptist Ch (1958: 140), Nairobi Undenominational Ch (Open Brethren) (c1930; 45), Restoration (House-Church Movement/Pyramid Ch/Ch of the Great Shepherd; neo-charismatic split ex mainline Charismatic Renewal), Scriptural Holiness Mission (1948; 150 members; member of NCCK), Seventh-day Adventist Reform Movement (c1968; 400), World-Wide Missions (1961).

OTHER ORTHODOX CHURCHES. After several years of contact with indigenous federations of churches in Kenya, 2 churches have opened teaching missions and churches in Nairobi: in 1973, the Ethiopian Orthodox Church (HQ Addis Ababa); and in 1976, the Coptic Orthodox Church (HQ Cairo), registered in Kenya as the Apostolic Church of St Mark, with an Egyptian bishop set aside solely for ministry with African indigenous churches.

OTHER MARGINAL PROTESTANT BODIES. These include Branhamites (Kenya Local Believers, End Time Believers; begun 1970 from HQ Jeffersonville, IN, USA; Jesus-Only Unitarians), Worldwide Ch of God (Radio Ch of God, USA; begun 1975; visiting teams from Japan et al), et alia.

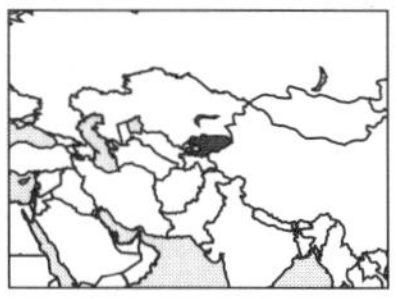

KIRGHIZIA

SECULAR DATA, AD 2000

STATE

Official name: Kyrgyz Respublikasy (The Kyrgyz Republic).
Short name: Kyrgyzstan. **Adjective of nationality:** Kyrgyz.
Flag: Red field with stylized sun in center.
Area: 198,500 sq. km. (76,600 sq. mi.).
Government: Unitary multiparty republic with two legislative houses (1921 Russian republic, 1936 Soviet rule).
Legislature: Assembly of People's Representatives, 70 members; Legislative Assembly, 35 members.
Official language: Kirghiz, Russian.
Monetary unit: 1 som = 100 tyiyn. **US$1=** 21.60 som.
Chief cities: BISHKEK (Pishpek, Frunze) 743,601; Os (Osh) 276,066; Dzalal-Abad 92,601; Tokmak (Bolshoy Tokmak) 82,518; Karakol (Przevalsk) 74,521.
Political divisions: 7 provinces.
Armed forces: 12,000.

DEMOGRAPHY

Population: 4,699,000.
Population density: 23.6/sq. km. (61.3/sq. mi.).
Under 15 years: 1,645,000.
Growth rate p.a.: 0.90% (births 23.07, deaths 6.83).
Mortality: Infant, per 1,000: 35.9; **Maternal per 100,000:** 110.0.
Life expectancy: 69 (male 65, female 73).
Household size: 4.2. **Floor area per person, sq.m:** 15.0.
Major languages: Kirghiz, Russian, Uzbek, German, Kazakh.
Urban dwellers: 40.08%. **Urban growth rate p.a.:** 1.8%.
Labor force: 41%.

ETHNOLINGUISTIC PEOPLES

59.8% Kirghiz; 16.0% Russian; 13.2% Uzbek; 1.9% Ukrainian; 1.6% Tatar.

ECONOMY

National income p.a. per person: US$700; **per family:** US$2,940.

EDUCATION

Adult literacy: 97% (male 99%, female 95%). **Schools:** 3,359.
Universities: 12. **School enrolment:** female/male: 96%/93%.

HEALTH

Access to health services: 70%. **Access to safe water:** 75%.
Hospitals: 396 (99 beds per 10,000). **Doctors:** 14,674.
Blind: 4,000. **Deaf:** 272,600. **Murder rate:** 10.
Lepers: 1,000.

LITERATURE

New book titles p.a.: 330 (70 p.a. per million). **Periodicals:** 70.
Newspapers: 2 dailies.

COMMUNICATION (per 1,000 people)

Phones: 77 (0% mobile). **Radios:** 183. **TV sets:** 238.
Daily newspaper circulation: 11. **Computers:** 25.

HUMAN LIFE AND LIBERTY (optimum condition=100.0%)

HDI: 63.5. **HSI:** 30.0. **HFI:** 15.0. **EFL:** 15.0.

Country status. Kirghizia, a former republic of the Soviet Union, is a mountainous, landlocked country in Central Asia bordering China. The economy is based on the production of cotton, tobacco, sugar beets, and opium.

HUMAN LIFE AND LIBERTY

Human rights and freedoms. Kirghizia became an independent nation in 1991 and adopted a new constitution in 1993 establishing a unitary, democratic and secular republic and guaranteeing all civil and political rights. However, the legal and judicial systems remain largely unchanged from the Soviet period and contain provisions inimical to the growth of personal freedoms. Concerns are also raised by observers regarding the government's policy toward

Country Table 1. Religious adherents in Kirghizia, AD 1900-2025.

Year	1900		1970		mid-1990		Annual change, 1990-2000				mid-1995		mid-2000		mid-2025	
Name	Adherents	%	Adherents	%	Adherents	%	Natural	Conversion	Total	Rate	Adherents	%	Adherents	%	Adherents	%
Muslims	541,000	96.3	1,005,187	33.9	2,366,000	53.8	16,397	32,577	48,974	1.90	2,663,300	58.3	2,855,736	60.8	4,688,000	76.9
Nonreligious	500	0.1	860,000	29.0	1,063,000	24.2	7,353	-12,176	-4,823	-0.46	1,030,000	22.5	1,014,770	21.6	800,000	13.1
Christians	**17,000**	**3.0**	**340,813**	**11.5**	**505,850**	**11.5**	**3,499**	**-5,260**	**-1,761**	**-0.35**	**510,000**	**11.2**	**488,245**	**10.4**	**450,000**	**7.4**
PROFESSION																
crypto-Christians	0	0.0	50,000	1.7	30,000	0.7	208	792	1,000	2.92	35,000	0.8	40,000	0.9	55,000	0.9
professing Christians	**17,000**	**3.0**	**290,813**	**9.8**	**475,850**	**10.8**	**3,291**	**-6,052**	**-2,761**	**-0.60**	**475,000**	**10.4**	**448,245**	**9.5**	**395,000**	**6.5**
AFFILIATION																
unaffiliated Christians	1,000	0.2	0	0.0	21,650	0.5	150	-57	93	0.42	18,800	0.4	22,580	0.5	25,500	0.4
affiliated Christians	**16,000**	**2.9**	**340,813**	**11.5**	**484,200**	**11.0**	**3,349**	**-5,203**	**-1,854**	**-0.39**	**491,200**	**10.7**	**465,665**	**9.9**	**424,500**	**7.0**
Orthodox	10,000	1.8	274,000	9.2	390,000	8.9	2,698	-5,392	-2,694	-0.71	384,450	8.4	363,065	7.7	320,000	5.3
Independents	0	0.0	23,200	0.8	59,400	1.4	411	699	1,110	1.73	69,750	1.5	70,500	1.5	70,000	1.2
Protestants	1,000	0.2	43,413	1.5	33,000	0.8	228	-528	-300	-0.95	35,050	0.8	30,000	0.6	30,000	0.5
Roman Catholics	5,000	0.9	200	0.0	1,400	0.0	10	10	20	1.34	1,500	0.0	1,600	0.0	3,500	0.1
Marginal Christians	0	0.0	0	0.0	400	0.0	3	7	10	2.26	450	0.0	500	0.0	1,000	0.0
Trans-megabloc groupings																
Evangelicals	800	0.1	1,200	0.0	2,600	0.1	18	22	40	1.44	3,378	0.1	3,000	0.1	3,000	0.1
Pentecostals/Charismatics	0	0.0	2,000	0.1	13,100	0.3	91	379	470	3.11	15,985	0.4	17,800	0.4	25,000	0.4
Great Commission Christians	**15,000**	**2.7**	**118,000**	**4.0**	**246,000**	**5.6**	**1,702**	**-3,786**	**-2,084**	**-0.88**	**250,000**	**5.5**	**225,162**	**4.8**	**255,000**	**4.2**
Atheists	0	0.0	700,000	23.6	420,000	9.6	2,905	-15,396	-12,491	-3.47	325,000	7.1	295,093	6.3	100,000	1.6
Buddhists	500	0.1	5,000	0.2	16,000	0.4	111	330	441	2.46	18,500	0.4	20,411	0.4	32,000	0.5
Ethnoreligionists	2,000	0.4	50,000	1.7	18,000	0.4	125	-80	45	0.25	17,900	0.4	18,448	0.4	16,000	0.3
Jews	1,000	0.2	4,000	0.1	5,300	0.1	37	2	39	0.72	5,400	0.1	5,694	0.1	8,000	0.1
Zoroastrians	0	0.0	0	0.0	850	0.0	6	3	9	1.01	900	0.0	940	0.0	2,000	0.0
World A (unevangelized persons)	504,114	89.7	2,223,375	75.0	2,601,840	59.2	17,984	-30,674	-12,690	-0.50	2,500,573	54.7	2,471,674	52.6	2,901,696	47.6
World B (evangelized non-Christians)	40,886	7.3	400,312	13.5	1,287,310	29.3	8,950	35,934	44,884	3.05	1,560,858	34.1	1,739,081	37.0	2,744,304	45.0
World C (Christians)	17,000	3.0	340,813	11.5	505,850	11.5	3,499	-5,260	-1,761	-0.35	510,000	11.2	488,245	10.4	450,000	7.4
Country's population	**562,000**	**100.0**	**2,964,500**	**100.0**	**4,395,000**	**100.0**	**30,433**	**0**	**30,433**	**0.67**	**4,571,432**	**100.0**	**4,699,000**	**100.0**	**6,096,000**	**100.0**

COLUMNS, ROWS.
For meanings and definitions, see Codebook (Part 3). Note that, by definition, total 'Christians' = professing + crypto-Christians, which also = affiliated + unaffiliated Christians, and also = Great Commission Christians + latent Christians. Percentages may not always total exactly, due to rounding.

NOTES ON RELIGIONS
ATHEISTS. Rapid decline after 1989 with most ethnic Kirghiz reaffirming their Muslim faith.
BAHA'IS. Expanding since collapse of Communism in 1991, to 12 local spiritual assemblies by 1996.
BUDDHISTS. Koreans and Kalmyks.
ORTHODOX. Decline after 1989 due to emigration of Russians & Ukrainians.
PROTESTANTS. Decline after 1989 due to emigration of Germans.

Great Commission Instrument Panel: status of Kirghizia (for explanation see start of Part 4)

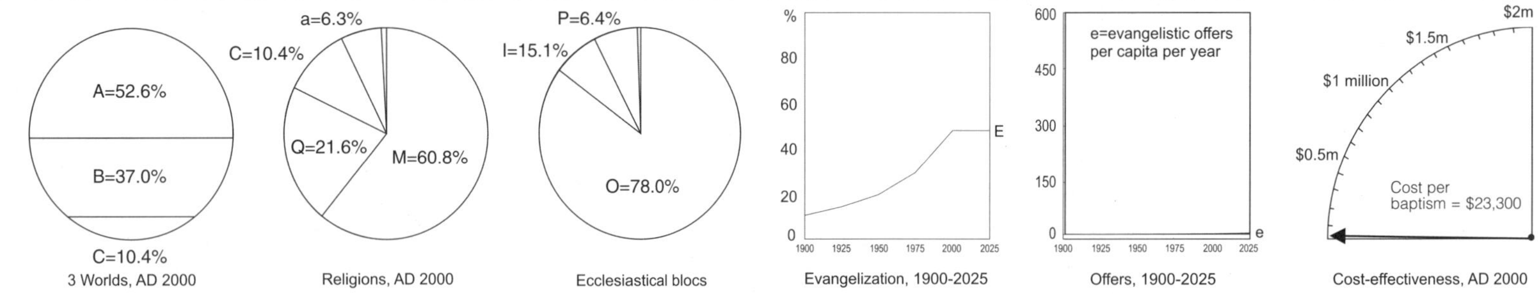

non-Kyrgyz minorities, especially Russians. A new law on press freedom was passed in 1992 and it conforms to internationally accepted standards. The daily press is often critical of the president and his government and have resisted attempts to muzzle its freedom to criticize official policies and actions. A number of human rights organizations are active in the country.

NON-CHRISTIAN RELIGIONS

Islam. The region that includes Kirghizia was opened to the entry of Islam following the defeat of the Chinese at a battle near Talas in AD 751. Few local people became Muslims, however, until the late 16th and early 17th centuries, when Muslim missionaries entered through the Fergana Valley. The expansion of Islam and its influence was stunted by the mountainous inaccessibility of most of the country. In the early 19th century Kirghizia was conquered by the Uzbek khan of Khokand (Kokand). Only then did the northern and eastern regions become largely Muslim. This expansion was led by Sufi orders, and Sufism remains influential. Also, Islam continues to be strongest in the south of the country. Nearly all the Muslims of Kirghizia are Hanafi Sunnis.

Between 1917 and 1930 Islam was brutally attacked in all of Soviet Central Asia. One estimate is that 80% of the mosques were closed. The work of 90% of the clergy was halted, often because they were executed or sent to labor camps. Another strong anti-religious crusade swept the country in the late 1950s, under Khruschev. Even then, nearly all citizens, party members, and even officials continued to participate in Muslim funeral rites, which were often as much shamanistic as Muslim. Officials responsible for atheist propaganda were frustrated to see even high officials honoring and using the Quran at times.

Muslim activities were organized and administered under the Central Asian Spiritual Directorate of Muslims (SADUM). Mullahs who registered with SADUM enjoyed certain privileges and endured certain restrictions. In the late 1980s, Kirghizia had only 33 officially registered mosques but, by one count, 296 unofficial ones (mosques or houses or prayer, often called 'study groups'). Most religious activity was led by unofficial, informally trained, volunteer mullahs. They held meetings in homes, tea-houses, and cemeteries, led unofficial Quran schools, preserved and restored shrines, and officiated at weddings, funerals, and circumcisions. Usually practitioners of folk Islam, they also supplied amulets and talismans with surahs from the Quran. The most overt opposition was sustained by the Sufi brotherhoods (*tariqat*) which have been anti-Modernist, anti-Communist, decentralized, and strongest among former nomadic communities. Worship at holy places has been an important feature of Muslim devotion in Kirghizia. According to one source, there were as many as 200 holy places or pilgrimage sites functioning quietly in the Soviet era, often with clandestine schools. Some bear names that connect them with Old Testament characters, considered a mere cover for pre-Islamic local deities.

SADUM ended abruptly with independence in 1991 and a mufti for Kirghizia was soon appointed. Shrines were allowed to re-open and relics were returned by the state. Construction of new mosques began immediately and soon accelerated. By 1994 the country had more than 160 open mosques, 7 madrasahs, and a new Islamic Center at Bishkek. Kirghiz have been invited to study Islam in Egypt, in Saudi Arabia, and at the International Islamic University in Malaysia. Some have received scholarships from Syria.

The Muslims of Kirghizia have the reputation of not being very devout. Through most of the country, few have contact with the larger Muslim world. Kirghiz women have not traditionally worn the veil, and—rare in Islamic practice—they often pray alongside the men. Fundamentalism has never gained much of a foothold in the country. It is common for Kirghiz and Kazakstanis to boast that they are the least Islamic and the most European of the Central Asian nations. That is true ethnically, as these 2 countries include larger Russian and other-European populations.

But Islam is strong in some areas, notably the Fergana Valley, most of which lies in Uzbekistan and Tajikistan. At the eastern end of the valley is the Kirghiz city of Os (also Osh or Oz), which in the 10th century was a major center of Islamic scholarship. A mountain there is called *Takht-e-Suleiman*, or 'the seat of Solomon', on the understanding that King Solomon once blessed it. It is the most important pilgrimage site in Kirghizia if not in all of Central Asia. Though officially closed in the Soviet era, it was still regularly visited by tens of thousands of faithful. Other important shrines at Os include the reputed tomb of the Old Testament character Job, and the Mosque of Babar. Babar, the emperor who founded the Muslim Mogul empire in India, is revered as a saint. Aging Kirgese Sufis preserve the stories of Babar and proclaim them at the recently-rebuilt shrine that replaces the one destroyed by Stalin. In the early 1990s the Wahabi reform movement spread rapidly in the Fergana Valley, touching Os and other southern Kirghiz towns. Wahabis have been active in building mosques, teaching in madrasahs, converting Kirgese to Islam or to deeper faith, and opposing Christian evangelization. With the help of generous Saudi funds, a large Wahabi mosque was built in Os and another begun in Bishkek.

Islam is an important facet of national identity, separating the nation from its bitter years of Russian domination, but it has yet to appear as a visible presence in national politics. That is partly because many clerics, probably most, are not ethnic Kirghiz. Many are Tatar immigrants. Often they are semi-literate, their teaching based on oral tradition. In the Soviet era it was forbidden to learn Arabic. In the first years after independence, Kirghiz were suspicious that clergy had been KGB agents. There was much turnover in the higher Islamic positions due to such distrust. The

Country summary. **Worlds A, B, C by ethnolinguistic peoples, cities, and major civil divisions in Kirghizia.**

	PEOPLES							CITIES							CIVIL DIVISIONS						
World	Num	Pop 2000	C%	Christians	E%	U%	Unevangelized	Num	Pop 2000	C%	Christians	E%	U%	Unevangelized	Num	Pop 2000	C%	Christians	E%	U%	Unevangelized
A	24	3,761,833	0.06	2,092	35	65	2,462,172	5	387,132	1.29	4,977	36	64	249,030	6	4,017,756	9.21	369,959	47	53	2,146,088
B	7	786,721	44.38	349,140	99	1	10,563	2	1,019,667	15.19	154,865	55	45	457,766	1	681,581	14.04	95,706	52	48	327,012
C	11	150,780	75.89	114,432	100	0	362	0	0	0.00	0	0	0	0	0	0	0.00	0	0	0	0
Total	**42**	**4,699,334**	**9.91**	**465,664**	**47**	**53**	**2,473,097**	**7**	**1,406,799**	**11.36**	**159,842**	**50**	**50**	**706,796**	**7**	**4,699,337**	**9.91**	**465,665**	**47**	**53**	**2,473,100**

Islamic Renaissance Party (IRP) exists only underground and with apparently little popularity. Political parties based on religion are banned. On the one hand, the government has welcomed the rising interest in Islam, and religion, as a positive moral force. On the other hand, any expression of Islamic political action has been quickly suppressed. Unlike some of its neighbors, Kirghizia has deliberately not joined the Islamic Conference Organization.

The Muslim community was rocked in 1992 when the Qu'ran appeared in Kirghiz for the first time, translated by the famous Kirghiz poet Ernest Tursunov. His life was threatened and Muslim clergy called for all copies to burned. Tursunov also worked on translating the New Testament, and was publicly quoted as saying that the New Testament was to the Qu'ran like light to darkness. Thousands of copies of the Kirghiz New Testament (not Tursunov's translation) sold out quickly. The local Writer's Union welcomed the publication of both holy books, and invited both Christians and Muslims to make formal presentations on national television.

Other religions. Shamans are active in the mountains of Kirghizia, helping the living speak with the dead, conducting funerals, wrestling against evil spirits (*jinns*), and serving as healers. The culture's ancient shamanistic heritage is also kept alive in the many epics, legends, and poems that each generation recounts to the next. These teach about the spiritual powers associated with the sun, the moon, certain rivers, and sacred mountains. In the most prominent spot in many yurts is a cradle made of wood from 'the eternal tree', the juniper. A kind of Totemism also survives, as various Kirghiz tribes are identified with animals and their powers—such as the deer, the white camel, the snake, or the bear.

Most Jews came to the country in World War II, and apparently now most hope to emigrate to Israel, despite the new freedoms since independence. The Society of Jewish Culture of Kirghizia was the first religious organization to register with the government when that became possible in 1991. Jews moved quickly to enjoy their new freedoms, importing copies of the Torah, celebrating religious events and holy days, and circumcising 80 males with the aid of a specialist from Europe. Because of persecution, many Jews hid their identity during the Communist era. Only 250 of the 980 Jews who emigrated to Israel in 1991 were identified as Jews on their passports.

CHRISTIANITY

The first Christians in the area were Italian and French monks who, on their way to China, visited Tokmak (near Bishkek) in the 12th century. Tokmak was later the seat of a Nestorian archbishopric.

ORTHODOX CHURCHES. Russians began colonizing present-day Kirghizia in the mid-19th century, and by 1876 the tsar controlled the region. Many Russians, Slavs and peoples of European ancestry poured into the area, most of them Orthodox and some of them Protestant.

The Christian presence in Kirghizia in the 20th century has waxed and waned according to immigration and, since 1991, emigration of Russians, Germans, Ukrainians, and other European peoples. The country was under Soviet power from 1919 to 1991. Christianity grew due to renewed emigration. Christianity also suffered under Communist anti-religious purges and persecution. However, even the officials responsible for atheist propaganda admitted their efforts met with little success in Kirghizia. The 1940s and 1950s brought renewed waves of immigration. Ethnic Kirghiz diminished from 52% of the national population to 40.5%.

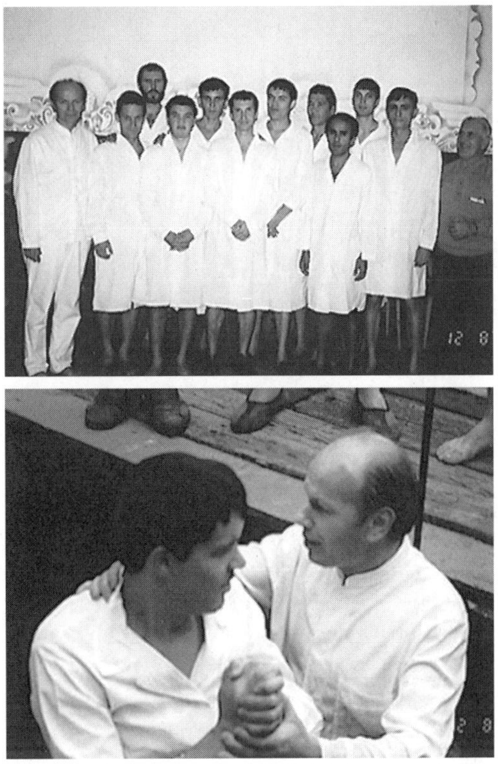

Good News Mission. Kirghiz Pastor Vladimir visits prisons, holds Bible class, (*bottom*) baptizes an inmate.

PROTESTANT CHURCHES. The Germans who were exiled there by Stalin, many of them Lutherans or Mennonites, were received better by the Kirghiz than the Russians, though almost no ethnic Central Asians ever converted to Christianity. Since independence the population of Kirghizia has been in dramatic flux. In 4 years 169,000 people emigrated, most of them Russian and German, many of them Christian. Then 61,000 of them returned. Ethnic Kirghiz have regained majority status in the country.

Some expatriate Evangelical Christians, most of them Korean, have entered the country since independence to help with various aspects of national development and to teach in the few officially registered Bible schools. Expatriate Christian groups have served in prison ministry, orphanages, schools for the blind, and other social ministry. A Korean mission has presented a series of well-advertised and well-attended orchestral concerts throughout the country. The main Baptist church of Bishkek has a large building, seating more than 1,000, but German emigration reduced the membership to 250 by the mid-1990s, reflecting the national trend. Undaunted, Baptists have joined with others to sponsor a Bible school and evangelistic activities. Soon Russian-language services were filling the building. From various evangelistic efforts, some conversions of ethnic Kirghiz have been noted.

CATHOLIC CHURCH. In the early 1990s a Catholic Church opened in Bishkek, the city's first for centuries, if not the first ever.

The Holy See has diplomatic relations with Kirghizia and in AD 2000 is represented to government and the Catholic hierarchy by a nuncio residing in Bishkek.

CHURCH AND STATE

The Law on Religious Freedom and Religious Organizations, enacted in 1991, outlines one of the strongest commitments to religious freedom in all of Central Asia. It guarantees 'the individual right of every citizen to freely and independently define his attitude toward religion, personally or with others, to profess any religion or none, to change religious convictions, and also to manifest and distribute religious convictions'. Religious organizations are given tax-free status. When the new national constitution was being drafted, a reference to the 'moral principles, national traditions, and spiritual values of Islam' attracted objections from other religious communities. In late 1992, before the constitution was adopted, the wording was changed, instead mentioning 'Islam and other religions' in a positive light. The constitution also guarantees complete freedom of religion and evangelization. All religions are equal before the law. Islam enjoys little preference in national life, and Christianity suffers almost no restrictions. The Orthodox Christmas day (January 6th) is a national holiday, as are 2 Muslim holy days. Churches can operate schools, while the government cannot finance religious—or atheistic—education. Open evangelistic events have been allowed, including large gatherings in stadiums organized by Baptists, Adventists, and Pentecostals. Muslim leaders have objected. At one point, mullahs threatened to kill any Kirghiz who converted, but no inter-religious violence was known.

BROADCASTING AND MEDIA

Programming in central Asian languages (Kazakh, Tajik, Uzbek, Kyrgyz) can be received from TWR (Guam), FEBC (Saipan), and HCJB (Ecuador), and in Turkish from TWR (Monaco) and TWR (Albania). HCJB planted a local radio ministry in Kirghizia in partnership with Ray of Hope.

Some 1.4 million have seen the 'Jesus' Film, mainly through broadcasts on television.

INTERDENOMINATIONAL ORGANIZATIONS

No such councils exist.

FUTURE TRENDS AND PROSPECTS

Christians seem likely to decline in the post-Communist period falling to 7.4% by AD 2025. The nonreligious and atheists, over 50% of the population in 1970, will fall to under 15% by AD 2025.

If there is no significant response to Christianity among the Kirghiz, Christians could fall to under 5% of the population by mid-century. Muslims are likely to grow past 90% in the same period with the nonreligious and atheists continuing to decline.

BIBLIOGRAPHY

Country profile, Kyrgyzstan. London: International Institute for the Study of Islam and Christianity, 1994. 91p.
Din zhana dinii kaldyktar. B. Amanaliev. Frunze: 'Ilim' basmasy, 1969. 177p.
Doislamskie verovaniia i ikh perezhitki u kirgizov. T. D. Baialiva. Frunze: 'Ilim', 1972. 170p.
In the Kirghiz steppes. J. W. Wardell. London: Galley Press, 1961.
Iz istorii religii i ateizma v Kyrgyzstane. M. Abdyldaev. Bishkek: 'Ilim', 1991. 127p.
Kirghizia. K. Omurkulov. Moscow: Novosti, 1987. 85p.
'Kirgizistan and the Kirgiz,' A. Hetmanek, in *Handbook of major Soviet nationalities*, p.238–61. Z. Katz (ed). London: Collier Macmillan, 1975. (With bibliography).

Country Table 2. **Organized churches and denominations in Kirghizia.**

Official name (bold type = church with over 10% of affiliated) 1	*Begun* 2	*Type* 3	*Counc* 4	*Congs* 5	*Adults* 6	*Affiliated 1970* 7	*Affiliated 1995* 8	*G%* 9	*Names, notes, and other statistics* (see Codebook, Part 3) 10
Armenian Apostolic Church		O-Arm	E....	2	1,920	2,000	2,500	0.05	Armenians.
Assembly Hall Churches	c1992	I-3nC	.....	1	20	–	100	33.33	*Local Churches. Little Flock.* Begun 1922 in China. Chinese.
Baptist Churches of Kirghizia	c1950	P-Bap	T....	29	3,460	313	5,600	12.23	Formerly AUCECB/EUUCB. Russians, Germans, 1 Kirghiz congregation.

Continued overleaf

Country Table 2–concluded

Official name (bold type = church with over 10% of affiliated) 1	*Begun* 2	*Type* 3	*Counc* 4	*Congs* 5	*Adults* 6	*Affiliated 1970* 7	*Affiliated 1995* 8	*G%* 9	*Names, notes, and other statistics* (see Codebook, Part 3) 10
Catholic Church in Kirghizia		R-LEr	P....	4	800	200	1,500	0.05	Largely Europeans: Lithuanians, Byelorussians, Estonians, a few Russians.
Church of Christ in Kirghizia	c1990	I-3cZ	.....	12	2,000	–	5,000	20.00	M=USA chs (Vineyard, Grace Fellowship, Presbyterians). 75% Russians, 10% Kirghiz. 200n.
Evangelical Lutheran Church	c1930	P-Lut	.....	80	10,000	40,000	20,000	-2.73	Germans, with massive emigration after 1989.
Georgian Orthodox Church		O-Geo	M....	1	300	400	450	0.05	Residents from Georgia.
Greek Orthodox Church		O-Gre	C....	2	800	1,600	1,500	0.05	Greek residents.
Independent Charismatic Churches	1990	I-3cZ	.....	2	240	–	600	20.00	Including several Kirghiz breakoff groups.
Jehovah's Witnesses	c1970	m-Jeh	.....	3	135	–	450	27.68	Active witnessing under way throughout Communist era.
Korean Methodist Church		I-Met	.....	5	1,000	500	2,000	0.05	Korean settlers from 1952 and earlier.
Old Mennonites		P-Men	.....	5	700	1,000	1,500	0.05	Germans. Farmers, businessmen.
Old Ritualist Church	c1900	I-OBe	x....	1	600	700	1,000	1.44	Old Believers. Byelorussians, Russians.
Pentecostal Church		P-Pe2	.....	20	2,300	2,000	3,600	0.05	95% Russians, 3% Kyrgyz, 10 other ethnic groups.
Presbyterian Church in Kirghizia	c1990	P-Ref	.....	1	300	–	600	20.00	Linked to Korean Presbyterian Ch in Korea. 90% Koreans, 5% Russians, 5% Kirghiz.
Russian Orthodox Ch: D Tashkent	c1800	O-Rus	.....	200	270,000	270,000	380,000	1.38	Diocese of Tashkent & Central Asia, ROC.
Seventh-day Adventist Church	c1985	P-Adv	.....	1	1,050	–	1,750	10.00	*SDA*. 90% Russians, 10% various ethnic group including Kirghiz.
Tree of Life	c1993	I-3cZ	.....	3	20	–	50	50.00	Kirghiz split from Church of Faith (Presbyterian).
Ukrainian Orthodox Church (P Kiev)	c1993	I-Ukr	.....	50	30,000	3,000	40,000	50.00	Ukrainian residents. Under Patriarchate of Kiev.
Other independent Orthodox chs		I-Ort	.....	40	13,000	19,000	21,000	0.05	Ukrainian Autocephalous OC, ROCOR, Bulgarian OC.
Other Protestant churches		P-	.....	50	1,000	100	2,000	0.05	Total 12: ELCE and MCE (Estonians), ERCL (Lithuanians), CEF, CWE (Polish), IPKh, CCECB.
Totals				**512**	**339,645**	**340,813**	**491,200**		

Churches, members, growth, 1900-2025	*Congs*	*Adults*	*Affiliated*	*G%*	*Total denominations*	*6 Megablocs:* *O*	*R*	*A*	*P*	*I*	*m*
Total churches, members, and denominations (mid-1900)	50	10,300	16,000	4.47	1	1	0	0	0	0	0
Total churches, members, and denominations (mid-1970)	178	218,935	340,813	4.47	20	4	1	0	9	6	0
Total churches, members, and denominations (mid-1990)	500	335,000	484,200	1.77	35	4	1	0	17	12	1
Total churches, members, and denominations (mid-1995)	512	339,645	491,200	0.29	37	4	1	0	18	13	1
Total churches, members, and denominations (mid-2000)	530	322,000	465,665	-1.06	39	4	1	0	19	14	1
Total churches, members, and denominations (mid-2025)	520	294,000	424,500	-0.37	78	6	1	0	30	40	1

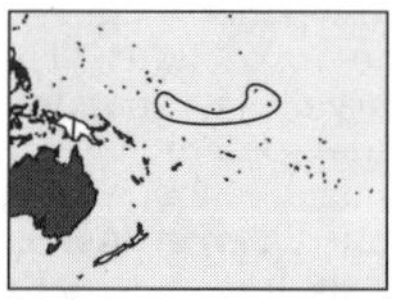

KIRIBATI

SECULAR DATA, AD 2000

STATE
Official name: Ribaberikin Kiribati (The Republic of Kiribati).
Short name: Kiribati. **Adjective of nationality:** of Kiribati.
Flag: (of the colony) British Blue Ensign with shield of the Colony in the fly. (1979) Sun, waves, bird.
Area: 811 sq. km. (313 sq. mi.).
Government: Parliamentary state, since 1979 (1892 British protectorate, 1916 British crown colony of the Gilbert and Ellice Islands; 1976 self-governing British crown colony, 1979 Independence).
Legislature: House of Assembly, 41 members.
Official language: English.
Monetary unit: 1 Australian Dollar (SA) = 100 cents. **US$1=** $A 1.70.
Chief cities: BAIRIKI (Tarawa) 2,686.
Political divisions: 3 provinces.

DEMOGRAPHY
Population: 83,000.
Population density: 102.8/sq. km. (266.4/sq. mi.).
Under 15 years: 27,000.
Growth rate p.a.: 1.60% (births 20.74, deaths 4.71).
Mortality: Infant, per 1,000: 9.3; **Maternal per 100,000:** 300.0.
Life expectancy: 76 (male 73, female 78).
Household size: 6.6. **Floor area per person, sq.m:** 20.0.
Major languages: English, Gilbertese, Chinese.
Urban dwellers: 37.29%. **Urban growth rate p.a.:** 3.0%.
Labor force: 45%.

ETHNOLINGUISTIC PEOPLES
97.3% Kiribertese (Gilbertese); 1.3% Euronesian; 0.5% British; 0.5% Tuvaluan; 0.1% Han Chinese.

ECONOMY
National income p.a. per person: US$923; **per family:** US$6,094.

EDUCATION
Adult literacy: 90% (male 93%, female 87%). **Schools:** 107.
Universities: 0. **School enrolment:** female/male: 90%/90%.

HEALTH
Access to health services: 90%. **Access to safe water:** 99%.
Hospitals: 4 (40 beds per 10,000). **Doctors:** 10.
Blind: 100. **Deaf:** 5,200. **Murder rate:** 5.
Lepers: 1,000.

LITERATURE
New book titles p.a.: 17 (200 p.a. per million). **Periodicals:** 14.
Newspapers: 0 dailies.

COMMUNICATION (per 1,000 people)
Phones: 26 (0% mobile). **Radios:** 79. **TV sets:** 25.
Daily newspaper circulation: 100. **Computers:** 100.

HUMAN LIFE AND LIBERTY (optimum condition=100.0%)
HDI: 53.2. **HSI:** 50.0. **HFI:** 60.0. **EFL:** 30.0.

Country Table 1. **Religious adherents in Kiribati, AD 1900-2025.**

Year / *Name*	*1900* *Adherents*	*%*	*1970* *Adherents*	*%*	*mid-1990* *Adherents*	*%*	*Annual change, 1990-2000* *Natural*	*Conversion*	*Total*	*Rate*	*mid-1995* *Adherents*	*%*	*mid-2000* *Adherents*	*%*	*mid-2025* *Adherents*	*%*
Christians	**20,500**	**100.0**	**48,940**	**97.7**	**68,540**	**94.8**	**1,052**	**-37**	**1,015**	**1.39**	**73,490**	**94.6**	**78,688**	**94.4**	**110,110**	**92.5**
PROFESSION																
professing Christians	**20,500**	**100.0**	**48,940**	**97.7**	**68,540**	**94.8**	**1,052**	**-37**	**1,015**	**1.39**	**73,490**	**94.6**	**78,688**	**94.4**	**110,110**	**92.5**
AFFILIATION																
unaffiliated Christians	100	0.5	20	0.0	900	1.3	14	32	46	4.19	1,090	1.4	1,357	1.6	2,110	1.8
affiliated Christians	**20,400**	**99.5**	**48,920**	**97.6**	**67,640**	**93.6**	**1,038**	**-69**	**969**	**1.35**	**72,400**	**93.2**	**77,331**	**92.7**	**108,000**	**90.8**
Roman Catholics	9,200	44.9	23,900	47.8	36,800	50.9	562	168	730	1.83	39,825	51.3	44,100	52.9	65,000	54.6
Protestants	11,200	54.6	24,780	49.5	33,500	46.3	512	-162	350	1.00	35,298	45.5	37,000	44.4	50,000	42.0
Marginal Christians	0	0.0	90	0.2	1,200	1.7	18	32	50	3.54	1,444	1.9	1,700	2.1	4,000	3.4
Independents	0	0.0	0	0.0	1,100	1.5	17	3	20	1.68	1,218	1.6	1,300	1.6	2,000	1.7
Anglicans	0	0.0	150	0.3	55	0.1	1	-2	-1	-0.95	55	0.1	50	0.1	50	0.0
doubly-affiliated	0	0.0	0	0.0	-5,015	-7.0	-77	-103	-180	3.12	-5,440	-7.0	-6,819	-8.2	-13,050	-11.0
Trans-megabloc groupings																
Evangelicals	5,100	24.9	1,800	3.6	4,900	6.8	75	30	105	1.96	5,354	6.9	5,950	7.2	8,000	6.7
Pentecostals/Charismatics	0	0.0	700	1.4	10,400	14.4	159	71	230	2.02	11,540	14.9	12,700	15.3	21,400	18.0
Great Commission Christians	**1,230**	**6.0**	**10,000**	**20.0**	**9,050**	**12.6**	**138**	**-20**	**118**	**1.23**	**9,635**	**12.4**	**10,228**	**12.3**	**14,280**	**12.0**
Baha'is	0	0.0	1,060	2.1	3,500	4.9	53	29	82	2.13	3,900	5.0	4,321	5.2	8,000	6.7
Nonreligious	0	0.0	100	0.2	250	0.4	4	8	12	3.91	300	0.4	367	0.4	850	0.7
Buddhists	0	0.0	0	0.0	10	0.0	0	0	0	0.96	10	0.0	11	0.0	40	0.0
World A (unevangelized persons)	0	0.0	50	0.1	72	0.1	1	0	1	1.84	77	0.1	83	0.1	119	0.1
World B (evangelized non-Christians)	0	0.0	1,060	2.2	3,688	5.1	56	37	93	2.24	4,090	5.3	4,229	5.5	8,771	7.4
World C (Christians)	20,500	100.0	48,940	97.7	68,540	94.8	1,052	-37	1,015	1.39	73,490	94.6	78,688	94.4	110,110	92.5
Country's population	**20,500**	**100.0**	**50,051**	**100.0**	**72,300**	**100.0**	**1,109**	**0**	**1,109**	**1.43**	**77,658**	**100.0**	**83,400**	**100.0**	**119,000**	**100.0**

COLUMNS, ROWS.
For meanings and definitions, see Codebook (Part 3). Note that, by definition, total 'Christians' = professing + crypto-Christians, which also = affiliated + unaffiliated Christians, and also = Great Commission Christians + latent Christians. Percentages may not always total exactly, due to rounding.

CENSUSES.
Figures for the Gilbert and Ellice Islands combined: **30.IV.1963:** 56.4% Protestants (54.9% LMS), 42.1% Roman Catholics, 1.0% Baha'is (508 persons), 0.3% Anglicans, 0.2% nonreligious. **6.XII.1968:** 55.6% Protestants (53.5% Congregationalists, 1.5% SD Adventists), 42.9% Roman Catholics, 0.8% Baha'is (440 persons), 0.4% Anglicans, 0.2% nonreligious.

NOTES ON RELIGIONS
BAHA'IS. Begun 1955. Rapid growth in the Gilbert and Ellice Islands from 16 local spiritual assemblies (1964) to 54 (1973) with 72 other isolated centers or groups (total localities in 1973, 126); with a total of 151 Baha'i centers by the end of 1973, including a Baha'i Temple site on Tarawa. In 1973 at the end of the worldwide Baha'i Nine Year Plan, Baha'i claimed 2,460 followers in the Gilbert and Ellice Islands, and asserted that the name of Baha'ullah was already universally known there. Converts are mostly former Congregationalists.
NONRELIGIOUS. Europeans and Chinese.
PROTESTANTS. Since 1900, Congregationalists have suffered losses to Catholicism, newer Protestant bodies, and since 1955 to Baha'i.

Country status. Kiribati consists of a group of islands in the southwest Pacific Ocean including the Gilbert Islands, the Line Islands, the Phoenix Islands, and Banaba. Formerly, the main product was phosphates but tuna fishing and copra are now the economic mainstays.

HUMAN LIFE AND LIBERTY

Human rights and freedoms. Kiribati, formerly Gilbert Islands, was a colony of the United Kingdom until independence, and British traditions of human rights have been maintained. It is a fully democratic society and there are no reports of violations of human rights.

NON-CHRISTIAN RELIGIONS

Baha'i has grown rapidly in numbers since its introduction into the Gilbert and Ellice Islands in 1955, though with a decline from 1963-68; in 1995, there were 55 local spiritual assemblies in Kiribati and 100 other isolated centers and groups.

Great Commission Instrument Panel: status of Kiribati (for explanation see start of Part 4)

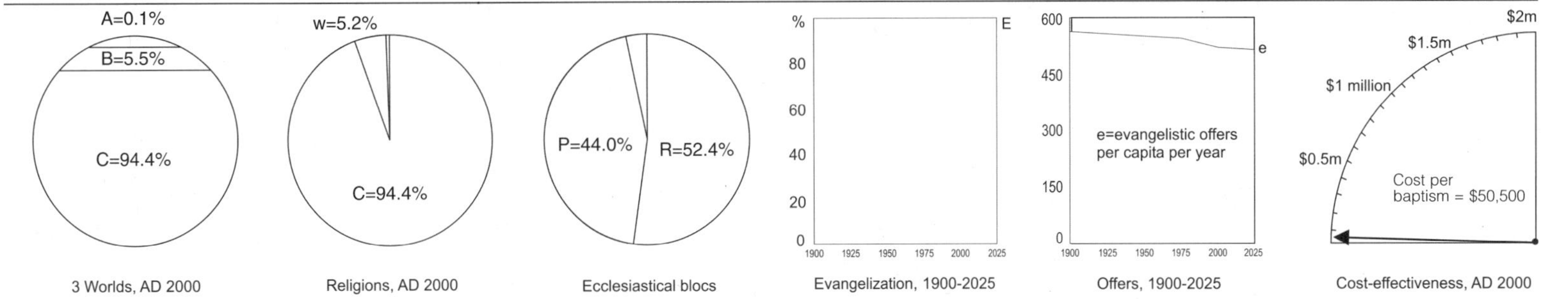

Country summary. **Worlds A, B, C by ethnolinguistic peoples, cities, and major civil divisions in Kiribati.**

	PEOPLES							CITIES							CIVIL DIVISIONS						
World	*Num*	*Pop 2000*	*C%*	*Christians*	*E%*	*U%*	*Unevangelized*	*Num*	*Pop 2000*	*C%*	*Christians*	*E%*	*U%*	*Unevangelized*	*Num*	*Pop 2000*	*C%*	*Christians*	*E%*	*U%*	*Unevangelized*
A	0	0	0.00	0	0	0	0	0	0	0.00	0	0	0	0	0	0	0.00	0	0	0	0
B	1	83	54.22	45	100	0	0	0	0	0.00	0	0	0	0	0	0	0.00	0	0	0	0
C	5	83,304	92.78	77,287	100	0	59	1	2,686	92.00	2,471	100	0	2	3	83,388	92.74	77,331	100	0	61
Total	**6**	**83,387**	**92.74**	**77,332**	**100**	**0**	**59**	**1**	**2,686**	**92.00**	**2,471**	**100**	**0**	**2**	**3**	**83,388**	**92.74**	**77,331**	**100**	**0**	**61**

Traditional Micronesian and Polynesian religions have ceased to exist as separate entities although local beliefs and customs continue to persist among Christians.

Kiribati Protestant Church. *Top.* A Sunday congregation. *Bottom.* Sunday school pupils on parade.

CHRISTIANITY

PROTESTANT CHURCHES. The pioneer missionary Hiram Bingham opened the first American Board station at Abaiang in 1856, thus beginning the evangelization of the northern Gilbert Islands. Before long, Samoan pastors had been placed on Arorae, Tamana, Onotoa and Beru in the southern Gilberts. In 1917, the American Board agreed to hand over all its work to the LMS, thereby providing for a single witness. Because of ethnic tensions, Congregationalists in the formerly united church of the Gilbert and Ellice Islands have since 1968 divided themselves into 2 separate autonomous churches, one serving the Gilbert Islands (now Kiribati) and the other the Ellice Islands (now Tuvalu). They form the largest single church tradition, with 38% of the population in the Gilberts in 1995.

Following World War II, Seventh-day Adventists built their first church at Abemama in the Gilbert Islands. By 1963, 497 persons claimed to be Adventists increasing to 1,160 by 1995. Two Church of God groups have been active since the mid-1950s, but growth has been slower.

Most LMS schools and medical institutions have now been taken over by government, there being only one primary school and one teacher-training college still under church sponsorship. However, Adventists continue to operate 8 primary schools and there is one Church of God school.

Catholic Church (*left*), **Diocese of Tarawa & Nauru** (*right*). Postage stamps of chapel in Tarawa

CATHOLIC CHURCH. Catholicism was introduced into the islands by 2 native Gilbertese, Petero and Tiroi, who were converted while working in Tahiti and who then brought their new faith back to Nonouti with them. When the first priests appeared in 1888, they found that there was already a Catholic community of 500 believers.

Catholics in the Gilbert Islands constitute 51.3% of the population. In the Gilbert archipelago, the vast distances make pastoral visits difficult and links between parishes tenuous.

The diocese of Tarawa, Nauru, and Funafuti encompasses all the Gilbert Islands (except for the Line Islands which belong to the diocese of Honolulu in the USA) as well as Tuvalu, Nauru, and Canton and Enderbury. Nevertheless, because the Line Islands are peopled by the same ethnic group, pastoral care in the form of Gilbertese catechists is provided by the bishop of Tarawa.

The Holy See has no diplomatic relations with Kiribati in AD 2000, but is represented there by an apostolic delegate for the Pacific Ocean residing in Wellington, New Zealand.

INDIGENOUS CHURCHES. Although nothing survives today, there was an indigenous religious movement in 1929 called Religion of Barane, or Swords of Gabriel. It was begun on Onotoa Island in the Congregational Church (now the GIPC) by Barane who was identified as the prophet of God, with a female prophetess Nei Kamaitia and Nei Baate. The movement lasted only a year or 2 before disappearing.

Indigenous missions. Although some Christians from the Gilbert Islands were involved in evangelizing neighboring islands in the 19th century, there are very few foreign missionaries sent out from Protestant or Catholic churches today.

CHURCH AND STATE

Theoretically, all denominations enjoy equal freedom before the law, but local anti-Catholic sentiment prevents the building of Catholic churches on the islands of Tamana and Arorae in the Gilberts.

Although many LMS schools were placed under government supervision after World War II, the churches continue to play an important role in education. Government subsidies are provided for their operation as well as for teachers' salaries.

The churches exert an important influence on the life of the islands and the surrounding area. In December 1970, the Catholic bishop of Tarawa placed before the pope and the bishops of the Pacific and Australia his concern at the over-population and lack of resources of the territory, in the hope that Australia might be requested to open its doors to Gilbertese immigration.

BROADCASTING AND MEDIA

Shortwave radio programs from KNLS have generated responses. Radio Kiribati airs WEC programs. Over a third of the population have seen the 'Jesus' Film. Kiribati is a member of UNDA: Catholics broadcast a daily 5-minute devotional each third week, and a 15-minute topical program 'Biblical Insight' each second Sunday.

INTERDENOMINATIONAL ORGANIZATIONS

No organizations exist at the national level. In 1969, the Catholic Church announced that intercommunion with Anglicans was permitted.

FUTURE TRENDS AND PROSPECTS

Baha'is, 2.1% of the population in 1970, are expected to grow to over 6% by AD 2025. Christians will likely experience a slow decline to 92.5% in the same period.

Though Christianity will probably remain above 85% for the indefinite future, Baha'is could grow to over 10% of the population within a few decades.

BIBLIOGRAPHY

A brief introduction to the Kiribati Protestant Church. N. Healey. Bairiki Tarawa, Republic of Kiribati: Kiribati Protestant Church, [1983]. 15p.

A pattern of islands. A. F. Grimble. 1952; reprint, Harmondsworth: Penguin, 1981. 264p.

'A study of corporate personality concept into the divine authority of the Maneaba in the southern Gilberts.' T. B. Kirata. B.D. thesis, Pacific Theological College, Suva, Fiji, 1978. 55p.

'A study of the two denominations in Tabiteuea, Kiribati: Kiribati Protestant Church and the Roman Catholic Church.' T. Toakai. B.D. thesis, Pacific Theological College, Suva, Fiji, 1980. 98p.

Christ and Kiribati culture: report of workshop on traditional Kiribati culture and Christian faith, Bonrik Village, Tarawa, Kiribati, July 12–24, 1981. Tarawa, Kiribati: Kiribati Protestant Church, 1981. 38p.

Nous mourons de te voir! = (Ti mate ni kan moriko!). G. Delbos. *Des Chrétiens.* [Paris]: Le Sarment, Fayard, 1987.

Sous l'équateur du Pacifique: les iles Gilbert et la mission Catholique. E. Sabatier. Issoudun, Indre, Archiconfrerie Paris: Éditions Dillen, [1939]. 292p.

S[outh] Gilbert Islands' Church manual: Taniani kaetieti n te ekaretia. W. E. Goward & F. S. Iupeli. Beru, 1908. 32p.

'The Swords of Gabriel,' H. E. Maude, *Journal of Pacific history*, 2 (1967), 113–36.

'The transmission of the Christian conception of God from one culture to the other.' M. R. Itaia. B.D. thesis, Pacific Theological College, Suva, Fiji, 1973. 97p.

Country Table 2. **Organized churches and denominations in Kiribati.**

Official name (bold type = church with over 10% of all affiliated) 1	*Begun* 2	*Type* 3	*Counc* 4	*Congs* 5	*Adults* 6	*Affiliated 1970* 7	*Affiliated 1995* 8	*G%* 9	*Names, notes, and other statistics* (see Codebook, Part 3) 10
Anglican Church (D Polynesia)		A-Hig	awPK.	1	36	150	55	0.05	In Diocese of Polynesia, Ch of the Province of New Zealand. Indians.
Assemblies of God	c1975	P-Pe2	Z....	9	950	–	1,400	5.00	M=AoG. 17 ministers, 1 missionary.
Catholic Ch: D Tarawa & Nauru	1850	R-Lat	P.PY.	21	25,000	23,900	39,825	2.06	Begun by 2 locals. 1888, M=MSC. 62 aliens. C=1+0+2. (1990) 8n,16x,44m,74w,2444Yy.
Christ Groups	c1980	I-3hP	x....	73	600	–	1,000	6.67	Home churches for converts after nationwide EHC campaign (M=Every Home for Christ).
Church of God	1954	P-Pe2	.....	1	100	100	200	2.81	M=South Carolina Memorial Church of God (USA). On Tarawa only. 1 school. 1f.
Church of God (Cleveland)	1955	P-Pe3	ZF...	30	1,035	500	2,070	5.85	M=CoG(Cleveland) (USA), based on Tarawa. 13 churches, 6 missions. 15n,2f,1p.
Ch of Jesus Christ of Latter-day Saints	c1960	m-LdS	x....	17	780	40	1,300	14.94	*Mormons.* M=CJCLdS.
Jehovah's Witnesses	c1960	m-Jeh	x....	1	36	50	144	4.32	*Watch Tower. IBSA.* Active witnessing under way by 1962. (1975) 2Y. (1995) 5Y.
Kiribati Protestant Church	1856	P-Con	.vP..	124	11,200	23,000	29,600	1.01	*GIPC.* 1857, M=ABCFM(USA); 1917, LMS(UK),CCWM. A=1968. 1972 applied to WCC. 1f,1j,1s.
New Apostolic Church	c1990	I-3aX	x....	2	100	–	218	20.00	*NAC/NAK.* M=Neuapostolische Kirche (HQ Zurich).
Presbyterian Church		P-Ref	.....	1	41	50	68	0.05	Small church of Presbyterian immigrants from other Pacific areas.
Seventh-day Adventist Church	1947	P-Adv	x....	5	815	730	1,160	1.87	*SDA, G & El Mission*, Central Pacific Union Mission. 2nx,25mw,1r,5t(510),52Y.
Other Protestant churches		P-	.....	10	500	400	800	0.05	In 4 recent denominations, including Elim FWM(USA).
Doubly-affiliated		2-aff			-2,900	0	-5,440		
Totals				**295**	**38,293**	**48,920**	**72,400**		

Churches, members, growth, 1900-2025	*Congs*	*Adults*	*Affiliated*	*G%*	*Total denominations*	*6 Megablocs:* O	R	A	P	I	m
Total churches, members, and denominations (mid-1900)	60	10,100	20,400	1.26	2	0	1	0	1	0	0
Total churches, members, and denominations (mid-1970)	171	24,296	48,920	1.26	11	0	1	1	7	0	2
Total churches, members, and denominations (mid-1990)	220	35,800	67,640	1.63	16	0	1	1	10	2	2
Total churches, members, and denominations (mid-1995)	295	38,293	72,400	1.37	16	0	1	1	10	2	2
Total churches, members, and denominations (mid-2000)	300	40,900	77,331	1.33	16	0	1	1	10	2	2
Total churches, members, and denominations (mid-2025)	400	57,200	108,000	1.35	32	0	1	1	15	10	5

NOTES ON TABLE ABOVE
NATIONAL COUNCILS (Column 4, 5th letter).
C = Protestant Churches in Tuvalu & Kiribati.

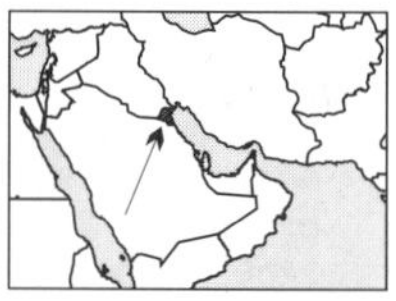

KUWAIT

SECULAR DATA, AD 2000

STATE
Official name: Dawlat al-Kuwayt (The State of Kuwait).
Short name: Kuwait. **Adjective of nationality:** Kuwaiti.
Flag: Green, white, and red stripes, with black trapezoid at flagstaff.
Area: 17,818 sq. km. (6,880 sq. mi.).
Government: Constitutional monarchy (emirate), since 1990 (1756 emirate, 1899 British quasi-protectorate, 1961 independence as monarchy).
Legislature: National Assembly, 64 members.
Official language: Arabic.
Monetary unit: 1 Kuwaiti dinar (DK) = 1,000 fils. **US$1=** $3.30.
Chief cities: AL-KUWAYT 1,187,000; Al-Ahmadi 301,293; Al-Salimiyah (Salmuja) 162,126; Hawalli 153,422; Qalib ash-Shuyukh 121,332.
Political divisions: 5 provinces.
Armed forces: 15,300.

DEMOGRAPHY
Population: 1,972,000.
Population density: 110.6/sq. km. (286.5/sq. mi.).
Under 15 years: 665,000.
Growth rate p.a.: 2.26% (births 20.20, deaths 2.39).
Mortality: Infant, per 1,000: 10.8; **Maternal per 100,000:** 29.0.
Life expectancy: 77 (male 75, female 79).
Household size: 7.4. **Floor area per person, sq.m:** 25.0.
Major languages: Arabic, Persian (Farsi), English, Kurdish.
Urban dwellers: 97.59%. **Urban growth rate p.a.:** 2.2%.
Labor force: 39%.

ETHNOLINGUISTIC PEOPLES
30.0% Kuwaiti Arab; 17.0% Palestinian Arab; 9.6% Kurdish (Kurd); 9.5% Jordanian Arab; 9.0% Najdi Bedouin.

ECONOMY
National income p.a. per person: US$17,390; **per family:** US$128,687.

EDUCATION
Adult literacy: 78% (male 82%, female 74%). **Schools:** 671.
Universities: 1. **School enrolment:** female/male: 66%/66%.

HEALTH
Access to health services: 100%. **Access to safe water:** 100%.
Hospitals: 22 (26 beds per 10,000). **Doctors:** 2,717.
Blind: 1,000. **Deaf:** 118,000. **Murder rate:** 1.
Lepers: 200. **Underweight prevalence under 5:** 6%.

LITERATURE
New book titles p.a.: 260 (130 p.a. per million). **Periodicals:** 102.
Newspapers: 9 dailies.

COMMUNICATION (per 1,000 people)
Phones: 226 (33% mobile). **Radios:** 591. **TV sets:** 373.
Daily newspaper circulation: 387. **Computers:** 85.

REFUGEES
Alien refugees from other countries: 55,000.

HUMAN LIFE AND LIBERTY (optimum condition=100.0%)
HDI: 84.4. **HSI:** 72.0. **HFI:** 20.0. **EFL:** 52.0.

Country Table 1. **Religious adherents in Kuwait, AD 1900-2025.**

Year	*1900*		*1970*		*mid-1990*		*Annual change, 1990-2000*				*mid-1995*		*mid-2000*		*mid-2025*	
Name	*Adherents*	*%*	*Adherents*	*%*	*Adherents*	*%*	*Natural*	*Conversion*	*Total*	*Rate*	*Adherents*	*%*	*Adherents*	*%*	*Adherents*	*%*
Muslims	66,800	99.7	700,550	94.1	1,920,000	89.6	-15,355	-12,894	-28,249	-1.58	1,410,900	83.5	1,637,507	83.0	2,407,000	80.9
Christians	**200**	**0.3**	**38,600**	**5.2**	**162,000**	**7.6**	**-1,293**	**10,048**	**8,755**	**4.42**	**210,800**	**12.5**	**249,546**	**12.7**	**410,000**	**13.8**
PROFESSION																
crypto-Christians	100	0.2	2,350	0.3	40,000	1.9	-319	2,319	2,000	4.14	42,000	2.5	60,000	3.0	110,000	3.7
professing Christians	**100**	**0.2**	**36,250**	**4.9**	**122,000**	**5.7**	**-973**	**7,728**	**6,755**	**4.50**	**168,800**	**10.0**	**189,546**	**9.6**	**300,000**	**10.1**
AFFILIATION																
unaffiliated Christians	0	0.0	2,025	0.3	2,120	0.1	-17	6	-11	-0.53	1,909	0.1	2,011	0.1	3,400	0.1
affiliated Christians	**200**	**0.3**	**36,575**	**4.9**	**159,880**	**7.5**	**-1,276**	**10,042**	**8,766**	**4.47**	**208,891**	**12.4**	**247,535**	**12.6**	**406,600**	**13.7**
Roman Catholics	100	0.2	17,700	2.4	100,000	4.7	-798	8,317	7,519	5.77	150,000	8.9	175,185	8.9	275,000	9.3
Independents	0	0.0	3,562	0.5	51,040	2.4	-407	1,703	1,296	2.29	51,040	3.0	64,000	3.3	120,000	4.0
Orthodox	100	0.2	12,150	1.6	7,500	0.4	-60	10	-50	-0.69	6,550	0.4	7,000	0.4	9,000	0.3
Protestants	0	0.0	1,650	0.2	1,100	0.1	-9	9	0	0.00	1,058	0.1	1,100	0.1	2,200	0.1
Anglicans	0	0.0	1,500	0.2	200	0.0	-2	2	0	0.00	200	0.0	200	0.0	200	0.0
Marginal Christians	0	0.0	13	0.0	40	0.0	0	1	1	2.26	43	0.0	50	0.0	200	0.0
Trans-megabloc groupings																
Evangelicals	0	0.0	2,100	0.3	18,000	0.8	-144	144	0	0.00	15,747	0.9	18,000	0.9	30,000	1.0
Pentecostals/Charismatics	0	0.0	2,400	0.3	60,000	2.8	-479	1,279	800	1.26	57,059	3.4	68,000	3.5	130,000	4.4
Great Commission Christians	**200**	**0.3**	**30,000**	**4.0**	**111,000**	**5.2**	**-886**	**6,181**	**5,295**	**3.98**	**136,000**	**8.1**	**163,948**	**8.3**	**284,000**	**9.6**
Hindus	0	0.0	3,800	0.5	39,000	1.8	-311	1,871	1,560	3.42	45,000	2.7	54,595	2.8	100,000	3.4
Nonreligious	0	0.0	0	0.0	15,000	0.7	-120	806	686	3.84	16,600	1.0	21,856	1.1	40,000	1.3
Baha'is	0	0.0	1,050	0.1	5,000	0.2	-40	57	17	0.34	4,200	0.3	5,172	0.3	12,000	0.4
Sikhs	0	0.0	0	0.0	2,000	0.1	-16	112	96	3.99	2,500	0.2	2,957	0.2	5,000	0.2
World A (unevangelized persons)	62,511	93.3	485,258	65.2	1,071,500	50.0	-8,584	-28,502	-37,086	-4.16	760,289	45.0	700,060	35.5	948,706	31.9
World B (evangelized non-Christians)	4,289	6.4	220,402	29.6	909,500	42.4	-7,258	18,454	11,196	1.18	718,443	42.5	1,022,394	51.8	1,615,294	54.3
World C (Christians)	200	0.3	38,600	5.2	162,000	7.6	-1,293	10,048	8,755	4.42	210,800	12.5	249,546	12.7	410,000	13.8
Country's population	**67,000**	**100.0**	**744,261**	**100.0**	**2,143,000**	**100.0**	**-17,135**	**0**	**-17,135**	**-0.83**	**1,689,533**	**100.0**	**1,972,000**	**100.0**	**2,974,000**	**100.0**

COLUMNS, ROWS.
For meanings and definitions, see Codebook (Part 3). Note that, by definition, total 'Christians' = professing + crypto-Christians, which also = affiliated + unaffiliated Christians, and also = Great Commission Christians + latent Christians. Percentages may not always total exactly, due to rounding.

CENSUSES.
28.II.1957: 94.4% Muslims, 4.7% Christians, 0.9% other religionists. **25.IV.1965:** 94.1% Muslims, 5.3% Christians (24,506 non-Kuwaitis, 134 Kuwaitis), 0.6% other religionists (all non-Kuwaitis). **19.IV.1970** (including 754 nationals abroad): 94.7% Muslims, 4.6% Christians (34,179 persons), 0.6% other religionists.

NOTES ON RELIGIONS
BAHA'IS. Growth from 3 local spiritual assemblies (1964) to 7 (1973). Including several Indians, former Hindus and Muslims. Since then there has been growth, largely due to huge numbers of immigrant Baha'is either as refugees or migrant workers.
COUNTRY'S POPULATION. The non-Kuwaiti population, mostly immigrant workers (30% Palestinian and Jordanian Arabs. 4.2% Persians, 3.5% Iraqis, 2.8% Lebanese, 9.5% Omanis, 0.5% Syrians) has risen from 92,800 in 1957 (40% of the population) to 980,000 in 1995 (58% of the population).
HINDUS. South Indians.
INDEPENDENTS. South Indian and Arab indigenous congregations, in 4 denominations or groupings in 1995 (see Table 2).
MUSLIMS. Kuwaitis are Sunnis of various rites including Malikite, at one time strongly influenced by the Wahhabi movement; foreign Muslims mostly Shias. There are over 300 mosques. Hajj pilgrims to Mecca. (1968) 8,783; (1970) 8,072; (1975) 8,808; (1976) 4,908.

Great Commission Instrument Panel: status of Kuwait (for explanation see start of Part 4)

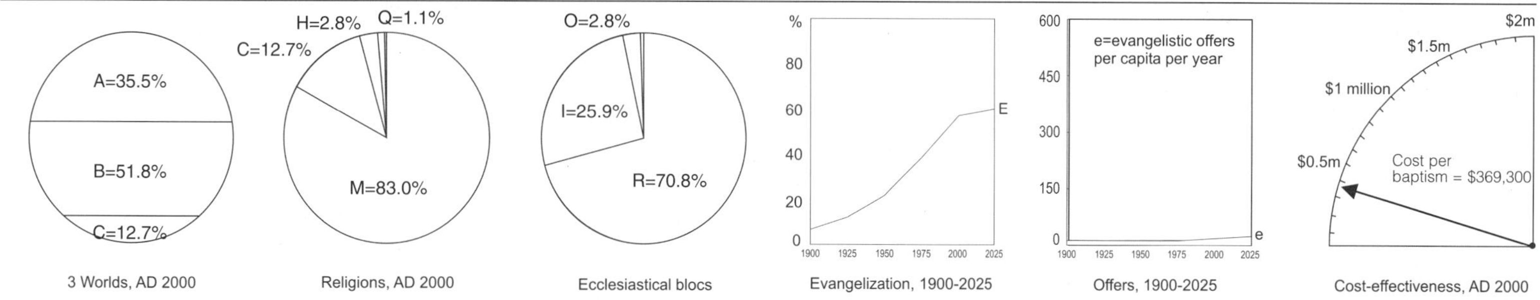

Country status. Kuwait is an oil-rich emirate in the Persian Gulf region bordering Iraq and Saudi Arabia. Its occupation by Iraq in 1990 was the casus belli of the Gulf War of 1991. Since the discovery of oil in the 1930s Kuwait has become one of the richest oil producing countries in the world.

HUMAN LIFE AND LIBERTY

Human need and development. Kuwait is one of the richest desert kingdoms in the Middle East. Much of its productive resources were destroyed in the Gulf War which was fought for its defense. The rebuilding of the country is expected to take years, but reparations from Iraq and the continuing flow of oil wealth are expected to speed the process. The per capita income of the average Kuwaiti is close to that of the United Kingdom.

Human rights and freedoms. The traditional ruling emirs of Kuwait are not particularly noted as defenders of human rights. The kingdom was more or less a fiefdom of the Al-Sabah family, and what rights its citizens enjoyed were at the sufferance of the rulers. After the Gulf War highlighted the general lack of popular participation in government, there was an attempt to introduce at least the semblance of parliamentary institutions. In 1992 elections were held in a free and open atmosphere, although the franchise was restricted to those narrowly defined as Kuwaiti citizens. Prepublication censorship was eliminated although other restrictions on freedom of speech and press remain. The group most subject to abuse is the large contingent of non-Kuwaiti guest workers, many of whom are harassed, detained, and subjected to physical mistreatment. There are reports of disappearances and deaths in police custody of non-nationals. Over 100,000 Palestinians were forced to leave the country or were deported. Non-Kuwaitis are harassed at checkpoints on major roads routinely manned by the police. The rights of Kuwaitis, both male and female, to marry non-Kuwaitis, are severely restricted. Although prepublication censorship was lifted in 1992, the press exercises self-censorship for fear of government reprisals. The press is free to criticize government officials and policies as long the criticism is not personal and is not directed against the emir. Political parties are banned, and public gatherings must receive prior government approval as must private gatherings of more than 5 people that result in the issuance of a public statement. The bidoons (bedouins) are subject to considerable discrimination and many of them were stripped of their civil identification cards. Being stateless, they are in a legal limbo without the legal right to work, attend school, or travel in and out of Kuwait. Foreign women working as maids and domestics are subjected to sexual abuse by their employers for which they have no legal recourse. Non-Muslims are not permitted to become citizens and foreign nationals are prohibited from owning property or businesses. The Shi'as face some discrimination in public service employment.

Human environment. The Gulf War in 1991 did extensive damage to Kuwait's environment. About 1,000 oil fields were set on fire by retreating Iraqis, and the flames sent billowing black clouds of soot which were later deposited on the vegetation and soil. Tank and troop movements damaged and eroded the fragile desert soils. The Iraqis also deliberately spilled millions of barrels of oil into the Gulf poisoning the fisheries and the ecosystem. Recovery from this damage may take decades.

NON-CHRISTIAN RELIGIONS

Islam is the religion of virtually all Kuwaitis, who are Muslim Sunnis of the Malikite rite and are strongly influenced by the Wahhabi movement. Foreign Muslims are mainly Shi'as. There is a total of over 300 mosques.

Muslims. Kuwaiti headmaster of village school at Fahaheel, with 120 pupils.

CHRISTIANITY

The massive influx of workers into the oil fields from both western and eastern countries has included a wide variety of Christians of different denominations and rites. Seven of Kuwait's 42 private schools are under Christian management (4 Catholic, plus one each serving the Greek, Armenian, and Protestant communities), and there is also a Catholic hospital.

CATHOLIC CHURCH. Although an American Catholic priest entered Kuwait as early as 1795, the first resident cleric did not arrive until 1948. Individual Catholics represent many Eastern-rite traditions (Melkites, Maronites, Chaldeans, and others), but all are part of the Latin-rite vicariate of Kuwait. Aided by OCD priests and 3 congregations of sisters, Catholicism is the principal Christian denomination in Kuwait.

The Holy See has diplomatic relations with Kuwait and in AD 2000 is represented to government and the Catholic hierarchy by a nuncio residing in Harissa, Lebanon.

ORTHODOX CHURCHES. Five different Orthodox groups are present, 3 belonging to the Oriental Orthodox (Non-Chalcedonean) tradition: Armenian, Coptic and Syrian churches.

The Greek Orthodox are Kuwait's largest Orthodox body and only representative of Eastern Orthodoxy. Although having had resident priests since 1962, they continue to hold services in the Protestant churches of Kuwait and Ahmadi. The church also sponsors Al Salam School, which was begun in 1968 and has 700 pupils.

The Armenian Apostolic Church, Kuwait's second largest Orthodox community, built its own church in 1958 and has had a resident priest since that time. In addition, the church operates a school with 600 pupils. Coptics and Syrians also have resident priests.

The Ancient church of the East (Assyrians or Nestorians), forms a small community led by a resident deacon.

OTHER CHURCHES. The Protestant pioneer was Samuel Zwemer of the Reformed Church in America who entered Kuwait in 1903. The first Arabic church service of the National Evangelical Church was held in 1926 and the first building constructed in 1931. The church consists of Arabic, English and Indian congregations, each with their own resident ministers.

The first Anglican services were held in Ahmadi in 1947, and a permanent building, St Paul's church, was completed there in 1956.

A large Mar Thoma congregation serving South Indian Christians and a small Brethren group are also active.

Renewal movements. In the 1990s the Pentecostal/Charismatic Renewal continued to spread rapidly across most older churches, and numbered over 53,000 adherents (of whom none are Pentecostals, 11% Charismatics, and 89% Independents).

Indigenous missions. Very few missionaries have been sent out by the churches in Kuwait.

A remedial reading lesson for a deaf-mute, a perennial Christian concern.

CHURCH AND STATE

According to the 1962 constitution, Islam is the religion of the state and the Islamic Sharia constitutes one of the principal sources of legislation (Article 2). Religious liberty is guaranteed,and the state protects the free practice of religion in conformity with established customs (Article 35). Relations between Christian churches and the government are amicable, but by implicit agreement with the Kuwaiti authorities, no overt attempt is made to convert Muslims.

The government agency responsible for religion is the Ministry of Awqaf and Religious Affairs. It has a large staff numbering over 2,500.

BROADCASTING AND MEDIA

FEBA (Seychelles) has shortwave radio programs in Arabic, Azeri and Farsi. Other shortwave programs from KNLS, HCJB (Ecuador), AWR (Slovakia), Voice of Hope (Lebanon) and TWR (Monaco) can be heard.

Satellite TV programs are received mainly in Arabic.

INTERDENOMINATIONAL ORGANIZATIONS

The Anglican, Catholic, and Evangelical churches work closely together through the Council of Churches in Kuwait, which was founded in 1960. Cooperation is also maintained with the Orthodox in the joint use of church buildings in Kuwait and Ahmade.

FUTURE TRENDS AND PROSPECTS

During the Iraqi invasion (1990-91) most expatriate Christians fled Kuwait causing the Christian community to drop below 2% (from 7% right before the invasion). However, an influx of Christian immigrant workers will in all probability boost the Christian percentage to near 11% by 2025.

Christianity could grow to over 15% before AD 2050 as the result of an increase in Christian immigrant workers. Muslim converts to Christianity may continue to represent less than 1% of Kuwait's pop-

Country summary. **Worlds A, B, C by ethnolinguistic peoples, cities, and major civil divisions in Kuwait.**

World	PEOPLES Num	Pop 2000	C%	Christians	E%	U%	Unevangelized
A	8	484,036	0.04	204	29	71	343,985
B	13	1,449,348	14.81	214,582	75	25	356,600
C	6	38,249	85.62	32,749	100	0	55
Total	**27**	**1,971,633**	**12.55**	**247,535**	**64**	**36**	**700,640**

World	CITIES Num	Pop 2000	C%	Christians	E%	U%	Unevangelized
A	0	0	0.00	0	0	0	0
B	2	1,488,293	12.68	188,777	65	35	517,995
C	0	0	0.00	0	0	0	0
Total	**2**	**1,488,293**	**12.68**	**188,777**	**65**	**35**	**517,995**

World	CIVIL DIVISIONS Num	Pop 2000	C%	Christians	E%	U%	Unevangelized
A	0	0	0.00	0	0	0	0
B	5	1,971,634	12.55	247,535	64	36	700,639
C	0	0	0.00	0	0	0	0
Total	**5**	**1,971,634**	**12.55**	**247,535**	**64**	**36**	**700,639**

ulation. Muslims, in the same period, could drop to less than 80% for the first time in centuries due to an expected increase of the nonreligious.

BIBLIOGRAPHY

'An ethnic geography of Kuwait: a study of eight ethnic groups.' A. B. Al-Ostad. Ph.D. dissertation, Kent State University, Kent, OH, 1986. 257p.

Analytical guide to the bibliographies on the Arabian Peninsula. C. L. Geddes. *Bibliographic series*, no. 4. Denver, CO: American Institute of Islamic Studies, 1974.

Back to the Indian mission: via Kuwait. V. Sanmiguel. Vemsur, India: Christ the King Church, 1984. 135p.

Christians in Kuwait. V. Sanmiguel. Beirut: Beirut Printing Press, 1970. 107p. (By the Catholic bishop).

Kuwait. F. A. Clements. *World bibliographical series*, vol. 56. Oxford, UK: CLIO Press, 1985. 198p. (See especially 'Religion,' p.55–6).

'Kuwait: religion and politics.' M. H. Ali. Ph.D. dissertation, Michigan State University, East Lansing, MI, 1986. 2 vols.

Persian Gulf states: country studies. H. C. Metz (ed). 3rd ed. *Area handbook series*. Lanham, MD: Bernan, 1994. 501p.

'Present–day Christianity in the Gulf states of the Arabian Peninsula,' N. A. Horner, *Occasional bulletin of missionary research*, 2 (April 1978), 53–63.

Source book on Arabian Gulf States, Arabian Gulf in general, Kuwait, Bahrain, Qatar and Oman. S. Kabeel. Kuwait: Kuwait University, Libraries Department, 1975. 427p. (With over 3,000 item bibliography).

The Arab of the desert. H. R. P. Dickson. Ed., R. D. Wilson & Z. D. Freeth. 3rd ed. London: Allen & Unwin, 1983. 271p.

The evolving culture of Kuwait. Edinburgh: Royal Scottish Museum H.M.S.O, 1985. 166p.

The Grahams report on Kuwait. L. Graham & M. Graham. Richmond, VA: Southern Baptist Foreign Mission Board, 1991. (25 min. videocassette on couple trapped in Kuwait during Iraqi invasion in 1990).

Country Table 2. **Organized churches and denominations in Kuwait.**

Official name (bold type = church with over 10% of all affiliated) 1	*Begun* 2	*Type* 3	*Counc* 4	*Congs* 5	*Adults* 6	*Affiliated 1970* 7	*Affiliated 1995* 8	*G%* 9	*Names, notes, and other statistics* (see Codebook, Part 3) 10
Ancient Church of the East		O-Nes	Yw...	1	95	450	150	0.05	*Assyrians (Nestorians)*. Patriarch in USA. 1 congregation with resident deacon.
Anglican Church (D Cyprus & the Gulf)	1947	A-plu	aw..C	1	60	1,500	200	-7.74	In Episcopal Ch in Jerusalem & the Middle East. 77% British, 23% Arabs. W=10%.
Armenian Apostolic Church: V Kuwait	1958	O-Arm	Sw.N.	1	1,280	5,600	2,000	-4.03	Under P Cilicia (Lebanon). Since 1958, own church and priest. 1 school (600).
Assemblies (Jehova Shammah)		I-CBr	x....	1	20	50	40	0.05	Indian missionaries (Brother Bakht Singh), HQ Hyderabad, AP (India).
Catholic Church: VA Kuwait	1795	R-Lat	P..LC	4	70,000	17,700	150,000	8.92	58% Latins (31% Indian, 21% Arab). C=1+0+3. (1970) 5x,303Y. (1990) 3n,4x,4m,12w,314Yy.
Christian Brethren		P-CBr	x....	2	80	200	200	0.05	*Plymouth Brethren. Open Brethren.* 50% Arabs, 50% Indians.
Coptic Orthodox Church (P Alexandria)	1960	O-Cop	Nwa..	2	1,890	950	3,000	4.71	By 1977, 600 families. Resident priest, with Coptic papal representative.
Greek Orthodox Church (P Antioch)		O-Ara	Cw...	2	384	4,200	600	0.05	Resident priest since 1962, using Protestant buildings. 1 school (700), 1 bishop.
Isolated radio churches	c1950	I-3rS	.....	2,200	30,000	1,900	50,000	13.97	Isolated radio believers (students) R=500 (FEBA,TWR &c) T=4000 (RSB,ICI)
Jehovah's Witnesses	1956	m-Jeh	.....	1	30	13	43	4.90	*Watchtower.*
Mar Thoma Syrian Ch (D Bahya Kerala)		I-ReO	xwe..	1	310	1,150	500	0.05	In Diocese of Outside Kerala.
National Evangelical Church in Kuwait	1903	P-Ref	...NC	2	294	1,200	700	-2.13	Arab, Indian, USA congregations. M=RCA(USA). 3x,4f,1H (until 1968),1k,1t(50).
Orthodox Syrian Church of India		O-SyM	Dwe..	1	496	950	800	0.05	Malayalis. Resident priest since 1959, using National Ev Ch building.
Pentecostal Churches	c1962	I-3pS	.....	2	325	462	500	0.32	Various indigenous Arab evangelists at work.
Other Protestant churches		P-	.....	1	69	250	158	0.05	Total about 4.
Totals				**2,222**	**105,333**	**36,575**	**208,891**		

Churches, members, growth, 1900-2025	*Congs*	*Adults*	*Affiliated*	*G%*	*Total denominations*	*6 Megablocs:* O	R	A	P	I	m
Total churches, members, and denominations (mid-1900)	3	120	200	7.73	1	0	1	0	0	0	0
Total churches, members, and denominations (mid-1970)	74	21,957	36,575	7.73	16	5	1	1	4	4	1
Total churches, members, and denominations (mid-1990)	1,500	80,600	159,880	7.65	18	5	1	1	6	4	1
Total churches, members, and denominations (mid-1995)	2,222	105,333	208,891	5.49	18	5	1	1	6	4	1
Total churches, members, and denominations (mid-2000)	2,300	125,000	247,535	3.45	18	5	1	1	6	4	1
Total churches, members, and denominations (mid-2025)	3,800	205,000	406,600	2.00	55	7	1	1	20	25	1

NOTES ON TABLE ABOVE
NATIONAL COUNCILS (Column 4, 5th letter).

C = Council of Churches in Kuwait.

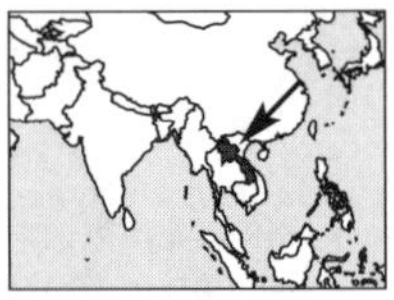

LAOS

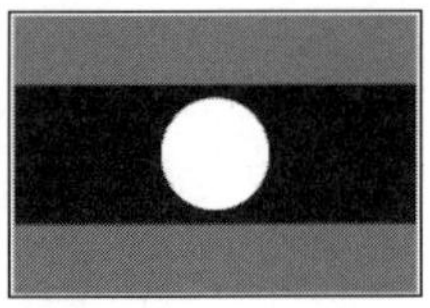

SECULAR DATA, AD 2000

STATE
Official name: Saathiaranarath Prachhathipatay Prachhachhon Lao (The Lao People's Democratic Republic).
Short name: Laos. **Adjective of nationality:** Lao.
Flag: Narrow red stripes top and bottom; wide blue stripe in middle with large white circle.
Area: 236,800 sq. km. (91,429 sq. mi.).
Government: One-party Communist state, since 1975 (14th century kingdom of Laos, 1893 French protectorate, 1947 constitutional monarchy, 1949 Independence).
Legislature: National Assembly, 85 members.
Official language: Lao.
Monetary unit: 1 kip (KN) = 100 at. **US$1=** KN 3,408.
Chief cities: VIANGCHAN (Vientiane) 588,244; Savannakhet 98,177; Pakxe (Pakse) 73,270; Louangphrabang (Luang Prabang) 70,556; 0.
Political divisions: 18 provinces.
Armed forces: 37,000.

DEMOGRAPHY
Population: 5,433,000.
Population density: 22.9/sq. km. (59.4/sq. mi.).
Under 15 years: 2,388,000.
Growth rate p.a.: 2.51% (births 37.04, deaths 11.85).
Mortality: Infant, per 1,000: 82.7; **Maternal per 100,000:** 650.0.
Life expectancy: 56 (male 55, female 57).
Household size: 6.0. **Floor area per person, sq.m:** 5.0.
Major languages: Lao, French, Thai, Chinese, Vietnamese, English, and 70 other languages.
Urban dwellers: 23.46%. **Urban growth rate p.a.:** 5.2%.
Labor force: 49%.

ETHNOLINGUISTIC PEOPLES
48.6% Lao (Laotian Tai, Lao-Lu); 10.8% Khmu (Lao-Theng); 2.6% Chinese Shan; 2.5% Phu Thai (Phuthai); 2.1% So (Kah So, So Makon).

ECONOMY
National income p.a. per person: US$350; **per family:** US$2,100.

EDUCATION
Adult literacy: 56% (male 69%, female 44%). **Schools:** 9,250.
Universities: 9. **School enrolment:** female/male: 56%/78%.

HEALTH
Access to health services: 67%. **Access to safe water:** 39%.
Hospitals: 1,074 (25 beds per 10,000). **Doctors:** 1,173.
Blind: 10,000. **Deaf:** 341,600. **Murder rate:** 15.
Lepers: 20,000. **Underweight prevalence under 5:** 40%.

LITERATURE
New book titles p.a.: 70 (13 p.a. per million). **Periodicals:** 4.
Newspapers: 3 dailies.

COMMUNICATION (per 1,000 people)
Phones: 4 **(18% mobile). Radios:** 121. **TV sets:** 7.
Daily newspaper circulation: 3. **Computers:** 10.

HUMAN LIFE AND LIBERTY (optimum condition=100.0%)
HDI: 45.9. **HSI:** 13.0. **HFI:** 5.0. **EFL:** 5.0.

Country status. Laos is a small landlocked country in Southeast Asia bordering Thailand, China, Myanmar, Cambodia, and Vietnam. Like Vietnam, it has a Communist government and, as a result, has been isolated from the rest of the world for many decades. Subsistence farming is the main economic activity.

HUMAN LIFE AND LIBERTY

Human needs and development. Laos exhibits the combination of a landlocked country with poor natural resources isolated from the rest of the world under a Marxist government—and thus locked into a state of nondevelopment. Consumption patterns are simple. Food, clothing, and housing follow tradition, and require little or no largescale production. For example, houses are erected by the householders with no outside help with materials, like bamboo and thatch, supplied from neighboring forests. Rice makes up 90% of the daily diet. Milk and meat are used sparingly. Modern medicine is making only slow progress. Only a few villages and towns have sanitary water supplies and there is no adequate system of sewage disposal. The climate favors insects and other disease-carrying vectors constantly threatening the health of the average Laotians. There has been some improvement in the standards of living after the government abandoned its socialist policies in 1985 and reintroduced private enterprise and a market-oriented economy.

Human rights and freedoms. A new constitution was promulgated in 1991, but it significantly omits any reference to such basic rights as freedom of the press, the freedom of assembly and the right of privacy and it restricts freedom of religion. Arbitrary arrest and detention and denial of fair public trial continue to characterize the criminal justice system even after the publication of a new penal code. As there are no private lawyers, legal assistance is not available to those accused of any crime. Government owns the media, and expression of political dissent by any means is a punishable criminal offense. The new

Country Table 1. Religious adherents in Laos, AD 1900-2025.

Year / Name	1900 Adherents	1900 %	1970 Adherents	1970 %	mid-1990 Adherents	mid-1990 %	Annual change, 1990-2000 Natural	Conversion	Total	Rate	mid-1995 Adherents	mid-1995 %	mid-2000 Adherents	mid-2000 %	mid-2025 Adherents	mid-2025 %
Buddhists	905,000	60.3	1,566,490	57.8	2,033,650	49.0	62,750	-1,109	61,641	2.68	2,330,575	48.8	2,650,061	48.8	4,510,600	46.7
Ethnoreligionists	581,000	38.7	917,080	33.8	1,720,000	41.4	53,066	1,558	54,624	2.80	1,985,000	41.6	2,266,239	41.7	4,080,600	42.3
Nonreligious	0	0.0	90,000	3.3	175,000	4.2	5,399	597	5,996	2.99	204,000	4.3	234,962	4.3	500,000	5.2
Christians	**8,000**	**0.5**	**51,330**	**1.9**	**91,500**	**2.2**	**2,823**	**-712**	**2,111**	**2.10**	**102,825**	**2.2**	**112,609**	**2.1**	**236,400**	**2.5**
PROFESSION																
crypto-Christians	3,000	0.2	21,330	0.8	55,000	1.3	1,697	603	2,300	3.56	65,000	1.4	78,000	1.4	165,000	1.7
professing Christians	**5,000**	**0.3**	**30,000**	**1.1**	**36,500**	**0.9**	**1,126**	**-1,315**	**-189**	**-0.53**	**37,825**	**0.8**	**34,609**	**0.6**	**71,400**	**0.7**
AFFILIATION																
unaffiliated Christians	0	0.0	0	0.0	50	0.0	2	-2	0	-0.83	50	0.0	46	0.0	100	0.0
affiliated Christians	**8,000**	**0.5**	**51,330**	**1.9**	**91,450**	**2.2**	**2,821**	**-710**	**2,111**	**2.10**	**102,775**	**2.2**	**112,563**	**2.1**	**236,300**	**2.5**
Independents	0	0.0	300	0.0	33,000	0.8	1,018	243	1,261	3.29	40,031	0.8	45,613	0.8	110,000	1.1
Protestants	0	0.0	9,150	0.3	25,000	0.6	771	169	940	3.24	29,650	0.6	34,400	0.6	80,000	0.8
Roman Catholics	8,000	0.5	41,480	1.5	33,000	0.8	1,018	-1,118	-100	-0.31	32,594	0.7	32,000	0.6	45,000	0.5
Marginal Christians	0	0.0	100	0.0	250	0.0	8	2	10	3.42	300	0.0	350	0.0	1,000	0.0
Anglicans	0	0.0	300	0.0	200	0.0	6	-6	0	0.00	200	0.0	200	0.0	300	0.0
Trans-megabloc groupings																
Evangelicals	0	0.0	9,200	0.3	32,500	0.8	1,003	-253	750	2.10	38,245	0.8	40,000	0.7	85,000	0.9
Pentecostals/Charismatics	0	0.0	500	0.0	32,800	0.8	1,012	708	1,720	4.31	40,815	0.9	50,000	0.9	115,836	1.2
Great Commission Christians	**6,000**	**0.4**	**46,000**	**1.7**	**82,000**	**2.0**	**2,530**	**-672**	**1,858**	**2.06**	**92,000**	**1.9**	**100,576**	**1.9**	**210,000**	**2.2**
Chinese folk-religionists	3,000	0.2	30,000	1.1	62,000	1.5	1,913	139	2,052	2.90	73,000	1.5	82,519	1.5	170,000	1.8
Atheists	0	0.0	28,000	1.0	47,000	1.1	1,450	38	1,488	2.79	55,000	1.2	61,878	1.1	122,000	1.3
Muslims	3,000	0.2	30,000	1.1	18,000	0.4	555	-399	156	0.83	17,500	0.4	19,560	0.4	32,000	0.3
New-Religionists	0	0.0	0	0.0	8,000	0.2	247	-123	124	1.45	8,700	0.2	9,236	0.2	12,000	0.1
Hindus	0	0.0	0	0.0	5,000	0.1	154	25	179	3.10	6,000	0.1	6,787	0.1	12,000	0.1
Baha'is	0	0.0	100	0.0	900	0.0	28	5	33	3.16	1,100	0.0	1,229	0.0	3,000	0.0
Taoists	0	0.0	0	0.0	950	0.0	29	-8	21	2.01	1,100	0.0	1,159	0.0	2,400	0.0
doubly-counted religionists	0	0.0	0	0.0	-10,000	-0.2	-309	-11	-320	2.82	-11,800	-0.3	-13,202	-0.2	-28,000	-0.3
World A (unevangelized persons)	1,440,000	96.0	1,898,820	70.0	2,350,032	56.6	72,511	-22,564	49,947	1.95	2,601,461	54.5	2,852,325	52.5	4,845,806	50.2
World B (evangelized non-Christians)	52,000	3.5	762,450	28.1	1,710,468	41.2	52,771	23,276	76,047	3.73	2,069,036	43.3	2,468,066	45.4	4,570,794	47.3
World C (Christians)	8,000	0.5	51,330	1.9	91,500	2.2	2,823	-712	2,111	2.10	102,825	2.2	112,609	2.1	236,400	2.5
Country's population	**1,500,000**	**100.0**	**2,712,600**	**100.0**	**4,152,000**	**100.0**	**128,105**	**0**	**128,105**	**2.73**	**4,773,323**	**100.0**	**5,433,000**	**100.0**	**9,653,000**	**100.0**

COLUMNS, ROWS.
For meanings and definitions, see Codebook (Part 3). Note that, by definition, total 'Christians' = professing + crypto-Christians, which also = affiliated + unaffiliated Christians, and also = Great Commission Christians + latent Christians. Percentages may not always total exactly, due to rounding.

CENSUSES.
The religion question has not been asked.

NOTES ON RELIGIONS
ATHEISTS. Lao People's Party (Phak Passaon Lao, LPP) (Communist; neutral in Sino-Soviet dispute).
BAHA'IS. Despite Communist opposition, Baha'i has expanded somewhat and by 1996 had 21 local spiritual assemblies.
BUDDHISTS. Theravada (or Hinayana, Little Vehicle); predominantly Lao, with 80,000 Vietnamese and about 34,000 Chinese (Mandarin-speaking).
ETHNORELIGIONISTS. Animists among non-Lao ethnic minorities and Montagnard tribes. Tribes over 95% animist: Alak (population 4,500), Brao (14,800), Jeng 8,000), Kasseng (9,000), Loven (29,000), Makong (3,000), Nyaheun (6,000), Oi (15,700), and Phu Thai (122,000).
INDEPENDENTS. Isolated radio believers scattered across the nation (see Table 2).
MUSLIMS. Mainly Sunnis of the Shafiite rite among the Cham and other peoples from Cambodia, Viet Nam and surrounding countries.
NONRELIGIOUS. Communist forces and sympathizers, also Chinese (Mandarin-speaking), including 30,000 Chinese engaged on road-building, and (in 1976) 30,000 North Vietnamese troops.
PROTESTANTS. In 1975-76, 450 Protestant families with 17 pastors (about 2,500 persons) fled from Laos and settled as a community in central Thailand.

Great Commission Instrument Panel: status of Laos (for explanation see start of Part 4)

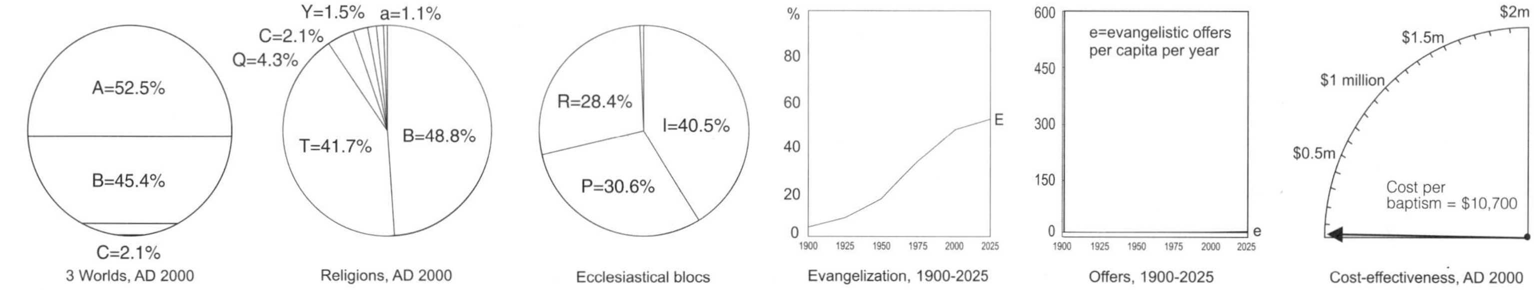

penal code bans slandering the state or its leaders, distorting state or party policies, and spreading false rumors. All associations are party controlled. The government and the party are controlled by the ethnic Lao, also called Lowland Lao, who have a historical animosity with other minorities, such as the Hmong. However, there is no legal discrimination against the Hmong, some of whom occupy important positions in government. Women have fared well under the Communists, and have a greater role than in the past in political and economic activity.

Human environment. Once heavily forested, Laos faces loss of its forest cover and resources. Because of deforestation, Laos has lost 71% of its original, natural wildlife habitat, and two-thirds of its wetlands are threatened.

NON-CHRISTIAN RELIGIONS

Theravada or ***Hinayana Buddhism*** is the principal and official religion and that professed by about 49% of the Laotian population. The head of the Buddhist community is the Phra Sangharaja, who is advised by the Religious Council consisting of 5 members known as Chao Rajakhana. Two Buddhist monastic orders are active, the Thammayut and the Mahanakay, the latter being the more important. Village life is generally centered around a pagoda. In 1966, the number of pagodas in Laos was estimated to be about 1,900. The principal national institution is the Buddhist Institute in Vientiane, founded in 1947, which makes available religious information and supervises Pali schools for training future monks. In 1958, some 100 Pali schools were functioning, with a total enrollment of 5,000 students.

Buddhists. Buddha Garden at Sienkhuan, a suburb of Vientiane; images are donated for deceased relatives.

Country summary. **Worlds A, B, C by ethnolinguistic peoples, cities, and major civil divisions in Laos.**

	PEOPLES							CITIES							CIVIL DIVISIONS						
World	Num	Pop 2000	C%	Christians	E%	U%	Unevangelized	Num	Pop 2000	C%	Christians	E%	U%	Unevangelized	Num	Pop 2000	C%	Christians	E%	U%	Unevangelized
A	82	2,239,460	2.64	59,049	34	66	1,486,761	3	242,003	0.50	1,210	47	53	128,310	18	5,433,037	2.07	112,563	48	52	2,849,471
B	12	3,184,943	1.49	47,492	57	43	1,362,447	1	588,244	4.00	23,530	51	49	285,416	0	0	0.00	0	0	0	0
C	3	8,630	69.77	6,021	97	3	268	0	0	0.00	0	0	0	0	0	0	0.00	0	0	0	0
Total	**97**	**5,433,033**	**2.07**	**112,562**	**48**	**52**	**2,849,476**	**4**	**830,247**	**2.98**	**24,740**	**50**	**50**	**413,726**	**18**	**5,433,037**	**2.07**	**112,563**	**48**	**52**	**2,849,471**

Traditional tribal religion remains important among the non-Lao ethnic minorities: Alak, Brao, Galler, Jeng, Kasseng, Loven, Makong, Ngeq, Nyaheun, Oi, Phu Thai, So, and Ta-oi. Buddhist missionary attempts among them have met with a mixed reaction, some tribes being more resistant than others. Traditionalists numbered over 32% of the population in 1995. The belief in spirits, Phi, is fundamental to tribal religions, and ancestor veneration forms an essential part of the cult of such groups as the Black Tai. The Black Tai affirm that each person has 32 souls, some of which go 'beyond the sky' at death while others remain on the ancestral altar. Of special concern are spirits of the soil (called ten), which exist at the district (pi muong) and village (pi ban) levels, in addition to the chief of soil spirit (ten luong). The priests of the soil cult are known as Mo.

Ethnoreligionists. Keeping funeral vigil after death of village schoolteacher in Laos.

CHRISTIANITY

CATHOLIC CHURCH. The first efforts by the Catholic Church to evangelize the country were begun in 1630 and were concentrated among the Tahi Lao of the plains, the major ethnic group of Laos. All the mission centers are located along the border with Thailand, and the Tahi Lao faithful are dominant (59 percent) in the 3 vicariates of Vientiane, Savannakhet, and Pakse. Beginning in 1950, due to the increase in missionaries and insufficient evangelistic results among the Lao, the attention of the church has been turned increasingly to the tribal mountain peoples. In 1970, they were 21% of all Catholics but their catechumens made up 80% of the total catechumens in the country. Foreigners have also traditionally constituted a significant part of the Catholic community: French (1%), American Filipinos (0.2%), Chinese (1.2%) and Vietnamese (15%). Since 1974, the foreign community has decreased. The first Lao priest was ordained in 1963 and the first Lao bishop consecrated in 1974, the latter as auxiliary bishop of Vientiane.

The Holy See has no diplomatic relations with Laos in AD 2000, but an apostolic delegate resides in Bangkok.

PROTESTANT CHURCH. The Protestant pioneers in Laos were Swiss Brethren. They began work in 1902 and translated the entire Bible into Lao, their work being strengthened by the arrival of Overseas Missionary Fellowship workers after 1957. However, the Gospel church of Laos, affiliated with the CMA, which entered in 1929, has had the greatest numerical success. After World War II, missionary effort was intensified. Although the Lao have been resistant to Christian evangelization, there has been considerable penetration among the Montagnard tribal groups, largely due to the increase in numbers of native catechists. Christian work is also carried on among the thousands of refugees created by the prolonged fighting.

Indigenous missions. Laotian Christians have not deliberately initiated foreign missionary work. However, thousands of Laotian Christians are living as expatriates in many other countries, including Thailand, Australia, New Zealand, USA, Canada, and several European countries.

CHURCH AND STATE

The constitution, promulgated in May 1947 and amended in 1956 and 1961, 'recognizes as fundamental principles and rights of the Lao, notably equality before the law, legal protection of the means of existence, freedom of conscience . . .' (Preamble). 'Buddhism is the State religion. The King is its official protector' (Article 7), and he 'should be a fervent Buddhist' (Article 8). There is a certain imprecision in the constitution, lacking as it does any declaration regarding freedom of religion or worship. Successive amendments have tended to be more restrictive than the initial text adopted in 1947 which declared: 'Laos recognizes as the fundamental rights of Laotians individual freedom, freedom of conscience . . . and freedom of meeting and association . . . ' However, although the Christian churches have enjoyed considerable freedom, the slogan 'A good patriot follows the religion of his King' is still heard.

The statute relating to church property depends on a law passed by the Ministry of Colonies of the French Republic in January 1939, which was incorporated into Laotian legislation. Congregations and associations, having as their purpose the exercise of public worship, are directed by administrative councils and endowed with a religious and moral personality. Since 1970, the government has refused to recognize the ecclesiastical ownership of Catholic and Protestant schools but rather considers them private schools under the names of individual priests and pastors. Property used for worship, education, medical, and social service is not subject to fiscal legislation, and in practice, priests and nuns, as with Buddhist bonzes, are exempt from personal taxes.

Until its reorganization in 1967, the Ministry of Religion only concerned itself with Buddhist questions. In 1967, the Department of Religious Administration (Kom Pokkhong Satsana) was established to cater for other religions, although no director was appointed until 1971. Church registration is not required. Administrative councils are free to be registered or not at will.

In the government of national union which came to power on 5 April 1974, following the agreement of 22 February 1973, providing for the reconciliation of rightist and leftist elements in Laos, the Ministry of Religion was given to a representative of the Pathet Lao. A Buddhist monk, the minister was at first flanked, as with all the ministers of the left and right (with the exception of the 2 neutralist ministries), by a secretary of state representing the opposite political tendency. This pattern subsequently became less significant as the Pathet Lao has increasingly assumed control of the government.

By 1976, the Communist regime had taken over all Catholic schools, orphanages, residences and churches, and religious eduction had been eliminated. Only 2 of Vientiane's 87 Buddhist pagodas remained open also.

BROADCASTING AND MEDIA

FEBC (Philippines) broadcasts in Hmong, Khmu and Lao with good response. Shortwave radio programs from KNLS have generated responses.

The 'Jesus' Film has been shown to 72,000 people, mainly by film teams.

INTERDENOMINATIONAL ORGANIZATIONS

No council of churches exists. In 1971, the Catholic Church established an Office of Buddhism with the purpose of stimulating Buddhist-Christian dialogue.

FUTURE TRENDS AND PROSPECTS

Expected declines in Buddhism (57.7% in 1970 to 46.7% in 2025) could be made up partially in Christian growth (1.9% in 1970 to 2.5% in 2025).

Christianity is expected to remain less than 5% of the population until AD 2050. Buddhism could remain near 50% in that same period. The nonreligious could reach 10%.

BIBLIOGRAPHY

1972 Mission directory of Thailand, Cambodia and Laos. B. Bray (ed). Bangkok: Newsasia, 1972.

A bibliography of the Hmong (Miao) of Southeast Asia and the Hmong refugees in the United States. D. P. Olney. 2nd ed. *Southeast Asian refugee studies, Occasional papers,* no. 1. Minneapolis, MN: Center for Urban and Regional Affairs, University of Minnesota, 1983. 75p.

As the rock flower blooms. R. A. Watson. Sevenoaks, UK: Overseas Missionary Fellowship, 1984. 315p.

'Buddhism in Laos,' T. N. Abhay, in *Kingdom of Laos: the land of the million elephants and of the white parasol,* p.237–56. R. de Berval. Saigon: France Asie, 1959.

Ethnic groups of French Indochina. L. Malleret. Washington, DC: US Joint Publications Research Service, 1962. 110p. (Translation of 1937 French edition).

Folk stories of the Hmong: peoples of Laos, Thailand, and Vietnam. N. J. Livo & D. Cha. Englewood, CO: Libraries Unlimited, 1991. 147p.

'Hmong ethnohistory: an historical study of Hmong culture and its implications for ministry.' J. Davidson. D.Miss. thesis, Fuller Theological Seminary, Pasadena, CA, 1993. 230p.

I am a shaman: a Hmong life story with ethnographic commentary. D. Conquergood & P. Thao. *Southeast Asian refugee studies, Occasional paper,* no. 8. Minneapolis, MN: Center for Urban and Regional Affairs, University of Minnesota, 1989. 90p. (Related to the documentary film *Between two worlds: the Hmong shaman in America,* produced by D. Conquergood and T. Siegel [Chicago: Siegel Productions, 1985]).

In the valley of the Mekong: an American in Laos. M. J. Menger. Patterson, NJ: St. Anthony Guild Press, 1970. 226p. (By an American missionary).

Laos. H. Cordell. *World bibliographical series,* vol. 133. Oxford, UK: CLIO Press, 1991. 254p. (See especially 'Religion and shamanism,' p.80–5).

Laos, no turning back: the story of Lungh Singh. J. Pitt & D. Wooding. *The Church in areas of conflict.* Basingstoke, UK: Marshalls and Open Doors, 1985. 127p.

Les cetiya de sable au Laos et en Thailande: les textes. L. Gabaude. *Publications de l'École Française d'Extrême-Orient,* vol. 118. Paris: École Française d'Extrême-Orient, 1979. 338p.

Les fêtes profanes et religieuses au Laos. P. S. Nginn. 2nd ed. Vientiane, Laos: Editions du Comité Littéraire, 1967. 61p.

Life after liberation: the church in the Lao People's Democratic Republic. Nakhon Sawan, Thailand: Lao Christian Service, 1987. 50p.

Lokapâla: génies, totems et sorciers du Nord Laos. H. Deydier. Paris: Plon, 1954. 242p.

'Notes sur le bouddhisme populaire lao en milieu rural lao,' G. Condominas, *Archives de sociologie des religions,* 25/26 (1968), 81–110.

'Phiban cults in rural Laos,' G. Condominas, in *Change and persistence in Thai society: essays in honor of Lauriston Sharp,* p.252–73. G. W. Skinner & A. T. Kirsch (eds). Ithaca, NY: Cornell University Press, 1975.

'Religion,' in *Area handbook for Laos.* D. P. Whitaker et al. Washington, DC: US Government Printing Office, 1972.

Religion and legitimation of power in Thailand, Laos and Burma. B. L. Smith. Chambersburg, PA: Anima, 1978.

'Religious structures in Laos,' C. Archaimbault, *Journal of the Siam society,* 52, 1 (1964), 57–74.

Rites et ceremonies en milieu bouddhiste lao. M. Zago. *Documenta missionalia,* no. 6. Rome: Università Gregoriana Editrice, 1972. 408p.

'Ritual and social hierarchy: an aspect of traditional religion in Buddhist Laos,' F. E. Reynolds, in *Religion and legitimation of power in Thailand, Laos, and Burma,* p.166–74. B. L. Smith (ed). Chambersburg, PA: Anima Books, 1978.

Structures religieuses lao: rites et mythes. C. Archaimbault. *Documents pour le Laos,* vol. 2. Vientiane, Laos: Vithagna, 1973. 289p.

The Hmong: an annotated bibliography, 1983–1987. J. C. Smith. *Southeast Asian refugee studies, Occasional papers,* no. 7. Minneapolis, MN: Center for Urban and Regional Affairs, University of Minnesota, 1988. 67p.

'The way of the monk and the way of the world: Buddhism in Thailand, Laos and Cambodia,' J. Bunnag, in *The world of Buddhism: Buddhist monks and nuns in society and culture,* p.159–70. H. Bechert & R. Gombrich (eds). London: Thames & Hudson, 1984.

Un après–goût de bonheur: une ethnologie de la spiritualité lao. A. Doré. *Documents pour le Laos,* no. 4. Vientiane, Laos: Vithagna, 1974. 99p.

'Yao religion and society,' J. Lemoine, in *Highlanders of Thailand,* p.195–211. J. McKinnon & W. Bhruksasri (eds). Kuala Lumpur, Malaysia: Oxford University Press, 1983.

Country Table 2. **Organized churches and denominations in Laos.**

Official name (bold type = church with over 10% of all affiliated) 1	*Begun* 2	*Type* 3	*Counc* 4	*Congs* 5	*Adults* 6	*Affiliated 1970* 7	*Affiliated 1995* 8	*G%* 9	*Names, notes, and other statistics* (see Codebook, Part 3) 10
Eglise Adventiste du Septième Jour	1957	P-Adv	x....	2	100	100	250	3.73	*SDA, Seventh-day Adventists.* In Thailand Mission. Meos, some Chinese. 1x,W=99%,10Y.
Eglise Anglicane (D Singapore)		A-Cen	awaA.	2	80	300	200	0.05	*Church of the Holy Spirit*, Vientiane; in D Singapore. 99% expatriates (UK,USA).
Eglise Catholique au Laos:	1630	R-Lat	P.F.P	76	18,200	41,480	32,594	-0.96	*Catholic Ch. Phrakristachak Katolik.* C=2+0+6. 15n 40x 45m 96w 2075Yy
VA Luang Prabang	1963	R-Lat	Pomi	14	1,300	3,134	2,500	-0.90	Royal/Buddhist centre. Montagnards; 26 dialects. 1n 25x 28m 11w 100Yy
VA Paksé	1967	R-Lat	Pmep	26	6,000	7,700	10,372	1.20	South. Rural. 50% from ethnic minorities. M=MEP. 4n 0x 0m 22w 475Yy
VA Savannakhet	1950	R-Lat	Pmep	19	3,900	7,494	7,722	0.12	Centre of country. Rural, one mining centre. M=MEP. 7n 6x 6m 51w 300Yy
VA Vientiane	1938	R-Lat	Pomi	17	7,000	23,152	12,000	-2.59	Capital; vast influx of refugees. Many tribes. M=OMI. 3n 9x 11m 12w 1200Yy
Eglise Evangélique du Laos	1929	P-Hol	xFE..	160	8,000	6,000	16,000	4.00	*Gospel Ch of Laos.* M=CMA(USA). 90% tribal (Meo, Khmu) in north, 39n,27f,2h,1s.
Eglise Neo-Apostolique	c1992	I-3aX	x....	1	20	–	31	33.33	*New Apostolic Church. NAC/NAK.* M=Neuapostolische Kirche (HQ Zurich).
Eglise radiophoniques isolées	1952	I-3rZ	.....	200	16,700	300	30,000	20.23	Isolated radio believers (FEBC), mostly students and youths, across nation.
Hidden Buddhist believers in Christ	c1970	I-Bud	.....	200	6,000	–	10,000	44.54	Converted Buddhists who choose to stay in Buddhism as witnesses to Christ.
Mission Evangélique au Laos	1902	P-CBr	xM...	90	6,500	3,000	13,000	6.04	*Ev Mission.* M=Swiss Brethren(Open) and 1957, OMF. Hill tribes in south. 20f,1H.
Témoins de Jéhovah	c1955	m-Jeh	x....	3	100	100	300	4.49	*Jehovah's Witnesses, Watch Tower. IBSA.* Active witnessing from 1959. 6Y.
Other Protestant denominations		P-	.....	10	220	50	400	0.05	ERF,FMB-SBC (1971),LEF/GCL,ACCM,Christian Association,TSPM(China),NTM,CCT.
Totals				**744**	**55,920**	**51,330**	**102,775**		

Churches, members, growth, 1900-2025	*Congs*	*Adults*	*Affiliated*	*G%*	*Total denominations*	*6 Megablocs:* *O*	*R*	*A*	*P*	*I*	*m*
Total churches, members, and denominations (mid-1900)	30	4,500	8,000	2.69	1	0	1	0	0	0	0
Total churches, members, and denominations (mid-1970)	232	28,896	51,330	2.69	14	0	1	1	10	1	1
Total churches, members, and denominations (mid-1990)	500	49,800	91,450	2.93	23	0	1	1	18	2	1
Total churches, members, and denominations (mid-1995)	744	55,920	102,775	2.36	24	0	1	1	18	3	1
Total churches, members, and denominations (mid-2000)	900	61,200	112,563	1.84	24	0	1	1	18	3	1
Total churches, members, and denominations (mid-2025)	1,600	129,000	236,300	3.01	43	0	1	1	30	10	1

NOTES ON TABLE ABOVE
NATIONAL COUNCILS (Column 4, 5th letter).
P = Conférence Episcopale du Laos et du Cambodge (CELAC) (Episcopal Conference of Laos & Cambodia) (Sapha (Sangharat) Lao-Kmen).

LATVIA

SECULAR DATA, AD 2000

STATE
Official name: Latvijas Republika (The Republic of Latvia).
Short name: Latvia. **Adjective of nationality:** Latvian.
Flag: Brown field bisected by white stripe.
Area: 64,610 sq. km. (24,946 sq. mi.).
Government: Unitary multiparty republic with a single legislative body, since 1991 (1721 Russian empire, 1939 Soviet rule).
Legislature: Parliament, or Saeima, 100 members.
Official language: Latvian.
Monetary unit: 1 lats (Ls; plural lati) = 100 santimi. **US$1=** 0.59 lats.
Chief cities: RIGA 921,000; Daugavpils (Dvinsk) 119,886; Liepaja (Liepaya, Libau) 106,782; Jelgava (Mitava) 69,237; Jurmala 61,802.
Political divisions: 33 provinces.
Armed forces: 4,500.

DEMOGRAPHY
Population: 2,357,000.
Population density: 36.4/sq. km. (94.4/sq. mi.).
Under 15 years: 416,000.
Growth rate p.a.: -1.10% (births 9.13, deaths 13.97).
Mortality: Infant, per 1,000: 15.3; **Maternal per 100,000:** 40.0.
Life expectancy: 70 (male 64, female 75).
Household size: 3.1. **Floor area per person, sq.m:** 19.4.
Major languages: Latvian, Latgalian, Russian, Belorussian, Ukrainian.
Urban dwellers: 74.30%. **Urban growth rate p.a.:** -0.4%.
Labor force: 55%.

ETHNOLINGUISTIC PEOPLES
32.8% Russian; 32.5% Latvian (Lett, Lettish); 21.7% Latgalian (Upper Latvian); 4.0% Byelorussian; 2.9% Ukrainian.

ECONOMY
National income p.a. per person: US$2,269; **per family:** US$7,036.

EDUCATION
Adult literacy: 99% (male 99%, female 99%). **Schools:** 978.
Universities: 14. **School enrolment:** female/male: 86%/84%.

HEALTH
Access to health services: 90%. **Access to safe water:** 90%.
Hospitals: 170 (121 beds per 10,000). **Doctors:** 7,714.
Blind: 2,000. **Deaf:** 143,800. **Murder rate:** 14.
Lepers: 200.

LITERATURE
New book titles p.a.: 1,650 (700 p.a. per million). **Periodicals:** 238.
Newspapers: 22 dailies.

COMMUNICATION (per 1,000 people)
Phones: 280 (14% mobile). **Radios:** 547. **TV sets:** 482.
Daily newspaper circulation: 228. **Computers:** 40.

REFUGEES
Alien refugees from other countries: 100.

HUMAN LIFE AND LIBERTY (optimum condition=100.0%)
HDI: 71.1. **HSI:** 55.0. **HFI:** 35.0. **EFL:** 39.0.

Country Table 1. **Religious adherents in Latvia, AD 1900-2025.**

Year	*1900*		*1970*		*mid-1990*		*Annual change, 1990-2000*				*mid-1995*		*mid-2000*		*mid-2025*	
Name	*Adherents*	*%*	*Adherents*	*%*	*Adherents*	*%*	*Natural*	*Conversion*	*Total*	*Rate*	*Adherents*	*%*	*Adherents*	*%*	*Adherents*	*%*
Christians	**1,199,500**	**99.5**	**1,214,900**	**51.2**	**1,693,000**	**63.1**	**-20,677**	**9,164**	**-11,513**	**-0.70**	**1,649,600**	**65.0**	**1,577,870**	**66.9**	**1,509,000**	**77.9**
PROFESSION																
crypto-Christians	0	0.0	300,000	12.6	220,000	8.2	-2,680	-19,320	-22,000	-70.77	0	0.0	0	0.0	0	0.0
professing Christians	**1,199,500**	**99.5**	**914,900**	**38.5**	**1,473,000**	**54.9**	**-17,997**	**28,484**	**10,487**	**0.69**	**1,649,600**	**65.0**	**1,577,870**	**66.9**	**1,509,000**	**77.9**
AFFILIATION																
unaffiliated Christians	80,000	6.6	0	0.0	1,500	0.1	-18	12	-6	-0.37	1,600	0.1	1,445	0.1	2,000	0.1
affiliated Christians	**1,119,500**	**92.8**	**1,214,900**	**51.2**	**1,691,500**	**63.0**	**-20,608**	**9,100**	**-11,508**	**-0.70**	**1,648,000**	**65.0**	**1,576,425**	**66.9**	**1,507,000**	**77.8**
Protestants	542,500	45.0	372,800	15.7	570,000	21.2	-6,944	5,944	-1,000	-0.18	562,900	22.2	560,000	23.8	500,000	25.8
Orthodox	177,000	14.7	503,900	21.2	585,000	21.8	-7,127	4,127	-3,000	-0.53	577,100	22.8	555,000	23.6	480,000	24.8
Roman Catholics	400,000	33.2	340,000	14.3	500,000	18.6	-6,092	5,092	-1,000	-0.20	500,000	19.7	490,000	20.8	450,000	23.2
Independents	0	0.0	60,000	2.5	110,000	4.1	-1,340	1,840	500	0.45	111,364	4.4	115,000	4.9	150,000	7.8
Marginal Christians	0	0.0	200	0.0	2,300	0.1	-28	48	20	0.84	2,400	0.1	2,500	0.1	5,000	0.3
doubly-affiliated	0	0.0	-62,000	-2.6	-75,800	-2.8	923	-7,951	-7,028	6.78	-105,764	-4.2	-146,075	-6.2	-78,000	-4.0
Trans-megabloc groupings																
Evangelicals	220,000	18.2	110,000	4.6	162,000	6.0	-1,974	2,574	600	0.36	165,150	6.5	168,000	7.1	156,000	8.1
Pentecostals/Charismatics	0	0.0	6,000	0.3	88,800	3.3	-1,082	1,202	120	0.13	93,577	3.7	90,000	3.8	110,000	5.7
Great Commission Christians	**73,000**	**6.1**	**332,000**	**14.0**	**500,000**	**18.6**	**-6,092**	**3,249**	**-2,843**	**-0.58**	**500,000**	**19.7**	**471,566**	**20.0**	**460,000**	**23.8**
Nonreligious	1,000	0.1	736,100	31.0	762,770	28.4	-9,293	-5,626	-14,919	-2.15	706,650	27.9	613,584	26.0	343,300	17.7
Atheists	500	0.0	394,000	16.6	198,000	7.4	-2,412	-3,157	-5,569	-3.25	157,000	6.2	142,308	6.0	60,000	3.1
Jews	5,000	0.4	24,000	1.0	21,000	0.8	-256	-501	-757	-4.37	14,400	0.6	13,432	0.6	10,000	0.5
Muslims	0	0.0	5,000	0.2	8,800	0.3	-107	112	5	0.06	8,900	0.4	8,854	0.4	13,000	0.7
Ethnoreligionists	0	0.0	0	0.0	330	0.0	-4	5	1	0.39	340	0.0	343	0.0	500	0.0
Buddhists	0	0.0	0	0.0	100	0.0	-1	3	2	1.67	110	0.0	118	0.0	200	0.0
World A (unevangelized persons)	1,206	0.1	142,440	6.0	34,892	1.3	-426	-814	-1,240	-4.28	27,903	1.1	23,570	1.0	13,552	0.7
World B (evangelized non-Christians)	5,294	0.4	1,016,660	42.8	956,108	35.6	-11,647	-8,350	-19,997	-2.33	859,190	33.9	755,560	32.0	413,448	21.4
World C (Christians)	1,199,500	99.5	1,214,900	51.2	1,693,000	63.1	-20,677	9,164	-11,513	-0.70	1,649,600	65.0	1,577,870	67.0	1,509,000	77.9
Country's population	**1,206,000**	**100.0**	**2,374,000**	**100.0**	**2,684,000**	**100.0**	**-32,750**	**0**	**-32,750**	**-1.29**	**2,536,694**	**100.0**	**2,357,000**	**100.0**	**1,936,000**	**100.0**

COLUMNS, ROWS.
For meanings and definitions, see Codebook (Part 3). Note that, by definition, total 'Christians' = professing + crypto-Christians, which also = affiliated + unaffiliated Christians, and also = Great Commission Christians + latent Christians. Percentages may not always total exactly, due to rounding.

NOTES ON RELIGIONS
ATHEISTS. Large-scale decline after 1989 with most Russians returning to Orthodoxy and most Latvians becoming either Catholic or Protestant.
BAHA'IS. In 1995 there were 2 local spiritual assemblies (LSAs).
JEWS. Decline after 1989 due to emigration to Israel.
MUSLIMS. Azerbaijanis, Chuvash, and Tatars.

Country status. Latvia, a former republic of the Soviet Union, is a country on the eastern shore of the Baltic Sea between Estonia and Lithuania. The country's main agricultural products are related to pig-breeding and dairy farming.

HUMAN LIFE AND LIBERTY

Human rights and freedoms. Latvia regained its independence in 1991 after 50 years of Soviet rule. It has

Great Commission Instrument Panel: status of Latvia (for explanation see start of Part 4)

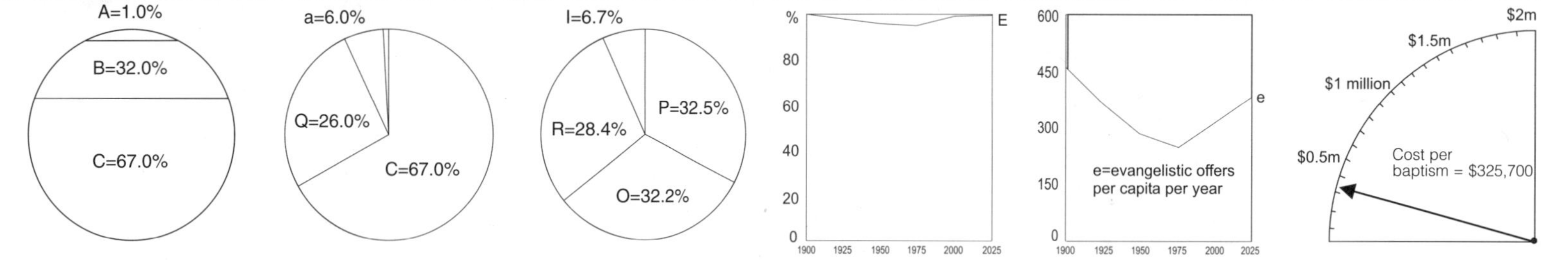

3 Worlds, AD 2000 | Religions, AD 2000 | Ecclesiastical blocs | Evangelization, 1900-2025 | Offers, 1900-2025 | Cost-effectiveness, AD 2000

moved toward a full parliamentary and democratic form of government (although with a limited franchise) and a market economy. In 1991 a new Constitutional law was passed providing for human rights and freedoms.There are few restrictions on press freedom but a new law on the press and broadcast media contains certain provisions inimical to a free press. The major human rights problem relates to discrimination against ethnic Russians who form about one-third the population and are in the majority in all the cities.

NON-CHRISTIAN RELIGIONS

Judaism still survives in Latvia. The Jewish community of Latvia was nearly annihilated during the Nazi occupation of 1940-45. After the war Jews emigrated from other parts of the USSR, fleeing Stalinist persecution. Many Latvian synagogues were confiscated by the state and converted to other purposes. The religious renewal that came with *glasnost* and independence brought new life to the Jewish community as well as the Christian. A survey in 1994 counted 5 Jewish congregations in Latvia. By 1995 there were 14,000 Jews in the country, with their numbers slowly declining, mainly due to emigration to Israel.

Atheists and ***nonreligious*** form the largest non-Christian group in Latvia. Comprising only about 1,500 individuals at the start of the 20th century, by 1970 these constituted more than 47% of the population, a drastic shift resulting from the forces of modernity, Communist education, and official atheist and anti-church propaganda. In the late 1980s and early 1990s, as the country quickly turned its back on Communism and Soviet domination, the people just as quickly turned their faces again toward the Christian faith of their ancestors. By 1995 atheists and nonreligious had dropped to 6.2 and 27.9% of the population, respectively.

CHRISTIANITY

After the Russian conversion to Orthodox Christianity in 988, clans in the eastern sections of Latvia made tribute payments to principalities in the further east; thus came the first contact with Christianity. The pioneer missionary to Latvia was Meinhard, a monk from Holstein. He arrived in 1180, following German merchants, and was named bishop of Üxküll (Ikskile) 6 years later. Christianity made little progress until the third bishop, Albert of Buxhoevden, arrived in the country with 23 ships and 500 Saxon soldiers, believing that evangelization could only proceed behind a vanguard of protection and under a canopy of domination. He was given permission from pope Innocent III to found the Order of the Brothers of the Sword (Schwertbrüderorden), also known as the Livonian Order, in 1202. These soldier-missionaries spread the gospel and conquered until the tribal kingdoms were all beaten. Albert granted parcels of territory (fiefs) to his knights for them to govern, thus essentially setting the country's civil as well as spiritual rule under the bishop. From 1282 Riga was an archbishopric. By the end of the 15th century, 70 churches served the land. Through the Middle Ages clergy were frustrated at how the people mixed their Christian faith with practices and beliefs from the local pre-Christian paganism. Even as late as the 18th century Lutheran pastors complained of how much the treasured ancient songs, tales, and fables affected the beliefs of their parishioners.

CATHOLIC CHURCH. The Jesuits were active in parts of modern-day Latvia in the 16th century. Thanks to their efforts a majority of the churches in some areas remained Catholic. The southeastern province of Latgale has been the historic Catholic stronghold. In the mid-17th century nearly all the Catholic clergy spoke Polish and the ecclesiastical leadership were all Poles. Catholic clergy have played an important cultural role in Latvia, participating in and encouraging the intelligentsia, and standing against Russification. In 1935, 24.5% of Latvia was Roman Catholic. Catholics were encouraged in 1983 when the Communist government permitted bishop Julijans Vaivods to receive from Rome elevation to cardinal status. This was unprecedented in all of Latvian history and in all of the USSR. Though he was 87 at the time, he lived and led for 7 years, stubbornly opposing Communist pressure. In the late 1970s and 1980s priests were trained in Latvia for other Soviet republics. One sign of the revitalization of the Catholic church was the increase in baptisms, from 5,167 in 1985 to 10,661 in 1991. The Catholic presence became spread more evenly throughout the country, so that by 1995 only 42% of Latvia's Catholics lived in Latgale.

The Holy See has diplomatic relations with Latvia and in AD 2000 is represented to government and the Catholic hierarchy by a nuncio residing in Vilnius (Lithuania).

PROTESTANT CHURCHES. Luther's ideas came early to Latvia. In the 1520s some of Riga's leading citizens were supporting and promoting the nascent Reformation. Soon people everywhere were debating what reform should come to the church and how. Mobs attacked monasteries and churches. For the first time, Christian worship was conducted in the Latvian language, and ethnic Latvians became clergy—though both of those reforms remained extremely rare for many decades. By the middle of the 16th century most of the German nobility had forsaken Rome for reform and carried their vassals with them. The Catholic Teutonic Knights, who were then suffering defeat in various places, lost control of Livonia (approximate predecessor to modern Latvia) in 1558 and the land was partitioned between Sweden and Poland-Lithuania. The area under Swedish control soon had a strong and well-organized Protestant church.

For centuries Latvians were considered to hold only mild loyalty to their Lutheran faith. The clergy lived in a different cultural world than their parishioners. They were almost entirely German, and almost entirely under the control of the German landowners. Even after the country came under Russian power in the 18th century, German landowners continued to control pastoral appointments. Renewal came to the Lutheran church in the 18th century through German Pietist missionaries, notably Moravian Brethren from Herrnhut. By 1738 they had established a seminary to train leaders, and soon had 4,000 members in their own congregations. Their emphasis on education served to spread literacy.

The Lutheran church was reorganized in 1922 and enjoyed a season of relative health and growth during Latvia's independence that ended in 1940. Reformers sought to give the church a more indigenous flavor by composing new Latvian hymns, publishing a new Latvian translation of the New Testament, and recruiting more Latvian clergy who then became the leaders of the denomination. In 1935, 68.35% of ethnic Latvians were Lutheran, and 55.2% of the nation overall. During and following the Nazi occupation, the Lutheran church suffered the loss of much of its leadership—through death, escape to the West, or deportation to Siberia—and many of its church buildings were destroyed. The Evangelical Lutheran Church had an estimated 600,000 members in 1956, but then suffered drastic decline under Soviet persecution. An internal memo in 1987 estimated only 25,000 active members (likely measured by attendance; the statistics below reflect all adult members, both active and inactive).

A group of young, well-educated theologians and clergy in the Evangelical Lutheran Church organized the Rebirth and Renewal movement (Atdzimsana un Atjaunosana) in 1987. They worked for parish renewal, for structural renewal of their stuffy and timid denomination, and even dared to confront Communist officials. Though their numbers were small, their influence was large in the life of the church and, eventually, in the life of the nation. At the denominational synod of 1989, the entire leadership of the denomination was voted out, including the archbishop, and members of Rebirth and Renewal were voted in. Some of the movement's members also helped in the founding of the Popular Front of Latvia (*Latvijas Tautas Fronte,* LFT), the party that played the leading role in the newly-independent country.

Evangelical Lutheran Church of Latvia. Worship service of Resurrection Church, Riga.

As Communism fell and the religious climate of Latvia quickly changed, the Lutheran church came alive in new ways. Church buildings were rebuilt or restored, Sunday Schools opened, Christian instruction was given in schools, and sermons were published in the media. Various Protestant groups, notably Baptists and Pentecostals, launched into vigorous evangelism and grew. Ethnic Russians were a majority in the Pentecostal churches, while the Baptist churches tended to be Latvian. One evangelistic event, HOPE '91, reported 2,000 professions of faith. At the same time, Baptists and others were hurt by emigration of lay and pastoral leadership. The Lutheran Cathedral Church in the Old Town of Riga holds the world's largest pipe organ, played by the most noted organists of Europe. Choral singing is the national hobby of Latvia and a beautiful part of her Christian worship.

OTHER CHURCHES. In 1710 Peter the Great captured Riga. Russia continued to win Latvian territory until by 1795 the entire country was under the tsar, though local rule remained under the German nobility. The Orthodox church grew both from Slavic immigration and from Latvian conversion. Some Latvians decided to cast their lot with the Russians as a gesture of opposition to the German nobility that had ruled over them for centuries. Latvia's Orthodox church was independent prior to the Nazi occupation, but then was forced under the Moscow Patriarchate when the country was taken into the Soviet Union. A large number of Russians immigrated, with clergy also coming from Russia. By 1989, of all the Soviet republics only Russia had a larger percentage of ethnic Russians than Latvia. The Orthodox cathedral in Riga was confiscated and converted to a planetarium and coffee shop. In 1992 Latvia's Orthodox church regained both its independence and its cathedral. Old Believers, a different Orthodox group, fled from tsarist persecution to Latvia in the 17th century when the

Country summary. **Worlds A, B, C by ethnolinguistic peoples, cities, and major civil divisions in Latvia.**

	PEOPLES							CITIES							CIVIL DIVISIONS						
World	*Num*	*Pop 2000*	*C%*	*Christians*	*E%*	*U%*	*Unevangelized*	*Num*	*Pop 2000*	*C%*	*Christians*	*E%*	*U%*	*Unevangelized*	*Num*	*Pop 2000*	*C%*	*Christians*	*E%*	*U%*	*Unevangelized*
A	8	25,498	2.11	539	44	56	14,235	0	0	0.00	0	0	0	0	0	0	0.00	0	0	0	0
B	8	872,686	50.91	444,287	99	1	5,099	0	0	0.00	0	0	0	0	0	0	0.00	0	0	0	0
C	19	1,458,326	77.60	1,131,600	100	0	3,266	5	1,263,744	65.12	822,938	99	1	13,416	33	2,356,510	66.90	1,576,425	99	1	22,605
Total	**35**	**2,356,510**	**66.90**	**1,576,426**	**99**	**1**	**22,600**	**5**	**1,263,744**	**65.12**	**822,938**	**99**	**1**	**13,416**	**33**	**2,356,510**	**66.90**	**1,576,425**	**99**	**1**	**22,605**

country was under Swedish and Polish control. They had 56 churches in 1994.

Renewal movements. In the 1990s the Pentecostal/Charismatic Renewal continued to spread rapidly across most older churches, and numbered over 84,000 adherents (of whom 12% Pentecostals, 88% Charismatics, and 0% Independents).

Indigenous missions. Latvian Christians, long oppressed, are slowly beginning to gain a vision for sending missionaries to other peoples.

CHURCH AND STATE

As Latvia was independent from 1920 to 1940, its church was spared the worst of Stalin's purges. Just before the German invasion of 1941 the Soviets arrested and deported 15,000 Latvian leaders, including many clergymen, most of whom died in exile. When the Communists re-gained power in 1945, all church properties were taken by the state, local committees determined when or if congregations needed to meet, and high rents were charged. Russification and Sovietization programs were intense in Latvia, more so than in the other Baltic republics. All Christian activity suffered severely. Since independence in 1991 the country has enjoyed complete freedom of religious belief and worship. Expatriate and local Christians have evangelized freely, though it will likely be difficult to gain permission for more high-profile, large-scale evangelistic events after the one in 1991. Only native Latvians are permitted to register new religious organizations.

BROADCASTING AND MEDIA

IBRA-produced programs in Latvian and Russian can be heard daily on local radio station RIGA. Shortwave radio programs from KNLS, TWR (Guam), HCJB (Ecuador) and AWR (Slovakia), as well as other international broadcasters, can also be received. HCJB is planting a local radio ministry in Latvia in partnership with Latvia Christian Radio.

Some 1.3 million (46%) have seen the 'Jesus' Film, mainly on television. Satellite TV programs are received mainly in Arabic.

FUTURE TRENDS AND PROSPECTS

In the post-Communist period, Christianity will probably grow to 78% of the population by AD 2025.

Christianity could then continue to grow as atheists and the nonreligious decline. By AD 2050, Christians could represent 85% of the population.

BIBLIOGRAPHY

'Baltic Protestantism,' W. Kahle, *Religion in Communist lands*, 7, 4 (Winter 1979), 220–25. (Deals with Estonia, Latvia, and Lithuania).

Dawn in dark Latgalia. O. A. Blumit. : Hulbert Publishing Co., [1928].

Germanische und Baltische Religion. A. V. Strom & H. Biezais. *Die Religionen der Menschheit.* Stuttgart: Verlag W. Kohlhammer, 1975. 391p.

Gli inizi del cristianesimo in Livonia–Lettonia. Vatican City: Libreria Editrice Vaticana, 1989. 290p.

Gorbachev, glasnost and the gospel. M. A. Bourdeaux. London: Hodder & Stoughton, 1990. 226p.

Latviesu trimdas izdevumu bibliografija. B. Jegers. Stockholm: Daugava, 1968–1988. 4 vols.

'Lutheranism in Latvia: a struggle between "Kultur" and faith,' J. C. Wohlrabe Jr., *Concordia journal*, 11 (May 1985), 82–93.

Lutherans in Latvia and Estonia. D. Krueger. Lansing, IL: D. Krueger, 1984. 36p.

'"Rebirth and renewal" in the Latvian Lutheran Church,' M. Sapiets, *Religion in Communist lands*, 16, 3 (Autumn 1988), 237–49.

Studien über die Anfänge der Mission in Livland. M. Hellmann. *Vorträge und Forschungen*, Sonderband 37. Sigmaringer, Germany: Jan Thorbecke Verlag, 1989. 167p.

'Suffering and hope: two recurrent ideas among Latvian Lutherans in exile,' E. Grislis, *Lutheran quarterly*, 22 (Aug 1970), 298–318.

The Baltic States: Estonia, Latvia, Lithuania. I. A. Smith & M. V. Grunts. *World bibliographical series*, vol. 161. Oxford, UK: CLIO Press, 1993.

The Latvian Orthodox church. Protopresbyter Alexander Cherney. Welshpool, Wales, UK: Stylite Publishing, 1985. 143p.

'The revival in Latvia during the 1920s and subsequent Baptist immigration to Brazil.' O. Bruvers. Ph.D. dissertation, Fuller Theological Seminary, Pasadena, CA, 1991. 297p.

'The spiritual influence of the Moravian Brethren in Latvia in the eighteenth century.' O. Bruvers. M.A. thesis, Fuller Theological Seminary, Pasadena, CA, 1982. 90p.

These ruins accuse: a record of religious suppression of the Evangelical Lutheran Church in occupied Latvia. Stockholm: Latvian National Foundation, [1975]. 24p.

'Vignettes of faith experiences.' A. J. Liepkalns. Diss., Lutheran School of Theology, Chicago, 1992. 212p. (Stories of Latvian Lutherans).

'Which way to the church?,' J. Rubenis, *Religion in Communist lands*, 17, 1 (Spring 1989), 81–86.

Country Table 2. **Organized churches and denominations in Latvia.**

Official name (bold type = church with over 10% of affiliated) 1	*Begun* 2	*Type* 3	*Counc* 4	*Congs* 5	*Adults* 6	*Affiliated 1970* 7	*Affiliated 1995* 8	*G%* 9	*Names, notes, and other statistics* (see Codebook, Part 3) 10
Armenian Apostolic Church		O-Arm	E....	2	1,200	500	2,000	0.05	Gregorians. Armenian immigrants.
Catholic Church in Latvia:	1207	R-Lat	B....	349	360,100	340,000	500,000	1.55	Minority. (1970) 132n,13x,13m,50w,5263Yy. (1995) 126n 20x 31m 92w 12000Yy
M Riga	c1250	R-Lat	Bs	145	90,000	260,000	170,000	-1.69	In capital city. 60n 13x 13m 62w 6657Yy
D Jelgaba (Jelgava)	1995	R-Lat	B....	60	72,500	–	90,000	0.05	Population is 21% Roman Catholic. 16n 1149Yy
D Liepaja	1937	R-Lat	Bs	25	24,700	80,000	30,000	-3.85	Catholics 9.5%. 4n 1x 1m 348Yy
D Rezekne-Aglona	1995	R-Lat	B....	90	172,900	–	210,000	0.05	Population is 51% Roman Catholic. 46n 6x 17m 30w
Estonian Apostolic Orthodox Church		O-Est	C....	4	2,000	1,000	3,000	0.05	1990-98 argument: Constantinople or Moscow jurisdiction.
Evangelical Lutheran Ch of Latvia	c1550	P-Lut	LWC..	291	300,000	350,000	500,000	1.44	Membership fell from 600,000 in 1956 under Soviet persecution and deportations to Siberia. 92n
Ev Reformed Ch in Lithuania	1557	P-Ref	R....	20	1,500	1,000	2,500	3.73	Presbyterian lifestyle from Lithuania.
Georgian Orthodox Church		O-Geo	M....	1	100	100	200	0.05	Migrants and residents from Georgia.
Jehovah's Witnesses	1930	m-Jeh	x....	10	270	200	2,400	10.45	(1995) 314Y.
Latvian Orthodox Ch: D Riga	c1130	O-Lav	M....	100	200,000	200,000	250,000	0.90	Before 1990, 67% Russians, Ukrainians, and other Slavs, 33% Latvians.
Methodist Church in Latvia	c1970	P-Met	.....	3	150	–	400	27.08	*MCL.* Links to British Methodism.
Moldavian Orthodox Ch		O-Mol	M....	3	1,000	1,000	2,100	0.05	Canonical part related to Romanian Orthodox Patriarchate.
New Apostolic Church	c1985	I-3aX	x....	10	400	–	764	10.00	*NAC/NAK.* M=Neuapostolische Kirche (HQ Zurich, Switzerland).
Old Ritualist Church	c1670	I-OBe	.....	56	50,000	60,000	110,000	2.45	*Old Believers.* 17th-century Russian refugees from tsarist persecution in Russia.
Pentecostal Church of Latvia		P-Pe2	.....	49	4,000	6,000	10,000	0.05	Mainline Pentecostals with Europe and USA links. 1939: 1,500 believers.
Romanian Orthodox Ch		O-Rum	.....	1	400	200	800	0.05	Under P Bucharest.
Reformed Church in Latvia		P-Ref	R....	2	300	300	1,000	0.05	*RCL.*
Russian Orth Ch: D Riga & Latvia	1836	O-Rus	.....	100	200,000	300,000	289,000	-0.15	Mainly Russians. Under ROC, Patriarchate of Moscow.
Seventh-day Adventist Church	c1970	P-Adv	x....	33	2,000	–	4,000	39.34	*SDA.*
Ukrainian Orthodox Ch		O-Ukr	.....	30	20,000	1,100	30,000	0.05	Under P Moscow.
Union of Baptist Churches in Latvia		P-Bap	T....	66	27,800	13,500	35,000	0.05	Formerly AUCECB. Rapid growth since 1988.
Other independent churches		I-	.....	10	300	–	600	0.05	Including: Assembly Hall Churches (Chinese).
Other Protestant denominations		P-	.....	100	6,000	2,000	10,000	0.05	Total 20 denominations including several very recent arrivals.
Doubly-affiliated		2-aff			-71,000	-62,000	-105,764		Pentecostals and Evangelicals who are also baptized Orthodox or Lutherans.
Totals				**1,240**	**1,106,520**	**1,214,900**	**1,648,000**		

Churches, members, growth, 1900-2025	*Congs*	*Adults*	*Affiliated*	*G%*	*Total denominations*	*6 Megablocs:* O	R	A	P	I	m
Total churches, members, and denominations (mid-1900)	300	762,000	1,119,500	0.12	7	3	1	0	3	0	0
Total churches, members, and denominations (mid-1970)	610	827,170	1,214,900	0.12	25	8	1	0	14	1	1
Total churches, members, and denominations (mid-1990)	1,100	1,136,000	1,691,500	1.67	43	8	1	0	26	7	1
Total churches, members, and denominations (mid-1995)	1,240	1,106,520	1,648,000	-0.52	44	8	1	0	27	7	1
Total churches, members, and denominations (mid-2000)	1,000	1,058,000	1,576,425	-0.88	45	8	1	0	28	7	1
Total churches, members, and denominations (mid-2025)	900	1,012,000	1,507,000	-0.18	82	15	1	0	35	30	1

NOTES ON TABLE ABOVE

NATIONAL COUNCILS (Column 4, 5th letter).

R = Conferentia Episcopalis Lettoniae (CEL, Latvian Episcopal Conference).

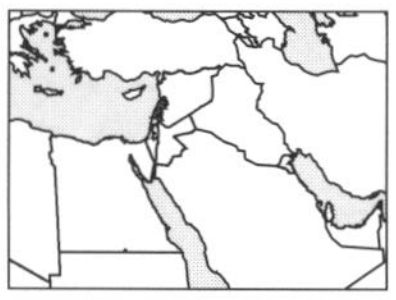

LEBANON

SECULAR DATA, AD 2000

STATE
Official name: Al-Jumhouriya al-Lubnaniya (The Lebanese Republic).
Short name: Lebanon. **Adjective of nationality:** Lebanese.
Flag: Red, white, and red stripes, with green cedar tree in centre.
Area: 10,230 sq. km. (3,950 sq. mi.).
Government: Parliamentary republic, since 1941 (1919 French mandate, 1926 republic, 1941 Independence proclaimed).
Legislature: National Assembly, 128 members.
Official language: Arabic.
Monetary unit: 1 Lebanese pound (£L) = 100 piastres. **US$1=** £L 1,512.
Chief cities: BAYRUT (Beirut) 2,058,000; Zahlah (Zahle) 282,787; Tarabulus (Tripoli) 270,000; Sayda (Sidon) 129,487.
Political divisions: 5 provinces.
Armed forces: 55,000.

DEMOGRAPHY
Population: 3,282,000.
Population density: 320.8/sq. km. (830.8/sq. mi.).
Under 15 years: 1,073,000.
Growth rate p.a.: 1.37% (births 19.77, deaths 6.11).
Mortality: Infant, per 1,000: 25.4; **Maternal per 100,000:** 300.0.
Life expectancy: 71 (male 69, female 73).
Household size: 5.3. **Floor area per person, sq.m:** 18.0.
Major languages: Arabic, French, English, Armenian, Kurdish, Greek, Turkish, Italian, Chaldean (Aramaic), and numerous others.
Urban dwellers: 89.74%. **Urban growth rate p.a.:** 1.8%.
Labor force: 27%.

ETHNOLINGUISTIC PEOPLES
71.2% Lebanese Arab; 12.1% Palestinian Arab; 6.8% Armenian (Ermeni, Armiane); 6.1% Northern Kurd (Kermanji); 0.8% Syrian Arab.

ECONOMY
National income p.a. per person: US$2,660; **per family:** US$14,098.

EDUCATION
Adult literacy: 92% (male 94%, female 90%). **Schools:** 2,100.
Universities: 20. **School enrolment:** female/male: 95%/92%.

HEALTH
Access to health services: 95%. **Access to safe water:** 100%.
Hospitals: 25 (50 beds per 10,000). **Doctors:** 6,638.
Blind: 5,000. **Deaf:** 197,300. **Murder rate:** 4.
Lepers: 1,000.

LITERATURE
New book titles p.a.: 130 (40 p.a. per million). **Periodicals:** 84.
Newspapers: 16 dailies.

COMMUNICATION (per 1,000 people)
Phones: 89 (44% mobile). **Radios:** 601. **TV sets:** 291.
Daily newspaper circulation: 135. **Computers:** 35.

REFUGEES
Alien refugees from other countries: 348,300.
Internal displacement: 400,000.

HUMAN LIFE AND LIBERTY (optimum condition=100.0%)
HDI: 79.4. **HSI:** 39.0. **HFI:** 30.0. **EFL:** 41.0.

Country Table 1. **Religious adherents in Lebanon, AD 1900-2025.**

Year	*1900*		*1970*		*mid-1990*		*Annual change, 1990-2000*				*mid-1995*		*mid-2000*		*mid-2025*	
Name	*Adherents*	*%*	*Adherents*	*%*	*Adherents*	*%*	*Natural*	*Conversion*	*Total*	*Rate*	*Adherents*	*%*	*Adherents*	*%*	*Adherents*	*%*
Christians	**317,400**	**77.4**	**1,541,743**	**62.4**	**1,370,000**	**53.6**	**38,959**	**-2,124**	**36,835**	**2.41**	**1,604,000**	**53.3**	**1,738,354**	**53.0**	**2,246,000**	**51.1**
PROFESSION																
crypto-Christians	0	0.0	215,943	8.8	180,000	7.1	5,122	-6,122	-1,000	-0.57	175,000	5.8	170,000	5.2	150,000	3.4
professing Christians	**317,400**	**77.4**	**1,325,800**	**53.7**	**1,190,000**	**46.6**	**33,837**	**3,952**	**37,835**	**2.80**	**1,429,000**	**47.5**	**1,568,354**	**47.8**	**2,096,000**	**47.6**
AFFILIATION																
unaffiliated Christians	0	0.0	52,927	2.1	4,000	0.2	114	-161	-47	-1.23	3,500	0.1	3,533	0.1	3,000	0.1
affiliated Christians	**317,400**	**77.4**	**1,488,816**	**60.3**	**1,366,000**	**53.5**	**38,868**	**-1,986**	**36,882**	**2.42**	**1,600,500**	**53.2**	**1,734,821**	**52.9**	**2,243,000**	**51.0**
Roman Catholics	300,000	73.2	1,088,695	44.1	1,100,000	43.1	31,299	-1,799	29,500	2.40	1,290,000	42.9	1,395,000	42.5	1,825,000	41.5
Orthodox	12,300	3.0	356,500	14.4	410,000	16.1	11,666	834	12,500	2.70	487,800	16.2	535,000	16.3	720,000	16.4
Independents	0	0.0	10,600	0.4	87,000	3.4	2,475	625	3,100	3.09	104,412	3.5	118,000	3.6	240,000	5.5
Protestants	5,000	1.2	28,095	1.1	22,000	0.9	626	-826	-200	-0.95	20,597	0.7	20,000	0.6	20,000	0.5
Marginal Christians	0	0.0	3,126	0.1	5,300	0.2	151	119	270	4.20	6,760	0.2	8,000	0.2	16,000	0.4
Anglicans	100	0.0	1,800	0.1	250	0.0	7	-12	-5	-2.21	233	0.0	200	0.0	200	0.0
doubly-affiliated	0	0.0	0	0.0	-258,550	-10.1	-7,357	-926	-8,283	2.82	-309,302	-10.3	-341,379	-10.4	-578,200	-13.1
Trans-megabloc groupings																
Evangelicals	4,000	1.0	17,000	0.7	43,000	1.7	1,224	276	1,500	3.04	51,829	1.7	58,000	1.8	90,000	2.1
Pentecostals/Charismatics	0	0.0	8,000	0.3	125,000	4.9	3,557	643	4,200	2.94	150,133	5.0	167,000	5.1	250,000	5.7
Great Commission Christians	**37,000**	**9.0**	**494,000**	**20.0**	**560,000**	**21.9**	**15,934**	**144**	**16,078**	**2.56**	**660,000**	**21.9**	**720,781**	**22.0**	**968,000**	**22.0**
Muslims	84,300	20.6	874,257	35.4	1,074,850	42.1	30,584	1,038	31,622	2.61	1,271,450	42.3	1,391,068	42.4	1,881,000	42.8
Nonreligious	0	0.0	37,000	1.5	85,000	3.3	2,419	1,069	3,488	3.50	104,000	3.5	119,879	3.7	200,000	4.6
Atheists	0	0.0	12,000	0.5	21,000	0.8	598	36	634	2.67	25,000	0.8	27,343	0.8	65,000	1.5
Baha'is	100	0.0	1,000	0.0	2,500	0.1	71	6	77	2.73	2,800	0.1	3,272	0.1	6,000	0.1
Jews	8,200	2.0	3,000	0.1	1,650	0.1	47	-25	22	1.26	1,750	0.1	1,871	0.1	2,000	0.1
World A (unevangelized persons)	74,210	18.1	496,269	20.1	275,940	10.8	7,825	-8,658	-833	-0.31	291,844	9.7	265,842	8.1	299,200	6.8
World B (evangelized non-Christians)	18,390	4.5	430,988	17.5	909,060	35.6	25,894	10,782	36,676	3.46	1,112,859	37.0	1,277,804	38.9	1,854,800	42.1
World C (Christians)	317,400	77.4	1,541,743	62.4	1,370,000	53.6	38,959	-2,124	36,835	2.41	1,604,000	53.3	1,738,354	53.0	2,246,000	51.1
Country's population	**410,000**	**100.0**	**2,469,000**	**100.0**	**2,555,000**	**100.0**	**72,678**	**0**	**72,678**	**2.54**	**3,008,704**	**100.0**	**3,282,000**	**100.0**	**4,400,000**	**100.0**

COLUMNS, ROWS.
For meanings and definitions, see Codebook (Part 3). Note that, by definition, total 'Christians' = professing + crypto-Christians, which also = affiliated + unaffiliated Christians, and also = Great Commission Christians + latent Christians. Percentages may not always total exactly, due to rounding.

CENSUSES.
The last government census of religion was held in **1932**, as follows: 53.7% Christians (29.0% Maronites, 10% Greek Orthodox, 6.3% Greek Catholics, 6.2% Armenians, 2.2% other Christians), 39.0% Muslims (excluding Druzes; 20.8% Sunnis, 18.2% Shias), 6.3% Druzes, 1% other religionists including Jews. **1958** (semi-official estimate): 55.0% Christians (29.9% Maronites, 10.6% Greek Orthodox, 7.5% other Catholics, 4.9% Armenian Orthodox, 1.0% Protestants), 37.9% Muslims (20.2% Sunnis, 17.7% Shias) 6.2% Druzes, 0.5% Jews (6,600 persons).

NOTES ON RELIGIONS
ATHEISTS. Lebanese Communist Part (LCP) (only legal party in Arab world (since 1970); split on Sino-Soviet dispute). There is also an illegal Armenian Communist Party.
BAHA'IS. Reached Lebanon before 1892. Growth of local spiritual assemblies; 1964, none: 1973, 8; but then decline, to 5 in 1996.
CHRISTIANS. The column 'Natural change' includes considerable annual emigration by Maronites and others. The column 'Conversion change' indicates that many young persons abandon Christianity each year to become agnostics or atheists.
COUNTRY'S POPULATION. (a) There has long been large-scale emigration of Lebanese. In 1963 Lebanese emigrants living abroad (in North and South America, Africa, Australia) numbered 1,214,000. (b) During the civil war between Muslims and Christians from 1975 onwards, hundreds of thousands fled the country temporarily, and many thousands of others were killed (60,000 in the 24 months from April 1975). The column 'Annual change' above gives averages for the whole decade 1990-2000; the column 'Natural' includes considerable annual emigration by Christians (mainly Maronites) and annual immigration by Muslims (Palestinians, refugees, guerrillas, and others); it also includes higher Muslim than Christian fertility (birth-rate).
CRYPTO-CHRISTIANS. Christians unknown to and unrecognized by the state. They are mainly Roman Catholics, who have increased their proportion considerably since the 1932 census, although their proportion of the total population has decreased.
JEWS. Decline from 10,000 in 1956, by emigration to Israel.
MUSLIMS. There has been large-scale immigration of Muslims in the 20th century (especially by 300,000 Palestinian Arabs). In 1975, 46% of all Muslims were Sunnis (along the coast and in Beirut, Tripoli, Sidon), 40% of all Muslims were Shias (mountainous east (Bekaa) and south; mostly Twelvers or Ithna-Asharis); and 14% of all Muslims were Druzes (included here under Muslims though not usually counted as Muslims in Lebanon), followers of Hakimiya, an 11th-century Muslim Shia Ismaili schism with Christian and Jewish elements. Druzes are Arabic-speaking and regard themselves as the pure Monotheists. They are treated here as a sect within the wider Muslim community, and in Lebanon they form 14% of all Muslims (6.3% of total population). There is also a small Ahmadiya Mission (enumerated here under Muslims although declared non-Muslim by Pakistan). Muslims are mainly Arabs with some Kurds, Turks and others. In addition to Muslims as enumerated here (46.1% in 1995) there are a further 3% or 4% of the population in Muslim areas who profess publicly to be Muslims but who are affiliated to churches and so are classified here as crypto-Christians. As the column 'Conversion change' shows, many Muslim youths abandon Islam each year to become agnostics, atheists, or (a growing number) crypto-Christians. *Hajj pilgrims to Mecca.* (1970) 6,712; (1974) 9,528; (1975) 1,208; (1976) 1,069.
ORTHODOX. In the 20th century, there has been massive immigration into Lebanon of Orthodox from Syria, Israel, Egypt, Jordan and Turkey. In 1905, there were only 1,000 Armenian Apostolics in the diocese of Beirut, but after 1915 vast numbers of refugees arrived from Turkey.

Great Commission Instrument Panel: status of Lebanon (for explanation see start of Part 4)

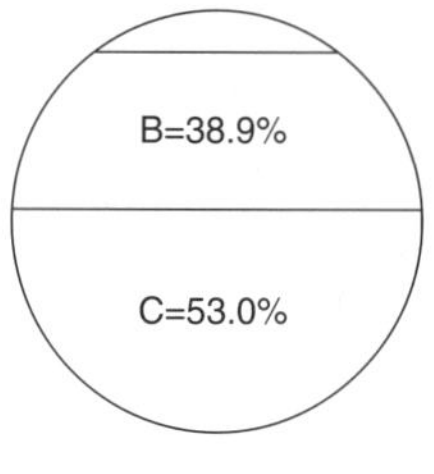

3 Worlds, AD 2000

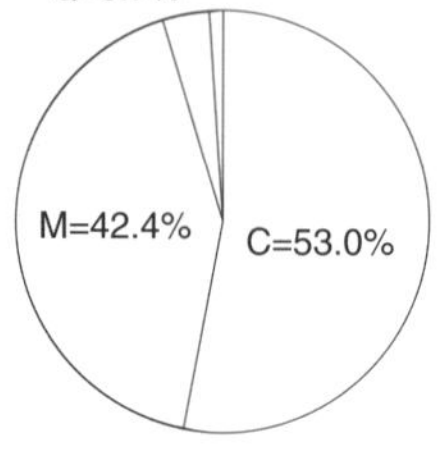

Religions, AD 2000

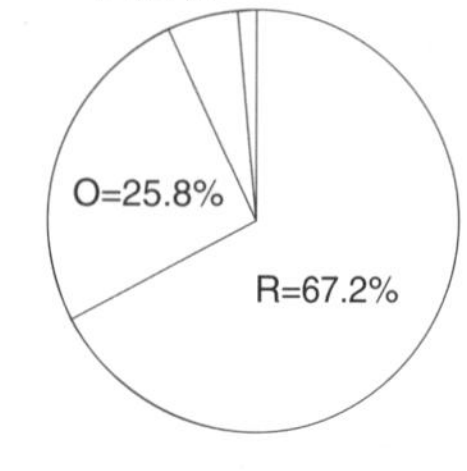

Ecclesiastical blocs

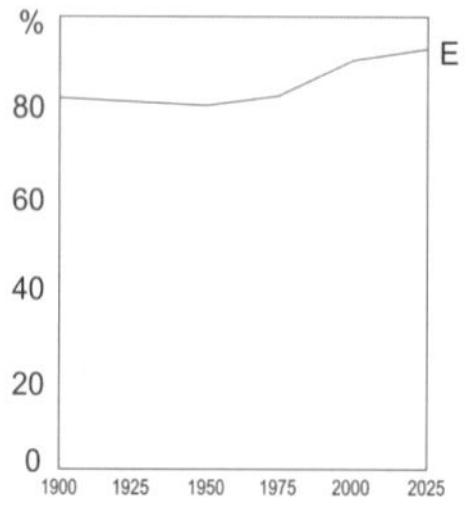

Evangelization, 1900-2025

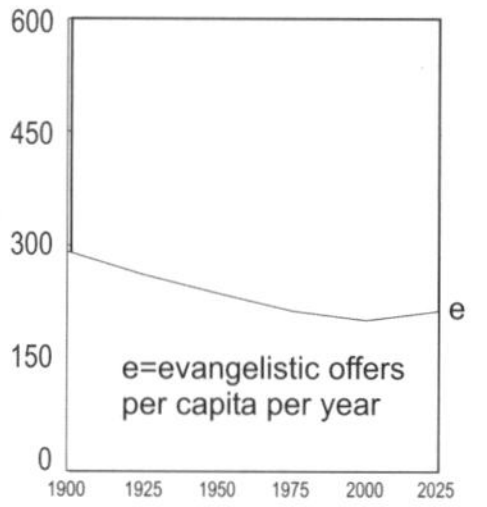

Offers, 1900-2025

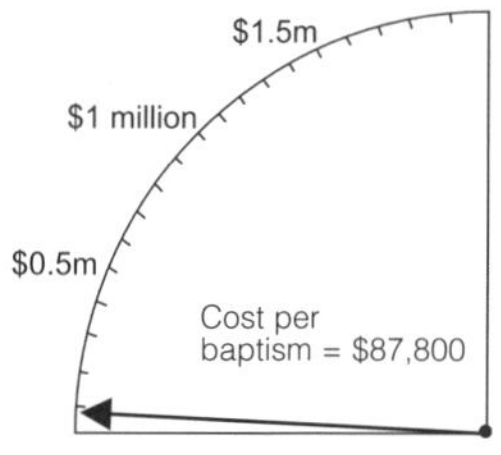

Cost-effectiveness, AD 2000

Country summary. **Worlds A, B, C by ethnolinguistic peoples, cities, and major civil divisions in Lebanon.**

	PEOPLES							CITIES							CIVIL DIVISIONS						
World	*Num*	*Pop 2000*	*C%*	*Christians*	*E%*	*U%*	*Unevangelized*	*Num*	*Pop 2000*	*C%*	*Christians*	*E%*	*U%*	*Unevangelized*	*Num*	*Pop 2000*	*C%*	*Christians*	*E%*	*U%*	*Unevangelized*
A	3	215,154	1.14	2,463	29	71	152,229	0	0	0.00	0	0	0	0	0	0	0.00	0	0	0	0
B	5	441,236	8.57	37,830	76	24	105,244	4	2,740,274	54.01	1,480,159	94	6	159,499	5	3,281,787	52.86	1,734,821	92	8	266,666
C	11	2,625,398	64.54	1,694,530	100	0	9,191	0	0	0.00	0	0	0	0	0	0	0.00	0	0	0	0
Total	**19**	**3,281,788**	**52.86**	**1,734,823**	**92**	**8**	**266,664**	**4**	**2,740,274**	**54.01**	**1,480,159**	**94**	**6**	**159,499**	**5**	**3,281,787**	**52.86**	**1,734,821**	**92**	**8**	**266,666**

Country status. An embattled country originally carved out of the French Mandate in the Middle East, Lebanon occupies the Mediterranean coast north of Israel. After a swift rise as the 'Switzerland of the East', in the 1950s, it became an arena in the struggle between Christians and Muslims in the late 1970s and 1980s. The civil war nearly brought the country to the verge of extinction. Banking, food processing, and textiles are the main industries.

HUMAN LIFE AND LIBERTY

Human need and development. Until the Civil War, Lebanon was one of the most developed countries in the Middle East. Beirut's fabled high-rise apartments and hotels and commercial buildings rivaled those of Cairo and Tel Aviv. The ravages of the civil war are best seen in these buildings, many of them now charred and scarred shells. The civil war also took a heavy toll in terms of manpower as most of the enterprising Lebanese left for safer havens abroad, leaving the country to military generals and Muslim fundamentalists. The financial and physical infrastructure also have been damaged heavily, much of the commerce being limited to the black market. Many public structures were caught in the crossfire between the warring factions. Nevertheless, housing continues to be of high standard, especially in Mount Lebanon (Jabal Lubnan). Traditionally, private welfare activity (directed by the churches in the case of Christians and by the wakfs in the case of Muslims) has been a major factor in caring for those who have lost their possessions or have been stricken by major calamities. By and large, the Lebanese are well fed with adequate daily caloric intake and healthy dietary habits. Supply of water varies from plentiful along the coast and the mountain areas to short in the Biqa Valley and the Anti-Lebanon Mountains. Poor sanitation and contaminated water are the most common causes of diseases. Lebanon has a large supply of doctors and its medical facilities are so well reputed that patients come to them from all over the Arab world.

Human rights and freedoms. Much of Lebanon operates outside of government control. Palestinian groups in the south run their own autonomous government. Israel has 1,000 troops in southern Lebanon where the Christian-led South Lebanon Army (SLA) holds sway. Syria controls much of Beirut, North Lebanon and Biqa Valley according to the Taif Agreement. In between the Hezbollah, the Druzes and their allies maintain their own private armies and defy the central government with impunity. The general anarchy notwithstanding, the Military Security makes periodical arrests of those who are not too powerful to retaliate, such as students, journalists and civilians, but the net effect of these arrests on public safety is not known. Lebanon has a long heritage of freedom of press and speech. The press is nominally independent, but virtually all newspapers and magazines are financed or subsidized by sectarian groups, many of them foreign, and thus present the views of their owners. Attacks on the dignity of the presidents of Lebanon and Syria are serious crimes. The numerous radio and television stations are not even registered with the government, and carry on their propaganda activities without any check or restraint. The amended Constitution of 1990 attempts to abolish confessionalism in public life and employment, but no practical steps have been taken toward this end. Also suffering from legal discrimination are Palestinians, about 180,000 other stateless persons, and homeless children. Hundreds of abandoned children are found each year in the streets, and juvenile delinquency is rising. Many of the delinquent juveniles are detained in ordinary prisons.

Human environment. Lebanon's beautiful landscape has become one of the casualties of the civil war. Much of Lebanon's famed forests have been cut down for military and other reasons. The Mediterranean Coast has become a junkyard as the weakness of the civil authorities encourages polluters to dump everything into the sea.

Young militant of fundamentalist Hezbollah wears strict Islamic dress but with machine gun ready.

NON-CHRISTIAN RELIGIONS

The principal religions of Lebanon are divided internally into communities which although not always coinciding with Lebanon's different ethnic groups nevertheless form coherent social groups each with their own property, hierarchy, courts, and representatives in parliament. The state recognizes 15 of these communities.

Islam is represented by both Sunnis and Shias. Sunnis are found along the coast, with very important groups also in Beirut, Tripoli, and Sidon. Shias occupy for the most part the mountainous area in the east (Bekaa) and the south. Community councils and diverse associations for schools, hospitals, dispensaries, and clubs all contribute to the vitality and unity of the Muslim community. Religious leaders are known as muftis among the Sunnis and imams among the Shias. The Near East regional bureau of the World Muslim Congress, with its international headquarters in Pakistan, is located in Beirut. For the first time in Lebanon's history, a national Islamic Congress met from 3 June-10 June 1974. This congress was mainly concerned with analyzing Lebanese Islamic institutions and with setting out possible reforms to deal with the impact of the Western world in the social and pastoral fields. Sunnis, Shias, and Druzes were all represented at the congress.

Druze religion is an off-shoot from Islam and is a Muslim sect which originated in the 11th century through the preaching of Darasi, who identified the Egyptian Fatimid caliph al-Hakim as the incarnation of Allah. Druzes are governed by a council of judges whose supreme head is known as the Cheikh-al-Aql. As well as being numerous in Lebanon, Druzes are also found in Syria, Jordan, and Israel.

Judaism is known as the Community of Moses, the name adopted by the Jewish community in 1973. Numbering now about 1,800, Jews have lived in peace in Lebanon for centuries.

CHRISTIANITY

Christianity came to Lebanon in the 1st century AD and over the centuries has continued to play an important role in the country in spite of the numerical encroachment of Islam. Lebanon has the highest proportion of Christians of any country in the Middle East, and their influence in government and commercial life is even greater than their size would indicate. Christianity in Lebanon displays great variety. Catholics, the predominant Christian body, are represented by 6 different rites: Maronite, Melkite, Armenian, Syrian, Chaldean, and Latin. The Orthodox include both Chalcedonians (Greek and Russian) and non-Chalcedonians (Armenian, Syrian, and Coptic), as well as Nestorians in the Ancient Church of the East. There are also significant Anglican and Protestant communities, in addition to marginal Protestant groups including Jehovah's Witnesses and Mormons.

In the past 50 years, Lebanon has passed from a feudal to a commercial capitalistic economy which is increasingly secular in outlook. This in turn offers new challenges to ancient church structures which are no longer adequate in the new situation. A significant element is the role assumed by youth, especially Catholic Action and the Orthodox Youth Movement, in the renewal of the churches.

Catholic Church in Lebanon. Recently proclaimed saint Sharbel of Na'ba to whom cures and miracles are attributed.

CATHOLIC CHURCH. The largest community is that of the Maronites, who formed their own hierarchy in the 7th century. At that time, Greek Orthodox, centered on the 5th century monastery of Mar Maroun (St Maron) in the Apamee region in northern Syria, detached themselves from the Orthodox patriarch of Antioch in order to elect their own patriarch and form a church embodying the Syriac culture. Fleeing from harassment by various Orthodox and Muslim groups, they took refuge in the deep valleys of northern Lebanon where they mixed with the indigenous population. Qadisha (Holy Valley) being their principal location. Moving gradually to the south, they formed with the Druzes the nucleus of Mt Lebanon's resistance to the Ottoman occupation. This was the historic role of the Maronite patriarchate in the rise of the Lebanese nation during the 19th century, until the creation of Great Lebanon in 1920. Lebanon was under French mandate until 1943 when full independence was granted. By that time, the Maronite community, which had united with Rome in 1357, had become the major part of the Roman Catholic community.

Maronites are mostly land owners and small farmers in the mountains, merchants at the coast, civil servants or members of the professions. Although deeply rooted in Lebanon, they are also found in neighboring Arab countries as well as in other parts of the world. The Maronite community enjoys certain privileges in national life. By common agreement, a Maronite is always president of the republic and commander-in-chief of the army, and other key posts in several ministries are reserved for Maronites. Maronite bishops form the majority in the commissions of the Assembly of Catholic Patriarchs and Bishops of Lebanon, the principal inter-rite Episcopal organization in the country.

The Greek Catholics or Melkites form that part of the Orthodox patriarchate of Antioch which united with Rome in the 18th century. It includes faithful in Lebanon, Syria, Jordan, Palestine, Egypt, the Americas, Australia, Europe, and Africa. Its head has the title of patriarch of Antioch, Alexandria, and Jerusalem, with residences at Damascus and Beirut. Melkites are found equally in the towns of the coast and in the mountains and form the third largest Christian community in Lebanon (after the Catholic Maronites and the Greek Orthodox). They play a dynamic part in both inter-Catholic and interdenominational relations. The Congress of Melkite Catholic Clergy, which was founded in 1969 and holds an annual general assembly, is an organ of dialogue between elected representatives of secular and religious clergy and the episcopate for all questions concerning the priestly ministry. A Synodal Commission for Renewal, created in August 1974, is the principal force for renewal in the Melkite Catholic Church.

Other Catholic rites participating in the Assembly of Catholic Patriarchs and Bishops of Lebanon include Armenians and Syrians, for the most part refugees since World War I who have their patriarchs in Lebanon (Charfeh and Mount Lebanon); Chaldeans, a branch originating from the Assyrian (Nestorian) Church, who have one diocese for the whole of Lebanon, with their patriarchal see at Baghdad, and Latins, who first became fully organized in Lebanon in 1953 and have been represented by a Lebanese vicar apostolic since 1973. The Latin bishop of Beirut is a member of the Conference of Latin Bishops of the Arab Regions (CELRA), with its headquarters in East Jerusalem.

The Holy See has diplomatic relations with Lebanon and in AD 2000 is represented to government and the Catholic hierarchy by a nuncio residing in Harissa (Kesrouan).

ORTHODOX CHURCHES. The Greek Orthodox Patriarchate of Antioch consists almost entirely of Arabs and uses Arabic in its liturgy. Beginning with the rise of the Maronites in the 7th century, and the Melkites in the 18th century, it has continued to lose members both to Latin-rite Catholicism and to Protestantism. Nevertheless, the patriarchate as a whole, with its see in Damascus, numbers more than 500,000 faithful, not counting its dioceses which serve immigrants to North and South America and Australia. The church in Lebanon has a total community of 200,000. With members consisting of rural agricultural communities in the north and south of Lebanon, as well as urban merchants, officials and members of the liberal professions, the church has experienced a significant renewal since World War II. This has been manifested in several ways: creation of the Orthodox Youth Movement (OYM) in 1942; reorganization of the basic statutes of the patriarchate, the Holy Synod and diocesan councils; appointment of a new generation of bishops; reestablishment of monastic life through the new convent of Mar Yacoub-Dedde in northern Lebanon and the monastery at Dei al-Harf, Mt Lebanon; a new emphasis on catechesis in liaison with Syndesmos, the World fellowship of Orthodox Youth Organizations; promotion of the ecumenical movement regionally, nationally and worldwide; establishment of a theological seminary at Blamand near Tripoli in 1970; and the participation of Orthodox in Arab nationalist, progressive socialist, and Palestinian movements. The Antioch patriarchate maintains 25 elementary schools, 12 secondary schools, a hospital in Beirut, together with clinics, homes for the aged and orphanages.

Armenian Apostolic Church, Catholicate of Cilicia. Cathedral, Antelias (*right*), with (*center*) martyrion, and (*left*) burial chapel of former patriarchs.

The non-Chalcedonian Armenian Apostolic Church, officially termed the Catholicate (or Catholicossate) of Cilicia (Sis), has its see at Antelias, a suburb of Beirut. Originating from Armenia and established in Cilicia, southern Asia Minor, in AD 1441, Armenian Orthodox flooded into northern Syria and Lebanon as refugees from the Turkish massacres of 1915-1920. They are now fully integrated into Lebanese society, with 4 deputies in parliament in addition to one for the Armenian Catholic community and are well represented in skilled industry, commerce, and liberal professions. They have also been involved in the creation of secondary schools, cultural associations, hospitals, and housing projects. Their School of Theology at Antelias, founded in 1930, provides for renewal of the clergy and also furnishes priests to serve the diaspora communities of Cyprus, Syria, Iraq, Iran, USA, Canada, and Australia. The Catholicate of Cilicia, which has long recognized the spiritual primacy of the Catholicate of Echmiadzin in the USSR severed relations with Echmiadzin in 1956 in a dispute over Cilicia's right to appoint its own catholicos. In Lebanon, Cilicia has also played an important role in helping to develop relations between Chalcedonian and non-Chalcedonian churches, as well as between Orthodox and Catholics. Its vitality as a church was not seriously weakened by the separation of the Uniate Armenian Catholics who submitted to Rome in the 16th century, nor by the creation of the Armenian Evangelical Union in the 19th century.

Other smaller Orthodox churches represented in Lebanon include the Russian Orthodox Church, and its rival the Russian Orthodox Church Outside of Russia; 2 Oriental bodies, the Coptic and Syrian Orthodox Churches; and the ancient Church of the East (Nestorians).

Syrian Orthodox Patriarchate of Antioch, Diocese of Beirut. Class at Mar Ephrem seminary, Atshana.

PROTESTANT CHURCHES. The National Evangelical Synod of Syria and Lebanon, which owes its origin to the missionary outreach of the American board (ABCFM) as early as 1823 and later American United Presbyterians, has the largest Protestant constituency in both countries, with a Christian community of 10,000 in Syria and the same in Lebanon. The church became autonomous in 1920 and has its headquarters in Beirut. It sponsors 2 hospitals, 12 primary schools, 11 secondary schools, Beirut University College for Women, in addition to being the original sponsor in 1866 of the American University of Beirut. Church union discussions with the third largest Protestant body, the National Evangelical Church of Beirut, failed in 1958, but were begun again and broadened to include Anglicans in 1973. The National Evangelical Church has the most important Protestant parish in Beirut, plus 2 small village congregations.

There are 2 Armenian Protestant churches, the Union of Armenian Evangelical Churches and the Armenian Evangelical Spiritual Brethren. American Board work among the Armenian Orthodox in Istanbul resulted in the formation of the first Armenian Evangelical congregation in 1846. Taking refuge in Lebanon in 1918 during the Turkish massacres, the Union of Armenian Evangelical Churches is the second strongest Protestant community in the country with an extensive primary and secondary school program serving 20% of the entire Armenian school population. The Armenian Evangelical Spiritual Brethren, formed in 1920 in Aleppo, consists of a small community of Plymouth Brethren-type which separated from the various Evangelical, Catholic, and Orthodox Armenian communities.

Although a small community, the Lebanese Baptist Convention (related to USA Southern Baptists) has established an important theological school, Arab Baptist Seminary, in Mansourieh.

Other groups include those formed through the missionary activity of Seventh-day Adventists, Church of God (Anderson), Pentecostal Church of God, Assemblies of God, Christian and Missionary Alliance and several smaller bodies.

Renewal movements. In the 1990s the Pentecostal/Charismatic Renewal continued to spread rapidly across most older churches, and numbered over 167,000 adherents (of whom 1% Pentecostals, 29% Charismatics, and 71% Independents).

Indigenous missions. Though Lebanese Christians have been active in mission throughout the 20th century, their numbers have been greatly reduced by the civil war.

CHURCH AND STATE

The Lebanese political regime rests on an original system called 'confessionalism' which guarantees each religious community participation in the government proportional to its numerical importance. In Article 9 of the constitution, amended several times since its promulgation on 23 May 1926, the state guarantees freedom of conscience and respect for all faiths in these words: 'The state in rendering homage to the Most High shall respect all religions and creeds'. Article 95 stipulates that 'Provisionally in order to further justice and concord, the communities shall be equally represented in public employment and in the composition of ministries'. The basic agreement, constantly enforced and invoked, was enshrined in an unwritten National Pact (Al Mithak al-Watani) concluded in 1943 at the beginning of independence.

As a result, confessional representation is continuously maintained at all levels of public service up to the highest positions of state. Thus, the president of the republic must be a Maronite, the president of the legislative assembly a Shia, the premier a Sunni, and vice-presidents of both the assembly and government must be Greek Orthodox. The distribution of parliamentary seats is governed by the same system, with the electoral reorganization of 1960 maintaining the previously existing proportion of 6 Christian deputies to 5 Muslims. Distribution of ministerial portfolios is also made on the basis of religious affiliation, somewhat differently from that of parliament because of the small number of posts. There is no government ministry of religions, but each ministry has an ad hoc section charged with the application within itself of proportional community representation.

No new government census of population has been taken since 1932. The system of proportional community representation remains therefore based on an official numerical estimate published by the Ministry of the Interior and expressed (in the 1932 percentages) as follows: Christians 53.7% (Maronites 29%, Greek Orthodox 10%, Greek Catholics 6.3%, Armenians 6.2%, other Christians 2.2%), Muslims 39.0% (Sunnis 20.8%, Shias 18.2%), Druzes 6.3% and 1% for others including Jews.

By virtue of Article 9 of the constitution, religious communities are recognized by the state as juridical personalities with specific prerogatives, notably in the field of law. Thus, religious courts enact laws concerning marriage, separation, divorce, and inheritance. Each head of a community is assisted by a community council. The religion of each citizen is registered with the state as well as on his identity card. As yet, there is no civil marriage although campaigns have been conducted for it. Religious chanceries issue certificates of baptism and death, which have official validity, and in the Muslim community, judicial officers are civil servants of the state. All communities receive subsidies for their social work, courts, and schools. Article 10 of the constitution, which concerns educational freedom, provides for the involvement of the various religious communities in education. At the present time, there are in Lebanon approximately 1,500 confessional or private schools as contrasted with 1,300 government schools.

In addition to demands for 'participation' by those

communities which feel left out, as well as for 'deconfessionalization' of the state by recent political parties, especially the younger generation, other problems include government bureaucracy, financial distribution, economic development, social justice, cultural unity and plurality, integration with the Arab world, unemployment, emigration and relations with immigrant groups including Syrian workers, stateless Kurds and expelled Palestinians.

The fact that the Christian population, though only slightly the majority block in the country, has continued over the years to dominate Lebanon's political and economic scene has led to increasing unrest on the part of the Muslim minority and was the principal cause of the outbreak of civil war between Christian and Muslim factions during 1975.

BROADCASTING AND MEDIA

The Voice of Hope transmitter is located in southern Lebanon and broadcasts 8.5 hours of daily programming in a variety of languages, including Tatar, Turkish, Russian, Ukrainian and Arabic. These can be received in the CIS, Lebanon, most of Israel and Jordan, part of Syria, and along the coast of Egypt and Cyprus. Some are produced by IBRA. Shortwave radio programs from FEBA (Seychelles) in Arabic and English can be received, as can programs from KNLS, AWR (Slovakia), TWR (Monaco, Albania) and HCJB (Ecuador).

The Middle East Television station is situated in south Lebanon and broadcasts a large number of programs throughout the Middle East. METV uses a strategy of general-interest programs to attract attention to a core of Christian programming. Satellite TV programs are received mainly in Arabic.

Some 3.7 million have seen the 'Jesus' Film, mainly through a television broadcast watched by 3.6 million.

INTERDENOMINATIONAL ORGANIZATIONS

Ecumenical agencies are numerous in Lebanon, considering the small size of the country. Several are mainly national with extensions to the Middle East region. Others ar for the most part regional with national branches.

At the national level, there are 4 official commissions for ecumenical relations. The first emanates from the Armenian Catholicate of Cilicia; the second from the Assembly of Catholic Patriarchs and Bishops of Lebanon; the third from the Greek Orthodox patriarchate; and the fourth from the Supreme Council of Evangelical Churches in Lebanon and Syria. Their joint executive secretariat is the Ecumenical Pastoral Group (Groupe Oecumenique de Pastorale, GOP), founded in 1968, which coordinates the activities of the following 8 mixed working groups some of which were operating prior to the creation of the official commissions. (1) The Center for Religious Sociology conducts studies on specific problems of the country and its institutions, in collaboration with the WCC. (2) Common Prayer (Priere Commune) is a service which publishes and distributes each year material used for the Week of Prayer for Unity, in conjunction with the ad hoc commissions in Rome and Geneva. (3) Joint Catechesis (Catechese Harmonisee) is a group which develops catechetical programs for Christian students in government schools and prepares curricula and lessons for catechists. (4) Evangelization Teams for different age groups and milieux handle the problem of the reevangelization of modern Lebanese society, in collaboration with the Catholic center for Catechesis and Pastoralia (Centre de Catechese et de Pastorale Notre Dame des Dons). (5) Parables and Symbols for Today (Paraboles et Symboles pour Aujourd'hui, PSA) is an ecumenical service for audiovisual catechesis, in collaboration with the Catholic Center for Catechesis and Pastoralia, which produces notable material on liturgical renewal especially for Maronites and Orthodox. (6) The Lebanese Ecumenical Committee for Development, Justice and Peace, founded in 1972, serves as the executive office of the Ecumenical Secretariat for Youth and Students of the Middle East in conjunction with Sodepax and ad hoc international Catholic organizations. (7) The Coordination Committee for Christian Movements promotes the training of lay leaders. Lastly, there is (8) the Assembly of Involved Christians (Rassemblement des Chretiens Engages), founded in 1974, which joins together Christians with a social and political orientation who seek to discover a new Christian identity through their solidarity in the liberation struggle of the Arab world.

Several monasteries and convents have become ecumenical prayer centers, notably the Orthodox monastery of St Georges at Dei el'Harf, create through the efforts of the Orthodox Youth Movement; the Orthodox Convent of St James the Persian at Dedde near Tripoli; the Catholic monastery of Our Lady of Unity at Yarze; and the Carmelites of Harissa Catholic convent near Jounieh.

Ecumenical pastoral survey by MECC and WCC, with (*right*) Swedish Lutheran Archbishop Olof Sundby.

At the regional level, with headquarters in Beirut, an organization which has played an especially important role is the Middle East Council of Churches (MECC), an organization founded in Nicosia in May 1974, replacing the Near East Council of Churches (NECC) which was formed in 1927 as the Council of Western Asia and Northern Africa, later called the Near East Christian Council and, finally in 1944, the Near East Council of Churches with a new constitution in 1967. The MECC represents the interests of 3 church families: the Chalcedonian (Eastern Orthodox), Non-Chalcedonian (Oriental Orthodox), and Anglican/Protestant churches; and each of these 3 groups is accorded an equal number of delegates in the general assembly. The council carries on its work through 4 divisions: (1) Radio Broadcasting, which includes program production in the main studio in Beirut and in 2 associated studios in Egypt and the Sudan and, until 1977, broadcast over Radio Voice of the Gospel in Ethiopia; (2) Literature, which coordinates the publishing and distribution policy of member churches through their publishing houses and bookshops throughout the Middle East; (3) Christian Education, which seeks to train leaders and teachers and produces the Faith and Work curriculum; and (4) Outreach and Witness, which is involved in training Christians for dialogue with non-Christians and undertakes research and studies in Christian-Muslim relations.

Other specialized organizations and institutions include the following: (1) the Ecumenical Secretariat for Youth and Students of the Middle East (ESYSME), founded in 1962, with a subregional secretariat in Cairo, which is involved in research, leadership training, development programs (conscientization and literacy) and consultations concerning the role of Christianity in the Middle East; (2) Association for Theological Education in the Near East (ATENE), with headquarters in Cairo and a sub-secretariat in Beirut; (3) Near East School of Theology (NEST), founded in Beirut in 1931 to serve the Protestant churches; (4) World Conference of Christians for Palestine, with headquarters in Paris and a Secretariat for Arab countries in Beirut; (5) Near East Ecumenical Information and Interpretation Bureau (NEEBII), founded in 1971, which provides information and theological insight for the Christian world concerning the region, especially Palestine; (6) Common Translation Service for the Bible in Arabic, initiated by the regional secretariat of the United Bible Societies; (7) Near East Ecumenical Committee for Palestinian Refugees (NEECPR), with headquarters in Nicosia and a subsecretariat in Beirut; and (8) the Middle East secretariat of the World Student Christian Federation (WSCF or FUACE).

FUTURE TRENDS AND PROSPECTS

Muslims will continue to trail Christians in Lebanon by 2025 (43% and 51% respectively). The greatest growth is expected among the nonreligious (1.5% in 1970 to 4.6% by 2025).

Lebanon will likely be 50% Christian, 40% Muslim, and 10% nonreligious by AD 2050.

BIBLIOGRAPHY

Aliens at home: a socio–religious analysis of the Protestant Church in Lebanon and its backgrounds. W. A. Semaan. Beirut: Librairie du Liban, 1986. 183p.

Amal and the Shi'a: a struggle for the soul of Lebanon. A. R. Norton. *Modern Middle East series*, 13. Austin, TX: University of Austin Press, 1987. 210p.

American interests in Syria, 1800–1901: a study of educational, literary, and religious work. A. L. Tibawi. Oxford, UK: Clarendon Press, 1966. 333p.

Baptist beginnings in Lebanon, 1893–1956. J. Graham. 1986. 202p.

Christ au Liban. V. Gheorghiu. Monaco: Éditions du Rocher, 1989. 217p.

Christliche Gruppen im Libanon: Kampt um Ideologie und Herrschaft in einer unfertigen Nations. M. Kuderna. Wiesbaden, Germany: Franz Steiner, 1983. 453p.

Class and client in Beirut: the Sunni Muslim community and the Lebanese state 1840–1985. M. Johnson. London: Atlantic Highlands, 1986. 227p.

Die Christen im Libanon. W. Sanders (ed). *Publikationen der Katholischen Akademie Hamburg*, Bd. 9. Hamburg: Katholische Akademie Hamburg, 1990. 176p.

Die Kirche im Libanon. Stimmen der Weltkirche, 20. Bonn: Catholic Church Deutsche Bischofskonferenz Sekretariat, [1983]. 29p.

Die Koexistenz der Religionsgemeinschaften im Libanon. W. A. Kewenig. Berlin: De Gruyter, 1965. 221p.

Encyclopédie maronite. Kaslik, Lebanon: Université Saint Esprit, 1992–. (Multivolume).

'English and Irish reaction to the massacres in Lebanon and Syria, 1860,' A. P. Saab, *Muslim world*, 74, 1 (1984), 12–25.

History of the Maronite Church. P. Dib. Trans., S. Beggiani. Beirut: Imprimerie Catholique, 1971. 257p. (Originally published as a 2-volume work in French).

'Le dialogue islamo–chrétien au Liban et sa fécondité,' Y. Moubarac & S. Saleh, *Conférences du Cénacle* (Lebanon), 19 (1965), 17–72.

'Le Protestantisme contemporain au Liban,' F. E. Accad, *Travaux et Jours* (Lebanon), 22 (1967), 17–26.

'Le statut personnel des communautés chrétiennes en Syrie et au Liban,' P. Mazas, *En Terre d'Islam* (France), 21 (1937), 133–45.

Lebanese Christian nationalism: the rise and fall of an ethnic resistance. W. Phares. Boulder, CO: L. Rienner, 1995. 260p.

Lebanon. C. H. Bleaney. 2nd ed. *World bibliographical series*, vol. 2. Oxford, UK: CLIO Press, 1991. 264p. (See especially 'Religion,' p.43f).

Lebanon: the land and the Lady. J. Goudard & H. Jalabert. Trans., E. P. Burns. Beirut: Catholic Press, 1966. 364p.

L'école catholique au Liban et ses contradictions. J. Brun. *Hommes et sociétés du Proche-Orient*, 5. Beyrouth: Dar el-Machreq, 1973. 320p.

L'église maronite jusqu'à la fin du moyen âge. P. Dib. Paris: Letouzey, 1930. 276p.

Les Chrétiens d'Orient. P. Rondot. *Cahiers de l'Afrique et de l'Asie*, 4. Paris: Peyronnet, 1955. 322p.

Les communautés confessionnelles du Liban. L. de Bar. Paris: Editions Recherche sur les Civilisations, 1983. 215p.

Les conciles de l'église maronite de 1557–1644. P. Dib. Le Puy, France: Imprimerie Haute Loire, 1926. 47p.

Les Maronites sous les Ottomans: histoire civile d'après les principaux témoins contemporains. P. Dib. Beirut: Editions La Sagesse, 1962. 628p.

Minorities in the Arab world. A. H. Hourani. London: Oxford University Press for the Royal Institute of International Affairs, 1947. 140p. (Chapter 9 on Lebanon).

Notables and clergy in Mount Lebanon: the Khoazin Sheikhs and the Maronite Church, 1736–1840. R. van Leeuwen. Leiden: E. J. E.J. Brill, 1994. 299p.

Rediscovering Christianity where it began: a survey of contemporary churches in the Middle East and Ethiopia. N. A. Horner. Beirut: Near East Council of Churches, 1974. 110p.

'Religion,' in *Area handbook for Lebanon*, p.123–33. Washington, DC: US Government Printing Office, 1969.

Religious, cultural and political history of the Maronites. B. Dau. Lebanon: [Dau], 1984. 840p.

'Religious groups in Lebanon: a descriptive investigation,' J. Chamie, *International journal of Middle East studies*, 11 (1980), 175–87.

'Shia movements in Lebanon: their formation, ideology, social basis, and links with Iran and Syria,' M. Deeb, *Third world quarterly*, 10, 2 (1988), 683–98.

Shi'i thought from the south of Lebanon. C. Mallat. *Papers on Lebanon*, 7. Oxford: Centre for Lebanese Studies, 1988. 42p.

The Catholic Church in the Middle East. B. Etteldorf. New York: Macmillan, 1958.

The Druze. R. B. Betts. New Haven, CT: Yale University Press, 1988. 147p.

'The effect of twentieth–century Arab nationalism on the Christian witness in the Near East.' C. Smith. Thesis, Wheaton College, Wheaton, IL, 1970.

'The Greek Orthodox community in Lebanon: historical and contemporary perspectives.' C. C. Attie. M.A. thesis, University of Texas at Austin, 1988. 188p.

The Lebanese in the world: a century of emigration. A. Hourani & N. Shehadi (eds). London: Center for Lebanese Studies/I. B. Tauris, 1993. 741p.

The legal status of non–Moslem communities in the Near East, and especially in Syria and Lebanon. I. A. Khairallah. Beirut: American University of Beirut, 1965. 187p.

The Maronites in history. M. Moosa. New York: Syracuse University Press, 1986. 361p.

The vanished Imam: Musa al Sadr and the Shia of Lebanon. F. Ajami. London: Tauris, 1986. 228p.

Country Table 2. Organized churches and denominations in Lebanon.

Official name (bold type = church with over 10% of all affiliated) 1	Begun 2	Type 3	Counc 4	Congs 5	Adults 6	Affiliated 1970 7	Affiliated 1995 8	G% 9	Names, notes, and other statistics (see Codebook, Part 3) 10
Ancient Church of the East: D Beirut		O-Nes	Yw...	3	2,000	6,000	4,000	0.05	*Assyrian Church. Nestorians.* Under Tehran Patriarchate. No dissidents as in Iraq. 3n.
Armenian Apostolic Ch: C Cilicia (Sis)	1440	O-Arm	SW.N.	280	84,000	135,000	175,000	1.04	*Catholicate of Sis.* Broke with C Echmiadzin in 1956, restored 1995. 12 Dioceses, 19 bps, 120n.
Armenian Ev Spiritual Brethren	1920	I-CBr	x....	5	500	250	1,000	5.70	Beirut. Split ex-Armenian Evangelicals. Holiness Brethren. 1r.
Assemblies of God	c1920	P-Pe2	ZF...	2	135	400	300	-1.14	M=AoG(USA). 1972, university campaign; 9,000 student attenders. 3n,10f,1s(13).
Assyrian Evangelical Church	c1985	I-Eva	.....	1	25	–	83	10.00	Indigenous evangelical body.
Bible Baptist Churches	1956	I-Bap	.....	1	27	150	55	-3.93	Arabic and English services; 1 Lebanese pastor. Formerly M=BBFI(USA). Aided by BIM.
Beirut Community Church		P-com	.....	1	100	400	300	0.05	English-speaking community church. 1 North American pastor. W=75%.
Catholic Church in Lebanon:	c 300	R-LEr	O...R	1,078	726,000	1,088,695	1,290,000	0.68	*Al-Kanissa al-Kathoulikiah.* C=21+2+53. 671n 668x 948m 2655w 14436Yy
P Antioch (EP Batrun: *Maronite)*	1848	R-Mar	Os	137	137,000	184,763	298,000	1.93	*Maronite Patriarchal Diocese* 69 schools. 2H. 130n 44x 155m 107w 2943Yy
AD Antelias *(Maronite)*	1988	R-Mar	Os	82	62,000	75,000	102,310	14.29	Before 1968 was 95% of AD Cyprus. 12 schools. 66n 51x 64m 317w 1500Yy
D Baalbek-Deir El-Ahmar *(Maronite)*	1671	R-Mar	Os	19	16,800	91,200	35,000	-3.76	Heliopolis. Rapid growth. 80 schools. 1H. 11n 2x 2m 10w 250Yy
AD Beirut *(Maronite)*	1577	R-Mar	Os	125	196,000	190,000	350,000	2.47	*Al-Mawarinah* (Maronites). 101 schools, 3H. 92n 37x 37m 137w 2386Yy
D Jbeil (Byblos) *(Maronite)*	1990	R-Mar	Oomm	89	168,000	–	300,000	20.00	Founded AD 360; 1990, reorganized. M=OMM. 44n 21x 41m 54w 1560Yy
D Jounieh *(Maronite)*	1977	R-Mar	Os	64	103,000	–	191,928	5.56	Sizable emigration of Maronites (from all dioceses). 62n 49x 80m 78w 1396Yy
D Saida (Sidon) *(Maronite)*	1900	R-Mar	Os	127	53,800	103,970	65,000	-1.86	Sidon. Rapid growth. 40 schools. Covers Israel also. 26n 18x 18m 62w 260Yy
AD Tripoli (Tarabulus) *(Maronite)*	c1650	R-Mar	Os	124	55,200	176,000	80,828	-3.06	Rapid growth, then rapid emigration. 208 schools. 96n 9x 9m 51w 1030Yy
AD Tur (Tyre) *(Maronite)*	1838	R-Mar	Os	20	13,100	22,000	18,000	-0.80	Sour. Rapid expansion. HQ Tyr. 12 schools. 20n 9x 9m 35w 320Yy
D Zahleh *(Maronite)*	1990	R-Mar	Os	30	27,000	–	48,850	20.00	History of linking with D Baalbek. 6n 12x 12m 47w 300Yy
P Antiochia (VP Lebanon) *(Syrian)*	c1650	R-Syr	Os	9	12,900	18,000	23,000	0.99	*Patriarchal Vicariate.* Growing numerically. 6 schools. 14n 0x 0m 10w 95Yy
P Cilicia (M Beirut) *(Armenian)*	1742	R-Arm	Obs	13	6,700	24,300	12,000	-2.78	*Patriarchal Diocese*, Armenian P Cilicia. 12 schools. 2n 20x 20m 33w 115Yy
M Beirut & Gibail *(Melkite)*	c 350	R-Mel	Os	80	84,000	80,000	150,000	2.55	First founded c350. Rapid expansion. 26 schools. 4h. 45n 122x 225m 271w 1129Yy
M Tyr (Sur, Tyre) *(Melkite)*	c 150	R-Mel	Os	10	4,600	6,000	8,298	1.31	Sour. *Al-Rounn al-Malakioun al-Kathoulik.* M=BS. 5n 2x 2m 4w 45Yy
AD Baniyas *(Melkite)*	c 350	R-Mel	Os	12	3,300	4,162	3,600	-0.58	Paneas. Caesarea Philippi. Golan area. M=BC. 2n 0x 2m 10w 25Yy
AD Saida (Sidon) *(Melkite)*	1683	R-Mel	Os	31	10,600	26,000	20,000	-1.04	Sidon & Deir el Qamar. Expanding. M=BS. 15n 11x 11m 21w 190Yy
AD Tripoli *(Melkite)*	c 350	R-Mel	Os	11	3,300	6,500	6,000	-0.32	Tarabulus (4th century) HQ Tripoli. M=BA. 11 schools. 10n 1x 1m 16w 140Yy
AD Baalbek *(Melkite)*	c 350	R-Mel	Os	10	12,900	15,000	25,000	2.06	Heliopolis, dating from c350. 27 schools. 9n 2x 2m 43w 145Yy
AD Zahleh & Furzol *(Melkite)*	1724	R-Mel	Obs	48	71,000	40,000	126,000	4.70	Formerly suffragan, AD Damascus.. 21 schools. 1H. 11n 20x 20m 33w 492Yy
D Beirut *(Chaldean)*	1957	R-Cha	Os	4	5,600	5,800	10,000	2.20	*Al-Kaldan al-Kathoulik.* Under P Babylon. 1 school. 2n 4x 4m 0w 61Yy
VA Beirut *(Latin)*	1953	R-Lat	Oocd	33	11,200	20,000	20,000	0.00	*Al-Latinn (Latins).* M=OCD,OFMConv. 189 schools. 3n 234x 234m 1316w 54Yy
Doubly-counted Catholics		R-Lat		0	-332,000	–	-603,814		Catholics counted in an older diocese and also in a new diocese.
Christian Brethren (Exclusive)		P-EBr	x....	2	80	200	160	0.05	*Plymouth (Closed) Brethren (Kelly-Continental)*, in 2 meetings.
Christian Brethren (Open)		P-CBr	x....	3	260	400	330	0.05	*Plymouth (Open) Brethren, Gospel Halls.* M=CMML(USA,UK). 6f.
Church of Christ		I-Dis	x....	3	70	200	150	0.05	M=CC(Non-Instrumental) (USA). Independents. Mainly USA expatriates. 1p.
Church of God (Anderson)	1910	P-Hol	x...C	14	1,000	500	2,000	5.70	M=CoG(Anderson) (USA). No missionaries now except visitors from Egypt. 4n,W=55%.
Ch of Jesus Christ of Latter-day Saints		m-LdS	x....	3	385	426	700	0.05	*Mormons.* M=CJCLdS(Utah, USA). Mostly USA expatriates.
Coptic Orthodox Church		O-Cop	NwaN.	1	300	300	500	0.05	Under P Cairo. Egyptians. Congregation in Beirut, new building. 1 deacon, 1x.
Epis Ch in Jerusalem & ME (D Jerusalem)		A-Low	aw.NC	1	140	1,800	233	0.05	ECJME. Formerly Jerusalem Archbishopric. 67% Arab, 33% British, M=JEM. 1n,2x,W=50%,13y.
Evangelical Baptist Church		I-Bap	.....	1	200	100	300	0.05	Independent Lebanese congregation in Beirut. No foreign missionaries.
Evangelical Church of the Nazarene	1952	P-Hol	xF..C	2	130	400	195	-2.83	*Kniset Innasari Il Injiliyeh.* M=CoN(USA). 1n,1x,39m,6f,1p(4),6t(268),W=39%.
French Evangelical Church		P-Ref	.....	1	30	30	50	0.05	French-speaking. In Beirut, for francophone expatriates. 1 Armenian pastor. 1r.
German Evangelical Church in Beirut		P-Lut	.....	1	100	150	200	0.05	*Deutschsprachige Evangelische Kirche.* German-speaking congregation. 1x (German).
Gospel Preaching Church		I-Eva	.....	1	100	100	200	0.05	Arabic and English. Small independent congregation. 1 Lebanese pastor.
Greek Orth Patriarchate of Antioch:	33	O-Ara	Cw.N.	350	150,000	200,000	300,000	0.05	Arabic-speaking. Patriarch in Damascus. 210n,15d,1H,P=60%,12r,1s(Tripoli),W=10%.
D Akkar (Arkadia)		O-Ara	Cm	53	22,500	30,000	45,000	0.05	HQ Archevêché Grec-Orthodoxe, Halba. 2 monasteries (6 monks), 40n.
D al-Hadath (Byblos & Botrus)		O-Ara	Cm	130	56,200	75,000	112,500	0.05	*Diocese of Mount Lebanon.* HQ Hadeth. 5 monasteries (12 monks), 65n.
D Beirut (Berytos)		O-Ara	Cm	15	7,500	10,000	15,000	0.05	Seat of archbishop in Beirut. Summer residence Souk El-Gharb. 15n,3d(30).
D Marj Uyun (Tyre & Sidon)		O-Ara	Cm	38	15,000	20,000	30,000	0.05	HQ Archevêché Grec-Orthodoxe, Marj Uyun (in southeast near Israel border). 28n.
D Tripoli		O-Ara	Cm	84	37,500	50,000	75,000	0.05	HQ Archêveché Grec-Orthodoxe, Tripoli, 40n,5d,1s (in monastery).
D Zahla (Heliopolis & Seleucia)		O-Ara	Cm	30	11,300	15,000	22,500	0.05	HQ Zahlah, in Lebanon Mountains east of Beirut. 22 parish priests.
Independent Evangelical Church		I-Fun	.T.T.	1	100	100	200	0.05	One congregation in Beirut. Fundamentalist. 1 American pastor.
Internat Ch of the Foursquare Gospel	1962	P-Pe2	ZF...	5	200	200	500	3.73	M=ICFG(USA). Classical Pentecostals (2-stage). 2nm,2f,1p(8),W=41%,12Y.
Isolated radio churches	c1950	I-3rS	.....	1,000	60,000	5,100	100,000	12.64	Isolated radio believers in Muslim areas. R=1200,T=180000(ICI & 17 others).
Jehovah's Witnesses	c1930	m-Jeh	x....	56	2,726	2,700	6,060	3.29	*Watch Tower.* Witnessing under way by 1940. HQ Beirut. (1975) 74Y. (1995) 157Y.
Lebanese Baptist Convention	1895	P-Bap	T...C	28	1,200	1,540	3,600	3.45	1948, M=SBC. 13 Arabic-speaking congs. 10n,4x,30f,1r,1s,W=95%,50Y,50z.
Lebanon Evangelical Mission	1860	P-Eva	.G...	10	1,400	2,000	2,500	0.90	M=IEM(UK)/MECO, formerly British Syrian Mission; 1963, expelled. 104n,32f,1p,1s,2r.
National Ev Christian Alliance Church	1890	P-Hol	xF..C	3	270	275	592	3.11	M=CMA. 50% Arabic-speaking, 50% English-speaking. 1n,9f,1p,W=45%,5Y,3z.
National Evangelical Union	c1950	I-Ref	...NC	3	1,000	3,500	1,300	-3.88	Arabs. Beirut, and 2 mountain village churches. 1958, refused to join NESynod. 3r.
National Ev Synod of Syria & Lebanon	1823	P-Ref	RW.NC	13	1,200	10,000	1,870	-6.49	M=UPUSA,UCBWM. A=1920. Emigration 4%pa,9n,2x,25f,2H,8r,1u,W=70%,39Yy.
New Apostolic Church		I-3aX	x....	1	10	1,000	24	0.05	*NAC.* In Wiesbaden Bezirk (District); world HQ Zurich. Germans.
Pentecostal Church of God of America	1950	P-Pe2	Z....	3	200	500	400	-0.89	M=PCG(USA). Classical Pentecostals. Work with Jews in Beirut. 1 school. 3f,1p.
Religious Society of Friends	1869	P-Qua	Q...C	2	50	100	100	0.00	In Near East Yearly Meeting. Quakers. 1 high school by HQ in Broumana.
Russian Orthodox Church		O-Rus	Mwc..	1	150	200	300	0.05	Under P Moscow. Uses Greek Orthodox building in Beirut. 1x (sent from Russia).
Russian Orthodox Ch Outside of Russia		I-Rus	x....	1	70	100	100	0.05	Related to ROCOR(New York). 1 Russian priest. In Ain Mraissé, Beirut.
Seventh-day Adventist Church	1908	P-Adv	x...C	2	500	3,000	1,110	-3.90	*SDA*, East Mediterranean Field, Middle East Union. 8nx,51f,1j,6r,14t(1000),40Y.
Syrian Orth Patr of Antioch: D Beirut	33	O-Syr	Dw.N.	5	4,800	15,000	8,000	0.05	*Jacobites.* Patriarch in Damascus. Summer residence, Zahle. 1r,1s(Atshana),W=10%.
Union of Armenian Ev Chs in Near East	1918	P-Con	RW.NC	5	2,140	7,000	2,390	-4.21	Refugees and descendents from 1914-18 massacres. 1918, M=AMAA(USA). HQ Beirut. 28n.
Other independent charismatic chs	1990	I-3cS	.....	30	500	–	1,000	20.00	Including Association of Vineyard Chs (3 chs).
Other Protestant denominations		P-	.....	40	2,000	1,000	4,000	0.05	Total about 20, including Coptic Evangelical Ch.
Doubly-affiliated		2-aff			-169,000	0	-309,302		Evangelicals and Pentecostals who are also baptized Orthodox or Catholics.
Totals				**2,963**	**875,098**	**1,488,816**	**1,600,500**		

Churches, members, growth, 1900-2025	*Congs*	*Adults*	*Affiliated*	*G%*	*Total denominations*	*6 Megablocs:* *O*	*R*	*A*	*P*	*I*	*m*
Total churches, members, and denominations (mid-1900)	600	177,000	317,400	2.23	10	4	1	0	5	0	0
Total churches, members, and denominations (mid-1970)	1,911	831,698	1,488,816	2.23	46	6	1	1	26	10	2
Total churches, members, and denominations (mid-1990)	2,400	747,000	1,366,000	-0.43	67	6	1	1	37	20	2
Total churches, members, and denominations (mid-1995)	2,963	875,098	1,600,500	3.22	68	6	1	1	37	21	2
Total churches, members, and denominations (mid-2000)	3,100	948,000	1,734,821	1.62	69	6	1	1	37	22	2
Total churches, members, and denominations (mid-2025)	4,500	1,226,000	2,243,000	1.03	129	15	1	1	50	55	7

NOTES ON TABLE ABOVE
NATIONAL COUNCILS (Column 4, 5th letter).
C = Supreme Council of Evangelical Churches in Lebanon & Syria (Conseil Suprème des Eglises Evangéliques au Liban et en Syrie).
R = Assembly of Catholic Patriarchs and Bishops of Lebanon (Assemblée des Patriarches et Evêques Catholiques du Liban).

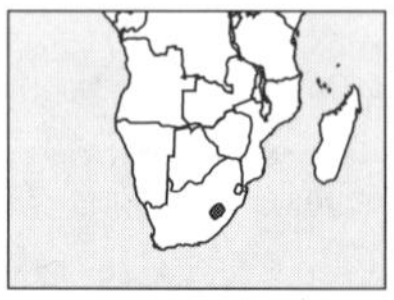

LESOTHO

SECULAR DATA, AD 2000

STATE
Official name: Lesotho/The Kingdom of Lesotho.
Short name: Lesotho. **Adjective of nationality:** of Lesotho.
Flag: Field of white with shield, spear and club cut by blue and green diagonal fields.
Area: 30,355 sq. km. (11,720 sq. mi.).
Government: Parliamentary constitutional monarchy, since 1966 (1818 Basotho nation, 1868 under British protection as Basutoland, 1959 self-government, 1966 Independence, 1991 military coup, 1993 new constitution).
Legislature: Parliament: National Assembly, 65 members; Senate, 33 members.
Official language: English and Sesotho.
Monetary unit: 1 loti (plural maloti (M) = 100 lisente. **US$1=** M 5.83.
Chief cities: MASERU-Roma-Morija 159,012.
Political divisions: 10 provinces.
Armed forces: 2,000.

DEMOGRAPHY
Population: 2,153,000.
Population density: 70.9/sq. km. (183.6/sq. mi.).
Under 15 years: 858,000.
Growth rate p.a.: 1.93% (births 33.92, deaths 13.98).
Mortality: Infant, per 1,000: 87.6; **Maternal per 100,000:** 610.0.
Life expectancy: 52 (male 51, female 53).
Household size: 4.8. **Floor area per person, sq.m:** 10.0.
Major languages: Sotho (Sesotho), English, Afrikaans, Zulu, Xhosa, French.
Urban dwellers: 27.96%. **Urban growth rate p.a.:** 5.1%.
Labor force: 32%.

ETHNOLINGUISTIC PEOPLES
80.3% Southern Sotho (Sutu); 14.4% Zulu; 2.0% Phuthi; 1.5% Taung; 1.0% Xhosa (Tembu, Thembu).

ECONOMY
National income p.a. per person: US$769; **per family:** US$3,694.

EDUCATION
Adult literacy: 71% (male 81%, female 62%). **Schools:** 1,397.
Universities: 1. **School enrolment:** female/male: 78%/67%.

HEALTH
Access to health services: 80%. **Access to safe water:** 52%.
Hospitals: 22 (15 beds per 10,000). **Doctors:** 136.
Blind: 3,000. **Deaf:** 137,600. **Murder rate:** 33.
Lepers: 40,000. **Underweight prevalence under 5:** 21%.

LITERATURE
New book titles p.a.: 650 (300 p.a. per million). **Periodicals:** 28.
Newspapers: 2 dailies.

COMMUNICATION (per 1,000 people)
Phones: 9 (20% mobile). **Radios:** 569. **TV sets:** 7.
Daily newspaper circulation: 7. **Computers:** 40.

HUMAN LIFE AND LIBERTY (optimum condition=100.0%)
HDI: 45.7. **HSI:** 30.0. **HFI:** 40.0. **EFL:** 27.0.

Country Table 1. **Religious adherents in Lesotho, AD 1900-2025.**

Year	1900		1970		mid-1990		Annual change, 1990-2000				mid-1995		mid-2000		mid-2025	
Name	*Adherents*	*%*	*Adherents*	*%*	*Adherents*	*%*	*Natural*	*Conversion*	*Total*	*Rate*	*Adherents*	*%*	*Adherents*	*%*	*Adherents*	*%*
Christians	**33,800**	**11.1**	**913,900**	**85.9**	**1,556,070**	**90.4**	**38,902**	**1,488**	**40,390**	**2.33**	**1,745,700**	**90.6**	**1,959,972**	**91.0**	**3,303,400**	**94.2**
PROFESSION																
professing Christians	**33,800**	**11.1**	**913,900**	**85.9**	**1,556,070**	**90.4**	**38,902**	**1,488**	**40,390**	**2.33**	**1,745,700**	**90.6**	**1,959,972**	**91.0**	**3,303,400**	**94.2**
AFFILIATION																
unaffiliated Christians	6,100	2.0	136,356	12.8	350,070	20.3	8,762	7,695	16,457	3.93	433,949	22.5	514,643	23.9	843,400	24.1
affiliated Christians	**27,700**	**9.1**	**777,544**	**73.1**	**1,206,000**	**70.0**	**30,185**	**-6,252**	**23,933**	**1.83**	**1,311,751**	**68.1**	**1,445,329**	**67.1**	**2,460,000**	**70.2**
Roman Catholics	4,000	1.3	410,600	38.6	660,000	38.3	16,519	-1,866	14,653	2.03	726,330	37.7	806,529	37.5	1,350,000	38.5
Protestants	20,200	6.6	223,844	21.0	260,000	15.1	6,508	-4,608	1,900	0.71	265,644	13.8	279,000	13.0	400,000	11.4
Independents	1,000	0.3	62,000	5.8	185,000	10.7	4,630	2,270	6,900	3.22	216,417	11.2	254,000	11.8	540,000	15.4
Anglicans	2,500	0.8	80,000	7.5	98,000	5.7	2,453	-2,053	400	0.40	100,000	5.2	102,000	4.7	160,000	4.6
Marginal Christians	0	0.0	1,100	0.1	3,000	0.2	75	5	80	2.39	3,360	0.2	3,800	0.2	10,000	0.3
Trans-megabloc groupings																
Evangelicals	18,000	5.9	47,000	4.4	62,000	3.6	1,552	-152	1,400	2.06	69,621	3.6	76,000	3.5	120,000	3.4
Pentecostals/Charismatics	0	0.0	54,000	5.1	257,000	14.9	6,432	2,068	8,500	2.90	297,682	15.5	342,000	15.9	645,000	18.4
Great Commission Christians	**25,000**	**8.2**	**200,000**	**18.8**	**405,000**	**23.5**	**10,137**	**437**	**10,574**	**2.35**	**455,000**	**23.6**	**510,738**	**23.7**	**876,500**	**25.0**
Ethnoreligionists	271,200	88.9	140,210	13.2	145,700	8.5	3,647	-1,579	2,068	1.34	157,170	8.2	166,379	7.7	150,000	4.3
Baha'is	0	0.0	8,700	0.8	14,400	0.8	360	106	466	2.84	16,500	0.9	19,062	0.9	36,000	1.0
Nonreligious	0	0.0	500	0.1	3,400	0.2	85	9	94	2.47	4,000	0.2	4,338	0.2	12,000	0.3
Hindus	0	0.0	60	0.0	1,100	0.1	28	-9	19	1.62	1,200	0.1	1,292	0.1	2,000	0.1
Muslims	0	0.0	530	0.1	850	0.1	21	-7	14	1.56	930	0.1	992	0.1	1,600	0.1
Atheists	0	0.0	100	0.0	480	0.0	12	-8	4	0.78	500	0.0	519	0.0	1,000	0.0
World A (unevangelized persons)	215,025	70.5	22,351	2.1	8,610	0.5	193	-149	44	0.56	7,705	0.4	8,612	0.4	17,530	0.5
World B (evangelized non-Christians)	56,175	18.4	128,082	12.0	157,320	9.1	3,960	-1,339	2,621	1.60	173,003	9.0	184,416	8.5	185,070	5.3
World C (Christians)	33,800	11.1	913,900	85.9	1,556,070	90.4	38,902	1,488	40,390	2.33	1,745,700	90.6	1,959,972	91.1	3,303,400	94.2
Country's population	**305,000**	**100.0**	**1,064,334**	**100.0**	**1,722,000**	**100.0**	**43,055**	**0**	**43,055**	**2.26**	**1,926,409**	**100.0**	**2,153,000**	**100.0**	**3,506,000**	**100.0**

COLUMNS, ROWS.
For meanings and definitions, see Codebook (Part 3). Note that, by definition, total 'Christians' = professing + crypto-Christians, which also = affiliated + unaffiliated Christians, and also = Great Commission Christians + latent Christians. Percentages may not always total exactly, due to rounding.

CENSUSES.
1904 (Census of the British Empire) Basutoland: 85.5% ethnoreligionists, 11.7% Protestants, 1.6% Roman Catholics, 1.0% Anglicans, 0.2% African indigenous (AMEC). **23.IV.1911:** 82.4% ethnoreligionists, 17.6% Christians (11.5% Protestants, 3.3% Roman Catholics, 2.1% Anglicans, 0.7% African indigenous). **1921:** 72.2% ethnoreligionists, 14.7% Protestants (13.5% French Reformed, 0.3% Methodists, 0.1% Dutch Reformed), 7.9% Roman Catholics, 4.0% Anglicans, 1.2% African indigenous. **1936:** 54.2% ethnoreligionists, 20.1% Roman Catholics, 17.5% Protestants (14.8% French Reformed, 0.7% Methodists), 6.7% Anglicans, 1.5% African indigenous. **7.V.1946** (Basutoland): 38.2% ethnoreligionists, 26.9% Roman Catholics, 23.4% Protestants, 8.9% Anglicans, 2.2% African indigenous, 0.4% non-Christians. **8.IV.1956:** 33.7% Roman Catholics, 28.8% ethnoreligionists, 23.0% Protestants (21.9% PEMS), 9.5% Anglicans, 5.0% African indigenous. **14-24.IV.1966** (Africans only): 38.7% Roman Catholics, 26.7% Protestants, 18.2% ethnoreligionists, 10.4% Anglicans, 6.0% African indigenous.

NOTES ON RELIGIONS
ATHEISTS. Lesotho Communist Party (proscribed 1970).
BAHA'IS. Rapid growth from 1 local spiritual assembly (1964) to 37 (1973), then declining to 25 LSAs (1996).
COUNTRY'S POPULATION. The figures, as with official censuses in Lesotho since 1966, do not include temporarily absentee workers. The massive labor migration of men to the Rand and OFS in South Africa amounts to 12% of the entire population; as a result there are far more women than men in the churches throughout Lesotho.
INDEPENDENTS. There were 798 members of the AME Church in the 1904 census, 6,181 in the 1921 census, and 8,642 in the 1936 census. In 1995, there were over 210 indigenous denominations (see Table 2).
MUSLIMS. About 400 Asian traders with their families, with a mosque at Butha-Buthe since 1972.

Great Commission Instrument Panel: status of Lesotho (for explanation see start of Part 4)

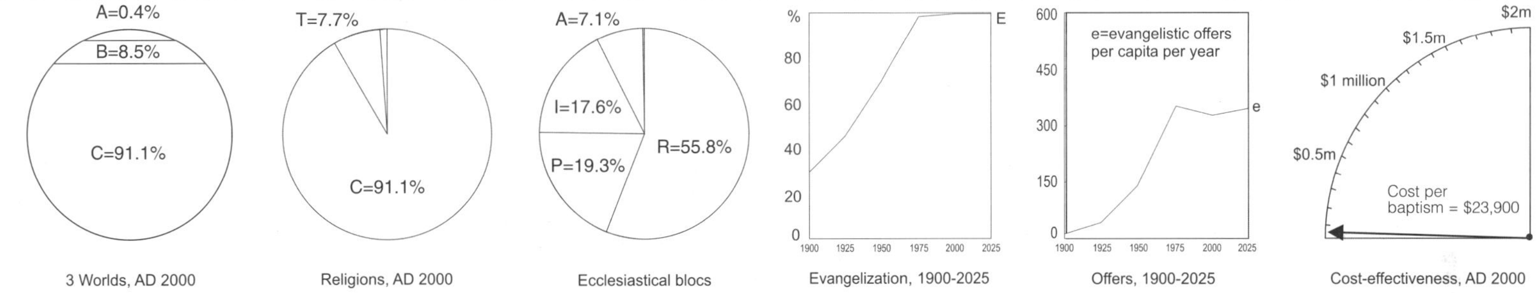

Country status. Lesotho is a mountainous and landlocked country completely surrounded by South Africa. Though some of the population is involved in subsistence farming, the majority are employed several months of the year in mining, farming, and industries in South Africa.

HUMAN LIFE AND LIBERTY

Human need and development. Lesotho is an underdeveloped country with hosts of developmental needs that have grown rather than diminished since independence. About 60% of the male population is at work in South Africa, and the bulk of the GNP is derived from migrant wages. The country's dependence on South Africa is absolute. The budget is financed mostly by the South African Customs Union. Only 9% of the land is arable. Agriculture employs 80% of the resident labor force, but about 70% is subsistence farming. The land has more livestock than it can support, as a result of which there is serious land degradation.

Human rights and freedoms. With the return of civilian rule, Lesotho has more freedom than it has enjoyed since 1986 when a military coup overthrew the legitimate government. The new Constitution includes a lengthy section on protection of fundamental rights and freedoms. There are periodical reports of police brutality coupled with illegal and arbitrary detention of suspects and their incarceration under inhuman conditions. Freedom of the press and speech are observed even though the government controls the official media, including the 2 main newspapers. There is considerable discrimination against Asian businessmen who, as elsewhere in Africa, have monopolized the retail trade. In 1991 Asian shops were attacked and looted by rioters.

Human environment. A harsh and inhospitable land, Lesotho has become even more so as a result of uncontrolled deforestation and overgrazing. About 2% of the arable land is lost every year to soil erosion. The Caledon River system is polluted as a result of the discharge of industrial waste and municipal sewage.

NON-CHRISTIAN RELIGIONS

African traditional religions are practiced by a minority of under 8% of the population. The Sotho name for God is Molimo, and the Balimo are ancestral spirits. Another term, Medimo, is used to refer to such divinities as Cosa who is responsible for fixing man's destiny, and Nape to whom appeal is made during divination. A diviner is called moitse-a-Nape, one who knows Nape. Other Medimo associated with the initiation ceremonies are Tintibane, Thobege-a-phachwa, and Thanakana. Mathuela, a spirit-possession cult among women, utilizes dancing, drumming, songs, and medicines and places emphasis on divination.

Islam has made no gains among the indigenous peoples, but a small group of about 100 Asian traders built a mosque at Butha-Buthe in 1972. There are now 1,000 Muslims.

CHRISTIANITY

CATHOLIC CHURCH. French OMI priests arrived in 1862 and, in 1930, turned over their work to Canadian OMI missionaries. The Catholic population grew from 60,000 in 1930, when the first Mosotho priest was ordained, to 205,000 in 1953, the latter year being notable for the consecration of Lesotho's first indigenous bishop. Catholics are spread very evenly over all areas and over all types and groups of people. For the coming years, one of the primary needs of the church is to hand over to lay leadership institutions which are now largely managed, directed, and administered by clergy.

The Holy See has diplomatic relations with Lesotho and in AD 2000 is represented to government and the Catholic hierarchy by a pro-nuncio residing in Pretoria (South Africa).

Catholic Church in Lesotho. French pioneer missionary Joseph Gerand OMI, born 1831.

PROTESTANT CHURCHES. The Lesotho Evangelical Church is the oldest Christian denomination in the country, tracing its history to the arrival of the Paris Mission in 1833. The church became autonomous in 1964 and is strongly ecumenical in

Country summary. Worlds A, B, C by ethnolinguistic peoples, cities, and major civil divisions in Lesotho.

	PEOPLES							CITIES							CIVIL DIVISIONS						
World	Num	Pop 2000	C%	Christians	E%	U%	Unevangelized	Num	Pop 2000	C%	Christians	E%	U%	Unevangelized	Num	Pop 2000	C%	Christians	E%	U%	Unevangelized
A	0	0	0.00	0	0	0	0	0	0	0.00	0	0	0	0	0	0	0.00	0	0	0	0
B	3	314,274	57.31	180,101	99	1	2,486	0	0	0.00	0	0	0	0	0	0	0.00	0	0	0	0
C	10	1,838,281	68.83	1,265,231	100	0	5,653	1	159,012	70.00	111,308	100	0	509	10	2,152,553	67.14	1,445,329	100	0	8,139
Total	**13**	**2,152,555**	**67.14**	**1,445,332**	**100**	**0**	**8,139**	**1**	**159,012**	**70.00**	**111,308**	**100**	**0**	**509**	**10**	**2,152,553**	**67.14**	**1,445,329**	**100**	**0**	**8,139**

outlook, with membership in the Christian Council of Lesotho, All Africa Conference of Churches, World Council of Churches and World Alliance of Reformed Churches. The church's commitment to education is large: 541 primary, 3 secondary and 3 junior-secondary schools, 2 teacher-training colleges, a trades school and training colleges for boys and girls. Other activities include 2 hospitals, one dispensary, the Mophato oa Morija youth center, a church newspaper called Leselinyana and several development projects conducted along ecumenical lines through Sodepax.

The Methodist and Dutch Reformed churches of South Africa have initiated work in Lesotho, as have several North American Pentecostal groups: Assemblies of God, Church of God (Cleveland), and Pentecostal Holiness Church. Seventh-day Adventists are also active.

Anglican Church in Lesotho. *Upper.* Bishop arrives on horseback at Lereko's. *Lower.* After robing, he administers confirmation.

ANGLICAN CHURCH. The third largest church in Lesotho, dating from 1875, is the Anglican Church, which is of Anglo-Catholic tradition and is a diocese in the Church of the Province of Southern Africa. Among social service activities may be mentioned a number of primary and 2 secondary schools, one teacher-training college, one hospital, and a clinic.

INDIGENOUS CHURCHES. Lesotho was the scene of the first independent church in southern Africa, a secession in 1872 from the Herman congregation of the Paris Mission. Although this group later went out of existence, many more have been formed since then, and there are now estimated to be about 210 such bodies spread throughout the country. The largest Lesotho-originated indigenous church continues to be the Moshoeshoe Berean Bible Readers' Church, a schism from the Paris Mission in 1909, in spite of the fact that it has of late lost many of its supporters. Some indigenous churches have entered Lesotho from South Africa, including Zion Christian Church; whereas, others owe their origin to the outreach of such USA-based Black denominations as the African Methodist Episcopal Church and the National Baptist Convention.

Renewal movements. In the 1990s the Pentecostal/Charismatic Renewal continued to spread rapidly across most older churches, and numbered over 342,000 adherents (of whom 7% Pentecostals, 20% Charismatics, and 73% Independents).

Independents. *Upper.* African Federal Church Council. *Lower.* Moshoeshoe Berean Bible Readers' Church: white robed Nazarite women leaders process in silence except for Bible quoting or singing.

Indigenous missions. Due to poor communications and difficult economic circumstances, Lesotho Christians have sent out only a few missionaries, and these mainly to surrounding African countries.

CHURCH AND STATE

During the political crisis of 1970, the 1965 constitution was suspended, and a state of emergency was declared. The first step in the crisis was the imprisonment by the ruling prime minister (a Roman Catholic, as was his Nationalist Party) of the leftist opposition which appeared about to win the national elections. The Catholic Church is still identified with this party. The other Christian denominations have no such affiliations. In 1970, when riots spread throughout the country, the Christian Council's call for reconciliation achieved little due to lack of Catholic support. However, the Catholic Church itself joined the council in 1972, and this has had its effect on the church-state situation. In April 1973, the Lesotho Ecumenical Association (with Catholic, Protestant and Anglican membership) launched an appeal for reconciliation between government and the opposition party. Following the riots of 1974, 32 members of the opposition Basotho Congress Party were imprisoned without trial, and the Christian Council hired a lawyer to defend them. Although 17 were convicted, the sentences meted out were lighter than expected, a fact which Christian leaders hope will open the door to dialogue.

There is no official government ministry or department dealing with religion, but 2 cabinet members have had special responsibility for church affairs. The 1965 constitution guaranteed freedom of religion, which has remained unaltered by events since 1970.

BROADCASTING AND MEDIA

Lesotho is a member of UNDA. Catholics air a Sunday worship program, and another program featuring prayers and reflections on Scriptures during the week.

TBN programs appear in Maseru on national television. Film teams have presented the 'Jesus' Film to 94,000, 14,000 have made decisions for Christ.

INTERDENOMINATIONAL ORGANIZATIONS

The Christian Council of Lesotho was founded in 1964 as a successor to the General Missionary Conference. It is a member of the AACC and an associate council of the South African Council of Churches. Member churches subscribe to the doctrinal basis of the World Council of Churches, and other Christian bodies prepared to cooperate are associate members. The Catholic Church also had associate status for many years prior to becoming a full member in November 1972. The council carries on its work through 3 commissions: (1) Lesotho Sodepax Commission, which is related to Sodepax in Switzerland and is a member of the Movement for Ecumenical Action in National Development (MEND) in Malawi, and whose projects include the establishment of an ecumenical agricultural school at Thaba Khupa in 1972; (2) Social Services Commission, which is especially concerned for the integration of political refugees from South Africa; and (3) Lesotho Ecumenical Association, which studies such topics as peace and justice and attempts to influence the government to take a Christian position.

Other signs of ecumenical progress in Lesotho are: joint study by Anglican and Catholic seminarians at the Catholic major seminary in Roma since 1971; the establishment of a nursing school to train Catholic, Protestant, and Anglican nurses; and the opening of the first ecumenical primary school at Ntsane in 1971.

FUTURE TRENDS AND PROSPECTS

Christians are expected to grow to 94% of the population by 2025. Ethnoreligionists, near 90% in 1900, will probably diminish to under 5% by 2025.

With the continuing decline of tribal religion into the 21st century, Christianity is expected to grow to 98% of the population by AD 2050. An increase in the nonreligious could cause gradual decline of Christians around this time.

BIBLIOGRAPHY

A century of mission work in Basutoland (1833–1933). V. F. Ellenberger. Morija, Lesotho: Sesuto Book Depot, 1938. 382p.

A decade with the Basotho. H. Sleath. Ed., T. Coggin. Johannesburg: Dept. of Public Relations and Communication of the Methodist Church of Southern Africa, 1988. 127p.

'A history of Christian missions in Lesotho.' G. M. Haliburton. Mimeographed paper, History Workshop, Gaborone, Botswana, 1973. 38p.

A history of Christian missions in South Africa. J. Du Plessis. 1911; reprint, Cape Town: Struik, 1965. 494p.

A history of the church in Southern Africa: a select bibliography of published material. J. W. Hofmeyr & K. E. Cross. Pretoria, South Africa: University of South Africa, 1986. 2 vols.

Anglican pioneers in Lesotho: some account of the Diocese of Lesotho, 1876–1930. R. Dove. , [1975]. 217p.

Basotho religion and Western thought. L. B. B. Machobane. Edinburgh: Centre of African Studies, Edinburgh University, 1995. 57p.

Essai d'histoire de littérature catholique en Sesotho. M. Ferragne. Roma, Lesotho: The Social Centre, [1970]. 36p.

From mission to church: fifty years of the work of the Paris Evangelical Missionary Society and the Lesotho Evangelical Church, 1933–1983. J. M. Mohapeloa. Morija, Lesotho: Morija Sesuto Book Depot, 1985. 77p.

Histori ea Kereke ea Roma naheng ea Lesotho, 1862–1937. F. Laydevant. *Lesotho documents.* Roma, Lesotho: The Social Centre, [1977]. 68p.

Lesotho: a comprehensive bibliography. S. M. Willet & D. P. Ambrose. *World bibliographical series,* 3. Oxford: CLIO Press, 1980. 538p. (See especially 'Religion,' p.125f).

Lesotho Catholic directory. Mazenod, Lesotho: Mazenod Institute, 1972. 192p.

Lesotho Christian handbook, 1992–93. M. Froise (ed). Johannesburg: Christian Info, 1992. 72p.

L'expérience de la conversion chez les Basotho. J. L. Richard. *Documata Missionalia 12.* Rome: Università Gregoriana Editrice, 1977.

Politics and religion in Lesotho: a survey. G. M. Haliburton. Dalhousie, Canada, 1973. 61p. (Mimeograph).
'Social organizational aspects of religious change among Basotho.' D. Bosko. Ph.D. dissertation, New York University, New York, 1983. 368p.
'Spirituality of the Basotho: the values of the reign of God.' M. R. A. Khiba. M.T.S. thesis, Catholic Theological Union, Chicago, 1991. 97p.
The biblical concept of messianism and messianism in Southern Africa. M. Martin. Morija, Lesotho: Sesuto Book Depot, 1964.
The Catholic Church of Lesotho at the hour of independence, 4 October 1966. Maseru, Lesotho: Lesotho Catholic Information Bureau, 1966. 30p.
The Mabilles of Basutoland. E. W. Smith. London: Hodder & Stoughton, 1939.
'The Sotho notion of the Supreme Being and the impact of the Christian proclamation,' K. Nürnberger, *Journal of religion in Africa*, 7 (1975).
'Walter Matitta and Josiel Lefela: a prophet and a politician in Lesotho,' G. M. Haliburton, *Journal of religion in Africa*, 7 (1975).

Country Table 2. **Organized churches and denominations in Lesotho.**

Official name (bold type = church with over 10% of all affiliated) 1	*Begun* 2	*Type* 3	*Counc* 4	*Congs* 5	*Adults* 6	*Affiliated 1970* 7	*Affiliated 1995* 8	*G%* 9	*Names, notes, and other statistics* (see Codebook, Part 3) 10
African Methodist Episcopal Church	c1892	I-Met	Vw..K	48	7,319	16,000	13,100	-0.80	*AMEC*. USA Black mission. In 18th Episcopal District, AMEC. 1 USA bishop. HQ Maseru.
Anglican Church in Lesotho	1875	A-ACa	AwaVK	400	60,000	80,000	100,000	0.90	*Kereke ea Chache*. In CPSA (diocese 1950). M=SSM,USPG. 25n,14x,1H,W=40%,692Y,21531y.
Apostolic Faith Mission of South Africa	1904	P-Pe3	Z....	25	1,500	1,500	3,000	2.81	M=AFM(SA). Mission of large South African body. Classical Pentecostals (2-stage). 2f.
Assemblies of God in Lesotho	1916	P-Pe2	ZF..K	236	7,300	2,000	14,266	8.18	M=AoG(USA,SA),PAoC,NPY,SPM. Classical Pentecostals. HQ Maseru. 17n,2f,1s(14).
Bantu Baptist Church	1961	I-Bap	.....	9	270	1,000	900	-0.42	Links with African United National Baptist Ch (SA). & NBCUSA. HQ Maseru. 4n,1r,1s.
Baptist Churches of Lesotho	1987	P-Bap	.....	2	35	–	50	12.50	M=FMB-SBC.
Catholic Church in Lesotho:	1862	R-Lat	P.SSS	76	445,000	410,600	726,330	2.31	*Kereke ea Roma*. C=1+1+7. (1970) 37n,109x, (1990) 36n,79x,157m,582w,23657Yy.
M Maseru	1894	R-Lat	Pomi	31	164,000	243,292	264,750	0.34	Densely-populated lowlands. 1p,1s. 15n 46x 105m 261w 10332Yy
D Leribe	1952	R-Lat	Ps	18	102,000	89,563	165,000	2.47	Agricultural, most fertile part of country. 12n 10x 19m 136w 3925Yy
D Mohalés Hoek	1977	R-Lat	Pomi	14	83,500	–	138,340	5.56	M=OMI. 4n 12x 17m 85w 6567Yy
D Qacha's Nek	1961	R-Lat	Pomi	13	95,500	77,745	158,240	2.88	Mountainous, arid. Large % pagan. M=OMI. 1p. 5n 11x 16m 100w 2833Yy
Dutch Reformed Church	1957	P-Ref	F....	4	150	200	300	1.64	*NGK. Nederduitse Gereformeerde Kerk*, from Orange Free State, SA. White Afrikaners.
Dutch Reformed Church in Africa	1957	P-Ref	F....	8	2,500	1,000	7,396	8.33	*NGK in Afrika* (mission body from South Africa); Bantu work. 1r.
Ethiopian Catholic Ch of South Africa	c1920	I-3pA	I	2	600	1,000	1,100	0.38	Branch of indigenous body in South Africa. Sotho, Xhosa members.
Fill the Gap Ministries	1985	I-3cA	.....	14	600	–	1,000	10.00	Agency working among the 500,000 mountain people accessible only on horseback.
Full Gospel Church of God	1951	P-Pe3	ZF...	40	2,400	5,000	4,032	-0.86	Branch from South Africa. M=CoG(Cleveland) (USA),FGCoG(SA). 32n.
Galilean Mission Church		I-3pA	I	5	1,000	1,000	1,600	0.05	Basotho United church. Small body in FCAC. Local Sotho members.
Heralds of Christ	1987	I-3oA	.....	1	150	–	250	12.50	Oneness pentecostals.
Jehovah's Witnesses	c1945	m-Jeh	x....	45	1,304	1,000	3,260	4.84	*Watch Tower. IBSA*. Active witnessing under way by 1949. (1975) 25Y. (1995) 200Y.
Joy to the World	1988	I-3cA	.....	1	70	–	150	14.29	Indigenous charismatics.
Lesotho Evangelical Church	1833	P-Ref	RWA.K	550	67,500	200,000	211,000	0.21	M=PEMS,SM,UCCan. A=1964. 541 schools (83,000). 36n,8x,38f,2H,1h,1j,1p,17r,1s.
Mahon Mission	1966	P-Bap	.....	15	1,800	1,200	3,600	4.49	Baptist Mission from USA teaching pastors of Zion Christian Church.
Maseru United Church	1908	P-com	.....	1	82	500	150	-4.70	Union church in capital. Expatriate Whites, mainly.
Methodist Church of South Africa	c1900	P-Met	Vwa.K	8	5,000	5,000	10,000	2.81	Part of Northern Free State & Lesotho district. All Sotho. Numerical decline.
Moshoeshoe Berean Bible Readers' Ch	1909	I-3zA	I.I.I	25	4,500	5,500	10,000	2.42	*MBBRC. Kereke ea Moshoeshoe*. Founder prophet Mattita, ex PEMS. 5 schisms. 3n,3m.
New Apostolic Church	c1985	I-3aX	x....	5	200	–	317	10.00	*NAC*. M=Neuapostolische Kirche (HQ Zurich, Switzerland).
New Church of South Africa		m-Swe	x....	1	40	100	100	0.05	*Swedenborgians*. From mother church in South Africa.
Pentecostal Fellowship	1990	I-3pA	.....	3	1,500	–	2,500	20.00	Indigenous pentecostals.
Pentecostal Holiness Church		P-Pe3	ZF...	2	300	400	600	0.05	M=IPHC(USA), from South Africa. Holiness Pentecostals (3-stage).
St Paul's Church of Africa	c1960	I-Non	.v..I	2	500	500	1,000	2.81	Indigenous group based on Lefihlile Mission, Maseru. Leader termed cardinal.
Salvation Army	1969	P-Sal	x....	2	95	44	200	6.24	M=Salvation Army(South Africa,Britain).
Seventh-day Adventist Church	1899	P-Adv	x....	22	2,427	2,000	4,050	2.86	*Lesotho Field*, southern Union (Black),SAfrican UC (White). 7nx,2f,1H,23t(1700),130Y.
Union Apostolic Church		I-3pA	I	5	1,000	1,000	2,000	0.05	*Union Apostole Mission*. In FCAC. Birettas, stoles. Local Sotho members.
Zion Christian Church	c1920	I-3zA	x....	20	5,000	1,000	10,000	9.65	*ZCC*. Lekganyane's church, from South Africa. Strong in Teyateeaneng.
Zion Foundation Church of Lesotho	c1965	I-3zA	I	60	6,000	7,000	12,000	2.18	A merger/union of 45 small Zionist bodies. Member of FCAC.
Zoe Bible Church	1986	I-3cA	.....	7	300	–	500	11.11	Indigenous charismatics.
Other African indigenous churches		I-3pA	.....	350	89,400	28,000	150,000	0.05	Total about 200 (see list below), including many Zulu bodies from South Africa.
Other independent charismatic chs	c1985	I-3cA	.....	50	0	–	10,000	10.00	Indigenous charismatic networks and denominations.
Other Protestant denominations		P-	.....	60	2,500	5,000	7,000	0.05	Total about 40 (see list below), many based in South Africa.
Totals				**2,104**	**724,354**	**777,544**	**1,311,751**		

Churches, members, growth, 1900-2025	*Congs*	*Adults*	*Affiliated*	*G%*	*Total denominations*	*6 Megablocs:* *O*	*R*	*A*	*P*	*I*	*m*
Total churches, members, and denominations (mid-1900)	40	14,500	27,700	4.88	6	0	1	1	3	1	0
Total churches, members, and denominations (mid-1970)	1,278	407,188	777,544	4.88	132	0	1	1	30	98	2
Total churches, members, and denominations (mid-1990)	2,000	666,000	1,206,000	2.22	272	0	1	1	53	215	2
Total churches, members, and denominations (mid-1995)	2,104	724,354	1,311,751	1.70	317	0	1	1	53	260	2
Total churches, members, and denominations (mid-2000)	2,200	798,000	1,445,329	1.96	322	0	1	1	53	265	2
Total churches, members, and denominations (mid-2025)	4,000	1,358,000	2,460,000	2.15	377	0	1	1	70	300	5

NOTES ON TABLE ABOVE
NATIONAL COUNCILS (Column 4, 5th letter).
E = Evangelical Alliance of Lesotho.
I = Federal Council of African Churches (FCAC) (Federation of African Independent Churches; links with AICA of South Africa); begun 1925-27; 23 members (1980).
K = Christian Council of Lesotho (CCL) (Lekhotla la Likereke la Lesotho).
S = Lesotho Catholic Bishops' Conference, or Episcopal Conference of Lesotho (ECL), and also full member of CCL.

OTHER AFRICAN INDIGENOUS CHURCHES. There are many immigrant groups from the republic of South Africa, especially Zulu bodies, in addition to many scores of short-lived Zionist groupings indigenous to Lesotho in remote areas. The total includes: Apostolic Ch in Zion of the New Jerusalem (1919, ex AFM of South Africa), Basuto Redemption Episcopal Ch, Christian Apostolic Catholic Church in Zion (member of FCAC), Ethiopian Ch of Lesotho, Melchizedek Ch of Salem (member of FCAC), St Joseph's Apostolic Ch, The Lord's New Church.
OTHER PROTESTANT DENOMINATIONS. These smaller bodies, many related to denominations in South Africa, include: Metropolitan Church Association, United Missionary Ch of South Africa.

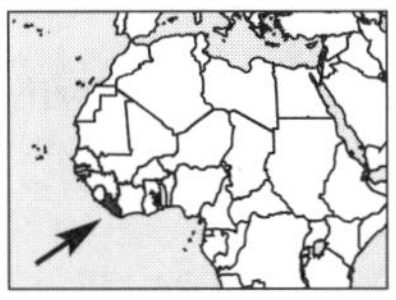

LIBERIA

SECULAR DATA, AD 2000

STATE
Official name: The Republic of Liberia.
Short name: Liberia. **Adjective of nationality:** Liberian.
Flag: Alternative stripes of red and white, with blue square containing white star in upper hoist corner.
Area: 99,067 sq. km. (38,250 sq. mi.).
Government: Republic under military junta (1822 colony founded by ex-slaves, 1847 Independence as republic, 1980 military coup, 1984 new constitution).
Legislature: Congress: Senate, 26 members; House of Representatives, 64 members.
Official language: English.
Monetary unit: 1 Liberian dollar (L$) = 100 cents. **US$1=** L$1.00.
Chief cities: MONROVIA 1,413,000.
Political divisions: 12 provinces.
Armed forces: 3,000.

DEMOGRAPHY
Population: 3,154,000.
Population density: 31.8/sq. km. (82.4/sq. mi.).
Under 15 years: 1,329,000.
Growth rate p.a.: 3.59% (births 47.66, deaths 11.87).
Mortality: Infant, per 1,000: 75.1; **Maternal per 100,000:** 560.0.
Life expectancy: 55 (male 54, female 56).
Household size: 5.0. **Floor area per person, sq.m:** 8.0.
Major languages: English, Kpelle, Bassa, Kru, Grebo, Kissi, Mandingo, Arabic, Yoruba, and over 25 other tribal languages.
Urban dwellers: 47.91%. **Urban growth rate p.a.:** 4.5%.
Labor force: 34%.

ETHNOLINGUISTIC PEOPLES
18.9% Kpelle; 13.0% Bassa; 6.9% Kru; 6.0% Mano (Mah, Maa, Mawe); 5.3% Loma (Toma, Bouze).

ECONOMY
National income p.a. per person: US$770; **per family:** US$3,850.

EDUCATION
Adult literacy: 38% (male 53%, female 22%). **Schools:** 2,076.
Universities: 3. **School enrolment:** female/male: 45%/45%.

HEALTH
Access to health services: 39%. **Access to safe water:** 30%.
Hospitals: 92 (13 beds per 10,000). **Doctors:** 89.
Blind: 15,000. **Deaf:** 195,400. **Murder rate:** 20.
Lepers: 39,000. **Underweight prevalence under 5:** 20%.

LITERATURE
New book titles p.a.: 60 (20 p.a. per million). **Periodicals:** 42.
Newspapers: 8 dailies.

COMMUNICATION (per 1,000 people)
Phones: 2 (3% mobile). **Radios:** 275. **TV sets:** 25.
Daily newspaper circulation: 14. **Computers:** 20.

REFUGEES
Citizen refugees in other countries: 725,000.
Alien refugees from other countries: 120,000.
Internal displacement: 1,000,000.

HUMAN LIFE AND LIBERTY (optimum condition=100.0%)
HDI: 31.1. **HSI:** 24.0. **HFI:** 17.5. **EFL:** 20.0.

Country Table 1. **Religious adherents in Liberia, AD 1900-2025.**

Year	1900		1970		mid-1990		Annual change, 1990-2000				mid-1995		mid-2000		mid-2025	
Name	Adherents	%	Adherents	%	Adherents	%	Natural	Conversion	Total	Rate	Adherents	%	Adherents	%	Adherents	%
Ethnoreligionists	271,000	87.4	690,000	49.8	1,142,250	44.3	25,467	-4,270	21,197	1.72	900,000	43.1	1,354,220	42.9	2,500,000	37.8
Christians	**32,800**	**10.6**	**430,000**	**31.0**	**974,750**	**37.8**	**21,734**	**4,663**	**26,397**	**2.43**	**820,200**	**39.2**	**1,238,721**	**39.3**	**2,848,000**	**43.0**
PROFESSION																
professing Christians	**32,800**	**10.6**	**430,000**	**31.0**	**974,750**	**37.8**	**21,734**	**4,663**	**26,397**	**2.43**	**820,200**	**39.2**	**1,238,721**	**39.3**	**2,848,000**	**43.0**
AFFILIATION																
unaffiliated Christians	4,500	1.5	139,200	10.1	304,000	11.8	6,778	-6,512	266	0.09	241,979	11.6	306,661	9.7	748,000	11.3
affiliated Christians	**28,300**	**9.1**	**290,800**	**21.0**	**670,750**	**26.0**	**14,956**	**11,175**	**26,131**	**3.34**	**578,221**	**27.7**	**932,060**	**29.6**	**2,100,000**	**31.7**
Independents	11,000	3.6	134,906	9.7	380,000	14.7	8,472	7,378	15,850	3.55	342,347	16.4	538,500	17.1	1,200,000	18.1
Protestants	15,000	4.8	119,697	8.6	320,000	12.4	7,135	3,865	11,000	3.00	286,326	13.7	430,000	13.6	920,000	13.9
Roman Catholics	0	0.0	23,697	1.7	98,000	3.8	2,185	3,015	5,200	4.35	96,864	4.6	150,000	4.8	350,000	5.3
Anglicans	2,200	0.7	11,000	0.8	24,000	0.9	535	515	1,050	3.70	26,000	1.2	34,500	1.1	75,000	1.1
Marginal Christians	100	0.0	1,500	0.1	4,500	0.2	100	250	350	5.92	4,790	0.2	8,000	0.3	25,000	0.4
doubly-affiliated	0	0.0	0	0.0	-155,750	-6.0	-3,473	-3,846	-7,319	3.93	-178,106	-8.5	-228,940	-7.3	-470,000	-7.1
Trans-megabloc groupings																
Evangelicals	3,000	1.0	70,000	5.1	250,000	9.7	5,574	2,926	8,500	2.97	214,554	10.3	335,000	10.6	850,000	12.8
Pentecostals/Charismatics	0	0.0	79,000	5.7	415,000	16.1	9,253	1,247	10,500	2.28	341,906	16.4	520,000	16.5	1,250,000	18.9
Great Commission Christians	**25,000**	**8.1**	**152,000**	**11.0**	**405,000**	**15.7**	**9,030**	**4,739**	**13,769**	**2.97**	**350,000**	**16.8**	**542,686**	**17.2**	**1,314,000**	**19.9**
Muslims	6,200	2.0	262,000	18.9	420,000	16.3	9,364	-955	8,409	1.84	331,500	15.9	504,087	16.0	1,100,000	16.6
Nonreligious	0	0.0	0	0.0	35,000	1.4	780	522	1,302	3.21	32,300	1.6	48,017	1.5	140,000	2.1
Baha'is	0	0.0	3,000	0.2	7,000	0.3	156	40	196	2.49	6,000	0.3	8,955	0.3	30,000	0.5
World A (unevangelized persons)	225,990	72.9	761,832	55.0	778,858	30.2	17,390	-8,679	8,711	1.06	599,872	28.7	867,350	27.5	1,541,994	23.3
World B (evangelized non-Christians)	51,210	16.5	193,317	13.9	825,392	32.0	18,377	4,016	22,393	2.42	670,074	32.1	1,047,929	33.2	2,228,006	33.7
World C (Christians)	32,800	10.6	430,000	31.1	974,750	37.8	21,734	4,663	26,397	2.43	820,200	39.2	1,238,721	39.3	2,848,000	43.0
Country's population	**310,000**	**100.0**	**1,385,150**	**100.0**	**2,579,000**	**100.0**	**57,501**	**0**	**57,501**	**2.03**	**2,090,147**	**100.0**	**3,154,000**	**100.0**	**6,618,000**	**100.0**

COLUMNS, ROWS.
For meanings and definitions, see Codebook (Part 3). Note that, by definition, total 'Christians' = professing + crypto-Christians, which also = affiliated + unaffiliated Christians, and also = Great Commission Christians + latent Christians. Percentages may not always total exactly, due to rounding.

CENSUSES.
The religion question has not been asked in any census or sample survey.

NOTES ON RELIGIONS
ANGLICANS. In 1885 there were 419 communicants and 30 preaching places; in 1895, 1,237 communicants and 63 preaching places; in 1900, 1,507 communicants; in 1930, 6,152 communicants and a total baptized community of 8,190. These data indicate that from 1900-1990 this church remained the same size, numerically, relative to the total population of the country.
BAHA'IS. Growth from 3 local spiritual assemblies (1964) to 20 (1973). Expansion was particularly rapid among youth, but by 1995 during the civil war organized LSAs had fallen to only 3.
ETHNORELIGIONISTS. The Loma and Kpelle (in which the Poro and Sande secret societies have been especially powerful) have resisted Islam. Tribes over 60% traditionalist (animist) in 1995: Gio (90%), Mano (95%), Gbande (80%), Loma (Toma) (60%), Sapo (80%). Pagan areas unreached by Christian mission include a Loma clan, Gola, several clans of Bush Grebo, 2 clans of Belle, et alia.
INDEPENDENTS. Originally begun by Black denominations from the USA, by 1995 there were 125 denominations of which the great majority were African indigenous bodies unrelated to USA Black missions (see Table 2).
MUSLIMS. Africans, mostly Sunnis (of the Malikite rite), with some Ahmadis (Qadianis; enumerated here under Muslims, though declared non-Muslim by Pakistan) with missionaries from Pakistan; Qadiriya and Tijaniya orders; and numerous Mandingo (Wangara) traders. Muslims in tribes: Gola and Vai (75%), both recently islamized; Kissi, Gbande (10%), and Mande and other Guinean, Sierra Leonian and Ivorian tribesmen. Since 1955 numbers of whole Gbande villages have become Muslim; and conversions to Islam have been numerous among the Gio (Dan, Yakuba). In addition, Mandingo small traders from Guinea, all Muslims, have been infiltrating from the north (3% of the population); and there are Lebanese Arabs (1.0%) and alien migrant workers from Muslim areas in Ghana and Nigeria. *Hajj pilgrims to Mecca.* (1970) 85; (1975) 61; (1976) 98.
PROFESSING CHRISTIANS. Persons publicly professing to be Christians. Amongst other Christian and quasi-Christian groups, this category includes the quasi-religious movement Freemasonry, a worldwide male secret brotherhood. Most of its members in Liberia are Protestants, and its influence on Liberia is very strong.
UNAFFILIATED CHRISTIANS. As in Nigeria and Ghana, this category is very numerous due to widespread Christian schools and complete freedom of religion, and consists of persons professing to be Christians but not affiliated to or known by the churches.

Great Commission Instrument Panel: status of Liberia (for explanation see start of Part 4)

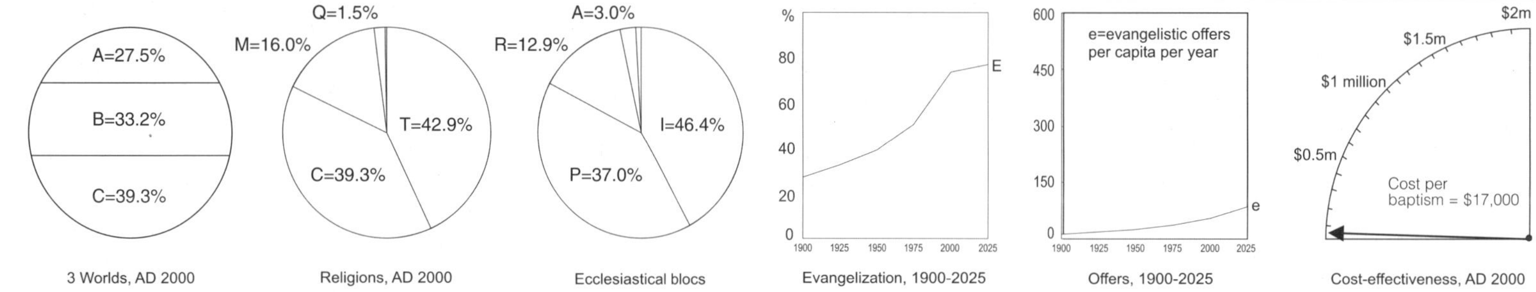

Country status. A war-ravaged country on the great western bulge of Africa, Liberia is a nation in name only. In reality, it exists as 3 nations, one, the Interim Government of National Unity under president Amos Sawyer, supported by the Economic Community of West African States, one under Charles Taylor's National Patriotic Front of Liberia, and one under the United Liberation Movement for Democracy in Liberia, a Sierra-Leone based group. The first controls the city of Monrovia and its environs; the second controls the remaining national territory with the exception of the 2 southwestern counties which are controlled by the third. Another warring faction is the AFL, Armed Forces of Liberia, the remnants of former president Samuel Doe's army. Liberia is rich in natural resources including diamonds, gold, rubber, and timber.

HUMAN LIFE AND LIBERTY

Human need and development. As in every country riven by civil war, economic development has virtually ceased while each rival faction is trying to destroy the lives and property of the other. In many areas, all productive non-military activities are at a standstill and there is no acknowledged governmental authority. Roads are blocked by soldiers at various checkpoints and passage is permitted after the payment of extortionate amounts of money. Each faction has imposed an embargo on the movement of goods and people into or out of its territory. The cost of such essential commodities as are available in the market has risen astronomically since the beginning of the civil war. Soldiers of all factions commandeer food and possessions from civilians and rob and abuse those who do not comply. Health services are available only in Monrovia and on a very limited scale.

Human rights and freedoms. Public executions, beating and torture of civilians, extortion of money, confiscation of property, arbitrary arrests, and other violations of human rights have become commonplace in Liberia and are indicative of the general state of anarchy in the country. Conditions in the regular jails as well as military camps are abysmal and hundreds are reported to have died of starvation and lack of medical care. In the absence of a strong national government, there are few functioning constitutional safeguards for human rights. Vigilante squads have a field day passing summary sentences and executing enemy collaborators and settling ethnic scores. Each faction publishes its own newspaper and operates radio and television stations and are intolerant of any opposition. Children are conscripted by force into the 3 armies. Women are subjected to the gamut of abuses, including rape by unruly soldiers. Ethnic rights are in serious jeopardy as each faction is dominated by one group and is bent on destroying the others. The worst affected are the Krahns, the tribe of former president Samuel Doe, whose excesses triggered the present civil war. Thousands of Krahns have fled to neighboring countries.

Human environment. With human rights in such sad disarray and human needs mounting every day, the environment is faring poorly. Because of political instability, most communal forests are being cut indiscriminately. Liberia's former rich biodiversity has been lost.

NON-CHRISTIAN RELIGIONS

Traditional religions are the living faith of well over 40% of the population and are strongest among the inland peoples. Tribes over three-quarters traditionalist are: Gbande 80%, Grio 95%, Kpelle 90%, Loma 80%, Mano 95%, Sapo 80% and Tchien 80%. Names for God include Zra (among the Dan), Kamba (Vai), Hala (Kissi), Yala (Kpelle), and Gala (Loma). Nevertheless, veneration of ancestors forms the core of Liberian traditional religious experience. The Mandingo are especially noted as diviners, their principal method being the observation of the pattern formed by bones thrown in the sand. Medicine men (zo in Loma) are active, and belief in witchcraft is strong. Secret societies (Poro for men, Sande for women among the Loma) also play a dominant role and are characterized by elaborate initiation ceremonies.

Islam is strongest among the Vai who are more than 90% islamized. Muslim minorities are also found among the northwestern peoples, especially the Kissi and Gbande, largely due to the influence of Mandingo traders. Muslims make up 16% of the population, and Ahmadiya missionaries from Egypt and Pakistan have been active since 1956.

CHRISTIANITY

PROTESTANT CHURCHES. Methodists were among the pioneer settlers from America in 1822, but the church generally dates its origin to the arrival of the first missionary in 1833. For many years, during this century, the church was served by black bishops from the USA, the first Liberian bishop being elected in 1965. In Monrovia, Methodists have active

Country summary. **Worlds A, B, C by ethnolinguistic peoples, cities, and major civil divisions in Liberia.**

	PEOPLES							CITIES							CIVIL DIVISIONS						
World	Num	Pop 2000	C%	Christians	E%	U%	Unevangelized	Num	Pop 2000	C%	Christians	E%	U%	Unevangelized	Num	Pop 2000	C%	Christians	E%	U%	Unevangelized
A	5	599,092	3.01	18,005	40	60	361,247	0	0	0.00	0	0	0	0	0	0	0.00	0	0	0	0
B	31	2,352,207	32.54	765,298	79	21	505,319	1	1,413,000	36.00	508,680	79	21	297,295	12	3,154,001	29.55	932,060	73	27	867,108
C	11	202,702	73.39	148,759	100	0	539	0	0	0.00	0	0	0	0	0	0	0.00	0	0	0	0
Total	**47**	**3,154,001**	**29.55**	**932,062**	**73**	**27**	**867,105**	**1**	**1,413,000**	**36.00**	**508,680**	**79**	**21**	**297,295**	**12**	**3,154,001**	**29.55**	**932,060**	**73**	**27**	**867,108**

Americo-Liberian communities, but attention has also been given to the peoples of the interior. Ganta mission station was opened on the northern border in 1925, followed by Gbarnga in 1948, and important evangelistic initiatives have also been taken on the Kru coast. Methodists maintain 13 primary and 4 secondary schools, including the College of West Africa which was established in Monrovia in 1939. They also sponsor a hospital, a nursing school, and an extensive leprosy program.

United Methodist Church in Liberia. Choir in Ganta church.

The Lutheran Church had its beginnings in a mission to the interior tribes in 1860 undertaken by the United Lutheran Church in America. The work produced few conversions, although a school system was developed. In 1908, a new expansion into the interior began with the opening of a mission at Kpoloelle, and during the next 50 years, 6 more stations were begun. In 1947, the Evangelical Lutheran Church in Liberia was organized. By 1965, the Lutheran mission ceased to exist as a separate entity, and the church changed its name to the Lutheran Church in Liberia. The church is still basically rural although new work has been started in urban areas where educated tribal peoples have gone to find employment. The Lutheran Church is responsible for 9 primary schools, 4 secondary schools, 2 hospitals, 8 dispensaries, a nursing school, 3 literacy centers, 3 community centers, and an agricultural extension program.

Pentecostal missionaries from the USA opened the first of their mission stations at Newaka in 1908. Since then, more than a dozen stations have been established in the eastern part of the country. Churches are completely indigenous, and response to the gospel from tribal peoples has been marked, with entire villages burning their traditional charms. There are 3 Bible schools, a coeducational school in Monrovia, a girls' school at Newaka, a leper colony in New Hope Town and a new work begun on a Firestone rubber plantation. Several other Pentecostal groups are also working in Liberia including the United Pentecostal Church and Free Pentecostal Church.

Seventh-day Adventists entered Liberia in 1927, and the United Liberia Inland Church was started by the Worldwide Evangelization Crusade in 1938. In addition to medical, educational, literacy, and evangelistic work in the interior, the latter has a ministry at one of the large Firestone plantations, and operates a bookstore in Monrovia and an aircraft service.

In 1954, the Sudan Interior Mission built the first mission radio station in Africa, ELWA (Eternal Love Winning Africa). It broadcasted in 40 languages covering Africa and the Middle East and, in addition, ran a hospital before being destroyed in the civil war.

A number of other small Protestant societies and churches are also at work in Liberia.

INDIGENOUS CHURCHES. The first church built in Liberia, and the oldest Baptist congregation in Africa, was the Providence Baptist Church in Monrovia, begun by two USA black Baptist missionaries, Lott Carey and Colin Teague, who took part in the expedition of American Negro settlers to Liberia in 1822. The church later received support from the Lott Carey Baptist Foreign Mission Convention, a Negro society formed in 1897. A second black society was the National Baptist Convention USA which established missions in 1897 at Brewerville and Monrovia and later took over the work of the independent Klay Mission. Today, these various initiatives are combined in the Liberian Baptist Convention, the largest denomination in Liberia. Aid is also received from Southern Baptists who entered Liberia in 1960. The Convention sponsors 14 primary schools, 3 secondary schools, a hospital and industrial academy in Monrovia and a rubber farm at Bamboota. In addition to their work with the Convention, Southern Baptists also provide support for the churches begun by independent Baptist missionaries including Mother George, who founded 13 congregations in the area of Greenville in Simoe Country prior to 1961, and Daniel Horton who was originally a missionary of the National Baptist Convention. Horton organized a separate conference among Bassa tribesmen in 1938 which included 71 congregations by 1990.

The influence of Blacks from the USA has also been felt in the creation of the African Methodist Episcopal Church (1873), AME Zion Church (1876), Pentecostal Assemblies of the World (1919), and other smaller groups. Independent churches from other parts of west Africa have also spread to Liberia. The Church of the Lord (Aladura) is a Nigerian body which entered Liberia in 1947 at the request of a Liberian judge who had visited Nigeria for healing the previous year. Healing has in fact been a major emphasis in the witness of many independent churches. Contrary to the situation in other parts of West Africa, no large or powerful indigenous churches have arisen within Liberia itself. Prophet Harris was himself a native Grebo but his ministry in 1914-15 was carried on almost entirely in neighboring Ivory Coast. Nevertheless, many small denominations exist.

Independents. African Christians Fellowship, among Kru, Bassa, Mano, and Krahn peoples.

CATHOLIC CHURCH. Although the coast of Liberia was first touched by Portuguese mariners as early as 1462 and was included in the diocese of Cape Verde in 1533, no permanent Catholic work was established until the present century. When the first Negroes emigrated to Liberia in 1822, Catholic bishops in the USA attempted to begin a mission. Edward Barron and 2 others went to Monrovia in 1841 but were unsuccessful in gaining a foothold. In 1848, Holy Ghost priests opened a church and school in Monrovia, but the project was abandoned in 1887 due to opposition. The church today is the outgrowth of work established in 1906 by a different body, the Society of African Missions. Attention was at first given to Monrovia and Kakata. However, when the Kru coast appeared to be more receptive, other missions were closed and efforts were concentrated on the Kru. Catholics have also had some success with the Grebo in the southeastern part of the country, the Bassa and the Mano to the north. At present, there are 3 vicariates. Great success has attended Catholic educational work in schools.

The Holy See has diplomatic relations with Liberia and in AD 2000 is represented to government and the Catholic hierarchy by a pro-nuncio residing in Freetown.

ANGLICAN CHURCH. The Protestant Episcopal Church of the USA opened a station among the Grebo at Cape Palmas in 1836. The first black bishop was appointed in 1885 and was largely responsible for developing the extensive educational program which today includes 41 primary schools, 10 secondary schools and a university, Cuttington College and Divinity School. Since the 1920s, the church has given more attention to evangelistic work at Cape Mount in western Liberia and at Bolahun among the Gbande and other northwestern peoples. The church is an extra-provincial missionary diocese of the Episcopal Church in the USA and resisted joining in the Anglican Province of West Africa until 1975.

Renewal movements. In the 1990s the Pentecostal/Charismatic Renewal continued to spread rapidly across most older churches, and numbered over 520,000 adherents (of whom 29% Pentecostals, 9% Charismatics, and 62% Independents).

Indigenous missions. Though Liberian Christians are active in evangelism, only a few have been sent out as foreign missionaries, mainly to surrounding African countries.

Modern communications: Light aircraft used by Evangelical missionary societies.

CHURCH AND STATE

Founded and organized by the American Colonization Society in the early part of the 19th century in order to resolve the problem of blacks in the USA, Liberia was first led by Protestant ministers. In the beginning, the laws and regulations were based on Christian principles and often legislative, executive and judicial powers were exercised by churchmen.

In the history of the country, 4 of the presidents of the republic have been pastors, including president Tolbert who was an ordained Baptist minister. The latter announced in 1971 that the teaching of religion would henceforth form part of the program of all schools.

The constitution of 1847, which is still in force, provides for liberty of conscience and worship. It specifies that 'No sect of Christians shall have exclusive privileges or preference over any other sect; but all shall be alike tolerated' (Article 1, section 3). The civil authorities stress that Liberia terms itself a Christian country but that all religions are protected. The churches receive financial help of various kinds from the government. There is no ministry charged with religious affairs, and churches are not required to register with government.

BROADCASTING AND MEDIA

Prior to its destruction in 1996 during civil disorder, the ELWA station in Liberia blanketed much of Africa with regular Christian radio programming in numerous languages (including Arabic, Baoule, English, French, Kpelle, Krio, Fulfulde, Hausa, Kanuri,

Menenka, Djoula, Bambara, Mende, Moore, Nupe, Senoufo, Themne, Twi, and Yoruba). Since it went off the air, Lutherans have been purchasing air time on secular radio stations to try to make up some of the lost broadcasting. Liberia is a member of UNDA and there are 2 Catholic radio stations: ELCM in Monrovia, and ELSM in Sanniquellie, broadcasting in English, Mano, and Gio. Shortwave radio programs from KNLS have generated responses.

Over 3.3 million have seen the 'Jesus' Film, chiefly due to widespread showings by film teams. Some 300,000 have responded with decisions.

INTERDENOMINATIONAL ORGANIZATIONS

Liberia has had no national Christian council or other ecumenical body fostering cooperation among the churches.

The United Ecumenical Organization (UEO), founded in 1970, is a lay group composed mostly of Methodists and Episcopalians, with some Catholic participation, whose major interest is social work. There is also an ad hoc National Interdenominational Conference of Bishops which provides an opportunity for Catholics, Episcopalians, Methodists, and Lutherans to discuss together the special problems of Christian presence in slum areas. The Christian Rural Fellowship was begun in 1967. In 1968, a conservative grouping, the Liberian Evangelical Fundamental Fellowship was formed, which 6 years later joined the AEAM as the Liberian Evangelical Fellowship.

FUTURE TRENDS AND PROSPECTS

Tribal religionists are expected to experience modest but continuing decline through 2025 ending up at about 38% (down from near 90% in 1900). Christians will reach 43% by 2025. Muslims are likely to level off at about 16.5% in the same period.

By AD 2050 it is possible that Christians will claim over 50% of the population. Tribal religionists are expected to fall below 15% in the near future.

BIBLIOGRAPHY

'A cross–cultural communication of Biblical truth in Grebo villages of Maryland County, Liberia.' R. J. Martin. D.Min. thesis, Southeastern Baptist Theological Seminary, Wake Forest, NC, 1990. 130p.

A history of the Episcopal Church in Liberia, 1821–1980. D. E. Dunn. *ATLA monograph series*, no. 30. Metuchen, NJ: American Theological Library Association and The Scarecrow Press, 1992. 499p.

Alexander Crummell (1819–1898) and the creation of an African–American church in Liberia. J. R. Oldfield. *Studies in the history of missions*, vol. 6. Lewiston, NY: E. Mellen Press, 1990. 165p.

Catholic missionaries and Liberia: a study of Christian enterprise in West Africa, 1842–1950. E. M. Hogan. Cork, Ireland: Cork University Press, 1981. 286p.

'Change strategies initiated in the Protestant Episcopal Church in Liberia from 1836 to 1950 and their effects.' D. A. Holt. Ph.D. dissertation, Boston University School of Education, Boston, 1970.

Christianity and politics in Doe's Liberia. P. Gifford. *Cambridge studies in ideology and religion*, vol. 2. Cambridge: Cambridge University Press, 1993. 365p.

God's impatience in Liberia. J. C. Wold. Grand Rapids, MI: Eerdmans, 1968. 227p.

'History of the Methodist Church mission in Liberia.' W. J. King. Monrovia, Liberia: Methodist Church, [1950]. 77p. (Mimeographed; by the Methodist bishop).

Liberia. D. E. Dunn. *World bibliographical series*, vol. 157. Oxford, UK: CLIO Press, 1994. 152p.

Lutherans in Liberia, 1860–1960. E. Otto. : United Lutheran Church women and the Board of Foreign Missions of the United Lutheran Church in America, 1960. 23p.

Organisation und gesellschaftliche Funktion unabhängiger Kirchen in Afrika: Beispiele aus Liberia und Ansätze zu einer allgemeinen Theorie. W. Korte. *Studien und Materialien der anthropologischen Forschung*, Bd. 2, Nr. 1. Wiesbaden: B. Heymann, 1977. 253p.

Secret societies and the church: an evaluation of the Poro and Sande secret societies and the missionary among the Mano of Liberia. P. J. Harrington. Rome: Pontificia Universitas Gregoriana, Facultas Scientiarum Socialium, 1975. 71p.

'Spiritual and secular activities of the Methodist Episcopal Church in Liberia, 1833–1933.' J. M. D'Amico. Ph.D. dissertation, St. John's University, 1977. 482p.

The Bassa of Liberia: a study of culture, historical development, and indigenization of the Gospel. L. Vanderaa. N.p., 1982. 138p.

The Catholic story of Liberia. M. J. Bane. New York: Declan MacMullen, 1950.

'The cultural politics of religious change: a study of the Kpelle of Liberia.' R. Stakeman. Ph.D. dissertation, Stanford University, Stanford, CA, 1982. 355p.

'The dual legacy: government authority and mission influence among the Glebo of eastern Liberia, 1834–1910.' J. J. Martin. Ph.D. dissertation, Boston University, Boston, 1978. 479p.

The Episcopal Church of Liberia under indigenous leadership: reflections on a twenty year episcopate. G. D. Browne. Stone Mountain, GA: Strugglers' Community Press, 1992.

'The growth of Christianity in the Liberian environment.' J. W. Cason. Ph.D. dissertation, Columbia University, New York, 1962. 484p.

'The Presbyterian mission to Liberia, 1832–1900.' E. N. Hodgson. Ph.D. dissertation, Columbia University, New York, 1980. 382p.

'Theological education by extension among the Bassa tribe of Liberia.' H. B. Goeh. M.A. thesis, Columbia Graduate School of Bible and Missions, Columbia, SC, 1986. 71p.

Theological education in Liberia: problems and opportunities. A. F. Kulah. Lithonia, GA: SCP/Third World Literature, 1994. 135p.

'Toward a theology of mission for Liberia: an appropriation of David Bosch's model.' E. G. D. Nyakoon. Th.M. thesis, Southern Baptist Theological Seminary, Louisville, KY, 1993. 125p.

'Transcending boundaries: an anthropological study of the African Methodist Episcopal Church in Monrovia, Liberia.' B. P. Bruce. Ph.D. dissertation, Harvard University, Cambridge, MA, 1978. 208p.

Country Table 2. **Organized churches and denominations in Liberia.**

Official name (bold type = church with over 10% of all affiliated) 1	*Begun* 2	*Type* 3	*Counc* 4	*Congs* 5	*Adults* 6	*Affiliated 1970* 7	*Affiliated 1995* 8	*G%* 9	*Names, notes, and other statistics* (see Codebook, Part 3) 10
African Christians Fellowship	1986	I-3cA	.....	43	3,610	–	7,000	11.11	Largest congregations among Kru; also Bassa, Mano, Krahn. M=CAM.
African Disciples of Christ	1968	I-Dis	.....	20	1,500	2,000	3,000	1.64	*Soul-Winning Mission Ch of Liberia.* 74% Bassa, 16% Kru, 10% Kpelle. 9n,4m,72Y,60y.
African Methodist Episcopal Church	1873	I-Met	VwA..	75	5,590	8,576	13,000	1.68	M=AMEC(USA). Part of 14th Episcopal District. 16 schools. 71n,3w,1h,3r.
African Methodist Episcopal Zion Ch	1876	I-Met	Vw...	12	2,200	7,500	5,000	-1.61	In 9th Episcopal District. M=AMEZC(USA). 20 schools. HQ Monrovia. 20n.
African Salvation Army Church	1964	I-Sal	.....	5	300	1,000	800	-0.89	A Bassa church on Firestone plantation. HQ Buchanan. Declining. 5n,4m,54Y,34y.
Apostolic God of Mercy Church	1957	I-3pA	.....	15	900	1,569	2,000	0.98	On Firestone Plantation. Bassa. Buchanan area. HQ Owensgrove. 25n,15w,160Y.
Army of the Cross of Christ Church	c1950	I-3sA	.....	20	1,000	585	1,500	3.84	*MDCC. Musama Disco Christo Ch.* Immigrant church from Ghana (Fante).
Assoc of Independent Chs in Africa	1965	I-Non	.....	175	7,000	800	14,000	12.13	Helped by Partners International.
Bafu Bay Church	1952	I-Bap	.....	50	3,000	4,000	7,000	2.26	Begun by USA roadbuilder, continued by Sapo tribesmen. HQ Juarzon. 5n,5m,288Y.
Believe in God Healing Church	1960	I-3pA	.....	10	200	200	500	3.73	*Poe Yonswah-tah un jae por* (Sapo) Woman bishop. 60% Sapo. 75% lost in splits.
Bethel World Outreach	1986	I-3fA	.....	35	6,000	–	10,000	11.11	In first 3 years began 31 churches. Faith gospel of prosperity ('Name it, Claim it').
Catholic Church in Liberia:	1906	R-Lat	P.SGP	62	58,200	23,697	96,864	5.79	3 failed starts; 1906 M=SMA. C=2+2+7. (1970) 5n,1277Yy,1s. (1990) 21n,29x,51m,50w,4192Yy.
M Monrovia	1903	R-Lat	Ps	21	47,800	13,317	80,000	7.44	Heavy Catholic immigration from VA Cape Palmas. 9n 19x 26m 28w 3600Yy
D Cape Palmas	1950	R-Lat	Psma	29	6,000	10,380	9,700	-0.27	80% Kru, 15% Grebo, 5% Kran, Lebanese Maronites. 11n 3x 9m 11w 428Yy
D Gbarnga	1986	R-Lat	Ps	12	4,400	–	7,164	11.11	M=SMA. 1n 7x 16m 11w 164Yy
Church of God by Faith	1959	I-3pA	.....	10	1,000	1,000	2,000	2.81	25% Bassa, 23% Kpelle, 23% Mano, 18% Dei, 11% Gio. HQ Barnardsville. 1n,5m,1s(6),23Y.
Church of God (Cleveland)	1974	P-Pe3	.....	30	1,992	–	3,320	4.76	M=CoG(Cleveland).
Church of God in Christ	c1945	I-3pB	Z...I	40	2,000	500	3,000	7.43	M=CoGiC(Black mission from USA). Main work among Grebo, Bassa. HQ Monrovia.
Church of God—Liberia	c1970	I-3oA	.....	10	1,000	–	3,000	37.75	Oneness churches; member of AWCF. HQ Monrovia. Presiding bishop.
Church of God of Prophecy	1979	P-Pe3	.....	2	300	–	750	6.25	M=CGP.
Ch of the Lord JC of Apostolic Faith	1963	I-3oA	x...I	36	1,190	1,000	3,050	4.56	Linked with M=COLJCAF(USA). Black pentecostals. 90% Bassa. HQ Fortsville. 2n,135Y.
Church of the Lord (Aladura)	1947	I-3pA	xwi..	100	20,000	10,000	30,000	4.49	M=CLA(Nigeria). 9 Districts. Widespread Bassa, Kru, Kpelle. 60n,70m,20w,5h,3r.
Church of the Nazarene	1990	P-Hol	.....	5	510	–	850	20.00	M=CoN.
Church of the Twelve Apostles	1956	I-3sA	.....	20	2,000	1,000	3,000	4.49	Part of original Harrist Church begun in 1914 in Ivory Coast. Bassa members.
Churches of Christ	1966	I-Dis	x....	43	3,150	1,500	4,890	4.84	M=CCCC(Instrumental) (USA). 5 churches in Monrovia. School, mobile clinic. 4f,1p.
Episcopal Church of Liberia	1836	A-Cen	awAV.	129	13,000	11,000	26,000	3.50	D in PECUSA Prov 11. M=OHC. Grebo, Kru, Kissi. 22n,4x,3h,1p,10r,1s,1v,202Y,356y.
Evangelical Church of Christ	c1968	I-Eva	.T...	50	1,000	800	2,000	3.73	Begun by former ELWA radio programmer. 7 churches in Muslim areas. Most Bassa.
Evangelical Chs of West Africa	1951	P-Eva	xMG.G	19	1,700	590	3,700	7.62	*ECWA.* M=SIM. 1954 radio station ELWA, 43 languages. 29% White. 1n,4x,80f,1H,W=78%.
Ev Congregational Ch of Christ	1971	P-Hol	xFG.G	30	1,500	–	3,000	4.17	M=Ev Congregational Ch(USA). Formerly East Pennsylvania Conference. 2f.
Evangelical Lutheran Church	1978	P-Lut	.....	45	508	–	1,086	5.88	M=ELC(USA).
Fellowship of Christian Assemblies	c1960	I-3pA	x....	10	1,000	200	2,000	9.65	*FOCA.* Begun by M=FOCA(Seattle, USA). Mostly in southeast Liberia. 5f,1p.
Fire-Baptized Holiness CoG of Africa		I-3pA	x...I	150	5,000	6,000	10,000	0.05	M=FBHC(USA). 4 Districts across nation. Mainly Kru, Bassa, Gola, Kran. 60nm,75Y.
Free Pentecostal Church	1920	P-Pe2	Z...I	30	1,500	5,000	4,550	-0.38	M=SFM(Sweden). Mass movement. 40% Kissi, 40% Loma, 20% Gbande. 3 schools.
Free Protestant Episcopal Church	1957	I-ARo	xv...	50	4,000	3,800	6,000	1.84	*D W Africa, ECF.* M=FPEC(UK,USA). 50% Nigerians. 3n,6x,8r,1s(10),W=39%,615Y,200y.
Gethsemane Church of Liberia	1959	I-3pA	.....	40	2,000	1,500	3,500	3.45	54% Bassa, 27% Kpelle, 14% Mano, 5% Gio. 2 schools 19n,10m,9w,W=75%.
Intern Ch of the Foursquare Gospel	1983	P-Pe2	.....	1	18	–	30	8.33	M=ICFG(USA).
Jehovah's Witnesses	1887	m-Jeh	x....	39	1,914	1,500	4,790	4.75	1887, Grebo secession Russelite Ch, ex PECUSA. HQ Monrovia. (1975) 101Y. (1995) 158Y.
Liberia Assemblies of God	1908	P-Pe2	ZFG.G	395	45,000	20,000	85,000	5.96	M=AoG(USA),PAoC(Canada). A=1967. 95% Kru. 4 schools. 242n,21f,1H,3p,1s(63).
Liberian Baptist Convention	1822	I-Bap	T.A..	229	59,222	50,000	98,700	2.76	*LBMEC.* M=NBCUSA,LCBFMC; 1960 SBC(USA). Grebo. 140n,39f,1H,7h,4r,2s,1318Y.
Liberian Christian Assemblies of God	1920	I-3pA	I	80	2,000	500	5,000	9.65	*Sinoe Bible Institute.* M=IAoG(Scandinavians from USA). 5 schools. 33f,2h,1p.
Liberian Gospel Crusade Church	1952	I-3pA	.....	20	1,800	2,000	4,000	2.81	*LGCC.* Director in Liberian senate. Mainly Bassa; Kpelle. 23n,30m,10w,W=75%,46Y.
Lighthouse Fellowship of Churches	1936	I-3pA	.T...	40	2,000	2,000	4,000	2.81	*Mother Blatch's Chs.* M=Lighthouse Full Gospel Ch (USA). Americo-Liberians. Monrovia.
Lutheran Church in Liberia	1860	P-Lut	LWA..	119	31,200	20,507	69,779	5.02	*LCL.* First M=Muhlenberg M, LCA(USA). A=1947. Kpelle, Loma. 39f,2H,8h,4r,1s,W=20%.
Mary Sharp Memorial Church	1876	I-Met	.....	3	500	300	1,000	4.93	Kru. Begun by USA missionary M. Sharp. Aid from M=Defenders of the Faith (USA).
Mid-Liberia Baptist Mission	1938	P-Fun	xT...	75	3,750	600	7,500	10.63	M=BMM,GARB(Canada,USA). HQ Monrovia. Gio, Mano, Bassa, Kran, Kpelle. 44f,1H,2h,2s.
New Apostolic Church		I-3aX	x....	20	2,000	–	3,577	0.05	*NAC,NAK.* M=Neuapostolische Kirche (HQ Zurich, Switzerland).
Open Bible Standard Churches	1935	I-3pW	ZFG.G	21	917	800	1,830	3.37	Schism ex AoG by a USA woman missionary. HQ River Cess. 2 schools. 11f,1h,1p.
Pentecostal Assemblies of the World	1919	I-3aO	xv..I	70	10,000	10,000	20,000	2.81	M=PAW(USA Blacks). 90% Kru, 3% Dey, 2% Bassa. 43n,2x,24m,17w,3f,1H,1h,W=87%,153Y.
Pillar of Fire	1961	P-Hol	x....	50	2,000	500	3,000	7.43	M=Pillar of Fire West African Missions (USA). At River Cess. 2 schools. 45n,5f,1h,1s.
Presbytery of Liberia in West Africa	1831	P-Ref	RuA..	15	1,500	2,000	3,750	2.55	*Presbyterian Ch in Liberia.* M=UPUSA. A=1890. Many women evangelists. 16n (5 women).
Seventh-day Adventist Church	1927	P-Adv	x....	34	9,355	7,000	18,700	4.01	*Liberian Mission.* 67% Bassa, 29% Kpelle, 4% Gio. 7n,13f,1s(7),1v,W=60%,529Y.
Star of Bethlehem Church	1960	I-Ang	.....	20	2,000	1,776	4,000	3.30	Sinoe, Gedeh countries. 84% Sapo, 11% Kran, 4% Kru. 18n,26m,10w,1p,W=75%,32Y,17y.
Transcea	1983	I-3nA	.....	20	5,000	–	9,000	8.33	*Transcontinental Evangelical Association Church.* No buildings, only rented halls.
United Liberia Inland Church	1938	P-Non	xFG.G	71	7,800	5,000	20,000	5.70	*LIM. Liberia Inland Mission.* M=WEC. Bassa, Mano, Gio, Kpelle. 9m,9w,40f,6h,1p,1r.
United Methodist Church of Liberia	1823	P-Met	VwA..	420	21,800	50,000	43,681	-0.54	*Liberia CC,* UMC(USA). 33% Bassa, 19% Kru. 75n,5x,34f,1H,10h,4r,W=25%,931Y,1205y.
United Pentecostal Church of Liberia	1936	P-Pe1	x...I	70	4,200	5,000	6,360	0.97	*Jesus Only Ch.* Unitarians. M=UPC(USA). Belle. 1 school. 29n,4f,1h,1p(30),1r.
Wesleyan Church	1978	P-Hol	.....	15	2,400	–	5,270	5.88	M=WC(USA).
World-Wide Missions of Liberia	1961	I-Non	x.G.G	50	2,500	4,000	5,000	0.90	M=World-Wide Missions (USA). Evangelicals with base in Pasadena, CA(USA).
Other African indigenous churches		I-3pA	.....	200	20,000	10,000	40,000	0.05	Total about 200 (see below), including National Baptist Ch, Harrist Ch, and 100 other Bassa ICs.
Other independent charismatic chs		I-3cA	.....	50	5,000	–	10,000	0.05	Indigenous charismatics.

Continued opposite

Country Table 2–concluded

Official name (bold type = church with over 10% of affiliated) 1	*Begun* 2	*Type* 3	*Counc* 4	*Congs* 5	*Adults* 6	*Affiliated 1970* 7	*Affiliated 1995* 8	*G%* 9	*Names, notes, and other statistics* (see Codebook, Part 3) 10
Other Protestant denominations		P-	.....	40	3,000	3,500	6,000	0.05	Total about 15 (see list below).
Doubly-affiliated		2-aff			-94,400	0	-178,106		Evangelicals and Pentecostals who are also baptized Catholics or others.
Totals				**3,538**	**306,326**	**290,800**	**578,221**		

Churches, members, growth, 1900-2025	*Congs*	*Adults*	*Affiliated*	*G%*	*Total denominations*	*6 Megablocs:*	*O*	*R*	*A*	*P*	*I*	*m*
Total churches, members, and denominations (mid-1900)	200	14,000	28,300	3.38	7	....	0	0	1	3	2	1
Total churches, members, and denominations (mid-1970)	1,962	143,671	290,800	3.38	139	....	0	1	1	18	118	1
Total churches, members, and denominations (mid-1990)	3,000	355,000	670,750	4.27	315	....	0	1	1	32	280	1
Total churches, members, and denominations (mid-1995)	3,538	306,326	578,221	-2.93	320	....	0	1	1	33	284	1
Total churches, members, and denominations (mid-2000)	5,000	494,000	932,060	10.02	327	....	0	1	1	34	290	1
Total churches, members, and denominations (mid-2025)	12,000	1,113,000	2,100,000	3.30	567	....	0	1	1	60	500	5

NOTES ON TABLE ABOVE
NATIONAL COUNCILS (Column 4, 5th letter).
E = Association of Evangelicals of Liberia (AEL), or Liberia Evangelical Fellowship (LEF) (formerly Liberian Ev Fundamental Fellowship, LEFF).
H = Pentecostal Fellowship Union of Liberia.
K = Liberian Council of Churches (LCC).
P = Inter-Territorial Catholic Bishops' Conference of the Gambia, Liberia & Sierra Leone, ITCABIC.
Other national or plurinational councils. National Interdenominational Conference of Bishops. Association of Independent Churches of Africa (supported by Peoples Church, Toronto, Canada). National Union of Christian Alliance of Liberia. United Pentecostal Assemblies of the World in Liberia & Sierra Leone (HQ Monrovia).
OTHER AFRICAN INDIGENOUS CHURCHES. In addition to immigrant groups from Ghana and Nigeria, there are at least 50 more Liberian-founded churches. The dominant tribe of each, together with date of founding, are given in parentheses below where known. The total includes: Abosso Apostolic Faith Ch of Jesus Christ (Kru, 1938), African Faith Tabernacle Ch, African Glory Prophet Ch Number One (Bassa, 1955), African National Pentecostal Ch (Kru, 1945), Assemblies of God Kissi Ch (Kissi, 1963, Cavalla River Ch (Krahn, 1966), Cherubim & Seraphim (Nigeria), Christ Apostolic Ch (Nigeria), Ch of Heaven (Kru, 1955), Emissaries of Divine Light (Ghana), First United Ch of Jesus Christ (Apostolic) (Jamaica pentecostals), Grace Pentecostal Ch (Kru, 1949), Healing Ch of Christ (Bassa, 1969), House of Prayer (Grebo, 1953), Morning Star Ch of God in Christ (Bassa, 1945), Mount Hermon Holy Ch (Kru, 1969), Mount Sanai Ch (Bassa, 1968), Shepherd looking for Lost Sheep Ch (Bassa, 1966), Twelve Apostles Ch (Bassa, 1956), Universal House of Prayer (Gbande, 1955), Zion Christian Ch (Bassa, 1948). There are in addition a number of other USA Black pentecostal missions, including: Bible Way Chs of Our Lord Jesus Christ World Wide (1958), Ch of the Living God (1947), Kodesh Ch of Immanuel (1956), United Holy Ch of America; there is also the National Baptist Convention of America.
OTHER PROTESTANT DENOMINATIONS. The many smaller bodies are mostly missions from the USA. Among these and other foreign bodies are: American Soul Clinic (1959), Baptist International Missions (1972), Baptist Mid-Missions (mid-Liberian Mission), Christian Nationals' Evangelism Commission (1965), Christian Reformed Ch, Christian Union General Mission Board (1969), International Gospel League (1947), Voice of Africa Mission (1966), West African Gospel Mission (1954).

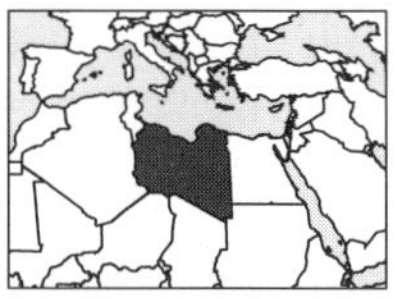

LIBYA

SECULAR DATA, AD 2000

STATE
Official name: Al-Jamahiriya Al-Arabiya Al-Libiya Ash-Shabiya Al-Ishtirakiya Al-Uzma (The Socialist People's Libyan Arab Jamahiriya).
Short name: Libya. **Adjective of nationality:** Libyan.
Flag: Green.
Area: 1,757,000 sq. km. (678,400 sq. mi.).
Government: Socialist military junta, since 1969 (1911 Italian colony, 1943 under British military rule, 1951 Independence as United Kingdom of Libya).
Legislature: General People's Congress, 760 members.
Official language: Arabic.
Monetary unit: 1 Libyan dinar (LD) = 1,000 dirhams. **US$1=** U.S. $2.59.
Chief cities: TARABULUS (Tripoli) 2,041,000; Banghazi (Benghazi) 975,000; Misratah (Misurata) 183,516; Tubruq (Tobruk) 132,322; Al-Bayda (Beida) 117,976.
Political divisions: 13 provinces.
Armed forces: 70,000.

DEMOGRAPHY
Population: 5,605,000.
Population density: 3.1/sq. km. (8.2/sq. mi.).
Under 15 years: 2,109,000.
Growth rate p.a.: 2.33% (births 27.84, deaths 4.58).
Mortality: Infant, per 1,000: 25.1; **Maternal per 100,000:** 220.0.
Life expectancy: 71 (male 69, female 73).
Household size: 5.4. **Floor area per person, sq.m:** 12.0.
Major languages: Arabic, English, Italian, Tuareg, Maltese, French, Berber, and 5 others.
Urban dwellers: 87.63%. **Urban growth rate p.a.:** 3.5%.
Labor force: 25%.

ETHNOLINGUISTIC PEOPLES
30.9% Tripolitanian Arab; 26.2% Cyrenaican Arab; 9.2% Sanusi Bedouin; 7.7% Egyptian Arab; 4.2% Arabized Berber.

ECONOMY
National income p.a. per person: US$6,510; **per family:** US$35,154.

EDUCATION
Adult literacy: 76% (male 87%, female 63%). **Schools:** 4,494.
Universities: 10. **School enrolment:** female/male: 103%/107%.

HEALTH
Access to health services: 45%. **Access to safe water:** 30%.
Hospitals: 75 (41 beds per 10,000). **Doctors:** 4,749.
Blind: 10,000. **Deaf:** 383,200. **Murder rate:** 1.
Lepers: 7,700. **Underweight prevalence under 5:** 5%.

LITERATURE
New book titles p.a.: 2,240 (400 p.a. per million). **Periodicals:** 3.
Newspapers: 4 dailies.

COMMUNICATION (per 1,000 people)
Phones: 59 (40% mobile). **Radios:** 190. **TV sets:** 138.
Daily newspaper circulation: 13. **Computers:** 25.

REFUGEES
Alien refugees from other countries: 28,100.

HUMAN LIFE AND LIBERTY (optimum condition=100.0%)
HDI: 80.1. **HSI:** 49.0. **HFI:** 2.5. **EFL:** 6.0.

Country Table 1. **Religious adherents in Libya, AD 1900-2025.**

Year / *Name*	*1900* *Adherents*	*%*	*1970* *Adherents*	*%*	*mid-1990* *Adherents*	*%*	*Annual change, 1990-2000* *Natural*	*Conversion*	*Total*	*Rate*	*mid-1995* *Adherents*	*%*	*mid-2000* *Adherents*	*%*	*mid-2025* *Adherents*	*%*
Muslims	749,980	93.8	1,924,610	96.9	4,234,980	95.9	114,026	972	114,998	2.43	4,759,330	95.8	5,384,964	96.1	8,234,850	95.2
Christians	**10,020**	**1.3**	**58,750**	**3.0**	**147,000**	**3.3**	**3,929**	**-1,081**	**2,848**	**1.79**	**168,500**	**3.4**	**175,478**	**3.1**	**292,300**	**3.4**
PROFESSION																
crypto-Christians	5,020	0.6	51,150	2.6	105,000	2.4	2,827	-327	2,500	2.16	125,000	2.5	130,000	2.3	200,000	2.3
professing Christians	**5,000**	**0.6**	**7,600**	**0.4**	**42,000**	**1.0**	**1,131**	**-783**	**348**	**0.80**	**43,500**	**0.9**	**45,478**	**0.8**	**92,300**	**1.1**
AFFILIATION																
unaffiliated Christians	0	0.0	1,166	0.1	5,300	0.1	143	-160	-17	-0.33	4,775	0.1	5,126	0.1	6,000	0.1
affiliated Christians	**10,020**	**1.3**	**57,584**	**2.9**	**141,700**	**3.2**	**3,815**	**-950**	**2,865**	**1.86**	**163,725**	**3.3**	**170,352**	**3.0**	**286,300**	**3.3**
Orthodox	0	0.0	47,000	2.4	95,000	2.2	2,558	-1,394	1,164	1.16	107,600	2.2	106,642	1.9	180,000	2.1
Roman Catholics	10,000	1.3	3,650	0.2	33,000	0.8	889	311	1,200	3.15	40,000	0.8	45,000	0.8	70,000	0.8
Independents	0	0.0	2,670	0.1	9,300	0.2	250	220	470	4.18	11,570	0.2	14,000	0.3	30,000	0.4
Protestants	20	0.0	3,850	0.2	4,200	0.1	113	-83	30	0.69	4,350	0.1	4,500	0.1	6,000	0.1
Anglicans	0	0.0	380	0.0	150	0.0	4	-4	0	0.00	150	0.0	150	0.0	200	0.0
Marginal Christians	0	0.0	34	0.0	50	0.0	1	0	1	1.84	55	0.0	60	0.0	100	0.0
Trans-megabloc groupings																
Evangelicals	10	0.0	1,600	0.1	4,200	0.1	113	17	130	2.73	4,874	0.1	5,500	0.1	13,000	0.2
Pentecostals/Charismatics	0	0.0	700	0.0	13,800	0.3	372	48	420	2.69	15,663	0.3	18,000	0.3	35,000	0.4
Great Commission Christians	**9,600**	**1.2**	**33,000**	**1.7**	**80,000**	**1.8**	**2,154**	**-839**	**1,315**	**1.53**	**84,400**	**1.7**	**93,153**	**1.7**	**150,000**	**1.7**
Buddhists	0	0.0	400	0.0	15,200	0.3	409	-35	374	2.23	16,870	0.3	18,944	0.3	55,000	0.6
Nonreligious	0	0.0	2,000	0.1	11,000	0.3	296	157	453	3.51	13,000	0.3	15,525	0.3	40,000	0.5
Hindus	0	0.0	0	0.0	3,800	0.1	102	22	124	2.87	4,700	0.1	5,044	0.1	13,000	0.2
Sikhs	0	0.0	0	0.0	1,700	0.0	46	-14	32	1.73	1,900	0.0	2,018	0.0	5,000	0.1
Chinese folk-religionists	0	0.0	0	0.0	1,400	0.0	38	-22	16	1.11	1,560	0.0	1,564	0.0	4,000	0.1
Baha'is	0	0.0	200	0.0	400	0.0	11	5	16	3.42	520	0.0	560	0.0	1,000	0.0
Ethnoreligionists	0	0.0	0	0.0	340	0.0	9	0	9	2.35	420	0.0	429	0.0	1,200	0.0
Jews	40,000	5.0	40	0.0	100	0.0	3	-2	1	1.14	110	0.0	112	0.0	250	0.0
Atheists	0	0.0	0	0.0	80	0.0	2	-2	0	0.49	90	0.0	84	0.0	400	0.0
World A (unevangelized persons)	750,400	93.8	1,709,946	86.1	2,499,456	56.6	67,312	-15,352	51,960	1.91	2,731,803	55.0	3,021,095	53.9	4,401,323	50.9
World B (evangelized non-Christians)	39,580	4.9	217,304	10.9	1,769,544	40.1	47,630	16,433	64,063	3.13	2,066,611	41.6	2,408,427	43.0	3,953,377	45.7
World C (Christians)	10,020	1.3	58,750	3.0	147,000	3.3	3,929	-1,081	2,848	1.79	168,500	3.4	175,478	3.1	292,300	3.4
Country's population	**800,000**	**100.0**	**1,986,000**	**100.0**	**4,416,000**	**100.0**	**118,871**	**0**	**118,871**	**2.41**	**4,966,915**	**100.0**	**5,605,000**	**100.0**	**8,647,000**	**100.0**

COLUMNS, ROWS.
For meanings and definitions, see Codebook (Part 3). Note that, by definition, total 'Christians' = professing + crypto-Christians, which also = affiliated + unaffiliated Christians, and also = Great Commission Christians + latent Christians. Percentages may not always total exactly, due to rounding.

CENSUSES.
30.VII.1954: 95.5% Muslims, 4.0% Christians (43,888 persons: 37,954 Italians, 1,849 British, 688 Greeks, 590 USA), 0.4% Jews (4,743 persons). **31.VII.1964** (de jure): 97.2% Muslims, 2.4% Christians (38,274 persons: 21,167 Italians, 6,737 USA, 6,672 British, 1,554 Greeks), 0.2% Jews (3,866 persons), 0.1% other religionists.

NOTES ON RELIGIONS
BAHA'IS. 1973, 1 local spiritual assembly; no subsequent growth by 1998.
BUDDHISTS. Chinese.
COUNTRY'S POPULATION. At the beginning of 1970 the bulk of the Italian population, and other expatriates, finally left or were expelled. By 1978, large numbers of expatriates had returned as technical advisers and other foreign workers.

Continued overleaf

Country Table 1–concluded

CRYPTO-CHRISTIANS. Arab Christians. In general the state has tended either to ignore or not to recognize the existence of Arab Christians (mostly from Egypt).
INDEPENDENTS. Isolated radio believers (see Table 2).
JEWS. Decline from 30,000 in 1931 and 35,000 in 1948, to 6,300 in 1964 (all in Tripolitania), to 40 in 1970, due to mass emigration to Israel. Languages used: Hebrew, also Arabic and Italian.
MUSLIMS. Almost all Sunnis of the Hanafite and Shafiite rites, with Sanusis (a militant reform order inaugurated in Cyrenaica in 1843; Sunnis of the Malikite rite) still predominant in Cyrenaica. Libyan Berbers, few in number, belong to a rival Ibadi (Kharijite) sect, in Zuwara (12,000) and Jabal Nafusa (30,000) in Tripolitania. Missionaries. There is a fluctuating number of Egyptians sent by Al-Azhar University (Cairo). Hajj pilgrims to Mecca. (1964) 6,000; (1968) 10,444; (1969) 13,547; (1970) 11,835; (1971) 16,861; (1972) 23,774; (1973) 30,705; (1974) 30,715; (1975) 52,718; (1976) 18,057.
NONRELIGIOUS. Expatriate Europeans and some Chinese.
ORTHODOX. In the 1964 census, only 8,521 alien Arabs were enumerated. By 1995 the number of immigrant Arabs from Egypt was estimated to be over 400,000, of whom 80,000 were Christians (75,000 Coptic Orthodox). The latter however remained largely unorganized and the Coptic Orthodox Church in Egypt was able to open for them only a handful of parishes with priests
ROMAN CATHOLICS. Italian settlers since their beginnings in 1912 reached a peak of 110,000 in 1941. After 1945 most were expelled, and in 1963 there were only 22,840 Catholics left in Tripoli, 2,000 in Bengazi and 300 in Derna. By mid-1990 this had risen again to 40,000.

Great Commission Instrument Panel: status of Libya (for explanation see start of Part 4)

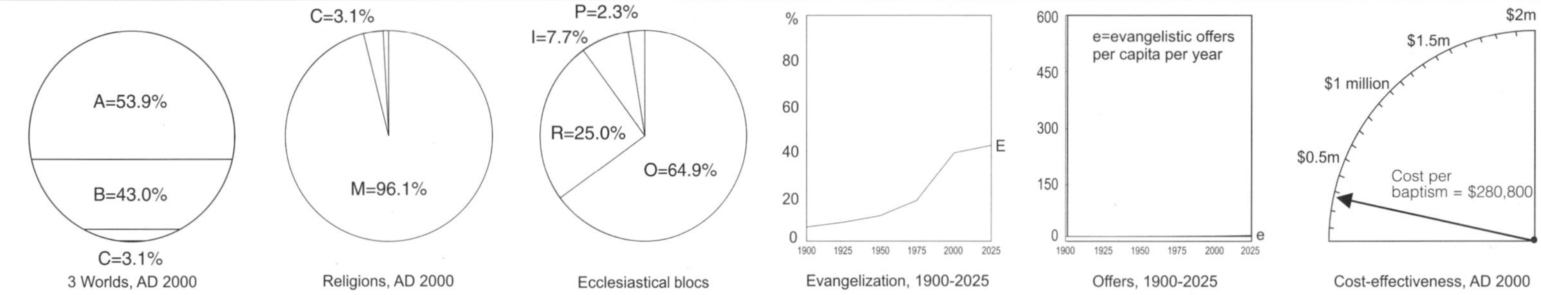

Country status. Libya is an oil rich Islamic nation in North Africa with the longest coastline of any country on the southern shore of the Mediterranean Sea. The country is largely desert and semidesert with no permanent rivers. With scarce natural resources, Libya is dependent on the sale of crude oil, discovered in the late 1950s.

HUMAN LIFE AND LIBERTY

Human need and development. For a country with a small population and coffers full of petro-dollars, Libya presents the picture of a primitive country in an Arabian Nights setting. Although the per capita income is high, there are significant differences in the standards of life of the elite ruling class and the immigrant workers on the one hand and the lower income groups and the blacks on the other. Oil wealth has made little difference to the lives of the poorer Arabs, the Berbers, and the Blacks. The expatriates lead a more affluent life style and receive substantial benefits and generous pay. Living standards on the whole have improved since 1970. Free medical care is available to all, the number of physicians and medical facilities have increased severalfold, and malnutrition has become a thing of the past, at least in the cities. The social security program, instituted in 1957, provides all Libyans with social protection far superior to that available in most developing countries.

Human rights and freedoms. Since 1969, Libya has been an Islamic dictatorship. Operating without a Constitution and based only on the Green Book, Libya is ruled by a junta headed by Muammar Qaddafi and aided by an extensive security apparatus, using terror, assassination, intimidation and other tactics to keep all Libyans under a tight leash. The economy is entirely state-controlled. Worst affected in terms of human rights are Black African workers, thousands of whom were expelled in 1991 after being detained and tortured. Various means of torture are used, such as clubbing, electric shock, corkscrews in the back, suffocation with plastic bags, and beatings on the soles of the feet. Noncitizens are often summarily expelled without reason. Security forces may judge 'traitors to the people' guilty without any trial. The private practice of law is prohibited and all attorneys are employees of the Secretariat of Justice. Freedom of speech is severely limited, especially with regard to criticism of Qaddafi. Political speech is repressed through legislation banning all political activities not sanctioned by the government. Almost any form of communication may be deemed illegal under a law which makes 'dissemination of hostile information' a crime. All media are owned and controlled by the state. Travel abroad by Libyans is tightly controlled, and Libyans who live abroad are monitored by the Libyan Security Forces. As in all Islamic societies, women play a subordinate role in society.

Human environment. Libya has an inhospitable environment that is also very fragile, and subject to quick degradation. Desertification has increased in recent years as a result of overgrazing and extension of farming. Excessive pumping of water from underground wells is causing salt-water intrusion into the aquifers. Effluents from untreated sewage, oil, mining and industrial operations are contaminating coastal areas.

NON-CHRISTIAN RELIGIONS

Islam spread to Libya from Arabia and Egypt in the second half of the 7th century. Almost the entire Libyan population are Sunnis of the Hanafite and Shafite rites, with Sanusis (Malikite rite) predominant in Cyrenaica. Sanusiya, a militant reform order founded in 1843, plays a significant role in Libyan life. Important Islamic institutions and organizations in Libya are the Faculty of Arabic Language and Islamic Studies of the University of Libya in Bengazi, created in 1970 to replace the Ali Sanusi Islamic University and the Islamic Vocation Association (Jamiat al-Dawah al-Islamiah), founded by the government in Tripoli in 1973, which fosters Islam's international missionary role.

Muslims. Sunni Muslims meet on market day in coastal village of Garbulli 25 miles east of Tripoli.

CHRISTIANITY

In North Africa, Christianity has had an ancient history, being the scene of the church's early expansion and the home of some of its most distinguished theologians. However, the combination of a failure to convert the Berbers and internal divisions due in part to Donatism weakened the church and made it impotent in the face of Muslim expansion in the 7th century. There are today almost no indigenous professing Christian believers, and Christianity is made up of Catholics and Orthodox from Greece and the Near East, in addition to a decreasing number of Protestants and Anglicans from Europe and North America.

CATHOLIC CHURCH. Before the departure of Italians at the beginning of 1970, the Catholic Church was divided into 4 ecclesiastical jurisdictions: the vicariates of Bengazi, Derna, Tripoli, and the prefecture of Misurata. In 1969, there were 39,300 faithful of the Latin rite in 23 parishes, served by 30 Franciscan priests, 20 brothers and 200 sisters of different congregations. By 1972, 3 of the 4 jurisdictions had been closed, leaving the vicariate of Tripoli, and only 2 churches remained open for worship: St Francis in Tripoli and another in the Berka quarter of Bengazi. Between 1970 and 1976, when Egyptians were expelled from Libya en masse, Coptic Catholics made up a substantial proportion of the Catholic community.

The Holy See has no diplomatic relations with Libya in AD 2000, but is represented by an apostolic delegate residing in Algiers.

ORTHODOX CHURCH. During 1970-76, the principal Christian tradition present in Libya was that of the Coptic Orthodox Church. For many years, Coptic Orthodox, estimated to number in 1995 up to 90,000 in Libya, had no formal church structures or worship centers. However, following the visit of patriarch Shenouda in 1971, authorization was granted by the government to form 2 Coptic congregations, one in Bengazi using a Greek Orthodox church and another in Tripoli using a former Catholic church. Greek Orthodox, most expatriate residents, have organized churches in both Tripoli and Bengazi.

OTHER CHURCHES. The North Africa Mission entered Tripoli in 1889, and for many years, an Anglican body, Church Missions to Jews (now the Church's Ministry among the Jews) carried on work in the country. All non-Catholic missionaries were expelled by the Italians in 1936 but were allowed reentry in 1946 after Libya was placed under United Nations' trusteeship. Seventh-day Adventists followed, and between 1960 and 1970, 10 Protestant churches existed serving the expatriate community, the largest being the Union Church in Tripoli with 1,500 members. Since the 1969 revolution, which resulted in the evacuation of British and American military bases, missionaries are no longer permitted, and expatriate Protestants and Anglicans have been greatly reduced in numbers.

In Tripoli, 4 congregations continue active: the Union Church which has its own building, Anglicans who use the Union Church building, Southern Baptists who have a rented hall and the Church of Christ which uses the Baptist hall. In Bengazi, the Anglican community worships in a Catholic church building. All these congregations in both Tripoli and Bengazi are composed of expatriates. The Union Church has been substantially weakened by the exodus of military personnel and oil company employees and the more recent expulsion of Egyptians (including Coptic Evangelicals) in 1976.

Beginning in 1972, the Children of God International, an outgrowth of the Jesus Movement in the USA, have visited Libya on over 12 missions and been received several times by the Muslim president Qaddafi, whom the groups regards as a latter-day prophet and who has given them permission to stage musical tours, has supported them financially and has even composed a religious song they perform.

Indigenous missions. There has been virtually no foreign missionary enterprise from the fledgling Libyan church.

CHURCH AND STATE

The provisional constitution of 1970 stipulates that 'Islam is the religion of the State' and that 'The State protects freedom of worship according to observed traditions' (Article 2). There are also a number of articles dealing with the foundations of the family and Article 8 with inheritance.

The Libyan revolution which came to power on 1 September 1969, has adopted as its national anthem Allah Akbar (Allah is Great) and confers upon Islam an ideological role, considering it as a radically different alternative to both capitalism and communism. It insists on total respect for all Islamic religious regulations and traditions. By a 1971 law, the Libyan government called for the submission of all existing laws to the Muslim Sharia (Holy Law), even if this required their abolition. Another 1971 law institutionalized zakat (giving of alms), one of the 5 ritual oblig-

Country summary. **Worlds A, B, C by ethnolinguistic peoples, cities, and major civil divisions in Libya.**

	PEOPLES							CITIES							CIVIL DIVISIONS						
World	Num	Pop 2000	C%	Christians	E%	U%	Unevangelized	Num	Pop 2000	C%	Christians	E%	U%	Unevangelized	Num	Pop 2000	C%	Christians	E%	U%	Unevangelized
A	26	4,949,640	0.26	12,905	42	58	2,889,505	6	3,559,105	3.41	121,258	47	53	1,877,989	13	5,604,723	3.04	170,352	46	54	3,019,597
B	5	556,604	14.16	78,819	77	23	129,892	0	0	0.00	0	0	0	0	0	0	0.00	0	0	0	0
C	9	98,476	79.84	78,627	100	0	199	0	0	0.00	0	0	0	0	0	0	0.00	0	0	0	0
Total	**40**	**5,604,720**	**3.04**	**170,351**	**46**	**54**	**3,019,596**	**6**	**3,559,105**	**3.41**	**121,258**	**47**	**53**	**1,877,989**	**13**	**5,604,723**	**3.04**	**170,352**	**46**	**54**	**3,019,597**

ations of the Muslim believers, under the form of an additional tax of 2.5% on land, flocks, money deposits, and other possessions. In a speech delivered at Zware on 15 April 1973, to mark the birthday of the Prophet Mohammed, president Qaddafi, a Muslim fundamentalist, called for the suspension of all existing laws and the implementation of the thoughts of the Prophet. The austerity of life of the chief of state and members of government, as well as that imposed on the entire population (such as the prohibition of alcohol), are due directly to the influence of the Sanusiya.

An agreement between the Holy See and the Libyan government was signed in Tripoli on 10 October 1970, whereby the Catholic Church renounced all its property including churches, convents, schools, and welfare projects. In return, the Libyan government conceded use of 2 churches for worship and also permission for 10 priests to reside in Libya (6 at Tripoli and 4 at Bengazi) to serve the spiritual needs of Catholics. These church buildings are used by other Christian communities as well. The Ministry of Unity and Foreign Affairs (Wizarat al-Wihda wa al-Kharijia) is the branch of government responsible for all matters relating to Christian churches.

By 1975, the government was once more recognizing the value of foreign missionaries. In 1975, 12 Catholic nurse sisters were invited in by government, and in 1976, 23 sisters and 2 priests arrived from Poland.

BROADCASTING AND MEDIA

Shortwave radio programs from FEBA (Seychelles) in Arabic and English can be received, as can programs from AWR (Slovakia), TWR (Monaco, Albania), and HCJB (Ecuador). Although there has been response, security issues make it very difficult to contact seekers and incorporate them into churches.

At least 166,000 have seen the 'Jesus' Film, mainly through radio/TV broadcasts. Satellite TV programs are received mainly in Arabic.

FUTURE TRENDS AND PROSPECTS

Growing Christian immigrant populations could increase Christians to 3.4% of Libya's population by 2025.

Without a breakthrough among native Libyans, Christianity is likely to remain below 5% well into the 21st century—an expression primarily of the expatriate community. Islam should remain above 90% throughout this period.

BIBLIOGRAPHY

Baal, Christ and Mohammed: religion and revolution in North Africa. J. K. Cooley. New York: Holt, Rinehart & Winston, 1965. 369p.

Children of Allah. A. N. Keith. Boston: Little, Brown, [1966]. 479p.

Die innere und äussere islamische Mission Libyens: historisch–politischer Kontext, innere Struktur, regionale Ausprägung am Beispiel Afrikas. H. Mattes. *Entwicklung und Frieden Wissenschaftliche Reihe,* 44. Mainz: Grünewald, 1986. 419p.

I Frati minori Lombardi in Libia: la missione di Tripoli (1908–1991). F. Sabbadin. *Quaderni della Provincia Lombarda dei Frati Minori,* no. 6. Milano: Edizioni Biblioteca Francescana, 1991. 184p.

Islam and the Third Universal Theory: the religious thought of Muhammar al–Qadhdhafi. M. Ayoub. London: Kegan Paul, 1991. 155p.

Islam in Qadhafi's Libya: religion and politics in a developing country. C. Kooij. *Papers on European and Mediterranean societies,* no. 13. Amsterdam: Antropologisch-Sociologisch Centrum, Universiteit van Amsterdam, 1980. 53p.

Island of the Blest: Islam in a Libyan oasis community. J. P. Mason. *Papers in international studies: Africa series,* no. 31. Athens, OH: Ohio University, Center for International Studies, 1977. 173p.

Jewish life in Muslim Libya: rivals and relatives. H. E. Goldberg. Chicago: University of Chicago Press, 1990. 197p.

Libya. R. I. Lawless. *World bibliographical series,* vol. 79. Oxford, UK: CLIO Press, 1987. 246p. (See especially, 'Religion,' p.79–81).

L'Islam dans les cinq pays du maghreb arabe. L. Pruvost. *Dossiers de la C.R.R.M,* no. 6. : Commission pour les Relations Religieuses avec les Musulmans, Conseil Pontifical pour le Dialogue Interreligieux, 1993. 18p.

Living among the Bedouin Arabs. A. R. Johnson. New York: Vantage Press, 1985. 99p.

The Bedouin of Cyrenaica: studies in personal and corporate power. E. L. Peters. Ed., J. Goody & E. Marx. *Cambridge studies in social and cultural anthropology,* no. 72. Cambridge, UK: Cambridge University Press, 1990. 329p.

'The social history and anthropology of the Arabized Berbers of the Augila oasis in the Libyan Sahara desert.' J. P. Mason. Ph.D. dissertation, Boston University, Boston, 1971. 555p.

Volksmacht und Islam: eine terminologie– und ideologieanalytische Untersuchung zum Politik– und Religionsverständnis bei Muhammar al–Qaddafi. E. Hager. *Islamkundliche Untersuchungen,* Bd. 107. Berlin: K. Schwarz, 1985. 281p.

Country Table 2. **Organized churches and denominations in Libya.**

Official name (bold type = church with over 10% of all affiliated) 1	Begun 2	Type 3	Counc 4	Congs 5	Adults 6	Affiliated 1970 7	Affiliated 1995 8	G% 9	*Names, notes, and other statistics* (see Codebook, Part 3) 10
Anglican Church (D Egypt)	c1900	A-Cen	aw.U.	1	83	380	150	-3.65	In Episcopal Ch in Jerusalem & M East. M=ICS(UK). Use of Union building. Expatriates 2x.
Baptist Church in Tripoli	1965	P-Bap	T....	1	50	500	100	-6.23	M=SBC(USA). Expatriate Americans with oil companies. 2f,17Y.
Bulgarian Orthodox Church	c1970	O-Bul	M....	2	1,000	–	1,700	34.65	Bulgarian migrant workers. Under P Sofia.
Catholic Church in Libya:	1642	R-Lat	P.SH.	10	22,700	3,650	40,000	10.05	Italians, French, Egyptians, Maltese,Croats. C=1+0+1. 1n 12x 12m 93w 154Yy
VA Benghazi (Bengasi)	1927	R-Lat	Pofm	9	5,700	350	10,000	14.35	Large-scale immigration of Croats. M=OFM,SDB. 0n 7x 7m 64w 29Yy
VA Derna (Cyrenaica)	1939	R-Lat	Pofm	0	0	200	0	-19.10	1969: 2,500 expatriates. Closed since 1972. 0n 0x 0m 0w 0Yy
VA Tripoli	1927	R-Lat	Pofm	1	17,000	3,000	30,000	9.65	Decline from 39,300 expatriates in 1969. M=OFM. 1n 5x 5m 29w 125Yy
PA Misurata	1939	R-Lat	Pofm	0	0	100	0	-16.82	1969: 1,146 expatriates. Closed since 1972. 0n 0x 0m 0w 0Yy
Church of Christ in Tripoli		I-Dis	x....	1	10	50	20	0.05	Among USA military, strong until US Wheelus air base closed.
Coptic Evangelical Church	c1968	P-Ref	RwaN.	5	1,800	2,500	3,600	1.47	Part of the growing Egyptian immigrant worker community.
Coptic Orthodox Ch: D North Africa	c1968	O-Cop	NwaN.	40	60,000	42,000	90,000	3.10	Under P Cairo. Egyptian workers. Requisitioned churches, 2 resident priests.
Greek Orth P Alexandria: D Carthage		O-Ara	Cw.N.	20	2,300	2,000	3,900	0.05	16 parishes (8 Russian Orthodox chapels). Greeks, Arabs. Archbishop, 6 priests.
Isolated radio churches	c1950	I-3rS	.....	200	5,000	620	10,000	11.76	Isolated radio believers, mostly students and youths. R=50,T=2200(GMU,ICI,RSB).
Jehovah's Witnesses	1950	m-Jeh	.....	1	44	34	55	1.94	*Watch Tower.*
Korean Presbyterian churches	c1970	I-Ref	.....	40	1,200	–	1,500	33.98	Korean immigrant workers.
Serbian Orthodox Church	c1970	O-Ser	C....	10	6,000	–	10,000	44.54	Serbian migrant workers. Under P Belgrade.
Seventh-day Adventist Church	c1950	P-Adv	x....	1	50	50	100	2.81	Formerly in SDA, North African Union. Hospital in Benghazi now commandeered. 37f.
Union Church of Tripoli		P-com	.....	1	100	700	150	0.05	Expatriate Americans, declining rapidly in membership. 1x.
Other Orthodox churches		O-	.....	10	1,300	3,000	2,000	0.05	Migrant workers from Armenian Apostolic Ch, Russian OC, Macedonian OC, Ukrainian OC.
Other Protestant denominations		P-	.....	5	200	100	400	0.05	NAM/AWM (1889; a few believers left), Tripoli Bible Ch, WEC.
Other independent bodies		I-	x....	3	30	2,000	50	0.05	Other bodies including Children of God (1972).
Totals				**351**	**101,867**	**57,584**	**163,725**		

Churches, members, growth, 1900-2025	*Congs*	*Adults*	*Affiliated*	*G%*	*Total denominations*	*6 Megablocs:* O	R	A	P	I	m
Total churches, members, and denominations (mid-1900)	30	4,500	10,020	2.53	2	0	1	1	0	0	0
Total churches, members, and denominations (mid-1970)	152	26,045	57,584	2.53	20	6	1	1	7	4	1
Total churches, members, and denominations (mid-1990)	300	88,200	141,700	4.61	35	14	1	1	10	8	1
Total churches, members, and denominations (mid-1995)	351	101,867	163,725	2.93	35	14	1	1	10	8	1
Total churches, members, and denominations (mid-2000)	370	106,000	170,352	0.80	35	14	1	1	10	8	1
Total churches, members, and denominations (mid-2025)	540	178,000	286,300	2.10	78	20	1	1	30	25	1

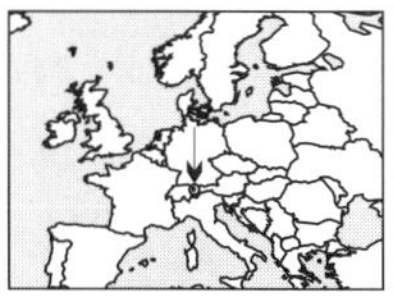

LIECHTENSTEIN

SECULAR DATA, AD 2000

STATE

Official name: Fürstentum Liechtenstein (The Principality of Liechtenstein).
Short name: Liechtenstein. **Adjective of nationality:** of Liechtenstein.
Flag: Blue and red: gold crown in blue stripe.
Area: 160 sq. km. (62 sq. mi.).
Government: Constitutional principality, created 1719 (1342 country of Vaduz).
Legislature: Diet, 25 members.
Official language: German (Deutsch).
Monetary unit: 1 Swiss franc (Sw F) = 100 centimes. **US$1=** Sw F 1.38.
Chief cities: VADUZ 5,473.
Political divisions: 2 provinces.

DEMOGRAPHY

Population: 33,000.
Population density: 205.2/sq. km. (529.7/sq. mi.).
Under 15 years: 6,000.
Growth rate p.a.: 0.40% (births 10.07, deaths 8.90).
Mortality: Infant, per 1,000: 5.5; **Maternal per 100,000:** 9.0.
Life expectancy: 79 (male 76, female 82).
Household size: 3.0. **Floor area per person, sq.m:** 45.0.
Major languages: German (Alemannish).
Urban dwellers: 22.66%. **Urban growth rate p.a.:** 3.2%.
Labor force: 49%.

ETHNOLINGUISTIC PEOPLES

65.0% Austrian; 20.7% German Swiss; 4.8% German (High German); 3.8% Italian; 0.1% Jewish.

ECONOMY

National income p.a. per person: US$33,005; **per family:** US$99,016.

EDUCATION

Adult literacy: 100% (male 100%, female 100%). **Schools:** 23.

Universities: 0. **School enrolment:** female/male: 100%/100%.

HEALTH
Access to health services: 95%. **Access to safe water:** 95%.
Hospitals: 1 (35 beds per 10,000). **Doctors:** 32.
Blind: 30. **Deaf:** 2,000. **Murder rate:** 5. **Lepers:** 50.

LITERATURE
New book titles p.a.: 33 (1,000 p.a. per million). **Periodicals:** 111.
Newspapers: 2 dailies.

COMMUNICATION (per 1,000 people)
Phones: 638 (45% mobile). **Radios:** 384. **TV sets:** 371.

Daily newspaper circulation: 581. **Computers:** 2.

HUMAN LIFE AND LIBERTY (optimum condition=100.0%)
HDI: 92.7. **HSI:** 85.0. **HFI:** 80.0. **EFL:** 55.0.

Country Table 1. **Religious adherents in Liechtenstein, AD 1900-2025.**

Year	*1900*		*1970*		*mid-1990*		*Annual change, 1990-2000*				*mid-1995*		*mid-2000*		*mid-2025*	
Name	*Adherents*	*%*	*Adherents*	*%*	*Adherents*	*%*	*Natural*	*Conversion*	*Total*	*Rate*	*Adherents*	*%*	*Adherents*	*%*	*Adherents*	*%*
Christians	**9,380**	**99.8**	**20,860**	**98.7**	**27,120**	**94.5**	**393**	**-52**	**341**	**1.19**	**28,860**	**93.7**	**30,530**	**93.0**	**37,040**	**89.7**
PROFESSION																
professing Christians	**9,380**	**99.8**	**20,860**	**98.7**	**27,120**	**94.5**	**393**	**-52**	**341**	**1.19**	**28,860**	**93.7**	**30,530**	**93.0**	**37,040**	**89.7**
AFFILIATION																
unaffiliated Christians	50	0.5	460	2.2	2,890	10.1	40	19	59	1.87	3,183	10.3	3,479	10.5	4,260	10.4
affiliated Christians	**9,330**	**99.3**	**20,400**	**96.6**	**24,230**	**84.4**	**353**	**-71**	**282**	**1.11**	**25,677**	**83.4**	**27,051**	**82.4**	**32,780**	**79.4**
Roman Catholics	9,150	97.3	19,000	89.9	22,000	76.7	322	-84	238	1.03	23,250	75.5	24,381	74.2	28,500	69.0
Protestants	180	1.9	1,385	6.6	2,140	7.5	30	8	38	1.65	2,313	7.5	2,520	7.7	3,800	9.2
Marginal Christians	0	0.0	15	0.1	70	0.2	1	3	4	4.62	85	0.3	110	0.3	360	0.9
Independents	0	0.0	0	0.0	20	0.1	0	2	2	7.18	29	0.1	40	0.1	120	0.3
Trans-megabloc groupings																
Evangelicals	50	0.5	40	0.2	110	0.4	2	0	2	1.29	116	0.4	125	0.4	200	0.5
Pentecostals/Charismatics	0	0.0	100	0.5	600	2.1	8	12	20	2.92	715	2.3	800	2.4	1,500	3.7
Great Commission Christians	**850**	**9.0**	**6,600**	**31.2**	**12,050**	**42.0**	**166**	**46**	**212**	**1.64**	**13,200**	**42.9**	**14,173**	**43.2**	**18,000**	**43.6**
Nonreligious	0	0.0	170	0.8	870	3.0	12	30	42	3.98	1,060	3.4	1,285	3.9	2,400	5.9
Muslims	0	0.0	0	0.0	600	2.1	8	20	28	3.89	760	2.5	879	2.7	1,500	3.7
Baha'is	0	0.0	40	0.2	70	0.2	1	3	4	4.33	80	0.3	107	0.3	300	0.7
Jews	20	0.2	30	0.1	40	0.1	1	-1	0	0.73	40	0.1	43	0.1	60	0.2
World A (unevangelized persons)	0	0.0	21	0.1	377	1.3	5	13	18	4.10	431	1.4	528	1.6	779	1.9
World B (evangelized non-Christians)	20	0.2	248	1.2	1,203	4.2	17	39	56	2.60	1,498	4.9	1,942	5.4	3,481	8.4
World C (Christians)	9,380	99.8	20,860	98.7	27,120	94.5	393	-52	341	1.19	28,860	93.7	30,530	93.0	37,040	89.7
Country's population	**9,400**	**100.0**	**21,129**	**100.0**	**28,700**	**100.0**	**415**	**0**	**415**	**1.30**	**30,790**	**100.0**	**32,800**	**100.0**	**41,300**	**100.0**

COLUMNS, ROWS.
For meanings and definitions, see Codebook (Part 3). Note that, by definition, total 'Christians' = professing + crypto-Christians, which also = affiliated + unaffiliated Christians, and also = Great Commission Christians + latent Christians. Percentages may not always total exactly, due to rounding.

CENSUSES.
1.XII.**1960**: 92.3% Roman Catholics, 6.8% Protestants, 0.7% nonreligious, 0.2% Jews. 1.XII.**1970**: 90.1% Roman Catholics, 8.8% Protestants, 0.9% others (nonreligious, Baha'is), 0.1% Jews (also 4 Old Catholics). **1990:** 84.9% Roman Catholics, 9.2% Protestants, 2.7% others (nonreligious, Baha'is), 2.4% Muslims, 0.75% Independents, 0.05% Jews (also 4 Old Catholics).

NOTES ON RELIGIONS
MUSLIMS. North African immigrant workers since 1980.

Great Commission Instrument Panel: status of Liechtenstein (for explanation see start of Part 4)

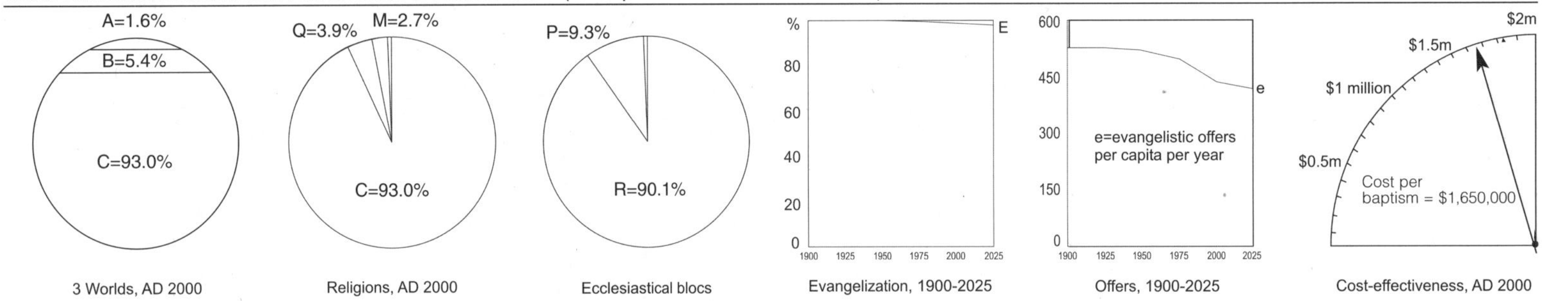

Country status. Liechtenstein is a small landlocked country in the Alps between Switzerland and Austria. It has a strong economy based on banking, tourism, and the manufacture of specialized machinery.

HUMAN LIFE AND LIBERTY

Human rights and freedoms. The principality of Liechtenstein is a constitutional monarchy with a historic record of maintaining and fostering human rights. Because of its small population, the principality has not faced any major social or political problems. Although Roman Catholicism is the official religion, there is full religious freedom.

NON-CHRISTIAN RELIGIONS

With increasing mobility and movement of migrant labor, numbers of non-Christians, including Baha'is and Jews, reside in the country.

Katholische Kirche. Catholic nun works the fields with 2 peasant women.

CHRISTIANITY

CATHOLIC CHURCH. As Liechtensteinis surrounded on 3 sides by Switzerland, the development of the Catholic Church in the principality corresponds to that in Switzerland, the earliest Christian contacts taking place during the Roman occupation in the first centuries of the Christian era. At the present time the principality forms a single deanery within the diocese of Church in Switzerland. In 1990 it consisted of 13 parishes, with 31 priests (10 religious), one Italian mission and several sisters.

The Holy See has diplomatic relations with Liechtenstein and in AD 2000 is represented to government and the Catholic hierarchy by a nuncio residing in Bern.

PROTESTANT CHURCHES. The major Protestant body is the interdenominational Evangelical Church in the Principality of Liechtenstein, which consists of one parish with about 1,500 active members. It was formed in 1881 by skilled textile workers immigrating from neighboring countries, most being members of Lutheran of Reformed churches. Following World War II, there was an influx of trained artisans and university graduates to meet the needs of industrial expansion, and the parish now consists of young families occupying relatively high positions in the country. In 1954 the Evangelical Church entered into a patronage agreement (Patronatsvertrag) with the Protestant Church of the Canton of St Gallen in Switzerland. This agreement assures support and help, especially in pastoral appointments, but leaves the church free to arrange its own affairs in conformity with its interdenominational character. A separate Lutheran congregation was formed in 1954 and belongs to the Association of Evangelical Lutheran Churches in Switzerland and the Principality of Liechtenstein, a body of 13,400 Lutherans based in Zurich. There also is a small Seventh-day Adventist community.

Indigenous missions. Only a few Christians from Liechtenstein have served overseas as missionaries, some in Africa, but most in other European countries.

CHURCH AND STATE

According to the constitution of 1921, 'The Roman Catholic Church is the State church (Landeskirche) and as such enjoys the full protection of the State'; nevertheless, freedom of religion and of conscience is guaranteed to all (Article 37). Article 39 states: 'The exercise of national and political rights is independent of one's religious confession; national duties shall not be prejudiced on account of an individual's religious profession'. Also safeguarded are the rights to ownership and utilization of property by religious communities and groups, for worship, education or charitable activity (Article 38). The state guarantees to protect the 'religious and moral interests' of the populace (Article 14); and in collaboration with family, school, and church, it assumes responsibility for insuring to the younger generation a moral and religious education (Article 15). Religious education is therefore placed under state supervision (Article 16).

In conformity with the law of 1 August 1870 concerning the administration of church property in parishes, such property is administered by a church council composed of the parish priest, members designated by the community council and one member elected by the local citizens.

Katholische Kirche. Parish church (center), under Vaduz Castle (left).

Country summary. **Worlds A, B, C by ethnolinguistic peoples, cities, and major civil divisions in Liechtenstein.**

	PEOPLES							CITIES							CIVIL DIVISIONS						
World	Num	Pop 2000	C%	Christians	E%	U%	Unevangelized	Num	Pop 2000	C%	Christians	E%	U%	Unevangelized	Num	Pop 2000	C%	Christians	E%	U%	Unevangelized
A	1	43	0.00	0	49	51	22	0	0	0.00	0	0	0	0	0	0	0.00	0	0	0	0
B	1	1,757	40.30	708	73	27	469	0	0	0.00	0	0	0	0	0	0	0.00	0	0	0	0
C	4	31,043	84.86	26,343	100	0	46	1	5,473	81.00	4,433	97	3	164	2	32,843	82.36	27,051	98	2	538
Total	**6**	**32,843**	**82.36**	**27,051**	**98**	**2**	**537**	**1**	**5,473**	**81.00**	**4,433**	**97**	**3**	**164**	**2**	**32,843**	**82.36**	**27,051**	**98**	**2**	**538**

BROADCASTING AND MEDIA

Shortwave radio programs in European languages can be received from AWR (Slovakia), TWR (Monaco, Albania), and HCJB (Ecuador). Satellite TV and radio programs are received in English, Arabic, German and Italian.

FUTURE TRENDS AND PROSPECTS

The nonreligious, 0.8% of the population in 1970, are expected to grow to 6% by 2025 accompanied by a decline in the Christian percentage to 90% in the same period.

Secularization will potentially cause a steady decline in the Christian percentage, perhaps dropping well under 80% after AD 2050.

BIBLIOGRAPHY

Brauchtum in Liechtenstein. A. P. Goop. Vaduz: Liechtensteinische Trachtenvereinigung, 1986. 415p.

In Christo. Benderen: Dekanat Liechtenstein, 1936–. (Semimonthly).

Liechtenstein. R. A. Meier. *World bibliographical series*, vol. 159. Oxford, UK: CLIO Press, 1993. 146p. (See especially 'The Catholic church,' p.38–9).

Staat und Kirche im Fürstentum Liechtenstein. H. Wille. *Freiburger Veröffenlichungen aus dem Gebiete von Kirche und Staat*, vol. 15. Freiburg, Switzerland: University of Freiburg, 1972. 503p.

'Zur Kirchen– und Pfarreigeschichte,' W. Müller, in *Das Fürstentum Liechtenstein: Ein landeskundliches Portrait*, p.33–61. W. Müller (ed). *Veröffentlichung des Alemannischen Instituts Freiburg i. Br.*, no. 50. Bühl/Baden, Germany: Konkordia, 1981.

Country Table 2. **Organized churches and denominations in Liechtenstein.**

Official name (bold type = church *with over 10% of all affiliated)* 1	*Begun* 2	*Type* 3	*Counc* 4	*Congs* 5	*Adults* 6	*Affiliated 1970* 7	*Affiliated 1995* 8	*G%* 9	*Names, notes, and other statistics* (see Codebook, Part 3) 10
Evangelische Kirche im Furstentum L	1881	P-Uni	Rwc..	2	900	1,100	1,500	1.25	*EKFL. Ev Ch in Liechtenstein.* Linked to Protestant Ch of St Gallen. Many Austrians. 1x.
Evangelische Gemeinschaft	c1985	I-3cW	.....	1	20	–	29	10.00	*Evangelical Fellowship.* Informal gathering of Evangelicals from several denominations.
Evangelisch-Lutherische Kirche	1954	P-Lut	l....	2	304	185	400	3.13	*AELCSL. Assoc of Ev Lutheran Chs in Switzerland & L.* HQ Zurich. 1x,W=20T,3Yy.
Katholische Kirche (D Chur)	c 450	R-Lat	b.B..	13	15,000	19,000	23,250	0.81	*Catholic Ch..* One deanery in D Chur (Switz), one Italian mission. (1990). , 21n, 13x, 18m, 84w, 280Yy
Siebenten-Tags-Adventisten		P-Adv	x....	1	45	100	113	0.05	*SDA. Seventh-day Adventists*, part of German Swiss Conference, Swiss Union Conference.
Zeugen Jehovas	c1960	m-Jeh	.....	1	51	15	85	7.18	*Jehovah's Witnesses. Watch Tower.*
Other Protestant churches	c1980	P-	.....	15	200	–	300	6.67	Total about 10 bodies.
Totals				**35**	**16,520**	**20,400**	**25,677**		

Churches, members, growth, 1900-2025	*Congs*	*Adults*	*Affiliated*	*G%*	*Total denominations*	*6 Megablocs:* O	R	A	P	I	m
Total churches, members, and denominations (mid-1900)	6	7,100	9,330	1.12	2	0	1	0	1	0	0
Total churches, members, and denominations (mid-1970)	16	15,489	20,400	1.12	5	0	1	0	3	0	1
Total churches, members, and denominations (mid-1990)	30	15,600	24,230	0.86	16	0	1	0	13	1	1
Total churches, members, and denominations (mid-1995)	35	16,520	25,677	1.17	16	0	1	0	13	1	1
Total churches, members, and denominations (mid-2000)	40	17,400	27,051	1.05	16	0	1	0	13	1	1
Total churches, members, and denominations (mid-2025)	50	21,100	32,780	0.77	39	0	1	0	20	15	3

LITHUANIA

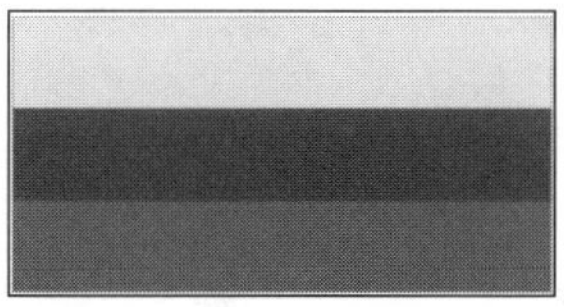

SECULAR DATA, AD 2000

STATE

Official name: Lietuvos Respublika (The Republic of Lithuania).
Short name: Lithuania. **Adjective of nationality:** Lithuanian.
Flag: Orange, green, and red stripes.
Area: 65,301 sq. km. (25,213 sq. mi.).
Government: Unitary multiparty republic with a single legislative body, since 1991 (1795 Russian empire, 1939 Soviet rule).
Legislature: The Seimas, 141 members.
Official language: Lithuanian.
Monetary unit: 1 litas (plural litai) = 100 centai. **US$1=** 4.00 litai.
Chief cities: VILNIUS (Wilno) 581,359; Kaunas (Kovno) 422,534; Klaipeda (Memel) 203,775; Siauliai (Shaulyay) 144,840; Panavezys (Panevezhis) 125,861.
Political divisions: 10 provinces.
Armed forces: 5,300.

DEMOGRAPHY

Population: 3,670,000.
Population density: 56.2/sq. km. (145.5/sq. mi.).
Under 15 years: 705,000.
Growth rate p.a.: -0.32% (births 9.82, deaths 11.89).
Mortality: Infant, per 1,000: 14.1; **Maternal per 100,000:** 36.0.
Life expectancy: 71 (male 66, female 76).
Household size: 3.2. **Floor area per person, sq.m:** 16.2.
Major languages: Lithuanian, Russian, Polish, Ukrainian, Belorussian.
Urban dwellers: 74.67%. **Urban growth rate p.a.:** 0.3%.
Labor force: 49%.

ETHNOLINGUISTIC PEOPLES

75.8% Lithuanian; 9.3% Russian; 7.0% Polish (Pole); 3.8% Samogit (Lithuanian); 1.7% Byelorussian.

ECONOMY

National income p.a. per person: US$1,900; **per family:** US$6,080.

EDUCATION

Adult literacy: 99% (male 99%, female 99%). **Schools:** 2,485.
Universities: 14. **School enrolment:** female/male: 88%/86%.

HEALTH

Access to health services: 90%. **Access to safe water:** 90%.
Hospitals: 198 (117 beds per 10,000). **Doctors:** 14,670.
Blind: 3,000. **Deaf:** 221,400. **Murder rate:** 6.
Lepers: 100.

LITERATURE

New book titles p.a.: 4,000 (1,090 p.a. per million). **Periodicals:** 332.
Newspapers: 16 dailies.

COMMUNICATION (per 1,000 people)

Phones: 254 (19% mobile). **Radios:** 381. **TV sets:** 364.
Daily newspaper circulation: 136. **Computers:** 40.

REFUGEES

Alien refugees from other countries: 400.

HUMAN LIFE AND LIBERTY (optimum condition=100.0%)

HDI: 76.2. **HSI:** 65.0. **HFI:** 55.0. **EFL:** 30.0.

Country status. Lithuania, a former republic of the Soviet Union, is a Baltic country between Latvia and Poland in northern Europe. It has a diversified economy with a strong agricultural base (meat, dairy, and timber) as well as manufacturing (steel, ships, paper, and textiles).

HUMAN LIFE AND LIBERTY

Human rights and freedoms. These were ignored throughout the Soviet period. Since the collapse of Communism, full rights have been restored.

NON-CHRISTIAN RELIGIONS

Islam. The small Muslim community in Lithuania, descended from Tatars who settled there in the fourteenth century, is very ignorant of their religion, having been suppressed for 50 years under the Communist regime. Some selected passages from the Quran have recently been published in Lithuanian.

CHRISTIANITY

Around the fifth century, the pagan tribes of the region that is now Lithuania formed a loose confederation. But it was not until the early thirteenth century, under the threat of invasion from the German Teutonic Knights, that the groups coalesced into an effective political union. Its leader Mendog was baptized in 1251 and 2 years later was named king by the pope. His conversion seemed motivated by strategic concerns more than spiritual ones, however, and he repudiated Christianity in 1263.

CATHOLIC CHURCH. Traditionally, Lithuania has been a Roman Catholic country. In the nineteenth century Roman Catholic clerics feared that the rise of a Lithuanian national movement directed against Polish cultural dominance would also undermine the position of the Catholic Church. In the period following World War I, Lithuanian politics continued to be characterized by major conflicts between the Catholic Church and anticlerical nationalists. However, the annexation of the country by the Soviet Union transformed the church into a key element of the national resistance movement during the 1940s. Although severely affected by Soviet repression, the Roman Catholic Church remains the dominant and the most influential denomination. Lithuania's Roman Catholic Church consisted in 1992 of 2 archdioceses (Vilnius and Kaunas) and 4 dioceses (Kaisiadorys, Panevezys, Vilkaviskis, and Telsiai). The church is presided over by cardinal Vincentas Sladkevicius in Kaunas, who was held in internal exile by the Soviets for 30 years. The church has 688 parishes, 2 theological seminaries, and several convents and monasteries.

The Holy See has diplomatic relations with Lithuania and in AD 2000 is represented to government and the Catholic hierarchy by a nuncio residing in Vilnius.

OTHER CHURCHES. Among the small number of other traditions, the largest denominations are the Russian Orthodox, Lutherans, and Old Believers.

Renewal movements. In the 1990s the Pentecostal/Charismatic Renewal continued to spread rapidly across most older churches, and numbered over 51,300 adherents (of whom 6% were Pentecostals, 70% Charismatics and 24% Independents).

Indigenous missions. There have been very few Lithuanian foreign missionaries but new opportunities have arisen in the wake of the collapse of Communism.

Country Table 1. Religious adherents in Lithuania, AD 1900-2025.

Year	1900		1970		mid-1990		Annual change, 1990-2000				mid-1995		mid-2000		mid-2025	
Name	Adherents	%	Adherents	%	Adherents	%	Natural	Conversion	Total	Rate	Adherents	%	Adherents	%	Adherents	%
Christians	**2,053,500**	**99.7**	**2,212,800**	**70.3**	**3,180,000**	**85.1**	**-5,675**	**9,121**	**3,394**	**0.11**	**3,223,800**	**86.5**	**3,213,940**	**87.6**	**3,158,000**	**92.9**
PROFESSION																
crypto-Christians	0	0.0	400,000	12.7	0	0.0	0	0	0	0.00	0	0.0	0	0.0	0	0.0
professing Christians	**2,053,500**	**99.7**	**1,812,800**	**57.6**	**3,180,000**	**85.1**	**-5,675**	**9,121**	**3,394**	**0.11**	**3,223,800**	**86.5**	**3,213,940**	**87.6**	**3,158,000**	**92.9**
AFFILIATION																
unaffiliated Christians	120,000	5.8	0	0.0	600	0.0	-1	-5	-6	-0.99	600	0.0	543	0.0	1,000	0.0
affiliated Christians	**1,933,500**	**93.9**	**2,212,800**	**70.3**	**3,179,400**	**85.1**	**-5,674**	**9,126**	**3,400**	**0.11**	**3,223,200**	**86.5**	**3,213,397**	**87.6**	**3,157,000**	**92.9**
Roman Catholics	1,853,500	90.0	2,060,000	65.5	3,100,000	83.0	-5,532	6,084	500	0.02	3,119,400	83.7	3,105,000	84.6	3,000,000	88.3
Orthodox	70,000	3.4	100,000	3.2	112,000	3.0	-201	401	200	0.18	112,000	3.0	114,000	3.1	120,000	3.5
Protestants	10,000	0.5	36,500	1.2	43,300	1.2	-78	148	70	0.16	43,400	1.2	44,000	1.2	80,000	2.4
Independents	0	0.0	16,000	0.5	28,000	0.8	-50	450	400	1.34	31,105	0.8	32,000	0.9	38,000	1.1
Marginal Christians	0	0.0	300	0.0	3,000	0.1	-5	135	130	3.67	3,500	0.1	4,300	0.1	9,000	0.3
doubly-affiliated	0	0.0	0	0.0	-106,900	-2.9	192	1,908	2,100	-2.16	-86,205	-2.3	-85,903	-2.3	-90,000	-2.7
Trans-megabloc groupings																
Evangelicals	9,000	0.4	7,400	0.2	8,800	0.2	-16	26	10	0.11	8,790	0.2	8,900	0.2	10,000	0.3
Pentecostals/Charismatics	0	0.0	1,500	0.1	44,800	1.2	-80	730	650	1.36	50,026	1.3	51,300	1.4	65,000	1.9
Great Commission Christians	**62,000**	**3.0**	**252,000**	**8.0**	**435,000**	**11.6**	**-780**	**273**	**-507**	**-0.12**	**436,000**	**11.7**	**429,935**	**11.7**	**500,000**	**14.7**
Nonreligious	1,000	0.1	605,200	19.2	487,380	13.0	-874	-7,721	-8,595	-1.92	444,300	11.9	401,435	10.9	210,600	6.2
Atheists	500	0.0	314,000	10.0	55,000	1.5	-99	-1,400	-1,499	-3.13	43,000	1.2	40,013	1.1	15,000	0.4
Muslims	0	0.0	6,000	0.2	7,500	0.2	-13	72	59	0.76	8,000	0.2	8,093	0.2	10,000	0.3
Jews	5,000	0.2	9,000	0.3	7,000	0.2	-13	-22	-35	-0.51	6,770	0.2	6,653	0.2	5,000	0.2
Ethnoreligionists	0	0.0	0	0.0	120	0.0	0	2	2	1.26	130	0.0	136	0.0	400	0.0
World A (unevangelized persons)	0	0.0	160,507	5.1	18,685	0.5	-36	-502	-538	-3.08	18,627	0.5	14,680	0.4	13,596	0.4
World B (evangelized non-Christians)	6,500	0.3	773,892	24.6	538,315	14.4	-963	-8,567	-9,530	-1.97	483,167	13.0	441,380	12.0	227,404	6.7
World C (Christians)	2,053,500	99.7	2,212,800	70.3	3,180,000	85.1	-5,675	9,121	3,394	0.11	3,223,800	86.5	3,213,940	87.6	3,158,000	92.9
Country's population	**2,060,000**	**100.0**	**3,147,200**	**100.0**	**3,737,000**	**100.0**	**-6,674**	**0**	**-6,674**	**-0.18**	**3,725,595**	**100.0**	**3,670,000**	**100.0**	**3,399,000**	**100.0**

COLUMNS, ROWS
For meanings and definitions, see Codebook (Part 3). Note that, by definition, total 'Christians' = professing + crypto-Christians, which also = affiliated + unaffiliated Christians, and also = Great Commission Christians + latent Christians. Percentages may not always total exactly, due to rounding.

NOTES ON RELIGIONS
ATHEISTS. Sharp decline with collapse of Communism (1989) and the dissolution of the USSR.
CRYPTO-CHRISTIANS. Only from 1940-1990.
MUSLIMS. Mainly Tatars, Uzbeks, and Azerbaijanis.

Great Commission Instrument Panel: status of Lithuania (for explanation see start of Part 4)

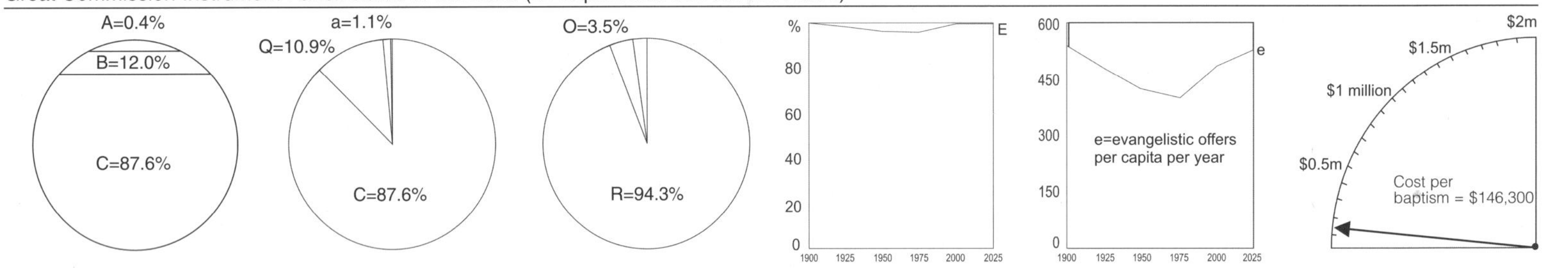

3 Worlds, AD 2000 | Religions, AD 2000 | Ecclesiastical blocs | Evangelization, 1900-2025 | Offers, 1900-2025 | Cost-effectiveness, AD 2000

Country summary. Worlds A, B, C by ethnolinguistic peoples, cities, and major civil divisions in Lithuania.

	PEOPLES							CITIES							CIVIL DIVISIONS						
World	Num	Pop 2000	C%	Christians	E%	U%	Unevangelized	Num	Pop 2000	C%	Christians	E%	U%	Unevangelized	Num	Pop 2000	C%	Christians	E%	U%	Unevangelized
A	7	17,047	0.46	79	41	59	9,983	0	0	0.00	0	0	0	0	0	0	0.00	0	0	0	0
B	3	1,763	30.18	532	78	22	391	0	0	0.00	0	0	0	0	0	0	0.00	0	0	0	0
C	14	3,651,458	87.99	3,212,787	100	0	4,248	6	1,550,241	85.66	1,327,926	100	0	6,743	10	3,670,268	87.55	3,213,397	100	0	14,619
Total	**24**	**3,670,268**	**87.55**	**3,213,398**	**100**	**0**	**14,622**	**6**	**1,550,241**	**85.66**	**1,327,926**	**100**	**0**	**6,743**	**10**	**3,670,268**	**87.55**	**3,213,397**	**100**	**0**	**14,619**

CHURCH AND STATE

Relations have swung full circle from the pre-1989 stifling control under the Soviet regime to a post-1990 recognition of full rights for all religions and the Catholic Church in particular.

Catholic Church in Lithuania. John Paul II visits Hill of Crosses, 1994.

BROADCASTING AND MEDIA

Shortwave radio programs in European languages can be received from AWR (Slovakia), KNLS, TWR (Monaco, Albania), and HCJB (Ecuador). IBRA-produced programs can be heard on local radio stations. Lithuania is a member of UNDA.

Over 3 million have seen the 'Jesus' Film, mainly through cinematic showings and television broadcasts. Satellite TV programs are received mainly in Arabic.

FUTURE TRENDS AND PROSPECTS

The nonreligious and atheists, representing over 50% of the population in 1970, are expected to decline dramatically through AD 2025 (to just over 6%). Christianity will be the main recipient of these losses growing to over 90% by AD 2025.

Before AD 2050 it is probable that atheists and the nonreligious will decline to under 5%. Christianity will likely claim most of the remaining 95%.

Scriptures in Lithuania and other languages sell briskly at Conference on Family and Responsibility, Vilnius.

BIBLIOGRAPHY

A Lithuanian bibliography: a check–list of books and articles held by the major libraries of Canada and the United States. A. Kantautas & F. Kantautas. Edmonton: University of Alberta Press, 1975. 725p.
Atlaidai: Lithuanian pilgrimages. R. Pozerskis, A. Kezys & L. Skeiviene. Chicago: Loyola University Press, 1990. 208p.
'Baltic Protestantism,' W. Kahle, *Religion in Communist lands,* 7, 4 (Winter 1979), 220–25. (Deals with Estonia, Latvia, and Lithuania).
Catholic Church in Lithuania 1917–1940: collection of documents. V. Kazakevicius (ed). Vilnius: Mintis Publishers, 1986. 257p.
'Catholicism and nationalism in Lithuania,' K. K. Girnius, in *Religion and nationalism in Soviet and East European politics,* p.109–137. P. Ramet (ed). 2nd ed. Durham, NC: Duke University Press, 1989.
Catholics in Soviet–occupied Lithuania: faith under persecution. El Toro, CA: Aid to the Church in Need, 1981. 120p.
Die katholische Kirche in Litauen. G. Simon. Cologne: Bundesinstitut für Ostwissenschaftliche und Internationale Studien, 1982. 20p. (Summary in English).
Germanische und Baltische Religion. A. V. Strom & H. Biezais. *Die Religionen der Menschheit.* Stuttgart: Verlag W. Kohlhammer, 1975. 391p.
Gorbachev, glasnost and the gospel. M. A. Bourdeaux. London: Hodder & Stoughton, 1990. 226p.
La Cristianizzazione della Lituania: atti del colloquio internazionale di storia ecclesiastica in occasione del VI centenario della Lituania cristiana (1387–1987), Roma, 24–26 giugno 1987. P. Rabikauskas (ed). Vatican City: Libreria Editrice Vaticana, 1989. 307p.
Land of crosses: the struggle for religious freedom in Lithuania, 1939–1978. M. Bourdeaux. Devon, UK: Augustine Publishing Company, 1979. 359p.
Lithuania and Lithuanians: a selected bibliography. J. Balys. New York: Praeger for the Lithuanian Research Institute, 1961.
Lituanica collections in European research libraries: a bibliography. A. Sesplaukis. Chicago: Lithuanian Research & Study Centre, 1986. 215p.

Litwa: 600–lecie chrzescijanstwa, 1387–1987. M. Kaluski. London: Veritas, 1987. 108p.
Religion in Lithuania. J. Rimaitis. [Vilnius: Gintaras, 1971]. 33p.
The Baltic States: Estonia, Latvia, Lithuania. I. A. Smith & M. V. Grunts. World bibliographical series, vol. 161. Oxford, UK: CLIO Press, 1993.
The Catholic Church, dissent and nationality in Soviet Lithuania. V. S. Vardys. *East European Monographs*, no. 43. London: E. J. Brill, 1978. 336p.
The chronicle of the Catholic Church in Lithuania: underground journal of human rights violations. N. Grazulis (trans and ed). Chicago: Loyala University Press, 1981–.
The establishment of socialism in Lithuania and the Catholic Church. J. Aniμcas. Vilnius: Mintis, 1975. 126p.
The Reformation in Lithuania: religious fluctuations in the sixteenth century. A. Musteikis. *East European monographs*, no. 246. Boulder, CO: East European Monographs, 1988.
The resistance of the Catholic Church in Lithuania against religious persecution. P. Dauknys. Rome: Pontificia Studiorum Universitas A.S. Thoma Aq. in Urbe, 1984. 195p.
The sword and the cross: a history of the Church in Lithuania. S. Suziedelis. Huntington, IN: Our Sunday Visitor, Inc., 1988. 264p.

Country Table 2. **Organized churches and denominations in Lithuania.**

Official name (bold type = church with over 10% of all affiliated) 1	*Begun* 2	*Type* 3	*Counc* 4	*Congs* 5	*Adults* 6	*Affiliated 1970* 7	*Affiliated 1995* 8	*G%* 9	*Names, notes, and other statistics* (see Codebook, Part 3) 10
Baptist Union of Lithuania		P-Bap	T....	6	335	1,200	1,500	0.05	*Union of Ev Christians-Baptists of L.* Formerly part of AUCECB (Moscow).
Bible Way	1974	I-3pW	.....	4	400	–	1,000	4.76	Independent pentecostals in Vilnius. Persecuted by Catholic Church.
Catholic Church in Lithuania:		R-Lat	B....	715	2,061,000	2,060,000	3,119,400	0.05	Strong national church, vicious persecution till 1991. 625n 101x 203m 1228w 51349Yy
M Kaunas (Samogit)	1417	R-Lat	Bs	135	412,000	560,000	750,000	1.18	1971-2, massive protests by laity and priests. 139n 17x 32m 418w 13786Yy
D Telsiai (& Klaipeda)	1926	R-Lat	Bs	154	467,000	470,000	680,000	1.49	Port (formerly Memel). 1970, 53% Catholic. 114n 14x 17m 65w 11733Yy
D Vilkaviskis	1926	R-Lat	Bs	123	279,000	350,000	406,000	0.60	1970, opposed by vast network of atheistic centers. 101n 18x 20m 65w 5967Yy
M Vilnius	1388	R-Lat	Bs	112	412,000	50,000	600,000	10.45	1963, Communist attempt to secularize rites. 84n 24x 25m 269w 8615Yy
D Kaisiadorys	1926	R-Lat	Bs	68	155,000	220,000	228,400	0.15	Virtually all children baptized, attendance very high. 63n 16w 3148Yy
D Panevezys	1926	R-Lat	Bs	123	336,000	410,000	455,000	0.42	In 1944, area was 93% Catholic. 124n 28x 109m 411w 8100Yy
Ev Lutheran Ch of Lithuania		P-Lut	.....	33	12,800	25,000	32,000	0.05	*ELCL.* Germans, Lithuanians, Latvians.
Ev Reformed Church in Lithuania	1557	P-Ref	.....	11	2,100	10,000	3,500	-4.11	*ERCL.* Lithuanians, Latvians. Severe attrition by persecution, emigration. M=PCUSA.
Jehovah's Witnesses	c1940	m-Jeh	x....	10	420	300	3,500	10.33	(1995) 345Y.
New Apostolic Church	c1990	I-3aX	x....	5	2,000	–	4,705	20.00	*Neuapostolische Kirche.* M=NAK(HQ Zurich, Switzerland).
Old Ritualist Church	c1700	I-OBe	x....	51	10,200	16,000	20,400	0.98	*Old Believers (Raskolniki).* Byelorussians, Russians.
Pentecostal Churches in Lithuania	1906	P-Pe2	.....	36	1,200	1,000	3,000	0.05	1906 first church in Birzai, many by 1910. M=AoG.
Russian Orthodox Ch: D Vilnius & L	1321	O-Rus	M....	45	71,500	100,000	110,000	0.38	Under P Moscow. Largely Russians, Byelorussians.
Seventh-day Adventist Church		P-Adv	x....	2	200	–	400	0.05	M=SDA(USA).
Word of Life	c1990	I-3cW	x....	10	500	–	1,000	20.00	Charismatic body from M=Word of Life (Sweden). Very rapid growth since 1991.
Other independent churches	c1980	I-	.....	20	3,000	–	4,000	6.67	Total 10, including CBI,BBFI,CCECB,CWE,IPKH,ROCOR.
Other Protestant churches	c1985	P-	.....	20	2,000	–	3,000	10.00	Total 10, including Estonians (ELCE, MCE), CB,UMC,MCC.
Other Orthodox churches	c1975	O-	.....	5	1,000	–	2,000	5.00	Total 4, including Moldavian Orthodox Ch, also Georgian Orthodox Ch,UAOC.
Doubly-affiliated		2-aff			-56,500	0	-86,205		Evangelicals and Pentecostals who are also baptized Roman Catholics.
Totals				**943**	**2,113,020**	**2,212,800**	**3,223,200**		

Churches, members, growth, 1900-2025	*Congs*	*Adults*	*Affiliated*	*G%*	*Total denominations*	*6 Megablocs:* O	R	A	P	I	m
Total churches, members, and denominations (mid-1900)	500	1,319,000	1,933,500	0.19	4	1	1	0	1	1	0
Total churches, members, and denominations (mid-1970)	654	1,509,800	2,212,800	0.19	8	1	1	0	4	1	1
Total churches, members, and denominations (mid-1990)	800	2,084,000	3,179,400	1.83	24	2	1	0	15	5	1
Total churches, members, and denominations (mid-1995)	943	2,113,020	3,223,200	0.27	27	5	1	0	15	5	1
Total churches, members, and denominations (mid-2000)	910	2,107,000	3,213,397	-0.06	28	6	1	0	15	5	1
Total churches, members, and denominations (mid-2025)	900	2,070,000	3,157,000	-0.07	62	10	1	0	30	20	1

NOTES ON TABLE ABOVE
NATIONAL COUNCILS (Column 4, 5th letter).
K = National Council of Churches in Lithuania (NCCL).
R = Conferentia Episcopalis Lituaniae (CEL, Episcopal Conference of Lithuania).

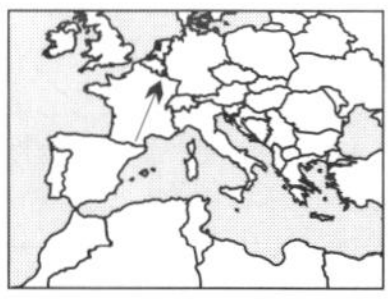

LUXEMBOURG

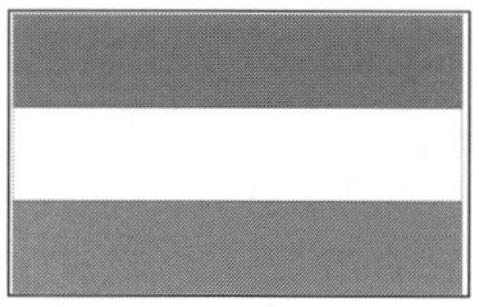

SECULAR DATA, AD 2000

STATE
Official name: Grousherzogtum Lëtzebuerg/Le Grand-Duché de Luxembourg (The Grand Duchy of Luxembourg).
Short name: Luxembourg. **Adjective of nationality:** of Luxembourg.
Flag: Red, white, and light blue stripes.
Area: 2,586 sq. km. (999 sq. mi.).
Government: Parliamentary constitutional grand duchy, since 1839 (1354 duchy, 1839 autonomy).
Legislature: Council of State, 21 members; Chamber of Deputies, 60 members.
Official language: Luxemburgish (Lezebuurjes).
Monetary unit: 1 Luxembourg franc (Lux F) = 100 centimes. **US$1=** Lux F 34.47.
Chief cities: LUXEMBOURG-Ville 150,040; Esch-sur-Alzette 91,568.
Political divisions: 3 provinces.
Armed forces: 800.

DEMOGRAPHY
Population: 431,000.
Population density: 166.5/sq. km. (431.0/sq. mi.).
Under 15 years: 78,000.
Growth rate p.a.: 0.76% (births 11.54, deaths 9.41).
Mortality: Infant, per 1,000: 6.6; **Maternal per 100,000:** 8.0.
Life expectancy: 77 (male 74, female 81).
Household size: 2.8. **Floor area per person, sq.m:** 40.0.
Major languages: Luxemburgish, French, Italian, German, English.
Urban dwellers: 91.06%. **Urban growth rate p.a.:** 1.1%.
Labor force: 44%.

ETHNOLINGUISTIC PEOPLES
67.9% Luxemburger; 12.6% Portuguese; 7.3% Italian; 2.4% German (High German); 2.1% French.

ECONOMY
National income p.a. per person: US$41,210; **per family:** US$115,390.

EDUCATION
Adult literacy: 100% (male 100%, female 100%). **Schools:** 100.
Universities: 1. **School enrolment:** female/male: 80%/82%.

HEALTH
Access to health services: 95%. **Access to safe water:** 95%.
Hospitals: 34 (115 beds per 10,000). **Doctors:** 848.
Blind: 204. **Deaf:** 25,800. **Murder rate:** 13. **Lepers:** 50.

LITERATURE
New book titles p.a.: 750 (1,750 p.a. per million). **Periodicals:** 711.
Newspapers: 5 dailies.

COMMUNICATION (per 1,000 people)
Phones: 550 (24% mobile). **Radios:** 586. **TV sets:** 593.
Daily newspaper circulation: 384. **Computers:** 250.

HUMAN LIFE AND LIBERTY (optimum condition=100.0%)
HDI: 89.9. **HSI:** 93.0. **HFI:** 85.0. **EFL:** 61.0.

Country Table 1. **Religious adherents in Luxembourg, AD 1900-2025.**

Year	*1900*		*1970*		*mid-1990*		*Annual change, 1990-2000*				*mid-1995*		*mid-2000*		*mid-2025*	
Name	*Adherents*	*%*	*Adherents*	*%*	*Adherents*	*%*	*Natural*	*Conversion*	*Total*	*Rate*	*Adherents*	*%*	*Adherents*	*%*	*Adherents*	*%*
Christians	**234,560**	**99.4**	**323,000**	**95.3**	**358,800**	**94.2**	**4,670**	**-111**	**4,561**	**1.20**	**382,600**	**94.0**	**404,414**	**93.9**	**430,400**	**93.0**
PROFESSION																
professing Christians	**234,560**	**99.4**	**323,000**	**95.3**	**358,800**	**94.2**	**4,670**	**-111**	**4,561**	**1.20**	**382,600**	**94.0**	**404,414**	**93.9**	**430,400**	**93.0**
AFFILIATION																
unaffiliated Christians	3,300	1.4	17,490	5.2	2,600	0.7	34	-120	-86	-3.94	2,000	0.5	1,740	0.4	3,400	0.7
affiliated Christians	**231,260**	**98.0**	**305,510**	**90.1**	**356,200**	**93.5**	**4,636**	**12**	**4,647**	**1.23**	**380,600**	**93.5**	**402,674**	**93.4**	**427,000**	**92.2**
Roman Catholics	227,960	96.6	296,500	87.4	360,000	94.5	4,724	-24	4,700	1.23	386,270	94.9	407,000	94.4	430,000	92.9
Protestants	3,300	1.4	6,760	2.0	7,200	1.9	94	-64	30	0.41	7,309	1.8	7,500	1.7	8,500	1.8
Marginal Christians	0	0.0	1,000	0.3	2,200	0.6	29	51	80	3.15	2,570	0.6	3,000	0.7	6,000	1.3
Independents	0	0.0	850	0.3	1,820	0.5	24	14	38	1.91	1,979	0.5	2,200	0.5	3,500	0.8
Orthodox	0	0.0	200	0.1	900	0.2	12	8	20	2.03	1,000	0.3	1,100	0.3	1,600	0.4
Anglicans	0	0.0	200	0.1	450	0.1	6	9	15	2.92	500	0.1	600	0.1	900	0.2
doubly-affiliated	0	0.0	0	0.0	-16,370	-4.3	-215	-21	-236	1.35	-19,028	-4.7	-18,726	-4.3	-23,500	-5.1
Trans-megabloc groupings																
Evangelicals	2,000	0.9	540	0.2	950	0.3	12	3	15	1.48	1,026	0.3	1,100	0.3	1,400	0.3
Pentecostals/Charismatics	0	0.0	600	0.2	16,000	4.2	210	170	380	2.15	18,171	4.5	19,800	4.6	25,000	5.4
Great Commission Christians	**14,000**	**5.9**	**40,000**	**11.8**	**64,000**	**16.8**	**840**	**302**	**1,142**	**1.66**	**69,000**	**17.0**	**75,421**	**17.5**	**82,000**	**17.7**
Nonreligious	100	0.0	10,800	3.2	13,100	3.4	172	128	300	2.08	14,860	3.7	16,102	3.7	20,000	4.3
Muslims	80	0.0	500	0.2	3,900	1.0	51	-7	44	1.08	4,100	1.0	4,343	1.0	6,000	1.3
Atheists	0	0.0	3,000	0.9	3,200	0.8	42	-11	31	0.94	3,300	0.8	3,513	0.8	4,000	0.9
Baha'is	0	0.0	1,000	0.3	1,300	0.3	17	8	25	1.75	1,440	0.4	1,546	0.4	2,000	0.4
Jews	1,210	0.5	700	0.2	700	0.2	9	-9	0	-0.03	700	0.2	698	0.2	600	0.1
World A (unevangelized persons)	0	0.0	1,017	0.3	1,905	0.5	25	178	203	7.54	2,848	0.7	3,879	0.9	5,093	1.1
World B (evangelized non-Christians)	1,390	0.6	15,156	4.4	20,295	5.3	266	-69	197	1.13	21,451	5.3	22,707	5.2	27,507	5.9
World C (Christians)	234,560	99.4	323,000	95.3	358,800	94.2	4,670	-111	4,561	1.20	382,600	94.0	404,414	93.9	430,400	93.0
Country's population	**235,950**	**100.0**	**339,174**	**100.0**	**381,000**	**100.0**	**4,961**	**0**	**4,961**	**1.24**	**406,900**	**100.0**	**431,000**	**100.0**	**463,000**	**100.0**

Continued overleaf

Country Table 1–concluded

COLUMNS, ROWS.
For meanings and definitions, see Codebook (Part 3). Note that, by definition, total 'Christians' = professing + crypto-Christians, which also = affiliated + unaffiliated Christians, and also = Great Commission Christians + latent Christians. Percentages may not always total exactly, due to rounding.

CENSUSES.
1871: 99.5% Roman Catholics, 0.3% Jews, 0.2% Protestants. **1.XII.1900:** 98.5% Roman Catholics, 0.9% Protestants, 0.5% Jews. **1922:** 97.4% Roman Catholics, 1.1% Protestants, 0.5% Jews. **1935:** 97.0% Roman Catholics, 1.1% Protestants, 1.1% Jews. **31.XII.1947** (de jure): 98.3% Roman Catholics, 0.9% Protestants, 0.3% Jews, 0.2% nonreligious, 0.2% other religionists. **31.XII.1960** (de jure): 98.2% Roman Catholics, 1.0% Protestants, 0.2% Catholics (non-Roman), 0.2% Jews, 0.2% nonreligious, 0.1% marginal Protestants, 0.1% Orthodox. **31.XII.1970:** 93.9% Roman Catholics, 4.1% nonreligious and atheists, 1.2% Protestants, 0.2% Jews, 0.6% other Christians and non-Christian religionists.

NOTES ON RELIGIONS
ATHEISTS. Parti Communiste de Luxembourg (PCL) (legal; pro-Soviet). Communists are mostly urban, and are found in the heavily industrialized south near the French border. Many consider themselves still Roman Catholics.
BAHA'IS. Growth from 4 local spiritual assemblies (1964) to 7 (1973), and eventually to 11 LSAs (1995).
MUSLIMS. Recent North African immigrant workers.
PROTESTANTS. In the 20th century there has been a gradual increase in the number of Protestants (and other non-Catholics) largely due to immigration. Many however remain nominal only and are unaffiliated to churches.

Great Commission Instrument Panel: status of Luxembourg (for explanation see start of Part 4)

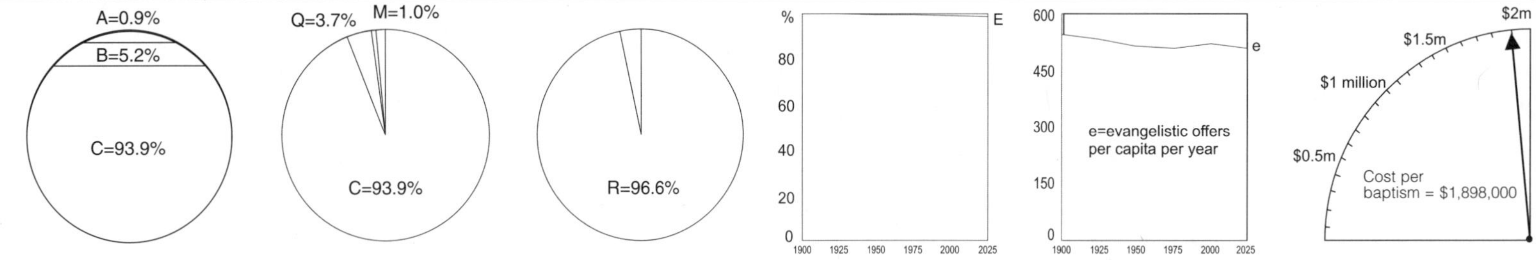

3 Worlds, AD 2000 | Religions, AD 2000 | Ecclesiastical blocs | Evangelization, 1900-2025 | Offers, 1900-2025 | Cost-effectiveness, AD 2000

Country summary. **Worlds A, B, C by ethnolinguistic peoples, cities, and major civil divisions in Luxembourg.**

	PEOPLES							CITIES							CIVIL DIVISIONS						
World	*Num*	*Pop 2000*	*C%*	*Christians*	*E%*	*U%*	*Unevangelized*	*Num*	*Pop 2000*	*C%*	*Christians*	*E%*	*U%*	*Unevangelized*	*Num*	*Pop 2000*	*C%*	*Christians*	*E%*	*U%*	*Unevangelized*
A	1	5,297	0.18	953	36	64	3,390	0	0	0.00	0	0	0	0	0	0	0.00	0	0	0	0
B	1	775	0.00	2	59	41	315	0	0	0.00	0	0	0	0	0	0	0.00	0	0	0	0
C	13	424,545	0.95	401,719	100	0	224	2	241,608	93.07	224,861	99	1	2,215	3	430,615	93.51	402,674	99	1	3,931
Total	**15**	**430,617**	**0.94**	**402,674**	**99**	**1**	**3,929**	**2**	**241,608**	**93.07**	**224,861**	**99**	**1**	**2,215**	**3**	**430,615**	**93.51**	**402,674**	**99**	**1**	**3,931**

Country status. Luxembourg is a small principality in northwestern Europe situated between Belgium, Germany, and France. It is the smallest member of the European Union. It is rich in iron ore and has developed large iron and steel industries.

HUMAN LIFE AND LIBERTY

Human rights and freedoms. All human rights are guaranteed and protected by the Constitution. Judicial and penal systems are open, efficient, and fair. There is universal suffrage for all citizens aged 18 and above. There is no risk or danger in dissent. Although foreigners make up 20% of the national population, antiforeign incidents are few.

Human environment. Because of the small size of the country, environmental problems are limited and manageable.

NON-CHRISTIAN RELIGIONS

Baha'i has a small following in 11 local spiritual assemblies.

Judaism, with a population of 2,000 in 1940, was decimated by the Nazi occupation in World War II. The Jewish community numbered 700 in 1995 of whom 30% were non-citizens.

Eglise Catholique. Capital city with (left) late-Gothic Cathedral of Notre-Dame, built 1613-21, and other churches. During the Octave (national pilgrimage) for 2 weeks after 3rd Sunday after Easter, tens of thousands flock to its miraculous shrine.

CHRISTIANITY

CATHOLIC CHURCH. Catholicism, organized in Luxembourg by the French missionary Willibroard who built the monastery of Echternach in 698, is the traditional religion of Luxembourg, although the proportion of professing Catholics has decreased slightly since World War II. Catholics represented 94.9% of the total population in 1995 as contrasted with 98.3% in 1947. The role played by Christian labor unions, the Christian Socialist Party (which has been in power for more than 50 years and claims to represent the 'social doctrine of the church') and the newspaper Luxemburger Wort (the largest daily in the country whose 70,000 copies are said to reach 80% of all Luxembourg readers), all witness to the institutional force of Catholicism in the Grand Duchy. The diocese of Luxembourg is administratively directly under the Holy See.

The Holy See has diplomatic relations with Luxembourg and in AD 2000 is represented to government and the Catholic hierarchy by a nuncio residing in Brussels.

OTHER CHURCHES. The Protestant community is a small minority, composed mostly of non-citizens or those of foreign extraction whose numbers have grown slightly with the founding of the European Economic Community. There are English, Dutch, French, and German-speaking congregations in the country. Protestants are found mostly in the urban areas of Luxembourg city and in the mining basin. The largest denomination is the Protestant Church of the Grand Duchy, which is Lutheran and Reformed in tradition and owes its origin to Prussian soldiers who occupied Luxembourg after 1813. German Mennonites built farms near Echternach in eastern Luxembourg in 1844 and since 1951 American Mennonite missionaries have carried on urban industrial work in Esch-sur-Alzette and Dudelange. Of the denominations established more recently, most success has been recorded by Jehovah's Witnesses and the New Apostolic Church.

Small Russian and Greek Orthodox groups also exist.

Indigenous missions. Luxembourg has supported a steady stream of Roman Catholic missionaries throughout the 20th century.

CHURCH AND STATE

The Napoleon concordat of 1801, concluded well before the independence of the country in 1839, has never been expressly abolished, with the exception of a few articles which have been superseded by subsequent laws. Nevertheless, because the context of the document has little utility today, one may conclude that for all practical purposes the concordat no longer exists.

The legal status of the churches, as found in the constitution of 1868 (Articles 19, 20, 21, 26) and other legislative texts, follows essentially the provisions of the constitution of Belgium: reciprocal independence of state and church and protection of the freedom of the latter, payment of clergy by the state, and the like. The only difference is the law of 30 April 1873 concerning the nomination of the Catholic bishop, who must pledge his oath to the crown, and the recognition of the Bishopric of Luxembourg created in 1870. Article 26 of the constitution, which provides that 'the establishment of all religious corporations must be authorized by law', has given rise to divergent interpretations. However, ancient practice dictates that legal authorization is only required for obtaining juridical personality. In such cases, where the buying and selling of property is involved, the state treats religious congregations in the same way as public benevolent organizations.

In state primary education, a course in the Catholic religion is obligatory, except where parents specifically request that their children be excused. In secondary schools, since 1968 parents have been able to choose between a course in the Catholic religion (85% so choose), non-confessional ethics (12.5%) or no course at all (2.5%). Beyond its role in the secondary education of girls, the Catholic Church has not generally established schools. However, one of the 5 persons termed curators exercising supervision over state schools represents the Catholic Church. Moreover, 5 'episcopal dormitories' are attached to the country's main secondary schools and many such schools have priests teaching both secular and religious courses.

Ecclesiastical affairs are handled by the Ministry of Religions (Ministere des Cultes).

Eglise Catholique, Diocése de Luxembourg. Postage stamp commemorating 1870 founding of Diocese.

BROADCASTING AND MEDIA

Shortwave radio programs in European languages can be received from AWR (Slovakia), KNLS, TWR (Monaco, Albania) and HCJB (Ecuador).

Satellite TV and radio programs are received in English, Arabic, German and Italian. Luxembourg is a member of UNDA.

INTERDENOMINATIONAL ORGANIZATIONS

The Luxembourg Interconfessional Association, founded in 1965 as the Interconfessional Luxembourg Committee and reorganized in 1970, brings together Catholics, Protestants and Jews for the study of common problems and to promote mutual understanding. The association, which is a member of the International Council of Christians and Jews in London, enjoys the moral and financial support of the 3 communities, each of which appoints to the association a theological counselor. There is also an Ecumenical Homestead (Oekumenische Heimstatte) run by Protestants, and the Benedictine abbey of Cleraux serves as a center for study and reflection oriented towards the Scandinavian countries.

FUTURE TRENDS AND PROSPECTS

The nonreligious and immigrant Muslims, 3.4% of the population in 1970, are expected to grow to nearly 6% by AD 2025 with a corresponding decline in the Christian percentage.

Christians could decline to less than 90% by AD 2050 with the nonreligious and Muslims making up the bulk of the remaining 10%.

BIBLIOGRAPHY

Annuaire diocésain de Luxembourg, 1971. Luxembourg: Evêché, 1971.

Aspects of religious sociology of the diocese of Luxembourg. A. Heiderscheid. Luxembourg: Editions de l'Imprimerie Saint-Paul, 1961–62. 2 vols.

Die Kirche in Luxemburg von den Anfängen biz sur Gegenwart. E. Donckel. Luxembourg: Sankt-Paulus-Druckerei, 1950. 248p.

Die Luxemburger Kirche im 2. Weltkrieg: Dokumente, Zeugnisse, Lebensbilder. R. Fisch (ed). Luxembourg: Editions Saint-Paul, 1991. 733p.

La communauté juive du Luxembourg dans le passé et dans le présent: histoire illustrée. C. Lehrmann & G. Lehrmann. Esch-sur-Alzette, Luxembourg: Imprimerie Coopérative Luxembourgeoise, 1953. 155p.

Les sectes en Belgique et au Luxembourg. A. Lallemand. Brussels: Editions EPO, 1994. 238p.

Luxembourg. C. Hury & J. Christophory. *World bibliographical series*, vol. 23. Oxford, UK: CLIO Press, 1981. 206p. (See especially 'Religion,' p.98–101).

Umfrage zur Luxemburger Synode: Überblick über Ergebnisse und Motivzusammenhänge. Allensbach, Luxembourg: Institut für Demoskopie Allensbach, 1973. 46p.

Country Table 2. **Organized churches and denominations in Luxembourg.**

Official name (bold type = church with over 10% of all affiliated) 1	*Begun* 2	*Type* 3	*Counc* 4	*Congs* 5	*Adults* 6	*Affiliated 1970* 7	*Affiliated 1995* 8	*G%* 9	*Names, notes, and other statistics* (see Codebook, Part 3) 10
Assemblées de Dieu	1981	P-Pe2	Z....	2	129	–	180	7.14	Assemblies of God. M=AoG(France,Belgium,UK,USA).
Communauté des Protestants CECA	c1960	P-LuR	.....	5	300	250	500	2.81	CP-CECA. *Protestant Community for CECA.* In capital. Mostly Germans. 1n,W=20%,10Yy,31z.
Communauté Protestante Anglaise	c1900	P-com	.....	2	400	200	600	4.49	CPA. English-speaking Protestant Community. Expatriates, mostly temporary residents.
Eglise Adventiste du Septième Jour	c1900	P-Adv	x....	1	35	50	78	1.79	*SDA. Seventh-day Adventists, Belgium-Luxembourg Conference.* 1x,W=99%,3Y.
Eglise Anglicane (D Europe)	c1910	A-plu	awc..	1	300	200	500	3.73	*Anglican Ch.* English-speaking chaplaincy, for 900 UK citizens. 1 chapel.
Eglise Catholique: AD Luxembourg	c 250	R-Lat	bzB.h	274	280,000	296,500	386,270	1.06	*Katoulesch Kiirch.* C=8+2+17. (1970) 535nx,4318Yy. (1990) 243n,71x,91m,837w,3650Yy.
Eglise Evangélique Libre	c1960	P-Eva	.....	3	80	37	119	4.78	Free Evangelical Ch.
Eglise Mennonite	c1830	P-Men	G....	2	100	200	167	-0.72	*Mennonite Ch.* M=EMBMC(USA). Agricultural, German-speaking. 2x,2f,1k,W=67%,5Y,4z.
Eglise Néo-Apostolique	c1900	I-3aX	x....	1	1,000	400	1,419	5.20	NAK. *New Apostolic Ch.* Schism ex Catholic Apostolic Ch. World HQ Zurich. Germans.
Eglise Orthodoxe Grecque (D Belgique)	c1925	O-Gre	Cwe..	1	600	200	1,000	6.65	*D Belgique, Hollande et Luxembourg. Greek Orthodox Ch.* Under EP Constantinople.
Eglise Orth Russe Hors-Frontieres	c1920	I-Rus	x....	1	150	150	200	1.16	*Russian Orthodox Ch Outside Russia.* M=ROCOR(New York). Russian exiles after 1917.
Eglise Protestante du Canton d'Esch	c1940	P-Non	.....	3	170	400	340	-0.65	*Consistory of the Protestant Ch of Esch Canton.* HQ Esch-sur-Alzette. Independent.
Eglise Prot du Grand-Duché de L	1813	P-LuR	.v..h	5	1,400	4,843	2,325	-2.89	EPGDL. *Protestant Ch.* 1918 influx from Netherlands. A state church. 85% Reformed. 4n.
Eglise Protestante Européenne	c1939	P-com	.....	1	200	200	300	1.64	*European Protestant Ch* (French-speaking). Expatriates, mostly temporary residents.
Eglise Protestante Néerlandaise	1958	P-Ref	.....	1	100	80	200	3.73	EPN. NPG. *Nederlandse Protestantse Gemeenschap.* Dutch. 1x,W=56%,8Yy,2z.
Mission Intérieure au Luxembourg		I-Non	.....	1	80	200	160	0.05	MIL. *Inner Luxembourg Mission.* Independent body with congregation in Luxembourg city.
Témoins de Jéhovah	1929	m-Jeh	x....	22	1,541	1,000	2,570	3.85	*Jehovah's Witnesses. Watch Tower.* First activity 1929, then expansion. (1975) 37Y. (1995) 92Y.
Other Protestant denominations		P-	.....	5	1,000	500	2,500	0.05	Total about 10 (see list below).
Other independent churches		I-3	.....	3	100	100	200	0.05	Manna Ch (Portugal); Reformiert-Apostolischen Gmb (and other schisms ex NAK).
Doubly-affiliated		2-aff			-13,700	0	-19,028		Evangelicals and Pentecostals who are also baptized Roman Catholics.
Totals				**334**	**273,985**	**305,510**	**380,600**		

Churches, members, growth, 1900-2025	*Congs*	*Adults*	*Affiliated*	*G%*	*Total denominations*	*6 Megablocs:* O	R	A	P	I	m
Total churches, members, and denominations (mid-1900)	200	181,000	231,260	0.40	5	0	1	0	2	2	0
Total churches, members, and denominations (mid-1970)	318	239,542	305,510	0.40	22	1	1	1	13	5	1
Total churches, members, and denominations (mid-1990)	320	256,000	356,200	0.77	32	1	1	1	20	8	1
Total churches, members, and denominations (mid-1995)	334	273,985	380,600	1.33	32	1	1	1	20	8	1
Total churches, members, and denominations (mid-2000)	360	290,000	402,674	1.13	32	1	1	1	20	8	1
Total churches, members, and denominations (mid-2025)	400	307,000	427,000	0.23	76	3	1	1	30	40	1

NOTES ON TABLE ABOVE

NATIONAL COUNCILS (Column 4, 5th letter).

h = Association Interconfessionnelle du Luxembourg (formerly Comité Interconfessionnelle Luxembourgeois) (Luxembourg Interconfessional Association); includes also Jews.

Other national councils. Alliance of the Protestant Churches in Luxembourge, 1993. Council of Christian Churches in Luxembourg, 1997.

OTHER PROTESTANT DENOMINATIONS. These small groups include: Assemblies of God, Christian Ch of North America (Pentecostal), Eglise Libre du Grand-Duché, Free Ev Ch, Worldwide European Fellowship, and a few chaplaincies and union congregations for other language groups.

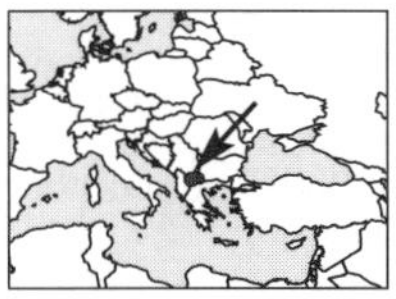

MACEDONIA

SECULAR DATA, AD 2000

STATE

Official name: Republika Makedonija (The Republic of Macedonia).
Short name: Macedonia. **Adjective of nationality:** Macedonian.
Flag: Red field with small sun in center and yellow rays emanating outward.
Area: 25,713 sq. km. (9,928 sq. mi.).
Government: Unitary multiparty republic with a unicameral legislature, since 1992 (1918 Yugoslavia).
Legislature: Assembly, 120 members.
Official language: Macedonian.
Monetary unit: denar. **US$1=** 52.13 denar.
Chief cities: SKOPJE 623,267; Bitola (Bitol) 162,977; Kumanovo 147,466.
Political divisions: 30 provinces.
Armed forces: 16,000.

DEMOGRAPHY

Population: 2,024,000.
Population density: 78.7/sq. km. (203.8/sq. mi.).
Under 15 years: 464,000.
Growth rate p.a.: 0.60% (births 15.57, deaths 8.12).
Mortality: Infant, per 1,000: 20.8; **Maternal per 100,000:** 70.0.
Life expectancy: 74 (male 72, female 76).
Household size: 4.4. **Floor area per person, sq.m:** 32.0.
Major languages: Macedonian, Albanian, Aromanian, Turkish, Serbo-Croatian.
Urban dwellers: 62.00%. **Urban growth rate p.a.:** 1.3%.
Labor force: 45%.

ETHNOLINGUISTIC PEOPLES

53.8% Macedonian; 18.0% Kosovar (Albanian); 5.2% Balkan Gypsy (Jerides); 5.0% Aromanian (Aromunen); 4.8% Turk.

ECONOMY

National income p.a. per person: US$859; **per family:** US$3,783.

EDUCATION

Adult literacy: 89% (male 94%, female 83%). **Schools:** 1,145.
Universities: 27. **School enrolment:** female/male: 77%/77%.

HEALTH

Access to health services: 80%. **Access to safe water:** 80%.
Hospitals: 61 (52 beds per 10,000). **Doctors:** 4,528.
Blind: 2,000. **Deaf:** 134,000. **Murder rate:** 3. **Lepers:** 200.

LITERATURE

New book titles p.a.: 690 (340 p.a. per million). **Periodicals:** 104.
Newspapers: 3 dailies.

COMMUNICATION (per 1,000 people)

Phones: 179 **(2% mobile). Radios:** 179. **TV sets:** 179.
Daily newspaper circulation: 21. **Computers:** 45.

REFUGEES

Alien refugees from other countries: 7,000.

HUMAN LIFE AND LIBERTY (optimum condition=100.0%)

HDI: 74.8. **HSI:** 65.0. **HFI:** 50.0. **EFL:** 25.0.

Country status. Macedonia, a former province of Yugoslavia, is a landlocked country in the Balkans surrounded by Greece, Albania, Serbia, and Bulgaria. It has a mixed Mediterranean-continental weather pattern with cold, moist winters and hot, dry summers. The economy is predominantly agricultural, however there are a variety of natural resources including zinc, lead, manganese, nickel, chromium, and tungsten.

HUMAN LIFE AND LIBERTY

Human need and development. Macedonia is a poverty-stricken nation which has suffered under recent economic and political woes. The transport of goods, raw materials, and semi-manufactured goods via the poorly passable east-west corridor has resulted in a drastic rise in business costs. There is a freeway and railway system that run North to South; however, travelling from east to west is often a formidable task because of the lack of decent roads and no rail system. These obstacles have resulted in many companies facing bankruptcy while others have been forced to stop production. On 16 February 1994, the Greek government cancelled all trade links with Macedonia and began an embargo. Six weeks after the blockade, Macedonian authorities estimated the monthly cost of the blockade at $80 million equivalent to 85% of the country's total export earnings.

The minimum wage set in 1993 was equivalent to US$50 per month and the average salary as of October 1994 was about $200. Despite this rise in income, the cost of living far exceeds the minimum wage. Farmers and land labor help are found predominantly working with hand tools instead of machinery. Macedonia has under 1 telephone per 6 persons.

Human rights and freedoms. Following its declaration of independence from Yugoslavia on 20 November 1991, the Macedonian government began drafting the content of a democratic regime. Its parliament had previously been elected in free and fair elections in 1990. Human rights follow closely to that of other democratic constitutions allowing freedom of

Country Table 1. **Religious adherents in Macedonia, AD 1900-2025.**

Year	*1900*		*1970*		*mid-1990*		*Annual change, 1990-2000*				*mid-1995*		*mid-2000*		*mid-2025*	
Name	*Adherents*	*%*	*Adherents*	*%*	*Adherents*	*%*	*Natural*	*Conversion*	*Total*	*Rate*	*Adherents*	*%*	*Adherents*	*%*	*Adherents*	*%*
Christians	**540,000**	**90.6**	**1,282,400**	**81.8**	**1,310,700**	**68.7**	**7,855**	**-10,175**	**-2,238**	**-0.17**	**1,352,200**	**68.9**	**1,288,319**	**63.7**	**1,400,000**	**62.0**
PROFESSION																
crypto-Christians	0	0.0	125,000	8.0	25,000	1.3	151	-2,651	-2,500	-63.67	0	0.0	0	0.0	0	0.0
professing Christians	**540,000**	**90.6**	**1,157,400**	**73.8**	**1,285,700**	**67.4**	**7,701**	**-7,442**	**262**	**0.02**	**1,352,200**	**68.9**	**1,288,319**	**63.7**	**1,400,000**	**62.0**
AFFILIATION																
unaffiliated Christians	22,000	3.7	0	0.0	1,000	0.1	6	7	13	1.20	1,056	0.1	1,127	0.1	2,000	0.1
affiliated Christians	**518,000**	**86.9**	**1,282,400**	**81.8**	**1,309,700**	**68.6**	**7,849**	**-10,100**	**-2,251**	**-0.17**	**1,351,144**	**68.8**	**1,287,192**	**63.6**	**1,398,000**	**61.9**
Orthodox	512,500	86.0	1,240,123	79.1	1,240,000	65.0	7,470	-11,470	-4,000	-0.33	1,273,800	64.9	1,200,000	59.3	1,272,000	56.3
Roman Catholics	5,000	0.8	40,000	2.6	57,000	3.0	343	1,017	1,360	2.16	63,200	3.2	70,600	3.5	100,000	4.4
Independents	0	0.0	300	0.0	5,800	0.3	35	204	239	3.51	6,500	0.3	8,192	0.4	12,000	0.5
Protestants	500	0.1	1,584	0.1	6,000	0.3	36	64	100	1.55	6,644	0.3	7,000	0.4	10,000	0.4
Marginal Christians	0	0.0	393	0.0	900	0.1	5	45	50	4.52	1,000	0.1	1,400	0.1	4,000	0.2
Trans-megabloc groupings																
Evangelicals	400	0.1	640	0.0	2,450	0.1	15	52	67	2.45	2,778	0.1	3,120	0.2	5,100	0.2
Pentecostals/Charismatics	0	0.0	300	0.0	6,800	0.4	41	49	90	1.25	7,189	0.4	7,700	0.4	10,000	0.4
Great Commission Christians	**36,000**	**6.0**	**157,000**	**10.0**	**196,600**	**10.3**	**1,184**	**412**	**1,596**	**0.78**	**204,000**	**10.4**	**212,563**	**10.5**	**275,000**	**12.2**
Muslims	50,000	8.4	177,600	11.3	427,000	22.4	2,572	12,011	14,583	2.98	443,400	22.6	572,825	28.3	671,700	29.8
Nonreligious	0	0.0	78,000	5.0	138,340	7.3	833	-1,350	-517	-0.38	135,400	6.9	133,168	6.6	160,000	7.1
Atheists	0	0.0	30,000	1.9	32,000	1.7	193	-562	-369	-1.22	31,000	1.6	28,308	1.4	25,000	1.1
Jews	6,000	1.0	0	0.0	960	0.1	6	-6	0	0.01	1,000	0.1	961	0.1	1,300	0.1
World A (unevangelized persons)	29,800	5.0	141,117	9.0	246,261	12.9	1,482	-1,904	-422	-0.17	245,436	12.5	242,880	12.0	250,638	11.1
World B (evangelized non-Christians)	26,200	4.4	144,452	9.2	352,039	18.4	2,122	11,997	14,119	3.42	365,852	18.6	492,801	24.3	607,362	26.9
World C (Christians)	540,000	90.6	1,282,400	81.8	1,310,700	68.7	7,855	-10,175	-2,238	-0.17	1,352,200	68.9	1,288,319	63.7	1,400,000	62.0
Country's population	**596,000**	**100.0**	**1,567,970**	**100.0**	**1,909,000**	**100.0**	**11,459**	**0**	**11,459**	**0.59**	**1,963,488**	**100.0**	**2,024,000**	**100.0**	**2,258,000**	**100.0**

COLUMNS, ROWS.
For meanings and definitions, see Codebook (Part 3). Note that, by definition, total 'Christians' = professing + crypto-Christians, which also = affiliated + unaffiliated Christians, and also = Great Commission Christians + latent Christians. Percentages may not always total exactly, due to rounding.

NOTES ON RELIGIONS
CRYPTO-CHRISTIANS. Only before 1995.
MUSLIMS. Mainly Albanians, with 120,000 Macedonians, and Rumelian Turks, Balkan Gypsies, and Bosnians.

Great Commission Instrument Panel: status of Macedonia (for explanation see start of Part 4)

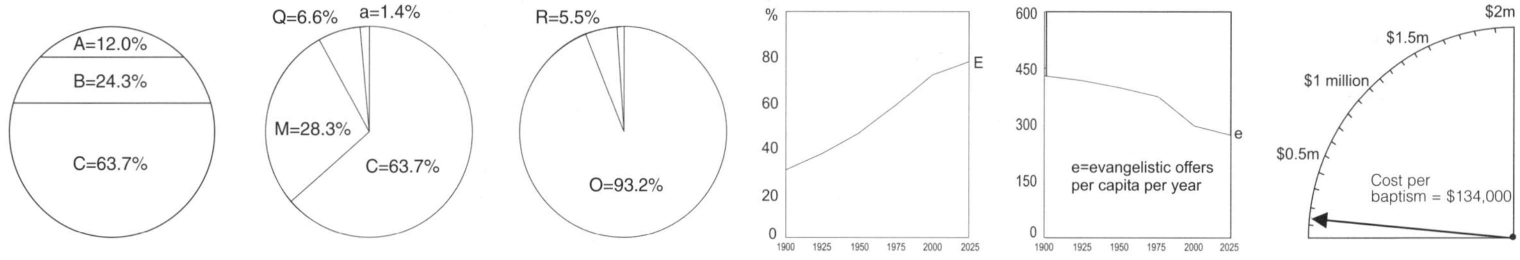

3 Worlds, AD 2000 | Religions, AD 2000 | Ecclesiastical blocs | Evangelization, 1900-2025 | Offers, 1900-2025 | Cost-effectiveness, AD 2000

religion, speech, public address, and all pertaining to individualistic freedoms. With human right to life irrevocable, there is currently no death penalty in the Republic of Macedonia.

The Utopian concept wrought by constitutions such as these is often less than ideal because of the lack of internal security, poor economic conditions, and official corruption. The government generally respects these rights; however there have been credible reports of police abuse of prisoners. Violent acts and discrimination against women are problems.

Minorities which include ethnic Albanians, ethnic Turks, and ethnic Serbs protest about various human rights infringements and discriminations. Due to the large composition of national and ethnic groups there are constant demonstrations protesting the abuse of freedom, rights, and discrimination levied against each group.

In April of 1993 Macedonia was approved for UN admission by the Security Council after months of haggling with Greece over the name and flag of the former Yugoslav republic. Though this admission does not heighten internal freedoms per se, it does boost the enforcement of strict human rights and freedoms.

Human environment. The country's vast natural resources have led to a poisoning of the environment which has escalated in recent times. Mining operations have left indelible scars on the landscape and with their metallurgical factory counterparts they pollute the air and waterways. Pro-active groups have risen to thwart these effects which have been wreaking havoc on the biology of lakes Ohrid and Prespa.

NON-CHRISTIAN RELIGIONS

Islam remains widespread in the 1990s. The end of the 14th century heralded the Ottoman conquest which introduced large numbers of Turkish and Turkic-speaking settlers to Macedonia, and with them, Islam. It is by far the major non-Christian religious community in the country. Some 425 mosques are dispersed throughout the land, and well over half a million Muslims comprise nearly 30% of the population. Turks and Albanians compose the majority of Muslims within the country and these constitute an ethnic, cultural, and religious minority while maintaining a formidable degree of internal significance. Data gathered by village birth registers shows that 120,000 Macedonians are of the Islamic religion. This would make them 6% of the population, significantly more Macedonians being Muslims than Turkish Muslims.

Muslims. Pashah Mustafa mosque in Skopje, with 424 other mosques, Muslims have increased twelve-fold since 1900.

Atheism is thinly spread throughout the region with 1.4% of the population claiming to be atheists.

Judaism has long been prevalent in Macedonia dating their arrival to the 6th century BC when they were brought in by Phoenician merchants as slaves. The Apostle Paul in the first century AD mentions Jewish communities in Salonika (Thessaloniki). Jews fled here from persecution in the mid 15th century from all parts of Europe to the umbrella of amnesty under the Ottoman empire, only to be nearly wiped out by the insidious genocidal attempt on Jews some 500 years later by Hitler's Nazi regime.

Consisting of only 0.1% of the population today, their presence is hardly recognized but prevalent nonetheless.

CHRISTIANITY

Christianity was introduced into Macedonia by the Apostle Paul in the first century on his journey from Asia Minor when he landed in Neapolis and journeyed on to Thessaloniki. The Christian faith took hold and slowly spread. The second decade of the 4th century saw strong Christian development acquiring political weight with the conversion of Constantine and the declaration of his entire empire for Christianity. The Macedonian church was organized with its center at Thessaloniki because of that city's importance in the imperial administration. It was under the ecclesiastical jurisdiction of Rome and functioned as papal vicar especially from the time of Innocent I.

ORTHODOX CHURCH. The first autocephalous Slav church was the archbishopric of Ohrid, established by Naum and Clement. These were students of Cyril and Methodius who developed an alphabet for use by the Slavs which was used to translate scripture into the dialect of Macedonian Slavs.

The Macedonian archbishopric of Ohrid became the ecclesiastical center from which the Eastern Orthodox faith was spread throughout Serbia, Bulgaria, and Kievan Russia. For most of the early twentieth century the Macedonian Orthodox Church was under the authority of the Serbian Orthodox Church, but shortly after World War II they proclaimed themselves independent under the leadership of the archbishop of Ohrid and Macedonia. At the June 1994 session, the Holy Synod of the Macedonian Orthodox Church affirmed that 'the autocephalous status of the Macedonian Church and the interests of the Macedonian people and state are Holy and inalienable values, which it has no intention of ever giving up'. Today the Macedonian Orthodox Church is headed by a Holy Synod of Bishops under 6 bishops.

CATHOLIC CHURCH. Catholics have a small diocese, which is partly in Serbia, and a small minority of 40,000 members.

The Holy See has diplomatic relations with Macedonia and in AD 2000 is represented to government and the Catholic hierarchy by a nuncio.

Country summary. **Worlds A, B, C by ethnolinguistic peoples, cities, and major civil divisions in Macedonia.**

World	PEOPLES Num	Pop 2000	C%	Christians	E%	U%	Unevangelized	CITIES Num	Pop 2000	C%	Christians	E%	U%	Unevangelized	CIVIL DIVISIONS Num	Pop 2000	C%	Christians	E%	U%	Unevangelized
A	3	156,828	0.04	63	46	54	84,018	0	0	0.00	0	0	0	0	0	0	0.00	0	0	0	0
B	6	524,107	20.22	105,966	70	30	156,149	0	0	0.00	0	0	0	0	0	0	0.00	0	0	0	0
C	15	1,342,648	87.97	1,181,165	100	0	1,615	3	933,710	61.67	575,773	87	13	117,274	30	2,023,581	63.61	1,287,192	88	12	241,782
Total	**24**	**2,023,583**	**63.61**	**1,287,194**	**88**	**12**	**241,782**	**3**	**933,710**	**61.67**	**575,773**	**87**	**13**	**117,274**	**30**	**2,023,581**	**63.61**	**1,287,192**	**88**	**12**	**241,782**

OTHER CHURCHES. As well as the 1.2 million adherents of the Orthodox Church, there are approximately 100,000 other Christians in other denominations and independent churches in the country. Most are indigenous or regional parts of other Orthodox jurisdictions. Methodists form the largest Protestant church. In the Strumica region of the Greek-Bulgarian border, several villages have Methodist groups nearly as numerous as the Orthodox. Though they are far more free now than under the Communist regime, they are still concerned about the power wielded by the dominant Orthodox Church. Macedonian Methodists are the product of American missionary activity in European Turkey prior to the Balkan wars.

Indigenous missions. Missionaries from Macedonia were active in the first centuries after the Apostle Paul's work there but few Macedonians have served as missionaries since that era.

CHURCH AND STATE

The new Macedonian constitution was adopted on 8 September 1991. Article 19 states plainly and succinctly that freedom of religious confession is guaranteed. The right to express one's faith freely and publicly, individually or with others is guaranteed. The Macedonian Orthodox Church and other religious communities and groups are free to establish schools and other social and charitable institutions, by ways of a procedure regulated by law.

Members of the Macedonian Internal Revolutionary Party and younger parliamentarians who are faithful Orthodox dissatisfied with the church-state arrangements defined in the constitution, argue that the constitution should re-establish the Orthodox Church's dominant place within the state as the hinge of the Macedonian nation and there should be interaction with religion and political authorities. While the Macedonian Orthodox Church alone is mentioned by name in the constitution it does not receive official status. However, other religious communities charge that the government favors it, citing the ease with which it can obtain property and building permits for new construction. In 1995, 2 or 3 houses that that did not have such permits and were being used as mosques were destroyed by authorities. Protestant groups complain also about harassment and vandalism to which police fail to respond. Objections also include their inability to register their churches and obtain regular employment status for employees. On several occasions they have been prevented from having religious meetings in venues outside churches. Shades of gray tend to shroud the whole issue as is noted by the statement of bishop Mikhail who became metropolitan on 5 December 1993. He explicitly stated that while he supported the separation of church and state, his church could not countenance the removal of references to it in the constitution.

BROADCASTING AND MEDIA

Shortwave radio programs in European languages can be received from AWR (Slovakia), TWR (Monaco, Albania) and HCJB (Ecuador). IBRA-produced programs can be heard on local radio stations in 5 cities.

The 'Jesus' Film has had some distribution on videocassette; half of the 20,000 viewers to date have responded with decisions for Christ. Satellite TV programs are received mainly in Arabic.

FUTURE TRENDS AND PROSPECTS

Unlike in surrounding countries, Christianity is expected to decline in Macedonia, falling to 62% by AD 2025. Islam could grow to near 30% in the same period.

Christianity probably will continue to decline, perhaps falling below 60% before AD 2050. Muslims and the nonreligious will likely make up the bulk of the other 40% well into the 21st century.

BIBLIOGRAPHY

'A history of Baptists in Yugoslavia, 1862–1962.' J. D. Hopper. Ph.D. dissertation, Southwestern Baptist Theological Seminary, Fort Worth, TX, 1977. 180p.

'A history of the Congregational and Methodist Churches in Bulgaria and Yugoslavia.' P. B. Mojzes. Ph.D. dissertation, Boston University, Boston, 1965. 674p.

A history of the Jews in Macedonia. A. Matkovski. Skopje, Macedonia: Macedonian Review Editions, 1982. 223p.

'A tour of Ohrid,' A. Isaacs, *Sacred art journal*, 11 (March 1990), 23–26. (On Macedonian churches).

'Changing functions of religion in a socialist society: the case of Catholicism in Yugoslavia,' S. Vrcan, *Social compass*, 28, 1 (1981), 43–61.

Church and state in Yugoslavia since 1945. S. Alexander. Cambridge, UK: Cambridge University Press, 1979. 351p.

'Church–state relations in Yugoslavia since 1967,' S. Alexander, *Religion in Communist lands*, 4, 1 (Spring 1976), 18–27.

'Denominational affiliation in Yugoslavia, 1930–1989,' S. Flere, *East European quarterly*, 25 (June 1991), 145–65.

Die unierte Kirche in Mazedonien (1856–1919). R. Grulich. *Das östliche Christentum*, N.f., Bd. 29. Würzburg: Augustinus-Verlag, 1977. 155p.

In the claws of the red dragon: ten years under Tito's heel. W. Gruber. Toronto: St. Michaelswerk, 1988. 208p.

Islam in the Balkans: religion and society between Europe and the Arab World. H. T. Norris. Columbia, SC: University of South Carolina Press, 1993. 326p. (Deals with Bosnia, Albania, Macedonia).

'Islam in Yugoslavia today,' S. Ramet, *Religion in Communist lands*, 18, 3 (Autumn 1990), 226–35.

Islamizacijata i etnickite promeni vo Makedonija. N. Limanoski. Skopje, Macedonia: Makedonska kniga, 1993. 456p. (Summary in English and French).

Istorija na Makedonskata pravoslavna crkva. S. Dimevski. Skopje, Macedonia: Makedonska kn, 1989. 1,155p.

'La situación religiosa en Yugoslavia,' G. Canders, *Revista de estudios politicos*, 161 (1968), 259–67.

Nations and nationalities of Yugoslavia. K. Joncic (ed). Belgrade: Medjunarodna politika, 1974. 549p.

Opci sematizam katolicka crkve u Jugoslaviji, cerkerv Jugoslaviji, 1974 (General survey of the Catholic Church in Yugoslavia). Zagreb: Biskupska konferencija Jugoslavije, 1975. 1,166p. (Parts in Croat, Slovenian, Latin, English, French, German).

'Recent developments in church–state relations in Yugoslavia,' C. Criic, *Religion in Communist lands*, 1, 1 (Spring 1973), 6–8.

'Religion and nationality in Yugoslavia,' P. Ramet, in *Religion and nationalism in Soviet and East European politics*, p.299–327. P. Ramet (ed). 2nd ed. Durham, NC: Duke University Press, 1989.

'Religion in Yugoslavia: the background,' J. Broun, *America*, 165 (November 30, 1991), 414–16.

Religions in Yugoslavia: historical survey, legal status, church in socialism, ecumenism, dialogue between Marxists and Christians, etc. Z. Frid (ed). Zagreb: Binoza, 1971. 168p.

'Skopje from the Serbian to Ottoman Empires: conditions for the appearance of a Balkan Muslim city.' E. Fraenkel. Ph.D. dissertation, University of Pennsylvania, Philadelphia, 1986. 311p.

'Some social expectations of Christians in Yugoslavia with primary emphasis on the Protestant churches,' N. G. Shenk, *Occasional papers on religion in Eastern Europe*, 1 (November 1981), 1–10.

'The church of Macedonia: "limited autocephaly" or schism?,' S. K. Pavlowitch, *Sobornost*, n.s. 9, 1 (1987), 42–59.

'The Gypsy population of Yugoslavia,' T. P. Vukanovic, *Journal of the Gypsy Lore Society*, 42, 1/2 (1963), 10–27.

The Macedonian Orthodox Church: the road to independence. D. Ilievski. Trans., J. L. Leech. *Macedonian heritage collection.* Skopje, Macedonia: Macedonian Review Editions, 1973. 131p.

'The position of believers as second–class citizens in Socialist countries: the case of Yugoslavia,' Z. Roter, *Occasional papers on religion in Eastern Europe*, 9 (June 1989), 1–17.

The position of the Church in Yugoslavia. R. Vidic. Belgrade: Izdavac, 1962.

'The social role of religion in contemporary Yugoslavia.' N. G. Shenk. Ph.D. dissertation, Northwestern University, Evanston, IL, 1987. 264p.

'Yugoslavia,' A. Fiamengo, in *Western religion: a country by country sociological enquiry*, p.587–99. H. Mol (ed). The Hague: Mouton, 1972.

Yugoslavia. J. J. Horton. 2nd ed. *World bibliographical series*, vol. 1. Oxford, UK: CLIO Press, 1990. 304p. (See especially 'Religion,' p.72f, and 'Nationalities,' p.97–103).

Yugoslavia: a comprehensive English–language bibliography. F. Friedman (ed). Wilmington, DE: Scholarly Resources, Inc., 1993. 547p. (Section on 'Religion,' p.453–61).

Yugoslavia: the church and the state. London: Information Office, Embassy of the Federal People's Republic of Yugoslavia, 1953. 92p.

'Yugoslavie aujourd'hui: une église entre l'est et l'ouest,' *Information catholique internationale* (Paris), 400 (January 1972), 7–15.

Country Table 2. **Organized churches and denominations in Macedonia.**

Official name (bold type = church with over 10% of all affiliated) 1	*Begun* 2	*Type* 3	*Counc* 4	*Congs* 5	*Adults* 6	*Affiliated 1970* 7	*Affiliated 1995* 8	*G%* 9	*Names, notes, and other statistics* (see Codebook, Part 3) 10
Albanian Orthodox Church		O-Alb	C....	7	4,200	5,000	6,000	0.05	Albanians now resident citizens.
Baptist Church of Macedonia		P-Bap	.....	2	33	30	50	0.05	Formerly in Union of Baptist Churches in Yugoslavia.
Bulgarian Orthodox Church		O-Bul	M....	5	3,500	5,000	5,000	0.05	Under P Sofia. Bulgarian migrant workers.
Catholic Ch: D Skopje-Prizren	c 350	R-Lat	P....	25	27,000	40,000	63,200	1.85	Northern part in Serbia. HQ Skopje. Many Byzantine-rite. (1990) 51n,8x,13m,109w,1398Yy.
Congregational Church	c1980	P-Ref	.....	1	60	–	86	6.67	Schism ex-Methodist Church.
Evangelical Church in Macedonia	c1980	P-Pe2	.....	1	120	–	200	6.67	Pentecostals formerly in Yugoslavian churches.
Greek Orthodox Church	c1900	O-Gre	C....	2	3,200	2,000	5,300	3.98	Greeks, and migrant Arabs from North Africa and Middle East.
Gypsy Evangelical Movement		I-3pE	.....	5	900	300	1,000	0.05	Many varieties of Gypsies, including Balkan Gypsy, Serbian Rom Gypsy.
Jehovah's Witnesses		m-Jeh	x....	8	400	393	1,000	0.05	*Watch Tower. IBSA.* (1995) 106Y.
Macedonian Orthodox Church:	60	O-Mac	c....	960	877,000	1,120,000	1,200,000	0.05	1919 integrated into Serbian Orthodox Ch, 1967 declared its independence. 7 bishops.
M Skopje	c 350	O-Mac	cm	340	307,000	380,000	420,000	0.40	Part of old diocese is in Serbian Orthodox Ch. 1s(92) in Dracevo (Skopje).
D Debar-Kicevo	c1000	O-Mac	cb	140	139,000	190,000	190,000	0.00	Original church center. HQ Ochrid, cradle of Slav Orthodoxy.
D Palagonia		O-Mac	cb	80	73,000	90,000	100,000	0.05	On Yugoslavia/Greece border. Macedonians with some Serbs, Greeks, Albanians.
D Prespa-Bitda	1018	O-Mac	cb	150	146,000	180,000	200,000	0.42	Originally called Pelagonia, then (to 1959) Ochrid-Bitola. HQ Bitola.
D Zletovo-Strumica	c1350	O-Mac	cb	250	212,000	280,000	290,000	0.14	HQ Stip. In this area also are 5,000 Roman Catholics of Macedonian ethnic sub-rite.
Methodist Church of Macedonia	1890	P-Met	.....	10	1,000	1,400	3,000	3.10	Formerly in Methodist Church in Yugoslavia.
New Apostolic Church	c1970	I-3aX	x....	6	200	–	500	28.22	*Neuapostolische Kirche. NAK*
Romanian Orthodox Church		O-Rum	.....	3	4,000	1,000	7,000	0.05	Under P Bucharest. Romanian, Aromanians.
Serbian Orthodox Ch: D Skopje	c1250	O-Ser	C....	20	30,000	107,123	50,000	-3.00	Remnants of SOC diocese after 1967 secession of Macedonian Orthodox Church.
Seventh-day Adventist Church		P-Adv	x....	5	200	154	308	0.05	M=SDA(USA).
Ukrainian Orthodox Church	c1975	O-Ukr	.....	1	300	–	500	5.00	UOC. Ukrainian residents and migrant workers.
Other Protestant bodies	c1985	P-	.....	20	1,500	–	3,000	10.00	Total 10, including ECCBHV, PCCY, RCCY, CNC, COGY, AoG, CGP.
Other independent Catholic churches	c1970	I-CCa	.....	5	1,000	–	2,000	35.53	Including OCCBH.
Other independent charismatic chs	1985	I-3cW	.....	20	1,000	–	3,000	10.00	Including Association of Vineyard Chs (1 ch).
Totals				**1,106**	**955,613**	**1,282,400**	**1,351,144**		

Churches, members, growth, 1900-2025	*Congs*	*Adults*	*Affiliated*	*G%*	*Total denominations*	*6 Megablocs:* *O*	*R*	*A*	*P*	*I*	*m*
Total churches, members, and denominations (mid-1900)	400	381,000	518,000	1.30	5	3	1	0	1	0	0
Total churches, members, and denominations (mid-1970)	1,052	942,677	1,282,400	1.30	12	6	1	0	3	1	1
Total churches, members, and denominations (mid-1990)	1,100	926,000	1,309,700	0.11	36	7	1	0	15	12	1
Total churches, members, and denominations (mid-1995)	1,106	955,613	1,351,144	0.63	37	7	1	0	15	13	1
Total churches, members, and denominations (mid-2000)	1,000	910,000	1,287,192	-0.97	38	7	1	0	15	14	1
Total churches, members, and denominations (mid-2025)	1,100	989,000	1,398,000	0.33	77	10	1	0	25	40	1

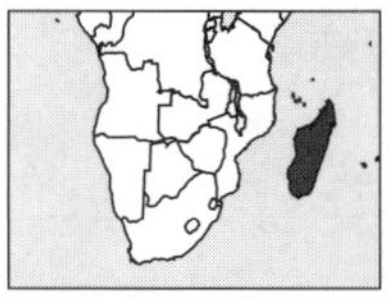

MADAGASCAR

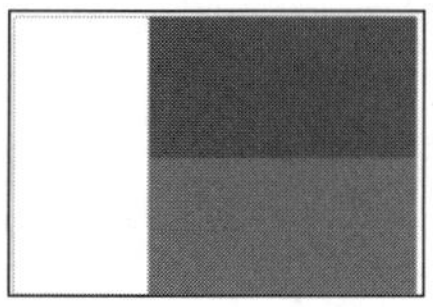

SECULAR DATA, AD 2000

STATE
Official name: Republikan'i Madagasikara (The Republic of Madagascar).
Short name: Madagascar. **Adjective of nationality:** Malagasy.
Flag: White bar; stripes of red over green.
Area: 587,041 sq. km. (226,658 sq. mi.).
Government: Multiparty republic, since 1993 (16th century monarchy, 1896 French colony, 1958 self-government, 1960 Independence, 1972 military junta, 1975 one-party Socialist state).
Legislature: National Assembly, 138 members.
Official language: Malagasy and French (Français).
Monetary unit: 1 Malagasy franc (FMG)) = 100 centimes. **US$1=** FMG 5,300.
Chief cities: ANTANANARIVO (Tananarive) 1,128,000; Fianarantsoa 440,312; Toamasina (Tamatave) 337,573; Antsiranana (Diego-Suarez) 322,896; Mahajanga (Majunga) 293,541.
Political divisions: 6 provinces.
Armed forces: 21,000.

DEMOGRAPHY
Population: 15,942,000.
Population density: 27.1/sq. km. (70.3/sq. mi.).
Under 15 years: 7,088,000.
Growth rate p.a.: 2.69% (births 36.19, deaths 9.33).
Mortality: Infant, per 1,000: 73.0; **Maternal per 100,000:** 490.0.
Life expectancy: 60 (male 58, female 61).
Household size: 4.7. **Floor area per person, sq.m:** 5.8.
Major languages: Malagasy, French, English, Swahili, Hindi, Arabic, Chinese.
Urban dwellers: 29.51%. **Urban growth rate p.a.:** 5.1%.
Labor force: 43%.

ETHNOLINGUISTIC PEOPLES
16.2% Merina (Hova, Imerina); 11.3% Betsileo; 7.6% Betsimisaraka; 7.6% Merina (Vakinankaratra); 7.0% Tsimihety.

ECONOMY
National income p.a. per person: US$230; **per family:** US$1,081.

EDUCATION
Adult literacy: 80% (male 87%, female 72%). **Schools:** 14,766.
Universities: 5. **School enrolment:** female/male: 42%/43%.

HEALTH
Access to health services: 65%. **Access to safe water:** 29%.
Hospitals: 250 (9 beds per 10,000). **Doctors:** 1,392.
Blind: 40,000. **Deaf:** 1,043,700. **Murder rate:** <1.
Lepers: 120,000. **Underweight prevalence under 5:** 34%.

LITERATURE
New book titles p.a.: 640 (40 p.a. per million). **Periodicals:** 88.
Newspapers: 7 dailies.

COMMUNICATION (per 1,000 people)
Phones: 2 (8% mobile). **Radios:** 173. **TV sets:** 24.
Daily newspaper circulation: 4. **Computers:** 15.

HUMAN LIFE AND LIBERTY (optimum condition=100.0%)
HDI: 35.0. **HSI:** 25.0. **HFI:** 40.0. **EFL:** 33.0.

Country Table 1. **Religious adherents in Madagascar, AD 1900-2025.**

Year	1900		1970		mid-1990		Annual change, 1990-2000				mid-1995		mid-2000		mid-2025	
Name	*Adherents*	*%*	*Adherents*	*%*	*Adherents*	*%*	*Natural*	*Conversion*	*Total*	*Rate*	*Adherents*	*%*	*Adherents*	*%*	*Adherents*	*%*
Christians	**1,010,200**	**39.2**	**3,366,700**	**49.1**	**5,730,000**	**49.3**	**212,288**	**3,748**	**216,036**	**3.25**	**6,780,000**	**49.3**	**7,890,359**	**49.5**	**15,000,000**	**51.8**
PROFESSION																
professing Christians	**1,010,200**	**39.2**	**3,366,700**	**49.1**	**5,730,000**	**49.3**	**212,288**	**3,748**	**216,036**	**3.25**	**6,780,000**	**49.3**	**7,890,359**	**49.5**	**15,000,000**	**51.8**
AFFILIATION																
unaffiliated Christians	140,000	5.4	223,133	3.3	282,500	2.4	10,467	-12,607	-2,140	-0.78	265,028	1.9	261,096	1.6	340,000	1.2
affiliated Christians	**870,200**	**33.7**	**3,143,567**	**45.8**	**5,447,500**	**46.8**	**201,821**	**16,355**	**218,176**	**3.43**	**6,514,972**	**47.4**	**7,629,263**	**47.9**	**14,660,000**	**50.6**
Protestants	480,000	18.6	1,351,040	19.7	2,825,000	24.3	104,675	21,825	126,500	3.77	3,433,000	25.0	4,090,000	25.7	8,000,000	27.6
Roman Catholics	387,000	15.0	1,595,241	23.3	2,670,000	23.0	98,931	305	99,236	3.21	3,133,697	22.8	3,662,363	23.0	6,800,000	23.5
Independents	200	0.0	145,532	2.1	320,000	2.8	11,857	7,143	19,000	4.77	409,685	3.0	510,000	3.2	1,150,000	4.0
Anglicans	3,000	0.1	50,414	0.7	163,000	1.4	6,040	9,660	15,700	6.98	270,000	2.0	320,000	2.0	780,000	2.7
Marginal Christians	0	0.0	800	0.0	17,000	0.2	630	420	1,050	4.93	20,160	0.2	27,500	0.2	70,000	0.2
Orthodox	0	0.0	540	0.0	2,500	0.0	93	97	190	5.82	3,430	0.0	4,400	0.0	10,000	0.0
doubly-affiliated	0	0.0	0	0.0	-550,000	-4.7	-20,379	-23,121	-43,500	6.00	-755,000	-5.5	-985,000	-6.2	-2,150,000	-7.4
Trans-megabloc groupings																
Evangelicals	310,000	12.0	308,000	4.5	625,000	5.4	23,158	9,342	32,500	4.28	776,000	5.7	950,000	6.0	2,317,000	8.0
Pentecostals/Charismatics	0	0.0	40,000	0.6	475,000	4.1	17,600	8,400	26,000	4.46	611,181	4.5	735,000	4.6	1,880,000	6.5
Great Commission Christians	**258,000**	**10.0**	**1,030,000**	**15.0**	**1,791,000**	**15.4**	**66,362**	**3,298**	**69,660**	**3.34**	**2,130,000**	**15.5**	**2,487,601**	**15.6**	**4,750,000**	**16.4**
Ethnoreligionists	1,556,000	60.3	3,366,050	49.1	5,597,000	48.1	207,385	-2,281	205,104	3.17	6,590,770	48.0	7,648,041	48.0	12,823,600	44.3
Muslims	13,000	0.5	111,900	1.6	239,700	2.1	8,882	-1,833	7,049	2.61	286,500	2.1	310,187	2.0	900,000	3.1
Nonreligious	100	0.0	4,000	0.1	32,000	0.3	1,186	694	1,880	4.73	47,000	0.3	50,796	0.3	150,000	0.5
Baha'is	0	0.0	4,000	0.1	12,000	0.1	445	-118	327	2.44	14,200	0.1	15,270	0.1	36,000	0.1
Hindus	100	0.0	1,250	0.0	7,000	0.1	259	-34	225	2.82	8,800	0.1	9,246	0.1	20,000	0.1
Chinese folk-religionists	400	0.0	4,000	0.1	6,500	0.1	241	-94	147	2.06	7,500	0.1	7,971	0.1	17,000	0.1
Atheists	0	0.0	0	0.0	4,600	0.0	170	-67	103	2.04	5,300	0.0	5,632	0.0	8,000	0.0
Buddhists	200	0.0	2,000	0.0	3,000	0.0	111	-12	99	2.88	3,700	0.0	3,985	0.0	9,000	0.0
Jews	0	0.0	100	0.0	200	0.0	7	-3	4	1.80	230	0.0	239	0.0	400	0.0
World A (unevangelized persons)	1,161,000	45.0	1,715,075	25.0	2,396,192	20.6	88,927	-57,693	31,234	1.23	2,625,155	19.1	2,710,140	17.0	3,997,032	13.8
World B (evangelized non-Christians)	408,800	15.8	1,778,525	25.9	3,505,808	30.1	129,759	53,945	183,704	4.30	4,339,112	31.6	5,341,501	33.5	9,966,968	34.4
World C (Christians)	1,010,200	39.2	3,366,700	49.1	5,730,000	49.3	212,288	3,748	216,036	3.25	6,780,000	49.3	7,890,359	49.5	15,000,000	51.8
Country's population	**2,580,000**	**100.0**	**6,860,300**	**100.0**	**11,632,000**	**100.0**	**430,974**	**0**	**430,974**	**3.20**	**13,744,268**	**100.0**	**15,942,000**	**100.0**	**28,964,000**	**100.0**

COLUMNS ROWS.
For meanings and definitions, see Codebook (Part 3). Note that, by definition, total 'Christians' = professing + crypto-Christians, which also = affiliated + unaffiliated Christians, and also = Great Commission Christians + latent Christians. Percentages may not always total exactly, due to rounding.

CENSUSES.
The religion question has not been asked.

NOTES ON RELIGIONS
ATHEISTS. Malagasy Communist Party (MCP) (pro-Soviet): membership negligible.
BAHA'IS. Founded 1955; growth from 3 local spiritual assemblies (1964) to 27 (1973) and then to 48 LSAs (1995). Peoples: Hova, Betsileo, Comorians, Antaimoro, Antaifasy, Antambahoaka, and Antaisaka.
CHRISTIANS. After the mass conversion of the Merina from 1869-1900, growth by conversions has been very small during the 20th century.
ETHNORELIGIONISTS. Animists, especially among the Sihanaka (72% animist in 1995) and Antanosy (45%). Among the southern Betsimisaraka, cult leaders known as Tangalamena officiate at the cult of the ancestors.
HINDUS. Originally immigrants from India. In 1975 a new Hindu sect, the Divine Light Mission led by Guru Maharaj Ji, began to spread and obtained 500 young converts before being banned by the military government in August 1975.
INDEPENDENTS. In 24 denominations in 1995 (see Table 2).
MUSLIMS. Strongest on northwest coast among the Sakalava. About 15,000 are Asians (Indo-Pakistanis and others). There are at least 75 mosques. Among Malagasy peoples, the Antanosy, Antaimoro, Antambahoaka, and Sakalava have been superficially islamized to some extent; the Antankarana (100,000; mixture of Sakalava, Betsimisaraka and Arabs) have been strongly islamized. *Hajj pilgrims to Mecca.* (1970) 31; (1976) 13.
NONRELIGIOUS. Mainly French.
PROTESTANTS. As a result of the mass movement among the Merina, LMS adherents grew from 5,000 in 1861 (the end of Ranavalona I's persecution) to 13,000 with 100 congregations in 1867, 37,112 in 1868 (7,066 being communicants), 230,000 with 600 congregations by 1870, and 455,000 by 1895. After 1900, the mass conversions ceased, and the proportion of affiliated Protestants (known to the churches) in the total population increased only slightly from 18.6% in 1900 to 19.7% in 1990.
ROMAN CATHOLICS. The 19th-century mass movement produced growth from 1,150 Catholics in 1870 to 387,000 (112,000 baptized including 3,000 French, 3,500 Reunionese, and 1,000 Mauritians; and 275,000 catechumens) by 1900. Thereafter, annual conversions rapidly slowed down.

Great Commission Instrument Panel: status of Madagascar (for explanation see start of Part 4)

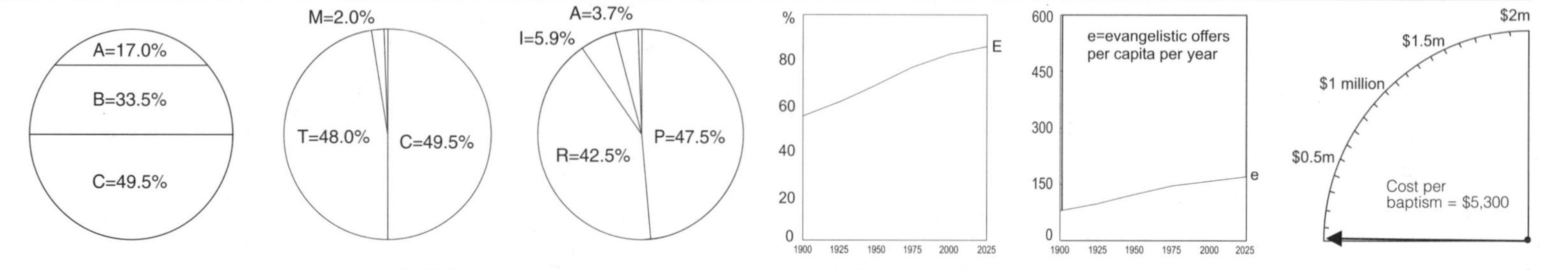

3 Worlds, AD 2000 | Religions, AD 2000 | Ecclesiastical blocs | Evangelization, 1900-2025 | Offers, 1900-2025 | Cost-effectiveness, AD 2000

Country status. Madagascar, the world's 4th largest island, lies in southwestern Indian Ocean, separated from the mainland of Africa by the Mozambique Channel. The island is rich in minerals including graphite, and its chief exports are vanilla and coffee.

HUMAN LIFE AND LIBERTY

Human need and development. Living conditions in urban centers differ from those in the countryside so that it may be said that Madagascar has 2 societies.

Country summary. **Worlds A, B, C by ethnolinguistic peoples, cities, and major civil divisions in Madagascar.**

World	PEOPLES Num	Pop 2000	C%	Christians	E%	U%	Unevangelized	CITIES Num	Pop 2000	C%	Christians	E%	U%	Unevangelized	CIVIL DIVISIONS Num	Pop 2000	C%	Christians	E%	U%	Unevangelized
A	11	475,526	5.15	24,471	43	57	272,588	0	0	0.00	0	0	0	0	0	0	0.00	0	0	0	0
B	35	9,623,794	26.89	2,588,108	75	25	2,431,528	6	1,761,248	41.21	725,781	79	21	371,830	6	15,941,725	47.86	7,629,263	83	17	2,712,335
C	9	5,842,404	85.87	5,016,683	100	0	8,221	1	1,128,000	65.00	733,200	94	6	66,214	0	0	0.00	0	0	0	0
Total	**55**	**15,941,724**	**47.86**	**7,629,262**	**83**	**17**	**2,712,337**	**7**	**2,889,248**	**50.50**	**1,458,981**	**85**	**15**	**438,044**	**6**	**15,941,725**	**47.86**	**7,629,263**	**83**	**17**	**2,712,335**

In the countryside, patterns of life have hardly changed for centuries, and herders live in huts built with their own hands, wear garments woven and dyed at home and eat the produce of his own field. Income levels also differ between rich provinces, such as Tananarive and poor provinces, such as Tulear. In rural areas, houses are small mud or bamboo thatch-covered huts. All share certain customary features linked to astrological beliefs. They are always built north-south, with two-sided roofs, and also serve as sun dials because of their orientation. Where rainfall is heavy houses are raised on posts and the floors are often up to 2 feet above ground. Houses have 3 or more openings of which one is reserved for carrying out the dead. The northeastern corner of the house also is devoted to dead ancestors. The diet of the average Malagasy is based almost entirely on rice. Few have a balanced diet throughout the year. Caloric intake drops by half during winter months when most people subsist mainly on tubers, maize, wild grains and fruits. Some 40% of the people experience hunger during the 5 winter months. Two bad harvests in succession will lead to serious famines. Lack of adequate sanitation is one of the major causes of the low life expectancy, but lack of animal proteins in diets also play their part. On the other hand, Malagasy are relatively free from many of the scourges of Africa, such as sleeping sickness, cholera, brucellosis, smallpox and yellow fever, and heart attacks are almost unknown.

Human rights and freedoms. The end of former president Didier Ratsiraka's oppressive rule has led to the establishment of the so-called Third Republic. Human rights are protected under the new constitution, but there are sporadic incidents of political violence, generally pitting supporters of Ratsiraka against his opponents. Prison conditions are notoriously inhuman, and most prisoners are expected to receive food from their relatives. Legal safeguards against arbitrary arrests and detention are ineffective. Average pretrial detention is anywhere between one year and 4 years, and 60% of the prisoners are in pretrial detention. Since 1989 when press censorship was ended, the press has been relatively free. The state-owned radio faces competition from 4 pirate stations. Ethnic rivalries among 18 distinct groups spill over into politics and religion, complicating the exercise of many of the human rights.

Human environment. Separated from the African mainland a millennia ago, Madagascar is a rich repository of some of the rarest animal and plant species, numbering over 200,000, three-fourths of which exist nowhere else in the world. Madagascar is home to 5% of the world's total species, including 1,000 types of chameleons and 1,000 species of orchids. But even this tropical paradise is not immune to pollution. Surface water is contaminated with untreated sewage and other organic wastes. In rural areas charcoal and firewood are used for household cooking, and to meet the demand for both, forests are being clear cut indiscriminately. Clearcut areas are set on fire and converted into grazing areas.

Ethnoreligionists. Witchdoctor and accomplice practicing divination and traditional medicine. Traditional Malagasy religion is still followed by 48% of the population.

NON-CHRISTIAN RELIGIONS

Traditional religions retained the allegiance of nearly half of the population in 1995 and are especially strong among the Sihanaka and Antanosy. In spite of tribal differences, a certain unity of belief and religious practice exists among the various tribal religions. The central element is a belief in the spiritual survival of the personality after death and the continuation of relations between the living and the dead. God the creator (Zahahary) exists, but the most important rituals are those concerned with maintaining the proper relationship of the living to their ancestral spirits (Razana). The ceremony of turning the corpses of the dead (famadihana) is a major occasion, when corpses are wrapped in cloths are moved around, fed, and even danced with. Belief in the negative effects of witchcraft (mpamosavy) and the beneficial function of amulets (ody) is less strong today than previously, but the ancestral cult has been little affected by modern developments in the country.

Islam is strongest on the northwest coast among the Sakalava of the Majunga region. In addition to the indigenous peoples, there are also Muslim immigrants from the Comoro Islands, forced to emigrate because of the overpopulation of their homeland, and Indo-Pakistani Muslims scattered throughout the country. In 1995 there were approximately 265,000 Sunnis. Among other smaller Muslim groups are 4,000 Ithna-Asharis, 4,000 Khojas (Ismailis), 7,000 Bohoras, and 5,000 Yemeni Zaydis.

Other religions include 8,800 Hindus, 200 Jews, a number of followers of Chinese folk religion, some Chinese Buddhists, and a rapidly-growing number of Baha'is.

1968 postage stamp commemorating 150 years of permanent Christian presence.

CHRISTIANITY

The dominant people, the Merina, immigrated to the islands from the south Pacific, beginning before the Christian era and continuing up to the 15th century. While they were settling in the central highlands, newcomers from Africa and Arabia were occupying the coastal areas. Europeans first sighted the island in 1500. During the 17th century, sporadic efforts were made to establish Catholic mission, and a number of missionaries died or were killed, but little was accomplished. King Radama (1810-28) introduced European culture and welcomed missionaries who opened schools and churches and developed a written form of the Malagasy language. The translation of the Bible completed in 1836 is still used. Queen Ranavalona I (1828-61) turned against Christianity in 1836, expelling all Europeans and ordering the death of hundreds of Christians. However, the Christian community continued to grow, and their numbers actually increased by the time the missionaries returned in 1861. Queen Ranavalona II became a Christian at her coronation in 1869 and welcomed new missionary activity. Indeed Christianity was then recognized as the faith of the island. For the next 30 years a phenomenal mass movement into the churches began, and professing Christians increased from 5,000 in 1861 to over a million by 1900 (39% of the total population). After 1900, however, mass conversions ceased, and 95 years later the proportion of Christians had only increased slightly to 49.3%.

Meanwhile, dissension between Merina rulers and the Grench caused the wars of 1883-85 and 1895-96 and resulted in the Grench taking possession of the island and making it a French colony in 1896. A new wave of terror followed with more Christians killed and many churches destroyed. Moreover, French anticlericalism resulted in severe restrictions being placed on church work. This was alleviated to some degree by the entrance of the Paris Mission in 1897, whose strong protests to the French government helped to bring about a more stable situation.

Approximately 50% of the population now consider themselves Christians, with varying degrees of commitment, some being third-generation Christians, some being recent converts from traditional religion. Most are found in the highlands, among the progressive Merina and Betsileo, with Catholics slightly more numerous than Protestants. Most Protestant clergy are Malagasy, whereas only a quarter of the Catholic clergy are nationals, celibacy being a major stumbling block. Politically, Protestants have been more nationalistic, particularly in the north, and the leader of the main opposition party during the 1960s was a Protestant pastor. However, one of the earliest church statements in favor of political independence was issued by the Catholic episcopate in 1953.

CATHOLIC CHURCH. Following the failure of the Catholic efforts to establish missions in Madagascar during the 17th century, work was quietly resumed in the southern part of the island during the 19th century persecution, although the later arrival of more Jesuits in 1861 is generally given as the official date for the beginning of the present Malagasy Catholic Church. By 1875 there were 15,000 Catholics. Catholic missions benefitted for a time after Madagascar became a French colony but later suffered from the anti-religious bias of the French government. A vicariate was established in the south in 1896, and 2 others were formed in 1900. At the turn of the century 78 priests and 100 religious were serving 112,000 baptized Catholics and 275,000 catechumens. In 1925, 9 Malagasy priest were ordained, and in 1939 the first Malagasy bishop was consecrated. The Malagasy hierarchy was established in 1955 and divided into 3 provinces, and a Malagasy became archbishop in 1960. An attempt to involve the wider Catholic communities in the affairs of the church was evident in 1972 when the bishops decided to call a National Synod to be prepared by diocesan synods; this Synod was in fact begun in 1975.

With Protestantism firmly rooted in the high plateau and among the upper classes of Merina society, the Catholic Church has orientated its work towards the peasant masses and the coastal religions. This continues to characterize Catholicism, although it has also penetrated the intellectual and social elites through its schools.

The Holy See has diplomatic relations with Madagascar and in AD 2000 is represented to government and the Catholic hierarchy by a pro-nuncio residing in Tananarive.

Eglise du Réveil Spirituelle Malgache. White-robed priests and faithful meet after Sunday liturgy in their headquarters church, a converted mansion, in Tananarive. The Spiritual Head of the church stands in background under a Malagasy text which reads simply: *Mibebaha ('Repent')*.

PROTESTANT CHURCH. The London Missionary Society was the first mission to arrive, in 1818. Through its efforts, by 1836, 30,000 had learned to read, 2,000 had become Christians and the translation of the Bible had been completed. All missionaries were expelled in 1836 and none were permitted to return until the death of the anti-Christian queen in 1861. At that time the LMS found 5,000 disciples who had retained their faith throughout the persecution. The baptism of the new queen and her husband in 1869 resulted in a mass movement into the church, membership rising from 13,000 in 1867 to 230,000 in 600 congregations by 1870. By 1895 there were 455,000 Merina Protestants, 74 missionary pastors and 1,313 catechists. The entrance of French Catholics and other missions in the 1860s resulted in growing tension between Christians associated with English missions and those of French missions. French Jesuits actually took over most of the schools for a time, after Madagascar became a French colony. British Friends arrived in 1869 and the Paris Mission in 1897; and when comity agreements were reached among Protestants in 1913, the LMS released 1,290 schools and 500 of its 700 churches to these other societies. All of these groups have been concentrated in the northern half of the island, and in 1968, they united to form the Church of Jesus Christ in Madagascar, which in 1995 includes nearly two-thirds of all Malagasy Protestants.

Eglise Luthérienne Malgache. *Top.* Antaimoro revivalist prophetess Nenilava ('My tall Mother'), Mrs. Volahavana Germaine, catechist's widow who leads 40-year-old Lutheran revival at Ankaramalaza. *Lower.* Nenilava conducts healings in Ankaramalaza Lutheran Church, assisted by 2 Lutheran foreign missionaries. On the wall are the words of Jesus concerning John the Baptist: 'What did you go out to see? Someone dressed in fine clothes? A prophet? Yes, I tell you and far more than a prophet'.

In 1866 the Norwegian Missionary Society sent workers to the southern part of the island, and 2 American Lutheran bodies entered in 1892 and 1895. In 1950 these 3 Lutheran groups united to form the Malagasy Lutheran Church with 6 independent synods. In 1967, at their centenary, there were 344 ordained national pastors and 1,440 trained evangelists. In 1995, with 852,000 members, it is Madagascar's second largest Protestant church.

Seventh-day Adventists entered in the 1920s, and 2 small Pentecostal groups are also at work: Swedish Free Missions, and the United Pentecostal Church.

Protestants have always placed great emphasis on the development of schools and now operate more than 800 primary schools and nearly 300 secondary schools.

INDIGENOUS CHURCHES. A total of about 21 independent churches have been founded by Malagasy leaders, both as a result of schisms from parent mission-related bodies and also from the numerous revival movements since the Soatanana revival in 1895. The first to emerge was the Malagasy Protestant Church Tranozozoro Antranobiriky, a schism from the LMS in 1894. Many others have subsequently broken from LMS and Lutheran missions. Of the Revivalists (Fifohazana), the best known are the Disciples of the Lord who, after remaining for 60 years inside the Lutheran Church, finally seceded in 1955. Another important schism in 1955 from the LMS was that of the Evangelical Reformed Church. In 1966, the Bible Baptist Church, which split from the LMS in 1930, invited Conservative Baptists from the USA to send missionaries to aid them in their work.

ANGLICAN CHURCH. Both the SPG and CMS arrived in 1863, but the latter withdrew after 10 years. The SPG began along the east coast and later expanded its work to the far north and the general area of the capital. The Anglican Church is found throughout the country and has shown remarkable growth since 1965. The 3 Madagascar dioceses are part of the Church of the Province of the Indian Ocean since the latter's formation in 1973.

ORTHODOX CHURCH. The Greek Orthodox Church was established in Madagascar in 1927 and is under the Patriarchate of Alexandria. There are 3 churches, but no priest has been resident for several years.

Renewal movements. In the 1990s the Pentecostal/Charismatic Renewal continued to spread rapidly across most older churches, and numbered over 735,000 adherents (of whom 2% Pentecostals, 64% Charismatics, and 34% Independents).

Indigenous missions. Some Christians from Madagascar were sent to the mainland as missionaries at the end of the 19th century. However, in the twentieth century most of the Roman Catholic missionaries have gone to France and Reunion, while most Protestants go to surrounding African countries.

CHURCH AND STATE

Since the end of the persecutions in 1861, freedom of religion and worship has been consistently recognized. The constitution of 1959 was suspended by the new military regime in 1972 and replaced for 5 years by a 'Referendary Law', but no radical changes in the government's attitude towards religion have appeared. The constitution of 1959 made reference to God, guaranteed freedom of worship in the preamble and affirmed the 'neutrality' of the state with regard to the various religions (Article 2). After Madagascar achieved independence, the Malagasy government passed legislation on specifically Malagasy religions, taking into account local factors, which differs slightly from the old French legislation. According to Ordinance 62-117 of October 1962, followed by the present regime: (1) the state provides no salaries or subsidies to any religion; (2) it is not necessary to secure authorization for holding religious meetings, whether public or private; (3) when the number of faithful who regularly attend private religious meetings reaches one hundred, a religious association may be formed and can obtain legal recognition; (4) a religious association can always integrate itself with a recognized church if the majority of the members so desire; (5) several religious associations may group themselves together to form a church to whose juridical existence and moral personality the government, through the Ministry of the Interior, may give recognition. An amendment to Ordinance 62-117 recognized at the outset the juridical existence and moral personality of 6 churches each of which had a long history in Madagascar and had proved its vitality and carried out activities judged profitable to the country in the cultural and social domains. These included the Catholic Church (Eglizy Katolika Apostolika Romana), Anglicans (Fiangonana Episkopal Malagasy), LMS (Fianfonan'i Kristy eto Madagasikara), Lutherans (Fiangonana Loterana Malagasy), PEMA (Fiangonana Ara-Pilazantsara eto Madagasikara), and the Friends (Fiangonana Frengy Malagasy). In addition, Decrees 63-586 (15 October 1963) and 73-6127 (18 May 1973) recognize 3 other churches: the Church of the Revival (Fifohazan' ny Mpianatrty ny Tompo), the FMTA (Fiangonana Protestanta Malagasy Tranozozoro Antranobiriky), and the Seventh-day Adventist Church.

Each year there is held a census of worship places, which are exempt from taxation, and their personnel. Each denomination may provide religious instruction within the primary or secondary school system; and the provincial budget subsidizes Christian schools according to the number of teachers employed and their level of education. In 1974 following the publication of an open letter from the president of the Episcopal Commission for Catholic Education, the Malagasy government decided to subsidize private schools, both confessional and non-confessional, of which many were in serious financial difficulties.

Until May 1972 when riots put an end to the concentration of power in the hands of president Tsiranana, the Protestant churches were considered more autonomous and less tied to the state than the Catholic Church. Protestants seemed less concerned than Catholics about state subsides for private schools. They also followed a teaching program more closely in touch with the realities of the situation. The Catholic Church followed the official program but saw its own influence over educational policy decrease after independence. In the face of the arbitrary regime of Tsiranana, the Catholic hierarchy adopted a policy of not involving itself in politics, explicable in part by the slow rate of malgachisation (indigenization of leadership). At the end of 1971, 10 of the 16 bishops were Europeans and only one of the 4 bishops consecrated between 1967 and 1971 was Malagasy; and by 1973, 9 out of 19 were expatriates. Nevertheless, 2 Catholic journals, Lumiere and Lakroan'i Madagasikara, are noted for their freedom of expression. Several Catholics and Protestants, including priests, were arrested in 1971; and the leaders of the Hery Malagasy Association (HEMA), a program for the social and political training of young Catholic adults modeled after the New Life Movement in France, were thrown into prison for alleged 'Maoist subversion'. Because of the political troubles which shook the country in 1972, and also due to the influence of Vatican II, the Catholic bishops have called for wide-ranging reforms in the area of development (pastoral letter of 26 March 1972 on 'The Church and development in Madagascar') and the involvement of Christians in politics (Christmas pastoral letter of 1973 on 'The Church and politics'). In a joint pastor letter published at the end of 1972, the Catholic episcopate broke all ties with the old order; and in 1975, in a decision unique among Catholic hierarchies, the bishops refused to organize a national pilgrimage to Rome to celebrate the Holy Year, arguing that because of the poverty of Madagascar such would be a negative witness.

BROADCASTING AND MEDIA

Shortwave programs in French and Malagasy can be received from KNLS, FEBA (Seychelles), and TWR (Swaziland). HCJB World Radio helped start local stations in Madagascar in cooperation with ministries like Island Mission. The Lutheran World Federation has a studio in Madagascar that produces programs in Malagasi and French. Madagascar is a member of UNDA.

Over 158,000 have seen the 'Jesus' Film, mainly through film team showings. Around 33,000 have responded with decisions.

INTERDENOMINATIONAL ORGANIZATIONS

The Christian Council of Madagascar (Fiomban' ny Fiangonana Protestanta eto Madagasikara, FFPM) was created in 1958, replacing the Missionary Conference formed in 1913 by the LMS and 2 Lutheran missions. It consists of the 2 major churches, the Church of Jesus Christ in Madagascar in the north and the Malagasy Lutheran Church in the south. Anglicans were members of the former missionary conference until 1927 when comity conflicts caused their withdrawal. However, relations between the FFPM and both the Anglican and Catholic churches are good, and the council sponsors a Commission for the Study of Church Unity. In addition to denominational seminaries, a united theological college has been established. There is also a Mixed Commission of Theologians which includes Catholics. The Catholic Episcopal Conference has attached to it a Commission for Ecumenism.

FUTURE TRENDS AND PROSPECTS

Significant Christian gains are likely to be made in the wake of waning tribal religions, projected to fall below 45% by 2025 (Christians rising to 52% in the same period).

Though ethnic religions have displayed remarkable tenacity in light of the growth of the Christian church, it is possible that as a percentage they will decline to less than 40% of the population by AD 2050. Christianity, on the other hand, will then reach 60% by mid-century.

BIBLIOGRAPHY

2000 titres: littératures de l'océan indien: Comores, Madagascar, Maurice, Réunion, Seychelles. Notre Librairie, no. 116. [Paris: CLEF, 1994]. 174p.

'A historical and missiological account of the pioneer missionaries in the establishment of the American Lutheran mission in southeast Madagascar, 1887–1911: John P. and Oline Hogstad.' J. B. Vigen. Th.D. thesis, Lutheran School of Theology, Chicago, 1991. 292p.

'A study in the self–propagating church: Madagascar,' C. W. Forman, in *Frontiers of the Christian world mission since 1938*, p.115–70. W. C. Harr (ed). New York: Harper, 1962. (The Soatanana Revival, p. 150-65).

Annuaire de l'Eglise Catholique à Madagascar. Antananarivo, Madagascar: Impr. Catholique, 1971.

'Church and world in Madagascar: a Lutheran perspective.' J. Fenomanana. M.S.T. thesis, Trinity Lutheran Seminary, Columbus, OH, 1979. 114p.

'Church growth on the island of Madagascar.' L. D. Jacobsen. M.A. thesis, Fuller Theological Seminary, Pasadena, CA, 1967. 105p.

Contes et mythes de Madagascar et des Comores. Paris: Institut des langues et civilisations orientales, 1987. 152p.

Diary Malagasy 1966. Antananarivo, Madagascar: Imprimerie Luthérienne, 1965.

'Factors underlying accelerated growth trends as reflected in the history of the Malagasy Baptist Church.' M. Neumann. D.Min. thesis, Fuller Theological Seminary, Pasadena, CA, 1990. 409p.

Friends in Madagascar, 1867–1967: a short account drawn up to mark the centenary of Quaker work in the island and the beginning of a new era. London: Friends Service Council, 1967. 59p.

'John Ratsizehena: a self–ordained Malagasy bishop,' B. A. Bow, *Journal of religious history* (North Ryde, NSW, Australia), (December 1976), 158–172.

La Mission Luthérienne à Madagascar. P. Buchsenschutz. Antananarivo, Madagascar: Imprimerie de la Mission Norvégienne, 1938. 34p.

Langues, cultures et sociétés de l'océan Indien. Asie du sud-est et monde insulindien, vol. 8, nos. 3-4. Paris: A.S.E.M.I, 1977. 263p.

Le mort et les coutumes funéraires à Madagascar. R. Decary. Paris: G.-P. Maisonneuve et Larose, 1962. 305p. (Excellent illustrations of ancestral cult).

L'Église Catholique à Madagascar EKAR. Antananarivo, Madagascar: Imprimerie Catholique, 1990. 215p.

Les esprits de la vie à Madagascar. J. Faublée. Paris: Presses Universitaires, 1954. 139p.

Les îles de l'Océan indien: Comores, Madagascar, Maurice, Réunion, Seychelles: bibliographie réalisée à partir de la Banque de données IBISCUS, triée par grands domaines. P. Hue. *Collection Réseaux documentaires sur le développement, Série Références bibliographiques.* Paris: Ministère de la coopération et du développement, [1991]. 285p.

Les Musulmans à Madagascar et aux Iles Comores. G. Ferrand. *Algiers Université Faculté des lettres Publications*, Ser. 1, t. 9. Paris: E. Leroux, 1891–1902. 3 vols.

L'inculturation de l'Eglise catholique dans le nord de Madagascar. J. M. Aubert. Antsiranana, Madagascar: Institut supérieur de théologie et de philosophie de Madagascar, Etablissement d'Antsiranana, [1986]. 43p.

'Madagascar,' in *Annuaire des missions catholiques, 1968-1969: Afrique francophone et al*, p.1070–1156. Paris: ONPC, 1969.

Madagascar. H. Bradt. *World bibliographical series*, vol. 165. Oxford, UK: CLIO Press, 1993. 137p. (See especially 'Religion,' p.53–7).

Madagascar and the Protestant impact: the work of the British missions, 1818–95. B. A. Gow. *Dalhousie African studies series.* London: Longman, 1979. 283p.

Madagascar et le Christianisme. Histoire œcumenique. Paris: Agence de coopération culturelle et technique, 1993. 518p.

Madagascar on the move. J. T. Hardyman. London: Livingstone Press, 1950.

Madagascar's miracle story. F. Richardson. Hazelwood, MO: Word Aflame Press, 1989. 176p.

Norwegian missions in African history. J. Simensen & F. Fuglestad (eds). Oxford, UK: Oxford University Press, 1986. (Volume 2 is on Madagascar).

Taboo: a study of Malagasy customs and beliefs. J. Rund. Oslo: Oslo University Press, 1960. 324p. (By a Norwegian Lutheran missionary).

Taboo: a study of Malagasy customs and beliefs. J. Ruud. London: George Allen & Unwin, 1960.

'The Church and Christians in Madagascar today,' P. Gérard, *Pro Mundi Vita*, Africa Dossier 6 (July–August, 1978), 1–39.

The martyr church: a narrative of the introduction, progress, and triumph of Christianity in Madagascar. W. Ellis. London: John Snow, 1869. 406p.

The possessed and the dispossessed: spirits, identity, and power in a Madagascar migrant town. L. A. Sharp. *Comparative studies of health systems and medical care*, no. 37. Berkeley, CA: University of California Press, 1993. 364p.

The waiting isle: Madagascar and its church. G. F. Burton. London: Livingstone Press, 1953.

'Theologien–prêtre africain et developpement de la culture negro–africaine,' P. R. Ralibera, in *Cahiers Présence Africaine*, p.155–87. Paris: Présence Africaine, 1964.

Triumph in death: the story of the Malagasy martyrs. F. G. Smith. Welwyn, UK: Evangelical Press, 1987. 128p.

Un culte de possession à Madagascar: le tromba. J. Estrade. Paris: Editions Anthropos, 1977. 391p.

Vingt ans après Vatican II: recherches dans l'Eglise catholique à Madagascar. Antsiranana, Madagascar: Institut supérieur de théologie et de philosophie de Madagascar, Etablissement d'Antsiranana, [1987]. 62p.

Country Table 2. **Organized churches and denominations in Madagascar.**

Official name (bold type = church with over 10% of all affiliated) 1	*Begun* 2	*Type* 3	*Counc* 4	*Congs* 5	*Adults* 6	*Affiliated 1970* 7	*Affiliated 1995* 8	*G%* 9	*Names, notes, and other statistics* (see Codebook, Part 3) 10
Assemblées de Dieu	c1968	I-3pA	.....	76	9,000	1,000	13,800	11.07	*Assemblies of God.* Schism of 50% ex FPM after founder deported. M=SFM(Sweden).
Eglise Adventiste du Septième Jour	1926	P-Adv	x....	144	26,000	20,700	65,000	4.68	*Seventh-day Adventists,* Indian Ocean Union Mission. 31nx,1h,1j,5r,164t(10504),520Y.
Eglise Apostolique de Madagascar	1968	I-Ang	IT...	123	14,000	15,000	25,000	2.06	*Apostolic Ch.* Schism ex Episcopal Ch. M=AOC(USA). 5n,25m,1p,1s(5),W=50%,22Y,90y.
Eglise Baptiste Biblique à Madagascar	1930	I-Bap	IF...	30	1,200	5,000	4,000	-0.89	*FBMB. Bible Baptist Ch in M.* Schism ex LMS. 1966, former M=CBFMS(USA). Mail courses. 10f.
Eglise Catholique au Madagascar:	1540	R-Lat	P.S.S	312	1,565,900	1,595,241	3,133,697	2.74	*Eglizy Katolika..* C=14+5+55. (1975) 61345Yy. (1990) 266n 486x 1072m 2581w 237170Yy
M Antananarivo (Tananarive)	1643	R-Lat	Ps	56	295,000	309,201	579,917	2.55	Catholics 90%, Merina. M=SJ,OSB,Car. 1p,1s. 57n 114x 287m 731w 17941Yy
D Ambatondrazaka	1959	R-Lat	Posst	16	102,000	58,909	195,000	4.90	34% Merina, 32% Sihanaka, 20% Bezanozano. 1p. 4n 20x 30m 140w 4900Yy
D Antsirabé	1913	R-Lat	Pms	25	272,000	291,833	504,643	2.21	95% Merina, 5% Betsileo, 678 Whites. 38n 30x 131m 211w 156687Yy
D Miarinarivo	1933	R-Lat	Ps	14	66,000	73,989	139,839	2.58	95% Merina, 5% Betsileo, 34 Whites. 11n 7x 9m 32w 6747Yy
D Tsiroanomandidy	1949	R-Lat	Posst	14	52,000	50,906	114,173	3.28	Sakalava, 1,095 Whites M=OSST(Spain). MS. 1p. 8n 11x 17m 67w 3209Yy
M Antsirarana (Diégo-Saurez)	1896	R-Lat	Ps	21	105,000	83,257	330,115	5.66	55% Betsimisaraka, 25% Tsimihety. M=CSSp. 31n 16x 47m 122w 6219Yy
D Ambanja	1848	R-Lat	Pofmc	18	24,000	26,822	51,929	2.68	50% Tsimihety, 35% Sakalava, 10% Makoa. 19n 17x 26m 86w 2924Yy
D Mahajanga (Majunga)	1923	R-Lat	Ps	18	34,000	46,003	65,130	1.40	Sakalava, Betsileo, Tsimihety. M=CSSp. 1p. 16n 20x 29m 101w 1984Yy
D Port-Bergé	1993	R-Lat	Ps	3	10,000	–	12,979	50.00	Formerly in D Mahajanga. 5n 1x 1m 20w 527Yy
D Toamasina (Tamatave)	1935	R-Lat	Psmm	17	85,000	77,714	151,420	2.70	Betsimisaraks, 2,8a54 Whites. 1p. 6n 29x 49m 92w 2318Yy
M Fianarantsoa	1913	R-Lat	Psj	7	339,000	365,740	645,827	2.30	82% Betsileo, 8% Merina, 7% Tanala. M=SJ. 1p. 49n 79x 234m 356w 20678Yy
D Farafangana	1923	R-Lat	Ps	19	30,600	69,500	53,511	-1.04	38% Antaimoro, 32% Antaisaka, 9% Antaifasy. M=SJ. 7n 22x 31m 93w 2094Yy
D Ihosy	1967	R-Lat	Pms	9	18,600	15,697	27,508	2.27	Bara tribe, 36 Whites. M=CM(Italy),MS. 1n 17x 26m 57w 1071Yy
D Mananjary	1968	R-Lat	Ps	12	34,800	32,732	68,518	3.00	Antaimoro tribe, 500 Whites. M=SJ,MEP. 5n 22x 24m 69w 1907Yy
D Morombe	1960	R-Lat	Pmsf	10	12,600	12,917	23,448	2.41	44% Betsileo, 31% Sakalava, 14% Bara. M=MSF. 0n 15x 16m 22w 857Yy
D Morondava	1938	R-Lat	Pms	20	20,500	22,871	34,000	1.60	Sakalava, Bara, 210 Whites. M=MS(USA). 1n 20x 30m 36w 1484Yy
D Tolagnaro (Fort-Dauphin)	1896	R-Lat	Pcm	14	33,500	21,000	72,818	5.10	Very poor. Antandroy, Antanosy. 1971 riots. 5n 25x 37m 113w 3846Yy
D Toliara (Tuléar)	1957	R-Lat	Paa	19	31,300	36,150	62,922	2.24	50% Sakalava, 17% Mahafalv, 4% Betsileo. 3n 21x 48m 233w 1777Yy
Eglise de Jésus-Christ à Madagascar	1818	P-Uni	RWA.N	4,492	1,200,000	881,487	2,500,000	4.26	*FJKM.* 1968 union of FKM, FPM. M=CCWM,PEMS,FSC. 830n,75r(61000),4s,1u,W=34%.
E du Réveil des Disciples du Seigneur	1955	I-3pA	I....	400	10,000	11,534	27,000	3.46	*Fifohazana.* 1895, Soatanana Revival; 1955, schism ex FLM. Betsileo. 104n.
Eglise du Réveil Spirituelle Malgache	1958	I-3pA	I....	300	12,000	10,000	25,000	3.73	*FPPM. Malagasy Spiritual Ch of Revival. Vomiters.* Schism ex Mandoa Revival in FLM.
Eglise Episcopale de Madagascar	1864	A-Hig	AW.V.	500	110,000	50,414	270,000	6.94	*EEM. Eklesia Episkopaly Malagasy.* 1973, in CPIO. 3 Dioceses. M=USPG. 57n,4x,163Y,1959y.
Eglise Evangélique Libre	c1965	I-Eva	.....	135	10,800	1,000	24,000	13.56	*Free Evangelical Church.*
Eglise FSSM		I-Non	.....	197	15,800	25,000	35,000	0.05	Indigenous Nondenominationalists.
Eglise Neo-Apostolique	c1965	I-3aX	.....	150	17,000	10,000	25,685	3.85	*NAC/NAK. New Apostolic Ch.* M=Neuapostolische Kirche(HQ Zurich).
Eglise Orthodoxe Grecque	1927	O-Gre	Cw...	3	378	540	630	0.62	*Greek Orthodox Ch,* AD Rhodesia (P Akexandria). In Majunga. Greeks. No priest.
Eglise Orthodoxe Russe	c1970	O-Rus	.....	3	1,500	–	2,800	37.37	*ROC. Russian Orthodox Ch,* under P Moscow. Originally military and political advisers.
Eglise Orthodoxe Russe en Exil	c1980	I-Rus	.....	1	100	–	200	6.67	*ROCOR. Russian Orthodox Ch Outside of Russia.*
Eglise Luthérienne Malgache	1866	P-Lut	LWA.N	4,096	478,000	448,253	852,000	2.60	*FLM. Malagasy Lutheran Ch.* M=NMS,ALC(USA). 444nx,128f,6p,1s(52),1943Y,14290y.
Eglise Malgache du Réveil	1962	I-3pA	I....	200	18,000	1,000	40,000	15.90	*Malagasy Revivalist Ch, Jesus Saves. Jesosy Mamonjy.* Pentecostals. Banned 1970.
Eglise Malgache Luthérienne Evangile	c1960	I-Lut	.....	10	1,500	1,000	3,000	4.49	*FALM. Lutheran Gospel Ch. Fiangonana Ara-pilazantsara Loterana Malagasy.* Ex FLM.
Eglise Pentecostale Unie	1969	P-Pel	x....	160	4,800	600	12,000	12.73	*United Pentecostal Ch. Jesus Only Church.* Unitarians. M=UPC(USA). 2n,4f,1p(58).
Eglise Pentecôtiste en Madagascar	1961	I-3pA	.....	5	500	200	1,000	6.65	*FPM. Pentecostal Full Gospel Ch.* Lebanese founder M A Daoud; healings, deported.
Eglise Protestante Malgache TA	1894	I-Con	IvI..	120	15,000	23,401	32,000	1.26	*FMTA.* Ex LMS. 1967, applied to join WCC. 36n,10m,5w,1s(5),W=25%,5000Yy.
Eglise Protestante Témoin à Jésus	1967	I-Ref	.....	106	9,500	100	19,000	23.35	*FPVJ. Vavolombelon'i Jesosy. Protestant Witness to Jesus Church.* Schism ex FJKM.
Eglise Réformée Evangélique de M	1955	I-Con	IT...	500	87,500	36,297	105,000	4.34	*Mission Ev de Tananarive. MET.* Ex LMS Museum. 33n,124m,1p,1s(8),60Y,126y.
Témoins de Jehovah	1933	m-Jeh	x....	90	3,673	800	20,160	13.78	*Jehovah's Witnesses. Vavolombelon'i Jehovah.* Banned 1970. (1975) 41Y. (1995) 1438Y.
Other Malagasy indigenous churches		I-3pA	.....	300	10,000	5,000	30,000	0.05	Total about 10 AICs (see list below).
Other Protestant bodies	c1970	P-	.....	75	2,000	–	4,000	39.34	Around 15 recent missions from Europe, America, India, Indonesia: total 15.
Doubly-affiliated		2-aff			-376,000	0	-755,000		Evangelicals and Pentecostals who are also baptized Roman Catholics.
Totals				**12,528**	**3,248,151**	**3,143,567**	**6,514,972**		

Churches, members, growth, 1900-2025	*Congs*	*Adults*	*Affiliated*	*G%*	*Total denominations*	*6 Megablocs:* O	R	A	P	I	m
Total churches, members, and denominations (mid-1900)	2,000	470,000	870,200	1.85	5	0	1	1	2	1	0
Total churches, members, and denominations (mid-1970)	9,672	1,699,337	3,143,567	1.85	26	1	1	1	4	18	1
Total churches, members, and denominations (mid-1990)	11,000	2,716,000	5,447,500	2.79	49	2	1	1	19	25	1
Total churches, members, and denominations (mid-1995)	12,528	3,248,151	6,514,972	3.64	49	2	1	1	19	25	1
Total churches, members, and denominations (mid-2000)	14,000	3,803,000	7,629,263	3.21	49	2	1	1	19	25	1
Total churches, members, and denominations (mid-2025)	30,000	7,308,000	14,660,000	2.65	96	3	1	1	30	60	1

NOTES ON TABLE ABOVE

NATIONAL COUNCILS (Column 4, 5th letter).

- C = Fédération des Eglises Protestants de Madagascar (FFPM), 1913.
- I = Fédération des Eglises Indépendantes de Madagascar (FFKMMT).
- N = Conseil Chrétien des Eglises à Madagascar (CCEM, Christian Council of Churches in Madagascar), (Fiombonan'ny Fiongonana Kristiana eto Madagasikara, FFKM) (Christian Council of Madagascar), 1980.
- S = Conférence Episcopal de Madagascar (CEM) (Episcopal Conference of Madagascar), also member of FFKM.

OTHER MALAGASY INDIGENOUS CHURCHES. In addition to those listed in the table, there are about 10 others, including those following. Schisms ex LMS: Malagasy Christian Ch, Ankazomasina, Malagasy Christian Protestant Ch Ankadilalana, Malagasy Protestant Church Antanimena (1916). Schism ex FMTA: Malagasy Protestant Tranozozoro Antanifotsy Ch. Schisms ex Lutheran Church: Malagasy Christian Protestant Church Antanetikely (c1960), Malagasy Christian Protestant Church Morarano II (c1960). Many of the 50,000 adults in the Soatanana revival (Disciples of the Lord) are still members of Protestant churches (FJKM, FLM). Other Third-World indigenous bodies: in 1975 the Korean movement, Holy Spirit Association for the Unification of World Christianity, began work; but, soon after, was suppressed by the state and its workers expelled.

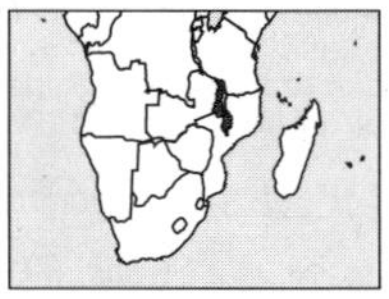

MALAWI

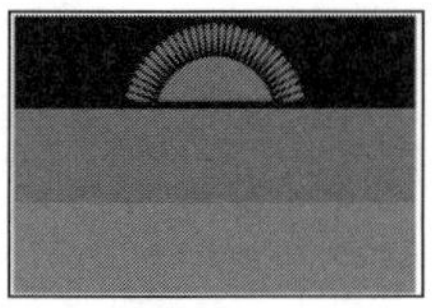

SECULAR DATA, AD 2000

STATE
Official name: Dziko la Malawi (The Republic of Malawi).
Short name: Malawi. **Adjective of nationality:** Malawian.
Flag: Black, red, and green stripes, with red rising sun on black stripe.
Area: 118,484 sq. km. (45,747 sq. mi.).
Government: Multiparty republic, since 1993 (1891 British protectorate of British Central Africa later Nyasaland, 1953 in Central African Federation, 1963 self-government, 1964 Independence, 1966 republic, 1970 one-party republic).
Legislature: National Assembly, 177 members.
Official language: Chichewa and English.
Monetary unit: 1 Malawi kwacha (MK) = 100 tambala. **US$1=** MK 40.05.
Chief cities: Blantyre-Limbe 501,836; LILONGWE 354,102.
Political divisions: 24 provinces.
Armed forces: 10,000.

DEMOGRAPHY
Population: 10,925,000.
Population density: 92.2/sq. km. (238.8/sq. mi.).
Under 15 years: 5,151,000.
Growth rate p.a.: 2.37% (births 45.11, deaths 21.43).
Mortality: Infant, per 1,000: 126.5; **Maternal per 100,000:** 560.0.
Life expectancy: 40 (male 40, female 41).
Household size: 4.3. **Floor area per person, sq.m:** 7.0.
Major languages: Chewa (Chichewa, similar to Chinyanja), English Tumbuka (Chitumbuka), Yao, Ngoni (Zulu), Hindi, Portuguese and 10 smaller languages.
Urban dwellers: 15.35%. **Urban growth rate p.a.:** 5.2%.
Labor force: 30%.

ETHNOLINGUISTIC PEOPLES
34.7% Chewa (Western Nyanja); 12.1% Southern Nyanja (Maravi); 9.0% Ngoni (Mombera, Gomani); 7.8% Yao (Ajao, Ajawa); 7.8% Tumbuka (Phoka).

ECONOMY
National income p.a. per person: US$169; **per family:** US$730.

EDUCATION
Adult literacy: 56% (male 71%, female 41%). **Schools:** 3,225.
Universities: 4. **School enrolment:** female/male: 83%/92%.

HEALTH
Access to health services: 80%. **Access to safe water:** 45%.
Hospitals: 395 (16 beds per 10,000). **Doctors:** 186.
Blind: 18,400. **Deaf:** 659,000. **Murder rate:** 3.
Lepers: 70,000. **Underweight prevalence under 5:** 30%.

LITERATURE
New book titles p.a.: 330 (30 p.a. per million). **Periodicals:** 20.
Newspapers: 1 daily.

COMMUNICATION (per 1,000 people)
Phones: 3 (21% mobile). **Radios:** 112. **TV sets:** 70.
Daily newspaper circulation: 2. **Computers:** 5.

REFUGEES
Alien refugees from other countries: 2,000.

HUMAN LIFE AND LIBERTY (optimum condition=100.0%)
HDI: 32.0. **HSI:** 21.0. **HFI:** 35.0. **EFL:** 32.0.

Country Table 1. **Religious adherents in Malawi, AD 1900-2025.**

Year	1900		1970		mid-1990		Annual change, 1990-2000				mid-1995		mid-2000		mid-2025	
Name	Adherents	%	Adherents	%	Adherents	%	Natural	Conversion	Total	Rate	Adherents	%	Adherents	%	Adherents	%
Christians	**13,500**	**1.8**	**2,665,400**	**59.0**	**7,006,000**	**75.1**	**119,353**	**18,858**	**138,211**	**1.82**	**7,342,000**	**75.9**	**8,388,107**	**76.8**	**15,770,900**	**79.0**
PROFESSION																
professing Christians	**13,500**	**1.8**	**2,665,400**	**59.0**	**7,006,000**	**75.1**	**119,353**	**18,858**	**138,211**	**1.82**	**7,342,000**	**75.9**	**8,388,107**	**76.8**	**15,770,900**	**79.0**
AFFILIATION																
unaffiliated Christians	3,000	0.4	391,038	8.7	1,122,350	12.0	19,117	4,233	23,350	1.91	1,182,382	12.2	1,355,847	12.4	2,270,900	11.4
affiliated Christians	**10,500**	**1.4**	**2,274,362**	**50.3**	**5,883,650**	**63.0**	**100,236**	**14,625**	**114,861**	**1.80**	**6,159,618**	**63.7**	**7,032,260**	**64.4**	**13,500,000**	**67.6**
Roman Catholics	500	0.1	993,448	22.0	2,240,000	24.0	38,153	7,633	45,786	1.88	2,349,704	24.3	2,697,860	24.7	5,100,000	25.6
Protestants	6,800	0.9	960,356	21.3	1,850,000	19.8	31,510	-2,510	29,000	1.47	1,907,285	19.7	2,140,000	19.6	3,912,000	19.6
Independents	100	0.0	187,758	4.2	1,500,000	16.1	25,549	7,451	33,000	2.01	1,584,579	16.4	1,830,000	16.8	3,700,000	18.5
Anglicans	3,100	0.4	76,500	1.7	179,000	1.9	3,049	2,051	5,100	2.54	200,000	2.1	230,000	2.1	500,000	2.5
Marginal Christians	0	0.0	55,300	1.2	112,000	1.2	1,908	-108	1,800	1.50	115,400	1.2	130,000	1.2	280,000	1.4
Orthodox	0	0.0	1,000	0.0	2,650	0.0	45	130	175	5.20	2,650	0.0	4,400	0.0	8,000	0.0
Trans-megabloc groupings																
Evangelicals	6,400	0.9	384,030	8.5	800,000	8.6	13,626	374	14,000	1.63	830,032	8.6	940,000	8.6	2,000,000	10.0
Pentecostals/Charismatics	0	0.0	85,000	1.9	1,600,000	17.1	27,252	6,748	34,000	1.95	1,689,262	17.5	1,940,000	17.8	3,800,000	19.0
Great Commission Christians	**12,500**	**1.7**	**994,000**	**22.0**	**2,091,000**	**22.4**	**35,615**	**988**	**36,603**	**1.63**	**2,166,000**	**22.4**	**2,457,034**	**22.5**	**4,600,000**	**23.1**
Muslims	22,500	3.0	725,000	16.1	1,394,120	14.9	23,746	-2,054	21,692	1.46	1,428,000	14.8	1,611,040	14.8	2,900,000	14.5
Ethnoreligionists	714,000	95.2	1,113,220	24.6	876,000	9.4	14,921	-17,559	-2,638	-0.31	834,750	8.6	849,620	7.8	1,100,000	5.5
Nonreligious	0	0.0	500	0.0	20,000	0.2	341	413	754	3.25	22,000	0.2	27,544	0.3	70,000	0.4
Baha'is	0	0.0	8,400	0.2	18,000	0.2	307	343	650	3.13	21,600	0.2	24,501	0.2	70,000	0.4
Hindus	0	0.0	5,000	0.1	20,000	0.2	341	-5	336	1.57	20,700	0.2	23,363	0.2	45,000	0.2
Sikhs	0	0.0	200	0.0	410	0.0	7	1	8	1.72	430	0.0	486	0.0	1,000	0.0
Jews	0	0.0	80	0.0	170	0.0	3	0	3	1.48	180	0.0	197	0.0	300	0.0
Other religionists	0	0.0	200	0.0	300	0.0	5	3	8	2.37	340	0.0	379	0.0	800	0.0
World A (unevangelized persons)	623,250	83.1	677,670	15.0	457,415	4.9	7,835	-10,684	-2,849	-0.64	454,504	4.7	437,000	4.0	498,950	2.5
World B (evangelized non-Christians)	113,250	15.1	1,174,730	26.0	1,871,585	20.0	31,836	-8,174	23,662	1.16	1,873,810	19.4	2,099,893	19.2	3,688,150	18.5
World C (Christians)	13,500	1.8	2,665,400	59.0	7,006,000	75.1	119,353	18,858	138,211	1.82	7,342,000	75.9	8,388,107	76.8	15,770,900	79.0
Country's population	**750,000**	**100.0**	**4,517,800**	**100.0**	**9,335,000**	**100.0**	**159,024**	**0**	**159,024**	**1.59**	**9,670,315**	**100.0**	**10,925,000**	**100.0**	**19,958,000**	**100.0**

COLUMNS, ROWS.
For meanings and definitions, see Codebook (Part 3). Note that, by definition, total 'Christians' = professing + crypto-Christians, which also = affiliated + unaffiliated Christians, and also = Great Commission Christians + latent Christians. Percentages may not always total exactly, due to rounding.

CENSUSES.
None have included the religion question for the whole population. **8.V.1956** (non-Africans): 7,523 Christians, 5,748 Muslims, 2,506 Hindus, 378 nonreligious, 134 Sikhs, 37 Jews, 109 other religionists. **26.IX.1861** (non-Africans): 7,730 Christians, 7,570 Muslims, 3,010 Hindus, 720 nonreligious, 1,850 other religionists.

NOTES ON RELIGIONS
BAHA'IS. Growth from 1 local spiritual assembly (1964) to 27 (1973); including numerous Indians formerly Muslims or Hindus; then a massive demographic surge to (1995) 21,000 in 121 LSAs.
CHRISTIANS. In 1921, some 103,001 Africans claimed to be Christians (8.6% of the known population then).
COUNTRY'S POPULATION. From 1965-75, around 500,000 Mozambican refugees, mostly Catholics and traditional religionists, with some Anglicans, Protestants and Muslims, fled from Mozambique, settled in Malawi and have become absorbed into Malawian life. From 1969-76, over 10,000 Jehovah's Witnesses fled the country to Mozambique, then were deported back to Malawi.
ETHNORELIGIONISTS. Animistic remnants among various tribes, including Kunda and Mpoto (both over 50% pagan with no Muslims).
HINDUS. Indians, mostly traders.
INDEPENDENTS. In about 92 denominations in 1995 (see Table 2), this number increasing annually.
MUSLIMS. The first effective Muslim proselytism did not begin till 1890 after the defeat of the slave traders; by 1921, 73,015 (6% of the population, mostly Yao and Lakeside Chewa) claimed to be Muslims. Africans are Sunnis (of the Shafiite rite), including 82% of the Yao who still form the majority of Muslims. There has been no spread of Islam for a long time, no Muslim militancy, and there is among the Yao considerable interconversion between both Islam and Christianity. There are also several thousand Indo-Pakistani Muslims, as well as some Arabs and Swahili. *Hajj pilgrims to Mecca* (figures for all Central Africa). (1970) 121; (1974) 232.
NONRELIGIOUS. Europeans.
OTHER RELIGIONISTS. Including Rosicrucians (AMORC).

Great Commission Instrument Panel: status of Malawi (for explanation see start of Part 4)

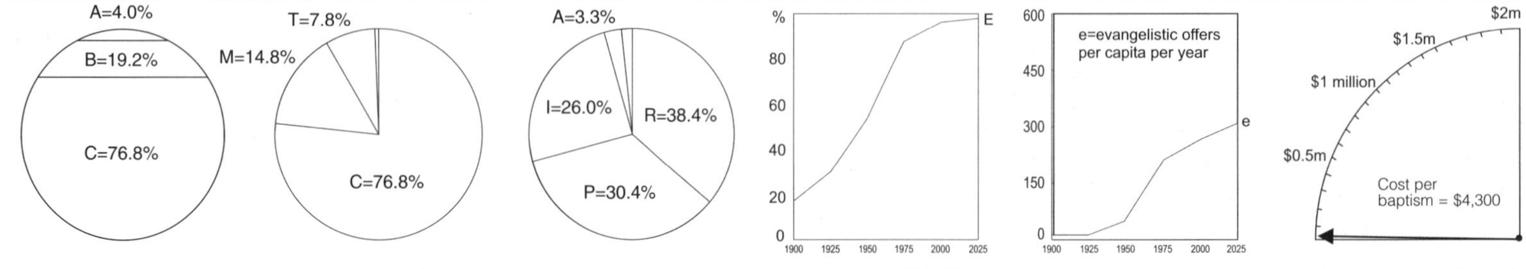

3 Worlds, AD 2000 | Religions, AD 2000 | Ecclesiastical blocs | Evangelization, 1900-2025 | Offers, 1900-2025 | Cost-effectiveness, AD 2000

Country summary. **Worlds A, B, C by ethnolinguistic peoples, cities, and major civil divisions in Malawi.**

	PEOPLES							CITIES							CIVIL DIVISIONS						
World	*Num*	*Pop 2000*	*C%*	*Christians*	*E%*	*U%*	*Unevangelized*	*Num*	*Pop 2000*	*C%*	*Christians*	*E%*	*U%*	*Unevangelized*	*Num*	*Pop 2000*	*C%*	*Christians*	*E%*	*U%*	*Unevangelized*
A	3	34,830	0.09	32	49	51	17,893	0	0	0.00	0	0	0	0	0	0	0.00	0	0	0	0
B	11	1,925,006	30.40	585,290	80	20	388,366	0	0	0.00	0	0	0	0	0	0	0.00	0	0	0	0
C	17	8,965,401	71.91	6,446,937	100	0	25,251	2	855,938	70.59	604,175	98	2	17,025	24	10,925,237	64.37	7,032,260	96	4	431,510
Total	**31**	**10,925,237**	**64.37**	**7,032,259**	**96**	**4**	**431,510**	**2**	**855,938**	**70.59**	**604,175**	**98**	**2**	**17,025**	**24**	**10,925,237**	**64.37**	**7,032,260**	**96**	**4**	**431,510**

Country status. Malawi is a small landlocked country in southeast Africa, extending along the western shores of Lake Malawi, the third-largest lake in Africa. The climate is subtropical and its chief exports are tobacco, tea, and coffee.

HUMAN LIFE AND LIBERTY

Human need and development. About 80% of Malawians are agriculturists living in rural hamlets and villages. Most of them are poor, but not destitute or starving, and are generally better off than rural people in neighboring countries. Only a small percentage of household income is in the form of cash. There is a steady drain of manpower from the villages into the towns, especially Blantyre. Those who move into the towns are forced to adapt lifestyles alien to the traditional ways. Because urban life is precarious and expensive, men arrive without their families and send them back to ease the financial burdens. In any case, women go home periodically to help with farm chores during the busy season. Most rural Malawians live in houses they build themselves with local materials, such as wattle and daub, bamboo, and thatch. Rural houses require constant repair, as the ants eat away the bamboo poles, wind and rain erode the plaster, and the thatched roofs begin to leak. Urban housing ranges from shanties to Western-style dwellings built of brick and wood. In rural and urban areas, many people live in insanitary conditions. Thatched roofs are havens for rodents and insects. The houses are poorly ventilated, livestock is kept close to the house, and water sources are contaminated. Preventive health is given low priority in official budgets, and government and Christian mission facilities are overburdened. Christian missions provide a major part of medical services, and they receive grants from the Ministry of Health. Prevailing social taboos and the prestige attached to folk medicine also hamper extension of healthcare in rural areas.

Human rights and freedoms. Malawi's poor human rights record stands in sharp contrast to its economic achievements and humanitarian handling of Africa's largest refugee population. Even after a political referendum on the future of one party rule in 1993, the government keeps a tight rein on all aspects of public life with continued restrictions on freedoms of press and speech and assembly. There is persistent police abuse of prisoners and credible reports of torture. Government also uses arbitrary detention under the Preservation of Public Security Act to silence political opponents, although such detentions are of shorter duration and less frequent than in the past. However, the judiciary is not totally subservient to the president and on occasion asserts the rights of political prisoners. Police may enter houses of suspects at will to conduct searches. Telephones are routinely tapped, domestic and international mail may be opened, and a network of informers monitor the activities of political opponents. Freedom of the press is circumscribed, and it is a criminal offense to publish anything 'likely to undermine the authority of, or public confidence in, the government'. Foreign journalists covering events in Malawi face numerous restrictions. Political meetings are not permitted other than under the auspices of the Malawi Congress Party, and any gathering of more than 3 people may be construed as an unlawful assembly. Northern Malawians experience discrimination in employment. Asian Malawians are the target of considerable hostility from the government as well as the public. Strict rules dictate where they may own property, and they have been compelled to transfer ownership of rural shops to ethnic Africans. A strict dress code is maintained for women. Pants and shorts are not permitted in public and dress length must be below the knees.

Human environment. About 8% of the country, including the southern tip of Lake Malawi, has been set aside as wilderness area. But largescale poaching is threatening rhino and elephant populations in this area. Because of the pressure on land, deforestation is a serious problem, and Malawi has the second highest rate of deforestation in Africa, after Ivory Coast. Farmland degradation has followed intensive cultivation of marginal lands.

NON-CHRISTIAN RELIGIONS

Traditional religions continue to exist among all tribes, but among none are they the dominant influence. Tribal religionists have dwindled from 95.2% of the population in 1900 to only 8.6% by 1995. God is known among many peoples as Mulungu, but other names are also prevalent: Ciuta (among the Tumbuka and Matengo), Kyala (Ngonde), Unkurukuru (Ngoni), Tilo (Tonga) and Chisumphi (northern Chewa). In an earlier day the Chisumphi cult was highly developed, with its main center at Kaphirintiwa. The symbol of God was a sacred drum, and Chisumphi regularly possessed the Makewana, cultic spirit wives who served as mediums at the shrine. The shrine was also cared for by a priesthood whose chief was called Mfumu ya Chisumphi. During the slave-raiding days of the middle of the 19th century, the sacred drum was removed to Msekere in Mozambique and was later returned to a new shrine at Tsang'oma in Nyasaland. The cult still exists but in attenuated form. A more durable movement is the M'Bona cult of the southern Chewa which is centered in the divinity M'Bona who was once human. Since the arrival of Christianity, the cult has taken on syncretistic elements including the identification of M'Bona as a Black Jesus. There is also a strong emphasis among the Chewa on secret societies (Nyau), with a cultic use of masks representing ancestral spirits and elaborate ceremonies (pembero lalikulu) performed at burials and tribal initiations. In 1930 a highly important witchcraft eradication movement, Mchape (Medicine), arose in Nyasaland and ultimately spread through Northern and Southern Rhodesia, Tanganyika, and Mozambique.

Islam is strongest among the Yao tribesmen of eastern Malawi, with 83% of the 875,000 Yao claiming to be Muslims. Malawi Muslims, who are Sunnis and almost all Africans, number about 15% of the population. Because of their numerical strength and vitality, they form the southern frontier of Islam in Africa.

Baha'i has spread considerably in the last 30 years and in 1995 had grown to 121 local spiritual assemblies.

CHRISTIANITY

PROTESTANT CHURCHES. David Livingstone explored the Zambesi and Shire rivers during 1858-64 and attracted others to begin missionary work in Malawi. Protestant pioneers were Presbyterians from the Free Church of Scotland in 1875 and the Church of Scotland the following year, the former concentrating its work at the renowned Livingstonia station in the north, with the latter active in the southern region of Blantyre. The next to arrive (1888) were Dutch Reformed missionaries from South Africa at Nkhoma. These 3 groups joined together in 1926 to create the large Church of Central Africa Presbyterian (CCAP), now with 2,172 churches in 3 synods. The church as a whole has continued to grow at a rapid rate, and this is especially true of the Blantyre Synod.

Seventh-day Adventists opened their first mission in 1891 and have shown significant gains since then. Malawi Adventists form the South-East Africa Union of the SDA Church, which was organized in 1925. At present the church has 3 fields covering the northern, central, and southern regions of the country.

Two groups of Disciples entered Malawi in the early part of the century, the Church of Christ (Non-Instrumental) from the USA in 1907, the Churches of Christ from the UK in 1909. The latter is larger although both have succeeded in establishing sizeable communities in Malawi.

Notable by their relative absence are Pentecostals, there being only 7 relatively small Pentecostal denominations. Exceptions are the Assemblies of God which tripled in size from 1970 to 1990, and the Apostolic Faith Mission which grew from 1,500 to 16,700 in the same period. In 1978, the Pentecostal Fellowship of Malawi was formed to co-ordinate them.

Other Protestant denominations include the Zambesi Evangelical Church, Evangelical Church of Malawi, Seventh Day Baptist Church, and several smaller bodies.

Protestants on the churches' rolls make up about 30% of the population and have been heavily involved in education, medical, and social service. Churches belonging to the Christian Council of Malawi, which is mostly Protestant, operate 22 hospitals, 36 clinics, one school for the blind, 5 teacher-training colleges, one technical school, one village co-operative, 3 lay training centers, 4 printing presses, and 24 bookshops, in addition to 8 Bible schools and 2 theological colleges.

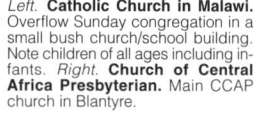

Left. **Catholic Church in Malawi.** Overflow Sunday congregation in a small bush church/school building. Note children of all ages including infants. *Right.* **Church of Central Africa Presbyterian.** Main CCAP church in Blantyre.

CATHOLIC CHURCH. Catholic missionaries entered what is now Malawi from Mozambique during the 16th century but established no permanent stations until the arrival of the White Fathers in 1889. The first indigenous priest was ordained in 1937 and the church now has over 70 national priests in addition to 288 Malawian sisters and 1,580 catechists. An African bishop was consecrated in 1956 and the hierarchy established in 1959. Three indigenous religious congregations have been formed for sisters and in 1929 one for brothers, although the latter had only 2 members remaining by 1972. The Catholic Church has increased enormously in size since 1950 and its members are now 29% of the total population of the country. The church is heavily involved in education and social service.

The Holy See has diplomatic relations with Malawi and in AD 2000 is represented to government and the Catholic hierarchy by a pro-nuncio residing in Lusaka.

OTHER CHURCHES. The Anglican UMCA, heeding the call of David Livingstone, appeared briefly in Malawi during 1861 and definitively after 1879. The work is now organized into 2 dioceses which are part of the Church of the Province of Central Africa.

Jehovah's Witnesses have built up an important community since their arrival from South Africa in 1907. Following a government ban on their activities in 1969, many fled to Mozambique but have attempted to return since Mozambique obtained its independence in 1975. Witnesses continue to suffer from virulent state persecution both in Mozambique and Malawi.

Some 90 African indigenous churches are active in Malawi. The first and still the most important is the Providence Industrial Mission, begun in 1898. Other early groups include the Achewa Church (1920), African Covenant Church (1923), and the Last Church of God and His Christ (1924). The influence of Black churches from the USA has been felt through the African Methodist Episcopal Church. Another foreign church is the African Apostolic Church of Johane Maranke, which entered Malawi from Rhodesia in 1958.

Renewal movements. In the 1990s the Pentecostal/Charismatic Renewal continued to spread rapidly across most older churches, and numbered over 1,940,000 adherents (of whom 7% Pentecostals, 18% Charismatics, and 75% Independents).

Indigenous missions. Missionaries from Malawi have been growing in number and mostly confined to contiguous African countries.

CHURCH AND STATE

The constitution of 1963 adheres to the United Nation's Declaration of Human Rights and so affirms freedom of conscience for all. There is no established church and Malawi leans towards the principle of separation of church and state. Because of its extreme poverty, the state accepts the churches as partners in development. Hospitals and clinics in operation when the Federation of Rhodesia and Nyasaland was disbanded in 1963 still receive a small grant-in-aid, but new medical institutions since that date receive no subsidies. Teachers' salaries are paid by government and church institutions are not taxed. Religious instruction is a compulsory subject in primary schools; in post-primary institutions, provision is made for the religious instruction of teachers of religion. Churches are not required to register, and no government body is specifically charged with responsibility for religious affairs.

In June 1969 the government banned the Jehovah's Witnesses as 'dangerous to the good government of the state'. In 1976 some 5,000 were estimated to be held in prison or prison camps, often subjected to torture, others having suffered the loss of their jobs or similar privations. The Youth League of the ruling Malawi Congress Party has been involved in deliberate harassment of the Witnesses, which has caused many to flee to Mozambique. Others attempting to return to Malawi from the increasingly hostile situation in Mozambique have experienced even more serious persecution. By 1976 their plight had aroused widespread international protest.

BROADCASTING AND MEDIA

One in 8 people have radios. Shortwave programs in Yao can be received from FEBA (Seychelles) and in Chewa from TWR (Swaziland). Broadcasts from KNLS have had responses. HCJB World Radio helped start local stations in Malawi in cooperation with ministries like the African Bible College. Malawi is a member of UNDA.

Some 2.8 million have have seen the 'Jesus' Film: through film teams (2 million) and videocassettes (622,000), with 167,000 responding.

INTERDENOMINATIONAL ORGANIZATIONS

The Christian Council of Malawi was founded in 1939, building on foundations laid earlier by the Consultative Board of Federative Missions of Nyasaland. At present 13 churches and several other bodies are members, including a wide spectrum of church traditions from high-church Anglicans to African indigenous churches. The council is affiliated to CWME of the World Council of Churches and 5 of its Protestant members also belong to the Evangelical Association of Malawi, a constituent member body of the Association of Evangelicals of Africa and Madagascar. The principal Catholic body responsible for interdenominational relations is the National Catholic Commission for Ecumenism.

Two national committees co-ordinating the work of CCM churches and the Catholic Church are: (1) the Private Hospital Association of Malasi (PHAM), established in 1965 with the support of the WCC, which provides for co-operation in Christian medical work with the Ministry of Health; and (2) the Christian Service Committee of the Churches with Malawi (CSC), founded in Blantyre in 1968, which sponsors social service and development projects in liaison with government and Sodepax in Switzerland. The CSC is a member of CIDSE in Belgium. An important institution fostering a spirit of ecumenism is the Chilema Training Centre, sponsored by the Anglican and Presbyterian churches, with a Catholic member on its board of government. A regional Sodepax-type group based in Blantyre (but serving also Botswana, Lesotho, Kenya, Tanzania, Uganda, and Zambia) is the Movement for Ecumenical Action in National Development (MEND).

FUTURE TRENDS AND PROSPECTS

Christians will probably grow to 79% by AD 2025, primarily due to conversions of ethnoreligionists.

Christianity could reach 85% by AD 2050 if tribal religionists continue to decline. After that Christians and Muslims will share the country's population 85/15.

BIBLIOGRAPHY

A general survey of the history of Independent Churches in Malawi, 1900–1976. H. J. Sindima. Nairobi: AACC, 1977. 10p.

'A missionary strategy for evangelism in central Africa: an examination of people–movement strategy in the historical–cultural context of Malawi.' H. B. Bickers. Ph.D. dissertation, Southwestern Baptist Theological Seminary, Fort Worth, TX, 1977. 334p.

An annotated bibliography on religion. S. F. Chinyamu. Zomba, Malawi: Malawi Library Association, [1993]. 36p.

An annotated list of independent churches in Malawi, 1900–1981 (Rev. ed.). J. C. Chakanza. *Sources for the study of religion in Malawi*, no. 10. [Zomba, Malawi: Dept. of Religious Studies, Chancellor College, University of Malawi, 1983]. 71p.

Biblical exegesis in African independence churches in Malawi. H. B. P. Mijoga. *Sources for the study of religion in Malawi*, no. 14. Zomba, Malawi: Dept. of Theology and Religious Studies, Chancellor College, University of Malawi, 1991. 56p.

Catholic directory of Malawi, 1970. Limbe, Malawi: Catholic Secretariat in Malawi, 1970.

Catholics, peasants, and Chewa resistance in Nyasaland, 1889–1939. I. Linden & J. Linden. Berkeley, CA: University of California Press, 1974. 235p.

'Christian stewardship in the Synod of Livingstonia.' O. P. Mazunda. D.Min. thesis, Columbia Theological Seminary, Decatur, GA, 1984. 175p.

Christianity in Malawi: a source book. K. R. Ross (ed). Gweru, Zimbabwe: Mambo Press; Bonn, Germany: Verlag für Kultur und Wissenschaft, 1996. 253p.

Christianity in northern Malawi: Donald Fraser's missionary methods and Ngoni culture. T. J. Thompson. *Studies in Christian mission*, vol. 15. New York: E. J. Brill, 1995.

'Contextual factors in church growth in Malawi.' P. L. Capp. M.Div. thesis, Western Evangelical Seminary, 1979. 252p.

Five years in the life of the Christian Service Committee of the churches in Malawi, 1968–1972. J. D. Mein. Blantyre: Christian Council of Malawi, 1972.

Independent African: John Chilembwe and the origins, setting and significance of the Nyasaland native rising of 1915. G. Shepperson & T. Price. Edinburgh: Edinburgh University Press, 1958. 564p.

Mainstream Christianity to 1980 in Malawi, Zambia, and Zimbabwe. J. C. Weller et al. Gweru, Zimbabwe: Mambo Press, 1984. 235p.

'Malawian churches and the struggle for life and personhood: crisis and rupture of Malawian thought and society.' H. J. Sindima. Ph.D. dissertation, Princeton Theological Seminary, Princeton, NJ, 1987. 488p.

Missiology in Malawi. J. C. Chakanza, K. Fiedler & K. R. Ross. *Sources for the study of religion in Malawi*, no. 16. Zomba, Malawi: Chancellor College, [1993]. 41p.

Missions and politics in Malawi. K. N. Mufuka. *Modern Africa series*, no. 1. Kingston, Ontario: Limestone Press, 1977. 300p.

'Missions to Malawi.' F. Alexander. Thesis, Fuller Theological Seminary, Pasadena, CA, 1969.

Pentecostalism and neo–traditionalism: the religious polarization of a rural district in southern Malawi. J. M. Schoffeleers. Amsterdam: Free University Press, 1985. 54p.

'Political removal and deportation of African separatist church leaders in Nyasaland, 1909–1925.' K. Lohrentz. Seminar paper, Syracuse University, Syracuse, NY, 1970.

Politics and Christianity in Malawi, 1875–1940: the impact of the Livingstonia Mission in the northern province. J. McCracken. London: E. J. Brill, 1977. 324p.

Religion in Malawi (Zomba, Malawi), 1987-. (Periodical).

Religion in Malawi: current research, 1983. D. S. Bone. *Sources for the study of religion in Malawi*, no. 6. Zomba, Malawi: Dept. of Religious Studies, Chancellor College, University of Malawi, 1983. 29p.

Religious independency in Nyasaland: a typology of origins. J. Parratt. [Zomba, Malawi]: Dept. of Religious Studies, Chancellor College, University of Malawi, 1979. 29p.

Religious pluralism in contemporary Malawi. J. C. Chakanza. *Sources for the study of religion in Malawi*, no. 15. [Zomba, Malawi: Dept. of Theology and Religious Studies, Chancellor College, University of Malawi, 1992]. 59p.

Sectarianism in Southern Nyasaland. R. L. Wishlade. London: Oxford University Press, 1964. 162p.

The beginnings of Nyasaland and North–Eastern Rhodesia, 1859–95. A. J. Hanna. Oxford, UK: Oxford University Press, 1956.

The Christian missionary response to the development of Islam in Malawi, 1875–1940. D. S. Bone. *History seminar*, 1983/84, paper no. 11. [Zomba, Malawi]: History Dept, Chancellor College, University of Malawi, [1984]. 29p.

The legacy of Scottish missionaries in Malawi. H. J. Sindima. *Studies in the history of missions*, vol. 8. Lewiston, NY: E. Mellen Press, 1992. 158p.

The message of mainstream Christianity in Malawi: an analysis of contemporary preaching. K. R. Ross. *Sources for the study of religion in Malawi*, no. 17. [Zomba, Malawi: Dept. of Theology and Religious Studies, Chancellor College, University of Malawi, 1993]. 33p.

'The Nyasaland Government's policy toward African Muslims, 1900–1925.' R. Greenstein. 27p. (Duplicated).

Country Table 2. Organized churches and denominations in Malawi.

Official name (bold type = church with over 10% of all affiliated) 1	*Begun* 2	*Type* 3	*Counc* 4	*Congs* 5	*Adults* 6	*Affiliated 1970* 7	*Affiliated 1995* 8	*G%* 9	*Names, notes, and other statistics* (see Codebook, Part 3) 10
Achewa Baptist Church	1920	I-Bap	.....	33	5,000	2,500	12,000	6.48	Schism ex PIM, Dedza district; Chewa (Achewa) tribe. 9 ministers (unsalaried).
Africa Evangelical Church of Malawi	1900	P-Eva	xMG.a	50	6,000	5,000	15,000	4.49	M=AEF(SAGM). 55% Mang'anja, 30% Sena, 9% Zimba. 5n,3x,10f,2h,2k,2p,W=80%,60Y.
African Apostolic Ch of Johane Maranke	1934	I-3aA	x....	60	8,000	2,000	15,000	8.39	*AACJM. Mpingo wa Apositoli.* Shonas from Umtali (Rhodeis). 14 pasakas held.
African Baptist Assembly Malawi	1898	I-Bap	T...N	1,160	56,694	25,258	72,500	4.31	*Providence Industrial Mission.* M=NBCUSA(Black). 70% Lomwe,10% Yao,2f,2H,2h.
African Covenant Church	1923	I-Ref	.....	200	13,200	10,000	25,000	3.73	*Chipangano (Covenant), or Ch of Abraham.* Ex CCAP(CSM). All over north. Tumbuka.
African Methodist Episcopal Church	1924	I-Met	Vw..N	180	9,000	4,000	18,000	6.20	M=AMEC(Black mission from USA). Chewa-speaking. HQ Kasungu.
African National/International Church	1928	I-Ref	.....	30	3,000	4,000	5,000	0.90	*ANC.* Schism ex CCAP(Free Ch of Scotland). OT theology, polygamous. Also in Tanzania.
Anglican Church in Malawi	1861	A-ACa	AWAVN	500	90,000	76,500	200,000	3.92	In Anglican *CPCA.* 2 Dioceses. M=USPG. Rural. 60 schools. 26f,10H,P=60%.
Apostolic Ch of Pentecost of Malawi	1947	I-3oA	.....	150	4,500	4,000	11,300	4.24	M=ACP(Canada). North of Lilongwe. HQ Mponela. 5n,3x,56m,42,4f,105Y.
Apostolic Faith Mission of Malawi	1933	P-Pe2	Z....	83	7,500	1,500	16,700	10.12	M=AFM(South Africa). 8 Bantu congregations, one White missionary pastor.
Assemblies of God in Malawi	1930	P-Pe2	ZFG.a	819	26,000	10,000	40,000	5.70	M=AoG(USA). HQ Limbe. 80% Chewa, 20% Tumbuka. 10n,5x,50m,16f,1j,4k,1s(115),200Y.
Baptist Convention of Malawi	1926	P-Bap	T.G.a	763	89,889	10,000	108,000	9.99	1959,M=SBC(USA). 67% Lomwe, 13% Chewa, 13%Nyanja. 1 school. 61n,28f,6h,2s,1609Y.
Blackman's Presbyterian Ch of Africa	1933	I-Ref	.....	10	1,400	1,500	2,700	2.38	*Mpingo wa Afipa wanu Africa.* Ex FCSM. Also Zambia, Tanzania, Tonga, Tumbuka. M=TEEM.
Brethren in Christ Church	1985	P-Men	.....	1	200	–	400	10.00	M=BiCC(USA).
Broadsheet Readers' Clubs	c1980	I-3nA	.....	59	1,600	–	3,000	6.67	Readers of Gospel Broadsheets produced by M=WEC(UK).
Catholic Church in Malawi:	1561	R-Lat	PzSER	144	1,212,000	993,448	2,349,704	3.50	C=4+3+10. (1970) 70n,235x,37143Yy. (1990) 219n 156x 252m 717w 83666Yy
M Blantyre	1903	R-Lat	Ps	46	358,000	330,078	692,478	3.01	60% Lomwe, 25% Ngoni, 15% Yao. 1p. 53n 26x 57m 183w 20927Yy
D Chikwawa	1965	R-Lat	Ps	12	152,000	64,043	287,747	6.19	40% Sena, 30% Lomwe, 30% Nyanja. M=SMM. 11n 6x 8m 34w 5863Yy
D Dedza	1956	R-Lat	Ps	16	148,000	130,164	289,342	3.25	65% Ngoni, 35% Nyanja. 1p. 33n 15x 31m 107w 11861Yy
D Lilongwe (Nyassa, Likuri)	1889	R-Lat	Ps	28	300,000	244,305	582,549	3.54	New capital. 90% Chewa, 10% Ngoni. M=WF. 1s. 43n 43x 52m 193w 25342Yy
D Mangochi (Fort Johnston)	1969	R-Lat	Psmm	14	78,000	56,794	157,703	4.17	In south. 1973,elevated as D Mangochi. M=SMM. 20n 23x 49m 58w 6562Yy
D Mzuzu	1947	R-Lat	Pwf	14	82,000	67,469	160,000	3.51	80% Tumbuka, 20% Tonga. M=WF,SPS. 1p. 30n 30x 35m 89w 8000Yy
D Zomba	1952	R-Lat	Ps	14	94,000	100,595	179,885	2.35	30% Muslims. 50% Lomwe, 20% Ngoni, 10% Yao. 29n 13x 20m 53w 5111Yy
Christadelphian Ecclesias	1960	m-Ade	x....	10	200	300	400	1.16	M=Christadelphian Bible Mission. Pacifist. 1973, Abale a Yesu (Brothers of Jesus) secede.
Christian Brethren	1964	P-CBr	.....	80	10,600	1,560	20,000	10.74	Open Brethren. Plymouth Brethren.
Christian Churches and Chs of Christ	c1970	I-Dis	.....	20	12,629	–	21,000	48.90	M=CCCC. Disciples
Church of Central Africa Presbyterian	1875	P-Ref	RvA.N	2,500	400,000	766,000	900,000	0.65	*CCAP*, formed 1926. 3 Synods. (1990) 151nx,15148Y,14291y,51670z.
Church of Christ (Non-Instrumental)	1907	I-Dis	x....	1,200	30,000	50,000	70,000	1.35	1957,M=CC(Non-Instrumental) (USA). 80% Chewa, 20% Tumbuka. 10f,1H,2p.
Church of Disciples Mission in Malawi	1974	I-3pA	.....	283	9,850	–	20,000	4.76	Work in: Sena, Cewa, Chikwawa, Lomwe. M=CAM.
Church of God of Prophecy	1977	P-Pe3	.....	40	6,000	–	12,000	5.56	M=CGP.
Church of the Ancestors	1942	I-Adv	.....	5	1,000	1,000	2,000	2.81	*Calici ca Makolo. Ethiopian Ch.* Nyanja-speaking schism ex Seventh-day Adventists.
Church of the Nazarene in Malawi	1957	P-Hol	xFG.G	81	7,496	3,000	14,515	6.51	M=CoN(USA).99% Nyanja, 1% Yao. HQ Limbe. 2n,4x,10f,1s,W=76%,567z.
Church of the Watch Tower/Mikael Ch	1908	I-Jeh	.....	10	1,500	4,000	3,000	-1.14	Tonga mass revival; collapsed. 1937, restarted as Mikael Church. Banned 1969.
Churches of Christ	1909	I-Dis	x...N	2,500	50,000	20,000	83,300	5.87	M=CC(UK). 2 Synods. 20% Lomwe, 20% Tumbuka, 20% Nyanja.16n,4f,1H,227Y.
Congregation of the Lamb	1932	I-Non	.....	3	300	500	500	0.00	*Kagula ka Nkhosa.* Indigenous body ex Zambesi Industrial Mission. Nyanja. Mlanje.
Courage for Christian Living Ch	c1990	I-3oA	.....	20	2,000	–	4,000	20.00	HQ Blantyre. Oneness body, member of AWCF.
Evangelical Baptist Ch of Malawi	1973	P-Bap	T....	250	17,000	–	26,700	4.55	Yao-speakers. M=CAM.
Evangelical Brethren	1980	P-Bap	.....	33	5,000	–	11,100	6.67	M=Evangelical Brethren.
Evangelical Church of Malawi	1893	P-Eva	xMG.a	150	8,000	15,000	25,000	2.06	Formerly Nyasa Industrial M, Nyasa Ev Ch. M=TEAM(USA, SA). Cholo. Nyanja. 1h,1k,1p.
Faith Bible Ministries	c1970	I-3cA	.....	35	3,500	–	7,780	43.10	Indigenous Malawian Charismatics.
Faithful Church of Christ	1949	I-Non	.....	40	1,000	1,000	2,000	2.81	*Wendewende Mission.* Schism ex African Chs of Christ. Nyanja. Many splits.
Forward in Faith	1974	I-3pA	.....	62	4,115	–	10,000	4.76	Languages: Sena, Yao, Cewa, Lomwe.
Free Baptist Church	c1970	I-Bap	.....	32	3,824	–	8,500	43.61	Independent Baptists.
Free Methodist Church	1973	I-Hol	.....	171	7,624	–	25,400	4.55	M=FMC.
Free Pentecostal Church of Christ	c1980	I-3oA	.....	50	4,000	–	8,000	6.67	Oneness teaching, member of AWCF.
Full Gospel Ch of God	1930	P-Pe3	ZF...	165	5,306	2,000	13,400	7.91	M=CoG(Cleveland) (USA), Full Gospel Ch of God (South Africa). 6n.
Greek Orth Archbishopric of Rhodesia	c1920	O-Gre	Cw...	1	1,325	1,000	2,650	3.98	In AD Rhodesia, under Greek P Alexandria. No resident priest. Greek settlers.
Independent Assemblies of God	1958	I-3pA	....N	40	2,000	3,000	6,000	2.81	Formerly African Gospel Ch, AoG in S&C Africa. Ex AoG, led by White missionary.
Independent Baptist Convention	c1970	I-Bap	.....	100	15,000	–	30,000	51.04	Independent Fundamentalist Baptists.
Intern Ch of the Foursquare Gospel	c1970	P-Pe2	.....	10	613	–	1,750	34.81	M=ICFG(USA).
Jehovah's Witnesses	1906	m-Jeh	x....	500	12,500	55,000	90,000	1.99	1972, 1975 vicious persecutions of 36,000 to Mozambique. (1975) 1577Y. (1995) 3180Y.
Last Church of God & His Christ	1924	I-Ref	.....	70	10,000	5,000	15,000	4.49	Schism ex Chipangano; many ex CCAP. Growing fast north of Mzimba, also Tanzania. Tumbuka.
Lilongwe Pentecostal Church	c1975	I-3pA	.....	8	5,000	–	8,330	5.00	Indigenous pentecostals.
Living Waters Church	1984	I-3cA	.....	175	23,200	–	44,000	9.09	10,000-member mother church in Blantyre. Work in Mozambique, Tanzania, Kenya, Uganda.
Lutheran Church of Central Africa	1962	P-Lut	x....	76	4,620	796	14,000	12.15	LCCA. *African Lutheran Ch.* M=Wisconsin ELSynod (USA). Chewa. 3x,2m,5f,3p,W=69%,46Y,68.
Mennonite Brethren	1986	P-Men	.....	25	420	–	800	11.11	*Mpingo Wa Abale Mwa Yesu.*
New Apostolic Church	1923	I-3aX	x....	30	15,000	10,000	22,969	3.38	*Zambia-Malawi Church District.* M=NAC(Chief Apostle in Dortmund, Germany).
New Jerusalem Church	c1980	I-3oA	.....	30	2,500	–	6,000	6.67	Oneness body, member of AWCF. HQ Blantyre.
Pentecostal Assemblies of God	c1970	P-Pe2	.....	40	630	–	1,050	32.08	M=PAoC(Canada).
Pentecostal Holiness Church	1932	P-Pe3	ZFG.G	95	3,000	2,000	5,700	4.28	Lambya, Winamwanga from PHA in Zambia; extreme north. M=IPHC(USA). 4n,2f,1p,19Y.
Seventh Day Baptist Church	1899	P-Bap	Tw..N	90	4,500	8,000	10,000	0.90	Central Africa Conf. Ex FCSM.1947,M=SDB(USA). 50% Lomwe, 20% Ngoni. 4f,1H,2h,1k.
Seventh-day Adventist Church	1891	P-Adv	x...N	441	84,763	100,000	188,000	2.56	South-East Africa U. 86% Chewa. 63n,9x,40f,2H,12h,1j,3k,3r,454t(47831),W=72%,3513Y.
United Apostolic Faith Church		P-Pe2	x....	40	6,000	5,000	15,000	0.05	M=UAFC(UK). HQ Pretoria (SA). British-Israelite Pentecostals. All Africans.
United Evangelical Church	1977	P-Eva	.....	106	10,600	–	32,000	5.56	M=Zambezi Evangelical Mission & Nyasa Mission.
United Pentecostal Church	1980	P-Pe1	.....	110	5,500	–	9,170	6.67	UPC(USA).
Zambesi Evangelical Church	1892	P-Eva	..G.a	300	15,000	30,000	45,000	1.64	M=ZM(UK), formerly Zambesi Industrial Mission. HQ Blantyre. 9f,1H,2h,1j,2k,1p.
Other African indigenous churches		I-3pA	.....	1,000	560,000	40,000	1,000,000	0.05	Total about 300 (see list below), including many small bodies, also Zion Christian Ch, CCACZ.
Other marginal Christian bodies		m-	.....	156	12,000	–	25,000	0.05	Total around 10 bodies from UK and USA.
Other Protestant denominations		P-	.....	50	204,000	500	382,000	0.05	Total about 15 (see list below), including ELCT (Tanzania), PHA/IPHC,Moravian Ch.
Other charismatic churches	c1975	I-3cA	.....	48	14,500	–	22,300	5.00	Agape Ch, Ebenezer Ch, Holy Cross Ministries Ch, Christian Ambassadors Ministry Ch.
Totals				**15,523**	**3,137,598**	**2,274,362**	**6,159,618**		

Churches, members, growth, 1900-2025	*Congs*	*Adults*	*Affiliated*	*G%*	*Total denominations*	*6 Megablocs:* O	R	A	P	I	m
Total churches, members, and denominations (mid-1900)	100	4,800	10,500	7.99	9	0	1	1	6	1	0
Total churches, members, and denominations (mid-1970)	7,291	1,032,070	2,274,362	7.99	177	1	1	1	22	150	2
Total churches, members, and denominations (mid-1990)	12,000	2,997,000	5,883,650	4.87	393	1	1	1	38	340	12
Total churches, members, and denominations (mid-1995)	15,523	3,137,598	6,159,618	0.92	396	1	1	1	39	342	12
Total churches, members, and denominations (mid-2000)	17,000	3,582,000	7,032,260	2.69	401	1	1	1	40	346	12
Total churches, members, and denominations (mid-2025)	32,000	6,877,000	13,500,000	2.64	579	1	1	1	60	500	16

NOTES ON TABLE ABOVE

NATIONAL COUNCILS (Column 4, 5th letter).

- a = member of both CCM and EFM.
- E = Evangelical Fellowship of Malawi (EFM), formerly Evangelical Association of Malawi (EAM).
- H = Pentecostal Fellowship of Malawi (PFM).
- I = Reformed Independent Churches Association of Malawi (RICAM).
- J = Followers of Christ Association of Malawi (FCAM).
- N = Christian Council of Malawi (CCM).
- R = Episcopal Conference of Malawi (ECM).

OTHER AFRICAN INDIGENOUS CHURCHES. These, some of which are branches of Zambian or Rhodesian or South African bodies, include: African Abraham Ch (1929; Tonga), African Assemblies of God (1969; ex IAoG), African Ch (c1953, ex Zambesi Industrial Mission), African Ch Crucified Mission (1960), African Chs of Christ (1933; ex Ch of Christ; several small factions), African Emmanuel Ch (1927; 10 congregations in north), African Nyasa Mission (1946, in south, ex Nyasa Industrial Mission), African Pentecostal Ch (in north), African United Baptist Ch (1946, in south, ex PIM), Apostolic Zion Ch (1928), Bantu Ch (Tonga), Chitemwano cha Chiuta Ch, Christian Catholic Apostolic Ch in Zion (1923), Ch of God in Africa (1931; ex Ch of Christ), Emmanuel Chs of Christ, Episcopal Holiness Ch, Full Gospel Ch (Zionist, pentecostal; ex CCAP), Galilea Ch (ex RCC), Gospel of God Ch (Apostolic Ch of Johane Masowe; 1946; 4 congregations, 2,000 followers), Independent Baptist Convention (1971; split ex PIM; 10 churches, 20 ministers), Jordan Ch (1961, ex CCAP Blantyre Synod), Last Reformed Ch, Light African Ch (1970, ex CCAP), New Jerusalem of God Ch, Presbyterian Ch of Africa (from South Africa), Sent of the Holy Ghost Ch/Holy Ghost Evangelical Ch in Africa (1927, ex ZIM), Sons of god (1929; ex Ch of Christ), Sons of God/Ana a Mulungu (1935; ex SDA), Watchman Healings Mission/Ine wa Jehova ndi Mikaeli (1937), Yesu Ch, Zion Christian Ch, Zion Ch (ex SDA Ch), Zion Prophet Ch (1978), Zion Restoration Ch. Many others are small schisms from ZEC, CCAP, Ch of Christ, Baptist. In 1975 a Korean movement began work, with 2 Japanese missionaries: Holy Spirit Association for the Unification of World Christianity.

OTHER PROTESTANT DENOMINATIONS. These smaller bodies include: Religious Society of Friends, Salvation Army (1967).

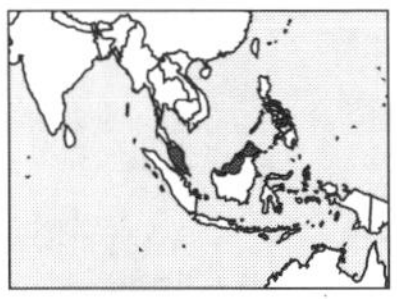

MALAYSIA

SECULAR DATA, AD 2000

STATE

Official name: Persekutuan Tanah Malaysia (The Federation of Malaysia).
Short name: Malaysia. **Adjective of nationality:** Malaysian.
Flag: Red and white stripes with blue field containing gold crescent and 14-pointed gold star.
Area: 330,442 sq. km. (127,584 sq. mi.).
Government: Federal constitutional monarchy, since 1963 (by 1900 British-protected, 1946 Union of Malaya, 1948 Federation of Malaya, 1957 Independence).
Legislature: Parliament: Senate (Dewan Negara), 70 members; House of Representatives (Dewan Ra'ayat), 192 members.
Official language: Malay and English.
Monetary unit: 1 ringgit, or Malaysian dollar. **US$1=** RM 3.80.
Chief cities: KUALA LUMPUR 1,378,000; Pinang (George Town, Penang) 801,967; Ipoh 476,075; Johor Bharu (Johore, Johor Baharu) 399,193; Petaling Jaya 336,672.
Political divisions: 15 provinces.
Armed forces: 115,000.

DEMOGRAPHY

Population: 22,244,000.

Population density: 67.3/sq. km. (174.3/sq. mi.).
Under 15 years: 7,565,000.
Growth rate p.a.: 1.69% (births 21.51, deaths 4.65).
Mortality: Infant, per 1,000: 10.2; **Maternal per 100,000:** 80.0.
Life expectancy: 73 (male 71, female 75).
Household size: 4.9. **Floor area per person, sq.m:** 12.0.
Major languages: Malay, English, Chinese (Fukienese), Tamil, Javanese, Iban, Dusun, Banjarese, Telugu, Punjabi, Arabic, Dayak, and about 170 smaller languages.
Urban dwellers: 57.25%. **Urban growth rate p.a.:** 2.9%.
Labor force: 38%.

ETHNOLINGUISTIC PEOPLES
33.0% Malay (Melaju, Melayu); 8.7% Han Chinese (Hokkien); 7.1% Han Chinese (Hakka); 7.1% Tamil; 5.4% Han Chinese (Cantonese).

ECONOMY
National income p.a. per person: US$3,889; **per family:** US$19,060.

EDUCATION
Adult literacy: 83% (male 89%, female 78%). **Schools:** 8,379. **Universities:** 54. **School enrolment:** female/male: 79%/76%.

HEALTH
Access to health services: 70%. **Access to safe water:** 90%.
Hospitals: 264 (22 beds per 10,000). **Doctors:** 7,012.
Blind: 50,000. **Deaf:** 1,337,900. **Murder rate:** 2.
Lepers: 30,000. **Underweight prevalence under 5:** 20%.

LITERATURE
New book titles p.a.: 7,560 (340 p.a. per million). **Periodicals:** 2,283. **Newspapers:** 44 dailies.

COMMUNICATION (per 1,000 people)
Phones: 166 (27% mobile). **Radios:** 476. **TV sets:** 226.
Daily newspaper circulation: 142. **Computers:** 113.

REFUGEES
Alien refugees from other countries: 5,300.

HUMAN LIFE AND LIBERTY (optimum condition=100.0%)
HDI: 83.2. **HSI:** 60.0. **HFI:** 22.5. **EFL:** 52.0.

Country Table 1. **Religious adherents in Malaysia, AD 1900-2025.**

Year	1900		1970		mid-1990		Annual change, 1990-2000				mid-1995		mid-2000		mid-2025	
Name	Adherents	%	Adherents	%	Adherents	%	Natural	Conversion	Total	Rate	Adherents	%	Adherents	%	Adherents	%
Muslims	1,024,000	48.8	5,388,000	49.7	8,508,000	47.7	209,741	-625	209,116	2.22	9,588,200	47.7	10,599,160	47.7	14,770,000	47.7
Chinese folk-religionists	525,000	25.0	2,698,373	24.9	4,325,000	24.2	106,616	-2,759	103,857	2.18	4,862,000	24.2	5,363,569	24.1	6,850,000	22.1
Christians	**32,000**	**1.5**	**581,827**	**5.4**	**1,440,000**	**8.1**	**35,498**	**5,201**	**40,699**	**2.52**	**1,640,000**	**8.2**	**1,846,985**	**8.3**	**3,050,000**	**9.9**
PROFESSION																
crypto-Christians	7,000	0.3	101,327	0.9	398,500	2.2	9,823	6,327	16,150	3.46	490,000	2.4	560,000	2.5	960,000	3.1
professing Christians	**25,000**	**1.2**	**480,500**	**4.4**	**1,041,500**	**5.8**	**25,674**	**-1,125**	**24,549**	**2.14**	**1,150,000**	**5.7**	**1,286,985**	**5.8**	**2,090,000**	**6.8**
AFFILIATION																
unaffiliated Christians	0	0.0	12,000	0.1	62,700	0.4	1,546	-236	1,310	1.91	65,767	0.3	75,796	0.3	117,000	0.4
affiliated Christians	**32,000**	**1.5**	**569,827**	**5.3**	**1,377,300**	**7.7**	**33,952**	**5,437**	**39,389**	**2.55**	**1,574,233**	**7.8**	**1,771,189**	**8.0**	**2,933,000**	**9.5**
Roman Catholics	20,000	1.0	301,449	2.8	570,000	3.2	14,051	1,138	15,189	2.39	645,181	3.2	721,889	3.3	1,190,000	3.8
Protestants	2,000	0.1	159,178	1.5	520,000	2.9	12,819	1,181	14,000	2.41	590,510	2.9	660,000	3.0	1,100,000	3.6
Anglicans	10,000	0.5	69,600	0.6	155,000	0.9	3,821	1,179	5,000	2.84	180,000	0.9	205,000	0.9	280,000	0.9
Independents	0	0.0	37,200	0.3	128,000	0.7	3,155	1,845	5,000	3.35	153,372	0.8	178,000	0.8	350,000	1.1
Marginal Christians	0	0.0	900	0.0	2,200	0.0	54	126	180	6.16	2,970	0.0	4,000	0.0	10,000	0.0
Orthodox	0	0.0	1,500	0.0	2,100	0.0	52	-32	20	0.91	2,200	0.0	2,300	0.0	3,000	0.0
Trans-megabloc groupings																
Evangelicals	2,000	0.1	128,000	1.2	360,000	2.0	8,874	5,126	14,000	3.34	440,402	2.2	500,000	2.3	947,000	3.1
Pentecostals/Charismatics	0	0.0	40,000	0.4	420,000	2.4	10,353	1,647	12,000	2.54	479,725	2.4	540,000	2.4	870,000	2.8
Great Commission Christians	**29,500**	**1.4**	**434,000**	**4.0**	**981,000**	**5.5**	**24,183**	**13,248**	**37,431**	**3.28**	**1,126,000**	**5.6**	**1,355,307**	**6.1**	**2,150,000**	**6.9**
Hindus	210,000	10.0	804,500	7.4	1,315,000	7.4	32,416	-965	31,451	2.17	1,478,000	7.4	1,629,511	7.3	2,350,000	7.6
Buddhists	105,000	5.0	689,800	6.4	1,160,000	6.5	28,595	3,273	31,868	2.46	1,325,000	6.6	1,478,676	6.7	2,200,000	7.1
Ethnoreligionists	200,000	9.5	553,000	5.1	670,000	3.8	16,516	-7,712	8,804	1.24	710,000	3.5	758,043	3.4	800,000	2.6
New-Religionists	0	0.0	50,000	0.5	240,000	1.3	5,916	1,796	7,712	2.83	285,000	1.4	317,124	1.4	500,000	1.6
Nonreligious	0	0.0	16,000	0.2	75,000	0.4	1,849	1,167	3,016	3.44	89,600	0.5	105,156	0.5	200,000	0.7
Baha'is	0	0.0	42,700	0.4	78,000	0.4	1,923	-15	1,908	2.21	88,200	0.4	97,078	0.4	170,000	0.6
Atheists	0	0.0	8,000	0.1	28,000	0.2	690	586	1,276	3.83	35,000	0.2	40,755	0.2	60,000	0.2
Sikhs	4,000	0.2	20,000	0.2	30,000	0.2	740	-56	684	2.07	33,300	0.2	36,836	0.2	60,000	0.2
Other religionists	0	0.0	800	0.0	3,000	0.0	74	52	126	3.58	3,700	0.0	4,264	0.0	8,000	0.0
doubly-counted religionists	0	0.0	0	0.0	-27,000	-0.2	-666	57	-609	2.06	-30,000	-0.2	-33,093	-0.2	-50,000	-0.2
World A (unevangelized persons)	1,850,100	88.1	6,511,500	60.0	7,548,435	42.3	186,116	-132,983	53,133	0.68	8,224,333	40.9	8,074,572	36.3	9,011,688	29.1
World B (evangelized non-Christians)	217,900	10.4	3,759,173	34.6	8,856,565	49.6	218,294	127,782	346,076	3.36	10,244,061	50.9	12,322,443	55.4	18,906,312	61.0
World C (Christians)	32,000	1.5	581,827	5.4	1,440,000	8.1	35,498	5,201	40,699	2.52	1,640,000	8.2	1,846,985	8.3	3,050,000	9.9
Country's population	**2,100,000**	**100.0**	**10,852,500**	**100.0**	**17,845,000**	**100.0**	**439,908**	**0**	**439,908**	**2.23**	**20,108,395**	**100.0**	**22,244,000**	**100.0**	**30,968,000**	**100.0**

COLUMNS, ROWS.
For meanings and definitions, see Codebook (Part 3). Note that, by definition, total 'Christians' = professing + crypto-Christians, which also = affiliated + unaffiliated Christians, and also = Great Commission Christians + latent Christians. Percentages may not always total exactly, due to rounding.

CENSUSES.
(a) *Malaya* (West Malaysia). **1931:** 45.1% Muslims, 38.4% Chinese folk-religionists and buddhists, 12.0% Hindus, 2.3% Christians, 0.7% ethnoreligionists, 0.4% Sikhs. **23.IX.1947:** 44.0% Muslims, 43.8% Chinese folk-religionists and Buddhists, 8.7% Hindus, 2.1% Christians, 0.6% ethnoreligionists, 0.3% Sikhs. **24.VIII.1970:** 53.2% Muslims, 34.9% Chinese folk-religionists and Buddhists, 8.7% Hindus, 2.5% Christians, 0.4% ethnoreligionists, 0.2% Sikhs. (b) *Sabah* (formerly North Borneo). **1921:** 52.5% ethnoreligionists, 31.8% Muslims, 13.0% Chinese folk-religionists and Buddhists, 2.7% Christians. **1931:** 48.7% ethnoreligionists, 32.1% Muslims, 15.3% Chinese folk-religionists and Buddhists, 3.9% Christians. **3.IV.1951:** 40.3% ethnoreligionists, 34.5% Muslims, 16.5% Chinese folk-religionists and Buddhists, 8.7% Christians. **9.VIII.1960:** 37.9% Muslims, 29.0% ethnoreligionists, 16.5% Chinese folk-religionists and Buddhists, 16.6% Christians. **24.VIII.1970:** 40.1% Muslims, 9.7% Christians (rest incorrectly recorded: probably 33.7% ethnoreligionists, 16.5% Chinese folk-religionists and Buddhists). (c) *Sarawak*. **23.IX.1947:** 45.7% ethnoreligionists, 24.6% Muslims, 21.8% Chinese folk-religionists and Buddhists, 7.9% Christians (3.7% Protestants, 2.4% Roman Catholics, 1.8% Anglicans). **14.VI.1960:** 37.3% ethnoreligionists, 23.5% Chinese folk-religionists and Buddhists, 23.4% Muslims, 15.8% Christians. **23.VIII.1970:** 30.9% ethnoreligionists, 25.8% Muslims, 24.0% Chinese folk-religionists and Buddhists, 19.3% Christians. (d) *Malaysia* (all parts). **24.VIII.1970:** 50.0% Muslims, 32.8% Buddhists and Chinese folk-religionists, 7.4% Hindus, 5.1% ethnoreligionists, 4.4% Christians, 0.2% Sikhs, 0.2% nonreligious.

NOTES ON RELIGIONS
ATHEISTS. Communist Party of Malaya (proscribed; pro-Chinese).
BAHA'IS. 1962, mass conversions in Sarawak of 6,000 in 4 months to Baha'i, then rapid growth from 97 local spiritual assemblies (1964; 70 in Sarawak) to 287 (1973; 165 in Sarawak), then to 332 LSAs by 1995 (124 in West Malaysia, 187 in Sarawak, and 21 in Sabah). There are many Iban teachers.
BUDDHISTS. Chinese adherents of Mahayana and Tantric Buddhism, with small areas of Theravada (Sinhalese et alii).
CRYPTO-CHRISTIANS. Mostly unorganized individuals in legal or recognized churches in Sabah; in the 1960 census there, 16.6% Christians were recorded, but in 1970 (under strong state-aided Muslim pressure) only 9.7% publicly professed to be Christians. There are also numerous organized and unorganized isolated radio believers.
ETHNORELIGIONISTS. Animists in East Malaysia among the Dusun, Iban (Sea Dayak), Land Dayak and other tribes.
HINDUS. Mostly Tamils from South India. Every year 200,000 Hindus make the pilgrimage to the Batu Caves for the Thaipusam festival, doing penance by carrying spiked cages (*Kavadis)* whilst in a trance. Sects include the Ramakrishna Mission.
INDEPENDENTS. In 17 denominations or groupings in 1995 (see Table 2); Chinese, Indian and Malay indigenous Christians.
MUSLIMS. Sunnis (with Shia and Sufi elements), consisting of: all Malays (all Shafiite), all Pakistanis, most Javanese, 50,000 Indians in West Malaysia, 10,200 Indonesians in Sabah, and 33% of the Aboriginal population of East Malaysia. There are also a few Ahmadis (enumerated here although declared non-Muslim by Pakistan). *Hajj pilgrims to Mecca.* (1968) 6,236; (1969) 8,353; (1970) 10,361; (1971) 10,650; (1972) 10,395; (1973) 12,983; (1974) 15,366; (1975) 15,835; (1976) 3,373. *Conversions.* With state support many Aboriginals and others in Sabah are being converted to Islam, and state pressure on the Iban to become Muslim is particularly strong. A Chinese Muslim trained at Al-Azhar University (Cairo, Egypt) is training Chinese Muslim missionaries in Kuala Lumpur. At the same time, many Muslims in West Malaysia are being converted to Baha'i, atheism and non-religion (with a few to Christianity), so that the net balance is a small annual numerical loss to Islam in Malaysia.
NEW-RELIGIONISTS. Adherents of (1) Heavenly Virtue Holy Church (T'ien Te Sheng Hui), a syncretistic combination of Confucianism, Taoism, Buddhism, Islam and Christianity, begun in 1920 in China and widespread among the Chinese diaspora; and (2) Soka Gakkai (Nichiren Shoshu) from Japan.
NONRELIGIOUS. Mainly Chinese.
OTHER RELIGIONISTS. Including Rosicrucians (1 AMORC center).

Great Commission Instrument Panel: status of Malaysia (for explanation see start of Part 4)

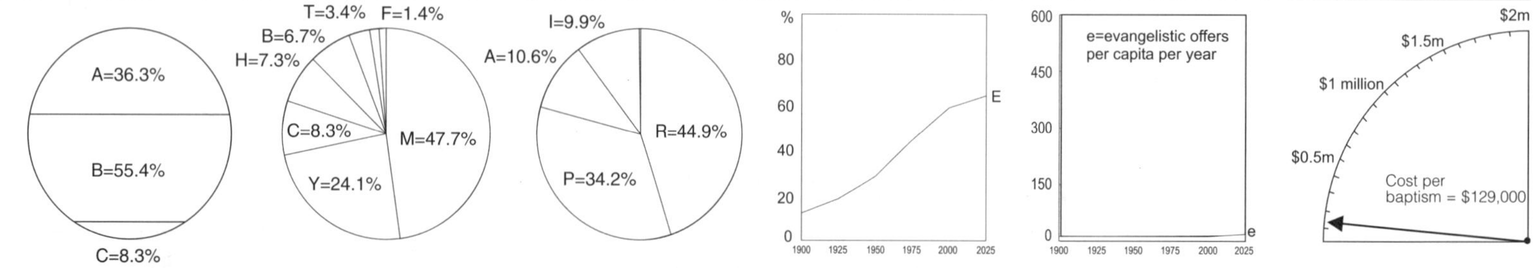

3 Worlds, AD 2000 | Religions, AD 2000 | Ecclesiastical blocs | Evangelization, 1900-2025 | Offers, 1900-2025 | Cost-effectiveness, AD 2000

Country status. Malaysia, a country in Southeast Asia, consists of the southern part of the Malayan peninsula and the northern part of Borneo. West Malaysia is the world's leading producer of both palm oil and rubber. Oil is an important product of East Malaysia.

HUMAN LIFE AND LIBERTY

Human need and development. Malaysia is generally considered as among the second tier of emerging powers of Asia. Its economic performance is high by Third World standards, but still falls short of those of Singapore, Korea, Taiwan or Hong Kong. What holds it back is social disharmony and the lack of single-minded dedication to growth. There is also a marked distortion between the politically powerful Muslim Malays and the economically powerful Chinese who, like the Indians, are numerically in the minority and thus targets of legal discrimination. The result is that the nation is divided along all possible lines, religiously, socially, economically, linguistically, and culturally. There are pockets of wealth everywhere in the towns and pockets of poverty in the rural areas. Differentials in living conditions between urban and rural areas have become more accentuated in recent years. A major consequence of increased urban density has been the growth in squatter communities on

Country summary. **Worlds A, B, C by ethnolinguistic peoples, cities, and major civil divisions in Malaysia.**

PEOPLES

World	Num	Pop 2000	C%	Christians	E%	U%	Unevangelized
A	95	2,912,494	3.64	105,904	32	68	1,968,963
B	59	19,086,365	7.83	1,494,186	68	32	6,111,346
C	20	245,200	69.78	171,094	100	0	1,021
Total	**174**	**22,244,059**	**7.96**	**1,771,184**	**64**	**36**	**8,081,330**

CITIES

World	Num	Pop 2000	C%	Christians	E%	U%	Unevangelized
A	0	0	0.00	0	0	0	0
B	21	5,766,208	8.50	489,840	65	35	2,019,739
C	0	0	0.00	0	0	0	0
Total	**21**	**5,766,208**	**8.50**	**489,840**	**65**	**35**	**2,019,739**

CIVIL DIVISIONS

World	Num	Pop 2000	C%	Christians	E%	U%	Unevangelized
A	0	0	0.00	0	0	0	0
B	15	22,244,061	7.96	1,771,189	64	36	8,081,331
C	0	0	0.00	0	0	0	0
Total	**15**	**22,244,061**	**7.96**	**1,771,189**	**64**	**36**	**8,081,331**

the outskirts of towns. Most Malays prefer to live on kampongs limited to their own ethnic group. Housing in rural areas range from simple split-bamboo frame and thatched roof houses elevated on poles to wooden dwellings with tile roofs. In Sarawak and Sabah tribal people commonly live in what are known as longhouses, built on stilts. As many as 60 families live in one longhouse. In contrast to the earlier part of the 20th century when many kinds of diseases were widespread, the general level of health in the country has become second only to that of Singapore The overall improvement in health is reflected in vital statistics. Infant mortality has dropped from 82 deaths per 1,000 live births in 1957 to 11 in 1995, crude death rate from 12.7 per 1,000 in 1957 to 4.8 in 1995. Life expectancy has grown from 52 at the time of independence to 72 in 1995.

Human rights and freedoms. Malaysia's human rights record is mixed. Although democratic in its formal governmental and judicial structure, citizens are arrested and detained without trial, and the freedoms of association and expression are limited. The principal means of human rights violations are the 1960 Internal Security Act, the Emergency (Essential Powers) Act of 1969, and the Dangerous Drugs Act of 1985. Under each of these Acts, the government may detain suspects without judicial review or formal charges The government does not publish statistics on the number of detainees under these Acts. The right to a fair trial is restricted when these Acts are invoked in criminal cases. The independence of the judiciary was jeopardized in 1988 when the government dismissed the Supreme Court lord president and 2 other justices after they had ruled against it in a Constitutional case. This was followed by a Constitutional amendment and legislation restricting judicial review. Press freedom is subject to important limitations under the Seditions Act and in the interests of security. Under the Printing Presses and Publications Act of 1984, domestic and foreign publications must apply annually to the government for a permit. The Act was amended in 1987 to make the publication of malicious news a crime, expand the government's right to ban or restrict publications, and prohibit court challenges to suspension or revocation of publication permits. Press freedom is also restricted in practice by the fact that the government and its political party supporters own all the major newspapers as well as all radio and television stations. The state-owned Malaysian News Agency (Bernama) is the sole distributor of foreign news in the country. Right of peaceful assembly is restricted by the need for police permits and the right of association by the Societies Act of 1966, under which any association with 7 or more members must be registered with the government. The Malays dominate government and all public institutions, although they make up only 33% of the population. There are few opportunities for non-Malays in government and they are discriminated against in higher education, and in the grant of business permits and licenses.

Human environment. East Malaysia is heavily forested, but indiscriminate logging is permitted in order to earn foreign currency. Many of the rivers and much of the coastal waters are polluted with runoff from industrial plants and tin mines. The estuaries are heavily silted and coral reefs are absent.

NON-CHRISTIAN RELIGIONS

Islam is the state religion and is adhered to by virtually all Malays, who constitute 50% of the population of West Malaysia, by all Pakistanis, and by about 50,000 Indians in West Malaysia; the latter being low-caste farmer immigrants from southern India; approximately one-third of the aboriginal population of East Malaysia also are Muslims. In 1995 Malaysia was 48% Muslim, Sabah 40%, and Sarawak 26%.

Islam was brought to Malaya by Arab traders in the 13th century, and within the next 200 years became the predominant religion of the region. By the end of the 16th century Malayan Islam tended to be Sunni in form, although today Shia elements and a Sufi spirit are also evident. Malays are attracted to the more mystical aspect of Islam but freely retain and adapt them to early Hindu and animistic traditions. Ancestor veneration, belief in the omnipresence of spirits, sacrifices, astrology, amulets, magicians and shamans all have a place in popular devotion. As elsewhere, Muslim religious education tends to concentrate on memorizing passages from the Quran; but in recent years educated Malay Muslims, influenced by British secular education, have turned to various modern Islamic movements such as those expounded at the University of Al-Azhar in Cairo or the Muhammadiyah party of Indonesia. The Southeast Asia regional bureau of the World Muslim Congress, with headquarters in Pakistan, is located in Kuala Lumpur.

Muslims. One of the most modern mosques in Asia, the National Mosque (Masjid Negara) in Kuala Lumpur, opened in 1965, accommodates 15,000 worshippers. Its spire and roof depict, respectively, a folded umbrella and unfurled parasol, both symbolic of Malaysian royalty.

Chinese folk religion and ***Buddhism*** are the predominant religions among the Chinese, who make up 40% of the population of West Malaysia and 25% in Sarawak. Buddhism arrived in Malaya in the 3rd century, the original Hinayana form being displaced in the 12th century by Mahayana. A still later manifestation is Tantric Buddhism, a result of the influence of early Malayan Hinduism. Most Chinese immigrants, however, have come from the lower classes of south and central China and observe a popular folk religion centered in ancestral veneration rituals and magical practices together with elements taken from Buddhism, Confucianism, and Taoism.

Hinduism was introduced during the first century AD. Immigrants from the Indian sub-continent, most of whom have come since the end of the 19th century, make up 11% of the population of West Malaysia and are predominantly Hindus. There is also a significant community of Sikhs originating in the Punjab of northwest India.

Hindus. Thaipusam festival in Batu Caves (14 miles from Kuala Lumpur): devotee in trance carries a kavadi (cage of metal spikes) to shrine of Hindu deity Lord Subramaniam, the Spotless One. Every year 200,000 Hindus make this pilgrimage.

Tribal religions are still strong among the indigenous peoples of Sarawak and Sabah. Although there are variations between the different tribes (Dusan, Iban or Sea Dayak, Land Dayak), they share many beliefs and rituals in common. All believe in the existence of good and evil spirits whose favor is sought or whose anger must be placated. Omens, tabus, divination, and magical practice are also important, and elaborate rites are performed at burials as well as at rice-planting and harvesting seasons. Traditional tribal religions, including head-hunting customs, continue to exist among the Dayaks in Sarawak. Possession of a skull is believed to ensure fertility of the soil, safe arrival of the deceased to the land of the dead, and enlistment of the spirit of the dead enemy in the service (after death) of the one possessing his skull. Among some Dayaks, marriage arrangements cannot be formalized until a skull has been captured.

Heavenly Virtue Holy Church (T'ien Te Sheng Hui) is a syncretistic new religion widespread among the Chinese diaspora, especially in Hong Kong (100,000 adherents) and in Malaysia where it is supported by wealthy Chinese and has a following among medical doctors because of its emphasis on healing. It was founded in Yunnan (China) in 1920 by a Chinese Buddhist, and it attempts to combine the 5 major religions of Confucianism, Taoism, Buddhism, Islam, and Christianity. It stresses ethical conduct, virtue, and wisdom, and aims to establish harmony between heaven and earth. It has a cosmological concept of history and a low level of folk-religion content.

Baha'i has grown rapidly since its mass conversion of 6,000 in Sarawak in 4 months in 1962. Growth has been largely due to population natural increase. By 1995 there were 332 local spiritual assemblies.

CHRISTIANITY

The first Christians were Catholics who arrived in the 16th century after the conquest of Malacca by the Portuguese. Protestantism appeared in the 17th century with the Dutch occupation, but Protestant missions made little advance until the arrival of the British in the early part of the 19th century. Christianity is most highly developed among the Chinese, somewhat less so among the Indians and Aboriginals, and has made no inroads at all among the Malays who remain almost entirely Muslim. By 1995 Christians made up 8% of the total population of Malaysia, with Catholics 3.2% and Protestants 2.9%. In 1995 Christians formed 10% of the population of Sabah and 19% in Sarawak. Several denominations consist of jurisdictions covering both Malaysia and Singapore, a state of affairs which remained unaltered even after Singapore's withdrawal from the Federation in 1965. A few have since redrawn their ecclesiastical boundaries to accord with the new political situation. However, the Council of Churches of Malaysia and Singapore remained undivided and based in Singapore, as one of the major centers of Christian activity in southeast Asia, until 1975 when it split up into 2 separate national councils, one for each nation.

CATHOLIC CHURCH. The first Catholic priest arrived in Malacca with the Portuguese in 1511, and Francis Xavier spent 3 years there in the 1540s. Malacca became a diocese in 1557, but the bishop was forced to leave in 1641 when the Dutch took over Malaysia. In 1841 the area was formed into the vicariate of West Siam. The diocese of Malacca was reconstituted in 1888 with Singapore as its seat, and in 1953 an archdiocese was established. Singapore became a separate archdiocese in 1972.

In West Malaysia the majority of Catholics are Indians with a substantial number of Chinese and Eurasians; in fact, almost all Eurasians are Catholics. The present diocese of Malacca-Johore has a Catholic population of 18,000 Chinese, 5,000 Indians and 3,000 Eurasians. Of its 21 priest, 12 are Chinese, 3 Indians, 2 Eurasians, and 4 Europeans (MEP). In East Malaysia most Catholics are either Aboriginal or Chinese. In the state of Sabah, whose Catholic population consists of 50,000 Aboriginals and 40,000 Chinese, plus a few in other ethnic groups, the Catholic Church has been under attack by provincial authorities, which has not been the case in the adjoining state of Sarawak with its larger Chinese constituency. The vicar apostolic of Kota Kinabalu, although a naturalized Malaysian citizen, has in fact never been granted permission to reside permanently in Sabah. While living in the neighboring vicariate of Miri (Sarawak), he is authorized to make only one pastoral visit to Sabah every 2 weeks. A general problem for the church has been its failure to develop local clergy to replace foreign missionaries, in contrast to Protestant churches which are well provided with local leaders.

According to the Office of the Apostolic Visitor for the Chinese of the Diaspora in Singapore, in 1969 there were in Malaysia, Brunei, and Singapore an estimated 166,900 Chinese Catholics among a total Chinese population of 5,802,000, with 183 Chinese priests working among them in 85 churches.

An anachronistic vestige of the old Portuguese patronage system is the presence of a Portuguese parish within the diocese of Malacca-Johore but under the jurisdiction of the diocese of Macao.

The Holy See has no diplomatic relations with Malaysia in AD 2000, but an apostolic delegate residing in Bangkok.

PROTESTANT CHURCHES. Protestant missions and churches have been characterized by great diversity since the arrival of numerous new missionaries after World War II, including many forced out of mainland China and others sent by autonomous national churches in Japan, Korea, and the Philippines. Many congregations are composed of immigrants from China and India, which has militated against unity within denominations as well as between them. The various conservative ethnic churches, particularly among the large Chinese population, generally give more attention to their national traditions and the social needs of their members than to broader Christian concerns. This pattern of ethnic isolation has been further aggravated by certain government policies. Out of fear of infiltration by Chinese communists in the early 1950s, new inland villages were created in West Malaysia composed of Chinese who had formerly been living in slum settlements along the Thailand border. In East Malaysia, rapid conversion to Christianity took place among Aboriginals, which did not preclude the continuation of many traditional beliefs. This is also true of conversions to Islam. In both East and West Malaysia, the influence of Christian mission schools and hospitals far outweighs their numerical significance.

Protestantism first entered Malaya with the conquest of Malacca by the Dutch in 1641 but was confined to the European population. When Malacca passed into the hands of the British at the beginning of the 19th century, a first Protestant missionary was sent by the London Missionary Society in 1814. Soon after, the Anglo-Chinese College was established in Malacca to train Chinese missionaries for work in China, which was then closed to Europeans. The LMS left Malaya for China when the door opened for missionary work in 1843.

Another early LMS missionary, a Presbyterian, worked among Malays but with little success. Presbyterian growth has been slow due to the restriction of its sphere of activity to the east coast of the Malay peninsula, and also due to Presbyterian Chinese immigrants importing their own structures. Nevertheless, the Presbyterian Church in Singapore and Malaysia, also called the Chinese Christian Church began to register important gains during the 1960s and in fact doubled in size between 1970 and 1990.

Methodists have the largest Protestant church in Malaysia. The first American Methodist missionaries arrived in Singapore in 1885, followed later by others from Australia and Britain. Chinese and Tamil pastors came from China, India, and Ceylon; and the first annual conference was held in 1902. The Sarawak Annual Conference was formed in 1956 and the Sarawak Iban Provisional Annual Conference in 1962. The church has 35 primary and 43 secondary schools, but these are now coming increasingly under government control. There are also 5 medical institutions (one hospital and 4 clinics), an agricultural extension service and a rural community development program for Ibans in Sarawak and a community center in Kuala Lumpur. The Methodist Church of Malaysia and Singapore became autonomous in 1968, with its first local bishop elected at that time.

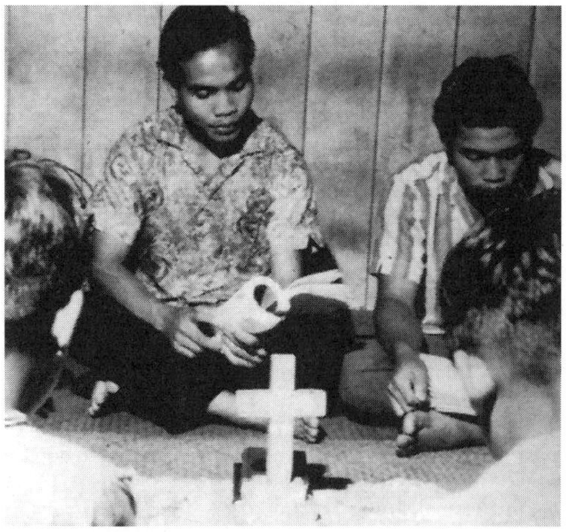

Methodist Church in Malaysia. Iban pastor conducts service on longhouse verandah in Sarawak.

The second largest Protestant denomination is the Evangelical church of Borneo, which was founded in 1963 and has 510 local congregations in more than 10 tribes. This church owes its beginnings to the outreach of the Borneo Evangelical Mission from Australia among East Malaysian tribesmen, particularly the Dusuns, in 1928. From the beginning emphasis was placed on indigenous principles of evangelization, and its Central Bible School now has a largely local staff and 150 students.

Seventh-day Adventists are growing rapidly in East Malaysia, particularly in Sabah; church membership quintupled in size from 1970 to 1990. The Basel Mission opened work among Chinese Christian Hakka families in Northern Borneo in 1882. There congregations have grown through continual Chinese immigration, as well as by conversion and natural increase; and the Basel Christian Church was formally established in 1926.

Pentecostal bodies include the Assemblies of God and the Finnish Free Foreign Mission. Also present are Baptists, Brethren, Lutherans, Salvation Army, and several smaller denominations.

OTHER CHURCHES. The first Anglican touched Malaysia in 1809. An Anglican opened the first English-speaking school in 1816, but systematic work did not begin for another 30 years. In 1841 Sarawak was ceded to the British settler James Brook, who arranged for the arrival of the first SPG missionaries in 1848. The missionary staff was later enlarged by the addition of CMS members from the UK and Australia. Evangelistic, educational, and medical work was undertaken among Chinese residents, Tamil immigrants from India, and the Sea Dayaks whose language was then reduced to writing. The church is now responsible for 59 primary schools, 6 secondary schools, 3 clinics, and an agricultural program in Kuching. The 3 Anglican dioceses in Malaysia are missionary dioceses under the archbishop of Canterbury, England, and in 1974 they formed part of the Council of the Church of South East Asia (from 1975 renamed East Asia).

Several independent churches have been formed in Malaysia, especially among the Chinese. The major group is the True Jesus Church which was brought to Malaysia by immigrants from mainland China. Other immigrant bodies are the Tamil-speaking Ceylon Pentecostal Church of Malaya, which was established in 1936, and the Mar Thoma Syrian Church which serves Indians from Kerala. Of groups entirely indigenous to Malaysia, the largest is the Bible Presbyterian Church which was created through a schism in the Chinese Christian Church.

There is also a small community of the Orthodox Syrian Church composed of immigrants from Kerala, South India.

Renewal movements. In the 1990s the Pentecostal/Charismatic Renewal continued to spread rapidly across most older churches, and numbered over 540,000 adherents (of whom 9% Pentecostals, 61% Charismatics, and 30% Independents).

Indigenous missions. In recent years, some Chinese Christians have been sent out from Malaysia to surrounding countries as missionaries.

CHURCH AND STATE

According to the constitution of 1957 (Article 3, item 1), 'Islam is the religion of the Federation'; but when Sabah and Sarawak joined the federation in 1963, safeguards covering their special interests were included. The head of state or king is the recognized head of Islam (the Muslim community) in his home state and also in 2 other states, Malacca and Penang. These latter states have no Muslim sultans but governors are appointed by the king, and their provincial constitutions provide that the king will also serve as the head of Islam in their areas. In Sabah and Sarawak there is no head of Islam, but Article 3 is also applicable there. Although the constitution does not specifically enjoin that the head of state should be a Muslim, as a matter of fact only a Muslim can be elected because he is always chosen from the Muslim sultans of the 9 states of West Malaysia. Furthermore, while it is not stated in the constitution that the king is officially the defender of the faith or head of Islam throughout the federation, nevertheless when taking the oath of office the king declares that he will 'at all times protect the Muslim religion', and he is constitutionally empowered to undertake action in minor matters such as fixing uniform dates for religious functions and festivals.

Article 11, item 1, stipulates: 'Every person has the right to profess and practise his religion and, subject to clause 4, to propagate it'. Clause 4 provides that any state law may control and restrict the propagation of any religious doctrine or belief among persons professing the Muslim religion. Nevertheless, Article 161D affirms that in the 2 Borneo states no law controlling or restricting the propagation of any religious doctrine or belief among Muslims may be passed, except with the consent of a two-thirds majority in the state legislature.

Islamic state religion. Muslim court musicians at installation of King of Malaysia.

In each state there is a council of religion, called by various names, to advise the sultan in the exercise of his functions as head of Islam. In Malacca and Penang, the council advises the king and in Sabah and Sarawak the state governments. To provide for a more efficient co-ordination of religious affairs, on 17 October 1968 the national Council for Islamic Affairs of West Malaysia was established. Usually the prime minister is appointed chairman of this council, and the secretariat with a small staff works at the prime minister's office in Kuala Lumpur. Its function are, firstly, to advise and make recommendations concerning any religious matters referred to it by any state government or state religious council; and secondly, to advise the Conference of Rulers, state governments, and state religious councils on matters concerning islamic law, the administration of Islam, and islamic education. Nevertheless, the National Council has no jurisdiction over the position, privileges, rights, sovereignty or other powers of any ruler as head of Islam in his state.

Although Islam is the official religion of the whole federation, the power to legislate on matters of Islamic law is vested solely in the state legislatures. Today Islamic law in Malaysia is restricted entirely to religious matters and the personal status and rights of Malays.

Recently the Catholic Church has had a prolonged dispute with the state government of Sabah. Between March 1970 and December 1974, 37 Mill Hill priests and all expatriate sisters were deported and others were refused permits to enter Sabah. At the same time there has been since 1969 an upsurge in Muslim missionary activities with the formation of the United

Sabah Islamic Association (USIA). The secretary-general of the USIA, a prominent lawyer, recently claimed that 'leaders of the USIA have made tremendous progress in winning converts all over Sabah, particularly in the interior'. There have been allegations that some conversions to Islam from among the Aboriginal and Christian populations have been based on coercion or bribery. The Sabah chief minister in 1972 held that Islam alone could bring national unity to Malaysia and did not hide his antipathy towards Christian conversions in his state. These anti-Catholic developments do not have the approval of Kuala Lumpur, but the federal government is unwilling to involve itself in Sabah's internal religious affairs. By 1977 all Protestant missionaries also had been deported or withdrawn from Sabah.

BROADCASTING AND MEDIA

Programs from KNLS can be heard, and FEBC (Philippines, Saipan) broadcast in Malay. Malaysia is a member of UNDA.

Some 1.5 million have seen the 'Jesus' Film, mainly through film team presentations and the wide use of videocassette copies.

INTERDENOMINATIONAL ORGANIZATIONS

The Council of Churches of Malaysia and Singapore, begun in 1948, had its headquarters in Singapore until 1975. It operated through 11 regional councils, 10 in Malaysia, and one in Singapore. The council continued to have difficulty in breaking through denominational self-sufficiency due to the large number of national and tribal churches and the multiplicity of languages and dialects, both foreign and local. Other problems included divisions created by pro- and anti-ecumenical factions, the conservative attitude of the large Chinese Christian population, and the government's uncompromising opposition to mission work among Malays. The latter policy also restricted co-operative efforts in radio broadcasting. Finally in 1975 the Council split into 2 separate national councils, one for Malaysia and one for Singapore.

Church union discussions among several members of the Council have been in progress for a number of years. In both Malaysia and Singapore, discussions have begun concerning the creation of a Sodepax committee.

FUTURE TRENDS AND PROSPECTS

Christians will likely grow to 10% of the population primarily due to conversions of young English-speaking Chinese. Muslims will remain at 47.7% through 2025.

Christianity could reach 15% by AD 2050 if growth among ethnoreligionists and Chinese folk-religionists continues into the middle of the 21st century. Islam will probably continue to dominate with Hinduism, Buddhism, and ethnic religions all declining.

BIBLIOGRAPHY

A bibliography of bibliographies on Malaysia. D. C. Ming. Petaling Jaya, Malaysia: Hexagon Elite Publications, 1981. 184p.

A bibliography of Christianity in Malaysia. J. Roxborogh. *Malaysian church history series*, no. 2. Kuala Lumpur: Seminari Theoloji Malaysia and the Catholic Research Centre for the Malaysian Church History Study Group, 1990. 68p.

'A comparison of Tamil and Chinese Lutheran churches in peninsular Malaysia and Singapore.' D. W. Vierow. D.Miss. thesis, Fuller Theological Seminary, Pasadena, CA, 1976. 283p.

A history of Baptists in Malaysia & Singapore. L. O. Rogers (ed)., [1971]. 146p.

'A model of pastoral leadership development in a local church in Malaysia.' P. Y. Tang. D.Min. thesis, Dallas Theological Seminary, Dallas, TX, 1989. 286p.

A short introduction to Malaysian church history: a guide to the story of Christianity in Malaysia and how to go about discovering the history of your church. J. Roxborogh. 2d ed. *Malaysian church history series*, no. 1. Kuala Lumpur: Seminari Theoloji Malaysia Catholic Research Centre, 1989. 38p.

'Adat and Islam in Malaya,' M. B. Hooker, *Bijdragen tot de Taal-, Land- en Volkenkunde*, 130, pt. 1 (1974), 69–90.

An analysis of Malay magic. K. M. Endicott. Kuala Lumpur: Oxford University Press, 1970. 188p.

Are Christians ignoring the Malays?: Islam in Malaysia. S. Amin. Leicester, UK: Universities and Colleges Christian Fellowship, [1982?]. 22p.

Batek negrito religion: the world–view and rituals of a hunting and gathering people of Peninsular Malaysia. K. Endicott. Oxford, UK: Clarendon Press, 1979. 234p.

Bibliography of Malaysia and Singapore. R. S. Karni. Kuala Lumpur: Penerbit Universiti Malaya, 1980. 649p.

Bishops and Brookes: the Anglican mission and the Brooke raj in Sarawak, 1848–1941. G. E. Saunders. *South-East Asian historical monographs.* Singapore: Oxford University Press, 1992. 323p.

Buddhism in Malaya. C. McDougall. Singapore: Donald Moore, 1956. 61p.

Catholic directory and diary 1973. Kuala Lumpur: Bishop's House, 1973.

'Christ in tribal culture: a study of the interaction between Christianity and Semai society of peninsular Malaysia in the context of the history of the Methodist Mission (1930–1983).' H. P. Shastri. Thesis, Universität Heidelberg, 1989. 213p.

Christian mission and Islamic dawah in Malaysia. Ghazali Basri. Kuala Lumpur: Nurin Enterprise, 1990. 80p.

Christianity in Malaysia: a denominational history. R. Hunt, L. K. Hing & J. Roxborogh (eds). Selangor Darul Ehran, Malaysia: Pelanduk Publications, 1992. 410p.

Church structure issues in Asian ecumenical thought with particular reference to Malaysia and Singapore. K. H. Yap. Ann Arbor, MI: University Microfilms, 1970. 260p. (Dissertation).

'Communicating the Gospel among the Iban: a resource manual for new cross–cultural missionaries.' J. A. Fowler. D.Min. thesis, Southern Methodist University, Dallas, TX, 1976. 148p.

Contemporary issues on Malaysian religions. T. A. R. Putra et al. Petaling Jaya: Pelanduk Publications, 1984. 212p.

'Diaspora Indians: church growth among Indians in West Malaysia.' C. D. Thomas. D.Miss. thesis, Fuller Theological Seminary, Pasadena, CA, 1976. 337p.

'Explaining the crucifixion to Muslims: with special reference to Indonesia and Malaysia.' K. Tan. Ph.D. dissertation, Fuller Theological Seminary, Pasadena, CA, 1993. 293p.

'Folk religion among the Chinese in Singapore and Malaysia.' L. Tjandra. D.Miss. thesis, Fuller Theological Seminary, Pasadena, CA, 1988. 392p. (Text in Chinese with extended summary in English).

Heaven in transition: non–Muslim religious innovation and ethnic identity in Malaysia. S. E. Ackerman & R. Lee. Honolulu, HI: University of Hawaii Press, 1988. 211p.

Indian Christians in Peninsular Malaysia. J. R. Daniel. Kuala Lumpur: Tamil Annual Conference, Methodist Church, Malaysia, 1992. 271p.

Indian festivals in Malaya. S. Arasaratnam. Kuala Lumpur: Department of Indian Studies, University of Malaya, 1966. 51p.

'Into a new age.' R. Nyce. Area Research Report, Kuala Lumpur, 1972. (Mimeographed).

'Islamic revivalism and the political process in Malaysia,' M. A. Bakar, *Asian Survey*, 21, 10 (1981), 1040–1059.

Khabar Gembira (the Good News): A history of the Catholic Church in East Malaysia and Brunei. J. Rooney. London: Burns & Oates with Mill Hill Missionaries, 1981. 292p.

Malaya: what of the church? F. G. Healey. London: Edinburgh House Press, 1951. 27p.

Malaysia. I. Brown & R. Ampalavanar. *World bibliographical series*, vol. 12. Oxford, UK: CLIO Press, 1986. 343p. (See especially 'Religion,' p.97–106).

'Malaysia: Islam and multiethnic politics,' F. R. von der Mehden, in *Islam in Asia: religion, politics, & society*, p.177–201. J. L. Esposito (ed). New York: Oxford University Press, 1987.

'New dawn over Sarawak: the church and its mission in Sarawak, East Malaysia.' B. W. Newton. M.A. thesis, Fuller Theological Seminary, Pasadena, CA, 1988. 207p.

'Public policy toward religion in Malaysia,' G. P. Means, *Pacific affairs*, 51, 3 (1978), 384–405.

Readings in Malaysian church & mission. Goh Keat Peng (ed). Malaysia: Pustaka SUFES, 1992. 163p.

'Redefine the theology and practice of worship for Malaysian Baptists.' C. Kang. D.Min. thesis, San Francisco Theological Seminary, San Anselmo, CA, 1986. 155p.

Redemptorists in Singapore–Malaysia. K. J. O'Brien. Singapore: Navjiwan Press, 1985. 227p.

Religion and modernization: a study of changing rituals among Singapore's Chinese, Malays & Indians. S. C. Tham. Singapore: Graham Brash, 1985. 204p.

Religion in West Malaysia and Singapore: a bibliography. J. J. Corfield. *Bibliography and literature*, no. 8. Hull, UK: Centre for South-East Asian Studies, University of Hull, 1991. 150p.

Sacred tension: modernity and religious transformation in Malaysia. R. L. M. Lee & S. E. Ackerman. Columbia: University of South Carolina Press, 1997.

'Sai Baba, salvation and syncretism: religious change in a Hindu movement in urban Malaysia,' R. L. M. Lee, *Contributions to Indian sociology*, n.s., 16, 1 (1982), 125–40.

'Singapore, Malaysia and Brunei: the Church in a racial melting pot,' J. R. Fleming, in *Christ and crisis in Southeast Asia*, p.81–106. G. H. Anderson (ed). New York: Friendship Press, 1968.

'Some aspects of Chinese religious practices and customs in Singapore and Malaysia,' T. Sakai, *Journal of Southeast Asian studies*, 12, 1 (1981), 133–41.

Studies in Chinese folk religion in Singapore and Malaysia. J. R. Clammer (ed). *Contributions to Southeast Asian ethnography*, no. 2. Singapore: National University of Singapore, 1983. 178p.

Taming the wind of desire: psychology, medicine, and aesthetics in Malay shamanistic performance. C. Laderman. *Comparative studies of health systems and medical care.* Berkeley, CA and Los Angeles: University of California Press, 1991. 382p.

'Teams multiply churches in Malaysia/Singapore,' L. Childs, *Urban mission*, 2, 5 (May 1985), 33–39.

The 15th anniversary of the Lutheran Church in Malaysia & Singapore, 1963–1978. Selangor, Malaysia: Lutheran Church in Malaysia and Singapore, 1979. 46p. (Text in English and Chinese).

The 20th anniversary of the Lutheran Church in Malaysia & Singapore, 1963–1983. Kuala Lumpur: Academe Art & Printing, 1983. 48p.

The Catholic Church in Malaya. F. G. Lee. Singapore: D. Moore for Eastern Universities Press, [1963]. 56p.

The Centenary of the Methodist Church in Southeast Asia. J. N. Hollister. Lucknow, India: Lucknow Publishing House, 1956.

'The church in West Malaysia and Singapore: a study of the Catholic Church in West Malaysia and Singapore regarding her situation as an indigenous church.' K. M. Williams. Ph.D. dissertation, Katholieke Universiteit te Leuven, 1976. 259p.

'The form of a North Borneo nativistic behavior,' T. R. Williams, *American anthropologist*, 65, 3 (1963), Part I, 543–51. (During Japanese contact in 1941).

'The impact of Christianity on power relationships and social exchanges: a case study of change among the Tagal Murut, Sabah, Malaysia.' A. S. Harris. D. Miss. thesis, School of Intercultural Studies, Biola University, La Mirada, CA, 1995. 307p.

The march of Methodism in Singapore and Malaysia, 1885–1980. T. R. Doraisamy. Singapore: Methodist Book Room, 1982. 123p.

'The new fundamentalism: Islam in contemporary Malaysia,' J. Nagata, *Asian thought and society: an international review*, 5, 14 (1980), 128–41.

'The Orang Asli: an outline of their progress in modern Malaya,' A. Jones, *Journal of Southeast Asian history*, 9, 2 (1968), 286–305.

The Portuguese missions in Malacca and Singapore (1511–1958). M. Teixeira. Lisbon: Agência Geral do Ultramar, 1961–1963. 3 vols.

'The potential of the Methodist Tamil Church in West Malaysia for evangelism and church planting.' E. J. Thoraisingam. Th.M. thesis, Fuller Theological Seminary, Pasadena, CA, 1977. 169p.

Country Table 2. **Organized churches and denominations in Malaysia.**

Official name (bold type = church with over 10% of all affiliated) 1	*Begun* 2	*Type* 3	*Counc* 4	*Congs* 5	*Adults* 6	*Affiliated 1970* 7	*Affiliated 1995* 8	*G%* 9	*Names, notes, and other statistics* (see Codebook, Part 3) 10
Advent Christian Church	1959	P-Adv	xF...	4	200	200	500	3.73	M=American Advent Mission Society (USA). Begun from India. Tamils.
Anglican Church of Malaysia	1809	A-Cen	AwEAW	300	110,000	69,600	180,000	3.87	In *CPSEA* (South East Asia). 3 Dioceses. 3h.
Apostolic Bible Christian Church	1960	I-3pI	.....	5	100	100	300	4.49	Small group of indigenous pentecostals. Members all South Indians. 1n,W=80%,10Y.
Asia Evangelistic Fellowship	1980	I-Non	.....	25	450	–	900	6.67	M=Asia Evangelistic Fellowship. Tamils. 1s.
Assemblies of God	1928	P-Pe2	ZF...	231	28,952	6,000	40,000	7.88	*Sidang Jumat Allah.* M=AoG(USA,UK). Classical Pentecostals. 1 school 61n,12f,1s(39).
Assembly Hall Churches	c1960	I-3nC	.....	44	7,324	8,000	15,000	2.55	*Local Churches. Little Flock.* Chinese. Begun 1922 in China.
Bible Presbyterian Church		I-Ref	.TT.T	50	1,000	1,500	2,000	0.05	Schism ex Chinese Christian Ch. Sponsors Malaysia Christian Pioneer Mission.
Calvary Charismatic Centres	c1990	I-3dZ	.....	12	1,200	–	3,000	20.00	Mission sent from CCC (Singapore). Nominal link with AoG.
Catholic Church in Malaysia:	1511	R-Lat	P.F.P	164	312,800	301,449	645,181	3.09	53% West. C=7+4+12. (1970) 13606Yy. (1990) 176n 57x 125m 515w 20000Yy
M Kuala Lumpur	1955	R-Lat	Ps	34	42,000	53,885	81,952	1.69	*Diocesi Agong Kuala L.* Indian, Chinese, Eurasian. 48n 26x 60m 147w 1888Yy
D Melaka-Johor (Malacca-Johore)	1972	R-Lat	Ps	20	15,000	25,975	29,570	4.35	69% Chinese, 19% Indian, 12% Eurasian. M=MEP. 1p. 24n 2x 9m 59w 956Yy
D Penang	1955	R-Lat	Ps	29	35,000	61,237	63,000	0.11	*Diocesi Penang.* Major centre of Buddhism. 1p,1s. 35n 3x 29m 97w 1361Yy
M Kuching	1927	R-Lat	Ps	9	51,500	65,380	105,800	1.94	Sarawak. 1976, archdiocese. Majority Chinese. M=MHM. 17n 3x 7m 65w 3633Yy
D Keningau	1992	R-Lat	Ps	9	31,300	–	64,935	33.33	Formerly part of D Kota Kinabolu. M=MHM. 7n 5x 5m 15w 2173Yy
D Kota Kinabalu (Jesselton)	1927	R-Lat	Ps	19	77,000	80,837	158,150	2.72	Sabah. 55% Aborigines, 45% Chinese. M=MHM. 25n 5x 8m 117w 5913Yy

Continued overleaf

Country Table 2–concluded

Official name (bold type = church with over 10% of affiliated) 1	*Begun* 2	*Type* 3	*Counc* 4	*Congs* 5	*Adults* 6	*Affiliated 1970* 7	*Affiliated 1995* 8	*G%* 9	*Names, notes, and other statistics* (see Codebook, Part 3) 10
D Miri	1959	R-Lat	Ps	33	23,000	14,135	64,774	6.28	Chinese, Indian, European. Includes Brunei. M=MHM. 10n 6x 7m 15w
D Sibu	1986	R-Lat	Ps	11	38,000	–	77,000	11.11	Formerly part of M Kuching. M=MHM. 10n 7x 7m 0w 2467Yy
Christian Brethren	c1865	P-CBr	x....	74	3,000	5,000	6,500	1.05	*Open Brethren.* M=CMML(UK, NZ, Australia). Chinese in West Malaysia. 11f.
CNEC Churches	1951	P-Non	xF...	23	1,500	265	2,000	8.42	*CNEC. Keristen Nasionals Pengar Injil.* 5 schools. Fast growth. 1n,1p,W=62%.
Church of God of Prophecy	1983	P-Pe3	Z....	2	80	–	160	8.33	M=CGP(USA).
Ch of Jesus Christ of Latter-day Saints		m-LdS	x....	3	180	500	300	0.05	*Mormons.* M=CJCLdS(Utah, USA). Mainly expatriates (Asians, USA, Oceanians).
Churches of Christ		I-Dis	x....	20	1,000	1,000	2,000	0.05	M=CC(Non-Instrumental) (USA). In Ipoh, Penang, Seremban, Kuala Lumpur, et alia.
Evangelical Church of Borneo	1928	P-Eva	.H...	510	110,000	40,000	190,000	6.43	*Sidang Injil Borneo.* M=BEM. 60% in Sabah. All ex-animists. 150n,46f,6p,2s.
Evangelical Free Ch of Malaysia	1957	P-Con	KF...	14	850	200	1,750	9.06	M=EFCA(USA). Several preaching points, related to 2 churches in Singapore. 10f.
Ev Lutheran Church in Malaysia	1907	P-Lut	L...W	22	1,300	1,831	2,500	1.25	M=Tamil ELC(India). 1961, M=SKM(Sweden). A=1962. Tamils. 9n,1p(2),57Yy.
Evangelize China Fellowship	1951	I-Non	x....	5	200	100	300	4.49	Begun in China by a Chinese, 1947. M=ECF(HQ, USA). Chinese members. HQ Singapore.
Full Gospel Churches of Malaysia	1978	I-3fZ	.....	17	6,000	–	9,000	5.88	Mainly Chinese members, a few Indians.
Hidden Hindu Believers in Christ	c1970	I-Hin	.....	900	13,000	–	21,500	49.04	Converted Hindus who choose to remain in Hinduism as witnessing to Christ.
Hidden Muslim believers in Christ	c1970	I-Mus	.....	100	3,000	–	5,500	41.13	Converted Muslims who stay within Islam to be witnesses for Christ.
Isolated radio churches	1952	I-3rZ	.....	1,000	30,000	13,800	60,000	6.05	Isolated believers, R=2400 (FEBC,&c), T=31000 (ICI,FEBC). ICI: S=5000,V=1500.
Jehovah's Witnesses	1932	m-Jeh	x....	20	1,201	400	2,670	7.89	Under Australian branch 1932. Activity by 1957 in Sarawak. (1975) 32Y. (1995) 215Y.
Jemaluang Community Church Mission		P-Non	..T.T	2	100	100	200	0.05	Mission from Kaimuki Community Church, Hawaii(USA), In Johore (West Malaysia).
Latter Rain Church of Malaysia	1975	I-3pZ	....E	27	1,200	–	1,500	5.00	*Gereja Hujan Akhir.* A fully indigenous church under Malay origin and leadership.
Lutheran Ch in Malaysia & Singapore	1949	P-Lut	L...W	30	2,390	1,476	5,320	5.26	*Ma Sin Tsue Dtuk Tsau Sin Yi Whei.* M=ULCA (now LCA)(USA). Some Aborigines. 16f,1s.
Malaysia Baptist Convention	1951	P-Bap	T....	88	7,000	4,000	12,780	4.76	Begun from China. M=FMB-SBC(USA). In west. 8 schools. SS=2,076. 16n,40f,1s,269Y.
Mar Thoma Syrian Church in Malaysia	1926	I-ReO	xwe.W	17	1,300	2,200	3,000	1.25	In Diocese of Bahya Kerala (Outside Kerala). Syrians from South India. 2 priests.
Methodist Church in Malaysia	1885	P-Met	VWE.W	300	77,692	65,000	230,000	5.18	M=UMC(USA)45f, MMS(UK)9f. 50% West, 50% Sarawak (Chinese, Iban). 50n,1H,43r,1s.
New Apostolic Church	1965	I-3aX	x....	15	3,000	200	4,872	13.62	In Canada Bezirk, Neuapostolische Kirche. M=NAK(world HQ Zurich, Switzerland).
Orthodox Syrian Church in Malaya		O-SyM	Dwe.W	7	880	1,500	2,200	0.05	In Diocese of Bahya Kerala (Outside Kerala). Syrians from South India. 3x.
Overseas Missionary Fellowship	1952	P-Non	xM...	20	1,000	1,000	2,500	3.73	OMF has a few congregations but mostly works with BEM and other denominations. 66f.
Pentecostal Church of Malaya	1936	I-3pI	Z....	25	1,000	1,000	3,000	4.49	CPM. M=Ceylon Pentecostal Mission (Sri Lanka). Tamil-speaking. HQ Singapore.
Pentecostal Evangelical Churches		P-Pe2	Z....	15	2,000	1,000	4,000	0.05	*Free Ev Pentecostal Ch. Glad Tidings Ch.* M=FFFM(Finland) Classical Pentecostals.
Pentecostal Holiness Church	c1985	P-Pe3	Z....	2	240	–	600	10.00	M=IPHC(USA).
Presbyterian Church in Malaysia	1851	P-Ref	Rw..W	5	700	1,000	1,200	0.73	*Malaysia Presbytery, Presbyterian Ch of England.* British expatriate chaplaincy.
Presbyterian Church in Singapore & M	1881	P-Ref	R...W	72	6,500	4,106	10,000	3.62	*Chinese Christian Ch.* M=LMS,PCE(UK). Doubled 1960-70. 10n,6x,W-43%,136Yy.
Protestant Church in Sabah	1882	P-LuR	lW..w	320	15,000	13,000	25,000	2.65	*Basel Christian Ch.* Hakka Chinese, Rungus. M=BM. 64n,2x,200m,7f,W=56%,155Yy.
Salvation Army in Malaya	1935	P-Sal	xwe.W	5	300	2,000	500	-5.39	*Bala Keselamatan* (Malay). *Chiu Shi Chen* (Mandarin). Singapore/M Command. 20n,5f.
Seventh-day Adventist Church	1911	P-Adv	x....	200	30,000	10,000	50,000	6.65	*Masehi Advent Hari Ketujah. SDA Chs.* Kadazans. 3n,3x,10f,1H,3r,W=85%,400Y.
True Jesus Church	1927	I-3oC	x....	50	10,000	8,000	15,000	2.55	*Gereja Jesus Jang Sejati.* Chinese. Begun China 1917. 33 churches in Sabah.
World-Wide Missions of Malaysia	1961	I-Non	x....	10	300	300	500	2.06	M=World-Wide Missions (USA). Evangelicals with base in Pasadena, CA (USA).
Other Protestant denominations		P-	.....	60	2,500	3,000	5,000	0.05	Total about 20 (see list below).
Other indigenous churches		I-3pZ	.....	100	3,000	1,000	6,000	0.05	About 10 (see below), incl Jesus is Lord Fellowship (Philippines), Trinity CC (Singapore).
Totals				**4,915**	**799,439**	**569,827**	**1,574,233**		

Churches, members, growth, 1900-2025	*Congs*	*Adults*	*Affiliated*	*G%*	*Total denominations*	*6 Megablocs:* O	R	A	P	I	m
Total churches, members, and denominations (mid-1900)	100	17,500	32,000	4.20	7	0	1	1	5	0	0
Total churches, members, and denominations (mid-1970)	1,985	311,608	569,827	4.20	45	1	1	1	27	13	2
Total churches, members, and denominations (mid-1990)	4,000	699,000	1,377,300	4.51	66	1	1	1	39	22	2
Total churches, members, and denominations (mid-1995)	4,915	799,439	1,574,233	2.71	67	1	1	1	40	22	2
Total churches, members, and denominations (mid-2000)	6,000	899,000	1,771,189	2.39	70	1	1	1	41	24	2
Total churches, members, and denominations (mid-2025)	12,000	1,489,000	2,933,000	2.04	118	1	1	1	60	50	5

NOTES ON TABLE ABOVE

NATIONAL COUNCILS (Column 4, 5th letter).

- E = Persaudaraan Kristian Evangelikal Nasional, Malaysia (National Evangelical Christian Fellowship of Malaysia).
- P = Catholic Bishops' Conference of Malaysia, Singapore, and Brunei (BCMSB).
- T = Malaysia Council of Christian Churches.
- W = Council of Churches of Malaysia (CCM) (until 1975 'and Singapore').

Local councils. 10 regional councils.

OTHER PROTESTANT DENOMINATIONS. These include: American Baptist Convention FMS (1967), Baptist Churches, Christian & Missionary Alliance (31 missionaries), Malaysia Evangelistic Fellowship, Malaysia Faith Mission, New Tribes Mission, Peniel Chs of VOCA (Voice of China & Asia Missionary Society) (1963), Worldwide Evangelization Crusade.

OTHER INDIGENOUS CHURCHES. These include: Ch of Christ of Malaya, Fishermen of Christ Fellowship, Jesus Saves Mission, Trinity Christian Center (Singapore).

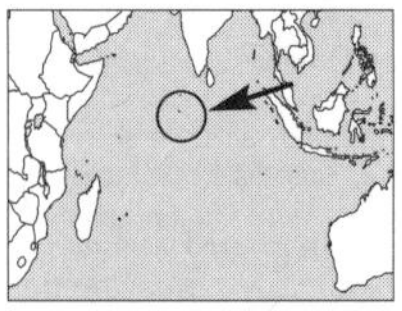

MALDIVES

SECULAR DATA, AD 2000

STATE
Official name: Divehi Raajjeyge Jumhooriyyaa (The Republic of Maldives).
Short name: Maldives. **Adjective of nationality:** Maldivian.
Flag: Red field with green panel containing white crescent.
Area: 298 sq. km. (115 sq. mi.).
Government: Republic with no political parties, since 1975 ruled by decree (1887 British protectorate, 1965 Independence as constitutional monarchy, 1968 republic, 1975 rule by decree).
Legislature: Majlis, 48 members.
Official language: Divehi (Maldivian Sinhale).
Monetary unit: 1 Maldivian rufiyaa (Rf) = 100 laari. **US$1=** Rf 11.77.
Chief cities: MALE 76,022.
Political divisions: 19 provinces.
Armed forces: 1,000.

DEMOGRAPHY
Population: 286,000.
Population density: 960.4/sq. km. (2,488.9/sq. mi.).
Under 15 years: 123,000.
Growth rate p.a.: 2.70% (births 33.28, deaths 6.28).
Mortality: Infant, per 1,000: 40.8; **Maternal per 100,000:** 200.0.
Life expectancy: 67 (male 68, female 66).
Household size: 7.1. **Floor area per person, sq.m:** 10.0.
Major languages: Divehi, Arabic, Sinhalese, Tamil.
Urban dwellers: 28.33%. **Urban growth rate p.a.:** 4.6%.
Labor force: 27%.

ETHNOLINGUISTIC PEOPLES
98.4% Maldivian (Malki, Mahl); 0.6% Sinhalese; 0.2% Gujarati; 0.1% Malayali; 0.1% Tamil.

ECONOMY
National income p.a. per person: US$988; **per family:** US$7,020.

EDUCATION
Adult literacy: 93% (male 93%, female 93%). **Schools:** 262.
Universities: 0. **School enrolment:** female/male: 89%/91%.

HEALTH
Access to health services: 50%. **Access to safe water:** 89%.
Hospitals: 5 (8 beds per 10,000). **Doctors:** 45.
Blind: 128. **Deaf:** 18,100. **Murder rate:** 1.
Lepers: 100. **Underweight prevalence under 5:** 39%.

LITERATURE
New book titles p.a.: 9 (30 p.a. per million). **Periodicals:** 90.
Newspapers: 2 dailies.

COMMUNICATION (per 1,000 people)
Phones: 57 (6% mobile). **Radios:** 99. **TV sets:** 40.
Daily newspaper circulation: 12. **Computers:** 15.

HUMAN LIFE AND LIBERTY (optimum condition=100.0%)
HDI: 61.1. **HSI:** 30.0. **HFI:** 10.0. **EFL:** 8.0.

Country status. Maldives is an archipelago of 1,190 coral islands in 26 natural atolls 415 miles southwest of Sri Lanka and 372 miles from the southern tip of India. About 200 of the islands are inhabited. The islands are only a few feet above water and many of them are just tiny banks washed by the ocean. Fishing and tourism are the main economic activities of the islands.

HUMAN LIFE AND LIBERTY

Human need and development. Maldives is on the same level of development as Sri Lanka, although less exposed to Western influences. Not surprisingly, most Maldivians are fishermen, and fishing is the principal economic activity. Although the atolls are not fertile and fresh water is in short supply, there is some farming, but almost all rice, the staple food, is imported. Tourism is the major revenue earner. There are few modern health facilities or educational institutions in the conventional sense. Some public services are offered on the main island of Male, but the absence of such services is hardly felt by the people. The majority of the people live in crudely built huts. The small size of the islands precludes the need for roads and there is little traffic to justify them.

Muslims. The country converted to Islam in AD 1153.

Human rights and freedoms. Maldives is an autocracy where a repressive Islamic regime has been in power since independence. Under the guise of the Sharia, the government restricts human rights in many areas including free speech, religion, elections, and women's and workers' rights. Other violations of human rights include arbitrary arrest and incommunicado detention of political opponents winked at by a subservient judiciary. An independent press has ceased to exist as a result of the revocation of press permits. House arrests and banishments to isolated atolls are common punishments. There is no limit on the detention of persons suspected of such crimes as drug abuse, terrorism, and attempted overthrow of government. The trials are conducted not by trained jurists but by Islamic kadi, all appointed by the president and serving at his pleasure. There are few professional lawyers and most defendant are left to their devices. There are no legal requirements for arrest

Country Table 1. Religious adherents in Maldives, AD 1900-2025.

Year	1900		1970		mid-1990		Annual change, 1990-2000				mid-1995		mid-2000		mid-2025	
Name	Adherents	%	Adherents	%	Adherents	%	Natural	Conversion	Total	Rate	Adherents	%	Adherents	%	Adherents	%
Muslims	72,000	100.0	120,760	99.5	214,260	99.2	6,965	-30	6,935	2.84	246,685	99.1	283,613	99.2	495,800	99.0
Buddhists	0	0.0	0	0.0	1,100	0.5	36	39	75	5.33	1,600	0.6	1,849	0.7	3,600	0.7
Christians	**0**	**0.0**	**220**	**0.2**	**340**	**0.2**	**11**	**-8**	**3**	**0.82**	**370**	**0.2**	**369**	**0.1**	**800**	**0.2**
PROFESSION																
crypto-Christians	0	0.0	0	0.0	20	0.0	1	1	2	7.18	30	0.0	40	0.0	200	0.0
professing Christians	**0**	**0.0**	**220**	**0.2**	**320**	**0.2**	**10**	**-9**	**1**	**0.28**	**340**	**0.1**	**329**	**0.1**	**600**	**0.1**
AFFILIATION																
unaffiliated Christians	0	0.0	0	0.0	50	0.0	2	-6	-4	-14.05	3	0.0	11	0.0	100	0.0
affiliated Christians	**0**	**0.0**	**220**	**0.2**	**290**	**0.1**	**9**	**-2**	**7**	**2.13**	**367**	**0.2**	**358**	**0.1**	**700**	**0.1**
Protestants	0	0.0	90	0.1	180	0.1	6	2	8	3.67	262	0.1	258	0.1	500	0.1
Roman Catholics	0	0.0	120	0.1	90	0.0	3	-4	-1	-1.17	85	0.0	80	0.0	100	0.0
Independents	0	0.0	10	0.0	20	0.0	1	-1	0	0.00	20	0.0	20	0.0	100	0.0
Trans-megabloc groupings																
Evangelicals	0	0.0	20	0.0	50	0.0	2	-1	1	1.84	55	0.0	60	0.0	100	0.0
Pentecostals/Charismatics	0	0.0	10	0.0	25	0.0	1	2	3	7.18	46	0.0	50	0.0	70	0.0
Great Commission Christians	**0**	**0.0**	**100**	**0.1**	**240**	**0.1**	**8**	**-2**	**6**	**2.26**	**265**	**0.1**	**300**	**0.1**	**600**	**0.1**
Hindus	0	0.0	0	0.0	190	0.1	6	-2	4	2.10	210	0.1	234	0.1	500	0.1
Nonreligious	0	0.0	0	0.0	60	0.0	2	2	4	5.03	80	0.0	98	0.0	200	0.0
Baha'is	0	0.0	20	0.0	50	0.0	2	-1	1	1.84	55	0.0	60	0.0	100	0.0
World A (unevangelized persons)	72,000	100.0	110,838	91.3	174,960	81.0	5,693	-178	5,514	2.78	200,991	80.7	229,944	80.4	394,788	78.8
World B (evangelized non-Christians)	0	0.0	10,341	8.5	40,700	18.8	1,319	186	1,505	3.18	47,698	19.1	55,687	19.5	105,412	21.0
World C (Christians)	0	0.0	220	0.2	340	0.2	11	-8	3	0.82	370	0.2	369	0.1	800	0.2
Country's population	**72,000**	**100.0**	**121,400**	**100.0**	**216,000**	**100.0**	**7,022**	**0**	**7,022**	**2.85**	**249,060**	**100.0**	**286,000**	**100.0**	**501,000**	**100.0**

COLUMNS, ROWS.
For meanings and definitions, see Codebook (Part 3). Note that, by definition, total 'Christians' = professing + crypto-Christians, which also = affiliated + unaffiliated Christians, and also = Great Commission Christians + latent Christians. Percentages may not always total exactly, due to rounding.

CENSUSES.
18.VI.1965: 100% Muslims.

NOTES ON RELIGIONS.
BAHA'IS. In 1 isolated group.
CHRISTIANS. All expatriate Sinhalese from Sri Lanka, and South Indians
MUSLIMS. Sunnis (of the Shafiite rite), since the conversion of the Maldives to Islam in 1153.

Great Commission Instrument Panel: status of Maldives (for explanation see start of Part 4)

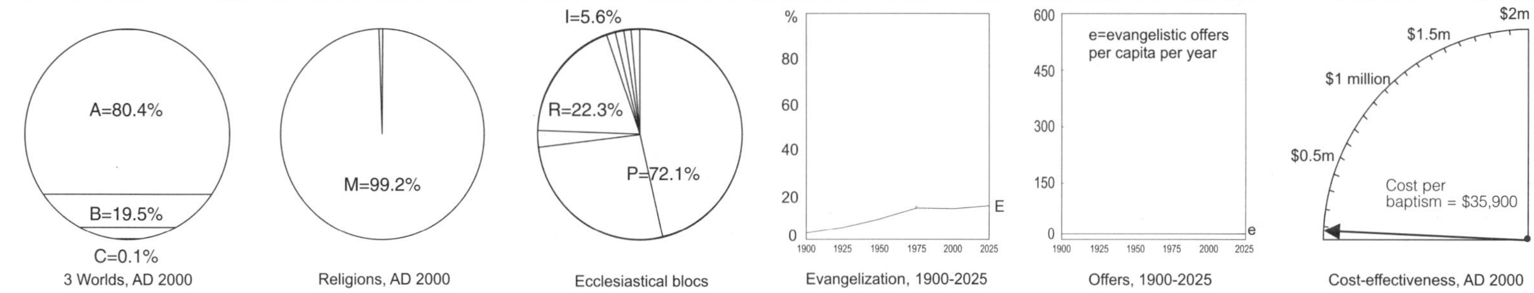

warrants or searches, and residences may be searched by police officials without prior warning. Press freedom is sharply restricted. The only 2 dailies are published by government ministers, and so are 11 of the 74 periodicals. The Department of Information and Broadcasting applies constant pressure on journalists and printers to toe the government line and avoid publishing anything that might bring official wrath on their heads. Political parties are not permitted. The present president, Maumoon Abdul Gayoom, has been elected thrice without opposition, and wields a tight control on the island. Women play a subordinate role in society, as they do in most Islamic societies.

Human environment. Tourism is the main threat to the Maldivian environment. The atolls have a fragile ecology, and are easily degraded by the kind of activities that tourists have introduced into the islands, and which the government promotes in order to bring in foreign exchange.

NON-CHRISTIAN RELIGIONS

Islam is the religion of virtually the entire indigenous population. Originally Buddhists, the Maldivian people were converted to Islam in 1153.

CHRISTIANITY

MAJOR CHURCHES. The Maldive Islands have historical links with the Catholic Church in Sri Lanka. In 1995 there were 100 Catholics, mostly Ceylonese teachers, working in the islands. There are no priests assigned there, and no parish structures. Catholic religious services consist largely of informal Bible readings. Small groups of expatriate Protestants, mostly Adventists, also meet together for worship.

The Holy See has no diplomatic relations with Maldives in AD 2000.

Indigenous missions. With virtually no Christian community, there have been no missionaries sent out from the Maldives.

CHURCH AND STATE

Following the conversion to Islam in 1314 of the Buddhist ruler of the Maldives, Dharumasantha Rasgefanu, he took the name Sultan Muhammed bin Abdullah, and the islands were ruled as a Muslim sultanate until the 20th century. In 1953 the sultanate was abolished and attempts were made to initiate progressive social legislation. However, Muslim traditionalists strongly opposed the changes, and the sultanate was restored. On 11 November 1968 the sultan was deposed once more and a republic proclaimed. According to the constitution of 1964, revised in 1968, Islam is the official religion of the Maldives; and the fundamental rights of individuals are recognized, provided that they do not contradict the stipulations of Islam. The nation's legal system has its basis in Islamic law, the Sharia.

BROADCASTING AND MEDIA

Various foreign Christian agencies broadcast Christian programs. For many years this was regularly advertised by a USA Black pentecostal body, the Bible Way Church of Our Lord Jesus Christ Worldwide.

FUTURE TRENDS AND PROSPECTS

Few changes are expected in religious affiliation in the Maldives in the next 30 years.

It is unlikely that Christianity will reach even 1% of the population before AD 2050. Immigration from India and Sri Lanka could add to Buddhists, Hindus, and Christians.

Christians. Several Maldivian postage stamps carry Christian themes: (*from left*), 1953, Coronation in England; Michelangelo; and his portraits of Apostles Peter and Paul.

BIBLIOGRAPHY

Maldive and and Minicoy Islands bibliography with the Laccadive Islands. L. Vilgon. 2nd ed. Stockholm: 1993. 119p. (Available through British Library).

Maldives. C. H. B. Reynolds. *World bibliographical series*, vol. 158. Oxford, UK: CLIO Press, 1993. 116p. (See especially 'Religion,' p.46–7).

Mysticism in the Maldives: eyewitness accounts of supernatural encounters. A. Husain. Trans., I. Khaleel et al. Male, Maldives: Novelty Printers and Publishers, 1991. 110p.

People of the Maldive Islands. C. Maloney. Bombay: Orient Longman, 1980. 462p.

'Southern Arabia and the Islamicisation of the Indian Ocean archipelagoes,' A. D. W. Forbes, *Archipel*, 21 (1981), 55–92.

The Islamic history of the Maldive islands. H. Yajima (ed). *Studia culturae Islamicae*, nos. 16, 22. Tokyo: Institute for the Study of Languages and Cultures of Asia and Africa, 1982–1984. 2 vols.

'The mosque in the Maldive Islands: a preliminary historical survey,' A. D. W. Forbes, *Archipel*, 26 (1983), 44–74.

Country summary. **Worlds A, B, C by ethnolinguistic peoples, cities, and major civil divisions in Maldives.**

	PEOPLES							CITIES							CIVIL DIVISIONS						
World	Num	Pop 2000	C%	Christians	E%	U%	Unevangelized	Num	Pop 2000	C%	Christians	E%	U%	Unevangelized	Num	Pop 2000	C%	Christians	E%	U%	Unevangelized
A	5	283,274	0.03	75	19	81	229,109	1	76,022	0.30	228	26	74	56,431	19	286,221	0.13	358	20	80	230,135
B	3	2,833	7.31	207	64	36	1,029	0	0	0.00	0	0	0	0	0	0	0.00	0	0	0	0
C	1	114	65.79	75	100	0	0	0	0	0.00	0	0	0	0	0	0	0.00	0	0	0	0
Total	**9**	**286,221**	**0.12**	**357**	**20**	**80**	**230,138**	**1**	**76,022**	**0.30**	**228**	**26**	**74**	**56,431**	**19**	**286,221**	**0.13**	**358**	**20**	**80**	**230,135**

Country Table 2. **Organized churches and denominations in Maldives.**

Official name (bold type = church with over 10% of all affiliated) 1	*Begun* 2	*Type* 3	*Counc* 4	*Congs* 5	*Adults* 6	*Affiliated 1970* 7	*Affiliated 1995* 8	*G%* 9	*Names, notes, and other statistics* (see Codebook, Part 3) 10
Catholic Church (M Colombo)		R-Lat	P.F..	1	49	120	85	0.05	95% Ceylonese (mostly teachers). No parish or priest. Lay-led Bible studies.
Church of South India		P-Uni	.....	2	70	70	150	0.05	Tamils and Malayalis from South India.
Evangelical Mennonite Ch	1991	P-Men	.....	1	30	–	50	25.00	Mission related to Mennonites in Europe and USA.
Isolated radio believers		I-3rI	.....	3	10	10	20	0.05	Isolated believers following radio programs.
Seventh-day Adventist Church		P-Adv	x....	1	10	20	12	0.05	Under SDA, Ceylon Union, Southern Asia Division. Expatriates, occasional meetings.
Other Protestant bodies	c1980	P-	.....	1	35	–	50	6.67	Expatriates.
Totals				**9**	**204**	**220**	**367**		

Churches, members, growth, 1900-2025	*Congs*	*Adults*	*Affiliated*	*G%*	*Total denominations*	*6 Megablocs:* O	R	A	P	I	m
Total churches, members, and denominations (mid-1900)	0	0	0	0.00	0	0	0	0	0	0	0
Total churches, members, and denominations (mid-1970)	4	115	220	2.00	4	0	1	0	2	1	0
Total churches, members, and denominations (mid-1990)	8	160	290	1.39	7	0	1	0	5	1	0
Total churches, members, and denominations (mid-1995)	9	204	367	4.82	8	0	1	0	6	1	0
Total churches, members, and denominations (mid-2000)	10	200	358	-0.50	8	0	1	0	6	1	0
Total churches, members, and denominations (mid-2025)	20	390	700	2.72	12	0	1	0	10	1	0

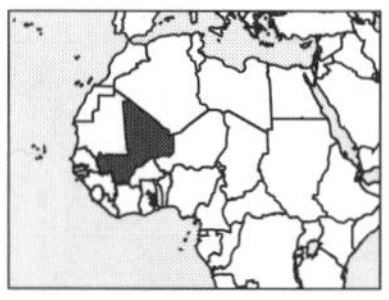

MALI

SECULAR DATA, AD 2000

STATE
Official name: République du Mali (The Republic of Mali).
Short name: Mali. **Adjective of nationality:** Malian.
Flag: Bars of green, yellow, and red.
Area: 1,248,574 sq. km. (482,077 sq. mi.).
Government: Multiparty republic, since 1997 (1904 French Soudan, 1958 self-government, 1960 Independence, 1968 military junta).
Legislature: National Assembly, 147 members.
Official language: French (Français).
Monetary unit: 1 CFA franc (CFAF) = 100 centimes. **US$1=** CFAF 560.38.
Chief cities: BAMAKO 1,160,000; Segou 132,840; Mopti 110,573; Sikasso 109,184; Gao 82,017.
Political divisions: 8 provinces.
Armed forces: 8,000.

DEMOGRAPHY
Population: 11,234,000.
Population density: 9.0/sq. km. (23.3/sq. mi.).
Under 15 years: 5,199,000.
Growth rate p.a.: 2.53% (births 44.65, deaths 14.39).
Mortality: Infant, per 1,000: 109.9; **Maternal per 100,000:** 1,200.0.
Life expectancy: 55 (male 54, female 57).
Household size: 5.6. **Floor area per person, sq.m:** 7.0.
Major languages: French, Bambara, Fulani, Senufo, Soninke, Dioula, Dogon, Tuareg, Mandingo, Arabic, Mossi, and 15 smaller languages.
Urban dwellers: 30.04%. **Urban growth rate p.a.:** 5.0%.
Labor force: 45%.

ETHNOLINGUISTIC PEOPLES
30.5% Bambara (Bamanakan); 9.5% Fula Macina (Niafunke); 7.4% Soninke (Sarakole); 6.5% Northwestern Maninka; 6.3% Songhai (Sonrhai).

ECONOMY
National income p.a. per person: US$249; **per family:** US$1,399.

EDUCATION
Adult literacy: 31% (male 39%, female 23%). **Schools:** 1,821.
Universities: 7. **School enrolment:** female/male: 15%/26%.

HEALTH
Access to health services: 30%. **Access to safe water:** 37%.
Hospitals: 15 (4 beds per 10,000). **Doctors:** 435.
Blind: 110,000. **Deaf:** 753,600. **Murder rate:** 6.
Lepers: 270,000. **Underweight prevalence under 5:** 31%.

LITERATURE
New book titles p.a.: 110 (10 p.a. per million). **Periodicals:** 10.
Newspapers: 2 dailies.

COMMUNICATION (per 1,000 people)
Phones: 1 (14% mobile). **Radios:** 176. **TV sets:** 12.
Daily newspaper circulation: 4. **Computers:** 4.

REFUGEES
Citizen refugees in other countries: 90,000.
Alien refugees from other countries: 15,000.
Internal displacement: 10,000.

HUMAN LIFE AND LIBERTY (optimum condition=100.0%)
HDI: 22.9. **HSI:** 30.0. **HFI:** 10.0. **EFL:** 38.0.

Country Table 1. **Religious adherents in Mali, AD 1900-2025.**

Year	*1900*		*1970*		*mid-1990*		*Annual change, 1990-2000*				*mid-1995*		*mid-2000*		*mid-2025*	
Name	*Adherents*	*%*	*Adherents*	*%*	*Adherents*	*%*	*Natural*	*Conversion*	*Total*	*Rate*	*Adherents*	*%*	*Adherents*	*%*	*Adherents*	*%*
Muslims	390,312	30.0	4,278,300	78.0	7,163,200	81.0	193,768	9,401	203,169	2.53	8,085,700	81.3	9,194,893	81.9	18,060,000	84.8
Ethnoreligionists	909,000	69.9	1,120,000	20.4	1,500,000	17.0	40,579	-10,519	30,060	1.84	1,650,000	16.6	1,800,595	16.0	2,724,500	12.8
Christians	**688**	**0.1**	**85,164**	**1.6**	**168,500**	**1.9**	**4,558**	**1,136**	**5,694**	**2.95**	**196,000**	**2.0**	**225,440**	**2.0**	**475,000**	**2.2**
PROFESSION																
crypto-Christians	388	0.0	42,764	0.8	90,000	1.0	2,435	1,565	4,000	3.75	110,000	1.1	130,000	1.2	310,000	1.5
professing Christians	**300**	**0.0**	**42,400**	**0.8**	**78,500**	**0.9**	**2,124**	**-430**	**1,694**	**1.97**	**86,000**	**0.9**	**95,440**	**0.9**	**165,000**	**0.8**
AFFILIATION																
unaffiliated Christians	0	0.0	3,984	0.1	900	0.0	24	-6	18	1.79	1,234	0.0	1,075	0.0	2,000	0.0
affiliated Christians	**688**	**0.1**	**81,180**	**1.5**	**167,600**	**1.9**	**4,534**	**1,143**	**5,677**	**2.96**	**194,766**	**2.0**	**224,365**	**2.0**	**473,000**	**2.2**
Roman Catholics	688	0.1	60,740	1.1	96,700	1.1	2,616	271	2,887	2.65	110,033	1.1	125,565	1.1	230,000	1.1
Protestants	0	0.0	20,124	0.4	59,000	0.7	1,596	704	2,300	3.35	69,163	0.7	82,000	0.7	200,000	0.9
Independents	0	0.0	300	0.0	11,600	0.1	314	156	470	3.46	15,170	0.2	16,300	0.2	42,000	0.2
Marginal Christians	0	0.0	16	0.0	300	0.0	8	12	20	5.24	400	0.0	500	0.0	1,000	0.0
Trans-megabloc groupings																
Evangelicals	0	0.0	20,400	0.4	61,000	0.7	1,650	1,040	2,690	3.72	73,740	0.7	87,900	0.8	245,750	1.2
Pentecostals/Charismatics	0	0.0	500	0.0	21,200	0.2	574	226	800	3.25	24,397	0.3	29,200	0.3	80,000	0.4
Great Commission Christians	**650**	**0.1**	**73,000**	**1.3**	**152,000**	**1.7**	**4,112**	**709**	**4,821**	**2.79**	**174,000**	**1.8**	**200,207**	**1.8**	**450,000**	**2.1**
Nonreligious	0	0.0	0	0.0	8,800	0.1	238	0	238	2.42	10,650	0.1	11,176	0.1	30,000	0.1
Baha'is	0	0.0	436	0.0	900	0.0	24	-11	13	1.36	990	0.0	1,030	0.0	2,500	0.0
Other religionists	0	0.0	100	0.0	600	0.0	16	-7	9	1.36	660	0.0	687	0.0	3,000	0.0
World A (unevangelized persons)	1,250,600	96.2	4,113,288	75.0	5,296,358	59.9	143,363	-39,335	104,028	1.81	5,767,508	58.0	6,335,976	56.4	10,711,385	50.3
World B (evangelized non-Christians)	48,712	3.7	1,285,932	23.4	3,377,142	38.2	91,262	38,199	129,461	3.30	3,980,471	40.0	4,672,584	41.6	10,108,615	47.5
World C (Christians)	688	0.1	85,164	1.6	168,500	1.9	4,558	1,136	5,694	2.95	196,000	2.0	225,440	2.0	475,000	2.2
Country's population	**1,300,000**	**100.0**	**5,484,384**	**100.0**	**8,842,000**	**100.0**	**239,183**	**0**	**239,183**	**2.42**	**9,943,980**	**100.0**	**11,234,000**	**100.0**	**21,295,000**	**100.0**

COLUMNS, ROWS.
For meanings and definitions, see Codebook (Part 3). Note that, by definition, total 'Christians' = professing + crypto-Christians, which also = affiliated + unaffiliated Christians, and also = Great Commission Christians + latent Christians. Percentages may not always total exactly, due to rounding.

CENSUSES.
1960-61: 76.4% Muslims, 22.8% ethnoreligionists, 0.5% Roman Catholics, 0.2% Protestants.

NOTES ON RELIGIONS
BAHA'IS. In 3 local spiritual assemblies (1973), growing to 30 LSAs (1995).
CRYPTO-CHRISTIANS. In 1961, the government census reported 20,100 Roman Catholics and 7,300 Protestants, whereas soon after (1963) the Catholic Church reported 28,653 baptized Catholics and 18,247 catechumens, which total 46,900; and Protestants reported about 12,000. Crypto-Christians (Christians unknown to the state) therefore amount to over half the total Christian community.
ETHNORELIGIONISTS. Animists. Tribes over 30% traditionalist in 1995: Kagoro (98% animist), Bobo (50%), Minianka (43%). Fetish altars are still prominent in many villages.
MUSLIMS. Almost all Sunnis (of the Malikite rite). Hamaliya (using an 11-bead rosary) is still especially strong in Mali. Conversions to Islam are taking place among ethnoreligionists, through family conversion in areas remote from Western influence, and by individual conversion in urban areas. *Hajj pilgrims to Mecca.* (1970) 113; (1974) 2,628; (1975) 2,719; (1976) 2,072.
OTHER RELIGIONISTS. Including Rosicrucians (1 AMORC center).
ROMAN CATHOLICS. In the year 1900, there were 101 baptized Catholics and 587 catechumens.

Great Commission Instrument Panel: status of Mali (for explanation see start of Part 4)

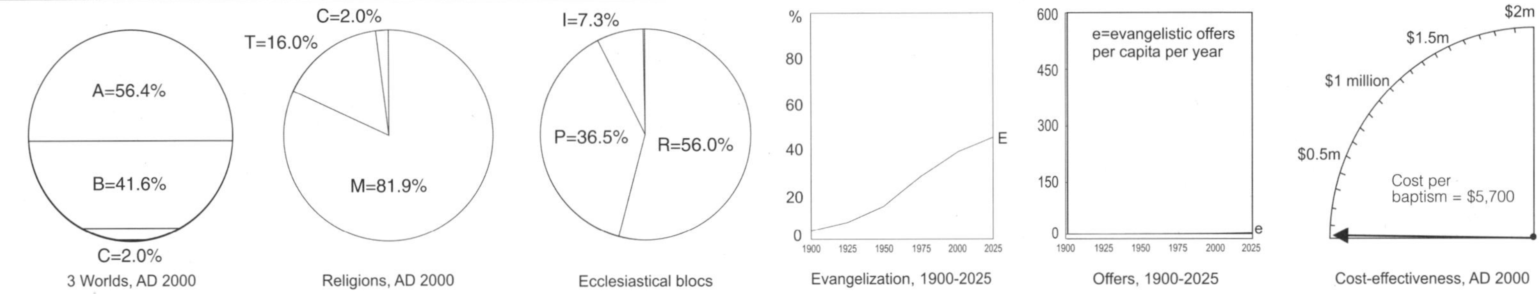

Country status. Mali is a landlocked country in northwestern Africa. The northern part of Mali lies within the Sahara Desert, and the central part is filled by the floodplains of the Niger Delta. Its exports include livestock, peanuts, cotton, and fish.

HUMAN LIFE AND LIBERTY

Human need and development. Mali is one of the poorest and most arid countries in the world with a per capita income of $249. Only the southern part of the country is inhabitable, and even so the desert dominates the lifestyles of all Malians. Much of the land is scarred with dry wells, abandoned villages and withered vegetation. The economy is based on subsistence farming which is highly vulnerable to lack of rainfall. Rural communities experience what is known as sodure, or a period of dire famine just before the harvest. If the harvest should fail any year, a whole year of scarcity is assured, and if it should fail for successive years, it is a disaster. Medical facilities are limited to the few towns, and serve only the relatively well to do. For the others folk doctors and folk medicine are the only recourse. Only about 10% have access to adequate and sanitary water supplies. Rivers and open wells are heavily contaminated with organisms that cause onchocerciasis and schistosomiasis. Malian houses are extremely primitive, built mostly with earth, and afford little protection to their residents against the harsh climate.

Human rights and freedoms. In 1992 Mali became a democracy ending many decades of dictatorship. The transition to a democracy was followed by a distinct improvement in human rights, a series of free and direct elections, and a new constitution. The state of human rights remains subject to the insurgency in the north by Tuareg rebels and also ravages of bandits roving the countryside. Rebels frequently abducted civilians, including government officials, during their raids. The new government has made serious efforts to improve the conditions of the jails, and to curb police brutality and torture. The new constitution has expanded the rights of arrested persons, and also provides for the independence of the judiciary. The inviolability of the home is respected in practice. Malians enjoy complete freedom of speech and press. The new Constitution contains strong affirmations of these freedoms. The press vigorously criticizes the government, including the president. There are nearly 30 independent newspapers and journals, 3 independent radio stations, and an independent television station. Political parties operate freely, and permits for meetings and demonstrations are granted routinely. Virtually all ethnic groups are represented at all levels of government. There are social conflicts between the nomads, such as Tuaregs and Moors, and other Malians which periodically break out in the open. By tradition, women are disadvantaged legally and socially, and there are few educational or economic opportunities for them. Violence against women in the home, including wife beating, is considered socially acceptable.

Muslims. Village mosque with mud walls in Sikasso region (Minianka tribe, 10% Muslims).

Human environment. Mali has a harsh environment, equally hard on humans as on animals and nature. Recurring draught has led to growing desertification and soil degradation, which are further promoted by overgrazing and use of firewood for domestic use. The Manantali Dam has greatly reduced the area available for pasture. Wildlife resources are declining rapidly.

Ethnoreligionists. *Upper.* Animistic Minianka with their fetish house (a form of pagan temple) in Koutiala region. *Lower.* A massive fetish in Koutiala, covered with libations.

NON-CHRISTIAN RELIGIONS

Islam was first propagated in the 11th century and is now the principal religion of Mali, claiming the allegiance of 82% of the population. Important cities include Timbuktu, one of the most famous holy places of African Islam, Djenne, a law school center, Oualata and Nioro, the cradle of Hamaliya, a 20th century sect which split from Tijaniya. In 1976 a large new mosque in Mamako was completed, paid for by Saudi Arabia.

Traditional African religions retain the allegiance of about 16% of the population and are especially strong among the Dogon, Bobo, Kagoro, and Minianka, all of whom are more than 60% traditionalist. The Bambara name for God is Jalang while the Dogon term is Amma, Creator. Dogon myths of creation are extremely complex and essential for understanding traditional conceptions of the individual, family, and society. Key elements are the creation of the primordial egg (aduno tal) with twin placenta, each with twin male and female Nommo, recognized as children of God and ideal models of man. The key event revolves around the premature emergence of the first man (Yurugu) from the male principle of one of the egg's placentas, resulting in imperfection and impurity, with a fragment of Uyrugu's placenta forming each. Secret societies, with extensive rituals and rich mask symbolism, play an important role in the life of the Dogon.

Eglise Catholique au Mali. Small rural church in Mandiakui.

CHRISTIANITY

CATHOLIC CHURCH. Bamako was reached in 1895 by White Fathers coming from Senegal, and White Sisters followed soon afterwards. The vicariate of Bamako was erected in 1921 and the first African priest ordained in 1936. New vicariates were formed at Gao in 1942 and at Kayes and Sikasso in 1947; and the archdiocese of Bamako was established in 1955. The first Malian bishop was consecrated in 1962. Numerically, the progress of the Catholic Church is slow, only one half of 1% of the population being affiliated Catholics. The most christianized ethnic groups are the Bobo and Wala in the diocese of San and the Dogon in the diocese of Mopti.

The Holy See has diplomatic relations with Mali and in AD 2000 is represented to government and the Catholic hierarchy by a nuncio residing in Dakar.

PROTESTANT CHURCHES. Of the 7 Protestant groups at work in Mali, the first to arrive was the Gospel Missionary Union in 1919. The most significant success has been recorded by the Evangelical Christian Church of Mali in its work among the Dogon people. Aided by the CMA, which began work in southeastern Mali in 1923, this church is now active throughout the country and maintains Bible schools for training church leaders. Several other missions have entered since World War II and the Protestants form less than 0.7% of the population. Three indigenous church movements have appeared in Mali all in the 1980s.

Indigenous missions. There has been little missionary outreach from the Mali Christian community with only 1 or 2 Catholic priests serving in surrounding countries.

CHURCH AND STATE

According to the constitution of September 1960, modified in January 1961, the republic is secular, and equality before the law without distinction of religion is assured for all (Article 1). Law 86 AN-RM of 21 July 1961, 'On the organization of religious liberty and the exercise of cult in the Republic of Mali', specifies that the creation of religious establishments, missions, and congregations must be submitted for authorization beforehand to the Ministry of the Interior (Article 4). Duly-recognized councils of administration represent such religious bodies in all the affairs of civil life (Article 8), and religious education may be given to children frequenting the public schools outside the time scheduled for classes (Article 25).

Country summary. **Worlds A, B, C by ethnolinguistic peoples, cities, and major civil divisions in Mali.**

	PEOPLES							CITIES							CIVIL DIVISIONS						
World	Num	Pop 2000	C%	Christians	E%	U%	Unevangelized	Num	Pop 2000	C%	Christians	E%	U%	Unevangelized	Num	Pop 2000	C%	Christians	E%	U%	Unevangelized
A	39	6,890,000	0.91	62,452	32	68	4,698,049	6	578,438	1.61	9,298	43	57	327,119	8	11,233,822	2.00	224,365	44	56	6,340,284
B	4	4,331,800	3.52	152,308	62	38	1,642,213	1	1,160,000	4.40	51,040	52	48	561,904	0	0	0.00	0	0	0	0
C	2	12,020	79.93	9,608	100	0	24	0	0	0.00	0	0	0	0	0	0	0.00	0	0	0	0
Total	**45**	**11,233,820**	**2.00**	**224,368**	**44**	**56**	**6,340,286**	**7**	**1,738,438**	**3.47**	**60,338**	**49**	**51**	**889,023**	**8**	**11,233,822**	**2.00**	**224,365**	**44**	**56**	**6,340,284**

A convention dealing with Catholic education in Mali called 'Catholic private education' (Enseignement prive catholique', EPC), was concluded on 8 August 1973 between the minister of National Education and the archbishop of Bamako in the name of the Episcopal Conference of Mali. Renewable every 3 years, the convention deals with all Catholic educational institutions except kindergartens, catechetical schools and training centers for religious personnel. EPC is defined as being 'of private service in the general interest'; and while retaining its specific organization and its relationship to the Episcopal Conference (Article 8), it remains part of the national school system (article 3). EPC accepts control by the state (Article 13) and pledges fidelity to official programs and recognizes that Mali is a secular state (Article 5). It cannot give diplomas, since all its students are required to take official examinations (Article 16). EPC is entitled to regular financial subsidies for teachers' salaries; at least 70% of the amount available for those in state schools; and occasionally receives personnel and supplementary financial grants for equipment and the administrative costs of lycees and second-cycle schools (Articles 21 and 29).

BROADCASTING AND MEDIA

HCJB World Radio helped start local stations in Mali. Mali is a member of UNDA, and Catholics air a 30 minute radio program <chaque semaine>. Television: <une emission tous les 15 jours>.

Of the 6.9 million who have seen the 'Jesus' Film, film teams made presentations to 3.6 million and the other half viewed it on television.

INTERDENOMINATIONAL ORGANIZATIONS

The Association of Evangelical Protestant Churches and Missions in Mali, with 4 member churches, is a member of the Association of Evangelicals of Africa and Madagascar (AEA) based in Nairobi, Kenya.

FUTURE TRENDS AND PROSPECTS

Ethnoreligionists will likely continue to fall drastically from a high of 70% in 1900 to less than 13% by 2025. Most of these are converting to Islam with small gains among Christians. By 2025 Muslims are expected to grow to 84.8% and Christians to 2.2%.

Christians could reach 4% of the population before AD 2050. Muslims will probably grow to above 90% in the 21st century.

BIBLIOGRAPHY

7 ans de vie soudanaise. Religieuse missionnaire de Notre-Dame d'Afrique. Lyon: G.-L. Arlaud, 1935 printing. 204p.

Conversations with Ogotemmeli: an introduction to Dogon religious ideas. M. Griaule. London: Oxford University Press, 1965. (1948, in French).

Divination bei den Kafibele–Senufo: zur Aushandlung und Bewältigung von Alltagskonflikten. T. Förster. Berlin: Reimer, 1985. 370p.

Eglise et pouvoir colonial au Soudan français: les relations entre les administrateurs et les missionnaires catholiques dans la Boucle du Niger, de 1885 à 1945. J.-R. de Benoist. *Hommes et sociétés.* Paris: Karthala, 1987. 539p.

Essai sur la religion bambara. G. Dieterlen. Paris: Presses Universitaires de France, 1950.

Études sur l'Islam et les tribus du Soudan. P. Marty. Paris: E. Leroux, 1920–21. 4 vols.

Guérisseurs et magiciens du Sahel. J. Gibbal. Paris: Presses universitaires de France, 1984. 160p.

'Le Nya: changements spirituels modernes d'une société ouest–africaine,' B. Holas, *Acta tropica* (Basel), 12, 2 (1955), 97–122. (Nya and Massa cults among the Minianka).

Le recontre de Jésus–Christ en milieu Bambara. S. P. M. Sidibe. Leiden: E. J. Brill, 1978. 318p.

Les chemins de Nya: culte de possession au Mali. J. P. Colleyn. *Anthropologie visuelle,* 1. Paris: Editions de l'Ecole des Hautes Études en Sciences Sociales, 1988. 221p.

L'Islam et le terroir africain. M. Cardaire. Bamako-Koulouba, Mali: IFAN, 1954.

Mali. R. A. Myers. *World bibliographical series.* Oxford, UK: CLIO Press, 1994. ca. 275p.

'Mali: prestige du passé, destin nouveau,' *Vivant univers* (Namur), 267 (1970), 1–47.

Paroles de nouvel an: témoignages de l'Eglise catholique malienne. L. Sangaré. [Bamako, Mali]: Editions Jamana, [1988]. 216p.

Status of Christianity profile: Mali. Nairobi: Daystar University College, [1988]. 54p.

'The Dogon,' M. Griaule & G. Dieterlen, in *African worlds,* p.83–110. D. Forde (ed). London: Oxford University Press, 1954.

'The expansion of Islam among the Bambara under French rule, 1890–1940.' S. A. Harmon. Ph.D. dissertation, University of California, Los Angeles, 1988. 562p.

The making of Bamana sculpture: creativity and gender. S. C. Brett-Smith. *RES monographs in anthropology and aesthetics.* Cambridge, UK: Cambridge University Press, 1994. 372p.

Country Table 2. **Organized churches and denominations in Mali.**

Official name (bold type = church with over 10% of all affiliated) 1	*Begun* 2	*Type* 3	*Counc* 4	*Congs* 5	*Adults* 6	*Affiliated 1970* 7	*Affiliated 1995* 8	*G%* 9	*Names, notes, and other statistics* (see Codebook, Part 3) 10
Assemblées de Dieu	1983	P-Pe2	Z....	20	690	–	1,300	8.33	*Assemblies of God.* M=AoG.
Eglise Adventiste du 7me Jour	c1980	P-Adv	.....	2	100	–	200	6.67	*Seventh-day Adventist Church.* M=SDA(USA).
Eglise Baptiste	1983	P-Bap	.....	1	46	–	120	8.33	*Baptist Church.* M=SBC.
Eglise Baptiste du Septième Jour	1986	P-Bap	.....	1	32	–	53	11.11	*Seventh Day Baptist Church.* M=SDB.
Eglise Catholique au Mali:	1895	R-Lat	P.SFR	41	54,100	60,740	110,033	2.41	*Catholic Ch.* Minority ch. C=1+1+16. (1970) 14n,2231Yy. (1990) 64n,105x,128m,206w,3990Yy
M Bamako	1921	R-Lat	Ps	7	20,100	13,374	38,200	4.29	65% Muslim, 34% animist. Catholics 70% Bambara. 12n 35x 40m 91w 1180Yy
D Kayes	1947	R-Lat	Pwf	8	3,600	5,649	6,497	0.56	60% Muslim, 40% animist. 50% Bambara, Kasonke. 5n 16x 18m 19w 186Yy
D Mopti (Gao)	1942	R-Lat	Pwf	6	7,300	14,739	13,711	-0.29	81% Muslim, 19% animist. Catholics 80% Dogon. 5n 12x 16m 13w 730Yy
D San	1962	R-Lat	Pwf	5	11,800	17,548	26,000	1.59	76% animist, 18% Muslim, 90% Bobo Oule. M=WF. 17n 8x 16m 34w 801Yy
D Ségou	1962	R-Lat	Ps	5	5,900	5,853	10,951	2.54	79% Muslim, 20% animist. Mostly Bambara. M=WF. 6n 4x 5m 16w 262Yy
D Sikasso	1947	R-Lat	Ps	10	5,400	3,577	14,674	5.81	50% Muslim, 49% animist. Catholics Minianka. 19n 30x 33m 33w 831Yy
Eglise Chrétienne Ev du Mali	1923	P-Hol	xFG.G	579	14,026	14,074	41,698	4.44	*ECEM. Ev Christian Ch.* M=CMA. 80% Dogon (Kado). 65n,6x,27f,6h,2s(3),W=68%,1384Y.
Eglise Chrétienne Réformée	1984	P-Ref	.....	1	2	–	7	9.09	*Christian Reformed World Mission.* M=CRWM(USA).
Eglise du Christ Apostolique		I-3pA	.....	2	50	–	100	0.05	*Christ Apostolic Ch.* M=CAC(Nigeria).
Eglise Ev Protestante au Mali	1919	P-Hol	xMG.G	278	14,690	5,000	24,200	6.51	*EEPM. Ev Protestant Ch.* M=GMU(USA). Bambara. 2 schools. 5n,12x,16m,45f,4h,1s,23Y.
Eglise Protestante de Kayes	1953	P-Non	xFG.G	16	300	1,000	1,000	0.00	EPK. *United World Mission.* M=UWM(USA). 86% Malinke, 15% Kasonke. 16f,1H,2h,1s,45Y.
Mission Alliance	1984	P-Con	.....	7	130	–	325	9.09	M=Allianz Mission(Germany).
Isolated radio believers	c1970	I-3rA	.....	300	5,000	–	10,000	44.54	Isolated house churches in scattered remote areas.
Mission Evangélique du Sahel	1980	P-Eva	.....	1	6	–	20	6.67	*Evangelical Mission of the Sahel.* M=RSMT.
Mission Frontières	1984	I-Non	.....	1	20	–	50	9.09	M=Frontiers (USA).
Mission Pioneers	1987	I-Non	.....	1	8	–	20	12.50	M=Pioneers (USA).
Mission Protestante Norvégienne	1981	P-Lut	.....	3	40	–	100	7.14	*Norwegian Protestant Mission.* M=NPM.
Témoins de Jéhovah	1965	m-Jeh	.....	4	88	16	400	13.74	*Jehovah's Witnesses. IBSA.* (1995)12Y.
Union des Eglises Ev Baptistes	1950	P-Bap	xTG.G	4	70	50	140	4.20	*Ev Baptist Missions.* M=UEEB(Niger),EBM(USA). Gao area (99% Muslim). Songhais,Tuaregs.14f
Other independent denominations		I-	....G	20	1,000	300	3,000	0.05	CBFMS/CBI(Ivory Coast migrants), Coopération Ev Mondiale, World-Wide Missions (1964).
Other African indigenous churches	c1975	I-3pA	.....	15	900	–	2,000	5.00	Labor migrants from West African indigenous churches, including CAC,COTLA,C&S,CCC.
Totals				**1,297**	**91,298**	**81,180**	**194,766**		

Churches, members, growth, 1900-2025	*Congs*	*Adults*	*Affiliated*	*G%*	*Total denominations*	*6 Megablocs:* O	R	A	P	I	m
Total churches, members, and denominations (mid-1900)	10	380	688	7.05	1	0	1	0	0	0	0
Total churches, members, and denominations (mid-1970)	402	44,953	81,180	7.05	9	0	1	0	4	3	1
Total churches, members, and denominations (mid-1990)	800	78,600	167,600	3.69	39	0	1	0	12	25	1
Total churches, members, and denominations (mid-1995)	1,297	91,298	194,766	3.05	39	0	1	0	12	25	1
Total churches, members, and denominations (mid-2000)	1,400	105,000	224,365	2.87	39	0	1	0	12	25	1
Total churches, members, and denominations (mid-2025)	3,000	222,000	473,000	3.03	77	0	1	0	25	50	1

NOTES ON TABLE ABOVE

NATIONAL COUNCILS (Column 4, 5th letter).

G = Association des Groupements des Eglises et Missions Protestantes du Mali (AGEMPEM) (Association of Evangelical Protestant Churches & Missions in Mali).

R = Conférence Episcopale du Mali (CEM) (Episcopal Conference of Mali).

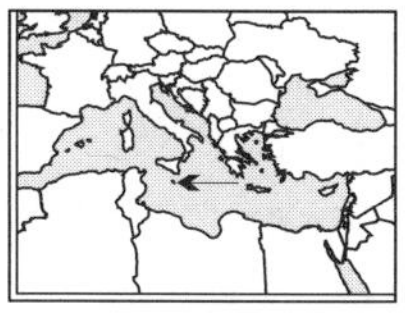

MALTA

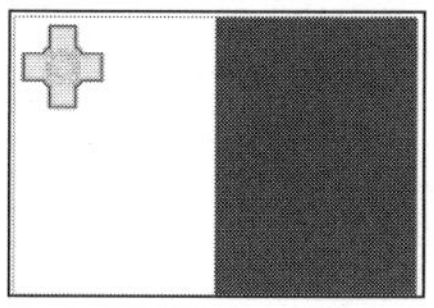

SECULAR DATA, AD 2000

STATE
Official name: Repubblika ta' Malta (The Republic of Malta).
Short name: Malta. **Adjective of nationality:** Maltese.
Flag: White and red bars, with George Cross in silver on white bar.
Area: 316 sq. km. (122 sq. mi.).
Government: Parliamentary republic, since 1974 (1814 British crown colony, 1962 self-government, 1964 Independence, 1974 republic)
Legislature: House of Representatives, 69 members.
Official language: Maltese and English.
Monetary unit: 1 Maltese lira (Lm) = 100 cents = 1,000 mils. **US$1=** Lm 0.38.
Chief cities: VALLETTA (Valetta) 227,610.
Political divisions: 6 provinces.
Armed forces: 2,000.

DEMOGRAPHY
Population: 389,000.
Population density: 1,229.5/sq. km. (3,184.7/sq. mi.).
Under 15 years: 79,000.
Growth rate p.a.: 0.66% (births 13.19, deaths 7.78).
Mortality: Infant, per 1,000: 7.6, ; **Maternal per 100,000:** 10.0.
Life expectancy: 78 (male 76, female 80).
Household size: 3.6. **Floor area per person, sq.m:** 17.0.
Major languages: Maltese, English, Italian, Arabic, Greek.
Urban dwellers: 90.53%. **Urban growth rate p.a.:** 0.8%.
Labor force: 37%.

ETHNOLINGUISTIC PEOPLES
93.8% Maltese; 2.1% British; 2.0% Arab; 1.4% Italian; 0.2% USA White.

ECONOMY
National income p.a. per person: US$12,001; **per family:** US$43,204.

EDUCATION
Adult literacy: 96% (male 96%, female 95%). **Schools:** 192.
Universities: 1. **School enrolment:** female/male: 94%/101%.

HEALTH
Access to health services: 95%. **Access to safe water:** 100%.
Hospitals: 7 (58 beds per 10,000). **Doctors:** 900.
Blind: 570. **Deaf:** 22,700. **Murder rate:** 3. **Lepers:** 500.

LITERATURE
New book titles p.a.: 450 (1,150 p.a. per million). **Periodicals:** 503.
Newspapers: 3 dailies.

COMMUNICATION (per 1,000 people)
Phones: 459 (10% mobile). **Radios:** 260. **TV sets:** 448.
Daily newspaper circulation: 145. **Computers:** 250.

HUMAN LIFE AND LIBERTY (optimum condition=100.0%)
HDI: 88.7. **HSI:** 80.0. **HFI:** 70.0. **EFL:** 39.0.

Country Table 1. **Religious adherents in Malta, AD 1900-2025.**

Year	1900		1970		mid-1990		Annual change, 1990-2000				mid-1995		mid-2000		mid-2025	
Name	Adherents	%	Adherents	%	Adherents	%	Natural	Conversion	Total	Rate	Adherents	%	Adherents	%	Adherents	%
Christians	**207,910**	**100.0**	**301,300**	**99.5**	**350,140**	**98.9**	**3,419**	**-229**	**3,190**	**0.88**	**369,560**	**98.5**	**382,039**	**98.3**	**419,570**	**97.6**
PROFESSION																
professing Christians	**207,910**	**100.0**	**301,300**	**99.5**	**350,140**	**98.9**	**3,419**	**-229**	**3,190**	**0.88**	**369,560**	**98.5**	**382,039**	**98.3**	**419,570**	**97.6**
AFFILIATION																
unaffiliated Christians	12,910	6.2	99	0.0	8,770	2.5	87	102	189	1.97	9,579	2.6	10,658	2.7	10,600	2.5
affiliated Christians	**195,000**	**93.8**	**301,201**	**99.5**	**341,370**	**96.4**	**3,332**	**-331**	**3,001**	**0.85**	**359,981**	**96.0**	**371,381**	**95.5**	**408,970**	**95.1**
Roman Catholics	184,000	88.5	297,261	98.2	338,000	95.5	3,300	-350	2,950	0.84	356,300	95.0	367,501	94.5	403,920	93.9
Anglicans	10,000	4.8	3,000	1.0	1,300	0.4	13	-33	-20	-1.66	1,200	0.3	1,100	0.3	800	0.2
Protestants	800	0.4	210	0.1	650	0.2	6	29	35	4.40	890	0.2	1,000	0.3	1,600	0.4
Marginal Christians	0	0.0	230	0.1	700	0.2	7	13	20	2.54	791	0.2	900	0.2	1,500	0.4
Independents	0	0.0	400	0.1	600	0.2	6	9	15	2.26	680	0.2	750	0.2	1,000	0.2
Orthodox	200	0.1	100	0.0	120	0.0	1	0	1	0.80	120	0.0	130	0.0	150	0.0
Trans-megabloc groupings																
Evangelicals	600	0.3	250	0.1	500	0.1	5	0	5	0.96	518	0.1	550	0.1	800	0.2
Pentecostals/Charismatics	0	0.0	500	0.2	82,000	23.2	811	689	1,500	1.69	90,438	24.1	97,000	24.9	112,000	26.1
Great Commission Christians	**21,000**	**10.1**	**79,000**	**26.1**	**149,000**	**42.1**	**1,473**	**633**	**2,106**	**1.33**	**158,000**	**42.1**	**170,064**	**43.7**	**185,000**	**43.0**
Nonreligious	0	0.0	1,000	0.3	2,000	0.6	20	164	184	6.74	3,090	0.8	3,839	1.0	6,000	1.4
Muslims	0	0.0	0	0.0	1,250	0.4	12	58	70	4.53	1,700	0.5	1,947	0.5	3,000	0.7
Atheists	0	0.0	500	0.2	300	0.1	3	4	7	1.98	330	0.1	365	0.1	700	0.2
Baha'is	0	0.0	100	0.0	220	0.1	2	2	4	1.49	230	0.1	255	0.1	600	0.1
Jews	60	0.0	50	0.0	50	0.0	0	1	1	1.32	50	0.0	57	0.0	80	0.0
Hindus	30	0.0	50	0.0	40	0.0	0	0	0	0.25	40	0.0	41	0.0	50	0.0
World A (unevangelized persons)	0	0.0	0	0.0	354	0.1	2	1	3	1.48	375	0.1	389	0.1	430	0.1
World B (evangelized non-Christians)	-20	0.0	1,410	0.5	3,506	1.0	35	228	263	6.49	5,089	1.4	6,572	1.6	10,000	2.3
World C (Christians)	207,910	100.0	301,300	99.5	350,140	98.9	3,419	-229	3,190	0.88	369,560	98.5	382,039	98.3	419,570	97.6
Country's population	**207,890**	**100.0**	**302,710**	**100.0**	**354,000**	**100.0**	**3,456**	**0**	**3,456**	**0.95**	**375,025**	**100.0**	**389,000**	**100.0**	**430,000**	**100.0**

COLUMNS, ROWS.
For meanings and definitions, see Codebook (Part 3). Note that, by definition, total 'Christians' = professing + crypto-Christians, which also = affiliated + unaffiliated Christians, and also = Great Commission Christians + latent Christians. Percentages may not always total exactly, due to rounding.

CENSUSES.
1901 Census of the British Empire: as in 1900 column above, adjusted to include the 23,000 resident British military personnel. No question on religion has been asked recently.

NOTES ON RELIGIONS
ANGLICANS. Mostly expatriate British military and civilians.
ATHEISTS. Communist Party of Malta (CPM) (founded 1970, legal; pro-Soviet) It is assumed in Malta that good Christians cannot be communists, and vice versa.
BAHA'IS. In 1 local spiritual assembly, over 30 years to 1995.
COUNTRY'S POPULATION. In 1968 there were 1,608 foreign residents; of these 480 were Italians, almost all Roman Catholics. Many more Maltese citizens are of Italian origin.
HINDUS. Indian traders.
JEWS. With a synagogue in Valletta.
MUSLIMS. Mainly North African immigrant workers.
NOMINAL CHRISTIANS. Largely British military.
NONRELIGIOUS. Mainly British military.
PENTECOSTALS (or, Catholic charismatics). The first meetings were held in mid-1975. 1980: 35 prayer groups.
PENTECOSTALS/CHARISMATICS. The first Catholic Charismatic Renewal meetings were held in mid-1975. Subsequently, numbers have become large and very significant, with Malta playing a global role in its creation and support of schools of evangelization under ICPE (International Catholic Program for Evangelization).
ROMAN CATHOLICS. About 3,000 emigrate annually, mostly to Australia.

Great Commission Instrument Panel: status of Malta (for explanation see start of Part 4)

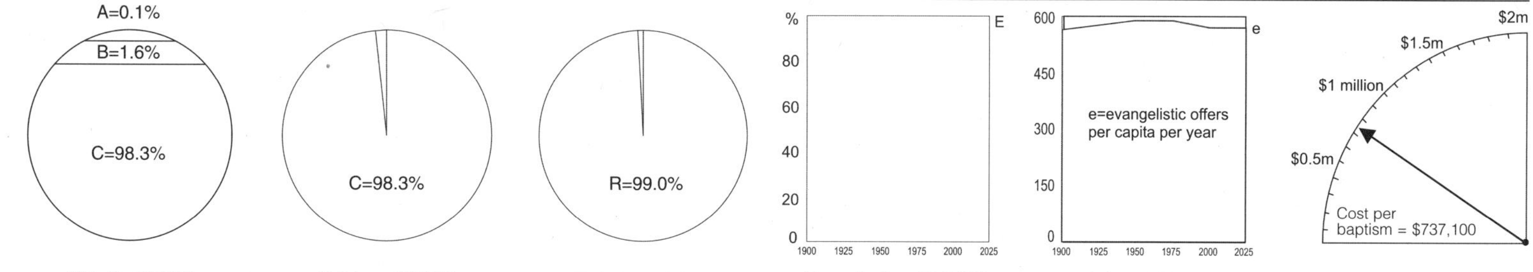

3 Worlds, AD 2000 | Religions, AD 2000 | Ecclesiastical blocs | Evangelization, 1900-2025 | Offers, 1900-2025 | Cost-effectiveness, AD 2000

Country status. Malta is a small island in the Mediterranean Sea about 60 miles south of Sicily. An important British naval base in the past, the economy today is supplemented by tourism.

HUMAN LIFE AND LIBERTY

Human need and development. Despite its small size, Malta shares many of the characteristics of a developed country. Heavily urbanized, it has a good infrastructure, including a fine port and a flourishing economy based on tourism and light industry. Although there is no social security, the Maltese enjoy many medical and other benefits. The educational system is well funded.

Human rights and freedoms. The Maltese government is strongly committed to human rights, and constitutional rights are upheld by an independent judiciary. These rights include freedom from arbitrary arrest and a fair and public trial. The press is entirely free and includes a number of private newspapers, journals and radio and television stations. A constitutional amendment banning discrimination based on sex was passed in 1991 and came into effect in 1993.

Human environment. As in other small islands, the environment is sensitive to heavy maritime and urban activities. Coastal pollution is causing official concern. The lack of rivers limits the supply of water to wells.

NON-CHRISTIAN RELIGIONS

Islam exists in the significant expatriate Arab community.

Baha'i has grown steadily from 100 in 1970 to 230 in 1995.

Small ***Jewish*** and ***Hindu*** groups are found among the expatriate community, and there is a Jewish synagogue in Valletta.

Country summary. **Worlds A, B, C by ethnolinguistic peoples, cities, and major civil divisions in Malta.**

	PEOPLES							CITIES							CIVIL DIVISIONS						
World	Num	Pop 2000	C%	Christians	E%	U%	Unevangelized	Num	Pop 2000	C%	Christians	E%	U%	Unevangelized	Num	Pop 2000	C%	Christians	E%	U%	Unevangelized
A	0	0	0.00	0	0	0	0	0	0	0.00	0	0	0	0	0	0	0.00	0	0	0	0
B	2	116	1.72	2	51	49	57	0	0	0.00	0	0	0	0	0	0	0.00	0	0	0	0
C	9	388,428	95.61	371,380	100	0	162	1	227,610	95.60	217,595	100	0	91	6	388,545	95.58	371,381	100	0	221
Total	**11**	**388,544**	**95.58**	**371,382**	**100**	**0**	**219**	**1**	**227,610**	**95.60**	**217,595**	**100**	**0**	**91**	**6**	**388,545**	**95.58**	**371,381**	**100**	**0**	**221**

Catholic Church in Malta. St Publius Church, Floriana, Valetta. The numerous silos are granaries in use during the Knights occupation (1530-1802).

CHRISTIANITY

CATHOLIC CHURCH. According to the Acts of the Apostles, the apostle Paul was shipwrecked on Malta and remained there for 3 months on his way to Rome. A bishop from Malta was later in attendance at the Council for Chalcedon in 451. The island fell to the Arabs in 870 but was recaptured by Normans in 1090 and given to the Knights of St John of Jerusalem in 1530. Virtually all native Maltese are baptized Roman Catholics.

Catholicism is practiced in Malta in the Italian manner, with its religious ceremonies such as the celebration of the apostle Paul's shipwreck on 10 February being transformed into popular feasts with decorated streets and lights. Catholicism is an institutional power of exceptional significance in Malta. In addition to publishing the influential daily newspaper, *Il-Hajj*, the church organizes social and cultural movements, credit unions, and immigration services. Annual emigration figures are about 3,000, mostly to Australia.

In 1970, 351 Maltese priests were working outside the islands in foreign lands: 138 as foreign missionaries, 61 as chaplains for Maltese communities abroad, and 152 in other work including service as priests in Europe or the USA. In 1966, there were also 395 nuns serving abroad. The church has its own institute for foreign missions, the Missionary Society of St Paul, which had 45 priests in 1969 and received pontifical recognition in 1973.

The church in Malta owns large properties, a fact which has become increasingly controversial in recent years. In 1973 the pope approved the proposals of a commission set up in 1971 under the chairmanship of a Vatican diplomat to carry out reforms in Maltese church administration. The commission reached its conclusions on the basis of recommendations made by a USA management consultant firm which had been called in to establish the relevant facts. The annual income of the Catholic Church in Malta was revealed to be approximately US $840,000. It owns 17% of the island's urban and 18% of the rural property. A major problem noted in the report is that 'financial administration is the uncontrolled and undirected responsibility of about 1,500 administrations that are in turn the responsibility of 280 separate administrators'. Recent financial scandals in Malta involving church funds have highlighted the need for reform.

The Holy See has diplomatic relations with Malta and in AD 2000 is represented to government and the Catholic hierarchy by a nuncio residing in Attard.

OTHER CHURCHES. Several denominations serve the expatriate community: Greek Orthodox, Anglicans and Church of Scotland in Valletta; Methodists, Gospel Hall and Salvation Army in Floriana; Anglicans in Sliema; and Christian Scientists in Marsa. Jehovah's Witnesses are also active.

Renewal movements. In the 1990s the Pentecostal/Charismatic Renewal continued to spread rapidly across most older churches, and numbered over 97,000 adherents (of whom <1% Pentecostals, 100% Charismatics, and <1% Independents).

Indigenous missions. Malta has one of the longest histories of missionary sending of any country in the world. Throughout most of Christian history it has also had an unusually high per-capita rate of missionary sending. Today, with over 750 missionaries, Malta continues its leadership in commitment to the missionary enterprise.

CHURCH AND STATE

The constitution which became effective at Independence on 21 September 1964 affirms that 'The religion of Malta is the Roman Catholic and Apostolic Religion' (Article 2, item 1), but guarantees full freedom to all other religions (Article 41). It stipulates that the Catholic Church is entitled to run its own affairs (Article 2, item 2) and that the Catholic religion is to be taught in state schools (Article 10). State legislation on marriage runs parallel with canon law, since there is no provision for civil marriage nor for divorce.

There is no concordat between church and state, which remain in practice quite separate. Catholic and other religious bodies, as well as their clergy and personnel, receive neither remuneration nor subsidies from the state, although they are usually exempt from tax. The only exceptions to this are secular clergy who have to pay taxes and private Catholic schools which receive small subsidies.

The Catholic Church largely controls social and cultural life in Malta. Before Independence the church was the natural representative of the people vis-á-vis both the French imperial and British colonial governments. At the local level, parish priests are still community leaders in the absence of nonreligious local authorities. During the early years of the movement seeking national independence, Catholic clergy led political movements and were elected to parliament. This is now no longer the case; and the most important episcopal statement in recent years, that of Easter 1969, both announced the settlement of the dispute between the church and the Labour Party, and at the same time affirmed the separation of ecclesiastical and political affairs. During 1974-75 contacts were made between the Maltese government and the Vatican to discuss the possibility of constitutional change effecting the Church in Malta.

There is no ministry or government department in charge of religious matters, and churches are not obliged to register with any state office.

BROADCASTING AND MEDIA

There has been some response to KNLS shortwave radio programs. Malta is a member of UNDA. Catholics air a variety of programs, including 2 30-minute magazine programs (on Thursdays and Fridays), a 3-minute 'Thought for the day' aired each morning and evening, and 30 minutes of Scripture reading and prayers each Friday. One each fortnight a special program discusses themes mentioned in speeches by prominent religious leaders.

RTK is a local Catholic radio station, broadcasting in Maltese and English.

Satellite TV and radio programs are received in English, Arabic, German and Italian. 'Dawlilhajja' is a Catholic 20-minute magazine-format program broadcast on television on Wednesday evening, and repeated on Sunday. The mass is broadcast on Sundays as well.

Since 1889, Malta's stamps have commemorated St. Paul's shipwreck; here in 1960, its 19th centenary and that of episcopal consecration of Publius.

INTERDENOMINATIONAL ORGANIZATIONS

The Catholic Episcopal conference has an Ecumenical Commission, and there is also a wider Ecumenical Group including other bodies which meets periodically in Valletta.

FUTURE TRENDS AND PROSPECTS

Christianity will probably decline to 97.6% of the population by AD 2025 with small inroads made by the nonreligious and immigrant Muslims.

If immigration patterns and secularization continue into the middle of the 21st century, Christianity could decline below 95% before AD 2040 and below 90% shortly after.

Many Malta postage stamps have biblical themes. *Left.* Star of Bethlehem, shepherds. *Below.* The Nativity.

BIBLIOGRAPHY

A bibliography of Maltese bibliographies. P. Xuereb. Valletta, Malta: University of Malta Library, 1978. 18p.

Brief historical notes on some smaller churches in Valletta. M. Galea. Valletta, Malta: Veritas Press, 1972. 49p.

Catholic directory of Malta and Gozo, 1963. Floriana, Malta: Empire Press, 1963.

Catholic life in Malta AD60–1960. Floriana, Malta: Catholic Institute, 1963. 52p.

Friendly refuge: a study of St. Paul's shipwreck and his stay in Malta. G. H. Musgrave. Heathfield, UK: Heathfield Publications, 1979. 120p.

From lordship to stewardship: religion and social change in Malta. M. Vassallo. *Religion and society series*, no. 15. The Hague: Mouton, 1979. 272p.

History of the Church in Malta. M. A. Bonnici. Vols. 1 & 2, Valletta, Malta: Empire Press—Catholic Institute, 1967-68; vol. 3, Zabbar, Malta: Veritas Press, 1975. 3 vols.

Malta. J. R. Thackrah. *World bibliographical series*, vol. 64. Oxford, UK: CLIO Press, 1985. 184p. (See especially 'Religion,' p.57–61).

Prelates and politicians in Malta: changing power–balances between church and state in a Mediterranean island fortress, 1800–1976. A. Koster. *Studies of developing countries*, 29. Assen, The Netherlands: Van Gorcum, 1984. 327p.

Regular and secular clergy in Malta: cooperation or infighting in a Mediterranean Catholic regime. A. Koster. Amsterdam: Institute of Cultural Anthropology, Free University, 1983. 26p.

Report on the Sunday mass census of 17 December 1967. B. Tonna & A. Depasquale. Valletta, Malta: Pastoral Research Services, 1969. 156p.

Sacred art in Malta 1890–1960. G. Gauci (ed). Valletta, Malta: Said International, 1990. 111p.

Saints and fireworks: religion and politics in rural Malta. J. Boissevain. London: Athlone Press, 1969. 162p.

The Maltese church amid social and political upheaval. London: Herder Correspondence, 1966.

The Order of St. John in Malta. M. Preti (ed). Valletta, Malta: St. Paul's Press, 1971. 333p.

What is happening to religion in Malta? M. Gonzi. Valletta, Malta: Pastoral Research Services, 1969. 38p. (By the Catholic archbishop).

Country Table 2. Organized churches and denominations in Malta.

Official name (bold type = church with over 10% of all affiliated) 1	Begun 2	Type 3	Counc 4	Congs 5	Adults 6	Affiliated 1970 7	Affiliated 1995 8	G% 9	*Names, notes, and other statistics* (see Codebook, Part 3) 10
Bible Baptist Church	1983	I-Bap	.....	1	48	–	80	8.33	Independent Baptists.
Catholic Church in Malta:	60	R-Lat	BxB.R	107	230,300	297,261	356,300	0.05	*Il-Knisja Kattolika.* C=10+1+2. (1970) 1038n. (1990). 512n 449x 568m 1363w 5494Yy
M Malta	1831	R-Lat	Bs	65	213,100	271,000	329,000	0.78	*Arcidjocesi ta' Malta.* Industries, tourism. 1s. 347n 430x 538m 1228w 5045Yy
D Gozo	1864	R-Lat	Bs	42	17,200	26,261	27,300	0.16	*Djocesi ta' Ghaiodex.* Rural island. 99.8% RC. 1s. 165n 19x 30m 135w 449Yy
Christian Evangelical Church	1984	P-Pe2	.....	6	155	–	220	9.09	M=AoG(UK,USA).
Church of Christ, Scientist		m-Sci	x....	1	15	30	20	0.05	*Christian Science.* One informal group in Marsa. M=CCS(Boston, USA).
Church of England (D Europe)	1798	A-plu	awc..	2	940	3,000	1,200	-3.60	British residents and military. Has co-cathedral of diocese. 6x,W=50%,29Yy.
Church of Scotland		P-Ref	Rwc..	1	80	50	150	0.05	St Andrew's Church. Valletta. Expatriate Scots, mostly temporary. 1f.
Evangelical Baptist Church	c1926	P-CBr	x....	1	56	30	80	4.00	Former Brethren Gospel Hall. Formerly expatriate British; now Maltese. W=99%,20Y.
Greek Orthodox Church (AD Thyateira)		O-Gre	Cwc..	1	60	100	120	0.05	St George's Church, Valletta. Under jurisdiction of EP Constantinople. 1 bishop.
Int Pentecostal Holiness Ch	1988	P-Pe3	.....	2	100	–	200	14.29	M=IPHC(USA). Holiness Pentecostals.
Jehovah's Witnesses	c1939	m-Jeh	x....	5	424	200	771	5.55	*Watch Tower.* 1939, under Syrian branch; active witnessing since 1952. (1975) 3Y. (1995) 21Y.
Methodist Church		P-Met	Vwc..	1	30	30	40	0.05	Under Methodist Church of GB. Church in Floriana. Mostly expatriate British.
Salvation Army	1896	P-Sal	xwc..	3	100	100	200	2.81	Under British Territory. Red Shield work, Floriana (British armed forces).
Other independent churches		I-	.....	5	300	400	600	0.05	Including New Apostolic Ch (19 members).
Totals				**136**	**232,608**	**301,201**	**359,981**		

Churches, members, growth, 1900-2025	*Congs*	*Adults*	*Affiliated*	*G%*	*Total denominations*	*6 Megablocs:* O	R	A	P	I	m
Total churches, members, and denominations (mid-1900)	40	129,000	195,000	0.62	3	0	1	1	1	0	0
Total churches, members, and denominations (mid-1970)	91	199,523	301,201	0.62	11	1	1	1	4	2	2
Total churches, members, and denominations (mid-1990)	120	221,000	341,370	0.63	17	1	1	1	6	6	2
Total churches, members, and denominations (mid-1995)	136	232,608	359,981	1.07	17	1	1	1	6	6	2
Total churches, members, and denominations (mid-2000)	160	240,000	371,381	0.63	17	1	1	1	6	6	2
Total churches, members, and denominations (mid-2025)	190	264,000	408,970	0.39	42	1	1	1	15	20	4

NOTES ON TABLE ABOVE
NATIONAL COUNCILS (Column 4, 5th letter).
R = Konferenza Episkopali Maltija (KEM, Malta Episcopal Conference, MEC).

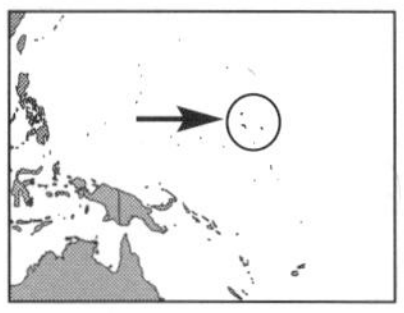

MARSHALL ISLANDS

SECULAR DATA, AD 2000

STATE
Official name: Majol/Republic of the Marshall Islands.
Short name: Marshall Islands. **Adjective of nationality:** of the Marshall Islands, Marshallese.
Flag: Blue field with white sun and narrow yellow and white stripes.
Area: 181 sq. km. (70 sq. mi.).
Government: Unitary republic with two legislative houses, since 1979 (1886 German protectorate, 1947 UN Trust Territory).
Legislature: Council oflroij, 12 members; Nitijela, 33 members.
Official language: Marshallese, English.
Monetary unit: 1 US dollar (U.S.$) = 100 cents. **US$1=** 100 cents.
Chief cities: MAJURO (D.U.D. or Darrit-Uliga-Dalap) 15,531.
Political divisions: 24 provinces.

DEMOGRAPHY
Population: 64,000.
Population density: 354.8/sq. km. (917.4/sq. mi.).
Under 15 years: 21,000.
Growth rate p.a.: 1.60% (births 20.74, deaths 4.71).
Mortality: Infant, per 1,000: 9.3, ; **Maternal per 100,000:** 100.0.
Life expectancy: 76 (male 73, female 78).
Household size: 8.7. **Floor area per person, sq.m:** 15.0.
Major languages: Marshallese, English.
Urban dwellers: 71.85%. **Urban growth rate p.a.:** 4.1%.
Labor force: 27%.

ETHNOLINGUISTIC PEOPLES
88.5% Marshallese; 6.5% USA White; .

ECONOMY
National income p.a. per person: US$1,884; **per family:** US$16,392.

EDUCATION
Adult literacy: 91% (male 92%, female 90%). **Schools:** 115.
Universities: 0. **School enrolment:** female/male: 75%/75%.

HEALTH
Access to health services: 70%. **Access to safe water:** 31%.
Hospitals: 2 (14 beds per 10,000). **Doctors:** 20.
Blind: 50. **Deaf:** 3,900. **Murder rate:** 7. **Lepers:** 50.

LITERATURE
New book titles p.a.: 13 (200 p.a. per million). **Periodicals:** 0.
Newspapers: 1 daily.

COMMUNICATION (per 1,000 people)
Phones: 44 **(8% mobile). Radios:** 500. **TV sets:** 20.
Daily newspaper circulation: 20. **Computers:** 200.

HUMAN LIFE AND LIBERTY (optimum condition=100.0%)
HDI: 57.8. **HSI:** 70.0. **HFI:** 70.0. **EFL:** 40.0.

Country Table 1. Religious adherents in the Marshall Islands, AD 1900-2025.

Year	*1900*		*1970*		*mid-1990*		*Annual change, 1990-2000*				*mid-1995*		*mid-2000*		*mid-2025*	
Name	*Adherents*	*%*	*Adherents*	*%*	*Adherents*	*%*	*Natural*	*Conversion*	*Total*	*Rate*	*Adherents*	*%*	*Adherents*	*%*	*Adherents*	*%*
Christians	**5,000**	**62.5**	**24,000**	**95.3**	**44,468**	**96.7**	**1,733**	**24**	**1,757**	**3.39**	**52,695**	**96.3**	**62,042**	**96.6**	**122,800**	**96.7**
PROFESSION																
professing Christians	**5,000**	**62.5**	**24,000**	**95.3**	**44,468**	**96.7**	**1,733**	**24**	**1,757**	**3.39**	**52,695**	**96.3**	**62,042**	**96.6**	**122,800**	**96.7**
AFFILIATION																
unaffiliated Christians	0	0.0	7,662	30.4	2,668	5.8	104	-177	-73	-3.14	2,295	4.2	1,939	3.0	2,100	1.7
affiliated Christians	**5,000**	**62.5**	**16,338**	**64.9**	**41,800**	**90.9**	**1,629**	**201**	**1,830**	**3.70**	**50,400**	**92.1**	**60,103**	**93.6**	**120,700**	**95.0**
Protestants	4,300	53.8	14,000	55.6	47,124	102.4	1,844	187	2,031	3.65	57,399	104.9	67,431	105.0	124,460	98.0
Independents	0	0.0	0	0.0	5,400	11.7	211	59	270	4.14	6,700	12.3	8,100	12.7	16,000	12.6
Roman Catholics	700	8.8	2,000	8.0	3,700	8.0	145	10	155	3.56	4,400	8.0	5,250	8.2	11,000	8.7
Marginal Christians	0	0.0	338	1.3	1,500	3.3	59	41	100	5.24	1,900	3.5	2,500	3.9	6,500	5.1
doubly-affiliated	0	0.0	0	0.0	-15,924	-34.6	-623	-102	-725	3.83	-19,999	-36.6	-23,178	-36.2	-37,260	-29.3
Trans-megabloc groupings																
Evangelicals	3,200	40.0	4,500	17.9	13,860	30.1	542	62	604	3.68	16,730	30.6	19,900	31.1	38,500	30.3
Pentecostals/Charismatics	0	0.0	4,000	15.9	20,790	45.2	814	127	941	3.80	25,374	46.4	30,200	47.2	62,230	49.0
Great Commission Christians	**560**	**7.0**	**4,300**	**17.1**	**5,300**	**11.5**	**207**	**-7**	**200**	**3.25**	**6,240**	**11.4**	**7,300**	**11.4**	**14,000**	**11.0**
Baha'is	0	0.0	300	1.2	682	1.5	27	7	34	4.14	865	1.6	1,023	1.6	2,500	2.0
Ethnoreligionists	3,000	37.5	800	3.2	720	1.6	28	-38	-10	-1.41	700	1.3	625	1.0	500	0.4
Nonreligious	0	0.0	100	0.4	330	0.7	13	7	20	4.85	440	0.8	530	0.8	1,200	0.9
World A (unevangelized persons)	1,760	22.0	327	1.3	92	0.2	3	-6	-3	-4.98	54	0.1	64	0.1	0	0.0
World B (evangelized non-Christians)	1,240	15.5	844	3.5	1,440	3.5	65	-18	47	2.78	1,950	3.6	1,894	3.3	4,200	3.3
World C (Christians)	5,000	62.5	24,000	95.2	44,468	96.3	1,733	24	1,757	3.39	52,695	96.3	62,042	96.6	122,800	96.7
Country's population	**8,000**	**100.0**	**25,172**	**100.0**	**46,000**	**100.0**	**1,801**	**0**	**1,801**	**3.36**	**54,700**	**100.0**	**64,200**	**100.0**	**127,000**	**100.0**

COLUMNS, ROWS.
For meanings and definitions, see Codebook (Part 3). Note that, by definition, total 'Christians' = professing + crypto-Christians, which also = affiliated + unaffiliated Christians, and also = Great Commission Christians + latent Christians. Percentages may not always total exactly, due to rounding.

NOTES ON RELIGIONS
BAHA'IS. Rapid expansion to 15 local spiritual assemblies.
ETHNORELIGIONISTS. 1.5% of the Marshallese.

Country status. The Marshall Islands are a group of 34 islands in the Pacific Ocean east of the Caroline Islands. Formerly used as a site for the USA to test atomic and hydrogen bombs, today its chief economic activities are the production of copra and tourism.

HUMAN LIFE AND LIBERTY

Human rights and freedoms. Formerly a Trust Territory under U S administration, Marshall Islands became a republic in 1986 but retains free association with the United States under a compact. The Constitution provides for all the basic human rights and there are no reported violations of these rights.

NON-CHRISTIAN RELIGIONS

Traditional polytheism still has followers.

Baha'i has been spreading rapidly for some years and each year has numerous new adherents.

CHRISTIANITY

PROTESTANT CHURCHES. Missionaries came in strength in the 1850s, mainly through the American

Great Commission Instrument Panel: status of the Marshall Islands (for explanation see start of Part 4)

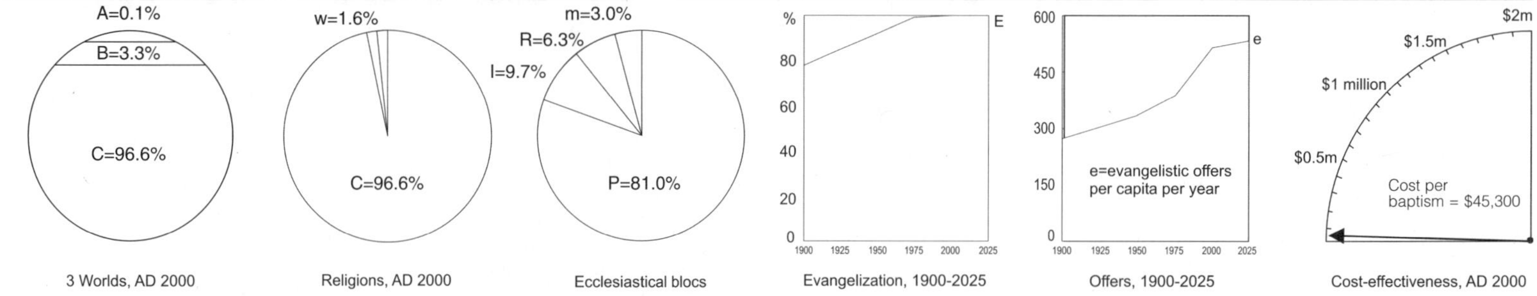

Country summary. **Worlds A, B, C by ethnolinguistic peoples, cities, and major civil divisions in the Marshall Islands.**																					
	PEOPLES							*CITIES*							*CIVIL DIVISIONS*						
World	*Num*	*Pop 2000*	*C%*	*Christians*	*E%*	*U%*	*Unevangelized*	*Num*	*Pop 2000*	*C%*	*Christians*	*E%*	*U%*	*Unevangelized*	*Num*	*Pop 2000*	*C%*	*Christians*	*E%*	*U%*	*Unevangelized*
A	0	0	0.00	0	0	0	0	0	0	0.00	0	0	0	0	0	0	0.00	0	0	0	0
B	0	0	0.00	0	0	0	0	0	0	0.00	0	0	0	0	0	0	0.00	0	0	0	0
C	3	64,220	93.59	60,103	100	0	41	1	15,531	93.00	14,444	100	0	14	24	64,220	93.59	60,103	100	0	42
Total	**3**	**64,220**	**93.59**	**60,103**	**100**	**0**	**41**	**1**	**15,531**	**93.00**	**14,444**	**100**	**0**	**14**	**24**	**64,220**	**93.59**	**60,103**	**100**	**0**	**42**

Board of Commissions for Foreign Missions. By the 1990s Protestants were still in the majority, but with several other rival groupings.

CATHOLIC CHURCH. Missionaries began in 1902 in what is now the Prefecture Apostolic of the Marshall Islands.

The Holy See has diplomatic relations with Marshall Islands and in AD 2000 is represented to government and the Catholic hierarchy by a nuncio residing in Wellington, New Zealand.

Indigenous missions. Despite a predominately Christian population, only a handful of missionaries have been sent out from the Marshall Islands.

FUTURE TRENDS AND PROSPECTS

Few changes are expected before 2025 except that Baha'is, 1.2% in 1970, will likely reach 2% of the population by 2025.

Christianity will potentially continue above 90% well into the 21st century but Baha'is and the nonreligious could represent 5% of the population before AD 2050.

BIBLIOGRAPHY

'A new dawn: Christianity in the Marshall Islands, 1857—1885.' H. Sam. B.D. thesis, Pacific Theological College, Suva, Fiji, [1988]. 77p.

Auf den Marshall–Inseln (Deutsche Südsee): Land und Leute katholische Missionstätigkeit. H. Linckens. Freilassing: Herz-Jesu-Kloster, 1911. 111p.

'Indigenization as a missionary goal in the Caroline and Marshall Islands,' F. X. Hezel, in *Mission, church, and sect in Oceania*, p.251–74. J. A. Boutilier, D. T. Hughes & S. W. Tiffany (eds). *Association for Social Anthropology in Oceania monograph*, 6. Ann Arbor, MI: University of Michigan Press, 1978.

Missions in the Carolines and Marshall Islands. F. Hernandez. Madrid, 1955. 28p.

Position papers and consensus statements: plenary meeting of all Jesuit missionaries, Caroline and Marshall Islands Mission of the New York Province, held at Xavier High School, Truk August 22–25, 1968. [Truk, 1968]. 91p.

'The concepts of God among the people of Marshall Islands.' P. Johnny. Thesis, Pacific Theological College, Suva, Fiji, 1978. 67p.

The first taint of civilization: a history of the Caroline and Marshall Islands in pre–colonial days, 1521–1885. F. X. Hezel. , 1983.

United Church of Christ in the Marshall Islands. A local church.

Country Table 2. **Organized churches and denominations in the Marshall Islands.**									
Official name (bold type = church with over 10% of all affiliated) 1	*Begun* 2	*Type* 3	*Counc* 4	*Congs* 5	*Adults* 6	*Affiliated 1970* 7	*Affiliated 1995* 8	*G%* 9	*Names, notes, and other statistics* (see Codebook, Part 3) 10
Assemblies of God	1960	P-Pe2	.....	38	10,100	4,000	14,200	5.20	M=AOG(USA). Regional HQ Majuro. 5f. 110 ministers.
Catholic Ch: PA Marshall Islands	1902	R-Lat	P...F	3	2,000	2,000	4,400	3.20	Prefecture created 1993. M=SJ. (1990) 5x,5m,17w,157Yy. , 0n, 5x, 5m, 17w, 157Yy
Ch of Jesus Christ of Latter-day Saints	c1960	m-LdS	x....	7	780	200	1,300	7.77	M=CJCLdS(USA). Mormons.
Gospel Fellowship Association	c1970	I-Fun	.....	2	50	–	100	20.23	M=GFA(USA). 4f.
Jehovah's Witnesses	1968	m-Jeh	x....	3	167	138	600	6.05	*Watch Tower.* 29Y.
Looking for Jesus Church	1985	I-3pP	.....	2	1,000	–	2,400	10.00	*Bakot Non Jesus.* Schism ex AoG, affiliated to UPC.
New Apostolic Church		I-3aX	x....	2	40	–	50	0.05	M=NAC/NAK(Switzerland).
Reformed Congregational Church	1986	I-Ref	.....	27	2,000	–	4,000	11.11	Schism ex UCCMI.
Salvation Army		P-Sal	x....	5	200	–	400	0.05	M=Salvation Army(USA).
Seventh-day Adventist Church	1930	P-Adv	.....	15	700	–	1,200	32.79	M=SDA(USA).
United Ch of Christ in the Marshall Is	1857	P-Uni	.vP.F	180	26,200	10,000	38,599	5.55	*UCCMI. Jarin Rarik Dron.* 1857. M=ABCFM, later UCBWM(UCC,USA). 4f.
United Pentecostal Church		P-Pe1	x....	10	1,000	–	2,000	0.05	*UPC.* Jesus Only Church (Oneness).
Other Protestant denominations	c1980	P-	....F	5	500	–	1,000	6.67	From a variety of traditions; total 3.
Other independent churches		I-Bap	.....	6	80	–	150	0.05	Independent Baptist churches; total 2.
Doubly-affiliated		2-aff			-12,700	0	-19,999		Pentecostals who are also baptized Catholics or Protestants.
Totals				**305**	**32,117**	**16,338**	**50,400**		

Churches, members, growth, 1900-2025	*Congs*	*Adults*	*Affiliated*	*G%*	*Total denominations*	*6 Megablocs:* *O*	*R*	*A*	*P*	*I*	*m*
Total churches, members, and denominations (mid-1900)	30	2,400	5,000	1.71	1	0	0	0	1	0	0
Total churches, members, and denominations (mid-1970)	112	7,823	16,338	1.71	5	0	1	0	2	0	2
Total churches, members, and denominations (mid-1990)	260	26,600	41,800	4.81	12	0	1	0	8	1	2
Total churches, members, and denominations (mid-1995)	305	32,117	50,400	3.81	17	0	1	0	8	6	2
Total churches, members, and denominations (mid-2000)	400	38,300	60,103	3.58	17	0	1	0	8	6	2
Total churches, members, and denominations (mid-2025)	800	76,800	120,700	2.83	42	0	1	0	15	20	6

NOTES ON TABLE ABOVE
NATIONAL COUNCILS (Column 4, 5th letter).

C = Micronesian Council of United Churches of Christ (MCUCC), 1958.

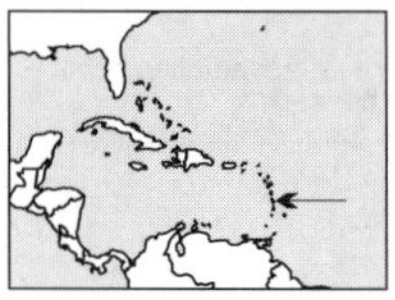

MARTINIQUE

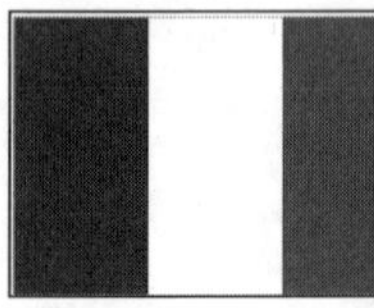

SECULAR DATA, AD 2000

STATE

Official name: Le Département de la Martinique (The Department of Martinique).
Short name: Martinique. **Adjective of nationality:** of Martinique.
Flag: That of France.
Area: 1,128 sq. km. (436 sq. mi.).
Government: Overseas department of France, since 1946 (1635 French possession).
Legislature: General Council, 45 members; Regional Council, 41 members.
Official language: French (Français).
Monetary unit: 1 French franc (F) = 100 centimes. **US$1=** F 5.60.
Chief cities: FORT-DE-FRANCE 139,488.
Political divisions: 3 provinces.
Armed forces: 1,500.

DEMOGRAPHY
Population: 395,000.
Population density: 350.5/sq. km. (906.7/sq. mi.).
Under 15 years: 89,000.
Growth rate p.a.: 0.68% (births 13.39, deaths 6.61).
Mortality: Infant, per 1,000: 7.0, ; **Maternal per 100,000:** 20.0.
Life expectancy: 79 (male 76, female 83).
Household size: 3.3. **Floor area per person, sq.m:** 12.0.
Major languages: French, French Creole, Tamil, English, Chinese, Arabic, Vietnamese.
Urban dwellers: 94.89%. **Urban growth rate p.a.:** 1.1%.
Labor force: 46%.

ETHNOLINGUISTIC PEOPLES
93.4% Mulatto; 2.3% French; 1.9% Tamil (East Indian); 0.7% French Creole; 0.3% West Indian Black.

ECONOMY
National income p.a. per person: US$10,000; **per family:** US$33,003.

EDUCATION
Adult literacy: 92% (male 91%, female 93%). **Schools:** 361.
Universities: 1. **School enrolment:** female/male: 90%/90%.

HEALTH
Access to health services: 75%. **Access to safe water:** 80%.
Hospitals: 20 (103 beds per 10,000). **Doctors:** 625.
Blind: 100. **Deaf:** 23,900. **Murder rate:** 5.
Lepers: 4,000.

LITERATURE
New book titles p.a.: 90 (240 p.a. per million). **Periodicals:** 6.
Newspapers: 1 daily.

COMMUNICATION (per 1,000 people)
Phones: 381 (24% mobile). **Radios:** 187. **TV sets:** 137.
Daily newspaper circulation: 84. **Computers:** 120.

HUMAN LIFE AND LIBERTY (optimum condition=100.0%)
HDI: 91.2. **HSI:** 65.0. **HFI:** 50.0. **EFL:** 35.0.

Country Table 1. Religious adherents in Martinique, AD 1900-2025.

Year	1900		1970		mid-1990		Annual change, 1990-2000				mid-1995		mid-2000		mid-2025	
Name	Adherents	%	Adherents	%	Adherents	%	Natural	Conversion	Total	Rate	Adherents	%	Adherents	%	Adherents	%
Christians	**207,500**	**99.8**	**320,900**	**98.6**	**350,630**	**97.4**	**3,446**	**-179**	**3,267**	**0.89**	**368,210**	**97.2**	**383,296**	**97.0**	**430,040**	**95.6**
PROFESSION																
professing Christians	**207,500**	**99.8**	**320,900**	**98.6**	**350,630**	**97.4**	**3,446**	**-179**	**3,267**	**0.89**	**368,210**	**97.2**	**383,296**	**97.0**	**430,040**	**95.6**
AFFILIATION																
unaffiliated Christians	4,200	2.0	5,827	1.8	9,030	2.5	88	1	89	0.95	8,610	2.3	9,924	2.5	10,040	2.2
affiliated Christians	**203,300**	**97.7**	**315,073**	**96.8**	**341,600**	**94.9**	**3,358**	**-180**	**3,177**	**0.89**	**359,600**	**94.9**	**373,372**	**94.5**	**420,000**	**93.3**
Roman Catholics	203,300	97.7	306,000	94.0	333,500	92.6	3,279	-29	3,250	0.93	351,000	92.7	366,000	92.7	410,000	91.1
Protestants	0	0.0	11,340	3.5	20,520	5.7	200	118	318	1.45	22,311	5.9	23,700	6.0	30,000	6.7
Marginal Christians	0	0.0	2,000	0.6	6,800	1.9	66	54	120	1.64	7,400	2.0	8,000	2.0	15,000	3.3
Independents	0	0.0	1,733	0.5	3,700	1.0	36	29	65	1.63	4,056	1.1	4,349	1.1	6,500	1.4
doubly-affiliated	0	0.0	-6,000	-1.8	-22,920	-6.4	-223	-353	-576	2.27	-25,167	-6.6	-28,677	-7.3	-41,500	-9.2
Trans-megabloc groupings																
Evangelicals	0	0.0	3,650	1.1	12,500	3.5	122	228	350	2.50	14,363	3.8	16,000	4.1	25,000	5.6
Pentecostals/Charismatics	0	0.0	300	0.1	12,900	3.6	125	125	250	1.79	14,048	3.7	15,400	3.9	23,000	5.1
Great Commission Christians	**2,000**	**1.0**	**9,800**	**3.0**	**36,800**	**10.2**	**358**	**241**	**599**	**1.52**	**40,000**	**10.6**	**42,790**	**10.8**	**54,000**	**12.0**
Nonreligious	0	0.0	2,700	0.8	4,080	1.1	40	89	129	2.78	4,700	1.2	5,366	1.4	9,000	2.0
Baha'is	0	0.0	1,000	0.3	1,300	0.4	13	60	73	4.56	1,700	0.5	2,031	0.5	3,500	0.8
Atheists	0	0.0	1,000	0.3	1,600	0.4	16	7	23	1.35	1,700	0.5	1,829	0.5	2,500	0.6
Hindus	0	0.0	0	0.0	800	0.2	8	6	14	1.61	900	0.2	939	0.2	1,600	0.4
Muslims	500	0.2	200	0.1	700	0.2	7	9	16	2.06	800	0.2	858	0.2	1,600	0.4
Spiritists	0	0.0	0	0.0	340	0.1	3	5	8	2.11	400	0.1	419	0.1	700	0.2
Chinese folk-religionists	0	0.0	0	0.0	200	0.1	2	2	4	1.71	220	0.1	237	0.1	400	0.1
Buddhists	0	0.0	0	0.0	140	0.0	1	1	2	1.22	150	0.0	158	0.0	300	0.1
New-Religionists	0	0.0	0	0.0	10	0.0	0	1	1	7.18	20	0.0	20	0.0	60	0.0
Other religionists	0	0.0	200	0.1	200	0.1	2	-1	1	0.44	200	0.1	209	0.1	300	0.1
World A (unevangelized persons)	0	0.0	325	0.1	360	0.1	3	15	18	4.39	378	0.1	395	0.1	900	0.2
World B (evangelized non-Christians)	500	0.2	4,274	1.3	9,010	2.5	89	164	253	2.30	10,230	2.7	11,309	2.9	19,060	4.2
World C (Christians)	207,500	99.8	320,900	98.6	350,630	97.4	3,446	-179	3,267	0.89	368,210	97.2	383,296	97.0	430,040	95.6
Country's population	**208,000**	**100.0**	**325,500**	**100.0**	**360,000**	**100.0**	**3,538**	**0**	**3,538**	**0.93**	**378,819**	**100.0**	**395,000**	**100.0**	**450,000**	**100.0**

COLUMNS, ROWS.
For meanings and definitions, see Codebook (Part 3). Note that, by definition, total 'Christians' = professing + crypto-Christians, which also = affiliated + unaffiliated Christians, and also = Great Commission Christians + latent Christians. Percentages may not always total exactly, due to rounding.

CENSUSES.
The religion question has not been asked.

NOTES ON RELIGIONS
ATHEISTS. Communist Party of Martinique (legal; pro-Soviet).
BAHA'IS. Rapid growth in local spiritual assemblies: 1964, none; 1973, 10; then a marked decline to 3 LSAs (1995).
BUDDHISTS. Vietnamese.
HINDUS. East Indian Tamils.
MUSLIMS. Syrian Arabs.
NONRELIGIOUS. Mostly metropolitan French, French Creoles, a few Chinese, with Martiniquan communists and sympathizers.
OTHER RELIGIONISTS. Including Rosicrucians (3 AMORC centers).
SPIRITISTS. Martinique East Indians (originally 25,000 Tamils from South India, declining through repatriation by 1900 to 10,000) are now all Roman Catholics, speaking Creole, but they follow the cult of Maldevidan, a hybrid Hindu-Catholic spirit-possession religion based on the worship of a pantheon of Tamil Hindu village gods, centered on Maldevidan as chief deity (identified as Vishnu Christ or St Michael), and Mari-eman (the Virgin Mary, also Mari the South Indian goddess of disease). There are many temples, and the northern half of the island is dotted with small masonry structures (*chapelles*) and statues, to which on Sundays during the cane harvest several hundred East Indians come to participate in rites devoted to *les bons dieux coolies*. The rites include drumming, animal sacrifice (sheep, goats, cocks), ecstatic possession, and dancing on sharpened machettes.

Great Commission Instrument Panel: status of Martinique (for explanation see start of Part 4)

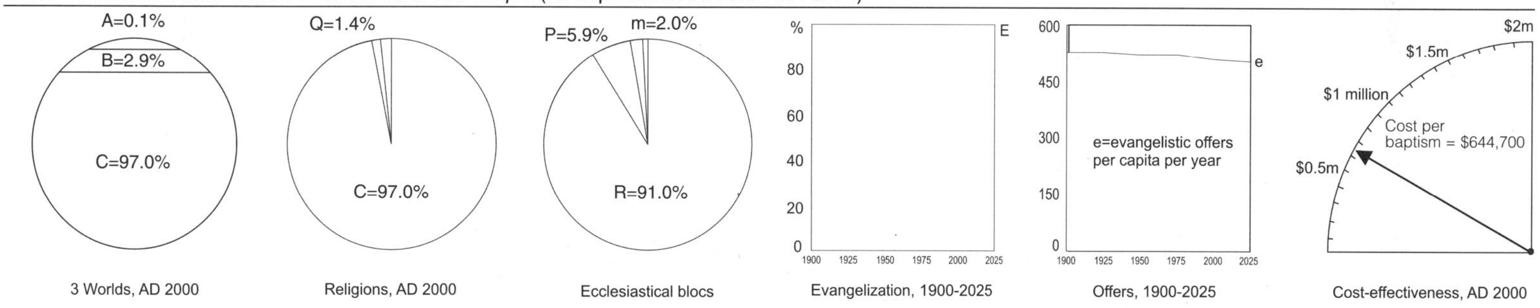

Country status. Martinique, a French overseas department, is a volcanic island in the Lesser Antilles in the Caribbean Sea. Its chief economic activities are tourism and oil refining.

HUMAN LIFE AND LIBERTY

Human rights and freedoms. The situation is as well-developed as in metropolitan France.

NON-CHRISTIAN RELIGIONS

Maldevidan Spiritism in the form of a syncretistic mixture of Hinduism and Catholicism is found among East Indians, who were commonly referred to at an earlier period of history as 'coolies'. Virtually all are now Roman Catholics, but claim to be Hindus as well. Scores of temples are found in the northern part of the island, where Sunday ceremonies are led by a ritual leader known as l'abbé coolie, the rites performed being devoted to 'the good coolie gods' (les bons dieux coolies). The principal deity of the pantheon is Maldevidan who is represented as riding on a horse and is commonly identified with Jesus Christ. The second most important is Mari-eman, a female divinity corresponding to the Virgin Mary except that she is not the mother of Maldevidan. The extensive pantheon also includes Katarai, identified as St Michael, and Buminaman, who is said to be an evil saint. Ritual ceremonies, which are most common during the harvest season (January to June), involve drumming, dancing, spirit possession, the sacrifice of a sheep and cock, and an elaborate community feast.

Islam exists among a small community of Syrian Muslims.

CHRISTIANITY

CATHOLIC CHURCH. There was missionary activity by Dominicans, Jesuits, and Capuchins during the 16th century, but the first apostolic prefect was not appointed until 1816. The island was made a diocese in 1850. Because of the difficulty of obtaining clergy, Martinique was placed under the jurisdiction of Propaganda Fide in Rome at the beginning of the twentieth century and confided to the Holy Ghost Fathers in 1909. Although often at a superficial level, the majority of the people are Catholics.

The Holy See has no diplomatic relations with Martinique in AD 2000.

PROTESTANT CHURCHES. Protestant activity is recent and not extensive although Protestants nearly doubled from 11,300 in 1970 to 22,300 in 1995. Independent Baptists have developed a limited work in 4 areas since their arrival in 1945, and the Reformed Church caters almost entirely for metropolitan Frenchmen. The greatest advance is being made by Seventh-day Adventists who entered in 1924 and have both an urban and a rural following among the lower classes.

Indigenous missions. Though many Christians (especially Roman Catholics) have served overseas, most of these have been in French-speaking countries like French Guiana, Guadeloupe, and France.

CHURCH AND STATE

Legal statutes regarding religious liberty are the same as in metropolitan France. In practice, the hierarchy has more influence than in France since the civil authorities tend to seek their support. It appears to public opinion that the interventions of the hierarchy in burning social and political questions (immigration, political status of the island, unemployment) remain rather cautious by contrast with the initiatives of in-

Country summary. **Worlds A, B, C by ethnolinguistic peoples, cities, and major civil divisions in Martinique.**

	PEOPLES							*CITIES*							*CIVIL DIVISIONS*						
World	*Num*	*Pop 2000*	*C%*	*Christians*	*E%*	*U%*	*Unevangelized*	*Num*	*Pop 2000*	*C%*	*Christians*	*E%*	*U%*	*Unevangelized*	*Num*	*Pop 2000*	*C%*	*Christians*	*E%*	*U%*	*Unevangelized*
A	0	0	0.00	0	0	0	0	0	0	0.00	0	0	0	0	0	0	0.00	0	0	0	0
B	3	1,581	41.37	654	94	6	94	0	0	0.00	0	0	0	0	0	0	0.00	0	0	0	0
C	6	393,781	94.65	372,717	100	0	414	1	139,488	94.40	131,677	100	0	181	3	395,362	94.44	373,372	100	0	507
Total	**9**	**395,362**	**94.44**	**373,371**	**100**	**0**	**508**	**1**	**139,488**	**94.40**	**131,677**	**100**	**0**	**181**	**3**	**395,362**	**94.44**	**373,372**	**100**	**0**	**507**

dividual priests and laymen. However, this has tended to change since 1973, when for the first time a Martinique national became archbishop.

BROADCASTING AND MEDIA

Shortwave programs from KNLS, HCJB (Ecuador), TWR (Antilles), and AWR (Costa Rica) can be easily received. There are 2 local Catholic radio programs each 30 minutes long. Radio Saint-Louis is a local Catholic radio station. Martinique is a member of UNDA.

There are 2 15-minute weekly Catholic television programs. Additional programming can be received via satellite.

INTERDENOMINATIONAL ORGANIZATIONS

A group made up of Catholics and French Reformed was constituted in November 1970 and meets regularly for dialogue and Bible study, though not as an organized council.

FUTURE TRENDS AND PROSPECTS

Christians are expected to decline as a percentage through 2025 to 95.6% (from nearly 100% in 1900). The nonreligious, 0.8% in 1970, are projected to reach 2.0% in 2025.

The nonreligious and non-Christian religions could grow well into the 21st century, possibly reaching 10% of the population by AD 2050.

BIBLIOGRAPHY

Annuaire ecclésiastique 1971. Fort-de-France, Martinique: Imprimerie Antillaise Saint-Paul, 1971.

Le clergé: dictionnaire biographique de la Martinique (1635–1848). B. David. Fort-de-France: Société d'histoire de la Martinique, 1984. 3 vols.

Martinique. J. Crane. *World bibliographical series*, vol. 175. Oxford, UK: CLIO Press, 1995.

Martinique de mon coeur: chroniques d'un prêtre québécois aux îles. A. Lafortune. , 1980. 187p.

Origine des paroisses et des quartiers de la Martinique d'après des documents inédits. J. Rennard. Fort-de-France: Imprimerie antillaise, [1927]. 78p.

'The French presence and the church in Martinique and Guadeloupe,' O. La Croix, in *New mission for a new people: voices from the Caribbean*, p.30–34. D. I. Mitchell (ed). New York: Friendship Press, 1977.

The incredible rescue operation: church planting in Martinique. L. Seaman. *Missionary reading books*, 1987-88. Kansas City, MO: Nazarene Publishing House, 1987. 115p.

'The Martiniquan East Indian cult of Maldevidan,' M. Horowitz & M. Klass, *Social and economic studies*, 10, 1 (1961), 93–100.

'The Seventh–day Adventists in Martinique: a church growth study.' J. E. Seaman. M.A. thesis, Nazarene Theological Seminary, Kansas City, MO, 1977. 88p.

'Theological education by extension: a proposal for ministerial training in Martinique, French West Indies for the Church of the Nazarene.' J. E. Seaman. M.R.E. thesis, Nazarene Theological Seminary, Kansas City, MO, 1979. 42p.

Eglise Catholique, Archdiocèse de Fort-de-France. Cathedral in Fort-de-France.

Country Table 2. **Organized churches and denominations in Martinique.**

Official name (bold type = church with over 10% of all affiliated) *1*	*Begun 2*	*Type 3*	*Counc 4*	*Congs 5*	*Adults 6*	*Affiliated 1970 7*	*Affiliated 1995 8*	*G% 9*	*Names, notes, and other statistics* (see Codebook, Part 3) *10*
Assemblées de Dieu	c1975	P-Pe2	.....	21	1,500	–	3,000	5.00	M=AoG(France, USA).
Assoc des Eglises Ev Baptistes	c1980	P-Bap	.....	5	200	–	308	6.67	Association of Evangelical Baptist Chs.
Communautés Evangéliques Libres		I-CBr	x....	14	700	1,000	1,170	0.05	Indigenous congregations, Plymouth (Open) Brethren influence. Fort-de-France.
Eglise Adventiste du Septième Jour	1924	P-Adv	x....	55	7,360	10,000	11,318	0.50	*Seventh-day Adventists, Martinique Mission.* Working-class. 8nx,1r,63t(5819),279Y.
Eglise Baptiste	1977	P-Bap	.....	2	200	–	300	5.56	M=FMB-SBC.
Eglise Baptiste Indépendante	1945	I-Bap	.....	10	500	400	769	2.65	*Independent Baptist Ch.* M=Ev Baptist Missions (USA). Bible shops, radio work. 10f.
Eglise Catholique: M Fort-de-France	1635	R-Lat	PxNMr	49	180,000	306,000	351,000	0.55	*Catholic Ch in M.* 2.0% East Indian. C=2+0+6. 39n,29x,40m,199w,4992Yy.
Eglise de Dieu	c1975	P-Pe3	.....	1	261	–	746	5.00	M=CoG(Cleveland) (USA).
Eglise de Dieu de Prophétie	1986	P-Pe3	.....	1	50	–	83	11.11	Church of God of Prophecy. M=CGP.
Eglise du Nazarène	1976	P-Hol	.....	5	146	–	206	5.26	M=CoN.
Eglise Réformée de France		P-Ref	Rwc..	1	100	200	200	0.05	ERF. Serving almost entirely short-term metropolitan French, military and civilian.
Fédération des Eglises Ev Baptistes	c1985	P-Bap	.....	1	20	–	40	10.00	*Federation of Evangelical Baptist Churches.*
Mission Chrétienne Ev de Martinique	c1955	P-Eva	.....	31	4,275	1,140	6,110	6.95	*Evangelical Christian Mission of Martinique.*
Témoins de Jéhovah	c1945	m-Jeh	x....	30	2,961	2,000	7,400	5.37	*Jehovah's Witnesses, Watch Tower..* Activity first reported 1950. (1975) 97Y. (1995) 249Y.
Other independent denominations		I-3pW	.....	18	550	200	917	0.05	Including Streams of Power, World-Wide Missions.
Other single congregations		I-Non	.....	18	720	133	1,200	0.05	Including New Apostolic Church (34 members).
Doubly-affiliated			2-aff			-13,100	-6,000	-25,167	Evangelicals who are also baptized Roman Catholics.
Totals				**262**	**186,443**	**315,073**	**359,600**		

Churches, members, growth, 1900-2025	*Congs*	*Adults*	*Affiliated*	*G%*	*Total denominations*	*6 Megablocs:* *O*	*R*	*A*	*P*	*I*	*m*
Total churches, members, and denominations (mid-1900)	80	113,000	203,300	0.63	1	0	1	0	0	0	0
Total churches, members, and denominations (mid-1970)	122	174,750	315,073	0.63	11	0	1	0	3	6	1
Total churches, members, and denominations (mid-1990)	200	177,000	341,600	0.41	23	0	1	0	10	11	1
Total churches, members, and denominations (mid-1995)	262	186,443	359,600	1.03	23	0	1	0	10	11	1
Total churches, members, and denominations (mid-2000)	290	194,000	373,372	0.75	47	0	1	0	15	30	1
Total churches, members, and denominations (mid-2025)	340	218,000	420,000	0.47	47	0	1	0	15	30	1

NOTES ON TABLE ABOVE
NATIONAL COUNCILS (Column 4, 5th letter).

r = member of Conférence Episcopale de France (CEF) (Episcopal Conference of France).

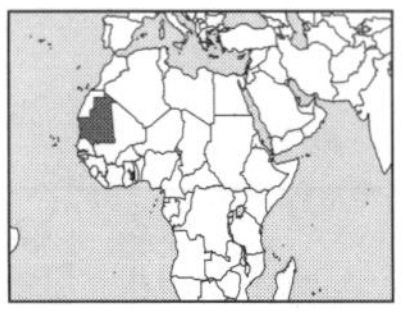

MAURITANIA

SECULAR DATA, AD 2000

STATE

Official name: La République Islamique Arabe et Africaine de Mauritanie (The Islamic Republic of Mauritania).
Short name: Mauritania. **Adjective of nationality:** Mauritanian.
Flag: Gold star and crescent on green field.
Area: 1,030,700 sq. km. (398,000 sq. mi.).
Government: Multiparty republic, since 1991 (1903 French protectorate, 1920 colony in French West Africa, 1958 self-government, 1960 Independence, 1964 one-party republic).
Legislature: Senate, 56 members, National Assembly, 79 members.
Official language: French (Français).
Monetary unit: 1 ouguiya (UM) = 5 khoums. **US$1=** UM 208.83.
Chief cities: NOUAKCHOTT 395,785.
Political divisions: 13 provinces.
Armed forces: 16,000.

DEMOGRAPHY

Population: 2,670,000.
Population density: 2.5/sq. km. (6.7/sq. mi.).
Under 15 years: 1,158,000.
Growth rate p.a.: 2.67% (births 38.61, deaths 11.99).
Mortality: Infant, per 1,000: 83.9, ; **Maternal per 100,000:** 930.0.
Life expectancy: 56 (male 54, female 57).
Household size: 5.0. **Floor area per person, sq.m:** 4.0.
Major languages: French, Hassaniyah (Arabic), Fulani (Poulah), Berber, Spanish, Soninke, Zenaga, and about 5 others.
Urban dwellers: 57.74%. **Urban growth rate p.a.:** 4.1%.
Labor force: 31%.

ETHNOLINGUISTIC PEOPLES

24.0% Black Moor (Maure); 20.0% White Moor (Bidan); 9.6% Arabized Berber; 8.5% Trarza (Brakna); 7.2% Tukulor (Takarir).

ECONOMY

National income p.a. per person: US$460; **per family:** US$2,300.

EDUCATION
Adult literacy: 37% (male 49%, female 26%). **Schools:** 1,696. **Universities:** 4. **School enrolment:** female/male: 38%/50%.

HEALTH
Access to health services: 63%. **Access to safe water:** 76%. **Hospitals:** 16 (7 beds per 10,000). **Doctors:** 135. **Blind:** 15,000. **Deaf:** 154,800. **Murder rate:** 1. **Lepers:** 9,000. **Underweight prevalence under 5:** 23%.

LITERATURE
New book titles p.a.: 3 (1 p.a. per million). **Periodicals:** 1. **Newspapers:** 1 daily.

COMMUNICATION (per 1,000 people)
Phones: 4 (2% mobile). **Radios:** 444. **TV sets:** 58. **Daily newspaper circulation:** 0. **Computers:** 3.

REFUGEES
Citizen refugees in other countries: 80,000.
Alien refugees from other countries: 35,000.

HUMAN LIFE AND LIBERTY (optimum condition=100.0%)
HDI: 35.5. **HSI:** 23.0. **HFI:** 5.0. **EFL:** 24.0.

Country Table 1. **Religious adherents in Mauritania, AD 1900-2025.**

Year	1900		1970		mid-1990		Annual change, 1990-2000				mid-1995		mid-2000		mid-2025	
Name	Adherents	%	Adherents	%	Adherents	%	Natural	Conversion	Total	Rate	Adherents	%	Adherents	%	Adherents	%
Muslims	214,950	97.7	1,213,100	99.3	2,005,560	99.0	63,705	370	64,075	2.81	2,308,080	99.1	2,646,306	99.1	4,737,620	99.4
Ethnoreligionists	5,000	2.3	1,000	0.1	11,000	0.5	350	-61	289	2.36	11,800	0.5	13,890	0.5	15,000	0.3
Christians	**50**	**0.0**	**6,200**	**0.5**	**6,930**	**0.3**	**220**	**-256**	**-36**	**-0.53**	**6,520**	**0.3**	**6,569**	**0.3**	**7,580**	**0.2**
PROFESSION																
crypto-Christians	0	0.0	1,200	0.1	2,000	0.1	64	-14	50	2.26	2,200	0.1	2,500	0.1	4,300	0.1
professing Christians	**50**	**0.0**	**5,000**	**0.4**	**4,930**	**0.2**	**157**	**-243**	**-86**	**-1.90**	**4,320**	**0.2**	**4,069**	**0.2**	**3,280**	**0.1**
AFFILIATION																
unaffiliated Christians	0	0.0	0	0.0	30	0.0	1	0	1	3.67	30	0.0	43	0.0	50	0.0
affiliated Christians	**50**	**0.0**	**6,200**	**0.5**	**6,900**	**0.3**	**219**	**-256**	**-37**	**-0.56**	**6,490**	**0.3**	**6,526**	**0.2**	**7,530**	**0.2**
Roman Catholics	50	0.0	6,160	0.5	5,000	0.3	159	-237	-78	-1.69	4,386	0.2	4,216	0.2	4,000	0.1
Independents	0	0.0	0	0.0	1,500	0.1	48	-28	20	1.26	1,600	0.1	1,700	0.1	2,500	0.1
Protestants	0	0.0	40	0.0	400	0.0	13	7	20	4.14	500	0.0	600	0.0	1,000	0.0
Marginal Christians	0	0.0	0	0.0	0	0.0	0	1	1	25.89	4	0.0	10	0.0	30	0.0
Trans-megabloc groupings																
Evangelicals	0	0.0	40	0.0	400	0.0	13	7	20	4.14	500	0.0	600	0.0	1,100	0.0
Pentecostals/Charismatics	0	0.0	50	0.0	1,500	0.1	48	12	60	3.42	1,748	0.1	2,100	0.1	4,000	0.1
Great Commission Christians	**45**	**0.0**	**4,900**	**0.4**	**4,000**	**0.2**	**127**	**-136**	**-9**	**-0.22**	**3,500**	**0.2**	**3,914**	**0.2**	**5,500**	**0.1**
Nonreligious	0	0.0	600	0.1	2,200	0.1	70	-59	11	0.51	2,200	0.1	2,314	0.1	5,000	0.1
Baha'is	0	0.0	100	0.0	150	0.0	5	7	12	5.94	220	0.0	267	0.0	500	0.0
Atheists	0	0.0	0	0.0	160	0.0	5	-1	4	2.26	180	0.0	200	0.0	300	0.0
World A (unevangelized persons)	217,800	99.0	1,123,442	92.0	1,489,110	73.5	47,317	-14,491	32,826	2.01	1,651,412	70.9	1,818,270	68.1	3,002,580	63.0
World B (evangelized non-Christians)	2,150	1.0	91,490	7.5	529,960	26.2	16,818	14,747	31,565	4.78	671,281	28.8	845,161	31.6	1,755,840	36.8
World C (Christians)	50	0.0	6,200	0.5	6,930	0.3	220	-256	-36	-0.53	6,520	0.3	6,569	0.3	7,580	0.2
Country's population	**220,000**	**100.0**	**1,221,133**	**100.0**	**2,026,000**	**100.0**	**64,355**	**0**	**64,355**	**2.80**	**2,329,214**	**100.0**	**2,670,000**	**100.0**	**4,766,000**	**100.0**

COLUMNS, ROWS.
For meanings and definitions, see Codebook (Part 3). Note that, by definition, total 'Christians' = professing + crypto-Christians, which also = affiliated + unaffiliated Christians, and also = Great Commission Christians + latent Christians. Percentages may not always total exactly, due to rounding.

NOTES ON RELIGIONS
BAHA'IS. In 2 local spiritual assemblies (1973), with much alternation but no growth in the subsequent 25 years.
CHRISTIANS. The total has fluctuated considerably during the 1990s due to arrivals and departures of expatriates, French and Africans (net immigration is included in the column 'Natural change'). The projection to AD 2025 envisages a leveling off of the number of African expatriates from francophone Africa, mainly Catholics.
CRYPTO-CHRISTIANS. African expatriates and a few nationals who attend church services.
ETHNORELIGIONISTS. A few pockets of animists among Blacks (Negroes), following pre-Islamic customs.
MUSLIMS. Sunnis (of the Malikite rite). The majority follow Qadiriya (Sufi) maraboutism, which is widespread; others follow Tijaniya, and a few Shadhiliya. The Black minorities are all Muslims but are opposed to arabization. *Hajj pilgrims to Mecca.* (1970) 724; (1975) 914; (1976) 1,654.
NONRELIGIOUS. Mainly French.

Great Commission Instrument Panel: status of Mauritania (for explanation see start of Part 4)

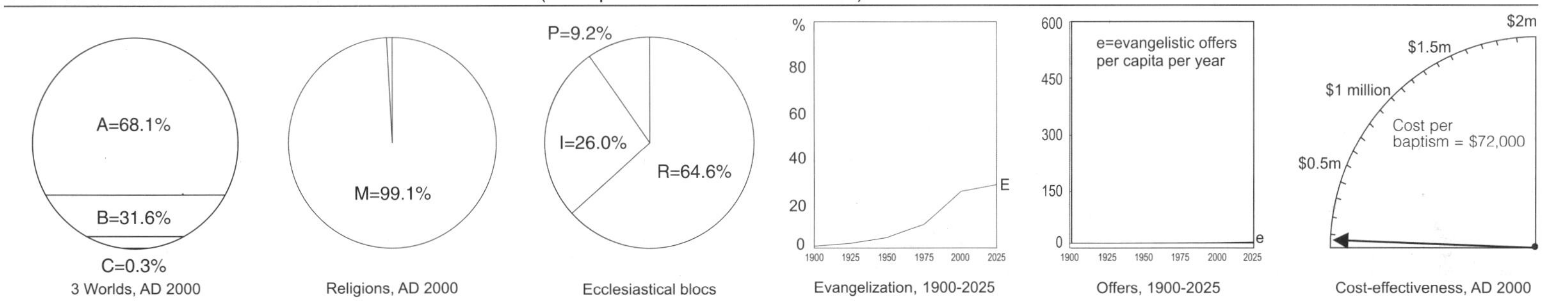

Country status. Mauritania is a large country on the Western bulge of Africa. About 80% of the land is within the Sahara Desert, and is sparsely inhabited. Culturally, Mauritania is a bridge between Arab-Berber North Africa and Black Africa. Its main exports are iron ore and fish.

HUMAN LIFE AND LIBERTY

Human need and development. Most of the population is concentrated along the Senegal River in the extreme southern part. The rest of the country is desert, where living conditions have become intolerable after the continuous drought since the 1970s. Water holes have dried up, the cattle have perished, and grazing lands have turned barren of all vegetation. Nomadic pastoralists, who make up one-third of the population, have been resettled in suburban areas. Even in the dryland along the Senegal River, productive activities have been curtailed by drought and clashes between farmers and nomads. Mauritania's quality of life indicators are among the lowest in the world: Life expectancy is 57 for females and 54 for males, infant mortality rate is 84 per 1,000 live births, 30% of children are malnourished, the adult literacy rate is 37%, and the per capita income is only $460. There is little or no industrial production, and the vast majority live at bare subsistence levels. Medical facilities are limited to Nouakchott and a few other towns, but medical intervention is rarely sought by the nomads and farmers in rural areas. Much of education is carried out by Islamic schools which only serve to keep the children in a state of intellectual underdevelopment.

Human rights and freedoms. Although the regime of Maaouya Ould Sid'Ahmed Taya transformed itself from a military dictatorship into a civilian one through a staged election, nothing has really changed in the country. A newly elected puppet parliament has replaced the old Military Committee. Serious human rights abuses continue, most of them related to the expulsion of Black Mauritanians in 1989-90. Many of them still live in Senegalese camps. More than 500 Blacks are believed to have died in the purge, and many hundreds more were tortured and maimed. Further, Mauritania is one of the few countries of the modern world where slavery is still practiced. Security forces regularly engage in extrajudicial killings of blacks, and there are credible reports of disappearances and drownings, as well as torture and inhuman and degrading treatment. Dissidents are denied due process, access to legal counsel and right to appeal. Even in ordinary criminal cases, the traditional 'ghissas', retributory justice as in eye for an eye, and blood money compensation are applied more often than modern concepts of justice. Prisoners are held incommunicado for prolonged periods without being charged with any crime, and then released after influential palms have been greased. The legal system is based on the sharia, tempered by tribal and familial traditions. There are reports of government surveillance of dissidents and the existence of a wide network of informers. The 1991 Constitution provides for freedom of the press and freedom of assembly, and, in comparison with previous years, Mauritanians enjoy a greater degree of freedom in these areas. Although the government publishes the nation's only daily, there are a number of independent periodicals which are often very critical of the government. However, since most Mauritanians are illiterate, they depend on radio and television for their news, both of which are operated by the state. All newspapers are required to register with the government, and journalists are frequently threatened with libel action by the government. Similarly, the right of assembly is restricted by the requirement that all political groups must be registered and permission must be obtained for large gatherings. Such permission is sometimes denied, or granted in an inconsistent fashion. Since independence, the government has been pursuing an active policy of

Postage stamps with religious themes: (*top*) Nouakchott Mosque. (*bottom*) 90th anniversary of birth of Protestant missionary Albert Schweitzer.

Country summary. **Worlds A, B, C by ethnolinguistic peoples, cities, and major civil divisions in Mauritania.**

	PEOPLES							CITIES							CIVIL DIVISIONS						
World	*Num*	*Pop 2000*	*C%*	*Christians*	*E%*	*U%*	*Unevangelized*	*Num*	*Pop 2000*	*C%*	*Christians*	*E%*	*U%*	*Unevangelized*	*Num*	*Pop 2000*	*C%*	*Christians*	*E%*	*U%*	*Unevangelized*
A	21	2,648,990	0.09	2,304	32	68	1,811,946	1	395,785	0.38	1,504	36	64	253,184	13	2,669,548	0.24	6,526	32	68	1,818,259
B	2	16,018	5.00	801	61	39	6,300	0	0	0.00	0	0	0	0	0	0	0.00	0	0	0	0
C	3	4,538	75.41	3,422	100	0	11	0	0	0.00	0	0	0	0	0	0	0.00	0	0	0	0
Total	**26**	**2,669,546**	**0.24**	**6,527**	**32**	**68**	**1,818,257**	**1**	**395,785**	**0.38**	**1,504**	**36**	**64**	**253,184**	**13**	**2,669,548**	**0.24**	**6,526**	**32**	**68**	**1,818,259**

Arabization, leading to the dominance of the Whites (beydane) over the Blacks (haratine), although the latter are numerically in the majority. Few blacks are represented in the government or in the economy. The government promotes Arabic at the expense of French, the former official language which has been demoted in the new Constitution. This policy also discriminates against the Blacks, almost all of whom are French-speaking. The 1983 Land Reform Law is used to allow the beydane to encroach on Black-owned lands in the Senegal River Valley.

Human environment. Sahelian Mauritania is increasingly becoming all desert. Bereft of vegetation, the soil is being subjected to heavy wind erosion, and desert conditions are creeping into settled lands. The Senegal River dam is expected to increase the land under irrigation, but its long-term ecological impact will be adverse on wetlands, forests, and fishing.

NON-CHRISTIAN RELIGIONS

Islam reached the nomadic Berbers of this region in the 10th century and a century afterwards produced the warrior-like Almoravides who later took control of Morocco and Spain for a period. Arabs appeared in the 15th century and the present population is a mixture of Berbers and Arabs who speak a dialect of Arabic similar to the language used in the Quran. The southern region is inhabited by Blacks, but all are united by Islam which is the official religion of the country. All Mauritanians, Moors and Blacks are Sunnis of the Malikite rite, although Mauritanians also continue to follow some pre-Muslim customs. An institute of higher Islamic studies has been established at Boutilimit.

CHRISTIANITY

CATHOLIC CHURCH. The Catholic Church dating from the beginning of the present century is the only organized Christian body existing in Mauritania at the present time. All Catholics are foreigners. Most are French, a transitory group generally spending terms of 3 years' service in government institutions. Other Christians include some Senegalese, Togolese, Dahomeans, and Spanish from the Canary Islands, who form a sub-proletariat at the port of Nouadhibou. Ten Holy Ghost Fathers are divided between Nouakchott, Nouadhibou, Atar, Zouerate, Rosso and Kaedi. Living in a country whose citizens are virtually 100% Muslims, their pastoral efforts are directed largely towards immigrant workers from Black Africa. This involves literacy work and, for a small number of adults, catechetical study leading to baptism.

The Holy See has no diplomatic relations with Mauritania in AD 2000, but is represented an apostolic delegate residing in Dakar.

PROTESTANT CHURCH. Protestants have on several occasions attempted to begin activity in Mauritania, but without success. The last Protestant group to work in the country, the Worldwide Evangelization Crusade, withdrew its missionaries in 1965. A small expatriate congregation exists in the capital.

Indigenous missions. The small Christian community in Mauritania has not sent missionaries to other countries.

CHURCH AND STATE

The preamble to the constitution of May 1961 invokes the All-Powerful God. Article 2 stipulates that Islam is the religion of the Mauritanian people and guarantees to each person liberty of conscience and the right to practice his religion. In practice, conversion from Islam is prohibited and virtually non-existent.

BROADCASTING AND MEDIA

Remarkably, over a quarter of the households have TVs (often homes are shanties equipped with a TV, an antenna, and a car battery).

FUTURE TRENDS AND PROSPECTS

Muslims will likely maintain 99% of the population through the early part of the 21st century. The percentage of Christians is not expected to change much through 2025.

As long as the Christian community is primarily expatriate it is unlikely that Christians will grow to represent 1% of the population, even as late as AD 2050. Muslims will probably remain around 99% over the next few decades.

BIBLIOGRAPHY

Breve estudio sobre las tribus moras de Mauritania. A. C. de Laiglesia. *Primer informe*, 10. Madrid: Instituto Hispano-Arabe de Cultura, [1985]. 120p.

Eléments d'histoire de la Mauritanie. A. W. Ould Cheikh. *Collection 'Connaissance de la Mauritanie'.* Nouakchott [Mauritania]: Institut mauritanien de recherche scientifique, Centre culturel français Antoine de St-Exupéry, [1988]. 135p.

Historical dictionary of Mauritania. A. G. Pazzanita. *African historical dictionaries*, no. 68. Lanham, MD: Scarecrow Press, 1996.

Islam and social order in Mauritania: a case study from the nineteenth century. C. C. Stewart with E. K. Stewart. Oxford, UK: Clarendon Press, 1973. 204p.

La littérature religieuse mauritanienne. M. A. Sakho. Nouakchott, Mauritania: Imprimerie Nouvelle, 1986. 127p.

Les hommes qui cueillent la vie: les Imragen. F. Pelletier. *L'Aventure vécue.* Paris: Flammarion, 1986. 246p.

L'étrier, la houe et le livre: sociétés traditionnelles au Sahara et au Sahel occidental. F. de Chassey. Paris: L'Harmattan, 1993. 312p.

L'Islam dans les cinq pays du maghreb arabe. L. Pruvost. *Dossiers de la C.R.R.M*, no. 6. : Commission pour les Relations Religieuses avec les Musulmans, Conseil Pontifical pour le Dialogue Interreligieux, 1993. 18p.

'L'Islam en Mauritanie,' A. Leriche, *Bulletin de l'Institut Français d'Afrique Noire*, 11 (1949), 458–70.

L'Islam en Maurtianie et en Sénégal. P. Marty. Paris: E. Leroux, 1915–16. 483p.

Mauritania. S. Calderini, D. Cortese & J. L. A. Webb Jr. *World bibliographical series*, vol. 141. Oxford, UK: CLIO Press, 1992. 184p. (See especially 'Religion,' p.69–73).

'Nomadisme, Islam et pouvoir politique dans la société maure precoloniale (XIème siècle–XIXème siècle): essai sur quelques aspects du tribalisme.' A. W. Ould Cheikh. Université de Paris V, René Descartes, 1985. 3 vols.

Status of Christianity profile: Mauritania. Nairobi, Kenya: Daystar University College, [1988]. 31p.

Tribus, ethnies et pouvoir en Mauritanie. P. Marchesin. Paris: Karthala, 1992. 437p.

Country Table 2. **Organized churches and denominations in Mauritania.**

Official name (bold type = church with over 10% of all affiliated) 1	*Begun* 2	*Type* 3	*Counc* 4	*Congs* 5	*Adults* 6	*Affiliated 1970* 7	*Affiliated 1995* 8	*G%* 9	*Names, notes, and other statistics* (see Codebook, Part 3) 10
Eglise Catholique: D Nouakchott	c1900	R-Lat	p.SPP	11	2,500	6,160	4,386	-1.35	*Catholic Ch.* 90% French. C=1+0+1. M=CSSp. (1990) 2n,9x,12m,32w,44Yy.
Eglise Evangélique	c1964	P-Eva	.....	3	150	40	200	6.65	Expatriate Protestant believers in Nouakchott. Links with M=WEC(UK),WVI,et alia.
Isolated radio believers	c1970	I-3rA	.....	20	200	–	500	28.22	Isolated house church hearing radio programs.
Korean Full Gospel Church	c1985	I-3fK	Z....	1	90	–	100	10.00	Korean fishermen.
Témoins de Jéhovah	c1975	m-Jeh	x....	1	4	–	4	5.00	*Jehovah's Witnesses. Watch Tower.*
Other Protestant bodies	c1980	P-	.....	5	200	–	300	6.67	Mainly West African migrant laborers and traders. AoG,SDA,ECWA,etc.
Other African indigenous churches	1971	I-3pA	.....	15	700	–	1,000	4.17	Labor migrants in West African AICs, mainly Yoruba, Ibo, Kru, Bassa; total 18.
Totals				**56**	**3,844**	**6,200**	**6,490**		

Churches, members, growth, 1900-2025	*Congs*	*Adults*	*Affiliated*	*G%*	*Total denominations*	*6 Megablocs:* *O*	*R*	*A*	*P*	*I*	*m*
Total churches, members, and denominations (mid-1900)	1	29	50	7.13	1	0	1	0	0	0	0
Total churches, members, and denominations (mid-1970)	8	3,620	6,200	7.13	2	0	1	0	1	0	0
Total churches, members, and denominations (mid-1990)	40	4,100	6,900	0.54	29	0	1	0	8	19	1
Total churches, members, and denominations (mid-1995)	56	3,844	6,490	-1.22	30	0	1	0	8	20	1
Total churches, members, and denominations (mid-2000)	70	3,900	6,526	0.11	31	0	1	0	8	21	1
Total churches, members, and denominations (mid-2025)	80	4,500	7,530	0.57	44	0	1	0	12	30	1

NOTES ON TABLE ABOVE
NATIONAL COUNCILS (Column 4, 5th letter).

P = Conférence des Evêques du Sénégal, de la Mauritanie, du Cap-Vert, et de Guinée-Bissau (Episcopal Conference of Senegal, Mauritania, Cape Verde, and Guinea-Bissau).

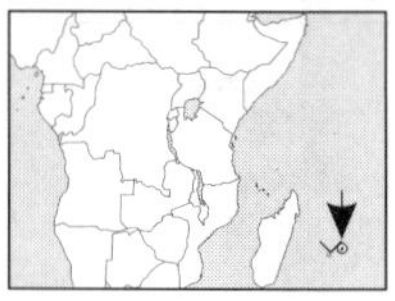

MAURITIUS

SECULAR DATA, AD 2000

STATE

Official name: The Republic of Mauritius.
Short name: Mauritius. **Adjective of nationality:** Mauritian.
Flag: Red, blue, yellow, and green stripes.
Area: 2,040 sq. km. (788 sq. mi.).
Government: Parliamentary state (constitutional monarchy), since 1968 (1589 Dutch settlement, 1810 British protectorate, 1903 British colony, 1968 Independence).
Legislature: National Assembly, 66 members.
Official language: English.
Monetary unit: 1 Mauritian rupee (Mau Re; plural Mau Rs) = 100 cents. **US$1=** Mau Rs 24.26.
Chief cities: PORT LOUIS 472,752; Beau Bassin-Rose Hill 106,072; Curepipe 75,082; Quatre Bornes 74,018; Vacoas-Phoenix 63,410.
Political divisions: 11 provinces.
Armed forces: 1,000.

DEMOGRAPHY

Population: 1,156,000.
Population density: 566.9/sq. km. (1,467.6/sq. mi.).
Under 15 years: 293,000.

Growth rate p.a.: 0.83% (births 15.78, deaths 6.55).
Mortality: Infant, per 1,000: 13.9, ; **Maternal per 100,000:** 120.0.
Life expectancy: 73 (male 69, female 76).
Household size: 5.3. **Floor area per person, sq.m:** 7.0.
Major languages: English, Creole, Hindi, Urdu, French, Tamil, Punjabi, Bihari, Telugu, Chinese (Cantonese), Malagasy.
Urban dwellers: 41.29%. **Urban growth rate p.a.:** 1.8%.
Labor force: 45%.

ETHNOLINGUISTIC PEOPLES
30.8% Indo-Mauritian (Hindi); 21.6% Franco-Mauritian Mulatto; 20.3% Indo-Mauritian; 5.8% Indo-Mauritian (Urdu); 5.7% Franco-Mauritian.

ECONOMY
National income p.a. per person: US$3,380; **per family:** US$17,914.

EDUCATION
Adult literacy: 82% (male 87%, female 78%). **Schools:** 421.
Universities: 2. **School enrolment:** female/male: 80%/79%.

HEALTH
Access to health services: 100%. **Access to safe water:** 98%.
Hospitals: 23 (28 beds per 10,000). **Doctors:** 941.
Blind: 250. **Deaf:** 70,600. **Murder rate:** 3.
Lepers: 400. **Underweight prevalence under 5:** 16%.

LITERATURE
New book titles p.a.: 130 (110 p.a. per million). **Periodicals:** 87.
Newspapers: 6 dailies.

COMMUNICATION (per 1,000 people)
Phones: 131 **(19% mobile). Radios:** 353. **TV sets:** 187.
Daily newspaper circulation: 68. **Computers:** 50.

HUMAN LIFE AND LIBERTY (optimum condition=100.0%)
HDI: 83.1. **HSI:** 60.0. **HFI:** 35.0. **EFL:** 15.0.

Country Table 1. **Religious adherents in Mauritius, AD 1900-2025.**

Year	1900		1970		mid-1990		Annual change, 1990-2000				mid-1995		mid-2000		mid-2025	
Name	Adherents	%	Adherents	%	Adherents	%	Natural	Conversion	Total	Rate	Adherents	%	Adherents	%	Adherents	%
Hindus	206,000	54.5	379,380	46.0	474,400	45.0	4,542	-1,158	3,384	0.69	492,320	44.3	508,236	44.0	529,100	38.4
Christians	**126,600**	**33.5**	**296,820**	**36.0**	**339,000**	**32.1**	**3,295**	**520**	**3,815**	**1.07**	**359,600**	**32.3**	**377,154**	**32.6**	**490,000**	**35.6**
PROFESSION																
crypto-Christians	600	0.2	19,840	2.4	25,800	2.5	247	273	520	1.85	28,000	2.5	31,000	2.7	45,000	3.3
professing Christians	**126,000**	**33.3**	**276,980**	**33.6**	**313,200**	**29.7**	**3,048**	**247**	**3,295**	**1.01**	**331,600**	**29.8**	**346,154**	**29.9**	**445,000**	**32.3**
AFFILIATION																
unaffiliated Christians	0	0.0	0	0.0	7,400	0.7	71	-39	32	0.43	7,600	0.7	7,722	0.7	20,000	1.5
affiliated Christians	**126,600**	**33.5**	**296,820**	**36.0**	**331,600**	**31.4**	**3,225**	**558**	**3,783**	**1.09**	**352,000**	**31.7**	**369,432**	**32.0**	**470,000**	**34.1**
Roman Catholics	118,300	31.3	280,000	34.0	287,850	27.3	2,756	-541	2,215	0.74	302,000	27.2	310,000	26.8	340,000	24.7
Protestants	4,200	1.1	5,880	0.7	95,000	9.0	909	591	1,500	1.48	102,090	9.2	110,000	9.5	150,000	10.9
Anglicans	4,100	1.1	8,000	1.0	5,400	0.5	52	-92	-40	-0.77	5,200	0.5	5,000	0.4	4,500	0.3
Independents	0	0.0	1,300	0.2	2,700	0.3	26	44	70	2.33	3,577	0.3	3,400	0.3	6,000	0.4
Marginal Christians	0	0.0	1,640	0.2	2,200	0.2	21	9	30	1.29	2,350	0.2	2,500	0.2	3,300	0.2
doubly-affiliated	0	0.0	0	0.0	-61,550	-5.8	-589	597	8	-0.01	-63,217	-5.7	-61,468	-5.3	-33,800	-2.5
Trans-megabloc groupings																
Evangelicals	3,000	0.8	3,000	0.4	89,500	8.5	857	393	1,250	1.32	96,726	8.7	102,000	8.8	145,000	10.5
Pentecostals/Charismatics	0	0.0	2,000	0.2	263,750	25.0	2,525	700	3,225	1.16	281,990	25.4	296,000	25.6	399,000	29.0
Great Commission Christians	**27,000**	**7.1**	**62,000**	**7.5**	**73,800**	**7.0**	**707**	**786**	**1,493**	**1.86**	**81,100**	**7.3**	**88,727**	**7.7**	**115,000**	**8.4**
Muslims	41,200	10.9	131,800	16.0	175,000	16.6	1,675	307	1,982	1.08	187,000	16.8	194,822	16.9	240,000	17.4
Nonreligious	80	0.0	1,600	0.2	26,000	2.5	249	78	327	1.19	28,000	2.5	29,273	2.5	50,000	3.6
Baha'is	0	0.0	6,500	0.8	18,000	1.7	172	213	385	1.96	21,000	1.9	21,848	1.9	35,000	2.5
Chinese folk-religionists	1,000	0.3	1,600	0.2	13,800	1.3	132	27	159	1.10	14,700	1.3	15,393	1.3	20,000	1.5
Buddhists	3,100	0.8	5,800	0.7	2,700	0.3	26	-9	17	0.61	2,800	0.3	2,868	0.3	2,500	0.2
Sikhs	0	0.0	0	0.0	2,200	0.2	21	13	34	1.46	2,450	0.2	2,544	0.2	3,600	0.3
Ethnoreligionists	0	0.0	0	0.0	2,100	0.2	20	1	21	0.97	2,200	0.2	2,313	0.2	2,800	0.2
Atheists	20	0.0	400	0.1	1,200	0.1	11	8	19	1.47	1,300	0.1	1,388	0.1	3,000	0.2
Other religionists	0	0.0	100	0.0	600	0.1	6	0	6	0.94	630	0.1	659	0.1	1,000	0.1
World A (unevangelized persons)	210,279	55.6	290,163	35.2	324,940	30.8	3,111	-6,539	-3,428	-1.11	322,484	29.0	290,156	25.1	269,892	19.6
World B (evangelized non-Christians)	41,320	10.9	237,343	28.8	391,060	37.1	3,743	6,019	9,762	2.25	429,932	38.7	488,690	42.3	617,108	44.8
World C (Christians)	126,600	33.5	296,820	36.0	339,000	32.1	3,295	520	3,815	1.07	359,600	32.3	377,154	32.6	490,000	35.6
Country's population	**378,200**	**100.0**	**824,327**	**100.0**	**1,055,000**	**100.0**	**10,149**	**0**	**10,149**	**0.92**	**1,112,017**	**100.0**	**1,156,000**	**100.0**	**1,377,000**	**100.0**

COLUMNS, ROWS.
For meanings and definitions, see Codebook (Part 3). Note that, by definition, total 'Christians' = professing + crypto-Christians, which also = affiliated + unaffiliated Christians, and also = Great Commission Christians + latent Christians. Percentages may not always total exactly, due to rounding.

CENSUSES.
1881. 56.6% Hindus, 30.0% Roman Catholics, 9.9% Muslims, 1.5% Protestants, 1.0% Anglicans, 0.9% Buddhists, 0.1% Parsis. **1891:** 56.5% Hindus, 31.2% Roman Catholics, 9.4% Muslims, 1.0% Protestants, 1.0% Anglicans, 0.9% Buddhists. **1901** (excluding foreign military personnel): 55.0% Hindus, 31.2% Roman Catholics, 11.0% Muslims, 0.9% Protestants, 0.9% Anglicans, 0.9% Buddhists. (The figures for 1900 in the above table are adjusted to 1900 and to include 2,313 foreign military personnel). **19.VI.1952:** 47.0% Hindus (41.1% self-termed Sanatanists, 5.6% Arya Samajists), 34.6% Roman Catholics, 15.0% Muslims (1.3% Ahmadis), 1.5% Buddhists, 1.0% Anglicans, 0.5% Protestants, 0.2% nonreligious, 0.2% Chinese folk-religionists, 0.1% marginal Protestants. **30.VI.1962** (including European military): 47.6% Hindus (23.0% self-termed Sanatanists, 13.7% Arya Samajists), 33.8% Roman Catholics, 15.8% Muslims, 1.0% Anglicans, 0.9% Buddhists, 0.5% Protestants, 0.2% Chinese folk-religionists, 0.1% Baha'is, 0.1% nonreligious. **30.VI.1972:** 49.7% Hindus (30.4% self-termed Sanatanists, 11.8% Arya Samajists), 33.3% Christians (31.8% Roman Catholics, 0.8% Anglicans, 0.7% Protestants, 0.1% marginal Protestants), 16.1% Muslims, 0.6% Buddhists, 0.1% Baha'is, 0.1% nonreligious. **1990:** 50.8% Hindus, 32.3% Christians (27.2% Roman Catholics, 4.5% Protestants, 0.4% Anglicans, 0.2% Marginal Christians), 16.3% Muslims, 0.3% Buddhists, 0.2% nonreligious, 0.1% Baha'is.

NOTES ON RELIGIONS
ATHEISTS. Mauritian Communist Party (MCP) (legal): membership very small.
BAHA'IS. Growth from 18 local spiritual assemblies (1964) to 57 (1973), and to 141 LSAs (1995). Many are Indians converted from Hinduism.
BUDDHISTS. Chinese.
COUNTRY'S POPULATION. There has been heavy emigration since 1966, mainly of Catholics leaving for Australia.
CRYPTO-CHRISTIANS. As always in a majority non-Christian society, a small number of Christians affiliated to churches are recorded in government censuses as, or are regarded as, or profess in those censuses to be (for family or employment reasons), non-Christians (in this case Hindus).
HINDUS. 75% Sanatanists (Orthodox, or idol-worshippers), with (in 1956) 178 temples (48 Northern Hindu, 2 Marathi, 25 Telugu, 103 Tamil), and 25% Arya Samaj (Reform) (of whom over 90% are Northern Hindu). Hare Krishna (ISKCON) has 1 centre, the Ramakrishna Mission others.
MARGINAL CHRISTIANS. In the 1901 census, 138 adherents of the New Jerusalem Church were recorded; in the 1990 census, 1,663 Jehovah's Witnesses.
MUSLIMS. Mainly Indians; 88.9% Urdu-speaking Sunnis (82% Hanafite, 6.9% Shafiite), 0.8% Shias, 0.3% Bohras, 10.0% adherents of Ahmadiya. Begun in 1915; Qadianis (the main body in Pakistan), with a small Lahori faction. There are 6 mosques, and considerable proselytizing activity with many converts claimed (the latter enumerated here under Muslims, though declared non-Muslim by Pakistan). Hajj pilgrims to Mecca. (1975) 214; (1976) 315.
NONRELIGIOUS. Largely Chinese abandoning traditional folk religion.
OTHER RELIGIONISTS. Including Rosicrucians (1 AMORC centre).
PENTECOSTALS/CHARISMATICS. The Catholic Charismatic Renewal began in 1975, with by 1998 a sizeable percentage of baptized Catholics participating. There are many committed members of covenant communities.
ROMAN CATHOLICS. Declining since 1960 by emigration, largely to Australia. The column 'Natural change' includes about 650 Catholic emigrants a year.

Great Commission Instrument Panel: status of Mauritius (for explanation see start of Part 4)

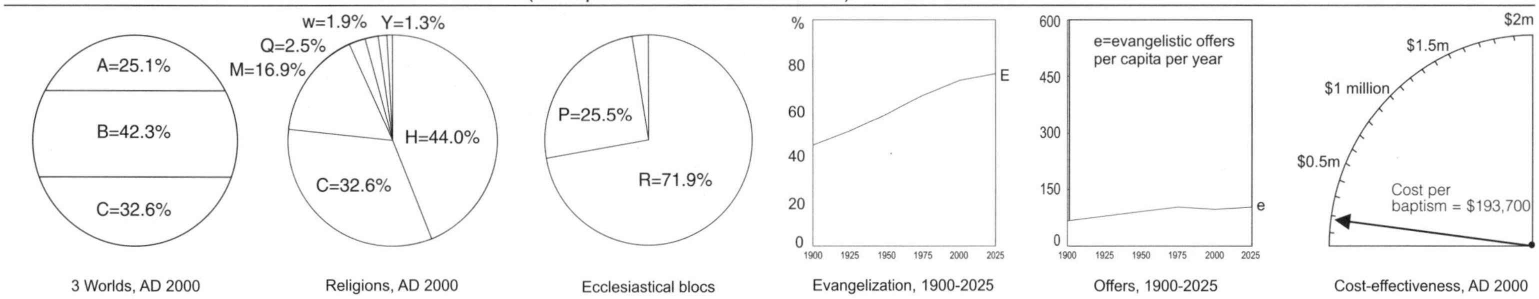

Country status. Mauritius is a group of islands in the Indian Ocean, about 500 miles to the east of Madagascar. Its economy is almost entirely dependent on sugar.

HUMAN LIFE AND LIBERTY

Human need and development. Although small, Mauritius stands out among African countries as one of the most progressive with its rating in many quality of life indicators comparable to those of developed countries. Its per capita GNP of $3,380 is growing at the rate of 6.1%. Life expectancy is a high 73, the literacy rate is 82%, infant mortality rate is only 14 per 1,000 live births, the population per physician is 1,180, and primary school enrollment is virtually complete. The population is split among a number of ethnic groups, yet there is little ethnic animosity. The economy is anchored by tourism and sugarcane.

Human environment. Like Madagascar, its closest neighbor, Mauritius has many unique endemic plants and animals, but they are endangered as a result of illegal logging and deforestation. Rapid economic development has also led to the overuse of pesticides and fertilizers in agriculture and chemicals in industries. Coastal waters are threatened by untreated wastewater and sewage.

NON-CHRISTIAN RELIGIONS

Hinduism is the principal religion of Mauritius, the professed faith of 44% of the population. Hindus can be divided into 2 groups: Sanatanists (Orthodox, or idol-worshipper) and Arya Samaj (Reform). The latter, present in Mauritius since 1913, number over 100,000. They do not frequent temples and they use simplified rites. Many Hindus however participate in the ceremonies and activities of both groups. In 1956, there were 48 temples for northern Indians, 25 for Telugus and 103 for Tamils, although northern Indians are more numerous. By 1954 the rural Hindus had established 416 *baitkas* (sitting-places) which are religious and mutual aid societies, used for religious conferences and teaching courses in Indian languages. In cities, the baitkas are generally replaced by clubs. The caste system is less complex than in India and can be reduced to 2 principal classes: the 'great nations',

Country summary. **Worlds A, B, C by ethnolinguistic peoples, ,and major civil divisions in Mauritius.**

	PEOPLES							CITIES							CIVIL DIVISIONS						
World	Num	Pop 2000	C%	Christians	E%	U%	Unevangelized	Num	Pop 2000	C%	Christians	E%	U%	Unevangelized	Num	Pop 2000	C%	Christians	E%	U%	Unevangelized
A	1	4,626	0.11	5	44	56	2,586	0	0	0.00	0	0	0	0	0	0	0.00	0	0	0	0
B	18	828,861	8.58	71,102	65	35	287,887	1	472,752	40.10	189,574	85	15	70,818	11	1,156,497	31.94	369,432	75	25	290,719
C	5	323,009	92.36	298,323	100	0	246	0	0	0.00	0	0	0	0	0	0	0.00	0	0	0	0
Total	**24**	**1,156,496**	**31.94**	**369,430**	**75**	**25**	**290,719**	**1**	**472,752**	**40.10**	**189,574**	**85**	**15**	**70,818**	**11**	**1,156,497**	**31.94**	**369,432**	**75**	**25**	**290,719**

including the priestly caste of the Marazes and the old warrior caste of the Baboojee; and the 'little nations' where are gathered the old servile castes. In between one finds a middle class or bourgeoisie composed of those who have acquired property or high governmental positions. There are no pariahs (untouchables).

Hindus. Cavadee festival procession, Port Louis: penitent, bodies pierced with needles, walk toward temple.

Islam is primarily of Indian origin, about 15% of the population considering itself Muslim. Although Muslims come from different parts of India, 90% are Sunnis whose common language is Urdu. The remaining 10% belong to the Ahmadiya Muslim Mission, considered heretical by Sunnis, plus some descendants of merchants of Surat and Gujarat on the northwestern coast of India. Speaking Gujarati, they belong to 2 different sects: Dutchi Maiman and Sunni Surti. Their imams are trained at the Jummah mosque in Port-Louis, but some continue to come from abroad in which case they often do not know English.

Buddhism is still practiced by a few aged Chinese, but is tending to disappear.

Chinese folk-religionists now account for 1.3% of the population due to its popularity among Sino-Mauritians.

CHRISTIANITY

CATHOLIC CHURCH. Lazarist Fathers began the evangelization of Mauritius in 1722, which they then carried on for nearly a century. In 1819 the work was given to the Benedictines and Port-Louis was made the center of a vicariate which included Madagascar, South Africa, and Australia until 1837 and the Seychelles and St Helena until 1852. In 1847 Port-Louis was made a diocese, and the first Holy Ghost (CSSp) and Jesuit priests appeared after the middle of the century. The Catholic Church counts in its membership about 27% of the total population of the territory, including 98% of Rodriguez Island. Catholics are 60% urban, and there are a disproportionate number of Catholic emigrants, mostly to Australia. In recent years there has developed inter-island collaboration between the 3 dioceses of the Seychelles, Reunion, and Mauritius, in the areas of pastoral work, catechesis, and mass-media communications. These exchanges, which require a new style of pastoral endeavor with certain tasks done co-operatively, undoubtedly are having their effect on the mentality of the clergy and are helping to create new forms of ministry.

The Holy See has diplomatic relations with Mauritius and in AD 2000 is represented to government and the Catholic hierarchy by a pro-nuncio residing in Tananarive, Madagascar.

OTHER CHURCHES. The Church of God (Cleveland) first entered Mauritius in 1983 and by 1990 had 43 congregations and 18,000 members, making it the largest non-Catholic Christian community. Assemblies of God have also seen marked growth-from 800 members in 1970 to 75,900 by 1995. Anglicans first entered in 1810. The Anglican diocese of Mauritius is part of the Church of the Province of the Indian Ocean. The first Protestant missionaries to Mauritius were LMS in 1814, a work which is now incorporated into the Church of Scotland. Seventh-day Adventists, who belong to the Indian Ocean Union Mission, have built up 24 congregations and a substantive community since their arrival in 1914. Several small marginal Protestant groups are also active.

Indigenous missions. The number of missionaries sent out from Mauritius has been small and most have served in surrounding countries in Africa.

Catholic Church, Diocese of Port-Louis. Catholic parish at Curepipe.

CHURCH AND STATE

The constitution of Mauritius of March 1968, incorporated in the Mauritius Independence Order 1968, presents in detail in 5 paragraphs of Article 11 the multiple aspects of liberty of conscience recognized in the country, especially liberty of thought and of religion and the right to manifest and propagate one's belief and religion. Article 14 gives to any body or grouping, religious or not, the right to found and maintain schools at its own expense. In 1810, when Mauritius passed from French to British control, the Napoleonic concordat of 1801 was implicitly maintained by the English governor. Article 8 of the act of capitulation stipulated that all 'the religious establishments in the colony will be maintained with their privileges and revenues, without any change'; and the validity of this agreement was never contested by the colonial authorities. The independent state of Mauritius does not recognize explicitly the existence of a state religion in its constitution of 1968, and no other document recognizes any differences between the Catholic Church and other churches or religions. Nevertheless, the budget includes each year an allocation to the Catholic and Anglican churches under the headings 'personal emoluments' and 'other recurrent charges'. The Church of Scotland gets only the second of these. Under the title 'subsidization of religions', other registered religious associations also receive government funds. Religious matters are dealt with by the office of the prime minister.

BROADCASTING AND MEDIA

Mauritius is a member of UNDA. Catholics air 3 half-hour religious programs each Sunday and 2 other programs during the week. A half-hour weekly program is prepared especially for Rodrigues Island. During Lent, an additional 30 minute program is broadcast. Religious news from Radio Vatican is also broadcast. Shortwave programs in Creole and French can be received from FEBA (Seychelles). Shortwave radio programs from KNLS have generated responses. Christian television programming can be viewed via satellite.

INTERDENOMINATIONAL ORGANIZATIONS

A Mixed Committee, composed of ecclesiastical and lay representatives of the Ecumenical Commission of the Catholic Church, the Church of England and the Church of Scotland, meets 4 times yearly for discussion and prayer. A conference and spiritual retreat center in the south of the island, called Centre Unita, is directed by a Catholic priest but serves all religions and churches. In 1974 on the island of Rodrigues, the Catholic and Anglican colleges joined to form one ecumenical institution, Rodrigues College, with 400 students.

Mauritius is unusual in having a multi-religious council, the Mauritius Interreligious Committee (Comité Interreligieux Mauricien), also known as World Fraternal Solidarity (Solidarité Fraternelle Mondiale). It is composed of representatives of 17 churches and religious groups, including the Catholic, Anglican, Presbyterian, Adventist, and Christian Science churches, and the principal Hindu and Muslim associations. Its aim is the promotion of contacts, understanding, and peace among Mauritians.

FUTURE TRENDS AND PROSPECTS

Muslims and Hindus, representing 60% of the population in 1970, will likely fall below 56% jointly before 2025. Christians are projected to decline from 36.0% in 1970 to 34.1% by AD 2025.

In the distant future it is possible that Christians could claim 40% of the population while Hindus and Muslims claim 35% and 20% respectively.

BIBLIOGRAPHY

2000 titres: littératures de l'océan indien: Comores, Madagascar, Maurice, Réunion, Seychelles. Notre Librairie, no. 116. [Paris: CLEF, 1994]. 174p.

A short history of Mauritius. P. J. Barnwell & A. Toussaint. London: Longmans, Green for the Government of Mauritius, 1949. 276p.

Annuaire du Diocèse de Port–Louis, 1971. Port-Louis, Ile Maurice, Mauritius: Evêché, 1971.

Approches de la pratique missionnaire catholique à l'Ile Maurice entre 1840 et 1895. D. Colson. Toulouse, France: University of Toulouse, 1980. 800p.

Bibliography of Mauritius (1502–1954). A. Toussaint & H. Adolphe. Port Louis, Mauritius: Mauritius Archives, 1956. 884p.

Blessed Jacques Laval: apostle of Mauritius. E. Cowper. London: Catholic Truth Society, 1984. 27p.

Catholic life. M. Dinan (ed). Port Louis, Mauritius: L'Union Catholique de l'Ile Maurice, 1930–. (Weekly).

Diocese of Mauritius (1810–1973). G. Emmanuel. , 1975. 367p.

Festivals of Mauritius. R. Ramdoyal. Rose Hill, Mauritius: Editions de l'Océan Indien, 1990. 169p.

Festivals, religious practices, and traditions of Telugus in Mauritius. R. Sokappadu. N.p., 1992. 64p.

Hindi in Mauritius. S. Bhuckory. 2nd ed. Rose Hill, Mauritius: Editions de l'Océan Indien, 1988. 147p.

Hindu festivals in Mauritius. C. S. Seewoochurn. *Festivals in Mauritius.* Quatre Bornes, Mauritius: Editions Capucines, 1995. 159p.

Historical dictionary of Mauritius. S. Selvon & L. Rivière. 2nd ed. *African historical dictionaries*, no. 49. Metuchen, NJ: Scarecrow Press, 1991. 285p.

History of the Muslims in Mauritius. M. Emrith. Vacoas, Mauritius: Editions Le Printemps, 1994. 387p.

Le mouvement Ahmadiyya dans l'Islam. H. M. B. Ahmad. Port Louis, Mauritius: Ahmadiyya Association of Mauritius, 1964. 86p.
L'Eglise à Maurice 1810–1841. A. Nagapen. Port Louis, Mauritius: Port Louis Diocese, 1984. 454p.
Les îles de l'Océan indien: Comores, Madagascar, Maurice, Réunion, Seychelles: bibliographie réalisée à partir de la Banque de données IBISCUS, triée par grands domaines. P. Hue. *Collection Réseaux documentaires sur le développement, Série Références bibliographiques.* Paris: Ministère de la coopération et du développement, [1991]. 285p.
Les pratiques, rites et croyances de la religion populaire chinoise: 25 ans de la mission catholique chinoise à l'Ile Maurice. La mission catholique chinoise de l'Ile Maurice. Port Louis, Mauritius: The Author, 1975. 56p.
L'Islam à Maurice. R. N. Gassita. Paris: Ernest Leroux, 1913. 44p.
Mauritius. P. R. Bennett. *World bibliographical series*, vol. 140. Oxford, UK: CLIO Press, 1992. 179p.
Problems of Muslims in Mauritius. G. Beegun. Port Louis: [The Mauritius Urdu Academy, 1968]. 36p.
The Indian Christian community in Mauritius. A. Nagapen. Port Louis, Mauritius: Roman Catholic Diocese of Port Louis/Mahatma Handhi Institute, 1984. 25p.
The Mauritian kaleidoscope: languages and religion. M. Dinan. Port Louis, Mauritius: Best Graphics, 1986. 74p.
'The Mauritian Muslim family in transition structural and ideological changes: a cultural diffusion approach.' M. S. Rajah. Ph.D. dissertation, University of California, San Diego, 1987. 342p.
The Muslims in Mauritius. M. Emrith. Goodlands, Mauritius: Regent Press, 1966. 172p.
The religion and culture of Indian immigrants in Mauritius and the effect of social change. K. Hazareesingh. Port Louis, Mauritius: Indian Cultural Association, 1966.

Country Table 2. **Organized churches and denominations in Mauritius.**

Official name (bold type = church with over 10% of all affiliated) 1	*Begun* 2	*Type* 3	*Counc* 4	*Congs* 5	*Adults* 6	*Affiliated 1970* 7	*Affiliated 1995* 8	*G%* 9	*Names, notes, and other statistics* (see Codebook, Part 3) 10
Anglican Church: D Mauritius	1810	A-Hig	Aw.Vh	21	3,380	8,000	5,200	-1.71	1973, in Ch of the Province of the Indian Ocean, Poverty, cyclones. 10n,10x,2r,1s.
Assemblies of God		P-Pe2	Z....	110	59,000	800	75,900	0.05	Assemblées de Dieu. M=AdD(France). On Mauritius and Rodriguez.
Baptist Association of Mauritius	1977	P-Bap	.....	1	116	–	232	5.56	M=FMB-SBC.
Catholic Church: D Port-Louis	1722	R-Lat	pxS.r	49	162,000	280,000	302,000	0.30	Includes Rodriguez Is. 98% RC. M=CSSp. C=3+2+7. (1990) 57n,32x,61m,277w,6186Yy.
Chinese Christian Fellowship of M	c1960	I-Non	.....	6	300	100	500	6.65	Chinese in nondenominationalist grouping.
Church of Christ		I-Dis	x....	11	280	500	560	0.05	Eglise du Christ. M=CC(Non-Instrumental) (USA). Rose Hill. 1p(12) (Indian Ocean BS).
Church of Christ, Scientist		m-Sci	x...h	1	10	40	20	0.05	Christian Science. M=CCS(Boston, USA). Rose Hill Society.
Church of God (Cleveland)	1983	P-Pe3	.....	43	9,000	–	18,000	8.33	M=CoG(Cleveland).
Ch of Jesus Christ of Latter-day Saints	c1985	m-LdS	.....	2	140	–	200	10.00	*Mormons.* M=CJCLdS.
Church of the New Jerusalem	c1850	m-Swe	x....	1	15	100	30	-4.70	Swedenborgian Ch. M=GCNJ(South Africa, USA). Decline from 140 adherents in 1900.
Dutch Reformed Church	c1975	P-Ref	.....	1	60	–	100	5.00	Members of DRC (South Africa).
Evangelical Church of Mauritius	1968	P-Eva	.....	3	300	80	600	8.39	M=AEF.
Jehovah's Witnesses	1933	m-Jeh	x....	13	904	1,500	2,100	1.35	Association Les Témoins de Jehovah. IBSA Rose Hill. Hindi, Telugu, Tamil.(1975)49Y.(1995)43Y.
New Apostolic Church	c1980	I-3aX	.....	5	100	–	142	6.67	*NAC.* M=Neuapostolische Kirche. HQ Zurich (Switzerland).
Pentecostal Church		I-3pA	.....	15	1,000	700	2,000	0.05	English-speaking Pentecostals on both Mauritius and Rodriguez.
Presbyterian Church of Mauritius	1814	P-Ref	Rwc.h	5	500	1,000	1,000	0.00	*Eglise Reformée Indépendante de l'Ile Maurice.* Ch of Scotland. 1814, M=LMS(UK).
Seventh-day Adventist Church	1914	P-Adv	x...h	24	1,330	3,000	2,658	-0.48	SDA, Mauritius Mission, Indian Ocean Union Mission, 4nx,34mw,1r,13t(1141),109Y.
Sino-Mauritian Evangelical Church	1975	I-Hol	.....	1	30	–	75	5.00	Holiness independents of Chinese-Mauritian background.
United Pentecostal Church	1982	P-Pel	.....	14	1,170	–	2,600	7.69	M=UPC(USA).
Voice of Deliverance Church	c1975	I-3pA	.....	1	150	–	300	5.00	*Eglise de la Voix de la Délivrance.* Schism ex AoG.
Other Protestant denominations		P-	.....	10	500	1,000	1,000	0.05	Total about 5 (see list below), including FJKMK,FLM.
Doubly-affiliated		2-aff			-36,600	0	-63,217		Evangelicals who are also baptized Roman Catholics.
Totals				**337**	**203,685**	**296,820**	**352,000**		

Churches, members, growth, 1900-2025	*Congs*	*Adults*	*Affiliated*	*G%*	*Total denominations*	*6 Megablocs:* O	R	A	P	I	m
Total churches, members, and denominations (mid-1900)	40	70,300	126,600	1.22	4	0	1	1	1	0	1
Total churches, members, and denominations (mid-1970)	139	164,772	296,820	1.22	14	0	1	1	6	3	3
Total churches, members, and denominations (mid-1990)	210	192,000	331,600	0.56	25	0	1	1	13	6	4
Total churches, members, and denominations (mid-1995)	337	203,685	352,000	1.20	25	0	1	1	13	6	4
Total churches, members, and denominations (mid-2000)	380	214,000	369,432	0.97	25	0	1	1	13	6	4
Total churches, members, and denominations (mid-2025)	500	272,000	470,000	0.97	59	0	1	1	20	30	7

NOTES ON TABLE ABOVE
NATIONAL COUNCILS (Column 4, 5th letter).
h = Mauritius Inter-Religious Committee/Comité Inter-religieux Mauricien (World Fraternal Solidarity); its 17 members also include the Catholic Church, and Hindu and Muslim associations.
r = attached to Conférence Episcopale de Madagascar (Episcopal Conference of Madagascar).
OTHER PROTESTANT DENOMINATIONS. Including: Africa Evangelical Fellowship (1969), Christadelphian Ecclesias, Methodist Ch, Mission Salut et Guérison (on Rodriguez).

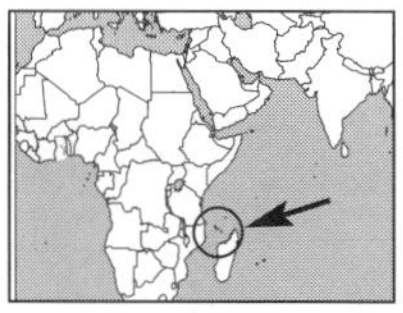

MAYOTTE

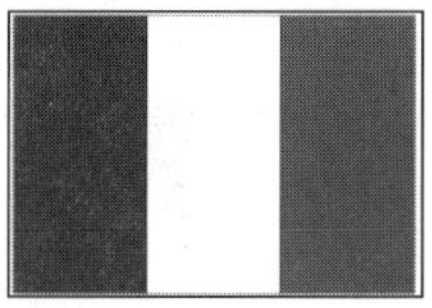

SECULAR DATA, AD 2000

STATE
Official name: Le Département de Mayotte (The Territorial Collectivity of Mayotte).
Short name: Mayotte. **Adjective of nationality:** of Mayotte.
Flag: That of France.
Area: 373 sq. km. (144 sq. mi.).
Government: Overseas department of France, since 1976 (1843 annexed by France, 1886 part of Comoros, 1975 secession)
Legislature: General Council 17 members.
Official language: French (Français).
Monetary unit: 1 French franc (F) = 100 centimes. **US$1=** F 5.60.
Chief cities: MAMOUNDZOU 12,500.
Political divisions: 2 provinces.

DEMOGRAPHY
Population: 102,000.
Population density: 272.4/sq. km. (705.7/sq. mi.).
Under 15 years: 43,000.
Growth rate p.a.: 2.64% (births 34.81, deaths 8.41).
Mortality: Infant, per 1,000: 67.0, ; **Maternal per 100,000:** 600.0.
Life expectancy: 61 (male 59, female 62).
Household size: 4.9. **Floor area per person, sq.m:** 8.0.
Major languages: French, Swahili, Arabic, French Creole, Malagasy.
Urban dwellers: 33.23%. **Urban growth rate p.a.:** 2.00%.
Labor force: 29%.

ETHNOLINGUISTIC PEOPLES
92.3% Comorian (Mauri,Mahorais); 3.2% Swahili; 1.7% French; 1.0% Makua (Makhua); 0.6% Makonde.

ECONOMY
National income p.a. per person: US$600; **per family:** US$2,941.

EDUCATION
Adult literacy: 91% (male 95%, female 87%). **Schools:** 95.
Universities: 1. **School enrolment:** female/male: 40%/40%.

HEALTH
Access to health services: 50%. **Access to safe water:** 60%.
Hospitals: 2 (11 beds per 10,000). **Doctors:** 9.
Blind: 80. **Deaf:** 6,100. **Murder rate:** 11.
Lepers: 200.

LITERATURE
New book titles p.a.: 10 (100 p.a. per million). **Periodicals:** 0.
Newspapers: 0 dailies.

COMMUNICATION (per 1,000 people)
Phones: 48 (15% mobile). **Radios:** 427. **TV sets:** 1.
Daily newspaper circulation: 15. **Computers:** 2.

HUMAN LIFE AND LIBERTY (optimum condition=100.0%)
HDI: 49.3. **HSI:** 35.0. **HFI:** 20.0. **EFL:** 20.0.

Country status. Mayotte, administered by France, is a small group of islands in the Indian Ocean east of the Comoro Islands. Its chief exports are coffee, cinnamon, and copra.

HUMAN LIFE AND LIBERTY

Human rights and freedoms. These are as guaranteed and as strict as in metropolitan France.

NON-CHRISTIAN RELIGIONS

Islam, the predominant religion, dates back to Arab settlement 6 centuries ago. Muslims are Sunnis of the Shafiite rite.

CHRISTIANITY

Catholics are metropolitan French and Reunionese with some Malagasy. Mayotte is part of the apostolic administration of the Comoro Islands. Protestants are mostly Malagasy with a few French.

The Holy See has no diplomatic relations with Mayotte in AD 2000.

Indigenous missions. Christians, mainly expatriates, have not sent any missionaries to other countries.

CHURCH AND STATE

Since the secession of Mayotte in 1975, the island has, as a French territory, come under French law with its separation of church and state.

FUTURE TRENDS AND PROSPECTS

Christians are projected to grow from 0.8% of the population in 1970 to 2.6% by AD 2025.

Christianity could reach up to 5% of the population before AD 2050 if native Mayottens become Christians in significant numbers. Islam will likely dominate for the indefinite future.

BIBLIOGRAPHY

'An ethnography of the Mahorais (Mayotte, Comoro Islands).' J. Breslar. Ph.D. dissertation, University of Pittsburgh, Pittsburgh, PA, 1981. 3 vols
Bibliographie des Comores: sciences humaines. M. Girardin et al. Paris: Institut des langues et civilisations orientales, 1992. 49p.
Human spirits: a cultural account of trance in Mayotte. M. Lambek. *Cambridge studies in cultural systems*, 6. Cambridge, UK: Cambridge University Press, 1981. 238p.
La vie quotidienne à Mayotte, archipel des Comores. S. Blanchy. *Repères pour Madagascar et l'océan Indien.* Paris: L'Harmattan, 1990. 239p.
'Spirit possession/spirit succession: aspects of social continuity among Malagasy speakers in Mayotte,' M. Lambek, *American ethnologist*, 15 (November 1988), 710–31.
'The practice of Islamic experts in a village on Mayotte,' M. Lambek, *Journal of religion in Africa/Religion en Afrique*, 20 (February 1990), 20–40.

Country Table 1. Religious adherents in Mayotte, AD 1900-2025.

Name	1900 Adherents	%	1970 Adherents	%	mid-1990 Adherents	%	Annual change, 1990-2000 Natural	Conversion	Total	Rate	mid-1995 Adherents	%	mid-2000 Adherents	%	mid-2025 Adherents	%
Muslims	9,970	99.7	42,640	99.2	75,250	96.5	2,330	-13	2,317	2.72	87,240	96.9	98,415	96.5	180,100	96.3
Christians	**30**	**0.3**	**360**	**0.8**	**1,600**	**2.1**	**49**	**13**	**62**	**3.34**	**1,900**	**2.1**	**2,222**	**2.2**	**4,900**	**2.6**
PROFESSION																
professing Christians	**30**	**0.3**	**360**	**0.8**	**1,600**	**2.1**	**49**	**13**	**62**	**3.34**	**1,900**	**2.1**	**2,222**	**2.2**	**4,900**	**2.6**
AFFILIATION																
unaffiliated Christians	0	0.0	0	0.0	310	0.4	10	-5	5	1.39	342	0.4	356	0.4	400	0.2
affiliated Christians	**30**	**0.3**	**360**	**0.8**	**1,290**	**1.7**	**40**	**18**	**58**	**3.76**	**1,558**	**1.7**	**1,866**	**1.8**	**4,500**	**2.4**
Roman Catholics	30	0.3	260	0.6	880	1.1	27	11	38	3.62	1,050	1.2	1,256	1.2	3,000	1.6
Protestants	0	0.0	100	0.2	250	0.3	8	2	10	3.42	300	0.3	350	0.3	800	0.4
Independents	0	0.0	0	0.0	100	0.1	3	3	6	4.81	130	0.1	160	0.2	400	0.2
Marginal Christians	0	0.0	0	0.0	60	0.1	2	2	4	5.24	78	0.1	100	0.1	300	0.2
Trans-megabloc groupings																
Evangelicals	0	0.0	30	0.1	80	0.1	2	2	4	4.14	101	0.1	120	0.1	300	0.2
Pentecostals/Charismatics	0	0.0	20	0.1	125	0.2	4	4	8	4.81	163	0.2	200	0.2	500	0.3
Great Commission Christians	**30**	**0.3**	**250**	**0.6**	**660**	**0.9**	**20**	**7**	**27**	**3.48**	**790**	**0.9**	**929**	**0.9**	**2,400**	**1.3**
Ethnoreligionists	0	0.0	0	0.0	550	0.7	17	-1	16	2.60	630	0.7	711	0.7	1,200	0.6
Nonreligious	0	0.0	0	0.0	200	0.3	6	1	7	3.12	230	0.3	272	0.3	800	0.4
World A (unevangelized persons)	9,900	99.0	34,388	80.0	50,700	65.0	1,567	-587	980	1.79	56,250	62.5	60,486	59.3	100,045	53.5
World B (evangelized non-Christians)	70	0.7	8,237	19.2	25,700	32.9	786	574	1,360	4.34	31,850	35.4	39,292	38.5	82,055	43.9
World C (Christians)	30	0.3	360	0.8	1,600	2.1	49	13	62	3.34	1,900	2.1	2,222	2.2	4,900	2.6
Country's population	**10,000**	**100.0**	**42,985**	**100.0**	**78,000**	**100.0**	**2,402**	**0**	**2,402**	**2.72**	**90,000**	**100.0**	**102,000**	**100.0**	**187,000**	**100.0**

COLUMNS, ROWS.
For meanings and definitions, see Codebook (Part 3). Note that, by definition, total 'Christians' = professing + crypto-Christians, which also = affiliated + unaffiliated Christians, and also = Great Commission Christians + latent Christians. Percentages may not always total exactly, due to rounding.

Great Commission Instrument Panel: status of Mayotte (for explanation see start of Part 4)

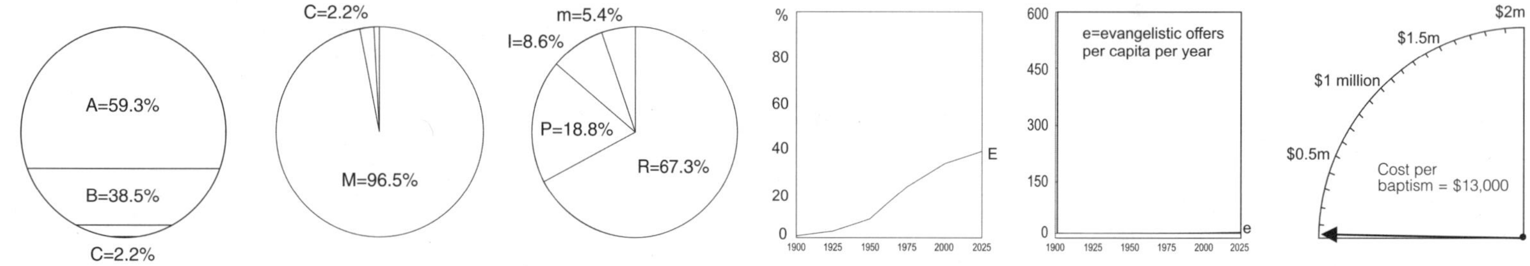

3 Worlds, AD 2000 — Religions, AD 2000 — Ecclesiastical blocs — Evangelization, 1900-2025 — Offers, 1900-2025 — Cost-effectiveness, AD 2000

Country summary. Worlds A, B, C by ethnolinguistic peoples, cities, and major civil divisions in Mayotte.

World	PEOPLES Num	Pop 2000	C%	Christians	E%	U%	Unevangelized	CITIES Num	Pop 2000	C%	Christians	E%	U%	Unevangelized	CIVIL DIVISIONS Num	Pop 2000	C%	Christians	E%	U%	Unevangelized
A	7	99,020	0.12	117	39	61	60,243	1	12,500	4.50	563	48	52	6,454	2	101,621	1.84	1,866	41	59	60,252
B	1	610	52.95	323	100	0	3	0	0	0.00	0	0	0	0	0	0	0.00	0	0	0	0
C	2	1,992	71.54	1,425	100	0	6	0	0	0.00	0	0	0	0	0	0	0.00	0	0	0	0
Total	**10**	**101,622**	**1.84**	**1,865**	**41**	**59**	**60,252**	**1**	**12,500**	**4.50**	**563**	**48**	**52**	**6,454**	**2**	**101,621**	**1.84**	**1,866**	**41**	**59**	**60,252**

Country Table 2. Organized churches and denominations in Mayotte.

Official name (bold type = church with over 10% of all affiliated) 1	Begun 2	Type 3	Counc 4	Congs 5	Adults 6	Affiliated 1970 7	Affiliated 1995 8	G% 9	Names, notes, and other statistics (see Codebook, Part 3) 10
Eglise Catholique (AA Comores)	1517	R-Lat	P.S.r	4	600	260	1,050	5.74	*Parish of Dzaoudzi* (begun 1845). French, Reunionese. M=OFMCap. 1x, 2m, 7w, 19Yy.
Eglise de Jésus-Christ aux Comores		P-Ref	.....	1	200	100	300	0.05	*EJCC.* Malagasy Protestants (seasonal workers, officials), French military. M=AIM.
Témoins de Jéhovah	1980	m-Jeh	.....	1	31	–	78	6.67	*Jehovah's Witnesses. Watch Tower.* Baptisms: 1Y.
Other Malagasy churches	1970	I-	.....	2	65	–	130	21.49	Malagasy immigrants and labor migrants, from 2 groupings.
Totals				**8**	**896**	**360**	**1,558**		

Churches, members, growth, 1900-2025	*Congs*	*Adults*	*Affiliated*	*G%*	*Total denominations*	*6 Megablocs:* O	R	A	P	I	m
Total churches, members, and denominations (mid-1900)	1	16	30	3.61	1	0	1	0	0	0	0
Total churches, members, and denominations (mid-1970)	4	190	360	3.61	2	0	1	0	1	0	0
Total churches, members, and denominations (mid-1990)	6	740	1,290	6.59	5	0	1	0	1	2	1
Total churches, members, and denominations (mid-1995)	8	896	1,558	3.85	5	0	1	0	1	2	1
Total churches, members, and denominations (mid-2000)	10	1,100	1,866	3.67	5	0	1	0	1	2	1
Total churches, members, and denominations (mid-2025)	20	2,600	4,500	3.58	16	0	1	0	7	5	3

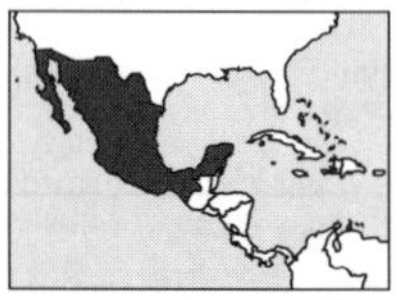

MEXICO

SECULAR DATA, AD 2000

STATE

Official name: Les Estados Unidos Mexicanos (The United Mexican States).
Short name: Mexico. **Adjective of nationality:** Mexican.
Flag: Green, white, and red bars; coat of arms in centre (eagle devouring serpent, and Aztec legend).
Area: 1,958,201 sq. km. (756,066 sq. mi.).
Government: Federal republic, since 1823 (1519 Spanish possession (New Spain), 1821 Independence as empire, 1823 republic).
Legislature: Congress: Senate, 128 members; Chamber of Deputies, 500 members.
Official language: Spanish (Español/Castella).
Monetary unit: 1 Mexican peso (Mex$) = 100 centavos. **US$1=** Mex$10.25.
Chief cities: CIUDAD DE MEXICO (Mexico City) 18,131,000; Guadalajara 3,908,000; Monterrey 3,416,000; Puebla 1,968,000.
Political divisions: 32 provinces.
Armed forces: 175,000.

DEMOGRAPHY

Population: 98,881,000.
Population density: 50.5/sq. km. (130.7/sq. mi.).
Under 15 years: 32,779,000.
Growth rate p.a.: 1.42% (births 22.17, deaths 5.07).
Mortality: Infant, per 1,000: 28.2, ; **Maternal per 100,000:** 110.0.
Life expectancy: 73 (male 70, female 76).
Household size: 5.1. **Floor area per person, sq.m:** 6.0.
Major languages: Spanish, English, Nahuatl, Maya, Otomí, Zapotec, Mixtec, Arabic, Chinese, Yiddish. There are in addition over 200 other Indian languages. Usage: 92.2% Spanish-speaking only, 5.6% bilingual Indian, 2.1% monolingual Indian (no Spanish).
Urban dwellers: 74.39%. **Urban growth rate p.a.:** 1.7%.
Labor force: 39%.

ETHNOLINGUISTIC PEOPLES

54.6% Mexican Mestizo; 15.0% Mexican White; 10.5% Detribalized Amerindian; 9.7% Part-Indian (Half-Indian); 0.8% Yucatec (Maya).

ECONOMY
National income p.a. per person: US$3,320; **per family:** US$16,932.

EDUCATION
Adult literacy: 89% (male 91%, female 87%). **Schools:** 112,624.
Universities: 13,000. **School enrolment:** female/male: 85%/86%.

HEALTH
Access to health services: 78%. **Access to safe water:** 83%.
Hospitals: 1,539 (10 beds per 10,000). **Doctors:** 149,432.
Blind: 60,000. **Deaf:** 5,932,900. **Murder rate:** 7.
Lepers: 40,000. **Underweight prevalence under 5:** 14%.

LITERATURE
New book titles p.a.: 8,900 (90 p.a. per million). **Periodicals:** 255.
Newspapers: 309 dailies.

COMMUNICATION (per 1,000 people)
Phones: 96 (25% mobile). **Radios:** 230. **TV sets:** 192.
Daily newspaper circulation: 113. **Computers:** 60.

REFUGEES
Alien refugees from other countries: 38,500.

HUMAN LIFE AND LIBERTY (optimum condition=100.0%)
HDI: 85.3. **HSI:** 47.0. **HFI:** 37.5. **EFL:** 33.0.

Country Table 1. **Religious adherents in Mexico, AD 1900-2025.**

Year	*1900*		*1970*		*mid-1990*		*Annual change, 1990-2000*				*mid-1995*		*mid-2000*		*mid-2025*	
Name	*Adherents*	*%*	*Adherents*	*%*	*Adherents*	*%*	*Natural*	*Conversion*	*Total*	*Rate*	*Adherents*	*%*	*Adherents*	*%*	*Adherents*	*%*
Christians	**13,493,600**	**99.2**	**49,602,000**	**98.0**	**80,254,500**	**96.4**	**1,509,633**	**-18,180**	**1,491,453**	**1.72**	**87,791,000**	**96.3**	**95,169,034**	**96.3**	**123,979,000**	**95.2**
PROFESSION																
professing Christians	**13,493,600**	**99.2**	**49,602,000**	**98.0**	**80,254,500**	**96.4**	**1,509,633**	**-18,180**	**1,491,453**	**1.72**	**87,791,000**	**96.3**	**95,169,034**	**96.3**	**123,979,000**	**95.2**
AFFILIATION																
unaffiliated Christians	1,089,800	8.0	1,851,696	3.7	1,404,500	1.7	26,419	-30,658	-4,239	-0.31	1,396,000	1.5	1,362,107	1.4	479,000	0.4
affiliated Christians	**12,403,800**	**91.2**	**47,750,304**	**94.4**	**78,850,000**	**94.7**	**1,483,219**	**12,479**	**1,495,693**	**1.75**	**86,395,000**	**94.8**	**93,806,927**	**94.9**	**123,500,000**	**94.9**
Roman Catholics	12,380,200	91.0	47,028,524	93.0	78,070,000	93.8	1,468,514	1,486	1,470,000	1.74	85,500,000	93.8	92,770,000	93.8	121,200,000	93.1
Protestants	55,800	0.4	692,126	1.4	2,600,000	3.1	48,907	19,093	68,000	2.35	2,967,213	3.3	3,280,000	3.3	5,500,000	4.2
Independents	0	0.0	1,178,662	2.3	2,350,000	2.8	44,204	10,796	55,000	2.13	2,612,880	2.9	2,900,000	2.9	5,200,000	4.0
Marginal Christians	1,800	0.0	212,432	0.4	1,580,000	1.9	29,720	7,280	37,000	2.13	1,770,150	1.9	1,950,000	2.0	3,600,000	2.8
Anglicans	5,000	0.0	8,881	0.0	149,800	0.2	2,818	982	3,800	2.29	163,900	0.2	187,800	0.2	260,000	0.2
Orthodox	1,000	0.0	54,000	0.1	87,000	0.1	1,636	-336	1,300	1.40	90,800	0.1	100,000	0.1	130,000	0.1
doubly-affiliated	-40,000	-0.3	-1,424,321	-2.8	-5,986,800	-7.2	-112,613	-26,794	-139,407	2.12	-6,709,943	-7.4	-7,380,873	-7.5	-12,390,000	-9.5
Trans-megabloc groupings																
Evangelicals	55,000	0.4	400,000	0.8	1,331,000	1.6	25,036	15,864	40,900	2.72	1,542,421	1.7	1,740,000	1.8	2,650,000	2.0
Pentecostals/Charismatics	0	0.0	1,260,000	2.5	10,650,000	12.8	200,329	39,671	240,000	2.05	11,967,772	13.1	13,050,000	13.2	19,000,000	14.6
Great Commission Christians	**410,000**	**3.0**	**2,023,000**	**4.0**	**4,161,000**	**5.0**	**78,269**	**17,976**	**96,245**	**2.10**	**4,648,000**	**5.1**	**5,123,454**	**5.2**	**8,800,000**	**6.8**
Nonreligious	10,160	0.1	838,900	1.7	2,451,100	3.0	46,106	15,676	61,782	2.27	2,769,900	3.0	3,068,920	3.1	5,170,000	4.0
Muslims	1,000	0.0	15,000	0.0	210,000	0.3	3,950	767	4,717	2.05	230,000	0.3	257,168	0.3	500,000	0.4
Jews	150	0.0	35,000	0.1	105,000	0.1	1,975	-275	1,700	1.51	112,400	0.1	122,001	0.1	130,000	0.1
Atheists	0	0.0	20,000	0.0	80,000	0.1	1,505	1,047	2,552	2.81	96,000	0.1	105,523	0.1	200,000	0.2
Ethnoreligionists	100,000	0.7	50,000	0.1	53,000	0.1	997	948	1,945	3.18	66,700	0.1	72,450	0.1	60,000	0.1
Baha'is	0	0.0	15,100	0.0	28,000	0.0	527	63	590	1.93	31,000	0.0	33,903	0.0	60,000	0.1
Buddhists	2,090	0.0	15,000	0.0	19,000	0.0	357	37	394	1.90	21,000	0.0	22,940	0.0	40,000	0.0
New-Religionists	0	0.0	1,000	0.0	9,000	0.0	169	-41	128	1.34	9,500	0.0	10,284	0.0	20,000	0.0
Chinese folk-religionists	0	0.0	3,000	0.0	8,500	0.0	160	-1	159	1.73	9,200	0.0	10,086	0.0	20,000	0.0
Hindus	0	0.0	0	0.0	5,400	0.0	102	-41	61	1.08	5,600	0.0	6,010	0.0	10,000	0.0
Other religionists	0	0.0	1,000	0.0	2,500	0.0	47	0	47	1.72	2,700	0.0	2,966	0.0	7,000	0.0
World A (unevangelized persons)	27,214	0.2	101,192	0.2	166,452	0.2	2,822	-3,030	-208	-0.14	182,290	0.2	197,762	0.2	260,392	0.2
World B (evangelized non-Christians)	86,485	0.6	893,008	1.8	2,805,048	3.4	53,073	21,210	74,283	2.28	3,171,981	3.5	3,514,204	3.5	5,956,608	4.6
World C (Christians)	13,493,600	99.2	49,602,000	98.0	80,254,500	96.4	1,509,633	-18,180	1,491,453	1.72	87,791,000	96.3	95,169,034	96.3	123,979,000	95.2
Country's population	**13,607,300**	**100.0**	**50,596,201**	**100.0**	**83,226,000**	**100.0**	**1,565,528**	**0**	**1,565,528**	**1.74**	**91,145,272**	**100.0**	**98,881,000**	**100.0**	**130,196,000**	**100.0**

COLUMNS, ROWS.
For meanings and definitions, see Codebook (Part 3). Note that, by definition, total 'Christians' = professing + crypto-Christians, which also = affiliated + unaffiliated Christians, and also = Great Commission Christians + latent Christians. Percentages may not always total exactly, due to rounding.

CENSUSES.
1900: 99.4% Roman Catholics, 0.4% Evangelicals, 0.2% nonreligious and pagans. **1910:** 99.2% Roman Catholics, 0.5% Evangelicals, 0.3% nonreligious, pagans and others. **1921:** 97.1% Roman Catholics, 0.5% Evangelicals, 0.8% nonreligious. **1930:** 97.7% Roman Catholics, 1.0% nonreligious and pagans, 0.8% Evangelicals, 0.3% other religionists. **1940:** 96.6% Roman Catholics, 2.3% nonreligious and pagans, 0.9% Evangelicals, 0.1% Jews, 0.2% other religionists. **6.VI.1950** (de jure): 98.2% Roman Catholics, 1.3% Evangelicals, 0.4% others religionists, 0.1% Jews. **8.VI.1960:** 97.1% Roman Catholics, 1.8% Evangelicals, 0.6% nonreligious, 0.3% Jews, 0.3% marginal Protestants. **28.I.1970** (de jure): 96.2% Roman Catholics, 1.8% Evangelicals (Protestants, Mexican indigenous, marginal Protestants, Anglicans), 1.6% nonreligious, 0.3% other religionists, 0.1% Jews. Exact interpretation and comparison of these censuses is difficult because the census term 'Evangélicos' includes Protestants, Anglicans, marginal Protestants and some Mexican indigenous, but some of the latter appear under other categories also ('Católicos', 'Otros', 'Ninguna').'Otra' is defined in the census as 'Islam, Buddhism, Taoism, Shinto, Confucianism, Brahmanism, Orthodoxy, etc'.

NOTES ON RELIGIONS
ATHEISTS. Partido Comunista de México (PCM) (legal; no longer pro-Soviet).
BAHA'IS. Rapid growth from 10 local spiritual assemblies (1964) to 96 (1973), followed by slow growth to 108 LSAs (1995). Converts include Seri and Tarahumara Indians.
BUDDHISTS. Chinese and Japanese; mainly in Lower California and Sonorá.
DOUBLY-AFFILIATED. The term covers those affiliated to, or claimed by, both the Catholic Church and also a church termed by the state Evangélica (Protestant, Mexican indigenous, Anglican or marginal Christian) or other church, i.e. baptized Catholics who have recently become Evangelicals or others. Because their statistics represent a duplication, they are shown in the table as a negative quantity (with a minus sign).
ETHNORELIGIONISTS. A small proportion of monolingual Amerindians in 100 tribes have resisted and still resist both Catholicism, christo-paganism and also Protestant missions; among them are 13,800 Huichols in western Mexico who eventually forced missions to give up and now live with their own culture and religion, and the Tepehuans of northern Mexico who in 1956 began a traditionalist fertility cult movement of reaction away from both christo-paganism and Mexican culture.
EVANGELICALS. The English term is used here in the sense understood within the churches (not as understood by the state), and embraces the following 4 groupings: (1) Conservative Evangelicals, namely all persons affiliated to Protestant denominations which are Conservative Evangelical in theology and emphasis, (2) Conciliar Evangelicals, within the non-Evangelical or conciliar Protestant denominations usually affiliated to the Ecumenical Movement, (3) Fundamentalists, namely all persons affiliated to Protestant denominations linked with the ICCC or other fundamentalist councils, and (4) Anglican (Episcopalian) Evangelicals. This definition excludes non-Protestant groupings such as the Mexican indigenous pentecostal churches.
INDEPENDENTS. In about 130 denominations in 1995 (see Table 2). The 1990 total above was obtained by totalling column 7 in Table 2 for the indigenous churches listed there (coded 'I' in column 3).
JEWS. Mostly in Mexico City. Ashkenazi and Sefardi synagogues, and one congregation of Indian Jews; 55% Yiddish-speaking Ashkenazi, 15% Spanish-speaking Sefardi, 10% Arabic-speaking.
MUSLIMS. Lebanese, Palestinian and Syrian Arab immigrants.
NEW-RELIGIONISTS. By 1995, 9,000 converts to the Japanese movement Nichiren Shoshu (Soka Gakkai).
OTHER RELIGIONISTS. Adherents of other non-Christian religions and syncretistic cults, including Rosicrucians (AMORC, 22 Lodges and centers), and Theosophists.
PENTECOSTALS/CHARISMATICS. Over 60% are in the Catholic Charismatic Renewal, begun in 1971 with (in June) one prayer group of 40 people in Mexico City. Totals (January 1974): 3,000 involved adults (over 15 years old) in 100 prayer groups; total charismatic community including children, 6,000. By mid-1975 there were 10,000 adults involved (20,000 total community). In January 1976, over 5,000 attended a National Day of Renewal in Mexico City; in 1978, 7,000 attended the national renewal conference in San Luis. In 1991, over 70,000 met in Azteque stadium. A recent CCR clergy retreat was attended by 700 priests and 53 bishops.
ROMAN CATHOLICS. Over 95% of Mexico's 2.1% monolingual Amerindians, and around 30% of the 5.6% bilingual Amerindians, still practice strong christo-paganism, which is the term usually given to their syncretistic folk-Catholicism as a religion combining 17th-century Spanish Catholicism with traditional Amerindian religion (in particular, Aztec and Mayan religious concepts and worldviews). At the same time, however, they remain baptized Roman Catholics, and are enumerated as such by the Catholic Church and also by the state and its census enumerators.

Great Commission Instrument Panel: status of Mexico (for explanation see start of Part 4)

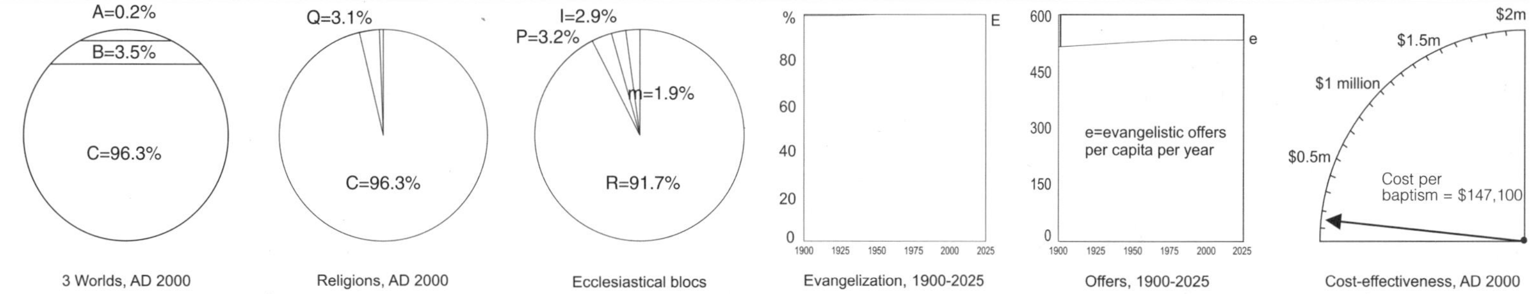

Country status. Mexico is located on the southern part of North America and extends like a cone to Central America. It is the largest Spanish-speaking nation in the world and the oldest nation in the Western Hemisphere. Its chief exports are coffee, cotton, and shrimp. Oil also plays an important role in the economy.

HUMAN LIFE AND LIBERTY

Human need and development. Mexico is characterized by very uneven economic and living conditions. About half the nation may be considered as slightly more advanced than Third World, and the other half as below or near Third World conditions. In the cities, especially in Mexico City, there are facilities and amenities comparable to those of the United States and Europe, while in rural villages life has changed only slightly since the Revolution and families live at subsistence level. The dichotomy between the 2 Mexicos makes it difficult to make generalizations. For example, there is a small rural elite with high incomes and consumption patterns and there is an urban poor who are worse off than their rural counterparts. In general labor is cheap, and even middle class people are able to maintain servants. Life is generally slower and less stressful than in industrialized countries. There is an extensive Social Security system, and its benefits are supple-

Country summary. **Worlds A, B, C by ethnolinguistic peoples, cities, and major civil divisions in Mexico.**

	PEOPLES						
World	Num	Pop 2000	C%	Christians	E%	U%	Unevangelized
A	4	111,320	0.89	987	45	55	61,548
B	4	685,248	45.61	312,570	94	6	40,664
C	270	98,084,795	95.32	93,493,369	100	0	45,705
Total	**278**	**98,881,363**	**94.87**	**93,806,926**	**100**	**0**	**147,917**

	CITIES						
World	Num	Pop 2000	C%	Christians	E%	U%	Unevangelized
A	0	0	0.00	0	0	0	0
B	0	0	0.00	0	0	0	0
C	132	56,508,258	93.09	52,601,908	100	0	131,171
Total	**132**	**56,508,258**	**93.09**	**52,601,908**	**100**	**0**	**131,171**

	CIVIL DIVISIONS						
World	Num	Pop 2000	C%	Christians	E%	U%	Unevangelized
A	0	0	0.00	0	0	0	0
B	0	0	0.00	0	0	0	0
C	32	98,881,289	94.87	93,806,927	100	0	147,917
Total	**32**	**98,881,289**	**94.87**	**93,806,927**	**100**	**0**	**147,917**

mented by a peculiarly Mexican institution known as the Civil Association. The closeness of the ties that bind the Mexican family has considerable welfare significance. Aged parents are cared for unquestioningly. The rate of child abandonment is far lower than in most other Latin American countries.

Human rights and freedoms. Although a democratic country, Mexico has a long history of human rights violations. Police brutality is widespread, and is often condoned by the ruling political party. There is a culture of impunity in which violators usually go unpunished. Several political and human rights activists are murdered every year. In rural states, violent disputes over land result in clashes in which many are killed. Paramilitary bands called madrinas and local police controlled by political bosses and landowners carry out their own brand of summary justice against their opponents. Torture is prohibited by the Constitution, yet it is used widely by the police to produce 'confessions'. Incidents of arbitrary arrest and imprisonment occur frequently, despite the constitutional provision of amparo, which is similar to habeas corpus. Judges are overly dependent on the executive for tenure, and therefore tend to bow to government pressure. Low pay and high caseloads also contribute to widespread corruption. Because of language and cultural barriers, poor Indians receive less justice than others. People who convert to the evangelical churches are expelled from their villages with the tacit permission of officials. There are no formal restrictions on the press, but government control of advertising budgets and under-the-counter payments to journalists significantly restrict expressions of dissent. Violence and threats against journalists are common as a means of muzzling them. The electoral system is designed to perpetuate the regime of the Institutional Revolutionary Party (PRI) which has been in power since 1929. To maintain their monopoly of power, PRI relies on extensive public patronage, the use of state funds and resources for party promotion, and plain electoral fraud. Indian groups remain outside the political and economic mainstream, but nevertheless support the PRI, and, in turn, are treated benevolently.

Human environment. Air, water, and land pollution are severe in all industrial areas, but particularly in and around Mexico City, which suffers from atmospheric inversions that trap smog, lead, and other toxic materials in the air. There are few environmental regulations, and lax controls and corruption enables polluters to go scot-free. There is a severe shortage of water because 85% of the water resources lie at altitudes of less than 1,600 feet, and yet more than half of Mexico's population and industry and much of its cropland are at higher altitudes.

Iglesia Catolica. French conservative schismatic, archbishop M. Lefebvre confirms hundreds of Oaxaca Indians.

NON-CHRISTIAN RELIGIONS

Traditional Indian religions retain a strong attraction for the more than 100 tribes in Mexico, each of which has its own distinctive language (Aztec, Ch'ol Sabanilla, Chamula, Huave, Mixteco, Otomi, Yaqui, Zinacanteco, et elia). The vast majority of all monolingual Indians still practice strong christo-paganism, namely a syncretistic folk-Catholicism combining 17th century Spanish Catholicism with traditional Amerindian religion, and in particular with Aztec and Mayan religious concepts and worldviews. A further small proportion of monolingual Indians including the Huichols and Tepehuans have resisted and still resist both Catholicism, christo-paganism and Protestant missions and retain their traditional religions.

Judaism is represented in Mexico by about 115,000 Jews who reside mostly in Mexico City. There are both Ashkenazi and Sefardi synagogues and also one congregation of Indian Jews. The principal Jewish co-ordinating organization is the Israelite Central Committee of Mexico (Comite Central Israelita de Mexico).

Baha'i has experienced rapid growth, from 15,000 followers in 1970 to 31,000 by 1995.

Islam also has followers, mostly immigrant Lebanese, Palestinian and Syrian Arabs.

Buddhism and other Asiatic religions are found among small groups of immigrant Asians in the northwestern part of the country in Lower California and Sonora.

Iglesia Católica en México. *Above.* At right, old Basilica of Our Lady of Guadalupe (dedicated 1709; accommodating 2,000 worshipers), north of Mexico City, which is rapidly tilting and subsiding into ground, to which came 500,000 pilgrims a year up to 1970; and (*left*) ultramodern new Basilica inaugurated 12 October 1976 in presence of half a million pilgrims from around the world, to which greatly increased crowds have since come (in 1976, 2 million). *Below.* Interior of new basilica during inaugural mass with 100 Mexican and other bishops present; it accommodates 20,000 people with visibility unobstructed by a single pillar.

CHRISTIANITY

CATHOLIC CHURCH. Amerigo Vespucci landed near Tampico in 1497, and the first Spanish settlers arrived in 1518. Franciscan missionaries came in 1522, soon followed by other religious orders. The first bishop was appointed in 1528, and by 1551 the University of Mexico had been founded. The Catholic Church has been the principal organized influence in Mexico for nearly 5 centuries. Today it is the major example of self-support and self-propagation of all the Catholic communities in Latin America, with the highest proportion of citizen personnel in the continent. The majority of the church's clergy are nationals. By 1974 there were 11 archdioceses, 48 dioceses and 7 other jurisdictions.

There are 26 diocesan or interdiocesan major seminaries in addition to a Mexican major seminary in New Mexico (USA) and a seminary for missionaries in Mexico. The work of catechists is being taken over increasingly by sisters, aided by young girls.

The religious attitudes and customs of Mexican Catholics are extremely varied, differing from region to region. Over 90% of the population are baptized Catholics; more than 80% have been confirmed and 77% married in the church.

Apart from christo-paganism among Amerindians, Mexican Catholicism among Mestizos also has syncretistic elements in it, of which one of the best-known is the cult of the Virgin of Guadalupe. From 9-12 December 1531, an Indian, Juan Diego, claimed visions of the Virgin Mary. Today this has grown into an intense and impassioned cult, a uniquely Mexican creation with a vast iconography, in which the Aztec worship of the earth goddess Cuauhtli (Coatlicue, or Tonantzin, Madre Antigua) has become fused with veneration of Virgin Mary (Madre Nueva, Madre Nuestra). Each year hundreds of thousands of pilgrims from across the world visit the shrine and basilica.

The Holy See has diplomatic relations with Mexico and in AD 2000 is represented to government and the Catholic hierarchy by a nuncio residing in Mexico City.

PROTESTANT CHURCHES. Protestant efforts began with the distribution of scriptures by the American Bible Society in 1824; but until the revolution of 1857 Mexico was virtually closed to Protestant missions. Juarez, the new president at that time, encouraged Protestant activities and several independent missionaries entered Monterrey during the late 1850s. Lutheran immigrants formed a German-speaking congregation in 1861, and the following year the first Baptist church was begun. Encouraged by their success, the American Baptist Home Mission Society established a station in 1870; and 2 years later American Board missionaries were also found in Monterrey and Guadalajara. American Presbyterians entered Mexico City in 1872 and the Methodists a year later. In 1901 the Presbyterian Synod of Mexico was formed and the autonomous Methodist Church of Mexico in 1930. The Southern Baptist Convention came to Mexico in 1880, its first Latin American field; and another important early arrival was the Seventh-day Adventist church in 1893.

The number of Protestant churches continued to grow until 1910 when anti-church laws, created to continue the government's attack on the Catholic Church, limited equally the activities of all the other churches. Many missions left. Membership in established Protestant churches fell noticeably during the next 25 years. In contrast, however, church groups originating during this period grew in membership.

A comity arrangement, agreed upon by 9 of the earliest missions in 1917 to prevent overlapping of effort, created bitterness as congregations were separated from their original sponsoring bodies. Several missions refused to observe the new lines of demarcation.

Since the mid-1930s, with greater social stability in Mexico and a shift in attitude of government and the Catholic Church towards Protestants, the number of Evangelicals (Evangelicos) or Protestants has increased. In one instance, the government attempted to eradicate them completely in the state of Tabasco in 1930; but 5 years later when the persecution ceased, there were twice as many Presbyterians as before.

The National Presbyterian Church increased eightfold between 1935 and 1960 and quadrupled again by 1990, making this the third largest Protestant denomination in Mexico today after Assemblies of God and Seventh-day Adventists. Presbyterianism is especially strong in the states of Chiapas and Tabasco. Of the many USA-based groups which have entered Mexico since World War II, some of the most significant gains have been registered by the Church of God (Anderson).

Pentecostalism was brought by Mexicans returning from the USA as early as 1915 and has grown very rapidly during the present century. Much of the growth of such Pentecostal groups as the Assemblies of God is due to strong leadership-training programs carried on in numerous Bible schools and to the fact that churches have been completely autonomous since their origin.

Work among the large Indian population of Mexico has been slow because of the over 100 different languages spoken by them. Wycliffe Bible Translators, with their main training center for Latin America in Mexico, has published portions of the Bible in many of these languages. The Mexican Indian Mission has trained 30 national evangelists in its Bible school. An aid in this work has been the Mission Aviation Fellowship which opened its first field in Mexico in 1946.

INDIGENOUS CHURCHES. Numerous independent churches, large and small, have developed in Mexico, particularly during the government persecution in the first third of this century. Some were started by migrant Mexican workers returning from the USA, while others are the result of local schisms. Most are pentecostal and are characterized by an apostolic and biblical faith built on the Catholic culture they inherited. The earliest, the Apostolic Church of the Faith in Jesus Christ, begun in 1914, has churches in all but one of Mexico's 29 states.

The largest of these churches is the Union of Evangelical Independent Churches, which began in 1923 and has its strength among the Otomi Indians.

The largest schism from Catholicism took place in 1926, leading to the formation of the Orthodox Catholic Apostolic Mexican Church, also known as the National Church.

Union de Iglesias Evangélicas Independientes. Otomî Indians (theological students under Rev. Ramundo Ramirez, center) redecorate rural Bible institute near pentecostal stronghold of Pachuca. This indigenous pentecostal church is the second largest denomination in Mexico.

OTHER CHURCHES. Two marginal Protestant bodies from the USA have built up large constituencies in Mexico during the present century, namely the Mormons and Jehovah's Witnesses who arrived respectively in 1879 and 1893. Mormons have had spectacular successes among Indians.

Three Eastern Orthodox groups are active, representing the Russian, Greek, and Antiochene traditions. The Russian Orthodox community is the largest and is an exarchate of the Orthodox Church in America (OCA).

The Episcopal Church traces its origins to 1857 as a mass secession from the Roman Catholic Church demanding ecclesiastical reforms, named Iglesia de Jesus and supported by several leading government officials. By 1865 there were 72 congregations, with over 7,000 members in Mexico City alone. Their appeal for bishops to the Episcopal Church in the USA met with interminable delays during which time the movement declined catastrophically before an Englishman was consecrated as the first bishop in 1879. Finally in 1904 the church became a missionary district of the Episcopal Church in the USA, with 34 Mexican and 27 English-speaking congregations, with 16 Mexican and 12 USA clergy.

Renewal movements. In the 1990s the Pentecostal/Charismatic Renewal continued to spread rapidly across most older churches, and numbered over 13,050,000 adherents (of whom 7% Pentecostals, 73% Charismatics, and 21% Independents).

Indigenous missions. Mexican Christians, both Roman Catholic and Protestant, have served in large numbers overseas, though most of these went to surrounding Latin American countries. Recently, some are targeting World A peoples in the Middle East and North Africa, as well as in Asia.

Tzeltal Christians at service for their first Old Testament translation, 1993.

CHURCH AND STATE

The federal constitution of the United States of Mexico, ratified in 1917, recognizes in Article 24 freedom of conscience and freedom of the practice of religion, both public and private. Nevertheless, the law recognizes no juridical personality for either the Catholic Church or other churches (Article 130). Building on this basic principle, a series of precise constitutional dispositions have been developed, tending to regulate the internal structure of the churches especially the Catholic Church, and to limit their function as social entities. (1) The religious ministry is considered as a profession, subject to regulation by the state. The government has the power to determine the maximum number of clergy and to authorize the opening of any place of worship. Clergy do not have the right to vote nor to participate in politics; they may not criticize in public or at religious meetings either the laws of the country or public authorities. Their right to inheritance is limited (Article 130). (2) The nation is assured complete control of all landed property that churches may hold in their own right or that of an intermediary. Churches thus do not have any property rights (Article 27). (3) All activities in education are forbidden to clergy and religious associations (Article 3). The establishment of monastic orders by any denomination for any purpose is also forbidden (Article 5).

These constitutional dispositions put into a general framework all the anti-clerical laws developed in Mexico after Independence in 1821. They testify to the violence and past scars of the struggle between the Catholic Church, which was the state religion until 1857, and the revolutionary forces which became victorious in 1910. Today the majority of these anti-clerical laws are rarely applied, but the legislation continues to exist. Relations between the state and the Catholic Church may therefore be interpreted as a kind of modus vivendi, translated in practice into peace-existence without reconciliation.

Since 1971 several bishops have publicly denounced institutionalized oppression and violence, and the modus vivendi has been placed in jeopardy by the move towards the right by government and towards the left by a section of the Catholic Church which includes several bishops as well as progressivist priests and laymen. Bishop Mendes Arceo of Cuernavaca has been considered the leader of this Latin American emphasis which has become known as Christians for Socialism.

In 1974 the Mexican parliament over, Catholic objections, adopted an education law which establishes state control over private schools and prohibits religious authorities from intervening in any way in any type of degree of education. The same law warns that the state may withdraw the licenses of private schools if they contravene Article 3 of the constitution prohibiting clergy and religious associations from involvement in educational activities.

BROADCASTING AND MEDIA

Daily programs produced by IBRA can be received from local radio stations in the United States and Mexico. There are 2 Catholic FM radio stations, and 13 Catholic university centers for media studies. Shortwave radio programs from KNLS, HCJB (Ecuador), TWR (Antilles), and AWR (Costa Rica) can also be received. Mexico is a member of UNDA.

CBN's *700 Club* can be seen on local television and cable channels on weekdays in the late afternoons and evenings. LeSEA programs can be seen on the World Harvest Satellite network.

INTERDENOMINATIONAL ORGANIZATIONS

The Evangelical Federation of Mexico (Federacion Evangelica de Mexico), begun in 1927, includes 13 churches, of which the largest is the Methodist Church. Also members of the federation are a number of interdenominational bodies including the National Anti-Alcoholic Association (Asociacion Nacional Antialcoholica), Audio-Visual Education Centre (Centro Audiovisual Educativo, CAVE), Christian Student Movement (Movimiento Estudiantil Cristiano), Evangelical Literature Committee (Comite de Literatura Evangelica), and National Union of Christian Women's Societies (Union Nacional de Sociedades Femeniles Cristianas).

A significant number of indigenous pentecostal churches are grouped in the Pentecostal Fraternal Association (Asociacion Fraternal de Iglesias Pentecostales, also known as the Asociacion Fraternal Pentecostes).

Catholic involvement in the ecumenical movement is maintained through the National Secretariat for Ecumenism (Secretariado Nacional de Ecumenismo), founded in 1963 under the name Centre for Christian Unity, which is dependent on the Episcopal Commission for the Doctrine of the Faith (Comision Episcopal para la Doctrina de la Fe).

The Centre for Ecumenical Studies (Centro de Estudios Ecumenicos), founded in 1969, provides for dialogue and co-operation between Catholics and Protestants, as well as sponsoring research and programs of social action.

FUTURE TRENDS AND PROSPECTS

Christians are projected to decline steadily through 2025 as the nonreligious, 1.7% in 1970, rise to over 4% by 2025.

Though Christianity is expected to predominate, the nonreligious could grow beyond 10% of the population by mid-21st century.

BIBLIOGRAPHY

'A guide for church planting in rural Mexico.' T. S. Puckett. D.Min. thesis, Dallas Theological Seminary, Dallas, TX, 1984. 400p.

A guide to Mexican witchcraft. W. Madsen & C. Madsen. *Minutiae Mexicana series.* Mexico City: Editorial Minutiae Mexicana, 1972. 96p.

'A strategy for planting churches in the Mexican context.' D. R. Kuiper. D.Min. thesis, Westminster Theological Seminary, Chestnut Hill, PA, 1990. 2 vols

'A study of the number, distribution and growth of the Protestant population in Mexico.' J. C. Bridges. Thesis, University of Florida, Gainesville, FL, 1969. 108p.

Anuario de la Iglesia en México, 1970. Mexico: Secretariado General del Episcopado, 1970.

Book of the gods and rites and the ancient calendar. D. Durán. Trans. and ed., F. Horcasitas & D. Heyden. *Civilization of the American Indian series,* no. 102. Norman, OK: University of Oklahoma Press, 1971. 502p.

'Christo–paganism: a study of Mexican religious syncretism,' W. Madsen. New Orleans: Middle American Research Institute, Tulane University, 1957. (Publication 19: 105-80).

Church growth in Mexico. D. A. McGavran, J. Huegel & J. Taylor. Grand Rapids, MI: Eerdmans, 1963. 136p. (Protestantism).

Directorio evangélico de la Ciudad de México, 1969–70. Mexico: CINCOMEX, 1970. 72p.

Directorio evangélico de México, 1970. Mexico City: Mexico Missionary Services, 1970.

El guadalupanismo mexicano. F. de la Maza. Mexico: Porrúa y Obregón, 1953. 130p. (Aztec/Catholic syncretism in the Guadalupe cult).

Encyclopedia of Mexico. M. Werner (ed). : Fitzroy Dearborn, 1997. 2 vols.

Evangelism and apostacy: the evolution and impact of evangelicals in modern Mexico. K. Bowen. Montreal: McGill-Queen's University Press, 1996. 288p.

La Iglesia en Méjico: estructuras eclesiásticas. R. Rama, I. Alonso & D. Garre. Fribourg: Feres, 1963. 119p. (Roman Catholic).

La serpiente y la paloma. M. Gaxiola. South Pasadena, CA: William Carey Library, 1970. 177p. (On IAFCJ indigenous church).

Los disidentes: sociedades Protestantes y revelución en México, 1872–1911. J. P. Bastian. Mexico: Fondo de Cultura Econoómica, 1989.

Mary, Michael and Lucifer: folk Catholicism in central Mexico. J. M. Ingham. *Latin American monographs*, no. 69. Austin, TX: Institute of Latin American Studies, University of Texas, 1986. 216p.

Mexican celebrations. E. Porter et al. Albuquerque, NM: University of New Mexico Press, 1990. 115p.

Mexican churches. E. Porter & E. Auerbach. Albuquerque, NM: University of New Mexico Press, 1987. 20. (Illustrated).

Mexican costume. C. Sayer. London: British Museum Publications, 1985. 240p.

Mexican folk toys: festival decorations and ritual objects. F. H. Pettit & R. M. Pettit. New York: Hastings House, 1978. 185p.

'Mexican popular religion: a way of spirituality.' F. González-Galarza. M.A. thesis, Catholic Theological Union, Chicago, 1990. 161p.

'Mexican Protestantism: the struggle for identity and relevance in a pluralistic society.' M. J. Gaxiola-Gaxiola. Ph.D. dissertation, University of Birmingham, 1989. 370p.

'Mexico,' *Pro Mundi Vita* (Brussels), 7 (1965).

Mexico. G. D. E. Philip. Rev. ed. *World bibliographical series*, vol. 48. Oxford, UK: CLIO Press, 1993. 196p. (See especially 'Religion,' p.72–4).

Mexico mystique: the coming sixth world of consciousness. F. Waters. Chicago: Sage Books, 1975. 326p. (Study of mythology and religious symbolism of Mexico).

Missionaries, miners, and Indians: Spanish contact with the Yaqui nation of Northwestern New Spain, 1533–1820. E. H. Hart. Tuscon, AZ: University of Arizona Press, 1981. 152p.

Mito y magia del mexicano. J. Carrión. Mexico: Porrúa y Obregón, 1952. 104p.

Mormons in Mexico: the dynamics of faith and culture. F. L. Tullis. Logan, UT: Utah State University Press, 1987. 286p.

'Pagan and Christian concepts in a Mexican Indian culture,' W. L. Wonderly, *Practical anthropology*, 5, 5-6 (1958), 197–202. (Review of W. Madsen, *op. cit.*).

'Peyote: giver of visions,' R. Shonle, *American anthropologist*, 27 (1925), 53–75. (Peyote cult in Mexico and Oklahoma; bibliography).

Protestantismo y sociedad en México. J. P. Bastian. Mexico: CUPSA, 1983.

Protestants and the Mexican revolution: missionaries, ministers, and social change. D. J. Baldwin. Chicago: University of Illinois Press, 1990.

Religious aspects of the conquest of Mexico. C. S. Brader. New York: AMS Press, 1966. 344p.

River of light. Worcester, PA: Gateway Films. (2 videocassettes; total of 228 minutes; history of Christianity in Spain, Portugal and Mexico after the conquistadors).

'Seventh–day Adventism in a Mexican village: a study in motivation and culture change,' O. Lewis, in *Process and pattern*, p.63–83. Chicago: 1960.

Spanish Jesuit churches in Mexico's Tarahumara. P. M. Roca. Tuscon, AZ: University of Arizona Press, 1979. 369p.

The Catholic Church in Mexico: historical essays for the general reader. Vol. 1, 1519–1910. P. Murray. Mexico City: Editorial E.P.M., 1965. 398p.

The Church in contemporary Mexico. G. W. Grayson. *Significant issues series*, vol. 14, no. 5. Washington, DC: Center for Strategic and International Studies, 1992. 114p.

'The cult of the Holy Cross: an analysis of cosmology and Catholicism in Quintana Roo,' C. Zimmerman, *History of religions*, 3, 1 (1963), 50–71.

The gods and symbols of ancient Mexico and the Maya: an illustrated dictionary of Mesoamerican religion. M. Miller & K. Taube. London: Thames and Hudson, 1993. 216p.

The gods of Mexico. C. A. Burland. New York: Putnam, 1967. 219p.

'The history of the Church of Jesus Christ of Latter–day Saints in Mexico.' B. J. McNeil. M.A. thesis, San Jose State University, San Jose, CA, 1990. 105p.

'The "Luz del Mundo" movement in Mexico,' R. S. Greenway, *Missiology*, 1, 2 (1973), 113–24.

The Mexican Kikapoo Indians. F. A. Latorre & D. L. Latorre. *Texas Pan–American series.* Austin, TX: University of Texas Press, 1976. 401p.

The Mexican revolution and the Catholic Church 1910–1929. R. E. Quirk. Bloomington, IN: Indiana University Press, 1973. 276p.

The myth of ritual: a native's ethnography of Zapotec life–crisis rituals. F. E. Gundi & A. H. Jiménez. Tucson, AZ: University of Arizona Press, 1986. 147p.

'The sign of the cross: folk Catholicism in a rural Yucatecan community.' A. C. Woodrick. Ph.D. dissertation, University of California, San Diego, 1989. 454p.

The skeleton at the feast: the Day of the Dead in Mexico. E. Carmichael. London: British Museum Publications, 1991. 160p.

The spiritual conquest of Mexico: an essay on the apostolate and the evangelizing methods of the mendicant orders in New Spain 1523–1572. R. Ricard. Trans., L. B. Simpson. Berkeley and Los Angeles: University of California Press, 1966. 423p.

They sought a country: Mennonite colonization in Mexico. H. L. Sawatzky. London: University of California Press, 1971. 387p.

Tinder in Tabasco: a study of church growth in tropical Mexico. C. Bennet. Grand Rapids, MI: Eerdmans, 1968. 213p.

Todos Santos in rural Tlaxcala: a syncretistic, expressive and symbolic analysis of the cult of the dead. H. G. Nutini. Princeton, NJ: Princeton University Press, 1988. 471p.

Traditional papermaking and paper cult figures of Mexico. A. R. Sandstrom & P. E. Sandstrom. Norman, OK: University of Oklahoma Press, 1986. 327p.

Country Table 2. **Organized churches and denominations in Mexico.**

Official name (bold type = church with over 10% of all affiliated) 1	*Begun* 2	*Type* 3	*Counc* 4	*Congs* 5	*Adults* 6	*Affiliated 1970* 7	*Affiliated 1995* 8	*G%* 9	*Names, notes, and other statistics* (see Codebook, Part 3) 10
Asambleas de Dios de México	1915	P-Pe2	ZF..I	3,400	350,000	100,000	570,334	7.21	Begun by Mexicans. M=AoG. Aids Igl Cri Nacional. Rapid growth. 950n.23f,14s(450).
Asambleas Locales	c1980	I-3nC	.....	37	1,851	–	4,000	6.67	*Local Churches. Little Flock. Assembly Hall Churches.* Chinese.
Asociación de Igls Cristianas Ev en M	1895	P-Dis	x.u.N	35	3,900	3,000	9,750	4.83	*Igl Cristiana Discipulos. Disciples of Christ.* M=UCMS. 1960 expansion. 6f,1s,1u.
Bando Evangelistico Gedeón	1938	I-3gL	.....	100	3,000	3,000	7,000	3.45	*Gideon's Ev Band.* White suits, ties, dresses. Mass bible distributors. HQ Jalapa.
Centros Culturas Calacoaya	1976	I-3gL	.....	2	3,000	–	7,000	5.26	F=Gonzalo Vega. Tent on edge of Mexico City. 60 self-help ministries. Former RC Charismatics.
Centros de Amistad Cristiana	1963	I-3hL	x....	100	19,400	–	30,000	51.04	*Centers of Christian Love. Christian Fellowship Chs.* South Mexico among Mixtecs. M=MRC.
Centros de Fe, Esperanza, y Amor	c1970	I-3cL	.....	200	28,000	–	75,000	56.68	*Centers of Faith, Hope, & Love.* Mixtec. M=Missionary Revival Crusade. Also in Nicaragua. 30f.
Concilio Latino-Americana de Igls Cris	c1925	I-3gL	I	80	4,000	5,000	10,000	2.81	*Latin American Council of Christian Chs.* Begun in USA (Los Angeles) by Mexicans.
Congregación Escandinava en México	1953	P-Lut	l...N	1	640	1,100	920	-0.71	*Scandinavian Congregation in Mexico.* Set up with support from LWF. 2n.W=15%,10Yy.
Congreg Ev Lut de habla Alemana	1861	P-Lut	L.u.N	20	2,400	4,613	3,900	-0.67	*German Ev Congs in Mexico.* German immigrants. 3 parish districts. 4x,58Yy,324z.
Conv Nacional Bautista de México	1862	P-Bap	T....	913	68,497	35,000	140,000	5.70	*National Baptists* (1902). 1880, M=SBC(USA): 1971, CBHMS. 172n,73f,1H,1s,1276Y.
Cruzada Evangelistica Mundial	1950	P-Hol	xF...	9	318	200	1,060	6.90	*World Gospel Crusade. World Gospel Church.* M=WGM(USA). HQ Tijuana. 7m.5f,1p.
Ejército de Salvación	1937	P-Sal	xwu.N	103	5,200	5,000	8,000	1.90	*Salvation Army, Mexico Division.* USA Southern Territory. In 25 cities. 1s.
Fraternidad Cristiana Int de M	c1950	I-3oL	.....	20	2,000	2,000	4,000	2.81	*International Christian Brotherhood of Mexico.* Oneness body, in AWCF. HQ Guadalajara.
Grupos de Cristo	c1970	I-3hL	x....	63	6,000	–	12,000	45.60	*Christ Groups.* Home churches for isolated converts after nationwide EHC campaign.
Hermanos Menonitas	1950	P-Men	GF...	5	400	300	700	3.45	M=Mennonite Brethren Ch of NAmerica(USA). HQ Durango. 5f,1H,1h.
Iglesia Adventista del Séptimo Día	1893	P-Adv	x....	994	328,000	100,000	547,000	7.03	*Seventh-day Adventists, Mexico Union Mission.* 88nx,651m,26f,1H,6h,5r,1376t(76491),5415Y.
Iglesia Alianza Cristiana y Misionera	1954	P-Hol	xF...	37	3,000	200	7,000	15.28	*Christian & Missionary Alliance Ch.* M=CMA(USA). HQ Mexico City 15, 14m,2f.
Iglesia Apostólica de la Fe en CJ	1914	I-3oL	x....	1,520	138,000	48,192	176,000	5.32	*IAFCJ, Apost Ch of Faith in CJ.* Mestizos. In 10 countries. 441n,776m,14s(100),1115Y.
Iglesia Bautista Americana	1870	P-Bap	.....	35	2,700	13,100	6,000	-3.08	M=ABCIM(USA).
Iglesia Bautista del Séptimo Día	1976	P-Bap	Tw...	23	820	1,000	1,640	5.26	*Seventh Day Baptist Ch.* Ch of Christ of the 7th Day. Under Gen Conf. SDBC(USA).
Iglesia Bautista Internacional	1965	I-Bap	.....	33	4,800	870	9,600	10.08	Baptist International Mission. M=BIM(USA).
Igl Católica Apostólica Ortodoxa en M	1926	I-CCa	.....	12	16,000	18,000	32,000	2.33	*Catholic Apostolic Orth Ch.* Ex RCC. Lebanese Arabs. 12n,1s(5),W=68%,208Yy.
Iglesia Católica en México:	1518	R-Lat	B.L.R	11,357	45,740,800	47,028,524	85,500,000	2.42	*Catholic Ch.* C=37+3+146. 8725n 3075x 7061m 20176w 1712611Yy
M Acapulco	1958	R-Lat	Bs	70	1,511,500	460,800	2,725,000	7.37	Towns, ports, tourism and seasonal influx. 1s. 66n 15x 21m 127w 26376Yy
D Chilpancingo-Chilapa	1863	R-Lat	Bs	65	561,000	798,825	1,050,000	1.10	50% urban. Subsistence level rural Indians. 1s. 92n 8x 138m 150w 11550Yy
D Ciudad Altamirano	1964	R-Lat	Bs	26	369,000	349,000	690,000	2.76	80% rural. Traditional Indian catholicism. M=OP. 47n 6x 6m 50w 13096Yy
D Ciudad Lazaro Cardenas	1985	R-Lat	Bs	18	275,000	–	514,000	10.00	Population is 89% Catholic. 23n 10x 13m 48w 7803Yy
D Tlapa	1992	R-Lat	Bs	21	224,000	–	420,000	33.33	93% Catholics. 21n 0x 0m 18w 8891Yy
M Antequera (Oaxaca)	1535	R-Lat	Bs	139	787,000	1,399,618	1,472,100	0.20	50% urban, Indians: many monolingual. W=5%. 141n 40x 51m 276w 39470Yy
D San Cristóbal de las Casas	1539	R-Lat	Bs	2,275	590,000	725,632	1,104,000	1.69	90% rural. 80% Indian. Strong christo-paganism. 34n 27x 42m 130w 26980Yy
D Tapachula	1957	R-Lat	Bs	38	490,000	453,318	917,512	2.86	80% rural. 70% Indian. 80% RC. New farming areas. 48n 4x 4m 105w 14133Yy
D Tehuantepec	1891	R-Lat	Bs	33	676,000	287,850	1,264,000	6.10	90% rural. 30% monolingual Indians. 35n 7x 9m 120w 9922Yy
D Tuxtepec	1979	R-Lat	Bs	19	328,000	–	614,000	6.25	M=MVM. 18n 8x 8m 37w 10182Yy
D Tuxtla Gutiérrez	1964	R-Lat	Bs	34	532,000	402,000	995,500	3.69	80% rural, 70% Indian. New farming areas. 51n 14x 22m 204w 22660Yy
PN Huautla	1972	R-Lat	Bmj	191	60,800	–	113,764	4.35	M=MJ. 6n 6x 11m 5w 2457Yy
PN Mixes (Mixe)	1964	R-Lat	Bsdb	15	90,000	90,360	169,085	2.54	Entirely rural, all Indian (monolingual). M=SDB. 3n 21x 25m 28w 3061Yy
M Chihuahua	1891	R-Lat	Bs	317	490,000	825,843	917,728	0.42	Rapid urban growth, rich agricultural areas. 1s. 82n 25x 34m 204w 23665Yy
D Ciudad Juárez	1957	R-Lat	Bs	45	601,000	552,908	1,124,000	2.88	80% urban. Industrial expansion very recent. 53n 18x 28m 166w 18029Yy
D Parral	1992	R-Lat	Bs	197	254,000	–	475,000	33.33	89% Catholic. 12n 7x 8m 51w 5135Yy
D Tarahumara	1950	R-Lat	Ps	22	124,000	145,000	233,268	1.92	Rural. 40% monolingual Indians. Poor economy. 8n 18x 36m 112w 5084Yy
PN Madera (Ciudad Madera)	1966	R-Lat	Bs	17	169,000	163,000	317,000	2.70	In northwest. 90% rural. M=OAR. 14n 13x 14m 38w 4438Yy
PN Nuevo Casas Grandes	1977	R-Lat	Bs	24	145,000	–	271,000	5.56	95% Catholic. 18n 13x 18m 32w 2740Yy
M Durango	1620	R-Lat	Bs	131	811,000	651,371	1,517,402	3.44	50% urban, mass city immigration. Tepehuanas. 1s. 190n 19x 43m 402w 52346Yy
D Culiacán (Sinaloa)	1883	R-Lat	Bs	81	877,000	728,935	1,641,000	3.30	Prosperous rural areas, intensively farmed. 1s. 116n 6x 13m 300w 26200Yy
D Mazatlán	1958	R-Lat	Bs	44	334,000	336,000	625,000	2.51	Recent tourist industry. Insufficient clergy. 1s. 63n 10x 11m 122w 11042Yy
D Torreón	1957	R-Lat	Bs	33	612,000	456,142	1,145,000	3.75	Rural, farming, industries. Clergy inadequate. 67n 42x 47m 136w 15010Yy
PN El Salto	1968	R-Lat	Bs	58	96,000	94,090	180,000	2.63	100% rural. 90% Indian. Underdeveloped. M=OCD. 13n 0x 0m 15w 3050Yy
M Guadalajara	1548	R-Lat	Bs	1,182	2,425,000	2,474,168	4,535,000	2.45	90% urban. Traditional catholicism. 1p,2s. 787n 150x 543m 3021w 85615Yy
D Aguascalientes	1899	R-Lat	Bs	169	627,000	438,936	1,174,500	4.02	Little development, mass emigration elsewhere. 1s. 162n 30x 57m 581w 30850Yy
D Autlán	1961	R-Lat	Bs	60	147,000	227,581	275,600	0.77	Intensively farmed. Very high practice: W=75%. 97n 1x 2m 157w 6849Yy
D Ciudad Guzman	1972	R-Lat	Bs	280	307,000	–	575,000	4.35	98% Catholic. 104n 9x 56m 203w 9496Yy
D Colima	1881	R-Lat	Bs	76	265,000	379,570	495,447	1.07	Tourism. Rural. High religious practice. 1s. 111n 7x 7m 203w 14710Yy
D San Juan de los Lagos	1972	R-Lat	Bs	118	529,000	–	989,000	4.35	99% Catholic. 213n 16x 44m 350w 18026Yy
D Tepic	1891	R-Lat	Bs	101	644,000	591,000	1,205,000	2.89	60% urban. Rich new farming. Few Indians. 1s. 162n 6x 13m 189w 21463Yy
D Zacatecas	1863	R-Lat	Bs	112	750,000	1,010,000	1,403,000	1.32	50% urban. Much emigration. Some Indians. M=SM. 179n 5x 8m 348w 29378Yy
PN Jesús María (Nayar)	1962	R-Lat	Bofm	18	85,000	53,000	160,000	4.52	100% rural, 95% monolingual Indians. M=OFM. 4n 15x 24m 24w 2518Yy
M Hermosillo (Sonora)	1779	R-Lat	Bs	355	516,000	549,119	966,000	2.29	Mass immigration from other parts of Mexico. 1s. 79n 8x 14m 158w 31316Yy
D Ciudad Obregón	1959	R-Lat	Bs	51	601,000	497,125	1,125,000	3.32	Very rapid urban expansion and immigration. 78n 19x 34m 140w 24500Yy
D La Paz en la Baja California Sur	1957	R-Lat	Ps	24	163,000	144,200	305,000	3.04	Area recently opened to colonization. M=FACJ. 23n 27x 30m 182w 4240Yy
D Mexicali	1966	R-Lat	Bs	48	777,000	662,707	1,453,000	3.19	80% urban. Immigration, rapid industrialization. 67n 26x 32m 152w 20548Yy
D Tijuana	1874	R-Lat	Bs	71	1,058,000	572,000	1,978,000	5.09	90% urban. Intensive industrialization, 1s. 109n 65x 123m 477w 26313Yy
M Jalapa (Veracruz)	1863	R-Lat	Bs	127	963,000	1,084,140	1,801,312	2.05	Rich farming areas, expanding urban areas. 1s. 209n 13x 19m 491w 44426Yy
D Coatzacoalcos	1984	R-Lat	Bs	24	629,000	–	1,176,000	9.09	98% Catholic. 36n 12x 17m 63w 10639Yy
D Papantla	1922	R-Lat	Bs	42	1,032,000	550,000	1,931,110	5.15	70% rural. Bilingual (Indian/Spanish) Indians. 59n 2x 2m 143w 20398Yy
D San Andrés Tuxtla	1959	R-Lat	Bs	44	368,000	705,000	689,000	-0.09	60% urban. Rich farm land, petroleum. Few Indians. 43n 3x 3m 86w 14480Yy
D Tuxpan	1962	R-Lat	Bs	41	564,000	695,812	1,055,000	1.68	50% urban. Area in farm land, petroleum. 58n 0x 0m 55w 17352Yy
D Veracruz	1962	R-Lat	Bs	52	1,176,000	604,000	2,200,000	5.31	70% urban. Port, tourism, 20% Pesquera Indians. 62n 25x 25m 210w 18667Yy
M México	1530	R-Lat	Bs	557	9,732,000	7,250,000	18,203,000	3.75	Capital. 100% urban. 93% RC. 5p,1s. 679n 1172x 2257m 4840w 8998Yy
D Atlacomulco	1984	R-Lat	Bs	38	372,000	–	696,672	9.09	98% Catholic. 50n 4x 5m 87w 24950Yy
D Cuernavaca	1891	R-Lat	Bs	85	878,000	620,000	1,642,000	3.97	Tourism. Diocesan experiments. HQ of CIDOC. 94n 47x 56m 416w 17550Yy
D Toluca	1950	R-Lat	Bs	120	980,000	891,112	1,834,000	2.93	60% urban, immigrants. Monolingual Indians. 1s. 195n 37x 37m 335w 38260Yy
D Tula	1961	R-Lat	Bs	35	414,000	397,000	775,000	2.71	80% rural, 30% monolingual Indians. Subsistence. 42n 11x 13m 128w 15014Yy
D Tulancingo	1863	R-Lat	Bs	66	642,000	679,384	1,201,000	2.31	60% rural. Metals, mining, Indians monolingual. 118n 4x 13m 185w 26948Yy

Continued opposite

Country Table 2–continued

Official name (bold type = church with over 10% of affiliated) 1	*Begun* 2	*Type* 3	*Counc* 4	*Congs* 5	*Adults* 6	*Affiliated 1970* 7	*Affiliated 1995* 8	*G%* 9	*Names, notes, and other statistics* (see Codebook, Part 3) 10
M Monterrey (Linares, Nueva Leon)	1777	R-Lat	Bs	155	2,545,000	1,353,251	4,761,000	5.16	70% urban. Rich farming areas. 1s, W=70%. 237n 96x 233m 598w 41660Yy
D Ciudad Valles	1960	R-Lat	Bs	36	389,000	440,000	728,000	2.03	80% rural. Recent petroleum industry. Huastecos. 43n 11x 11m 123w 16829Yy
D Ciudad Victoria	1964	R-Lat	Bs	30	401,000	279,994	750,000	4.02	50% urban. Rural areas subsistence level. M=OFM. 29n 16x 18m 95w 4522Yy
D Linares	1962	R-Lat	Bs	17	228,000	248,200	427,000	2.19	80% rural. Subsistence farming. Indian groups. 33n 0x 0m 58w 4315Yy
D Matamoros	1958	R-Lat	Bs	48	763,000	590,000	1,428,000	3.60	Rich farming and petroleum areas. Rapid growth. 55n 7x 8m 73w 22413Yy
D Nuevo Laredo	1989	R-Lat	Bs	29	411,000	–	769,800	16.67	D=MSpS. 30n 14x 19m 92w 10041Yy
D Saltillo	1891	R-Lat	Bs	718	688,000	720,000	1,287,000	2.35	80% urban, rapid industrialization; coal mining. 105n 30x 58m 432w 31208Yy
D Tampico	1870	R-Lat	Bs	53	442,000	465,120	827,570	2.33	60% urban. Rich petroleum area. Few Indians. 75n 18x 25m 155w 24378Yy
M Morelia (Michoacan)	1536	R-Lat	Bs	294	1,307,000	1,900,000	2,445,022	1.01	Formerly M Michoacán. 2p,1s. 428n 98x 177m 1100w 75717Yy
D Apatzingán	1962	R-Lat	Bs	25	363,000	288,145	680,000	3.49	80% rural. Recently-opened farming areas. M=MSF. 49n 3x 6m 123w 9227Yy
D Tacámbaro	1913	R-Lat	Bs	44	193,000	215,903	361,294	2.08	70% rural. Traditional Indian catholicism. 1s. 71n 4x 4m 112w 9681Yy
D Zamora	1863	R-Lat	Bs	121	966,000	776,774	1,807,606	3.44	50% urban. Rich farms. Monolingual Indians. 251n 25x 51m 836w 35243Yy
M Puebla de los Angeles (Tlaxcola)	1525	R-Lat	Bs	360	2,041,000	1,832,141	3,818,756	2.98	60% urban. Traditional catholicism. 1s. W=60%. 351n 99x 253m 1055w 36475Yy
D Huajuápan de León	1903	R-Lat	Bs	100	287,000	336,000	538,000	1.90	Rural; Indian groups. Unevangelized areas. 1s. 105n 0x 0m 161w 7197Yy
D Huejutla	1922	R-Lat	Bs	38	253,000	280,000	474,100	2.13	Rural, Indian groups. Insufficient clergy. 72n 6x 6m 76w 8300Yy
D Tehuacan	1962	R-Lat	Bs	52	237,000	265,000	444,000	2.09	60% rural. Intensive colonization. Some Indians. 74n 8x 8m 137w 12182Yy
D Tlaxcala	1959	R-Lat	Bs	69	588,000	409,340	1,100,000	4.03	50% urban. Traditional Indian catholicism. 1s. 115n 20x 42m 324w 28389
M San Luis Potosí	1854	R-Lat	Bs	84	1,015,000	782,106	1,898,053	3.61	50% urban. Traditional Indian catholicism. 1s. 183n 49x 117m 512w 36577Yy
D Celaya	1973	R-Lat	Bs	53	578,000	–	1,081,546	4.55	92% Catholic. 119n 49x 74m 528w 29397Yy
D León	1863	R-Lat	Bs	250	1,430,000	1,193,819	2,675,000	3.28	80% urban. Moderate urbanization. 1p,1s,W=60%. 224n 115x 180m 1005w 42319Yy
D Querétaro	1863	R-Lat	Bs	81	590,000	544,800	1,103,388	2.86	60% urban, Impoverished Indians. 1s. 139n 100x 206m 810w 33685Yy
M Tlalnepantla	1964	R-Lat	Bs	309	1,520,000	1,475,000	2,843,387	2.66	90% urban, rapid industrialization. 1s. 225n 45x 71m 455w 38681Yy
D Cuautitlan	1979	R-Lat	Bs	105	724,000	–	1,354,000	6.25	91% Catholic. 111n 53x 131m 248w 46275Yy
D Netzahualcoyotl	1979	R-Lat	Bs	105	2,060,000	–	3,854,000	6.25	90% Catholic. Huge city. 134n 34x 64m 21w 76450Yy
D Texcoco	1960	R-Lat	Bs	128	1,463,000	847,411	2,736,000	4.80	80% urban, immigration, industry. Rural Indians. 166n 19x 22m 261w 57368Yy
M Yucatán	1561	R-Lat	Bs	124	649,000	716,182	1,214,000	2.13	Mérida. 60% urban. Major tourist centre of future. 150n 32x 47m 298w 23341Yy
D Campeche	1895	R-Lat	Bs	44	229,000	254,000	428,000	2.11	Towns, ports, tourism. Rich farming. W=60%. 36n 10x 25m 139w 14000Yy
D Tabasco	1880	R-Lat	Bs	50	969,000	728,792	1,812,000	3.71	50% urban. Immigration; farms, petroleum. W=10%. 72n 16x 19m 185w 13428Yy
PN Chetumal	1970	R-Lat	Bs	25	361,000	90,000	675,000	8.39	Prelature formed out of M Yucatan. M=LC. 2n 25x 26m 48w 12950Yy
D Nuestra Señora del Paraiso (*Melkite*)	1988	R-Mel	os	1	1,500	–	2,500	14.29	Greek Melkite Diocese. 0n 1x 1m 0w 926Yy
Doubly-counted Catholics		R-Lat		0	-15,602,000	–	-29,163,022		Persons in new dioceses still counted in old.
Iglesia Católica Romana Antigua	1935	I-CCa	.v...	2	100	200	300	1.64	*Ecclesia Veteris Romanae Catholicae. Old Roman CC.* 1965 applied to WCC, rejected.
Iglesia Cristiana Bethel	1953	I-3pL	I	40	1,500	2,000	3,000	1.64	*Bethel Assemblies of Latin America.* Ex CoG in RM. 1956. M=BFMF(USA). 20f.
Igl Cristiana Fundamental de M	c1980	I-Fun	.....	50	6,000	–	12,000	6.67	Half of church members are now pentecostals. 1 missionary in Italy.
Iglesia Cristiana Interdenominacional		I-3pL	I	400	26,000	50,000	75,000	0.05	*Interdenominational Christian Ch.* Rapidly expanding. 10 churches in Mexico City.
Igl Cristiana Nacional de las AdD	1934	I-3pL	Z....	756	34,000	30,000	68,000	3.33	*National Christian Ch of the Assemblies of God.* Indigenous, working with M=AoG.
Iglesia Cristiana Reformada	1959	P-Ref	.....	35	3,150	900	6,300	8.09	*Christian Reformed Church.* M=CRWM.
Iglesia Cristiana Unida	c1938	P-Non	..u.N	30	3,000	4,000	4,100	0.10	*United Christian Ch.* Spanish refugees from 1936 Spanish civil war. HQ Mexico 12.
Iglesia de Dios de la Profecía	1944	P-Pe3	Z...I	252	8,820	4,000	19,600	6.56	*Ch of God of Prophecy.* M=CGP(USA). Holiness Pentecostals. HQ Mexico City 8.
Iglesia de Dios del Séptimo Día	1920	I-Adv	.....	200	9,000	15,000	20,000	1.16	*Ch of God (Seventh-day).* Ex SDAs. Link with M=CGSD(USA). Rapidly growing. 185n.
Iglesia de Dios en Cristo	1933	P-Men	G....	20	1,000	2,000	2,500	0.90	*Ch of God in Christ.* M=Ch of God in Christ, Mennonite (USA). 48f.
Iglesia de Dios en Cristo por El ES	1969	I-3pL	.....	30	1,000	400	2,000	6.65	ES=Espiritu Santo. *Ch of God in Christ through the Holy Spirit.* 8n,W=90%,86Y,18z.
Igl de Dios en la República Mexicana	1920	I-3pL	I	625	75,000	80,000	150,000	2.55	*Ch of God in Republic of M.* Schism ex AoG and 1946 CoG(Cleveland). 9 Districts.
Iglesia de Dios en México	1893	P-Hol	x.u.N	440	11,000	50,000	22,000	-3.23	*Ch of God in Mexico.* M=CoG(Anderson) (USA). In 5 states. HQ Mexico 14. 7f,2h,2s.
Iglesia de Dios Pentecostal	1942	P-Pe2	Z...I	80	2,000	2,000	5,000	3.73	*Igl de Dios Pentecostés.* M=Pentecostal Ch of God of America (USA). HQ Veracruz. 4f.
Iglesia de Dios (Evangelio Completo)	1932	P-Pe3	ZF..I	825	41,959	50,000	105,000	3.01	*Ch of God (Full Gospel).* Begun by Mexicans. M=CoG(Cleveland). Schisms. 568n,7f,5s.
Iglesia de JC de los Santos de los UD	1879	m-LdS	x....	1,231	285,000	112,232	570,000	6.72	*Latter-day Saints. Mormons.* M=CjCLdS(USA). Indians. 900f,40000Yy(in 1976).
Iglesia de los Amigos	1871	P-Qua	QF...	4	400	300	600	2.81	*Ch of the Friends. Quakers.* M=California YMF,FUM(USA). HQ Mexico City 1. 2f.
Iglesia del Evangelio Cuadrangular	1943	P-Pe2	ZF..I	120	9,600	10,000	32,000	4.76	*International Ch of the Foursquare Gospel.* M=ICFG. HQ Monterrey. 57nm,8f.3p(32),170Y.
Iglesia del Nazareno en México	1903	P-Hol	xFu.N	333	27,604	30,000	39,340	1.09	*Ch of the Nazarene.* M=CoN(USA). 4 Districts. Very rapid growth. HQ Guadalajara. 74n.
Iglesia El Buen Pastor	1942	I-3oL	.....	100	5,000	5,000	12,000	3.56	*Church of the Good Shepherd.* Schism ex Iglesia La Luz del Mundo (Aaronistas). 75n.
Iglesia Episcopal Mexicana	1857	A-Low	awuRN	216	50,800	8,881	163,900	12.37	Ex Ch of Rome. 8 Dioceses. 31n,11x,2s(14),W=75%,213Yy.
Igl Evangélica de los Hermanos Libres	c1895	P-CBr	x....	110	6,600	5,000	11,000	3.20	*Ev Ch of Open Brethren.* Plymouth Brethren. M=CMML(USA,UK). HQ Mexico 3. 19f,1p.
Iglesia Ev de los Peregrinos	1920	P-Hol	VF...	203	5,700	16,000	8,881	-2.33	M=Pilgrim Holiness (Wesleyan) Ch. HQ San Luis Potosi. 28n,1f,1s(24),W=44%,742Y.
Igl Ev del Consejo Espiritual Mexicano	1928	I-3oL	.....	150	5,500	18,000	15,000	-0.73	*Mexican Ch of Spiritual Council.* Schism ex IAFCJ. Many splits. Declining. Rural.
Igl Ev Menonita de los Mesa Central	1954	P-Men	GF...	10	200	300	500	2.06	M=Ev Mennonite Ch (USA). South central Mexico. Rapid growth. 1n,5x.12f,W=50%,8Y,5z.
Iglesia Ev Menonita del Noroeste de M	1961	P-Men	.....	12	200	106	300	4.25	*Ev Mennonite Ch of NE Mexico.* M=EMC.
Iglesia Evangélica Misionera	1954	P-Eva	.....	5	300	500	600	0.73	*Ev Missionary Ch.* M=Mexican Militant Mission (Texas, USA). Mestizos only. 1p.
Iglesia Evangélica Misionera del Pacto	1946	P-Con	.....	46	2,589	3,000	5,180	2.21	*Evangelical Covenant Church.* M=ECCA.
Iglesia Gracia Hermanos	1951	P-Dun	x....	3	300	300	600	2.81	M=Grace Brethren Church.
Iglesia La Luz del Mundo (Aaronistas)	1940	I-3oL	x....	400	258,000	230,000	400,000	2.24	*Light of the World Ch.* Messiah Aaron, died 1964. Vast tabernacle Guadalajara. 1h.
Iglesia Luterana Mexicana	1947	P-Lut	L.u.N	10	450	1,000	840	-0.69	*Mexican Lutheran Ch.* Begun by 2 Nazarene pastors with M=ALC(USA). A=1957. 1s.
Iglesia Menonita	1922	P-Men	G....	300	20,000	32,000	40,000	0.90	11,750 Old Colony Mennonites (first settlers in Latin America) from Canada. Germans.
Iglesia Metodista de México	1873	P-Met	VWu.N	489	44,000	70,000	73,300	0.18	*Methodist Ch* (A=1930), affiliated UMC(USA). 2 Confs. 79n,37f,1H,13r,1s,178t,1u.
Iglesia Metodista Libre Mexicana	1912	I-Hol	VF..N	50	1,629	2,000	3,260	1.97	*Mexican Free Meth Ch.* M=FMC(USA). HQ Nogales. 11n,6f,1h,1p,1s(18),206z.
Iglesia Misionera Mexicana	1951	I-3gL	.....	20	2,000	1,000	3,000	4.49	*Mexican Missionary Ch.* Founded by Methodist woman. Charismatic, enthusiastic.
Igl Nacional Presbiteriana de México	1872	P-Ref	R....	4,800	500,000	120,000	1,200,000	9.65	*IPNM. National Presb Ch.* M=PCUS,UPUSA,RCA. Many Indians. 8 synods,700n,85f.
Iglesia Nueva Apostólica		I-3aX	x....	30	13,200	1,000	20,411	0.05	*New Apostolic Ch,* USA Bezirk (District). Germans. World HQ Dortmund (Germany).
Igl Ortodoxa Cat Apostólica Mexicana	1926	I-CCa	.....	516	25,800	60,000	43,000	-1.32	National Ch. State-aided schism ex RCC. Decline since 1940. 10 bishops. 200n.
Iglesia Ortodoxa Católica de México	c1890	O-Rus	Mwo..	35	35,000	30,000	50,000	2.06	*Orth Cath Ch.* Exarchate of OCA(USA), 1972. Russians. Veracruz. Bishop, 7n,11f,15i.
Iglesia Ortodoxa Griega	c1970	O-Gre	Cwo..	2	3,500	4,000	6,800	2.15	In 12th Archdiocesan District, Greek Orthodox AD of N&SAmerica. Greeks, Arabs.
Igl Ortodoxa: D México & CAmerica	c1890	O-Ara	Cwo..	21	21,000	20,000	34,000	2.15	Under Antiochian Orth Ch (USA), & Greek P Antioch. Lebanese Arab emigres.
Igl Presbiteriana Asociada Reformada	1878	I-Ref	R.u.N	250	7,500	5,000	13,600	4.08	M=ARPC(USA). A=1964. 1975, left WARC. 14n,3x,6f,1H,1s(3),W=25%,340Yy.
Igl Presbiteriana Independiente de M	1962	P-Ref	JF...	150	2,000	2,000	4,000	2.81	Indep Presb Ch of Mexico. M=Iglesia Cristiana Reformada (CRC)(USA). 40f,1p,3s.
Iglesia Santa Pentecostés Mexicana	1931	P-Pe3	ZF..I	450	12,381	5,000	20,600	5.83	*Pentecostal Holiness Ch.* M=IPHC(USA). Holiness Pentecostals (3-stage). 95nm.12f,2s.
Iglesia Unidad Cristiana	1982	I-3pL	.....	3	6,000	–	18,000	7.69	*IUC. Christian Unity Church.* HQ Tijuana. Social programs, disaster relief.
Iglesias Avivamiento	c1985	I-3fL	.....	300	30,000	–	75,000	10.00	*Miracle Revival Crusade Chs.* M=MRC,GSMA(USA).
Iglesias Biblicos de México	1955	P-Non	xM...	36	1,600	250	2,670	9.94	M=Central American Mission (USA). Interdenominational. 1 school. 54f,1s.
Iglesias Congregationales de México	1872	P-Con	..u.N	25	1,500	1,110	2,500	3.30	*Junta General de IC. Congregational Ch in M.* M=UCBWM(USA). 5n,2f,1u,W=93%,47Y.
Iglesias de Cristo	1933	I-Dis	x....	180	7,000	5,000	11,700	3.46	M=Churches of Christ (Non-Instrumental) (USA). HQ Mexico City 7. 12f,2s,W=88%.
Iglesias de Cristo (Instrumental)	1902	I-Dis	x....	220	7,500	10,000	15,000	1.64	M=CCCC(Instrumental) (USA). Splits ex UCMS. Independents. 89f.
Iglesias Evangélicas Independientes	c1930	I-3pL	I	727	80,000	70,000	160,000	3.36	*Independent Chs.* Vast grouping of separate bodies under SFM (Sweden) influence.
Iglesias Evangélicas Independientes	1961	I-Eva	.....	20	20,000	20,000	30,000	1.64	*Independent Evangelical Churches.* M=Mexican Border Missions (USA). 8m,4f.
Misión Cristiana, México Poniente	1950	P-Non	.....	20	1,000	1,000	1,500	1.64	*Western Mexico Christian M.* HQ Hermosillo, Sonora. 6n,2x,1p(9),50Y,25z.
Misión Evangelistica Mexicana	1926	I-Hol	.....	250	3,000	4,000	6,000	1.64	*MEM. Mexican Ev M.* 1946, M=EMC(USA). Tarahumaras. 23n,10x,1j,1s(6),W=82%,45Y.
Misión Evangelización	1971	P-Non	.....	133	8,500	–	17,000	4.17	Unevangelized Fields Mission. M=UFM.
Misiones Mundiales de México	1960	I-Non	x....	30	2,000	3,000	4,000	1.16	M=World-Wide Missions (USA). Evangelicals based in Pasadena, CA (USA).
Movimiento Igls Ev Pentecostales Indep	1930	I-3pW	.....	1,567	47,000	40,000	85,500	3.09	*MIEPI. Movement of Ev Indep Pentecostal Chs.* In 12 states. Rapid growth. 115n.
Niños de Dios	c1980	I-mar	.....	20	226	–	509	6.67	*Children of God.* M=ChG.
Sinodo Luterano de México	1940	P-Lut	e....	13	487	1,502	1,211	-0.86	Formerly Conferencia Concordia de México. M=LCMS(USA). 17m,2f,16t(581),42Yy.
Sociedad de la Ciencia Cristiana		m-Sci	x....	2	90	200	150	0.05	*Ch of Christ, Scientist. Christian Science.* M=CCS(Boston, USA). 1w.
Testigos de Jehová	1893	m-Jeh	x....	9,800	304,756	100,000	1,200,000	10.45	*Jehovah's Witnesses.* Mass literature from 1929. (1975) 5683Y. (1995) 37454Y.
Unión de Iglesias Ev Independientes	1923	I-3pR	Z...I	1,000	300,000	350,000	500,000	1.44	*Union of Ev Independent Chs. Igl Cristiana Indep Pentecostés.* Otomí Indians. HQ Pachuca
Unión de Iglesias Ev Mexicanas	1930	P-Eva	.M...	300	4,000	6,000	8,000	1.16	*Union of Ev Mexican Chs.* M=Mexican Indian M (USA). Aztecs, others. 45mn,18f,1p.
Unión Evangelica Misionera	1956	P-Hol	.....	4	125	45	187	5.86	Gospel Missionary Union. M=GMU.
Unión Menonita de Mexico	1958	P-Men	G....	19	400	300	600	2.81	Union of IGM-MC and IGM-N of Mexico. M=Mennonite Ch of NAmerica, 3 schools. 14f,1H,1h.
Other independent charismatic chs	c1975	I-3cL	.....	3,400	60,000	–	100,000	5.00	Association of Vineyard Chs (13 chs), Tree of Life Ch (42 chs), house churches everywhere.
Other indigenous pentecostal chs		I-3pL	.....	600	200,000	100,000	400,000	0.05	Total about 100 (see list below).
Other Protestant denominations		P-	.....	60	15,000	10,000	35,000	0.05	Total about 200 (see list below).
Doubly-affiliated		2-aff			-3,560,000	-1,424,321	-6,709,943		Evangelicals who also are or were baptized Roman Catholics.
Totals				**51,679**	**45,842,692**	**47,750,304**	**86,395,000**		

Churches, members, growth, 1900-2025	*Congs*	*Adults*	*Affiliated*	*G%*	*Total denominations*	*6 Megablocs:* O	R	A	P	I	m
Total churches, members, and denominations (mid-1900)	4,000	6,678,000	12,403,800	1.94	18	2	1	1	11	1	2
Total churches, members, and denominations (mid-1970)	17,627	25,706,832	47,750,304	1.94	154	3	1	1	73	73	3
Total churches, members, and denominations (mid-1990)	46,000	41,839,000	78,850,000	2.54	291	3	1	1	113	170	3
Total churches, members, and denominations (mid-1995)	51,679	45,842,692	86,395,000	1.84	294	3	1	1	113	173	3
Total churches, members, and denominations (mid-2000)	65,000	49,775,000	93,806,927	1.66	297	3	1	1	114	175	3
Total churches, members, and denominations (mid-2025)	85,000	65,531,000	123,500,000	1.11	574	12	1	1	150	400	10

NOTES ON TABLE ABOVE

NATIONAL COUNCILS (Column 4, 5th letter).

C = Alianza de Iglesias Presbiterianas y Reformadas de la Republica Mexicana (AIPREM, 1995).

E = Confraternidad Evangélica Mexicana (CONEMEX).

I = Asociación Fraternal de Iglesias Pentecostales en la República de México (Asociación Fraternal Pentecostés) (Pentecostal Fraternal Association), representing over 200,000 adult pentecostals, including a number of bodies listed below under 'Other indigenous pentecostal churches'.

N = Federación Evangélica de México (FEM) (Evangelical Federation of Mexico).

R = Conferencia del Episcopado Mexicano (CEM) (Conference of the Mexican Episcopate).

OTHER INDIGENOUS PENTECOSTAL CHURCHES. There are at least 100 other distinct Mexican denominations and para-denominations, in addition to a large number of independent single congregations. A number belong to the Asociación Fraternal

Continued overleaf

Country Table 2–concluded

Pentecostés. Among this total of 100 are the following: Acción Cristiana Independiente de Nuevos Pentecostés, Pente-Asambleas Pentecostés Beteles de México, Comunión Iglesias costales Libres, Comunión de los Creyentes, Iglesia Apostólica de Dios, Iglesia Berea de Pentecostales, Iglesia de Dios Separado, Iglesia de la Fe en Jesucristo Dios (Mexicana), Iglesia Defensores de la Fe, Iglesia Ev Independiente, Iglesia Gideon Cristiana, Iglesia Libre Pentecostés, Iglesia Presbiteriana Nacional Independiente (member of ICCC), Iglesia Pentecostés La Hermosa, Iglesia Universal de Jesucristo, Iglesias del Aposento Alto (Chs of the Upper Room), Movimiento Cristiano Independiente Pentecostés, Movimiento Ev Independiente Pentecostés Debora, Movimiento Libre Pentecostés.
OTHER PROTESTANT DENOMINATIONS. About 70 other smaller Protestant denominations are at work, most being missions from denominations in the USA retaining their identity as separate bodies. They include the following: American Advent Mission Society (1956), American Baptist Association (1955; 10 churches), Apostolic Ch of Pentecost of Canada (1963), Apostolic Faith Mission (Oregon) (1966), Associated Brotherhood of Christians, Baptist Bible Fellowship International (1950), Baptist International Missions (1968), Baptist Mid-Missions (1960), Baptist Missionary Association of America (1950), Baptist World Mission (1965), Bethany Fellowship Missions (1971), Bible Missionary Ch, Children of God International (from USA), Christian Nationals Evangelism Commission (1968), Ch of Christ (Holiness), Ch of God Holiness (1967), Chs of Christ in Christian Union (1944; 6 churches), Congregational Holiness Ch (1963), Congregational Methodist Ch, Conservative Baptist Home Mission Society (1951), Elim Missionary Assemblies (1960), Ev Congregational Ch (1965), Exclusive Brethren (Continuing Tunbridge Wells), Free Will Baptist Mission, Gospel Missionary Union (1956), Independent Bible Baptist Missions (1960), International Pentecostal Assemblies (1952), Maranatha Baptist Mission (1966), Metropolitan Ch Association, Mexican Mission of the Churches of Christ (1917), Mexican Missions (Pentecostal) (1960). National Fellowship of Brethren Chs (1951), New Testament Missionary Union, Open Bible Standard Chs (1965), Pentecostal Free Will Baptist Ch (1963), Reformed Baptists (USA), Southern Methodist Ch, Spanish America Inland Mission (1955), Unevangelized Fields Mission (1971), Union Ev Ch (English-speaking), United Ev Chs (16 missionaries), United Pentecostal Ch (1974), Wisconsin Ev Lutheran Synod (1968), World Baptist Fellowship Mission Agency (1956), World Mission (1959).
OTHER MARGINAL BODIES. The Reorganized Ch of Jesus Christ of Latter-day Saints (USA) has a small work based in Mexico City 10 (358 members); also Friends of Man (Switzerland), Ch of Our Lord Jesus Christ (Bickertonites), Ch of Christ (Temple Lot) (200 members among Indians).

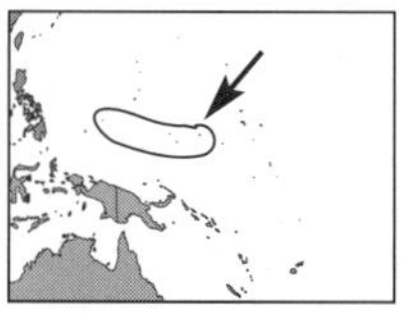

MICRONESIA

SECULAR DATA, AD 2000

STATE
Official name: The Federated States of Micronesia.
Short name: Micronesia. **Adjective of nationality:** of the Federated States of Micronesia.
Flag: Blue field with four white stars in center.
Area: 701 sq. km. (271 sq. mi.).
Government: Federal republic in free association with the United States with one legislative house, since 1979 (1899 German protectorate, 1947 UN Trust Territory).
Legislature: Congress, 14 members.
Official language: English.
Monetary unit: 1 U.S. dollar (U.S.$) = 100 cents. **US$1=** 100 cents.
Chief cities: KOLONIA 9,576.
Political divisions: 4 provinces.

DEMOGRAPHY
Population: 119,000.
Population density: 169.3/sq. km. (437.9/sq. mi.).
Under 15 years: 39,000.
Growth rate p.a.: 1.60% (births 20.74, deaths 4.71).
Mortality: Infant, per 1,000: 9.3, ; **Maternal per 100,000:** 700.0.
Life expectancy: 76 (male 73, female 78).
Household size: 7.0. **Floor area per person, sq.m:** 12.0.
Major languages: Trukese, Ponapean, Yapese, Mortlock, Kosraen.
Urban dwellers: 29.70%. **Urban growth rate p.a.:** 4.5%.
Labor force: 30%.

ETHNOLINGUISTIC PEOPLES
28.0% Trukese; 24.9% Ponapean; 10.6% Yapese; 5.6% Mortlockese; 5.2% Kosraen (Kusaie).

ECONOMY
National income p.a. per person: US$2,013; **per family:** US$14,095.

EDUCATION
Adult literacy: 76% (male 67%, female 87%). **Schools:** 193.
Universities: 1. **School enrolment:** female/male: 90%/90%.

HEALTH
Access to health services: 70%. **Access to safe water:** 100%.
Hospitals: 4 (31 beds per 10,000). **Doctors:** 50.
Blind: 200. **Deaf:** 8,500. **Murder rate:** 6.
Lepers: 600.

LITERATURE
New book titles p.a.: 36 (300 p.a. per million). **Periodicals:** 0.
Newspapers: 2 dailies.

COMMUNICATION (per 1,000 people)
Phones: 74 (20% mobile). **Radios:** 667. **TV sets:** 21.
Daily newspaper circulation: 25. **Computers:** 70.

HUMAN LIFE AND LIBERTY (optimum condition=100.0%)
HDI: 55.5. **HSI:** 65.0. **HFI:** 65.0. **EFL:** 35.0.

Country Table 1. **Religious adherents in Micronesia, AD 1900-2025.**

Year	1900		1970		mid-1990		Annual change, 1990-2000				mid-1995		mid-2000		mid-2025	
Name	Adherents	%	Adherents	%	Adherents	%	Natural	Conversion	Total	Rate	Adherents	%	Adherents	%	Adherents	%
Christians	**22,700**	**63.1**	**57,290**	**93.7**	**90,010**	**93.2**	**2,061**	**-9**	**2,052**	**2.07**	**99,660**	**92.9**	**110,528**	**93.1**	**175,800**	**92.5**
PROFESSION																
professing Christians	**22,700**	**63.1**	**57,290**	**93.7**	**90,010**	**93.2**	**2,061**	**-9**	**2,052**	**2.07**	**99,660**	**92.9**	**110,528**	**93.1**	**175,800**	**92.5**
AFFILIATION																
unaffiliated Christians	185	0.5	9,737	15.9	1,510	1.6	34	2	36	2.14	1,660	1.6	1,866	1.6	2,000	1.1
affiliated Christians	**22,515**	**62.5**	**47,553**	**77.8**	**88,500**	**91.6**	**2,027**	**-11**	**2,016**	**2.07**	**98,000**	**91.4**	**108,662**	**91.5**	**173,800**	**91.5**
Roman Catholics	4,400	12.2	20,000	32.7	55,500	57.5	1,279	629	1,908	3.00	64,089	59.8	74,578	62.8	120,000	63.2
Protestants	18,115	50.3	27,233	44.6	37,000	38.3	839	161	1,000	2.42	41,320	38.5	47,000	39.6	76,000	40.0
Marginal Christians	0	0.0	320	0.5	2,350	2.4	53	42	95	3.45	2,730	2.6	3,300	2.8	9,000	4.7
Independents	0	0.0	0	0.0	1,100	1.1	25	35	60	4.45	1,890	1.8	1,700	1.4	4,200	2.2
doubly-affiliated	0	0.0	0	0.0	-7,450	-7.7	-169	-878	-1,047	9.17	-12,029	-11.2	-17,916	-15.1	-35,400	-18.6
Trans-megabloc groupings																
Evangelicals	12,000	33.3	4,200	6.9	10,250	10.6	232	133	365	3.09	11,840	11.0	13,900	11.7	32,700	17.2
Pentecostals/Charismatics	0	0.0	400	0.7	7,000	7.2	159	81	240	2.99	8,251	7.7	9,400	7.9	20,000	10.5
Great Commission Christians	**4,300**	**11.9**	**5,500**	**9.0**	**16,400**	**17.0**	**372**	**232**	**604**	**3.19**	**19,000**	**17.7**	**22,442**	**18.9**	**40,000**	**21.1**
Ethnoreligionists	13,300	36.9	3,000	4.9	3,600	3.7	82	-29	53	1.38	3,750	3.5	4,128	3.5	6,000	3.2
Baha'is	0	0.0	610	1.0	1,250	1.3	28	38	66	4.33	1,500	1.4	1,909	1.6	3,600	1.9
Nonreligious	0	0.0	0	0.0	550	0.6	12	13	25	3.84	730	0.7	802	0.7	1,800	1.0
Buddhists	0	0.0	0	0.0	450	0.5	10	-1	9	1.80	560	0.5	538	0.5	1,000	0.5
New-Religionists	0	0.0	0	0.0	400	0.4	9	-6	3	0.66	440	0.4	427	0.4	1,000	0.5
Chinese folk-religionists	0	0.0	200	0.3	340	0.4	8	-6	2	0.46	360	0.3	356	0.3	800	0.4
World A (unevangelized persons)	3,600	10.0	305	0.5	485	0.5	12	-20	-8	-1.63	536	0.5	476	0.4	760	0.4
World B (evangelized non-Christians)	9,700	26.9	3,524	5.7	6,105	6.3	137	29	166	2.09	7,043	6.6	7,996	6.5	13,440	7.1
World C (Christians)	22,700	63.1	57,290	93.7	90,010	93.2	2,061	-9	2,052	2.07	99,660	92.9	110,528	93.1	175,800	92.5
Country's population	**36,000**	**100.0**	**61,119**	**100.0**	**96,600**	**100.0**	**2,210**	**0**	**2,210**	**2.07**	**107,239**	**100.0**	**118,700**	**100.0**	**190,000**	**100.0**

COLUMNS, ROWS.
For meanings and definitions, see Codebook (Part 3). Note that, by definition, total 'Christians' = professing + crypto-Christians, which also = affiliated + unaffiliated Christians, and also = Great Commission Christians + latent Christians. Percentages may not always total exactly, due to rounding.

CENSUSES.
18.IX.1973: 49.2% Protestants, 45.4% Roman Catholics, 2.9% traditionalist (Micronesian indigenous Christians), 1.2% non-religious (tribal or traditional religionists), 1.3% other religionists.

NOTES ON RELIGIONS
BAHA'IS. Rapid growth from 1 local spiritual assembly (1964) to 20 (1973; 17 on Carolines, and 114 other isolated centers or groups; but then declining to 5 LSAs in Eastern Carolines by 1995.
ETHNORELIGIONISTS. Polytheists, animists, and ancestor-venerators among the indigenous Micronesian population. In Yap and some atolls of the central Carolines, traditional Micronesian religions continued to be practiced until around 1950, and are still regarded as major alternatives to Christianity in the western and central Carolines. Elements of traditional local religions survive widely in traditional medical practices.
INDEPENDENTS. In one marginal body in 1995 (see Table 2), regarded as traditional religionists in the government census.
ROMAN CATHOLICS. In 1900, 1,700 on Caroline Islands.

Great Commission Instrument Panel: status of Micronesia (for explanation see start of Part 4)

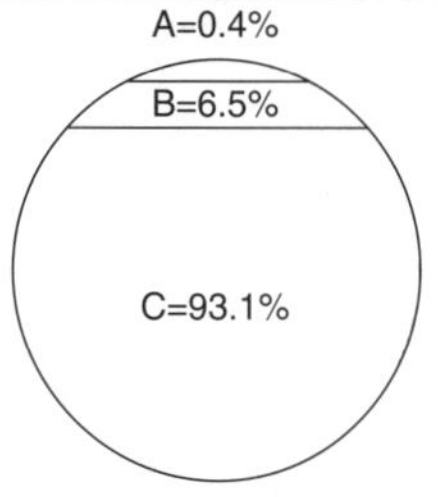

3 Worlds, AD 2000

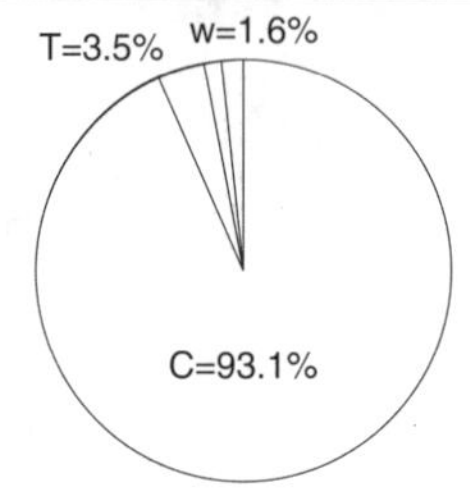

Religions, AD 2000

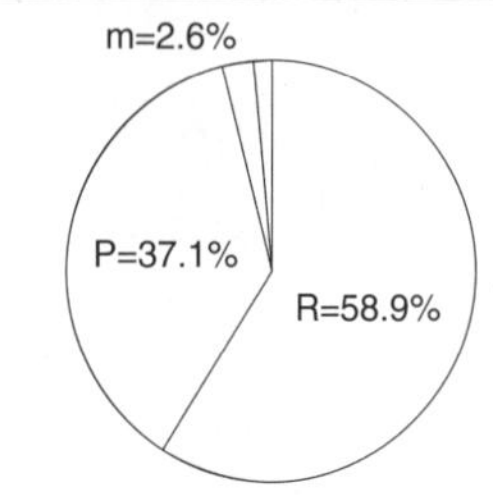

Ecclesiastical blocs

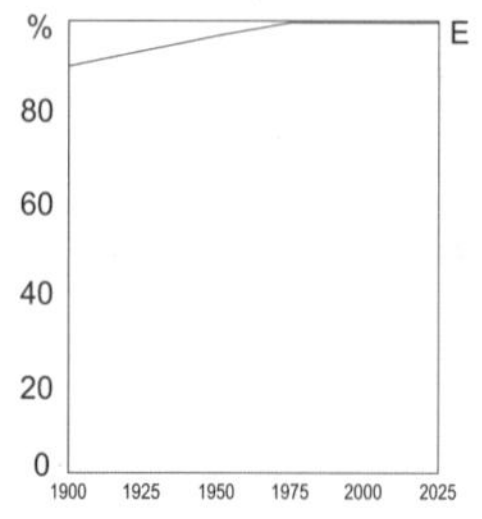

Evangelization, 1900-2025

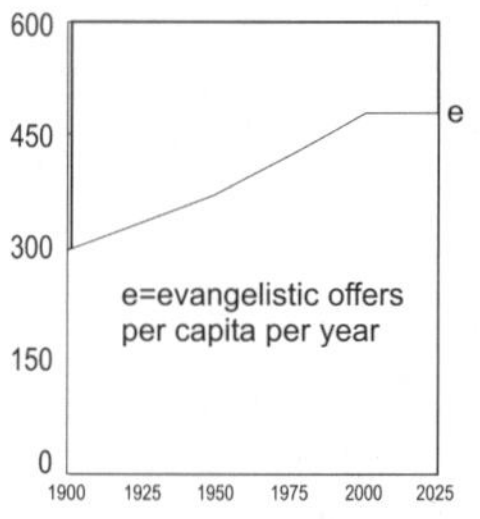

Offers, 1900-2025

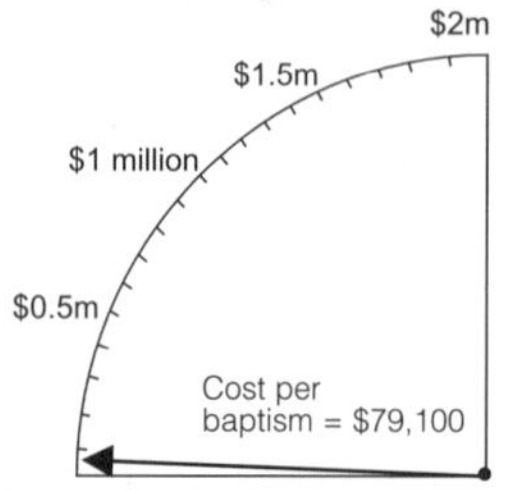

Cost-effectiveness, AD 2000

Country summary. **Worlds A, B, C by ethnolinguistic peoples, cities, and major civil divisions in Micronesia.**

World	PEOPLES Num	Pop 2000	C%	Christians	E%	U%	Unevangelized
A	0	0	0.00	0	0	0	0
B	2	1,543	18.47	285	77	23	356
C	20	117,148	92.51	108,379	100	0	88
Total	**22**	**118,691**	**91.55**	**108,664**	**100**	**0**	**444**

World	CITIES Num	Pop 2000	C%	Christians	E%	U%	Unevangelized
A	0	0	0.00	0	0	0	0
B	0	0	0.00	0	0	0	0
C	1	9,576	90.00	8,618	99	1	88
Total	**1**	**9,576**	**90.00**	**8,618**	**99**	**1**	**88**

World	CIVIL DIVISIONS Num	Pop 2000	C%	Christians	E%	U%	Unevangelized
A	0	0	0.00	0	0	0	0
B	0	0	0.00	0	0	0	0
C	4	118,689	91.55	108,662	100	0	441
Total	**4**	**118,689**	**91.55**	**108,662**	**100**	**0**	**441**

Protestant Church of East Truk. Villagers with their simple church in Penia village, Moen Island, Truk District.

United Church of Christ in Ponape. Congregationalist women's association meets outside church at Kolonia, Ponape District.

Country status. Micronesia, an independent state in free association with the USA, is a group of 600 islands in the Caroline Islands in the western Pacific north of the equator. Its chief economic activity is fishing.

HUMAN LIFE AND LIBERTY

Human rights and freedoms. The situation is similar to that in the USA.

NON-CHRISTIAN RELIGIONS

Ethnic religion continues to exist as a sub-stratum, although most of the indigenous residents of the islands have accepted Christianity. On Ulithi atoll in the Caroline Islands magic is still important, there being typhoon and navigation, community, fish, house, and grave magicians, as well as diviners. A form of ancestor veneration is also practiced, with special attention to 2 great community divinities: Iongolap and Marespa. The Great Spirit, Ialulep is known across the Carolines, as is Solal, lord of the nether regions.

CHRISTIANITY

CATHOLIC CHURCH. Catholicism began in the islands in 1668 and the population is now about 40% Catholic. There are no mission hospitals, Catholic or Protestant in the territory, but church schools are common.

The Holy See has diplomatic relations with Micronesia and in AD 2000 is represented to government and the Catholic hierarchy by a nuncio residing in Wellington, New Zealand.

PROTESTANT CHURCHES. American Board missionaries first began work in the Caroline Islands in 1852 and later spread to other parts of Micronesia. From this early activity have grown autonomous Congregationalist churches on Ponape, Truk, and the Marshall Islands, which continue to receive support from the United Church of Christ in the USA.

The Liebenzell Mission entered Truk in the eastern Carolines in 1906, meeting the request of the American Board for German missionaries after Germany had claimed sovereignty over the islands in 1885. By 1914, 7 stations had opened manned by 11 missionaries and 50 nationals. Although all German missionaries were evacuated during World War I, they returned again in 1925 and opened new stations on Ponape and Palau by 1928. Following World War II, the work was further extended to Yap.

More recent arrivals have been Seventh-day Adventists and Assemblies of God, the latter with headquarters at Majuro in the Marshall Islands

INDIGENOUS CHURCHES. Small indigenous religious movements have existed in the islands since the early part of the 20th century.

Indigenous missions. From the introduction of Christianity, Islanders have traveled to other islands with the gospel. In recent times, Micronesian Christians have been sent to distant parts of Oceania and farther afield to Asia.

CHURCH AND STATE

From the 16th to the 19th centuries the islands were Spanish possessions. Germany was sovereign between 1885 and World War I, after which Micronesia became a Japanese territory. Since World War II, the islands have been governed as a trust territory of the USA. The early Spanish period was favorable to the growth of Catholicism; the Liebenzell Mission owes its origin in the Carolines to the political conditions created by German colonial expansion in 1885; but the present policy of the USA is to maintain complete separation of church and state.

FUTURE TRENDS AND PROSPECTS

Christians, 93.4% of the population in 1970, are expected to decline to 92.5% by 2025. Ethnoreligionists will probably remain at around 3.5% through the same period.

Nonetheless, Micronesia is projected to remain over 90% Christian well into the 21st century.

BIBLIOGRAPHY

'Civilizing the heathen: missionaries and social change in the Mortlock Islands,' J. D. Nason, in *Mission, church, and sect in Oceania*, p.109–37. J. A. Boutilier, D. T. Hughes & S. W. Tiffany (eds). *Association for Social Anthropology in Oceania monograph*, 6. Ann Arbor: University of Michigan Press, 1978.

'Confess therefore your sins: status and sin on Kusaie.' P. D. Schaefer. Ph.D. dissertation, University of Minnesota, 1976. 240p.

'Cultural values in a Micronesian society.' J. L. Caughey. Thesis, University of Pennsylvania, Philadelphia, 1970. 292p.

Die Bewohner der Truk–Inseln: Religion, Leben und kurze Grammatik eines Mikronesiervolkes. L. Bollig. *Anthropos-ethnologische Bibliothek*, Bd. 3, Heft 1. Münster: Aschendorff, 1927. 309p. (Microfiche; has English translation).

'God versus gods: the first years of the Micronesian mission on Ponape, 1852–1859,' D. L. Hanlon, *Journal of Pacific history*, 19 (January 1984), 41–59.

'Indigenization as a missionary goal in the Caroline and Marshall Islands,' F. X. Hezel, in *Mission, church, and sect in Oceania*, p.251–74. J. A. Boutilier, D. T. Hughes & S. W. Tiffany (eds). *Association for Social Anthropology in Oceania monograph*, 6. Ann Arbor, MI: University of Michigan Press, 1978.

'Introduction of Christianity to the island people of Yap with special emphasis on the work of the Liebenzell Mission.' H. O. Hengstler. M.A. thesis, Columbia Graduate School of Bible and Missions, Columbia, SC, 1983. 152p.

Kapingamarangi, social and religious life of a Polynesian atoll. K. P. Emory. Honolulu, HI: The Museum, 1965. 357p.

Micronesia, 1975–1987: a social science bibliography. N. J. Goetzfridt & W. L. Wuerch. *Bibliographies and indexes in anthropology*, no. 5. New York: Greenwood Press, 1989. 207p.

Micronesian religion and lore: a guide to sources, 1526–1990. D. E. Haynes & W. L. Wuerch. *Bibliographies and indexes in religious studies*, no. 32. Westport, CT: Greenwood Press, 1995. 321p.

Religious beliefs and practices of the inhabitants of Yap (German South Seas). S. Walleser. [Buffalo: Jesuit Bureau, 1967]. (Also in German).

'Sky world and this world: the place of Kachaw in Micronesian cosmology,' W. H. Goodenough, *American anthropologist*, 88 (Sept 1986), 551–68.

The Catholic Church in Micronesia: historical essays on the Catholic Church in the Caroline–Marshall Islands. F. X. Hezel. Chicago: Micronesian Seminar, Loyola University Press, 1991.

'The effects of missionization on cultural identity in two societies,' D. T. Hughes, in *Missionaries and anthropologists*, p.167–82. F. Salamone (ed). *Studies in Third World societies*, no. 26. Williamsburg, VA: College of William and Mary, 1985. (Deals with Philippines and Ponape).

The first taint of civilization: a history of the Caroline and Marshall Islands in pre–colonial days, 1521–1885. F. X. Hezel. , 1983.

'The influence of Christianity among the people of Ponape.' J. Shem. B.D. thesis, Pacific Theological College, Suva, Fiji, 1972. 169p.

'The Protestant mission work on the Truk Islands in Micronesia: a missiological analysis and evaluation.' K. W. Mueller. M.A. thesis, Fuller Theological Seminary, Pasadena, CA, 1981. 395p. (also in German).

Country Table 2. **Organized churches and denominations in Micronesia.**

Official name (bold type = church with over 10% of all affiliated) 1	*Begun* 2	*Type* 3	*Counc* 4	*Congs* 5	*Adults* 6	*Affiliated 1970* 7	*Affiliated 1995* 8	*G%* 9	*Names, notes, and other statistics* (see Codebook, Part 3) 10
Assemblies of God	1960	P-Pe2	.....	5	440	233	650	4.19	M=AoG(USA). Classical Pentecostals.
Catholic Ch: D Caroline Islands	1902	R-Lat	P....	35	30,000	20,000	64,089	4.77	M=SJ. Yapese, Chamorro, Chinese, Carolinian, Mortlockese. (1990) 10n,20x,24m,37w,2521Yy.
Church of Christ		I-Dis	.....	5	100	–	170	0.05	On Truk and Ponape.
Ch of Jesus Christ of Latter-day Saints		m-LdS	.....	19	1,140	100	1,900	0.05	Yapese, Palauans, Pomapeans.
Congregational Church	1984	I-Con	.....	2	200	–	500	9.09	Pohnpe, Kosrae. M=Conservative Cong Chr Conference (USA). School. 2f.
Independent Baptist Churches	1972	I-Bap	.....	10	400	–	670	4.35	On Truk, also Ponape. M=BBFI(USA),BIM(USA). BMM(USA). 10f.
Jehovah's Witnesses		m-Jeh	.....	6	400	220	830	0.05	*Watch Tower.*
Nukuono Protestant Church	c1990	I-3pP	.....	5	100	–	150	20.00	Schism on Truk island.
Pentecostal Churches	c1975	I-3pP	.....	4	200	–	400	5.00	Indigenous pentecostals.
Protestant Ch of the Caroline Islands	1906	P-Non	.....	100	6,000	2,000	12,000	7.43	M=Liebenzell M (German, USA).
Protestant Church of East Truk	1885	P-Uni	.....	28	8,350	15,000	16,700	0.43	Language name: Chuuk. M=ABCFM, now UCBWM(USA). Trukese.
Seventh-day Adventist Church		P-Adv	.....	10	300	–	520	0.05	M=SDA(USA).
United Churches of Christ in Pohnpe	1852	P-Uni	.....	22	5,600	10,000	11,200	0.45	M=ABCFM, now BWM(USA).
United Pentecostal Church	1981	P-Pe1	.....	5	100	–	250	7.14	M=UPC(USA). Working on Ponape and Truk.
Doubly-affiliated		2-aff			-5,800	0	-12,029		Evangelicals who are also baptized Roman Catholics.
Totals				**256**	**47,530**	**47,553**	**98,000**		

Churches, members, growth, 1900-2025	*Congs*	*Adults*	*Affiliated*	*G%*	*Total denominations*	*6 Megablocs:* O	R	A	P	I	m
Total churches, members, and denominations (mid-1900)	50	11,200	22,515	1.07	2	0	0	0	2	0	0
Total churches, members, and denominations (mid-1970)	121	23,718	47,553	1.07	7	0	1	0	4	0	2
Total churches, members, and denominations (mid-1990)	230	42,900	88,500	3.15	11	0	1	0	6	2	2
Total churches, members, and denominations (mid-1995)	256	47,530	98,000	2.06	14	0	1	0	6	5	2
Total churches, members, and denominations (mid-2000)	270	52,700	108,662	2.09	14	0	1	0	6	5	2
Total churches, members, and denominations (mid-2025)	360	84,200	173,800	1.90	38	0	1	0	12	20	5

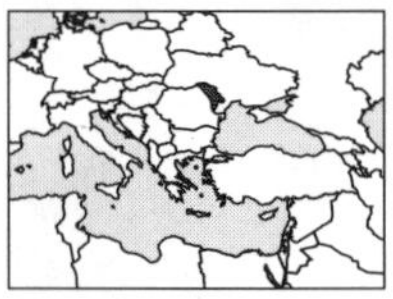

MOLDAVIA

SECULAR DATA, AD 2000

STATE
Official name: Republica Moldoveneasca (The Republic of Moldavia).
Short name: Moldavia. **Adjective of nationality:** Moldavian.
Flag: Blue, yellow, and red bars with coat of arms in center.
Area: 33,700 sq. km. (13,000 sq. mi.).
Government: Unitary multiparty republic with a single legislative body, since 1991 (1924 Moldovian ASSR, 1940 Soviet rule).
Legislature: Parliament, 104 members.
Official language: Romanian.
Monetary unit: 1 Moldovan leu (plural lei) = 100 bani. **US$1=** 4.95.
Chief cities: KISIN'OV (Kishinev) 830,000; Tiraspol' 191,497; Bel'cy (Beltsy) 169,773; Bendery (Bender) 145,682; Rybnica 64,759.
Political divisions: 50 provinces.
Armed forces: 11,000.

DEMOGRAPHY
Population: 4,380,000.
Population density: 129.9/sq. km. (336.9/sq. mi.).
Under 15 years: 1,020,000.
Growth rate p.a.: 0.03% (births 12.88, deaths 10.74).
Mortality: Infant, per 1,000: 24.8, ; **Maternal per 100,000:** 60.0.
Life expectancy: 69 (male 65, female 73).
Household size: 3.4. **Floor area per person, sq.m:** 18.4.
Major languages: Moldavian, Russian, Ukrainian, Bulgarian.
Urban dwellers: 55.18%. **Urban growth rate p.a.:** 1.4%.
Labor force: 47%.

ETHNOLINGUISTIC PEOPLES
48.2% Moldavian; 13.8% Ukrainian; 12.9% Russian; 8.1% Bulgarian; 4.2% Gagauzi Turk.

ECONOMY
National income p.a. per person: US$919; **per family:** US$3,127.

EDUCATION
Adult literacy: 96% (male 98%, female 94%). **Schools:** 1,700.
Universities: 18. **School enrolment:** female/male: 81%/79%.

HEALTH
Access to health services: 75%. **Access to safe water:** 80%.
Hospitals: 335 (122 beds per 10,000). **Doctors:** 18,000.
Blind: 3,700. **Deaf:** 267,500. **Murder rate:** 8. **Lepers:** 500.

LITERATURE
New book titles p.a.: 770 (175 p.a. per million). **Periodicals:** 95.
Newspapers: 4 dailies.

COMMUNICATION (per 1,000 people)
Phones: 131 (1% mobile). **Radios:** 358. **TV sets:** 300.
Daily newspaper circulation: 24. **Computers:** 45.

HUMAN LIFE AND LIBERTY (optimum condition=100.0%)
HDI: 61.2. **HSI:** 60.0. **HFI:** 40.0. **EFL:** 31.0.

Country Table 1. **Religious adherents in Moldavia, AD 1900-2025.**

Year	*1900*		*1970*		*mid-1990*		*Annual change, 1990-2000*				*mid-1995*		*mid-2000*		*mid-2025*	
Name	*Adherents*	*%*	*Adherents*	*%*	*Adherents*	*%*	*Natural*	*Conversion*	*Total*	*Rate*	*Adherents*	*%*	*Adherents*	*%*	*Adherents*	*%*
Christians	**1,310,400**	**99.1**	**1,665,000**	**46.3**	**2,726,200**	**62.5**	**1,048**	**27,727**	**28,775**	**1.01**	**2,900,000**	**66.3**	**3,013,953**	**68.8**	**3,726,500**	**82.0**
PROFESSION																
crypto-Christians	0	0.0	500,000	13.9	200,000	4.6	73	-20,073	-20,000	-70.49	0	0.0	0	0.0	0	0.0
professing Christians	**1,310,400**	**99.1**	**1,165,000**	**32.4**	**2,526,200**	**57.9**	**974**	**47,801**	**48,775**	**1.78**	**2,900,000**	**66.3**	**3,013,953**	**68.8**	**3,726,500**	**82.0**
AFFILIATION																
unaffiliated Christians	100,000	7.6	5,700	0.2	171,200	3.9	63	4,357	4,420	2.32	195,700	4.5	215,395	4.9	101,500	2.2
affiliated Christians	**1,210,400**	**91.6**	**1,659,300**	**46.2**	**2,555,000**	**58.6**	**985**	**23,371**	**24,356**	**0.91**	**2,704,300**	**61.8**	**2,798,558**	**63.9**	**3,625,000**	**79.7**
Orthodox	1,175,400	88.9	1,545,300	43.0	1,800,000	41.3	660	14,396	15,056	0.81	1,896,500	43.3	1,950,558	44.5	2,400,000	52.8
Independents	0	0.0	6,000	0.2	600,000	13.8	220	6,780	7,000	1.11	645,100	14.7	670,000	15.3	1,000,000	22.0
Protestants	15,000	1.1	32,800	0.9	70,000	1.6	26	774	800	1.09	73,000	1.7	78,000	1.8	125,000	2.8
Roman Catholics	20,000	1.5	75,000	2.1	65,000	1.5	24	776	800	1.17	66,000	1.5	73,000	1.7	100,000	2.2
Marginal Christians	0	0.0	200	0.0	20,000	0.5	7	693	700	3.05	23,700	0.5	27,000	0.6	50,000	1.1
Trans-megabloc groupings																
Evangelicals	13,000	1.0	9,200	0.3	18,800	0.4	7	113	120	0.62	19,500	0.5	20,000	0.5	24,400	0.5
Pentecostals/Charismatics	0	0.0	6,000	0.2	43,000	1.0	16	584	600	1.31	46,410	1.1	49,000	1.1	65,000	1.4
Great Commission Christians	**66,000**	**5.0**	**251,000**	**7.0**	**800,000**	**18.3**	**293**	**3,356**	**3,649**	**0.45**	**831,000**	**19.0**	**836,487**	**19.1**	**1,000,000**	**22.0**
Nonreligious	2,000	0.2	1,068,000	29.7	970,000	22.2	356	-7,946	-7,590	-0.81	944,740	21.6	894,104	20.4	450,000	9.9
Muslims	1,000	0.1	7,000	0.2	222,000	5.1	81	1,759	1,840	0.80	230,000	5.3	240,403	5.5	280,000	6.2
Atheists	800	0.1	800,000	22.3	387,000	8.9	142	-20,537	-20,395	-7.21	249,000	5.7	183,052	4.2	50,000	1.1
Jews	7,800	0.6	55,000	1.5	58,550	1.3	21	-1,005	-984	-1.82	52,000	1.2	48,711	1.1	40,000	0.9
Ethnoreligionists	0	0.0	0	0.0	250	0.0	0	2	2	0.74	260	0.0	269	0.0	500	0.0
World A (unevangelized persons)	1,322	0.1	359,450	10.0	305,480	7.0	112	-5,320	-5,208	-1.85	275,672	6.3	254,040	5.8	195,521	4.3
World B (evangelized non-Christians)	10,278	0.8	1,570,050	43.7	1,332,320	30.5	488	-22,407	-21,919	-1.79	1,200,077	27.4	1,112,007	25.4	624,979	13.7
World C (Christians)	1,310,400	99.1	1,665,000	46.3	2,726,200	62.5	1,048	27,727	28,775	1.01	2,900,000	66.3	3,013,953	68.8	3,726,500	82.0
Country's population	**1,322,000**	**100.0**	**3,594,500**	**100.0**	**4,364,000**	**100.0**	**1,648**	**0**	**1,648**	**0.04**	**4,375,750**	**100.0**	**4,380,000**	**100.0**	**4,547,000**	**100.0**

COLUMNS, ROWS.
For meanings and definitions, see Codebook (Part 3). Note that, by definition, total 'Christians' = professing + crypto-Christians, which also = affiliated + unaffiliated Christians, and also = Great Commission Christians + latent Christians. Percentages may not always total exactly, due to rounding.

NOTES ON RELIGIONS
BAHA'IS. From 1990 on, gradual growth including immigration, to (1995) 4 local spiritual assemblies.
MUSLIMS. Mainly Gypsies and Turks.

Country status. Moldavia, a former republic of the Soviet Union, is a landlocked country in southeast Europe bordering Romania and Ukraine. The economy is primarily agricultural, focused on fruits, grains, vegetables, and wines.

HUMAN LIFE AND LIBERTY

Human need and development. Moldavia is that part of the countries of Eastern Europe and the Commonwealth of Independent States where the highest increase in poverty and misery is noted. In a public opinion poll conducted in 1995 by the sociological service Opinia (opinion) the quality of life in Moldavia was confirmed to be unfavorable for a majority of the population. Of those questioned, thirty-two percent considered themselves to be living below the poverty line, 57% declared a rather low quality of life, and only 10.5% were satisfied with their quality of life.

Moldavia ranks 98th of the 174 countries in the UN's Human Development Index, placing it in the low medium human development range. Many in-

Great Commission Instrument Panel: status of Moldavia (for explanation see start of Part 4)

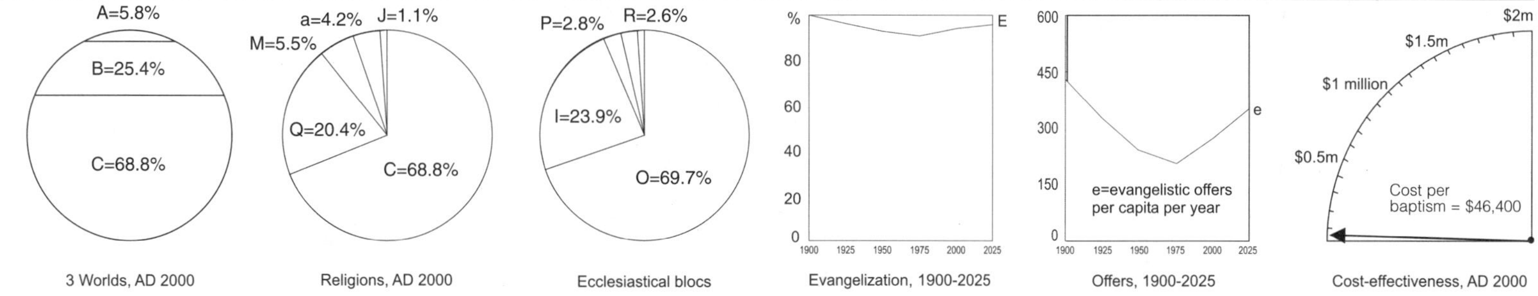

ternal factors contribute to this sisyphian march towards progress. The existence of the self-proclaimed Moldavian Transnistrian Republic including state attributes of president, parliament, army, and the like continues to enhance ongoing disintegration of the Republic of Moldavia and Moldavian society. The Transnistrians are pro-Russian whilst the Republic of Moldavia is pro-democratization independence. The leadership of the ROM have offered Transnistria the status of an autonomous unit. This offer has been supported by all international organizations including the Commonwealth of Independent States. Unfortunately, it was rejected by the leadership of Transnistria. With such internal strife, there remains a stifling of human development.

The majority of industrial regions lie within Transnistria which has led to the development of 2 separate financial systems, only furthering the economic crisis. Contrary to industry, most of the region's higher education institutions and those which specialize in training for health and sciences are located within ROM. The political and ideological atmosphere created by leaders of Transnistria has inhibited the population of the self-proclaimed republic to leave the region and make use of these institutions, which has deterred their development.

The GDP for Moldavia has dropped by around 65% since independence, and according to estimates of the State Department of Statistics , the GDP registered a drop of 8% in 1996. They estimate the drop in agricultural output in that year to be around 13% and that of industrial output 8.5%. Total unemployment is 20% of the labor force. Also noteworthy is the average monthly salary which is equivalent to US $40 per month.

Human rights and freedoms. Moldavia became independent in 1991, and since then has moved slowly toward a full democratic regime. Much of the republic was part of Romania between 1918 and 1940 and the majority of the population is Romanian-speaking. The major human rights problems arise from the 2 separatist movements that have been smoldering for over 3 years. One is led by a pro-Russian group in the Trans-nistria region and the other by the Gagauz or Christian Turks. The Russian minority also is restive, alleging that they are discriminated against in the courts and in public institutions. The former Soviet code on penal procedure remains in force, with some amendments. The local human rights group, the Helsinki Watch, operates without government interference. Religious freedom has been completely restored with a new 1992 law on religion. However, the law requires that religious groups can function only after they are recognized by the government and that they hire non-Moldavians only with government approval. The law also prohibits proselytizing, causing Protestant denominations to complain that it is directed against them. The law is not implemented in practice and street preaching has flourished. Although the Orthodox Church under the authority of the patriarch of Moscow is not designated as the official church, it is virtually one. It is opposed by the pro-Romanian Metropolitanate of Bessarabia-Old Style which has not received official recognition.

Human environment. An overuse of pesticides, herbicides, and artificial fertilizers was intended to bring about increase of agricultural output at any cost, with no regard for consequences. As a result, soil and groundwater have been contaminated by lingering chemicals, some including DDT which has been banned in the West. In the early 1990s the use of pesticides per hectare averaged 20 times that of other former Soviet republics and Western nations. In addition, poor farming methods including the destruction of forests for vineyard planting have enhanced the extensive soil erosion already prevalent in the country.

NON-CHRISTIAN RELIGIONS

Judaism. Moldavian Jews have managed to retain their identity despite the Soviet government's prior suppression and harassment. About a dozen Jewish newspapers have begun since the early 1990s and a synagogue in Chisinau has been opened. In addition, Moldavia's government created the Department of Jewish Studies at Chisinau State University, mandated the opening of a Jewish high school and at several schools in various cities classes on Judaism were offered. There is also governmental financial support for the Society for Jewish Culture.

Islam represents a small portion of the religious groups within Moldavia and Muslims are widely dispersed.

Atheism is also represented due to the roots of Communism that prevailed for so long.

Baptist Union of Moldova. Kishinev congregation

CHRISTIANITY

Moldavia's Latin origins can be traced to the period of Roman occupation of nearby Dacia from AD 105-271. The region's history closely parallels Romanian's as a number of ethnic groups fought their way through the area including Huns, Ostrogoths, Mongols, and Bulgarians. In the midst of this, Christianity reached the shores of the Black Sea and by the third century had become a strong presence. Moldavia's Christian tradition has primarily been influenced by its roots in Romanian culture and its regional contact with such forces as the Byzantine empire, Ottoman Turks, and neighboring Slav and Magyar populations. Although historically a republic of Russia, the Moldavian people have long considered themselves as ethnic Romanians.

Between the 10th and 12th centuries, Moldavia belonged to Kievan Rus. Prince Vladimir ruled Rus from 978 to 1015 and his greatest achievement was the christianization of this region. He built large cathedrals, patronized monasticism and native clergy, and started a school system. His choice of Eastern Orthodox mirrored his ties with Constantinople, and thus facilitated the conversion of the region to Christianity.

Moldavian Orthodox Church. Centenary of Church of St Panteleimon (1992).

ORTHODOX CHURCHES. Nearly 70% of Moldavians are professing Christians with some 45% of these adherents of the Orthodox religion. Before Soviet power was established in Moldavia, the majority of Moldavians (ethnic Romanians) belonged to the Romanian Orthodox Church, but today the Russian Orthodox Church has jurisdiction. The Soviet government strictly limited the activities of the Orthodox Church seeking at times to exploit it with the ultimate goal of bringing an end to all religious activity. Most Orthodox churches and monasteries were demolished or converted to other uses and clergy punished for holding services. In 1991, Moldavia had 853 Orthodox churches and 11 monasteries, with the Old Ritualist Church having 14 churches and one monastery.

After the recent religious revival in Russia, most clergy wanted to return to the Bucharest Patriarchate but were prevented from doing so. Because there was no resolution to this matter, in 1993 a major schism occurred and so Moldavia now has two rival bodies, one for each patriarch.

CATHOLIC CHURCH. A sizeable Latin-rite minority church remains. There is also an Eastern-rite minority, mainly among ethnic Ukrainians. This Uniate church was declared illegal in 1946 by the Soviet government and was forced to unite with the Russian Orthodox Church. It survived underground, outlasting the Soviet Union.

The Holy See has diplomatic relations with Moldavia and in AD 2000 is represented to government and the Catholic hierarchy by a nuncio residing in Budapest.

Indigenous missions. Since the introduction of Christianity in the 7th century there has been a steady stream of Moldavian Christians who have worked as missionaries in surrounding countries. This trend was interrupted in the 20th century under Soviet rule but has begun again with Moldavian independence.

Pentecostal Union. Service in Kishinev.

CHURCH AND STATE

Moldavia adopted its constitution on 27 August 1994 and thus made its step towards democratization and individual human freedoms. The preamble mentions that irreversible processes are under way in Europe and in the democratic world leading to a consolidation of freedom, independence, and national unity. It refers to the UN charter and the Helsinki Document among its reasons for independence. Along with these claims comes the guarantee of individual freedoms, but as is so often the case there are many outstanding variables which impede the fulfillment of such freedoms. Article 30 guarantees the freedom of spirit essentially guaranteeing the freedom of religion. Section 4 of Article 30 states: 'The religious faiths are autonomous in respect to the state and benefit of its support. The State facilitates the religious ac-

Country summary. **Worlds A, B, C by ethnolinguistic peoples, cities, and major civil divisions in Moldavia.**

	PEOPLES							CITIES							CIVIL DIVISIONS						
World	*Num*	*Pop 2000*	*C%*	*Christians*	*E%*	*U%*	*Unevangelized*	*Num*	*Pop 2000*	*C%*	*Christians*	*E%*	*U%*	*Unevangelized*	*Num*	*Pop 2000*	*C%*	*Christians*	*E%*	*U%*	*Unevangelized*
A	10	364,215	3.26	11,858	35	65	238,010	0	0	0.00	0	0	0	0	0	0	0.00	0	0	0	0
B	6	8,405	32.67	2,746	68	32	2,669	0	0	0.00	0	0	0	0	0	0	0.00	0	0	0	0
C	16	4,007,871	69.46	2,783,956	100	0	12,243	5	1,401,711	62.73	879,227	93	7	93,055	50	4,380,501	63.89	2,798,558	94	6	252,932
Total	**32**	**4,380,491**	**63.89**	**2,798,560**	**94**	**6**	**252,922**	**5**	**1,401,711**	**62.73**	**879,227**	**93**	**7**	**93,055**	**50**	**4,380,501**	**63.89**	**2,798,558**	**94**	**6**	**252,932**

tivity in the army, in hospitals, in penitentiaries, asylums, and orphanages'. Prior to the adoption of the constitution, legislation passed in 1992 guaranteed religious freedom but required that all religious groups be officially recognized by the government.

BROADCASTING AND MEDIA

IBRA-produced programs can be heard on local radio channels, and there have been responses to shortwave radio programming from KNLS. Satellite TV programs are received mainly in Arabic. HCJB is planting a local radio ministry in Moldavia in partnership with Little Samaritan Mission.

Some 2.8 million (60%) have seen the 'Jesus' Film, most through TV broadcasts (2.4 million) and also cinema showings (325,000).

FUTURE TRENDS AND PROSPECTS

Christianity is projected to increase to 82.0% of the population by AD 2025. Nonreligious and atheists, on the other hand, representing nearly 60% of the population in 1970, are projected to jointly fall to only 11% by AD 2025.

Christianity could reach 90% of the population later in the 21st century if current declines among atheists and nonreligious continue.

BIBLIOGRAPHY

Crestinismul la est de Carpati: de la origini si pîna în secolul al XIV–lea. D. G. Teodor. Mitropoliei Moldovei si Bucovinei: IASI, 1991. 229p.

Religioznaia filosofiia v Moldavii nachala XX veka. V. M. Topilina. Kishinev: Shtiintsa, 1990. 131p.

Stifterrecht und Kirchenpatronat im fürstentum Moldau und in der Bukowina: eine historisch–dogmatische Studie aum Morgenländischen Kirchenrecht. N. Cotlarciuc. Stuttgart: F. Enke, 1907. 221p.

Country Table 2. **Organized churches and denominations in Moldavia.**

Official name (bold type = church with over 10% of all affiliated) 1	*Begun* 2	*Type* 3	*Counc* 4	*Congs* 5	*Adults* 6	*Affiliated 1970* 7	*Affiliated 1995* 8	*G%* 9	*Names, notes, and other statistics* (see Codebook, Part 3) 10
Armenian Apostolic Church	1900	O-Arm	E....	1	1,500	2,800	4,000	0.05	Gregorians. Armenians, under C Echmiadzin.
Assembly Hall Churches	1990	I-3nC	M....	1	35	–	100	20.00	*Local Churches. Little Flock.* Chinese. Begun 1922 in China.
Baptist Union of Moldova		P-Bap	T....	265	17,800	26,000	50,000	0.05	Formerly related to AUCECB(Moscow). Russians, Ukrainians, Moldavians, and 1,000 Gagauz.
Bulgarian Orthodox Church		O-Bul	M....	10	39,000	37,000	60,000	0.05	Mainly Bulgarian, also Gagauz.
Catholic Ch in Moldova:		R-LEr	b....	14	40,000	75,000	66,000	0.05	History of persecution and murders throughout Communist era. 6n,7x,20w,130Yy.
D Tiraspol	1848	R-LEr	bs	10	30,000	75,000	51,000	-1.53	Latin-rite and Eastern-rite Catholics, originally across Volga to Caucasus, now in Moldavia only.
AA Moldova	1993	R-Lat	bs	4	10,000	–	15,000	50.00	Newest administrative jurisdiction.
Evangelical Lutheran Ch in Moldova	c1950	P-Lut	.....	10	1,200	300	2,000	7.88	Mainly Germans.
Followers of Innocent		I-Ort	.....	10	4,500	2,000	5,000	0.05	An Orthodox sect from Russia.
Jehovah's Witnesses	c1950	m-Jeh	x....	70	10,510	200	23,700	21.05	*Jehovah's Christian Witnesses.* Rapid growth in 1990s of 11% per year. (1995) 1917Y.
Metropolitan Church of Bessarabia	1993	I-Mol	.....	40	400,000	–	630,000	50.00	Schism of 33% of Orthodox Church from P Moscow, aided by P Bucharest. 25n.
Moldovan Orthodox Ch: D Chisinau	1401	O-Mol	M....	150	900,000	1,150,000	1,300,000	0.05	Ethnic Moldavians & Romanians under Russian P Moscow; autonomy 1992. 4 Dioceses, 4 bps.
Old Ritualist Church	c1900	I-OBe	.....	14	6,500	4,000	10,000	0.05	*Old Believers.* Mostly Russians, Byelorussians. 1 monastery.
Pentecostal Union of Moldova.	c1930	P-Pe2	.....	172	6,000	6,000	15,000	0.05	*Christians of the Evangelical Faith.* Mostly Romanians and Ukrainians. M=AoG (USA).
Romanian Orthodox Church	1401	O-Rum	C....	6	7,000	5,000	10,000	0.05	Churches of ethnic Romanians resident in Moldavia, under P Bucharest.
Russian Orthodox Church	1800	O-Rus	.....	130	364,000	350,000	520,000	0.05	D Kishinev (Chisinau) & Moldova. Ethnic Russians & Ukranians, under Patriarchate of Moscow.
Seventh-day Adventist Church	c1970	P-Adv	.....	4	400	–	1,000	31.83	M = SDA supported by Europe and USA.
Other Orthodox churches		O-	.....	4	1,630	500	2,500	0.05	Including Georgian Orthodox Ch.
Other Protestant churches		P-	.....	25	2,000	500	5,000	0.05	Independent Reformed Ch, Reformed Adventist Ch.
Totals				**926**	**1,802,075**	**1,659,300**	**2,704,300**		

Churches, members, growth, 1900-2025	*Congs*	*Adults*	*Affiliated*	*G%*	*Total denominations*	*O*	*R*	*A*	*P*	*I*	*m*
Total churches, members, and denominations (mid-1900)	200	862,000	1,210,400	0.45	6	4	1	0	0	1	0
Total churches, members, and denominations (mid-1970)	478	1,181,900	1,659,300	0.45	18	9	1	0	5	2	1
Total churches, members, and denominations (mid-1990)	800	1,703,000	2,555,000	2.18	28	13	1	0	9	4	1
Total churches, members, and denominations (mid-1995)	926	1,802,075	2,704,300	1.14	28	13	1	0	9	4	1
Total churches, members, and denominations (mid-2000)	1,100	1,865,000	2,798,558	0.69	28	13	1	0	9	4	1
Total churches, members, and denominations (mid-2025)	1,400	2,416,000	3,625,000	1.04	54	20	1	0	17	15	1

(6 Megablocs: O, R, A, P, I, m)

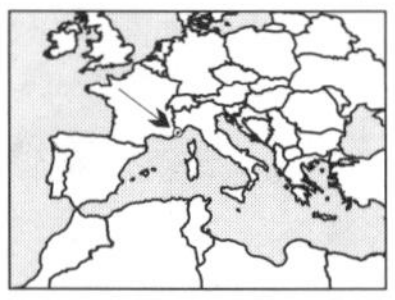

MONACO

SECULAR DATA, AD 2000

STATE

Official name: Le Principauté de Monaco (The Principality of Monaco).
Short name: Monaco. **Adjective of nationality:** Monegasque.
Flag: Red stripe over white stripe.
Area: 2 sq. km. (1 sq. mi.).
Government: Constitutional principality, since 1911 (1524 Spanish protectorate, 1641 French protectorate).
Legislature: National Council, 18 members.
Official language: French (Français).
Monetary unit: 1 French franc (F) = 100 centimes. **US$1=** F 5.60.
Chief cities: MONACO-Ville 33,601.
Political divisions: 1 province.

DEMOGRAPHY

Population: 34,000.
Population density: 16,798.5/sq. km. (33,597.0/sq. mi.).
Under 15 years: 6,000.
Growth rate p.a.: 0.28% (births 11.85, deaths 9.51).
Mortality: Infant, per 1,000: 5.9, ; **Maternal per 100,000:** 10.0.
Life expectancy: 79 (male 75, female 83).
Household size: 2.2. **Floor area per person, sq.m:** 35.0.
Major languages: French, English, Italian, Monegasque.
Urban dwellers: 100.00%. **Urban growth rate p.a.:** 1.1%.
Labor force: 42%.

ETHNOLINGUISTIC PEOPLES

45.8% French; 17.2% Ligurian (Genoan); 16.9% Monegasque (Provencal); 4.5% British; 3.0% USA White.

ECONOMY

National income p.a. per person: US$25,002; **per family:** US$55,004.

EDUCATION

Adult literacy: 99% (male 99%, female 99%). **Schools:** 6.
Universities: 0. **School enrolment:** female/male: 100%/100%.

HEALTH

Access to health services: 95%. **Access to safe water:** 100%.
Hospitals: 1 (168 beds per 10,000). **Doctors:** 112.
Blind: 15. **Deaf:** 2,000. **Murder rate:** <1.
Lepers: 0.

LITERATURE

New book titles p.a.: 24 (700 p.a. per million). **Periodicals:** 4.
Newspapers: 1 dailies.

COMMUNICATION (per 1,000 people)

Phones: 876 (40% mobile). **Radios:** 987. **TV sets:** 670.
Daily newspaper circulation: 263. **Computers:** 300.

HUMAN LIFE AND LIBERTY (optimum condition=100.0%)

HDI: 94.0. **HSI:** 95.0. **HFI:** 85.0. **EFL:** 60.0.

Country status. Monaco, an enclave with France, is in southern Europe on the Mediterranean coast. Tourism is the principal economic activity.

HUMAN LIFE AND LIBERTY

Human rights and freedoms. The Principality of Monaco, the world's smallest secular sovereign state, is essentially a fiefdom of the Rainier royal family. Nevertheless, the principality respects all human and civil rights of its residents, who are outnumbered at any given time by tourists and expatriates. Those who hold Monegasque nationality number only about 5,000 and they have special rights and privileges.

Eglise Catholique, Diocèse de Monaco. Cathedral in Monaco.

NON-CHRISTIAN RELIGIONS

Judaism has been represented by a cultural association since 1947. A resident rabbi serves the Jewish community, with Sabbath and feast days celebrated in a chapel built in 1960. The construction of a synagogue is anticipated.

Baha'i also has a small community.

CHRISTIANITY

CATHOLIC CHURCH. Catholicism is the majority religion of Monaco. A parish was formed in 1247 as part of the diocese of Nice. It became a diocese in its own right in 1887 and is, ecclesiastically, immediately subject to the Holy See. Diocesan clergy and several religious congregations are active in 5 Catholic

Country Table 1. Religious adherents in Monaco, AD 1900-2025.

Year / Name	1900 Adherents	1900 %	1970 Adherents	1970 %	mid-1990 Adherents	mid-1990 %	Annual change, 1990-2000 Natural	Conversion	Total	Rate	mid-1995 Adherents	mid-1995 %	mid-2000 Adherents	mid-2000 %	mid-2025 Adherents	mid-2025 %
Christians	**15,300**	**98.7**	**23,270**	**98.3**	**28,400**	**94.7**	**337**	**-46**	**291**	**0.98**	**29,920**	**94.1**	**31,313**	**93.2**	**37,100**	**91.2**
PROFESSION																
professing Christians	**15,300**	**98.7**	**23,270**	**98.3**	**28,400**	**94.7**	**337**	**-46**	**291**	**0.98**	**29,920**	**94.1**	**31,313**	**93.2**	**37,100**	**91.2**
AFFILIATION																
unaffiliated Christians	110	0.7	45	0.2	250	0.8	3	-7	-4	-1.64	260	0.8	212	0.6	100	0.2
affiliated Christians	**15,190**	**98.0**	**23,225**	**98.2**	**28,150**	**93.8**	**333**	**-38**	**295**	**1.00**	**29,660**	**93.2**	**31,101**	**92.6**	**37,000**	**90.9**
Roman Catholics	14,640	94.5	21,675	91.6	27,000	90.0	318	-18	300	1.06	28,530	89.7	30,000	89.3	35,800	88.0
Protestants	450	2.9	1,000	4.2	720	2.4	10	-14	-4	-0.56	700	2.2	681	2.0	800	2.0
Anglicans	100	0.7	450	1.9	340	1.1	5	-6	-1	-0.30	340	1.1	330	1.0	300	0.7
Orthodox	0	0.0	100	0.4	90	0.3	1	-1	0	0.00	90	0.3	90	0.3	100	0.2
Trans-megabloc groupings																
Evangelicals	150	1.0	80	0.3	60	0.2	1	0	1	0.80	62	0.2	65	0.2	80	0.2
Pentecostals/Charismatics	0	0.0	100	0.4	900	3.0	12	4	16	1.65	977	3.1	1,060	3.1	1,500	3.7
Great Commission Christians	**1,100**	**7.1**	**4,300**	**18.2**	**7,800**	**26.0**	**104**	**-5**	**99**	**1.20**	**8,270**	**26.0**	**8,786**	**26.1**	**10,800**	**26.5**
Nonreligious	0	0.0	0	0.0	940	3.1	13	44	57	4.83	1,160	3.7	1,506	4.4	2,500	6.1
Jews	200	1.3	400	1.7	500	1.7	7	0	7	1.32	530	1.7	570	1.7	700	1.7
Muslims	0	0.0	0	0.0	120	0.4	2	1	3	2.32	140	0.4	151	0.4	280	0.7
Baha'is	0	0.0	30	0.1	40	0.1	1	1	2	3.61	50	0.2	57	0.2	120	0.3
World A (unevangelized persons)	15	0.1	47	0.2	300	1.0	4	5	9	2.71	349	1.1	408	1.2	492	1.2
World B (evangelized non-Christians)	184	1.2	345	1.4	1,300	4.3	19	41	60	5.77	1,543	4.8	2,279	5.6	3,108	7.6
World C (Christians)	15,300	98.7	23,270	98.3	28,400	94.7	337	-46	291	0.98	29,920	94.1	31,313	93.2	37,100	91.2
Country's population	**15,500**	**100.0**	**23,662**	**100.0**	**30,000**	**100.0**	**360**	**0**	**360**	**1.26**	**31,813**	**100.0**	**33,600**	**100.0**	**40,700**	**100.0**

COLUMNS, ROWS.
For meanings and definitions, see Codebook (Part 3). Note that, by definition, total 'Christians' = professing + crypto-Christians, which also = affiliated + unaffiliated Christians, and also = Great Commission Christians + latent Christians. Percentages may not always total exactly, due to rounding.

CENSUSES.
10.III.1946: 94.6% Roman Catholics, 3.2% Protestants, 1.0% Orthodox, 0.9% Jews, 0.2% Muslims, 0.1% nonreligious. The religion question was not asked in subsequent censuses.

NOTES ON RELIGIONS
BAHA'IS. Begun 1955. In 1 local spiritual assembly (1964, 1973, and the same in 1995).
JEWS. In over 150 families, using an equipped oratory but with no synagogue.
MUSLIMS. North African immigrant workers.

Great Commission Instrument Panel: status of Monaco (for explanation see start of Part 4)

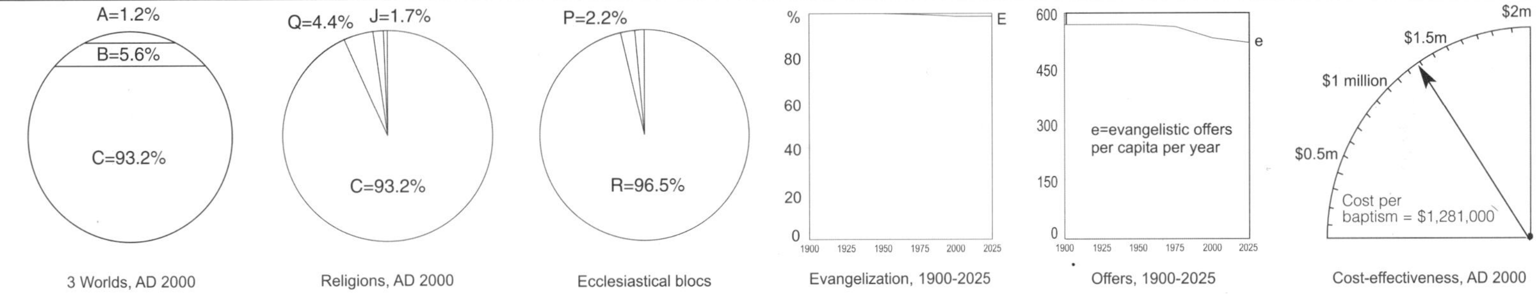

parishes, as well as in the official schools and social service institutions of the principality.

The Holy See had no diplomatic relations with Monaco in AD 2000.

Eglise Catholique. 1958 postage stamp: centenary of Lourdes apparition in 1858.

OTHER CHURCHES. Monaco's large English-speaking community is served by St Paul's Church, which was built in 1925 and is attached to the Anglican diocese of Gibraltar. The building is also used by Greek Orthodox who are part of the Parish of the Riviera and the Principality, and under the ecumenical patriarch of Constantinople, services being conducted by an archimandrite from Nice. The Reformed Church of Monaco also made use of the Anglican building until 1959 when their own was opened.

Indigenous missions. Despite a long Christian history only a handful of missionaries have been sent out from Monaco, and most of these to surrounding Christian countries.

CHURCH AND STATE

The constitution of 17 December 1962 stipulates that 'The Catholic Apostolic and Roman religion is the religion of the State' (Article 9). Since the preceding constitution lacked such a declaration, the Department of the Interior of the Ministry of State justified this inclusion by reference to the following: (1) the papal bull 'Quemadmodum sollicitus pastor' of 15 March 1887, which listed the guarantees, endowments, and juridical status accepted by the state prior to the creation of the diocese; and (2) the 'organic law' of 28 September 1887, which gave legal sanction to this bull. The government considers that these texts bear the significance of a concordat, in contrast to the ecclesiastical authorities for whom, according to canon law, a concordat is a solemn bilateral treaty, and who do not speak of Catholicism as the state religion. Nevertheless, the prince plays the role of patron; and when there is a vacancy in the episcopal see, he presents a list of 3 candidates for papal selection. In return the Catholic Church receives financial compensation including salaries of many clergy, upkeep of buildings, and the covering of parish deficits by the state. Article 23 of the constitution guarantees freedom of religion and expression of opinion. For the construction or opening of a building destined for worship, authorization from the Department of the Interior is required. All official community schools, the hospital as well as 2 hostels and 3 orphanages, are run by Catholic religious personnel.

Headquarters of Trans World Radio on Mount Agel, Monaco.

BROADCASTING AND MEDIA

TWR broadcasts from Monte Carlo in 23 languages, with an emphasis on those spoken in the Middle East. Some of these programs are produced by IBRA and ERF. Shortwave radio programs can be received from KNLS, AWR (Slovakia), and HCJB (Ecuador). Monaco is a member of UNDA, and Catholics broadcast 3 15-minute programs (2 on Sunday) and a daily 2-minute morning meditation.

Satellite TV and radio programs are received in English, Arabic, German and Italian. Catholics broadcast occasional short programs on local television.

INTERDENOMINATIONAL ORGANIZATIONS

Although no formal organizations exist, there are good relations between Monaco's religious confessions. The Anglican building is available to other denominations, and the Catholic bishop has on numerous occasions participated in ecumenical services at the Anglican and Reformed churches.

FUTURE TRENDS AND PROSPECTS

The nonreligious, nonexistent in 1970, are expected to number over 6% by 2025.

The nonreligious are projected to grow throughout the 21st century, perhaps reaching 10% of the population before AD 2050. Christianity would then fall well below 90% in the same period.

BIBLIOGRAPHY

Eglise de Monaco/Gieija de Munegu: revue diocésaine mensuelle. Monaco: Evêché de Monaco, March 1963—. (Monthly).
Essai sur l'autonomie religieuse de la Principauté de Monaco jusqu'à la création de l'évêché. H. Chobaut. Monaco: Imprimerie de Monaco, 1913. 163p.
Essai sur le droit de patronat et de collation des bénéfices ecclésiastiques dans la Principauté de Monaco. L. Baudoin. Monaco: Editions de Fontvieille, 1955. 223p.
Fête populaire et tradition religieuse en pays niçois. P. Canestrier. Nice, France: Serre, 1978. 208p.
Histoire de Monaco. J. B. Robert. Paris: Presses universitaires de France, 1973. 126p.
La musique religieuse dans la Principauté de Monaco. G. Favre. Paris: La Pensée universelle, 1981. 168p.
'La Révolution et le catholicisme dans le département des Alpes Maritimes (1792–1799),' M. Sifre, *Annales du Midi*, 81, 92 (1969), 197–209.

La situation religieuse de la Principauté de Monaco. A. J. Rance-Bourrey. Nice, France: Les Annales du Comté de Nice, 1934. 31p.
Les confréries, leur origine: les pénitents de Monaco. J. Baud. Monaco: Imprimerie de Monaco, 1913. 79p.
Les diocèses de Nice et Monaco. F. Hildesheimer (ed). *Histoire des diocèses de France*, n.s., 17. Paris: Beauchesne, 1984. 387p.
Monaco. G. L. Hudson. *World bibliographical series*, vol. 120. Oxford, UK: CLIO Press, 1991. 230p. (See especially 'Religion,' p.55–8).
'Quelques anciennes chapelles de Monaco,' L. Baudoin, *Annales Monégasques*, 7 (1983), 9–31.

Country summary. **Worlds A, B, C by ethnolinguistic peoples, cities, and major civil divisions in Monaco.**

	PEOPLES							CITIES							CIVIL DIVISIONS						
World	*Num*	*Pop 2000*	*C%*	*Christians*	*E%*	*U%*	*Unevangelized*	*Num*	*Pop 2000*	*C%*	*Christians*	*E%*	*U%*	*Unevangelized*	*Num*	*Pop 2000*	*C%*	*Christians*	*E%*	*U%*	*Unevangelized*
A	1	202	20.79	42	41	59	119	0	0	0.00	0	0	0	0	0	0	0.00	0	0	0	0
B	1	571	0.18	1	55	45	256	0	0	0.00	0	0	0	0	0	0	0.00	0	0	0	0
C	13	32,824	94.62	31,057	100	0	17	1	33,601	92.57	31,104	99	1	393	1	33,597	92.57	31,101	99	1	392
Total	**15**	**33,597**	**92.57**	**31,100**	**99**	**1**	**392**	**1**	**33,601**	**92.57**	**31,104**	**99**	**1**	**393**	**1**	**33,597**	**92.57**	**31,101**	**99**	**1**	**392**

Country Table 2. **Organized churches and denominations in Monaco.**

Official name (bold type = church with over 10% of all affiliated) 1	*Begun* 2	*Type* 3	*Counc* 4	*Congs* 5	*Adults* 6	*Affiliated 1970* 7	*Affiliated 1995* 8	*G%* 9	*Names, notes, and other statistics* (see Codebook, Part 3) 10
Eglise Anglicane (D Europe)	1925	A-plu	awc..	1	270	450	340	-1.11	*St Paul's Anglican Ch.* Chaplaincy in D Gibraltar. English residents, tourists. 1x.
Eglise Catholique: AD Monaco	1247	R-Lat	bxB..	8	20,000	21,675	28,530	1.11	Under Holy See. M=TD. C=5+1+7. (1970) 32nx,274Yy. (1990) 13n,13x,13m,23w,268Yy.
Eglise Orthodoxe Grecque	1957	O-Gre	Cwc..	1	54	100	90	-0.42	*Parish of Monte Carlo, Greek Orthodox Ch.* Greek residents. Use Anglican building.
Eglise Réformée de Monaco	1959	P-Ref	Rwc..	1	560	1,000	700	-1.42	*Reformed Ch of M.* Chapel of Eglise Réformée de France (Menton).
Totals				**11**	**20,884**	**23,225**	**29,660**		

Churches, members, growth, 1900-2025	*Congs*	*Adults*	*Affiliated*	*G%*	*Total denominations*	*6 Megablocs:* *O*	*R*	*A*	*P*	*I*	*m*
Total churches, members, and denominations (mid-1900)	4	11,000	15,190	0.61	1	0	1	0	0	0	0
Total churches, members, and denominations (mid-1970)	8	16,850	23,225	0.61	4	1	1	1	1	0	0
Total churches, members, and denominations (mid-1990)	10	19,800	28,150	0.97	4	1	1	1	1	0	0
Total churches, members, and denominations (mid-1995)	11	20,884	29,660	1.05	4	1	1	1	1	0	0
Total churches, members, and denominations (mid-2000)	12	21,900	31,101	0.95	4	1	1	1	1	0	0
Total churches, members, and denominations (mid-2025)	20	26,100	37,000	0.70	16	3	1	1	6	5	0

NOTES ON TABLE ABOVE
OTHER MARGINAL BODIES. Société des Antoinistes (12 adherents in 1946).

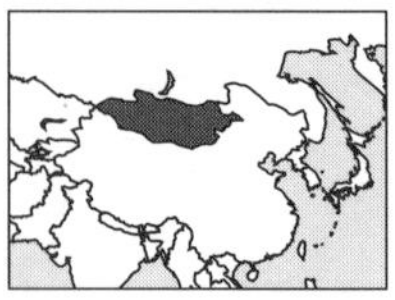

MONGOLIA

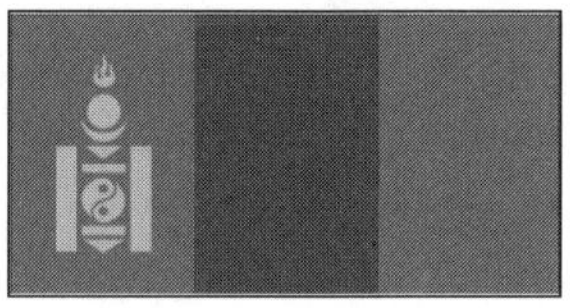

SECULAR DATA, AD 2000

STATE
Official name: Mongol Uls (The State of Mongolia).
Short name: Mongolia. **Adjective of nationality:** Mongolian.
Flag: Red, blue, and red bars, with national emblem (soyombo symbol) in gold below 5-pointed gold star.
Area: 1,566,500 sq. km. (604,800 sq. mi.).
Government: Multiparty republic, since 1992 (1200 Mongolian empire, 1691 Chinese province, 1911 autonomy, 1921 republic, 1924 one-party Communist state).
Legislature: State Great, 76 members.
Official language: Mongolian (Khalka Mongol).
Monetary unit: 1 tugrik (Tug) = 100 möngö. **US$1=** Tug 840.56.
Chief cities: ULAANBAATAR (Ulan Bator) 686,374; Darchan (Darhan) 97,293.
Political divisions: 21 provinces.
Armed forces: 21,000.

DEMOGRAPHY
Population: 2,662,000.
Population density: 1.7/sq. km. (4.4/sq. mi.).
Under 15 years: 921,000.
Growth rate p.a.: 1.50% (births 20.91, deaths 5.94).
Mortality: Infant, per 1,000: 44.5, ; **Maternal per 100,000:** 65.0.
Life expectancy: 68 (male 66, female 69).
Household size: 4.8. **Floor area per person, sq.m:** 10.0.
Major languages: Mongolian (Khalka), Russian, Kazakh, Buryat, Chinese.
Urban dwellers: 63.51%. **Urban growth rate p.a.:** 2.8%.
Labor force: 47%.

ETHNOLINGUISTIC PEOPLES
63.5% Khalkha Mongol; 9.1% Western Mongol (Oirat); 5.4% Kazakh (Qazaq); 5.0% Southeastern Mongolian; 2.9% Durbet (Dorwot).

ECONOMY
National income p.a. per person: US$309; **per family:** US$1,487.

EDUCATION
Adult literacy: 82% (male 88%, female 77%). **Schools:** 708.
Universities: 9. **School enrolment:** female/male: 75%/60%.

HEALTH
Access to health services: 95%. **Access to safe water:** 54%.
Hospitals: 475 (105 beds per 10,000). **Doctors:** 5,911.
Blind: 4,000. **Deaf:** 164,200. **Murder rate:** 19.
Lepers: 200. **Underweight prevalence under 5:** 12%.

LITERATURE
New book titles p.a.: 290 (110 p.a. per million). **Periodicals:** 63.
Newspapers: 1 daily.

COMMUNICATION (per 1,000 people)
Phones: 32 (**2% mobile**). **Radios:** 121. **TV sets:** 59.
Daily newspaper circulation: 88. **Computers:** 2.

HUMAN LIFE AND LIBERTY (optimum condition=100.0%)
HDI: 66.1. **HSI:** 57.0. **HFI:** 5.0. **EFL:** 30.0.

Country Table 1. **Religious adherents in Mongolia, AD 1900-2025.**

Year	*1900*		*1970*		*mid-1990*		*Annual change, 1990-2000*				*mid-1995*		*mid-2000*		*mid-2025*	
Name	*Adherents*	*%*	*Adherents*	*%*	*Adherents*	*%*	*Natural*	*Conversion*	*Total*	*Rate*	*Adherents*	*%*	*Adherents*	*%*	*Adherents*	*%*
Ethnoreligionists	316,450	60.6	438,500	34.9	700,000	31.6	14,089	-1,064	13,025	1.72	768,000	31.3	830,246	31.2	1,015,000	27.4
Nonreligious	0	0.0	494,000	39.3	700,750	31.6	14,104	-2,535	11,569	1.54	754,850	30.8	816,444	30.7	1,115,900	30.1
Buddhists	200,000	38.3	27,000	2.2	465,000	21.0	9,359	4,018	13,377	2.56	542,000	22.1	598,772	22.5	950,000	25.6
Atheists	0	0.0	268,000	21.3	220,000	9.9	4,428	-2,415	2,013	0.88	232,000	9.5	240,134	9.0	300,000	8.1
Muslims	5,000	1.0	22,000	1.8	95,000	4.3	1,912	1,236	3,148	2.90	110,000	4.5	126,483	4.8	250,000	6.7
Christians	**550**	**0.1**	**3,500**	**0.3**	**26,500**	**1.2**	**533**	**209**	**742**	**2.50**	**30,000**	**1.2**	**33,915**	**1.3**	**62,900**	**1.7**
PROFESSION																
crypto-Christians	550	0.1	3,200	0.3	22,160	1.0	446	74	520	2.13	24,600	1.0	27,360	1.0	48,600	1.3
AFFILIATION																
unaffiliated Christians	0	0.0	0	0.0	600	0.0	12	-20	-8	-1.38	550	0.0	522	0.0	200	0.0
affiliated Christians	**550**	**0.1**	**3,500**	**0.3**	**25,900**	**1.2**	**521**	**228**	**749**	**2.57**	**29,450**	**1.2**	**33,393**	**1.3**	**62,700**	**1.7**
Protestants	0	0.0	0	0.0	17,310	0.8	348	78	426	2.23	19,000	0.8	21,573	0.8	40,000	1.1
Independents	0	0.0	100	0.0	6,700	0.3	135	195	330	4.09	8,600	0.4	10,000	0.4	20,000	0.5
Orthodox	500	0.1	3,350	0.3	1,600	0.1	32	-52	-20	-1.33	1,500	0.1	1,400	0.1	1,500	0.0
Roman Catholics	50	0.0	50	0.0	250	0.0	5	5	10	3.42	300	0.0	350	0.0	600	0.0
Marginal Christians	0	0.0	0	0.0	40	0.0	1	2	3	5.76	50	0.0	70	0.0	600	0.0
Trans-megabloc groupings																
Evangelicals	0	0.0	0	0.0	800	0.0	16	14	30	3.24	900	0.0	1,100	0.0	2,000	0.1
Pentecostals/Charismatics	0	0.0	100	0.0	7,700	0.4	155	65	220	2.54	8,870	0.4	9,900	0.4	20,000	0.5
Great Commission Christians	**550**	**0.1**	**2,500**	**0.2**	**19,800**	**0.9**	**399**	**579**	**978**	**4.10**	**23,000**	**0.9**	**29,582**	**1.1**	**55,800**	**1.5**
Chinese folk-religionists	0	0.0	3,000	0.2	8,710	0.4	175	551	726	6.25	14,100	0.6	15,972	0.6	15,000	0.4
Baha'is	0	0.0	0	0.0	40	0.0	1	0	1	2.85	50	0.0	53	0.0	200	0.0
World A (unevangelized persons)	502,164	96.2	1,054,744	84.0	1,500,232	67.7	30,191	-27,988	2,203	0.15	1,556,660	63.5	1,522,664	57.2	1,891,590	51.0
World B (evangelized non-Christians)	19,286	3.7	197,403	15.7	689,268	31.1	13,877	27,779	41,656	4.84	864,773	35.3	1,105,421	41.5	1,754,510	47.3
World C (Christians)	550	0.1	3,500	0.3	26,500	1.2	533	209	742	2.50	30,000	1.2	33,915	1.3	62,900	1.7
Country's population	**522,000**	**100.0**	**1,255,648**	**100.0**	**2,216,000**	**100.0**	**44,601**	**0**	**44,601**	**1.85**	**2,451,434**	**100.0**	**2,662,000**	**100.0**	**3,709,000**	**100.0**

COLUMNS, ROWS.
For meanings and definitions, see Codebook (Part 3). Note that, by definition, total 'Christians' = professing + crypto-Christians, which also = affiliated + unaffiliated Christians, and also = Great Commission Christians + latent Christians. Percentages may not always total exactly, due to rounding.

CENSUSES.
No census has ever included religion.

NOTES ON RELIGIONS
ATHEISTS. Mongolian People's Revolutionary Party (MPRP) (Communist; in power; pro-Soviet).
BAHA'IS. After the collapse of Communism in 1991, Baha'i workers initiated organized centers, with by 1995 a total of 15 local spiritual assemblies.
BUDDHISTS. 1900: 200,000 Lamaists (followers of Tibetan Tantrism). 1920: 120,000 lamas in 2,648 temples, and 85,000 followers of the Living Buddha (Bogdo-Guegen) of Urga. 1929: all

Continued opposite

Country Table 1–concluded

lamaseries suppressed or destroyed, then nationalized and secularized. 1960: new lamasery permitted at Gandan Djoo, with 40 young monks by 1977.
CRYPTO-CHRISTIANS. The existence of Christians has never been recognized by the state, so all Christians are properly termed crypto-Christians. There are 4 groupings (see Table 2).
INDEPENDENTS. This term is used here to describes the very small number of scattered and completely isolated indigenous radio believers (see Table 2).
MUSLIMS. Mostly Sunnis (of the Hanafite rite) in the west, including Kazaks, Uighurs, and Uzbeks.
NONRELIGIOUS. Mongolians and Chinese.
SHAMANISTS. Unorganized traditional religionists, functioning at the family level without public temples or centers; declining since 1930, but increasing again in influence.

Great Commission Instrument Panel: status of Mongolia (for explanation see start of Part 4)

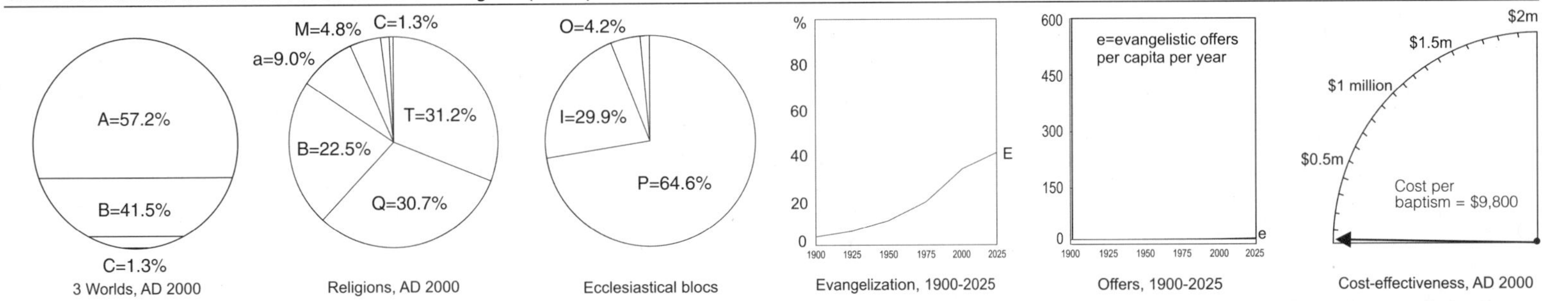

Country status. Mongolia is a large and sparsely populated country in East Asia bordered by Russia and China. It is rich in natural resources such as coal and oil. Much of the population is nomadic pastoralists.

HUMAN LIFE AND LIBERTY

Human need and development. The 7 decades of Soviet hegemony had helped to transform Mongolia from one of the most primitive economies in the world based almost entirely on livestock to a moderately developed one with a small industrial sector and a reasonably good educational and technological infrastructure. The end of Soviet dominance has forced Mongolia to rely on its own resources in any effort toward further modernization. The urban sector is still small and beset with problems of housing and communication. But public health and education, objects of intense development during the Soviet era, are comparable to those of developed nations while literacy is nearly universal among the younger generation. The population is no longer declining in numbers, as it was during the pre-Soviet decades, and such blights as venereal diseases, formerly widely prevalent, have been wiped out.

Human rights and freedoms. Mongolia has made the transition from a communist state to a democracy far more rapidly and completely than Russia. The first multiparty legislative elections were held in 1990 and the government that came to power is committed to dismantling the former apparatus of terror. The new constitution, which came into force in 1992, has restructured the legislature (replacing the former bicameral legislature with a unicameral State Great Hural) and also the judiciary. Procedural changes are being made in the legal system in order to provide more rights to prisoners and defendants. The new Constitution provides for freedoms of the press, speech, and assembly, and these are respected in practice. Newspapers circulate freely and there is a free-ranging discussion of political and social issues. Women were emancipated under the Communist regime, and continue to play a strong role in national politics and in the economy

During the Communist period, Christian themes occasionally appeared on postage stamps. *Left.* The Transfiguration of Christ (Bellini).

Human environment. Only 1% of the national territory is arable, and about 90% is pasture or desert. The Gobi Desert in the southeast contains almost no natural vegetation. The climate is arid and the soils fragile, with the result that overgrazed pastureland easily turns into desert. There are serious shortages of water in areas near the Gobi Desert.

NON-CHRISTIAN RELIGIONS

Shamanism is Mongolia's traditional religion. Devoid of public temples, it has its center in family worship. Although strongly challenged at one time by Tibetan Tantrism, and ruthlessly suppressed by the Communist regime since 1921, it has by no means disappeared; in 1995 it still claimed over 30% of the population.

Buddhists (Lamaists). *Upper.* Bogdo-Guegen (Living Buddha) Temple. *Lower.* Major service in progress in Ulaanbaatar monastery.

Tibetan Tantrism, or ***Lamaism,*** is a form of Buddhism which was introduced in 1575. Encouraged by the Manchu emperors, it exercised great economic, social, political, and cultural influence. In 1920 there were 2,648 temples and monasteries with 120,000 lamas, in addition to 85,000 disciples of the Living Buddha, Bogdo-Guegen of Urga (now Ulan Bator), who was monarch and head of the Buddhist clergy. In 1929 the Communist government suppressed or destroyed all lamaseries, nationalized temple properties and integrated the lamas forcibly into civic life; but by 1960 the situation had improved sufficiently to permit the construction of a new temple at Ulan Bator, the lamasery of Gandan Djoo. Tantrism has witnessed a remarkable resurgence since the collapse of Communism.

Islam is represented by 126,000 Muslims in the western part of the country, mostly Sunnis of the Hanafite rite.

Bible Society kiosk in downtown capital.

CHRISTIANITY

Nestorian missionaries from China touched Mongolia as early as the 7th century, but Christianity had disappeared there by the 10th century. Franciscans and Dominicans entered in the 13th century, and Lazarists in the 1830s. From 1817-41 the London Missionary Society had 2 missionaries working among the Buryats; they translated the Bible into literary Mongolian. In 1870 the LMS missionary James Gilmour began a ministry which ended 21 years later without having seen a single baptism.

A Russian Orthodox congregation existed at Mai-mai-ch'eng until the mid-1930s. The government of China, which controlled the country until 1921, and from 1924-1990 the Communist government of Mongolia made overt Christian evangelization impossible. In 1922 the Holy See established the mission sui juris of Urga and placed it under the theoretical authority of the Scheut Fathers (CICM). Since the jurisdiction had no active work, it was never officially suppressed. The bulk of Mongolian Christians are the 5,000 isolated radio believers and the 19,000 believers newly organized into churches by Protestant missionaries, working mainly in Ulan Bator. There are also remnants of Russian Orthodox believers both from settlement and from the Soviet military occupation which ended in 1990.

The Holy See has diplomatic relations with Mongolia and in AD 2000 is represented to government and the Catholic hierarchy by a nuncio residing in Seoul, Korea.

Indigenous missions. The first Mongolian Christian missionaries were Nestorian Christians who traveled widely throughout the Mongol empire in the 13th and 14th century. Since the disappearance of this community, there have been very few Mongolian Christians, and hence, virtually no missionaries from Mongolia.

CHURCH AND STATE

The constitution of September 1960 proclaims the separation of religion from state and school, and Article 86 guarantees freedom of religion as well as the right to disseminate anti-religious propaganda. However, these guarantees mean little or nothing. Government pressure is in fact exerted against all religious profession except among old people. The only religious center recognized is the new lamasery, Gandan Djoo, at Ulan Bator. Its 130 monks live at the expense of the state, serving as propaganda for friendly Buddhist countries.

Country summary. **Worlds A, B, C by ethnolinguistic peoples, cities, and major civil divisions in Mongolia.**

	PEOPLES							CITIES							CIVIL DIVISIONS						
World	*Num*	*Pop 2000*	*C%*	*Christians*	*E%*	*U%*	*Unevangelized*	*Num*	*Pop 2000*	*C%*	*Christians*	*E%*	*U%*	*Unevangelized*	*Num*	*Pop 2000*	*C%*	*Christians*	*E%*	*U%*	*Unevangelized*
A	18	2,627,278	0.95	24,875	42	58	1,517,460	2	783,667	1.50	11,765	48	52	410,787	20	1,947,596	0.31	5,941	38	62	1,201,176
B	2	34,606	24.31	8,412	87	13	4,571	0	0	0.00	0	0	0	0	1	714,423	3.84	27,452	55	45	320,853
C	1	133	78.95	105	100	0	0	0	0	0.00	0	0	0	0	0	0	0.00	0	0	0	0
Total	**21**	**2,662,017**	**1.25**	**33,392**	**43**	**57**	**1,522,031**	**2**	**783,667**	**1.50**	**11,765**	**48**	**52**	**410,787**	**21**	**2,662,019**	**1.25**	**33,393**	**43**	**57**	**1,522,029**

BROADCASTING AND MEDIA

IBRA-produced radio programs can be heard in Mongolia. Shortwave programs in Mongolian can be received from FEBC (Saipan).

Over 220,000 have seen the 'Jesus' Film, mainly through film team presentations.

FUTURE TRENDS AND PROSPECTS

Though Christianity is expected to make inroads into Mongolia, it is not expected to grow to 2% of the population by 2025. Resurgence among Buddhists, on the other hand, will likely cause growth from only 2% in 1970 to over 25% by AD 2025.

Translators work on Old Testament in Halh language.

Christianity could grow beyond 2% as early as AD 2050 but it is Buddhism and Shamanism that are likely to grow in the light of significant losses by atheism and the nonreligious. By AD 2050 the latter could be less than 30% combined, down from over 60% in 1970.

BIBLIOGRAPHY

Beckoning fortune: a study of the Mongol dalalga ritual. K. Chabros. *Asiatische Forschungen*, Bd. 117. Wiesbaden, Germany: Harassowitz, 1992. 332p.

Die Religionen Tibets und der Mongolei. G. Tucci & W. Heissig. *Die Religionen der Menschheit*, Bd. 20. Stuttgart: W. Kohlhammer, [1970]. 455p.

Dieux et démons: lamas et sorciers de Mongolie. M. Percheron. Paris: Denoël, [1953]. 267p.

'Dreams and paranormal experiences among contemporary Mongolians,' D. C. Lewis, *Journal of the Anglo-Mongolian Society*, 13, 1-2 (1991), 48–55.

Geschichte der Missionsreisen nach Mongolei während des dreizehnten und vierzehnten Jahrhunderts. P. H. Külb. *Die Reisen der Missionäre*, Abt. 1. Regensburg: G .J. Manz, 1860. 3 vols

Historical dictionary of Mongolia. A. J. K. Sanders. *Asian historical dictionaries*, no. 19. Lanham, MD: Scarecrow Press, 1996.

Introduction to Mongolian history and culture. L. W. Moses & S. A. Halkovic Jr. Bloomington, IN: Research Institute for Inner Asian Studies, Indiana University, 1985. 309p.

James Gilmour of Mongolia. R. Lovett. London: Religious Trust Society, 1895.

Kumiss ceremonies and horse races: three Mongolian texts. H. Serruys. *Asiatische Forschungen*, Bd. 37. Wiesbaden, Germany: Harrassowitz, 1974. 124p.

Manual of Mongolian astrology and divination. F. W. Cleaves (ed). Cambridge, MA: Harvard University Press, 1969. 127p.

Monasteries and culture change in Inner Mongolia. R. J. Miller. *Asiatische Forschungen*, Band 2. Wiesbaden, Germany: Harrassowitz, 1959. 152p.

Mongolia. J. Nordby. *World bibliographical series*, vol. 156. Oxford, UK: CLIO Press, 1993. 226p. (See especially 'Religion,' p.71–9).

Mongolia challenge report: a summary of current spiritual needs and a strategy for response. Challenge report, 3. Seattle, WA: Issachar Frontier Missions Research, 1984.

Religion and ritual in society: Lamaist Buddhism in late 19th–century Mongolia. A. M. Pozdneyev. Ed., J. R. Krueger, trans., A. Raun and L. Raun. Bloomington, IN: Mongolia Society, 1978. 694p.

'Revolutionary Mongolia chooses a faith: Lamaism or Leninism.' L. W. Moses. Thesis, Indiana University, Bloomington, IN, 1972. 209p.

Service social de l'Eglise en Mongolie. C. van Melckebeke. Brussels: Editions de Scheut, [1968]. 140p.

The challenge of Central Asia: a brief survey of Tibet and its borderlands, Mongolia, NW Kansu, Chinese Turkestan and Russian Central Asia. M. Cable et al. London: World Dominion Press, 1932. 141p.

The changing world of Mongolia's nomads. M. C. Goldstein & C. M. Beall. Berkeley and Los Angeles: University of California Press, 1994. 176p.

'The Dalai Lamas and the Mongols,' P. V. Hyer, *Tibet journal*, 6, 4 (1981), 3–12.

The Diluv Khutagt: memoirs and autobiography of a Mongol reincarnation in religion and revolution. O. Lattimore & F. Isono. *Asiatische Forschungen*, Band 74. Wiesbaden, Germany: Harrassowitz, 1982. 279p.

The modern history of Mongolia. C. R. Bawden. 2nd ed. London: Kegan Paul International, 1989. 519p.

The Mongol mission: narratives and letters of the Franciscan missionaries in Mongolia in the 13th century. C. H. Dawson. New York: Sheed and Ward, 1955. 285p.

The Mongols of the West. S. A. Halkovic Jr. Bloomington, IN: Research Institute for Inner Asian Studies, Indiana University, 1985. 226p.

The religions of Mongolia. W. Heissig. Trans., G. Samuel. Berkeley and Los Angeles: University of California Press, 1980. 146p.

'The shamanism of the Mongols,' M. Even, in *Mongolia today*, p.183–205. S. Akiner (ed). London: Kegan Paul International, 1991.

Country Table 2. **Organized churches and denominations in Mongolia.**

Official name (bold type = church with over 10% of all affiliated) 1	*Begun* 2	*Type* 3	*Counc* 4	*Congs* 5	*Adults* 6	*Affiliated 1970* 7	*Affiliated 1995* 8	*G%* 9	*Names, notes, and other statistics* (see Codebook, Part 3) 10
Assembly Hall Churches	c1980	I-3nC	.....	16	310	–	800	6.67	*Local Churches. Little Flock.* Witness Li's Shouters. Begun 1922 in China.
Catholic Church: m Urga (Ulan Bator)	1798	R-Lat	P....	2	200	50	300	7.43	Jurisdiction erected in 1922, confided to M=CICM. Scattered secret believers. (1990) 3x,3m,3w.
Ch of Jesus Christ of Latter-day Saints		m-LdS	.....	1	10	–	20	0.05	Mostly expatriates.
Isolated radio churches	1969	I-3rZ	.....	200	2,000	100	5,000	16.94	Isolated radio believers (through FEBC), mostly youths and students.
Jehovah's Witnesses	c1990	m-Jeh	.....	1	20	–	30	20.00	*Watch Tower.* Witnessing permitted in 1990s.
Mongolian Partnership	1991	P-Eva	....E	40	7,000	–	17,000	25.00	Begun from Hong Kong. By 1996, 40 agencies from 50 nations with 120 workers (42% local).
Russian Orthodox Church		O-Rus	M....	1	370	50	600	0.05	Remnants of numbers of Russian settlers; last church building suppressed 1937.
Russian military groups	1921	O-Rus	.....	10	400	3,000	500	-6.92	Small private prayer groups among mainly Orthodox believers in USSR armed forces.
Russian Orthodox Ch in Exile	c1991	I-Rus	.....	10	1,000	–	2,500	25.00	One parish in Ulan Bator. Russians, formerly Orthodox.
Other Protestant churches	c1980	P-	.....	20	1,000	–	2,000	6.67	Begun by several Western indep missionaries.
Other Orthodox churches		O-	.....	15	200	300	400	0.05	Mostly expatriates, with services held in embassies.
Other indigenous denominations	1990	I-3nZ	.....	2	150	–	300	20.00	Including a few house churches.
Totals				**318**	**12,660**	**3,500**	**29,450**		

Churches, members, growth, 1900-2025	*Congs*	*Adults*	*Affiliated*	*G%*	*Total denominations*	*6 Megablocs:* O	R	A	P	I	m
Total churches, members, and denominations (mid-1900)	5	360	550	2.68	1	0	1	0	0	0	0
Total churches, members, and denominations (mid-1970)	113	2,270	3,500	2.68	5	3	1	0	0	1	0
Total churches, members, and denominations (mid-1990)	250	11,100	25,900	10.53	13	4	1	0	2	6	0
Total churches, members, and denominations (mid-1995)	318	12,660	29,450	2.60	25	4	1	0	11	7	2
Total churches, members, and denominations (mid-2000)	350	14,400	33,393	2.54	27	4	1	0	12	8	2
Total churches, members, and denominations (mid-2025)	800	27,000	62,700	2.55	51	6	1	0	20	20	4

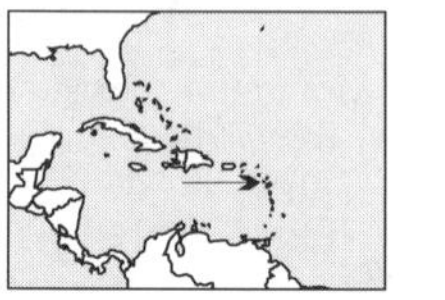

MONTSERRAT

SECULAR DATA, AD 2000

STATE

Official name: The Crown Colony of Montserrat.
Short name: Montserrat. **Adjective of nationality:** of Montserrat.
Flag: British Blue Ensign with shield of the Colony in the fly.
Area: 102 sq. km. (39 sq. mi.).
Government: Self-governing crown colony of United Kingdom (Britain), since 1960 (1493 Spanish influence, 1782 French rule).
Legislature: Executive Council, 6 members; Legislative Council, 10 members.
Official language: English.
Monetary unit: 1 East Caribbean dollar (EC$) = 100 cents. **US$1=** EC$2.70.
Chief cities: PLYMOUTH 1,449.
Political divisions: 1 province.

DEMOGRAPHY

Population: 11,000.
Population density: 104.2/sq. km. (272.5/sq. mi.).
Under 15 years: 3,000.
Growth rate p.a.: 1.19% (births 15.26, deaths 5.77).
Mortality: Infant, per 1,000: 7.8, ; **Maternal per 100,000:** 35.0.
Life expectancy: 78 (male 75, female 82).
Household size: 4.0. **Floor area per person, sq.m:** 18.0.
Major languages: English.
Urban dwellers: 18.37%. **Urban growth rate p.a.:** 2.7%.
Labor force: 40%.

ETHNOLINGUISTIC PEOPLES

95.3% Black; 2.7% British; 0.7% Mulatto; 0.5% French; 0.2% German.

ECONOMY

National income p.a. per person: US$12,512; **per family:** US$50,051.

EDUCATION

Adult literacy: 82% (male 86%, female 78%). **Schools:** 15.
Universities: 1. **School enrolment:** female/male: 90%/90%.

HEALTH

Access to health services: 90%. **Access to safe water:** 90%.
Hospitals: 2 (55 beds per 10,000). **Doctors:** 10.
Blind: 10. **Deaf:** 600. **Murder rate:** 4.
Lepers: 0.

LITERATURE

New book titles p.a.: 1 (100 p.a. per million). **Periodicals:** 4.
Newspapers: 0 dailies.

COMMUNICATION (per 1,000 people)

Phones: 350 (**10% mobile**). **Radios:** 1,935. **TV sets:** 125.
Daily newspaper circulation: 150. **Computers:** 150.

HUMAN LIFE AND LIBERTY (optimum condition=100.0%)

HDI: 84.2. **HSI:** 70.0. **HFI:** 65.0. **EFL:** 45.0.

Country Table 1. Religious adherents in Montserrat, AD 1900-2025.															
Year	1900		1970		mid-1990		Annual change, 1990-2000				mid-1995		mid-2000		mid-2025
Name	Adherents	%	Adherents	%	Adherents	%	Natural	Conversion	Total	Rate	Adherents	%	Adherents	%	Adherents	%
Christians	**12,200**	**100.0**	**10,920**	**97.2**	**10,540**	**96.7**	**-32**	**-1**	**-33**	**-0.32**	**10,400**	**96.6**	**10,209**	**96.1**	**10,000**	**93.5**
PROFESSION																
professing Christians	**12,200**	**100.0**	**10,920**	**97.2**	**10,540**	**96.7**	**-32**	**-1**	**-33**	**-0.32**	**10,400**	**96.6**	**10,209**	**96.1**	**10,000**	**93.5**
AFFILIATION																
unaffiliated Christians	1,340	11.0	1,220	10.9	60	0.6	-1	-1	-2	-4.22	50	0.5	39	0.4	30	0.3
affiliated Christians	**10,860**	**89.0**	**9,700**	**86.4**	**10,480**	**96.2**	**-20**	**-11**	**-31**	**-0.30**	**10,350**	**96.2**	**10,170**	**95.9**	**9,970**	**93.2**
Protestants	3,660	30.0	4,350	38.7	5,500	50.5	0	0	0	0.00	5,462	50.7	5,500	51.9	5,500	51.4
Anglicans	6,100	50.0	4,000	35.6	3,400	31.2	-10	-20	-30	-0.92	3,300	30.7	3,100	29.2	2,400	22.4
Roman Catholics	1,100	9.0	1,300	11.6	1,400	12.8	0	0	0	0.00	1,400	13.0	1,400	13.2	1,450	14.0
Independents	0	0.0	0	0.0	900	8.3	12	3	15	1.55	1,000	9.3	1,050	8.9	1,500	13.6
Marginal Christians	0	0.0	50	0.5	90	0.8	3	1	4	3.75	111	1.0	130	1.2	200	1.8
doubly-affiliated	0	0.0	0	0.0	-810	-7.4	-10	-10	-20	2.23	-923	-8.6	-1,010	-9.5	-1,080	-10.1
Trans-megabloc groupings																
Evangelicals	3,000	24.6	2,800	24.9	2,730	25.1	-8	-2	-8	-0.30	2,701	25.1	2,650	25.0	2,500	23.4
Pentecostals/Charismatics	0	0.0	1,300	11.6	3,550	32.6	-1	0	-1	-0.03	3,546	32.9	3,540	33.4	3,700	34.6
Great Commission Christians	**700**	**5.7**	**900**	**8.0**	**1,950**	**17.9**	**0**	**0**	**0**	**-0.02**	**1,950**	**18.1**	**1,946**	**18.4**	**2,070**	**19.4**
Nonreligious	0	0.0	130	1.2	185	1.7	4	1	5	2.51	220	2.0	237	2.2	410	3.8
Baha'is	0	0.0	150	1.3	150	1.4	1	0	1	0.39	155	1.4	156	1.4	220	2.1
Spiritists	0	0.0	0	0.0	15	0.1	0	0	0	0.65	15	0.1	16	0.2	40	0.4
Hindus	0	0.0	0	0.0	10	0.1	0	0	0	0.96	10	0.1	11	0.1	30	0.3
World A (unevangelized persons)	0	0.0	11	0.1	11	0.1	0	0	0	-3.50	10	0.1	11	0.1	11	0.1
World B (evangelized non-Christians)	0	0.0	302	2.7	349	3.2	5	1	6	5.68	354	3.3	380	3.8	689	6.4
World C (Christians)	12,200	100.0	10,920	97.2	10,540	96.7	-32	-1	-33	-0.32	10,400	96.6	10,209	96.1	10,000	93.5
Country's population	**12,200**	**100.0**	**11,233**	**100.0**	**10,900**	**100.0**	**27**	**0**	**-27**	**0.00**	**10,764**	**100.0**	**10,600**	**100.0**	**10,700**	**100.0**

COLUMNS, ROWS.
For meanings and definitions, see Codebook (Part 3). Note that, by definition, total 'Christians' = professing + crypto-Christians, which also = affiliated + unaffiliated Christians, and also = Great Commission Christians + latent Christians. Percentages may not always total exactly, due to rounding.

CENSUSES.
7.IV.1960: 48.8% Protestants (28.2% Methodists 10% Pentecostals, 6.5% SDAs), 38.8% Anglicans, 10.4% Roman Catholics, 1.2% non-Christian religionists, 0.7% nonreligious, 0.1% marginal Protestants. 7.IV.1970: 47.8% Protestants (28.3% Methodists, 9.5% Pentecostals, 7.0% SDAs), 37.8% Anglicans, 11.6% Roman Catholics, 1.3% non-Christian religionists, 1.1% nonreligious, 0.4% marginal Protestants.

NOTES ON RELIGIONS
BAHA'IS. In 2 local spiritual assemblies (1973), with little progress in subsequent 25 years.

Great Commission Instrument Panel: status of Montserrat (for explanation see start of Part 4)

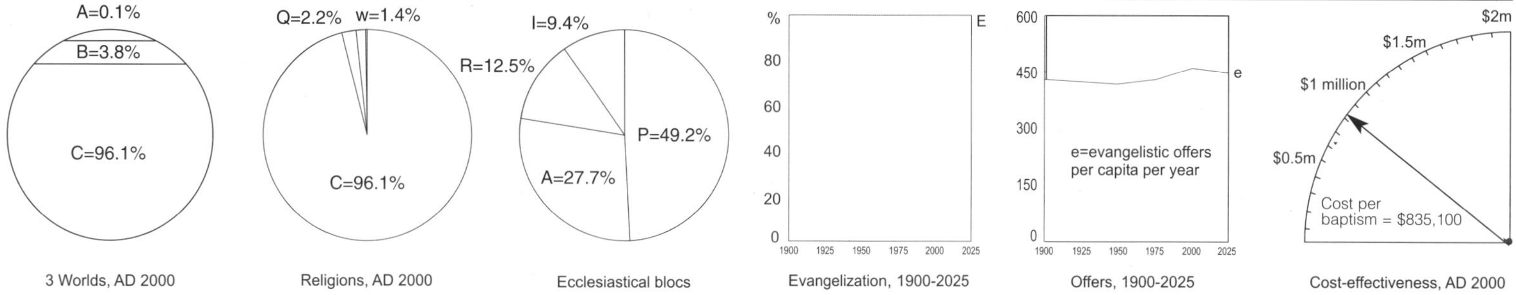

Country status. Montserrat is one of the Leeward Islands in the West Indies in the Caribbean Sea. Offshore finance is the country's leading economic activity. The country was half destroyed in 1997 by volcanic eruption.

HUMAN LIFE AND LIBERTY

Human rights and freedoms. Montserrat is a dependent territory of the United Kingdom where British laws apply. All human rights and civil liberties are guaranteed in theory and respected in practice.

NON-CHRISTIAN RELIGIONS

Baha'i has a small following. In addition, a few claim allegiance to other religions or no religion.

CHRISTIANITY

ANGLICAN CHURCH. As is true of all the Leeward Islands, the Anglican Church is the principal denomination. Its strength is about the same as the Church of England on Antigua and greater than that of St Kitts-Nevis and Anguilla. All of these islands form the diocese of Antigua, which was founded in 1842 and its part of the Church of the Province of the West Indies.

PROTESTANT CHURCHES. In spite of declining membership in recent years, Methodism remains the largest Protestant body in Montserrat, having had its West Indies beginnings in nearby Antigua as early as 1760. The Methodist Church is now more influential in Montserrat than in Antigua although not quite as much so as in St Kitts-Nevis or Anguilla, the other members of the Leeward chain.

Canadian Pentecostals and American Adventists have been active respectively since 1910 and 1926. Adventists, who lost members during the 1960s, belong to the SDA East Caribbean Conference. The Church of God of Prophecy is also at work, as is the Wesleyan Church, formerly known as the Pilgrim Holiness Church; the latter body has not been as successful here as in St Kitts-Nevis.

CATHOLIC CHURCH. Montserrat belongs to the diocese of Saint John's with its seat in Antigua. Montserrat has one parish, 2 stations, 2 priests, and several Missionary Sisters of the Immaculate Heart of Mary engaged in teaching commercial courses, in addition to school and social work.

The Holy See has no diplomatic relations with Montserrat in AD 2000, but an apostolic delegate residing in Port of Spain

Indigenous missions. Since the introduction of Christianity to Montserrat there have been only a handful of missionaries sent out, with these almost exclusively to other islands in the Caribbean.

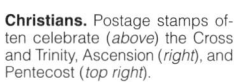

Christians. Postage stamps often celebrate (*above*) the Cross and Trinity, Ascension (*right*), and Pentecost (*top right*).

CHURCH AND STATE

Unlike Antigua, St Kitts-Nevis and Anguilla, Montserrat has so far not sought either full or partial independence from Great Britain. However, such political differences have little effect on church-state relations, and all the Leeward Islands have similar policies regarding religion: there are no established churches and there is equal status for all religious bodies before the law.

BROADCASTING AND MEDIA

Shortwave programs from HCJB (Ecuador), TWR (Antilles) and AWR (Costa Rica) can be easily received. Christian television programs can be received via satellite.

INTERDENOMINATIONAL ORGANIZATIONS

The Anglican, Methodist, and Catholic churches belong to the Montserrat Council for Social Action.

FUTURE TRENDS AND PROSPECTS

Baha'is and the nonreligious together accounted for 2.5% of the population in 1970 but by 2025 are expected to grow to 5.7%.

Though Christians could continue to represent well above 90% of the population in the 21st century, there could be an ongoing trend of double affiliation among church members.

BIBLIOGRAPHY

Montserrat. R. Berleant-Schiller. World bibliographical series, vol. 134. Oxford, UK: CLIO Press, 1991. 102p. (See especially 'Religion,' p.76–8).
Montserrat and its Methodism. G. E. Lawrence. [Bristol, UK: The Author, 1967]. 3 vols
Montserrat: history of a Caribbean colony. H. A. Fergus. London: Macmillan, 1994. 304p.
Montserrat, West Indies: a chronological history. M. M. Wheeler. Montserrat, West Indies: Montserrat National Trust, 1988. 77p.
'Religion and cultural identity: the Montserratian case,' J. D. Dobbin, Caribbean issues, 4, 1 (1980), 71–83.
Saint Anthony's Church, Montserrat, W.I. F. E. Peters. Bridgetown, Barbados: Advocate Co., 1931. 11p. (History of the first recorded church in Montserrat).

The Catholic Church in Montserrat, West Indies, 1756–1980. B. A. Demets. Plymouth, Montserrat: Montserrat Printery, 1980. 92p.
The jombee dance of Montserrat: a study of trance ritual in the West Indies. J. D. Dobbin. Columbus, OH: Ohio State University Press, 1986. 202p.
The origin of Judy Piece Methodism in the island of Montserrat, BWI. G. E. Lawrence. Plymouth, Montserrat, 1944. 29p.
Thomas O'Garra: a West Indian local preacher. G. E. Lawrence. London: Epworth Press. 59p. (A Judy Piece Methodist minister in Montserrat).

Country summary. **Worlds A, B, C by ethnolinguistic peoples, cities, and major civil divisions in Montserrat.**

PEOPLES

World	*Num*	*Pop 2000*	*C%*	*Christians*	*E%*	*U%*	*Unevangelized*
A	0	0	0.00	0	0	0	0
B	1	21	28.57	6	86	14	3
C	7	10,606	95.81	10,162	100	0	4
Total	**8**	**10,627**	**95.68**	**10,168**	**100**	**0**	**7**

CITIES

World	*Num*	*Pop 2000*	*C%*	*Christians*	*E%*	*U%*	*Unevangelized*
A	0	0	0.00	0	0	0	0
B	0	0	0.00	0	0	0	0
C	1	1,449	89.99	1,304	100	0	4
Total	**1**	**1,449**	**89.99**	**1,304**	**100**	**0**	**4**

CIVIL DIVISIONS

World	*Num*	*Pop 2000*	*C%*	*Christians*	*E%*	*U%*	*Unevangelized*
A	0	0	0.00	0	0	0	0
B	0	0	0.00	0	0	0	0
C	1	10,629	95.68	10,170	100	0	7
Total	**1**	**10,629**	**95.68**	**10,170**	**100**	**0**	**7**

Country Table 2. **Organized churches and denominations in Montserrat.**

Official name (bold type = church with over 10% of all affiliated) 1	*Begun* 2	*Type* 3	*Counc* 4	*Congs* 5	*Adults* 6	*Affiliated 1970* 7	*Affiliated 1995* 8	*G%* 9	*Names, notes, and other statistics* (see Codebook, Part 3) 10
Anglican Church (D Antigua)	1842	A-ACa	awMRC	7	1,950	4,000	3,300	-0.77	*CPWI.* In Ch of the Province of the West Indies. M=USPG. 95% West Indian Blacks. Declining.
Baptist Association	c1975	P-Bap	.....	1	200	–	333	5.00	M=FMB-SBC. Southern Baptist Convention (USA).
Catholic Church (D Saint John's)		R-Lat	P.NMC	4	1,000	1,300	1,400	0.05	In D Saint John's (Antigua). M=FSC. 1 parish, 1 school (120). 2nx,4w,P=47%.
Church of God of Prophecy	1951	P-Pe3	Z....	10	300	250	500	2.81	M=CGP(USA). Schism in USA ex Ch of God (Cleveland). Holiness Pentecostals.
Jehovah's Witnesses		m-Jeh	x....	1	30	50	111	0.05	*Watch Tower.* Small congregation with in 1972 one baptism only. (1995) 1Y.
Meth Ch in Caribbean & Americas	1820	P-Met	VvM.C	7	700	2,000	1,400	-1.42	In MCCA (1967) union, Leeward Islands District. M=MMS(UK). Declining rapidly. 2n.
Pentecostal Assemb of the W Indies	1910	P-Pe2	ZF...	9	600	1,000	1,200	0.73	*PAWI.* M=PAoC(Canada). Expanding. Many emigrants to UK (Anglo-West-Indian Assembly).
Seventh-day Adventist Church	1926	P-Adv	x....	2	650	800	929	0.60	*SDA*, East Caribbean Conference, Caribbean Union Conference. Decline since 1960.
Wesleyan Church		P-Hol	VF...	2	150	300	300	0.05	Before 1968 merger, M=Pilgrim Holiness Church (USA). Holiness denomination.
Other Protestant bodies	c1975	P-	.....	10	300	–	800	5.00	Total about 5.
Other Black indigenous churches	c1970	I-3nU	.....	20	500	–	1,000	31.83	Total about 6, from neighboring Caribbean islands.
Doubly-affiliated		2-aff			-520	0	-923		Pentecostals who are also baptized Catholics, Anglicans, or Methodists.
Totals				**73**	**5,860**	**9,700**	**10,350**		

Churches, members, growth, 1900-2025	*Congs*	*Adults*	*Affiliated*	*G%*	*Total denominations*	*6 Megablocs:* O	R	A	P	I	m
Total churches, members, and denominations (mid-1900)	30	5,900	10,860	-0.16	2	0	0	1	1	0	0
Total churches, members, and denominations (mid-1970)	40	5,275	9,700	-0.16	8	0	1	1	5	0	1
Total churches, members, and denominations (mid-1990)	60	5,900	10,480	0.39	19	0	1	1	10	6	1
Total churches, members, and denominations (mid-1995)	73	5,860	10,350	-0.25	20	0	1	1	11	6	1
Total churches, members, and denominations (mid-2000)	80	5,800	10,170	-0.35	21	0	1	1	12	6	1
Total churches, members, and denominations (mid-2025)	120	5,600	9,970	-0.08	38	0	1	1	20	15	1

NOTES ON TABLE ABOVE
NATIONAL COUNCILS (Column 4, 5th letter).
C = Montserrat Council for Social Action.

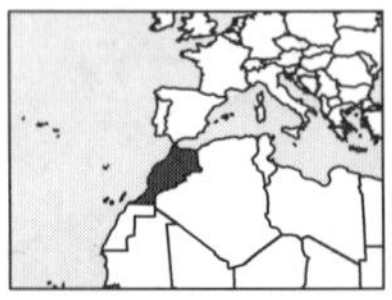

MOROCCO

SECULAR DATA, AD 2000

STATE
Official name: Al-Mamlaka al-Maghrebia (The Kingdom of Morocco).
Short name: Morocco. **Adjective of nationality:** Moroccan.
Flag: Red field with green 5-pointed star.
Area: 458,730 sq. km. (177,117 sq. mi.).
Government: Absolute (de facto) or constitutional (de jure) monarchy, since 1956 (1912 French and Spanish protectorates, 1956 Independence).
Legislature: House of Representatives, 333 members.
Official language: Arabic.
Monetary unit: 1 Moroccan dirham (DH) = 100 Moroccan francs.
US$1= DH 9.28.
Chief cities: Casablanca (Dar el Beida) 3,535,000; RABAT-Sale 1,493,000; Marrakech 780,186; Fes (Fez) 780,186; Meknes 546,859.
Political divisions: 43 provinces.
Armed forces: 196,000.

DEMOGRAPHY
Population: 28,221,000.
Population density: 61.5/sq. km. (159.3/sq. mi.).
Under 15 years: 9,186,000.
Growth rate p.a.: 1.57% (births 22.83, deaths 6.13).
Mortality: Infant, per 1,000: 41.0, ; **Maternal per 100,000:** 610.0.
Life expectancy: 69 (male 67, female 71).
Household size: 5.8. **Floor area per person, sq.m:** 10.0.
Major languages: Arabic, Berber (Ghomara, Rif, Shilha, Tamazigt), French, Spanish, English, and a few others.
Urban dwellers: 55.32%. **Urban growth rate p.a.:** 2.7%.
Labor force: 29%.

ETHNOLINGUISTIC PEOPLES
41.6% Moroccan Arab; 12.3% Arabized Berber; 8.9% Southern Shilha (Shleuh); 8.0% White Moor (Bidan); 7.3% Central Shilha (Berraber).

ECONOMY
National income p.a. per person: US$1,110; **per family:** US$6,437.

EDUCATION
Adult literacy: 43% (male 56%, female 31%). **Schools:** 6,474.
Universities: 50. **School enrolment:** female/male: 50%/68%.

HEALTH
Access to health services: 70%. **Access to safe water:** 52%.
Hospitals: 203 (11 beds per 10,000). **Doctors:** 7,695.
Blind: 35,000. **Deaf:** 1,731,200. **Murder rate:** 1.
Lepers: 40,000. **Underweight prevalence under 5:** 10%.

LITERATURE
New book titles p.a.: 710 (25 p.a. per million). **Periodicals:** 21.
Newspapers: 13 dailies.

COMMUNICATION (per 1,000 people)
Phones: 43 (7% mobile). **Radios:** 194. **TV sets:** 145.
Daily newspaper circulation: 13. **Computers:** 10.

HUMAN LIFE AND LIBERTY (optimum condition=100.0%)
HDI: 56.6. **HSI:** 41.0. **HFI:** 17.5. **EFL:** 46.0.

Country status. Morocco is a country in Northwest Africa on both the Mediterranean Sea and the Atlantic Ocean. It is one of the leading exporters of phosphates. Fishing, tourism, and agriculture are also important.

HUMAN LIFE AND LIBERTY

Human need and development. Morocco is on the edge of the developed world, both physically and economically, but is nevertheless rooted in the world of Islam. Human needs are great in certain regions, but there is no stark poverty or deprivation. Rather, social norms act as a drag on economic growth and provide no incentive for modernization. There are bidonvilles or slums in almost all large towns. The percentage of the poor and the wealthy have remained stationary for decades. The relation between the 2 classes is mediated by the wakfs or charities which constitute an effective welfare system. In economic terms it is classified as a lower middle income country with a per capita income of less than $1,110. More than half the Moroccans are illiterate. There are no major health problems. The infant mortality rate has been halved since 1970 to 41 per 1,000 live births.

Human rights and freedoms. Morocco has a long history of authoritarian and repressive government and violation of human rights. The king, as the ultimate authority, rules in a feudal fashion, sometimes by decree and sometimes with a token prime minister and a subservient parliament. Widespread human rights abuses, including torture and incommunicado detention are practiced by the security apparatus, which reports directly to the palace. There are periodical deaths in police custody, which are rarely investigated. Police sometimes 'kidnap' victims in unmarked cars, and then report them as disappearances. The government maintains 6 clandestine detention centers, including the military fortress of Ahermoumou and another at Tazmamart. There are no procedural safeguards or due process for defendants. The judiciary is at the beck and call of the king, and generally bows to his dictates. An extensive informant system exists along with surveillance of communications. Press freedom is significantly restricted, though the limits are not clearly defined. The 3 forbidden topics are the person of the king, the Moroccan claims over Western Sahara, and Islam. The government controls the licensing of newspapers and journals through a registration procedure. Domestic and foreign newspapers offending the government or not heeding its guidelines on certain matters may be seized and destroyed. A new Constitutional amendment was passed in 1992 with a 99.96% approval, largely through electoral fraud. The elections are managed by the Ministry of Interior, and the results are generally predictable. Blacks suffer various forms of social and economic discrimination. The civil law status of Moroccan women is governed by the Moudouwana, or code of personal status, based on the Koran. Moudouwana treats women as chattels, but efforts to reform it have been stymied by the fundamentalists. One Muslim cleric has issued a fatwa saying that all attempts to provide equal treatment for women should be punishable by death. The sharia-based criminal law prescribes the death penalty for a number of offenses, including adultery.

Human environment. Although an underdeveloped country, Morocco suffers from all the environ-

Country Table 1. **Religious adherents in Morocco, AD 1900-2025.**

Name	1900 Adherents	%	1970 Adherents	%	mid-1990 Adherents	%	Annual change, 1990-2000 Natural	Conversion	Total	Rate	mid-1995 Adherents	%	mid-2000 Adherents	%	mid-2025 Adherents	%
Muslims	5,012,920	96.4	15,012,500	98.9	23,396,350	98.3	434,120	-170	433,950	1.72	25,392,000	98.3	27,735,853	98.3	37,733,000	97.9
Nonreligious	1,000	0.0	3,000	0.0	230,000	1.0	4,268	132	4,400	1.77	250,000	1.0	273,995	1.0	500,000	1.3
Christians	**30,080**	**0.6**	**131,000**	**0.9**	**146,250**	**0.6**	**2,714**	**205**	**2,919**	**1.84**	**161,700**	**0.6**	**175,435**	**0.6**	**248,000**	**0.6**
PROFESSION																
crypto-Christians	5,080	0.1	36,580	0.2	123,500	0.5	2,292	358	2,650	1.96	136,000	0.5	150,000	0.5	220,000	0.6
professing Christians	**25,000**	**0.5**	**94,420**	**0.6**	**22,750**	**0.1**	**422**	**-153**	**269**	**1.12**	**25,700**	**0.1**	**25,435**	**0.1**	**28,000**	**0.1**
AFFILIATION																
unaffiliated Christians	0	0.0	703	0.0	850	0.0	16	-5	11	1.21	866	0.0	959	0.0	1,700	0.0
affiliated Christians	**30,080**	**0.6**	**130,297**	**0.9**	**145,400**	**0.6**	**2,698**	**210**	**2,908**	**1.84**	**160,834**	**0.6**	**174,476**	**0.6**	**246,300**	**0.6**
Independents	0	0.0	23,250	0.2	115,000	0.5	2,134	1,066	3,200	2.49	131,700	0.5	147,000	0.5	220,000	0.6
Roman Catholics	30,000	0.6	100,000	0.7	24,750	0.1	459	-726	-267	-1.14	23,600	0.1	22,076	0.1	20,000	0.1
Protestants	30	0.0	5,047	0.0	4,300	0.0	80	-100	-20	-0.48	4,211	0.0	4,100	0.0	5,000	0.0
Orthodox	0	0.0	900	0.0	780	0.0	14	-18	-4	-0.53	760	0.0	740	0.0	600	0.0
Anglicans	50	0.0	600	0.0	450	0.0	8	-8	0	0.00	450	0.0	450	0.0	500	0.0
Marginal Christians	0	0.0	500	0.0	120	0.0	2	-3	-1	-0.87	113	0.0	110	0.0	200	0.0
Trans-megabloc groupings																
Evangelicals	20	0.0	7,900	0.1	32,000	0.1	594	526	1,120	3.05	37,584	0.2	43,200	0.2	70,000	0.2
Pentecostals/Charismatics	0	0.0	24,000	0.2	115,000	0.5	2,134	1,366	3,500	2.69	130,805	0.5	150,000	0.5	240,000	0.6
Great Commission Christians	**26,000**	**0.5**	**75,900**	**0.5**	**92,800**	**0.4**	**1,722**	**-27**	**1,695**	**1.69**	**100,700**	**0.4**	**109,745**	**0.4**	**154,000**	**0.4**
Baha'is	0	0.0	2,200	0.0	23,600	0.1	438	74	512	1.98	26,800	0.1	28,719	0.1	50,000	0.1
Jews	156,000	3.0	31,100	0.2	16,000	0.1	297	-218	79	0.48	15,700	0.1	16,790	0.1	12,000	0.0
Atheists	0	0.0	1,200	0.0	2,600	0.0	48	-12	36	1.32	2,800	0.0	2,963	0.0	5,000	0.0
doubly-counted religionists	0	0.0	0	0.0	-10,800	-0.1	-200	-11	-211	1.80	-12,000	-0.1	-12,913	-0.1	-18,000	-0.1
World A (unevangelized persons)	4,799,600	92.3	10,930,086	72.0	14,258,596	59.9	264,403	-57,938	206,465	1.36	15,114,787	58.5	16,311,738	57.8	20,189,720	52.4
World B (evangelized non-Christians)	370,320	7.1	4,119,589	27.1	9,399,154	39.5	174,568	57,733	232,301	2.24	10,560,756	40.9	11,733,827	41.6	18,092,280	47.0
World C (Christians)	30,080	0.6	131,000	0.9	146,250	0.6	2,714	205	2,919	1.84	161,700	0.6	175,435	0.6	248,000	0.6
Country's population	**5,200,000**	**100.0**	**15,180,676**	**100.0**	**23,804,000**	**100.0**	**441,685**	**0**	**441,685**	**1.72**	**25,837,244**	**100.0**	**28,221,000**	**100.0**	**38,530,000**	**100.0**

COLUMNS, ROWS.
For meanings and definitions, see Codebook (Part 3). Note that, by definition, total 'Christians' = professing + crypto-Christians, which also = affiliated + unaffiliated Christians, and also = Great Commission Christians + latent Christians. Percentages may not always total exactly, due to rounding.

CENSUSES.
31.XII.1950-15.IV.1952 (excluding military personnel): 92.8% Muslims, 4.9% Christians, 2.3% Jews. **18.VI.1960:** 95.2% Moroccan Muslims, 1.4% Moroccan Jews (160,000 persons), 3.4% 'others' (Christians, alien Jews and alien Muslims). **20.VII.1971** (de jure): 99.1% Muslims, 0.7% 'unknown' (111,909 persons, mainly Christians), 0.2% Jews (31,119 persons).

NOTES ON RELIGIONS
ATHEISTS. Moroccan Communist Party (MCP) (outlawed 1959), now Party of Liberation and Socialism (PLS) (banned 1969. A number of intellectuals however are atheists, as well as many French expatriates.
BAHA'IS. Severe persecution since 1962. Local spiritual assemblies: 10 (1964), 13 (1973). Many Baha'is are Berbers.
COUNTRY'S POPULATION. After France declared Morocco a protectorate in 1912, French and Spanish settlers arrived in growing numbers. At Independence in 1956 they numbered 500,000, mostly Roman Catholics; most then left for Europe or (Jews) for Israel. In the 1990s, some one million Moroccans lived in Europe (France, Belgium, Germany, Netherlands) as migrant workers, mostly from the Atlas, Rif and Tafilalt regions.
CRYPTO-CHRISTIANS. Christians affiliated to churches but not known to the state or censuses, of 3 kinds: (a) a few hundred Moroccan nationals in the recognized churches who have been baptized but are not allowed to practice their faith openly, (b) expatriates in the churches who prefer not to be publicly known as Christians, and (c) isolated radio and correspondence course believers.
INDEPENDENTS. Isolated Moroccan radio and correspondence course believers (see Table 2).
JEWS. Maghreb Jews. Decline from 250,000 in 1952 (2.7% of the population), and 160,000 in 1960 (1.4%), to 25,000 in 1990 (0.1%), due to emigration to Israel. Most are urban, descendants of Sefardic Jews from Spain and Portugal. There are several ancient Berber-speaking groups, and Arabic-speaking communities.
MUSLIMS. Sunnis (of the Malikite rite). Sufi brotherhoods remain strong, including Qadiriya and Kattaniya. *Hajj pilgrims to Mecca.* (1968) 8,208; (1969) 10,943, (1970) 10,640; (1971) 15,463; (1972) 22,425; (1973) 14,923; (1974) 26,632; (1975) 16,176; (1976) 15,044.
Missionaries. There are a number of Egyptians sent by Al-Azhar University (Cairo).
NONRELIGIOUS. French, also some Arab intellectuals.
ROMAN CATHOLICS. In the year 1900, all French and Spanish except 6,260 indigenous Catholics.

Great Commission Instrument Panel: status of Morocco (for explanation see start of Part 4)

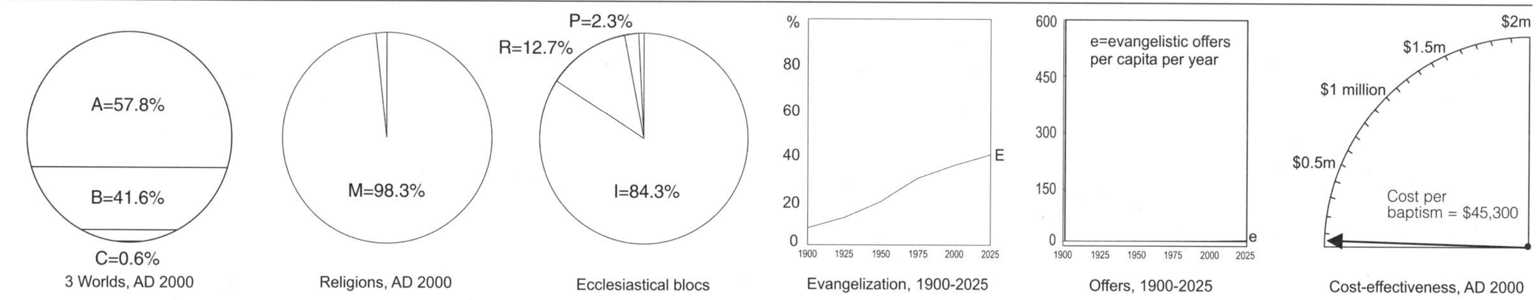

mental problems associated with development: wildlife habitat destruction, overconsumption of water, pollution from untreated urban sewage and industrial effluents, soil erosion, soil degradation, and depletion of vegetation.

NON-CHRISTIAN RELIGIONS

Islam is the state religion and, with a few exceptions, Moroccans are Sunnis almost all of the Malikite rite. The islamization of the country has been profound, including the Berbers, although in the exercise of religion Berbers often depart from Muslim orthodoxy. There are only a few small dissident sects; but the Sufi brotherhoods and religious congregations remain strong, as was evident during the nationalist revival which led to Independence in 1956. The most important national leader at that time was Allal El-Fassi, the Moroccan representative of the Maghribian Salafiya, a reformist movement advocating a return to Islamic sources, the purification of maraboutistic distortions and the integration of Islamic religion with the forces of modern progress. As a whole, however, Islam has made little accommodation to the secular forces which are increasingly evident in Moroccan life. If the majority of youth still submit to collective religious obligations, a minority, especially among intellectuals and in the cities, call in question the very foundations of Islam.

Two universities are dedicated exclusively to Arabic and Islamic studies: the Université Ben Youssef at Marrakech with more than 1,000 students; and the Université al-Qarawiyin at Rabat, Fez and Marrakech with 400 students. The latter institution was founded in AD 859 and has faculties of Quranic law, theology, Arabic language and literature; an Institute of Islamic Studies; and offers a master's degree in the study of the Quran.

Muslims. Hassan II mosque in Casablanca, newest in North Africa (cost $500 million).

Judaism was represented in 1995 by about 15,700 persons as contrasted with 250,000 in 1952, most of whom subsequently emigrated to Israel. Jews have virtually disappeared from the rural areas, and in the cities they are progressively losing their identity as organized groups.

Baha'i has a growing number of followers but many have been severely persecuted and imprisoned over the past 3 decades.

CHRISTIANITY

CATHOLIC CHURCH. By the end of the 2nd century AD, 4 bishoprics had been established in the Tangier-Rabat-Fez triangle, but in the centuries which followed the church suffered successively from the Diocletian persecution, the Donatist schism, the Arian vandal invasion and finally the triumph of Islam throughout North Africa. A new missionary effort was begun by Franciscans in 1220, and in 1234 the diocese of Marrakech was formed. The diocese was suppressed in 1566; and in spite of attempts by Capuchins in 1624 and Andalusian Franciscans in 1639, the church remained weak. In 1822 there was only one Catholic priest resident in the country, at Tangiers. Nevertheless, a new start was made in 1859 with the creation of the prefecture of Morocco, which was made a vicariate in 1908. In 1923 the vicariate of Rabat was established, becoming an archdiocese in 1955.

The Catholic population, mostly French and Spanish at the time of the protectorate, has tended since Independence to become more diversified and other nations have developed co-operative relations with Morocco. Numbering 420,000 in 1955, Catholics declined to 100,000 in 1970, and continued to decline to less than 25,000 by 1995.

The positive attitude of Christian leaders, notably Catholics, towards the movement which led to na-

Country summary. **Worlds A, B, C by ethnolinguistic peoples, cities, and major civil divisions in Morocco.**

	PEOPLES							CITIES							CIVIL DIVISIONS						
World	*Num*	*Pop 2000*	*C%*	*Christians*	*E%*	*U%*	*Unevangelized*	*Num*	*Pop 2000*	*C%*	*Christians*	*E%*	*U%*	*Unevangelized*	*Num*	*Pop 2000*	*C%*	*Christians*	*E%*	*U%*	*Unevangelized*
A	24	27,477,505	0.17	45,888	41	59	16,082,040	26	10,638,377	0.71	75,066	45	55	5,869,077	42	27,590,593	0.56	154,106	42	58	16,029,784
B	2	620,859	6.87	42,627	63	37	232,243	0	0	0.00	0	0	0	0	1	630,248	3.23	20,370	55	45	284,859
C	6	122,478	70.18	85,961	100	0	361	0	0	0.00	0	0	0	0	0	0	0.00	0	0	0	0
Total	**32**	**28,220,842**	**0.62**	**174,476**	**42**	**58**	**16,314,644**	**26**	**10,638,377**	**0.71**	**75,066**	**45**	**55**	**5,869,077**	**43**	**28,220,841**	**0.62**	**174,476**	**42**	**58**	**16,314,643**

tional independence in 1956 has undoubtedly helped the churches. Nevertheless, one cannot speak of any significant influence exercised by them in the country, either as institutions or by means of their doctrine and teaching. The churches, and especially the Catholic Church, tend to reduce to a minimum only outward manifestations which call attention to their presence. Moreover, during the past 30 years, numerous Catholic places of worship have been secularized or closed as expatriate Catholics have left the country.

The Holy See has diplomatic relations with Morocco and in AD 2000 is represented to government and the Catholic hierarchy by a nuncio residing in Rabat.

OTHER CHURCHES. The Bible Churchmen's Missionary Society has had the largest church work in Morocco, beginning in the central area in 1929 as part of the Anglican diocese of Sierra Leone. In 1968 the government closed down 3 stations, but 5 others remain open. Anglicans in Morocco are virtually all expatriates, their first chaplaincy work dating from the British occupation of Tangiers in 1662.

Eastern Orthodox are also expatriates and are divided in a Russian Orthodox congregation in Rabat under the Moscow Patriarchate, a White Russian congregation in Casablanca opposed to the Moscow Patriarchate and 3 Greek Orthodox communities under the Patriarchate of Alexandria.

The first Protestants were from the north Africa Mission which entered Morocco in 1884, establishing the widely-known Tullock Memorial Hospital and Nurses Training School in Tangiers. In 1959 the NAM merged with the Southern Morocco Mission, a Scottish society. These missions have always given special emphasis to health care, 7 of their 9 centers being devoted to medical work. Attention has recently been given to Bible correspondence courses and radio broadcasts from Marseilles, France. Missionaries of 2 Protestant groups were expelled in the late 1960s, those of the Gospel Missionary Union and the Emmanuel Mission Sahara, which had been in the country respectively since 1894 and 1926. The GMU was at the time engaged in a successful Bible correspondence course program which it then continued to operate from Malaga, Spain, in addition to radio broadcasts from Monaco. Nevertheless, Moroccans originally associated with these missions continue to remain Christians.

The largest Protestant denomination at the present time is the Evangelical Church of Morocco (Eglise Evangelique au Maroc) related to the Reformed Church of France, although this consists almost entirely of French citizens involved in technical assistance in the country. A few expatriate American congregations form the Church of Christ composed of USA military personnel.

A large number of other mission bodies and individual missionaries have entered to work in social service or development projects and have gathered small groups of expatriates and Moroccans into loosely-organized Christian communities. In spite of legal prohibitions against Moroccans becoming Christians, it is estimated that there are now over 130,000 indigenous Christians, some 5% of whom have openly manifested their religious allegiance through public baptism.

Renewal movements. In the 1990s the Pentecostal/Charismatic Renewal continued to spread rapidly across most older churches, and numbered over 150,000 adherents (of whom none are Pentecostals, 1% are Charismatics, and 99% Independents).

Indigenous missions. Berber Christians in early centuries played a missionary role in the region but since the Islamic conquest, very few Moroccan Christians have been sent out as missionaries.

CHURCH AND STATE

The Alawite dynasty has ruled Morocco since the 17th century, its rulers having combined the role of political monarch with that of supreme chief in the religious domain. At the present time the Moroccan state is founded on the following 3 attributes of its head of state: (1) sharif, which confers on him a special legitimacy because of his being a descendant of the prophet Mohammed's family; (2) king, a title used since 1956 in place of the traditional appellation, sultan; (3) commander of the faithful (Amir al-Muminin), or caliph, because he is the heir of the prestigious historical caliphates of Cordoba, an Arab dynasty, and Marrakech, a Berber dynasty. The king's authority derives from the holy character of his person, which is described in the constitution of 1972 (Article 23) as 'inviolable and sacred'. Article 19 reads: 'The King, Commander of the Faithful, supreme representative of the nation, symbol of its unity, guarantor of the perpetuation and continuity of the state, insures that Islam and the constitution are properly respected'. Finally, Article 6 of the constitutional text of 1972 establishes, in a manner similar to the earlier constitutions of 1962 and 1970, that 'Islam is the religion of the state which guarantees to all the free exercise of religion'.

The government is moreover dedicated to the preservation of Islam. As one instance, the practice of Ramadan enters into the Penal Code (Article 222); as another, Muslim prayers in primary and secondary schools have been obligatory since 1966. In October 1968, king Hassan II inaugurated a campaign in favor of Quranic schools. A few months later, he invited Moroccan women to create a National Union, one of whose objects would be 'the advancement of women within the limits of Quranic tradition'. Apart from Islam, other confessions receive no legal recognition but are in fact tolerated by the state so long as their activities are confined to serving strictly the religious needs of their essentially expatriate members. Authority granted to the churches to administer their various properties is part of the common right of every group or association, each in its capacity as a moral person. However, proselytism is outlawed, and conversion from Islam to Christianity is prohibited by law. In September 1974, a missionary couple of the North Africa Mission received a 6-month prison sentence for allegedly 'bribing' 2 Moroccan youth to convert to Christianity. While pending appeal in June 1975 they were suddenly expelled from the country. Later during 1975 a baptized Moroccan Christian, Mustapha Jabiri, was given a 6-month prison term for breaking the Muslim fast of Ramadan, an action which discouraged other Moroccan believers from openly acknowledging their faith. The situation has changed little by 1998.

BROADCASTING AND MEDIA

Shortwave radio programs can be received from KNLS, AWR (Slovakia), HCJB (Ecuador), and TWR (Monaco, Albania). Berber-language programs have met with great success. Satellite TV and radio programs are received in English, Arabic, German and Italian. Christian television programming can be received via satellite, and has met with good results.

INTERDENOMINATIONAL ORGANIZATIONS

Catholics, Protestants, Orthodox and Anglicans have been members of an informal ecumenical council in Casablanca and have engaged in co-operative relief and development projects through the Ecumenical Interchurch-Aid Committee of Morocco (Comite Oecumenique d'Entr'aide au Maroc, COEM). In 1977 this relationship was formalized with the formation of the Morocco Council of Christian Churches, with 5 members. There is also an ecumenical group called the College Oecumenique au Maroc which provides for dialogue between the Christian, Muslim, and Jewish communities.

FUTURE TRENDS AND PROSPECTS

Isolated radio believers will probably continue to represent the majority Christian community through 2025 when 0.6% of the population is expected to be Christian. Muslims still dominate in that year at near 98%.

Without more indigenous church growth, the number of Christians in Morocco will have difficulty reaching even 1% of the population. Islam will likely predominate well into the 21st century. A growing number of nonreligious could eventually pass the 10% mark.

BIBLIOGRAPHY

Baal, Christ and Mohammed: religion and revolution in North Africa. J. K. Cooley. New York: Holt, Rinehart & Winston, 1965. 369p.

'Beliefs and practices at or in relation to a Moroccan tribal market,' W. Fogg, *Folklore*, 51, 2 (1940), 132–38.

'Celebration of the body: spirituality and corporeality in Muslim Morocco.' M. G. Messina. Ph.D. dissertation, State University of New York at Stony Brook, 1991. 408p.

'Chrétienté et Islam au Maroc (du XVIe à XXe siècle),' G. Matringe, *Revue historique de droit français et étranger*, 4 (1943), 588–643.

'Eglises chrétiennes en terre d'Islam: essai sur la liberté de culte et la pratique religieuse au Maroc depuis le XIIe siècle,' G. Matringe, in *Etudes d'histoire de droit canonique dédiées à Gabriel le Bras*, p.341–49. Paris: 1965.

Extinction of the Christian Churches in North Africa. L. R. Holme. New York: Burt Franklin, 1969.

Fasting and feasting in Morocco: women's participation in Ramadan. M. Buitelaar. *Mediterranea series.* Oxford, UK: Berg, 1993. 219p.

Fez: city of Islam. T. Burckhardt. Trans., W. Stoddart. : Islamic Texts Society, 1992. 175p.

'Ideological change and regional cults: maraboutism and ties of closeness in western Morocco,' D. F. Eickelman, in *Regional cults*, p.3–28. R. P. Werbner (ed). London: Academic Press, 1977.

'Islam in Morocco,' R. Landau, *Geographical magazine*, 22, 8 (1949), 320–34.

Islam observed: religious development in Morocco and Indonesia. C. Geertz. New Haven, CT: Yale University Press, 1968. 136p.

'Islamic revival fuels Maghreb discontent,' P. Blum, *Middle East Economic Digest*, 24, 9 (1980), 6–8.

La Archdiocesis de Tanger: Anuario 1970. Tangier: Curia Pastoral, 1970.

L'église chrétienne du Maroc et la mission franciscaine, 1221–1790. H. Koehler. [Paris]: Société d'éditions franciscaines, [1935]. 274p.

L'Islam dans les cinq pays du maghreb arabe. L. Pruvost. *Dossiers de la C.R.R.M*, no. 6. : Commission pour les Relations Religieuses avec les Musulmans, Conseil Pontifical pour le Dialogue Interreligieux, 1993. 18p.

Looking at French Morocco. J. E. Seddon. *Look on the Fields Series.* London: Bible Churchmen's Missionary Society, 1954. 24p.

'Maghribi brotherhoods.' K. L. Brown. Paper presented at the annual meeting of the American Historical Association, New York, 1968. (Mimeographed).

Missionary romance in Morocco. J. Haldane. London: Pickering & Inglis, 1937. 189p.

Moroccan Islam: tradition and society in a pilgrimage centre. D. Eickelman. *Modern Middle East Series*, 1. Austin, TX: University of Texas Press, 1976.

Morocco. A. M. Findlay & A. M. Findlay. 2nd ed. *World bibliographical series*, vol. 47. Oxford: CLIO Press, 1994. ca. 350p. (Complements 1st edition, focusing upon material since 1984).

'Morocco and the Near East: reflections on some basic differences,' E. B. III, *Archives Européennes de Sociologie*, 10, 1 (1969), 70–94.

Pagan survivals in Mohammedan civilisation. E. A. Westermarck. London: Macmillan, 1933. 190p.

Pélerinages au Maroc: fête, politique et échange dans l'Islam populaire. F. Reysoo. Neuchâtel, Switzerland: Editions de l'Institut d'ethnologie, 1991. 227p.

'Political and religious organization of the Berbers of the central High Atlas,' E. Gellner, in *Arabs and Berbers: from tribe to nation in North Africa*, p.59–66. E. Gellner & C. Micaud (eds). London: Duckworth, 1973.

Religion and power in Morocco. H. Munson Jr. New Haven, CT: Yale University Press, 1993. 251p.

Saints and spirits. M. Llewlyn-Davies, E. W. Fernea & A. Abbassi. Chicago: Films Incorporated Video, 1991. (25 min videocassette).

Saints of the Atlas. E. Gellner. London: Weidenfeld & Nicolson, 1969. 317p. (Charismatic Muslim leaders in holy villages among the contemporary Berbers [Rif, Tamazigt, Tashlehait] of the High Atlas).

'Situation actuelle de l'Islam maghrébin,' *Maghreb*, 47 (September–October 1971), 30–46.

Some women of Marrakech. M. L. Davies. Rexdale, Ontario: Thomas Howe Associates. (53 min videocassette).

'Symbol and sanction: social change and the vitality of Moroccan Islam.' S. B. Swensen. Ph.D. dissertation, University of Virginia, Charlottesville, VA, 1983. 113p.

The Hamadsha: a study in Moroccan ethnopsychiatry. V. Crapanzano. Berkeley and Los Angeles: University of California Press, 1973. 258p.

'The logic of analogy and the role of the Sufi shaykh in post–Marinid Morocco,' V. J. Cornell, *International Journal of Middle Eastern Studies*, 15 (1983), 67–93.

'The Moorish concept of holiness *(baraka)*,' E. Westermarck, *Ofversigt af Finska Vetenskaps Societetens, B*, 58, 1 (1916), 1–153.

'The restitution of Islam: a comparative study of the Islamic movements in contemporary Tunisia and Morocco.' E. E. A. Shahin. Ph.D. dissertation, Johns Hopkins University, Baltimore, MD, 1990. 314p.

'The role of Islam in modern North Africa,' L. C. Brown, in *State and society in independent North Africa*, p.96–122. L. C. Brown (ed). Washington, DC: Middle East Institute, 1966.

'The Salafiyya movement in Morocco: the religious bases of the Moroccan nationalist movement,' J. Abun-Nasr, *St. Anthony's Papers*, 16 (1963), 90–105.

The victim and its masks: an essay on sacrifice and masquerade in the Maghreb. A. Hammoudi. Chicago: University of Chicago Press, 1993. 214p. (Also in French).

Trekking among Moroccan tribes. J. Haldane. London: Pickering & Inglis, 1948. 192p.

Un cycle oral hagiographique dans le Moyen–Atlas marocain. J. Drouin. *Série Sorbonne*, 2. Paris: Publications de la Sorbonne, 1975. 270p.

'Women, Sufism and decision–making in Moroccan Islam,' D. H. Dwyer, in *Women in the Muslim world*, p.585–98. L. Beck & N. Keddie (eds). London: Harvard University Press, 1978.

Country Table 2. **Organized churches and denominations in Morocco.**

Official name (bold type = church with over 10% of all affiliated) 1	*Begun* 2	*Type* 3	*Counc* 4	*Congs* 5	*Adults* 6	*Affiliated 1970* 7	*Affiliated 1995* 8	*G%* 9	*Names, notes, and other statistics* (see Codebook, Part 3) 10
Assemblées de Dieu	1945	P-Pe2	Z....	2	50	50	83	2.05	M=Swedish Free Mission (Sweden),NPM(Norway). Based on Tangiers, radio work.
Baptist Convention	1966	P-Bap	T....	3	100	17	167	9.57	M=FMB-SBC. Southern Baptist Convention (USA).
Eglise Adventiste du Septième Jour	1928	P-Adv	x....	3	32	50	51	0.08	*Seventh-day Adventists*, in NAfrica M, Euro-Africa Division. Some work in south.
Eglise Anglicane (D Europe)	1662	A-Cen	aw.UK	5	290	600	450	-1.14	Till 1974 in D Egypt. English chaplaincies; M=CMJ(1832),BCMS(1929), D Gibraltar. 9f.
Eglise Catholique au Maroc:	1220	R-Lat	pzSHK	42	13,800	100,000	23,600	-5.61	*Cath Ch.* French, Spanish. C=11+3+28. 15n 52x 68m 305w 68Yy
AD Rabat	1923	R-Lat	ps	32	12,300	80,000	21,000	-5.21	Massive, ongoing emigration. M=OFM. C=8+2+21. 15n 39x 50m 188w 58Yy
AD Tanger (Tangiers)	1630	R-Lat	pofm	10	1,500	20,000	2,600	-7.84	*Arquidiocesis (Iglesia Católica).* Spanish. C=3+1+7. 0n 13x 18m 117w 10Yy
Eglise Chrétienne de Réveil		I-3pS	.....	3	50	50	150	0.05	*Christian Revival Ch.* In Casablanca and Rabat. Foreigners, 4 Moroccans. 1x.
Eglise du Christ		I-Dis	x....	2	20	100	50	0.05	*Ch of Christ.* M=CC(Non-Instrumental) (USA). Tangiers, Kenitra. USA naval personnel.
Eglise Emmanuel	1926	P-Hol	x....	3	100	300	200	-1.61	*Emmanuel Holiness Ch. Sahara Mission.* M=EHC(UK) until banned 1968. Meknes. 8f.
Eglise Evangélique au Maroc	1910	P-Ref	R.A.K	9	280	3,000	700	-5.65	*EEAM. Ev Ch.* In Reformed Ch of France until 1958. All French. 3x,W=20%,5Y,20y.
Eglise Orthodox Belorusse		O-Bye	M....	1	70	150	130	0.05	*Byelorussian Orthodox Ch.* White Russian refugee congregation in Casablanca.
Eglise Orthodox Grecque		O-Ara	Cw.NK	3	350	600	500	0.05	*Greek Orthodox Ch.* Under P Alexandria. Half in Casablanca. Arab immigrants. 1x.
Eglise Orthodox Russe		O-Rus	Mwc.K	1	70	150	130	0.05	*Russian Orthodox Ch.* Under P Moscow. 1 congregation in Rabat. Russian emigres.
Eglises radiophoniques isolées	1958	I-3rS	.....	1,000	60,000	22,400	120,000	6.94	Isolated radio believers, most under 25. R=2300,S=4400,T=110000 (RSB,GMU,ICI).
Frères Larges		P-CBr	x....	5	150	200	300	0.05	*Christian Brethren (Open).* M=CMML(UK, USA). Tangiers. Marrakesh. 3f.
Hidden Muslim believers in Christ	c1970	I-Mus	.....	700	6,000	–	10,800	44.99	Converted Muslims who choose to remain in Islam as witnesses to Christ.
Mission du Monde Arabe	1884	P-Non	xMg..	10	200	150	350	3.45	M=AWM/North Africa M(UK). 70% Moroccans, in legal building. 28f (in secular jobs),1H.
Mission Israel	1950	P-Lut	l....	1	40	30	60	2.81	M=Swedish Israel Mission. Small group in Casablanca for Hebrew Christians.
Témoins de Jéhovah	c1950	m-Jeh	x....	3	51	500	113	-5.78	*Jehovah's Witnesses.* Active witnessing under way by 1952. All foreigners. 37Y.
Union Evangélique Missionnaire	1894	P-Hol	xM...	10	100	50	300	7.43	*UEM.* M=Gospel Missionary Union (USA). 50 Moroccans. Radio courses. Banned 1969. 4f.
Other Protestant denominations		P-	.....	25	1,000	1,200	2,000	0.05	Total about 10 (see list below).
Other indigenous charismatic chs		I-3aS	x....	10	400	700	700	0.05	Including Tree of Life Church (5 churches, 200 members).
Totals				**1,841**	**83,153**	**130,297**	**160,834**		

Churches, members, growth, 1900-2025	*Congs*	*Adults*	*Affiliated*	*G%*	*Total denominations*	*6 Megablocs:* *O*	*R*	*A*	*P*	*I*	*m*
Total churches, members, and denominations (mid-1900)	200	16,600	30,080	2.12	4	0	1	1	2	0	0
Total churches, members, and denominations (mid-1970)	725	71,753	130,297	2.12	23	3	1	1	13	4	1
Total churches, members, and denominations (mid-1990)	1,600	75,200	145,400	0.55	32	3	1	1	19	7	1
Total churches, members, and denominations (mid-1995)	1,841	83,153	160,834	2.04	32	3	1	1	19	7	1
Total churches, members, and denominations (mid-2000)	1,900	90,200	174,476	1.64	32	3	1	1	19	7	1
Total churches, members, and denominations (mid-2025)	2,300	127,000	246,300	1.39	59	10	1	1	26	20	1

NOTES ON TABLE ABOVE

NATIONAL COUNCILS (Column 4, 5th letter).

K = Conseil des Eglises du Maroc, formerly Conseil des Eglises Chrétiennes au Maroc (Morocco Council of Christian Churches), formed 1977, formerly Comité Oecuménique d'Entr'aide au Maroc (COEM) (Ecumenical Interchurch-Aid Committee of Morocco).

OTHER PROTESTANT DENOMINATIONS. These consist of (1) small para-denominations begun by foreign mission bodies but now with few or no followers, including: Action Biblique de Genève, Berean Mission (1966, among Berbers), Ch of the Brethren (1959), Fellowship of Independent Missions (1950: formerly Morocco Evangelistic Fellowship), Light of Africa Mission, Mennonite Central Committee (1958), Southern Baptist Convention (1966, Rabat), Swedish Church Seamen's Mission; and (2) USA military chaplaincies among 1,000 USA servicemen and dependents.

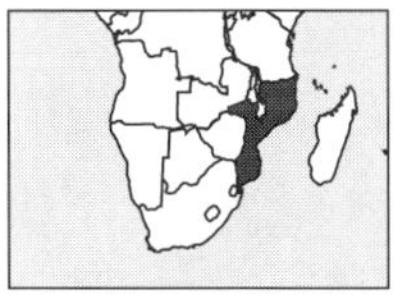

MOZAMBIQUE

SECULAR DATA, AD 2000

STATE

Official name: La República de Moçambique (The Republic of Mozambique).
Short name: Mozambique. **Adjective of nationality:** Mozambican.
Flag: Three equal horizontal bands of green (top), black, and yellow with a red isosceles triangle based on the hoist side; the black band is edged in white; centered in the triangle is a yellow five-pointed star bearing a crossed rifle and hoe in black superimposed on an open white book.
Area: 812,379 sq. km. (313,661 sq. mi.).
Government: Multiparty republic, since 1990 (1505 Portuguese possession, 1952 overseas province of Portugal, 1975 Independence, 1975 one-party Marxist state).
Legislature: Legislative Assembly, 250 members.
Official language: Portuguese (Português).
Monetary unit: 1 metical (Mt; plural meticals) = 100 centavos. **US$1=** Mt 11,495.
Chief cities: MAPUTO (Lourenco Marques) 3,017,000; Beira 395,257; Nampula 267,539; Nacala 137,735; Chimoio (Vila Pery) 120,530.
Political divisions: 11 provinces. **Armed forces:** 12,000.

DEMOGRAPHY

Population: 19,680,000.
Population density: 24.2/sq. km. (62.7/sq. mi.).
Under 15 years: 8,835,000.
Growth rate p.a.: 1.73% (births 41.21, deaths 23.93).
Mortality: Infant, per 1,000: 115.7, ; **Maternal per 100,000:** 1,500.0.
Life expectancy: 38 (male 37, female 39).
Household size: 4.4. **Floor area per person, sq.m:** 8.0.
Major languages: Portuguese, Makua, Tsonga, Lomwe, Karanga, Chopi, Ronga, Sena, Shona, Ndau (Chishanga), Chewa (Nyanja), Makonde, Yao, and about 20 smaller languages.
Urban dwellers: 40.23%. **Urban growth rate p.a.:** 4.8%.
Labor force: 49%.

ETHNOLINGUISTIC PEOPLES

15.2% Makuana; 9.0% Makua (Makhua, Meto); 8.5% Tsonga (Shangaan); 7.9% Sena; 7.0% Lomwe (Ngulu, Nguru).

ECONOMY

National income p.a. per person: US$79; **per family:** US$351.

EDUCATION

Adult literacy: 40% (male 57%, female 23%). **Schools:** 4,035.
Universities: 2. **School enrolment:** female/male: 29%/41%.

HEALTH

Access to health services: 39%. **Access to safe water:** 32%.
Hospitals: 238 (9 beds per 10,000). **Doctors:** 388.
Blind: 28,000. **Deaf:** 1,173,800. **Murder rate:** 4.
Lepers: 20,000. **Underweight prevalence under 5:** 27%.

LITERATURE

New book titles p.a.: 200 (10 p.a. per million). **Periodicals:** 4.
Newspapers: 2 dailies.

COMMUNICATION (per 1,000 people)

Phones: 3 (8% mobile). **Radios:** 36. **TV sets:** 3.
Daily newspaper circulation: 5. **Computers:** 8.

REFUGEES

Citizen refugees in other countries: 97,000.
Internal displacement: 500,000.

HUMAN LIFE AND LIBERTY (optimum condition=100.0%)
HDI: 28.1. **HSI:** 7.0. **HFI:** 15.0. **EFL:** 19.0.

Country status. Mozambique, a former Portuguese colony, is located on the east coast of Africa, opposite the island of Madagascar. The economy is almost entirely based on agriculture supplemented by a small coal output.

HUMAN LIFE AND LIBERTY

Human need and development. Mozambique, in addition to being one of the poorest nations in Africa, was until recently wracked by a civil war between rival factions. The scars of violence inflicted by both sides may take decades to heal. Meanwhile, the vast majority of Mozambicans live in substandard conditions with little or no health care, scanty food resources and few social services. Malnutrition and diseases take a heavier toll each year than all the years of the civil war. Educational facilities, hard hit by the civil war, are at the same level as existed in the West about 200 years ago. In the major cities, most people displaced by the civil war live in squatter settlements with makeshift water or sewage services. The GNP per capita is the lowest in the world at $80; life expectancy, also the lowest in the world, is 38, and the percentage of adult illiterates is 60. Death toll in the civil war is estimated at one million and several millions have been rendered homeless. As both the government and the rebels blocked deliveries of international relief supplies and diverted them for private gain, tens of thousands have died from starvation.

Human rights and freedoms. With the signing of a peace accord between the FRELIMO led government of President Joaquin Chissano and the insurgent Mozambique National Resistance (RENAMO) in 1992, there was an apparent end to the indiscriminate violence and human rights abuses that had brought havoc to the country for 16 years. The terms of the ceasefire commited the government to hold democratic elections within a year, amnesty all combatants, and dissolve the infamous Mozambican National Security Service (SNASP). Press freedom has expanded with the appearance of a number of privately published news bulletins and labor unions have been permitted to operate outside FRELIMO control. But the legacies of war continue to haunt the country. There were unexplained disappearances, kidnappings, assaults on innocent civilians, forcible relocations, and summary executions, as routine episodes during the civil war which the peace accord has done little to erase. Ethnic rivalries have been accentuated by the civil war. The FRELIMO government is dom-

Country Table 1. **Religious adherents in Mozambique, AD 1900-2025.**

Year	1900		1970		mid-1990		Annual change, 1990-2000				mid-1995		mid-2000		mid-2025	
Name	*Adherents*	*%*	*Adherents*	*%*	*Adherents*	*%*	*Natural*	*Conversion*	*Total*	*Rate*	*Adherents*	*%*	*Adherents*	*%*	*Adherents*	*%*
Ethnoreligionists	2,504,900	96.3	5,430,300	57.8	7,222,000	50.9	278,849	-10,149	268,700	3.21	8,820,000	50.7	9,908,997	50.4	14,226,000	46.5
Christians	**16,700**	**0.6**	**2,807,000**	**29.9**	**5,384,000**	**37.9**	**207,882**	**8,936**	**216,818**	**3.44**	**6,606,850**	**38.0**	**7,552,177**	**38.4**	**13,000,000**	**42.5**
PROFESSION																
professing Christians	**16,700**	**0.6**	**2,807,000**	**29.9**	**5,384,000**	**37.9**	**207,882**	**8,936**	**216,818**	**3.44**	**6,606,850**	**38.0**	**7,552,177**	**38.4**	**13,000,000**	**42.5**
AFFILIATION																
unaffiliated Christians	3,400	0.1	757,644	8.1	786,500	5.5	30,368	146	30,514	3.33	961,039	5.5	1,091,644	5.6	1,384,000	4.5
affiliated Christians	**13,300**	**0.5**	**2,049,356**	**21.8**	**4,597,500**	**32.4**	**177,514**	**8,789**	**186,303**	**3.46**	**5,645,811**	**32.5**	**6,460,533**	**32.8**	**11,616,000**	**38.0**
Roman Catholics	12,000	0.5	1,552,723	16.5	2,290,000	16.1	88,419	-6,419	82,000	3.11	2,767,090	15.9	3,110,000	15.8	4,800,000	15.7
Protestants	1,000	0.0	358,333	3.8	1,200,000	8.5	46,333	8,667	55,000	3.85	1,490,282	8.6	1,750,000	8.9	3,300,000	10.8
Independents	100	0.0	46,300	0.5	975,000	6.9	37,646	7,057	44,703	3.85	1,230,439	7.1	1,422,033	7.2	3,200,000	10.5
Anglicans	200	0.0	45,000	0.5	75,000	0.5	2,896	604	3,500	3.90	95,000	0.6	110,000	0.6	215,000	0.7
Marginal Christians	0	0.0	45,000	0.5	57,000	0.4	2,201	-1,101	1,100	1.78	62,500	0.4	68,000	0.4	100,000	0.3
Orthodox	0	0.0	2,000	0.0	500	0.0	19	-19	0	0.00	500	0.0	500	0.0	1,000	0.0
Trans-megabloc groupings																
Evangelicals	800	0.0	230,000	2.5	950,000	6.7	36,681	3,319	40,000	3.58	1,180,743	6.8	1,350,000	6.9	2,835,000	9.3
Pentecostals/Charismatics	0	0.0	134,000	1.4	1,635,000	11.5	63,129	5,871	69,000	3.58	2,040,623	11.7	2,325,000	11.8	4,000,000	13.1
Great Commission Christians	**15,600**	**0.6**	**1,128,000**	**12.0**	**2,520,000**	**17.8**	**97,300**	**6,182**	**103,482**	**3.50**	**3,110,000**	**17.9**	**3,554,815**	**18.1**	**6,300,000**	**20.6**
Muslims	78,300	3.0	1,145,000	12.2	1,500,640	10.6	57,989	-1,204	56,785	3.26	1,832,000	10.5	2,068,491	10.5	3,030,700	9.9
Nonreligious	0	0.0	5,000	0.1	55,000	0.4	2,124	1,890	4,014	5.63	81,380	0.5	95,140	0.5	250,000	0.8
Hindus	0	0.0	6,500	0.1	22,000	0.2	849	120	969	3.72	27,700	0.2	31,686	0.2	50,000	0.2
Atheists	0	0.0	0	0.0	12,000	0.1	463	373	836	5.43	17,000	0.1	20,364	0.1	50,000	0.2
Baha'is	0	0.0	1,000	0.0	2,200	0.0	85	36	121	4.46	2,900	0.0	3,405	0.0	5,000	0.0
Jews	100	0.0	200	0.0	160	0.0	6	-2	4	2.10	170	0.0	197	0.0	300	0.0
World A (unevangelized persons)	2,314,000	89.0	3,757,900	40.0	3,847,658	27.1	148,267	-80,137	68,130	1.65	4,346,955	25.0	4,526,400	23.0	5,510,160	18.0
World B (evangelized non-Christians)	269,300	10.4	2,829,851	30.1	4,966,342	35.0	192,098	71,201	263,299	4.35	6,434,017	37.0	7,601,423	38.6	12,101,840	39.5
World C (Christians)	16,700	0.6	2,807,000	29.9	5,384,000	37.9	207,882	8,936	216,818	3.44	6,606,850	38.0	7,552,177	38.4	13,000,000	42.5
Country's population	**2,600,000**	**100.0**	**9,394,752**	**100.0**	**14,198,000**	**100.0**	**548,247**	**0**	**548,247**	**3.32**	**17,387,823**	**100.0**	**19,680,000**	**100.0**	**30,612,000**	**100.0**

COLUMNS, ROWS.
For meanings and definitions, see Codebook (Part 3). Note that, by definition, total 'Christians' = professing + crypto-Christians, which also = affiliated + unaffiliated Christians, and also = Great Commission Christians + latent Christians. Percentages may not always total exactly, due to rounding.

CENSUSES.
21.X.1950 (de jure): 81.3% ethnoreligionists, 10.7% Muslims, 6.2% Roman Catholics, 1.7% Protestants & Anglicans, 0.1% Hindus, 0.1% nonreligious. **21.IX.1950** (civilized population only, 91,954 total): 71.8% Roman Catholics, 24.9% non-Christians (Muslims, Hindus, also nonreligious), 3.3% Protestants. **1955** (non-Africans only, 117,405 totals): 73.0% Roman Catholics, 13.9% Muslims, 4.0% Hindus, 3.3% Protestants, 5.6% nonreligious and other religionists.

NOTES ON RELIGIONS
AFRICAN INDIGENOUS. In around 210 denominations in 1995 (see Table 2).
ATHEISTS. In February 1977, the broad Liberation movement FRELIMO (Frente de Libertação de Moçambique) was changed to become a Marxist-Leninist party, cancelling existing membership lists and reducing membership to a revolutionary core of about 5,000.
BAHA'IS. In 1973, in 7 local spiritual assemblies, increasing to 18 LSAs (1995).
HINDUS. Indians, numbering 4,731 at the 1955 census.
MUSLIMS. Sunnis (of the Shafiite rite). Mainly among the Yao (80%), Makonde (44%), Makua (18%), in the northern districts of Delgado, Moçambique, Niassa and Zambezia. In 1955, there were also 16,348 Muslim Indo-Pakistanis and others from the Comoro Islands and Mauritius. *Hajj pilgrims to Mecca.* (1976) 47.
NOMINAL CHRISTIANS. Under Portuguese rule until 1975, many Africans professed to be Christians in censuses, although not yet affiliated to churches, thus forming part of a sizeable nominal fringe. After 1975 this fringe steadily decreased in size.
NONRELIGIOUS. As in Portugal itself, in 1995 about 7% of the 186,000 Portuguese settlers were nonreligious; so were numbers of the Chinese from Macau. As the Portuguese emigrated, workers from the People's Republic of China arrived, most being nonreligious.
ROMAN CATHOLICS. After experiencing phenomenal numerical growth from 6.2% of the population in 1950 to about 30% in 1970 and 35% in 1975, professing Catholics ceased to grow so rapidly due to the 1974-76 emigration of 250,000 Portuguese, the state's nationalization of all Catholic schools, and the subsequently-increasing government restrictions placed on Catholic missions.
ETHNORELIGIONISTS. All tribes north of the Save river were over 60% traditionalist in 1995, except the Yao, Makonde (12%) and Makua (59%). These included: Chuabo (60% animist), Ndau (63%), Sena (60%); Kunda (72%), Nsenga (73%), and Tawara (63%).

Great Commission Instrument Panel: status of Mozambique (for explanation see start of Part 4)

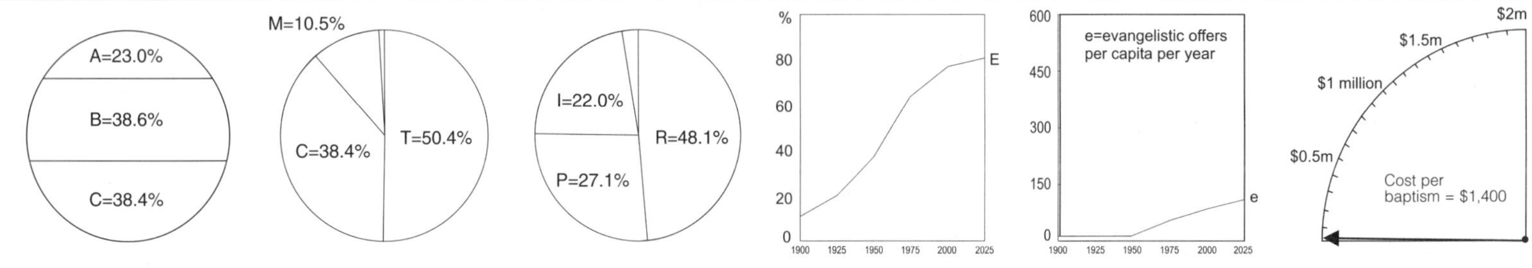

3 Worlds, AD 2000 — Religions, AD 2000 — Ecclesiastical blocs — Evangelization, 1900-2025 — Offers, 1900-2025 — Cost-effectiveness, AD 2000

inated by southerners, especially by members of the Shangana ethnic group while RENAMO is led by members of the Shona-speaking ethnic group. Women and children have fared badly during the civil war. Mozambican women have the highest maternal mortality rates and the lowest rates of literacy in the world.

Human environment. The environment has deteriorated since independence, because of the civil war and also because of neglect. The mangrove forests which once comprised 48% of the coastline have been reduced by 70%. Mangrove wood is used as firewood in rural areas, and is being cut down indiscriminately. As a result, there is severe coastal erosion.

NON-CHRISTIAN RELIGIONS

Traditional religions are followed by more than half the African population. With the exception of 3 tribes (Yao, Makonde and Makua) where Islam is a significant feature, all peoples north of the Save river are at least 70% traditionalist. The most common names for God are Mulungu north of the Zambezi (among the Yao, Nyanja, Chewa) and Tilo (Sky) among the Chopi and Tsonga of southern Mozambique. The Tsonga do not attribute creation to Tilo, but they insist that he is responsible for such celestial phenomena as thunder and lightning, as well as death. Rain on the other hand is given or withheld by the Psikwembu, the ancestral spirits, who must be placated in time of drought. Part of the rain-making rite is a purification ceremony, mbelele, administered by women. Revitalization movements playing an important role during the 20th century include the Murimi of 1915 and Mchape of 1934. The former was a cult of the supreme being Mwirimi (in Hlengwe) who was believed to possess the movement's prophets. Beginning among the Hlengwe, it spread south, the immediate cause being a severe famine in the area between 1913 and 1915. It ultimately took on the characteristics of a witchcraft eradication campaign, the active cleansing agent being the snuffing of tobacco. Mchape (Medicine), another witchcraft eradication movement, began in Nyasaland and spread quickly to Tanganyika, Northern and Southern Rhodesia and among the Ndau of Mozambique, although it never became as important in Mozambique as in the other areas. Mchape took the form of water or maize meal doctored with blood, hair and fingernail clippings. Both movements were suppressed by the Portuguese authorities.

Islam has a long history in Mozambique. Arab and Persian traders reached the northern coast about AD 1000; and until the arrival of the Portuguese, the coastal area was controlled by Muslim sultans centered on Zanzibar. The Yao, who inhabit the region east of Lake Malawi, are 80% islamized, the only interior tribe below the equator to experience such a mass conversion to Islam. This is explained by their role as traders between the lake and Kilwa since the 19th century. The northern Makonde are 43% Muslim and the Makua 18% with greatest concentration of Muslims in the coastal area. Islamic influence is also evident along the Zambezi river.

CHRISTIANITY

CATHOLIC CHURCH. Dominican missionaries arrived in Mozambique as early as 1506 accompanying the advance of Portuguese maritime discoveries. In 1560 came the Jesuits, and during the next century and a half Dominicans, Jesuits and Augustinians were active on the southern coast and in the region of the Zambezi river. This early activity was followed by a period of decline. Sustained work among most of the tribes north of the Save river was not begun until the end of the 19th and early 20th centuries. The northwestern Yao were not reached until 1930.

The war of liberation which began in 1964 took its toll, a number of missions having been abandoned in the northern area of hostilities. Many were established in villages later destroyed by the Portuguese army.

The Holy See has no diplomatic relations with Mozambique in AD 2000, but an apostolic delegate residing in Maputo.

PROTESTANT CHURCHES. Protestant efforts began in 1879 with the arrival of the first American Board missionaries; and although this work was turned over to American Methodists in 1888, there still exists a Congregationalist church dating its origin to 1879. Today United Methodists have a large following in the Inhambane area. Other early Methodist groups include Free Methodists from the USA and Wesleyan Methodists from South Africa. Swiss Presbyterians arrived in 1881 and directed their attention to the Tsonga and Shangaan people northwest of Lourenco Marques.

Country summary. **Worlds A, B, C by ethnolinguistic peoples, cities, and major civil divisions in Mozambique.**

	PEOPLES							CITIES							CIVIL DIVISIONS						
World	*Num*	*Pop 2000*	*C%*	*Christians*	*E%*	*U%*	*Unevangelized*	*Num*	*Pop 2000*	*C%*	*Christians*	*E%*	*U%*	*Unevangelized*	*Num*	*Pop 2000*	*C%*	*Christians*	*E%*	*U%*	*Unevangelized*
A	7	227,348	7.10	16,133	44	56	127,412	0	0	0.00	0	0	0	0	0	0	0.00	0	0	0	0
B	38	16,214,382	25.09	4,067,392	73	27	4,385,323	10	4,352,701	42.18	1,835,928	88	12	532,541	11	19,680,455	32.83	6,460,533	77	23	4,521,299
C	12	3,238,721	73.39	2,377,007	100	0	8,568	0	0	0.00	0	0	0	0	0	0	0.00	0	0	0	0
Total	**57**	**19,680,451**	**32.83**	**6,460,532**	**77**	**23**	**4,521,303**	**10**	**4,352,701**	**42.18**	**1,835,928**	**88**	**12**	**532,541**	**11**	**19,680,455**	**32.83**	**6,460,533**	**77**	**23**	**4,521,299**

Igrejia Metodista Unida. Woman pastor Olga Marie Raimundo.

Following World War I, there was a new missionary upsurge with the entry of Scandinavian Baptists in 1918, now the largest Protestant denomination in Mozambique, International Holiness Mission in 1921, SAGM and Nazarenes in 1922, Seventh-day Adventists in 1933, and 2 Pentecostal bodies from the USA and Canada during the 1930s. The latter group, the Pentecostal Assemblies of God, has now built up the third largest Protestant community in Mozambique. The International Holiness work north of Tete has been taken over by Nazarenes who have added this field to the work northeast of Maputo. Baptists are located north of Maputo and Inhambane and Adventists north of the Zambezi among the Lomwe and Chuabo peoples.

Around 1960 the Assemblies of God entered the country planting 3 congregations with 3,200 members by 1970. By 1995, following phenomenal growth, they had 396 congregations with 380,000 members.

In 1962 the Africa Evangelical Fellowship (formerly SAGM) was expelled from Mozambique, but its work among the Lomwe west of Nampula was carried on by its daughter church, the Evangelical Church of Mozambique, with support from the Christian Council of Mozambique. The latter is also responsible for founding the Church of Christ in Manica & Sofala in 1965.

ANGLICAN CHURCH. Although Anglicans exist in the districts of Maputo and Gaza, they exert their greatest influence among the Yao of northwestern Mozambique, the only predominantly Muslim tribe in the country. High Church Anglican missionaries of the UMCA were in fact the Christian pioneers in Yao country. Bishop Steere visited them in 1875, but it was not until 1893 that a permanent mission station was established at Unango. At the present time there are about twice as many Yao Anglicans as Catholics.

INDIGENOUS CHURCHES. Because of strong government opposition, African indigenous churches have had difficulty in establishing themselves in Mozambique. There exist today over 100 small semi-clandestine bodies, most owing their origin to outside influences. Many have been brought home by Mozambican miners working in South Africa. Several, including the African Apostolic Church of Johane Maranke, have been imported from neighboring Rhodesia; and the African Methodist Episcopal Church was begun by Blacks from the USA as early as 1883. Several have a purely Mozambican origin, beginning with the Igreja Luso-Africana which split from the Swiss Mission in 1921.

Renewal movements. In the 1990s the Pentecostal/Charismatic Renewal continued to spread rapidly across most older churches, and numbered over 2,325,000 adherents (of whom 40% Pentecostals, 14% Charismatics, and 46% Independents).

Indigenous missions. Although some Mozambican Christians have served as missionaries, the number has been very small and most of these served in surrounding countries.

Varying urban church architectural styles: (*from top*) Roman Catholic (Maputo), Roman Catholic (Inhambane), Methodist (Maputo), Presbyterian (Maputo).

CHURCH AND STATE

Prior to Independence in June 1975, the juridical bases of the relationship of the Catholic Church to the Portuguese government were contained in the Missionary Concordat of 1940 and the Missionary Statute of 1941. By their declarations and acts, the local Catholic hierarchy closely identified the interests of the church with those of the Portuguese state, thereby sanctioning the colonial status quo and remaining silent in the face of injustices perpetrated in the name of 'defence of Christian civilization'. In their pastoral letter of 1970 entitled 'Christian message for ordering right relations in Mozambique' (Mensagem Crista nas Coordenadas de Mocambique), the bishops noted 'the total absence of racial discrimination in Portuguese laws', condemned 'every kind of guerrilla action (terrorismo)' and expressed the wish that social injustices be resolved in a progressive mutual assumption of social, economic, and political responsibility.

After 1971, this attitude of the hierarchy was increasingly rejected by European clergy. In May of that year, the 48 White Fathers (natives of 9 Western countries but with none from Portugal) who worked in the dioceses of Beira and Tete withdrew en masse in protest against the identification of the hierarchy with the politics of colonialism. This decision, taken by the general council of the missionary congregation after consultation with the missionaries, was strongly criticized by the Portuguese government and the Episcopal Conference of Mozambique who 'did not believe it to be dictated by an authentic evangelical spirit' and who, on the same occasion, re-emphasized their support of government policy. The exodus of White Fathers had repercussions on other congregations serving in Mozambique, especially those of the Burgos, Consolata, and Combonian Fathers, of whom some (including Portuguese) felt constrained to leave the country. Moreover, 4 priests (2 diocesan Portuguese and 2 Spanish IEME), accused of being in contact with Frelimo, were arrested and sentenced to prison in 1972. Only 2 bishops were known for this non-conformist attitude towards Portuguese colonialism; Sebastiao Soares Rezenda, former bishop of Beira (died 1967) who courageously defended the rights of Africans (although within the context of integration rather than political independence) and Manuel Vieira Pinto, bishop of Nampula, who was ultimately exiled on 14 April 1974 because of his criticism of the colonial war. About 100 other Catholic missionaries were expelled from Mozambique prior to the coup d'etat in Portugal on 25 April 1974. In addition, many catechists were killed during the hostilities generated by the colonial war.

The Protestant churches had been much more independent than the Catholic Church with respect to the colonial administration, without however serving as any real or effective opposition. This independence, made possible by the absence of privileges, and the educational role of Protestant missions in training an African elite, served indirectly to promote the idea of national emancipation, which explains the attachment of large numbers of Protestants to the liberation movement and the Portuguese police repression of which these churches were often the object, a repression which amounted to religious persecution. Significant elements within Frelimo were of Protestant origin. In 1972 during a police raid that produced several hundred arrests, 31 African Presbyterian leaders were imprisoned, including Zedequias Manganhela and Jose Sidumo who later died in Machava prison.

Since the coup d'etat of April 1974 in Portugal and especially following Mozambique's Independence on 25 June 1975, a radical change has taken place in church-state relations. On its part, the Catholic Church has made an effort to adjust to the new situation. The episcopal conference, in a pastoral letter of 30 August 1974 entitled 'The Church in an independent Mozambique', expressed its 'profound joy' at the proclamation of the right to independence. Later the Portuguese archbishop of Maputo was replaced by an

African in December 1974. In a statement of support for the Mozambique Revolution issued in mid-1975, the Burgos Fathers affirmed: 'We dissociate ourselves from any reactionary and reformist attitude or activity of the Church. In the life of the Church, also, there exists class struggle, often hidden behind a facade of unity. By participating in the revolutionary struggle, we are working for the true unity of the Church, since that unity can only be achieved through the unity of Mankind'. An editorial in the July issue of the Catholic magazine *Nova vida* acknowledged the past errors of the Catholic Church and promised support for the cause of liberation.

For its part the transitional government extended an invitation to return to bishop Manuel Vieira Pinto and other Catholic missionaries who had left in protest against Portuguese policy or been expelled.

Article 19 of the new constitution affirms: 'The People's Republic of Mozambique is a secular State, in which there is an absolute separation between the State and religious organizations. In the People's Republic of Mozambique all activities of religious bodies must conform to the laws of the State.' Article 26 assures to all citizens the same rights and duties 'independent of their colour, race, sex, ethnic, origin, place of birth, religion, rank of instruction, social position and profession', with the further proviso that 'all acts with the goal of prejudice, creating divisions or situations of privilege' because of these things 'will be punished by the law'. Article 33 affirms that 'the State guarantees citizens the freedom to practice a religion'.

The president of Mozambique, Samora Machel, although from a Free Methodist background, is known for his Marxist sentiments and his attempt to equate religion with superstition, exploitation and divisiveness. Before Independence, in a speech on 4 June 1975, he stated: 'Another factor which divides our people is religion... Therefore, there will be no privileges for any church here in Mozambique. The privileged will be the Mozambican people, and only Frelimo will organize the peoples of Mozambique, noone else'. Elsewhere, Machel held that 'Religion, and especially Roman Catholicism, contributed enormously towards the cultural and human alienation of the Mozambican, in order to make him into a submissive instrument and the object of exploitation, to smother any manifestation of resistance by appealing to the Christian doctrine of abnegation'. On yet another occasion, before 100,000 people in Maputo's Machava stadium, Machel castigated the churches for allowing themselves to be ruled from outside Mozambique: Catholics from Rome, Presbyterians from Switzerland, and Methodists from America.

Muslims likewise have also been strongly criticized for allegedly allowing themselves to be used by the Portuguese in order to gain material benefits and official recognition.

A major move to reduce the influence of the churches was the nationalization of all educational and social service institutions of the churches, including schools and hospitals. Missionary doctors and teachers wishing to stay were required to sign contracts with government and were in most cases relocated to different areas.

Many missionaries in fact left the country and others were expelled. Three, including 2 Nazarenes and one WEC, were imprisoned and held for trial, though later released. New missionaries are not being sought by churches.

The last of Machel's attacks on the churches was made in a speech on 11 November 1975, Angola's day of independence. Subsequently he has shown a more conciliatory attitude, and on 31 January 1976 received a delegation representing the Catholic and Protestant churches, and the Christian Council of Mozambique, who sought clarification of the role of the churches in newly-independent Mozambique.

Subsequently the churches have become recognized as a voice of sanity, reconciliation, and concrete assistance, and have moved into the servant role now widespread in developing countries.

BROADCASTING AND MEDIA

IBRA-produced radio programs can be heard on local radio channels. FEBA (Seychelles) broadcasts programs in Portuguese and Yao, and TWR (Swaziland) broadcasts in Lomwe, Portuguese, Makua, Shangaan and Tshwa. Mozambique is a member of UNDA. Film teams have shown the 'Jesus' Film to 53,000.

INTERDENOMINATIONAL ORGANIZATIONS

The Christian Council of Mozambique (Conselho Cristão de Mocambique), with 8 member churches, was organized in 1944 to implement with church as well as mission representation the work begun by the Evangelical Missionary Association of Mozambique in 1923. In addition to sponsorship of an evangelical newspaper, a youth hostel in Maputo, literature and audio-visual programs, the CCM has been engaged in evangelistic work in the districts of Manica e Sofala and Zambezia. A direct product of this activity is the Church of Christ in Manica & Sofala. The CCM was also instrumental in the establishment of a united seminary at Ricatla in 1958. Ecumenical affairs for the Catholic episcopal conference are handled by the Episcopal Commission on Ecumenism (Commissao Episcopal do Ecumenismo). Thus far contacts between Anglicans and Catholics have been more cordial than the relations of either of these churches with Protestants.

Bible society executive secretary distributes scripture portions near Xai-Xai.

FUTURE TRENDS AND PROSPECTS

Tribal religions, waning at the end of the 20th century, will likely continue their decline through the year 2025 when they are projected to fall to 46.5%, down from near 100% in 1900. Christians are expected to rise to 42.5% in the same period.

Tribal religion has remained surprisingly strong in Mozambique but is certain to decline significantly throughout the 21st century. Most of these are likely to become Christians, resulting in a probable 50% by AD 2050.

BIBLIOGRAPHY

A history of Mozambique. M. Newitt. Bloomington, IN: Indiana University Press, 1993.

A Igreja das Palhotas: Génese da Igreja em Moçambique, entre o colonialismo e a independência. J. Luzia. *Cadernos de Estudos Africanos*, vol. 2, no. 4. Lisbon: Edição do Centro de Relexão Cristã, 1989. 128p.

'A presença protestante em Moçambique,' in *Protestantismo em Africa: contribuição para o estudo do protestantismo na Africa Portuguesa*, p.109–36. J. J. Gonçalves. Lisbon: Junta de Investigações do Ultramar, 1960.

Africains, missionnaires et colonialistes: les origines de l'Eglise presbytérienne du Mozambique (Mission suisse), 1880–1896. J. van Butselaar. *Studies on religion in Africa*, 5. Leiden: E. J. Brill, 1984. 239p.

Anuário católico de Moçambique, 1971. R. Dias. Lourenço Marques: Conferência Episcopal de Moçambique, 1971.

Cent ans au Mozambique: le parcours d'une minorité: reportage sur l'histoire de l'Eglise presbytérienne du Mozambique. C. Biber. Lausanne: Editions du Soc, 1987. 158p.

Church, state, and people in Mozambique: an historical study with special emphasis on Methodist developments in the Inhambane Region. A. Helgesson. *Studia missionalia Upsaliensia*, 54. Uppsala: Uppsala University Swedish Institute of Missionary Research, 1994. 455p.

'Developing a strategy for the spreading of a missionary vision among the Igreja Uniao Baptista.' R. H. Comrie. M.A. thesis, Columbia Biblical Seminary and Graduate School of Missions, Columbia, SC, 1988. 105p.

Historia de Moçambique cristão. A. Garcia. Lourenço Marques: Diario Grafica, 1969. 208p.

Igreja Católica em Moçambique. [Viseu, Portugal: Delfos, 1972]. 173p.

La Iglesia en Mozambique hoy, entre el colonialismo y la revolución. Madrid: Instituto de Estudios Políticos para América Latina y Africa, 1979. 119p.

'Le mouvement de mourimi: un réveil au sein de l'animisme thonga,' H. A. Junod, *Journal de psychologie normale et patholigique* (Paris), 21, 10 (1924), 55–69. (Murimi witchfinding movement).

Life out of death in Mozambique. P. Thompson. : Hodder & Stoughton, 1989. 169p.

Missão em Moçambique. E. D. Nogueira. Vila Cabral, Mozambique, 1970. 480p.

Missões franciscanas em Moçambique, 1898–1970. F. F. Lopes. Braga, 1972. 655p.

Moçambique milestones. L. O. Schultz. *Missionary reading books.* Kansas City, MO: Nazarene Publishing House, 1982. 112p.

Mozambique. C. Darch with C. Pacheleke. *World bibliographical series*, vol. 78. Oxford, UK: CLIO Press, 1987. 388p. (See especially 'Religion,' p.110f).

'Mozambique: a church in a socialist state in a time of radical change,' L. Hertsens, *Pro Mundi Vita* (Brussels), Africa Dossier 3 (January–February 1977), 1–42.

Mozambique: the cross and the crown. E. Hein & R. Hein. Dallas: Christ for the Nations, 1989. 166p.

Mozambique, une église, signe de salut ... pour qui? 2d ed. Rome, 1973. 422p.

'New England merchants and missionaries in coastal nineteenth century Portuguese East Africa.' C. B. White. Ph.D. dissertation, Boston University, Boston, 1974. 317p.

Os Jesuítas em Moçambique, 1541–1991: no cinquentenário do 4o. período da nossa missão. J. A. A. de Sousa. *Colecção 'História da Companhia de Jesus'.* Braga: Livraria A.I., [1991]. 213p.

Portuguese East Africa: a study of its religious needs. E. Moreira. London: World Dominion Press, 1936. 104p.

Questões Cristãs à religão tradicional africana, Moçambique. A. Langa. 2nd ed. Braga: Edorial Franciscana, 1992. 256p.

'Seitas religiosas gentilicas de Moçambique,' A. I. F. De Freitas, *Estudos ultramarinos* (Lisbon), 1 (1961), 91–122. (Pagan sects).

'The challenge of Mozambique: the unreached five million.' P. Johnstone. Pretoria: Dorothea Mission, 1965. 26p.

The Church in Mozambique: the colonial inheritance: minutes of a discussion between the Roman Catholic bishops and the government of Mozambique. Rome: IDOC International, 1979. 84p.

'The history and political role of the M'Bona cult among the Mang'anja,' M. Schoffeleers, in *The historical study of African religion*, p.73–94. T. O. Ranger & I. N. Kimambo (eds). Berkeley and Los Angeles: University of California Press, 1972.

The Mozambique story. F. Howie. *NWMS reading books.* Kansas City, MO: Nazarene Publishing House, 1993. 78p.

'The Tshwa response to Christianity: a study of the religious and cultural impact of Protestant Christianity on the Tshwa of Southern Mocambique.' A. Helgesson. M.A. thesis, University of the Witwatersrand, Johannesburg, 1971. 296p.

Country Table 2. **Organized churches and denominations in Mozambique.**

Official name (bold type = church with over 10% of all affiliated) *1*	*Begun* *2*	*Type* *3*	*Counc* *4*	*Congs* *5*	*Adults* *6*	*Affiliated 1970* *7*	*Affiliated 1995* *8*	*G%* *9*	*Names, notes, and other statistics* (see Codebook, Part 3) *10*
Assembleias de Deus	c1960	P-Pe2	Z...C	396	120,000	3,200	380,000	21.06	*Assemblies of God.* M=AoG. Main body related to AoG (USA).
Assembleias de Deus Africanas	1970	I-3pA	.....	120	40,000	–	70,000	56.24	*ADDA. African Assembies of God.* M=ZAOGA(Zimbabwe).
Assembleias de Deus Internacionales	c1970	I-3pA	.....	400	10,000	–	20,000	48.61	*International Assemblies of God.* Rival mission to AoG (USA), claiming its churches.
Assembleias Ev de Deus Pentecostales	1938	P-Pe2	ZF..C	600	60,000	70,000	150,000	3.10	*Pentecostal Assemblies of God.* M=PAoC(Canada). HQ Maputo. 385n,4x.
Convenção Baptista de Moçambique	1957	P-Bap	T...C	17	10,492	1,000	12,200	10.52	M=CBP,CBB(Brazil). 50% Shangaan, 50% Portuguese. 4n,1f,1p(6),W=65%,26Y.
Exército de Salvação	1916	P-Sal	xwa.C	18	3,500	2,000	7,000	5.14	*Salvation Army.* Pioneers Bantu miners converts from SAfrica. Organized 1923. Banned.
Igreja Adventista do Séptimo Dia	1933	P-Adv	x...C	402	49,323	20,733	82,200	5.66	*Seventh-day Adventists, Mozambique UM.* 57% Chuabo. 10n,1h,1j,1s,W=69%,1270Y.
Igreja Africana Metodista Episcopal	1883	I-Met	Vw..C	1	280	1,000	500	-2.73	*African Methodist Episcopal Church*, 18th Episcopal District. M=Amecu (USA Black).
Igreja Aguas Vidas	c1990	I-3cA	x....	10	500	–	1,000	20.00	M=Living Waters Church (based in Blantyre, Malawi). Rapidly-spreading charismatic churches.

Continued opposite

Country Table 2–concluded

Official name (bold type = church with over 10% of affiliated) 1	*Begun* 2	*Type* 3	*Counc* 4	*Congs* 5	*Adults* 6	*Affiliated 1970* 7	*Affiliated 1995* 8	*G%* 9	*Names, notes, and other statistics* (see Codebook, Part 3) 10
Igreja Anglicana: D Lebombo	1893	A-ACa	AwaVC	118	52,400	45,000	95,000	3.03	In CPSA. M=USPG. 30% Nyanja, 20% Shangaan. 30n,3x(2 Brazilian),2H,P=57%,544Y,799y.
Igreja Apostólica de Johane Maranke	c1950	I-3aA	x....	33	10,000	5,000	25,000	6.65	*AACJM.* M=African Apostolic Ch of Johane Maranke (Rhodesia). Shonas. 5 pasakas held.
Igreja Católica em Moçambique:	1506	R-Lat	P.SSR	290	1,590,800	1,552,723	2,767,090	2.34	C=15+2+32. (1970) 27n,548x,204m,1224w,44591Yy. 39n,290x,409m,561w,125150Yy.
M Beira	1940	R-Lat	Ps	23	35,000	215,207	80,500	-3.86	Rural. Commercial, new industries. Shona, Sena. 1p. 4n 29x 63m 84w 2478Yy
D Chimoio	1990	R-Lat	Puf	15	34,800	–	58,801	20.00	M=WF,OFM. 2n 9x 10m 38w 2030Yy
D Gurue	1993	R-Lat	Ps	13	64,000	–	158,400	50.00	Formerly part of D Quelimane. 0n 17x 18m 4w 3000Yy
D Quelimane	1954	R-Lat	Pofmc	36	232,000	162,322	260,000	1.90	North of Beira. Makua, Sena, Nyanja. M=OFMCap. 6n 52x 63m 62w 79170Yy
D Tete	1962	R-Lat	Ps	29	80,000	97,681	155,000	1.86	Maravi, Angoni. Cobara Bassa dam. War area. 3n 14x 20m 40w 6200Yy
M Maputo (Lourenço Marques)	1940	R-Lat	Ps	36	247,000	253,519	432,000	2.15	Urban. Tsonga majority, 50,000 Europeans in 1974. 8n 84x 122m 63w 3834Yy
D Inhambane	1962	R-Lat	Ps	21	118,000	186,381	194,200	0.16	Southern coast. Rural. Tsonga, Chopi. 1p. 0n 15x 16m 31w 1706Yy
D Xai-Xai (João Belo)	1970	R-Lat	Ps	19	120,000	212,613	250,000	0.65	Formed from M Maputo. Rural. Tsonga. M=SMP. 2n 9x 10m 29w 990Yy
M Nampula	1940	R-Lat	Ps	34	117,000	247,811	211,458	-0.63	95% Makua. Army HQ. M=SMP. 1p. 5n 24x 35m 98w 8976Yy
D Lichinga (Vila Cabral)	1963	R-Lat	Ps	19	74,000	70,435	130,125	2.49	80% Makua, 12% Yao, 8% Nyanja. M=SJ,IC. 2n 13x 17m 38w 2954Yy
D Nacala	1991	R-Lat	Pcm	19	93,000	–	155,606	25.00	M=CM. 1n 14x 21m 34w 5862Yy
D Pemba (Porto Amélia)	1957	R-Lat	Ps	26	376,000	106,754	681,000	7.69	50% Makua, 50% Makonde. 1970s, guerilla area. 6n 10x 14m 40w 7950Yy
Igreja CCAP	1913	P-Ref	R...C	18	3,500	3,000	7,000	3.45	Malawians from CCAP, and their Mozambique missions (formerly Lomweland Mission).
Igreja Congregacional Unida de M	1879	P-Con	Rwa.c	32	4,200	7,000	7,000	0.00	*Mozambique Region, UCCSA.* M=ABCFM(UCBWM). Tswa, Tsonga, Chopi. 4n,W=98%,40Y,80y.
Igreja da Nova Aliança	c1970	I-3pA	.....	120	12,000	12,000	30,000	3.73	*Ch of the New Covenant. Ch of Christ in Zambezi.* Ex AFMSA. 70% Sena, 10% Manyika.
Igreja de Cristo em Manica e Sofala	c1965	P-Uni	C	75	6,000	5,000	15,000	4.49	*Ch of Christ in M&S.* Joint CCM project, M=UMC,Swiss Mission. HQ Beira.
Igreja de Cristo em Zambezia		P-Non	C	141	10,000	15,000	25,000	0.05	*Church of Christ in Zambezia.*
Igreja de Deus Profecia	c1975	P-Pe3	Z....	24	1,320	–	2,930	5.00	*Church of God of Prophecy.* M=CGP(USA).
Igreja do Evangelho Completo de Deus	1931	P-Pe3	ZF...	149	18,113	20,000	51,800	3.88	*Assembleias de Deus.* M=FGCoG(SA),AoG(Portugal),CoG(Cleveland)(USA). 724n.
Igreja do Nazareno	1922	P-Hol	xF..C	214	13,734	20,000	28,907	1.48	M=CoN. 80% Shangaan, 20% Tsonga. 27n,9x23f,1H,1h,1s(115),245t(8986),W=81%,65Y.
Igreja Evangélica	c1980	P-Eva	.....	112	5,603	–	14,000	6.67	*Evangelical Church.* M=TEAM.
Igreja Evangélica Cuadrangular	c1965	P-Pe2	Z....	5	363	1,000	725	-1.28	*International Church of the Foursquare Gospel.* M=ICFG(USA).
Igreja Evangélica dos Irmãos		P-CBr	x....	3	160	200	320	0.05	*Christian Brethren.* Plymouth (Open) Brethren. Small independent congregations.
Igreja Evangélica Portuguesa	1933	P-Eva	....f	1	100	200	200	0.00	*Portuguese Ev Ch.* Protestants from Portugal. 30 families before 1976 evacuation.
Igreja Luso-Africana	1921	I-Ref	.....	4	200	300	625	2.98	*African Portuguese Ch.* First separatist movement; ex Swiss Mission. Tsonga.
Igreja Metodista Unida	1879	P-Met	VwA.C	900	30,000	60,000	60,000	0.00	*United Meth Ch, Africa Central Conference.* M=UMC(USA). Tswa. 60n,20f,1H,1r,1s.
Igreja Metodista Livre	1885	I-Hol	VF..C	93	10,218	10,000	20,000	2.81	M=Free Meth(USA),ABCFM. Tswa,Chopi,Shangaan. 62n, 16f,1H,1h,2s(44),1153z.
Igreja Metodista Wesleyana	1880	P-Met	C	178	8,000	6,000	16,000	4.00	M=Meth Ch of South Africa. Returning miners from Rand. 65% Ronga, 35% Tsonga.
Igreja Nova Apostolica	c1980	I-3aX	.....	40	4,000	–	8,314	6.67	*NAC/NAK. M=Neuapostolische Kirchurich (Switzerland).*
Igreja Ortodoxa		O-Gre	Cw...	2	150	2,000	500	0.05	Part of Greek AD Rhodesia, under P Alexandria. Beira, Maputo. 2x.
Igreja Pentecostal Santidad	c1985	P-Pe3	Z....	28	4,400	–	8,000	10.00	*Pentecostal Holiness Church.* M=IPHC(USA).
Igreja Presbiteriana de Moçambique	1881	P-Ref	R.A.C	1,049	43,000	50,000	100,000	2.81	M=Swiss M/Tsonga PC(SA). A=1948. 62% Tsonga, 35% Ronga, 3% Chopi. 20n,2H,1u,671Yy.
Igreja Reformada em Moçambique	1908	P-Ref	x...C	121	14,500	5,000	30,000	7.43	*Reformed Ch.* Formerly M=DRC(Transvaal Synod) until 1922, then CCAP(Nkhoma).
Igreja União Baptista de Moçambique	1918	P-Bap	C	1,778	160,000	65,000	400,000	7.54	*United Baptist Ch of M.* 1970 merger: Ev Bap Ch in N, Scandinavian Bap Mission in S. M=AEF.
Igrejas de Cristo	1992	I-Dis	x....	100	3,000	–	5,000	33.33	*Churches of Christ.* Based on support from bodies in Malawi.
Missão da Fé Apostólica		P-Pe2	Z....	50	6,000	3,000	12,000	0.05	M=Apostolic Faith Mission of South Africa, AFMSA African Ch (Rhodesia), Umtali.
Testemunhas de Jeová	1933	m-Jeh	x....	400	25,000	45,000	62,500	1.32	*Jehovah's Witn.* 1973, 36,000 persecuted Malawians; 1975, expelled. (1975) 438Y. (1995)2936Y.
Other independent charismatic chs	1980	I-3cA	x....	2,000	200,000	–	300,000	6.67	Total over 20, foreign missions: huge Rhema Bible Ch , Word of Life World Outreach, &c.
Other African indigenous churches		I-3pA	.....	2,500	375,000	18,000	750,000	0.05	Total about 200, including Amazioni (Zion Christian Church of SA).
Other Protestant denominations		P-	.....	800	40,000	1,000	80,000	0.05	Total about 40; others since 1984 AIM,FMB/IMB,YWAM,OD.
Totals				**13,342**	**2,945,856**	**2,049,356**	**5,645,811**		

Churches, members, growth, 1900-2025	*Congs*	*Adults*	*Affiliated*	*G%*	*Total denominations*	*6 Megablocs:* *O*	*R*	*A*	*P*	*I*	*m*
Total churches, members, and denominations (mid-1900)	20	7,700	13,300	7.46	8	0	1	1	4	2	0
Total churches, members, and denominations (mid-1970)	4,037	1,181,809	2,049,356	7.46	136	1	1	1	38	94	1
Total churches, members, and denominations (mid-1990)	10,000	2,399,000	4,597,500	4.12	296	1	1	1	62	230	1
Total churches, members, and denominations (mid-1995)	13,342	2,945,856	5,645,811	4.19	303	1	1	1	63	236	1
Total churches, members, and denominations (mid-2000)	15,000	3,371,000	6,460,533	2.73	308	1	1	1	64	240	1
Total churches, members, and denominations (mid-2025)	35,000	6,061,000	11,616,000	2.37	536	3	1	1	80	450	1

NOTES ON TABLE ABOVE

NATIONAL COUNCILS (Column 4, 5th letter).

C = Conselho Cristão de Moçambique (CCM) (Christian Council of Mozambique) (begun 1948; unrelated to WCC and AACC until 1976).

E = Associação Evangélica de Moçambique (AEM, Evangelical Association of Mozambique).

f = formerly member of CCM.

R = Conferência Episcopal de Moçambique (CEM) (Episcopal Conference of Mozambique).

OTHER AFRICAN INDIGENOUS CHURCHES. There are a number of branches of churches from the republic of South Africa, Malawi, Zimbabwe and Swaziland which have not been permitted to become organized or centralized in Mozambique. These include: African Abraham Ch, African Assemblies of God (Malawi), African Catholic Ch of Gaza, African United Gaza Ch, Apostolic Ch of Johane Masowe (1969), Ch of the Holy Ghost, Ch of the Lost Christians (from Rhodesia), Emmanuel Chs of Christ (Malawi), Gazaland Zimbabwe Ethiopian Ch, Igreja Luso-Africana Eti (Mal, Igreja Luz Episcopal, Luso African Congregational Ch, United Ch of Ethiopian South Africa, VaZioni (Zionists), & 80 unorganized groups.

OTHER PROTESTANT DENOMINATIONS. These include: Pentecostal Holiness Ch (from SA), Southern Baptist Convention (1970), Worldwide Evangelization Crusade (1966).

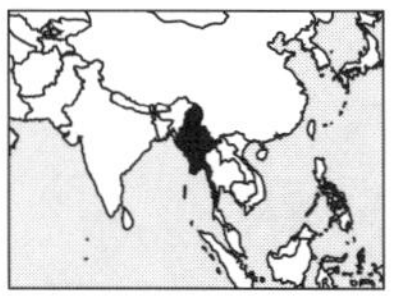

MYANMAR

SECULAR DATA, AD 2000

STATE

Official name: Pyidaungzu Myanma Naingngandaw (The Union of Myanmar).
Short name: Myanmar. **Adjective of nationality:** Myanmarese.
Flag: Red field, blue rectangle with 14 white stars.
Area: 676,577 sq. km. (261,228 sq. mi.).
Government: Military regime, since 1988 (1826 British possession, 1885 province of British India, 1948 Independence as Union of Burma, 1962 socialist military dictatorship, 1974 socialist republic).
Legislature: National Assembly, 485 members.
Official language: Burmese, with use of English.
Monetary unit: 1 Myanmar kyat (K) = 100 pyas. **US$1=** K 6.25.
Chief cities: YANGON (Rangoon) 4,458,000; Mandalay 763,098; Karnbe (Kanbe) 370,695; Mawlamyine (Moulmein) 314,949; Bago (Pegu) 215,532.
Political divisions: 14 provinces. **Armed forces:** 429,000.

DEMOGRAPHY

Population: 45,611,000.
Population density: 67.4/sq. km. (174.6/sq. mi.).
Under 15 years: 12,726,000.
Growth rate p.a.: 1.13% (births 19.87, deaths 8.61).
Mortality: Infant, per 1,000: 69.9, ; **Maternal per 100,000:** 580.0.
Life expectancy: 63 (male 61, female 64).
Household size: 5.2. **Floor area per person, sq.m:** 7.0.
Major languages: Burmese, Shan, Karen, Kuki-Chin, English, Chinese, and over 100 smaller tribal languages.
Urban dwellers: 27.69%. **Urban growth rate p.a.:** 3.4%.
Labor force: 40%.

ETHNOLINGUISTIC PEOPLES

55.8% Burmese (Myen, Bhama); 6.5% Burmese Shan (Thai Yai); 4.2% Arakanese (Maghi, Mogh); 3.5% Sgaw Karen (Paganyaw); 3.3% White Karen (Pwo Karen).

ECONOMY

National income p.a. per person: US$1,790; **per family:** US$9,308.

EDUCATION

Adult literacy: 83% (male 88%, female 77%). **Schools:** 38,754.
Universities: 40. **School enrolment:** female/male: 61%/63%.

HEALTH

Access to health services: 60%. **Access to safe water:** 38%.
Hospitals: 717 (6 beds per 10,000). **Doctors:** 12,245.
Blind: 210,000. **Deaf:** 2,960,500. **Murder rate:** 4.
Lepers: 880,000. **Underweight prevalence under 5:** 43%.

LITERATURE

New book titles p.a.: 4,110 (90 p.a. per million). **Periodicals:** 28.
Newspapers: 5 dailies.

COMMUNICATION (per 1,000 people)

Phones: 3 **(3% mobile). Radios:** 72. **TV sets:** 76.
Daily newspaper circulation: 23. **Computers:** 1.

REFUGEES

Citizen refugees in other countries: 160,400.
Internal displacement: 1,000,000.

HUMAN LIFE AND LIBERTY (optimum condition=100.0%)

HDI: 47.5. **HSI:** 19.0. **HFI:** 7.0. **EFL:** 14.0.

Country status. Myanmar, formerly known as Burma, is the largest country in southeast Asia and is located on the Bay of Bengal. Rice and teak are the country's 2 main products.

HUMAN LIFE AND LIBERTY

Human need and development. Under the military dictatorship, Myanmar has made hardly any progress and there has been no material improvement in the standards of life during the past 40 years. Although ostensibly socialist, and committed to the welfare of the common people, the regime has adopted policies that have achieved the opposite result. Ne Win's 26-year rule has reduced what was once the richest country in southeast Asia to the least developed. The so-called Burmese way of Socialism adopted in 1988 has produced a further decline in the quality of life. Myanmar is the only large country whose statistics are excluded from publications like the World Bank's

Country Table 1. **Religious adherents in Myanmar, AD 1900-2025.**

Year	1900		1970		mid-1990		Annual change, 1990-2000				mid-1995		mid-2000		mid-2025	
Name	Adherents	%	Adherents	%	Adherents	%	Natural	Conversion	Total	Rate	Adherents	%	Adherents	%	Adherents	%
Buddhists	9,055,280	86.7	21,308,900	78.6	29,358,400	72.5	368,883	9,743	378,626	1.22	31,003,760	72.3	33,144,660	72.7	40,018,000	68.9
Ethnoreligionists	522,500	5.0	3,000,000	11.1	5,483,000	13.5	68,889	-42,293	26,596	0.47	5,550,000	12.9	5,748,958	12.6	6,977,000	12.0
Christians	**232,500**	**2.2**	**1,350,000**	**5.0**	**3,080,000**	**7.6**	**38,698**	**30,638**	**69,336**	**2.05**	**3,450,000**	**8.1**	**3,773,362**	**8.3**	**6,382,000**	**11.0**
PROFESSION																
crypto-Christians	85,500	0.8	255,149	0.9	500,000	1.2	6,282	13,718	20,000	3.42	600,000	1.4	700,000	1.5	1,200,000	2.1
professing Christians	**147,000**	**1.4**	**1,094,851**	**4.0**	**2,580,000**	**6.4**	**32,416**	**16,920**	**49,336**	**1.77**	**2,850,000**	**6.7**	**3,073,362**	**6.7**	**5,182,000**	**8.9**
AFFILIATION																
unaffiliated Christians	0	0.0	3,851	0.0	31,000	0.1	389	-299	90	0.29	31,342	0.1	31,898	0.1	50,000	0.1
affiliated Christians	**232,500**	**2.2**	**1,346,149**	**5.0**	**3,049,000**	**7.5**	**38,308**	**30,938**	**69,246**	**2.07**	**3,418,658**	**8.0**	**3,741,464**	**8.2**	**6,332,000**	**10.9**
Protestants	132,000	1.3	962,836	3.6	2,040,000	5.0	25,631	21,535	47,166	2.10	2,295,305	5.4	2,511,664	5.5	4,200,000	7.2
Roman Catholics	70,000	0.7	267,513	1.0	510,000	1.3	6,408	1,592	8,000	1.47	538,921	1.3	590,000	1.3	1,050,000	1.8
Independents	0	0.0	86,800	0.3	445,000	1.1	5,591	7,409	13,000	2.60	521,652	1.2	575,000	1.3	1,000,000	1.7
Anglicans	30,000	0.3	27,000	0.1	48,600	0.1	611	329	940	1.78	56,700	0.1	58,000	0.1	70,000	0.1
Marginal Christians	0	0.0	2,000	0.0	5,400	0.0	68	72	140	2.33	6,080	0.0	6,800	0.0	12,000	0.0
Orthodox	500	0.0	0	0.0	0	0.0	0	0	0	0.00	0	0.0	0	0.0	0	0.0
Trans-megabloc groupings																
Evangelicals	115,000	1.1	385,000	1.4	910,000	2.3	11,433	9,567	21,000	2.10	1,019,657	2.4	1,120,000	2.5	2,030,000	3.5
Pentecostals/Charismatics	0	0.0	80,000	0.3	770,000	1.9	9,674	9,326	19,000	2.23	853,767	2.0	960,000	2.1	1,700,000	2.9
Great Commission Christians	**210,000**	**2.0**	**1,100,000**	**4.1**	**2,300,000**	**5.7**	**28,898**	**-33,152**	**-4,254**	**-0.19**	**2,490,000**	**5.8**	**2,257,465**	**5.0**	**5,000,000**	**8.6**
Muslims	338,000	3.2	1,000,000	3.7	1,080,000	2.7	13,569	-14,010	-441	-0.04	1,086,000	2.5	1,075,593	2.4	1,250,000	2.2
Hindus	284,000	2.7	250,000	0.9	660,000	1.6	8,292	14,986	23,278	3.07	850,000	2.0	892,783	2.0	1,500,000	2.6
Confucianists	0	0.0	0	0.0	600,000	1.5	7,538	94	7,632	1.20	660,000	1.5	676,320	1.5	1,250,000	2.2
Nonreligious	0	0.0	50,000	0.2	210,000	0.5	2,638	1,066	3,704	1.64	229,510	0.5	247,043	0.5	650,000	1.1
Chinese folk-religionists	10,000	0.1	100,000	0.4	118,000	0.3	1,483	-1,568	-85	-0.07	122,000	0.3	117,154	0.3	150,000	0.3
Baha'is	100	0.0	11,200	0.0	55,000	0.1	691	1,713	2,404	3.69	68,000	0.2	79,044	0.2	150,000	0.3
Atheists	0	0.0	26,000	0.1	24,700	0.1	310	-464	-154	-0.64	22,900	0.1	23,162	0.1	45,000	0.1
Sikhs	6,600	0.1	5,000	0.0	7,600	0.0	95	-61	34	0.43	7,800	0.0	7,936	0.0	12,000	0.0
Jains	100	0.0	500	0.0	2,700	0.0	34	-12	22	0.78	2,800	0.0	2,919	0.0	5,000	0.0
Jews	680	0.0	200	0.0	350	0.0	4	-3	1	0.31	370	0.0	361	0.0	500	0.0
Zoroastrians	240	0.0	200	0.0	250	0.0	3	-1	2	0.58	260	0.0	265	0.0	500	0.0
doubly-counted religionists	0	0.0	0	0.0	-160,000	-0.4	-2,010	172	-1,838	1.09	-176,400	-0.4	-178,382	-0.4	-270,000	-0.5
World A (unevangelized persons)	8,401,800	80.4	17,616,162	65.0	19,003,880	46.9	238,738	-353,511	-114,773	-0.62	18,522,679	43.2	17,833,901	39.1	18,017,200	31.0
World B (evangelized non-Christians)	1,815,700	17.4	8,135,625	30.0	18,436,120	45.5	231,681	322,873	554,554	2.67	20,903,892	48.7	24,003,737	52.6	33,720,800	58.0
World C (Christians)	232,500	2.2	1,350,000	5.0	3,080,000	7.6	38,698	30,638	69,336	2.05	3,450,000	8.1	3,773,362	8.3	6,382,000	11.0
Country's population	**10,450,000**	**100.0**	**27,101,788**	**100.0**	**40,520,000**	**100.0**	**509,117**	**0**	**509,117**	**1.19**	**42,876,572**	**100.0**	**45,611,000**	**100.0**	**58,120,000**	**100.0**

COLUMNS, ROWS.
For meanings and definitions, see Codebook (Part 3). Note that, by definition, total 'Christians' = professing + crypto-Christians, which also = affiliated + unaffiliated Christians, and also = Great Commission Christians + latent Christians. Percentages may not always total exactly, due to rounding.

CENSUSES.
1.III.1901: 87.5% Buddhists, 5.0% tribal religionists, 3.2% Muslims, 2.7% Hindus, 1.4% Christians (0.8% Baptists, 0.3% Roman Catholics, 0.2% Anglicans), 0.1% Sikhs. **24.II.1931:** 84.3% Buddhists, 5.2% ethnoreligionists, 4.0% Muslims, 3.9% Hindus, 2.3% Christians. **1.II.1953** (de jure; urban areas of nation only): 82.6% Buddhists, 8.0% Muslims, 5.0% Hindus, 2.4% Christians, 1.5% ethnoreligionists, 0.4% Chinese folk-religionists. **1953-54:** 88.5% Buddhists, 5.5% Muslims, 3.1% Hindus, 1.8% Christians, 0.9% ethnoreligionists, 0.2% Chinese folk-religionists. **31.XII.1969** (government registration, but not a census): 89.4% Buddhists, 3.9% Christians, 3.6% Muslims, 2.1% ethnoreligionist, 1.0% Hindus. **1983:** 89.4% Buddhists, 4.9% Christians (3.2% Baptists, 1.0% Roman Catholics, 0.6% other Christians, 0.1% Anglicans), 3.9% Muslims, 1.2% animists, 0.5% Hindus, 0.1% other religionists.

NOTES ON RELIGIONS
ATHEISTS. 2 parties, both illegal and underground since 1964: Burma Communist Party (White Flag) (Chinese-supported); mainly in the Shan and Kachin states; and Communist Party of Burma (Red Flag) (Trotskyist).
BAHA'IS. Begun from India in 1878; rapid growth from 11 local spiritual assemblies (1964) to 75 (1973), then massive growth to (1995) 223 LSAs. Converts include Chin, Karen and Shan.
BUDDHISTS. Most ethnic Burmese and Shan are Theravada (or Hinayana, Little Vehicle) Buddhists. Sects: Thudhamma, Shewgyin, Dwara. The Chinese practice Mahayana (Great Vehicle) Buddhism; the Sino-Burmese practice Theravada. The center of Burmese Buddhism is Manadalay.
CRYPTO-CHRISTIANS. Christians affiliated to churches but not known as such in censuses or to society or the state, of 3 kinds: (1) persons in the recognized churches who prefer not to reveal their commitment publicly, (2) members of clandestine churches, and (3) isolated radio and correspondence course believers.
ETHNORELIGIONISTS. Animists, known as *nat* (spirit-worshippers), among over 100 ethnic groups. Animism is widely practiced among Montagnard groups (Moken, Naga); also, the larger northern tribes (including Karen, Chin-Lushai, Kachin-Lisu) still have large numbers of traditionalists, as do the Shan, Mon and Arakanese.
HINDUS. South Indians, mainly Tamil and Telugu. Numbers decreased rapidly by forced emigration in the 1960s.
INDEPENDENTS. In over 60 denominations in 1995 (see Table 2), including isolated radio believers.
JEWS. With one synagogue in Rangoon.
MUSLIMS. Sunnis (of the Hanafite rite). Islam is practiced by half of the Arakan peoples, by Bengalis, and by Yunnan immigrants. There is also a small Ahmadiya mission based on Rangoon. Qadianis from Pakistan since 1938, with a mission established in 1952. There are 2 mosques.
ORTHODOX. In the 1901 census, there were 240 Armenian Apostolics and 67 Greek Orthodox, all Europeans. With the repatriation of Indians, their Orthodox churches in Burma were closed, although a handful of them still remain.
PARSIS. Zoroastrians; originally Indians from Bombay or Persians.
PROFESSING CHRISTIANS. In the census of 1931, the ethnic composition of Christians was as follows: 66.1% Karen, 9.3% European and Anglo-Indian, 9.1% Indian (Tamil, Telugu), 4.7% Kachin, 4.4% Burmese, 2.4% Kuki Chin, 0.7% Shan, 0.4% Chinese, 3.6% others.
PROTESTANTS. In 1900, Baptist members (adults) numbered 42,000. In 1990, about 95% of all Baptists were from animistic backgrounds, and only 5% were from Buddhism.
SIKHS. Punjabis from India; decreasing by repatriation.

Great Commission Instrument Panel: status of Myanmar (for explanation see start of Part 4)

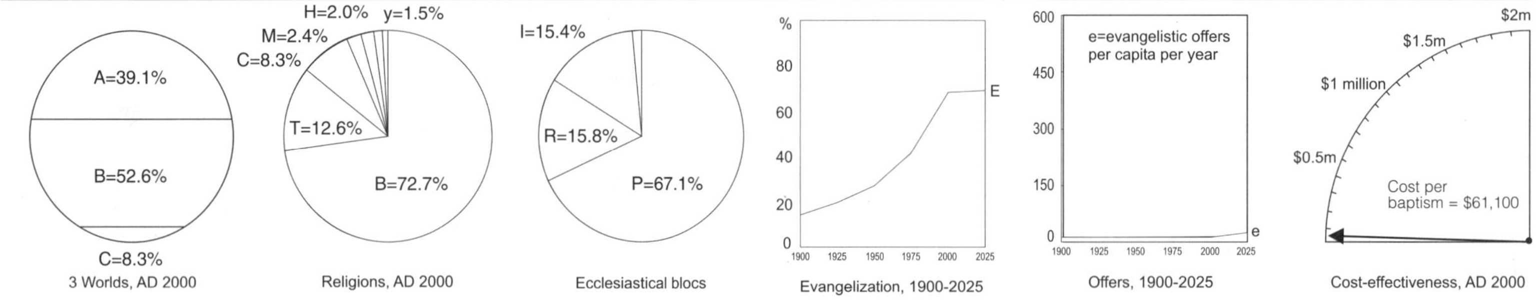

World Development Report because such statistics are generally not collected, and where available are not published. In the 1950s and 1960s the government initiated a social welfare program and also a public housing program, but both were seriously underfunded, and much of their impetus was lost during the political unrest of the 1980s.

Human rights and freedoms. Myanmar has been described as one of the major human rights violators in the post-Communist world. The State Law and Order Restoration Council which seized power after the fall of Ne Win wields tight control over the nation and has shown no inclination to allow free elections or constitutional government. The primary agent of the reign of terror is the pervasive security apparatus. It is estimated that over 1,000 political prisoners remain in custody, including Nobel Laureate Aung San Suu Kyi. Over 100 members of the National League for Democracy, which won 80% of the seats in the National Assembly, have been forced to resign, flee into exile, or convicted of trumped up charges. In remote areas there are reports of a number of extrajudicial killings and also of forced labor camps. Dissidents sometimes disappear. Prisoners are subjected to torture, or other cruel, inhuman and degrading punishment. To instill fear in people, the government routinely and arbitrarily arrests and detains people . There is no provision in Myanmarese law for judicial determination of the legality of detention. Since the government rules by decree it is not bound by any constitutional guarantee of public trials and due process. Forced entry into and unannounced warrantless searches of private homes are common. A ubiquitous system of neighborhood informers reports on dissidents. Almost all the major minorities remain in a state of insurgence, providing a pretext for largescale human rights violations in remote areas. The government owns and operates all media. As a result private citizens have no forum for expressing opposing views or criticism. Military officials appoint editors and approve editorials in advance. All forms of communication—domestic and imported books, periodicals, motion pictures, and musical recordings—are officially controlled and censored. Criticism is permitted only of minor officials. The official media are used as tools of a government propaganda campaign against 'decadent' Western culture, which, nevertheless, remains extremely popular. Professors and professionals, like doctors, are subject to political indoctrination. Teachers are forbidden to discuss politics in class, join political parties, engage in political activity or meet foreign officials. Periodically, teachers, as well as other civil servants, accused of political disloyalty, are fired from their jobs in mass purges. All outdoor assemblies of more than 5 persons are banned as are political demonstrations of any kind. Trade unions and professional groups need government sanction to function. An estimated half million poor urban residents have been forcibly relocated to rural areas since 1989. Citizens traveling outside their homes have to continuously report to officials their temporary places of residence. Until 1992 the government enforced a nationwide nighttime curfew. The right to emigrate is seriously curtailed. Passports are issued only after protracted administrative delays, and denied to those

Country Summary Table. **Worlds A, B, C by ethnolinguistic peoples, cities and major civil divisions in Myanmar.**

	PEOPLES							CITIES							CIVIL DIVISIONS						
World	Num	Pop 2000	C%	Christians	E%	U%	Unevangelized	Num	Pop 2000	C%	Christians	E%	U%	Unevangelized	Num	Pop 2000	C%	Christians	E%	U%	Unevangelized
A	64	10,927,447	1.32	143,760	39	61	6,674,107	0	0	0.00	0	0	0	0	1	5,914,898	4.00	236,596	46	54	3,165,653
B	36	32,653,593	6.94	2,264,997	66	34	11,170,561	29	8,400,400	4.92	413,532	59	41	3,439,898	13	39,696,276	8.80	3,495,117	57	43	17,059,641
C	33	2,030,136	65.65	1,332,712	100	0	7,603	0	0	0.00	0	0	0	0	0	0	0.00	0	0	0	0
Total	**133**	**45,611,176**	**8.20**	**3,741,469**	**61**	**39**	**17,852,271**	**29**	**8,400,400**	**4.92**	**413,532**	**59**	**41**	**3,439,898**	**14**	**45,611,174**	**8.18**	**3,731,713**	**56**	**44**	**20,225,294**

suspected of dissidence. In 1992 alone, 270,000 Muslim Arakanese fled the country to Bangladesh and another 70,000 Myanmarese fled to Thailand. Ethnic minorities, among whom a substantial number are Christians, are underrepresented in government. Areas where minorities are numerically strong are discriminated against in development funds. Myanmarese of Indian and Chinese origin are denied citizenship. Arakanese Muslims have suffered most, with unconfirmed reports that they have been subjected to brutal treatment, including arrests, beatings, and rapes. There are no organizations devoted to the promotion of women's rights.

Human environment. Other than extensive deforestation (which has led to the disappearance of two-thirds of the nation's tropical forests) Myanmar has remained free of major environmental problems. Relative underdevelopment has been a blessing for the country. The agricultural system is unintensive, and does not overburden the soils. Population pressures are low enough to prevent other environmental problems.

Buddhists. The Kaba E (World Peace) Pagoda, dedicated to cause of world peace; 7 miles from Yangon, it was completed in 1952 near Great Sacred Cave where 6th Great Buddhist Synod was held from 1954-56.

NON-CHRISTIAN RELIGIONS

Theravada Buddhism, also called Hinayana or Little Vehicle, entered Myanmar in the first century of the Christian era. During subsequent centuries, it absorbed a number of elements from Burmese traditional religions. It has been the dominant religion since the 9th century and has exerted great influence on the development of Burmese culture. Today, over 72% of the population is Buddhist, including the overwhelming majority of ethnic Burmese and Shan peoples. In most villages, there is a monastery (kyaung) occupied by monks (pongyi). The principal sect is the Thudhamma; others include the Shewgyin and Dwara sects. The Buddhist University of Pali, established in 1950 with state support, sets as one of its goals the training of Buddhist missionaries. The fifth world synod in the history of Buddhism took place in 1871, and the sixth synod was held in Burma during 1954-56. Its purpose was to revise the official edition of the Dhamma, the teaching of the Buddha. The Shwe Dagon pagoda in Rangoon is one of the most important sanctuaries of all Buddhism and is believed to contain authentic relics of the Buddha himself.

Mahayana Buddhism, or Great Vehicle, is practiced by a part of the Chinese community, but the Sino-Burmese, now assimilated into the local population, are adherents of Theravada Buddhism.

Islam is the religion of approximately half the Arakan peoples who inhabit the southwest near the border with Bangladesh. It is also practiced by Bengali communities south of Prome and the Panthay immigrants from Yunnan province in China.

Traditional religions are still widely practiced among Montagnard groups (including the Moken and Naga) and continue to influence Buddhism. Wooden statues serving as the abode of spirits (Nats) play an important role in family worship. Traditional beliefs and practices also remain significant for the Karens, of whom 80% have not become Christians. The success of Christianity among the 20% has been due in part to an ancient Karen prophecy that the Golden Book of Y'wa, their supreme being, would be returned to them by a White man. Karens also manifest a strong tendency toward syncretism, as seen in several cults beginning with that of Hpo Pai San in 1866.

Hinduism, Taoism and ***Confucianism*** are largely confined to the Indian and Chinese communities.

Judaism is followed by a few expatriates. There is one synagogue in Rangoon.

CHRISTIANITY

There were Nestorians in Pegu by the 10th century, Roman Catholics by 1544, and Protestants by 1813. Response to the Christian faith has varied widely in the different ethnic groups. Several tribes, notably the Karen, Chin, and Kachin peoples, have embraced Christianity for many years and have built up strong indigenous Christian communities. Others have ignored or rejected the Christian message. There are very few Bhama (ethnic Burmese) converted to Christianity. Christians, in fact, represent no more than a small minority who are found largely in the Irrawaddy delta region and in the border areas. Baptists and Catholics are the 2 principal Christian groups. Prior to the nationalization of private schools in 1965-66, numerous secondary schools were run by churches.

Kachin Baptist Convention. Baptism of 6,215 converts in Irrawaddy river on single occasion in December 1977, during centennial celebration at Naung Nang, Myitkyina, in presence of 100,000

PROTESTANT CHURCHES. The largest Christian force in Myanmar is the Myanmar Baptist Convention, which owes its origin to the pioneering activity of the American Baptist missionary, Adoniram Judson, in 1813. Beginning in Rangoon, church headquarters was transferred to Moulmein in 1826, from where it spread out to the borders of Myanmar in every direction. The Karen tribe was the first reached in 1827, followed by Chins in 1845 and Kachins in 1876, and these 3 ethnic groups continue to make up the bulk of Baptist membership. Of the 16 member bodies of the convention, 3 represent more than 75% of the Baptist community: Kachin Baptist Convention, Karen Baptist Convention (Sgaw), and Zomi (Chin) Baptist Convention. The Burma Baptist Convention (BBC) was organized in 1865 and has met annually since, except for a brief period during World War II. After 1945, responsibility for the convention's work was transferred from the American mission to indigenous leadership. Subsequently, this work has grown to number nearly 3,000 congregations with a Christian community of 900,000. Prior to the nationalization of Christian institutions in 1965-66, there were 12 hospitals and dispensaries and more than 600 schools with 45,000 pupils.

Methodist Church, Burma. Minister and family outside Tahan Methodist Church.

The next Protestant groups to arrive were Lutherans and Methodists. American Methodist missionaries first came to Myanmar from India in 1879 and settled in the south. They were followed 7 years later by British Methodists who concentrated their attention on northern Burma. Both churches are autonomous today.

Twentieth-century efforts include the work of the Salvation Army begun in 1915, Seventh-day Adventists in 1919, Assemblies of God in 1930, Church of Christ in 1949 and Presbyterianism in 1954. Whereas the first 3 groups were begun by western missionaries, the Presbyterian Church of Burma was formed by immigrant Lushais from Assam, India, who migrated to Myanmar after World War II and brought their church with them. The Church of Christ is composed primarily of Chinese immigrants from the north.

CATHOLIC CHURCH. The first Catholic contacts with Myanmar were established by the Portuguese in the 16th century. The Bayingyi, a group of ancient Eurasian origin, descendants of Portuguese and Burmese, are the oldest Catholic community, but 90% of the faithful are Karen, Kachin, Chin, Shan, and Kaw. The lack of priests is compensated for by the large number of seminary students, catechists, and nuns, all of whom teach catechism and are involved in liturgical and sacramental functions. The Ne Win government has allowed Catholics to retain a limited network of charitable institutions, which are concentrated mostly in the diocese of Kengtung. In 1969, these included 3 leprosaria with 1,361 lepers, 24 orphanages with 959 children, 8 homes for 281 infants, 7 homes for the aged with 424 persons and one home for the infirm with 13 patients.

The Holy See has no diplomatic relations with Myanmar in AD 2000, but apostolic delegate residing in Bangkok.

ANGLICAN CHURCH. Although there were Anglican chaplains in Myanmar as early as 1825 and an increased number after British annexation of the territory in 1853, the first USPG missionaries did not begin at Moulmein until 1859. Nevertheless, Anglicans usually date the founding of the church in Myanmar to 1877 when the first bishop of Rangoon was appointed. The USPG began its work among ethnic Burmese and later extended it to Karens and Chins. In 1924, a second Anglican mission arrived, the BCMS, who directed their attention to upper Myanmar and the Khumis of west Myanmar. The church formed part of the Church of India, Pakistan, Burma, and Ceylon (CIPBC) until the India and Pakistan dioceses were incorporated into united churches in 1970. Since the corresponding Burma union negotiations were not so advanced, an autonomous Church of the Union of Burma was then formed.

INDIGENOUS CHURCHES. Independent churches begun by Burmese nationals have been formed from many of the major traditions working in Myanmar The first was the Self-Supporting Karen Baptist Missionary Society, a split in 1912 from the Karen Baptist Convention. Other Baptists schisms have produced the People's Church Movement and the Brethren. The latter has developed new relationships with several overseas Brethren groups. In 1962, disturbances were caused among Baptist Zomi Chins by the Dancing Christian Movement (Hlimsang). Two independent Anglican churches have been at St Gabriel's Church Union, a large Tamil-speaking congregation in Rangoon and the Independent Anglican Church which broke from BCMS work among the Kachins of upper Myanmar The Independent Methodist Church of Burma is a recent schism from the Methodists of lower Burma historically related to American Methodism.

The Independent Church of Burma, is a schism from the Indo-Burma Pioneer Mission which first opened work in India in 1910. The immediate cause was a conflict in 1929 between the missionary founder and the home board in the USA over his insistence upon the development of national leadership. The Independent Church of India was thus formed in 1930 disassociating itself from the mission, though subsequently supported by it, and later, followers over the border began the Independent Church of Burma.

Evangelical Baptist Church. Annual conference attenders.

Renewal movements. In the 1990s the Pentecostal/Charismatic Renewal continued to spread rapidly across most older churches, and numbered over 960,000 adherents (of whom 31% Pentecostals, 26% Charismatics, and 43% Independents).

Indigenous missions. Christians in Myanmar have been surprisingly active in sending out missionaries, first to peoples within their own country and then to surrounding countries.

CHURCH AND STATE

The relationship between the Burmese state and the religions, particularly Buddhism, has been strongly influenced by the political evolution of the country since Independence, especially by the governments of U Nu (1948-58, 1960-62) and Ne Win (1958-60, 1962 to the 1970s). Throughout its existence, the U. Nu regime followed a policy of giving increasing support to Buddhism which it considered compatible with the process of Burmese modernization. During its reign, the following parliamentary acts were successively adopted: (1) the Vinasaya Act (1949), establishing a system of ecclesiastical courts and requiring all members of the Sangha (community of monks) to register, a measure which was meant to improve governmental financial assistance to the Sangha and to draw attention to those who were not members; (2) the Dhammacuriya Act (1950), establishing the University of Pali; and (3) the Union Buddha Sasana Council Act (1950), creating the governmental organization for Buddhist affairs (UBSC). Finally, in 1961, Buddhism was declared the state religion, although the rights of minority religions were guaranteed. The U. Nu government consistently supported the Buddhist Council, which groups together laymen and monks, and favored the creation in the suburbs of Rangoon of a vast complex including an Institute of Higher Buddhist Studies and a large institution for the production of Buddhist religious literature.

In contrast, the military regime of Ne Win showed considerable reluctance to involve the government in religious affairs. Working for the establishment of a 'Burmese way towards socialism', the regime in 1962 withdrew from Buddhism recognition as the state religion and decreed that all religions would be equally respected. In 1964-65, it abolished all previous parliamentary acts concerning Buddhism and reorganized and then finally suppressed the UBSC in favor of a new and unique Organization of the Council for the Buddhist Community, embracing all Buddhist sects. After an initial attempt at resistance, the Sangha gave in and has adopted a position of patient waiting. The establishment of a one-party state in 1964 forced on all groups, including religious organizations, the obligation to register with the authorities. In a move more nationalist and socialist than anti-Christian, Christian schools and hospitals were nationalized in 1965-66, with the exception of seminaries and a few homes and medical institutions. Lastly in 1966, again for the same nationalistic reasons, the government refused to renew the residence permits of all foreign missionaries who had not worked in the country before Independence, which resulted in the expulsion of 234 Catholic missionaries (priests, brothers, and sisters), 56 American Baptists, 29 BCMS and USPG Anglicans, 18 American Methodists, 15 British Methodists, 8 Salvation Army and 7 Assemblies of God workers. In all, nearly 375 missionaries were evicted by this decree.

Subsequently, the churches have not been interfered with by the state. In 1976, the president in fact agreed to authorize the government printing press to provide paper for and to print 10,000 Bibles in Burmese.

BROADCASTING AND MEDIA

IBRA-produced radio programs can be heard on local radio channels. Shortwave radio programs in 17 languages can be received from FEBC (Philippines), in Burmese from FEBC (Saipan) and TWR (Guam), and from VERITAS. AWR has a studio in Yangoon that produces Burmese programs. Myanmar is a member of UNDA.

At least 10% of the country has seen the 'Jesus' Film, including 4 million who have seen it on television.

INTERDENOMINATIONAL ORGANIZATIONS

In 1914, a Regional Council for Burma was formed under the National Christian Council of India, which in 1949 became the independent Burma Christian Council, and by 1975, the Burma Council of Churches. This is an associate council of the WCC and is also affiliated to its Commission on World Mission and evangelism, as well as being a member of the Christian Conference of Asia (formerly EACC). Several of Myanmar's churches are also members of the WCC and the CCA. Local councils of churches are being formed in towns where there are 2 or more denominations. Of the 15 regional councils, the Rangoon Council of Churches is the largest.

FUTURE TRENDS AND PROSPECTS

Buddhism is expected to decline after the year 2000 to 68.9% by AD 2025. Christianity may pass the 10% mark by 2025 primarily due to conversions and church growth among minorities and the falling off of animistic practices.

Though Buddhists will likely continue to claim over 60% of the population well into the 21st century, Christians could grow to over 15% before AD 2050.

BIBLIOGRAPHY

'A brief history and development factors of the Karen Baptist Church of Burma (Myanmar).' S. D. Say. Th.M. thesis, Fuller Theological Seminary, Pasadena, CA, 1990. 206p.

'A brief history of the planting and growth of the church in Burma.' K. T. Vuta. D. Miss. thesis, Fuller Theological Seminary, Pasadena, CA, 1983. 363p.

A century of growth: the Kachin Baptist Church of Burma. H. G. Tegenfeldt. South Pasadena, CA: William Carey Library, 1974. 512p.

'A messianic Buddhist association in Upper Burma,' E. M. Mendelson, *Bulletin of the School of Oriental & African Studies*, 24, 4 (1961), 560–80.

'A renewal strategy of the Karen Baptist Church of Myanmar (Burma) for mission.' S. G. Taw. Th.M. thesis, Fuller Theological Seminary, Pasadena, CA, 1992. 182p.

'A study of Karen Baptist Church growth in Myanmar.' L. Zan. Th.M. thesis, Fuller Theological Seminary, Pasadena, CA, 1993. 115p.

A thousand lives away: Buddhism in contemporary Burma. W. L. King. Cambridge, MA: Harvard University Press, 1964. 238p.

'Biblical basis of church growth and its application to the Kachin Baptist church of Burma.' H. Naw. D.Miss. thesis, Trinity Evangelical Divinity School, 1990. 209p.

'Buddhism and animism in a Burmese village,' J. F. Brohm, *Journal of Asian studies*, 22 (February 1963), 155–67.

Buddhism and society: a great tradition and its Burmese vicissitudes. M. E. Spiro. 2nd ed. Berkeley and Los Angeles: University of California Press, 1980. 510p.

Buddhist backgrounds of the Burmese revolution. E. Sarkisyanz. The Hague: Nijhoff, 1966.

Burma. P. M. Herbert. *World bibliographical series*, vol. 132. Oxford, UK: CLIO Press, 1991. 354p. (See especially 'Religion,' p.144–57).

Burma Baptist chronicle: Judson Sesquicentennial edition. M. S. Wa et al. Rangoon: Burma Baptist Convention, 1963. 448p. (42 historical essays).

Burma through missionary eyes: views of the Burmese in the nineteenth century. H. G. Trager. New York: Praeger, 1966. 239p.

'Burmese religion and the Burmese religious revival.' J. F. Brohm. PhD thesis, Cornell University, Ithaca, NY, 1957. 507p.

Burmese supernaturalism: a study in the explanation and reduction of suffering. M. E. Spiro. 2nd ed. Philadelphia: Institute for the Study of Human Issues, 1978. 300p.

'Catholic directory of Burma, 1969'. Rangoon: Catholic Archdiocese, 1969 (Duplicated).

Christian missions in Burma. W. C. B. Purser. 2nd ed. Westminster, UK: Society for the Propagation of the Gospel in Foreign Parts, 1913.

Christian progress in Burma. A. McLeish. London: World Dominion Press, 1929. 100p.

'Christianizing the Karen.' K. M. Dettmer. M.A. thesis, Arizona State University, 1987. 113p.

Folk elements in Burmese Buddhism. H. Aung. 1962; Westport, CT: Greenwood Press, 1978. 140p.

History of the American Baptist Chin Mission: a history of the introduction of Christianity into the Chin Hills of Burma by missionaries of the American Baptist Foreign Mission Society during the years 1899 to 1966. R. G. Johnson. Valley Forge, PA: R. G. Johnson, 1988. 2 vols

'In search of the Karen king: a study in Karen identity with special reference to 19th century Karen evangelism in Northern Thailand.' A. P. Hovemyr. Doctoral thesis, University of Uppsala, 1989. 207p.

'Innocent pioneers and their triumphs in a foreign land: a critical look at the work of the American Baptist Mission in the Chin Hills, 1899–1966 in Burma from a missiological perspective.' Cung Lian Hup. Th.D. thesis, Lutheran School of Theology at Chicago, 1993. 204p.

Methodism in Burma. Halifax, UK: Halifax Methodist Circuit, 1986. 24p.

Mission in Burma: the Columban Fathers' forty–three years in Kachin country. E. Fischer. New York: Seabury, 1980. 164p.

Religion and legitimation of power in Thailand, Laos and Burma. B. L. Smith. Chambersburg, PA: Anima, 1978.

Religion and nationalism in Southeast Asia: Burma, Indonesia, the Philippines. F. R. Von der Mehden. Madison, WI: University of Wisconsin Press, 1963. 253p.

Religion, culture and political economy in Burma. B. Matthews (ed). Vancouver: Institute of Asian Research, University of British Columbia, 1993. 62p.

Sketches from the Karen hills. A. Bunker. New York: Revell, 1910. 215p. (Treats American Baptist missionary work).

Soo Thah: a tale of the making of the Karen nation. A. Bunker. London: Anderson & Ferrier, 1902. 280p. (Deals with a Karen convert to Christianity).

'The acculturation of the Burmese Muslims.' K. K. Su. M.A. thesis, Rangoon University, Rangoon, 1960. 135p.

'The adoption and diffusion of Christianity amongst the Khumi–Chin people of the Upper Kaladan river area of Arakan, North–West Burma from 1900 to 1966 (with an appendix up–date to 1988).' A. N. Nason. M.A. thesis, University of Warwick, Coventry, UK, 1988. 170p.

'The Baptist missionaries and the evangelization of Burmese society.' A. Myint. M.T.S. thesis, Garrett-Evangelical Theological Seminary, Chicago, 1989. 103p.

The Church alive in Burma. Valley Forge, PA: American Baptist Films, 1988. 1 videocassette (13 min.)

'The fifteen years of crisis, 1960–1975.' V. S. Lone. Th.M. thesis, South East Asia Graduate School of Theology, 1977. 281p. (Baptist work in Burma).

'The history and growth of the churches in Chin State, Myanmar (Burma).' Khuang Nawni. Th.M. thesis, Fuller Theological Seminary, Pasadena, CA, 1990. 184p.

The initiation of novicehood and the ordination of monkhood in the Burmese Buddhist culture. H. H. Win. Rangoon: Department of Religious Affairs, 1986. 172p.

The Kachins: religion and custom. C. Gilhodes. Calcutta: Catholic Orphan Press, 1922. 304p.

The Kachins: their customs and traditions. O. Hanson. 1913. New York: AMS, 1982. 225p.

'The last Burmese Jews,' R. F. Cernea, *B'nai B'rith international Jewish monthly*, 102, 10 (1988), 26–30.

The Muslims of Burma: a study of a minority group. M. Yegar. *Schriftenreihe des Südasien-Instituts der Universität Heidelberg.* Wiesbaden, GFR: Otto Harrassowitz, 1972.

'The symbolic dimensions of the Burmese Sangha.' J. P. Ferguson. Ph.D. dissertation, Cornell University, Ithaca, NY, 1976. 298p.

The Talaings. R. Halliday. Rangoon: Superintendent, Government Printing, 1917. 164p. (Treats religion).

The thirty–seven nats: a phase of spirit worship prevailing in Burma. R. C. Temple. London: W. Griggs, 1906. 71p. (Illustrated).

To the golden shore: the life of Adoniram Judson. C. Anderson. 1956. Grand Rapids, MI: Zondervan, 1972. 530p.

'Toward a new missionary impulse of the Karen Baptist Church of Myanmar.' S. D. Say. D. Miss. thesis, Fuller Theological Seminary, Pasadena, CA, 1993. 276p.

Understanding a state and its minorities from a religious and cultural perspective: the case of Siam and Burma. Sulak Sivaraksa. [Bangkok]: Sathoaban Santi Prachoatham, [1988]. 20p.

Country Table 2. **Organized churches and denominations in Myanmar.**

Official name (bold type = church with over 10% of all affiliated) 1	*Begun* 2	*Type* 3	*Counc* 4	*Congs* 5	*Adults* 6	*Affiliated 1970* 7	*Affiliated 1995* 8	*G%* 9	*Names, notes, and other statistics* (see Codebook, Part 3) 10
Assemblies of God of Myanmar	1924	P-Pe2	....E	1,324	185,400	50,000	223,000	6.16	Begun by Lisu. Kachin State. Fusion with Tibet Border Mission (China). 956n, 4s (520).
Assembly Hall Churches		I-3nC	.....	6	20	–	100	0.05	*Local Churches. Little Flock.* Chinese. Begun 1922 in China.
Bethany Evangelical Mission	1985	P-Eva	....E	5	809	–	1,618	10.00	Evangelicals from USA.
Catholic Church in Myanmar:	1544	R-Lat	P.F.R	249	322,500	267,513	538,921	2.84	*Catholic Athindaw.* 55% Karen. C=5+5+8. (1990) 338n 24x 104m 1057w 28586Yy
M Mandalay	1866	R-Lat	Ps	19	12,000	39,744	21,504	-2.43	Chins. Rapid growth from 23,410 (1960): until division. 30n 4x 19m 76w 483Yy
D Hakha	1992	R-Lat	Ps	20	37,600	–	63,097	33.33	Formerly in M Mandalay. 21n 1x 4m 43w 1125Yy
D Kengtung	1927	R-Lat	Ps	18	33,700	29,035	51,748	2.34	*Thathana Kengtung.* Kachins. 7,000 converts a year. 26n 0x 3m 98w 10655Yy
D Lashio	1975	R-Lat	Psdb	19	16,900	–	29,605	5.00	Until 1975 part of D Kengtung. M=SDB. 11n 17x 30m 84w 919Yy
D Myitkyina	1939	R-Lat	Ps	21	48,000	36,089	82,250	3.35	*Thathana Myitkyina.* Kaws, Lahus. M=SSCME. 28n 0x 2m 74w 4806Yy
M Yangon (Rangoon)	1866	R-Lat	Ps	46	45,300	48,868	75,763	1.77	*Thathanabaing Rangoon.* Capital. M=MEP. 2p,1s. 43n 1x 15m 181w 1307Yy
D Loikaw	1988	R-Lat	Ps	22	30,200	–	51,937	14.29	Formerly in D Taunggyi. 51n 1x 5m 89w 2695Yy
D Mawlamyine	1993	R-Lat	Ps	11	3,100	–	5,925	50.00	Until 1993 part of M Yangon. 10n 0x 0m 26w 255Yy
D Pathein (Bassein)	1955	R-Lat	Ps	20	38,300	37,778	61,980	2.00	Extreme southwest. Karens, Indians, Chinese. 1p. 33n 0x 17m 93w 1907Yy
D Pyay (Prome, Akyab)	1940	R-Lat	Ps	20	12,000	9,468	20,885	3.22	Formerly PA Akyab. Central west. Chins. M=MS. 20n 0x 2m 55w 400Yy
D Taunggyi	1961	R-Lat	Ps	16	22,800	41,373	37,377	-0.41	Karens. Formerly M=PIME. 1988, D Loikaw formed. 30n 0x 2m 115w 1694Yy
D Toungoo	1870	R-Lat	Ps	17	22,600	25,158	36,850	1.54	Adjoining Rangoon. Catholics almost entirely Karens. 35n 0x 5m 123w 2340Yy
Christian Brethren	c1965	I-CBr	x....	41	4,085	300	10,200	15.15	Schisms ex Burma Baptist Convention, with overseas Open Brethren links.
Christian & Missionary Alliance	1985	P-Hol	....E	27	1,553	–	2,813	10.00	M=CMA(USA).
Christian Reformed Church	1985	P-Ref	.....	65	3,420	–	5,700	10.00	M=CRCWM(USA).
Church of God (Cleveland)	1980	P-Pe3	.....	17	2,300	–	5,543	6.67	M=CoG(Cleveland). Most in Kachin State. 13n,1s.
Church of God in Myanmar	1961	I-3pZ	.....	5	190	100	281	4.22	Small indigenous group at Insein, a few kilometres north of Rangoon.
Church of God of Myanmar	1985	P-Hol	.....	5	310	–	620	10.00	M=CoG(Anderson).
Church of Jesus Christ	1970	I-Non	.....	55	9,000	–	15,000	46.91	Mainly Lushai, Haka Chin, Falam Chin.
Church of the Nazarene	1984	P-Hol	....E	6	540	–	870	9.09	M=CoN.
Church of the Province of Myanmar	1825	A-plu	AWEAW	150	29,000	27,000	56,700	3.01	In CIPBC until 1970. M=SPG,BCMS, until 1965. 6 Dioceses. 157n,48m,5w,98pp,2s(20),2000y.
Churches of Christ	1933	P-Non	....w	1,000	51,889	50,000	104,000	2.97	M=OMF(formerly CIM). Refugees from China: Chinese, Wa, Lahu, Lisu, Rawang. 80n.
Disciples of Christ	1980	P-Dis	x....	8	500	–	833	6.67	Mainline Disciples (USA).
Evangelical Baptist Church	1975	I-Bap	....E	50	5,500	–	12,200	5.00	Fundamentalists from USA.
Evangelical Believers Conference	1974	I-3nZ	.....	200	17,938	–	25,000	4.76	Work among Tiddim Chin mainly, also Lahu, Akha.
Evangelical Free Church of Myanmar	1955	I-Con	.....	352	8,000	6,900	20,500	4.45	Independent Congregationalists.
Evangelical Presbyterian Church	1983	I-Ref	.....	24	1,800	–	3,000	8.33	Independent Presbyterians.
Full Gospel Assembly	1987	I-3fZ	.....	7	1,500	–	3,000	12.50	Schism ex AoGM. Many Chins. In Yangon. Fast growing. 50nm, 1s.
Gospel Baptist Churches of Myanmar	1983	I-Bap	.....	77	5,434	–	10,900	8.33	Independent Baptists.
Hidden Buddhist believers in Christ	c1970	I-Bud	.....	900	80,000	–	192,300	62.69	Converted Buddhist who choose to stay in Buddhism as witnesses to Christ.
Independent Anglican Church	1958	I-Ang	.....	15	1,500	1,500	2,830	2.57	Split from Anglicans (BCMS mission). Kachins. HQ Mohnyin, Upper Burma. 1n.
Independent Church of Myanmar	1938	I-Non	....w	29	1,250	20,000	2,500	-7.98	Lushai split ex Indo-Burma Pioneer Mission, now in 3 factions. HQ Tahan. 82m.
Independent Methodist Ch of Myanmar	1967	I-Met	.....	20	1,000	500	1,430	4.29	*Free Methodist Ch.* Split ex Methodist Ch of Union of Burma. 2n,W=80%,17Y.
Intern Ch of the Foursquare Gospel	1988	P-Pe2	Z...E	22	3,000	–	6,000	14.29	Among the Vaiphei and other peoples in Shan state. M=ICFG(USA). Chins. 15n.
Isolated radio churches	1952	I-3rZ	.....	1,000	40,000	4,800	70,000	11.32	Isolated radio believers, mostly aged 12-25. (1970) R=3930 (FEBC,FEBA),S=10(ICI).
Jehovah's Witnesses	1910	m-Jeh	x....	86	1,763	2,000	6,080	4.55	Active witnessing under way by 1926. Re-established 1946. (1975) 63Y. (1995) 94Y.
Lakher Independent Evangelical Church	1907	I-Eva	.....	16	1,600	3,000	4,850	1.94	Members are 95% of whole Lakher former headhunting tribe, mostly in India. M=LPM(UK).
Lisu Christian Church		I-Non	....W	233	14,000	20,000	35,000	0.05	Lisu Christians from China, often migrating in order to obtain Lisu Bibles.
Lutheran Church in Myanmar	1878	P-Lut	Lwe.W	6	365	400	913	3.36	Originally of 2 Indian churches: Andhra ELC (Telugus), Tamil ELC (Tamils).
Mara Christian Church	1969	I-Con	.....	50	10,000	4,000	20,000	6.65	Strong across border in Assam as Mara Independent Ev Ch. Manipuris, Khumi, Rakhine.
Methodist Ch of the Union of Myanmar	1879	P-Met	VwE.W	25	3,104	5,000	5,540	0.41	*Methodist Ch. Lower Burma.* M=UMC(USA). Many Chinese, including bishop. 15n,21t.
Methodist Church, Myanmar	1886	P-Met	V.E.W	215	43,004	18,771	71,700	5.51	*Methodist Ch, Upper Burma.* M=MMS(US). 80% Lushai, 17% Khongsai (Kuki Chins). 140n.
Myanmar Baptist Convention	1813	P-Bap	TWE.W	3,551	1,195,000	798,560	1,750,000	3.19	*BBC*, organized 1865. M=ABFMS. 16 Conferences. 19p(827),P=75%,4s,1300t.
Myanmar Gospel Outreach	1955	I-3pI	.....	220	23,200	1,000	35,000	15.28	Work among Khumi, Tiddim Chin.
New Apostolic Church	c1975	I-3aX	x....	20	1,000	–	2,871	5.00	Southwest Shan state, and elsewhere. Several Karen tribes. M=NAK(Germany).
People's Church Movement		I-Bap	.....	10	1,000	2,000	3,330	0.05	In Chin Hills, ex Zomi Baptists; led by Chin prophet. Catholic features.
Presbyterian Church of Myanmar	1954	P-Ref	R...W	200	25,000	14,605	50,000	5.05	Lushai migrants from Mizo Presbyterian Ch, Assam. 15n,19m,1s(5),W=60%,646Yy.
St Gabriel's Church Union, CIB	1925	I-Ang	....W	1	100	200	300	1.64	*CIB=Ch of India & Burma.* Rangoon Anglican split. Tamils, returning to India.
Salvation Army	1915	P-Sal	xwE.W	15	340	500	855	2.17	*Ke-tin-gyin Tut.* SA, Burma Command. 2 Districts. Officers 12, institutions 4.
Self-Supporting Karen Baptist Miss Soc	1912	I-Bap	....W	105	10,500	10,000	21,000	3.01	*SSKBS.* Split from Karen work of BBC. Sgaw and Pwo Karen. HQ Rangoon. 40n.
Seventh Day Baptist Church	1965	I-Bap	T....	15	820	1,500	2,560	2.16	Chins who affiliated with SDB Ch (USA) through correspondence courses. HQ Tahan.
Seventh-day Adventist Church	1919	P-Adv	x....	139	12,798	15,000	32,000	3.08	*SDA, Burma Union* (4 Sections). HQ Rangoon. 34n,132mw,1j,1s,142t(6927),507Y.
United Pentecostal Church of Myanmar	1966	P-Pe1	x....	150	12,139	10,000	30,300	0.05	*Jesus Only Church.* M=UPC(India, then USA). Unitarian Pentecostals. Chins, 200n,1p(10).
Zo Christian Church	c1960	I-Non	.....	10	1,500	1,000	2,500	3.73	Nondenominationalists.
Other indigenous churches		I-3nZ	.....	150	12,000	10,000	25,000	0.05	Numerous small independent groups (over 40), especially among Karens. 50n.
Other Protestant bodies	c1970	P-	.....	30	2,000	–	3,000	37.75	Total about 20, including several from India, Thailand, China.
Totals				**10,906**	**2,149,671**	**1,346,149**	**3,418,658**		

Churches, members, growth, 1900-2025	*Congs*	*Adults*	*Affiliated*	*G%*	*Total denominations*	*6 Megablocs: O*	*R*	*A*	*P*	*I*	*m*
Total churches, members, and denominations (mid-1900)	200	94,600	232,500	2.54	6	0	1	1	4	0	0
Total churches, members, and denominations (mid-1970)	4,925	547,495	1,346,149	2.54	51	0	1	1	10	38	1
Total churches, members, and denominations (mid-1990)	8,000	1,917,000	3,049,000	4.17	114	0	1	1	37	74	1
Total churches, members, and denominations (mid-1995)	10,906	2,149,671	3,418,658	2.32	116	0	1	1	38	75	1
Total churches, members, and denominations (mid-2000)	12,000	2,353,000	3,741,464	1.82	118	0	1	1	39	76	1
Total churches, members, and denominations (mid-2025)	30,000	3,982,000	6,332,000	2.13	153	0	1	1	50	100	1

NOTES ON TABLE ABOVE
NATIONAL COUNCILS (Column 4, 5th letter).
E = Myanmar Evangelical Christian Fellowship (MECF).
R = Myanmar Catholic Bishops Conference (MCBC).
W = Myanmar Council of Churches (MCC), 1965.
w = associate member of MCC.

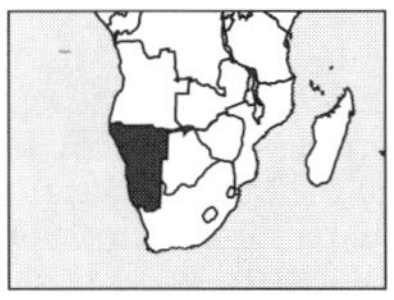

NAMIBIA

SECULAR DATA, AD 2000

STATE
Official name: The Republic of Namibia.
Short name: Namibia. **Adjective of nationality:** Namibian.
Flag: That of the Republic of South Africa.
Area: 825,118 sq. km. (318,580 sq. mi.).
Government: Republic with two legislative houses, since 1990 (1884 German colony, 1920 South African mandated territory, 1949 annexed by South Africa, 1966 named Namibia by UN, 1990 Independence).
Legislature: National Assembly, 72 members; National Council, 26 members.
Official language: English and Afrikaans.
Monetary unit: 1 Namibian dollar (N$) = 100 cents. **US$1=** N$5.83.
Chief cities: WINDHOEK 157,013.
Political divisions: 13 provinces.
Armed forces: 8,000.

DEMOGRAPHY
Population: 1,726,000.
Population density: 2.0/sq. km. (5.4/sq. mi.).
Under 15 years: 717,000.
Growth rate p.a.: 1.22% (births 34.19, deaths 22.02).
Mortality: Infant, per 1,000: 74.1, ; **Maternal per 100,000:** 370.0.
Life expectancy: 41 (male 41, female 41).
Household size: 4.8. **Floor area per person, sq.m:** 3.5.
Major languages: English, Afrikaans, Ovambo, Nama, Herero, German, Bushman, Tswana (Setswana), and 10 smaller languages.
Urban dwellers: 40.86%. **Urban growth rate p.a.:** 4.5%.
Labor force: 35%.

ETHNOLINGUISTIC PEOPLES
23.1% Ndonga (Ambo, Ovambo); 14.5% Coloured (Eurafrican); 11.2% Kwanyama (Ovambo); 9.1% Luyana (Kwangali, Kavango; 8.1% Afrikaner.

ECONOMY
National income p.a. per person: US$2,000; **per family:** US$9,600.

EDUCATION
Adult literacy: 75% (male 77%, female 74%). **Schools:** 1,064.
Universities: 7. **School enrolment:** female/male: 112%/106%.

HEALTH
Access to health services: 62%. **Access to safe water:** 57%.
Hospitals: 47 (45 beds per 10,000). **Doctors:** 324.
Blind: 1,400. **Deaf:** 104,000. **Murder rate:** 72.
Lepers: 1,500. **Underweight prevalence under 5:** 26%.

LITERATURE
New book titles p.a.: 190 (110 p.a. per million). **Periodicals:** 35.
Newspapers: 4 dailies.

COMMUNICATION (per 1,000 people)
Phones: 51 (16% mobile). **Radios:** 136. **TV sets:** 29.
Daily newspaper circulation: 93. **Computers:** 40.

REFUGEES
Alien refugees from other countries: 1,000.

HUMAN LIFE AND LIBERTY (optimum condition=100.0%)
HDI: 57.0. **HSI:** 60.0. **HFI:** 60.0. **EFL:** 25.0.

Country Table 1. Religious adherents in Namibia, AD 1900-2025.

Year	1900		1970		mid-1990		Annual change, 1990-2000				mid-1995		mid-2000		mid-2025	
Name	Adherents	%	Adherents	%	Adherents	%	Natural	Conversion	Total	Rate	Adherents	%	Adherents	%	Adherents	%
Christians	**12,400**	**8.7**	**749,000**	**94.6**	**1,248,000**	**92.4**	**34,745**	**-314**	**34,431**	**2.47**	**1,425,600**	**92.4**	**1,592,308**	**92.3**	**2,121,800**	**90.8**
PROFESSION																
professing Christians	**12,400**	**8.7**	**749,000**	**94.6**	**1,248,000**	**92.4**	**34,745**	**-314**	**34,431**	**2.47**	**1,425,600**	**92.4**	**1,592,308**	**92.3**	**2,121,800**	**90.8**
AFFILIATION																
unaffiliated Christians	4,200	3.0	150,966	19.1	203,000	15.0	5,654	-1,644	4,010	1.82	224,309	14.5	243,097	14.1	234,800	10.0
affiliated Christians	**8,200**	**5.8**	**598,034**	**75.5**	**1,045,000**	**77.4**	**29,091**	**1,330**	**30,421**	**2.59**	**1,201,291**	**77.8**	**1,349,211**	**78.2**	**1,887,000**	**80.7**
Protestants	8,000	5.6	401,681	50.7	645,000	47.8	17,950	-450	17,500	2.43	732,380	47.5	820,000	47.5	1,090,000	46.6
Roman Catholics	200	0.1	116,353	14.7	227,000	16.8	6,322	1,599	7,921	3.04	268,829	17.4	306,211	17.7	450,000	19.3
Independents	0	0.0	59,200	7.5	141,400	10.5	3,938	622	4,560	2.83	165,746	10.7	187,000	10.8	300,000	12.8
Anglicans	0	0.0	20,000	2.5	28,000	2.1	780	-480	300	1.02	30,000	1.9	31,000	1.8	35,000	1.5
Marginal Christians	0	0.0	800	0.1	3,600	0.3	100	40	140	3.34	4,336	0.3	5,000	0.3	12,000	0.5
Trans-megabloc groupings																
Evangelicals	7,000	4.9	58,000	7.3	128,400	9.5	3,576	-416	3,160	2.22	143,825	9.3	160,000	9.3	200,000	8.6
Pentecostals/Charismatics	0	0.0	18,000	2.3	171,000	12.7	4,763	1,137	5,900	3.01	200,519	13.0	230,000	13.3	370,000	15.8
Great Commission Christians	**8,500**	**6.0**	**95,000**	**12.0**	**224,100**	**16.6**	**6,242**	**871**	**7,113**	**2.79**	**262,000**	**17.0**	**295,226**	**17.1**	**467,600**	**20.0**
Ethnoreligionists	129,600	91.3	42,100	5.3	80,900	6.0	2,253	-46	2,207	2.44	92,400	6.0	102,970	6.0	139,000	6.0
Nonreligious	0	0.0	0	0.0	12,800	1.0	357	303	660	4.25	15,260	1.0	19,401	1.1	55,000	2.4
Baha'is	0	0.0	300	0.0	6,500	0.5	181	55	236	3.15	7,700	0.5	8,864	0.5	18,000	0.8
Jews	0	0.0	600	0.1	1,600	0.1	45	-6	39	2.19	1,770	0.1	1,988	0.1	3,500	0.2
Muslims	0	0.0	0	0.0	200	0.0	6	8	14	5.36	270	0.0	337	0.0	700	0.0
World A (unevangelized persons)	122,972	86.6	23,756	3.0	32,400	2.4	919	-303	616	1.73	35,498	2.3	39,698	2.3	49,098	2.1
World B (evangelized non-Christians)	6,628	4.7	19,138	2.4	69,600	5.2	1,923	617	2,540	3.05	82,312	5.3	93,994	5.4	167,102	7.1
World C (Christians)	12,400	8.7	749,000	94.6	1,248,000	92.4	34,745	-314	34,431	2.47	1,425,600	92.4	1,592,308	92.3	2,121,800	90.8
Country's population	**142,000**	**100.0**	**791,895**	**100.0**	**1,350,000**	**100.0**	**37,587**	**0**	**37,587**	**2.49**	**1,543,411**	**100.0**	**1,726,000**	**100.0**	**2,338,000**	**100.0**

COLUMNS, ROWS.
For meanings and definitions, see Codebook (Part 3). Note that, by definition, total 'Christians' = professing + crypto-Christians, which also = affiliated + unaffiliated Christians, and also = Great Commission Christians + latent Christians. Percentages may not always total exactly, due to rounding.

CENSUSES.
(South West Africa) **9.IV.1960** 60.9% Protestants (40.0% Lutherans, 8.4% NGK), 15.1% ethnoreligionists, 13.6% Roman Catholics, 7.4% Non-White indigenous (Bantu, Coloured), 2.8% Anglicans, 0.1% Jews. In 1980, estimated population was given as 1,024,000 in some quarters.

NOTES ON RELIGIONS
BAHA'IS. In 3 local spiritual assemblies (1973). Members include Ovambo, Herero and some Bushmen.
ETHNORELIGIONISTS. Animists among the Heikum and Kung Bushmen (over 80%), and a minority of the Ambo and Herero (less than 10% animist).
INDEPENDENTS In about 40 denominations in 1995, among both Bantu and Coloured races (see Table 2 below).
PROTESTANTS. The Rhenish Mission, begun in 1842, had 2,200 converts by 1874 and 3,600 by 1888; in 1908 alone there were 1,700 baptisms. The Finnish Mission grew from its origin in 1870 to 21 native Christians and 5 missionaries in 1890, to 2,000 baptized Christians and 24 missionaries by 1910.
ROMAN CATHOLICS. By 1907 there were 970 Catholics (800 Europeans, 170 natives).

Great Commission Instrument Panel: status of Namibia (for explanation see start of Part 4)

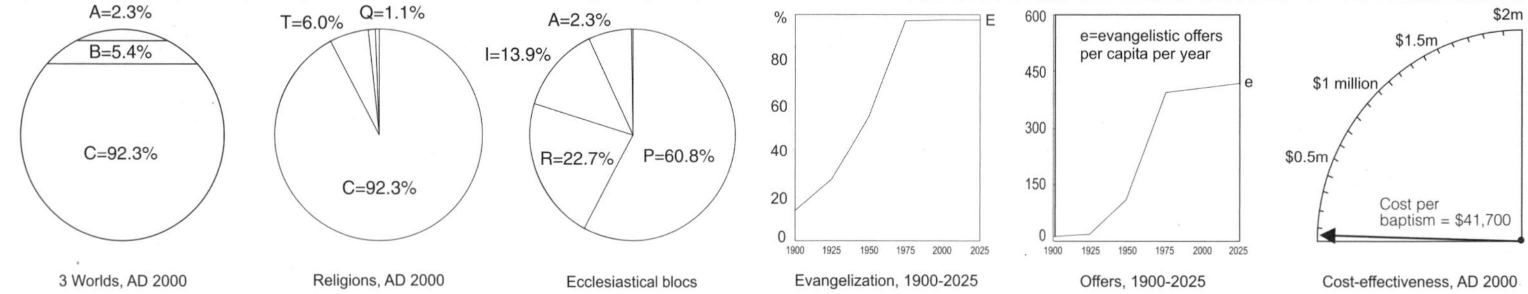

Country status. Namibia is a county in southwest Africa between South Africa and Angola. Diamond and uranium mining are the primary economic activities along with livestock raising and fishing.

HUMAN NEED AND LIBERTY

Human rights and freedoms. Namibia, which achieved independence later than most African nations, has made more significant progress than others in extending full civil and political rights to its citizens. However, certain pre-independence problems, such as disparities and racial discrimination in education, health, employment, and working conditions, have persisted because a number of apartheid laws remain on the statute books. Discrimination against women also is the norm rather than the exception. Members of defense and police forces are often guilty of offenses against civilians, including theft, murder, and assault.

NON-CHRISTIAN RELIGIONS

Traditional religions are still followed by a small minority of Ambo and Herero, most of whom have become Christian, as well as by over 90% of the Heikum and Kung bushmen. The traditional name for God among the Ambo is Kalunga, and Nijambi Kalunga among the Herero. In both cases God is conceived as distant, and so men's attention is centered on the ancestral spirits called Ovakuamungu by the Ambo and Ovakuru by the Herero. Belief in the efficacy of charms and the reality of witchcraft is also prevalent. Among the Amgo, the medicine man is called ondudu and the sorcerer omulodi. The Heikum and Kung appellation for God is Xu. Prayers are offered to him on the occasions of drought, illness, hunting, and before travel, and offerings are sometimes given following the hunt. The principal minister of Xu is Nawa who is the head of the spirits (Gouab) and executes God's will on earth.

Ethnoreligionists. Ovambo local herdsman at Osandi, dressed up for traditional religious cattle festivities. Some 6% of the Ovambo still adhere to tribal religion.

CHRISTIANITY

PROTESTANT CHURCHES. The Hottentots in southwest Africa were first reached by the London Missionary Society in 1805. At the request of LMS, the Rhenish Missionary Society (German Lutheran) arrived in 1842, followed by Finnish Lutherans in 1870. The largest church today, now under African leadership, is the direct result of this early activity.

In 1971 the Evangelical Lutheran Church in South West Africa (outgrowth of the Rhenish Society) and the Evangelical Lutheran Ovambokavango Church (related to the Finnish Lutheran Mission) came together to form the United Evangelical Church of South West Africa. The Christian community of this federated church (over 573,000) formed 37% of the total population of Namibia in 1995. A separate body, the German Evangelical Lutheran Church, serves the German-speaking White community; in 1975 they reluctantly agreed to join the United Church but the latter had by then itself become reluctant to accept them. The Reformed tradition is represented by 6 denominations all owing their origin to South Africa and reflecting the racial separation existing within their mother churches. Their impact on South West Africa has been much less than within the republic to the south. The largest of these is the Dutch Evangelical Reformed Church which is working among Herero, Kwangali, and Bushmen.

Other groups affiliated to South African denominations are the Methodist and Congregationalist churches and a Pentecostal body with strength among the Afrikaner population, the Apostolic Faith Mission. Seventh-day Adventists have been in Namibia since 1954 and 2 small Baptist communities have also been formed, one originating from South Africa and the other begun by Southern Baptists from the USA. Several other small missions are also at work.

Country summary. **Worlds A, B, C by ethnolinguistic peoples, cities, and major civil divisions in Namibia.**																					
	PEOPLES							*CITIES*							*CIVIL DIVISIONS*						
World	*Num*	*Pop 2000*	*C%*	*Christians*	*E%*	*U%*	*Unevangelized*	*Num*	*Pop 2000*	*C%*	*Christians*	*E%*	*U%*	*Unevangelized*	*Num*	*Pop 2000*	*C%*	*Christians*	*E%*	*U%*	*Unevangelized*
A	11	44,942	9.75	4,381	42	58	25,977	0	0	0.00	0	0	0	0	0	0	0.00	0	0	0	0
B	2	54,192	50.00	27,096	81	19	10,103	0	0	0.00	0	0	0	0	0	0	0.00	0	0	0	0
C	20	1,626,734	81.00	1,317,732	100	0	3,083	1	157,013	75.00	117,760	96	4	6,987	13	1,724,725	78.23	1,349,211	98	2	38,018
Total	**33**	**1,725,868**	**78.18**	**1,349,209**	**98**	**2**	**39,163**	**1**	**157,013**	**75.00**	**117,760**	**96**	**4**	**6,987**	**13**	**1,724,725**	**78.23**	**1,349,211**	**98**	**2**	**38,018**

United Evangelical Lutheran Church of Namibia. Arriving, worshiping, and fellowshipping members of Ephisius church, Windhoek.

CATHOLIC CHURCH. The Portuguese touched the coast of southwest Africa as early as 1485, but no sustained Catholic influence was felt until the end of the 19th century. Originally part of the prefecture of Cimbebasia in Portuguese Angola, the area south of the Angola border was designated a prefecture in its own right in 1892 and received its first Oblates of Mary Immaculate missionaries after 1896. The vicariate of Windhoek was erected in 1926. The growth of Catholics in the vicariate can be seen from the following statistics: 3,402 in 1921, 15,607 in 1946, 62,000 in 1965, 96,000 in 1970, and 218,000 in 1990. Catholic membership is largely Ovambo with a minority of Whites. The Keetmanshoop mission, entrusted to Oblates of St Francis de Sales, became a prefecture in 1909 and was elevated to a vicariate in 1940.

The Holy See has diplomatic relations with Namibia in AD 2000.

ANGLICAN CHURCH. The Anglican diocese of Damaraland is part of the Church of the Province of Southern Africa and is 77% Ambo in membership. Anglicans are the fourth largest Christian community in Namibia after the Lutheran, Catholic, and Dutch Reformed churches.

INDIGENOUS CHURCHES. Three important schisms from the Rhenish Mission have occurred since World War II. The first, among the Nama Hottentots in 1946 who were dissatisfied with the progress of Lutheran pastoral training, became a branch of the AME Church, a Black denomination from the USA which had been at work in South Africa since 1892. In 1955, unrest in the Herero community erupted, resulting in the establishment of the Herero Church, commonly called Oruuano (Community), which subsequently produced 2 further schisms, the Church of Africa and the Protestant Unity Church. Then in 1959, a majority of the Baster Coloureds at Rehoboth broke off to form the Independent Rhenish Mission of South Africa, protesting Bantu domination of the Evangelical Lutheran Church after 1957. Numerous independent churches from South Africa have also migrated to Namibia since World War I, but none has a large following.

Indigenous missions. Although Christians from Namibia have served as missionaries in foreign countries, most of these went to South Africa and other surrounding countries. This continues to be the pattern in the present.

Renewal movements. In the 1990s the Pentecostal/Charismatic Renewal continued to spread across most older churches, and numbered over 230,000 adherents (of whom 10% were Pentecostals, 38% Charismatics, and 52% Independents).

CHURCH AND STATE

The territory was a German colony until World War I, after which it was transferred as a trust territory to South Africa by the League of Nations in 1919, a mandate later disputed by the United Nations. Unrest under South African rule has manifested itself within the country and in the churches. In 1971, African leaders of the principal church of Namibia, the United Evangelical Church of South West Africa, published a pastoral letter, condemning the politics of apartheid, which received the support of Anglican and Catholic leaders as well. Moreover, in another 'Open Letter' in 1971 the Lutheran bishop called for the granting of independence to Namibia. These attitudes and actions caused SWAPO (South West African People's Organization, a national liberation movement) to write in its bulletin *Namibia today*, in November 1971, that clergy and other persons with religious responsibilities should be considered, along with guerrillas of the bush and workers in the towns, as one of the 3 elements of the Namibian revolution. On 4 March 1972, the Anglican bishop of Damaraland and 2 of his co-workers, all Whites, were expelled from the country. The bishop later declared that during the 3 years of his episcopal ministry, the South African authorities had refused 17 residence permits for Anglican missionaries. Some time later, his successor as bishop (another Englishman) was also deported. The churches today find themselves the sole institutions able to form a bridge between the African masses and their White rulers.

BROADCASTING AND MEDIA

Shortwave radio programs in German can be received from TWR (Swaziland).

Christian television programming is also available. CBN's *International 700 Club* and *Another Life* programs can be seen on Sundays. TBN programs are aired in Windhoek on national television. The 'Jesus' Film has been shown to 14,000, mainly through film teams.

INTERDENOMINATIONAL ORGANIZATIONS

Five of Namibia's churches are represented as members and 5 others as observers on the South African Council of Churches founded in 1936. In August 1978 the Namibian Council of Churches was inaugurated.

FUTURE TRENDS AND PROSPECTS

Ethnoreligionists will probably remain at 6% through 2025 (falling from over 90% in 1900). Christianity will begin to decline to 90.8% by 2025 (due to the rise of the nonreligious).

Christianity is expected to decline below 85% in the middle of the 21st century. The nonreligious could reach 10% before AD 2050.

BIBLIOGRAPHY

A history of the church in Southern Africa: a select bibliography of published material. J. W. Hofmeyr & K. E. Cross. Pretoria, South Africa: University of South Africa, 1986. 2 vols.

'Christ at the center of culture: the Namibian experience.' Z. K. Mujoro. S.T.M. thesis, Wartburg Theological Seminary, Dubuque, IA, 1984. 81p.

'Christian education among the Ovambo people: the house as the center of transmitting culture and tradition.' B. Haileka. S.T.M. thesis, Lutheran Theological Seminary at Gettysburg, Gettysburg, PA, 1994. 245p.

Church and liberation in Namibia. P. H. Katjavivi, P. Frostin & K. Mbuende (eds). : Pluto, 1990. 240p.

'Church and state in Namibia, 1806–1989.' S. V. V. Nambala. Th.D. thesis, Luther Northwestern Theological Seminary, St. Paul, MN, 1990. 329p.

'Die Gemeinschaft der Ahnen and die Gemeinde Jesu Christi bei den Herero.' W. A. Wienecke. Ph.D. dissertation, University of Hamburg, 1962.

Eingeborenenkirchen in Sud– und Sudwestafrika: ihre Geschichte und Sozialstruktur. K. Schlosser. Kiel, Germany: W. G. Mühlau, 1958. 355p.

Good magic in Ovambo. M. Hiltunen. Helsinki: Suomen Antropologinen Seura, 1993. 234p.

History of the church in Namibia. S. V. V. Nambala. Ed., O. K. Olson. : Lutheran Quarterly, 1994. 178p.

Mission and colonialism in Namibia. J. L. De Vries. Johannesburg: Ravan Press, 1978. 216p.

Namibia. S. Schoeman & E. Schoeman. *World bibliographical series*, vol. 53. Oxford, UK: CLIO Press, 1984. 212p. (See especially 'Religion,' p.63–4).

Namibia. C. O. Winter. London: Lutterworth, 1977. (By exiled Anglican bishop).

Otjikango or Gross Bermen: the history of the first Rhenish Herero mission station in South West Africa, 1844–1904. N. Mossolow. Windhoek: Meinert, 1979. 90p.

Schwarze Christen, weisse Christen: Lutheraner in Namibia und ihre Auseinandersetzung um den christlichen Auftrag in der Gesellschaft. W. F. Krüger. *Erlanger Monographien aus Mission und Ökumene*, Bd. 3. Erlangen: Verlag der Ev.-Luth. Mission, 1985. 246p.

'South East Africa (Namibia): a human tapestry,' E. du Pisani, *Namibiana*, 2, 2 (1980), 55–62.

'South West Africa and its indigenous people,' O. Levinson, *South Africa International*, 3 (1972), 19–27.

'The half–opened door,' G. Reeh, *International review of mission*, 50, 199 (1961), 293–96. (The Herero Church).

The Kalunga concept in Ovambo religion from 1870 onwards. T. Aarni. Stockholm: Almquist & Wicksell, 1982. 166p.

The Kavango peoples. G. D. Gibson, T. J. Larson & C. R. McGurk. Wiesbaden, Germany: Franz Steiner Verlag, 1981. 275p. (Treats religion).

'The Kavango: the country, its people and history,' K. F. R. Budack, *Namib und Meer*, 7 (1976), 29–42.

The Naron: a Bushman tribe of the central Kalahari. D. F. Bleek. Cambridge, UK: University of Cape Town, Publications of the School of African Life and Language, 1928. 67p.

The native tribes of South West Africa. C. H. L. Hahn. Cape Town: Cape Times, 1928. 214p.

'The Ovambo sermon: a study of the preaching of the Evangelical Lutheran Ovambo–Kavango Church in South West Africa.' S. Löytty. Tampereen Keskuspaino thesis, University of Helsinki, Tampere, Finland, 1971. 175p.

'The role and function of the pastor in the transition of the Namibian community.' M. T. Kapolo. S.T.M. thesis, Wartburg Theological Seminary, Dubuque, IA, 1991. 192p.

The role of the church in the transformation of the Namibian society: Conference on the Future Role of the Church in Namibia, held in Windhoek 27–31 March 1990. T. Mbako (ed). Katutura, Windhoek: Council of Churches in Namibia, 1990. 59p.

Witchcraft and sorcery in Ovambo. M. Hiltunen. Helsinki: Finnish Anthropological Society, 1986. 178p.

Zwischen Namib und Kalahari: 75 Jahre katholische Mission in Südwestafrika. Windhoek: Roman Catholic Mission, 1971. 250p.

Country Table 2. Organized churches and denominations in Namibia.

Official name (bold type = church with over 10% of all affiliated) 1	*Begun* 2	*Type* 3	*Counc* 4	*Congs* 5	*Adults* 6	*Affiliated 1970* 7	*Affiliated 1995* 8	*G%* 9	*Names, notes, and other statistics* (see Codebook, Part 3) 10
African Church	c1965	I-Lut	.....	12	1,200	1,000	3,000	4.49	One of 3 factions split ex Herero Church. Some Lutheran polity retained.
African Methodist Episcopal Church	1946	I-Met	Vw..K	44	3,500	15,000	10,600	-1.38	Nama Hottentot secession ex Rhenish Mission (RM). Later, affiliated to AMEC.
Anglican Ch: D Damaraland/Namibia	1924	A-Hig	AwaVK	123	16,000	20,000	30,000	1.64	In CPSA. 77% Ovambo, 18% White 5% Coloured. 17n,3x,15f,1h,P=32%,3r,1s1382Y,2379y.
Apostolic Faith Mission of S Africa		P-Pe2	Z....	29	2,000	1,400	5,000	0.05	M=AFM(SA). 83% White (Afrikaners), 13% Bantu, 4% Coloured. HQ Lyndhurst, SA. 2f.
Assemblies of God	1979	P-Pe2	....E	6	725	–	1,668	6.25	M=AoG.
Association of Vineyard Chs	c1990	I-3cW	.....	1	100	–	300	20.00	Supported by M=AVC(USA, SA).
Baptist Convention of Namibia	1968	P-Bap	T....	60	3,355	200	7,710	15.73	M=FMB-SBC(USA). Recent independent Baptist work. 16f,7Y.
Baptist Union of South Africa		P-Bap	T...w	3	200	200	400	0.05	*BUSA.* In Walvis Bay and Windhoek. All Whites. HQ Johannesburg, South Africa.
Catholic Church in Namibia:	1880	R-Lat	P.SSK	85	202,300	116,353	268,829	3.41	87% African, 10% Coloured. C=2+1+6. 9n 68x 114m 311w 8358Yy
M Windhoek (Cimbebasia)	1892	R-Lat	Pomi	55	133,300	97,576	154,163	1.85	37% Ambo, 34% Kwangare, 15% Damara. M=OMI,SCC. 6n 37x 74m 217w 5461Yy
D Keetmanshoop (Namaqualand)	1909	R-Lat	Posfs	22	20,400	18,777	34,646	2.48	South. Catholics mostly Basters; 5% Whites. 0n 21x 27m 57w 897Yy
VA Rundu	1994	R-Lat	Pomi	8	48,600	–	80,020	50.00	M=OMI. 3n 10x 13m 37w 2000Yy
Christian Assemblies	c1950	I-3pN	.....	22	4,200	5,000	10,500	3.01	*Christen Gemeente* (South). 80% Coloured. Strong in N & W Cape, Natal (SA).
Christian Reformed Church		P-Ref	x....	4	700	2,500	1,500	0.05	*NHK. Nederduitsch Hervormde Kerk van Afrika.* 99% White Afrikaners, in NHK(SA).
Church of Africa	c1965	I-Lut	.....	25	2,000	2,000	4,000	2.81	West Hereros. Schism ex Herero Church by members of Mbanderu sub-tribe.
Ch of Jesus Christ of Latter-day Saints		m-LdS	x....	1	130	100	186	0.05	*Mormons.* M=CJCLdS(Utah, USA). Mainly USA expatriates. HQ Johannesburg, SA.
Church of the Nazarene	1973	P-Hol	.....	4	168	–	402	4.55	M=CoN.
Dutch Reformed Church in SWA		P-Ref	F....	260	13,000	40,000	20,000	0.05	*NGK. Nederduitse Gereformeerde Kerk in SWA.* Mother Ch. White Afrikaners only.
Dutch Ref Ch in SWA (Coloured Ch)		P-Ref	F....	50	4,000	3,000	6,000	0.05	*NGK vir SWA.* Coloured section of NGK, based in Kakamas, CP, South Africa.
Evangelical Bible Church	1981	P-Eva	.....	25	2,500	–	5,000	7.14	M=AEF. Many Angolan refugees.
Evangelical Reformed Church in Africa	1955	P-Ref	F...w	88	27,500	3,000	44,000	11.34	*Ev Gereformeerde Kerk in Afrika.* M=NGK(SA). Herero, Kwangali, Bushmen. 2n,5x.
Full Gospel Ch of God in Southern A		P-Pe3	ZF...	44	6,509	2,000	13,000	0.05	M=FGCoG(South Africa),CoG(Cleveland) (USA). HQ Irene (Transvaal, SA). 1p.
German Ev Lutheran Church in Namibia	1896	P-Lut	L..JK	21	5,000	14,000	10,000	-1.34	One of 4 synods of UELCSA. German-speaking Whites only. HQ Oranjezicht, CP. 11nx.
Herero Church	1955	I-Lut	.....	54	5,400	5,000	9,000	2.38	*Oruuano (Community).* Schism of Herero tribe ex Rhenish Mission; now splintered. M=AIM(USA)
Independent Rhenish Mission of SA	1959	I-Lut	.....	10	7,500	4,000	15,000	5.43	Anti-Bantu schism ex Rhenish Mission by 80% all Basters (Coloureds) at Rehoboth.
Jehovah's Witnesses	c1945	m-Jeh	x....	15	644	600	2,150	5.24	Active witnessing under way by 1949. Literature in Kwanyama (Ambo). (1975) 14Y. (1995) 63Y.
Methodist Church of South Africa		P-Met	Vwa.K	12	960	5,000	3,200	0.05	Part of MCSA. HQ Cape Town. 45% White, 37% Coloured, 18% Bantu.
New Apostolic Church	c1910	I-3aX	x....	27	4,000	4,000	11,186	4.20	M=NAC(World HQ Zurich). Ex Catholic Apostolic Ch. German immigrants.
Ovambo Independent Church	c1970	I-Lut	.....	39	5,850	–	13,000	46.07	Schism of Ovambo Lutherans ex UELCN.
Presbyterian Church of Southern Africa		P-Ref	Rwa.W	3	400	500	1,000	0.05	*PCSA.* Attached to PCSA in South Africa. HQ Johannesburg. 90% White.
Protestant Unity Church	c1965	I-Lut	.....	174	17,400	18,000	29,000	1.93	Hereros. Largest faction to split ex Herero Church.
Reformed Church	1937	P-Ref	J....	18	2,520	5,000	3,600	-1.31	*Gereformeerde (Dopper) Kerk.* 2 Classis: Nossob, Etosha. 97% Afrikaners. W=50%.
Rhenish Evangelical Lutheran Ch		P-Lut	.....	25	2,000	1,500	4,000	0.05	Lutheran mission from Germany.
Seventh-day Adventist Church	1954	P-Adv	x....	38	5,700	600	19,000	14.82	SDA, SW Africa Field, South African UC (White, Coloured). 3nx,5mw,5t(211),34Y.
United Congr Ch in Southern Africa	1805	P-Con	Rwa.K	33	2,160	1,500	3,600	3.56	Part of Western Cape Region, UCCSA. 73% Coloured, 22%, Bantu, 5%, White. 1n.
United Ev Lutheran Ch of Namibia:	1791	P-Lut	L...K	600	229,000	319,281	573,000	2.37	1971 federation of 2 of the 3 Lutheran churches in SWA; both retain autonomy. 1s.
Evangelical Lutheran Ch in Namibia	1842	P-Lut	L..JK	200	60,000	115,391	150,000	1.05	M=RM,VEM(Germany). 39% Bergdama, 20% Nama, 17% Herero, 12% Colored. 54f,150Y,3300y
Ev Lutheran Ovambokavango Church	1870	P-Lut	L..JK	400	169,000	203,890	423,000	2.96	ELOC. M=Finnish Missionary Society. A=1954. 90%,10x,200m,81f,13H,24h.
United Pentecostal Church	1986	P-Pe1	.....	3	100	–	300	11.11	*Jesus Only Church.* M=UPC(USA). 2f.
Other Non-White indigenous churches		I-3nN	.....	300	30,000	5,000	60,000	0.05	Total over 30, mainly migrant groups from South African bodies (see list below)
Other Protestant denominations		P-	.....	100	5,000	2,000	10,000	0.05	Several recent smaller missions (see list below).
Other Independent Catholic churches		I-CCa	.....	2	80	200	160	0.05	Including Old Apostolic Church (from Europe).
Other marginal Protestant bodies		m-	.....	20	1,000	100	2,000	0.05	Small groups of German and other, including Horpenites (from Saxony).
Totals				**2,380**	**614,801**	**598,034**	**1,201,291**		

Churches, members, growth, 1900-2025	*Congs*	*Adults*	*Affiliated*	*G%*	*Total denominations*	*6 Megablocs:* O	R	A	P	I	m
Total churches, members, and denominations (mid-1900)	40	4,800	8,200	6.32	4	0	1	0	3	0	0
Total churches, members, and denominations (mid-1970)	1,529	350,461	598,034	6.32	59	0	1	1	25	27	5
Total churches, members, and denominations (mid-1990)	2,900	535,000	1,045,000	2.83	100	0	1	1	39	51	8
Total churches, members, and denominations (mid-1995)	2,380	614,801	1,201,291	2.83	102	0	1	1	40	52	8
Total churches, members, and denominations (mid-2000)	3,100	691,000	1,349,211	2.35	104	0	1	1	41	53	8
Total churches, members, and denominations (mid-2025)	5,600	966,000	1,887,000	1.35	134	0	1	1	50	70	12

NOTES ON TABLE ABOVE

NATIONAL COUNCILS (Column 4, 5th letter).

E = Namibia Evangelical Fellowship (NEF).
K = Namibian Council of Churches (formed 1978), also member of SACC.
w = member of South African Council of Churches (SACC), or observer member

OTHER NON-WHITE INDIGENOUS CHURCHES. Including: Afrikaans Protestant Ch, Apostolic Spiritual Healing Ch (Tswana leaders from Botswana), Orujano Ch (schism ex Herero Ch), St John's Apostolic Faith Ch, St Philip Apostolic Ch, Spiritual Healing Ch (Branch of Botswana church, with bishop for Namibia; Herero members; linked with Lesotho body, Moshoeshoe Berean Bible Readers' Ch).

OTHER PROTESTANT DENOMINATIONS. These include: Christian Brethren, Ch of the Latter Rain (Afrikaner Pentecostals, called Blourokkies because of women's blue dresses), Free Gospel Ch, Salvation Army (began 1932).

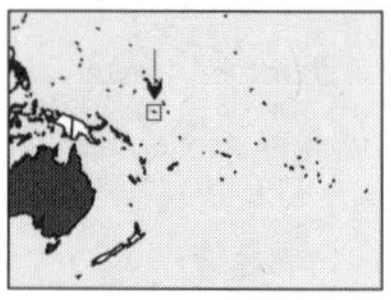

NAURU

SECULAR DATA, AD 2000

STATE
Official name: The Republic of Nauru.
Short name: Nauru. **Adjective of nationality:** Nauruan.
Flag: Blue field halved by horizontal gold stripe, 12-pointed white star at lower hoist corner (representing the 12 tribes from which Nauruans are descended).
Area: 21 sq. km. (8 sq. mi.).
Government: Republic, since 1968 (1888 German colony, 1914 Australian occupation, then mandated territory, 1947 trust territory of the UN, 1968 Independence).
Legislature: Legislative Assembly, 18 members.
Official language: English.
Monetary unit: 1 Australian dollar ($A) = 100 cents. **US$1=** $A 1.70.
Chief cities: YARAN (Yaren) 539.
Political divisions: 1 province.

DEMOGRAPHY
Population: 12,000.
Population density: 548.5/sq. km. (1,439.8/sq. mi.).
Under 15 years: 4,000.
Growth rate p.a.: 1.60% (births 20.74, deaths 4.71).
Mortality: Infant, per 1,000: 9.3, ; **Maternal per 100,000:** 100.0.
Life expectancy: 76 (male 73, female 78).
Household size: 8.0. **Floor area per person, sq.m:** 10.0.
Major languages: English, Nauruan, Gilbertese, Chinese (Cantonese).
Urban dwellers: 100.00%. **Urban growth rate p.a.:** 2.2%.
Labor force: 31%.

ETHNOLINGUISTIC PEOPLES
48.0% Nauruan; 19.2% Kiribertese (Gilbertese); 13.0% Han Chinese (Cantonese); 6.8% Tuvaluan; 6.2% Anglo-Australian.

ECONOMY
National income p.a. per person: US$8,073; **per family:** US$64,588.

EDUCATION
Adult literacy: 99% (male 99%, female 99%). **Schools:** 6.
Universities: 1. **School enrolment:** female/male: 70%/70%.

HEALTH
Access to health services: 70%. **Access to safe water:** 60%.
Hospitals: 1 (40 beds per 10,000). **Doctors:** 5.
Blind: 10. **Deaf:** 700. **Murder rate:** 25. **Lepers:** 100.

LITERATURE
New book titles p.a.: 2 (200 p.a. per million). **Periodicals:** 3.
Newspapers: 0 dailies.

COMMUNICATION (per 1,000 people)
Phones: 250 (20% mobile). **Radios:** 577. **TV sets:** 300.
Daily newspaper circulation: 20. **Computers:** 50.

HUMAN LIFE AND LIBERTY (optimum condition=100.0%)
HDI: 86.4. **HSI:** 65.0. **HFI:** 65.0. **EFL:** 30.0.

Country status. Nauru is an oval-shaped tropical island in the South Pacific near the equator. The island has the world's richest deposits of phosphates.

HUMAN LIFE AND LIBERTY

Human rights and freedoms. Nauru, formerly a Trust Territory of Australia, is a small republic in the Pacific. A notable feature is its high per capita income as a result of the revenues from phosphate mining. The Australian legacies of human and civil rights continue to be honored. Foreign workers, especially from Vanuatu, Kiribati, and Tuvalu, complain of discrimination because they enjoy no political rights.

Christian themes appear frequently on Nauru's postage stamps: here, Christmas theme with verses in English and Nauru language.

Country Table 1. Religious adherents in Nauru, AD 1900-2025.

Year	1900		1970		mid-1990		Annual change, 1990-2000				mid-1995		mid-2000		mid-2025	
Name	Adherents	%	Adherents	%	Adherents	%	Natural	Conversion	Total	Rate	Adherents	%	Adherents	%	Adherents	%
Christians	**300**	**20.0**	**4,450**	**79.3**	**7,270**	**75.7**	**147**	**-10**	**137**	**1.74**	**7,900**	**75.2**	**8,637**	**75.0**	**13,100**	**73.6**
PROFESSION																
professing Christians	**300**	**20.0**	**4,450**	**79.3**	**7,270**	**75.7**	**147**	**-10**	**137**	**1.74**	**7,900**	**75.2**	**8,637**	**75.0**	**13,100**	**73.6**
AFFILIATION																
unaffiliated Christians	0	0.0	400	7.1	270	2.8	5	-2	3	0.92	280	2.7	296	2.6	300	1.7
affiliated Christians	**300**	**20.0**	**4,050**	**72.1**	**7,000**	**72.9**	**142**	**-8**	**134**	**1.77**	**7,620**	**72.6**	**8,341**	**72.5**	**12,800**	**71.9**
Protestants	300	20.0	2,700	48.1	4,850	50.5	97	2	99	1.87	5,320	50.7	5,840	50.8	9,200	51.7
Roman Catholics	0	0.0	1,200	21.4	2,360	24.6	47	9	56	2.15	2,600	24.8	2,920	25.4	4,800	27.0
Independents	0	0.0	0	0.0	300	3.1	6	2	8	2.39	333	3.2	380	3.3	900	5.1
Anglicans	0	0.0	150	2.7	260	2.7	5	1	6	2.10	285	2.7	320	2.8	540	3.0
Marginal Christians	0	0.0	0	0.0	30	0.3	1	0	1	2.92	35	0.3	40	0.3	100	0.6
doubly-affiliated	0	0.0	0	0.0	-800	-8.3	-16	-20	-36	3.78	-953	-9.1	-1,159	-10.0	-2,740	-15.4
Trans-megabloc groupings																
Evangelicals	250	16.7	200	3.6	300	3.1	6	-5	1	0.33	276	2.6	310	2.6	400	2.2
Pentecostals/Charismatics	0	0.0	60	1.1	890	9.3	18	3	21	2.14	990	9.4	1,100	9.2	2,000	11.2
Great Commission Christians	**180**	**12.0**	**840**	**15.0**	**1,750**	**18.2**	**35**	**9**	**44**	**2.25**	**1,950**	**18.6**	**2,187**	**19.0**	**3,950**	**22.2**
Chinese folk-religionists	0	0.0	600	10.7	1,020	10.6	20	-1	19	1.70	1,110	10.6	1,207	10.5	1,700	9.6
Baha'is	0	0.0	100	1.8	840	8.8	17	10	27	2.79	965	9.2	1,106	9.4	2,000	11.2
Nonreligious	0	0.0	300	5.3	320	3.3	6	3	9	2.51	370	3.5	410	3.5	800	4.4
Buddhists	0	0.0	150	2.7	150	1.6	3	-2	1	0.58	155	1.5	159	1.4	200	1.1
Ethnoreligionists	1,200	80.0	0	0.0	0	0.0	0	0	0	0.00	0	0.0	0	0.0	0	0.0
World A (unevangelized persons)	750	50.0	561	10.0	500	5.0	10	-17	-7	-1.56	472	4.5	432	3.6	612	3.4
World B (evangelized non-Christians)	450	30.0	603	10.7	1,830	19.3	36	27	63	2.77	2,127	20.3	2,431	21.4	4,088	23.0
World C (Christians)	300	20.0	4,450	79.3	7,270	75.7	147	-10	137	1.74	7,900	75.2	8,637	75.0	13,100	73.6
Country's population	**1,500**	**100.0**	**5,614**	**100.0**	**9,600**	**100.0**	**193**	**0**	**193**	**1.84**	**10,500**	**100.0**	**11,500**	**100.0**	**17,800**	**100.0**

COLUMNS, ROWS.
For meanings and definitions, see Codebook (Part 3). Note that, by definition, total 'Christians' = professing + crypto-Christians, which also = affiliated + unaffiliated Christians, and also = Great Commission Christians + latent Christians. Percentages may not always total exactly, due to rounding.

CENSUSES.
30.IV.1961: 54.2% Protestants (44.1% Congregationalists), 26.0% Roman Catholics, 16.3% Chinese folk-religionists and Buddhists, 3.0% Anglicans, 0.5% non-religious. **30.VI.1966:** 51.6% Protestants (31.1% Congregationalists), 21.8% Roman Catholics, 19.1% Chinese folk-religionists and Buddhists, 4.0% non-religious, 3.0% Anglicans, 0.4% other religionists.

NOTES ON RELIGIONS
BAHA'IS. In 3 isolated groups.
BUDDHISTS. Chinese (from Hong Kong).
CHINESE FOLK-RELIGIONISTS. From Hong Kong; mostly laborers without their families.
COUNTRY'S POPULATION. The proportion of Nauruans has remained constant at around 50% since 1930; however, Chinese have decreased from 41% in 1930 (43% in 1950) to 16% in 1961, 19% in 1966, 15% in 1968 and 13% in 1995; and other Pacific islanders have increased in numbers from 2.4% in 1950 to 24% in 1961 and 36% in 1995.
ETHNORELIGIONISTS. Pre-Christian traditional Micronesian religion, embracing polytheism and the ancestor cult, did not finally disappear until well into the 20th century.
NON-RELIGIOUS. Mainly Chinese from Hong Kong who have abandoned their family religion.

Great Commission Instrument Panel: status of Nauru (for explanation see start of Part 4)

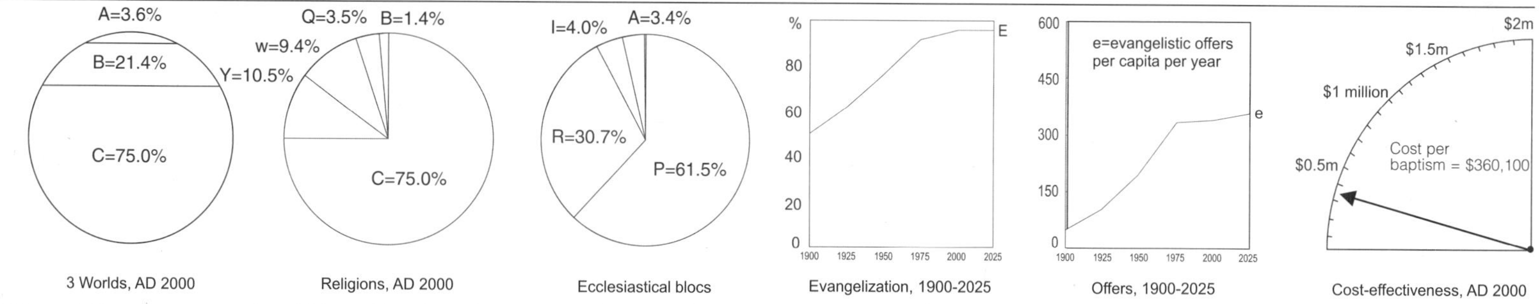

NON-CHRISTIAN RELIGIONS

Chinese folk religion is adhered to by most of the Chinese, who are imported laborers from Hong Kong.

Buddhism also has followers among the Chinese.

Baha'i, begun in the late 1960s, has experienced phenomenal growth with 1,100 followers by AD 2000.

Nauru Congregational Church. *Above.* Two young Christians celebrate Nauru's Independence in 1968.

CHRISTIANITY

PROTESTANT CHURCHES. The main denomination is the Nauruan Protestant Church (NPC), which was begun by Congregationalist missionaries of the London Missionary Society after Germany assumed control of the island in 1888. By 1902 scripture portions had been translated into the Nauru language, by 1907 the New Testament, and by 1918 the whole Bible. Although the church is basically congregational in polity, the membership includes also those of Presbyterian, Lutheran, Methodist, and Baptist background.

CATHOLIC CHURCH. Nauru forms part of the diocese of Tarawa, Nauru, and Funafuti, with its seat in the Gilbert Islands. The population identifies itself as about 25% Catholic.

The Holy See has diplomatic relations with Nauru and in AD 2000 is represented to government and the Catholic hierarchy by a nuncio residing in Wellington, New Zealand.

ANGLICAN CHURCH. Anglicans make up Nauru's smallest church. They belong to the diocese of Polynesia, formed in 1908, which is part of the Church of the Province of New Zealand and the South Pacific Anglican Council (SPAC).

Indigenous missions. Christians from Nauru have engaged in very little foreign mission work.

CHURCH AND STATE

Nauru was discovered by the British whaling captain, John Fearn, in 1798. Germany annexed the island in 1888 after which European settlement began. Between World War I and independence in 1968, Australia administered the territory. Religion has never been an issue vis-á-vis government. Prior to 1923 all education was in the hands of mission schools which were subsidized by government; and to this day Catholic schools continue to receive state aid. The independent state of Nauru, however, specifically recognizes God in its constitution: 'We the people of Nauru acknowledge God as the almighty and everlasting Lord and the giver of all good things...'

Nauru Congregational Church. *Above, left.* Church in Orro.

Catholic Church, Diocese of Tarawa, Nauru, and Funafuti. *Above, right.* Fr. Kayser and Nauru's first Catholic Church (1902). *Left.* Catholic Church, Arubo.

INTERDENOMINATIONAL ORGANIZATIONS

Relations between Protestants, Catholics and Anglicans are informal but cordial.

FUTURE TRENDS AND PROSPECTS

Christianity is projected to continue a slow decline to 72.8% by AD 2025.

With probable increases in the nonreligious and Baha'is, Christianity is likely to continue to decline through the 21st century, dropping to under 70% by AD 2050.

BIBLIOGRAPHY

'God's will first.' N. Billeam. 3rd year project, Pacific Theological College, Suva, Fiji, 1978. 70p.

Nauru bibliography. N. J. Pollock. Wellington, NZ: Dept. of Anthropology, Victoria University of Wellington, 1989. 26p.

The Nauruans. S. Petit-Skinner. San Francisco: MacDuff Press, c1981. 304p.

Country summary. **Worlds A, B, C by ethnolinguistic peoples, cities, and major civil divisions in Nauru.**

PEOPLES

World	Num	Pop 2000	C%	Christians	E%	U%	Unevangelized
A	0	0	0.00	0	0	0	0
B	1	1,497	6.81	102	74	26	392
C	8	10,021	82.21	8,238	100	0	17
Total	**9**	**11,518**	**72.41**	**8,340**	**96**	**4**	**409**

CITIES

World	Num	Pop 2000	C%	Christians	E%	U%	Unevangelized
A	0	0	0.00	0	0	0	0
B	0	0	0.00	0	0	0	0
C	1	539	72.91	393	97	3	16
Total	**1**	**539**	**72.91**	**393**	**97**	**3**	**16**

CIVIL DIVISIONS

World	Num	Pop 2000	C%	Christians	E%	U%	Unevangelized
A	0	0	0.00	0	0	0	0
B	0	0	0.00	0	0	0	0
C	1	11,519	72.41	8,341	96	4	410
Total	**1**	**11,519**	**72.41**	**8,341**	**96**	**4**	**410**

Country Table 2. **Organized churches and denominations in Nauru.**

Official name (bold type = church *with over 10% of all affiliated)* 1	*Begun* 2	*Type* 3	*Counc* 4	*Congs* 5	*Adults* 6	*Affiliated 1970* 7	*Affiliated 1995* 8	*G%* 9	*Names, notes, and other statistics* (see Codebook, Part 3) 10
Anglican Church (D Polynesia)		A-Hig	awpK.	2	122	150	285	0.05	In Ch of the Province of New Zealand. Small chaplaincy work.
Catholic Ch (D Tarawa and Nauru)	1902	R-Lat	P.PY.	2	900	1,200	2,600	3.14	Nauruans, many Gilbertese. M=MSC. 1x,4w (one Chinese),1r.
Jehovah's Witnesses	c1985	m-Jeh	x....	1	20	–	35	10.00	Actively witnessing small congregation.
Methodist Church of Samoa		P-Met	VuP.C	1	50	–	80	0.05	Recent immigrants from original church in Samoa.
Kiribati Protestant Church		P-Con	.vP..	5	300	–	500	0.05	*GIPC.* Immigrants from main Gilbertese church.
Nauru Congregational Church	1888	P-Con	..P..	18	1,580	1,500	3,140	3.00	*NCC/NPC. Nauruan Protestant Ch.* M=LMS(UK). 66% Nauruans, 30% Gilbertese, Tuvaluans.
Nauru Independent Church	c1975	I-3cP	.....	1	200	–	333	5.00	Recent schism ex NCC/NPC.
Tuvalu Church		P-Con	.....	4	350	–	500	0.05	*Ekalesia Kelisiano Tuvalu.*
Other Protestant bodies	c1960	P-	.....	6	440	1,200	1,100	-0.35	Total about 4 introduced through migrant workers, including, Seventh-day Adventists.
Doubly-affiliated		2-aff			-440	0	-953		Evangelicals who are also baptized Roman Catholics or Congregationalists.
Totals				**40**	**3,522**	**4,050**	**7,620**		

Churches, members, growth, 1900-2025	*Congs*	*Adults*	*Affiliated*	*G%*	*Total denominations*	*6 Megablocs: O*	*R*	*A*	*P*	*I*	*m*
Total churches, members, and denominations (mid-1900)	2	140	300	3.79	1	0	0	0	1	0	0
Total churches, members, and denominations (mid-1970)	14	1,930	4,050	3.79	4	0	1	1	2	0	0
Total churches, members, and denominations (mid-1990)	20	3,200	7,000	2.77	12	0	1	1	8	1	1
Total churches, members, and denominations (mid-1995)	40	3,522	7,620	1.71	12	0	1	1	8	1	1
Total churches, members, and denominations (mid-2000)	50	3,900	8,341	1.82	12	0	1	1	8	1	1
Total churches, members, and denominations (mid-2025)	70	5,900	12,800	1.73	19	0	1	1	10	6	1

NOTES ON TABLE ABOVE
NATIONAL COUNCILS (Column 4, 5th letter).
C = Protestant Churches in Tuvalu & Kiribati.

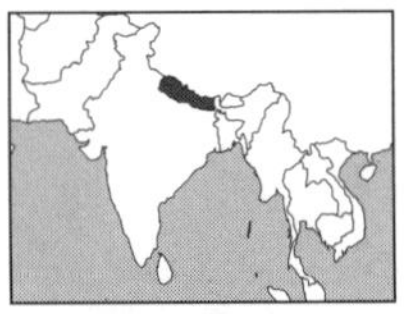

NEPAL

SECULAR DATA, AD 2000

STATE
Official name: Nepal Adhirajya (The Kingdom of Nepal).
Short name: Nepal. **Adjective of nationality:** Nepalese.
Flag: Red bordered in blue with white moon in upper triangle and white sun below.
Area: 147,181 sq. km. (56,827 sq. mi.).
Government: Constitutional monarchy with a bicameral parliament, since 1990 (absolute (de facto) or constitutional (de jure) monarchical Hindu state, since 1700s).
Legislature: National Council, 60 members; House of Representatives, 205 members.
Official language: Nepali.
Monetary unit: 1 Nepalese rupee (NRs) = 100 paisa (pice).
US$1= NRs 67.93.
Chief cities: KATHMANDU 520,281; Biratnagar (Wiratnagar) 153,801; Lalitpur (Patan) 131,326; Bhaktapur (Bhatgaon, Bhadgaon) 78,809.
Political divisions: 14 provinces.
Armed forces: 46,000.

DEMOGRAPHY
Population: 23,930,000.
Population density: 162.5/sq. km. (421.1/sq. mi.).
Under 15 years: 9,807,000.
Growth rate p.a.: 2.23% (births 31.85, deaths 9.53).
Mortality: Infant, per 1,000: 70.9, ; **Maternal per 100,000:** 1,500.0.
Life expectancy: 60 (male 60, female 60).
Household size: 5.5. **Floor area per person, sq.m:** 14.4.
Major languages: Nepali (Pahari), Tibetan, Hindi, English, Newari, Tharuhati, and 70 other minor languages.
Urban dwellers: 11.88%. **Urban growth rate p.a.:** 5.2%.
Labor force: 45%.

ETHNOLINGUISTIC PEOPLES
55.7% Nepalese (Eastern Pahari); 10.8% Maitili (Tirahutia); 7.8% Bhojpuri Bihari; 2.9% Newar; 2.6% Awadhi (Abadhi, Ambodhi).

ECONOMY
National income p.a. per person: US$200; **per family:** US$1,099.

EDUCATION
Adult literacy: 27% (male 40%, female 14%). **Schools:** 26,835.
Universities: 3. **School enrolment:** female/male: 57%/91%.

HEALTH
Access to health services: 35%. **Access to safe water:** 44%.
Hospitals: 114 (3 beds per 10,000). **Doctors:** 1,497.
Blind: 60,000. **Deaf:** 1,460,800. **Murder rate:** 2.
Lepers: 120,000. **Underweight prevalence under 5:** 49%.

LITERATURE
New book titles p.a.: 240 (10 p.a. per million). **Periodicals:** 4.
Newspapers: 28 dailies.

COMMUNICATION (per 1,000 people)
Phones: 3 **(4% mobile). Radios:** 29. **TV sets:** 3.
Daily newspaper circulation: 8. **Computers:** 4.

HUMAN LIFE AND LIBERTY (optimum condition=100.0%)
HDI: 34.7. **HSI:** 31.0. **HFI:** 10.0. **EFL:** 30.0.

Country status. A landlocked kingdom ringed by the Himalayan Mountains, Nepal is noted for the breath-taking beauty of its natural scenery. It is the only Hindu monarchy in the world. Its chief exports are clothing, carpets, and leather goods.

HUMAN LIFE AND LIBERTY

Human need and development. The majority of Nepalese are desperately poor, reflecting the subsistence level of the economy as a whole, the geographical isolation of the countryside, and the concentration of wealth in the hands of a privileged few. The quality of life is depressed by the unavailability of proper medical care, except in a few urban centers, poor diet, inadequate housing, and lack of social services. Floods, droughts, and landslides add to the general misery of the inhabitants periodically. Despite 4 major rivers and their tributaries, pure water is in short supply for both rich and poor, because public water supply systems making use of these resources are nonexistent. Poverty is most acute in the west, especially in the Piuthan district, about 145 miles west of Katmandu. On the other hand, the Sherpa settlements to the east are relatively prosperous. Most peasants live in dwellings of mud, wattle or stone, and produce all their food, but still must find money to buy commodities such as salt, cloth, and kerosene. Most farmers are heavily in debt to the Brahman moneylenders. Shortages of food develop in some areas from time to time because of drought or floods. Most people resort to traditional medicine and shamans or astrologers. Hospitals in general are crowded, ill-equipped, and understaffed. The annual per capita income is $200, average life expectancy is 60 and the percentage of illiterates in the population is 73.

Human rights and freedoms. The human rights situation has improved since 1990 when a new constitution guaranteeing a broad range of rights was passed. However, the constitutional provisions do not reflect the closed nature of society with built-in social and religious barriers and discriminatory practices. Political demonstrations are the occasion for excessive use of force by the police, and ending, generally, in the deaths of civilians. Prison conditions are inhuman, and beating and torture are historically part of law enforcement strategies. Laws under the Public Security Act allow arbitrary detention for extended periods. Freedoms of the press and expression exist on paper, but are circumscribed in practice. The Press and Publications Act provides for the licensing of publications and the granting of credentials to journalists. Both may be revoked if certain types of materials are published that, for example, foment disrespect toward the king, undermine security, peace and order, and promote religious and ethnic discord, or immorality. Both the untouchable Hindu castes and women as a whole suffer various forms of caste-engendered discrimination. The female literacy rate is only 14% compared to a male literacy rate of 40%. Wife beating is common as also dowry deaths.

Human environment. The major environmental problem is deforestation as a result of indiscriminate cutting of trees for firewood. The pressure on land is so great that vast areas are being denuded and converted to farmland and grazing areas or for housing. Saplings and branches of living trees are used as fodder for cattle. The timber industry also contributes to the problem. Deforestation promotes soil erosion, and millions of cubic feet of top soil are lost every year. Untreated sewage is dumped into the rivers and then used for drinking, bathing, and other purposes.

Country Table 1. Religious adherents in Nepal, AD 1900-2025.

Year / *Name*	*1900* *Adherents*	*%*	*1970* *Adherents*	*%*	*mid-1990* *Adherents*	*%*	*Annual change, 1990-2000* *Natural*	*Conversion*	*Total*	*Rate*	*mid-1995* *Adherents*	*%*	*mid-2000* *Adherents*	*%*	*mid-2025* *Adherents*	*%*
Hindus	3,410,000	77.0	9,100,150	80.3	14,502,600	77.3	398,539	-13,405	385,134	2.38	16,348,100	76.9	18,353,935	76.7	28,460,500	74.9
Ethnoreligionists	90,000	2.0	1,000,000	8.8	1,750,000	9.3	48,085	1,348	49,433	2.52	1,990,000	9.4	2,244,330	9.4	3,600,000	9.5
Buddhists	886,000	20.0	842,400	7.4	1,540,000	8.2	42,315	345	42,660	2.48	1,747,000	8.2	1,966,602	8.2	3,150,000	8.3
Muslims	44,000	1.0	331,500	2.9	710,000	3.8	19,509	2,123	21,632	2.70	820,000	3.9	926,316	3.9	1,500,000	4.0
Christians	**0**	**0.0**	**7,450**	**0.1**	**374,000**	**2.0**	**10,276**	**9,992**	**20,268**	**4.43**	**489,000**	**2.3**	**576,683**	**2.4**	**1,525,000**	**4.0**
PROFESSION																
crypto-Christians	0	0.0	5,000	0.0	150,000	0.8	4,122	5,878	10,000	5.24	200,000	0.9	250,000	1.0	700,000	1.8
professing Christians	**0**	**0.0**	**2,450**	**0.0**	**224,000**	**1.2**	**6,155**	**4,113**	**10,268**	**3.85**	**289,000**	**1.4**	**326,683**	**1.4**	**825,000**	**2.2**
AFFILIATION																
unaffiliated Christians	0	0.0	0	0.0	500	0.0	14	-2	12	2.21	562	0.0	622	0.0	1,000	0.0
affiliated Christians	**0**	**0.0**	**7,450**	**0.1**	**373,500**	**2.0**	**10,263**	**9,993**	**20,256**	**4.43**	**488,438**	**2.3**	**576,061**	**2.4**	**1,524,000**	**4.0**
Independents	0	0.0	5,690	0.1	360,000	1.9	9,892	9,208	19,100	4.35	469,846	2.2	551,000	2.3	1,450,000	3.8
Protestants	0	0.0	600	0.0	8,000	0.0	220	436	656	6.17	11,060	0.1	14,561	0.1	50,000	0.1
Roman Catholics	0	0.0	300	0.0	3,600	0.0	99	241	340	6.88	5,072	0.0	7,000	0.0	15,000	0.0
Orthodox	0	0.0	800	0.0	1,400	0.0	38	72	110	5.97	1,800	0.0	2,500	0.0	6,000	0.0
Marginal Christians	0	0.0	60	0.0	500	0.0	14	36	50	7.18	660	0.0	1,000	0.0	3,000	0.0
Trans-megabloc groupings																
Evangelicals	0	0.0	500	0.0	131,400	0.7	3,610	1,750	5,360	3.48	156,995	0.7	185,000	0.8	405,000	1.1
Pentecostals/Charismatics	0	0.0	3,700	0.0	320,000	1.7	8,793	10,007	18,800	4.73	427,137	2.0	508,000	2.1	1,300,000	3.4
Great Commission Christians	**0**	**0.0**	**5,200**	**0.1**	**343,600**	**1.8**	**9,441**	**10,533**	**19,974**	**4.69**	**426,000**	**2.0**	**543,340**	**2.3**	**1,435,000**	**3.8**
Nonreligious	0	0.0	30,000	0.3	60,000	0.3	1,649	9	1,658	2.47	68,000	0.3	76,577	0.3	160,000	0.4
Atheists	0	0.0	10,000	0.1	14,500	0.1	398	-158	240	1.54	15,100	0.1	16,898	0.1	30,000	0.1
Chinese folk-religionists	0	0.0	0	0.0	14,800	0.1	407	-217	190	1.22	15,200	0.1	16,701	0.1	30,000	0.1
Sikhs	0	0.0	0	0.0	7,100	0.0	195	-67	128	1.67	7,700	0.0	8,376	0.0	15,000	0.0
Baha'is	0	0.0	3,000	0.0	5,000	0.0	137	-21	116	2.11	5,500	0.0	6,163	0.0	11,000	0.0
Jains	0	0.0	2,500	0.0	4,000	0.0	110	-31	79	1.82	4,400	0.0	4,791	0.0	8,500	0.0
doubly-counted religionists	0	0.0	0	0.0	-210,000	-1.1	-5,770	82	-5,688	2.43	-238,000	-1.1	-266,881	-1.1	-480,000	-1.3
World A (unevangelized persons)	4,430,000	100.0	8,630,793	76.2	11,657,412	62.1	320,158	-198,380	121,678	1.00	12,295,084	57.8	12,874,340	53.8	18,092,760	47.6
World B (evangelized non-Christians)	0	0.0	2,688,257	23.7	6,740,588	35.9	185,416	188,488	373,904	4.51	8,487,687	39.9	10,478,977	43.8	18,392,240	48.4
World C (Christians)	0	0.0	7,450	0.1	374,000	2.0	10,276	9,992	20,268	4.43	489,000	2.3	576,683	2.4	1,525,000	4.0
Country's population	**4,430,000**	**100.0**	**11,326,500**	**100.0**	**18,772,000**	**100.0**	**515,850**	**0**	**515,850**	**2.46**	**21,271,772**	**100.0**	**23,930,000**	**100.0**	**38,010,000**	**100.0**

COLUMNS, ROWS.
For meanings and definitions, see Codebook (Part 3). Note that, by definition, total 'Christians' = professing + crypto-Christians, which also = affiliated + unaffiliated Christians, and also = Great Commission Christians + latent Christians. Percentages may not always total exactly, due to rounding.

CENSUSES.
22.VI.1961: 87.7% Hindus, 9.3% Buddhists, 3.0% Muslims (also 831 Jains, 458 Christians, 5,716 other religionists). **22.VI.1971:** 89.4% Hindus, 7.5% Buddhists, 3.0% Muslims, 0.1% other religionists (2,541 Jains, 5,836 others including Christians). **1981:** 89.5% Hindus, 5.3% Buddhists, 2.7% Muslims, 2.41% other religionists, 0.06% Jains, 0.03% Christians (3,891 persons). **1991:** 86.6% Hindus, 7.8% Buddhists, 3.55% Muslims, 1.7% Kirats, 0.17% Christians (31,280 persons), 0.14% other religionists, 0.04% Jains.

NOTES ON RELIGIONS
ATHEISTS. 2 parties: Communist Party of Nepal/Right, Communist Party of Nepal/Left (both proscribed 1960; internal factions; pro-Chinese).
BAHA'IS. Rapid growth from 2 local spiritual assemblies (1964) to 21 (1973); mainly Indians, formerly Hindus and a few ex-Christians.
BUDDHISTS. Both Mahayana and Tentrayana (Tantrism, Lamaism) have large followings, mostly in the north.
CRYPTO-CHRISTIANS. Nepali believers in the legal or recognized (expatriate) churches, and also in organized Nepali churches; together with organized and unorganized isolated radio and correspondence course believers.
ETHNORELIGIONISTS. Animists among the hill tribes.
MUSLIMS. Sunnis, mainly expatriate traders, also settlers, from India.
INDEPENDENTS. In 19 groupings in 1995 (see Table 2); mostly Nepali indigenous Christians and isolated radio believers, with 5 denominations from India.
NONRELIGIOUS. Mainly Nepali and Indian intellectuals also Europeans, also Nepali communist sympathizers.
PROFESSING CHRISTIANS. Europeans and some of the Indian Christians only ; Nepali believers are not recognized by the state and so exist as crypto-Christians.

Great Commission Instrument Panel: status of Nepal (for explanation see start of Part 4)

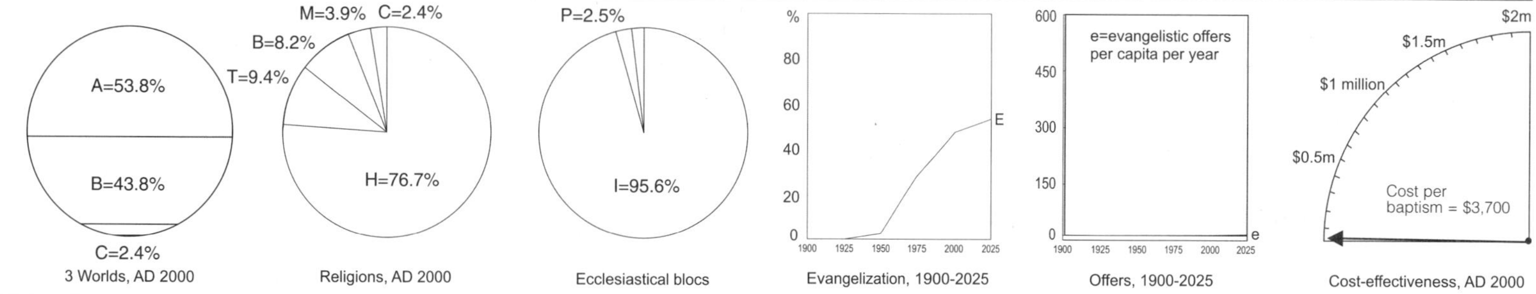

NON-CHRISTIAN RELIGIONS

Hinduism is the state religion and the religion of the great majority of the population. The king of Nepal is considered by the Hindu faithful to be a reincarnation of Vishnu. An unusual feature is the fertility cult revolving around the worship of the mother goddess Kumari in the form of a human child. This is in fact a cult of female energy as the source of the universe, and the king of Nepal is Kumari's trustee. The human goddess is possessed by Kumari only after her first menstruation when she becomes an ordinary human being, and a successor is then chosen.

Buddhists. *Left.* Bodhnath Stupa, pilgrimage center. *Right.* Pilgrim turns prayer wheels.

Mahayana Buddhism and ***Tantrism*** (Lamaism) have large followings in Nepal, mostly in the northern regions bordering Tibet. The founder of Buddhism, Gautama Buddha, was born about 567 BC in Lumbini near Padaria village in Nepal's Tarai district.

Islam is professed by a minority of Indian settlers and foreign traders.

Traditional tribal religions are still found among the hill peoples.

CHRISTIANITY

INDIGENOUS CHURCHES. Churches indigenous to India have been working in Nepal for many years. The first of all missionary societies to arrive was the Peace of Christ Brotherhood of the Mar Thoma Syrian Church, in 1952. The Assemblies (Jehova Shamma) also have work. Both have been expected to confine their ministries to Indians. Since foreign missions are not permitted to open churches among Nepalis, Nepali Christians organized in 1966 their own indigenous body, the Church of Christ in Nepal, which they keep separate from the missions and unrelated to them. This church is a loosely-knit organization consisting in 1995 of approximately 6,000 baptized members in 60 small congregations with a number of house churches scattered across the land. In addition to baptized Nepalis, there are many unbaptized believers, more fringe members who would call themselves Christians, and a sizeable number of secret believers. When Gurkhas served in the British Army in Malaysia, Singapore and elsewhere, many became Christians and on their return to Nepal moved back to remote areas. The church owes its origin to a Nepalese army officer, Prem Pradhan, who was converted to Christianity in India and returned to Nepal in 1959. His evangelistic activity led to conversions and 8 baptisms in Tansen in 1960, which being illegal resulted in the 9 of them being imprisoned for nearly 5 years. More conversions were recorded while he was in prison, and since his release he has continued to preach and baptize.

The largest group in Nepal is the National Churches Fellowship which started in 1951 growing from 1,000 members in 1970 to 80,000 by 1995.

Another independent group is the Nepali Christian Congregation, a well-attended church in Kathmandu.

PROTESTANT CHURCHES. Over 50 Protestant foreign missionary societies have been involved in education, medical, and community development work since the early 1950s. In 1954 the United Mission to Nepal opened its first medical center in Kathmandu. Beginning as a co-operative venture of 10 boards, the mission in 1990 had 300 missionaries, with over 700 national staff in its institutions, and was supported in work grants, capital grants, and personnel by 30 societies from 15 different countries. The mission operates 7 primary schools, one middle and 3 high schools (a girls' high school in Kathmandu with 630 students, a boys' boarding school in Pokhara and a third high school in Gorkha district), 5 hospitals, a leprosarium, an extensive public health program, a nurses' training school, a training school for auxiliary nurses and midwives, an industrial training center and hydro-

Country summary. **Worlds A, B, C by ethnolinguistic peoples, cities, and major civil divisions in Nepal.**

PEOPLES

World	Num	Pop 2000	C%	Christians	E%	U%	Unevangelized
A	101	9,266,674	0.19	17,599	26	74	6,822,905
B	12	14,650,651	3.74	548,207	59	41	6,043,845
C	5	13,162	77.91	10,254	100	0	29
Total	**118**	**23,930,487**	**2.41**	**576,060**	**46**	**54**	**12,866,779**

CITIES

World	Num	Pop 2000	C%	Christians	E%	U%	Unevangelized
A	3	752,891	3.00	22,593	48	52	389,975
B	0	0	0.00	0	0	0	0
C	0	0	0.00	0	0	0	0
Total	**3**	**752,891**	**3.00**	**22,593**	**48**	**52**	**389,975**

CIVIL DIVISIONS

World	Num	Pop 2000	C%	Christians	E%	U%	Unevangelized
A	14	23,930,490	2.41	576,061	46	54	12,866,777
B	0	0	0.00	0	0	0	0
C	0	0	0.00	0	0	0	0
Total	**14**	**23,930,490**	**2.41**	**576,061**	**46**	**54**	**12,866,777**

electric scheme (Butwal Technical Institute), and Nepal's first plywood factory. The Gorkha Community Service project, with heavy emphasis on agriculture, was taken over by the government in 1971.

Other foreign missions, engaging mostly in medical work, include the following: Seventh-day Adventists, with a hospital at Bhanipa 15 miles from the capital; International Nepal Fellowship (which combines the work of the Nepal Evangelistic Band, International Christian Fellowship, and Worldwide Evangelization Crusade) with a hospital, a leprosarium (Green Pastures) and several dispensaries in the Pokhara area; TEAM (Evangelical Alliance Mission) with a hospital in the extreme west at Dandeldhura; Operation Mobilization with 12 missionaries engaged in literature work; Summer Institute of Linguistics (Wycliffe Bible Translators); and a children's mission from over the border in India, Gorakhpur Nurseries, with a clinic, and dispensaries at Semri and Pyersingh run by independent missionaries.

Small Protestant congregations, consisting mostly of expatriates, are sponsored by several of these missions, in addition to Unitarian and Assemblies of God groups and the united English-speaking Protestant Church in Kathmandu.

CATHOLIC CHURCH. Nepal is part of the Catholic diocese of Patna in India. In Nepal in 1990 there were about 5,000 Catholics, some among foreign personnel with embassies and aid groups, and some from India, Pakistan, and Bangladesh. Among those from India are about 30 Nepali-speaking families from the Darjeeling area of West Bengal. There are no Catholic parish priests, sisters, brothers, catechists or catechumens; but 15 American-born Jesuit priests, of whom 5 are now Nepali citizens, came in 1951 at the government's invitation to open a school. There are also 14 sisters from the Institute of the Blessed Virgin Mary (Mary Ward, German branch), 10 of whom are Indians, who came to Nepal in 1954 and are involved in education. Two Jesuits, one with a doctorate in Nepali history, live and teach at the University Research Centre, doing research in Himalayan religions, particularly Buddhism and Tantrism. All activities of Catholic priests and sisters are restricted to Kathmandu Valley, although they are allowed to minister to foreign Catholics in other parts of Nepal.

The Holy See has diplomatic relations with Nepal and in AD 2000 is represented to government and the Catholic hierarchy by a pro-nuncio residing in New Delhi.

Independents. *Top.* Church in Letang. *Lower.* Easter March with banner 'Christ is Risen'.

Renewal movements. In the 1990s the Pentecostal/Charismatic Renewal continued to spread rapidly across most older churches, and numbered over 508,000 adherents (of whom 1% Pentecostals, <1% Charismatics, and 99% Independents).

Indigenous missions. Although Nepalese Christians have sent only a few missionaries outside of the country, significant numbers have been involved in home missions work among the various peoples of Nepal.

Hindus. Krishna temple square during Hindu festival in Patan.

CHURCH AND STATE

The 1967 constitution, Article 3, states that Nepal is 'a monarchical Hindu State', and in fact it is the world's only Hindu kingdom. According to Article 14, 'Every person may profess and practice his own religion as handed down from ancient times, provided that no person shall be entitled to convert another person from one religion to another'. The baptism of Hindu converts is thus illegal, and the United Mission to Nepal has strictly adhered to observance of the law since their arrival. However, Nepali Christians themselves have baptized converts, resulting in imprisonments. In 1973, 7 Christians in Pokhara were given 3-month prison sentences for changing their ancestral faith to Christianity, but the government generally overlooks the law. In fact, prosecution takes place only if a citizen makes a definite charge against a newly-baptized Christian. Foreign residents of Nepal are free to practice their own religions but not to engage in proselytism. The Christian witness of missionaries is restricted to educational and medical work and to pastoral activities among those foreign Christians.

There is no separate government ministry in charge of religious affairs, although the government-supported Guthi Corporation (Guthi Sansthan) looks after the maintenance of Hindu temples, religious buildings, and their landed property.

In 1972, a proposition to liberalize the constitution with respect to religion was discussed in parliament but finally rejected. The prohibition against converting Nepalese is directed not only at Christianity but also at Islam.

In August 1973 the government nationalized the administration of 15 hospitals (2 being leprosaria) maintained by Christian missionaries, but their foreign personnel continue to work under the control of the state. In 1976, the government moved against the Wycliffe Bible Translators, ordering its Summer Institute of Linguistics to withdraw its 90 overseas workers.

In 1978, the government requested missionary societies to move into areas previously closed to them.

In 1991, religious freedom was granted for all to practice and profess their faith but not to proselytize others.

BROADCASTING AND MEDIA

IBRA-produced radio programs can be heard on local radio channels. Programs in Hindi and Nepali can be received from FEBA (Seychelles), and shortwave programs from KNLS have had responses. AWR's Banepa studio produces Nepali-language programs.

The 'Jesus' Film has been shown to 3.3 million people, mainly by film teams. Videocassettes have also been useful.

Coordinating plans for nationwide Every Home Crusade.

INTERDENOMINATIONAL ORGANIZATIONS

Nepali and foreign Christians, and almost all missionaries, participate in the Nepali-run Nepal Christian Fellowship, which operates an annual Bible school and evangelistic trips. Among missions, the United Mission to Nepal is supported by more foreign societies than any other co-operative missionary venture in the world. Difficulties confronting missionary and evangelistic work have caused these missions to adopt a united front, but there are still other missions not actively co-operating.

FUTURE TRENDS AND PROSPECTS

Christianity is expected to grow steadily to 4.0% by 2025, primarily among Nepalese (Eastern Pahari) and a few minority peoples.

Christianity will likely grow to 6% of the population before AD 2050 and could reach 10% soon after. Other significant increases may be expected among Buddhists and Muslims, collectively growing to over 15% by the end of the 21st century.

BIBLIOGRAPHY

A heart for Nepal: the Dr. Helen Huston story. G. W. Hankins. Winnipeg: Windflower Communications, 1992. 249p.

'A select bibliography of works on the Tamangs of Nepal,' A. Höfer, *Bulletin of the Nepal Studies Association*, 10 (1976), 34–36.

'An annotated bibliography of the Thakalis,' M. Vinding & K. B. Bhattachan, *Contributions to Nepalese studies*, 12, 3 (1985), 1–24. (140 titles).

Atlas of South Asia. A. K. Dutt & M. M. Geib. Boulder, CO, and London: Westview Press, 1987. 255p.

Better than the witch doctor. M. Cundy. Crowborough, UK: Monarch, 1994. 288p.

Bibliographie du Népal, volume 1: sciences humaines—références en langues européenes. L. Boulnois & H. Millot. Paris: Centre Nationale de la Recherche Scientifique, 1969. 289p.

Bibliography of Nepal. K. M. Malla. Kathmandu: Royal Nepal Academy, 1975. 529p.

Buddhist monasteries of Nepal: a survey of the bahas. J. K. Locke. Kathmandu: Sahayogi, 1985. 542p.

Buddhist traditions and culture of the Kathmandu valley (Nepal). K. Vaidya. Kathmandu: Sajha, 1986. 299p.

Christian settlements in Nepal during the eighteenth century. F. Vannini. Agra: Capuchin Ashram, 1977. 167p.

'Consultations with Himalayan gods: a study of oracular reli-

gion and alternative values in Hindu Jumla.' J. G. Campbell. Ph.D. dissertation, Columbia University, New York, 1978. 560p. (Deals with both Brahminical Hinduism and spirit possession).
Cultural patterns and economic change (anthropological study of Dhimals of Nepal). R. R. Regmi. Delhi: Motilal Banarsidass, 1985. 218p.
'Culture and religion: its historical background,' P. R. Sharma, in *Nepal in perspective*, p.65–77. P. S. J. Rana & K. P. Malla (eds). Kathmandu: Centre for Economic Development and Administration, 1973.
Dictionary of Himalayan people. J. C. Regmi & S. Shiwakothi. *Nepal Antiquary*, nos. 50-55. Kathmandu: Office of the Nepal Antiquary, 1983. 220p.
'Dieux souverains et rois dévots dans l'ancienne royauté de la vallée du Népal,' G. Toffin, *L'homme*, 26, 3 (1986), 71–95. (Deals with Newar kingship).
Don't let the goats eat the loquat trees: the extraordinary adventures of a surgeon in Nepal. T. Hale. London: MARC Europe, 1986. 257p.
'Ethnographic notes on the Tamangs of Nepal,' C. von Fürer–Haimendorf, *Eastern anthropologist*, 9 (3–4 March 1956), 166–77.
First fruits of the forest: amongst the Tharus of North India. B. Pritchard. London: Regions Beyond Missionary Union, 1962. 14p.
Guide to enjoying Nepalese festivals: an introductory survey of religious celebration in Kathmandu Valley. J. Goodman. Kathmandu: Kali, 1981. 118p.
Gurkhas. C. J. Morris. 2nd ed. *Handbooks for the Indian Army.* Delhi: Government of India, 1936; reprint, B. R. Publishing, 1985. 182p.
Himalayan pilgrimage, a study of Tibetan religion by a traveller through western Nepal. D. L. Snellgrove. 2nd ed. Oxford, UK: Bruno Cassirer, 1981. 304p.
'Hinduism and Buddhism in the Kathmandu Valley (Nepal),' D. N. Gellner, in *The world's religions*, p.739–55. S. Sutherland et al. (eds). London: Croom Helm, 1988. (Deals with Newars).
Introducing Nepal & the United Mission to Nepal. E. H. Glassman. , 1987. 80p.
Le paysan limbu, sa maison et ses champs. P. Sagant. *Le monde d'outre mer passé et présent*, 1st series, 41. Paris: Mouton with Ecole des Hautes Etudes en Sciences Sociales, 1976. 404p.
Lepcha, my vanishing tribe. A. R. Foning. Delhi: Sterling, 1987. 314p. (Treats religion).
Les Gurungs—une population himalayenne du Népal. B. Pignède. Ed., L. Dumont. *Le monde d'outre mer passé et present*, 3rd series, 21. Paris: Mouton, 1966. 414p.
Les Tamangs du Népal—usages et religion. B. Steinman. Paris: Edition Recherche sur les Civilisations, 1987. 310p.
Life among the Magars. G. Shepherd. Kathmandu: Sahayogi, 1982. 269p.
Living stones of the Himalayas. T. Hale. Crowborough: MARC, 1994. 255p.
Maîtres et possédés: les dieux, les rites et l'organisation sociale chez les Tharu. G. Krauskopff. Paris: Editions du Centre Nationale de la Recherche Scientifique, 1989. 276p.
'Mission and evangelism in Nepal.' C. Retnadas. M.T.S. thesis, Garrett-Evangelical Theological Seminary, Evanston, IL, 1990. 156p.
'Monk, householder and priest: Newar Buddhism and its hierarchy of ritual.' D. N. Gellner. D.Phil. dissertation, Oxford University, Oxford, UK, 1987. 586p.
Nepal. J. Whelpton. *World bibliographical series*, vol. 38. Oxford, UK: CLIO Press, 1990. 322p. (See especially 'Religion,' p.87–99).
Nepal and the Gospel of God. J. Lindell. Kathmandu, Nepal: United Mission to Nepal, 1979.
Nepal bibliography. H. B. Wood. Tillamook, OR: America—Nepal Education Foundation, 1957. 108p.
Nepal et ses populations. M. Gaborieau. *Pays et Populations.* Brussels: Editions Complexe, 1978. 308p.
Nepal: on the potter's wheel. Kathmandu, Nepal: United Mission to Nepal, 1970. 50p.
Nepal: the early years. M. F. Foyle. 2nd ed. London: Bible and Medical Missionary Fellowship, [1961]. 48p.
Nepal, the land of festivals (religious, cultural, social and historical festivals). T. C. Majupuria & S. P. Gupta. New Delhi: S. Chand, 1981. 152p.
Nepalese customs and manners. K. Lall. Kathmandu: Ratna Pustak Bhandar, 1976. 59p.
'Newar Buddhist initiation rites,' J. K. Locke, *Contributions to Nepalese studies*, 2, 2 (1975), 1–23.
'Observations on the reform of Buddhism in Nepal,' H. Bechert & J. V. Hartmann, *Journal of the Nepal Research Centre*, 8 (1988), 1–30.
On the threshold of three closed lands: the guild outpost in the Eastern Himalayas. J. A. Graham. Edinburgh: T & T Clark, 1897. 166p. (Church of Scotland work in Tibet, Nepal, and Bhutan).
Order in paradox: myth, ritual, and exchange among Nepal's Tamang. D. H. Homberg. Ithaca, NY and London: Cornell University Press, 1989. 283p.
Religion in Nepal. No. 15 in section 13, *Indian religions*, in *Iconography of religions.* K. R. van Kooij. Leiden: E. J. Brill, 1978. 33p.
'Research on Nepal 1975–1983: a bibliography,' K. Seeland, H. Fritz & R. Olsen, in *Recent research on Nepal*, p.219–351. K. Seeland (ed). *Shriftenreihe—Internationales Asienforum*, Band 3. Munich: Weltforum, 1986. (2,300 titles).
Rhythms of a Himalayan village. H. R. Downs. San Francisco: Harper & Row, 1980. 228p. (Deals with Sherpa religion).
'Ritual paradoxes in Nepal: comparative perspectives on Tamang religion,' D. Holmberg, *Journal of Asian studies*, 43 (August 1984), 197–222.
Sherpas through their rituals. S. Ortner. *Cambridge studies in cultural systems*, no. 2. Cambridge, UK: Cambridge University Press, 1978. 195p.
Société et religion chez les Newar du Népal. G. Toffin. Paris: Centre Nationale de la Recherche Scientifique, 1984. 668p.
Spirit possession in the Nepal Himalayas. J. T. Hitchcock & R. L. Jones. Trans., H. L. Beegun. Warminster, UK: Aris & Philips, 1976. 401p.
Still in Nepal. E. W. Oliver. London: RBMU, 1961.
Tamang ritual texts, I: preliminary studies in the folk–religion of an ethnic minority in Nepal. A. Höfer. *Beiträge zur Südasienforschung*, vol. 65. Wiesbaden, Germany: Franz Steiner, 1981. 184p.
'Tharus of Dang: rites de passage and festivals,' D. P. Rajaure, *Kailash*, 9, 2–3 (1982), 177–258.
'Tharus of Dang: Tharu religion,' D. P. Rajaure, *Kailash*, 9, 1 (1982), 61–96.
'Tharus of Dang: the people and the social context,' D. P. Rajaure, *Kailash*, 8, 3–4 (1981), 155–82.
The cult of Kumari—virgin worship in Nepal. M. R. Allen. 2nd ed. Kathmandu: Madhab Lal Maharjan, 1986. 114p.
The Gurkhas. B. Farwell. New York: W. W. Norton, 1984. 317p.
The Gurungs of Nepal. D. A. Messerschmidt. Warminster, UK: Aris & Philips, 1976. 151p.
'The history of the Church in Nepal.' C. L. Perry. Intercultural studies graduate project, Wheaton College, Wheaton, IL, 1990. 177p.
'The history of the Thakaalis according to the Thakaali tradition,' S. Gauchan & M. Vinding, *Kailash*, 5, 2 (1977), 97–184.
The Indian Buddhist iconography, mainly based on the Sadhanamala and cognate tantric texts of rituals. B. Bhattacharya. 2nd ed. Calcutta: K. L. Mukhopadhyay, 1959. 478p.
The Nepal festivals: with some articles enquiring into Nepalese arts, religion and culture. D. K. Deep. Kathmandu: Ratna Pustak Bhandar, [1982]. 128p.
'The people,' D. B. Bista, in *Nepal in perspective*, p.35–45. P. S. J. Rana & K. P. Malla (eds). Kathmandu: Centre for Economic Development and Administration, 1973.
The people of Nepal. D. B. Bista. 5th ed. Kathmandu: Ratna Pustak Bhandar, 1987. 210p.
The people of the stones: the Chepangs of central Nepal. N. Rai. Kathmandu: Centre for Nepal and Asian Studies, 1985. 125p.
'The Raute: notes on a nomadic hunting and gathering tribe of Nepal,' J. Reinhard, *Kailash*, 2, 4 (1974), 233–71.
The sacred complex in Janakpur—Indological, sociological, anthropological and philosophical study of Hindu civilization. M. Jha. *Social Studies*, no. 1. Allahabad, India: United Publishers, 1971. 152p. (Southern province of Nepal).
The Sherpas of Nepal—Buddhist highlanders. C. von Fürer–Haimendorf. 1972; reprint, New Delhi: Sterling, 1979. 298p.
'Theravada Buddhism in Nepal,' R. Kloppenberg, *Kailash*, 5, 4 (1977), 301–321.

Country Table 2. **Organized churches and denominations in Nepal.**

Official name (bold type = church with over 10% of all affiliated) 1	*Begun* 2	*Type* 3	*Counc* 4	*Congs* 5	*Adults* 6	*Affiliated 1970* 7	*Affiliated 1995* 8	*G%* 9	*Names, notes, and other statistics* (see Codebook, Part 3) 10
Agape Fellowship	1982	I-3cI	.....	100	9,000	–	15,000	7.69	M=INF. Linked with Nepali Christian Congregation. Charismatics. 1994, Toronto Blessing.
Asian Outreach Churches	c1990	I-3cI	x....	3	50	–	100	20.00	New emphasis by M=AO(Hong Kong) on church planting. Based in Kathmandu.
Assemblies of God	1956	P-Pe2	Zf...	70	2,000	100	4,000	15.90	c1960,M=AoG(USA) had a station for a time. 1971, re-opened; 2 missionaries.
Assemblies (El Shaddai)	1972	I-CBr	x...C	21	1,200	60	2,400	4.35	*Jehovah Shammah.* Missionaries from India (Brother Bakht Singh); HQ Hyderabad, AP.
Baptist Association of Churches	c1975	P-Bap	T....	5	100	–	200	5.00	M=Mizo Baptists, Nagaland Baptists, FMB-SBC.
Bethel Church	c1991	I-3cI	.....	10	3,000	–	5,000	25.00	An indigenous Nepali church with large outreach ministries.
Brethren in Christ	1955	P-Men	.....	10	300	50	500	9.65	*BiCC.* Work mainly among Santal and Uraon, few Nepali. 9f.
Calvary Churches	1976	I-3pI	....E	240	8,000	–	20,000	5.26	HQ Katmandu. Heavy persecution, underground until 1990. Expansion in west. Many schools.
Catholic Church (D Patna)	1951	R-Lat	P.F..	30	3,000	300	5,072	11.98	70% French, Germans, Indians, 30% Nepali-speaking citizens. M=SJ. 5n,10x,14w. 4 schools.
Christ Groups	c1985	I-3hI	xE...	1,978	20,200	–	60,300	10.00	House cell churches formed through M=EHC campaigns in areas without churches.
Church of Christ in Nepal	1952	I-Non	C	60	3,000	2,000	6,000	4.49	*Mashi Mandali.* Entirely Nepali-run though begun as Mar Thoma Ch. 50% Nepali, 30% Indian.
Church of Christ	c1983	I-Non	.....	3	100	–	200	8.33	Indigenous Nondenominationalists.
Church of God	c1990	P-Pe3	.....	1	50	–	100	20.00	M=COG(USA). Holiness Pentecostals.
Churches of Nepal	1960	I-3cI	.....	122	17,200	200	30,000	22.19	Among Western Tamang (5,000 members), Newari, Chepang, Dhanwar.
Evangelical Alliance Mission	c1980	P-Eva	.....	3	115	–	210	6.67	M=TEAM. Noncharismatic, mainly supports churches in INF, NCF.
Evangelical Christian Alliance of Nepal	1985	I-3pI	ZF...	30	800	–	1,500	10.00	*Church of the Foursquare Gospel.* Begun as indigenous group, later called in M=ICFG(USA).
Ev Christian Fellowship of Nepal	c1985	I-3cI	.....	90	2,000	–	3,000	10.00	Network of churches. M=Christian Aid (USA), et alia. 1p.
Evangelical Convention Church	c1990	I-Eva	.....	2	30	–	100	20.00	*ECC.* Indian mission from ECC in Manipur. Several evangelists in eastern Nepal.
Evangelical Friends Church	1994	P-Qua	.....	2	30	–	50	100.00	Quaker mission from USA.
Evangelical Lutheran Ch in Nepal	1958	P-Lut	.....	5	300	100	600	7.43	*Nepal Mission.* M=NELC(India).
Hidden Hindu believers in Christ	c1980	I-Hin	.....	800	120,000	–	210,000	6.67	Converted Hindus who choose to stay in Hinduism as witnesses to Christ.
India Evangelical Church	c1980	I-Eva	.....	2	100	–	200	6.67	*IEC. New Life League.* M=IEM(India).
Isolated BCC believers	c1985	I-3hI	.....	20	400	–	600	10.00	*BCC*=Bible correspondence courses: M=Nepal EHC,NGOC,ICI,NBCI.
Isolated radio believers	1955	I-3rI	.....	300	6,000	600	10,000	11.91	T=6000 (Bible Correspondence Institute, India; FEBC,TWR,IBRA,GFA,FEBA,ICI,&c).
Jehovah's Witnesses	c1965	m-Jeh	x....	2	63	10	600	17.79	*Watch Tower, IBSA.* M=JWs from India, Europe, America. 47Y.
Kathmandu Bible College Chs	c1985	I-3cI	.....	20	500	–	1,000	10.00	Indigenous charismatics.
Korean Presbyterian Churches	c1990	I-Ref	.....	5	300	–	500	20.00	*KPC.* M=Hosanna. In Kathmandu and East Nepal.
Mar Thoma Syrian Ch (D Bahya Kerala)	1952	I-ReO	xwe.C	1	200	100	400	5.70	M=Peace of Christ Brotherhood, MTS Evangelistic Association (HQ Tiruvalla, India). In NCF.
Methodist Ch in Kathmandu	c1980	P-Met	.....	1	50	–	100	6.67	Related to Methodist Church of South Asia.
National Churches Fell of Nepal	1951	I-3cI	.E...	200	50,000	1,000	80,000	19.16	*NCF/N* (1960), formerly Nepal Christian Fellowship. M=INF,CCCI,NEB.
Nepal Baptist Church Council	1994	P-Bap	.....	50	500	–	1,000	100.00	Mainline Baptists.
Nepali Christian Congregation	1956	I-3cI	C	4	1,000	300	2,000	7.88	*Gyaneshwar Church.* Begun by a Nepali Lepcha. Packed services; 95% Nepali.
New Apostolic Church	c1990	I-3aX	x....	20	900	–	1,396	20.00	*NAC/NAK.* M=Neuapostolische Kirche (India). World HQ Zurich.
Orthodox Syrian Ch of the East	c1960	O-SyM	D....	1	1,000	800	1,800	3.30	*OSCE.* Long-time passive presence as agricultural and other assistants. Malayalis.
Presbyterian Free Church	c1990	I-Ref	.....	2	86	–	150	20.00	*EPC,* based in Kalimpong, India. M=Himalayan Evangelical Fellowship. In eastern Nepal.
Protestant Internat Ch in Kathmandu	c1969	P-com	C	1	700	300	1,000	4.93	English-speaking union church, for expatriates; Indians, British, USA, Germans.
Seventh-day Adventist Church	1954	P-Adv	x....	8	400	50	800	11.73	*SDA.* Under Northern Union (India), Southern Asia Division. Hospital, Bhanipa. 6f.
Unitarian Universalist Assoc of K	c1968	m-Unt	.....	3	30	50	60	0.73	K=Kathmandu. Links with Unitarian Universalist Association (USA).
Other independent charismatic chs	c1950	I-3cI	....	100	10,000	1,430	20,000	11.13	Independent locally-founded churches not in NCF; M=Nagaland Revival Ch.
Other Protestant churches	c1980	P-	.....	25	1,600	–	2,500	6.67	Total about 10, including UMN chapels (300f), CNI, GELC, Mizo Baptist Ch, EPC, Mizo PC.
Totals				**4,350**	**264,304**	**7,450**	**488,438**		

Churches, members, growth, 1900-2025	*Congs*	*Adults*	*Affiliated*	*G%*	*Total denominations*	*6 Megablocs:* *O*	*R*	*A*	*P*	*I*	*m*
Total churches, members, and denominations (mid-1900)	0	0	0	0.00	0	0	0	0	0	0	0
Total churches, members, and denominations (mid-1970)	100	3,524	7,450	25.00	19	1	1	0	5	10	2
Total churches, members, and denominations (mid-1990)	4,000	202,000	373,500	21.62	53	1	1	0	20	29	2
Total churches, members, and denominations (mid-1995)	4,350	264,304	488,438	5.51	55	1	1	0	21	30	2
Total churches, members, and denominations (mid-2000)	4,700	312,000	576,061	3.36	57	1	1	0	22	31	2
Total churches, members, and denominations (mid-2025)	15,000	825,000	1,524,000	3.97	147	1	1	0	40	100	5

NOTES ON TABLE ABOVE
NATIONAL COUNCILS (Column 4, 5th letter).
C = Nepal Christian Fellowship (NCF).
E = National Churches Fellowship of Nepal (NCFN).

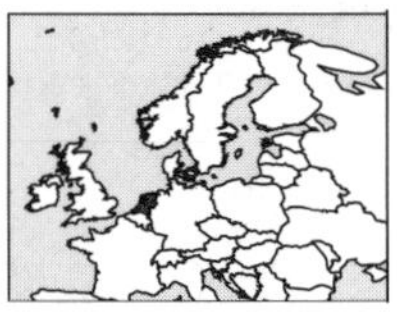

NETHERLANDS

SECULAR DATA, AD 2000

STATE
Official name: Het Koninkrijk der Nederlanden (The Kingdom of the Netherlands).
Short name: Netherlands. **Adjective of nationality:** Netherlands, a Netherlander.
Flag: Red, white, and blue stripes.
Area: 41,526 sq. km. (16,033 sq. mi.).
Government: Constitutional monarchy, since 1815 (1581 republic 1806 Napoleonic kingdom, 1815 independent monarchy).
Legislature: First Chamber, 75 members; Second Chamber, 150 members.
Official language: Dutch.
Monetary unit: 1 Netherlands guilder (f.) = 100 cents. **US$1=** f. 1.88.
Chief cities: AMSTERDAM 1,149,000; Rotterdam 1,078,000; 'S-GRAVENHAGE (The Hague) 816,843; Utrecht 557,612; Eindhoven 406,305.
Political divisions: 12 provinces.
Armed forces: 71,000.

DEMOGRAPHY
Population: 15,786,000.
Population density: 380.1/sq. km. (984.5/sq. mi.).
Under 15 years: 2,859,000.
Growth rate p.a.: 0.20% (births 10.34, deaths 9.00).
Mortality: Infant, per 1,000: 5.7, ; **Maternal per 100,000:** 12.0.
Life expectancy: 78 (male 76, female 81).
Household size: 2.4. **Floor area per person, sq.m:** 48.0.
Major languages: Dutch, Frisian, Turkish, Creole, Indonesian, Arabic, German, French, English, Chinese (Cantonese), Hindustani, Sranang Tongo (Surinamese).
Urban dwellers: 89.35%. **Urban growth rate p.a.:** 0.4%.
Labor force: 42%.

ETHNOLINGUISTIC PEOPLES
81.0% Dutch; 5.0% Frisian (Western Frisian); 3.7% Groningen Dutch; 1.4% Surinamese Creole; 1.2% Turk.

ECONOMY
National income p.a. per person: US$24,000; **per family:** US$57,600.

EDUCATION
Adult literacy: 100% (male 100%, female 100%). **Schools:** 10,888.
Universities: 206. **School enrolment:** female/male: 108%/112%.

HEALTH
Access to health services: 85%. **Access to safe water:** 100%.
Hospitals: 236 (57 beds per 10,000). **Doctors:** 39,069.
Blind: 8,000. **Deaf:** 952,300. **Murder rate:** 24.
Lepers: 500.

LITERATURE
New book titles p.a.: 35,520 (2,250 p.a. per million). **Periodicals:** 514. **Newspapers:** 46 dailies.

COMMUNICATION (per 1,000 people)
Phones: 525 (16% mobile). **Radios:** 775. **TV sets:** 495.
Daily newspaper circulation: 299. **Computers:** 450.

REFUGEES
Alien refugees from other countries: 39,300.

HUMAN LIFE AND LIBERTY (optimum condition=100.0%)
HDI: 94.0. **HSI:** 98.0. **HFI:** 92.5. **EFL:** 63.0.

Country Table 1. **Religious adherents in the Netherlands, AD 1900-2025.**

Year	1900		1970		mid-1990		Annual change, 1990-2000				mid-1995		mid-2000		mid-2025	
Name	Adherents	%	Adherents	%	Adherents	%	Natural	Conversion	Total	Rate	Adherents	%	Adherents	%	Adherents	%
Christians	**4,998,700**	**96.5**	**11,650,600**	**89.4**	**12,128,500**	**81.1**	**67,624**	**-11,080**	**56,544**	**0.46**	**12,485,000**	**80.8**	**12,693,943**	**80.4**	**12,199,000**	**77.3**
PROFESSION																
professing Christians	**4,998,700**	**96.5**	**11,650,600**	**89.4**	**12,128,500**	**81.1**	**67,624**	**-11,080**	**56,544**	**0.46**	**12,485,000**	**80.8**	**12,693,943**	**80.4**	**12,199,000**	**77.3**
AFFILIATION																
unaffiliated Christians	56,320	1.1	1,354,251	10.4	2,259,500	15.1	12,603	2,556	15,159	0.65	2,328,284	15.1	2,411,090	15.3	2,361,500	15.0
affiliated Christians	**4,942,380**	**95.4**	**10,296,349**	**79.0**	**9,869,000**	**66.0**	**55,021**	**-13,636**	**41,385**	**0.41**	**10,156,716**	**65.7**	**10,282,853**	**65.1**	**9,837,500**	**62.3**
Roman Catholics	1,816,770	35.1	5,366,919	41.2	5,350,000	35.8	29,841	-19,841	10,000	0.19	5,491,444	35.5	5,450,000	34.5	5,200,000	33.0
Protestants	3,113,730	60.1	4,688,965	36.0	4,080,000	27.3	22,758	-6,873	15,885	0.38	4,183,067	27.1	4,238,853	26.9	3,900,000	24.7
Independents	8,880	0.2	160,220	1.2	344,000	2.3	1,919	12,681	14,600	3.60	382,485	2.5	490,000	3.1	600,000	3.8
Marginal Christians	3,000	0.1	67,245	0.5	80,000	0.5	446	354	800	0.96	84,300	0.6	88,000	0.6	120,000	0.8
Anglicans	0	0.0	8,000	0.1	8,400	0.1	47	-27	20	0.24	8,500	0.1	8,600	0.1	9,000	0.1
Orthodox	0	0.0	5,000	0.0	6,600	0.0	37	43	80	1.15	6,920	0.0	7,400	0.1	8,500	0.1
Trans-megabloc groupings																
Evangelicals	1,554,000	30.0	625,000	4.8	598,000	4.0	3,336	-1,736	1,600	0.26	616,188	4.0	614,000	3.9	564,000	3.6
Pentecostals/Charismatics	0	0.0	200,000	1.5	940,000	6.3	5,243	4,757	10,000	1.02	993,786	6.4	1,040,000	6.6	1,300,000	8.2
Great Commission Christians	**777,000**	**15.0**	**4,560,000**	**35.0**	**6,145,000**	**41.1**	**34,276**	**2,791**	**37,067**	**0.59**	**6,369,100**	**41.2**	**6,515,668**	**41.3**	**6,500,000**	**41.2**
Nonreligious	65,000	1.3	1,158,700	8.9	1,900,000	12.7	10,598	2,596	13,194	0.67	1,970,430	12.8	2,031,935	12.9	2,221,850	14.1
Muslims	200	0.0	60,000	0.5	533,000	3.6	2,973	3,204	6,177	1.10	570,000	3.7	594,765	3.8	762,000	4.8
Atheists	10,000	0.2	100,000	0.8	181,070	1.2	1,010	1,381	2,391	1.25	190,000	1.2	204,978	1.3	250,000	1.6
Hindus	0	0.0	1,000	0.0	80,000	0.5	446	785	1,231	1.44	86,000	0.6	92,307	0.6	140,000	0.9
Buddhists	0	0.0	4,000	0.0	48,000	0.3	268	2,576	2,844	4.76	70,000	0.5	76,439	0.5	100,000	0.6
Jews	105,530	2.0	30,000	0.2	26,000	0.2	145	-251	-106	-0.41	25,500	0.2	24,941	0.2	20,000	0.1
Spiritists	0	0.0	3,000	0.0	18,000	0.1	100	424	524	2.59	22,000	0.1	23,237	0.2	29,000	0.2
New-Religionists	0	0.0	3,000	0.0	20,000	0.1	112	161	273	1.29	21,200	0.1	22,731	0.1	26,000	0.2
Chinese folk-religionists	0	0.0	15,000	0.1	6,000	0.0	33	22	55	0.88	6,000	0.0	6,551	0.0	14,000	0.1
Baha'is	0	0.0	2,700	0.0	3,800	0.0	21	150	171	3.78	4,800	0.0	5,506	0.0	9,000	0.1
Ethnoreligionists	0	0.0	0	0.0	580	0.0	3	2	5	0.85	620	0.0	631	0.0	1,000	0.0
Zoroastrians	0	0.0	0	0.0	50	0.0	0	1	1	0.96	50	0.0	55	0.0	150	0.0
Other religionists	570	0.0	4,000	0.0	7,000	0.1	39	29	68	0.93	7,400	0.1	7,680	0.1	10,000	0.1
World A (unevangelized persons)	25,900	0.5	260,646	2.0	343,896	2.3	1,896	1,460	3,356	0.95	355,551	2.3	378,864	2.4	489,242	3.1
World B (evangelized non-Christians)	155,400	3.0	1,121,054	8.6	2,479,604	16.6	13,852	9,620	23,472	0.90	2,618,198	16.9	2,713,193	17.2	3,093,758	19.6
World C (Christians)	4,998,700	96.5	11,650,600	89.4	12,128,500	81.1	67,624	-11,080	56,544	0.46	12,485,000	80.8	12,693,943	80.4	12,199,000	77.3
Country's population	**5,180,000**	**100.0**	**13,032,300**	**100.0**	**14,952,000**	**100.0**	**83,372**	**0**	**83,372**	**0.54**	**15,458,750**	**100.0**	**15,786,000**	**100.0**	**15,782,000**	**100.0**

COLUMNS, ROWS.
For meanings and definitions, see Codebook (Part 3). Note that, by definition, total 'Christians' = professing + crypto-Christians, which also = affiliated + unaffiliated Christians, and also = Great Commission Christians + latent Christians. Percentages may not always total exactly, due to rounding.

CENSUSES.
In contrast to most other countries, the Netherlands in its official censuses of religion since 1830, and in its public opinion polls, has not asked about religious preference ('What is your religion?') but has phrased it to cover only *kerkelijke gezindte*, church denominational affiliation ('With which church are your affiliated ?' (census), 'What is your religious affiliation?' (NIPO)). Consequently, the census categories, 'Roman Catholics', 'Protestants', etc imply formal church affiliation or membership; and the category of non-affiliated (*geen kerkelijke gezindte*) does not mean atheists and agnostics alone, but includes both (1) nominal Christians who lack formal membership requirements (baptism, confirmation, etc) or formal affiliation to churches; (2) nonreligious and atheists, and those who have withdrawn from Christian profession; and (3) adherents of non-Christian religions. In Table 1 above, nominal Christians are estimated to form half of this category of non-affiliated. Official censuses of religion have been held every 10 years since 1830. **1830:** 59.1% Protestants, 39.0% Roman Catholics, 1.8% Jews, 0.1% other religionists. **1840:** 59.6% Protestants, 38.5% Roman Catholics, 1.8% Jews, 0.1% other religionists. **1869:** 62.5% Protestants (54.7% NHK), 36.5% Roman Catholics, 1.9% Jews, 0.1% other religionists. **1889:** 60.7% Protestants (48.7% NHK), 35.4% Roman Catholics, 2.1% Jews, 1.5% non-affiliated, 0.3% other religionists. **1899:** 60.1% Protestants (48.4% NHK), 35.1% Roman Catholics, 2.3% non-affiliated, 2.0% Jews, 0.2% Old Catholics (Jansenists). **1909:** 56.9% Protestants (44.2% NHK), 35.0% Roman Catholics, 5.0% non-affiliated, 1.8% Jews, 1.1% other religionists, 0.2% Old Catholics. **1920:** 53.3% Protestants (41.2% NHK), 35.6% Roman Catholics, 7.8% non-affiliated, 1.7% Jews, 0.2% Old Catholics. **1930:** 45.5% Protestants (34.4% NHK), 36.4% Roman Catholics, 14.4% non-affiliated, 1.4% Jews, 0.1% Old Catholics. **31.V.1947** (de jure): 42.3% Protestants (31.0% NHK, 7.0% GK), 38.5% Roman Catholics, 17.1% non-affiliated, 1.9% other religionists, 0.1% Jews, 0.1% Old Catholics. **31.V.1960** (de jure): 41.0% Protestants (28.3% NHK, 6.9% GK), 40.4% Roman Catholics, 18.3% non-affiliated, 0.1% Jews, 0.1% Old Catholics, 0.1% marginal Protestants. **28.II.1971** 39.4% Roman Catholics, 37.9% Protestants (22.9% NHK, 7.0% GK), 22.7% non-affiliated. As explained above, the latter figure for Christians (77.3%) appears in the table above for 1970 under 'affiliated', and the figure for non-affiliated (22.7%) is broken down in the table in 1970 into 12.1% nominal Christians, 8.9% nonreligious, 0.8% atheists and 0.9% other religionists.

NOTES ON RELIGIONS
ATHEISTS. Communist Party of the Netherlands (Communistische Partij van Nederland, CPN) (legal; independent on Sino-Soviet dispute) and minuscule Maoist splinter groups.
BAHA'IS. Entered before 1921. Growth from 9 local spiritual assemblies (1964) to 18 (1973).
BUDDHISTS. Among the 60,000 Chinese with some Dutch converts.
DOUBLY-AFFILIATED. Members of newer Protestant denomination who are still enumerated by the NHK also.
EVANGELICALS. As documented for each province in Table 2 below, the NHK classifies 16% of all its churches as Conservative (i.e. Evangelical) in theology, as opposed to Liberal or Central. In addition, Evangelicals are found in over 130 other Protestant denominations of Conservative Evangelical theology.
HINDUS. Hindustani-speaking East Indians from Surinam, mostly immigrants (up to 12,000 a month) during 1975 immediately before Surinam's Independence. The column 'Natural change' includes this immigration, averaged over the decade 1990-2000. Among Hindu sects, ISKCON (Hare Krishna) operates 1 center, and Ananda Marga (Path of Bliss) operates others. A neo-Hindu movement is the Theosophical Society.
INDEPENDENTS. In about 15 denominations in 1995 (see Table 2).
JEWS. In 46 communities; Portuguese as well as Dutch Jews.
MUSLIMS. Mainly migrant workers, rapidly rising after 1960 to 25,083 registered workers in 1968, to 30,000 in 1970, to over 600,000 by 1995. Largest groups in 1995: 160,000 Turks, 107,000 Moroccans, 125,000 Indonesians, 190,000 from Surinam and the Netherlands Antilles, and 4,600 Tunisians. Almost all are Sunnis. There is also an Ahmadiya community (enumerated here under Muslims although declared non-Muslim by Pakistan). (The Ahmadiya Muslim Mission (Qadianis, from Pakistan) was begun in 1949 and now has a mosque in the Hague, with some Dutch converts).The totals in the table include these adult workers together with their dependents including children, and also other non-worker groups of Muslims. *Hajj pilgrims to Mecca.* (1976) 29.
NONRELIGIOUS. In addition to post-Christian Europeans, this includes a large number of Ambonese (Indonesians) formerly animists but now with no religion; also 30,000 organized humanists.
OTHER RELIGIONISTS. Adherents of other non-Christian religions and cults, including Rosicrucians (Rozekruisers Genootschap/Lectoriuum Rosicrucianum, world HQ in Haarlem, with 10 centers; also AMORC with 12 centers.
PENTECOSTALS. Charismatics within the non-Pentecostal Protestant denominations numbered in 1974 around 25,000 adults, mostly in the NHK, and also 10,000 young Jesus People (1973). Until 1974 the neo-pentecostal movement emphasized demon-possession and exorcism, and experienced little growth. From 1973 the charismatic movement also began to spread within the Old Catholic Church. By 1977 the agency Charismatische Werkgemeenschap Nederland was serving all charismatics including Classical Pentecostals and Roman Catholics. By 1992 CCR has 150 prayer groups; by 1997, 180.
UNAFFILIATED CHRISTIANS. Mainly Protestants who regard themselves as such but who are non-affiliated (unaffiliated to any church).

Great Commission Instrument Panel: status of the Netherlands (for explanation see start of Part 4)

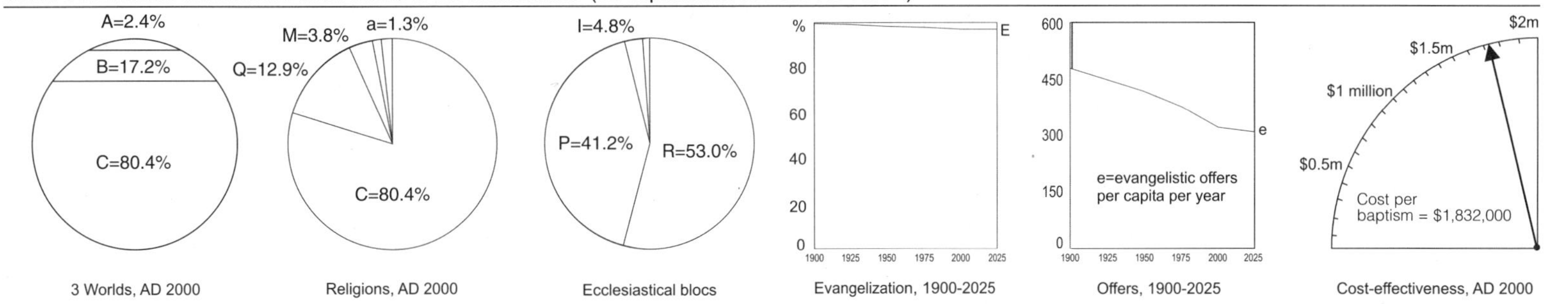

Country status. The Netherlands, one of the Low Countries in northeast Europe, is bordered by the North Sea to the west, by Belgium to the south and Germany to the east. It is one of the most densely populated countries in Europe. Its chief exports are food products, chemicals, and textiles.

HUMAN LIFE AND LIBERTY

Human need and development. The Netherlands is a developed country with one of the most prosperous economies in the world. However, the majority of the guest workers, asylees, and immigrants from former Dutch colonies in Indonesia and South America live in substandard conditions.

Human rights and freedoms. As in functioning multiparty democracies, human rights are fully guaranteed by Constitution and legislation. Preventive detention is permitted for a limited time, but only during emergencies. There are no prepublication restraints on the media. Privacy rights of the accused are respected during criminal investigations.

Human environment. The Netherlands suffers from all the environmental problems to which developed nations are subject: water, air, and noise. It is the estuary of 3 rivers susceptible to heavy pollution, the Rhine, Meuse, and Schelde. Further, since Dutch farmers are among the heaviest users of fertilizers in Europe, groundwater contains increasing amounts of nitrates. Air pollution is caused by the fact that the Dutch drive the most cars per mile and burn the most fossil fuels per capita in Europe, with the exception of Luxembourgers. However, the government is sensitive to the issue and has cut air pollution by half from the 1980 levels.

NON-CHRISTIAN RELIGIONS

Nonreligion and ***atheism*** are the largest non-Christian populations. These are those commonly regarded as secularists, materialists, communists, or similar terms. Numbers have grown dramatically since 1900 to over 15% of the country at present, with many organizations and activities.

Islam has a growing following; has expanded from 60,000 in 1970 to 595,000 in the last 30 years. Most Muslims come from 3 countries furnishing the Netherlands with manual labor: Turkey, Morocco and Tunisia, together with nationals from other Arab, Asian and African countries (including many Muslim Indonesians). Numerous Dutch born in Holland have converted to Islam. Today's massive Muslim presence is therefore due primarily to the recruitment of manual labor, beginning with Turks in 1960, followed later by the Moroccans and most recently the Tunisians. Their numbers have continued to increase.

Muslims are concentrated in the urbanized and industrialized west, in the provinces of Noord Holland and Zuid Holland. Worship places consist of a few prayer halls and mosques in The Hague (built by Ahmadiya in 1950) and others in the eastern part of the country, with others in the west. Quranic teaching is given privately and Turkish Islamic schools exist.

Judaism was severely decimated during the Nazi occupation, decreasing from 140,000 members before World War II to about 25,000 by 1995. Half of Holland's Jews live in Amsterdam where the Anne Frank House and the Jewish Historical Museum are widely visited. Other cities with Jewish communities include Eindhoven, Groningen, Haarlem, The Hague's-Hertogenbosch, Hilversum, Leeuwarden, Middelburn, Nijmegen, Rotterdam, Scheveningen, and Utrecht.

Buddhism has about 76,000 adherents, mostly Chinese. Holland's principal Buddhist center is a Theravada shrine, Dhammasucharitanucharee Temple administered by Thai monks at Waalwijk in North Brabant. Other small groups are located in Amsterdam (an Indonesian Theravada group), Utrecht (Tibetan Lamaism) and Amersfoort (Zen). An unusual feature of Dutch Buddhism is its sponsorship of Kosmos in Amsterdam, a meditation center serving all non-Christian religions. A movement to unify all Buddhists is in progress under the influence of the Stichting Nederlands Buddhistisen Centrum at Hengelo.

CHRISTIANITY

Evangelization began in the 7th century, with the Franks establishing a church at Utrecht; but little progress was made before the arrival of the English missionaries Willibroard and Boniface, during the first half of the 8th century. The Netherlands remained under the Holy Roman Empire until its disintegration when such local principalities as Utrecht became dominant; and the cities of Amsterdam and Haarlem rose to prominence following the Crusades. German mysticism became dominant in the 14th century through the influence of John of Ruysbroeck, Gerhard Groot, and Thomas a Kempis, with emphasis on union with God as contrasted with churchly observance or good works. Many banded themselves together as Brethren of the Common Life, living essentially a monastic life with common rules but without permanent vows. The Netherlands came under the control of the dukes of Burgundy in the 15th century, followed by the Hapsburgs and then by Spain in 1555. At the same time, Holland became a place of refuge for the followers of Luther, Zwingli, and Calvin, the latter ultimately taking precedence. With the attempt by Philip II of Spain to force Catholicism on Europe, the Dutch reformation became closely associated with its struggle for freedom, which lasted from 1568 to 1648. In 1581, 7 Protestant northern provinces began fighting under William of Orange, in turn persecuting Catholics of the southern provinces once Spanish rule had ended at the conclusion of the Thirty Years War.

The Golden Era of the 17th century saw Holland emerge as a great sea and commercial power, with colonies in the East Indies and North and South America. Dutch Reformed missions were established in the East Indies (1598), Formosa (1624), New York (1626), India (1633), Brazil (1640) and South Africa (1652); and the Dutch Reformed Church became Holland's official religion in 1651.

During the 18th century domestic quarrels and competitive wars with France, Britain, and Spain brought about a decline, the Netherlands becoming a French dependency from 1795 to 1815. During this period the Catholic Church began once again to gain recognition. The constitution of 1848 affirmed religious liberty for all, and the Catholic hierarchy was re-established in 1853.

CATHOLIC CHURCH. The Dutch Roman Catholic population has remained relatively stable since the middle of the last century. At that time Catholics numbered 38% of the total, which increased slightly to 38.5% in 1947 and 40.4% in 1960, decreasing to 39.3% in 1971 and further declining to 35.5% by 1995. In the years 1955-1964, the Catholic birth rate was still 2.7% above that of the population taken as a whole; but by 1970 the difference had been reduced to 0.7%, indicating that Catholics have by and large adopted family planning as have the rest of the population. The tendency towards non-attachment to a church, long apparent among the Reformed community, is also becoming more prevalent among Catholics.

The geographic spread of the Catholic population is uneven. The 3 northern provinces (Groningen, Drente, and Friesland), which make up the diocese of Groningen, are 8% Catholic and form only 2% of the Catholic population of the country. The center (dioceses of Utrecht, Haarlem, and Rotterdam) are 25 to 30% Catholic, but the percentage is weaker in the strongly urbanized west center (including Amsterdam and Rotterdam) than in the east. The south (dioceses of 's-Hertogenbosch, Breda, and Roermond) is mostly Catholic between 85% and 90%.

Catholic Church in the Netherlands, Diocese of Haarlem. Parish church of St. Vitus, Hilversum.

Catholic religious practice is still high if one compares it with the situation in other countries or that of the Dutch Reformed Church. Nevertheless, the tendency is towards a weakening of practice, even if it appears to be stabilized in the large cities. Some 6.5% of children born to Catholic parents are no longer baptized.

At the beginning of 1995 the Catholic Church in the Netherlands had a total strength of 3,728 secular and 8,583 regular priests. Not counting those retired or sick, about one-third were in the active parish ministry, one-third working overseas (mostly in missions) and one-third involved in administrative or teaching posts. More than a third of the parish priests were over 55 years of age.

Dutch Catholicism has experienced recent changes which have radically altered its character and spirit. After the re-establishment of the Catholic hierarchy in 1853, the Catholic Church tended to emphasize spirituality and was characterized by a defensive attitude towards Protestants, Socialists, and liberal Humanists. The effort to reintegrate the Catholic community into the main stream of the country's life, through the achievements of political and cultural equality, resulted in the formation of a system of organizations whose presence continues to be felt: press and media services (Catholic newspapers, radio and TV station), a political party (Katholieke Volkspartij), a trade union, and numerous social and professional

Country summary. **Worlds A, B, C by ethnolinguistic peoples, cities, and major civil divisions in the Netherlands.**

	PEOPLES							*CITIES*							*CIVIL DIVISIONS*						
World	*Num*	*Pop 2000*	*C%*	*Christians*	*E%*	*U%*	*Unevangelized*	*Num*	*Pop 2000*	*C%*	*Christians*	*E%*	*U%*	*Unevangelized*	*Num*	*Pop 2000*	*C%*	*Christians*	*E%*	*U%*	*Unevangelized*
A	3	70,247	0.92	645	41	59	41,188	0	0	0.00	0	0	0	0	0	0	0.00	0	0	0	0
B	18	844,364	11.63	98,222	66	34	285,497	0	0	0.00	0	0	0	0	0	0	0.00	0	0	0	0
C	25	14,871,091	68.48	10,183,989	100	0	46,872	40	8,610,193	63.79	5,492,728	97	3	255,250	12	15,785,697	65.14	10,282,853	98	2	373,555
Total	**46**	**15,785,702**	**65.14**	**10,282,856**	**98**	**2**	**373,557**	**40**	**8,610,193**	**63.79**	**5,492,728**	**97**	**3**	**255,250**	**12**	**15,785,697**	**65.14**	**10,282,853**	**98**	**2**	**373,555**

unions of various types. A similar compartmentalization (known as verzuiling) existed also among Protestants and Socialists, a vertical pluralism assuring social equilibrium and reciprocal tolerance. In the Catholic Church, this compartmentalization contributed to a tendency towards introversion, inherent in the theology of the Counter-Reformation, and a deep fidelity to the Roman pontiff whose anti-liberal and anti-Socialist position served to reinforce the existing system.

This traditional situation has changed radically since World War II through the development of urbanization and improvements in the standard of living. The questioning of authority in all sectors of society (family, factory, school, administration of justice) and the growth in desire for co-responsibility helped to prepare the way in 1954 for the first public criticism of the church by a group of Catholic Socialist laymen who refuse to obey the episcopate's demand forbidding the faithful from leaving their political and trade union organizations. This was followed by the evolution of intellectuals pleading for an 'open' Catholicism and a new spirit evident in priests returned from studies in foreign universities, especially Louvain (Belgium). At the same time the ideas of theologians, sociologists, and psychologists came increasingly to convergence. Thus, under the guidance of the episcopate aided by a special office of scientific counselors, began the development of a new image of the church, strongly reinforced by Vatican II. Other events of importance were the creation of the international theological journal Concilium in 1965, the first European episcopal conference in 1967, and the publication of the New Catechism for adults which attempted to bridge the gap between theology and exegesis on the one side and popular catechesis on the other. This work has enjoyed a wide success. However, 3 small groups of conservative Dutch Catholics (Confrontation, Leion of St Michael, and Truth and Life) with the aid of a part of the Roman Curia, attacked the catechism and received support from Vatican appointments in 1970 of conservative bishops to the dioceses of Rotterdam and Roermond.

An important event contributing to Catholic renewal in the Netherlands was the pastoral council held between 1966 and 1970. Creating it largely under the inspiration of the conciliar decree 'Cristus Dominus' of Vatican II, the Dutch bishops invited the faithful to assume a new form of co-responsibility for the church. The pastoral council, which became a deliberative assembly, set for itself 3 objectives: (1) the continuation of work begun at Vatican II, (2) an open study of the situation of the Catholic Church in the Netherlands; and (3) the elaboration of new options for the future. Such a meeting was made possible by the readiness of the Dutch bishops for open dialogue. Six plenary sessions, each of 3 days' during, were held at Noordwijkerhour between 1968 and 1970. In addition to the bishops, there were 70 members elected by the 7 diocesan pastoral councils, 10 religious personnel, 15 members appointed by the bishops, and 5 members of the Catholic secretariat, in addition to Catholic experts and delegates from other churches, religious communities and the Humanist Union. Among its more startling declarations were the Affirmation that the papal encyclical 'Humanae Vitae' was not convincing in its refusal to sanction contraceptives, and its recommendation that the requirement of celibacy for the priesthood be abolished. The council also requested a greater latitude for experiments in intercommunion with other Christian denominations and asked that a permanent body be set up to continue its work. In 1971 the bishops created a National Pastoral Council, with wide deliberative powers (although they retained the right of final decision), an action that was vetoed by Rome. In its place was established in 1972 a National Pastoral Committee (Landelijk Pastoraal Overleg), which would be informal and purely consultative.

The Dutch Catholic Church thus has attempted to transpose to the level of a national church the model of the universal church created at Vatican II. In addressing itself to the pastoral situation, it has not been able to avoid conflicts with Rome. Indeed, 2 different ecclesiologies are opposed: one in which Rome is united vertically with each national church, and the other in which the accent is placed on the horizontal communion of national churches forming together the universal church whose center of unity is the church in Rome and its bishop the pope. Many Dutch Catholics consider this a test case for other national churches which have not yet gone as far as they have, although the National Pastoral Council model has been followed in the Federal Republic of Germany, Austria, and Switzerland.

The Holy See has diplomatic relations with the Netherlands and in AD 2000 is represented to government and the Catholic hierarchy by a nuncio residing in The Hague.

PROTESTANT CHURCHES. The principal Protestant tradition in the Netherlands is the Dutch Reformed community which is at present divided into 6 different major denominations, together with the Moluccan Protestant Church formed in 1950 by Indonesians resident in Holland. The total affiliated Reformed community is 3.9 million. The mother church is the Netherlands Reformed Church (Nederlandse Hervormde Kerk, NHK) which traces its tradition to the Reformation in 1568 and retains a balance between orthodox and liberal Calvinists. The NHK is divided into 11 church provinces with 2,275 congregations, in addition to 16 Walloon (French-speaking) parishes. Its central legislative body is the general synod, with the administrative functions carried on by its general secretariat. Numerous boards and commissions have been established to handle the church's finances, publicity, personnel, missions, youth work, church schools, theological education, catechesis, social service, and ecumenical relations. Most NHK ministers are trained in the non-denominational theological faculties (Faculteiten der Godgeleerheid) in the state universities (Rijksuniversiteiten) of Leiden (founded in 1575, Groningen (1614) and Utrecht (1636), with the NHK Theological Seminary (Theologisch Seminarium vamwege de NHK) in Driebergen.

Reaction against liberalism and state influence in the mother church have produced a number of neo-Calvinist schisms from the NHK beginning in the early part of the 19th century. The first of these movements (called the Afscheiding or Secession) took place in the village of Ulrum in Groningen in 1834, and within 2 years 100 other so-called free churches had been formed throughout the country. More schisms followed during the 1840s, and in 1886 another large exodus (called the Doleantie or Dissensin) took place, with its center in Amsterdam. The most recent schism in the Reformed community was in 1944, resulting in the formation of the Liberated Reformed Churches. Several groups established during the 19th century have retained their identity as separate denominations, notably the Christian Reformed Churches who date their founding to 1834 and the Old Reformed Churches begun in 1841. However, there have also been unifying forces at work among the neo-Calvinists, and these came together in the creation of the Reformed Churches in the Netherlands (Gereformeerde Kerden in Nederland) in 1892 and the Reformed Communities in the Netherlands (Gereformeerde Gemeeenten) in 1907. The Gereformeerde Kerden is now the second largest Protestant denomination after the NHK, with nearly 1,200 parishes in 14 synods in Holland, and an affiliated body (Altreformierte Kirchen in Niedersachsen) in Germany. The church's general synod meets every 2 years with sessions lasting up to 8 weeks in duration. One of the church's most impressive institutions is the Free Reformed University of Amsterdam with 10,000 students.

Calvinism was made the state religion in 1651 but lost its special status in 1795 under the French occupation. Nevertheless, the NHK continues to regard itself as the Dutch folk church. Although there was a basis for the claim prior to the 19th century when nearly 60% of the population professed allegiance to the NHK, since that time this percentage has declined continuously from 48.4% (1899), to 44.2% (1909), 41.2% (1920), 34.4% (1930), 31.0% (1947), 28.3% (1960), and 22.9% (1971). During the same period the neo-Calvinist churches have tended to retain a more stable membership of 8% to 9% of the population; the Gereformeerde Kerken, for instance, formed 7.0% of the total population in 1947, 6.9% in 1960 and 7.0% in 1971. The decrease in adherents to the NHK has been accompanied by a continuous increase in those claiming to be without any church allegiance. These trends are due to the declining appeal of the NHK, and the much smaller birth rate (until recently at least) of its members as contrasted with Catholics. The degree of non-allegiance varies considerably from region to region, it being most significant in the industrial area west of Amsterdam.

Of Holland's other Protestant communities, the most important are the Congregationalists, who are divided into 2 groups, the Remonstrant Brotherhood dating from 1618 and the Association of Free Evangelical Congregations from 1834; Mennonites, who entered Holland from West Germany in 1811; Salvation Army, who arrived from England in 1887; and Lutherans, who owe their origin to the early Reformation period. At least 12 distinct Pentecostal bodies are present, the largest being the Apostolic Church in the Netherlands.

OTHER CHURCHES. The Old Catholic Church in the Netherlands traces its history to the 18th century Jansenist controversy which resulted in schism from Rome and its creation in 1724 as an independent Catholic church, with an archbishop in Utrecht. This church has also provided episcopal succession for other European Old Catholic churches established after 1870 by German and Swiss Catholics who rejected papal infallibility and other decisions of Vatican Council I. All these churches are related through acceptance of the common doctrinal basis contained in the 1889 Declaration of Utrecht. A more recent split from Catholicism is the Old Roman Catholic Church, formed in 1970.

The Catholic Apostolic (Irvingite) Church spread from England to Holland in 1869 and has given rise to numerous schisms: the New Apostolic Church and 3 of its splinter groups, the Restored Apostolic Church and the Restored Apostolic Missionary Church, and the Liberal Catholic Church.

Three Orthodox traditions are represented in Holland (Greek, Syrian, and Russian), and there are also Anglican chaplaincy services for the British expatriate community.

Novel architecture in Cross Church, Amstelveen.

Art and architecture. In Amsterdam, the center of Dutch culture, is the seven-towered church of St Willibrord, the largest in the country. Also in Amsterdam are the Beguinage, the only one of more than 20 monasteries that existed before the Reformation, the modern Opstanding Church, and St Nicholas Church. The Church of St Servatius in Maastricht is the oldest in the country. There are other notable cathedrals in Utrecht and s'Hertogenbosch.

Renewal movements. In the 1990s the Pentecostal/Charismatic Renewal continued to spread across most older churches, and numbered over 1,040,000 adherents (of whom 5% Pentecostals, 52% Charismatics, and 43% Independents).

Indigenous missions. The Netherlands has a long history of foreign missionary sending which began in the 7th century shortly after Christianity was introduced there. Missionaries were sent throughout the surrounding countries up until the Age of Discovery when Dutch missionaries could be found in South Africa, India, and Indonesia. Today Roman Catholics and Protestants send several thousand missionaries to countries all over the world.

CHURCH AND STATE

According to the constitution of 1814 (amended on numerous occasions), each person is free to teach his religious opinions (Article 181) and 'All religious communities enjoy equal protection' (Article 182). No discrimination is tolerated between citizens for religious reasons (Article 183). Religious services of all types are permitted inside buildings and private houses, and the same is true outside 'to the extent that they are authorized by laws and regulations' (Article 184). This last article was introduced in 1848, and Catholic processions are at present allowed only in places where permission was granted prior to that date, although this is not considered an important issue today. Correspondence with superiors of religious communities is free of postal charge, as is the issuing of ecclesiastical instructions (Article 187). In general, religious freedom is not restricted beyond the limitations established in the penal code (Article 181), or in common laws promulgated by the sovereign (Article 186), or in measures necessary to maintain peace and public order (Article 184).

The Netherlands has no concordat with the Holy See nor privileged religion or 'religious community' (Kerkgenootschap in official terminology). In this sense church and state are separate, and there has been no specific government ministry for religious affairs since 1871. An 1853 law, promulgated shortly after the restoration of the Catholic hierarchy, gives to a department of the Ministry of Justice responsibility for verifying that the organization and administration of the various religious communities are in conformity with the law. Thus state approval is required when a church confers an ecclesiastical office on an expatriate (Article 12). Following the Napoleonic Code of France, it has been prohibited since the beginning of the 19th century for clergy to celebrate a religious marriage prior to the civil ceremony, the officiating minister being liable for punishment in case of infraction.

Protection is accorded to religious communities through sanctions related to Sunday observance, prosecution of those who offend religious scruples, and state payment of the salaries of military and prison chaplains. The state provides for legal recognition of the juridical personality of religious communities and their autonomous associations, which are not subject to the laws of 22 May 1855 (concerning the regulation and limitation of the right of association and meeting) and 31 May 1956 (dealing with foundations). In virtue of a law relating to broadcasting, many religious communities are accorded radio and TV time, which may be used by them or be transferred to others. A law of 1962 concerning the construction of churches created temporarily the possibility of state subsidies of up to 30% of the value for such construction. The law was extended until 1 March 1975.

The Netherlands has 14 political parties represented in parliament, of which 2 are Roman Catholic and 4 Protestant. On 17 April 1962, parliament, acting on the preliminary proposal of an ad hoc commission formed in 1946 whose final report was submitted in 1967, repealed Article 185 of the constitution. This article was introduced in 1815 and provided certain religious communities with subsidies in the form of salaries and pensions of ministers and other financial benefits. In reality, since the amounts had remained unchanged for a century and a half, such aid had become negligible in value. The commission's proposal that future financial relations between the state and the churches be regulated by law has been accepted by the government and by parliament, but no concrete decisions have yet been taken. Several denominations, particularly the Netherlands Reformed and Catholic churches, have maintained that an annual contribution by the state would not compromise the freedom of the churches.

Since 1876, 3 theological faculties have been attached to the state universities of Groningen, Leiden, and Utrecht, serving primarily the NHK, and the state also meets supplementary costs relating to professional posts for training ministers of other religious communities. Since 1963, the theological faculties of the Free Reformed University of Amsterdam and the Catholic University of Nijmegen have been subsidized by the state. In 1970 these subsidies were extended to other higher schools of Reformed theology of Kampen and the Catholic theological training centers of Amsterdam, Heerlen, Tilburg, and Utrecht.

Public education is regulated by law, with due respect for the religious principles of each person. Private primary schooling is subsidized on an equal basis with that of the public sector. Private secondary education receives partial state subsidies in accordance with prevailing legal dispositions. Thus, in the domain of education as in the realm of social organizations in general, there exists a triple system of parallel institutions: public, Protestant and Catholic. Nevertheless, these social and cultural organizations are now in the process of deconfessionalization, a slow but seemingly irreversible movement. This is evident in the increasing separation of these organizations from the ecclesiastical hierarchy and their integration into comparable organizations outside the churches. This form of deconfessionalization goes back to the first decade following World War II when the reconstruction of social life required the co-operation of every element in society. The emancipation of the laity in the Catholic Church has also contributed to this evolution. At the same time, Christian organizations are attempting to conserve and deepen the Christian and evangelical foundations for their activities.

Broadcasting studios in Hilversum near Raadhuis, including NCRV (Netherlands Christian Broadcasting Corporation) and KRO (Catholic Broadcasting Corporation), being the situation in 1970.

BROADCASTING AND MEDIA

The largest public broadcasting company is the 'Evangelische Omroep' (EO) (Evangelical broadcasting Company) with more than 600,000 members. Shortwave radio programs in European languages can be received from KNLS, AWR (Slovakia), TWR (Monaco, Albania), and HCJB (Ecuador). Satellite TV and radio programs are received in English, Arabic, German and Italian. The Netherlands is a member of UNDA. Catholics broadcast 160 hours a year on radio, and 90 hours a year on television.

INTERDENOMINATIONAL ORGANIZATIONS

The Council of Churches in the Netherlands (Raad van Kerken in Nederland) was founded in 1946 as the Ecumenical Council of Churches and received its new name in 1968 when the Catholic Church became a full member. Since then the council has become the principal co-ordinating body of the Dutch churches and has absorbed all the bilateral consultative commissions between the churches, except one (the Rome-Utrecht Commission between the Roman Catholic and Old Catholic churches), transforming them into multilateral organs of the council. In 1973 member churches numbered 11 including associates. The Council carries on its work through 8 sections, working groups and commissions, dealing with social affairs, ecumenical actions, theological questions, international affairs (with a Sodepax-type structure), worship, inter-communion and ministry, ecumenical evangelization, and press and publicity.

Amsterdam hosts many international conferences: here, 1986 International Conference for Itinerant Evangelists.

Seven provincial councils have been formed for Drente, Friesland, Groningen, Limburg, Noord-Holland, Zeeland, and Zuid-Holland, together with 2 inter-provincial councils: Noord-Brabant, Zeeland en Limburg; and Overijssel, Gelderland en Utrecht. There are also about 200 local Christian councils. The Netherlands Missionary Council (Nederlandse Zendingsraad), founded in 1929 and re-organized in 1947, is dedicated to promoting fellowship and co-operation between the mission boards of its member churches (NHK, Gereformeerde, Moravian, Lutheran, Free Evangelical, Baptist, Remonstrant) and other missionary bodies (Reformed Missions League, Netherlands Bible Society, Etype Mission, Near East Mission). The council is affiliated to the CWME/WCC.

Another body, Inter-ecclesial Advent Action for Latin America (Interkerkelijke Adventsactie voor Latijns Amerika), formed in The Hague by the Catholic episcopate in 1966, with its membership broadened to include Protestants (NHK, Mennonites, Moravians, Remonstrants, Baptists, Netherlands Protestant League) in 1969, provides financial aid for social work to churches and Christian organizations in Latin America.

Regular consultation and joint activities are also carried on between the Catholic and Protestant missionary councils; Catholic and Protestant Bible societies; Catholic Foundation for the Business Apostolate and the Reformed 'Gospel and Industry' Foundation; theological faculties of the state and free universities; and the Catholic theological schools of Amsterdam and Utrecht.

Numerous ecumenical institutes and centers have been established; 6 may be mentioned here. (1) The Interuniversitair Instituut voor Missiologie en Oecumenica (IIMO), founded in 1969, has departments for ecumenism (Afdeling Oecumenica) at Utrecht and missiology at Leiden. (2) The Instituut voor Byzantijnse en Oecumenische Studies, founded in Nijmegen in 1948 by Catholic Assumptionist priests, organizes conferences and encounters on ecumenism with special emphasis on Eastern Orthodoxy. (3) The Ecumenical Research Exchange (ERE), founded in Rotterdam in 1971, is an independent institute related to the Inter-university Institute on Value Research in Rotterdam and the Forschungstatte der Evangelischen Studiengemeinschaft in Heidelberg, West Germany. Its special interest is work for peace. (4) The Liturgisch Oecumenisch Centrum, founded in Rotterdam in 1969, promotes ecumenical dialogue on the liturgy. (5) The Oekumenische Pastorie Oudezijds 100 (OZ 100), founded in Amsterdam in 1955, is an ecumenical pastoral center serving all churches in Amsterdam. (6) The Hospitium Oecumenicum San Luchesio, founded in Amsterdam in 1967, is a hostel for Catholic and Protestant clergy in Amsterdam, which also organizes pilgrimages to Rome, Taize, Assisi, Geneva, and Moscow.

Other ecumenical organizations include: (1) St Willibrord Vereniging, in 's-Hertogenbosch, which is the official Catholic agency for contacts with Protestants, Jews, and non-believers; (2) the Apostolate of Reconciliation (Apostolaat den Hereniging), founded in 1927 in Boxtel, which is the official Catholic agency for contacts with the Eastern churches; (3) the Interecclesiastical Council for Peace (Inter Kerkelijk Vredesberaad, IKV), founded in The Hague in 1966, which organizes annually a Week for Peace (Vredes Week) and includes in its membership 9 churches: Catholic, NHK, Gereformeerde, Baptist, Lutheran, Old Catholic, Quaker, Moravian, and Remonstrant; (4) the International League of Religious Socialists, founded in Switzerland in 1922, which has 600 members in Holland and associations in 7 other European countries; (5) the International Fellowship of Reconciliation (IFOR), established in the Netherlands in 1919, a pacifist organization dedicated to influencing the churches concerning their attitude to peace, war, and social justice; and (6) the Ecumenical Co-operative Society for Development, a World Council of Churches organization which was approved in August 1974 and established in Holland in 1976.

Dutch organizations dedicated to the advancement of dialogue between the world religions are numerous, of which 13 may be mentioned: (1) Wereldgesprek der Godsdiensten (WGG), founded in Driebergen in 1948, a branch of the World Congress of Faiths with headquarters in London, which was responsible for establishing in Rotterdam in 1972 the Instituut vood Godsdienstcommunicatie 'Interreligio'; (2) Permanent Comite van Joden, Christenen en Moslims in Europa in Amsterdam, which is a branch of the Standing Conference of Jews, Christians, and Muslims in Europe (JCM) in England; (3) Interkerkelijk Contact Israel (ICI) in Utrecht, which promotes Protestant and Catholic dialogue with Jews; (4) Raad voor de Verhouding van Kerk en Israel, in Utrecht, which sponsors Dutch Reformed dialogue with Jews; (5) Katholieke Raad voor Israel (KRI) in 's Hertogenbosch, which promotes Catholic dialogue with Jews; (6) Nederlandse Vereniging van Jesjoea Hammasjiach-belijdende Joden 'Hadderech', in The Hague, which is a Jewish organization related to the Christian Alliance; (7) Stichting 'Het Leerhuis', in Hilversum, which serves as a Beth NaMidzash for Jews, Christians and others and is a member of the International Council of Christians and Jews in London; (8) Anne Frank Stichting, in Amsterdam; (9) Contactorgaan van Levensovertuigingen, which promotes contacts between the churches and the Humanist Union; (10) Landelijk Werkgroep 'Samenleven Buitenlandse Werknemers', which is responsible for contacts between the churches and foreign workers (especially by White Fathers in Santpoort, which provides for relations between Christians and Muslims); (12) Muslim Foreign Workers section of the Catholic National Pastoral Committee; and (13) numerous local action groups (Rotterdam, Utrecht, Leiderdorp) seeking to aid foreign workers.

FUTURE TRENDS AND PROSPECTS

Christian affiliation will probably continue a downward trend to 62.3% by 2025 while the nonreligious increase from only 8.9% in 1970 to 14.1% by 2025.

Despite renewal movements within Christianity, the percentage of church members will likely continue to decline throughout the 21st century, perhaps dipping below 50% by AD 2050. The nonreligious could grow to over 25% in the same period.

BIBLIOGRAPHY

Aanzien kerk en godsdienst in Nederland en België 1945–1985. G. Klaasen. Utrecht: Spectrum, [1985]. 192p.

'Acts and reports of the Reformed Ecumenical Synod.' Amsterdam, 1968.

Catholica: informatiebron voor het Katholieke leven. Hilversum, The Netherlands: Stichting Catholica, 1968. Tomes I, II

Christelijk handboek Nederland: Netherlands Christian handbook. P. W. Brierley & E. Merckx-Stringer (eds). Bromley: MARC Europe, 1986. 352p.

De religieuze kaart van Nederland: omvang en geografische spreiding van de godsdienstige gezindten vanaf de Reformatie tot heden. H. Knippenberg. Assen: Van Gorcum, 1992. 313p.

De Tegenbeweging. R. Kranenborg (ed). *Religieuze bewegingen in Nederland*, vol. 24. Amsterdam: VU Uitgeverij, 1992. 168p.

Dutch Anabaptism: origin, spread, life and thought (1450–1600). C. Drahn. The Hague: Nijhoff, 1968. 303p.

'Dutch Jews in a segmented society,' H. Daalder, *Acta Historiae Neerlandicae*, 10 (1978), 175–94.

Dutch religion: the religious consciousness of the Netherlands after the cultural revolution. A. Felling, J. Peters & O. Schreuder. *Serie Sociaal-culturele ontwikkelingen in Nederland.* Nijmegen: Instituut voor toegepaste Sociale Wetenschappen, 1991. 121p.

Handboek godsdienst in Nederland. H. Schaeffer. Amersfoort: De Horstink, 1992. 613p.

Iconography of the Counter–Reformation in the Netherlands: heaven on earth. J. B. Knipping. Nieuwkoop, The Netherlands: Sijthoff, 1974. 2 vols.

Islam in Dutch society: current developments and future prospects. W. A. R. Shadid & P. S. van Koningsveld. Kampen, The Netherlands: Kok Pharos, 1992. 213p.

Katholiek en Protestant: een historisch en contemporain onderzoek naar confessionele culturen. J. Peters & O. Schreuder. *Serie Sociaal-culturele ontwikkelingen in Nederland.* Nijmegen: ITS, [1987?]. 226p.

Kerk in Nederland: een landelijk onderzoek naar kerkbetrokkenheid en kerkverlating. T. Schepens. *TFT studies*, 15. Tilburg: Tilburg University Press, 1991. 86p.

Lowland highlights: church and oecumene in the Netherlands. J. A. Hebly (ed). Kampen: Kok, 1972. 134p.

Memorbook: a history of Dutch Jewry from the Renaissance to 1940. M. H. Gans. Trans., A. J. Pomerans. Baarn, The Netherlands: Bosch & Kenning, 1977. 852p.

Mental, religious and social forces. H. Bavinck. *A general view of the Netherlands*, no. 17. The Hague: Ministry of Agriculture, Industry and Commerce, 1915. 63p.

'Netherlands,' L. Layendecker, in *Western religion: a country by country sociological enquiry*, p.325–63. H. Mol (ed). The Hague: Mouton, 1972.

Nieuw Kerkelijk Handboek 1972–1973. Gouda, The Netherlands: N. V. Drukkerij Koch & Knuttel, 1972. 613p.

Pillars of piety: religion in the Netherlands in the nineteenth century 1813–1901. M. J. Wintle. *Occasional Papers in Modern Dutch Studies*, no. 2. Hull, UK: Hull University Press, 1987. 91p.

Pius Almanak: Jaarboek van Katholiek Nederland, 1971. Amsterdam: N. V. Drukkerij De Tifd, 1971.

'Plurlisme religieux et chrétienté,' W. Goddijn, *Social compass*, 10, 1 (1963), 53–74.

'Prophetic ministry in a post–Christian culture: a program of Biblical education by extension in the Netherlands.' R. H. Matzken. D. Miss. thesis, Trinity Evangelical Divinity School, Deerfield, IL, 1982. 265p.

Protestantse zendingsperiodieken uit de negentiende en twintigste eeuw in Nederland, Nederlands–indie, Suriname en de Nederlandse Antillen: een bibliografische catalogus met inleiding (Protestant missionary periodicals from the nineteenth and twentieth century in the Netherlands, the Dutch East Indies and the Dutch West Indies: a bibliographical catalogue with introduction). J. A. B. Jongeneel. Leiden: Interuniversitair Instituut voor Missiologie en Oecumenica, 1990. 145p.

Religion in Dutch society 85: documentation of a national survey on religious and secular attitudes in 1985. A. Felling, J. Peters & O. Schreuder. Amsterdam: Steinmetz Archive, [1985?]. 444p.

Surinaamse religies in Nederland: Hindoeisme, Winti, Hindostaanse Islam. C. J. G. van den Burg (ed). *Religieuze bewegingen in Nederland*, 12. Amsterdam: VU Uitgeverij, 1986. 155p.

'The case of Dutch Catholicism: a contribution to the theory of the pluralistic society,' J. M. G. Thurlings, *Sociologia Neerlandica*, 7, 2 (1971), 118–36.

The deferred revolution: a social experiment in church innovation in Holland, 1960–1970. W. Goddijn. New York: Elsevier Scientific Publishing Co., 1975. (Dutch origin 1973).

'The development of sociology of religion in the Netherlands since 1960,' L. Layendecker, *Social compass*, 14 (1967).

The evolution of Dutch Catholicism, 1958–1974. J. A. Coleman. Berkeley and Los Angeles: University of California Press, 1978. 328p.

The liberation: causes and consequences: the struggle in the Reformed Churches in the Netherlands in the 1940's. C. Van Dam (ed). Winnipeg: Premier Publishing, 1995.

The Netherlands. P. King & M. Wintle. *World bibliographical series*, vol. 88. Oxford, UK: CLIO Press, 1987. 330p. (See especially 'Religion,' p.77–87).

'The relevance of secularization for interpreting and nurturing spirituality in Dutch Churches of Christ: an analysis of the relation of pre–modern, modern, and post–modern paradigms of faith and the practice of prayer.' P. D. Krumrei. D.Min. thesis, Harding Graduate School of Religion, Memphis, TN, 1992. 374p.

'The revolt of the Netherlands: the part played by religion in the process of nation building,' J. E. Ellemers, *Social compass*, 14 (1967).

Tussen geest en tijdgeest: denken en doen van vrijzinnig protestanten in de afgelopen honderd jaar. C. W. Mönnich et al. Utrecht: De Ploeg, 1989. 540p.

Vijf jaar Kerkontwikkeling in Nederland, 1967–1971 (Five years in the life of the Dutch Church, 1967-71). Amersfoort, Netherlands: KASKI, 1973. 152p.

Voor God en vaderland: nationalisme en religie. G. ten Berge. Kampen: J.H. Kok, 1992. 109p.

Wegwijs in gelovig Nederland: een alfabetische beschrijving van Nederlandse kerken en religieuze groeperingen. E. G. Hoekstra & M. H. Ipenburg. Kampen: J.H. Kok, [1987?]. 279p.

Wereldgodsdiensten in Nederland: christenen in gesprek met moslims, hindoes en boeddhisten. J. Slomp & R. van Kerken (eds), at Nederland Sektie Interreligieuze Ontmoeting. Amersfoort Voorburg: De Horstink Publivorm, 1991. 234p.

Country Table 2. **Organized churches and denominations in the Netherlands.**

Official name (bold type = church with over 10% of all affiliated) 1	*Begun* 2	*Type* 3	*Counc* 4	*Congs* 5	*Adults* 6	*Affiliated 1970* 7	*Affiliated 1995* 8	*G%* 9	*Names, notes, and other statistics* (see Codebook, Part 3) 10
Apostolic Church in the Netherlands	1905	P-PeA	Z....	40	10,000	32,600	25,000	-1.06	*Apostolische Kerk in Nederland.* Centralized hierarchy. Linked to Apostolic Ch (GB).
Apostolic Society	1940	I-3aX	x....	125	10,000	25,000	25,000	0.00	*Apostolisch Genootschap.* Schism of 80% ex New Apostolic Ch. In VAC (Switzerland).
Association of Free Ev Congregations	1834	P-Con	KTT.f	46	7,302	30,000	13,500	-3.14	*Bond van Vrije Evangelische Gemeenten.* In WCC 1947-49. 35n,1s.W=65%,160Y.
Bible Christian Union	1946	P-Non	.....	2	50	50	83	2.05	M=BCU.
Brotherhood of Baptist Churches		I-Bap	.....	26	2,350	1,000	4,700	0.05	*Baptisten Gemeenten.* Independent congregations of Baptist polity.
Baptist Mid-Missions	1954	I-Fun	x....	10	100	100	200	2.81	M=BMM(USA). Fundamentalist Baptist. Small autonomous congregations. 4f.
Catholic Apostolic Church	1867	I-3aX	x....	16	326	500	480	-0.16	*Katholiek-Apostolische Gemeenten. Irvingites.* Rapidly declining. HQ The Hague.
Catholic Church in the Netherlands:	c 650	R-Lat	B.B.S	1,850	3,867,600	5,366,919	5,491,444	0.09	*Rooms-Katholieke Kerk.* C=36+16+128. 7q,5s. 1781n 2875x 4867m 12227w 41904Yy
M Utrecht	c 650	R-Lat	Bs	366	626,000	906,000	900,000	-0.03	Overijssel, Utrecht, part Gelderland. D=PC(22). 328n 475x 703m 2080w 1301Yy
D Breda	1803	R-Lat	Bs	162	377,000	509,073	545,667	0.28	Zeeland, part Noord-Brabant. D=PC(76). 181n 251x 540m 1746w 5163Yy
D Groningen	1559	R-Lat	Bs	85	93,000	125,600	130,502	0.15	Groningen, Friesland, Drente. D=PC(19),pc(17). 33n 43x 54m 166w 1353Yy
D Haarlem	1559	R-Lat	Bs	210	459,000	747,972	601,272	-0.87	Noord-Holland, Amsterdam. D=PC(80),pc(20). 215n 267x 406m 1555w 4968Yy
D Roermond	1559	R-Lat	Bs	352	745,000	914,625	1,077,991	0.66	Suppressed 1801-53. Limburg province. D=PC(100). 444n 567x 959m 3000w 10354Yy
D Rotterdam	1955	R-Lat	Bs	200	520,000	805,927	719,560	-0.45	*Bisdom Rotterdam.* Zuid-Holland province. D=PC(33). 227n 305x 463m 760w 5367Yy
D 's-Hertogenbosch (Bois-le-Duc)	1559	R-Lat	Bs	370	1,015,000	1,327,722	1,476,452	0.43	Part N-Brabant, Gelderland; 76% Roman Catholic. 353n 967x 1742m 5000w 14699Yy
OM Netherlands	1957	R-Lat	Bs	105	32,600	30,000	40,000	1.16	Military Ordinariate of the Netherlands. HQ Rotterdam. 21 ordinaries. 3Yy.
Children of God	c1985	I-mar	.....	2	80	–	171	10.00	Former members of Jesus Movement (USA).
Christadelphian Ecclesia	1960	m-Ade	x....	1	40	100	100	0.00	*Broeders in Christus. Christadelphian Bible Mission.* Ecclesia (church). The Hague.
Christian Brethren		P-CBr	x....	37	2,800	7,500	4,670	0.05	*Vergadering van Gelovigen (Assembly of Believers).* Plymouth (Open) Brethren. 2f.
Christian & Missionary Alliance	1952	P-Hol	.....	10	1,200	500	1,522	4.55	*Parousia.* M=CMA.
Christian Reformed Churches in the N	1834	P-Ref	Jt...	194	45,000	70,051	76,000	0.33	*Christelijke Geref Kerken.* 1834, secession ex NHK. 121n,1s,W=65%,1508Yy.
Church of Christ, Scientist		m-Sci	x....	15	1,000	1,900	1,500	0.05	*Vereniging der Christelijke Wetenschap. Christian Science.* M=CCS(USA). 3m,17w.
Church of England (D Europe)	1586	A-plu	awc..	3	6,900	8,000	8,500	0.24	*Anglikaans Kerkgenootschap.* CCCS chaplaincies (some seasonal), MTS in ports. 8x.
Church of the Foursquare Gospel	c1985	P-Pe2	....E	1	150	–	250	10.00	M=ICFG. Mainline Pentecostals from USA.
Church of God (Cleveland)	1969	P-Pe3	.....	13	1,250	148	1,920	10.80	M=CoG(Cleveland) (USA). Holiness Pentecostals.
Church of the Nazarene	1967	P-Hol	....E	8	724	72	1,042	11.28	*Kerk van der Nazarener.* M=CoN.
Ch of Jesus Christ of Latter-day Saints	1864	m-LdS	x....	33	4,760	7,245	6,800	-0.25	*Kerk van Jezus Christus van de Heiligen der Laatste Dagen.* M=CJCLdS. 80f.
Churches of Christ		I-Dis	x....	7	500	500	1,000	0.05	*Gemeente van Christus.* M=CC(Non-Instrumental) (USA). In Amsterdam, Haarlem, Hague.
Dutch Evangelical Churches		P-Ref	xv...	9	300	1,000	900	0.05	*Evangelische Gemeenten.* HQ Haarlem, Amsterdam. 1972 applied to join WCC.
Evangelical Church in Germany	1857	P-LuR	lwc..	60	30,000	1,200	40,000	15.06	*Duitse Evangelische Gemeenten.* Germans, from EKD. The Hague. 4n,W=16%,16Yy,8z.
Exclusive Brethren		P-EBr	.....	78	6,200	8,360	8,860	0.05	*Vergadering van Gelovigen(gesloten).*
Fellowship of Pentecostal Churches	1905	P-Pe2	ZF..E	65	9,050	10,000	13,700	1.27	*Broederschap van Pinkstergemeenten.* M=AoG(USA, UK),SFM. 70n,4f,1j,1s(85),W=75%.
Free Evangelical Churches		I-Eva	.....	80	12,000	20,000	16,000	0.05	*Vrije Evangelische Gemeenten.* Independent groupings of congregations.

Continued opposite

Country Table 2–concluded

Official name (bold type = church with over 10% of affiliated) 1	*Begun* 2	*Type* 3	*Counc* 4	*Congs* 5	*Adults* 6	*Affiliated 1970* 7	*Affiliated 1995* 8	*G%* 9	*Names, notes, and other statistics* (see Codebook, Part 3) 10
Greek Orth Ch (D Belgium,Neth,Lux)		O-Gre	Cwc..	1	3,500	3,000	5,000	0.05	*Grieks-Orthodoxe Kerk.* Under EP Constantinople. 1 church in Rotterdam. 1x.
Jehovah's Witnesses	1908	m-Jeh	x....	329	31,359	30,000	53,200	2.32	*Getuigen van Jehovah.* Active witnessing under way by 1925. (1975) 1647Y. (1995) 896Y.
Johan Maasbach Foundation	1952	I-3pW	.....	10	3,600	30,000	12,000	-3.60	*Stichting Johan Maasbach Wereldzending.* The Hague. Radio. 12n,W=50%,275Y.
Liberal Catholic Church	1916	I-Lib	xv...	10	500	1,120	700	-1.86	*Vrije-Katholieke Kerk* (Centrum London). Decline. 40n,W=50%,20Yy.
Mennonite Brotherhood	1811	P-Men	GWC.W	150	18,000	62,000	32,700	-2.53	*Algemene Doopsgezinde Broederschap.* Rural. Also in NWGermany. Pacifist. 114n,1s.
Moluccan Protestant Church in the N	1952	P-Ref	Rwe..	85	29,400	20,000	36,000	2.38	*Molukse Evangelische Kerk in Nederland* (GPM, from Indonesia). Ambonese separatists.
Moravian Church in the Netherlands	1746	P-Mor	xwc.W	7	3,900	2,000	5,570	4.18	*Evangelische Broedergemeente. Hernhutters.* UB, European Continental Province. 5n.
Netherlands Free Reformed Churches		P-Ref	.....	104	18,300	26,200	30,000	0.05	*Nederlands Gereformeerde Kerden.*
Netherlands Orthodox Church		O-Gre	Cwc..	1	380	500	500	0.05	*Nederlandse Orthodoxe Kerk.* Under EP Constantinople. Bishop in The Hague.
New Apostolic Ch in the Netherlands	c1900	I-3aX	x....	102	10,200	12,000	12,694	0.23	*Nieuw-Apostolische Kerk in Nederland.* Chief Apostle in Zurich (Switzerland). HQ Amsterdam.
Old Catholic Church in the Netherlands	1724	I-OCa	UWC.W	11	2,660	11,000	7,000	-1.79	*Oud-Katholieke Kerk. Ch of Utrecht.* Schism ex Ch of Rome. 2 Dioceses. 35n,1s.
Old Reformed Churches	1841	P-Ref	.....	66	5,800	19,000	17,100	-0.42	*Oud-Gereformeerde Gemeenten.* Ledeboer schism 1841 ex NHK. 57 churches vacant. 9n.
Old Roman Catholic Church	1970	I-CCa	.....	5	600	1,000	1,200	0.73	*Oud-Roomsch Katholieke Kerk.* Recent schism ex Ch of Rome opposing centralization.
Protestant Union of the Netherlands	1870	m-Unt	....w	60	9,000	23,000	12,700	-2.35	*Vereniging Nederlandse Protestantenbond.* Unitarians. Radio VPRO. 40n.
Reformed Churches (Liberated)	1944	P-Ref	.....	270	62,000	86,451	116,000	1.18	*Gereformeerde Kerken (Vrijgemaakt).* Schism over baptismal regeneration. 159n,1s.
Reformed Churches in the N & Antilles	1907	P-Ref	.....	165	42,000	73,049	84,000	0.56	*Gereformeerde Gemeenten in Nederland.* Merger of 1840 NHK schisms. HQ Gouda. 43n,1s.
Reformed Congregations in the N		P-Ref	.....	47	7,000	15,946	14,000	0.05	Split ex Christian Reformed Ch. Conservative, 18th-century sermons. 3n.
Religious Society of Friends	1677	P-Qua	Q...W	13	150	200	250	0.90	*Genootschap der Vrienden.* Quaker-centrum, Amsterdam. Quakers. W=50%.
Remonstrant Brotherhood	1618	P-Con	RWC.W	44	11,800	40,000	26,200	-1.68	*Remonstrantse Broederschap.* 1618, NHK expelled 200 clergy. 60n,1s,330Yy.
Restored Apostolic Church	1897	I-3aX	.....	17	2,800	9,000	7,000	-1.00	*Hersteld Apostolische Gemeenten in de Eenheid der Apostolen.* Ex New Apostolic Ch.
Restored Apostolic Missionary Church	1897	I-3aX	.....	10	700	3,000	1,560	-2.58	*Hersteld Apostolische Zendingskerk. Stam Juda.* Ex New Apostolic Ch. HQ Amsterdam.
Russian Orthodox Church in the N		O-Rus	Mwc..	5	650	1,000	1,020	0.05	*Russisch-Orthodoxe Kerk*, AD Belgie & Nederland. Patriarchal Exarchate, Moscow.
Russian Orthodox Ch Outside Russia		I-Rus	x....	3	1,040	1,500	1,530	0.05	In D Western Europe & Austria, ROCOR (HQ New York). 1972, bishop defects.
Salvation Army	1887	P-Sal	xwc.W	189	22,000	60,000	47,000	-0.97	*Leger des Heils. Netherlands Territory*, 39 institutions. 428n,1s,W=33%,618Y.
Scandinavian Seamen's Churches		P-Lut	.....	20	2,000	600	3,000	0.05	*Scandinaafse Gemeenten.* Rotterdam: Danish, Finnish, Norwegian, Swedish churches.
Seventh Day Baptist Church		P-Bap	Tv...	5	100	200	300	0.05	*Zevendedags Baptisten. Netherlands Conference.* M=SDBC(USA). HQ Rotterdam.
Seventh-day Adventist Church	1898	P-Adv	x....	45	6,579	5,000	12,200	3.63	*Zevende Dags Adventisten. Netherlands UC(N,S Confs).* 31nx,1j,1s,W=80%,175Y.
Streams of Power Movement	1948	I-3pW	x....	16	2,500	5,000	6,250	0.90	*Stromen van Kracht.* Dutch Pentecostalism. Also in West Indies. 8n,350Y.
Syrian Orthodox Church: M Nederland		O-Syr	Dw.N.	3	200	500	400	0.05	*Oosters-Orthodoxe Kerk, Syro-Chaldeeuwse Successic.* In P Antioch. Arabs. 1 bishop.
Union of Baptist Churches in the N	1845	P-Bap	T...f	86	12,676	18,000	21,100	0.64	*Unie van Baptisten Gemeenten in Nederland.* In northeast. 54n,1s(10),W=45%,264Y.
United Pentecostal Church	1962	P-Pel	x....	5	1,000	200	1,500	8.39	*Tolie Evangelie Gemeenschappen Filadelfia. Jesus Only Ch.* M=UPC(USA). 2f.
United Protestant Ch in the N:	1995	P-LuR	.....	2,840	2,382,000	4,078,638	3,508,700	-0.60	*VPKN.* 1995, merger of NHK, GKN, and ELKN under way, aiming to finish by AD 2000.
Evangelical Lutheran Church in the N	c1520	P-Lut	LWC.W	40	12,000	50,355	24,700	-2.81	*ELKN. Evangelisch-Lutherse Kerk.* HQ Arnhem. 74n,1s. Declining. 1995, merger in VPKN.
Netherlands Reformed Church	c 690	P-Ref	RWC.W	1,800	1,900,000	3,147,000	2,700,000	-0.61	*NHK, Nederlandse Hervormde Kerk.* 11 Church Provinces. 1775n,1s. Uniting with ELK,GKN.
Reformed Churches in the Netherlands	1892	P-Ref	FWC.W	1,000	470,000	881,283	784,000	-0.47	*Geref Kerken in N.* 1886, the Dissension ex NHK. 1995, merger in VPKN. 1100n,1s,10997Yy.
Other Protestant denominations		P-	.....	300	20,000	20,000	40,000	0.05	Total over 130 (see list below).
Other marginal Protestant bodies		m-	.....	80	5,000	5,000	10,000	0.05	Total over 30 (see list below).
Other Third-World indigenous churches		I-3pG	.....	70	10,000	4,000	20,000	0.05	Several Indonesian, Korean and other bodies (see below); mainly pentecostal.
Other independent Catholic churches		I-CCa	.....	30	1,000	1,000	2,000	0.05	Total about 7 bodies (see below), mostly under episcopi vagantes.
Other independent single congregations	c1900	I-sin	.....	375	30,000	22,000	54,000	3.66	In around 40 loose geographical networks.
Other pentecostal churches	c1930	I-3pW	.....	583	70,000	12,500	109,000	9.05	Large number (about 50) of independent networks of pentecostal bodies.
Other independent charismatic chs	c1975	I-3cW	.....	300	70,000	–	100,000	5.00	Including Association of Vineyard Chs, Manna Church (Portugal).
Totals				**9,193**	**6,920,076**	**10,296,349**	**10,156,716**		

Churches, members, growth, 1900-2025	*Congs*	*Adults*	*Affiliated*	*G%*	*Total denominations*	*6 Megablocs:* *O*	*R*	*A*	*P*	*I*	*m*
Total churches, members, and denominations (mid-1900)	3,000	3,327,000	4,942,380	1.05	26	0	1	1	13	7	4
Total churches, members, and denominations (mid-1970)	8,501	6,844,522	10,296,349	1.05	207	4	1	1	91	87	23
Total churches, members, and denominations (mid-1990)	8,400	6,724,000	9,869,000	-0.21	387	4	1	1	170	166	45
Total churches, members, and denominations (mid-1995)	9,193	6,920,076	10,156,716	0.58	389	4	1	1	170	168	45
Total churches, members, and denominations (mid-2000)	10,000	7,006,000	10,282,853	0.25	393	4	1	1	171	170	46
Total churches, members, and denominations (mid-2025)	12,000	6,703,000	9,837,500	-0.18	572	10	1	1	200	300	60

NOTES ON TABLE ABOVE

CONFESSIONAL COUNCILS. The Remonstrant Brotherhood is a member of WARC and also of IARF.

NATIONAL COUNCILS (Column 4, 5th letter).

- E = Evangelische Alliantie.
- f = formerly in Ecumenical Council of Churches.
- S = Netherlands Bishops' Conference (Nederlandse Bisschoppen Konferentie), also member of CCN.
- W = Council of Churches in the Netherlands (CCN) (Raad van Kerken in Nederland, Conseil des Eglises aux Pays-Bas), replacing 1946-68 Ecumenical Council of Churches.
- w = associate (guest) member of CCN.

Other councils. 200 local councils and 7 provincial councils are affiliated to CCN.

OTHER PROTESTANT DENOMINATIONS. A large number of these smaller bodies are Reformed schisms which seceded for theological reasons; many others are Pentecostal bodies. Names are given here in Dutch or English depending on which is better known. They include: Bethel Pentecostal Temple, Children of God International (from USA), Christelijk Afgescheiden Gemeenten, Ch of God of Prophecy, Ch of God (Anderson) (3 isolated congregations), Ch of Norway, Ch of Sweden, Communidad Evangélica Espafrom USA), onder het Kruis (under the Cross), Gospel Missionary Union (1966), Hervormde Gereformeerde Gemeente, Independent Assemblies of God, Latter Rain Assemblies (from South Africa), Oud-Lutherse Gemeente (Amsterdam), Oud-Baptisten Gemeenten, Portuguese Kerk, Presbyteriaanse Gemeente (Rotterdam), Reformiert-Apostolischer Gemeindebund, Seventh-day Adventist Reform Movement, South-East Moluccan Protestant Ch, Vereniging van Uitgetredenen der NHK (Union of Separatists from NHK), Volle-Evangelie Gemeenten, Vrije Baptisten Gemeenten, Vrije Ev Broedergemeente, Vrije Gereformeerde Gemeenten, Vrije Hervormde Gemeenten, World Baptist Fellowship Mission Agency (1969), World Gospel Crusades (1968), World-Wide Missions (1969). There are also USA military chaplaincies among the 2,000 USA troops (1970).

OTHER MARGINAL PROTESTANT BODIES. These include: Amis de l'Homme (Groupe Sayerce), Anthroposophical Society (Christian Community Ch), Centrale Commissie voor het Vrijzinning Protestantisme in Nederland, Ch of the New Jerusalem (1 church), Gralsbewegung, Lord's New Ch, Lou-Gruppe or Lou-mensen (1950 movement begun by Lourens van Voorthuizen, fisherman prophet claiming to be divine, with 12 wives, died 1968), Reorganized Ch of Jesus Christ of Latter-day Saints (USA; 470 members), Universal Life Church in the Netherlands (HQ Modesto, USA; 1971 applied to join WCC); and other Unitarian bodies.

OTHER THIRD-WORLD INDIGENOUS CHURCHES. Several Indonesian indigenous movements have followers among the Moluccans and others in the Netherlands. There are also: Holy Spirit Association for the Unification of World Christianity in the Netherlands (from Korea; 2,000 adherents by 1976), Moluccan Evangelical Ch (member of ICCC).

OTHER CATHOLIC (NON-ROMAN) CHURCHES. Including Antoinists (from Belgium), Broederschap van het Heilig Sacrament (ex Liberal Catholic Ch), Free Apostolic Ch, and 6 bodies operated by bishops-at-large.

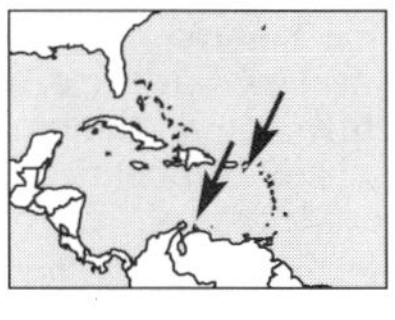

NETHERLANDS ANTILLES

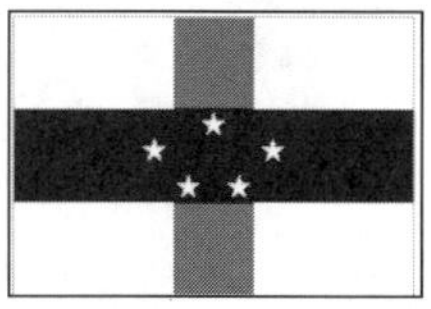

SECULAR DATA, AD 2000

STATE

Official name: De Nederlandse Antillen (The Netherlands Antilles).
Short name: Netherlands Antilles. **Adjective of nationality:** of Netherlands Antilles.
Flag: White background, vertical red stripe, horizontal blue stripe with 6 white stars.
Area: 800 sq. km. (308 sq. mi.).
Government: Self-governing integral part of the Kingdom of the Netherlands, since 1954 (1634 Dutch possession, 1954 co-equal part of kingdom).
Legislature: States, 27 members.
Official language: Dutch (Nederlands-Vlaams).
Monetary unit: Netherlands guilder. **US$1=** 1.79.
Chief cities: WILLEMSTAD 153,879.
Political divisions: 5 provinces.

DEMOGRAPHY

Population: 217,000.
Population density: 270.9/sq. km. (703.8/sq. mi.).
Under 15 years: 54,000.
Growth rate p.a.: 0.92% (births 15.32, deaths 6.11).
Mortality: Infant, per 1,000: 12.6, ; **Maternal per 100,000:** 15.0.
Life expectancy: 76 (male 73, female 79).
Household size: 3.7. **Floor area per person, sq.m:** 40.0.
Major languages: Dutch, Papiamento, English, French, Spanish, Chinese, Hindustani, Sranang Tongo (Surinamese).
Urban dwellers: 70.42%. **Urban growth rate p.a.:** 1.2%.
Labor force: 46%.

ETHNOLINGUISTIC PEOPLES

81.1% Antillean Creole; 5.3% Dutch; 2.9% Surinamese Creole; 2.9% West Indian Black; 2.0% French West Indian.

ECONOMY

National income p.a. per person: US$10,397; **per family:** US$38,472.

EDUCATION

Adult literacy: 93% (male 94%, female 93%). **Schools:** 142.
Universities: 1. **School enrolment:** female/male: 95%/95%.

HEALTH

Access to health services: 85%. **Access to safe water:** 90%.
Hospitals: 11 (73 beds per 10,000). **Doctors:** 291.
Blind: 500. **Deaf:** 12,100. **Murder rate:** 7.
Lepers: 30.

LITERATURE

New book titles p.a.: 170 (800 p.a. per million). **Periodicals:** 17.
Newspapers: 6 dailies.

COMMUNICATION (per 1,000 people)

Phones: 374 (25% mobile). **Radios:** 1,009. **TV sets:** 325.
Daily newspaper circulation: 260. **Computers:** 150.

HUMAN LIFE AND LIBERTY (optimum condition=100.0%)

HDI: 88.9. **HSI:** 80.0. **HFI:** 70.0. **EFL:** 35.0.

Country status. The Netherlands Antilles is 2 groups of Dutch islands; one group in the Lesser Antilles and one group off the coast of Venezuela, both in the Caribbean Sea. The primary industries are tourism and oil refining.

HUMAN LIFE AND LIBERTY

Human rights and freedoms. Rights are similar to the situation in the Netherlands itself.

NON-CHRISTIAN RELIGIONS

Judaism has a number of followers, with a notable synagogue on Curaçao.

Islam is followed by a small Muslim minority composed mostly of immigrants from Syria, Lebanon and Surinam. They are organized into the Association of the Muslim Community of Curaçao (Vereniging van der Moslem Gemeente op Curaçao).

Baha'i also has a few adherents.

Country Table 1. Religious adherents in the Netherlands Antilles, AD 1900-2025.

Year	1900		1970		mid-1990		Annual change, 1990-2000				mid-1995		mid-2000		mid-2025	
Name	Adherents	%	Adherents	%	Adherents	%	Natural	Conversion	Total	Rate	Adherents	%	Adherents	%	Adherents	%
Christians	**32,000**	**100.0**	**153,950**	**96.8**	**179,040**	**95.2**	**2,741**	**-172**	**2,569**	**1.35**	**194,590**	**94.8**	**204,730**	**94.4**	**240,840**	**93.4**
PROFESSION																
professing Christians	**32,000**	**100.0**	**153,950**	**96.8**	**179,040**	**95.2**	**2,741**	**-172**	**2,569**	**1.35**	**194,590**	**94.8**	**204,730**	**94.4**	**240,840**	**93.4**
AFFILIATION																
unaffiliated Christians	1,600	5.0	820	0.5	16,790	8.9	259	44	303	1.67	18,670	9.1	19,818	9.1	25,840	10.0
affiliated Christians	**30,400**	**95.0**	**153,130**	**96.3**	**162,250**	**86.3**	**2,482**	**-216**	**2,266**	**1.32**	**175,920**	**85.7**	**184,912**	**85.2**	**215,000**	**83.3**
Roman Catholics	24,960	78.0	133,700	84.1	132,800	70.6	2,028	-222	1,806	1.28	143,800	70.1	150,862	69.5	170,800	66.2
Protestants	5,440	17.0	17,130	10.8	20,100	10.7	310	-20	290	1.36	21,860	10.7	23,000	10.6	26,000	10.1
Marginal Christians	0	0.0	1,000	0.6	5,350	2.9	83	22	105	1.81	5,960	2.9	6,400	3.0	11,000	4.3
Anglicans	0	0.0	1,000	0.6	2,300	1.2	35	-10	25	1.04	2,400	1.2	2,550	1.2	3,600	1.4
Independents	0	0.0	300	0.2	1,700	0.9	26	14	40	2.14	1,900	0.9	2,100	1.0	3,600	1.4
Trans-megabloc groupings																
Evangelicals	5,000	15.6	3,000	1.9	5,700	3.0	88	42	130	2.08	6,465	3.2	7,000	3.2	10,000	3.9
Pentecostals/Charismatics	0	0.0	300	0.2	8,460	4.5	131	43	174	1.89	9,421	4.6	10,200	4.7	15,000	5.8
Great Commission Christians	**1,900**	**5.9**	**15,900**	**10.0**	**32,000**	**17.0**	**494**	**119**	**613**	**1.77**	**35,400**	**17.3**	**38,128**	**17.6**	**48,700**	**18.9**
Nonreligious	0	0.0	2,900	1.8	4,100	2.2	63	146	209	4.20	5,170	2.5	6,185	2.9	9,200	3.6
Spiritists	0	0.0	0	0.0	1,600	0.9	25	4	29	1.66	1,760	0.9	1,886	0.9	2,800	1.1
Buddhists	0	0.0	400	0.3	850	0.5	13	10	23	2.39	940	0.5	1,076	0.5	1,600	0.6
Jews	0	0.0	600	0.4	700	0.4	11	0	11	1.43	720	0.4	807	0.4	800	0.3
Baha'is	0	0.0	250	0.2	400	0.2	6	12	18	3.77	460	0.2	579	0.3	660	0.3
Hindus	0	0.0	100	0.1	380	0.2	6	1	7	1.73	400	0.2	451	0.2	600	0.2
Muslims	0	0.0	250	0.2	360	0.2	6	1	7	1.67	380	0.2	425	0.2	800	0.3
Chinese folk-religionists	0	0.0	500	0.3	320	0.2	5	-5	0	0.12	300	0.2	324	0.2	200	0.1
Atheists	0	0.0	0	0.0	100	0.1	2	2	4	3.20	120	0.1	137	0.1	200	0.1
Other religionists	0	0.0	50	0.0	150	0.1	2	1	3	1.61	160	0.1	176	0.1	300	0.1
World A (unevangelized persons)	0	0.0	318	0.2	1,128	0.6	19	16	35	2.57	1,436	0.7	1,519	0.7	3,096	1.2
World B (evangelized non-Christians)	0	0.0	4,791	3.0	7,832	4.2	120	156	276	3.22	9,158	4.5	10,751	4.9	14,064	5.4
World C (Christians)	32,000	100.0	153,950	96.8	179,040	95.2	2,741	-172	2,569	1.35	194,590	94.8	204,730	94.4	240,840	93.4
Country's population	**32,000**	**100.0**	**159,060**	**100.0**	**188,000**	**100.0**	**2,890**	**0**	**2,880**	**1.44**	**205,184**	**100.0**	**217,000**	**100.0**	**258,000**	**100.0**

COLUMNS, ROWS.
For meanings and definitions, see Codebook (Part 3). Note that, by definition, total 'Christians' = professing + crypto-Christians, which also = affiliated + unaffiliated Christians, and also = Great Commission Christians + latent Christians. Percentages may not always total exactly, due to rounding.

CENSUSES.
27.VI.1960, 31.XII.1960 (de jure): 82.7% Roman Catholics, 10.5% Protestants, 4.9% other religionists, 1.8% nonreligious. (Aruba 81.1% Roman Catholics; Curaçao 83.3% Roman Catholics; Bonaire 94.0% Roman Catholics). **31.XII.1971**. 86.9% Roman Catholics, 10.0% Protestants (including Anglicans and marginal Protestants), 1.5% nonreligious, 0.3% Jews, 0.1% Muslims, 0.1% Buddhists. **1992:** 73.9% Roman Catholics, 7.7% Protestants (3.1% Methodists, 2.2% Adventists), 9.1% other religionists, 6.3% nonreligious, 1.5% Marginal Christians, 1.0% Anglicans, 0.3 Jews, 0.2% Muslims.

NOTES ON RELIGIONS
BUDDHISTS. Chinese.
JEWS. The synagogue on Curaçao is a striking edifice.
MUSLIMS. Immigrants from Syria, Lebanon and Surinam, grouped in the Association of the Muslim Community of Curaçao, have a mosque on Curaçao.
OTHER RELIGIONISTS. Including Rosicrucians (2 AMORC centers).

Great Commission Instrument Panel: status of the Netherlands Antilles (for explanation see start of Part 4)

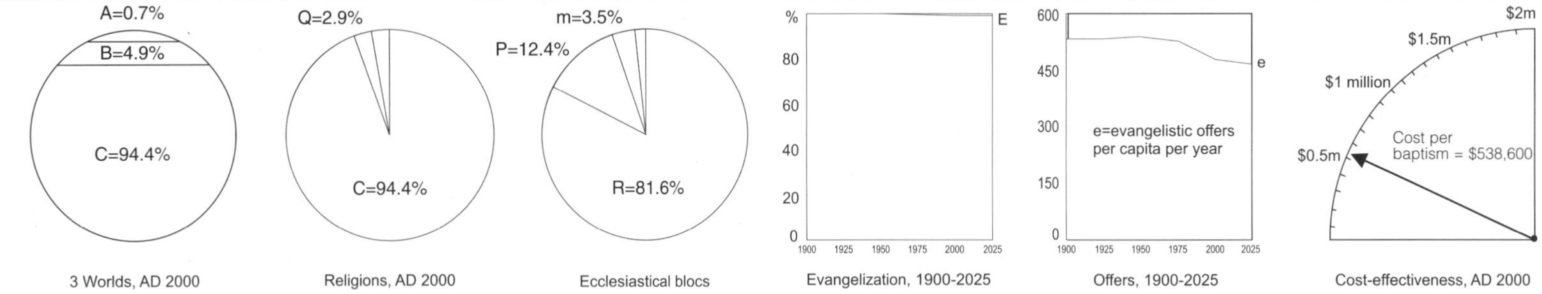

Catholic Church, Diocese of Willemstad. 'Goed Nieuws!' (Good News). Bible bookstall in Catholic church on Curaçao.

CHRISTIANITY

CATHOLIC CHURCH. Catholic clergy from the island of Santo Domingo began work during the 16th century, but in 1634 they were expelled and Catholicism prohibited by the Dutch. A few Jesuits were allowed to return in 1705, followed by Augustinians, Flemish secular priests, and Franciscans. The vicariate of Curaçao was erected in 1842 and became the diocese of Willemstad in 1958. Catholics, being preponderant in the Windward Islands, have 85% of the population of Curaçao, 80% of Aruba and 94% of Bonaire. Their influence in the Leeward Islands is less, only 37% of the population. The Catholic Church has 20 parishes on Curaçao, 8 on Aruba, 3 on Bonaire, and one each on St Maarten (Dutch part), Saba, and St Eustatius.

The Holy See has no diplomatic relations with Netherlands Antilles in AD 2000, but an apostolic delegate.

OTHER CHURCHES. The principal Protestant denomination of the islands is the United Protestant Church of Curaçao which is united Lutheran and Reformed in tradition and traces its origin to early Dutch settlement in 1650. Other churches of the Reformed tradition include the Protestant Church of the Netherlands Antilles in Aruba and Bonaire and 2 smaller Reformed churches on Curaçao. Methodism had its beginnings on St Eustatius which was evangelized by an African slave, Black Henry, and visited by Thomas Coke in 1787. The first missionary was sent to St Maarten in 1819, but it was not until 1929 and 1930 that Methodist work was begun on Aruba and Curaçao. Other active denominations include Seventh-day Adventists, Salvation Army, Anglicans, Moravians, and several smaller groups.

Jehovah's Witnesses began work in the 1940s and by 1995 had gained nearly 6,000 adherents, making them the second largest denomination in the islands.

Indigenous missions. A few missionaries from the Netherlands Antilles have been sent out to surrounding islands and a few have worked back in the Netherlands but missionary vision has never been strong.

CHURCH AND STATE

As in Surinam, there is no law regarding religious societies, nor any government ministry specifically charged with religious affairs. However, all denominations receiving government subsidies must be officially registered. The state provides subsidies for the salaries of Catholic bishops and some priests, as well as ordained Protestant ministers, and aids in the administration of private church-sponsored schools but not their construction. Schools may offer courses in religious education if there is a request for such instruction.

BROADCASTING AND MEDIA

TWR maintains a transmitter at Bon Aire which covers the Caribbean and South America with radio programs in Spanish, English, Portuguese and Banius. Shortwave radio programs can also be received from AWR (Costa Rica), HCJB (Ecuador), and KNLS. TBN programs are aired in Curaçao.

INTERDENOMINATIONAL ORGANIZATIONS

Four separate church councils serve the Netherlands Antilles: Aruba Council of Churches, Curaçao Ecumenical Council of Churches, St Eustatius Council of Christian Churches, and St Maarten Inter-Church Council. Although 9 churches are involved, membership varies from one council to another. Thus Catholics are not members in Curaçao, whereas the chairman of the St Eustatius council in 1975 was a Catholic priest.

Country summary. **Worlds A, B, C by ethnolinguistic peoples, cities, and major civil divisions in the Netherlands Antilles.**

	PEOPLES							*CITIES*							*CIVIL DIVISIONS*						
World	*Num*	*Pop 2000*	*C%*	*Christians*	*E%*	*U%*	*Unevangelized*	*Num*	*Pop 2000*	*C%*	*Christians*	*E%*	*U%*	*Unevangelized*	*Num*	*Pop 2000*	*C%*	*Christians*	*E%*	*U%*	*Unevangelized*
A	0	0	0.00	0	0	0	0	0	0	0.00	0	0	0	0	0	0	0.00	0	0	0	0
B	4	3,296	4.00	132	63	37	1,225	0	0	0.00	0	0	0	0	0	0	0.00	0	0	0	0
C	11	213,481	86.56	184,780	100	0	321	1	153,879	85.00	130,797	99	1	1,246	5	216,775	85.30	184,912	99	1	1,547
Total	**15**	**216,777**	**85.30**	**184,912**	**99**	**1**	**1,546**	**1**	**153,879**	**85.00**	**130,797**	**99**	**1**	**1,246**	**5**	**216,775**	**85.30**	**184,912**	**99**	**1**	**1,547**

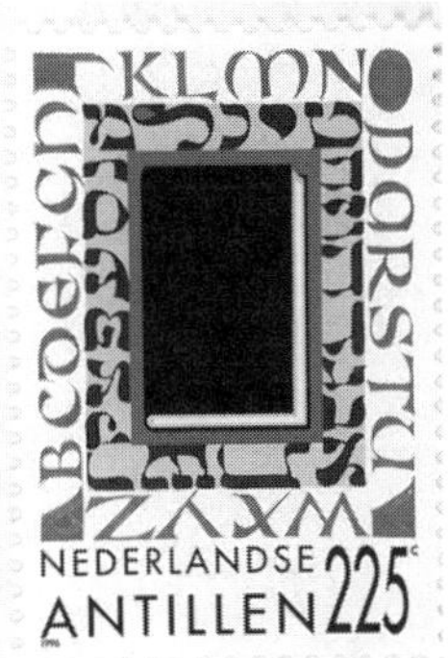

Postage stamps often have Christian themes: here, celebrating 1995 publication of Bible in Papiamentu language.

FUTURE TRENDS AND PROSPECTS

The nonreligious, 1.8% in 1970, are expected to grow to 3.6% by 2025 causing a decline in the Christian percentage to 93.4% in the same period.

Christianity will probably continue its decline through the 21st century, falling perhaps as low as 90% by AD 2050. The nonreligious could grow to 10% in the same period.

BIBLIOGRAPHY

'Balia ku Almasola or "dance with the lone soul": social transformations and symbolic representations in Afro–Curaçaoan religions,' R. Ansano, in *Op de bres voor eigenheid: Afhankelijkheid en dominantie in de Antillen*, p.165–89. R. Allen (ed). Amsterdam: Caraïbische Werkgroep AWIC, Universiteit van Amsterdam, 1990.

Bibliografie Nederlandse Antillen Aruba. S. R. Criens. Amsterdam: Universiteit van de Nederlandse Antillen, Stichting voor Culturele Samenwerking, Bibliotheek der Rijksuniversiteit Utrecht, 1989. (Contains 23,625 entries).

Brua. P. van Venlo. *Zjozjolí*, 2. [Curaçao]: P. Brenneker, 1986. 67p.

De Fraters van Zwijsen: 100 jaar fraters op de Nederlandse Antillen. Zutphen: Walburg Pers, 1986. 191p.

De Zusters Dominicanessen van Voorschoten: 100 jaar op St. Maarten, Nederlandse Antillen, 1890–1990. M. S. Voges. [Curaçao]: M.S. Voges, 1990. 100p.

'Evangelical church congregational survey ABC islands, Netherlands Antilles.' D. Christensen. Communications graduate project, Wheaton College, Wheaton, IL, 1977. 54p.

Geloven op de Nederlandse Antillen: een politiek–culturele analyse in historisch perspectief. M. P. Liberia-Peters. Utrecht: De Bazuin, 1993. 23p.

Kerk en Maatschappij op Curaçao. A. Lampe (ed). Caraçao, Netherlands Antilles: Typografix, 1991. 117p.

Kerkgeschiedenis der Bovenwindes Eilanden. W. M. Brada. Willemstad: Boekhandel St. Augustinus, 1952. 48p.

Morgen de eilanden zich verheugen. J. Hartog. Curaçao: Fortkerk, 1969. 268p. (History of 200 years of Protestantism in the Netherlands Antilles).

Netherlands Antilles and Aruba. K. Schoenhals. *World bibliographical series*, vol. 168. Oxford, UK: CLIO Press, 1993. 186p. (See especially 'Religion,' p.61–3).

Protestantse zendingsperiodieken uit de negentiende en twintigste eeuw in Nederland, Nederlands–indie, Suriname en de Nederlandse Antillen: een bibliografische catalogus met inleiding (Protestant missionary periodicals from the nineteenth and twentieth century in the Netherlands, the Dutch East Indies and the Dutch West Indies: a bibliographical catalogue with introduction). J. A. B. Jongeneel. Leiden: Interuniversitair Instituut voor Missiologie en Oecumenica, 1990. 145p.

The history of the Jews of the Netherlands Antilles. I. S. Emmanuel & S. A. Emmanuel. Cincinnati, OH: American Jewish Archives, 1970. 2 vols.

'The lost Catholic house of prayer of Curaçao,' C. Schunck, in *Building up the future from the past: studies on the architecture and historic monuments in the Dutch Caribbean*, p.128–35. H. A. Coomans, M. A. Newton & Coomans-Eustatia (eds). Zutphen, The Netherlands: Walburg Pers, 1990.

Country Table 2. **Organized churches and denominations in the Netherlands Antilles.**

Official name (bold type = church with over 10% of all affiliated) 1	*Begun* 2	*Type* 3	*Counc* 4	*Congs* 5	*Adults* 6	*Affiliated 1970* 7	*Affiliated 1995* 8	*G%* 9	*Names, notes, and other statistics* (see Codebook, Part 3) 10
Anglican Church (D Antigua)	c1960	A-ACa	awMRK	1	840	1,000	2,400	3.56	In Ch of the Province of the West Indies. 95% West Indians (90% Black). W=58%.
Assemblies of God	c1975	P-Pe2	.....	15	394	–	1,160	5.00	M=AoG.
Baptist Association	1983	P-Bap	.....	8	646	–	1,080	8.33	M=FMB-SBC.
Catholic Church: D Willemstad	c1580	R-Lat	P.NMK	30	70,000	133,700	143,800	0.29	*Rooms-Katholieke Kerk. M=OP.* C=4+3+7. 20n,20x,35m,55w,2700Yy.
Christian Brethren		P-CBr	x....	2	100	100	200	0.05	*Plymouth (Open) Brethren.* M=CMML. Small group influenced from Britain.
Church of God of Prophecy	1959	P-Pe3	Z....	3	300	100	500	6.65	M=CGP(USA). Holiness Pentecostals, split ex CoG(Cleveland). On Aruba. 2f.
Church of God (Anderson)		P-Hol	x....	7	280	400	560	0.05	*Genereal Assembly of the Church of God (Curaçao).* M=CoG(Anderson) (USA). 3n,W=50%.
Church of God (Cleveland)		P-Pe3	ZF...	5	200	100	400	0.05	M=CoG(Cleveland) (USA). Holiness Pentecostals. On Aruba & St. Martins. Blacks.
Evangelical Church	1931	P-Eva	xM...	12	472	500	1,200	3.56	M=TEAM. Papiamento work on Curaçao. Aruba, Bonaire. Radio Victoria (Aruba). 10f.
Jehovah's Witnesses	c1940	m-Jeh	x....	26	2,085	1,000	5,960	7.40	*Getuigen van Jehovah.* 5 congregations on Curaçao, 4 Aruba, 1 Bonaire. 90Y.
Largo Community Church		I-com	....K	1	100	100	200	0.05	Small independent congregation on Aruba, mainly European and other expatriates.
Liberal Catholic Church		I-Lib	x....	2	100	200	200	0.05	*Vrije-Katholieke Kerk.* In Netherlands, UK, USA, Australia, New Zealand, et alia.
Methodist Church in Curaçao	1787	P-Met	VwM.K	3	1,150	3,000	2,560	-0.63	In MCCA, Leeward Islands District. M=MMS(UK). First work St. Eustatius. 5n,1x,1f.
Moravian Church in Curaçao		P-Mor	xwM.K	2	600	700	1,000	0.05	In Surinam Province, Unity of Brethren. Work spread from Moravians in Surinam.
Reformed Church		P-Ref	....K	1	120	500	600	0.05	*Gereformeerde Kerk. Re-reformed Church.* On Curaçao. Dutch Calvinist origin.
Reformed Church (Liberated)	c1950	P-Ref	.....	1	440	90	100	0.42	*Gereformeerde Kerk (Vrijgemaakt).* 1944 schism in Holland over baptism. On Curacao.
Salvation Army in Curaçao	1927	P-Sal	xwM.K	16	800	2,000	1,140	-2.22	*Leger des Heils. Curaçao Region*, Caribbean & CAmerica Territory (HQ Jamaica).
Seventh-day Adventist Church	1925	P-Adv	x....	21	1,470	3,000	3,500	0.62	*Advent-Zendings Genootschap.* NA Mission. 4n,13mw,1h,1p,14t(1498),W=83%,125Y.
United Pentecostal Church	1974	P-Pe1	.....	4	300	–	700	4.76	*Jesus Only Church.* Oneness Pentecostals. M=UPC(USA). 4f.
United Protestant Church of Curaçao	1650	P-LuR	.uM.K	3	3,700	5,500	5,000	-0.38	*Verenigde Protestantse Gemeente van Curaçao.* M=NHK(Netherlands). 4x,2r.
Wesleyan Holiness Church	1902	P-Hol	VF...	1	80	140	160	0.54	Originally M=Pilgrim Holiness Mission (USA); now Wesleyan Ch (USA). 1n,W=93%,7Y,4z.
Other independent churches		I-3pU	.....	14	1,100	–	1,500	0.05	Including New Apostolic Church (45 members), also several Afro-Caribbean bodies.
Other Protestant denominations		P-	.....	20	1,000	1,000	2,000	0.05	Total about 10 (see list below).
Totals				**198**	**86,227**	**153,130**	**175,920**		

Churches, members, growth, 1900-2025	*Congs*	*Adults*	*Affiliated*	*G%*	*Total denominations*	*6 Megablocs:* O	*R*	*A*	*P*	*I*	*m*
Total churches, members, and denominations (mid-1900)	20	21,900	30,400	2.34	4	0	1	0	3	0	0
Total churches, members, and denominations (mid-1970)	123	110,326	153,130	2.34	22	0	1	1	17	2	1
Total churches, members, and denominations (mid-1990)	160	79,500	162,250	0.29	44	0	1	1	25	16	1
Total churches, members, and denominations (mid-1995)	198	86,227	175,920	1.63	46	0	1	1	26	17	1
Total churches, members, and denominations (mid-2000)	210	90,600	184,912	1.00	48	0	1	1	27	18	1
Total churches, members, and denominations (mid-2025)	260	105,000	215,000	0.60	88	0	1	1	40	45	1

NOTES ON TABLE ABOVE

NATIONAL COUNCILS (Column 4, 5th letter).

K = Curaçao Ecumenical Council of Churches (Oecumenische Raad van Kerken op Curaçao), also Aruba Council of Churches, St Eustatius Council of Christian Churches, St Maarten Inter-Church Council; 1962.

OTHER PROTESTANT DENOMINATIONS. These include: Bible Ch (Bethesda Mission), Ch of Christ (Non-Instrumental), Norwegian Seamen's Ch, PEMS (St Martin), Streams of Power.

UNITING CHURCHES. Negotiations for organic union were under way in 1974 between: Methodist Ch, United Protestant Ch of Curaçao; and also between the United Protestant Ch and the Reformed Ch.

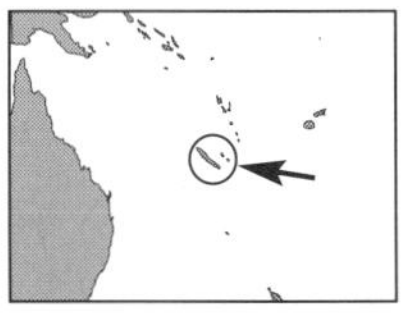

NEW CALEDONIA

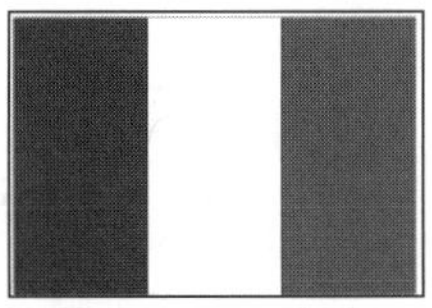

SECULAR DATA, AD 2000

STATE

Official name: La Nouvelle Calédonie et Dépendances (The Overseas Territory of New Caledonia).
Short name: New Caledonia. **Adjective of nationality:** New Caledonian.
Flag: That of France.
Area: 18,576 sq. km. (7,172 sq. mi.).
Government: Overseas territory of France, since 1946 (1853 annexed by France, 1864-94 used as penal colony).
Legislature: Territorial Congress, 54 members.
Official language: French (Français).
Monetary unit: CFA franc. **US$1=** 91.99.
Chief cities: NOUMEA (Numea) 115,236.
Political divisions: 3 provinces.

DEMOGRAPHY

Population: 214,000.
Population density: 11.5/sq. km. (29.8/sq. mi.).
Under 15 years: 64,000.
Growth rate p.a.: 1.53% (births 20.63, deaths 5.36).
Mortality: Infant, per 1,000: 9.8, ; **Maternal per 100,000:** 40.0.
Life expectancy: 74 (male 70, female 77).
Household size: 4.1. **Floor area per person, sq.m:** 30.0.
Major languages: French, Melanesian (Houailou, Iai, Lifu, Maré, Ponérihouen), Uvean, Javanese, Tahitian, Vietnamese, and about 20 other local languages.
Urban dwellers: 64.15%. **Urban growth rate p.a.:** 2.0%.
Labor force: 40%.

ETHNOLINGUISTIC PEOPLES

24.0% French; 8.8% Lifuan (Dehu, Deu); 6.4% Wallisian (East Uvean); 5.4% Half-Melanesian; 5.0% Euronesian.

ECONOMY

National income p.a. per person: US$7,998; **per family:** US$32,795.

EDUCATION
Adult literacy: 57% (male 57%, female 58%). **Schools:** 342. **Universities:** 6. **School enrolment:** female/male: 102%/100%.

HEALTH
Access to health services: 70%. **Access to safe water:** 90%. **Hospitals:** 8 (62 beds per 10,000). **Doctors:** 370. **Blind:** 30. **Deaf:** 11,700. **Murder rate:** 5. **Lepers:** 3,500.

LITERATURE
New book titles p.a.: 43 (200 p.a. per million). **Periodicals:** 10. **Newspapers:** 3 dailies.

COMMUNICATION (per 1,000 people)
Phones: 236 (20% mobile). **Radios:** 495. **TV sets:** 380. **Daily newspaper circulation:** 123. **Computers:** 200.

HUMAN LIFE AND LIBERTY (optimum condition=100.0%)
HDI: 71.3. **HSI:** 80.0. **HFI:** 75.0. **EFL:** 40.0.

Country Table 1. **Religious adherents in New Caledonia, AD 1900-2025.**

Year	1900		1970		mid-1990		Annual change, 1990-2000				mid-1995		mid-2000		mid-2025	
Name	Adherents	%	Adherents	%	Adherents	%	Natural	Conversion	Total	Rate	Adherents	%	Adherents	%	Adherents	%
Christians	**38,900**	**71.1**	**99,100**	**91.6**	**147,150**	**87.6**	**4,031**	**-126**	**3,905**	**2.38**	**168,560**	**87.3**	**186,195**	**87.0**	**244,500**	**85.5**
PROFESSION																
professing Christians	**38,900**	**71.1**	**99,100**	**91.6**	**147,150**	**87.6**	**4,031**	**-126**	**3,905**	**2.38**	**168,560**	**87.3**	**186,195**	**87.0**	**244,500**	**85.5**
AFFILIATION																
unaffiliated Christians	800	1.5	610	0.6	17,430	10.4	477	232	709	3.47	21,142	11.0	24,516	11.5	30,250	10.6
affiliated Christians	**38,100**	**69.7**	**98,490**	**91.1**	**129,720**	**77.2**	**3,554**	**-358**	**3,196**	**2.23**	**147,418**	**76.4**	**161,679**	**75.6**	**214,250**	**74.9**
Roman Catholics	34,000	62.2	76,500	70.7	92,800	55.2	2,543	-221	2,322	2.26	105,601	54.7	116,019	54.2	150,000	52.5
Protestants	4,000	7.3	17,940	16.6	24,500	14.6	671	-121	550	2.05	27,970	14.5	30,000	14.0	36,000	12.6
Independents	0	0.0	3,000	2.8	9,000	5.4	246	-46	200	2.03	9,807	5.1	11,000	5.1	18,000	6.3
Marginal Christians	100	0.2	1,000	0.9	3,280	2.0	90	32	122	3.21	3,890	2.0	4,500	2.1	10,000	3.5
Anglicans	0	0.0	50	0.1	140	0.1	4	-2	2	1.34	150	0.1	160	0.1	250	0.1
Trans-megabloc groupings																
Evangelicals	3,000	5.5	6,000	5.6	8,800	5.2	241	-41	200	2.07	10,073	5.2	10,800	5.1	17,850	6.2
Pentecostals/Charismatics	0	0.0	500	0.5	9,100	5.4	249	21	270	2.63	11,050	5.7	11,800	5.5	20,000	7.0
Great Commission Christians	**3,300**	**6.0**	**13,000**	**12.0**	**30,200**	**18.0**	**827**	**177**	**1,004**	**2.91**	**35,500**	**18.4**	**40,236**	**18.8**	**60,000**	**21.0**
Nonreligious	1,000	1.8	3,300	3.1	9,000	5.4	246	85	331	3.18	10,700	5.5	12,312	5.8	20,000	7.0
Muslims	0	0.0	4,400	4.1	4,700	2.8	129	-15	114	2.20	5,300	2.8	5,842	2.7	7,000	2.5
New-Religionists	0	0.0	0	0.0	2,700	1.6	74	6	80	2.63	3,100	1.6	3,499	1.6	5,000	1.8
Buddhists	0	0.0	400	0.4	2,100	1.3	58	27	85	3.46	2,500	1.3	2,950	1.4	4,500	1.6
Atheists	0	0.0	0	0.0	1,100	0.7	30	14	44	3.45	1,350	0.7	1,544	0.7	2,500	0.9
Baha'is	0	0.0	400	0.4	700	0.4	19	4	23	2.90	830	0.4	932	0.4	1,400	0.5
Ethnoreligionists	14,800	27.1	300	0.3	250	0.2	7	-5	2	0.88	260	0.1	273	0.1	300	0.1
Other religionists	0	0.0	100	0.1	300	0.2	8	10	18	4.86	400	0.2	482	0.2	800	0.3
World A (unevangelized persons)	10,994	20.1	540	0.5	2,016	1.2	55	41	96	3.96	2,509	1.3	2,996	1.4	5,148	1.8
World B (evangelized non-Christians)	4,805	8.8	8,514	7.9	18,834	11.2	516	85	601	2.79	21,938	11.4	24,809	11.6	36,352	12.7
World C (Christians)	38,900	71.1	99,100	91.6	147,150	87.6	4,031	-126	3,905	2.38	168,560	87.3	186,195	87.0	244,500	85.5
Country's population	**54,700**	**100.0**	**108,154**	**100.0**	**168,000**	**100.0**	**4,602**	**0**	**4,602**	**2.45**	**193,008**	**100.0**	**214,000**	**100.0**	**286,000**	**100.0**

COLUMNS, ROWS.
For meanings and definitions, see Codebook (Part 3). Note that, by definition, total 'Christians' = professing + crypto-Christians, which also = affiliated + unaffiliated Christians, and also = Great Commission Christians + latent Christians. Percentages may not always total exactly, due to rounding.

CENSUSES.
1961: 73.1% Roman Catholics, 20.1% Protestants, 5.4% other religionists.

NOTES ON RELIGIONS
BAHA'IS. Begun 1952. Growth from 1 local spiritual assembly (1964) to 3 (1973).
BUDDHISTS. Vietnamese.
ETHNORELIGIONISTS. In 1995, animists in remote mountain areas, and adherents of occasional traditionalist Melanesian cargo cults, usually introduced from New Hebrides.
INDEPENDENTS. In one denomination in 1995 (see Table 2).
MUSLIMS. Mostly Javanese immigrants from Indonesia, who are Sunnis (of the Shafiite rite), with some Arabs.
NONRELIGIOUS. In 1900, mainly French long-term political prisoners and other Europeans. In 1995, mainly French settlers.
OTHER RELIGIONISTS. Including Rosicrucians (1 AMORC centre).
ROMAN CATHOLICS. In 1900, Catholics consisted of almost all the 23,000 French (including a majority of the total of 40,000 French political prisoners taken to Ile Nou penal settlement from 1864-1897), many of the 27,700 Melanesians, and some of the 3,280 Chinese and other Asiatics.

Great Commission Instrument Panel: status of New Caledonia (for explanation see start of Part 4)

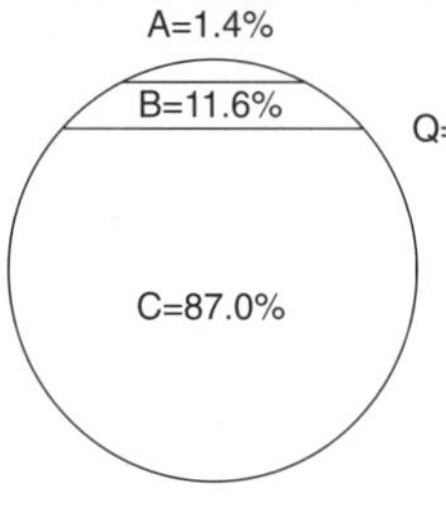

3 Worlds, AD 2000

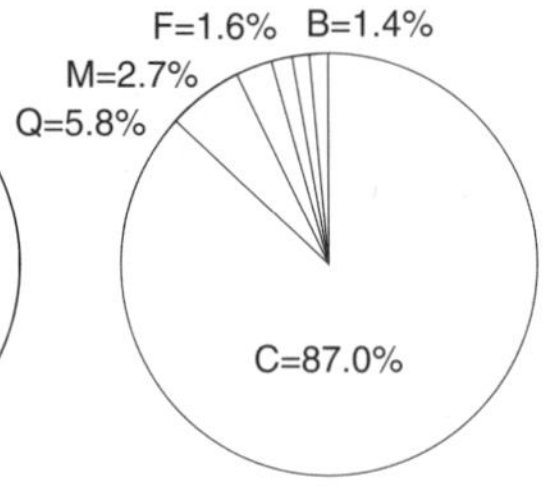

Religions, AD 2000

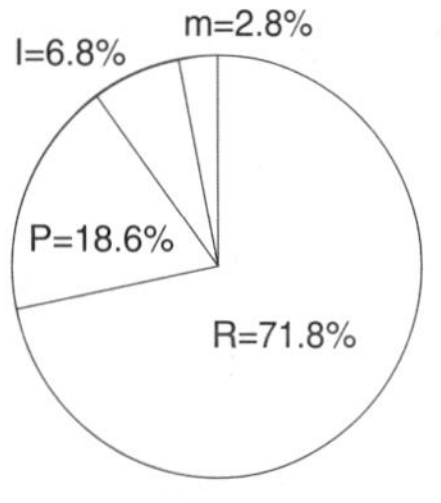

Ecclesiastical blocs

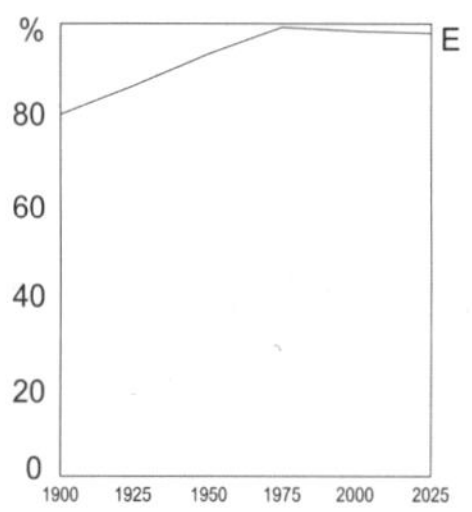

Evangelization, 1900-2025

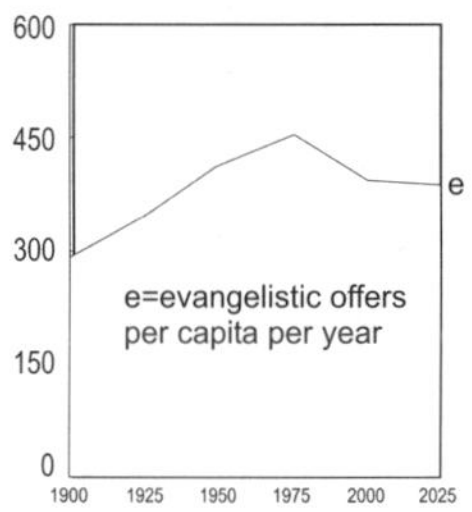

Offers, 1900-2025

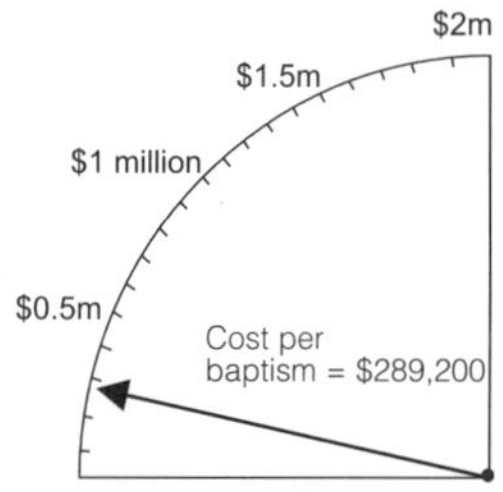

Cost-effectiveness, AD 2000

Country status. New Caledonia, a French Overseas Territory, is an island in the southwest Pacific Ocean east of Australia. Its chief exports are coffee, copra, and nickel.

Eglise Evangélique en Nouvelle-Calédonie et Iles Loyauté. Administration of communion.

HUMAN LIFE AND LIBERTY

Human rights and freedoms. The situation is similar to that in France, although militant Melanesians have clashed repeatedly with police and military.

NON-CHRISTIAN RELIGIONS

Islam has over 4,000 adherents, mostly Javanese immigrants from Indonesia, who are Sunnis of the Shafiite rite, with some Arabs.

Traditional religions exist only among a few tribes in remote mountain areas. Social rites, during which celebrations give way to orgiastic dancing called Pilou-pilou, are gradually disappearing. Melanesian cargo cults have touched New Caledonia at times, usually from New Hebrides.

CHRISTIANITY

CATHOLIC CHURCH. Catholic missionaries entered New Caledonia in 1843, and by 1884 the first 4 native priests had been ordained. The majority of the population is now Catholic and includes a large number of Europeans. Parishes with resident priests are found on New Caledonia itself, the islands of Bélep and Pines and the Loyalty Islands of Ouvea, Lifou, and Maré. A Vietnamese priest is in charge of a Vietnamese parish in Nouméa, the capital. The majority of the Wallis Islanders (11,600 in 1995) are Catholics. Coming to work in the nickel mines, they are poorly integrated into the local population and remain particularly dependent on the church.

The Holy See has no diplomatic relations with New Caledonia in AD 2000, but is represented there by an apostolic delegate for the Pacific Ocean residing in Wellington, New Zealand.

OTHER CHURCHES. Christianity was first brought to New Caledonia by a native Tongan in 1834. In 1841 the London Missionary Society sent 2 Samoans as teachers and the first White LMS missionaries arrived during the 1850s. The LMS turned over its work to the Paris Mission in 1922. The Evangelical Church, the result of this early effort, is the largest of the non-Catholic churches. A schism by 3 pastors in 1960 produced the country's first indigenous denomination, called the Free Church. Seventh-day Adventists have been active since 1925, with the Assemblies of God entering the field later. There are also Jehovah's Witnesses, and a Mormon schism. The small Anglican community, mostly British nationals, is part of the diocese of New Hebrides in the Church of the Province of Melanesia.

Indigenous missions. A few missionaries have been sent out to surrounding islands and some served back in France but New Caledonia has not had a strong missionary sending agenda.

CHURCH AND STATE

The island was named by Captain James Cook in 1774 and annexed by France in 1853. It served as a penal colony from 1864 to 1894. As a French overseas territory, church-state relations are the same as those in metropolitan France. The large Catholic and Protestant school programs receive government subsidies.

Country summary. **Worlds A, B, C by ethnolinguistic peoples, cities, and major civil divisions in New Caledonia.**

	PEOPLES							CITIES							CIVIL DIVISIONS						
World	Num	Pop 2000	C%	Christians	E%	U%	Unevangelized	Num	Pop 2000	C%	Christians	E%	U%	Unevangelized	Num	Pop 2000	C%	Christians	E%	U%	Unevangelized
A	0	0	0.00	0	0	0	0	0	0	0.00	0	0	0	0	0	0	0.00	0	0	0	0
B	4	17,561	25.95	4,557	85	15	2,571	0	0	0.00	0	0	0	0	0	0	0.00	0	0	0	0
C	46	196,468	79.97	157,124	100	0	391	1	115,236	76.00	87,579	99	1	1,072	3	214,030	75.54	161,679	99	1	2,966
Total	**50**	**214,029**	**75.54**	**161,681**	**99**	**1**	**2,962**	**1**	**115,236**	**76.00**	**87,579**	**99**	**1**	**1,072**	**3**	**214,030**	**75.54**	**161,679**	**99**	**1**	**2,966**

BROADCASTING AND MEDIA

Shortwave radio programs from KNLS have had responses. The 'Jesus' Film has been shown to 60,000, with a total of 19,500 responding. New Caledonia is a member of UNDA.

FUTURE TRENDS AND PROSPECTS

The nonreligious, 3.1% in 1970, will probably grow to over 7% by 2025. Buddhists and New-Religionists are also expected to increase significantly.

Christianity could continue its decline through the 21st century. The nonreligious, Buddhists, and New-Religionists could grow to jointly include 25% of the population by AD 2050.

BIBLIOGRAPHY

Archives of the Catholic Archdiocese of Noumea, 1843–1972. Catholic Church, Archdiocese of Noumea. *Oceania Marist Province Archives*, vol. 179-360. 82 reels. (Microfilm; available from Pacific Manuscripts Bureau).

Christianity in New Caledonia and the Loyalty Islands: sociological profile. J. M. Kohler. Noumea, New Caledonia: Office de la Recherche Scientifique et Technique Outre-Mer, 1981. 32p.

Église de Nouvelle Calédonie, (1976–). (weekly).

'Forerunners of Melanesian nationalism,' J. Guiart, *Oceania*, 22, 2 (1951), 81–90. (Cargo cults in New Hebrides and New Caledonia).

Histoire des catholiques dans l'île de Lifou. J. Izoulet. Lifou, New Caledonia: Mission de Nathalo, 1993–.

Kanaké: the Mélanésian way. J. M. Tjibaou & P. Missotte. Papeete: Editions du Pacifique, 1978. 120p.

La Sorcellerie canaque actuelle étude de l angoisse de mort et du mal–ajustement social dans une tribu. E. Métais. Bordeaux: Union française d'impression, 1967. 421p.

L'Eglise catholique en Nouvelle–Calédonie: un siècle et demi d'histoire. G. Delbos. Paris: Editions Desclée, 1993. 455p.

Moeurs et coutumes des indigènes. H. Mayet. 52p.

'Naissance et avortement d'un messianisme: colonisation et décolonisation en Nouvelle Calédonie,' J. Guiart, *Archives de sociologie des religions*, 7 (January–June, 1959), 3–44.

New Caledonia: towards Kanak independence: reports of an ecumenical visit to New Caledonia, 27 April–11 May 1984. E. Weingärtner & F. Trautmann. *Background information*, vol. 1984 no. 2. Geneva: Commission of the Churches on International Affairs, World Council of Churches, 1984. 51p.

Nouvelles protestantes: Journal mensuel de l'Eglise protestante de Nouméa et de Nouvelle-Calédonie, (n.s. 1952–). (monthly).

Petit essai bibliographique des ouvrages executes a Noumea et a St. Louis et sortis des presses de l'imprimerie Catholique de la mission de Nouvelle–Calédonie, 1885–1939. P. O'Reilly. Paris: The Author, 1951. 53p.

Sectes et dénominations en Nouvelle–Calédonie. Noumea: Eglise évangélique en Nouvelle-Calédonie et aux Iles Loyauté, Commission d'éducation chrétienne, 1973. 87p. (Text in French and Lifou).

'The development of the political awareness of the Kanak Evangelical Church in New Caledonia and the Loyalty Islands from 1960 to 1987 and its theological implications: possibility for a Kanak liberation theology.' P. Wete. B.D. thesis, Pacific Theological College, Suva, Fiji, 1988. 115p.

The Loyalty Islands: a history of culture contacts, 1840–1900. K. R. Howe. Canberra: Australian University Press, 1977. 222p.

Country Table 2. **Organized churches and denominations in New Caledonia.**

Official name (bold type = church with over 10% of all affiliated) 1	Begun 2	Type 3	Counc 4	Congs 5	Adults 6	Affiliated 1970 7	Affiliated 1995 8	G% 9	*Names, notes, and other statistics* (see Codebook, Part 3) 10
Assemblées de Dieu de Nouméa	1969	P-Pe2	ZF...	55	2,500	400	3,500	9.06	*Assemblies of God.* M=AdD(France),AoG(USA). 18n,2f,1s(10),W=50%,18Y,35z.
Eglise Adventiste du Septième Jour	1925	P-Adv	x....	4	339	800	900	0.47	*Seventh-day Adventists, NC Mission.* Declining 7% pa. 1n,2x,4t(549),W=85%.47Y.
Eglise Anglicane (D New Hebrides)		A-ACa	awpK.	1	90	50	150	0.05	*Anglican Ch.* Under D New Hebrides, Ch of the Province of Melanesia. British.
Eglise Catholique: M Nouméa	1843	R-Lat	P.PY.	37	60,000	76,500	105,601	1.30	M=SM2. C=2+2+5. (1970) 8n,51x,73m,244w,2220Yy. (1990) 10n,41x,85m,163w,1876Yy.
Eglise de J-C des Saints des D J	c1955	m-LdS	.....	4	280	200	700	5.14	*Ch of JC of Latter-day Saints. Mormons.*
Eglise Neo-Apostolique	c1990	I-3aX	x....	2	40	–	57	20.00	*NAC/NAK.* M=Neuapostolische Kirche (HQ Zurich, Switzerland).
Eglise Evangélique Libre	1957	I-Ref	.....	5	3,520	3,000	9,750	4.83	*Free Ch. French Protestant Ch.* Split ex EENC by 3 pastors. Mission in New Hebrides.
Eglise Sanito (Saints)	c1885	m-LdS	x....	4	193	500	350	-1.42	*Sanitos, Kanitos (Saints).* M=Reorganized Ch of JC of LdS(ex CJCLdS, USA). Noumea.
Eglises Evangéliques Autonomes	1841	P-Ref	.WP..	121	16,300	16,700	23,370	1.35	*EENC. Ev Ch in NC & Loyalty Is.* M=LMS,PEMS. Several schisms. 6n,1s(6),195Yy,135z.
Témoins de Jéhovah	c1950	m-Jeh	x....	11	1,165	300	2,840	9.41	*Jehovah's Witnesses.* Active witnessing under way by 1954. (1975) 37Y. (1995) 85Y.
Other Protestant bodies		P-	.....	4	120	40	200	0.05	In 2 recent mission arrivals.
Totals				**248**	**84,547**	**98,490**	**147,418**		

Churches, members, growth, 1900-2025	*Congs*	*Adults*	*Affiliated*	*G%*	*Total denominations*	*6 Megablocs:* O	R	A	P	I	m
Total churches, members, and denominations (mid-1900)	60	22,000	38,100	1.37	3	0	1	0	1	0	1
Total churches, members, and denominations (mid-1970)	148	56,795	98,490	1.37	10	0	1	1	4	1	3
Total churches, members, and denominations (mid-1990)	200	74,400	129,720	1.39	12	0	1	1	5	2	3
Total churches, members, and denominations (mid-1995)	248	84,547	147,418	2.59	12	0	1	1	5	2	3
Total churches, members, and denominations (mid-2000)	260	92,700	161,679	1.86	12	0	1	1	5	2	3
Total churches, members, and denominations (mid-2025)	320	123,000	214,250	1.13	30	0	1	1	10	12	6

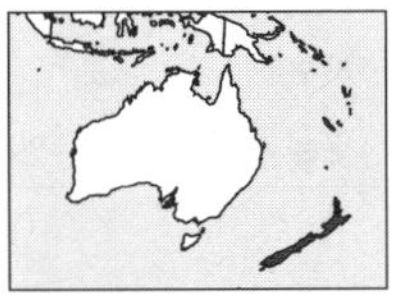

NEW ZEALAND

SECULAR DATA, AD 2000

STATE
Official name: The Dominion of New Zealand/Aotearoa.
Short name: New Zealand. **Adjective of nationality:** of New Zealand, a New Zealander.
Flag: Blue field with British Union Jack at upper hoist corner; 4 red stars outlined in white.
Area: 270,534 sq. km. (104,454 sq. mi.).
Government: Parliamentary state (constitutional monarchy), since 1947 (1840 British possession, 1907 self-governing dominion, 1947 Independence).
Legislature: House of Representatives, 120 members (4 being Maoris).
Official language: English.
Monetary unit: 1 New Zealand dollar ($NZ) = 100 cents. **US$1=** $NZ 2.02.
Chief cities: Auckland 1,014,000; WELLINGTON 387,292; Christchurch 339,909; Manukau 250,243; Hamilton 164,461.
Political divisions: 16 provinces.
Armed forces: 10,000.

DEMOGRAPHY
Population: 3,862,000.
Population density: 14.2/sq. km. (36.9/sq. mi.).
Under 15 years: 875,000.
Growth rate p.a.: 0.88% (births 14.20, deaths 7.90).
Mortality: Infant, per 1,000: 6.3, ; **Maternal per 100,000:** 25.0.
Life expectancy: 78 (male 75, female 81).
Household size: 2.9. **Floor area per person, sq.m:** 45.0.
Major languages: English, Maori, Dutch, Irish, Samoan, Tongan, Chinese (Cantonese), and other languages.
Urban dwellers: 86.91%. **Urban growth rate p.a.:** 1.3%.
Labor force: 49%.

ETHNOLINGUISTIC PEOPLES
69.4% Anglo-New Zealander; 9.9% Maori (Rotorua-Taupo); 7.0% British (English); 2.1% British (Scottish); 2.0% Samoan.

ECONOMY
National income p.a. per person: US$14,340; **per family:** US$41,586.

EDUCATION
Adult literacy: 100% (male 100%, female 100%). **Schools:** 2,772. **Universities:** 7. **School enrolment:** female/male: 108%/107%.

HEALTH
Access to health services: 95%. **Access to safe water:** 100%.
Hospitals: 330 (77 beds per 10,000). **Doctors:** 11,413.
Blind: 3,687. **Deaf:** 225,600. **Murder rate:** 3.
Lepers: 50.

LITERATURE
New book titles p.a.: 1,930 (500 p.a. per million). **Periodicals:** 8,103.
Newspapers: 31 dailies.

COMMUNICATION (per 1,000 people)
Phones: 479 (**23% mobile). Radios:** 866. **TV sets:** 506.
Daily newspaper circulation: 297. **Computers:** 499.

HUMAN LIFE AND LIBERTY (optimum condition=100.0%)
HDI: 93.7. **HSI:** 92.0. **HFI:** 90.0. **EFL:** 65.0.

Country status. New Zealand is a Commonwealth country consisting of 2 main islands in the South Pacific. Meat, wool, and dairy products are the main exports.

HUMAN LIFE AND LIBERTY

Human need and development. New Zealand is a developed country where the standards of life are close to those of the United Kingdom and Western Europe. Somewhat underpopulated, and also isolated from the rest of the world, New Zealand has the aura of being an outsider in the comity of nations, but this has not affected the quality of life of the average New Zealander. In fact, life on the 2 main islands is a replica of that of the United Kingdom. Like Australia, New Zealand adopted the concept of welfare state early in the 20th century, and thus has an advanced Social Security system. New Zealand has been particularly generous to the small nations of the South Pacific, and has tried to share with them both expertise and developmental funds.

Human rights and freedoms. New Zealand's Anglo-Saxon heritage assures full respect of all human rights. The legal system is based on British Common Law. The official but highly independent New Zealand Human Rights Commission adjudicates complaints relating to human rights. As a sig-

Country Table 1. **Religious adherents in New Zealand, AD 1900-2025.**

Year / Name	1900 Adherents	1900 %	1970 Adherents	1970 %	mid-1990 Adherents	mid-1990 %	Annual change, 1990-2000 Natural	Conversion	Total	Rate	mid-1995 Adherents	mid-1995 %	mid-2000 Adherents	mid-2000 %	mid-2025 Adherents	mid-2025 %
Christians	**801,930**	**98.3**	**2,690,080**	**95.4**	**2,830,080**	**84.2**	**42,273**	**-2,847**	**39,426**	**1.31**	**3,082,000**	**84.0**	**3,224,340**	**83.5**	**3,800,000**	**80.9**
PROFESSION																
professing Christians	**801,930**	**98.3**	**2,690,080**	**95.4**	**2,830,080**	**84.2**	**42,273**	**-2,847**	**39,426**	**1.31**	**3,082,000**	**84.0**	**3,224,340**	**83.5**	**3,800,000**	**80.9**
AFFILIATION																
unaffiliated Christians	60,040	7.4	440,413	15.6	531,780	15.8	7,945	5,089	13,034	2.22	610,685	16.6	662,121	17.1	782,000	16.7
affiliated Christians	**741,890**	**90.9**	**2,249,667**	**79.8**	**2,298,300**	**68.4**	**34,328**	**-7,936**	**26,392**	**1.09**	**2,471,315**	**67.3**	**2,562,219**	**66.3**	**3,018,000**	**64.3**
Protestants	309,600	37.9	851,895	30.2	840,000	25.0	12,550	-3,428	9,122	1.04	909,976	24.8	931,219	24.1	1,050,000	22.4
Anglicans	320,000	39.2	876,570	31.1	735,000	21.9	10,981	-1,981	9,000	1.16	800,000	21.8	825,000	21.4	850,000	18.1
Roman Catholics	110,100	13.5	426,128	15.1	470,000	14.0	7,022	-4,522	2,500	0.52	479,656	13.1	495,000	12.8	550,000	11.7
Independents	1,000	0.1	42,218	1.5	152,000	4.5	2,271	1,529	3,800	2.26	170,356	4.6	190,000	4.9	359,000	7.7
Marginal Christians	1,000	0.1	48,856	1.7	96,000	2.9	1,434	466	1,900	1.82	105,727	2.9	115,000	3.0	200,000	4.3
Orthodox	190	0.0	4,000	0.1	5,300	0.2	79	-9	70	1.25	5,600	0.2	6,000	0.2	9,000	0.2
Trans-megabloc groupings																
Evangelicals	424,000	52.0	600,000	21.3	595,000	17.7	8,890	-2,390	6,500	1.04	645,121	17.6	660,000	17.1	750,000	16.0
Pentecostals/Charismatics	0	0.0	25,000	0.9	500,000	14.9	7,470	1,530	9,000	1.67	556,246	15.2	590,000	15.3	820,000	17.5
Great Commission Christians	**82,000**	**10.1**	**705,000**	**25.0**	**1,310,000**	**39.0**	**19,572**	**3,589**	**23,161**	**1.64**	**1,450,000**	**39.5**	**1,541,611**	**39.9**	**1,878,000**	**40.0**
Nonreligious	4,800	0.6	84,360	3.0	412,700	12.3	6,166	1,784	7,950	1.78	457,630	12.5	492,200	12.7	700,000	14.9
Buddhists	430	0.1	1,360	0.1	26,700	0.8	399	693	1,092	3.49	33,500	0.9	37,616	1.0	55,000	1.2
Atheists	400	0.1	15,000	0.5	29,500	0.9	441	-1	440	1.40	31,200	0.9	33,898	0.9	45,000	1.0
Hindus	0	0.0	3,800	0.1	17,800	0.5	266	179	445	2.26	20,000	0.5	22,254	0.6	33,000	0.7
Ethnoreligionists	4,000	0.5	9,000	0.3	17,000	0.5	254	-24	230	1.28	17,800	0.5	19,298	0.5	21,000	0.5
Muslims	40	0.0	1,000	0.0	5,800	0.2	87	61	148	2.29	6,500	0.2	7,276	0.2	10,000	0.2
Chinese folk-religionists	2,000	0.3	7,000	0.3	7,000	0.2	105	-86	19	0.27	7,000	0.2	7,190	0.2	7,000	0.2
New-Religionists	0	0.0	0	0.0	3,000	0.1	45	192	237	5.99	4,100	0.1	5,368	0.1	6,000	0.1
Jews	1,600	0.2	3,800	0.1	4,600	0.1	69	-4	65	1.33	4,900	0.1	5,252	0.1	7,000	0.2
Baha'is	0	0.0	2,600	0.1	2,900	0.1	43	55	98	2.95	3,300	0.1	3,878	0.1	6,000	0.1
Spiritists	500	0.1	1,000	0.0	1,200	0.0	18	-4	14	1.11	1,240	0.0	1,340	0.0	2,000	0.0
Sikhs	0	0.0	0	0.0	320	0.0	5	2	7	1.89	350	0.0	386	0.0	700	0.0
Other religionists	300	0.0	1,000	0.0	1,400	0.0	21	0	21	1.39	1,480	0.0	1,608	0.0	2,300	0.1
World A (unevangelized persons)	1,632	0.2	14,098	0.5	30,240	0.9	433	266	699	2.18	33,042	0.9	34,758	0.9	75,120	1.6
World B (evangelized non-Christians)	12,637	1.5	115,423	4.1	499,680	14.9	7,486	2,581	10,067	1.90	556,308	15.1	602,902	15.6	819,880	17.5
World C (Christians)	801,930	98.3	2,690,080	95.4	2,830,080	84.2	42,273	-2,847	39,426	1.31	3,082,000	84.0	3,224,340	83.5	3,800,000	80.9
Country's population	**816,200**	**100.0**	**2,819,602**	**100.0**	**3,360,000**	**100.0**	**50,193**	**0**	**50,192**	**1.40**	**3,671,351**	**100.0**	**3,862,000**	**100.0**	**4,695,000**	**100.0**

COLUMNS, ROWS.
For meanings and definitions, see Codebook (Part 3). Note that, by definition, total 'Christians' = professing + crypto-Christians, which also = affiliated + unaffiliated Christians, and also = Great Commission Christians + latent Christians. Percentages may not always total exactly, due to rounding.

CENSUSES.
1901 (adjusted to include 43,143 Maoris): 42.0% Protestants (21.6% Presbyterians, 10.3% Methodists, 2.0% Baptists), 41.8% Anglicans, 14.2% Roman Catholics, 0.6% nonreligious, 0.3% Chinese folk-religionists and Buddhists, 0.2% Jews. **25.IX.1945** (excluding foreign military personnel): 80.7% Anglicans & Protestants, 14.8% Roman Catholics, 1.5% Polynesian indigenous (1.2% Ratana, 0.3% Ringatu), 1.3% nonreligious, 1.0% marginal Protestants, 0.2% Jews, 0.2% other religionists. **17.IV.1951:** 80.8% Anglicans & Protestants, 14.8% Roman Catholics, 1.3% Polynesian indigenous (1.0% Ratana, 0.3% Ringatu), 1.2% nonreligious, 1.0% marginal Protestants, 0.8% other religionists, 0.2% Jews. **17.IV.1956:** 96.8% Christians (including 1.3% Polynesian indigenous (1.0% Ratana, 0.3% Ringatu)), 1.0% nonreligious, 0.8% other religionists, 0.2% Jews, 0.1% Hindus. **18.IV.1961** (excluding foreign military): 41.4% Protestants (24.6% Presbyterians), 38.0% Anglicans, 16.6% Roman Catholics, 1.3% marginal Protestants, 1.3% Polynesian indigenous (1.0 Ratana, 0.2% Ringatu), 1.0% nonreligious, 0.2% Jews, 0.2% Orthodox, 0.1% Hindus. **22.III.1966** (excluding foreign military): 39.8% Protestants (23.8% Presbyterians, 7.6% Methodists), 36.9% Anglicans, 17.4% Roman Catholics, 1.5% nonreligious, 1.4% marginal Protestants, 1.4% Polynesian indigenous (1.1% Ratana, 0.2% Ringatu), 0.3% atheists, 0.2% Jews, 0.1% Orthodox, 0.1% Hindus. **23.III.1971:** 38.2% Protestants (23.1% Presbyterians, 7.2% Methodists, 1.9% Baptists), 35.4% Anglicans, 17.8% Roman Catholics, 3.0% nonreligious, 1.7% marginal Protestants, 1.5% Polynesian indigenous (1.2% Ratana, 0.2% Ringatu). **1981:** 36.2% Protestants (18.3% Presbyterians, 4.8% Methodists, 2.1% Baptists), 25.7% Anglicans, 16.5% Roman Catholics, 17.7% nonreligious, 1.7% Marginal Christians, 1.4% Polynesian indigenous (1.2% Ratana, 0.2% Ringatu), 0.3% Hindus, 0.2% Buddhists, 0.1% Muslims, 0.1% Baha'is, 0.1% Jews. **1991:** 34.9% Protestants (16.3% Presbyterians, 4.2% Methodists, 2.1% Baptists), 23.1% Anglicans, 21.1% nonreligious, 16.0% Roman Catholics, 2.0% Marginal Christians, 1.6% Polynesian indigenous (1.4% Ratana, 0.2% Ringatu), 0.5% Hindus, 0.4% Buddhists, 0.2% Muslims, 0.1% Baha'is, 0.1% Jews.

NOTES ON RELIGIONS
ATHEISTS. In 1970, New Zealand Communist Party (NZCP) (legal; pro-Chinese) and Socialist Unity Party (SUP) (pro-Soviet).
BAHA'IS. Rapid growth from 3 local spiritual assemblies (1964) to 17 (1973).
BUDDHISTS. Chinese.
ETHNORELIGIONISTS. A small minority of the Maoris do not identify themselves as Christians but follow traditional Maori religion.
HINDUS. Indians, with a handful of White converts to Hindu sects. ISKCON (Hare Krishna) operates 1 center, and Ananda Marga (Path of Bliss) operates 6 centers. Also, the Theosophical Society, a neo-Hindu movement.
INDEPENDENTS. In about 22 denominations in 1995 (see Table 2).
MUSLIMS. Arabs and Indo-Pakistanis.
NONRELIGIOUS. In the 1901 census, 2,856 freethinkers were recorded, 910 of no religion, 552 agnostics, et alia. In 1995, nonreligious were mostly Whites but with small numbers of Chinese.
OTHER RELIGIONISTS. Adherents of a number of small groups, including Rosicrucians (AMORC) with 7 Lodges.
PENTECOSTALS. Although late-starting by comparison with Anglican churches elsewhere, the Anglican charismatic movement has rapidly spread since 1972. It also includes many Anglican youth in the Jesus movement. By 1977 the Charismatic Renewal claimed to involve over 40% of all active Anglicans in New Zealand. (Catholic charismatics): totals (January 1974): 2,500 involved adults (over 15 years old) in 31 prayer groups; total charismatic community including children, 5,000. By 1997 CCR prayer groups had multiplied to 140.
ROMAN CATHOLICS. In 1900, including 3,600 Maoris.
SPIRITISTS. Adherents of non-Christian Spiritism or Spiritualism.

Great Commission Instrument Panel: status of New Zealand (for explanation see start of Part 4)

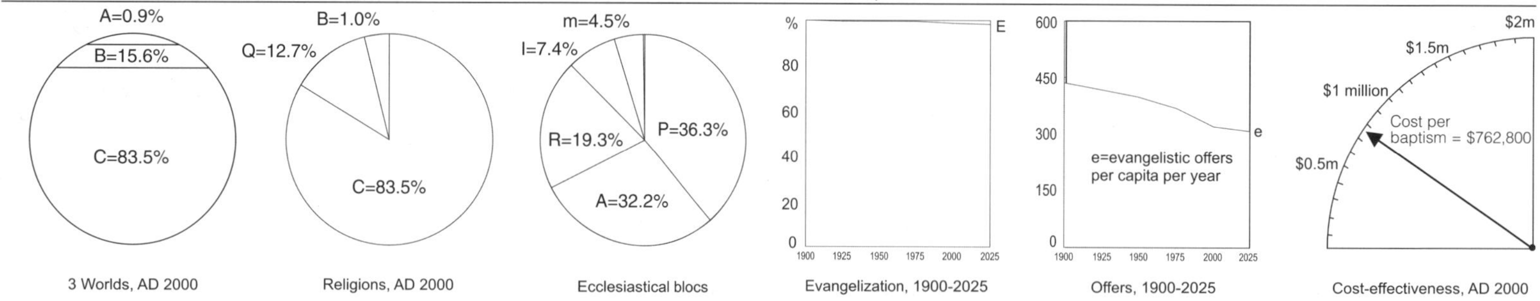

natory to the U N Convention on the Rights of the Child, New Zealand gives careful attention to the rights of children. There is an independent commissioner for children under the 1989 Children, Young Persons, and their Families Act. The Race Relations Conciliator hears complaints about racial discrimination.

Human environment. Only one-third of the original forest stands remain in their pristine state. Some of the islands' unique plants and animal species are threatened with extinction as a result of encroachments on the wilderness.

The country's postage stamps often celebrate Christian history. *Far Right.* Samuel Marsden conducting first Christian service, 1814. *Right.* Centenary of translation of Maori Bible in 1858.

NON-CHRISTIAN RELIGIONS

Traditional religion continues to exist among the Maoris, who make up 10% of the population, although a majority today call themselves Christians. In Maori mythology, Rangi, the supreme sky deity, emerged from an initial chaos and, together with Papa (old Mother Earth), was responsible for the propagation of men and other divinities.

Other religions include a sizeable Hindu community and small numbers of Chinese folk-religionists, Jews, Baha'is, Buddhists, and others.

CHRISTIANITY

The history of Christianity in New Zealand includes missions to the oldest of the present inhabitants, the Maoris, and also churches working among White settler immigrants. Maoris are a Malaysian-Polynesian people who came to the islands before 1350 and who later were more militantly opposed to European settlers than the Aborigines of Australia. Dutch explorers visited the islands in 1642 and the British in 1769. In the 1790s several English whaling establishments were begun.

ANGLICAN CHURCH. An Anglican chaplain in New South Wales named Samuel Marsden opened the first permanent Anglican mission in 1814. Marsden persuaded the CMS to send missionaries to the Maoris, and by 1838 there was a staff of 35, 21 schools, 178 communicants, and 2,176 attending services. A written language was also developed and portions of the Bible and other Christian literature translated. Missionaries had already been working among the Maoris for 25 years before the colonial problem became acute. The CMS attempted to protect

Country summary. **Worlds A, B, C by ethnolinguistic peoples, cities, and major civil divisions in New Zealand.**

	PEOPLES							CITIES							CIVIL DIVISIONS						
World	*Num*	*Pop 2000*	*C%*	*Christians*	*E%*	*U%*	*Unevangelized*	*Num*	*Pop 2000*	*C%*	*Christians*	*E%*	*U%*	*Unevangelized*	*Num*	*Pop 2000*	*C%*	*Christians*	*E%*	*U%*	*Unevangelized*
A	0	0	0.00	0	0	0	0	0	0	0.00	0	0	0	0	0	0	0.00	0	0	0	0
B	9	114,892	24.47	28,116	79	21	23,852	0	0	0.00	0	0	0	0	0	0	0.00	0	0	0	0
C	39	3,747,014	67.63	2,534,101	100	0	12,135	11	2,483,919	65.04	1,615,570	99	1	28,005	16	3,861,422	66.35	2,562,219	99	1	35,505
Total	**48**	**3,861,906**	**66.35**	**2,562,217**	**99**	**1**	**35,987**	**11**	**2,483,919**	**65.04**	**1,615,570**	**99**	**1**	**28,005**	**16**	**3,861,422**	**66.35**	**2,562,219**	**99**	**1**	**35,505**

the Maoris from British colonization, and when this failed they assisted in the Treaty of Waitangi of 1840, in which the Maoris acknowledged British sovereignty in return for the promise of continued possession of their land. The promise was not kept, and Maori uprisings took place during 1845-48 and 1860-70, to the dismay and demoralization of the missions. Discovery of gold in 1861 and rapidly-expanding commerce in meat and wool soon attracted large numbers of White settlers.

Among the Maoris who remained in the Anglican mission, 23 had been ordained by 1872, and 69 by 1900. In 1883 CMS withdrew and left its responsibilities to the Church of New Zealand which had been developed within the White community. Some time after 1914, Maoris requested and were granted an Anglican organization of their own, with a Maori clergyman consecrated as suffragan bishop. In 1926 a third of all Maoris were Anglicans. Many of the settlers who came to New Zealand following the 1840 treaty were Anglicans. The first bishop was appointed in 1841 with headquarters at Auckland on North Island, originally the most heavily populated. In 1851 a large body of colonists, almost all Anglicans arrived to establish what is now Christchurch in South Island, which continues to maintain the atmosphere of an English cathedral and university town. Originally the church was part of the diocese of Calcutta, but in 1844 a synod was convened and another in 1847; and finally an ecclesiastical province was created in 1858. A proposal in 1844 that the colonial government should pay part of the bishop's salary was defeated by Presbyterians and Catholics, and the Anglican church was at no time established by law. It remains the largest church in New Zealand, though the number of professing Anglicans has declined from 42% of the population in 1901 to 24% in 1995. The Church of the Province of New Zealand has 8 dioceses including the missionary diocese of Polynesia with its seat in Fiji. The church administers 25 primary schools, 18 secondary schools, and one hospital in New Zealand.

PROTESTANT CHURCHES. Wesleyan Methodists opened a mission on the northern coast of North Island in 1822. The violence of Maori reaction caused them to leave a few years later, but they returned within a year and the first baptism took place in 1930. Missions expanded along the western coast. In 1872 there were 3 districts, 29 circuits, 119 churches, 45 ministers, 181 local preachers and 2,658 members, including Methodists who had arrived as new settlers. In 1874 the first Methodist conference was held in Christchurch, and in 1913 a union took place of several Methodist bodies which had entered New Zealand during the 19th century. Methodists identified themselves as 8.9% of the population in 1926 and 7.2% in 1971, falling under 5% by 1995; Methodists operate one primary and one secondary school.

The first Presbyterian minister came to New Zealand in 1839 among a shipload of colonists to North Island. In 1843 a minister of the Church of Scotland arrived, and in 1850 one from the Free Church of Scotland. The rapid growth of the Presbyterian Church in New Zealand is attributable in part to church disruptions in Scotland in the middle of the 19th century, with New Zealand providing an outlet for the Free Church's outburst of energy. Presbyterians settled in 1844 at what is now Dunedin, in the southern part of South Island, desiring to establish a model Christian community similar to that of the Anglicans at Christchurch. In 1861 gold was discovered in the vicinity and a mixed population grew rapidly. Although most Presbyterians continued to be found in this area, Presbyterian ministers from Scotland, Ireland, and Canada spread throughout New Zealand; 17 arrived in 1871-72 from the Free Church alone. Two Presbyterian churches arose, one in the north and other in the south, which were finally united in 1901. New Zealand Presbyterians began to send out foreign missionaries in 1967, first to the New Hebrides, later to South China and to the Punjab in India. Presbyterians form the second largest church in New Zealand with 23.5% of the population in 1926, declining to 23.1% in 1971, and further declining to 16.4% by 1990. The Presbyterian Church sponsors 9 primary and 12 secondary schools.

Baptist colonists received their first pastor in 1851, and the Baptist Union of New Zealand was formed in 1882, and then undertook both home and foreign missions. Most Baptists are found in the north in the vicinity of Auckland.

The Baptist proportion of the population was 1.6% in 1926, 1.9% in 1971, declining to 1% by 1990.

Other smaller denominations include the Christian Brethren, Salvation Army, Disciples, Seventh-day Adventists, Lutherans, and Assemblies of God. Adventists have 13 primary and 2 secondary schools.

CATHOLIC CHURCH. An Irish priest entered New Zealand in 1828, although little progress was made until the arrival of French Marists in 1838. A vicariate was established in 1842 and a mission begun also among the Maoris with 1,000 conversions taking place by 1853. Friction developed between Catholics and Protestants, but more serious problems arose with the arrival of European settlers, the Maori revolt, and the eventual closing to all Europeans of the area in which Catholics worked. White Catholics were predominantly Irish, and numerous religious orders were sent to serve them. In 1848 Wellington was made a diocese and in 1887 an archdiocese. By 1892 there were 90,000 Catholics of whom more than 3,000 were Maoris, growing to 115,900 by the turn of the century. The Catholic Church is third in size among the churches. Catholics numbered 12.9% of the population in 1926, 17.4% in 1966, 17.8% in 1971, declining to 14.6% in 1990.

The Catholic population is very evenly distributed both geographically and throughout the income range of the population. The ethnic background of most Catholics is European, predominantly British, with a higher proportion of Irish than in the general population. But there are also substantial racial minorities, the largest being Maori. In recent years Maoris have shown a strong tendency to move from rural to urban areas, with resultant destruction of their traditional style of life and values. About half the Maoris live in Auckland diocese, which also has substantial Samoan and Cook Islands minorities as well. Maoris are served by a separate organized Maori Mission, staffed in Auckland by Mill Hill priests, whereas the rest of New Zealand is served by Marist priests.

The Holy See has diplomatic relations with New Zealand and in AD 2000 is represented to government and the Catholic hierarchy by a nuncio residing in Wellington.

Church of Jesus Christ of Latter-day Saints. One of the fastest-growing churches in New Zealand, expanding at 3.3% per year. Mormon Maori girls from New Zealand perform dance at Polynesian Cultural Centre, Hawaii.

MARGINAL CHURCHES. Marginal Protestant bodies from the Western world have a wide following. Mormons grew in numbers from 4,060 (0.3% of the population) in 1926 to 25,564 (1.0%) in 1966 and 2.3% in 1990. Their work is found mostly among Maoris, who increased from 5.4% Mormon in 1926 to 7.2% Mormon in 1961, and to 7.6% by 1971. They also have a secondary school. Jehovah's Witnesses began in New Zealand in 1904. By 1951 they numbered 1,756 (0.1%), in 1966 had increased to 7,455 (0.3%), and by 1995 had increased to 19,200 (0.6%). Christian Scientists on the other hand have decreased both in numbers and percentage over the period since 1951.

Ratana Church. Large central temple in Maori holy city Ratanapa, with archway commemorating Maori founder-healer T.W. Ratana and his 3 sons. Other Ratana churches elsewhere are replicas.

INDIGENOUS CHURCHES. Several churches not begun by Whites are found among the Maoris. During the last half of the 19th century when the Maoris were dying out through inter-tribal warfare and continued encroachment by White settlers, one reaction was the development of indigenous cults including the King movement of the 1850s and 1860s. It used biblical ideas to attempt to unite all Maoris under one king. The result however was a colonial war which further weakened them. Later, Hau Hau or Pai Marire, which included indigenous, Protestant, Catholic, and Old Testament elements, was stated by a Maori who claimed to receive guidance from the archangel Gabriel. Magic associated with the movement was believed to render its members safe from bullets. Two other movements still survive today as organized bodies. The Ratana Church is the third largest denomination among Maoris and was begun in 1918 by a Maori named Takapotiki Ratana. After a vision, Ratana urged his fellow tribesmen to leave their superstitions, with the assurance that God would send angels to help them. Ratana's followers developed their own socio-economic structures and in 1925 became a separate church. Since 1943 they have frequently held all 4 Maori seats in the New Zealand national legislature. The second body is Ringatu, which was founded in the 1860s by Te Kooti Rikirangi, a member of the Rongowhakaota tribe of Poverty Bay, and has a specialized liturgy which all members memorize and are permitted to conduct.

ORTHODOX CHURCHES. The Greek and Russian Orthodox churches have followings in New Zealand, mostly of immigrants from Europe since World War II. There is also a community of Old Believers.

Renewal movements. In the 1990s the Pentecostal/Charismatic Renewal continued to spread rapidly across most older churches, and numbered over 590,000 adherents (of whom 6% Pentecostals, 71% Charismatics, and 23% Independents).

Indigenous missions. Throughout the evangelization of the South Pacific, New Zealand was a strategic sending base for foreign missionaries. Today, both Protestants and Roman Catholics send significant numbers of missionaries abroad.

CHURCH AND STATE

New Zealand has 3 sources: the common law of England as it existed in 14 January 1840 when New Zealand became a British colony; certain statutes of the United Kingdom parliament enacted prior to 1947; and statutes of the New Zealand parliament. However, there has been from the beginning one significant difference from English law; there is and has been no established church in New Zealand. Although the Anglican Church has the largest membership, it has no special rights before the law, nor has any special legislation been passed regulating relations between church and state. No church receives direct financial aid from the state, although charitable institutions are exempt from some forms of taxation and ministers of religion are exempt from military service. Church schools receive financial aid from the state; and church charitable institutions including homes for the aged and hospitals are given state subsidies. In all cases of state assistance, however, aid is given on an equal interdenominational or secular basis; there is no religious basis for the granting or withholding of state aid.

Ministers of religion are gazetted as officiating ministers for the purpose of acting on behalf of the registrar of marriages. There is no ministry or government department in charge of religious or ecclesiastical affairs, nor do the churches have to register themselves with any government body.

There has been very little church-state conflict in New Zealand, except during the period when the Catholic and other churches were trying to obtain state aid for their schools.

BROADCASTING AND MEDIA

Shortwave radio programs from KNLS have had responses. Over half the residents have seen the 'Jesus' Film, most on television or in a movie theater. New Zealand is a member of UNDA. Catholics broadcast 'Call to Worship' each Sunday night, and Connections', exploring aspects of Catholic faith & responsibility, for an hour each Sunday morning.

INTERDENOMINATIONAL ORGANIZATIONS

The National Council of Churches in New Zealand was established in 1941 and now has 10 member denominations, including the Greek Orthodox Church and the Cook Islands Christian Church. An earlier body, the National Missionary Council of New Zealand, was formed in 1926 and became part of the NCC in 1957 as its Commission on Overseas Mission and Inter-Church Aid. There is a joint working group between the National Council and the Catholic Episcopal Conference.

In 1970 an interdenominational parish council was set up in the district of Dunedin. Its 6 member denominations (Anglican, Catholic, Baptist, Presbyterian, Church of Christ, and Salvation Army) undertake joint action in youth activities, social problems, relief services, and Bible study groups.

There is also the Evangelical Alliance of New Zealand, and the Associated Pentecostal Churches of New Zealand formed in 1975.

The Catholic Episcopal Conference created a National Commission on Ecumenism in 1967.

FUTURE TRENDS AND PROSPECTS

The nonreligious are expected to continue to grow to about 15% by 2025 while Christians drop to 81%.

Christianity could continue to decline well into the 21st century. The nonreligious could make up more than 25% of the population well before AD 2050.

BIBLIOGRAPHY

A brief history of the Catholic Church in New Zealand. E. R. Simmons. Auckland: Catholic Publications Centre, 1978. 119p.

A family affair: a brief survey of New Zealand Methodism's involvement in mission overseas, 1822–1972. G. G. Carter. [Auckland]: Wesley Historical Society of New Zealand, 1973. 245p.

A history of the charismatic movements in New Zealand: including a Pentecostal perspective and a breviate of the Catholic Apostolic Church in Great Britain. J. E. Worsfold. Wellington, NZ: Julian Literature Trust, 1974. 388p.

An ordered faith: faith and order in the Methodist Church of New Zealand, 1950–1984. D. Pratt. *Wesley Historical Society of New Zealand*, no. 53. Rotorua, NZ: Wesley Historical Society, 1989. 100p.

Be ye separate: fundamentalism and the New Zealand experience. B. Gilling (ed). *Waikato studies in religion*, vol. 3. Hamilton, NZ: University of Waikato Press, 1992. 177p.

Christianity in Aotearoa: a history of church and society in New Zealand. A. K. Davidson. Wellington, NZ: New Zealand Education for Ministry Board, 1991. 236p.

Churches and people in Australia and New Zealand, 1860–1930. H. R. Jackson. Wellington, NZ: Allen & Unwin, 1987. 219p.

Early Wellington churches. C. J. Fearnley. Ed., J. Bremner. Wellington, NZ: Millwood Press, 1977. 232p.

Finding the way: New Zealand Christians look forward. M. R. Martin (ed). Melbourne: Joint Board of Christian Education of Australia and New Zealand, 1983. 123p.

God's gentlemen: a history of the Melanesian Mission, 1849–1942. D. Hilliard. St. Lucia: University of Queensland Press, 1978. 357p.

Iconography of New Zealand Maori religion. No. 1 of section 2, *New Zealand,* of *Iconography of religions.* D. R. Simmons. Leiden: E. J. Brill, 1986. 33p.

In and out of the world: Seventh-day Adventists in New Zealand. P. H. Ballis (ed). Palmerston North, NZ: Dunmore Press, 1985. 178p.

Initial findings of a research analysis of the people and the church of New Zealand. B. Hall. Waikanae, NZ: Dawn Strategy, 1987. 54p.

New Zealand. R. Grover. *World bibliographical series*, vol. 18. Oxford, UK: CLIO Press, 1980. 254p. (See especially 'Religion,' p.63–5).

'New Zealand,' H. Mol, in *Western religion: a country by country sociological enquiry.* The Hague: Mouton, 1972.

New Zealanders and the Methodist evangel: an interpretation of the policies and performance of the Methodist Church of New Zealand. P. J. Lineham. Rotorua, NZ: Wesley Historical Society, 1983. 48p.

People movements in Southern Polynesia: studies in the dynamics of church–planting and growth in Tahiti, New Zealand, Tonga, and Samoa. A. R. Tippett. Chicago: Moody Press, 1971. 288p.

'Ratana: the origins and the story of the movement.' J. Henderson. Polynesian Society memorandum 36, Wellington, NZ, 1963.

Religion and race in New Zealand. H. Mol. Christchurch, NZ: National Council of Churches, 1966. 80p.

Religion in New Zealand. C. Nichol & J. Veitch (eds). 2nd ed. Wellington, NZ: Victoria University, 1983. 313p.

Religious history of New Zealand: a bibliography. P. J. Lineham. 4th ed. Palmerston North, NZ: Dept. of History, Massey University, 1993. 260p.

Rua and the Maori millennium. P. Webster. Wellington, NZ: Price Milburn, for the Victoria University Press, 1979. 328p.

Survey: a survey of religious opinions and attitudes. Christchurch, NZ: National Council of Churches, 1969. 77p.

Te Hahi Weteriana: three half centuries of the Methodist Maori Mission, 1822–1972. G. I. Laurenson. *Proceedings of the Wesley Historical Society of New Zealand*, vol. 27, nos. 1-2. [Auckland: Institute Press, 1972]. 267p.

The Anglican Church in New Zealand: a history. W. P. Morrell. Dunedin, NZ: Anglican Church of the Province of New Zealand, 1973. 277p.

'The claim of Maori identity on the cultural structure of church and society in New Zealand.' C. B. Turley. D.Min. thesis, School of Theology at Claremont, Claremont, CA, 1977. 141p.

'The growth of the Church of the Nazarene in New Zealand.' N. R. Bartle. M.A. thesis, Fuller Theological Seminary, Pasadena, CA, 1988. 193p.

'The island broken in two halves: sacred land and religious renewal movements among the Maori of New Zealand.' J. E. Rosenfeld. Ph.D. dissertation, University of California, Los Angeles, 1994. 474p.

'The Maori web,' chapter 2 in *People movements in Southern Polynesia*, p.40–75. A. R. Tippett. Chicago: Moody Press, 1971.

The Marist Brothers in New Zealand, Fiji and Samoa, 1876–1976. P. O. Gallagher. Tuakau, NZ: New Zealand Marist Brother Trust Fund, 1976. 210p.

The state of the churches in Great Britain, Ireland, Australia and New Zealand, 1986. Peoria, AZ: Ecumenism Research Agency, 1987. 6 microfilm reels.

'The upraised hand or the spiritual significance of the rise of the Ringatu faith,' *Journal of the Polynesian Society*, 51, 1 (1942), 1–80.

Transplanted Christianity: documents illustrating aspects of New Zealand church history. A. K. Davidson & P. J. Lineham. 2d ed. Palmerston North, NZ: Dunmore Press, 1989. 361p.

Women of spirit: life–stories of New Zealand Salvation Army women from the last 100 years. B. Sampson. Wellington, NZ: Salvation Army, 1993. 227p.

Zion in New Zealand: a history of the Church of Jesus Christ of Latter–day Saints in New Zealand, 1854–1977. B. W. Hunt. Temple View, NZ: Church College of New Zealand, 1977. 116p.

Country Table 2. **Organized churches and denominations in New Zealand.**

Official name (bold type = church with over 10% of all affiliated) 1	*Begun* 2	*Type* 3	*Councl* 4	*Congs* 5	*Adults* 6	*Affiliated 1970* 7	*Affiliated 1995* 8	*G%* 9	*Names, notes, and other statistics* (see Codebook, Part 3) 10
Absolute Maori Established Church	1941	I-Non	.....	2	50	130	100	-1.04	Maori indigenous church. Decline from 149 adherents (1966 census) to 128 (1971).
Angl Ch in Aotearoa, NZ, & Polynesia	1814	A-plu	AWE.W	1,500	616,000	876,570	800,000	-0.36	*CPNZ.* 9 Dioceses. 94% White, 6% Maori, Polynesian. (1990) 885n,37x,300Y.
Apostolic Church of Australia & NZ	1933	P-PeA	Z...H	74	3,740	3,000	6,804	3.33	Begun by Apostolic Ch (Australia). Has Maori mission. 31n,1sW=44%,62Y.
Assemblies of God in New Zealand	1922	P-Pe2	Z...H	149	10,300	6,000	17,226	4.31	M=AoG(UK,Austr). HQ Lower Hutt. 10% Samoan. 42n,4x(Samoan),1p,1s(70),W=95%,300Y.
Assembly Hall Churches	c1980	I-3nC	.....	19	1,238	–	2,000	6.67	*Local Churches. Little Flock.* Chinese. Begun 1922 in China.
Associated Churches of Christ in NZ	1844	P-Dis	xWE.W	39	760	10,000	1,767	-6.70	*ACCNZ. Disciples.* Decline since 1951. HQ Lower Hutt. 39n,3x,1s(7),W=38%,107Y.
Association of Vineyard Chs	c1980	I-3sW	.....	14	700	–	2,000	6.67	Assisted by M=AVC(USA).
Baptist International Missions	1979	I-Bap	.....	2	100	–	167	6.25	M=BIM(USA).
Baptist Union of New Zealand	1851	P-Bap	TWE.W	217	24,600	45,000	31,299	-1.44	*BUNZ.* Pakeha (Whites). Strongest at Auckland. 198n,1s(22),W=76%,589Y,17177z.
Bible Baptist Church	1971	I-Bap	.....	12	576	–	960	4.17	M=BBFI(USA).
Bible Presbyterian Ch of New Zealand		I-Ref	.TT.T	1	50	100	100	0.05	Schism ex Presbyterian Church of New Zealand. Fundamentalists. 1n.
Catholic Church in New Zealand:	1828	R-Lat	P...R	332	329,300	426,128	479,656	0.47	92% White, 8% Maori. C=12+4+22. 8376Yy. 349n 235x 431m 1248w 8376Yy
M Wellington	1848	R-Lat	Ps	53	58,000	147,000	85,566	-2.14	Capital. South of North Islands. 7 Maori missions. 80n 62x 86m 285w 1479Yy
D Auckland	1848	R-Lat	Ps	65	98,000	176,197	149,525	-0.65	North of North Island. Home of half of all Maoris. 66n 71x 173m 382w 2774Yy
D Christchurch	1887	R-Lat	Ps	50	42,000	61,162	64,800	0.23	Centre of South Island. Urban, rural. 59n 38x 59m 211w 977Yy
D Dunedin	1869	R-Lat	Ps	80	26,000	41,769	38,985	-0.28	Southern third of South Island. Urban, rural. 61n 7x 25m 147w 1012Yy
D Hamilton in New Zealand	1980	R-Lat	Ps	40	54,000	–	81,400	6.67	M=SM. 31n 13x 18m 66w 1075Yy
D Palmerston North	1980	R-Lat	Ps	35	50,000	–	57,380	6.67	Divided off from M Wellington. 52n 44x 70m 157w 1059Yy
OM New Zealand	1976	R-Lat	Ps	9	1,300	–	2,000	5.26	Military Ordinariate of New Zealand. 2 ordinaries, 14 auxiliaries. 13Yy.
Children of God	c1985	I-mar	.....	1	31	–	70	10.00	Former members of USA Jesus Movement.
Christadelphian Ecclesias		m-Ade	x....	18	1,110	1,700	1,845	0.05	*Christadelphian Bible Mission.* 16 ecclesias. Pacifist, adventists. 8n,1s.
Christian Brethren	1853	P-CBr	x....	240	13,200	23,000	20,337	-0.49	*Brethren Assemblies*(Open). Sends out 210 foreign missionaries. 118m,W=99%.
Christian Brethren	c1955	P-CBr	x...E	40	6,000	15,220	13,000	-0.63	Plymouth (Open) Brethren. M=CMML(NZ, Australia, USA). Southern Highlands. 69f.
Christian City Churches	1988	I-3cW	.....	5	770	–	1,540	14.29	Independent charismatics.
Christian Fellowships	c1975	I-3cW	.....	52	3,120	–	6,243	5.00	Independent charismatics.
Christian & Missionary Alliance	1972	P-Hol	.....	7	131	–	358	4.35	M=CMA(USA). 4f.
Christian Revival Crusade	1941	I-3pW	x...H	12	455	450	759	2.11	*CRC.* Related to CRC (Australia). On North Island. 11n,1s,W=72%,18Y,9z.
Church of Christ (Life & Advent)		P-Adv	.....	8	1,260	–	3,606	0.05	In fellowship with Advent Christian Church, USA.
Church of Christ, Scientist		m-Sci	x....	20	400	1,100	1,000	0.05	*Christian Science.* M=CCS(Boston, USA). Declining (1951: 4,586 adherents). 3m,18w.
Church of God (Cleveland)	1987	P-Pe3	.....	8	814	–	1,050	12.50	M=CoG(Cleveland) (USA). Holiness Pentecostals.
Church of God of Prophecy		P-Pe3	Z....	1	50	50	100	0.05	M=CGP(USA). White Pentecostals, split in USA ex CoG(Cleveland). In Christchurch.
Ch of Jesus Christ of Latter-day Saints	1851	m-LdS	x....	158	50,900	33,256	76,000	3.36	*Mormons* (USA). 70% Maori,30% White. Temple: Hamilton. 141n,500f,1r,W=50%.
Church of the Nazarene	1952	P-Hol	xF...	12	540	1,100	703	-1.77	Home mission area of M=CoN(USA). HQ Auckland. 9n,SS=907,W=75%.
Churches of Christ (Non-Instrumental)	1956	I-Dis	x....	20	1,300	2,000	2,500	0.90	M=CC(Non-Instrumental) (USA). In largest cities. 1 school. 18f.
Churches of Christ, New Zealand		I-3pW	.....	20	1,500	700	2,000	0.05	Pentecostals, based on HQ in Christchurch. Independent congregations.
Commonwealth Covenant Church		I-3pP	.....	10	600	506	1,000	0.05	Includes Maori mission with 123 members. Pentecostals, based on HQ Lower Hutt.
Congregational Chr Ch of Samoa in NZ		P-Con	Rwp..	100	11,000	3,000	21,000	0.05	*CCCSNZ.* Samoan immigrants from CCCS. HQ Otara. Mainly Auckland, Wellington. 15x.
Congregational Union of New Zealand	1840	P-Con	RWE.W	8	3,200	1,050	4,197	5.70	*CUNZ.* Union 1884. 1969, 67% of churches join Presbyterian Ch. 67% Pacific islanders. 8n.
Cook Islands Christian Church		P-Con	.wp.W	60	6,800	12,000	15,600	0.05	*CICC.* Cook Islanders working in New Zealand. 3 pastors. Linked with Presb Ch of NZ.
Elim Pentecostal Ch of New Zealand	1952	P-Pe2	Z...H	47	1,650	220	2,352	9.94	Pentecostals. Based on Wellington. 2 missionaries in Japan. 7n,W=50%,7Y.

Continued opposite

Country Table 2–concluded

Official name (bold type = church with over 10% of affiliated) 1	*Begun* 2	*Type* 3	*Counc* 4	*Congs* 5	*Adults* 6	*Affiliated 1970* 7	*Affiliated 1995* 8	*G%* 9	*Names, notes, and other statistics* (see Codebook, Part 3) 10
Evangelistic Church of Christ		I-3pW	.....	2	200	152	300	0.05	Small independent Pentecostal group based on Christchurch.
Free Wesleyan Church of Tonga	c1970	P-Met	.....	10	472	–	786	30.56	Methodist body.
Greater World Chr Spiritualist League		m-Spi	x....	2	70	200	150	0.05	*Greater World Sanctuary.* Christian spiritists. Auckland, Christchurch.
Greek Orthodox Ch: D New Zealand	1924	O-Gre	Cw..W	6	2,400	3,000	3,600	0.73	Under EP Constantinople. Created Diocese in 1970, includes E India, Japan, Korea.
Harvest	1988	I-3cW	.....	5	325	–	650	14.29	Independent charismatics.
Jehovah's Witnesses	1904	m-Jeh	x....	151	11,515	10,000	22,182	3.24	1973 International Assembly in Christchurch. (1975) 40m,555Y. (1995) 473Y.
Liberal Catholic Church	1916	I-Lib	x....	2	200	462	300	-1.71	Theosophist. Linked to churches and bishops in Australia, UK, USA. HQ Auckland.
Lutheran Church of New Zealand	1843	P-Lut	.....	20	3,800	6,255	4,965	-0.92	*LCNZ.* In Luth Ch of Australia. Germans in 1843, now Maoris. 1n,12x,W=35%,102Yy.
Methodist Church of New Zealand	1822	P-Met	VWE.W	197	107,000	160,000	138,705	-0.57	*MCNZ.* A=1913 (from Australia). 92% White, 8% Maori. 351n,669m,1r,W=36%.
Maori Evangelical Fellowship	1959	I-Eva	.....	12	265	–	408	27.18	*NAC/NAK.* M=Neuapostolische Kirche (HQ Zurich, Switzerland).
National Revival Church in NZ	1960	I-3pW	Z....	1	100	100	200	2.81	*NRC.* HQ Lower Hutt. Revivalist Pentecostals. Begun in Australia: split ex CRC.
New Apostolic Church		I-3aX	x....	4	100	–	182	0.05	M=NAC/NAK. Neuapostolische Kirche (Switzerland).
New Life Churches of New Zealand	c1970	I-3cW	.....	98	7,550	–	12,600	45.89	Latter Rain breakaway from Pentecostal Ch of NZ.
Niue Christian Church	c1900	P-Con	..P..	15	2,000	1,000	3,600	5.26	Members: 25% of NZ's 14,400 Niueans; the other 75% belong to CUNZ or to no church.
Old Believers Russian Orthodox Ch		I-OBe	x....	1	100	200	250	0.05	*Old Ritualists.* Immigrants from USSR church begun in 1667. HQ Christchurch.
Presbyterian Church of New Zealand	1839	P-Ref	RWE.W	1,392	416,000	500,000	540,675	0.31	*PCNZ.* A=1901. 23 White Presbyteries (99%). Maori Synod (1%). South. 635n,12r,1s,W=38%.
Ratana Church	1918	I-Met	.....	143	28,600	28,000	47,595	2.14	Maori. Begun by Ratanaan, ex-Methodist. 95% Maori. 141 apostles. W=20%.
Reformed Baptist Churches	c1980	I-Bap	.....	5	355	–	592	6.67	Independent Baptists.
Reformed Churches of New Zealand	1953	P-Ref	JtT.T	18	1,710	2,000	2,439	0.80	*RCNZ.* Conservative schism ex Presbyterian Ch of New Zealand. Dutch origin. HQ Auckland.
Religious Society of Friends	1909	P-Qua	Q...W	16	731	900	1,260	1.35	*New Zealand Yearly Meeting.* Established 1964. Quakers. HQ Christchurch. 1 school.
Reorganized Ch of JC of Latter-day S		m-LdS	x....	1	100	152	150	0.05	S=Saints (Sanitos, Kanitos). Schism in USA ex CJCLdS(Utah) Mormons.
Ringatu Church	1867	I-Non	.....	32	4,830	5,800	8,052	1.32	*Ch of the Upraised Hand.* Christian version of Hau Hau. Maori Bible ritual. 73n.
Russian Orthodox Ch Outside Russia	c1950	I-Rus	x....	4	800	1,500	1,000	-1.61	*ROCOR.* AD Australia & NZ, ROCOR(USA). Auckland, Christchurch. Dunedin, Wellington. 1n.
Salvation Army	1883	P-Sal	xwE.W	102	6,400	18,000	19,992	0.42	*SA, New Zealand Territory.* 5 Divisions. Officers 356, institutions 47. 6H,1s.
Seventh Day Baptist Church of NZ		P-Bap	Tw...	5	128	100	150	0.05	Related to M=SDBC(USA). Sabbatarian Baptists under Australasian Conference.
Seventh-day Adventist Church	1887	P-Adv	x....	87	9,750	10,000	13,005	1.06	SDA. *N & South NZ Confs.* 60n,G=1.4%pa,1H,3r,1s,70t(7401),W=90%,1000Y.
South Pacific Churches	c1965	I-Non	.....	29	2,300	818	4,188	6.75	Independent Nondenominationalists.
True Jesus Church	c1980	I-3oC	.....	6	300	–	1,000	6.67	*TJC.* Evangelized from Fujian and Taiwan. HQ Auckland.
Unitarian Free Churches	1898	m-Unt	.....	2	150	448	400	-0.45	In General Assembly, UFCC(UK). Churches: Auckland, Wellington. Declining. 1n.
United Pentecostal Church	1969	P-Pel	x....	50	2,500	4,000	5,000	0.90	*Jesus Only Church.* M=UPC(USA). Unitarian Pentecostals. 40n,2f,1p(25).
Other Protestant denominations		P-	.....	220	25,000	30,000	40,000	0.05	Total over 30 (see list below), including EEPF, Tuvalu Church.
Other marginal Protestant bodies		m-	.....	30	2,000	2,000	4,000	0.05	Total 7 (see below), including Ch of Scientology, New Ch, Worldwide Ch of God.
Other Orthodox churches		O-	.....	10	1,000	1,000	2,000	0.05	Parishes: Antiochian, Coptic, Free Serbian, Romanian, Serbian, Ukrainian AOC(2).
Other Polynesian indigenous chs		I-	.....	25	1,000	1,000	3,000	0.05	Total about 7 (see list below), mostly Maori in membership.
Other Catholic independent chs		I-CCa	.....	20	200	300	600	0.05	About 5, incl Antoinists, Catholic Tridentine Ch.
Other independent charismatic chs		I-3cW	.....	200	40,000	–	70,000	0.05	In about 30 geographical networks loosely associated: Rhema Ch.
Totals				**6,131**	**1,772,196**	**2,249,667**	**2,471,315**		

Churches, members, growth, 1900-2025	*Congs*	*Adults*	*Affiliated*	*G%*	*Total denominations*	*6 Megablocs:* O	R	A	P	I	m
Total churches, members, and denominations (mid-1900)	2,000	476,000	741,890	1.60	22	1	1	1	12	2	5
Total churches, members, and denominations (mid-1970)	5,903	1,443,152	2,249,667	1.60	81	8	1	1	42	19	10
Total churches, members, and denominations (mid-1990)	6,000	1,648,000	2,298,300	0.11	168	16	1	1	70	66	14
Total churches, members, and denominations (mid-1995)	6,131	1,772,196	2,471,315	1.46	172	16	1	1	71	69	14
Total churches, members, and denominations (mid-2000)	6,200	1,837,000	2,562,219	0.73	175	16	1	1	72	71	14
Total churches, members, and denominations (mid-2025)	7,000	2,164,000	3,018,000	0.66	337	25	1	1	90	200	20

NOTES ON TABLE ABOVE

NATIONAL COUNCILS (Column 4, 5th letter).

- E = Evangelical Fellowship of New Zealand (EFNZ), or Evangelical Alliance of New Zealand (member of WEF; 9 branches; no churches as members).
- H = Associated Pentecostal Churches of New Zealand (formed 1975).
- I = Maori Council of Churches (MCC).
- R = New Zealand Episcopal Conference (NZEC).
- T = New Zealand Consultative Council of the ICCC (with 8 local committees).
- W = Conference of Churches in Aotearoa/New Zealand (CCANZ); formerly, National Council of Churches in New Zealand (NCCNZ), 1941.

Other national councils. Maori Evangelical Alliance.

Local councils. 28 councils linked with NCCNZ.

OTHER PROTESTANT DENOMINATIONS. There are at least 30 other smaller organized denominations. These include: Baptist Bible Fellowship International (1971), Chinese Ch, Ch of NZ, Churches of God in the British Isles & Overseas (1 church), Exclusive Brethren (groups: Raven-Taylor, Kelly-Continental, Stuarts), Full Gospel Ch, Independent Assemblies of God, United Ch, United Ev Chs, Worldwide Evangelization Crusade.

OTHER MARGINAL PROTESTANT BODIES. These include: Branhamites (HQ Singapore; Jesus-Only Unitarians), Ch of Scientology (1973 licensed for weddings), Ch of the Mystic Christ, New Ch, Order of the Cross (2 centers), Spiritualists, Unity School of Christianity (1 church), Worldwide Ch of God.

OTHER POLYNESIAN INDIGENOUS CHURCHES. There are a small number of other Maori bodies, also a few followers of other Pacific indigenous groups. The former include: Ch of Te Kooti Rikirangi (47 members in 1966), United Maori Mission. There are also a few adherents of other Non-White indigenous churches including the Father Divine Peace Mission Movement (USA Blacks).

UNITING CHURCHES. Negotiations for organic union were under way in 1980 between: Associated Churches of Christ in NZ, Ch of the Province of NZ, Congregational Union of NZ, Methodist Ch of NZ, Presbyterian Ch of NZ.

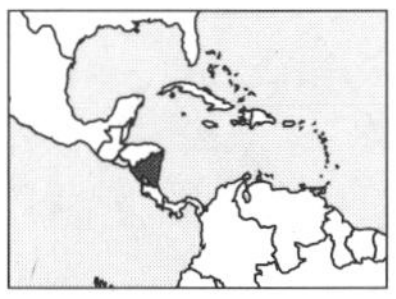

NICARAGUA

SECULAR DATA, AD 2000

STATE

Official name: La República de Nicaragua (The Republic of Nicaragua).
Short name: Nicaragua. **Adjective of nationality:** Nicaraguan.
Flag: Blue, white, and blue stripes, with coat of arms in centre.
Area: 131,670 sq. km. (50,838 sq. mi.).
Government: Republic under military rule, since 1936 (1523 Spanish possession, 1821 Independence, 1838 republic, several dictatorships).
Legislature: National Assembly, 93 members.
Official language: Spanish (Español/Castella).
Monetary unit: 1 córdoba oro (C$) = 100 centavos. **US$1=** C$10.86.
Chief cities: MANAGUA 1,319,000; Leon 161,719; Masaya 120,088; Chinandega 120,088; Granada 115,839.
Political divisions: 17 provinces. **Armed forces:** 17,000.

DEMOGRAPHY

Population: 5,074,000.
Population density: 38.5/sq. km. (99.8/sq. mi.).
Under 15 years: 2,169,000.
Growth rate p.a.: 2.68% (births 32.80, deaths 5.36).
Mortality: Infant, per 1,000: 38.9, ; **Maternal per 100,000:** 160.0.
Life expectancy: 69 (male 67, female 72).
Household size: 6.9. **Floor area per person, sq.m:** 25.0.
Major languages: Spanish, English, Miskito, Chinese, and over 12 others.
Urban dwellers: 64.71%. **Urban growth rate p.a.:** 3.1%.
Labor force: 35%.

ETHNOLINGUISTIC PEOPLES

63.1% Mestizo (Ladino); 14.0% Nicaraguan White; 5.0% Zambo (Mulatto); 4.0% Nicaraguan Black; 4.0% West Indian Black.

ECONOMY

National income p.a. per person: US$379; **per family:** US$2,621.

EDUCATION

Adult literacy: 65% (male 64%, female 66%). **Schools:** 7,544.
Universities: 4. **School enrolment:** female/male: 81%/76%.

HEALTH

Access to health services: 83%. **Access to safe water:** 61%.
Hospitals: 56 (12 beds per 10,000). **Doctors:** 2,554.
Blind: 1,800. **Deaf:** 281,700. **Murder rate:** 25.
Lepers: 900. **Underweight prevalence under 5:** 12%.

LITERATURE

New book titles p.a.: 1,120 (220 p.a. per million). **Periodicals:** 35.
Newspapers: 4 dailies.

COMMUNICATION (per 1,000 people)

Phones: 23 (12% mobile). **Radios:** 222. **TV sets:** 170.
Daily newspaper circulation: 30. **Computers:** 15.

REFUGEES

Citizen refugees in other countries: 16,150.
Alien refugees from other countries: 450.

HUMAN LIFE AND LIBERTY (optimum condition=100.0%)

HDI: 53.0. **HSI:** 34.0. **HFI:** 50.0. **EFL:** 28.0.

Country status. Nicaragua is the largest of the Central American republics with a coastline on both the Atlantic and Pacific Oceans. Until the late 1980s, it was torn by a bloody civil war. Its chief exports are coffee, bananas, sugar, and cotton.

HUMAN LIFE AND LIBERTY

Human need and development. The civil war was the single most important event in Nicaraguan history in the 20th century, and it has served to depress living conditions in the country to a level that prevailed in the years before World War II. Much of the infrastructure has been damaged, several sectors of the economy have been hard hit, and the general quality of life has deteriorated in urban as well as rural areas. The rebuilding of the country has been painfully slow because of continuing political discord and limited resources. As a result, most of the economic support systems have collapsed, and the common people are expected to fend for themselves as best as they can. The gap between the poor campesinos and the moderately affluent urban dwellers has widened. Even in better times, the campesinos were subsistence farmers and laborers, living at the margins of the cash economy. They generally live in one-room houses made of poles and mud and straw roofs. Water supply and sanitation are primitive. The daily calorie and protein intakes are below standards mandated by WHO. Medical facilities and personnel are concentrated in the urban areas. The per capita income of $379 is the lowest in the Western Hemisphere outside Haiti.

Human rights and freedoms. Persistent human rights problems are extrajudicial killings of political opponents, mistreatment of detainees, violence by paramilitary bands, and a backlogged and often partisan judiciary. Arbitrary arrest and detention by the police are common. The family members of detainees are rarely informed of the whereabouts of those in detention, and detainees do not have recourse to legal counsel until they have been formally charged with a crime. Soldiers convicted of murder and other hu-

Country Table 1. **Religious adherents in Nicaragua, AD 1900-2025.**

Year	*1900*		*1970*		*mid-1990*		*Annual change, 1990-2000*				*mid-1995*		*mid-2000*		*mid-2025*	
Name	*Adherents*	*%*	*Adherents*	*%*	*Adherents*	*%*	*Natural*	*Conversion*	*Total*	*Rate*	*Adherents*	*%*	*Adherents*	*%*	*Adherents*	*%*
Christians	**489,000**	**97.8**	**2,107,500**	**99.3**	**3,694,220**	**96.5**	**120,395**	**-1,244**	**119,151**	**2.83**	**4,268,160**	**96.4**	**4,885,732**	**96.3**	**8,289,200**	**95.3**
PROFESSION																
professing Christians	**489,000**	**97.8**	**2,107,500**	**99.3**	**3,694,220**	**96.5**	**120,395**	**-1,244**	**119,151**	**2.83**	**4,268,160**	**96.4**	**4,885,732**	**96.3**	**8,289,200**	**95.3**
AFFILIATION																
unaffiliated Christians	15,000	3.0	184,438	8.7	26,000	0.7	847	-617	230	0.85	26,832	0.6	28,300	0.6	49,200	0.6
affiliated Christians	**474,000**	**94.8**	**1,923,062**	**90.6**	**3,668,220**	**95.9**	**119,548**	**-627**	**118,921**	**2.85**	**4,241,328**	**95.8**	**4,857,432**	**95.7**	**8,240,000**	**94.8**
Roman Catholics	473,000	94.6	1,780,995	83.9	3,275,300	85.6	106,745	-2,275	104,470	2.81	3,790,000	85.6	4,320,000	85.1	7,050,000	81.1
Protestants	6,000	1.2	118,138	5.6	435,000	11.4	14,174	1,326	15,500	3.09	509,848	11.5	590,000	11.6	1,150,000	13.2
Independents	0	0.0	16,230	0.8	112,000	2.9	3,649	651	4,300	3.30	134,857	3.1	155,000	3.1	330,000	3.8
Marginal Christians	0	0.0	4,499	0.2	36,000	0.9	1,173	327	1,500	3.54	43,010	1.0	51,000	1.0	110,000	1.3
Anglicans	0	0.0	3,200	0.2	6,600	0.2	215	-45	170	2.32	7,320	0.2	8,300	0.2	15,000	0.2
doubly-affiliated	-5,000	-1.0	0	0.0	-196,680	-5.1	-6,409	-610	-7,019	3.10	-243,707	-5.5	-266,868	-5.3	-415,000	-4.8
Trans-megabloc groupings																
Evangelicals	1,000	0.2	70,400	3.3	324,700	8.5	10,580	1,550	12,130	3.23	383,648	8.7	446,000	8.8	850,000	9.8
Pentecostals/Charismatics	0	0.0	35,000	1.7	530,000	13.9	17,270	1,730	19,000	3.11	616,897	13.9	720,000	14.2	1,375,000	15.8
Great Commission Christians	**15,000**	**3.0**	**124,000**	**5.8**	**231,530**	**6.1**	**7,544**	**34**	**7,578**	**2.87**	**268,200**	**6.1**	**307,306**	**6.1**	**556,500**	**6.4**
Spiritists	1,000	0.2	4,000	0.2	51,000	1.3	1,662	387	2,049	3.43	60,600	1.4	71,485	1.4	140,000	1.6
Nonreligious	0	0.0	3,800	0.2	47,000	1.2	1,531	556	2,087	3.74	56,000	1.3	67,866	1.3	180,000	2.1
Ethnoreligionists	10,000	2.0	2,000	0.1	18,520	0.5	603	221	824	3.75	22,750	0.5	26,764	0.5	40,000	0.5
Baha'is	0	0.0	2,800	0.1	7,300	0.2	238	-6	232	2.79	8,200	0.2	9,616	0.2	20,000	0.2
Buddhists	0	0.0	1,000	0.1	4,200	0.1	137	27	164	3.34	4,700	0.1	5,835	0.1	12,000	0.1
Atheists	0	0.0	500	0.0	1,200	0.0	39	74	113	6.86	1,800	0.0	2,329	0.1	6,000	0.1
Chinese folk-religionists	0	0.0	1,000	0.1	1,700	0.0	55	3	58	2.99	1,800	0.0	2,283	0.0	4,500	0.1
Muslims	0	0.0	0	0.0	710	0.0	23	-8	15	1.97	760	0.0	863	0.0	1,500	0.0
Jews	0	0.0	200	0.0	400	0.0	13	-3	10	2.19	430	0.0	497	0.0	800	0.0
Other religionists	0	0.0	200	0.0	750	0.0	24	-7	17	2.11	800	0.0	924	0.0	2,000	0.0
World A (unevangelized persons)	5,000	1.0	2,123	0.1	3,827	0.1	130	183	313	5.94	4,425	0.1	5,074	0.1	17,392	0.2
World B (evangelized non-Christians)	6,000	1.2	13,453	0.6	128,953	3.4	4,195	1,061	5,256	3.57	153,041	3.5	183,194	3.6	389,408	4.5
World C (Christians)	489,000	97.8	2,107,500	99.3	3,694,220	96.5	120,395	-1,244	119,151	2.83	4,268,160	96.4	4,885,732	96.3	8,289,200	95.3
Country's population	**500,000**	**100.0**	**2,123,077**	**100.0**	**3,827,000**	**100.0**	**124,720**	**0**	**124,720**	**2.86**	**4,425,627**	**100.0**	**5,074,000**	**100.0**	**8,696,000**	**100.0**

COLUMNS, ROWS.
For meanings and definitions, see Codebook (Part 3). Note that, by definition, total 'Christians' = professing + crypto-Christians, which also = affiliated + unaffiliated Christians, and also = Great Commission Christians + latent Christians. Percentages may not always total exactly, due to rounding.

CENSUSES.
31.V.1950: 95.9% Roman Catholics, 4.0% Evangelicals (Protestants and Anglicans), 0.1% other religionists. **1963** (partial census): 96.0% Roman Catholics, 3.6% Protestants (1.8% Moravians, 0.2% Baptists), 0.2% Anglicans, 0.1% ethnoreligionists and others.

NOTES ON RELIGIONS
ATHEISTS. 2 parties: Communist Party of Nicaragua, Socialist Party of Nicaragua (PSN) (banned since 1945).
BAHA'IS. Growth from 11 local spiritual assemblies (1964) to 19 (1973).
BUDDHISTS. Chinese.
DOUBLY-AFFILIATED. The term covers those affiliated to, or claimed by, both the Catholic Church and also a church termed Evangélica by the state (Protestant, marginal Christian, Anglican, or Independents), i.e. baptized Catholics who have recently become Evangelicals or others. Because their statistics represent a duplication, they are shown in the table as a negative quantity (with a minus sign).
ETHNORELIGIONISTS. In 1900, many of the 40,000 Amerindians were pagans. Of the 125,000 Amerindians in 1995, small clusters still adhered to their traditional animistic religion, including among the Miskito, Sumu, Ulva, and Matagalpa.
INDEPENDENTS. In over 30 denominations in 1995 (see Table 2).
OTHER RELIGIONISTS. Including Rosicrucians (2 AMORC centers).
PENTECOSTALS (or, Catholic charismatics). After the 1972 earthquake, cursillo members visited Catholic charismatics in Honduras, then began the charismatic renewal in Nicaragua. In 1975 they numbered 7,000 adults (4,000 in Managua, increasing in June 1974 alone by 500 new Catholics baptized in the Spirit); total charismatic community, including children, 15,000. By 1977 there were 150 prayer groups in Managua alone. In April 1977 was held in Managua the First Central American Charismatic Conference, with 4,000 attenders. At each evening service, 2 rows were reserved for 30 lepers. During the Sandinista regime, hundred of new CCR prayer groups were formed.
PROTESTANTS. In 1950, professing Protestants were strongest (36.8% of inhabitants) in Zelaya department, and in Comarca del Cabo Gracias a Dios (63.8%). Table 2 below represents the 1995 situation. Many Protestant bodies doubled in size in the 3 years after the 1972 earthquake.
ROMAN CATHOLICS. Many are Christo-pagans—Amerindians whose syncretistic folk-Catholicism combines a 17th-century Spanish Catholicism with their own traditional pre-Columbian animism, concepts, and world-views. Roman Catholics actively and regularly involved in the practice of high or low spiritism, mainly Afro-American low spiritism.
SPIRITISTS. Non-Christian adherents of Afro-Caribbean spirit-possession cults (low spiritism) syncretizing Christianity with African religion; mostly Jamaicans and other Blacks. Also, in 1930 a large new spiritist movement began among the Miskito and Sumu Indians.

Great Commission Instrument Panel: status of Nicaragua (for explanation see start of Part 4)

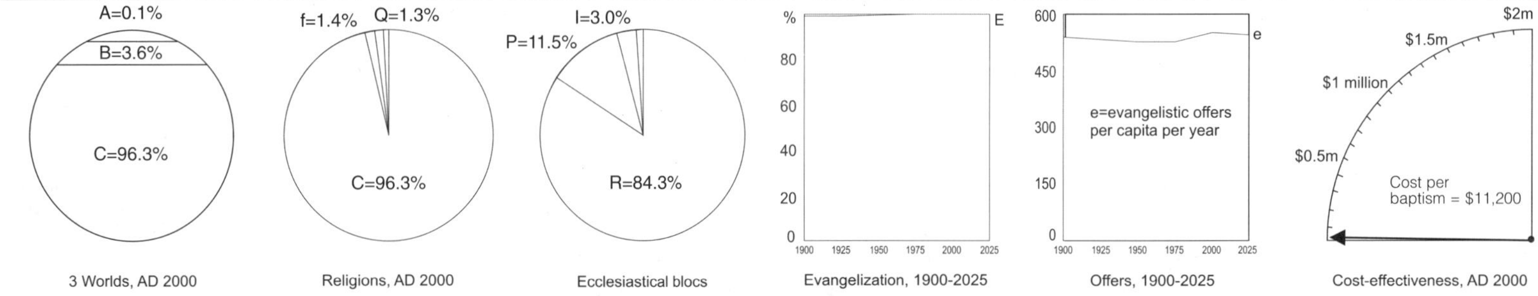

man rights violations are tried in military courts where they receive only light sentences. Freedoms of speech and press are guaranteed by the Constitution, but are, at the same time, restricted by other Constitutional provisions, requiring that the press present only 'accurate', 'socially responsible', information serving 'national interest', which terms may be defined variously, depending on whose ox is being gored. Women suffer economic, but not political, discrimination. About 72% of them live in poverty. The English-speaking Mesquites of the Atlantic Coast also suffer various forms of discrimination.

Human environment. Nicaragua is home to 44 species of birds, 45 species of fish and over 10,000 known species of flora. It has the most extensive Central American tropical forests covering some 40% of the territory, almost all of it in the east. No natural forests remain in the west. Soil erosion is a serious problem in areas where the forests have been cut down or where farming has been extended to steeply sloping areas.

NON-CHRISTIAN RELIGIONS

Less than 5% of the population are non-Christians, mainly small clusters of Miskito, Sumu, Ulva, and Matagalpa Indians adhering to traditional religion, and a steadily growing community of Baha'is.

Iglesia Católica en Nicaragua, Diocesis de León. State postage stamps of Stations of the Cross in Leon Cathedral, in Holy Week 1975.

CHRISTIANITY

CATHOLIC CHURCH. The population of Nicaragua is 85% Catholic. Evangelization began on the Atlantic coast in 1522, with missionaries from 4 religious orders arriving in 1526. The following year the diocese of Nicaragua was established by the king of Spain. Christianity did not reach the Pacific coast until 1689, leading to a 'golden age' of the church prior to expulsion of the Jesuits a hundred years later. Under Spanish rule, Nicaragua was part of Guatemala. Nicaragua's first independent constitution in 1826, following its separation from Spain, proclaimed Catholicism as the state religion. During the remainder of the century, foreign efforts to gain control of Nicaraguan territory for a proposed canal connecting Atlantic and Pacific oceans, together with internal unrest and civil strife, resulted in periodic shifts in the status of the church. At times the church was placed under the protection of the state: at other times its property was confiscated, religious orders suppressed, and clergy exiled. Nicaragua became an ecclesiastical province in 1912.

The Holy See has diplomatic relations with Nicaragua and in AD 2000 is represented to government and the Catholic hierarchy by a nuncio residing in Managua.

PROTESTANT CHURCHES. Protestants affiliated to churches numbered 11.5% of the population in 1995, with a higher percentage in the states along the east coast which were at one time under British control. These states have a large number of Indians and Negroes from Jamaica and include Zelaya (with 36.8% professing Protestants in 1950) and Comarca del Cabo Gracias a Dios (with 63.3% then). The other states averaged less than 2% in 1950, with the exception of Managua (2.5%) and Rio San Juan (2.2%), which continue to show a Protestant increase in growing urban areas. Subsequently Protestant denominations have risen dramatically, and since 1970 many have doubled or tripled in size.

Country summary. **Worlds A, B, C by ethnolinguistic peoples, cities, and major civil divisions in Nicaragua.**

	PEOPLES							CITIES							CIVIL DIVISIONS						
World	Num	Pop 2000	C%	Christians	E%	U%	Unevangelized	Num	Pop 2000	C%	Christians	E%	U%	Unevangelized	Num	Pop 2000	C%	Christians	E%	U%	Unevangelized
A	1	507	0.00	0	40	60	304	0	0	0.00	0	0	0	0	0	0	0.00	0	0	0	0
B	3	19,484	13.12	2,557	74	26	4,986	0	0	0.00	0	0	0	0	0	0	0.00	0	0	0	0
C	18	5,054,201	96.06	4,854,874	100	0	1,834	6	1,945,614	93.99	1,828,711	100	0	3,606	17	5,074,194	95.73	4,857,432	100	0	7,125
Total	**22**	**5,074,192**	**95.73**	**4,857,431**	**100**	**0**	**7,124**	**6**	**1,945,614**	**93.99**	**1,828,711**	**100**	**0**	**3,606**	**17**	**5,074,194**	**95.73**	**4,857,432**	**100**	**0**	**7,125**

Nicaragua was first entered in 1849 by German Moravians, who formed one of the earliest Protestant missions in Central America. Moravians are the fourth largest Protestant denomination in the country and are concentrated along the east coast among the Miskito Indians and the English-speaking Black population. Moravians direct a Bible institute and schools for 2,400 students. The Central American Mission came in 1900, but its growth has been slow, reduced in recent years through schisms, which produced the indigenous Central American Convention in 1955 and the National Evangelical Missionary Association in 1965.

Assemblies of God missionaries arrived in 1936, building on the efforts of independent pentecostal missionaries as early as 1912. With 1,370 congregations and its strength in eastern Nicaragua, this is now the largest of Nicaragua's Protestant churches. Other important Pentecostal bodies are the International Church of the Foursquare Gospel and the Church of God (Cleveland). The latter octupled in membership between 1970 and 1990.

In 1923 American Baptists took up work begun earlier by an independent Baptist missionary. Heavily involved in education and medical work, including a nurses training program, the National Baptist Conventino also have a large and growing membership. Three other Baptist societies from the USA are also active.

Seventh-day Adventists, who entered in 1904, increased their membership by 10 times between 1970 and 1990 making them the second largest Protestant denomination in Nicaragua. The Nazarenes have built up an important community since their arrival in 1943.

INDIGENOUS CHURCHES. As in most Latin American countries, there are a number of Non-White indigenous churches begun on Nicaraguan initiative. In 1970 these numbered 90 denominations with over 115,000 adherents.

Renewal movements. In the 1990s the Pentecostal/Charismatic Renewal continued to spread rapidly across most older churches, and numbered over 720,000 adherents (of whom 53% Pentecostals, 33% Charismatics, and 14% Independents).

Indigenous missions. Nicaraguan Christians have been active missionaries in surrounding Latin American countries since the Spanish conquest. In the 20th century, Roman Catholic and some Protestant missionaries have served in Europe, Africa, and Asia.

CHURCH AND STATE

The state invokes the name of God in the Preamble to its constitution in these words: 'Under the protection of God, we, the representatives of the people of Nicaragua...', although Article 8 affirms that 'The State has no official religion'.

The institutional separation of the Catholic Church from the state took place in 1893 with the liberal revolution of general Zelaya. The constitution of 1894 elaborated on the meaning of this separation for education, marriage, the financial involvement of the state, and the like, and subsequent constitutions have reflected the same attitude. The constitutions of 1911, 1939, and 1948 contained provisions guaranteeing religious freedom for all.

From 1934 when the Somoza family came to power in Nicaragua, the Catholic Church played an important role in supporting the regime. In 1936 the archbishop of Managua obtained financial concessions from the government including salaries for priests and bishops and a number of other privileges. Twenty years later the church was granted the right to teach catechism in public schools, at its own expense, as an optional subject when requested by parents, and this right was confirmed by the constitutional revision of 1965 (Article 100). It was not until 1969 that the church for the first time withdrew its support from the Somoza regime, with a declaration from the first National Pastoral Meeting supported by CELAM and the apostolic administrator of the archdiocese of Managua. In June 1972, the archbishop of Managua convened a meeting of the Episcopal Conference to take a position concerning the intention expressed by general Somoza to maintain himself in power until 1980 through an illegal amendment to the constitution. A pastoral letter followed, signed by all but one of the bishops, asking for a total change in the political, economic, and social structures of the country. Since then, the Catholic Church has been anxious to affirm and consolidate its independence and to avoid any compromise with the Somoza government. Thus, the absence of episcopal representatives at the ceremonies marking the beginning of the second presidential mandate of general Anastasio Somoza Debayle was widely noted, as well as the reduced influence of those priests well-known for their unconditional support of the regime. Such an attitude has caused the state to withdraw Catholic political and financial privilege and to oppose its pastoral program, which is increasingly oriented to the liberation of man.

Churches are expected to register with government, and orders gazetting their date of registration are published regularly.

Continente '75 3-week mass-communication crusade, involving 56 radio and 100 TV stations in 23 countries, with, Argentinian evangelist Luis Palau, then 41 years old. In earthquake-shattered Managua, there were 200,000 attenders and 6,000 decisions for Christ.

BROADCASTING AND MEDIA

Shortwave radio programs in European languages can be received from AWR (Slovakia), TWR (Monaco, Albania) and HCJB (Ecuador). Radio Catolica in Managua provides daily Catholic programs on medium-wave frequencies. Nicaragua is a member of UNDA.

CBN's *700 Club* can be seen on local television and cable channels on weekdays in the late afternoons and evenings. A ministry center follows-up response with weekly Bible studies. Other Christian television programs can be received via satellite.

The 'Jesus' Film has been shown to 6.7 million, including second time attenders; chiefly through TV (3.3 million) and radio broadcasts (3 million), with responses from 9,500.

INTERDENOMINATIONAL ORGANIZATIONS

A national evangelical council of churches was formed in 1966 by 9 denominations. In 1972, 5 days after the devastating earthquake of 27 December which levelled the capital and killed nearly 10,000 people, a much larger Evangelical body was formed, the Evangelical Committee for Development Aid (Comite Evangelico Pro-Ayuda al Desarrollo, CEPAD). After 2 months, it had members from 30 Evangelical denominations, and after 3 years, 35 members, of which 15 were Nicaraguan Non-White indigenous denominations. It has mainly supplied relief aid, medicines, food and clothing.

FUTURE TRENDS AND PROSPECTS

Christianity is expected to decline slowly to 2025, falling to 95.3% of the population compared to 99.3% in 1970.

Christianity will probably decline, albeit slowly, throughout the 21st century. The nonreligious could grow to over 5% of the population shortly before AD 2050.

BIBLIOGRAPHY

Anthropological bibliography of aboriginal Nicaragua. J. A. Lines, E. M. Shook & M. D. Olien. *Tropical Science Center occasional paper*, no. 3. San Jose: Tropical Science Center, 1965. 98p.

Anuario eclesiástico de Nicaraugua, 1967. Managua: Conferencia Episcopal de Nicaragua, 1967.

Apuntes para una teología nicaragüense. Centro Antonio Valdivieso, with the Instituto Histórico Centroamericano, Universidad Centroamericana. San José: Departamento Ecuménico de Investigación, 1981. 198p.

Bolivien und Nicaragua: Modelle einer Kirche im Aufbruch. M. Hofmann. Münster: Edition Liberación, 1987. 364p.

Breaking faith: the Sandinista revolution and its impact on freedom and Christian faith in Nicaragua. H. Belli. Westchester, IL: Crossway Books, 1985. 271p.

Breve historia de la iglesia en Nicaragua, 1523–1979. J. E. Arellano. 4th ed. Managua: Manolo Morales, 1986. 153p.

Ethnographical survey of the Miskito and Sumu Indians of Honduras and Nicaragua. E. Conzemius. Washington, DC: Bureau of American Ethnology, 1932. Bulletin no. 106. 191p.

Evangelism–in–depth; experimenting with a new type of evangelism; as told by team members of the Latin American Mission. Moody Bible Institute. Chicago: Moody Press, 1961. 126p.

Evangelizadores laícos para América Latina. G. Smutko. Quito: Don Bosco, 1970.

Fe cristiano y revolución sandinista en Nicaragua. A. Argüello (ed). *Apuntes para el Estudio de la Realidad Nacional*, no. 3. Managua: Instituto Histórico Centroamericano, 1979. 375p.

Folklore de Nicaragua. E. P. Hernández. Masaya, Nicaragua: Editorial Unión, 1968. 410p.

Historia del pueblo de Dios en Nicaragua. A. A. Quintana. *Historia Mínima de la Comisión de Estudios de Historia de la Iglesia en Latinoamérica*, no. 11. Managua: Centro Ecuméncio Antonio Valdivieso, 1990. 191p.

Iglesia Católica y revolución en Nicaragua. Tomo I. De la conquista a la liberación (1503–1979). O. G. Gary. Mexico City: Claves Latinoamericanas, 1986. 399p.

Is Latin America turning Protestant? The politics of evangelical growth. D. Stoll. Berkeley & Los Angeles: University of California Press, 1990. 445p. (Focuses especially on Guatemala, Nicaragua, and Ecuador).

Los nicaro y los chorotega según las fuentes históricas. A. M. Chapman. *Serie historia y geografía*, no. 4. San José: Universidad de Costa Risa, 1960. 115p.

Ministers of God, ministers of the people: testimonies of faith from Nicaragua. T. Cabestrero. Trans., R. B. Barr. Maryknoll, NY: Orbis Books, 1983. 130p.

Nicaragua. R. L. Woodward Jr. 2nd ed. *World bibliographical series*, vol. 44. Oxford, UK: CLIO Press, 1994. 322p. (See especially 'Religion,' p.84–93).

Nicaraguan national bibliography, 1800–1978. G. Elmendorf. Redlands, CA: Latin American Bibliographic Foundation, 1987–87. 3 vols.

Nicaragua's other revolution: religious faith and political struggle. M. Dodson & L. N. O'Shaughnessy. Chapel Hill, NC: University of North Carolina Press, 1990. 292p.

'Nuevo estudio sobre la religión de los Nicaraos,' A. Esqueva, *Boletín Nicaragüense de bibliografía y documentación*, 25 (September–October 1978), 1–9.

Obra morava en Nicaragua: trasfondo y breve historia. J. F. Wilson. Managua: Editorial Unión, 1990. 189p.

'Of MAULI, macaws, and other things: what it means to be human among the Rama Indians of eastern Nicaragua,' F. O. Loveland, *Journal of Latin American Indian literatures*, 1, 2 (1985), 137–47.

'Political dependence and religious policy: Protestants and the state in pre–revolutionary Nicaragua (1937–1979),' J. Daudelin, *Journal of Church and State*, 34 (Spring 1992), 229–58. (Deals with relations between US Protestant missionaries and Somoza government).

Politics and the Catholic Church in Nicaragua. J. M. Kirk. Gainesville, FL: University Press of Florida, 1992. 246p.

'Protestantism in Nicaragua: its historical roots and influences affecting its growth.' G. I. Ferris Jr. Ph.D. dissertation, Temple University, Philadelphia, 1981. 287p.

'Religion and the struggle for hegemony in Nicaragua.' K. Deonandan. Ph.D. dissertation, Queen's University at Kingston, Ontario, 1990. 330p.

Saints and Sandinistas: the Catholic Church in Nicaragua and its response to the revolution. A. Bradstock. London: Epworth, 1987. 86p.

Steadfastness of the saints: a journal of peace and war in Central and North America. D. Berrigan. Maryknoll, NY: Orbis Books, 1985. 142p.

Thanks to God and the revolution: popular religion and class consciousness in the new Nicaragua. R. N. Lancaster. New York: Columbia University Press, 1988.

The Catholic Church and politics in Nicaragua and Costa Rica. P. J. Williams. *Pitt Latin American series.* Pittsburgh: University of Pittsburgh Press, 1989. 244p.

The CEPAD report: news and analysis from the Evangelical Church in Nicaragua. Council of Evangelical Churches of Nicaragua. Managua, 1989- . Bi-monthly.

The church and revolution in Nicaragua. L. N. O'Shaughnessy & L. H. Serra. *Monographs in international studies: Latin*

American series, no. 11. Athens, OH: Ohio University, Center for International Studies, 1986. 118p.
The Evangelism in Depth of the Latin American Mission: a description and evaluation. R. S. Rosales. *Sondeos No. 21.* Cuernavaca, Mexico: CIDOC, 1968. 204p.
The Nicaraguan church and the revolution. J. Mulligan. Kansas City, MO: Sheed & Ward, 1991. 320p.
Veinticinco años de labor Bautista en Nicaragua, 1917–1942. A. Parajón. Managua, 1942.

Country Table 2. **Organized churches and denominations in Nicaragua.**

Official name (bold type = church with over 10% of all affiliated) 1	*Begun* 2	*Type* 3	*Counc* 4	*Congs* 5	*Adults* 6	*Affiliated 1970* 7	*Affiliated 1995* 8	*G%* 9	*Names, notes, and other statistics* (see Codebook, Part 3) 10
Asambleas de Dios	1912	P-Pe2	ZF..C	1,614	185,800	20,000	220,000	10.07	*Assemblies of God.* M=AoG(USA). In east. Very rapid growth. 115n11f.1s(57).
Asambleas Locales	c1985	I-3nC	.....	2	30	–	100	10.00	*Local Churches. Little Flock.* Chinese. Begun 1922 in China.
Associación Misionera Ev Nacional	1965	I-Eva	C	16	1,600	1,000	4,000	5.70	*National Ev Missionary Association.* Schism ex CAM over delay in self-government.
Conv Evangélica Centroamericana	1955	I-Eva	C	31	2,500	2,000	6,250	4.66	*Central American Convention.* 1955 schism of half all CAM's 22 churches. HQ Managua.
Conv Nacional Bautista de Nicaragua	1917	P-Bap	T...C	79	9,200	10,350	20,000	2.67	*National Baptist Convention of N.* M=ABHMS(USA). 11f,1s,178Y,195z.
Fraternidad de Igs Ev Menonita de N	1974	P-Men	.....	8	150	–	400	4.76	*Brotherhood of Evangelical Mennonite Chs of N.* M=EMC.
Hermanos Unidos en Cristo	1965	P-Hol	.....	7	260	60	578	9.48	United Brethren in Christ. M=UBC.
Iglesia Adventista del Séptimo Día	1904	P-Adv	x....	48	27,000	5,000	51,900	9.81	*Seventh-day Adventists, Nicaragua Mission,* CAmerican UM. 4nx,10f,1H,1r,30t,357Y.
Iglesia Apostólica de la Fe en CJ	1949	I-3oL	x...C	263	1,500	2,000	4,000	2.81	*IAFCJ. Apostolic Ch of the Faith in Christ Jesus.* Mexican Mestizos. 18n,110z.
Iglesia Apostolica Libre	1953	I-3oL	.....	70	7,000	3,330	11,700	5.15	*Free Apostolic Church. Jesus Only Church.*
Iglesia Apostolica Nicaragua		I-3oL	.....	10	500	–	1,000	0.05	Indigenous Oneness movement.
Iglesia Bando Evangelistico Gedeon	c1960	I-3pL	.....	5	600	50	1,000	12.73	*Gideon's Evangelistic Band.* Indigenous; HQ Mexico. White suits, dresses.
Iglesia Bautista El Buen Samaritano	1972	I-Bap	.....	100	8,000	–	20,000	4.35	Good Samaritan Baptist Church.
Iglesia Bautista Internacional	1959	I-Bap	x...C	42	6,000	1,400	9,380	7.91	M=Bapt Int Missions (USA). 1 school. 4n,2x,14f,1p,1s(8),W=43%,165Y,50z.
Iglesia Católica en Nicaragua:	1522	R-Lat	B.LDR	268	1,890,500	1,780,995	3,790,000	3.07	*Catholic Ch in N.* Shortage of vocations. C=5+1+9. 168n 136x 201m 731w 94465Yy
M Managua	1913	R-Lat	Bs	74	959,000	572,000	1,961,000	5.05	70% urban. 1972 earthquake disaster. M=SDB. 55n 62x 77m 260w 22300Yy
D Estelí	1962	R-Lat	Bs	32	151,000	195,939	422,000	3.12	75% rural. Most priests, citizens. M=SDB,OSA. 14n 9x 19m 36w 9442Yy
D Granada	1913	R-Lat	Bs	71	175,000	177,971	335,000	2.56	South coast adjoining Costa Rica. 62% rural. M=CM. 30n 17x 35m 140w 10827Yy
D Jinotega	1982	R-Lat	Bs	12	103,000	–	208,000	7.69	Population is 80% baptized Catholics. 9n 2x 9m 23w 7588Yy
D Juigalpa	1962	R-Lat	Bs	17	85,500	110,000	174,852	1.87	Area north of Lake Nicaragua. Rural. 6n 9x 9m 12w 6258Yy
D León en Nicaragua	1534	R-Lat	Bs	35	309,000	317,085	500,000	1.84	Extreme west of country. 48% urban. 37n 8x 17m 110w 15440Yy
D Matagalpa	1924	R-Lat	Bs	14	158,000	288,000	302,000	0.19	Central part of country. 83% rural. 9n 12x 13m 76w 11885Yy
VA Bluefields	1913	R-Lat	Pofmc	13	152,000	120,000	293,000	3.64	Rural. Poor communications, transport. M=OFMCap. 8n 17x 22m 74w 10725Yy
Doubly-counted Catholics		R-Lat		–	-202,000	–	-405,852		Catholics counted in older diocese and also in newer diocese.
Iglesia de Dios (Cleveland)	1950	P-Pe3	ZF..C	281	14,121	5,000	40,300	8.71	M=Ch of God(Cleveland) (USA). 42 churches, 24 missions. HQ Managua. 49n,2f,1p.
Iglesia de Dios de la Profecía	1962	P-Pe3	Z....	177	9,500	188	23,800	21.37	*Ch of God of Prophecy.* M=CGP(USA).
Iglesia de JC de los Santos de los UD		m-LdS	x....	9	1,110	1,499	2,100	0.05	*Ch of JC of Latter-day Saints. Mormon.* M=CJCLdS(USA). 20f.
Iglesia de los Hermanos en Cristo	1965	P-Men	GF..C	55	4,300	400	7,870	12.66	*Brethren in Christ Ch.* M=BiCC(USA). HQ Managua. Expanding. 1x,6f1H,W=80%,5Y,7z.
Iglesia del Evangelio Cuadrangular	1954	P-Pe2	ZFxxC	67	2,100	4,000	3,220	-0.86	*Internat Ch of the Foursquare Gospel.* M=ICFG(USA). 22nm,3f,1k,1p(5),W67%,61Y.
Iglesia del Nazareno	1943	P-Hol	xF..C	75	4,166	5,000	6,428	1.01	M=CoNazarene (USA). In west. 33n,5x,18f,2h,1s(32),51t(4089),W=67%,208Y.
Iglesia del Príncipe de Paz		I-3pL	x....	5	600	200	1,000	0.05	*Ch of the Prince of Peace.* Pentecostals from Guatemala. Exorcism. In Managua.
Iglesia Episcopal: D Nicaragua		A-ACa	aw.RC	56	3,000	3,200	7,320	0.05	*Episcopal Ch. ECUSA, Province IX.* 70% Black, 20% Miskito, 5% Carib. 4n,4x,P=70%,156y.
Iglesia Ev Luterana de CR,ES,H,N,P	1955	P-Lut	l...C	1	27	300	40	-7.74	*ELC of Costa Rica,El Sal,Hond,Nic,Pan.* German, Scandinavian diaspora. 1x,W=12%.
Iglesia Ev Menonita de Nicaragua	1968	P-Men	G...C	53	1,749	140	2,916	12.91	M=Conservative Mennonite BMC (USA). 2x,19f,1p,8Y,12z. 1977 formed a united convention.
Iglesia Evangélica Nacional		I-Eva	C	1	100	50	200	0.05	*National Ev Ch.* Small indigenous congregation in Managua.
Iglesia Morava de Nicaragua	1849	P-Mor	xw..C	135	12,100	32,000	36,596	0.54	*Moravian Ch, Nicaragua Prov.* UoB. 95% Black. 20n,7x,211m,14f,2H,29i,1s,19Y,1308y.
Iglesia Nacional del Nazareno	1976	I-Hol	.....	4	400	–	1,330	5.26	*National Church of the Nazarene.* Schism ex Church of the Nazarene.
Iglesia Nueva Apostolica	c1985	I-3aX	x....	10	600	–	897	10.00	*NAC/NAK.* M=Neuapostolische Kirche (HQ Zurich, Switzerland).
Iglesia Pentecostal Unida	1970	P-Pe1	x...C	141	12,000	200	30,000	22.19	*United Pentecostal Ch. Jesus Only Church.* M=UPC(USA). Unitarians. 2m,2f,1p(10).
Iglesias de Cristo		I-Dis	x...C	21	3,000	1,200	6,000	0.05	*Ch of Christ.* M=CC(Non-Instrumental)(USA). Congs in Managua, Masatepe. 8m,2f.
Ig de Cristo de la Misión Pentecostal	1975	I-3pL	.....	100	8,000	–	16,000	5.00	*Pentecostal Mission of Christ Churches.*
Iglesia Universal Cristiana	c1980	I-3oL	O....	10	1,000	–	2,000	6.67	*Universal Christian Church.* Oneness body, in AWCF. HQ Direamba, Carazo.
Iglesias Ev Misión Centroamericana	1900	P-Eva	xM..f	70	2,900	2,000	5,800	4.35	M=Central American Mission. Mainly Indians. Major schisms 1955, 1965. 9f,1s.
Testigos de Jehová	1934	m-Jeh	x....	160	4,900	3,000	40,910	11.02	*Jehovah's Witnesses.* 1934, visits; 1943, literature; 1945, missions. (1975) 204Y, (1995)1198Y.
Other Protestant denominations		P-	.....	400	30,000	33,500	60,000	0.05	Total about 30 (see list below).
Other Non-White indigenous churches		I-	.....	300	30,000	5,000	50,000	0.05	Total over 20 (see list below), including several Jamaican bodies.
Doubly-affiliated		2-aff			-124,000	0	-243,707		Evangelicals who also are or were baptized Roman Catholics.
Totals				**4,694**	**2,162,313**	**1,923,062**	**4,241,328**		

Churches, members, growth, 1900-2025	*Congs*	*Adults*	*Affiliated*	*G%*	*Total denominations*	*6 Megablocs:* O	R	A	P	I	m
Total churches, members, and denominations (mid-1900)	300	249,000	474,000	2.02	3	0	1	0	2	0	0
Total churches, members, and denominations (mid-1970)	1,140	1,009,338	1,923,062	2.02	53	0	1	1	27	22	2
Total churches, members, and denominations (mid-1990)	4,000	1,870,000	3,668,220	3.28	93	0	1	1	45	44	2
Total churches, members, and denominations (mid-1995)	4,694	2,162,313	4,241,328	2.95	94	0	1	1	45	45	2
Total churches, members, and denominations (mid-2000)	5,000	2,476,000	4,857,432	2.75	95	0	1	1	45	46	2
Total churches, members, and denominations (mid-2025)	7,000	4,200,000	8,240,000	2.14	167	0	1	1	60	100	5

NOTES ON TABLE ABOVE
NATIONAL COUNCILS (Column 4, 5th letter).
- C = Comité Evangélico Pro-Ayuda al Desarrollo (CEPAD) (Evangelical Committee for Development Aid), with 35 Evangelical denominations as members by 1976.
- E = Consejo Nacional Evangelico de Nicaragua (CNEN).
- f = formerly a member of CEPAD.
- R = Conferencia Episcopal de Nicaragua (CEN) (Episcopal Conference of Nicaragua).

Other national councils. Although there is no nation-wide council of churches, there are 2 local ones: Asociación de Iglesias Cristianas (ADIC), in Puerto Cabezas (members: Baptist, Episcopalian, Pentecostal, Roman Catholic); and Asociación de Cleros, in Bluefields.

OTHER PROTESTANT DENOMINATIONS. These include: American Baptist Association (2 churches), Baptist Bible Fellowship International (1969), Baptist Missionary Association of America (1964), Ev Mennonite Ch (1966), Iglesias Berea (Asociación Cristiana Nicaraguense), Iglesia Cristiana Reformada, Reformada, Salvation Army (1928), Union Ch (Managua), United Brethren in Christ (1966), United World Mission (1969): and a number of West Indian denominations. Of these, in 1976 over 7 belonged to CEPAD.

OTHER NON-WHITE INDIGENOUS CHURCHES. These include: Apostólica Libre, Asamblea Apostólica, Asambleas de Iglesias Cristianas (Assemblies of Christian Churches) (Puerto Rican pentecostals; 1964), Cristiana Misionera, Embajadora de Cristo, Iglesia Bautista Pentecostal, Iglesia Bíblica Nacional, Iglesia Ev Primitiva, Iglesia Fuente de Jacob, Iglesia Pentecostal Libre, Iglesia Poder Pentecostal, Iglesia Sinaí, Misión Cristiana, Misión Obreros de Cristo, Templo Bíblico. Of these, in 1976 about 11 belonged to CEPAD. Several Jamaican bodies have members among the 70,000 Jamaican residents. A USA Black mission is also at work: National Baptist Convention USA (1964).

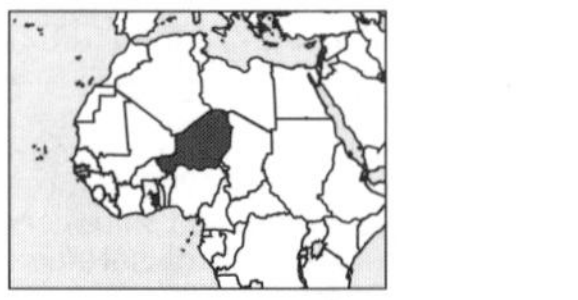

NIGER

SECULAR DATA, AD 2000

STATE
Official name: La République du Niger (The Republic of the Niger).
Short name: Niger. **Adjective of nationality:** of the Niger.
Flag: Orange, white, and green stripes with centered orange disc, the sun.
Area: 1,287,000 sq. km. (496,900 sq. mi.).
Government: Multiparty republic, since 1993 (1890 French penetration, 1922 French colony in French West Africa, 1958 autonomous, 1960 Independence as republic, 1974 military junta).
Legislature: National Assembly, 83 members.
Official language: French (Français).
Monetary unit: 1 CFA franc (CFAF) = 100 centimes. **US$1=** CFAF 560.38.
Chief cities: NIAMEY 593,012; Zinder 180,006; Maradi 168,203; Tahoua 73,334; Agadez 71,284.
Political divisions: 7 provinces.
Armed forces: 5,300.

DEMOGRAPHY
Population: 10,730,000.
Population density: 8.3/sq. km. (21.5/sq. mi.).
Under 15 years: 5,171,000.
Growth rate p.a.: 3.05% (births 45.57, deaths 15.12).
Mortality: Infant, per 1,000: 105.5, ; **Maternal per 100,000:** 1,200.0.
Life expectancy: 51 (male 49, female 52).
Household size: 6.4. **Floor area per person, sq.m:** 10.0.
Major languages: Hausa, Djemar, Fulani, Tuareg, French, Kanuri, Arabic, and about 10 smaller languages.
Urban dwellers: 20.57%. **Urban growth rate p.a.:** 5.6%.
Labor force: 32%.

ETHNOLINGUISTIC PEOPLES
25.7% Zerma (Dyerma); 14.9% Tazarawa; 11.1% Sokoto Fulani; 6.6% North Hausa (Arewa, Arawa; 6.0% Adarawa Hausa.

ECONOMY
National income p.a. per person: US$220; **per family:** US$1,408.

EDUCATION
Adult literacy: 13% (male 20%, female 6%). **Schools:** 2,768.
Universities: 3. **School enrolment:** female/male: 13%/23%.

HEALTH
Access to health services: 32%. **Access to safe water:** 53%.
Hospitals: 15 (5 beds per 10,000). **Doctors:** 142.
Blind: 50,000. **Deaf:** 648,300. **Murder rate:** <1.
Lepers: 75,000. **Underweight prevalence under 5:** 43%.

LITERATURE
New book titles p.a.: 210 (20 p.a. per million). **Periodicals:** 3.
Newspapers: 4 dailies.

COMMUNICATION (per 1,000 people)
Phones: 1 (6% mobile). **Radios:** 48. **TV sets:** 23.
Daily newspaper circulation: 1. **Computers:** 3.

REFUGEES
Citizen refugees in other countries: 20,000.
Alien refugees from other countries: 17,000.

HUMAN LIFE AND LIBERTY (optimum condition=100.0%)
HDI: 20.6. **HSI:** 30.0. **HFI:** 20.0. **EFL:** 26.0.

Country Table 1. **Religious adherents in the Niger, AD 1900-2025.**

Year / *Name*	*1900* *Adherents*	*%*	*1970* *Adherents*	*%*	*mid-1990* *Adherents*	*%*	*Annual change, 1990-2000* *Natural*	*Conversion*	*Total*	*Rate*	*mid-1995* *Adherents*	*%*	*mid-2000* *Adherents*	*%*	*mid-2025* *Adherents*	*%*
Muslims	410,000	45.1	3,580,010	86.0	6,986,000	90.4	271,012	3,563	274,575	3.37	8,291,900	90.6	9,731,745	90.7	20,145,500	93.7
Ethnoreligionists	500,000	55.0	565,300	13.6	695,900	9.0	26,995	-3,649	23,346	2.94	800,000	8.7	929,362	8.7	1,200,000	5.6
Christians	**0**	**0.0**	**18,890**	**0.5**	**42,100**	**0.5**	**1,633**	**15**	**1,648**	**3.36**	**49,700**	**0.5**	**58,577**	**0.6**	**123,500**	**0.6**
PROFESSION																
crypto-Christians	0	0.0	4,600	0.1	23,300	0.3	904	366	1,270	4.45	29,000	0.3	36,000	0.3	98,500	0.5
professing Christians	**0**	**0.0**	**14,290**	**0.3**	**18,800**	**0.2**	**729**	**-351**	**378**	**1.85**	**20,700**	**0.2**	**22,577**	**0.2**	**25,000**	**0.1**
AFFILIATION																
unaffiliated Christians	0	0.0	0	0.0	300	0.0	12	-11	1	0.23	304	0.0	307	0.0	500	0.0
affiliated Christians	**0**	**0.0**	**18,890**	**0.5**	**41,800**	**0.5**	**1,622**	**25**	**1,647**	**3.38**	**49,396**	**0.5**	**58,270**	**0.5**	**123,000**	**0.6**
Independents	0	0.0	1,030	0.0	15,000	0.2	582	418	1,000	5.24	18,762	0.2	25,000	0.2	60,000	0.3
Roman Catholics	0	0.0	13,360	0.3	17,600	0.2	683	-476	207	1.12	19,000	0.2	19,670	0.2	30,000	0.1
Protestants	0	0.0	4,450	0.1	8,800	0.1	341	79	420	3.98	11,134	0.1	13,000	0.1	32,000	0.2
Marginal Christians	0	0.0	50	0.0	400	0.0	16	4	20	4.14	500	0.0	600	0.0	1,000	0.0
Trans-megabloc groupings																
Evangelicals	0	0.0	2,400	0.1	8,500	0.1	330	40	370	3.68	9,844	0.1	12,200	0.1	29,000	0.1
Pentecostals/Charismatics	0	0.0	1,000	0.0	16,300	0.2	632	438	1,070	5.18	20,765	0.2	27,000	0.3	67,000	0.3
Great Commission Christians	**0**	**0.0**	**14,500**	**0.4**	**31,800**	**0.4**	**1,234**	**5**	**1,239**	**3.34**	**37,400**	**0.4**	**44,186**	**0.4**	**105,000**	**0.5**
Nonreligious	0	0.0	0	0.0	4,800	0.1	186	78	264	4.48	5,800	0.1	7,439	0.1	20,000	0.1
Baha'is	0	0.0	800	0.0	2,200	0.0	85	-7	78	3.07	2,600	0.0	2,978	0.0	6,000	0.0
World A (unevangelized persons)	910,000	100.0	3,540,139	85.0	4,777,758	61.8	185,437	-42,613	142,824	2.65	5,453,513	59.6	6,212,670	57.9	11,306,370	52.6
World B (evangelized non-Christians)	0	0.0	605,840	14.5	2,911,142	37.7	112,841	42,598	155,439	4.36	3,646,977	39.9	4,458,753	41.5	10,065,130	46.8
World C (Christians)	0	0.0	18,890	0.5	42,100	0.5	1,633	15	1,648	3.36	49,700	0.5	58,577	0.6	123,500	0.6
Country's population	**910,000**	**100.0**	**4,164,870**	**100.0**	**7,731,000**	**100.0**	**299,911**	**0**	**299,911**	**3.33**	**9,150,191**	**100.0**	**10,730,000**	**100.0**	**21,495,000**	**100.0**

COLUMNS, ROWS.
For meanings and definitions, see Codebook (Part 3). Note that, by definition, total 'Christians' = professing + crypto-Christians, which also = affiliated + unaffiliated Christians, and also = Great Commission Christians + latent Christians. Percentages may not always total exactly, due to rounding.

CENSUSES.
X.1959-III.1960 (Niger Africans only, de jure): 98.5% Muslims, 1.4% ethnoreligionists, 0.04% Christians. (This survey covered only half the population).

NOTES ON RELIGIONS
BAHA'IS. By 1973, 5 local spiritual assemblies established.
CHRISTIANS. About 5% citizens (Africans), 95% expatriates (in 1995, 7,000 French and other Europeans, and 40,000 Nigerians and other African expatriates).
CRYPTO-CHRISTIANS. Unorganized individuals in the recognized churches, including many citizens and some African expatriates.
ETHNORELIGIONISTS. Animists in the south, especially among the Kurfei (95% traditionalist in 1995) and Mauri (95%).
INDEPENDENTS. In 5 denominations in 1995 (see Table 2).
MUSLIMS. Sunnis (of the Malikite rite), mostly linked to the Tijaniya brotherhood. *Hajj pilgrims to Mecca.* (1970) 1,827; (1974) 7,030; (1975) 685; (1976) 139.

Great Commission Instrument Panel: status of Niger (for explanation see start of Part 4)

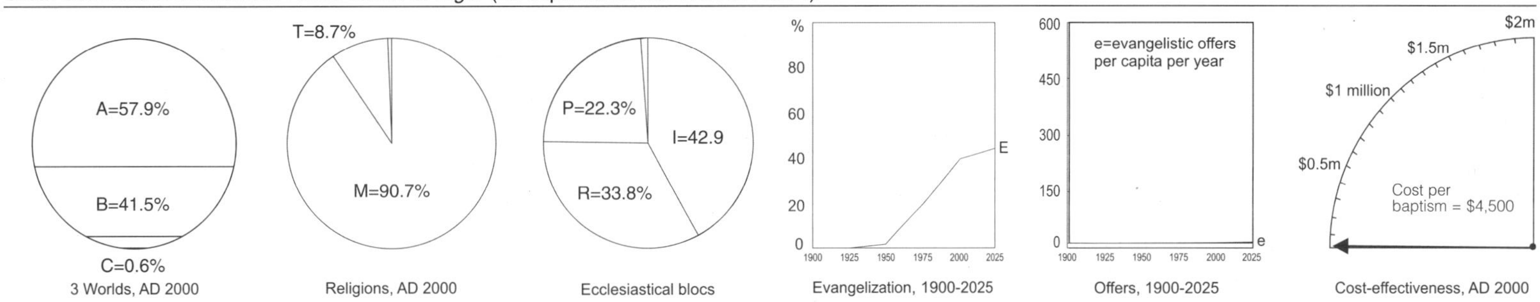

Country status. Niger is a landlocked country in West Africa between the Sahara Desert and the Sahel. It is the largest country in West Africa. The northern half of the country is too hot and dry to be habitable. Virtually, the entire population is crowded into the southern one-fifth along the Niger river.

Muslims. Tuareg dance.

HUMAN LIFE AND LIBERTY

Human need and development. Niger is one of the poorest countries in the world, and ranks near the bottom of the economic scale even among African countries. Having driven out all forms of life from the north the scorching desert is encroaching on the south. Periodic droughts have killed much of the livestock from which the vast majority of the people of Niger obtain their livelihood. During a 6-year period from 1967 to 1973, half the national cattle herd was wiped out, and the economy has never recovered from this disaster. Medical facilities are available only in Niamey, the capital. Most of the nomads live in makeshift dwellings and have no access to any but the most primitive tools. The per capita GNP is $220, the life expectancy 51 years, and the adult illiteracy rate 87%.

Human rights and freedoms. Niger is ruled by a transitional government outwardly committed to constitutional rule. However, the civilian-run transitional government has little control over the military and the police, especially over a rebellious element in the rank and file called La Troupe. The insurgent staged abductions of public officials attempted to put down a Tuareg uprising by harsh reprisals. The Tuaregs themselves provoked much violence by attacking civilian personnel and vehicles on the major road arteries in the north and cutting off food supplies. In other areas the new government has achieved solid gains in establishing human rights. The Crimes and Abuses Commission created in 1991 continued its investigations into the crimes committed by previous regimes. The process of democratization also ended the traditional dominance of the Zerma ethnic group who make up only 25% of the population, and gave a fairer share of and larger role in government to the Hausa who make up 33%, as well as the Fulani (Peul) and the Tuareg. Prevailing Islamic traditions discriminate against females.

Human environment. Niger has an environment that is unfriendly to man and beast. The desert is encroaching steadily from the north while human settlements are despoiling what is left. Drought, devegetation, and soil erosion wreak havoc on the fragile ecological system of the Sahel. Niger has one of the largest national parks in West Africa, but poaching, hunting, and mining have combined to decimate the wildlife in it and destroy their habitat.

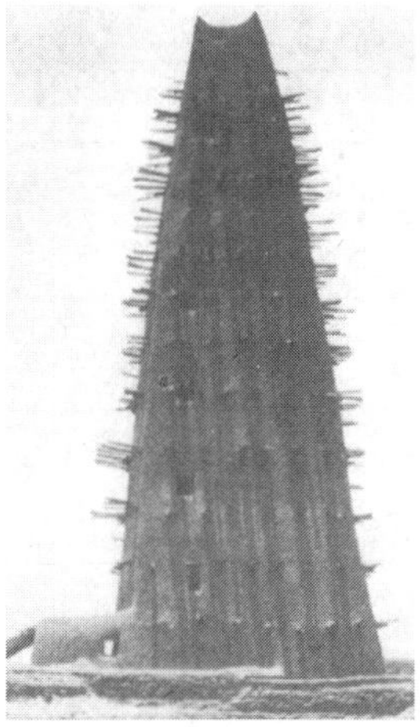

Muslims. Thousand-year-old mosque.

NON-CHRISTIAN RELIGIONS

Islam was first propagated in Niger in the 11th century and is the predominant religion in the country. Today most Muslims are linked through their clerics to the Tijaniya brotherhood, which is strong among the Tuareg, Kanuri, Fulani, and Hausa city-dwellers, whilst a mixture of Islamic and traditional beliefs is found among the Zerma-Songhai, Beriberi and rural Hausa. A training school for marabouts exists at Say, the principal Muslim holy city in the Niger. A recent development is a powerful Muslim radio station, funded by Arab governments.

Country summary. **Worlds A, B, C by ethnolinguistic peoples, cities, and major civil divisions in the Niger.**

	PEOPLES							CITIES							CIVIL DIVISIONS						
World	Num	Pop 2000	C%	Christians	E%	U%	Unevangelized	Num	Pop 2000	C%	Christians	E%	U%	Unevangelized	Num	Pop 2000	C%	Christians	E%	U%	Unevangelized
A	24	6,350,436	0.15	9,354	35	65	4,153,205	5	1,085,839	1.13	12,286	45	55	598,318	7	10,730,103	0.54	58,269	42	58	6,208,245
B	9	4,369,686	0.95	41,421	53	47	2,055,015	0	0	0.00	0	0	0	0	0	0	0.00	0	0	0	0
C	4	9,979	75.10	7,494	100	0	26	0	0	0.00	0	0	0	0	0	0	0.00	0	0	0	0
Total	**37**	**10,730,101**	**0.54**	**58,269**	**42**	**58**	**6,208,246**	**5**	**1,085,839**	**1.13**	**12,286**	**45**	**55**	**598,318**	**7**	**10,730,103**	**0.54**	**58,269**	**42**	**58**	**6,208,245**

African traditional religions retain the allegiance of about 8% of the people, most of whom are located in the southern part of the country. The Kurfei and Mauri peoples are almost totally resistant to the claims of both Christianity and Islam.

CHRISTIANITY

In the 7th century, Berber Christians who had been driven out of North Africa by nascent Islam migrated into the Air region and reached as far southwest as the Niger river. They were however isolated from any other Christian support and eventually disappeared without a trace. Christianity did not return again to Niger until the 20th century.

CATHOLIC CHURCH. Catholicism spread from Dahomey to Niger in 1931. The prefecture of Niamey was erected in 1942 and was raised to a diocese in 1961. The first indigenous priest was ordained in 1972 in the presence of senior government officials and the Muslim great imam of Niamey. Of all Catholics, 95% are expatriates from Europe, North America, Lebanon and West Africans from Togo, Benin, and Upper Volta. Local African Catholics include Hausas from the region of Dogondoutchi, Zerma-Songhai from Dolbel, mixed-race persons, and naturalized citizens from Togo and Benin (Dahomey). The number today is considerably smaller than in 1963 when the government deported all Dahomeans, although some subsequently returned clandestinely.

The Holy See has diplomatic relations with Niger and in AD 2000 is represented to government and the Catholic hierarchy by a nuncio residing in Abidjan.

PROTESTANT CHURCHES. The main Protestant work is being carried on by the Evangelical Churches of Niger, supported by the Sudan Interior Mission since its arrival in 1923. Active in the Maradi and Dogondoutchi areas, the church is involved in an extensive school and social service program including a large hospital at Galmi, a leprosarium at Maradi and numerous dispensaries. The Evangelical Baptist Church is located in southwest Niger at Niamey and along the Niger river. The small Methodist Church confines its activities largely to expatriates from Togo and Dahomey.

INDIGENOUS CHURCHES. There have been no indigenous schismatic churches in Niger, but immigrant Nigerians and Dahomeans have introduced 2 bodies: the Cherubim and Seraphim from the Nigerian coast have made some progress west of Niamey, and the Heavenly Christian Church from Benin works in Niamey. Both of these bodies had grown to over 1,000 members by 1995.

Indigenous missions. Only a select few missionaries have been sent out from Niger to other countries.

CHURCH AND STATE

According to the constitution of November 1960, modified in July 1961, Niger is a secular republic (Article 2) which respects all beliefs (Article 6). The churches are neither subsidized nor taxed except for a small basic tax for occupation of land. The state contributes, nonetheless towards the expenses involved in the functioning of private schools. Courses of religions instruction are given outside school hours and premises. There is no government ministry charged with religious affairs nor any obligation for the churches to register with government.

BROADCASTING AND MEDIA

The Niger is a member of UNDA. Each Sunday, 15-minute Catholic programs are aired in French, Zarma, and Hawson. Shortwave radio programs from KNLS have had responses.

The 'Jesus' Film has been shown to 2.3 million, mainly on television broadcasts.

FUTURE TRENDS AND PROSPECTS

Christianity will potentially only make small gains into the 21st century with most church members found in expatriates and in small tribes. Islam, on the other hand, is expected to increase in strength to 94% by 2025.

Ethnoreligionists will likely decline throughout the 21st century, most of these becoming Muslims. Christianity may remain below 1% of the population up to and beyond AD 2050.

BIBLIOGRAPHY

Ambivalence et culte de possession: contribution à l'étude du Bori hausa. J. Monfouga-Nicolas. Paris: Anthropos, [1972]. 403p.

Croyants dans la ville propos. R. Deniel. *Chemins de chrétiens africains*, 7. Abidjan, Ivory Coast: INADES, 1982. 36p.

Embodying colonial memories: spirit possession, power, and the Hausa in West Africa. P. Stoller. New York: Routledge, 1995.

Girkaa: une cérémonie d'initiation au culte de possession bòorii des Hausa de la région de Maradi (Niger). V. Erlmann & H. Magagi. Berlin: Dietrich Reimer Verlag, 1989. 173p.

Hausa women in the twentieth century. C. Coles & B. Mack (eds). Madison, WI: University of Wisconsin Press, 1991. 308p.

In sorcery's shadow: a memoir of apprenticeship among the Songhay of Niger. P. Stoller & C. Olkes. Chicago: University of Chicago Press, 1987. 252p.

L'Eglise au Niger: une pastorale en pays islamique d'Afrique noire. P. Prevot. Paris: Institut catholic, 1967. 67p.

'L'Islam et les tribus dans la colonie du Niger,' P. Marty, *Revue des études islamiques*, (1930), 333–429.

Niger. L. F. Zamponi. *World bibliographical series*, vol. 164. Oxford, UK: CLIO Press, 1994. 431p. (See especially 'Religion,' p.93–99).

Origins of the Niger Mission, 1841–1891: a paper read at the centenary of the mission at Christ Church, Onitsha, on 13 November 1957. K. O. Dike. [Ibadan]: Ibadan University Press for the Church Missionary Society Niger Mission, 1957. 21p.

Spirit possession and personhood among the Kel Ewey Tuareg. S. J. Rasmussen. Cambridge, UK: Cambridge University Press, 1995. 189p.

Sufi mystics of the Niger desert: Sidi Mahmud and the hermits of Air. H. T. Norris. Oxford, UK: Clarendon Press, 1990. 180p.

The C.M.S. Niger mission centenary, 1857–1957. J. O. Onwuteaka. Onitsha, Nigeria: Mbidokwu Press, [1957]. 23p.

The Hausa people: a bibliography. F. A. Salamone with the assistance of J. A. McCain. New Haven, CT: Human Relations Area Files, 1983. 2 vols.

The spirits and their cousins: some aspects of belief, ritual, and social organization in a rural Hausa village in Niger. R. H. Faulkingham. Amherst, MA: Dept. of Anthropology, University of Massachusetts, 1975. 57p.

'The Sudanese 'Mahdiyya' and the Niger–Chad region,' S. Biobaku & M. al-Hajj, in *Islam in tropical Africa: studies presented and discussed at the Fifth International African Seminar, Ahmadu Bello University, Zaria, January 1964*, p.226–39. I. M. Lewis (ed). 2nd ed. Bloomington, IN: International African Institute in association with Indiana University Press, 1988.

'Trance and music in the Hausa "bòorii" spirit possession cult in Niger,' V. Erlmann, *Ethnomusicology*, 26, 1 (1982), 49–58.

'Un aspect historique des rapports de l'animisme et de l'Islam au Niger,' H. Raulin, *Journal de la Société des Africanistes*, 32, 2 (1962–63), 249–74. (Syncretism between animism and Islam, hidden by apparent conversions to Islam).

'Women, ecology and Islam in the making of modern Hausa cultural history.' M. W. Bivins. Ph.D. dissertation, Michigan State University, East Lansing, MI, 1994. 265p.

Country Table 2. **Organized churches and denominations in the Niger.**

Official name (bold type = church with over 10% of all affiliated) 1	Begun 2	Type 3	Counc 4	Congs 5	Adults 6	Affiliated 1970 7	Affiliated 1995 8	G% 9	Names, notes, and other statistics (see Codebook, Part 3) 10
Assemblées de Dieu	c1985	P-Pe2	Z....	2	214	–	400	10.00	*Assemblies of God*. M=AoG(USA).
Chérubin et Séraphin	c1960	I-3aA	x.I..	10	500	50	1,000	12.73	*Cherubim and Seraphim* (Nigeria). Schism at Tera of EBM converts among Songhai.
Eglise Baptiste	1973	P-Bap	.....	1	70	–	117	4.55	Southern Baptist Mission. M=FMB-SBC.
Eglise Baptiste Internationale	1966	I-Bap	.....	1	32	30	64	3.08	Baptist International Missions. M=BIM(USA).
Eglise Catholique: D Niamey	1931	R-Lat	p.SFP	21	10,000	13,360	19,000	1.42	C=1+1+7. 95% expatriate, 380 Songhai,Hausa. (1970) 26x,177Yy. (1990) 6n, 35x,540Yy.
Eglise de la Porte Ouverte	c1965	I-3pA	.....	1	36	50	120	3.56	Church of the Open Door.
Eglise du Christianisme Céleste	c1968	I-3aA	x.I..	12	600	200	1,100	7.06	*Celestial Ch of Christ. Heavenly Christianity Ch.* Ex C & S. Niamey. HQ Porto Novo (Benin).
Eglise Méthodiste		P-Met	Vwa..	1	50	50	100	0.05	*Methodist Ch.* Migrants from church in Togo and Benin (HQ Contonou, Benin).
Eglise Neo-Apostolique	c1980	I-3aX	x....	50	2,500	–	3,478	6.67	*NAC/NAK*. M=Neuapostolische Kirche (HQ Zurich, Switzerland).
Eglises Evangéliques du Niger	1923	P-Eva	xM...	80	2,800	2,000	5,500	4.13	M=EMS(Nigeria),SIM(USA). 98% Hausa; Tuareg, Beriberi. 4n,16m,30f,2H,5h,1p(14).
Eglises radiophoniques isolées	c1960	I-3rA	.....	1,000	6,000	700	10,000	11.22	Isolated radio believers, mostly youths aged 12-25. T=50 (ELWA,SIM,ICI).
Mission Evangélique Saharienne	c1980	P-Eva	.....	1	10	2,000	17	6.67	Evangelical mission from Europe and USA.
Témoins de Jéhovah	c1960	m-Jeh	x....	7	141	50	500	9.65	*Jehovah's Witnesses*. Active witnessing under way by 1965. (1975) 1Y. (1995) 26Y.
Union des Egls Evangéliques Baptistes	1927	P-Bap	xT...	9	500	200	1,000	6.65	*Ev Baptist Missions*. M=EBM(USA). 90% Yoruba immigrants, 10% Zerma. 26f,2h,1p.
Other African indigenous churches	c1975	I-3pA	.....	40	0	–	3,000	5.00	Total about 15 bodies from Nigeria.
Other Protestant denominations		P-	.....	50	3,000	200	4,000	0.05	Total about 30 (see list below), including EEPM (Moli), SDA(from 1987.
Totals				**1,286**	**28,007**	**18,890**	**49,396**		

Churches, members, growth, 1900-2025	Congs	Adults	Affiliated	G%	Total denominations	6 Megablocs: O	R	A	P	I	m
Total churches, members, and denominations (mid-1900)	0	0	0	0.00	0	0	0	0	0	0	0
Total churches, members, and denominations (mid-1970)	137	9,970	18,890	10.00	24	0	1	0	17	5	1
Total churches, members, and denominations (mid-1990)	1,000	23,700	41,800	4.05	44	0	1	0	36	6	1
Total churches, members, and denominations (mid-1995)	1,286	28,007	49,396	3.40	64	0	1	0	36	26	1
Total churches, members, and denominations (mid-2000)	1,400	33,000	58,270	3.36	65	0	1	0	37	26	1
Total churches, members, and denominations (mid-2025)	2,100	69,700	123,000	3.03	88	0	1	1	50	35	1

NOTES ON TABLE ABOVE

NATIONAL COUNCILS (Column 4, 5th letter).

P = Conférence Episcopale de Haute-Volta et Niger (CEHVN) (Episcopal Conference of Upper Volta & Niger).

OTHER PROTESTANT DENOMINATIONS. These smaller bodies include: Coopération Evangélique Mondiale, Sahara Desert Mission (work among Tuaregs), Southern Methodist Ch, World-Wide Missions.

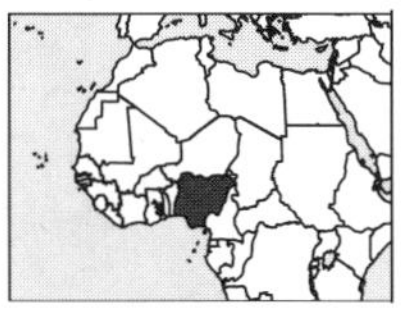

NIGERIA

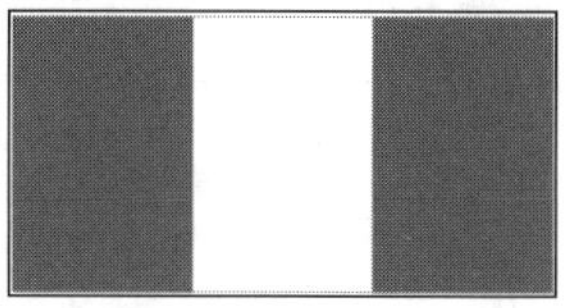

SECULAR DATA, AD 2000

STATE
Official name: The Federal Republic of Nigeria.
Short name: Nigeria. **Adjective of nationality:** Nigerian.
Flag: Green, white, and green bars.
Area: 923,768 sq. km. (356,669 sq. mi.).
Government: Democracy from 1998; previously, military regime, since 1995 (1861 British colony, 1883 Niger Coast protectorate, 1914 unified British colony and protectorate, 1954 federation, 1960 Independence, 1963 republic, 1966 military rule, 1979 republic).
Legislature: Provisional Ruling Council.
Official language: English.
Monetary unit: 1 Nigerian naira (N) = 100 kobo. **US$1=** N90.00.
Chief cities: Lagos 13,488,000; Ibadan 1,739,000; Ogbomosho 852,835; Kano 787,581; Oshogbo 557,145.
Political divisions: 31 provinces.
Armed forces: 77,000.

DEMOGRAPHY
Population: 111,506,000.
Population density: 120.7/sq. km. (312.6/sq. mi.).
Under 15 years: 48,037,000.
Growth rate p.a.: 2.24% (births 37.15, deaths 14.36).
Mortality: Infant, per 1,000: 76.2, ; **Maternal per 100,000:** 1,000.0.
Life expectancy: 50 (male 49, female 52).
Household size: 5.0. **Floor area per person, sq.m:** 12.0.
Major languages: English, Hausa, Yoruba, Ibo, Fulani, Tiv, Kanuri, Efik, Bini, Nupe, Pidgin English, and over 510 other tribal languages.
Urban dwellers: 43.99%. **Urban growth rate p.a.:** 4.6%.
Labor force: 31%.

ETHNOLINGUISTIC PEOPLES
17.5% Yoruba (Oyo, Ekiti, Ijebu; 17.2% Hausa (Hausawa); 13.3% Igbo (Ibo); 4.9% Toroobe Fulani; 3.0% Yerwa Kanuri (Beriberi).

ECONOMY
National income p.a. per person: US$260; **per family:** US$1,300.

EDUCATION
Adult literacy: 57% (male 67%, female 47%). **Schools:** 44,723.
Universities: 31. **School enrolment:** female/male: 56%/70%.

HEALTH
Access to health services: 66%. **Access to safe water:** 39%.
Hospitals: 11,588 (12 beds per 10,000). **Doctors:** 17,954.
Blind: 420,000. **Deaf:** 7,727,100. **Murder rate:** 15.
Lepers: 1,000,000. **Underweight prevalence under 5:** 35%.

LITERATURE
New book titles p.a.: 6,690 (60 p.a. per million). **Periodicals:** 129.
Newspapers: 27 dailies.

COMMUNICATION (per 1,000 people)
Phones: 3 (15% mobile). **Radios:** 170. **TV sets:** 38.
Daily newspaper circulation: 18. **Computers:** 8.

REFUGEES
Alien refugees from other countries: 8,000.

HUMAN LIFE AND LIBERTY (optimum condition=100.0%)
HDI: 39.3. **HSI:** 30.0. **HFI:** 32.5. **EFL:** 35.0.

Country Table 1. **Religious adherents in Nigeria, AD 1900-2025.**

Year	1900		1970		mid-1990		Annual change, 1990-2000				mid-1995		mid-2000		mid-2025	
Name	Adherents	%	Adherents	%	Adherents	%	Natural	Conversion	Total	Rate	Adherents	%	Adherents	%	Adherents	%
Christians	**176,000**	**1.1**	**21,728,000**	**43.8**	**39,550,000**	**45.4**	**1,112,242**	**45,075**	**1,157,317**	**2.60**	**45,200,000**	**45.7**	**51,123,167**	**45.9**	**86,000,000**	**47.0**
PROFESSION																
professing Christians	**176,000**	**1.1**	**21,728,000**	**43.8**	**39,550,000**	**45.4**	**1,112,242**	**45,075**	**1,157,317**	**2.60**	**45,200,000**	**45.7**	**51,123,167**	**45.9**	**86,000,000**	**47.0**
AFFILIATION																
unaffiliated Christians	77,100	0.5	7,420,539	15.0	250,000	0.3	7,031	-16,215	-9,184	-4.48	200,000	0.2	158,165	0.1	100,000	0.1
affiliated Christians	**98,900**	**0.6**	**14,307,461**	**28.9**	**39,300,000**	**45.2**	**1,105,211**	**61,309**	**1,166,500**	**2.63**	**45,000,000**	**45.5**	**50,965,002**	**45.7**	**85,900,000**	**46.9**
Independents	5,000	0.0	3,307,472	6.7	17,406,200	20.0	489,500	167,380	656,880	3.25	20,644,944	20.9	23,975,000	21.5	34,000,000	18.6
Anglicans	35,000	0.2	2,941,000	5.9	14,800,000	17.0	416,208	110,792	527,000	3.09	17,500,000	17.7	20,070,000	18.0	34,770,000	19.0
Protestants	40,000	0.3	3,979,001	8.0	10,700,000	12.3	300,907	34,093	335,000	2.76	12,268,591	12.4	14,050,000	12.6	25,000,000	13.7
Roman Catholics	18,900	0.1	3,889,688	7.8	10,100,000	11.6	284,034	45,966	330,000	2.87	11,689,038	11.8	13,400,000	12.0	25,500,000	13.9
Marginal Christians	0	0.0	188,300	0.4	400,000	0.5	11,249	8,751	20,000	4.14	508,100	0.5	600,000	0.5	1,400,000	0.8
Orthodox	0	0.0	2,000	0.0	3,000	0.0	84	-74	10	0.33	3,050	0.0	3,100	0.0	4,000	0.0
doubly-affiliated	0	0.0	0	0.0	-14,109,200	-16.2	-396,781	-305,609	-702,390	4.12	-17,613,723	-17.8	-21,133,098	-19.0	-34,774,000	-19.0
Trans-megabloc groupings																
Evangelicals	73,000	0.5	4,750,000	9.6	16,100,000	18.5	452,767	167,233	620,000	3.31	19,061,850	19.3	22,300,000	20.0	42,100,000	23.0
Pentecostals/Charismatics	96,000	0.6	3,600,000	7.3	26,950,000	31.0	757,892	135,608	893,500	2.90	31,385,667	31.7	35,885,000	32.2	61,940,000	33.8
Great Commission Christians	**162,000**	**1.0**	**3,471,000**	**7.0**	**8,442,000**	**9.7**	**237,407**	**43,674**	**281,081**	**2.92**	**9,800,000**	**9.9**	**11,252,805**	**10.1**	**21,964,000**	**12.0**
Muslims	4,200,000	25.9	21,750,000	43.9	38,199,700	43.9	1,074,258	5,738	1,079,996	2.52	43,435,000	43.9	48,999,663	43.9	82,107,000	44.9
Ethnoreligionists	11,824,000	73.0	5,970,000	12.0	9,000,000	10.3	253,099	-56,718	196,381	1.99	9,959,150	10.1	10,963,809	9.8	14,000,000	7.7
Nonreligious	0	0.0	100,000	0.2	200,000	0.2	5,624	7,010	12,634	5.02	270,000	0.3	326,339	0.3	700,000	0.4
Atheists	0	0.0	20,000	0.0	32,500	0.0	914	-233	681	1.92	34,000	0.0	39,313	0.0	100,000	0.1
Baha'is	0	0.0	11,400	0.0	25,000	0.0	703	-500	203	0.78	27,000	0.0	27,031	0.0	80,000	0.0
Buddhists	0	0.0	500	0.0	5,000	0.0	141	-46	95	1.76	5,900	0.0	5,953	0.0	15,000	0.0
Chinese folk-religionists	0	0.0	0	0.0	3,000	0.0	84	-55	29	0.93	3,300	0.0	3,291	0.0	7,000	0.0
Jews	0	0.0	0	0.0	800	0.0	22	-22	0	0.04	850	0.0	803	0.0	2,000	0.0
Other religionists	0	0.0	11,100	0.0	15,000	0.0	422	-249	173	1.10	16,800	0.0	16,726	0.0	30,000	0.0
World A (unevangelized persons)	13,494,600	83.3	20,927,525	42.2	21,583,688	24.8	607,439	-511,485	95,954	0.44	22,462,073	22.7	22,524,212	20.2	28,188,314	15.4
World B (evangelized non-Christians)	2,529,400	15.6	6,935,767	14.0	25,897,312	29.8	727,828	466,410	1,194,238	3.87	31,289,791	31.6	37,858,621	33.9	68,852,686	37.6
World C (Christians)	176,000	1.1	21,728,000	43.8	39,550,000	45.4	1,112,242	45,075	1,157,317	2.60	45,200,000	45.7	51,123,167	45.9	86,000,000	47.0
Country's population	**16,200,000**	**100.0**	**49,591,293**	**100.0**	**87,031,000**	**100.0**	**2,447,509**	**0**	**2,447,509**	**2.51**	**98,951,865**	**100.0**	**111,506,000**	**100.0**	**183,041,000**	**100.0**

COLUMNS, ROWS.
For meanings and definitions, see Codebook (Part 3). Note that, by definition, total 'Christians' = professing + crypto-Christians, which also = affiliated + unaffiliated Christians, and also = Great Commission Christians + latent Christians. Percentages may not always total exactly, due to rounding.

CENSUSES.
1921: 56.8% ethnoreligionists, 39.0% Muslims, 1.6% Protestants, 1.0% Anglicans, 0.9% Roman Catholics, 0.8% African indigenous. **1921** (Northern Nigeria): 65.0% Muslims, 34.8% tribal religionists, 0.2% Christians. **1931:** 50.0% ethnoreligionists, 43.6% Muslims, 2.4% Protestants, 1.4% Anglicans, 1.3% Roman Catholics, 1.2% African indigenous. **1931** (Northern Nigeria): 66.0% Muslims, 33.2% ethnoreligionists, 0.6% Christians (0.5% Protestants). **VII.1952-VI.1953** (Africans only): 45.3% Muslims, 32.8% ethnoreligionists, 21.9% Christians. **1952** (by regions): Western: 36.9% Christians, 32.8% Muslims, 30.3% ethnoreligionists; Eastern: 49.2% Christians, 50.2% ethnoreligionists, 0.6% Muslims; Northern: 73.0% Muslims, 24.3% ethnoreligionists, 2.7% Christians. **5-8.XI.1963** (modified by UN to correct overenumeration): 43.4% Muslims, 37.9%, Christians, 18.7% ethnoreligionists. By plotting the latter census' figure for Christians on a graph together with figures from all previous censuses, and by comparing the result with parallel graphs from other tropical African countries, it may be seen that Christianity is expanding in Nigeria in the 20th century in the manner shown in the table above with its future projections.

POLLS.
Public-opinion polls of religious preference have been conducted only in cities and urban areas (Lagos, Enugu, et alia).

NOTES ON RELIGIONS
ATHEISTS. Socialist Workers and Farmers Party (SWAFP) (banned since 1966). Many intellectuals also are atheists.
BAHA'IS. Growth from 15 local spiritual assemblies (1964) to 76 (1973) to over 140 (1996).
BUDDHISTS. Chinese.
ETHNORELIGIONISTS. Strongest in the central plateau. Peoples over 90% traditionalist (animist) in 1995: Afo (94%), Awak (90%), Bada (90%), Duguza (90%), Dulbu (90%), Gengle (94%), Guduf (96%), Guruntum (90%), Jaba (95%), Jibu (90%), Ju (95%), Kamantan (91%), Kamo (90%), Lungu (90%), Luri (90%), Maguzawa (Hausa) (90%), Matakam (91%), Miya (96%), Ogori-Magongo (90%), Piti (90%).
INDEPENDENTS. In over 1,800 denominations in 1995 (see Table 2).
MUSLIMS. Mainly Sunnis (of the Malikite rite), and mainly in the north among the Hausa, Fulani, Kanuri, and Nupe; strongest brotherhoods are Qadiriya, Tijaniya, and Ahmadiya (the latter enumerated here under Muslims though declared non-Muslim by Pakistan).(The Ahmadiya Mission, begun in 1916, has its adherents mainly in the south among the Yoruba, with some of the 40 mosques also in eastern Nigeria. There are 10 schools. Many of the large number of adherents claimed are children and others influenced by the mission's institutions). There are also Lebanese and Syrian Arabs who are mainly Shias. *Conversions to Islam.* These have been continuing since 1880 among ethnoreligionists particularly in Northern Nigeria, and among the Yoruba and a few other southern peoples. The major period for conversions was 1890-1920, whole tribes becoming islamized. In 1964 the Sardauna of Sokoto conducted massive campaigns in Zaria and Niger provinces which converted over 100,000 pagan Maguzawa and other peoples to Islam (187,216 from December 1963 to June 1965), the largest single-day figure being 7,400 on 8 May 1965. *Missionaries.* There are a large number of Egyptian missionaries sent by Al-Azhar University (Cairo). *Hajj pilgrims to Mecca.* (1968) 10,790; (1969) 24,185; (1970) 35,187; (1971) 44,061; (1972) 48,981; (1973) 38,869; (1974) 51,764; (1975) 92,593; (1976) 66,873; (1977) 140,000.
OTHER RELIGIONISTS. Including religions of expatriates. Occultist and similar non-Christian religions from Europe and Asia have growing followings. Rosicrucians (AMORC) have 29 Lodges and centers.
PENTECOSTALS (or, Anglican charismatics). The movement has been especially strong among young people; in one diocese (Benin), such youth groups have been excommunicated, and in others have become separatist bodies. The strongest areas are: Mid-West, Eastern (strong among Ibo since 1971), Western (new para-denominations among the Yoruba, especially around Oyo).
PENTECOSTALS/CHARISMATICS. From 1970 onwards Charismatics mushroomed in all the major denominations, especially among youths and youth organizations. By 1998 the total involved was just over 20 million (see above and Country Table 2).
UNAFFILIATED CHRISTIANS. These are persons professing in censuses to be Christians, but not affiliated to or known by the churches. In Nigeria they are of 2 kinds: (1) past and present pupils in the vast network of Protestant, Anglican and Roman Catholic schools who have nevertheless not joined those churches, and (2) ethnoreligionists who have made a clear break with pagan society and regard themselves as Christians but who have not as yet been contacted or initiated by the churches. After 1980 the percentage size of this large nominal fringe around the churches can be seen to decrease as the churches catch up with the vast influx.
UNAFFILIATED CHRISTIANS IN 1900. At that time large numbers of Nigerians belonged to the early African Independent Churches but were unknown to the mainline mission bodies, hence regarded as 'nominal' or 'unaffiliated'. They can be regarded as early pentecostals, charismatics, and neocharismatics, and are so treated in Part 5 "GeoRenewal" and its Tables 5-8 and 5-9, where they are classified as in the Independent megabloc, Neocharismatics of type I-3nA.

Country status. Nigeria, the most populous country in Africa, is also notable as one of the richest. It is an anglophone country on the coast of West Africa that became independent in 1960. The discovery of oil in the 1960s has led Nigeria to become one of the world's leading exporters of oil.

HUMAN LIFE AND LIBERTY

Human need and development. Although a rich country in terms of its resources, Nigeria is not much different economically from other African countries and the standards of living are only slightly higher. The per capita income of $260 is lower than that of even smaller countries, such as Togo, while the average life expectancy of 50 and the illiteracy rate of 43% place it squarely in the league of less developed countries. The distribution of wealth is also uneven, both geographically and among classes. The economy of the heavily Islamic north which had spurned Western education until recently is quite depressed while that of the more christianized south is quite prosperous. There are also strong class-driven inequities which have created a ruling elite living off the

Great Commission Instrument Panel: status of Nigeria (for explanation see start of Part 4)

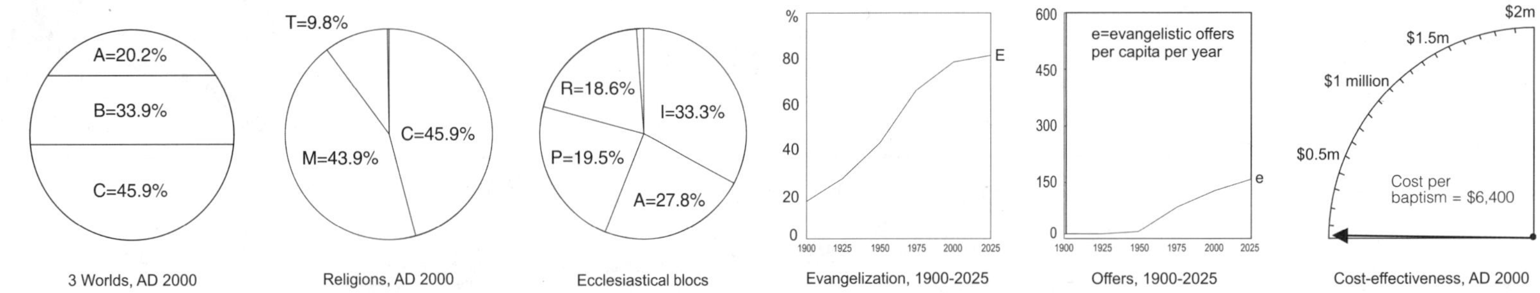

fat of the land while the average Nigerian ekes a bare subsistence. The social value system encourages consumption rather than production, with the result that few Nigerians save money. Standards of health and diet have markedly improved in recent years, but housing remains substandard in many towns and cities. Much of the population of Lagos lives in a labyrinth of tin-roofed houses on narrow, twisting alleys which have open sewers.

Human rights and freedoms. In an era when many African governments are renouncing authoritarian rule and adopting a democratic form of government, Nigeria also has once again replaced military rule by an elected president. Human rights were previously circumscribed by numerous decrees issued by the Armed Forces Ruling Council. Extrajudicial killings and excessive use of police force are still common occurrences. More persons are killed in Nigeria, according to the president of the Nigeria Labour Congress, by the police than by armed robbers. Policemen guilty of these killings generally go unpunished. Citizens are generally harassed at police checkpoints, if they refuse to pay bribes to those manning them. Conditions in prisons are life-threatening. Lack of water and sewage facilities and medical supplies causes diseases to run rampant. About 8% of the prison population—or about 5,000—die annually as a result of diseases. There are considerable delays, often stretching several years, in bringing suspects to trial. During this period they are generally held incommunicado. Approximately 20,000 of Nigeria's 60,000 prisoners are awaiting trial at any given time. Sometimes relatives and friends of wanted suspects are detained in order to induce an accused to present himself or herself to the police. The so-called Decree Two of 1984 enabled the government to detain persons without charge and without judicial remedies for acts prejudicial to state security and harmful to the country's economic welfare. Judicial independence, dating back to the Colonial times, has been under attack from the military governments which have sought to circumvent due process. Law enforcement officials sometimes search private premises without search warrants. Although the 1989 Constitution provides for freedom of the press and of speech, the authorities pressure journalists to exercise self-censorship under Decree Two, especially relating to certain sensitive subjects, as corruption and criminal activity by government officials and ethnoreligious strife. There is no official policy of discrimination against any of the 250 ethnic groups and laws do not favor one group over another. Public service in the federal government is apportioned to reflect ethnic and regional distribution of the population. However, there is a long tradition of discrimination against non-Muslims in certain northern states. Women face customary and religious disabilities in the northern states where a woman cannot own property in her own right or inherit her husband's property which generally reverts to the husband's family.

Human environment. Overpopulation exerts an enormous pressure for land, which in turn encourages indiscriminate use of existing resources. Intensive farming has resulted in widespread soil erosion. Water is contaminated in rural and urban areas because of the lack of treatment and sewage facilities. The country loses about 5% of its forest lands every year and only about 20% of the original forest stands remain.

NON-CHRISTIAN RELIGIONS

Islam is numerically parallel to Christianity in Nigeria. Muslims are dominant in the northern states, and they are also important in Western Nigeria. The Hausa, Fulani, Kanuri, Nupe and a significant number of Yoruba provide most of the country's Muslim strength. Islamic influence was first felt in the 11th and 12th centuries, and by the 15th century, Kano had become a flourishing center for Muslim culture and commerce. A new thrust came in the 19th century when a Fulani crusade swept over the Hausa area leaving permanent marks on the culture and social system. Following a period of disintegration, the British policy of indirect rule through existing Muslim chiefs succeeded in strengthening Islam as well as hindering the entrance of Christian missions. The Qadiriya, Tijaniya and Ahmadiya are the strongest brotherhoods today. The spiritual head of Islam in Nigeria is the Sardauna of Sokoto. In 1962, a faculty of arts and Islamic studies was established at the Amadu Bello University in Zaria, and in the same year, the Abdullahi Bavero College, founded in Kano in 1960, was attached to the Amadu Bello University as its Kano-based Faculty of Arts and Islamic Studies.

Traditional religions have their main strength in the central plateau. The following peoples are estimated to be more than 90% traditionalist: Afo, Ankwe, Bunu, Chawai, Daka, Dibo, Gade, Ibaji, Jaba, Jerawa, Jukun, Kadara, Kamantan, Kamuku, Lungu, Maguzawa, Mumuye, Ngamo, Shanga, Vere, and Warjawa. As in other parts of Africa, Nigerian traditional religions place considerable emphasis on the importance of ancestral spirits and magical practices, while retaining the idea of a supreme being. God is called Olodumare (among the Yoruba), Chuku (Ibo), Soko (Nupe, Bgari), Abassi (Ibibio), Kashiri (Binawa, Butawa, Dungi, Kaibi, Kitimi, Rishuwa, Rumaiya, Srubu), Gwaza (Kagoro, Katab), Owo (Idoma, Iyala), with other names common among Nigeria's many smaller tribes. A distinctive element is the emphasis placed on divinities, who serve as God's ministers in the theocratic rule of the world. Among the Yoruba, there are more than a thousand such divinities each with his own name and function and collectively called orisa.

Methodist Church, Nigeria. In 1976 major reorganization to make their church more indigenous, Methodists appointed 6 bishops (5 shown standing here), 4 archbishops (seated), and a patriarch, His Pre-Eminence Bolaji Idowu (centre), complete with vestments.

CHRISTIANITY

PROTESTANT CHURCHES. British Wesleyan Methodists first came to Yoruba country in 1842, beginning work at Badagry and Abeokuta; and towards the end of the century (1893), Primitive Methodists entered Calabar from Fernando Poo. Today, the membership of the autonomous Methodist Church is about equally divided among the Yoruba, Ibibio, Ijebu, and Ibo. In January 1976, Methodists completely reorganized their church in an effort to make it more indigenous. The denomination's leadership now includes 6 bishops and 4 archbishops with a patriarch as overall head of the church.

The first Presbyterian missionaries were Jamaicans who settled in Calabar, eastern Nigeria, in 1846. They were soon followed by Scottish members of the CSM and more recently (1954) Canadian Presbyterians. The Presbyterian Church of Nigeria has been autonomous since 1954.

Church of Nigeria, Diocese of Northern Nigeria. Anglican workers conduct evangelism among Nupe and other pagans around Bida.

Southern Baptists came to Western Nigeria in 1850, and this remains their oldest field anywhere in the world. Although progress was slow in the early years, this has now become one of the most important of Nigeria's churches. The Yoruba Baptist Association was formed in 1914 which later changed its name to the Nigerian Baptist Convention.

In 1887, the interdenominational Qua Iboe Mission of Belfast opened a station at Ibuno on the Qua Iboe river; and in spite of later evangelistic thrusts among the Igala in 1931 and the Bassa in 1936, the strength of the church is still found among the Ibibio.

The Evangelical Churches of West Africa (ECWA), autonomous since 1956, stem from the outreach of the Sudan Interior Mission as early as 1893. One of the largest denominations in Nigeria, this church both receives and sends missionaries. SIM maintains nearly 800 workers in Nigeria, while ECWA has sent more than 500 Africans to other parts of Africa. The church has had considerable success in northern Nigeria.

Another body is the Fellowship of Churches of Christ in Nigeria (TEKAN) which was formed in 1955 as TEKAS, a loose federation of 8 separate groups, 4 of which were begun by the Sudan United Mission beginning in 1904. Others owe their origin to the missionary activity of the Church of the Brethren, Dutch Reformed Church of South Africa, EUB (now United Methodists) in the USA and independent Nigerians.

Two important Pentecostal churches entered Nigeria during the 1930s, the Apostolic Church from UK in 1931 and Assemblies of God from the USA in 1939. Of groups coming after World War II, the greatest progress has been made by the Churches of Christ. A number of smaller but still significant churches include Seventh-day Adventists, Lutherans, and the Salvation Army.

CATHOLIC CHURCH. Catholicism first came to Nigeria with the Portuguese in the 15th century, but it had virtually disappeared by the end of the 17th century. The modern era of Catholic missions began in 1865 with the arrival in Lagos of priests belonging to the Society of African Missions of Lyons. Other important groups have been Holy Ghost priests in eastern Nigeria and St. Patrick's Society after 1932. A vicariate was erected for Benin in 1870, and in 1950, the archdioceses of Kaduna, Lagos, and Onitsha were

Country summary. **Worlds A, B, C by ethnolinguistic peoples, cities, and major civil divisions in Nigeria.**

	PEOPLES							*CITIES*							*CIVIL DIVISIONS*						
World	*Num*	*Pop 2000*	*C%*	*Christians*	*E%*	*U%*	*Unevangelized*	*Num*	*Pop 2000*	*C%*	*Christians*	*E%*	*U%*	*Unevangelized*	*Num*	*Pop 2000*	*C%*	*Christians*	*E%*	*U%*	*Unevangelized*
A	189	16,084,518	2.45	393,482	39	61	9,738,173	2	972,223	12.43	120,850	46	54	529,466	4	18,143,591	18.96	3,440,296	48	52	9,430,768
B	162	55,649,729	26.76	14,893,230	77	23	12,716,901	89	31,522,439	40.28	12,696,646	80	20	6,200,933	20	69,525,690	44.36	30,841,730	82	18	12,655,687
C	140	39,771,835	89.71	35,678,310	100	0	104,462	19	3,188,194	70.93	2,261,384	99	1	39,497	7	23,836,813	69.99	16,682,976	98	2	473,079
Total	**491**	**111,506,082**	**45.71**	**50,965,022**	**80**	**20**	**22,559,536**	**110**	**35,682,856**	**42.26**	**15,078,880**	**81**	**19**	**6,769,896**	**31**	**111,506,094**	**45.71**	**50,965,002**	**80**	**20**	**22,559,534**

established. The Catholic Church in Nigeria consisted in 1995 of 38 ecclesiastical divisions.

Intertribal rivalries and the resulting 1967-70 civil war had a serious effect on Catholicism. The mass killings of southerners (mostly Christian Ibos) in the North where they had settled sparked a mass migration homeward which left many northern areas with no Christian community; while in other areas non-Ibo Christians also disappeared. Estimates of the total massacred range from 10,000 to 30,000, and the migration affected around one million people. The diocese of Sokoto in northwestern Nigeria, which had 15,000 Ibo Catholics in 1965, had only 1,650 left in 1970. Nearly two-thirds of the country's Catholics in 1967 were found in 8 dioceses located in eastern Nigeria, which caused a widespread impression that the war was a religious one of Muslims versus Christians. However, the religious aspect of Nigerian intercultural rivalries was in fact not important. The subsequent defeat and collapse of the east resulted in a serious interruption in the social and economic development of what was formerly the most dynamic and most Christian part of the country.

At the end of the civil war in January 1970, the church in eastern Nigeria experienced important changes including the expulsion of most foreign missionaries (about 300 priests and 200 sisters) and the nationalization of all primary and secondary schools which had previously played a significant role in evangelization. Nigerian church personnel were relatively numerous, with some 760 priests, brothers and sisters in 1970. Nevertheless, they were inadequate for the task since many priests were responsible for a pastoral charge of more than 5,000 faithful. Nevertheless, vocations continue to be very promising, and among the faithful, especially youth, has emerged the spontaneous Black Rosary Movement which has expanded with great rapidity. This movement gathers people together by house blocks for prayer, singing, Bible study and religious instruction. The movement has been officially recognized by the hierarchy and integrated into parish and diocesan structures.

The Holy See has diplomatic relations with Nigeria and in AD 2000 is represented to government and the Catholic hierarchy by a pro-nuncio residing in Lagos.

Catholic Charismatics. Residential ACCSE School of Evangelism in Issele-Uku diocese, 1991.

ANGLICAN CHURCH. The first Anglicans in Nigeria were freed slaves from Sierra Leone, and in 1842, the CMS followed. By 1853, work had begun at Abeokuta, Lagos, and Ibadan. In 1864, the first African bishop was consecrated, although he was replaced by a European in 1891. The Church of the Province of West Africa, formed in 1952, now consists of dioceses in Ghana, Gambia, and Sierra Leone, as well as 11 dioceses within Nigeria itself.

Anglican communicant membership exceeds that of every Nigerian denomination. The exceptionally large numbers of adult and infant baptisms are proof of the continued vitality and growth of the Anglican Church in Nigeria.

INDIGENOUS CHURCHES. The first in a long line of independent groups in Nigeria was the Native Baptist Church, splitting from Southern Baptist work among the Yoruba in 1888; however, by 1914, almost the entire body of seceders has been reintegrated into the Nigerian Baptist Convention. The first permanent schism was the United Native African Church, a break precipitated by the consecration of a European to replace the first African Anglican bishop in 1891. Other important Anglican schisms include the African Church and the Christ Army Church, begun respectively in 1901 and 1915. A conflict among Yoruba Methodists in 1917 resulted in the creation of the United African Methodists Church, commonly called Eldja (Fishmongers). A number of important independent churches owe their origin indirectly to a virulent influenza epidemic which ravaged West Africa in 1918. Believing the mission churches to be impotent in the fact of this disaster, Yoruba Christians formed prayer and healing groups which ultimately resulted in the formation of the Cherubim and Seraphim, Church of the Lord (Aladura, or Praying), and Christ Apostolic Church, in addition to a series of other bodies which subsequently split from them. The Cherubim and Seraphim movement itself has spawned some 200 distinct denominations including several of Nigeria's largest churches: the Eternal Sacred Order of Cherubim and Seraphim, Cherubim and Seraphim Church of Zion of Nigeria and the Holy Order of Cherubim and Seraphim. A large Pentecostal prayer-healing church in the eastern sector is the Nigerian Christian Fellowship. Several black denominations from the USA have also been influential, including the AME and AME Zion Churches.

Nigeria has been fertile soil for the growth of independent Christian bodies. The number of distinct denominations or bodies, in most cases registered with government, was around 1,000 in 1990 and has increased steadily each year.

Deeper Life Bible Church. Headquarters church, Lagos, with 150,000 attenders each Sunday.

Catholic Church in Nigeria. On papal visit in February 1982, pope John Paul II ordains 92 new clergy from Nigeria's ever-expanding number of dioceses.

Renewal movements. In the 1990s the Pentecostal/Charismatic Renewal continued to spread rapidly across most older churches, and numbered over 35,885,000 adherents (of whom 8% Pentecostals, 27% Charismatics, and 64% Independents).

Indigenous missions. Nigerian Christians have shown a remarkable commitment to the missionary enterprise. They can be found all over West Africa. Nonetheless, about 90% of these are working within Nigeria, often among non-Christian peoples.

CHURCH AND STATE

The federal constitution of Oct. 1, 1963, (chapter III, 'Fundamental Rights', Section 24) provides for freedom of religious belief and practice, including the freedom to observe, teach and propagate one's beliefs and also to change one's religion. Religious communities are free to provide religious instruction in educational institutions which they maintain, but no pupil may be required to attend religious ceremonies or receive religious instruction contrary to his wishes. Historically, Christian bodies have provided a major part of Nigeria's basic educational and medical facilities, and the federal, regional and state governments have assumed financial responsibility for a great deal of maintenance and assistance to church-sponsored schools and hospitals. However, this has now been changing as the government has increasingly assumed control over Christian schools.

The government attitude towards church schools varies from state to state. The first to take over all schools was the East Central State (formerly Biafra) on 26 May 1970. By May 1975, all private schools in the following states were in government hands: Mid-Western State, South Eastern State, Rivers State, North

Western State, and North Central State. In Lagos and in Western and Kwara States, the governments have not in principle taken over schools, but in practice, the state school boards appoint teachers and transfer them indiscriminately. Religion is taught in all schools, but the content and time allowed for it vary. Thus, in East Central State, one free period a week is made available during which teachers may give religious instruction to willing pupils of their own denomination; in Mid-Western State, 5 periods of religious instruction per week are available also on a denominational basis; and in South Eastern State, the Joint Agreed Christian Syllabus of Religious Education is taught for 2 periods a week.

In the largely theocratic northern area where the powers of Muslim emirs remain as strong as under former British colonial policy, non-Islamic religious movements have been limited. Nevertheless, Muslim Nigeria represents a wide spectrum, and numerous Muslim leaders cooperate in the matter of Christian religious education and even over the evangelization of peoples still largely traditionalist.

Religious bodies must be officially recognized by government in order to acquire property and clergy must be authorized to officiate at legally-registered marriages. Religious groups are exempt from some taxes and a number of other regulations. Until recently, the policy of permitting the entrance of foreign missionaries was quite liberal. However, during and following the Biafra war, with its emotional overtones and the search for culprits, the government frequently expressed strong criticism of the churches, notably the Catholic Church. Church relief work on behalf of the Biafran people and the involvement of many locally-based missionaries in propaganda work for them, was especially resented; and one result has been the restriction of visas for further missionaries. Many Catholic expatriate priests in Ibo country indeed were deported after the conflict. Nevertheless, even with the indignation of federal authorities, church-state tensions have been far less serious than might have been expected.

In 1977, with wide support from the churches, the regime introduced a federal government ban on

Independents. Members have mushroomed spectacularly to 23 million by AD 2000 (Above, in Ibadan).

membership in secret societies including Freemasonry for all publicly-employed persons.

BROADCASTING AND MEDIA

Nigeria is a member of UNDA. There is a Catholic Media Service Center in Kaduna. IBRA-produced radio programs can be received on local radio stations. The Lutheran World Federation maintains a studio in Nigeria that produces English-language radio programs. Shortwave radio programming can be received from KNLS. In addition to radio, Christian television programming can be received and CBN's programs can be seen on a weekly, and in some areas daily, basis. A full-time ministry center in Abuja follows-up response with discipleship training, video ministries, and church referrals.

INTERDENOMINATIONAL ORGANIZATIONS

The Christian Council of Nigeria (CCN), founded in 1930, has 9 member bodies, including the large Anglican, Methodist, Baptist, Presbyterian, and Qua Iboe churches. Methodists, Anglicans, and Presbyterians are also members of the WCC, and several of Nigeria's churches belong to the AACC. The Nigerian Evangelical Fellowship has 10 member churches and belongs to AEAM, the Association of Evangelicals of Africa and Madagascar. The Catholic Episcopal Conference has no ecumenical commission. Responsibility for ecumenical relations is lodged with the Pastoral Commission, which handles also the lay apostolate, religious education, and liturgy.

In 1976, a new ecumenical body was formed, the Christian Association of Nigeria (CAN), with a secretary general the secretary of the CCN and as members Roman Catholic, Protestant, Anglican, and indigenous churches.

Another powerful council of churches is the Nigeria Association of Aladura Churches, founded in 1960, with as members over 200 indigenous denominations and a total constituency of 2 million Christians. There are over 10 other similar councils linking indigenous churches.

Three ecumenical institutes have been established: (1) the Institute of Church and Society, founded in 1964 by the Christian Council of Nigeria, which engages in study and dialogue on the church and the world; (2) the Pastoral Institute in Bodija, which is basically Catholic but works in close relationship with the Institute for Church and Society; and (3) the National Institute for Religious Sciences founded in Lagos in 1971, which is involved in the training of secondary school teachers of religion. The latter institution is sponsored and maintained jointly by the Catholic Episcopal Conference and the Christian Council of Nigeria, with help from the WCC.

Four interdenominational associations have been formed to promote medical work and Christian education: (1) Christian Health Association of Nigeria, to review the Christian commitment in health services; (2) Christian Education Review Council (CERC), to discuss with government whenever necessary the church's involvement in education; (3) Association for Christian Higher Education (ACHEN), to influence policy and promote standards of religious education in post-secondary educational institutions; and (4) National Institute of Moral and Religious education, founded in 1971 in the vicinity of the University of Lagos. The latter institution is sponsored and supported jointly by the Catholic Episcopal Conference and the Christian Council of Nigeria and is formally affiliated to the Institute of Education of the University of Ibadan. It promotes a program called Project TIME (Teachers in Moral Education) held each year, in addition to a research and experimentation center, a specialist library and a model audiovisual center. In December 1974, leaders of both the Catholic and Protestant churches held a Retreat of National Concern centered on the moral decadence of Nigeria, at which time they agreed to set up a Moral Leadership Foundation to inspire Christian and moral ideals among the nation's leaders.

Several organizations are dedicated to the promotion of interreligious contacts and dialogue. The Islam in Africa Project Council began in 1959 and is a joint undertaking of several church groups to prepare Christians for their encounter with and responsibility towards Muslims in Africa south of the Sahara. It has personnel working in Sierra Leone, Liberia, Ghana, Nigeria, Cameroon, Ethiopia, and Kenya and is active in other territories including Upper Volta and Malawi. Part of the project is the Study Center for Islam and Christianity (formerly the Pierre Benignus Study Center) founded in 1965 in Ibadan. Here Christian students from many parts of Africa study the Quran, Islam and the Christian approach to Muslims. Another body, the Community Development Group (CDG), formerly the Christian Community Development Group, is a private interdenominational body which includes Catholic participation. Open to people of all religions, it functions as a mutual-help society for those involved in community development and social work.

Nigeria Association of Aladura Churches (NAAC), linking 200 denominations, in Okeseni, Ibadan.

FUTURE TRENDS AND PROSPECTS

Declines in tribal religions (73% in 1900 to 7.7% by 2025) are picked up as gains shared between Christians and Muslims. Christians are expected to grow from 43.8% in 1970 to 47.0% by 2025, and Muslims are expected to grow from 43.9% in 1970 to 44.9% by 2025.

Ethnoreligionists will certainly continue their decline throughout the 21st century. Both Christians and Muslims are expected to grow in the same period. By AD 2050, however, it is possible that Christians will have a slight edge of perhaps 50-55% to Islam's 45-50%.

BIBLIOGRAPHY

150 years of Christianity in Nigeria, 1842–1992. , 1992. 151p. (Anglican).

40 years of the Dominicans in Nigeria, [1991]. 38p.

'A family life education for the Church's ministry to urban migrants in Nigeria.' Y. Y. Akpem. D.Miss. thesis, Fuller Theological Seminary, Pasadena, CA, 1982.

'A hundred years of change in Kalabari religion,' R. Horton, in *Black Africa: its peoples and their cultures today*, p.192–211. J. Middleton (ed). London: Macmillan, 1970.

'A select periodical bibliography on African traditional religion, with special emphasis on Nigeria, 1900–1970,' H. O. Emezi, *A current bibliography on African affairs*, 12, 3 (1979–80), 329–39.

A study of conversion among the Angas of Plateau State of Nigeria with emphasis on Christianity. D. N. Wambutda. Frankfurt am Main: P. Lang, 1992. 238p.

African independent church. H. W. Turner. London: Oxford University Press, 1967. 2 vols. (On the Church of the Lord [Aladura]).

'African traditional religion in transition.' D. S. Gilliland. Ph.D. dissertation, Hartford Seminary Foundation, Hartford, CT, 1971. (On Northern Nigeria).

Aladura: a religious movement among the Yoruba. J. D. Y. Peel. London: Oxford University Press for the International African Institute, 1968. 338p.

An introduction to the history of SIM/ECWA in Nigeria, 1893–1993. Y. Turaki. , [1993]. 310p.

Baptist churches in Nigeria, 1850–1950: accounts of their foundation and growth. J. A. Atanda (ed). Ibadan: University Press, 1988. 360p.

'Bridging the missionary communication gap: a study of cross–cultural communications between the Sudan Interior Mission and the Evangelical Churches of West Africa.' A. F. Temmesfeld. Th.M. thesis, Dallas Theological Seminary, Dallas, TX, 1973. 60p.

Brotherhood of the cross and star: a new religious movement in Nigeria. F. M. Mbon. *Studies in the Intercultural History of Christianity*, 78. Frankfurt am Main: Peter Lang, 1992.

Cherubim & Seraphim Organisation: a critical perspective on prophethood. H. O. Atansuyi. [Lagos, 1989]. 132p.

Christian missionary enterprise in the Niger delta, 1864–1918. G. O. M. Tasie. *Studies of religion in Africa*, vol. 3. Leiden: E. J. Brill, 1978. 287p.

Christianity in Northern Nigeria. E. P. T. Crampton. 3rd ed. London: G. Chapman, 1975. 251p.

Christian–Muslim relations in Africa: the cases of northern Nigeria and Tanzania compared. L. Rasmussen. London: British Academic Press, 1993. 143p.

Church growth in central and southern Nigeria. J. B. Grimley & G. E. Robinson. Grand Rapids, MI: Eerdmans, 1966.

Development of Christianity and Islam in modern Nigeria. G. M. Okafor. Würzburg: Echter, 1992. 240p.

'Emerging themes in Nigerian and West African religious history,' J. F. A. Ajayi & E. A. Ayandele, *Journal of African studies*, 1 (1974), 1–39.

Fifty years of the Student Christian Movement in Nigeria. M. Oduyoyo (ed). Ibadan: Daystar Press for SCM of Nigeria, 1990. 152p.

Frontier peoples of central Nigeria and a strategy for outreach. G. O. Swank. South Pasadena, CA: William Carey Library, 1977. 192p.

God: ancestor or creator? Aspects of traditional beliefs in Ghana, Nigeria and Sierra Leone. H. Sawyerr. London: Longman, 1970. 118p.

'Growth of Churches of Christ among Ibibios of Nigeria.' W. W. Broom. Thesis, Fuller Theological Seminary, Pasadena, CA, 1970. 268p.

Hausa studies: a selected bibliography of B.A., M.A., and Ph.D. papers available in Northern Nigerian universities. E. L. Powe. 2nd ed. Kano, Nigeria: Bayero University, 1983. 29p. (330 items; religion is a main heading).

Hausa women in the twentieth century. C. Coles & B. Mack (eds). Madison, WI: University of Wisconsin Press, 1991.

Healing and exorcism: the Nigerian experience: (Proceedings, lectures, discussions and conclusions of the First Missiology Symposium on Healing and exorcism—the Nigerian experience, organised by the Spiritan International School of Theology (SIST), Attakwu, Enugu, from May 18–20, 1989). U. C. Manus, L. N. Mbefo & E. E. Uzukwu (eds). *SIST symposium series*, no. 1. Enugu: Snapp Press, 1992. 174p.

Hegemony and culture: politics and religious change among the Yoruba. D. D. Laitin. Chicago: University of Chicago, 1986. 252p.

Horses, musicians, & gods: the Hausa cult of possession–trance. F. E. Besmer. South Hadley, MA: Bergin & Garvey, 1983. 290p.

Islamic in Nigeria. A. R. I. Doi. Zaria, Nigeria: Gaskiya Corporation Limited, 1984. 379p.

Methodism in Nigeria, 1842–1992. M. M. Familusi. Ibadan: NPS Educational Publishers, 1992. 333p.

My conversion: from a witchdoctor to an evangelist. E. O. Omoobajesu. : O'Dine, 1987. 82p.

New life for all: thrilling stories of evangelism in West Africa. E. Lageer. : Lakeland. 144p.

New religious movements in Nigeria. R. I. J. Hackett (ed).

African studies, vol. 5. Lewiston, NY: E. Mellen Press, 1987. 245p.

Nigeria. R. A. Myers. *World bibliographical series*, vol. 100. Oxford, UK: CLIO Press, 1989. 496p. (See especially 'Religion,' p.183–90).

Nigeria: a comprehensive bibliography in the humanities and social sciences, 1900–1971. C. C. Aguolu. Boston: G. K. Hall, 1973. 620p.

Nigerian life and culture: a book of readings. O. Y. Oyeneye & M. O. Shoremi (eds). Ago-Iwoye, Nigeria: Ogun State University, 1985. 373p.

Nigerian studies, or the religious and political system of the Yoruba. R. E. Dennett. *Cass library of African studies, General studies*, no. 48. 1910; reprint, London: Frank Cass, 1968. 235p.

'Northern Nigeria,' M. Hiskett, in *Islam in Africa*, p.287–300. J. Kritzeck & W. H. Lewis (eds). New York: Van Nostrand-Reinhold, 1969.

Nupe religion. S. F. Nadel. Glencoe, IL: Free Press, 1954.

Official Nigeria Catholic directory, 1973. Lagos: Catholic Secratariat of Nigeria, 1973. 163p.

Olódùmarè: god in Yoruba belief. E. B. Idowu. New York: Praeger, 1963. 222p.

Origins of the Niger Mission, 1841–1891: a paper read at the centenary of the mission at Christ Church, Onitsha, on 13 November 1957. K. O. Dike. [Ibadan]: Ibadan University Press for the Church Missionary Society Niger Mission, 1957. 21p.

Orisha: the gods of Yorubaland. J. Gleason. New York: Atheneum, 1971. 122p.

Pentecostalism and the Catholic church in Nigeria. E. Bassey. Calabar, Nigeria: Mariana Publications, 1993. 99p.

Proliferation of churches in Nigeria. S. A. Adewale (ed). Ibadan, Nigeria: Nigerian Association for Christian Studies, 1989. 298p.

Religion and national integration in Africa: Islam, Christianity, and politics in the Sudan and Nigeria. J. O. Hunwick. *Series in Islam and society in Africa*. Evanston, IL: Northwestern University Press, 1992. 188p.

Religion and political culture in Kano. J. N. Paden. Berkeley, CA and Los Angeles: University of California Press, 1973.

Religion and politics in Nigeria: a study in Middle Belt Christianity. N. Kastfelt. London: British Academic Press, 1994. 216p.

Religion in an African city. G. Parrinder. Reprint; Westport, CT: Negro Universities Press, 1974. 211p. (Deals with Ibadan, Nigeria).

Religion in Calabar: the religious life and history of a Nigerian town. R. I. J. Hackett. *Religion and society*, no. 27. Berlin: Mouton de Gruyter, 1989. 499p.

'Religion, legitimacy and conflict in Nigeria,' H. Bienen, *Annals of the American Academy of Political and Social Science*, 483 (January 1986), 50–60.

'Religious disturbances in Nigeria: a guide to sources of information.' E. E. Ahmodu. Certificate in Librarianship thesis, Ahmadu Bello University, Zaria, Nigeria, 1989. 65p.

Religious pluralism and the Nigerian state. S. O. Ilesanni. *Religions in Africa*, vol. 2. Athens: Ohio University Center for International Studies, 1997. 330p.

Sacrifice in Ibo religion. F. A. Arinze. Ed., J. S. Boston. Ibadan, Nigeria: Ibadan University, 1970. 129p.

'Seventh–day Adventism in Western Nigeria, 1914–1981: a study in the relationship between Christianity and African culture from the missionary era to the introduction of African leadership.' A. A. Kuranga. Ph.D. dissertation, Miami University, Miami, OH, 1991. 337p.

'Shariah in Northern Nigeria: its implication and problem for the Christian.' J. N. Aeneas. M.A. thesis, Hartford Seminary Foundation, Hartford, CT, 1992. 138p.

Sixteen cowries: Yoruba divination from Africa to the New World. W. Bascom. Bloomington, IN: Indiana University, 1980. 790p.

Sons of Tiv: a study of the rise of the church among the Tiv of central Nigeria. E. Rubingh. Grand Rapids, MI: Baker, 1969. 263p.

Tekas Fellowship of Churches: its origin and growth. E. H. Smith. Jos, Nigeria: Tekas Literature Committee, 1969. 68p. (Now renamed TEKAN).

The African churches among the Yoruba, 1888–1922. J. B. Webster. Oxford, UK: Clarendon, 1964. 217p.

'The Celestial Church of Christ: an African independent church.' R. Duckworth. Thesis, London School of Economics, 1978.

'The charismatic movement in Nigeria today,' M. A. Ojo, *International bulletin of missionary research*, 19, 3 (July 1995), 114–118.

'The Christ Apostolic Church: its history, beliefs and organization,' *Ecumenical review*, 28, 4 (1976), 418–28.

The Church of Christ in The Sudan Among the Tiv: a sociological perspective. A. Dzurgba. Ibadan, Nigeria: Dept. of Religious Studies, University of Ibadan, 1992. 145p.

The cult of Ifá among the Yoruba. Vol. 1: folk practice and the art. E. M. McClelland. London: Ethnographica, 1982.

The Hausa people: a bibliography. F. A. Salamone with the assistance of J. A. McCain. New Haven, CT: Human Relations Area Files, 1983. 2 vols.

The heritage of Islam: women, religion, and politics in West Africa. B. Callaway & L. E. Creevey. Boulder, CO: Lynne Rienner, 1994. 231p.

The Holy Ghost Fathers and Catholic worship among the Igbo people of eastern Nigeria. D. E. O. Ogudo. Paderborn, Germany: Verlag Bonifatius-Druckerei, 1988. 331p.

The influence of Islam on a Sudanese religion. J. Greenberg. *Monographs of the American Ethnological Society*, no. 10. Seattle, WA: University of Washington, 1966. 73p.

The missionary impact on modern Nigeria, 1842–1914: a political and social analysis. E. A. Ayandele. London: Longmans Green, 1966. 393p.

'The Nigerian Islamic view of state and its effects on the mission of the Christian church in Nigeria.' J. O. Folaranmi. D.Miss. thesis, Reformed Theological Seminary, 1994.

The proposed constitutions and standing orders: Methodist Church. Lagos: Methodist Church, 1974. 115p. (Introducing patriarchal and archepiscopal hierarchies).

The school in the service of evangelization: the Catholic educational impact in Eastern Nigeria 1886–1950. N. I. Omenka. Leiden: E. J. Brill, 1989. 317p.

'The Shango cult in Nigeria and in Trinidad,' G. E. Simpson, *American anthropologist*, 64, 2 (1963), 1204–19.

The Wesleyan presence in Nigeria, 1842–1962: an exploration of power, control, and partnership in mission. M. A. Oduyoye. Ibadan: Sefer, 1992. 171p.

Towards a mature African Christianity. L. N. Mbefo. Enugu, Nigeria: Spiritan Publications, 1989. 122p.

'Traditional religion in Nigeria with particular reference to the Yoruba,' E. A. Odumuyinwa, in *Nigerian life and culture: a book of readings*. O. Y. Oyeneye & M. O. Shoremi (eds). Ago–Iwoye, Nigeria: Ogun State University, 1985.

West African traditional religion. J. O. Awolalu & P. A. Dopamu. Ibadan, Nigeria: Onibonoje, 1979. 310p.

'Women, ecology and Islam in the making of modern Hausa cultural history.' M. W. Bivins. Ph.D. dissertation, Michigan State University, East Lansing, MI, 1994. 265p.

'Women in religion and development in Nigeria: a comparative study of Roman Catholic Church and an African independent church.' M. V. N. Asoegwu. Ph.D. dissertation, Loyola University of Chicago, 1993. 288p.

Year book of Nigerian churches. A. A. Akinkusote (ed). Ibadan, Nigeria: Akinniola Associates, 1969. 169p.

Yoruba beliefs and sacrificial rites. J. O. Awolalu. London: Longman, 1979. 203p.

Yoruba religion and medicine in Ibadan. G. E. Simpson. Ibadan, Nigeria: Ibadan University, 1980. 195p.

Yoruba religious carving: pagan and Christian sculpture in Nigeria and Dahomey. K. Carroll. London: G. Chapman, 1967. 184p.

Country Table 2. **Organized churches and denominations in Nigeria.**

Official name (bold type = church with over 10% of all affiliated) 1	*Begun* 2	*Type* 3	*Counc* 4	*Congs* 5	*Adults* 6	*Affiliated 1970* 7	*Affiliated 1995* 8	*G%* 9	*Names, notes, and other statistics* (see Codebook, Part 3) 10
Acts of Apostles Christ Ch, Nigeria	1961	I-3pA	I....	10	1,000	1,000	2,000	2.81	Indigenous pentecostals. Vision 1957 by founder, ex RCC. HQ Mushin, Lagos. 1p.
African Apostolic Ch of Nigeria & Benin	1942	I-3aA	Iv..I	220	6,000	10,000	12,000	0.73	*AAC*. Schism ex CAC by illiterate protesting discrimination. 55% Yoruba. 40% Ibo.
African Church, The	1901	I-Ang	IvA.K	1,000	30,000	48,709	60,000	0.84	Schism ex CMS Lagos. 7 Dioceses (4 Yoruba). Applied to join WCC. 91n,1215m,37r,1s.
African Methodist Episcopal Church	c1920	I-Met	Vw...	450	45,000	5,000	110,000	13.16	M=AMEC(Black mission from USA). Attached to small local indigenous churches.
African Methodist Episcopal Zion Ch	1930	I-Met	Vw...	492	25,100	15,000	76,000	6.71	M=AMEZC. 12th Episcopal District. 100 Ibo churches in east. 2 in Lagos. 2 schools.
American Orthodox Cath Ch in Nigeria	c1970	I-ReO	x....	15	300	500	750	1.64	M=AOCC(AD N&SAmerica), Egl Vielle-Cath (Branche Francaise). Ukrainian origin.
Anglican Church of Nigeria	1842	A-Low	AWAVK	9,000	9,688,000	2,941,000	17,500,000	7.39	In CPWA until 1979 when ACN formed. Mushrooming to 63 Dioceses. M=CMS(UK).68f,1p,1s,1u
Apostolic Church of Light	1957	I-3aA	.....	10	1,000	1,500	2,000	1.16	Schism ex African Apostolic Church by superintendent bishop Aboge. HQ Mushin.
Apostolic Church of Nigeria	1931	P-PeA	ZG..J	5,135	380,000	400,000	844,000	3.03	*TAC*. M=ACMM(UK). 1931, invited to assist Aladura churches. Southeast. 6 Areas. 5f,3s.
Apostolic Faith Church	1945	I-3aA	I...I	200	25,000	4,000	50,000	10.63	*Jehovah Jireh Christ Ch*. Schism ex Saviour's Apostolic Ch. Anti-medicine. 1s.
Apostolic Life Mission Church	1942	I-3aA	I...I	20	8,000	10,000	17,000	2.15	Founded by group of government officials who became evangelists. Yoruba. Ibadan.
Apostolic Temple Ch of Nigeria	c1980	I-3oA	.....	10	1,000	–	3,000	6.67	Oneness body, member of AWCF. In Abak, Cross River State.
Assemblies of God	1939	P-Pe2	ZFG.G	4,317	820,694	150,000	1,200,000	8.67	M=AoG(USA). A=1960. 48% Ibo, 8% Ishan. 667n,31x,8f,3h,1j,5s(296),W=50%,2593Y.
Assembly Hall Churches		I-3nC	.....	5	550	–	1,000	0.05	*Local Churches. Little Flock*. Begun 1922 in China.
Baptist International Missions	1966	I-Bap	.....	5	942	376	1,880	6.65	M=BIM(USA). Small body with American connections.
Believers' Assemblies of Nigeria	1970	I-3cA	I....	45	19,400	–	40,000	52.79	Work among: Ibibio, Anaang, Efik, Hausa. M=CAM.
Benin United Baptist Mission of N	1942	I-Bap	.....	4	1,500	2,000	3,000	1.64	Schism ex Nigerian Baptist Convention opposing missionary decisions. Declining in influence.
Bible Missionary Church	1952	P-Hol	x....	100	9,000	10,000	18,000	2.38	M=BHM(Canada). 1972 after civil war, merger. HQ Ikot. Ibo, Yoruba. 12n,2f, W=95%.
Broadsheet Readers' Clubs	c1970	I-3nA	.....	788	10,000	–	20,000	48.61	Readers of Gospel Broadsheets produced by M=WEC(UK).
Brotherhood of the Cross and Star	1956	I-3nA	..I..	3,200	600,000	330,000	1,074,000	4.83	Vast expanding movement with numerous churches abroad. F=Olumba Olumba Obu.
Calvary Church of God in Christ	c1965	I-3pB	Z....	15	1,500	1,500	3,000	2.81	M=CoGiC(Jamaican and CoGiC (USA Blacks) support).
Calvary Ministries	1985	I-Eva	.....	18	403	–	1,340	10.00	Indigenous body with sizable outreach activities.
Catholic Church in Nigeria:	1487	R-Lat	PzSGV	1,305	5,702,900	3,889,688	11,689,038	4.50	C=11+4+23. 5p,4s(546). 1904n 592x 1436m 2602w 362040Yy
M Abuja	1981	R-Lat	Ps	12	15,600	–	34,419	7.14	Federal Capitol Territory. 21n 67x 167m 30w 1577Yy
D Idah	1968	R-Lat	Ps	15	36,800	36,466	79,904	3.19	Kosi State. Mostly Igala; (87% pagan). M=CSSp. 1H. 18n 14x 31m 75w 5188Yy
M Bomadi	1991	R-Lat	Psps	5	5,400	–	10,435	25.00	Delta State. Relates to M Benin City. M=SPS. 1n 9x 12m 2w 140Yy
M Calabar	1934	R-Lat	Ps	40	99,000	239,480	191,605	-0.89	Cross River State. Port. 50% Ibibio. 24n 3x 3m 57w 11500Yy
D Ikot Ekpene	1963	R-Lat	Ps	23	36,000	62,780	79,784	0.96	Akwa Ibom State. 95% Annang Ibibio. 1s. 51n 4x 26m 110w 2425Yy
D Ogoja	1938	R-Lat	Ps	20	116,500	91,510	228,139	3.72	Cross River State. 85% animist. 48% Ibo, 17% Boki. 25n 5x 8m 68w 7515Yy
D Port Harcourt	1961	R-Lat	Ps	25	56,000	61,497	108,822	2.31	Rivers State. Major sea/river port. Ibo dominance. 98n 9x 11m 56w 2918Yy
D Uyo	1989	R-Lat	Ps	38	321,000	–	597,826	16.67	Akwa-Ibom State. Formerly in M Colabar. M=SPS. 59n 5x 5m 52w 2530Yy
M Ibadan	1952	R-Lat	Ps	23	66,000	56,700	140,000	3.68	Oyo State. Vast ancient city. 80% Yoruba. M=SMA. 37n 31x 158m 100w 32500Yy
D Ekiti (Ado-Ekiti)	1972	R-Lat	Ps	33	66,000	–	130,000	4.35	Ondo State. Formed out of D Ondo. 27n 3x 3m 52w 2350Yy
D Ondo	1943	R-Lat	Ps	22	88,000	88,000	169,000	2.64	Ondo State. 99% Yoruba, Urhobo, Ijaw. Many AICs. 25n 12x 30m 54w 16951Yy
D Oyo	1949	R-Lat	Ps	37	44,000	50,424	100,000	2.78	Oshun State. 88% Yoruba, 7% Ishan, 5% Ibo. M=WF. 22n 24x 26m 89w 2021Yy
M Jos	1934	R-Lat	Ps	44	297,000	120,000	342,976	4.29	Plateau State. 20% Birom, 13% Angas, 13% Ankwe. 65n 21x 36m 80w 24610Yy
D Jalingo	1995	R-Lat	Ps	23	98,100	–	172,345	50.00	New diocese, mainly rural. 20n 6x 11m 19w 16024Yy
D Maiduguri	1953	R-Lat	Posa	19	46,000	27,696	91,084	4.88	Borno State. 70% Muslim, 22% pagan. 65% Margi. 12n 10x 11m 26w 4736Yy
D Yola	1950	R-Lat	Posa	35	50,000	37,733	93,987	3.72	Adamawa. 30% Chamba, 20% Higi, 20% Mumuye. 33n 17x 23m 41w 14228Yy
M Kaduna	1911	R-Lat	Ps	44	159,000	95,000	274,391	4.33	55% Katab, 10% Koro, 5% Kadara, Gbari. M=SMA. 46n 14x 14m 18w 16839Yy
D Ilorin	1960	R-Lat	Ps	18	27,200	16,000	56,149	5.15	Kwara State. Predominantly Muslim. M=OP,SMA. 10n 11x 11m 27w 1255Yy
D Minna	1964	R-Lat	Ps	20	51,500	6,350	82,525	10.80	Niger State. 75% animist, 20% Muslim. M=SPS. 14n 13x 13m 13w 5846Yy
D Sokoto	1953	R-Lat	Ps	9	15,000	5,400	28,001	6.80	Sokoto. 1966: 15,000 Ibo Catholics massacred. 15n 4x 5m 6w 2486Yy
VA Kano	1991	R-Lat	Psma	19	18,700	–	35,000	25.00	M=SMA. 10n 6x 6m 7w 1524Yy
M Lagos	1860	R-Lat	Ps	54	689,000	141,000	1,951,000	11.08	Mainly urban. 87% Yoruba, 6% Ibo. M=SMA. 1p. 54n 57x 58m 170w 16270Yy
D Ijebu-Ode	1969	R-Lat	Ps	16	16,300	11,450	45,900	5.71	Ogun State. Yoruba, Ijebu. Strongly Muslim area. 8n 17x 17m 20w 1947Yy
M Onitsha	1889	R-Lat	Ps	91	471,000	515,783	1,193,714	3.41	Anambra State. On Niger. 90% Ibo. 10% Ijaw. 161n 29x 92m 287w 10762Yy
D Abakaliki	1973	R-Lat	Ps	34	93,000	–	199,800	4.55	Anambra State. Formerly in D Ogoja. M=SPS. 43n 8x 8m 54w 11359Yy
D Lokoja (Kabba)	1955	R-Lat	Ps	17	19,500	22,147	32,960	1.60	87% pagan. 40% Igala, 30% Yoruba, 29% Igbira. 20n 2x 2m 28w 1933Yy
D Awka	1977	R-Lat	Ps	82	268,000	–	538,517	5.56	Anambra State. 163n 0x 4m 105w 11867Yy
D Enugu	1962	R-Lat	Ps	52	300,000	458,000	553,378	0.76	Anambra State. Dying coal industry. M=CSSp. 1s. 96n 34x 284m 212w 24115Yy
D Nsukka	1990	R-Lat	Ps	27	153,000	–	361,000	20.00	Anambra State. Formerly in D Enugu. 71n 25x 59m 55w 14502Yy
M Owerri	1934	R-Lat	Ps	54	279,000	861,798	525,837	-1.96	Imo. Dense Ibo heartland. 22% of all Nigerian RCs. 88n 27x 108m 126w 12218Yy
D Aba	1990	R-Lat	Ps	29	157,000	–	298,410	20.00	Abia State. Formerly in D Umuahia. M=CSSp. 64n 9x 9m 49w 10171Yy
D Ahiara	1987	R-Lat	Ps	35	226,000	–	421,000	12.50	Imo State. Formerly part of M Owerri. 59n 2x 2m 33w 4486Yy
D Okigwe	1981	R-Lat	Ps	37	200,000	–	465,559	7.14	Imo State. Previously part of D Umuahia. 98n 0x 30m 43w 4701Yy
D Orlu	1980	R-Lat	Ps	66	280,000	–	512,840	6.67	94n 32x 37m 79w 9488Yy
D Umuahia	1958	R-Lat	Ps	28	52,300	478,201	99,576	-6.08	Abia State. 99% Ibo. No foreign priests. M=CSSp. 48n 4x 8m 67w 3587Yy
D Makurdi (Oturkpo, Benue)	1934	R-Lat	Ps	60	469,000	111,273	799,105	8.21	Benue State. RCs all Tiv; many animists. M=CSSp. 112n 28x 37m 101w 42352Yy
M Benin City	1884	R-Lat	Ps	48	127,000	179,000	262,109	1.54	Bendel. 34% Ibo, 25% Ishan, 25% Afemai, 15% Bini. 53n 24x 64m 134w 13027Yy
D Issele-Uku	1973	R-Lat	Ps	23	102,000	–	196,941	4.55	Bendel State. 34n 7x 13m 46w 3516Yy
D Warri	1964	R-Lat	Ps	28	88,000	116,000	185,000	1.88	Bendel State. Oil industry. Ijaw, Urhobo. M=SPS. 25n 5x 5m 30w 6600Yy
Celestial Church of Christ	1952	I-3aA	IvI.F	1,140	1,708,000	65,000	3,085,000	16.70	*Heavenly Christianity*. Begun Dahomey 1947. Yoruba elites. Rapid growth also in 20 countries.

Continued overleaf

Country Table 2–continued

Official name (bold type = church with over 10% of all affiliated) 1	Begun 2	Type 3	Counc 4	Congs 5	Adults 6	Affiliated 1970 7	Affiliated 1995 8	G% 9	Names, notes, and other statistics (see Codebook, Part 3) 10
Chad Brothers	c1900	I-CBr	.....	15	400	1,000	1,200	0.73	*Gidan Bishara (House of the Gospel).* Hausa Chad group antedating White missions.
Charismatic youth movements	1975	I-3cA	.....	500	60,000	10,000	120,000	5.00	Begun 1971 among Isoko, Ibo. M=SU(UK). 1974, excommunications ex Anglican Church.
Cherubim & Seraphim Ch of Zion of N	1948	I-3aA	I.I.I	1,087	250,000	100,000	500,000	6.65	Begun by colleague of Orimolade. 62% West, 23% Mid-West, 13% Lagos, 2% East. 1s.
Christ Apostolic Church	1917	I-3aA	I.I.Z	4,952	520,000	400,000	1,300,000	4.83	*CAC*(1942). 1920 Faith Tabernacle. 39 Districts. 74% Yoruba. 281n,1224m,284,2s,12630Y.
Christ Apostolic Mission Church	1952	I-3aA	I....	20	8,000	8,000	17,000	3.06	Indigenous pentecostal apostolics. Schism ex CAC and AAC. Yoruba. HQ Mushin. 1s.
Christ Apostolic Universal Church	1962	I-3aA	.....	17	10,000	10,000	21,000	3.01	Indigenous pentecostal apostolics. Schism ex CAC by pastor. Yoruba. HQ Mushin. 1s.
Christ Army Church	1915	I-Ang	.T.T.	40	22,100	45,760	40,000	-0.54	Ex CMS founded by Garrick Braide. Annang Ibibio. Many schisms. 12n,6m,W=85%,620Y.
Christ Chapel (Lagos)	c1970	I-3pA	.....	400	50,000	–	70,000	56.24	Began in Lagos, then 1985 vast expansion takes place. Prosperity gospel taught.
Christ Chosen Ch of God of N	1976	I-3pA	.....	70	180,000	–	250,000	5.26	30,000 members in HQ church, Benin City. Branches across WAfrica, SEAsia, Europe.
Christ Church of the Lord	1941	I-3pA	I...I	10	1,100	2,000	2,000	0.00	Schism in Ilesha ex Anglican Ch and CL(Aladura). Yoruba. HQ Yaba.
Christ Gospel Apostolic Ch of Nigeria	1947	I-3aA	I...I	50	12,000	20,000	25,000	0.90	*CGAC.* Schism ex Christ Apostolic Ch. Yoruba. HQ Ibadan. Work across Nigeria.
Christian Brethren	c1925	P-CBr	x....	300	17,000	20,000	28,300	1.40	Plymouth (Open) Brethren. Gospel Halls. M=CMML(USA, UK). 30f.
Christian Churches & Chs of Christ	1955	I-Dis	x....	45	1,000	–	2,500	36.75	M=CCCC(Instrumental) (USA). Independent congregations. 4f.
Christian Fellowship (Evangelical) in N	1972	I-3cA	.....	45	1,000	–	2,500	4.35	HQ Uyo, Akwa Ibom State. F=Mary Awa, a nurse. Ex RCC. Bible school, conference center.
Christian Methodist Episcopal Church		I-Met	Vw...	10	500	500	1,000	0.05	M=CMEC(Black mission from USA): until 1956. Colored ME Ch. 4 churches in Abak.
Christian & Missionary Alliance	c1970	P-Hol	.....	20	3,500	–	4,000	39.34	M=CMA(USA). 2f..
Christian Union of Nigeria	1977	I-Con	.....	20	3,500	–	4,000	5.56	Recent independent church.
Church of Christ, Scientist		m-Sci	x....	4	100	200	200	0.05	*Christian Science.* M=CCS(Boston, USA). 2 Societies.
Church of God in Christ (Mennonite)	1963	P-Men	G....	10	660	8,000	1,200	-7.31	M=Ch of God in Christ, Mennonite (USA). HQ Ile Ife. 6f.
Church of God Mission International	1968	I-3aA	.....	3,200	880,000	50,000	1,200,000	13.56	*Miracle Centre*, Benin City. International seminary, led by archbishop B. Idahosa.
Church of God in Nigeria	1949	P-Pe3	ZFG.G	175	17,400	7,000	31,500	6.20	M=CoG(Cleveland) (USA). SEastern Nigerian. 93% Efik, 7% Ibo. 28n,1s,100Y.
Church of God of Prophecy	1971	P-Pe3	Z....	16	720	–	1,800	4.17	M=CGP(USA). Small mission unable to secure a foothold.
Ch of Jesus Christ of Latter-day Saints	1953	m-LdS	.....	72	7,200	8,000	12,000	1.64	Begun by Ibos & Efiks using Mormon literature. M=CJCLdS(USA) not allowed in for many years.
Church of the Lord (Aladura)	1930	I-3pA	IWI.b	2,888	462,000	30,000	1,400,000	16.62	Aladura=Praying (Yoruba). Revival ex CMS. In 17 West African nations, also UK, USA, &c).
Church of the Nazarene	1977	P-Hol	.....	40	8,767	–	10,799	5.56	M=CoN. Relations with overseas aid and influence.
Churches of Christ	1947	I-Dis	x....	1,050	99,800	100,000	200,000	2.81	Begun by Africans. 1950, M=CC(Non-Instrumental) (USA). In SE. 80% Efik,Ibo. 10x,2H,3s.
Congregational Holiness Church		I-3pA	x....	50	7,000	10,000	15,000	0.05	M=CHC(USA). Holiness Pentecostals (3-stage). Work in South Eastern State.
Coptic Orthodox Church (P Alexandria)	c1970	O-Cop	NwaN.	3	300	500	750	1.64	Under P Alexandria (Egypt). 200 Egyptian families.1 priest for short period.
Deeper Life Bible Church of Nigeria	1973	I-3pA	x...K	5,733	348,980	–	612,641	4.55	F=W.F. Kumuyi. HQ church, Lagos: has 150,000 attenders, 5,000 cells. Missions in 45 countries.
Divine Healing Church of Israel	c1960	I-3pA	.v...	4	500	2,000	1,000	-2.73	Supreme Headquarters, Ibadan. Yoruba pentecostals. 1968, applied to join WCC.
Divine Love Gospel Church	c1980	I-3cA	.....	11	1,350	–	3,000	6.67	One of many small indigenous churches.
Edo National Church of God	1945	I-mar	.....	10	8,000	10,000	15,000	1.64	*Aruosa (Holy Place).* Begun by Oba of Benin Akenzua II (ex CMS). Bini syncretism.
El-Bethel Church (Mt Silloh)	1926	I-3aA	.....	25	2,000	2,000	3,000	1.64	Pentecostals. Founded by colleague of Moses Orimolade (C&S). HQ Agege.
Elim Church	1975	P-Pe2	Z....	11	1,100	–	2,750	5.00	M=Elim Pentecostal Ch (UK).
Emmanuel Church Mission of Nigeria	c1980	I-3cA	.....	9	1,200	–	3,000	6.67	Small charismatic indigenous church.
Eternal Sacred Order of Cherubim & S	1925	I-3aA	I.I.b	3,500	350,000	300,000	1,000,000	4.93	Original main body of Cherubim & Seraphim. Many schisms, lawsuits. HQ Ebute-Meta.
Eternal Sacred Order of C&S, Mt Zion	1929	I-3aA	I...I	600	25,000	20,000	50,000	3.73	Cherubim & Seraphim. One of many factions claiming first founder. Many schisms.
Ethiopian National Church, Nigeria	1919	I-3pA	I...I	20	7,000	10,000	15,000	1.64	Founded by prophet Adeniran Oke; attempt to introduce Ifa Oracle. 1r,1s.
Evangel Baptist Church	c1980	I-Bap	.....	6	1,000	–	2,860	6.67	Small body with Baptist polity
Evangelical Baptist Church	1986	I-Bap	.....	1	75	–	167	11.11	M=EBM(USA).
Evangelical Church of God	c1975	I-3pA	.....	22	4,000	–	10,000	5.00	Indigenous pentecostal body.
Evangelical Churches of West Africa	1893	P-Eva	xMG.G	2,547	1,384,000	500,000	2,500,000	6.65	*ECWA.* M=SIM. A=1956. 800n,500m,50w,672f,3H,88h,31k,22p(692),1s,W=80%,2000Y.
Evangelical Lutheran Church of Nigeria	1936	P-Lut	L....	320	29,000	46,501	68,000	1.53	Begun by M=Ev Luth Synodical Conf (USA); 1964 LC Missouri S. Ibibio. 26f,2p,1r,1s.
Fellowship of Chs of Christ of Nigeria	1904	P-Uni	.....	5,000	1,384,000	1,746,000	2,500,000	1.45	*TEKAN.* 1955 Federation, in north, of 8 major denominations (UK, USA origins). 140f,6H,177h.
Free Protestant Episcopal Church	1946	I-ARo	xv...	20	5,000	6,225	8,000	1.01	*Ecumenical Ch Foundation*, D WAfrica. M=FPEC(UK, USA). Ibibio. 3n,8m,1s(5),520Y,189y.
God's Kingdom Society	1934	I-Jeh	.....	130	40,000	10,000	50,000	6.65	*GKS.* Urhobos. Strong emphasis on Second Coming of Christ. Schism ex Jehovah's Witnesses.
Gospel Assemblies of Nigeria	c1970	I-3pA	.....	50	4,500	–	11,300	45.25	Small body, indigenous leadership.
Gospel Faith Mission	1953	I-3aA	..G.G	6,000	642,000	2,000	1,185,000	29.09	*GFM.* Schism ex CAC. HQ Ibadan, Benin. M=CAM. Kambari, Ibo, Yoruba, Gongola. 3859Y.
Greater World Chr Spiritualist League		m-Spi	x....	1	250	300	500	0.05	*Redemptive Church Mission*, Enugu. Specifically Christian spiritists. M=GWCSL(UK).
Greek Orthodox P Alexandria (D Accra)		O-Gre	Cw...	1	1,500	1,500	2,300	0.05	HQ Yaoundé (Cameroon). In P Alexandria. Lebanese, Greek traders. 720 in Kaduna. 1x.
Holiness Evangelical Mission		I-3cA	.....	15	1,000	–	2,000	0.05	*HEM.* Recent mission with work in Northern Nigeria among Margi and other peoples.
Holy Apostles Community (Aiyetoro)	1947	I-Non	.....	7	3,500	5,000	6,000	0.73	*Happy City.* 6 self-contained Yoruba fishing communities built over sea. Declining. 1h, 1r.
Holy Assembly of Christ Church	1951	I-3aA	I...I	20	2,000	2,000	4,000	2.81	Schism in Lagos ex Holy Flock of Christ Ch. 2s (Lagos, Ibadan).
Holy Flock of Christ	1932	I-3aA	I...I	40	20,000	20,000	40,000	2.81	Indigenous pentecostal apostolics. Split ex Cherubim & Seraphim. HQ Lagos.
Holy Order of Cherubim & Seraphim	1927	I-3aA	I.I.I	400	120,000	80,000	200,000	3.73	One of several Cherubim & Seraphim groupings of pentecostals. HQ Kaduna. 1p.
Holy Saviour's Church	1948	I-3aA	.....	15	3,000	4,000	7,000	2.26	Schism ex Church of the Lord (Aladura). 1945, praying band. HQ Ile Ife. 15n.
Holy Spirit Ministries International	c1990	I-3wA	.....	100	116,000	–	210,000	20.00	Prosperity gospel teaching, elements of traditional medicine.
Household of God Fellowship	c1985	I-3pA	.....	60	6,000	–	12,000	10.00	Exponents of Prosperity gospel ('Claim riches by faith'): schism ex Christ Chapel.
Internat Ch of the Foursquare Gospel	1954	P-Pe2	ZFG.a	1,360	219,800	3,000	543,994	23.12	M=ICFG(USA). 2 Divisions. HQ Yaba, Lagos. 25n,3x,6m,2p(42),W=59%,84Y.
Jehovah's Witnesses	1921	m-Jeh	x....	3,200	142,073	170,000	440,000	3.88	Witnessing by 1925. 1972: 200,193 at annual Memorial. (1975) 10492Y. (1995) 13184Y.
Light of Christ Church	1963	I-3aA	I....	2	500	1,000	1,500	1.64	Begun in 1963 revival in Ibadan by young woman, ex Christ Apostolic Ch.
Living Faith World Outreach Centre	1983	I-3wA	.....	90	35,000	–	90,000	8.33	F=D. Oyedepo. Faith prosperity gospel—cars, costly clothing. Missions in 20 countries.
Mambilla Baptist Convention	1961	P-Bap	TF...	171	18,588	8,000	30,100	5.44	M=CBC(Cameroon),NABGMS(USA). Station at Wuwar. 12f,1H,1h,1s.
Methodist Church, Nigeria	1842	P-Met	VWA.K	3,000	600,000	160,000	1,500,000	9.37	M=MMS(UK). 25% Yoruba, 23% Ibibio, 20% Ijebu, 20% Ibo. 40f,15H,33r,1u,4435Y,6401y.
National Church of Christ (Aladura)	1965	I-3aA	I....	30	3,000	5,000	7,000	1.35	*Mount Pisgah.* Ex Cherubim. Name revealed to founder in vision. HQ Lagos.
National Evangelical Mission	c1975	I-3nA	.....	96	5,000	–	10,000	5.00	Small African indigenous body.
New Apostolic Church	c1980	I-3aX	x....	600	110,000	–	256,046	6.67	*NAC.* M=Neuapostolische Kirche (Switzerland, HQ Zurich).
New Assembly Christian Church	c1950	I-3pA	.T.T.	25	3,100	4,000	7,500	2.55	Linked with Apostolic Faith (Portland, Oregon, USA). HQ Uyo, South East state. 5n.
New Church in West Africa		m-Swe	x....	10	1,200	4,000	3,000	0.05	M=GCNC(UK). 38% Efik, 30% Yoruba, 18% Ibo. Decline due to secessions.
New Eden Light of Jesus Christ	1958	I-3aA	I...I	10	3,000	4,000	5,000	0.90	Ex Cherubim & Seraphim. HQ Ibadan. Witchcraft eradication. 1s.
New Life Church of Christ in Nigeria		I-Non	.T.T.	10	1,000	1,000	2,000	0.05	In Vom, Northern Nigeria. Fundamentalists, supported by USA bodies.
New Salem Church (Aladura)	1956	I-3aA	.....	20	1,600	4,227	4,000	-0.22	Schism ex Holy Saviour's Ch led by founder's wife Lucy Adeoti. HQ Ile Ife.
New Testament Apostolic Movement	c1970	I-3oA	.....	20	2,000	–	5,000	40.59	Oneness body, in AWCF. HQ Azumini, Aba, Imo State.
New Testament Gospel Church	1952	I-Non	.v...	20	3,000	8,175	7,000	-0.62	Indigenous independents. Ibibio, in Ikot Ekpene area. 1962 applied to join WCC.
Nigeria Mennonite Church	1957	P-Men	G....	57	6,634	15,000	10,008	-1.61	M=Mennonite Ch of NAmerica. Churches in SE state (Abak, Ibiono, Itam, Ubium). 2f,1s.
Nigerian Baptist Convention	1850	P-Bap	TWA.K	4,512	1,050,000	300,000	1,250,000	5.87	*NBC*(1914). M=FMB-SBC(USA). Yoruba, Gude, Fali, Kamberi. 780n,187f,5H,3s,7852Y.
Nigerian Christian Fellowship		I-3pA	.....	5,375	430,000	400,000	956,000	0.05	A loosely-organized grouping of pentecostal bodies in eastern Nigeria. HQ Uyo.
Open Bible Standard Church	c1990	I-3pW	Z....	1	80	–	160	20.00	M=OBSC(USA). Support and influence from abroad.
Pentecostal Assemblies of the World	1930	I-3oA	x....	100	10,000	3,000	20,000	7.88	M=PAOW(USA). Oneness pentecostals, member of AWCF. HQ Uyo.
Pentecostal Holiness Church	1955	P-Pe3	ZFG.G	30	2,919	5,000	5,840	0.62	M=IPHC(USA). South Eastern state. National HQ Mushin, Lagos. 11n.
Pilgrim Baptist Mission		I-Bap	T...K	60	20,000	30,000	45,000	0.05	M=Lott Carey BFMC,NBCUSA(USA Blacks). West of Niger among Ibo. 11f,1h.
Powerline Bible Church	c1990	I-3pA	.....	50	4,000	–	8,000	20.00	Schism ex Christ Chapel (Lagos). Prosperity gospel teaching.
Presbyterian Ch in West Cameroon	1959	P-Ref	Rwa..	3	500	500	1,000	2.81	Extension of PCWC(Basel Mission) work from Cameroon. Station at Gavva.
Presbyterian Church of Nigeria	1846	P-Ref	RWA.K	617	262,000	100,000	474,000	6.42	M=CSM(UK),PCC(Canada). 45% Ibo, 26% Ibibio, 22% Efik. 46n,11f,2p,W=85%,2325Y,1953y.
Qua Iboe Church	1887	P-Non	.G..K	1,065	150,000	90,000	429,000	6.45	80% Ibibio, Efik, on Qua Iboe river; Igala, Bassa. M=QIM(NIreland). 25f,5H,8r,2s.
Redeemed Christian Church of God	1952	I-3aA	I...I	2,220	635,618	2,000	2,100,000	32.08	Ex C&S. Abortive aid: 1957, M=AFM(SAfrica), 1963 Velberter M(Germany). 1p. 18 chs in USA.
Redeemed People's Mission	c1985	I-3nA	.....	10	10,000	–	16,000	10.00	Small indigenous movement.
Reorganized Ch of Jesus Christ of LDS		m-LdS	x....	10	1,000	1,500	2,000	0.05	Ex Mormons/CJCLdS(Utah) aiding Nigerians in Abak. World HQ Independence, MO/USA.
Salvation Army	1920	P-Sal	xwA.z	225	25,000	35,000	83,300	3.53	In Efik, Nka Erinyana. SA, Nigeria Territory. 70% Ibibio. 154n,7x,2r,1s,W=80%.
Saviour's Apostolic Ch of Nigeria	1941	I-3aA	I...I	150	20,000	20,000	40,000	2.81	Indigenous pentecostal apostolics. Schism ex Christ Apostolic Ch. HQ Ibadan. 1s.
Saviour's Evangelical Church		I-3nA	.....	50	3,000	–	5,000	0.05	*SEC.* An Ibo independent church in Eastern Nigeria. From 1983, M=CMA(USA).
Seventh-day Adventist Church	1914	P-Adv	x....	434	80,648	50,000	161,000	4.79	*WAfr UM(ECentral, NNig, Rivers-SE, WNig Missions).* 64nx,45f,2H,2h,4r,W=80%,3569Y.
True Assemblies of God Ch of N	c1970	I-3oA	.....	100	10,000	–	25,000	49.94	*TAGCN.* Oneness pentecostals, member of AWCF. HQ Aba, Imo State.
Undenominational Ch of the Lord in N	1958	I-Hol	.....	25	2,000	2,000	4,000	2.81	In southeast Nigeria. USA missionaries. 4n,1p,W=85%,82Y,70z.
Unitarian Brotherhood Church	1919	m-Unt	.....	2	200	300	400	1.16	In General Assembly, Unitarian & Free Christian Chs (UK). One church in Lagos.
United African Methodist Church	1917	I-Met	I.I.F	320	6,000	10,000	15,000	1.64	*Eledja (Fishmongers)*, because near Lagos fish market). Schism ex MMS. Yoruba.
United Ch of the Cherubim & Seraphim	1948	I-3aA	I...I	150	15,000	30,000	50,000	2.06	Split ex C&S. 5 Dioceses: Oyo, Ondo, Mid-West, Lagos, Kwara. 8 schools. 1s.
United Gospel Apostolic Church	1943	I-3aA	.....	10	4,000	5,000	7,000	1.35	1000 adults in HQ congregation. Ebute-Meta, Lagos. Revival crusades. Yoruba. 8n.
United Missionary Church of Africa	1901	P-Hol	xFG.G	193	13,500	15,000	30,000	2.81	M=UMS,MC(USA). 60% Yoruba,30% Nupe,10% Hausa-speaking. 20n,7x,49f,1H,16h,4s,W=40%.
United Native African Church	1891	I-Ang	I.I.F	300	17,000	31,000	45,000	1.50	*UNAC.* Ex CMS. 36% Ibo, 18% Ijaw, 15% Yoruba. Also in Dahomey. 36n,W=50%,2000Yy.
United Pentecostal Church	1970	P-Pe1	.....	100	20,000	10,000	40,000	5.70	*Jesus Only Church.* M=UPC(USA). Unitarian Pentecostals. 30n,6f,1p(32).
Word of Faith Ministries	c1985	I-3wA	.....	300	277,000	–	500,000	10.00	Prosperity gospel message. M=Rhema Bible Churches (USA).
Word of Life Church	c1975	I-3cA	.....	35	5,000	–	11,100	5.00	Christ for the Rural Areas Ministries.
World Evangelical Crusaders in Christ	c1970	I-3pA	.....	30	3,000	–	6,000	41.62	*WECC Ministries.* HQ Benin City.
World-Wide Missions of Nigeria	1957	I-Non	x....	100	25,000	30,000	45,000	1.64	M=World-Wide Missions(USA). Evangelicals linked to HQ in Pasadena, CA (USA).
Zion Methodist Church in Nigeria	1942	I-Met	.T.T.	30	15,000	20,000	25,000	0.90	Methodist schism based on Owerri. 99% Ibo. 6n,35m,28w,4p,1r,W=87%,158Y,450z.
Other African indigenous churches		I-3pA	.....	5,000	1,200,000	940,000	3,000,000	0.05	Total over 1,500 (see below), including CMF, and Dominion Cathedral (huge; in 40 nations).
Other indigenous Oneness bodies	c1970	I-3oA	.....	200	15,000	–	30,000	51.04	Total 30: Apos Assem Our Lord & Savior JC, Holy Ch of Pentecost, True AOG Ch, True Zion Ch.
Other Protestant denominations		P-	.....	2,000	200,000	300,000	500,000	0.05	Total over 100 (see list below).
Other marginal Protestant bodies		m-	.....	100	25,000	4,000	50,000	0.05	Including COLJCB, Unity School of Christianity.
Other independent Catholic churches		I-CCa	.....	20	10,000	2,000	15,000	0.05	Including numerous bodies from Europe and USA under Episcopi Vagantes.
Other independent charismatic chs	1970	I-3cA	.....	3,000	60,000	–	100,000	58.49	Geographical networks, including large numbers of youth churches meeting in secular halls.
Doubly-affiliated		2-aff			-9,003,000	0	-17,616,223		Evangelicals and charismatics who are also baptized Roman Catholics.
Totals				**102,939**	**23,001,251**	**14,307,461**	**45,000,000**		

Churches, members, growth, 1900-2025	Congs	Adults	Affiliated	G%	Total denominations	6 Megablocs: O	R	A	P	I	m
Total churches, members, and denominations (mid-1900)	300	54,600	98,900	7.36	37	0	1	1	5	30	0
Total churches, members, and denominations (mid-1970)	32,869	7,904,357	14,307,461	7.36	880	2	1	1	75	785	16
Total churches, members, and denominations (mid-1990)	95,000	20,087,000	39,300,000	5.18	1,976	2	1	1	145	1,800	27
Total churches, members, and denominations (mid-1995)	102,939	23,001,251	45,000,000	2.75	2,030	2	1	1	146	1,853	27
Total churches, members, and denominations (mid-2000)	109,000	26,049,000	50,965,002	2.52	2,079	2	1	1	147	1,900	28
Total churches, members, and denominations (mid-2025)	190,000	43,905,000	85,900,000	2.11	4,229	7	1	1	180	4,000	40

Continued opposite

Country Table 2–concluded

NOTES ON TABLE ABOVE
NATIONAL COUNCILS (Column 4, 5th letter).
a = member of NEF and can.
b = member of NAAC and CAN
F = Christian Association of Nigeria (CAN), only.
G = Nigeria Evangelical Fellowship (NEF).
I = Nigeria Association of Aladura Churches (NAAC) (Isokan Ijo Aladura Nigeria (IIAN)/Communion of Aladura Churches, formerly National Council of Aladura Churches (NCAC), founded in 1960, with over 70 denominations as members by 1976 and 95 by late 1977).
K = Christian Council of Nigeria (CCN), and through it, member of CAN.
V = National Episcopal Conference of Nigeria (NECN), also full member of CAN.
Z = member of NAAC, CAN and associate member of CCN.
z = member of NEF, CCN and CAN.

*Other national councils (*mostly African indigenous). Christian Council of Praying Bands. Confederation of Nigerian Churches. Federation of Aladura. Inter-denominational Church Council of Nigeria (1962). Prophets' Union of Nigeria (Non-denominational), Reformed Ecumenical Council of Nigeria (RECON, 1991), Spiritual Union of Aladura Churches (1961). Union of Christian Praying Bands. United Independent Churches Fellowship (1959).

OTHER AFRICAN INDIGENOUS CHURCHES. There are a vast number of other churches, mostly each with under 1,000 adult followers in 1970, including an estimated 200 offshoots of the Cherubim and Seraphim. Among the total are the following (with in parenthesis year of origin, and 1970 membership statistics): Abosso Apostolic Faith Ch of Christ, African Ch of the Lord (1959; 72 adults), Agbala Imole Mission Ch Aladura (1964; 500 adults), Apostolic Ch of God (1964; 150 adults), Apostolic Gospel Ch (1964), Army of the Cross of Christ Ch (MDCC from Ghana, begun when leader deported), Associated Gospel Tabernacle Mission Chs (member of ICCC), Bible Methodist Ch (member of ICCC), Bible Presbyterian Ch (member of ICCC), Bible Reformed Ev Ch, Bible Way Baptist Ch (member of ICCC), Blood of Jesus Christ Apostolic Ch International, Brotherhood of the Cross and Star (in Calabar; Efik, Ibibio), Calvary Association of Baptist Chs (member of ICCC), Christ Ch of Jerusalem (1967; 150 adults), Christ Devotional Independent African Ch (120 adults), Christ Ecumenical Ch, Christ Flock of Light, Christ Gospel Apostolic Ch (1956), Christ Healing Ch (1960; 400 adults), Christ Living Ch (member of ICCC), Christ Spiritual Ch (Imisi Jesu) (1964; 250 adults), Christ Temple Baptist Ch (member of ICCC), Church Army of Africa, Ch of Christ (Ijo Enia Krist) (1931; 800 adults), Ch of Philadelphia (member of ICCC), Ebenezer Apostolic Ch (1940), Emissaries of Divine Light Ch (Ilesha, 400 members, 8 groups, bishop, USA missionaries), Evangelical Ch of Apostles Nigeria (1964; 500 adults), First United Ch of Jesus Christ (Apostolic) (Jamaican pentecostals), Free Christian Ch (member of ICCC), God's The Hosts Tabernacle, Gospel Ch or Light (1964; 350 adults), Gospel Pentecostal Assembly (Voice of Deliverance) (1960) (member of NEF), Gospel Team Ch of Nigeria (1950; 400 adults), Holy Assembly Ch (1960; 500 adults), Idapo Mimo Cherubim & Seraphim (1954; 750 adults), Ijo Irapada Kristi (1967; 250 adults), Ijo Ore Ofe Olorun (1965; 100 pentecostals), Latter Rain Assemblies Mission (member of ICCC), Light of the World Ch (1955; 500 adults), Lutheran Bible Reformed Ch (member of ICCC), New Heaven Bible Ch (member of ICCC), Open Door Ch (member of ICCC), Pentecostal Ch of Christ (1954; 580 adults), St Johns' United African Christian Ch (1946; 500 member), St Joseph Gospel Ch of Christ (1968; 200 adults), St Joseph's Chosen Ch of God (1975, applied to join WCC), Saint Moses Ch (1964; 600 adults), Spiritual Ch of Christ (1955), Temple Ch (member of ICCC), Unity Ch of Truth of Nigeria, Universal Christian Ch (member of ICCC), Universal Ch of the Holy Spirit in Nigeria (in south-east), West African Episcopal Ch (1903). Since 1970, 6 of these have applied to join the WCC. In 1976, at least 55 more bodies, in addition to those shown in the table itself, belonged to the Nigeria Association of Aladura Churches. In addition, there is a small number of other UK and USA Black missions, including: Father Divine Peace Mission Movement (USA), Pentecostal Assemblies of the World, Progressive National Baptist Convention USA (1963).

OTHER PROTESTANT DENOMINATIONS. The vast proliferation of smaller Protestant bodies includes: American Advent Mission Society (1966), Brethren Ch (Ashland, USA; 1948), Children of God International (USA; ministry to drug addicts), Christian Nationals Evangelism Commission (1961), Christian Union (USA; 1943), Ch of God General Conference (Abrahamic Faith) (USA; 1967), Ch of God (Queen's Village, USA; 1969, 483 adults), Ch of God (Seventh-day), Ch of the Lutheran Confession (USA) (35 churches), Chs of God in the British Isles & Overseas (7 churches), International Pentecostal Assemblies, Mennonite Brethren Ch of North America (1944), Seventh-day Adventist Reform Movement, Seventh-day Baptist Ch, Southern Methodist Ch (USA), World Missions (1972). There are also a large number of independent single congregations.

UNITING CHURCHES. Negotiations for organic union were under way in 1974 between: Ch of the Province of West Africa (11 dioceses), Methodist Ch Nigeria, Presbyterian Ch of Nigeria (negotiations began 1933, broke down 1966, resume 1973).

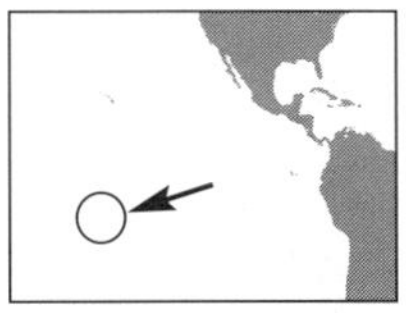

NIUE ISLAND

SECULAR DATA, AD 2000

STATE
Official name: The Territory Overseas of Niue Island.
Short name: Niue Island. **Adjective of nationality:** of Niue.
Flag: That of New Zealand.
Area: 260 sq. km. (100 sq. mi.).
Government: Territory overseas of New Zealand, since 1903.
Legislature: Island Assembly, 20 members.
Official language: English.
Monetary unit: 1 New Zealand dollar ($NZ) = 100 cents. **US$1=** $NZ 2.02.
Chief cities: ALOFI 585.
Political divisions: 1 province.

DEMOGRAPHY
Population: 2,000.
Population density: 7.2/sq. km. (18.7/sq. mi.).
Under 15 years: 1,000.
Growth rate p.a.: 1.85% (births 27.33, deaths 4.64).
Mortality: Infant, per 1,000: 19.3, ; **Maternal per 100,000:** 50.0.
Life expectancy: 73 (male 71, female 75).
Household size: 5.0. **Floor area per person, sq.m:** 17.0.
Major languages: English, Niuean, Chinese.
Urban dwellers: 29.40%. **Urban growth rate p.a.:** -1.4%.
Labor force: 40%.

ETHNOLINGUISTIC PEOPLES
93.3% Niuean; 2.6% Anglo-New Zealander; 0.6% Han Chinese.

ECONOMY
National income p.a. per person: US$2,665; **per family:** US$13,326.

EDUCATION
Adult literacy: 96% (male 97%, female 95%). **Schools:** 2.
Universities: 0. **School enrolment:** female/male: 70%/70%.

HEALTH
Access to health services: 70%. **Access to safe water:** 80%.
Hospitals: 1 (10 beds per 10,000). **Doctors:** 5.
Blind: 15. **Deaf:** 100. **Murder rate:** 5.
Lepers: 120.

LITERATURE
New book titles p.a.: 1 (300 p.a. per million). **Periodicals:** 3.
Newspapers: 0 dailies.

COMMUNICATION (per 1,000 people)
Phones: 100 **(20% mobile). Radios:** 700. **TV sets:** 150.
Daily newspaper circulation: 0. **Computers:** 200.

HUMAN LIFE AND LIBERTY (optimum condition=100.0%)
HDI: 70.0. **HSI:** 70.0. **HFI:** 70.0. **EFL:** 40.0.

Country Table 1. **Religious adherents in Niue, AD 1900-2025.**

Year	1900		1970		mid-1990		Annual change, 1990-2000				mid-1995		mid-2000		mid-2025	
Name	Adherents	%	Adherents	%	Adherents	%	Natural	Conversion	Total	Rate	Adherents	%	Adherents	%	Adherents	%
Christians	**4,200**	**100.0**	**4,995**	**99.1**	**2,267**	**98.6**	**-40**	**-4**	**-44**	**-2.16**	**2,056**	**97.9**	**1,823**	**97.2**	**1,310**	**93.6**
PROFESSION																
professing Christians	**4,200**	**100.0**	**4,995**	**99.1**	**2,267**	**98.6**	**-40**	**-4**	**-44**	**-2.16**	**2,056**	**97.9**	**1,823**	**97.2**	**1,310**	**93.6**
AFFILIATION																
unaffiliated Christians	0	0.0	510	10.1	112	4.9	-1	-2	-3	-2.49	95	4.6	87	4.6	55	3.9
affiliated Christians	**4,200**	**100.0**	**4,485**	**89.0**	**2,155**	**93.7**	**-41**	**-2**	**-42**	**-2.14**	**1,961**	**93.4**	**1,736**	**92.5**	**1,255**	**89.6**
Protestants	4,200	100.0	3,730	74.0	1,460	63.5	-38	0	-38	-3.01	1,267	60.3	1,076	57.4	705	50.4
Marginal Christians	0	0.0	505	10.0	460	20.0	-2	0	-2	-0.44	470	22.4	440	23.4	320	22.9
Roman Catholics	0	0.0	220	4.4	175	7.6	-3	0	-3	-1.53	160	7.6	150	8.0	130	9.3
Anglicans	0	0.0	30	0.6	40	1.7	0	0	0	0.00	40	1.9	40	2.1	40	2.9
Independents	0	0.0	0	0.0	20	0.9	1	0	1	4.14	24	1.2	30	1.6	60	4.3
Trans-megabloc groupings																
Evangelicals	0	0.0	200	4.0	70	3.0	0	0	0	0.00	69	3.4	70	3.7	70	5.0
Pentecostals/Charismatics	0	0.0	50	1.0	210	9.1	1	0	1	0.47	216	10.3	220	11.7	250	17.9
Great Commission Christians	**250**	**6.0**	**600**	**11.9**	**390**	**17.0**	**-4**	**-2**	**-6**	**-1.69**	**360**	**17.1**	**329**	**17.5**	**265**	**18.9**
Baha'is	0	0.0	5	0.1	20	0.9	-2	3	1	3.79	25	1.2	29	1.6	50	3.6
Nonreligious	0	0.0	0	0.0	10	0.4	0	1	1	7.70	15	0.7	21	1.2	30	2.1
Chinese folk-religionists	0	0.0	0	0.0	3	0.2	0	0	0	2.92	4	0.2	4	0.2	10	0.7
World A (unevangelized persons)	0	0.0	0	0.0	0	0.0	0	0	0	0.00	2	0.1	2	0.1	1	0.1
World B (evangelized non-Christians)	0	0.0	44	0.9	33	1.4	-2	4	2	67.61	41	2.0	75	2.7	89	6.3
World C (Christians)	4,200	100.0	4,995	99.1	2,267	98.6	-40	-4	-44	-2.16	2,056	97.9	1,823	97.2	1,310	93.6
Country's population	**4,200**	**100.0**	**5,039**	**100.0**	**2,300**	**100.0**	**-42**	**0**	**-42**	**0.00**	**2,100**	**100.0**	**1,900**	**100.0**	**1,400**	**100.0**

COLUMNS, ROWS.
For meanings and definitions, see Codebook (Part 3). Note that, by definition, total 'Christians' = professing + crypto-Christians, which also = affiliated + unaffiliated Christians, and also = Great Commission Christians + latent Christians. Percentages may not always total exactly, due to rounding.

CENSUSES.
25.IX.1945: 99.5% Protestants, 0.5% other religionists. **25.IX.1956:** 99.9% Christians. **25.IX.1961:** 84.9% Protestants (84.1% LMS), 9.5% marginal Protestants (8.8% Mormons, 0.7% Jehovah's Witnesses), 4.3% Roman Catholics, 1.2% Anglicans, 0.1% nonreligious. **28.IX.1966** 84.7% Protestants (83.4% LMS), 9.8% marginal Protestants (8.2% Mormons, 1.6% Jehovah's Witnesses), 4.7% Roman Catholics 0.7% Anglicans, 0.1% Baha'is. **28.IX.1971:** 81.1% Protestants (77.8% LMS), 12.1% marginal Protestants (10.4% Mormons, 1.7% Jehovah's Witnesses), 5.7% Roman Catholics, 1.0% Anglicans, 0.1% Baha'is. **1991:** 73.1% Protestant (70.9% LMS), 12.8% Marginal Christians (10.6% Mormons, 2.1% Jehovah's witnesses), 6.2% Roman Catholics, 5.0% other religionists, 3.1% nonreligious.

NOTES ON RELIGIONS
BAHA'IS. A selection of Baha'i prayers was published in the Niuean language soon after 1970.
COUNTRY'S POPULATION. There is a large Niuean community living in New Zealand (6,500 in 1995), and each year about 50 more emigrate there from Niue.

Country status. Niue is an island in the South Pacific east of Tonga. It is the largest coral island in the world. Its chief export is coconut cream.

HUMAN LIFE AND LIBERTY

Human rights and freedoms. Niue is a self-governing territory in free association with New Zealand which is responsible for external affairs. The Niue Islanders enjoy all basic human rights and civil liberties

NON-CHRISTIAN RELIGIONS

Niue is almost entirely Christian, except for a few individuals. In the 1991 census, 25 persons claimed to belong to the Baha'i World Faith.

CHRISTIANITY

PROTESTANT CHURCHES. The first attempt to evangelize Niue was made in 1830 by the pioneer John Williams of the London Missionary Society. Unsuccessful at the time, the LMS continued to make periodic visits to the island. In 1846 a Niuean, trained as a teacher in an LMS school in Samoa, returned home and was followed 3 years later by a Samoan

Great Commission Instrument Panel: status of Niue (for explanation see start of Part 4)

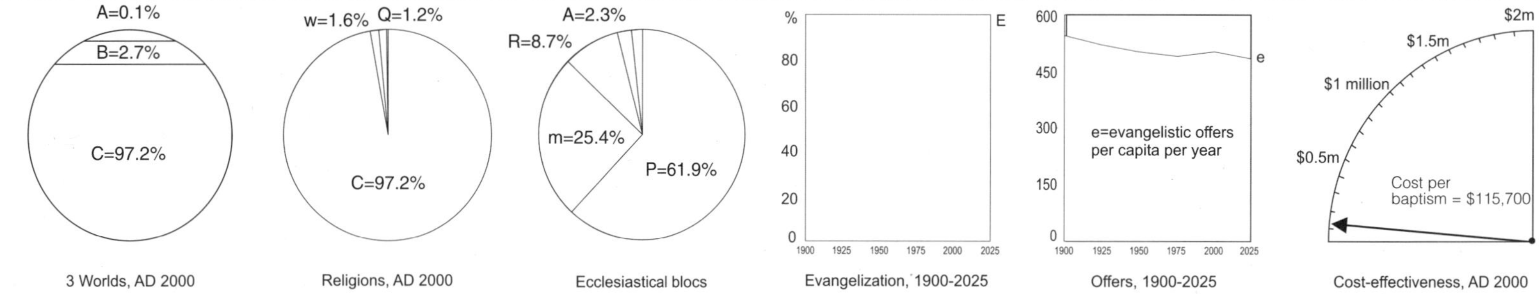

Country summary. **Worlds A, B, C by ethnolinguistic peoples, cities, and major civil divisions in Niue.**

World	PEOPLES Num	Pop 2000	C%	Christians	E%	U%	Unevangelized	CITIES Num	Pop 2000	C%	Christians	E%	U%	Unevangelized	CIVIL DIVISIONS Num	Pop 2000	C%	Christians	E%	U%	Unevangelized
A	0	0	0.00	0	0	0	0	0	0	0.00	0	0	0	0	0	0	0.00	0	0	0	0
B	1	11	36.36	4	100	0	0	0	0	0.00	0	0	0	0	0	0	0.00	0	0	0	0
C	3	1,865	92.82	1,731	100	0	1	1	585	90.09	527	100	0	1	1	1,876	92.54	1,736	100	0	1
Total	**4**	**1,876**	**92.48**	**1,735**	**100**	**0**	**1**	**1**	**585**	**90.09**	**527**	**100**	**0**	**1**	**1**	**1,876**	**92.54**	**1,736**	**100**	**0**	**1**

named Paulo who was instrumental in establishing the church in Niue. There was no resident European missionary until 1861. The early LMS influence was decisive, and Niueans still consider themselves predominantly Congregationalists. There is also a small Seventh-day Adventist church.

MARGINAL CHURCHES. As in other parts of Oceania, Mormons have met with marked success, and the Church of Jesus Christ of Latter-day Saints is now the second largest church on the island. Jehovah's Witnesses are also present.

CATHOLIC CHURCH. The small Catholic community is served by a Marist priest at Alofi. In May 1972 Niue was separated from the diocese of Tonga and attached instead to the diocese of Rarotonga with its seat in the Cook Islands.

The Holy See has no diplomatic relations with Niue in AD 2000, but is represented there by an apostolic delegate for the Pacific Ocean residing in Wellington, New Zealand.

Indigenous missions. Some marginal Christians have been sent to other islands in the Pacific but there is little missionary vision in the churches.

CHURCH AND STATE

Niue was reached by Captain James Cook in 1774 but did not come under British protection until 1889. In 1901 the island was annexed to New Zealand. Religion has not been an issue between church and state and the latter is effectively secular. A resident commissioner and the Niue Island Assembly, with 14 elected members, handle administrative and legislative affairs. Freedom of religion is guaranteed by the constitution of New Zealand.

A number of Niue's postage stamps have Christian motifs; here in Easter 1978, (left) The Descent from the Cross (Caravaggio), and (right) The Burial of Christ (Bellini).

FUTURE TRENDS AND PROSPECTS

Baha'is and the nonreligious seem likely to grow from just 0.1% jointly to 5.7% by 2025. Christianity is expected to decline to 93.6% in the same period.

Christianity will thus predominate throughout the 21st century. Baha'is and the nonreligious could together reach 15% by AD 2050.

BIBLIOGRAPHY

Bibliographies of the Kermadec Islands, Niue, Swains Island and the Tokelau Islands. W. G. Coppell. Honolulu, HI: Pacific Islands Studies Program, University of Hawaii, 1975. 102p.

Bibliography of Niué, South Pacific. N. L. H. Krauss. Honolulu, HI, 1970. 16p.

Diocesan archives, 1891–1993. Catholic Church Diocese of the Cook Islands and Niue. Canberra, Australia: Pacific Manuscripts Bureau, Australian National University, [1994]. (53 microfilm reels).

Ear piercing ceremony in Niue. G. Jowitt. *Focus on the Pacific.* Auckland: Longman Paul, 1990. 16p.

History and traditions of Niue. E. M. Loeb. 1926; reprint, New York: Kraus Reprint, 1978. 232p.

'Island church/island state: a study of the impact of the Christian mission on constitutional development in Niue.' S. Carney. Paper, University of Hawaii, 1973. 36p.

Niue: a history of the island. T. M. Chapman et al. : Published jointly by the Institute of Pacific Studies of the University of the South Pacific and the Government of Niue, 1982. 159p.

Niue: the island and its people. S. P. Smith. 1902-1903; reprint, Suva, Fiji: Institute of Pacific Studies & the Niue Extension Centre of the University of the South Pacific, 1983. 141p.

'Symbolic slaying in Niue: post–European changes in a dramatic ritual complex,' K. Luomala, in *The changing Pacific: essays in honour of H. E. Maude,* p.142–62. N. Gunson (ed). Melbourne: Oxford University Press, 1978.

Torea Katorika. Catholic Church Diocese of the Cook Islands and Niue. , 1982–. (Monthly periodical; published bimonthly before 1982).

Country Table 2. **Organized churches and denominations in Niue.**

Official name (bold type = church with over 10% of all affiliated) 1	*Begun* 2	*Type* 3	*Counc* 4	*Congs* 5	*Adults* 6	*Affiliated 1970* 7	*Affiliated 1995* 8	*G%* 9	*Names, notes, and other statistics* (see Codebook, Part 3) 10
Anglican Church (D Polynesia)		A-Hig	awpK.	1	7	30	40	0.05	Under Diocese of Polynesia, Ch of the Province of New Zealand. Expatriates.
Catholic Church (D Rarotonga)		R-Lat	P.PY.	1	50	220	160	0.05	Part of D Rarotonga (Cook Is) since 1972; previously under D Tonga. M=SM2. 1x.
Ch of Jesus C of Latter-day Saints	1953	m-LdS	x....	7	135	425	400	-0.24	*Mormons.* M=CJCLdS(Utah, USA). Many expatriates. 2f.
Jehovah's Witnesses	c1960	m-Jeh	x....	1	21	80	70	-0.53	*Watch Tower. IBSA.* First activity reported 1961 (36 adherents). (1975) 1Y. (1995) 2Y.
New Apostolic Church	c1975	I-3aX	x....	1	12	–	24	5.00	M=Neuapostolische Kirche (Germany).
Niue Christian Church	1846	P-Con	..P..	14	730	3,700	1,200	-4.40	*Ekalesia Niue.* 1861, M=LMS(UK). Massive emigration to New Zealand. 12n,1x.
Seventh-day Adventist Church		P-Adv	x....	1	20	30	67	0.05	*SDA.* Part of Tonga Mission, Central Pacific Union Mission.
Totals				**26**	**975**	**4,485**	**1,961**		

Churches, members, growth, 1900-2025	*Congs*	*Adults*	*Affiliated*	*G%*	*Total denominations*	*6 Megablocs:* *O*	*R*	*A*	*P*	*I*	*m*
Total churches, members, and denominations (mid-1900)	20	2,100	4,200	0.09	1	0	0	0	1	0	0
Total churches, members, and denominations (mid-1970)	24	2,235	4,485	0.09	6	0	1	1	2	0	2
Total churches, members, and denominations (mid-1990)	20	1,100	2,155	-3.60	7	0	1	1	2	1	2
Total churches, members, and denominations (mid-1995)	26	975	1,961	-1.87	7	0	1	1	2	1	2
Total churches, members, and denominations (mid-2000)	20	860	1,736	-2.41	7	0	1	1	2	1	2
Total churches, members, and denominations (mid-2025)	20	620	1,255	-1.29	15	0	1	1	4	6	3

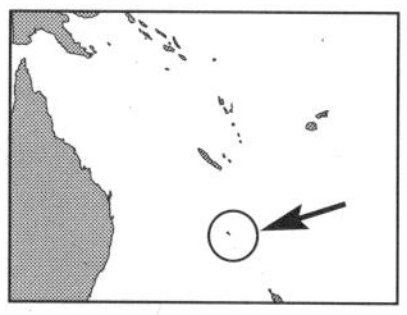

NORFOLK ISLAND

SECULAR DATA, AD 2000

STATE
Official name: The Territory of Norfolk Island.
Short name: Norfolk Island. **Adjective of nationality:** Norfolk Islander.
Flag: Vertical green stripes on right and left, tree on white in center.
Area: 40 sq. km. (15 sq. mi.).
Government: Territory of Australia, since 1913 (1856 settlement).
Legislature: Norfolk Island Council, 9 members.
Official language: English.
Monetary unit: 1 Australian dollar ($A) = 100 cents. **US$1=** $A 1.70.
Chief cities: KINGSTON-NORFOLK 1,228.
Political divisions: 1 province.

DEMOGRAPHY
Population: 2,100.
Population density: 51.8/sq. km. (138.3/sq. mi.).
Under 15 years: 420.
Growth rate p.a.: 0.91% (births 12.57, deaths 7.65).
Mortality: Infant, per 1,000: 5.5, ; **Maternal per 100,000:** 40.0.
Life expectancy: 79 (male 76, female 82).
Household size: 4.0. **Floor area per person, sq.m:** 25.0.
Major languages: English.
Urban dwellers: 70.00%. **Urban growth rate p.a.:** 0.00%.
Labor force: 35%.

ETHNOLINGUISTIC PEOPLES
41.4% Norfolker (Pitcairner); 31.0% Anglo-Australian; 13.8% Anglo-New Zealander; 10.1% British; 3.2% Euronesian.

ECONOMY
National income p.a. per person: US$2,409; **per family:** US$9,638.

EDUCATION
Adult literacy: 95% (male 96%, female 94%). **Schools:** 1.
Universities: 0. **School enrolment:** female/male: 85%/85%.

HEALTH
Access to health services: 75%. **Access to safe water:** 85%.
Hospitals: 1 (20 beds per 10,000). **Doctors:** 5.
Blind: 20. **Deaf:** 100. **Murder rate:** 4.
Lepers: 0.

LITERATURE
New book titles p.a.: 1 (300 p.a. per million). **Periodicals:** 0.
Newspapers: 0 dailies.

COMMUNICATION (per 1,000 people)
Phones: 150 (15% mobile). **Radios:** 800. **TV sets:** 200.
Daily newspaper circulation: 0. **Computers:** 500.

HUMAN LIFE AND LIBERTY (optimum condition=100.0%)
HDI: 80.0. **HSI:** 80.0. **HFI:** 75.0. **EFL:** 45.0.

Country Table 1. **Religious adherents in Norfolk Island, AD 1900-2025.**

Year	1900		1970		mid-1990		Annual change, 1990-2000				mid-1995		mid-2000		mid-2025	
Name	Adherents	%	Adherents	%	Adherents	%	Natural	Conversion	Total	Rate	Adherents	%	Adherents	%	Adherents	%
Christians	**1,000**	**100.0**	**981**	**87.9**	**1,400**	**77.8**	**23**	**-3**	**20**	**1.35**	**1,550**	**77.5**	**1,601**	**77.2**	**1,800**	**72.0**
PROFESSION																
professing Christians	**1,000**	**100.0**	**981**	**87.9**	**1,400**	**77.8**	**23**	**-3**	**20**	**1.35**	**1,550**	**77.5**	**1,601**	**77.2**	**1,800**	**72.0**
AFFILIATION																
unaffiliated Christians	100	10.0	151	13.5	190	10.6	7	-1	6	2.70	226	11.3	248	11.8	210	8.4
affiliated Christians	**900**	**90.0**	**830**	**74.4**	**1,210**	**67.2**	**16**	**-2**	**14**	**1.12**	**1,324**	**66.2**	**1,353**	**64.4**	**1,590**	**63.6**
Anglicans	720	72.0	360	32.3	580	32.2	4	-1	3	0.51	600	30.0	610	29.0	700	28.0
Protestants	160	16.0	290	26.0	420	23.3	9	-3	6	1.24	460	23.0	475	22.6	580	23.2
Roman Catholics	20	2.0	180	16.1	240	13.3	1	0	1	0.33	250	12.5	248	11.8	250	10.0
Marginal Christians	0	0.0	0	0.0	10	0.5	1	0	1	7.18	14	0.7	20	1.0	60	2.4
doubly-affiliated	0	0.0	0	0.0	-40	-2.2	4	0	4	-30.85	0	0.0	0	0.0	0	0.0
Trans-megabloc groupings																
Evangelicals	100	10.0	250	22.4	390	21.7	4	0	4	0.86	413	20.7	425	20.2	480	19.2
Pentecostals/Charismatics	0	0.0	10	0.9	85	4.7	2	1	3	2.61	98	4.9	110	5.2	160	6.4
Great Commission Christians	**80**	**8.0**	**200**	**17.9**	**510**	**28.3**	**6**	**3**	**9**	**1.55**	**570**	**28.5**	**595**	**28.3**	**730**	**29.2**
Nonreligious	0	0.0	119	10.7	400	22.2	4	3	7	1.71	450	22.5	474	22.8	700	28.0
World A (unevangelized persons)	0	0.0	2	0.2	6	0.3	0	0	0	1.55	8	0.4	6	0.3	12	0.6
World B (evangelized non-Christians)	0	0.0	132	11.8	394	21.9	4	3	7	-4.05	442	22.1	493	22.5	188	27.4
World C (Christians)	1,000	100.0	981	87.9	1,400	77.8	23	-3	20	1.35	1,550	77.5	1,601	77.2	1,800	72.0
Country's population	**1,000**	**100.0**	**1,116**	**100.0**	**1,800**	**100.0**	**27**	**0**	**27**	**0.00**	**2,000**	**100.0**	**2,100**	**100.0**	**2,500**	**100.0**

COLUMNS, ROWS.
For meanings and definitions, see Codebook (Part 3). Note that, by definition, total 'Christians' = professing + crypto-Christians, which also = affiliated + unaffiliated Christians, and also = Great Commission Christians + latent Christians. Percentages may not always total exactly, due to rounding.

CENSUSES.
30.VI.1947: 92.8% Anglicans & Protestants, 6.9% Roman Catholics, 0.3% non-religious. **30.VI.1954:** 92.8% Anglicans & Protestants, 6.9% Roman Catholics, 0.4% non-religious. **30.VI.1961:** 59.6% Anglicans, 32.8% Protestants (17.2% Methodists, 9.1% SD Adventists, 4.5% Presbyterians), 7.1% Roman Catholics, 0.5% non-religious. **30.VI.1966:** 55.7% Anglicans, 31.8% Protestants (15.8% Methodists, 7.7% SD Adventists, 5.9% Presbyterians), 9.8% Roman Catholics, 2.6% non-religious. **30.VI.1971:** 47.0% Anglicans, 33.9% Protestants (15.8% Methodists, 7.9% Presbyterians, 5.6% SD Adventists, and followers of about 10 other denominations), 12.1% Roman Catholics, 7.0% non-religious. This census enumerates the population by 20 different categories of religion.

NOTES ON RELIGIONS
ANGLICANS. These have decreased rapidly since 1960, whilst Roman Catholics and non-religious have increased markedly.
NONRELIGIOUS. Europeans of British origin.
PROTESTANTS. Although only 2 denominations have organized congregations, the 1971 census lists the following additional denominational traditions to which persons professed to belong: Baptist, Brethren, Churches of Christ, Congregational, Lutheran, and Salvation Army.

Great Commission Instrument Panel: status of Norfolk Island (for explanation see start of Part 4)

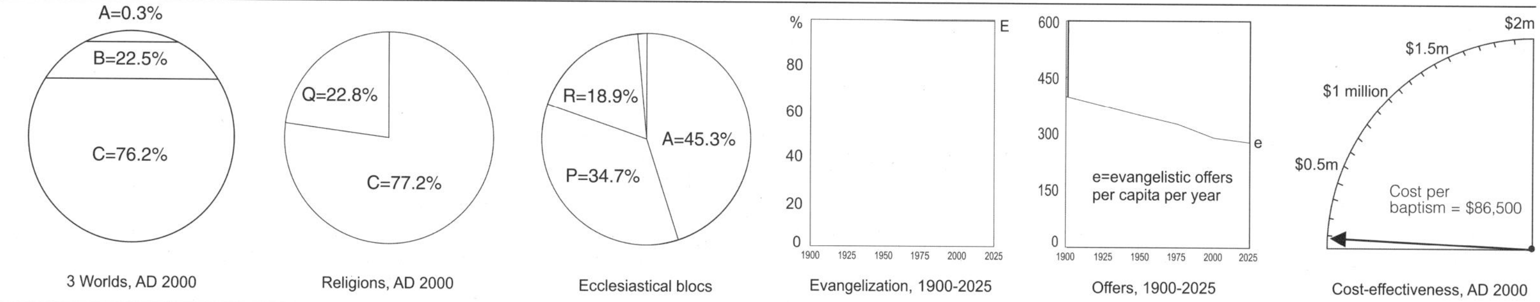

The Island's postage stamps often illustrate Christian themes: (*left*) the first Christmas service, 1788; (*right*) St. Barnabas Chapel, exterior and interior.

Country status. Norfolk Island, an external territory of Australia since 1913, is an island in the Pacific Ocean off the east coast of Australia. The island was originally settled by descendants of the mutineers from the *Bounty*.

NON-CHRISTIAN RELIGIONS

As the inhabitants of the island are either of British stock or Euronesian, non-Christian religions have gained no foothold. Persons without religion however have increased rapidly from one census to the next since 1947 and now number 23%.

CHRISTIANITY

ANGLICAN CHURCH. The first Christmas service was held in 1788. The Melanesian Mission established its main headquarters on the island in 1867, and St Barnabas chapel there was consecrated as a church in 1880. By 1896 the church claimed 230 members. In 1919 the headquarters were moved to Siota in the British Solomon Islands, but the territory has remained mainly Anglican in denomination, though Anglicans have recently declined in numbers. They form part of the diocese of Sydney in the Church of England in Australia.

PROTESTANT CHURCHES. Methodists and Adventists have organized congregations on the island. Both are related to their churches in Australia.

CATHOLIC CHURCH. A Marist priest serves one parish, which is attached to the archdiocese of Sydney (Australia). Catholics are growing in numbers, chiefly at the expense of Anglicans.

The Holy See has no diplomatic relations with Norfolk Island in AD 2000.

CHURCH AND STATE

In 1774 Captain James Cook discovered an uninhabited island which he named after the English duke of Norfolk. The island was annexed by Great Britain in 1788, the second of Britain's possessions in the Pacific. Settlement began in 1856 from Pitcairn Island, and in 1914 it became a territory of the Australian

Commonwealth. Religion has never been an issue between church and state. Norfolk Island is today governed by an administrator named by the governor-general of Australia. There is also a Norfolk Island Council, elected every 2 years from the resident community, which acts in an advisory capacity to the administrator. The Australian constitution guarantees freedom of religion.

FUTURE TRENDS AND PROSPECTS

Christianity is expected to steadily decline but remain above 70% of the population through AD 2025. The nonreligious, 10.7% in 1970, would then grow to 28% by 2025. Correspondingly, Christians will likely decline from 87.9% in 1970 to 72% by 2025.

The nonreligious will likely continue to increase, perhaps growing to 40% before AD 2050.

BIBLIOGRAPHY

Gathering jewels, or, life and labors of Mr. and Mrs. A. H. Phelps in New Zealand, Norfolk island and their native land. A. H. Phelps. Meriden, CT: Journal Pub. Co, 1896. 410p. (Treats Methodist mission work).

George Hunn Nobbs, 1799–1884: chaplain on Pitcairn and Norfolk Island. R. Nobbs. Norfolk Island: Pitcairn Descendants Society, 1984. 166p.

Norfolk Island: an outline of its history, 1774–1987. M. Hoare. 4th ed. St. Lucia: University of Queensland Press, 1988.

Pitcairn hymns and Norfolk favourites. Norfolk Island: Church of England, [1974]. 42p.

Pitcairn und Norfolk. A. Petersen-Roil. *Bibliographie einer Insel*, Bd. 3. Munich: Verlag A. Petersen-Roil, 1987. 76p. (Bibliographical work).

St. Barnabas and the Melanesian Mission, Norfolk Island. R. Nobbs. [North Ryde, NSW]: Macquarie University Australian History Resources Centre, for The Friends of St. Barnabas Chapel, Norfolk Island, 1990. 20p.

'The history of the Methodist Church on Norfolk Island.' E. Smart. Paper, Methodist Historical Society, Sydney, 1974.

Country summary. **Worlds A, B, C by ethnolinguistic peoples, cities, and major civil divisions in Norfolk Island.**

World	PEOPLES Num	Pop 2000	C%	Christians	E%	U%	Unevangelized	CITIES Num	Pop 2000	C%	Christians	E%	U%	Unevangelized	CIVIL DIVISIONS Num	Pop 2000	C%	Christians	E%	U%	Unevangelized
A	0	0	0.00	0	0	0	0	0	0	0.00	0	0	0	0	0	0	0.00	0	0	0	0
B	0	0	0.00	0	0	0	0	0	0	0.00	0	0	0	0	0	0	0.00	0	0	0	0
C	6	2,074	65.24	1,353	100	0	7	1	1,228	64.98	798	100	0	5	1	2,075	65.20	1,353	100	0	7
Total	**6**	**2,074**	**65.24**	**1,353**	**100**	**0**	**7**	**1**	**1,228**	**64.98**	**798**	**100**	**0**	**5**	**1**	**2,075**	**65.20**	**1,353**	**100**	**0**	**7**

Country Table 2. **Organized churches and denominations in Norfolk Island.**

Official name (bold type = church with over 10% of all affiliated) 1	*Begun* 2	*Type* 3	*Counc* 4	*Congs* 5	*Adults* 6	*Affiliated 1970* 7	*Affiliated 1995* 8	*G%* 9	*Names, notes, and other statistics* (see Codebook, Part 3) 10
Catholic Church (M Sydney)		R-Lat	P....	1	100	180	250	0.05	Attached to M Sydney (Australia). M=SM2. One parish. 1x.
Ch of England in Australia (D Sydney)	1788	A-plu	awe..	1	319	360	600	2.06	*Parish of All Saints*, in Diocese of Sydney (Australia). M=Melanesian Mission (UK).
Jehovah's Witnesses	1985	m-Jeh	x....	1	6	–	14	10.00	*Watch Tower.*
Methodist Church		P-Met	Vwe..	1	120	200	260	0.05	Related to Methodist Church of Australasia. Migrant workers and transients.
Seventh-day Adventist Church	c1900	P-Adv	x....	1	50	90	100	0.42	In Greater Sydney Conference, Trans-Tasman UC. Pitcairn Islanders.
Other Protestant churches		P-	.....	3	60	–	100	0.05	A handful of recent arrivals.
Totals				**8**	**655**	**830**	**1,324**		

Churches, members, growth, 1900-2025	*Congs*	*Adults*	*Affiliated*	*G%*	*Total denominations*	*6 Megablocs:* O	R	A	P	I	m
Total churches, members, and denominations (mid-1900)	4	600	900	-0.12	3	0	1	1	1	0	0
Total churches, members, and denominations (mid-1970)	4	550	830	-0.12	4	0	1	1	2	0	0
Total churches, members, and denominations (mid-1990)	8	600	1,210	1.90	8	0	1	1	5	0	1
Total churches, members, and denominations (mid-1995)	8	655	1,324	1.82	8	0	1	1	5	0	1
Total churches, members, and denominations (mid-2000)	8	670	1,353	0.43	8	0	1	1	5	0	1
Total churches, members, and denominations (mid-2025)	12	790	1,590	0.65	11	0	1	1	7	0	2

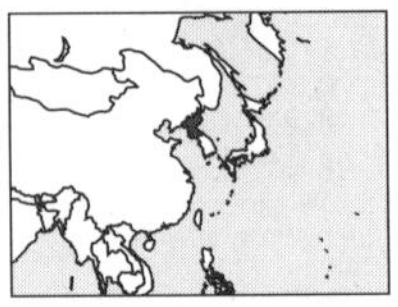

NORTH KOREA

SECULAR DATA, AD 2000

STATE
Official name: Chosun Minchu-chui Inmin Konghwa-guk (The Democratic People's Republic of Korea).
Short name: North Korea. **Adjective of nationality:** North Korean.
Flag: Large red centre stripe bordered by thin white stripes and wider blue stripes; white circle near hoist enclosing red 5-pointed star.
Area: 122,762 sq. km. (47,399 sq. mi.).
Government: One-party Communist state, formed 1948 (1910 Japanese possession).
Legislature: Supreme People's Assembly, 687 members.
Official language: Korean (Chosenmal).
Monetary unit: 1 won = 100 chon. **US$1=** 2.20 won.
Chief cities: PYONGYANG 2,726,000; Chongjin 685,081; Wonsan 556,453; Kimchaek (Songjin) 519,348; Sinuiju 426,428.
Political divisions: 13 provinces.
Armed forces: 1,128,000.

DEMOGRAPHY
Population: 24,039,000.
Population density: 195.8/sq. km. (507.1/sq. mi.).
Under 15 years: 6,640,000.
Growth rate p.a.: 1.13% (births 16.78, deaths 5.45).
Mortality: Infant, per 1,000: 19.1, ; **Maternal per 100,000:** 70.0.
Life expectancy: 73 (male 70, female 76).
Household size: 4.8. **Floor area per person, sq.m:** 14.0.
Major languages: Korean, Chinese (Mandarin), Russian.
Urban dwellers: 62.81%. **Urban growth rate p.a.:** 1.8%.
Labor force: 45%.

ETHNOLINGUISTIC PEOPLES
99.0% North Korean; 0.7% Han Chinese (Mandarin); 0.0% Khalka Mongol; 0.0% Russian; 0.0% French.

ECONOMY
National income p.a. per person: US$949; **per family:** US$4,559.

EDUCATION
Adult literacy: 95% (male 96%, female 94%). **Schools:** 6,122.
Universities: 281. **School enrolment:** female/male: 80%/80%.

HEALTH
Access to health services: 40%. **Access to safe water:** 100%.
Hospitals: 2,500 (135 beds per 10,000). **Doctors:** 57,690.
Blind: 48,000. **Deaf:** 1,434,800. **Murder rate:** 5. **Lepers:** 40,000.

LITERATURE
New book titles p.a.: 240 (10 p.a. per million). **Periodicals:** 0.
Newspapers: 11 dailies.

COMMUNICATION (per 1,000 people)
Phones: 46 (10% mobile). **Radios:** 211. **TV sets:** 115.
Daily newspaper circulation: 213. **Computers:** 1.

HUMAN LIFE AND LIBERTY (optimum condition=100.0%)
HDI: 76.5. **HSI:** 63.0. **HFI:** 35.0. **EFL:** 2.0.

Country Table 1. **Religious adherents in North Korea, AD 1900-2025.**

Year / *Name*	*1900* Adherents	%	*1970* Adherents	%	*mid-1990* Adherents	%	*Annual change, 1990-2000* Natural	Conversion	Total	Rate	*mid-1995* Adherents	%	*mid-2000* Adherents	%	*mid-2025* Adherents	%
Nonreligious	0	0.0	6,316,000	44.3	11,327,000	55.4	198,094	5,347	203,441	1.67	12,360,320	55.6	13,361,406	55.6	16,446,000	56.0
Atheists	0	0.0	2,253,000	15.8	3,160,000	15.4	55,259	3,276	58,535	1.71	3,440,000	15.5	3,745,348	15.6	4,600,000	15.7
New-Religionists	20,000	0.5	2,100,000	14.7	2,700,000	13.2	47,215	-7,684	39,531	1.38	2,900,000	13.0	3,095,313	12.9	3,500,000	11.9
Ethnoreligionists	3,766,100	94.2	3,165,000	22.2	2,522,800	12.3	44,116	-1,151	42,965	1.59	2,725,000	12.3	2,952,452	12.3	3,000,000	10.2
Christians	**13,900**	**0.4**	**142,000**	**1.0**	**415,000**	**2.0**	**7,257**	**1,508**	**8,765**	**1.93**	**456,000**	**2.1**	**502,646**	**2.1**	**1,425,000**	**4.9**
PROFESSION																
crypto-Christians	0	0.0	142,000	1.0	354,000	1.7	6,190	310	6,500	1.70	387,000	1.7	419,000	1.7	1,250,000	4.3
professing Christians	**13,900**	**0.4**	**0**	**0.0**	**61,000**	**0.3**	**1,067**	**1,198**	**2,265**	**3.21**	**69,000**	**0.3**	**83,646**	**0.4**	**175,000**	**0.6**
AFFILIATION																
unaffiliated Christians	0	0.0	0	0.0	2,000	0.0	35	8	43	1.98	2,000	0.0	2,433	0.0	15,000	0.1
affiliated Christians	**13,900**	**0.4**	**142,000**	**1.0**	**413,000**	**2.0**	**7,222**	**1,499**	**8,721**	**1.93**	**454,000**	**2.0**	**500,213**	**2.1**	**1,410,000**	**4.8**
Independents	0	0.0	8,000	0.1	355,000	1.7	6,208	1,533	7,741	1.99	392,000	1.8	432,413	1.8	900,000	3.1
Roman Catholics	1,000	0.0	15,000	0.1	46,000	0.2	804	96	900	1.80	50,000	0.2	55,000	0.2	300,000	1.0
Protestants	12,900	0.3	118,000	0.8	10,000	0.1	175	-175	0	0.00	10,000	0.0	10,000	0.0	200,000	0.7
Marginal Christians	0	0.0	1,000	0.0	2,000	0.0	35	45	80	3.42	2,000	0.0	2,800	0.0	10,000	0.0
Trans-megabloc groupings																
Evangelicals	11,000	0.3	7,500	0.1	16,300	0.1	285	85	370	2.07	16,620	0.1	20,000	0.1	30,000	0.1
Pentecostals/Charismatics	0	0.0	8,000	0.1	350,000	1.7	6,120	3,880	10,000	2.54	393,060	1.8	450,000	1.9	1,100,000	3.7
Great Commission Christians	**12,000**	**0.3**	**130,000**	**0.9**	**388,000**	**1.9**	**6,785**	**1,282**	**8,067**	**1.91**	**427,000**	**1.9**	**468,670**	**2.0**	**1,200,000**	**4.1**
Buddhists	200,000	5.0	288,000	2.0	320,000	1.6	5,596	-1,131	4,465	1.31	341,000	1.5	364,648	1.5	380,000	1.3
Chinese folk-religionists	0	0.0	0	0.0	14,000	0.1	245	-147	98	0.68	14,400	0.1	14,976	0.1	32,000	0.1
Muslims	0	0.0	0	0.0	2,200	0.0	38	-18	20	0.89	2,280	0.0	2,404	0.0	5,000	0.0
World A (unevangelized persons)	3,400,000	85.0	11,254,267	78.9	11,151,245	54.5	194,999	-107,367	87,632	0.76	11,742,008	52.8	12,019,500	50.0	11,755,200	40.0
World B (evangelized non-Christians)	586,100	14.6	2,867,696	20.1	8,894,755	43.5	155,564	105,859	261,423	2.62	10,040,644	45.1	11,516,854	47.9	16,207,800	55.1
World C (Christians)	13,900	0.4	142,000	1.0	415,000	2.0	7,257	1,508	8,765	1.93	456,000	2.1	502,646	2.1	1,425,000	4.9
Country's population	**4,000,000**	**100.0**	**14,263,964**	**100.0**	**20,461,000**	**100.0**	**357,820**	**0**	**357,820**	**1.62**	**22,238,653**	**100.0**	**24,039,000**	**100.0**	**29,388,000**	**100.0**

Continued opposite

Country Table 1–concluded

COLUMNS, ROWS.
For meanings and definitions, see Codebook (Part 3). Note that, by definition, total 'Christians' = professing + crypto-Christians, which also = affiliated + unaffiliated Christians, and also = Great Commission Christians + latent Christians. Percentages may not always total exactly, due to rounding.

CENSUSES.
No religion question has ever been asked in population censuses.

NOTES ON RELIGIONS
ATHEISTS. Korean Workers' Party (KWP) (in power; neither pro-Soviet nor pro-China): Communist membership (1970) 1,600,000. Of party members about a third are atheists and the rest nonreligious.
BUDDHISTS. Mahayana.
COUNTRY'S POPULATION. After the Korean war (1950-53) in which about 5 million persons were killed, a further 2 million fled from North to South Korea, including vast numbers of Protestants.
CRYPTO-CHRISTIANS. Since 1950 all Christians have been forced underground. Although there is now no organized religion, there is much private activity including radio listening. In 1957, 2,000 active Christians in 500 small units were discovered by the regime and 10 leaders were executed.
INDIGENOUS. Organized and unorganized isolated radio believers (see Table 2) exist across the nation even though radio sets are relatively few in number.
NEW-RELIGIONISTS. Chondogyo (Religion of the Heavenly Way), begun in 1860, had 2 million followers in North Korea in 1945. In 1948, 10,000 of its leaders and members were arrested. In 1995 its members were believed to be still as numerous and active as in 1945, though the leadership is underground.
NONRELIGIOUS. Agnostics, secularists, indifferent to religion, including most communists.
PROFESSING CHRISTIANS. Since 1950, there have been no professing Christians, because so far as the state is concerned Christianity has been eradicated and completely destroyed. Our survey projects that by 2025 this situation will have changed and 500,000 will be professing Christians.
SHAMANISTS (ethnoreligionists). Unorganized remnants of earlier folk religion blending animism, spirit-worship and folk-healing.

Great Commission Instrument Panel: status of North Korea (for explanation see start of Part 4)

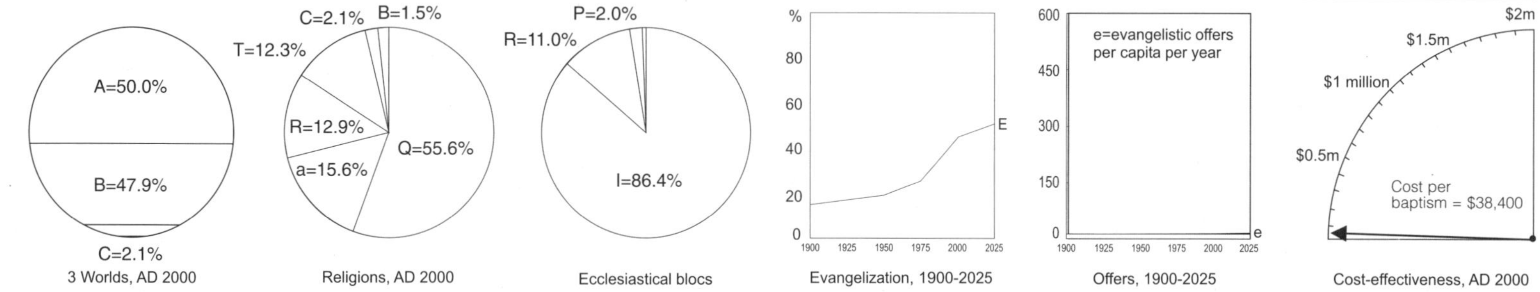

Country status. North Korea occupies the northern part of the Korean Peninsula. Ruled for the past 40 years by Kim Il-Sung, and then his son, it is one of the last relics of Stalinism in the world. The marked isolation of the country under Kim Il-Sung and the ideological constraints of Communism have led North Korean society to develop in a radically different fashion relative to South Korea. Its chief export is iron ore.

HUMAN LIFE AND LIBERTY

Human need and development. Although Marxism is an egalitarian and materialistic ideology, in practice it works against both equality and material prosperity. The result in North Korea has been a society that is more and more grotesquely nonegalitarian and an economy that is stunted. The government is responsible for maintaining standards of living and for providing food, clothing, housing and health care at no cost or low cost. No one pays income tax, direct taxation having been abolished in 1974. Traditionally Koreans place considerable value on houses with tiled roofs, silk clothing, and white rice unmixed with other grain. Kim Il-Sung promised all 3 in the 1960s and made much progress in keeping that promise. But there it rested. Because of the low wages, very few North Koreans are able to afford anything else in life. Consumer goods, when they are available, are generally of poor quality. The national ideology of chuch'e (self-reliance) discourages conspicuous consumption of luxuries and mandates involuntary austerity. Most workers live in drab apartments, but party chieftains live in luxurious structures with small gardens, central heating, and plumbing. Food is rationed under a system in which rice and other essentials are available at very low cost, and additional purchases at 8 to 10 times that cost. Producers have no right to sell their crops or produce directly but have to deliver everything they produce to the state stores. Medical facilities combine modern or Western medicine with the traditional tonguihak, or Chinese medicine. There is a national medical insurance system under the Ministry of Public Health which also controls the nationalized hospitals. The North Korean economy on the whole has contracted significantly after the loss of subsidies from the former Soviet Union. About one-fourth of GNP is devoted to the military, leaving little to development.

Human rights and freedoms. North Korea has a repressive system of government. As the country does not have diplomatic representation with any Western nation, and since journalists are denied entry, it is difficult to assess actual human rights conditions. The Penal Code is notorious as one of the most draconian in the world. It is believed that there are over 150,000 political prisoners in maximum security camps, or gulags, in remote areas, although the government calls them 're-education centers'. The Communist Party exercises pervasive control over the criminal justice system and the judiciary, ordering judges to impose certain types of punishment in each case. Defense attorneys are not representatives of the accused but of the court, and they are expected to help the accused confess their crimes. Political crimes are subject to deterrent punishment. The press is tightly controlled. Radios and television sets are built to receive only government programming. There is considerable discrimination against disabled people who are reportedly not allowed to live within the city limits of Pyongyang.

Human environment. Little information is available on the environment except that industrial pollution is severe in Pyongyang because of the absence of environmental controls

NON-CHRISTIAN RELIGIONS

Shamanism, belief in the existence of good and evil spirits residing in material objects such as rocks and trees, which may be controlled by priests (mudang), combined with Confucianist concepts, is still widespread in the rural north. Propitiatory rites are centered in the exorcism of evil spirits in times of illness and misfortune. Shamanism's individualistic mixture of ancestor veneration and magical practices and its lack of central organization are assets for survival in an antireligious state.

Chondogyo, the Religion of the Heavenly Way, began in 1860 and had 2 million followers in North Korea in 1945. Despite the arrest of 10,000 of its members in 1948, it continues underground with somewhat the same numerical strength in 1995 as 50 years previously.

Buddhism continues to exist among a small minority of the population in spite of the suppression of Buddhist temples and monasteries.

CHRISTIANITY

The earliest Catholic contacts with North Korea were through China at the end of the 18th century. In 1831, a vicariate was erected, and the following year the first Protestant missionary made a short visit to Korea. Religious freedom became a reality after the signing of the Korean treaty with the USA in 1882, and within 3 years, Presbyterian and Methodist missionaries were at work. Catholics also took up their duties with renewed vigour, having suffered severely from persecution and martyrdom for most of a century.

Tracts and literature are sent by balloon across skies of North Korea and China by Christian Mission to the Communist World (Christ to Far East's Millions), based in Seoul. Each balloon scatters 250,000 small paper tracts. In return, the regime sends Communist propaganda material to the South in covers disguised as gospels.

PROTESTANT CHURCHES. Prior to 1945, the Christian population of Korea was second in size in Asia only to that of the Philippines. The Presbyterian Church was the largest denomination, followed by the Methodists, with smaller numbers of adherents belonging to the Salvation Army, Holiness Church, and Seventh-day Adventists. The strongest sections of the Presbyterian church were found in North and South Pyongan provinces, an area which forms part of present-day North Korea. Reports during the 1930s listed entire rural villages as having become Christian, with 50% of the whole population of Sonchon and 10% of Pyongyang cities worshipping in Presbyterian churches on Sundays.

After the coming of the Communist regime to power following World War II, many Christians fled south; those who remained suffered severe persecution in the government's antireligion campaign. Towards the end of the Korean war in 1953, migrations southward increased again and rose to massive proportions. In 1990, Seventh-day Adventists estimated that there were 20 SDA congregations and churches in North Korea. Although no other organized churches can be identified today, many crypto-Christians are known to exist.

CATHOLIC CHURCH. In 1945, North Korea had 2 dioceses, suffragans of Seoul: Ham Heung and Pyongyang, founded respectively in 1920 and 1927. In addition, Korean Catholics in southeastern Manchuria (China) were served by the Chinese diocese of Yenki (founded 1937) and the abbey nullius of Deok Weon established at Tokwon, North Korea, in 1940. All of these have been suppressed, and their administrators and priests now reside in South Korea or abroad. Half the Catholic population fled south after World War II, leaving only 25,000 adherents in 1950; and of these, a large proportion subsequently fled as well.

The Holy See has no diplomatic relations with North Korea in AD 2000.

Renewal movements. In the 1990s the Pentecostal/Charismatic Renewal continued to spread across most older churches, and numbered over 450,000 adherents (of whom none were Pentecostals, 1% Charismatics, and 99% Independents).

Indigenous missions. In the early history of Christianity North Korean Christians were active in evangelism in the region but since 1948 have been totally isolated.

CHURCH AND STATE

Less is known about Christianity in North Korea than in any other Communist country. Christianity was subject to considerable persecution during the

Country summary. **Worlds A, B, C by ethnolinguistic peoples, cities, and major civil divisions in North Korea.**																					
	PEOPLES							*CITIES*							*CIVIL DIVISIONS*						
World	*Num*	*Pop 2000*	*C%*	*Christians*	*E%*	*U%*	*Unevangelized*	*Num*	*Pop 2000*	*C%*	*Christians*	*E%*	*U%*	*Unevangelized*	*Num*	*Pop 2000*	*C%*	*Christians*	*E%*	*U%*	*Unevangelized*
A	3	223,564	1.15	2,576	37	63	139,928	11	4,236,521	0.98	41,641	49	51	2,166,008	5	7,298,989	1.36	99,278	42	58	4,220,409
B	2	23,814,907	2.09	497,029	50	50	11,886,386	1	2,726,000	3.50	95,410	55	45	1,216,069	8	16,740,204	2.40	400,934	53	47	7,805,906
C	2	721	84.33	608	100	0	2	0	0	0.00	0	0	0	0	0	0	0.00	0	0	0	0
Total	**7**	**24,039,192**	**2.08**	**500,213**	**50**	**50**	**12,026,316**	**12**	**6,962,521**	**1.97**	**137,051**	**51**	**49**	**3,382,077**	**13**	**24,039,193**	**2.08**	**500,212**	**50**	**50**	**12,026,315**

Japanese occupation (1910-45), especially so during the 1930s with the increase of Japanese pressure to adopt Shinto as the national religion. During the short period between the fall of Japan and the introduction of the Communist regime, Presbyterians formed a temporary northern General Assembly. They also launched a country-wide Freedom Memorial Evangelistic Campaign and reopened the Presbyterian theological seminary in Pyongyang which in 1947 had 164 students. Communist suppression of religion took place in several stages. In 1946, Christian organizations seeking political freedom were suppressed, and their leaders were imprisoned or disappeared. A Christian League was organized by the government to foster church support for the new regime, and in 1950, the Methodist and Presbyterian seminaries were combined into one 'Christian seminary'. When the League was consistently boycotted by the Christian population, a systematic attempt to exterminate Christianity was initiated. Church buildings were confiscated and leaders imprisoned. As the Korean war progressed, retreating Communist soldiers massacred many Christians to prevent their liberation. When United Nations forces temporarily gained control of North Korea and the Communist capital fell, many Christians were observed attending church. However, when these forces later withdrew and over 2 million fled south, a virtually complete blackout on the fate of remaining Christians descended which has continued to the present day.

BROADCASTING AND MEDIA

Korean-language programs are can be received from FEBC's radio stations in South Korea, as well as from KNLS, TWR (Guam), AWR (Guam), FEBC, (Philippines) and Radio Veritas.

FUTURE TRENDS AND PROSPECTS

Increased contact with Christian South Korea could result in massive church growth in the 21st century. Christians are expected to increase from 2.0% in 1990 to 4.9% by 2025.

If North Korea opens to South Korea in the early part of the 21st century, Christianity could grow rapidly to 30-40% before AD 2050. If the North remains closed, then Christians will remain few, perhaps growing to 5% before AD 2050. The nonreligious will remain dominant in this second scenario.

BIBLIOGRAPHY

A history of the church in Korea. A. D. Clark. Seoul: Christian Literature Society of Korea, 1971.

Ancestor worship and Christianity in Korea. J. Y. Lee (ed). New York: E. Mellen Press, 1988. 94p.

Caring, growing, changing: a history of the Protestant mission in Korea. M. Huntley. New York: Friendship Press, 1984. 212p.

Catholic Korea, yesterday and now. J. C. Kim & J. J. Chung. Seoul: Catholic Korean Publishing Co., 1964.

Cheonjugyo Pyeongyang kyogusa. Kyeongbuk Chilgok-kun: Pundo Chulpansa, 1981. 565p.

Earth without heaven: how religion was extinguished in North Korea. J. Kong. [3d] ed. Seoul: Korea Religions Research Institute, [1983]. 54p.

Fire beneath the frost: the struggles of the Korean people and the church. P. Billings et al. New York: Friendship Press, 1984.

Haebang hu Pukhan kyohoesa: yeongu, cheungeon, charyo. Chopan ed. Seoul: Tasan Keulpang, 1992. 540p.

Haneul eomneun ttang: Pukhan eui chonggyo malsal kwa wijang cheongchaek. C. Kong. [Chaepan] ed. Seoul: Kwangmyeong Chulpansa, 1983. 108p.

Kim Hyeon–seok changno chongi. K. Kim. Seoul Teukpyeolsi: Maengmillan, 1982. 409p.

Perspectives on Christianity in Korea and Japan: the Gospel and culture in East Asia. M. Mullins & R. F. Young (eds). Lewiston, NY: E. Mellen Press, 1995. 253p.

Pukhan eui chonggyo cheongchaek. T. Ko. Chopan ed. *Chonggyo sahoe chongseo*, 1. Seoul: Minjok Munhwasa, 1988. 298p.

Pukkoe neun mueoseul norigo inna: chonggyo mit nocho chimtu. [Seoul]: Chayu Pyeongnonsa, 1978. 128p.

Religion in the Pacific Era. F. K. Flinn & T. Hendricks (eds). *Studies in the Pacific Era series.* New York: Paragon House, 1985. 242p. (See chapters 5, 6, and 8).

Seo Majeon–dong Yesu kkun: Paek In–suk Cheondosa saengae. S. Cheong. Chopan ed. Seoul: Hyeseon Chulpansa, 1984. 220p.

The history of Protestant missions in Korea, 1832–1910. I. G. Park. Seoul: Yonsei University Press, 1970.

The iconography of Korean Buddhist painting. No. 9 of section 12, *East and Central Asia*, of *Iconography of religions.* H. H. Sorensen. Leiden: Brill, 1988. 21p.

The Zen monastic experience: Buddhist practice in contemporary Korea. R. E. Buswell Jr. Princeton, NJ: Princeton University Press, 1994. 280p.

Tongil kwa Pukhan seongyo cheollyak. P. An. *Seongseojeok tongillon*, 2. Seoul: Pedeuro Seoweon, 1991. 319p.

Country Table 2. **Organized churches and denominations in North Korea.**

Official name (bold type = church with over 10% of all affiliated) 1	*Begun* 2	*Type* 3	*Counc* 4	*Congs* 5	*Adults* 6	*Affiliated 1970* 7	*Affiliated 1995* 8	*G%* 9	*Names, notes, and other statistics* (see Codebook, Part 3) 10
Catholic Church in Korea	1777	R-Lat	P....	1	35,000	15,000	50,000	4.93	Formerly M=MM(USA). 1950, 25,000 Catholics remain in 3 jurisdictions; suppressed.
Church of the New Jerusalem	1933	m-Swe	x....	20	1,000	1,000	2,000	2.81	Before 1950, 40 congregations in the North. Suppressed, underground.
House Church movement	c1970	I-3hK	.....	20,000	170,000	–	300,000	65.61	Underground churches, cells, house churches. M=Cornerstone (USA).
Isolated radio churches		I-3rK	.....	550	69,000	8,000	80,000	0.05	Isolated radio believers (students, youths). FEBC is heard 2.5 hours per day.
Korean Christian Federation	1970	I-3hK	C	2	9,600	–	12,000	45.60	Officially recognized grouping.
Methodist Church	1888	P-Met	.....	50	500	5,000	1,000	-6.23	Slow growth in 1930s. Suppressed from 1945 onwards, but underground activity.
Presbyterian Church of Korea	1887	P-Ref	.....	40	2,000	108,000	5,000	-11.57	Mass influx 1907-10. In 1940, 85,115 communicants in North. Suppressed after 1945.
Seventh-day Adventist Church	1934	P-Adv	x....	20	400	3,000	1,000	-4.30	*North Korean Mission*, Korean Union Mission. 2,265 enrolled in sabbath schools.
Other Protestant denominations		P-	.....	25	1,500	2,000	3,000	0.05	Remnants of other bodies strong before 1945: Holiness Ch (OMS), et alia.
Totals				**20,708**	**289,000**	**142,000**	**454,000**		

Churches, members, growth, 1900-2025	*Congs*	*Adults*	*Affiliated*	*G%*	*Total denominations*	*6 Megablocs:* *O*	*R*	*A*	*P*	*I*	*m*
Total churches, members, and denominations (mid-1900)	10	5,800	13,900	3.38	3	0	1	0	2	0	0
Total churches, members, and denominations (mid-1970)	432	59,100	142,000	3.38	10	0	1	0	7	1	1
Total churches, members, and denominations (mid-1990)	15,000	263,000	413,000	5.48	18	0	1	0	13	3	1
Total churches, members, and denominations (mid-1995)	20,708	289,000	454,000	1.91	18	0	1	0	13	3	1
Total churches, members, and denominations (mid-2000)	20,900	318,000	500,213	1.96	18	0	1	0	13	3	1
Total churches, members, and denominations (mid-2025)	50,000	898,000	1,410,000	4.23	53	1	1	1	20	26	4

NOTES ON TABLE ABOVE
NATIONAL COUNCILS (Column 4, 5th letter).
C = Korean Christian Federation (KCF, 1980).

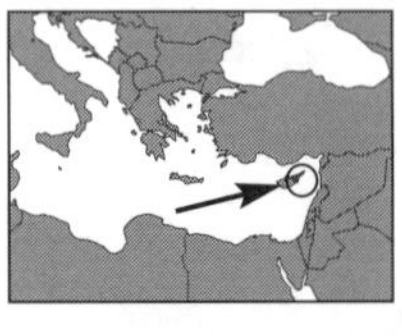

NORTHERN CYPRUS

SECULAR DATA, AD 2000

STATE

Official name: Kuzey Kibris Türk Cumhuriyeti (The Turkish Republic of Northern Cyprus.
Short name: Northern Cyprus. **Adjective of nationality:** Northern Cypriot.
Flag: White with a red crescent and star in the center, lined by two red horizontal stripes, on top and at the bottom.
Area: 3,335 sq. km. (1,288 sq. mi.).
Government: Republic, since 1974 (1925 British crown colony, 1960 Independence).
Legislature: Legislative Assembly, 50 members.
Official language: Turkish.
Monetary unit: 1 Cyprus pound = 100 cents. **US$1=** ª1.20.
Chief cities: LEFKOSE (Levkosia-2, Nicosia-2) 42,085.
Political divisions: 1 province.
Armed forces: 500.

DEMOGRAPHY

Population: 185,000.
Population density: 55.4/sq. km. (143.6/sq. mi.).
Under 15 years: 43,000.
Growth rate p.a.: 0.79% (births 13.64, deaths 7.58).
Mortality: Infant, per 1,000: 8.1, ; **Maternal per 100,000:** 40.0.
Life expectancy: 78 (male 76, female 81).
Household size: 3.0. **Floor area per person, sq.m:** 18.0.
Major languages: Turkish, Greek.
Urban dwellers: 56.77%. **Urban growth rate p.a.:** 1.00%.
Labor force: 40%.

ETHNOLINGUISTIC PEOPLES

89.5% Turkish Cypriot; 8.0% Greek Cypriot; 0.5% Yoruk.

ECONOMY

National income p.a. per person: US$12,402; **per family:** US$37,207.

EDUCATION

Adult literacy: 85% (male 87%, female 83%). **Schools:** 80.
Universities: 2. **School enrolment:** female/male: 90%/90%.

HEALTH

Access to health services: 70%. **Access to safe water:** 100%.
Hospitals: 25 (15 beds per 10,000). **Doctors:** 250.
Blind: 150. **Deaf:** 11,100. **Murder rate:** 20. **Lepers:** 500.

LITERATURE

New book titles p.a.: 19 (100 p.a. per million). **Periodicals:** 0.
Newspapers: 0 dailies.

COMMUNICATION (per 1,000 people)

Phones: 350 (25% mobile). **Radios:** 220. **TV sets:** 100.
Daily newspaper circulation: 90. **Computers:** 50.

HUMAN LIFE AND LIBERTY (optimum condition=100.0%)

HDI: 88.2. **HSI:** 45.0. **HFI:** 25.0. **EFL:** 15.0.

Country Table 1. **Religious adherents in Northern Cyprus, AD 1900-2025.**

Year / Name	1900 Adherents	1900 %	1970 Adherents	1970 %	mid-1990 Adherents	mid-1990 %	Annual change, 1990-2000 Natural	Conversion	Total	Rate	mid-1995 Adherents	mid-1995 %	mid-2000 Adherents	mid-2000 %	mid-2025 Adherents	mid-2025 %
Muslims	51,050	99.8	132,790	92.5	155,270	90.3	1,179	-56	1,123	0.70	162,190	90.1	166,496	90.0	188,900	89.1
Christians	**150**	**0.3**	**10,210**	**7.1**	**15,000**	**8.7**	**113**	**27**	**140**	**0.90**	**15,860**	**8.8**	**16,402**	**8.9**	**19,500**	**9.2**
PROFESSION																
crypto-Christians	0	0.0	0	0.0	2,360	1.4	18	36	54	2.08	2,600	1.4	2,900	1.6	5,000	2.4
professing Christians	**150**	**0.3**	**10,210**	**7.1**	**12,640**	**7.4**	**96**	**-10**	**86**	**0.66**	**13,260**	**7.4**	**13,502**	**7.3**	**14,500**	**6.8**
AFFILIATION																
unaffiliated Christians	0	0.0	0	0.0	300	0.2	2	-2	0	-0.13	300	0.2	296	0.2	500	0.2
affiliated Christians	**150**	**0.3**	**10,210**	**7.1**	**14,700**	**8.6**	**111**	**30**	**141**	**0.92**	**15,560**	**8.6**	**16,106**	**8.7**	**19,000**	**9.0**
Orthodox	150	0.3	10,000	7.0	12,850	7.5	97	5	102	0.77	13,500	7.5	13,870	7.5	15,000	7.1
Independents	0	0.0	210	0.2	1,850	1.1	14	25	39	1.91	2,060	1.1	2,236	1.2	4,000	1.9
Trans-megabloc groupings																
Evangelicals	0	0.0	20	0.0	180	0.1	1	3	4	2.03	200	0.1	220	0.1	350	0.2
Pentecostals/Charismatics	0	0.0	210	0.2	1,720	1.0	13	33	46	2.40	2,060	1.1	2,180	1.2	2,700	1.3
Great Commission Christians	**150**	**0.3**	**2,750**	**1.9**	**3,970**	**2.3**	**30**	**21**	**51**	**1.21**	**4,200**	**2.3**	**4,479**	**2.4**	**5,600**	**2.6**
Nonreligious	0	0.0	1,000	0.7	1,730	1.0	13	29	42	2.18	1,950	1.1	2,147	1.2	3,600	1.7
World A (unevangelized persons)	48,950	95.7	114,727	79.9	84,968	49.4	647	-1,010	-363	-0.44	84,060	46.7	81,400	44.0	76,532	36.1
World B (evangelized non-Christians)	2,049	4.0	18,651	13.0	72,032	41.9	545	983	1,528	1.93	80,080	44.5	87,198	47.1	115,968	54.7
World C (Christians)	150	0.3	10,210	7.1	15,000	8.7	113	27	140	0.90	15,860	8.8	16,402	8.9	19,500	9.2
Country's population	**51,150**	**100.0**	**143,589**	**100.0**	**172,000**	**100.0**	**1,305**	**0**	**1,305**	**0.73**	**180,000**	**100.0**	**185,000**	**100.0**	**212,000**	**100.0**

COLUMNS, ROWS.
For meanings and definitions, see Codebook (Part 3). Note that, by definition, total 'Christians' = professing + crypto-Christians, which also = affiliated + unaffiliated Christians, and also = Great Commission Christians + latent Christians. Percentages may not always total exactly, due to rounding.

NOTES ON RELIGION
MUSLIMS. Almost all Hanafi Sunnis, with a very few Shias.
ORTHODOX. Mainly Greek merchants and their families.

Great Commission Instrument Panel: status of Northern Cyprus (for explanation see start of Part 4)

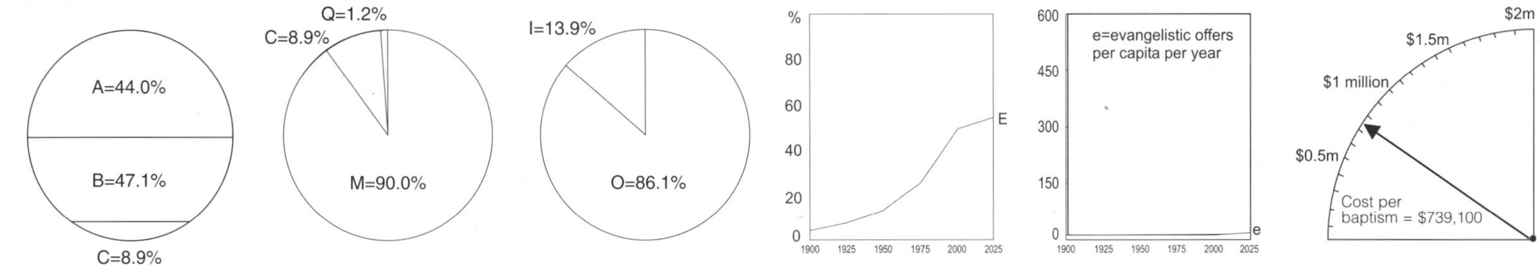

3 Worlds, AD 2000 | Religions, AD 2000 | Ecclesiastical blocs | Evangelization, 1900-2025 | Offers, 1900-2025 | Cost-effectiveness, AD 2000

Country status. Northern Cyprus is the northern 37% of the island of Cyprus in the Mediterranean Sea south of Turkey. Its principal exports are fruits and clothing.

HUMAN LIFE AND LIBERTY

Human rights and freedoms. The Republic of Northern Cyprus is a puppet state created by Turkey after the Turkish invasion of the island in 1974. The illegal state has not been recognized by any government other than Turkey. The republic has the distinction of being one of the most heinous violators of human rights in the world, committing all kinds of atrocities against the Greek Cypriots, including confiscation of property, rape, murder, pillage and plunder of artistic treasures, destruction of churches, arrest and detention without cause and torture. The republic is run arbitrarily by Turks who also have looted the public treasury. Because no other nation in the world trades with this state, its economy is in ruins. The UN has been present since 1964 as a peace keeping presence. Christian presence has nearly disappeared.

Human environment. The Mesaoria is a broad plain that runs east to west on the island and opens to the sea at either end. This was once rich with forests whose timber was the prize of ancient conquerors for sailing vessels. Centuries-long deforestation has damaged the islands drainage system and its year round water supply access. In the summer all of the island's rivers are dry. Dams and waterways are being constructed to bring water to farming areas.

NON-CHRISTIAN RELIGIONS

Islam is dominant. Virtually the entire Turkish population is Islamic, consisting of nearly 90% of the population of TRNC. Most of its adherents are Sunnis of the Hanafi sect. The few Shias belong for the most part to dervish orders, mainly the Ticani, Mevlevi, and Bektasi. The office of the Evkaf serves the religious needs of the Muslims of the republic. Muslim influence was birthed from the Ottoman Empire reign of the island from 1571-1878.

Oratory in Buyuk Han, Nicosia.

CHRISTIANITY

ORTHODOX CHURCH. The apostles Paul and Barnabas visited Salamis, Barnabas' birthplace, in AD 46, and Barnabas later became the first bishop of Cyprus. In 441 the third ecumenical council of Ephesus discussed the separation of the Church of Cyprus from the Church of Antioch, and during the reign of the eastern emperor Zeno (474-491) the Cypriot church received autocephalous status along with the patriarchates of Antioch, Jerusalem, Alexandria, and Constantinople. From the 8th to the 10th centuries, Cyprus was subjected to a series of Arab raids, after which a considerable number of monasteries were built. In 1054, the schism between the Eastern and Western churches became a reality. At the invitation of the Latin king Gui de Lusignan, the initial immigration of Maronites from Lebanon to Cyprus occurred during the Crusades at the end of the 12th century. Their number ultimately reached 80,000 divided into 60 villages. The Maronite archdiocese of Cyprus was founded in 1352. From the 12th to the 15th centuries Cyprus was ruled by followers of the Latin rite, the Franks and then the Genoese, who placed a Latin hierarchy over both the Latin and Orthodox churches. When Venice gained control of Cyprus in 1489, it relaxed many of the former restrictions on the Eastern church, but antagonism between the 2 churches continued. Many Gothic churches and cathedrals were built during this period of domination by the Latin church. When the Turks invaded the island in 1572, they restored the Orthodox church to its former position in recognition of its help in the war against Venice. The Latin church was banished. The Maronites were also persecuted because of their alliances with the Lusignan dynasty and later the Venetians. Some returned to Lebanon, including the Maronite bishop, while other converted to the Orthodox church or Islam. Only a small minority of Maronites remained in Cyprus. Franciscans, who had first come to Cyprus in 1226 during the lifetime of Francis of Assisi, were later given permission to re-establish the Latin rite at Nicosia and Larnaca. Through the Muslim policy of using the religious leader of a conquered people as their political leader, the archbishop (ethnarch) of the Orthodox church increased in power, being given responsibility for collecting taxes and maintaining law and order. By the beginning of the 19th century both Greeks and Turks were restive under this growing domination, and in 1821 following the Greek war of independence the ethnarch and several of his closest collaborators were executed. In 1878 Cyprus came under British influence, formal annexation following in 1914. Agitation for union with Greece (enosis) gradually increased among the Greeks under British rule, with church leaders playing an active part; and in 1956 the ethnarch, archbishop Makarios, was banished from the island. He was later allowed to return and was elected president in 1959. Formal independence was declared in August 1960.

OTHER CHURCHES. Four Christian groups are present in the TRNC serving the community. They are the Anglican church of St Andrew in Kyrenia, the Roman Catholic Church also in Kyrenia, the Maronite Church of Ayios Georgios in Korucam, and the Greek Orthodox Church at Dipkarpaz

The Holy See has no diplomatic relations with Northern Cyprus in AD 2000.

Indigenous missions. Though today predominately Muslim, Northern Cyprus has a long and significant history of missionary sending. Missionaries were sent out from Northern Cyprus for many centuries, interrupted by the Turkish invasion in 1572. Though the Orthodox church sent some missionaries after this time, relatively few have been sent out in the 20th century, virtually stopping completely with declared independence in 1974.

CHURCH AND STATE

Article 23 of the Constitution of the Turkish Republic of Northern Cyprus states in section one that all have the freedom of conscience, religious faith, and opinion. This guarantees everyone in TRNC the right of religious freedom without interference from the State. Section 4 states that religious education and teaching is to be carried out by the supervision and control of the State. Islam is the recognized religion of the TRNC and Turkish Cypriots have joined the Islamic Conference Organization. While freedom of religion is stated, no open Christian activity is permitted.

Country summary. **Worlds A, B, C by ethnolinguistic peoples, cities, and major civil divisions in Northern Cyprus.**

	PEOPLES							CITIES							CIVIL DIVISIONS						
World	Num	Pop 2000	C%	Christians	E%	U%	Unevangelized	Num	Pop 2000	C%	Christians	E%	U%	Unevangelized	Num	Pop 2000	C%	Christians	E%	U%	Unevangelized
A	1	925	0.00	0	45	55	509	0	0	0.00	0	0	0	0	0	0	0.00	0	0	0	0
B	2	169,316	1.82	3,079	52	48	80,848	1	42,085	11.00	4,629	58	42	17,541	1	185,045	8.70	16,106	56	44	81,374
C	1	14,804	88.00	13,028	100	0	18	0	0	0.00	0	0	0	0	0	0	0.00	0	0	0	0
Total	**4**	**185,045**	**8.70**	**16,107**	**56**	**44**	**81,375**	**1**	**42,085**	**11.00**	**4,629**	**58**	**42**	**17,541**	**1**	**185,045**	**8.70**	**16,106**	**56**	**44**	**81,374**

BROADCASTING AND MEDIA

Turkish Cypriot media is free and the publishing and airing of any views and ideas is permitted without restriction. Christian radio is broadcast over Greek Cyprus radio and TV station BRT has daily broadcast in Greek, English, and Turkish. News, music, current affairs, movies, and docu-dramas make up the program content.

FUTURE TRENDS AND PROSPECTS

Christianity is expected to grow slowly but remain below 10% of the population through AD 2025. Christianity is not expected to grow beyond 15% of the population in the foreseeable future. Islam will likely dominate throughout the 21st century.

BIBLIOGRAPHY

Cyprus: a country study. E. Solsten (ed). *Area handbook series, U.S. Army*. Washington, DC: Federal Research Division, Library of Congress, 1993. 336p. (See section on Northern Cyprus, p.82–103; p.93–9 deal with religion).

Excerpta Cypria for today: a source book in the Cyprus problem. A. Faulds MP (ed). London: K. Rusten and Brother, 1988. 224p.

Greek–Turkish relations and U.S. foreign policy. T. Bahcheli et al. *Peaceworks*, 17. Washington, D.C.: U.S. Institute of Peace, 1997. 53p.

Negotiating for survival: the Turkish Cypriot quest for a solution to the Cyprus problem. P. Oberling. : Princeton, NJ, Aldington Press. 64p.

The road to Bellapais: the Turkish Cypriot exodus to northern Cyprus. P. Oberling. *Atlantic studies*, no. 25. Boulder, CO and New York: Social Science Monographs, Columbia University Press, 1982. 268p.

Country Table 2. **Organized churches and denominations in Northern Cyprus.**

Official name (bold type = church with over 10% of all affiliated) 1	Begun 2	Type 3	Counc 4	Congs 5	Adults 6	Affiliated 1970 7	Affiliated 1995 8	G% 9	Names, notes, and other statistics (see Codebook, Part 3) 10
Greek Orthodox Church	46	O-Gre	C....	6	9,000	10,000	13,500	0.05	2 Dioceses: Kyrenia, Morphou. Residual Greeks, especially merchants, subject to Turkish law.
Independent home meetings	c1965	I-3hZ	.....	2	40	10	60	7.43	Turkish Cypriot converts, some expatriates.
Isolated radio churches	c1960	I-3rW	.....	100	1,300	200	2,000	9.65	Turkish Cypriots.
Totals				**108**	**10,340**	**10,210**	**15,560**		

Churches, members, growth, 1900-2025	Congs	Adults	Affiliated	G%	Total denominations	6 Megablocs: O	R	A	P	I	m
Total churches, members, and denominations (mid-1900)	2	90	150	6.21	1	1	0	0	0	0	0
Total churches, members, and denominations (mid-1970)	16	6,106	10,210	6.21	3	1	0	0	0	2	0
Total churches, members, and denominations (mid-1990)	100	9,800	14,700	1.84	3	1	0	0	0	2	0
Total churches, members, and denominations (mid-1995)	108	10,340	15,560	1.14	3	1	0	0	0	2	0
Total churches, members, and denominations (mid-2000)	120	10,700	16,106	0.69	3	1	0	0	0	2	0
Total churches, members, and denominations (mid-2025)	140	12,600	19,000	0.66	11	1	0	0	0	10	0

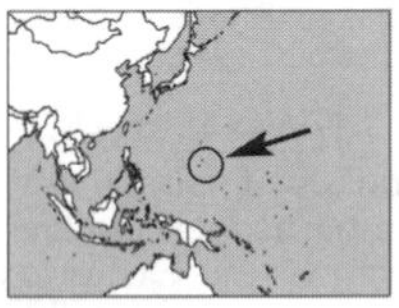

NORTHERN MARIANA ISLANDS

SECULAR DATA, AD 2000

STATE
Official name: The Commonwealth of the Northern Mariana Islands.
Short name: Northern Mariana Islands. **Adjective of nationality:** Northern Mariana Islanders.
Flag: Blue field with coat of arms and white star in center.
Area: 477 sq. km. (184 sq. mi.).
Government: Unitary multiparty republic with two legislative houses, since 1978 (1889 German protectorate, 1947 UN Trust Territory).
Legislature: Senate, 9 members; House of Representatives, 15 members.
Official language: English.
Monetary unit: 1 dollar (U.S.$) = 100 cents. **US$1=** 1.00.
Chief cities: SUSUPE (Saipan) 12,443.
Political divisions: 1 province.

DEMOGRAPHY
Population: 78,000.
Population density: 164.2/sq. km. (425.8/sq. mi.).
Under 15 years: 26,000.
Growth rate p.a.: 1.60% (births 20.74, deaths 4.71).
Mortality: Infant, per 1,000: 9.3, ; **Maternal per 100,000:** 20.0.
Life expectancy: 76 (male 73, female 78).
Household size: 4.6. **Floor area per person, sq.m:** 15.0.
Major languages: Chamorro, Filipino, Mandarin Chinese.
Urban dwellers: 54.77%. **Urban growth rate p.a.:** 2.43%.
Labor force: 35%.

ETHNOLINGUISTIC PEOPLES
33.6% Filipino; 29.0% Chamorro; 9.0% Han Chinese; 8.1% Korean; 5.4% Carolinian.

ECONOMY
National income p.a. per person: US$10,503; **per family:** US$48,315.

EDUCATION
Adult literacy: 96% (male 96%, female 95%). **Schools:** 27.
Universities: 1. **School enrolment:** female/male: 90%/90%.

HEALTH
Access to health services: 75%. **Access to safe water:** 70%.
Hospitals: 1 (19 beds per 10,000). **Doctors:** 23.
Blind: 40. **Deaf:** 3,200. **Murder rate:** 3. **Lepers:** 100.

LITERATURE
New book titles p.a.: 16 (200 p.a. per million). **Periodicals:** 0.
Newspapers:0 dailies.

COMMUNICATION (per 1,000 people)
Phones: 100 (20% mobile). **Radios:** 190. **TV sets:** 82.
Daily newspaper circulation: 20. **Computers:** 10.

HUMAN LIFE AND LIBERTY (optimum condition=100.0%)
HDI: 83.6. **HSI:** 55.0. **HFI:** 70.0. **EFL:** 40.0.

Country Table 1. **Religious adherents in the Northern Mariana Islands, AD 1900-2025.**

Year	1900		1970		mid-1990		Annual change, 1990-2000				mid-1995		mid-2000		mid-2025	
Name	Adherents	%	Adherents	%	Adherents	%	Natural	Conversion	Total	Rate	Adherents	%	Adherents	%	Adherents	%
Christians	**2,400**	**60.0**	**12,440**	**98.3**	**38,640**	**89.2**	**3,127**	**-28**	**3,099**	**6.07**	**52,400**	**89.1**	**69,631**	**88.9**	**213,000**	**86.9**
PROFESSION																
professing Christians	**2,400**	**60.0**	**12,440**	**98.3**	**38,640**	**89.2**	**3,127**	**-28**	**3,099**	**6.07**	**52,400**	**89.1**	**69,631**	**88.9**	**213,000**	**86.9**
AFFILIATION																
unaffiliated Christians	0	0.0	40	0.3	200	0.5	16	1	17	6.37	320	0.5	371	0.5	1,000	0.4
affiliated Christians	**2,400**	**60.0**	**12,400**	**97.9**	**38,440**	**88.8**	**3,111**	**-29**	**3,082**	**6.06**	**52,080**	**88.5**	**69,260**	**88.5**	**212,000**	**86.5**
Roman Catholics	2,000	50.0	11,080	87.5	38,280	88.4	3,100	-2	3,102	6.11	52,000	88.4	69,300	88.6	213,100	87.0
Independents	0	0.0	0	0.0	3,100	7.2	252	104	356	7.95	4,675	7.9	6,660	8.5	24,500	10.0
Protestants	400	10.0	1,320	10.4	4,100	9.5	334	-94	240	4.72	5,270	9.0	6,500	8.3	14,700	6.0
Marginal Christians	0	0.0	0	0.0	1,000	2.3	81	6	87	6.46	1,400	2.4	1,870	2.4	6,120	2.5
doubly-affiliated	0	0.0	0	0.0	-8,040	-18.7	-654	-49	-703	6.48	-11,265	-19.1	-15,070	-19.3	-46,420	-19.0
Trans-megabloc groupings																
Evangelicals	360	9.0	200	1.6	1,600	3.7	130	39	169	7.48	2,291	3.9	3,290	4.2	13,800	5.6
Pentecostals/Charismatics	0	0.0	200	1.6	4,300	10.0	350	50	400	6.80	6,079	10.3	8,300	10.6	29,400	12.0
Great Commission Christians	**120**	**3.0**	**500**	**4.0**	**3,800**	**8.8**	**309**	**34**	**343**	**6.64**	**5,290**	**9.0**	**7,226**	**9.3**	**25,700**	**10.5**
Buddhists	0	0.0	0	0.0	2,250	5.2	183	4	187	6.23	3,060	5.2	4,118	5.3	13,750	5.6
Chinese folk-religionists	0	0.0	20	0.2	800	1.9	65	-4	61	5.83	1,070	1.8	1,410	1.8	6,100	2.5
Nonreligious	0	0.0	0	0.0	510	1.2	42	19	61	8.14	740	1.3	1,115	1.4	4,800	2.0
New-Religionists	0	0.0	0	0.0	450	1.1	37	6	43	6.96	640	1.1	882	1.1	3,400	1.4
Ethnoreligionists	1,600	40.0	200	1.6	370	0.9	30	-3	27	5.55	490	0.8	635	0.8	1,700	0.7
Baha'is	0	0.0	40	0.3	140	0.3	11	6	17	8.34	210	0.4	312	0.4	1,400	0.6
Confucianists	0	0.0	0	0.0	140	0.3	11	0	11	6.14	190	0.3	254	0.3	850	0.4
World A (unevangelized persons)	800	20.0	75	0.6	602	1.4	49	-25	24	3.37	706	1.2	858	1.1	2,450	1.0
World B (evangelized non-Christians)	800	20.0	147	1.1	4,058	9.4	330	53	383	7.17	5,739	9.7	7,811	10.0	29,550	12.1
World C (Christians)	2,400	60.0	12,440	98.3	38,640	89.2	3,127	-28	3,099	6.07	52,400	89.1	69,631	88.9	213,000	86.9
Country's population	**4,000**	**100.0**	**12,662**	**100.0**	**43,300**	**100.0**	**3,506**	**0**	**3,506**	**6.14**	**58,846**	**100.0**	**78,300**	**100.0**	**245,000**	**100.0**

COLUMNS, ROWS.
For meanings and definitions, see Codebook (Part 3). Note that, by definition, total 'Christians' = professing + crypto-Christians, which also = affiliated + unaffiliated Christians, and also = Great Commission Christians + latent Christians. Percentages may not always total exactly, due to rounding.

NOTES ON RELIGIONS
BUDDHISTS. Mainly Chinese and Japanese.

Great Commission Instrument Panel: status of the Northern Mariana Islands (for explanation see start of Part 4)

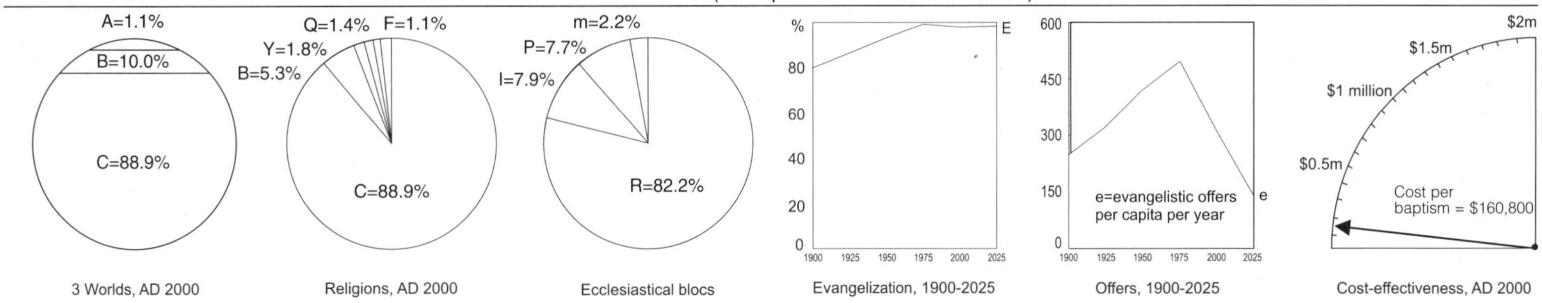

Country summary. **Worlds A, B, C by ethnolinguistic peoples, cities, and major civil divisions in the Northern Mariana Islands.**

	PEOPLES							*CITIES*							*CIVIL DIVISIONS*						
World	*Num*	*Pop 2000*	*C%*	*Christians*	*E%*	*U%*	*Unevangelized*	*Num*	*Pop 2000*	*C%*	*Christians*	*E%*	*U%*	*Unevangelized*	*Num*	*Pop 2000*	*C%*	*Christians*	*E%*	*U%*	*Unevangelized*
A	0	0	0.00	0	0	0	0	0	0	0.00	0	0	0	0	0	0	0.00	0	0	0	0
B	2	9,011	32.39	2,919	91	9	806	0	0	0.00	0	0	0	0	0	0	0.00	0	0	0	0
C	8	69,344	95.67	66,340	100	0	30	1	12,443	85.00	10,577	98	2	231	1	78,356	88.39	69,260	99	1	836
Total	**10**	**78,355**	**88.39**	**69,259**	**99**	**1**	**836**	**1**	**12,443**	**85.00**	**10,577**	**98**	**2**	**231**	**1**	**78,356**	**88.39**	**69,260**	**99**	**1**	**836**

Country status. The Northern Mariana Islands is a self-governing territory of mountainous islands in the northwest Pacific Ocean. Its chief economic activities are fishing and tourism.

HUMAN LIFE AND LIBERTY

Human rights and freedoms. The inhabitants of the islands were granted US citizenship in 1990 and CNMI's constitution closely follows that of the US with essential human rights copying those of the citizens of the USA. CNMI citizens do not vote in US presidential elections but do elect their own political leaders including a governor, lieutenant governor, and attorney general.

Widespread reports concerning the abuse of factory workers and the abuse of foreign workers have been prevalent. Such abuses occur because of the lax labor and immigration laws which govern the islands. These abuses are often uninvestigated and left unprosecuted.

NON-CHRISTIAN RELIGIONS

Baha'is and followers of Confucianism represent a small portion of the population.

Traditional folk religion beliefs are often intermingled even among those who are considered committed Christians. Spiritism and Animism are also found mixed in with Christianity.

Buddhism. Over one million Japanese tourist visit annually, mainly to worship at Shinto and Buddhist shrines.

CHRISTIANITY

CATHOLIC CHURCH. The Holy See has no diplomatic relations with Northern Mariana Islands in AD 2000, but is represented there by an apostolic delegate for the Pacific Ocean residing in Wellington, New Zealand.

Indigenous missions. Since the introduction of Christianity to the islands in 1668 there have been some missionaries sent to other islands but the number is small.

CHURCH AND STATE

Chamarros migrated here from Malaysia, Philippines, and other south pacific islands first, followed by the Spanish who named the islands the Marianas. Their claim on the islands lasted for hundreds of years. Germany later acquired the Marianas only to lose them to the Japanese in WWI. The Japanese in turn relinquished control to the US during WWII in whose control in remains today. Through all these claims and exchange of forces, the freedom of religion has not been usurped in any way and is now officially recognized by the CNMI Constitution adopted in January of 1978.

BROADCASTING AND MEDIA

FEBC maintains several transmitters which broadcast in 8 languages, including Kazakh, Uzbek, Mongolian, Uighur, and Hui. Some of the programs are produced by IBRA. Shortwave radio programs from KNLS have seen some response.

FUTURE TRENDS AND PROSPECTS

Immigrant Buddhists, Chinese folk-religionists, and new religionists are expected to represent over 10% of the population by 2025.

Christianity will likely remain above 80% well into the 2040s.

BIBLIOGRAPHY

History of the Northern Mariana Islands. D. A. Farrell. Ed., P. Koontz. [Saipan]: Public School System, Commonwealth of the Northern Mariana Islands, 1991. 718p.

Country Table 2. **Organized churches and denominations in the Northern Mariana Islands.**

Official name (bold type = church with over 10% of all affiliated) 1	*Begun* 2	*Type* 3	*Counc* 4	*Congs* 5	*Adults* 6	*Affiliated 1970* 7	*Affiliated 1995* 8	*G%* 9	*Names, notes, and other statistics* (see Codebook, Part 3) 10
Assemblies of God	c1975	P-Pe2	Z....	1	200	–	500	5.00	M=MoG(USA). Classical Pentecostals.
Catholic Church: D Chalan Kanoa	1668	R-Lat	P....	13	19,000	11,080	52,000	6.38	Diocese erected 1984 out of M Agaña. M=SJ. C=1+0+2. (1990) 7n,5x,29m,27w,970Yy.
Chinese Churches	c1975	I-Non	.....	3	200	–	333	5.00	Chinese Nondenominationalists.
Church of Christ	c1980	I-	x....	1	500	–	1,000	6.67	*Iglesia ni Cristo (Manalista).* Filipino migrant laborers.
Ch of Jesus Christ of Latter-day Saints	c1980	m-LdS	.....	1	120	–	200	6.67	*Mormons.* M=CJCLdS(USA).
Chuuk Church	c1980	P-Uni	.....	3	400	200	800	6.67	Protestant Chs of East Truk, West Truk. Nomoneas (East) Association. M=ABCFM(UCBWM).
Filipino Baptist Churches	c1985	I-Bap	.....	2	1,000	–	1,670	10.00	Independent Baptists from Philippines.
General Baptist Church	1947	P-Bap	TF...	1	250	120	500	5.87	M=Gen. Bap. For. Miss. Soc(USA).
Independent Baptist Chs	c1975	I-Bap	.....	4	100	–	222	5.00	2 groups.
International Church	c1975	P-Non	.....	1	120	–	160	5.00	Nondenominationalists.
Jehovah's Witnesses	c1980	m-Jeh	.....	2	400	–	1,200	6.67	*Watch Tower.* 14Y.
Korean Baptist Church	c1985	I-Bap	.....	2	250	–	400	10.00	Korean Independent Baptists.
Korean Methodist Church	c1985	I-Met	.....	1	150	–	200	10.00	Korean Independent Methodists.
Korean Presbyterian Church	c1980	I-Ref	.....	4	500	–	850	6.67	Korean Independent Presbyterians.
Methodist Church	c1985	P-Met	.....	1	15	–	50	10.00	Mainline Methodists.
Palau Evangelical Church	c1980	P-Eva	.....	1	300	–	600	6.67	Immigrants from Palau.
Seventh-day Adventist Church	c1980	P-Adv	.....	2	130	–	260	6.67	M=SDA(USA).
United Church of Christ	c1950	P-Uni	..P..	10	1,000	1,000	2,000	2.81	M=UCBWM(USA).
United Pentecostal Church	c1975	P-Pel	x....	2	100	–	200	5.00	M=UPC(USA). Oneness Pentecostals.
Other Protestant denominations		P-	.....	6	150	–	200	0.05	In 3 recently-arrived denominations.
Doubly-affiliated		2-aff			-4,400	0	-11,265		Evangelicals who are also baptized Roman Catholics.
Totals				**61**	**20,485**	**12,400**	**52,080**		

Churches, members, growth, 1900-2025	*Congs*	*Adults*	*Affiliated*	*G%*	*Total denominations*	*6 Megablocs:* *O*	*R*	*A*	*P*	*I*	*m*
Total churches, members, and denominations (mid-1900)	2	1,500	2,400	2.37	1	0	1	0	0	0	0
Total churches, members, and denominations (mid-1970)	17	7,654	12,400	2.37	4	0	1	0	3	0	0
Total churches, members, and denominations (mid-1990)	50	15,100	38,440	5.82	19	0	1	0	11	5	2
Total churches, members, and denominations (mid-1995)	61	20,485	52,080	6.26	22	0	1	0	12	7	2
Total churches, members, and denominations (mid-2000)	70	27,200	69,260	5.87	23	0	1	0	13	7	2
Total churches, members, and denominations (mid-2025)	200	83,300	212,000	4.58	32	0	1	0	20	7	4

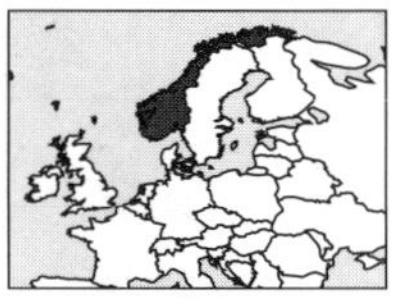

NORWAY

SECULAR DATA, AD 2000

STATE
Official name: Det Kongeriket Norge (The Kingdom of Norway).
Short name: Norway. **Adjective of nationality:** Norwegian.
Flag: Blue Latin cross bordered in white on red field.
Area: 323,878 sq. km. (125,050 sq. mi.).
Government: Constitutional monarchy, since AD 900 (1319 united with Sweden, 1905 Independence from Sweden).
Legislature: Storting, 165 members.
Official language: Norwegian (Norsk).
Monetary unit: 1 Norwegian krone (NKr) = 100 øre. **US$1=** NKr 7.40.
Chief cities: OSLO 761,463; Bergen 252,763; Trondheim 142,784; Stavanger 140,711; Baerum 88,477.
Political divisions: 19 provinces.
Armed forces: 34,000.

DEMOGRAPHY
Population: 4,461,000.
Population density: 13.7/sq. km. (35.6/sq. mi.).
Under 15 years: 876,000.
Growth rate p.a.: 0.45% (births 12.23, deaths 9.97).
Mortality: Infant, per 1,000: 4.9, ; **Maternal per 100,000:** 6.0.
Life expectancy: 79 (male 76, female 82).
Household size: 2.2. **Floor area per person, sq.m:** 38.3.
Major languages: Norwegian (Bokmal (urban) and Nynorsk (rural) dialects), Lapp, Swedish, Finnish, Danish, English, German.
Urban dwellers: 74.18%. **Urban growth rate p.a.:** 0.6%.
Labor force: 49%.

ETHNOLINGUISTIC PEOPLES
69.7% Norwegian (Dano-Norwegian); 24.0% Norwegian (New Norse); 2.4% Vietnamese; 0.5% Swedish (Swede); 0.3% Punjabi.

ECONOMY
National income p.a. per person: US$31,249; **per family:** US$68,749.

EDUCATION
Adult literacy: 100% (male 100%, female 100%). **Schools:** 4,096.
Universities: 195. **School enrolment:** female/male: 107%/109%.

HEALTH
Access to health services: 95%. **Access to safe water:** 100%.
Hospitals: 350 (53 beds per 10,000). **Doctors:** 14,497.
Blind: 4,000. **Deaf:** 264,200. **Murder rate:** 1.
Lepers: 200.

LITERATURE
New book titles p.a.: 7,000 (1,570 p.a. per million). **Periodicals:** 9,814. **Newspapers:** 83 dailies.

COMMUNICATION (per 1,000 people)
Phones: 558 (43% mobile). **Radios:** 767. **TV sets:** 561.
Daily newspaper circulation: 498. **Computers:** 515.

REFUGEES
Alien refugees from other countries: 11,200.

HUMAN LIFE AND LIBERTY (optimum condition=100.0%)
HDI: 94.3. **HSI:** 96.0. **HFI:** 87.5. **EFL:** 51.0.

Country Table 1. **Religious adherents in Norway, AD 1900-2025.**

Year	1900		1970		mid-1990		Annual change, 1990-2000				mid-1995		mid-2000		mid-2025	
Name	Adherents	%	Adherents	%	Adherents	%	Natural	Conversion	Total	Rate	Adherents	%	Adherents	%	Adherents	%
Christians	**2,207,060**	**99.4**	**3,828,900**	**98.8**	**4,031,760**	**95.1**	**21,217**	**-3,582**	**17,635**	**0.43**	**4,114,000**	**94.7**	**4,208,114**	**94.3**	**4,441,000**	**92.3**
PROFESSION																
professing Christians	**2,207,060**	**99.4**	**3,828,900**	**98.8**	**4,031,760**	**95.1**	**21,217**	**-3,582**	**17,635**	**0.43**	**4,114,000**	**94.7**	**4,208,114**	**94.3**	**4,441,000**	**92.3**
AFFILIATION																
unaffiliated Christians	6,700	0.3	13,500	0.4	7,400	0.2	39	-94	-55	-0.77	7,000	0.2	6,852	0.2	5,000	0.1
affiliated Christians	**2,200,360**	**99.1**	**3,815,400**	**98.5**	**4,024,360**	**95.0**	**21,178**	**-3,488**	**17,690**	**0.43**	**4,107,000**	**94.5**	**4,201,262**	**94.2**	**4,436,000**	**92.2**
Protestants	2,207,000	99.4	3,924,465	101.3	3,995,000	94.3	21,023	-523	20,500	0.50	4,095,663	94.3	4,200,000	94.2	4,400,000	91.4
Independents	0	0.0	20,477	0.5	125,000	3.0	658	442	1,100	0.85	133,266	3.1	136,000	3.1	180,000	3.7
Roman Catholics	2,070	0.1	10,059	0.3	38,500	0.9	203	447	650	1.57	41,180	1.0	45,000	1.0	60,000	1.3
Marginal Christians	500	0.0	13,383	0.4	20,000	0.5	105	295	400	1.84	21,600	0.5	24,000	0.5	40,000	0.8
Anglicans	0	0.0	2,000	0.1	2,000	0.1	11	-11	0	0.00	2,000	0.1	2,000	0.0	2,000	0.0
Orthodox	0	0.0	400	0.0	1,400	0.0	7	13	20	1.34	1,500	0.0	1,600	0.0	2,500	0.1
doubly-affiliated	-9,210	-0.4	-155,384	-4.0	-157,540	-3.7	-829	-4,151	-4,980	2.78	-188,209	-4.3	-207,338	-4.7	-248,500	-5.2
Trans-megabloc groupings																
Evangelicals	1,340,000	60.3	949,500	24.5	478,000	11.3	2,515	-1,815	700	0.15	488,370	11.2	485,000	10.9	466,000	9.7
Pentecostals/Charismatics	0	0.0	70,000	1.8	1,144,000	27.0	6,020	4,480	10,500	0.88	1,155,730	26.6	1,249,000	28.0	1,450,000	30.1
Great Commission Christians	**200,000**	**9.0**	**931,000**	**24.0**	**1,018,000**	**24.0**	**5,357**	**307**	**5,664**	**0.54**	**1,045,000**	**24.1**	**1,074,638**	**24.1**	**1,164,500**	**24.2**
Nonreligious	12,300	0.6	30,400	0.8	73,000	1.7	384	776	1,160	1.49	76,960	1.8	84,601	1.9	130,000	2.7
Buddhists	0	0.0	100	0.0	48,000	1.1	253	1,669	1,922	3.42	62,000	1.4	67,219	1.5	100,000	2.1
Muslims	0	0.0	4,000	0.1	38,000	0.9	200	573	773	1.87	41,300	1.0	45,730	1.0	70,000	1.5
Atheists	1,000	0.1	10,000	0.3	23,000	0.5	121	78	199	0.83	24,000	0.6	24,988	0.6	30,000	0.6
New-Religionists	0	0.0	0	0.0	17,500	0.4	92	308	400	2.08	19,900	0.5	21,502	0.5	30,000	0.6
Baha'is	0	0.0	1,200	0.0	1,700	0.0	9	39	48	2.51	1,850	0.0	2,179	0.1	3,000	0.1
Ethnoreligionists	0	0.0	0	0.0	950	0.0	5	20	25	2.40	1,100	0.0	1,204	0.0	1,400	0.0
Chinese folk-religionists	0	0.0	0	0.0	900	0.0	5	16	21	2.08	960	0.0	1,106	0.0	1,200	0.0
Jews	640	0.0	900	0.0	820	0.0	4	-4	0	0.01	810	0.0	821	0.0	800	0.0
Spiritists	0	0.0	0	0.0	370	0.0	2	7	9	2.09	420	0.0	455	0.0	600	0.0
Other religionists	0	0.0	500	0.0	2,000	0.1	11	100	111	4.52	2,700	0.1	3,112	0.1	4,000	0.1
World A (unevangelized persons)	0	0.0	15,502	0.4	50,856	1.2	276	592	868	1.54	56,492	1.3	62,454	1.4	96,240	2.0
World B (evangelized non-Christians)	13,940	0.6	31,238	0.8	155,384	3.7	810	2,990	3,800	2.05	175,100	4.0	190,432	4.3	274,760	5.7
World C (Christians)	2,207,060	99.4	3,828,900	98.8	4,031,760	95.1	21,217	-3,582	17,635	0.43	4,114,000	94.7	4,208,114	94.3	4,441,000	92.3
Country's population	**2,221,000**	**100.0**	**3,875,641**	**100.0**	**4,238,000**	**100.0**	**22,303**	**0**	**22,303**	**0.51**	**4,345,593**	**100.0**	**4,461,000**	**100.0**	**4,812,000**	**100.0**

COLUMNS, ROWS.
For meanings and definitions, see Codebook (Part 3). Note that, by definition, total 'Christians' = professing + crypto-Christians, which also = affiliated + unaffiliated Christians, and also = Great Commission Christians + latent Christians. Percentages may not always total exactly, due to rounding.

CENSUSES.
3.XII.1900 (not strictly a census, but a government-sponsored survey of dissenters): 99.3% Protestants (97.6% state church, 1.6% others), 0.6% nonreligious, 0.1% Roman Catholics. **3.XII.1946** (de jure): 99.0% Protestants, 0.7% nonreligious, 0.2% Roman Catholics. **1.XII.1950** (de jure): 99.1% Protestants, 0.7% nonreligious, 0.1% Roman Catholics, 0.1% other religionists. **1.XI.1960** (de jure): 98.8% Protestants (96.3% state church), 0.8% nonreligious, 0.2% Roman Catholics, 0.2% marginal Protestants. There was no similar religion question asked in the 1970 census, but church bodies were asked to submit figures of membership. Government estimates are therefore based on church returns and consist of statistics of both professing and affiliated, and also of adults only mixed with adults and children.

NOTES ON RELIGIONS
ATHEISTS. Norwegian Communist Party (Norges Kommunistiske Parti, NKP) (legal; independent in Sino-Soviet dispute): declining. Among other atheistic organizations, the Human-Etisk Forbund (founded 1956) specifically aims to promote unbelief and since 1951 has provided an annual civic nonreligious confirmation ceremony (200 youths each year).
BAHA'IS. Growth from 4 local spiritual assemblies (1964) to 7 (1973).
BUDDHISTS. With a Tibetan center in Oslo, based on headquarters in Copenhagen.
DOUBLY-AFFILIATED. A large majority of members of Protestant free churches (especially the Salvation Army) are also regarded as members of the state church which therefore enumerates them all as such.
EVANGELICALS. Although there are many Evangelical free churches, the bulk of all Evangelicals remain within the state church. Conservative or anti-ecumenical attitudes are stronger in Norway than elsewhere in Scandinavia.
JEWS. Recognized since 1851. Most live in Oslo.
MUSLIMS. Mostly migrant laborers from the Balkans, Turkey and Pakistan, with a small Ahmadiya Mission (enumerated here under Muslims though declared non-Muslim by Pakistan). Begun about 1960. Qadianis from Pakistan (Ahmadiya Muslim Mission), with a handful of Norwegian converts. Muslims are found mostly in Oslo, aided by the Muslim Union of Oslo which has asked both for legal recognition and also for land for a mosque.
PENTECOSTALS/CHARISMATICS. The total (1975) includes 1,000 lay charismatics and 15 clergy within the state church in 50 organized prayer groups, in a renewal which gathered momentum in 1971 and is now served by the Agape Society; and also about 4,000 in other non-Pentecostal Protestant churches. Total charismatic community including children, 10,000. The Inner Missions in the state church have tended to be anti-charismatic. By 1998 there were several hundred thousand Charismatics.
OTHER RELIGIONISTS. Including Rosicrucians (2 AMORC centers) and a growing number of cultists.
PROTESTANTS. 83% of children born in 1995 were then baptized in the Church of Norway.

Great Commission Instrument Panel: status of Norway (for explanation see start of Part 4)

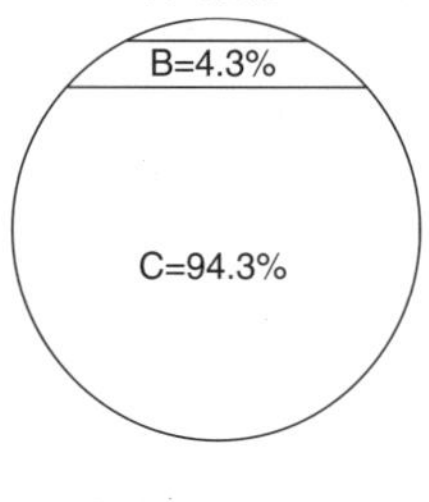

3 Worlds, AD 2000

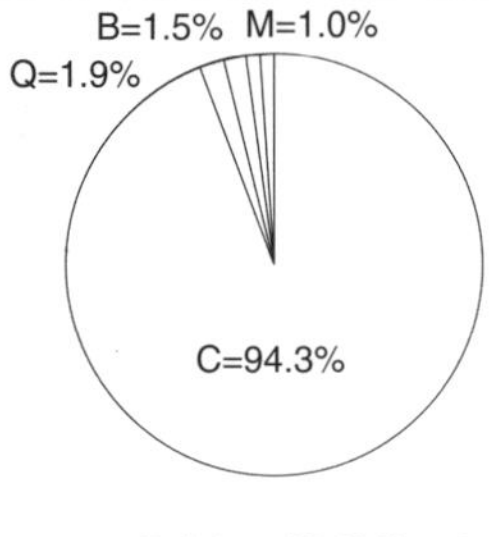

Religions, AD 2000

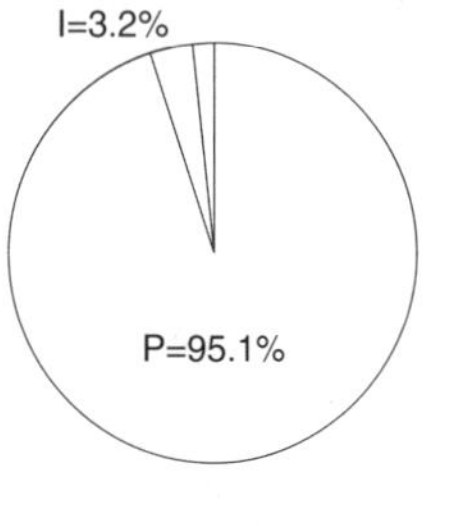

Ecclesiastical blocs

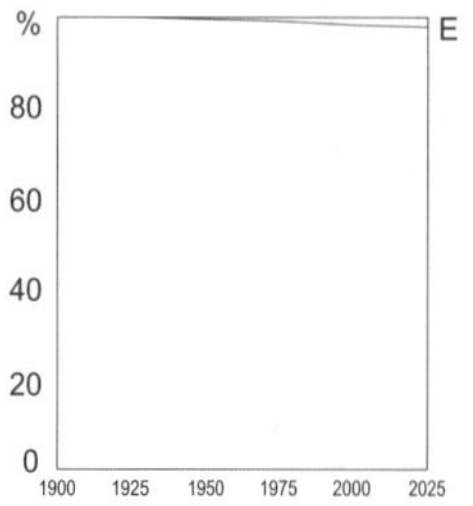

Evangelization, 1900-2025

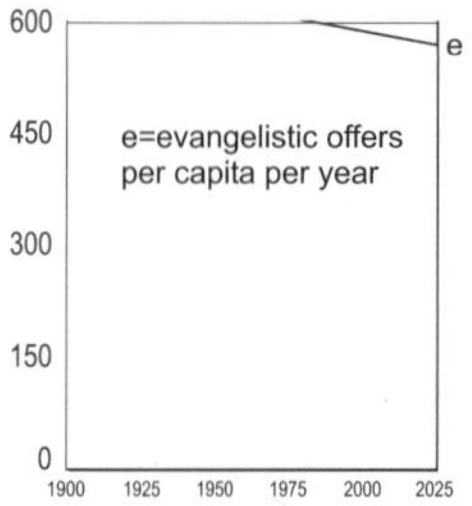

Offers, 1900-2025

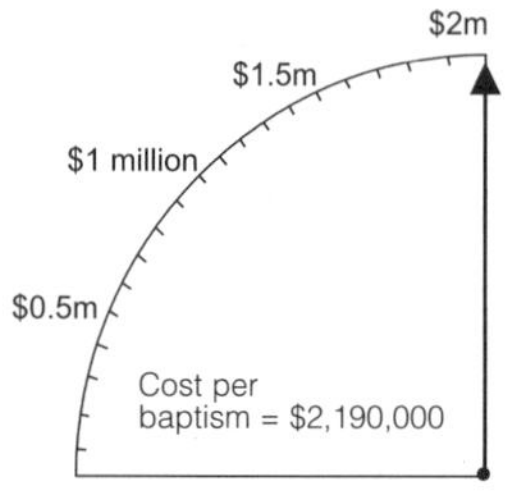

Cost-effectiveness, AD 2000

Country summary. **Worlds A, B, C by ethnolinguistic peoples, cities, and major civil divisions in Norway.**

	PEOPLES							CITIES							CIVIL DIVISIONS						
World	*Num*	*Pop 2000*	*C%*	*Christians*	*E%*	*U%*	*Unevangelized*	*Num*	*Pop 2000*	*C%*	*Christians*	*E%*	*U%*	*Unevangelized*	*Num*	*Pop 2000*	*C%*	*Christians*	*E%*	*U%*	*Unevangelized*
A	3	21,903	0.23	51	37	63	13,725	0	0	0.00	0	0	0	0	0	0	0.00	0	0	0	0
B	7	150,472	15.11	22,738	69	31	46,343	0	0	0.00	0	0	0	0	0	0	0.00	0	0	0	0
C	22	4,288,659	97.43	4,178,474	100	0	1,008	9	1,631,732	93.34	1,523,120	98	2	26,858	19	4,461,033	94.18	4,201,262	99	1	61,076
Total	**32**	**4,461,034**	**94.18**	**4,201,263**	**99**	**1**	**61,076**	**9**	**1,631,732**	**93.34**	**1,523,120**	**98**	**2**	**26,858**	**19**	**4,461,033**	**94.18**	**4,201,262**	**99**	**1**	**61,076**

Country status. Norway is the northernmost country in Europe. It is part of Scandinavia and has strong cultural ties with Finland, Sweden, Denmark, and Iceland. It is a leading exporter of fish, ships, pulp, paper, and aluminum.

HUMAN LIFE AND LIBERTY

Human need and development. Norway is a developed country with living standards comparable to those of other European countries. Its per capita income of $31,249 is the fourth highest in the world, and far ahead of the United States. In recent years it has acquired a substantial minority of asylees from the Middle East and Asia. Their standards of living are significantly lower.

Human rights and freedoms. Deeply rooted democratic traditions, a historic attachment to egalitarianism, an independent press and highly developed social welfare and educational systems have helped to make Norway an exemplar of human rights at home and a strong defender of these rights abroad. Asylees are not subject to any form of discrimination and receive generous social welfare benefits while their applications are being considered. Qualified foreigners who have resided in the country for at least 3 years may vote in local elections only. The Sami (Lapp) minority elected their own constituent assembly, the Sameting, in 1989.

Human environment. Norway has more unspoiled wilderness than any country in Europe. The Nature Conservation Act protects about 4.4% of the country in national parks and forests. Nevertheless, acid rain has affected parts of southern Norway where the lakes have become too acidified to support fish life. Air pollution is also a problem near urban areas.

NON-CHRISTIAN RELIGIONS

Islam was represented in Norway by about 26,500 Muslims in 1995, most of them in the capital city. In the late '70s, the Muslim Union of Oslo built a mosque, and they were recognized as a religious congregation.

Judaism, which has been accepted since 1851, had some 800 adherents in 1995, the majority of whom live in Oslo.

Baha'is and ***New Religionists*** each had over 1,700 adherents in 1995.

Church of Norway. One of 30 remaining 11th-12th-century stave churches (made of timber with intricate carving), at Borgund, Sognefjord area, western Norway.

Church of Norway. Pastor Gunn Berit Guldbrandsen in Biskopshavn Church, Bergen.

CHRISTIANITY

PROTESTANT CHURCHES. Christianity was introduced about A.D. 900 in the region of the Oslo-fjord through the missionary activity of the Bremen-Hambourg archbishopric, but the greatest influence came from Norwegian kings of the 10th and 11th centuries (the first being Hakon the Good who reigned during 945-960) whose early Christian education took place in England. Resistance to Christianity gradually gave way both in Norway and among those who had established themselves on the islands of the North Atlantic, including Iceland and Greenland. This secular establishment of Christianity led to repeated conflicts between the Norwegian kings and the ecclesiastical authorities in Denmark, who were appointed by Rome to administer the whole of Scandinavia, conflicts which were heightened by the Danish and Swedish political domination of Norway. There was little hesitancy on the part of royalty, therefore, at the time of the Protestant Reformation, in establishing a state church system based on the Lutheran Confession. The evangelical fervor that characterized other European countries during this period did not appear in Norway until the middle of the 19th century. Leaders advocating church reform tended more to emigrate with their followers to America, contributing to the proliferation of Scandinavian Lutheran synods and missionary societies in the USA.

Lay movements within the state church, leading ultimately to the establishment of free churches as well as a renewal of the Church of Norway, began with a layman and farmer, Hans Nielsen Hauge, at the beginning of the 19th century. After a personal experience of Christ, he began to preach and encouraged the formation of societies of believers, bound together by the Holy Spirit and practicing their own fervent devotions while remaining loyal members of the Lutheran Church. In the middle of the century, a second awakening took place reaching all social classes through the preaching of Giles Johnson, who also made use of lay evangelists. Small groups were organized throughout the country, frequently calling upon state church ministers to be their leaders. Out of this movement grew the Luther Foundation in 1868, with a strong mission emphasis, which in 1891 became the Lutheran Inner Mission Society (Indremisjon). A similar society developed in western Norway as a result of emigrants returning from America and Britain. In 1891 also, the Norwegian Lutheran Mission society was created, after a revival in 1880-90, to train young people for foreign service. The 20th century has not witnessed renewal movements of comparable intensity to those which characterized the earlier period. Nevertheless, the Church of Norway continues to be a dominant force in Norwegian life.

As compared with other Western nations, membership (96% of the total population) and orthodox religious belief remain high in the Church of Norway, while attendance at weekly worship services is low (about 3%). The origin of this paradox can be traced to patterns established early in Norwegian history, when the population was more scattered and communications difficult or almost non-existent, in which situation habitual churchgoing never developed on a wide scale. Popular religious feeling and practice is therefore evidenced today in the high level of listener attendance to religious radio broadcasts.

When the church became Lutheran in 1537, it retained a diocesan and parish structure basically identical with the prereformation Catholic organization, which explains its present high church tradition evidenced in use of vestments and the like. Nevertheless, the Church of Norway defines itself in accordance with the constitution of 1814 as Evangelical Lutheran based on the Apostles' Creed, the Augustana Confession, and Luther's Little Catechism. During the German occupation of Norway in World War II, the church was made independent of the state. When its previous relationship with the state was restored after the war, a number of democratic policies were introduced in church administration.

The first free churches established in Norway owed their origin to foreign, though Scandinavian, influences. A Danish missionary founded a Norwegian Baptist church in 1850, and by 1879, some 18 separate congregations had joined together to form the Baptist Union. Methodism came to Norway in 1853 through the instrumentality among others of a returned Norwegian seaman who was converted and ordained in the USA. With 45 congregations in 1905, Norway's Methodism has grown to be the largest Methodist body in Scandinavia.

Other free churches of Lutheran tradition grew out of the renewal within the state church at the end of the 19th century; these included the Evangelical Lutheran Free Church and the Mission Covenant Church. The latter emerged in 1884, though its roots went back to 1856, following the example of the Swedish Bible Readers' movement which had broken ties with the Swedish state church in 1878. These churches wanted all people to be loyal Lutherans but free-thinking in 'non-essential' doctrines. In the beginning, emphasis was placed on Christ as personal Savior and membership in the state church was retained, but gradually they emerged as separate and exclusive denominations.

Scandinavian Pentecostalism began in Norway when a former Methodist pastor, on a money-raising trip to the USA, came under Pentecostal influence. His meetings in Oslo in 1906 drew large crowds, which disturbed the Methodist Conference and forced his resignation from it. Norwegian Pentecostalism has subsequently grown steadily, from 8,000 adult members in 1930 to 30,000 in 1950, 34,100 in 1960 and 65,000 in 1990. For many years now, Pentecostals, with the Salvation Army, still ranked highest in membership among non-established religious bodies.

Over the last decade, the main free churches have shown considerable growth.

CATHOLIC CHURCH. The first Roman Catholic parish was organized in 1842, after the liberalization of the state church system had begun. By 1890, the number of Catholics had reached a thousand, and by 1995, they still represent only 1% of the population. The Catholic community consists of 15% converts from other churches, 20% foreign-born immigrants and 65% native-born Catholics, most of the latter being still minors and children of mixed marriages. Because of its small numbers, its high immigrant membership and its foreign-born clergy (75% of the total) and expatriate personnel (90% of the total), the Catholic Church in Norway has not played an important role in national life. Nevertheless, there are signs of change. The widespread prejudice which for so long tended to isolate Catholics is abating, and the number of active Norwegian-born priests is high in relation to the number of Catholics.

In 1977, Norway was transferred from the jurisdiction of Propaganda to that of the Congregation for Bishops.

The Holy See has diplomatic relations with Norway and in AD 2000 is represented to government and the Catholic hierarchy by a nuncio residing in Denmark.

Renewal movements. In the 1990s the Pentecostal/Charismatic Renewal continued to spread across most older churches, and numbered over 1,249,000 adherents (of whom 6% Pentecostals, 83% Charismatics, and 12% Independents).

Indigenous missions. The first Norwegian missionaries were descendants of the Vikings who converted to Christianity in the 9th and 10th centuries. In the Age of Discovery, Norwegian missionaries could be found in Africa and Asia. Today, Norwegian missionaries are found all over the world and Norway has one of the highest per capita sending ratios in the world.

Church of Norway. *Top left.* Lomskyrkja, old stave church at Lom, dating back to 1270, with (*top right*) interior. *Lower.* Cathedral of Diocese of Nidaros, in Trondheim; outstanding example of Gothic style in full flowering.

CHURCH AND STATE

A state church system was introduced in 1537 with a royal decree that made the king of Denmark and Norway the head of the church on the basis of the Lutheran Confession. When Norway declared its independence from Denmark in 1814, its constitution specified 'the Evangelical-Lutheran Religion' as the 'official Religion of the State' (Article 2). This provision is still preserved, while various other constitutional terms have been eliminated, including the ban against 'monkish Priests, Jesuits and Jews'. Article 4 states that the king most profess and uphold the state religion, and article 12 rules that at least half the king's cabinet must do the same.

The principal law governing church structure (Norske Kirkes Ordning) dates from 29 April 1953, and prescribes the elements of a self-governing structure: pastors (sogneprest), elected parish councils responsible for administration, bishops, and diocesan councils. On the national level, the law recognizes the existence of a regular bishops' meeting and a meeting every 4 years of all diocesan councils. A Central Council of Diocesan Councils (Bispedommeradenes Fellesrad) was established by law in 1969. The real power in church affairs, including the appointment of ministers and bishops and control over finance, is still vested in the government through the Ministry of Church Affairs and Education (Kongelige Kirkeog Undervisnings-departement) which occupies itself mainly with the state church and public education.

Following the elections of 1973, parliament had for the first time 2 Catholic deputies, one of whom was elected president of the parliamentary Commission for Church Affairs and Education. This election provoked unrest given the fact that the commission is responsible for preparing a new canon law for the Lutheran state church.

The financial needs of the state church are provided for partly by the state, with the salaries of state-appointed clergy as its main item; partly by the 440 municipalities which build churches, appoint and pay minor church officials and provide clergy housing; and also partly by voluntary collections among church members.

The principle that denominations outside the state church system should receive a proportional amount of public money was not recognized until the promulgation of the law of 13 June 1969, (Trudomssamfunn og Ymist Anna, Article 19) which regulates relations between the state and non-established denominations, especially in that which concerns the state budget.

Other salient points of the 1969 law are: (1) complete freedom of religion is assured for all religions, Christian and non-Christian; (2) religious bodies must register with the county where their central authority or administration is situated; (3) anyone of 15 years or over may freely join or leave any religious body; (4) it is forbidden for persons under 20 to take perpetually-binding religious vows; (5) children born in wedlock belong to the religion of their parents, but if the parents belong to different bodies, they must choose after birth to which group the child shall belong; (6) children born out of wedlock follow the religion of the mother; and (7) none is permitted to belong to more than one religious body at the same time.

BROADCASTING AND MEDIA

Shortwave radio programs in European languages can be received from KNLS, AWR (Slovakia), TWR (Monaco, Albania), and HCJB (Ecuador). NOREA Radio produces programs in Norwegian for local radio stations. These programs are also translated into 15 other languages for use by TWR, FEBA, and private stations in Japan, Taiwan, Indonesia, Bolivia, and Peru. AWR has a studio in Oslo that produces Norwegian programs. Norway is a member of UNDA.

CBN's *700 Club* and *Studio 7* are both available four days a week in Oslo. Satellite TV and radio programs are received in English, Arabic, German and Italian. Norway produces and transmits satellite TV.

INTERDENOMINATIONAL ORGANIZATIONS

Conservative and anti-ecumenical forces are stronger in Norway than in most other Scandinavian countries, which accounts for the fact that there is no national ecumenical council of churches in the country. Pentecostal opposition to a recent proposal to establish such a council proved decisive. Of note also was the refusal of the Norwegian Missionary Council (Norsk Misjonsrad), founded in 1921, to join the CWME at the time of merger in 1961 of the International Missionary Council with the World Council of Churches. Nevertheless, the Church of Norway is a member of both the Lutheran World Federation and the WCC, and Methodists are also members of the WCC through their association with American Methodism. The Free Church Council (Norsk Frikirkerad) groups non-established Protestant denominations, and the Norwegian Evangelical Alliance is also active. A more inclusive ecumenical collaboration exists at the parish level in conjunction with the Week of Prayer for Christian Unity.

The Center for Ecumenical Theology (Centrum for Okumenisk Teologi) is an interdenominational research institute, founded in 1967, where theologians of different denominations, including Catholics, work together to promote spiritual and social ecumenism. Emphasis is given to 'church in the world' dialogue and youth training. There is an Ecumenical Institute attached to the University of Oslo; and the Egede Institute (Egede Instituttet), which is affiliated to the International Association for Mission Studies, is also found in Oslo.

FUTURE TRENDS AND PROSPECTS

Christianity is expected to drop off only slightly into the 21st century (92.3% by 2025) with most of this loss related to the growth of the nonreligious (up to 2.7% by 2025 from 0.8% in 1970).

The nonreligious, atheists, and immigrant non-Christians could represent over 15% of population in the 21st century. Christianity will likely remain above 80% in the same period.

BIBLIOGRAPHY

'A theological foundation to design a strategy for the renewal and growth of the Norwegian Pentecostal Movement.' F. M. Matre. D.Min. thesis, Fuller Theological Seminary, Pasadena, CA, 1985. 272p.

'A twofold structural model for renewal and mission with special reference to the Church of Norway.' B. R. Eriksen. D.Min. thesis, Fuller Theological Seminary, Pasadena, CA, 1983. 136p.

'An anthology of Norwegian religious music.' R. E. Hovey. Ed.D. diss., New York University, 1967. 2 vols.

'An investigation into the determinative factors behind the missionary movement within the Norwegian Lutheran Church.' D. Solheim. D.Min. thesis, Fuller Theological Seminary, Pasadena, CA, 1978. 259p.

Arbok for den Norske Kirke, 1970. Oslo: Forlaget Land og Kirke, 1970.

'Catholicism in Norway,' *The month*, n. s., 21, 2 (1959), 69–128.

Clash of cultures: the Norwegian experience with Mormonism, 1842–1920. G. M. Haslam. *American University studies, Series IX: History*, vol. 7. New York: P. Lang, 1984. 372p.

Den Norske Kirke. I. Lonning et al. Oslo: Studier i Norge, 1966. 64p.

Fra Hans Nielsen Hauge til Eivind Berggrav. E. Molland. Oslo: Gyldendal, 1951. (Translated as *Church life in Norway 1800-1950*, Minneapolis, MN: Augsburg, 1957).

History of the Baptists in Norway. P. Stiansen. Chicago: Blessing Press, 1933. 176p.

History of the church and state in Norway from the tenth to the sixteenth century. T. B. Willson. St. Clair Shores, MI: Scholarly Press, 1971. 382p.

Methodism as a carrier of the holiness tradition in Norway, 1850–1910. T. Meistad. Alta, Norway: Finnmark College, [1994]. 290p.

Nordic democracy: ideas, issues, and institutions in politics, economy, education, social and cultural affairs of Denmark, Finland, Iceland, Norway, and Sweden. E. Allardt et al. (eds). Copenhagen: Det Danske Selskab, 1981. (See articles on 'Ethnic minorities' on p. 627-49 and 'The popular revival movements' on p. 589-608).

Nordnorsk religiøsitet og identitet. T. Meistad. Alta, [Norway]: Alta laererhøgskole, [1994]. 108p.

Norway. L. B. Sather. Ed., H. H. Wellisch. *World bibliographical series*, vol. 67. Oxford, UK: CLIO Press, 1986. 320p. (See especially 'Religion,' p.98–104).

'Norway,' E. D. Vogt, in *Western religion: a country by country sociological enquiry*, p.381–401. H. Mol (ed). The Hague: Mouton, 1972.

'Norway's Gypsy minority,' U. Jørstad, *Scandinavian review*, 58, 2 (1970), 129–37.

Norway's stave churches: architecture, history, and legends. E. Valebrokk & T. Thiis-Evensen. Trans., A. C. Zwick. [Norway]: Boksenteret, 1993. 104p.

Norwegian Christian handbook. P. W. Brierley (ed). : MARC Europe, 1990. 48p.

Norwegian religious pluralism: a trans–Atlantic comparison. F. Hale. *Texts and studies in religion*, vol. 59. Lewiston, NY: E. Mellen Press, 1992. 237p.

Oversikt over den Katolske Kirke i Norden, 1971. Oslo: Nordiske Bispekonferanse, 1971.

Pulpit under the sky: a life of Hans Nielsen Hauge. J. M. Shaw. Minneapolis, MN: Augsburg, 1955. 250p.

'Rebuilding the infra–structure of an old inner–city church by establishing a network of relational groups.' I. Øvergaard. D.Min. thesis, Trinity Evangelical Divinity School, Deerfield, IL, 1993. 221p.

'Religion,' T. Mathiesen & O. Hauglin, in *Norwegian society*, p.226–59. N. R. Ramsøy (ed). Oslo: Universitetsforlaget, 1974.

Religion and power: the case of Methodism in Norway. A. Hassing. Lake Junaluska, NC: General Commission on Archives and History, United Methodist Church, 1980. 323p.

'Religious change in eleventh–century Norway,' P. Hassing, *Missiology*, 3, 4 (1975).

Scandinavian churches: a picture of the development and life of the churches of Denmark, Finland, Iceland, Norway and Sweden. L. S. Hunter (ed). London: Faber & Faber, 1965. 200p.

The Catholic Church in the North. E. D. Vogt. Bergen, Norway, 1962.

The church beneath the northern lights: Fenno–Scandian historical theology. A. J. Kristoffersen. , [1990]. 105p.

'The Church in Norway,' O. Lang, in *Norway year book 1967*. Oslo: S. Mortensen, 1967.

The Church of Norway. Hegdehaugen, Norway: Church of Norway Information Service, [1990]. 46p.

The Lapps. R. Bosi. *Ancient people and places.* London: Thames & Hudson, 1960. 220p. (Discusses Lapp religion).

'The witness of the church of Norway,' G. Ostenstad, *International review of mission*, 62, 245 (1973), 43–50.

'Working together towards growth: a plan for renewal and growth in the Norwegian Lutheran State Church.' J. T. Hanssen. D.Min. thesis, Fuller Theological Seminary, Pasadena, CA, 1990. 279p.

Country Table 2. **Organized churches and denominations in Norway.**

Official name (bold type = church with over 10% of all affiliated) 1	*Begun* 2	*Type* 3	*Counc* 4	*Congs* 5	*Adults* 6	*Affiliated 1970* 7	*Affiliated 1995* 8	*G%* 9	*Names, notes, and other statistics* (see Codebook, Part 3) 10
Apostolic Church		P-PeA	Z....	10	200	100	400	0.05	*Apostolske Kirke.* M=Apostolic Ch of Great Britain(UK). Pentecostals.
Apostolic Faith		P-Pe3	x....	15	1,000	500	2,000	0.05	*Apostoliske Tro.* M=AFM(Portland, Oregon, USA). Holiness Pentecostals. HQ Stavanger.
Association of Vineyard Churches		I-3cW	.....	6	300	–	1,000	0.05	Assisted by M=AVC(USA).
Catholic Apostolic Church	c1880	I-3aX	x....	1	50	375	100	-5.15	*Katolsk Apostolisk Menighet.* Remnant of Irvingite church from Britain. Dying out.
Catholic Church in Norway:	1842	R-Lat	b.BQ.	32	28,200	10,059	41,180	5.80	*Romersk Katolske Kirke.* 20% immigrants. C=8+0+9. 18n 46x 54m 228w 627Yy
D Oslo	1868	R-Lat	bsscc	20	25,900	9,127	37,536	5.82	*Oslo Katolske Bispedömme.* M=SSCC,OCSO,OFM. 16n 30x 35m 196w 569Yy
PN Trondheim (Central Norway)	1931	R-Lat	bsscc	5	1,500	579	2,285	5.64	*Apostoliske Vikariat Mellom-Norge.* M=SSCC. 1n 7x 9m 4w 46Yy
PN Tromso (Northern Norway)	1931	R-Lat	bmsf	7	800	353	1,359	5.54	*Nord-Norge.* Also Svalbard, Jan Mayen. M=MSF. 1n 9x 10m 28w 12Yy
Christadelphian Ecclesias	1955	m-Ade	x....	2	50	100	100	0.00	*Christadelphian Bible Mission.* 2 ecclesias (churches) in Bergen.
Christian Brethren	c1880	P-CBr	x....	3	200	300	350	0.62	*Plymouth Brethren. Open Brethren. Gospel Halls.* Links with UK Brethren.
Church of Christ, Scientist		m-Sci	x....	1	100	200	200	0.05	*Christian Science.* M=CCS(Boston,USA). First Church, Oslo. Many expatriates. 2w.
Church of England (D Europe)	c1850	A-plu	awc..	6	1,000	2,000	2,000	0.00	English-speaking Anglican Chaplaincies, including 4 seasonal and 7 occasional. 1x.
Ch of Jesus Christ of Latter-day Saints	1850	m-LdS	x....	23	2,410	3,083	3,700	0.73	*Jesu Kristi Kirke av Siste Dagers Hellige. Mormoner.* M=CJCLdS(USA). 60f.
Church of Norway	c 900	P-Lut	LWX.K	1,360	2,800,000	3,740,000	3,900,000	0.17	*Norske Kirke*, reformed 1536. Now 11 Dioceses. 1280n,65012Yy.
Church of Sweden		P-Lut	Lwc..	20	1,000	1,500	2,000	0.05	Swedish citizens and residents belonging to Sweden's national church.
Churches of Christ		I-Dis	x....	3	100	100	300	0.05	*Kristi Kirke.* M=CC(Non-Instrumental) (USA). In Oslo, Bergen. Mainly Americans.
Congregation of God at Vegardshei		I-Lut	.....	1	1,355	2,000	1,780	0.05	*Guds Menighet pa Vegardshei.* Ex Ch of Norway; Old Lutheran, old Bible versions.
Congregation of Jesus Christ	1880	P-Dis	x....	3	600	1,000	1,100	0.38	*Kristi Menighet. Disciples of Christ.* Conservative. From USA via Denmark.
Evangelical Assembly		I-Dis	.....	1	235	462	362	0.05	*Evangeliske Forsamling.*
Evangelical Lutheran Ch Community	1871	P-Lut	.....	6	1,980	3,618	2,680	-1.19	*Evangelisk-Lutherske Kirkesamfunn.* Conservative schism ex Church of Norway.
Evangelical Lutheran Free Church of N	1877	P-Lut	..D.e	72	7,200	19,109	20,600	0.30	*Evangelisk Lutherske Frikirke i Norge.* Ex Ch of Norway. 69n,1s(6),151Yy.
Free Evangelical Assemblies	c1895	P-Con	..D.e	74	5,400	6,000	7,940	1.13	*Frie Evangeliske Forsamlinger.*Schism ex MCCN. 1967, pentecostal trends emerge.
Free Pentecostal Friends	1959	I-3pW	.....	6	1,500	2,000	3,000	1.64	*Frie Pinsevenner.* Schism ex Maranatha Revival Ch and ex Pentecostal Revival of Norway.
Greek Orthodox Church (D Swedia)		O-Gre	Cwc..	1	1,200	400	1,500	0.05	*Gresk-Ortodokse Kirke.* Under jurisdiction of EP Constantinople. Growing.
Gypsy Evangelical Movement		I-3pE	.....	18	3,100	2,540	3,820	0.05	Gypsies in independent pentecostal body.
Jehovah's Witnesses	1891	m-Jeh	x....	176	9,671	10,000	17,600	2.29	*Jehovas Vitner.* Active witnessing 1926. HQ Oslo 2. (1975) 546Y. (1995) 264Y.
Maranatha Revival Church	c1955	I-3pW	x....	5	700	500	1,500	4.49	Schism from Pentecostal Revival of Norway, similar to that in Sweden. M=MBM(USA).
Methodist Church of Norway	1853	P-Met	Vwx.x	56	6,300	17,702	14,700	-0.74	*Norway Annual Conf*, NEurope CC, UMC(USA). 75n,1x,21f,3H,1j,1s,139Yy.
Mission Covenant Church of Norway	1856	P-Con	K...C	133	8,110	11,000	16,200	1.56	*Norske Misjonsforbund.* Declining slowly. HQ Oslo 1. 83n,1p,1s(43),W=70%.
Nardus Church	1983	I-3oU	.....	14	400	–	1,000	8.33	An Afro-Caribbean denomination of Oneness theology. In Grimstad.
National Church of Denmark		P-Lut	LWX..	3	700	800	1,000	0.05	Residents and citizens from Denmark who are members of its state church.
New Apostolic Church		I-3aX	x....	8	70	500	104	0.05	*NAC.* Schism ex Catholic Apostolic Ch. World HQ Zurich. Germans.
Norwegian Baptist Union	1850	P-Bap	T.D.x	59	5,900	12,300	11,800	-0.17	*Norske Baptistsamfunn.* Africa missions. Declining. 61n,24x,1s,W=50%,127Y.
Norwegian Pentecostal Movement	1906	P-Pe2	Z.D.x	279	40,200	55,500	61,800	0.43	*Pinsebevegelsen/Pente Revival of N. Filadelfia.* NPY. 250n,1j,3p,2s,3000Y.
Religious Society of Friends	1818	P-Qua	Q...C	3	122	200	203	0.06	*Vennenes Samfunn (Kvekerne). Quakers.* In 1900, 175 adherents. W=34%.
Salvation Army	1888	P-Sal	xwx.x	128	27,900	44,836	42,900	-0.18	*Frelsesarméen. Norway & Iceland Terr.* 6 Divs. 70 institutions. 518n,1s.
Seventh-day Adventist Church	1887	P-Adv	x....	72	5,450	10,000	6,990	-1.42	*Adventistsamfunnet.* East & North & West Norway Confs. 24nx,75mw,4H,1j,1r,187Y.
Other independent charismatic chs	c1975	I-3cW	.....	300	60,000	–	100,000	5.00	Total 30 networks and denominations, including Assembly Hall Churches (Chinese).
Other independent denominations		I-	.....	19	1,000	2,000	1,500	0.05	Total about 15. IPHC(USA).
Other independent single churches		I-sin	.....	58	10,361	10,000	18,800	0.05	Loosely associated in 10 geographical networks.
Other Pentecostal denominations	c1970	P-Pen	.....	20	1,000	–	3,000	37.75	Total about 6 including International Pente Holiness Ch, UPC (USA).
Doubly-affiliated		2-aff			-133,000	-155,384	-188,209		Salvation Army and other Free Church members who retain state church membership.
Totals				**2,997**	**2,902,064**	**3,815,400**	**4,107,000**		

Churches, members, growth, 1900-2025	*Congs*	*Adults*	*Affiliated*	*G%*	*Total denominations*	*6 Megablocs:* *O*	*R*	*A*	*P*	*I*	*m*
Total churches, members, and denominations (mid-1900)	1,000	1,611,000	2,200,360	0.79	19	0	1	1	13	2	2
Total churches, members, and denominations (mid-1970)	2,643	2,793,186	3,815,400	0.79	43	1	1	1	17	19	4
Total churches, members, and denominations (mid-1990)	2,800	2,844,000	4,024,360	0.27	88	1	1	1	18	63	4
Total churches, members, and denominations (mid-1995)	2,997	2,902,064	4,107,000	0.41	90	1	1	1	18	65	4
Total churches, members, and denominations (mid-2000)	3,000	2,969,000	4,201,262	0.45	92	1	1	1	18	67	4
Total churches, members, and denominations (mid-2025)	3,900	3,135,000	4,436,000	0.22	244	2	1	1	30	200	10

NOTES ON TABLE ABOVE
NATIONAL COUNCILS (Column 4, 5th letter).
C = Norwegian Free Church Council (NFCC) (Norske Frikirkerad).
E = Norwegian Evangelical Alliance (NEA) (Evangeliske Allianse i Norge) (founded about 1850; affiliated to EAA but not to WEF).
K = Christian Council of Norway (CCN).
x = member of both NFCC and NEA.
OTHER PROTESTANT DENOMINATIONS. These smaller bodies include: Baptist Bible Fellowship International (1971), Baptist Missionary Association of America, Christian Society (Kristensamfunnet), Ch of the Brethren (1972), Exclusive Brethren (Raven-Taylor), World-Wide Missions.
OTHER MARGINAL BODIES. The General Ch of the New Jerusalem has a Circle in Oslo.

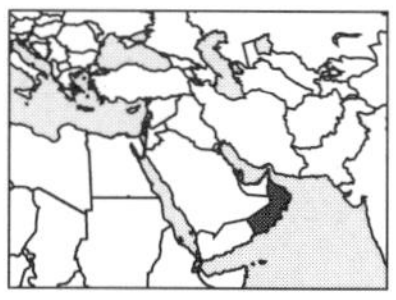

OMAN

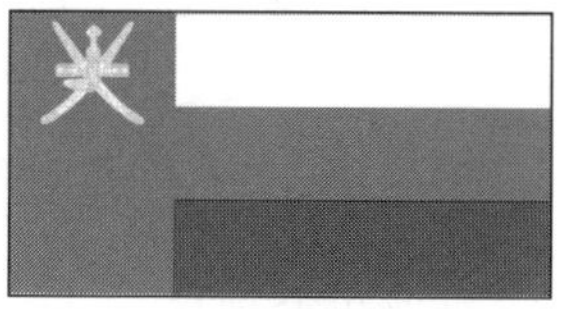

SECULAR DATA, AD 2000

STATE
Official name: Sultanat 'Uman (The Sultanate of Oman).
Short name: Oman. **Adjective of nationality:** Omani.
Flag: Red bar with crossed white swords next to staff; white, red, and green stripes.
Area: 309,500 sq. km. (119,500 sq. mi.).
Government: Absolute monarchy, since 1741 (Muscat and Oman before 1970; de facto British protectorate).
Legislature: Consultative Council, 82 members.
Official language: Arabic.
Monetary unit: 1 rial Omani (RO) = 1,000 baizas. **US$1=** 1 RO = U.S.$2.6.
Chief cities: MASQAT 61,892.
Political divisions: 8 provinces.
Armed forces: 44,000.

DEMOGRAPHY
Population: 2,542,000.
Population density: 8.2/sq. km. (21.2/sq. mi.).
Under 15 years: 1,121,000.
Growth rate p.a.: 3.27% (births 35.77, deaths 3.90).
Mortality: Infant, per 1,000: 21.1, ; **Maternal per 100,000:** 190.0.
Life expectancy: 72 (male 70, female 75).
Household size: 3.7. **Floor area per person, sq.m:** 24.0.
Major languages: Arabic, Persian, Baluchi, Hindi, Tamil, English, Mahri, and a number of minor language.
Urban dwellers: 83.98%. **Urban growth rate p.a.:** 5.0%.
Labor force: 38%.

ETHNOLINGUISTIC PEOPLES
48.1% Omani Arab; 15.0% Southern Baluch; 4.4% Bengali; 3.2% Gulf Arab; 2.8% Persian.

ECONOMY
National income p.a. per person: US$4,819; **per family:** US$17,833.

EDUCATION
Adult literacy: 59% (male 71%, female 46%). **Schools:** 568.
Universities: 5. **School enrolment:** female/male: 72%/77%.

HEALTH
Access to health services: 96%. **Access to safe water:** 63%.
Hospitals: 180 (23 beds per 10,000). **Doctors:** 2,095.
Blind: 23,000. **Deaf:** 163,000. **Murder rate:** <1.
Lepers: 250. **Underweight prevalence under 5:** 14%.

LITERATURE
New book titles p.a.: 31 (12 p.a. per million). **Periodicals:** 21.
Newspapers: 4 dailies.

COMMUNICATION (per 1,000 people)
Phones: 79 (31% mobile). **Radios:** 416. **TV sets:** 61.
Daily newspaper circulation: 30. **Computers:** 40.

HUMAN LIFE AND LIBERTY (optimum condition=100.0%)
HDI: 71.8. **HSI:** 50.0. **HFI:** 20.0. **EFL:** 43.0.

Country status. Oman is an Arab sultanate at the southeastern corner of the Arabian Peninsula. It consists of 2 inhabited regions separated by a vast expanse of desert. The discovery of oil in 1964 transformed the economy into one entirely dependent on this industry.

HUMAN LIFE AND LIBERTY

Human need and development. Oman is an arid country with only 1% of its land area under cultivation. It also suffers from permanent drought, as the rainfall is sparse, and the aquifers are shallow. The oil-based economy has introduced an artificial prosperity limited mainly to the ruling class, but has not affected the common Omanis, many of whom follow the nomadic lifestyle of their forefathers. In the towns, there are signs of affluence. Both the bedouin in the interior and the urban dwellers enjoy a balanced and healthy diet in which meat and fish are prominent. Traditional housing in the interior is of 2 kinds. One is built of stone and mud with deep windows with bars but no glass. The deep-set windows provide air circulation without admitting the sun, and the mud permits the rooms to breathe so that the homes are comfortable despite the ferocious heat. The other type known as *barastis* is built like a stockade with wooden corner posts and walls of woven palm fronds. In the towns good medical facilities are available to all, and are staffed by expatriates from developed Arab countries and the Indian subcontinent.

Human rights and freedoms. The sultan is an absolute monarch who rules without parliamentary institutions of any kind. Basic human rights have never been codified and are tightly restricted in practice. However, there is no opposition to the sultan or to the current order, and therefore, the absence of human rights does not imply repression. There is a certain degree of royal benevolence implicit in the system, and abuses of power are infrequent. The trial system is relatively fair, being governed by tribal customs and Islamic injunctions. There are no rules for admission of evidence during trials or codified procedures for

Country Table 1. Religious adherents in Oman, AD 1900-2025.

Year	1900		1970		mid-1990		Annual change, 1990-2000				mid-1995		mid-2000		mid-2025	
Name	Adherents	%	Adherents	%	Adherents	%	Natural	Conversion	Total	Rate	Adherents	%	Adherents	%	Adherents	%
Muslims	279,980	100.0	716,125	99.1	1,583,040	88.7	67,111	-3,282	63,829	3.45	1,885,810	87.5	2,221,328	87.4	4,538,300	84.8
Hindus	0	0.0	2,000	0.3	90,000	5.0	3,817	1,699	5,516	4.90	122,000	5.7	145,159	5.7	350,000	6.5
Christians	**20**	**0.0**	**3,850**	**0.5**	**78,400**	**4.4**	**3,325**	**1,248**	**4,573**	**4.70**	**104,110**	**4.8**	**124,127**	**4.9**	**318,000**	**5.9**
PROFESSION																
crypto-Christians	20	0.0	900	0.1	15,000	0.8	636	364	1,000	5.24	19,400	0.9	25,000	1.0	90,000	1.7
professing Christians	**0**	**0.0**	**2,950**	**0.4**	**63,400**	**3.6**	**2,689**	**884**	**3,573**	**4.57**	**84,710**	**3.9**	**99,127**	**3.9**	**228,000**	**4.3**
AFFILIATION																
unaffiliated Christians	0	0.0	5	0.0	2,700	0.2	115	-164	-49	-1.98	2,224	0.1	2,211	0.1	2,000	0.0
affiliated Christians	**20**	**0.0**	**3,845**	**0.5**	**75,700**	**4.2**	**3,210**	**1,412**	**4,622**	**4.88**	**101,886**	**4.7**	**121,916**	**4.8**	**316,000**	**5.9**
Roman Catholics	0	0.0	470	0.1	35,000	2.0	1,484	316	1,800	4.24	43,800	2.0	53,000	2.1	130,000	2.4
Independents	0	0.0	775	0.1	25,000	1.4	1,060	832	1,892	5.80	34,597	1.6	43,916	1.7	120,000	2.2
Orthodox	0	0.0	1,000	0.1	10,000	0.6	424	226	650	5.14	13,000	0.6	16,500	0.7	45,000	0.8
Protestants	20	0.0	500	0.1	3,300	0.2	140	100	240	5.62	7,089	0.3	5,700	0.2	15,000	0.3
Anglicans	0	0.0	1,100	0.2	2,400	0.1	102	-62	40	1.55	3,400	0.2	2,800	0.1	6,000	0.1
Trans-megabloc groupings																
Evangelicals	20	0.0	400	0.1	4,600	0.3	195	5	200	3.68	5,526	0.3	6,600	0.3	21,400	0.4
Pentecostals/Charismatics	0	0.0	600	0.1	29,000	1.6	1,230	570	1,800	4.95	37,094	1.7	47,000	1.9	133,800	2.5
Great Commission Christians	**20**	**0.0**	**2,500**	**0.4**	**36,000**	**2.0**	**1,527**	**425**	**1,952**	**4.43**	**45,300**	**2.1**	**55,517**	**2.2**	**160,560**	**3.0**
Buddhists	0	0.0	0	0.0	13,000	0.7	551	92	643	4.10	16,500	0.8	19,432	0.8	55,000	1.0
Sikhs	0	0.0	0	0.0	11,000	0.6	466	112	578	4.31	14,000	0.7	16,775	0.7	40,000	0.8
Baha'is	0	0.0	300	0.0	5,500	0.3	233	129	362	5.19	7,700	0.4	9,123	0.4	25,000	0.5
Nonreligious	0	0.0	1,600	0.2	3,800	0.2	161	8	169	3.75	4,600	0.2	5,490	0.2	25,000	0.5
Ethnoreligionists	0	0.0	0	0.0	120	0.0	5	-2	3	2.46	130	0.0	153	0.0	300	0.0
Atheists	0	0.0	0	0.0	80	0.0	3	-3	0	-0.51	80	0.0	76	0.0	200	0.0
New-Religionists	0	0.0	0	0.0	60	0.0	3	-1	2	2.39	70	0.0	76	0.0	200	0.0
World A (unevangelized persons)	279,880	100.0	628,962	87.0	1,060,290	59.4	44,972	-16,285	28,687	2.42	1,209,034	56.1	1,347,260	53.0	2,397,696	44.8
World B (evangelized non-Christians)	100	0.0	90,132	12.5	646,310	36.2	27,378	15,037	42,415	5.18	841,997	39.1	1,070,613	42.1	2,636,304	49.3
World C (Christians)	20	0.0	3,850	0.5	78,400	4.4	3,325	1,248	4,573	4.70	104,110	4.8	124,127	4.9	318,000	5.9
Country's population	**280,000**	**100.0**	**722,945**	**100.0**	**1,785,000**	**100.0**	**75,675**	**0**	**75,675**	**3.60**	**2,155,142**	**100.0**	**2,542,000**	**100.0**	**5,352,000**	**100.0**

COLUMNS, ROWS.
For meanings and definitions, see Codebook (Part 3). Note that, by definition, total 'Christians' = professing + crypto-Christians, which also = affiliated + unaffiliated Christians, and also = Great Commission Christians + latent Christians. Percentages may not always total exactly, due to rounding.

NOTES ON RELIGIONS
BUDDHISTS. Sinhala labor migrants from Sri Lanka.
BAHA'IS. In 3 local spiritual assemblies (1973).
CRYPTO-CHRISTIANS. Unorganized individual nationals either in the recognized churches, in unrecognized churches, or in isolated radio churches.
HINDUS. Indian merchants, from Gujarat and Bombay.
INDEPENDENTS. South Indian and Arab indigenous congregations, in 7 groupings in 1995, mushrooming to 13 by 1997 (see Table 2).
MUSLIMS. Mostly Hinawis who are Ibadi Kharijites (fundamentalist seceders from both Sunnis and Shias), with Ghafiris in Sunni minorities (Shafiite, Hanbalite, and Wahhabi), and 7% Shias (Persians, Arabs, who are Ithna-Asharis or Ismailis) near Muscat. Most Muslims are Arabs (Omani and expatriate), with some Iranians, Baluchis, Indo-Pakistanis and Zanzibari Blacks. There is also, since 1950, a small Ahmadiya Mission (enumerated here under Muslims although declared non-Muslim by Pakistan). *Hajj pilgrims to Mecca.* (1970) 1,569; (1975) 3,377; (1976) 2,251.
NONRELIGIOUS. British and Americans.
PROFESSING CHRISTIANS. Mainly Europeans and USA personnel; fluctuating in the 1990s due to replacement of expatriate technicians by Omanis.

Great Commission Instrument Panel: status of Oman (for explanation see start of Part 4)

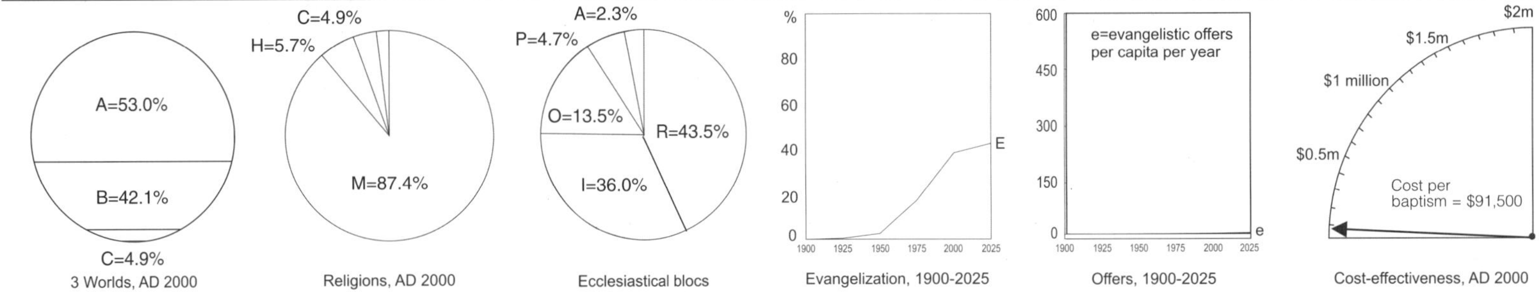

reaching verdicts. The government maintains strict control over the media through a law requiring prepublication censorship. The government also owns 2 of the 4 dailies and subsidizes the other two. Legal discrimination against women exists but is based on the Sharia, rather than on governmental decrees.

Human environment. Although an arid country, Oman has a rich and varied bird population, including 372 bird species and 63 species of butterflies. The major environmental problem is water scarcity which may become more serious in the future as the present aquifers are depleted. Extensive use of water pumps in the northern coastal areas has led to seawater intrusion in the shallow aquifers. Oil tanker traffic through the Gulf of Oman and the Strait of Hormuz has polluted the Omani beaches.

NON-CHRISTIAN RELIGIONS

Islam is the official religion, the majority being Ibadi Kharijites. Shafite, Hanbalite and Wahhabi Sunnis make up important minorities.

Oman Christian Fellowship. Notice-board offering Full Gospel ministry.

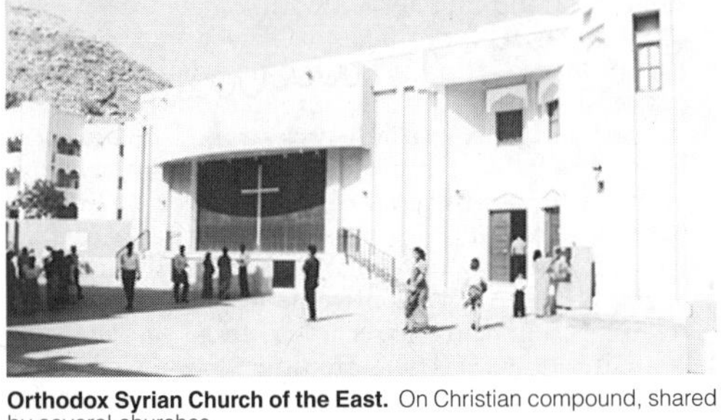

Orthodox Syrian Church of the East. On Christian compound, shared by several churches.

CHRISTIANITY

CATHOLIC CHURCH. Although tradition holds that the Apostle Bartholomew brought Christianity to Arabia, and unquestionably Christian communities were active there in the first centuries of the Christian era, this almost certainly did not include Oman. With the triumph of Islam in the 7th century, Christianity was completely eclipsed in Arabia proper until the 19th century. Meanwhile, Portuguese lived in Muscat from 1508. The first Catholic missionary of the modern era returned to Aden in 1841. Aden became a prefecture in 1854 and a vicariate in 1888, and the following year, the vicariate of Arabia was formed. The vicariate which has been administered from Abu Dhabi since 1973, exercises ecclesiastical supervision over the Catholic community of Oman, which in 1995 consisted of 44,000 Catholics, all foreigners. There are no Catholic institutions, but an American Capuchin has been resident in the capital, Muscat. In November 1977, the first Catholic church building in the Sultanate of Oman was consecrated in Muscat on land donated by the sultan of Oman himself.

The Holy See has no diplomatic relations with Oman in AD 2000, but is represented there by an apostolic delegate residing in Lebanon.

OTHER CHURCHES. The pioneer Protestant missionaries to Oman were James Cantine and Samuel Zwemer who set out respectively in 1889 and 1890 under the American Arabian Mission. In 1894, their work was taken over by the Reformed Church in America which continues to support 16 missionaries and 2 clinics in the country. The Reformed Church also operates a school at Muscat. Anglican chaplaincy is organized as part of the Episcopal Church in Jerusalem and the Middle East.

Bible Centre and volunteer staffer, Muscat.

Country summary. **Worlds A, B, C by ethnolinguistic peoples, cities, and major civil divisions in Oman.**																						
	PEOPLES							*CITIES*							*CIVIL DIVISIONS*							
World	*Num*	*Pop 2000*	*C%*	*Christians*	*E%*	*U%*	*Unevangelized*	*Num*	*Pop 2000*	*C%*	*Christians*	*E%*	*U%*	*Unevangelized*	*Num*	*Pop 2000*	*C%*	*Christians*	*E%*	*U%*	*Unevangelized*
A	13	854,026	0.68	5,776	29	71	605,131	0	0	0.00	0	0	0	0	7	1,850,089	3.97	73,500	45	55	1,023,444
B	10	1,626,714	3.65	59,358	54	46	742,693	1	61,892	5.50	3,404	51	49	30,531	1	691,650	7.00	48,416	53	47	324,422
C	3	61,002	93.08	56,783	100	0	42	0	0	0.00	0	0	0	0	0	0	0.00	0	0	0	0
Total	**26**	**2,541,742**	**4.80**	**121,917**	**47**	**53**	**1,347,866**	**1**	**61,892**	**5.50**	**3,404**	**51**	**49**	**30,531**	**8**	**2,541,739**	**4.80**	**121,916**	**47**	**53**	**1,347,866**

Indigenous missions. There are very few indigenous Christians in Oman and no missionaries have been sent to other countries.

CHURCH AND STATE

With one of the largest proportions of nomadic populations in the world and few oil resources, Oman remains the least-developed state in the Persian gulf. Although the country is still ruled directly without benefit of a constitution, the new sultan has promised to establish a modern government. Islam is the state religion, and the country's judicial system conforms to Islamic law. Nevertheless, Oman places fewer restrictions on Christian activity than most of its neighbors. In 1973, sultan Qabous officially accorded to the Catholic and Protestant churches the right to found Christian communities in the sultanate.

BROADCASTING AND MEDIA

Programs in Arabic and English can be received from FEBA (Seychelles) and HCJB (Ecuador).

FUTURE TRENDS AND PROSPECTS

Christianity is projected to grow from 1970 (0.5%) to 2025 (5.9%) but gains are primarily due to increased use of foreign labor (Indians, British, and Americans).

Christianity could reach 10% before AD 2050, but only with significant response from Omani Muslims or with an increase in expatriate labor. Islam is likely to remain well above 80% throughout the 21st century.

BIBLIOGRAPHY

A bibliography of Oman, 1900–1950. R. King & J. H. Stevens. *Occasional paper series*, no. 2. Durham, UK: University of Durham, Centre for Middle Eastern and Islamic Studies, 1973. 141p.

'A prevalence of furies: tribes, politics and religion in Oman and Trucial Oman,' J. B. Kelly, in *The Arabian peninsula: society and politics*, p.107–141. D. Hopwood (ed). London: Allen & Unwin, 1972.

Analytical guide to the bibliographies on the Arabian Peninsula. C. L. Geddes. *Bibliographic series*, no. 4. Denver, CO: American Institute of Islamic Studies, 1974.

Behind the veil in Arabia: women in Oman. U. Wikan. Chicago: University of Chicago Press, 1991. 327p.

Grace in the gulf: the autobiography of Jeanette Boersma, missionary nurse in Iraq and the Sultanate of Oman. J. Boersma & D. De Groot. *Historical series of the Reformed Church in America*, no. 20. Grand Rapids, MI: Eerdmans, 1991. 315p.

Nomads in the Sultanate of Oman: tradition and development in Dhofar. J. Janzen. *Westview special studies on the Middle East.* Boulder, CO: Westview Press, 1986. 338p.

Oman. F. A. Clements. 2nd ed. *World bibliographical series*, vol. 29. Oxford, UK: CLIO Press, 1994. 290p. (See especially 'Religion,' p.117–8).

Oman and Ibadhism. A. H. Maamiry. 2nd ed. New Delhi: Lancers Books, 1989. 129p.

Oman and southeastern Arabia: a bibliographic survey. M. O. Shannon. Boston: G. K. Hall, 1978. 165p.

Persian Gulf states: country studies. H. C. Metz (ed). 3rd ed. *Area handbook series.* Lanham, MD: Bernan, 1994. 501p.

'Present–day Christianity in the Gulf states of the Arabian Peninsula,' N. A. Horner, *Occasional bulletin of missionary research*, 2 (April 1978), 53–63.

Religion and political structure: remarks on Ibadism in Oman and the Mzab (Algeria). T. Bierschenk. Bielefeld, Germany: University of Bielefeld, 1983. 27p.

Source book on Arabian Gulf States, Arabian Gulf in general, Kuwait, Bahrain, Qatar and Oman. S. Kabeel. Kuwait: Kuwait University, Libraries Department, 1975. 427p. (With over 3,000 item bibliography).

The countries and tribes of the Persian Gulf. S. B. Miles. 2nd ed. London: Cass, 1966. 643p.

'The Ibadites in Arabia and Africa,' T. Lewicki, *Journal of world history*, 13, 1 (1971), 51–130.

The imamate tradition of Oman. J. C. Wilkinson. *Cambridge Middle East Library.* Cambridge, UK: Cambridge University Press, 1987. 427p.

The Sultanate of Oman: a twentieth century history. M. Joyce. Westport, CT: Praeger, 1995.

'Tradition and change among the pastoral Harasiis in Oman,' D. Chatty, in *Anthropology and development in North Africa and the Middle East.* Boulder, CO: Westview Press, 1990.

Tribes in Oman. J. R. L. Carter. London: Peninsular, 1982. 176p.

Water and tribal settlement in South–east Arabia: a study of the Afloaj of Oman. J. C. Wilkinson. Oxford, UK: Clarendon Press, 1977. 292p.

Women and community in Oman. C. Eickelman. New York: New York University Press, 1984. 270p.

The Passion of Christ, on official postage stamps: from left, Gethsemane, Before Pilate, Carrying the Cross, Behold your Son, Entombment.

Country Table 2. **Organized churches and denominations in Oman.**									
Official name (bold type = church with over 10% of all affiliated) 1	*Begun* 2	*Type* 3	*Counc* 4	*Congs* 5	*Adults* 6	*Affiliated 1970* 7	*Affiliated 1995* 8	*G%* 9	*Names, notes, and other statistics* (see Codebook, Part 3) 10
Anglican Church (D Cyprus & the Gulf)	c1910	A-plu	aw...	3	1,600	1,100	3,400	4.62	Chaplaincy, in Episcopal Ch in Jerusalem & ME. For 2,000 UK citizens.
Arab indigenous churches	c1968	I-3cS	.....	3	1,070	25	2,117	19.43	Jordanian, Lebanese, Egyptian.
Bread of Life Church	1993	I-3cS	.....	2	200	–	400	50.00	Recent fellowship centered on Bible reading and distribution.
Brethren Assemblies	c1960	I-CBr	.....	5	200	100	300	4.49	Longstanding Plymouth Brethren assemblies; mainly Indians (Tamils, Malayalis).
Catholic Church (VA Arabia)	1508	R-Lat	P..L.	30	20,300	470	43,800	19.89	All expatriates (including Arab Catholics) mainly Filipino migrant laborers. 1 Capuchin in Muscat.
Other charismatic house groups	c1976	I-3cS	.....	20	1,210	–	3,280	5.26	Arab networks of charismatics.
Church of South India	c1970	P-Uni	.....	4	1,300	–	2,429	36.59	*CSI.* Members: Tamil, Telugu, Hindi, Malayali, Gujerati.
Coptic Orthodox Church	1970	O-Cop	N....	10	4,500	1,000	6,000	7.43	*P Alexandria.* Egyptian labor migrants.
Filipino Christian Fellowship	1993	I-3pF	.....	4	250	–	700	50.00	Filipino pentecostals: labor migrants from Philippines.
Isolated radio churches	c1950	I-3rS	.....	100	7,000	300	15,000	16.94	Isolated radio believers, mostly aged 12-25 (ICI, WEC, FEBA, RVOG, RVatican).
Mar Thoma Syrian Ch (D Behya Kerala)	c1968	I-ReO	xwe..	4	2,300	150	4,300	14.37	In Diocese of Outside Kerala. South Indians (Malayalis) in Muscat. 1x.
New Christian Fellowship	1993	I-3cS	.....	3	100	–	300	50.00	Young church members; charismatic healings and ministries.
Oman Christian Fellowship	1992	I-3fF	.....	5	500	–	1,000	33.33	Full Gospel Ministry. Mainly Filipinos, also Indians, Sri Lankans.
Orthodox Syrian Church of the East	1976	O-SyM	Dw...	8	1,500	–	5,000	5.26	*OSCE.* In D Bahya Kerala (Outside Kerala). South Indians. Meet in RCA church, Muscat.
Pentecostal Fellowship	1990	I-3pS	.....	5	300	–	600	20.00	In Muscat. M=Toledo Pentecostal Fellowship.
Protestant Church in Oman	1889	P-Ref	Rw...	20	1,300	500	3,660	8.29	*PCO.* M=RCA(USA). Ref Ch Synod (Denmark). School in Muscat. HQ Muscat. 16f(1 Dutch). 2h.
Revival Prayer Fellowship	1994	I-3cS	.....	5	200	–	500	100.00	Small groupings of Arab charismatics.
Seventh-day Adventist Ch	1970	P-Adv	x....	10	500	–	1,000	31.83	*SDA.* Recognized for quality of social service endeavors.
St Thomas Evangelical Ch	c1975	I-ReO	.....	1	200	–	500	5.00	Split in Kerala ex Mar Thoma Syrian Church. Malayalis.
Syrian Orthodox Church	1980	O-Syr	D....	2	1,000	–	2,000	6.67	*Jacobite Church.* Indians formerly in OSCE, but now directly under P Antioch (HQ Damascus).
Other independent churches		I-3pI	.....	5	3,000	200	5,600	0.05	Indian Pentecostals, Christian Brethren (Indian), New Apostolic Church (60 members), et alii.
Totals				**249**	**48,530**	**3,845**	**101,886**		

Churches, members, growth, 1900-2025	*Congs*	*Adults*	*Affiliated*	*G%*	*Total denominations*	*6 Megablocs:* *O*	*R*	*A*	*P*	*I*	*m*
Total churches, members, and denominations (mid-1900)	2	11	20	7.80	2	0	1	0	1	0	0
Total churches, members, and denominations (mid-1970)	31	2,065	3,845	7.80	15	1	1	1	1	11	0
Total churches, members, and denominations (mid-1990)	200	36,100	75,700	16.07	33	3	1	1	3	25	0
Total churches, members, and denominations (mid-1995)	249	48,530	101,886	6.12	35	3	1	1	3	27	0
Total churches, members, and denominations (mid-2000)	300	58,100	121,916	3.65	37	3	1	1	3	29	0
Total churches, members, and denominations (mid-2025)	1,400	151,000	316,000	3.88	83	6	1	1	15	60	0

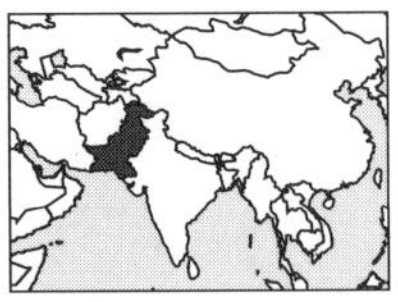

PAKISTAN

SECULAR DATA, AD 2000

STATE
Official name: Islami Jamhuriya e Pakistan (The Islamic Republic of Pakistan).
Short name: Pakistan. **Adjective of nationality:** of Pakistan, a Pakistani.
Flag: Green field with white crescent and star; white bar along hoist.
Area: 796,095 sq. km. (307,374 sq. mi.).
Government: Socialist Islamic republic, since 1971 (1859 British supremacy, 1947 Partition and Independence as dominion, 1956 republic, 1958 military rule).
Legislature: Parliament: Senate, 87 members; National Assembly, 217 members.
Official language: Urdu and English.
Monetary unit: 1 Pakistan rupee (PRs) = 100 paisa. **US$1=** PRs 50.07.
Chief cities: Karachi 11,774,000; Lahore 6,030,000; Faisalabad (Lyallpur) 2,228,000; Peshawar 2,094,000; Gujranwala 2,048,000.
Political divisions: 6 provinces.
Armed forces: 587,000.

DEMOGRAPHY
Population: 156,483,000.
Population density: 196.5/sq. km. (509.1/sq. mi.).
Under 15 years: 65,441,000.
Growth rate p.a.: 2.50% (births 32.91, deaths 6.75).
Mortality: Infant, per 1,000: 65.2, ; **Maternal per 100,000:** 340.0.
Life expectancy: 66 (male 65, female 67).
Household size: 6.3. **Floor area per person, sq.m:** 1.3.
Major languages: Urdu, English, Punjabi, Sindhi, Pushtu, Baluchi, Kashmiri, Brahui, Gujarati, Hindi, and 40 smaller languages.
Urban dwellers: 37.04%. **Urban growth rate p.a.:** 4.2%.
Labor force: 28%.

ETHNOLINGUISTIC PEOPLES
42.6% Western Punjabi (Lahnda); 11.6% Sindhi; 9.8% Southern Punjabi; 7.9% Eastern Pathan; 7.4% Urdu.

ECONOMY
National income p.a. per person: US$460; **per family:** US$2,897.

EDUCATION
Adult literacy: 37% (male 50%, female 24%). **Schools:** 156,450.
Universities: 804. **School enrolment:** female/male: 28%/56%.

HEALTH
Access to health services: 55%. **Access to safe water:** 60%.
Hospitals: 10,905 (6 beds per 10,000). **Doctors:** 63,033.
Blind: 900,000. **Deaf:** 9,360,400. **Murder rate:** 6.
Lepers: 150,000. **Underweight prevalence under 5:** 38%.

LITERATURE
New book titles p.a.: 630 (4 p.a. per million). **Periodicals:** 395.
Newspapers: 273 dailies.

COMMUNICATION (per 1,000 people)
Phones: 16 (4% mobile). **Radios:** 76. **TV sets:** 22.
Daily newspaper circulation: 22. **Computers:** 5.

REFUGEES
Alien refugees from other countries: 1,200,000.

HUMAN LIFE AND LIBERTY (optimum condition=100.0%)
HDI: 44.5. **HSI:** 33.0. **HFI:** 12.5. **EFL:** 39.0.

Country Table 1. **Religious adherents in Pakistan, AD 1900-2025.**

Year	1900		1970		mid-1990		Annual change, 1990-2000				mid-1995		mid-2000		mid-2025	
Name	Adherents	%	Adherents	%	Adherents	%	Natural	Conversion	Total	Rate	Adherents	%	Adherents	%	Adherents	%
Muslims	20,910,900	82.2	63,585,450	96.8	114,591,100	96.2	3,589,841	-12,420	3,577,421	2.75	130,935,700	96.1	150,365,313	96.1	251,594,000	95.7
Christians	**90,000**	**0.4**	**1,160,000**	**1.8**	**2,836,000**	**2.4**	**88,844**	**12,616**	**101,460**	**3.11**	**3,335,000**	**2.5**	**3,850,596**	**2.5**	**7,450,000**	**2.8**
PROFESSION																
crypto-Christians	25,000	0.1	208,482	0.3	1,000,000	0.8	31,327	8,673	40,000	3.42	1,180,000	0.9	1,400,000	0.9	2,900,000	1.1
professing Christians	**65,000**	**0.3**	**951,518**	**1.5**	**1,836,000**	**1.5**	**57,517**	**3,943**	**61,460**	**2.93**	**2,155,000**	**1.6**	**2,450,596**	**1.6**	**4,550,000**	**1.7**
AFFILIATION																
unaffiliated Christians	0	0.0	5,218	0.0	33,000	0.0	1,034	-499	535	1.51	36,945	0.0	38,351	0.0	46,000	0.0
affiliated Christians	**90,000**	**0.4**	**1,154,782**	**1.8**	**2,803,000**	**2.4**	**87,810**	**13,115**	**100,925**	**3.12**	**3,298,055**	**2.4**	**3,812,245**	**2.4**	**7,404,000**	**2.8**
Protestants	50,000	0.2	562,000	0.9	1,310,700	1.1	41,061	7,469	48,530	3.20	1,558,940	1.1	1,796,000	1.2	3,700,000	1.4
Roman Catholics	20,000	0.1	341,231	0.5	860,000	0.7	26,941	3,559	30,500	3.08	1,008,742	0.7	1,165,000	0.7	2,100,000	0.8
Independents	0	0.0	251,251	0.4	631,500	0.5	19,783	2,067	21,850	3.02	729,376	0.5	850,000	0.5	1,600,000	0.6
Marginal Christians	0	0.0	300	0.0	800	0.0	25	20	45	4.52	997	0.0	1,245	0.0	4,000	0.0
Anglicans	20,000	0.1	0	0.0	0	0.0	0	0	0	0.00	0	0.0	0	0.0	0	0.0
Trans-megabloc groupings																
Evangelicals	25,000	0.1	230,000	0.4	453,000	0.4	14,191	3,109	17,300	3.29	531,875	0.4	626,000	0.4	1,315,000	0.5
Pentecostals/Charismatics	0	0.0	140,000	0.2	631,500	0.5	19,783	6,067	25,850	3.49	745,038	0.6	890,000	0.6	1,841,000	0.7
Great Commission Christians	**80,000**	**0.3**	**900,000**	**1.4**	**2,575,000**	**2.2**	**80,668**	**13,926**	**94,594**	**3.18**	**3,000,000**	**2.2**	**3,520,938**	**2.3**	**6,575,000**	**2.5**
Hindus	3,560,000	14.0	890,000	1.4	1,420,000	1.2	44,485	319	44,804	2.78	1,625,000	1.2	1,868,039	1.2	3,130,000	1.2
Ethnoreligionists	130,000	0.5	35,000	0.1	135,000	0.1	4,229	-714	3,515	2.34	148,000	0.1	170,150	0.1	280,000	0.1
Nonreligious	0	0.0	10,000	0.0	90,000	0.1	2,819	226	3,045	2.96	104,000	0.1	120,452	0.1	360,000	0.1
Buddhists	0	0.0	2,000	0.0	75,000	0.1	2,350	-206	2,144	2.55	86,000	0.1	96,443	0.1	160,000	0.1
Baha'is	100	0.0	15,100	0.0	55,000	0.1	1,723	643	2,366	3.64	68,500	0.1	78,658	0.1	140,000	0.1
Zoroastrians	4,000	0.0	5,200	0.0	19,000	0.0	595	9	604	2.80	22,000	0.0	25,037	0.0	47,000	0.0
Atheists	0	0.0	2,000	0.0	5,000	0.0	157	-31	126	2.27	5,500	0.0	6,259	0.0	10,000	0.0
Chinese folk-religionists	0	0.0	1,000	0.0	1,700	0.0	53	-6	47	2.49	1,900	0.0	2,173	0.0	4,000	0.0
Sikhs	760,000	3.0	0	0.0	1,500	0.0	47	-9	38	2.27	1,650	0.0	1,878	0.0	4,000	0.0
Jews	0	0.0	250	0.0	700	0.0	22	-6	16	2.10	750	0.0	862	0.0	1,000	0.0
doubly-counted religionists	0	0.0	0	0.0	-75,000	-0.1	-2,350	-421	-2,771	3.19	-90,000	-0.1	-102,706	-0.1	-180,000	-0.1
World A (unevangelized persons)	23,011,320	90.4	42,708,900	65.0	68,514,125	57.5	2,145,933	-665,156	1,480,777	1.98	76,024,351	55.8	83,248,956	53.2	130,185,000	49.5
World B (evangelized non-Christians)	2,353,680	9.2	21,837,100	33.2	47,804,875	40.1	1,498,038	652,540	2,150,578	3.80	56,885,005	41.7	69,383,448	44.3	125,365,000	47.7
World C (Christians)	90,000	0.4	1,160,000	1.8	2,836,000	2.4	88,844	12,616	101,460	3.11	3,335,000	2.5	3,850,596	2.5	7,450,000	2.8
Country's population	**25,455,000**	**100.0**	**65,706,000**	**100.0**	**119,155,000**	**100.0**	**3,732,815**	**0**	**3,732,815**	**2.76**	**136,244,357**	**100.0**	**156,483,000**	**100.0**	**263,000,000**	**100.0**

COLUMNS, ROWS.
For meanings and definitions, see Codebook (Part 3). Note that, by definition, total 'Christians' = professing + crypto-Christians, which also = affiliated + unaffiliated Christians, and also = Great Commission Christians + latent Christians. Percentages may not always total exactly, due to rounding.

CENSUSES.
28.II.1951 (West Pakistan; excluding foreigners): 96.9% Muslims, 1.7% Hindus (1.2% scheduled castes), 1.4% Christians (432,706 persons), 5,320 Parsis, 680 Buddhists. 1.II.1961 (West Pakistan; excluding foreigners and nomads): 97.2% Muslims, 1.5% Hindus (1.0% scheduled castes), 1.4% Christians (583,884 persons), 5,219 Parsis, 2,445 Buddhists. **1981**: 96.7% Muslims, 1.56% Christians, 1.52% Hindus, 0.008% Parsis, 0.003% Sikhs, 0.003% Buddhists, 0.206% other religionists.

NOTES ON RELIGIONS
ANGLICANS. Formerly one of the larger denominations, the Anglican church disappeared as a separate entity in 1970 when it joined the Protestant union, the Church of Pakistan.
ATHEISTS. Pakistan Communist Party: membership negligible. There are a few intellectuals and humanists.
BAHA'IS. Reached area before 1892. Rapid growth from 19 local spiritual assemblies (1964) to 97 (1973). Baha'is are mostly Persian residents.
BUDDHISTS. Chinese and some low-caste Hindu converts.
CHRISTIANS. Recent conversions have been from among 30 Hindu scheduled castes in Sindh and southern Punjab (8,000 Catholic baptisms and 5,000 Protestant baptisms since 1940).
COUNTRY'S POPULATION. At Partition in 1947, about 5.5 million Hindus and 2.5 million Sikhs fled to India, and about 8 million Muslims fled from India to Pakistan. A total of at least 200,000 were killed en route.
CRYPTO-CHRISTIANS. Christians affiliated to churches but not known as such to state or society, mainly unorganized individual nationals in the recognized churches, or members of Pakistani indigenous churches, or isolated radio believers. There are a lot of secret believers because of family pressure on converts.
HINDUS. Still strong in rural areas of Sindh (500,000) despite continuing emigration to India; strong also in Lahore, Rawalpindi, Peshawar and Karachi. Hindu peoples include: Bagri (250,000), Bajania (840,000), Balmiki (25,000), Bhil (200,000), Kutchi Kohli (82,000), Lohar, Meghwar (100,000), Od (52,000), Parkari Kohli (250,000), Sochi, Tharadari Kohli (50,000), and Wadiara Kohli (120,000). Since 1900 the Hindu community has decreased in size continuously relative to the Muslim community due to (1) lower Hindu fertility resulting from the prohibition of widow remarriage, (2) the mass emigration of 5.5 million at Partition in 1947, and (3) a steady trickle of emigration to India subsequently.
INDEPENDENTS. In about 12 denominations in 1995 (see Table 2).
JEWS. With a synagogue in Karachi.
MUSLIMS. Mostly Sunnis (of the Hanafiite rite, 67% being under Sufi influence via the 2 major orders Qadiriya and Naqshabandiya) except for 18% Shias mainly in business and banking (Ismailis and Ithna-Asharis), and a few Wahhabi reform movement centers in the northwest. The totals here also include adherents of the 2 Ahmadiya factions (Qadianis and Lahoris) who in 1974 were formally declared by the state to be heretical and so non-Muslim. *Ahmadis.* A messianic movement out of Shia Islam, the Ahmadiya Movement was founded in 1889 and was based in Qadian (present Punjab in India) until forced to emigrate en masse from India to Pakistan in 1947, to its present headquarters in Rabwah. In 1900 there were about 40,000 adult Ahmadis from Afghanistan right across India, the majority from Orissa, Mysore, Kashmir, the Punjab and Hyderabad (Deccan). Although declared non-Muslim by the state, Ahmadis (who are in majority called Qadianis, with a small faction of 10,000 called Lahoris) regard themselves as devout Muslims and are engaged in Muslim proselytism in 100 countries of the world. Since 1973, social and political discrimination against Ahmadis has increased markedly in Pakistan. An annual convention at Rabwah has attracted 100,000 regularly. *Muslim practice.* About 30% of all Muslims are estimated to actually practice all required Muslim duties. *Conversions to Islam.* Since 1965, several low-caste Hindu tribes have become Muslim, including the Batwal (in Sialkot area), Bazigar (in Sindh) and Gagare. *Hajj pilgrims to Mecca.* Pakistan (East and West): (1968) 25,052; (1969) 28,535; (1970) 38,256; (1971) 23,344. West Pakistan only: (1972) 89,373; (1973) 60,688; (1974) 66,534; (1975) 45,017; (1976) 48,327.
PARSIS. Mainly in Karachi.
PENTECOSTALS (or, Charismatics). Mainly in Church of Pakistan (begun in 1966 among Anglicans) and in the Catholic Church (begun in 1972). By 1997 the latter had 10,000 attenders in 50 weekly prayer groups. The first National Charismatic Renewal Conference (using English) took place in Murree in July 1975 with 150 Catholics and Protestants (particularly from the Church of Pakistan) present; the first using Urdu, with 150 participants, was held in Lahore in January 1977.
SIKHS. At Partition in 1947, every one of the 2.5 million Sikhs either left the newly-formed Pakistan or remained and was killed.
ETHNORELIGIONISTS. Animists among the tribal peoples including the Gagre (60,000), Kohlis, several thousand Kafir animists in Chitral, Bhils, et alii. The 4,000 Black Kafirs in Chitral are animists with priest-shamans, worshipping Imra as supreme creator.

Country status. Pakistan is in the northwestern part of the Indian subcontinent bordering Afghanistan and India. It extends from the Arabian Sea to the Himalayas. Wheat, cotton, and rice are the principal crops, much which is grown in semiarid areas with the aid of the world's largest contiguous irrigation system.

HUMAN LIFE AND LIBERTY

Human need and development. In terms of development, Pakistan is in the same league as India, although its per capita income of $460 is slightly better than India's $340. But in many other respects, it trails India. The average life expectancy of 66 is higher than that of India's 64, and the percentage of adult illiterates is higher at 63 compared to India's 48. But in education and health the Pakistanis fare worse. Infant and maternal mortality rates remain high. Nutritional deficiencies are more widely prevalent today than under British rule. Housing and sanitation are deplorable in both rural and urban areas; slums and shanty towns predominate in the major cities, such as Karachi and Lahore. There are more households than there are houses in the country. About 70% of the houses in the rural areas are made of sun-baked mud and in the cities the shacks are made of a variety of

Great Commission Instrument Panel: status of Pakistan (for explanation see start of Part 4)

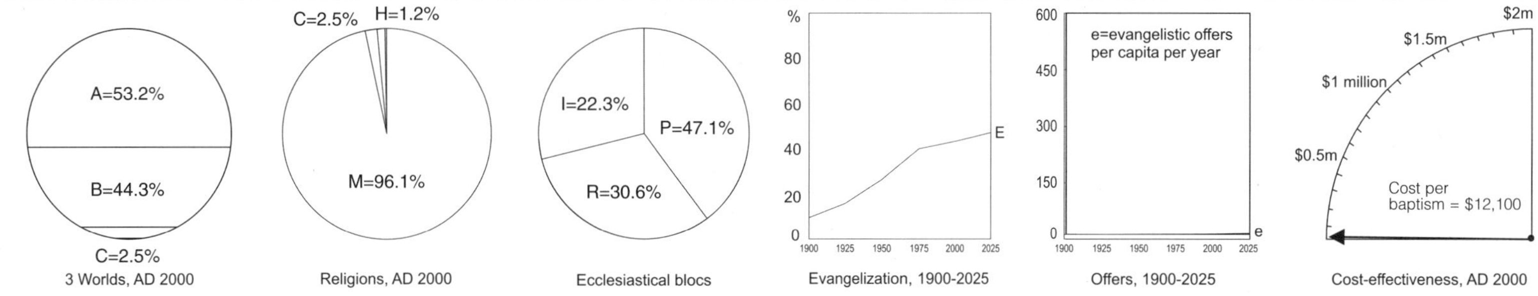

materials—cardboard, corrugated tin, or pieces of gunnysack. Very little public funding goes into social services, which are left to the *wakfs*, or Islamic charitable agencies. Numerous endemic and epidemic diseases have always been prevalent in the country, and inadequate diet, poor sanitation, and absence of adequate health facilities help to spread the diseases. The very high birth rate does not help any of these problems. Inequality of income has been increasing since independence, and the poor are worse off today than they were ever before.

Human rights and freedoms. Throughout its short history, Pakistan has suffered a deficit in human rights. For much of the post-independence period it has been under military rule. During the brief intervals of freedom, there were neither the political or legal mechanisms in place to ensure that people's rights would not be violated again. Arbitrary arrests, torture, and extrajudicial killings have become so routine that they do not even generate public outrage. There are few watchdogs of freedom; the media are controlled by one or other political group, Islamic extremists or economic interests. Corruption has become institutionalized in politics, police, government, and judiciary. Political violence has extended to the highest echelons of leadership; including the prime minister's office. Sectarian clashes result in numerous murders every week. Religious zealots make life unbearable for non-Muslim minorities, and they are encouraged in this effort by the government whose own attention is focused on turning the country into an Islamic state. Police shootouts are staged to cover up deaths of prisoners tortured to death while in police custody. In some cases persons shot to death by police are labeled as suicides or terrorists and saboteurs. Police torture prisoners routinely to elicit confessions or compel them to incriminate others. More than 70% of women in police custody are sexually assaulted or subjected to other physical violence. Police accused of offenses are seldom tried and punished, but are generally transferred to another district. The Hadood Ordinances promulgated by the central government in 1979 provided harsh punishments for violating the Islamic code of behavior. They apply to Muslims and non-Muslims alike, but weigh most heavily on women. A women who reports a case of rape to the authorities can find herself charged with adultery under these ordinances, and then imprisoned and flogged. Under a preventive detention law, hundreds of political opponents are detained for long periods without charge or implicated in false criminal charges. The police sometimes detain citizens without charge in order to extort money from them for their release. Such detainees are held incommunicado in prisons far from their homes. In many cases, bail, although provided for by law, is arbitrarily denied or set unreasonably high. Although the justices of high courts have a reasonable degree of security, those at lower levels are beholden to their political patrons and try to defend their interests. They may be transferred or denied tenure if they decide cases against those in executive authority. In 1990 the government promulgated 2 Islamic concepts as law: qisas (an eye for an eye) and diyat (blood money). In 1987 the government established the so-called 'speedy trial' courts where due process was seriously abridged. In 1991 the federal cabinet accepted the Sharia court's decision to apply death penalty to anyone convicted of intentionally uttering contemptuous remarks or offering insults to the prophet Muhammad. The first person to be so sentenced was a Christian. After the passage of the Sharia law there has been a significant increase in censorship. Women are required to cover their heads with a long scarf in all locally produced television programming. Government is able to pressure the press into submission through its control of advertising support and allotments of newsprint. Charges of sedition are sometimes brought against journalists who defy government 'advice' on publication of certain types of materials. Police attacks are common against journalists and photographers who record police violence against the people. In addition, fundamentalist Islamic groups enforce their own brand of justice against those who do not conform to Quranic injunctions on public conduct. After the passage of the Sharia law, the position of women has deteriorated. In rural areas the adult female literacy rate is only 4%, and in urban areas, women are encouraged to remain at home or veil their faces when going out. Divorce and inheritance laws are heavily weighted against women. Under the Hadood Ordinances, the testimony of one man was equal to those of 2 women. Rape of women is condoned because it is regarded as a private matter. Burning of women by husbands or in-laws is generally reported as kitchen stove accidents. Women suspected of adultery may be stoned publicly, but not men charged with the same offense.

Human environment. Northern Pakistan is rich in wildlife, and is home to more than 6,000 species of plants, including 2,000 medicinal plants. Yet much of Pakistan's ecological resources are at risk because of the enormous pressure of population growth. Water is scarce in most parts of the country as the major rivers have been dammed and their water diverted to irrigation. Unlike India, Pakistan does not receive the monsoons. Water quality is deteriorating, because of inadequate sewage facilities, and barely one-half of the population has access to safe water. There is severe coastal pollution around the Karachi area. Fuelwood supplies the energy needs of rural families, and this has led to the indiscriminate cutting of trees. The nation's forest resources are shrinking by more than 1% each year. Even in arable areas, erosion and poor agricultural practices have combined to degrade the land, once noted as among the most fertile in Asia.

NON-CHRISTIAN RELIGIONS

Islam was proclaimed in 1956 to be the state religion of Pakistan; and in fact, the nation had been created in 1947 on the basis of the common Muslim religious identity shared by the peoples inhabiting the eastern and western parts of the Indian subcontinent. Until the outbreak of civil war between East and West Pakistan in 1971, strenuous efforts had been made to remind the population of the earlier struggle for independence and to stress that Pakistan was the most populous Muslim country in the world. Since the secession of the East as Bangladesh, the Islamic character of Pakistan has been even more accentuated, although there are also serious tensions between the rival claims of traditionalism and modernism in providing solutions for present-day problems. Both in mosques and in religious schools, maulvi (religious leaders) warn of the dangers of modernism and call for the preservation of traditional religious values. On the other hand, secularizing tendencies are clearly evident and can be seen in the growing influence of socialists, especially in the political parties. The Central Institute of Islamic Research established by the government contributes to this modernizing tendency, particularly through its training programs for teachers of Islam in government schools. Two Muslim international organizations are based in Pakistan: (1) the World Federation of Islamic Missions, including also the Ahimia Institute of Islamic Studies, the function of which is to prepare Muslim missionaries; and (2) the World Muslim Congress (Motamar al-Alam al-Islami), in Karachi, whose origin goes back to 1926 but which did not become a permanent organization until 1951. The latter is one of the most important of

Ahmadis. Annual convention at Rabwah, with in attendance 100,00 devout Ahmadis (who regard themselves as Muslims, though declared non-Muslims by the state), listening to speech by leader Hazrat Hafiz Mirza Nasir Ahmad, Khalifat-ul-Massih III. At 1974 convention, 15,000 converts were made.

Country summary. **Worlds A, B, C by ethnolinguistic peoples, cities, and major civil divisions in Pakistan.**

	PEOPLES							*CITIES*							*CIVIL DIVISIONS*						
World	*Num*	*Pop 2000*	*C%*	*Christians*	*E%*	*U%*	*Unevangelized*	*Num*	*Pop 2000*	*C%*	*Christians*	*E%*	*U%*	*Unevangelized*	*Num*	*Pop 2000*	*C%*	*Christians*	*E%*	*U%*	*Unevangelized*
A	80	115,171,832	2.64	3,042,135	44	56	64,497,057	56	15,340,556	1.29	197,682	43	57	8,710,977	4	64,421,626	1.14	737,417	40	60	38,809,217
B	11	41,295,670	1.83	757,495	54	46	18,810,681	7	23,355,532	4.25	993,492	51	49	11,358,304	2	92,061,528	3.34	3,074,829	52	48	44,498,548
C	2	15,649	80.60	12,613	100	0	30	0	0	0.00	0	0	0	0	0	0	0.00	0	0	0	0
Total	**93**	**156,483,151**	**2.44**	**3,812,243**	**47**	**53**	**83,307,768**	**63**	**38,696,088**	**3.08**	**1,191,174**	**48**	**52**	**20,069,281**	**6**	**156,483,154**	**2.44**	**3,812,246**	**47**	**53**	**83,307,765**

Islam's international organizations, along with the Muslim World League (from the religious point of view) and the Islamic Conference (from the political point of view), both with headquarters in Saudi Arabia. The World Muslim Congress is principally a cultural organization although also religious, whose purpose is to promote unity and cooperation among Muslims. It is a member of the Muslim World League and tends to confine its attention principally to matters internal to the Muslim world. It has affiliated organizations in some 50 countries with 5 regional offices in Senegal, Somalia, Lebanon, Malaysia, and the Philippines.

Ahmadiya, begun as a Shia Muslim sect near Lahore in 1889, has grown dramatically in Pakistan and has sent missionaries to spread its doctrines throughout the world. Long considered heretical by other Muslims, it was formally and officially excluded from Islam in 1974 by the Muslim World League in Saudi Arabia and also declared non-Muslim by the Pakistan parliament. Known also as Qadianis, Ahmadis have their strength in the region of Lahore, on the northeast frontier with India and Indian Kashmir. At present, there are over 3 million Ahmadis in Pakistan.

Hinduism is still strong in Sindh in spite of the continuing tendency, evident since 1947, of Hindus to emigrate to India.

Traditional religions are practiced by several tribal peoples, including the Gagre, Kohli, Bhil, and others.

Church of Pakistan. *Top.* Inauguration service in 1970, with clergy at left. *Lower.* Khudian Village church (Diocese of Lahore) whose members have more than doubled since church was built.

CHRISTIANITY

The first missionaries and Christians were Nestorians who came to the Punjab during the 8th century, although no permanent work resulted. In 1594, Jesuit missionaries arrived at the court of Akbar in Lahore, but no lasting Roman Catholic work was begun until much later.

In the 20th century, the churches are mainly working among Punjabis, and 83% of all Christians in Pakistan are from this ethnic group. This is a result of a mass movement of illiterate low-caste Hindus into Christianity which began after the turn of the century. As Christians form no more than a small minority in a dominant Muslim society, they usually identify themselves first as a community in the religio-caste sense of the term. Their primary loyalties are to families and relatives and to their caste and ethnic coreligionists who speak the same language. Participation in national life and civil activities has little attraction for them. In general, Protestants have developed deeper roots than Catholics among rural illiterate communities; and their democratically oriented ecclesiastical policy has contributed to a more rapid pakistanization of church leadership. Catholicism, on the other hand, is strongest in the cities, especially among the Goan merchant class. There is today a small but rapidly growing number of well-educated indigenous clergy calling for more dynamic policies to help the churches face the challenge of the modern world.

PROTESTANT CHURCH. The Church of Pakistan was inaugurated in 1970 through a union of Anglicans, Methodists, Lutherans, and Sialkot Presbyterians. The largest of these was the Anglican Church. The Church Missionary Society entered Karachi in 1850, and the Anglican diocese of Lahore was organized in 1877. In 1960, the diocese of Karachi was formed under the first Pakistani Anglican bishop. American Methodists established themselves in Karachi in 1873 and, after 1900, were involved in a mass movement among Hindu outcasts in central Punjab. Between 1902 and 1915, Methodists increased from 1,200 to 15,000 and numbered 60,000 at the time of union. Meanwhile, Lutheran work had been begun in the northwest in 1903 by the Danish Pathan Mission, with additional workers from the Finnish Missionary Society lending support in 1959 and the World Mission Prayer League from the USA. Although all 3 were involved in the Pakistan Lutheran Church, the Danish Pathan Mission group refused to go into union in 1970. The Sialkot Church Council was formed through the missionary activity of Scottish Presbyterians and was formerly a member of the United Church of North India and Pakistan.

American Presbyterian missionaries opened their first station at Lahore in 1849 and moved westward outside the Lahore area in 1855. Since this early period, the work has been organized separately, and ultimately, 2 churches were formed known as the Lahore Church Council and the United Presbyterian Church of Pakistan. The latter church subsequently grew to be the largest Protestant denomination in Pakistan. Widely involved in education, United Presbyterians founded 5 institutions of higher learning, 3 of which are more than 100 years old. The church suffered from a schism in 1968 which carried a portion of the church into the fold of the International Council of Christian Churches (ICCC). It was hoped that the United Presbyterian Church of Pakistan would join the union scheme which produced the Church of Pakistan, but the schisms the church had suffered earlier militated against this. The Lahore Church Council also suffered a schism related to the ICCC in 1968 which played a role in its withdrawal from church union in 1970. Another smaller Presbyterian group is the Associate Reformed Presbyterian Church.

A number of Adventist, Baptist, Pentecostal, and other bodies have also begun work in the country, the most important being the Salvation Army. A Pentecostal body, the Full Gospel Assemblies of Pakistan, was of indigenous origin in 1943 but is now been part of the Swedish and North American mission work.

Church of Pakistan. Attending this village church on Sundays is the high point of the week for members.

CATHOLIC CHURCH. In 1594, Jesuits reached the court of the Mongol emperor Akbar, through whom subsidies were received for the construction of the first Christian church in Lahore. However, few conversions took place. Augustinians and Carmelites were involved in evangelistic activity in Sindh in the 17th century, but their work was interrupted by the persecution of 1672. Work was not begun again until after the conquest of Sindh by the British in 1842. In 1880, the vicariate of the Punjab was erected, being detached from the vicariate of Hindustan; and it became the vicariate of Lahore in 1886. The diocese of Karachi was made an archdiocese in 1950. The Catholic Church is served by 3 indigenous congregations of sisters in addition to 10 foreign orders and congregations of priests, brothers and sisters.

The Holy See has diplomatic relations with Pakistan and in AD 2000 is represented to government and the Catholic hierarchy by a nuncio residing in Islamabad.

Indigenous churches. During 1968, major Pakistani-led schisms occurred among the Lahore Presbyterians, United Presbyterians, Methodists, and Anglicans, influenced by the International Council of Christian Churches. The following year, an even larger split appeared among the United Presbyterians, resulting in the formation of the National Virgin Church of Pakistan. Several other small groups have also come into existence.

Renewal movements. In the 1990s the Pentecostal/Charismatic Renewal continued to spread rapidly across most older churches, and numbered over 890,000 adherents (of whom 9% Pentecostals, 33% Charismatics, and 58% Independents).

Indigenous missions. Only a few Christians from Pakistan have served as missionaries abroad, and these mainly in surrounding countries. There is a growing movement of home missionaries within Pakistan.

Church and state. Christians are frequently arrested, tied up, beaten by hostile police.

CHURCH AND STATE

On 23 March 1956, Pakistan was proclaimed an Islamic republic, and this has been reemphasized in the constitutions of 1962 and 1973. Article 2 of the latter affirms: 'Islam shall be the State religion of Pakistan'. Article 20 guarantees that 'Every citizen shall have the right to profess, practice and propagate his religion; and every religious denomination and every sect thereof shall have the right to establish, maintain and manage its religious institutions'. The constitution outlaws any levy of special taxes for 'the propagation or maintenance of any religion' other than one's own (Article 20) and guarantees that no student will be required to receive religious instruction or attend worship ceremonies against his will (Article 21). Article 31 calls upon the state to take steps to enable Muslims to live in accordance with the fundamental principles of Islam, including the compulsory 'teaching of the Holy Quran and Islamiat'. Article 36 affirms: 'The State shall safeguard the legitimate rights and interests of minorities, including their due representation in the Federal and Provincial services'. In Article 40, mention is made of the need 'to preserve and strengthen fraternal relations among Muslim countries based on Islamic unity', while Article 41 requires that the president of the republic be a Muslim. According to Article 106, a few seats are reserved for members of the minority religions in the provincial assemblies of Baluchistan (one seat), Punjah (3), North-West Frontier (one) and Sindh (2). Articles 227-231 in part IX of the constitution deal with 'Islamic Provisions', matters relating to the Holy Quran and Sunnah and the Islamic Council.

In order to demonstrate that its laws are in line with the Quran and with tradition, the government has established the Central Institute of Islamic Research, with the aim of promoting Islamic studies.

All matters concerning minorities, including religious questions, come under the Ministry of Minority Affairs, a ministry created after 1970. Christians, Hindus, scheduled castes, Sikhs, Parsis, Buddhists, Ahmadis, and tribal groups are all defined as minorities. Ahmadis or Qadianis were included in the list of non-Muslim minorities by an amendment to Article 106 of the constitution on 7 September 1974. At the same time, the following new clause was added as an amendment to Article 260: 'A person who does not believe in the absolute and unqualified finality of the prophethood of Mohammed (Peace Be Upon Him), the last of the prophets, or claims to be a prophet in any sense of the word or of any description whatsoever, after Mohammed (Peace Be Upon Him) or recognizes such a claimant as a prophet or a religious reformer, is not a Muslim for the purposes of the Constitution or Law'.

Churches are not obliged to register officially with government, but as a matter of policy, most dioceses and denominations have been registered in the names of individuals, some of whom are foreigners.

Since 1969, the government has exercised increasing control over Christian institutions and the activities of foreign missionaries, it being feared that they are evangelizing and converting people. All private schools and colleges were nationalized after a government decision taken in 1972. Although this law affects Muslims as well as Christian schools, Christians believe that its main purpose is to weaken Christian influence in Pakistan in contradiction to Article 20 of the constitution. It is necessary to emphasize that the government has not taken over the ownership of nationalized Christian institutions. They continue to belong to the churches and are rented by the government.

Nevertheless, the situation of Christians in Pakistan is becoming increasingly precarious due to both a generalized anti-Christian agitation and a growing feeling among numerous members of the federal government that Christianity should be suppressed.

Scripture distribution. *Bottom.* Printing Pashtu New Testament in Lahore. *Top.* Brisk sales of scriptures outside village church.

BROADCASTING AND MEDIA

Shortwave radio programs in Baloch, Hindko, Punjabi, Pashto, Sindhi, Siraiki, and Urdu can be received from FEBA (Seychellese), and in Urdu from TWR (Swaziland). Shortwave radio programs from KNLS have seen some response. AWR's Lahore studio produces programs in Urdu and Dari (Farsi). Pakistan is a member of UNDA. Catholics air a 90-minute Christmas story on Christmas day, and a 90-minute Easter story on Good Friday. Similar Christmas and Easter plays (each 15 minutes) air on television. Media courses are taught in Lahore.

Despite its low distribution, the 'Jesus' Film has been an extremely useful tool: of the 8 million who have viewed it (6% of the population), 3 million—nearly half—have responded.

INTERDENOMINATIONAL ORGANIZATIONS

Cooperation between Protestant and Anglican missions crystallized in 1913 with the formation of the Punjab Representative Council of Missions. After a visit by John R. Mott, it became known in 1923 as the Punjab Christian Council and was associated with other Christian councils in India. Following national independence in 1947, the name was changed in 1949 to the West Pakistan Christian Council, which in 1971 had as members 6 churches, 6 missions and 9 other Christian organizations. After Bangladesh gained its independence, the name was changed to the Pakistan Christian Council, then again to the National Council of Churches in Pakistan. Another more conservative council is the Evangelical Fellowship of Pakistan, organized in 1956 and composed of 4 mission and churches. The International Council of Christian Churches (ICCC) has 5 member churches. The Catholic Bishop's Conference sponsors a Commission for Ecumenism.

Cooperative ecumenical institutions and organizations include: (1) Institute for Religious and Social Studies/Ecumenical Section, founded by Franciscans in 1962, which aims at fostering an ecumenical attitude among Catholics, better relations between Catholics and Protestants and common projects and studies, including the compilation of a joint Dictionary of Christian Terminology, in Urdu; (2) Pakistan Christian Industrial Service, founded in 1969 as an autonomous body by the Catholic, Anglican, and Methodists churches of Karachi, which seeks to promote Christian concern for the social, economic, and spiritual dimensions of urbanization and industrialization in Pakistan; (3) Adult Basic Education office, an autonomous group organized by Protestant churches with the help of Catholics and Muslims for the purposes of planning, organizing and promoting adult education programs for illiterate and newly literate adults; and (4) Christian Medical Association, which helps to coordinate the medical programs of the various churches.

Three Christian institutes or centers have been established to promote a better understanding of Islam: (1) Christian Study Center, founded in 1967 by the West Pakistan Christian Council with 2 Catholic members on its board of managers, which aims at creating among the churches an appreciation for Islam and seeks to build up contacts with Muslim schools; (2) Loyola Hall, founded by Jesuits, which is largely academic in nature; and (3) Institute for Religions and Social studies Islamic Section, founded by Franciscans in 1962, which seeks to encourage dialogue between Christians and Muslims.

FUTURE TRENDS AND PROSPECTS

Christianity will in all probability grow to 2.8% by 2025, primarily through the establishment of small but viable indigenous churches among the Pathan, Sindhi, and Urdu peoples. Islam consequently would drop to 95.7% by 2025, down from 96.8% in 1970.

Christianity will probably not reach 4% by AD 2050 without a significant number of conversions among Muslims. Islam will likely remain over 90% throughout the 21st century.

BIBLIOGRAPHY

A century for Christ in India and Pakistan, 1855–1955. Lahore, Pakistan: United Presbyterian Church, 1958.

A glossary of the tribes and castes of the Punjab and North–West Frontier Province. D. Ibbetson, E. Maclagan & H. A. Rose. Reprint, New Delhi: Rima, 1985. 3 vols.

A people of migrants: ethnicity, state, and religion in Karachi. O. Verkaaik. *Comparative Asian studies*, 15. Amsterdam: VU University Press, 1994. 89p.

A select bibliography of periodical literature on India and Pakistan, 1947–70. P. I. Cheema. Islamabad, Pakistan: National Commission on Historical and Cultural Research, 1976–84. 3 vols. (Over 5,000 titles).

A short history of the Catholic Diocese of Lahore. E. Blondeel. [Lahore: n.p., 197]. 6p.

A united church: faith and order in the North India/Pakistan unity plan: a theological assessment. W. J. Marshall. Delhi: I.S.P.C.K, 1987. 159p.

Atlas of South Asia. A. K. Dutt & M. M. Geib. Boulder, CO, and London: Westview Press, 1987. 255p.

'Church growth in West Pakistan with special emphasis upon the United Presbyterian Church.' F. E. Stock. Thesis, Fuller Theological Seminary, Pasadena, CA, 1968.

'Eine sozio–ethno–religiöse Minderheit: die Christen West–Pakistans,' K. H. Pfeffer, *Sociologus*, n.s., 12, 2 (1962), 113–27.

Focus on Pakistan. V. Stacey. London: Bible and Medical Missionary Fellowship, 1969. 124p.

Frontier challenge. L. T. Daniels. : Bridge Publications, 1987. 184p. (Missionary biography).

I dared to call Him Father. B. Sheikh with R. Schneider. Eastbourne, UK: Kingsway, 1979. 169p. (By a convert from Islam).

Into deserts: a history of the Catholic Diocese of Lahore, 1886–1986. J. Rooney. *Pakistan Christian history*, no. 4. Rawalpindi: Christian Study Centre, 1986. 149p.

Islam and Pakistan. F. Abbott. Ithaca, NY: Cornell University Press, 1968. 242p.

'Islam and Pakistan: a descriptive study.' A. M. Williams. M.A. thesis, Columbia Bible College, Columbia, SC, 1953. 125p.

Islam in India and Pakistan. No. 9 in section 22, *Islam*, in *Iconography of religions.* A. Schimmel. Leiden: E. J. Brill, 1982. 34p.

Islam in India and Pakistan: a religious history in India and Pakistan. M. T. Titus. *Christian students' library*, no. 20. Madras: Christian Literature Society, 1959. 328p.

Islamic modernism in India and Pakistan 1857–1964. A. Ahmad. London: Oxford University Press, 1967. 294p.

Islamic movements in Egypt, Pakistan, and Iran: an annotated bibliography. A. Hussain. London: Mansell, 1983. 168p.

'Islamic revival: an evangelical response in Pakistan.' W. T. Dalton. M.A.M. thesis, Talbot Theological Seminary, La Mirada, CA, 1984. 67p.

Islamic studies (Islamabad, Pakistan: International Islamic University), (1962–). (Quarterly journal).

Islamisation of Pakistan. A. Iqbal. Lahore, Pakistan: Vanguard Books, 1986. 198p.

'Islamization: an analysis of religious, political and social change in Pakistan,' R. Hassan, *Middle Eastern studies*, 21, 3 (1985), 263–84.

Millennium and charisma among Pathans: a critical essay in social anthropology. A. S. Ahmed. *International Library of Anthropology.* London and Boston: Routledge and Kegan Paul, 1976. 192p.

News from the country, Pakistan. Christian Study Centre series, no. 21. Rawalpindi, Pakistan: Christian Study Centre, 1985. 232p.

On heels of battles: a history of the Catholic Church in Pakistan, 1780–1886. J. Rooney. Rawalpindi, Pakistan: Christian Study Centre, 1986. 129p.

On rocky ground: the Catholic Church in the North West Territories, 1887–1987. J. Rooney. Rawalpindi, Pakistan: Christian Study Centre, 1987. 181p.

Pakistan. D. Taylor. *World bibliographical series*, vol. 10. Oxford, UK: CLIO Press, 1990. 290p. (See especially 'Religion,' p.92–101).

Pakistan Catholic directory, 1966. Karachi, Pakistan: Archbishop's House, 1966.

'Pakistan: Islamic government and society,' K. A. Faruki, in *Islam in Asia: religion, politics, & society*, p.53–78. J. L. Esposito (ed). New York: Oxford, 1987.

'Parliament, parties, polls and Islam: issues in the current debate on religion and politics in Pakistan,' M. Ahmad, *American journal of Islamic social sciences*, 2, 1 (1985), 15–28.

'People movements in the Punjab with special reference to the United Presbyterian Church.' F. E. Stock. Thesis, Fuller Theological Seminary, Pasadena, CA, 1974. (Also in published form, South Pasadena, CA: William Carey Library, 1975).

Reaching for the crescent moon: the Michael and Mary Cawthorne story. H. Rogers. Fearn: Christian Focus, 1995. 272p.

Religion and Asian politics: national dialogue: Pakistan. C. Amjad-Ali (ed). Hong Kong: Christian Conference of Asia International Affairs, 1987. 73p. (Papers from workshop at the Pastoral Institute in Multan, Pakistan).

Religion and society in Arab Sind. D. N. Maclean. *Monographs and theoretical studies in sociology and anthropology*, no. 25. Leiden: E. J. Brill, 1989. 201p.

Religion and society in Pakistan. A. Ahmad (ed). Leiden: E. J. Brill, 1971. 105p.

'Secularizing trends in West Pakistan,' R. A. Butler, *Al-Mushir* (Rawalpindi, Pakistan), 13, 1-2 (1971), 1–31. (Bibliography of 143 items).

Shadows in the dark: a history of Christianity in Pakistan up to the 10th century. J. Rooney. *Pakistan Christian history*, no. 1. Rawalpindi, Pakistan: Christian Study Centre, 1984. 120p.

'South Asia: the Baluch frontier tribes of Pakistan,' R. G. Wirsing, in *Protection of ethnic minorities: comparative perspectives*, p.277–312. R. G. Wirsing (ed). New York: Pergamon Press, 1981.

'State Islamicity in the 20th century: a case study of Pakistan.' M. Shafiq. Ph.D. dissertation, Temple University, Philadelphia, 1982. 300p.

Survey report of the Church in West Pakistan: a study of the economic, educational and religious condition of the Church, 1955–59. Lahore, Pakistan: West Pakistan

Christian Council, 1960. 55p.

Symphony on Sands: a history of the Catholic Church in Sind & Baluchistan. J. Rooney. *Pakistan Christian history*, nos. 6-7. Rawalpindi: Christian Study Centre, 1988. 202p.

The Christian community and change in nineteenth century North India. J. C. B. Webster. Delhi: Macmillan, 1976. 293p.

The Christian minority in the North West Frontier Province of Pakistan. L. Vemmelund. *CSC series*, no. 6. Rawalpindi, Pakistan: Christian Study Centre, 1973. 110p.

The concept of an Islamic state: an analysis of the ideological controversy in Pakistan. I. Ahmed. London: Frances Pinter, 1987. 235p.

The desert shall bloom: a drama of water in Pakistan. J. B. White. : Associate Reformed Presbyterian Church. 80p.

The hesitant dawn: Christianity in Pakistan 1579–1760. J. Rooney. *Pakistan Christian history monograph*, no. 2. Rawalpindi, Pakistan: Christian Study Centre, 1984. 120p.

The population of India and Pakistan. K. Davis. Princeton, NJ: Princeton University Press, 1951. 279p.

The religions of the Hindukush. K. Jettmar. Wiltshire, UK: Aris & Phillips, 1986. 3 vols.

The story of the Christian Church in India and Pakistan. S. C. Neill. Grand Rapids, MI: Eerdmans, 1970. 183p.

The sweepers of Slaughterhouse: conflict and survival in a Karachi neighbourhood. P. H. Streefland. *Studies of developing countries*, 23. Assen, The Netherlands: Van Gorcum, 1979. 162p. (Study of a Christian socioeconomic class).

'Theological education in Pakistan: a case study of the Gujranwala Theological Seminary.' R. Masih. M.A. thesis, Fuller Theological Seminary, Pasadena, CA, 1974. 200p.

Through the blood and the fire: a Muslim fanatic becomes a fiery evangelist for Jesus Christ. C. Alam. Chichester: New Wine, 1994. 128p.

Träger medialer Begabung im Hindukusch und Karakorum. E. Friedl. *Acta Ethnologica et Linguistica*, 8. Vienna: Österreichische Ethnologische Gesellschaft, 1965. 127p.

Country Table 2. **Organized churches and denominations in Pakistan.**

Official name (bold type = church with over 10% of all affiliated) 1	*Begun* 2	*Type* 3	*Councl* 4	*Congs* 5	*Adults* 6	*Affiliated 1970* 7	*Affiliated 1995* 8	*G%* 9	*Names, notes, and other statistics* (see Codebook, Part 3) 10
Anglican Orthodox Church: D Pakistan	1967	I-ReA	xT..T	150	8,600	18,057	15,000	-0.74	*Episcopal Ch of Pakistan.* Schism ex Anglican Ch, Sialkot. M=AOC(USA). 19n,1p(3).
Assemblies (Jehova Shammah)		I-CBr	x....	250	5,800	6,000	17,500	0.05	Associated with evangelist Brother Bakht Singh (HQ Hyderabad, India).
Associate Reformed Presbyterian Ch	1906	I-Ref	FT..a	176	63,000	18,000	110,000	7.51	M=ARPC(USA),GKN. 3 Presbyteries; Montgomery, Multan. 17 schools. 26f,1H.
Baptist Convention	1957	P-Bap	T....	14	400	500	1,140	3.35	M=Southern Baptist Convention (USA). Sunday-school enrolment 235. 5n,22Y.
Bhai Mission	1892	P-CBr	x...E	150	5,800	5,000	14,500	4.35	*Brethren Mission.* M=Brethren Missionary Fellowship (Germany, UK). Multan area. 20f.
Catholic Church in Pakistan:	1594	R-Lat	P.F.s	239	510,000	341,231	1,008,742	4.43	*Romai Katholik Kalisia.* C=9+6+18. (1970) 74n,159x. 133n 121x 255m 746w 23092Yy
M Karachi	1948	R-Lat	Ps	18	44,000	42,000	122,721	4.38	*Usqufia-e-Uzma Karachi.* Goans, Punjabis. M=OFM. 52n 18x 30m 183w 3409Yy
D Hyderabad in Pakistan	1958	R-Lat	Ps	15	27,000	23,421	58,100	3.70	*Usqufia Hyderabad.* Very poor. Sindhi, Urdu. M=OFM. 4n 25x 29m 58w 1531Yy
M Lahore	1886	R-Lat	Ps	25	270,000	148,382	500,567	4.98	Most Catholics in 2,506 scattered villages. M=OFM. 28n 31x 110m 217w 3846Yy
D Faisalabad (Lyallpur)	1960	R-Lat	Ps	144	61,000	64,875	124,446	2.64	Mainly rural. Urdu and Punjabi. 1p. 28n 17x 37m 97w 4887Yy
D Islamabad-Rawalpindi	1887	R-Lat	Ps	20	62,000	39,249	110,308	4.22	Mostly in villages; many in Islamabad. M=MHM. 10n 18x 22m 143w 4307Yy
D Multan	1936	R-Lat	Pop	17	46,000	23,304	92,600	5.67	Centre. Rural. Mostly Punjabi. M=OCar,OP. 11n 12x 27m 48w 5112Yy
Church of God (Anderson)	1918	P-Hol	x....	5	500	500	1,000	2.81	M=CoG(Anderson) (USA). Holiness denomination aiming to unite all churches.
Church of God (Cleveland)	1977	P-Pe3	Z....	17	2,900	–	5,100	5.56	M=CoG(Cleveland).
Church of Pakistan	1850	P-Uni	VWE.N	550	500,000	250,000	1,160,000	6.33	1970 union of CIPBC, UCNIP(part), MCSA(UMC), Pakistan Lutheran Ch. 8 Dioceses. 600n,128f.
Churches of Christ	c1960	I-Dis	x....	5	200	100	300	4.49	M=CC(Non-Instrumental) (USA). In Karachi, Lahore. Expatriate Americans. 3f.
Churches of God	1911	P-Ref	x....	15	400	1,000	800	-0.89	M=Churches of God in North American, General Eldership (USA).
Cooneyites (Two-by-Twos)		I-Fun	x....	50	400	300	600	0.05	*Christian Undenominational Church. Go-Preachers.* Irish itinerants from USA, UK.
Danish Pathan Mission	1903	P-Lut	....N	10	690	1,000	1,200	0.73	*Tent Mission.* In Pakistan Lutheran Ch until policy split. M=DPM,FMS,WMPL. 3f.
Evangelical Alliance Churches	1946	P-Eva	xM..E	8	690	700	1,200	2.18	M=TEAM(USA). In north, adjoining Kashmir. 3 schools. HQ Rawalpindi. 52f,1H,5h.
Full Gospel Assemblies of Pakistan	1943	P-Pe2	.....	63	5,000	8,000	16,100	2.84	*Scandinavian Free Ch.* M=SFM(Sweden), AoG(UK, USA), CAM. 16n,20f,W=83%.
Hidden Hindu believers in Christ	c1970	I-Hin	.....	800	12,000	–	28,200	50.66	Converted Hindus who choose to stay in Hinduism as witnesses to Christ.
Hidden Muslim believers in Christ	c1970	I-Mus	.....	200	40,000	–	82,400	57.27	Converted Muslims who remain in Islam to witness there for Christ.
Independent Evangelical Church	1990	I-Eva	....	100	15,300	–	26,700	20.00	M=an independent group (Lancashire, UK).
Indus Christian Fellowship	1954	I-Bap	xF..2	6	1,208	799	3,020	5.46	ICF. M=CBInternational (USA). Work in Sind. HQ Jacobabad. 2n,1m,1w,25f,1H,62Y.
Intern Ch of the Foursquare Gospel	1928	P-Pe2	Z....	9	204	300	510	2.15	M=ICFG (USA).
International Missions	1954	P-Non	xM...	36	900	2,000	3,000	1.64	*Pakistan Mission of IM.* M=IM(USA). In Muzaffargah, Dera Ghazi Khan. 12f.
Isolated radio churches	c1960	I-3rZ	....	1,500	40,000	17,500	70,000	5.70	Isolated radio believers. R=213 (FEBA,IBRA),T=120000 (90002 PBCS,SFM,VOP,CBFMS,ICI).
Jehovah's Witnesses	c1924	m-Jeh	x....	6	281	250	937	5.43	*Watch Tower Bible & Tract Society.* First missionaries 1926. Little impact. (1975) 6Y. (1995) 27Y.
Lahore Church Council (ICCC)	1968	I-Ref	.T..T	20	2,500	5,000	7,000	1.35	LCC Sharakpur. Schism ex ICC 1968. M=IBPFM(USA). 10n,1p,W=60Y,300Yy,500z.
National Church of Pakistan		I-3pZ	.....	8	1,500	1,000	3,000	0.05	Pakistani pentecostals. Headquarters Clarkabad, District Lahore. 1f.
National Methodist Church of Pakistan	1968	I-Met	.T..T	148	13,300	22,294	38,000	2.16	Schism ex UMC(USA) in Lahore. M=independents(USA). 11n,7f,220Yy.
National Virgin Church of Pakistan	1969	I-Ref	.v...	96	24,000	44,701	60,000	1.18	*Saint Council.* Ex UPCP. HQ Pasrur, Sialkot. 1969, applied to WCC. 52n,168Yy,230z.
New Apostolic Church	c1940	I-3aX	x....	1,000	150,000	100,000	231,656	3.42	*NAC/NAK.* M=Neuapostolische Kirche (HQ Zurich, Switzerland).
Pakistan Christian Fellowship	1954	P-Non	xM...	6	910	2,000	1,590	-0.91	M=International Christian Fellowship (Ceylon & India General Mission). 19f,1p.
Philadelphia Pentecostal Church		P-Pe2	Z....	15	1,600	1,000	3,000	0.05	M=Swedish Baptist (Orebro) Mission (Sweden). HQ Murree. 4n,7t(290),26Y.
Salvation Army	1883	P-Sal	xwE.N	668	25,200	60,000	42,000	-1.42	*Muktifauj. Pakistan Territory.* 7 Divisions. 2 hostels. 192n,21f,5h,4r,1s.
Seventh-day Adventist Church	1913	P-Adv	x....	45	6,579	8,000	18,800	3.48	*Pak Union (& Punjab Section)*, SAsia Div. 17nx,307m,58f,1H,1h,1j,1r,87Y.
Unitarian Universalist Fellowship		m-Unt	.....	1	30	50	60	0.05	*UUF of Lahore.* Small fellowship of expatriates. Links with M=UUA(USA).
United Ch in Pakistan: Lahore Ch C	1849	P-Ref	....N	82	14,000	35,000	40,000	0.54	C=Council. In former UCNIP. M=UPUSA. 1968, major schism, property lost. 30n.
United Pentecostal Church	c1960	P-Pe1	x....	200	16,000	10,000	40,000	5.70	*Jesus Only Church.* M=UPC(USA). Unitarian Pentecostals. 29n,4f,2p(33).
United Presbyterian Church in Pakistan	1968	I-Ref	.T..T	200	14,800	15,000	25,000	2.06	*Synod of UP Ch.* Ex UPCP, opposing WCC, claiming name, property. M=IBPFM(USA). 1s.
United Presbyterian Church of Pakistan	1849	P-Ref	RWE.N	200	70,000	175,000	200,000	0.54	*UPCP.* M=UPUSA. A=1961. 1968, schisms. 1970, union scheme rejected. 158n,48f.
World-Wide Missions	1962	I-Non	x....	10	500	200	1,000	6.65	M=World-Wide Missions(USA). Evangelicals with links in Pasadena, CA (USA).
Other Pakistani indigenous churches		I-	.....	100	5,000	2,300	10,000	0.05	Total about 3 small groupings begun by Pakistanis.
Other Protestant denominations		P-	.....	70	4,000	2,000	9,000	0.05	Total about 15 (see list below), including Moravian Ch (among Kanauri, Ladakh), CoG Prophecy.
Totals				**7,228**	**1,564,192**	**1,154,782**	**3,298,055**		

Churches, members, growth, 1900-2025	*Congs*	*Adults*	*Affiliated*	*G%*	*Total denominations*	*6 Megablocs:* *O*	*R*	*A*	*P*	*I*	*m*
Total churches, members, and denominations (mid-1900)	200	46,800	90,000	3.71	8	0	1	1	6	0	0
Total churches, members, and denominations (mid-1970)	2,819	600,369	1,154,782	3.71	42	0	1	0	24	15	2
Total churches, members, and denominations (mid-1990)	5,500	1,329,000	2,803,000	4.53	56	0	1	0	33	20	2
Total churches, members, and denominations (mid-1995)	7,228	1,564,192	3,298,055	3.31	56	0	1	0	33	20	2
Total churches, members, and denominations (mid-2000)	8,000	1,808,000	3,812,245	2.94	56	0	1	0	33	20	2
Total churches, members, and denominations (mid-2025)	18,000	3,512,000	7,404,000	2.69	156	1	1	0	50	100	4

NOTES ON TABLE ABOVE

NATIONAL COUNCILS (Column 4, 5th letter).

a = member of both NCCP and EFP.
E = Evangelical Fellowship of Pakistan (EFP).
N = National Council of Churches in Pakistan (NCCP) (formerly West Pakistan Christian Council).
s = Catholic Bishops' Conference of Pakistan (CBCP), and also official observer member of NCCP.
T = Pakistan Council of Christian Churches.

Local councils. Frontier Regional Conference, Peshawar; Southern Regional Conference, Karachi.

OTHER PROTESTANT DENOMINATIONS. These include: Afghan Border Crusade (1940), Baptist Bible Fellowship International (1954), Central Asian Mission, Christ-Bearers (Christusträger, from West Germany, 1961; 9 missionaries), Evangelical Methodist Ch, Fellowship of Ev Baptist Chs in Canada, Religious Society of Friends (Quakers), Worldwide Evangelization Crusade (1935).

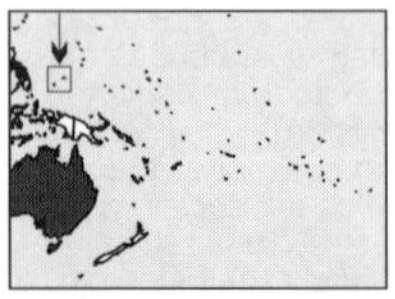

PALAU

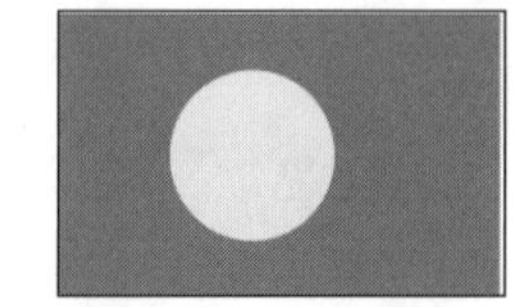

SECULAR DATA, AD 2000

STATE

Official name: Belu'u er a Belau/The Republic of Belau.
Short name: Palau. **Adjective of nationality:** Palauan.
Flag: .Yellow disc on light blue field.
Area: 1,632 sq. km. (630 sq. mi.).
Government: Unitary republic with a national congress composed of two legislative houses, since 1981 (1899 German protectorate, 1947 UN Trust Territory).
Legislature: Senate, 14 members; House of Delegates, 16 members.
Official language: Palauan, English.
Monetary unit: 1 U.S. dollar (U.S.$) = 100 cents. **US$1=** 100 cents.
Chief cities: KOROR (Corrora) 11,889.
Political divisions: 1 province.

DEMOGRAPHY

Population: 19,000.
Population density: 11.9/sq. km. (30.8/sq. mi.).
Under 15 years: 6,000.
Growth rate p.a.: 1.60% (births 20.74, deaths 4.71).
Mortality: Infant, per 1,000: 9.3, ; **Maternal per 100,000:** 20.0.
Life expectancy: 76 (male 73, female 78).
Household size: 6.0. **Floor area per person, sq.m:** 10.0.
Major languages: Palauan, English.
Urban dwellers: 72.84%. **Urban growth rate p.a.:** 2.4%.
Labor force: 35%.

ETHNOLINGUISTIC PEOPLES

77.3% Palauan; 9.7% Filipino; 5.0% Sonsorolese; 3.0% USA White.

ECONOMY

National income p.a. per person: US$4,993; **per family:** US$29,959.

EDUCATION

Adult literacy: 97% (male 98%, female 96%). **Schools:** 32.
Universities: 1. **School enrolment:** female/male: 90%/90%.

HEALTH

Access to health services: 75%. **Access to safe water:** 90%.
Hospitals: 1 (45 beds per 10,000). **Doctors:** 10.
Blind: 10. **Deaf:** 1,100. **Murder rate:** 5.
Lepers: 0.

LITERATURE

New book titles p.a.: 2 (100 p.a. per million). **Periodicals:** 0.
Newspapers: 0 dailies.

COMMUNICATION (per 1,000 people)

Phones: 90 (20% mobile). **Radios:** 536. **TV sets:** 89.
Daily newspaper circulation: 15. **Computers:** 20.

HUMAN LIFE AND LIBERTY (optimum condition=100.0%)

HDI: 66.9. **HSI:** 60.0. **HFI:** 75.0. **EFL:** 40.0.

Country Table 1. **Religious adherents in Palau, AD 1900-2025.**

Name	1900 Adherents	%	1970 Adherents	%	mid-1990 Adherents	%	Annual change, 1990-2000 Natural	Conversion	Total	Rate	mid-1995 Adherents	%	mid-2000 Adherents	%	mid-2025 Adherents	%
Christians	**2,080**	**65.0**	**9,270**	**97.4**	**14,630**	**96.3**	**408**	**-12**	**396**	**2.43**	**16,530**	**96.0**	**18,593**	**95.7**	**31,260**	**94.2**
PROFESSION																
professing Christians	**2,080**	**65.0**	**9,270**	**97.4**	**14,630**	**96.3**	**408**	**-12**	**396**	**2.43**	**16,530**	**96.0**	**18,593**	**95.7**	**31,260**	**94.2**
AFFILIATION																
unaffiliated Christians	20	0.6	18	0.2	130	0.9	3	6	9	5.50	180	1.0	222	1.2	410	1.2
affiliated Christians	**2,060**	**64.4**	**9,252**	**97.2**	**14,500**	**95.4**	**405**	**-18**	**387**	**2.39**	**16,350**	**94.9**	**18,371**	**94.7**	**30,850**	**93.1**
Roman Catholics	500	15.6	3,000	31.5	6,400	42.1	171	49	220	3.00	7,500	43.5	8,600	44.3	15,500	47.0
Protestants	1,560	48.8	2,214	23.3	4,200	27.6	112	28	140	2.92	4,900	28.5	5,600	28.9	10,000	30.3
Independents	0	0.0	4,000	42.0	3,700	24.3	99	-59	40	1.03	3,842	22.3	4,100	21.1	6,000	18.2
Marginal Christians	0	0.0	38	0.4	450	3.0	12	8	20	3.75	550	3.2	650	3.4	1,400	4.2
doubly-affiliated	0	0.0	0	0.0	-250	-1.7	-7	-26	-33	8.76	-442	-2.6	-579	-3.1	-2,050	-6.2
Trans-megabloc groupings																
Evangelicals	1,300	40.6	1,000	10.5	1,560	10.3	42	-3	39	2.26	1,750	10.2	1,950	10.2	3,000	9.1
Pentecostals/Charismatics	0	0.0	100	1.1	980	6.5	26	3	29	2.63	1,117	6.5	1,270	6.7	2,400	7.3
Great Commission Christians	**100**	**3.1**	**380**	**4.0**	**2,050**	**13.5**	**55**	**21**	**76**	**3.22**	**2,400**	**13.9**	**2,814**	**14.5**	**4,980**	**15.1**
Nonreligious	0	0.0	50	0.5	170	1.1	5	13	18	7.46	240	1.4	349	1.8	1,000	3.0
Buddhists	0	0.0	0	0.0	120	0.8	3	2	5	3.24	140	0.8	165	0.9	350	1.1
Baha'is	0	0.0	30	0.3	120	0.8	3	0	3	2.26	130	0.8	150	0.8	400	1.2
Ethnoreligionists	1,120	35.0	130	1.4	130	0.9	3	-4	-1	-0.80	120	0.7	120	0.6	100	0.3
Chinese folk-religionists	0	0.0	20	0.2	30	0.2	1	1	2	5.03	40	0.2	49	0.3	90	0.3
World A (unevangelized persons)	499	15.6	9	0.1	15	0.1	0	0	0	0.96	17	0.1	19	0.1	33	0.1
World B (evangelized non-Christians)	620	19.4	237	2.5	555	3.6	15	12	27	0.89	678	3.9	788	4.2	1,707	5.7
World C (Christians)	2,080	65.0	9,270	97.4	14,630	96.3	408	-12	396	2.43	16,530	96.0	18,593	95.7	31,260	94.2
Country's population	**3,200**	**100.0**	**9,516**	**100.0**	**15,200**	**100.0**	**423**	**0**	**423**	**2.39**	**17,225**	**100.0**	**19,400**	**100.0**	**33,000**	**100.0**

COLUMNS, ROWS.
For meanings and definitions, see Codebook (Part 3). Note that, by definition, total 'Christians' = professing + crypto-Christians, which also = affiliated + unaffiliated Christians, and also = Great Commission Christians + latent Christians. Percentages may not always total exactly, due to rounding.

NOTES ON RELIGIONS
BUDDHISTS. Japanese and Koreans.

Great Commission Instrument Panel: status of Palau (for explanation see start of Part 4)

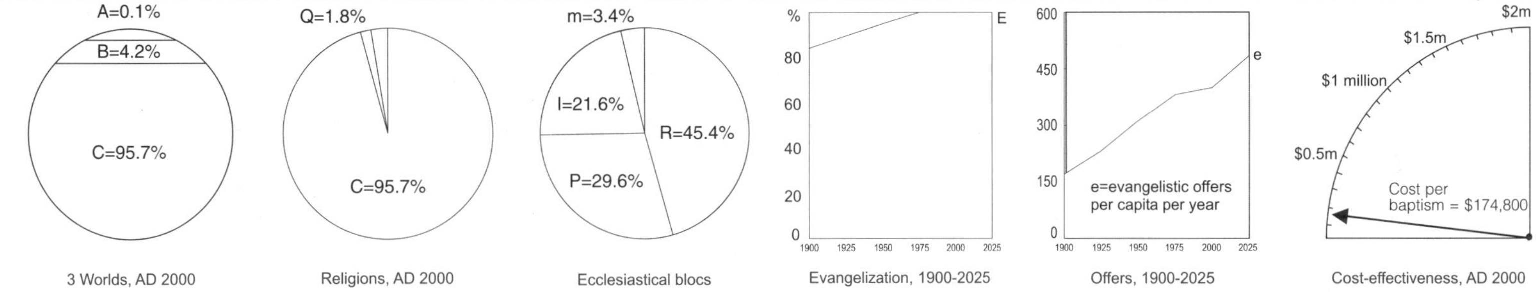

Country status. Palau is a group of 26 islands and over 300 small islets in the western Pacific Ocean. Fishing is the primary economic activity.

HUMAN LIFE AND LIBERTY

Human rights and freedoms. Similar guarantees and practice as in the USA are observed.

NON-CHRISTIAN RELIGIONS

The indigenous Palauan people are more than 95% Christian, but a small Asian immigration in recent decades has introduced a few dozen Buddhists and Chinese folk-religionists to the islands. By 1995 the Baha'i faith had won about 150 converts. Only about 100 citizens continue to follow the pre-Christian tribal religion.

CHRISTIANITY

CATHOLIC CHURCH. Spanish explorers first reached Palau in 1710. Though it was under Spanish control from the 16th to the 19th century, the first Catholic missionaries arrived and began evangelizing only in 1891.

The Holy See has no diplomatic relations with Palau in AD 2000, but an apostolic delegate for the Pacific Ocean residing in Wellington, New Zealand.

PROTESTANT CHURCHES. The Spanish priests were replaced by German Capuchins after 1899. The latter were instrumental in bringing an end to tribal warfare and concubinage. German control of Micronesia, which began in 1855, opened the way for the entry of missionaries from the Liebenzell Mission in 1929. The initial team, a Liebenzell missionary couple and a Trukese man, sailed in on a Japanese ship from Truk. Christianity spread rapidly. Their first congregation, in the village of Ngiual, was still a healthy church and a regional center for evangelism in the mid-1980s. In 1968 they initiated a boat ministry to Yap. Liebenzell missionary Hildegard Thiena finished the first translation of the New Testament into Palauan in 1950. The United Bible Societies completed the Old Testament in 1985. By the mid-1980s, 21 indigenous pastors and evangelists worked with 4 long-term missionaries and Bible women under the Liebenzell Mission in the country. The mission also runs Christian boarding schools, one for boys and one for girls, that draw students from all over Micronesia. Youth With A Mission has a base in Palau that is stimulating the Church's missionary vision and action. The Assemblies of God began work about 1980, and the Seventh-day Adventists have also planted churches.

INDIGENOUS CHURCHES. The third major church in Palau (after the Roman Catholics and the Liebenzell-related Koror Evangelical Church) is that connected with the Modekne movement. Based on new revelations from the ancient gods, it began in 1912 as a syncretic religion, combining Christianity with revived traditional Palauan beliefs. It became one of the most important indigenous religious movements in Micronesia, popular due to its emphasis on healing, and its commercial enterprises. Modekne was strongest in 1937, under the Japanese. In 1945 it was banned by the government. It then declined in strength but continues to function quietly. Later, its leaders adopted Christian symbols and made overtures to the other churches, seeking to be accepted as genuinely Christian.

Indigenous missions. Until recently very little outreach beyond Micronesia was attempted by Palauan Christians. In the last decade a small number of Palauans have been sent through YWAM, mainly to Asian countries.

Christians. A set of stamps covering a century of history.

Country summary. **Worlds A, B, C by ethnolinguistic peoples, cities, and major civil divisions in Palau.**																						
	PEOPLES							**CITIES**							**CIVIL DIVISIONS**							
World	Num	Pop 2000	C%	Christians	E%	U%	Unevangelized	Num	Pop 2000	C%	Christians	E%	U%	Unevangelized	Num	Pop 2000	C%	Christians	E%	U%	Unevangelized	
A	0	0	0.00	0	0	0	0	0	0	0.00	0	0	0	0	0	0	0.00	0	0	0	0	
B	0	0	0.00	0	0	0	0	0	0	0.00	0	0	0	0	0	0	0.00	0	0	0	0	
C	5	19,425	94.56	18,369	100	0	11	1	11,889	94.00	11,176	100	0	8	1	19,426	94.57	18,371	100	0	11	
Total	**5**	**19,425**	**94.56**	**18,369**	**100**	**0**	**11**	**1**	**11,889**	**94.00**	**11,176**	**100**	**0**	**8**	**1**	**19,426**	**94.57**	**18,371**	**100**	**0**	**11**	

CHURCH AND STATE

When the Japanese took control after WWI they expelled all Catholic and Protestant missionaries. Later, realizing the important role of Christianity in the moral and spiritual order of Palauan society, Japanese authorities asked Rome for help. After several orders declined the invitation, 22 Spanish Jesuits finally were sent to the islands. After 1927 German Liebenzell missionaries were also allowed to return. The 1930s and 1940s were difficult times for Palauan Christians. The Japanese government, violating their League of Nations mandate, fortified the islands. Many islanders were forced into hard labor. Missionaries came under pressure when they defended the islanders' rights. Palau has followed the American pattern of complete separation between church and state since the USA trusteeship of Micronesia following WWII. It became a self-governing republic in 1981. Since then relations have been stable.

INTERDENOMINATIONAL ORGANIZATIONS

No council of churches exists.

FUTURE TRENDS AND PROSPECTS

The nonreligious in Palau will likely continue a dramatic increase from only 0.2% of the population to 3.0% by 2025.

Nonetheless, Christians could remain over 90% over the next few decades.

BIBLIOGRAPHY

Essays on Palau. H. E. Charles. Pasadena, CA: Fuller Theological Seminary School of World Mission, 1976. 168p.

'Islands of change in Palau church, school, and elected government, 1891–1981.' D. R. Shuster. Ed.D. thesis, University of Hawaii, 1982. 441p.

The religion of the Palauans. J. S. Kubary. Woodstock, MD: Micronesian Seminar, Woodstock College, 1969. 40p. (Translation of original 1888 edition).

The sacred remains: myth, history, and polity in Belau. R. J. Parmentier. Chicago: University of Chicago Press, 1987. 364p.

'Transformation of traditional religion under the influence of Christianity.' M. Aoyagi. Paper, [1970]. 12p.

Country Table 2. **Organized churches and denominations in Palau.**

Official name (bold type = church with over 10% of all affiliated) 1	*Begun* 2	*Type* 3	*Counc* 4	*Congs* 5	*Adults* 6	*Affiliated 1970* 7	*Affiliated 1995* 8	*G%* 9	*Names, notes, and other statistics* (see Codebook, Part 3) 10
Assemblies of God	c1980	P-Pe2	.....	2	115	–	200	6.67	M=AoG(USA). Mainline Pentecostals.
Catholic Church (D Caroline Is)		R-Lat	P....	12	2,400	3,000	7,500	0.05	Local church in independent nation; part of wider diocese.
Church of Christ	c1975	I-3pF	x....	1	25	–	42	5.00	*Iglesia ni Cristo (Manalista).*
Ch of Jesus Christ of Latter-day Saints	c1975	m-LdS	.....	4	90	–	300	5.00	*Mormons.* M=CJCLdS(USA).
Jehovah's Witnesses	c1965	m-Jeh	x....	1	62	38	250	7.83	*Watch Tower.* (1995) 4Y.
Koror Evangelical Church	1906	P-Eva	.....	15	1,200	2,000	2,500	0.90	*Liebenzell Protestant Church.* M=LM.
Modekne	1912	I-mar	.....	10	3,000	4,000	3,800	-0.20	Nativistic healing movement (Christianity, animism, magic). Banned 1945, underground.
Seventh-day Adventist Church		P-Adv	x....	3	1,200	214	1,800	0.05	M=SDA(USA).
Other Protestant churches	c1970	P-	.....	8	200	–	400	27.08	In 3 missions or denominations.
Doubly-affiliated		2-aff			-220	0	-442		Evangelicals who are also baptized Roman Catholics.
Totals				**56**	**8,072**	**9,252**	**16,350**		

Churches, members, growth, 1900-2025	*Congs*	*Adults*	*Affiliated*	*G%*	*Total denominations*	*6 Megablocs:* O	*R*	*A*	*P*	*I*	*m*
Total churches, members, and denominations (mid-1900)	20	930	2,060	2.17	1	0	1	0	0	0	0
Total churches, members, and denominations (mid-1970)	46	4,165	9,252	2.17	5	0	1	0	2	1	1
Total churches, members, and denominations (mid-1990)	50	7,200	14,500	2.27	10	0	1	0	6	2	1
Total churches, members, and denominations (mid-1995)	56	8,072	16,350	2.43	11	0	1	0	6	2	2
Total churches, members, and denominations (mid-2000)	60	9,100	18,371	2.36	11	0	1	0	6	2	2
Total churches, members, and denominations (mid-2025)	120	15,200	30,850	2.10	28	0	1	0	12	10	5

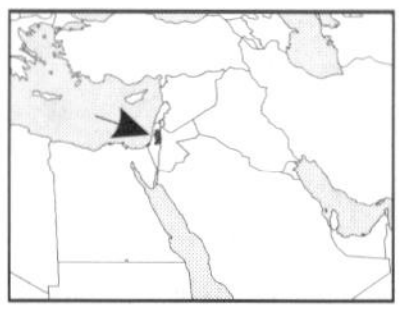

PALESTINE

SECULAR DATA, AD 2000

STATE
Official name: The Palestine Authority.
Short name: Palestine. **Adjective of nationality:** Palestinian.
Flag: Stripes of black (top), white, and green, with red triangle in the hoist.
Area: 6,242 sq. km. (2,410 sq. mi.).
Government: Provisional republic in exile, Status in 1978: Israeli-occupied territory, since 1967; 1994 Palestinian Authority. Possible future: independence under UN auspices.
Legislature: Legislative Council, 88 members.
Official language: Arabic.
Monetary unit: shekel. **US$1=** 3.10.
Chief cities: Ghazzah (Gaza) 303,353; Al Quds (EAST JERUSALEM) 183,489; Nabulus (Nablus) 150,529; Khan Yunus 135,930; Rafah 127,761.
Political divisions: 2 provinces.
Armed forces: 30,000.

DEMOGRAPHY
Population: 2,215,000.
Population density: 354.9/sq. km. (919.2/sq. mi.).
Under 15 years: 1,145,000.
Growth rate p.a.: 4.01% (births 43.76, deaths 3.83).
Mortality: Infant, per 1,000: 20.4, ; **Maternal per 100,000:** 200.0.
Life expectancy: 73 (male 71, female 75).
Household size: 6.0. **Floor area per person, sq.m:** 12.0.
Major languages: Arabic, English, Hebrew, French, German, Armenian, Aramiac.
Urban dwellers: 94.56%. **Urban growth rate p.a.:** 1.00%.
Labor force: 40%.

ETHNOLINGUISTIC PEOPLES
82.9% Palestinian/Gazan Arab; 10.5% Jewish; 3.0% Russian Jew; 1.5% Egyptian Arab; 0.5% Syrian Arab.

ECONOMY
National income p.a. per person: US$14,583; **per family:** US$87,503.

EDUCATION
Adult literacy: 72% (male 80%, female 64%). **Schools:** 500.
Universities: 1. **School enrolment:** female/male: 85%/85%.

HEALTH
Access to health services: 70%. **Access to safe water:** 85%.
Hospitals: 100 (50 beds per 10,000). **Doctors:** 9,000.
Blind: 2,000. **Deaf:** 124,200. **Murder rate:** 20.
Lepers: 500.

LITERATURE
New book titles p.a.: 330 (150 p.a. per million). **Periodicals:** 42.
Newspapers: 5 dailies.

COMMUNICATION (per 1,000 people)
Phones: 300 (25% mobile). **Radios:** 300. **TV sets:** 150.
Daily newspaper circulation: 200. **Computers:** 210.

REFUGEES
Citizen refugees in other countries: 3,286,100.

HUMAN LIFE AND LIBERTY (optimum condition=100.0%)
HDI: 78.8. **HSI:** 30.0. **HFI:** 25.0. **EFL:** 25.0.

Country status. Palestine is an incipient state in the Middle East on the eastern coast of the Mediterranean Sea bordering Israel. It is made up of the West Bank, Gaza Strip, and East Jerusalem. Many places sacred to Christians, Muslims, and Jews attract large numbers of pilgrims and tourists.

HUMAN LIFE AND LIBERTY

Human rights and freedoms. After many decades in limbo as a state without a country, Palestine is emerging as a reality following the Israeli-PLO peace accord of 1994, the subsequent Oslo accords, agreement on a Palestinian Authority, and the Camp David failed talks of AD 2000. Because of the unsettled conditions in the area and the fluid nature of its boundaries, it may still be many months before a firm civil state is established. Meanwhile, both Israelis and Arabs are guilty of continued terrorist acts and violations of human rights.

Palestine has issued its own stamps since 1918. *Left.* 1922. *Right.* Many countries have recognized Palestine as a state for 20 years or more.

NON-CHRISTIAN RELIGIONS

Islam makes up 73.5% of the population of the West Bank, Gaza Strip, and East Jerusalem. Muslims are mostly Shafiites, but there are also some Hanafites and Hanbalites and a small community of Ahmadis.

Judaism is represented by large numbers of settlers who have set up their homes in Palestine in the 1980s and 1990s.

Samaritan religion has existed as a sect separate from Judaism since BC 432. Samaritans number 260 on the West Bank and worship on Mount Gerizim.

Country Table 1. **Religious adherents in Palestine, AD 1900-2025.**

Year	1900		1970		mid-1990		Annual change, 1990-2000				mid-1995		mid-2000		mid-2025	
Name	*Adherents*	*%*	*Adherents*	*%*	*Adherents*	*%*	*Natural*	*Conversion*	*Total*	*Rate*	*Adherents*	*%*	*Adherents*	*%*	*Adherents*	*%*
Muslims	206,700	79.5	747,400	92.3	1,137,100	74.1	50,413	-1,329	49,084	3.65	1,453,070	74.3	1,627,941	73.5	2,937,000	71.1
Jews	23,000	8.9	1,000	0.1	173,000	11.3	7,664	2,331	9,995	4.67	230,130	11.8	272,947	12.3	520,000	12.6
Christians	**30,300**	**11.7**	**56,930**	**7.0**	**142,100**	**9.3**	**6,295**	**-1,541**	**4,754**	**2.93**	**168,900**	**8.6**	**189,641**	**8.6**	**370,000**	**9.0**
PROFESSION																
crypto-Christians	4,300	1.7	11,630	1.4	94,000	6.1	4,164	-264	3,900	3.53	115,000	5.9	133,000	6.0	280,000	6.8
professing Christians	**26,000**	**10.0**	**45,300**	**5.6**	**48,100**	**3.1**	**2,131**	**-1,277**	**854**	**1.65**	**53,900**	**2.8**	**56,641**	**2.6**	**90,000**	**2.2**
AFFILIATION																
unaffiliated Christians	0	0.0	507	0.1	1,000	0.1	44	-9	35	3.06	1,134	0.1	1,352	0.1	2,000	0.1
affiliated Christians	**30,300**	**11.7**	**56,423**	**7.0**	**141,100**	**9.2**	**6,251**	**-1,532**	**4,719**	**2.93**	**167,766**	**8.6**	**188,289**	**8.5**	**368,000**	**8.9**
Independents	0	0.0	5,300	0.7	68,000	4.4	3,012	523	3,535	4.27	88,700	4.5	103,349	4.7	240,000	5.8
Orthodox	23,000	8.9	27,500	3.4	41,000	2.7	1,816	-1,102	714	1.62	45,160	2.3	48,140	2.2	75,000	1.8
Roman Catholics	6,000	2.3	19,443	2.4	25,400	1.7	1,125	-865	260	0.98	26,225	1.3	28,000	1.3	40,000	1.0
Protestants	300	0.1	2,380	0.3	3,100	0.2	137	-57	80	2.32	3,481	0.2	3,900	0.2	6,000	0.2
Anglicans	1,000	0.4	1,400	0.2	2,600	0.2	115	-25	90	3.02	3,200	0.2	3,500	0.2	4,000	0.1
Marginal Christians	0	0.0	400	0.1	1,000	0.1	44	-4	40	3.42	1,000	0.1	1,400	0.1	3,000	0.1
Trans-megabloc groupings																
Evangelicals	700	0.3	1,900	0.2	9,400	0.6	416	4	420	3.76	11,965	0.6	13,600	0.6	28,000	0.7
Pentecostals/Charismatics	0	0.0	6,000	0.7	73,000	4.8	3,234	166	3,400	3.90	93,454	4.8	107,000	4.8	240,000	5.8
Great Commission Christians	**21,000**	**8.1**	**32,400**	**4.0**	**114,000**	**7.4**	**5,050**	**504**	**5,554**	**4.05**	**146,600**	**7.5**	**169,540**	**7.7**	**340,000**	**8.2**
Nonreligious	0	0.0	2,000	0.3	80,000	5.2	3,544	608	4,152	4.27	100,000	5.1	121,515	5.5	300,000	7.3
Atheists	0	0.0	1,000	0.1	1,800	0.1	80	-35	45	2.24	1,900	0.1	2,247	0.1	4,000	0.1
Baha'is	0	0.0	1,670	0.2	1,000	0.1	44	-34	10	0.98	1,000	0.1	1,102	0.1	2,000	0.1
World A (unevangelized persons)	177,060	68.1	424,263	52.4	600,185	39.1	26,620	-21,577	5,043	0.81	643,277	32.9	651,210	29.4	1,000,186	24.2
World B (evangelized non-Christians)	52,640	20.2	328,470	40.6	792,715	51.6	35,125	23,118	58,243	5.66	1,143,073	58.5	1,374,149	62.0	2,762,814	66.8
World C (Christians)	30,300	11.7	56,930	7.0	142,100	9.3	6,295	-1,541	4,754	2.93	168,900	8.6	189,641	8.6	370,000	9.0
Country's population	**260,000**	**100.0**	**809,664**	**100.0**	**1,535,000**	**100.0**	**68,040**	**0**	**68,040**	**3.74**	**1,955,251**	**100.0**	**2,215,000**	**100.0**	**4,133,000**	**100.0**

COLUMNS, ROWS.
For meanings and definitions, see Codebook (Part 3). Note that, by definition, total 'Christians' = professing + crypto-Christians, which also = affiliated + unaffiliated Christians, and also = Great Commission Christians + latent Christians. Percentages may not always total exactly, due to rounding.

CENSUSES.
(Holy Land). **1800** (estimate): 14,000 Christians (about 11,800 being Greek Orthodox). **1919:** 81.7% Muslims, 9.4% Jews (65,000), 8.9% Christians (62,000). **23.X.1922:** 78.0% Muslims, 11.1% Jews, 9.6% Christians (73,024). **1926:** 73% Muslims, 17% Jews, 9.7% Christians (80,000). **18.XII.1931:** 73.3% Muslims, 16.9% Jews, 8.9% Christians (91,938). **1939:** 61.5% Muslims, 30.8% Jews, 7.7% Christians (100,000). **18.XI.1961** (West Bank and Jerusalem): 5.7% Christians (46,000). Gaza Strip, **14.IX.1967:** 99.0% Muslims, 0.6% Christians (2,480), 0.4% others. East Jerusalem, **27.IX.1967:** 10,795 Christians. West Bank (Judea and Samaria), **1967:** 29,434 Christians.

NOTES ON RELIGIONS
ANGLICANS. In the year 1900, there were 1,000 faithful (Arab converts from Greek Orthodoxy and Catholicism); there were also 1,762 pupils in 31 Anglican schools.
ATHEISTS. Many Arabs belong to the New Communists (RAKAH), most of whom remain practicing Muslims or Christians.
CHRISTIANS. The total includes 11,000 Christians in East Jerusalem, a disputed area claimed by Israel since 1967 as part of the state of Israel. Other concentrations of Christians (1969): Ramallah and Bira 7,300, Bethlehem 6,400, Beit Sahour 3,730, Beit Jala 2,270, Gaza 1,650, Bir Zeit 1,350. Over the years since 1948, large numbers of Palestinian Arabs have emigrated, including a high proportion of Christians. Altogether, among all Palestinians in Palestine or abroad, Christians number about 12% (a total of over 300,000) compared with only 4.7% in Palestine itself. The total of all Palestinian Arab Christians in 1975 is made up to 49,000 in Palestine, 50,000 in Jordan, 64,000 in Israel, over 80,000 in Arab countries outside Palestine and Jordan, and over 50,000 outside the Arab world (in the USA, Europe, Latin America, et alia).By 1998 emigration was still a major concern.
COUNTRY'S POPULATION. The statistics in the table refer to the de facto territory and population of West Bank, East Jerusalem and the Gaza Strip. Large numbers of Palestinians fled the territory between 1948 and 5 June 1967, including refugees to Jordan who by 1970 numbered 305,000 (a fair number of whom were Christians) and had become permanent residents in Jordan; but also after the 1967 war a further 433,866 fled to Jordan, almost all Muslims with only a very few Christians. In addition there has been steady emigration of Palestinians to the USA, Canada, Australia, Saudi Arabia, Kuwait, Libya, Lebanon, Syria, et alia. Hence the population of West Bank fell from over 830,000 in 1960 to 680,000 in 1970. In 1970, the population consisted of 680,000 (58% of Palestine as here defined) in West Bank and East Jerusalem, and 501,000 (42%) in Gaza Strip (UN estimates published in 1975).Even with the Palestine Authority's new status after 1994, the overall situation remains unstable.
CRYPTO-CHRISTIANS. Secret believers, i.e. Christians affiliated to churches but not known as such to state or society nor recorded in censuses.
INDEPENDENTS. Isolated radio and correspondence course believers scattered across the country (see Table 2).
JEWS. In the year 1900, residents from throughout Ottoman rule, mainly in Jerusalem, Hebron and Gaza. In 1970, there remained only Israeli military, administrative and some civilian personnel.By 1990, large numbers of Jews settled in the West Bank and East Jerusalem. *Samaritans*, or As-Samarah. Around Nablus, West Bank, where their high priest lives.
MUSLIMS. Palestinian Arabs with a few Bedouin, all Sunnis (mainly of Shafiite rite, also some of Hanafite and Hanbalite rites); also an Ahmadiya Mission (enumerated here under Muslims, though declared non-Muslim by Pakistan).Arab Qadianis. There is also a large Palestinian Arab community of Ahmadis in Haifa, Israel. *Hajj pilgrims to Mecca.* (1970) 838; (1975) 1,445; (1976) 656.
ORTHODOX. The Greek Orthodox Church has since 1850 lost many members as converts to Catholicism, Protestantism and Anglicanism, also by emigration, also by conversion to Islam or nonreligion.
PENTECOSTALS. An ecumenical charismatic renewal began in 1970, initially among English-speaking Anglican expatriates, later among Arab Christians.

Great Commission Instrument Panel: status of Palestine (for explanation see start of Part 4)

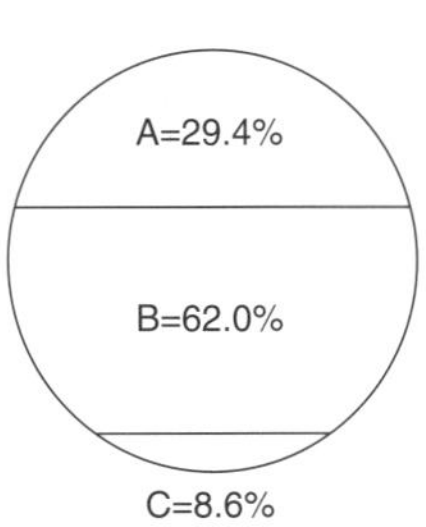

3 Worlds, AD 2000

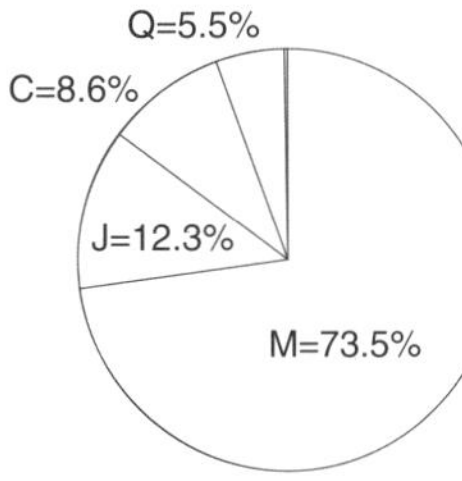

Religions, AD 2000

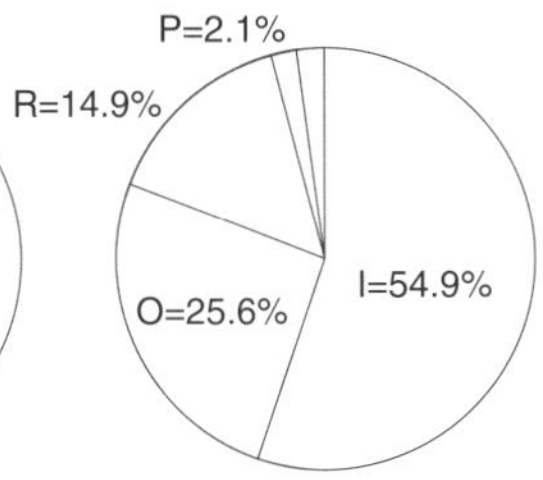

Ecclesiastical blocs

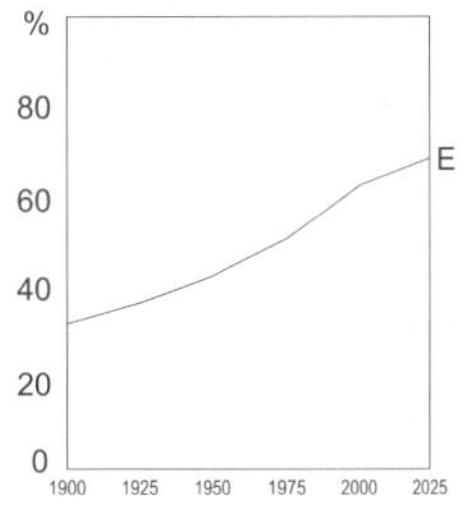

Evangelization, 1900-2025

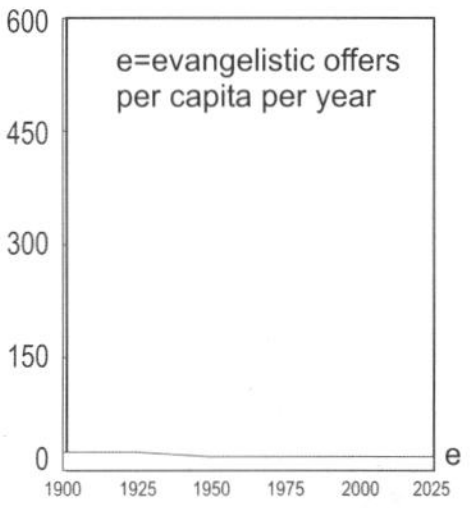

Offers, 1900-2025

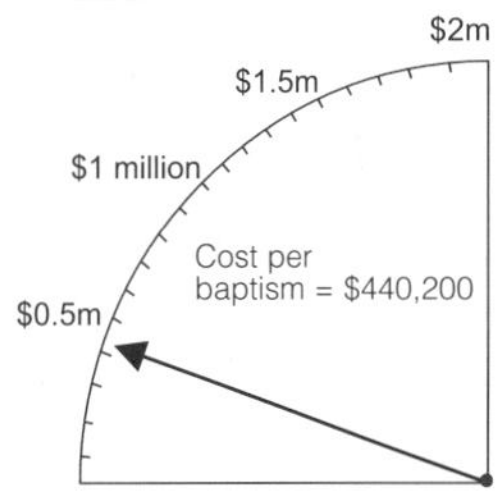

Cost-effectiveness, AD 2000

Church of the Nativity, Bethlehem. Traditional cave birthplace of Jesus, with first church building dating back from AD 290; long a source of conflict between Christian traditions, and now divided among Greek Orthodox, Roman Catholic and Armenian Apostolic jurisdictions.

CHRISTIANITY

As the scene of the birth, death, and resurrection of Jesus and the birth and expansion of the early church, Palestine has a long and complex history. Colonized and occupied by Romans, Arabs, and Turks for centuries, it was followed by the British mandate (1917-48). Palestine was the scene of Arab-Jewish hostilities in 1948 as a result of which over 600,000 Palestinians fled the country. In 1949, it was divided between the newly formed state of Israel and Jordan, the latter annexing Jerusalem and the West Bank, while the Gaza coastal strip was placed under Egyptian administration. In the 1967 war, Israel occupied the latter 3 territories, which provoked a further exodus of Palestinians. By 1970, the total number of Palestinians had reached 3,250,000, divided as follows: Jordan (Transjordan) 850,000; Palestine (West Bank and Gaza) 1,171,000; Israel 450,000; Lebanon 300,000; Syria 180,000; Kuwait 140,000; Egypt 33,000; Gulf countries 30,000; Saudi Arabia 20,000; West Germany 15,000; Iraq 14,000; Libya 10,000; USA 7,000; U.K. 7,000; and Latin America 5,000.

About 88% of Palestinians are Sunni Muslims, and 12% of the entire Palestinian people are Christians of different denominations. Benefitting from a higher level of education than Muslims, Christian Palestinians have moved quickly into the urban middle class and the professions. Few are in refugee camps, because as doctors, engineers and other professionals, they quickly become candidates for emigration. It is estimated that Christians compose almost half of those actively engaged in the Palestinian resistance. In 1974, a Protestant pastor, Elie Khoury, was a member of the executive committee of the Palestine Liberation Organization (PLO), which served to represent all Palestinian resistance organizations as well as leaders of mass movements. Other members and leaders in the PLO are also Christians. At the international and interdenominational level, there is a World Conference of Christians for Palestine, with its principal center in Paris and an office in Beirut.

The vast Palestinian Christian diaspora is a recent phenomenon of very great importance to the Christian presence in the Muslim world. A majority of Palestinians abroad are Christians. About 40% of all Palestinian Roman Catholic religious personnel now live and work outside Palestine, especially in Jordan, Lebanon, Kuwait, United Arab Emirates, and Syria. Some 15% have Jordanian citizenship. Among the most notable congregations are the Holy Rosary Sisters with widespread work in the diaspora.

ORTHODOX CHURCHES. The Greek Orthodox Church is the second largest Christian denomina-

Country summary. **Worlds A, B, C by ethnolinguistic peoples, cities, and major civil divisions in Palestine.**																								
	PEOPLES							*CITIES*							*CIVIL DIVISIONS*									
World	*Num*	*Pop 2000*	*C%*	*Christians*	*E%*	*U%*	*Unevangelized*	*Num*	*Pop 2000*	*C%*	*Christians*	*E%*	*U%*	*Unevangelized*	*Num*	*Pop 2000*	*C%*	*Christians*	*E%*	*U%*	*Unevangelized*			
A	5	12,540	8.86	1,111	39	61	7,616	0	0	0.00	0	0	0	0	0	0	0.00	0	0	0	0			
B	5	2,180,634	7.75	169,067	71	29	642,768	5	901,062	8.70	78,413	71	29	257,860	2	2,215,393	8.50	188,289	71	29	650,425			
C	11	22,219	81.51	18,111	100	0	41	0	0	0.00	0	0	0	0	0	0	0.00	0	0	0	0			
Total	**21**	**2,215,393**	**8.50**	**188,289**	**71**	**29**	**650,425**	**5**	**901,062**	**8.70**	**78,413**	**71**	**29**	**257,860**	**2**	**2,215,393**	**8.50**	**188,289**	**71**	**29**	**650,425**			

tion, although its community is decreasing slowly due to the emigration of Orthodox Christians to other parts of the world. A source of tension exists between priests and laity, who are mostly Palestinian Arabs and the patriarch and bishops who are Greeks.

Three other Eastern Orthodox communities are the Romanians who come under the Patriarchate of Bucharest and 2 Russian groups, one of which is under the Patriarchate of Moscow, the other representing the Russian Orthodox Church Outside of Russia which is opposed to the Moscow Patriarchate.

Five Oriental Orthodox or Monophysite bodies are active: Syrian, Coptic, and Ethiopian Orthodox and the 2 rival Armenian bodies. One of the latter is part of the Catholicate of Cilicia in Lebanon, while the other is related to the Catholicate of Echmiadzin in the Soviet Union through the Armenian Patriarchate of Jerusalem.

The Ancient Church of the East (Nestorians) are also present in the West Bank.

CATHOLIC CHURCH. Seven different Catholic rites are present in Palestine. (1) Latin Catholics predominate. All are under the jurisdiction of the Latin Patriarchate of Jerusalem whose patriarch resides in East Jerusalem. Twelve groups of Latin-rite priests are at work, the most important of whom are the OFM who have been granted the Custody of the Holy Places. A host of other orders and congregations of brothers and sisters are also active. (2) Melkite Catholics number 3,000. The Greek Melkite patriarch of Antioch, who lives in Damascus, has a patriarchal vicar in Jerusalem. (3) Maronite Catholics form a small community of 375. Maronites belong to the archbishopric of Tyre in Lebanon. (4) Syrian Catholics come under the patriarchal vicar of Jerusalem, who is dependent on the Syrian Catholic patriarch of Antioch and the East in Beirut, Lebanon. There are 2 parishes, Jerusalem and Bethlehem, and one other priest. (5) Armenian Catholics are found at Jerusalem, Ramleh, Beirut, Jamal, and Haifa (in Israel). They are served

Armenian Apostolic Patriarchate of Jerusalem. A huge throng of 4,000 Armenians follows Catholicos of Echmiadzin (USSR), His Holiness Vasken I, Supreme Catholicos of All Armenians (followed by Patriarch of Jerusalem), to Church of the Holy Sepulchre in Jerusalem in 1963. Over quarter of a million Christians visit Jerusalem each year.

by 2 priests, including a patriarchal vicar. (6) Chaldean Catholics are dependent on the Chaldean vicariate of Jerusalem under the Chaldean patriarch in Iraq. (7) Coptic Catholics are ministered to by a Franciscan priest attached to the Custody of the Holy Places.

The Holy See has no diplomatic relations with Palestine in AD 2000, but an apostolic delegate residing in Jerusalem.

OTHER CHURCHES. Anglicans arrived in 1820 to work with the Jews and were followed in 1860 by Lutherans. The latter are related to German Lutheranism and are confined to the West Bank; while the former, previously in the Jerusalem Archbishopric, now belong to the diocese of Jerusalem of the Episcopal Church in Jerusalem and the Middle East.

Southern Baptists have been at work since 1911 and cater for an extensive program in Gaza. The Church of the Nazarene entered in 1921 and has Arab and Armenian congregations in East Jerusalem. Pentecostalism is widely represented through the presence of 12 denominations, though none has a large membership. The same is true of 30 other small missions mostly from the USA who have appeared on the scene since World War II.

Renewal movements. In the 1990s the Pentecostal/Charismatic Renewal continued to spread across most older churches, and numbered over 107,000 adherents (of whom 2% Pentecostals, 4%

Many Christians have become involved in political and guerilla activities.

Charismatics, and 94% Independents).

Indigenous missions. Some of Christianity's first missionaries were sent out from what is now the borders of present-day Palestine. This country has a long and nearly unbroken record of sending missionaries to other countries. Even today, Palestinian Christians can be found preaching the gospel in foreign countries, particularly in the Middle East.

CHURCH AND STATE

The PLO has as its objective the establishment of a Palestinian secular state assuring equal rights for Jews, Christians, and Muslims. Parallel political organizations also exist in Israel and neighboring Arab countries. A large number of Arab Christians, both those living in cities (such as the Arab town of Nazareth in Israel proper, which is half Christian and half Muslim) and rural areas, vote for the Arab Communist party RAKAH, because they believe it to be the only officially tolerated party which is concerned about the Palestinian cause. Arab communists are generally religious believers at the same time and insist that their party defends more effectively than others the rights of the disinherited. It is not unusual for militant lay Christians to exercise responsibility within the body of the party.

Because Gaza, the West Bank, and East Jerusalem have been under Israeli control since the 1967 Middle East war, church-state relations follow a pattern similar to that of Israel itself.

According to Israeli law, persons are considered to be under specific religious communities much as in the old Turkish millet system, their religious communities in turn being responsible for decisions relating to marriage, divorce, and other matters of a personal nature. Recognized community religious authorities report to Israel's Ministry of the Interior which keeps a record of all decisions made.

The occupying Israeli regime also maintains a Ministry of Religions (Misrad Hadtoth), within which are located departments of Muslim affairs and Christian affairs.

BROADCASTING AND MEDIA

Satellite TV programs are received mainly in Arabic.

INTERDENOMINATIONAL ORGANIZATIONS

Anglicans, Baptists, Lutherans and Nazarenes are members of the United Christian Council in Israel (UCCI).

Considerable influence is wielded by the various ecumenical centers and organizations in Israel. In West Bank itself, a significant ecumenical role is played by the first Catholic university in the Holy Land, Bethlehem Regional University, which was established in 1974. With faculties of arts and sciences, pedagogy and commerce and schools of nursing and hotel administration, it provides the possibility for young Palestinians to pursue higher studies without leaving Palestine or Israel. It is not a Catholic University in the usual sense of the term, for although the funds and decision to build have come principally from Catholics, local committees composed of Christians of all confessions and Muslims have been formed to assure its development. Courses are given in Arabic.

FUTURE TRENDS AND PROSPECTS

Christianity is projected to continue to grow slowly reaching 9.0% of the population by 2025. Jews, numerous since the 1960s, are expected to remain about 12.5% in the same period.

Christians could grow beyond 10% of the population before AD 2050. Muslims will likely predominate in the same period.

BIBLIOGRAPHY

A history of the Christian presence in the Holy Land. S. P. Colbi. Lanham, MD: University Press of America, 1988. 343p.

Annuaire de l'Eglise Catholique en Terre Sainte, 1972. Jerusalem: Franciscan Printing Press, 1972.

Blessed are the peacemakers: a Palestinian Christian in the occupied West Bank. A. G. Rantisi. Grand Rapids, MI: Zondervan, 1990. 172p.

Christian communities in Jerusalem and the West Bank since 1948: an historical, social, and political study. D. Tsimhoni. Westport, CT: Praeger, 1993.

Christianity in the Holy Land, past and present. S. P. Colbi. Tel Aviv: Am Hassefer, 1969. 272p.

Christians in the Holy Land. M. Prior & W. Taylor (eds). London: World of Islam Festival Trust, 1994. 253p.

Faith and the Intifada: Palestinian Christian voices. N. S. Ateek, M. H. Ellis & R. Radford Ruether (eds). Maryknoll, NY: Orbis Books, 1992. 204p.

I am a Palestinian Christian. M. Raheb. Trans., R. C. L. Gritsch. Minneapolis, MN: Fortress, 1995. 175p.

Israel and the West Bank and Gaza Strip. C. H. Bleaney. 2nd ed. *World bibliographical series*, vol. 58. Oxford, UK: CLIO Press, 1994. 390p. (Complements 1st edition, focusing upon materials since 1984).

Jerusalem blessed, Jerusalem cursed: Jews, Christians, and Muslims in the Holy City from David's time to our own. T. A. Idinopulos. Chicago: Ivan R. Dee, 1991. 343p.

Jerusalem, the Holy City: a bibliography. J. D. Purvis. *ATLA bibliography series*, no. 20. : American Theological Library Association, 1988–91. 2 vols.

Les minorités chrétiennes de Palestine à travers les siècles: étude historico–juridique et développement moderne international. A. O. Issa. Jerusalem: Franciscan Printing Press, 1978. 363p.

The forgotten faithful: the Christians of the Holy Land. S. Aburish. London: Quartet, 1993.

The historic role of the Christian Arabs of Palestine. S. Runciman. *Carreras Arab lecture, 1968.* Harlow, UK: Longmans, 1970. 44p.

The land called holy: Palestine in Christian history and thought. R. L. Wilken. New Haven, CT: Yale University Press, 1992. 371p.

The Palestinians and the churches. M. C. King & L. Ekin. Geneva: Commission on Inter-Church Aid, Refugee and World Service, World Council of Churches, 1981–1985. 2 vols.

We belong to the land: the story of a Palestinian Israeli who lives for peace and reconciliation. E. Chacour. San Francisco: HarperSanFrancisco, 1990. 205p. (By a Melkite priest).

Country Table 2. Organized churches and denominations in Palestine.

Official name (bold type = church with over 10% of all affiliated) 1	*Begun* 2	*Type* 3	*Counc* 4	*Congs* 5	*Adults* 6	*Affiliated 1970* 7	*Affiliated 1995* 8	*G%* 9	*Names, notes, and other statistics* (see Codebook, Part 3) 10
Ancient Church of the East (P Tehran)	c1000	O-Nes	Yw...	1	280	1,000	400	-3.60	Under P Tehran. *Nestorians*, Assyrians, East Syrians. Mostly in Jerusalem, Bethlehem and area.
Apostolic Church of Pentecost		P-Pel	x....	3	100	100	200	0.05	M=ACP(Canada). Unitarian Pentecostals (Jesus Only). In Bethlehem, Ramallah. 1f.
Armenian Apostolic Ch (C Cilicia)	c1500	O-Arm	Sw.N.	1	200	50	300	7.43	*Gregorians*, related to C Cilicia (Sis) in Lebanon. In Gaza Strip. Armenians.
Armenian Apostolic P of Jerusalem	c 500	O-Arm	Ew.N.	6	1,000	1,500	2,000	1.16	Under C Echmiadzin. *Gregorians.* Since 1950, 90% of faithful have emigrated. 8 bps,1d,1j,1s(40)
Assemblies of God	1908	P-Pe2	ZF...	4	130	–	200	23.61	M=AoG(USA). Classical Pentecostals (2-stage). Correspondence courses. 5n.
Baptist Churches in Palestine	1911	P-Bap	T...K	5	300	300	500	2.06	M=SBC(USA). Ramallah, Jerusalem. In Gaza: 1x,18f,1H. In Jerusalem: 1k.
Bible Presbyterian Church	1946	I-Ref	.T.T.	1	50	50	100	2.81	*Baraka BPC.* M=IBPFM(USA). Educational centre and hospital in Bethlehem.
Catholic Church in Palestine:	33	R-LEr	O..P.	40	13,700	19,443	26,225	0.05	*Al-Kanisa al-Kathoulikiah.* C=17+2+32. 90n 255x 557m 1229w 1395Yy
P Jerusalem *(Latin)*	1099	R-Lat	Os	20	10,000	13,750	20,000	1.51	*Latin Patriarchate* restored 1847. M=OFM Custody. 82n 250x 546m 1196w 1325Yy
EP Jerusalem (*Armenian* C Cilicia)	1742	R-Arm	Os	1	100	100	200	2.81	*Exarchate Patriarchal*, Armenian C Cilicia.
EP Jerusalem (*Chaldean* P Babylon)	c250	R-Cha	Os	1	100	100	200	0.06	*Exarchate Patriarchal*, Chaldean P Babylon.
EP Jerusalem (*Maronite* P Antioch)	1848	R-Mar	Os	2	200	400	375	-0.26	*Exarchate Patriarchal*, Maronite P Antioch.
EP Jerusalem (*Melkite* P Antioch)	1932	R-Mel	Os	8	1,800	3,200	3,000	-0.26	*Patriarchal Vicariate.* Includes 300 in Gaza. 6n 5x 11m 33w 68Yy
EP Jerusalem (*Syrian* P Antioch)	c1660	R-Syr	Os	3	500	893	950	0.25	*Exarchate Patriarchal*, Syrian P Antioch. 2n 0x 0m 0w 2Yy
Catholics affiliated abroad		R-Lat	Bs	5	1,000	1,000	1,500	0.05	Roman Catholic residents affiliated abroad, but not locally in Palestine.
Church of God of Prophecy	1965	P-Pe3	Z....	5	500	300	1,000	4.93	M=CGP(USA). Holiness Pentecostals. In East Jerusalem, Beit Jala, Ramallah.
Church of God (Cleveland)	1946	P-Pe3	ZF...	4	45	80	113	1.39	M=CoG(Cleveland) (USA). Holiness Pentecostals. In East Jerusalem. 2n3f,1p,W=69%,5Y,6z.
Church of the Nazarene	1921	P-Hol	xF..K	2	50	100	150	1.64	M=CoN(USA). Jerusalem: Armenian and Arab congregations. 2m,4f,1t(92),W=70%.
Coptic Orthodox Church: D Jerusalem	c 850	O-Cop	NwaN.	6	600	1,200	1,000	-0.73	Under P Alexandria. Egyptians. In Bethlehem, Jericho; 500 in Gaza Strip. 2 schools.
Episcopal Ch in Jeru & ME: D Jerusalem	1820	A-plu	AW.NK	12	2,000	1,400	3,200	3.36	Formerly Jerusalem Archbishopric. M=CMS,JEM. Arabs (Evangelical Episcopalians).
Ethiopian Orthodox Ch: D Jerusalem	1172	O-Eth	Nwa..	4	50	50	60	0.73	Under P Addis Ababa. In Jerusalem. Mostly priests and monks 25x,1d(12),4y.
Evangelical Lutheran Ch in Jordan	1860	P-Lut	l..NK	2	121	1,300	318	-5.48	First M=BJ(Germany). West Bank. Arabs, some Germans. 4n,1x,W+18%21Yy.
Free Pentecostal Church	1966	I-3pS	.....	10	1,000	400	2,000	6.65	*Free Grace Pentecostal Church.* In Beit Jala, Beit Sahour. W=33%.
Greek Orthodox Church: P Jerusalem	33	O-Ara	CW.N.	15	16,000	21,950	40,000	0.05	99% Arab (laity, priests); Greek bishops, monks. 19 bps,19d(18),4e(20),1s.
Isolated radio churches	c1950	I-3rS	.....	2,000	40,000	4,500	80,000	12.20	Isolated Arab radio believers, mostly aged 12-25. S-10000,T=33000 (ICI,GMU,&c).
Jehovah's Witnesses	c1920	m-Jeh	x....	4	500	400	1,000	3.73	*Watch Tower. IBSA.* Active witnessing under way in Palestine by 1926. 10Y.
Native Church of God	1959	I-3pS	.....	2	100	150	200	1.16	*Native Ch (Holy Land) Crusade.* M=Voice of Healing (Christ for the Nations) (USA).
New Apostolic Church	c1970	I-3aX	x....	3	500	–	1,000	31.83	*NAC. Neuapostolische Kirche.* World headquarters in Zurich (Switzerland).
Romanian Orthodox Church	1935	O-Rum	Cwc..	1	213	350	300	-0.61	*Biserica Ortodoxa Romana.* Under jurisdiction of P Bucharest. 3nx,2d,W=70%.
Russian Orthodox Church	1848	O-Rus	Mwc..	5	300	300	500	2.06	Under P Moscow. In 1918, 100 schools, 12,000 pupils. Now token clergy. 1e(50 nuns).
Russian Orthodox Ch Outside Russia	1920	I-Rus	x....	5	200	200	400	2.81	M=FROC, formerly ROCOR(USA). Many pre-1917 institutions; some property still. 3e(40 nuns).
Syrian Orthodox Church: D Jerusalem	33	O-Syr	Dw.M.	3	300	1,100	600	0.05	Under Syrian P Antioch. *Jacobites.* Largest congregation in Bethlehem, also Jerusalem. 5x,2d.
Other independent charismatic chs	c1970	I-3cS	.....	10	2,000	–	5,000	40.59	Several networks of Arab charismatics.
Other Protestant denominations	c1950	P-	.....	40	500	200	1,000	6.65	Total about 20 including Seventh-day Adventist Ch.
Totals				**2,194**	**80,739**	**56,423**	**167,766**		

Churches, members, growth, 1900-2025	*Congs*	*Adults*	*Affiliated*	*G%*	*Total denominations*	*6 Megablocs:* *O*	*R*	*A*	*P*	*I*	*m*
Total churches, members, and denominations (mid-1900)	100	18,200	30,300	0.89	10	7	1	1	1	0	0
Total churches, members, and denominations (mid-1970)	294	33,870	56,423	0.89	32	9	1	1	15	5	1
Total churches, members, and denominations (mid-1990)	2,000	67,900	141,100	4.69	69	9	1	1	27	30	1
Total churches, members, and denominations (mid-1995)	2,194	80,739	167,766	3.52	70	9	1	1	27	31	1
Total churches, members, and denominations (mid-2000)	2,300	90,600	188,289	2.34	71	9	1	1	27	32	1
Total churches, members, and denominations (mid-2025)	4,700	177,000	368,000	2.72	173	25	1	1	45	100	1

NOTES ON TABLE ABOVE

NATIONAL COUNCILS (Column 4, 5th letter).
C = International Christian Committee in Jerusalem.
E = Evangelical Fellowship of Palestine.
K = United Christian Council in Israel (UCCI).

OTHER PROTESTANT DENOMINATIONS. A number of other bodies, especially USA missions, have small followings and church services, and so may be considered as denominations or para-denominations: American Baptist Association (1967), Apostolic Faith Ch of Canada (Bethlehem), Christian Catholic Ch USA; 1948; 2 groups in Bethlehem area), Ch of Faith (Ramallah), Ch of God (Seventh-day), Churches of Christ (East Jerusalem), Ev Missions to the Muslims (1964), Exclusive Brethren (Kelly-Continental), First Baptist Bible Ch (chapels in East Jerusalem and Ramallah), Independent Assemblies of God, Norwegian Pentecostal Mission, Religious Society of Friends (USA) (1869; in Ramallah), Seventh-day Adventist Ch (East Jerusalem), Slavic Gospel Association (1959), Swedish Free Mission, Swiss Pentecostal Mission, United Evangelical Chs, United Fundamentalist Ch (USA; 1952), World-Wide Missions (1961).

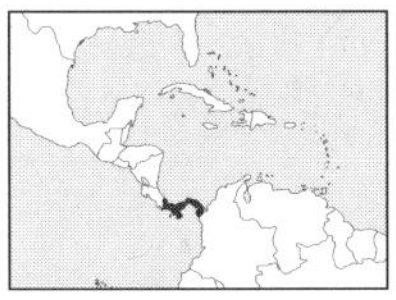

PANAMA

SECULAR DATA, AD 2000

STATE
Official name: La Républica de Panamá (The Republic of Panama).
Short name: Panama. **Adjective of nationality:** Panamanian.
Flag: Quarters of blue, red, and white, with blue and red stars on the 2 white portions.
Area: 75,517 sq. km. (29,157 sq. mi.).
Government: Multiparty republic, since 1994 (1502 Spanish possession, 1821 province of Colombia, 1903 Independence from Colombia, 1968 republic under military rule).
Legislature: Legislative Assembly, 72 members.
Official language: Spanish (Español/Castella).
Monetary unit: 1 balboa (B) = 100 cents. **US$1=** B 1.00.
Chief cities: PANAMA (Panama City) 1,088,000; San Miguelito 288,875; Colon 114,345; David 78,177.
Political divisions: 11 provinces.
Armed forces: 12,000.

DEMOGRAPHY
Population: 2,856,000.
Population density: 37.8/sq. km. (97.9/sq. mi.).
Under 15 years: 894,000.
Growth rate p.a.: 1.43% (births 20.34, deaths 5.09).
Mortality: Infant, per 1,000: 18.6, ; **Maternal per 100,000:** 55.0.
Life expectancy: 74 (male 73, female 77).
Household size: 4.4. **Floor area per person, sq.m:** 14.0.
Major languages: Spanish, English, Guaymi, Cuna, Choco, Hindi, Chinese, Arabic.
Urban dwellers: 57.75%. **Urban growth rate p.a.:** 2.2%.
Labor force: 37%.

ETHNOLINGUISTIC PEOPLES
58.1% Panamanian Mestizo; 9.4% Panamanian Mulatto; 4.6% Panamanian White; 4.6% Jamaican Black; 4.0% USA White.

ECONOMY
National income p.a. per person: US$2,749; **per family:** US$12,099.

EDUCATION
Adult literacy: 90% (male 91%, female 90%). **Schools:** 3,141.
Universities: 8. **School enrolment:** female/male: 85%/85%.

HEALTH
Access to health services: 80%. **Access to safe water:** 83%.
Hospitals: 60 (29 beds per 10,000). **Doctors:** 3,168.
Blind: 2,000. **Deaf:** 171,300. **Murder rate:** 13.
Lepers: 850. **Underweight prevalence under 5:** 7%.

LITERATURE
New book titles p.a.: 570 (200 p.a. per million). **Periodicals:** 11.
Newspapers: 7 dailies.

COMMUNICATION (per 1,000 people)
Phones: 116 **(4% mobile). Radios:** 200. **TV sets:** 229.
Daily newspaper circulation: 62. **Computers:** 30.

REFUGEES
Alien refugees from other countries: 800.

HUMAN LIFE AND LIBERTY (optimum condition=100.0%)
HDI: 86.4. **HSI:** 62.0. **HFI:** 52.5. **EFL:** 52.0.

Country status. Panama is located in Central America on a narrow isthmus connecting North and South America. Much of the economy is related to the Panama Canal. Panama's chief exports are bananas, coffee, and fish.

HUMAN LIFE AND LIBERTY

Human need and development. Panama has 3 economic systems, each with its own level of development. At the top is the Canal-related economy which, because of its U. S. association, is relatively well-developed. At the middle is the urban economy which has prospered as a result of commerce, banking and other sectors. At the bottom is the Indian and tribal economy which is virtually outside the pale. However, Indians and Blacks, who are the neediest people in Panama, form only 10% of the population. Among the Spanish-speaking mestizo majority, there is a further distinction between rural and urban people. The former, who make up half the population, are mainly poor peasants who live isolated lives in villages. Urban Panamanians enjoy many of the comforts of civilized society, but yet there are slums that serve as pockets of poverty and deprivation.

Human rights and freedoms. After the U. S.-led Operation Just Cause ended many years of misrule in Panama, there have been few cases of overt abuse of human rights. The main human rights problems relate to prolonged pretrial detention, an inefficient criminal justice system, and an overcrowded prison system. There have been scattered cases of police brutality, despite legislation against the excessive use of force. The Constitution prohibits discrimination against indigenous groups as well as women, but in practice there are subtle, cultural barriers to their progress.

Human environment. Panama has a variety of habitats, including tropical rainforests, savannahs and coastal mangroves. However, many of these habitats are threatened by colonization projects. Every year, some 90,000 acres of tropical rainforests are being lost. Coastal fisheries are at risk because of the loss of mud flats and mangrove forests. Deforestation promotes soil erosion. Annually, some 2,000 tons of top soil are being washed down to the sea.

Country Table 1. Religious adherents in Panama, AD 1900-2025.

Year	*1900*		*1970*		*mid-1990*		*Annual change, 1990-2000*				*mid-1995*		*mid-2000*		*mid-2025*	
Name	*Adherents*	*%*	*Adherents*	*%*	*Adherents*	*%*	*Natural*	*Conversion*	*Total*	*Rate*	*Adherents*	*%*	*Adherents*	*%*	*Adherents*	*%*
Christians	**193,000**	**96.5**	**1,394,600**	**92.6**	**2,129,000**	**88.8**	**40,631**	**-1,715**	**38,916**	**1.69**	**2,327,500**	**88.5**	**2,518,164**	**88.2**	**3,231,500**	**85.5**
PROFESSION																
professing Christians	**193,000**	**96.5**	**1,394,600**	**92.6**	**2,129,000**	**88.8**	**40,631**	**-1,715**	**38,916**	**1.69**	**2,327,500**	**88.5**	**2,518,164**	**88.2**	**3,231,500**	**85.5**
AFFILIATION																
unaffiliated Christians	4,000	2.0	24,600	1.6	40,000	1.7	764	1,346	2,110	4.33	56,400	2.1	61,100	2.1	31,500	0.8
affiliated Christians	**189,000**	**94.5**	**1,370,000**	**91.0**	**2,089,000**	**87.1**	**39,867**	**-3,061**	**36,806**	**1.64**	**2,271,100**	**86.3**	**2,457,064**	**86.0**	**3,200,000**	**84.7**
Roman Catholics	164,000	82.0	1,316,421	87.4	1,880,000	78.4	35,907	-2,907	33,000	1.63	2,047,901	77.8	2,210,000	77.4	2,850,000	75.4
Protestants	18,000	9.0	84,001	5.6	280,000	11.7	5,348	652	6,000	1.96	309,245	11.8	340,000	11.9	490,000	13.0
Independents	1,000	0.5	13,800	0.9	53,000	2.2	1,012	988	2,000	3.25	64,510	2.5	73,000	2.6	142,000	3.8
Marginal Christians	0	0.0	7,146	0.5	31,500	1.3	602	448	1,050	2.92	37,150	1.4	42,000	1.5	90,000	2.4
Anglicans	6,000	3.0	15,000	1.0	21,000	0.9	401	-151	250	1.13	22,000	0.8	23,500	0.8	24,000	0.6
Orthodox	0	0.0	1,000	0.1	1,300	0.1	25	-15	10	0.74	1,350	0.1	1,400	0.1	2,000	0.1
doubly-affiliated	0	0.0	-67,368	-4.5	-177,800	-7.4	-3,396	-2,108	-5,504	2.73	-211,056	-8.0	-232,836	-8.2	-398,000	-10.5
Trans-megabloc groupings																
Evangelicals	17,000	8.5	53,500	3.6	211,000	8.8	4,030	1,170	5,200	2.23	236,534	9.0	263,000	9.2	400,000	10.6
Pentecostals/Charismatics	0	0.0	42,000	2.8	400,000	16.7	7,640	1,360	9,000	2.05	446,304	17.0	490,000	17.2	718,000	19.0
Great Commission Christians	**8,000**	**4.0**	**120,500**	**8.0**	**347,000**	**14.5**	**6,627**	**3,179**	**9,806**	**2.52**	**395,000**	**15.0**	**445,061**	**15.6**	**680,000**	**18.0**
Muslims	1,000	0.5	65,000	4.3	105,000	4.4	2,005	150	2,155	1.88	116,000	4.4	126,551	4.4	170,000	4.5
Nonreligious	0	0.0	8,500	0.6	50,200	2.1	959	1,249	2,208	3.71	60,760	2.3	72,283	2.5	150,000	4.0
Baha'is	0	0.0	14,400	1.0	28,500	1.2	544	138	682	2.17	32,000	1.2	35,318	1.2	56,000	1.5
Buddhists	0	0.0	2,000	0.1	18,300	0.8	350	4	354	1.78	20,100	0.8	21,835	0.8	30,000	0.8
Ethnoreligionists	6,000	3.0	8,000	0.5	17,000	0.7	325	-37	288	1.58	18,300	0.7	19,876	0.7	27,500	0.7
New-Religionists	0	0.0	1,000	0.1	12,000	0.5	229	50	279	2.11	13,600	0.5	14,789	0.5	30,000	0.8
Spiritists	0	0.0	0	0.0	11,000	0.5	210	50	260	2.15	12,500	0.5	13,604	0.5	20,000	0.5
Atheists	0	0.0	2,000	0.1	10,000	0.4	191	162	353	3.07	12,000	0.5	13,527	0.5	35,000	0.9
Hindus	0	0.0	5,000	0.3	8,000	0.3	153	-39	114	1.34	8,400	0.3	9,138	0.3	14,000	0.4
Chinese folk-religionists	0	0.0	3,000	0.2	3,600	0.2	69	-12	57	1.48	3,850	0.2	4,169	0.2	6,000	0.2
Jews	0	0.0	2,000	0.1	3,400	0.1	65	-27	38	1.06	3,550	0.1	3,778	0.1	4,000	0.1
Other religionists	0	0.0	500	0.0	2,000	0.1	38	27	65	2.85	2,440	0.1	2,650	0.1	5,000	0.1
World A (unevangelized persons)	2,000	1.0	22,594	1.5	38,368	1.6	745	66	811	1.91	42,095	1.6	48,552	1.7	94,475	2.5
World B (evangelized non-Christians)	5,000	2.5	89,107	5.9	230,632	9.6	4,393	1,649	6,042	2.29	261,397	9.9	289,284	10.1	453,025	12.0
World C (Christians)	193,000	96.5	1,394,600	92.6	2,129,000	88.8	40,631	-1,715	38,916	1.69	2,327,500	88.5	2,518,164	88.2	3,231,500	85.5
Country's population	**200,000**	**100.0**	**1,506,302**	**100.0**	**2,398,000**	**100.0**	**45,769**	**0**	**45,769**	**1.76**	**2,630,993**	**100.0**	**2,856,000**	**100.0**	**3,779,000**	**100.0**

COLUMNS, ROWS.
For meanings and definitions, see Codebook (Part 3). Note that, by definition, total 'Christians' = professing + crypto-Christians, which also = affiliated + unaffiliated Christians, and also = Great Commission Christians + latent Christians. Percentages may not always total exactly, due to rounding.

CENSUSES.
1930: 86.8% Roman Catholics, 7.7% Evangelicals, 3.6% Muslims (with some Hindus), 1.7% nonreligious and ethnoreligionists, 0.2% Jews. Subsequent censuses have not asked the religion question.

NOTES ON RELIGIONS
ATHEISTS. Partido del Pueblo (PDP) (Communist; banned 1968, suppressed; pro-Soviet) and small factions.
BAHA'IS. Rapid growth from 27 local spiritual assemblies (1964) to 96 (1973). Many Indians (Guaymí, Cuna, et alii). Panama City has the first and so far the only Baha'i House of Worship (temple) in Latin America.
BUDDHISTS. Chinese, Japanese.
COUNTRY'S POPULATION. From 1855-1900, 30,000 Black immigrants from the Antilles arrived as laborers; but in the 1880s during the French attempts to build a canal some 20,000 workers died of yellow fever.
DOUBLY-AFFILIATED. The term covers those affiliated to, or claimed by, both the Catholic Church and also a church termed Evangélica by the state (Protestant, marginal Christian, Anglican, or Independents), i.e. baptized Catholics who have recently become Evangelicals or others. Because their statistics represent a duplication, they are shown in the table as a negative quantity (with a minus sign).
ETHNORELIGIONISTS. Of the 170,000 Amerindians, a proportion still retain traditional animism, including among the Cuna (northeastern coast) and the Guaymi and Terraba (in the west).
HINDUS. East Indians.
INDEPENDENTS. In about 9 denominations in 1995 (see Table 2). There have been a number of other marginal Christian movements, including from 1962-65 the Mama Chi (Little Mother) movement among the Ngawbe or western Guaymi begun by Delia Atencio and now in decline.
MUSLIMS. There is a very heavy population of merchants from the Indian sub-continent, many of whom have contracted mixed marriages. There are also many Palestinian, Syrian, Lebanese and other Arabs from the Middle East. From 1975 Muslim missionaries from Egypt (Sunnis) have been sent by agreement between the governments of Panama and Egypt.
NEW-RELIGIONISTS. By 1995, there were 13,000 converts to the Japanese movement Nichiren Shoshu (Soka Gakkai).
OTHER RELIGIONISTS. Including Rosicrucians (5 AMORC centers).
PENTECOSTALS. By 1976 one bishop was involved in the Catholic Charismatic Renewal, and numerous clergy and laymen.
PENTECOSTALS/CHARISMATICS. The Catholic Charismatic Renewal began in 1973, has been supported by a bishop since 1976, and has held many large youth rallies since 1979. From 9-12 March 1995, 4,000 young people attended the 16th Catholic Charismatic Youth Conference, in Chitne. Over 40,000 youth have done evangelization work throughout Panama. There are 100 weekly prayer groups, supported by 30 priests and 10 bishops.
ROMAN CATHOLICS. Many Christo-Pagans Amerindians whose syncretistic folk-Catholicism combines 17th-century Spanish Catholicism with their own traditional animism, concepts and world-views.

Great Commission Instrument Panel: status of Panama (for explanation see start of Part 4)

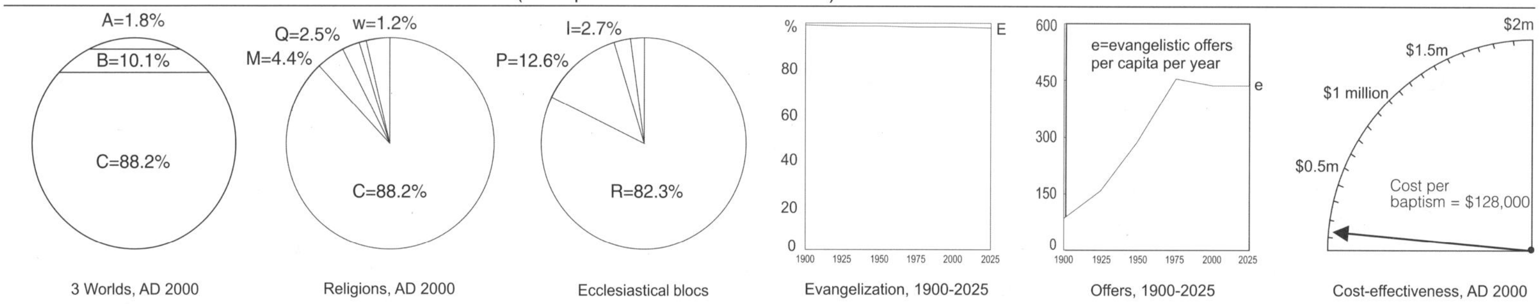

NON-CHRISTIAN RELIGIONS

Islam is represented by merchants from the Indian subcontinent and Arabs from the Middle East who make up about 4.4% of the population.

Baha'i has over 100 local spiritual assemblies, and the first Baha'i temple in Latin America has been built outside Panama City.

Baha'is. Worshipers in front of one of 9 doors of Baha'i House of Worship (Temple) on Cerro Sonsonate, just outside Panama City, first and so far only temple in Latin America.

Traditional religions from pre-Hispanic times still exist in the forms of rites and beliefs among the Cuna Indians of the northeastern coast and the Guaymi and Terraba Indians of western Panama.

CHRISTIANITY

CATHOLIC CHURCH. Panama formed a part of the first Latin Catholic diocese, that of Antigua in 1513. Franciscans began the task of evangelization and were followed later by Dominicans, Jesuits (1582), Capuchins and Augustinians in 1648. St Francis Xavier University was founded in 1674 but closed again in 1763 when the Jesuits were expelled from Panama. The ecclesiastical province of Panama was erected in 1925, and in the same year, the vicariate of Darien was formed. The diocese of David was created in 1955.

Nearly 65% of Panama's priests, 65% of its brothers and 55% of its sisters are concentrated in the archdiocese of Panama. This pastoral imbalance is further accentuated by the extensive involvement of clergy and religious personnel in education, amounting to 45% of all priests, 90% of brothers and 72% of sisters and by the small number of students whom they teach. The development of indigenous vocations has been slow in Panama. In 1995, Panamanian priests and sisters numbered respectively 44 and 46 as contrasted with 221 expatriate priests and 424 expatriate sisters.

The Holy See has diplomatic relations with Panama and in AD 2000 is represented to government and the Catholic hierarchy by a nuncio residing in Panama City.

Altarpiece in Darien featuring a Black Christ. Most parishioners are Afro-Americans.

Country summary. **Worlds A, B, C by ethnolinguistic peoples, cities, and major civil divisions in Panama.**

	PEOPLES							CITIES							CIVIL DIVISIONS						
World	Num	Pop 2000	C%	Christians	E%	U%	Unevangelized	Num	Pop 2000	C%	Christians	E%	U%	Unevangelized	Num	Pop 2000	C%	Christians	E%	U%	Unevangelized
A	0	0	0.00	0	0	0	0	0	0	0.00	0	0	0	0	0	0	0.00	0	0	0	0
B	10	310,554	32.82	101,918	85	15	45,066	0	0	0.00	0	0	0	0	0	0	0.00	0	0	0	0
C	23	2,545,129	92.54	2,355,150	100	0	2,048	3	1,280,522	84.42	1,081,053	98	2	28,474	11	2,855,683	86.04	2,457,064	98	2	47,114
Total	**33**	**2,855,683**	**86.04**	**2,457,068**	**98**	**2**	**47,114**	**3**	**1,280,522**	**84.42**	**1,081,053**	**98**	**2**	**28,474**	**11**	**2,855,683**	**86.04**	**2,457,064**	**98**	**2**	**47,114**

OTHER CHURCHES. The first Protestants in Panama were immigrant Methodists from the Caribbean as early as 1815, and Protestantism was strengthened through the arrival of 30,000 Black immigrants from the Antilles as rural and contract workers between 1855 and 1900. In 1882, the Methodist Synod in Jamaica sent missionaries to care for its members and these were followed later by others from the SPG (UK) and the Jamaica Baptist Missionary society (JBMS). After Panama's declaration of independence from Colombia in 1903, with strong support from the USA, a number of new and mostly North American denominations made their appearance: the Salvation Army in 1904; Church of God (Anderson), American Methodists and Seventh-day Adventists in 1905; and American Episcopalians in 1906, the latter taking over the work of the SPG. Three Pentecostal groups entered after World War I: the International Church of the Foursquare Gospel in 1927 and the Church of God (Cleveland) in 1935 and later, in 1967, the Assemblies of God. The latter has continued to grow rapidly during the 1980s and is now the largest Protestant denomination in the country. Southern Baptists arrived in 1943 to work with the Panama Baptist Convention, formed earlier through the activity of the JBMS. A large number of smaller missionary societies have taken up work in Panama since World War II.

Iglesia Metodista. Site for Resurrection Methodist Church.

Renewal movements. In the 1990s the Pentecostal/Charismatic Renewal continued to spread rapidly across most older churches, and numbered over 490,000 adherents (of whom 46% Pentecostals, 42% Charismatics, and 12% Independents).

Indigenous missions. From the introduction of Christianity to Panama in the 16th century there have been Christians from Panama serving in the surrounding countries. In the 20th century some Roman Catholics began to venture abroad. Recently, Protestants have sent Panamanian Christians to North Africa, Europe, and other places overseas.

CHURCH AND STATE

Church and state are partially separate in Panama. The constitution of 11 October 1972, stipulates: 'Freedom of religion and worship for all faiths exists with no other limitation than respect for Christian morality and public order. It is recognized that the Catholic religion is that of the majority of Panamanians' (Article 34); and 'Religious associations have authority to direct and administer their property as do other organizations holding juridical personality' (Article 35). Clergy and members of religious orders may not hold public office with the exception of those engaged in social service, public education or scientific research (Article 41). The same article also affirms that 'Leaders of the Catholic Church in Panama, including bishops, vicars-general, episcopal vicars, apostolic administrators and prelates nullius, must be Panamanian citizens by birth. this holds true also for clergymen of other faiths having similar responsibilities and equivalent jurisdictions'. Since this latter disposition was not made retroactive, it did not alter the status of bishops in office at the time the constitution went into effect. Article 101 states that 'The Catholic religion shall be taught in public schools, but attendance at classes or religious worship shall not be obligatory for students whose parents or guardians request exemption'.

Relations between the state and the Catholic Church have been strained since the military coup d'etat of 1968. Although the bishops have publicly supported the claims of the new government concerning Panama's sovereignty over the Canal Zone, at the same time they have criticized (as for example in their joint declaration of 2 August 1973) the general lack of freedom in the country and the marginal economic life of the masses living in poverty. The episcopate has also protested against the obstacles placed by government in the way of efforts by the church to promote social justice, as in its 1973 Lentin Letter. One incident evocative of this tension took place on 9 June 1971, when the police seized Hector Gallego, a Colombian priest actively engaged in programs of conscientization and development in the diocese of Veraguas which had been begun by bishop MacGrath prior to becoming archbishop of Panama. Gallego disappeared without trace, and several priests who persisted in demanding information about him were expelled from the country. The episcopate was unanimous in expressing its concern about the affair.

BROADCASTING AND MEDIA

Shortwave radio programs in European languages can be received from AWR (Slovakia), TWR (Monaco, Albania) and HCJB (Ecuador). Panama is a member of UNDA. There are 3 local Catholic radio stations, and a Catholic television program producer (FETV). Panama is a member of UNDA.

LeSEA programming can be seen on the World Harvest satellite network.

INTERDENOMINATIONAL ORGANIZATIONS

The Panama Evangelical Alliance (Alianza Evangelical de Panama), building on the work of the earlier Isthmian Religious Workers Federation begun in 1941, has 5 members: Assemblies of God, Missouri Lutherans, United Methodists, Conservative Baptists, and the Evangelical Mission. For Catholics, the Archdiocesan Department of Ecumenism (Departmento Arquidiocesano de Ecumenismo) coordinates interest and activities relating to ecumenism. On the interdenominational level, there is the Pacific religious Workers' League which engages in cooperative projects.

FUTURE TRENDS AND PROSPECTS

Christianity will probably continue a steady decline through 2025, to a low of 85.5% (from 92.6% in 1970). Most of these losses are picked up by nonreligious (0.6% in 1970 to 4% in 2025).

Christianity could continue its decline throughout the 21st century. Non-Christians will probably make up more than 15% of the population before AD 2050 and grow to over 20%. Major groups will include Muslims, Baha'is and the nonreligious.

BIBLIOGRAPHY

Anuario Eclesiástico de Panamá, 1965. Panama City: Curia Arzobispal, 1965.

Breve historia de la Iglesia panameña: episcopologios de la Diócesis de Panamá. E. J. C. Reyes. [Panama: Arquidiócesis de Panamá], 1965. 93p.

'Church and politics in time of crisis: Noriega's Panama.' S. M. Muschett Ibarra. Ph.D. dissertation, University of Notre Dame, South Bend, IN, 1992. 159p.

'Leadership in the Choco church,' J. A. Loewen, *Missiology*, 1 (January 1973), 73–90.

Option für die Anderen: Kirche und ursprüngliche Religionen am Beispiel der Kuna–Indianer. A. Wagua. Lucerne, Switzerland: Romero-Haus, 1992. 18p.

Panama. E. D. Langstaff. Ed., S. R. Herstein. 2nd ed. *World bibliographical series*, vol. 14. Oxford, U.K.: CLIO Press, 1982. 184p. (See especially 'Religion,' p. 59–61).

Panamá: la Iglesia y la lucha de los pobres. A. Opazo Bernales. San José, Costa Rica: Departamento Ecuménico de Investigaciones, 1988. 213p.

'Protestant growth and a changing Panama: a study of Foursquare Gospel and Methodist patterns.' C. O. Butler. Thesis, Fuller Theological Seminary, Pasadena, CA, 1964.

Ser cristiano en Panamá: testimonios: IV Congreso Eucarístico Bolivariano. Panama, 1982. 116p.

'The Church in Central America and Panama,' *Pro Mundi Vita* (Brussels), 46 (1973).

Country Table 2. **Organized churches and denominations in Panama.**

Official name (bold type = church with over 10% of all affiliated) 1	Begun 2	Type 3	Counc 4	Congs 5	Adults 6	Affiliated 1970 7	Affiliated 1995 8	G% 9	*Names, notes, and other statistics* (see Codebook, Part 3) 10
Asambleas de Dios	1967	P-Pe2	ZF..C	258	38,071	2,500	115,000	16.55	M=Assemblies of God (USA). Classical Pentecostals.
Consejo de Igls Luteranas en CA & P	1942	P-Lut	x...C	5	400	705	600	-0.64	*Council of Lutheran Chs in CAmerica & Panama.* M=LCMS(USA). 2x,2t(100),5Yy,10z.
Convención Bautista de Panamá	c1855	P-Bap	T....	85	8,511	10,000	21,300	3.07	1943, M=FMB-SBC. 39% Black, 31% Indian, 30% Indian, 30% USA. 23n,15x,1h,1s(15),374Y.
Ecclesias Cristadelfianas		m-Ade	x....	3	100	100	150	0.05	M=Pacific Coast of America Bible Mission (USA). 2 ecclesias (churches) in Colon.
Ejército de Salvación	1904	P-Sal	xwM..	12	400	1,000	1,330	1.15	*Salvation Army, Panama Division.* Caribbean & CAmerica Territory (HQ Jamaica).
Hermanos Libres		P-CBr	x....	2	100	100	200	0.05	*Christian Brethren.* Plymouth Brethren (Open). Gospel Halls.
Hermanos Menonitas (Iglesia Ev Unida)	1958	P-Men	GF...	16	700	730	1,560	3.08	M=Mennonite Brethren (USA). Indians: Choco (Waunana, Empera) in southeast. 2f.
Icthus Internacional	1983	I-3cL	.....	28	840	–	2,400	8.33	*Icthus International.* Panamanian charismatics.
Iglesia Adventista del Séptimo Día	1905	P-Adv	x....	120	30,000	15,000	50,000	4.93	*Seventh-day Adventists, Panama Conference, CAmerican UM.* 41% Black,20% Indian.4f,1r,350Y
Igl Apostólica Pentecostal Nacional		I-3pL	.....	70	3,000	2,000	5,000	0.05	*National Apostolic Pentecostal Ch.* Indigenous grouping of Mestizos and WI Blacks.
Iglesia Bautista Libre	1962	P-Bap	xF...	5	780	500	1,170	3.46	*Free Will Baptist Ch.* M=NAFWB(USA). Darien Indians. 2x,6f,W=81%,30Y,12z.
Iglesia Católica en Panamá:	1513	R-Lat	B.LDR	278	1,145,000	1,316,421	2,047,901	1.78	C=13+3+22. (1970) 44n,221x,470w,3223Yy, (1990). 149n 201x 260m 515w 32014Yy
M Panamá	1513	R-Lat	Bs	90	506,000	675,000	901,144	1.16	Southern Canal Zone. 1,236 Cuna Indians. M=CSC. 82n 114x 147m 297w 14020Yy
D Chitré	1962	R-Lat	Bs	13	96,000	144,000	170,000	0.67	Semi-urban, rural. No Amerindian population. M=OAR. 11n 8x 8m 13w 2455Yy
D Colon	1988	R-Lat	B cmf	23	79,000	–	142,336	14.29	Formed out of VA Darien. M=CMF. 17n 15x 25m 71w 2848Yy
D David	1955	R-Lat	Bs	31	207,000	213,000	367,064	2.20	Urban, rural. 11% Indian (25,190 Guaymis). M=SVD. 6n 31x 43m 54w 5103Yy
D Penonome	1993	R-Lat	B	8	87,000	–	159,507	50.00	Population is 92% Catholic. 9n 8x 8m 25w 2000Yy
D Santiago de Veraguas	1963	R-Lat	Bs	14	121,000	149,874	219,000	1.53	Semi-urban, rural. 2.5% Indian (3,380 Guaymis). 24n 4x 5m 21w 3935Yy
PN Bocas del Toro	1962	R-Lat	B oar	84	27,000	21,600	48,850	3.32	Rural. 32% Indian (29,700 Guaymis). M=OAR. 0n 10x 10m 13w 691Yy
VA Darién	1925	R-Lat	Pcmf	15	22,000	112,947	40,000	-4.07	18% Indian (28,930 Cunas). P=4%,2295z. 0n 11x 14m 21w 962Yy
Iglesia Centroamericana	1944	P-Non	xM...	17	1,100	1,000	1,680	2.10	M=CAM International (USA). Interdenominational mission with HQ Panama 5.8f.
Iglesia de Dios (Anderson)	1905	P-Hol	x....	9	700	5,000	1,400	-4.96	Ch of God. M=CoG(Anderson) (USA). 3n,2f,1h(medical boat),W=73%,255Y,500z.
Iglesia de Dios (Cleveland)	1935	P-Pe3	ZF...	122	7,833	3,500	26,100	8.37	M=CoG(USA). 47% Mestizos, 35% Indians. 57n,4x,4f,1p(15),W=43%,260Y.
Iglesia de Dios de la Profecía	1962	P-Pe3	.....	39	1,100	183	2,750	11.45	*Church of God of Prophecy.*
Iglesia de JC de los Santos de los UD		m-LdS	x....	37	7,950	1,146	15,000	0.05	*Ch of JC of Latter-day Saints. Mormons.* Many Indians. M=CJCLdS(USA). 20f.

Continued overleaf

Country Table 2–concluded

Official name (bold type = church with over 10% of affiliated) 1	*Begun* 2	*Type* 3	*Counc* 4	*Congs* 5	*Adults* 6	*Affiliated 1970* 7	*Affiliated 1995* 8	*G%* 9	*Names, notes, and other statistics* (see Codebook, Part 3) 10
Iglesia del Evangelio Cuadrangular	1927	P-Pe2	ZF...	327	16,000	25,000	49,000	2.73	*Foursquare.* M=ICFG(USA). 95% Mestizos, 3% Indians. 202nm,7f,2p(28),W=58%,180Y.
Iglesia del Nazareno	1953	P-Hol	xF...	24	1,377	2,000	2,556	0.99	*Nazarenes.* M=CoN(USA). 1n,11mw,12f,1s(36),16t(1670),W=67%,75Y,60z.
Iglesia Episcopal: D Panama	c1855	A-Cen	aw.R.	25	14,700	15,000	22,000	1.54	c1870,M=SPG(UK). 1919, Missionary District, Province IX, PECUSA. 77% Black. 10x,1H.
Iglesia Evangelica	1970	I-3pL	.....	16	1,600	–	4,000	39.34	*Evangelical Church.* Local evangelicals.
Iglesia Evangelica Pentecostal	1940	I-3pL	.....	25	3,000	2,700	7,500	4.17	*Evangelical Pentecostal Church.*
Iglesia Evangelica do Nova Vida	1967	I-Hol	.....	6	700	750	1,750	3.45	*New Life Evangelical Church.*
Iglesia Evangelica Unido Choco	1971	P-Uni	.....	4	450	–	1,360	4.17	*Choco United Evang Church.* Indian congregations.
Iglesia Ev Luterana de CR,ES,H,N,P	c1950	P-Lut	l....	1	100	130	200	1.74	*Ev Luth Ch in Costa Rica, El Sal,Hond,Nic,Pan.* German-speaking. 1x,W=17%.
Iglesia Luterana El Redentor	c1985	P-Lut	.....	1	270	–	450	10.00	*Redeemer Lutheran Church.*
Iglesia Metodista	1815	P-Met	VwV.C	56	4,000	7,500	8,300	0.41	M=MMS, UMC(USA). 1974 3 Methodist denoms merge. 3n,3x.
Iglesia Nueva Apostolica		I-3aX	x....	20	600	300	1,160	0.05	*NAC. New Apostolic Church.* M=Neuapostolische Kirche. HQ Zurich (Switzerland).
Iglesia Ortodoxa Griega		O-Gre	Cwo..	2	675	1,000	1,350	0.05	In 12th Archidiocesan District, Greek Orthodox AD N&S America. Panama City, Colon.
Iglesia Pentecostal Unida	1980	P-Pe1	.....	40	2,000	–	4,440	6.67	M=UPC. Oneness Pentecostals from USA.
Iglesia Santa Pentecostés	c1985	P-Pe3	.....	1	75	–	167	10.00	*International Pentecostal Holiness Church.* M=IPHC.
Iglesia Unificación	c1970	m-HSA	x....	10	300	–	500	28.22	*Unification Ch. Holy Spirit Association for Unification of World Christianity.* Koreans.
Iglesias Unión		P-com	.....	3	600	1,603	1,000	0.05	*Union Churches.* Formerly in Canal Zone, English speaking. Interdenominational.
Iglesias de Cristo	1945	I-Dis	x....	63	5,000	3,000	12,500	5.87	*Churches of Christ.* M=CC(Non-Instrumental) (USA). Panama City. USA personnel.
Misión Bautista Conservadora	1962	I-Bap	xF..C	10	100	50	200	5.70	*Conservative Baptist Mission.* M=MAM(USA). In Panama City. 2x,6Y,20z.
Misión Evangélica de Panamá	1958	P-Eva	C	35	700	1,000	1,400	1.35	M=Pan-American MS(USA). 150 San Blas Indians. 6n,1x,7f,3p(30),W=90%,120Y.
Misión Nuevas Tribus	1952	P-Fun	x....	46	4,000	4,250	10,000	3.48	M=New Tribes Mission.
Testigos de Jehová	1929	m-Jeh	x....	133	6,451	5,900	21,500	5.31	*Jehovah's Witnesses.* (1975) 164Y. (1995) 635Y.
Unión Misionera Evangélica de Panamá	1953	P-Hol	xM...	42	855	300	1,282	5.98	M=Gospel Missionary Union(USA). 1 school. 2x,18f,1h,1p,1s,W=36%,6Y.
Other Non-White indigenous churches		I-3pL	.....	200	10,000	5,000	20,000	0.05	Jamaicans, FDPMM(USA),ICAB(Brazil) with bishop, NBCA(USA),Black pentecostals.(CoGiC,&c)
Other Protestant denominations		P-	.....	100	3,000	2,000	6,000	0.05	Total about 15 (see list below).
Other independent charismatic chs	c1980	I-3cL	.....	50	5,000	–	10,000	6.67	In several grassroots charismatic networks.
Doubly-affiliated		2-aff			-113,000	-67,368	-211,056		Evangelicals and Pentecostals who are also baptized Roman Catholics.
Totals				**2,346**	**1,215,138**	**1,370,000**	**2,271,100**		

Churches, members, growth, 1900-2025	*Congs*	*Adults*	*Affiliated*	*G%*	*Total denominations*	*6 Megablocs:* *O*	*R*	*A*	*P*	*I*	*m*
Total churches, members, and denominations (mid-1900)	500	104,000	189,000	2.87	5	0	1	1	3	0	0
Total churches, members, and denominations (mid-1970)	1,138	751,025	1,370,000	2.87	48	1	1	1	27	15	3
Total churches, members, and denominations (mid-1990)	2,100	1,118,000	2,089,000	2.13	84	1	1	1	38	39	4
Total churches, members, and denominations (mid-1995)	2,346	1,215,138	2,271,100	1.69	86	1	1	1	39	40	4
Total churches, members, and denominations (mid-2000)	2,500	1,315,000	2,457,064	1.59	88	1	1	1	40	41	4
Total churches, members, and denominations (mid-2025)	3,800	1,712,000	3,200,000	1.06	203	3	1	1	70	120	8

NOTES ON TABLE ABOVE

NATIONAL COUNCILS (Column 4, 5th letter).
- C = Alianza Evangélica de Panamá (AEP) (Panama Evangelical Alliance).
- E = Confraternidad Evangelica Panameña (CEP).
- R = Conferencia Episcopal de Panamá (CEP) (Episcopal Conference of Panama).

OTHER PROTESTANT DENOMINATIONS. These smaller bodies include: Exclusive Brethren (Kelly-Continental), Free Methodist Ch, Iglesia de Dios Pentecostal (1946; from Puerto Rico), New Tribes Mission (1953; 32 missionaries).

UNITING CHURCHES. The Iglesia Metodista Unida was expected to join the Methodist Church in the Caribbean & the Americas after 1974.

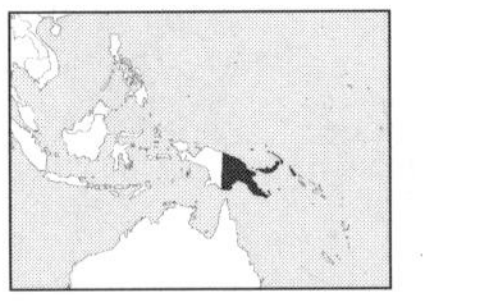

PAPUA NEW GUINEA

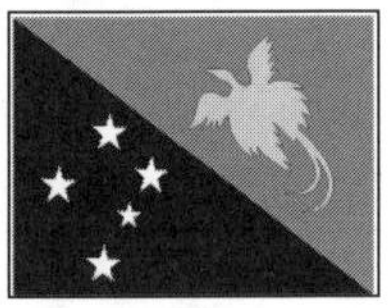

SECULAR DATA, AD 2000

STATE
Official name: The Independent State of Papua New Guinea.
Short name: Papua New Guinea. **Adjective of nationality:** of Papua New Guinea, a Papua New Guinean.
Flag: Five-star constellation on black triangle on lower left; gold bird of paradise on red triangle on upper right.
Area: 462,840 sq. km. (178,704 sq. mi.).
Government: Parliamentary state (constitutional monarchy), since 1975 (1884 British protectorate, 1906 Australian territory of Papua, 1920 Australian territory of New Guinea, 1973 self-government, 1975 Independence).
Legislature: House of Assembly, 109 members.
Official language: English, Tok Pisin.
Monetary unit: 1 Papua New Guinea kina (K) = 100 toea. **US$1=** K 2.28.
Chief cities: PORT MORESBY 242,549; Lae 98,235.
Political divisions: 20 provinces.
Armed forces: 4,300.

DEMOGRAPHY
Population: 4,608,000.
Population density: 9.9/sq. km. (25.7/sq. mi.).
Under 15 years: 1,782,000.
Growth rate p.a.: 2.14% (births 30.39, deaths 9.00).
Mortality: Infant, per 1,000: 54.8, ; **Maternal per 100,000:** 930.0.
Life expectancy: 60 (male 59, female 61).
Household size: 4.6. **Floor area per person, sq.m:** 8.0.
Major languages: English, Pidgin English (Neo-Melanesian), Motu, Chinese. In addition there are over 950 tribal and other languages.
Urban dwellers: 17.41%. **Urban growth rate p.a.:** 4.0%.
Labor force: 25%.

ETHNOLINGUISTIC PEOPLES
5.8% Detribalized; 4.9% Enga (Endakali, Wabag); 3.2% Medlpa (Melpa, Hagen); 1.9% Chimbu (Kuman, Nagane); 1.8% Huli (Tari, Huri).

ECONOMY
National income p.a. per person: US$1,159; **per family:** US$5,335.

EDUCATION
Adult literacy: 72% (male 81%, female 62%). **Schools:** 3,073.
Universities: 2. **School enrolment:** female/male: 46%/55%.

HEALTH
Access to health services: 96%. **Access to safe water:** 28%.
Hospitals: 150 (40 beds per 10,000). **Doctors:** 301.
Blind: 9,000. **Deaf:** 276,700. **Murder rate:** 8.
Lepers: 20,000. **Underweight prevalence under 5:** 35%.

LITERATURE
New book titles p.a.: 690 (150 p.a. per million). **Periodicals:** 42.
Newspapers: 2 dailies.

COMMUNICATION (per 1,000 people)
Phones: 10 (15% mobile). **Radios:** 72. **TV sets:** 163.
Daily newspaper circulation: 15. **Computers:** 10.

REFUGEES
Alien refugees from other countries: 9,500.

HUMAN LIFE AND LIBERTY (optimum condition=100.0%)
HDI: 52.5. **HSI:** 34.0. **HFI:** 75.0. **EFL:** 38.0.

Country status. Papua New Guinea occupies the eastern half of the island of New Guinea as well as several smaller islands to the east and north in the southwestern Pacific Ocean north of Australia. Though most of the inhabitants are involved in agriculture, timber and minerals are the major source of income for the country.

HUMAN LIFE AND LIBERTY

Human need and development. As in other countries in Oceania modernization and improvement in living standards have not been unmixed blessings in Papua New Guinea. Progress has been characterized by decrease in mortality and a population explosion. This, in turn, has created overcrowding and worsening environmental sanitation. Subsistence production has been neglected in favor of cash-earning pursuits, placing further strains on the fragile economy. Change in eating habits from fresh, unrefined foods to polished rice, white bread, and convenience foods has brought about new problems of tooth decay and malnutrition. There is no organized public welfare system other than those organized by Christian missionaries. Nevertheless, Papua New Guinea is not by any means a poor country. The economy is sustained by rich mineral resources and by generous economic aid from Australia. Although parts of the interior remain primitive, coastal areas and towns have prospered in recent years. The per capita income is $1,159, life expectancy 60 and the adult literacy rate 72%.

Human rights and freedom. The principal human rights problems arise from the long-standing Bougainville secessionist uprising. There are occasional reports of torture, disappearances, and police abuses, but judicial redress is available to victims of official misconduct. The law guarantees a public trial and the Constitution provides for due process, and an independent judiciary enforces both. However, Papua New Guinea has a very high crime rate, and the police have a tendency to be highhanded in dealing with criminals. Because of the extreme ethnic diversity of Papua New Guineans, no one tribe or clan is dominant. Governments are generally based on loose parliamentary coalitions in which most ethnic groups are represented. Although discrimination against women is illegal, traditional society relegates them to second-class status. Violence against women, especially rape, is widely prevalent. Attacks on women are common during the frequent inter-tribal warfare.

Human environment. Straddling the Wallace Line, Papua New Guinea is rich in fauna and flora. There are over 11,000 plant species, including 2,000 ferns. The country claims the world's largest and smallest parrots, the smallest frogs, and the largest lizards, doves, and butterflies. Over 85% of the country remains under forest cover. However, logging and open-pit mining operations are gradually reducing the forested area.

NON-CHRISTIAN RELIGIONS

Traditional religions are followed by only about 3% of the population, decreasing rapidly each year, although their influence continues to be felt also among professing Christians. These tribal religions are centered primarily on ancestor veneration coupled with a strong belief in good and evil spirits and the efficacy of magical charms.

Cargo cults, the term describing a long series of messianic and syncretistic movements combing traditional elements with Christian and Western secular elements, have arisen under the impact of Western culture since around 1890 and especially since the military campaigns of World War II. Among the earliest of these sects were the Cult of the Prophet Tokerau at Milne Bay in 1893, the Cult of the Three Prophets of Saibai of Torres Strait in 1914, the 'Vailala Madness' among the Orokolo peoples of the Gulf of

Country Table 1. **Religious adherents in Papua New Guinea, AD 1900-2025.**

Year	1900		1970		mid-1990		Annual change, 1990-2000				mid-1995		mid-2000		mid-2025	
Name	Adherents	%	Adherents	%	Adherents	%	Natural	Conversion	Total	Rate	Adherents	%	Adherents	%	Adherents	%
Christians	**45,000**	**4.0**	**2,184,900**	**94.4**	**3,491,500**	**95.0**	**88,775**	**67**	**88,842**	**2.29**	**3,912,700**	**95.0**	**4,379,915**	**95.1**	**6,902,400**	**96.2**
PROFESSION																
professing Christians	**45,000**	**4.0**	**2,184,900**	**94.4**	**3,491,500**	**95.0**	**88,775**	**67**	**88,842**	**2.29**	**3,912,700**	**95.0**	**4,379,915**	**95.1**	**6,902,400**	**96.2**
AFFILIATION																
unaffiliated Christians	15,400	1.4	572,228	24.7	525,300	14.3	13,354	-6,445	6,909	1.24	563,957	13.7	594,387	12.9	573,600	8.0
affiliated Christians	**29,600**	**2.6**	**1,612,672**	**69.7**	**2,966,200**	**80.7**	**75,420**	**6,513**	**81,933**	**2.47**	**3,348,743**	**81.3**	**3,785,528**	**82.2**	**6,328,800**	**88.2**
Protestants	10,000	0.9	910,278	39.3	2,002,000	54.5	50,895	9,905	60,800	2.69	2,278,756	55.4	2,610,000	56.6	4,133,000	57.6
Roman Catholics	19,300	1.7	606,544	26.2	1,075,000	29.3	27,329	3,171	30,500	2.53	1,214,038	29.5	1,380,000	30.0	2,400,000	33.5
Anglicans	200	0.0	60,000	2.6	235,000	6.4	5,974	1,326	7,300	2.74	270,000	6.6	308,000	6.7	550,000	7.7
Independents	100	0.0	30,650	1.3	200,000	5.4	5,084	1,916	7,000	3.05	232,349	5.6	270,000	5.9	505,000	7.0
Marginal Christians	0	0.0	5,000	0.2	11,300	0.3	287	123	410	3.14	13,300	0.3	15,400	0.3	40,000	0.6
Orthodox	0	0.0	200	0.0	300	0.0	8	2	10	2.92	300	0.0	400	0.0	800	0.0
doubly-affiliated	0	0.0	0	0.0	-557,400	-15.2	-14,170	-9,917	-24,087	3.66	-660,000	-16.0	-798,272	-17.3	-1,300,000	-18.1
Trans-megabloc groupings																
Evangelicals	8,500	0.8	290,000	12.5	617,000	16.8	15,685	3,615	19,300	2.76	711,685	17.3	810,000	17.6	1,470,000	20.5
Pentecostals/Charismatics	0	0.0	110,000	4.8	558,000	15.2	14,185	5,115	19,300	3.02	650,135	15.8	751,000	16.3	1,400,000	19.5
Great Commission Christians	**40,000**	**3.6**	**104,000**	**4.5**	**400,000**	**10.9**	**10,169**	**2,141**	**12,310**	**2.72**	**461,000**	**11.2**	**523,096**	**11.4**	**1,016,000**	**14.2**
Ethnoreligionists	1,074,000	95.9	114,300	4.9	136,140	3.7	3,461	-368	3,093	2.07	151,400	3.7	167,068	3.6	150,000	2.1
Baha'is	0	0.0	9,300	0.4	27,000	0.7	686	108	794	2.61	30,500	0.7	34,939	0.8	65,000	0.9
Nonreligious	0	0.0	2,000	0.1	9,000	0.2	229	114	343	3.28	10,250	0.3	12,427	0.3	32,000	0.5
Buddhists	0	0.0	2,000	0.1	5,500	0.2	140	52	192	3.03	6,600	0.2	7,415	0.2	13,000	0.2
Chinese folk-religionists	0	0.0	2,200	0.1	2,600	0.1	66	8	74	2.55	2,950	0.1	3,344	0.1	4,800	0.1
New-Religionists	0	0.0	0	0.0	900	0.0	23	14	37	3.50	1,100	0.0	1,270	0.0	3,000	0.0
Muslims	0	0.0	0	0.0	900	0.0	23	7	30	2.94	1,000	0.0	1,203	0.0	3,000	0.0
Jews	0	0.0	300	0.0	460	0.0	12	-2	10	2.06	500	0.0	564	0.0	800	0.0
World A (unevangelized persons)	929,102	83.0	115,750	5.0	95,524	2.6	2,382	-356	2,026	1.98	102,918	2.5	115,200	2.5	143,480	2.0
World B (evangelized non-Christians)	145,298	13.0	14,350	0.6	86,976	2.4	2,258	289	2,547	2.64	101,109	2.5	112,885	2.4	128,120	1.8
World C (Christians)	45,000	4.0	2,184,900	94.4	3,491,500	95.0	88,775	67	88,842	2.29	3,912,700	95.0	4,379,915	95.1	6,902,400	96.2
Country's population	**1,119,400**	**100.0**	**2,315,000**	**100.0**	**3,674,000**	**100.0**	**93,415**	**0**	**93,415**	**2.29**	**4,116,728**	**100.0**	**4,608,000**	**100.0**	**7,174,000**	**100.0**

COLUMNS, ROWS.
For meanings and definitions, see Codebook (Part 3). Note that, by definition, total 'Christians' = professing + crypto-Christians, which also = affiliated + unaffiliated Christians, and also = Great Commission Christians + latent Christians. Percentages may not always total exactly, due to rounding.

CENSUSES.
20.VI-9.VII.1966 (Papua New Guinea, including North Solomons i.e. Bougainville and Buka): 55.5% Protestants (27.4% Lutherans, 14.7% United Church of PNGSI, 3.3% SDA), 31.3% Roman Catholics, 7.5% ethnoreligionists, 5.2% Anglicans, 0.1% nonreligious.**1980**: 49.8% Protestants (25.7% Lutherans, 11.1% United Church of PNGSI, 6.2% SDA), 38.6% Roman Catholics, 7.8% Anglicans, 2.1% other religionists, 1.4% nonreligious, 0.3% marginal Christians.

NOTES ON RELIGIONS
BAHA'IS. Very rapid growth from 2 local spiritual assemblies (1964) to 67 (1973). Strongest in Gulf district of Papua, Eastern Highlands of New Guinea, and among the Talasea of New Britain.
BUDDHISTS. Chinese.
ETHNORELIGIONISTS. Animists in several hundred New Guinea mainland tribes following traditional religions including the ancestral cult, together with modern nativistic or syncretistic revitalization movements termed cargo cults. Beginning in 1893, there have been (by 1990) over 115 distinct non-Christian cargo cults (see description in article below).
INDEPENDENTS. In about 38 christianized Melanesian (including Papuan) cargo-cult type movements in 1995 (see Table 2).
NONRELIGIOUS. Europeans and Chinese.

PENTECOSTALS/CHARISMATICS. By 1975 The Catholic renewal was rapidly growing, with numerous priests and sisters involved; with the archbishop of Madang a charismatic leader. By 1998 there were thousands of prayer group attenders in all 18 dioceses.
UNAFFILIATED CHRISTIANS. During the 20th century, the enormous influx into the churches found them unable to provide adequate instruction in Christian initiation, and as a result a huge nominal fringe grew up of professing Christians unaffiliated to churches. By 1970 when remaining ethnoreligionists numbered under 5%, the nominal fringe stopped expanding, and by began to decrease in size as the churches caught up with the expansion of professing Christians.

Great Commission Instrument Panel: status of Papua New Guinea (for explanation see start of Part 4)

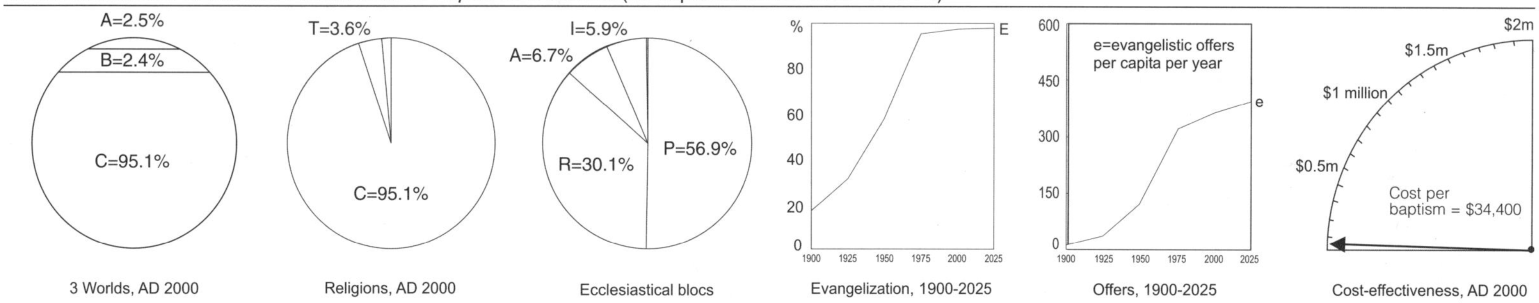

Ethnoreligionists. Mudmen from Asaro river dance to scare off evil spirits.

Papua at the time of World War I and the cult of Baigona the Snake among the Orokaivas of New Guinea. Most of these have now been superseded by the rapid spread of the Taro cult initiated in 1914 by Buninia, a Bunadele prophet. After receiving a vision of his slain father's spirit, Buninia developed rites for improving the production of taro crops. Beginning among the Orokaiva, the cult has now spread north and south among neighboring peoples. Great emphasis is placed on ecstatic singing, dancing, communal meals, and spirit possession. Taro spirits substituted for the traditional spirits of the dead are expected to bring prosperity in the form of native-grown produce or European goods. By 1973, a total of over 115 distinct cargo cults had arisen in different areas of the territory, about 30 in Papua, 70 in New Guinea (mostly in the east) and the rest on New Britain, New Ireland, and the Admiralty islands.

Baha'i has a large following, growing rapidly between 1970-1990 and now strongest in the Gulf district of Papua and in the Eastern Highlands of New Guinea.

CHRISTIANITY

By 1995, 95% of the total population had become Christians, 30% being Catholics and 65% in other denominations. Catholicism was strongest in New Guinea with 36% as against only 20% in Papua.

PROTESTANT CHURCHES. A pioneer of the London Missionary Society entered southern Papua in 1871 with several Lifu Christians from the Loyalty Islands. During the next few years, they were joined by LMS missionaries and Christians from other Pacific islands to the east, including the Cook Islands, and a training school was established at the mouth of the Fly River. A large Christian community resulted. In 1962, the LMS, Presbyterian Church of New Zealand, and Kwato Mission joined to form the Papua Ekalesia, at the time the largest single church in Papua. In 1966, 20% of Papua's population were adherents of the Ekalesia. A further union took place in 1968 involving the Papua Ekalesia, the Methodists Church, and the Union Church in Port Moresby, producing the United Church of Papua New Guinea in the Solomon Islands. Australian Methodists entered into an early comity arrangement with the LMS and Anglicans, whereby the Methodists were allocated islands to the southeast of Papua. A team including Christians from Fiji and Samoa arrived at the Duke of York Islands in 1875, later moving on to New Britain and New Ireland and finally to Papua itself in 1890. Missionary losses due to cannibalism were not uncommon in the early days; and during World War II, other missionaries together with their Christian followers were killed and their buildings destroyed. The stone-age peoples of the Highlands were not reached until 1950, and little progress was made for another decade. By 1961, there were only 200 Methodist members, but by 1967, the figure had risen to 3,000. Of the local men who serve as pastors and evangelists in this area, 90% are preliterate. At the time of the merger creating the United Church in 1968, 8.5% of the population professed to be Methodists, 16% in Papua and 5% in New Guinea.

Country summary. **Worlds A, B, C by ethnolinguistic peoples, cities, and major civil divisions in Papua New Guinea.**

PEOPLES

World	Num	Pop 2000	C%	Christians	E%	U%	Unevangelized
A	27	23,162	14.16	3,280	38	62	14,263
B	113	257,952	37.96	97,917	66	34	88,001
C	722	4,327,050	85.15	3,684,385	100	0	11,680
Total	**862**	**4,608,164**	**82.15**	**3,785,582**	**98**	**2**	**113,944**

CITIES

World	Num	Pop 2000	C%	Christians	E%	U%	Unevangelized
A	0	0	0.00	0	0	0	0
B	0	0	0.00	0	0	0	0
C	2	340,784	80.58	274,592	98	2	7,225
Total	**2**	**340,784**	**80.58**	**274,592**	**98**	**2**	**7,225**

CIVIL DIVISIONS

World	Num	Pop 2000	C%	Christians	E%	U%	Unevangelized
A	0	0	0.00	0	0	0	0
B	0	0	0.00	0	0	0	0
C	20	4,608,146	82.15	3,785,528	98	2	113,958
Total	**20**	**4,608,146**	**82.15**	**3,785,528**	**98**	**2**	**113,958**

Lutheran pioneers to New Guinea were German missionaries of the Neuendettelsau and Rhenish missions. Beginning in 1886, the work saw little advance in the early years, but since the turn of the century, the church has grown rapidly until now Lutherans form the largest sector of the non-Catholic population. Assistance has also been received from Lutheran churches in Australia and the USA and since 1951 from the Leipzig Mission. The Evangelical Lutheran Church of New Guinea (ELCONG) became autonomous in 1956. Another Lutheran body is the Wabag Lutheran Church, organized in 1961 as the result of the work of Missouri Synod Lutherans (USA) among the Enga people of the Central Highlands.

Other denominations include the Australian Assemblies of God, Australian Baptists, Plymouth Brethren, Apostolic Church Mission, and Seventh-day Adventists. The first interdenominational or faith missions were also from Australia: the Unevangelized Fields Missions among the Gongodala people of the south coast of Papua in 1931 and the South Sea Evangelical Mission at the Sepik River of New Guinea in 1948. These were followed by the New Tribes Mission in 1949, Nazarenes in 1955 and numerous other missions after 1960.

Catholic Church in Papua New Guinea. *Top.* Cathedral, Port Moresby. *Below.* Penitential procession carrying huge cross in Diocese of Wabag.

CATHOLIC CHURCH. Although Catholic missionaries first came to the Bismark archipelago in 1847, little success was recorded prior to the arrival of Sacred Heart missionaries in 1881. In 1885, the first service was held on Papua itself, and the vicariate of British New Guinea was established in 1889. There are now 4 archdioceses and 13 dioceses (excluding Bougainville), the largest in terms of membership being those on mainland New Guinea. The Catholic Church grew enormously during the 1960s, from 432,481 in 1963 to 606,000 in 1970, an average increase of more than 5% per year. From 1970 to 1990 the church grew a more modest 3.1% per annum.The first Papuan priest was not ordained until 1937 and became also the first Papuan bishop in 1970. The first ordinations of indigenous priests in New Guinea were in 1953.

The Holy See has diplomatic relations with Papua New Guinea and in AD 2000 is represented to government and the Catholic hierarchy by a nuncio residing in Port Moresby.

Anglican Church of Papua New Guinea. Cathedral of St. Peter, Dogura.

ANGLICAN CHURCH. Anglican missions began in 1892 at Dogura in eastern Papua. The diocese of Papua New Guinea was erected in 1898 and was a missionary diocese of the Church of England in Australia until the formation in 1977 of an autonomous Anglican province, the Church of the Province of Papua New Guinea with 5 dioceses.

INDIGENOUS CHURCHES. A number of cargo cults, 35 or so, have incorporated sufficiently strong Christian elements for them properly to be classified as Christian movements, though mostly of a marginal kind. Most also have been short-lived. Among several which began as revivals within mission churches was Eemasang (Cleanup movement) among Kate-speaking tribes in 1927, which lasted as a renewal movement within the Lutheran church until by 1936 it had become a cargo cult which later collapsed. New cults by 1990 included: among Lutherans, a prophet among the Atzera tribe up the Markham river who reintroduced the ancestral cult and promised cargo; and among Baining-speaking United Church adherents near Rabaul, kivung (meetings) featuring military drilling, testimonies and simultaneous audible prayer. The only cult to survive for any length of time as an organized church so far is the Paliau Church on Manus Island, a schism from the Catholic Church which has now established cooperative links with the Manus Evangelical Church and other Protestant missions. There are also a number of former cargo-cult groups that have become independent Pentecostal congregations.

Indigenous missions. Missionaries have been sent out from PNG since the earliest days of its penetration. The indigenous Papua New Guinea Missionary Association has been very active and many denominations are now sending missionaries.

Renewal movements. In the 1990s the Pentecostal/Charismatic Renewal continued to spread rapidly across most older churches, and numbered over 751,000 adherents (of whom 32% Pentecostals, 41% Charismatics, and 27% Independents).

Catholic Charismatics. 1972 procession led by (in center) Archbishop A.A Noser of Madang.

CHURCH AND STATE

According to the Papua and New Guinea Act 1949-66, Article 8, the Australian administrative authority guaranteed to the inhabitants of the territory 'freedom of conscience and worship and freedom of religious teaching'. There was and is no state church or religion. Neither the administration nor the new state assist the churches or pay clergy engaged in religious work, except army and police chaplains; but churches are exempt from taxation. There is no ministry or government department responsible for religious affairs. Churches must register as corporate bodies in order to obtain titles of property, but they do not have to register as religious organizations.

In accordance with the Education (Papua and New Guinea) Ordinance of 1970, the Australian administration paid the salaries of all qualified teachers in the territory's education system. The Weeden Report which brought about this Ordinance expressed appreciation for the efforts of churches and missions in the field of education. Religious instruction then and subsequently has been provided by church teachers in state schools as well as in church schools.

After their annual conferences of 1969 and 1970, the Catholic bishops issued documents calling for the acceleration of the process leading to independence and opposing labor conditions with kept indigenous workers away from their families for lengthy periods of time.

The president of the drafting committee for the new constitution was an indigenous Catholic priest who was also an elected deputy in parliament.

BROADCASTING AND MEDIA

Shortwave radio programs from KNLS have seen some response. Papua New Guinea is a member of UNDA. Catholics broadcast 4 hours of programming on 13 stations, including Scripture readings, youth programs, drama, music and interviews.

The 'Jesus' Film has been presented to 20% of the country by film teams.

Catholics air a 30-minute youth program and a meditation on Genesis each Sunday. Training courses are offered at 3 institutes.

Early missionaries (from top left, clockwise): bishop Verjus, pastor Ruatoka (from 1872), Dr. Fuerl, Copeland King.

INTERDENOMINATIONAL ORGANIZATIONS

The Melanesian Council of Churches (MCC), which covers also the Solomon Islands, was founded at Port Moresby in 1965 and included the Anglican Church, Australian Baptist mission, evangelical Lutheran Church, Salvation Army and the bodies which in 1968 merged into the United Church. The Catholic Church joined in 1971 and local ecumenical councils have been established in the main towns of Papua New Guinea, one of which is the Lae Kristen Kaunsil. The MCC is not affiliated with the WCC (though in working relationship with it) but has strong fraternal ties with the Evangelical Alliance of the South Pacific Islands, Australian Council of Churches, Pacific Conference of Churches and the Solomon Islands Christian Association. Of the churches working in Papua New Guinea, 20 are members of the Evangelical Alliance of the South Pacific. In 1969, the Melanesian Association of Theological Schools was formed by the theological colleges of the Anglican, Catholic, Lutheran and United churches. Other ecumenical initiatives are the Churches Education Council, which consists of the various denominational education officers responsible for church interests in the newly formed Education System and Sodepang (Sodepax Papua New Guinea) which works in collaboration with Sodepax, New Guinea in the field of human development.

FUTURE TRENDS AND PROSPECTS

Christians, only 4% of the population in 1900, are expected to plateau at about 96% by 2025. Ethnoreligionists, 95.9% in 1900, are expected to fall to 2% by 2025.

Tribal religions would then continue a slow decline throughout the 21st century. Christianity, already claiming the vast majority, will continue strong in the same period. Only Baha'is and the nonreligious will likely grow to 3-4% of the population jointly by mid-century.

BIBLIOGRAPHY

75 years in New Guinea: Divine Word Missionaries, 1896–1971. Divine Word Missionaries. Wewak, New Guinea: Wantok Publications, 1971. 56p.

'A cargo movement in the East Central Highlands of New Guinea', R. M. Berndt, *Oceania*, 23, 1 (1952-53), 40-63, and 23, 3 (1952-53), 137-158.

A church is born: a history of the Evangelical Church of Papua New Guinea. J. Prince & M. Prince. [Preston, Victoria: Asia Pacific Christian Mission], 1991. 142p.

A church self–study in Papua New Guinea, 1972–75. Brussels: Pro Mundi Vita, 1976. (PMV dossier).

'A comparison between the Begesin Rebellion and the present Christian Revival movement in the Kein area of the Begesin region.' A. Yagas. Typescript, University of PNG, 1976.

'A history of Cargoism in Sio, Northeast New Guinea,' T. G. Harding, *Oceania*, 38, 1 (1967), 1–23.

A short history of the Anglican Church in Papua New Guinea. A. Chittleborough. Stanmore, Australia: Australian Board of Commissions, 1976. 24p.

'An approach for measuring and improving church indigeneity in Papua New Guinea.' D. J. Price. Th.M. thesis, Fuller Theological Seminary, Pasadena, CA, 1979. 129p.

An introduction to Melanesian religions. E. Mantovani (ed). *Point Series*, no. 6. Goroka, Papua New Guinea: Melanesian Institute, 1984. 306p.

An introduction to ministry in Melanesia. B. Schwarz (ed). *Point Series*, no. 7. Goroka, Papua New Guinea: Melanesian Institute, 1985. 304p.

'Cargo cults and religious beliefs among the Garia,' P. Lawrence, *Internationalis Archiv für Ethnographie*, 47 (1955), 1–20.

Catholic Church in Papua New Guinea. R. Walei. *Pagini bibliography*, no. 3. : University of Papua New Guinea Library, 1975. 3p.

Charles W. Abel: Papuan Pioneer. M. K. Abel. London: Oliphants, 1957. (On the 1891 founder of the Kwato Church).

Christ, the life of Papua New Guinea. E. Mantovani & M. N. MacDonald. *Occasional papers of the Melanesian Institute*, no. 1. Goroka, Papua New Guinea: Melanesian Institute for Pastoral and Socio-Economic Service, 1988. 61p.

Christian stewardship in the South Pacific. J. Sharpe. Madang, Papua New Guinea: Kristen Pres, 1972. 77p.

'Christianity, cargo cults and politics among the Toaripi of Papua,' D. Ryan, *Oceania*, 40, 2 (1969), 99–118.

Christianity in Papua New Guinea. Pacific Conference of Churches research paper, no. 1. Port Villa, New Hebrides: Pacific Churches Research Centre, 1980. 12p.

Church and people in New Guinea. G. F. Vicedom. London: Lutterworth, 1961. 79p.

'Church growth and urbanization in New Guinea.' G. Fugmann. Thesis, Fuller Theological Seminary, Pasadena, CA, 1969. 244p.

Contextualization of Christianity and Christianization of language: a case study from the highlands of Papua New Guinea. G. L. Renck. *Erlanger Monographien aus Mission und Ökumene*, Bd. 5. Erlangen, Germany: Verlag der Ev.-Luth. Mission, 1990. 330p.

Directory of the Catholic churches in Papua New Guinea and Solomon Islands. Port Moresby, Papua New Guinea: Catholic Church Bishops' Conference of the Papua New Guinea and Solomon Islands, 1985. 204p.

God, ghosts and men in Melanesia: some religions of Australian New Guinea and the New Hebrides. P. Lawrence & M. J. Meggitt (eds). London: Oxford University Press, 1965.

Hidden people: how a remote New Guinea culture was brought back from the brink of extinction. L. F. Oates. Sutherland, Australia: Albatross Books, 1992. 352p.

'Housing for urban settlement communities in Papua New Guinea: strategic issues for effective ministry.' M. A. Jelliffe. M.A. thesis, Fuller Theological Seminary, Pasadena, CA, 1992. 167p.

I have a strong belief: the Reverend Leslie Boseto's own story of his eight years as the first Melanesian moderator of the United Church in Papua New Guinea and the Solomon Islands. L. Boseto. Rabaul, Papua New Guinea: Unichurch Books, 1983. 215p.

'Inculturation of rites of Christian initiation of the Kewabi people of Papua New Guinea.' M. T. Dwan. M.T.S. thesis, Catholic Theological Union, Chicago, 1993. 81p.

Like people you see in a dream: first contact in six Papuan societies. E. L. Schieffelin & R. Crittenden. Stanford, CA: Stanford University Press, 1991. 343p.

Lutheran Church in Papua New Guinea: the first hundred years, 1886–1986. H. Wagner & H. Reiner (eds). Adelaide, Australia: Lutheran Publishing House, 1986. 677p.

'Maisin Christianity: an ethnography of the contemporary religion of a seaboard Melanesian people.' J. Barker. Ph.D. dissertation, University of British Columbia, 1985. 578p.

Mambu: a Melanesian millennium. K. Burridge. London: Methuen, 1961. 296p.

Manus religion: an ethnological study of the Manus natives of the Admiralty Islands. R. F. Fortune. Philadelphia: American Philosophical Society, 1935. 391p.

Melanesian cargo cults: new salvation movements in South Pacific. F. Steinbauer. Trans., M. Wohlwill. St. Lucia, Australia: University of Queensland Press, 1979. 215p.

'Melanesian understanding of the church: historical and theological perspectives.' Z. N. Kemung. S.T.M. thesis, Wartburg Theological Seminary, Dubuque, IA, 1986. 162p.

Methodist Church in Papua New Guinea. E. Maiuka. *Pagini bibliography*, no. 4. : University of Papua New Guinea Library, 1975. 5p.

'Methodist missionary influence on native education in Tonga, Fiji and Papua–New Guinea with special reference to government–mission relationships since 1942.' R. C. Wilkinson. M.Ed. thesis, University of Sydney, Sydney, Australia, 1959. 372p.

Missionsbeginn in Neuguinea: die Anfänge der Rheinischen, Neuendettelsauer und Steyler Missionsarbeit in Neuguinea. P. Steffen. *Studia Instituti Missiologici Societatis Verbi Divini*, Nr. 61. Nettetal, Germany: Steyler, 1995. 312p.

'Native Christianity in a New Guinea village,' H. I. Hogbin, *Oceania*, 18 (1947), 1–35.

One hundred years in the islands: the Methodist–United Church in the New Guinea Islands Region, 1875–1975. N. A. Threlfall. Rabaul, Papua New Guinea: The United Church, 1975. 288p.

Orokaiva magic. F. E. Williams. London: Oxford, 1928.

Papua New Guinea. F. McConnell. *World bibliographical series*, vol. 90. Oxford, UK: CLIO Press, 1988. 379p. (See especially 'Religion,' p.178–93).

Pigs for the ancestors: ritual in the ecology of a New Guinea people. R. A. Rappaport. New Haven, CT: Yale University Press, 1967.

Religious movements in Melanesia today. W. Flannery (ed). *Point Series*, nos. 2-4. Goroka, Papua New Guinea: Melanesian Institute, 1983–84. 3 vols.

Reluctant mission: the Anglican Church in Papua New Guinea, 1891–1942. D. Wetherell. St. Lucia, Australia: University of Queensland Press, 1977. 344p.

'Revival Christianity among the Urat of Papua New Guinea: some possible motivational and perceptual antecedents.' S. L. Eyre. Ph.D. dissertation, University of California, San Diego, 1988. 300p.

Romans and Anglicans in Papua New Guinea. [Goroka, Papua New Guinea]: Liturgical Catechetical Institute, [1991]. 144p. (Also published as vol. 7 of the *Melanesian journal of theology*).

The Anglican Church in Papua New Guinea. M. B. Aiahu. *Pagini bibliography*, no. 6. : University of Papua New Guinea Library, 1975. 5p.

The birth of an indigenous church: letters, reports and documents of Lutheran Christians of Papua New Guinea. G. Fugmann (ed). *Point series*, no. 10. Goroka, Papua New Guinea: The Melanesian Institute, 1986. 291p.

'The ecclesiological frontier: an ethnohistorical study of Catholic missionaries in the Sepik Region of Papua New Guinea.' M. T. Huber. Ph.D. dissertation, University of Pittsburgh, 1986. 386p.

'The mission of God in the Wabag area of New Guinea.' E. L. Spruth. Thesis, Fuller Theological Seminary, Pasadena, CA, 1970. 471p.

The mustard seed: from a French mission to a Papuan church, 1885–1985. G. Delbos. Port Moresby, Australia: Institute of Papua New Guinea Studies, 1985. 465p.

'The Paliau movement in the Admiralty Islands, 1946–1954,' T. Schwartz, *Anthropological papers of the American Museum of Natural History*, 40, Part 2 (1962), 211–413. (Many photographs).

'The Remnant Church: a separatist church.' M. Mauliu. Christian Leader's Training College, Banz, Papua New Guinea,

The trumpet shall sound: a study of 'cargo' cults in Melanesia. P. Worsley. London: MacGibbon & Kee, 1957. 290p.

The United Church in Papua, New Guinea, and the Solomon Islands: the story of the development of an indigenous church on the occasion of the centenary of the L. M. S. in Papua, 1872–1972. R. G. Williams. Rabaul, Papua New Guinea: Trinity Press, [1972]. 350p.

'The view from Hurun: the Peli Association of the East Sepik District.' R. J. May. New Guinea Research Unit, Port Moresby, Papua New Guinea, 1975.

Towards a Melanesian theology. Port Moresby, Papua New Guinea: Melanesian Institute.

United Church directory. Port Moresby, Papua New Guinea: UCPNGSI, 1975. (Annual).

Country Table 2. **Organized churches and denominations in Papua New Guinea.**

Official name (bold type = church with over 10% of all affiliated) 1	*Begun* 2	*Type* 3	*Counc* 4	*Congs* 5	*Adults* 6	*Affiliated 1970* 7	*Affiliated 1995* 8	*G%* 9	*Names, notes, and other statistics* (see Codebook, Part 3) 10
Anglican Church of Papua New Guinea	1891	A-Hig	AWPKK	667	163,000	60,000	270,000	6.20	1977, 5 Dioceses. 92% Papuan. 55n,47x,166f,3H,27h,2p,3r,1s(20),=W70%,2CCOYy.
Apostolic Christian Church	1960	P-Hol	x....	130	15,700	5,000	26,000	6.82	M=ACC(USA). Members Wala tribe. Very rapid growth 20% pa. 2x,6f,9p,W=80%,500Y.
Apostolic Church	1954	P-PeA	Z...E	300	25,000	17,000	50,000	4.41	M=Apostolic Church of Australia & New Zealand. Western Highlands. HQ Kandep.
Assemblies of God	1948	P-Pe2	ZH..E	350	18,000	20,000	37,000	2.49	*New Guinea Miss.* M=AoG(Australia, UK). Wewak. 14n,15x,100f,3p,W=28%,2COY.
Assoc of Baptists for World Evangelism	1967	I-Bap	x....	15	860	1,000	1,720	2.19	M=ABWE(USA). Regular Baptists. Fundamentalists. 2f.
Bamu River Mission	1936	P-Non	.H..E	20	1,300	2,000	2,200	0.38	M=BRM(Aust). Members: Kuvai, Bamu, Duvani tribes. 1 launch. 1n,1x,3f,1H,1p,W=75%,3Y.
Baptist Bible Fellowship International	1961	I-Bap	x....	2	200	150	300	2.81	M=BBFI(USA). Fundamentalist Baptists. 6f.
Baptist International Missions	c1970	I-Bap	.....	35	5,000	–	12,500	45.84	M=BIM(USA).
Baptist Union of PNG	1949	P-Bap	TH..a	360	35,270	17,000	78,400	6.31	M=ABMS(Australia). Sepik. Engas. 96n,10x,49f,1H,1s(15),W=79%,250Y,300z.
Bible Missionary Church		I-Non	x....	100	4,000	3,000	11,400	0.05	M=BMC(USA). Southern Highlands. HQ Kagua, via Mt Hagen. 3f.
Bethel Pentecostal Temple	1948	P-Pe2	.....	267	40,000	40,000	88,000	3.20	M=BPC(Seattle,USA). Classical Pentecostals (2-stage). Growth 7.5%pa,1p,2300Y.
Catholic Ch in Papua New Guinea:	1847	R-Lat	P...Q	416	664,300	606,544	1,214,038	2.81	Many institutions. C=12+8+31. 97H,3q,3s. 88n 382x 709m 845w 32838Yy
M Madang	1913	R-Lat	Ps	28	60,000	55,475	123,328	3.25	NG, between Catholic and Lutheran spheres. M=SVD. 6n 25x 60m 96w 3710Yy
D Aitape	1952	R-Lat	Pofm	20	34,000	37,337	58,521	1.81	NG mainland, extreme north. Underdeveloped. 2n 21x 44m 61w 2024Yy
D Lae	1959	R-Lat	Pcmn	9	17,700	11,450	30,000	3.93	NG Mainland. Lutheran sphere, few Catholics. 3n 9x 17m 4w 572Yy
D Vanimo	1963	R-Lat	Ps	11	11,000	5,700	26,000	6.26	NG mainland. Remote, primitive. M=CP,PIME,CMI. 0n 14x 24m 29w 992Yy
D Wewak	1913	R-Lat	Psvd	27	47,600	75,871	95,000	0.90	NG mainland. 43% RC, widespread schools. 11n 44x 90m 67w 3645Yy
M Mount Hagen	1959	R-Lat	Psvd	23	68,500	90,255	119,479	1.13	NG mainland, rural highlands. Catholics strong. 4n 26x 41m 29w 2970Yy
D Goroka	1959	R-Lat	Psvd	10	11,000	83,341	13,800	-6.94	NG rural highlands. Catholics very strong. 3n 14x 22m 26w 293Yy
D Kundiawa	1982	R-Lat	Psvd	18	56,000	–	94,279	7.69	M=SVD. 9n 15x 25m 21w 1574Yy
D Mendi	1958	R-Lat	Pofmc	14	41,000	26,636	74,562	4.20	P rural highlands. White influence very recent. 2n 21x 31m 45w 2280Yy
D Wabag	1982	R-Lat	Psvd	18	35,000	–	61,736	7.69	Formerly in M Mount Hagen. 4n 16x 23m 15w 1195Yy
M Port Moresby	1946	R-Lat	Ps	23	59,000	23,112	123,000	6.92	Papua. Catholics most from other areas. M=MSC-1. 7n 29x 118m 154w 2290Yy
D Alotau-Sideia	1946	R-Lat	Pmscl	98	16,000	11,500	27,084	3.49	Papua: many widely scattered islands. 1n 18x 28m 43w 1125Yy
D Bereina	1959	R-Lat	Pmscl	17	34,000	39,862	58,600	1.55	Papua mainland. 199 expatriate Catholics. 6n 17x 34m 3w 2510Yy
D Daru-Kiunga	1959	R-Lat	Psmn	26	15,000	2,805	27,857	9.62	P mainland. Vast wasteland; large mining works. 1n 8x 19m 29w 556Yy
D Kerema	1971	R-Lat	Pmscl	11	7,500	–	13,656	4.17	Formerly in D Bereina and D Mendi. M=MSC-1. 2n 7x 15m 23w 801Yy

Continued overleaf

Country Table 2–concluded

Official name (bold type = church with over 10% of affiliated) 1	Begun 2	Type 3	Counc 4	Congs 5	Adults 6	Affiliated 1970 7	Affiliated 1995 8	G% 9	*Names, notes, and other statistics* (see Codebook, Part 3) 10
M Rabaul	1889	R-Lat	Pmscl	43	118,000	109,000	209,120	2.64	New Britain. Rich. First RC mission in PNG. 1p. 19n 64x 95m 198w 6301Yy
D Kavieng	1957	R-Lat	Pmscl	20	33,000	34,200	58,016	2.14	NG: New Ireland etc. Fishing, agriculture. 8n 13x 23m 23w 0Yy
Christian Brethren	c1955	P-CBr	x...E	352	20,000	15,220	42,500	4.19	*Plymouth (Open) Brethren.* M=CMML(NZ, Australia, USA). Southern Highlands. 69f.
Christian Revival Crusade	1963	I-3pW	x....	138	18,000	1,000	45,000	16.45	M-CRC(Australia). Works also with International Ch of the Foursquare Gospel. 2n,1s.
Ch of Jesus Christ of Latter-day Saints	1979	m-LdS	.....	13	1,260	–	2,100	6.25	Mormons. M=CJCLdS(USA).
Church of the Nazarene	1955	P-Hol	xF..E	111	4,850	3,000	6,780	3.32	M=CoN(USA). HQ Banz. 7x,109m,33f,1H,1h,1s(23),16t(1945),W=67%,30Y.
Churches of Christ in Christian Union	1963	P-Hol	xF..E	70	8,000	9,200	14,800	1.92	M=CCCU(USA). Wesleyan doctrine. Southern Highlands. 1 school. 15f,3h.
Churches of Christ	1958	I-Dis	x...E	160	12,800	7,000	32,000	6.27	M=Australian Churches of christ Mission. HQ Tung, Wewak. New Guinea. 10f.
Evangelical Bible Mission	1948	P-Hol	....E	165	6,600	2,000	13,200	7.84	M=EBM(USA),East & West Indies Bible Mission,Gospel Tidings Mission. 24f,5h,1s.
Evangelical Ch of Papua New Guinea	1931	P-Eva	xM..E	160	19,500	12,601	48,800	5.57	M=Asia Pacific Christian Mission,UFM(USA,UK). 160n,139f,7p*80),W=98%,349Y.
Ev Lutheran Ch of Papua New Guinea	1886	P-Lut	L.p.K	2,050	358,000	365,137	575,000	1.83	*ELCONG.* 200 tribes. 275n,98x,2255m,130f,34h,8p,3s(150),W=62%,5161Y,10710y.
Faith Mission		P-Non	.....	60	7,000	8,730	15,000	0.05	Interdenominational mission. In Gono, Goroka, Eastern Highlands. 13f.
Greek Orthodox Church: AD Australia		O-Gre	Cw...	1	150	200	300	0.05	Greeks. Under jurisdiction of EP Constantinople, in AD Australia & E All Oceania.
Independent Christian Missionary Soc	1965	I-3pP	....E	20	3,000	3,000	8,000	4.00	Port Moresby. Pentecostal. Very rapid growth: 35% pa. 10n,4x,W=99%,21Y.
Indigenous cargo-cult churches	1893	I-mar	.....	25	1,300	1,000	2,000	2.81	Long series of over 30 christianized movements, 1893-1980 (e.g. Wok belong Yali).
Indigenous pentecostal congregations		I-3pP	.....	40	2,000	1,000	4,000	0.05	Christian pentecostal groups arising from cargo-cult manifestations.
Internat Ch of the Foursquare Gospel	1955	P-Pe2	ZF..E	328	20,004	20,000	33,300	2.06	M=ICFG(USA), CRC(Australia). Rapid growth in 5 tribes. 64n,21x,2p,(55),W=76%,359Y.
Jehovah's Witnesses	1938	m-Jeh	x....	58	2,471	5,000	11,200	3.28	Churches: Papua 16; NG 11; Manus 1; New Britain 1; New Ireland 1. (1975) 100Y. (1995) 220Y.
Kein Independence Group	1969	I-Lut	.....	6	400	500	1,000	2.81	Ex ELCONG. HQ Kein, Begesin District, Madang. '7 Steps and 7 Keys'.
Kwato Church	1917	I-3pP	.....	40	3,000	4,000	5,000	0.90	Ex LMS; 1977, ex UCPNG. Strong MRA influence. Milne Bay Province.
Manus Evangelical Church	1914	P-Eva	xM..E	18	1,840	4,000	4,600	0.56	M=MEM(Liebenzell) (USA). Manus Island, 31 languages. 5n,2x,9f,W=42%,122Y.
National Revival Church Mission		I-3pP	Z....	25	800	500	2,000	0.05	M=National Revival Crusade(Australia). Pentecostals (2-stage).
New Apostolic Church	c1970	I-3aX	x....	200	40,000	–	60,339	55.32	*NAC.* M=NAK (HQ Zurich). 1978 took over huge Peli movement.
New Guinea Gospel Mission	1960	P-Non	.H..E	15	1,000	1,000	1,500	1.64	M-NGGM(Australia). Interdenominational. HQ Wewak. Schools, medical work. 9f.
New Tribes Mission Churches	1949	P-Fun	x....	109	13,100	10,000	32,700	4.85	M=NTM(USA). HQ Goroka, EHD. 1 school. 21n,37x,88f,1h,2p,W=43%,100Y.
Open Bible Standard Church	c1980	I-3pW	.....	24	1,156	–	2,890	6.67	M=OBSC(USA).
Paliau Church	1946	I-ReC	.....	10	600	1,000	1,200	0.73	Schism 25% of RCC on Manus, begun by policeman, Paliau; now links with Manus Ev Ch.
Peli (Hawk) Association	1971	I-mar	.....	10	2,000	500	5,000	4.17	HQ Yangoru, East Sepik. 1972: 200,000 members. 1978: M=New Apostolic Ch (Canada).
Pentecostal Church	1968	P-Pe2	Z....	20	1,000	850	2,500	4.41	M=SFM(Sweden),FFFM(Finland). Classical Pentecostals. 2n,3x,1p,W=47%,10Y,20z.
Pioneers	c1985	P-Non	.....	2	67	–	150	10.00	M=Pioneers(USA).
Salvation Army	1956	P-Sal	xwe.K	80	2,000	2,000	5,000	3.73	*PNG Region*, in Eastern Territory, Australia. 24n,22x,1p,1s(11),W=60%,82Y.
Seventh-day Adventist Church	1908	P-Adv	x....	484	62,100	72,000	103,546	1.46	*Coral Sea & Bismarck-Solomons UMs.* 100nx,1127mw,21f,3H,41h,2r,2s,839t(52570),2666Y.
South Seas Evangelical Church	1948	P-Eva	xH..E	193	5,400	5,000	9,000	2.38	*SSEC.* M=SSEM(Australia). Losses to cargo cult. 10x,2p,W=80%,250Y,120z.
Sovereign Grace Baptist Mission		P-Bap	.....	50	1,600	3,000	3,100	0.05	Southern Highlands. HQ Tanggi, Koroba, via Mt Hagen; and Goroka EHD. 1f.
Swiss Evangelical Brotherhood Mission		P-Eva	.....	260	4,000	7,000	8,000	0.05	HQ Lae. Districts: Chimbu, Eastern & Western Highlands, New Guinea. 45f.
United Ch in Papua New Guinea	1871	P-Uni	VWP.K	3,000	600,000	210,540	1,000,000	6.43	1968 union: Papua Ekalesia (M=LMS), 4 Methodist areas. 276n,58x,5p,2s(80),19138z.
Wabag (Gudnius/Good News) Luth Ch	1948	P-Lut	L...K	417	33,081	48,000	63,000	1.09	M=NGLM(LCMS,USA). Enga tribe. 23 schools. 80n,17x,58f,1p,2s(35),1696Yy.
Wesleyan Church	1961	P-Hol	VF..E	53	2,154	5,000	4,680	-0.26	M=WC(USA). HQ Pangia. 2 schools. Rapid growth. 4x,6f,2p,W=87%,17Y,25z.
World-Wide Missions	1971	I-Non	x....	40	4,000	7,000	8,000	4.17	M=WWM(USA). Evangelicals based on Pasadena, CA (USA). In Goroka territory, NG. 1f.
Other Protestant denominations		P-	.....	100	5,000	5,000	10,000	0.05	Total over 20 (see list below).
Other independent charismatic chs	c1975	I-3cP	.....	150	10,000	–	30,000	5.00	
Doubly-affiliated		2-aff			-371,000	0	-660,000		Evangelicals who are also baptized Roman Catholics, Anglicans, or Lutherans.
Totals				**11,719**	**1,880,863**	**1,612,672**	**3,348,743**		

Churches, members, growth, 1900-2025	*Congs*	*Adults*	*Affiliated*	*G%*	*Total denominations*	*6 Megablocs:* O	R	A	P	I	m
Total churches, members, and denominations (mid-1900)	300	15,800	29,600	5.88	5	0	1	1	2	1	0
Total churches, members, and denominations (mid-1970)	8,212	859,518	1,612,672	5.88	57	1	1	1	39	14	1
Total churches, members, and denominations (mid-1990)	10,000	1,666,000	2,966,200	3.09	98	1	1	1	57	36	2
Total churches, members, and denominations (mid-1995)	11,719	1,880,863	3,348,743	2.46	99	1	1	1	57	37	2
Total churches, members, and denominations (mid-2000)	13,000	2,126,000	3,785,528	2.48	100	1	1	1	57	38	2
Total churches, members, and denominations (mid-2025)	27,000	3,555,000	6,328,800	2.08	190	2	1	1	80	100	6

NOTES ON TABLE ABOVE
NATIONAL COUNCILS (Column 4 5th letter).
- a = member of both MCC and EASPI. In addition, the Highland Synod, United Church in PNG & SI, is a member of both.
- C = Papua New Guinea Council of Churches (PNGCC, 1970).
- E = Evangelical Alliance of Papua New Guinea (EAPNG).
- H = National Council of Pentecostal Churches (NCPC, 1979).
- K = Melanesian Council of Churches (MCC) (member churches are all in Papua New Guinea).
- Q = Bishops' Conference of Papua New Guinea & the Solomon Islands, also member of MCC.

Local councils. Lae Kristen Kaunsil, and others (related to MCC).
OTHER PROTESTANT DENOMINATIONS. Among the over 20 smaller denominations are the following: Baptist Ch (Boroko), Christadelphians (1 ecclesia), Churches of Christ (USA), Ev Wesleyan Ch, Highlands Christian Mission, Hohola Gospel Mission, Independent Assemblies of God, Independent Baptist Mission, Independent Nazarene Ch, New Guinea Christian Mission, Sola Fide Mission, United Ev Chs, Village Church Mission, Wewak Christian Fellowship.

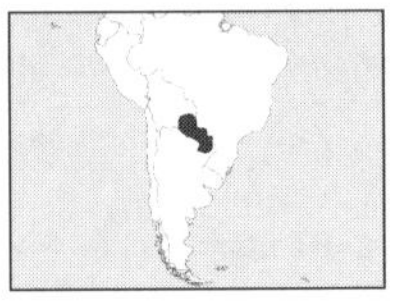

PARAGUAY

SECULAR DATA, AD 2000

STATE
Official name: La República del Paraguay/Tetã Paraguáype (The Republic of Paraguay).
Short name: Paraguay. **Adjective of nationality:** Paraguayan.
Flag: Red, white, and blue stripes; national coat of arms in centre.
Area: 406,752 sq. km. (157,048 sq. mi.).
Government: Multiparty republic, since 1954 (1524 Spanish possession, 1811 Independence, several dictatorships and republics, 1992 new constitution).
Legislature: Senate, 45 members. Chamber of Deputies, 80 members.
Official language: Spanish (Español/Castella).
Monetary unit: 1 Paraguayan Guaraní (G) = 100 céntimos. **US$1=** G2,810.
Chief cities: ASUNCION 1,262,000; Ciudad del Este 164,354; San Lorenzo 163,636; Lambare 122,356; Fernando de la Mora 116,962.
Political divisions: 18 provinces.
Armed forces: 20,000.

DEMOGRAPHY
Population: 5,496,000.
Population density: 13.5/sq. km. (35.0/sq. mi.).
Under 15 years: 2,173,000.
Growth rate p.a.: 2.46% (births 29.64, deaths 5.07).
Mortality: Infant, per 1,000: 37.0, ; **Maternal per 100,000:** 160.0.
Life expectancy: 71 (male 69, female 73).
Household size: 4.7. **Floor area per person, sq.m:** 10.0.
Major languages: Guaraní, Spanish, Lengua, German, Portuguese, Italian, Ukrainian, and 20 other languages. Usage: 90% speak Guaraní, 75% speak Spanish.
Urban dwellers: 55.98%. **Urban growth rate p.a.:** 3.6%.
Labor force: 34%.

ETHNOLINGUISTIC PEOPLES
82.9% Paraguayan Mestizo; 3.4% Latin American White; 3.1% German; 2.0% Mestizo; 1.7% Half-Indian.

ECONOMY
National income p.a. per person: US$1,690; **per family:** US$7,943.

EDUCATION
Adult literacy: 92% (male 93%, female 90%). **Schools:** 6,282.
Universities: 2. **School enrolment:** female/male: 78%/79%.

HEALTH
Access to health services: 63%. **Access to safe water:** 8%.
Hospitals: 100 (12 beds per 10,000). **Doctors:** 2,924.
Blind: 4,000. **Deaf:** 329,800. **Murder rate:** 15.
Lepers: 14,000. **Underweight prevalence under 5:** 4%.

LITERATURE
New book titles p.a.: 170 (31 p.a. per million). **Periodicals:** 28.
Newspapers: 5 dailies.

COMMUNICATION (per 1,000 people)
Phones: 34 **(27% mobile). Radios:** 144. **TV sets:** 144.
Daily newspaper circulation: 42. **Computers:** 35.

HUMAN LIFE AND LIBERTY (optimum condition=100.0%)
HDI: 70.6. **HSI:** 37.0. **HFI:** 25.0. **EFL:** 47.0.

Country status. Paraguay is a landlocked country in central South America, south of Brazil and north of Argentina. Its main industries are meat-packing, vegetable-oil processing, and textiles.

HUMAN LIFE AND LIBERTY

Human need and development. Although conditions vary widely between towns and villages, Paraguayans in general enjoy a reasonably good standard of living. They are among the best fed in Latin America and have access to a wide variety of foods and a nutritious diet. Housing also is adequate and no segment of the population has an absolute lack of regular shelter. Paraguay does not face the serious housing problems common to many developing countries. A small proportion of the families live as squatters. About 65% of the housing units are ranchos or roughly constructed small shacks. There are no serious health problems, and both medical facilities and medical personnel are adequate. Piped water is available only in Asuncion, which also has the only municipal sewer system. Most Paraguayans are covered by state social welfare programs, first initiated in 1946.

Human rights and freedoms. Paraguay has been almost continuously under authoritarian rule since 1811, but in 1989, a new government, the leaders of which had deposed dictator Alfred Stroessner, committed itself to democracy, and took important steps toward that goal. But many of the legacies of the Stroessner era continue to haunt the country. Among them are extrajudicial killings, police torture of suspects, beatings and mistreatment of prisoners, police corruption, detention of suspects without judicial orders, firings of labor organizers, violent evictions of squatters, and military intrusions into the civilian arena. The significant Korean and Chinese minorities experience social and economic discrimination as do the indigenous people. The new constitution guarantees women many rights they were previously denied under the old Penal Code, especially in matters of property and employment.

Human environment. The Chaco region is flat and arid, and has suffered from heavy deforestation. Most farmers burn wood for their domestic needs. Water

Country Table 1. **Religious adherents in Paraguay, AD 1900-2025.**

Year	1900		1970		mid-1990		Annual change, 1990-2000				mid-1995		mid-2000		mid-2025	
Name	Adherents	%	Adherents	%	Adherents	%	Natural	Conversion	Total	Rate	Adherents	%	Adherents	%	Adherents	%
Christians	**580,000**	**96.7**	**2,299,700**	**97.8**	**4,134,900**	**98.0**	**125,199**	**-1,606**	**123,593**	**2.65**	**4,725,000**	**97.9**	**5,370,826**	**97.7**	**9,118,800**	**97.5**
PROFESSION																
professing Christians	**580,000**	**96.7**	**2,299,700**	**97.8**	**4,134,900**	**98.0**	**125,199**	**-1,606**	**123,593**	**2.65**	**4,725,000**	**97.9**	**5,370,826**	**97.7**	**9,118,800**	**97.5**
AFFILIATION																
unaffiliated Christians	0	0.0	37,000	1.6	160,800	3.8	4,867	-1,225	3,642	2.06	180,000	3.7	197,224	3.6	218,800	2.3
affiliated Christians	**580,000**	**96.7**	**2,262,700**	**96.3**	**3,974,100**	**94.2**	**120,332**	**-382**	**119,950**	**2.67**	**4,545,000**	**94.1**	**5,173,602**	**94.1**	**8,900,000**	**95.1**
Roman Catholics	580,000	96.7	2,304,591	98.1	3,835,000	90.9	116,077	-4,577	111,500	2.59	4,360,217	90.3	4,950,000	90.1	8,300,000	88.7
Protestants	100	0.0	42,413	1.8	143,446	3.4	4,342	1,313	5,655	3.38	171,981	3.6	200,000	3.6	500,000	5.3
Independents	0	0.0	10,932	0.5	51,000	1.2	1,544	436	1,980	3.33	60,364	1.3	70,800	1.3	140,000	1.5
Marginal Christians	0	0.0	3,070	0.1	18,000	0.4	545	255	800	3.75	21,840	0.5	26,000	0.5	60,000	0.6
Anglicans	100	0.0	3,000	0.1	12,500	0.3	378	132	510	3.48	15,015	0.3	17,600	0.3	33,600	0.4
Orthodox	0	0.0	1,000	0.0	1,800	0.0	54	-34	20	1.06	1,900	0.0	2,000	0.0	3,400	0.0
doubly-affiliated	-200	0.0	-30,006	-1.3	-37,646	-0.9	-1,139	1,124	-15	0.04	-34,317	-0.7	-37,798	-0.7	-67,000	-0.7
disaffiliated	0	0.0	-72,300	-3.1	-50,000	-1.2	-1,513	1,013	-500	0.96	-52,000	-1.1	-55,000	-1.0	-70,000	-0.8
Trans-megabloc groupings																
Evangelicals	200	0.0	31,000	1.3	114,000	2.7	3,451	1,049	4,500	3.38	135,002	2.8	159,000	2.9	390,000	4.2
Pentecostals/Charismatics	0	0.0	9,000	0.4	177,000	4.2	5,357	1,143	6,500	3.18	213,732	4.4	242,000	4.4	550,000	5.9
Great Commission Christians	**18,000**	**3.0**	**188,000**	**8.0**	**329,000**	**7.8**	**9,958**	**88**	**10,046**	**2.70**	**376,500**	**7.8**	**429,463**	**7.8**	**748,400**	**8.0**
Nonreligious	0	0.0	9,800	0.4	30,000	0.7	908	2,099	3,007	7.19	43,000	0.9	60,072	1.1	140,000	1.5
Ethnoreligionists	20,000	3.3	32,000	1.4	29,500	0.7	893	-849	44	0.15	29,250	0.6	29,942	0.5	25,000	0.3
Buddhists	0	0.0	2,000	0.1	6,200	0.2	188	297	485	5.95	9,700	0.2	11,048	0.2	24,000	0.3
Atheists	0	0.0	3,000	0.1	6,800	0.2	206	106	312	3.84	8,000	0.2	9,916	0.2	13,000	0.1
Baha'is	0	0.0	2,100	0.1	6,800	0.2	206	15	221	2.86	7,900	0.2	9,011	0.2	25,000	0.3
New-Religionists	0	0.0	200	0.0	2,400	0.1	73	-22	51	1.94	2,600	0.1	2,908	0.1	6,000	0.1
Jews	0	0.0	1,200	0.1	2,400	0.1	73	-40	33	1.30	2,550	0.1	2,731	0.1	3,200	0.0
World A (unevangelized persons)	12,000	2.0	11,751	0.5	8,438	0.2	225	36	261	3.05	9,656	0.2	10,992	0.2	18,710	0.2
World B (evangelized non-Christians)	8,000	1.3	38,938	1.6	75,662	1.8	2,322	1,570	3,892	4.20	93,821	1.9	114,182	2.1	217,490	2.3
World C (Christians)	580,000	96.7	2,299,700	97.9	4,134,900	98.0	125,199	-1,606	123,593	2.65	4,725,000	97.9	5,370,826	97.7	9,118,800	97.5
Country's population	**600,000**	**100.0**	**2,350,390**	**100.0**	**4,219,000**	**100.0**	**127,746**	**0**	**127,746**	**2.68**	**4,828,478**	**100.0**	**5,496,000**	**100.0**	**9,355,000**	**100.0**

COLUMNS, ROWS.
For meanings and definitions, see Codebook (Part 3). Note that, by definition, total 'Christians' = professing + crypto-Christians, which also = affiliated + unaffiliated Christians, and also = Great Commission Christians + latent Christians. Percentages may not always total exactly, due to rounding.

CENSUSES.
14.X.1962 (excluding 35,000 jungle Indians): 96.7% Roman Catholics, 2.3% other Christians, 0.6% other religionists, 0.4% non-religious.

NOTES ON RELIGIONS
ATHEISTS. Communist Party of Paraguay (PCP) (proscribed, suppressed) and factions. Many remain Roman Catholics, a number practicing.
BAHA'IS. Growth from 3 local spiritual assemblies (1964) to 14 (1973). Many converts are Indians (Yanaigua, Chulupi, Maka).
BUDDHISTS. Among Japanese (since 1956; in Itapua and Alto Paraná) and Korean immigrants.
COUNTRY'S POPULATION. From 1955-70, about 650,000 Paraguayans (450,000 being men) emigrated principally to Argentina, including large numbers of Catholics and some Protestants.
DISAFFILIATED. This term is used here to describe persons who, although baptized Roman Catholics and therefore regarded by the Catholic Church as still affiliated to it (and hence enumerated as such), have recently disaffiliated themselves from Christianity and now regard themselves as non-Christians. In the 1990s the Catholic Church claimed over 99.5% of the whole population, although 2.1% regarded themselves as non-Christians. Because their statistics represent a duplication, they are shown in the table above as a negative quantity (with a minus sign).
DOUBLY-AFFILIATED. The term covers those affiliated to, or claimed by, both the Catholic Church and also an Evangelical or other non-Catholic church, i.e. baptized Catholics who have recently become Evangelicals or others. Because their statistics represent a duplication, they are shown in the table as a negative quantity (with a minus sign).
ETHNORELIGIONISTS. Of the 80,000 tribal lowland Amerindians in 6 linguistic families and 198 tribes, a large proportion remain animists.
INDEPENDENTS. In Paraguayan, Chilean and Brazilian indigenous churches; about 13 denominations in 1995 (see Table 2).
NEW-RELIGIONISTS. By 1995, converts to the Japanese movement Nichiren Shoshu (Soka Gakkai) numbered 2500.
PENTECOSTALS. A charismatic renewal began in 1972 among the Disciples of Christ and other Protestants, and also within the Anglican Church.
ROMAN CATHOLICS. Many are Christo-Pagans Amerindians whose syncretistic folk-Catholicism combines 17th-century Spanish Catholicism with their own traditional pre-Christian animism, concepts and world-views.

Great Commission Instrument Panel: status of Paraguay (for explanation see start of Part 4)

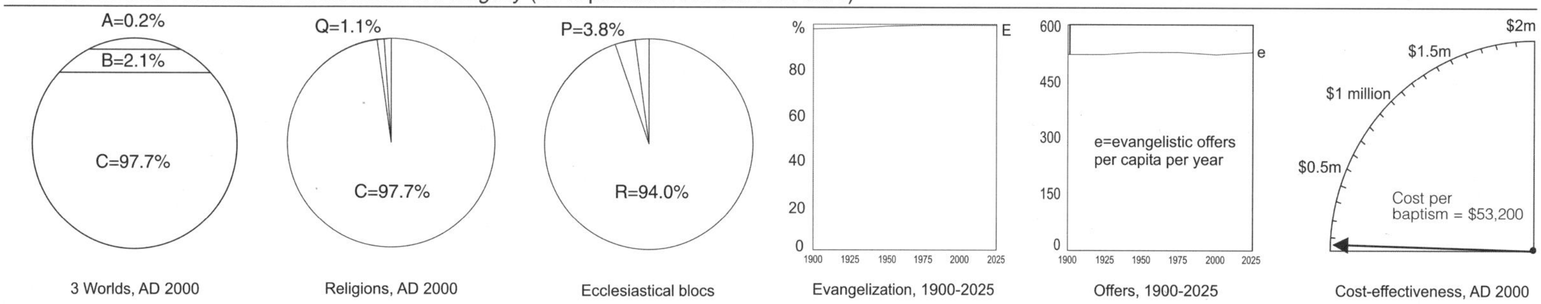

pollution is a major problem affecting Asuncion. Solid waste is generally dumped into landfills which have a negative impact on the environment.

NON-CHRISTIAN RELIGIONS

Traditional Indian religions still exist among the tribal lowland Amerindians, over a third of whom remain animists.

There are also a few Baha'is, Buddhists, and Jews.

Independents. Under construction, Iglesia de Cristo Misionera.

CHRISTIANITY

CATHOLIC CHURCH The Spanish arrived in Paraguay in 1524 and founded Asuncion in 1537. The diocese of Asuncion was erected in 1547, received a bishop in 1556 and 2 years later Jesuits arrived to evangelize the Indian population. In the western Chaco plains of Paraguay, the Jesuits established settlements known as reductions among the Guarani Indians similar to those at that period in Brazil, Argentina, and Bolivia. Each consisted of a small town centered on a large church, with the population engaged in cultivation of crops and cattle raising. About 100 such reductions were created and a million Indians baptized before the Jesuits were expelled in 1767. A written form of the Guarani language was also developed, and this is still widely used. In fact, more people understand this language than Spanish (90% for Guarani as contrasted with 75% for Spanish). The paternalistic system enshrined in the reductions left Indians poorly prepared to continue the communities after the Jesuit expulsion, and they therefore disintegrated. Paraguay achieved independence from Spain in 1811 without upheaval, but during the 19th century, the country was involved in several disastrous wars. More than half of the population died in the war of 1865-70. The Catholic Church remained subservient to the state, with the government appointing bishops, and the clergy were inadequate to meet the needs of the people. Between 1881 and 1911, only 60 priests were ordained, and only one third of the population was registered on parish rolls.

Today the great majority of Paraguayans have been baptized as Catholics, but sacramental life continues to be impeded by the situation in which many find themselves.

In contrast to the position of the Catholic Church in most Latin American countries, the church in Paraguay owns very little property. Its relative poverty explains in part its present sensitivity to social problems.

The Holy See has diplomatic relations with Paraguay and in AD 2000 is represented to government and the Catholic hierarchy by a nuncio residing in Asuncion.

PROTESTANT CHURCHES. The American Bible Society was the first Protestant body to make contact with Paraguay in 1856, and in 1886, an American Methodist missionary began work there. German Lutheran immigrants organized their first congregations as early as 1893, which came together to form a Lutheran union in 1899. Seventh-day Adventists arrived in 1900, followed by the New Testament Missionary Union 2 years later, the latter directing its attention to the planting of self-supporting churches rather than institutional work. In 1916, the Disciples of Christ (USA) initiated a few small service institutions and later took over Methodist work. The first Mennonites were refugees from Russia following the 1917 Bolshevik revolution. Seeing the needs of local Chaco Indians, they opened work among them and appealed to North American Mennonite groups for assistance. Mennonites at present have the second

Country summary. **Worlds A, B, C by ethnolinguistic peoples, cities, and major civil divisions in Paraguay.**

	PEOPLES							CITIES							CIVIL DIVISIONS						
World	Num	Pop 2000	C%	Christians	E%	U%	Unevangelized	Num	Pop 2000	C%	Christians	E%	U%	Unevangelized	Num	Pop 2000	C%	Christians	E%	U%	Unevangelized
A	2	3,872	0.59	23	45	55	2,111	0	0	0.00	0	0	0	0	0	0	0.00	0	0	0	0
B	8	53,729	39.20	21,060	90	10	5,297	0	0	0.00	0	0	0	0	0	0	0.00	0	0	0	0
C	35	5,438,850	94.74	5,152,514	100	0	2,656	5	1,662,211	92.51	1,537,753	100	0	4,691	18	5,496,454	94.13	5,173,602	100	0	10,064
Total	**45**	**5,496,451**	**94.13**	**5,173,597**	**100**	**0**	**10,064**	**5**	**1,662,211**	**92.51**	**1,537,753**	**100**	**0**	**4,691**	**18**	**5,496,454**	**94.13**	**5,173,602**	**100**	**0**	**10,064**

largest Christian community outside the Catholic Church, including over a thousand Indian converts. Another group of German Mennonites from the USSR, Mennonite Brethren, was formed in 1930. The first Baptists (1920) were missionaries of the Baptist Convention of Argentina, and since 1945, the Evangelical Baptist Convention of Paraguay has been aided by Southern Baptist missionaries from the USA. In 1953, they opened the first Baptist hospital in South America. They are now the largest non-Catholic denomination in Paraguay.

Assemblies of God missionaries came to Paraguay in 1945 to assist Pentecostal Christians who had left Slavic countries in eastern Europe. Literature, Bible correspondence courses, and radio programs have helped develop a small national church, established in 1958. The Church of God (Cleveland) began in 1954 and has also experienced steady growth. Working in close cooperation with the government's Indian Affairs Department, the New Tribes Mission has since 1946 been active among 6 tribes.

A Lengua family with just-published Northern Lengua Bible, in Pozo, Amarillo.

ANGLICAN CHURCH. Following the death of its founder Allen Gardiner among Patagonia Indians in southern Argentina, the South American Missionary Society in 1888 moved its work to the Chaco region of Paraguay. Anglian missionaries were the first to live among the Lengua Indians where the language was reduced to writing, scriptures translated and grammars prepared, in addition to evangelistic and social service activity.

Renewal movements. In the 1990s the Pentecostal/Charismatic Renewal continued to spread rapidly across most older churches, and numbered over 242,000 adherents (of whom 32% Pentecostals, 44% Charismatics, and 24% Independents).

Indigenous missions. Although significant numbers of Roman Catholics missionaries have been sent out from Paraguay, most of these have served in neighboring countries or in Europe. Recently some organizations have been planning outreach to non-Christian countries.

CHURCH AND STATE

The legal relations between church and state rest on Law 863 of 1963 and on the constitution of 25 August 1967. Law 863 brings together various scattered dispositions made over the years concerning the Catholic Church. The state recognizes the 'perfect character' of the church, confers on it a juridical personality, confirms certain important privileges including exemption from tax on donations and properties and makes provision for financial contributions to it from the national budget. The constitution of 1967 guarantees respect for religion freedom but in Article 6 recognizes Roman Catholicism as the official religion of the country, requires that the president be a Roman Catholic and envisages also that concordats or bilateral treaties should regulate relations between Paraguay and the Holy See. However, no such agreement has yet been negotiated. Article 189, item 2, makes the archbishop of Asuncion a legal member of the Council of State, as the representative of the Catholic Church. In 1972, the archbishop took the oath of office but then publicly renounced his post citing existing institutional injustice throughout the country.

For several hundred years, the Catholic Church in Paraguay has existed in a state of subjection to the political power. The patronage system, which was not abolished until 1967, not only conferred on the government the right of nominating bishops but also the right to censor edicts of the hierarchy with which it did not agree. For many years, even the rank and file of priests had been considered officially as chaplains, i.e., religious functionaries of a nominally Catholic government. When general Stroessner disbanded political parties, trade unions and student activities in 1954, only Catholic Action managed to escape suppression, due to its markedly decentralized structure. At the time, Law 863 and its acceptance by the hierarchy was judged anachronistic by Catholic Action militants and lay apostolate activists who saw this as a maneuver on the part of government to secure the silence and support of the church at a time when it was preparing for the unconstitutional renewal of Stroessner's presidential mandate. Nevertheless, at this period in 1963, the Catholic bishops published several documents criticizing the new constitution: 'Doctrinal orientations concerning constitutional reform' of 25 December 1966, and 'Letter to members of the National Convention' in 1967. The first incidents calling into question existing church-state relations took place in 1969, when there were 3 attempts by the government to intimidate the church: on the occasion of the inauguration of the Paraguayan major seminary, after a sermon given at the cathedral concerning political prisoners and during a national pilgrimage to Caacupe. These incidents, together with the previous acts of repression against Agrarian Leagues and the Christian Federation of Workers (CCT), made the church decide to take a firm attitude against the abuse of power, not only concerning Christians but also all classes of citizens. Use was therefore made of the refusal to offer Te Deum prayers at government functions, protests against violation of the rights of political prisoners and the excommunication of government officials. The latter, in 1971, involved principally the minister of the Interior and the chief of police. The excommunication was not lifted until the end of 1974 and had a profound effect upon the populace who are unusually religious. This same attitude has also led the church to oppose international Catholic collaboration with the Stroessner regime and to the suspension in 1972 of food distribution by Catholic Relief Services. In its side, the government has attacked foreign clergy. In October 1969, the editor of Communidad was deported although he was a naturalized citizen, and other priests and laymen attached to the Department of Laity of CELAM, Agrarian Leagues and CCT have also suffered imprisonment, torture and deportation.

Several particularly brutal events became widely known because foreigners were witnesses and victims. On 8 February 1975, the army attacked the village of San Isidro de Jejui, headquarters of the Agrarian League, burning the houses of peasants and sacking the cooperative Experiencia de Fraternidad Campesina. Eight peasants were killed, numerous others wounded and about 50 were arrested. Two American directors of Catholic Relief Services visiting the cooperative at the time and 2 French priests were also arrested although later released. The Episcopal Conference, which is responsible for the cooperative, was not officially informed until several days later and then published a declaration accusing the army's anti-subversion brigade of murder and the theft of more than a million guaranis that had been in the cooperative treasury. Shortly after this attack, several other villages were also victims of similar excesses by the army.

The change in attitude of the hierarchy and clergy since 1954 is due largely to the profound impact on Paraguay of Vatican II and the Medellion conference in 1968. Four of the 10 Paraguayan bishops participated actively in the latter. The unanimity of the bishops in the face of state power constitutes an important factor within the context of present church-state conflicts in Latin American and reinforces the image of the church as the only structured force opposing the Stroessner regime. In 1973, the episcopate created a consultative organism for relations between church and state.

BROADCASTING AND MEDIA

Shortwave broadcasts from TWR (Antilles), HCJB (Ecuador), and AWR (Costa Rica) can be received. IBRA broadcasts 3.5 hours of programming weekly from 4 local radio stations. Shortwave radio programs from KNLS have seen some response. Radio Curitas is a local AM Catholic radio station with 20 hours of daily programs. Radio Carlos A. Lopez has regular Catholic programs each Sunday. Paraguay is a member of UNDA. Communications training courses are offered through the Asociacion de Comunicacion of Educacion RadioFonica.

CBN's *700 Club* can be seen on local television and cable channels on weekdays in the late afternoons and evenings, and other Christian television programs can be received via satellite. There is a 45-minute Catholic program 'Santa Misa' broadcast weekly on 2 television channels.

Virtually everyone in the country has seen the 'Jesus' Film due to multiple showings on television and wide use of the film by mission agencies, with 72,000 responses.

INTERDENOMINATIONAL ORGANIZATIONS

The Paraguayan Episcopal Conference of the Catholic Church maintains a Department of Ecumenism. There is no ecumenical council of churches, but an Evangelical Coordinating Commission of Paraguay (Comision Coordinadora Evangelica de Paraguay), with 5 member churches, has been formed.

FUTURE TRENDS AND PROSPECTS

Roman Catholicism seems certain to remain strong into the 21st century, with Christian affiliation remaining around 98% from 1990-2025.

Christianity could continue above 95% throughout the 21st century. The nonreligious could grow beyond 3% before AD 2050.

BIBLIOGRAPHY

A church in the wilds: the remarkable story of the establishment of the South American mission amongst the hitherto savage and intractable natives of the Paraguayan Chaco. W. B. Grubb. London: Seeley Service, Dutton, 1914. 287p.

An unquenchable flame. W. Mann & H. Sutton. London: South American Missionary Society, 1968. 94p. (History of Anglican South American Missionary Society).

Anuario eclesiástico del Paraguay, 1981. Asunción, Paraguay: Conferencia Episcopal Paraguaya, 1981. 176p.

'Church growth in Paraguay.' J. T. Shumaker. Thesis, Fuller Theological Seminary, Pasadena, CA, 1972. 158p.

Community in Paraguay: a visit to the Bruderhof. B. Wagoner & S. Wagoner. Farmington, PA: Plough, 1991. 292p.

Die Kirche in Paraguay: von der Kolonialzeit bis zum Ende des Stroessner–Staates. M. Krischer. Mettingen: Brasilienkunde-Verlag, [1991]. 211p.

Die Missionsarbeit der katholischen Kirche bei den Indianern in Paraguay. A. Brachetti. *Mundus Reihe Ethnologie*, Bd. 39. Bonn: Holos, 1990. 119p.

El protestantismo en el Paraguay: su aporte cultural económico y espiritual. R. Plett. Asunción, Paraguay: Instituto Bíblico Asunción, 1987. 200p.

'Evangelism–in–depth in Paraguay.' V. M. Monterro. D.Miss. thesis, Fuller Theological Seminary, Pasadena, CA, 1976.

Guia de las iglesias evangélicas en el Paraguay. 3rd ed. Asunción, Paraguay: Asociación de Obreros, Pastores y Misioneros del Paraguay, 1964. 20p.

La evangelización en el Paraguay: cuatro siglos de historia. L. Cano et al. Asunción, Paraguay: Ediciones Loyola, 1979.

La Iglesia en el Paraguay: una historia mínima. M. Durán Estragó. [Asunción, Paraguay]: RP Ediciones. 158p.

La religiosidad popular paraguaya: aproximación a los valores del pueblo. R. Domínguez et al. Asunción, Paraguay: Ediciones Loyola, 1981. 234p.

Los judíos en el Paraguay. A. M. Seiferheld. Asunción, 1981.

Paraguay. R. A. Nickson. *World bibliographical series*, vol. 84. Oxford, UK: CLIO Press, 1987. 214p. (See especially 'Religion,' p.68–71).

'Paraguay: the church confronted by a country in evolution,' *Pro Mundi Vita* (Brussels), 38 (1971), 1–32.

'Patterns of church growth within the Seventh–day Adventist Church in the River Platte Republics.' J. C. Viera-Rossano. M.A. thesis, Fuller Theological Seminary, Pasadena, CA, 1988. 165p. (Text in Spanish with extended summary in English).
Pilgrims in Paraguay: the story of Mennonite civilization in South America. J. W. Fretz. Scottdale, PA: Herald Press, 1953. 247p.
The River Plate republics: a survey of the religious, economic and social conditions in Argentina, Paraguay and Uruguay. W. E. Browning. London: World Dominion Press, 1928.

Country Table 2. **Organized churches and denominations in Paraguay.**

Official name (bold type = church with over 10% of all affiliated) 1	*Begun* 2	*Type* 3	*Counc* 4	*Congs* 5	*Adults* 6	*Affiliated 1970* 7	*Affiliated 1995* 8	*G%* 9	*Names, notes, and other statistics* (see Codebook, Part 3) 10
Asambleas de Dios en el Paraguay	1945	P-Pe2	ZF..C	216	27,620	2,000	44,950	13.26	*Assemblies of God in P.* M=AoG(USA). Russians. Poles, Germans. 23n,7f,1s(12).
Asambleas Locales	c1980	I-3nC	.....	9	275	–	400	6.67	*Local Churches. Little Flock.* Chinese. Begun 1922 in China.
Asociación de Cristianos Unidos	c1965	P-Uni	.....	12	1,725	250	5,130	12.85	*Assoc of United Christians.*
Convención Evangélica Bautista del P	1920	P-Bap	T....	92	13,000	4,000	22,275	7.11	CEBP. *Baptist Conv of P.* 1945, M=FMB-SBC(USA). 18n,12x,27f,1H,3h,1s(8),W=40%,225Y.
Ejército de Salvación en el Paraguay	1910	P-Sal	xw...	1	40	1,000	120	-8.13	*Salvation Army, Paraguay District,* South America East Territory. HQ Asuncion. 2f.
Hermanos Menonitas	1930	P-Men	GF...	10	3,000	5,000	8,000	1.90	1935 M=MBCNA(USA). Begun USSR Germans: now 87% Lengua, Chulupi, Guarani. 1H,1h,1s.
Iglesia Adventista del Séptimo Día	1900	P-Adv	x....	23	5,200	2,000	13,000	7.77	*Seventh-day Adventists, Paraguay M,* Austral UC. 6% Japanese. 2n,15m,6f,2H,79Y.
Iglesia Alianza Cristiana y Misionera	1966	P-Hol	xF...	3	115	50	378	8.43	*Christian & Missionary Alliance.* M=CMA(USA). Small holiness body. In Asuncion.
Iglesia Anglicana Paraguaya	1889	A-Eva	Aw.CC	30	5,178	3,000	15,015	6.65	*D Paraguay* (begun 1964). In CASA, ACSCA. M=SAMS(UK). Indians. 15n,4x,25f,W=58%.
Igl Bautista Independiente Maranatha	1965	I-Bap	.....	1	590	200	1,013	6.70	*Maranatha Independent Baptist Church.*
Iglesia Católica en el Paraguay:	1524	R-Lat	B.L.R	1,339	2,341,000	2,304,591	4,360,217	2.58	*Catholic Ch in Paraguay.* C=17+1+29. 1p,2q,1s(218). 212n 343x 607m 1189w 91231Yy
M Asunción	1547	R-Lat	Bs	77	620,000	690,020	1,080,000	1.81	Capital, and rural Central department. M=SDB. 1s. 69n 168x 336m 572w 25657Yy
D Alto Paraná	1968	R-Lat	Bs	27	292,000	80,000	524,800	7.81	Recent rapid colonization; Japanese. M=SVD. 3n 49x 53m 101w 11363Yy
D Benjamin Aceval	1980	R-Lat	Bs	6	38,000	–	72,400	6.67	M=OMI. 5n 3x 9m 7w 832Yy
D Caacupé	1960	R-Lat	Bs	21	77,000	190,000	194,800	0.10	National shrine Virgen de los Milagros. M=CSSR. 31n 1x 2m 38w 4227Yy
D Carapegua	1978	R-Lat	Bs	17	171,000	–	322,000	5.88	Population 330,000, 97% Roman Catholic. 12n 8x 16m 61w 4480Yy
D Concepción en Paraguay	1929	R-Lat	Bs	13	159,000	284,727	232,000	-0.82	Breeding, forestry, tea, coffee plantations. W=20%. 12n 15x 16m 0w 7200Yy
D Coronel Oviedo	1961	R-Lat	Bsci	417	273,000	200,000	521,000	3.90	East of capital. Forests and mountains. M=TOR,SCI. 7n 18x 28m 54w 3286Yy
D Encarnación	1957	R-Lat	Bs	632	208,000	197,953	398,417	2.84	Population concentrated around Itapua. M=SVD. 14n 29x 45m 111w 11385Yy
D San Juan Bautista de las Misiones	1957	R-Lat	Bs	30	83,000	143,241	167,000	0.62	M=Misiones. Area of 18th-century Jesuit reductions. 14n 17x 23m 69w 7150Yy
D San Pedro	1978	R-Lat	Bsvd	20	136,000	–	308,000	5.88	M=SVD. 7n 7x 7m 14w 5231Yy
D Villarrica del Espiritu Santo	1929	R-Lat	Bs	32	231,000	418,500	456,000	0.34	Breeding, forestry, sugar cane. 1p,W=25%. 37n 10x 43m 118w 9310Yy
VA Chaco Paraguayo	1948	R-Lat	Psdb	7	10,500	32,150	20,800	-1.73	Forest. In western depopulated area. M=SDB. 1n 8x 9m 15w 527Yy
VA Pilcomayo	1925	R-Lat	Pomi	9	17,500	58,000	33,000	-2.23	Western depopulated region of country. 10% pagans. 0n 10x 20m 29w 583Yy
OM Paraguay	1961	R-Lat	Bs	31	25,000	10,000	30,000	4.49	Military Ordinariate of Paraguay. M=CSSR. 10 ordinaries, 8 auxiliaries, 3 w,1769Yy.
Ig Cristiano Evang Bautista Eslava	c1955	P-Bap	.....	12	2,100	500	3,645	8.27	*Christian Evangelical Slavic Baptist Ch.*
Iglesia de Biblia Abierta	c1985	I-3pL	.....	1	33	–	83	10.00	Open Bible Standard Church. M=OBSC(USA).
Iglesia de Dios de la Profecía	1977	P-Pe3	.....	8	173	–	540	5.56	*Church of God of Prophecy.* M=CGP(USA).
Iglesia de Dios en el Paraguay	1954	P-Pe3	ZF..C	80	3,471	2,000	7,800	5.59	*Ch of God.* M=CoG(Cleveland) (Chile, USA). German, Spanish, Guarani. 38n,1s.
Iglesia de JC de los Santos de los UD	c1946	m-LdS	x....	46	5,830	1,070	11,000	9.77	*Latter-day Saints. Mormons.* M=CJCLdS(USA). Indians. Rapid Growth, 7.5%pa. 10f.
Iglesia de los Hermanos Libres	1919	P-CBr	x....	45	1,380	870	4,050	6.35	IHL. *Free (Open) Brethren.* M=CMML(NZ, USA, UK). Strong in south. HQ Asuncion. 13f.
Iglesia del Evangelio Cuadrangular	c1985	P-Pe2	Z....	5	125	–	250	10.00	*International Church of the Foursquare Gospel.* M=ICFG(USA).
Iglesia de Nazareno	1980	P-Hol	x....	13	528	–	945	6.67	*Church of the Nazarene.* M=CoN.
Iglesia Discipulos de Cristo del P	1886	P-Dis	x.U..	8	1,400	528	2,430	6.30	*Disciples of Christ.* 1886 Methodists (USA): 1916 takeover by M=UCMS(USA). 3n,8f,1r.
Iglesia Ev Asambleas de Dios en el P	1970	I-3pL	.....	12	920	–	2,835	37.44	*Evangelical Assemblies of God Ch.*
Igl Ev Asambleas de Dios Misionera	c1970	I-3pL	.....	33	4,945	–	10,230	44.68	*Evangelical Missionary Assemblies of God Ch.*
Iglesia Evangélica del Nuevo Pacto	c1950	I-Eva	.....	3	200	100	400	5.70	*Ev Ch of the New Covenant.* Schism ex NTMU. in Asuncion. Small indigenous body.
Iglesia Evangélica del Río de la Plata	1893	P-LuR	L....	100	8,000	3,900	12,000	4.60	1899 union of German diaspora congs (10% Reformed). 2n,3x,1s,W=30%,83Yy.
Iglesia Ev Filadelfia de Asunción	1938	P-Pe2	Z...C	27	805	645	2,295	5.21	*Philadelphia Ev Ch.* M=NPY(Norway),SFM(Sweden). Guarani. 3n,1x,1H,1s,W=62%,46Y,45z.
Iglesia Evangélica Gracia y Gloria	c1950	P-Pe2	.....	43	2,990	600	8,775	11.33	*Ev Ch of Grace and Glory.* From USA, UK. In Asuncion, also among Guaranis. 2n,8m,5x.
Iglesia Evangélica Menonita en el P	1921	P-Men	GF...	50	10,000	12,000	20,000	2.06	IEMP. M=GCMC,MCNA. 7 colonies, Germans from USSR, also Lenguas. 35n,1f,5H,2h,1p.
Iglesia Evangélica Paraguaya		I-Eva	.....	1	50	50	150	0.05	*Ev Ch of Paraguay.* Schism ex NTMU, in Villa Aurelia. Small indigenous group. 1n.
Iglesia Ev Filadelfia de la Incamación	c1965	I-3gL	.....	23	1,127	571	3,038	6.91	*Philadelphia Evangelical Ch of the Incarnation.*
Iglesia Ev Pentecostal Paraguaya	c1975	I-3pL	.....	7	863	–	2,100	5.00	*Paraguay Evang Pentecostal Church.*
Iglesia Evangélica Plenitud		I-3pL	.....	4	500	400	1,500	0.05	*Fullness Ev Church.* Small group of indigenous pentecostals. In Asuncion. 1n.
Iglesia Evangélica Unida de Corea		P-Eva	.....	3	200	100	300	0.05	*Korean United Ev Ch.* Community of immigrants from Korea, with a Korean pastor.
Iglesia Luterana (Misuri)	1936	P-Lut	e....	13	2,200	600	3,800	7.66	*Ev Luth Congr of Holy Cross.* M=LC Missouri Synod (USA). 1x,W=80%,12Yy,14z.
Iglesia Metodista Libre en el Paraguay	1946	I-Hol	VF..C	16	1,200	301	2,020	7.91	FMCP. M=Free Methodist Ch(USA). Some Japanese. HQ Asuncion. 2n,3f,1h,1p,1r,65z.
Iglesia Mondial Evangélica	c1985	P-Hol	.....	1	14	–	35	10.00	World Gospel Church. M=WGM.
Iglesia Nueva Apostolica	c1980	I-3aX	x....	10	500	–	749	6.67	New Apostolic Church. Neuapostolische Kirche. Mainly Germans. M=NAC(Germany).
Iglesia Ortodoxa Griega	c1970	O-Gre	Cwo..	1	1,000	1,000	1,900	2.60	Part of 11th Archidiocesan District, Greek Orthodox AD of N&S America. Greeks.
Iglesia Ortodoxa Russa (D Argentina)	1918	I-Rus	x....	2	100	100	200	2.81	*Russian Orthodox Ch Outside of Russia.* M=ROCOR (New York, USA). Exile church since 1917.
Iglesia Ortodoxa Ucrania	c1925	I-Ukr	x....	2	3,000	3,000	5,700	2.60	Branch of Ukrainian Orthodox Ch in the USA. Refugee Ukrainians after 1945. 1n.
Iglesia Paraguaya Misionera	1935	I-3gL	.....	21	3,860	3,500	5,000	1.44	*Paraguay Missionary Church.* Among Northern Lengua.
Iglesia Pentecostal de Chile		I-3pL	xw...	50	7,000	500	15,000	0.05	*Pentecostal Ch of Chile.* Chileans, from large indigenous body in Chile.
Iglesia Pentecostal Unida	1973	P-Pe1	x....	20	500	200	1,000	4.55	*United Pentecostal Ch. Jesus Only Church.* M=UPC(USA). Unitarian Pentecostals. 2f.
Iglesias Evangelicas Coreanes	c1960	I-Ref	.....	8	1,183	1,110	3,240	4.38	Korean Protestant churches.
Iglesias Pentecostales Coreanas	c1960	I-3pK	.....	3	1,000	600	2,000	4.93	Korean Pentecostal churches.
Misión a las Tribus Nuevas	1946	P-Fun	x....	34	1,200	170	2,025	10.42	M=New Tribes Mission(USA). Work among 7 Indian tribes of the north. HQ Asuncion. 68f,1h.
Misión Alemana entre los Nativos del P	c1970	P-Non	.....	9	510	–	878	31.14	*German Mission among the natives of P.* M=German Indian Pioneer Mission (DIPM)(Germany).
Sociedad Fraternal Hutterianá	1941	P-Men	x....	6	600	700	1,200	2.18	*Sociedad de Hermanos, Hutterian Brethren, Hutterites.* Primavera Bruderhof.
Testigos de Jehová	1924	m-Jeh	x....	60	3,501	2,000	10,840	6.99	*Jehovah's Witnesses. Watch Tower.* Begun by Argentinian in 1925. (1975) 121Y. (1995) 405Y.
Union de Igs Ev Pentecostales	c1970	I-3pL	.....	7	1,000	–	1,706	34.67	*Union of Evang Pentecostal Chs.*
Unión Misionera Neotestamentaria	1902	P-Non	x....	10	690	3,000	2,160	-1.31	M=New Testament Miss Union (UK). In 5 departments: Central, Guiara, et al. 12n,4f.
Other Protestant denominations		P-	.....	30	2,000	2,300	4,000	0.05	Total about 25 (see list below).
Other Non-White indigenous churches		I-3pL	.....	25	1,600	500	3,000	0.05	Including ICAB (with missionary bishop) from Brazil, and similar bodies.
Doubly-affiliated		2-aff			-18,300	-30,006	-34,317		Evangelicals who also are or were baptized Roman Catholics.
Disaffiliated		X-Aff			-27,800	-72,300	-52,000		Baptized Catholics now disaffiliated agnostics, atheists or traditionalists.
Totals				**2,588**	**2,429,941**	**2,262,700**	**4,545,000**		

Churches, members, growth, 1900-2025	*Congs*	*Adults*	*Affiliated*	*G%*	*Total denominations*	*6 Megablocs:* *O*	*R*	*A*	*P*	*I*	*m*
Total churches, members, and denominations (mid-1900)	200	308,000	580,000	1.96	4	0	1	1	2	0	0
Total churches, members, and denominations (mid-1970)	751	1,199,731	2,262,700	1.96	58	1	1	1	32	21	2
Total churches, members, and denominations (mid-1990)	2,200	2,125,000	3,974,100	2.86	92	1	1	1	50	37	2
Total churches, members, and denominations (mid-1995)	2,588	2,429,941	4,545,000	2.72	95	1	1	1	51	39	2
Total churches, members, and denominations (mid-2000)	2,800	2,766,000	5,173,602	2.62	96	1	1	1	52	39	2
Total churches, members, and denominations (mid-2025)	5,000	4,758,000	8,900,000	2.19	188	1	1	1	70	110	5

NOTES ON TABLE ABOVE
NATIONAL COUNCILS (Column 4, 5th letter).
C = Comisión Coordinadora Evangélica de Paraguay (CCEP) (Evangelical Co-ordinating Commission of Paraguay).
E = Asociación de Pastores del Paraguay.
R = Conferencia Episcopal Paraguaya (CEP) (Paraguay Episcopal Conference).
OTHER PROTESTANT DENOMINATIONS. These smaller bodies include: Christ-Bearers (Christusträger, WGermany), Chs of Christ, Ev Mennonite Conference (1962), Ev Methodist Ch (1960), Iglesia Cristiana de la Fe, Iglesia Ev Bautista Independiente, Slavic Baptist Chs (Russian), World-Wide Missions (1971).

PERU

SECULAR DATA, AD 2000

STATE
Official name: La República del Perú (The Republic of Peru).
Short name: Peru. **Adjective of nationality:** Peruvian.
Flag: Red, white, and red bars, with centered coat of arms.
Area: 1,285,216 sq. km. (496,225 sq. mi.).
Government: Multiparty republic, since 1993 (1533 Spanish conquest, 1821 Independence as republic, several dictatorships, 1968 Socialist military rule).
Legislature: Congress, 120 members.
Official language: Spanish (Español/Castella).
Monetary unit: 1 nuevo sol (S/.) = 100 céntimos. **US$1=** S/. 3.04.
Chief cities: LIMA-Callao (Gran Lima) 7,443,000; Arequipa 656,251; Barrio Obrero Industrial 641,379; San Martin de Porras 594,456; Trujillo 520,225.
Political divisions: 14 provinces.
Armed forces: 125,000.

DEMOGRAPHY
Population: 25,662,000.
Population density: 19.9/sq. km. (51.7/sq. mi.).
Under 15 years: 8,568,000.
Growth rate p.a.: 1.60% (births 22.56, deaths 6.16).
Mortality: Infant, per 1,000: 37.4, ; **Maternal per 100,000:** 280.0.
Life expectancy: 70 (male 67, female 72).
Household size: 5.1. **Floor area per person, sq.m:** 12.0.
Major languages: Spanish, Quechua, Aymara, Jivaro, Japanese, Chinese, English, and around 100 minor languages.
Urban dwellers: 72.77%. **Urban growth rate p.a.:** 2.1%.
Labor force: 36%.

ETHNOLINGUISTIC PEOPLES
31.9% Peruvian Mestizo; 28.0% Detribalized Quechua; 12.0% Peruvian White; 7.1% Cuzco Quechua; 5.3% Ayacucho Quechua (Chanka).

ECONOMY
National income p.a. per person: US$2,309; **per family:** US$11,780.

EDUCATION
Adult literacy: 88% (male 94%, female 83%). **Schools:** 63,551. **Universities:** 655. **School enrolment:** female/male: 101%/101%.

HEALTH
Access to health services: 75%. **Access to safe water:** 60%. **Hospitals:** 427 (17 beds per 10,000). **Doctors:** 23,771. **Blind:** 23,000. **Deaf:** 1,539,700. **Murder rate:** 9. **Lepers:** 12,000. **Underweight prevalence under 5:** 11%.

LITERATURE
New book titles p.a.: 2,260 (88 p.a. per million). **Periodicals:** 63. **Newspapers:** 48 dailies.

COMMUNICATION (per 1,000 people)
Phones: 47 (20% mobile). **Radios:** 225. **TV sets:** 100. **Daily newspaper circulation:** 86. **Computers:** 44.

REFUGEES
Alien refugees from other countries: 700. **Internal displacement:** 480,000.

HUMAN LIFE AND LIBERTY (optimum condition=100.0%)
HDI: 71.7. **HSI:** 37.0. **HFI:** 40.0. **EFL:** 40.0.

Country Table 1. **Religious adherents in Peru, AD 1900-2025.**

Year	1900		1970		mid-1990		Annual change, 1990-2000				mid-1995		mid-2000		mid-2025	
Name	Adherents	%	Adherents	%	Adherents	%	Natural	Conversion	Total	Rate	Adherents	%	Adherents	%	Adherents	%
Christians	**3,589,200**	**94.7**	**12,933,400**	**98.0**	**21,047,200**	**97.6**	**399,365**	**-9,171**	**390,194**	**1.72**	**22,917,000**	**97.4**	**24,949,143**	**97.2**	**34,227,500**	**96.4**
PROFESSION																
professing Christians	**3,589,200**	**94.7**	**12,933,400**	**98.0**	**21,047,200**	**97.6**	**399,365**	**-9,171**	**390,194**	**1.72**	**22,917,000**	**97.4**	**24,949,143**	**97.2**	**34,227,500**	**96.4**
AFFILIATION																
unaffiliated Christians	0	0.0	0	0.0	204,200	1.0	3,875	414	4,289	1.92	227,000	1.0	247,094	1.0	377,500	1.1
affiliated Christians	**3,589,200**	**94.7**	**12,933,400**	**98.0**	**20,843,000**	**96.6**	**395,566**	**-9,641**	**385,905**	**1.71**	**22,690,000**	**96.4**	**24,702,049**	**96.3**	**33,850,000**	**95.3**
Roman Catholics	3,589,200	94.7	12,888,702	97.7	20,770,000	96.3	394,171	-16,171	378,000	1.69	22,590,000	96.0	24,550,000	95.7	33,000,000	92.9
Protestants	5,000	0.1	296,992	2.3	1,210,000	5.6	22,961	4,039	27,000	2.03	1,338,536	5.7	1,480,000	5.8	2,800,000	7.9
Independents	0	0.0	54,990	0.4	366,000	1.7	6,945	2,055	9,000	2.22	403,508	1.7	456,000	1.8	775,000	2.2
Marginal Christians	0	0.0	23,931	0.2	230,000	1.1	4,365	5,635	10,000	3.68	276,200	1.2	330,000	1.3	700,000	2.0
Orthodox	0	0.0	2,500	0.0	4,800	0.0	91	-21	70	1.37	5,100	0.0	5,500	0.0	8,000	0.0
Anglicans	100	0.0	2,500	0.0	2,000	0.0	38	-38	0	0.00	2,000	0.0	2,000	0.0	2,000	0.0
doubly-affiliated	-5,100	-0.1	-136,215	-1.0	-1,289,800	-6.0	-24,476	-4,689	-29,165	2.06	-1,425,344	-6.1	-1,581,451	-6.2	-2,635,000	-7.4
disaffiliated	0	0.0	-200,000	-1.5	-450,000	-2.1	-8,539	-461	-9,000	1.84	-500,000	-2.1	-540,000	-2.1	-800,000	-2.3
Trans-megabloc groupings																
Evangelicals	4,500	0.1	200,000	1.5	885,000	4.1	16,794	7,606	24,400	2.46	1,001,205	4.3	1,129,000	4.4	2,131,000	6.0
Pentecostals/Charismatics	0	0.0	150,000	1.1	2,700,000	12.5	51,236	22,764	74,000	2.45	3,044,598	12.9	3,440,000	13.4	5,327,700	15.0
Great Commission Christians	**114,000**	**3.0**	**500,000**	**3.8**	**817,460**	**3.8**	**15,512**	**-365**	**15,147**	**1.71**	**889,500**	**3.8**	**968,929**	**3.8**	**1,420,000**	**4.0**
Nonreligious	0	0.0	39,000	0.3	190,000	0.9	3,605	8,639	12,244	5.10	249,430	1.1	312,438	1.2	700,000	2.0
Ethnoreligionists	200,000	5.3	160,000	1.2	143,000	0.7	2,714	-1,429	1,285	0.86	145,000	0.6	155,850	0.6	180,000	0.5
New-Religionists	0	0.0	5,000	0.0	60,000	0.3	1,139	974	2,113	3.06	72,700	0.3	81,128	0.3	130,000	0.4
Buddhists	1,000	0.0	20,000	0.2	45,000	0.2	854	419	1,273	2.52	52,000	0.2	57,731	0.2	100,000	0.3
Atheists	0	0.0	12,800	0.1	30,000	0.1	569	230	799	2.39	34,700	0.2	37,986	0.2	75,000	0.2
Baha'is	0	0.0	13,500	0.1	28,000	0.1	531	315	846	2.68	33,000	0.1	36,463	0.1	60,000	0.2
Chinese folk-religionists	500	0.0	3,000	0.0	14,000	0.1	266	23	289	1.89	15,400	0.1	16,889	0.1	22,000	0.1
Jews	0	0.0	5,000	0.0	8,000	0.0	152	-44	108	1.28	8,500	0.0	9,083	0.0	12,000	0.0
Muslims	300	0.0	300	0.0	500	0.0	9	6	15	2.61	570	0.0	647	0.0	1,500	0.0
Other religionists	0	0.0	1,000	0.0	3,300	0.0	63	38	101	2.71	3,700	0.0	4,311	0.0	10,000	0.0
World A (unevangelized persons)	113,730	3.0	131,926	1.0	64,707	0.3	1,228	-855	373	0.56	70,595	0.3	76,986	0.3	106,554	0.3
World B (evangelized non-Christians)	88,070	2.3	127,345	1.0	457,093	2.1	8,674	10,026	18,700	3.36	544,089	2.3	635,871	2.5	1,183,946	3.3
World C (Christians)	3,589,200	94.7	12,933,400	98.0	21,047,200	97.6	399,365	-9,171	390,194	1.72	22,917,000	97.4	24,949,143	97.2	34,227,500	96.4
Country's population	**3,791,000**	**100.0**	**13,192,672**	**100.0**	**21,569,000**	**100.0**	**409,267**	**0**	**409,267**	**1.75**	**23,531,685**	**100.0**	**25,662,000**	**100.0**	**35,518,000**	**100.0**

COLUMNS, ROWS.
For meanings and definitions, see Codebook (Part 3). Note that, by definition, total 'Christians' = professing + crypto-Christians, which also = affiliated + unaffiliated Christians, and also = Great Commission Christians + latent Christians. Percentages may not always total exactly, due to rounding.

CENSUSES.
1940: 98.6% Roman Catholics, 0.9% Evangelicals, 0.2% Buddhists, 0.1% Chinese folk-religionists, 0.1% nonreligious. **2.VII.1961**: 98.1% Roman Catholics, 1.6% Evangelicals, 0.2% nonreligious and ethnoreligionists. **4.VI.1972** (excluding jungle Amerindians): 96.4% Roman Catholics, 2.5% Evangelicals, 0.7% other religionists, 0.4% nonreligious and atheists. **II.VII.1993**: 88.9% Roman Catholics, 7.2% Evangelicals, 2.5% other religionists, 1.4% nonreligious and atheists.

NOTES ON RELIGIONS
ATHEISTS. 2 parties: Communist Party of Peru (pro-Soviet), Communist Party of Peru (pro-Chinese).
BAHA'IS. Very rapid growth from 13 local spiritual assemblies (1964) to 82 (1973), particularly among the Quechua Indians in the Cuzco area.
BUDDHISTS. Mostly Japanese immigrants, with a few Chinese. Mass conversions to Soka Gakkai have been taking place.
ROMAN CATHOLICS. Many Christo-Pagans Amerindians syncretizing folk-Catholicism with traditional pre-Columbian animism.
DISAFFILIATED. This term is used here to describe persons who, although either baptized Roman Catholics or claimed and enumerated as affiliated by the Catholic Church in its totals, have recently withdrawn or disaffiliated themselves completely from Christianity and now profess to be or regard themselves as either nonreligious (agnostics), atheists, or adherents of non-Christian religions. In particular, it may be noted that in jungle areas Catholic jurisdictions still claim almost the entire population, although a majority of jungle Amerindians there regard themselves as followers of their own tribal religions.
DOUBLY-AFFILIATED. The term covers those affiliated to, or claimed by, both the Catholic Church and also a church termed Evangélica by the state (Protestant, Anglican, Independents, marginal Christians), i.e. baptized Catholics who have recently become Evangelicals or others. Because their statistics represent a duplication, they are shown in the table as a negative quantity (with a minus sign).
ETHNORELIGIONISTS. A large proportion of the 350,000 lowland or jungle Amerindians in the interior in 1900, and the 200,000 in 1995, were still animists, including among the Augaruna and Chayahuita.
INDEPENDENTS. In about 30 denominations or groupings in 1995 (see Table 2).
NEW-RELIGIONISTS. Japanese adherents of Soka Gakkai (one hall in Lima in 1969) and other New Religions. By 1995, converts to Soka Gakkai, mainly from orthodox Buddhism, numbered 65,000.
OTHER RELIGIONISTS. Adherents of other non-Christian religions and syncretistic cults, including Rosicrucians (AMORC, 4 Lodges).
PENTECOSTALS/CHARISMATICS. The Catholic renewal began in 1973. Totals (January 1974): around 7,000 involved adults, including many priests and sisters, in over 400 prayer groups; total charismatic community including children, 15,000. By 1997 these had increased to 650 weekly prayer groups with 19,500 regular attenders. Annual rallies have exceeded 20,000 attenders since 1990.

Great Commission Instrument Panel: status of Peru (for explanation see start of Part 4)

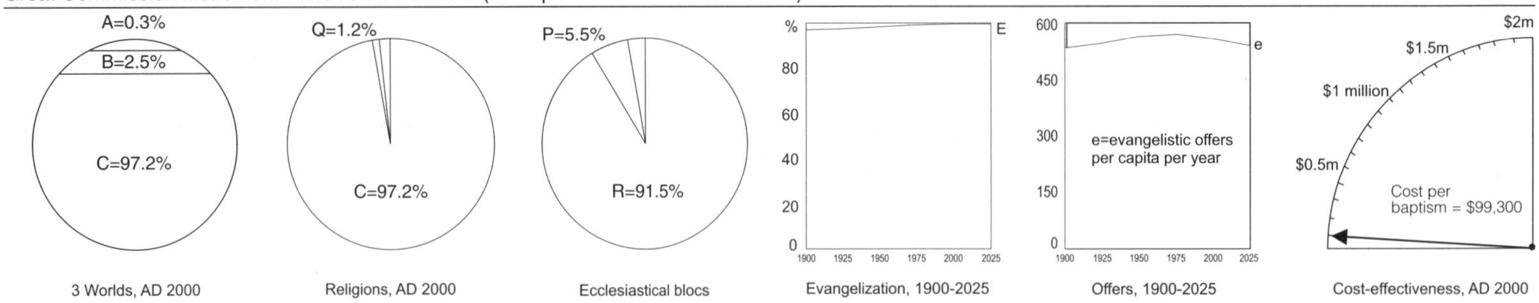

Country status. Peru is located in western South America on the Pacific Ocean and is the fourth largest in size in the continent. Agriculture is the most important economic activity though fish-meal and minerals are exported.

HUMAN LIFE AND LIBERTY

Human need and development. Peruvian society, like its geography, is marked by contrasts. There are pockets of wealth, but, in contrast, the vast majority of the Indians live in poverty, although not in dire poverty as their forefathers did. One-third of Peruvians are estimated to live below the poverty level. The sweeping land reforms of 1969 did much to improve the lot of the Peruvian peasant; it clipped the powers of the hacienda owners, and gave the thousands of landless some small parcels of land. But since then progress has been slow; budgetary constraints have hobbled official attempts to bring basic modern amenities outside the cities. In the cities themselves, squatter settlements have become permanent as the squatters transformed them into pueblos jovenes (young towns). They fill a critical need for low-income housing that the government itself is unable to provide. Nevertheless, Peru has been able to achieve a modest degree of success in raising the standards of living. Life expectancy is 70 and the illiteracy rate is about 12%.

Human rights and freedoms. After 12 years of democratic government, Peru relapsed into autocracy when President Fujimori staged an autogolpe, dissolved parliament and began ruling under emergency powers. He claimed that the old political system was not capable of fighting terrorism. The crisis was precipitated by the fact that the Sendero Luminoso (Shining Path) had been waging a campaign of terror against the government as well as the majority of the people. They, as well as the Tupac Amaru Revolutionary Movement, are reported to have committed 723 political assassinations until Fujimori's autogolpe. The security forces generally retaliate in kind, and there are credible reports of summary executions, disappearances, arbitrary detentions, torture and rape by the military and police. The Peruvian Code of Military Justice contains no provision for dealing with cases of killing, kidnaping or torture, and thus security forces generally escape punishment for atrocities they commit. The Sendero terrorists are guilty of even more heinous crimes against people. A number of killings against teachers, clergy, engineers, development workers and other

Country summary. **Worlds A, B, C by ethnolinguistic peoples, cities, and major civil divisions in Peru.**

	PEOPLES							*CITIES*							*CIVIL DIVISIONS*						
World	*Num*	*Pop 2000*	*C%*	*Christians*	*E%*	*U%*	*Unevangelized*	*Num*	*Pop 2000*	*C%*	*Christians*	*E%*	*U%*	*Unevangelized*	*Num*	*Pop 2000*	*C%*	*Christians*	*E%*	*U%*	*Unevangelized*
A	15	89,795	6.77	6,080	46	54	48,303	0	0	0.00	0	0	0	0	0	0	0.00	0	0	0	0
B	21	274,347	45.84	125,758	95	5	12,554	0	0	0.00	0	0	0	0	0	0	0.00	0	0	0	0
C	75	25,297,529	97.12	24,570,219	100	0	7,578	24	12,050,560	95.27	11,480,630	100	0	45,885	14	25,661,669	96.26	24,702,049	100	0	68,433
Total	**111**	**25,661,671**	**96.26**	**24,702,057**	**100**	**0**	**68,435**	**24**	**12,050,560**	**95.27**	**11,480,630**	**100**	**0**	**45,885**	**14**	**25,661,669**	**96.26**	**24,702,049**	**100**	**0**	**68,433**

civilians are carried out in gruesome fashion in order to intimidate others. Many of their victims are reported to have been mutilated, tortured, strangled, stoned, or burned. All constitutional freedoms against arbitrary arrest and detention are suspended in areas under a state of emergency. The judiciary is not independent of the executive. One of the first acts of President Fujimori after his coup was to dismiss 14 Supreme Court justices charged with corruption. Nevertheless, there still are widespread charges of corruption in the judicial system, including suborning of justices and witnesses. The judiciary also suffers from heavy backlogs, ranging from an estimated 28,000 for the Supreme Court and 250,000 to 500,000 for the entire system. Intimidation of judges by the Senderoso accounts for a low conviction rate (estimated at only 10%) of terrorists. Freedom of speech and the press is seriously abridged by the pressures of the civil conflict. Terrorists sometimes occupy newspaper and radio offices and kill journalists and broadcasters. Sendero conducts numerous armed strikes in various parts of the country during which civilians are obliged to stay home or risk reprisals. They also ambush vehicles, especially buses, killing their civilian passengers. Sexual violence is a chronic problem in Peruvian society. Only about 10% of rapes are reported and only 10% of the cases tried result in convictions.

Human environment. Peru's government is environmentally active and strong legislation is on the statute books to avert environmental degradation. The coastal waters, once famous for their fisheries, have become polluted by industrial and municipal wastes.

NON-CHRISTIAN RELIGIONS

Traditional religions are still practiced by some Indian peoples including the Chayahuita, usually in combination with Roman Catholic practices.

Aymara religion is centered in beliefs concerning guardian, nature, and evil spirits and the means of controlling them. The divinity of good luck (Ekeko) and old Mother Earth (Pachamama) are also widely venerated. Traditional beliefs once recognized the existence of a supreme being known as Viracocha, who was creator of all things. However, this name is no longer used, traditional concepts having been supplanted by Catholic ideas of God. Jungle Amerindians also remain largely animist.

Iglesia Catolica en el Peru. John Paul II visits jungle missions in Iquitos, 1985.

CHRISTIANITY

CATHOLIC CHURCH. Pizarro reached Peru in 1533. At the request of Spain, the diocese of Cuzco was erected in 1536 followed by the diocese of Lima in 1541, and by 1546, Lima had become the metropolitan see for the Pacific coast from Nicaragua to Chile. The 17th century, called 'the religious century' of Peru with 2 canonized saints, was followed by a general decline in monastic and religious life.

In 1845, Catholicism was made the official state religion. Foreigners were given permission to conduct Protestant services, provided that no Peruvians attended. A notable shift in social attitudes away from positions of extreme conservatism has characterized the Catholic clergy in recent years. This is clearly reflected in a document issued by the Peruvian episcopate in 1971, entitled 'Justice in the world'. Some consider this to be the most audacious document on the subject yet to have been issued by any episcopal body. It asserts that evangelization cannot exist 'without engaging in the fight against domination'. It asked the second Synod of Bishops in Rome to condemn the repressive methods of those who imply violence in the name of Christian civilization and to denounce 'the withdrawal of capital by developed nations as well as the pseudoneutrality of those countries which, by their banking systems, favor the flight of wealth and its accumulation' by a few. A further shift in the practice and attitudes of Catholics is reflected in the results of a census taken in Lima in May 1967, which revealed that only 20% of the Catholic population attended Sunday mass weekly. Among these, 18% were boys, 16% girls, 22% men and 44% women.

Pastoral work has been severely hampered by the lack of priests, there being only one priest for every 6,000 inhabitants. The proportion of Peruvian to expatriate priests has decreased steadily from 1901, when 82% of all priests were nationals, to 39% in 1970. Expatriate brothers are more numerous than Peruvians; whereas, there are slightly more Peruvian sisters than expatriates.

The Holy See has diplomatic relations with Peru and in AD 2000 is represented to government and the Catholic hierarchy by a nuncio residing in Lima.

PROTESTANT CHURCH. The earliest Protestant mission workers in Peru, as in surrounding countries, were agents of the Bible societies. These initial efforts dating from 1822 were carried out in collaboration with sympathetic Catholic clergy whose purpose was to promote a 'spontaneous reformation' from within the church. The first Methodists from the USA arrived in 1877, but little penetration among the Peruvian people was made until the arrival in 1888 of Francisco Penzotti, another Bible society agent. Jailed several times with his Peruvian assistants, he ultimately succeeded in bringing many to a commitment to Christ. In 1891, his work was followed up by the Methodists, whose contribution included the development of an extensive school program. Independent Brethren missionaries began services in Lima in 1896, a work which was later associated with the Regions Beyond Missionary Union (1897), Evangelical Union of South America (1911), and the Christian and Missionary alliance (1933) and resulted in the establishment of the Peruvian Evangelical Church, the fourth largest church in Peru at the present time. John Ritchie, perhaps the strongest force in the development of the church, was sent by the RBMU in 1907 and remained influential until his death in 1952. This work included the establishment of a press to address the nation at large, as well as a large farm project where Indians could receive training in agriculture. However, as a result of different mission theories and conflicting personalities, the history of the church has been marked by disagreement and schism. Several foreign missions eventually found it expedient to withdraw from direct and indirect assistance, continuing their efforts with congregations which chose to remain with them.

Independents. School of missions conducted by AMEN, 1989.

Seventh-day Adventists, beginning in 1898, have found their greatest response among the Aymara Indians, their schools having a special appeal. While subject to schism, it remains one of the 2 largest Protestant churches. The rapidly growing Pentecostal movement is divided into a number of separate denominations, the Assemblies of God having the second largest membership, and indeed, along with the Adventists, the largest Protestant constituency in Peru. Two holiness churches, Wesleyans and Nazarenes, began work in 1903 and 1914 respectively, and the first of several small Baptist missions entered Peru in 1927. Since 1921, the South American Indian Mission has centered most of its work in the jungle lowlands of the east, while the Wycliffe Bible Translators, with a team of 236 in Peru, one of their larger fields, are active in approximately 40 tribes. Small groups from Europe work in Peru, usually in cooperation with other Evangelical bodies, but the major missionary thrust has been from North America.

iNDIGENOUS CHURCHES. Many indigenous bodies have been formed during the present century. Most are Pentecostal in emphasis, and several have come into existence as schisms from the Assemblies of God. The largest of these independent Pentecostal bodies is the Autonomous Pentecostal Churches which receives assistance from Swedish Pentecostals. Another important independent group, resulting from a schism within the Seventh-day Adventist community, is the Evangelical Israelite Church of the New Covenant, whose members are popularly known as Cabanistas or Tabernaclers.

OTHER CHURCHES. The first of Peru's non-Catholic denominations was the Anglican Church which entered the country in 1849. The church's small constituency forms part of the diocese of Chile, Bolivia and Peru under the Anglican Council for South America, CASA.

Two marginal bodies which have had striking success during the present century are Jehovah's Witness and the Mormons.

Renewal movements. In the 1990s the Pentecostal/Charismatic Renewal continued to spread rapidly across most older churches, and numbered over 3,440,000 adherents (of whom 13% Pentecostals, 76% Charismatics, and 11% Independents).

Iglesia Catolica, VA Puerto Maldonado. Welcome for visiting missionaries.

Indigenous missions. Although Roman Catholic missionaries from Peru have long served in surrounding countries, many Roman Catholics and Protestants are now working in North Africa, Europe, and the Middle East.

CHURCH AND STATE

The constitution of 1933, with several amendments added in 1940 and 1961, was the first in Peruvian history to declare that the state is no longer officially and formally Catholic. It continues, nevertheless, to accord a special status to the Catholic Church, which is placed juridically in the domain of public law. Article 32 states: 'Respecting the feelings of the majority of the nation, the state protects the Roman and Apostolic Catholic religion. The other religions enjoy the freedom of exercising their respective worship'. Article 234 says: 'The rapport between the State and the Catholic Church is governed by the concordats concluded by the executive power and approved by Congress' (Law 9166 of 5 September 1940). Article 235 states that 'To exercise the responsibilities of an archbishop or bishop, it is necessary to be Peruvian by birth or to have had Peruvian national citizenship for at least three years before the appointment, with continuous residence in the country during that time' (Law 13739 of 29 November 1961). Article 154 defines the duties of the president as including the power (a) to nominate archbishops and bishops for presentation to the Holy See and to ensure observance of papal bulls (Law 13739); and (b) to nominate candidates for priestly and other ecclesiastical posts. Finally, Article 123 gives to Congress the authority for 'creating new dioceses and archdioceses, or of suppressing those in existence on the order of the executive power' (Law 9166).

With regard to the constitution and its application, it should be noted that freedom of religion is proclaimed only as the right of individuals; in virtue of Article 232 (by decree since 1945) all meetings and acts of worship or propaganda in public areas are strictly forbidden to non-Catholics. Vatican II caused a definite relaxation in this area, and the decree of 1945 is rarely observed today. Furthermore, Article 233 confirms the national patronage (Patronato Nacional) conceded to the Peruvian government by the 1874 papal bull 'Preclarainter beneficia', which takes the place of a concordat. The text of Articles 123 and 154 also confirms the right of patronage. To evade the problems posed by the intervention of the state in the nomination of priests, the bishops have substituted for the latter the category of 'stewart curates', but this subterfuge caused the withholding of salaries to parish clergy. Nevertheless, the state continues to pay the salaries of bishops in office and canons as well as subsidizing seminaries, schools, and Catholic hospitals.

Since the 1941 law on public education, Catholic religious instruction is obligatory in all educational institutions in the country, public or private, including penal institutions. Students wishing a dispensation from this must make an explicit request. The National Bureau of Catholic Education (Oficina Nacional de Educacion Catolica, ONEC), which is recognized and subsidized by the state, supervises religious education at the national level, controls its programs and licenses teachers. An undersecretariat for religion is in charge of all religious and church affairs, but there is no obligatory registration of churches.

BROADCASTING AND MEDIA

Shortwave broadcasts from KNLS, TWR (Antilles), HCJB (Ecuador), and AWR (Costa Rica) can be received. IBRA broadcasts 10 hours of programming weekly from 4 local radio stations.

Peru is a member of UNDA. On local radio channels Catholics broadcast a dozen programs hanging in length from 5 minutes to 2 hours.

The 'Jesus' Film has been shown to 19 million (73%), mainly through TV (18.6 million) and film team presentations, with 432,000 responding.

CBN's *700 Club*, *Answers*, and *Superbook* programs can be seen on local television and cable channels, and response is followed up from a full-time ministry center. TBN can be received in Lima on channel 54.

Catholics broadcast 8 programs, half of which use a 30-minute magazine format.

INTERDENOMINATIONAL ORGANIZATIONS

The National Evangelical Council of Peru (Concilio Nacional Evangelico del Peru) was formed in 1940 by Protestant missions and their national churches. The Methodists withdrew in 1966, asserting it to be a mission-dominated organization. The council in turn remains apprehensive of ecumenical organizations in which Methodists among others participate. An association for theological education was initiated in 1965 with 10 theological colleges in its membership. The Catholic Episcopal Conference maintains a Secretariat for the Union of Christians (Secretariado para la Union de los Cristianos).

Iglesia Catolica, VA Iquitos. In Amazonian jungle, an Achual Indian hears the gospel.

FUTURE TRENDS AND PROSPECTS

The nonreligious will no doubt make slight gains from 0.3% in 1970 to nearly 2% by 2025, while Christians continue to claim about 97% of the population through 2025.

Though Christians are expected to remain above 90% well into the 21st century, the nonreligious could grow to more than 5% of the population in the same period. Immigrant non-Christians could also affect the percentage of Christians in this period.

BIBLIOGRAPHY

'A friendship evangelism course for Peru.' L. B. Del Pozo. D.Min. thesis, Biola University, La Mirada, CA, 1991. 213p.

'A Quechua messiah in eastern Peru,' A. Metraux, *American Anthropologist*, 44, 4 (1942), 721–25.

A study of the older Protestant missions and churches in Peru and Chile: with special reference to the problems of division, nationalism and native ministry. J. B. A. Kessler Jr. Goes, Netherlands: Oosterbaan & Le Cointre, 1967. 369p.

Anuario Eclesiástico del Perú, 1969. Lima, Peru: Secretariado del Episcopado Nacional, 1969.

'Born in the fire: the history of the first ten years of the Assemblies of God in Peru.' R. E. Leslie. M.A. thesis, Fuller Theological Seminary, Pasadena, CA, 1988. 89p.

'Campa cosmology,' G. Weiss, *Ethnology*, 11, 2 (1972), 157–72.

Christian communities in Chile and Peru. M. Fleet. Notre Dame, IN: Helen Kellogg Institute for International Studies, University of Notre Dame, 1992. 40p.

Church growth in the high Andes. K. E. Hamilton. Lucknow, India: Lucknow Publishing House, 1962. 146p.

Cosmovisión andina y catolicismo: lo sobrenatural en la vida cotidiana a partir de una biografía religiosa. A. G. Buitrón Aranda. Lima, Peru: Cultural Cuzco, 1992. 131p.

Directorio eclesiástico. Lima, Peru: Conferencia Episcopal Peruana, 1993. 504p.

Fishers of men or founders of empire: the Wycliffe Bible Translators in Latin America. D. Stoll. London: Zed, 1982. 344p.

'God hears the cry of the poor: the emerging spirituality in the Christian communities in Peru (1965–1986).' M. O'Neill. Ph.D. dissertation, Pontificiae Universitatis Gregorianae, Rome, 1990. 328p.

Gracias!: a Latin American journal. H. J. M. Nouwen. San Francisco: Harper & Row, 1983. 202p.

Guerreros de la oración: las nuevas iglesias en el Perú. W. Kapsoli Escudero. Lima, Peru: SEPEC, 1994. 505p.

'Ideological change and internal cleavages in the Peruvian Church: change, status quo and the priest; the case of ONIS.' M. G. Macaulay. Ph.D. dissertation, University of Notre Dame, [1972]. 172p.

La Iglesia en Perú y Bolivia: estructuras eclesiásticas. I. Alonso et al. Madrid: Oficina Internacional de Investigaciones Sociales, 1961. 271p.

La religión en el Perú: aproximación bibliográfica 1900–1983. C. Rivera. Lima, Peru: Comisión Evangélica Latinoamericana de Educación Cristiana, 1985. 251p.

La religión popular en el Perú: informe y diagnóstico. J. L. G. Martínez. Cuzco, Peru: Instituto de Pastoral Andina, 1987. 397p.

La transformación religiosa peruana. M. Marzal. Lima, Peru: Universidad Católica del Perú, 1983. 458p.

Las nuevas sectas en el Perú. J. M. Carreras. Lima, Peru: Compañia de Jesus, 1983. 79p.

Methodist education in Peru: social gospel, politics, and American ideological and economic penetration, 1888–1930. R. del Carmen Bruno-Jofré. Waterloo: Wilfrid Laurier University Press, 1988.

Peace and hope in the corner of the dead. J. Maust. Miami: Latin America Mission, 1987. 189p.

Peru. J. R. Fisher. *World bibliographical series*, vol. 109. Oxford, UK: CLIO Press, 1990. 194p. (See especially 'Religion,' p.92f).

Pilgrims of the Andes: regional cults in Cusco. M. J. Sallnow. Washington, DC: Smithsonian Institution Press, 1987. 351p.

'Protestant missionary activity and freedom of religion in Ecuador, Peru, and Bolivia.' P. E. Kuhl. Ph.D. dissertation, Southern Illinois University at Carbondale, 1982. 500p.

Radicalización y conflicto en la iglesia peruana. L. Pasará. Lima, Peru: El Virrey, 1986. 172p.

Religion and revolution in Peru, 1824–1976. J. L. Klaiber. Notre Dame, IN: University of Notre Dame Press, 1977. 259p.

'Religion, collectivism, and intrahistory: the Peruvian ideal of dependence,' F. B. Pike, *Journal of Latin American studies*, 10, 2 (1978), 239–62.

Religion in the Andes: vision and imagination in early colonial Peru. S. MacCormack. Princeton, NJ: Princeton University Press, 1991. 504p.

Religiosidad popular en el Perú: bibliografía. J. L. González & T. M. von Ronzelen. Lima, Peru: Centro de Estudios y Publicaciones, 1983. 375p.

Religious regimes in Peru: religion and state development in a long-term perspective and the effects in the Andean village of Zurite. F. Spier. [Amsterdam]: Amsterdam University Press, 1994. 328p.

'Renewal in the Latin American Church: a study of the Peruvian dioceses of Cajamarca and Ica.' J. N. Steidel. Ph.D. dissertation, University of Southern California, 1975. 327p.

Rituales en las regiones andinas de Bolivia y Peru. L. Girault. La Paz, Bolivia: Don Cosco, 1988. 467p.

The Catholic Church in Peru, 1821–1985: a social history. J. L. Klaiber. Washington, DC: Catholic University of America Press, 1992. 428p.

The church and the option for the poor in Peru. A. Quinn. *Catholic Institute for International Relations justice papers*, no. 3. London: Catholic Institute for International Relations, 1982. 15p.

'The emergent Andean church inculturation and liberation in southern Peru, 1968–1986.' S. P. Judd. Ph.D. dissertation, Graduate Theological Union, San Francisco, 1987. 348p.

'"The heart has its reasons": predicaments of missionary Christianity in early colonial Peru,' S. MacCormack, *Hispanic American historical review*, 65, 3 (1985), 443–66.

'The Protestant movement in Ecuador and Peru: a comparative socio-anthropological study of the establishment and diffusion of Protestantism in two central highland regions.' R. E. Paredes-Alfaro. Ph.D. dissertation, University of California at Los Angeles, 1980. 278p.

Theologies and liberation in Peru: the role of ideas in social movements. M. Peña. Philadelphia: Temple University Press, 1995. 234p.

'Towards an Aymara church.' D. Llanque Chana. M.Th. thesis, St. John's Seminary, 1979. 146p.

Voices like thunder: a journalist's account of Christianity among the people of Peru. C. H. Gervais. Windsor, Ontario: Third World Resource Centre, 1984. 66p.

Volksreligiosität und Pastoral im andinen Peru: Zugänge und Perspektiven einer Pastoral der Volksreligiosität. H. Gimpl. *Dissertationen Theologische Reihe*, Bd. 60. St. Ottilien: EOS, 1993. 367p.

Country Table 2. **Organized churches and denominations in Peru.**

Official name (bold type = church with over 10% of affiliated) 1	*Begun* 2	*Type* 3	*Counc* 4	*Congs* 5	*Adults* 6	*Affiliated 1970* 7	*Affiliated 1995* 8	*G%* 9	*Names, notes, and other statistics* (see Codebook, Part 3) 10
Asambleas de Dios del Perú	1911	P-Pe2	ZF..E	2,305	173,814	100,000	341,000	5.03	*Assemblies of God of Peru.* 1919, M=AoG(USA). HQ Lima. 807n,16f,1j,3s(154).
Asambleas Locales	1960	I-3nL	.....	22	758	150	2,000	10.92	*Local Assemblies. Local Church. Little Flock.* Begun in China in 1922. Chinese.
Asociación Bautista Maranatha	1964	P-Bap	x...E	3	300	300	1,000	4.93	M=Maranatha Baptist Mission (USA). Radical Baptists. HQ Ica. 4f.
Asoc Bautistas para Ev Mundial	1931	I-Bap	xT..E	87	3,454	1,000	6,910	8.04	Ev=Evangelismo. M=Assoc of Baptists for World Evangelism (USA). 6n,18x,33f,1s(29).
Asoc de Igs Bíblicas Ev de Lima	c1975	P-Eva	.....	4	172	–	491	5.00	*Assoc of Evangelical Bible Chs of Lima.* M=TEAM,RBMU.

Continued opposite

Country Table 2–continued

Official name (bold type = church with over 10% of affiliated) 1	Begun 2	Type 3	Counc 4	Congs 5	Adults 6	Affiliated 1970 7	Affiliated 1995 8	G% 9	Names, notes, and other statistics (see Codebook, Part 3) 10
Asoc de Igs Ev del Nor-Oriente Peruano	1897	P-Eva	xM..E	91	5,000	1,800	12,500	8.06	Northeast. M=RBMU(UK, USA)(Misión de Perú Interior). 26f,1p,1s(16),128Y.
Asoc Iglesia Evangélica Aguaruna	c1965	I-Eva	.....	64	1,600	833	5,330	7.71	*Aguaruna Assoc of Evangelical Chs.*
Asoc de Igs Ev Libres del Peru	1965	P-Con	.....	6	115	50	275	7.06	*Assoc of Evangelical Free Chs. of Peru.* M=EFCA.
Asoc de Igs Pentecostales Autonomas	c1970	I-3pL	.....	79	7,900	–	23,900	49.67	*Assoc of Independent Pentecostal Chs.*
Asociación Misionera Ev Nacional	1946	I-Eva	.....	50	1,000	150	2,000	10.92	*AMEN. Nat Ev Missionary Assoc.* Ex IEP, but new churches join IEP. 9n,W=60%,9Y,10z.
Comunidad Cristiana El Agua Viva	c1976	I-3kL	.....	20	25,000	–	60,000	5.26	*Christian Community of the Living Water.* Cell-based (weekly in homes). HQ Lima. Satellites.
Convención Evangélica Bautista del P	1950	P-Bap	T...E	115	7,712	3,000	22,000	8.30	*Ev Baptist Convention of Peru.* M=FMB-SBC(USA). 16n,34f,1s,162Y.
Ejército de Salvación	1910	P-Sal	xw..E	20	800	2,000	2,500	0.90	*Ejercituman Salvacionman* (Quechua). *Peru District.* 5n,4x,1s,W=78%.
Hermanos Libres	c1925	P-CBr	x...E	100	4,000	1,000	8,890	9.13	*Open Brethren. Free Brethren. Brethren Assemblies.* M=CMML(USA, UK). HQ Lima. 33f.
Ig Ev Misionera de los Herm Menonitas	1946	P-Men	GF...	4	150	777	300	-3.74	M=Mennonite Brethren Ch of NAmerica. HQ Atalaya, via pucallpa. 4f.
Iglesia Adventista del Séptimo Día	1898	P-Adv	x....	424	187,151	100,000	374,000	5.42	*7th-day Adv. Inca UM.* 50% Aymara. 60n,20x,38f,3H,4p,1s,1143t(65270),9159Y.
Iglesia Alianza Cristiana y Misionera	1923	P-Hol	xF..E	176	20,730	2,930	37,313	10.71	M=CMA(USA). 1954, major split from 1EP. HQ Lima. 4n,25x,1k,1s(20),250Y.
Iglesia Anglicana: D Peru	1849	A-Low	Aw.CE	15	600	2,500	2,000	-0.89	*Anglican Ch,* in ACSCA. 70% English. M=CMS(Austr),SAMS,BCMS. 2x,8f,W=50%,1Y,12y.
Iglesia Autonoma Pentecostal del Perú	c1952	I-3pL	.....	80	2,000	2,000	4,000	2.81	*Autonomous Pentecostal Ch of Peru.* Schism ex AoG by American missionary.
Iglesia Bautista Independiente		I-Bap	.....	152	7,600	1,000	19,000	0.05	*Independent Baptist Church.*
Iglesia Bautista Internacional	1970	I-Bap	.....	28	1,400	–	4,000	39.34	*Baptist International Mission.* M=BIM(USA).
Iglesia Bautista Mid-Mission	c1955	I-Fun	.....	28	1,570	857	4,480	6.84	*Baptist Mid-Missions.* M=BMM(USA).
Iglesia Católica en el Perú:	1536	R-Lat	B.I.R	3,903	12,699,300	12,888,702	22,590,000	2.27	*Catholic Ch.* 9 Zones. C=40+6+110. 10p,4q,9x(115). 1090n 1167x 1844m 4019w 345701Yy
M Arequipa	1577	R-Lat	Bs	141	516,000	378,000	952,000	3.76	Z:7. Industry, farming. Strong religious. M=SJ. 1p,1s. 77n 86x 159m 255w 10163Yy
D Puno	1861	R-Lat	Bs	45	342,000	350,000	660,000	2.57	8 Rural. Quechua, Aymara. Popular religiosity. M=OP. 23n 12x 17m 57w 8640Yy
D Tacna y Moquegua	1944	R-Lat	Bs	33	187,000	190,000	334,000	2.28	7 Urban. Important copper-mining area. M=SM. 6n 16x 18m 22w 4115Yy
PN Ayaviri	1958	R-Lat	Bs	31	103,000	190,000	194,000	0.08	8 Quechua, Aymara. Very religious. M=SDB,SSCC. 8n 9x 12m 37w 2648Yy
PN Chuquibamba	1962	R-Lat	Bs	25	83,000	98,000	145,000	1.58	7 Rural, farming. West of Arequipa. M=OP. 6n 6x 6m 42w 2403Yy
PN Juli	1957	R-Lat	Bs	30	176,000	400,000	328,000	-0.79	8 Rural poverty; Aymara. Religious. M=MM,CM. 3n 11x 11m 21w 5583Yy
M Ayacucho (Huamanga)	1609	R-Lat	Bs	51	204,000	300,000	396,000	1.12	4 Rural Quechua. Superficial catholicism. M=SDB,OFM. 25n 11x 15m 120w 13300Yy
D Huancavelica	1944	R-Lat	Bs	27	261,000	303,263	491,000	1.95	4 Rural Quechua, very poor. Religious. M=CSSR. 25n 0x 0m 41w 15050Yy
PN Caravelí	1957	R-Lat	Bs	22	82,000	122,000	154,000	0.94	7 Coast, in south. Rural. Partly Quechua. M=MSC. 3n 8x 11m 60w 1992Yy
M Cuzco	1536	R-Lat	Bs	98	496,000	446,559	1,000,000	3.28	8 Ancient Inca capital. Quechua. 1p,1s. M=OdeM 64n 58x 109m 279w 5320Yy
D Abancay	1958	R-Lat	Bs	34	159,000	256,000	285,808	0.44	8 Impoverished Quechua. Traditional religion. 28n 0x 3m 132w 12260Yy
PN Chuquibambilla	1968	R-Lat	Bs	8	43,000	175,000	78,500	-3.16	8 Quechua, very poor; christo-paganism. M=OSA. 3n 9x 19m 32w 2587Yy
PN Sicuani	1959	R-Lat	Bs	24	176,000	230,000	324,000	1.38	8 Poor rural Quechua; christo-paganism. M=OCer. 16n 5x 6m 30w 4301Yy
M Huáncayo	1944	R-Lat	Bs	42	458,000	600,000	782,000	1.07	4 90% rural Quechua. Transport, mining. 1s. 32n 23x 33m 64w 10557Yy
D Huanuco	1865	R-Lat	Bs	31	319,000	405,000	602,000	1.60	4 Rural, mountains, forest. M=SDB. 18n 23x 28m 42w 14690Yy
D Tarma	1958	R-Lat	Bs	19	272,000	260,000	500,000	2.65	4 Rural. Cultivation, produce. M=SM. 14n 12x 12m 29w 4951Yy
M Lima	1541	R-Lat	Bs	475	2,027,000	2,731,488	3,163,256	0.59	5 39% live in barriadas (slums). M=SJ. 1p,1s. 241n 509x 797m 1111w 20949Yy
D Callao	1967	R-Lat	Bs	53	308,000	290,000	586,000	2.85	5 Port, industry, commerce. Immigrants. M=SJ,CP. 55n 22x 92m 149w 7949Yy
D Carabayllo	1996	R-Lat	Bs	36	749,200	–	1,124,830	0.05	Served by M=OFM. 52n 116x 116m 200w 5000Yy
D Chosica	1996	R-Lat	Bs	17	423,900	–	636,440	0.05	New diocese with M=MSC. 18n 96x 96m 100w 2000Yy
D Huacho	1958	R-Lat	Bs	285	268,000	322,000	498,000	1.76	6 Urban, rural with agriculture, fisheries. M=OdeM. 29n 8x 15m 43w 4700Yy
D Ica	1946	R-Lat	Bs	42	368,000	311,648	681,000	3.18	6 55% urban, with large farming region. 23n 26x 30m 91w 19270Yy
D Lurin	1996	R-Lat	Bs	22	531,200	–	797,474	0.05	New diocese. M=SDB. 45n 12x 12m 50w 5000Yy
PN Yauyos	1957	R-Lat	Bs	25	115,000	161,083	248,545	1.75	6 Rural, agriculture, impoverished. 1p,2s. 31n 1x 1m 46w 5544Yy
M Piura	1940	R-Lat	Bs	44	610,000	531,891	1,154,000	3.15	2 Urban; major petroleum area of Peru. 50n 39x 49m 150w 19405Yy
D Chachapoyas (Maynas)	1805	R-Lat	Bs	25	149,000	141,120	337,041	3.54	1 Poor peasantry, living by agriculture. M=SJ. 22n 6x 11m 97w 18652Yy
D Chiclayo	1956	R-Lat	Bs	105	460,000	370,500	883,280	3.54	2 80% urban. Commercial, sugar, rice. M=Opus Dei. 57n 22x 26m 114w 15854Yy
D Chulucanas	1964	R-Lat	Bs	16	267,000	370,000	412,883	0.44	1 Rural, agricultural, poor. M=OSA. 11n 25x 26m 49w 10766Yy
PN Chota	1963	R-Lat	Bs	432	237,000	260,000	452,000	2.24	1 Rural, agricultural, poor. M=OAR. 16n 8x 9m 12w 5529Yy
M Trujillo	1577	R-Lat	Bs	64	512,000	630,000	1,036,306	2.01	2 Major commercial city, old colonial; sugar. M=SJ. 53n 41x 96m 214w 17360Yy
D Cajamarca	1908	R-Lat	Bs	51	316,000	380,000	574,050	1.66	1 Rural. Agriculture. Poor area. 30n 5x 12m 89w 13330Yy
D Chimbote	1962	R-Lat	Bs	432	261,000	177,000	444,000	3.75	2 Mass urban immigration; fishing port. M=SJ,OP. 27n 10x 14m 97w 10808Yy
D Huaraz	1899	R-Lat	Bs	9	198,000	278,150	255,979	-0.33	3 Quechuas. Earthquake disaster 1970. M=SDB. 26n 6x 9m 38w 6420Yy
PN Huamachuco	1961	R-Lat	Bs	482	115,000	165,000	217,000	1.10	1 Rural, agricultural, poor. M=TOR. 3n 7x 12m 18w 1648Yy
PN Huari	1958	R-Lat	Bs	21	154,000	277,000	289,000	0.17	3 Rural; very impoverished Quechuas. M=OSI. 3p. 16n 5x 5m 17w 6868Yy
PN Moyobamba	1948	R-Lat	Bs	387	198,000	221,500	373,000	2.11	1 Mountainous, rural. Quechuas. M=CP. 6n 25x 29m 59w 4852Yy
VA Iquitos	1900	R-Lat	Posa	26	302,000	160,000	571,000	5.22	9 27% Amazon tribes: Jivaro, Arabela. M=OSA. 6n 17x 31m 32w 7350Yy
VA Jaen en Peru (S Francisco Javier)	1946	R-Lat	Psj	32	268,000	108,000	512,000	6.42	1 Aguaruna, Hambisa; genocide tried 1971. M=SJ. 13n 15x 24m 94w 7703Yy
VA Pucallpa	1956	R-Lat	Ppme	22	118,000	113,500	284,000	3.74	9 Urban, rural. Cashibo and Shipibo. M=PME. 0n 17x 17m 25w 5239Yy
VA Puerto Maldonado	1900	R-Lat	Pop	13	124,000	90,000	228,000	3.79	9 Poverty. Huarayo, Mashco, Huachipairi. M=OP. 5n 25x 29m 47w 3852Yy
VA Requena	1956	R-Lat	Pofm	8	54,000	88,000	99,000	0.47	9 Rural, urban. Dispersed tribes: Cocama. M=OFM. 1n 6x 8m 26w 5325Yy
VA San José de Amazonas	1945	R-Lat	Pofm	11	46,000	100,000	85,400	-0.63	9 Forest. Huitoto, Bora, Ocaina, Orejon. M=OFM. 5n 8x 13m 30w 1580Yy
VA San Ramón	1900	R-Lat	Pofm	31	337,000	175,000	637,000	5.30	9 Urban, forest. Campa, Amuesha tribes. M=OFM. 9n 13x 14m 54w 3478Yy
VA Yurimaguas	1921	R-Lat	Pcp	34	77,000	52,000	142,550	4.12	9 Forest. Scattered small Indian tribes. M=CP. 4n 12x 16m 54w 2710Yy
OM Peru	1943	R-Lat	Bs	42	100,000	30,000	190,000	7.66	*Military Ordinariate of Peru.* 43 ordinaries, 1 auxiliary. 9m, 5223Yy.
Doubly-counted Catholics		R-Lat		0	-871,000	-350,000	-1,549,342		Catholics in newer dioceses also counted in parent dioceses.
Iglesia de Cristo	1935	I-3pL	.....	30	1,000	500	2,000	5.70	*Ch of Christ.* Schism ex Assemblies of God. In Lima, Callao, Chimbote.
Iglesia de Cristo Pentecostal	c1965	I-3pL	.....	59	2,950	1,000	7,380	8.32	*Pentecostal Church of Christ.*
Iglesia de Dios de la Profecía	1955	P-Pe3	Z....	191	7,260	1,000	20,700	12.89	M=Ch of God of Prophecy (USA). Holiness Pentecostals (3-stage). HQ Chimbote. 2f.
Iglesia de Dios del Perú	1947	P-Pe3	ZF..E	127	4,866	5,000	12,200	3.63	*Ch of God of P.* M=CoG(Cleveland) (USA). Begun by Chilean missionaries. 25n,4f,1k.1p.
Iglesia de Dios en el Perú	1968	P-Hol	x....	30	640	500	1,000	2.81	*Ch of God in Peru.* M=CoG(Anderson) (USA). Growing. 1n,1x,4f,1s,W=99%,10Y,5z.
Iglesia de JC de los Santos de los UD	c1956	m-LdS	x....	370	87,500	13,831	159,000	10.26	*Latter-day Saints. Mormons.* M=CJCLdS(USA). Indians. Rapid growth, 7.9%pa. 250f.
Iglesia de la Biblia Abierta	c1980	I-3pL	.....	4	135	–	338	6.67	*Open Bible Standard Church.* M=OBSC(USA).
Iglesia del Evangelio Cuadrangular	1983	P-Pe2	.....	2	440	–	683	8.33	*Church of the Foursquare Gospel.* M=ICFG.
Iglesia de los Marineros Escandinavos		P-Lut	l....	10	1,000	300	2,000	0.05	*Scandinavian Seamens Ch.* Ministry to Norwegian, Swedish &c visiting ships' crews.
Iglesia de los Peregrinos del Perú	1903	P-Hol	VF..E	159	3,975	5,492	11,400	2.96	*Ch of Pilgrims.* M=Wesleyan Ch (USA). HQ Chiclayo. 17n,2x,7f,1p,1p.W=79%,778Y.
Iglesia del Nazareno	1914	P-Hol	xF..E	296	22,917	15,000	52,734	5.16	*Nazarenes.* M=CoN(USA). 2 schools. 15n,8x,80m,21f,1h,1s,166t(12040),W=70%.
Iglesia Evangélica Cristiana Libre	c1970	I-Con	.....	54	2,160	–	5,400	41.02	*Free Evangelical Christian Church.*
Iglesia Evangélica de Cristo		I-3pL	.....	2	200	200	500	0.05	*Ev Ch of Christ.* Indigenous pentecostal split ex Southern Baptists. HQ Chimbote.
Iglesia Ev Israelita del Nuevo Pacto		I-Adv	.....	170	17,000	10,000	34,000	0.05	*Ev Israelite Ch of the New Covenant. Cabañistas (Tabernaclers).* Schism ex SDAs.
Iglesia Evangélica Luterana en el Perú	1897	P-Lut	Lv...	5	180	2,500	300	-8.13	1966, M=LCA(USA). Germans. Norwegians, Mestizos. 1n,4x,6f,1h,W=17%,69Yy.
Iglesia Ev Pentecostal de Jesu Cristo		I-3pL	x....	89	4,540	1,000	11,300	0.05	*Ev Pentecostal Ch of Jesucristo* former *Ev Pent Ch of Chile.* Mission of Chilean indigenous body.
Iglesia Ev Pentecostal del Perú	1950	I-3pL	.....	137	2,740	1,000	7,830	8.58	*Ev Pentecostal Ch of Peru.* Schism ex AoG. Lima area, Ica, Ayacusho.
Iglesia Ev Pentecostal Misionera	1945	I-3pL	.....	48	25,600	2,000	40,000	12.73	*Missionary Pentecostal Ev Ch. Iglesia Pentecostal Avanzada.* Schism ex AoG.
Iglesia Evangélica Peruana	1894	P-Ref	.G..E	1,600	80,000	25,000	250,000	9.65	*IEP.* M=EUSA. 60% Quechua. 8 schisms. 30n,10x,100w,34f,1s(54),W=70%,1000Y.
Iglesia Evangélica Presbiteriana del P	1975	P-Ref	.G..E	54	1,350	1,863	4,500	5.00	*Ev Presbyterian Ch of Peru.* M=Iglesia Libre de Escocia (Free Ch of Scotland) (UK).
Iglesia La Luz del Mundo (Aaronistas)	1940	I-3oL	x....	100	3,000	3,000	7,000	3.45	*Light of the World Ch.*(Mexico). Revivalists in La Convención jungles. Beards, brown/white robes
Iglesia Metodista del Peru	1877	P-Met	VuU.f	70	12,000	7,000	18,700	4.01	*Methodist Ch of Peru.* 1887, M=UMC(USA). HQ Brena. A=1970. 28n,15f,6r(4000),52t,1u.
Iglesia Misionera de la Biblia	1981	I-Hol	.....	2	80	–	242	7.14	*Bible Missionary Church.* M=BMC(USA).
Iglesia Nacional Ev Los Amigos	1961	P-Qua	QF..E	60	2,500	700	6,250	9.15	*National Ev Friends Ch.* M=Oregon YM of Friends (USA). Lake Titicaca. 3x,8f.
Iglesia Nueva Apostólica		I-3aX	x....	210	16,500	1,000	25,526	0.05	In Canada Bezirk, *New Apostolic Ch.* M=NAC(Germany). World HQ Zurich (Switzerland).
Iglesia Ortodoxa Griega	c1970	O-Gre	Cwo..	1	2,100	2,000	4,500	3.30	In 11th Archidiocesan District, Greek Orthodox AD of N&S America. Greeks. Lima.
Iglesia Ortodoxa Russa		O-Rus	Mwo..	1	400	500	600	0.05	*Russian Orthodox Ch.* In D SAmerica, Orthodox Ch in America (USA). Russians. 1x.
Iglesia Pentecostal Autónoma del Centro	1961	I-3pL	.....	30	1,300	700	2,000	4.29	*Autonomous Pentecostal Ch of the Centre.* HQ Huancayo. 4n,13x,1p,W=90%,19Y,45z.
Iglesia Pentecostal Unida	1962	P-Pe1	x....	100	3,000	3,000	8,000	4.00	*United Pentecostal Ch. Jesus Only.* Unitarians. M=UPC(USA). 23n,6f,1p(75).
Iglesia Presbiteriana Nacional del P	1937	P-Ref	.T..E	80	1,000	2,000	3,000	1.64	*Misión Presb Peruana.* M=WPM(RPCES). Quechuas. 4n,6x,17f,1p,W=50%,40Yy.
Iglesia Unión de Lima	1924	P-com	.....	1	150	300	300	0.00	*Union Church of Lima.* English-speaking expatriates 1n,W=50%,6Yy.
Iglesias de Cristo	1965	I-Dis	x....	54	2,160	2,000	7,200	5.26	*Chs of Christ.* M=CCCC(Instrumental) (USA). Independent congregations. 3x,90Y.
Iglesias Pentecostales Autónomas		I-3pL	.....	130	11,000	10,000	22,000	0.05	*Autonomous Pentecostal Churches.* Some aid from M=SFM(Sweden), and USA.
Iglesias radiofónicas solitarias	c1950	I-3rL	.....	1,000	10,000	600	15,000	13.74	Isolated radio believers (HCJB, FEBC) across Amazon jungles. T=3000(ICI).
Misión a los Indios de Sud-América	1921	P-Non	xN..E	34	2,900	2,000	4,500	3.30	*South America Indian Mission.* M=SAIM(USA). HQ Pucallpa. 4 schools. 50f,3h,2s.
Misión Alianza Evangélica	1962	P-Eva	xM..E	4	500	500	1,000	2.81	M=TEAM(Ev Alliance Mission)(USA). HQ Lima. 13f,1p.
Misión Suiza de Cooperación Evangélica	1963	P-Pe2	Z....	30	1,000	780	2,000	3.84	*Swiss Mission for Ev Cooperation.* M=SPM(Switz). 4n,3x,1p,1s(5),W=65%,100Y,150z.
Movimiento Evangelistico Misionero		I-3gL	.....	114	22,800	8,000	45,600	0.05	*Missionary Evangelistic Movement.* M=MEM.
Niños de Dios	c1985	I-mar	.....	2	83	–	172	10.00	*Children of God.* Former Jesus Movement followers from USA.
Sociedad de la Ciencia Cristiana		m-Sci	x....	2	100	100	200	0.05	*Christian Science. Ch of Christ, Scientist.* M=CCS(Boston, USA). First Church, Lima.
Sinodo Evangélico Luterano	1968	P-Lut	.....	2	200	200	300	1.64	M=Ev Lutheran Synod(USA). Small mission in Trinidad (Lima). 5f.
Templos de Avivamiento	1965	I-3pL	.....	200	3,000	2,000	5,000	3.73	*Revival Temples. MEM.* Mestizo,Aymara,Quechua. 28n,5x,1s(10),W=90%,221Y.
Testigos de Jehová	c1930	m-Jeh	x....	673	34,978	10,000	117,000	10.34	*Jehovah's Witnesses.* Active witnessing under way by 1932. (1975) 974Y. (1995) 4506Y.
Unión Bautista del Sur	1927	P-Bap	....E	133	56,800	2,000	88,700	16.38	*Union of Baptists of South Peru.* M=IBFM(Baptist Union of Ireland). Indians. 6x.13f,200Y.
Other Protestant denominations		P-	.....	100	20,000	10,000	50,000	0.05	Total about 30 (see list below).
Other independent single congregations		I-sin	.....	221	5,530	4,000	18,400	0.05	In about 25 loose geographical networks.
Other indigenous pentecostal churches		I-3pL	.....	50	6,000	2,000	15,000	0.05	Total about 10 (see list below).
Doubly-affiliated		2-aff			-790,000	-136,215	-1,425,344		Evangelicals who also are or were baptized Roman Catholics.
Disaffiliated		X-Aff			-277,000	-200,000	-500,000		Baptized Catholics now disaffiliated agnostics, atheists, or traditionalists.
Totals				**14,617**	**12,570,660**	**12,933,400**	**22,690,000**		

Churches, members, growth, 1900-2025	*Congs*	*Adults*	*Affiliated*	*G%*	*Total denominations*	*6 Megablocs: O*	*R*	*A*	*P*	*I*	*m*
Total churches, members, and denominations (mid-1900)	1,500	1,970,000	3,589,200	1.85	8	0	1	1	6	0	0
Total churches, members, and denominations (mid-1970)	5,170	7,097,525	12,933,400	1.85	86	2	1	1	42	37	3
Total churches, members, and denominations (mid-1990)	14,000	11,548,000	20,843,000	2.41	133	2	1	1	61	65	3
Total churches, members, and denominations (mid-1995)	14,617	12,570,660	22,690,000	1.71	132	2	1	1	61	64	3
Total churches, members, and denominations (mid-2000)	15,000	13,686,000	24,702,049	1.71	134	2	1	1	61	66	3
Total churches, members, and denominations (mid-2025)	19,000	18,754,000	33,850,000	1.27	225	7	1	1	80	130	6

Continued overleaf

Country Table 2–concluded

NOTES ON TABLE ABOVE
NATIONAL COUNCILS (Column 4, 5th letter).
E = Concilio Nacional Evangélico del Perú (CNEP, CONEP) (National Evangelical Council of Peru), 1940.
f = member of CNEP until withdrawal in 1966.
R = Conferencia Episcopal Peruana (CEP) (Peru Episcopal Conference).
OTHER PROTESTANT DENOMINATIONS. These smaller bodies include: American Baptist Association (1960; 5 churches), Andes Ev Mission (1969; 8 missionaries), Asociación de Iglesias Bautistas de la Selva (member of ICCC), Asociación Misionera de Iglesias Ev de la Selva (member of ICCC), Baptist Bible Fellowship International (1959), Baptist Faith Missions (1935), Baptist Gospel Fellowship, Bethany Missionary Association, Children of God International (over 1 million letters distributed), Chinese Christian (Gospel) Fellowship, Elim Missionary Assemblies (1964), Exclusive Brethren (Continuing Tunbridge Wells, Kelly-Continental), German Ev Ch, Iglesia de Dios Pentecostal, International Ch of the Foursquare Gospel, Mid-Peruvian Mission, Misión a los Andes, Peruvian Fellowship (1933), United Ev Chs, United World Mission (1955), World Baptist Fellowship Mission Agency (1961), World Missions (1963).
OTHER INDIGENOUS PENTECOSTAL CHURCHES. These include: Iglesia Pentecostal Independiente, and other immigrant bodies from Chile. In addition, there is a USA Black pentecostal mission, Ch of God (Holiness).
OTHER MARGINAL BODIES. The Reorganized Ch of Jesus Christ of Latter-day Saints (USA) maintains a small work based on Miraflores, Lima (65 members).

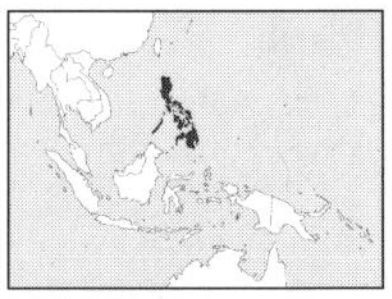

PHILIPPINES

SECULAR DATA, AD 2000

STATE
Official name: Republika ng Pilipinas (The Republic of the Philippines).
Short name: Philippines. **Adjective of nationality:** Philippine, a Filipino.
Flag: Blue and red stripes bordered by white triangle containing yellow stars and sun.
Area: 300,076 sq. km. (115,860 sq. mi.).
Government: Multiparty republic, since 1987 (1564 Spanish colony, 1898 independence declared but USA rule established, 1946 Independence as republic, 1972 one-party republic).
Legislature: Congress: Senate, 24 members; House of Representatives, 221 members.
Official language: Filipino and English.
Monetary unit: 1 Philippine peso (P) = 100 centavos. **US$1=** P43.78.
Chief cities: MANILA-Quezon (Metro Manila) 10,818,000; Manila 2,595,840; Quezon City 2,002,452; Davao 1,196,000; Cebu (Cebu City) 1,012,268.
Political divisions: 16 provinces.
Armed forces: 110,000.

DEMOGRAPHY
Population: 75,967,000.
Population density: 253.1/sq. km. (655.6/sq. mi.).
Under 15 years: 27,872,000.
Growth rate p.a.: 1.88% (births 25.63, deaths 5.34).
Mortality: Infant, per 1,000: 29.7, ; **Maternal per 100,000:** 280.0.
Life expectancy: 70 (male 68, female 72).
Household size: 5.7. **Floor area per person, sq.m:** 22.8.
Major languages: Filipino, English, Spanish, Cebuano, Tagalog, Ilocan, Ilongo, Bicol, Pampango, Chinese. In addition, there are about 150 local languages. Usage: Tagalog 44%, English 39%, Spanish 2%, Chinese 0.5%.
Urban dwellers: 58.62%. **Urban growth rate p.a.:** 3.1%.
Labor force: 40%.

ETHNOLINGUISTIC PEOPLES
20.4% Tagalog (Pilipino); 19.0% Visayan (Bisayan, Cebu); 11.1% Ilocano; 9.3% Hiligaynon (Visaya); 4.6% Waray-Waray (Binisaya).

ECONOMY
National income p.a. per person: US$1,050; **per family:** US$5,985.

EDUCATION
Adult literacy: 94% (male 95%, female 94%). **Schools:** 42,228.
Universities: 809. **School enrolment:** female/male: 99%/99%.

HEALTH
Access to health services: 76%. **Access to safe water:** 85%.
Hospitals: 1,723 (11 beds per 10,000). **Doctors:** 78,445.
Blind: 80,000. **Deaf:** 4,502,200. **Murder rate:** 30.
Lepers: 67,000. **Underweight prevalence under 5:** 30%.

LITERATURE
New book titles p.a.: 2,280 (30 p.a. per million). **Periodicals:** 2,198.
Newspapers: 42 dailies.

COMMUNICATION (per 1,000 people)
Phones: 25 (38% mobile). **Radios:** 116. **TV sets:** 129.
Daily newspaper circulation: 65. **Computers:** 21.

REFUGEES
Alien refugees from other countries: 450.

HUMAN LIFE AND LIBERTY (optimum condition=100.0%)
HDI: 67.2. **HSI:** 50.0. **HFI:** 25.0. **EFL:** 42.0.

Country Table 1. **Religious adherents in the Philippines, AD 1900-2025.**

Year	*1900*		*1970*		*mid-1990*		*Annual change, 1990-2000*				*mid-1995*		*mid-2000*		*mid-2025*	
Name	*Adherents*	*%*	*Adherents*	*%*	*Adherents*	*%*	*Natural*	*Conversion*	*Total*	*Rate*	*Adherents*	*%*	*Adherents*	*%*	*Adherents*	*%*
Christians	**6,550,000**	**86.2**	**35,359,600**	**94.2**	**54,664,800**	**90.1**	**1,376,320**	**-27,658**	**1,348,662**	**2.23**	**61,452,000**	**89.9**	**68,151,424**	**89.7**	**96,610,800**	**89.3**
PROFESSION																
professing Christians	**6,550,000**	**86.2**	**35,359,600**	**94.2**	**54,664,800**	**90.1**	**1,376,320**	**-27,658**	**1,348,662**	**2.23**	**61,452,000**	**89.9**	**68,151,424**	**89.7**	**96,610,800**	**89.3**
AFFILIATION																
unaffiliated Christians	570,000	7.5	1,317,600	3.5	1,259,800	2.1	31,720	-2,563	29,157	2.10	1,437,000	2.1	1,551,367	2.0	1,610,800	1.5
affiliated Christians	**5,980,000**	**78.7**	**34,042,000**	**90.7**	**53,405,000**	**88.0**	**1,344,600**	**-25,094**	**1,319,506**	**2.23**	**60,015,000**	**87.8**	**66,600,057**	**87.7**	**95,000,000**	**87.8**
Roman Catholics	5,980,000	78.7	30,860,093	82.2	50,600,000	83.4	1,274,026	-77,026	1,197,000	2.15	56,553,712	82.7	62,570,000	82.4	87,400,000	80.7
Independents	1,800,000	23.7	6,829,726	18.2	11,170,000	18.4	281,242	34,758	316,000	2.52	12,795,165	18.7	14,330,000	18.9	22,000,000	20.3
Protestants	100	0.0	1,447,143	3.9	2,913,000	4.8	73,345	12,855	86,200	2.63	3,324,550	4.9	3,775,000	5.0	6,800,000	6.3
Marginal Christians	0	0.0	166,925	0.4	500,000	0.8	12,589	4,411	17,000	2.97	574,400	0.8	670,000	0.9	1,200,000	1.1
Anglicans	0	0.0	63,276	0.2	95,000	0.2	2,392	108	2,500	2.36	110,000	0.2	120,000	0.2	160,000	0.2
doubly-affiliated	-1,800,100	-23.7	-5,325,163	-14.2	-11,873,000	-19.6	-298,943	-251	-299,194	2.27	-13,342,827	-19.5	-14,864,943	-19.6	-22,560,000	-20.8
Trans-megabloc groupings																
Evangelicals	100	0.0	600,000	1.6	1,370,000	2.3	34,494	11,006	45,500	2.91	1,583,482	2.3	1,825,000	2.4	3,230,000	3.0
Pentecostals/Charismatics	0	0.0	3,050,000	8.1	15,750,000	26.0	396,559	33,441	430,000	2.44	17,854,537	26.1	20,050,000	26.4	30,310,000	28.0
Great Commission Christians	**456,000**	**6.0**	**2,252,400**	**6.0**	**3,216,000**	**5.3**	**80,974**	**-10,978**	**69,996**	**1.99**	**3,554,000**	**5.2**	**3,915,959**	**5.2**	**5,950,000**	**5.5**
Muslims	266,000	3.5	1,553,000	4.1	3,700,000	6.1	93,160	9,750	102,910	2.48	4,207,700	6.2	4,729,095	6.2	7,000,000	6.5
Ethnoreligionists	760,000	10.0	338,400	0.9	1,600,000	2.6	40,285	4,728	45,013	2.51	1,831,000	2.7	2,050,129	2.7	2,600,000	2.4
Nonreligious	2,000	0.0	78,000	0.2	300,000	0.5	7,554	12,458	20,012	5.24	390,000	0.6	500,124	0.7	1,100,000	1.0
Baha'is	0	0.0	67,500	0.2	170,000	0.3	4,280	1,672	5,952	3.05	200,000	0.3	229,522	0.3	420,000	0.4
Atheists	0	0.0	20,000	0.1	110,000	0.2	2,770	274	3,044	2.47	125,400	0.2	140,442	0.2	300,000	0.3
Buddhists	7,000	0.1	50,000	0.1	80,000	0.1	2,014	-240	1,774	2.02	87,300	0.1	97,744	0.1	160,000	0.2
Chinese folk-religionists	15,000	0.2	70,000	0.2	44,000	0.1	1,108	-1,050	58	0.13	39,800	0.1	44,582	0.1	20,000	0.0
New-Religionists	0	0.0	1,000	0.0	11,000	0.0	277	66	343	2.75	12,800	0.0	14,434	0.0	25,000	0.0
Confucianists	0	0.0	0	0.0	1,550	0.0	39	-12	27	1.64	1,650	0.0	1,823	0.0	3,000	0.0
Hindus	0	0.0	1,000	0.0	1,200	0.0	30	2	32	2.39	1,350	0.0	1,519	0.0	3,500	0.0
Jews	0	0.0	500	0.0	850	0.0	21	-6	15	1.62	900	0.0	998	0.0	1,200	0.0
Other religionists	0	0.0	1,000	0.0	3,600	0.0	91	16	107	2.63	4,100	0.0	4,665	0.0	7,500	0.0
World A (unevangelized persons)	532,000	7.0	1,126,200	3.0	3,337,785	5.5	83,265	8,314	91,579	2.47	3,759,472	5.5	4,254,152	5.6	5,845,554	5.4
World B (evangelized non-Christians)	518,000	6.8	1,054,200	2.8	2,684,415	4.4	68,364	19,344	87,708	2.87	3,142,581	4.6	3,561,424	4.7	5,794,646	5.3
World C (Christians)	6,550,000	86.2	35,359,600	94.2	54,664,800	90.1	1,376,320	-27,658	1,348,662	2.23	61,452,000	89.9	68,151,424	89.7	96,610,800	89.3
Country's population	**7,600,000**	**100.0**	**37,540,000**	**100.0**	**60,687,000**	**100.0**	**1,527,949**	**0**	**1,527,949**	**2.27**	**68,354,054**	**100.0**	**75,967,000**	**100.0**	**108,251,000**	**100.0**

COLUMNS, ROWS.
For meanings and definitions, see Codebook (Part 3). Note that, by definition, total 'Christians' = professing + crypto-Christians, which also = affiliated + unaffiliated Christians, and also = Great Commission Christians + latent Christians. Percentages may not always total exactly, due to rounding.

CENSUSES.
1939: 78.8% Roman Catholics, 10.0% Filipino indigenous (9.8% Aglipayans), 4.2% Muslims, 4.0% ethnoreligionists, 2.4% Protestants and Anglicans, 0.3% Buddhists, 0.1% Shintoists, 0.1% nonreligious, 0.1% Chinese folk-religionists. **1.X.1948:** 83.0% Roman Catholics, 8.0% Filipino indigenous (7.6% Aglipayans, 0.3% Iglesia ni Cristo), 4.1% Muslims, 2.2% Protestants, 1.8% ethnoreligionists, 0.5% other religionists, 0.2% Buddhists, 0.1% Anglicans. **15.II.1960:** 83.8% Roman Catholics, 6.7% Filipino indigenous (5.2% Aglipayans, 1.0% Iglesia ni Cristo), 4.9% Muslims, 2.7% Protestants, 1.3% ethnoreligionists, 0.2% Anglicans, 0.2% Chinese folk-religionists, 0.1% Buddhists, 0.1% nonreligious. **6.V.1970:** 85.0% Roman Catholics, 5.6% Filipino indigenous (3.9% Aglipayans, 1.3% Iglesia ni Cristo, 0.4% others), 4.3% Muslims, 3.1% Protestants, 0.1% Episcopalians, 0.1% Buddhists, 1.8% other religionists or nonreligious (0.9% ethnoreligionists). **1990:** 82.9% Roman Catholics, 5.5% Independents (2.6%Aglipayans, 2.3%Iglesia ni Cristo, 0.6% others), 4.6% Muslims, 5.2% Protestants, 0.58% marginal Christians, 0.2% Episcopalians, 0.04% Buddhists, 0.99 other religionists or nonreligious.

NOTES ON RELIGIONS
ATHEISTS. Communist Party of the Philippines (PKP) (illegal 1932, outlawed 1957) and several factions: (many in the New People's Army, People's Liberation Army (Huks), and Maoist New People's Army).
BAHA'IS. 1961, only 200 Baha'is in 40 centers, then rapid growth to 1,600 Baha'is in 182 centers within year, then from 150 local spiritual assemblies (1964) to 268 (1973), with 3,110 other isolated centers or groups. From 1967-72, 64 young Persian pioneers from Iran entered as students; by 1971, 3,100 students in 5 universities had become Baha'is. Over 4,000 were enrolled in 1973 in Baha'i correspondence courses. Many Baha'is are former Hindus.
BUDDHISTS. About 10% of all Chinese are Buddhists.
DOUBLY-AFFILIATED. The term covers those affiliated to, or claimed by, both the Roman Catholic Church and also a church termed or regarded as Evangelical by the state (Protestant, Aglipayan or other Filipino indigenous, Anglican, or marginal Christian), i.e. baptized Catholics who have recently become Evangelicals or others. Because their statistics represent a duplication, they are shown in the table as a negative quantity (with a minus sign).
ETHNORELIGIONISTS. Animists or shamanists among mountain tribes, especially the Ifugao (150,000), Igorot and Bontoc (17,000) of Luzon. Other pagan tribes and peoples: Apayao, Atta (1,800), Bagobo, Bukidnon, Dumagat (12,000), Gadang (37,000), Kalagan (138,000), Kalinga, Mandaya, Mangyan (22,000), Manobo (480,000), Negritos, Subanon, (66,000), Tagbanua (Palawan), Tboli (93,500), Tinggian, and Tiruray.
EVANGELICAL CATHOLICS. This term is used here to describe persons who are affiliated to churches termed or regarded by the state as Evangélica or Evangelical (Protestant, Aglipayan or other Filipino indigenous, Anglican, or marginal Christian churches), but who in government censuses are regarded as, or who profess publicly to be, Roman Catholics. Many Aglipayans regard themselves as Evangélica or Evangelical.
HINDUS. Increasing adherents of the Ananda Marga sect; and a neo-Hindu movement, the Theosophical Society. Many Hindus have become Baha'is.
INDEPENDENTS. After its founding in 1890, the Philippine Independent Church (PIC) numbered at its peak nearly half of all Roman Catholics in the Philippines. Since 1906, however, this Aglipayan segment with its splinter groups has declined rapidly with each successive decade. After 1960, other types of Filipino indigenous churches began to increase markedly, especially the Iglesia ni Cristo (INC). By 1995 there were over 330 such indigenous denominations (see Table 2), and the PIC itself was again increasing.
JEWS. With a synagogue in Manila.
MUSLIMS. All Sunnis (of the Shafiite rite); commonly termed Moros (Moors). Mainly in the south on Mindanao, Suly archipelago and Palawan. Of all Muslims, 96.0% belong to these predominantly-Muslim peoples: Sulu-Samal (875,000, including 525,000 Tau Sug), Magindanao (1,060,000), Maranao (960,000), Yakan (72,000), Sangir (11,000), Melebuganon, Bajau (Sea Gypsies). There is also an Ahmadiya Mission (Qadianis; enumerated here under Muslims though declared non-Muslim by Pakistan). Begun about 1950; Qadianis from Pakistan, mainly on Sulu and Mindanao (HQ Bongao, Sulu).*Hajj pilgrims to Mecca.* (1970) 150; (1974)

Continued opposite

Country Table 1–concluded

1,564; (1975) 1,154; (1976) 357.
NEW-RELIGIONISTS. Adherents of Asian syncretistic New Religions from China, Japan, Korea and Indonesia, including by 1995, 10,000 converts to the Japanese movement Nichiren Shoshu (Soka Gakkai).
OTHER RELIGIONISTS. Followers of numerous other smaller Western cults including Rosicrucians (1 AMORC center).
PENTECOSTALS/CHARISMATICS. The Catholic renewal began in 1972, with the first wave (from the USA) touching an estimated 10 million people.Totals (January 1974): 15,000 involved adults (over 15 years old), including 100 priests and 500 nuns, in over 200 prayer groups; total charismatic community including children, 30,000. In March 1978, 380 leaders attended a National Leaders Conference in Manila. By 1997, there were 2 million Catholics regularly attending 500 weekly prayer groups (or 175 covenant communities), with 500 priests and 30 bishops involved. The largest rally recently had over 1 million present; total Catholic Charismatics are estimated at 7 million.

Great Commission Instrument Panel: status of the Philippines (for explanation see start of Part 4)

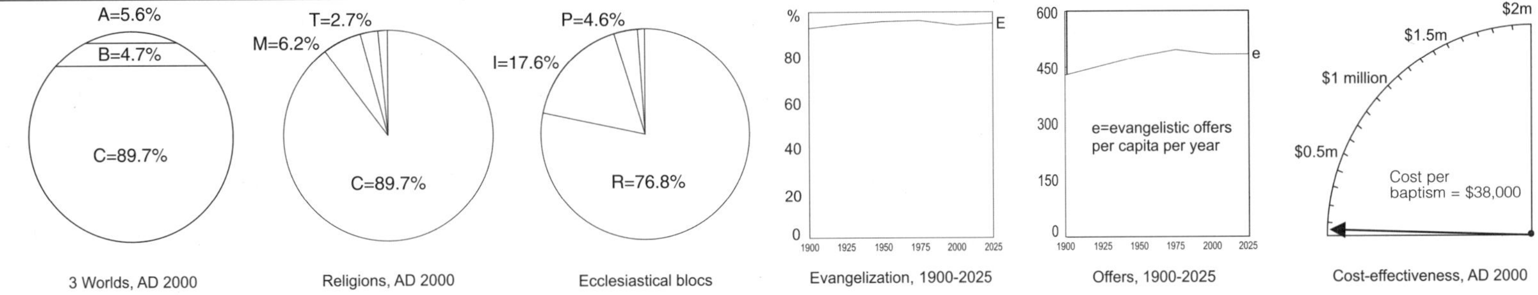

Country status. The Philippines comprises 7,107 islands between the Pacific Ocean and the South China Sea. Extending 1,000 miles north to south, it is the second largest archipelagic nation in the world. Luzon in the north and Mindanao in the south comprise 65% of the land area. Its chief products are timber, copper, and nickel.

HUMAN LIFE AND LIBERTY

Human need and development. The end of the Marcos dictatorship and the transition to a democratic society has not been smooth. It has brought about numerous changes in the economic structure, but not all of these changes have improved the living standards of the average Filipino. While the glaring income inequalities of the earlier era have disappeared, this has not meant a transfer of wealth to the less fortunate. About 80% of Filipinos live beneath the poverty level. Women in this group tend to suffer not only poverty but also the allied evils of incest, rape, prostitution, and exploitation. There is a growing scarcity of adequate housing. Squatter settlements are a blight in all major cities, but particularly in Manila. Developmental activities are concentrated in urban areas which also account for most commercial and industrial enterprises. Only a few of the barrios or villages have shared in this development. Rural areas, particularly in the outlying islands, have inferior health and sanitation services, educational facilities, and infrastructure. Lower levels of income in rural areas have also led to malnutrition. Steady progress in the health sector, which began with the US occupation in the early 20th century, has been maintained since independence. However, medical facilities are concentrated in the urban areas and reach only two-thirds of the population. Social Security was introduced in 1957 and covers all wage and salary workers.

Human rights and freedoms. The Philippines is a democratic country, but the state of insurgency that has prevailed for many decades provides the backdrop to a wide range of human rights abuses by the police. These abuses include extrajudicial killings, disappearances, arbitrary arrest, and torture. The label of insurgents is used very casually to include opponents of government, including labor union activists and civil rights attorneys. Generally, the campaign against guerrillas in remote areas is carried on with little regard to the value of life or property. Muslims and other smaller minorities suffer some discrimination in public life. Muslims prefer to educate their children in Islamic schools, which deprives them of many of the skills needed to advance in some occupations. Many of the disabilities suffered previously by women were removed by the Women in Development Act passed under president Aquino in 1992.

Human environment. Like other countries in Southeast Asia, the Philippines has suffered considerable environmental damage after World War II. One of the principal sources of this damage is deforestation as a result of indiscriminate logging. At the end of World War II, about one-half of the country was covered by forests. Within the next 40 years, this percentage has been reduced to one-fifth. Coastal degradation and silting has led to a deterioration of the marine environment. River systems near urban and industrial areas have suffered water pollution through the disposal of sewage and industrial wastes.

1980 Commemoration of 600 years of Islam in the Philippines.

NON-CHRISTIAN RELIGIONS

Islam was introduced in 1380 by Malay immigrants. Filipino Muslims are Sunnis of the Shafiite rite. They are commonly referred to as Moros (the Spanish word for Moor), but this term is not acceptable to most because of its negative connotations dating from the Spanish occupation of the islands. Filipino Muslims are concentrated in the relatively undeveloped islands of Mindanao, the Sulu archipelago and Palawan in the south of the nation. The Muslim population in 1995 was over 4 million. There are 9 different filipino linguistic groups professing Islam, all belonging to the Central Philippine subgroup and closely related to the major languages spoken by Filipinos, namely Tagalog and Cebuano. The following groups account for 92% of all Muslims: Magindanao, the largest group of Muslims in the country, living along the banks of Rio Grande de Cotabato, Mindanao; Maranao, of whom 90% live in the province of Lanao del Sur and 10% in Lanao del Norte, Mindanao; and Tau Sug, who occupy the archipelago and province of Sulu where Muslims constitute 95% of the total population. Other Muslim groups are the Samals, Bajaus and Yakan. The Bajaus, often called Sea Gypsies, are of Arab and Malay ancestry and live in southern Sulu; the Yakan of Basilan island are part Polynesian in origin. Other provinces with a Muslim minority are Zamboanga del Sur, Davao del Norte, Davao del Sur, and Davao Oriente. Ethnically, Filipino Muslims along with most other Filipinos are of Malaysian and Indonesian stock.

Muslims showed unyielding resistance to Spanish military domination and attempts at christianization and were not completely conquered by Spanish forces until 1876, nor were they ever integrated into Philippine political life. In 1938, the head of state, president Quezon, coined the mottos 'Land for the landless' and 'Go south, young man' and offered farms in the Muslim south to Christian Filipinos from the nation's more congested areas. Cotabato was first chosen for this settlement, and other areas in the south were opened to the influx of settlers beginning in 1939. With a pause during World War II, this influx has continued up to the present time. Although they had occupied the land for centuries, most Muslims lacked written titles for their property; consequently, many lost their land to thousands of new Christian settlers.

In 1970, the bitterness of Muslims on Mindanao broke out in armed revolt directed against both government and Christian colonists. The resulting civil war has spread to other predominantly Muslim regions and, aggravated by massive and indiscriminate military repression, has threatened to cause the secession of all Muslims from the Filipino state. The conflict has continued now since 1945 and has taken on new vitality recently as a result of the cultural awakening of the elite, more thorough training for Muslim religious leaders (imams) some of whom have studied abroad in Egypt and other countries, interference by president Quaddafi of Libya and recent increases in the numbers of Quranic schools and Muslim religious associations.

In certain regions, such as Sulu and Cotabato, the Muslim insurrection has lost its character as a religious conflict, either because it has the support of the Catholic clergy or because it is directed equally against the ruling Muslim class (the Datus) who hold vast properties and enjoy government support. In other areas, however, where the Ilagas (Catholic terrorists dedicated to hunting Muslims) carry on their savage activities, many bishops fear that Muslims will hold the Catholic Church responsible for atrocities committed against them. The government created a loan bank without interest and accepted the installation of a permanent delegation for the South from the Islamic Conference, the major Muslim political body with headquarters in Saudi Arabia, which would divide the aid and prepare plans for the development of those regions inhabited by Muslims.

The Far East regional office of the World Muslim Congress, with its headquarters in Pakistan, is located in Manila.

Traditional religions are still prevalent among the mountain dwellers dispersed throughout the nation, including the Bontoc, Gadang, Ifugao and Igorot of Luzon, Mangyan of Mindoro, Tagbanua of Palawan, and Atta, Manoboand Subanon of Mindanao. Tribal religion,with emphasis on magic, spirits and an originator supreme being, is followed by the nomadic Negritos who inhabit the wooded mountains of the smaller islands. The Kalinga of Northern Luzon, with a population of 100,000, are still headhunters, although a few have now become Christians. Their religion consists of 3 principal elements: (1) the work of the medium or shaman (Mangalisig) who is usually a woman and wears a turban; (2) belief in spirits (Anitos); and (3) a creator God (Kaboniyan). Traditionalists fell from 4% of the population in 1939 to 1.3% in 1060 and to 0.8% by 1975 but climbed over 2% in a resurgence of tribal identity in the 1980s. The influence of these religions persists however in popular Christianity.

Baha'i is steadily growing, from 40 centers in 1961 to several thousand by 1995. Agents in producing many conversions are Persian missionaries from Iran and extensive correspondence courses.

Other religions include Buddhism, Taoism and Confucianism, often mixed. There are also some Hindus and Jews.

Country summary. **Worlds A, B, C by ethnolinguistic peoples, cities, and major civil divisions in the Philippines.**

	PEOPLES							CITIES							CIVIL DIVISIONS						
World	*Num*	*Pop 2000*	*C%*	*Christians*	*E%*	*U%*	*Unevangelized*	*Num*	*Pop 2000*	*C%*	*Christians*	*E%*	*U%*	*Unevangelized*	*Num*	*Pop 2000*	*C%*	*Christians*	*E%*	*U%*	*Unevangelized*
A	91	5,977,584	1.81	108,423	37	63	3,761,670	7	1,416,357	25.67	363,585	33	67	950,178	0	0	0.00	0	0	0	0
B	34	1,477,268	30.63	452,442	72	28	410,022	4	1,060,337	49.60	525,924	64	36	380,911	1	2,237,517	35.00	783,131	57	43	967,279
C	58	68,511,650	96.39	66,039,203	100	0	51,097	40	19,449,000	87.83	17,081,257	95	5	949,485	15	73,728,982	89.27	65,816,926	96	4	3,255,507
Total	**183**	**75,966,502**	**87.67**	**66,600,068**	**94**	**6**	**4,222,789**	**51**	**21,925,694**	**81.96**	**17,970,766**	**90**	**10**	**2,280,574**	**16**	**75,966,499**	**87.67**	**66,600,057**	**94**	**6**	**4,222,786**

Upper. Stamp commemorating first resident missionaries, 1565. *Lower.* First mass in Limasawa, AD 1521.

CHRISTIANITY

CATHOLIC CHURCH. The explorer Magellan's world expedition brought the first priest to the Philippines in 1521, and the first Augustinian missionary arrived in 1565. Dominicans established the University of St Thomas in 1611 and Jesuits their first college in 1695. During the 17th and 19th centuries, the Philippines served as a base for missions to Japan, China, and Cambodia. For much of the 19th century, the church retained its Spanish character and discriminated against the few national priests. The latter participated in various revolutionary efforts, and 3 priests were shot in 1872. Following the war of 1898, 500 missionary priests were expelled and the church lost its favored position. From 1890 onwards, a leading Filipino priest, Gregorio Aglipay, with others rebelled against the continued failure to indigenize the Catholic Church and founded the Philippine Independent Church. The Catholic hierarchy was reorganized in 1907 and several new missionary congregations arrived for new work in mountainous regions. In 1905, the first Filipino bishop was consecrated, followed in 1934 by the first archbishop and in 1960 by the first cardinal.

The republic of the Philippines has the highest percentage of Catholics of all countries of Asia (84%). Nevertheless, traditional beliefs retain much of their vigor and give to the practice of Christianity the quality of a folk religion.

Several characteristics of the Catholic Church in the Philippines are similar to those found in Latin American countries. Its triumphalism, long autocratic tradition and social and theological conservatism have created for it an image which was widely criticized by the press and the student world prior to the promulgation of martial law in September 1972. The former cardinal-archbishop, Rufino J. Santos, who died in September 1973, became the principal focus of criticism and indeed the object of public demonstrations in the streets of the capital during 1969 and 1970.

The forces of change are, however, also at work, especially since 1965 when priests and lay persons began to become involved in social action. This movement consists essentially of groups not recognized by the majority of bishops and often in conflict with them. A number of Jesuits figure among the principal progressivist leaders of the church, which has led president Marcos to state that the Society of Jesus 'foments violent revolution' in the country. A new factor is the active involvement of several younger bishops in the committees of the Federation of Asian Bishops' Conferences (FABC), formed in Hong Kong in 1972, which may in the long run aid the Catholic Church in the Philippines to discover its Asian identity and to depart from the model of Western Christianity which has characterized it to date. It was with this in view that the Office for Human Development of the FABC was located in Manila.

The Holy See has diplomatic relations with the Philippines and in AD 2000 is represented to government and the Catholic hierarchy by a nuncio residing in Manila.

Top. **Philippine Independent Church.** Noticeboard for Manila cathedral; largest of Filipino indigenous denominations. *Below.* **Banner of the Race Church.** Catholic-type hierarchy of Iglesia Watawat ng Lahi (a Rizalist spiritist body with 50,000 members) in front of their church in Calamba, Laguna.

INDIGENOUS CHURCHES. In 1840, the first peasant protest movement against Spanish Catholicism took place, with the formation of an independent brotherhood, the Confraternity of St Joseph. It won thousands of followers in Tayabas, Laguna, and Batangas before the leader, known as king of the Tagalogs, was captured and executed in 1841. Subsequently, many similar movements of religious protest and independence have arisen, most becoming institutionalized as independent churches. By 1995, there were over 500 such denominations begun by Filipinos in the Philippines, as well as some pseudo-Christian groups which mix Christian, tribal, and nationalistic traditions, including cults deifying the nationalist leader Jose Rizal, who was executed in 1896.

The largest of these churches is the Philippine Independent Church which was founded in 1890 and organized in 1902 by a Catholic priest Gregorio Aglipay and a nationalist leader Isabelo de Los Reyes. The PIC attracted a vast following in its early years, including many priests and nearly 50% of the entire Catholic community. However, when the Supreme Court in 1906 ordered the return of all Catholic properties appropriated by the PIC, peoples' attachment to their parish churches resulted in large numbers returning to Catholicism. The PIC went into decline with only a few poorly trained clergy, no funds, inadequate buildings and a liturgy and dogma which became increasingly unitarian and rationalist. Following the death of its 2 founders in the late 1930s, a new Declaration of Faith and Articles of Religion were prepared and arrangements made for the consecration of bishops by the Philippine Episcopal Church (Anglican) in 1948. Priests are now trained in the Episcopalian seminary, and in 1961, the 2 churches entered into full communion with each other. As with other churches, the PIC has experienced a series of schisms, several of which arose from its new direction in 1948. While over the years it declined in influence from 14% of the population in 1918 to 7% in 1948 and to 6% in 1960, it is now experiencing rapid growth and has nearly 5 million members.

The Church of Christ (Iglesia ni Cristo), which also has a larger membership than any mission-founded Protestant church, was begun by Felix Manalo, a Catholic who entered and left several other churches before declaring that he had been divinely appointed to revive the original Christian church, outside of which there is no salvation. Its aggressive nationalistic emphasis, authoritarian organization and all-Filipino leadership have attracted many followers, who form a major force in politics by practicing block voting in government elections. The church now has 8,400 congregations. Other important indigenous churches include Crusaders of the Divine Church of Christ.

Church of Christ (Manalista). Second largest Filipino indigenous church (1.5 million members), organized like an army, with some ministers carrying revolvers. *Above.* One of its 35 cathedrals, in Manila. *Below.* Executive Minister (and son of 1913 founder), Brother Eraño G. Manalo (centre), greets and blesses followers after packed church service in House of Worship, Moriones (Tondo, Manila), before he drives off.

PROTESTANT CHURCHES. American Protestant missionaries entered the Philippines following its annexation by the USA in 1898. The first Presbyterian began in 1899, founding the well-known Silliman University in 1901. Presbyterians early involved themselves in ecumenical dialogue with other churches and jointly formed, with Congregationalists, the United Evangelical Church in 1929. This church in turn became part of the United Church of Christ in the Philippines in 1948.

American Methodists arrived in 1899, and the first annual conference was held in 1908. Schisms took place in the Methodist Church in 1905, 1909 and 1933, the result in part of the Filipino desire for independence which was frustrated by American rule. The first Filipino Methodist bishop was elected in 1944, and all key administrative positions are now held by nationals. Methodists continue their heavy involvement in education, medicine, social service, and agricultural development. Among their many institutions are a large hospital in Manila and a school of nursing.

American Baptists entered in 1900 for work on the islands of Panay and Negros. They opened several hospitals, completed translation of the Bible in Panayan Visayan and began an industrial center which later became the Central Philippine University. The Convention of Philippine Baptist Churches was organized in 1935 and now has over 1,000 full-time workers.

Disciples of Christ sent missionaries in 1901 to work in northern Luzon. In 1943, their church joined with the United Brethren to form the Evangelical Church which in 1948 joined the United Church of Christ. Churches established by missionaries of the American Board also became part of the United Church in 1948.

Entering in 1902, the Christian and Missionary Alliance grew into an autonomous church in 1947 and in 1995 had 1,600 congregations, preaching in 30 dialects. It has a publishing center and is also involved in radio.

Seventh-day Adventists have since 1906 built up the largest Protestant church membership. They continue to sponsor a large number of secondary schools and hospitals, in addition to having more than 2,400 churches.

Pentecostals are also active, the largest group at present being the Assemblies of God, which began with the return of Filipino converts from the U.S.A. in the 1920s; there are now over 1,500 national workers.

The United Church of Christ came into being in 1948 as a reorganization of a union of evangelical churches created during the Japanese occupation. Participating churches included the United Evangelical Church, the independent Philippine Methodist Church, and the Evangelical Church.

A large number of other small mostly American missions work in the Philippines, the majority of which have made their appearance since World War II. There are now several times as many foreign missionaries serving nonecumenical churches in the Philippines as those serving ecumenical churches. This represents a clear reversal of the distribution prior to World War II. Comity lines have broken down with the influx of new missions and shifting populations, and no common strategy for the location of new work has been developed among Evangelicals. On the other hand, these new bodies have contributed to Protestant growth which has been extremely rapid since 1948.

ANGLICAN CHURCH. The Episcopal Church in the USA sent its first missionaries to the Philippines in 1902, directing their attention to unchurched and minority groups such as Chinese in greater Manila, tribal groups in northern Luzon and tribal people and Muslims in western Mindanao and Sulu. The Philippine Episcopal Church continues to maintain elementary and secondary schools, hospitals and St Andrew's Seminary. The first Filipino bishop was consecrated in 1967, and 80% of his clergy are nationals. From 1945-61, the number of Filipino clergy increased from 3 to 48 and the number of baptized members more than doubled. In 1961, the church entered into full communion with the Philippine Independent Church.

Renewal movements. In the 1990s the Pentecostal/Charismatic Renewal continued to spread rapidly across most older churches, and numbered over 20,050,000 adherents (of whom 4% Pentecostals, 58% Charismatics, and 38% Independents).

Church of Jesus Christ of Latter-day Saints. A Filipino Mormon family.

Indigenous missions. Filipino Christians have been involved in outreach to the Pacific Islands and Asia since Christianity was introduced there in the 16th century. In the middle part of the nineteenth century Roman Catholic missionaries were sent out by the hundreds. More recently, Protestants have also begun to send significant numbers of Filipino Christians as missionaries. In addition, large numbers work as home missionaries, many cross-culturally.

28th Seekers Conference, Unida Center, Carite, 1990, designed to appeal to non-Christians.

CHURCH AND STATE

Separation of church and state in the Philippines coincides with the beginning of American rule, as delineated in the Treaty of Paris of December 1898. It is stated as follows in the constitution of January 1973: 'The separation of Church and State shall be inviolable' (Article XV, section 15). According to the constitution, the state guarantees freedom of religion and worship 'without discrimination or preference' (Article IV, section 8) and it also affords protection in employment and ensures equal work opportunities for all regardless of sex, race or creed (Article II, section 9). No public money or property may be paid to or used by any religious institution or any priest, minister or other religious teacher, except clergy assigned to armed forces, penal institutions, government orphanages or leprosaria (Article VIII, section 18, 2). The property of churches, mosques, non-profit cemeteries and other charitable institutions is exempt from taxation (Article VIII, section 17, 3), and this includes denominationally owned institutions such as radio and TV stations. An exception to this is the recent requirement that private and confessional schools must now pay taxes. Finally, the constitution stipulates that 'At the option expressed in writing by the parents or guardians and without cost to them and the government, religion shall be taught to their children or wards in public elementary and high schools as may be provided by law' (Article XV, section 8, 8). This religious education, the sanction for which came from the former constitution of 1935, was approved by vote of parliament in 1965.

Being the only predominantly Christian country in Asia, the Philippines has always tended towards a loose interpretation of the separation of church and state. Consequently, the preamble of the new constitution begins with this invocation: 'We, the sovereign Filipino people, imploring the aid of the Divine Providence . . . .'One result of this religious milieu is that seminarians in San Jose Major Seminary, who are enrolled in four-year courses at Ateneo University, are exempt from military training, although all able-bodied male citizens are required by law to follow a two-year basic course in the Reserve Officers' Training Corps.

The influence of the Catholic Church remains preponderant. On the one hand, the government hesitates to oppose the hierarchy openly in such fields as divorce and birth control; on the other hand, the Catholic Church has successfully expressed opposition to several proposed laws of a nationalistic character, including the proposal in 1956 to make compulsory in schools the study of the 2 principal literary works of Jose Rizal, 'The Father of the Nation' who was executed in 1896. Catholics opposed this because Rizal had often attacked the church. They also opposed the proposal of a Catholic senator who in 1958 wished to place Filipinos as heads of all Catholic schools run by foreign missionaries. On this subject, the constitution of 1973 states that 'Educational institutions other than those established by religious orders and mission boards shall be owned solely by citizens of the Philippines' (Article XV, section 8, 8).

By virtue of the separation of church and state, there is no governmental department in charge of religious or ecclesiastical affairs. According to Section 154 of the Corporation Law, Action 1459, as amended on 1 April 1906, for the administration of the temporal affairs of any religious denomination or church and the management of the estates and properties thereof, it is lawful for the bishop, chief priest or other leader to become a corporation in himself. According to Section 155, for purposes of affording public notice of the existence of such a corporation, the head of the religious body must file with the government's Securities and Exchange Commission articles of incorporation setting forth the facts required by law. Further, in order to be legally permitted to solemnize marriages, priests, ministers, and rabbis must register their names with the National Library.

Brisk business is done in selling print and cassette scriptures at Bible House, Manila.

BROADCASTING AND MEDIA

The Philippines is a member of UNDA, and there are 36 local Catholic AM and FM stations, along with 3 TV stations, they comprise the Philippines Federation of Catholic Broadcasters.

Several local radio stations carry Christian programming, including *Back to the Bible* and IBRA programs (Burmese, Khmer, Mandarin), particularly in the late evenings.

FEBC maintains several shortwave radio transmitters which blanket the islands and transmit to several other Asian nations. Shortwave programming can also be received from other transmitters in Eastern Asia, including TWR (Guam), as well as shortwave transmitters in other parts of the world (KNLS). AWR operates 3 studios: Manila (Tagalog), Cagayan de Ora (Ilonggo), and Cebu City (Cebuano).

Radio Veritas is a powerful shortwave Catholic transmitter covering nearly all of Asia, broadcasting in 15 languages with a two-fold mission of evangelism and development.

Christian television programming is also readily available. There are 3 local Catholic TV stations. CBN's *700 Club, International 700 Club* and *Superbook* programs can be seen every day throughout the country. A third of the country has seen the 'Jesus' Film: some 29 million, most of whom watched it on television. TBN programs appear in Zamboanga on Destiny Cable. Broadcasts are also available via satellite.

INTERDENOMINATIONAL ORGANIZATIONS

The National Council of Churches in the Philippines (NCCP), founded in 1963, evolved out of 4 previous changes in the original Evangelical union of 1901, Filipino leaders assuming greater control with each change in name and structure. The NCCP has as members 9 churches and 4 associate organizations. There is also an Inter-Church Commission on Medical Care and an Association of Christian Schools and Colleges, the latter being affiliated with the NCCP. Two other more conservative councils are the Philippine Council of Evangelical Churches (PCEC) and the Philippine Council of Fundamental Evangelical Churches.

The John XXIII Ecumenical Center (JEC) was founded in 1968 and functions as the permanent secretariat of the Roman Catholic Bishops' Commission for Promoting Christian Unity (BCPCU) and deals directly with the NCCP in all joint ecumenical endeavors. This service center also promotes ecumenical study and research through the training of personnel who teach ecumenical subjects and are involved in ecumenical activities and also by theological and pastoral reflection on those problems which are of interest to the ecumenical movement in general and to the Philippine situation in particular.

The Cardinal Bea Institute for Ecumenical Studies (CBI), founded by Jesuits in 1968, is involved in research, dialogue, and ecumenical training in connection with the Ateneo de Manila University. The CBI shares the same offices and personnel as the JEC. As a research center, it provides materials and personnel for both the Philippines and also southeast Asia. Special emphasis is given to doctrinal and theological questions.

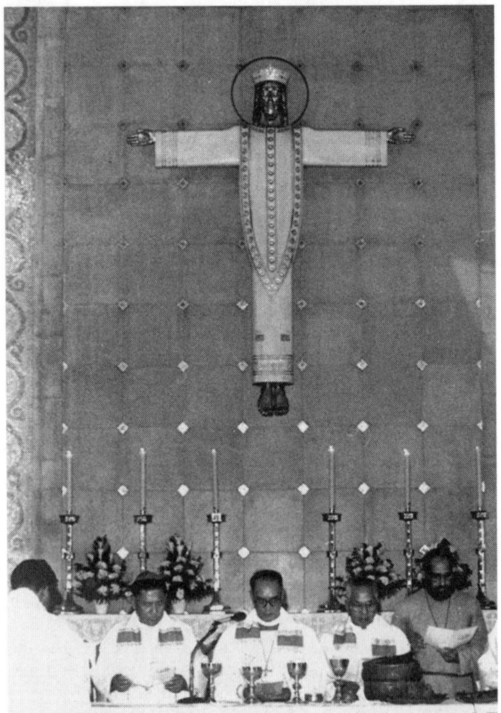

Ecumenical service in Manila celebrating 25 years of National Council of Churches in the Philippines.

The Interchurch committee on Urban Squatter Resettlement (ICUSR) was founded in 1969 by Catholic, Independent, and Protestant leaders. The ICUSR is a cooperative agency which complements and strengthens the government program to resettle squatters and ameliorate the living conditions of slum dwellers in greater Manila.

FUTURE TRENDS AND PROSPECTS

Ethnoreligionists are now projected to remain at about 2.5% of the population through 2025 while Islam is expected to grow from 4.1% in 1970 to 6.5% by 2025.

Christianity would then drop to less than 85% of the population around AD 2050. Islam and the nonreligious are both expected to grow well into the 21st century, jointly reaching 10% early in that period.

BIBLIOGRAPHY

1983 Catholic directory of the Philippines. P. S. de Achutegui (ed). Manila: Catholic Bishops Conference of the Philippines, 1983. 857p.

'A Christian response to Philippine liberation movements.' A. San Pedro Agtarap. Ph.D. dissertation, Fuller Theological Seminary, Pasadena, CA, 1991. 304p.

A history of Christianity in the Philippines: the initial encounter. T. V. Sitoy Jr. Quezon City, Philippines: New Day, 1985. 384p.

'A study of the Iglesia Ni Cristo: a political–religious sect in the Philippines,' H. Ando, *Pacific affairs*, 42, 3 (1969), 334–45.

'An analysis of growth among Southern Baptist churches on Mindanao, Philippines, 1951–1985.' J. M. Terry. Ph.D. dissertation, Southwestern Baptist Theological Seminary, Fort Worth, TX, 1986. 264p.

Awakening to mission: the Philippine Catholic church, 1965–1981. P. T. Giordano. Quezon City, Philippines: New Day, 1988. 391p.

Catholic directory of the Philippines, 1971. Manila: Catholic Trade School, 1971.

Christ in the Philippines. L. N. Mercado. Tacloban City, Philippines: Divine Word University, 1982. 128p.

Church persecution in the Philippines. P. Geremia. Davao City, Philippines: Philippine International Forum, [1988]. 8p.

Church profiles: basic information on member churches and associate members. Quezon City, Philippines: National Council of Churches in the Philippines, Research and Documentation Office, [1989]. 75p.

Church truly alive: journey to the Filipino revolution. J. H. Kroeger. 2nd ed. Davao City, Philippines: Mission Studies Institute, 1988. 68p.

Churches and sects in the Philippines: a descriptive study of contemporary religious group movements. D. J. Elwood. Dumaguete City, Philippines: Silliman University, 1968. 213p.

Contextual evangelization in the Philippines: a Filipino Franciscan experience. O. A. Ante. Kampen: Kok, 1991. 204p.

'Developing Christian men for leadership in evangelism and church growth in the Philippine context.' T. M. Pajaron. D.Miss. thesis, Western Conservative Baptist Seminary, Denver, CO, 1992. 251p.

Filipino religious psychology. L. N. Mercado (ed). Tacloban City, Philippines: Divine World University Publications, 1977. 224p.

Folk Christianity: a preliminary study of conversion and patterning of Christian experience in the Philippines. F. L. Jocano. Quezon City, Philippines: Trinity Research Institute, Trinity College of Quezon City, 1981. 122p.

History of the Church in the Philippines (1521–1898). P. Fernandez. *Orientalia Dominicana Philippines*, no. 8. Manila: Life Today Publications, 1988. 468p.

'Iglesia ni Cristo: an angel and his church,' A. L. Tuggy, in *Dynamic religious movements*, p.85–101. D. J. Hesselgrave (ed). Grand Rapids, MI: Baker, 1978.

Islands under the Cross: the story of the church in the Philippines. P. G. Gowing. Manila: National Council of Churches in the Philippines, 1967. 286p.

'Kamuning, Philippines—an urban church–planting model,' F. W. Allen, *Urban mission*, 6, 2 (November 1988), 56–60.

Muslim Filipinos: heritage and horizon. P. G. Gowing. Quezon City, Philippines: New Day, 1979. 285p.

Nationalism and Christianity in the Philippines. R. L. Deats. Dallas: Southern Methodist University Press, 1967.

New Testament fire in the Philippines. J. H. Montgomery. Manila: Church Growth Research in the Philippines, 1972. 209p. (On Pentecostal growth).

Philippine church history. C. Sabado. Manila: Salesiana, 1990. 178p.

Philippine ethnography: a critically annotated and selected bibliography. S. Saito. *East–West bibliographic series*, no. 2. Honolulu, HI: University Press of Hawaii, 1972. 512p.

Philippines. J. Richardson. *World bibliographical series*, vol. 106. Oxford, UK: CLIO Press, 1989. 402p. (See especially 'Religion,' p.123–36).

Protestant missionaries in the Philippines, 1898–1916: an inquiry into the American colonial mentality. K. J. Clymer. Urbana and Chicago: University of Illinois Press, 1986. 281p.

Readings in Philippine church history. J. N. Schumacher. Quezon City, Philippines: Loyola School of Theology, Ateneo de Manila University, 1979. 428p.

Religion and nationalism in Southeast Asia: Burma, Indonesia, the Philippines. F. R. Von der Mehden. Madison, WI: University of Wisconsin Press, 1963. 253p.

Religion and society among the Tagbanuwa of Palawan Island, Philippines. R. B. Fox. *Monograph series*, no. 9. Manila: National Museum, 1982. 262p.

Revolt in Mindanao: the rise of Islam. T. J. S. George. Leiden: E. J. Brill, 1980. 290p.

Sacrifice and sharing in the Philippine highlands: religion and society among the Buid of Mindoro. T. Gibson. *London School of Economics monographs in social anthropology*, no. 57. London: Athlone, 1986. 262p.

'Some theological aspects of Roman Catholic responses to lowland Filipino spirit–world beliefs.' D. J. Schneider. Thesis, Concordia Lutheran Seminary, St. Louis, MO, 1971.

Split–level Christianity and Christian renewal of Philippine values. J. C. Bulatao & V. R. Gorospe. Quezon City, Philippines: Ateneo de Manila University Press, 1966.

Studies in Philippines church history. G. H. Anderson. Ithaca, NY: Cornell University Press, 1969. 421p.

'Syncretism in Philippine Catholicism: its historical causes,' J. N. Schumacher, *Philippine studies*, 32 (3rd quarter, 1984), 251–72.

The Catholic Church in the Philippines today. I. Alonso et al. Manila: Bookmark (Historical Conservation Society), 1968. 139p.

The contemporary Muslim movement in the Philippines. C. A. Majul. Berkeley, CA: Mizan Press, 1985. 162p.

The discipling of a nation. J. H. Montgomery & D. A. McGavran. [Santa Clara, CA]: Global Church Growth Bulletin, 1980. 175p.

'The effects of missionization on cultural identity in two societies,' D. T. Hughes, in *Missionaries and anthropologists*, p.167–82. F. Salamone (ed). *Studies in Third World societies*, no. 26. Williamsburg, VA: College of William and Mary, 1985. (Deals with Philippines and Ponape).

'The Filipino spirit world: in–church or out–of–church?' R. L. Henry. Th.M. thesis, Fuller Theological Seminary, Pasadena, CA, 1984. 118p.

The Iglesia ni Kristo: its Christology and ecclesiology. F. G. Elesterio. *Cardinal Bea studies*, no. 5. Quezon City, Philippines: Cardinal Bea Institute, Loyola School of Theology, Ateneo de Manila University, 1977. 217p.

'The Iglesia Watawat ng Lahi: an anthropological study of a social movement in the Philippines.' P. R. Covar. Ph.D. dissertation, University of Arizona, 1975. 162p.

The J.I.L. love story: the church without a roof. M. Wourms. El Cajon, CA: Christian Services Publishing, 1992. 224p. (History of the Jesus Is Lord Fellowship).

The Philippine Church and evangelization, 1965–1984. J. H. Kroeger. Rome: Pontifical Gregorian University, 1985. 595p.

The Philippine church: growth in a changing society. A. L. Tuggy. Grand Rapids, MI: Eerdmans. 191p.

'The Philippine Iglesia ni Cristo: a study in independent church dynamics.' A. L. Tuggy. Ph.D. dissertation, Fuller Theological Seminary, Pasadena, CA, 1974.

'The Philippines: autonomy for the Muslims,' L. G. Noble, in *Islam in Asia: religion, politics, & society*, p.97–124. J. L. Esposito (ed). New York: Oxford University Press, 1987.

'The Sapilada religion: reformation and accommodation among the Igorots of Northern Luzon,' F. Eggan & A. Pacyaya, *Southwestern journal of anthropology*, 18, 2 (1962).

'The spread of fire: a study of ten growing churches in Metro–Manila.' O. C. Baldemor. Th.M. thesis, Fuller Theological Seminary, Pasadena , CA, 1990. 178p.

The story of Methodism in the Philippines. R. L. Deats. Manila: National Council of Churches in the Philippines for Union Theological Seminary, 1964. 129p.

Theological themes for the Philippine church. A. Dominguez & E. Dominguez. Quezon City, Philippines: New Day, 1989. 268p.

'Toward an urban strategy for Mindanao, Philippines,' M. Shelley, *Urban mission*, 4, 5 (May 1987), 21–31.

Country Table 2. **Organized churches and denominations in the Philippines.**

Official name (bold type = church with over 10% of affiliated) 1	*Begun* 2	*Type* 3	*Counc* 4	*Congs* 5	*Adults* 6	*Affiliated 1970* 7	*Affiliated 1995* 8	*G%* 9	*Names, notes, and other statistics* (see Codebook, Part 3) 10
Advent Christian Church	1953	P-Adv	xF...	30	1,500	2,000	3,500	2.26	M=AAM(ACC)(USA). HQ Lagonglong, Misamis Oriental. 11f,1s.
Alaph Divine Temple		I-mar	.....	150	35,000	90,000	70,000	0.05	*Alaph Catolico Filipino.* Split ex RCC. HQ Sagay, Negros Occidental. 1p.
Alpha & Omega Christian Church	1966	I-3pF	.....	100	1,000	1,000	3,000	4.49	M=AOCC(Honolulu,USA). Churches in Ilocos Norte (Luzon). 6n,1s(40),W=75%,180Y.
Anchor Bay Evangelistic Assoc of the P	1955	I-3pW	.....	115	2,300	3,600	4,600	0.99	M=ABEA(USA). Fundamentalists. HQ Kabacan, Cotabato. 2p,2s.
Apostolic Church of God Christians	1964	I-3oF	.....	30	1,000	1,421	3,000	3.03	HQ Initao, Misamis Oriental. Indigenous. 20n,W=80%,1010Y,200z.
Apostolic Door of Faith	1965	I-3aF	.....	15	600	500	1,000	2.81	Indigenous pentecostals. All members Ilocanos. 6n,1p,W=25%,80Y.
Apostolic Faith Mission	1962	P-Pe3	x....	50	1,000	1,000	3,000	4.49	M=AFM(Portland,Oregon,USA). HQ Cabanatuan City. 4n,W=60%,64Y,40z.
Apostolic Independent Missions	c1980	I-3oF	.....	200	15,000	–	30,000	6.67	Indigenous group of Oneness theology
Assemblies of Christians	1956	I-Non	.....	20	1,600	2,000	2,500	0.90	Independent groups with no central organization. HQ Rosales, Pangasinan.
Assemblies of God	1926	P-Pe2	ZF...	1,900	230,845	87,100	297,840	5.04	*Philippine General Council.* M=AoG(USA). Rapid growth. 621n,47f,6s(255).
Assemblies of the Lord Jesus Christ	1949	I-3oF	x....	15	1,000	800	2,000	3.73	M=COLJCAF(USA) Black pentecostals. In central Luzon. 17n,1p,W=80%,506Y,100z.

Continued opposite

Country Table 2–continued

Official name (bold type = church with over 10% of all affiliated) 1	*Begun* 2	*Type* 3	*Counc* 4	*Congs* 5	*Adults* 6	*Affiliated 1970* 7	*Affiliated 1995* 8	*G%* 9	*Names, notes, and other statistics (see Codebook, Part 3)* 10
Assembly Hall Churches	c1940	I-3nC	.....	700	60,000	20,000	200,000	9.65	*Local Churches. Little Flock.* Chinese. Begun 1922 in China.
A of BC in Luzon, Visayas, Mindanao	1965	P-Bap	.TT.T	92	14,000	30,000	34,100	0.51	*A of BC=Association of Baptist Chs. ABCLVM.* Rapidly-growing church-planting body.
Assoc of Bible Chs of the Philippines	1951	P-Non	xM..E	232	15,000	2,000	37,500	12.44	ABCOP. M=OMF(formerly CIM). HQ Calapan, Oriental Mindoro: also Manila. 51f,1s.
Assoc of Fundamental Baptist Chs in P	1927	P-Fun	xTT.T	817	47,000	12,100	58,800	6.53	*Doane Baptists.* M=ABWE(Regular Baptists) (USA). Growing very rapidly. 76f,3h,2s.
Banner of the Race Church	1936	I-Lib	.....	100	35,000	50,000	70,000	1.35	*Iglesia Watawat ng Lahi.* Ex RCC. Catholic-type hierarchy. Rizalist, spiritist.
Baptist Bible Fellowship of the P	1950	I-Bap	x.T.T	100	7,000	10,000	16,000	1.90	Fundamentalist Baptists. M=BBFI(USA). HQ Manila. 38f,6s.
Baptist General Conference of the P	1949	P-Bap	TF..E	172	10,315	2,250	22,500	9.65	M=BGCA(USA). HQ Cebu. Cebuano. 10n,13x,26f,1s(30),W=65%,210Y,150z.
Baptist International Churches	c1970	I-Bap	.....	110	10,000	–	16,700	47.54	M=BIM(USA). Fundamentalist Baptists.
Believers in Christ	1957	I-Non	.....	100	2,000	2,000	3,000	1.64	HQ Tondo, Manila. Small local grouping of independents.
Bethel Temples	1952	P-Pe2	.....	20	6,000	7,000	12,000	2.18	M=Lester Sumrall Evangelistic Association(USA), formerly World Temples. Manila
Bible Holiness Movement	1960	P-Hol	x....	12	400	800	1,200	1.64	M=Bible Holiness Movement (Canada). Body with holiness doctrines. 6n,W=99%.
Bible Missionary Church	1978	P-Hol	.....	6	300	–	667	5.88	M=BMC(USA).
Bumila Fellowship of Baptist Churches	1951	P-Bap	.....	40	500	800	1,300	1.96	M=International Missions(USA). On Mindanao. 4n,W=75%,32Y,30z.
Catholic Church in the Philippines:	1521	R-Lat	B.F.R	7,851	30,030,200	30,860,093	56,553,712	2.45	*Iglesia Catolica.* C=34+3+66. 3799n 1964x 245m 8728w1776476Yy
M Cáceres	1595	R-Lat	Bs	903	486,000	1,086,739	919,068	-0.67	SLuzon. Rural, poor. Strongly Catholic. M=OP. 1s. 108n 8x 43m 106w 26883Yy
D Daet	1974	R-Lat	Bs	20	219,000	–	421,000	4.76	In Camarines Norte. 28n 2x 2m 21w 13000Yy
D Legazpi	1951	R-Lat	Bs	42	493,000	789,610	937,066	0.69	SLuzon. Densely populated. Many priests vocations. 78n 19x 22m 104w 244675Yy
D Masbate	1968	R-Lat	Bs	373	299,000	434,652	548,516	0.94	An island. Poor (including priests) exploited. 37n 9x 0m 21w 21583Yy
D Sorsogón	1951	R-Lat	Bs	26	361,000	391,560	541,056	1.30	Southern end of Luzon. Poor, especially priests. 58n 7x 7m 81w 14197
D Virac	1974	R-Lat	Bs	17	112,000	–	182,090	4.76	Recent diocese in Catanduanes. 27n 1x 2m 7w 6265Yy
PN Libmanan	1989	R-Lat	Bs	17	210,000	–	397,451	16.67	In Camarines Sur. 24n 0x 0m 11w 13587Yy
M Cagayán de Oro	1933	R-Lat	Bs	118	475,000	484,038	735,133	1.69	NMindanao. Catholics from Visayan islands. 1s. 56n 40x 42m 180w 8574Yy
D Butuan	1967	R-Lat	Bs	32	398,000	421,705	729,763	2.22	Mindanao. Recent Visayan Christian immigrants. 40n 19x 20m 40w 22710Yy
D Malaybalay	1969	R-Lat	Bs	39	408,000	357,659	884,722	3.69	Primitive pagans in interior of Bukidnon. M=SJ. 40n 12x 26m 88w 24381Yy
D Surigao	1939	R-Lat	Bs	34	209,000	425,000	399,465	-0.25	Mindanao, coast. Visayan immigrants. M=SVD,MSC. 20n 25x 29m 39w 7070Yy
D Tandag	1978	R-Lat	Bs	21	217,000	–	378,301	5.88	M=CSSR. 19n 5x 5m 25w 2780Yy
M Capiz	1951	R-Lat	Bs	26	341,000	759,644	626,700	-0.77	MPanay. Developed farms. Many priest vocations. 71n 0x 0m 96w 15905Yy
D Kalibo	1976	R-Lat	Bs	22	193,000	–	364,000	5.26	In Aklan. 36n 0x 1m 46w 9759Yy
D Romblon	1974	R-Lat	Bs	236	108,000	–	182,567	4.76	Area is 75% Roman Catholics. 28n 1x 1m 3w 4597Yy
M Cebú	1595	R-Lat	Bs	124	1,352,000	1,828,759	2,561,265	1.36	M Cebú (Nominis Iesu) Cradle of Christianity. 1s. 225n 175x 362m 675w 63400Yy
D Dumaguete	1955	R-Lat	Bs	43	405,000	833,581	799,312	-0.17	Eastern Negros is. Developed; rich-poor cleavage. 70n 10x 10m 75w 19457Yy
D Maasin	1968	R-Lat	Bs	32	284,000	379,000	544,702	1.46	SLeyte. Poor, very religious (site of first mass). 42n 0x 0m 124w 10632Yy
D Tagbilaran	1941	R-Lat	Bs	38	220,000	620,718	404,453	-1.70	Bohol Island. Strongly religious. 80n 0x 0m 65w 10600Yy
D Talibon	1986	R-Lat	Bs	23	229,000	–	410,994	11.11	Recent diocese, in Bohol. 42n 0x 1m 35w 14548Yy
M Cotabato	1950	R-Lat	Bs	32	406,000	648,714	874,652	1.20	Southwest Mindanao. Strong Muslims. M=OMI. 23n 36x 66m 121w 16807Yy
D Kidapawan	1976	R-Lat	Bs	18	167,000	–	356,822	5.26	Recently opened, in North Cotabato. 14n 12x 19m 38w 5771Yy
D Marbel	1960	R-Lat	Bs	24	517,000	389,790	993,050	3.81	Catholic immigrants from Luzon, Visayas. M=CD. 41n 13x 31m 70w 18584Yy
M Davao	1949	R-Lat	Bs	26	451,000	827,249	851,076	0.11	SMindanao. Catholic immigrants from Luzon. 1s. 50n 57x 126m 349w 10000Yy
D Digos	1979	R-Lat	Bpme	15	320,000	–	902,743	6.25	M=PME. 29n 16x 18m 47w 17045Yy
D Mati	1984	R-Lat	Bs	12	191,000	–	387,291	9.09	Recent diocese. 72% Roman Catholic. 21n 3x 3m 50w 8017Yy
D Tagum	1962	R-Lat	Bs	25	484,000	565,000	887,120	1.82	East Mindanao. Muslims. Catholic immigrants. 47n 2x 7m 67w 19700Yy
M Jaro	1865	R-Lat	Bs	79	913,000	1,033,934	1,708,094	2.03	SPanay. Mostly very poor. Original RC centre. 1s. 149n 51x 84m 367w 27121Yy
D Bacolod	1932	R-Lat	Bs	827	521,000	1,134,637	984,740	-0.57	NNegros. Social unrest due to sugar magnates. 1s. 69n 51x 137m 124w 24709Yy
D Kabankalan	1987	R-Lat	Bs	27	329,000	–	615,795	12.50	Recently opened, in Negros Occidental. 27n 16x 17m 22w 15427Yy
D San Carlos	1987	R-Lat	Bs	25	412,000	–	807,254	12.50	Negros Occidental. 31n 14x 57m 30w 21264Yy
D San José de Antique	1962	R-Lat	Bs	24	168,000	211,820	286,097	1.21	Many sects due to lengthy shortage of priests. 26n 13x 19m 84w 8128Yy
M Lingayen-Dagupan	1928	R-Lat	Bs	26	475,000	1,110,244	852,000	-1.05	CLuzon. Rural prosperity. Many Protestants. M=SVD. 66n 12x 19m 30w 35281Yy
D Alaminos	1985	R-Lat	Bs	19	201,000	–	349,400	10.00	In Pangasinan. 13n 7x 7m 44w 6076Yy
D Cabanatuan	1963	R-Lat	Bs	25	423,000	679,120	826,801	0.79	CLuzon. Prosperity and poverty. Little religiosity. 33n 0x 0m 50w 24847Yy
D San Fernando de la Unión	1970	R-Lat	Bs	26	200,000	328,000	489,220	1.61	NWCLuzon. Hocan-speaking. Emigration. 36n 7x 7m 22w 8504Yy
D San Jose	1984	R-Lat	Bs	16	283,000	–	476,748	9.09	M=SDB. 11n 8x 8m 20w 8651Yy
D Urdaneta	1985	R-Lat	Bs	21	290,000	–	531,970	10.00	In Pangasinan. 36n 6x 50m 20w 9558Yy
M Lipa	1910	R-Lat	Bs	50	904,000	888,247	1,664,240	2.54	Near Manila. Very progressive farmers. 95n 22x 85m 100w 54126Yy
D Boac	1977	R-Lat	Bs	12	98,000	–	179,912	5.56	In Marinduque. 20n 0x 0m 10w 5566Yy
D Gumaca	1984	R-Lat	Bs	21	329,000	–	616,636	9.09	In Quezon. 34n 0x 0m 32w 13704Yy
D Lucena	1950	R-Lat	Bs	599	383,000	901,121	750,862	-0.73	SLuzon. Mountainous, self-supporting. Religious. 65n 0x 0m 235w 20772Yy
PN Infanta	1950	R-Lat	Bs	16	132,000	110,142	237,080	3.11	Eastern coast Luzon. Poor roads, economy. M=OCD. 24n 4x 4m 35w 7385Yy
M Manila	1579	R-Lat	Bs	242	3,883,000	3,682,435	7,508,525	2.89	SLuzon. Vast slums, little church action. 2p. 2s. 461n 797x 2412m 2335w 250479Yy
D Antipolo	1983	R-Lat	Bs	35	637,000	–	1,168,000	8.33	In Rizal. 85% Roman Catholic. 46n 45x 328m 235w 47528Yy
D Imus	1961	R-Lat	Bs	46	495,000	364,057	934,000	3.84	Very backward province near Manila. No industry. 64n 33x 328m 194w 50244Yy
D Malolos	1961	R-Lat	Bs	72	902,000	833,220	1,752,000	3.02	Near Manila. Very developed, industry. 136n 0x 2m 290w 51564Yy
D San Pablo	1966	R-Lat	Bs	534	740,000	635,723	1,371,776	3.12	SLuzon. Big landowners. Farming. Religious area. 76n 57x 164m 289w 44021Yy
M Nueva Segovia	1595	R-Lat	Bs	40	260,000	328,307	478,744	1.52	Early Catholic area. Farming, backward. M=OMI. 55n 10x 10m 149w 8785Yy
D Bangued	1955	R-Lat	Bsvd	224	101,000	115,327	165,094	1.45	NLuzon. Poor. Hocos: Fingians in mountains. M=SVD. 18n 17x 22m 18w 4429Yy
D Laoag	1961	R-Lat	Bs	79	216,000	177,337	410,065	3.41	NLuzon. Emigration due to poverty. PIC stronghold. 33n 7x 17m 93w 6312Yy
M Ozamis	1951	R-Lat	Bs	18	166,000	223,758	338,463	1.67	NMindanao. Visayan immigrants. M=CM,SSCME. 25n 10x 11m 47w 7737Yy
D Dipolog	1967	R-Lat	Bs	930	325,000	350,112	585,730	2.08	North of Zamboanga. Poor, mountainous, bad roads. 45n 3x 9m 27w 16195Yy
D Iligan	1971	R-Lat	Bs	22	313,000	237,577	499,000	4.17	Mindanao Moroland. Politico-religious disturbances. 22n 9x 13m 53w 10313Yy
D Pagadían	1971	R-Lat	Bs	26	278,000	288,884	467,939	4.17	New diocese covering east of Zamboanga del Sur. 30n 13x 15m 36w 8230Yy
PN Marawi	1976	R-Lat	Bs	4	15,600	–	30,000	5.26	M=SSCME. 3n 8x 8m 13w 1245Yy
M Palo	1937	R-Lat	Bs	45	556,000	877,865	1,107,286	0.93	NLeyte. Developed. First island christianized. 1s. 105n 15x 16m 84w 32313Yy
D Borongan	1960	R-Lat	Bs	27	217,000	358,203	398,857	0.43	SSamar. Poorest province, isolated. 34n 4x 4m 27w 8385Yy
D Calbayog	1910	R-Lat	Bs	28	371,000	580,802	540,190	-0.29	NSamar. Populace very poor but strongly Catholic. 39n 6x 20m 43w 18369Yy
D Catarman	1974	R-Lat	Bs	21	201,000	–	365,967	4.76	Northern Samar. 27n 0x 0m 43w 11283Yy
D Naval	1988	R-Lat	Bs	17	113,000	–	226,009	14.29	In Biliran Sub-Province. 90% Catholic. 18n 5x 5m 5w 3288Yy
M San Fernando	1948	R-Lat	Bs	493	854,000	657,289	1,470,601	3.27	CLuzon. Very developed. Communism began here. 122n 15x 74m 99w 112963Yy
D Balanga	1975	R-Lat	Bs	206	211,000	–	461,174	5.00	In Bataan. 86% Catholic. 25n 2x 5m 15w 10998Yy
D Iba	1955	R-Lat	Bs	25	347,000	217,814	608,871	4.20	Coast of western Luzon. No industry, poor farmland. 23n 14x 15m 57w 11009Yy
D Tarlac	1963	R-Lat	Bs	28	396,000	419,831	797,475	2.60	Land owned by 2%; Huku communist hotbed. 36n 4x 4m 50w 20421Yy
M Tuguegarao	1910	R-Lat	Bs	39	435,000	471,740	798,875	2.13	Northern end of Luzon. Still mostly uncultivated. 51n 16x 16m 146w 21991Yy
D Bayombong	1966	R-Lat	Bs	220	178,000	145,000	412,449	4.27	Undeveloped, mountains. Immigrant Hocanos. M=CICM. 10n 16x 16m 18w 7427Yy
D Ilagan	1970	R-Lat	Bs	39	478,000	520,000	929,225	2.35	NELuzon. Many immigrants. PIC, Protestants strong. 23n 22x 22m 56w 16857
PN Batanes & Babuyán Islands	1950	R-Lat	Bop	7	12,000	17,922	22,315	0.88	Islands north of Luzon. Marginal subsistence. M=OP. 0n 8x 8m 3w 626Yy
M Zamboanga	1910	R-Lat	Bs	20	227,000	698,376	434,935	-1.88	WMindanao. Poor. Visayan Catholics. Rest Muslims. 42n 15x 28m 24w 10357Yy
PN Ipil	1979	R-Lat	Bsj	16	194,000	–	315,187	6.25	M=SJ. 12n 20x 22m 36w 9237Yy
PN Isabela	1963	R-Lat	Bs	8	37,000	40,000	73,398	2.46	Basilian City, island. Badly neglected area. 8n 7x 9m 40w 1700Yy
VA Baguio (Mountain Provinces)	1932	R-Lat	Ps	21	239,000	324,480	500,814	1.75	Montasñosa. Mines. 30% pagan. Headhunters. M=CICM. 23n 31x 208m 183w 9921Yy
VA Bontoc-Lagawe	1992	R-Lat	Ps	12	92,000	–	180,156	33.33	New diocese. 61% Catholic. 14n 3x 3m 19w 4022Yy
VA Calapan	1936	R-Lat	Ps	22	312,000	396,090	524,699	1.13	Vast Mindoro island, stone-age Mangyans. M=SVD. 28n 28x 46m 68w 16876Yy
VA Jolo (Sulu)	1953	R-Lat	Pomi	11	7,600	10,500	14,500	1.30	Southwest. Mostly Muslims; Catholics 2%. M=OMI. 0n 12x 17m 41w 521Yy
VA Palawan	1910	R-Lat	Ps	34	246,000	196,761	453,229	3.39	West of Visayas. Many mines. M=ORSA. 43n 4x 4m 31w 17980Yy
VA San Jose in Mindoro	1983	R-Lat	Psvd	13	136,000	–	267,929	8.33	M=SVD. 11n 16x 18m 33w 6585Yy
VA Tabuk	1992	R-Lat	Pcicm	13	83,000	–	163,008	33.33	M=CICM. 2n 9x 9m 19w 5673Yy
OM Philippines	1950	R-Lat	Bs	63	140,000	50,000	180,000	5.26	Military Ordinariate of the Philippines. 73 ordinaries, 1 auxiliary, 8897Yy.
Children of God	1965	I-mar	.....	12	149	300	208	-1.45	Filipinos unrelated to USA body. HQ San Juan. Rizal. 8n,1p,W=25%,25Y.
Chinese Christian Gospel Centre	1931	I-EBr	x....	30	2,000	3,000	6,000	2.81	*Chu Hui So. Little Flock.* Chinese indigenous body. HQ Santa Cruz, Manila.
Christ Centered Church	c1990	I-3nF	....W	20	1,500	–	3,000	20.00	*CCC.*
Christ Jesus' Holy Church	1958	I-CCa	.....	15	3,500	7,000	10,000	1.44	Indigenous Catholic-type body, split ex Church of Rome. HQ Sta Maria, Pangasinan.
Christ to the Philippines	c1975	I-3cF	.....	100	10,000	–	28,600	5.00	Filipino charismatics.
Christian & Missionary Alliance Chs	1902	P-Hol	xF..z	2,167	113,430	56,354	249,500	6.13	M=CAM(USA). 1,000 Indonesians. 101n,45f,1h,2p,1s(12),W=73%,500Y,5142z.
Christian Catholic Ch (Evangelical)	1947	P-Con	x....	30	2,500	3,500	4,000	0.54	M=CCC(Zion City, Illinois, USA). Congregationalist polity. HQ Ormoc City. 1p.
Christian Ecumenical Faith of the P	1966	I-ReC	.....	10	5,500	10,000	9,000	-0.42	Filipino attempt to unite all Catholic and Protestant churches in world. 55nm.
Christian Evangelical Mission	1950	I-Eva	.....	75	9,000	20,000	16,400	-0.79	HQ Davao City. M=Midwest Evangelistic Assoc (USA), 94n,104Y,60z. Koronadal Blaan.
Christian Fellowship Churches	1974	I-3pF	.....	82	5,660	–	11,000	4.76	Work among Cebuano, Ilongo
Christian Fell Gospel Ministries	1975	I-3pF	.....	116	8,168	–	15,000	5.00	Work among Surigaonon, Mandaya, Visayan.
Christian Mission in the Far East	1946	I-Non	....E	20	10,000	20,000	21,000	0.20	An indigenous Filipino pioneer mission organization. HQ Singalong, Manila, 1p.
Christian Missions in the Philippines	1922	P-CBr	x....	86	9,300	3,000	16,900	7.16	*Christian Brethren. Plymouth (Open) Brethren.* M=CMML(USA, NZ, UK). HQ Rizal. 26f.
Christian Reformed Church of the P	1962	P-Ref	xF...	19	3,010	225	5,020	13.22	M=CRC(USA). HQ Bacolod City. 3x,12f,1s(7),W=98%,40Y,25z.
Christian Settlement Association	1945	I-EBr	.....	25	5,000	7,000	10,000	1.44	*Christohanon.* A Filipino version of the Chinese Little Flock. Rapid growth.
Christian Spiritist Union of the P	1920	I-Spi	.....	180	60,000	100,000	110,000	0.38	*Union Espiritista Cristiana de Filipinas.* Spiritualist body. HQ Malabon, Rizal.
Christian Union for True Knowledge	1950	I-mar	.....	15	600	2,000	1,900	-0.20	*CUTK and Spiritual Living.* Indigenous body, marginal doctrines. HQ Dagupan City.
Church of Christ (Manalista)	1913	I-3nF	x....	8,400	1,050,000	1,500,000	1,750,000	0.62	*INC. Iglesia ni Cristo (Manalista).* 35 cathedrals, 2 radio stations. Not charismatic. 1902n.
Church of Christ upon the Rock	1932	I-Adv	.....	5	100	300	200	-1.61	*Iglesia ni Cristo sa Ibabaw ng Bato.* Declining. 7n,1p,1s(2),W=60%,23Y.
Church of Christ (Matt 16.18) in the P	1949	I-Non	.....	10	1,000	2,000	2,000	0.00	Indigenous body based on Tondo, Manila; independents. 1p.
Church of Christ, Scientist		m-Sci	x....	5	150	300	400	0.05	*Christian Science.* M=CCS(Boston, USA). In Manila and Baguio.
Ch of Father of Fathers & Mother of Ms	1951	I-mar	.....	12	8,000	15,457	12,000	-1.01	Ms=Mothers. *Samahan ng Amang Ka-Amahan at Inang Ka-Inainahan.* Rizalist. Bongabon.
Church Founded by JC in the Far East	1923	I-Non	.....	10	650	1,000	1,100	0.38	*Iglesia ng Itinayo ni Jesucristo sa Malayong Silangan.* HQ Cabanatuan City.
Church of God	1956	I-Non	.....	9	800	2,000	1,600	-0.89	*Iglesia ng Dios.* Indigenous group in Manila.
Church of God in Christ Jesus	1922	I-Non	.....	20	10,000	30,000	20,000	-1.61	*Iglesia ng Dios kay Kristo Jesus.* Indigenous group based on Tondo, Manila.
Church of God in Christ, Mennonite	c1975	P-Men	.....	21	235	–	470	5.00	M=Ch of God in Christ, Mennonite.
Church of God of Prophecy	1952	P-Pe3	Z....	44	1,140	433	1,910	6.12	M=CGP(USA). Mission split in USA from CoG (Cleveland) (USA). HQ Ilocos Sur. 2f.
Church of God (Anderson)	1963	P-Hol	x....	59	2,070	1,000	5,160	6.78	M=CoG(Anderson) (USA). HQ Valenzuela, Bulacan. No missionaries remain. 3n,W=17%.
Church of God (Cleveland)	1947	P-Pe3	ZF...	305	24,222	17,000	60,600	5.22	Formerly called New Testament Ch of God. M=Ch of God(Cleveland) (USA). 140 chs. 250n.

Continued overleaf

Country Table 2–continued

Official name (bold type = church with over 10% of affiliated) 1	*Begun* 2	*Type* 3	*Counc* 4	*Congs* 5	*Adults* 6	*Affiliated 1970* 7	*Affiliated 1995* 8	*G%* 9	*Names, notes, and other statistics* (see Codebook, Part 3) 10
Church of God (Ecclesiae Dei)	1957	I-3pF	....E	150	70,000	83,000	100,000	0.75	Indigenous pentecostals. 300n,10x,1s(300),W=70%,5000Y,5000z.
Church of God (Seventh-day)		P-Adv	x....	14	1,100	2,000	2,100	0.05	M=CGSD(USA). Mission from one of several small USA bodies using same name.
Church of Jesus Christ New Jerusalem	1918	I-Non	.....	50	35,000	50,000	60,000	0.73	*Iglesia ni Jesucristo Bagong Jerusalem.* Indigenous body based on Tondo, Manila.
Ch of Jesus Christ of Latter-day Saints	1955	m-LdS	x....	638	149,000	11,625	213,000	12.34	*Mormons.* M=CJCLdS. HQ Pasay City. Many Filipino missionaries abroad. 240f.
Church of the Holy Trinity	1952	I-3pF	.....	30	2,000	2,000	4,000	2.81	Indigenous pentecostal group based on Cebu City.
Church of the Living God	1962	I-3pF	.....	350	80,000	100,000	160,000	1.90	*Iglesia ti Dios a Sibibiag. Revival Fellowship. Daily radio ministry. 126n,2p.*
Church of the Nazarene	1942	P-Hol	xF...	172	10,310	6,000	16,790	4.20	M=CoN(USA). Across nation. 21n,8x,28mw,13f,2s(60),93t(4948),W=37%,350z.
Churches of Christ	1901	I-Dis	x....	70	2,000	2,500	4,000	1.90	M=CCCC(USA). Rejected 1948 UCCP merger. Luzon, Mindanao. 24n,22f,1s(19),W=90%,151Y.
Churches of Christ (New Testament)	1966	I-Non	.....	200	12,000	10,000	25,000	3.73	One of many indigenous Churches of Christ groupings. HQ Caloocan City.
Churches of Christ, Philippine Mission	1924	I-Dis	x....	281	85,000	100,000	121,000	0.77	*Wolfe Group* (split ex Disciples). M=CC(USA). Growing very rapidly. 21f,2p.
Conservative Baptist Assoc of the P	1952	I-Bap	xF..Z	258	30,000	5,713	75,000	10.85	*CBAP.* M=CBFMS(USA). Mainly Tagalog-speaking. 19n,9x,35f,1p,1p,1s(25),W=46%,189Y.
Convention of Philippine Baptist Chs	1900	P-Bap	T...W	691	94,713	60,000	166,000	4.15	M=ABFMS(USA). Organized 1935. 2 schools. 66n,5x,16f,2H,1h,1p,1s(19),1v,1499Y.
Corpus Cristi Community Foundation	c1975	I-3cF	.....	35	10,000	–	20,000	5.00	Filipino charismatics.
Crusaders of the Divine Ch of Christ	1955	I-ind	.....	1,692	225,000	300,000	375,000	0.90	Very rapid expansion until 1970. HQ Pangasinan. 60% Ilocano. 200n,1p(3),W=66%,3000Y.
Davao Fell of Fundamental Baptist Chs	1952	I-Fun	.TT.T	30	1,500	2,000	3,000	1.64	Regular Baptists. Fundamentalists. HQ Davao City. 11n,W=85%,50Y.
Divine Filipino Catholic Church	1954	I-CCa	.....	20	7,000	10,000	15,000	1.64	Aglipayan. Widespread. HQ Valenzuela, Bulacan. 15n,5s(20),W=80%,800Y,1000z.
Divine Trinity of Jesus (Catholic Ch)	1962	I-CCa	.....	40	10,000	15,000	20,000	1.16	Indigenous Catholic-type body, Catholic elements. HQ San Francisco. Agusan.
Edified Church of Jesus Christ	1956	I-Non	.....	35	12,500	20,000	21,000	0.20	*Iglesia Edificada de Jesucristo.* Independents. HQ Malabon, Rizal.
Equifrilibricum World Religion	1925	I-mar	.....	10	5,000	16,000	10,000	-1.86	*Equality-Fraternity-Liberty Church. Moncadistas.* Begun 1925 by Filipinos in USA.
Ev Christian Catholic Apostolic Ch	1957	I-CCa	.....	2	400	1,000	1,000	0.00	Indigenous group in Davao City. Catholic features, beliefs and rituals.
Evangelical Church of Christ	1956	I-Eva	.....	5	300	600	500	-0.73	Small Filipino indigenous group. On Mindanao. Cebu. 11n,1x,W=75%,20Y.
Evangelical Church of God	1955	I-ind	.....	20	2,200	4,000	4,100	0.10	*Philippine District Council.* M=Ev Bible Ch (Maryland, USA). 1p.
Evangelical Free Philippine Church	1951	P-Con	KF..E	42	1,600	750	2,600	5.10	*EFPC.* M=EFCA(USA). First pastors 1969. 2n,4x,14f,1p(5),W=53%,46Yy,30z.
Evangelical Friends Mission	1978	P-Qua	.....	7	300	–	400	5.88	M=Evan Friends Mission.
Evangelical Full Gospel Revival Center	1965	I-3fF	.....	150	10,000	7,000	20,000	4.29	Indigenous pentecostal group based on Davao City. 10n,1s(57),600Y,5000z.
Evangelical Methodist Church in the P	1909	I-Met	VWE.W	295	44,964	70,000	112,000	1.90	*IEMELIF. Iglesia Ev Metodista en las Islas F.* First Filipino schism. HQ Tondo. 1p.
Evangelical Presbyterian Church	c1980	I-Ref	.....	6	1,100	–	2,200	6.67	M=Korean Interest Mission (Korea).
Evangelical Spiritist Church	1946	I-Spi	.....	1	200	1,000	500	-2.73	*Iglesia Evangelica Espiritista.* Spiritualist group in Caloocan City.
Faith Tabernacle	c1975	I-3wF	.....	38	15,000	–	25,000	5.00	Filipinos teaching Word of Faith/Prospering Gospel.
Far Eastern Gospel Crusade	1947	P-Non	xM..E	40	1,000	2,500	3,000	0.73	M=FEGC(USA). Members Tagalog-speaking. 25n,84f,1H,2s(40),W=76%,163Y,200z.
Fell of Indig Fundamental Chs of the P	c1965	I-Fun	.....	17	1,500	875	3,750	5.99	*FIFCOP.*
Fellowship of Missionary Chs	1974	I-3pF	.....	24	2,100	–	4,000	4.76	Work in Cebuano and Ilongo.
Filipino Christian Church	1928	I-ReC	.....	2	400	1,500	1,000	-1.61	Indigenous group based on Quezon City. Catholic beliefs and practices.
Free Methodist Ch in the Philippines	1949	I-Hol	VF..E	114	11,209	3,000	18,700	7.59	M=FMC(USA). Members Cebuano, Samareno, Manobo. 20n,10f,1s(25),W=83%,222Y,250z.
General Baptist Ch of the Philippines	1957	P-Bap	TF..Z	400	13,270	1,147	24,000	12.93	M=GBFMS(USA). HQ Davao City. 19n,9x,3s(48),W=70%,37Y,142z.
Glorious Seventh-day Adventist Mission	1921	I-Adv	.....	15	1,000	2,000	3,000	1.64	*Iglesia Adventista del Septimo Dia Glorioso.* Schism ex SDAs. HQ Manila.
God of the World Association	1952	I-mar	.....	30	2,000	8,000	5,000	-1.86	*Ang Bathala ng Daigdig Asosasyon.* Based on Tondo, Manila. Marginal in doctrine.
God, Mysterious Mother	1948	I-mar	.....	200	70,000	200,000	150,000	-1.14	Bathalismo (Inang Mahiwaga). *Large Rizalist movement. HQ Nueva Ecija.*
Golden Harvest Fellowship	c1980	I-3cF	.....	40	5,000	–	10,000	6.67	Network, with new congregation in Las Vegas (USA) among 48,000 Filipinos there.
Good Shepherd's Fold	1946	I-Bap	.....	50	1,000	1,200	3,000	3.73	Radio station, M=FEBC(USA). HQ Buenavista, Iloilo. 2n,2p,W=99%,26Y,180z.
Gospel Mission	1960	I-Eva	.....	15	1,500	2,000	3,000	1.64	Indigenous grouping. HQ Valenzuela, Bulacan. 4n,W=25Y,100z.
Grace & Truth Tabernacle	1936	I-3pF	.....	50	3,000	5,000	8,000	1.90	Open-air crusades begun 1969. HQ Mlang, Cotabato. 10n,1p,W=50%,450Y,200z.
Grace Gospel Church of Christ	1958	P-Adv	.....	120	3,500	5,000	7,000	1.35	M=Things to Come Mission (USA). HQ Ozamis City. 8f,2p.
Grace Gospel Church of Manila	1952	I-Bap	....E	2	500	760	1,500	2.76	Chinese body. Sends out Grace Mission, 33 missionaries. 1n,W=66%,74Y,10z.
Holy Stone of Cath Apost Ch of Spirit	1938	I-Lib	.....	3	1,000	2,000	2,500	0.90	Began among migrant settlers from the Visayas to Davao province. HQ Mati, Davao.
Independent Baptist Church		I-Bap	.....	87	5,200	3,000	13,000	0.05	Independent Baptists with USA ties.
Independent Ch of Filipino Christians	1946	I-Lib	.....	5	2,000	1,700	3,000	2.30	*Fonacier Group.* Schism ex Philippine Independent Ch by deposed primate Fonacier.
Independent Republican Christian Ch	c1960	I-Non	.....	70	43,200	50,000	70,000	1.35	Rapidly-growing indigenous group. 20n,2p,1s(20),1000Y,2000z.
Internat Ch of the Foursquare Gospel	1927	P-Pe2	ZF..E	745	35,836	25,000	70,000	4.20	M=ICFG(USA). Rapid growth. 213n,5x,13f,11p,3s(117),W=74%,3197Y,7716z.
International Pentecostal Holiness Ch	1975	P-Pe3	.....	125	6,000	–	13,300	5.00	M=IPHC(USA). Holiness Pentecostals.
Jehovah's Witnesses	1912	m-Jeh	x....	2,981	104,519	150,000	348,000	3.42	*Watch Tower.* Active witnessing by 1929. Rapid growth. (1975) 6224Y. (1995) 7987Y.
Jesus is Lord Fellowship	1978	I-3fF	.....	3,000	1,200,000	–	2,000,000	5.88	*JILF. Philippines for Jesus.* Mass movement. F=E. Villanueva. In 25 countries.
Kingdom of God through Jesus Christ	1958	I-Non	.....	2	700	1,000	2,000	2.81	Indigenous body. HQ Butuan City. Baptism not until 30 years of age. 3n,3p,W=50%
Leyte Agape Evangelistic Ministries	1966	I-3pF	.....	29	2,230	500	4,000	8.67	Work among Sorsogonon (Hanunoo), in Southern Oriental Mindoro..
Light & Spirit of Truth	1907	I-mar	.....	150	7,000	20,000	15,000	-1.14	*Tipan ng Panginoon.* Marginal group based on Caloocan City.
Living Rock Ministries	1975	I-3pF	.....	68	3,041	–	6,000	5.00	Work among Waray-Waray.
Lutheran Church in the Philippines	1946	P-Lut	L...W	175	7,800	10,200	21,740	3.07	*LCP.* M=LCMS(USA). A=1963. Radio, TV. 17n,20x,30f,1s(11),612Yy,624z.
Luzon Conv of Southern Baptist Chs	1948	P-Bap	T....	380	29,200	4,000	35,000	9.06	M=SBC-IMB(USA).
March of Faith	1970	I-3pF	.....	208	25,000	–	62,500	55.54	Filipino pentecostals.
Mennonite Missions Now Chs	1974	P-Men	.....	13	431	–	1,003	4.76	Mennonite mission from USA.
Mindanao Baptist Conv of SB Chs	1948	P-Bap	T....	889	52,166	5,000	60,000	10.45	*SBC=Southern Baptist Churches.* M=IMB(USA).
Mount Olive Gospel Churches	1972	I-3pF	.....	27	3,280	–	7,000	4.35	Working among Bukidnon.
National Catholic Apostolic Church	1930	I-CCa	.....	100	18,500	35,000	30,000	-0.61	*Iglesia Catolica Apostolica Nacional.* Ex RCC. HQ Cabanatuan City. 85n,1s(7),250Yy.
National Catholic Church	1930	I-CCa	.....	20	6,000	10,000	11,000	0.38	*Iglesia Catolica Nacional.* Catholic-type body based on Ormoc City, Leyte.
National Schismatic Church of the P	1938	I-CCa	.....	14	5,000	10,000	9,000	-0.42	*Iglesia Cismatica Filipina Nacional.* Schism ex Ch of Rome, Misamis Occidental.
New Apostolic Church	c1980	I-3aX	x....	200	90,000	–	140,267	6.67	*NAC/NAK.* M=Neuapostolische Kirche (HQ Zurich, Switzerland).
New Tribes Mission of the Philippines	1951	P-Fun	x...E	115	2,300	2,967	6,570	3.23	M=NTM(USA). Work among jungle tribes. 10n,20x,62f,1h,1p,W=95%,66Y,348z.
Open Bible Standard Church	c1970	I-3pW	.....	20	722	–	1,440	33.76	M=OBSC.
Oriental Missionary Crusade	1958	P-Pe2	.....	25	7,000	10,000	15,000	1.64	Pentecostals with USA links. M=OMC(USA). HQ Sampaloc, Manila. 40m,3f.
Patriotic Ch of Our Lord Jesus Christ	1938	I-3pF	.....	70	20,000	40,000	30,000	-1.14	*Iglesia Patriota de Nuestro Senor JC.* Rizalist. 45n,1s(20),W=27%,500Y.
Pentecostal Bible Way Church	1948	I-3oF	.....	30	1,000	1,000	3,000	4.49	M=BWCOLJCWW(USA Black pentecostals). 5n,1p,W=50%,50Y.
Pentecostal Church of God of the P	1950	P-Pe2	Z....	200	2,000	3,000	5,000	2.06	M=PCG(USA). Classical Pentecostals. HQ Caudon, Ilocos Sur. 2 schools. 4f.
Pentecostal Ev Assembly of Christ Elect	1962	I-3pF	.....	150	3,000	4,000	6,000	1.64	Indigenous Filipino pentecostal group based on Quezon City.
People's Missionary Church	1964	I-3pF	.....	30	1,000	1,500	3,000	2.81	Indigenous churches around HQ Sampaloc. Manila. 8n,1p,1p,W=90%,65Y,18z.
Philippine Church (Adarnista)	1901	I-mar	.....	90	12,000	15,000	25,000	2.06	*Iglesia Filipina (Adarnistas).* Followers of bishop Adarna. Rizalist. HQ La Union.
Philippine Episcopal Church	1898	A-ACa	awEAW	457	48,000	63,276	110,000	2.24	*PEC. Igl Epis.* M=ECUSA. 5 Dioceses. 83n,9x,15f,3H,12r,1u(135),147Y,1875y.
Philippine Independent Catholic Church	1981	I-ReC	.....	3,000	1,000,000	–	2,000,000	7.14	*PICC. Iglesia Filipina Catolica Independiente.* Schism of 40% of ICI by primate M.V.Ga. In north.
Philippine Independent Church	1890	I-ReC	UWRAW	5,751	2,000,000	3,500,000	2,800,000	-0.89	*PIC. Iglesia Filipina Independiente, IFI.* Ex RCC. Many breakoffs. 470n.
Philippine Missionary Fellowship	1956	I-Non	....E	50	4,000	4,000	10,000	3.73	An indigenous Filipino pioneer mission organization. HQ Silang. Cavite. 1p.
Philippine Unitarian Church	1955	I-Lib	.....	1	400	1,000	1,000	0.00	Catholic-type independent church: unitarian doctrines. HQ Urdaneta, Pangasinan.
Sacred Church of the Race	1949	I-mar	.....	20	10,000	35,000	25,000	-1.34	*Iglesia Sagrada ng Lahi.* Christian rites, traditional beliefs, Rizalist. HQ Tondo.
Sacred Philippine Ch of the 5 Vowels	1926	I-mar	.....	2	500	1,000	1,100	0.38	*SPC5V and Virtues. Iglesia Sagrada Filipina.* Rizalist. HQ Candelaria, Quezon.
Salvation Army	1937	P-Sal	xwE.W	52	15,400	20,000	25,000	0.90	*Hukbo ng Kaligtasan. SA, Philippines Command.* Officers 64, 1 girls' home, 1s.
Seventh-day Adventist Church	1906	P-Adv	x....	2,405	438,329	200,000	548,000	4.11	*CN&S Philip Unions.* 4 launches. 190n,30f,6H,3h,1j,18r,2s,2027t,10211Y.
Seventh-day Adv Reform Movement	1957	I-Adv	x....	5	1,000	1,000	1,500	1.64	M=SDARM(USA). Schism ex SDAs. HQ Manila. World HQ Charlottenlund, Denmark.
Teachings of God the Father	1953	I-mar	.....	5	3,100	10,000	5,000	-2.73	*Pagtulun-an sa Dios nga Amahan (Iglesia ni Tinago).* San Carlos, Negros Occidental.
Temple of God, Jehovah's Witnesses JC	1960	I-Jeh	.....	1	400	1,000	800	-0.89	JC=for Jesus Christ. *Templo ng Dios (Mga Saksi ni Jehovah kay Kristo Jesus).* Rizal.
The Church, the Body of Christ	1966	I-Non	.....	1	200	2,000	500	-5.39	Indigenous group in Pagadian. Zamboanga del Sur.
The Rock, Christ Jesus	1957	I-mar	.....	2	1,000	4,000	3,000	-1.14	*White Rock,* Rizalist tendencies. HQ Rizal, Zamboanga del Norte.
Things To Come Mission	1958	I-Adv	.....	290	12,800	12,000	32,000	4.00	Independent Adventists.
True Spiritual Ch of the Holy Spirit	1904	I-Spi	.....	10	1,000	6,000	3,000	-2.73	*Iglesia Espirita Veridica del Espiritu Santo.* HQ Caloocan City. Spiritists.
Unevangelized Fields Mission	c1980	P-Non	.....	4	100	–	200	6.67	M=UFM.
United Church of Christ in the P	1899	P-Uni	WWE.W	2,486	586,000	500,000	950,000	2.60	*UCCP.* 1948 union 4 bodies. M=P Interboard Comm (USA). 342n,47f,10H,16r,2s,1u,1v.
United Evangelical Church of Christ	1931	I-Eva	.v..W	96	18,500	15,000	30,000	2.81	*Iglesia Ev Unida de Cristo.* Filipino attempt at united church. 1973 applied to WCC.
United Evangelical Church (Reformed)	1929	I-Eva	.....	220	17,000	30,000	35,000	0.62	Chinese independent indigenous church. HQ Manila. 1p.
United Filipino Church	1962	I-CCa	.....	20	10,000	25,000	30,000	0.73	*Iglesia Filipinista.* Expanding. HQ Labazon. 4n,1s(7),W=63%,1800Yy,5000z.
United Methodist Church in the P	1899	P-Met	VwE.W	1,120	155,000	300,000	282,000	-0.25	*Philippines Central Conf, UMC(USA).* 6 Annual Confs. 750n,33f,5H,lj,2p,14r,lu.
United Pentecostal Church	1957	P-Pe1	x....	733	110,000	40,000	183,000	6.27	*Jesus Only Ch.* M=UPC(USA). Unitarians. HQ Pampanga. 1 school. 220n,52m,8f,4p(98).
United World Mission	1952	P-Non	.....	19	800	467	1,780	5.50	M=UWM.
Universal Church of Christ	1924	P-Non	.....	20	1,000	1,000	2,000	2.81	*Iglesia Universal de Cristo (Carlson Group).* Mission from USA. HQ Cebu City.
Universal Family of Yahweh of the FB	1956	I-3pF	.....	30	1,000	2,000	2,500	0.90	FB=Firstborn. Pentecostal, holiness. HQ Manila. 25n,W=60%,70Yy.
Universalist Church of the Philippines	1955	m-Unt	.....	5	1,000	4,000	3,000	-1.14	M=Unitarian Universalist Association (USA). HQ San Carlos. Negros Occidental.
Visayan Associated Gospel Chs of the P	1948	P-Bap	.....	25	1,100	2,000	2,100	0.20	M=Associated Gospel M(USA). HQ Cauayan. 2n,1p,2r,W=80%,270Y,250z.
Way of Salvation Church of the P	1948	I-3pF	.....	30	6,000	10,000	12,000	0.73	M=WSC(founded Honolulu,Hawaii). HQ Narvacan, Ilocos Sur. 4n,1p,W=85%.
Wesleyan Church of the Philippines	1932	P-Hol	VF..E	168	15,000	6,550	25,000	5.50	1936 Pilgrim Holiness(USA), 1950 WMC; 1968 union. 42n,5x,11f,3p,W=46%,222Y.
World Wide Pentecostal Ch of Christ	c1970	I-3oF	.....	40	8,000	–	15,000	46.91	Indigenous pentecostal network with Oneness theology. HQ Manila.
Other Filipino indigenous churches		I-3nF	.....	1,000	100,000	50,000	250,000	0.05	Total about 250 (see list below).
Other independent Oneness bodies	c1970	I-3oF	.....	400	15,000	–	46,000	53.64	Total about 30, including Philippines Apostolic Christian Fellowship.
Other Protestant denominations		P-	.....	100	20,000	13,000	40,000	0.05	Total about 50 (see list below), including USA military chaplaincies.
Other marginal bodies		m-	.....	40	5,000	1,000	10,000	0.05	Incl: New Ch. Reorganized Ch of Jesus Christ of Latter Day Saints (on Pangasinan).
Other independent Catholic chs	c1930	I-CCa	.....	30	4,000	500	8,000	11.73	Including a few related to European Episcopi Vagantes.
Other independent charismatic chs	c1975	I-3cF	.....	1,200	600,000	–	1,200,000	5.00	Including Association of Vineyard Chs (1 ch).
Doubly-affiliated		2-aff			-7,243,000	-5,325,163	-13,342,827		Evangelicals, Aglipayans and others who also are or were baptized Roman Catholics.
Totals				**61,189**	**32,576,164**	**34,042,000**	**60,015,000**		

Churches, members, growth, 1900-2025	*Congs*	*Adults*	*Affiliated*	*G%*	*Total denominations*	*6 Megablocs:* O	R	A	P	I	m
Total churches, members, and denominations (mid-1900)	2,000	3,196,000	5,980,000	2.52	7	0	1	1	3	2	0
Total churches, members, and denominations (mid-1970)	23,686	18,195,708	34,042,000	2.52	296	0	1	1	62	215	17
Total churches, members, and denominations (mid-1990)	53,000	28,989,000	53,405,000	2.28	592	0	1	1	96	460	34
Total churches, members, and denominations (mid-1995)	61,189	32,576,164	60,015,000	2.36	595	0	1	1	96	463	34
Total churches, members, and denominations (mid-2000)	65,000	36,151,000	66,600,057	2.10	598	0	1	1	96	466	34
Total churches, members, and denominations (mid-2025)	98,000	51,567,000	95,000,000	1.43	982	0	1	1	120	800	60

Continued opposite

Country Table 2–concluded

NOTES ON TABLE ABOVE
NATIONAL COUNCILS (Column 4, 5th letter).
E = Philippine Council of Evangelical Churches (PCEC).
I = Philippines for Jesus Movement (1983: umbrella organization for over 4,000 independent charismatic fellowships and churches).
R = Catholic Bishops' Conference of the Philippines (CBCP).
T = Philippine Council of Fundamental Evangelical Churches.
W = National Council of Churches in the Philippines (NCCP) (Sangguniang Pambansa ng mga Simbahan sa Pilipinas).
Other national councils. Joint Council of the Philippine Episcopal Church & the Philippine Independent Church.
OTHER FILIPINO INDIGENOUS CHURCHES. The table lists 69 bodies with 1,000 or more adherents, and 6 with under 1,000. In addition, there are over 250 other Filipino indigenous churches, about 180 being small bodies with under 1,000 but over 100 adherents. These latter include: Apostolic Philippine Pentecostal Mission, Association of the Holy Family, Association of Three Persons One God, Brotherhood of Faith, Christian Brethren of the Gospel of St John, Ch in the Community, Ch of Christ (Pilipino Movement), Ch of God Christ Buildeth, Ch of God (Acts 20.28), Ch of Liberty, Ch of Philadelphia, Ch of the Holy Family, Ch of the Mystic City of God, Churches of the Saints, Ev Catholic Ch of the Philippines, Free Faith Organisation, God of Truth Ch, Holy Catholic Apostolic Christian Ch, Independent Ch of Free Independent Christians d(Unitarian), Independent Filipino Ch of the Most Holy Trinity (c1935 schism ex Philippine Independent Ch), Kingdom of God, March of Faith (begun 1970 ex AoG), Moncadian Ch of God, Mystic Ch of the Philippines, New Testament Ch, Philippine Liberal Ch, Sacred Family of God, Spirit and Life, Spiritual Filipino Catholic Ch, Temple of the Holy Spirit, True Ch, Universal Christian Ch, Universal Dei Ecclesia, World Christian Movement.
OTHER PROTESTANT DENOMINATIONS. The table gives bodies with 200 or more adherents (total 48). In addition, there are over 40 others including: American Baptist Association (1961), Assembly of Yahvah, Berean Mission (1952), Bethany Fellowship Missions (1971), Bethany Home, Bible Protestant Ch of the Philippines, Christadelphian Ecclesias, Christian Ch of North America, Christian Nationals Evangelism Commission (1968), Church of God (Abrahamic Faith), Free Gospel Ch, International Missions (1951), Liebenzell Mission (1970), Missionary Ch, Peniel Chs of VOCA (Voice of China & Asia MS, 1948), Philippine Miracle Missions, Slavic Gospel Association, Union Ch of Manila, United Followers of Christ Ch, World Baptist Fellowship Mission Agency (1972), World-Wide Missions (1962). In addition to these bodies with Filipino membership, there were in 1970 about 10,000 Protestants in USA military chaplaincies.
OTHER MARGINAL PROTESTANT BODIES. The Reorganized Ch of Jesus Christ of Latter-day Saints (USA) maintains a small work based on Pangasinan (283 members); and the New Ch (Swedenborgian) has a society in Malabon, Rizal.

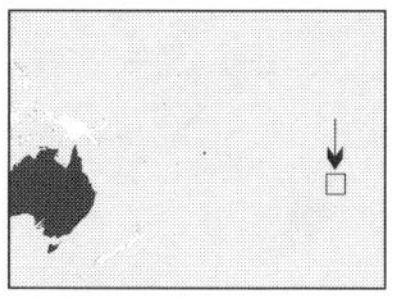

PITCAIRN ISLANDS

SECULAR DATA, AD 2000

STATE
Official name: The Colony of the Pitcairn Islands
Short name: Pitcairn Islands. **Adjective of nationality:** Pitcairn Islanders.
Flag: That of the UK (Britain).
Area: 4 sq. km. (1.5 sq. mi.).
Government: British colony, since 1898 (1790 founded by Bounty mutineers).
Legislature: Council, 10 members.
Official language: English.
Monetary unit: 1 New Zealand dollar ($NZ) = 100 cents. **US$1=** $NZ 2.02.
Chief cities: ADAMSTOWN 47.
Political divisions: 1 province.

DEMOGRAPHY
Population: 47.
Population density: 11.7/sq. km. (4.5/sq. mi.).
Under 15 years: 10.
Growth rate p.a.: 1.85% (births 27.33, deaths 4.64).
Mortality: Infant, per 1,000: 19.3, ; **Maternal per 100,000:** 30.0.
Life expectancy: 73 (male 71, female 75).
Household size: 3.0. **Floor area per person, sq.m:** 30.0.
Major languages: English.
Urban dwellers: 0.00%. **Urban growth rate p.a.:** 0.00%.
Labor force: 60%.

ETHNOLINGUISTIC PEOPLES
94.0% Pitcairner; 3.0% British; .

ECONOMY
National income p.a. per person: US$21,276; **per family:** US$63,829.

EDUCATION
Adult literacy: 90% (male 92%, female 88%). **Schools:** 1.
Universities: 0. **School enrolment:** female/male: 90%/90%.

HEALTH
Access to health services: 80%. **Access to safe water:** 80%.
Hospitals: 1 (20 beds per 10,000). **Doctors:** 1.
Blind: 2. **Deaf:** 2. **Murder rate:** 1. **Lepers:** 0.

LITERATURE
New book titles p.a.: 0 (0 p.a. per million). **Periodicals:** 0.
Newspapers: 0 dailies.

COMMUNICATION (per 1,000 people)
Phones: 500 (20% mobile). **Radios:** 1,000. **TV sets:** 100.
Daily newspaper circulation: <1. **Computers:** 10.

HUMAN LIFE AND LIBERTY (optimum condition=100.0%)
HDI: 85.0. **HSI:** 85.0. **HFI:** 80.0. **EFL:** 50.0.

Country Table 1. **Religious adherents in the Pitcairn Islands, AD 1900-2025.**

Year	*1900*		*1970*		*mid-1990*		*Annual change, 1990-2000*				*mid-1995*		*mid-2000*		*mid-2025*	
Name	*Adherents*	*%*	*Adherents*	*%*	*Adherents*	*%*	*Natural*	*Conversion*	*Total*	*Rate*	*Adherents*	*%*	*Adherents*	*%*	*Adherents*	*%*
Christians	**150**	**100.0**	**90**	**100.0**	**62**	**93.9**	**-2**	**0**	**-2**	**-3.82**	**43**	**91.5**	**42**	**89.4**	**42**	**89.4**
PROFESSION																
professing Christians	**150**	**100.0**	**90**	**100.0**	**62**	**93.9**	**-2**	**0**	**-2**	**-3.82**	**43**	**91.5**	**42**	**89.4**	**42**	**89.4**
AFFILIATION																
affiliated Christians	**150**	**100.0**	**90**	**100.0**	**62**	**93.9**	**-2**	**0**	**-2**	**-3.82**	**43**	**91.5**	**42**	**89.4**	**42**	**89.4**
Protestants	150	100.0	90	100.0	62	93.9	-2	0	-2	-3.82	43	91.5	42	89.4	42	89.4
Trans-megabloc groupings																
Evangelicals	100	66.7	10	11.1	5	7.6	0	0	0	0.00	4	8.5	5	10.6	5	10.6
Pentecostals/Charismatics	0	0.0	0	0.0	2	3.0	0	0	0	0.00	2	4.3	2	4.3	3	6.4
Great Commission Christians	**15**	**10.0**	**20**	**22.2**	**26**	**39.4**	**-1**	**0**	**-1**	**-3.09**	**19**	**40.4**	**19**	**40.4**	**20**	**42.6**
Nonreligious	0	0.0	0	0.0	4	6.1	0	0	0	2.26	4	8.5	5	10.6	5	10.6
World A (unevangelized persons)	0	0.0	0	0.0	0	0.0	0	0	0	0.00	0	0.0	0	0.0	0	0.0
World B (evangelized non-Christians)	0	0.0	0	0.0	4	6.1	0	0	0	2.26	4	8.5	5	10.6	5	10.6
World C (Christians)	150	100.0	90	100.0	62	93.9	-2	0	-2	-3.82	43	91.5	42	89.4	42	89.4
Country's population	**150**	**100.0**	**90**	**100.0**	**66**	**100.0**	**-2**	**0**	**-2**	**-3.34**	**47**	**100.0**	**47**	**100.0**	**47**	**100.0**

COLUMNS, ROWS.
For meanings and definitions, see Codebook (Part 3). Note that, by definition, total 'Christians' = professing + crypto-Christians, which also = affiliated + unaffiliated Christians, and also = Great Commission Christians + latent Christians. Percentages may not always total exactly, due to rounding.

NOTES ON RELIGIONS
CHRISTIANS. Anglicans until 1887; since then, all Seventh-day Adventists.

Great Commission Instrument Panel: status of the Pitcairn Islands (for explanation see start of Part 4)

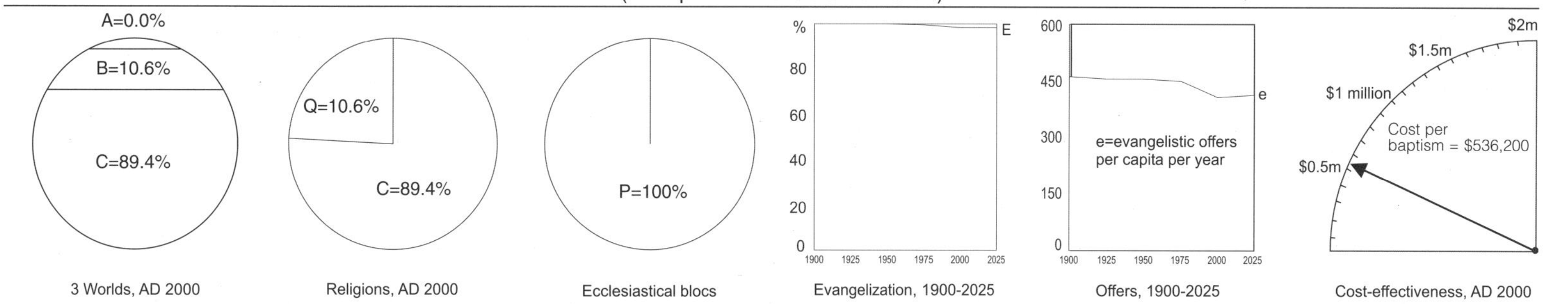

Country status. Pitcairn Islands is a British dependency made up of a group of volcanic islands in the South Pacific, east of French Polynesia. The islands were originally settled in 1790 by mutineers from the HMS *Bounty* and their Tahitian companions.

Bounty Bible on postage stamp.

HUMAN LIFE AND LIBERTY

Human rights and freedoms. Pitcairn Islands is a dependent territory of the United Kingdom where UK laws guarantee all human rights and civil liberties.

CHRISTIANITY

Pitcairn Island was uninhabited when a party of mutineers from the ship *Bounty* with some Tahitians arrived to settle it in 1790. The leader of the group, John Adams, was a zealous Christian and helped to form a highly-disciplined Church of England community. In 1877 Seventh-day Adventist literature arrived from the USA which transformed the life of the island. Within a decade the Church of England had been supplanted, and the SDA Pitcairn Island Mission was organized in 1895. To this day Pitcairn

Country summary. **Worlds A, B, C by ethnolinguistic peoples, cities, and major civil divisions in Pitcairn Islands.**

World	PEOPLES Num	Pop 2000	C%	Christians	E%	U%	Unevangelized	CITIES Num	Pop 2000	C%	Christians	E%	U%	Unevangelized	CIVIL DIVISIONS Num	Pop 2000	C%	Christians	E%	U%	Unevangelized
A	0	0	0.00	0	0	0	0	0	0	0.00	0	0	0	0	0	0	0.00	0	0	0	0
B	2	2	100.00	2	100	0	0	0	0	0.00	0	0	0	0	0	0	0.00	0	0	0	0
C	1	44	93.18	41	100	0	0	1	47	89.36	42	100	0	0	1	47	89.36	42	100	0	0
Total	**3**	**46**	**93.48**	**43**	**100**	**0**	**0**	**1**	**47**	**89.36**	**42**	**100**	**0**	**0**	**1**	**47**	**89.36**	**42**	**100**	**0**	**0**

remains completely Adventist in its religious allegiance. The single congregation in Adamstown is served by a resident pastor.

The Holy See has no diplomatic relations with Pitcairn Islands in AD 2000.

Indigenous missions. There is no mission activity from the Pitcairn Islands.

CHURCH AND STATE

All education was organized by the SDA Mission until 1948 when the New Zealand Department of Education sent its first schoolmaster to the island. The government makes secondary education available to Pitcairn residents in both Fiji and New Zealand.

FUTURE TRENDS AND PROSPECTS

The nonreligious, few in 1970, are expected to maintain 10% of the population through 2025.

Christianity, though impacted by the growth of the nonreligious, is likely to predominate throughout the 21st century.

Librarian examines Bounty Bible, original copy used for strict theocratic government by John Adams and crew of British ship HMS Bounty after 1789 mutiny.

BIBLIOGRAPHY

George Hunn Nobbs, 1799–1884: chaplain on Pitcairn and Norfolk Island. R. Nobbs. Norfolk Island: Pitcairn Descendants Society, 1984. 166p.

Mutineers on Pitcairn Island. H. M. S. Richards. Nashville, TN: Southern Pub. Association, 1980. 64p.

Pitcairn harvest 1890-1990. Sydney: Adventist Media Centre, 1990. (58 minute videocassette).

Pitcairn hymns and Norfolk favourites. Norfolk Island: Church of England, [1974]. 42p.

Pitcairn Island, the first 200 years. S. Murray. La Canada, CA: Bounty Sagas, 1992. 188p.

Pitcairn und Norfolk. A. Petersen-Roil. *Bibliographie einer Insel*, Bd. 3. Munich: Verlag A. Petersen-Roil, 1987. 76p. (Bibliographical work).

'Selected bibliography on the Pitcairn Islanders, University of Hawaii collection.' R. Starker. 1991. 9p.

The Pitcairn people. New York: Radim Films, 1963-64. (27 minute, 16mm film).

Country Table 2. **Organized churches and denominations in the Pitcairn Islands.**

Official name (bold type = church with over 10% of all affiliated) 1	*Begun* 2	*Type* 3	*Counc* 4	*Congs* 5	*Adults* 6	*Affiliated 1970* 7	*Affiliated 1995* 8	*G%* 9	*Names, notes, and other statistics* (see Codebook, Part 3) 10
Seventh-day Adventist Church	1895	P-Adv	x....	1	40	90	43	-2.91	*PI Mission*, Central Pacific Union Mission. 95% SDA. In Adamstown. 3n,1t(64).
Totals				**1**	**40**	**90**	**43**		

Churches, members, growth, 1900-2025	*Congs*	*Adults*	*Affiliated*	*G%*	*Total denominations*	*6 Megablocs:* O	R	A	P	I	m
Total churches, members, and denominations (mid-1900)	2	110	150	-0.73	1	0	0	0	1	0	0
Total churches, members, and denominations (mid-1970)	1	64	90	-0.73	1	0	0	0	1	0	0
Total churches, members, and denominations (mid-1990)	1	58	62	-1.85	1	0	0	0	1	0	0
Total churches, members, and denominations (mid-1995)	1	40	43	-7.06	1	0	0	0	1	0	0
Total churches, members, and denominations (mid-2000)	1	39	42	-0.47	1	0	0	0	1	0	0
Total churches, members, and denominations (mid-2025)	3	39	42	0.00	1	0	0	0	3	0	0

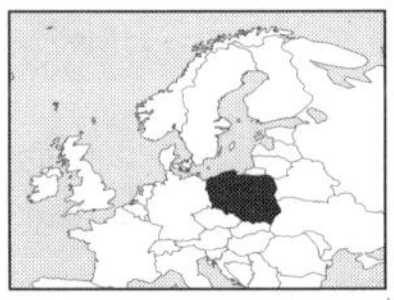

POLAND

SECULAR DATA, AD 2000

STATE

Official name: Rzeczpospolita Polska (The Republic of Poland).
Short name: Poland. **Adjective of nationality:** Polish, a Pole.
Flag: White stripe over red stripe.
Area: 312,685 sq. km. (120,728 sq. mi.).
Government: Multiparty republic, since 1991 (1918 Independence as republic, 1926 dictatorship, 1947 one-party Communist state).
Legislature: Senate, 100 members; Diet, 460 members.
Official language: Polish (Polski).
Monetary unit: 1 zloty (Zl) = 100 groszy. **US$1=** Zl 3.55.
Chief cities: Katowice 3,488,000; WARSZAWA (Warsaw) 2,269,000; Lodz 1,055,000; Gdansk (Danzig) 893,000; Krakow (Cracow) 857,000.
Political divisions: 49 provinces.
Armed forces: 241,000.

DEMOGRAPHY

Population: 38,765,000.
Population density: 123.9/sq. km. (321.0/sq. mi.).
Under 15 years: 7,524,000.
Growth rate p.a.: 0.09% (births 11.08, deaths 9.89).
Mortality: Infant, per 1,000: 13.6, ; **Maternal per 100,000:** 19.0.
Life expectancy: 74 (male 69, female 78).
Household size: 3.6. **Floor area per person, sq.m:** 18.2.
Major languages: Polish, Ukrainian, Russian, Kashubian, Byelorussian, German, Yiddish, et alia.
Urban dwellers: 65.56%. **Urban growth rate p.a.:** 0.7%.
Labor force: 45%.

ETHNOLINGUISTIC PEOPLES

89.9% Polish (Pole, Silesian); 4.0% German (High German); 4.0% Ukrainian; 0.5% Byelorussian; 0.4% Kashubian (Cashubian).

ECONOMY

National income p.a. per person: US$2,790; **per family:** US$10,044.

EDUCATION

Adult literacy: 98% (male 99%, female 98%). **Schools:** 31,813.
Universities: 140. **School enrolment:** female/male: 97%/98%.

HEALTH

Access to health services: 90%. **Access to safe water:** 100%.
Hospitals: 752 (63 beds per 10,000). **Doctors:** 87,706.
Blind: 21,523. **Deaf:** 2,323,600. **Murder rate:** 3.
Lepers: 1,000.

LITERATURE

New book titles p.a.: 14,730 (380 p.a. per million). **Periodicals:** 4,130. **Newspapers:** 66 dailies.

COMMUNICATION (per 1,000 people)

Phones: 148 **(18% mobile). Radios:** 421. **TV sets:** 408.
Daily newspaper circulation: 141. **Computers:** 95.

REFUGEES

Alien refugees from other countries: 800.

HUMAN LIFE AND LIBERTY (optimum condition=100.0%)

HDI: 83.4. **HSI:** 67.0. **HFI:** 25.0. **EFL:** 39.0.

Country status. Poland is located in east-central Europe on the Baltic Sea bordering Germany and Ukraine. Its chief exports are products of heavy industry. Poland has large deposits of coal, copper, iron, and other minerals.

HUMAN LIFE AND LIBERTY

Human need and development. After its emergence from Communist dictatorship in the late 1980s, Poland has made tentative strides in establishing a free-market economy. The transition from a centrally planned system has proved slower and more uneven than anticipated but, nevertheless, the economic reform program is on course. Although little headway has been made in privatizing large state-owned enterprises, the share of the private sector has continued to grow. However, the country is plagued by high inflation and unemployment, and standards of living have not materially improved since the collapse of Communism. There are shortages of all basic necessities and foodstuffs, most of which find their way into a flourishing black market. In the cities, apartments are cramped even when they are available. The social services and subsidized amenities available under the Communists have been scrapped without any effort to replace them. The poor and the elderly bear the brunt of economic dislocations brought about by the transitional state of affairs.

Human rights and freedoms. Most of the human rights violations that characterized the former Communist rule have disappeared. But society still grapples with the intractable problems of social, gender and ethnic intolerance. New laws passed by the Sejm have expanded freedoms of the media, and a new penal code has strengthened the framework of human rights. Discrimination against national minorities is prohibited by law, but, nevertheless, exists in covert forms. Prejudice is strong against Germans and Romanian Gypsies. There are also scattered anti-Semitic incidents.

Human environment. Like most ex-Communist countries, Poland suffers from considerable ecological damage and is considered one of the most polluted countries in the world. About 11% of the land has been designated as environmentally hazardous, including the provinces of Krakow and Katowice. Much of the hazardous wastes generated by industries are not disposed of properly. Air pollution from coal-fired power plants is severe as is water pollution from industrial and municipal wastes.

Country Table 1. **Religious adherents in Poland, AD 1900-2025.**

Year / Name	1900 Adherents	1900 %	1970 Adherents	1970 %	mid-1990 Adherents	mid-1990 %	Annual change, 1990-2000 Natural	Conversion	Total	Rate	mid-1995 Adherents	mid-1995 %	mid-2000 Adherents	mid-2000 %	mid-2025 Adherents	mid-2025 %
Christians	**21,989,500**	**90.9**	**29,631,585**	**91.1**	**36,900,000**	**96.8**	**62,542**	**23,274**	**85,816**	**0.23**	**37,462,000**	**97.0**	**37,758,156**	**97.4**	**38,264,000**	**97.9**
PROFESSION																
crypto-Christians	0	0.0	2,026,685	6.2	250,000	0.7	424	-25,424	-25,000	-71.15	0	0.0	0	0.0	0	0.0
professing Christians	**21,989,500**	**90.9**	**27,604,900**	**84.9**	**36,650,000**	**96.2**	**62,118**	**48,698**	**110,816**	**0.30**	**37,462,000**	**97.0**	**37,758,156**	**97.4**	**38,264,000**	**97.9**
AFFILIATION																
unaffiliated Christians	606,000	2.5	0	0.0	342,000	0.9	580	-8,770	-8,190	-2.70	333,326	0.9	260,097	0.7	104,000	0.3
affiliated Christians	**21,383,500**	**88.4**	**29,631,585**	**91.1**	**36,558,000**	**95.9**	**61,963**	**32,043**	**94,006**	**0.25**	**37,128,674**	**96.2**	**37,498,059**	**96.7**	**38,160,000**	**97.7**
Roman Catholics	18,656,500	77.1	28,783,085	88.5	35,000,000	91.8	59,322	14,984	74,306	0.21	35,475,061	91.9	35,743,059	92.2	36,360,000	93.1
Orthodox	2,020,000	8.4	527,500	1.6	950,000	2.5	1,610	6,390	8,000	0.81	1,000,600	2.6	1,030,000	2.7	1,050,000	2.7
Independents	0	0.0	133,700	0.4	265,000	0.7	449	6,051	6,500	2.22	294,013	0.8	330,000	0.9	350,000	0.9
Marginal Christians	0	0.0	23,000	0.1	150,000	0.4	254	4,746	5,000	2.92	165,500	0.4	200,000	0.5	300,000	0.8
Protestants	707,000	2.9	164,300	0.5	193,000	0.5	327	-127	200	0.10	193,500	0.5	195,000	0.5	230,000	0.6
Trans-megabloc groupings																
Evangelicals	110,000	0.5	46,000	0.1	114,000	0.3	193	2,407	2,600	2.08	128,360	0.3	140,000	0.4	225,000	0.6
Pentecostals/Charismatics	0	0.0	30,000	0.1	1,890,000	5.0	3,203	9,297	12,500	0.64	1,953,956	5.1	2,015,000	5.2	2,500,000	6.4
Great Commission Christians	**968,000**	**4.0**	**2,602,000**	**8.0**	**2,897,000**	**7.6**	**4,910**	**1,242**	**6,152**	**0.21**	**2,934,000**	**7.6**	**2,958,523**	**7.6**	**3,515,000**	**9.0**
Nonreligious	20,000	0.1	1,897,015	5.8	1,040,850	2.7	1,764	-19,426	-17,662	-1.84	980,530	2.5	864,235	2.2	700,000	1.8
Atheists	5,000	0.0	969,200	3.0	150,000	0.4	254	-3,709	-3,455	-2.58	140,500	0.4	115,452	0.3	72,100	0.2
Spiritists	0	0.0	0	0.0	6,800	0.0	12	37	49	0.69	7,000	0.0	7,285	0.0	9,000	0.0
Jews	2,180,000	9.0	8,000	0.0	9,000	0.0	15	-277	-262	-3.39	7,000	0.0	6,377	0.0	6,000	0.0
Muslims	500	0.0	100	0.0	4,500	0.0	8	51	59	1.25	4,800	0.0	5,094	0.0	7,500	0.0
Buddhists	0	0.0	0	0.0	900	0.0	2	9	11	1.14	950	0.0	1,008	0.0	1,400	0.0
Baha'is	0	0.0	100	0.0	450	0.0	1	4	5	1.14	470	0.0	504	0.0	1,000	0.0
Other religionists	5,000	0.0	20,000	0.1	6,500	0.0	11	37	48	0.71	6,750	0.0	6,975	0.0	8,000	0.0
World A (unevangelized persons)	242,000	1.0	650,516	2.0	38,119	0.1	64	-2,193	-2,129	-7.89	38,610	0.1	16,713	0.1	16,000	0.0
World B (evangelized non-Christians)	1,968,500	8.1	2,243,699	6.9	1,180,881	3.1	2,003	-21,081	-19,078	-1.58	1,109,562	2.9	1,006,844	2.6	805,000	2.1
World C (Christians)	21,989,500	90.9	29,631,585	91.1	36,900,000	96.8	62,542	23,274	85,816	0.23	37,462,000	97.0	37,758,156	97.4	38,264,000	97.9
Country's population	**24,200,000**	**100.0**	**32,525,800**	**100.0**	**38,119,000**	**100.0**	**64,609**	**0**	**64,609**	**0.17**	**38,610,173**	**100.0**	**38,765,000**	**100.0**	**39,069,000**	**100.0**

COLUMNS, ROWS.
For meanings and definitions, see Codebook (Part 3). Note that, by definition, total 'Christians' = professing + crypto-Christians, which also = affiliated + unaffiliated Christians, and also = Great Commission Christians + latent Christians. Percentages may not always total exactly, due to rounding.

CENSUSES.
30.XI.1921 (within 1921 boundaries): 74.3% Roman Catholics (11.8% Greek Catholics), 11.1% Orthodox, 10.8% Jews, 3.7% Protestants, 0.1% Mariavites.

NOTES ON RELIGIONS
ATHEISTS. Polish United Workers' Party (Communist; pro-Soviet): Only about 15% of party members are estimated to be committed atheists, the rest being nonreligious with a considerable number of professing (and many practicing) Catholics also.
CRYPTO-CHRISTIANS. Before 1995 Christians affiliated to churches but not known as such to the state. Since there is relative, if controlled, religious freedom in Poland, there is no organized underground church related to the main Protestant or Catholic traditions. Crypto-Christians exist, however, in 2 forms: (1) unregistered or prohibited denominations including Jehovah's witnesses, who have a strong underground organization; and (2) Catholics, often practicing, who do not reveal their affiliation publicly or to the state. There is also a tiny handful of isolated radio believers.
JEWS. In 1939, 3,500,000, of whom the Nazi Third Reich exterminated 3,350,000. In 1963, 31,000, declining rapidly by emigration. In 1968, 18 congregations and 11 synagogues. There is also a small Karaite (Readers of the Scriptures) community, the Religious Karaite Union.
MUSLIMS. Tatars and 10% of Lovari and Rom Gypsies.
NONRELIGIOUS. Agnostics, indifferent to religion, including most Communist party members. In addition, there were in 1970 another 6.2% of the population whom the polls record as non-religious but who are affiliated to the churches and so are classified here as crypto-Christians.
OTHER RELIGIONISTS. Including young Polish adherents of Occultists, adherents of Yoga, and also several thousand non-Christian Gypsies.
PENTECOSTALS/CHARISMATICS. The Catholic renewal began in 1975, with 500 involved adults in 20 prayer groups, including loosely-structured temporary student groups, also hundreds of young Jesus people and Jesus revolutionaries; total charismatic community including children, 3,000. In October 1975, 400 attended a first Polish charismatic conference, in Lublin. In 1980, 80,000 copies of a weekly youth-oriented Oasis-type magazine *Hight-Life* were being circulated. In 1992, 10,000 attended CCR's 10th Congress, with over 100 priests professing renewal. By 1997, 20,850 adults (9,700 being under 25) were regularly attending 711 weekly prayer groups, with 540 involved priests and 4 bishops. The Czestochowa-Jasna Gora annual pilgrimage is attended by 1,000 CCR leaders and around 200,000 adults. Detailed statistics are kept for all dioceses.
UNAFFILIATED CHRISTIANS. Only before 1945, and after 1990.

Great Commission Instrument Panel: status of Poland (for explanation see start of Part 4)

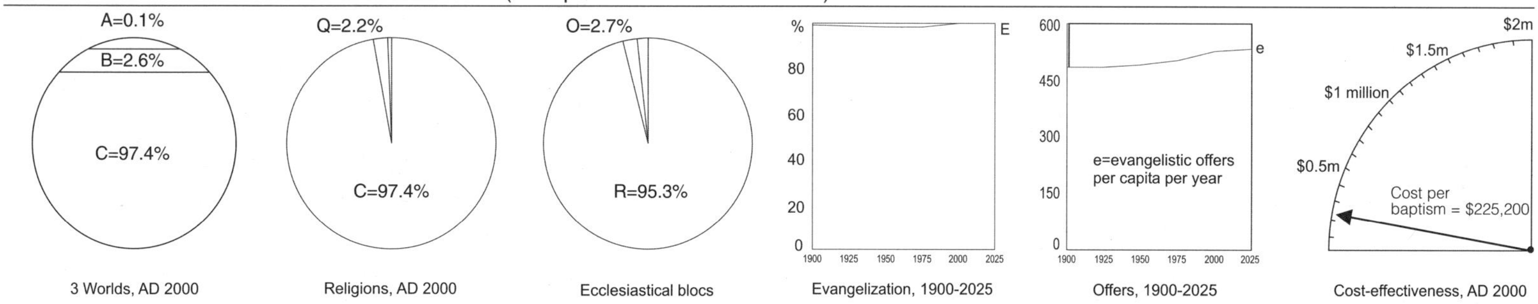

NON-CHRISTIAN RELIGIONS

Judaism consisted in 1939 of a large community of about 3.5 million Polish Jews. As a result of the World War II massacres which claimed 3 million victims, flight to the West and Russia and post-war emigration to Israel, Jews were reduced to about 31,000 by 1963. Subsequently, the anti-Zionist policy of the government provoked even greater emigration, reducing the Jewish community to about 8,000 by 1970. The community has subsequentially declined to nearly 7,000 at the present time. Among the Jews, authority is centralized in the Union Congress Assembly in Warsaw.

Islam had 5,000 adherents in 1995, 3 imams, 2 mosques and 6 religious communities. The supreme authority for Islam in Poland is the Muslim College with a lay chairman.

CHRISTIANITY

In the year 966, the duke of Mieszka was converted to Christianity through his Christian wife, and in 968 the first bishopric was established in Poznan. Under Mieszka's son Boleslaw Chrobry, who reigned until 1025, the power of both the kingdom and the church grew, and missionaries were sent out to other countries. German missionaries brought about much of the early development of Poland, and Boleslaw had to contend with German imperialistic designs. In AD 1000, however, Gniezno was made an independent archepiscopal see with 3 suffragan bishoprics. After Boleslaw's death, a reaction set in against Christianity and foreign clergy and the country itself began to disintegrate. Some progress was made in restoring church-state relations during the next century, but Christianity in Poland for a long period failed to achieve the strength it had attained in western Europe. In 1364, the university of Krakow was established, and the pagan Lithuanian duke Jagiello became ruler of both Poland and Lithuania following his baptism in 1386. Once again, the state took an interest in promoting the Christian faith, though Christianity in Poland seemed to owe as much to German missionary work and the eastward expansion of German settlers as to the conversion of the Polish rulers. The 15th century became known as the century of saints, and the 16th century was regarded as Poland's gold age with such men as Nicholas Copernicus among its scholars.

Lutheranism spread to Poland in 1518 and Poznan became the center for those of the nobility who adopted this faith. Calvinism appeared in 1548, and exiled Moravians also began entering Poland. The result was the development of over 900 Protestant centers, with Protestants holding important posts in the government. A national church was requested by Roman Catholics but refused at the Council of Trent in 1564. Popular reaction against the Catholic Church accompanied similar dissatisfaction with royal authority. The Jagiello regime was finally overthrown in 1572, the throne became elective and a parliament was established. Shortly after, however, the Catholic Church was in 1587 given official recognition and Protestantism was restricted. Disputes continued among noblemen espousing the different faiths, and in 1772 Russia, Austria, and Prussia took advantage of these internal conflicts and divided Polish territory among themselves. Catholic dioceses remained, though several had to operate without bishops for long periods. A certain amount of religious freedom existed in the territories annexed by Austria but greater repression was experienced in the Russian sector, and a number of bishops, priests, and laymen were deported to Siberia.

Following World War I, Poland became an independent nation once again. At the same time, the influence of the Catholic Church was reestablished and religious instruction required in all schools. During World War II, the German Nazi regime liquidated 6 million Poles, half of them Jews, while Russia deported 1.7 million Poles.

CATHOLIC CHURCH. Since the creation of the Polish state in 966, the vigor and influence of Polish Catholicism have been closely linked with the fortunes of the Polish nation and people. The dismemberment of the nation in the 18th century again accentuated this link. It has been the church rather than the state which has traditionally served as the political and social focal point. Clergy, drawn from all levels of society, have played an active cultural and patriotic role. This fact is important in understanding the character of Polish Catholicism today. Although 6 bishops, 2,030 diocesan and religious priests, 127 seminarians, 173 brothers and 243 sisters were exe-

Country summary. **Worlds A, B, C by ethnolinguistic peoples, cities, and major civil divisions in Poland.**

	PEOPLES							CITIES							CIVIL DIVISIONS						
World	Num	Pop 2000	C%	Christians	E%	U%	Unevangelized	Num	Pop 2000	C%	Christians	E%	U%	Unevangelized	Num	Pop 2000	C%	Christians	E%	U%	Unevangelized
A	4	7,676	0.36	28	30	70	5,343	0	0	0.00	0	0	0	0	0	0	0.00	0	0	0	0
B	0	0	0.00	0	0	0	0	0	0	0.00	0	0	0	0	0	0	0.00	0	0	0	0
C	20	38,757,410	96.75	37,498,029	100	0	11,371	75	17,554,549	95.18	16,708,528	100	0	12,742	49	38,765,084	96.73	37,498,059	100	0	16,712
Total	**24**	**38,765,086**	**96.73**	**37,498,057**	**100**	**0**	**16,714**	**75**	**17,554,549**	**95.18**	**16,708,528**	**100**	**0**	**12,742**	**49**	**38,765,084**	**96.73**	**37,498,059**	**100**	**0**	**16,712**

cuted by the Nazis during World War II, the influence of the church since then has actually increased. This is due in no small part to the changes in the boundaries of Poland in 1945, when territory to the east was lost but territory to the west was gained. The shift in boundaries not only made Poland more homogeneous in nationality but also more uniform in religious profession.

Polish Catholicism is a popular and mass phenomenon based on a religiosity which believes that there is a kind of special link between God and the Polish people, a faith which is often blind and inflexible but which has resulted in a great attachment and fidelity to the church.

Today Catholics form the vast majority of the population and are served by a large and growing priesthood. There is little difference in religious practice from one social class to another. Religious traditions were developed among the working classes during the 19th century and new industrial centers have been populated by people from rural areas who brought their religious traditions with them. The percentage practicing their religion, generally high in rural areas and reduced in the cities, remains much higher than in Western Europe. This is not uniform in all areas: religious practice is comparatively weak in industrial regions and areas with long-standing traditions of socialism such as Zaglebie, Dabrowskie, Lodz, and Warsaw as well as in several rural areas of the eastern part of the country, including the Lublin region. There are, however, industrial centers with strong traditional religious conviction, as in Upper Silesia, and yet others where religious conviction has shaped their evolution, as in Nowa Huta. Some new urban and industrial communities as yet have no churches including Swidnik K/Lublina, Nowy Krasnik, and Nowy Konin.

Councils or senates of priests exist in almost all dioceses. Members consist of those in charge of the different diocesan offices, who serve ex-officio and also elected members representing various categories of priests including superiors, parish priests, vicars and chaplains in the armed forces. These senates in their meetings usually avoid major pastoral and theological problems in favor of practical problems such as relationships between parish priests and vicars, equalization of stipends and pensions for retired priests.

The Holy See has diplomatic relations with Poland and in AD 2000 is represented to government and the Catholic hierarchy by a nuncio residing in Warsaw.

ORTHODOX CHURCH. The autocephalous Orthodox Church of Poland traces its origin back to the 10th century, with further development taking place after the union of Lithuania and Poland in the 14th century. When Poland was dismembered among its neighbors in 1772, its Orthodox church was united with the Orthodox Church of Russia, and this state of affairs continued until 1918. In 1925, the ecumenical patriarch of Constantinople recognized the autocephality of the Polish church, but the Russian church withheld agreement until 1948. Because of this lack of Russian recognition, the Polish government refused to accord it full status, and its members suffered discrimination prior to and during the war years. Before World War I, the church had 10 bishops, 5 dioceses, about 2,000 parishes, 15 monasteries and around 4 million members. Its membership is now only 20% of its former size, part of this decrease being attributable to the church's past failures to involve itself in missionary activity of any kind. Clergy are trained at the Orthodox seminary and at the Orthodox Theological Department of the Christian Theology Academy. The latter institution is state-supported and jointly operated with various Protestant denominations.

PROTESTANT CHURCHES. Of the various Protestant denominations in Poland, only about a third are recognized by the government as churches. The rest are listed as religious organizations. Upper Silesia is the most Protestant part of the country.

The largest Protestant body has long been the Lutheran Church, although following the expulsion of Germans after World War II, its membership was reduced by a third. Lutherans in the former German territory of west Poland have formed their own church as well as Poles outside the country who have established the Polish Lutheran Church in exile. Pastors are trained at the ecumenical Christian Theology Academy. After the Helsinki Accord, 125,000 Lutherans and Reformed of German origin were allowed to emigrate to west German in 1975-76.

The Reformed Church traces its origin to the entry of Calvinism into Poland in 1548. It is active in the ecumenical movement in the country.

United Evangelical Church of the Gospel. Catechumens enter river for believer's baptism, 1974.

The United Evangelical Church of the Gospel was created in 1947 by the amalgamation of 3 distinct denominations with 2 more added in 1953: Union of Christian Evangelists, Free Christian Union, Committed Christian Union, Pentecostals, and Church of Christ. Just under half of all members are Pentecostals. The church sponsors a home for the aged in Ostroda.

Three denominations with fraternal ties outside Poland were granted recognition after World War II: the Methodist, Adventist, and Baptist churches. All are able to publish widely circulated journals. Each has its headquarters in Warsaw; Methodists also operate an English-language school there. The Epiphany Lay Missionary Movement has its seat in Poznan; the Free Union of Holy Scripture Seekers are entered in Krakow.

Evangelical Church of the Augsburg Confession. Main Lutheran church, in Warsaw.

CATHOLIC (INDEPENDENT) CHURCHES. Several bodies have broken off from the Roman Catholic Church. In 1906, a schism took place in Poland known as the Old Catholic Mariavite Church, which has since its inception placed emphasis on moral renewal and the cult of the Virgin Mary (Mariavite=Imitator of Mary).

From 1924, it was not regarded as genuinely Old Catholic and was excluded from the Union of Utrecht, but in 1973 it was once more accepted into the Old Catholic community. The church has founded a number of convents and also Plock seminary for training its clergy. In 1936, a further split from within this group produced the Catholic Mariavite Church.

A much larger schism originated in the USA in 1897 when the Polish National Catholic Church was founded as a protest against domination by German and Irish priests in Roman Catholic dioceses with large Polish Catholic majorities. The movement spread to Poland following World War I and the church was officially recognized in 1922. The church is accepted as Old Catholic and belongs to the Union of Utrecht. There are now 4 dioceses in the USA, one in Canada and 3 in Poland. Education for the priesthood is carried on at the Old Catholic Theological Department of the Christian Theology Academy.

Catholic Church in Poland, Archdiocese of Krakow. *Above.* New church for Lenin Steelworks employees in Nowa Huta (New Foundry), finally completed despite massive bureaucratic opposition for 23 years. *Below.* Former Archbishop of Krakow returns to Warsaw as Pope John Paul II, June 1979.

Renewal movements. In the 1990s the Pentecostal/Charismatic Renewal continued to spread rapidly across most older churches, and numbered over 2,015,000 adherents (of whom 2% Pentecostals, 90% Charismatics, and 7% Independents).

Indigenous missions. Polish Christians have been active in missions since the gospel was introduced to the country in the 10th century. Missionary sending continued at a vigorous pace even under Communist rule. Today Polish Christian missionaries can be found all over the world.

CHURCH AND STATE

The constitution of 22 July 1952, Article 70, paragraph 1, 'guarantees freedom of conscience and religion to all citizens. The (Catholic) Church and other religious bodies may freely exercise their religious functions'. The same article proclaims the separation of church and state (paragraph 2), forbids citizens being prevented from taking part in religious activities or ceremonies (paragraph 1) and declares that it is punishable by law to 'abuse freedom of conscience and religion for ends contrary to the interests of the Popular Republic of Poland' (paragraph 3).

Relations between the Communist government emerging out of World War II and the Catholic Church were often strained; but in spite of administrative difficulties, the Polish church never experienced persecution comparable to that which has taken place in most other European Communist countries.

Strongly nationalistic and retaining the loyalty of the great majority of the population, the Polish church was the principal representative of the churches with the state Bureau of Religious Affairs (Urzad do Spraw

Wyznan). This bureau was under the president of the Council of Ministers with headquarters at Warsaw and branches in each province (voivodie). Since 1945, the principal sources of tension were the status of the former German dioceses (finally settled in 1972), taxation of the church (a 1962 decree ordering listing of church property with a view to taxation was rescinded in 1972), religious education in public schools (suppressed in 1951, restored in 1956, suppressed again in 1961) and the construction of new church buildings.

Five important events in these relations between the Communist state and the Catholic Church may be noted. First, was the unilateral denunciation by the state, on 14 September 1945, of the concordat of 1925 with the Holy See. Second, was the failure of the government's attempt to create a national church which it could manipulate and which was followed by the signing of an agreement between state and church on 14 April 1950, a compromise resulting in the government adopting a more conciliatory attitude and recognizing the pope as head of the church, with the church agreeing to support government foreign policies and to urge the Holy See to recognize Polish sovereignty over the former German territories in Oder-Neisse, Gdansk, and east Prussia. This agreement provided the basis for the church to name residential bishops replacing the existing apostolic administrators. The third event was the arrest of cardinal Wyszinski on 26 September 1953, and the fourth his release with numerous other priests in 1956 at the start of the Gomulka regime.

Fifth, a further agreement embodying a new modus vivendi was signed on 8 December 1956. Last, in May 1967, the Holy See appointed 4 apostolic administrators (ad nutum Sanctae Sedis) for the former German territories in the north and west and promoted them to titular bishops.

Although by 1973 church-state relations had greatly improved, there was still considerable tension due to the demands of cardinal Wysznski concerning educational reform, which he considered 'to place youth in danger'. In mid-1975, however, it was clear that the church had more reason for satisfaction than discontent. By this time, the principal concerns of the Polish episcopate had become: total freedom of association and meeting, since Catholic action groups were still nonexistent; more authorizations to build new churches; recognition of the full rights of Polish Catholics in the life of the nation; and assurance that the educational system of the schools would respect the beliefs of all.

The Catholic Church receives no subsidy from the government and relies solely on donations from its faithful, although it still owns some rural property. The agrarian reform of 1944 in fact resulted in the loss of no more than 50 hectares of Catholic property. The church and its institutions are not recognized as public bodies and are taxed in a way similar to private enterprises; but with the abolition of the compulsory annual listing, its taxes have been somewhat reduced. Nursery schools, primary schools and charitable institutions have now been taken over by government but the church continues to operate a few secondary schools, seminaries, and theological faculties as well as the Catholic University of Lublin. Because of the separation of religion and schools, religious instruction is conducted in churches, chapels and on parish and private premises. These catechetical centers must be registered and submit to public education authorities annual reports of their activities, including numbers of hours of courses, numbers of children, but without having to name personnel involved.

BROADCASTING AND MEDIA

Shortwave radio programs in European languages can be received from KNLS, AWR (Slovakia) and HCJB (Ecuador). AWR's Warsaw studio produces Polish programs. TWR launched a new transmitter in 1996. Poland is a member of UNDA. Catholics broadcast 12 regular weekly programs totalling over 6 hours, including evangelistic and Bible study programs.

The 'Jesus' Film has been shown to 13.3 million: 350,000 watched a broadcast on national television, and 13 million have seen it presented by a film team, with 90,000 responses. Satellite TV programs are received mainly in Arabic. Catholics air 4 regular television programs, each 20 to 30 minutes in length.

150th Anniversary of Bible Society in Poland, 1966, in Polish Ecumenical Center, hearing lecture by Bishop H. Hogsbro of Denmark.

INTERDENOMINATIONAL ORGANIZATIONS

The Polish Ecumenical Council was formed in 1945, but it traces its tradition of cooperation back to the Sandomierz Accord of 1570 when Lutherans, Calvinists, and Moravian Brethren began holding joint synods. The council consists of the 10 principal Old Catholic, Orthodox, and Protestant bodies. The Christian Theological Academy in Warsaw is also a member. The council's aims are to develop an awareness of ecumenical, evangelistic, and peace problems and to coordinate studies and pastoral work. It operates through 11 subsidiary regional bodies. A Joint Commission of the Polish Ecumenical Council and the Catholic Episcopal Commission for Ecumenism was formed in 1974.

FUTURE TRENDS AND PROSPECTS

With the collapse of Communism, the downward trend in Christian affiliation has been halted and an upward climb should now continue through 2025 reaching 98% of the population.

After AD 2025 Christianity could begin a slow decline throughout the 21st century. The nonreligious, declining in the wake of the collapse of Communism, then would begin to grow again by AD 2050.

BIBLIOGRAPHY

'Baptists in Poland: past and present,' R. E. Davies, *Religion in Communist lands*, 18, 1 (Spring 1990), 52–63.
Bibliography of books on Poland or relating to Poland (published outside Poland since 1 September 1939). J. Zabielska (ed, vols 1-3) & Z. Jagodzinski (ed, vol 4). London: Polish Library, 1953-85. 4 vols.
'Church and nation in socialist Poland,' M. Kennedy & M. D. Simon, in *Religion and politics.* P. H. Merkl & N. Smart (eds). New York: New York University Press, 1983.
'Church and nationality in postwar Poland,' V. C. Chrypinski, in *Religion and nationalism in Soviet and East European politics*, p.241–263. P. Ramet (ed). 2nd ed. Durham, NC: Duke University Press, 1989.
Culture in Poland. W. Gielzynski. Warsaw: Interpress Publishers, 1975. 93p.
Doctoral dissertations and master's theses regarding Polish subjects 1900–85: an annotated bibliography. B. Wielewinski (ed). *East European monographs*, no. 235. New York: Columbia University Press, 1988. 200p.
Encyklopedia Katolicka (Catholic encyclopedia). F. Gryglewicz et al. (eds). Lublin, Poland: Catholic University, 1973–. 12 vols. (In progress).
Five centuries of Lutheranism in Poland. A. Tokarczyk. Warsaw: Interpress, 1984. 56p.
'Five years underground: the opposition and the Church in Poland since martial law,' I. Korba, *Religion in Communist lands*, 15, 2 (Summer 1987), 167–81.
John Paul II in Poland, 2–10 June 1979. D. Le Corre & M. Sobotka. Trans., J. Sikorski & G. Lutos. London: Veritas Foundation, 1979. 120p.
Journeys to glory—a celebration of the human spirit. A. Bujak & M. Young. New York: Harper and Row, 1976. (Photographic collection of religious celebrations in Poland).
Katoliczym Ludowu w Polsce: studia socjologiczne (Catholic Church in Poland: sociological studies). E. Ciupak. Warsaw: Wiedza Powszechna, 1973.
L'église catholique en Pologne. P. Lenert. Paris: Centurion, 1962. 173p.
Light and life: renewal in Poland. G. Sikorska. Grand Rapids, MI: Eerdmans, 1989. 156p.
Next to God—Poland: politics and religion in contemporary Poland. B. Szajkowski. London: F. Pinter, 1983. 264p.
'Pastoral mobilization and symbolic politics: the Catholic Church in Poland, 1918–1966.' M. Osa. Ph.D. dissertation, University of Chicago, 1992. 184p.
'Poland,' J. Majka, in *Western religion: a country by country sociological enquiry*, p.403–25. H. Mol (ed). The Hague: Mouton, 1972.
Poland. G. Sanford & A. Gozdecka-Sanford. 2nd ed. *World bibliographical series*, vol. 32. Oxford, UK: CLIO Press, 1993. 292p. (See especially 'Religion,' p.70–8).
Poland: an annotated bibliography of books in English. A. G. Kanka. *Garland reference library of the humanities*, no. 743. London: Garland, 1988. 395p. (1,585 titles; see especially 'Religious conditions,' p.319–24).
Poland and the minority races. A. L. Goodhart.
Poland in Christian civilization. J. Braun (ed). London: Veritas Foundation, 1985. 633p.
Poland, past and present: a select bibliography of works in English. N. Davies. Newtonville, MA: Oriental Research Partners, 1977. 185p.
Poland's adventure in grace: one thousand years, 966–1966. Z. Peszkowski. Orchard Lake, MI: Orchard Lake Schools, 1966. 63p.
Poland's millennium of Catholicism. Lublin: Scientific Society of the Catholic University, 1969. 626p.
Poland's thousand years, the vanguard of Christendom. M. McLaren. London: Catholic Institute for International Relations, 1965. 62p.
Polish Jewry: history and culture. M. Fuks et al. Trans., B. Piotrowska & L. Petrowicz. Warsaw: Interpress, 1982. 196p.
'Polish Protestants: ecumenism in a dual diaspora,' P. Keim, *Religion in Communist lands*, 10, 3 (Autumn 1983), 295–309.
Politics and religion in Eastern Europe: Catholicism in Hungary, Poland, and Czechoslovakia. P. Michel. Oxford, UK: Polity, 1991. 329p.
Protestantism in Poland. C. E. Edwards. Philadelphia: Westminster Press, 1901. 61p.
Religious life in Poland. J. Walicki. Trans., L. Zembrzuski. Warsaw: Interpress Publishers, 1970. 82p.
Religiousness in the Polish society life: chosen problems. W. Zdaniewicz (ed). *Religious sociological studies*, vol. 3. Warsaw: Pallottinum, 1981. 169p.
'Sociology of religion in Poland,' *Social compass*, 15, 3-4 (1968).
Some questions of Polish religiosity in the 1980s. W. Zdaniewicz (ed). *Religious sociological studies*, vol. 10. Warsaw: Pallottinum, 1989. 92p.
Song, dance, and customs of peasant Poland. S. Benet. London: D. Dobson, 1951. 247p.
The Catholic Church in communist Poland 1945–85: forty years of church–state relations. R. C. Monticone. *East European monographs*, no. 205. New York: Columbia University Press, 1986. 227p.
'The character of Polish Catholicism,' J. Majka, *Social compass*, 15, 3-4 (1968), 185–208.
'The Christian Church in Poland: a history of church planting with strategies for future beginnings.' M. R. Householder. D.Min. thesis, Fuller Theological Seminary, Pasadena, CA, 1992. 289p.
The church and the state in Poland after World War II: the background. A. Korbonski. Washington, DC: National Council for Soviet and East European Research, [1994]. 26p.
The Church in Poland: facts, figures, information. A. Piekarski. Warsaw: International Publication Service, 1978. 238p.
The church in Poland under martial law. London: NSZZ Solidarnosc Information Office, 1983. 64p.
The Gypsies in Poland: history and customs. J. Ficowski. Trans., E. Healey. Warsaw: Interpress, 1989. 303p.
'The insoluble problem: church and state in Poland,' L. Blir, *Religion in Communist lands*, 1 (May–June, 1973).
The Jesuits in Poland. A. F. Pollard. 1892; reprint, New York: Haskell House Publishers, 1971. 98p.
The Orthodox Eastern Church in Poland: past and present. Ditchling, UK: Ditchling Press, 1942. 49p.
The Poles: how they live and work. M. E. Heine. New York: Praeger Publishers, 1975. 167p.
'The Polish Church under martial law,' J. Luxmore, *Religion in Communist lands*, 15, 2 (1987), 124–66.
The Pope in Poland. Munich: Radio Free Europe Research, 1979. 128p. (Deals with John Paul II's visit to Poland in 1979).
The priest who had to die: the tragedy of Father Jerzy Popieluszko. R. Boyes & J. Moody. London: Victor Gollancz, 1986. 204p.
The Protestant churches in Poland. London: Polish Research Centre, 1944. 66p.
'The Roman Catholic Church in 1944–89 Poland,' V. C. Chrypinski, in *Catholicism and politics in communist societies*, p.117–41. P. Ramet (ed). Durham, NC: Duke University Press, 1990.
'The situation of Protestants in today's Poland,' B. Tranda, *Religion in Communist lands*, 19, 1-2 (1991), 37–44.
The third Adam: the Mariavite experiment in mystical marriage. J. M. Pietrkiewicz. London: Oxford University Press, 1975. 243p.
The Ukrainians in Poland. M. Filinski. London: Reynolds and Co., 1931. 173pp.
Treasured Polish Christmas customs and traditions, carols, decorations and a Christmas play. Minneapolis, MN: Polanie Club, 1972. 198p.
'Ukrainian Catholics and Orthodox in Poland,' A. Sorokowski, *Religion in Communist lands*, 14, 3 (1986), 244–61.
Unser Weg: Vom Leben der Mitgliedskirchen des Polnischen Ökumenischen Rates. J. Niewieczerzal. Warsaw: Ökumenische Rat, 1966. 225p.
Wspolczesne chrzescijanstwo w Polsce (Contemporary Christianity in Poland). S. Markiewicz. Warsaw: Ksiazka i Wiedza, 1967.

Country Table 2. **Organized churches and denominations in Poland.**

Official name (bold type = church *with over 10% of all affiliated)* 1	*Begun* 2	*Type* 3	*Counc* 4	*Congs* 5	*Adults* 6	*Affiliated 1970* 7	*Affiliated 1995* 8	*G%* 9	*Names, notes, and other statistics* (see Codebook, Part 3) 10
Assemblies of God	c1930	P-Pe2	.....	252	25,487	4,900	36,500	0.05	M=AoG. 1987, registered separately as Pentecostal Ch of Poland.
Assembly Hall Churches	c1990	I-3nC	.....	10	191	–	500	20.00	*Little Flock. Local Churches.* Begun 1922 in China. Chinese.
Catholic Church in Poland:	c 950	R-Lat	B.B.R	10,539	23,456,000	28,783,085	35,475,061	0.84	*Kosciól Rzymsko-katolicki.* C=35+7+99. 26q,24s. 19130n 4746x 8120m24242w 476116Yy
M Bialystok	c1350	R-Lat	Bs	108	254,000	283,348	385,274	1.24	*Archidiecezja w Bialymstoku.* Suppressed1945-91. 304n 10x 11m 175w 5746Yy
D Drohiczyn	1925	R-Lat	Bs	177	146,000	92,572	221,080	3.54	In D Pinsk, suppressed 1945-91. M=OFMCap. 163n 11x 14m 108w 3299Yy
D Lomza	1925	R-Lat	Bs	236	381,000	570,000	576,638	0.05	Population is 98% baptized Catholics. 365n 18x 24m 183w 9992Yy
M Czestochowa	1925	R-Lat	Bs	286	551,000	1,318,000	835,500	-1.81	North rural, south dechristianized. Cult of Mary. 556n 157x 236m 999w 10512Yy
D Radom	1992	R-Lat	Bs	289	680,000	–	1,030,000	33.33	98% baptized Catholics. 561n 80x 92m 304w 12656Yy
D Sosnowiec	1992	R-Lat	Bs	154	496,000	–	751,500	33.33	M=SDB. 326n 31x 37m 177w 7687Yy
M Gdansk (Danzig)	1925	R-Lat	Bs	155	635,000	515,600	961,718	2.52	Port, industry. Large pastoral activity. M=CM. 422n 197x 290m 496w 11886Yy
D Pelplin (Chelmno)	1243	R-Lat	Bs	287	520,000	1,221,132	788,281	-1.74	*Diecezja Chelminska.* Traditional religiosity. 444n 83x 96m 328w 10894Yy
D Torun	1992	R-Lat	Bs	183	445,000	–	675,000	33.33	M=CSMA. 308n 64x 70m 438w 9304Yy
M Gniezno	1000	R-Lat	Bs	328	664,000	937,028	1,006,268	0.29	*Archidiecezja Gnieznienska.* Primatial see. 608n 87x 96m 381w 14733Yy
D Wloclawek (Wladislavia, Cujavia)	996	R-Lat	Bs	368	571,000	1,001,028	866,184	0.10	Rural, being industrialized. Active practice. 486n 91x 270m 464w 13364Yy
M Katowice	1925	R-Lat	Bs	308	1,015,000	1,600,000	1,538,000	-0.16	Working-class, religious. Protestant bloc in south. 849n 91x 155m 1025w 21364Yy
D Gliwice	1992	R-Lat	Bs	146	492,000	–	745,900	33.33	92% baptized Catholics. 295n 136x 144m 300w 8881Yy
D Opole (formerly Oppeln)	1972	R-Lat	Bs	389	574,000	1,540,000	870,000	4.35	Detached from M Breslau. Settlers from all Poland. 596n 141x 208m 899w 11592Yy
M Kraków	c960	R-Lat	Bs	373	1,080,000	1,899,729	1,637,000	0.10	Centre of national culture, strongly religious. 959n 784x 1726m 2224w 21895Yy
D Bielsko-Zywiec	1992	R-Lat	Bs	202	481,000	–	728,550	33.33	90% baptized Catholics. 439n 69x 88m 528w 9478Yy
D Kielce	1805	R-Lat	Bs	284	544,000	898,074	825,000	-0.34	Industrial, becoming dechristianized. 556n 62x 80m 427w 11248Yy
D Tarnów	1786	R-Lat	Bs	433	750,000	1,143,600	1,137,000	-0.02	Many religious and priestly vocations. 1086n 147x 269m 1300w 18226Yy
M Lublin	1805	R-Lat	Bs	241	678,000	1,216,100	1,028,000	-0.67	Difficult pastorally, low religious practice. 776n 172x 329m 943w 14464Yy
D Sandomierz	1818	R-Lat	Bs	227	463,000	1,175,000	701,000	-2.04	Industrial centers, becoming dechristianized. 439n 45x 50m 489w 10494Yy
D Siedlce	1918	R-Lat	Bs	233	461,000	780,550	699,124	-0.44	East of Warsaw. Very active religious practice. 490n 57x 69m 358w 13361Yy
M Poznan	968	R-Lat	Bs	804	1,024,000	1,600,000	1,552,000	0.10	Industrial and cultural centre. High practice. 815n 236x 621m 1572w 30419Yy
D Kolisz	1992	R-Lat	Bs	258	493,000	–	747,000	33.33	Population is 99% baptized Catholics. 415n 70x 82m 517w 10731Yy
M Przemysl of the Latins	1375	R-Lat	Bs	377	543,000	1,371,293	823,916	-2.02	99% baptized Catholics. 736n 118x 142m 971w 12331Yy
D Rzeszow	1992	R-Lat	Bs	202	399,000	–	604,054	33.33	98% Catholic. 491n 101x 201m 257w 8433Yy
D Zamosc-Lubaczów	1412	R-Lat	Bs	167	328,000	77,734	497,000	7.70	Formerly in AD Lvov (USSR) suppressed 1945-92. 311n 13x 14m 116w 7384Yy
M Szczecin-Kamien (Stettin)	1972	R-Lat	Bs	251	660,000	847,000	1,000,000	4.35	Detached from D Berlin. Northern port. M=OFMConv. 390n 158x 165m 180w 12925Yy
D Koszalin-Kolobrzeg	1972	R-Lat	Bs	209	570,000	818,690	863,000	4.35	Formed from D Berlin, PN Schneidemuhl. 344n 114x 126m 292w 11812Yy
D Zielona Gora-Gorzów (Landsberg)	1972	R-Lat	Bs	246	587,000	948,500	890,300	4.35	Formed from Breslau, Berlin, Schneidemuhl. M=CM. 453n 102x 107m 325w 13871Yy
M Warmia	1243	R-Lat	Bs	429	452,000	1,150,000	685,000	-2.05	Rural. Ex East Prussia, with Polish settlers. 337n 104x 185m 258w 9405Yy
D Elblag	1992	R-Lat	Bs	183	307,000	–	466,346	33.33	98% Catholic. 199n 61x 69m 150w 7910Yy
D Elk	1992	R-Lat	Bs	141	320,000	–	485,000	33.33	92% Catholic. 198n 46x 48m 133w 8175Yy
M Warszawa (Warsaw)	1798	R-Lat	Bs	180	957,000	2,800,000	1,450,000	-2.60	Capital; attached to Gniezno. Dechristianization. 548n 372x 665m 2425w 13824Yy
D Lowicz	1992	R-Lat	Bs	160	392,000	–	594,793	33.33	99.8% baptized Catholics. 295n 64x 99m 465w 7968Yy
D Plock	c950	R-Lat	Bs	235	538,000	840,000	815,000	0.10	Strongest area of Mariavite schismatics. 473n 57x 107m 297w 11342Yy
D Warszawa-Praga	1992	R-Lat	Bs	136	737,000	–	1,117,000	33.33	95% Catholic. 372n 103x 113m 1225w 10574Yy
M Wroclaw (Breslau, Breslavia)	1000	R-Lat	Bs	393	971,000	2,829,400	1,471,455	-2.58	1972, parts added from D Meissen, AD Prague. 765n 285x 515m 1422w 17815Yy
D Legnica	1992	R-Lat	Bs	276	752,000	–	1,140,000	33.33	97% Catholic. 430n 29x 100m 341w 11377Yy
AD Lódz	1920	R-Lat	Bs	198	1,000,000	1,250,000	1,516,180	0.78	Socialist traditions. Shortage of priests. 480n 164x 382m 734w 14849Yy
D Przemysl (*Ukrainian*)	1087	R-Ukr	os	108	79,000	1,150,000	120,000	-8.64	Longstanding Byzantine tradition. 50n 16x 25m 16w 3895Yy
O Poland	1991	R-Ori	Os	20	66,000	–	100,000	25.00	Ordinariate for all Eastern-rite Catholics (Melkite, Armenian, et alia).
OM Poland	1919	R-Lat	Bs	159	400,000	100,000	530,000	6.90	Military Ordinariate of Poland. 115 ordinaries, 68 auxiliaries. 11w,2090Yy.
Doubly-counted Catholics		R-Lat		0	0	-3,191,293	0		Catholics counted in newer dioceses but also in parent dioceses.
Christ Groups	c1990	I-3hW	x....	19	500	–	1,000	20.00	Home churches for isolated converts after nationwide EHC campaign.
Ch of Jesus Christ of Latter-day Saints		m-LdS	x....	2	240	500	600	0.05	*Mormons*, related to CJCLdS(Utah, USA). Neither recognized by state nor banned.
Churches of Christ		I-Dis	xv...	24	1,200	2,000	2,000	0.05	M=CCCC(Instrumental)(USA). Warsaw, Breslau and 10 other cities. Rapid growth. 2f.
Epiphany Lay Missionary Movement		P-Non	.....	90	1,800	3,000	3,000	0.05	Lay movement linked to USA body. HQ Poznan. 87 houses of prayer, 274 elders.
Ev Ch of the Augsburg Confession in P	1518	P-Lut	LWC.W	352	68,300	120,000	91,000	-1.10	*Kosciól Ewangelicko-Augsburski w PRL.* 6 Dioceses. Germans. 107n,125b,1j,214t,1u.
Free Evangelical Church	1988	I-Eva	.....	18	1,800	–	3,000	14.29	Independent Evangelicals.
Free Union of Holy Scripture Seekers		I-Non	.....	109	2,400	5,000	4,000	0.05	Independents centered on Bible study. HQ Krakow. 320 preachers.
Indep Autonom Roman Cath Parishes	1962	I-CCa	.....	2	7,920	15,000	12,000	-0.89	Schisms ex RCC by 2 parishes: Wierzbica (11 villages, 9000), & Kamionka Wielka.
Isolated radio churches	1939	I-rad	.....	3,000	100,000	600	150,000	24.71	Isolated believers in non-religious families. R=9600(SGA, TWR, Radio Vatican, &c).
Jehovah's Witnesses	1905	m-Jeh	x....	1,248	96,841	20,000	161,000	8.70	1920, 700 attending meetings. Active witnessing under way by 1926. (1995) 7502Y.
Mariavite Ch of Ancient Catholic Rite	1936	I-CCa	....w	31	3,450	4,000	4,600	0.56	*Catholic Mariavite Ch.* Schism ex Old Catholic Mariavite Ch. HQ Felicjanow. 70n,24b.
Methodist Ch in the Polish Republic	1922	P-Met	VvC.W	50	3,500	12,000	7,000	-2.13	*Kosciól Metodystyczny.* Linked C&S Europe CC, UMC(USA). 5 Districts 26n,1r(6000).
New Apostolic Church		I-3aX	x....	3	480	500	713	0.05	*Neo-Apostolic Association.* Bezirk Schweiz. World HQ (Zurich). Germans.
Old Catholic Church of Poland	1946	I-CCa	.....	2	600	1,000	1,200	0.73	Schism ex RCC. Joined by Mariavite remnants Links with NAORCC (USA).
Old Catholic Mariavite Ch of Poland	1906	I-CCa	UWC.W	194	15,500	24,000	25,000	0.16	*Staro-Katolickiego Koscióla Mariawitów. Imitators of Mary.* 3 Dioceses. 39n,200w,1s.
Old Ritualist Church (Priestless)	1634	I-OBe	.....	3	3,600	5,000	6,000	0.73	*Philippians. Old Believers.* Schism ex Russian OC. HQ Wojnowo. 6-hour services.
Orthodox Church of Poland:	c 990	O-Pol	MWC.W	345	626,000	527,000	1,000,000	2.60	*Autokefaliczny Kosciol Prawoslawny.* 1939, 4 million. 6 bps. (1970) 216n,216b,1d,1e,1s,1u.
D Warszawa (Warsaw) & Bielsk	1370	O-Pol	Mm	130	246,000	207,000	393,000	2.60	Mainly Ukrainians and Russians. 1 monastery for men (Jableczna). 94n (in 1977), 430n (1985).
D Bialystok & Gdansk (Danzig)		O-Pol	Mb	125	226,000	190,000	360,000	0.05	North and northeast. Many White Russians (Byelorussians), Ukrainians, Russians.
D Lódz & Poznan		O-Pol	Ma	50	95,000	80,000	152,000	0.05	Centre of country, west of Warsaw. Byelorussians, Ukrainians. 16 priests in 1977.
D Wroclaw & Szczecin		O-Pol	Mb	40	59,000	50,000	95,000	0.05	Formerly Breslau and Stettin in Germany, now settled by Poles. 27 priests in 1977.
Polish Baptist Union	1858	P-Bap	TvC.W	56	3,150	8,000	5,000	-1.86	*Polski Kosciol Chrzescijan Baptystów.* 10,000 adults in 1939. Declining. 64n,1s.
Polish National Catholic Church	1920	I-OCa	UWC.W	67	20,100	56,600	38,000	-1.58	*Kosciól Polskokatolicki.* USA schism ex RCC. Dioc: Warsaw, Krakow, Wroclaw. 126n,1u.
Reformed Evangelical Church in Poland	1548	P-Ref	RvC.W	17	2,800	4,900	4,000	-0.81	*Kosciól Ewangelicko-Reformowany.* 1939-45, almost obliterated. Declining. 6n.
Seventh-day Adventist Church	1912	P-Adv	x...w	130	30,900	8,500	40,000	6.39	*Kosciól Adwentystow Ds w Polsce. SDA, Polish UC.* 25n,75mw,1j1s,120t(4801),189Y.
Union of Polish Brethren		m-Unt	.....	1	240	500	400	0.05	Unitarian tendencies. Links with Unitarian Universalist Association (USA).
United Evangelical Ch of the Gospel	1909	I-3pW	ZFC.W	350	21,000	20,000	42,000	3.01	Zjednoozony Kosciol Ewangeliezny. 1947 5 church merger. 65% Pentecostals. 125n,1s.
Other Protestant denominations		P-	.....	31	4,690	3,000	7,000	0.05	Total about 6 others (see list below).
Other marginal Protestant bodies		m-	.....	12	1,750	2,000	3,500	0.05	Total about 10 others (see list below).
Other Orthodox churches		O-	.....	2	240	500	600	0.05	Isolated groups, including Armenian Apostolics (Gregorians).
Other pentecostal churches	c1980	I-3pW	.....	38	2,660	–	4,000	6.67	In about 15 recent loose networks.
Totals				**16,997**	**24,503,339**	**29,631,585**	**37,128,674**		

Churches, members, growth, 1900-2025	*Congs*	*Adults*	*Affiliated*	*G%*	*Total denominations*	*6 Megablocs:* *O*	*R*	*A*	*P*	*I*	*m*
Total churches, members, and denominations (mid-1900)	5,000	14,102,000	21,383,500	0.47	6	1	1	0	3	1	0
Total churches, members, and denominations (mid-1970)	11,714	19,541,191	29,631,585	0.47	34	5	1	0	10	11	7
Total churches, members, and denominations (mid-1990)	16,000	24,127,000	36,558,000	1.06	64	9	1	0	13	28	13
Total churches, members, and denominations (mid-1995)	16,997	24,503,339	37,128,674	0.31	65	9	1	0	13	29	13
Total churches, members, and denominations (mid-2000)	17,000	24,747,000	37,498,059	0.20	66	9	1	0	13	30	13
Total churches, members, and denominations (mid-2025)	19,000	25,184,000	38,160,000	0.07	214	20	1	0	25	150	18

NOTES ON TABLE ABOVE

NATIONAL COUNCILS (Column 4, 5th letter).

R = Polish Episcopal Conference (Konferencja Episkopatu Polski, KEP).

W = Polish Ecumenical Council (Polska Rada Ekumeniczna, PRE), 1946.

w = associate member of PRE.

Local councils. 11 subsidiary regional bodies of PRE.

OTHER PROTESTANT DENOMINATIONS. In addition to those listed in the table, there are around 15 others not recognized by the state as churches but as either registered religious associations, other associations, or unregistered. These include: Apostolic See in Jesus Christ, Association of Bible Students, Association for Christian Education, Ch of God, Ch of Sabbath-Day Christians in Poland, Ch of the Brethren (1946; 7 missionaries, USA), Communities of Non Confessional Christians, Disciples of Christ, Evangelical Association of Prayer, Exclusive Brethren (Kelly-Continental), Friends (Quakers), Mennonites.

OTHER MARGINAL PROTESTANT BODIES. These include: Amis de l'Homme 'Ange du Seigneur' (Friends of Man 'Angel of the Lord') Lay Movement (schism ex Jehovah's Witnesses), Ch of Christ Scientist, Divine See of the Lamb of the Apostles in the Spirit and the Truth of Alpha & Omega The Beginning and The End, Pan-Monistic Community, Rustres (Clowns or Louts).

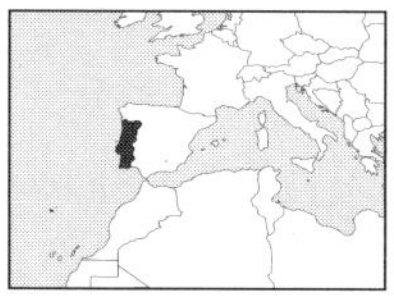

PORTUGAL

SECULAR DATA, AD 2000

STATE
Official name: La República Portuguesa (The Portuguese Republic).
Short name: Portugal. **Adjective of nationality:** Portuguese.
Flag: Green and red bars with national coat of arms.
Area: 92,135 sq. km. (35,574 sq. mi.).
Government: Parliamentary socialist republic, since 1976 (12th century independence as monarchy, 1910 republic, 1932 dictatorship, 1974 military junta, 1982 new constitution).
Legislature: National Assembly, 230 seats.
Official language: Portuguese (Portugués).
Monetary unit: 1 escudo (Esc) = 100 centavos. **US$1=** Esc 171.31.
Chief cities: LISBOA (Lisbon) 1,971,000; Porto (Oporto) 1,220,563; Amadora 95,172; Setubal (Saint Yves) 77,602; Coimbra 74,345.
Political divisions: 20 provinces.
Armed forces: 59,000.

DEMOGRAPHY
Population: 9,875,000.
Population density: 107.1/sq. km. (277.5/sq. mi.).
Under 15 years: 1,614,000.
Growth rate p.a.: -0.06% (births 10.00, deaths 10.87).
Mortality: Infant, per 1,000: 8.1, ; **Maternal per 100,000:** 15.0.
Life expectancy: 76 (male 73, female 80).
Household size: 3.8. **Floor area per person, sq.m:** 30.0.
Major languages: Portuguese, Spanish, English.
Urban dwellers: 38.00%. **Urban growth rate p.a.:** 1.3%.
Labor force: 48%.

ETHNOLINGUISTIC PEOPLES
91.8% Portuguese; 1.1% Marrano (Crypto-Jew); 1.1% Brazilian; 0.9% Han Chinese; 0.8% Angolan Mestico.

ECONOMY
National income p.a. per person: US$9,739; **per family:** US$37,011.

EDUCATION
Adult literacy: 90% (male 92%, female 87%). **Schools:** 14,140.
Universities: 250. **School enrolment:** female/male: 93%/90%.

HEALTH
Access to health services: 95%. **Access to safe water:** 100%.
Hospitals: 335 (42 beds per 10,000). **Doctors:** 24,499.
Blind: 8,225. **Deaf:** 587,300. **Murder rate:** 4.
Lepers: 4,000.

LITERATURE
New book titles p.a.: 8,100 (820 p.a. per million). **Periodicals:** 1,312.
Newspapers: 23 dailies.

COMMUNICATION (per 1,000 people)
Phones: 362 (42% mobile). **Radios:** 224. **TV sets:** 333.
Daily newspaper circulation: 41. **Computers:** 160.

REFUGEES
Alien refugees from other countries: 350.

HUMAN LIFE AND LIBERTY (optimum condition=100.0%)
HDI: 89.0. **HSI:** 75.0. **HFI:** 75.0. **EFL:** 48.0.

Country Table 1. **Religious adherents in Portugal, AD 1900-2025.**

Year	1900		1970		mid-1990		Annual change, 1990-2000				mid-1995		mid-2000		mid-2025	
Name	Adherents	%	Adherents	%	Adherents	%	Natural	Conversion	Total	Rate	Adherents	%	Adherents	%	Adherents	%
Christians	**5,420,800**	**100.0**	**8,835,100**	**97.7**	**9,183,320**	**93.1**	**544**	**-6,771**	**-6,227**	**-0.07**	**9,125,000**	**92.6**	**9,121,054**	**92.4**	**8,460,300**	**90.5**
PROFESSION																
professing Christians	**5,420,800**	**100.0**	**8,835,100**	**97.7**	**9,183,320**	**93.1**	**544**	**-6,771**	**-6,227**	**-0.07**	**9,125,000**	**92.6**	**9,121,054**	**92.4**	**8,460,300**	**90.5**
AFFILIATION																
unaffiliated Christians	5,500	0.1	365,812	4.0	56,000	0.6	3	-1,521	-1,518	-3.11	50,000	0.5	40,823	0.4	35,300	0.4
affiliated Christians	**5,415,300**	**99.9**	**8,469,288**	**93.6**	**9,127,320**	**92.5**	**541**	**-5,250**	**-4,709**	**-0.05**	**9,075,000**	**92.1**	**9,080,231**	**92.0**	**8,425,000**	**90.1**
Roman Catholics	5,412,800	99.8	8,379,224	92.7	9,050,000	91.7	536	-8,536	-8,000	-0.09	9,000,000	91.3	8,970,000	90.8	8,300,000	88.8
Independents	0	0.0	10,920	0.1	266,000	2.7	16	1,084	1,100	0.41	272,765	2.8	277,000	2.8	350,000	3.7
Protestants	2,000	0.0	53,644	0.6	125,000	1.3	8	992	1,000	0.77	130,436	1.3	135,000	1.4	170,000	1.8
Marginal Christians	0	0.0	20,000	0.2	87,500	0.9	5	1,045	1,050	1.14	90,500	0.9	98,000	1.0	180,000	1.9
Anglicans	500	0.0	4,500	0.1	3,200	0.0	0	-15	-15	-0.48	3,190	0.0	3,050	0.0	2,700	0.0
Orthodox	0	0.0	1,000	0.0	1,200	0.0	0	0	0	0.00	1,200	0.0	1,200	0.0	1,200	0.0
doubly-affiliated	0	0.0	0	0.0	-405,580	-4.1	-25	181	156	-0.04	-423,091	-4.3	-404,019	-4.1	-578,900	-6.2
Trans-megabloc groupings																
Evangelicals	1,500	0.0	37,000	0.4	94,000	1.0	6	1,394	1,400	1.40	99,287	1.0	108,000	1.1	140,000	1.5
Pentecostals/Charismatics	0	0.0	34,000	0.4	612,000	6.2	37	2,963	3,000	0.48	628,384	6.4	642,000	6.5	700,000	7.5
Great Commission Christians	**542,000**	**10.0**	**3,075,000**	**34.0**	**3,555,000**	**36.0**	**216**	**1,303**	**1,519**	**0.04**	**3,548,000**	**36.0**	**3,570,189**	**36.2**	**3,320,000**	**35.5**
Nonreligious	2,000	0.0	175,000	1.9	495,880	5.0	30	4,045	4,075	0.79	524,470	5.3	536,634	5.4	617,100	6.6
Atheists	0	0.0	30,000	0.3	95,000	1.0	6	1,502	1,508	1.48	105,000	1.1	110,075	1.1	120,000	1.3
Buddhists	0	0.0	0	0.0	50,000	0.5	3	527	530	1.01	52,500	0.5	55,299	0.6	70,000	0.8
Muslims	0	0.0	800	0.0	20,000	0.2	1	402	403	1.85	22,000	0.2	24,033	0.2	45,000	0.5
Chinese folk-religionists	0	0.0	0	0.0	18,000	0.2	1	243	244	1.28	20,000	0.2	20,441	0.2	26,000	0.3
Spiritists	0	0.0	0	0.0	3,000	0.0	0	46	46	1.43	3,200	0.0	3,456	0.0	5,000	0.1
Baha'is	0	0.0	1,800	0.0	1,800	0.0	0	5	5	0.25	1,820	0.0	1,845	0.0	2,000	0.0
Ethnoreligionists	0	0.0	0	0.0	1,500	0.0	0	8	8	0.52	1,550	0.0	1,580	0.0	2,200	0.0
Jews	200	0.0	1,300	0.0	500	0.0	0	-7	-7	-1.38	460	0.0	435	0.0	400	0.0
World A (unevangelized persons)	0	0.0	45,221	0.5	39,476	0.4	2	-352	-350	-0.92	39,424	0.4	39,500	0.4	46,740	0.5
World B (evangelized non-Christians)	2,200	0.0	163,978	1.8	646,204	6.5	39	7,123	7,162	1.01	691,730	7.0	714,446	7.2	840,960	9.0
World C (Christians)	5,420,800	100.0	8,835,100	97.7	9,183,320	93.1	544	-6,771	-6,227	-0.07	9,125,000	92.6	9,121,054	92.4	8,460,300	90.5
Country's population	**5,423,000**	**100.0**	**9,044,300**	**100.0**	**9,869,000**	**100.0**	**585**	**0**	**585**	**0.01**	**9,856,155**	**100.0**	**9,875,000**	**100.0**	**9,348,000**	**100.0**

COLUMNS, ROWS.
For meanings and definitions, see Codebook (Part 3). Note that, by definition, total 'Christians' = professing + crypto-Christians, which also = affiliated + unaffiliated Christians, and also = Great Commission Christians + latent Christians. Percentages may not always total exactly, due to rounding.

CENSUSES.
15.XII.1950: 96.7% Roman Catholics, 2.6% nonreligious, 0.7% other religionists. **15.XII.1960** (de jure): 97.9% Roman Catholics, 1.7% nonreligious, 0.4% Protestants. **15.XII.1970:** 96.5% Roman Catholics, 2.4% nonreligious and atheists, 0.5% Protestants, 0.5% other Christians (including some here termed Protestants), 1,300 Jews, 365 Muslims, 2,220 other non-Christians.

NOTES ON RELIGIONS
ATHEISTS. Partido Communista Português (PCP) banned and underground until 1974; pro-Soviet) and pro-Peking faction FAP. Most Communist voters regard themselves also as Roman Catholics, and many are still practicing Catholics.
BAHA'IS. Local spiritual assemblies: 1964, 9; 1973, 14.
DOUBLY-AFFILIATED. The term covers those affiliated to, or claimed by, both the Catholic Church and also another church: Evangelical (Protestant, marginal Christian, Anglican, Independents) or Catholic (non-Roman) or Orthodox; i.e. baptized Roman Catholics who have recently became Evangelicals or others. Because their statistics represent a duplication, they are shown in the table as a negative quantity (with a minus sign).
INDEPENDENTS. In 1991, The Universal Church of the Kingdom of God (IURD) from Brazil began work in Portugal, growing to 200,000 members by 1996.
JEWS. With 2 synagogues in Lisbon and one in Oporto. There are also 100,000 Marranos (Crypto-Jews), whose ancestors adopted Catholicism under duress in and after 1497 but who still secretly keep the Passover and other Jewish practices. In northern Portugal they number up to 10% of all Catholics in some towns. In the table above, they are enumerated as Roman Catholics.
MUSLIMS. Originally from Pakistan, Mozambique, Guinea-Bissau, Timor, Macao and North Africa. A number are present illegally (hence unregistered in censuses). *Hajj pilgrims to Mecca.* (1970) 79; (1976) 8.
PENTECOSTALS/CHARISMATICS. The Catholic renewal began in 1974. In mid-1978, 1,500 people from all parts of Portugal attended the Second National Conference of the Charismatic Renewal, held at Vila Nova de Gaia, organized by prayer groups in the diocese of Porto, and supported by the bishops of Porto and Setubal. From 1992, CCR television programs have been aired. By 1997, Charismatics numbered 12,000 adult regular attenders at 280 weekly prayer groups (and one covenant community), with 120 priests involved and 5 bishops. The XIXth Interdiocesan National Congress in 1996 attracted 3,000 participants.
ROMAN CATHOLICS. Including 100,000 Marranos (Crypto-Jews, Ansuim, New Christians, Conversos) who are baptized and outwardly-practicing Catholics mainly in the north.

Great Commission Instrument Panel: status of Portugal (for explanation see start of Part 4)

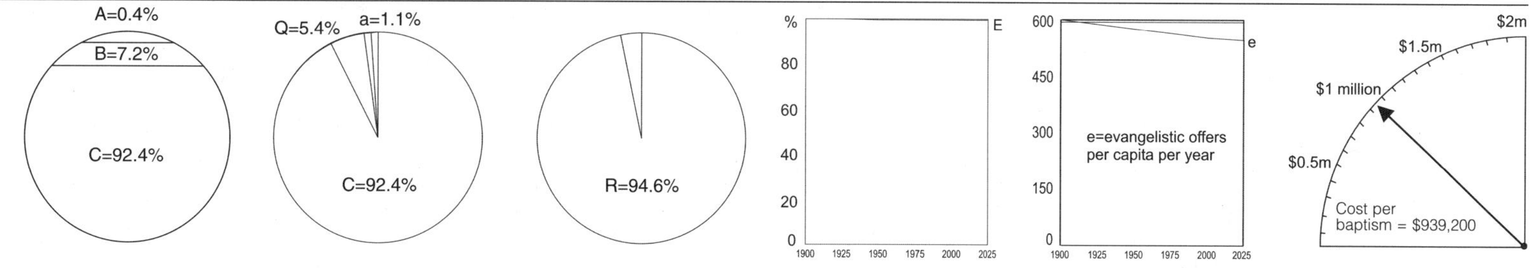

3 Worlds, AD 2000 | Religions, AD 2000 | Ecclesiastical blocs | Evangelization, 1900-2025 | Offers, 1900-2025 | Cost-effectiveness, AD 2000

Country status. Portugal is on the western Iberian peninsula in south-west Europe bordering the Atlantic Ocean and Spain. The economy is based on agriculture with the chief exports being cork, timber, fish, and wine.

HUMAN LIFE AND LIBERTY

Human need and development. In terms of population Portugal is a slow growing country gaining only one million between 1960 and 1990; even this growth was limited to coastal areas while other areas actually lost population. Heavy emigration to Western European countries accounted for the loss of people in rural areas. The proportion of women in the population grew as most of the emigrants were young men. Their departure has created serious social and

Country summary. **Worlds A, B, C by ethnolinguistic peoples, cities, and major civil divisions in Portugal.**

World	PEOPLES Num	Pop 2000	C%	Christians	E%	U%	Unevangelized
A	1	148	0.00	0	38	62	92
B	6	132,274	20.46	27,060	78	22	28,749
C	23	9,742,432	92.93	9,053,175	100	0	7,159
Total	**30**	**9,874,854**	**91.95**	**9,080,235**	**100**	**0**	**36,000**

World	CITIES Num	Pop 2000	C%	Christians	E%	U%	Unevangelized
A	0	0	0.00	0	0	0	0
B	0	0	0.00	0	0	0	0
C	6	3,427,424	88.48	3,032,650	99	1	29,240
Total	**6**	**3,427,424**	**88.48**	**3,032,650**	**99**	**1**	**29,240**

World	CIVIL DIVISIONS Num	Pop 2000	C%	Christians	E%	U%	Unevangelized
A	0	0	0.00	0	0	0	0
B	0	0	0.00	0	0	0	0
C	20	9,874,854	91.95	9,080,231	100	0	36,000
Total	**20**	**9,874,854**	**91.95**	**9,080,231**	**100**	**0**	**36,000**

economic problems. The shortage of men has affected patterns of marriage and fertility since many women spend long periods of time separated from their husbands. Nevertheless, birthrates remain high as also infant mortality rates. Portugal ranks at the bottom or near it on almost all significant quality of life indicators. Life expectancy is lower because many contagious diseases are prevalent. The numbers of doctors and medical facilities are small by European standards and maldistributed in favor of Lisbon and other large cities. Wages have not kept pace with inflation which ran over 17% during the 1980s. Sometimes there are shortages even of fish and eggs, the staples of Portuguese diet. Housing conditions also are among the poorest in Europe. The influx of migrants from rural areas as well as returnees from Portuguese colonies abroad created a housing shortage which was never solved. Soaring rents forced poorer families into substandard housing without electricity, running water or sewage system. *Barracas* or shantytowns sprang up around Lisbon and other cities. When the *barracas* were demolished, the tenants were merely distributed to dormitories on the periphery of the cities. Rural housing is in a worse shape, with most houses lacking basic amenities.

Human rights and freedoms. Portugal became a democracy soon after the death of the dictator Salazar, and has remained one since then, although its progress has been bumpy. Portuguese citizens are guaranteed all basic civil rights. There are constitutionally mandated organizations that serve as watchdogs of these rights. For example, the ombudsman, chosen by the Assembly of the Republic, monitors complaints of human rights violations and the High Commissioner for Social Communications monitors freedom of the press and access to the media. The African community suffers from some forms of social discrimination, but officially enjoys all basic rights.

Human environment. Water pollution in coastal areas and air pollution around cities are the most serious ecological problems. Nearly 75% of the hazardous wastes are dumped on land.

Portugal's long history of Christianity is frequently on postage stamps. *Left.* The Fatima apparitions, with half a million pilgrims a year. *Right.* Jesuit missionaries, with Francis Xavier.

NON-CHRISTIAN RELIGIONS

Baha'i has a small and slowly-growing community of 1,800 people.

Judaism has a small but influential community centered primarily in Lisbon. After the Inquisition, their first synagogue was opened in 1813. There are at present about 400 Jews in Portugal, with 2 synagogues in Lisbon and one in Oporto. There are also 100,000 Marranos (Crypto-Jews), whose ancestors were forced to adopt Catholicism but who still keep Jewish practices.

Islam has about 24,000 followers in Portugal, mainly migrant workers from North Africa, with others coming from Pakistan, Mozambique, Guinea-Bissau, Timor, and Macao. Portuguese Muslims are members of the Islamic Community of Lisbon (Comunidade Islámica de Lisboa) which was officially recognized in March 1968. The community publishes a quarterly, *O Islão*, which is the only periodical in Portuguese dealing with Islamic culture.

CHRISTIANITY

CATHOLIC CHURCH. The Romans arrived in the western part of the Iberian peninsula in the 2nd century BC. Little is known of the introduction of Christianity other than that the Apostles James and Paul are said to have visited there. By the end of the 2nd century AD, Christianity was firmly established. Visigoths from the north who were proponents of Arian Christianity entered the peninsula in the 5th century. The indigenous population eventually had Catholicism declared their state religion at the Third Council of Toledo in 589, but friction with the Goths continued. In the 6th and 7th centuries the church began to flourish only to be oppressed under the Moors, Muslim Arabs who defeated the Visigoths in 711. In 1095 Henry of Burgundy was granted part of western Iberia because of his success against the Moors, and his son declared it an independent nation in 1139. Conflicts continued with Moors and Castilians until 1385 when, under John I, Portugal's era of maritime expansion began. At this time many Jews who were suffering persecution in Spain fled to Portugal, but in 1497 all Jews in Portugal were compelled to accept Christian baptism or to leave the country. The notorious Inquisition was then introduced in order to detect those secretly practicing the Jewish faith.

During the following century Portuguese explorers ranged extensively over the oceans; Bartholomeu Dias passed Africa's southern tip, Vasco da Gama sailed to India and Pedro Cabral discovered Brazil. Catholic missionaries usually accompanied such voyages. After a number of major discoveries by Portuguese and Spaniards, the Holy See issued a series of pronouncements the most important of which was the Demarcation Bull of 1493 which divided mission responsibilities across the world between Portugal and Spain, and under which Portugal was given authority over Africa and much of Asia and the East Indies, as well as, later, Brazil. The system known as the Patronato authorized civil authorities to make ecclesiastical appointments and to assume responsibility for the conversion of the heathen. In Africa the major mission was in the Congo; the first missionaries arrived in 1491, and more than a million Congolese were baptized within a century. Jesuits and Dominicans at the same time were beginning missions in Mozambique, and Francis Xavier and other Jesuits launched missions from Portuguese colonies in India and China, and many thousands were soon baptized. Portuguese missionary efforts, however, were often less successful than those of their Spanish counterparts. In many countries Portuguese Christianity later died out completely as a result of opposition from Asia's highly-developed cultures, Portugal's heavy involvement in the African slave trade, the decline of Portugal as a world power, and the decline of missionary fervor and recruiting at home.

From 1581 to 1640 Portugal itself came under the rule of Spain. Later in 1807 Napoleon entered Portugal and the royal family fled to Brazil whence the king returned in 1820. Political unrest continued during the 19th century, involving the church also. The Jesuits had been expelled from Portugal in 1759, and relations were broken with the Holy See between 1833 and 1841. Religious orders were suppressed in 1834. In 1857 a concordat concerning patronage privileges and responsibilities in the Orient was agreed upon with the Holy See. In 1910, the republic of Portugal was proclaimed, religious orders again suppressed, relations with the Holy See broken, the separation of church and state was declared, and the Catholic Church was disestablished. Following the Fátima appearances in 1917 a popular religious renewal took place, and in 1933 the church entered into a new alliance with Salazar's Estado Novo government. A further concordat with the Holy See in 1940 affirmed the separation of church and state but gave the church considerable autonomy in evangelization and education in overseas territories.

Portuguese Catholicism today still reflects the anticlerical movement which accompanied the revolution of 1910. Isolated, living in the past and fearful of the modern world, such are the characteristics of Portuguese Catholicism which shared in its long and close relationship with the Salazar and Caetano regimes. Indeed the Catholic Church aided these regimes, from the foundation of the Estado Novo in 1933 until its fall in 1974, to suffocate every semblance of liberty or cultural and political innovation. Exploited by Salazar in the name of anti-communism, even the spiritual movement resulting from the apparitions at Fátima in 1917 did no more than reinforce the conservatism of the Portuguese church.

The policy of the episcopate has always consisted, and still does consist, in attempting to create and maintain the cohesion and unity of Portuguese Catholics. Since the coup d'etat of 25 April 1974, the bishops have feared a repetition of the 1910 situation. Unquestionably, potential divisions have existed below the surface for a long time.

One such division is geographical, between North and South. The South is in many ways a dechristianized region, being earlier the fief of the regular clergy, who were driven out in 1834 and who preferred to install themselves in the ecclesiastical fortress of the North. A region of large farms and industrial conglomerations such as Setubal, Portugal south of the Tagus has an extremely low percentage of Sunday church attendance and a very unfavorable ratio of priests to inhabitants: one to 4,500. On the other hand, in the Centre and especially the North the church is powerful and firmly planted, with a priest for every 600 inhabitants. Weekly religious practice there is high and attains 100% in some villages, with clerical authority dominating the whole of life. Nevertheless, a factor bringing change is the large emigration of workers mostly from the North of Portugal, about a million of whom have made their way to other Western European countries, especially France. This has already affected recruitment to the priesthood, one of the traditions of the North.

A second divisive factor concerns the mentality of Portuguese Catholics. The mass of Portuguese, especially those of the rural areas of the Centre and North, practice a religion which is traditional, sociologically-conditioned and tainted with superstition and fatalism. This religiosity, far from being discouraged or corrected, has been encouraged by the hierarchy and indeed used to combat minority groups of priests and lay persons who are socially and politically involved.

The Holy See has diplomatic relations with Portugal and in AD 2000 is represented to government and the Catholic hierarchy by a nuncio residing in Lisbon.

Igreja Crista Mana, a fast-expanding global movement; leader leads meeting inside vast white tent in St Antão do Teja, Lisbon.

OTHER CHURCHES. Several of the first non-Catholic churches were built for citizens of other nations residing in Portugal, including German Lutherans (1763), Anglicans (1843) and Scottish Presbyterians (1871). These churches continue to function to the present day.

Early work with the Portuguese population during the 19th century was undertaken by missionaries from Great Britain and Brazil as well as by returned Portuguese emigrants. The first chapel was opened in 1838 by a returning Portuguese sent by the European Missionary Society. The first British missionary opened Brethren work in 1867 and by 1871 British Methodists were active in the north. A local Presbyterian church was also established in Lisbon in 1871 by another returned Portuguese. Baptists entered Portugal in 1888 and since then a number of different groups have been formed. Brazilian Baptist missionaries have been on the scene since 1908. Other early movements in Portugal were initiated by the Seventh-day Adventists and Assemblies of God.

The Lusitanian Church also owes its origin to the last century, being a schism from Catholicism by 11 Catholic priests in 1871. Its present bishop was consecrated by a Brazilian Episcopalian bishop in 1958, and the church has since 1980 been fully integrated into the Anglican Communion. Several other separatist bodies have been formed from the Methodist, Baptist, and Pentecostal churches.

Famed missionary ship MV Logos visits Lisbon.

North American missionary influences began to make their presence felt around the time of World War II. The Evangelical Alliance Mission (TEAM) began in 1936, and United Presbyterians from the USA have lent support to local Presbyterianism since World War II, especially in the Caravellos Seminary. Two new Baptist groups have also appeared, Conservative Baptists in 1946 to work with the Association of Portuguese Baptist Churches and more recently (1959) Southern Baptists who are under the Portuguese Baptist Convention.

While the Portuguese constitution guarantees freedom of religion and open opposition is minimal, Protestants have in fact been restricted in their public activities. The difficulties involved in obtaining official permission to own property and build churches have been important factors limiting church growth.

Renewal movements. In the 1990s the Pentecostal/Charismatic Renewal continued to spread across most older churches, and numbered over 642,000 adherents (of whom 14% Pentecostals, 40% Charismatics, and 46% Independents).

Indigenous missions. Christians from Portugal were active in the evangelization of the northern Barbarians and throughout Europe in the Medieval period. In the age of Discovery, Portuguese Christians took a leading role in global missions under the leadership of Prince Henry the Navigator. They spread the gospel throughout parts of Africa, Asia, and South America. In the nineteenth century both Roman Catholic and Protestants have been active in sending missionaries around the world.

CHURCH AND STATE

Prior to the coup d'etat of 25 April 1974 the church-state situation was as follows. Section X of the constitution of 1933 (which is still largely although provisionally in effect) entitled Religious freedom and relations between the State and the Catholic Church and other religious bodies contained 4 articles, 45-48. Of these the most important were the first 2: 'The State, recognizing its responsibilities before God and man assures freedom of worship and organization to those religious bodies whose doctrines are not contrary to the fundamental principles of the existing constitutional order, nor offend the social order or good morals, and whose worship respects the life, physical integrity and dignity of the person' (Article 45). 'The Roman Catholic Apostolic Religion is considered to be the traditional religion of the Portuguese nation. The Catholic Church possesses existence as a legal body. The principle regulating relations between the state and religious bodies is that of separation, without prejudice to the existence of concordats or agreements with the Holy See' (Article 46). A noteworthy paragraph stated: 'Portuguese Catholic missions in overseas provinces and training centers for their personnel shall be protected and aided by the State, both as institutions of education and social assistance and also as instruments of civilization'.

This legislation, already favorable to the Catholic Church, was made even more explicit by the concordat of 7 May 1940 consisting of 31 articles, the Missionary Agreement (Acordo Missionário) consisting of 21 articles annexed to the concordat, and the Missionary Statute (Estatuto Missionário) of 82 articles which became Law 31,207 on 5 April 1941.

The concordat stipulated that the appointment of bishops was subject to 'objections of a general political nature' which the Portuguese government might have against the candidates chosen by the Holy See (Article 10). The military service of priests was described as a 'religious presence given to the armed forces' (Articles 14 and 18), under which the church agreed to provide chaplains for the military, although this was not put into effect until the outbreak of the colonial wars in Africa (Decree 47,188 of September 1964). The church was free to own schools, which were put on a par with public schools and subsidized if they were located in missionary areas (Article 20). Education offered in public schools was to obey the principles of Christian doctrine and morals, since these are 'traditional principles in the country'; in consequence, the teaching of Catholic religion and morals was obligatory in public elementary and middle schools for all pupils whose parents did not request exemption (Article 21). The state recognized Catholic religious marriages as civil contracts and confirmed their indissoluble character (Articles 22 and 24), which gave rise to a dualism of marriage regulations since both secular marriage and secular divorce were authorized for non-Catholics. Missionary dioceses and jurisdictions were subsidized by the state (Article 27).

The Missionary Agreement and the Statute complemented each other, the second clarifying the first. (In the resume that follows, articles in the Agreement are identified by the letters MA and those in the Statute by MS). 'Portuguese Catholic missions are institutions of value from the imperial point of view, since they play an eminently civilizing role' (MS 2). In principle, all missionary personnel should be of Portuguese nationality (MS 15); at the request of bishops, however, the government may admit foreign junior personnel provided that they speak and write Portuguese fluently (MS 17). Bishops, vicars, and prefects must however be Portuguese (MA 3) and their nomination must be approved by the Lisbon government (MA 7). Missionaries are not officials of the state (MA 17) and do not receive salaries from it, but they have the right to various privileges including exemption from taxes, travel expenses (MA 14), free medical care (MS 30), and a retirement pension. Moreover, 'as head of the missions of their respective dioceses' bishops, vicars, and prefects have the right to an 'honourable salary' guaranteed by the Portuguese government (MA 12), equal to that of provincial governors (MS 19). Missionary organizations are subsidized by the governments of Metropolitan Portugal and of the colony (MA 9), and dioceses and missionary orders both in Portugal and in the colonies are exempt from taxes (MA 11). The education of native populations is placed entirely in the hands of missionary personnel (MS 66). The use of the Portuguese language is obligatory, except in the case of religious education where the local language is sanctioned (MA 16). This education is considered official and should be 'essentially nationalists' and obey the 'doctrinal orientation of the political constitution' (MS 68).

Portuguese religious legislation was further complemented by the Law on Religious Liberty of 22 July 1971, by which the way was opened for the state to officially recognize religious associations or organizations other than the Catholic Church, granting them also juridical personality (Article 9, paragraph 1). Recognition was secured by a church when it presented an application signed by at least 500 adult members (Article 9, paragraph 2). It could be refused or revoked by government if the latter considered the doctrine or activities of the organization to be contrary 'to the fundamental principles of constitutional order or to the interests of Portuguese sovereignty' (Article 8, paragraph 1). Only recognized religious bodies could build and operate places for worship (Article 17); they also had the right to hold meetings without previous authorization 'for community worship or for other specifically religious purposes'. At the time of formulation this statement was considered too restrictive by the more liberal members of parliament, because there was no clear definition of what was 'specifically religious', and also because the text restricted the understanding of religious life to acts of worship, without involvement in social action. Various amendments proposed by these members were all rejected so that the final text adopted was that presented by the government modified only by consideration of remarks made in an episcopal letter requesting that the unique position of the Catholic Church be even more strongly underlined.

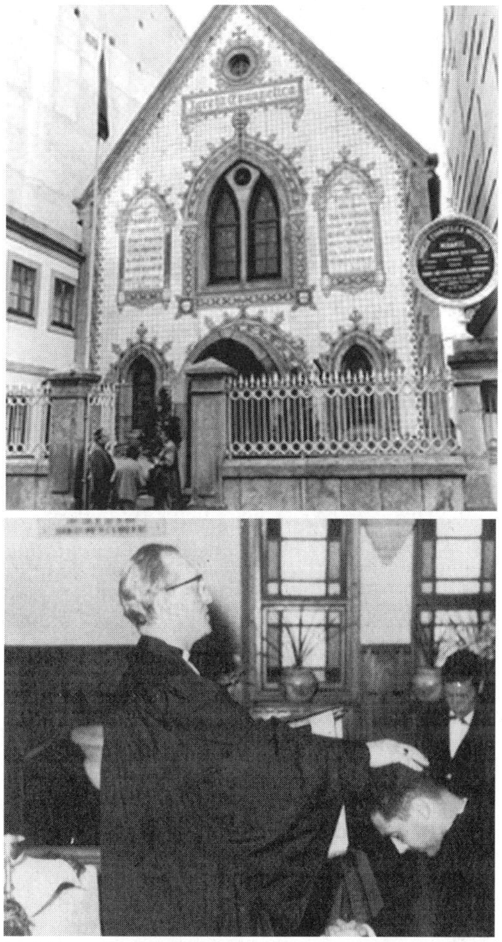
Igreja Evangelica Metodista Portuguesa. *Lower.* Confirmation service in Aleace taken by Rev. Albert Aspey. *Top.* Church in Porto.

Most Portuguese bishops did not provide open and whole-hearted support for the regime but nevertheless remained silent on political and social questions, especially those relating to colonial policy. An exception was the bishop of Porto, who was exiled from 1959 to 1969 and who demonstrated openness to the problems created by social injustice, emigration and the lack of fundamental liberties.

The first incident of open conflicts between Catholics and the government took place in 1955 at the time of a JOC congress. However, it was not until after 1958 that a tendency towards opposition, at the political as well as the ecclesiastical levels, began to make itself felt among militant Catholics and a small minority of the clergy. Anti-government hostility was especially pronounced within the ranks of Catholic Workers Action, which published 2 magazines, *Lar e Trabalho* (Home and Work) and *Voz do Trabalho* (Voice of Work), having a circulation of 44,000 copies in spite of the fact that the organization itself only had 8,000 members of whom 5,000 were women. A minority of the Portuguese Catholic intelligentsia attacked also the concordat especially because of the privileges given to the Catholic Church and because of Article 24 on divorce. To this the regime and hierarchy responded that Catholicism was not the religion of the state, that the clergy were not subsidized and that there was therefore no clericalism in Portugal. According to the former patriarch of Lisbon, who consistently supported the government in its policies, 'The concordat, is, as a document, a precursor and innovator which anticipated Vatican Council II' because it is a concordat of 'separation'. The new patriarch appointed in 1973 also assumed a position of support for the regime. The only exception to this was a declaration made in January 1973 in which he refused to dissociate himself entirely from a 'subversive' vigil for peace opposing the colonial war held by a group of Catholics in the Rato chapel on 30-31 December 1972. The vigil for peace had in fact been preceded by publication of a document criticizing the war, which originated from the Commission on Justice and Peace of the diocese of Porto, the only such commission existing in Portugal. However, when the Caetano regime continued its repression of such groups, the hierarchy maintained its silence.

It may be noted that relations between Portugal and the Vatican during this period were not devoid of paradox. The social encyclicals of pope John XXIII were censored in Portugal and in the colonies. The voyage of pope Paul VI to Bombay was boycotted by the Portuguese mass media because it followed so soon after the seizure of Goa by India. The audiences given by Paul VI in 1971 to leaders of African liberation movements from Mozambique, Angola and Guinea-Bissau also greatly irritated the Portuguese authorities. The latter, however, did not fail to exploit for political purposes the same pope's pilgrimage to Fatima in May 1967.

The church-state situation in Portugal has been significantly altered since the coup d'etat of 25 April 1974, when the ancient and close links between the former regime and the Portuguese church were broken and the army released from prison militant Christians (clergy and lay), communists, socialists,and leftists.

The church has continued to be characterized by dualism, a conservative majority led by the hierarchy, with its strength in the North and most priests and faithful under its control, and a minority of priests and laity dedicated to the revolution.

The first reaction by the episcopate to the coup was a declaration published on 28 April, expressing the hope that the events would contribute to the well-being of Portuguese society, to the cause of justice, reconciliation and respect for all persons. The public statements of the hierarchy which followed were so reserved that one (issued on 5 May 1974) was widely interpreted as support for members of the hated and discredited PIDE.

In May 1974 a group of about a thousand Christians meeting in Lisbon demanded the removal of bishops and the apostolic nuncio who were known to be sympathetic to the former regime.

A year after the coup the Catholic Church was the only major institution to withhold its support from the Armed Forces Movement (MFA). At the time of the elections to the constituent assembly of 25 April 1975, the bishops warned Catholics not to vote for the Communist party. Indeed following the election, where the communists gained only 12% of the vote, Catholics attacked Communist party headquarters throughout the North and were instrumental in provoking in late 1975 the fall of premier Vasco Conçalves for his Marxist leanings.

From a juridical standpoint, the MFA promulgated in May 1974 a provisional constitution, maintaining temporarily those stipulations of the constitution of 1933 not in conflict with the principles of the MFA program. The new regime did not denounce the concordat of 1940 but called for its revision. A partial agreement, called the 'Additional Protocol', was signed on 15 February 1975 between the Holy See and the Portuguese government which modified Article 24 allowing the courts to grant civil divorces for couples married in the church. The Missionary Agreement and Missionary Statute have become void by force of circumstance, at least as they relate to Portugal's former African colonies. On 31 December 1974, in signing the Indo-Portuguese Treaty of Reconciliation, Mario Soares, at that time Portugal's foreign minister, declared that the agreement requiring the Vatican to consult Lisbon before appointing religious authorities in Goa was 'obsolete'.

BROADCASTING AND MEDIA

Shortwave radio programs in European languages can be received from KNLS, AWR (Slovakia), TWR, (Monaco, Albania) and HCJB (Ecuador). Satellite TV and radio programs are received in English, Arabic, German and Italian. IBRA-produced programs can be received on local radio stations.

Portugal is a member of UNDA. Catholics air 16 regular weekly radio programs, of which are an hour in length. Radio Renascenca and ARIC are local Catholic radio stations.

Catholics air 'Misa Dominical' each Sunday for 50 minutes, followed by '70 X 7', for 25 minutes. TV1 is a local Catholic television station.

INTERDENOMINATIONAL ORGANIZATIONS

Co-operation among Protestants is carried on through the Portuguese Council of Christian Churches since 1974, and also through the following 13 organizations: (1) Portuguese Evangelical Alliance (Aliança Evangélica Portuguesa) with 2 sub-commissions, for northern and southern Portugal; (2) Portuguese Inter-Ecclesiastical Commission (Comissão Inter-Eclesiástica Portuguesa) composed of 3 members (Lusitanian, Methodist and Presbyterian churches); (3) Commission for Christian Literature (Comissão de Literatura Cristã); (4) Gypsy Evangelical Movement of Portugal (Movimento Evangélico Cigano de Portugal), which is de facto a denomination; (5) Beira-Vouga Convention (Convenção Beira-Vouga) founded in 1926 and modeled on the Keswick Convention of England; (6) Youth for Christ in Portugal (Moçidade para Cristo em Portugal); (7) Christian Businessmens' Movement (Movimento dos Homens Cristãos de Negóçios); (8) United Evangelical Women of Portugal (Senhoras Evangélicas Unidas de Portugal); (9) Women's Christian Union (União Cristã Feminina); (10) Evangelical Christian Medical Union (União Médica Cristã Evangélica); (11) Union of Sunday Schools of North Portugal (União das Escolas Dominicais do Norte de Portugal, UEDNOP) with Lusitanian, Methodist, and Presbyterian membership; (12) Portuguese Union for Christian Endeavour (União Portuguesa de Esforço Cristão, UPEC) composed of Lusitanians and Methodists; and (13) Evangelical League for Missionary and Educational Action (Liga Evangélica de Accão Missionária e Educacional).

The Ecumenical Centre for Reconciliation (Centro Ecumenico Reconciliação), founded in 1969, provides opportunities for co-operation between the Protestant churches and YMCAs of Spain and Portugal. Participant members from Portugal are the Lusitanian, Methodist and Presbyterian churches. The Evangelical League for Missionary and Educational Action coordinates, on an ecumenical basis, the training of foreign missionaries studying the Portuguese language in Lisbon. The League also maintains an ecumenical hostel in the capital.

With regard to the Catholic Church, there is no specific commission for ecumenism under the Episcopal Conference. Ecumenical questions are handled by the Episcopal Commission for the Doctrine of the Faith and Social Communications.

FUTURE TRENDS AND PROSPECTS

Roman Catholicism is expected to continue to lose members to Protestants through 2025 (expressed in the rise of the doubly-affiliated from none in 1970 to 6.2% by 2025). The nonreligious and atheists combined are expected to grow to over 10% after AD 2050.

Though Christianity will probably remain strong in Portugal, the nonreligious are expected to grow to over 10% before the middle of the 21st century. If this trend continues they could represent a major force for the foreseeable future.

Portugal's history returns continuously to biblical criteria; *left*, The White Horseman of Revelation.

BIBLIOGRAPHY

A history of the Marranos. C. Roth. Philadelphia: The Jewish Publication Society of America, 1932. 422p.

'A program to equip lay people to plant churches in Cascais, Portugal.' J. P. de Sousa. D.Min. thesis, Southwestern Baptist Theological Seminary, Fort Worth, TX, 1987. 160p.

A religião popular portuguesa. M. Espírito Santo. 2nd ed. *Peninsulares Especial*, 21. Lisbon: Assírio & Alvim, 1990.

A short history of the Portuguese evangelical church. G. C. Ericson. , 1983. 79p.

A situação religiosa de Portugal: conspecto e condiserações. E. Moreira. Lisbon: Edição do Portuagal Novo, 1935. 29p.

Anuário Católico de Portugal, 1968. Lisbon: Secretariado de Informação Religiosa, 1968.

Atlas missionário português, 1964. A. da Silva Rego & E. dos Santos (eds). 2nd ed. Lisbon: Junta de Investigações do Ultramar e Centro de Estudos Históricos Ultramarinos, 1964. 206p.

Churches of Portugal. C. de Azevedo. New York: Scala Books, 1985. 199p.

Comportamento religioso da população portuguesa. L. de França. *Colecção estudos para o desenvolvimento*, 4. Lisbon: Moraes, 1981. 163p.

Dicionário de história da Igreja em Portugal. A. A. B. de Andrade. Lisbon: Editorial Resistência, 1979–1983. 2 vols.

Evangelização, anúncio de liberdade: o futuro do evangelho em Portugal à luz do Sínodo. J. da Cruz Policarpo. Lisbon: Multinova, [1975]. 275p.

'Factors influencing evangelical church growth in Portugal since World War II.' G. C. Ericson. D.Min. thesis, Dallas Theological Seminary, Dallas, TX, 1988. 259p.

'Guidelines for the church planter in Portugal.' S. D. Faircloth. D.Miss. project, Trinity Evangelical School, Deerfield, IL, 1984. 267p.

História dos Batistas Nacionais: Documentário. E. Tognini. 2nd ed. Brasilia: Convenção Batista Nacional, 1993. 147p.

História eclesiástica de Portugal. M. de Oliveira. 2nd ed. *Biblioteca da história*, 11. Mem Martins: Publicações Europa-América, 1994. 327p.

Igreja e sociedade no Portugal contemporâneo. Studium generale Estudos contemporâneos. Porto, Portugal: Secretaria de Estado da Cultura, Centro de Estudos Humanísticos, 1979. 217p.

La Iglesia del siglo XX en España, Portugal y América Latina. Barcelona: Editorial Herder, 1987. 1364p.

'Making EE work: the cross–cultural adaption and local application of EEIII International in Lisbon, Portugal.' C. E. Quarterman. D.Min. thesis, Reformed Theological Seminary, Jackson, MS, 1986. 136p.

Origens do cristianismo português. M. Espirito Santo. Lisbon: Instituto de Sociologia e Etnologia das Religiões, Universidade Nova de Lisboa, [1993]. 225p.

Os evangélicos portugueses e a lei. E. Moreira. Lisbon, 1938.

Portugal. A. Querido. The Hague: Mouton, 1972.

Portugal. P. T. H. Unwin. *World bibliographical series*, vol. 71. Oxford, UK: CLIO Press, 1987. 311p. (See especially 'Religion,' p.97–101).

Portugal: a pioneer of Christianity. E. Prestage. 2nd ed. Lisbon: Empresa Nacional de Publicidade, 1945. 31p.

Prontuário de igrejas, organismos e obreiros evangélicos em Portugal. Lisbon: Movimento Promotor de Evangelização, 1967. 176p.

River of light. Worcester, PA: Gateway Films. (2 videocassettes; total of 228 minutes; history of Christianity in Spain, Portugal and Mexico after the conquistadors).

The church and revolution: Portugal. Rome: IDOC, 1975. 96p.

The Church Militant and Iberian expansion, 1440–1770. C. R. Boxer. *Johns Hopkins symposia in comparative history*, vol. 10. Baltimore, MD: Johns Hopkins University Press, 1978. 159p.

The making of an enterprise: the Society of Jesus in Portugal, its empire, and beyond: 1540–1750. D. Alden. Stanford, CA: Stanford University Press, 1995.

Vidas convergentes: história breve dos movimentos de reforma cristã em Portugal a partir do século XVIII. E. Moreira. Lisbon: Junta Prebiteriana de Cooperação em Portugal, 1957. 409p.

Country Table 2. **Organized churches and denominations in Portugal.**

Official name (bold type = church with over 10% of all affiliated) 1	*Begun* 2	*Type* 3	*Counc* 4	*Congs* 5	*Adults* 6	*Affiliated 1970* 7	*Affiliated 1995* 8	*G%* 9	*Names, notes, and other statistics* (see Codebook, Part 3) 10
Acção Bíblica	1930	I-Non	.....	12	400	220	667	4.54	*Biblical Action.* M=Action Biblique (Switzerland).
Assembleias de Deus em Portugal	1913	P-Pe2	Z...C	510	45,000	24,000	83,300	5.10	*Assemblies of God in Portugal.* M=AoG(UK). 35n,2x,1j,200t,715Y,400z.
Assambleias Locales	c1990	I-3nC	.....	3	18	–	50	20.00	*Local Churches. Little Flock.* Chinese. Begun 1922 in China.
Assoc de Batistas para Ev Mundial	1980	I-Bap	.....	7	350	–	538	6.67	M=ABWE. Fundamentalist Baptists from USA.
Assoc de Igrejas Batistas Portuguesas	c1930	I-Bap	xF...	21	315	2,000	630	-4.52	*AIBP. Assoc of Portuguese Baptist Chs.* Ex CBP. 1946, M=CBFMS(USA). 8n,2f,1s,W=60%.
Atos Igreja Crista	1987	I-3pW	.....	3	120	–	240	12.50	White-led Postdenominationalists. Split ex Mana-Igreja.
Centro Evan e Miss do Feijó e Missoes	1958	P-CBr	.....	5	150	–	250	24.71	Open Plymouth Brethren.
Congregação Cristã em Portugal	c1930	I-3pY	.....	102	3,000	1,800	5,000	4.17	*Christian Congregation in P.* Brazilians from church based on São Paulo. HQ Porto.

Continued opposite

Country Table 2–concluded

Official name (bold type = church with over 10% of affiliated) 1	*Begun* 2	*Type* 3	*Counc* 4	*Congs* 5	*Adults* 6	*Affiliated 1970* 7	*Affiliated 1995* 8	*G%* 9	*Names, notes, and other statistics* (see Codebook, Part 3) 10
Convenção Batista Portuguesa	1888	P-Bap	T...C	58	3,943	6,000	5,260	-0.53	*CBP. Portuguese Baptist Conv.* 1959, M=SBC(USA). SS=2336. 20n,6f,1s,120Y.
Criancas do Deus	c1985	I-mar	.....	2	42	–	72	10.00	*Children of God.*
Elim Igreja Crista	c1980	P-Pe2	.....	5	200	–	333	6.67	*Elim Ch of Christ.* M=Elim Pent Ch.
Exército de Salvação	1971	P-Sal	xwc..	10	131	100	187	4.17	*Salvation Army, Portugal Command.* Recent beginnings in Porto and Lisbon. 2nx.
Igreja Adventista do Sétimo Dia	1904	P-Adv	x....	100	7,000	6,000	16,000	4.00	*Seventh-day Adv, Port Mission,* SEurope UM. 14nx,1j,1s,35t(3346),W=94%,438Y.
Igreja Anglicana (D Europe)	1656	A-plu	awc..	18	1,500	4,500	3,190	-1.37	English-speaking Anglican chaplaincies, including one on Madeira. 4x.
Igreja Apostólica	1969	P-PeA	.....	4	80	31	123	5.67	M=Apostolic Ch (UK).
Igreja Católica em Portugal:	c 150	R-Lat	B.B.R	6,736	6,432,000	8,379,224	9,000,000	0.29	*Catholic Ch.* C=23+3+63. 6q,9x(312). 3301n 1077x 1698m 5346w 79812Yy
M Braga	c 350	R-Lat	Bs	679	597,000	949,772	844,000	-0.47	Semi-industrial. Traditional religiosity. 1s,W=60%. 494n 124x 234m 821w 13311Yy
D Aveiro	1774	R-Lat	Bs	196	192,000	233,750	270,000	0.58	Heavy rural emigration, especially to France. 116n 15x 29m 156w 3249Yy
D Braganca & Miranda	1545	R-Lat	Bs	324	118,000	176,800	155,800	-0.50	Almost entirely rural and agricultural. 118n 7x 12m 142w 2007Yy
D Coimbra	c 550	R-Lat	Bs	298	429,000	522,046	611,000	0.63	Tourism, fishing, major university. 1s. 188n 38x 60m 398w 5900Yy
D Lamego	c1150	R-Lat	Bs	223	107,000	174,000	148,060	-0.64	Impoverished. no industry Mass emigration. 164n 15x 17m 82w 1842Yy
D Porto (Oporto)	c 350	R-Lat	Bs	467	1,356,000	1,537,179	1,930,000	0.91	Wine industry, commerce, university. 1s. 415n 234x 341m 1404w 041Yy
D Viana do Castelo	1977	R-Lat	Bs	373	178,000	–	249,100	5.56	Population is 96% Catholic. 179n 24x 30m 142w 2780Yy
D Vila Real	1922	R-Lat	Bs	480	197,000	234,618	281,000	0.72	Farms, sheep, wine smoked meat. 70 married priests. 136n 22x 35m 137w 2389Yy
D Viseu	572	R-Lat	Bs	677	179,000	280,164	259,020	0.07	Mountainous, poor agriculture. Heavy emigration. 1s. 176n 14x 18m 107w 3694Yy
M Evora	c 350	R-Lat	Bs	163	194,000	290,000	246,325	-0.65	South. Old city, historic religious traditions. M=OFM. 88n 27x 43m 258w 1204Yy
D Beja	1770	R-Lat	Bs	116	138,000	220,000	190,000	-0.58	In south, landlordism (latifundia). Practice: W=5%. 43n 14x 16m 87w 1654Yy
D Fáro	1577	R-Lat	Bs	75	226,000	263,250	331,700	0.93	Fishing, tourism. Few vocations. M=OFM. Practice. 49n 14x 15m 103w 2207Yy
P Lisboa (Lisbon)	c 350	R-Lat	Bs	863	1,420,000	2,156,179	2,006,000	-0.29	Industry, port, commerce, university. 1s(24),W=26%. 372n 357x 612m 1347w 18506Yy
D Angra	1534	R-Lat	Bs	195	165,000	289,296	232,000	-0.88	Azores. Fishing. Very traditional religiosity. 1s. 163n 6x 16m 251w 3429Yy
D Funchal	1514	R-Lat	Bs	96	181,000	245,420	256,461	0.18	Madeira, 8 isles. Tourism. Traditional religiosity. 85n 32x 56m 484w 3347Yy
D Guarda	c 550	R-Lat	Bs	365	177,000	301,000	250,000	-0.74	Mountains. Heavy emigration. Many vocations. 1s. 192n 18x 21m 140w 2500Yy
D Leiria-Fatima	1545	R-Lat	Bs	73	174,000	189,000	273,800	1.49	Rural. Major pilgrimage centre at Fatima (1917). 1s. 107n 64x 82m 177w 3100Yy
D Portalegre-Castelo Branco	1550	R-Lat	Bs	475	217,000	286,750	236,178	-0.77	Rural north, W=80%; urban and rural south. M=CM. 110n 13x 15m 208w 2154Yy
D Santarem	1975	R-Lat	Bs	352	200,000	–	247,000	5.00	M=OFM. 66n 10x 12m 180w 2047Yy
D Setubal	1975	R-Lat	Bs	48	420,000	–	597,000	5.00	84% Roman Catholics in diocese. 40n 29x 34m 126w 4492Yy
OM Portugal	1966	R-Lat	Bs	198	75,000	30,000	96,000	4.76	Military Ordinariate of Portugal. 60 ordinaries, 12 auxiliaries. 139Yy.
Doubly-counted Catholics		R-Lat		0	-508,000	–	-710,444		Catholics counted in new dioceses but also in parent dioceses.
Igreja de Deus (Cleveland)	1965	P-Pe3	.....	3	77	20	128	7.71	*Church of God.* M=CoG(Cleveland) (USA).
Igreja de Deus de Profecia	c1980	P-Pe3	.....	2	50	–	83	6.67	*Church of God of Prophecy.* M=CGP.
Igreja de Deus Pentecostal	1966	P-Pe2	.....	9	500	93	833	9.17	*Church of God Pentecostal.* M=CoG Pentecostal.
Igreja de J C dos SUD	c1970	m-LdS	.....	105	11,500	–	23,000	49.44	*Ch of Jesus Christ of Latter-day Saints.*
Igrejas de Reavivamento	c1975	I-3cU	.....	10	400	–	600	5.00	*Churches of Revival.*
Igreja do Nazareno	1973	P-Hol	.....	16	661	–	1,075	4.55	*Church of the Nazarene.* M=CoN.
Igreja Evangélica Alfa	1988	I-3cU	.....	5	200	–	333	14.29	Independent charismatics from the Caribbean.
Igr Evangélica Luterana Portuguesa	1763	P-Lut	.....	5	160	100	229	3.37	*Portuguese Ev Lutheran Ch. Igreja Alemã.* Germans. 1x,W=63%,7Yy,10z.
Igr Evangélica Metodista Portuguesa	1871	P-Met	VvC.d	19	4,100	2,500	5,000	2.81	*Methodist Ch.* 1964, applied to join WCC, rejected. 5n,1x2f,W=80%,18Yy,185z.
Igreja Evangélica Presbiteriana de P	1838	P-Ref	RuC.d	35	1,700	3,500	5,000	1.44	*Ev Presbyterian Ch.* M=IPB(Brazil), UPUSA, PCUS. A=1952. 13n,1x,1H,24t(850),W=72%.
Igr Lusitana Católica Apostólica Ev	1656	I-3nW	UuC.d	17	4,100	4,500	5,000	0.42	*Lusitanian Ch.* Schism ex Ch of Rome by 11 RC priests. 16n,2s,W=45%,32Yy.
Igreja Metodista Wesleyana	1979	P-Hol	.....	23	483	–	805	6.25	*Wesleyan Methodist Church.*
Igreja Nova Apostolica	c1950	I-3aX	.....	100	5,000	900	8,572	9.43	*NAC/NAK.* M=Neuapostolische Kirche. HQ Zurich (Switzerland).
Igreja Ortodoxa Greca (D France)	1949	O-Gre	Cwc..	1	600	1,000	1,200	0.73	*Greek Orthodox Ch in Spain and Portugal.* Served from Madrid: HQ Paris.
Igreja Universal do Reino do Deus	1991	I-3pY	x....	320	90,000	–	170,000	25.00	*Universal Ch of the Kingdom of God.* M=IURD(Brazil). 200,000 members by 1996. Radio, TV.
Igrejas Alianca Evangélica	1936	P-Eva	xM..C	4	130	300	160	-2.48	M=Evangelical Alliance Mission(TEAM)(USA). HQ Lisbon. 2x,1m,7f,1k,1s,W=67%,31Y,5z.
Igrejas do Cristo		I-Dis	x....	5	740	200	1,230	0.05	*Churches of Christ.* M=CC(Non-Instrumental) (USA). Americans in Lisbon, Azores. 5f.
Igrejas Evangélicas dos Irmãos	1867	P-CBr	x...C	117	4,000	8,000	6,670	-0.72	*Ev Chs of Brethren.* Plymouth (Open) Brethren. M=CMML(UK, USA). HQ Coimbra. 69m,17f.
Mana-Igreja Crista	1980	I-3kW	x....	31	40,000	–	75,000	6.67	*Manna Christian Ch.* Cell-based megachurch in Lisbon. Abroad: work in 35 countries.
Missão Ev Mâranato de P	1965	I-3cW	.....	11	200	100	333	4.93	*Maranatha Evangelical Mission of P.*
Movimento Ev Cigano de Portugal	1960	I-3pE	x....	23	500	1,000	1,000	0.00	*MECP. Gypsy Ev Movement.* Philadelphia Church. Itinerant work. Porto.
Testemunhas de Jeová	1925	m-Jeh	x....	546	38,071	19,500	64,500	4.90	*Jehovah's Witnesses.* 3 congs in Azores, 2 in Madeira. (1975) 1228Y. (1995) 2512Y.
União de Igrejas Ev Congregacionales		P-Con	C	22	400	1,000	1,000	0.05	*Congregational Ch.* Rejected 1952 merger with Presbyterian Ch. M=Brazil CC. 2n.
Other Protestant denominations		P-	.....	40	2,000	2,000	4,000	0.05	Total about 20 (see list below).
Other marginal bodies	1976	m-	.....	30	2,000	500	3,000	5.26	Including CJCLdS (Mormons from USA, widespread by 1979), Unification Ch (HSAUWC), et alia
Other Third-World indigenous churches		I-	.....	35	1,700	200	3,500	0.05	Including EJCSK, OBPC.
Doubly-affiliated		2-aff			-299,000	0	-423,091		Evangelicals who also are or were baptized Roman Catholics.
Totals				**9,130**	**6,404,521**	**8,469,288**	**9,075,000**		

Churches, members, growth, 1900-2025	*Congs*	*Adults*	*Affiliated*	*G%*	*Total denominations*	*6 Megablocs:* *O*	*R*	*A*	*P*	*I*	*m*
Total churches, members, and denominations (mid-1900)	3,000	3,840,000	5,415,300	0.64	8	0	1	1	5	1	0
Total churches, members, and denominations (mid-1970)	5,142	6,006,010	8,469,288	0.64	44	1	1	1	22	17	2
Total churches, members, and denominations (mid-1990)	9,000	6,442,000	9,127,320	0.37	87	1	1	1	37	35	12
Total churches, members, and denominations (mid-1995)	9,130	6,404,521	9,075,000	-0.11	89	1	1	1	38	36	12
Total churches, members, and denominations (mid-2000)	9,200	6,409,000	9,080,231	0.01	91	1	1	1	39	37	12
Total churches, members, and denominations (mid-2025)	10,000	5,946,000	8,425,000	-0.30	241	1	1	1	50	170	18

NOTES ON TABLE ABOVE

NATIONAL COUNCILS (Column 4, 5th letter).

d = Conselho Português de Igrejas Cristãs (COPIC) (Portuguese Council of Christian Churches, in working relationship with WCC), and also a member of Comissão Inter-Eclesiástica Portuguesa.

E = Alianca Evangelica Portuguesa (AEP) (Portuguese Evangelical Christian Alliance).

R = Conferência Episcopal Portuguesa da Metrópole (CEPM) (Portuguese Metropolitan Episcopal Conference).

OTHER PROTESTANT DENOMINATIONS. These smaller bodies include: Apostolic Ch Missionary Movement (UK), Baptist Missionary Association of America (1954), Bible Christian Union (1966), Ch of Scotland (1871), Ch of the Nazarene (Madeira), Danske Sömandskirki (Marinheiros Dinamarqueses: Danish Seamen's Ch), European Missionary Fellowship, Igreja Ev Pentecostal, Igrejas Batistas Independentes, United Pentecostal Ch (1972), World Gospel Mission and USA military chaplaincies.

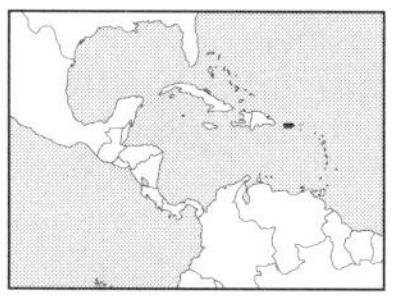

PUERTO RICO

SECULAR DATA, AD 2000

STATE

Official name: Estado Libre Asociado de Puerto Rico/The Commonwealth of Puerto Rico.
Short name: Puerto Rico. **Adjective of nationality:** Puerto Rican.
Flag: Three red and 2 white horizontal stripes, white star on blue triangle.
Area: 9,104 sq. km. (3,515 sq. mi.).
Government: Self-governing commonwealth in association with the USA, since 1952 (1492 Spanish possession, 1898 ceded to USA, 1917 US territory, 1952 commonwealth).
Legislature: Legislative Assembly: Senate, 29 members; House of Representatives, 53 members.
Official language: Spanish (Español) and English.
Monetary unit: 1 U.S. dollar (U.S.$) = cents. **US$1=** 100 cents.
Chief cities: SAN JUAN 1,381,000; Ponce 252,086; Bayamon 238,612; Mayaguez 217,312; Carolina 192,619.
Political divisions: 7 provinces.
Armed forces: 3,500.

DEMOGRAPHY

Population: 3,869,000.
Population density: 424.9/sq. km. (1,100.6/sq. mi.).
Under 15 years: 940,000.
Growth rate p.a.: 0.77% (births 16.63, deaths 8.13).
Mortality: Infant, per 1,000: 11.5, ; **Maternal per 100,000:** 12.0.
Life expectancy: 75 (male 70, female 79).
Household size: 3.6. **Floor area per person, sq.m:** 40.0.
Major languages: Spanish, English.
Urban dwellers: 75.22%. **Urban growth rate p.a.:** 1.4%.
Labor force: 34%.

ETHNOLINGUISTIC PEOPLES

72.0% Puerto Rican White; 15.0% Black; 10.0% Mulatto; 2.2% USA White; 0.2% Cuban White.

ECONOMY

National income p.a. per person: US$7,799; **per family:** US$28,079.

EDUCATION

Adult literacy: 89% (male 89%, female 89%). **Schools:** 1,989.
Universities: 45. **School enrolment:** female/male: 95%/95%.

HEALTH

Access to health services: 95%. **Access to safe water:** 95%.
Hospitals: 72 (26 beds per 10,000). **Doctors:** 6,269.
Blind: 4,500. **Deaf:** 232,600. **Murder rate:** 26.
Lepers: 1,800.

LITERATURE

New book titles p.a.: 1,930 (500 p.a. per million). **Periodicals:** 49.
Newspapers: 3 dailies.

COMMUNICATION (per 1,000 people)

Phones: 321 **(35% mobile). Radios:** 666. **TV sets:** 311.
Daily newspaper circulation: 184. **Computers:** 180.

HUMAN LIFE AND LIBERTY (optimum condition=100.0%)

HDI: 87.9. **HSI:** 85.0. **HFI:** 75.0. **EFL:** 50.0.

Country status. Puerto Rico is the most easterly island of the Greater Antilles in the West Indies. This Caribbean nation's chief exports are chemicals, electronic equipment, and clothing.

HUMAN LIFE AND LIBERTY

Human rights and freedoms. Puerto Rico is a commonwealth in free association with the United States but without electoral rights. Its constitution, ratified by the United States of America, is modeled on the US Constitution and contains all the provisions in the latter enshrining human rights and civil liberties.

Country Table 1. **Religious adherents in Puerto Rico, AD 1900-2025.**

Year	1900		1970		mid-1990		Annual change, 1990-2000				mid-1995		mid-2000		mid-2025	
Name	Adherents	%	Adherents	%	Adherents	%	Natural	Conversion	Total	Rate	Adherents	%	Adherents	%	Adherents	%
Christians	**951,800**	**99.9**	**2,672,800**	**98.4**	**3,432,540**	**97.3**	**33,137**	**-1,031**	**32,106**	**0.90**	**3,608,480**	**97.1**	**3,753,600**	**97.0**	**4,304,100**	**96.1**
PROFESSION																
professing Christians	**951,800**	**99.9**	**2,672,800**	**98.4**	**3,432,540**	**97.3**	**33,137**	**-1,731**	**32,106**	**0.90**	**3,608,480**	**97.1**	**3,753,600**	**97.0**	**4,304,100**	**96.1**
AFFILIATION																
unaffiliated Christians	300	0.0	7,800	0.3	27,000	0.8	261	170	431	1.49	28,480	0.8	31,309	0.8	54,100	1.2
affiliated Christians	**951,500**	**99.8**	**2,665,000**	**98.1**	**3,405,540**	**96.5**	**32,876**	**-1,201**	**31,675**	**0.89**	**3,580,000**	**96.4**	**3,722,291**	**96.2**	**4,250,000**	**94.9**
Roman Catholics	950,000	99.7	2,585,824	95.2	2,700,000	76.5	26,057	-6,057	20,000	0.72	2,801,500	75.4	2,900,000	75.0	3,250,000	72.6
Protestants	1,000	0.1	227,835	8.4	450,000	12.8	4,349	1,151	5,500	1.16	480,046	12.9	505,000	13.1	650,000	14.5
Independents	0	0.0	80,000	3.0	223,000	6.3	2,155	445	2,600	1.11	237,790	6.4	249,000	6.4	350,000	7.8
Marginal Christians	0	0.0	18,257	0.7	80,000	2.3	773	727	1,500	1.73	86,760	2.3	95,000	2.5	175,000	3.9
Anglicans	500	0.1	9,722	0.4	11,400	0.3	110	-10	100	0.84	12,000	0.3	12,400	0.3	14,500	0.3
Orthodox	0	0.0	1,000	0.0	1,200	0.0	12	-2	10	0.80	1,200	0.0	1,300	0.0	1,600	0.0
doubly-affiliated	0	0.0	-257,638	-9.5	-60,060	-1.7	-581	2,546	1,965	-3.89	-39,296	-1.1	-40,409	-1.0	-191,100	-4.3
Trans-megabloc groupings																
Evangelicals	800	0.1	140,000	5.2	306,000	8.7	2,958	1,242	4,200	1.29	325,519	8.8	348,000	9.0	485,000	10.8
Pentecostals/Charismatics	0	0.0	170,000	6.3	915,000	25.9	8,844	2,156	11,000	1.14	974,687	26.2	1,025,000	26.5	1,300,000	29.0
Great Commission Christians	**67,000**	**7.0**	**271,600**	**10.0**	**490,000**	**13.9**	**4,736**	**725**	**5,461**	**1.06**	**520,100**	**14.0**	**544,610**	**14.1**	**671,700**	**15.0**
Nonreligious	0	0.0	29,000	1.1	50,000	1.4	483	686	1,169	2.12	56,000	1.5	61,692	1.6	100,000	2.2
Spiritists	1,100	0.1	4,000	0.2	23,200	0.7	224	183	407	1.63	26,000	0.7	27,274	0.7	36,000	0.8
Atheists	0	0.0	5,000	0.2	12,000	0.3	116	99	215	1.66	13,300	0.4	14,150	0.4	18,000	0.4
Hindus	0	0.0	1,000	0.0	2,850	0.1	28	27	55	1.79	3,250	0.1	3,404	0.1	6,000	0.1
Baha'is	0	0.0	1,200	0.0	2,200	0.1	21	38	59	2.40	2,500	0.1	2,788	0.1	6,000	0.1
Jews	100	0.0	2,000	0.1	2,500	0.1	24	-6	18	0.71	2,600	0.1	2,683	0.1	2,800	0.1
Muslims	0	0.0	0	0.0	820	0.0	8	3	11	1.24	880	0.0	928	0.0	2,000	0.0
Buddhists	0	0.0	0	0.0	450	0.0	4	1	5	1.12	480	0.0	503	0.0	1,000	0.0
Chinese folk-religionists	0	0.0	0	0.0	400	0.0	4	2	6	1.50	440	0.0	464	0.0	800	0.0
Other religionists	0	0.0	1,000	0.0	1,040	0.0	10	-2	8	0.70	1,070	0.0	1,115	0.0	1,300	0.0
World A (unevangelized persons)	0	0.0	5,432	0.2	3,528	0.1	44	-118	-74	-1.73	3,715	0.1	3,869	0.1	4,478	0.1
World B (evangelized non-Christians)	1,400	0.1	38,067	1.4	91,932	2.6	878	1,149	2,027	1.95	102,943	2.8	111,531	2.9	169,422	3.8
World C (Christians)	951,800	99.9	2,672,800	98.4	3,432,540	97.3	33,137	-1,031	32,106	0.90	3,608,480	97.1	3,753,600	97.0	4,304,100	96.1
Country's population	**953,200**	**100.0**	**2,716,300**	**100.0**	**3,528,000**	**100.0**	**34,059**	**0**	**34,059**	**0.93**	**3,715,139**	**100.0**	**3,869,000**	**100.0**	**4,478,000**	**100.0**

COLUMNS, ROWS.
For meanings and definitions, see Codebook (Part 3). Note that, by definition, total 'Christians' = professing + crypto-Christians, which also = affiliated + unaffiliated Christians, and also = Great Commission Christians + latent Christians. Percentages may not always total exactly, due to rounding.

CENSUSES.
The religion question has not been asked.

NOTES ON RELIGIONS
ATHEISTS. Partido Comunista Puertorriquerants from Cuba, including practitioners of Mayombe (based on Congolese traditional rites). There are also a number of Rastafarians (from Jamaica).
BAHA'IS. Growth from 1 local spiritual assembly (1964) to 8 (1973). In 1970 over 300 new believers were enrolled.
DOUBLY-AFFILIATED. The term covers those affiliated to, or claimed by, both the Catholic Church and also a church termed Evangélica by the state (Protestant, marginal Christian, Anglican or Independents) or other church, i.e. baptized Catholics who have recently become Evangelicals or others. Because their statistics represent a duplication, they are shown in the table as a negative quantity (with a minus sign).
HINDUS. Immigrants from India, also converts to new sects including 200 in the Bengali movement, Sri Chinmoy Centre; and 1 center of ISKCON (Hare Krishna).
OTHER RELIGIONISTS. Adherents of other Western religions and cults, including Rosicrucians (6 AMORC centers).
INDEPENDENTS. In 38 denominations in 1995 (see Table 2).
PENTECOSTALS/CHARISMATICS. The Catholic renewal began in 1969. Totals (January 1974): 10,000 involved adults (over 15 years old) in over 100 prayer groups, rising to 15,000 in 200 prayer groups by mid-year; total charismatic community including children (mid-1974), 30,000. On several occasions 7,000 or more met for day-long prayer meetings. By 1976, 100 priests were in the movement, prayer groups had arisen in almost all Puerto Rican cities, and 14 retreat centers provided direction to the Renewal.By 1997, 216,000 adults (30% being under 25) were regularly attending the 850 weekly prayer meetings, with 75 involved priests and 1 bishop. The largest recent rally had 25,000 participants.
SPIRITISTS. Adherents of non-Christian forms of spiritism, which was begun in 1898.
SPIRITISTS. Mostly Black and Mulatto immigrants from Cuba, including practitioners of Mayombe (based on Congolese traditional rites). There are also a number of Rastafarians (from Jamaica).

Great Commission Instrument Panel: status of Puerto Rico (for explanation see start of Part 4)

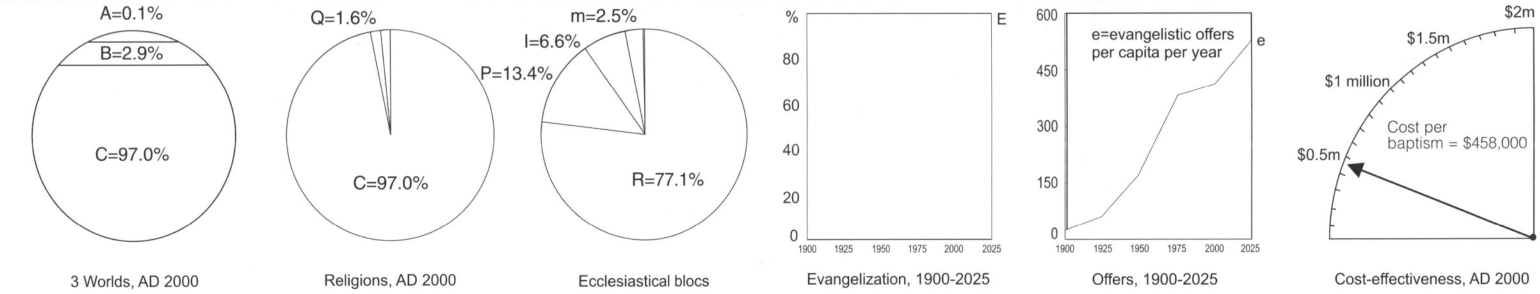

NON-CHRISTIAN RELIGIONS

Spiritism in various forms exists among some whose ties to the Catholic Church have become tenuous or even nonexistent. It involves the use of native herbs to cure illness and mediums to contact the dead and divine the cause and solution to problems. In remote villages where the existence of witches is believed in, bracelets (*asabache*) are placed on the arms of children to protect them from the evil eye (*mal del ojo*). There are also forms of Afro-American spiritism brought by immigrants from Cuba.

Judaism is represented by a small Jewish community concentrated for the most part in San Juan.

Baha'i and ***Hinduism*** number approximately 3,000 followers each.

CHRISTIANITY

CATHOLIC CHURCH. Columbus touched Puerto Rico in 1493, and in 1511 the first Catholic diocese in the New World was established there. At the end of the 17th century, smallpox killed 21 of the 25 priests on the island, and little further activity took place for a hundred years. The shortage of priests continued until the beginning of the Latin American wars of independence, when members of the hierarchy loyal to Spain fled from other South American countries and established themselves in Puerto Rico. The loyalty of the hierarchy to Spain again weakened the position of the church during the second half of the 19th century, when Puerto Ricans began their own search for independence. The first Protestants entered Puerto Rico in 1860, followed by Anglicans in 1872, but it was not until after the Spanish-American war that Protestantism made any appreciable impact on the scene. With the end of Spanish rule, the number of Catholic priests began to decline. In 1930, there were only 45 diocesan priests and the number did not return again to the 1910 level until 1955. A majority of Catholic priests continue to belong to missionary societies from the USA and Spain.

In Puerto Rico as with the rest of Latin America, Catholicism is very ancient, having arisen from the joint missionary and colonizing zeal of Spanish monarchism. But, unlike Latin America, Puerto Rico has become the battleground between 2 distinct cultural traditions, Hispanic and North American. Whatever elements may be common to both due to modernization, the fact is that each has a separate symbolic existence in the island.

The Catholic Church as an institution or structure has been particularly sensitive to these traditions. Historically, in the Hispanic tradition the church is the unilateral arbiter of the religio-temporal identities of mankind. While temporal and religious goods are differentiated, the latter are by definition the superior ones. In the relationship between church and state, the latter must be beholden to the former. In the North American historical experience, on the other hand, Catholicism was and still is considered as a foreign, retardative element within the social milieu of Protestant libertarianism. The Catholic Church has had to adapt to that milieu or risk the stigma of disloyalty and unpatriotism. Thus, it is beholden to the state to the extent that the latter is protective or nonantagonistic to its interests and prerogatives.

In both traditions, the result has been a symbiotic relationship between church and state structures. This relationship has been galling to clergy in search of an image of relevance. In the 1974 Episcopal view of the church situation in Puerto Rico 'Panorama of the Catholic Church in Puerto Rico since the Synod of Bishops', one finds an oft repeated theme of clerical desertion: priests who have abandoned their ministry are 'excessively lax in the discharge of their sacred obligations'; they 'provoke confrontation with the ecclesiastical structure'. One also notes the paternalism of the hierarchy in the suggestion that ex-priests be returned to the lay apostolate 'once they overcome their emotional crisis'. Enthusiasm for the priestly vocation is widely lacking among Puerto Ricans, even at the hierarchical level. Under both the Spanish and American colonial regimes, Puerto Rican clergy never stood out in number or quality. In 1960, at the height of the American episcopate in the island, there were relatively fewer native clergy (one Puerto Rican among nine clergy) than in 1897 near the end of Spanish rule, when one out of 5 clergy was Puerto Rican. By 1974, all Catholic bishops were native born. While most Catholic movements or groups are conservatively oriented and take their cue directly from the Catholic hierarchy, a certain number of these (Juventud Obrera Cristiana, Juventud Estudiantil Cristiana, Juventud Yniversitaria Catolica, Jornadas

Country summary. **Worlds A, B, C by ethnolinguistic peoples, cities, and major civil divisions in Puerto Rico.**

	PEOPLES							CITIES							CIVIL DIVISIONS						
World	Num	Pop 2000	C%	Christians	E%	U%	Unevangelized	Num	Pop 2000	C%	Christians	E%	U%	Unevangelized	Num	Pop 2000	C%	Christians	E%	U%	Unevangelized
A	0	0	0.00	0	0	0	0	0	0	0.00	0	0	0	0	0	0	0.00	0	0	0	0
B	5	16,364	34.56	5,656	85	15	2,454	0	0	0.00	0	0	0	0	0	0	0.00	0	0	0	0
C	7	3,852,238	96.48	3,716,634	100	0	1,411	4	2,024,269	95.48	1,932,786	100	0	2,430	7	3,868,601	96.22	3,722,291	100	0	3,863
Total	**12**	**3,868,602**	**96.22**	**3,722,290**	**100**	**0**	**3,865**	**4**	**2,024,269**	**95.48**	**1,932,786**	**100**	**0**	**2,430**	**7**	**3,868,601**	**96.22**	**3,722,291**	**100**	**0**	**3,863**

de Juventud, and segments of Cursillo de Cristiandad), together with their clerical sympathizers and mentors, have moved to active involvement in and for the cause of socio-political liberation in Puerto Rico. The reaction of church authorities has been either to withdraw recognition or to impose sanctions. Liberal and separatist clerics were forced out of their parishes and a number abandoned the ministry altogether, while others organized the Association of Priests (Asociación Puertorriquena de Sacerdotes) in Rio Pedras in 1972, which is the only Catholic organization wholly and openly in favor of political independence and socialism for Puerto Rico.

The Holy See has no diplomatic relations with Puerto Rico in AD 2000.

Iglesia Metodista Unida. Methodist Church in Jayuya.

PROTESTANT CHURCHES. Puerto Rico was included among other former Spanish territories in 1898 comity agreement among American Protestant churches, determining the location of their work after the Spanish-American war. The next year (1899) saw the arrival of 5 denominations (Baptists, Disciples, Lutherans, Presbyterians, and United Brethren), followed by Methodists in 1900 and Adventists in 1909. Of these, Methodists and Adventists have built up large constituencies. Both have given considerable attention to schools, and Adventists also maintain important medical work. Adventist missionaries make up 26% of all foreign Protestant church workers on the island at the present time. The Baptist Convention of Puerto Rico, which originated in 1899 and is related historically to Northern American Baptists in the USA, has also achieved a significant membership. Presbyterians are strongest in western Puerto Rico, beginning there with a small group which had first been introduced to independent worship by an English trader of Reformed faith in 1860. In 1904, they opened one of the finest hospitals on the island and, in 1919, contributed the first president to the new interdenominational evangelical seminary. Although Lutheran membership remains small, Lutherans are responsible for administering Puerto Rico's main Protestant bookstore. In 1931, the United Evangelical Church was formed by a merger of 3 denominations: United Brethren, Christian Church, and Congregational Church. Although the purpose of the merger was to build a strong united church, growth has been slow due in part to internal dissension over questions not resolved prior to union. The Disciples considered joining the UEC in 1933 but decided against it and remain an independent body.

Pentecostalism entered the island in 1916 with the return of Puerto Ricans who had come under the influence of the Assemblies of God while seeking work in Hawaii; and the Pentecostal Church of God is now the island's largest denomination outside Roman Catholicism. The church is fully self-supporting and maintains missionaries in Spain. Portugal and 9 other Latin American countries. Other Pentecostal groups include the Church of God (Cleveland), Church of God of Prophecy, International church of the Foursquare Gospel, and United Pentecostal Church. Protestantism has been able to penetrate all levels of social, economic, and political life, both rural and urban, more completely in Puerto Rico than in any other Latin American country; and largely as a result of their schools. Protestants are now widely represented in the professions, business and government.

OTHER CHURCHES. Four years after Spain decreed religious tolerance in 1868, the English bishop of Antigua received permission to build the first Anglican church in Puerto Rico, at Ponce. Responsibility for Anglican work was transferred to the Episcopal Church in the USA in 1901. In 1923, the independent Church of Jesus, founded in 1902, merged with it, and although membership remains small, the Episcopal Church maintains a strong educational and medical program.

A large number of indigenous churches have emerged in Puerto Rico, principally out of Pentecostalism. The most successful have been the Missionary Church of Christ, Defenders of the Faith Church, Pentecostal Church of Jesus Christ, and the Church of Christ in the Antilles. Jehovah's Witnesses also have experienced significant growth, becoming the fourth largest non-Catholic church by 1990.

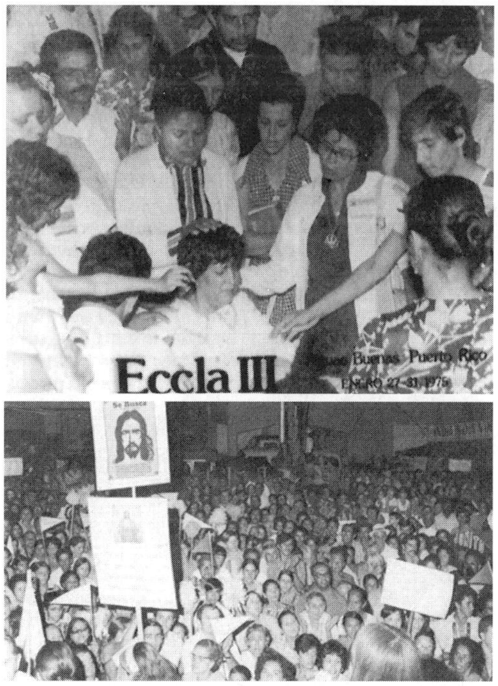

Catholic Charismatics. *Upper.* A healing in process at ECCLA 3 (Latin America-wide). *Lower.* 'Se busca (wanted)!' All night praise and prayer meeting and procession in Orcocovis, with 4,000 attenders.

Renewal movements. In the 1990s the Pentecostal/Charismatic Renewal continued to spread rapidly across most older churches, and numbered over 1,025,000 adherents (of whom 23% Pentecostals, 53% Charismatics, and 23% Independents).

Indigenous missions. Puerto Rican Christians were involved in evangelizing other islands in the Caribbean in the 16th and 17th centuries. In the 19th century many missionaries have been sent out but the vast majority of these work in the United States with Puerto Ricans living there.

CHURCH AND STATE

In Puerto Rico, church and state are regarded as separate, mutually independent entities. The definitive legal commitment for this view is set forth in the constitution of the Commonwealth of Puerto Rico of 1952. Article II, section 3 of that constitution states that 'No law shall be made respecting an establishment of religion or prohibiting the free exercise thereof. There shall be complete separation of Church and State'.

Except for the second statement, the religion clause quoted above is a replica of that found in the first amendment to the federal constitution of the USA. In fact, statutory nonestablishment and religious freedom were introduced into Puerto Rico with the transfer of sovereign rights over the island from Spain to the USA Article X of the Treaty of Paris of 1898, which ended the Spanish-American War and provided among other items for such transfer, reads thus: 'The inhabitants of the territories over which Spain relinquishes or cedes her sovereignty shall be secure in the free exercise of their religion'. The prescription proscribing any establishment, which is the other of 2 coordinate or parallel aspects of the separation principle within the USA's historical tradition of church-state relationships, was implicit in the USA's acquisition of that sovereignty. It was later incorporated explicitly in the Jones Law of 1917 which the USA Congress passed to provide a framework of government for Puerto Rico. The law also included specific clauses to ensure that separation be an actual fact in a colony which was predominantly Roman Catholic and where the Spanish notion of the oneness of church and state had been deeply rooted. The separation guarantees (paragraphs 18 and 19 of Article II) were worded thus: 'That the free exercise and enjoyment of religious profession and worship without discrimination or preference shall forever be allowed and that no political religious tests other than an oath to support the constitution of the United States and the laws of Puerto Rico shall be required as a qualification to any office or public trust under the government of Puerto Rico'; also 'That no public money or property shall ever be appropriated, applied, donated, used, directly or indirectly, for the use, benefit or support of any sect, church, denomination, sectarian institution, or association, or system of religion, or for the use, benefit or support of any priests, preacher, minister or other religious teacher or dignitary as such'.

The law, however, was unable to prevent church and state in Puerto Rico from becoming entangled in each other's domain. Relations between the 2 were further complicated by the presence of Protestants from the USA. From the beginning of American rule in the island, the Catholic Church fought a losing battle concerning the public schools which it criticized for their secularism and for depriving Catholics of their right to religious and moral instruction. The Catholic community was also critical of American Protestant evangelism and culturalism and the influence of Protestants both outside and inside the political community. Divorce was implanted within a few years after the advent of the Americans, while all attempts to provide moral instruction in the public schools proved fruitless.

In 1937, the Catholic conscience was outraged by the passage of so called neo-Malthusian or eugenic laws by the island's legislature. Ostensibly to fight over-population and its negative influence on the social economy, these laws allowed and facilitated birth control, particularly in the form of sterilization of the deranged, lunatics, mentally retarded, epileptics, alcoholics, drug addicts, and also persons 'whose state of economic penury or bad conditions of life do not allow them to attend to the rearing and education of their children'. Official Catholic opposition to the laws was put in moral terms, as contravening the sacred procreative end of matrimony. In November 1974 and May 1975, the Catholic bishops twice condemned the government's massive birth control program, including the sterilization of women, which they stated was not, as its sponsors officially claimed, entirely voluntary.

In 1942, under the new political leadership of the Populares, a law was passed recognizing, for all legal purposes, children born out of wedlock. By 1960, differences between church and state had been compounded not only by questions of the public schools and population control but also by personality conflicts between the Catholic hierarchy who were USA nationals and a vociferous native political leadership. The conflict came to a head when local political leader Munoz Marin refused to yield on his party's commitment to institutionalized family planning, and the Catholic hierarchy countered by hastily creating a Catholic party. This party failed to win a single seat in the island's legislature, while Marin's party, the Populares, received the largest electoral support ever. Four years later in 1964, the 2 USA bishops who had led the fight against Marin were recalled.

Since then the Puerto Rican bishops who have taken over the island's dioceses have avoided politics, particularly the issue of status for the island vis-a-vis the USA. At present, the main alternatives are defined as statehood, independence, and some form of commonwealth. Critics of the hierarchy, among them separatist Catholics, suggest that the present Catholic withdrawal from politics is proof of its alliance with the economic power structure of the island which, in turn, is seen as an extension of that on the mainland. In recent years, clergy and sisters who have given up their vocations have been mostly separatists or sympathizers with the independence movement.

Since the churches are regarded in law as nonprofit, private, corporate bodies, church income and property are tax-exempt, and donations to them are tax-deductible (Law number 74, 1 January 1924). The idea of such concessions, interpreted in some quarters as subsidies to organized religion, originated in the USA where they came into law in 1916 and 1917. In 1947, the decision of the United States Supreme Court on the case of Everson vs. Board of Education allowed state aid in the form of transportation to children of sectarian schools. The influence of this decision is seen in Section 5 of the Bill of Rights of the Puerto Rican constitution which, while providing for 'a system of free and wholly nonsectarian public instruction', does not forbid the state from 'furnishing to any child noneducational services established by law for the protection or welfare of children'. Thus, Catholic schools, like those of other religious groups, receive government aid in the form of transportation, lunches, dental service, scholarships, textbooks, and other services.

Of the religious denominations found on the island, all but the Catholic Church are registered in the archives of the Department of Justice. This fact derives from the legal attitude taken with regard to the nature of the island's Roman Catholic Church. Some maintain that the Catholic Church is a 'a juridical-sovereign ecclesiastical body', with a public right to enter into a pact on an equal footing with the state, and that this view was affirmed in canon law and was the basis of the concordats of the 19th century between the Vatican and the Spanish monarchy. It is further claimed that this is compensation from the people of Puerto Rico and the government of the USA for property which allegedly had been lost to and remained unrestored to Spain at the time of the assumption of government by the USA.

BROADCASTING AND MEDIA

Shortwave broadcasts from TWR (Antilles), HCJB (Ecuador), and AWR (Costa Rica) can be received. Puerto Rico is a member of UNDA.

CBN's talk show, news programs and children's programs can be seen on various days of the week throughout the country. TBN programming can be seen on local channel 54 in 5 cities. LeSEA's programming can be received via the World Harvest Satellite.

One million (32%) have seen the 'Jesus' Film: mainly on TV (600,000) and through cinematic showings (310,000).

In 1998 global evangelist Billy Graham, preaching from Puerto Rico, reached one billion listeners at a time.

INTERDENOMINATIONAL ORGANIZATIONS

The Evangelical Council of Puerto Rico (Concilio Evangélico de Puerto Rico) was begun in 1954 on the foundations laid earlier by the Evangelical Union in 1905 and the Association of Evangelical Churches of Puerto Rico in 1930. Full members include Baptists, Brethren, Disciples, Mennonites, Methodists, Presbyterians, Salvation Army, and United Evangelicals.

The Catholic Episcopal Conference maintains a Commission for Ecumenism.

The Evangelical Seminary of Puerto Rico is sponsored by 10 denominations and serves 12 countries. It also works closely with the Episcopal Seminary of the Caribbean and the Catholic Theological Faculty at the Central University of Bayamon. Co-operative activities of these 3 seminaries (especially the first 2) include joint faculty meetings and sharing of faculty and library facilities.

FUTURE TRENDS AND PROSPECTS

Christians, over 98% of the population in 1970, will probably decline to 96% by 2025 while the nonreligious grow from 1.1% in 1970 to 2.2% by 2025.

By the middle of the 21st century the nonreligious and atheists could comprise over 5% of the population. Christianity is expected to predominate throughout the next 50 years at least.

BIBLIOGRAPHY

'A comparative analysis of the attitudes of the graduates of Caribbean Christian College and Leadership Training by Extension in Puerto Rico.' E. F. Mathews. D.Miss. thesis, Fuller Theological Seminary, Pasadena, CA, 1980. 185p.

'A consideration of some factors involved in the development of church planning in Puerto Rico.' R. Morales-Alamo. Thesis, Butler University, Indianapolis, IN, 1964.

An annotated selected Puerto Rican bibliography. E. R. Bravo (ed). Trans., M. Cuevas. New York: Urban Center, Columbia University, 1972. 114p. (338 titles).

'Becoming a medium: the role of trance in Puerto Rican spiritism as an avenue to mazeway resynthesis.' M. Michtom. Ph.D. dissertation, New York University, 1975. 425p.

Bibliografía puertoriqueña de ciencias sociales, 1931–1960. Universidad de Puerto Rico, Centro de Investigaciones Sociales. Río Piedras, Puerto Rico: Editorial Universitaria, 1977. 600p.

Bibliografía puertorriqueña (1493–1930). A. S. Pedreira. *Monografías de la Universidad de Puerto Rico, series A, Estudios Hispánicos*, 1. Madrid: Imprenta de Hernando, 1932. 707p.

Brethren in Florida and Puerto Rico. E. S. Moyer. Elgin, IL: Brethren Press, 1975. 237p.

Breve historia de la Iglesia Presbiteriana en Puerto Rico. J. Aracelio Cardona. Río Piedras, Puerto Rico: Iglesia Presbiteriana Unida en los Estados Unidos de América, Sínodo de Puerto Rico, 1976. 147p.

'Cultural change and Protestantism in Puerto Rico, 1945–1966.' E. M. Baselga. Ph.D. dissertation, New York University, New York, 1971. 343p.

'Economic aspects of church development: a study of the policies and procedures of the major Protestant groups in Puerto Rico from 1897–1957.' M. Saenz. Thesis, University of Pennsylvania, Philadelphia, 1961.

Espiritismo (y curanderismo) para sacerdotes, monjas, seglares católicos, protestantes y espiritistas. J. P. Benabarre Vigo. Aler, España Humacao, Puerto Rico, 1991. 153p.

Festividades religiosas de conmemoración popular en Puerto Rico. J. Roca Rivera. , 1986. 19p.

'Group ministry for new converts in Puerto Rico.' M. A. Gonzalez. D.Min. project, Andrews University, Seventh-day Adventist Theological Seminary, Barrien Springs, MI, 1990. 280p.

Historia de la Iglesia de Dios Pentecostal, M.I.: una Iglesia Ungida da Para Hacer Misión. D. R. Torres. Puerto Rico: Editorial Pentecostal. 464p.

Historia de la Iglesia en Puerto Rico, 1511–1802. C. Campo Lacasa. San Juan, Puerto Rico: Instituto de Cultura Puertorriqueña, 1977. 333p.

Historia de los Bautistas de Puerto Rico. T. Rosario Ramos. 2nd ed. Santa Domingo, Dominican Republic: Editora Educativa Dominicana, 1979. 437p.

La Iglesia en Puerto Rico. A. Mendoza. *Informes de Pro Mundi Vita América Latina*, 40. Brussels, Belgium: Pro Mundi Vita, 1985. 31p.

Light of the Spirit: the Brethren in Puerto Rico, 1942 to 1992. M. S. H. Rosenberger. Elgin, IL: Association of Brethren Caregivers, [1992]. 96p.

Los Discipulos de Cristo en Puerto Rico: albores, crecimiento y madurez de un peregrinar de fe, constancia y esperanze, 1899–1987. J. Vargas. [Puerto Rico]: Iglesia Cristiana (Discipulos de Cristo) en Puerto Rico, 1988. 204p.

Los franciscanos en Puerto Rico. M. Errasti & V. Beaín. [Puerto Rico]: M. Errasti, [1994]. 114p.

María en la religiosidad popular de Puerto Rico. A. Dávila Rodríguez. *Colección V centenario*, 31. Bogota, Colombia: Consejo Episcopal Lationamericano, 1989. 59p.

Presbyterian missions to Trinidad and Puerto Rico. G. S. Mount. Hantsport, Canada: Lancelot Press, 1983. 356p.

'Presbyterianism in Puerto Rico: formative years, 1899–1914,' G. S. Mount, *Journal of Presbyterian history*, 55, 3 (1977), 241–54.

'Puerto Rican spiritism: contrasts in the sacred and profane,' W. P. Bradford, *Caribbean Quarterly*, 24, 3-4 (1978), 48–55.

Puerto Rico. E. Cevallos. *World bibliographical series*, vol. 52. Oxford, UK: CLIO Press, 1985. 195p. (See especially 'Religion,' p.33–6).

Puerto Rico: iglesia y sociedad, 1969–1971. A. Parilla-Bonilla. *Sondeos*, No. 84. Cuernavaca, Mexico: CIDOC, 1971. 550p.

Puerto Rico para Cristo: a history of the progress of the Evangelical missions on the island of Puerto Rico. D. T. Moore. Cuernavaca, Mexico: CIDOC, 1969. 332p.

'Religion and missions in Puerto Rico.' B. Alicea. M.A. thesis, New Brunswick Theological Seminary, New Brunswick, NJ, 1978. 127p.

'Religion and science divinely related: a case history of spiritism in Puerto Rico,' J. D. Koss, *Caribbean Studies*, 16, 1 (1976), 22–43.

Rx: spiritist as needed: a study of a Puerto Rican community mental health resource. A. Harwood. New York: Wiley-Interscience, 1977. 251p.

'Showcase for God: a study of evangelical church growth in Puerto Rico.' E. E. Carver. M.A. thesis, Fuller Theological Seminary, Pasadena, CA, 1972. 267p.

'Spiritism: the popular religion of Puerto Rico.' W. J. Callahan. M.T.S. thesis, Catholic Theological Union, Chicago, 1985. 78p.

St. James in the streets: the religious processions of Loiza, Puerto Rico. E. C. Zaragoza. *Drew studies in liturgy*, no. 2. Lanham, MD: Scarecrow Press, 1995.

The Catholic Church in colonial Puerto Rico. E. J. de Nieves. Río Piedras, Puerto Rico: Editorial Edil, 1982. 266p.

The Community of the Holy Spirit: a movement of change in a convent of nuns in Puerto Rico. J. Sánchez. Lanham, MD: University Press of America, 1983. 189p.

'The indigenous elements in popular religion of Puerto Ricans.' A. M. Stevens-Arroyo. Ph.D. dissertation, Fordham University, New York, 1981. 279p.

'The origins and growth of the Methodist Church in Puerto Rico, 1900–1970.' M. O. Ziegler. Immaculata College, Immaculata PA, 1988. 76p.

The Puerto Ricans: an annotated bibliography. P. Vivo (ed). New York: Bowker, 1973. 299p.

Una iglesia triunfante: 50 años de historia de la iglesia de Dios 'mission board' Puerto Rico. [Puerto Rico, 1994]. 102p.

Understanding the religious background of the Puerto Rican. J. Fenton. *Sondeos*, no. 52. Cuernavaca, Mexico: Centro Intercultural de Documentación, 1969. 72p.

Country Table 2. **Organized churches and denominations in Puerto Rico.**

Official name (bold type = church *with over 10% of all affiliated)* 1	*Begun* 2	*Type* 3	*Counc* 4	*Congs* 5	*Adults* 6	*Affiliated 1970* 7	*Affiliated 1995* 8	*G%* 9	*Names, notes, and other statistics* (see Codebook, Part 3) 10
Asamblea des Iglesias Cristianas	1940	I-3pL	x....	160	7,500	5,000	15,000	4.49	*Assembly of Christian Churches.* Begun 1939 by Puerto Ricans in New York, ex LACC.
Asambleas de Dios	1957	P-Pe2	ZF..E	146	39,000	3,000	70,900	13.49	*Assemblies of God.* M=AoG(USA), until 1956 working with Iglesia de Dios Pente. 1p.
Asambleas Locales	c1960	I-3nC	.....	24	1,370	200	2,000	9.65	*Local Churches. Little Flock.* Chinese. Begun 1922 in China.
Asociación Bautista	1956	P-Bap	T....	59	4,200	3,000	10,500	5.14	M=Southern Baptist Convention (Home Mission Board) (USA). 14f,642Y.
Congregacion Iglesia Ev Menonitas	1945	P-Men	G.U.N	14	868	2,000	950	-2.93	*Puerto Rico Mennonite Conference.* M=MCNA(USA). Non-Germans. 9f,1H,2r,1s.
Convención Bautista de Puerto Rico	1899	P-Bap	T.u.N	82	27,000	20,000	54,000	4.05	*Baptist Convention of PR.* 1899, M=ABHMS(USA). 4f,1u.
Ejército de Salvación	1961	P-Sal	xwu.N	5	824	500	1,270	3.80	*Salvation Army, PR Region*, USA Eastern Territory. San Juan. 1 emergency home. 1s.
Hermanos Libres		P-CBr	x....	8	250	500	714	0.05	*Christian Brethren. Plymouth (Open) Brethren. Gospel Halls.* M=CMML(USA, UK). 10f.
Hermanos de Ig Cr Carismaticos	c1975	I-3cL	.....	50	3,000	–	4,290	5.00	Latin American charismatics.
Iglesia Adventista del Séptimo Día	1901	P-Adv	x....	247	29,950	25,000	74,900	4.49	*Seventh-day Adv, East/West PR Confs.* 26nx,195mw,72f,1H,2r,1s,150t(9339),1479Y.

Continued opposite

Country Table 2–concluded

Official name (bold type = church with over 10% of affiliated) 1	*Begun* 2	*Type* 3	*Counc* 4	*Congs* 5	*Adults* 6	*Affiliated 1970* 7	*Affiliated 1995* 8	*G%* 9	*Names, notes, and other statistics* (see Codebook, Part 3) 10
Iglesia Alianza Cristiana y Misionera	1900	P-Hol	xF..E	51	5,631	7,000	14,100	2.84	*Christian & Missionary Alliance Ch.* M=CMA(USA). HQ Magnolia Gardens. 36m,1s.
Ig Bautistas Fund Indep	c1950	I-Fun	.....	51	5,000	3,000	10,000	4.93	*Independent Fundamental Baptist Churches.*
Iglesia Católica en Puerto Rico:	1509	R-Lat	B.L.R	1,075	1,661,000	2,585,824	2,801,500	0.32	*Catholic Ch in Puerto Rico.* C=24+3+75. 2q,2s. 376n 362x 433m 1130w 45059Yy
M San Juan de Puerto Rico	1511	R-Lat	Bs	305	571,000	1,025,000	1,002,080	-0.09	Northeast quarter of island. Capital. 1s. 135n 189x 237m 433w 13826Yy
D Arecibo	1960	R-Lat	Bs	59	256,000	524,819	484,420	-0.32	Northwest. Strong Charismatic Renewal. M=CP. 79n 41x 55m 180w 8008Yy
D Caguas	1964	R-Lat	Bs	272	327,000	500,000	515,000	0.12	Southeast, also Vieques islands (8,100), Culebra. 60n 49x 48m 133w 7610Yy
D Mayagüez	1976	R-Lat	Bs	177	252,000	–	360,000	5.26	New diocese; population 79% Roman Catholic. 38n 30x 37m 141w 5453Yy
D Ponce	1924	R-Lat	Bs	262	255,000	536,005	440,000	-0.79	Southwest quarter of island. Charismatics strong. 64n 53x 56m 243w 10162Yy
Iglesia de Cristo en las Antillas	1933	I-3pL	.....	48	3,200	7,100	6,400	-0.41	*Ch of Christ in Antilles.* Mission to New York (USA). 24n,1x,1s(76),150Y.
Iglesia de Cristo Misionera	1934	I-3pL	.....	81	8,000	10,000	13,300	1.15	*Missionary Ch of Christ.* Until 1938 Iglesia de Cristo en las Antillas.
Iglesia de Dios	1939	I-3pL	.....	120	7,000	7,000	15,000	3.10	*Ch of God.* Begun by 9 Puerto Ricans in east, expanded to west, SW, NE, SE.
Iglesia de Dios de la Profecia	1938	P-Pe3	Z....	25	1,030	2,000	1,710	-0.62	*Ch of God of Prophecy.* Ex CoG (Cleveland). HQ Rio Piedras. M=CGP(USA). 2f.
Iglesia de Dios Pentecostal	1916	P-Pe2	ZF...	480	66,953	60,000	112,000	2.53	*Pentecostal Ch of God.* Begun by Puerto Rican Catholics. M=AoG(USA). G=15%pa,1s.
Iglesia de Dios (Anderson)	1966	P-Hol	x....	5	150	100	400	5.70	*Ch of God.* M=CoG(Anderson) (USA). HQ Caguas, San José. 1 school. 1n,2f,W=50%.
Iglesia de Dios (Cleveland)	1944	P-Pe3	ZF...	199	14,689	20,000	24,500	0.82	M=CoG(Cleveland) (USA). Before 1944, Iglesia Roca de Salvación et al. 144n,4f,1p.
Iglesia de JC de los Santos de los UD		m-LdS	x....	49	11,200	507	16,000	0.05	*Ch of JC of Latter-day Saints. Mormons.* M=CJCLdS(USA). About 20 missionaries.
Iglesia de la Biblia Abierta	1958	I-3pW	ZF...	3	259	200	432	3.13	*Open Bible Chs.* M=OBSC(USA). Classical Pentecostals. HQ Rio Piedras. 2f,1j.
Iglesia de los Hermanos	1942	P-Dun	x.u.N	3	700	1,000	1,500	1.64	M=Church of the Brethren (USA). Small mission of German Baptist origins. 5f.
Iglesia Defensores de la Fe	1931	I-3pL	xT...	123	12,000	9,000	24,000	4.00	*Defenders of the Faith Ch.* Missions to Dominican Republic. HQ Santurce. 1s.
Iglesia del Evangelio Cuadrangular	1930	P-Pe2	ZF..E	18	1,530	1,000	5,100	6.73	M=Internat Ch of the Foursquare Gospel (USA). HQ Ponce. 14nm,2f,1p(11),W=56%,26Y.
Iglesia del Nazareno	1943	P-Hol	xF..E	37	2,636	3,000	4,513	1.65	*PR Distrito Nazareno.* M=Ch of the Nazarene (USA). 13n,9m,8f,1s,20t(2565).
Iglesia Discipulos de Cristo	1899	P-Dis	x.u.N	93	10,600	15,000	17,600	0.64	*Christian (Disciples) Convention of PR.* M=UCMS(USA). 1u.
Iglesia Episcopal: D Puerto Rico	1872	A-Cen	aw.R.	38	6,600	9,722	12,000	0.85	*Episcopal Ch.* In ECUSA, Prov IX. 95% nationals. 35n,12x,1H,1s,W=25%,29Y,414y.
Iglesia Ev Luterana Confessional	c1985	I-Lut	.....	4	153	–	219	10.00	*Evangelical Lutheran Confessing Church.*
Iglesia Evangélica Unida de PR	1899	P-Uni	..u.N	58	5,000	12,000	10,000	-0.73	*United Ch of PR.* 1931 union of UBC, Christian Ch, Congregationalists. Static. 1u.
Iglesia Luterana Puertorriqueña	1899	P-Lut	L.M..	26	5,049	8,000	8,609	0.29	Caribbean Synod, Lutheran Ch in America. Main Protestant book distributor. 25n.
Iglesia Metodista Unida	1900	P-Met	Vwu.N	70	10,000	25,000	25,000	0.00	*PR Provisional Annual Conference, United Methodist Ch* (USA). 58n,1r,1u.
Iglesia Mita	1942	I-mar	.....	10	4,000	5,000	10,000	2.81	Messianic schism ex AoG, female founder Mita as incarnation of Holy Spirit.
Iglesia Nueva Apostólica	c1950	I-3aX	x....	20	100	1,000	120	-8.13	*New Apostolic Ch*, USA Bezirk (District). M=NAC(Germany); world HQ Zurich.
Iglesia Ortodoxa		O-Ara	Cwo..	2	600	1,000	1,200	0.05	Under Antiochian Orth Ch (USA) and P Antioch, E America. Lebanese, Syrian Arabs.
Iglesia Pentecostal de Jesucristo	1938	I-3pL	.....	90	10,000	9,000	20,000	3.25	*Pentecostal Ch of Jesus Christ.* Ex Iglesia de Dios Pentecostal, in south & east.
Iglesia Pentecostal Unida	1962	P-Pe1	x....	20	1,000	1,000	3,000	4.49	*United Pentecostal Ch. Jesus Only Church.* Unitarians. M=UPC(USA). 8n,4f,2p(22).
Iglesia Presbiteriana	1860	P-Ref	..u.N	69	9,256	10,000	16,800	2.10	*Presbytery of Puerto Rico.* M=UPUSA. Mostly around Mayagüez. 1H,1u.
Iglesia Wesleyana	1952	P-Hol	VF...	16	1,401	735	1,925	3.93	1959 merger indigenous Tabernáculos de Dios. M=PHC,WC(USA). 5n,4x,19f,1s.
Iglesias de Cristo	1953	I-Dis	x....	30	1,100	1,000	2,000	2.81	*Churches of Christ.* M=CC(Non-Instrumental) (USA). In cities. 16f,1s.
Iglesias Metodistas Libres	c1980	I-Met	.....	2	90	–	129	6.67	*Free Methodist Ch.* M=FMC(USA).
Misión UFM	c1985	P-Non	.....	1	25	–	55	10.00	Unevangelized Fields Mission. M=UFM.
Samaria Iglesia Evangélica	1941	I-3pL	.....	40	2,000	1,500	4,000	4.00	*Samarian Ev Ch.* Begun Río Grande, ex Baptist Ch. Mission in New York state (USA).
Santa Iglesia Católica Apost Ortodoxa	1961	I-CCa	.v...	2	300	1,000	900	-0.42	*Holy Orth Cath Apost Ch.* RCC, aided by Polish NCC(USA). 1968 applied to WCC. 1s.
Sociedad de la Ciencia Cristiana		m-Sci	x....	1	30	50	60	0.05	*Christian Science.* First Ch of Christ, Scientist, San Juan. M=CCS(Boston, USA).
Testigos de Jehová	c1930	m-Jeh	x....	293	24,042	14,700	68,700	6.36	*Jehovah's Witnesses. Watch Tower.* Active witnessing by 1932. (1975) 786Y. (1995) 1139Y.
Other Non-White indigenous churches		I-3pN	.....	190	30,000	20,000	60,000	0.05	Total about 26 (see list below), almost all pentecostal.
Other Protestant denominations		P-	.....	300	10,000	8,000	20,000	0.05	Total about 25 (see list below).
Other marginal Protestant bodies		m-	.....	20	800	3,000	2,000	0.05	Incl: Unitarian Fellowship of San Juan, Unity School of Christianity (2 churches).
Other independent charismatic chs	c1975	I-3cL	.....	100	20,000	–	50,000	5.00	In about 20 loose networks.
Doubly-affiliated		2-aff			-22,400	-257,638	-39,296		Evangelicals who also are or were baptized Roman Catholics.
Totals				**4,658**	**2,044,686**	**2,665,000**	**3,580,000**		

Churches, members, growth, 1900-2025	*Congs*	*Adults*	*Affiliated*	*G%*	*Total denominations*	*6 Megablocs:* O	R	A	P	I	m
Total churches, members, and denominations (mid-1900)	900	535,000	951,500	1.48	10	0	1	1	8	0	0
Total churches, members, and denominations (mid-1970)	2,334	1,498,227	2,665,000	1.48	72	1	1	1	33	26	10
Total churches, members, and denominations (mid-1990)	4,000	1,945,000	3,405,540	1.23	129	1	1	1	48	60	18
Total churches, members, and denominations (mid-1995)	4,658	2,044,686	3,580,000	1.00	132	1	1	1	48	63	18
Total churches, members, and denominations (mid-2000)	5,000	2,126,000	3,722,291	0.78	135	1	1	1	48	66	18
Total churches, members, and denominations (mid-2025)	7,000	2,427,000	4,250,000	0.53	416	8	1	1	80	300	26

NOTES ON TABLE ABOVE

NATIONAL COUNCILS (Column 4, 5th letter).

- E = Evangelical Alliance of Puerto Rico.
- N = Concilio Evangélico de Puerto Rico (CEPR)/Evangelical Council of Puerto Rico, 1954.
- R = Conferencia Episcopal Puertorriqueña (CEP)/Puerto Rico Episcopal Conference.

OTHER NON-WHITE INDIGENOUS CHURCHES. These bodies, begun by Puerto Ricans and Blacks, are almost all pentecostal, and include: Asamblea Cristiana, Concilio Iglesia de Dios Apostólica, Iglesia Cristiana de Nazareth, Iglesia de Cristo Séptimo Día, Iglesia de Dios Hebreos, Iglesia de Dios Primitiva, Iglesia de Dios Sacrificada, Iglesia de Dios Singular, Iglesia Ev de Avivamiento, Iglesia Ev del Buen Pastor, Iglesia Mensajeros de Cristo, Iglesia Monte Sión, Iglesia Pentecostal del Nazareno, Iglesia Refugio de Sión.

OTHER PROTESTANT DENOMINATIONS. These include: Baptist Bible Fellowship International (1955), Baptist International Missions, Baptist Mid-Missions (1959), Bethany Fellowship Missions (1965), Children of God International, Christian Reformed Ch (1967), Conservative Baptist Home Missions Society (1958; 5 churches), Exclusive Brethren (Kelly-Continental), Fellowship of Independent Missions (1968), Go-Ye Fellowship, Grace Mission (1961), Independent Assemblies of God, International Gospel League (1961), International Pentecostal Assemblies (1962), National Fellowship of Brethren Chs (1959), Reformed Baptists (USA; 1 church), Union Churches (in 2 cities), United Missionary Fellowship (1968) (merger of Pioneer Bible Mission, United Faith Mission), Wisconsin Ev Lutheran Synod (1963), World Gospel Crusades (1969), World-Wide Missions (1962). There are also military chaplaincies for the USA armed forces.

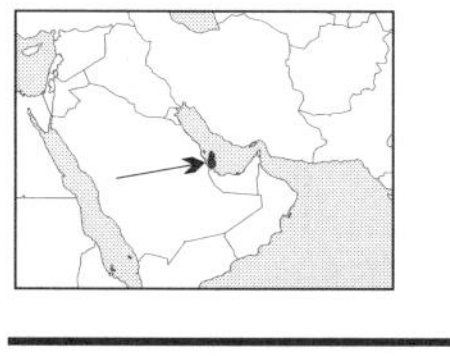

QATAR

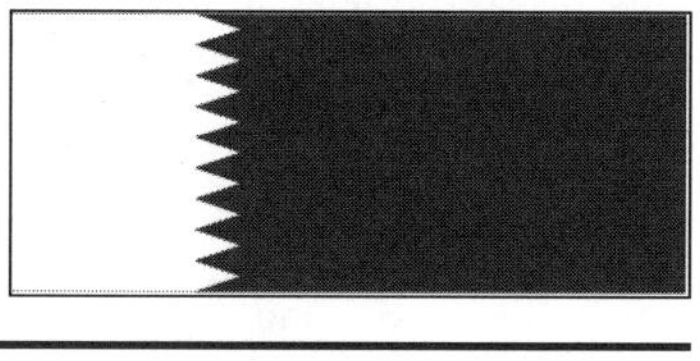

SECULAR DATA, AD 2000

STATE
Official name: Dawlat Qatar (The State of Qatar).
Short name: Qatar. **Adjective of nationality:** of Qatar.
Flag: Maroon field with broad white serrated band at hoist.
Area: 11,427 sq. km. (4,412 sq. mi.).
Government: Absolute monarchy (1916 British protectorate, 1971 Independence as emirate).
Legislature: Advisory Council, 30 members.
Official language: Arabic.
Monetary unit: 1 riyal (QR) = 100 dirhams. **US$1=** QR 3.64.
Chief cities: AD-DAWHAH (Doha) 486,037.
Political divisions: 9 provinces.
Armed forces: 12,000.

DEMOGRAPHY
Population: 599,000.
Population density: 52.4/sq. km. (135.7/sq. mi.).
Under 15 years: 156,000.
Growth rate p.a.: 1.53% (births 18.05, deaths 4.40).
Mortality: Infant, per 1,000: 15.2, ; **Maternal per 100,000:** 50.0.
Life expectancy: 73 (male 71, female 76).
Household size: 6.4. **Floor area per person, sq.m:** 25.0.
Major languages: Arabic, English, Persian.
Urban dwellers: 92.47%. **Urban growth rate p.a.:** 1.7%.
Labor force: 54%.

ETHNOLINGUISTIC PEOPLES
16.4% Persian (Irani); 13.4% Palestinian Arab; 13.2% Qatari Arab; 10.4% Lebanese Arab; 9.5% African Bantu.

ECONOMY
National income p.a. per person: US$11,599; **per family:** US$74,238.

EDUCATION
Adult literacy: 79% (male 79%, female 79%). **Schools:** 197.
Universities: 1. **School enrolment:** female/male: 83%/86%.

HEALTH
Access to health services: 90%. **Access to safe water:** 100%.
Hospitals: 3 (20 beds per 10,000). **Doctors:** 758.
Blind: 200. **Deaf:** 36,000. **Murder rate:** 1.
Lepers: 1,000. **Underweight prevalence under 5:** 6%.

LITERATURE
New book titles p.a.: 410 (690 p.a. per million). **Periodicals:** 266.
Newspapers: 4 dailies.

COMMUNICATION (per 1,000 people)
Phones: 212 (29% mobile). **Radios:** 311. **TV sets:** 451.
Daily newspaper circulation: 138. **Computers:** 60.

HUMAN LIFE AND LIBERTY (optimum condition=100.0%)
HDI: 84.0. **HSI:** 68.0. **HFI:** 20.0. **EFL:** 30.0.

Country status. Qatar is an Arab state on the Persian Gulf ruled by an emir from the Al Thani family. Oil and natural gas are the country's main products.

HUMAN LIFE AND LIBERTY

Human need and development. Qatar has an artificial economy based on oil, and the fall in oil prices in recent years has led to a reversal in the country's rapid development in the 1970s and 1980s. This downturn has affected primarily the large expatriate population which outnumbers nationals by 4 to one. As in other Arab countries faced with the same problem, the guest workers (mostly from South Asia) form a vast underclass, the precariousness of whose existence is compounded by officially sanctioned discriminatory policies. Oil wealth has helped to create an unreal air of prosperity with impressive public and private edifices created with little planning. The infrastructure is patchy and inefficient. The standards of health and education have risen in recent years as a result of substantial investments in those sectors in the 1980s.

Human rights and freedoms. The emir belongs to the strict Wahhabi sect of Islam, and the Basic Law (or constitution) has institutionalized the puritanical tenets of this sect. Further, the emir is an absolute ruler responsible to no one, although by tradition he cannot violate the sharia and must heed the religious establishment. The legal system, based on the sharia,

Country Table 1. Religious adherents in Qatar, AD 1900-2025.

Year	1900		1970		mid-1990		Annual change, 1990-2000				mid-1995		mid-2000		mid-2025	
Name	Adherents	%	Adherents	%	Adherents	%	Natural	Conversion	Total	Rate	Adherents	%	Adherents	%	Adherents	%
Muslims	17,930	99.6	105,750	95.0	406,400	83.8	9,559	-642	8,917	2.00	452,220	82.5	495,566	82.7	621,100	79.7
Christians	**70**	**0.4**	**4,850**	**4.4**	**47,000**	**9.7**	**1,105**	**421**	**1,526**	**2.85**	**58,500**	**10.7**	**62,259**	**10.4**	**94,000**	**12.1**
PROFESSION																
crypto-Christians	70	0.4	2,030	1.8	17,500	3.6	411	139	550	2.77	20,100	3.7	23,000	3.8	35,800	4.6
professing Christians	**0**	**0.0**	**2,820**	**2.5**	**29,500**	**6.1**	**693**	**283**	**976**	**2.90**	**38,400**	**7.0**	**39,259**	**6.6**	**58,200**	**7.5**
AFFILIATION																
unaffiliated Christians	0	0.0	0	0.0	2,000	0.4	47	15	62	2.75	2,287	0.4	2,624	0.4	5,000	0.6
affiliated Christians	**70**	**0.4**	**4,850**	**4.4**	**45,000**	**9.3**	**1,058**	**406**	**1,464**	**2.86**	**56,213**	**10.3**	**59,635**	**10.0**	**89,000**	**11.4**
Roman Catholics	50	0.3	680	0.6	25,000	5.2	588	522	1,110	3.74	34,000	6.2	36,100	6.0	55,000	7.1
Independents	0	0.0	570	0.5	8,000	1.7	188	36	224	2.49	9,188	1.7	10,235	1.7	15,000	1.9
Anglicans	20	0.1	700	0.6	7,200	1.5	169	-89	80	1.06	8,000	1.5	8,000	1.3	11,000	1.4
Protestants	0	0.0	1,400	1.3	3,500	0.7	82	-32	50	1.34	3,725	0.7	4,000	0.7	6,000	0.8
Orthodox	0	0.0	1,500	1.4	1,300	0.3	31	-31	0	0.00	1,300	0.2	1,300	0.2	2,000	0.3
Trans-megabloc groupings																
Evangelicals	0	0.0	600	0.5	2,960	0.6	70	64	134	3.80	3,803	0.7	4,300	0.7	7,000	0.9
Pentecostals/Charismatics	0	0.0	500	0.5	10,200	2.1	240	180	420	3.51	12,511	2.3	14,400	2.4	27,300	3.5
Great Commission Christians	**70**	**0.4**	**3,300**	**3.0**	**20,000**	**4.1**	**470**	**556**	**1,026**	**4.23**	**25,000**	**4.6**	**30,261**	**5.1**	**50,000**	**6.4**
Hindus	0	0.0	0	0.0	11,500	2.4	270	90	360	2.76	13,700	2.5	15,096	2.5	20,000	2.6
Nonreligious	0	0.0	100	0.1	10,000	2.1	235	116	351	3.06	12,000	2.2	13,513	2.3	22,000	2.8
Buddhists	0	0.0	0	0.0	9,000	1.9	212	26	238	2.38	10,400	1.9	11,382	1.9	20,000	2.6
Baha'is	0	0.0	300	0.3	900	0.2	21	-12	9	0.91	940	0.2	985	0.2	1,400	0.2
Atheists	0	0.0	0	0.0	200	0.0	5	1	6	2.82	240	0.0	264	0.0	500	0.1
World A (unevangelized persons)	17,640	98.0	72,589	65.2	250,260	51.6	5,883	-4,744	1,139	0.45	248,786	45.4	261,164	43.6	299,915	38.5
World B (evangelized non-Christians)	290	1.6	33,893	30.4	187,740	38.7	4,419	4,323	8,742	3.91	240,700	43.9	275,577	46.0	385,085	49.4
World C (Christians)	70	0.4	4,850	4.4	47,000	9.7	1,105	421	1,526	2.85	58,500	10.7	62,259	10.4	94,000	12.1
Country's population	**18,000**	**100.0**	**111,333**	**100.0**	**485,000**	**100.0**	**11,407**	**0**	**11,407**	**2.13**	**547,987**	**100.0**	**599,000**	**100.0**	**779,000**	**100.0**

COLUMNS, ROWS.
For meanings and definitions, see Codebook (Part 3). Note that, by definition, total 'Christians' = professing + crypto-Christians, which also = affiliated + unaffiliated Christians, and also = Great Commission Christians + latent Christians. Percentages may not always total exactly, due to rounding.

NOTES ON RELIGIONS
BAHA'IS. Growth from 1 local spiritual assembly (1964) to 3 (1973) and to 10 (1995).
CHRISTIANS. The rapid increase from 1970 is due to immigration of Arab, Indian, and other Asian Christians.
COUNTRY'S POPULATION. The population has grown very rapidly since 1970 through the arrival of large numbers of immigrant workers. The column 'Natural change' includes this immigration, for all rows in the table also.
CRYPTO-CHRISTIANS. Mainly immigrant Arab Christians whom the state regards as Muslims, together with Arab isolated radio believers.
HINDUS. Indians arriving in the massive influx after 1970.
INDEPENDENTS. Indians from the Mar Thoma Syrian Church, et alia; also Arab isolated radio believers (see Table 2).
MUSLIMS. Indigenous Qataris are Sunnis (primarily Wahhabis), with a small number of Shias; Arabs (Qatari and expatriate), with some Indians and Iranians. *Hajj pilgrims to Mecca* (1970) 1,392; (1975) 974; (1976) 847.
NONRELIGIOUS. Mainly Europeans.
PROFESSING CHRISTIANS. Although no census of religion has been held, the state regards Europeans as professing Christians and either ignores or does not recognize most Arab Christians.

Great Commission Instrument Panel: status of Qatar (for explanation see start of Part 4)

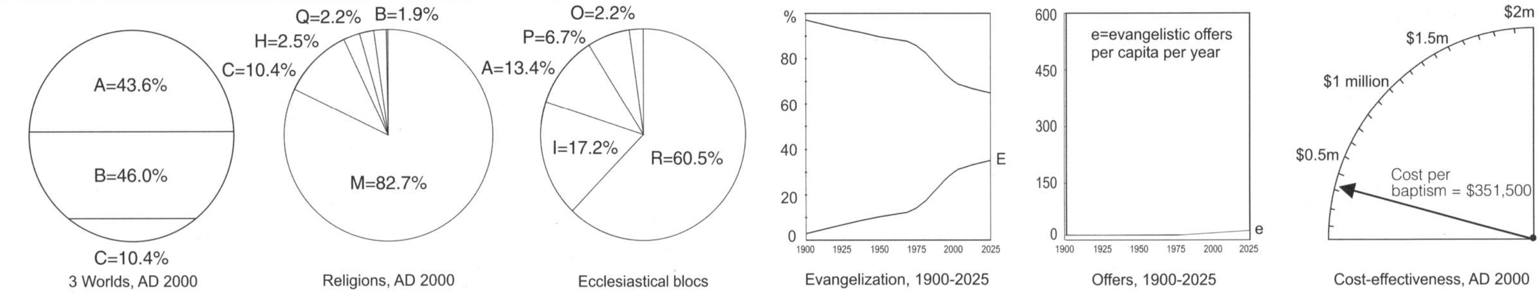

is biased in favor of Muslims and Qataris, since non-Muslims cannot bring a civil suit in a sharia court against a Muslim. Convicted persons are subject to corporal punishments prescribed by the sharia, although mutilation is uncommon. Further, non-Muslims are disadvantaged because lawyers are not permitted to assist defendants in court and all proceedings are in Arabic. There is little freedom of expression or of the press, and any public criticism of the emir is a punishable crime. Books and films are subject to clearance by a board of censors. Foreign guest workers are often harassed by the police, and they may be deported without the benefit of due process. Violence against women, particularly foreign domestic workers, is widespread and is rarely investigated by the police. Qatari women suffer a number of legal disabilities based on the Wahhabi system.

Human environment. Qatar's fragile desert environment has suffered as a result of the oil industry which has placed a heavy strain on the natural ecology of the country. The coastal areas are subject to pollution from oil tankers.

Muslims. Grand Mosque (foreground) and royal palace (left), Doha.

NON-CHRISTIAN RELIGIONS

Islam in Qatar as in Saudi Arabia is represented for the most part by Sunnis, primarily Wahhabis, although there are also a small number of Shias.

Baha'i has a small following in several local spiritual assemblies.

CHRISTIANITY

Christianity established itself in the Arabian Peninsula during the early centuries, with a hierarchy established in northwest Arabia before AD 244 but was completely eclipsed by Islam in the 7th century.

CATHOLIC CHURCH. The first Catholic of modern times returned to Aden in 1841, and by 1889 the whole of the peninsula was included in the vicariate of Arabia, which is now administered from Abu Dhabi. In 1995, there were 34,000 Catholics, mainly migrant workers including Arabs, but no Catholic institutions or religious congregations.

The Holy See has no diplomatic relations with Qatar in AD 2000.

OTHER CHURCHES. There are practically no indigenous professing Christians in Qatar, but a large interdenominational expatriate Christian community exists composed of Westerners (Anglicans, Episcopalians, Scottish Presbyterians, Lutherans, et alii), Indians (Syrian Orthodox, Mar Thoma Church, Church of South India) and Arabs from Palestine and Lebanon. Worship services are led by chaplains of the Arabian American Oil Company. Resident Christians also receive periodic visits from Anglican chaplains stationed at Abu Dhabi (United Arab Emirates), and there are 2 organized Brethren congregations.

Indigenous missions. Christians from Qatar were sent out as missionaries in the first few centuries of Christianity in the Arabian peninsula. In modern times, since the 19th century, very few Qatari Christians have served as foreign missionaries.

CHURCH AND STATE

Qatar came under British protection during the 19th century, largely through Britain's attempt to bring to an end the slave trade in the Gulf. Previously the country was a tribal patriarchal society under the firm control of the emir as chief of state, but a constitutional government was accepted when Independence was declared in 1970. The provisional constitution of 27 April 1970, makes Islam the official religion of the state and the source of its system of law, in addition to guaranteeing fundamental democratic rights for all. Government departments are gradually being developed to meet social and economic needs as they arise. Although any attempt at proselytism is prohibited, expatriate Christians are free to organize and publicize their worship services; and clergy can enter and travel in the country without impediment.

BROADCASTING AND MEDIA

Programs in Arabic and English can be received from FEBA (Seychelles) and HCJB (Ecuador). Shortwave radio programs from KNLS have seen some response.

FUTURE TRENDS AND PROSPECTS

Christians are expected to grow steadily to over 12% by 2025, primarily due to church growth among immigrant workers such as Lebanese Arabs (45% Christian and 15% of the population of Qatar by 2025).

Islam will likely predominate throughout the next 50 years. Christians could increase due to immigration or indigenous church growth to over 15% by mid-century.

BIBLIOGRAPHY

Analytical guide to the bibliographies on the Arabian Peninsula. C. L. Geddes. *Bibliographic series,* 4. Denver, CO: American Institute of Islamic Studies, 1974.

Country summary. **Worlds A, B, C by ethnolinguistic peoples, cities, and major civil divisions in Qatar.**																					
	PEOPLES							***CITIES***							***CIVIL DIVISIONS***						
World	*Num*	*Pop 2000*	*C%*	*Christians*	*E%*	*U%*	*Unevangelized*	*Num*	*Pop 2000*	*C%*	*Christians*	*E%*	*U%*	*Unevangelized*	*Num*	*Pop 2000*	*C%*	*Christians*	*E%*	*U%*	*Unevangelized*
A	9	327,088	1.51	4,951	43	57	185,649	0	0	0.00	0	0	0	0	7	97,045	4.11	3,987	47	53	51,085
B	8	236,631	9.83	23,262	68	32	75,701	1	486,037	10.50	51,034	58	42	204,524	2	502,019	11.08	55,648	58	42	210,303
C	4	35,345	88.90	31,422	100	0	39	0	0	0.00	0	0	0	0	0	0	0.00	0	0	0	0
Total	**21**	**599,064**	**9.95**	**59,635**	**56**	**44**	**261,389**	**1**	**486,037**	**10.50**	**51,034**	**58**	**42**	**204,524**	**9**	**599,064**	**9.95**	**59,635**	**56**	**44**	**261,388**

Bedouins of Qatar. K. Ferdinand. *Carlsberg Foundation Nomad Research Project.* London: Thames and Hudson, 1993. 399p.

Persian Gulf states: country studies. H. C. Metz (ed). 3rd ed. *Area handbook series.* Lanham, MD: Bernan, 1994. 501p.

'Present–day Christianity in the Gulf States of the Arabian Peninsula,' N. A. Horner, *Occasional bulletin of missionary research*, 2 (April 1978), 53–63.

Qatar. P. T. H. Unwin. *World bibliographical series*, vol. 36. Oxford, UK: CLIO Press, 1982. 162p.

Qatari women, past and present. A. Abu Saud. London: Longman, 1984. 216p.

Source book on Arabian Gulf States, Arabian Gulf in general, Kuwait, Bahrain, Qatar and Oman. S. Kabeel. Kuwait: Kuwait University, Libraries Department, 1975. 427p. (With over 3,000 item bibliography).

The heritage of Qatar. P. Vine & P. Casey. London: IMMEL, 1992. 159p.

Country Table 2. **Organized churches and denominations in Qatar.**

Official name (bold type = church with over 10% of all affiliated) 1	*Begun* 2	*Type* 3	*Counc* 4	*Congs* 5	*Adults* 6	*Affiliated 1970* 7	*Affiliated 1995* 8	*G%* 9	*Names, notes, and other statistics* (see Codebook, Part 3) 10
Anglican Ch (D Cyprus & the Gulf)	1916	A-plu	aw...	3	3,000	700	8,000	10.24	In Episcopal Ch in Jerusalem & ME. In Doha, Dukhan. Europeans, Indians, Arabs.
Arab Evangelical Church	c1970	I-Eva	.....	2	35	–	88	19.61	Independent Evangelicals.
Catholic Church (VA Arabia)	c1880	R-Lat	P..L.	4	24,700	680	34,000	16.94	Mainly Filipinos, also Arab Catholics. One Capuchin priest in Doha. M=OFMCap.
Christian Brethren	c1960	P-CBr	x....	3	50	200	125	-1.86	*Plymouth Brethren. Open Brethren. Gospel Halls.* Indians, British.
Isolated radio churches	c1950	I-3rS	.....	100	3,000	150	5,000	15.06	Isolated Arab radio believers, mostly aged 12-25, through RVOG, FEBA, RVatican, ICI.
Mar Thoma Syrian Church	c1960	I-ReO	.....	1	120	120	200	2.06	Migrant laborers from Kerala, South India. M=MTSC(India).
Other pentecostal congregations	c1970	I-3pS	.....	13	200	–	500	28.22	In about 3 loose Arabic-speaking networks.
Other Orthodox churches	c1950	O-	.....	3	850	1,500	1,300	-0.57	Expatriate Arabs (Greek, Syrian, Coptic), Armenians, et alii.
Other Protestant denominations	1940	P-	.....	12	2,600	1,200	3,600	4.49	Ch of Scotland, Free Ch (UK), USA, Lutherans, CSI (Indian), et al. House groups.
Other Non-White indigenous churches	c1965	I-3pS	.....	40	1,700	300	3,400	10.20	Mostly Indians from South India, also Arabs. House groups; also at Anglican services.
Totals				**181**	**36,255**	**4,850**	**56,213**		

Churches, members, growth, 1900-2025	*Congs*	*Adults*	*Affiliated*	*G%*	*Total denominations*	*6 Megablocs:* *O*	*R*	*A*	*P*	*I*	*m*
Total churches, members, and denominations (mid-1900)	2	40	70	6.24	1	0	1	0	0	0	0
Total churches, members, and denominations (mid-1970)	30	2,762	4,850	6.24	17	4	1	1	8	3	0
Total churches, members, and denominations (mid-1990)	160	29,000	45,000	11.78	33	8	1	1	13	10	0
Total churches, members, and denominations (mid-1995)	181	36,255	56,213	4.55	34	8	1	1	13	11	0
Total churches, members, and denominations (mid-2000)	200	38,500	59,635	1.19	35	8	1	1	13	12	0
Total churches, members, and denominations (mid-2025)	400	57,400	89,000	1.61	69	12	1	1	25	30	0

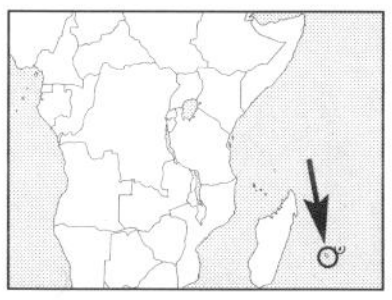

REUNION

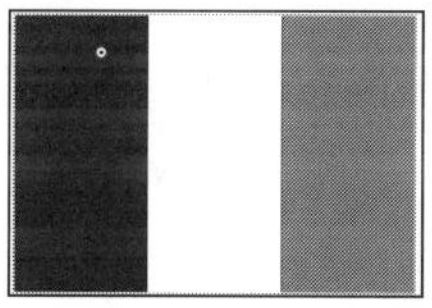

SECULAR DATA, AD 2000

STATE
Official name: Le Département de la Réunion (The Department of Reunion).
Short name: Reunion. **Adjective of nationality:** of Reunion.
Flag: That of France.
Area: 2,512 sq. km. (970 sq. mi.).
Government: Overseas department of France, since 1946 (1638 French possession).
Legislature: General Council, 47 members; Regional Council, 45 members.
Official language: French (Français).
Monetary unit: 1 French franc (F) = 100 CENTIMES. **US$1=** F 5.60.
Chief cities: SAINT-DENIS 112,736.
Political divisions: 4 provinces.
Armed forces: 4,000.

DEMOGRAPHY
Population: 699,000.
Population density: 278.4/sq. km. (721.0/sq. mi.).
Under 15 years: 192,000.
Growth rate p.a.: 1.14% (births 16.67, deaths 5.23).
Mortality: Infant, per 1,000: 8.0, ; **Maternal per 100,000:** 30.0.
Life expectancy: 77 (male 72, female 81).
Household size: 3.8. **Floor area per person, sq.m:** 20.0.
Major languages: French, French Creole, Chinese, Swahili, Gujarati, Malayalam, Malagasy.
Urban dwellers: 70.87%. **Urban growth rate p.a.:** 1.9%.
Labor force: 39%.

ETHNOLINGUISTIC PEOPLES
42.6% Reunionese Creole; 21.6% Reunionese White (French-speaking); 15.0% Tamil (Creole-speaking); 5.0% Tamil; 4.0% Reunionese White (Creole-speaking).

ECONOMY
National income p.a. per person: US$4,299; **per family:** US$16,337.

EDUCATION
Adult literacy: 78% (male 75%, female 80%). **Schools:** 445.
Universities: 1. **School enrolment:** female/male: 75%/75%.

HEALTH
Access to health services: 80%. **Access to safe water:** 90%.
Hospitals: 20 (44 beds per 10,000). **Doctors:** 1,061.
Blind: 1,000. **Deaf:** 41,900. **Murder rate:** 7.
Lepers: 1,400.

LITERATURE
New book titles p.a.: 80 (110 p.a. per million). **Periodicals:** 3.
Newspapers: 3 dailies.

COMMUNICATION (per 1,000 people)
Phones: 329 **(17% mobile). Radios:** 265. **TV sets:** 205.
Daily newspaper circulation: 83. **Computers:** 30.

HUMAN LIFE AND LIBERTY (optimum condition=100.0%)
HDI: 84.4. **HSI:** 55.0. **HFI:** 35.0. **EFL:** 35.0.

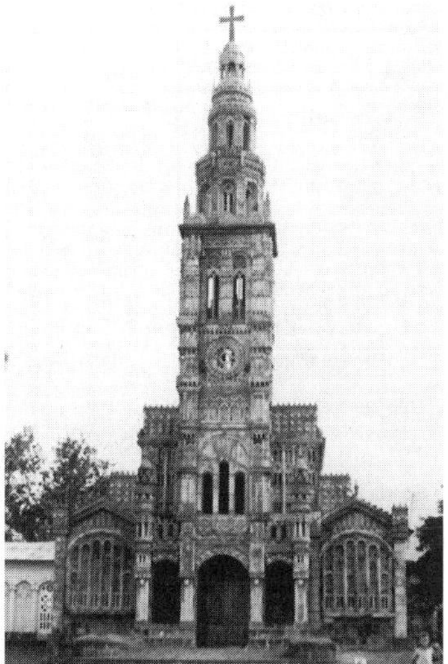

Eglise Catholique, Diocèse de la Réunion. *Left.* Extravagantly baroque parish church at Sainte-Anne.

Country status. Reunion, an overseas department of France, is a volcanically-active island in the Indian Ocean, east of Madagascar. Its chief export is sugar.

HUMAN LIFE AND LIBERTY

Human rights and freedoms. Although all basic human rights are vouchsafed by the French authorities and respected in practice, there is considerable social unrest as a result of the economic inequalities between the Whites and Indian elites on the one hand and the vast majority of Creoles or Blacks.

NON-CHRISTIAN RELIGIONS

Islam makes up 4.2% of the population, mainly Swahili and Bantu with some Indo-Pakistanis.

CHRISTIANITY

CATHOLIC CHURCH. Initial contacts were made at the beginning of colonization in 1653, and the island was afterwards served by visiting priests and sometimes by ships' chaplains. In 1712 a Lazarist was appointed prefect. The modern era of Catholic missions in Eastern Africa was initiated in 1817 by the arrival in Reunion of sisters of the Congregation of St Joseph of Cluny, and from here the evangelization of the East African coast was begun. The territory was placed under Holy Ghost priests in 1917. The diocese was divided into 12 deaneries, plus a Chinese mission founded in 1951 which is served by 2 Chinese secular priests. Reunion is overwhelmingly Catholic. The diocese covers the whole island but also works closely with other nearby islands including Mauritius.

The Holy See has no diplomatic relations with Reunion in AD 2000.

OTHER CHURCHES. Seventh-day Adventist work is small but growing. Begun in 1936, there are at present 15 congregations. The Assemblies of God (France) started work in the 1960s and have been the most successful of the non-Catholic churches, growing to 20,000 members in 130 congregations by 1995. The Africa Evangelical Fellowship (South Africa) has opened work, and the Reformed Church. Jehovah's Witnesses have 19 congregations.

Renewal movements. In the 1990s the Pentecostal/Charismatic Renewal continued to spread rapidly across most older churches, and numbered over 55,000 adherents (of whom 43% Pentecostals, 56% Charismatics, and 1% Independents).

Indigenous missions. Although overwhelmingly Christian, Reunion has only sent a handful of missionaries abroad, and these mainly to Madagascar and France.

Country Table 1. **Religious adherents in Reunion, AD 1900-2025.**																
Year	*1900*		*1970*		*mid-1990*		*Annual change, 1990-2000*				*mid-1995*		*mid-2000*		*mid-2025*	
Name	*Adherents*	*%*	*Adherents*	*%*	*Adherents*	*%*	*Natural*	*Conversion*	*Total*	*Rate*	*Adherents*	*%*	*Adherents*	*%*	*Adherents*	*%*
Christians	**90,000**	**52.0**	**445,300**	**96.7**	**535,090**	**88.6**	**8,455**	**-575**	**7,870**	**1.38**	**577,700**	**88.2**	**613,791**	**87.8**	**752,300**	**85.5**
PROFESSION																
professing Christians	**90,000**	**52.0**	**445,300**	**96.7**	**535,090**	**88.6**	**8,455**	**-575**	**7,870**	**1.38**	**577,700**	**88.2**	**613,791**	**87.8**	**752,300**	**85.5**
AFFILIATION																
unaffiliated Christians	30,000	17.3	15,072	3.3	7,200	1.2	113	-164	-51	-0.74	7,000	1.1	6,687	1.0	4,000	0.5
affiliated Christians	**60,000**	**34.7**	**430,228**	**93.4**	**527,890**	**87.4**	**8,342**	**-421**	**7,921**	**1.41**	**570,700**	**87.1**	**607,104**	**86.9**	**748,300**	**85.0**
Roman Catholics	60,000	34.7	427,028	92.7	532,000	88.1	8,407	-507	7,900	1.39	574,000	87.7	611,000	87.4	750,000	85.2
Protestants	0	0.0	2,200	0.5	26,000	4.3	409	141	550	1.94	29,010	4.4	31,500	4.5	49,000	5.6
Marginal Christians	0	0.0	1,000	0.2	4,650	0.8	73	62	135	2.58	5,250	0.8	6,000	0.9	12,300	1.4
Independents	0	0.0	0	0.0	580	0.1	9	3	12	1.90	627	0.1	700	0.1	1,100	0.1
doubly-affiliated	0	0.0	0	0.0	-35,340	-5.9	-556	-120	-676	1.76	-38,187	-5.8	-42,096	-6.0	-64,100	-7.3
Trans-megabloc groupings																
Evangelicals	0	0.0	1,200	0.3	21,800	3.6	343	167	510	2.12	24,457	3.7	26,900	3.9	47,000	5.3
Pentecostals/Charismatics	0	0.0	1,000	0.2	45,000	7.5	708	292	1,000	2.03	49,953	7.6	55,000	7.9	92,000	10.5
Great Commission Christians	**7,000**	**4.1**	**36,900**	**8.0**	**48,300**	**8.0**	**760**	**37**	**797**	**1.54**	**52,400**	**8.0**	**56,272**	**8.1**	**72,000**	**8.2**
Hindus	10,000	5.8	1,000	0.2	26,000	4.3	409	145	554	1.95	29,000	4.4	31,543	4.5	50,000	5.7
Muslims	20,000	11.6	10,900	2.4	25,400	4.2	400	-26	374	1.38	27,460	4.2	29,143	4.2	41,000	4.7
Nonreligious	0	0.0	1,000	0.2	7,000	1.2	110	403	513	5.65	9,000	1.4	12,130	1.7	15,000	1.7
Baha'is	0	0.0	1,200	0.3	5,000	0.8	79	14	93	1.72	5,500	0.8	5,927	0.9	10,000	1.1
Ethnoreligionists	53,000	30.6	1,000	0.2	2,400	0.4	38	16	54	2.04	2,750	0.4	2,938	0.4	4,000	0.5
Buddhists	0	0.0	0	0.0	1,000	0.2	16	14	30	2.64	1,150	0.2	1,298	0.2	2,400	0.3
Atheists	0	0.0	500	0.1	700	0.1	11	17	28	3.38	900	0.1	976	0.1	2,400	0.3
Jains	0	0.0	0	0.0	750	0.1	12	0	12	1.54	820	0.1	874	0.1	1,600	0.2
Sikhs	0	0.0	0	0.0	480	0.1	8	0	8	1.55	520	0.1	560	0.1	900	0.1
Other religionists	0	0.0	100	0.0	180	0.0	3	2	5	2.35	200	0.0	227	0.0	400	0.1
World A (unevangelized persons)	69,200	40.0	6,909	1.5	16,308	2.7	252	114	366	2.08	17,682	2.7	19,572	2.8	27,280	3.1
World B (evangelized non-Christians)	13,800	8.0	8,423	1.8	52,602	8.7	834	471	1,305	2.24	59,531	9.1	65,637	9.4	100,420	11.4
World C (Christians)	90,000	52.0	445,300	96.7	535,090	88.6	8,455	-575	7,870	1.38	577,700	88.2	613,791	87.8	752,300	85.5
Country's population	**173,000**	**100.0**	**460,633**	**100.0**	**604,000**	**100.0**	**9,541**	**0**	**9,541**	**1.47**	**654,914**	**100.0**	**699,000**	**100.0**	**880,000**	**100.0**

COLUMNS, ROWS.
For meanings and definitions, see Codebook (Part 3). Note that, by definition, total 'Christians' = professing + crypto-Christians, which also = affiliated + unaffiliated Christians, and also = Great Commission Christians + latent Christians. Percentages may not always total exactly, due to rounding.

CENSUSES.
The religion question has not been asked.

NOTES ON RELIGIONS
ATHEISTS. Reunion Communist Party (PCR) (legal).
BAHA'IS. Growth from 1 local spiritual assembly (1964) to 13 (1973), after which interest fell off leading to 6 reorganized LSAs by 1996.
CHRISTIANS. Including many expatriate French military and civilians.
COUNTRY'S POPULATION. This has increased from 1,200 (French settlers, Malagasy, Métis, Portuguese) in the year 1715, to 61,000 in 1789, to 225,000 in 1946. In 1848, 60,000 Black slaves were emancipated. Since 1945, there has been substantial emigration to France and Madagascar because of increasing unemployment and pressure on the land.
HINDUS. Indians, brought in temporarily as indentured laborers after 1848 emancipation of slaves.
MUSLIMS. Mainly Swahili (Bantu) with some Pakistanis and Indians; mostly Sunnis.
NONRELIGIOUS. Including many French military and civilians.
OTHER RELIGIONISTS. Including Rosicrucians (1 AMORC center).
ROMAN CATHOLICS. In 1900, 50,000 Catholics and many catechumens among freed slaves and their descendants.
ETHNORELIGIONISTS. From 1848 onwards, large numbers of Bantu and Malagasy freed slaves remained animist in religion, gradually being catechized and baptized by the Catholic Church, but with many remaining only nominal Christians.

Great Commission Instrument Panel: status of Reunion (for explanation see start of Part 4)

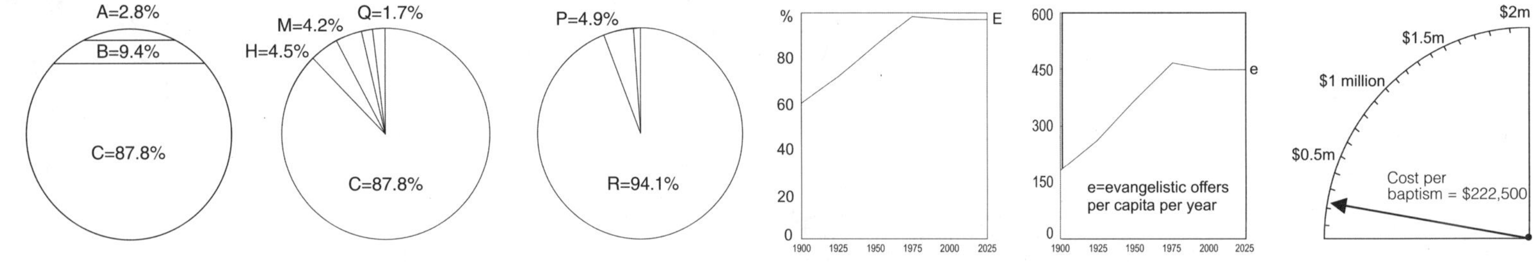

3 Worlds, AD 2000 | Religions, AD 2000 | Ecclesiastical blocs | Evangelization, 1900-2025 | Offers, 1900-2025 | Cost-effectiveness, AD 2000

Country summary. **Worlds A, B, C by ethnolinguistic peoples, cities, and major civil divisions in Reunion.**

	PEOPLES							***CITIES***							***CIVIL DIVISIONS***						
World	*Num*	*Pop 2000*	*C%*	*Christians*	*E%*	*U%*	*Unevangelized*	*Num*	*Pop 2000*	*C%*	*Christians*	*E%*	*U%*	*Unevangelized*	*Num*	*Pop 2000*	*C%*	*Christians*	*E%*	*U%*	*Unevangelized*
A	2	20,982	0.24	50	49	51	10,658	0	0	0.00	0	0	0	0	0	0	0.00	0	0	0	0
B	6	34,971	22.48	7,863	76	24	8,558	0	0	0.00	0	0	0	0	0	0	0.00	0	0	0	0
C	9	643,454	93.12	599,193	100	0	440	1	112,736	86.00	96,953	97	3	3,732	4	699,406	86.80	607,104	97	3	19,656
Total	**17**	**699,407**	**86.80**	**607,106**	**97**	**3**	**19,656**	**1**	**112,736**	**86.00**	**96,953**	**97**	**3**	**3,732**	**4**	**699,406**	**86.80**	**607,104**	**97**	**3**	**19,656**

CHURCH AND STATE
Since Reunion is a French overseas territory, separation of church and state, and freedom of religion, are guaranteed as in metropolitan France.

BROADCASTING AND MEDIA
French programs can be received from KNLS and FEBA (Seychelles). Reunion is a member of UNDA, and there is a Catholic FM radio station in Saint-Denis Cedex which broadcasts in French to the whole of the country. A Catholic religious program featuring news and liturgies is aired for 45 minutes each Sunday morning.

FUTURE TRENDS AND PROSPECTS
Christianity will probably continue to decline to under 86% by 2025 due to increases among Hindus, Muslims, and the nonreligious.

Christianity is expected to decline below 80% before AD 2050. Hindus and Muslims are both likely to grow in the same period.

BIBLIOGRAPHY

2000 titres: littératures de l'océan indien: Comores, Madagascar, Maurice, Réunion, Seychelles. Notre Librairie, no. 116. [Paris: CLEF, 1994]. 174p.

Annuaire ecclésiastique du Diocèse de la Réunion, 1971. Saint-Denis, Réunion: Evêché, 1971.

Brother Scubilion Rousseau, FSC: apostle of freedom and reconciliation. L. Salm. Romeoville, IL: Christian Brothers Publications, 1986. 143p.

Histoire des établissements religieux de Bourbon au temps de la Compagnie des Indes, 1664–1767. J. Barassin. [Saint-Denis]: Fondation pour la recherche et le développement de l'océan Indien, [1983]. 218p.

Histoire religieuse de la Réunion. C. Prudhomme. *Hommes et sociétés.* Paris: Editions Karthala, 1984. 369p.

Jean–Bernard Rousseau, frère Scubilion, 1797–1867: à l'île de la Réunion un évangile de liberté. A. Fermet. Paris: Desclée De Brouwer, 1985. 280p.

La religion populaire à la Réunion. P. Eve. [Sainte-Clotilde, Réunion]: Université de la Réunion, Institut de linguistique et d'anthropologie, 1985. 2 vols.

La vie religieuse: histoire. F. Lacpatia. : Association des écrivains réunionnais, 1990. 81p.

Le père Le Vavasseur. A. Le Roy. *Collection Mascarin.* Sainte Clotilde, Réunion: ARS terres créoles, [1989]. 219p.

Les îles de l'Océan indien: Comores, Madagascar, Maurice, Réunion, Seychelles: bibliographie réalisée à partir de la Banque de données IBISCUS, triée par grands domaines. P. Hue. *Collection Réseaux documentaires sur le développement, Série Références bibliographiques.* Paris: Ministère de la coopération et du développement, [1991]. 285p.

Les religions à la Réunion. A. Foulon. *Collection chroniques réunionnaises.* [Livry-Gargan, France]: Editions Orphie, 1989. 272p.

Les structures religieuses à la Réunion. [Saint-Denis, Réunion]: Association pour les études d'aménagement et d'urbanisme de la Réunion, [1981]. 18p.

Pour Dieu et pour l'homme réunionnais. G. Aubry. [Saint André, Réunion]: Océan éditions, [1988]. 491p.

Saint–André, ma paroisse. E. Baptiste. [Réunion]: The Author, 1990. 243p.

Country Table 2. Organized churches and denominations in Reunion.

Official name (bold type = church with over 10% of all affiliated) 1	Begun 2	Type 3	Counc 4	Congs 5	Adults 6	Affiliated 1970 7	Affiliated 1995 8	G% 9	Names, notes, and other statistics (see Codebook, Part 3) 10
Assemblées de Dieu	c1960	P-Pe2	Z....	130	12,000	800	20,000	13.74	*Assemblies of God.* M=Assemblées de Dieu(France). Centers throughout the island.
Centre Chrétien	c1985	I-3cA	.....	1	150	–	250	10.00	*Christian Centre.*
Eglise Adventiste du Septième Jour	1936	P-Adv	x....	15	1,200	1,000	3,000	4.49	*Seventh-day Adv, Reunion Mission,* Indian Ocean UM. 11n,6m,12t(670),W=80%,104Y.
Eglise Baptiste	1978	P-Bap	.....	8	625	–	1,040	5.88	*Baptist Church.* M=SBC.
Eglise Cath: D St-Denis-de-La Réunion	1653	R-Lat	Pz..r	75	301,000	427,028	574,000	1.19	13,000 Chinese. C=4+3+13. (1970) 43n,78x,13580Yy. (1990) 55n, 48x, 92m, 381w, 11206Yy
Eglise de la Pleine Evangile	c1985	I-3fA	.....	1	80	–	133	10.00	*Full Gospel Church.*
Eglise de J-C des Saints des DJ	c1975	m-LdS	x....	3	180	–	300	5.00	*Ch of JC of Latter-day Saints. Mormons.*
Eglise Evangélique de la Bible	c1985	I-Eva	.....	1	70	–	117	10.00	*Gospel Bible Church.*
Eglise Evangélique de la Réunion	1969	P-Eva	xM...	12	2,200	200	3,170	11.69	*Evangelical Ch of Reunion.* M=Africa Evangelical Fellowship (SAGM). 1m,3f.
Eglise Jésus Sauveur	c1985	I-3oA	.....	1	50	–	83	10.00	*Jesus Saves Church.*
Eglise Neo-Apostolique	c1993	I-3aX	x....	1	30	–	44	50.00	*New Apostolic Church. NAC.* HQ Zurich (Switzerland)
Eglise Réformée de la Réunion	c1968	P-Ref	.....	1	400	200	800	5.70	*Reformed Ch of Reunion.* Chaplaincy to military and civil French. In St-Denis.
Témoins de Jéhovah	c1955	m-Jeh	x....	19	1,833	1,000	4,950	6.61	*Jehovah's Witnesses.* Active witnessing under way by 1960. (1975) 27Y. (1995) 211Y.
Other Protestant denominations	1970	P-	.....	15	600	–	1,000	31.83	Total 4 bodies.
Doubly-affiliated		2-aff			-20,100	0	-38,187		Evangelicals who are also baptized Roman Catholics.
Totals				**283**	**300,318**	**430,228**	**570,700**		

Churches, members, growth, 1900-2025	*Congs*	*Adults*	*Affiliated*	*G%*	*Total denominations*	*6 Megablocs:* O	*R*	*A*	*P*	*I*	*m*
Total churches, members, and denominations (mid-1900)	20	33,500	60,000	2.85	1	0	1	0	0	0	0
Total churches, members, and denominations (mid-1970)	112	240,476	430,228	2.85	6	0	1	0	4	0	1
Total churches, members, and denominations (mid-1990)	220	278,000	527,890	1.03	12	0	1	0	5	4	2
Total churches, members, and denominations (mid-1995)	283	300,318	570,700	1.57	17	0	1	0	9	5	2
Total churches, members, and denominations (mid-2000)	290	319,000	607,104	1.24	17	0	1	0	9	5	2
Total churches, members, and denominations (mid-2025)	400	394,000	748,300	0.84	40	0	1	0	20	15	4

NOTES ON TABLE ABOVE
NATIONAL COUNCILS (Column 4, 5th letter).
r = attached to Conférence Episcopale de France (CEF) (Episcopal Conference of France).

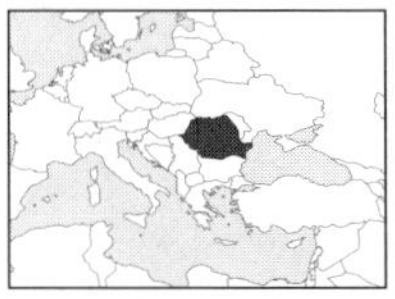

ROMANIA

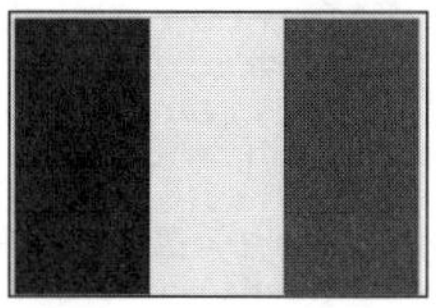

SECULAR DATA, AD 2000

STATE
Official name: România (The Republic of Romania).
Short name: Romania. **Adjective of nationality:** Romanian.
Flag: Blue, yellow, and red bars.
Area: 237,500 sq. km. (91,699 sq. mi.).
Government: Republic, since 1991 (1504 in Ottoman empire, 1861 Independence, 1881 constitutional monarchy, 1938 fascist dictatorship, 1947 People's Republic, 1947 one-party Communist state).
Legislature: Senate, 143 members; Assembly of Deputies, 343 members.
Official language: Romanian (Româneste).
Monetary unit: 1 Romanian leu (plural lei) = 100 bani. **US$1=** 9,098.
Chief cities: BUCURESTI (Bucharest) 2,130,000; Constanta 342,708; Iasi(Jassy) 335,391; Timisoara 326,869; Cluj-Napoca 320,738.
Political divisions: 41 provinces.
Armed forces: 231,000.

DEMOGRAPHY
Population: 22,327,000.
Population density: 94.0/sq. km. (243.4/sq. mi.).
Under 15 years: 3,963,000.
Growth rate p.a.: -0.35% (births 9.19, deaths 11.81).
Mortality: Infant, per 1,000: 19.0, ; **Maternal per 100,000:** 130.0.
Life expectancy: 71 (male 68, female 75).
Household size: 3.1. **Floor area per person, sq.m:** 22.0.
Major languages: Romanian, Hungarian, German, Romany, Yiddish, Turkish, Ukrainian, Serbo-Croatian, Russian, Slovak, Bulgarian, Czech, Greek, Armenian.
Urban dwellers: 58.21%. **Urban growth rate p.a.:** 0.6%.
Labor force: 46%.

ETHNOLINGUISTIC PEOPLES
82.5% Romanian; 11.5% Hungarian (Szekely, Sicul; 1.8% Romanian Gypsy (Bayash); 1.1% Kalderash Gypsy (Rom); 0.6% Rumelian Turk.

ECONOMY
National income p.a. per person: US$1,479; **per family:** US$4,587.

EDUCATION
Adult literacy: 96% (male 98%, female 95%). **Schools:** 16,769.
Universities: 63. **School enrolment:** female/male: 83%/83%.

HEALTH
Access to health services: 60%. **Access to safe water:** 100%.
Hospitals: 300 (95 beds per 10,000). **Doctors:** 42,808.
Blind: 15,918. **Deaf:** 1,350,300. **Murder rate:** 3.
Lepers: 4,500. **Underweight prevalence under 5:** 6%.

LITERATURE
New book titles p.a.: 7,810 (350 p.a. per million). **Periodicals:** 1,931.
Newspapers: 69 dailies.

COMMUNICATION (per 1,000 people)
Phones: 131 (5% mobile). **Radios:** 198. **TV sets:** 201.
Daily newspaper circulation: 297. **Computers:** 44.

REFUGEES
Alien refugees from other countries: 1,300.

HUMAN LIFE AND LIBERTY (optimum condition=100.0%)
HDI: 74.8. **HSI:** 56.0. **HFI:** 2.5. **EFL:** 26.0.

Country Table 1. Religious adherents in Romania, AD 1900-2025.

Year / Name	1900 Adherents	%	1970 Adherents	%	mid-1990 Adherents	%	Annual change, 1990-2000 Natural	Conversion	Total	Rate	mid-1995 Adherents	%	mid-2000 Adherents	%	mid-2025 Adherents	%
Christians	**10,384,000**	**94.4**	**16,840,000**	**83.2**	**19,948,400**	**86.0**	**-75,693**	**44,788**	**-30,905**	**-0.16**	**19,794,200**	**87.1**	**19,639,353**	**88.0**	**18,126,000**	**90.9**
PROFESSION																
crypto-Christians	0	0.0	1,620,000	8.0	0	0.0	0	0	0	0.00	0	0.0	0	0.0	0	0.0
professing Christians	**10,384,000**	**94.4**	**15,220,000**	**75.2**	**19,948,400**	**86.0**	**-75,693**	**44,788**	**-30,905**	**-0.16**	**19,794,200**	**87.1**	**19,639,353**	**88.0**	**18,126,000**	**90.9**
AFFILIATION																
unaffiliated Christians	330,000	3.0	0	0.0	20,100	0.1	-76	-735	-811	-5.04	17,000	0.1	11,990	0.1	6,000	0.0
affiliated Christians	**10,054,000**	**91.4**	**16,840,000**	**83.2**	**19,928,300**	**85.9**	**-75,616**	**45,522**	**-30,094**	**-0.15**	**19,777,200**	**87.0**	**19,627,363**	**87.9**	**18,120,000**	**90.9**
Orthodox	9,702,000	88.2	16,114,000	79.6	19,000,000	81.9	-72,047	72,047	0	0.00	19,204,900	84.5	19,000,000	85.1	17,000,000	85.2
Roman Catholics	152,000	1.4	2,833,880	14.0	3,330,000	14.4	-12,627	3,327	-9,300	-0.28	3,273,220	14.4	3,237,000	14.5	3,000,000	15.0
Protestants	143,000	1.3	1,585,511	7.8	2,350,000	10.1	-8,911	11,911	3,000	0.13	2,398,877	10.6	2,380,000	10.7	2,150,000	10.8
Independents	0	0.0	87,700	0.4	270,000	1.2	-1,024	3,024	2,000	0.72	285,256	1.3	290,000	1.3	320,000	1.6
Marginal Christians	57,000	0.5	59,000	0.3	140,000	0.6	-531	1,531	1,000	0.69	146,633	0.7	150,000	0.7	170,000	0.9
Anglicans	0	0.0	200	0.0	350	0.0	-1	11	10	2.54	400	0.0	450	0.0	600	0.0
doubly-affiliated	0	0.0	-3,840,291	-19.0	-5,162,050	-22.2	19,574	-46,378	-26,804	0.51	-5,532,086	-24.3	-5,430,087	-24.3	-4,520,600	-22.7
Trans-megabloc groupings																
Evangelicals	121,000	1.1	750,000	3.7	1,110,000	4.8	-4,209	32,739	28,530	2.31	1,313,036	5.8	1,395,302	6.3	1,550,000	7.8
Pentecostals/Charismatics	0	0.0	210,000	1.0	1,300,000	5.6	-4,930	9,930	5,000	0.38	1,319,812	5.8	1,350,000	6.1	1,795,000	9.0
Great Commission Christians	**220,000**	**2.0**	**506,000**	**2.5**	**1,500,000**	**6.5**	**-5,688**	**41,465**	**35,777**	**2.16**	**1,700,000**	**7.5**	**1,857,773**	**8.3**	**2,300,000**	**11.5**
Nonreligious	22,000	0.2	1,704,000	8.4	2,000,000	8.6	-7,584	-27,155	-34,739	-1.89	1,842,530	8.1	1,652,613	7.4	1,200,000	6.0
Atheists	6,000	0.1	1,356,000	6.7	958,500	4.1	-3,635	-18,457	-22,092	-2.59	795,000	3.5	737,577	3.3	300,000	1.5
Muslims	91,000	0.8	250,000	1.2	280,000	1.2	-1,062	1,219	157	0.06	282,000	1.2	281,570	1.3	300,000	1.5
Jews	496,000	4.5	100,000	0.5	15,000	0.1	-57	-457	-514	-4.11	12,000	0.1	9,859	0.0	10,000	0.1
Baha'is	0	0.0	0	0.0	1,700	0.0	-6	20	14	0.81	1,770	0.0	1,843	0.0	4,000	0.0
Other religionists	1,000	0.0	3,000	0.0	3,400	0.0	-13	42	29	0.81	3,500	0.0	3,687	0.0	5,000	0.0
World A (unevangelized persons)	110,000	1.0	1,012,625	5.0	232,070	1.0	-834	-4,874	-5,708	-2.96	204,577	0.9	156,289	0.7	139,615	0.7
World B (evangelized non-Christians)	506,000	4.6	2,399,888	11.8	3,026,530	13.0	-11,523	-39,914	-51,437	-1.77	2,732,099	12.0	2,531,358	11.3	1,679,385	8.4
World C (Christians)	10,384,000	94.4	16,840,000	83.2	19,948,400	86.0	-75,693	44,788	-30,905	-0.16	19,794,200	87.1	19,639,353	88.0	18,126,000	90.9
Country's population	**11,000,000**	**100.0**	**20,252,514**	**100.0**	**23,207,000**	**100.0**	**-88,050**	**0**	**-88,050**	**-0.39**	**22,730,877**	**100.0**	**22,327,000**	**100.0**	**19,945,000**	**100.0**

COLUMNS, ROWS.
For meanings and definitions, see Codebook (Part 3). Note that, by definition, total 'Christians' = professing + crypto-Christians, which also = affiliated + unaffiliated Christians, and also = Great Commission Christians + latent Christians. Percentages may not always total exactly, due to rounding.

CENSUSES.
XII.1899 (excluding Transylvania and northern parts of Romania): 91.5% Orthodox, 4.5% Jews, 2.9% Roman Catholics and Protestants, 0.8% Muslims, 0.4% other religionists. Subsequent censuses have not included the religion question.

NOTES ON RELIGIONS
ATHEISTS. Romanian Communist Party (independent over Sino-Soviet dispute). Of Communist party members, only around 15% are estimated to be committed and dedicatedly anti-religious atheists, the rest being nonreligious with a considerable minority of professing Christians (Orthodox) also.
BAHA'IS. Suppressed until the collapse of Communism in 1990, Baha'i experienced new interest and by 1996 had 29 organized local spiritual assemblies.
CRYPTO-CHRISTIANS. From 1945-1989, this bloc, usually

Continued overleaf

Country Table 1–concluded

referred to as the underground church, consisted of 3 different kinds of believers: (1) unorganized individuals who were not professing Christians but who were affiliated to the legal churches; (2) members of unrecognized or illegal denominations including Greek Catholics who refused to accept the liquidation of their church in 1948; and (3) a handful of isolated radio believers. After 1990 freedom of religion reduced these categories to zero.
DOUBLY-AFFILIATED. The majority of all Protestants and Roman Catholics (especially Uniates) are also counted or claimed as members by the Romanian Orthodox Church, mostly in sensitive areas where it would be unwise to attempt to clarify the situation by detailed enumeration.
JEWS. Decline from 500,000 in 1939. Under 25% have Yiddish as their mother tongue.
MUSLIMS. In 1899, Muslims were almost all in Constanta department and made up 37% of its population then. In 1995, they were more spread across the country, and consisted of Turks (all Turks being Hanafite Sunnis), Gypsies, Tatars, Bulgars, and others, who are now mainly Romanian nationals, with a mufti in Constanta.
NONRELIGIOUS. Agnostics, indifferent to religion, including most Communist party members. In addition to this total, in 1970 there was another 8.0% of the population regarded by state and society as nonreligious but who were affiliated to the churches and so classified here as crypto-Christians.
UNAFFILIATED CHRISTIANS. Only before 1947 and after 1990.

Great Commission Instrument Panel: status of Romania (for explanation see start of Part 4)

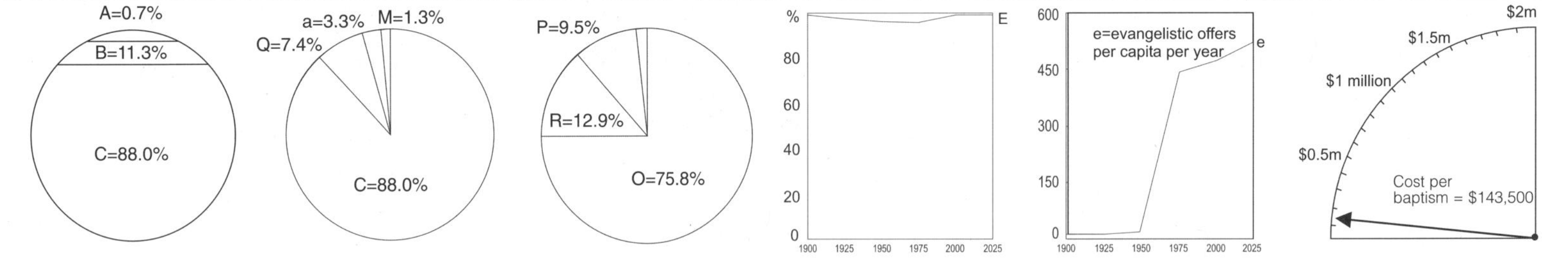

3 Worlds, AD 2000 | Religions, AD 2000 | Ecclesiastical blocs | Evangelization, 1900-2025 | Offers, 1900-2025 | Cost-effectiveness, AD 2000

Country status. Romania is the largest country in the Balkans in southeastern Europe. It borders Ukraine, Moldavia, Hungary, Yugoslavia, Bulgaria, and the Black Sea. Chief exports include oil, natural gas, and coal.

HUMAN LIFE AND LIBERTY

Human need and development. Romania emerged from the Communist era with a debilitated economy bled white by the excesses of the Ceaucesçu regime. Although the Communists had chalked up significant progress in public health, education, and housing, it was done at considerable human cost, and the collapse of the regime left the nation where it was some 40 years ago. The national government led by ex-Communists has emphasized its commitment to economic reform and the establishment of a free market economy. Most state-owned enterprises have been privatized, the exchange rate of the Romanian currency has been deregulated, and foreign investment has been welcomed. Despite these measures, the average Romanian has been hit hard by the transition. Inflation is high, and there are shortages even of essential foodstuffs which had previously been subsidized by the state. There are confirmed reports of thousands of abused children suffering malnutrition and poor medical care. Rents in cities are exorbitant. The housing area also is small, the per capita being about 82 square feet.

Human rights and freedoms. Since the fall of Ceaucesçu, Western human rights norms have been introduced successfully into the legal and constitutional system and democratic principles have been institutionalized. Complaints of human rights violations are mainly restricted to discrimination against Gypsies and ethnic Hungarians, and occasional intimidation of journalists. Parliament has passed a number of laws conforming to the new norms, including a new public order law, a National Security Law, and a law reorganizing the judiciary.

Human environment. Long neglect of the environment under the communists has produced a host of environmental problems, including soil degradation, water pollution, and industrial pollution. Some of the water pollution in the Danube is caused by cross-border activities. Industrial pollution is severe in towns, such as Copsa Mica, which have numerous chemical factories formerly exempt from environmental regulations.

NON-CHRISTIAN RELIGIONS

Islam is composed largely of Turks who are now Romanian nationals. As in Bulgaria, Muslims constitute an ethnic, cultural, and religious minority of relatively limited significance, underestimated and neglected. Several Muslim communities have been formed in Dobruja on the Black Sea coast, and there is a mufti at Constanta.

Judaism before World War II numbered around half a million Jews and formed a very dynamic minority in Moldavia, especially at Iasi and Czenovitz and in Transylvania in the region of Maramures. These numbers were drastically reduced by the Nazi massacres of 1940-44, but today Judaism continues to be important, although the flexible foreign policy adopted by the Ceaucesçu regime made possible large-scale emigration to Israel. Jews practice their strongly traditional Talmudic religion freely under the care of a grand rabbi in Bucharest. In 1995, there was a Jewish population of 12,000.

CHRISTIANITY

Historically, Romania emerged out of the Roman province of Dacia established by the emperor Trajan in the 2nd century. Overrun by Goths, Huns, Avars, Slavs, Mongols, and Bulgars in the following centuries, it remained basically a wedge of Latin culture between Slavs to the west and Mongols to the east. In the 10th century, it became known as Walachia and declared itself an independent principality in 1290. A second Romanian state, Moldavia, was established in 1363 to the north of Walachia, with the creation of Transylvania to the west following in 1526 as this part of Europe came under Turkish control. As the Turks were pushed back beginning in the 17th century, the peoples in this area found themselves driven back and forth between the armies of Austria, Hungary, Romania, and Russia, and this has been true of the modern period as well.

The life of the Christian church among Romanians reflects this turbulent history. Tradition holds that the first apostles, including Andrew, brought the Christian message to the Romanian peoples living on the shores of the Black Sea, and Christianity certainly existed there in strength by the beginning of the 3rd century. Romanians were among the martyrs of the emperor Diocletian's persecution of 303. At first, the liturgy was in Latin, but the formation of a Bulgarian state to the south and the introduction of a Slavic liturgy by Methodius and Constantine strongly influenced the Romanian people and drew them into the orbit of Constantinople. Catholic Hungarian and Polish immigrants during the 13th century, followed by Dominican missionaries brought about little change. The first Romanian metropolitan sees were created soon after the establishment of Wallachia and Moldavia, ultimately coming directly under the patriarch of Constantinople as the latter grew in authority in all areas under Turkish rule. When the Turks began to retreat along bordering territories, the Orthodox churches in these areas found themselves subjected to religious pressures from new conquerors: Austria, Hungary, and Russia. Thus, many of the Orthodox churches in Transylvania, which was captured by Austria and the Hapsburgs in 1688, became Uniate churches under Rome through Jesuit efforts. By 1733, there were in Transylvania 2,294 Uniate priests as opposed to 458 Orthodox priests and, in 1750, 569,000 Romanian Uniates as contrasted with only 25,000 Orthodox. Calvinism was also introduced into Transylvania during the 16th and 17th centuries during the influence of Hungary, while both countries were still under Turkish rule. Those who remained Orthodox in these annexed areas were placed under regional patriarchs, and autocephalous patriarchates were declared in the 19th century as the Balkan nations struggled for their independence. The Uniate churches consistently resisted the introduction of Latin in their liturgy; and in 1862 the Orthodox churches, resentful of Greek domination, replaced the Greek liturgy with a liturgy in the Romanian language. At the Congress of Parish in 1856, Moldavia and Walachia achieved virtual independence from Turkish rule. The Romanian Orthodox Church then declared itself autocephalous in 1865 and was recognized as such by Constantinople in 1885.

Romanian Orthodox Church. *Top.* Secu Monastery near Neamt, built 1602. *Center.* Believers outside Iasi cathedral with Metropolitan Daniel of Moldavia and Bukovina. *Lower center.* Packed believers standing inside Sibiu cathedral. *Bottom.* Family of believers in front of parish church in Moldavia.

Country summary. **Worlds A, B, C by ethnolinguistic peoples, cities, and major civil divisions in Romania.**

World	PEOPLES Num	Pop 2000	C%	Christians	E%	U%	Unevangelized
A	6	214,781	0.05	99	41	59	127,643
B	4	333,782	53.06	177,105	96	4	12,236
C	19	21,777,942	89.31	19,450,162	100	0	23,039
Total	**29**	**22,326,505**	**87.91**	**19,627,366**	**99**	**1**	**162,918**

World	CITIES Num	Pop 2000	C%	Christians	E%	U%	Unevangelized
A	0	0	0.00	0	0	0	0
B	0	0	0.00	0	0	0	0
C	49	8,927,646	86.90	7,758,537	99	1	93,331
Total	**49**	**8,927,646**	**86.90**	**7,758,537**	**99**	**1**	**93,331**

World	CIVIL DIVISIONS Num	Pop 2000	C%	Christians	E%	U%	Unevangelized
A	0	0	0.00	0	0	0	0
B	0	0	0.00	0	0	0	0
C	41	22,326,501	87.91	19,627,363	99	1	162,917
Total	**41**	**22,326,501**	**87.91**	**19,627,363**	**99**	**1**	**162,917**

ORTHODOX CHURCH. Following the establishment of new boundaries for Romania after World War I, the patriarchate of Bucharest was created in 1925 when the 2 Romanian metropolitanates of Walachia and Moldavia were united. In the Communist era, the Orthodox Church lived in a political situation which benefitted it more than the other churches. Its vitality was incontestable, with its seminaries having 3 times as many candidates as pastoral vacancies. Participation of the faithful in the sacraments and in regular public worship was significant and became massive at Easter. Equally impressive was the religious life of educated youth in the cities and also of the working classes. The national Orthodox Church administered its own property, lands presses and factories producing religious articles, operated a few minor seminaries, and produced 9 religious journals and a large number of books each year.

In the post-Communist era, the Orthodox Church is struggling with its new-found identity as the most influential religious body in the country. Relations with some non-Orthodox churches have been strained.

Other smaller Orthodox bodies in Romania include the Armenian, Bulgarian, Ancient Orthodox (Old Believers), Greek, Russian, Serbian, and Ukrainian Orthodox churches.

CATHOLIC CHURCH. Officially, all present day Catholics are of the Latin rite only. Although there are several thousand German and Moldavian Catholics dispersed throughout the south of Transylvania and in Bucharest, the majority of Romanian Catholics belong to the Hungarian minority and live in Transylvania, a region formally part of the Austro-Hungarian empire until 1919. The Hungarian language is predominant in the Catholic Church, and the church's fortunes are intimately bound up with those of this Hungarian minority.

As a result of its isolated situation, Romanian Catholicism tends to be introverted, concentrating its energy on survival and on interior spirituality. Apart from private visits by priests from Hungary and other countries, Catholics are completely cut off from the outside world. The only impact of Vatican II has been in the language of the liturgy and in a new edition of the missal, in which all feasts of Hungarian saints have been removed. Catholic organizations are notable by their absence. However, the Status of Transylvania (Erdelyi Status) is an old institution which continues to function as a pastoral council bringing together clergy and laity, but its activities are limited. Places of worship are well cared for due to government subsidies, and the 2 Catholic seminaries do not lack for vocations. Franciscans, the only religious order permitted, live in the convent of Csiksomlyo and maintain it as a lay pilgrimage center. Catholic schools have been suppressed, except for a minor seminary at Cluj which can take 100 pupils each year. There is a home for aged priests at Des.

The Byzantine-rite Uniate Catholic church has fared much worse. These are Catholics of Hungarian origin who live in Transylvania. In 1698, the Orthodox Church of Transylvania proclaimed its union with Rome, a few years after the principality came under Austrian domination. At the instigation of the Orthodox, they were declared in 1919 a national church with a status next in importance to that of the Orthodox Church. However, in December 1948, the church was formally declared by the new Communist regime to have voluntarily dissolved itself and to have rejoined the Orthodox Church. Although the latter accepts this thesis of 'auto-dissolution', the Uniate church was in fact forcibly suppressed. A synod was held at Cluj in October 1948 attended by 36 of the 1,818 Uniate priests, who ignored the local bishop's excommunication and, claiming to represent some 1,800 parishes and 1.6 million Uniates, decided on reunion with the Orthodox Church. At the time of its suppression, the Uniate church had a metropolitan see, Fagaras and Alba Julia founded in 1721 and 4 suffragan dioceses: Cluj-Cherla, Lugoj, Maramures and Oradea Mare. All these were forced into the Orthodox metropolitanate of Transylvania. Several hundred priests and laity were imprisoned, and the 6 bishops died in prison, the last being msgr Julio Hossu in 1970. An emissary from Rome, msgr Gerald O'Hara, consecrated other bishops, but these were arrested and later sent to monasteries from which they were only permitted to depart after promising that they would exercise no Episcopal function. A vast number of the faithful still continue to consider themselves attached to Rome.

The Holy See has diplomatic relations with Romania and in AD 2000 is represented to government and the Catholic hierarchy by a nuncio residing in Bucharest.

Pentecostal Church in the PRR. *Top.* Executive Council of the Pentecostal Churches in the PRR, 1974. *Bottom.* Sunday morning congregation of 1,500 members in a small village on border with USSR. The presence of police informers in all such congregations was always assumed.

PROTESTANT CHURCHES. The largest body is the Reformed Church of Romania (Biserica Reformata), which came into being in 1554 as the result of the work of Pierre Melius. Attached to the Hungarian Reformed church in 1881, it did not become autonomous again until after World War I, and most of its members still belong to the Hungarian minority in Romania. Lutheranism was introduced in 1519 and spread rapidly among Germans in Transylvania while it was under Turkish control. When Transylvania came under Austrian rule in 1691, the Lutherans were persecuted by the Hapsburg regime, although harassment gradually lessened over the next century. After World War I, the German Lutherans of Bessarabia were annexed again to Romania and united with those of Transylvania to form the Evangelical Protestant Church in Romania of the Augsburg Confession (Biserica Protestanta Evangelical din Romania dupa Confeiunea dela Ausburg). After World War II, Bessarabia was taken again from Romania, the Lutheran Church losing these Lutherans as well as the German Lutherans of Transylvania who were forced into exile at the same time.

Lutheran Hungarians had earlier formed their own church (Biserica Lutherana Ungara din Romania) after World War I.

The first Baptist community was established in Bucharest in 1856 among the German community, but there were no Romanian members until the beginning of the 20th century. The number increased greatly with the annexation of Transylvania and Bessarabia by Romania in 1918. A seminary was built in 1920, but between 1930 and 1944 the church was subject to state persecution.

During World War II the Baptist Church was dissolved by the Nazis. In 1945, the Baptist Convention of Romania was established, but the church suffered persecution again after 1947. Today Baptists are found mostly among the Romanians of Walachia. They are increasing in number and their church is officially recognized by the government. Considerable numbers are asking for baptism after hearing the gospel on foreign radio broadcasts. Adventists have been at work in Romania since 1911 and have built up a sizeable community organized into 4 conferences: Bacau, Bucharest, Cluj, and Sibiu.

Pentecostals began in 1922 and now have over 320,000 members with very many small communities scattered throughout Moldavia and Walachia.

Following the creation of the Popular Republic after World War II, all Protestant churches were cut off from the West, especially the bonds that they had maintained over the years with Germany and the Netherlands. Much cultural, linguistic, and political pressure was brought to bear, particularly upon the Hungarian minority. However, since the recent liberalization of governmental policies, contacts with other countries have been reestablished.

Since 1972, a large people movement to faith in Christ has taken place among the Gypsies, with thousands converted. There are also a few hundred Jewish Christians dating from the Norwegian Lutheran Church's 300 Jewish converts in the 1930s and 1940s.

MARGINAL CHURCHES. The Unitarian Church has an ancient history in Romania.

Followers of Michael Servet and successors to the alleged Arian heresy in their negation of the doctrines of the Trinity and the divinity of Jesus, the Unitarians were established in Transylvania in 1566 under the protection of the Hungarian nobility. Their ancient historic quarrels with Calvinists have long since receded into the background. Sustaining itself more on past tradition than on any ecumenical spirit, the Unitarian Church today has become a vehicle of local cultural values but without any great external influence.

Renewal movements. In the 1990s the Pentecostal/Charismatic Renewal continued to spread rapidly across most older churches, and numbered over 1,350,000 adherents (of whom 64% Pentecostals, 27% Charismatics, and 9% Independents).

Indigenous missions. The gospel was introduced to the area in the 3rd century and almost immediately these new Christians were witnessing outside of their borders. Waves of missionaries were sent out either deliberately, or as the result of displacement by warring tribes or barbarians. Later, under Orthodox direction, many Christians were sent to surrounding countries. Gypsy Christians also traveled widely in the region.

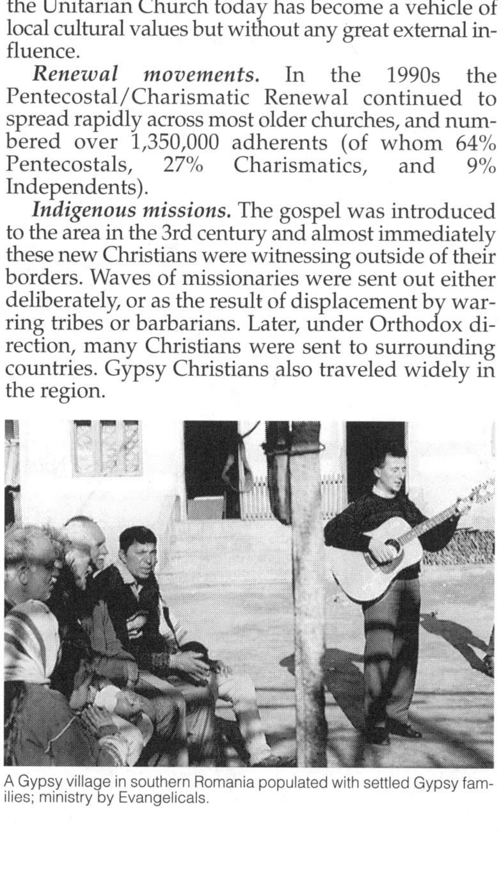

A Gypsy village in southern Romania populated with settled Gypsy families; ministry by Evangelicals.

CHURCH AND STATE

Before 1948, the Orthodox Church was often closely allied with the state. In fact, around 1930, the Orthodox patriarch was also prime minister, and the head of the government's Department of Cults was another Orthodox bishop. From 1940-44, the German Nazi regime dissolved the Baptist and Pentecostal churches. Consequently, Communist rule from 1948, with its removal of religious privilege or discrimination, has greatly benefitted the Protestant churches.

From 1950-1975, the Romanian government changed its constitution 4 times, but the statements regarding freedom of worship have undergone no modification. Article 30 of the constitution of 1969 affirms that everyone is free to hold or not to hold a religious belief. Freedom of conscience and worship is guaranteed. The organization and internal functioning of religious groups is unhampered, but their finances are regulated by law. The same article adds that schools are separated from churches, the only church-administered schools permitted being those 'especially aimed at the training of ministers of the denomination', which covers both major and minor seminaries.

In the Communist era, the state office of religious affairs, the Department of Cults (Departamentul Cultelor), maintained surveillance over the churches and their worship, which was more strict in the case of Catholics than in the case of others. The organization Priests for Peace was less structured here than in other Communist countries. The government paid one-third of the salaries of all clergy and the entire salaries of seminary teachers, including those of Catholic seminaries. Seminarians were not subject to military service. A system of Sunday Schools operated without hindrance in church buildings, and churches organized themselves freely.

The government passed a law in April 1974 prohibiting the reception or distribution of imported literature, including Bibles; and in July, Vasile Rascol, a Bucharest Pentecostal layman, was arrested and sentenced to 2 years in prison for being in possession of such Bibles and distributing them.

Christians appealed against the sentence stating that it infringed Romania's constitution and the UN Declaration of Human Rights and that in fact thousands of Christian believers are guilty of the same offense. The judge accepted the appeal and quashed the sentence, although the security police refused to release Rascol from prison. A prominent Baptist theologian, Iosif Ton, was also harassed for his writings, although not imprisoned.

In February 1975, msgr Luigi Poggi, apostolic nuncio for special assignments of the Holy See, visited Romania for the first time to begin a dialogue with the regime. In April 1975, the Romanian National Assembly adopted a law requiring all those holding cultural or artistic treasures (individuals, cultural organizations, and churches) to declare them before the Central Commission for National Cultural Treasures, which would in turn decide those objects to become state property with indemnity. Those items not commandeered at once were to be submitted for periodic examination and could be taken later if not maintained in a satisfactory condition. Objects of concern to the churches include works of art, manuscripts, rare books and other items used in worship. Before the adoption of the law, the archives of parishes under the jurisdiction of the Reformed bishop of Nagyvarat had been confiscated by state officials, after inventory; and so the measures decided by the Assembly were interpreted as a deliberate policy to deprive national minorities of their historic past.

Since the collapse of Communism, new legislation has appeared guaranteeing religious freedom. However, only certain religious bodies have been identified as eligible for state subsidies and there is widespread concern that this could encourage government control of denominations and evangelism.

BROADCASTING AND MEDIA

Shortwave radio programs in European languages can be received from KNLS, AWR (Slovakia), TWR (Monaco, Albania), and HCJB (Ecuador). Romanian programming can also be heard from FEBC (Saipan). IBRA-produced programs can be received on a local radio station in Cluj. HCJB is helping to plant a radio ministry in Romania in partnership with Radio Voice of the Gospel. AWR's Bucharest studio produces Romanian-language programs.

CBN's *Superbook* program can be received daily. Satellite TV programs are received mainly in Arabic. Over 2.5 million have seen the 'Jesus' Film: half in cinematic showings, and half through film team presentations.

INTERDENOMINATIONAL ORGANIZATIONS

Relations between the Orthodox and Romania's other religious bodies have improved markedly since 1965. Twice yearly, the Orthodox patriarch organizes meetings between theologians of different denominations. Patriarch Justinian established a personal relationship with the Catholic bishop of Alba Julia and permitted Catholics to use the Orthodox press for their publications. Nevertheless, Orthodox-Catholic relations continue strained due to the unresolved problem of the Catholic Uniates.

Protestants participate in the wider Christian alliance or council of churches.

FUTURE TRENDS AND PROSPECTS

With the collapse of Communism, a downward trend in church membership has been radically reversed with growth expected to increase the number of Christians to over 90% of the population by 2025, the first such apex since the 1930s.

Christianity will likely increase to well over 90% by AD 2050 and remain there at length. The nonreligious and atheists could jointly fall to less than 5% by AD 2050.

BIBLIOGRAPHY

Between hammer and sickle. M. Wurmbrand. Glendale, CA: Diane, 1972. 172p.

'Despre Inochentie si Inochentism,' H. H. Stahl, *Archiva pentru Stiinta si Reforma Sociala*, 10 (1932), 175–82. (Socio-psychological study of a new religious cult in Romania).

Die Reformation in Siebenbürgen. Ihr Verhältnis zu Wittenberg und der Schweitz. E. Roth. Cologne: Böhlau Verlag, 1962–64. 2 vols.

'Ecumenism in Eastern Europe: Romanian style,' E. A. Pope, *East European quarterly*, 13, 2 (1979), 185–212.

Faithfulness and renewal: contemporary realities in the life of the Romanian Orthodox Church. N. Vornicescu. Bucharest: Romanian Orthodox Church, 1989. 104p.

From suffering to triumph. R. Wurmbrand. Grand Rapids, MI: Kregel Publications, 1993. 159p.

In the eye of the Romanian storm: the heroic story of Pastor Laszlo Tokes. F. Corley & J. Eibner. Old Tappan, NJ: Revell, 1990. 280p.

Istoria bisericii ortodoxe române. M. Pacurariu. Sibiu, Romania: Editura Institutului Biblic si de Misiune al Bisericii Ortodoxe Române, 1972–81. 3 vols.

Orthodox Christianity: the Rumanian solution. New York: Time-Life Multimedia, 1978. (52 min. videocassette).

'Orthodox monasticism in Romania today,' S. E. Mary, *Religion in Communist lands*, 8, 1 (Spring 1980), 22–27.

Reformed Church in the Socialist Republic of Romania. [Bucharest]: The Church, 1976. 72p.

'Religion and nationality in Romania,' T. Gilberg, in *Religion and nationalism in Soviet and East European politics*, p.328–351. P. Ramet (ed). 2nd ed. Durham, NC: Duke University Press, 1989.

Religious life in Romania: essential information. Bucharest, Romania: Consultative Council of the Religious Denominations in the Socialist Republic of Romania, 1987.

Religious persecution in Romania. J. Ton. Wheaton, IL: Romanian Missionary Society, [1985?]. 39p.

'Religious persecutions in captive Romania,' R. Bossy, *Journal of Central European affairs*, 15, 2 (1955), 161–81.

Revolution in Romania: what God is doing in eastern Europe. S. Tippit. Chicago: Moody Press, 1990. 26p.

Romania. A. Deletant & D. Deletant. *World bibliographical series*, vol. 59. Oxford, UK: CLIO Press, 1985. 254p. (See especially 'Religion,' pp. 66-71).

Romania: its hesychast tradition and culture. Seraphim Joantea. Wildwood, CA: St. Xenia Skete, [1992]. 283p.

Romania: religion in a hardline state. Washington, DC: Puebla Institute, 1989. 57p.

Romania under pressure. C. Michael-Titus. London: Panopticum, 1979.

'Romanian Baptists and the state,' A. Scarfe, *Religion in Communist lands*, 4, 2 (Summar 1976), 14–20.

'Romanian Baptists under Marxism–Leninism: a study of the impact of Communist persecution on evangelism, 1945–1990.' J. Moldovan. Ph.D. dissertation, Southwestern Baptist Theological Seminary, Fort Worth, TX, 1994. 288p.

Stolen church, martyrdom in Communist Romania. A. Ratiu & W. Virtue. Huntington, IN: Our Sunday Visitor, 1979. 192p.

The atlas of religions and of religious historical monuments in Romania. C. Cuiuc. Trans., C. Dupu.

'The Evangelical wing of the Orthodox Church in Romania,' A. Scarfe, *Religion in Communist lands*, 3, 6 (1975), 15–19.

The fall of tyrants: the incredible story of one pastor's witness, the people of Romania, and the overthrow of Ceausescu. L. Tokes. Wheaton, IL: Crossway Books, 1990. 240p.

'The history of the Pentecostal Apostolic Church of God of Romania.' I. Ceuta. D.Min. thesis, Columbia Biblical Seminary and Graduate School of Missions, Columbia, SC, 1990. 154p.

The painted churches of Romania: a visitor's impressions. J. Fletcher. London: New Knowledge Books, 1971. 103p.

The Pentecostal Apostolic Church of God of the Socialist Republic of Romania. T. Sandru (ed). Bucharest, Romania: [The Pentecostal Apostolic Church of God of the Socialist Republic of Romania], 1982. 77p.

The present situation of the Baptist Church in Romania. I. Ton. *Religion in Communist lands*, no.1. [London: Jubal Multiwrite], 1973. 20p.

The Romanian church. M. Beza. London: Society for the Promotion of Christian Knowledge, 1943. 64p.

The Romanian Church in northwestern Romania under the Horthy scourge. N. Corneanu. Bucharest: Bible and Mission Institute of the Romanian Orthodox Church, 1986.

The Romanian Orthodox Church. 2nd ed. Bucharest: Orthodox Missionary Institute, 1968. 92p.

'The Romanian Orthodox Church and the state,' K. Hitchins, in *Religion and atheism in the USSR and Eastern Europe*, p.314–27. B. R. Bociurkiw & J. W. Strong (eds). Toronto: University of Toronto Press, 1975.

'The Romanian Orthodox Church today,' M. Villiers, *Religion in Communist lands*, 1, 3 (1973), 4–7.

'The Rumanian Orthodox Church and the West,' E. D. Tappe, in *The Orthodox Churches and the West*, p.277–91. D. Baker (ed). *Studies in Church History*, vol. 13. Oxford: Blackwell, 1976.

The Seventh–day Adventist Church in the Socialist Republic of Romania. D. Popa. Bucharest: Editura Curierul Adventist, 1983. 93p.

Through the fire without burning: the true story of a Romanian pastor facing Communist persecution. D. Duduman. 2nd ed. Fullerton, CA: Hand of Help, 1992. 204p.

'Zur Situation der Christlichen Kirchen in Rumanien,' *Herder Korrespondenz*, 25, 7 (1971), 321–25.

Country Table 2. **Organized churches and denominations in Romania.**

Official name (bold type = church with over 10% of all affiliated) 1	*Begun* 2	*Type* 3	*Counc* 4	*Congs* 5	*Adults* 6	*Affiliated 1970* 7	*Affiliated 1995* 8	*G%* 9	*Names, notes, and other statistics* (see Codebook, Part 3) 10
Apostolic Christian Ch (Nazarean)	1888	P-Hol	x....	100	2,000	2,000	4,000	2.81	Begun in Switzerland; long history of persecution in Romania.
Armenian Apostolic Ch: D Bucuresti		O-Arm	Ewc.K	19	8,400	10,000	11,400	0.05	*Gregorians.* Under C Echmiadzin (USSR). Covers Romania. Armenian emigres.
Assembly Hall Churches	c1990	I-3nC	.....	2	23	–	100	20.00	*Little Flock. Local Churches.* Chinese. Begun 1922 in China.
Association of Ancient Rite Christians	1852	I-OBe	.....	5	5,000	2,000	10,000	6.65	*Old Believers* (*Lippovans*,='Philippians'), under D Novosibirsk, in Belo-Krinitsa Concord.
Bulgarian Orthodox Church		O-Bul	Mwc..	10	3,500	2,000	7,000	0.05	*Balgarskata Pravoslavna Crkva.* Parishes in Bucharest and Galati. Under P Sofia.
Calvary Chapels International	c1990	I-3cW	x....	6	700	–	2,000	20.00	M=Calvary Chapels International (USA).
Catholic Church in Romania:	c1000	R-Lat	B.B.S	2,222	2,453,200	2,833,880	3,273,220	0.58	*Biserica Catolica Romana.* 68% Hungarian. C=1+0+0. 1213n 121x 369m 854w 13297Yy
M Bucuresti (Bucharest) *(Latin)*	1883	R-Lat	Bs	60	77,000	82,902	103,100	0.88	*Arch-Episcopia Bucuresti.* Diaspora Catholics. 60n 6x 8m 166w 417Yy
D Iasi	1884	R-Lat	Bs	119	190,000	208,999	253,989	0.78	In Moldavia, on border. 1s(Romanian-speaking). 215n 36x 219m 218w 4244Yy
D Oradea Mare (Gran Varadino)	1982	R-Lat	Bs	57	83,000	–	110,642	7.69	D Nagyvarad of the Latins, originating in AD 1077. 60n 2x 2m 55w 744Yy
D Satu Mare (Szatmar)	1804	R-Lat	bs	55	82,500	202,000	111,000	-2.37	*Szatmàr-Nagyvàradi Egyhazmegye.* Closed 1949-91. 64n 4x 5m 96w 1029Yy
D Timisoara	1930	R-Lat	Bs	72	109,000	320,000	145,104	-3.11	*Temesvàri Egyhàzmegye* (in Hungarian). Hungarians. 81n 9x 14m 60w 1912Yy
AD Alba Julia (Transilvania)	1009	R-Lat	bs	223	406,000	455,000	542,000	0.70	*Episcopia Alba Julia. Gyulafehervàri Egyhàzmegye.* 286n 39x 69m 139w 4160Yy
M Fagaras & Alba Julia *(Rumanian)*	1721	R-Rum	Os	1,200	371,000	412,486	495,000	0.73	*Greek Catholic Ch.* Rumanian rite, suppressed. 1948-90. 111n 6x 9m 41w 0Yy
D Cluj Gherla	1930	R-Rum	Os	100	379,000	421,652	505,000	0.72	D Claudiopoli-Armenopoli. Suppressed. 1948-90. 130n 12x 33m 71w 250Yy

Continued opposite

Country Table 2–concluded

Official name (bold type = church with over 10% of affiliated) 1	*Begun* 2	*Type* 3	*Counc* 4	*Congs* 5	*Adults* 6	*Affiliated 1970* 7	*Affiliated 1995* 8	*G%* 9	*Names, notes, and other statistics* (see Codebook, Part 3) 10
D Lugoj	1853	R-Rum	Os	202	375,000	127,763	500,000	5.61	1948-90 suppressed, forced into ROC. 42n 0x 0m 8w 17Yy
D Maramures	1930	R-Rum	Os	80	358,000	397,956	477,000	0.73	1948-90, suppressed. 90n 6x 6m 0w 479Yy
D Oradea Mare	1777	R-Rum	Os	50	22,000	203,122	29,385	-7.44	D Gran Varadino Rumanian rite. 1948-1990, suppressed. 73n 0x 3m 0w 40Yy
O Romania *(Armenian)*	1672	R-Arm	Os	4	700	2,000	1,000	-2.73	Ordinariate for Armenian-rite Catholics in Romania. 1n 1x 1m 0w 5Yy
Children of God (The Family)	1990	I-mar	x....	5	100	–	300	20.00	Linked to The Family (in USA and 57 other countries).
Christian Brethren (Ch of the Gospel)	1903	P-CBr	x...K	571	80,000	120,000	160,000	1.16	*Uniunea Cultului Crestin dupa Evanghelie. Christians According to the Gospel.* Ex ROC.2 groups
Church of England (D Europe)	1841	A-Cen	awc..	3	200	200	400	2.81	Anglican chaplaincy, Bucharest. Official relations with Orthodox patriarchate.
Ev Church of the Augsburg Confession	1519	P-Lut	LWC.K	141	37,500	184,000	45,000	-5.48	*Biserica Ev dupa Confeiunea dela Augsburg.* Germans. Saxon origin. Massive emigration.
Ev Lutheran Synodal Presbyterial Ch	1886	P-Lut	LW..K	30	15,000	32,000	21,000	-1.67	*Biserica Ev Sinodo-presbiteriala* (Augsburg Confession). Hungarian parishes except 4 Slovak.
Gypsy Evangelical Movement		I-3pE	x....	80	12,500	1,000	25,000	0.05	Nomadic caravan communities. 100% Gypsies. Aid from M=GGMS(Switzerland).
Hungarian Baptist Union	c1900	P-Bap	T....	99	26,500	9,000	33,300	5.37	Formed out of Baptist Union of Romania.
Isolated radio churches	c1955	I-3rW	.....	2,000	25,000	500	60,000	21.11	Isolated radio believers in nonreligious families. (1970) R=7900(RMS, HCJB, RVatican).
Jehovah's Witnesses	1911	m-Jeh	x....	410	19,030	4,000	70,300	12.15	Active witnessing by 1926. Prohibited, 10-year prison sentences prior to 1989. 2606Y.
Lord Jesus' Disciples	1946	I-3pW	.....	40	4,500	5,000	8,000	1.90	Strictly indigenous Romanian Pentecostalism.
New Apostolic Church		I-3aX	x....	10	2,000	1,000	4,066	0.05	In Canada Bezirk, *NAK.* World headquarters in Zurich. Underground before 1989.
Old Rite Romanian Orthodox Ch	1924	I-OCd	.....	45	15,000	3,000	23,600	8.60	Old Calendarists rejecting Romanian OC's change to Gregorian calendar. HQ Suceava.
Old Ritualist Ch of Ancient Orth Chr	c1800	I-OBe	x...K	60	46,900	60,000	70,000	0.62	Chr=Christians. HQ Braila. Ex Russian OC. Under Old Believers AD Moscow. In southeast.
Pentecostal Apostolic Ch of God in R	1922	P-Pe2	Z...K	18,000	508,000	200,000	820,000	5.81	*Biserica Pentecostala lui Dumnezeu Apostolica/Apostolic CoG.* 11% Hungarian. 200n,1s.
Reformed Church of Romania	1554	P-Ref	RWC.K	1,786	500,000	693,511	801,577	0.58	*Biserica Reformata din Romania.* Mostly Transylvania. Hungarians. 783n,1090mw,1s.
Reformed Pentecostal Church	c1980	I-3pW	.....	42	2,500	–	4,170	6.67	Sabbatarian pentecostals of indigenous Romanian origin.
Romanian Baptist Union	1856	P-Bap	Tv..K	1,523	110,000	250,000	330,000	1.12	*Uniunea Comunitatilor Crestine Baptiste* (Baptist Union of Romania). Walachia. 350n.
Romanian Evangelical Church	1920	P-CBr	.....	23	16,000	13,000	24,000	2.48	Revival in one ROC parish, 1923 excommunicated, 1940 in Brethren, 1990 broke off.
Romanian Orthodox Ch, P Bucuresti:	c 100	O-Rum	CWC.K	8,120	13,003,000	16,000,000	19,040,000	0.70	*Biserica Ortodoxa Romana.* The Lord's Army (300,000) is in Evangelical Alliance. 20 bps,8545n.
Metropolitanate of Ungrovlahia:	1359	O-Rum	Cp					0.00	Province of Oungro-Walachia (formerly Muntenia), with 3 dioceses. HQ Bucharest.
AD Bucuresti (Bucharest)		O-Rum	Cp	1,350	2,240,000	2,650,000	3,278,000	0.05	Capital. In city, 228 parish churches with 405 priests and 16 deacons 2s(454).
D Buzau	c1550	O-Rum	Cb	650	1,082,000	1,280,000	1,584,000	0.86	HQ Buzau. One minor seminary in Buzau. 1977: episcopal vicar dismissed by state.
D Dunarea de Jos (Lower Danube)	c1850	O-Rum	Cb	810	1,352,000	1,600,000	1,979,000	0.85	Lower Danube along USSR border. HQ Galati. Ancient monastery of Cocosu-Dobrogea.
Metropolitanate of Moldavia-Suceava:	1401	O-Rum	Cm					0.00	Province of Moldavia and Suceava, with 2 dioceses. HQ Jassy (26 km from USSR).
AD Iasi (Jassy)		O-Rum	Ca	700	1,157,000	1,370,000	1,694,000	0.05	Along USSR border. HQ Jassy. Courses on church buildings and church art.
D Roman & Husi	c1450	O-Rum	Cb	660	1,099,000	1,300,000	1,608,000	0.85	In Moldavia, northeast Romania. HQ Roman. Repairing of churches widespread.
Metropol of Transilvania (Ardeal):		O-Rum	Cm					0.05	Province of Transylvania. 1948, 1,560,000 Catholic Uniates forcibly re-absorbed until 1992.
AD Alba-Julia & Sibiu	1599	O-Rum	Ca	920	1,502,000	1,800,000	2,199,000	0.80	HQ Sibiu. Theological institute in Sibiu, 780 students. Very active press; 1j.
D Oradea		O-Rum	Cb	700	1,162,000	1,380,000	1,701,000	0.05	Northwest, along Hungary border. HQ Oradea. Repairs to churches under way.
D Vad, Fleac & Cluj		O-Rum	Cb	600	1,013,000	1,200,000	1,482,000	0.05	North centre of country. HQ Cluj. 589 parishes, 570 priests, 1s(246) at Cluj.
Metropolitanate of Oltenia:	1370	O-Rum	Cm					0.00	Province of Oltenia (formerly Severin), with 2 dioceses. HQ Craiova.
AD Craiova		O-Rum	Ca	570	947,000	1,120,000	1,386,000	0.05	Southern plains, west of Bucharest. HQ Craiova. One minor theological seminary.
D Ramnic & Arges	c1550	O-Rum	Cb	560	938,000	1,110,000	1,372,000	0.85	South of Transylvania Alps (Southern Carpathians). HQ Rimnicul Vilcea. 1s.
Metropolitanate of the Banat:		O-Rum	Cm					0.05	Province of the Banat, with 2 dioceses. HQ Timisoara. Very active press; 1j.
AD Timisoara & Caransebes		O-Rum	Ca	400	674,000	797,000	986,000	0.05	West (Yugoslavia border). HQ Timisoara. One minor seminary in Caransebes.
D Arad-Ienopolea & Halmagiului		O-Rum	Cb	200	332,000	393,000	486,000	0.05	Extreme west of Romania, on border with Hungary. HQ Arad.
Doubly-counted Orthodox		O-			-495,000	–	-715,000		Orthodox counted in 2 jurisdictions at same time.
Russian Orthodox Church	c1800	O-Rus	Mwc..	8	3,750	2,000	8,500	0.05	Under jurisdiction of P Moscow. Russian expatriates, almost all in Bucharest.
Serbian Orthodox Church: D Timisoara	1864	O-Ser	Cwc..	60	37,600	50,000	60,000	0.73	Under jurisdiction of P Belgrade. Many refugees from wars in former Yugoslavia. 47n,4d.
Seventh-day Adventist Church	1911	P-Adv	x...K	521	65,000	80,000	130,000	1.96	*Cultul Adventist de Ziua Saptea. Romanian UC.* 4 Confs. 172n,53mw,1s,512t(52857).
SDA Church, Reform Movement	1925	I-Adv	x....	2	175	200	350	2.26	Schism ex SDAs. HQ Charlottenlund, Denmark. Not officially recognized.
Traditionalist Christian Church	1934	I-OCd	.....	30	7,000	2,000	13,000	7.77	*Traditionalist Orthodox Ch.* 1934 schism ex Old Rite Romanian OC. Growing.
True Orthodox Ch of Romania		I-Tru	.....	20	10,000	3,000	20,000	0.05	*TOC.* Protest movement against main state church.
Ukrainian Orthodox Ch (P Kiev)	c1900	I-Ukr	.....	30	30,000	10,000	40,000	5.70	Schismatic church from Ukraine, over patriarchal claims.
Unitarian Churches in Romania	1566	m-Unt	....K	123	43,000	55,000	76,333	1.32	*Unitariani.* Hungarians in Transylvania. Bishop, 8 Districts. HQ Cluj. M=UUA(USA). 100n,1s.
Universal Church	c1975	I-3jW	.....	47	2,800	–	4,670	5.00	Radical Pentecostals.
Other Orthodox churches		O-	.....	40	51,000	50,000	78,000	0.05	Including: Greek Orthodox Ch, Moldavian Orthodox Church, ROCOR.
Other Protestant denominations		P-	.....	100	17,500	2,000	30,000	0.05	10 groups: Exclusive Brethren (Kelly-Continental), Methodists, Korean Presbyterians, IPHC.
Doubly-affiliated		2-aff			-3,752,000	-3,840,291	-5,532,086		Protestants and Catholics also counted or claimed as members by Orthodox Church.
Totals				**36,333**	**13,412,378**	**16,840,000**	**19,777,200**		

Churches, members, growth, 1900-2025	*Congs*	*Adults*	*Affiliated*	*G%*	*Total denominations*	*6 Megablocs:* O	R	A	P	I	m
Total churches, members, and denominations (mid-1900)	11,000	7,179,000	10,054,000	0.74	18	6	1	1	7	2	1
Total churches, members, and denominations (mid-1970)	22,531	12,024,376	16,840,000	0.74	38	9	1	1	14	11	2
Total churches, members, and denominations (mid-1990)	35,000	13,515,000	19,928,300	0.85	53	14	1	1	20	15	2
Total churches, members, and denominations (mid-1995)	36,333	13,412,378	19,777,200	-0.15	54	14	1	1	20	16	2
Total churches, members, and denominations (mid-2000)	38,000	13,311,000	19,627,363	-0.15	55	14	1	1	20	17	2
Total churches, members, and denominations (mid-2025)	43,000	12,289,000	18,120,000	-0.32	235	25	1	1	50	150	8

NOTES ON TABLE ABOVE
NATIONAL COUNCILS (Column 4, 5th letter).
E = Romanian Evangelical Alliance (REA).
K = Ecumenical Association of the Churches in Romania (AEBRom), or Romanian Council of Churches (unofficial; since 1974; all recognized churches, plus Jews and Muslims); links with European Evangelical Alliance.
S = Romanian Catholic Episcopal Conference (unofficial), also member of Romanian Council of Churches.

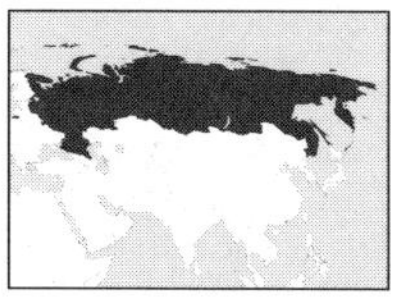

RUSSIA

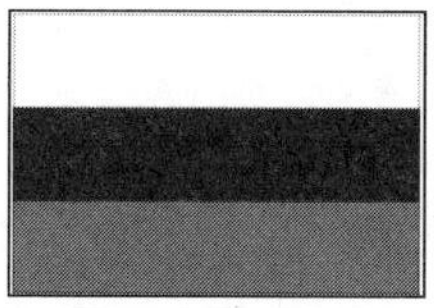

SECULAR DATA, AD 2000

STATE
Official name: Rossiiskaya Federatsiya (The Russian Federation).
Short name: Russia. **Adjective of nationality:** of the Russian Federation, Russian.
Flag: Currently: white (top), blue, and red horizontal bars as shown above. Formerly: red field with gold hammer and sickle below gold-bordered star in upper hoist corner.
Area: 17,075,400 sq. km. (6,592,800 sq. mi.).
Government: Federal multiparty republic, since 1990 (1547 empire, 1905 constitutional monarchy, 1917 Bolshevik revolution, 1917 one-party Communist state).
Legislature: Federation Council, 178 members; State Duma, 450 members.
Official language: Russian (Russki).
Monetary unit: 1 ruble (Rub) = 100 kopecks. **US$1=** Rub 16.12.
Chief cities: MOSKVA (Moscow) 9,299,000; Moskva (Moscow) 9,049,319; Sankt-Peterburg 5,132,000; Novosibirsk 1,476,000; Gor'kij (Gorky, Nizhni Novgorod) 1,461,000.
Political divisions: 21 provinces.
Armed forces: 1,240,000.

DEMOGRAPHY
Population: 146,934,000.
Population density: 8.6/sq. km. (22.2/sq. mi.).
Under 15 years: 26,683,000.
Growth rate p.a.: -0.19% (births 10.41, deaths 14.35).
Mortality: Infant, per 1,000: 17.5, ; **Maternal per 100,000:** 75.0.
Life expectancy: 67 (male 61, female 73).
Household size: 3.2. **Floor area per person, sq.m:** 17.7.
Major languages: Russian, Ukranian, Uzbek, Byelorussian, Tatar, Kazakh, Armenian, Azerbaijani, Georgian, Moldavian, Lithuanian, and over 120 other main languages; 65 being literary.
Urban dwellers: 77.68%. **Urban growth rate p.a.:** 0.1%.
Labor force: 49%.

ETHNOLINGUISTIC PEOPLES
80.1% Russian; 3.7% Tatar (Kazan Tatar, Tura); 2.3% Ukrainian; 1.1% Chuvash (Bolgar, Bulgar); 0.9% Bashkir (Bashkirian).

ECONOMY
National income p.a. per person: US$2,240; **per family:** US$7,168.

EDUCATION
Adult literacy: 98% (male 99%, female 96%). **Schools:** 72,574.
Universities: 569. **School enrolment:** female/male: 96%/91%.

HEALTH
Access to health services: 65%. **Access to safe water:** 90%.
Hospitals: 12,265 (119 beds per 10,000). **Doctors:** 612,400.
Blind: 350,000. **Deaf:** 8,771,700. **Murder rate:** 21.
Lepers: 20,000. **Underweight prevalence under 5:** 3%.

LITERATURE
New book titles p.a.: 39,670 (270 p.a. per million). **Periodicals:** 3,629. **Newspapers:** 17 dailies.

COMMUNICATION (per 1,000 people)
Phones: 170 (1% mobile). **Radios:** 341. **TV sets:** 380.
Daily newspaper circulation: 267. **Computers:** 60.

REFUGEES
Citizen refugees in other countries: 97,000.
Alien refugees from other countries: 500,000.
Internal displacement: 250,000.

HUMAN LIFE AND LIBERTY (optimum condition=100.0%)
HDI: 79.2. **HSI:** 69.0. **HFI:** 7.5. **EFL:** 30.0.

Country status. Russia occupies virtually all of northern Asia and the eastern parts of the European continent. It is the largest state to emerge out of the ruins of the Soviet Union. It has vast mineral resources of iron ore, gold, copper, and tin as well as natural resources such as oil, gas, and coal.

HUMAN LIFE AND LIBERTY

Human need and development. The new Russia has inherited all the serious economic problems of the old Soviet Union and has been unsuccessful in devising a set of policies to solve them. At the time of its demise, the economy of the Soviet Union was in tatters, and the country was in a general state of anarchy. Anarchy is nothing new to Russia, which has known extremes of every known form of disorder and chaos. But this time the collapse of the economy was so sudden and precipitous that it affected every individual and institution in Russia and sent shock waves through the whole social fabric. Ironically, it came after a 70 year experiment designed to modernize Russia and bring it out of the Dark Ages. The only rationale of Marxism was its promise of uni-

Country Table 1. **Religious adherents in Russia, AD 1900-2025.**

Year / Name	1900 Adherents	%	1970 Adherents	%	mid-1990 Adherents	%	Annual change, 1990-2000 Natural	Conversion	Total	Rate	mid-1995 Adherents	%	mid-2000 Adherents	%	mid-2025 Adherents	%
Christians	**61,544,600**	**83.4**	**50,000,000**	**38.4**	**81,929,800**	**55.3**	**-75,041**	**312,881**	**237,840**	**0.29**	**83,695,900**	**56.5**	**84,308,198**	**57.4**	**95,791,000**	**69.5**
PROFESSION																
crypto-Christians	0	0.0	12,900,000	9.9	0	0.0	0	0	0	0.00	0	0.0	0	0.0	0	0.0
professing Christians	**61,544,600**	**83.4**	**37,100,000**	**28.5**	**81,929,800**	**55.3**	**-75,041**	**312,881**	**237,840**	**0.29**	**83,695,900**	**56.5**	**84,308,198**	**57.4**	**95,791,000**	**69.5**
AFFILIATION																
unaffiliated Christians	5,033,400	6.8	8,466,600	6.5	729,800	0.5	-668	-3,328	-3,996	-0.56	708,900	0.5	689,841	0.5	741,000	0.5
affiliated Christians	**56,511,200**	**76.6**	**41,533,400**	**31.9**	**81,200,000**	**54.8**	**-74,373**	**316,209**	**241,836**	**0.29**	**82,987,000**	**56.0**	**83,618,357**	**56.9**	**95,050,000**	**68.9**
Orthodox	55,709,700	75.5	36,220,000	27.8	73,670,000	49.7	-67,464	295,464	228,000	0.31	74,572,000	50.4	75,950,000	51.7	85,500,000	62.0
Independents	0	0.0	4,321,000	3.3	7,414,600	5.0	-6,790	45,330	38,540	0.51	7,742,519	5.2	7,800,000	5.3	8,500,000	6.2
Protestants	550,000	0.8	927,700	0.7	1,400,000	0.9	-1,282	24,282	23,000	1.53	1,495,000	1.0	1,630,000	1.1	2,400,000	1.7
Roman Catholics	250,000	0.3	4,200	0.0	950,000	0.6	-870	55,870	55,000	4.67	1,311,200	0.9	1,500,000	1.0	1,800,000	1.3
Marginal Christians	0	0.0	60,000	0.1	150,000	0.1	-137	5,137	5,000	2.92	185,000	0.1	200,000	0.1	300,000	0.2
Anglicans	1,500	0.0	500	0.0	2,800	0.0	-3	53	50	1.66	3,000	0.0	3,300	0.0	6,000	0.0
doubly-affiliated	0	0.0	0	0.0	-2,387,400	-1.6	2,186	-109,940	-107,754	3.80	-2,321,719	-1.6	-3,464,943	-2.4	-3,456,000	-2.5
Trans-megabloc groupings																
Evangelicals	450,000	0.6	500,000	0.4	545,000	0.4	-499	1,999	1,500	0.27	551,560	0.4	560,000	0.4	660,000	0.5
Pentecostals/Charismatics	0	0.0	1,720,000	1.3	4,800,000	3.2	-4,396	171,896	167,500	3.04	6,020,675	4.1	6,475,000	4.4	8,275,000	6.0
Great Commission Christians	**7,375,000**	**10.0**	**22,167,000**	**17.0**	**29,065,000**	**19.6**	**-26,617**	**57,467**	**30,850**	**0.11**	**29,175,000**	**19.7**	**29,373,498**	**20.0**	**32,000,000**	**23.2**
Nonreligious	110,000	0.2	36,628,700	28.1	42,700,000	28.8	-39,103	-189,925	-229,028	-0.55	41,689,500	28.2	40,409,724	27.5	23,210,000	16.8
Muslims	6,575,700	8.9	10,100,000	7.8	11,250,000	7.6	-10,302	-994	-11,296	-0.10	11,250,000	7.6	11,137,043	7.6	11,500,000	8.3
Atheists	40,000	0.1	30,483,300	23.4	9,016,350	6.1	-8,257	-130,012	-138,269	-1.65	8,025,000	5.4	7,633,658	5.2	4,000,000	2.9
Ethnoreligionists	617,500	0.8	535,000	0.4	1,100,000	0.7	-1,007	3,770	2,763	0.25	1,140,000	0.8	1,127,627	0.8	1,000,000	0.7
Jews	4,470,000	6.1	2,168,000	1.7	1,050,000	0.7	-962	-8,930	-9,892	-0.98	980,000	0.7	951,076	0.7	600,000	0.4
Hindus	0	0.0	0	0.0	680,000	0.5	-623	9,233	8,610	1.20	730,000	0.5	766,096	0.5	900,000	0.7
Buddhists	400,000	0.5	475,000	0.4	550,000	0.4	-504	3,795	3,291	0.58	570,000	0.4	582,909	0.4	900,000	0.7
Baha'is	200	0.0	2,000	0.0	15,000	0.0	-14	173	159	1.01	15,700	0.0	16,586	0.0	30,000	0.0
Chinese folk-religionists	0	0.0	0	0.0	850	0.0	-1	9	8	0.91	900	0.0	931	0.0	2,000	0.0
World A (unevangelized persons)	7,302,042	9.9	19,558,770	15.0	13,346,280	9.0	-12,222	-330,030	-342,252	-2.92	11,551,527	7.8	9,991,512	6.8	6,620,784	4.8
World B (evangelized non-Christians)	4,911,358	6.7	60,833,030	46.6	53,015,920	35.7	-48,551	17,149	-31,402	-0.07	52,849,073	35.7	52,634,290	35.8	35,521,216	25.7
World C (Christians)	61,544,600	83.4	50,000,000	38.4	81,929,800	55.3	-75,041	312,881	237,840	0.29	83,695,900	56.5	84,308,198	57.4	95,791,000	69.5
Country's population	**73,758,000**	**100.0**	**130,391,800**	**100.0**	**148,292,000**	**100.0**	**-135,814**	**0**	**-135,814**	**-0.09**	**148,096,501**	**100.0**	**146,934,000**	**100.0**	**137,933,000**	**100.0**

COLUMNS, ROWS.
For meanings and definitions, see Codebook (Part 3). Note that, by definition, total 'Christians' = professing + crypto-Christians, which also = affiliated + unaffiliated Christians, and also = Great Commission Christians + latent Christians. Percentages may not always total exactly, due to rounding.

CENSUSES.
28.1.1897 (First General Census of the Empire, within 1897 boundaries including Finland): 72.0% Orthodox (69.3% Russian Orthodox (87,123,604 persons; including Ukrainian, Georgian), 1.8% Old Believers and other schismatics (2,204,596), 0.9% Armenian Apostolics (1,179,241), 11.1% Muslims, 9.1% Roman Catholics, 4.2% Jews (including Karaites), 2.9% Protestants (3,572,653 Lutherans, 85,400 Reformed, 66,564 Mennonites, 38,139 Baptists), 0.4% shamanists, 0.3% Buddhists. Some observers consider that around the year 1900 Orthodox dissenters and sectarians numbered up to 25 million, but here they are treated as revolts within Orthodoxy. In the **1937** census, the government included a question on religion; the results were suppressed and never published, but 33% of the urban population and 67% of the rural population were said to have called themselves 'believers' (i.e. in any religion), making 56% for the whole of the USSR; in 1945, it was said to be 50% for the entire Red Army. No subsequent census has enumerated religion. The figures for 1970 above give a total of 38.8% professing believers of all kinds (in any religion), which indicates both the long-term gradual erosion of professing belief caused by state hostility, and also the conservative nature of the estimates in this table.

NOTES ON RELIGIONS
ATHEISTS. There is a long history of militant atheism in the USSR, from the League of Militant Godless (1925-41; 3 million members by 1930, 5 million in 50,000 local groups by 1935), Groups of Godless Youth, and the All Union Society for the Dissemination of Scientific and Political Knowledge (founded in 1947), to the ongoing massive atheistic campaigns from 1964 onwards, symbolized in the contemporary journal *Nauka i Religia (Science and religion,* circulation 140,000), university departments and specialized schools of atheism (in a dozen universities) and at the more popular level, the Museums of Atheism in Leningrad and from 1966 in Vilnius. It is widely agreed by analysts and observers, however, that Marxist ideology and militant atheism as a pseudo-religion or quasi-religion in the USSR has been at an end since the 1950s, and that only a small minority among CPSU members even pretends to take Marxist ideology seriously. Most of what passes for 'scientific atheism' is very crude, a mere repetition of 18th- and 19th-century arguments. Nevertheless, it is possible to enumerate those holding this ideology even if in attenuated form. Atheists and anti-religious persons, defined in this Encyclopedia as those avowedly opposed to religion, were estimated at 56.5 million in 1970 by totalling membership of the CPSU (14.0 million party members and candidates, over 18 years (rising to 17 million members by 1980): 40% workers, 15% collective farmers, 45% engineers/scientists/teachers/bureaucrats/etc), Komsomol (VLKSM; All-Union Leninist Communist League of Youth, preparing people for party membership; over 28 million members, including 8 million aged 14 to 18; 160 newspapers with 64 million circulation), Pioneers (All-Union Lenin Pioneer Organization; militantly atheistic; 20 million members aged 10-15, increasing to 25 million by 1975), and Octoberists (14.5 million children aged 7-9). Distribution of CPSU membership by republics is shown in the table in the text below. Surveys of religion and atheism by Soviet scientists indicate that the proportion of atheists in the population declines gradually with age; it approaches 90% for the 16-19 years age-group but then falls evenly to around 20% for the over-70 age-group.
BAHA'IS. In about 12 isolated groups, Persians and others, in 1970, rising rapidly after 1991 to 42 organized local spiritual assemblies (1996). Baha'i entered before 1892 into Armenia, Azerbaijan, Georgia and Turkmenistan. The latter had the first of Baha'is 7 temples until it was demolished in 1963. There was severe persecution in 1928, 1938 and subsequently until 1991.
BUDDHISTS. Mahayana (Buryats, Kalymyks, and other Mongols; also Tuvinians, and a minority of the 450,000 Koreans), with Tantrayana in parts of Siberia.
CHRISTIANS. Only before the 1917 revolution and after the 1989 collapse of Communism.
COUNTRY'S POPULATION. During World War II, around 18,000,000 USSR military and civilians were killed.
CRYPTO-CHRISTIANS. (1917-1989) The term in this Russia context refers to 5 quite different groups, who in aggregate are popularly referred to as the underground church, clandestine church, catacomb church, church of silence, or church of the martyrs. (1) The first were unorganized masses of affiliated (baptized) Christians known individually to the legal churches (especially the Russian Orthodox Church) but who were unknown to (or regarded as nonreligious by) the state through their non-profession and nonpractice, irregular practice or secret practice. In 1970 these secret believers were mainly young persons and students preparing for future careers, and also the younger middle-aged classes and professionals. (2) There were several millions of Christians, especially Ukrainian Catholics, Jehovah's Witnesses and other sects, who have over the decades been imprisoned en mass, deported to Siberia, or otherwise scattered and dispersed in labor camps or in exile mostly across Siberia. Few were counted as Christians by the state, but many were believing and witnessing Christians and were remembered as such by families and friends in their home churches. (3) There were several unregistered denominations (the best-known being the CCECB), and numerous unregistered congregations in legal denominations, which were forced to remain illegal and to operate underground by the state's refusal to register them despite repeated requests. (4) There were a number of totally and deliberately clandestine bodies, namely the over 40 highly-organized illegal underground churches, with centrally-organized nation-wide networks of believers totalling in 1970 well over half a million adherents (see Table 2). Lastly (5) there were scattered across the entire Soviet Union several hundred thousand organized and unorganized isolated radio believers (see Table 2).
JEWS. Declined from 5.26 million in 1900 to 3.02 million in 1939, with 1.30 million massacred during 1941-45. In the 1970 official Soviet census, 2,151,000 Jews were recorded, but Western experts estimated the real figure at 3.0 million, the other 849,000 being either crypto-Jews unwilling to reveal their religion to the state, or secularized nonreligious Jews. Of the total in 1970, around 500,000 adults were practicing Jews (25%). By 1969, an average of 12,000 Jews a year were emigrating to Israel; in 1972 emigration increased to 35,500 and in 1973 to 34,750, rising dramatically with the collapse of the Soviet Union in 1989.
NONRELIGIOUS. Agnostics, indifferent to both religion and atheism, including large numbers of government officials.
PENTECOSTALS/CHARISMATICS (or, Orthodox charismatics). There has been a long charismatic of pentecostal tradition in Russian Orthodoxy. Large movements within Orthodoxy have often gone into schism, and other schismatic bodies have become charismatic when subjected to intense persecution by the Soviet regime (True Orthodox Christians, et alia). Before 1965, individual Orthodox who became charismatic or pentecostalist usually left the ROC and joined the AUCECB or other Pentecostal denominations. Since 1970, however, the tendency has been to remain within the ROC, where by 1995 a large but completely unorganized number of charismatics and charismatic house groups exist mostly underground, and often in contact with local Pentecostal congregations. A fair number of Orthodox priests are known to have had charismatic experience. In addition, there are thousands of unorganized Jesus movement youths and Jesus revolutionaries. Due to the sparse Catholic presence, there are few Catholic Charismatics. But after 1990 independent charismatics and Pentecostals have grown very rapidly to over 3 million.
PROTESTANTS. As shown in Table 2, the totals include over 3 million isolated radio believers scattered across the country, namely that portion of the total listening community for all religious radio broadcasts into the Soviet Union (Protestant, Catholic, BBC, and other secular stations, and also a number of clandestine stations within the USSR) who for a variety of reasons (mainly geographical) remain isolated from the organized denominations.
ROMAN CATHOLICS. The massive numerical decline from 1900-1970 is due to (1) forced mass conversions of Uniates and other Catholics to Orthodoxy, (2) heavy emigration, and (3) sustained and continuous state persecution against Catholic hierarchy, priests, and laity.
SHAMANISTS. Shamanism and tribal religion remain widespread among numerous peoples and tribes of northern Russia and Siberia, including the Chukchi, Tungus, and Samoyed peoples. Likewise, the suppression of Christianity and the destruction of churches after 1918 in the Caucasus caused widespread revivals of traditional shamanistic religion, especially in the inaccessible mountainous regions of Southern Ossetia, Khevsuria, and Svanetia (Georgia).

Great Commission Instrument Panel: status of Russia (for explanation see start of Part 4)

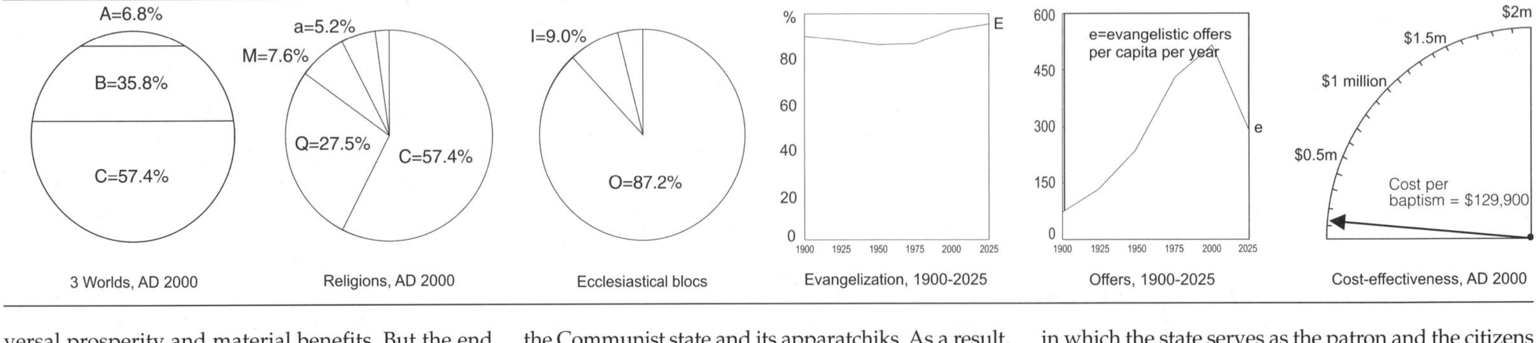

3 Worlds, AD 2000 | Religions, AD 2000 | Ecclesiastical blocs | Evangelization, 1900-2025 | Offers, 1900-2025 | Cost-effectiveness, AD 2000

versal prosperity and material benefits. But the end of Marxism brought Russia to a state worse than at the beginning. In many areas, Russia is a developed country, but the development is uneven and artificial. It was designed to serve not the Russian people but the Communist state and its apparatchiks. As a result, the net human balance sheet shows a large and frightening deficit, even though there are sectors in which Russia is still powerful. The thoroughness with which Czarist feudalism was swept away created a society in which the state serves as the patron and the citizens as clients or wards. Because of its enormous natural resources, Russia is self-sufficient in almost all raw materials and is capable of meeting the needs of its people in terms of food, clothing, shelter, and other

Country summary. Worlds A, B, C by ethnolinguistic peoples, cities, and major civil divisions in Russia.

	PEOPLES							CITIES							CIVIL DIVISIONS						
World	Num	Pop 2000	C%	Christians	E%	U%	Unevangelized	Num	Pop 2000	C%	Christians	E%	U%	Unevangelized	Num	Pop 2000	C%	Christians	E%	U%	Unevangelized
A	83	6,582,049	0.92	60,607	30	70	4,590,291	6	991,323	5.60	55,521	42	58	575,555	2	3,240,008	6.46	209,449	43	57	1,853,140
B	34	14,068,492	18.21	2,561,502	65	35	4,877,761	237	51,625,736	51.94	26,813,980	90	10	5,080,088	15	18,114,519	37.94	6,871,894	74	26	4,659,808
C	52	126,283,306	64.14	80,996,241	100	0	455,425	73	25,733,963	61.05	15,711,101	98	2	593,195	4	125,579,319	60.95	76,537,012	97	3	3,410,529
Total	**169**	**146,933,847**	**56.91**	**83,618,350**	**93**	**7**	**9,923,477**	**316**	**78,351,022**	**54.35**	**42,580,602**	**92**	**8**	**6,248,838**	**21**	**146,933,846**	**56.91**	**83,618,355**	**93**	**7**	**9,923,477**

basic necessities. But there are structural anomalies which have created shortages of virtually everything. Even though the factories, mines, and farms are highly productive, the stores are never full and consumers have little choice of goods. The quality of these goods is generally poor and the price extremely high. Another major weakness of the Russian economy is housing. The law guarantees every citizen living space. Government has been unable to provide new housing units to accommodate the increased urban population. The amount of living space is legally about 160 sq ft per person, but in practice is about 60 sq feet, less than what prevailed before the 1917 Revolution. Lavatory and kitchen facilities are frequently shared by several families. The consequences are severe for the average citizen. Sanitation facilities are overtaxed, personal privacy is limited, and consequently family relationships are strained. On the other hand, citizens still enjoy cradle-to-grave Social Security, and social and recreational services are extensive and well organized. Health and education sectors, on which the Communist attention and funds were concentrated for decades, are highly developed and are available free to all citizens.

Human rights and freedoms. Russia has made such a complete break with its Soviet past that it might be described as a new state. But the ghosts of Lenin and his successors still haunt the republic. For every 2 steps that it has taken on the road toward full democracy it has taken a step back. The repressive activities of the former KGB were ended in 1992 when it was split into 2 separate agencies, and both were required to respect human rights and be subject to legislative supervision. The human rights provisions of the temporary constitution have been strengthened to bring them in conformity with international norms. Freedom of speech and press, assembly and religion are largely respected. Restrictions on freedom of travel continue as also the residence permit system, a holdover from Communist days. The judiciary still operates under outdated rules. Persons may be arrested arbitrarily and detained without warrants. Detention and incarceration procedures inherited from the Soviet Union remain harsh. Prisoners are frequently placed in cells for violations of rules. Many judges are poorly trained in the new human rights procedures and have little understanding of the concept of an independent judiciary. Prosecutors continue to exercise powerful influence over the investigative process and over courtroom procedures. New constitutional amendments declare that the accused is innocent until proven guilty, a reversal of the old Soviet principle of the presumption of guilt. The most dramatic progress toward liberalization has been made in the area of freedom of speech and press as well as freedom of association, all of which are now accepted as normal elements in Russian society. Anti-Semitism is an occasional feature of political life but receives no official encouragement.

Human environment. Because environmental regulations were enforced loosely or not at all in the former Soviet Union, Russia's ecology has been subject over the years to irreversible degradation. In the drive toward rapid industrialization, little attention was paid to conservation or to reduction of pollution. In addition, agricultural policies also favored exploitation of natural resources at any cost. The Aral Sea, for example, has lost about two-thirds of its water since the 1970s as a result of the diversion of its water for agriculture. Lake Baikal, the largest freshwater lake in the world, is threatened with pollution. Russia's nuclear plants are an ever-present potential threat to the environment.

NON-CHRISTIAN RELIGIONS

Atheism dominated the USSR for 70 years, from the Bolshevik Revolution to the closing years of the Gorbachev regime. In effect, militant atheism was the official religion of the Soviet Union, having the Communist Party as its erstwhile church. Those days have come to an end. Though not eradicated from Russian culture, atheism does not have the relentless grasp it once monopolized. Only 5.2% of the population are adherents to atheism compared with a quarter of the population claiming atheism in 1970. Militant atheist groups are still in existence desiring a return to an atheistic communist regime.

Hindus. Large numbers of Hare Krishna followers in downtown Moscow, demonstrating but protected by police.

Islam is the professed religion of 7.6% of the population. The confrontation of the Slavic Russian and Muslim worlds is ancient. When Moscow entered modern history powerful Muslim kingdoms were camped at her doors, first the Great Bulgars of the Volga and then the Mongols of the Golden Horde. Ottoman domination was extended very late from Bessarabia to the Caucasus and over the peoples of Turkey and Central Asia, most of who then came under the Russian Empire during the 19th century.

A large majority of the 11.2 million Muslims are Sunnis, practically all of the Hanafite rite. In Russia today there is some 3000 Muslim associations that are registered with the government There are several organizations to govern certain regions of Muslim orders including the Moscow Muftiyat, which is responsible for 10 different regions and the Religious Board of the Muslims of Central Russia, known as the Dumser. Currently there are over 800 mosques and parishes.

Judaism had 980,000 adherents in 1995. Roughly 0.7% of the population as contrasted with 1.05 million in 1990, 2.1 million in 1970, 1.85 million in 1945, 3.02 million in 1939, and 5.2 million in 1897. About 1.3 million were massacred during World War II. The Jewish community is divided into 2 groups: (1) Western Jews, for the most part coming from Germany in the 17th and 18th centuries, and (2) Eastern Jews who are ancient inhabitants of southern and central Asia.

Although recognized officially, Judaism has had to begin the salvaging of cultural expression that was nearly lost during the 70 years of Soviet Socialist Regime coupled with the dread of anti-Semitism that so pervaded that period. Today foreign organizations openly disperse some $40 million into Jewish programming every year in the Former Soviet Union. More than 100 charity centers have opened throughout the FSU to serve the elderly and needy of the Jewish community as well as Jewish activists.

Still the enthusiasm for the heritage is not altogether the passion of the people. Gone are the hundreds of students of the early 1990's who competed to study courses on the Torah and Jewish history that had previously been banned for decades. No more than an estimated 5% of Jews in the FSU are religious. Only a third of those listed as Jewish nationality on their passport practice the Jewish faith.

Anti-Semitism is still a present force in Russia with several factions of neo-Nazi groups at the forefront of such demonstrations. Even before the Israeli-Arab war of 1967 but especially since then, authorities have shown increasing hostility towards the Jewish community. A 1996 survey of St Petersburg Jews showed that 12% had been physically attacked because they were Jewish, while some 54% had been the object of anti-Semitic name calling. The severe and often bloody history of anti-Semitism in Russia explains the desire of many to emigrate to Israel, and other established democratic nations, whose economic and cultural success are also important attractions. More than 600,000 Jews have emigrated to Israel from the FSU with others making new lives in the USA, Germany and other parts of the world. In 1996 some 5000 left for Israel with close to 2000 leaving for America every month.

Shamanism is still widely practiced by the Chukchi, Tungus, and Samoyed peoples of Siberia who believe in the existence of ancestral and free nature spirits, divinities of fire and the sun, and a supreme being who resides in the sky. In some areas the organization of hereditary magician-priests represents a high degree of sophistication. Roughly .8% of Russian population are adherents to shamanism.

Buddhism is officially recognized, though it also has a long history of repression since 1917. From 1933-38, all 120 Buddhist monasteries were destroyed or closed. Buddhists are principally Mongols, divided into different communities: Buryats in the Buryat autonomous republic where the headquarters of the Central Buddhist Office is located, Kalmyks located before 1941 in the Lower Volga but now widely dispersed, and Mongols of Chita region. There are currently 80 Buddhist religious associations, with 10 Datsan monasteries and the total monastic body comprising some 200 men. Ten additional monasteries are under construction.

CHRISTIANITY

The first Christians in all probability were Armenians, converted according to tradition by the Apostle Thaddeus a few years after the Day of Pentecost. Russia adopted Christianity under Prince Vladimir of Kiev in AD 988, in a ceremony patterned on Byzantine rites. This ceremony laid the pattern for the rise of the Russian Orthodox Church.

Left. Patriarch Tikhon, probably murdered by Stalin in 1925. *Right.* Modern-day Orthodox zealot.

ORTHODOX CHURCHES. (That were legal under Communist rule).

Orthodoxy was introduced into Russia in AD 988, and a Russian Orthodox patriarchate was instituted in 1589, after which the church called itself the Third Rome. During subsequent years relations between the Orthodox Church and the ruling authorities were close; thus from 1613-33 Filaret served as patriarch while his son Micahel ruled as the first Romanov tsar. In 1700 patriarch Adrian opposed a number of reforms instituted by Peter the Great, and as a result the patriarchate was abolished. Peter established a synod in 1721 composed of bishops and a tsar-appointed ober-procurator. From 1721-1917 the tsar ruled the church through the synod. From March 1917 with the abdication of tsar Nicholas II the relationship between church and state was terminated. During the provisional government in August 1917 a church council was convoked and the patriarchate re-established. From 1925 to 1944 there was no patriarch, but at the end of World War II a patriarch was appointed once again as part of Stalin's rapprochement with the church.

Since 1990 the Russian Orthodox Church has been led by patriarch Alexy II of Moscow and All Russia. He is the 15th patriarch in the church's history, who governs together with the Holy Synod. The ROC has survived for over a millennium as a formidable Christian force and it retains a vast reservoir of spirituality and courage, and in many areas is generating powerful new renewal movements. With the passing of the new Freedom of Conscience and Religious Associations bill signed into law by president Yeltsin in October of 1997, the ROC has risen to new heights and protection of its sacred heritage has been seemingly guaranteed.

The 56 million Russian Orthodox in 1900 (75% of the population) had fallen by 1970 to 38.8 million (29%) due to decades of repression and harassment. In mid 1995 there totaled 77.2 million (52%). The total number of open, active or registered churches declined from 80,792 in 1913 to 39,000 in 1925, and to only 1,000 in 1939; rising to 16,000 in 1945, to 20,000 by 1957, declining again to 5,100 by 1973. By 1988 it had risen to 6,893 and 10 years later some 17,000 parishes exist. Over 300 monasteries have been reopened totaling 395 compared to 18 in 1980. There are 147 Bishops, over 13,000 priests and over 1500 deacons. Presently there are 5 theological academies, 21 seminaries, 27 pre-seminaries. There are 2 Orthodox Universities and a theological institute.

Old Ritualist Church. Old Believers' Choir at Pokrovskaia church in Moscow.

The Old Believers are a unique regional group. Known in Siberia as Semieskie, they were founded more than 300 years ago by Orthodox dissenters who were in sharp disagreement with liturgical reforms proposed by the ROC in the 17th century. Led by Avvakum Petrovich, an archpriest who was executed soon thereafter, they were cruelly persecuted for their withdrawal by the church and the government. Eventually they divided into sects with some settling in the borderlands and the rest exiling to Siberia.

During the reign of Catherine the Great, Old Believers from Poland were taken into the wilds of what is the current day region of Buryat. Scattered here they preserved their heritage and traditions and began cultivating these new lands.

In 1971 the Council of the ROC officially recognized the rites and practices of the Old Believers. Modern day descendants still thrive and maintain the traditions and practices of their forefathers through folk tales, songs, dance, dialect, and unique style of dress.

ORTHODOX CHURCHES (That were illegal, unregistered or unrecognized under Communist rule). All of the above-mentioned Orthodox bodies were recognized by the Soviet regime; there were, however, in addition at least 34 unregistered, illegal and highly-clandestine Orthodox denominations, churches, sects and other dissenting bodies with at least 576,000 members in 1970, which until 1991 were (with their Protestant and Catholic counterparts) popularly known in the Western world as the underground church, the catacomb church, the church of silence, or the church of the martyrs. All totally rejected the Soviet regime and all churches which collaborated with it. Some, in particular the True Orthodox Church, adhere steadfastly to conservative Russian Orthodoxy in theology, liturgy, ritual, and church government. Others, unable to get priestly ministrations, are operated by lay leadership networks. These churches steadily increase their influence, often aided by nation-wide clandestine administrative networks, and there is no shortage of young recruits to their ranks.

Orthodox dissenting bodies and sub-Orthodox sects are also widespread.

Several groups of Spiritual Christians have sprung up out of the Orthodox milieu, rejecting Orthodox ritual. The Khlysty (Whippers), who had a vast geographical spread under the tsars, preserve most faithfully the traditions of the original sect formed in the 17th century. Further schisms have produced the New Israelites Brethren of Christ (also called Skoptsy or Castrated Ones), Dukhobors (Spirit-Wrestlers), and Molokans (Milkdrinkers) who were a million strong in 1917. All were highly clandestine and operated underground.

PROTESTANT CHURCHES. The Union of Evangelical Christians-Baptists (AUCECB) was formed in 1944 as a union of Baptists (who originated in 1841) and Evangelical Christians (Brethren, Stundists, from around 1870). Several Pentecostal groups joined in 1945 and 1947, some of whom later left, and some Mennonites have been members since 1963. The church is strongest in the Ukraine, Baltic states, and the Far East. Large numbers attend without seeking membership through adult baptism. During 1960-65 a schism resulted from the government anti-religious campaign leading to the formation of the Council of Churches of Evangelical Christians-Baptists, although this latter group was consistently refused legal recognition and remained critical of state atheistic policies under Communist rule. Its leaders were under constant harassment, with many imprisonments.

Lutherans are concentrated outside Russia in the Baltic states, particularly Latvia and Estonia, where recognized Lutheran denominations exist. Until recently there were only 2 official Lutheran congregations outside these states (Tselinograd and Karaganda, both in Kazakhstan), despite the fact that Lutherans are found in other parts particularly Siberia. Many worshipped as clandestine groups, while several congregations have obtained registration. The Lutheran Church of Russia was dissolved in 1938.

The Reformed Church of Russia which began in the 17th century was suppressed from 1917 to 1991. Subsequently, territorial acquisition brought within the Soviet Union other Reformed bodies, namely the churches of Carpatho-Ukraine, Lithuania, and Latvia.

Mennonites exist both within the AUCECB and outside. They first emigrated to Russia in the 18th century, mostly from Germany, but there has been considerable emigration out of Russia over the last hundred years, largely to the Americas. Many Old Mennonites exist in Asiatic Russia where they were forcibly resettled after World War II.

The Pentecostal movement began spreading in Russia during the 1920s. In 1944, 400 of the 700 known Pentecostal congregations (called Christians of Evangelical Faith) joined the AUCECB. By 1970, however, there were more Pentecostals outside the AUCECB than inside, though forced to operate clandestinely and underground.

About 80 other Protestant denominations exist, mostly unregistered.

CATHOLIC CHURCH. From over 4.5 million Roman Catholics in the USSR, concentrated primarily in Lithuania, western Ukraine and western Belorussi, today under half a million remain in the new Russia. Since the Stalin-Roosevelt accord of 1933 an American priest has resided permanently in Moscow to minister to diplomats and their families, a deceptive gesture which hid the desperate lack of pastoral care for Catholics across the whole of the USSR.

In the entire Soviet Union there remained no Catholic diocese with a legally-recognized residential bishop. Many were executed or killed after 1940. In 1971 there were only 5 titular bishops, apostolic administrators or their auxiliaries. During 1972 one new bishop was consecrated. There was no central leadership and virtually no official contact with the Vatican. Nevertheless, in May 1971 for the first time 3 Lithuanian bishops were given permission to travel together to Rome. Subsequent to 1991 the Vatican reorganized the reduced Catholic presence and appointed one archbishop for Russia. This was strongly objected to by the Orthodox Church and a long period of strained relations between Rome and Moscow began.

The Holy See has no diplomatic relations with Russia in AD 2000, but has an acting nuncio residing in Moscow.

Indigenous missions. Christians in the Crimea in the 3rd century sent missionaries outside of the region. When Russia became Orthodox in 988 hundreds of missionaries were sent not only within its borders but to surrounding territories. Throughout its history, the Russian Orthodox Church sent thousands of missionaries to dozens of countries outside of Russia. Russians continue to serve in foreign countries today, particularly in the former Soviet Union.

Renewal movements. Renewal movements. In the 1990s the Pentecostal/Charismatic Renewal continued to spread rapidly across most older churches, and numbered over 6,475,000 adherents (of whom 2% Pentecostals, 15% Charismatics, and 82% Independents).

CHURCH AND STATE

Article 124 of the constitution of 1936 stipulated that 'With the purpose of assuring the liberty of conscience of all citizens, the Church in the USSR is separated from the State and the school from the Church; all citizens enjoy the freedom to hold religious services and the freedom to engage in anti-religious propaganda.' The first Soviet constitution, that of Lenin in July 1918, had recognized equally the right of disseminating religious propaganda, but this was suppressed by constitutional changes effected under Stalin on 18 May 1929 which inter alia prohibited religious education for persons under 18 years old. The separation of church and state, and consequently church and school, rests ultimately on a decree of 23 January 1918 which deprived the Orthodox Church of the privileged position which it enjoyed under the tsars. The law concerning religious associations of 8 April 1929 makes their registration obligatory (Articles 2, 5, 6). These communities should be composed of a minimum of 20 persons (Article 3) whose names must be submitted (Article 8). The civil authorities have a month in which to accept or refuse the registration; and in case of refusal, they are not required to divulge their reasons (Article 7); in practice, however, they often fail to comply with the former requirement. Clergy must also be registered before they can exercise their offices. Article 17 contains a number of prohibitions limiting the life of the church to worship services. In general, the law virtually ignores the church as a hierarchical organization.

After 1960 there was a hardening in the attitude of the state vis-a-vis the church. The dispositions of the penal code were modified on 27 June 1961, increasing the penalties for infractions of laws, relating to religious activities. A new law concerning marriage and the family was passed containing passages which facilitate the practice already existent of removing children from believing parents. Subsequent to 1991 the dominant role of the Orthodox Church has been restored, resulting in bad feeling with both Catholics and Protestants.

From 1917-53, an estimated 60 million Soviet citizens were killed directly or indirectly as a result of the Bolshevik revolution (40% being executed or killed by communist officials), and a further 66 million were incarcerated in prisons or labor camps. At least half of these 2 totals were Christian believers, the great majority for alleged political offenses. From 1953-56 most of the survivors were released. Even so in 1976 there were still 10,000 political and about 1,000 religious prisoners in Soviet jails, out of a total of 10 million prisoners in 1,000 labor camps and jails. By 1995 most had been released.

BROADCASTING AND MEDIA

Both Russian and English are well saturated with programs from all the major broadcasters. TWR and IBRA broadcast in 34 other languages, including the major Central Asian and Eastern European languages (Kazakh, Kyrgyz, Tajik, Uzbek, German, Polish, Hungarian, etc). HCJB is helping to plant radio ministries throughout Russia in partnership with several Russian ministries. Most broadcasters have offices in Moscow or other locations to handle follow-up. AWR maintains a studio in Tula which produces Russian-language programs, and leases transmitters in Moscow and Sumara. KNLS, WORHAR and WYFR broadcast shortwave Russian programs from transmitters in the USA. IBRA broadcasts programs in Turkish and Arabic from Russian stations into the Middle East and Central Asia.

CBN did a nationwide media 'blitz' in the early 1990s, and continues to air the *700 Club*, animated specials and *Answers* program are available in virtually every viewing region on at least a weekly, and in some places a daily, basis. CBN maintains a mail response center in Russia and does followup with correspondence courses from there. A joint CBN/AIMS project trains pastors for plant churches among those who have responded to CBN's media programs. IBRA-produced programs in 12 languages are aired regularly on local television channels. Satellite TV programs are received mainly in Arabic.

The 'Jesus' Film has made a major impact. Over 52 million have watched it on television, joined by 4 million cinematic viewers, 3.9 million video viewers, and 4.4 million who saw film team presentations, with 600,000 responses.

Russian Orthodox Church. *Lower.* At monastic center Zagorsk, outside Moscow, in 1989 vast Thanksgiving service proceeds, led by (*upper*) procession of bishops and metropolitans.

INTERDENOMINATIONAL ORGANIZATIONS

International organizations were not permitted in the USSR, but 6 churches became members of the World Council of Churches between 1962-65. They and others were active participants in the 1969 Conference of Members of All Religions in the USSR for Co-operation and Peace among the Nations, held at Zagorsk, which is the nearest to an ecumenical council that the regime has permitted.

Further progress has been made since 1996-1999.

FUTURE TRENDS AND PROSPECTS.

Following both the collapse of Communism and the breakup of the Soviet Union, the church has begun to grow rapidly among Russians and minority peoples. This growth is expected to continue well into the 21st century so that Christians may consist of 70% of the population by AD 2025.

The nonreligious and atheists will probably continue their precipitous decline well beyond AD 2030, perhaps falling below 20% jointly before AD 2050. Christianity could grow to 75% by AD 2050.

BIBLIOGRAPHY

A history of Soviet atheism in theory and practice, and the believer. D. V. Pospielovsky. Basingstoke, UK: Macmillan, 1987–88. 3 vols.

A history of the people of Siberia. J. Forsyth. Cambridge, UK: Cambridge University Press, 1992.

A history of the Russian church to 1448. J. L. I. Fennell. London: Longman, 1995. 278p.

A pilgrimage of faith: the Mennonite Brethren Church in Russia and North America, 1860–1990. J. B. Toews. *Perspectives on Mennonite life and thought*, 8. Winnipeg: Kindred Press, 1993. 383p.

A thousand years of Russian Christianity: Kievan Rus' to present: comments and a survey of the literature. G. C. Jerkovich. Lawrence, KS: Soviet and East European Studies, University of Kansas, 1988. 65p.

A treasury of Russian spirituality. G. P. Fedotov (ed). London: Sheed & Ward, 1950. 501p.

Anti–religious propaganda in the Soviet Union: a study of mass persuasion. D. E. Powell. Cambridge, MA: Massachusetts Institute of Technology, 1975. 215p.

Aspects of religion in the Soviet Union, 1917–1967. R. H. Marshall (ed). Chicago: University of Chicago Press, 1971. 489p.

Christian prisoners in the USSR: a study by Keston College. 5th ed. *Keston book*, no. 11. [Keston, UK]: Keston College, 1985. 84p.

Christian religion in the Soviet Union: a sociological study. C. Lane. London: Allen and Unwin, 1978. 258p. (Analysis of the vast corpus of data from Soviet sociologists between 1955 and 1978).

Christianity after Communism: social, political, and cultural struggle in Russia. N. C. Nielsen Jr. Boulder, CO: Westview Press, 1994. 183p.

Christianity and the arts in Russia. W. C. Brumfield & M. Velimirovich (eds). Cambridge, UK: Cambridge University Press, 1991. 172p.

Christianity and the Eastern Slavs. B. Gasparov & O. Raevsky-Hughes. *California Slavic studies*, vol. 16. Berkeley, CA: University of California Press, 1993.

Christians and churches in Socialist countries: report of a visit by church leaders from South East Asia and Australia. J. S. Udy. Delhi: ISPCK, 1982. 204p.

Christians in contemporary Russia. N. Struve. London: Harvill Press, 1967.

Church handbook for the USSR. J. Innes. England, 1967–74. (Duplicated; loose-leaf; descriptions and rough maps of locations of open church buildings throughout the USSR.).

Church, nation and state in Russia and Ukraine. G. A. Hosking (ed). New York: St. Martin's Press, 1991. 372p.

Communist Russia and the Russian Orthodox Church, 1943–1962. W. B. Stroyen. Washington, DC: Catholic University of America, 1967. (See p.117-43 for texts of Soviet laws on religion).

Crescent in a red sky: the future of Islam in the Soviet Union. A. Taheri. London: Hutchinson, 1989. 287p.

Discretion and valour: religious conditions in Russia and Eastern Europe. T. Beeson. Glasgow: Collins, 1974. 348p.

Evangelical secularism in the Russian Empire and the USSR: a bibliographic guide. A. W. Wardin Jr. *ATLA bibliography series*, 36. Metuchen, NJ: Scarecrow Press, 1995. 906p.

Gorbachev, glasnost and the gospel. M. A. Bourdeaux. London: Hodder & Stoughton, 1990. 226p.

Handbook for Christian travelers to the CIS: reflections on Russian culture. R. LeClair, C. LeClair & L. Branitski. 2nd ed. Wheaton, IL: Slavic Gospel Association, 1993. 79p.

History of Evangelical Christianity in Russia. A. W. Olema. Katy, TX: Albert W. Olema, 1983. 240p.

Islam in the Soviet Union. A. Bennigsen & C. Lemercier-Quelquejay. Trans., G. E. Wheeler & H. Evans. London: Pall Mall Press in association with the Central Asian Research Centre, 1967. 285p.

Islamic peoples of the Soviet Union: an historical and statistical handbook. S. Akiner. 2nd ed. London: KPI, 1986. 462p.

Jews in the Soviet Union since 1917: paradox of survival. N. Levin. New York: New York University Press, 1988. 2 vols.

Kirchengeschichte Russlands der neuesten Zeit. C. P. Johannes. Munich: Anton Pustet, 1965–69. 3 vols.

Land of sickles and crosses: The United Methodist initiative in the Commonwealth of Independent States. M. B. Oden. Cincinnati, OH: United Methodist Church, [1992]. 111p.

Muslims of the Soviet Union: a guide. A. Bennigsen & S. E. Wimbush. London: Hurst, 1985. 294p.

Native peoples of the Russian far north. N. Vakhtin. London: Minority Rights Group, 1992. 38p.

Old Believers in modern Russia. R. R. Robson. DeKalb, IL: Northern Illinois University Press, 1998. 202p.

Opium of the people: the Christian religion in the USSR. M. A. Bourdeaux. London: Faber, 1965. 244p.

Patriarch and prophets: persecution of the Russian Orthodox Church today. M. A. Bourdeaux. London: Mowbrays, 1970.

Praying with the KGB: a startling report from the shattered empire. P. Yancey. Portland, OR: Multnomah, 1992. 106p.

Religion and atheism in the USSR and Eastern Europe. B. R. Bociurkiw & J. W. Strong (eds). London: Macmillan, 1975.

Religion and culture in early modern Russia and Ukraine. S. H. Baron & N. S. Kollmann (eds). DeKalb, IL: Northern Illinois University Press, 1998. 224p.

Religion and Soviet foreign policy, 1945–1970. W. C. Fletcher. London: Oxford University Press for the Royal Institute of International Affairs, 1973. 189p.

Religion and the search for new ideals in the USSR. W. C. Fletcher & A. J. Stover (eds). New York: Frederick A. Praeger, 1967.

Religion in the Soviet Union. W. Kolarz. London: Macmillan, 1961. 518p. (The most thorough overall study).

Religion in the U.S.S.R. R. Conquest (ed). *The contemporary Soviet Union series: institutions and policies*, 201. New York: Frederick A. Praeger, 1968. 135p.

Religious ferment in Russia: Protestant opposition to Soviet religious policy. M. A. Bourdeaux. London: Macmillan, 1968. 255p.

Religious minorities in the Soviet Union: a report. M. A. Bourdeaux. 4th ed. London: Minority Rights Group, 1984. 24p.

Religious policy in the Soviet Union. S. P. Ramet (ed). Cambridge, UK: Cambridge University Press, 1993. 361p.

'Religious problems in Russia today,' *Pro Mundi Vita* (Brussels), 58 (January 1976), 1–32.

Religioznoye sektantstvo i sovremennost (Religious sectarianism and the present). A. I. Klibanov. Moscow: Nauka, 1969. (Third volume of 3-vol history, 14th century to present).

Russian culture at the threshold of the third millennium of Christianity. Y. B. Pishchik. Moscow: Disput magazine, 1993. 126p.

Russian folk belief. L. J. Ivanits. Illustrated by S. Schiller. Armonk, NY: M. E. Sharpe, 1989. 256p.

Russian Orthodoxy and political culture transformation. J. W. Warhola. Pittsburgh, PA: Center for Russian & East European Studies, University of Pittsburgh, 1993. 53p.

Russian popular culture: entertainment and society. R. Stites. *Cambridge Soviet paperbacks*, no. 7. Cambridge, UK: Cambridge University Press, 1992. 269p.

Russian resurrection: strength in suffering: a history of Russia's evangelical church. M. Rowe. London: Marshall Pickering, 1994. 263p.

Russia/U.S.S.R. L. Pitman. 2nd ed. *World bibliographical series*, vol. 6. Oxford, UK: CLIO Press, 1994. (See especially 'Population, Nationalities,' pp. 76f, and 'Religion,' pp. 95-100).

Seeking God: the recovery of religious identity in Orthodox Russia, Ukraine, and Georgia. S. K. Batalden (ed). DeKalb, IL: Northern Illinois University Press, 1993. 299p.

Shamanism: Soviet studies of traditional religion in Siberia and Central Asia. M. M. Balzer (ed). Armonk, NY: M. E. Sharpe, 1990. 215p.

Shamans, lamas, and evangelicals: the English missionaries in Siberia. C. R. Bawden. London: Routledge & Kegan Paul, 1985. 424p.

Siberia and the Soviet Far East. D. Collins. *World bibliographical series*, vol. 127. Oxford, UK: CLIO Press, 1991.

'Sociology of religion in the USSR,' *Social compass*, 21, 2 (1974), 115–214.

Studies on shamanism. A. L. Siikala and M. Hoppál. *Ethnologica uralica*, 2. Helsinki: Finnish Anthropological Society, 1992. 230p.

The Christianization of ancient Russia, a millennium, 988–1988. Y. Hamant (ed). Paris: UNESCO, 1992. 336p.

The Cossacks. P. Longworth. London: Constable, 1969.

The Crimean Tartars. A. Fisher. Stanford, CA: Hoover Institution Press, 1978. 264p.

The grand strategy of the Soviet Union. E. N. Luttwak. London: Weidenfeld and Nicolson, 1983. 251p.

The icon handbook: a guide to understanding icons and the liturgy, symbols and practices of the Russian Orthodox Church. D. Coomler. Springfield, IL: Templegate, 1995. 319p.

The Jews of the Soviet Union: the history of a national minority. B. Pinkus. Cambridge, UK: Cambridge University Press, 1988. 397p.

The millennium: Christianity and Russia, A.D. 988–1988. A. Leong (ed). Crestwood, NY: St. Vladimir's Seminary Press, 1990.

The modern encyclopedia of religion in Russia and the Soviet Union. P. D. Steeves (ed). Gulf Breeze, FL: Academic International Press, 1988–. 5 vols.; in progress to 25 vols.

The Orthodox Church in the history of Russia. D. Pospielovsky. Crestwood, NY: St. Vladimir's Seminary Press, 1997. 406p.

The peoples of the Soviet Union. V. Kozlov. Trans., P. M. Tiffen. London: Hutchinson, 1988. 262p.

The politics of religion in Russia and the new states of Eurasia. M. A. Bourdeaux (ed). *International politics of Eurasia*, vol. 3. Armonk, NY: M.E. Sharpe, 1995. 334p.

The Russian church under the Soviet regime 1917–1982. D. Pospielovsky. Crestwood, NY: St. Vladimir's Seminary Press, 1984. 2 vols.

The Russian Orthodox Church: a contemporary history. J. Ellis. London: Croom Helm, 1986. 531p.

The Russian Orthodox Church: organization, situation, activity. Moscow: Orthodox Patriarchate, [1960]. (Official publication; very truncated historical section).

The Russian Orthodox Church underground, 1917–1970. W. C. Fletcher. London: Oxford University Press, 1971. 314p. (Detailed documentation on over 40 highly-organized clandestine movements).

The Russian Protestants: evangelicals in the Soviet Union, 1944–1964. S. Durasoff. Rutherford: Fairleigh Dickinson University Press, 1969. 312p.

The Russian religious mind. G. P. Fedotov. Cambridge, MA: Harvard University Press, 1966. 2 vols.

The Russian religious renaissance of the twentieth century. N. Zernov. London: Longman & Todd, 1963. 410p.

The Soviet Germans: past and present. I. Fleischhauer & B. Pinkus. London: Hurst, in association with the Marjorie Mayrock Center for Soviet and East European Research at the Hebrew University, Jerusalem, 1986. 185p.

The Soviet Union on the brink: an inside look at Christianity & glasnost. K. R. Hill. Portland, OR: Multnomah, 1991. 520p.

The Volga Tatars: a profile in national resilience. A. A. Rorlich. Stanford, CA: Hoover Institution Press, 1986. 288p.

The West in Russia and China: religions and secular thought in modern times. D. W. Treadgold. Cambridge, MA: Harvard University Press, 1973. 2 vols.

'USSR,' W. C. Fletcher, in *Western religion: a country by country sociological enquiry*, p.565–86. H. Mol (ed). The Hague: Mouton, 1972.

Voprosy istorii religii i ateizma (Problems of the history of religion and atheism). Academy of Sciences of USSR. Moscow: Academy Press, 1961. 12 vols.

Young Christians in Russia. M. A. Bourdeaux & K. Murray. *Keston books*, no. 5. London: Lakeland, 1976. 156p.

Country Table 2. **Organized churches and denominations in Russia.**

Official name (bold type = church with over 10% of all affiliated) 1	Begun 2	Type 3	Counc 4	Congs 5	Adults 6	Affiliated 1970 7	Affiliated 1995 8	G% 9	Names, notes, and other statistics (see Codebook, Part 3) 10
Adventists of the True Remnant	c1920	I-Adv	.....	200	15,000	30,000	20,000	-1.61	*Adventisty Vernogo Ostatka*. SDA split, rejecting state interference. Underground.
Ancient Church of the East (P Tehran)	c 400	O-Nes	Yw...	3	2,500	5,000	7,000	1.35	Syriac-speaking Assyrians in Armenia, Georgia; isolated, unorganized, attend ROC.
Anglican Ch (J North & Central Europe)	c1670	A-plu	awc.u	6	2,000	500	3,000	7.43	Chaplaincies in Kiev, Leningrad, Moscow. British expatriate personnel.
Apocalyptists	1923	I-Apo	.....	12	400	1,000	1,100	0.38	*Apokalipsisty*. Begun Vinnitsa by Catholic priest, spread to Far East; underground.
Armenian Apostolic Church:	c 35	O-Arm	EWc.u	60	250,000	70,000	400,000	7.22	*Gregorians*. Sizeable charismatics in Brotherhood of Lovers of the Church. 200n,6d,1s.
D Nor-Nakhichevan & Russia		O-Arm	Eb	40	170,000	40,000	250,000	0.05	Caucasus to South Russia, Don area. 24% urban. 76% rural. Armenian diaspora. 8n.
V Moskva		O-Arm	E	20	80,000	30,000	150,000	0.05	Armenians in Moscow and north Russia. One archimandrite.
Assembly Hall Churches	c1980	I-3nC	.....	25	3,103	–	6,000	6.67	*Little Flock. Local Churches*. Begun in China 1922. Chinese.
Association of Vineyard Chs	c1990	I-3sW	.....	5	600	–	2,000	20.00	Assisted by M=AVC(USA).
Bulgarian Orthodox Church		O-Bul	Mwc.u	10	6,000	1,000	12,000	0.05	*Balgarskata Prayoslavna Crkya*. Bulgarians in Moscow; resident bishop of Kropunich.
Catholic Church in Russia:	1084	R-LEr	B...u	186	1,033,700	4,200	1,311,200	25.83	*Rimsko-Katolicheskaya Tserkov*. (1970) 12n,45Yy. (1995) 31n,64x,30m,109w,1900Yy.
D Vladivostok	1923	R-Lat	bs	5	700	500	1,000	2.81	Formerly VA Siberia. Southeastern RSFSR.
EA Russia (*Russian-rite*)	1917	R-Rus	Os	2	6,900	3,000	10,000	4.93	For all Russians of Byzantine rite.
AA Sibiria (Siberia)	1921	R-Lat	Ps	118	789,000	500	1,000,000	35.53	North & Central Asia. Closed 1921, reopened 1991. Vast growth. 2n,35x,34w,506Yy.
PA Karafuto (Sakhalin)	1932	R-Lat	Ps	2	100	200	200	0.00	Formerly Japanese part of Sakhalin island, occupied by USSR since 1945.
AA Russia Europea	1991	R-Lat	Bs	59	237,000	–	300,000	25.00	European Russians of Latin and Eastern rites. (1991) 29n,29x,30m,75w,1343Yy.
Charismatic Assoc of Christian Chs of R	c1960	I-3cW	.....	500	50,000	9,000	100,000	10.11	Many ex AUCECB from 1961, central and northern Russia. 1,000 members in some churches.
Christ Groups	1991	I-3hW	x....	230	4,000	–	9,000	25.00	Isolated home churches after EHC (Every Home for Christ) campaign across Russia.
Christians of Evangelical Faith	1921	I-3pW	.....	500	40,000	150,000	100,000	-1.61	*CEF, Khristiane Evangel'skoy Very*. Underground. 65% of all CEF; rest are in AUCECB.
Christians of Zion	c1935	I-3fW	.....	40	1,600	5,000	4,000	-0.89	*Khristiane*.
Ch of Jesus Christ of Latter-day Saints	1990	m-LdS	.....	200	12,000	–	20,000	20.00	*Mormons*. Strong missionary force. Clashes with government.
Council of Churches of Ev Chr-Baptists	1961	I-3pW	.....	800	25,000	150,000	50,000	-4.30	*STEKhB/CCECB/Initsiativniki*. Anti-state schism ex AUCECB. Viciously harassed.
Evangelical Christian Brethren	c1870	P-CBr	x....	1,200	130,000	330,000	400,000	0.77	Open Brethren with links to Britain and Europe.
Ev Christians in the Apostolic Spirit	1913	I-3oW	.....	600	27,000	5,000	38,000	8.45	First Russian Pentecostals. Foot-washing, Oneness. 1947, loose union in AUCECB.
Evangelical Lutheran Ch of Ingria		P-Lut	.....	40	9,000	2,000	15,000	0.05	Northwest Russia bordering Finland. First language Finnish, second Russian. M=LCMS.
Evangelical Lutheran Church of Latvia	c1550	P-Lut	LWC.u	15	4,000	5,000	10,000	2.81	Parent church in Latvia has 15 dioceses, 102 pastors.
Ev Lutheran Ch of Russia & OS		P-LuR	.....	100	120,000	50,000	170,000	0.05	*ELCROS(OS=Other States)*. German-speaking farmers: Altai, refugees:Kirgizia, Kazakhstan.
Followers of John	c1883	I-Ose	.....	5	500	2,000	1,000	-2.73	*Ioannitsy*. Founder John Kronshtadtsky. Still active Ukraine, Voronezh, Krasnodar.
Free Russian Orthodox Church	1990	I-Rus	x....	50	30,000	–	50,000	20.00	*FROC*. M=ROCOR(Exile). Rapid growth ex True Orthodox Ch. Fierce opposition. 4 bps.
Georgian Orthodox Church		O-Geo	M....	60	42,300	49,000	65,000	0.05	Georgians in state Church of Georgia.
Global Strategy Christian Association	1991	I-3cW	x....	65	6,750	–	13,000	25.00	*GSCA*. M=Global Strategy Missions Assoc (GSMA, USA). Cell churches in largest cities.
Greek Orthodox Church		O-Gre	C....	12	30,000	10,000	70,000	0.05	Greeks. Members in Orthodox Church of Greece.
International Pentecostal Holiness Ch	c1980	P-Pe3	.....	25	2,000	–	3,000	6.67	*IPHC*. 21 churches in Moscow. M=IPHC(USA).
Isolated Messianic Jews	1995	I-3mJ	.....	1,000	30,000	–	50,000	49.28	After 1995 St Petersburg campaigns, 50,000 Russian/Ukrainian/Byelorussian Jews convert.
Isolated radio churches	1939	I-3rW	.....	50,000	2,000,000	800,000	3,000,000	5.43	Isolated radio believers. R=6000(2800 SGA,415 HCJB,300 FEBC,60 TWR,RVatican,BBC,&c).
Jehovah's Witnesses	c1920	m-Jeh	x....	250	70,000	10,000	110,000	10.07	*Svideteli Iegovi*. Mass deportations 1948-51 to Siberia, Arctic. Very rapid growth. 17269Y.
Mennonite Brethren (New Mennonites)	c1750	P-Men	.....	120	50,000	60,000	80,000	1.16	Mainline Mennonites; links with USA.
Messianic Congs & Synagogues	c1975	I-3mJ	x....	100	4,000	–	7,000	5.00	*Messianic Jews*. M=UMJC,IAMCS,JFJ(USA, UK), et alia.
New Apostolic Church	c1980	I-3aX	x....	200	20,000	–	29,919	6.67	*NAC. NAK. Neuapostolische Kirche*. Sizeable following in both European and Asiatic Russia.
New-Christian Union	c1940	I-Ose	.....	20	600	1,000	1,100	0.38	In Krasnodar and Stavropol in 1950-51; descended from New Israelites. Illegal for many years.
New Israelites	c1900	I-Ose	.....	15	1,500	5,000	3,000	-2.02	*Novy Izrail*. Spiritual Christians in Rostov region; many emigrated to Uruguay.
Old Ritualist Ancient Orth Christians	c1860	I-OBe	x...u	20	180,000	200,000	250,000	0.90	*AD Moscow. Beglopopovtsy (Ch of Fugitive Priests)*. Ex Popovtsy. Volga, Siberia. 18n.
Old Ritualist Ch Belokrinitsa Concord	1666	I-OBe	x...u	1,600	400,000	1,000,000	710,000	-1.36	*AD Moscow. Raskolniki (Schismatics), Popovtsy (Priestists)*. 5 Dioceses, 15 bishops. 200n.
Old Ritualist Church (Priestless)	c1710	I-OBe	....u	50	100,000	900,000	300,000	-4.30	*Bespopovtsy*. Old Believers. 46 factions (Pomortsy, &c) Also in Romania, Baltic, Byelorussia.
Old Ritualist Runaways	c1770	I-OBe	.....	4	500	2,000	1,000	-2.73	*Beguny (Runners), Bezdenezhniki (Moneyless)*. Totally reject Soviet state. Siberia.
Old Mennonites (Church Mennonites)	c1750	P-Men	.....	800	50,000	80,000	60,000	-1.14	German immigrants; forcibly resettled east and south east of Urals. Unregistered for many years.
Pentecostal Union of United Churches	1911	P-Pe2	.....	400	103,000	65,000	130,000	2.81	Ex AUCECB and unregistered Pentecostals in 1990. M=CoG,AoG. 5 bishops.
Redeemed Israelites	c1930	I-Ose	.....	15	400	1,000	900	-0.42	*Iskuplenny Izrail*. Founder Mother Mary; Spiritual Christians in Orenburg region.
Reformed Fundamental Church	1632	P-Ref	.....	40	3,000	2,700	5,000	2.50	Remnants of Latvian and Carpatho-Ukrainian Reformed Churches.
Russian Orthodox Church:	988	O-Rus	MWC.u	8,141	46,769,000	36,080,000	73,998,000	0.10	*ROC. Russkaya Pravoslavnaya Tserkov*. 93 Dioceses, 103 bps, 14000n,60de(5000),82s.
P Moskva (Moscow)	1325	O-Rus	Mp	880	5,055,000	3,900,000	7,999,000	2.92	Patriarchal diocese. 86% urban. 42 active churches in Moscow city. 6 bishops. 2s.
D Arkhangelsk & Kholmogory	1682	O-Rus	Mb	262	1,504,000	1,160,000	2,379,000	2.91	60% urban. Includes D Olonets & Petrozavodsk. Only 3 churches left in Lomi ASSR.
D Astrakhan & Enotaevka	1609	O-Rus	Mb	59	337,000	260,000	533,000	2.91	61% urban. Many Muslims. 1973, only 7 parishes open. Orthodox mostly Russians.
D Cheboksary & Chuvash	1853	O-Rus	Mb	83	480,000	370,000	759,000	2.92	Chuvash ASSR. Traditionally Orthodox. Theological samizdat circulation.
D Chelyabinsk & Zlatoust	1908	O-Rus	Mb	223	1,283,000	990,000	2,030,000	2.91	78% urban. Vacant since 1961. Administered by D Sverdlovsk, then D Perm.
D Gorkiy & Arzamas	1672	O-Rus	Ma	250	1,438,000	1,110,000	2,276,000	2.91	Nizhni Novgorod. 61% urban population get children baptized. 1968 protest to WCC.
D Irkutsk & Chita	1727	O-Rus	Ma	537	3,085,000	2,380,000	4,881,000	2.91	67% urban. East Siberia. Includes D Khabarovsk & D Vladivostok (suppressed 1958).
D Ivanovo & Kineshma	1866	O-Rus	Ma	90	518,000	400,000	820,000	2.91	75% urban. Regular harassment of believers of all denominations.
D Izhevsk & Udmurtia	1657	O-Rus	Mb	95	544,000	420,000	861,000	2.91	Udmurt ASSR. Traditionally Orthodox. 57% urban. Under D Kazan. Many pagans still.
D Kalinin & Kashin	1271	O-Rus	Mb	115	661,000	510,000	1,046,000	2.91	Formerly called D Tver. 57% urban. Determined state obstruction to all churches.
D Kaluga & Borovsk	1789	O-Rus	Ma	68	389,000	300,000	615,000	2.91	52% urban. 1965, archbishop in conflict with state and Holy Synod, dismissed.
D Kazan & Mari ASSR	1555	O-Rus	Ma	169	972,000	750,000	1,538,000	2.91	Traditionally Orthodox. 50% urban. 1960, archbishop given 3 years' prison.
D Kirov & Slobodskoy	1657	O-Rus	Ma	117	674,000	520,000	1,066,000	2.91	55% urban. 1960, 40 chs closed, massive protests. Diocese solidly reform-minded.
D Kostroma & Galich	1744	O-Rus	Ma	59	337,000	260,000	534,000	2.92	53% urban. Steady state pressure against all organized religion.
D Krasnodar & Kuban	1842	O-Rus	Ma	305	1,750,000	1,350,000	2,769,000	2.92	47% urban. 1959, 300 churches; 1971, reduced to 76 by unremitting state hostility.
D Kursk & Belgorod	1667	O-Rus	Mb	185	1,063,000	820,000	1,682,000	2.92	1667 D Belgorod founded; 1787 Kursk. Now 34% urban. Anti-religious state pressure.
D Kuybyshev & Syzran	1850	O-Rus	Mb	187	1,076,000	830,000	1,702,000	2.91	Formerly called D Samara. 72% urban. Severe repression.
D Leningrad & Novgorod	992	O-Rus	Mm	413	2,372,000	1,830,000	3,753,000	0.10	85% urban. Includes D Velikiye Luki & Toropets (suppressed 1957). 1s,1225Y,12941y.
D Novosibirsk & Barnaul	1908	O-Rus	Mb	350	2,009,000	1,550,000	3,179,000	2.91	55% urban. Includes D Krasnoyarsk, suppressed 1948. 1972 bishop forced to retire.
D Omsk & Tyumen	1895	O-Rus	Ma	219	1,257,000	970,000	1,989,000	2.91	Vast and important Siberian diocese. 52% urban. 1970 archbishop imprisoned.
D Orel & Bryansk	1799	O-Rus	Mm	169	972,000	750,000	1,538,000	2.91	44% urban. Vast samizdat circulation. Old Believers HQ.
D Orenburg & Buzuluk	1799	O-Rus	Ma	140	803,000	620,000	1,271,000	2.91	Chkalov. 53% urban. Long local history of sub-Orthodox sectarianism.
D Penza & Saransk	1799	O-Rus	Mb	174	998,000	770,000	1,579,000	2.91	40% urban. Mordvinians, traditionally Orthodox. 1970, bishop dismissed.
D Perm & Solikamsk	1383	O-Rus	Mb	284	1,633,000	1,260,000	2,584,000	2.91	Unremitting state obstruction. Perm cathedral closed 1960 on traffic-jam pretext.
D Pskov & Porkhov	1589	O-Rus	Mm	68	391,000	300,000	618,000	2.93	43% urban. Pskovo-Pechersky (Monastery of the Caves), 30,000 pilgrims regularly.
D Rostov-on-Don & Novocherkassk	1829	O-Rus	Mb	260	1,492,000	1,150,000	2,360,000	2.92	63% urban. Systematic campaign against overt religion; trials, imprisonments.
D Ryazan & Kasimov	1198	O-Rus	Mb	95	545,000	420,000	862,000	2.92	47% urban. Vacant until bishop appointed 1973. Long history of IPKh activity.
D Saratov & Volgograd	1828	O-Rus	Mb	323	1,854,000	1,430,000	2,933,000	2.92	Formerly Stalingrad. 65% urban. Steady state pressure against all denominations.
D Smolensk & Vyazma	1137	O-Rus	Mb	74	428,000	330,000	677,000	2.92	48% urban. 1965, diocese reported in chaotic disarray; bishop's reforms thwarted.
D Stavropol & Baku	1842	O-Rus	Mb	496	2,852,000	2,200,000	4,512,000	2.91	Azerbaijan SSR. 48% urban. Unremitting government hostility and obstruction.
D Sverdlovsk & Kurgan	1885	O-Rus	Mb	366	2,100,000	1,620,000	3,323,000	2.92	73% urban. Severe repression. 1976 appeal to WCC to oust absentee bishop.
D Tambov & Michurinsk	1682	O-Rus	Ms	102	583,000	450,000	923,000	2.92	39% urban. Regular circulation of samizdat theological literature. IPKh stronghold.
D Tula & Belev	1799	O-Rus	Ms	133	765,000	590,000	1,210,000	2.91	71% urban. Many Reform Baptists; severe persecution after 1969 Tula conference.
D Ufa & Sterlitamak	1799	O-Rus	Ma	169	971,000	750,000	1,537,000	2.91	Bashkir ASSR. 48% urban. 1967 formerly imprisoned Kazan bishop appointed to Ufa.
D Ulyanovsk & Melekess	1838	O-Rus	Mb	83	480,000	370,000	759,000	2.92	52% urban. Vacant since 1959. 1965, administered by bishop of Kuybyshev.
D Vladimir & Suzdal	1214	O-Rus	Ma	101	583,000	450,000	922,000	2.91	Monasteries built 11th and 12th centuries. Now 68% urban.
D Vologda & Velikiy Ustyug	1472	O-Rus	Ma	88	506,000	390,000	800,000	2.92	48% urban. Only 17 churches open. 1972, theologian bishop dismissed by Holy Synod.
D Voronezh & Lipetsk	1682	O-Rus	Mb	253	1,452,000	1,120,000	2,297,000	2.91	45% urban. Only 55 churches open. Continual state harassment. IPKh stronghold.
D Yaroslavl & Rostov	992	O-Rus	Mm	97	557,000	430,000	882,000	0.10	70% urban. 83 churches open, 85 priests. One of stronger Orthodox areas in RSFSR.
Russian Unified Fellowship of CEF	1913	I-3pW	.....	1,300	600,000	500,000	1,200,000	3.56	*CEF=Christians of the Evangelical Faith*. Formerly in AUCECB. 65 churches in Moscow.
Salvation Army	c1990	P-Sal	x....	15	1,500	–	3,000	20.00	Based in London (UK). Full range of social and evangelistic ministries.
Seventh-day Adventist Church	1883	P-Adv	x...u	205	50,000	46,000	90,000	2.72	*SDA*. Organized 1920. Strong in Ukraine, Siberia, Central Asia. 834t(46814),W=60%.
Seventh-day Christians	c1935	I-Adv	.....	5	600	2,000	1,000	-2.73	Schism ex SDAs on doctrinal issues. Suppressed, now active underground.
Spiritual Christians (Whippers)	c1650	I-Ose	.....	2	200	2,000	500	-5.39	*Khlysty*. Vast spread under tsars; now smallest surviving Spiritual Christians.
Spirit-Wrestlers (Dukhobors)	c1650	m-Ort	.....	450	40,000	50,000	55,000	0.38	Emigrations to Canada, then returns. Villages: Caucasus, Georgia, Siberia, CAsia.
True Orthodox Christians	1944	I-Tru	.....	5,000	60,000	200,000	100,000	-2.73	*IPKh*. Vast underground network, immune to detection. No clergy. Across USSR since 1944.
True Orthodox Christian Wanderers	1956	I-Tru	.....	1,000	10,000	30,000	20,000	-1.61	*IPKh Stranniki*. First nationally-organized totally-clandestine body. Across USSR for 50 years.
True Orthodox Christians in Hiding	c1900	I-OBe	.....	100	1,500	5,000	4,000	-0.89	*Skrytniki*. Since 1926, network of Old Believer ascetic hermits in northern forests.
True Orthodox Church	1927	I-Tru	.....	2,000	100,000	20,000	210,000	9.86	*IPTS. Istinno-Pravoslavnaya Tserkov*. Remnants of underground church smashed by KGB.
Ukrainian Orthodox Ch: P Kiev	1990	I-Ukr	.....	200	500,500	–	1,100,000	20.00	Ukrainians resident in Russia, but loyal to schismatic P-Kiev.
Union of Apostolic Chs of Russia	c1930	I-3oW	.....	520	25,000	23,000	60,000	3.91	Oneness churches, member of AWCF. Viciously persecuted in 1930s. HQ St Petersburg. 150n.
Union of Ev Chr-Baptists of the RF	1944	P-Bap	T....	1,200	339,000	257,000	429,000	2.07	*Euro-Asiatic Federation of Ev Christians-Baptists* (until 1992, AUCECB). Many Pentecostals left.
Victory Christian Centers	1993	I-3vW	x....	100	20,000	–	50,000	50.00	In St Petersburg, Moscow, other cities. M=VFM(Tulsa, USA).
Other independent Baptist churches		I-Bap	.....	80	10,000	18,000	30,000	0.05	In about 20 loose geographical networks.
Other Orthodox dissenting bodies		I-Ose	.....	600	60,000	200,000	100,000	0.05	Total about 20 (see list below), underground, organized, nationwide.
Other pentecostal bodies		I-3pW	.....	1,500	60,000	60,000	120,000	0.05	Total over 40 underground bodies, including Ev Christians in the Apostles' Faith.
Other Protestant denominations		P-	.....	1,000	70,000	30,000	100,000	0.05	Total about 300 (see list below), before 1990 unregistered, now just tolerated by the state.
Other Orthodox churches		O-	....u	40	9,000	5,000	20,000	0.05	Small congregations of immigrants from Eastern European countries.
Doubly-affiliated		2-aff			-1,458,000	0	-2,321,719		Pentecostals and Evangelicals who are also baptized Orthodox.
Totals				**82,741**	**52,128,753**	**41,533,400**	**82,987,000**		

Churches, members, growth, 1900-2025	*Congs*	*Adults*	*Affiliated*	*G%*	*Total denominations*	*6 Megablocs:* O	R	A	P	I	m
Total churches, members, and denominations (mid-1900)	30,000	38,101,000	56,511,200	-0.44	22	4	1	1	7	8	1
Total churches, members, and denominations (mid-1970)	50,407	28,002,320	41,533,400	-0.44	226	15	1	1	143	64	2
Total churches, members, and denominations (mid-1990)	80,000	51,006,000	81,200,000	3.41	467	26	1	1	312	124	3
Total churches, members, and denominations (mid-1995)	82,741	52,128,753	82,987,000	0.44	467	26	1	1	312	124	3
Total churches, members, and denominations (mid-2000)	84,000	52,525,000	83,618,357	0.15	470	28	1	1	312	125	3
Total churches, members, and denominations (mid-2025)	120,000	59,706,000	95,050,000	0.51	935	45	1	1	380	500	8

Continued opposite

Country Table 2–concluded

NOTES ON TABLE ABOVE
NATIONAL COUNCILS (Column 4 5th letter).
K = Christian Interconfessional Consultative Committee of CIS & Baltic Countries (CICC).
= Ecumenical Conference of Russia.
u = legally-registered or permitted bodies, participants in 1969 Conference of Members of All Religions in the USSR for Co-operation and Peace among the Nations (Zagorsk), and/or 1952 Zagorsk peace conference, and/or foreign chaplaincy churches.
. = illegal unregistered bodies, underground, non-participants in 1969 Zagorsk conference.
OTHER ORTHODOX DISSENTING BODIES. Around the year 1900, Orthodox sects numbered several million adherents, reduced by incessant persecution to under half a million today, found in over 20 distinct bodies. In addition to those listed in the table above, they include: God's People, Churikovtsy (c1920, 4,000 near Leningrad), Fyodorovtsy, Imyaslavtsy (begun 1910 from Greece), Malevantsy (begun 1889), Old Israel (Stary Izrail), Postniki (Fasters), Righteous Brotherhood (Zion Tidings), Trezvenniki (Teetotallers) (begun 1900), True Orthodox Christians-Silent Ones (Molchalniki) (begun 1955; 70% women; vow of total silence), Undergrounders. Many clandestine underground groups are ideally suited to avoiding detection and even thrive on severe pressure from the regime. Many other bodies have been completely suppressed, including the Russian Greek Catholic Church (former Roman Catholic Uniates who seceded in 1917 with tsarist encouragement but were destroyed in 1923). Another schism, the Living Church movement of 1922 (also known as Church of the Regeneration, Free Labour Church, Renovationists, Revival Church, Union of Communities of the Ancient Apostolic Church, Union of Religious Communal Societies), controlled 50% of all Russia's parishes in 1923, 21% in 1927, declining further thereafter until its extinction in 1946.
OTHER PROTESTANT DENOMINATIONS. There are at least 30 smaller Protestant non-Pentecostal groups, mostly unregistered and operating underground, including the following: Blue Cross Society, Brethren of Holy Zion, Disciples of Christ, Holiness Baptists, Holiness Ev Christians, Old Christians, Sabbathizers, True and Free Seventh-day Adventists (1924 split; 3 groups: Caucasian, Western, Central; savagely persecuted), Zionists, et alii.

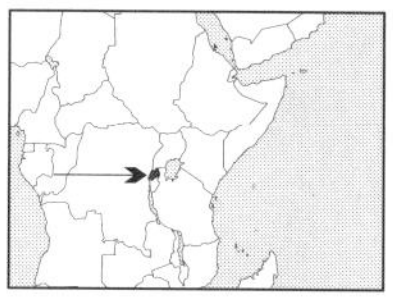

RWANDA

SECULAR DATA, AD 2000

STATE
Official name: Repubulika yu Rwanda/La République Rwandaise (The Rwandese Republic).
Short name: Rwanda. **Adjective of nationality:** Rwandese.
Flag: Red, yellow, and green bars with large "R" in the center.
Area: 26,338 sq. km. (10,169 sq. mi.).
Government: Transitional regime with one legislative body, since 1994 (c1500 kingdom, 1899 German colony, 1918 Belgian territory, 1961 Independence, 1973 military rule).
Legislature: Transitional National Assembly, 70 members.
Official language: Rwanda, French, English.
Monetary unit: 1 Rwanda franc (RF). **US$1=** RF 311.03.
Chief cities: KIGALI 301,448.
Political divisions: 10 provinces.
Armed forces: 55,000.

DEMOGRAPHY
Population: 7,733,000.
Population density: 293.6/sq. km. (760.4/sq. mi.).
Under 15 years: 3,509,000.
Growth rate p.a.: 2.11% (births 41.22, deaths 20.18).
Mortality: Infant, per 1,000: 115.7; **Maternal per 100,000:** 1,300.0.
Life expectancy: 41 (male 40, female 42).
Household size: 4.7. **Floor area per person, sq.m:** 10.0.
Major languages: Rwandan, Rundi.
Urban dwellers: 6.15%. **Urban growth rate p.a.:** 4.5%.
Labor force: 50%.

ETHNOLINGUISTIC PEOPLES
87.2% Hutu; 4.9% Rundi; 4.0% Tutsi; 1.8% Twa (Gesera) Pygmy; 1.0% Lingala (Zairian).

ECONOMY
National income p.a. per person: US$180; **per family:** US$846.

EDUCATION
Adult literacy: 60% (male 69%, female 51%). **Schools:** 1,724.
Universities: 3. **School enrolment:** female/male: 49%/51%.

HEALTH
Access to health services: 80%. **Access to safe water:** 66%.
Hospitals: 220 (9 beds per 10,000). **Doctors:** 272.
Blind: 7,000. **Deaf:** 460,400. **Murder rate:** 85.
Lepers: 80,000. **Underweight prevalence under 5:** 29%.

LITERATURE
New book titles p.a.: 39 (5 p.a. per million). **Periodicals:** 21.
Newspapers: 1 daily.

COMMUNICATION (per 1,000 people)
Phones: 2 (3% mobile). **Radios:** 78. **TV sets:** 2.
Daily newspaper circulation: <1. **Computers:** 8.

REFUGEES
Citizen refugees in other countries: 1,545,000.
Internal displacement: 500,000.

HUMAN LIFE AND LIBERTY (optimum condition=100.0%)
HDI: 18.7. **HSI:** 24.0. **HFI:** 15.0. **EFL:** 20.0.

Country Table 1. **Religious adherents in Rwanda, AD 1900-2025.**

Year	1900		1970		mid-1990		Annual change, 1990-2000				mid-1995		mid-2000		mid-2025	
Name	Adherents	%	Adherents	%	Adherents	%	Natural	Conversion	Total	Rate	Adherents	%	Adherents	%	Adherents	%
Christians	**100**	**0.0**	**2,283,600**	**61.3**	**5,696,444**	**81.5**	**60,833**	**9,219**	**70,052**	**1.17**	**4,308,000**	**81.9**	**6,396,966**	**82.7**	**10,787,000**	**86.8**
PROFESSION																
professing Christians	**100**	**0.0**	**2,283,600**	**61.3**	**5,696,444**	**81.5**	**60,833**	**9,219**	**70,052**	**1.17**	**4,308,000**	**81.9**	**6,396,966**	**82.7**	**10,787,000**	**86.8**
AFFILIATION																
unaffiliated Christians	0	0.0	95,580	2.6	55,944	0.8	597	-177	420	0.73	58,407	1.1	60,144	0.8	63,000	0.5
affiliated Christians	**100**	**0.0**	**2,188,020**	**58.7**	**5,640,500**	**80.7**	**60,235**	**9,397**	**69,632**	**1.17**	**4,249,593**	**80.8**	**6,336,822**	**82.0**	**10,724,000**	**86.3**
Roman Catholics	100	0.0	1,684,095	45.2	3,526,000	50.5	37,647	3,953	41,600	1.12	3,526,374	67.1	3,942,000	51.0	6,750,000	54.3
Protestants	0	0.0	328,926	8.8	1,415,000	20.3	15,108	5,374	20,482	1.36	1,669,970	31.8	1,619,822	21.0	2,710,000	21.8
Anglicans	0	0.0	161,899	4.3	600,000	8.6	6,406	-6,406	0	0.00	805,000	15.3	600,000	7.8	1,000,000	8.1
Independents	0	0.0	12,500	0.3	90,000	1.3	961	6,539	7,500	6.25	236,293	4.5	165,000	2.1	255,000	2.1
Marginal Christians	0	0.0	100	0.0	8,000	0.1	85	-85	0	0.00	8,000	0.2	8,000	0.1	5,000	0.0
Orthodox	0	0.0	500	0.0	1,500	0.0	16	34	50	2.92	1,500	0.0	2,000	0.0	4,000	0.0
disaffiliated	0	0.0	0	0.0	0	0.0	0	0	0	0.00	-1,997,544	-38.0	0	0.0	0	0.0
Trans-megabloc groupings																
Evangelicals	0	0.0	220,000	5.9	1,112,000	15.9	11,873	27,427	39,300	3.07	1,288,514	24.5	1,505,000	19.5	2,900,000	23.3
Pentecostals/Charismatics	0	0.0	86,000	2.3	1,048,000	15.0	11,189	7,711	18,900	1.67	1,149,751	21.9	1,237,000	16.0	2,235,000	18.0
Great Commission Christians	**100**	**0.0**	**149,000**	**4.0**	**792,000**	**11.3**	**8,456**	**8,406**	**16,862**	**1.95**	**611,000**	**11.6**	**960,617**	**12.4**	**1,800,000**	**14.5**
Ethnoreligionists	1,067,900	99.8	1,125,900	30.2	710,000	10.2	7,581	-9,074	-1,493	-0.21	520,200	9.9	695,074	9.0	600,000	4.8
Muslims	2,000	0.2	312,000	8.4	556,056	8.0	5,937	-234	5,703	0.98	412,130	7.8	613,083	7.9	980,000	7.9
Baha'is	0	0.0	5,500	0.2	12,500	0.2	133	38	171	1.29	9,500	0.2	14,211	0.2	30,000	0.2
Hindus	0	0.0	1,000	0.0	10,000	0.1	107	53	160	1.50	7,700	0.2	11,600	0.2	25,000	0.2
Nonreligious	0	0.0	0	0.0	2,000	0.0	21	-2	19	0.92	1,470	0.0	2,192	0.0	5,000	0.0
World A (unevangelized persons)	1,067,860	99.8	372,844	10.0	125,766	1.8	1,343	-5,084	-3,741	-3.47	84,137	1.6	85,063	1.1	124,270	1.0
World B (evangelized non-Christians)	2,040	0.2	1,072,004	28.7	1,164,790	16.7	12,436	-4,135	8,301	0.72	866,427	16.5	1,250,971	16.2	1,515,730	12.2
World C (Christians)	100	0.0	2,283,600	61.3	5,696,444	81.5	60,833	9,219	70,052	1.17	4,308,000	81.9	6,396,966	82.7	10,787,000	86.8
Country's population	**1,070,000**	**100.0**	**3,728,449**	**100.0**	**6,987,000**	**100.0**	**74,612**	**0**	**74,612**	**1.02**	**5,258,565**	**100.0**	**7,733,000**	**100.0**	**12,427,000**	**100.0**

COLUMNS, ROWS.
For meanings and definitions, see Codebook (Part 3). Note that, by definition, total 'Christians' = professing + crypto-Christians, which also = affiliated + unaffiliated Christians, and also = Great Commission Christians + latent Christians. Percentages may not always total exactly, due to rounding.

CENSUSES.
No religion question was asked until introduced in 1970. **5.XI.1970:** 47.4% Roman Catholics, 29.4% ethnoreligionists and others, 14.8% Protestants and Anglicans, 8.5% Muslims.

NOTES ON RELIGIONS
BAHA'IS. Rapid growth to 37 local spiritual assemblies by 1973, assisted by immigrant Ugandan Baha'is; then a plateau period of non-growth up to the 43 LSAs in 1993; then virtual obliteration in the massacres of 1994, recovery by 1995, and reorganized existence by 1998.
DISAFFILIATED. This negative number refers directly in the case of Rwanda to the 1994 genocide of around 700,000 affiliated church members and a similar number who fled the country as permanent refugees abroad.
ETHNORELIGIONISTS. Animists (also called Imanists or worshippers of the supreme being Imana), including the Twa pygmies (Gesera; 93,000), who are 90% animist. There is also the ancestor cult; a public initiation rite sacred to the hero Ryangombe king of the Imandwa (30 powerful spirits); and the cult of Nyabingi (a female spirit).
INDEPENDENTS. In 2 denomination in 1995 (see Table 2).
MUSLIMS. In 1995, Asian (Indo-Pakistani), Arab and Swahili merchants numbered 28,000. There are also many Africans (all Sunnis), Rwandese, also Ugandans, Tanzanians, Sudanese and others. Swahili is spoken in Arab and Arab-influenced town districts. There has been a steady stream of conversions of Rwandese to Islam over the years.
PENTECOSTALS/CHARISMATICS. Totals (mid-1975): 150 involved adults, in majority Rwandans, with many religious personnel; total Catholic Charismatic community including children, 400, increasing rapidly. (1991): 20,000 regular attenders in 705 weekly prayer groups, rising by 1993 to over 1,000 groups. Though large numbers of leaders were murdered in the 1994 genocide, by 1996 all 9 Catholic dioceses again had an organized CCR structure with parish prayer groups.

Country status. Rwanda is a small landlocked country just south of the equator in east central Africa bordering Zaire, Burundi, Tanzania, and Uganda. Its chief exports are agricultural products including coffee and tea. Waves of genocide have swept the country resulting in well over one million killings since independence in 1962 culminating in the Tutsi genocide of 1994.

HUMAN LIFE AND LIBERTY

Human need and development. The 2 most important facts about Rwanda are that it has one of the highest birth rates in the world, and it has no exploitable natural resources. These 2 facts explain why it is one of the poorest of African countries. The GNP per capita is $180, life expectancy is 41 and nearly half the population is illiterate. The vast majority of the people are engaged in subsistence agriculture, and all available land is used for either crops or pasture. The national diet is inadequate, running heavily to starch and deficient in fats and proteins. The continuing strife between the majority Hutu and the minority (although historically dominant) Tutsis has depressed the country even further and made it an economic basketcase. The bloodshed and the massive dislocations of the extended civil war may undo years of developmental work by Western and Christian agencies.

Human rights and freedoms. Like neighboring Burundi, Rwanda is subject to periodical outbursts of ethnic violence. The Tutsis, the principal minority ethnic group, have been engaged for many years in an armed struggle led by the Rwandan Patriotic Front (RPF). Although an uneasy truce was signed between the government and the rebels in 1992, violence erupted again in 1993 following the assassination of Juvenal Habyarimana, the popular Hutu president by Tutsi malcontents. There are unsubstantiated reports of the existence of death squads with possible links to the president. Hundreds of Rwandans have lost their

Great Commission Instrument Panel: status of Rwanda (for explanation see start of Part 4)

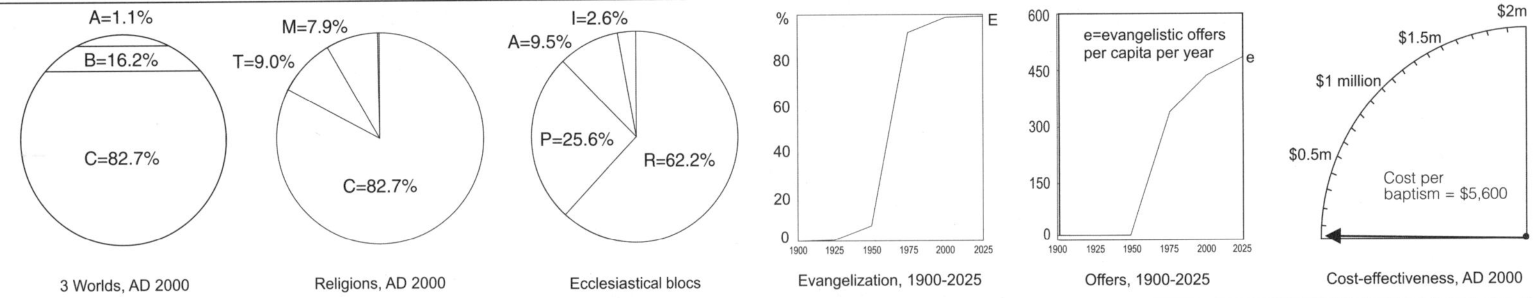

lives in terrorist incidents, involving land mine and bomb explosions and incidents of armed robbery involving grenades. Many observers believe that the so-called robberies are staged by the government as means of intimidation. Observers also suspect the military of involvement in land mine explosions in areas outside the war zone. Illegal detentions are common, and about 80% of the prisoners in Kigali were found to be illegally detained. The judicial system is susceptible to government influence and manipulation. Curbs on freedom of the press notwithstanding, there is a flourishing and independent private press. The government passed a new press law in 1991 providing stiff penalties for insulting the president. A number of journalists have suffered imprisonment for offending the government. Historically, the Tutsis have been singled out as targets for discrimination. An ethnic quota system has limited Tutsi access to education and employment. The Twa or Batwa of Pygmy origin are treated as second class citizens and exist on the margins of society. Women face serious de facto cultural and legal discrimination, and receive less schooling and less pay and fewer rights to property.

The final genocide of 1994 involved government-organized Hutu killing squads slaughtering around 700,000 Tutsis with some Hutu sympathizers. It was the most visible and horrific such genocide in history, being observed daily by the rest of the world.

Human environment. Rwanda's environmental problems are related to its overpopulation which has placed enormous strains on its agricultural land and encouraged deforestation as well as hunting and poaching in national parks.

NON-CHRISTIAN RELIGIONS

African traditional religions are practiced by a minority of the Hutu and Tutsi and the majority of the Twa, less than 10% of the latter having become Christian. Among the Banyarwanda, God is known as Imana. He is basically good but occasionally creates unsuccessfully, at which times he is identified as Ruremakwaci. The spirits of the dead (Bazimu) inhabit the underworld ruled by Nyamuzinda. The ancestral cult is aimed at appeasing the Bazimu who are mostly conceived of as malevolent. A particularly important group owes allegiance to Ryangombe who was once human. After death, Ryangombe's initiates (Imandwa) are believed to inhabit a paradise called Karisimbi. Ryangombe is Imana's servant and the intermediary between his initiates and God. His living followers are protected from harm by the deceased Imandwa. A more recent spirit possession cult is that of the female deity Nyabingi, who while living was a Karagwe queen named Kitami.

Islam has long been present in several small Indo-Pakistani, Arab, and Swahili merchant communities, numbering around 40,000 by 1995, mostly in the cities of Kigali and Butare. There are also large numbers of Rwandese Muslims, also Ugandans, Tanzanians, Sudanese and others, almost all Sunnis.

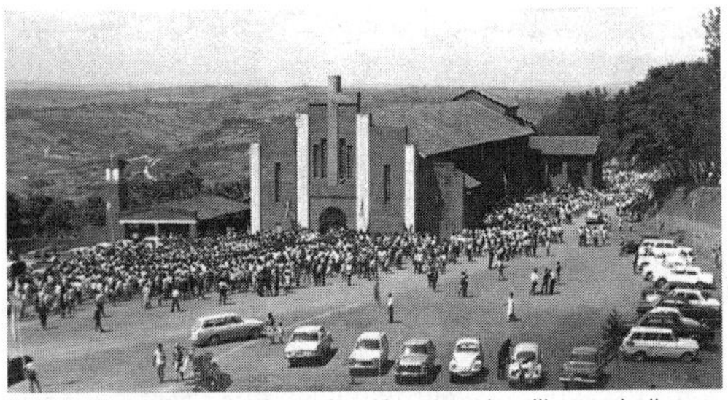

Eglise Catholique au Rwanda. Vast crowds still attend all open churches.

CHRISTIANITY

CATHOLIC CHURCH. While Fathers from the vicariate of Victoria Nyanza visited Rwanda as early as 1889, the first permanent missions were not established until 1900. In 1912, the vicariate of the Kivu was erected including Rwanda and Burundi (then Urundi), and 10 years later (1922) Rwanda became a vicariate in its own right. The first Rwanda priests were ordained in 1917. The Catholic Church grew rapidly during the 1930s and by the beginning of World War II had 300,000 members. In 1952, the first Rwanda bishop was consecrated, with the archdiocese of Kabgayi formed in 1959.

The success of the Catholic Church's missionary endeavor is evident in the fact that today more than half the population claims to be Catholic. The church's strength is its rural parish structure composed of branch establishments (chapels, schools) which are divided into elementary groups of Christians (inama). Each group consists of approximately 30 families and elects its own chief (mukuru) who, together with the catechists, form a liaison between the families and the visiting priest.

The Holy See has diplomatic relations with Rwanda and in AD 2000 is represented to government and the Catholic hierarchy by a nuncio residing in Kigali.

Eglise Catholique au Rwanda. *Lower.* Packed Sunday mass in Kigali, Archdiocese of Kigali. *Top.* A youth reads Sunday Epistle, in Rutongo church.

PROTESTANT CHURCHES. The first Protestants were Lutherans of the Bethel Mission who crossed the border from Tanzania in 1907 and built a station prior to World War I. All German missionaries were expelled in May 1916, and Belgium refused to allow them to return after the war. American Adventists came in 1919 although they were unable to establish themselves prior to 1921. Nevertheless, progress was rapid thereafter, and the Adventist community is now third in size behind the Catholic Church and Anglicans.

In 1921, the Belgian Society of Protestant Missions in the Congo, the missionary arm of the Reformed Church of Belgium, took over responsibility for part of the work of the Bethel Mission, helping to form the Presbyterian Church of Rwanda which became autonomous in 1959. Other Protestant groups in the pre-World War II period were American Free Methodists in 1935, Danish Baptists in 1938, and Swedish Pentecostals in 1940. Newer missions have been established by the Friends, Brethren, and Conservative Baptists since 1960, but all remain small. Except for the Adventists who are found in all parts of the country, Protestantism is for the most part characterized by a regional orientation: Free Methodists in southwest Rwanda, Pentecostals near Gisenyi, Baptists south of Butare, and Presbyterians near Kigali.

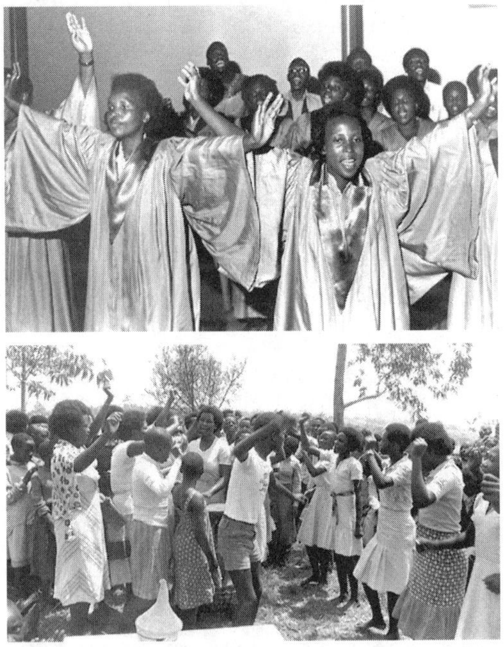

Protestants. *Top.* Worship at Presbyterian church in Kigali. *Lower.* Union des Eglises Baptistes.

ANGLICAN CHURCH. In 1920, an extensive medical and evangelistic program was begun by the Rwanda Mission (CMS), of Low Church Evangelical background. Together with the indigenous Revival Movement (Balokole, or Saved Ones) since 1927, CMS has contributed towards making the Anglican church the second largest Christian community in the country. The Rwanda church is part of the Church of the Province of Burundi, Rwanda, and Zaire, which had 7 dioceses in 1980.

Renewal movements. In the 1990s the Pentecostal/Charismatic Renewal continued to spread rapidly across most older churches, and numbered over 1,237,000 adherents (of whom 51% Pentecostals, 41% Charismatics, and 8% Independents).

Indigenous missions. Roman Catholics have been actively sending missionaries for much of the 20th century. Most of these serve in surrounding African countries.

Country summary. **Worlds A, B, C by ethnolinguistic peoples, cities, and major civil divisions in Rwanda.**

	PEOPLES							CITIES							CIVIL DIVISIONS						
World	Num	Pop 2000	C%	Christians	E%	U%	Unevangelized	Num	Pop 2000	C%	Christians	E%	U%	Unevangelized	Num	Pop 2000	C%	Christians	E%	U%	Unevangelized
A	3	41,758	0.34	142	45	55	23,102	0	0	0.00	0	0	0	0	0	0	0.00	0	0	0	0
B	1	139,196	7.60	10,579	64	36	50,667	0	0	0.00	0	0	0	0	0	0	0.00	0	0	0	0
C	9	7,552,171	83.77	6,326,100	100	0	14,616	1	301,448	80.00	241,158	98	2	6,270	10	7,733,126	81.94	6,336,822	99	1	88,386
Total	**13**	**7,733,125**	**81.94**	**6,336,821**	**99**	**1**	**88,385**	**1**	**301,448**	**80.00**	**241,158**	**98**	**2**	**6,270**	**10**	**7,733,126**	**81.94**	**6,336,822**	**99**	**1**	**88,386**

CHURCH AND STATE.

The constitution of Nov. 24, 1962, began in its Preamble: 'The National Assembly, Entrusting in Almighty God . . .' In Title 1, Article 3, the state declares that 'It respects all religions'. The constitution has since been suspended under military rule; but while awaiting the promulgation of a new one, Articles 37-39 from 1962 relating to religion, remain in vigor. The preamble to the 1962 constitution invokes confidence in the All-Powerfulness of God. Article 37 guarantees to all liberty of conscience, free profession, and practice of religion. Article 38 permits the establishment of religious institutions and communities who administer their affairs autonomously. Communist propaganda and activity are forbidden in Article 39.

Friction regarding education, relations between the churches and the state remains. The Catholic Church is very strong, and the churches play an important role in social action. The official University of Butare was created in 1964, served by Canadian Dominican priests.

East African Revival. Interpreters preach in 4 languages, alternately, to vast crowds up to 50,000 in number.

BROADCASTING AND MEDIA.

IBRA programming can be heard on Radio Rwanda (Kinyarwanda, French). Rwanda is a member of UNDA and a 30 minute Catholic religious program is broadcast each week.

Some 2.7 million have seen the 'Jesus' Film, mainly through film team presentations, with 675,000 responding with a decision for Christ.

INTERDENOMINATIONAL ORGANIZATIONS

The Protestant Council of Rwanda was established in 1935. Anglicans, Baptists, Free Methodists, and Presbyterians, are full members, with the following maintaining an associate member status: Friends, Pentecostals, and the Taize Community. Adventists cooperate in Bible translation work. The brothers of Taize and Benedictine priests of Gihindamuyaga form the Ecumenical Fraternity of Kigali which organizes regular meetings between Catholics, Anglicans, and Protestants with SDAs as observers.

FUTURE TRENDS AND PROSPECTS

Christianity is expected to once again make substantial gains with the continued precipitous drop of ethnoreligionists from 99.8% in 1900 to less than 5% by 2025. Christian profession could reach 87% by 2025.

Christianity would then grow to over 90% of the population before the middle of the 21st century. Muslims would likely remain between 8-9%.

BIBLIOGRAPHY

Annuaire ecclésiastique, Burundi et Rwanda, 1970–1971. Bujumbura, Burundi: SECOREB, 1970. (Roman Catholic).

Aperçu historique de l'évangélisation du Rwanda. F. Muvara. Kigali, Rwanda: Pallotti Presse, 1990. 54p.

Banyarwanda et Barundi. R. Bourgeois. Brussels: Institut Royal Colonial Belge, 1954–58. 4 vols. (Vol.1 treats 'ethnology,' vol. 2 'custom,' and vol. 3 'religion and magic').

Breath of life: the story of the Ruanda Mission. P. St. John. London: Norfolk Press, 1971. 238p.

Burundi et Rwanda, 1964–1968: plan quinquennal de développement. Usumbura, Burundi: COREB, 1963. 160p.

Ce don que nous avons reçu: histoire de l'Eglise presbytérienne au Rwanda (1907–1982). M. Twagirayesu & J. van Butselaar (eds). Kigali, Rwanda: L'Eglise, 1982. 191p.

Christianity in independent Africa. E. Fasholé-Luke (ed). London: Rex Collings, 1978. 630p. (Chapter on Roman Catholic Church in Rwanda by I. Linden).

'Christianity in Rwanda with special emphasis on the Seventh–day Adventist church.' A. M. Long. M.A. thesis, Andrews University, Barrien Springs, MI, 1973. 172p.

Church and revolution in Rwanda. I. Linden & J. Linden. London: E. J. Brill, 1977. 320p.

'De la religion subie au modernisme refusé: théophagie, ancêtres clandestins et résistance populaire au Rwandais,' C. Vidal, *Archives de sciences sociales des religions*, 35 (1974), 63–90.

Eglise et développement: inventaire commenté de la contribution de l'Eglise au développement économique et social au Rwanda et au Burundi. W. Hilgers. Bujumbura, Burundi: Centre de recherches et d'animation sociale, [1967]. 109p.

Imana et le culte des Mânes au Rwanda. M. Pauwels. Brussels: Académie Royale des Sciences Coloniales, 1958. 256p.

'Indifférence religieuse et neo–paganisme au Ruanda,' S. Bushayija, *Rythmes du monde*, 9, 1 (1961), 58–67.

La christianisation du Rwanda (1900–1945): méthode missionnaire et politique selon Mgr. Léon Classe. P. Rutayisire. [Fribourg]: Editions Universitaires Fribourg Suisse, 1987. 571p.

La philosophie bantu–rwandaise de l'être. A. Kagame. Brussels: Académie Royale des Sciences Coloniales, 1956.

Le catechumenat au Rwanda de 1900 à nos jours. J. van der Meersch. *Etude historique et pastorale.* Kigali: Pallotti-Presse, 1993. 244p.

Le catholicisme et la société rwandaise: 1900–1962. J. Kalibwami. Paris: Présence africaine, 1991. 597p.

'Le christianisme et la religion traditionelle au Rwanda.' L. J. Ndandali. M.A. thesis, Fuller Theological Seminary, Pasadena, CA, 1975. 232p.

'Le culte de Nyabingi (Rwanda),' M. Pauwels, *Anthropos* (Freiburg), 46, 3-4 (1951), 337–57.

Le défi des pauvres: de la fonction diaconale de l'eglise au Rwanda. C. M. Overdulve. Butare, Rwanda: Faculté de théologie protestante, 1991. 210p.

L'église du Rwanda vingt ans après le Concile Vatican II. Conférence Episcopale du Rwanda. [Kigali]: Pallotti-Presse, [1987]. 336p.

'Les peuples de la République démocratique du Congo, du Rwanda et du Burundi,' A. Dorsinfang-Smets, in *Ethnologie régionale*, p.566–661, vol. 1. J. Poirier (ed). Paris: Gallimard, 1972.

'L'idée de Dieu au Rwanda préchrétien.' F. Murekezi. Universite Catholique de Louvain, 1974. 225p.

L'Islam et les 'Swahili' au Rwanda. J. H. Kagabo. Paris: Editions de l'Ecole des Hautes Etudes en Sciences Sociales, 1988. 274p.

'Muslims in Rwanda: a status report,' O. H. Kasule, *Journal of the Institute of Muslim Minority Affairs*, 4, 1-2 (1982), 133–44.

'Mythe et société féodale: le culte de Kubandwa dans le Rwanda traditionnel,' L. de Heusch, *Archives de sociologie des religions*, 9, 18 (1964), 133–46.

Nyabingi: the social history of an African divinity. J. Freedman. Tervuren, Belgium: Musée Royal de l'Afrique Centrale, 1984. 119p.

Only one weapon: facing difficulty and danger with Christ in troubled Rwanda. H. W. Adeney. London: Ruanda Mission of the Church Missionary Society, 1963. 51p.

Petite histoire de l'Église Catholique au Rwanda. D. Nothomb. Kabgayi [Gitarama]: Imprimerie de l'Archidiocèse de Kabgayi, 1962. 190p.

Road to revival: the story of the Ruanda Mission. A. C. S. Smith. London: Church Missionary Society, 1946. 116p.

Rwanda. R. Fegley. *World bibliographical series*, vol. 154. Oxford, UK: CLIO Press, 1993. 200p. (See especially 'Religion and philosophy,' p.50-60).

'Rwanda: strength and weakness of the centre of Africa,' *Pro Mundi Vita* (Brussels), 6 (1965).

Rwandische Zivilisation und christlich–koloniale Herrschaft. H. Schürings. Frankfurt: Verlag für Interkulturelle Kommunikation, [1992]. 458p.

Société, culture et histoire du Rwanda: encyclopédie bibliographique 1863–1980/87. M. d'Hertefelt & D. de Lame. Tervuren, Belgium: Musée Royal de l'Afrique Centrale, 1987. 2 vols. (Includes entries on religion).

The angels have left us: the Rwanda tragedy and the churches. H. McCullum. *Risk book series*, no. 66. Geneva: WCC Publications, [1995]. 139p.

The Church of Uganda, Rwanda and Burundi: survey on administration and finance of the Church in Uganda. J. Bikangaga. Kampala, Uganda: Uganda Bookshop, 1969. 74p.

'The doctrine of God in Ruanda–Urundi,' R. Guillebaud, in *African ideas of God: a symposium*, p.180–200. E. Smith (ed). London: Edinburgh House Press, 1950.

'The kingdom of Ruanda,' J. J. Maquet, in *African worlds*, p.164–89. D. Forde (ed). London: Oxford, 1954.

Théologie et pastorale au Rwanda et au Burundi, 7, 1 (1967), 1–60.

Une réflexion théologique sur les données de la religion traditionnelle du Rwanda et du Burundi. B. Muzungu. , [1975]. 160p.

Country Table 2. **Organized churches and denominations in Rwanda.**

Official name (bold type = church with over 10% of affiliated) 1	*Begun* 2	*Type* 3	*Counc* 4	*Congs* 5	*Adults* 6	*Affiliated 1970* 7	*Affiliated 1995* 8	*G%* 9	*Names, notes, and other statistics* (see Codebook, Part 3) 10
Assemblée des Frères	1961	P-CBr	.....	3	128	100	320	4.76	*Assembly of Brethren, Open Brethren.* From Zaire via Burundi; 1961 in Kigali. 1k.
Assoc des Eglises Baptistes du R	c1965	I-Bap	xF...	67	31,700	2,000	60,000	14.57	*Assoc of Baptist Chs of Rwanda.* Former M=Conservative Baptist FMS(USA). 32m,2f,354Y.
Assoc des Eglises de Pentecôte du R	1940	P-Pe2	Z...k	2,141	331,000	85,000	572,000	7.92	*ADEPR. Chs of Pentecost.* M=SFM(Sweden). 91% Hutu. 45n,9x,369m,W=90%,7515Y,2225z.
Eglise Adventiste du Septième Jour	1919	P-Adv	x...	686	188,202	200,000	480,000	3.56	*Seventh-day Adv, N,E,S,W, Rwanda Fields.* 132nx,17f,1H,2h,1s,806t(185000),12688Y.
Eglise Anglicane du Rwanda	1920	A-Low	AwAVK	2,000	380,000	161,899	805,000	6.63	*EAR. Province of Rwanda*, with 9 Dioceses. M=RCMS(UK).
Eglise Catholique au Rwanda:	1889	R-Lat	P.S.P	277	1,939,000	1,684,095	3,526,374	3.00	C=6+8+29. (1970) 142n,245x, 766w,110587Yy. (1990) 366n 175x 466m 1245w 157358Yy
M Kigali	1976	R-Lat	Ps	18	349,000	–	635,451	5.26	First erected 1976, out of M Kabgayi. 44n 65x 115m 265w 30981Yy
D Butare (Astrida)	1961	R-Lat	Ps	137	288,000	487,191	522,668	0.28	Intellectual and religious hub. M=WF,OSB. 1s. 64n 40x 151m 342w 19302Yy
D Byumba	1981	R-Lat	Ps	11	183,000	–	333,485	7.14	Hutus are largely Francophone. 20n 17x 31m 74w 13014Yy
D Cyangugu	1981	R-Lat	Ps	9	140,000	–	254,986	7.14	Tutsis are largely Anglophone. 29n 11x 29m 94w 11977Yy
D Gikongoro	1992	R-Lat	Ps	37	121,000	–	219,613	33.33	Population is 27% Catholic. 22n 0x 0m 30w 8795Yy
D Kabgayi	1922	R-Lat	Ps	24	278,000	391,533	504,902	1.02	Metropolitan till 1976. 80% Hutu, 19% Tutsi. M=WF. 68n 9x 49m 173w 20299Yy
D Kibungo	1968	R-Lat	Ps	11	151,000	131,364	273,822	2.98	Formed out of M Kabgayi. M=WF. 64 alien RCs. 30n 7x 28m 78w 14800Yy
D Nyundo	1952	R-Lat	Ps	19	251,000	347,056	457,447	1.11	In west. M=WF. 383 expatriate Catholics. 1s. 62n 3x 28m 117w 25290Yy
D Ruhengeri	1960	R-Lat	Ps	11	178,000	326,951	324,000	-0.04	Densely populated. 90% Hutu, 9% Tutsi. M=WF. 27n 23x 35m 72w 12900Yy
Eglise de Dieu	1988	P-Pe3	.....	50	4,665	–	10,400	14.29	Church of God. M=CoG(Cleveland).
Eglise de Dieu de Prophétie	c1975	P-Pe3	.....	10	500	–	1,250	5.00	Church of God of Prophecy. M=CGP.
Eglise Ev Calvaire d'Afrique du R	1971	I-3pA	.....	50	1,000	400	3,000	4.17	*Calvary Ev Ch of Africa in Rwanda.* Ev Fraternity. M=PEFA,AIM (Kenya). HQ Gisenyi. 4n.
Eglise Kimbanguiste	c1965	I-3pA	xwi..	100	5,000	100	10,000	20.23	*Ch of Christ on Earth through the Prophet Simon Kimbangu.*
Eglise Libre Méthodiste au Rwanda	1935	I-Hol	VF..K	38	63,500	10,000	120,000	10.45	*ELMR. Free Methodist Ch.* M=FMC(USA). 11n,3x,94m,15f,1H,3h,1s,62t(2933),747Y.
Eglise Neo-Apostolique	c1980	I-3aX	x....	140	15,000	–	23,293	6.67	*NAC/NAK.* M=Neuapostolische Kirche. HQ Zurich (Switzerland).
Eglise Orth (AD Afrique Centrale)	1958	O-Gre	Cw...	2	900	500	1,500	4.49	*Orthodox Ch.* Parish of Bujumbura. Under Greek P Alexandria. Mostly Greeks.
Eglise Presbytérienne au Rwanda	1907	P-Ref	R.A.K	121	264,000	21,293	500,000	13.46	*EPR. Presb Ch.* M=BCMC(Belgium),RCN(Neth). A=1959. 95% Hutu, 5% Tutsi. 16n,1H,2h,1u.
Mission Evangélique des Amis	c1950	P-Qua	QF..k	12	1,100	500	2,000	5.70	M=Friends Africa Gospel Mission(Kansas YM,USA). In Burundi Quarterly Meeting.
Témoins de Jéhovah	c1965	m-Jeh	x....	40	2,480	100	8,000	19.16	*Jehovah's Witnesses.* In 1973, 5,150 hours of witnessing. (1975) 5Y. (1995) 923Y.
Union des Eglises Baptistes au Rwanda	1938	P-Bap	T.A.K	486	35,572	21,033	100,000	6.43	*UEBR.* M=Danish,Finnish BMs,FMB-SBC(USA). 11n,2x,94m,3893Y.
Other indigenous charismatic chs	1980	I-3cA	.....	100	10,000	–	20,000	6.67	Eglise Vivante; Restoration Church; Eglise Pentecôste Elim du R (EPER).

Continued overleaf

Country Table 2–concluded

Official name (bold type = church with over 10% of affiliated) 1	Begun 2	Type 3	Counc 4	Congs 5	Adults 6	Affiliated 1970 7	Affiliated 1995 8	G% 9	Names, notes, and other statistics (see Codebook, Part 3) 10
Other Protestant groups		P-	.....	30	2,000	1,000	4,000	0.05	Total over 20 smaller bodies.
Disaffiliated		X-Aff			-1,047,000	0	-1,997,544		Huge numbers lost in mass killings, genocide, refugee exodus.
Totals				**6,353**	**2,228,747**	**2,188,020**	**4,249,593**		

Churches, members, growth, 1900-2025	*Congs*	*Adults*	*Affiliated*	*G%*	*Total denominations*	*6 Megablocs:* O	R	A	P	I	m
Total churches, members, and denominations (mid-1900)	2	52	100	15.35	1	0	1	0	0	0	0
Total churches, members, and denominations (mid-1970)	2,633	1,148,659	2,188,020	15.35	26	1	1	1	18	4	1
Total churches, members, and denominations (mid-1990)	6,500	2,958,000	5,640,500	4.85	44	1	1	1	34	6	1
Total churches, members, and denominations (mid-1995)	6,353	2,228,747	4,249,593	-5.51	44	1	1	1	34	6	1
Total churches, members, and denominations (mid-2000)	7,000	3,323,000	6,336,822	8.32	44	1	1	1	34	6	1
Total churches, members, and denominations (mid-2025)	10,000	5,623,000	10,724,000	2.13	119	2	1	1	50	60	5

NOTES ON TABLE ABOVE
NATIONAL COUNCILS (Column 4, 5th letter).
E = Alliance Evangélique du Rwanda (AER).
K = Conseil Protestant du Rwanda (CPR) (Protestant Council of Rwanda).
k = associate member of CPR.
P = Conférence des Ordinaires du Rwanda et du Burundi (COREB) (Bishops' Conference of Rwanda & Burundi).

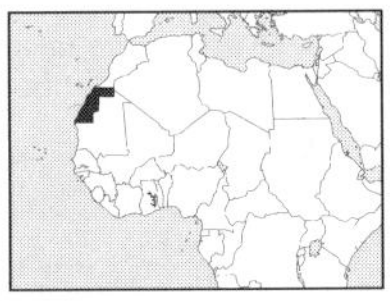

SAHARA

SECULAR DATA, AD 2000

STATE
Official name: Al-Jumhuriyah as-Sahra al-Arabiyah ad-Dimuqratiyah (The Sahara Arab Democratic Republic).
Short name: Sahara. **Adjective of nationality:** Saharan.
Flag: Stripes of green, white, and black, with red triangle on hoist, and red crescent and star on white band.
Area: 266,769 sq. km. (102,680 sq. mi.).
Government: (1) Socialist republic
(Polisario Front, supported by Algeria, Communist nations and leftist African countries). (2) Part of Morocco and Mauritania, annexed 1976 (1860).
Spanish colony of Spanish West Africa, 1958
province of Spanish Sahara, 1976 Independent.
Legislature: Moroccan Provincial government.
Official language: Arabic.
Monetary unit: 1 Moroccan dirham (DH) = 100 Moroccan francs.
US$1= DH 9.28.
Chief cities: EL AAIUN (Laayoun) 215,627.
Political divisions: 1 province.
Armed forces: 2,000.

DEMOGRAPHY
Population: 293,000.
Population density: 1.1/sq. km. (2.8/sq. mi.).
Under 15 years: 111,000.
Growth rate p.a.: 3.04% (births 28.57, deaths 7.55).
Mortality: Infant, per 1,000: 53.6; **Maternal per 100,000:** 800.0.
Life expectancy: 64 (male 62, female 66).
Household size: 5.0. **Floor area per person, sq.m:** 3.0.
Major languages: Arabic (Hassaniyah), Spanish.
Urban dwellers: 95.39%. **Urban growth rate p.a.:** 2.9%.
Labor force: 30%.

ETHNOLINGUISTIC PEOPLES
41.0% Delim Bedouin (Sahrawi); 20.0% Tekna Berber (Sahrawi); 13.0% Regeibat; 9.0% Moor (White, Black); 6.0% Izarguien.

ECONOMY
National income p.a. per person: US$207; **per family:** US$1,039.

EDUCATION
Adult literacy: 10% (male 15%, female 5%). **Schools:** 45.
Universities: 1. **School enrolment:** female/male: 30%/30%.

HEALTH
Access to health services: 25%. **Access to safe water:** 40%.
Hospitals: 2 (10 beds per 10,000). **Doctors:** 50.
Blind: 1,000. **Deaf:** 17,400. **Murder rate:** 25.
Lepers: 100.

LITERATURE
New book titles p.a.: 1 (4 p.a. per million). **Periodicals:** 1.
Newspapers: 1 daily.

COMMUNICATION (per 1,000 people)
Phones: 10 (20% mobile). **Radios:** 50. **TV sets:** 10.
Daily newspaper circulation: 1. **Computers:** 1.

REFUGEES
Citizen refugees in other countries: 80,000.

HUMAN LIFE AND LIBERTY (optimum condition=100.0%)
HDI: 24.2. **HSI:** 5.0. **HFI:** 5.0. **EFL:** 5.0.

Country Table 1. **Religious adherents in Sahara, AD 1900-2025.**

Year	1900		1970		mid-1990		Annual change, 1990-2000				mid-1995		mid-2000		mid-2025	
Name	Adherents	%	Adherents	%	Adherents	%	Natural	Conversion	Total	Rate	Adherents	%	Adherents	%	Adherents	%
Muslims	14,900	99.3	44,700	58.5	204,610	99.3	8,678	21	8,699	3.61	246,440	99.5	291,602	99.5	466,900	99.3
Nonreligious	0	0.0	0	0.0	600	0.3	25	3	28	3.93	750	0.3	882	0.3	1,800	0.4
Christians	**100**	**0.7**	**31,600**	**41.4**	**460**	**0.2**	**19**	**-16**	**3**	**0.57**	**460**	**0.2**	**487**	**0.2**	**700**	**0.2**
PROFESSION																
crypto-Christians	0	0.0	0	0.0	350	0.2	15	-10	5	1.34	380	0.2	400	0.1	650	0.1
professing Christians	**100**	**0.7**	**31,600**	**41.4**	**110**	**0.1**	**5**	**-7**	**-2**	**-2.32**	**80**	**0.0**	**87**	**0.0**	**50**	**0.0**
AFFILIATION																
unaffiliated Christians	0	0.0	1,600	2.1	0	0.0	0	0	0	0.00	0	0.0	0	0.0	0	0.0
affiliated Christians	**100**	**0.7**	**30,000**	**39.3**	**460**	**0.2**	**19**	**-16**	**3**	**0.57**	**460**	**0.2**	**487**	**0.2**	**700**	**0.2**
Independents	0	0.0	0	0.0	260	0.1	11	-2	9	2.93	300	0.1	347	0.1	600	0.1
Roman Catholics	100	0.7	30,000	39.3	200	0.1	8	-14	-6	-3.50	160	0.1	140	0.1	100	0.0
Trans-megabloc groupings																
Evangelicals	0	0.0	0	0.0	20	0.0	1	1	2	7.18	30	0.0	40	0.0	60	0.0
Pentecostals/Charismatics	0	0.0	50	0.1	225	0.1	10	5	15	5.10	305	0.1	370	0.1	600	0.1
Great Commission Christians	**100**	**0.7**	**11,500**	**15.1**	**290**	**0.1**	**12**	**-13**	**-1**	**-0.21**	**290**	**0.1**	**284**	**0.1**	**450**	**0.1**
Atheists	0	0.0	0	0.0	230	0.1	10	-6	4	1.43	240	0.1	265	0.1	400	0.1
Baha'is	0	0.0	100	0.1	100	0.1	4	-2	2	1.92	110	0.0	121	0.0	200	0.0
World A (unevangelized persons)	14,400	96.0	39,053	51.1	164,800	80.0	6,997	-1,365	5,632	2.98	190,774	77.0	220,922	75.4	320,070	68.1
World B (evangelized non-Christians)	500	3.3	5,771	7.5	40,740	19.8	1,720	1,381	3,101	5.80	56,524	22.8	71,591	24.4	149,230	31.7
World C (Christians)	100	0.7	31,600	41.4	460	0.2	19	-16	3	0.57	460	0.2	487	0.2	700	0.2
Country's population	**15,000**	**100.0**	**76,425**	**100.0**	**206,000**	**100.0**	**8,736**	**0**	**8,736**	**3.59**	**247,759**	**100.0**	**293,000**	**100.0**	**470,000**	**100.0**

COLUMNS, ROWS.
For meanings and definitions, see Codebook (Part 3). Note that, by definition, total 'Christians' = professing + crypto-Christians, which also = affiliated + unaffiliated Christians, and also = Great Commission Christians + latent Christians. Percentages may not always total exactly, due to rounding.

CENSUSES.
31.XII.1963: 79.2% Muslims (Arabs), 20.8% Roman Catholics (Spanish civilians). **31.XII.1970):** 78.2% Muslims (59,777 Arabs), 21.8% Roman Catholics (16,648 Spanish civilians). In addition, there were in 1970-75 around 15,000 Spanish military, not included in the census.

NOTES ON RELIGIONS
BAHA'IS. In 1973, in 3 isolated groups (1 in Rio de Oro). Numbers fell to zero after the 1976 exodus of Spanish military and civilians but picked up among Arabs and Berbers.
MUSLIMS. Sunnis (of the Malikite rite), largely nomadic Arabs.
ROMAN CATHOLICS. All Spanish; in 1970 civilian and military; in 1995 a few civilians only.
UNAFFILIATED CHRISTIANS. (in 1970) Spanish civilians and military.

Country status. Sahara is a former Spanish colony in northwest Africa on the Atlantic Ocean. It has the world's largest deposits of phosphate.

HUMAN LIFE AND LIBERTY

Human rights and freedoms. Sahara is under the de facto control of Morocco and its legal status and sovereignty remain unresolved. Its Polisario government maintains a shadowy existence in exile in Algiers.

NON-CHRISTIAN RELIGIONS

Islam is the principal religion, and virtually the entire indigenous population is Muslim. Most are Sunnis of the Malikite rite.

CHRISTIANITY

The Christian faith was known first around the end of the 2nd century, but all traces were eradicated during the years of Muslim rule.

CATHOLIC CHURCH. Spain first came into contact with the territory as early as 1476, but no protectorate was proclaimed until 1885 and no extensive Spanish settlement was begun until well into the 20th century. A Catholic prefecture was erected in 1954, confided to Oblates of Mary Immaculate with help from Salesian Sisters of the Sacred Heart of Jesus. Except for 11 indigenous wives of Spanish settlers who have become Catholics, the Catholic population is confined to the European (mostly Spanish) community, which has tended to diminish since Spain relinquished its authority over the colony in 1976. In 1975, there were 6 parishes: 3 in Aaiun, one at Bucraa, one at Villa Cisneros and one at Güera, but in subsequent years most fled to the Canary Islands or to mainland Spain.

The Holy See has no diplomatic relations with Sahara in AD 2000.

PROTESTANT CHURCHES. Seventh-day Adventists from Spain have attempted to open work in Spanish Sahara, but have not been successful.

Indigenous missions. No missionaries have been sent out from the fledgling Saharan church.

Great Commission Instrument Panel: status of the Sahara (for explanation see start of Part 4)

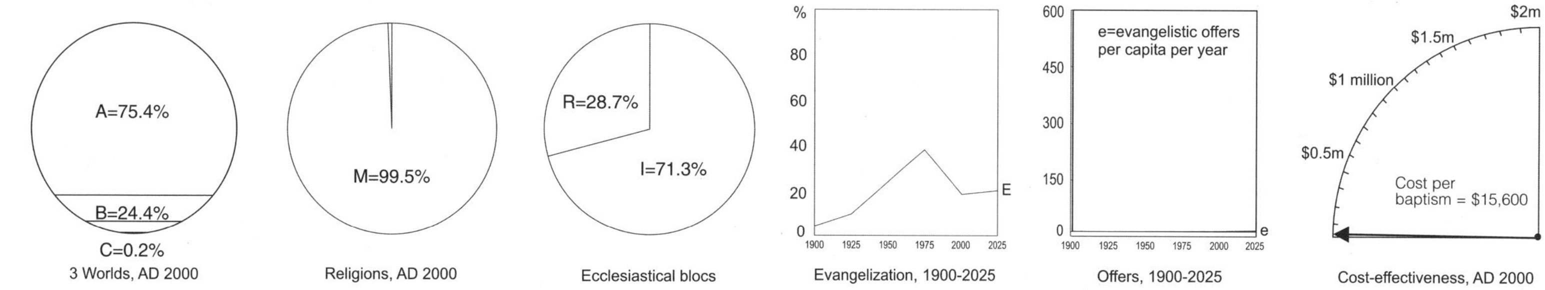

Country summary. **Worlds A, B, C by ethnolinguistic peoples, cities, and major civil divisions in Sahara.**

	PEOPLES							CITIES							CIVIL DIVISIONS						
World	*Num*	*Pop 2000*	*C%*	*Christians*	*E%*	*U%*	*Unevangelized*	*Num*	*Pop 2000*	*C%*	*Christians*	*E%*	*U%*	*Unevangelized*	*Num*	*Pop 2000*	*C%*	*Christians*	*E%*	*U%*	*Unevangelized*
A	10	293,033	0.06	185	25	75	221,119	1	215,627	0.18	388	25	75	161,656	1	293,357	0.17	487	25	75	221,118
B	0	0	0.00	0	0	0	0	0	0	0.00	0	0	0	0	0	0	0.00	0	0	0	0
C	2	322	93.48	301	100	0	0	0	0	0.00	0	0	0	0	0	0	0.00	0	0	0	0
Total	**12**	**293,355**	**0.17**	**486**	**25**	**75**	**221,119**	**1**	**215,627**	**0.18**	**388**	**25**	**75**	**161,656**	**1**	**293,357**	**0.17**	**487**	**25**	**75**	**221,118**

CHURCH AND STATE

Prior to the withdrawal of Spain in 1976, the concordat of the Spanish state with the Holy See was not considered applicable to the Muslim population of Spanish Sahara, and the government gave due respect to Muslim laws, customs, and practices. The legal system was a combination of Spanish civil law and customary law. Spanish courts were responsible for the handling of Spanish interest, while communal concerns of the indigenous population come under the jurisdiction of the Muslim court system with its source in the Quran. With the de facto division of the territory in 1976, the North is governed by Moroccan legislation and the South by Mauritania.

FUTURE TRENDS AND PROSPECTS

Little change is expected in Sahara before 2025 with Christians at 0.2% and Muslims at over 99% of the population.

Christianity is not expected to grow beyond 0.3% of the population before AD 2050. Islam will likely predominate throughout the indefinite future.

Christian themes occasionally appeared on Sahara postage stamps under Spanish rule in Spanish West Africa (of which Ifni was a part, from 1946-1958): (left): Church in Santa Cruze del Mar (1960), (right): Seville Cathedral (1963).

BIBLIOGRAPHY

Algérie et Sahara: Christianisme et Islam, Le Hoggar, Colomb–Béchar. R. Duvollet. Vesoul: R. Duvollet, [1982].
'El 'Aain' en el Sahara,' J. Cola Alberich, *Africa*, 158 (February 1955), 14–16.
'El culto a los 'Igurramen' (Santones),' E. Ibáñex, *Africa*, 99 (March 1950), 21–22.
Femmes sahraouies, femmes du désert. C. Perregaux. Paris: L'Harmattan, 1990. 191p.
Historia del Sahara español. J. R. Diego Aguirre. Madrid: Kaydeda, [1988]. 879p.
'La religión en el desierto,' A. Flores Morales, *Africa*, 119 (November 1951), 13–17.
Les populations du Sahara occidental: histoire, vie et culture. A. Gaudio. Paris: Karthala, 1993. 359p.
L'étrier, la houe et le livre: sociétés traditionnelles au Sahara et au Sahel occidental. F. de Chassey. Paris: L'Harmattan, 1993. 312p.
'Magia y superstición en el Sahara español,' J. Cola Alberich, *Africa*, 135 (March 1953), 21–23.
Missions des Pères Blancs en Tunisie, Algérie, Kabylie, Sahara. A. Philippe. Paris: Dillen, 1931. 146p.
Western Sahara: a comprehensive bibliography. L. F. Sipe. New York: Garland, 1984. 452p.

Country Table 2. **Organized churches and denominations in Sahara.**

Official name (bold type = church with over 10% of all affiliated) 1	*Begun* 2	*Type* 3	*Counc* 4	*Congs* 5	*Adults* 6	*Affiliated 1970* 7	*Affiliated 1995* 8	*G%* 9	*Names, notes, and other statistics* (see Codebook, Part 3) 10
Iglesia Católica: PA Sahara	1476	R-Lat	P...r	4	150	30,000	160	-18.89	*Catholic Ch.* M=OMI. Spaniards, Africans. 50% military. 2 schools.
Isolated radio believers	c1980	I-3rS	....	20	100	–	300	6.67	First known Sahrawi converts were baptized in 1995.
Totals				**24**	**250**	**30,000**	**460**		

Churches, members, growth, 1900-2025	*Congs*	*Adults*	*Affiliated*	*G%*	*Total denominations*	*6 Megablocs:* *O*	*R*	*A*	*P*	*I*	*m*
Total churches, members, and denominations (mid-1900)	1	80	100	8.49	1	0	1	0	0	0	0
Total churches, members, and denominations (mid-1970)	60	24,000	30,000	8.49	1	0	1	0	0	0	0
Total churches, members, and denominations (mid-1990)	30	250	460	0.00	2	0	1	0	0	1	0
Total churches, members, and denominations (mid-1995)	24	250	460	0.00	2	0	1	0	0	1	0
Total churches, members, and denominations (mid-2000)	30	260	487	1.15	2	0	1	0	0	1	0
Total churches, members, and denominations (mid-2025)	60	380	700	1.46	18	0	1	0	5	10	2

NOTES ON TABLE ABOVE
NATIONAL COUNCILS (Column 4, 5th letter).
r = attached to Conferencia Episcopal Española (CEE) (Spanish Episcopal Conference).

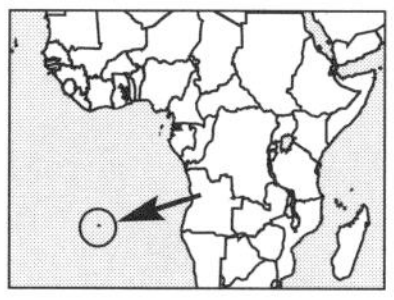

SAINT HELENA

SECULAR DATA, AD 2000

STATE
Official name: The Crown Colony of Saint Helena.
Short name: Saint Helena. **Adjective of nationality:** of Saint Helena.
Flag: British Blue Ensign with shield of the Colony in the fly.
Area: 122 sq. km. (47 sq. mi.).
Government: Crown colony of the United Kingdom, since 1834 (1633 Dutch possession, 1661 British colony).
Legislature: Legislative Council, 15 members.
Official language: English.
Monetary unit: 1 pound sterling (£) = 100 new pence. **US$1=** £ 0.59.
Chief cities: JAMESTOWN 1,575.
Political divisions: 1 province.

DEMOGRAPHY
Population: 6,000.
Population density: 51.5/sq. km. (133.8/sq. mi.).
Under 15 years: 1,000.
Growth rate p.a.: 0.11% (births 11.09, deaths 10.70).
Mortality: Infant, per 1,000: 6.6; **Maternal per 100,000:** 40.0.
Life expectancy: 78 (male 75, female 81).
Household size: 3.0. **Floor area per person, sq.m:** 20.0.
Major languages: English.
Urban dwellers: 70.64%. **Urban growth rate p.a.:** 2.3%.
Labor force: 40%.

ETHNOLINGUISTIC PEOPLES
79.0% Eurafrican White; 10.0% British; 10.0% USA White; .

ECONOMY
National income p.a. per person: US$9,057; **per family:** US$27,173.

EDUCATION
Adult literacy: 98% (male 98%, female 98%). **Schools:** 8.
Universities: 0. **School enrolment:** female/male: 75%/75%.

HEALTH
Access to health services: 75%. **Access to safe water:** 75%.
Hospitals: 1 (30 beds per 10,000). **Doctors:** 10.
Blind: 12. **Deaf:** 400. **Murder rate:** 4.
Lepers: 0.

LITERATURE
New book titles p.a.: 2 (350 p.a. per million). **Periodicals:** 3.
Newspapers: 0 dailies.

COMMUNICATION (per 1,000 people)
Phones: 100 (30% mobile). **Radios:** 600. **TV sets:** 150.
Daily newspaper circulation: <1. **Computers:** 700.

HUMAN LIFE AND LIBERTY (optimum condition=100.0%)
HDI: 75.0. **HSI:** 75.0. **HFI:** 70.0. **EFL:** 40.0.

Country Table 1. **Religious adherents in Saint Helena, AD 1900-2025.**

Name	1900 Adherents	1900 %	1970 Adherents	1970 %	mid-1990 Adherents	mid-1990 %	Annual change, 1990-2000 Natural	Conversion	Total	Rate	mid-1995 Adherents	mid-1995 %	mid-2000 Adherents	mid-2000 %	mid-2025 Adherents	mid-2025 %
Christians	**3,000**	**100.0**	**4,970**	**99.4**	**5,650**	**97.4**	**44**	**-3**	**41**	**0.70**	**5,810**	**96.3**	**6,061**	**96.2**	**7,420**	**95.1**
PROFESSION																
professing Christians	**3,000**	**100.0**	**4,970**	**99.4**	**5,650**	**97.4**	**44**	**-3**	**41**	**0.70**	**5,810**	**96.3**	**6,061**	**96.2**	**7,420**	**95.1**
AFFILIATION																
unaffiliated Christians	0	0.0	480	9.6	580	10.0	16	-1	15	2.31	614	10.2	729	11.6	840	10.8
affiliated Christians	**3,000**	**100.0**	**4,490**	**89.8**	**5,070**	**87.4**	**28**	**-2**	**26**	**0.51**	**5,196**	**86.1**	**5,332**	**84.6**	**6,580**	**84.4**
Anglicans	2,970	99.0	4,000	80.0	4,300	74.1	13	-2	11	0.26	4,350	72.1	4,412	70.0	5,200	66.7
Protestants	30	1.0	360	7.2	440	7.6	9	-1	8	1.68	488	8.1	520	8.3	650	8.3
Marginal Christians	0	0.0	100	2.0	170	2.9	2	1	3	1.64	182	3.0	200	2.2	400	5.1
Independents	0	0.0	0	0.0	120	2.1	3	1	4	2.92	136	2.3	160	2.6	250	3.2
Roman Catholics	0	0.0	30	0.6	40	0.7	0	0	0	0.00	40	0.7	40	0.6	80	1.0
Trans-megabloc groupings																
Evangelicals	30	1.0	120	2.4	145	2.5	1	0	1	0.67	156	2.6	155	2.5	200	2.6
Pentecostals/Charismatics	0	0.0	50	1.0	830	14.3	8	2	10	1.14	876	14.5	930	14.8	1,280	16.4
Great Commission Christians	**120**	**4.0**	**450**	**9.0**	**1,050**	**18.1**	**10**	**2**	**12**	**1.06**	**1,100**	**18.2**	**1,167**	**18.5**	**1,560**	**20.0**
Nonreligious	0	0.0	10	0.2	120	2.1	4	2	6	4.25	150	2.5	182	2.4	300	3.9
Baha'is	0	0.0	20	0.4	30	0.5	1	1	2	5.24	40	0.7	50	0.7	80	1.0
World A (unevangelized persons)	0	0.0	5	0.1	6	0.1	0	0	0	2.54	6	0.1	6	0.1	16	0.2
World B (evangelized non-Christians)	0	0.0	25	0.5	144	2.5	5	3	8	-4.93	219	3.6	233	3.7	364	4.7
World C (Christians)	3,000	100.0	4,970	99.4	5,650	97.4	44	-3	41	0.70	5,810	96.3	6,061	96.2	7,420	95.1
Country's population	**3,000**	**100.0**	**5,000**	**100.0**	**5,800**	**100.0**	**49**	**0**	**49**	**0.00**	**6,035**	**100.0**	**6,300**	**100.0**	**7,800**	**100.0**

COLUMNS, ROWS.
For meanings and definitions, see Codebook (Part 3). Note that, by definition, total 'Christians' = professing + crypto-Christians, which also = affiliated + unaffiliated Christians, and also = Great Commission Christians + latent Christians. Percentages may not always total exactly, due to rounding.

CENSUSES.
27.X.1946: 99.8% Christians. **21.X.1956:** 90.9% Anglicans, 7.6% Protestants (2.9% Baptists, 2.7% Salvation Army, 1.8% SD Adventists), 1.2% marginal Protestants (Jehovah's Witnesses), 0.3% Roman Catholics. **24.VII.1966:** 90.6% Anglicans, 6.7% Protestants (2.8% Baptists, 2.4% Salvation Army, 1.3% SD Adventists), 1.9% marginal Protestants (Jehovah's Witnesses), 0.5% Roman Catholics. **1987:** 87.5% Anglicans, 5.9% Protestants (2.7% Baptists, 1.3% SD Adventists, 1.2% Salvation Army), 4.4% marginal Christians (Jehovah's Witnesses), 1.7% nonreligious, 0.3% Roman Catholics, 0.2% other religionists.

NOTES ON RELIGIONS
BAHA'IS. In one isolated center in 1973, still the only presence 25 years later.
NONRELIGIOUS. Expatriate Whites.

Great Commission Instrument Panel: status of Saint Helena (for explanation see start of Part 4)

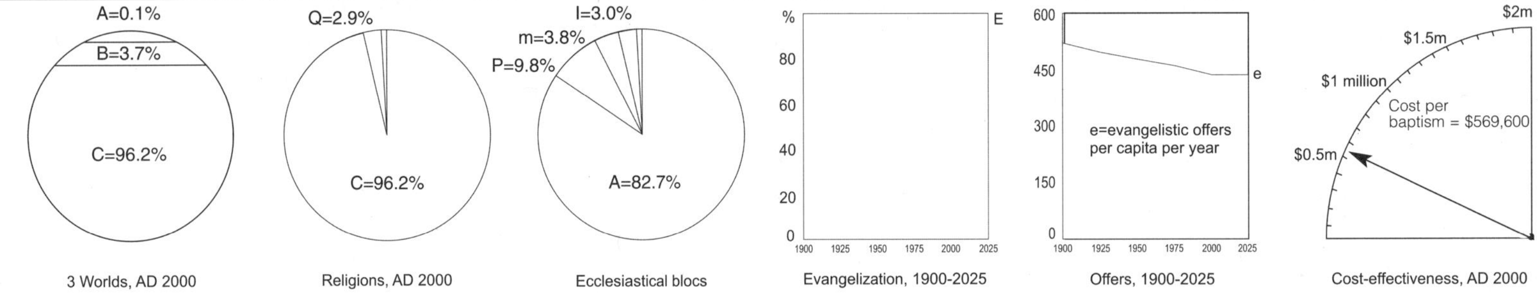

Country summary. **Worlds A, B, C by ethnolinguistic peoples, cities, and major civil divisions in Saint Helena.**

World	PEOPLES Num	Pop 2000	C%	Christians	E%	U%	Unevangelized	CITIES Num	Pop 2000	C%	Christians	E%	U%	Unevangelized	CIVIL DIVISIONS Num	Pop 2000	C%	Christians	E%	U%	Unevangelized
A	0	0	0.00	0	0	0	0	0	0	0.00	0	0	0	0	0	0	0.00	0	0	0	0
B	0	0	0.00	0	0	0	0	0	0	0.00	0	0	0	0	0	0	0.00	0	0	0	0
C	4	6,292	84.73	5,331	100	0	10	1	1,575	84.00	1,323	100	0	3	1	6,293	84.73	5,332	100	0	9
Total	**4**	**6,292**	**84.73**	**5,331**	**100**	**0**	**10**	**1**	**1,575**	**84.00**	**1,323**	**100**	**0**	**3**	**1**	**6,293**	**84.73**	**5,332**	**100**	**0**	**9**

Country status. St Helena, a British dependency, is an island of volcanic origin in the southern Atlantic Ocean. Its chief exports are handicrafts and fish, but it is also well-known as the place of Napoleon's exile and death.

HUMAN LIFE AND LIBERTY

Human rights and freedoms. St Helena is a dependency of the United Kingdom where British laws are in force. All human rights and civil liberties are fully respected by the colonial administration.

CHRISTIANITY

CATHOLIC CHURCH. A Catholic priest took up residence on St Helena in 1958, with annual trips to Ascension after 1965. St Helena belongs to the Catholic archdiocese of Cape Town, South Africa. Occasional visits by Catholic clergy are also made from Cape Town to Tristan da Cunha.

The Holy See has no diplomatic relations with St Helena in AD 2000.

ANGLICAN CHURCH. Residents of the islands are mostly Anglicans. The colony is covered by 2 dioceses, St Helena and Cape Town; the former is responsible for the islands of St Helena and Ascension, while the latter has jurisdiction over Tristan da Cunha island. Both dioceses belong to the Church of the Province of Southern Africa.

In 1995, St Helena island by itself was 80% Anglican and the total population 74% Anglican. There are 12 well-attended Anglican churches spread throughout the islands of St Helena and one on Ascension.

Anglican Church. *Left.* Origin in 1851. *Above.* Cathedral Church of St. Paul.

OTHER CHURCHES. Baptist, Salvation Army, Seventh-day Adventist, and Catholic churches are found at Jamestown, and there is a congregation of Jehovah's Witnesses at Levelwood. The Way International, a Pentecostal body, entered the islands in the 1980s and by 1990 had nearly 100 adherents.

Indigenous missions. The churches in St Helena have sent out very few missionaries.

CHURCH AND STATE

The Anglican Church has a special relationship to the colonial government dating back to the establishment of the diocesan see by the British sovereign. The original church ordinances, enshrined in colonial law are still valid. Other religions are required to register their buildings only for official marriage purposes.

INTERDENOMINATIONAL ORGANIZATIONS

The Anglican bishop has attempted to form a Christian council, but there has been disagreement regarding membership. The Baptists refused to join without the Adventists, who were in turn opposed by a number of Anglican clergy.

FUTURE TRENDS AND PROSPECTS

Little change is expected in Saint Helena except for the slow decline of Christians by percentage due to increases among Baha'is and the nonreligious.

Christianity will likely predominate for the next fifty years. However, non-Christians could reach 10% of the population around AD 2050, and Marginal Christians could represent 10% of the population in the same period.

BIBLIOGRAPHY

A history of the church in Southern Africa: a select bibliography of published material. J. W. Hofmeyr & K. E. Cross. Pretoria, South Africa: University of South Africa, 1986. 2 vols.
Churches of the South Atlantic Islands, 1502–1991. E. Cannan. Oswestry, UK: Anthony Nelson, 1992. 315p.
The emperor's last island: a journey to St Helena. J. Blackburn. London: Secker & Warburg, 1991. 244p.

Country Table 2. **Organized churches and denominations in Saint Helena.**

Official name (bold type = church *with over 10% of all affiliated)* 1	*Begun* 2	*Type* 3	*Counc* 4	*Congs* 5	*Adults* 6	*Affiliated 1970* 7	*Affiliated 1995* 8	*G%* 9	*Names, notes, and other statistics* (see Codebook, Part 3) 10
Anglican Church	1851	A-ACa	AwaV.	16	3,900	4,000	4,350	0.34	In Church of the Province of Southern Africa (CPSA). M=USPG(UK). 4f.
Baptist Church		P-Bap	.....	1	50	120	75	0.05	Congregation in Jamestown. Links with Baptist Union of South Africa.
Catholic Church (M Cape Town)	1958	R-Lat	P.S..	1	30	30	40	1.16	*Sacred Heart Church*, Jamestown, under M Cape Town. 1 resident priest since 1958.
Jehovah's Witnesses	c1930	m-Jeh	x....	2	109	100	182	2.42	Active witnessing under way by 1973. Congregation in Levelwood. (1975) 12Y. (1995) 7Y.
New Apostolic Church	c1980	I-3aX	.....	1	30	–	41	6.67	M=NAC/NAK(Zurich, Switzerland).
Salvation Army	1884	P-Sal	xwa..	1	70	120	108	-0.42	Attached to South Africa Territory. Congregation in Jamestown.
Seventh-day Adventist Church	1933	P-Adv	x....	1	70	70	105	1.64	*SDA*, Good Hope Conference, South African Union Conf. Congregation in Jamestown.
The Way International	c1980	I-3pW	.....	1	57	–	95	6.67	Small pentecostal movement from USA.
Other Protestant denominations		P-	.....	3	100	50	200	0.05	Including: Presbyterian Ch, Two-by-Two Mission (South Africa).
Totals				**27**	**4,416**	**4,490**	**5,196**		

Churches, members, growth, 1900-2025	*Congs*	*Adults*	*Affiliated*	*G%*	*Total denominations*	*6 Megablocs:* *O*	*R*	*A*	*P*	*I*	*m*
Total churches, members, and denominations (mid-1900)	10	2,300	3,000	0.58	2	0	0	1	1	0	0
Total churches, members, and denominations (mid-1970)	22	3,513	4,490	0.58	8	0	1	1	5	0	1
Total churches, members, and denominations (mid-1990)	25	4,300	5,070	0.61	12	0	1	1	7	2	1
Total churches, members, and denominations (mid-1995)	27	4,416	5,196	0.49	12	0	1	1	7	2	1
Total churches, members, and denominations (mid-2000)	30	4,500	5,332	0.52	12	0	1	1	7	2	1
Total churches, members, and denominations (mid-2025)	50	5,600	6,580	0.84	35	0	1	1	12	20	1

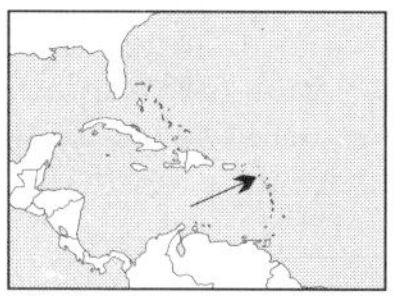

SAINT KITTS & NEVIS

SECULAR DATA, AD 2000

STATE
Official name: The Federation of Saint Kitts and Nevis.
Short name: Saint Kitts and Nevis. **Adjective of nationality:** of Saint Kitts and Nevis.
Flag: Green and red field bisected diagonally with black stripe with yellow edge and two white stars.
Area: 269 sq. km. (104 sq. mi.).
Government: Constitutional monarchy with one legislative house, since 1967 (1623 British colony).
Legislature: National Assembly, 15 members.
Official language: English.
Monetary unit: 1 Eastern Caribbean dollar (EC$) = 100 cents. **US$1=** EC$2.70.
Chief cities: BASSETERRE 13,727.
Political divisions: 2 provinces.

DEMOGRAPHY
Population: 38,000.
Population density: 143.0/sq. km. (369.9/sq. mi.).
Under 15 years: 9,000.
Growth rate p.a.: 1.19% (births 15.26, deaths 5.77).
Mortality: Infant, per 1,000: 7.8; **Maternal per 100,000:** 70.0.
Life expectancy: 78 (male 75, female 82).
Household size: 4.0. **Floor area per person, sq.m:** 15.0.
Major languages: English, Hindi.
Urban dwellers: 34.12%. **Urban growth rate p.a.:** 0.7%.
Labor force: 40%.

ETHNOLINGUISTIC PEOPLES
90.4% West Indian Black; 5.0% Mulatto; 3.0% East Indian; 1.0% British; 0.1% French.

ECONOMY
National income p.a. per person: US$5,172; **per family:** US$20,689.

EDUCATION
Adult literacy: 90% (male 90%, female 90%). **Schools:** 5.
Universities: 0. **School enrolment:** female/male: 95%/95%.

HEALTH
Access to health services: 90%. **Access to safe water:** 100%.
Hospitals: 1 (40 beds per 10,000). **Doctors:** 5.
Blind: 20. **Deaf:** 2,500. **Murder rate:** 14. **Lepers:** 100.

LITERATURE
New book titles p.a.: 8 (200 p.a. per million). **Periodicals:** 8.
Newspapers: 0 dailies.

COMMUNICATION (per 1,000 people)
Phones: 355 (1% mobile). **Radios:** 650. **TV sets:** 241.
Daily newspaper circulation: 600. **Computers:** 90.

HUMAN LIFE AND LIBERTY (optimum condition=100.0%)
HDI: 85.3. **HSI:** 75.0. **HFI:** 70.0. **EFL:** 45.0.

Country Table 1. **Religious adherents in Saint Kitts & Nevis, AD 1900-2025.**

Year	*1900*		*1970*		*mid-1990*		*Annual change, 1990-2000*				*mid-1995*		*mid-2000*		*mid-2025*	
Name	*Adherents*	*%*	*Adherents*	*%*	*Adherents*	*%*	*Natural*	*Conversion*	*Total*	*Rate*	*Adherents*	*%*	*Adherents*	*%*	*Adherents*	*%*
Christians	**42,300**	**100.0**	**46,130**	**99.0**	**39,940**	**95.3**	**-324**	**-23**	**-347**	**-0.90**	**38,000**	**95.0**	**36,471**	**94.8**	**32,700**	**93.2**
PROFESSION																
professing Christians	**42,300**	**100.0**	**46,130**	**99.0**	**39,940**	**95.3**	**-324**	**-23**	**-347**	**-0.90**	**38,000**	**95.0**	**36,471**	**94.8**	**32,700**	**93.2**
AFFILIATION																
unaffiliated Christians	3,300	7.8	655	1.4	540	1.3	-5	-2	-7	-1.36	480	1.2	471	1.2	300	0.9
affiliated Christians	**39,000**	**92.2**	**45,475**	**97.6**	**39,400**	**93.9**	**-319**	**-21**	**-340**	**-0.90**	**37,520**	**93.8**	**36,000**	**93.5**	**32,400**	**92.3**
Protestants	25,000	59.1	25,861	55.5	24,200	57.6	-230	37	-193	-0.83	23,151	57.9	22,270	57.8	20,000	57.0
Anglicans	12,000	28.4	17,500	37.6	11,500	27.4	-110	-70	-180	-1.69	10,500	26.3	9,700	25.1	8,000	22.8
Roman Catholics	2,000	4.7	4,000	8.6	5,200	12.4	-50	15	-35	-0.69	5,000	12.5	4,850	12.6	4,500	12.9
Independents	0	0.0	2,700	5.8	1,700	4.1	-16	-4	-20	-1.24	1,597	4.0	1,500	3.9	1,200	3.4
Marginal Christians	0	0.0	300	0.6	460	1.1	-4	9	5	1.04	480	1.2	510	1.3	700	2.0
doubly-affiliated	0	0.0	-4,886	-10.5	-3,660	-8.7	35	48	83	-2.54	-3,208	-8.0	-2,830	-7.5	-2,000	-5.7
Trans-megabloc groupings																
Evangelicals	20,700	48.9	9,800	21.0	7,900	18.8	-75	-5	-80	-1.06	7,470	18.7	7,100	18.7	6,000	17.1
Pentecostals/Charismatics	0	0.0	1,900	4.1	6,930	16.5	-66	88	22	0.31	7,003	17.5	7,150	18.8	7,500	21.3
Great Commission Christians	**1,000**	**2.4**	**1,400**	**3.0**	**2,225**	**5.3**	**-21**	**8**	**-13**	**-0.59**	**2,160**	**5.4**	**2,098**	**5.5**	**2,500**	**7.1**
Hindus	0	0.0	0	0.0	580	1.4	-6	6	0	-0.05	600	1.5	577	1.5	600	1.7
Spiritists	0	0.0	0	0.0	550	1.3	-5	2	-3	-0.46	555	1.4	525	1.4	550	1.6
Nonreligious	0	0.0	60	0.1	400	1.0	-4	12	8	1.90	420	1.1	483	1.3	650	1.9
Baha'is	0	0.0	200	0.4	200	0.5	-2	2	0	-0.15	205	0.5	197	0.5	300	0.9
Muslims	0	0.0	0	0.0	110	0.3	-1	2	1	0.45	120	0.3	115	0.3	200	0.6
New-Religionists	0	0.0	210	0.5	120	0.3	-1	-1	-2	-1.42	100	0.3	104	0.3	100	0.3
World A (unevangelized persons)	0	0.0	0	0.0	42	0.1	0	1	1	3.42	40	0.1	38	0.1	70	0.2
World B (evangelized non-Christians)	0	0.0	470	1.0	2,018	4.6	-19	22	3	-2.98	1,960	4.9	1,991	5.1	2,330	6.6
World C (Christians)	42,300	100.0	46,130	99.0	39,940	95.3	-324	-23	-347	-0.90	38,000	95.0	36,471	94.8	32,700	93.2
Country's population	**42,300**	**100.0**	**46,600**	**100.0**	**42,000**	**100.0**	**-343**	**0**	**-343**	**-1.00**	**40,000**	**100.0**	**38,500**	**100.0**	**35,100**	**100.0**

COLUMNS, ROWS.
For meanings and definitions, see Codebook (Part 3). Note that, by definition, total 'Christians' = professing + crypto-Christians, which also = affiliated + unaffiliated Christians, and also = Great Commission Christians + latent Christians. Percentages may not always total exactly, due to rounding.

CENSUSES.
1844 (St Kitts): 67.4% Protestants (43.9% Methodists, 23.5% Moravians), 32.2% Anglicans, 0.3% Roman Catholics. **4.IV.1881** (St Kitts): 65.3% Protestants (45.9% Methodists, 19.3% Moravians), 29.2% Anglicans, 5.5% Roman Catholics. **7.IV.1960** (St Kitts-Nevis; de jure): 54.4% Protestants (34.7% Methodists, 10.6% Moravians, 3.4% Pilgrim Holiness Church, 1.7% SDAs), 36.5% Anglicans, 8.1% Roman Catholics, 0.7% non-Christian religionists, 0.3% marginal Protestants, 0.1% nonreligious. **1991:** 51.4% Protestants (28.8% Methodists, 8.7% Moravians, 3.5% Church of God), 32.6% Anglicans, 7.2% Roman Catholics, 5.0% other Christians, 1.5% nonreligious, 1.3% other religionists, 1.0% marginal Christians (Jehovah's Witnesses).

NOTES ON RELIGIONS
BAHA'IS. In 2 local spiritual assemblies (1973), remaining the same 2 decades later.
HINDUS. Hindi-speaking East Indian traders.
INDEPENDENTS. In 7 denominations in 1995 (see Table 2).

Country status. St. Kitts & Nevis are 2 islands of the Leeward Islands in the West Indies. The economy is almost entirely dependent on tourism.

HUMAN LIFE AND LIBERTY

Human rights and freedoms. St Kitts & Nevis is a member of the Commonwealth. Its Constitution and the legal system are based on British models and ensure basic human rights and civil liberties. The media are government-controlled and do not provide access to the opposition parties. The island of Nevis has considerable self-government.

NON-CHRISTIAN RELIGIONS

Bahai's have a small work with 2 local spiritual assemblies.

CHRISTIANITY

PROTESTANT CHURCHES. The first Protestants in St Kitts were Moravians, in 1777, followed by the Methodist Thomas Coke and 2 others a decade later. Nevis was reached by Methodists in 1787. The respective strength of these 2 oldest and largest Protestant churches is reversed when one compares St Kitts-Nevis with Antigua. On Antigua the

Great Commission Instrument Panel: status of Saint Kitts & Nevis (for explanation see start of Part 4)

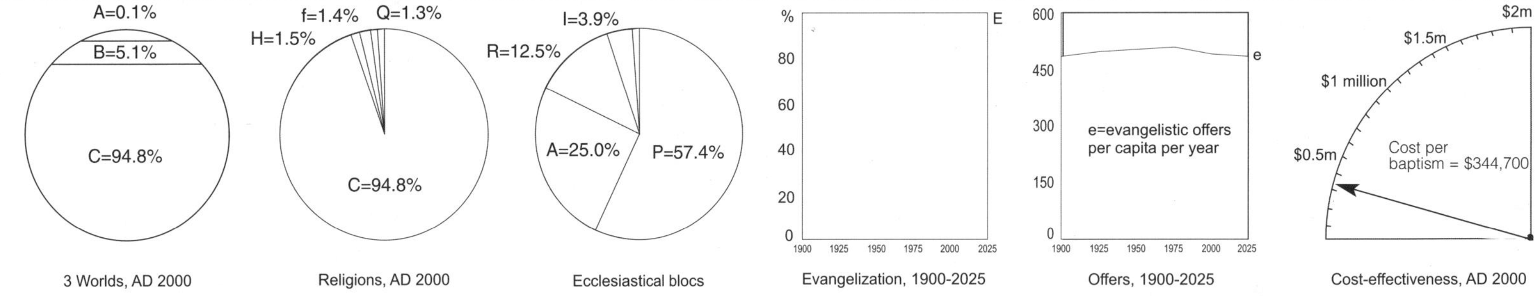

Country summary. **Worlds A, B, C by ethnolinguistic peoples, cities, and major civil divisions in Saint Kitts & Nevis.**

	PEOPLES							*CITIES*							*CIVIL DIVISIONS*						
World	*Num*	*Pop 2000*	*C%*	*Christians*	*E%*	*U%*	*Unevangelized*	*Num*	*Pop 2000*	*C%*	*Christians*	*E%*	*U%*	*Unevangelized*	*Num*	*Pop 2000*	*C%*	*Christians*	*E%*	*U%*	*Unevangelized*
A	0	0	0.00	0	0	0	0	0	0	0.00	0	0	0	0	0	0	0.00	0	0	0	0
B	1	1,154	35.01	404	99	1	12	0	0	0.00	0	0	0	0	0	0	0.00	0	0	0	0
C	5	37,319	95.39	35,597	100	0	17	1	13,727	91.00	12,492	100	0	19	2	38,473	93.57	36,000	100	0	28
Total	**6**	**38,473**	**93.57**	**36,001**	**100**	**0**	**29**	**1**	**13,727**	**91.00**	**12,492**	**100**	**0**	**19**	**2**	**38,473**	**93.57**	**36,000**	**100**	**0**	**28**

Moravian community is twice as large as that of the Methodists, whereas Methodists are 3 times as numerous as Moravians in St Kitts-Nevis. Of the other churches on the islands, most of which have been established by conservative American missionary societies in the present century, the largest is the Wesleyan Church.

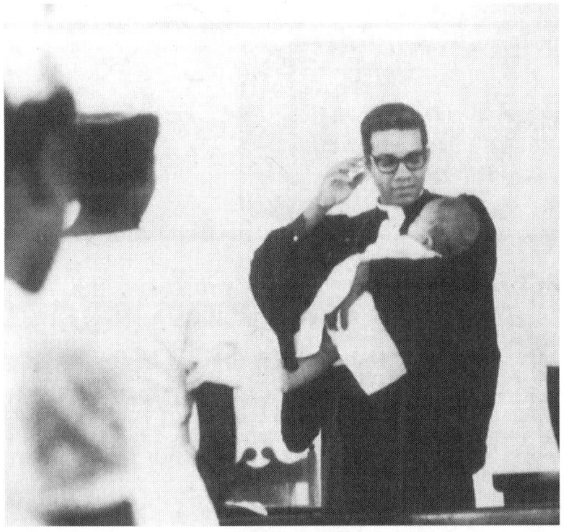

Methodist Church in the Caribbean & The Americas. *Top.* 1967 postage stamps commemorating Methodist founders John and Charles Wesley and Thomas Coke. *Lower.* Minister baptizes infant in a St. Kitts church.

ANGLICAN CHURCH. The Anglican Church is the original church of the islands, its first chaplains coming from England to serve the European settler community in the 17th century. The Leeward Islands were transferred from the bishopric of London to that of Barbados in 1824, and the archdeaconry of Antigua (including St Kitts-Nevis) was formed in the same year. The archdeaconry was elevated to a diocese in 1842 and since 1883 has been an integral part of the Church of the Province of the West Indies. Anglicans are not as strong in St Kitts-Nevis as in Antigua or Montserrat, and are now the second largest single denomination.

Anglican Church. Priest of Diocese of Antigua with young people in village of Cayon, St. Kitts.

CATHOLIC CHURCH. Catholicism is not strong in any of the Leeward Islands. St Kitts-Nevis forms part of the diocese of Saint John's in Antigua, which was detached from the diocese of Roseau, Dominica in 1971. On St Kitts there were 3 parishes served by Redemptorist priests, one mission station and several sisters (Canadian Daughters of Jesus) working in 3 Catholic schools and a non-Catholic general hospital. Nevis Island has one parish with a resident Redemptorist priests, in addition to Daughters of Jesus nuns who are engaged in hospital work.

The Holy See has diplomatic relations with St Kitts & Nevis and in AD 2000 is represented to government and the Catholic hierarchy by a pro-nuncio residing in Port of Spain.

INDIGENOUS CHURCHES. There are at least 6 denominations indigenous to the islands begun by Blacks, of which the best-known are the Spiritual Baptists. Several have spread by emigration to Britain and North America.

Indigenous missions. Only a few Christians have been sent out from St Kitts and most of these have served in the United Kingdom.

Renewal movements. In the 1990s the Pentecostal/Charismatic Renewal continued to spread rapidly across most older churches, and numbered over 7,100 adherents (of whom 36% Pentecostals, 50% Charismatics, and 14% Independents).

CHURCH AND STATE

St Kitts-Nevis is a secular state, associated with Great Britain, which assures complete freedom of religion for all. Churches are not obliged to register with government, but permission must be granted for new denominations to begin work in the islands. Such permission is not difficult to obtain, and recognized bodies may be licensed to perform marriages.

Through the auspices of the Christian Council of St Kitts, the churches compiled a syllabus for religious teaching in state schools. There is no separate government ministry or department dealing with religion.

BROADCASTING AND MEDIA

Shortwave broadcasts from TWR (Antilles), HCJB (Ecuador), and AWR (Costa Rica) can be received. Local station Radio Paradise carries Christian programming, including TBN programs. LeSEA's television broadcasts can be received via the World Harvest Satellite.

INTERDENOMINATIONAL ORGANIZATIONS

The Christian Council of St Kitts has in its membership Anglican, Catholic, Methodist, and Moravian churches, and the Salvation Army. The first 3 bodies, plus the Wesleyan Church and the Red Cross, are also members of the Coordinating Council for Social Action of Nevis.

FUTURE TRENDS AND PROSPECTS

Growth is expected among all non-Christian traditions with the result that Christians could decline from 99% in 1970 to less than 94% of the population by 2025.

Although Christianity is expected to predominate in the future, it is possible that it will decline below 90% before AD 2050. Hindus, Muslims, the nonreligious, and Spiritists are all expected to grow in the same period.

BIBLIOGRAPHY

Caribbean Quakers. H. F. Durham. Hollywood, FL: Dukane, 1972. 133p.
Guide to the archives of Nevis. L. Hanley (ed). Charlestown, Nevis: Nevis Historical and Conservation Society, 1989. 41p.
St. Kitts, Nevis, Anguilla archives. E. C. Baker. Mona, Jamaica: University of the West Indies, [1963]. 3 vols. (A catalogue of documents).
St. Kitts–Nevis. V. P. Moll. *World bibliographical series*, vol. 174. Oxford, UK: CLIO Press, 1995. 208p. (See especially 'Religion,' p.41-4).
Statistical digest 1989: Nevis. Charlestown, Nevis: Nevis Administration, 1990.
'Statistical survey of St Kitts–Nevis,' in *Europa yearbook, 1994.* London: Europa Publications, Ltd, 1994. (Includes information on religion, p.2525-9).
Statistics in brief, 1981–1988. Basseterre, St Kitts: St Kitts-Nevis Planning Unit, 1988. 22p.
Ten years of progress: Saint Kitts and Nevis, 10th anniversary of independence, September 19, 1993. [1993]. 72p.
The Christian Council and Evangelical Association call for fresh elections. Basseterre, St Kitts: St Kitts Christian Council, 1994. 1p.
The folklore of St. Christopher's island. L. Matheson. Basseterre, St. Kitts: Creole Graphics, 1985. 15p.

Country Table 2. **Organized churches and denominations in Saint Kitts & Nevis.**

Official name (bold type = church with over 10% of all affiliated) 1	*Begun* 2	*Type* 3	*Counc* 4	*Congs* 5	*Adults* 6	*Affiliated 1970* 7	*Affiliated 1995* 8	*G%* 9	*Names, notes, and other statistics* (see Codebook, Part 3) 10
Anglican Church (D Antigua)	1623	A-ACa	awMRC	13	6,270	17,500	10,500	-2.02	*CPWI.* In Ch of Province of the West Indies. M=USPG. 95% West Indians (90% Black). W=58%.
Antioch Baptist Church	1963	I-Bap	.T...	3	160	1,500	267	-6.67	Baptist body founded by Blacks. HQ Basseterre. 2n,W=99%,3Y,20z.
Baptist Association	1969	P-Bap	.....	5	900	286	1,290	6.21	M=SBC. Southern Baptist Convention, USA.

Continued opposite

Country Table 2–concluded

Official name (bold type = church with over 10% of affiliated) 1	*Begun* 2	*Type* 3	*Counc* 4	*Congs* 5	*Adults* 6	*Affiliated 1970* 7	*Affiliated 1995* 8	*G%* 9	*Names, notes, and other statistics* (see Codebook, Part 3) 10
Catholic Church (D Saint John's)	1861	R-Lat	P.NMC	4	3,500	4,000	5,000	0.90	In D Saint John's (Antigua). Assisted by CSSR priests.
Christian Brethren		P-CBr	x....	12	350	600	583	0.05	*Open Brethren. Gospel Halls.* M=CMML(UK, USA, Bermuda). 1 group on Nevis. 7f.
Church of God of Prophecy		P-Pe3	Z....	13	700	1,000	1,270	0.05	M=CGP(USA). Holiness Pentecostals (3-stage). Split in USA ex CoG (Cleveland).
Church of God (Anderson)	1946	P-Hol	x....	5	300	513	500	-0.10	*General Assembly of the CoG (St. Kitts).* M=CoG(Anderson) (USA). 3n,2f,W=99%.
Church of God (Cleveland)	1943	P-Pe3	ZF...	9	674	900	1,120	0.88	M=CoG(Cleveland)(USA). St. Kitts: 5 churches. Nevis: 2 churches, 1 mission. 7n.
Church of the Nazarene	1983	P-Hol	.....	2	68	–	98	8.33	M=CoN. Holiness body.
Jehovah's Witnesses	c1940	m-Jeh	x....	3	216	300	480	1.90	*Watch Tower.* Active witnessing under way by 1942. HQ Sandy Point. (1975) 5Y. (1995) 16Y.
Meth Ch in Caribbean & Americas	1787	P-Met	VwM.C	30	5,900	12,000	10,800	-0.42	In MCCA (1967), Leeward Islands District. M=MMS(UK). HQ Basseterre. 5n,1x,1f.
Moravian Church	1777	P-Mor	xwM.C	4	2,400	4,045	3,270	-0.85	*St Kitts Conference,* Eastern West Indies Province, Unity of Brethren. W=44%,94Y.
Salvation Army		P-Sal	xwM.C	1	60	70	100	0.05	SA. In Caribbean & CAmerican Territory (HQ Jamaica). In Basseterre.
Seventh-day Adventist Church		P-Adv	x....	9	720	1,300	1,200	0.05	*SDA,* East Caribbean Conference, Caribbean Union Conference. HQ Basseterre.
Wesleyan Church	1902	P-Hol	VF..C	22	780	2,647	1,420	-2.46	*Pilgrim Holiness Ch.* M=WC(USA). HQ Basseterre. 10n,2x,2f,W=31%,33Y,20z.
Other Protestant denominations		P-	.....	19	1,100	2,500	1,500	0.05	Total about 15 bodies (see list below).
Other Black indigenous churches		I-	.....	8	800	1,200	1,330	0.05	Total over 6 (see list below).
Doubly-affiliated		2-aff			-2,000	-4,886	-3,208		Pentecostals who are also baptized Anglicans, Methodists, or Catholics.
Totals				**162**	**22,898**	**45,475**	**37,520**		

Churches, members, growth, 1900-2025	*Congs*	*Adults*	*Affiliated*	*G%*	*Total denominations*	*6 Megablocs:* *O*	*R*	*A*	*P*	*I*	*m*
Total churches, members, and denominations (mid-1900)	100	21,200	39,000	0.22	4	0	1	1	2	0	0
Total churches, members, and denominations (mid-1970)	150	24,732	45,475	0.22	25	0	1	1	17	5	1
Total churches, members, and denominations (mid-1990)	160	24,100	39,400	-0.71	38	0	1	1	26	9	1
Total churches, members, and denominations (mid-1995)	162	22,898	37,520	-0.97	38	0	1	1	26	9	1
Total churches, members, and denominations (mid-2000)	160	22,000	36,000	-0.82	38	0	1	1	26	9	1
Total churches, members, and denominations (mid-2025)	200	19,800	32,400	-0.42	56	0	1	1	32	20	2

NOTES ON TABLE ABOVE
NATIONAL COUNCILS (Column 4, 5th letter).
C = Christian Council of St Kitts, and/or Co-ordinating Council for Social Action of Nevis.
E = St Kitts Evangelical Association (SKEA).

Other national councils. St Kitts Evangelical Association.
OTHER PROTESTANT DENOMINATIONS. These numerous smaller bodies include: Baptist Ch, Chs of Christ, Exclusive Brethren (Kelly-Continental), Missionary Ch, Pentecostal Assemblies of the West Indies (many emigrants to UK).

OTHER BLACK INDIGENOUS CHURCHES. These include: Assemblies of the First-Born, Ch of the Apostolic Faith, Evangelical Faith Ch, International Ministerial Council, Spiritual Baptist Churches. Several now have branches in Britain due to emigration of their members.

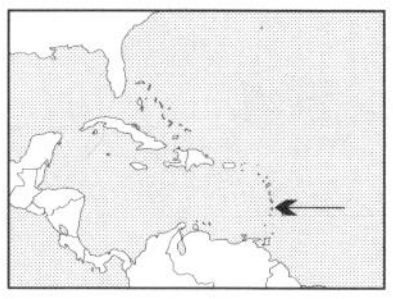

SAINT LUCIA

SECULAR DATA, AD 2000

STATE
Official name: The Realm of Saint Lucia.
Short name: Saint Lucia. **Adjective of nationality:** Saint Lucian.
Flag: Blue field, centered isosceles triangle in black, gold and white.
Area: 617 sq. km. (238 sq. mi.).
Government: Republic, formerly self-governing state in association with the United Kingdom (Britain) since 1967 (1814 British colony, Independence 1979).
Legislature: Senate, 11 members; House of Assembly, 17 members.
Official language: English.
Monetary unit: 1 Eastern Caribbean dollar (EC$) = 100 cents. **US$1=** EC$2.70.
Chief cities: CASTRIES 64,193.
Political divisions: 10 provinces.

DEMOGRAPHY
Population: 154,000.
Population density: 250.1/sq. km. (648.6/sq. mi.).
Under 15 years: 37,000.
Growth rate p.a.: 1.19% (births 15.26, deaths 5.77).
Mortality: Infant, per 1,000: 7.8; **Maternal per 100,000:** 50.0.
Life expectancy: 78 (male 75, female 82).
Household size: 4.0. **Floor area per person, sq.m:** 18.0.
Major languages: English, French patois, Dominican Creole, Hindi.
Urban dwellers: 37.78%. **Urban growth rate p.a.:** 1.9%.
Labor force: 37%.

ETHNOLINGUISTIC PEOPLES
44.6% Black; 44.4% Mulatto; 5.0% West Indian Black; 3.0% East Indian; 1.0% British.

ECONOMY
National income p.a. per person: US$3,368; **per family:** US$13,474.

EDUCATION
Adult literacy: 80% (male 82%, female 78%). **Schools:** 84.
Universities: 0. **School enrolment:** female/male: 90%/90%.

HEALTH
Access to health services: 95%. **Access to safe water:** 100%.
Hospitals: 4 (37 beds per 10,000). **Doctors:** 64.
Blind: 200. **Deaf:** 9,100. **Murder rate:** 17. **Lepers:** 100.

LITERATURE
New book titles p.a.: 39 (250 p.a. per million). **Periodicals:** 10.
Newspapers: 0 dailies.

COMMUNICATION (per 1,000 people)
Phones: 211 (4% mobile). **Radios:** 699. **TV sets:** 172.
Daily newspaper circulation: 700. **Computers:** 70.

HUMAN LIFE AND LIBERTY (optimum condition=100.0%)
HDI: 83.8. **HSI:** 80.0. **HFI:** 75.0. **EFL:** 48.0.

Country Table 1. **Religious adherents in Saint Lucia, AD 1900-2025.**

Year	*1900*		*1970*		*mid-1990*		*Annual change, 1990-2000*				*mid-1995*		*mid-2000*		*mid-2025*	
Name	*Adherents*	*%*	*Adherents*	*%*	*Adherents*	*%*	*Natural*	*Conversion*	*Total*	*Rate*	*Adherents*	*%*	*Adherents*	*%*	*Adherents*	*%*
Christians	**48,670**	**97.7**	**99,330**	**98.1**	**129,200**	**96.4**	**1,957**	**-39**	**1,918**	**1.39**	**138,650**	**96.2**	**148,380**	**96.1**	**198,950**	**95.7**
PROFESSION																
professing Christians	**48,670**	**97.7**	**99,330**	**98.1**	**129,200**	**96.4**	**1,957**	**-39**	**1,918**	**1.39**	**138,650**	**96.2**	**148,380**	**96.1**	**198,950**	**95.7**
AFFILIATION																
unaffiliated Christians	0	0.0	500	0.5	3,400	2.5	51	13	64	1.74	3,987	2.8	4,041	2.6	3,950	1.9
affiliated Christians	**48,670**	**97.7**	**98,830**	**97.6**	**125,800**	**93.9**	**1,907**	**-53**	**1,854**	**1.38**	**134,663**	**93.5**	**144,339**	**93.4**	**195,000**	**93.8**
Roman Catholics	40,970	82.3	92,510	91.3	101,500	75.8	1,515	-65	1,450	1.34	108,570	75.3	116,000	75.1	148,900	71.6
Protestants	1,730	3.5	6,130	6.1	17,500	13.1	261	39	300	1.59	18,808	13.1	20,500	13.2	33,500	16.1
Anglicans	5,970	12.0	3,000	3.0	3,900	2.9	58	-8	50	1.21	4,130	2.9	4,400	2.9	5,600	2.7
Independents	0	0.0	1,650	1.6	2,800	2.1	42	2	44	1.47	3,010	2.1	3,239	2.1	6,000	2.9
Marginal Christians	0	0.0	300	0.3	1,100	0.8	16	14	30	2.44	1,245	0.9	1,400	0.9	2,500	1.2
doubly-affiliated	0	0.0	-3,260	-3.2	0	0.0	0	0	0	0.00	0	0.0	0	0.0	0	0.0
disaffiliated	0	0.0	-1,500	-1.5	-1,000	-0.8	-15	-5	-20	1.84	-1,100	-0.8	-1,200	-0.8	-1,500	-0.7
Trans-megabloc groupings																
Evangelicals	1,500	3.0	2,900	2.9	8,600	6.4	128	52	180	1.92	9,421	6.5	10,400	6.8	17,000	8.2
Pentecostals/Charismatics	0	0.0	1,300	1.3	10,500	7.8	157	68	225	1.96	11,530	8.0	12,750	8.3	21,000	10.1
Great Commission Christians	**1,500**	**3.0**	**6,050**	**6.0**	**8,040**	**6.0**	**120**	**32**	**152**	**1.74**	**8,640**	**6.0**	**9,556**	**6.2**	**13,520**	**6.5**
Spiritists	0	0.0	1,500	1.5	2,020	1.5	30	24	54	2.38	2,300	1.6	2,555	1.7	4,000	1.9
Hindus	970	2.0	0	0.0	1,200	0.9	18	1	19	1.45	1,300	0.9	1,386	0.9	2,200	1.1
Muslims	160	0.3	0	0.0	600	0.5	9	2	11	1.63	660	0.5	705	0.5	1,000	0.5
New-Religionists	0	0.0	0	0.0	480	0.4	7	2	9	1.72	510	0.4	569	0.4	750	0.4
Baha'is	0	0.0	170	0.2	300	0.2	4	2	6	1.95	330	0.2	364	0.2	600	0.3
Nonreligious	0	0.0	0	0.0	200	0.2	3	8	11	4.41	250	0.2	308	0.2	500	0.2
World A (unevangelized persons)	99	0.2	202	0.2	1,206	0.9	18	17	35	2.57	1,296	0.9	1,540	1.0	2,496	1.2
World B (evangelized non-Christians)	1,030	2.1	1,762	1.7	3,594	2.7	53	22	75	1.28	4,154	2.9	4,080	2.9	6,554	3.1
World C (Christians)	48,670	97.7	99,330	98.1	129,200	96.4	1,957	-39	1,918	1.39	138,650	96.2	148,380	96.1	198,950	95.7
Country's population	**49,800**	**100.0**	**101,294**	**100.0**	**134,000**	**100.0**	**2,028**	**0**	**2,028**	**1.40**	**144,100**	**100.0**	**154,000**	**100.0**	**208,000**	**100.0**

COLUMNS, ROWS.
For meanings and definitions, see Codebook (Part 3). Note that, by definition, total 'Christians' = professing + crypto-Christians, which also = affiliated + unaffiliated Christians, and also = Great Commission Christians + latent Christians. Percentages may not always total exactly, due to rounding.

CENSUSES.
1901 Census of the British Empire (as in 1900 column above, adjusted), **7.IV.1960:** 92.5% Roman Catholics, 3.8% Anglicans, 3.6% Protestants (1.8% SD Adventists), 0.1% marginal Protestants. **7.IV.1970:** 90.5% Roman Catholics, 5.3% Protestants (2.4% SD Adventists), 3.4% Anglicans, 0.6% non-Christians, 0.2% marginal Protestants. **1980:** 85.6% Roman Catholics, 8.5% Protestants (4.3% SD Adventists, 1.4% Baptists, 1.3% Pentecostals), 2.7% Anglicans, 2.1% non-Christians, 0.7% nonreligious, 0.4% Jehovah's Witnesses. **1991:** 81.0% Roman Catholics, 13.6% Protestants (6.5% SD Adventists, 4.0% Pentecostals, 1.6% Baptists), 2.5% Anglicans, 1.3% nonreligious, 0.8% Jehovah's Witnesses, 0.6% Rastafarians, 0.13% Hindus, 0.07% Muslims.

NOTES ON RELIGIONS
BAHA'IS. In 2 local spiritual assemblies (1973), growing rapidly to 16 LSAs by 1995.

DISAFFILIATED. This term is used here to describe youths and other Black persons who, although baptized Roman Catholics and therefore regarded by the Catholic Church as still affiliated to it (and hence enumerated in Table 2 as such), have recently withdrawn or disaffiliated themselves from it and have become Rastafarians (Rastas). Because their statistics represent a duplication, they are shown in the table above as a negative quantity (with a minus sign).
HINDUS. Hindi-speaking East Indian traders.
INDEPENDENTS. In about 8 denominations in 1995 (see Table 2).
PENTECOSTALS/CHARISMATICS. Catholic totals (mid-1975): 200 involved adults (over 15 years) in 2 prayer groups; total charismatic

Continued overleaf

Country Table 1–concluded

community including children, 400. By 1995, Pentecostals/Charismatics had expanded to over 12,000.
SPIRITISTS. For some years there has been a growing movement among the poorer Black Catholics, youths in particular, to turn to the Ras Tafari Movement from Jamaica (here classified as one manifestation of Afro-American spiritism) and to become Rastas themselves. From being delinquents known as 'wharf rats', these youths have become productive craftsmen living communally. Unlike Jamaican Rastas, St Lucian Rastas do not hold repatriation to Ethiopia or Africa as an ideal, but regard Africa as being wherever they live. Other cults include Kele (Shango).

Great Commission Instrument Panel: status of Saint Lucia (for explanation see start of Part 4)

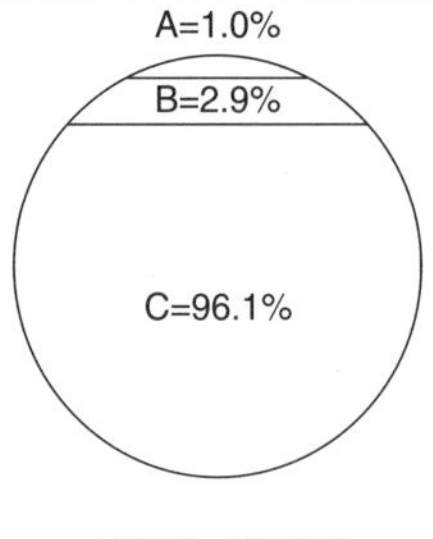

3 Worlds, AD 2000

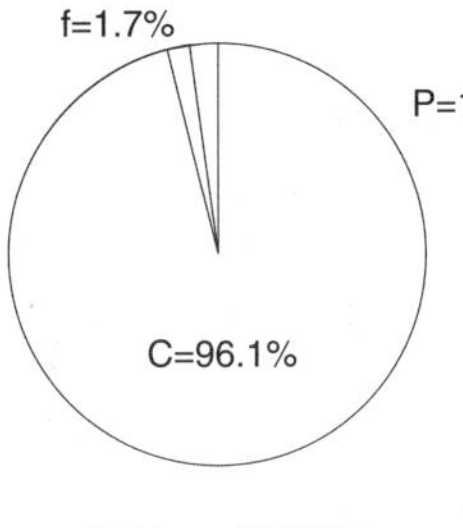

Religions, AD 2000

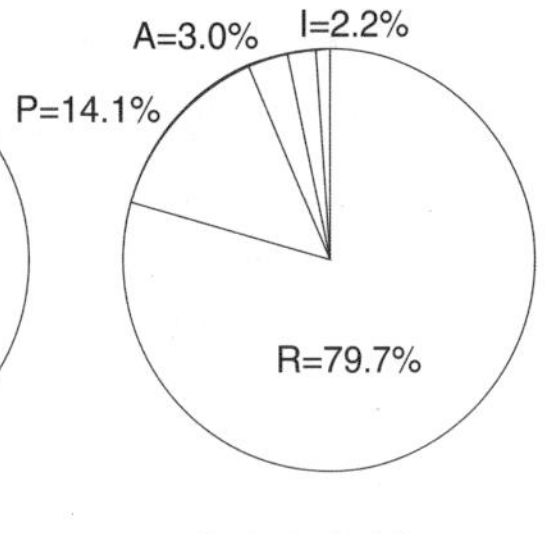

Ecclesiastical blocs

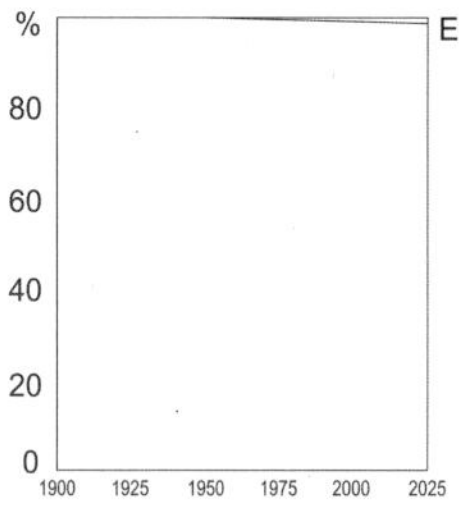

Evangelization, 1900-2025

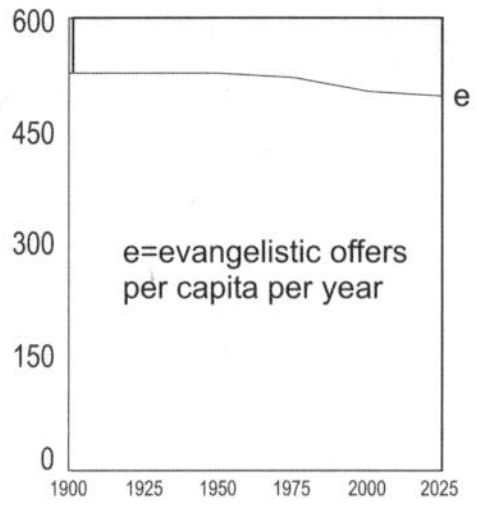

Offers, 1900-2025

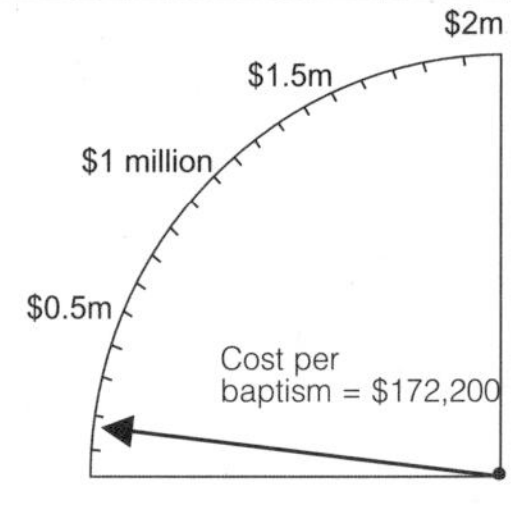

Cost-effectiveness, AD 2000

Country summary. **Worlds A, B, C by ethnolinguistic peoples, cities, and major civil divisions in Saint Lucia.**

	PEOPLES							CITIES							CIVIL DIVISIONS						
World	*Num*	*Pop 2000*	*C%*	*Christians*	*E%*	*U%*	*Unevangelized*	*Num*	*Pop 2000*	*C%*	*Christians*	*E%*	*U%*	*Unevangelized*	*Num*	*Pop 2000*	*C%*	*Christians*	*E%*	*U%*	*Unevangelized*
A	1	2,624	15.02	394	43	57	1,496	0	0	0.00	0	0	0	0	0	0	0.00	0	0	0	0
B	0	0	0.00	0	0	0	0	0	0	0.00	0	0	0	0	0	0	0.00	0	0	0	0
C	6	151,742	94.86	143,946	100	0	78	1	64,193	93.00	59,699	99	1	847	10	154,365	93.51	144,339	99	1	1,572
Total	**7**	**154,366**	**93.51**	**144,340**	**99**	**1**	**1,574**	**1**	**64,193**	**93.00**	**59,699**	**99**	**1**	**847**	**10**	**154,365**	**93.51**	**144,339**	**99**	**1**	**1,572**

Country status. St Lucia is one of the Windward Islands of the Lesser Antilles in the West Indies. Its chief exports are bananas and cocoa.

HUMAN LIFE AND LIBERTY

Human rights and freedoms. St Lucia, a member of the Commonwealth and a former British colony, is a multiparty parliamentary democracy. Aside from a few complaints of police brutality, there are no reported human rights violations.

NON-CHRISTIAN RELIGIONS.

Rastafarianism, an Afro-American cult from Jamaica, has made many converts from among unemployed young Blacks, particularly delinquents known as 'wharf rats'. Now trained as craftsmen, they live communally and stress development, thrift schemes, literacy, and so on. Baha'i has a small but growing following, with 2 assemblies in 1995.

Catholic Church, Archdiocese of Castries. Town and parish church of Soufrière at foot of Pitons mountains.

CHRISTIANITY

CATHOLIC CHURCH. Catholicism gained an early foothold in 1719 under the French, and this has never been relinquished. The archdiocese of Castries is today entrusted to the French FMI. St. Lucia is also served by Presentation Brothers and 3 congregations of sisters: St Joseph of Cluny, Sisters of the Sorrowful Mother and Corpus Christi Carmelites. The composition of the Catholic community is approximately 50% Negroes of African origin, 46% mixed race, three% East Indians, and 1% Whites.

The Holy See has diplomatic relations with St Lucia and in AD 2000 is represented to government and the Catholic hierarchy by a pro-nuncio residing in Port of Spain.

OTHER CHURCHES Anglicans form the second largest of the non-Catholic churches and are part of the diocese of the Windward Islands, in the Church of the Province of the West Indies. The diocese was created in 1878, the Windward Islands having been previously part of the diocese of Barbados. Seventh-day Adventists, who organized the East Caribbean Conference including St Lucia in 1926, are now the largest non-Catholic denomination with nearly 8,000 by 1990. Other smaller denominations include Baptist Mid-Missions, Church of God (Cleveland), and the Orthodox Baptist Church.

Indigenous missions. Only a handful of missionaries have been sent out and most of these to the surrounding islands.

CHURCH AND STATE

Although the state is secular, the government gives annual grants to the Roman Catholic, Anglican, and Methodist churches. Except for a vocational school for girls, all Catholic schools receive government aid.

BROADCASTING AND MEDIA

Shortwave broadcasts from TWR (Antilles), HCJB (Ecuador) and AWR (Costa Rica) can be received. Catholics broadcast daily Scripture readings over radio. St. Lucia is a member of UNDA.

Christian television programming can be seen on local channels and via satellite. CBN's programs can be seen each weekday. Catholic Television News is aired twice each week, and 'The Faith of Millions' (an explanation of the Catholic faith) is aired for 30 minutes each Monday. CTBS is a local Catholic TV station broadcasting in English and Creole.

Many postage stamps portray the story of Christ: (*left*) the Crucifixion, by Raphael, and (*right*) 'Noli me tangere (Do not touch me)', by Titian (Easter 1968).

INTERDENOMINATIONAL ORGANIZATIONS

There is an Inter-Church Council, with Catholic membership, whose purpose is to create good relations between the churches, to prepare joint services, to organize social work including feeding programs and to promote common interests in education, the family and other areas of concern.

FUTURE TRENDS AND PROSPECTS

Little change is expected in Saint Lucia over the next 30 years.

Although Christianity is expected to predominate in the future, it could decline below 90% some time around AD 2050 due to slight increases among non-Christians.

BIBLIOGRAPHY

A history of the Roman Catholic Church in St. Lucia. C. Gachet. Port of Spain, Trinidad: Key Publications, 1976.

Bibliography of St. Lucian material available at the NRDF Library. R. M. McDonald. *Research St. Lucia publications bibliographic series*, no. 1. Castries, St. Lucia: National Research and Development of St. Lucia, 1984. 28p.

Outlines of St Lucia's history. C. Jesse. 2d ed. Castries: St Lucia Archeological and Historical Society, 1964. 74p. (A history written by a priest. Concentrates on the role of the Catholic Church.).

'Political, religious and economic factors affecting language choice in St Lucia,' D. B. Frank, *International journal of the sociology of language*, 102 (1993), 39–56.

Research in ethnography and ethnohistory of St. Lucia: a preliminary report. M. Kremser & K. R. Wernhart (eds). Horn: F. Berger & Söhne, 1986. 170p.

St Lucia. J. H. Momsen. *World bibliographical series*, vol. 185. Oxford, UK: CLIO Press, 1996. (No specific chapter on religion, but see 'Language,' p.44-7, 'History of St. Lucia,' p.36f, 'Folklore,' p.143-4, and 'Bibliographies,' p.151-7).

St. Lucia, a bibliography. St. Augustine, Trinidad, West Indies: Library, University of the West Indies, [1980]. 21p.

St. Lucia: historical, statistical, descriptive. H. H. Breen. *Cass library of West Indian studies*. London: Longman, Brown, Green and Longmans, 1844; reprint ed., London: Frank Cass, 1970. 423p. (First major history of St. Lucia).

'St. Lucia in the time of Henry Breen,' J. Brown, *Chronicle of the West India Committee*, 80, 1404 (January 1965), 28–30. (Examines changes in crime and literacy rates after the placement of the first Church of England clergy in 1819).

'St. Lucian carnival: a Caribbean art form.' R. D. Dunstan. Ph.D. dissertation, State University of New York at Stony Brook, Stony Brook, NY, 1978. 373p. (A study of the preparations for and celebration of carnival, the pre–Lenten celebration. Includes consideration of the religious implications of carnival in St. Lucia).

The folk culture of St. Lucia. [St. Lucia: The Folk Research Centre, 1992–].

'The Kele (Chango) cult in St Lucia,' G. E. Simpson, *Caribbean studies*, 13 (October 1973), 110–16.

Country Table 2. **Organized churches and denominations in Saint Lucia.**

Official name (bold type = church with over 10% of all affiliated) 1	*Begun* 2	*Type* 3	*Counc* 4	*Congs* 5	*Adults* 6	*Affiliated 1970* 7	*Affiliated 1995* 8	*G%* 9	*Names, notes, and other statistics* (see Codebook, Part 3) 10
Anglican Church (D Windward Is)		A-ACa	awMRC	2	2,070	3,000	4,130	0.05	In Ch of Prov of West Indies. 90% Black. Decline from 5,980 in 1900. 1f,W=20%.
Apostolic Faith Church	c1970	P-Pe3	.....	4	800	–	2,000	35.53	Holiness Pentecostals.
Baptist Association	c1985	P-Bap	.....	2	58	–	120	10.00	M=SBC. Southern Baptist Convention, USA.
Baptist Mid-Missions	1946	I-Fun	x....	5	300	400	700	2.26	M=Baptist Mid-Missions (USA). Regular Baptists. Fundamentalists. 9f.

Continued opposite

Country Table 2–concluded

Official name (bold type = church with over 10% of affiliated) 1	*Begun* 2	*Type* 3	*Counc* 4	*Congs* 5	*Adults* 6	*Affiliated 1970* 7	*Affiliated 1995* 8	*G%* 9	*Names, notes, and other statistics* (see Codebook, Part 3) 10
Catholic Church: M Castries	1719	R-Lat	PxNMC	23	55,000	92,510	108,570	0.64	3% East Indian. C=2+1+3. , 20n, 22x, 25m, 37w, 2490Yy
Christian Brethren	1923	P-CBr	x....	5	90	200	300	1.64	*Open Brethren. Plymouth Brethren. Gospel Halls.* 2 missionaries from UK.
Christian Brethren (Exclusive)		P-EBr	x....	3	200	400	400	0.05	*Exclusive (Plymouth) Brethren.* Group: Kelly-Continental.
Church of Christ	c1970	I-Dis	.....	2	325	–	500	28.22	Independent Disciples from USA.
Church of God (Cleveland)	1940	P-Pe3	ZF...	19	1,264	200	2,110	9.88	M=CoG(Cleveland)(USA). Holiness Pentecostals (3-stage). 1 church, 1 mission. 1n.
Church of God (Seventh-day)	c1965	P-Hol	.....	4	250	250	500	2.81	Holiness body.
Ch of Jesus Christ of Latter-day Saints	c1985	m-LdS	.....	1	32	–	45	10.00	*Mormons.* M=CJCLdS(USA).
Church of the Nazarene	1972	P-Hol	.....	4	136	–	187	4.35	M=CoN(USA).
Evangelical Church of the West Indies	1949	P-Eva	xM...	11	543	1,200	1,085	-0.40	M=WIM(USA). Island base for evangelism in Windward Islands. 1 school. 7f.
Jehovah's Witnesses	1953	m-Jeh	x....	6	460	300	1,200	5.70	*Watch Tower. International Bible Students Association.* (1975) 24Y. (1995) 64Y.
Methodist Ch in Caribbean & Americas	1809	P-Met	VwM.C	2	302	600	480	-0.89	*MCCA,* South Caribbean Dist. Begun from Dominica. Decline (1,400 in 1900). 2x,17y.
Moravian Church	c1850	P-Mor	xwM..	1	108	200	180	-0.42	Eastern West Indies Province, Unity of Brethren. Blacks. In 1900, 130 Moravians.
New Apostolic Church	c1991	I-3aX	x....	2	40	–	90	25.00	*NAC/NAK.* M=Neuapostolische Kirche. HQ Zurich (Switzerland).
Orthodox Baptist Church		I-Bap	.....	4	200	250	400	0.05	Independent Baptist congregations. Also in Trinidad and Tobago. Blacks.
Pentecostal Assemblies of the W Indies		P-Pe2	ZF...	15	1,500	50	2,500	0.05	M=PAoC(Canada). Classical Pentecostals (2-stage). Emigration to UK. 1f.
Salvation Army		P-Sal	xwM..	3	75	30	107	0.05	In Barbados Division, Caribbean & CAmerica Territory (HQ Jamaica). HQ Castries.
Seventh-day Adventist Church	1926	P-Adv	x....	35	5,200	2,500	7,831	4.67	*SDA,* East Caribbean Conference, Caribbean Union Conference. 1r(SDA Academy).
Streams of Power	c1975	I-3pU	.....	1	98	–	150	5.00	Independent Afro-Caribbean pentecostals.
United Holy Church of America	c1965	I-3aB	x....	3	150	400	300	-1.14	*UHCA,* Barbados District. M=UHCA(USA Black pentecostals). Begun from Barbados.
Wesleyan Holiness Church	c1970	P-Hol	.....	1	65	–	108	20.60	Mainline Wesleyan Methodists.
Other Black indigenous churches		I-3nB	.....	4	350	600	870	0.05	Several bodies including Spiritual Baptists (Shouters, Shakers).
Other Protestant denominations		P-	.....	15	400	500	900	0.05	Total about 5, including Bible Missionary Church.
Doubly-affiliated		2-aff			0	-3,260	0		Evangelicals and others who also are or were baptized Roman Catholics.
Disaffiliated		X-Aff			-570	-1,500	-1,100		Baptized Catholics, mostly Black youths, who have recently become Rastafarians.
Totals				**177**	**69,446**	**98,830**	**134,663**		

Churches, members, growth, 1900-2025	*Congs*	*Adults*	*Affiliated*	*G%*	*Total denominations*	*6 Megablocs:* *O*	*R*	*A*	*P*	*I*	*m*
Total churches, members, and denominations (mid-1900)	30	26,000	48,670	1.02	4	0	1	1	2	0	0
Total churches, members, and denominations (mid-1970)	80	52,733	98,830	1.02	21	0	1	1	12	6	1
Total churches, members, and denominations (mid-1990)	150	64,900	125,800	1.21	36	0	1	1	19	13	2
Total churches, members, and denominations (mid-1995)	177	69,446	134,663	1.37	36	0	1	1	19	13	2
Total churches, members, and denominations (mid-2000)	180	74,400	144,339	1.40	36	0	1	1	19	13	2
Total churches, members, and denominations (mid-2025)	300	101,000	195,000	1.21	71	0	1	1	30	35	4

NOTES ON TABLE ABOVE
NATIONAL COUNCILS (Column 4, 5th letter).
C = St Lucia Inter-Church Council.
E = Evangelical Alliance of St Lucia.

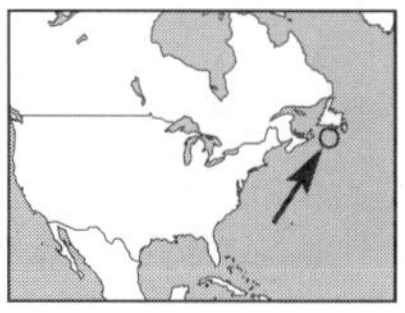

SAINT PIERRE & MIQUELON

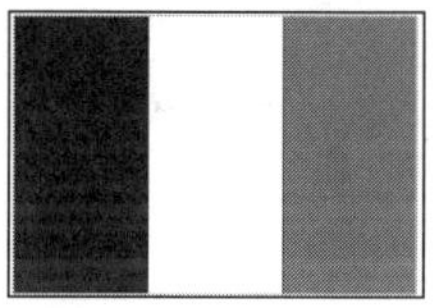

SECULAR DATA, AD 2000

STATE
Official name: Iles Saint-Pierre et Miquelon (The Territorial Collectivity of Saint Pierre & Miquelon).
Short name: Saint Pierre & Miquelon. **Adjective of nationality:** of Saint Pierre & Miquelon.
Flag: That of France.
Area: 242 sq. km. (93 sq. mi.).
Government: Overseas department of France, since 1975 (1535 French possession. 1946 overseas territory).
Legislature: General Council, 19 members.
Official language: French (Français).
Monetary unit: 1 French franc (F) = 100 centimes. **US$1=** F 5.60.
Chief cities: SAINT-PIERRE 5,987.
Political divisions: 1 province.

DEMOGRAPHY
Population: 7,000.
Population density: 27.1/sq. km. (70.6/sq. mi.).
Under 15 years: 1,000.
Growth rate p.a.: 0.28% (births 11.85, deaths 9.51).
Mortality: Infant, per 1,000: 5.9; **Maternal per 100,000:** 40.0.
Life expectancy: 79 (male 75, female 83).
Household size: 3.0. **Floor area per person, sq.m:** 22.0.
Major languages: French.
Urban dwellers: 92.02%. **Urban growth rate p.a.:** 0.7%.
Labor force: 40%.

ETHNOLINGUISTIC PEOPLES
95.2% French-Canadian; 3.7% Anglo-Canadian; .

ECONOMY
National income p.a. per person: US$10,963; **per family:** US$32,891.

EDUCATION
Adult literacy: 99% (male 99%, female 99%). **Schools:** 9.
Universities: 0. **School enrolment:** female/male: 80%/80%.

HEALTH
Access to health services: 80%. **Access to safe water:** 80%.
Hospitals: 1 (40 beds per 10,000). **Doctors:** 10.
Blind: 10. **Deaf:** 400. **Murder rate:** 4. **Lepers:** 0.

LITERATURE
New book titles p.a.: 3 (500 p.a. per million). **Periodicals:** 1.
Newspapers: 1 daily.

COMMUNICATION (per 1,000 people)
Phones: 150 (30% mobile). **Radios:** 900. **TV sets:** 200.
Daily newspaper circulation: 0. **Computers:** 1,000.

HUMAN LIFE AND LIBERTY (optimum condition=100.0%)
HDI: 75.0. **HSI:** 80.0. **HFI:** 75.0. **EFL:** 45.0.

Country Table 1. **Religious adherents in Saint Pierre & Miquelon, AD 1900-2025.**

Year / *Name*	*1900* *Adherents*	*%*	*1970* *Adherents*	*%*	*mid-1990* *Adherents*	*%*	*Annual change, 1990-2000* *Natural*	*Conversion*	*Total*	*Rate*	*mid-1995* *Adherents*	*%*	*mid-2000* *Adherents*	*%*	*mid-2025* *Adherents*	*%*
Christians	**6,500**	**100.0**	**5,350**	**99.1**	**6,260**	**97.8**	**15**	**-1**	**14**	**0.21**	**6,345**	**98.0**	**6,395**	**97.4**	**6,860**	**95.3**
PROFESSION																
professing Christians	**6,500**	**100.0**	**5,350**	**99.1**	**6,260**	**97.8**	**15**	**-1**	**14**	**0.21**	**6,345**	**98.0**	**6,395**	**97.4**	**6,860**	**95.3**
AFFILIATION																
unaffiliated Christians	1,200	18.5	17	0.3	5	0.1	0	0	0	3.42	5	0.1	7	0.1	10	0.1
affiliated Christians	**5,300**	**81.5**	**5,333**	**98.8**	**6,255**	**97.7**	**15**	**-2**	**13**	**0.21**	**6,340**	**97.9**	**6,388**	**96.8**	**6,850**	**95.2**
Roman Catholics	5,300	81.5	5,283	97.8	6,300	98.4	16	-1	17	0.26	6,403	98.9	6,465	98.1	7,090	98.5
Protestants	0	0.0	50	0.9	55	0.9	1	1	2	2.44	60	0.9	70	1.0	120	1.7
Marginal Christians	0	0.0	0	0.0	15	0.3	0	3	3	10.31	18	0.3	40	0.6	80	1.1
doubly-affiliated	0	0.0	0	0.0	-115	-1.9	-2	-5	-7	4.98	-141	-2.2	-187	-2.7	-440	-6.1
Trans-megabloc groupings																
Evangelicals	0	0.0	10	0.2	10	0.2	0	0	0	0.00	9	0.1	10	0.1	20	0.3
Pentecostals/Charismatics	0	0.0	10	0.2	120	2.0	2	2	4	2.92	134	2.1	160	2.3	280	3.9
Great Commission Christians	**600**	**9.2**	**1,620**	**30.0**	**2,150**	**33.6**	**9**	**1**	**10**	**0.46**	**2,210**	**34.1**	**2,251**	**34.1**	**2,520**	**35.0**
Baha'is	0	0.0	50	0.9	75	1.3	1	0	1	1.61	80	1.2	88	1.3	150	2.1
Nonreligious	0	0.0	0	0.0	55	0.9	1	1	2	3.15	65	1.0	75	1.1	150	2.1
Muslims	0	0.0	0	0.0	10	0.2	0	0	0	0.00	10	0.2	10	0.1	40	0.6
World A (unevangelized persons)	0	0.0	0	0.0	0	0.0	0	0	0	7.18	0	0.0	7	0.1	7	0.1
World B (evangelized non-Christians)	0	0.0	50	0.9	140	2.2	2	1	3	3.53	130	2.0	198	2.5	333	4.6
World C (Christians)	6,500	100.0	5,350	99.1	6,260	97.8	15	-1	14	0.21	6,345	98.0	6,395	97.4	6,860	95.3
Country's population	**6,500**	**100.0**	**5,400**	**100.0**	**6,400**	**100.0**	**17**	**0**	**17**	**1.55**	**6,475**	**100.0**	**6,600**	**100.0**	**7,200**	**100.0**

COLUMNS, ROWS.
For meanings and definitions, see Codebook (Part 3). Note that, by definition, total 'Christians' = professing + crypto-Christians, which also = affiliated + unaffiliated Christians, and also = Great Commission Christians + latent Christians. Percentages may not always total exactly, due to rounding.

CENSUSES.
20.IV.1962: 99.0% Roman Catholics, 1.0% Protestants.

NOTES ON RELIGIONS
BAHA'IS. Isolated adherents, with no local spiritual assembly by 1997.
PROTESTANTS. Individuals unaffiliated to churches.

Country status. Saint Pierre & Miquelon is a group of 8 islands in the northern Atlantic Ocean, south of Newfoundland. Its chief export is fish.

HUMAN LIFE AND LIBERTY

Human rights and freedoms. Saint Pierre & Miquelon, a French colony since 1763, is a territorial collectivity of France. As in other French overseas dependencies, all human rights are guaranteed and respected.

Great Commission Instrument Panel: status of Saint Pierre & Miquelon (for explanation see start of Part 4)

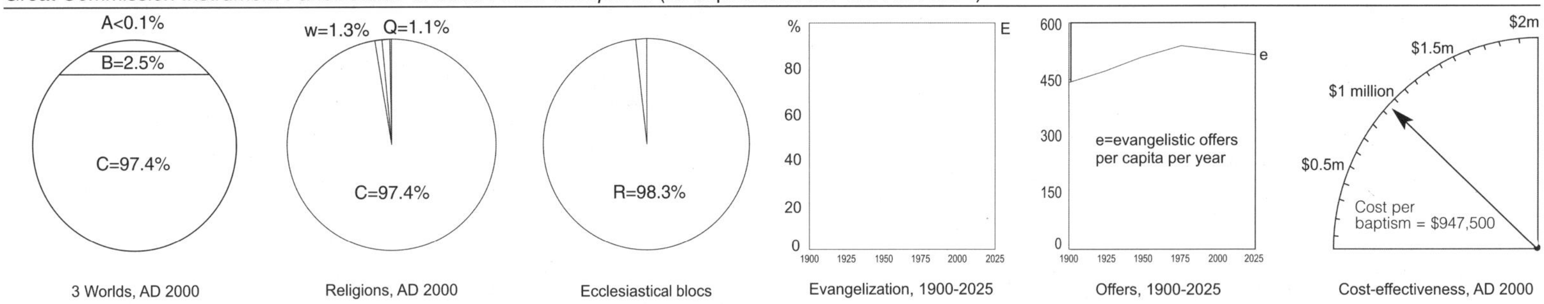

Country summary. **Worlds A, B, C by ethnolinguistic peoples, cities, and major civil divisions in Saint Pierre & Miquelon.**

	PEOPLES							CITIES							CIVIL DIVISIONS						
World	*Num*	*Pop 2000*	*C%*	*Christians*	*E%*	*U%*	*Unevangelized*	*Num*	*Pop 2000*	*C%*	*Christians*	*E%*	*U%*	*Unevangelized*	*Num*	*Pop 2000*	*C%*	*Christians*	*E%*	*U%*	*Unevangelized*
A	0	0	0.00	0	0	0	0	0	0	0.00	0	0	0	0	0	0	0.00	0	0	0	0
B	0	0	0.00	0	0	0	0	0	0	0.00	0	0	0	0	0	0	0.00	0	0	0	0
C	3	6,567	97.27	6,388	100	0	4	1	5,987	97.19	5,819	100	0	3	1	6,567	97.27	6,388	100	0	4
Total	**3**	**6,567**	**97.27**	**6,388**	**100**	**0**	**4**	**1**	**5,987**	**97.19**	**5,819**	**100**	**0**	**3**	**1**	**6,567**	**97.27**	**6,388**	**100**	**0**	**4**

NON-CHRISTIAN RELIGIONS

Baha'i has a small following on the islands.

CHRISTIANITY

Catholic work was begun in 1689, and this remains the only large church on the islands. The vicariate covers the whole territory and is attached, with consultative voice, to the Episcopal Conference of France. The islands are served by Holy Ghost priests, together with St Joseph de Cluny sisters.

The Holy See has no diplomatic relations with St Pierre & Miquelon in AD 2000.

OTHER CHURCHES. Jehovah's Witnesses, active since the late 1970s, have a small following. A few other Protestant denominations have made small inroads since the 1960s.

Indigenous missions. There have been few missionaries sent out from the islands.

CHURCH AND STATE

Legal statutes relating to the church are the same as for metropolitan France.

FUTURE TRENDS AND PROSPECTS

The nonreligious, Muslims, and Baha'is are expected to increase steadily through 2025 with a corresponding decline among Christians to 95% by 2025.

Christianity will probably predominate but Hindus, Muslims, and the nonreligious could grow beyond 10% of the population around mid-century and possibly as high as 20% after AD 2050.

BIBLIOGRAPHY

Saint Pierre and Miquelon. W. F. Rannie. Beamsville, Ontario: Rannie Publications, [1963]. 132p.

Eglise Catholique: VA Iles S-P & M. Postage stamps illustrating the main church buildings.

Country Table 2. **Organized churches and denominations in Saint Pierre & Miquelon.**

Official name (bold type = church with over 10% of all affiliated) 1	*Begun* 2	*Type* 3	*Counc* 4	*Congs* 5	*Adults* 6	*Affiliated 1970* 7	*Affiliated 1995* 8	*G%* 9	*Names, notes, and other statistics* (see Codebook, Part 3) 10
Eglise Catholique: VA Iles S-P & M	1689	R-Lat	P...r	3	3,800	5,283	6,403	0.77	98.6% Catholic. M=CSSp. C=1+0+1. (1970) 7x,1m,18w,131y. (1990) 3x, 3m, 7w, 105Yy. , 0n, 3x,
Jehovah's Witnesses	1977	m-Jeh	x....	1	7	–	18	5.56	*Watch Tower.* (1995) 1,510 hours of witnessing recorded.
Other Protestant congregations	c1960	P-	....	2	30	50	60	0.73	A few Protestants from elsewhere in Canada.
Doubly-affiliated		2-aff			-83	0	-141		Non-Catholics are counted in Catholic totals here.
Totals				**6**	**3,754**	**5,333**	**6,340**		

Churches, members, growth, 1900-2025	*Congs*	*Adults*	*Affiliated*	*G%*	*Total denominations*	*6 Megablocs: O*	*R*	*A*	*P*	*I*	*m*
Total churches, members, and denominations (mid-1900)	2	3,000	5,300	0.01	1	0	1	0	0	0	0
Total churches, members, and denominations (mid-1970)	3	3,025	5,333	0.01	2	0	1	0	1	0	0
Total churches, members, and denominations (mid-1990)	6	3,700	6,255	0.80	3	0	1	0	1	0	1
Total churches, members, and denominations (mid-1995)	6	3,754	6,340	0.27	3	0	1	0	1	0	1
Total churches, members, and denominations (mid-2000)	6	3,800	6,388	0.15	3	0	1	0	1	0	1
Total churches, members, and denominations (mid-2025)	20	4,100	6,850	0.28	9	0	1	0	1	5	2

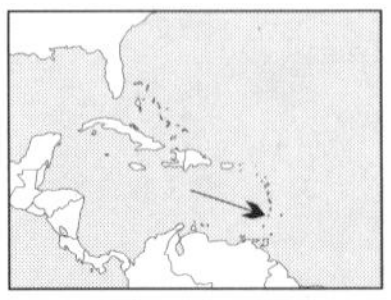

SAINT VINCENT & THE GRENADINES

SECULAR DATA, AD 2000

STATE
Official name: The Realm of Saint Vincent and the Grenadines.
Short name: Saint Vincent and the Grenadines. **Adjective of nationality:** of Saint Vincent & the Grenadines.
Flag: Blue, yellow, green and white bars, with Arms of St Vincent with motto 'Pax et Justitia'.
Area: 389 sq. km. (150 sq. mi.).
Government: Republic, formerly self-governing state in association with the United Kingdom (Britain), since 1969 (1783 British colony, 1979 Independence).
Legislature: House of Assembly, 21 members.
Official language: English.
Monetary unit: 1 Eastern Caribbean dollar (EC$) = 100 cents. **US$1=** EC$2.70.
Chief cities: KINGSTOWN 32,442.
Political divisions: 13 provinces.

DEMOGRAPHY
Population: 114,000.
Population density: 292.9/sq. km. (759.6/sq. mi.).
Under 15 years: 27,000.
Growth rate p.a.: 1.19% (births 15.26, deaths 5.77).
Mortality: Infant, per 1,000: 7.8; **Maternal per 100,000:** 40.0.
Life expectancy: 78 (male 75, female 82).
Household size: 4.0. **Floor area per person, sq.m:** 17.0.
Major languages: English, Hindi.
Urban dwellers: 54.79%. **Urban growth rate p.a.:** 2.8%.
Labor force: 39%.

ETHNOLINGUISTIC PEOPLES
65.1% West Indian Black; 19.9% Mulatto; 5.5% East Indian; 3.0% British; 2.0% Black Carib.

ECONOMY
National income p.a. per person: US$2,281; **per family:** US$9,126.

EDUCATION
Adult literacy: 96% (male 97%, female 95%). **Schools:** 60.
Universities: 0. **School enrolment:** female/male: 95%/95%.

HEALTH
Access to health services: 90%. **Access to safe water:** 100%.
Hospitals: 1 (44 beds per 10,000). **Doctors:** 40.
Blind: 100. **Deaf:** 7,000. **Murder rate:** 10.
Lepers: 100.

LITERATURE
New book titles p.a.: 23 (200 p.a. per million). **Periodicals:** 6.
Newspapers: 0 dailies.

COMMUNICATION (per 1,000 people)
Phones: 165 **(12% mobile). Radios:** 565. **TV sets:** 161.
Daily newspaper circulation: 500. **Computers:** 80.

HUMAN LIFE AND LIBERTY (optimum condition=100.0%)
HDI: 83.6. **HSI:** 75.0. **HFI:** 80.0. **EFL:** 46.0.

Country Table 1. **Religious adherents in Saint Vincent & the Grenadines, AD 1900-2025.**

Year	1900		1970		mid-1990		Annual change, 1990-2000				mid-1995		mid-2000		mid-2025	
Name	Adherents	%	Adherents	%	Adherents	%	Natural	Conversion	Total	Rate	Adherents	%	Adherents	%	Adherents	%
Christians	**46,500**	**98.9**	**84,700**	**96.8**	**96,800**	**91.3**	**727**	**-250**	**477**	**0.48**	**98,790**	**89.9**	**101,569**	**89.1**	**110,700**	**84.5**
PROFESSION																
professing Christians	**46,500**	**98.9**	**84,700**	**96.8**	**96,800**	**91.3**	**727**	**-250**	**477**	**0.48**	**98,790**	**89.9**	**101,569**	**89.1**	**110,700**	**84.5**
AFFILIATION																
unaffiliated Christians	4,250	9.0	20,113	23.0	22,750	21.5	172	-134	38	0.17	22,679	20.6	23,130	20.3	16,480	12.6
affiliated Christians	**42,250**	**89.9**	**64,587**	**73.8**	**74,050**	**69.9**	**555**	**-116**	**439**	**0.58**	**76,111**	**69.2**	**78,439**	**68.8**	**94,220**	**71.9**
Protestants	4,750	10.1	17,440	19.9	31,100	29.3	235	40	275	0.85	32,474	29.5	33,854	29.7	42,000	32.1
Anglicans	35,500	75.5	30,000	34.3	20,000	18.9	151	-180	-29	-0.14	20,000	18.2	19,715	17.3	20,600	15.7
Independents	100	0.2	2,617	3.0	11,800	11.1	89	61	150	1.20	12,477	11.4	13,300	11.7	18,000	13.7
Roman Catholics	1,900	4.0	14,330	16.4	10,300	9.7	78	-108	-30	-0.30	10,000	9.1	10,000	8.8	11,000	8.4
Marginal Christians	0	0.0	200	0.2	800	0.8	6	64	70	6.49	1,100	1.0	1,500	1.3	2,500	1.9
Orthodox	0	0.0	0	0.0	50	0.1	0	2	2	3.42	60	0.1	70	0.1	120	0.1
Trans-megabloc groupings																
Evangelicals	3,800	8.1	6,000	6.9	13,270	12.5	100	78	178	1.27	14,183	12.9	15,050	13.2	20,000	15.3
Pentecostals/Charismatics	0	0.0	3,400	3.9	20,870	19.7	158	155	313	1.41	23,011	20.9	24,000	21.1	32,000	24.4
Great Commission Christians	**1,900**	**4.0**	**7,000**	**8.0**	**22,260**	**21.0**	**168**	**14**	**182**	**0.79**	**23,200**	**21.1**	**24,080**	**21.1**	**31,500**	**24.1**
Hindus	0	0.0	0	0.0	3,450	3.3	26	11	37	1.03	3,650	3.3	3,823	3.4	5,800	4.4
Nonreligious	0	0.0	400	0.5	1,100	1.0	8	145	153	9.09	2,200	2.0	2,625	2.3	5,000	3.8
Spiritists	500	1.1	1,800	2.1	1,580	1.5	12	30	42	2.36	1,800	1.6	1,996	1.8	3,000	2.3
Muslims	0	0.0	0	0.0	1,500	1.4	11	9	20	1.25	1,600	1.5	1,698	1.5	2,800	2.1
Baha'is	0	0.0	600	0.7	1,200	1.1	9	37	46	3.31	1,500	1.4	1,662	1.5	3,000	2.3
New-Religionists	0	0.0	0	0.0	370	0.4	3	18	21	4.62	460	0.4	581	0.5	700	0.5
World A (unevangelized persons)	47	0.1	174	0.2	1,166	1.1	9	12	21	1.64	1,209	1.1	1,368	1.2	2,751	2.1
World B (evangelized non-Christians)	453	1.0	2,622	3.0	8,034	7.6	60	238	298	3.25	9,949	9.1	11,063	9.7	17,549	13.4
World C (Christians)	46,500	98.9	84,700	96.8	96,800	91.3	727	-250	477	0.48	98,790	89.9	101,569	89.1	110,700	84.5
Country's population	**47,000**	**100.0**	**87,497**	**100.0**	**106,000**	**100.0**	**796**	**0**	**796**	**0.73**	**109,949**	**100.0**	**114,000**	**100.0**	**131,000**	**100.0**

COLUMNS, ROWS.
For meanings and definitions, see Codebook (Part 3). Note that, by definition, total 'Christians' = professing + crypto-Christians, which also = affiliated + unaffiliated Christians, and also = Great Commission Christians + latent Christians. Percentages may not always total exactly, due to rounding.

CENSUSES.
7.IV.1960: 47.4% Anglicans, 40.6% Protestants (33.4% Methodists), 11.1% Roman Catholics, 0.5% Black indigenous (393 Spiritual Baptists), 0.3% nonreligious, 0.1% marginal Protestants.

NOTES ON RELIGIONS
BAHA'IS. Growth of local spiritual assemblies: 1964, none; 1973, 6 (2 on Grenadines). Converts include Carib Indians. By 1996 there were 16 LSAs.
INDEPENDENTS. In 9 denominations in 1995 (see Table 2).
PENTECOSTALS/CHARISMATICS (or, Catholic charismatics). Totals (mid-1975): 100 involved adults (over 15 years) in 3 prayer groups; total charismatic community including children, 200. By 1995 Pentecostals and Charismatics numbered over 23,000
SPIRITISTS. There are centers of Shango (Yoruba syncretism), including Obeah and other spirit-possession cults. There are also many Rastafarians (from Jamaica).
UNAFFILIATED CHRISTIANS. As in several other Caribbean countries, there are large numbers of persons professing in government censuses to be Anglicans, Methodists or other Protestants, but who have no church affiliation.

Great Commission Instrument Panel: status of Saint Vincent & the Grenadines (for explanation see start of Part 4)

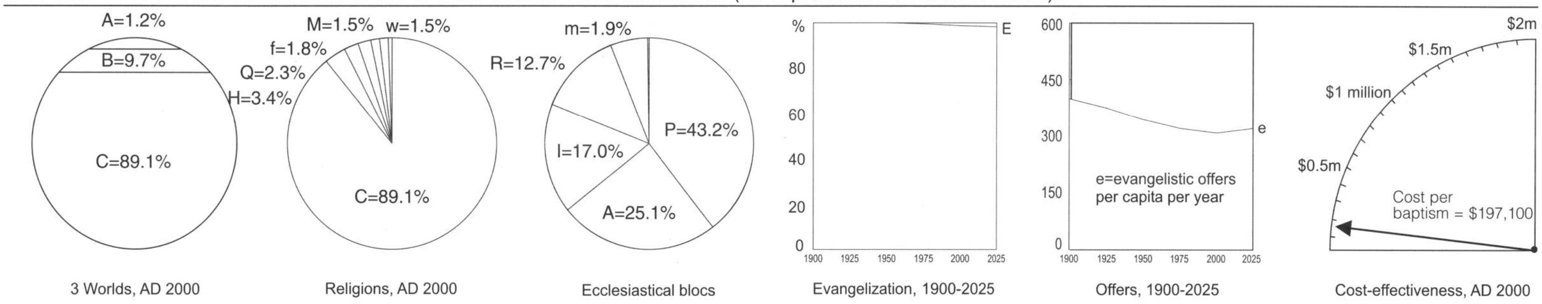

Country status. St Vincent and the Grenadines are islands in the Windward Islands in the West Indies. It is the world's chief producer of arrowroot, but tobacco, coconuts, and fruit are also important.

HUMAN LIFE AND LIBERTY

Human rights and freedoms. St Vincent and the Grenadines is a member of the Commonwealth and a parliamentary democracy where citizens enjoy all human rights and civil liberties.

NON-CHRISTIAN RELIGIONS

Afro-American spiritism is followed by a small number of persons of African descent.

Hinduism and ***Islam*** have a significant number of followers due to the presence of traders from India.

Baha'i has a number of followers, mostly former Hindus and Muslims among East Indians.

CHRISTIANITY

ANGLICAN CHURCH. Anglicanism has an ancient history in St Vincent dating back to the end of the 17th century and is still the principal church of the island. St Vincent belongs to the diocese of the Windward Islands, in the Church of the Province of the West Indies. The church is about 90% Black.

PROTESTANT CHURCHES. The Methodist Church, which first came to St Vincent in 1787, is the main Protestant body. Of some 14 smaller mostly American-based Protestant denominations begun in the present century, the largest are the Seventh-day Adventists and the Church of God (Cleveland).

CATHOLIC CHURCH. The territory of St Vincent belongs to the diocese of Bridgetown-Kingstown which is based on and includes Barbados. Catholicism has never gained a strong foothold in these islands, making up 9.1% in 1995.

The Holy See has diplomatic relations with St Vincent & the Grenadines and in AD 2000 is represented to government and the Catholic hierarchy by a nuncio.

Indigenous missions. There have been few missionaries sent out from the islands.

CHURCH AND STATE

St Vincent was granted home rule in 1969, 2 years after the other 3 islands of the Windward group. No special status is accorded to the Anglican Church in spite of its strength and its traditional relationship to the British Crown.

BROADCASTING AND MEDIA

Shortwave broadcasts from TWR (Antilles), HCJB (Ecuador), and AWR (Costa Rica) can be received. Christian television programming can be seen on local channels and via satellite. CBN's programs can be seen each weekday.

INTERDENOMINATIONAL ORGANIZATIONS

The Christian Council of St Vincent was founded in 1969 with 4 member bodies: Anglican, Catholic, and Methodist churches, and Salvation Army. The council works in close co-operation with the World Council of Churches; and in fact membership is restricted to churches who are members of the WCC, or whose parent bodies are, with the exception of the Catholic Church. Nevertheless, membership in the council's 5 commissions (ecumenism, family life, social action, communications, and youth) is open to denominations which have no WCC affiliation.

Anglican Church, Diocese of the Windward Isles. A series of government postage stamps commemorating Diocesan Centenary in 1977.

Country summary. **Worlds A, B, C by ethnolinguistic peoples, cities, and major civil divisions in Saint Vincent & the Grenadines.**

	PEOPLES							CITIES							CIVIL DIVISIONS						
World	Num	Pop 2000	C%	Christians	E%	U%	Unevangelized	Num	Pop 2000	C%	Christians	E%	U%	Unevangelized	Num	Pop 2000	C%	Christians	E%	U%	Unevangelized
A	0	0	0.00	0	0	0	0	0	0	0.00	0	0	0	0	0	0	0.00	0	0	0	0
B	2	6,837	17.42	1,191	84	16	1,094	0	0	0.00	0	0	0	0	0	0	0.00	0	0	0	0
C	11	107,119	72.12	77,251	100	0	296	1	32,442	68.00	22,061	98	2	665	13	113,953	68.83	78,439	99	1	1,388
Total	**13**	**113,956**	**68.84**	**78,442**	**99**	**1**	**1,390**	**1**	**32,442**	**68.00**	**22,061**	**98**	**2**	**665**	**13**	**113,953**	**68.83**	**78,439**	**99**	**1**	**1,388**

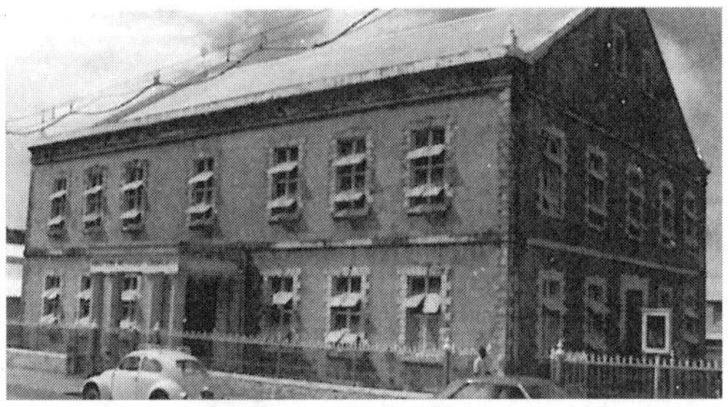

Pentecostal Assemblies of the West Indies. Noticeboard with times of regular services. Many St. Vincent Pentecostals have emigrated to Britain.

FUTURE TRENDS AND PROSPECTS

Christianity is expected to decline from 96.8% in 1970 to under 85% by AD 2025.

Christianity will potentially predominate but Hindus, Spiritists, Muslims, Baha'is, and the nonreligious will likely together grow beyond 20% of the population by the mid-21st century.

BIBLIOGRAPHY

Becoming West Indian: culture, self, and nation in St. Vincent. V. H. Young. *Smithsonian series in ethnographic inquiry.* Washington, DC: Smithsonian Institution Press, 1993. 239p.

Bibliography of material relating to St. Vincent and the Grenadines. Kingstown, St. Vincent: St. Vincent Public Library, 1982. 32p.

Black religions in the New World. G. E. Simpson. New York: Columbia University Press, 1978. 429p. (Chapter 4 deals with the Shakers and Streams of Power cult in St. Vincent).

Methodism in St. Vincent. Kingstown, St. Vincent: Kingstown Methodist Church, 1987. 57p.

'Spirit–possession belief and trance behaviour in two fundamentalist groups in St. Vincent,' J. H. Henney, in *Trance, healing and hallucination: three field studies in religious experience*, p.1–111. F. D. Goodman, J. H. Henney & E. Pressel (eds). New York: John Wiley & Sons, 1974. (Deals with Shakers and Streams of Power cult).

St. Vincent and the Grenadines. R. B. Potter. *World bibliographical series*, vol. 143. Oxford, UK: CLIO Press, 1992. 224p. (See especially 'Population,' p.56-8 and 'Religion,' p.71-3).

'The politics of ritual: the development of the Garifuna cult of the dead on St. Vincent,' B. Foster, in *Belize: ethnicity and development*, p.1–11. Society for the Promotion of Education and Research. Belize City: SPEAR, 1987.

The rise and fall of the Black Caribs of St. Vincent. I. E. Kirby & C. I. Martin. Kingstown, St. Vincent: St. Vincent Archaeological and Historical Society, 1972. 65p.

Country Table 2. **Organized churches and denominations in Saint Vincent & the Grenadines.**

Official name (bold type = church with over 10% of affiliated) 1	*Begun* 2	*Type* 3	*Counc* 4	*Congs* 5	*Adults* 6	*Affiliated 1970* 7	*Affiliated 1995* 8	*G%* 9	*Names, notes, and other statistics* (see Codebook, Part 3) 10
Anglican Church: D Windward Isles	c1700	A-ACa	AwMRK	23	15,000	30,000	20,000	-1.61	1878, Diocese in CPWI. M=USPG(UK). 95% WIndian (90% Black). 8n,12x12f,W+20%,1265y.
Baptist Association	1976	P-Bap	.....	5	290	–	488	5.26	M=FMB-SBC.
Baptist Churches	1946	I-Fun	x....	10	900	417	1,500	5.25	M=Baptist Mid-Missions (USA). Regular Baptists. Links with St. Lucia, 8f,1s.
Bible Missionary Church	1960	P-Hol	.....	3	180	100	300	4.49	M=BMC(USA).
Cath Ch in St Vincent: D Kingstown		R-Lat	P.NMK	16	6,000	14,330	10,000	0.05	C=1+1+2 (1970). 7x(SFM),5m(FSC),12w,1H,3r,500Yy. (1990). , 3n, 4x, 8m, 13w, 153Yy
Christian Brethren		P-CBr	x....	10	950	1,500	1,580	0.05	*Gospel Halls. Plymouth Brethren (Open).* M=CMML(UK,USA). 2f.
Christian Brethren (Exclusive)		P-EBr	x....	4	250	400	500	0.05	*Exclusive (Plymouth) Brethren.* Group: Kelly-Continental.
Christian Pilgrim Church of St Vincent		I-Non	.....	1	400	500	700	0.05	Indigenous Black church led by bishop. HQ Georgetown.
Church of God of Prophecy		P-Pe3	Z....	2	100	100	200	0.05	M=CGP(USA). Holiness Pentecostals. Schism in USA from CoG (Cleveland).
Church of God (Cleveland)	1940	P-Pe3	ZF...	19	1,330	600	2,960	6.59	M=CoG(Cleveland) (USA). Holiness Pentecostals. 11 churches, 6 missions. 13n.
Ch of Jesus Christ of Latter-day Saints	c1975	m-LdS	.....	2	200	–	400	5.00	*Mormons.* M=CJCLdS(USA).
Church of the Nazarene	1975	P-Hol	.....	5	164	–	204	5.00	M=CON. Holiness body.
Churches of Christ		I-Dis	x....	20	150	100	300	0.05	M=CC(Non-Instrumental) (USA). In most larger towns. Independent congregations. 6f.
Evangelical Church of the West Indies	1952	P-Eva	xM...	9	1,200	600	3,000	6.65	M=West Indies Mission(USA). Linked to WIM branches elsewhere in Caribbean. 3m,4f.
Jehovah's Witnesses	1932	m-Jeh	x....	5	200	200	700	5.14	*Watch Tower. IBSA.* Including Beguia Island (1956). (1975) 7Y. (1995) 22Y.
Meth Ch in Caribbean & Americas	1787	P-Met	VwM.K	29	4,320	10,000	12,000	0.73	In MCCA, South Caribbean District. M=MMS(UK). 72% women. 4n,518y.
New Apostolic Church	c1990	I-3aX	x....	4	100	–	143	20.00	*NAC/NAK.* M=Neuapostolische Kirche. HQ Zurich (Switzerland).
Open Bible Standard Church	1982	I-3pW	Z....	2	67	–	134	7.69	M=OBSC.
Pentecostal Assemblies of the W Indies		P-Pe2	Z....	5	500	500	833	0.05	PAoWI. Formerly M=PAoC(Canada). Classical Pentecostals (2-stage). Emigration to UK.
Salvation Army		P-Sal	xwM.K	1	120	200	250	0.05	In caribbean & CAmerica Territory (HQ Jamaica). HG Kingstown.
Seventh-day Adventist Church		P-Adv	x....	15	3,000	2,000	4,250	0.05	*SDA*, South Caribbean Conference, Caribbean UC. Increasing; many East Indians. 2r.
Spiritual Baptist Churches	c1860	I-3sU	.....	4	500	600	1,000	2.06	*Shouters, Shakers.* Banned 1913-65. White robes, vestments, RC ritual, Obeah. Bishop.
Syrian Orthodox Church	c1970	O-Syr	D....	1	40	–	60	17.79	Syrian Arab immigrants. Church under P Damascus.
Wesleyan Church		P-Hol	VF..	5	500	500	909	0.05	Before 1968 merger, M=Pilgrim Holiness Ch(USA). Holiness doctrines.
Other Black pentecostal churches	c1960	I-3pU	.....	35	4,000	1,000	8,700	9.04	Total 7 bodies.
Other Pentecostal denominations	c1960	P-Pe2	.....	20	2,000	540	4,000	8.34	Total 3. Pentecostal denominations.
Other Protestant denominations	c1965	P-	.....	10	400	400	1,000	3.73	Bible Missionary Ch, Ch of God (Anderson), Presbyterian Ch, Streams of Power (1965).
Totals				**265**	**42,861**	**64,587**	**76,111**		

Churches, members, growth, 1900-2025	*Congs*	*Adults*	*Affiliated*	*G%*	*Total denominations*	*6 Megablocs:* O	R	A	P	I	m
Total churches, members, and denominations (mid-1900)	80	22,100	42,250	0.61	4	0	1	1	1	1	0
Total churches, members, and denominations (mid-1970)	139	33,803	64,587	0.61	22	0	1	1	13	6	1
Total churches, members, and denominations (mid-1990)	230	41,700	74,050	0.69	42	1	1	1	23	14	2
Total churches, members, and denominations (mid-1995)	265	42,861	76,111	0.55	42	1	1	1	24	13	2
Total churches, members, and denominations (mid-2000)	300	44,200	78,439	0.60	42	1	1	1	23	14	2
Total churches, members, and denominations (mid-2025)	500	53,100	94,220	0.74	74	2	1	1	30	35	5

NOTES ON TABLE ABOVE
NATIONAL COUNCILS (Column 4, 5th letter).
E = Association of Evangelical Churches of St. Vincent & the Grenadines (AECSVG).
K = Christian Council of St Vincent (CCSV).

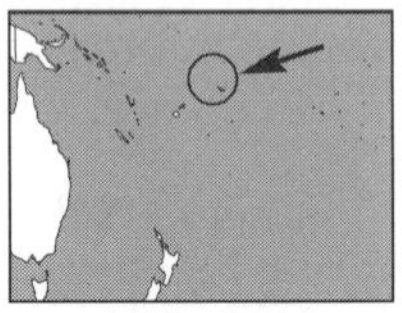

SAMOA

SECULAR DATA, AD 2000

STATE
Official name: Malo Sa'oloto Tuto'atasi o Samoa (The Independent State of Samoa).
Short name: Samoa. **Adjective of nationality:** Samoan.
Flag: Red field with blue rectangle in upper hoist corner; 5 white stars representing Southern Cross.
Area: 2,826 sq. km. (1,091 sq. mi.).
Government: Constitutional monarchy, since 1889 (1800 rival chiefdoms, 1900 German protectorate, 1919 New Zealand mandated territory, 1946 UN trusteeship, 1962 Independence).
Legislature: Legislative Assembly, 49 members.
Official language: Samoan and English.
Monetary unit: 1 tala (SA$, plural tala) = 100 sene. **US$1=** SA$3.09.
Chief cities: APIA 39,015.
Political divisions: 2 provinces.

DEMOGRAPHY
Population: 180,000.
Population density: 63.7/sq. km. (165.0/sq. mi.).
Under 15 years: 69,000.
Growth rate p.a.: 1.85% (births 27.33, deaths 4.64).
Mortality: Infant, per 1,000: 19.3; **Maternal per 100,000:** 35.0.
Life expectancy: 73 (male 71, female 75).
Household size: 7.8. **Floor area per person, sq.m:** 14.0.
Major languages: Samoan, English, Chinese.
Urban dwellers: 21.54%. **Urban growth rate p.a.:** 2.6%.
Labor force: 40%.

ETHNOLINGUISTIC PEOPLES
88.1% Samoan; 10.1% Euronesian (Part-Samoan); 0.6% USA White; 0.3% Anglo-New Zealander; 0.3% British.

ECONOMY
National income p.a. per person: US$1,121; **per family:** US$8,749.

EDUCATION
Adult literacy: 100% (male 100%, female 100%). **Schools:** 206.
Universities: 6. **School enrolment:** female/male: 75%/75%.

HEALTH
Access to health services: 80%. **Access to safe water:** 90%.
Hospitals: 16 (20 beds per 10,000). **Doctors:** 50.
Blind: 200. **Deaf:** 10,500. **Murder rate:** 7.
Lepers: 1,000.

LITERATURE
New book titles p.a.: 90 (500 p.a. per million). **Periodicals:** 20.
Newspapers: 1 daily.

COMMUNICATION (per 1,000 people)
Phones: 47 (15% mobile). **Radios:** 448. **TV sets:** 38.
Daily newspaper circulation: 122. **Computers:** 40.

HUMAN LIFE AND LIBERTY (optimum condition=100.0%)
HDI: 68.4. **HSI:** 60.0. **HFI:** 70.0. **EFL:** 44.0.

Country Table 1. **Religious adherents in Samoa, AD 1900-2025.**

Year	1900		1970		mid-1990		Annual change, 1990-2000				mid-1995		mid-2000		mid-2025	
Name	Adherents	%	Adherents	%	Adherents	%	Natural	Conversion	Total	Rate	Adherents	%	Adherents	%	Adherents	%
Christians	**32,800**	**100.0**	**143,200**	**99.1**	**155,670**	**97.3**	**1,953**	**-127**	**1,826**	**1.12**	**163,070**	**97.3**	**173,928**	**96.6**	**259,320**	**95.7**
PROFESSION																
professing Christians	**32,800**	**100.0**	**143,200**	**99.1**	**155,670**	**97.3**	**1,953**	**-127**	**1,826**	**1.12**	**163,070**	**97.3**	**173,928**	**96.6**	**259,320**	**95.7**
AFFILIATION																
unaffiliated Christians	600	1.8	7,983	5.5	4,270	2.7	53	0	53	1.17	4,770	2.9	4,799	2.7	6,320	2.3
affiliated Christians	**32,200**	**98.2**	**135,217**	**93.6**	**151,400**	**94.6**	**1,900**	**-127**	**1,773**	**1.11**	**158,300**	**94.4**	**169,129**	**94.0**	**253,000**	**93.4**
Protestants	28,770	87.7	82,500	57.1	116,000	72.5	1,450	-250	1,200	0.99	120,899	72.1	128,000	71.1	195,000	72.0
Roman Catholics	3,000	9.2	29,830	20.6	36,000	22.5	450	-100	350	0.93	37,203	22.2	39,500	21.9	59,000	21.8
Marginal Christians	330	1.0	21,737	15.0	17,200	10.8	215	-235	-20	-0.12	17,094	10.2	17,000	9.4	21,000	7.8
Independents	100	0.3	800	0.6	1,600	1.0	20	20	40	2.26	1,820	1.1	2,000	1.1	3,600	1.3
Anglicans	0	0.0	350	0.2	420	0.3	5	-2	3	0.69	430	0.3	450	0.3	700	0.3
doubly-affiliated	0	0.0	0	0.0	-19,820	-12.4	-248	448	200	-1.06	-19,146	-11.4	-17,821	-9.9	-26,300	-9.7
Trans-megabloc groupings																
Evangelicals	24,600	75.0	9,600	6.6	23,680	14.8	296	19	315	1.26	24,908	14.9	26,830	14.9	44,600	16.5
Pentecostals/Charismatics	0	0.0	4,000	2.8	24,320	15.2	304	94	398	1.53	26,213	15.6	28,300	15.7	46,000	17.0
Great Commission Christians	**5,000**	**15.2**	**49,300**	**34.1**	**72,000**	**45.0**	**900**	**435**	**1,335**	**1.72**	**77,280**	**46.1**	**85,350**	**47.4**	**135,500**	**50.0**
Baha'is	0	0.0	1,800	1.3	3,100	1.9	39	69	108	3.03	3,300	2.0	4,178	2.3	8,000	3.0
Nonreligious	0	0.0	0	0.0	1,200	0.8	15	58	73	4.87	1,600	1.0	1,930	1.1	3,600	1.3
Buddhists	0	0.0	0	0.0	15	0.0	0	0	0	1.84	15	0.0	18	0.0	40	0.0
Chinese folk-religionists	0	0.0	0	0.0	15	0.0	0	0	0	1.84	15	0.0	18	0.0	40	0.0
World A (unevangelized persons)	0	0.0	144	0.1	160	0.1	1	0	1	0.74	167	0.1	180	0.1	271	0.1
World B (evangelized non-Christians)	0	0.0	1,176	0.8	4,170	2.6	53	127	180	3.52	4,384	2.6	5,892	3.3	11,409	4.2
World C (Christians)	32,800	100.0	143,200	99.1	155,670	97.3	1,953	-127	1,826	1.12	163,070	97.3	173,928	96.6	259,320	95.7
Country's population	**32,800**	**100.0**	**144,521**	**100.0**	**160,000**	**100.0**	**2,007**	**0**	**2,007**	**1.18**	**167,622**	**100.0**	**180,000**	**100.0**	**271,000**	**100.0**

COLUMNS, ROWS.
For meanings and definitions, see Codebook (Part 3). Note that, by definition, total 'Christians' = professing + crypto-Christians, which also = affiliated + unaffiliated Christians, and also = Great Commission Christians + latent Christians. Percentages may not always total exactly, due to rounding.

CENSUSES.
25.IX.1945: 75.3% Protestants, 20.5% Roman Catholics, 4.2% marginal Protestants. **25.IX.1951:** 74.8% Protestants, 20.8% Roman Catholics, 4.4% marginal Protestants. **25.IX.1956:** 98.4% Christians, 1.6% other religionists. **25.IX.1961:** 71.3% Protestants (53.6% Congregationalists, 16.0% Methodists, 1.3% SD Adventists), 21.6% Roman Catholics, 6.3% marginal Protestants (Mormons), 0.5% Polynesian indigenous (Congregational Ch), 0.3% Anglicans. **21.XI.1966:** 69.1% Protestants (52.1% Congregationalists, 15.4% Methodists, 1.6% SD Adventists), 22.2% Roman Catholics, 7.2% marginal Protestants (Mormons), 0.5% Polynesian indigenous, 0.3% Anglicans, 0.8% other religionists. **3.XI.1971:** 69.4% Protestants (51.0% Congregationalists, 15.7% Methodists, 1.7% SD Adventists), 21.8% Roman Catholics, 7.8% marginal Protestants (Mormons), 0.2% Anglicans, 0.5% other religionists. **1976:** 67.3% Protestants (49.8% Congregationalists, 15.7% Methodists, 1.8% SD Adventists), 21.8% Roman Catholics, 7.8% marginal Christians (Mormons), 3.1% other Christians and religionists. **1981:** 65.8% Protestants (47.3% Congregationalists, 16.2% Methodists, 2.3% SD Adventists), 21.8% Roman Catholics, 8.3% marginal Christians (Mormons), 4.1% other Christians and religionists.

NOTES ON RELIGIONS
BAHA'IS. Rapid growth from 8 local spiritual assemblies (1964) to 26 (1973). In 1973, the malietoa (king) of Samoa announced his conversion to the Baha'i faith. In 1980, the world's 7th Baha'i Temple was under construction in Apia. By 1995, LSAs had expanded to 44 in Samoa, with another 8 on American Samoa.
INDEPENDENTS. In 3 denominations in 1995 (see Table 2).
MARGINAL CHRISTIANS. In the 1981 census, 8.3% of the population professed to be Mormons; however, by 1990 the Mormon mission claimed to have 40,000 adherents (25.0% of the population). It is clear therefore that, due to the exceptionally large Mormon missionary force and the extremely rapid growth in numbers of adherents, many persons who profess to be Congregationalists or Methodists in censuses have in fact joined and are still joining the Mormons.

Great Commission Instrument Panel: status of Samoa (for explanation see start of Part 4)

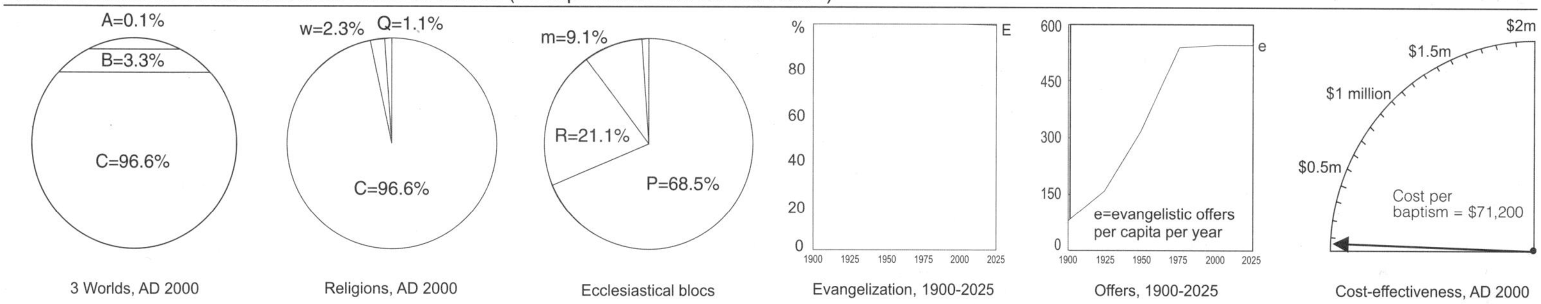

Country status. Samoa is a group of islands in the south-west Pacific Ocean. Its chief exports are coconut products, taro, and cocoa.

HUMAN LIFE AND LIBERTY

Human rights and freedoms. Samoa has had a relatively trouble-free history of rights, together with an ideal environment.

NON-CHRISTIAN RELIGIONS

Baha'i has a rapidly-growing community of recent origin and by 1995 numbered 3,300. In 1973, the malietoa (king) announced his conversion to the Baha'i faith.

CHRISTIANITY

PROTESTANT CHURCHES. The principal denomination is the Congregational Christian Church in Samoa, which owes its origin to the pioneer work of Tahitian teachers left by John Williams of the London Missionary Society in 1830. Williams and his Tahitian co-workers arrived at a particularly propitious time for the establishment of Christianity following a popular revolt against the despotic ruler Tamafaiga, who exercised the role of chief and high priest. Samoans not only accepted Christianity with enthusiasm but by 1840 had dedicated themselves to spreading the gospel to other South Sea islanders. They were in fact instrumental in taking Christianity to Tokelau, Niue, the Gilbert and Ellice Islands, and the New Hebrides, and by 1972 over 210 Samoan Congregationalists had gone overseas as foreign missionaries. At present the Congregational Christian Church, which is autonomous, fully supports 6 Samoan missionary couples in Papua New Guinea and has another couple in training in Australia. The church has in recent years been losing ground to such rapidly-growing groups as Mormons, Pentecostals, and Adventists. As a result the people of Samoa are now only 41% Congregationalist.

Methodism was introduced through the ministry of a Samoan who was converted in 1827 and brought his new faith back home with him. British missionaries appeared in 1835 and the church later developed a special relationship with Australian Methodism. Seventh-day Adventists have built up a substantial following since their arrival in 1895 and continue to grow. Other groups include Assemblies of God, Brethren, Nazarenes, and the United Pentecostal Church.

Congregationalists, Methodists, and Adventists are all heavily involved in education.

CATHOLIC CHURCH. The faith was first brought to Samoa by Wallisians (Uveans) from Wallis and Futuna Islands, now a completely Catholic territory. By 1966, Catholics numbered 22% of the population, a figure which has not altered significantly since the 1940s. The problem created by the lack of priests and the extensive area of the diocese has been resolved in part by the remarkable development of its system of catechists: 135 serving 23 parishes in 1974. In many cases several catechists and their families live together in communities. Although the diocese covers 3 different countries (Western Samoa, American Samoa, and Tokelau Islands), Western Samoa is the most heavily populated and has the most priests: 34 out of 42 for the whole diocese in 1974, of which 9 were nationals.

A series of postage stamps set illustrating (*from left to right*) Mormon Church, LMS church, RC Cathedral, and *below*, SDA sanatorium.

Country summary. **Worlds A, B, C by ethnolinguistic peoples, cities and major civil divisions in Samoa.**

	PEOPLES							*CITIES*							*CIVIL DIVISIONS*						
World	*Num*	*Pop 2000*	*C%*	*Christians*	*E%*	*U%*	*Unevangelized*	*Num*	*Pop 2000*	*C%*	*Christians*	*E%*	*U%*	*Unevangelized*	*Num*	*Pop 2000*	*C%*	*Christians*	*E%*	*U%*	*Unevangelized*
A	0	0	0.00	0	0	0	0	0	0	0.00	0	0	0	0	0	0	0.00	0	0	0	0
B	0	0	0.00	0	0	0	0	0	0	0.00	0	0	0	0	0	0	0.00	0	0	0	0
C	8	180,071	93.92	169,127	100	0	112	1	39,015	92.00	35,894	100	0	70	2	180,073	93.92	169,129	100	0	113
Total	**8**	**180,071**	**93.92**	**169,127**	**100**	**0**	**112**	**1**	**39,015**	**92.00**	**35,894**	**100**	**0**	**70**	**2**	**180,073**	**93.92**	**169,129**	**100**	**0**	**113**

The Holy See has diplomatic relations with Samoa and in AD 2000 is represented to government and the Catholic hierarchy by a nuncio residing in Wellington, New Zealand.

MARGINAL CHURCHES. Mormons are numerous in Western Samoa as in other parts of Oceania and are engaged in an extensive educational program. Their growth has been extraordinarily rapid; those professing in censuses to be Mormons rose from 4.2% in 1945 to 6.3% in 1961 to 7.8% in 1971 and to over 10% by 1991. However, the church itself claimed much larger numbers (24.7% by 1990), reflecting the large number of Congregationalists attending Mormon activities and becoming Mormons.

INDIGENOUS CHURCHES. There are 3 independent churches, Ponesi's Church (Congregational Church of Jesus Christ), an old split from the Congregational Church, and 2 small pentecostal groups, Makisua's Church (a schism from the Assemblies of God), and the Samoan Full Gospel Church.

Indigenous missions. After the early penetration of Christianity to the islands, Samoan Christians could be found working all over the Pacific spreading the gospel. By 1972, 210 Congregationalists had served overseas as foreign missionaries. Today there are Samoans serving in Asia, Europe, Africa, and South America.

Church of Jesus Christ of Latter-day Saints. Two native Samoan girls, who serve as Mormon missionaries, at a Zone Conference near Apia, with some of the other 350 missionaries contributing to this church's massive growth in Samoa.

CHURCH AND STATE

Western Samoa is a Christian state, as is indicated by the Preamble to the constitution of 28 October 1960: 'In the Holy Name of God, the Almighty, the Ever Loving: whereas sovereignty over the Universe belongs to the Omni-present God alone. Western Samoa (is) an Independent State based on Christian principles and Samoan custom and tradition'.

The constitution of January 1962 guarantees freedom of religion in Western Samoa. Although no government subsidies are provided, the churches operate numerous schools in close co-operation with the government Department of Education. Of 6 schools preparing students for New Zealand school certificate level in 1966, 5 belonged to the churches, the sole government school being Samoa College. The latter institution, along with 3 mission schools, also provides sixth-form instruction leading to New Zealand university entrance.

Samoan culture and Christianity have become so intertwined that it is virtually impossible to separate them. Not only does almost the entire population claim to be Christian, but also in some villages nonchurchgoing is regarded as anti-social and fines are still levied for failure to attend church services.

BROADCASTING AND MEDIA

Shortwave radio programs from KNLS have seen some response.

1986: 5th Assembly, Pacific Conference of Churches, held in Fale'Ula, Apia.

INTERDENOMINATIONAL ORGANIZATIONS

The Fellowship of Christian Churches in Samoa (FCCS) was formed, with Anglican, Catholic, Congregational, and Methodist churches as full members and Seventh-day Adventists as associates. A notable feature is the atmosphere of cordial relations being developed between Protestants and Catholics. The Week of Prayer for Christian Unity is observed, and there is a joint quarterly meeting of the leaders of Congregational, Methodist and Catholic theological colleges. These 3 denominations are also participating in a Christian Action Committee, the result of a visit to Samoa by the Pacific Islands Christian Education Curriculum Team.

FUTURE TRENDS AND PROSPECTS

Christianity will probably drop off only slightly by AD 2025 with most changes being within Christian traditions (Marginal Christians declining from 15% in 1970 to 7.8% by 2025).

Though both Baha'is and the nonreligious are expected to continue to grow, Christians could continue to claim more than 90% of the population throughout the next few decades.

BIBLIOGRAPHY

Archives of the Catholic Diocese of Samoa and Tokelau. : Catholic Church Diocese of Samoa and Tokelau, 1985. (49 reels of microfilm).

Die alte Religion und das Christentum Samoas. D. Schneider-Christians. [Bonn: Friedrich-Wilhelms-Universität], 1992. 608p.

'Educational role of the church: a study of the church and its concept of education, and how effective it is in the life and situation of the people, with special reference to the Congregational Christian Church in Samoa.' A. V. Maloo. B.D. thesis, Pacific Theological College, Suva, Fiji, 1980. 78p.

'Evangelical revival re–examined with reference to the present situation of Samoan Methodism.' L. L. Ofo'ia. B.D. thesis, Pacific Theological College, Suva, Fiji, 1973. 142p.

'From English mission to Samoan congregation: women and the church in rural Western Samoa.' E. M. Roach. Ph.D. dissertation, Columbia University, New York, 1984. 289p.

Overseas missions of the Australian Methodist Church. A. H. Wood. Melbourne: Aldersgate Press, [1975–78]. 3 vols.

'Patterns of leadership selection and church growth in the Samoa Mission of Seventh–day Adventists, 1967–1987.' E. F. Puni. M.A. thesis, Fuller Theological Seminary, Pasadena, CA, 1989. 161p.

People movements in Southern Polynesia: studies in the dynamics of church–planting and growth in Tahiti, New Zealand, Tonga, and Samoa. A. R. Tippett. Chicago: Moody Press, 1971. 288p.

'The great Samoan awakening of 1839,' A. G. Daws, *Journal of the Polynesian Society*, 70, 3 (1961), 326–37.

'The history, role and function of the contemporary Catholic Church in Western Samoa.' R. W. Franco. M.A. thesis, California State University, 1976. 95p.

'The Joe Gimlet or Siovili cult: an episode in the religious history of early Samoa,' in *Anthropology in the South Seas: essays presented to H. D. Skinner*, p.185–98. J. D. Freeman & W. R. Geddes (eds). New Plymouth, NZ: T. Avery, [1959].

The Marist Brothers in New Zealand, Fiji and Samoa, 1876–1976. P. O. Gallagher. Tuakau, NZ: New Zealand Marist Brother Trust Fund, 1976. 210p.

'The ministry in the making: a history of the emergence of the ministry of the Church in Samoa, 1830–1900.' F. Setu. Th.M. thesis, Pacific Theological College, Suva, Fiji, 1988. 130p.

'The ministry of the Congregational Christian Church in Samoa in a fa'a–Samoa (Samoan custom) framework.' L. Tuimaualuga. B.D. thesis, Pacific Theological College, Suva, Fiji, [1977]. 100p.

'The present worship of the Congregational Christian Church in Samoa in the light of the liturgical movement.' R. Ete. B.D. thesis, Pacific Theological College, Suva, Fiji, 1972. 150p.

'The theological appreciation of the 'faifeau' in the Congregational Christian Church in Samoa: is he Christian?: a project report.' F. Setu. B.D. thesis, Pacific Theological College, Suva, Fiji, 1986. 120p.

'Toward a contextualized organizational structure for the Seventh–Day Adventists in Samoa.' E. F. Puni. Ph.D. dissertation, Fuller Theological Seminary, Pasadena, CA, 1993. 330p.

Two Samoans: a cultural comparison. S. J. Burris. Hilo, HI: Samu Productions, 1984. (111 slide set with sound).

'Two webs meet,' chapter 4 in *People movements in Southern Polynesia*, p.111–36. A. R. Tippett. Chicago: Moody Press, 1971.

'Urbanisation and the church in Western Samoa: a general look at the influence of the West and its contribution to urbanisation which have resulted in rural change with special reference to the role of the Samoan Methodist Church.' P. Hakai. B.D. thesis, Pacific Theological College, Suva, Fiji, 1980. 162p.

Country Table 2. **Organized churches and denominations in Samoa.**

Official name (bold type = church with over 10% of all affiliated) 1	*Begun* 2	*Type* 3	*Counc* 4	*Congs* 5	*Adults* 6	*Affiliated 1970* 7	*Affiliated 1995* 8	*G%* 9	*Names, notes, and other statistics* (see Codebook, Part 3) 10
Anglican Church (D Polynesia)	c1950	A-Hig	awpKC	4	185	350	430	0.83	Part of CPNZ. 57% European, 35% part-Samoan, 6% Samoan. 1x,W=40%,3Y4y.
Assemblies of God in Samoa	1952	P-Pe2	ZF...	48	10,750	3,000	15,000	6.65	M=AoG(USA). Classical Pentecostals. Rapid expansion after 1970. HQ Apia. 70n,2f.
Catholic Church: M Samoa-Apia	1845	R-Lat	PzPYC	28	19,000	29,830	37,203	0.89	M=SM. C=1+1+4. (1970) 9n,25x,26m,109w,1837Yy. , 21n, 23x, 51m, 57w, 1466Yy
Christian Brethren		P-CBr	x....	5	250	300	500	0.05	*Plymouth Brethren. Open Brethren. Gospel Halls.*
Church of God (Cleveland)	1987	P-Pe3	Z....	2	114	–	228	12.50	M=CoG(Cleveland). Holiness Pentecostals from USA.
Church of God of Prophecy	1981	P-Pe3	Z....	4	80	–	200	7.14	M=CGP(USA). Holiness Pentecostals.
Ch of Jesus C of Latter-day Saints	1888	m-LdS	x....	93	11,000	21,537	16,394	-1.09	*Mormons.* M=CJCLdS(USA). 81% Samoans, 17% part-Samoans, 140 Whites.
Church of the Nazarene	1960	P-Hol	xF...	11	456	300	783	3.91	A home mission district of M=CoN(USA), still regarded as pioneer area. 4n,SS=350.
Congregational Christian Ch in S	1830	P-Con	RWP.C	244	41,600	60,000	68,651	0.54	*CCCS. Ekalesia Faapotopotoga Kerisiano i Samoa.* M=LMS/CWM(UK). 18n,3x,1s,W=95%.
Congregational Church of Jesus Christ	1846	I-Con	.v...	2	100	600	200	-4.30	*Ponesi's Church. Ch of JC in Samoa.* Schism ex CCCS. Many now returned to CCCS.
Jehovah's Witnesses	1938	m-Jeh	x....	5	226	200	700	5.14	Placed under Australian branch in 1938. First active witnessing 1951. (1975) 17Y. (1995) 37Y.
Makisua's Church		I-3pP	.....	1	100	100	150	0.05	Schism ex Assemblies of God. Small Samoan indigenous pentecostal group.
Methodist Church of Samoa	1827	P-Met	VuP.C	113	11,899	15,000	27,190	2.41	*Lotu Tonga/Ch of Tonga* (first workers Tongans). 161n,673m,3p,1s(34),W=93%,899Yy.
New Apostolic Church	c1980	I-3aX	x....	5	300	–	480	6.67	*NAC/NAK.* M=Neuapostolische Kirche. Zurich (Switzerland).
Samoan Full Gospel Church	c1965	I-3fP	.....	9	200	100	300	4.49	Indigenous pentecostal body. Ex AoG. Samoans. Branch also in American Samoa.
Samoan SDA Church	c1980	I-Adv	.....	4	240	–	340	6.67	*Ekalesia Asofitu.* Schism ex Seventh-day Adventists.
Seventh-day Adventist Church	1895	P-Adv	x...c	20	3,070	2,800	5,677	2.87	*SDA, Samoa Mission,* Central Pacific UM. Rapid growth. 6nx,41mw,2r,54t(2755),188Y.
United Pentecostal Church	c1965	P-Pe1	x....	5	1,000	600	1,670	4.18	*Jesus Only Church.* M=UPC(USA). Unitarian Pentecostals. 5n,2f,1p(16).
Other independent churches	c1980	I-3cP	.....	4	200	–	350	6.67	Including Apia Christian Fellowship (150).
Other Protestant denominations		P-	.....	10	600	500	1,000	0.05	Including Church of Christ, United Missionary Fellowship (1 church, 2 workers).

Continued opposite

Country Table 2–concluded

Official name (bold type = church with over 10% of affiliated) 1	*Begun* 2	*Type* 3	*Counc* 4	*Congs* 5	*Adults* 6	*Affiliated 1970* 7	*Affiliated 1995* 8	*G%* 9	*Names, notes, and other statistics* (see Codebook, Part 3) 10
Doubly-affiliated		2-aff			-10,900	0	-19,146		Evangelicals who are also baptized Roman Catholics.
Totals				**617**	**90,470**	**135,217**	**158,300**		

Churches, members, growth, 1900-2025	*Congs*	*Adults*	*Affiliated*	*G%*	*Total denominations*	*6 Megablocs:* *O*	*R*	*A*	*P*	*I*	*m*
Total churches, members, and denominations (mid-1900)	100	15,400	32,200	2.07	6	0	1	0	3	1	1
Total churches, members, and denominations (mid-1970)	531	64,536	135,217	2.07	16	0	1	1	9	3	2
Total churches, members, and denominations (mid-1990)	600	86,500	151,400	0.57	27	0	1	1	14	9	2
Total churches, members, and denominations (mid-1995)	617	90,470	158,300	0.90	27	0	1	1	14	9	2
Total churches, members, and denominations (mid-2000)	640	96,600	169,129	1.33	27	0	1	1	14	9	2
Total churches, members, and denominations (mid-2025)	950	145,000	253,000	1.62	52	0	1	1	25	20	5

NOTES ON TABLE ABOVE
NATIONAL COUNCILS (Column 4, 5th letter).
C = Samoa Council of Churches (SCC, 1994), formerly Fellowship of Christian Churches in Samoa (FCCS) or National Council of Christian Churches in Western Samoa; 1964.
c = related to FCCS.
E = Samoan Evangelical Fellowship (SEF).

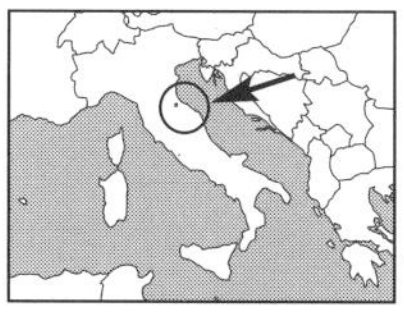

SAN MARINO

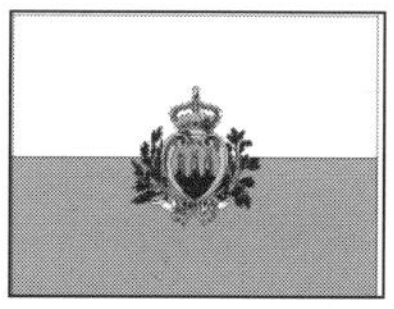

SECULAR DATA, AD 2000

STATE
Official name: Serenissima Repubblica di San Marino (The Most Serene Republic of San Marino).
Short name: San Marino. **Adjective of nationality:** of San Marino.
Flag: White stripe over blue stripe with national coat of arms in centre.
Area: 61 sq. km. (24 sq. mi.).
Government: Parliamentary republic, since Independence recognized by the pope in 1631 (AD 301 founded as republic).
Legislature: Grand and General Council, 60 members.
Official language: Italian (Italiano).
Monetary unit: 1 Italian lira (Lit; plural lire) = 100 centesimi. **US$1=** Lit 1,652.
Chief cities: SAN MARINO 3,264.
Political divisions: 9 provinces.

DEMOGRAPHY
Population: 27,000.
Population density: 434.6/sq. km. (1,104.7/sq. mi.).
Under 15 years: 4,000.
Growth rate p.a.: -0.18% (births 8.48, deaths 10.90).
Mortality: Infant, per 1,000: 6.6; **Maternal per 100,000:** 10.0.
Life expectancy: 79 (male 76, female 82).
Household size: 2.7. **Floor area per person, sq.m:** 40.0.
Major languages: Italian.
Urban dwellers: 95.73%. **Urban growth rate p.a.:** 1.4%.
Labor force: 55%.

ETHNOLINGUISTIC PEOPLES
91.0% Italian; 8.9% Sanmarinese.

ECONOMY
National income p.a. per person: US$24,703; **per family:** US$66,700.

EDUCATION
Adult literacy: 99% (male 99%, female 98%). **Schools:** 17.
Universities: 0. **School enrolment:** female/male: 100%/100%.

HEALTH
Access to health services: 95%. **Access to safe water:** 100%.
Hospitals: 5 (66 beds per 10,000). **Doctors:** 60.
Blind: 100. **Deaf:** 1,600. **Murder rate:** 4. **Lepers:** 0.

LITERATURE
New book titles p.a.: 19 (700 p.a. per million). **Periodicals:** 25.
Newspapers: 5 dailies.

COMMUNICATION (per 1,000 people)
Phones: 571 (30% mobile). **Radios:** 522. **TV sets:** 367.
Daily newspaper circulation: 82. **Computers:** 300.

HUMAN LIFE AND LIBERTY (optimum condition=100.0%)
HDI: 96.3. **HSI:** 95.0. **HFI:** 85.0. **EFL:** 60.0.

Country Table 1. **Religious adherents in San Marino, AD 1900-2025.**

Year	*1900*		*1970*		*mid-1990*		*Annual change, 1990-2000*				*mid-1995*		*mid-2000*		*mid-2025*	
Name	*Adherents*	*%*	*Adherents*	*%*	*Adherents*	*%*	*Natural*	*Conversion*	*Total*	*Rate*	*Adherents*	*%*	*Adherents*	*%*	*Adherents*	*%*
Christians	**8,000**	**100.0**	**17,630**	**95.9**	**21,595**	**93.1**	**302**	**-18**	**284**	**1.24**	**23,035**	**92.6**	**24,434**	**92.2**	**29,180**	**90.1**
PROFESSION																
professing Christians	**8,000**	**100.0**	**17,630**	**95.9**	**21,595**	**93.1**	**302**	**-18**	**284**	**1.24**	**23,035**	**92.6**	**24,434**	**92.2**	**29,180**	**90.1**
AFFILIATION																
unaffiliated Christians	0	0.0	200	1.1	476	2.1	8	10	18	3.24	489	2.0	655	2.5	680	2.1
affiliated Christians	**8,000**	**100.0**	**17,430**	**94.8**	**21,119**	**91.0**	**293**	**-27**	**266**	**1.19**	**22,546**	**90.6**	**23,779**	**89.7**	**28,500**	**88.0**
Roman Catholics	8,000	100.0	17,400	94.7	20,909	90.1	290	-30	260	1.18	22,310	89.7	23,509	88.7	28,000	86.4
Marginal Christians	0	0.0	30	0.2	210	0.9	4	2	6	2.54	236	1.0	270	1.0	500	1.6
Trans-megabloc groupings																
Pentecostals/Charismatics	0	0.0	50	0.3	405	1.8	7	1	8	1.82	446	1.8	485	1.8	755	2.4
Great Commission Christians	**1,400**	**17.5**	**5,520**	**30.0**	**10,440**	**45.0**	**182**	**64**	**246**	**2.13**	**11,700**	**47.0**	**12,895**	**48.7**	**16,500**	**50.9**
Nonreligious	0	0.0	500	2.7	1,070	4.6	19	9	28	2.36	1,220	4.9	1,351	5.1	2,000	6.3
Atheists	0	0.0	200	1.1	380	1.6	7	3	10	2.43	445	1.8	483	1.8	800	2.5
Baha'is	0	0.0	70	0.4	150	0.7	3	6	9	4.86	195	0.8	241	0.9	400	1.3
Muslims	0	0.0	0	0.0	5	0.0	0	0	0	0.00	5	0.0	5	0.0	20	0.1
World A (unevangelized persons)	0	0.0	36	0.2	23	0.1	1	-1	0	0.33	24	0.1	27	0.1	64	0.2
World B (evangelized non-Christians)	0	0.0	712	3.9	1,582	6.8	28	19	47	2.57	1,822	7.3	2,039	7.7	3,156	9.7
World C (Christians)	8,000	100.0	17,630	95.9	21,595	93.1	302	-18	284	1.24	23,035	92.6	24,434	92.2	29,180	90.1
Country's population	**8,000**	**100.0**	**18,379**	**100.0**	**23,200**	**100.0**	**331**	**0**	**331**	**1.62**	**24,882**	**100.0**	**26,500**	**100.0**	**32,100**	**100.0**

COLUMNS, ROWS.
For meanings and definitions, see Codebook (Part 3). Note that, by definition, total 'Christians' = professing + crypto-Christians, which also = affiliated + unaffiliated Christians, and also = Great Commission Christians + latent Christians. Percentages may not always total exactly, due to rounding.

NOTES ON RELIGIONS
ATHEISTS. Partito Comunista di San Marino (PCSM). Many members remain practicing Catholics.
BAHA'IS. In 1 local spiritual assembly (1973), and the same in 1996.
CHRISTIANS. The table enumerates residents only. In addition, large numbers of the 2 million tourists annually attend churches in San Marino during their visits.

Great Commission Instrument Panel: status of San Marino (for explanation see start of Part 4)

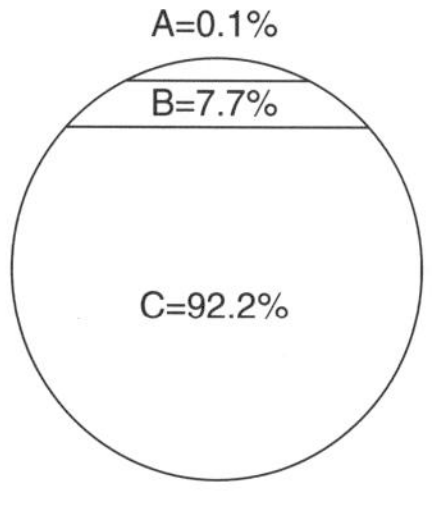

3 Worlds, AD 2000

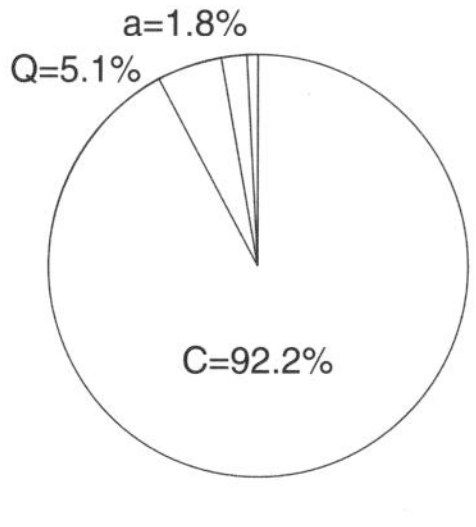

Religions, AD 2000

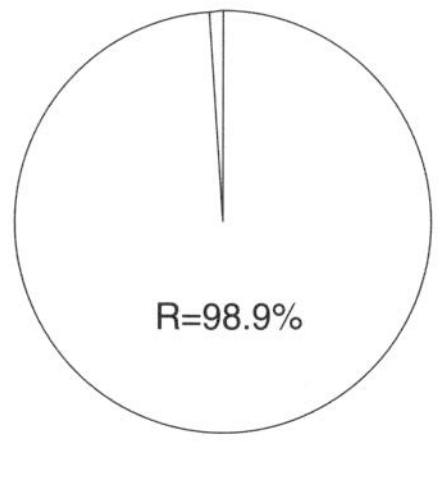

Ecclesiastical blocs

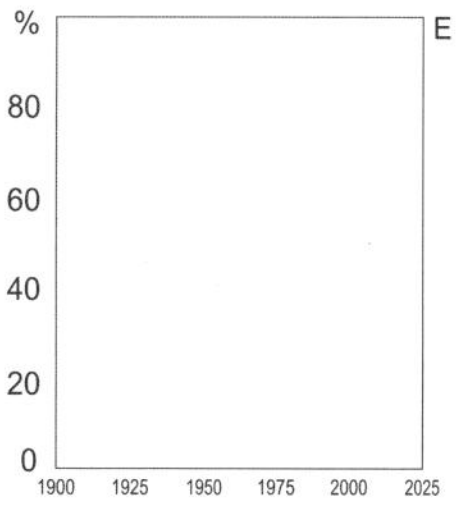

Evangelization, 1900-2025

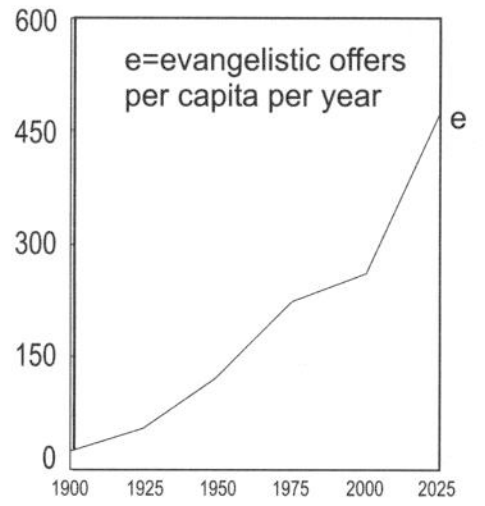

Offers, 1900-2025

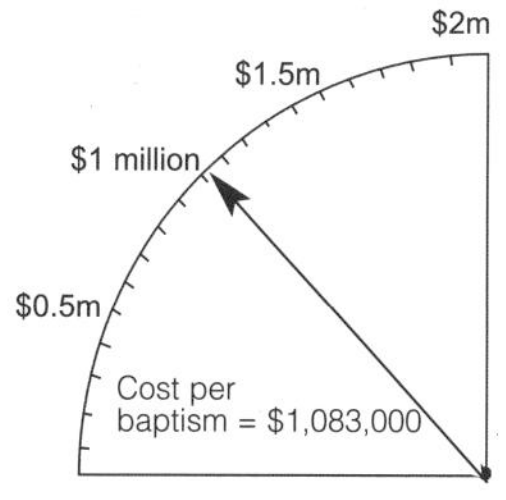

Cost-effectiveness, AD 2000

Country status. San Marino is a small, landlocked state within Italy near Rimini, Italy. It is considered Europe's oldest state and its chief products are grains, wines, and olive oil.

HUMAN LIFE AND LIBERTY

Human rights and freedoms. One of the world's smallest countries and oldest republics, San Marino has an exemplary commitment to the human rights and civil liberties of its citizens. The Legal Code of the Republic specifies and guarantees all these rights.

Country summary. Worlds A, B, C by ethnolinguistic peoples, cities, and major civil divisions in San Marino.

	PEOPLES							CITIES							CIVIL DIVISIONS						
World	Num	Pop 2000	C%	Christians	E%	U%	Unevangelized	Num	Pop 2000	C%	Christians	E%	U%	Unevangelized	Num	Pop 2000	C%	Christians	E%	U%	Unevangelized
A	0	0	0.00	0	0	0	0	0	0	0.00	0	0	0	0	0	0	0.00	0	0	0	0
B	1	27	55.56	15	85	15	4	0	0	0.00	0	0	0	0	0	0	0.00	0	0	0	0
C	3	26,488	89.72	23,764	100	0	28	1	3,264	89.49	2,921	100	0	4	9	26,514	89.68	23,779	100	0	31
Total	**4**	**26,515**	**89.68**	**23,779**	**100**	**0**	**32**	**1**	**3,264**	**89.49**	**2,921**	**100**	**0**	**4**	**9**	**26,514**	**89.68**	**23,779**	**100**	**0**	**31**

CHRISTIANITY

CATHOLIC CHURCH. The history of the church goes back at least to AD 441 when a hermitage was built. Today, the Republic of San Marino is part of the 2 Italian dioceses of Montefeltro (Conciliar Region of Marche) and of Rimini (Conciliar Region of Romagna/Flaminia). The population is almost entirely Catholic. In 1972 there were 12 parishes, 8 in the diocese of Montefeltro and 4 in the diocese of Rimini. Male religious congregations include OFM, OFMCap, OFMConv, and OSM. Female religious congregations include Clarisses (contemplative sisters), Maestre Pie dell'Addolorata, and Figlie di Santa Anna.

Chiesa Cattolica. Basilica of San Marino. The church's history dates back to AD 441.

The Holy See has diplomatic relations with San Marino and in AD 2000 is represented to government and the Catholic hierarchy by a nuncio based in the Vatican.

OTHER CHURCHES. Jehovah's Witnesses are the only organized non-Catholic religious body in the republic. Beginning in the 1960s, the Witnesses have built up a small community, but had grown to over 200 by 1990. Another body is the Seventh-day Adventist Church which, although it has no organized work, has since 1933 regularly sent in colporteurs to distribute SDA publications.

Indigenous missions. Since the establishment of a hermitage in San Marino in the 5th century few individuals have gone to surrounding countries to evangelize. Today very few missionaries are sent out from San Marino.

CHURCH AND STATE

The law as it relates to religious matters is more customary than codified. There is no specific treaty between the Republic of San Marino and the Holy See. Religious marriages have civil significance because they are recorded in state registers. Non-Catholic religious bodies are free to practice their worship without the requirement of government registration.

BROADCASTING AND MEDIA

Satellite TV and radio programs are received in English, Arabic, German and Italian.

Many postage stamps carry Christian themes; here (at Christmas 1967) the Cimabue Crucifix in Florence.

FUTURE TRENDS AND PROSPECTS

With expected growth among the nonreligious and atheists, Christians could fall to 90% of the population by 2025.

Though atheists and the nonreligious could continue to grow well into the 21st century, Christianity is expected to predominate with over 80% of the population through AD 2050.

BIBLIOGRAPHY

A short history of the Republic of San Marino. G. Rossi. Ed., C. N. Packett. , 1979. 91p.

Il diritto sovrano della Santa Sede sopra le Valli di Comacchio e sopra la repubblica di S. Marino difeso. Rome: Stamperia della Rev. Cam. Apost., 1834. 164p.

Country Table 2. Organized churches and denominations in San Marino.

Official name (bold type = church with over 10% of all affiliated) 1	Begun 2	Type 3	Counc 4	Congs 5	Adults 6	Affiliated 1970 7	Affiliated 1995 8	G% 9	Names, notes, and other statistics (see Codebook, Part 3) 10
Chiesa Cattolica	441	R-Lat	B.B..	12	12,000	17,400	22,310	0.06	*Catholic Ch.* Parts in D Montefeltro, D Rimini(Italy). C=4+0+3. 12nx,40w,1H.
Testimoni de Geova	c1965	m-Jeh	x....	2	132	30	236	8.60	*Jehovah's Witnesses.* 1971 Circuit Assembly: 1,749 present. (1975) 4Y. (1995) 3Y.
Totals				**14**	**12,132**	**17,430**	**22,546**		

Churches, members, growth, 1900-2025	*Congs*	*Adults*	*Affiliated*	*G%*	*Total denominations*	*6 Megablocs: O*	*R*	*A*	*P*	*I*	*m*
Total churches, members, and denominations (mid-1900)	4	4,600	8,000	1.12	1	0	1	0	0	0	0
Total churches, members, and denominations (mid-1970)	13	10,025	17,430	1.12	2	0	1	0	0	0	1
Total churches, members, and denominations (mid-1990)	14	11,400	21,119	0.96	2	0	1	0	0	0	1
Total churches, members, and denominations (mid-1995)	14	12,132	22,546	1.32	2	0	1	0	0	0	1
Total churches, members, and denominations (mid-2000)	14	12,800	23,779	1.07	2	0	1	0	0	0	1
Total churches, members, and denominations (mid-2025)	20	15,300	28,500	0.73	6	0	1	0	2	1	2

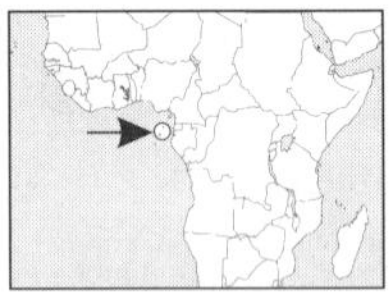

SAO TOME & PRINCIPE

SECULAR DATA, AD 2000

STATE

Official name: La República Democrática de São Tomé e Príncipe (The Democratic Republic of São Tomé and Príncipe).
Short name: São Tomé & Príncipe. **Adjective of nationality:** of São Tomé and Príncipe.
Flag: Stripes of green, yellow, and green with red triangle at hoist; 2 black stars on centre yellow stripe.
Area: 1,001 sq. km. (386 sq. mi.).
Government: Multiparty republic, since 1990 (1470 Portuguese possession, 1951 overseas province of Portugal, 1975 Independence, 1975 one-party Socialist state).
Legislature: National Assembly, 55 members.
Official language: Portuguese (Português).
Monetary unit: 1 dobra (Db) = 100 cêntimos. **US$1=** Db 2,390.
Chief cities: SAO TOME 34,902.
Political divisions: 7 provinces.
Armed forces: 900.

DEMOGRAPHY

Population: 147,000.
Population density: 146.6/sq. km. (380.2/sq. mi.).
Under 15 years: 62,000.
Growth rate p.a.: 1.80% (births 36.34, deaths 18.36).
Mortality: Infant, per 1,000: 92.3; **Maternal per 100,000:** 1,200.0.
Life expectancy: 45 (male 43, female 47).
Household size: 4.0. **Floor area per person, sq.m:** 10.0.
Major languages: Portuguese, Fang.
Urban dwellers: 46.71%. **Urban growth rate p.a.:** 3.3%.
Labor force: 32%.

ETHNOLINGUISTIC PEOPLES

75.9% Saotomense Mestico; 10.0% Fang (Pahouin); 7.6% Angolar; 3.3% Principense Mestico; 1.9% Portuguese.

ECONOMY

National income p.a. per person: US$347; **per family:** US$1,389.

EDUCATION

Adult literacy: 54% (male 70%, female 39%). **Schools:** 64.
Universities: 2. **School enrolment:** female/male: 50%/50%.

HEALTH

Access to health services: 30%. **Access to safe water:** 70%.
Hospitals: 5 (10 beds per 10,000). **Doctors:** 61.
Blind: 200. **Deaf:** 8,800. **Murder rate:** 4. **Lepers:** 200.

LITERATURE

New book titles p.a.: 15 (100 p.a. per million). **Periodicals:** 1.
Newspapers: 0 dailies.

COMMUNICATION (per 1,000 people)

Phones: 19 (20% mobile). **Radios:** 237. **TV sets:** 154.
Daily newspaper circulation: 20. **Computers:** 15.

HUMAN LIFE AND LIBERTY (optimum condition=100.0%)

HDI: 53.4. **HSI:** 20.0. **HFI:** 10.0. **EFL:** 20.0.

Country status. São Tomé & Príncipe, formerly an overseas province of Portugal, is a country made up of 2 islands in the Gulf of Guinea off the coast of west-central Africa. Its chief exports are copra, cocoa, and coffee.

HUMAN LIFE AND LIBERTY

Human rights and freedoms. São Tomé & Príncipe is among the few African nations that have successfully made the transition to a democratic and parliamentary form of government. Residual problems in this area include long delays in the legal system in bringing cases to trial and limited worker rights in an economic system dominated by plantations.

NON-CHRISTIAN RELIGIONS

Traditional religions have nearly disappeared, remaining mainly as a sub-stratum underlying the be-

Country Table 1. **Religious adherents in Sao Tome & Principe, AD 1900-2025.**

Year / Name	1900 Adherents	1900 %	1970 Adherents	1970 %	mid-1990 Adherents	mid-1990 %	Annual change, 1990-2000 Natural	Conversion	Total	Rate	mid-1995 Adherents	mid-1995 %	mid-2000 Adherents	mid-2000 %	mid-2025 Adherents	mid-2025 %
Christians	**1,250**	**3.1**	**70,850**	**97.1**	**114,500**	**96.2**	**2,673**	**-67**	**2,606**	**2.07**	**127,745**	**96.4**	**140,559**	**95.8**	**205,700**	**94.8**
PROFESSION																
professing Christians	**1,250**	**3.1**	**70,850**	**97.1**	**114,500**	**96.2**	**2,673**	**-67**	**2,606**	**2.07**	**127,745**	**96.4**	**140,559**	**95.8**	**205,700**	**94.8**
AFFILIATION																
unaffiliated Christians	250	0.6	5,130	7.0	5,100	4.3	120	216	336	5.19	7,264	5.5	8,456	5.8	12,700	5.9
affiliated Christians	**1,000**	**2.5**	**65,720**	**90.1**	**109,400**	**91.9**	**2,553**	**-283**	**2,270**	**1.90**	**120,481**	**90.9**	**132,103**	**90.1**	**193,000**	**88.9**
Roman Catholics	1,000	2.5	62,720	86.0	92,500	77.7	2,155	-350	1,805	1.80	101,182	76.4	110,553	75.3	160,000	73.7
Independents	0	0.0	2,000	2.7	12,300	10.3	289	31	320	2.34	13,939	10.5	15,500	10.5	27,000	12.4
Protestants	0	0.0	1,000	1.4	4,200	3.5	99	26	125	2.64	4,860	3.7	5,450	3.7	12,000	5.5
Marginal Christians	0	0.0	0	0.0	400	0.3	9	11	20	4.14	500	0.4	600	0.4	1,500	0.7
Trans-megabloc groupings																
Evangelicals	0	0.0	700	1.0	3,450	2.9	81	36	117	2.96	4,003	3.0	4,620	3.1	10,700	4.9
Pentecostals/Charismatics	0	0.0	730	1.0	16,300	13.7	384	96	480	2.61	18,604	14.0	21,100	14.4	35,500	16.4
Great Commission Christians	**1,200**	**3.0**	**8,750**	**12.0**	**16,900**	**14.2**	**398**	**75**	**473**	**2.50**	**19,285**	**14.6**	**21,628**	**14.7**	**34,720**	**16.0**
Baha'is	0	0.0	50	0.1	2,050	1.7	48	48	96	3.92	2,500	1.9	3,011	2.1	7,000	3.2
Ethnoreligionists	38,750	96.9	2,000	2.7	1,500	1.3	35	-10	25	1.54	1,600	1.2	1,748	1.2	1,200	0.6
Nonreligious	0	0.0	0	0.0	900	0.8	21	29	50	4.51	1,100	0.8	1,399	1.0	3,000	1.4
Muslims	0	0.0	0	0.0	50	0.0	1	0	1	1.67	55	0.0	59	0.0	100	0.1
World A (unevangelized persons)	34,400	86.0	364	0.5	119	0.1	3	-2	1	0.89	132	0.1	147	0.1	217	0.1
World B (evangelized non-Christians)	4,350	10.9	1,722	2.4	4,381	3.7	102	69	171	3.69	4,653	3.5	6,294	4.1	11,083	5.1
World C (Christians)	1,250	3.1	70,850	97.1	114,500	96.2	2,673	-67	2,606	2.07	127,745	96.4	140,559	95.8	205,700	94.8
Country's population	**40,000**	**100.0**	**72,937**	**100.0**	**119,000**	**100.0**	**2,778**	**0**	**2,778**	**2.14**	**132,531**	**100.0**	**146,800**	**100.0**	**217,000**	**100.0**

COLUMNS, ROWS.
For meanings and definitions, see Codebook (Part 3). Note that, by definition, total 'Christians' = professing + crypto-Christians, which also = affiliated + unaffiliated Christians, and also = Great Commission Christians + latent Christians. Percentages may not always total exactly, due to rounding.

NOTES ON RELIGIONS
BAHA'IS. From a minuscule presence in 1970, there has been rapid growth to 18 local spiritual assemblies by 1995.

ETHNORELIGIONISTS. Animists among the indigenous and immigrant Bantu population.
INDEPENDENTS. In 3 denominations in 1995 (see Table 2).

Great Commission Instrument Panel: status of Sao Tome & Principe (for explanation see start of Part 4)

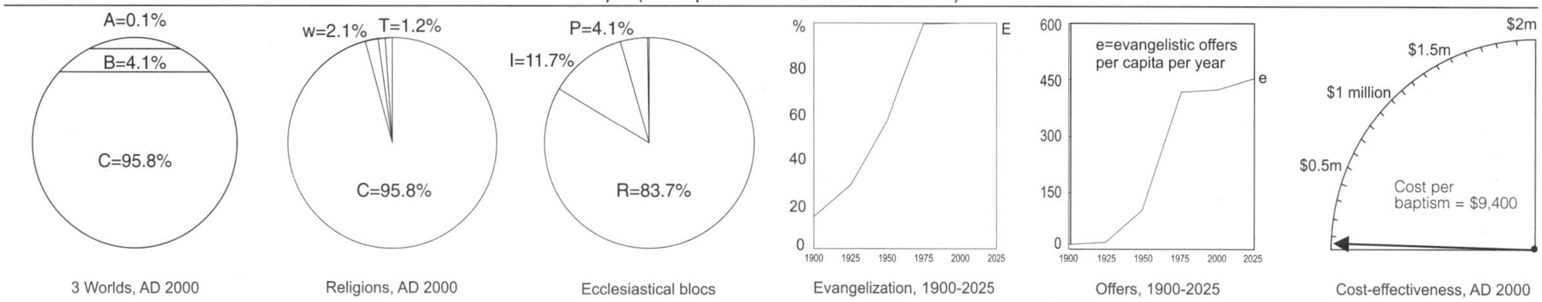

liefs of professing Christians. In 1900, adherents of traditional religions were estimated at 97% of the population, falling to 17% by 1964 and to 1.2% by 1995 as a result of Catholic evangelistic activity among immigrant Bantu.

Baha'i has expanded rapidly in the period 1970-2000.

Above. Emergency food from São Tome sent to Nigeria famine.

Official postage stamps depicting (*top*) a Roman Catholic village church (1960), and (*bottom*) 1951 Exhibition of Missionary Art.

CHRISTIANITY

CATHOLIC CHURCH. From the end of the 15th century, São Tomé and Príncipe served as a strategic supply center for the Portuguese exploration of southern Africa and the later trade route to India. Pope Paul III erected a diocese for the territory in 1534; at first it was attached to the ecclesiastical province of Funchal (Madeira); then it became a suffragan diocese of, successively, Lisbon, Baia de Todos-os-Santos (Brazil), Lisbon again, and finally Luanda in 1940. It was originally responsible for all islands from Cape Palmas to the Cape of Good Hope, but these were transferred to the new diocese of Angola and the Congo in 1596. There has been no resident bishop since 1816. The diocese has been administered since 1940 by the archbishop of Luanda through a vicar-general. Catholics made up 91% of the population in 1995.

From 1975, all Portuguese overseas territories, which were formerly under the Council for the Public Affairs of the Church, in Rome began to be transferred to Propaganda (SC for the Evangelization of Peoples).

The Holy See has diplomatic relations with São Tomé & Principe and in AD 2000 is represented to government and the Catholic hierarchy by a pronuncio residing in Luanda, Angola.

OTHER CHURCHES. The Evangelical Church was created entirely through indigenous efforts. The church was planted by an Angolan Christian exiled for penal servitude to São Tomé during the 1930s. The first scriptures and hymnbook were written down from memory. In 1957, an African Methodist missionary was sponsored by the Evangelical Alliance of Angola for work with indigenous Christians, and in 1960 another African missionary was sent from the Evangelical Church of Central Angola. Political conditions made further contacts between the 2 churches difficult. There were in 1995 3 congregations on São Tomé and on Príncipe totaling 2,400 members. In 1995 Protestants and African indigenous Christians numbered 6.5% of the population.

Portuguese Seventh-day Adventists first appeared on São Tomé in 1938, and in 1947 organized the St Thomas Island Mission as part of their Angola Union Mission. There are now 6 preaching places on São Tomé and one on Príncipe with over 1,000 members total.

Youth With A Mission (YWAM) began a work in 1990 with Brazilian missionaries that has grown to 150 members in a short time.

Indigenous missions. Very few Christians have been sent out as foreign missionaries.

CHURCH AND STATE

Prior to 1974 relations between church and state were governed, as with all Portuguese overseas territories, by the 1940 concordat signed between the Portuguese government and the Holy See. São Tomé was for many years the penal colony for Angola, a fact which contributed to the spread of Protestantism.

FUTURE TRENDS AND PROSPECTS

Christianity will probably continue to claim 95% of the population through AD 2025.

Christians could claim over 90% of the population around mid-century.

BIBLIOGRAPHY

A history of Sao Tome Island, 1470–1655: the key to Guinea. R. Garfield. San Francisco: Mellen Research University Press, 1992. 349p.
Atlas missionário português, 1964. A. da Silva Rego & E. dos Santos (eds). 2nd ed. Lisbon: Junta de Investigações do Ultramar e Centro de Estudos Históricos Ultramarinos, 1964. 206p.
Boletim eclesiástico de Angola e São Tomé, 1963–64. Luanda: Missões Católicas Portuguesas, 1965. 239p.
Mães de S. Tomé e Príncipe. F. Vaz. Lisboa: F. Vaz, 1993. 284p.
Os mensageiros da paz. J. G. Pereira. Lisbon: Colégio Universitário Pio XII, 1984. 181p.
São Tomé and Principe. C. S. Shaw. *World bibliographical series*, vol. 172. Oxford, UK: CLIO Press, 1994. ca 175p.
São Tomé and Príncipe: from plantation colony to microstate. T. Hodges & M. Newitt. Boulder, CO: Westview, 1988. 191p.
Subsídios para a história de S. Tomé e Príncipe. A. Ambrósio. [Lisbon]: Livros Horizonte, 1984. 285p.
The people of the Cape Verde islands: exploitation and emigration. A. Carreira. London: C. Hurst, 1982. 233p. (Deals with emigration and immigration, including slave trade and slavery in Sao Tome and Principe).

Country summary. **Worlds A, B, C by ethnolinguistic peoples, cities, and major civil divisions in Sao Tome & Principe.**

	PEOPLES							CITIES							CIVIL DIVISIONS						
World	Num	Pop 2000	C%	Christians	E%	U%	Unevangelized	Num	Pop 2000	C%	Christians	E%	U%	Unevangelized	Num	Pop 2000	C%	Christians	E%	U%	Unevangelized
A	0	0	0.00	0	0	0	0	0	0	0.00	0	0	0	0	0	0	0.00	0	0	0	0
B	0	0	0.00	0	0	0	0	0	0	0.00	0	0	0	0	0	0	0.00	0	0	0	0
C	7	146,776	90.00	132,104	100	0	141	1	34,902	88.00	30,714	100	0	35	7	146,775	90.00	132,103	100	0	142
Total	**7**	**146,776**	**90.00**	**132,104**	**100**	**0**	**141**	**1**	**34,902**	**88.00**	**30,714**	**100**	**0**	**35**	**7**	**146,775**	**90.00**	**132,103**	**100**	**0**	**142**

Country Table 2. **Organized churches and denominations in Sao Tome & Principe.**

Official name (bold type = church with over 10% of all affiliated) 1	Begun 2	Type 3	Counc 4	Congs 5	Adults 6	Affiliated 1970 7	Affiliated 1995 8	G% 9	Names, notes, and other statistics (see Codebook, Part 3) 10
Assembleias de Deus	c1960	P-Pe2	.....	12	1,400	500	3,500	8.09	*Assemblies of God.* Local leadership; large 800-seat temple in city.
Igreja Adventista do Sétimo Dia	1938	P-Adv	x....	1	430	500	1,080	3.13	*Seventh-day Adventists, St Thomas Island Mission*, Angola UM. 1x,7m,8t(495),30Y.
Igreja Católica: D São Tomé & Princ	1534	R-Lat	P.S.P	12	56,000	62,720	101,182	1.93	M=CSSp,CMF. C=1+0+2. (1970)15x,2m,16w,1250Yy. (1990) , 1n, 6x, 24m, 32w, 2681Yy
Igreja do Vida Profonda do Biblia	1990	I-3pA	.....	1	80	–	200	20.00	*Deeper Life Bible Church.* M=DLBC(Nigeria). Also Manna Church (Portugal).
Igreja Evangélica	c1935	I-Eva	.....	3	1,200	2,000	2,400	0.73	Begun by Angolan exiled to São Tomé. Later assisted by African Protestants.
Igreja Evangélica YWAM	1990	I-3cA	.....	1	60	–	150	20.00	M=YWAM.
Igreja Metodista	c1970	P-Met	.....	1	140	–	280	25.28	*Methodist Church.*
Igreja Nova Apostolica	c1980	I-3aX	x....	100	8,000	–	11,189	6.67	*New Apostolic Church. NAC.* HQ Zurich (Switzerland). Very rapid growth.
Testémunhas de Jeová	c1975	m-Jeh	x....	2	56	–	500	5.00	*Jehovah's Witnesses. Watch Tower.* 52Y.
Totals				**133**	**67,366**	**65,720**	**120,481**		

Churches, members, growth, 1900-2025	*Congs*	*Adults*	*Affiliated*	*G%*	*Total denominations*	*O*	*R*	*A*	*P*	*I*	*m*
Total churches, members, and denominations (mid-1900)	10	600	1,000	6.16	1	0	1	0	0	0	0
Total churches, members, and denominations (mid-1970)	31	39,500	65,720	6.16	4	0	1	0	2	1	0
Total churches, members, and denominations (mid-1990)	120	61,200	109,400	2.58	7	0	1	0	3	2	1
Total churches, members, and denominations (mid-1995)	133	67,366	120,481	1.95	9	0	1	0	3	4	1
Total churches, members, and denominations (mid-2000)	140	73,900	132,103	1.86	9	0	1	0	3	4	1
Total churches, members, and denominations (mid-2025)	250	108,000	193,000	1.53	33	0	1	0	10	20	2

(6 Megablocs: O R A P I m)

NOTES ON TABLE ABOVE
NATIONAL COUNCILS (Column 4, 5th letter).
P = Conferência Episcopal de Angola e São Tomé (CEAST) (Episcopal Conference of Angola & São Tomé).

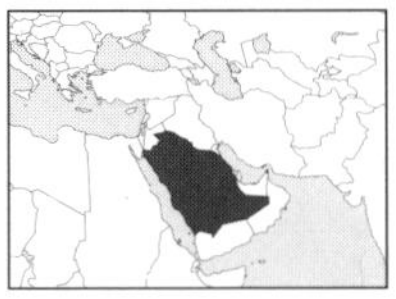

SAUDI ARABIA

SECULAR DATA, AD 2000

STATE
Official name: Al-Mamlaka al-'Arabiya as-Sa'udiya (The Kingdom of Saudi Arabia).
Short name: Saudi Arabia. **Adjective of nationality:** Saudi Arabian.
Flag: Green, with inscription 'There is no god but Allah and Mohammed is His prophet' in white Arabic characters above white sword.
Area: 2,248,000 sq. km. (868,000 sq. mi.).
Government: Absolute monarchy, since 1932 (7th century in Arab empire, c1500 under Ottoman empire, 1905 Nejd recaptured, 1927 Independence endorsed by Britain, 1932 unified Saudi Arabian Kingdom proclaimed).
Legislature: Council of Ministers, Legislative Assembly in Mecca, 90 members.
Official language: Arabic.
Monetary unit: 1 Saudi riyal (SRls) = 100 halalah. **US$1=** SRls 3.75.
Chief cities: Ar-RIYAD (Riyadh) 3,328,000; Jiddah (Jedda) 1,812,000; Makkah (Mecca) 920,000; At-Ta'if (Taif, Tayif) 663,986; Al-Madinah (Medina, Yathric) 641,853.
Political divisions: 5 provinces.
Armed forces: 158,000.

DEMOGRAPHY
Population: 21,607,000.
Population density: 9.6/sq. km. (24.8/sq. mi.).
Under 15 years: 8,757,000.
Growth rate p.a.: 2.97% (births 32.17, deaths 3.82).
Mortality: Infant, per 1,000: 18.3; **Maternal per 100,000:** 130.0.
Life expectancy: 73 (male 71, female 75).
Household size: 6.6. **Floor area per person, sq.m:** 15.0.
Major languages: Arabic, Persian, Hindi, Chinese, English, Korean, Turkish, Indonesian, Mahri, Shakari, and numerous smaller languages.
Urban dwellers: 85.74%. **Urban growth rate p.a.:** 3.5%.
Labor force: 36%.

ETHNOLINGUISTIC PEOPLES
74.2% Saudi Arab; 3.9% Bedouin Arab; 3.0% Gulf Arab; 2.4% Punjabi; 2.2% Urdu.

ECONOMY
National income p.a. per person: US$7,040; **per family:** US$46,463.

EDUCATION
Adult literacy: 62% (male 71%, female 50%). **Schools:** 17,338.
Universities: 72. **School enrolment:** female/male: 62%/69%.

HEALTH
Access to health services: 97%. **Access to safe water:** 93%.
Hospitals: 229 (21 beds per 10,000). **Doctors:** 25,543.
Blind: 230,000. **Deaf:** 1,299,700. **Murder rate:** <1.
Lepers: 2,000.

LITERATURE
New book titles p.a.: 1,510 (70 p.a. per million). **Periodicals:** 81.
Newspapers: 19 dailies.

COMMUNICATION (per 1,000 people)
Phones: 96 (17% mobile). **Radios:** 213. **TV sets:** 257.
Daily newspaper circulation: 54. **Computers:** 67.

REFUGEES
Alien refugees from other countries: 13,200.

HUMAN LIFE AND LIBERTY (optimum condition=100.0%)
HDI: 77.4. **HSI:** 56.0. **HFI:** 15.0. **EFL:** 42.0.

Country status. Saudi Arabia is a desert country in southwest Asia occupying most of the Arabian peninsula and bordering the Red Sea. Since the discovery of oil in 1938, the economy has become entirely based on this product which provides 85% of Saudi Arabia's revenues.

HUMAN LIFE AND LIBERTY

Human need and development. Although a rich country in terms of its gross national product, Saudi Arabia is an underdeveloped country both economically and socially. Despite enormous oil wealth, efforts to improve living conditions have been frustrated by a number of factors. Most of the oil wealth flows into the coffers of the royal family which prefers to spend money on showy palaces and public edifices. The economy is based solely on oil and there are virtually no other major productive sectors. There is a shortage of trained manpower, made more critical by the deliberate exclusion of a majority of the women from the work force. Knowledge of even elementary organizational and technological skills is lacking. Preoccupation with defense results in defense expenditures outweighing social expenditures in all national budgets. Much of the country is uninhabitable and without water. About two-thirds of the food supply is imported, although much of the imported food is subsidized. Virtually all citizens have access to a variety of free health services,. Education from primary to college is also free as also education at any institution of higher learning abroad.

Human rights and freedoms. Human rights are systematically violated in Saudi Arabia under the guise of religion. A combination of puritanism and authoritarianism, both built into the Saudi legal system, serves as the cover for some of the worst abuses. The sharia permits mutilation, whipping and other barbaric punishments for minor infractions and also executions for crimes against Islam. Torture of prisoners and incommunicado detention are routine features of the criminal justice system. Generally, detainees are beaten on the soles of the feet (a practice known as fallaqa), have their toenails pulled out, or burned by cigarettes. The Mutawwai'in (the religious police) and other religious zealots and vigilantes are encouraged to dispense their own brand of justice on people who have committed minor infractions. Women charged with adultery are stoned to death, while petty thieves may have their hands cut off. There are severe restrictions on freedoms of the press and speech, assembly and association as well as workers' rights. Criticism of Islam is punishable by death; criticism of the royal family and any call for reform are subject to imprisonment and torture. Foreign television programs, movies, books, magazines, and videos are censored with all references to politics,

Saudi Arabs. Traditional Arab tent with family in everyday dress.

Country Table 1. **Religious adherents in Saudi Arabia, AD 1900-2025.**

Year	1900		1970		mid-1990		Annual change, 1990-2000				mid-1995		mid-2000		mid-2025	
Name	*Adherents*	*%*	*Adherents*	*%*	*Adherents*	*%*	*Natural*	*Conversion*	*Total*	*Rate*	*Adherents*	*%*	*Adherents*	*%*	*Adherents*	*%*
Muslims	2,729,950	100.0	5,688,000	99.0	15,103,600	94.1	523,537	-8,704	514,833	2.98	17,140,200	93.9	20,251,925	93.7	36,318,000	90.9
Christians	**50**	**0.0**	**26,600**	**0.5**	**572,000**	**3.6**	**19,828**	**2,779**	**22,607**	**3.39**	**660,000**	**3.6**	**798,065**	**3.7**	**1,900,000**	**4.8**
PROFESSION																
crypto-Christians	50	0.0	16,900	0.3	100,000	0.6	3,467	533	4,000	3.42	115,000	0.6	140,000	0.7	350,000	0.9
professing Christians	**0**	**0.0**	**9,700**	**0.2**	**472,000**	**2.9**	**16,362**	**2,245**	**18,607**	**3.38**	**545,000**	**3.0**	**658,065**	**3.1**	**1,550,000**	**3.9**
AFFILIATION																
unaffiliated Christians	0	0.0	0	0.0	8,510	0.1	295	-38	257	2.67	8,940	0.1	11,080	0.1	21,800	0.1
affiliated Christians	**50**	**0.0**	**26,600**	**0.5**	**563,490**	**3.5**	**19,533**	**2,817**	**22,350**	**3.40**	**651,060**	**3.6**	**786,985**	**3.6**	**1,878,200**	**4.7**
Roman Catholics	50	0.0	2,600	0.1	450,000	2.8	15,599	1,989	17,588	3.35	520,000	2.9	625,875	2.9	1,500,000	3.8
Independents	0	0.0	13,050	0.2	60,000	0.4	2,080	420	2,500	3.54	68,560	0.4	85,000	0.4	200,000	0.5
Protestants	0	0.0	6,900	0.1	26,400	0.2	915	245	1,160	3.71	30,400	0.2	38,000	0.2	90,000	0.2
Orthodox	0	0.0	2,000	0.0	25,000	0.2	867	233	1,100	3.71	30,000	0.2	36,000	0.2	85,000	0.2
Anglicans	0	0.0	2,000	0.0	2,000	0.0	69	-69	0	0.00	2,000	0.0	2,000	0.0	3,000	0.0
Marginal Christians	0	0.0	50	0.0	90	0.0	3	-1	2	2.03	100	0.0	110	0.0	200	0.0
Trans-megabloc groupings																
Evangelicals	0	0.0	4,500	0.1	17,700	0.1	614	216	830	3.92	20,741	0.1	26,000	0.1	65,000	0.2
Pentecostals/Charismatics	0	0.0	12,500	0.2	72,000	0.5	2,496	1,954	4,450	4.93	93,033	0.5	116,500	0.5	300,000	0.8
Great Commission Christians	**50**	**0.0**	**20,000**	**0.4**	**288,800**	**1.8**	**10,011**	**2,871**	**12,882**	**3.76**	**346,800**	**1.9**	**417,623**	**1.9**	**1,125,000**	**2.8**
Hindus	0	0.0	1,000	0.0	160,000	1.0	5,546	2,437	7,983	4.13	200,000	1.1	239,834	1.1	600,000	1.5
Nonreligious	0	0.0	20,000	0.4	82,000	0.5	2,843	2,078	4,921	4.81	100,000	0.6	131,208	0.6	800,000	2.0
Buddhists	0	0.0	5,000	0.1	53,000	0.3	1,837	-85	1,752	2.90	61,000	0.3	70,524	0.3	150,000	0.4
Sikhs	0	0.0	0	0.0	30,000	0.2	1,040	109	1,149	3.29	35,000	0.2	41,485	0.2	90,000	0.2
Ethnoreligionists	0	0.0	0	0.0	17,000	0.1	589	1,643	2,232	8.75	27,000	0.2	39,324	0.2	40,000	0.1
Chinese folk-religionists	0	0.0	4,000	0.1	15,000	0.1	520	-84	436	2.58	17,000	0.1	19,360	0.1	34,000	0.1
New-Religionists	0	0.0	0	0.0	13,200	0.1	458	-59	399	2.67	14,500	0.1	17,186	0.1	35,000	0.1
Atheists	0	0.0	0	0.0	3,800	0.0	132	-16	116	2.69	4,400	0.0	4,957	0.0	10,000	0.0
Baha'is	0	0.0	400	0.0	2,900	0.0	101	14	115	3.38	3,400	0.0	4,045	0.0	8,000	0.0
doubly-counted religionists	0	0.0	0	0.0	-7,500	-0.1	-260	-112	-372	4.11	-9,500	-0.1	-11,222	-0.1	-20,000	-0.1
World A (unevangelized persons)	2,675,400	98.0	4,710,701	82.0	9,627,000	60.0	333,720	-322,889	10,831	0.11	9,801,611	53.7	9,744,757	45.1	14,986,875	37.5
World B (evangelized non-Christians)	54,550	2.0	1,007,456	17.5	5,846,000	36.4	202,623	320,110	522,733	6.59	7,790,924	42.7	11,064,178	51.2	23,078,125	57.7
World C (Christians)	50	0.0	26,600	0.5	572,000	3.6	19,828	2,779	22,607	3.39	660,000	3.6	798,065	3.7	1,900,000	4.8
Country's population	**2,730,000**	**100.0**	**5,744,758**	**100.0**	**16,045,000**	**100.0**	**556,171**	**0**	**556,171**	**3.02**	**18,252,536**	**100.0**	**21,607,000**	**100.0**	**39,965,000**	**100.0**

COLUMNS, ROWS.
For meanings and definitions, see Codebook (Part 3). Note that, by definition, total 'Christians' = professing + crypto-Christians, which also = affiliated + unaffiliated Christians, and also = Great Commission Christians + latent Christians. Percentages may not always total exactly, due to rounding.

NOTES ON RELIGIONS
BAHA'IS. Slow growth from 2 local spiritual assemblies in 1962 (Riyadh, Fahahil) with 5 other groups, to 4 local spiritual assemblies (1973); then considerable immigration. By 1995 presence was mainly clandestine.
BUDDHISTS. Chinese.
CHRISTIANS. Rapid growth since 1970, and especially 1975, is due to high immigration rate from Arab churches abroad, especially Palestine and Lebanon.
CRYPTO-CHRISTIANS. Arabs. In general the state regards Europeans as the only Christians and either ignores or does not recognize Arab Christians.
HINDUS. Expatriates from India.
INDEPENDENTS. Small indigenous congregations and groups of 2 kinds (see Table 2): among immigrant Christian Arabs, and isolated radio believers.
MUSLIMS. Almost all Sunnis (of the Shafiite rite dominant in the Hejaz and Asir, and Wahhabi (Hanbalite) reform movement in Nejd and Eastern Province, with a few Hanafite, Malikite, and other Hanbalite minorities); and also 130,000 Shias (Ismailis, known as Qarmatian schismatics, particularly Jafaris in the east, Makramis in southern Asir, and Zaydis near Mecca). Immigrant workers were initially restricted to persons from Pakistan (Sunnis) and 700,000 from North Yemen (Zaydi Shias), with Palestinians, a few Indians, Iranians, Indonesians and Turks. After 1975 Muslims were immigrating from many other countries, including 20,000 Chinese Muslims. *Hajj pilgrims to Mecca*. In 1912, these numbered 300,000; from 1920-40, the total averaged 70,000 a year (225,000 in 1927 of whom 90,662 from abroad), falling to 9,024 from abroad in 1940; 23,863 in 1941, rising to 99,069 in 1949, 164,072 in 1954, then to the following totals present during the 7-day Hajj in November-December each year: (1965), 294,118 from abroad, (1966) 316,226 from abroad, (1967) 318,507 from abroad, (1968) 692,784 total (318,000 from Saudi Arabia, 374,784 from abroad), (1969) 406,295 from abroad, (1970) 1,079,760 (648,490 from Saudi Arabia, 431,270 from abroad; of the total, 67.9% were men and 32.1% women), (1971) 1,042,027 total (562,688 from SA, 479339 from abroad), (1972) 1,216,951 total (571,769 from SA, 645,182 from abroad), (1973) 1,122,545 (514,790 from SA, 607,755 from abroad), (1974) 1,484,975 total (566,188 from Saudi Arabia, 918,777 from abroad), (1975) 1,557,867 total (306,159 Saudis and 357,135 non-Saudis from SA, 894,573 from abroad), (1976) 1,456,432 total (302,303 Saudis and 435,089 non-Saudis from SA, 719,040 from abroad), (1977) 1,627,589 total (392,129 Saudis and 496,141 non-Saudis resident in SA, 739,319 from abroad), (1978) 1,899,420 total (400,179 Saudis and 669,005 non-Saudis resident in SA, 830,236 from abroad), and thereafter increasing annually to 2,300,000 from 100 countries in 1998. These official statistics are divided up by immediate country of origin or departure (not by citizenship).
NONRELIGIOUS. Europeans, Chinese and other expatriates.
ORTHODOX. Many expatriate Arabs (Greek, Syrian, Coptic Orthodox), with some Indians (Syrian Orthodox) and Armenians. Most are unknown to or ignored by the state.
ROMAN CATHOLICS. In 1973 Jeddah had one Catholic church, and Catholic activity among European expatriates there and at Dhahran was tolerated but not officially recognized. After 1975 Catholic immigrants, mostly Arabs, became numerous, but official church structures (parishes) lagged a long way behind in the interests of caution.

Great Commission Instrument Panel: status of Saudi Arabia (for explanation see start of Part 4)

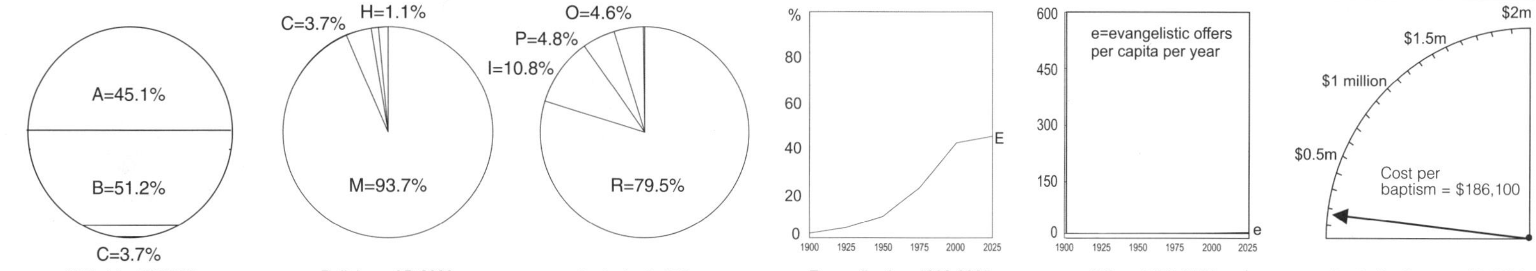

3 Worlds, AD 2000 | Religions, AD 2000 | Ecclesiastical blocs | Evangelization, 1900-2025 | Offers, 1900-2025 | Cost-effectiveness, AD 2000

non-Islamic religions, pigs, pork, Israel, alcohol, and sex deleted. Academic freedom likewise is limited. The study of evolution, psychology, socialism, Christianity, and Western philosophy is banned. There is an injunction against the study of music or art in any form. Cinemas and musical and theatrical performances do not exist. Although racial discrimination is theoretically unconstitutional. Blacks are treated as inferiors. Women generally are second class citizens, deprived by both Islam and the state of many of the rights they enjoy elsewhere in the world. Men may divorce easily, unlike women, and if divorced, a woman may keep her children only until they are 7 years of age when they revert to the husband's family. Employment opportunities for women are limited. They make up only 5% of the labor force, and this economic insecurity is used as a means to keep women in subjection to their husbands. There is no legal minimum wage. Saudis observe all the criminal punishments prescribed in the Quran, including execution by beheading, stoning and amputation. Confessions are generally forced. Apostasy like adultery is punishable by death or stoning, thievery by amputation of the right hand, and drunkenness by flogging. Saudi law makes no provision for bail or habeas corpus, neither are the detainee's family or friends informed of of his or her arrest.

Human environment. A desert environment in its natural state, Saudi Arabia is subject to creeping desertification. As a corollary, water is being depleted at a very fast rate. It is estimated that all the aquifers in the country will be dry within the next 20 years. Oil, the source of Saudi wealth, is itself a cause of much coastal pollution.

NON-CHRISTIAN RELIGIONS

Islam is the religion of 93.7% of the population. Muslims are mostly Sunnis; the Shafiite rite is dominant in the Hejaz and Asir while the Wahhabi reform movement is more important in Nejd and Eastern Province. There have always been a few Hanafiite and Malikite minorities, such as at the Hofuf Oasis. In Ahsa, the majority are semi-Wahhabite Hanbalites, but there also exist 60,000 Ismailis, known here as Qarmatian schismatics. Wahhabism, the Sunni sect which dominates the country, is a puritan reform movement and is intimately bound up with Saudi royalty. The Hejaz, where the holy places of Islam are located, has been increasingly closed to non-Muslims. It has become an extension of Haram, the holy land, where one comes to accomplish the Hajj, the obligatory pilgrimage of all Muslims.

Arabia is the heart of the Muslim world, Mecca and Medina being the 2 principal holy cities of Islam. The great mosque of Mecca, where the Kaaba is found, holds 300,000 people. The annual pilgrimage to Mecca attracts a growing number of foreign Muslims: 9,024 in 1940; 164,072 in 1954; 918,777 in 1974, falling to under 800,000 in 1990, then rising to 2,300,000 by 1998. This poses massive organizational programs for a pilgrimage which lasts for only 7 days.

Saudi Arabia is the headquarters for 2 of Islam's most important international organizations. (1) The Muslim World League (Rabita Al-Alam Al Islami), founded in Mecca in 1963, is the major Muslim religious organization in the world. Its purposes are to propagate the message of Islam, to make known its teaching and doctrine, and to strengthen the unity of the Muslim world. The members of its Constituent Council are chosen from among Islam's most eminent religious and cultural personalities. The League also maintains offices in a number of non-Muslim countries or countries where Islam is a minority, notably the USA (New York), Switzerland (Geneva), Denmark (Copenhagen), Nigeria, Madagascar, and Thailand. In 1975, the League decided to found a World Muslim Missionary Organization and to concern itself more actively with the Muslim diaspora.

1

4

PILGRIMAGE TO MECCA. The following 9 photographs illustrate this Encyclopedia's statistics of pilgrims of all kinds (Christian, Muslim, Hindu, et alia) by describing the major Islamic annual event, the 7-day Hajj to Mecca, birthplace of Muhammed, in the month of Dhu al-Hijjah (usually November). This pilgrimage is the last of the 5 Pillars (or absolute requirements) of Islam prescribed by the Quran, and is usually only performed once a lifetime by all Muslims who are able to afford it. Statistics of total pilgrims each year from 1912-1976 are given under Table 1 above, and for every country in the footnote MUSLIMS under its Table 1

1. Signpost on road to Mecca: no non-Muslims are permitted within the Haram, a sacred area 20 miles long by 6 miles wide with Mecca in its middle.

2. Logistics and progress of the Hajj, with its up to 2 million pilgrims at one time, are controlled by the governor, the Emir of Mecca (right) flying overhead by helicopter. Hajj control is now handled by an all-Arabic computer with 200 TV monitor screens. The government Ministry of Hajj was planning for 5 million pilgrims a year by 1980, but it increased less explosively up to 2.3 million in 1998.

3. The Emir's helicopter passes over the Mount of Mercy swarming with pilgrims, as he monitors the whole vast tented area accommodating 2 million pilgrims on the bare Arafat plain.

4. In the heart of the Sacred City of Mecca (normal population 376,000 in 35,000 houses covering 10 square miles) is Al-Masjid al-Haram, the Great or Sacred Mosque, covering an area of 1,724,032 square feet. At its right is the long al-Mas'a (Place of Running) within which pilgrims run 7 times.

5. Every available spot both within the Mosque and outside is crowded during prayers with (as here) 1.2 million worshippers in sacred robes (*ihram*). The inner courtyard holds over 500,000 worshippers at once, with a further 700,000 outside.

3

8

6

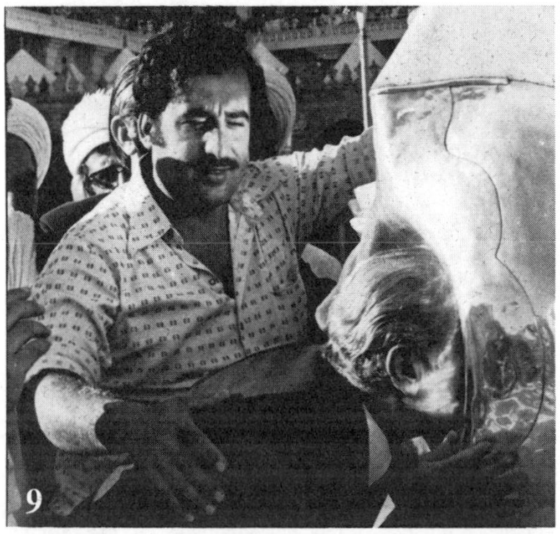

9

6. At the center of the inner courtyard is the Ka'bah (or Kaaba), the most sacred area in the entire Muslim world, the House of God first built by Abraham, and the physical axis of the Muslim world towards which 500 million Muslims world-wide face for prayer 5 times a day.
7. Worshippers individually circle the Kaaba 7 times, and this Tawaf or circling (3 times running, 4 times slowly, starting from and kissing the Black Stone each time) can be clearly seen in photographs taken at night (below. Not without reason, this area round the Kaaba with its running and jostling day and night (stopping only when prayers are said) has been called the most dangerous spot in Arabia.
8. The Kaaba is a structure of grey stone and marble, 45 feet high, cubical in shape, its 4 corners roughly aligned with the cardinal points of the compass, with one door and with an interior empty except for 3 pillars and suspended lamps. It is covered each year with a magnificent newly-woven covering of black silk brocade, the Kiswah, weighing 2.2 tons, on which are embroidered verses from the Quran in gold thread. At the southeastern corner (buttom right) is its focal point, the Black Stone (Hajar al-Aswad).
9. *The climax.* On each of his 7 circuits the devout pilgrim places his head inside the protective silver sheath to kiss or touch the Hajar al-Aswad, a simple 12-inch polished Black Stone placed there, according to tradition, by the Prophet Muhammed himself.

7

Country summary. **Worlds A, B, C by ethnolinguistic peoples, cities, and major civil divisions in Saudi Arabia.**

PEOPLES

World	Num	Pop 2000	C%	Christians	E%	U%	Unevangelized
A	18	2,763,497	1.56	43,239	39	61	1,698,365
B	14	18,477,177	2.35	435,003	57	43	8,036,370
C	7	366,018	84.35	308,742	100	0	573
Total	**39**	**21,606,692**	**3.64**	**786,984**	**55**	**45**	**9,735,308**

CITIES

World	Num	Pop 2000	C%	Christians	E%	U%	Unevangelized
A	0	0	0.00	0	0	0	0
B	17	9,853,298	3.96	390,548	56	44	4,313,343
C	0	0	0.00	0	0	0	0
Total	**17**	**9,853,298**	**3.96**	**390,548**	**56**	**44**	**4,313,343**

CIVIL DIVISIONS

World	Num	Pop 2000	C%	Christians	E%	U%	Unevangelized
A	0	0	0.00	0	0	0	0
B	5	21,606,690	3.64	786,984	55	45	9,735,309
C	0	0	0.00	0	0	0	0
Total	**5**	**21,606,690**	**3.64**	**786,984**	**55**	**45**	**9,735,309**

(2) The Islamic Conference with headquarters in Jeddah, is the major Muslim political organization in the world, extends to more than 40 member states including as follows: Afghanistan, Algeria, Bangladesh, Bahrain, Burkina Faso, Cameroon, Chad, Comoros, Djibouti, Egypt, Gabon, Gambia, Guinea, Guinea Bissau, Indonesia, Iran, Iraq, Jordan, Kuwait, Lebanon, Libya, Malaysia, Maldives, Mali, Mauritania, Morocco, Niger, Oman, Pakistan, Palestine Liberation Organization (PLO), Qatar, Saudi Arabia, Senegal, Sierra Leone, Somalia, Sudan, Syria, Tunisia, Turkey, Uganda, United Arab Emirates, and Yemen. Its purpose is to foster solidarity and cooperation between member states. Beyond its secretary general, there is a Conference of Monarchs, consisting of heads of state and government and a Conference of the Ministers of Foreign Affairs. In 1952, the Islamic Conference created an international Islamic press agency (IINA), with headquarters in Kuala Lumpur, Malaysia, to aid efforts in maintaining the activities of Islamic cultural centers in non-Muslim countries.

Since about 1950, Saudi Arabia has developed a vast network of teaching and religious training institutions, of which a number are open to foreigners. Of special importance are the following: (1) the Islamic University of Medina, founded in 1961, whose purpose is essentially missionary and which has admitted since its foundation students from more than 70 countries of Asia, Africa, Europe, and North America; (2) Faculty of the Sharia and Islamic Studies in Mecca, which is part of the king Abdul Aziz University of Jeddah, founded in 1967; (3) Higher Institute of Judiciary, founded in Riyadh in 1965, which trains judges with specialized competence in the diverse Islamic Sharia law rules; and (4) Islamic Jurisprudence College (or Sharia College), founded in Mecca in 1949, which trains teachers in religious and Arabic language subjects, as well as judges and missionaries. All of these institutions are self-governing or under the control of the Ministry of Education. In addition, there are 2 other colleges in Riyadh and institutes in 34 different cities and towns of Saudi Arabia, under the control of the General Presidency for Institutes and colleges, the first of these institutes being founded in 1950. Some 2 dozen Muslim organizations cooperated in the construction of a powerful radio station in Mecca called The Voice of Islam to counter the influence of Christian radio programs in Africa.

The Kingdom of Saudi Arabia has long espoused the Palestinian cause (Dome of the Rock, Jerusalem).

CHRISTIANITY

According to tradition, the Apostle Bartholomew was the first missionary to Arabia. Christianity was firmly established by AD 525, but in the 7th century, it was completely vanquished by Islam.

PROTESTANT CHURCHES. Protestant work was begun in Aden as early as 1885 and carried on after 1890 in several countries of the Persian gulf by Samuel Zwemer of the American Arabian Mission. Missions have never been permitted in Saudi Arabia, however. In 1970, there were 2 small congregations of Brethren and a Church of Christ group in Dhahran, all serving expatriates, together with a large number of house groups. Since 1970, however, the situation was dramatically altered by the enormous influx of several hundred thousand immigrant workers from many lands. A significant proportion of these have been Arab Protestants from Lebanon, Syria, and Palestine, followed later by Indian Protestants, Korean Protestants, and others. By 1990 over 30,000 Protestants were living in Saudi Arabia.

CATHOLIC CHURCH. The first Catholic of the modern era was a Servite priest who arrived in Aden in 1841. Aden was included in the vicariate of Galla in Africa in 1851, becoming a separate prefecture in 1854 and a vicariate in 1888. The vicariate of Arabia, to which Saudi Arabia belongs, was formed in 1889 and is now administered from Abu Dhabi. In 1970, there were only some 2,600 Catholics, mostly Americans or foreign Arabs working for the ARAMCO oil company. Since 1970, there was a large influx of Arab and other Catholics from many lands, so that by 1990 there were over 500,000 living and working in Saudi Arabia.

The Holy See has no diplomatic relations with Saudi Arabia in AD 2000, but has an apostolic delegate residing in Harissa (Lebanon).

OTHER CHURCHES. Because of severely anti-Christian measures, prohibitions and social pressures in the past, there now exist large numbers of Arabs, expatriate and citizen, who have either entered as immigrants holding privately to Christian beliefs or have become Christians through house groups or through radio programs, all of whom prefer to remain as secret believers.

Renewal movements. In the 1990s the Pentecostal/Charismatic Renewal continued to spread rapidly across most older churches, and numbered over 116,500 adherents (of whom none were Pentecostals, 28% Charismatics, and 72% Independents).

Indigenous missions. The Church of the East sent large numbers of missionaries out from the Arabian peninsula in the 6th and 7th centuries before the Islamic conquest. Very few Christians have been sent out as missionaries since.

CHURCH AND STATE

The king of Saudi Arabia is also the imam or spiritual leader of all Muslim believers. He holds all power: executive, legislative, judicial and religious. In addition, at the pan-Islamic level, he benefits from the prestige accorded Saudi Arabia because the Muslim holy places Mecca and Medina, of which he is the recognized guardian, are located there and because of the pilgrims they attract. Indeed, each year on the day following the Aid el Kebir (feast on the Sacrifices), the king washes the interior of the Kaaba and changes the cloth of black brocade which envelopes it. He is the only person allowed to enter the shrine.

The supreme law of the land is the Sharia, Islamic religious law. Although in recent years civic administrative courts have ben set up, the religious tribunals continue to retain a virtual monopoly over judicial decisions. The highest office is held by the grand mufti, supreme judge and head of the department of Sharia affairs. There exists, in addition, a Ministry of Pilgrimage and Religious Trusts, concerned with the welfare of pilgrims in such matters as food, transportation, and medical services, in addition to the construction and upkeep of mosques, the safe guarding of archeological ruins of religious interest and the promotion of tourism.

All religions other than Islam are prohibited. Christian worship services are held for foreign personnel, but it is important to stress that these meetings are completely private. Although tacitly tolerated by Saudi authorities, they are not officially recognized, nor is the presence of non-Muslim clergy within Arabia officially admitted.

The faithful practice of Islam is encouraged by rewards, such as the edict of November 1954 offering US$200 for every Muslim able to repeat the Quran by heart, as well as by enforcement and surveillance on the part of the authorities. One of the most feared of government agencies is the corps of Mujahidun, in ancient times known as the Ikhwans. The Mujahidun make up the personal militia of the king and are especially charged with maintaining public respect for the morals and the practice of Muslim rituals according to the principle of Wahhabism. They are also used on occasion in the suppression of strikes. Ancient Quranic punishments have been carried over in modernized form such as the surgical severing of the hand of a thief.

The policy of the king in general is to maintain an equilibrium between the Ulama, Muslim theologians who are traditionally conservative and the new bourgeoisie whose influence is slowly growing.

BROADCASTING AND MEDIA

No Christian programming is permitted to be broadcast from within the country. Shortwave radio programs in Arabic can be received from FEBA (Seychelles) and HCJB (Ecuador), and programming from KNLS has also generated some response Satellite TV programs are received mainly in Arabic.

The 'Jesus' Film has been broadcast in its radio version with an estimated audience of 166,000.

FUTURE TRENDS AND PROSPECTS

Christianity could grow to 4.8% (by 2025) for the first time in centuries as a higher proportion of the Saudi Arabian population is represented by immigrant workers and indigenous church growth becomes a reality.

Christians will likely remain primarily expatriates and below 7% of the population well into the 21st century.

BIBLIOGRAPHY

'A local church study of the Middle East: two approaches.' W. E. Otter. D.Min. thesis, Concordia Theological Seminary, Fort Wayne, IN, 1982. 197p.

'A rising tide in Meccaq,' G. H. Blake, *Middle East International*, no. 58 (1976), 16–18.

Analytical guide to the bibliographies on the Arabian Peninsula. C. L. Geddes. *Bibliographic series*, 4. Denver, CO: American Institute of Islamic Studies, 1974.

Arabia: the cradle of Islam: studies in the geography, people and politics of the Peninsula, with an account of Islam and mission–work. S. M. Zwemer. 2d ed. New York: Revell, 1900. 437p.

'Basic statistics on Hajj.' Hajj Research Centre, King Abdulaziz University, Jeddah, Saudi Arabia, 1978. 18p.

'Communicating God's love in Saudi Arabia.' N. Colaco. M.A.M. thesis, Talbot Theological Seminary, La Mirada, CA, 1981. 97p.

Der christliche Kult an der vorislamischen Kaaba als Problem der Islamwissenschaft und christlichen Theologie. G. Lüling. 2nd ed. Erlangen: Lüling, 1992. 100p.

Golden roads: migration, pilgrimage and travel in mediaeval and modern Islam. I. R. Netton (ed). Richmond, UK: Curzon Press, 1993. 210p.

'Permanence and change: an analysis of the Islamic political culture of Saudi Arabia with special reference to the Royal Family.' M. A. T. Al Saud. Ph.D. dissertation, Claremont Graduate School, Claremont, CA, 1982. 206p.

Pilgrimage to Mecca. M. Amin. London: Visnews, 1977. 256p. (Pictorial description of Hajj of 1975 and 1976).

Religion and state in the Kingdom of Saudi Arabia. A. Al-Yassini. *Westview special studies on the Middle East.* Boulder, CO: Westview, 1985. 183p.

'Revival and reform in Islam,' F. Rohman, in *The further Islamic lands; Islamic society and civilization*, p.632–56. P. M. Holt, A. K. S. Lanbton & B. Lewis (eds). *Cambridge history of Islam*, vol. 2. Cambridge, UK: Cambridge University Press, 1970.

Saudi Arabia. F. A. Clements. 2nd ed. *World bibliographical series*, vol. 5. Oxford, UK: CLIO Press, 1988. 386p. (Extensive chapter on religions).

Saudi Arabia: religious intolerance: the arrest, detention, and torture of Christian worshippers and Shi'a Muslims. New York: Amnesty International, [1993]. 28p.

'Saudi Arabia: the Islamic island,' G. Rentz, *Journal of International Affairs*, 19, 1 (1965), 115–25.

Source book on Arabian Gulf States, Arabian Gulf in general, Kuwait, Bahrain, Qatar and Oman. S. Kabeel. Kuwait: Kuwait University, Libraries Department, 1975. 427p. (With over 3,000 item bibliography).

The Arab at home. P. W. Harrison. London: Hutchinson, 1924. 345p.

The Arab of the desert. H. R. P. Dickson. Ed., R. D. Wilson & Z. D. Freeth. 3rd ed. London: Allen & Unwin, 1983. 271p.

The golden milestone: reminiscences of pioneer days fifty years ago in Arabia. S. M. Zwemer & J. Cantine. New York: Revell, 1938. 157p.

The Hadj: a pilgrimage to Mecca. M. Wolfe. London: Secker & Warburg, 1994. 343p.

The hajj: the Muslim pilgrimage to Mecca and the holy places. F. E. Peters. Princeton, NJ: Princeton University Press, 1994. 452.
'The Islamic content of the foreign policy of Saudi Arabia: King Faisal's call for Islamic solidarity, 1965–1975.' N. O. Madani. Ph.D. dissertation, American University, Washington, DC, 1977. 230p.
'The Islamic pilgrimage to Mecca: a study of distribution of Muslim pilgrims.' A. M. N. Ghazali. M.A. thesis, California State University, Chico, CA, 1981. 108p.
'The pilgrimage to Mecca: some geographical and historical aspects,' R. King, *Erdkunde*, 26 (1972), 61–72.
Women in Muslim family law. J. L. Esposito. Syracuse, NY: Syracuse University Press, 1982. 167p.
'Women of Saudi Arabia,' M. Alireza, *National geographic*, (1987).

Country Table 2. **Organized churches and denominations in Saudi Arabia.**

Official name (bold type = church with over 10% of all affiliated) 1	*Begun* 2	*Type* 3	*Counc* 4	*Congs* 5	*Adults* 6	*Affiliated 1970* 7	*Affiliated 1995* 8	*G%* 9	*Names, notes, and other statistics* (see Codebook, Part 3) 10
Anglican Church (D Cyprus & the Gulf)		A-plu	aw...	1	1,200	2,000	2,000	0.05	In Episcopal Church of Jerusalem & the Middle East. Mostly British expatriates.
Catholic Church (VA Arabia)	1875	R-Lat	P..L.	34	350,000	2,600	520,000	23.61	99% expatriates: Filipinos, Koreans, Melkites, Arabs, Indians, Europeans. M=OFMCap.
Christian Brethren		P-CBr	x....	4	200	200	400	0.05	*Plymouth Brethren. Open Brethren. Gospel Halls.* Also M=RSMT. All expatriates.
Church of Christ		I-Dis	x....	1	30	50	60	0.05	M=Churches of Christ (Non-Instrumental) (USA). In Dhahran. Mainly Americans.
Hidden Muslim believers in Christ	c1960	I-Mus	.....	500	6,000	500	7,500	11.44	Converted Muslims who remain within Islam as witnesses to Christ.
Isolated radio churches	c1950	I-3rS	.....	1,000	18,000	8,300	32,000	5.55	Isolated Arab believers, mostly ages 12-25. (1970) R=350(TWR, RVOG, RV, FEBA),T=2000(ICI).
Saudi Arab house churches	c1950	I-3hS	.....	1,100	12,000	1,200	18,000	11.44	Saudi Arab believers organized into private house meetings; no foreign contacts.
Unitarian Fellowship of Dhahran	c1960	m-Unt	.....	1	50	50	100	2.81	Small fellowship of expatriate Whites. In 1964, 33 members, 56 total community.
Other Protestant denominations	1938	P-	.....	200	20,000	6,700	30,000	6.18	USA and European Protestants (ARAMCO, etc), CSI (India), Arabs. House churches.
Other independent churches	c1965	I-3cS	.....	500	5,500	3,000	11,000	5.33	Small groups, begun by immigrant Arab Christians; also New Apostolic Ch (13 members).
Other Orthodox churches	c1965	O-	.....	40	21,000	2,000	30,000	11.44	Expatriate Arabs (Greek, Syrian, Coptic), Indians (Syrian); private meetings.
Totals				**3,381**	**433,980**	**26,600**	**651,060**		

Churches, members, growth, 1900-2025	*Congs*	*Adults*	*Affiliated*	*G%*	*Total denominations*	*6 Megablocs:*	*O*	*R*	*A*	*P*	*I*	*m*
Total churches, members, and denominations (mid-1900)	2	27	50	9.38	1		0	1	0	0	0	0
Total churches, members, and denominations (mid-1970)	616	14,430	26,600	9.38	20		2	1	1	9	6	1
Total churches, members, and denominations (mid-1990)	3,000	376,000	563,490	16.49	42		9	1	1	16	14	1
Total churches, members, and denominations (mid-1995)	3,381	433,980	651,060	2.93	42		9	1	1	16	14	1
Total churches, members, and denominations (mid-2000)	4,000	525,000	786,985	3.86	42		9	1	1	16	14	1
Total churches, members, and denominations (mid-2025)	6,000	1,252,000	1,878,200	3.54	138		15	1	1	50	70	1

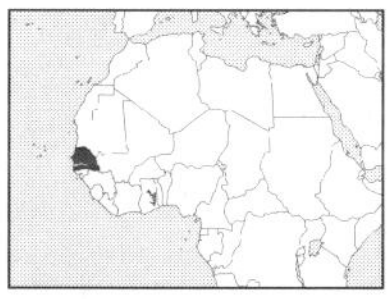

SENEGAL

SECULAR DATA, AD 2000

STATE
Official name: La République du Sénégal (The Republic of Senegal).
Short name: Senegal. **Adjective of nationality:** Senegalese.
Flag: Bars of green, gold, and red, with centered green star.
Area: 196,712 sq. km. (75,951 sq. mi.).
Government: Multiparty republic, since 1974 (1857 French possession, 1960 Independence as republic, 1962 one-party republic).
Legislature: National Assembly, 120 members.
Official language: French (Français).
Monetary unit: 1 CFA franc (CFAF) = 100 centimes. **US$1=** CFAF 560.38.
Chief cities: DAKAR 2,077,000; Thies 252,982; Saint-Louis (Ndar) 219,854; Kaolack 207,975; Ziguinchor 170,043.
Political divisions: 10 provinces.
Armed forces: 13,000.

DEMOGRAPHY
Population: 9,481,000.
Population density: 48.2/sq. km. (124.8/sq. mi.).
Under 15 years: 4,236,000.
Growth rate p.a.: 2.54% (births 37.91, deaths 11.58).
Mortality: Infant, per 1,000: 58.3; **Maternal per 100,000:** 1,200.0.
Life expectancy: 54 (male 53, female 56).
Household size: 8.8. **Floor area per person, sq.m:** 8.0.
Major languages: French, Wolof, Serer, Fulani, English, Tukulor, Diola, Mandingo, Bambara, and about 15 smaller languages.
Urban dwellers: 47.01%. **Urban growth rate p.a.:** 3.99%.
Labor force: 43%.

ETHNOLINGUISTIC PEOPLES
34.6% Wolof; 12.4% Fulakunda (Fula Cunda); 11.2% Serer-Sine; 8.7% Tukulor (Takarir); 5.9% Mandinka (Mandingo, Sose).

ECONOMY
National income p.a. per person: US$600; **per family:** US$5,280.

EDUCATION
Adult literacy: 33% (male 43%, female 23%). **Schools:** 2,832.
Universities: 18. **School enrolment:** female/male: 31%/44%.

HEALTH
Access to health services: 40%. **Access to safe water:** 50%.
Hospitals: 20 (10 beds per 10,000). **Doctors:** 520.
Blind: 22,000. **Deaf:** 569,700. **Murder rate:** 1.
Lepers: 100,000. **Underweight prevalence under 5:** 22%.

LITERATURE
New book titles p.a.: 1,420 (150 p.a. per million). **Periodicals:** 172.
Newspapers: 3 dailies.

COMMUNICATION (per 1,000 people)
Phones: 9 (20% mobile). **Radios:** 93. **TV sets:** 37.
Daily newspaper circulation: 6. **Computers:** 8.

REFUGEES
Citizen refugees in other countries: 17,000.
Alien refugees from other countries: 68,000.

HUMAN LIFE AND LIBERTY (optimum condition=100.0%)
HDI: 32.6. **HSI:** 34.0. **HFI:** 57.5. **EFL:** 32.0.

Country Table 1. **Religious adherents in Senegal, AD 1900-2025.**

Year	*1900*		*1970*		*mid-1990*		*Annual change, 1990-2000*				*mid-1995*		*mid-2000*		*mid-2025*	
Name	*Adherents*	*%*	*Adherents*	*%*	*Adherents*	*%*	*Natural*	*Conversion*	*Total*	*Rate*	*Adherents*	*%*	*Adherents*	*%*	*Adherents*	*%*
Muslims	699,600	70.0	3,615,000	86.9	6,427,000	87.7	188,958	-983	187,975	2.60	7,304,540	87.7	8,306,748	87.6	14,800,500	88.4
Ethnoreligionists	282,000	28.2	316,000	7.6	460,000	6.3	13,523	-398	13,125	2.54	520,000	6.2	591,249	6.2	800,000	4.8
Christians	**18,400**	**1.8**	**224,500**	**5.4**	**400,000**	**5.5**	**11,759**	**493**	**12,252**	**2.71**	**455,000**	**5.5**	**522,518**	**5.5**	**1,040,000**	**6.2**
PROFESSION																
professing Christians	**18,400**	**1.8**	**224,500**	**5.4**	**400,000**	**5.5**	**11,759**	**493**	**12,252**	**2.71**	**455,000**	**5.5**	**522,518**	**5.5**	**1,040,000**	**6.2**
AFFILIATION																
unaffiliated Christians	3,100	0.3	36,799	0.9	48,050	0.7	1,413	-695	718	1.40	52,861	0.6	55,227	0.6	64,680	0.4
affiliated Christians	**15,300**	**1.5**	**187,701**	**4.5**	**351,950**	**4.8**	**10,347**	**1,187**	**11,534**	**2.88**	**402,139**	**4.8**	**467,291**	**4.9**	**975,320**	**5.8**
Roman Catholics	15,000	1.5	183,021	4.4	333,000	4.5	9,790	1,013	10,803	2.85	380,432	4.6	441,031	4.7	920,000	5.5
Independents	0	0.0	100	0.0	9,800	0.1	288	132	420	3.63	11,331	0.1	14,000	0.2	30,100	0.2
Protestants	300	0.0	4,080	0.1	7,500	0.1	220	10	230	2.71	8,276	0.1	9,800	0.1	20,000	0.1
Marginal Christians	0	0.0	400	0.0	1,500	0.0	44	36	80	4.37	1,950	0.0	2,300	0.0	5,000	0.0
Anglicans	0	0.0	100	0.0	150	0.0	4	-3	1	0.65	150	0.0	160	0.0	220	0.0
Trans-megabloc groupings																
Evangelicals	200	0.0	2,700	0.1	4,400	0.1	129	31	160	3.15	5,382	0.1	6,000	0.1	12,000	0.1
Pentecostals/Charismatics	0	0.0	2,000	0.1	25,600	0.4	753	187	940	3.18	29,906	0.4	35,000	0.4	73,000	0.4
Great Commission Christians	**16,000**	**1.6**	**122,000**	**2.9**	**220,000**	**3.0**	**6,468**	**1,594**	**8,062**	**3.17**	**253,000**	**3.0**	**300,623**	**3.2**	**624,000**	**3.7**
Nonreligious	0	0.0	0	0.0	23,400	0.3	688	879	1,567	5.26	31,000	0.4	39,073	0.4	60,000	0.4
Baha'is	0	0.0	2,400	0.1	13,000	0.2	382	-2	380	2.60	15,200	0.2	16,804	0.2	32,000	0.2
Atheists	0	0.0	0	0.0	3,000	0.0	88	16	104	3.02	3,600	0.0	4,041	0.0	9,000	0.1
Other religionists	0	0.0	100	0.0	600	0.0	18	-5	13	1.95	660	0.0	728	0.0	1,500	0.0
World A (unevangelized persons)	900,000	90.0	2,702,834	65.0	4,191,044	57.2	123,194	-30,349	92,845	2.02	4,648,200	55.8	5,119,740	54.0	8,388,243	50.1
World B (evangelized non-Christians)	81,600	8.2	1,230,872	29.6	2,735,956	37.3	80,463	29,856	110,319	3.44	3,226,908	38.7	3,838,742	40.5	7,314,757	43.7
World C (Christians)	18,400	1.8	224,500	5.4	400,000	5.5	11,759	493	12,252	2.71	455,000	5.5	522,518	5.5	1,040,000	6.2
Country's population	**1,000,000**	**100.0**	**4,158,207**	**100.0**	**7,327,000**	**100.0**	**215,416**	**0**	**215,416**	**2.61**	**8,330,109**	**100.0**	**9,481,000**	**100.0**	**16,743,000**	**100.0**

Continued overleaf

Country Table 1–concluded

COLUMNS, ROWS.
For meanings and definitions, see Codebook (Part 3). Note that, by definition, total 'Christians' = professing + crypto-Christians, which also = affiliated + unaffiliated Christians, and also = Great Commission Christians + latent Christians. Percentages may not always total exactly, due to rounding.

CENSUSES.
IV.1960-VIII.1961 (de jure): 89.7% Muslims, 5.6% Roman Catholics, 4.6% ethnoreligionists, 0.06% Protestants. **1991:** 94.0% Muslims, 4.9% Christians (mainly Roman Catholics), 1.1% other religionists (including ethnoreligionists).

NOTES ON RELIGIONS
AFFILIATED CHRISTIANS. Although numbers of conversions from paganism to Christianity are taking place each year, the net total is negative because of losses from the churches to Islam, especially school children. In the Bignona region, 15,000 Catholics became Muslims from 1955-65.
ATHEISTS. None; only a small outlawed pro-Communist party, African Party of Independence (PAI); communist membership negligible.
BAHA'IS. From 1964, growth to 16 local spiritual assemblies (1973), then mushrooming increase to 81 LSAs by 1996.
ETHNORELIGIONISTS. Animists, usually strongly resistant to Islam, mainly among the Serer (8% traditionalist in 1995) and Diola (30%).
MUSLIMS. African Sunnis (of the Malikite rite). Islamic brotherhoods active (1957): Qadiriya with 304,000 members, the missionary order of Tijaniya with 1 million with one of its major Black African headquarters in Kaolack, Muridiya 423,000 (attaining overwhelming power during the 20th century), and 23,000 in others. Conversions to Islam are taking place among ethnoreligionists, particularly the Serer (420,000), who were entirely pagans up to 1870, resisted Islam through 2 brutal jihads against them, until 1900 when islamization began, remaining weak (due to resistance by the powerful Serer monarchy, tenacious fetishism and sacrificial religion) until 1950 when the traditional chieftainships disappeared; by 1995 the Serer had become 70% Muslim. Half of the Diola, 100,000 or so, became Muslims from 1940-70. *Missionaries.* A number of Egyptian missionaries sent by Al-Azhar University (Cairo) are at work, with several big building projects. *Hajj pilgrims to Mecca.* (1970) 2,422; (1974) 3,403; (1975) 3,832; (1976) 4,148.
OTHER RELIGIONISTS. Including Rosicrucians (1 AMORC center).
PENTECOSTALS/CHARISMATICS. Catholic charismatics (January 1975): 200 involved adults; total charismatic community including children, 400, increasing rapidly every month; (1997) 44 weekly prayer groups with 1,000 regularly attending adults (with 25 involved priests and 1 bishop).

Great Commission Instrument Panel: status of Senegal (for explanation see start of Part 4)

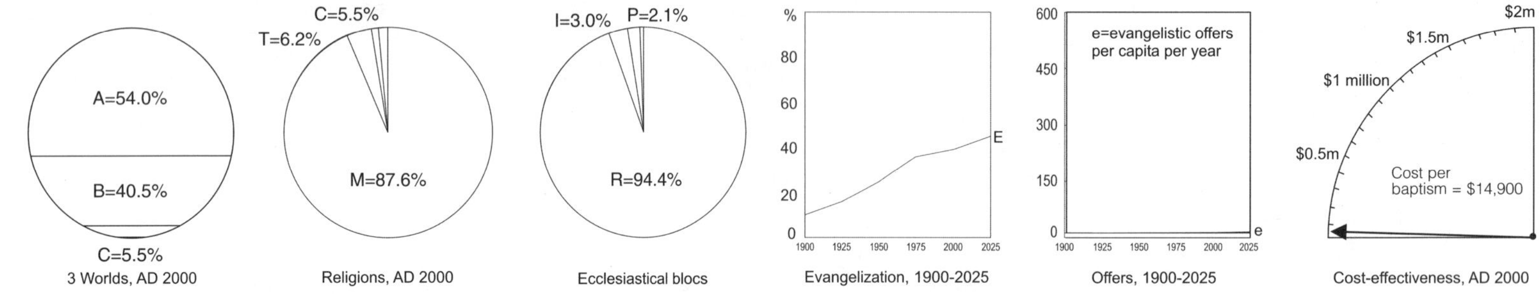

Country status. Senegal, part of Sahel in West Africa, is the westernmost country in Africa. It is also one of the leading Francophone countries in the region. Its chief exports are groundnuts, seafood, and rock phosphate.

HUMAN LIFE AND LIBERTY

Human need and development. Although Senegal is economically and socially more viable than other Sahelian countries, it is still a highly underdeveloped country and one in which the development process has only helped to accentuate the gulf between the vast majority of its rural population and the small urban elite. In the large towns, such as Dakar, there is a small minority of business people, officials and professionals who have access to some of the modern conveniences, such as cars, brick houses, and imported foods. But for most of the rural population, privation is a constant fact of life. Their survival hinges upon the level of rainfall. Even in the best years, there is a season, known as soudure, or famine, that precedes the harvest. In years when the rainfall is sparse, the soudure can be a disaster which can wipe out both man and beast. To escape the rigors of such a life, many rural dwellers have migrated to the towns where they are forced to live in cramped makeshift quarters. Only a third of the urban work force have full time jobs. Between the 2 extremes—the wealthy and the unemployed rural immigrants—are the majority of the urban residents. On the surface they appear somewhat better off than the average villager. But they too lead very monotonous lives, with poor diet, inadequate housing and few, if any, other amenities. In rural areas, many people live in huts made of branches, muds, reeds or straw. When these materials deteriorate after a few years, the houses are generally rebuilt. Sometimes sheep and goats live within the same compounds. Most towns have sections for the well-to-do, but the majority live in shantytowns crowded along narrow streets. Sewage and trash are commonly dumped along streets and on vacant land. Public sanitation is nonexistent except in certain parts of towns. The average diet is higher in protein content than the diet in many African countries, but because of poor dietary practices many children suffer from serious diseases, such as kwashiorkor, caused by nutritional deficiency. Despite significant advances in public health, Senegal is troubled by a variety of communicable diseases and parasitic infections exceeding any other country outside the Sahel. The most serious of these diseases are schistosomiasis and onchocerciasis. The vast majority of doctors and medical facilities are concentrated in Dakar. Social Security programs are limited to the small minority working for the government or in private enterprise.

Human rights and freedoms. Traditionally, Senegal has a strong record in human rights, but some serious abuses surfaced in 1993 against a background of political conflict over the elections, and extensive terrorist and military operations in the Casamance. There are credible reports that detainees are sometimes tortured and beaten despite a legal ban on such physical abuse. The press is free and criticism of the government is openly expressed in the independent publications. However, the broadcast media are totally controlled by the government. Elections are generally open and free with few flagrant irregularities. There is no discrimination based on gender, but women suffer extensive societal disabilities.

Human environment. Senegal has serious problems with the encroaching desert. Deforestation and overgrazing of livestock promotes desertification where the land is naturally arid. Senegal is the world's largest exporter of exotic birds, and, in turn, this has lead to poaching of wildlife areas.

Muslims. Serer converts to Islam at daily prayers outside their homestead, in region of Kaolack.

NON-CHRISTIAN RELIGIONS

Islam with its strength concentrated in the north (among the Wolofs) and east (among the Fulani) is the dominant religion of Senegal, with 87.6% of the population. Several brotherhoods are active: Qadiriya from Morocco with 300,000 members, the first to arrive: Tijaniya also from Morocco with one million members, many of its adherents having come from Qadiriya; and Muridiya with over 400,000 members whose headquarters is Touba. The Murid chiefs control about 50% of Senegal's peanut production through a feudal system. The conservatism and sectarianism of the Qadiriya and Tijaniya marabouts (called Serigue among the Wolofs and Tierno among the Fulani) has provoked a movement of resistance by youth and intellectuals centered in the Union Culturelle Musulmane, begun in 1953.

Arabic is widely spoken, encouraged by the civil authorities. A chair of Muslim languages and civilizations and an Islamic Institute exist at the University of Dakar. The West African regional office of the World Muslim Congress (headquarters in Pakistan) is found at Kaolack.

African traditional religions retain their vitality especially among the Diola of Casamance and the Serer of Sine-Salcum. Among the latter, God (Rog) is recognized as creator and is invoked in time of war. Nevertheless, appeal is made more often to departed ancestors who possess men, animals, and inanimate objects. For the Diola, ancestral veneration, directly by a separated priestly class, is also more widely practices than the worship of God (Emit). The Diola Felup believe in the existence of a satanic being, Buso, who epitomizes evil.

CHRISTIANITY

CATHOLIC CHURCH. The coast of Senegal was explored by Portuguese in 1445, providing the first Christian contacts with the local population. In 1486, the Senegalese chief Behemoi was baptized in Lisbon, and by 1490 the first religious establishments were set up in the region of Ziguinchor. The diocese of Funchal, including Senegal, was created in 1514, and although a prefecture of St Louis was erected in 1779, work was sporadic prior to the arrival of St Joseph of Cluny sisters in 1819. Three Senegalese priests were ordained in 1840, and Holy Ghost priests arrived in 1845. The vicariate of The Two Guineas was formed in 1847, becoming the vicariate of Senegambia in 1863 and of Dakar in 1936. The hierarchy was established in 1955, Dakar becoming an archdiocese, and its first African archbishop was consecrated in 1962. In 1972, the bishop in Senegal decided that all dioceses should have African priests, since the preceding year 3 dioceses had only expatriate clergy. Following this decision, newly ordained Senegalese priests were to consider themselves as 'national' rather than 'diocesan' priests.

Christians, as is the case also with traditionalists, are found mostly among the Serer and Diola in southwestern Senegal, with many living in the region of Dakar.

The Holy See has diplomatic relations with Senegal and in AD 2000 is represented to government and the Catholic hierarchy by a nuncio residing in Dakar.

PROTESTANT CHURCH. The Protestant Church of Dakar, whose membership is about 60% European, is the result of the activity of the Paris Mission as early as 1863. The Worldwide Evangelization Crusade from Britain arrived in 1935, and since World War II a number of small conservative missions, mostly from the USA, have taken up work in the country. The most successful of these new arrivals have been the Assemblies of God, who have done extensive evangelism through radio broadcasts.

The largest Protestant denomination is the Lutheran Church, started in 1974 by the Finnish Lutheran Mission, and growing to 3,000 members in 37 congregations by 1995.

Renewal movements. In the 1990s the Pentecostal/Charismatic Renewal continued to spread rapidly across most older churches, and numbered over 35,000 adherents (of whom 9% Pentecostals, 52% Charismatics, and 39% Independents).

Indigenous missions. Most of the missionaries sent out from Senegal are Roman Catholics serving in surrounding African countries and France.

Country summary. **Worlds A, B, C by ethnolinguistic peoples, cities and major civil divisions in Senegal.**

	PEOPLES							*CITIES*							*CIVIL DIVISIONS*						
World	*Num*	*Pop 2000*	*C%*	*Christians*	*E%*	*U%*	*Unevangelized*	*Num*	*Pop 2000*	*C%*	*Christians*	*E%*	*U%*	*Unevangelized*	*Num*	*Pop 2000*	*C%*	*Christians*	*E%*	*U%*	*Unevangelized*
A	38	7,583,843	0.34	25,494	41	59	4,448,489	3	578,937	3.01	17,409	45	55	320,640	7	5,712,179	2.19	125,139	43	57	3,276,319
B	14	1,676,976	16.10	269,921	60	40	669,470	3	2,455,018	9.38	230,212	55	45	1,101,093	3	3,768,981	9.08	342,151	51	49	1,842,126
C	6	220,343	78.00	171,875	100	0	485	0	0	0.00	0	0	0	0	0	0	0.00	0	0	0	0
Total	**58**	**9,481,162**	**4.93**	**467,290**	**46**	**54**	**5,118,444**	**6**	**3,033,955**	**8.16**	**247,621**	**53**	**47**	**1,421,733**	**10**	**9,481,160**	**4.93**	**467,290**	**46**	**54**	**5,118,445**

A 1972 postage series expounds the Nativity: Jesus and Mary, Joseph, and the 3 kings Melchior, Balthazar, and Gaspard (Caspar).

CHURCH AND STATE

According to the constitution of March 1963, modified by the constitutional law of 26 February 1970, the republic is secular, assuring equality for all citizens and freedom of religion (Title I, Article 1). Freedom of conscience and the profession and free practice of religion, are guaranteed to all. Institutions and religious communities not under state control may regulate and administer their affairs in an autonomous manner (Title II, Article 49). Private confessional education is subsidized provided it follows the government program, and religious instruction is given in state schools.

The government encourages the various churches and religious groups, without discrimination to play a positive role in development, manifesting an understanding of the importance of the spiritual dimension of life. Although Senegal is nearly 90% Muslim, it was led after Independence by a Catholic president, Leopold Sedar Senghor. In 1962, he imprisoned the Muslim prime minister, Mamadou Dia, and several other Muslim collaborators, because of their socialistic tendencies, but this provoked no religious animosity. The Muslim marabouts, especially the Murids, contribute significantly to a maintenance of the social status quo.

BROADCASTING AND MEDIA

Shortwave radio programs from KNLS have seen some response. Senegal is a member of UNDA. There is a regular 15-minute Catholic radio program which focuses on family-oriented topics.

Some 6.2 million have seen the 'Jesus' Film, chiefly through local broadcasts (5.6 million) and film team presentations (786,000).

INTERDENOMINATIONAL ORGANIZATIONS

The Evangelical Fellowship of Senegal (Fraternite Evangelique du Senegal) has in its membership most of the Evangelical groups working in Senegal at the present time. Among Protestant bodies, the principal non-members are the Protestant Church of Dakar and the Seventh-day Adventists.

FUTURE TRENDS AND PROSPECTS

In light of the continuing decline of ethnoreligionists, Christians could grow to 6.2% by 2025.

Muslims will likely claim over 90% of the population well into the 21st century. Christianity could reach 8% by AD 2050.

BIBLIOGRAPHY

'A project of prayer for renewal among missionaries and for spiritual awakening among the masses of Senegal.' A. R. Hodges. D.Min. thesis, Midwestern Baptist Theological Seminary, Kansas City, MO, 1994. 122p.

'Animisme, religion caduque: étude qualitative et quantitative sur les opinions et la pratique religieuse en Basse–Casamance (pays diola),' L. Thomas, *Bulletin de l'IFAN*, 27 (B), 1-2 (1965), 1–41.

Annuaire catholique du Sénégal pour l'année 1972. Dakar: Archevêché de Dakar, 1972. (Annual).

Colonisations et religions en Afrique noire: l'exemple de Ziguinchor. J. Trincaz. Paris: L'Harmattan, 1981. 360p.

Consultation of Lutheran Churches on work in West Africa among Fulani speaking people: Dakar, Senegal, January 14–21, 1979. R. Lehtonen (ed). Geneva: Lutheran World Federation, 1979. 108p.

Etudes sur l'Islam au Sénégal: vol. 1. Les personnes; vol. 2. Les doctrines et les institutions. P. Marty. *Collection de la Revue du Monde Musulman.* Paris: E. Leroux, 1917. 2 vols.

Eyes of the night: witchcraft among a Sengalese people. W. S. Simmons. Boston: Little, Brown & Co., 1971. 169p. (Treats Badyaranke).

Histoire religieuse du Sénégal. J. Delcourt. Dakar: Editions Clairafrique, [1976]. 126p.

'Identity conflict and ceremonial events in a Sereer community of Saalum, Senegal.' K. M. Marcoccio. Ph.D. dissertation, Brandeis University, Waltham, MA, 1987. 347p.

Islamic society and state power in Senegal: disciples and citizens in Fatick. L. A. Villalón. *African studies series*, 80. Cambridge, UK: Cambridge University Press, 1995. 357p.

La chrétienté africaine de Dakar. V. Martin. Dakar: Fraternité St-Dominique, 1964. 293p.

'La dimension thérapeutique du culte des rab: Ndop, tuuru et samp.,' A. Zempleni, *Psychopathologie Africaine*, 2, 3 (1966), 295–439.

La vie religieuse au Sénégal: instituts masculins. Dakar: Saint Paul, 1990. 67p.

'Lat–Dyor, Damel du Kayor (1842–86) et l'Islamisation des Wolofs du Sénégal,' V. Monteil, in *Islam in tropical Africa*, p.342–49. I. M. Lewis (ed). London: Oxford University Press, 1966.

'Le christianisme au Sénégal,' H. J. de Dianoux, *L'Afrique et l'Asie modernes*, no. 4 (1981), 3–22.

'Le Tidjanisme au Sénégal,' I. Marone, *Bulletin de l'IFAN*, 32(B), 1 (1970), 136–215.

Les Diola: essai d'analyse fonctionelle sur une population de Basse–Casamance. L. Thomas. *Mémoire*, 55. Dakar: IFAN, 1959. 2 vols.

L'Islam au Sénégal: demain les mollahs? La 'question' musulmane et les partis politiques au Sénégal de 1946 à nos jours. M. Magassouba. Paris: Karthala, 1985. 219p.

L'Islam en Maurtianie et en Sénégal. P. Marty. Paris: E. Leroux, 1915–16. 483p.

L'Islam et la culture dans la République du Sénégal. M. M. Ane. Dakar: Dar-Senegalia, 1973. 39p.

'L'Islam et l'histoire du Sénégal,' A. Samb, *Bulletin de l'IFAN*, 33 (B), 3 (1971), 461–507.

Muslim brotherhoods and politics in Senegal. L. C. Behrman. Cambridge, MA: Harvard University Press, 1970. 475p.

'Muslim brotherhoods and politics in Senegal in 1985,' L. E. Creevey, *Journal of modern African studies*, 23, 4 (1985), 715–21.

'Nomination, réincarnation et/ou ancêtre tutélaire? Un mode de survie: l'exemple des Sérèr Ndout (Sénégal),' M. Dupire, *L'Homme*, 22, 1 (1982), 5–31.

Notes d'instructions à une étude socio–religieuse des populations de Dakar et du Sénégal. V. Martin. Dakar: Fraternité St-Dominique, 1964. 82p.

Peace is everything: world view of Muslims in the Senegambia. D. E. Maranz. Dallas: Summer Institute of Linguistics, 1993. 316p.

'Religion traditionnelle et techniques thérapeutiques des Lëbou du Sénégal,' O. Silla, *Bulletin de l'IFAN*, 30 (B) (1968), 1566–80.

'Rites d'initiation et vie en société chez les Sérèrs du Sénégal,' H. Gravrand, *Afrique documents* (Dakar), 52 (1960), 129–44.

Senegal. R. Dilley & J. Eades. *World bibliographical series*, vol. 166. Oxford, UK: CLIO Press, 1994. 328p. (See especially 'Censuses,' p.40-1 and 'Religion,' p.167-80).

Spotlight on Senegal. B. MacIndoe. London: Worldwide Evangelization Crusade, [1964].

'The Catholic Mission and some aspects of assimilation in Senegal, 1817–1852,' D. H. Jones, *Journal of African history*, 21, 3 (1980), 323–40.

'The emergence of a Diola Christianity,' R. M. Baum, *Africa*, 60, 3 (1990), 370–98.

'The expansion of Islam among the Bambara under French rule, 1890–1940.' S. A. Harmon. Ph.D. dissertation, University of California, Los Angeles, 1988. 562p.

The heritage of Islam: women, religion, and politics in West Africa. B. Callaway & L. E. Creevey. Boulder, CO: Lynne Rienner, 1994. 231p.

'The impact of Islam on women in Senegal,' L. E. Creevey, *Journal of developing areas*, 25, 3 (1991), 347–68.

The Mourides of Senegal: the political and economic organization of an Islamic brotherhood. D. B. C. O'Brien. Oxford, UK: Clarendon Press, 1971. 321p.

'The supernatural world of the Badyaranké of Tonghia (Senegal),' W. Simmons, *Journal des africanistes*, 37, 1 (1967), 41–72.

'Un système philosophique sénégalais: la cosmologie des Diola,' L. V. Thomas, *Présence africaine*, 32/33 (1960), 64–76.

Country Table 2. **Organized churches and denominations in Senegal.**

Official name (bold type = church with over 10% of all affiliated) 1	*Begun* 2	*Type* 3	*Counc* 4	*Congs* 5	*Adults* 6	*Affiliated 1970* 7	*Affiliated 1995* 8	*G%* 9	*Names, notes, and other statistics* (see Codebook, Part 3) 10
Assemblées de Dieu	1956	P-Pe2	ZFG.R	55	1,213	1,500	2,910	2.69	*Assemblies of God.* M=AoG(USA). Polygamists baptized. 17n,15g,1h,1r,1s(14),40Y.
Association Baptiste	1969	P-Bap	T....	3	101	30	168	7.13	*Baptist Association.* M=SBC.
Eglise Adventiste du Septième Jour	1952	P-Adv	x....	3	138	200	345	2.20	*SDA, Seventh-day Adventists, Senegal Mission.* HQ Dakar. 1nx,20mw,1h,1r,3t(158),23Y.
Egl Anglicane (D Gambia & Rio Pongas)		A-ACa	awaV.	1	90	100	150	0.05	In CPWA. St Peter's Anglican congregation, Dakar. All expatriates.
Eglise Baptiste du Sénégal	1961	I-Bap	xFG.E	9	94	100	235	3.48	M=CBInternational (USA). Work among Wolof. 1 school. 14f.
Eglise Catholique au Sénégal:	1445	R-Lat	P.SFP	101	222,800	183,021	380,432	2.97	45% Serer. C=10+4+29. (1970) 43n,7654Yy. (1990) 154n 136x 312m 593w 15868Yy
M Dakar	1863	R-Lat	Ps	32	126,000	101,450	220,000	3.14	65% Serer,20% White,10% Cape Verdean,5% Wolof. 37n 67x 158m 314w 2700Yy
D Kaolack	1957	R-Lat	Ps	15	5,400	8,236	10,146	0.84	90% Serer,4% Diola,3% Wolof,1% Bassari. M=MSC. 9n 11x 25m 52w 427Yy
D Saint-Louis du Sénégal	1763	R-Lat	Pcssp	6	2,200	1,726	3,297	2.62	99% Muslim, Serer, Manjak, Diola, Europeans. 3n 12x 21m 22w 59Yy
D Tambacounda	1970	R-Lat	Ps	8	3,000	530	5,700	9.97	Bassari. Many Guinea (Conakry) refugees. M=CSSp. 8n 13x 23m 22w 237Yy
D Thiès	1969	R-Lat	Ps	18	25,400	21,171	33,289	1.83	Regions of Thies and Diourbel. 34n 24x 62m 60w 1002Yy
D Ziguinchor	1939	R-Lat	Ps	22	60,800	49,908	108,000	3.14	1970, Niaguis-Boffa mission: Guinea-B refugees. 63n 9x 23m 123w 11443Yy
Eglise du Nazarene	1987	P-Hol	.....	1	24	–	48	12.50	*Church of the Nazarene.* M=CoN.
Egl Ev Chrétienne de l'Ouest-Africain	1988	P-Eva	.....	1	20	–	40	14.29	*EECOA/ECWA. Evangelical Churches of West Africa.* M=SIM.
Eglise Luthérienne	1974	P-Lut	.....	37	1,800	–	3,000	4.76	*Lutheran Church.* M=Finnish Lutheran Mission.
Eglise Neo-Apostolique	c1980	I-3aX	x....	120	7,000	–	10,596	6.67	*NAC/NAK.* M=Neuapostolische Kirche. HQ Zurich (Switzerland).
Eglise Protestante du Sénégal	1863	P-Ref	R.A..	2	270	1,500	500	-4.30	*Protestant Church of Dakar.* 1863, M=PEMS(France). 60% White,40% Black. 1x,30Yy.
Eglises Baptistes Internationales	1975	I-Bap	.....	2	75	–	100	5.00	*Baptist International Mission.* M=BIM(USA).
Eglises Nouveaux Tribus	c1985	P-Fun	x....	3	18	–	60	10.00	*New Tribes Mission.* M=NTM.
Mission Ev de l'Afrique Occidentale	1935	P-Eva	.FG.E	7	70	200	230	0.56	M=Worldwide Evangelization Crusade (UK, USA). HQ Ziguinchor & Saint-Louis. 17f,1p.
Mission Mondiale Unie	1955	P-Non	.FG.E	2	140	250	175	-1.42	M=United World Mission (USA). Centre Evangelique, Dakar. Orphanage, radio. 18f.

Continued overleaf

Country Table 2–concluded

Official name (bold type = church with over 10% of affiliated) 1	*Begun* 2	*Type* 3	*Counc* 4	*Congs* 5	*Adults* 6	*Affiliated 1970* 7	*Affiliated 1995* 8	*G%* 9	*Names, notes, and other statistics* (see Codebook, Part 3) 10
Témoins de Jéhovah	c1930	m-Jeh	x....	14	585	400	1,950	6.54	*Jehovah's Witnesses.* HQ Dakar. Active witnessing by 1932. (1975) 41Y. (1995) 56Y.
Other Protestant denominations		P-	..C.E	40	400	400	800	0.05	Total about 8 (see list below).
Other African indigenous chs	c1970	I-3pA	.....	11	200	–	400	27.08	In about 10 pentecostal denominations from Nigeria, Ghana, Liberia.
Totals				**412**	**235,038**	**187,701**	**402,139**		

Churches, members, growth, 1900-2025	*Congs*	*Adults*	*Affiliated*	*G%*	*Total denominations*	*6 Megablocs:* O	*R*	*A*	*P*	*I*	*m*
Total churches, members, and denominations (mid-1900)	20	8,900	15,300	3.65	2	0	1	0	1	0	0
Total churches, members, and denominations (mid-1970)	124	108,639	187,701	3.65	14	0	1	1	10	1	1
Total churches, members, and denominations (mid-1990)	400	206,000	351,950	3.19	34	0	1	1	18	13	1
Total churches, members, and denominations (mid-1995)	412	235,038	402,139	2.70	34	0	1	1	18	13	1
Total churches, members, and denominations (mid-2000)	450	273,000	467,291	3.05	37	0	1	1	19	13	3
Total churches, members, and denominations (mid-2025)	900	570,000	975,320	2.99	76	1	1	1	30	40	3

NOTES ON TABLE ABOVE
NATIONAL COUNCILS (Column 4, 5th letter).
E = Fraternité Evangélique du Sénégal (FES).
P = Conférence Episcopale de Sénégal-Mauritanie (CESM) (Episcopal Conference of Senegal & Mauritania).
OTHER PROTESTANT DENOMINATIONS. These, most of which are members of FES, include: Action Biblique, Christian Brethren (UK), Mission Evangélique Indépendante, Mission Luthérienne Finlandaise, New Tribes Mission (1955; 10 missionaries), Southern Baptist Convention (1969), World-Wide Missions (1965).

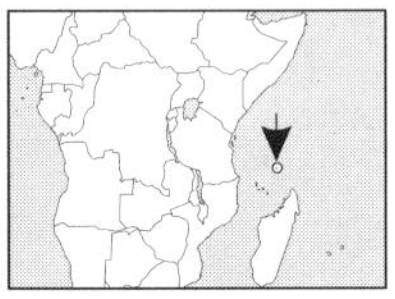

SEYCHELLES

SECULAR DATA, AD 2000

STATE
Official name: Repiblik Sesel/The Republic of Seychelles (The Republic of Seychelles).
Short name: Seychelles. **Adjective of nationality:** of Seychelles, a Seychellois.
Flag: White St Andrew's cross; blue triangles at top and bottom; red triangle at hoist and fly.
Area: 455 sq. km. (176 sq. mi.).
Government: Parliamentary republic, since 1976 (1768 French colony, 1794 British possession, 1903 British crown colony, 1970 self-government, 1976 Independence).
Legislature: National Assembly, 33 members.
Official language: English and French (Françias).
Monetary unit: 1 Seychelles rupee (SR) = 100 cents. **US$1=** SR 5.27.
Chief cities: PORT VICTORIA 27,470.
Political divisions: 5 provinces.
Armed forces: 200.

DEMOGRAPHY
Population: 77,400.
Population density: 170.1/sq. km. (439.9/sq. mi.).
Under 15 years: 20,000.
Growth rate p.a.: 0.83% (births 15.78, deaths 6.55).
Mortality: Infant, per 1,000: 13.9; **Maternal per 100,000:** 200.0.
Life expectancy: 73 (male 69, female 76).
Household size: 4.8. **Floor area per person, sq.m:** 10.0.
Major languages: English, French, French Creole, Gujarati, Tamil, Chinese.
Urban dwellers: 58.49%. **Urban growth rate p.a.:** 2.1%.
Labor force: 39%.

ETHNOLINGUISTIC PEOPLES
93.2% Seychellese Creole; 3.0% British; 1.8% French; 0.5% Han Chinese; 0.3% Hindi.

ECONOMY
National income p.a. per person: US$6,624; **per family:** US$31,799.

EDUCATION
Adult literacy: 84% (male 82%, female 85%). **Schools:** 45.
Universities: 1. **School enrolment:** female/male: 90%/90%.

HEALTH
Access to health services: 70%. **Access to safe water:** 97%.
Hospitals: 7 (56 beds per 10,000). **Doctors:** 72.
Blind: 150. **Deaf:** 4,600. **Murder rate:** 2. **Lepers:** 100.

LITERATURE
New book titles p.a.: 11 (140 p.a. per million). **Periodicals:** 3.
Newspapers: 1 daily.

COMMUNICATION (per 1,000 people)
Phones: 187 (25% mobile). **Radios:** 667. **TV sets:** 184.
Daily newspaper circulation: 40. **Computers:** 20.

Country Table 1. **Religious adherents in Seychelles, AD 1900-2025.**

Year / *Name*	*1900* Adherents	%	*1970* Adherents	%	*mid-1990* Adherents	%	*Annual change, 1990-2000* Natural	Conversion	Total	Rate	*mid-1995* Adherents	%	*mid-2000* Adherents	%	*mid-2025* Adherents	%
Christians	**18,740**	**97.3**	**52,400**	**98.3**	**67,635**	**97.3**	**775**	**-39**	**736**	**1.04**	**71,180**	**96.9**	**74,996**	**96.9**	**93,950**	**95.9**
PROFESSION																
professing Christians	**18,740**	**97.3**	**52,400**	**98.3**	**67,635**	**97.3**	**775**	**-39**	**736**	**1.04**	**71,180**	**96.9**	**74,996**	**96.9**	**93,950**	**95.9**
AFFILIATION																
unaffiliated Christians	240	1.3	2,150	4.0	2,735	3.9	27	20	47	1.59	2,830	3.9	3,201	4.1	4,100	4.2
affiliated Christians	**18,500**	**96.1**	**50,250**	**94.3**	**64,900**	**93.4**	**748**	**-58**	**690**	**1.01**	**68,350**	**93.1**	**71,795**	**92.8**	**89,850**	**91.7**
Roman Catholics	17,000	88.3	46,000	86.3	63,450	91.3	734	-79	655	0.99	66,650	90.8	70,000	90.4	84,000	85.7
Anglicans	1,500	7.8	3,900	7.3	4,800	7.0	48	-8	40	0.80	5,030	6.9	5,200	6.7	6,000	6.1
Protestants	0	0.0	250	0.5	1,550	2.2	16	24	40	2.32	1,739	2.4	1,950	2.5	3,000	3.1
Marginal Christians	0	0.0	100	0.2	220	0.3	2	3	5	2.07	240	0.3	270	0.4	500	0.5
Independents	0	0.0	0	0.0	30	0.0	0	2	2	5.24	40	0.1	50	0.1	120	0.1
doubly-affiliated	0	0.0	0	0.0	-5,150	-7.5	-52	-1	-53	0.98	-5,349	-7.3	-5,675	-7.3	-3,770	-3.9
Trans-megabloc groupings																
Evangelicals	0	0.0	800	1.5	2,200	3.1	22	13	35	1.49	2,370	3.2	2,550	3.3	4,000	4.1
Pentecostals/Charismatics	0	0.0	50	0.1	3,400	4.9	34	31	65	1.76	3,687	5.0	4,050	5.3	7,000	7.1
Great Commission Christians	**600**	**3.1**	**3,700**	**6.9**	**7,700**	**11.1**	**77**	**77**	**154**	**1.84**	**8,440**	**11.5**	**9,236**	**11.9**	**13,720**	**14.0**
Nonreligious	30	0.2	230	0.4	1,000	1.4	10	35	45	3.79	1,300	1.8	1,450	1.9	2,500	2.6
Hindus	390	2.0	310	0.6	380	0.5	4	-1	3	0.86	390	0.5	414	0.5	500	0.5
Baha'is	0	0.0	150	0.3	240	0.3	2	5	7	2.66	280	0.4	312	0.4	700	0.7
Muslims	60	0.3	170	0.3	160	0.2	2	-1	1	0.37	160	0.2	166	0.2	150	0.2
Chinese folk-religionists	0	0.0	20	0.0	35	0.1	0	1	1	1.59	40	0.1	41	0.1	90	0.1
Jains	80	0.4	10	0.0	30	0.0	0	0	0	0.65	30	0.0	32	0.0	50	0.1
Zoroastrians	0	0.0	10	0.0	20	0.0	0	0	0	1.41	20	0.0	23	0.0	60	0.1
World A (unevangelized persons)	19	0.1	53	0.1	280	0.4	3	4	7	2.20	293	0.4	385	0.5	490	0.5
World B (evangelized non-Christians)	500	2.8	837	1.6	1,585	2.3	15	35	50	2.45	1,963	2.7	2,019	2.6	3,560	3.6
World C (Christians)	18,740	97.1	52,400	98.3	67,635	97.3	775	-39	736	1.04	71,180	96.9	74,996	96.9	93,950	95.9
Country's population	**19,260**	**100.0**	**53,291**	**100.0**	**69,500**	**100.0**	**793**	**0**	**793**	**0.96**	**73,437**	**100.0**	**77,400**	**100.0**	**98,000**	**100.0**

COLUMNS, ROWS.
For meanings and definitions, see Codebook (Part 3). Note that, by definition, total 'Christians' = professing + crypto-Christians, which also = affiliated + unaffiliated Christians, and also = Great Commission Christians + latent Christians. Percentages may not always total exactly, due to rounding.

CENSUSES.
1901 Census of the British Empire: 83.4% Roman Catholics, 13.7% Anglicans and Protestants, 2.0% Hindus, 0.3% Muslims, 0.3% Chinese folk-religionists, 0.2% nonreligious. **4.V.1960:** 90.7% Roman Catholics, 7.8% Anglicans, 0.4% Hindus, 0.3% Protestants (0.3% SDAs), 0.3% Muslims, 0.1% Chinese folk-religionists, 0.1% Parsis, 0.1% Jains. **5.V.1971:** 90.0% Roman Catholics, 7.6% Anglicans, 0.6% Hindus, 0.4% marginal Protestants (Jehovah's Witnesses), 0.4% nonreligious, 0.3% Muslims, 0.3% Baha'is, 0.3% Protestants, 0.1% other religionists (Parsis, Jains, Chinese folk-religionists). **1997:** 90.0% Roman Catholics, 7.4% other Christians, 0.7% Hindus, 0.4% nonreligious, 0.3% Muslims, 0.3% other religionists.

NOTES ON RELIGIONS
BAHA'IS. Growth from 1 local spiritual assembly (1964) to 8 (1973), and from 15 adherents in 1960 census to 156 in 1971 census. (1996) 13 LSAs after reorganization. Since 1969, Baha'i teaching and singing over government radio has been permitted.

Country status. Seychelles, a member of the Commonwealth, consists of about 115 islands in the Indian Ocean northeast of Madagascar. Tourism is the major economic activity. Fish, copra, and cinnamon are exported.

HUMAN LIFE AND LIBERTY

Human rights and freedoms. Seychelles, as a member of the Commonwealth, has several inherent advantages. A new Constitution approved by the voters in 1993 provides for a multiparty government and free elections. It also reforms governmental institutions to accord with international standards of human rights practice. However, some traces of authoritarianism remain. The Constitutional Appointments Authority allows the ruling party to control appointments. The president sometimes intervenes directly with administrative officials to secure special favors for his friends. The government has a dominant position in the media, controlling the only local daily newspaper, The Nation, as well as the state-controlled radio and television. The economic and political system is dominated by Whites and Asians although Creoles of African origin constitute the majority.

NON-CHRISTIAN RELIGIONS

Hinduism is practiced by Indian traders and other settlers, and ***Islam*** by Muslims of Asian extraction.

Baha'i has a small community, and there are also a few Zoroastrians, Jains, and Chinese folk-religionists.

Great Commission Instrument Panel: status of Seychelles (for explanation see start of Part 4)

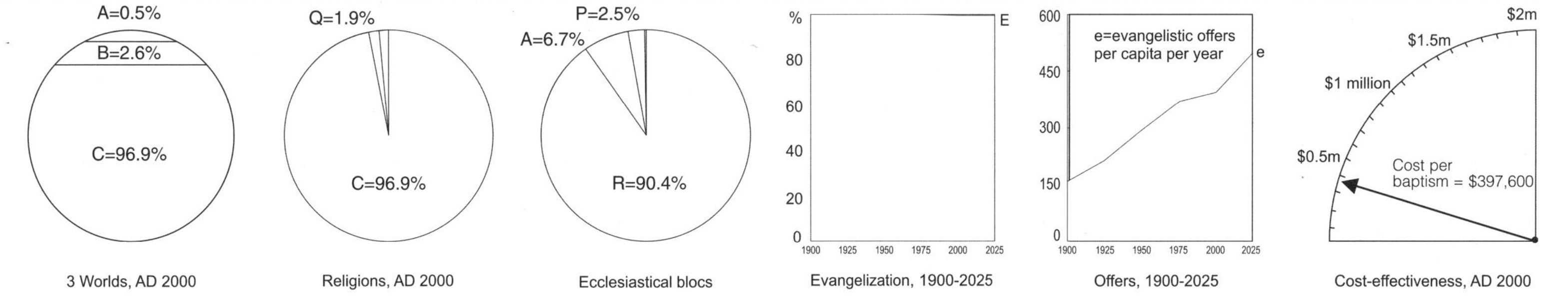

Country summary. **Worlds A, B, C by ethnolinguistic peoples, cities, and major civil divisions in Seychelles.**

	PEOPLES							CITIES							CIVIL DIVISIONS						
World	*Num*	*Pop 2000*	*C%*	*Christians*	*E%*	*U%*	*Unevangelized*	*Num*	*Pop 2000*	*C%*	*Christians*	*E%*	*U%*	*Unevangelized*	*Num*	*Pop 2000*	*C%*	*Christians*	*E%*	*U%*	*Unevangelized*
A	1	77	0.00	0	42	58	45	0	0	0.00	0	0	0	0	0	0	0.00	0	0	0	0
B	3	618	12.30	76	59	41	251	0	0	0.00	0	0	0	0	0	0	0.00	0	0	0	0
C	6	76,739	93.46	71,719	100	0	52	1	27,470	91.00	24,998	99	1	157	5	77,435	92.72	71,795	100	0	348
Total	**10**	**77,434**	**92.72**	**71,795**	**100**	**0**	**348**	**1**	**27,470**	**91.00**	**24,998**	**99**	**1**	**157**	**5**	**77,435**	**92.72**	**71,795**	**100**	**0**	**348**

CHRISTIANITY

CATHOLIC CHURCH. Catholics, whose origins date from 1770, make up 90% of the population of the Seychelles, and include Creoles, Europeans, Blacks (Bantu), and 3500 Chinese. There are parishes with resident priests at Mahé, Praslin, and La Digue; while other islands receive one or 2 pastoral visits each year, including the islands of the British Indian Ocean Territory. The diocese of Port Victoria is served by 7 national priests and 22 expatriates; and the first national bishop was consecrated in 1975. There is one indigenous congregation of nuns, the Sisters of St Elizabeth, which was formed in 1940.

The Holy See has diplomatic relations with Seychelles and in AD 2000 is represented to government and the Catholic hierarchy by a nuncio residing in Tananarive, Madagascar.

ANGLICAN CHURCH. Anglican work began in 1843 and now exists on both Mahé and Praslin Islands, the population of the latter being one-third Anglican. The Anglican diocese of the Seychelles has been since 1975 part of the Church of the Province of the Indian Ocean. The church has established 9 schools.

OTHER CHURCHES. There are 4 Seventh-day Adventist congregations, one at Mahé, one at Praslin and 2 others. Adventists have been in the Seychelles since 1929.

Indigenous missions. Very few missionaries are sent out from Seychelles but major missionary radio broadcasting is beamed from the islands.

CHURCH AND STATE

Relations are generally good in spite of continuing friction over the use of French by the Catholic Church. Since 1945 Catholic school personnel have been appointed and paid by government, with the church retaining control over appointments.

BROADCASTING AND MEDIA

FEBA maintains a strategic transmitter in Seychelles which reaches several east African, Middle East, and Asian nations. Some of its programs are produced by Back to the Bible and IBRA, and languages covered include Amharic, Portuguese, Swahili, Yao, Mekonde, Bhojpuri, Bengali, Dari, Hindi, Kannada, Nepali, Pushto, Punjabi, Telugu, Urdu, Azerbaijani, Baluch, Farsi, and Hazaragi. Shortwave radio programs from KNLS have seen some response. Seychelles is a member of UNDA. A 15 minute radio program featuring a family emphasis is aired.

INTERDENOMINATIONAL ORGANIZATIONS

An Ecumenical Committee, composed of 3 Catholic and 2 Anglican members, was formed in April 1970.

FUTURE TRENDS AND PROSPECTS

In light of the expected growth of the nonreligious, 0.4% of the population in 1970 to 2.6% by 2025, Christianity is expected to decline slightly to less than 96% in the same period.

Christianity will likely remain near 95% until AD 2050 when the nonreligious could grow beyond 4%. In the 21st century Christians could however decline to less than 90% if the secularization trend continues.

BIBLIOGRAPHY

2000 titres: littératures de l'océan indien: Comores, Madagascar, Maurice, Réunion, Seychelles. Notre Librairie, no. 116. [Paris: CLEF, 1994]. 174p.

Education in Seychelles: the government and the missions 1839–1944. I. R. Stone. Milton Keynes, UK: Open University, 1977.

L'Echo des îles. F. P. Giulio (ed). Victoria, Seychelles: Roman Catholic Mission, 1960—. (Monthly).

Les îles de l'Océan indien: Comores, Madagascar, Maurice, Réunion, Seychelles: bibliographie réalisée à partir de la Banque de données IBISCUS, triée par grands domaines. P. Hue. *Collection Réseaux documentaires sur le développement, Série Références bibliographiques.* Paris: Ministère de la coopération et du développement, [1991]. 285p.

Men, women, and money in Seychelles. M. Benedict & B. Benedict. Berkeley and Los Angeles: University of California Press, 1982. 300p.

Seychelles. G. Bennett with P. R. Bennett. *World bibliographical series*, vol. 153. Oxford, UK: CLIO Press, 1993. 148p. (Contains only a short section on religion).

Seychelles calling. D. Winter. Woking, UK: FEBA, 1971. 35p. (Describes founding of FEBA).

The history of the Catholic church in Seychelles. J. T. Bradley. Victoria, Seychelles: Clarion Press, 1940.

The Seventh–day Adventist Mission in Seychelles: a review of events from years 1930–1980. Victoria, Seychelles: The Mission, [1981].

Postage stamps showing Anglican and Roman Catholic cathedrals and churches in Victoria, Bel Ombre and Praslin.

Country Table 2. **Organized churches and denominations in Seychelles.**

Official name (bold type = church with over 10% of all affiliated) 1	*Begun* 2	*Type* 3	*Counc* 4	*Congs* 5	*Adults* 6	*Affiliated 1970* 7	*Affiliated 1995* 8	*G%* 9	*Names, notes, and other statistics* (see Codebook, Part 3) 10
Anglican Church: D Seychelles	1843	A-Hig	Aw.V.	11	1,910	3,900	5,030	1.02	In Ch of the Province of the Indian Ocean. Until 1973 in D Mauritius. M=USPG. 4n,3x.
Catholic Church: D Port Victoria	1770	R-Lat	pzSEr	22	38,000	46,000	66,650	1.49	*Eglise Catholique.* Mostly French-speaking. C=1+1+2. (1970) 7n,22x,1684Yy. (1990)
Evangelical Church	1980	P-Eva	.....	2	423	–	650	6.67	M=AIM.
Jehovah's Witnesses	c1960	m-Jeh	x....	2	81	100	240	3.56	Congregation in Victoria, Mahé. Active witnessing under way by 1964. (1975) 2Y. (1995) 23Y.
New Apostolic Church	1995	I-3aX	x....	1	20	–	40	31.95	*NAC/NAK.* M=Neuapostolische Kirche. HQ Zurich (Switzerland).
Pentecostal Church	c1980	P-Pe2	.....	1	325	–	650	6.67	M=PAoC(Canada).
Seventh-day Adventist Church	1929	P-Adv	x....	4	143	150	239	1.88	*SDA, Seycheles Field*, East African Union. Mahe; recently Praslin. 2x,2t(83),9Y.
Other Protestant denominations		P-	.....	4	100	100	200	0.05	Including: International Christian Fellowship (UK).
Doubly-affiliated		2-aff			-3,000	0	-5,349		Anglicans and Pentecostals who are also baptized Catholics.
Totals				**47**	**38,002**	**50,250**	**68,350**		

Churches, members, growth, 1900-2025	*Congs*	*Adults*	*Affiliated*	*G%*	*Total denominations*	*6 Megablocs:* O	R	A	P	I	m
Total churches, members, and denominations (mid-1900)	20	10,500	18,500	1.44	2	0	1	1	0	0	0
Total churches, members, and denominations (mid-1970)	33	28,656	50,250	1.44	6	0	1	1	3	0	1
Total churches, members, and denominations (mid-1990)	40	36,100	64,900	1.29	11	0	1	1	8	0	1
Total churches, members, and denominations (mid-1995)	47	38,002	68,350	1.04	12	0	1	1	8	1	1
Total churches, members, and denominations (mid-2000)	50	39,900	71,795	0.99	12	0	1	1	8	1	1
Total churches, members, and denominations (mid-2025)	80	50,000	89,850	0.90	39	0	1	1	20	15	2

NOTES ON TABLE ABOVE

NATIONAL COUNCILS (Column 4, 5th letter).

r = member, Kenya Episcopal Conference (KEC).

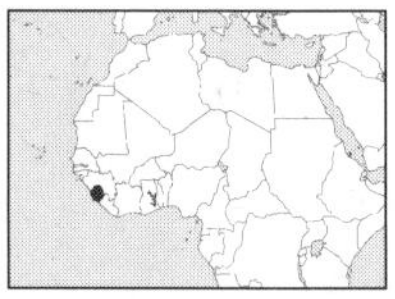

SIERRA LEONE

SECULAR DATA, AD 2000

STATE
Official name: The Republic of Sierra Leone.
Short name: Sierra Leone. **Adjective of nationality:** Sierra Leonean.
Flag: Stripes of green (top), white and blue.
Area: 71,740 sq. km. (27,699 sq. mi.).
Government: Military regime, since 1997 (1808 British colony and (1896) protectorate, 1961 Independence, 1967 military junta, 1971 one-party republic, 1991, multiparty republic).
Legislature: Military regime.
Official language: English.
Monetary unit: 1 leone (Le) = 100 cents. **US$1=** Le 1,550.
Chief cities: FREETOWN 743,063; Koindu (Koidu) 116,730; Bo 84,593; Kenema 74,268; Makeni 69,406.
Political divisions: 4 provinces.
Armed forces: 20,000.

DEMOGRAPHY
Population: 4,854,000.
Population density: 67.6/sq. km. (175.2/sq. mi.).
Under 15 years: 2,138,000.
Growth rate p.a.: 2.17% (births 43.93, deaths 22.27).
Mortality: Infant, per 1,000: 145.7; **Maternal per 100,000:** 1,800.0.
Life expectancy: 41 (male 39, female 42).
Household size: 4.7. **Floor area per person, sq.m:** 6.0.
Major languages: English, Krio (Pidgin English), Mende, Temne, Mandingo, Koranko, Susu, Limba, Kono, Fulani, Loko, Kissi, and about 10 other languages.
Urban dwellers: 36.64%. **Urban growth rate p.a.:** 4.0%.
Labor force: 36%.

ETHNOLINGUISTIC PEOPLES
26.0% Mende (Boumpe, Kossa); 24.6% Temne (Timne, Timmanee); 11.0% Krio (Creole); 7.0% West Central Limba; 5.5% Kuranko (Koranko).

ECONOMY
National income p.a. per person: US$180; **per family:** US$846.

EDUCATION
Adult literacy: 31% (male 45%, female 18%). **Schools:** 2,039.
Universities: 2. **School enrolment:** female/male: 29%/43%.

HEALTH
Access to health services: 38%. **Access to safe water:** 34%.
Hospitals: 219 (10 beds per 10,000). **Doctors:** 404.
Blind: 28,000. **Deaf:** 291,900. **Murder rate:** 12.
Lepers: 150,000. **Underweight prevalence under 5:** 29%.

LITERATURE
New book titles p.a.: 49 (10 p.a. per million). **Periodicals:** 21.
Newspapers: 1 daily.

COMMUNICATION (per 1,000 people)
Phones: 3 (3% mobile). **Radios:** 221. **TV sets:** 16.
Daily newspaper circulation: 2. **Computers:** 4.

REFUGEES
Citizen refugees in other countries: 363,000.
Alien refugees from other countries: 15,000.
Internal displacement: 1,000,000.

HUMAN LIFE AND LIBERTY (optimum condition=100.0%)
HDI: 17.6. **HSI:** 16.0. **HFI:** 35.0. **EFL:** 25.0.

Country Table 1. **Religious adherents in Sierra Leone, AD 1900-2025.**

Year	1900		1970		mid-1990		Annual change, 1990-2000				mid-1995		mid-2000		mid-2025	
Name	Adherents	%	Adherents	%	Adherents	%	Natural	Conversion	Total	Rate	Adherents	%	Adherents	%	Adherents	%
Muslims	102,600	10.0	1,011,000	38.1	1,831,460	45.9	39,474	357	39,831	1.99	1,922,030	45.9	2,229,768	45.9	3,754,600	46.4
Ethnoreligionists	876,600	85.4	1,425,950	53.7	1,652,000	41.4	35,571	-4,910	30,661	1.72	1,706,000	40.7	1,958,614	40.4	2,979,500	36.9
Christians	**46,800**	**4.6**	**216,800**	**8.2**	**427,500**	**10.7**	**9,205**	**3,612**	**12,817**	**2.66**	**467,190**	**11.2**	**555,673**	**11.5**	**1,070,000**	**13.2**
PROFESSION																
professing Christians	**46,800**	**4.6**	**216,800**	**8.2**	**427,500**	**10.7**	**9,205**	**3,612**	**12,817**	**2.66**	**467,190**	**11.2**	**555,673**	**11.5**	**1,070,000**	**13.2**
AFFILIATION																
unaffiliated Christians	4,520	0.4	26,096	1.0	38,000	1.0	818	-100	718	1.75	39,040	0.9	45,179	0.9	50,000	0.6
affiliated Christians	**42,280**	**4.1**	**190,704**	**7.2**	**389,500**	**9.8**	**8,387**	**3,712**	**12,099**	**2.74**	**428,150**	**10.2**	**510,494**	**10.5**	**1,020,000**	**12.6**
Protestants	19,000	1.9	97,787	3.7	142,000	3.6	3,058	-158	2,900	1.88	148,260	3.5	171,000	3.5	270,000	3.3
Roman Catholics	2,980	0.3	47,467	1.8	116,000	2.9	2,498	2,816	5,314	3.84	134,958	3.2	169,140	3.5	410,000	5.1
Independents	300	0.0	17,950	0.7	128,000	3.2	2,756	944	3,700	2.57	138,453	3.3	165,000	3.4	350,000	4.3
Anglicans	20,000	2.0	25,000	0.9	25,100	0.6	540	-550	-10	-0.04	25,040	0.6	25,000	0.5	25,000	0.3
Marginal Christians	0	0.0	2,000	0.1	2,450	0.1	53	-28	25	0.98	2,510	0.1	2,700	0.1	4,000	0.1
Orthodox	0	0.0	500	0.0	600	0.0	13	-12	1	0.17	600	0.0	610	0.0	800	0.0
doubly-affiliated	0	0.0	0	0.0	-24,650	-0.6	-531	700	169	-0.71	-21,671	-0.5	-22,956	-0.5	-39,800	-0.5
Trans-megabloc groupings																
Evangelicals	26,000	2.5	32,000	1.2	66,000	1.7	1,421	579	2,000	2.68	71,849	1.7	86,000	1.8	197,000	2.4
Pentecostals/Charismatics	0	0.0	13,000	0.5	155,000	3.9	3,338	1,162	4,500	2.58	167,175	4.0	200,000	4.1	492,000	6.1
Great Commission Christians	**41,000**	**4.0**	**159,000**	**6.0**	**311,000**	**7.8**	**6,697**	**1,113**	**7,810**	**2.27**	**330,000**	**7.9**	**389,099**	**8.0**	**815,000**	**10.1**
Nonreligious	0	0.0	0	0.0	72,300	1.8	1,557	739	2,296	2.80	80,000	1.9	95,261	2.0	250,000	3.1
Baha'is	0	0.0	750	0.0	8,000	0.2	172	167	339	3.59	9,600	0.2	11,385	0.2	25,000	0.3
Hindus	0	0.0	1,400	0.1	2,050	0.1	44	0	44	1.96	2,150	0.1	2,490	0.1	4,000	0.1
Atheists	0	0.0	0	0.0	90	0.0	2	1	3	3.26	100	0.0	124	0.0	300	0.0
Other religionists	0	0.0	100	0.0	600	0.0	13	34	47	5.94	930	0.0	1,068	0.0	1,600	0.0
World A (unevangelized persons)	845,424	82.4	1,327,778	50.0	1,801,294	45.1	38,796	-20,622	18,174	0.97	1,826,005	43.6	1,980,432	40.8	2,999,535	37.1
World B (evangelized non-Christians)	133,776	13.0	1,110,978	41.8	1,765,206	44.2	38,037	17,010	55,047	2.76	1,894,891	45.2	2,317,895	47.7	4,015,465	49.7
World C (Christians)	46,800	4.6	216,800	8.2	427,500	10.7	9,205	3,612	12,817	2.66	467,190	11.2	555,673	11.5	1,070,000	13.2
Country's population	**1,026,000**	**100.0**	**2,655,556**	**100.0**	**3,994,000**	**100.0**	**86,038**	**0**	**86,038**	**1.97**	**4,188,087**	**100.0**	**4,854,000**	**100.0**	**8,085,000**	**100.0**

COLUMNS, ROWS.
For meanings and definitions, see Codebook (Part 3). Note that, by definition, total 'Christians' = professing + crypto-Christians, which also = affiliated + unaffiliated Christians, and also = Great Commission Christians + latent Christians. Percentages may not always total exactly, due to rounding.

CENSUSES.
1891 (Colony only): 34.8% ethnoreligionists, 27.5% Anglicans, 27.1% Protestants, 9.9% Muslims, 0.8% Roman Catholics. **1901** (Colony): 31.4% ethnoreligionists, 29.2% Anglicans, 26.0% Protestants, 12.4% Muslims, 1.0% Roman Catholics, 0.4% African indigenous. **1911** (Colony): 32.5% ethnoreligionists, 25.0% Anglicans, 24.7% Protestants, 15.2% Muslims, 1.9% Roman Catholics, 0.6% African indigenous. **1921** (Colony): 32.7% ethnoreligionists, 23.7% Anglicans, 21.2% Protestants, 19.5% Muslims, 2.3% Roman Catholics, 0.6% African indigenous. **1931** (Colony): 28.8% ethnoreligionists, 26.3% Muslims, 21.4% Anglicans, 19.7% Protestants, 3.4% Roman Catholics, 0.4% African indigenous. **1931** (Protectorate): 86.5% ethnoreligionists, 11.6% Muslims, 1.9% Christians. **1931** (Colony and Protectorate): 83.4% ethnoreligionists, 12.4% Muslims, 4.2% Christians. Subsequently the religion question was not asked.

NOTES ON RELIGIONS
BAHA'IS. In 5 local spiritual assemblies (1973). Enormous growth then ensued, reaching 53 LSAs by 1996.
ETHNORELIGIONISTS. Animists, mainly among peoples in the east. Tribes with over 60% traditionalists in 1995: Kono (78% animist), Kissi (60%), Koranko (68%). Of the largest tribes, the Mende are 43% animist and the Temne 35%.
HINDUS. Indian traders.
INDEPENDENTS. In 17 denominations in 1995 (see Table 2).
MUSLIMS. Almost all Sunnis (of the Malikite rite). Islamized peoples: Bullom (80%), Fulbe, Koranko (30% Muslim), Krim (40%), Limba (35%), Loko (39%), Malinke, Mende (40%), Sherbro (40%), Susu (95%), Temne (30% in 1956, 60% by 1972), Vai (100%), Yalunka (60% Muslim). There is an Ahmadiya Mission (enumerated here as Muslims, though declared non-Muslim by Pakistan) in Bo and Freetown. Ahmadis: begun 1957; Qadianis from Pakistan, with missions in Freetown and Bo; 10% of adherents are in Temne country, 90% in Mende. An attempt to plant the mission in the diamond-mining Kono district had collapsed by 1959. The number of branches elsewhere grew from 25 in 1963 to 40 in 1970. There were also 17 primary schools in 1963, and a printing press and bookstore. The Muslim Brotherhood (Ikhwan al-Muslimin) is active in Freetown. *Hajj pilgrims to Mecca.* (1970) 353; (1971) 504; (1975) 377; (1976) 319.
OTHER RELIGIONISTS. Including Rosicrucians (1 AMORC center).
PENTECOSTALS/CHARISMATICS. By 1975, the Catholic charismatic renewal was under way, with its center in Port Loko. Steady growth followed thereafter.
ROMAN CATHOLICS. In 1900 there were 2,400 indigenous baptized Catholics and 575 catechumens.

Great Commission Instrument Panel: status of Sierra Leone (for explanation see start of Part 4)

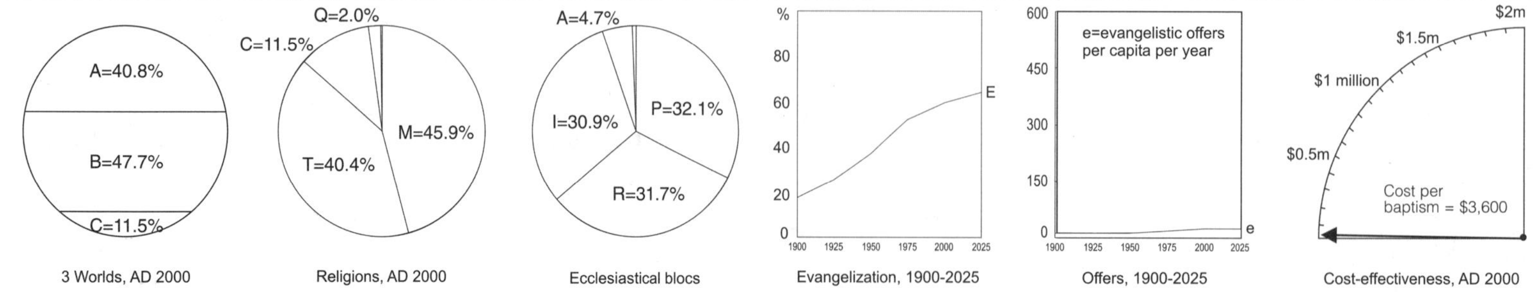

Country status. Sierra Leone is a small country on the coast of West Africa bounded by Guinea and Liberia. Though much of the population is engaged in subsistence farming, most of the revenue comes from exporting iron ore, bauxite, and diamonds.

HUMAN LIFE AND LIBERTY

Human need and development. The majority of the rural Sierra Leonians depend on subsistence agriculture for their living and struggle with the vagaries of nature to stave off famine. Both men and women share the backbreaking chores all year round. The monotony of the work and the exiguous income drive many of them to the cities in search of work that very often does not exist. Rural as well as urban areas suffer from a shortage of housing. In the towns, many

Country summary. **Worlds A, B, C by ethnolinguistic peoples, cities, and major civil divisions in Sierra Leone.**

	PEOPLES							*CITIES*							*CIVIL DIVISIONS*						
World	*Num*	*Pop 2000*	*C%*	*Christians*	*E%*	*U%*	*Unevangelized*	*Num*	*Pop 2000*	*C%*	*Christians*	*E%*	*U%*	*Unevangelized*	*Num*	*Pop 2000*	*C%*	*Christians*	*E%*	*U%*	*Unevangelized*
A	15	1,156,218	2.60	30,041	39	61	709,198	0	0	0.00	0	0	0	0	1	1,739,228	5.00	86,961	46	54	945,096
B	11	3,680,787	12.68	466,547	65	35	1,272,506	5	1,088,060	13.08	142,349	65	35	376,773	3	3,115,154	13.60	423,533	67	33	1,036,642
C	5	17,379	80.04	13,911	100	0	34	0	0	0.00	0	0	0	0	0	0	0.00	0	0	0	0
Total	**31**	**4,854,384**	**10.52**	**510,499**	**59**	**41**	**1,981,738**	**5**	**1,088,060**	**13.08**	**142,349**	**65**	**35**	**376,773**	**4**	**4,854,382**	**10.52**	**510,494**	**59**	**41**	**1,981,738**

houses are dilapidated shacks. The traditional rural houses are made of mud walls and thatched roofs. These houses are in constant need of repair, especially after heavy rains. Malnutrition is widespread, as meals are unbalanced in essential nutrients, and large sections of the population cannot afford better diet. The health infrastructure is characterized by a paucity of medical facilities and personnel and insufficient supplies of medicine. Life expectancy is 41 years. The prevalence of serious diseases is the result of widespread insanitary conditions. Thatched roofs harbor rodents and insects. Houses are poorly ventilated. Livestock are kept in the same compound. Food is sold in the open and exposed to dust and flies that breed in the open latrines and unprotected waste disposal sites. In rural areas water polluted with human and animal wastes is used for bathing, laundering, and drinking. There is no comprehensive Social Security system.

Human rights and freedoms. Sierra Leone is ruled by a military junta which led the coup against president Joseph Momoh in 1992. For a year after the coup, the regime was faced with an insurrection by malcontents and rebels along the border with Liberia. These events have led to increased human rights abuses in the country. Both government forces and rebels are reported to have engaged in looting, robbery, extortion, and extrajudicial killings of opponents. Military personnel physically abuse civilians and mutilate prisoners. There are credible reports of summary executions of rebels, and public humiliation and torture including disfigurement of captives. The judicial system is based on the British model, but the military junta has circumvented some of the authority of judicial institutions by setting up special commissions of inquiry. Under the guise of national security, freedom of press and speech has been curtailed and abridged. Criticizing government leaders and offending the dignity of the state are criminal offenses. Newspapers most critical of the government were forced to close down when their registrations were rescinded. In one incident, newspaper offices were ransacked by government agents and journalists kicked and physically abused. There is a broad pattern of legal and societal discrimination against women and people of non-African origin. Women do not have equal access to education, economic advancement, or health facilities. Tribal loyalties remain important factors in government and the junta is heavily Mende in composition.

Human environment. Over the past decade, forest lands have been lost to agriculture. Over 85% of the wildlife habitats also have been lost.

Ethnoreligionists. Kono wayside sacrificial stone. 95% of the Kono are traditionalists (pagans).

NON-CHRISTIAN RELIGIONS

African traditional religions are strongest in eastern Sierra Leone. The Kono remain 78% animist, the Kissi 60% and the Koranko 68%, while most of the Limba and Loko of the north central part of the country still follow their ancestral tribal religions. The Mende are 43% traditionalist, mostly concentrated in the east. The supreme being is identified as Kanu among the Limba and Kuru among the Temne. The Kono have 2 names for God, Meketa (Everlasting One) and Yataa (Omnipresent One), although the latter is more common today. Kono divinities include Dugbo (Mother Earth), the wife of Yataa; Kwigbe, who is believed to reside in a sacred stone at Gbamandu and provides aid to barren women; Nyalwe, a river spirit to whom animals are offered during initiation ceremonies; and Kaene, a river divinity who guides the affairs of chiefs' sons. Offerings are made to the ancestral spirits (Fuenu) at designated altars (kotina) throughout the region, and special ceremonies are performed periodically by priests (kongoyasoenu). The departed ancestors are believed to serve as intermediaries between the living community and God. This is also true of the Mende who conceive of God (Ngewo) as a great chief and approach him most commonly through the recent dead (Kekeni). The Kekeni in turn petition the distance ancestors (Ndebla) who pass the requests on to Ngewo. Both among the Kono and Mende there are strong beliefs in the efficacy of charms, medicine men, divination, and the reality of witchcraft. Secret societies have increased in importance in recent years.

Muslims (Ahmadis). Students at the Ahmadiya Missionary School, Freetown.

Islam is found principally in the north and west although the coastal peoples have also come under Muslim influence. The Susu, Vai, and Bullom are predominantly Muslim, and Islam is also strong among the Yalunka and Temne. There has recently been an upsurge in conversions to Islam among the Mende. The Ahmadiya Mission has been active since 1957; adherents now are 90% Mende, 10% Temne.

CHRISTIANITY

Christianity has had its greatest success near the coast; however, only the Creoles are fully christianized. The Mende and Temne have shown themselves partially responsive to the gospel, and the churches have made few converts among most of the other tribal peoples.

PROTESTANT CHURCHES. Protestantism came to Sierra Leone in 1785 with the arrival of Black settlers from Nova Scotia, who brought with them their own denominations. Methodist and Baptist churches and the Countess of Huntingdon's Connexion were established at that time. British Baptist missionaries entered in 1795, followed by British Methodists in 1796 and pioneers of the London, Edinburgh, and Glasgow missionary societies in 1799. The first North Americans (1842) belonged to the American Missionary Association. United Brethren entered in 1850 but divided in 1889 into United Brethren and EUB factions. The merger of the EUB with American Methodists in the USA in 1968 produced the present United Methodist Church. Another Methodist group was the Wesleyan Church which came from the USA in 1889. The present century has witnessed the arrival of Seventh-day Adventists, Assemblies of God, and many other smaller denominations.

The work of the various Protestant churches is widely spread throughout the country; and except among the northern Susu and the southeastern Vai, Christian work is carried on among all peoples. Assemblies of God, United Pentecostals, United Brethren, and Missionary Church Association have grown steadily over the past quarter century. Wesleyan Methodists have shown greater gains although these have been spasmodic. Methodists grew rapidly from 1945 to 1955 followed by a period of decline from which they have been trying to recover. United Methodists (formerly EUB), whose growth from 1955-1970 has been spectacular, have seen a great slowdown in growth in the past 2 decades. Almost all Methodist bodies in Sierra Leone, Dahomey, Gambia, Ghana, Ivory Coast, and Nigeria are linked in the Council of the Methodist Church in West Africa.

CATHOLIC CHURCH. Portuguese mariners first touched the coast of Sierra Leone in the 15th century and various unsuccessful attempts were made to open work during succeeding centuries. The vicariate of Sierra Leone was erected in 1858 and given to the Lyons Fathers, followed by Holy Ghost priests in 1860. Nevertheless, significant progress was not made until 1950 when the diocese of Freetown and Bo was erected and placed under the direct supervision of Propaganda. The first indigenous priest was ordained in 1939.

The Holy See has no diplomatic relations with Sierra Leone in AD 2000, but has an apostolic delegate residing in Freetown.

ANGLICAN CHURCH. Anglicans began work in 1804, but since the beginning attention has been focused on the Creole community with little concern for the surrounding tribal peoples. Numerically the church has barely increased at all since 1900.

INDIGENOUS CHURCHES. The West African Methodist Church was formed in 1844 when Africans were refused permission to preach in the Methodist Church founded by Nova Scotia settlers. For a period, missionaries were received from dissident British Methodist groups, but since Methodist union in Britain in 1932 this largely Creole Church has had no formal relations with any foreign denomination. In 1945, a schism from the EUB produced the God is Our Light Church which has close ties to Ghana, and the National Pentecostal Church split from the Assemblies of God in 1970. Outside influences from Blacks in the USA have formed the AMEC and the PAW churches, and the Church of the Lord (Aladura) has spread to Sierra Leone from Nigeria and Ghana.

Renewal movements. In the 1990s the Pentecostal/Charismatic Renewal continued to spread rapidly across most older churches, and numbered over 200,000 adherents (of whom 13% Pentecostals, 12% Charismatics, and 76% Independents).

Indigenous missions. A handful of Anglicans, Protestants, and Roman Catholics have served in surrounding countries as foreign missionaries. However, a significant home missionary force is active among many of the ethnic groups.

Independents. Worshipers at Nongousa Miracle Centre in Kenema.

CHURCH AND STATE

The constitution for April 1972 guarantees freedom of conscience, expression, assembly and association (Article 11). In 1971, parliament passed a resolution to the effect that all aid (technical, financial or otherwise, including all forms of food supplies, clothing, and medical supplies) received from foreign governments and organizations should be channeled through the Sierra Leone government. Recognized Christian schools receive partial grants from the Ministry of Education. There is no ministry or governmental department in charge of religious matters. Churches are not obliged to register with government; but for purposes of Christian marriage, 'places of worship' and ministers must be registered.

BROADCASTING AND MEDIA

Shortwave radio programs from KNLS have seen some response. Sierra Leone is a member of UNDA. An interdenominational program featuring a religious service from a local church is broadcast each Sunday. Sundays also feature a 30-minute program entitled 'Religious requests' and a 15-minute 'Deliverance Hour' featuring music, testimonies, reading, and preaching. A final 30-minute program 'Evensong' features singing on Sunday evening.

Some 4.3 million (80%) have seen the 'Jesus' Film: through film team showings (3.8 million), TV broadcasts (200,000) and mission agency use (242,000). Responses have come from 334,000.

INTERDENOMINATIONAL ORGANIZATIONS

Twelve denominations are full members of the United Christian Council of Sierra Leone (UCCSL), which was founded in 1924. The Church of the Lord (Aladura) is an affiliate member. The council's aims and functions are 'to restore the unity of the Church of Christ, preserve comity among the Churches and Missions, serve as spokesman of the Church on religious, educational, moral, social, and such other matters as affect the Christian cause in Sierra Leone; and where necessary, to take joint action'. In addition to its other activities, the council manages 327 primary schools. The Sierra Leone Evangelical Fellowship (SLEF) formed more recently with 6 members, all also members of the UCCSL.

In 1973, at the insistence of the government, one of the 2 Catholic teacher training colleges was united with a Protestant one to form a state institution, the Normal School of Bo, which is open to all without religious distinction. The director in 1975 was a lay Protestant and the assistant director a Catholic priest. Religious instruction is given separately to Protestants and Catholics.

FUTURE TRENDS AND PROSPECTS

Tribal religions are expected to continue to decline (from 54% in 1970 to 37% by 2025) due to urbanization and continued economic deprivation. Christians will likely grow to 13%, mainly within groups already penetrated with the gospel.

Christians could grow to over 15% of the population early in the 21st century. At the same time, Muslims are expected to grow well beyond 50%, perhaps as high as 60% around mid-century.

BIBLIOGRAPHY

'A history of church growth among the Yalunka tribe of Sierra Leone (1951–1983).' S. M. Harrigan. M.A. thesis, Columbia Graduate School of Bible and Missions, Columbia, SC, 1985. 110p.

'A history of the development of the Sierra Leone Missionary Church.' W. D. Gerig. M.A. thesis, Trinity Evangelical Divinity School, Deerfield, IL, 1974. 148p.

'Ahmadiyya in Sierra Leone,' H. Fisher, *Sierra Leone bulletin of religion*, 2, 1 (1960), 1–10.

'Ancestor worship,' H. Sawyerr, *Sierra Leone bulletin of religion*, 6, 2 (1964), 25–33.

'Case study: holistic ministry in Freetown, Sierra Leone,' S. Nikkel, *Urban mission*, 5, 4 (March 1988), 35–39.

Centenary souvenir of Holy Ghost Fathers in Sierra Leone, 1864–1964. E. Hamelberg (ed). Freetown, Sierra Leone: CSSP, 1965. 136p.

'Christ and West Africa: Africanization in the Northern Province of Sierra Leone.' A. Salicone. M.A. thesis, Catholic Theological Union, Chicago, 1981. 153p.

Church growth in Sierra Leone: a study of church growth in Africa's oldest Protestant mission field. G. W. Olson. Grand Rapids, MI: Eerdmans, 1969. 222p.

Deep Mende: religious interactions in a changing African rural society. D. Reeck. *Studies on religion in Africa*, 4. Leiden: E. J. Brill, 1976. 102p.

'Evangelization of the polygamous in Sierra Leone in the light of the local customary family life: a pastoral suggestion.' S. J. Kanneh. Thesis, Pontificia Universita' Lateranense, Rome, 1986. 170p.

'Formation of a mission church in an African culture: the United Brethren in Sierra Leone.' H. E. Mueller. Ph.D. dissertation, Northwestern University, Evanston, IL, 1973. 263p.

God: ancestor or creator? Aspects of traditional beliefs in Ghana, Nigeria and Sierra Leone. H. Sawyerr. London: Longman, 1970. 118p.

'Islam in Sierra Leone during the nineteenth century.' D. E. Skinner. Ph.D. dissertation, University of California, Berkeley, 1971. 270p.

'Islamic law in Sierra Leone.' J. J. Tully. M.A. thesis, Hartford Seminary, Hartford, CT, 1993. 209p.

'Mande settlement and the development of Islamic institutions in Sierra Leone,' D. E. Skinner, *International journal of African historical studies*, 11, 1 (1978), 32–62.

Mende religion: aspects of belief and thought in Sierra Leone. A. J. Gittins. *Studia Instituti Anthropos*, vol. 41. Nettetal, Germany: Steyler Verlag-Wort und Werk, 1987. 258p.

Peoples of Sierra Leone. M. McCulloch. *Ethnographic survey of Africa: Western Africa*, part 2. 1950; reprinted with supplementary bibliography, London: International African Institute, 1964. 102p.

'Religion and ethnicity in the arts of a Limba chiefdom,' S. Ottenberg, *Africa*, 58, 4 (1988), 437–65.

'Religion and social organization among a West African Muslim people: the Susu of Sierra Leone.' J. S. Thayer. Ph.D. dissertation, University of Michigan, Ann Arbor, MI, 1981. 386p.

Religion in an African society: a study of the religion of the Kono people of Sierra Leone in its social environment with special reference to the function of religion in that society. R. T. Parsons. Leiden: E. J. Brill, 1964. 245p.

Sierra Leone. M. Binns & J. A. Binns. *World bibliographical series*, vol. 146. Oxford, UK: CLIO Press, 1992. 282p. (See 'Religion,' p.79-81).

Sierra Leone bulletin of religion. Freetown: University of Sierra Leone, Fourah Bay College, Department of Theology, 1959—68. Semi–annual. N.S., 1980— . Annual.

'The Baptist churches in Sierra Leone,' M. Banton, *Sierra Leone bulletin of religion*, 5, 2 (1963), 55–60.

The Church of the United Brethren in Christ in Sierra Leone. E. D. Cox. South Pasadena, CA: William Carey Library, [1970]. 182p.

'The dynamics of Methodism in Sierra Leone, 1860–1911: western European influence and culture in church development.' L. E. T. Shyllon. Ph.D. dissertation, University of Aberdeen, 1983. 524p.

'The Martha Davies Confidential Benevolent Association,' I. M. Ndanema, *Sierra Leone bulletin of religion*, 3, 2 (1961), 64–67.

'The Mende in Sierra Leone,' K. L. Little, in *African worlds: studies in the cosmological ideas and social values of African peoples*, p.111–137. C. D. Forde (ed). London: Oxford University Press, 1954.

The redeemed say so: stories of witnessing Christians in Sierra Leone, West Africa. M. Lind. Marion, IN: Wesley Press, 1972. 175p.

The Sierra Leone Church: an independent Anglican church: a contemporary study. R. S. Foster. London: SPCK, 1961. 76p.

The springs of Mende belief and conduct: a discussion of the influence of the belief in the supernatural among the Mende. W. T. Harris & H. Sawyerr. Freetown: Sierra Leone University Press, 1968. 152p.

The story of a mission. The Sierra Leone Church: first daughter of C.M.S. T. S. Johnson. London: SPCK, 1953. 151p.

Trail blazers in Sierra Leone. G. D. Fleming. , 1971–1973. 2 vols. (United Brethren in Christ).

'Varieties of religion and religious specialists among the Susu of Sierra Leone,' J. S. Thayer, in *Sierra Leone studies at Birmingham, 1983: proceedings of the third Birmingham Sierra Leone Studies Symposium, 15th-17th July 1983, Fircroft College, Birmingham.* P. K. Mitchell & A. Jones (eds). Birmingham, UK: University of Birmingham, Centre of West African Studies, 1984.

Country Table 2. **Organized churches and denominations in Sierra Leone.**

Official name (bold type = church with over 10% of all affiliated) 1	*Begun* 2	*Type* 3	*Counc* 4	*Congs* 5	*Adults* 6	*Affiliated 1970* 7	*Affiliated 1995* 8	*G%* 9	*Names, notes, and other statistics* (see Codebook, Part 3) 10
African Methodist Episcopal Church	1886	I-Met	Vw..N	9	1,355	1,500	3,000	2.81	M=AMEC(Black mission from USA), Creoles, 2 elementary schools,6n,1x,6m,1r.
African Methodist Episcopal Zion Ch	c1955	I-Met	.....	2	300	500	600	0.73	M=AMEZC(USA).
Apostolic Church	c1970	P-PeA	.....	11	700	–	1,400	33.61	M=AC(Britain).
Assemblies of God	1916	P-Pe2	ZFC.a	109	6,500	4,000	16,679	5.88	M=AoG(UK, USA), 56% Limba, 19% Kissi, 9% Kru, 9% Loko, 6x,40m,16f,2s(33),156Y.
Baptist Convention of Sierra Leone	1984	P-Bap	T....	36	3,805	–	6,340	9.09	M=FMB-SBC(USA).
Catholic Church in Sierra Leone:	1858	R-Lat	P.SGP	49	66,000	47,467	134,958	4.27	Slow growth, C=2+1+4. (1970) 3n, 3199Yy. (1990) 37n 74x 111m 105w 4304Yy
M Freetown & Bo	1858	R-Lat	Ps	20	39,000	34,800	85,700	3.67	Mainly Temne, Mende. 1,120 expatriates. M=CSSp. 20n 18x 26m 54w 1973Yy
D Kenema	1970	R-Lat	Pcssp	14	11,000	6,322	16,598	3.94	In southeast. Kono and other smaller tribes. 9n 13x 18m 16w 822Yy
D Makeni	1952	R-Lat	Psx	15	16,000	6,345	32,660	6.77	71% Temne, 11% Limba, 5% Mende, 3% Loko. 8n 43x 67m 35w 1509Yy
Christ Apostolic Church	c1970	I-3aA	.....	6	900	–	1,500	33.98	M=CAC(Nigeria). Specializing in conversion of Muslims.
Christian Extension Services		I-Non	.....	55	1,300	–	2,890	0.05	An independent body with no denominational connections.
Christian Reformed Church	1980	P-Ref	.....	3	700	–	1,250	6.67	M=CRWM(USA).
Church of God of Prophecy	1934	P-Pe3	Z....	3	500	2,400	833	-4.14	M=CGP(USA). Members of Temne tribe at Port Loko and Magburaka. HQ Freetown.
Church of the Lord (Aladura)	1947	I-3pA	xwI.n	40	600	1,000	2,000	2.81	Aladura=Praying. Church from Nigeria, leaders Ghanaians. Mende, Kono, Creoles.
Churches of Christ	1961	I-Dis	x....	31	1,200	1,000	2,000	2.81	M=CC(Non-Instrumental) (USA). HQ Freetown. Creoles. 1 school. 12f,1s,63Y.
Countess of Huntingdon's Connexion	1792	P-Con	....N	10	1,380	2,000	2,300	0.56	Begun by Nova Scotia settlers. 1825, M=CHC; Sierra Leone Mission (UK). Creoles.
Evangelical Lutheran Church	1983	P-Lut	.....	4	200	–	360	8.33	M=LCMS(USA,Missouri Synod).
Free Gospel Church	1920	I-3fA	.....	7	360	300	1,030	5.06	M=FGC(HQ Turtle Creek, PA, USA). Pentecostals. 8m,4f,1h.
God is Our Light Church	1945	I-3pA	.....	40	900	1,500	2,100	1.35	*GIOL*. Indigenous church ex EUB, controlled from Ghana. Anti-medicine. Kono, Mende.
Greek Orthodox P Alexandria (D Accra)		O-Gre	Cw...	1	390	500	600	0.05	HQ Yaounde (Cameroon). Under P Alexandria (Egypt). Lebanese, Greek traders.
Jehovah's Witnesses	1923	m-Jeh	x....	18	752	2,000	2,510	0.91	First missionaries entered 1923. Strong among Temne in Makeni. (1975) 113Y. (1995) 86Y.
Maranatha Churches	c1970	I-3cA	.....	10	590	–	1,180	32.70	Independent charismatics.
Methodist Church, Sierra Leone	1792	P-Met	VWA.N	235	14,900	30,000	25,729	-0.61	*SL Conf.* M=MMS. 70% Creole, 27%Mende, 3% Kissi. 35n,12x,34f,1p,5r,W=60%,618Y,464y.
National Pentecostal Church	1970	I-3pA	.....	20	5,930	500	9,890	12.68	Schism ex Assemblies of God. Sierra Leonian indigenous pentecostals.
New Apostolic Church	c1960	I-3aX	x....	400	43,000	50	76,413	34.08	*NAC.* M=Neuapostolische Kirche. HQ Zurich. Massive growth.
Nigerian Baptist Convention	1960	P-Bap	Twa.a	16	1,467	600	2,450	5.79	M=NBC(Nigeria). Work among Limba at Magburaka. 1x,4m,6f,W=45%,16Y,25z.
Open Bible Standard Churches	1967	I-3pW	ZF...	2	180	100	450	6.20	M=OBSC(USA). Classical Pentecostals (2-stage). 4f.
Pentecostal Assemblies of the World		I-3aO	xv...	5	1,200	1,000	2,400	0.05	M=PAOW(USA Blacks). Strong in Liberia (HQ Monrovia). 1967 enquiry re joining WCC.
Seventh-day Adventist Church	1905	P-Adv	x....	117	5,320	4,854	8,859	2.44	*Sierra Leone Mission*, WAfrican UM. 75% Mende, 25% Temne. 8n,3x,21f,1H,1p,2r,168Y.
Sierra Leone Baptist Union	1785	P-Bap	..G.a	6	400	700	1,300	2.51	Begun by Nova Scotians. M=EBMS. 75% Bassa, Creole. 3n,3x,7f,1h,W=73%,9Y.
Sierra Leone Church	1804	A-Low	AwAVN	49	13,000	25,000	25,040	0.01	*Diocese of SL*, in CPWA. M=CMS(UK). 82% Creole,10% Mende, 5% Limba. 36n,2x,11f,1s.
Sierra Leone Missionary Church	1945	P-Hol	xFG.a	34	1,000	1,350	2,500	2.50	*SLMC.* M=Missionary Church Assoc, now MC(USA). Koranko, Yalunka. 3n,7x,25f,3h,1p.
Wesleyan Church of Sierra Leone	1889	P-Hol	VFG.a	108	4,850	5,383	15,090	4.21	M=WC. Limba, Temne,Loko. 20 schools. 9n,8x,38m,37f,1H,3h,1p,1s,W=65%,237Yy.
United Brethren in Christ	1850	P-Hol	xFG.a	53	5,577	4,000	11,200	4.20	M=UBC(USA). Holiness body. Mende. 32 schools. 21n,4x,106m,33w,28f,1H,1s.
United Methodist Church	1850	P-Met	VwA.N	226	27,733	40,000	46,200	0.58	Till 1968, EUB. SL Provisional CC, UMC(USA), EMK. Mende, Temne. 28n,6x,22f,1p.
United Pentecostal Church	c1960	P-Pe1	x.G.E	36	1,800	1,500	2,770	2.48	*Jesus Only Ch.* M=UPC(USA). Unitarians. HQ Magburaka. 95% Temne, 5% Limba.
West African Methodist Church	1844	I-Met	V...N	42	10,000	10,000	19,000	2.60	Ex Nova Scotia Methodists. A=1933. 83% Creole, 11% Kru, 5% Mende. 10n,1r,18Y,205y.
Other Protestant denominations		P-	.....	30	1,600	1,000	3,000	0.05	Total about 6, including: Calvary Baptist Ch, World-Wide Missions (1965).
Other African indigenous churches		I-3pA	.....	50	2,000	500	4,000	0.05	Total 20: Christ Apostolic Ch (Nigeria), Ch of Salvation, Salvation Band, Celestial Ch of Christ.
Other independent charismatic chs	c1985	I-3cA	.....	30	7,000	–	10,000	10.00	Total 7 networks.
Doubly-affiliated		2-aff			-11,300	0	-21,671		Evangelicals and Pentecostals who are also baptized Roman Catholics.

Continued opposite

Country Table 2–concluded

Official name (bold type = church with over 10% of affiliated) 1	*Begun* 2	*Type* 3	*Counc* 4	*Congs* 5	*Adults* 6	*Affiliated 1970* 7	*Affiliated 1995* 8	*G%* 9	*Names, notes, and other statistics* (see Codebook, Part 3) 10
Totals				**1,903**	**224,089**	**190,704**	**428,150**		

Churches, members, growth, 1900-2025	*Congs*	*Adults*	*Affiliated*	*G%*	*Total denominations*	*6 Megablocs:* *O*	*R*	*A*	*P*	*I*	*m*
Total churches, members, and denominations (mid-1900)	300	23,000	42,280	2.18	10	0	1	1	6	2	0
Total churches, members, and denominations (mid-1970)	1,601	103,731	190,704	2.18	39	1	1	1	15	20	1
Total churches, members, and denominations (mid-1990)	1,800	204,000	389,500	3.64	67	1	1	1	22	41	1
Total churches, members, and denominations (mid-1995)	1,903	224,089	428,150	1.91	67	1	1	1	22	41	1
Total churches, members, and denominations (mid-2000)	2,000	267,000	510,494	3.58	67	1	1	1	22	41	1
Total churches, members, and denominations (mid-2025)	4,000	534,000	1,020,000	2.81	136	3	1	1	40	90	1

NOTES ON TABLE ABOVE
NATIONAL COUNCILS (Column 4, 5th letter).
a = member of both UCCSL and SLEF.
E = Evangelical Fellowship of Sierra Leone.
N = United Christian Council of Sierra Leone (UCCSL).
n = associate member of UCCSL.
P = Inter-Territorial Episcopal Conference of the Gambia, Liberia & Sierra Leone.

Other national or plurinational councils. United Pentecostal Assemblies of the World in Liberia & Sierra Leone.

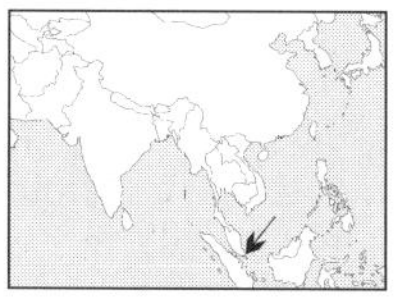

SINGAPORE

SECULAR DATA, AD 2000

STATE
Official name: Hsin-chia-p'o Kung-ho-kuo/The Republic of Singapore.
Short name: Singapore. **Adjective of nationality:** Singaporean.
Flag: Red and white stripes, with white crescent and 5 white stars on red stripe.
Area: 641 sq. km. (247 sq. mi.).
Government: Parliamentary republic, since 1965 (1000 Sumatran colony, 1824 British possession, 1867 British crown colony, 1959 self-government, 1963 in Federation of Malaysia, 1965 Independence).
Legislature: Parliament (Legislative Assembly), 90 members.
Official language: Malay (national language).
Monetary unit: 1 Singapore dollar (S$) = 100 cents. **US$1=** S$1.69.
Chief cities: SINGAPORE 3,587,000.
Political divisions: 1 province.
Armed forces: 70,000.

DEMOGRAPHY
Population: 3,567,000.
Population density: 5,564.1/sq. km. (14,439.7/sq. mi.).
Under 15 years: 788,000.
Growth rate p.a.: 1.03% (births 12.76, deaths 5.25).
Mortality: Infant, per 1,000: 4.8; **Maternal per 100,000:** 10.0.
Life expectancy: 78 (male 76, female 80).
Household size: 3.9. **Floor area per person, sq.m:** 25.0.
Major languages: Chinese (Fukienese/Hokkienese), English, Malay, Tamil, Malayalam, Punjabi, Hindi, Javanese.
Urban dwellers: 100.00%. **Urban growth rate p.a.:** 1.0%.
Labor force: 50%.

ETHNOLINGUISTIC PEOPLES
17.8% Han Chinese (Min Nan); 12.6% Malay; 11.5% Peranakan (Straits Chinese); 9.6% Han Chinese (Teochew); 8.5% Han Chinese (Cantonese).

ECONOMY
National income p.a. per person: US$26,730; **per family:** US$104,247.

EDUCATION
Adult literacy: 89% (male 95%, female 83%). **Schools:** 392.
Universities: 7. **School enrolment:** female/male: 86%/86%.

HEALTH
Access to health services: 100%. **Access to safe water:** 100%.
Hospitals: 22 (36 beds per 10,000). **Doctors:** 4,301.
Blind: 427. **Deaf:** 215,200. **Murder rate:** 1.
Lepers: 12,000.

LITERATURE
New book titles p.a.: 2,850 (800 p.a. per million). **Periodicals:** 35.
Newspapers: 8 dailies.

COMMUNICATION (per 1,000 people)
Phones: 478 (33% mobile). **Radios:** 275. **TV sets:** 218.
Daily newspaper circulation: 340. **Computers:** 412.

HUMAN LIFE AND LIBERTY (optimum condition=100.0%)
HDI: 90.0. **HSI:** 72.0. **HFI:** 27.5. **EFL:** 74.0.

Country Table 1. **Religious adherents in Singapore, AD 1900-2025.**

Year	*1900*		*1970*		*mid-1990*		*Annual change, 1990-2000*				*mid-1995*		*mid-2000*		*mid-2025*	
Name	*Adherents*	*%*	*Adherents*	*%*	*Adherents*	*%*	*Natural*	*Conversion*	*Total*	*Rate*	*Adherents*	*%*	*Adherents*	*%*	*Adherents*	*%*
Chinese folk-religionists	123,800	49.5	1,125,000	54.2	1,330,134	44.1	24,262	-5,146	19,116	1.35	1,428,870	43.0	1,521,289	42.7	1,458,300	35.0
Muslims	55,000	22.0	373,000	18.0	552,000	18.3	10,085	238	10,323	1.73	610,000	18.4	655,231	18.4	780,000	18.7
Buddhists	42,500	17.0	200,000	9.6	430,000	14.3	7,856	733	8,589	1.84	480,000	14.5	515,894	14.5	650,000	15.6
Christians	**10,000**	**4.0**	**161,700**	**7.8**	**352,000**	**11.7**	**6,431**	**2,128**	**8,559**	**2.20**	**400,000**	**12.1**	**437,593**	**12.3**	**660,000**	**15.8**
PROFESSION																
professing Christians	**10,000**	**4.0**	**161,700**	**7.8**	**352,000**	**11.7**	**6,431**	**2,128**	**8,559**	**2.20**	**400,000**	**12.1**	**437,593**	**12.3**	**660,000**	**15.8**
AFFILIATION																
unaffiliated Christians	1,450	0.6	19,081	0.9	27,300	0.9	499	237	736	2.41	31,982	1.0	34,657	1.0	42,000	1.0
affiliated Christians	**8,550**	**3.4**	**142,619**	**6.9**	**324,700**	**10.8**	**5,932**	**1,892**	**7,824**	**2.18**	**368,018**	**11.1**	**402,936**	**11.3**	**618,000**	**14.8**
Roman Catholics	5,000	2.0	80,000	3.9	119,500	4.0	2,183	167	2,350	1.81	132,425	4.0	143,000	4.0	210,000	5.0
Protestants	2,500	1.0	35,467	1.7	100,000	3.3	1,827	827	2,654	2.38	114,513	3.5	126,536	3.6	200,000	4.8
Independents	0	0.0	16,300	0.8	74,000	2.5	1,352	648	2,000	2.42	85,630	2.6	94,000	2.6	150,000	3.6
Anglicans	1,000	0.4	10,000	0.5	27,000	0.9	493	207	700	2.33	30,700	0.9	34,000	1.0	50,000	1.2
Marginal Christians	0	0.0	650	0.0	3,000	0.1	55	45	100	2.92	3,450	0.1	4,000	0.1	6,000	0.1
Orthodox	50	0.0	202	0.0	1,200	0.0	22	-2	20	1.55	1,300	0.0	1,400	0.0	2,000	0.1
Trans-megabloc groupings																
Evangelicals	2,000	0.8	30,000	1.5	90,000	3.0	1,644	1,156	2,800	2.75	108,932	3.3	118,000	3.3	190,000	4.6
Pentecostals/Charismatics	0	0.0	10,000	0.5	114,600	3.8	2,094	1,046	3,140	2.45	131,217	4.0	146,000	4.1	260,000	6.2
Great Commission Christians	**8,000**	**3.2**	**100,000**	**4.8**	**229,000**	**7.6**	**4,184**	**2,166**	**6,350**	**2.48**	**259,000**	**7.8**	**292,499**	**8.2**	**412,000**	**9.9**
Hindus	16,200	6.5	120,000	5.8	150,000	5.0	2,740	344	3,084	1.89	167,000	5.0	180,836	5.1	250,000	6.0
Nonreligious	0	0.0	62,000	3.0	125,000	4.1	2,284	1,613	3,897	2.75	150,000	4.5	163,965	4.6	250,000	6.0
New-Religionists	0	0.0	10,000	0.5	52,500	1.7	959	69	1,028	1.80	58,200	1.8	62,783	1.8	78,000	1.9
Sikhs	2,500	1.0	20,000	1.0	14,000	0.5	256	-91	165	1.12	14,600	0.4	15,650	0.4	19,500	0.5
Baha'is	0	0.0	700	0.0	4,400	0.2	80	28	108	2.22	5,100	0.2	5,482	0.2	9,000	0.2
Atheists	0	0.0	2,000	0.1	3,400	0.1	62	51	113	2.90	4,100	0.1	4,525	0.1	8,000	0.2
Shintoists	0	0.0	0	0.0	700	0.0	13	4	17	2.17	810	0.0	868	0.0	1,500	0.0
Ethnoreligionists	0	0.0	0	0.0	600	0.0	11	5	16	2.37	700	0.0	758	0.0	900	0.0
Jews	0	0.0	400	0.0	580	0.0	11	-1	10	1.57	630	0.0	678	0.0	800	0.0
Other religionists	0	0.0	200	0.0	686	0.0	13	25	38	4.47	990	0.0	1,062	0.0	2,000	0.1
World A (unevangelized persons)	200,000	80.0	1,078,792	52.0	1,049,568	34.8	19,141	-26,738	-7,594	-0.75	1,009,490	30.4	973,791	27.3	900,288	21.6
World B (evangelized non-Christians)	40,000	16.0	834,108	40.2	1,614,432	53.5	29,488	24,610	54,098	2.93	1,911,203	57.6	2,155,616	60.4	2,607,712	62.6
World C (Christians)	10,000	4.0	161,700	7.8	352,000	11.7	6,431	2,128	8,559	2.20	400,000	12.0	437,593	12.3	660,000	15.8
Country's population	**250,000**	**100.0**	**2,074,600**	**100.0**	**3,016,000**	**100.0**	**55,063**	**0**	**55,063**	**1.69**	**3,320,694**	**100.0**	**3,567,000**	**100.0**	**4,168,000**	**100.0**

COLUMNS, ROWS.
For meanings and definitions, see Codebook (Part 3). Note that, by definition, total 'Christians' = professing + crypto-Christians, which also = affiliated + unaffiliated Christians, and also = Great Commission Christians + latent Christians. Percentages may not always total exactly, due to rounding.

CENSUSES.
1990: (Percentage aged 10 and over) 31.1% Buddhists, 22.4% Chinese folk-religionists, 15.4% Muslims, 14.3% nonreligious, 12.5% Christians (4.7% Roman Catholics), 3.7% Hindus, 0.4% Sikhs, 0.4% Sikhs, 0.2% other religionists.

NOTES ON RELIGIONS
ANGLICANS. The Anglican proportion of the population remained unchanged from 1900 to 1970. After 1970, the church grew as the result of conversions among native Singaporeans, offsetting British emigration.
ASIAN INDIGENOUS. Mostly Chinese indigenous with some Indian indigenous Christians; in about 30 denominations in 1990 (see Table 2).
ATHEISTS. Communist Party of Malaya (illegal; pro-Chinese): all underground.
BAHA'IS. Growth from 1 local spiritual assembly (1964) to 5 (1973). Surprisingly for such a cosmopolitan city, adherents have little appeal and by 25 years later LSAs still numbered only 5.
BUDDHISTS. Chinese adherents to Mahayana Buddhism; with Sinhalese (Ceylonese), and a Chinese minority, following Theravada Buddhism; the latter are assisted by a number of Theravada missionaries from Thailand who have established several temples in Singapore.
CHINESE FOLK-RELIGIONISTS. The bulk are followers in varying degrees of the popular amalgam of Buddhism, Taoism, Confucianism, the ancestor-cult and spiritism, with numerous temples and deities. There are a number of spirit-medium cults (Shenism). Chinese folk-religionists are declining in proportion to the population as their children abandon the old beliefs and practices.
HINDUS. Tamils and Malayalees from south India, with 31 temples. A Hindu sect, Ananda Marga (Path of Bliss), also has a following.
JEWS. With 2 synagogues.
MUSLIMS. Mostly Malays, also Indians, Pakistanis, Javanese, Arabs, Buginese, and several hundred Chinese Muslims; with a total of 83 masjids and saraus. There is also an Ahmadiya Mission begun 1935; Qadianis (world HQ Rabwah, Pakistan) enumerated here as Muslims though declared non-Muslim by Pakistan. Hajj pilgrims to Mecca. (1974) 954; (1975) 1,152; (1976) 434.
NEW-RELIGIONISTS. Followers of various Chinese and Japanese syncretistic or salvationist New Religions, including the faith-healing Tao Yuan Organization (for Chinese only) and its related philanthropic association for non-members, the World Red Swastika Society (Singapore Association, begun 1936, membership falling from 1,331 in 1948 to 770 by 1970). Others are: T'ung-shan She (Fellowship of Goodness), universalistic in membership and attracting mainly middle-class Chinese, which was brought to Singapore in 1927; the Religion of the Void, which appeared in Singapore in 1900; Great Way of Former Heaven (Hsien-t'ien Ta Tao), a number of separate sects each with its own leader; and Soka Gakkai (Nichiren Shoshu) from Japan, with 10,000 adherents in Singapore in 1995.
NONRELIGIOUS. Chinese, especially youths, who have abandoned their former folk-religious beliefs and practices.
OTHER RELIGIONISTS. Adherents of other Western religions and cults, including Rosicrucians (1 AMORC center).
PENTECOSTALS/CHARISMATICS Anglican charismatics are very strong. The charismatic renewal, begun 1972, has centered on the

Continued overleaf

Country Table 1–concluded

Anglican cathedral, bishop's house and house churches, with the Anglican bishop as leader. By 1976, the Spiritual Renewal Fellowship also served a few hundred Protestants (Lutherans, Methodists) and also about 100 Catholic charismatics. By 1996, the Catholic Charismatic Renewal had 15 weekly prayer groups with 1,500 regular adult attenders (with 20 involved priests and 1 bishop), with over 8,000 at any one meeting.
SIKHS. Punjabis; with 4 temples.

Great Commission Instrument Panel: status of Singapore (for explanation see start of Part 4)

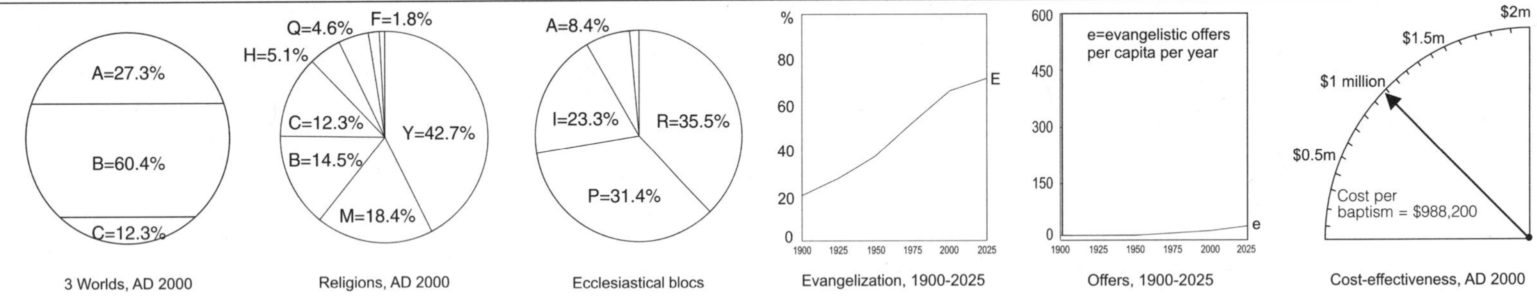

Country status. Singapore consists of one large and many smaller islands off the southern tip of the Malaysian Peninsula in Southeast Asia. It is one of the world's busiest ports and is a leading trade and financial center.

HUMAN LIFE AND LIBERTY

Human need and development. Although still classified as a developing country, Singapore is, in fact, a developed country ranking with most European nations in its standard of living. Further, as a city-state, it is able to mobilize its financial and economic resources within a small, well-defined land area. Singapore also ranks high in its social indicators, such as the quality of health and education. The national per capita income is $26,700. Over 90% of Singaporeans own their homes. Wealth is distributed almost equally in what is essentially a full-employment economy.

Human rights and freedoms. Singapore has been under authoritarian, albeit paternalistic, rule since independence in 1965. Intimidation of opposition politicians, restrictions on press freedom, and detention of people on politically motivated grounds have been used by the government in an effort to maintain itself in power. As a result, Singapore has had one-party rule longer than any non-Communist Asian country. Arrest without warrant is legally permitted under the Internal Security Act, and detainees may be confined indefinitely. The Penal Code mandates caning in addition to imprisonment for certain types of offenses against person, vandalism, and breach of immigration controls. Persons suspected of trafficking in narcotics are detained without trial. The state has wide discretionary powers in cases where it deems that national security is threatened. Warrantless searches can be conducted under the Misuse of Drugs Act. The Constitution permits official restrictions on freedom of the press and prohibits publication of materials that incite violence, provoke ethnic tensions, and threaten public order. The law has been interpreted broadly to restrict all kinds of political opposition and criticism. The electronic media are entirely owned by the government while newspapers are owned by a group with close ties to the ruling party. Foreign publications are required to post a bond equivalent to $118,000 and name a local resident to accept legal service. Those that arouse government ire are 'gazetted', or banned from selling more than a certain number of copies. Music, movies, and videos are censored for content. There is no legal or informal public discrimination based on gender, race or religion. Minorities are afforded equal rights and are well represented in government.

Human environment. As a total urban environment, Singapore has no natural forests or areas. With a limited land area, Singapore has been expanding vertically. Congestion has brought air, water, and noise pollution, which the city-state has attempted to combat by enforcing strong environmental laws. Singapore was one of the earliest Asian countries to establish a ministry of environment in 1972. Nevertheless, as a major oil refiner, Singapore is facing more severe oil-related pollution problems every year.

NON-CHRISTIAN RELIGIONS

Buddhism and ***Chinese folk religion*** are the most prevalent forms of religious expression in Singapore, involving rituals and moral regulations common to Chinese culture. There are about 515,000 Buddhists on the island in addition to over 1.5 million adherents of Chinese popular religion, which is a syncretistic mixture of Buddhism, Taoism, Confucianism, and traditional magical practices. The majority of Buddhists in Singapore are Chinese and belong to the Mahayana school. A small Chinese minority and the Ceylonese majority follow the Theravada school. These 2 schools have been brought closer together by the coordinating activities of the Singapore Buddhist Federation, the Singapore Buddhist Sangha Organization, and the Singapore Regional Center of the World Fellowship of Buddhists.

Islam is found primarily among the Malays, Indians, and Pakistanis. The Muslim population numbers 655,000, the second largest religious community in Singapore. The Muslim Religious Council (Majlis Ugama Islam), under the Ministry of Social Affairs, conducts and regulates the activities of the community under Islamic law.

Hinduism exists among the Tamils and Malayalees from South India. The Hindu population numbers over 180,000.

Judaism has 600 adherents who worship in 2 synagogues.

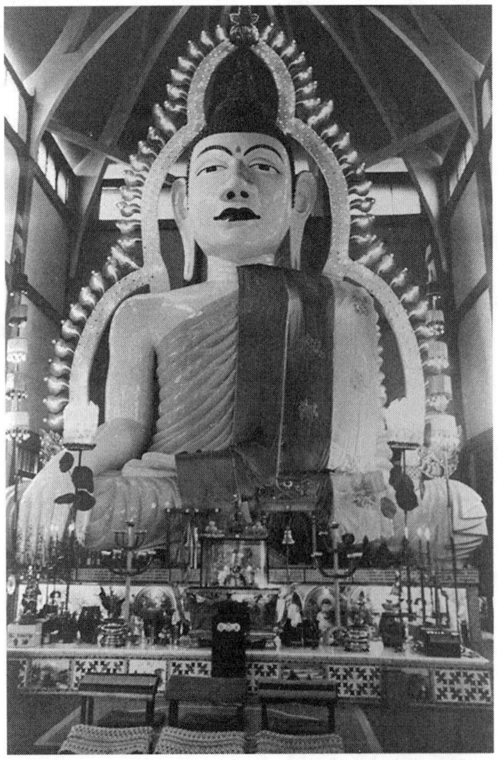

Mahayana Buddhists. Worshipers before vast 50-foot high statue of the Buddha in Temple of a Thousand Lights (Sakya Muni Buddh Gaya Temple), Singapore. A movie with this English title was made in 1965.

CHRISTIANITY

Although the majority of Singapore's churches are Chinese, Christianity is found among all the various ethnic groups on the island. The multiplicity of cultures and languages among Christians is a major problem; congregations worshipping in a single language may use Mandarin, Hokkien, Cantonese, Teochew, English, Malay, Tamil, Malayalam, Foochow, Hainan, Hakka, Hingwa, Matak, Punjabi, or several others. Despite their close proximity, efforts to coordinate denominational activities in Singapore and Malaysia have been hampered by this linguistic diversity.

CATHOLIC CHURCH. The first Catholic priests arrived in Malacca following the conquest by the Portuguese in 1511. Francis Xavier came in 1545 and the diocese of Malacca was established in 1557. Catholic activity was suppressed by the Dutch in 1641 from which it was slow to recover. In 1819, there were only 12 Catholics in Singapore, but by 1831 membership had risen to 300. Singapore and Malaya became an independent vicariate in 1841, and Singapore was made the seat of the diocese of Malacca in 1888 and an archdiocese in 1953. In December 1972, the metropolitan see of Singapore-Malacca covering Singapore and a part of West Malaysia was divided, one part being the area of the republic of Singapore which thus lost its metropolitan character. About 70% of the 135,000 Catholics in Singapore are Chinese. One relic of the Portuguese patronage system is the important Portuguese parish of Singapore which is part of the diocese of Macao and which consists of 9,000 Catholics with 4 priests from Portugal, Goa, and Macao. The Apostolic Visitor for the Chinese of the Diaspora lives in Singapore and has responsibility for all Chinese communities throughout the world with the exception of Taiwan, Hong Kong, and Macao. The visitor has the rank of bishop and his services are integrated into the archdiocese of Singapore. His work is to animate and coordinate the activities of some one million Chinese Catholics scattered over the 6 continents. Its central bureau includes such services as the press, correspondence courses on religion, a library, catechesis, and social assistance.

The Holy See has diplomatic relations with Singapore and in AD 2000 is represented to government and the Catholic hierarchy by a nuncio residing in Singapore.

PROTESTANT CHURCH. Protestantism began with the Dutch conquest of Malaysia in 1641 but was confined to Europeans until the London Missionary Society sent its first missionary, a Presbyterian, to Malacca in 1814. Singapore was reached in 1819, and during the following decades the LMS, the American Board (ABCFM), and the Parish Mission (PEMS) contributed much to the development of education on the island. In 1841, the LMS church members numbered only 10, rising to 60 by 1843. In 1846, LMS closed the mission in Singapore and transferred its work to China, but the church continued under indigenous leadership. Other Presbyterian missionaries appeared in 1850 and 1881, and by 1925 there were 800 Chinese members, primarily due to an influx of immigrants. Chinese immigrant congregations continued to use the name Church of Christ in China until 1949 when they became part of the Presbyterian Church in Singapore and Malaysia. The Presbyterian Church is the fifth largest denomination on the island. Presbyterian schools have a large enrollment.

Country summary. **Worlds A, B, C by ethnolinguistic peoples, cities, and major civil divisions in Singapore.**

	PEOPLES							*CITIES*							*CIVIL DIVISIONS*						
World	*Num*	*Pop 2000*	*C%*	*Christians*	*E%*	*U%*	*Unevangelized*	*Num*	*Pop 2000*	*C%*	*Christians*	*E%*	*U%*	*Unevangelized*	*Num*	*Pop 2000*	*C%*	*Christians*	*E%*	*U%*	*Unevangelized*
A	9	109,388	0.77	847	40	60	65,626	0	0	0.00	0	0	0	0	0	0	0.00	0	0	0	0
B	28	3,312,421	8.75	289,905	73	27	908,105	1	3,587,000	11.24	403,027	73	27	979,610	1	3,566,614	11.30	402,936	73	27	974,057
C	10	144,804	77.47	112,185	100	0	325	0	0	0.00	0	0	0	0	0	0	0.00	0	0	0	0
Total	**47**	**3,566,613**	**11.30**	**402,937**	**73**	**27**	**974,056**	**1**	**3,587,000**	**11.24**	**403,027**	**73**	**27**	**979,610**	**1**	**3,566,614**	**11.30**	**402,936**	**73**	**27**	**974,057**

The first Methodist missionary arrived in Singapore from India in 1885. In 1888, Malaysia became a separate mission, and the first session of the Malaya Annual Conference was held in Singapore in 1893. Two conferences were formed in 1936, one English-speaking and one Chinese speaking, and a Tamil Provisional Conference was added in 1968. The Malaysia and Singapore Methodist Church became autonomous in 1968 under its own local bishop and is the largest non-Catholic church in Singapore. From its beginning, the Methodist Church emphasized education and now has 7 educational institutions with 18,000 students. Church membership more than tripled between 1970 and 1990 in both the English and Chinese conferences.

The work of Brethren Assemblies was opened in 1856 by 2 independent couples. Chinese Baptist immigrants came to Singapore in 1905, worshipping at first in the Presbyterian Church, but in 1937 the first independent Baptist service was conducted. Since 1950, Southern Baptist missionaries from the USA had been at work with the church. Assemblies of God entered in 1933 and now have 36 congregations; they form one of the most rapidly growing denominations in Singapore at present.

Other Protestant bodies include Adventists, Evangelical Free Church, Lutherans, and Salvation Army.

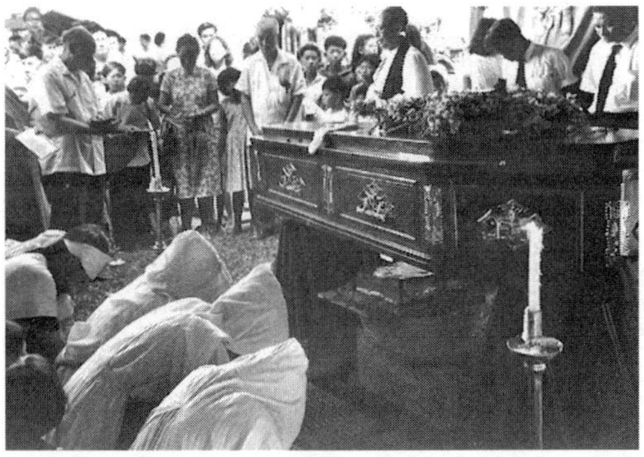

Anglican Church, Diocese of Singapore. Chinese funeral in Queenstown, with relatives of the deceased wearing off-white hoods. According to Chinese tradition, an elaborate and costly funeral shows a family's honor for its dead.

ANGLICAN CHURCH. Anglicanism, the fourth largest denomination after Catholicism, Methodism, and Assemblies of God entered Singapore with the appointment of an Anglican chaplain by the East India Company in 1826 to serve the European population. Missionary activity began in 1856 based on the first Singapore Anglican church, St Andrew's Church Mission, which worked in collaboration with SPG missionaries from England. During the next 50 years, work was carried out in the Hokkien, Tamil, Malay, and Cantonese languages. The first bishop was appointed for Singapore as a separate diocese in 1909. In 1966, the first local bishop was consecrated with Singapore becoming a diocese separate from Malaysia in 1970. The bishop has been the leader of a rapidly growing charismatic renewal among Anglicans, centered on the cathedral.

INDIGENOUS CHURCHES. Numerous small independent churches, mostly Chinese, are active in Singapore. The first was the True Jesus Church which dates from 1927, but the majority were established after the Christian exodus from China in 1949. A Ceylonese group using Tamil, the Ceylon Pentecostal Church of Malaya, was founded in 1936.

ORTHODOX CHURCH. There are 2 congregations, one of the Orthodox Syrian Church in Singapore and one for Armenians related to Echmiadzin.

Renewal movements. In the 1990s the Pentecostal/Charismatic Renewal continued to spread rapidly across most older churches, and numbered over 146,000 adherents (of whom 22% Pentecostals, 36% Charismatics, and 43% Independents).

Indigenous missions. The bulk of the foreign missionaries sent out from Singapore have been Protestants and Anglicans sent in the last 2 decades.

CHURCH AND STATE

Singapore is a secular state and its constitution of 1966 has little to say about religion. Religious minorities are protected in Article 89:1, in the following words: 'It shall be the responsibility of the government constantly to care for the interests of the racial and religious minorities in Singapore'. Islam is referred to in Article 6:2 which states that the legislature shall by law make provision for regulating Muslim religious affairs and for constituting a council to advise the president in matters relating to the Muslim religion. At the end of 1971, Jehovah's Witnesses were prohibited by the government on the grounds that they constitute a danger to 'public welfare and good order'. Christians have been commended by the prime minister for their interest in politics; 15 members of parliament out of 69 (22%) are Christians.

BROADCASTING AND MEDIA

Shortwave radio programs from KNLS have seen some response. Singapore is a member of UNDA: Catholics teach courses in media communications at the Catholic Audio Visual Centre. Some 650,000 have seen the 'Jesus' Film, mainly through cinematic showings: 3,300 have responded.

INTERDENOMINATIONAL ORGANIZATIONS

The Council of Churches of Malaysia and Singapore was created in 1948, the result of shared experiences of expatriate church leaders in prison camps during World War II. Its headquarters were in Singapore until it divided in 1975 into 2 separate councils, one in each nation. Its membership includes 9 churches and 4 agencies, and it represents 23% of Singapore's Christian community. Affiliated to the Singapore Regional Council are a Student Center, Churches' Counseling Service, Singapore Urban Industrial Mission Board (SUIM), Singapore Churches' Conference Center, Community Study Center and a Radio/TV Broadcasting Committee. The Counseling Service has a staff of 5 under the management of a board including Anglicans, Methodists, Lutherans, and Presbyterians; it now includes a 24-hour telephone counseling ministry. SUIM was set up in 1969 to pioneer community work in 2 large housing estates and a satellite town being built by government. Lutherans sponsor one housing unit on an ecumenical basis; Catholics and other Protestants cooperate in the other. The Institute for the Study of Religions and Society in Singapore and Malaysia, founded in 1968, is engaged in research on local religion and the social impact of industrialization, urbanization, and secularization. Activities include studies in rural and urban development of manpower and resources, folk religions, and local cultural patterns. Theological colleges (Trinity College, Singapore Bible College, and the Discipleship Training Center) are ecumenical in character. There is also an Inter-Religious Organizations Council, a private body recognized by government.

FUTURE TRENDS AND PROSPECTS

Young English-speaking Chinese are expected to continue to leave the religion of their parents, Chinese folk-religion (54% in 1970 declining to 35% by 2025), becoming Christians (7.8% in 1970 up to 15.8% by 2025) or nonreligious (3% in 1970 up to 6.0% by 2025).

Christianity will probably continue to grow, mainly due to conversions of Chinese folk-religionists. Christians could reach 20% by AD 2050.

BIBLIOGRAPHY

'A comparison of Tamil and Chinese Lutheran churches in peninsular Malaysia and Singapore.' D. W. Vierow. D.Miss. thesis, Fuller Theological Seminary, Pasadena, CA, 1976. 283p.

A handbook of churches and Christian organizations in Singapore. J. Y. K. Wong. Singapore: Study Group for Church Growth and Evangelism, 1971. 69p.

A history of Baptists in Malaysia & Singapore. L. O. Rogers (ed), [1971]. 146p.

'A study of the contemporary Protestant Christian ministry in Singapore.' P. S. K. Tow. Thesis, Trinity Evangelical Divinity School, Deerfield, IL, 1973. 244p.

'An investigation and evaluation of the growth of Singapore Baptist churches from 1970 onwards and a projection of growth to the years 1990 and 2000.' T. C. T. Lim. M.Div. thesis, Baptist Theological Seminary, Penang, Malaysia, 1982. 150p.

Banished: the expulsion of the Christian Conference of Asia from Singapore and its implications. R. O'Grady. Kowloon, Hong Kong: International Conference of Asia, 1990. 102p.

Bibliography of Malaysia and Singapore. R. S. Karni. Kuala Lumpur: Penerbit Universiti Malaya, 1980. 649p.

'Chinese religious festivals in Singapore,' C. H. Ming, in *Annual publication of the China Society.* Singapore: China Society, 1949.

Chinese spirit–medium cults in Singapore. A. J. A. Elliot. London: London School of Economics, 1955.

Chinese temples in Singapore. L. Comber. Singapore: Eastern Universities Press, 1958. 110p.

Chinese temples of Singapore. A. K. Tong. Singapore: Nanfong Commercial Publishing Bureau, 1949.

Church and society: Singapore context. B. E. K. Sng (ed). Singapore: Graduates Christian Fellowship, 1989. 93p.

'Church growth in Singapore.' H. J. K. Koo. Th.M. thesis, Columbia Theological Seminary, Decatur, GA, 1991. 135p.

'Church growth patterns and potential analytical study of two Methodist churches in Singapore.' C. K. Lim. Th.M. thesis, Fuller Theological Seminary, Pasadena, CA, 1982. 259p.

Conversions à Singapour: contribution à une sociologie de la mutation socio–religieuse. P. Lopez de Ceballas. Paris: Ecole Pratique des Hautes Etudes, 1974.

'Developing disciple–makers among Singaporean women: a case study.' F. P. Tan. D.Min. thesis, Dallas Theological Seminary, Dallas, TX, 1992. 306p.

Ethnicity and nationality in Singapore. C. S. Foon. *Southeast Asia series,* no. 78. Athens, OH: Ohio University Monographs in International Studies, 1987. 229p.

Evangelism in Singapore: a research analysis among Baptists. D. Finnell. Singapore: Singapore Baptist Book Store, 1986. 130p.

'Folk religion among the Chinese in Singapore and Malaysia.' L. Tjandra. D.Miss. thesis, Fuller Theological Seminary, Pasadena, CA, 1988. 392p. (Text in Chinese with extended summary in English).

Forever beginning II. One hundred years of Methodism in Singapore. T. R. Doraisamy. Singapore: Methodist Church in Singapore, 1986. 144p.

Growing churches Singapore style: ministry in an urban context. K. Hinton. Singapore: Overseas Missionary Fellowship, 1985. 234p.

Hinduism in Singapore: a guide to the Hindu temples of Singapore. J. Mialaret. Singapore: Donald Moore for Asia Pacific Press, 1969. 72p.

In his good time: the story of the church in Singapore, 1819–1978. B. E. K. Sng. Singapore: Graduates' Christian Fellowship, 1980. 343p.

Islam and society in Southeast Asia. T. Abdullah & S. Siddique (eds). Singapore: Institute of Southeast Asian Studies, 1986.

'Leadership development: implications for Singapore Methodism.' C. K. Lim. D.Miss. thesis, Fuller Theological Seminary, Pasadena, CA, 1983. 331p.

'Metamorphosis of a church: a study on the people of God in the Republic of Singapore: analysis and projection.' R. P. Balhetchet. Thesis, Pontificia Universitas St. Thomae, Rome, 1976. 281p.

'New Testament teachings on church discipline and its application to the Singapore church.' P. W. Tham. Th.M. thesis, Dallas Theological Seminary, Dallas, TX, 1991. 71p.

Redemptorists in Singapore–Malaysia. K. J. O'Brien. Singapore: Navjiwan Press, 1985. 227p.

'Religion and language among Singapore Indians,' J. Clammer, in *Proceedings of the Conference on Tamil Language and Literature in Singapore,* p.139–48. K. Anbalagan (ed). Singapore: Tamil Language Society, 1981.

Religion and modernization: a study of changing rituals among Singapore's Chinese, Malays & Indians. S. C. Tham. Singapore: Graham Brash, 1985. 204p.

Religion in West Malaysia and Singapore: a bibliography. J. J. Corfield. *Bibliography and literature,* no. 8. Hull, UK: Centre for South-East Asian Studies, University of Hull, 1991. 150p.

Religious switching in Singapore: a study of religious mobility. J. B. Tamney & R. Hassan. *Asian studies monograph,* 3. Singapore: Select Books, 1987. 63p.

Religious trends in Singapore with special reference to Christianity. B. E. K. Sng & P. S. You. Singapore: Graduates' Christian Fellowship, 1982. 86p.

Singapore. S. R. Quah & J. S. T. Quah. *World bibliographical series,* vol. 95. Oxford, UK: CLIO Press, 1988. 278p. (See 'Religion,' p.34-6).

'Singapore, Malaysia and Brunei: the Church in a racial melting pot,' J. R. Fleming, in *Christ and crisis in Southeast Asia,* p.81–106. G. H. Anderson (ed). New York: Friendship Press, 1968.

'Singapore Methodist churches: a critical analysis.' E. J. Thoraisingam. D.Miss. thesis, Fuller Theological Seminary, Pasadena, CA, 1978. 284p.

'Singapore: urbanism, culture, and the church,' J. Clammer, *Urban mission*, 7, 4 (March 1990), 6–20.

'Some aspects of Chinese religious practices and customs in Singapore and Malaysia,' T. Sakai, *Journal of Southeast Asian studies*, 12, 1 (1981), 133–41.

Studies in Chinese folk religion in Singapore and Malaysia. J. R. Clammer (ed). *Contributions to Southeast Asian ethnography*, no. 2. Singapore: National University of Singapore, 1983. 178p.

'Teams multiply churches in Malaysia/Singapore,' L. Childs, *Urban mission*, 2, 5 (May 1985), 33–39.

The 15th anniversary of the Lutheran Church in Malaysia & Singapore, 1963–1978. Selangor, Malaysia: Lutheran Church in Malaysia and Singapore, 1979. 46p. (Text in English and Chinese).

The 20th anniversary of the Lutheran Church in Malaysia & Singapore, 1963–1983. Kuala Lumpur: Academe Art & Printing, 1983. 48p.

'The administration of Islam in Singapore,' S. Siddique, in *Islam and society in Southeast Asia*, p.315–31. T. Abdullah & S. Siddique (eds). Singapore: Institute of Southeast Asian Studies, 1986.

'The church in West Malaysia and Singapore: a study of the Catholic Church in West Malaysia and Singapore regarding her situation as an indigenous church.' K. M. Williams. Ph.D. dissertation, Katholieke Universiteit te Leuven, 1976. 259p.

The march of Methodism in Singapore and Malaysia, 1885–1980. T. R. Doraisamy. Singapore: Methodist Book Room, 1982. 123p.

'The past contributions and future role of parachurch organizations in youth evangelism in Singapore.' A. Tan. M.A. thesis, Columbia Biblical Seminary and Graduate School of Missions, Columbia, SC, 1990. 152p.

The Portuguese missions in Malacca and Singapore (1511–1958). M. Teixeira. Lisbon: Agência Geral do Ultramar, 1961–1963. 3 vols.

The sociology of Singapore religion: studies in Christianity and Chinese culture. J. R. Clammer. *Asia Pacific monograph*, no. 4. Singapore: Chopmen Publishers, 1991. 125p.

'Towards a culturally relevant strategy of evangelism and church planting for Baptists among English–speaking Chinese in urban Singapore.' C. C. Carroll. Ph.D. dissertation, Southwestern Baptist Theological Seminary, Fort Worth, TX, 1989. 373p.

Country Table 2. **Organized churches and denominations in Singapore.**

Official name (bold type = church with over 10% of all affiliated) 1	*Begun* 2	*Type* 3	*Counc* 4	*Congs* 5	*Adults* 6	*Affiliated 1970* 7	*Affiliated 1995* 8	*G%* 9	*Names, notes, and other statistics* (see Codebook, Part 3) 10
Anglican Church: D Singapore	1826	A-Cen	awRAW	24	10,657	10,000	30,700	4.59	Language 60% English,34% Chinese,6% Tamil. 14n,16x,1u(5),W=50%,117Y,150y.
Apostolic Church of Singapore	1961	I-3aI	.....	3	500	200	1,000	6.65	South Indians, Chinese. Malayalam, Hokkien, English. 1n,1x,W=59%,13Y,11z.
Armenian Apostolic Church	c1850	O-Arm	Ew...	1	50	100	150	1.64	*Ch of St Gregory the Illuminator.* Few services, but still legally registered.
Assemblies of God	1933	P-Pe2	ZF...	36	17,332	4,000	25,119	7.63	*Elim Ch.* M=AoG(USA). One of fastest-growing bodies. 36n,10x,6f,1p,33z.
Assembly Hall Churches	c1970	I-3nC	.....	1	450	–	1,000	31.83	*Local Churches. Little Flock.* Chinese. Begun 1922 in China.
Batak Christian Protestant Church	1948	P-Lut	Lwe..	1	200	200	500	3.73	*Independent Lutheran Ch. Huria Kristen Batak Protestan. HKBP.* Bataks (Indonesia).
Bible Church	1958	I-Non	.....	5	300	300	600	2.81	Begun by Singaporeans. Till 1964, Sunday Bible School (SBS). Help from M=OMF.
Bible Presbyterian Churches	1950	I-Ref	.TT.T	25	6,079	2,000	13,500	7.94	Schism from Chinese Christian Ch. Official dissolution 1988.
Brethren Assemblies	1856	I-CBr	x....	20	5,243	5,000	10,500	3.01	*Gospel Halls.* Congs: 8 English,4 Hokkien,3 Malay,1 Cantonese. 18m,3f,W=69%,180Y.
Calvary Charismatic Centre	c1970	I-3dZ	.....	10	3,000	–	5,000	40.59	Centres in UK, Zambia, Malaysia, Brunei, USA, and 7 other countries. Nominally in AoG.
Cath Ch: AD Singapore (Malacca)	1511	R-Lat	pzF.P	30	70,000	80,000	132,425	2.04	70% Chinese. (1970) C=5+3+7. 37n, 3500Yy. (1990) , 74n, 36x, 100m, 226w, 4092Yy
Christian Assembly	1935	I-Non	.....	2	500	1,000	1,500	1.64	Independent congregation, Services in English, Mandarin, Hokkien, In Singapore 9.
Church of Christ of Malaya	1949	I-Non	.....	1	200	400	400	0.00	Independent church with work in Malaysia also. Services in Hakka, Mandarin.
Church of Christ, Scientist		m-Sci	x....	1	20	50	50	0.05	*Christian Science.* M=CCS(Boston USA). Singapore Society, in Singapore 10.
Ch of Jesus Christ of Latter-day Saints		m-LdS	x....	5	980	100	1,400	0.05	*Mormons.* M=CJCLdS(USA). Mainly USA expatriates. In Singapore 10.
Church of Singapore	1963	I-3cC	.....	4	1,000	700	2,000	4.29	Chinese charismatics, ex Brethren. House church. By 1978, 1,000 baptized. W=50%.
Churches of Christ	1956	I-Dis	x....	13	1,000	1,500	2,200	1.54	M=CC(Non-Instrumental) (USA). English, Mandarin, Cantonese services. 1p.
CNEC Churches	1951	P-Non	.F...	11	1,107	550	2,460	6.18	*Christian National Evangelism Commission. Keristen Nasionals Pengar Injil.* 5 schools. 2n,3x.
Evangelical Free Ch of Singapore	1957	I-Con	KF...	12	980	300	2,300	8.49	M=EFC of Canada. 2 organized churches; preaching points in Malaysia. 4f.
Evangelize China Fellowship	1951	I-Non	x....	2	200	100	400	5.70	Begun in China by a Chinese. M=ECF(HQ, USA). HQ Singapore 13. 3f.
Faith Community Baptist Church	1986	I-3kC	.....	20	12,000	–	23,000	11.11	*FCBC.* Schism ex Singapore Baptist Convention. F=Lawrence Khong. Large, cell-based.
Fisherman of Christ Church	1957	I-Non	.....	3	200	300	500	2.06	Indigenous church. Services in Mandarin and English. Located in Singapore 1 & 7.
Jehovah's Witnesses	1912	m-Jeh	x....	10	500	300	1,000	4.93	*Watch Tower. IBSA.* Small but active group, in Singapore districts 9 & 11. Banned 1971. 37Y.
Korean charismatic churches	c1980	I-3fK	.....	4	280	–	400	6.67	Full Gospel, Presbyterian background.
Lutheran Church: Singapore District	1966	P-Lut	L...W	6	1,910	800	3,180	5.68	M=ULCA(now LCA, USA). Chinese, Indians. 15f,1u.
Mar Thoma Syrian Church in Singapore	1936	I-ReO	xwe.W	2	450	600	1,130	2.56	In D Bahya Kerala (Outside Kerala). Malayali Indians. Declining. 1n,2x,W=60%,10Yy.
Methodist Church in Singapore	1885	P-Met	VuE.W	39	21,707	15,000	46,200	4.60	M=UMC(USA), 13f/MMS(UK)2f. A=1968. Confs: Engl, Chinese, Tamil. G=2.6%pa,74(1800),1u.
Orthodox Syrian Church in Singapore	1958	O-SyM	Dwe.W	1	770	102	1,150	10.18	In Diocese of Bahya Keralam (Outside Kerala). Syrians from South India. 1b.
Pentecostal Church of Malaya	1936	I-3pI	Z....	1	300	400	500	0.90	*CPM.* M=Ceylon Pentecostal Mission (Sri Lanka). Tamil-speaking. In Singapore 12.
Pentecostal Evangelical Churches	1957	P-Pe2	Z....	20	2,000	1,000	3,000	4.49	*Glad Tidings Free Pente Ch.* M=FFFM(Finland),GTMS(Canada). 1n,W=42%,34Y,15z.
Presbyterian Church in Singapore	1819	P-Ref	R...W	36	6,000	5,817	7,964	1.26	*Chinese Christian Ch.* Autonomous 1975. M=LMS,PCE. 12n,5x,1u,W=43%,198Yy.
Presbytery of Malaysia & Singapore	1851	P-Ref	Rw..W	1	60	100	150	1.64	*Presbyterian Ch of England.* Chaplaincy for British expatriates.
Salvation Army	1935	P-Sal	xwE.W	6	2,200	1,000	2,790	4.19	*Kiu Se Kun* (Amoy), *Kau Shai Kwan* (Cantonese). S & Malaysia Command. 20n,1s.
Seventh-day Adventist Church	1904	P-Adv	x....	7	2,072	3,000	3,450	0.56	*Gereja Maschi Advent Hari Ketujah.* In Malaya Mis, Southeast Asia UM. 65f,1H,1j,4r.
Singapore Baptist Convention	1937	P-Bap	T....	30	6,264	3,000	15,700	6.84	Begun by Chinese from South China. 1950, M=SBC(USA). 2 schools. 6n,20f,64Y.
Tabernacle Church and Missions	1975	I-3cC	.....	2	935	–	1,700	5.00	Schism ex CNEC/Bartley Christian Ch.
Trinity Bible Centre	c1980	I-3dZ	.....	5	1,000	–	2,000	6.67	Network, also in AoG. Own seminary, overseas missions program.
True Jesus Church	1927	I-3oC	x....	15	2,000	1,500	3,000	2.81	*Gereja Isa Benar Abadi.* Chinese; begun 1917 in China. Services in Mandarin.
Other independent charismatic chs	c1970	I-3cC	.....	10	3,000	–	8,000	43.26	Including: New Apostolic Church (81 members), JILF (Philippines).
Other Chinese indigenous churches		I-3cC	.....	40	2,000	2,000	5,000	0.05	Total about 15 (see list below).
Other Protestant denominations		P-	.....	3	3,100	1,000	4,000	0.05	Total about 12 (see list below).
Other marginal Protestant bodies		m-	.....	15	600	200	1,000	0.05	Including Asia HQ of Branhamites (Local Believers, End Time Believers) from USA.
Totals				**483**	**189,146**	**142,619**	**368,018**		

Churches, members, growth, 1900-2025	*Congs*	*Adults*	*Affiliated*	*G%*	*Total denominations*	*6 Megablocs:* O	R	A	P	I	m
Total churches, members, and denominations (mid-1900)	20	4,800	8,550	4.10	7	1	1	1	3	1	0
Total churches, members, and denominations (mid-1970)	271	79,603	142,619	4.10	48	2	1	1	16	21	7
Total churches, members, and denominations (mid-1990)	320	167,000	324,700	4.20	90	2	1	1	23	50	13
Total churches, members, and denominations (mid-1995)	483	189,146	368,018	2.54	91	2	1	1	23	51	13
Total churches, members, and denominations (mid-2000)	520	207,000	402,936	1.83	92	2	1	1	23	52	13
Total churches, members, and denominations (mid-2025)	1,000	318,000	618,000	1.73	272	10	1	1	40	200	20

NOTES ON TABLE ABOVE

NATIONAL COUNCILS (Column 4, 5th letter).

- E = Evangelical Fellowship of Singapore (EFOS)
- P = Catholic Bishops' Conference of Malaysia-Singapore.
- T = Malaysia Council of Christian Churches (Singapore & Malaysia).
- W = National Council of Churches of Singapore (until 1975 'of Malaysia & Singapore').

OTHER CHINESE INDIGENOUS CHURCHES. There are numerous independent congregations, as well as groupings. These include: Ch of God in Singapore, Free Christian Ch, Jehovah True God Ch, Jesus Saves Mission (1964), Revival Centre Ch (1953), Singapore Ch (Independent).

OTHER PROTESTANT DENOMINATIONS. Including Baptist Bible Fellowship International (1968), Ch of the Nazarene (1972), Overseas Missionary Fellowship (1951; 31 missionaries, but not church-planting), Religious Society of Friends (Quakers) (1958), Voice of China & Asia Missionary Society, Worldwide Evangelization Crusade, World-Wide Missions (1961).

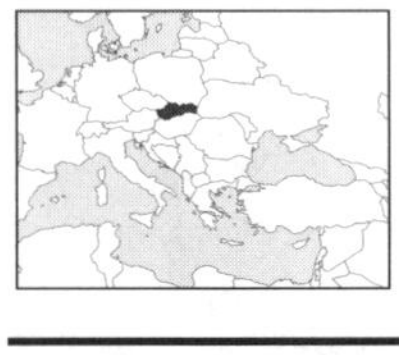

SLOVAKIA

SECULAR DATA, AD 2000

STATE

Official name: Slovenská Republika (The Slovak Republic).
Short name: Slovakia. **Adjective of nationality:** Slovak.
Flag: White, blue, and red stripes with shield on left.
Area: 49,035 sq. km. (18,933 sq. mi.).
Government: Unitary multiparty republic with one legislative house, since 1992 (1918 republic created, 1946 one-party Communist state).
Legislature: National Council, 150 members.
Official language: Slovak.
Monetary unit: 1 Slovak koruna (Sk) = 100 halura. **US$1=** Sk 34.84.
Chief cities: BRATISLAVA 457,521; Kosice 243,387; Nitra 93,159; Presov 90,983; Banska Bystrica 88,101.
Political divisions: 4 provinces.
Armed forces: 36,000.

DEMOGRAPHY

Population: 5,387,000.
Population density: 109.8/sq. km. (284.5/sq. mi.).
Under 15 years: 1,060,000.
Growth rate p.a.: 0.15% (births 11.13, deaths 9.63).
Mortality: Infant, per 1,000: 10.2; **Maternal per 100,000:** 17.0.
Life expectancy: 74 (male 70, female 78).
Household size: 3.0. **Floor area per person, sq.m:** 22.3.
Major languages: Slovak-Hungarian, Czech.
Urban dwellers: 61.11%. **Urban growth rate p.a.:** 0.9%.
Labor force: 47%.

ETHNOLINGUISTIC PEOPLES

83.7% Slovak; 11.1% Hungarian; 1.1% Carpathian Gypsy; 1.1% Czech (Bohemian); 0.6% Slovak Gypsy.

ECONOMY

National income p.a. per person: US$2,949; **per family:** US$8,849.

EDUCATION

Adult literacy: 100% (male 100%, female 100%). **Schools:** 3,386.
Universities: 14. **School enrolment:** female/male: 0%/0%.

HEALTH

Access to health services: 65%. **Access to safe water:** 90%.
Hospitals: 111 (91 beds per 10,000). **Doctors:** 15,767.
Blind: 4,500. **Deaf:** 322,300. **Murder rate:** 2.
Lepers: 700.

LITERATURE

New book titles p.a.: 3,930 (730 p.a. per million). **Periodicals:** 594.
Newspapers: 21 dailies.

COMMUNICATION (per 1,000 people)

Phones: 208 (23% mobile). **Radios:** 118. **TV sets:** 216.
Daily newspaper circulation: 256. **Computers:** 112.

REFUGEES

Alien refugees from other countries: 1,600.

HUMAN LIFE AND LIBERTY (optimum condition=100.0%)

HDI: 87.3. **HSI:** 60.0. **HFI:** 25.0. **EFL:** 41.0.

Country Table 1. Religious adherents in Slovakia, AD 1900-2025.

Year	1900		1970		mid-1990		Annual change, 1990-2000				mid-1995		mid-2000		mid-2025	
Name	Adherents	%	Adherents	%	Adherents	%	Natural	Conversion	Total	Rate	Adherents	%	Adherents	%	Adherents	%
Christians	**3,950,840**	**97.1**	**3,873,300**	**85.5**	**4,397,800**	**83.7**	**10,981**	**10,284**	**21,265**	**0.47**	**4,536,000**	**84.7**	**4,610,452**	**85.6**	**4,770,800**	**88.5**
PROFESSION																
crypto-Christians	0	0.0	861,200	19.0	0	0.0	0	0	0	0.00	0	0.0	0	0.0	0	0.0
professing Christians	**3,950,840**	**97.1**	**3,012,100**	**66.5**	**4,397,800**	**83.7**	**10,981**	**10,284**	**21,265**	**0.47**	**4,536,000**	**84.7**	**4,610,452**	**85.6**	**4,770,800**	**88.5**
AFFILIATION																
unaffiliated Christians	200,000	4.9	0	0.0	125,800	2.4	314	15,733	16,047	8.57	263,398	4.9	286,266	5.3	277,800	5.2
affiliated Christians	**3,750,840**	**92.2**	**3,873,300**	**85.5**	**4,272,000**	**81.3**	**10,667**	**-5,408**	**5,219**	**0.12**	**4,272,602**	**79.8**	**4,324,186**	**80.3**	**4,493,000**	**83.3**
Roman Catholics	3,445,840	84.7	3,533,058	78.0	3,620,000	68.9	9,022	-5,003	4,019	0.11	3,651,552	68.2	3,660,186	67.9	3,700,000	68.6
Protestants	300,000	7.4	806,900	17.8	588,000	11.2	1,466	-266	1,200	0.20	557,050	10.4	600,000	11.1	720,000	13.4
Independents	0	0.0	102,100	2.3	25,000	0.5	62	-262	-200	-0.83	24,000	0.5	23,000	0.4	23,000	0.4
Orthodox	5,000	0.1	216,000	4.8	23,000	0.4	57	-257	-200	-0.91	22,000	0.4	21,000	0.4	20,000	0.4
Marginal Christians	0	0.0	5,000	0.1	16,000	0.3	40	360	400	2.26	18,000	0.3	20,000	0.4	30,000	0.6
doubly-affiliated	0	0.0	-789,758	-17.4	0	0.0	0	0	0	0.00	0	0.0	0	0.0	0	0.0
Trans-megabloc groupings																
Evangelicals	50,000	1.2	160,000	3.5	120,000	2.3	299	-799	-500	-0.42	110,493	2.1	115,000	2.1	135,000	2.5
Pentecostals/Charismatics	0	0.0	2,500	0.1	231,000	4.4	576	924	1,500	0.63	235,362	4.4	246,000	4.6	300,000	5.6
Great Commission Christians	**81,000**	**2.0**	**181,000**	**4.0**	**630,000**	**12.0**	**1,570**	**11,630**	**13,200**	**1.92**	**700,000**	**13.1**	**761,996**	**14.2**	**870,000**	**16.1**
Nonreligious	5,160	0.1	400,000	8.8	636,350	12.1	1,586	-7,928	-6,342	-1.04	608,150	11.4	572,928	10.6	495,500	9.2
Atheists	2,000	0.1	250,200	5.5	216,300	4.1	539	-2,391	-1,852	-0.89	205,000	3.8	197,779	3.7	120,000	2.2
Jews	110,000	2.7	4,000	0.1	4,650	0.1	12	8	20	0.42	4,800	0.1	4,848	0.1	5,000	0.1
Baha'is	0	0.0	0	0.0	400	0.0	1	26	27	5.25	550	0.0	667	0.0	1,000	0.0
Muslims	0	0.0	500	0.0	500	0.0	1	1	2	0.33	500	0.0	517	0.0	700	0.0
World A (unevangelized persons)	40,680	1.0	226,423	5.0	63,072	1.2	157	-3,922	-3,765	-8.70	37,482	0.7	26,935	0.5	21,572	0.4
World B (evangelized non-Christians)	76,480	1.9	428,737	9.5	795,128	15.1	1,982	-6,362	-4,380	-0.59	781,169	14.6	749,613	13.9	600,628	11.1
World C (Christians)	3,950,840	97.1	3,873,300	85.5	4,397,800	83.7	10,981	10,284	21,265	0.47	4,536,000	84.7	4,610,452	85.6	4,770,800	88.5
Country's population	**4,068,000**	**100.0**	**4,528,460**	**100.0**	**5,256,000**	**100.0**	**13,120**	**0**	**13,120**	**0.25**	**5,354,652**	**100.0**	**5,387,000**	**100.0**	**5,393,000**	**100.0**

COLUMNS, ROWS.
For meanings and definitions, see Codebook (Part 3). Note that, by definition, total 'Christians' = professing + crypto-Christians, which also = affiliated + unaffiliated Christians, and also = Great Commission Christians + latent Christians. Percentages may not always total exactly, due to rounding.

CENSUSES.
3.III.1991: 70.9% Roman Catholic, 15.9% nonreligious, 9.5% Protestants (7.3% Slovak Evangelicals), 3.4% Greek Catholics, 0.2% marginal Christians (Jehovah's Witnesses), 0.1% other religionists.

NOTES ON RELIGIONS
BAHA'IS. In 1995 Slovakia had 3 local spiritual assemblies.

Great Commission Instrument Panel: status of Slovakia (for explanation see start of Part 4)

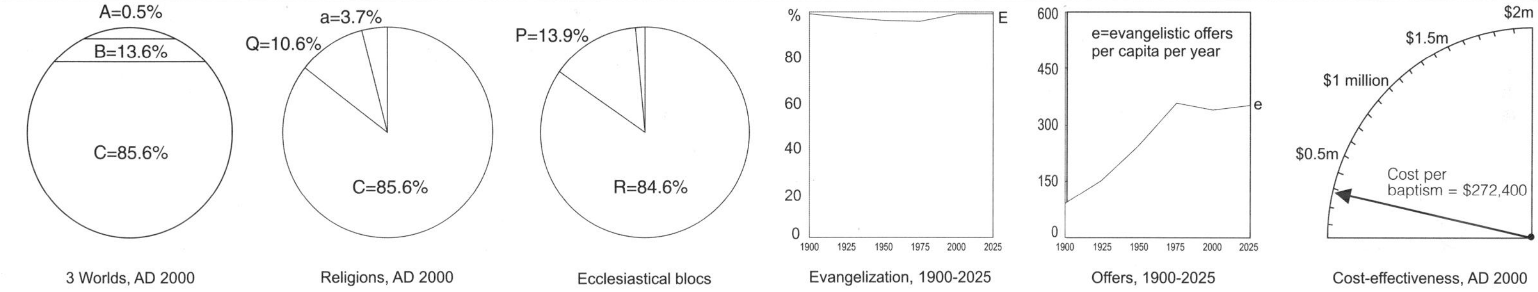

Country status. Slovakia, a former republic of Czechoslovakia, is a mountainous country in central Europe. Its chief exports are minerals including iron ore, copper, and mercury.

HUMAN LIFE AND LIBERTY

Human rights and freedoms. Slovakia became an independent republic on 1 January 1993 following the dissolution of the Czech and Slovak Federated Republic (CSFR). Even before the dissolution CSFR had dismantled much of the repressive security and legal apparatus and other paraphernalia of the old Communist regime. Among the minor problems that remain the most serious is the discrimination against Romanians, Hungarians, and other minorities. The government also has adversarial relations with the media and periodically tries to clamp down on journalists. The press is free and the Constitution prohibits censorship. But the media do their work as a watchdog so well that it provokes government ire occasionally. Anti-government newspapers tend to lose subsidies, and editors who do not hew the official line may tend to lose their jobs as well. The government is encouraging ethical self-regulation by journalists, an ominous term suggestive of self-censorship. Under existing law, only registered churches and religious organizations may conduct worship services or engage in educational, cultural, and social welfare activities. The state provides subsidies to such organizations. To receive subsidies, churches must have at least 20,000 adult members permanently resident in Slovakia. The Law on Reconciliation passed in 1991 calls for the return of all confiscated properties to the respective churches.

NON-CHRISTIAN RELIGIONS

Atheism and ***agnosticism*** have been significant forces in Slovakian life, especially prior to the collapse of communism in former Czechoslovakia in 1989. Communist Party membership already started decreasing prior to 1989, from 20% of the population in 1948 to 12% in the 1960s and 8% in the 1970s, with 7.3% of the population being atheist. In 1995, only 3.8 % of Slovakia's population described themselves as being atheist.

Judaism decreased in number by more than 85% as a result of the Nazi massacres of the 1930s and 1940s, and again decreased after 1989 because of the increased freedom for Jews to emigrate to Israel.

CHRISTIANITY

CATHOLIC CHURCH. Catholicism remains the majority religion of Slovakia in spite of the impediments imposed on it by the former Communist regime. Religious orders were dissolved in 1950 and were able to reconstitute themselves somewhat only in 1968. This included the creation of Czech and Slovak committees of religious congregations. However, since the fall of the Dubcek regime, they were again suppressed. Since the fall of communism the church has been freed from government and party controls. Theology faculties and seminaries have been reopened, and formerly banned religious orders have resumed parish, educational, and social work. Archbishop Jan Sokol has issued a call to bar the doors of seminaries to the West to prevent liberal theology from entering.

Typically Carpathian wooden church in Lietava, eastern Slovakia.

The Holy See has diplomatic relations with Slovakia and in AD 2000 is represented to government and the Catholic hierarchy by a nuncio residing in Bratislava.

A major ecumenical problem can be found in East Slovakia. In 1950 the 9,000 Orthodox were implicated in the suppression of the 225,000-strong Greek Catholic Church. The Prague Spring of 1968 brought partial rehabilitation of the Catholics, with the Orthodox returning more than 200 churches to their original occupants. In 1990 the Slovak government under pressure from the Greek Catholic Bishop Jan Hirta granted total restitution but also provided modest subsidies to enable the Orthodox to build new churches. Most church buildings were returned to the Catholic community, but this has not gone without dispute and in 1995, 20 churches had still not been handed over.

LUTHERAN CHURCH. Lutheranism is the predominant Protestant tradition in Slovakia, with the largest body being the Slovak Evangelical Church of the Augsburg Confession. The Reformed Christian Church in Slovakia was created in 1918 after Slovakia was severed from the Hungarian empire, and the Hungarian and Slovak languages are accorded equal status in the liturgical and administrative life of the church.

Indigenous missions. Many missionaries were sent out from Slovakia in the 5th century, after the introduction of Christianity to the region. These were successively under the guidance of Rome or Constantinople. Missions reached its apex under Cyril and Methodius. Later, under Protestant reform, new waves of missionaries were sent out. Roman Catholic and Protestant mission-sending slowed considerably under Communist rule in the 20th century.

Renewal movements. Renewal movements. In the 1990s the Pentecostal/Charismatic Renewal continued to spread rapidly across most older churches, and numbered over 246,000 adherents (of whom 2% Pentecostals, 96% Charismatics, and 2% Independents).

Country summary. **Worlds A, B, C by ethnolinguistic peoples, cities, and major civil divisions in Slovakia.**

	PEOPLES							CITIES							CIVIL DIVISIONS						
World	*Num*	*Pop 2000*	*C%*	*Christians*	*E%*	*U%*	*Unevangelized*	*Num*	*Pop 2000*	*C%*	*Christians*	*E%*	*U%*	*Unevangelized*	*Num*	*Pop 2000*	*C%*	*Christians*	*E%*	*U%*	*Unevangelized*
A	1	5,387	0.50	27	39	61	3,313	0	0	0.00	0	0	0	0	0	0	0.00	0	0	0	0
B	2	26,936	50.00	13,468	99	1	135	0	0	0.00	0	0	0	0	0	0	0.00	0	0	0	0
C	16	5,354,867	80.50	4,310,691	100	0	21,901	11	1,363,700	80.36	1,095,811	100	0	4,776	4	5,387,191	80.27	4,324,186	100	0	25,349
Total	**19**	**5,387,190**	**80.27**	**4,324,186**	**100**	**0**	**25,349**	**11**	**1,363,700**	**80.36**	**1,095,811**	**100**	**0**	**4,776**	**4**	**5,387,191**	**80.27**	**4,324,186**	**100**	**0**	**25,349**

CHURCH AND STATE

In 1969 the then Czechoslovakian Ministry of Culture published the 'Plan for limiting the activity of the Churches of Slovakia'. As a whole, this document indicates the will of the state in relation to the churches following the liberalization of 1968, especially a return to a stricter application of the laws of 1948-50 which were created for the purpose of forcing an exclusively religious character on the churches. Since 1989, with the Communist Party and government restrictions on churches and religious orders abolished, freedom of religion exists in Slovakia.

Catholic Church in Slovakia. Presov Church, on a 1943 postage stamp

BROADCASTING AND MEDIA

AWR leases a shortwave transmitting station in Slovakia which reaches most of Europe, Africa, Southern Asia, and the Middle East in 17 languages. Shortwave radio programs in European languages can also be received from KNLS, TWR (Monaco, Albania), and HCJB (Ecuador). Christian television programming can be received via satellite.

Some 582,000 have seen the 'Jesus' Film, most in cinematic showings.

FUTURE TRENDS AND PROSPECTS

In the wake of the collapse of Communism, Christians are expected to grow beyond 88% by AD 2025.

Christianity could grow well beyond 90% of the population as the nonreligious and atheists continue their decline throughout the 21st century. By AD 2050, Slovakia could be 95% Christian.

BIBLIOGRAPHY

Cesta kríza. A. Habovstiak. Trnava: Konfederácia politickych väznov Slovenska vo vyd-ve KON-PRESS, 1992. 120p.

'Christianity and national heritage among the Czechs and Slovaks,' P. Ramet, in *Religion and nationalism in Soviet and East European politics*, p.264–285. P. Ramet (ed). 2d ed. Durham, NC: Duke University Press, 1989.

Christians and churches in Socialist countries: report of a visit by church leaders from South East Asia and Australia. J. S. Udy. Delhi: ISPCK, 1982. 204p.

Church and state in Czechoslovakia: historically, juridically, and theologically documented. L. Nemec. New York: Vantage Press, 1955. 577p.

Church in a Marxist society: a Czechoslovak view. J. M. Lochman. New York: Harper & Row, [1970]. 198p.

Cirkev v dejinách Slovenska. J. C. Korec. Bratislava: Lúc, 1994. 800p.

'Czechoslovakia,' E. Kadlecovà, in *Western religion: a country by country sociological enquiry*, p.117–134. H. Mol (ed). The Hague: Mouton, 1972.

Czechoslovakia. D. Short. *World bibliographical series*, vol. 68. Oxford, UK: CLIO Press, 1986. 411p. (See especially 'Religion and theology,' p.103–8).

'Czechoslovakia: a church reborn in resistance,' G. Weigel, in *The final revolution: the resistance church and the collapse of Communism*, p.159–90. New York: Oxford University Press, 1992.

Die evangelischen Karpatendeutschen aus der Slowakei. A. Hudak, K. Kautz & E. Streck. *Die Unverlierbarkeit evangelischen Kirchentums aus dem Osten*, Bd. 2, Heft 2. Düsseldorf: Unser Weg, 1972. 50p.

Directorium officii divini persolvendi sacrique peragendi pro anno domini MCMLXXIX: in usum cleri omnium diocesium Slovaciae ab excellentissimis dominis ordinariis approbatum, continens propria necnon speciales instructiones. Bratislava: Spolok sv. Vojtecha, 1979. 308p.

Fellowship of service: life and work of Protestant churches in Czechoslovakia. D. Capek (ed). Prague: Ecumenical Council of Churches, 1961. 152p.

Freedom denied: Czechoslovakia after Helsinki. A. Hlinka. Trans., H. E. Oborg. [1977]. 36p.

Icons in Czechoslovakia. H. Skrobucha. London: Hamlyn, 1971. 155p.

Lutherans in Slovakia. A. A. Skodacek. 1982. 259p.

Our Lady of Hostyn: queen of the Marian Garden of the Czech, Moravian, Silesian and Slovak Madonnas. L. Nemec. New York: RCH Press, 1981. 171p.

Pilgrims. M. Luskacová. London: Victoria and Albert Museum, 1983. 48p. (Photographic collection, especially of religious life of East Slovakia).

Politics and religion in Eastern Europe: Catholicism in Hungary, Poland, and Czechoslovakia. P. Michel. Oxford, UK: Polity, 1991. 329p.

Prague winter: restrictions on religious freedom in Czechoslovakia twenty years after the Soviet invasion. Washington, DC: Puebla Institute, 1988. 59p.

Religion in Czechoslovakia. M. Navrat. Prague: Orbis Books, 1984. 108p.

Slovak bishops: martyrs of Christ. T. J. Zubek. Toronto: Canadian Slovak League, 1963. 16p.

Slovak Lutheran liturgy: past and present. A. A. Skodacek. [1968]. 212p.

Slovenská evanjelická cirkev a.v. J. Kmet. Prague: SPVC MK CSR, 1982. 146p.

SS. Cyril and Methodius among the Slovaks: observing the 1,000 anniversary of Saint Methodius' death. I. Kruzliak & F. L. Mizenko (eds). Saginaw, MI: Slovak Catholic Federation, 1985. 282p.

The development of church organization in Slovakia. J. Tomko. 1979. 86p.

'The forced liquidation of the Union of Uzhorod. Part II: The destruction of the diocese of Presov,' M. Lacko, *Slovak studies* (Rome), 1 (1961), 145–85.

'The Lutheran reformation in Slovakia, 1517–1618.' D. P. Daniel. Thesis, Pennsylvania State University, State College, PA, 1972. 348p.

'The Orthodox Church in Czechoslovakia,' G. Novak, *Orthodoxy*, (1964), 240–52.

'The position of the church in Czechoslovakia,' *Pro Mundi Vita* (Brussels), Special note 28 (1973).

'The re–establishment of the Greek Catholic Church in Czechoslovakia,' M. Lacko, *Slovak studies* (Rome), 11 (1971), 159–89.

'The religious situation in Czechoslovakia,' M. Kalinovska, *Religion in Communist lands*, 5, 3 (Autumn 1977), 148–57.

Yesterday and today: a survey of Czechoslovak Protestantism. Prague: Preparatory Committee, Ecumenical Council of Churches in Czechoslovakia, 1955. 56p.

Yugoslavia inferno: ethnoreligious warfare in the Balkans. P. Mojzes. 1994.

Country Table 2. **Organized churches and denominations in Slovakia.**

Official name (bold type = church with over 10% of all affiliated) 1	*Begun* 2	*Type* 3	*Counc* 4	*Congs* 5	*Adults* 6	*Affiliated 1970* 7	*Affiliated 1995* 8	*G%* 9	*Names, notes, and other statistics* (see Codebook, Part 3) 10
Baptist Union of Slovakia	1885	P-Bap	Tv..W	20	2,100	6,000	5,500	-0.35	*Ustredi Bratrske-Jednoty-Baptistu.* Slovaks. 12n,50m.
Catholic Church in Slovakia:	828	R-Lat	B....	1,427	2,914,870	3,533,058	3,651,552	0.09	Formerly in Czechoslavakia. 1420n 420x 814m 2659w 60653Yy
M Bratislava-Trnava	1922	R-Lat	Bs	469	955,900	1,415,910	1,190,169	-0.69	Many small villages, traditionally Catholic. 395n 198x 360m 1042w 18949Yy
D Banska Bystrica	1776	R-Lat	Bs	128	226,000	327,224	323,045	-0.05	Traditional Catholicism, declining. 132n 19x 37m 304w 5798Yy
D Kosice	1804	R-Lat	Bs	189	465,200	561,900	579,167	0.12	Eastern Slovakia. 50% Hungarians. 221n 49x 111m 283w 10313Yy
D Nitra	880	R-Lat	Bsj	159	627,900	636,309	781,693	0.09	Northwest Slovakia. Small villages, mountains. 190n 72x 132m 554w 10583Yy
D Roznava	1776	R-Lat	Bs	94	134,100	212,437	167,000	-0.96	Southeast Slovakia. 68n 18x 37m 68w 2926Yy
D Spis	1776	R-Lat	Bs	159	322,300	369,278	401,288	0.33	Northern Slovakia. Germans, Ruthenians. 210n 30x 66m 276w 8689Yy
D Presov (Prjasev, *Slovak*)	1818	R-Slo	os	229	150,000	10,000	209,190	12.93	'Church of Silence' liquidated 1945-50. 204n 34x 71m 132w 3395Yy
Evangelical Church of Czech Brethren	c1370	P-LuR	RWC.W	100	30,000	100,000	60,000	-2.02	*Ceskobratrska Circev Evangelicka.* Mainly urban.
Hussite Church of Slovakia	1920	I-ReC	.WC.W	100	13,000	100,000	20,000	-6.23	*Cirkev Husitska.* Los von Rom.
Isolated radio churches	c1950	I-3rW	.....	100	1,500	500	2,000	5.70	Believers through radio programs.
Jehovah's Witnesses	1912	m-Jeh	x....	120	11,000	5,000	18,000	5.26	*Watch Tower.* 1.7 million hours of preaching. (1995)814Y.
New Apostolic Church	c1890	I-3aX	x....	2	540	600	700	0.62	M=NAC/NAK. *Neuapostolische Kirche* (HQ Zurich).
Old Catholic Church in Slovakia	1898	I-OCa	U...W	3	500	1,000	1,000	0.00	*Starokatolicka Cirkev.* 1945 German members deported.
Orthodox Church of Slovakia:	1863	O-Slo	MWC.W	12	11,000	216,000	22,000	-8.73	*Cirkev Pravoslavna.*
D Mikhailov	1950	O-Slo	Mb	10	10,000	40,000	20,000	-2.73	East Slovakia. Gained from Catholic Uniates.
D Presov	1949	O-Slo	Mb	2	1,000	176,000	2,000	-16.40	1950, Greek Catholics forcibly annexed to Orthodoxy. 77n.
Pentecostal Movement	1917	P-Pe2	ZF...	95	3,200	1,000	4,250	0.05	Begun Novi Sad (Kosice) by returning deportee. M=AoG(USA,UK,France)..
Reformed Christian Ch in Slovakia	1918	P-Ref	RWC.f	403	40,000	165,000	120,000	-1.27	Mostly farmers with Hungarian origins.
Seventh-day Adventist Church	1919	P-Adv	x....	6	600	1,000	1,000	0.00	M=SDA(USA,UK,Germany). Union Conference.
Silesian Ev Ch of Augsburg Confession	1528	P-Lut	LWC.W	5	5,000	20,000	10,000	-2.73	*Slezka Cirkev Evangelicka Augsburskeho Vyznami.* Polish speaking.
Slovak Calvinist Church		P-Ref	.....	61	14,600	–	20,000	0.05	Reformed tradition and polity.
Slovak Ev Ch of Augsburg Confession	1530	P-Lut	LWC.f	327	271,000	510,000	330,000	-1.73	Main Lutheran body in Slovakia.
United Methodist Church	1930	P-Met	VwC.W	3	2,000	2,500	3,500	1.35	*Ev Cirkev Metodisticka.*
Unity of Brethren	1457	P-Mor	xv..W	2	700	1,000	2,200	3.20	*Jednota Bratrska. Moravian Church.*
Other Protestant denominations		P-	.....	33	400	400	600	0.05	In about 10 denominations with Czech roots.
Other independent charismatic chs	1988	I-3cW	.....	100	200	–	300	14.29	In 20 loose geographical networks or associations.
Doubly-affiliated		2-aff			0	-789,758	0		Protestants and Independents who are also baptized Catholics.
Totals				**2,919**	**3,340,402**	**3,873,300**	**4,272,602**		

Churches, members, growth, 1900-2025	*Congs*	*Adults*	*Affiliated*	*G%*	*Total denominations*	*6 Megablocs:* O	R	A	P	I	m
Total churches, members, and denominations (mid-1900)	2,000	2,721,000	3,750,840	0.05	10	1	1	0	6	2	0
Total churches, members, and denominations (mid-1970)	2,797	2,809,270	3,873,300	0.05	20	1	1	0	13	4	1
Total churches, members, and denominations (mid-1990)	2,850	3,340,000	4,272,000	0.49	45	1	1	0	19	23	1
Total churches, members, and denominations (mid-1995)	2,919	3,340,402	4,272,602	0.00	47	1	1	0	20	24	1
Total churches, members, and denominations (mid-2000)	3,100	3,381,000	4,324,186	0.24	49	1	1	0	21	25	1
Total churches, members, and denominations (mid-2025)	3,300	3,513,000	4,493,000	0.15	110	6	1	0	30	70	3

NOTES ON TABLE ABOVE
NATIONAL COUNCILS (Column 4, 5th letter).
E = Evangelical Alliance of Slovakia (EAS).
W = Ecumenical Council of Churches in Slovakia (ECCS).

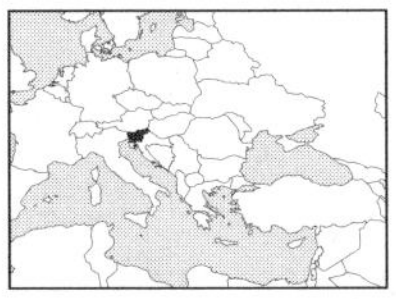

SLOVENIA

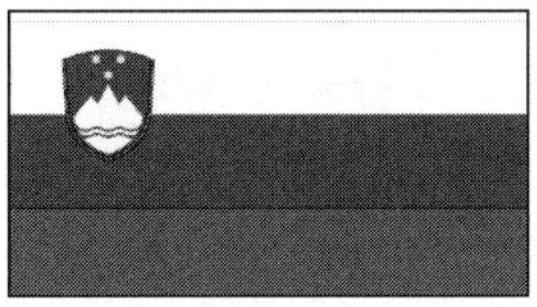

SECULAR DATA, AD 2000

STATE
Official name: Republika Slovenija (The Republic of Slovenia).
Short name: Slovenia. **Adjective of nationality:** Slovene.
Flag: White, blue, and red stripes with coat of arms in upper left.
Area: 20,256 sq. km. (7,821 sq. mi.).
Government: Unitary multiparty republic with two legislative houses, since 1990 (1918 kingdom of Serbs, Croats, and Slovenes, 1929 Yugoslavia).
Legislature: National Council, 40 members, National Assembly, 90 members.
Official language: Slovene.
Monetary unit: 1 Slovene tolar (SIT; plural tolarji) = 100 stotin. **US$1=** 158.77 tolarji.
Chief cities: LJUBLJANA 324,767; Maribor (Marburg) 192,487.
Political divisions: 12 provinces.
Armed forces: 10,000.

DEMOGRAPHY
Population: 1,986,000.
Population density: 98.0/sq. km. (253.8/sq. mi.).
Under 15 years: 316,000.
Growth rate p.a.: -0.11% (births 8.87, deaths 10.50).
Mortality: Infant, per 1,000: 6.4; **Maternal per 100,000:** 13.0.
Life expectancy: 75 (male 71, female 79).
Household size: 3.1. **Floor area per person, sq.m:** 21.0.
Major languages: Slovenian, Serbo-Croatian, German.
Urban dwellers: 52.61%. **Urban growth rate p.a.:** 0.4%.
Labor force: 48%.

ETHNOLINGUISTIC PEOPLES
89.8% Slovene; 4.9% Croat; 1.2% Austrian; 0.9% German; 0.6% Serb.

ECONOMY
National income p.a. per person: US$8,200; **per family:** US$25,420.

EDUCATION
Adult literacy: 99% (male 100%, female 100%). **Schools:** 1,067.
Universities: 28. **School enrolment:** female/male: 90%/90%.

HEALTH
Access to health services: 75%. **Access to safe water:** 95%.
Hospitals: 24 (58 beds per 10,000). **Doctors:** 4,086.
Blind: 1,600. **Deaf:** 114,800. **Murder rate:** 4.
Lepers: 1,000.

LITERATURE
New book titles p.a.: 3,570 (1,800 p.a. per million). **Periodicals:** 675.
Newspapers: 6 dailies.

COMMUNICATION (per 1,000 people)
Phones: 309 (11% mobile). **Radios:** 320. **TV sets:** 374.
Daily newspaper circulation: 183. **Computers:** 100.

REFUGEES
Alien refugees from other countries: 24,000.

HUMAN LIFE AND LIBERTY (optimum condition=100.0%)
HDI: 88.6. **HSI:** 55.0. **HFI:** 25.0. **EFL:** 33.0.

Country Table 1. **Religious adherents in Slovenia, AD 1900-2025.**

Year	1900		1970		mid-1990		Annual change, 1990-2000				mid-1995		mid-2000		mid-2025	
Name	Adherents	%	Adherents	%	Adherents	%	Natural	Conversion	Total	Rate	Adherents	%	Adherents	%	Adherents	%
Christians	**956,000**	**100.0**	**1,549,000**	**92.8**	**1,745,358**	**91.0**	**6,144**	**2,268**	**8,412**	**0.47**	**1,819,860**	**91.5**	**1,829,481**	**92.1**	**1,705,850**	**93.8**
PROFESSION																
crypto-Christians	0	0.0	130,000	7.8	0	0.0	0	0	0	0.00	0	0.0	0	0.0	0	0.0
professing Christians	**956,000**	**100.0**	**1,419,000**	**85.0**	**1,745,358**	**91.0**	**6,144**	**2,268**	**8,412**	**0.47**	**1,819,860**	**91.5**	**1,829,481**	**92.1**	**1,705,850**	**93.8**
AFFILIATION																
unaffiliated Christians	48,000	5.0	192	0.0	73,058	3.8	259	1,703	1,962	2.41	89,868	4.5	92,675	4.7	94,850	5.2
affiliated Christians	**908,000**	**95.0**	**1,548,808**	**92.8**	**1,672,300**	**87.2**	**5,885**	**566**	**6,451**	**0.38**	**1,729,992**	**86.9**	**1,736,806**	**87.5**	**1,611,000**	**88.6**
Roman Catholics	906,000	94.8	1,477,000	88.5	1,597,000	83.3	5,618	583	6,201	0.38	1,654,049	83.1	1,659,006	83.5	1,520,000	83.6
Protestants	1,000	0.1	35,030	2.1	32,500	1.7	115	-165	-50	-0.15	32,743	1.7	32,000	1.6	35,000	1.9
Independents	0	0.0	5,600	0.3	29,000	1.5	103	97	200	0.67	29,700	1.5	31,000	1.6	40,000	2.2
Orthodox	1,000	0.1	30,200	1.8	11,500	0.6	41	9	50	0.43	11,000	0.6	12,000	0.6	12,000	0.7
Marginal Christians	0	0.0	978	0.1	2,300	0.1	8	42	50	1.99	2,500	0.1	2,800	0.1	4,000	0.2
Trans-megabloc groupings																
Evangelicals	800	0.1	6,200	0.4	12,900	0.7	46	44	90	0.68	13,526	0.7	13,800	0.7	17,400	1.0
Pentecostals/Charismatics	0	0.0	4,000	0.2	53,700	2.8	190	1,390	1,580	2.61	64,953	3.3	69,500	3.5	90,900	5.0
Great Commission Christians	**38,000**	**4.0**	**117,000**	**7.0**	**240,000**	**12.5**	**851**	**1,584**	**2,435**	**0.97**	**255,000**	**12.8**	**264,345**	**13.3**	**270,000**	**14.9**
Nonreligious	0	0.0	69,900	4.2	111,900	5.8	397	-1,363	-966	-0.90	111,000	5.6	102,239	5.2	79,400	4.4
Atheists	0	0.0	50,000	3.0	59,192	3.1	210	-930	-720	-1.29	57,400	2.9	51,990	2.6	30,000	1.7
Muslims	0	0.0	1,000	0.1	1,350	0.1	5	3	8	0.58	1,380	0.1	1,430	0.1	2,000	0.1
Baha'is	0	0.0	0	0.0	100	0.0	0	20	20	11.50	250	0.0	297	0.0	600	0.0
Jews	0	0.0	100	0.0	100	0.0	0	2	2	1.75	110	0.0	119	0.0	150	0.0
World A (unevangelized persons)	0	0.0	66,789	4.0	3,836	0.2	13	0	13	0.34	3,980	0.2	3,972	0.2	1,818	0.1
World B (evangelized non-Christians)	0	0.0	53,940	3.2	168,806	8.8	599	-2,268	-1,669	-1.01	166,160	8.3	152,547	7.7	110,332	6.1
World C (Christians)	956,000	100.0	1,549,000	92.8	1,745,358	91.0	6,144	2,268	8,412	0.47	1,819,860	91.5	1,829,481	92.1	1,705,850	93.8
Country's population	**956,000**	**100.0**	**1,669,730**	**100.0**	**1,918,000**	**100.0**	**6,756**	**0**	**6,756**	**0.35**	**1,990,000**	**100.0**	**1,986,000**	**100.0**	**1,818,000**	**100.0**

COLUMNS, ROWS.
For meanings and definitions, see Codebook (Part 3). Note that, by definition, total 'Christians' = professing + crypto-Christians, which also = affiliated + unaffiliated Christians, and also = Great Commission Christians + latent Christians. Percentages may not always total exactly, due to rounding.

NOTES ON RELIGIONS
BAHA'IS. In 1996 Slovenia had 2 local spiritual assemblies.
MUSLIMS. Serbs and Bosnian Muslims.
PENTECOSTALS/CHARISMATICS. The Catholic Charismatic Renewal began in Slovenia in 1992, with over 1,000 participating in cathedral meetings. By 1997 there were 15 regular weekly prayer groups in the capital Lubljana

Great Commission Instrument Panel: status of Slovenia (for explanation see start of Part 4)

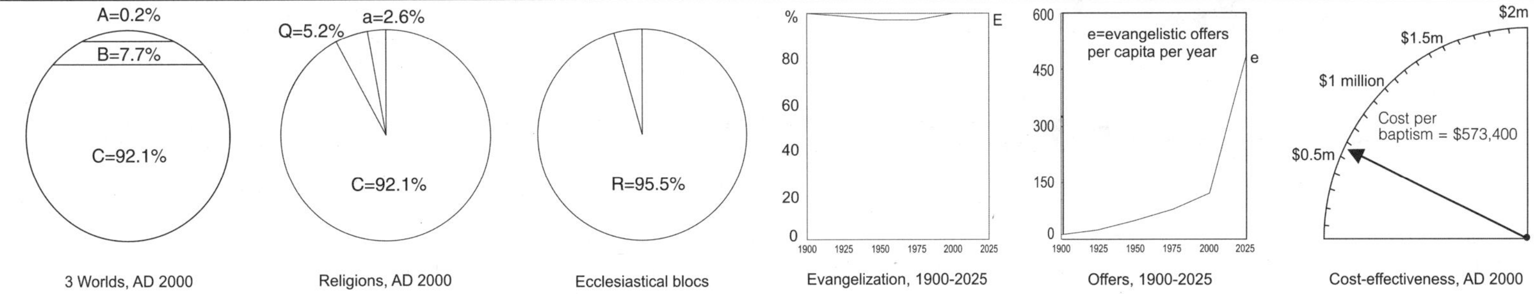

Country status. Slovenia, a former republic of the Yugoslavia, is a semimountainous state in central Europe bordered by Austria. It economy is based on its mineral resources including oil, coal, lead, and mercury. Tourism is also important.

HUMAN LIFE AND LIBERTY

Human rights and freedoms. Slovenia won its independence from the Socialist Federal Republic of Yugoslavia in 1991. Apart from a brief 10-day war, it has been relatively free of strife ever since. Slovenia is a functioning multiparty democracy without any major human rights problems. The Italian and Hungarian minorities as well as the Gypsies enjoy Constitutional protection. Legacies of the old Communist regime include a timid press. Spared the tragedies of the Bosnian conflict, Slovenia has granted political asylum to over 75,000 refugees, many of them Muslims.

CHRISTIANITY

Christianization of the Slovenes began in the 8th century, while Church organization in Slovenia was established during the 10th and 11th centuries. As Christianization spread, a network of parishes and dioceses evolved, with 2 archdioceses, Salzburg and Aquileia, including most of the lands with a Slovene population.

CATHOLIC CHURCH. The Catholic Church in Slovenia has been under Austrian influence in the past.

The education of Slovenes was closely connected to the Catholic Church from the early Middle Ages until almost the 20th century. During the period of the

Catholic Church. A noted Bishop of Maribor, A. M. Slomsek (1800-1862).

Country summary. **Worlds A, B, C by ethnolinguistic peoples, cities, and major civil divisions in Slovenia.**

	PEOPLES							CITIES							CIVIL DIVISIONS						
World	Num	Pop 2000	C%	Christians	E%	U%	Unevangelized	Num	Pop 2000	C%	Christians	E%	U%	Unevangelized	Num	Pop 2000	C%	Christians	E%	U%	Unevangelized
A	0	0	0.00	0	0	0	0	0	0	0.00	0	0	0	0	0	0	0.00	0	0	0	0
B	1	3,971	32.99	1,310	62	38	1,509	0	0	0.00	0	0	0	0	0	0	0.00	0	0	0	0
C	14	1,981,585	87.58	1,735,495	100	0	2,424	2	517,254	89.37	462,281	100	0	849	12	1,985,557	87.47	1,736,806	100	0	3,933
Total	**15**	**1,985,556**	**87.47**	**1,736,805**	**100**	**0**	**3,933**	**2**	**517,254**	**89.37**	**462,281**	**100**	**0**	**849**	**12**	**1,985,557**	**87.47**	**1,736,806**	**100**	**0**	**3,933**

'second Yugoslavia', the communist republic under president Tito, official adherence to the Catholic faith declined. A public opinion poll conducted in 1968 showed one-third of the population as traditional believers, one-third as non-conformist believers, and one-third as non-believers.

With the independence of Slovenia, the Catholic Church in Slovenia has once again started growing with currently 86.9% of the population being Catholic. The Slovene ecclesiastical province, established in 1968, encompasses the entire republic and consists of the Archdiocese of Ljubljana, and the dioceses of Maribor and Koper – altogether 66 deaneries and 792 parishes. Twelve male and 16 female religious orders were active in Slovenia in 1992.

The Holy See has diplomatic relations with Slovenia and in AD 2000 is represented to government and the Catholic hierarchy by a nuncio residing in Lubljana.

LUTHERAN CHURCH. The Evangelical Christian Church in Slovenia, which has its headquarters in Lendava and the majority of its parishes in the Prekmurje region, served as a Lutheran refuge during the Counter Reformation.

Indigenous missions. Christians were sent out from Slovenia shortly after the gospel arrived there in the early Christian centuries. Missionary activity increased along with influence from Constantinople. After Cyril and Methodius more missionaries were sent to surrounding countries. This continued through the 20th century, even under Communist rule. In the 1990s Roman Catholic missionaries form the bulk of the foreign missionary force sent out from Slovenia.

Renewal movements. In the 1990s the Pentecostal/Charismatic Renewal continued to spread rapidly across most older churches, and numbered over 69,000 adherents (of whom 1% Pentecostals, 52% Charismatics, and 47% Independents).

Meeting to elect board members for newly-formed Bible Society, Ljubljana, 1993.

CHURCH AND STATE

Social and political changes since Slovenia declared its independence have provided a freer atmosphere for Church activities. The new constitution provides for freedom of religion and guarantees churches the right to engage in a broad range of religious and secular activities.

BROADCASTING AND MEDIA

Shortwave radio programs in European languages can be received from AWR (Slovakia), TWR (Monaco, Albania), and HCJB (Ecuador). IBRA programs can be heard over local radio via Novomesto. Christian television programming can be received via satellite.

FUTURE TRENDS AND PROSPECTS

Few changes are expected in the religious situation in Slovenia in the next 30 years except for slight declines among the nonreligious and atheists and a slight increase among Christians.

The nonreligious and atheists could decline to less than 6% jointly before the middle of the 21st century. Christianity could grow to 95% of the population by AD 2050.

BIBLIOGRAPHY

'A history of Baptists in Yugoslavia, 1862–1962.' J. D. Hopper. Ph.D. dissertation, Southwestern Baptist Theological Seminary, Fort Worth, TX, 1977. 180p.
'A history of the Congregational and Methodist Churches in Bulgaria and Yugoslavia.' P. B. Mojzes. Ph.D. dissertation, Boston University, Boston, 1965. 674p.
'Changing functions of religion in a socialist society: the case of Catholicism in Yugoslavia,' S. Vrcan, *Social compass*, 28, 1 (1981), 43–61.
Church and state in Yugoslavia since 1945. S. Alexander. Cambridge, UK: Cambridge University Press, 1979. 351p.
'Church–state relations in Yugoslavia since 1967,' S. Alexander, *Religion in Communist lands*, 4, 1 (Spring 1976), 18–27.
'Denominational affiliation in Yugoslavia, 1930–1989,' S. Flere, *East European quarterly*, 25 (June 1991), 145–65.
Der Christliche Kulturverband bei den Kärntner Slowenen im Wandel der Zeit. P. Fantur (ed). *Veröffentlichungen des Internationalen Forschungszentrum für Grundfragen der Wissenschaften Salzburg*, n.F., Bd. 52. Innsbruck: Tyrolia, 1992. 292p.
In the claws of the red dragon: ten years under Tito's heel. W. Gruber. Toronto: St. Michaelswerk, 1988. 208p.
'Islam in Yugoslavia today,' S. Ramet, *Religion in Communist lands*, 18, 3 (Autumn 1990), 226–35.
Istria religiosa. P. Blasi & P. Zovatto. Trieste: [il Centro], 1989. 290p.
'La situación religiosa en Yugoslavia,' G. Canders, *Revista de estudios politicos*, 161 (1968), 259–67.
Nations and nationalities of Yugoslavia. K. Joncic (ed). Belgrade: Medjunarodna politika, 1974. 549p.
'Nature et structure de la religiosité en Slovénie,' Z. Roter, in *Religion and religiosity, atheism and non-belief in industrial and urban society*, p.145–67. J. Rouleau et al. Lille: Éditions C.I.S.R., 1971. (English and French).
Of whom the world was not worthy. M. Chapian. Minneapolis, MN: Bethany Fellowship, 1978. 256p. (Case studies of Christian witness in Yugoslavia during WW II).
Opci sematizam katolicka crkve u Jugoslaviji, cerkerv Jugoslaviji, 1974 (General survey of the Catholic Church in Yugoslavia). Zagreb: Biskupska konferencija Jugoslavije, 1975. 1,166p. (Parts in Croat, Slovenian, Latin, English, French, German).
'Our true Christianity—today and tomorrow,' F. Rode, *Religion in Communist lands*, 11, 2 (Summer 1983), 217–21. (Deals with Catholic Church in Slovenia).
'Recent developments in church–state relations in Yugoslavia,' C. Criic, *Religion in Communist lands*, 1, 1 (Spring 1973), 6–8.
'Religion and nationality in Yugoslavia,' P. Ramet, in *Religion and nationalism in Soviet and East European politics*, p.299–327. P. Ramet (ed). 2nd ed. Durham, NC: Duke University Press, 1989.
'Religion in Yugoslavia: the background,' J. Broun, *America*, 165 (November 30, 1991), 414–16.
Religions in Yugoslavia: historical survey, legal status, church in socialism, ecumenism, dialogue between Marxists and Christians, etc. Z. Frid (ed). Zagreb: Binoza, 1971. 168p.
Religious art in Slovenia. J. Anderlic & M. Zadnikar. : Ognjisce Koper, 1986. 272p.
Slovenska katoliska obzorja: izbor esejev, razprav, clankov. F. M. Dolinar. Buenos Aires: Slovenska kulturna akcija, 1990. 715p.
Slovenska kultura in versko izkustvo. T. Kermauner. Koper: TD Ognjisce, 1991. 191p.
'Some social expectations of Christians in Yugoslavia with primary emphasis on the Protestant churches,' N. G. Shenk, *Occasional papers on religion in Eastern Europe*, 1 (November 1981), 1–10.
'The Gypsy population of Yugoslavia,' T. P. Vukanovic, *Journal of the Gypsy Lore Society*, 42, 1/2 (1963), 10–27.
'The position of believers as second–class citizens in Socialist countries: the case of Yugoslavia,' Z. Roter, *Occasional papers on religion in Eastern Europe*, 9 (June 1989), 1–17.
The position of the Church in Yugoslavia. R. Vidic. Belgrade: Izdavac, 1962.
The Protestant movement of Slovenes in Pannonia. F. Sebjanic. Murska Sobota, Yugoslavia: Pomurska Zalozba, 1978. 60p.
'The social role of religion in contemporary Yugoslavia.' N. G. Shenk. Ph.D. dissertation, Northwestern University, Evanston, IL, 1987. 264p.
Thoughts of a Czech pastor. J. L. Hromádka. London: Student Christian Movement Press, 1970. 123p.
'Yugoslavia,' A. Fiamengo, in *Western religion: a country by country sociological enquiry*, p.587–99. H. Mol (ed). The Hague: Mouton, 1972.
Yugoslavia. J. J. Horton. 2nd ed. *World bibliographical series*, vol. 1. Oxford, UK: CLIO Press, 1990. 304p. (See especially 'Religion,' p.72f, and 'Nationalities,' p.97–103).
Yugoslavia: a comprehensive English–language bibliography. F. Friedman (ed). Wilmington, DE: Scholarly Resources, Inc., 1993. 547p. (Section on 'Religion,' p.453–61).
Yugoslavia inferno: ethnoreligious warfare in the Balkans. P. Mojzes. , 1994.
Yugoslavia: the church and the state. London: Information Office, Embassy of the Federal People's Republic of Yugoslavia, 1953. 92p.
'Yugoslavie aujourd'hui: une église entre l'est et l'ouest,' *Information catholique internationale* (Paris), 400 (January 1972), 7–15.

Country Table 2. **Organized churches and denominations in Slovenia.**

Official name (bold type = church *with over 10% of all affiliated)* 1	*Begun* 2	*Type* 3	*Counc* 4	*Congs* 5	*Adults* 6	*Affiliated 1970* 7	*Affiliated 1995* 8	*G%* 9	*Names, notes, and other statistics* (see Codebook, Part 3) 10
Catholic Church in Slovenia:	c500	R-Lat	B....	849	1,149,000	1,477,000	1,654,049	0.07	Majority church now freed of politics. 829n 247x 381m 939w 18248Yy
M Ljubljana	1461	R-Lat	Bs	356	495,000	660,000	702,922	0.25	Capital city. 352n 146x 236m 699w 7999Yy
D Koper (Capodistria)	c 550	R-Lat	Bs	207	142,000	102,075	208,599	2.90	Part of D Trieste (Italy) from 1828-1977. 166n 22x 28m 83w 1974Yy
D Maribor (Lavant)	1228	R-Lat	Bs	286	512,000	714,925	742,528	0.15	Formerly Lavant. 87% Catholic. 311n 79x 117m 157w 8275Yy
Christian Adventist Church in Slovenia	1909	P-Adv	x....	93	3,318	5,230	5,110	-0.09	*CACS.* Seventh-day Adventists.
Christian Brethren	1905	P-CBr	.....	2	50	140	100	-1.34	Open Brethren (Plymouth Brethren).
Church of United Brethren in Christ	1900	P-LuR	Rwc..	2	130	250	200	-0.89	*Ceskobratrska Cirkev Ev.* Moravians. *Unitas Fratrum.* Slovaks living in Slovenia.
Evangelical Christian Ch in Slovenia	1540	P-Lut	L...W	30	7,600	25,170	19,000	-1.12	*ECCS. Evangelical Ch of the Augsburg Confession.*
Gypsy Evangelical Movement	c1965	I-3pE	.....	20	1,500	500	2,000	5.70	Gypsy independent church, pentecostal basis.
Isolated radio churches	c1950	I-3rW	.....	500	13,000	3,000	25,000	8.85	Believers due to radio programs (house churches); also 3 independent charismatic chs.
New Apostolic Church	c1960	I-3aX	x....	4	500	100	1,000	9.65	*NAK. Neuapostolische Kirche.* HQ Zurich (Switzerland).
Old Catholic Church in Slovenia	1946	I-OCa	Uv...	3	850	2,000	1,700	-0.65	*OCCS.* Old Catholic Union of Utrecht.
Pentecostal Churches of Christ	c1965	P-Pe2	.....	16	1,680	50	2,833	11.91	*PCCs. Evangelical Church of Christ.* M=AoG.
Serbian Orthodox Church (M Zagreb)	1930	O-Ser	C....	10	5,000	30,000	9,000	-4.70	Remnant of former dominant church.
Ukrainian Orthodox Ch (P Kiev)	c1950	O-Ukr	.....	3	1,500	200	2,000	9.65	Ukrainian Church linked with P Moscow.
Union of Baptist Churches in Slovenia		P-Bap	.....	6	300	1,190	500	0.05	Mainline Baptists.
United Jehovah's Witnesses in Slovenia		m-Jeh	x....	29	1,496	978	2,500	0.05	*Watch Tower.* In 1995, 349,002 hours of preaching recorded. 87Y.
Other Protestant denominations		P-	.....	80	4,000	3,000	7,000	0.05	Total 25, including Christian Nazarene Community, Ch of God, Ch of the Spirit, Free Brethren.
Totals				**1,633**	**1,188,924**	**1,548,808**	**1,729,992**		

Churches, members, growth, 1900-2025	*Congs*	*Adults*	*Affiliated*	*G%*	*Total denominations*	*6 Megablocs:* O	R	A	P	I	m
Total churches, members, and denominations (mid-1900)	600	621,000	908,000	0.77	3	0	1	0	2	0	0
Total churches, members, and denominations (mid-1970)	1,017	1,059,014	1,548,808	0.77	25	2	1	0	17	4	1
Total churches, members, and denominations (mid-1990)	1,400	1,149,000	1,672,300	0.38	39	2	1	0	31	4	1
Total churches, members, and denominations (mid-1995)	1,633	1,188,924	1,729,992	0.68	39	2	1	0	31	4	1
Total churches, members, and denominations (mid-2000)	1,700	1,194,000	1,736,806	0.08	39	2	1	0	31	4	1
Total churches, members, and denominations (mid-2025)	1,800	1,107,000	1,611,000	-0.30	78	6	1	0	40	30	1

NOTES ON TABLE ABOVE
NATIONAL COUNCILS (Column 4, 5th letter).
W = Council of Christian Churches in Slovenia.

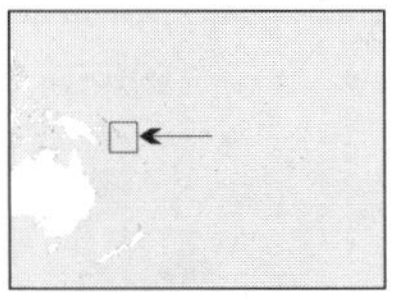

SOLOMON ISLANDS

SECULAR DATA, AD 2000

STATE
Official name: The Realm of the Solomon Islands.
Short name: Solomon Islands. **Adjective of nationality:** Solomon Islanders.
Flag: Two triangles with 5 stars.
Area: 28,370 sq. km. (10,954 sq. mi.).
Government: Parliamentary state (constitutional monarchy), since 1978 (1893 British protectorate, 1975 self-government, 1978 Independence).
Legislature: National Parliament, 50 members.
Official language: English.
Monetary unit: 1 Solomon Islands dollar (SI$) = 100 cents. **US$1=** S$4.99.
Chief cities: HONIARA 48,315.
Political divisions: 8 provinces.

DEMOGRAPHY
Population: 444,000.
Population density: 15.6/sq. km. (40.5/sq. mi.).
Under 15 years: 190,000.
Growth rate p.a.: 2.93% (births 33.00, deaths 3.73).
Mortality: Infant, per 1,000: 19.1; **Maternal per 100,000:** 70.0.
Life expectancy: 73 (male 71, female 75).
Household size: 5.6. **Floor area per person, sq.m:** 18.0.
Major languages: English, Pidgin English (Neo-Melanesian), Bambatana, Bugotu, Roviana, Nggela, Vaturanga, and about 85 other vernacular languages.
Urban dwellers: 19.67%. **Urban growth rate p.a.:** 5.8%.
Labor force: 14%.

ETHNOLINGUISTIC PEOPLES
8.0% Kwaraae; 7.0% Toambaita (Maluu, Mwala); 4.2% Kwaio; 4.2% Lau (Ndai); 4.0% Solomoni Creole.

ECONOMY
National income p.a. per person: US$910; **per family:** US$5,099.

EDUCATION
Adult literacy: 54% (male 62%, female 44%). **Schools:** 544.
Universities: 1. **School enrolment:** female/male: 58%/69%.

HEALTH
Access to health services: 60%. **Access to safe water:** 90%.
Hospitals: 8 (53 beds per 10,000). **Doctors:** 52.
Blind: 370. **Deaf:** 26,600. **Murder rate:** 10.
Lepers: 4,000. **Underweight prevalence under 5:** 21%.

LITERATURE
New book titles p.a.: 90 (200 p.a. per million). **Periodicals:** 11.
Newspapers: 2 dailies.

COMMUNICATION (per 1,000 people)
Phones: 17 (10% mobile). **Radios:** 117. **TV sets:** 16.
Daily newspaper circulation: 15. **Computers:** 50.

REFUGEES
Alien refugees from other countries: 1,000.

HUMAN LIFE AND LIBERTY (optimum condition=100.0%)
HDI: 55.6. **HSI:** 51.0. **HFI:** 30.0. **EFL:** 30.0.

Country Table 1. **Religious adherents in the Solomon Islands, AD 1900-2025.**

Year	1900		1970		mid-1990		Annual change, 1990-2000				mid-1995		mid-2000		mid-2025	
Name	Adherents	%	Adherents	%	Adherents	%	Natural	Conversion	Total	Rate	Adherents	%	Adherents	%	Adherents	%
Christians	**15,400**	**20.5**	**151,250**	**94.1**	**304,700**	**94.9**	**11,640**	**352**	**11,992**	**3.37**	**361,670**	**95.4**	**424,624**	**95.7**	**789,800**	**96.7**
PROFESSION																
professing Christians	**15,400**	**20.5**	**151,250**	**94.1**	**304,700**	**94.9**	**11,640**	**352**	**11,992**	**3.37**	**361,670**	**95.4**	**424,624**	**95.7**	**789,800**	**96.7**
AFFILIATION																
unaffiliated Christians	3,000	4.0	15,770	9.8	18,600	5.8	713	-431	282	1.42	19,137	5.1	21,421	4.8	46,300	5.7
affiliated Christians	**12,400**	**16.5**	**135,480**	**84.3**	**286,100**	**89.1**	**10,928**	**782**	**11,710**	**3.49**	**342,533**	**90.3**	**403,203**	**90.8**	**743,500**	**91.0**
Anglicans	12,000	16.0	50,000	31.1	115,000	35.8	4,407	1,043	5,450	3.96	142,000	37.5	169,503	38.2	323,000	39.5
Protestants	0	0.0	46,828	29.2	111,000	34.6	4,253	547	4,800	3.66	134,043	35.4	159,000	35.8	275,000	33.7
Roman Catholics	400	0.5	30,828	19.2	41,100	12.8	1,575	-885	690	1.56	43,743	11.5	48,000	10.8	90,000	11.0
Independents	0	0.0	4,878	3.0	15,000	4.7	575	175	750	4.14	18,667	4.9	22,500	5.1	50,000	6.1
Marginal Christians	0	0.0	2,946	1.8	4,000	1.3	153	-133	20	0.49	4,080	1.1	4,200	1.0	5,500	0.7
Trans-megabloc groupings																
Evangelicals	0	0.0	32,700	20.4	68,800	21.4	2,636	424	3,060	3.75	84,394	22.3	99,400	22.4	215,000	26.3
Pentecostals/Charismatics	0	0.0	5,200	3.2	41,900	13.1	1,606	404	2,010	4.00	51,361	13.6	62,000	14.0	125,000	15.3
Great Commission Christians	**2,300**	**3.1**	**8,000**	**5.0**	**40,000**	**12.5**	**1,533**	**456**	**1,989**	**4.12**	**49,000**	**12.9**	**59,890**	**13.5**	**120,000**	**14.7**
Ethnoreligionists	59,600	79.5	9,050	5.6	12,600	3.9	483	-370	113	0.86	12,900	3.4	13,726	3.1	15,300	1.9
Baha'is	0	0.0	400	0.3	1,450	0.5	56	-11	45	2.76	1,650	0.4	1,903	0.4	4,000	0.5
Buddhists	0	0.0	0	0.0	1,050	0.3	40	-4	36	2.96	1,200	0.3	1,405	0.3	2,500	0.3
Nonreligious	0	0.0	300	0.2	660	0.2	25	35	60	6.65	950	0.3	1,256	0.3	4,000	0.5
Muslims	0	0.0	0	0.0	440	0.1	17	-3	14	2.75	500	0.1	577	0.1	1,000	0.1
Atheists	0	0.0	0	0.0	100	0.0	4	1	5	4.21	130	0.0	151	0.0	400	0.1
World A (unevangelized persons)	57,000	76.0	803	0.5	642	0.2	25	-42	-17	-3.02	758	0.2	444	0.1	817	0.1
World B (evangelized non-Christians)	2,600	3.5	8,618	5.4	15,658	4.9	600	-310	290	1.92	16,715	4.4	18,932	4.2	26,383	3.2
World C (Christians)	15,400	20.5	151,250	94.1	304,700	94.9	11,640	352	11,992	3.37	361,670	95.4	424,624	95.7	789,800	96.7
Country's population	**75,000**	**100.0**	**160,672**	**100.0**	**321,000**	**100.0**	**12,265**	**0**	**12,265**	**3.30**	**379,144**	**100.0**	**444,000**	**100.0**	**817,000**	**100.0**

COLUMNS, ROWS.
For meanings and definitions, see Codebook (Part 3). Note that, by definition, total 'Christians' = professing + crypto-Christians, which also = affiliated + unaffiliated Christians, and also = Great Commission Christians + latent Christians. Percentages may not always total exactly, due to rounding.

CENSUSES.
1.XI.1959 (non-representative sample census): 48% Protestants (27% South Sea Ev Mission, 14% Methodists, 7% SDAs), 34% Anglicans, 14% Roman Catholics, 4% ethnoreligionists. **9.II.1970:** 37.6% Protestants (17.2% SSEC, 11.2% United Church, 9.2% SDAs), 33.5% Anglicans, 18.9% Roman Catholics, 4.8% ethnoreligionists (called in census 'heathen'), 2.8% Solomoni indigenous (Christian Fellowship Church), 1.8% marginal Protestants (Jehovah's witnesses), 0.2% nonreligious, 0.2% Baha'is, 0.2% other religionists. **1976:** 38.9% Protestants (16.9% SSEC, 11.3% United Church, 9.7% SDAs), 34.2% Anglicans, 18.7% Roman Catholics, 2.5% Independent Christians (Christian Fellowship Church), 1.8% marginal Christian (Jehovah's Witnesses), 0.4% Baha'is, 0.8% nonreligious, 2.7% ethnoreligionists. **1986:** 39.7% Protestants (17.7% SSEC, 11.0% United Church, 10.0% SDAs), 33.9% Anglicans, 19.2% Roman Catholics, 2.5% Independent Christians (Christian Fellowship Church), 1.8% marginal Christians (Jehovah's Witnesses), 0.4% Baha'is, 0.4% nonreligious, 2.1% ethnoreligionists.

NOTES ON RELIGIONS
BAHA'IS. Since beginning in 1954, there has been rapid growth from 8 local spiritual assemblies (1964) to 50 (1973). Then expansion mushroomed to 55 LSAs by 1996.
ETHNORELIGIONISTS. Animists, or adherents of custom (customary beliefs); 10,000 on Malaita mostly in the bush, and about 500 on Guadalcanal. This category, in both past and present, also covers the over 12 distinct non-Christian cargo cults (movements of revitalization based on traditional religion).
INDEPENDENTS. In 4 denominations in 1995 (see Table 2).
NONRELIGIOUS. Expatriates, mostly Europeans and Chinese in the towns.

Great Commission Instrument Panel: status of the Solomon Islands (for explanation see start of Part 4)

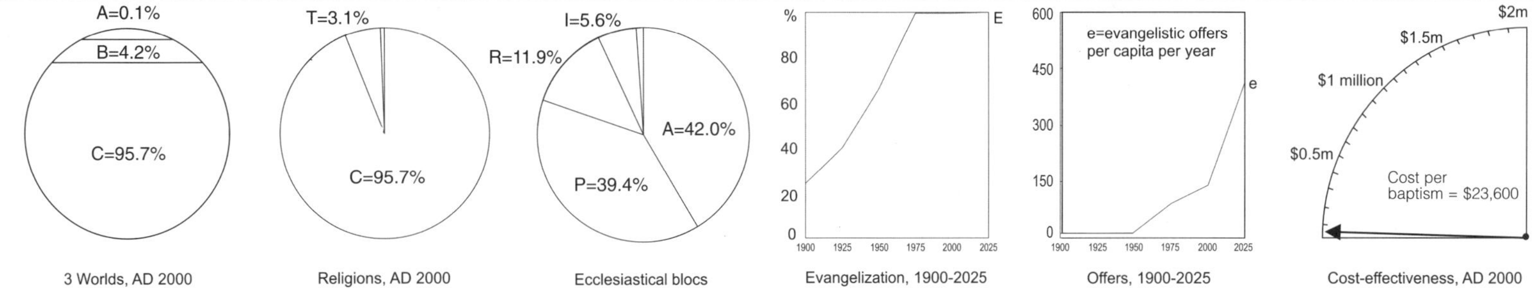

Country status. Solomon Islands is a sparsely-populated archipelago of densely forested, mountainous tropical islands about 1,000 miles northeast of Australia in the Pacific Ocean. Its chief exports are timber and copra.

HUMAN LIFE AND LIBERTY

Human need and development. Life in the Solomon Islands is leisurely. Most islanders work only intermittently and few work for the cash economy. They live in widely scattered settlements along the coast and engage in subsistence agriculture. The prevalence of numerous diseases has not made any impact on the growth of population because the birth rates are high. Population explosion has produced overcrowded conditions and has led to a deterioration in environmental sanitation and living standards in general. Traditional diets have changed since independence, and now consists increasingly of imported and canned foods. The change in diet has brought about malnutrition and tooth decay. As in the rest of Oceania, the scarcity of fresh water is a major problem and is an incidental cause for the decline in environmental sanitation.

Human rights and freedoms. Almost all basic human rights are provided for in the Constitution and respected by the authorities. Discrimination and violence against women and some restrictions on the press are the only blemishes on this record. The actual exercise of rights is monitored by an official ombudsman.

Human environment. Soil erosion is widespread on farming lands, particularly on steep slopes and clear-

Country summary. **Worlds A, B, C by ethnolinguistic peoples, cities, and major civil divisions in the Solomon Islands.**

	PEOPLES							CITIES							CIVIL DIVISIONS						
World	Num	Pop 2000	C%	Christians	E%	U%	Unevangelized	Num	Pop 2000	C%	Christians	E%	U%	Unevangelized	Num	Pop 2000	C%	Christians	E%	U%	Unevangelized
A	0	0	0.00	0	0	0	0	0	0	0.00	0	0	0	0	0	0	0.00	0	0	0	0
B	1	2,928	41.91	1,227	100	0	3	0	0	0.00	0	0	0	0	0	0	0.00	0	0	0	0
C	75	440,721	91.21	401,983	100	0	463	1	48,315	84.00	40,585	100	0	237	8	443,643	90.88	403,203	100	0	471
Total	**76**	**443,649**	**90.88**	**403,210**	**100**	**0**	**466**	**1**	**48,315**	**84.00**	**40,585**	**100**	**0**	**237**	**8**	**443,643**	**90.88**	**403,203**	**100**	**0**	**471**

ings in forests. Careless logging operations are damaging large areas of forests. Enforcement of environmental regulations is deficient in forest areas, and there is no adequate effort to replant cleared forests.

NON-CHRISTIAN RELIGIONS

Traditional tribal religions recognize the existence of a supreme being called Banara on Vella Lavella, Banara la'ata on Choiseul and Koevasi (who is female) on Guadalcanal. Although active in creation, the supreme being is little recognized and seldom worshiped. Attention is focused instead on departed ancestors and free spirits which were never human, as well as mana the impersonal power which pervades all things and may be manipulated for good or evil purposes. The desire for mana is the explanation for many of the customs of the islanders such as the collection of skulls and cannibalism. Mana is also fundamental for understanding sorcery, the antisocial side of magic, which is widely believed in. Other spirits are Nanama (those possessed of special power), Ndave (warrior spirits), Vi'ona (female snake spirits), Vaurangga (shark spirits) and clan spirits; the general term for spirits is Anggalo. Movements of revitalization based on traditional religion have been numerous.

Passion Play enacted by combined churches of Honiara, at Easter 1966.

CHRISTIANITY

PROTESTANT CHURCHES. There are 4 Protestant churches in the islands which together make up 35% of the population (1995). Over one-third of all Protestants (13% of the population) belong to the South Sea Evangelical Church, which owes its origin to the evangelization of Solomon Islands sugar plantation workers in Queensland (Australia) as early as 1882. SSEM missionaries from Australia first arrived in Malaita in 1904. The church is found mainly on Malaita, Guadalcanal, San Cristobal, Rennell, and Bellona. The United Church is a union of Methodists and Congregationalists; it is found in all parts of the Solomons but is strongest in the western islands. Seventh-day Adventists (9%) are concentrated on New Georgia, Guadalcanal, and Malaita and are also present on Rennell and Bellona.

Protestants sponsor 170 primary schools and 3 secondary schools, 4 hospitals, one maternity hospital, 9 clinics, a vocational training school, and various development projects and publications.

ANGLICAN CHURCH. Anglicans belong since 1975 to the province of Melanesia, previously a missionary diocese of the Church of the Province of New Zealand and now with 3 dioceses and a fourth for the New Hebrides. In 1995, they were the largest single religious body with 37% of the population. The church is strongest in the eastern islands: Santa Isabel, Malaita, Guadalcanal, and San Cristobal. Anglicans and Roman Catholics pioneered in education at the end of the 19th century; the first government school was not begun until after World War I. There are 100 Anglican primary schools, a secondary school and a teacher training college; a number of church schools are now being handed over to the government. Medical and social service institutions include 2 hospitals, one clinic, a leprosarium, and several community development centers.

Church of Melanesia. St. Barnabas cathedral, Honiara.

CATHOLIC CHURCH. The first Catholics were Marist priests in 1845, but the mission later had to be abandoned. Begun again, a prefecture was established in 1897 and elevated to a vicariate in 1912. Since 1966, the church has been organized into 2 jurisdictions, the diocese of Gizo in the western Solomons and the diocese of Honiara in the southern islands. Catholics in 1995 formed 11.5% of the population of the islands.

The Holy See has diplomatic relations with Solomon Islands and in AD 2000 is represented to government and the Catholic hierarchy by a nuncio residing in Port Moresby, Papua.

INDIGENOUS CHURCHES. The largest indigenous movement is the Christian Fellowship Church, also know as Etoism after its founder-messiah Silas Eto. It was the result of a schism on New Georgia from the former Methodist Church during 1959-61. Members number 4.9% of the population of the islands. They operate 11 primary schools.

Indigenous missions. After the early penetration of Christianity to the islands, Christians could be found working all over the Pacific spreading the gospel. By the 1970s, over 140 Solomon Islanders had served overseas as foreign missionaries. Today they can be found in Oceania, Asia, North America, and Europe.

CHURCH AND STATE

Guadalcanal was first discovered in 1568, but it was not considered an important island by Europeans during several subsequent centuries. The British declared a protectorate over the islands in 1893. There is no established church in the territory, and freedom of religion is protected. Since World War II, a number of religio-political bodies (notably the Pokokogoro Cult, Marching Rule and Hahalis Welfare Movement) have come into conflict with the government over the question of native rule. Internal self-rule was granted in November 1975 with full independence following in 1978.

BROADCASTING AND MEDIA

Shortwave radio programs from KNLS have seen some response. Two-thirds of the country have viewed the 'Jesus' Film through film team presentations. Solomon Islands is a member of UNDA. Catholics air a 5 minute devotional each morning and evening, and a 30-minute topical sermon one Sunday a month.

INTERDENOMINATIONAL ORGANIZATIONS

The Solomon Islands Christian Association was formed in 1967 with Anglican, Catholic, and United churches as members. The Solomon Islands Region of the United Church also belongs to the Melanesian Council of Churches (which covers Papua New Guinea and the Solomon Islands). The South Sea Evangelical Church is a member of the Evangelical Alliance of Papua New Guinea and the Solomon Islands and also an observer member of SICA.

FUTURE TRENDS AND PROSPECTS

Ethnoreligionists, 80% of the population in 1900, are expected to decline to less than 2% by AD 2025. Christianity will likely grow to over 96% in the same period.

If tribal religions continue their decline through the 21st century, Christians would continue to claim more than 98% of the population by AD 2050.

BIBLIOGRAPHY

'Catholic missions in the Solomon Islands.' H. M. Laracy. Ph.D. dissertation, Australia National University, Canberra, 1970.

'Comparative analysis of nativistic movements,' chapter 14 in *Solomon Islands Christianity: a study in growth and obstruction*, p.201–16. A. R. Tippett. New York: Friendship Press, 1967.

'Crisis and mass conversion on Rennell Island in 1938,' T. Monberg, *Journal of the Polynesian Society*, 71, 2 (1962), 145–50.

Directory of the Catholic churches in Papua New Guinea and Solomon Islands. Port Moresby, Papua New Guinea: Catholic Church Bishops' Conference of the Papua New Guinea and Solomon Islands, 1985. 204p.

Fire in the Islands! the acts of the Holy Spirit in the Solomons. A. Griffiths. Wheaton, IL: Harold Shaw, 1977. 208p.

I have a strong belief: the Reverend Leslie Boseto's own story of his eight years as the first Melanesian moderator of the United Church in Papua New Guinea and the Solomon Islands. L. Boseto. Rabaul, Papua New Guinea: Unichurch Books, 1983. 215p.

Isles of Solomon: a tale of missionary adventure. C. T. J. Luxton. [Auckland, New Zealand]: Methodist Foreign Missionary Society of New Zealand, [1955]. 220p.

'Kastom: stories and Christianity in the Solomon Islands.' D. C. Ryniker. M.A. thesis, Wichita State University, Wichita, KS, 1991. 135p.

'Le 'cargo cult' à Bougainville,' M. Lenormand, *Etudes melanésiennes*, n.s. no. 4 (July 1949), 82–83.

Marists and Melanesians: a history of Catholic missions in the Solomon Islands. H. Laracy. Canberra, Australia: Australian National University Press, 1976. 222p.

'Melanesians and missionaries: an ethnohistorical study of socio–religious change in the southwest Pacific.' D. L. Whiteman. Ph.D. dissertation, Southern Illinois University at Carbondale, 1980. 4 vols.

'Music in Pacific Island worship: with special reference to the Anglican Church in Lau, Malaita, Solomon Islands.' E. Suri. B.D. thesis, Pacific Theological College, Suva, Fiji, 1976. 84p.

Romance of Rennell Island. N. Deck. Westchester, IL: Good News Publishers, 1963. 64p. (Work of SSEM. Condensed from *South from Guadalcanal*, Zondervan).

'Silas Eto of New Georgia,' E. Tuza, in *Prophets of Melanesia: six essays.* G. W. Trompf (ed). Port Moresby, Papua New Guinea: Institute of Papua New Guinea Studies, 1977.

Solomon Islands Christianity: a study in growth and obstruction. A. R. Tippett. New York: Friendship Press, 1967. 424p.

'Sorcellerie et civilisation europèene aux Iles Salomon,' P. O'Reilly, in *La sorcellerie dans les pays de mission. Compte rendu de la XIVe Semaine de Missiologie de Louvain 1936.* Brussels: Desclee de Brouwer, 1937. (Account of an unsuccessful revolution in Buka).

'The Christian Fellowship Church: a revitalization movement in Melanesia.' F. H. Harwood. Ph.D. dissertation, University of Chicago, 1971. 337p.

'The continuity of the cults: Buka,' in *The trumpet shall sound: a study of cargo cults in Melanesia*, p.114–22. P. Worsley. New York: Schocken, 1968.

'The Hahalis Welfare Society,' H. Griffin, in *Melanesian and Judaeo-Christian traditions*, p.38f. G. W. Trompf (ed). Port Moresby, Papua New Guinea: University of PNG, 1976.

'The Hahalis Welfare Society of Buka.' M. R. Rimoldi. Ph.D. dissertation, Australian National University, Canberra, Australia, 1971.

'The history of the work of the Anglican Church in the Solomon Islands.' J. Naban. Thesis, Pacific Theological College, Suva, Fiji, 1976. 113p.

'The marching rule: a Christian revolution in the Solomon Islands.' T. C. Fulbright. M.A. thesis, University of British Columbia, 1986. 340p.

'The Remnant Church: a separatist church.' M. Mauliu. Christian Leader's Training College, Banz, Papua New Guinea.

The story of the Solomons. C. E. Fox. Honiara, Solomon Islands: Diocese of Melanesia Press, 1967.
'The transmission of the Christian conception of God from one culture to the other.' M. R. Itaia. B.D. thesis, Pacific Theological College, Suva, Fiji, 1973. 97p.
The United Church in Papua, New Guinea, and the Solomon Islands: the story of the development of an indigenous church on the occasion of the centenary of the L. M. S. in Papua, 1872–1972. R. G. Williams. Rabaul, Papua New Guinea: Trinity Press, [1972]. 350p.
'Towards localization of Anglican worship in the Solomon Islands.' R. Hagesi. B.D. thesis, Pacific Theological College, Suva, Fiji, 1972. 136p.

Country Table 2. Organized churches and denominations in the Solomon Islands.

Official name (bold type = church with over 10% of all affiliated) 1	*Begun* 2	*Type* 3	*Counc* 4	*Congs* 5	*Adults* 6	*Affiliated 1970* 7	*Affiliated 1995* 8	*G%* 9	*Names, notes, and other statistics* (see Codebook, Part 3) 10
Assemblies of God	1970	P-Pe2	ZF..E	22	1,800	700	3,600	6.77	M=AoG(USA). Honiara, Malaita. Rapid growth. 51n,2f.
Catholic Church in the Solomon Is:	1845	R-Lat	Px..Q	21	23,800	30,828	43,743	1.41	3.5% Gilbertese. C=2+1+3. (1970) 1408Yy. (1990) 7n 24x 42m 93w 1575Yy
M Honiara	1897	R-Lat	Psm2	14	18,600	27,354	35,315	1.03	M=SM. 5n 18x 31m 79w 1282Yy
D Gizo	1959	R-Lat	Pop	7	5,200	3,474	8,428	3.61	Northwest. M=OP. 2n 6x 11m 14w 293Yy
Christian Fellowship Church	1960	I-3nP	.....	49	5,400	3,878	8,963	3.41	*Etoism* (followers of prophet Eto). Schism ex Methodist Ch on New Georgia. W=90%.
Christian Outreach Centre	c1989	I-3cW	.....	30	2,000	–	2,800	16.67	Assisted by COCI (network based on Brisbane, Australia).
Christian Revival Church	c1980	I-3pW	.....	3	150	–	200	6.67	Aid from CRC(Australia). 38 full-time pastors.
Ch of Jesus Christ of Latter-day Saints	c1994	m-LdS	.....	1	30	–	50	100.00	*Mormons. M=CJCLdS(USA).*
Church of the Living Word	c1990	I-3wW	.....	10	500	–	800	20.00	Split ex Rhema Church by COM bishop's son.
Church of Melanesia	1848	A-ACa	AWPKK	1,120	67,200	50,000	142,000	4.26	91% Melanesian,8% Polynesian. 114n,12x,150m,50w,3H,18h,3p,1s(44),W=75%,2000y.
Jehovah's Witnesses	c1950	m-Jeh	x....	35	805	2,946	4,030	1.26	*Watch Tower.* Active Witnessing under way by 1953. (1975) 54Y. (1995) 89Y.
New Apostolic Church	c1980	I-3aX	x....	10	1,000	–	1,604	6.67	*NAC/NAK.* M=Neuapostolische Kirche. HQ Zurich (Switzerland).
Pentecostal Church	1970	I-3pP	.....	3	310	200	550	4.13	Small indigenous body begun by an Anglican islander. In eastern Solomons.
Rhema Church	1982	I-3wP	.....	10	400	–	700	7.69	Schism ex Church of Melanesia. M=RMAI (USA).
Remnant Church	1954	I-3pP	.....	4	300	300	850	4.25	Only survivor of several schisms ex SSEC. 2 special villages on Malaita: Heaven, and Radefasu.
Seventh-day Adventist Church	1914	P-Adv	x.p..	138	18,394	13,700	36,893	4.04	*SDA.* Missions: Eastern SI,Western SI, Malaita.19n,2x,4H,5h,1r,142t(10791),W=75%,436Y.
Solomons Baptist Association	c1965	I-Bap	x....	7	512	300	1,550	6.79	*ABA.* M=American Baptist Association (USA). Regular and independent Baptists. 6nm.
South Sea Evangelical Church	1904	P-Eva	xH..a	415	26,000	20,000	42,600	3.07	*SSEC.* M-SSEM(Australia). Malaita, Guadalcanal. 273mw,1H,9p,1s,W=90%,600Y,68Oz.
United Ch in the Solomon Islands	1902	P-Uni	VWP.K	440	23,000	12,428	50,000	5.73	*SI Region.* Methodist till 1968 union with LMS Papua. 13n,8x,4H,4h,1r,96t(4162),W=80%.
United Pentecostal Church		P-Pel	.....	2	100	–	150	0.05	M=UPC(USA). Oneness Pentecostals.
Worldwide Church of God	c1950	I-BrI	.....	3	70	–	100	20.23	Formerly Radio Church of God.
Other Melanesian indigenous chs		I-mar	.....	15	310	200	550	0.05	Remnants of cargo cults with Christian elements and christianized congregations.
Other Protestant churches	c1975	P-	.....	7	480	–	800	5.00	Total about 4 denominations.
Totals				**2,345**	**172,561**	**135,480**	**342,533**		

Churches, members, growth, 1900-2025	*Congs*	*Adults*	*Affiliated*	*G%*	*Total denominations*	*6 Megablocs:* *O*	*R*	*A*	*P*	*I*	*m*
Total churches, members, and denominations (mid-1900)	100	8,100	12,400	3.47	2	0	1	1	0	0	0
Total churches, members, and denominations (mid-1970)	1,351	88,199	135,480	3.47	16	0	1	1	4	9	1
Total churches, members, and denominations (mid-1990)	2,000	144,000	286,100	3.81	30	0	1	1	8	18	2
Total churches, members, and denominations (mid-1995)	2,345	172,561	342,533	3.67	35	0	1	1	9	22	2
Total churches, members, and denominations (mid-2000)	2,500	203,000	403,203	3.32	37	0	1	1	10	23	2
Total churches, members, and denominations (mid-2025)	4,100	375,000	743,500	2.48	81	0	1	1	25	50	4

NOTES ON TABLE ABOVE
NATIONAL COUNCILS (Column 4, 5th letter).
a = member of EASPI, also observer member of SICA.
E = Evangelical Alliance of the South Pacific Islands (EASPI) (all members are in Papua New Guinea except SSEC).
K = Solomon Islands Christian Association (SICA) (member of Pacific Conference of Churches).
Q = Bishops' Conference of Papua New Guinea and the Solomon Islands, also member of SICA.
Other national councils. The Solomon Islands Region, United Church, also belongs to the Melanesian Council of Churches.

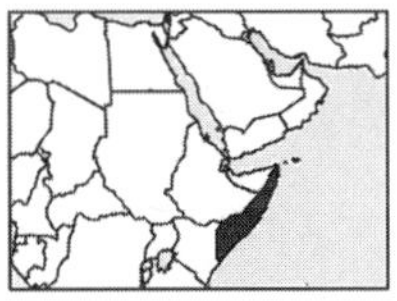

SOMALIA

SECULAR DATA, AD 2000

STATE
Official name: Jamhuriyadda Dimugradiga ee Soomaaliya (The Somali Democratic Republic).
Short name: Somalia. **Adjective of nationality:** Somali.
Flag: Light blue field with centered white star.
Area: 497,000 sq. km. (192,000 sq. mi.).
Government: One-party socialist state, since 1970 (1889 Italian protectorate, 1960 Independence as republic, 1969 leftist military junta).
Legislature: No central government.
Official language: Somali, Arabic.
Monetary unit: 1 Somali shilling (So.Sh.) = 100 cents. **US$1=** So.Sh. 2,620.
Chief cities: MUQDISHO (Mogadishu) 1,277,000; Kismaayo (Chismayu, Kismayu) 97,072; Merca (Marca, Marka, Merka) 83,205.
Political divisions: 13 provinces.

DEMOGRAPHY
Population: 7,265,000.
Population density: 14.6/sq. km. (37.8/sq. mi.).
Under 15 years: 3,484,000.
Growth rate p.a.: 3.60% (births 49.94, deaths 16.71).
Mortality: Infant, per 1,000: 112.4; **Maternal per 100,000:** 1,600.0.
Life expectancy: 49 (male 47, female 51).
Household size: 4.9. **Floor area per person, sq.m:** 4.0.
Major languages: Somali, Arabic, Italian, English, Bantu, Russian, Afar (Danakil), and others.
Urban dwellers: 27.49%. **Urban growth rate p.a.:** 4.8%.
Labor force: 41%.

ETHNOLINGUISTIC PEOPLES
74.3% Somali; 9.5% Juba Somali (Rahanwein); 3.5% Sab (Digil, Bimal); 3.0% Garre; 1.2% Amhara.

ECONOMY
National income p.a. per person: US$499; **per family:** US$2,449.

EDUCATION
Adult literacy: 25% (male 36%, female 14%). **Schools:** 1,125.
Universities: 1. **School enrolment:** female/male: 7%/13%.

HEALTH
Access to health services: 27%. **Access to safe water:** 25%.
Hospitals: 90 (7 beds per 10,000). **Doctors:** 450.
Blind: 10,000. **Deaf:** 521,800. **Murder rate:** 1.
Lepers: 14,000.

LITERATURE
New book titles p.a.: 22 (3 p.a. per million). **Periodicals:** 1.
Newspapers: 1 daily.

COMMUNICATION (per 1,000 people)
Phones: 1 (2% mobile). **Radios:** 41. **TV sets:** 13.
Daily newspaper circulation: 1. **Computers:** 2.

REFUGEES
Citizen refugees in other countries: 480,300.
Internal displacement: 300,000.

HUMAN LIFE AND LIBERTY (optimum condition=100.0%)
HDI: 22.1. **HSI:** 8.0. **HFI:** 5.0. **EFL:** 6.0.

Country status. Located in the Horn of Africa, Somalia is the easternmost country of the continent. It is an inland desert plateau and dry coastal plain that borders the Indian Ocean. Nomadic stock-raising and irrigated plantation farming are the principal economic activities.

HUMAN LIFE AND LIBERTY

Human need and development. In the early 1990s Somalia became a byword for political anarchy, economic destitution, and social atrophy. An arid country with a climate suited for neither man nor beast, Somalia has been a permanent feature on the UN list of the the world's poorest countries since the 1950s. In addition, it was burdened in the 1980s by a flood of refugees from strife-torn Ethiopia, and by ill-conceived Marxist economic experiments. The deterioration in its economic status was so precipitous that the World Bank has stopped providing data on it. Its per capita income, when last reported in the 1980s, was less than $100. Periodic droughts drive thousands of pastoralists into emergency camps. The overwhelming majority of the people are rural cattle raisers, camel nomads, fishermen and cultivators who try to wrest a living from an inhospitable land. The Somali have no urban tradition, and all major towns were founded by Arabs or Europeans. Nevertheless, the hard-pressed rural folks, facing starvation or death, fled to the towns whenever there was civil strife or drought. In the towns they face an existence far worse than the ones they escaped. Most of the urban poor are unemployed and are forced to live in portable dwellings (agal) on the outskirts of towns. Most of them therefore leave when the conditions in the villages improve. The majority of the dwellings in towns have neither electricity nor water. The average Somali diet is deficient even in good seasons. Diseases related to dietary deficiencies and undernourishment are widespread. Insufficient healthcare and a difficult environment combined with malnutrition make the entire population susceptible to a host of infectious and parasitic diseases, of which malaria and pulmonary tuberculosis are the major ones. Schistosomiasis exists particularly in riverine areas in the south where almost everyone is affected by it. About 75% of the population has one or more kinds of parasitic diseases. The absence of safe water and waste disposal facilities are the main reasons for the spread of diseases in the towns and villages. Almost all available water is contaminated. Most of the social welfare programs introduced after independence have become moribund as a result of the civil war.

Human rights and freedoms. Following the civil war, Somalia exists in a state of total anarchy without a central authority of any kind. Faction and clan militia and bandits routinely use intimidation, rape, kidnapping, murder, and looting to terrorize the people. All of them hold prisoners who are often executed summarily. The system of administration of justice

Country Table 1. **Religious adherents in Somalia, AD 1900-2025.**

Year	*1900*		*1970*		*mid-1990*		*Annual change, 1990-2000*				*mid-1995*		*mid-2000*		*mid-2025*	
Name	*Adherents*	*%*	*Adherents*	*%*	*Adherents*	*%*	*Natural*	*Conversion*	*Total*	*Rate*	*Adherents*	*%*	*Adherents*	*%*	*Adherents*	*%*
Muslims	599,400	99.9	2,221,090	99.6	5,409,300	97.7	169,023	4,450	173,473	2.82	5,538,700	97.7	7,144,028	98.3	16,074,600	99.1
Christians	**600**	**0.1**	**4,210**	**0.2**	**110,000**	**2.0**	**3,438**	**-4,250**	**-812**	**-0.76**	**115,000**	**2.0**	**101,881**	**1.4**	**120,000**	**0.7**
PROFESSION																
crypto-Christians	50	0.0	1,210	0.1	60,000	1.1	1,875	-375	1,500	2.26	70,000	1.2	75,000	1.0	75,000	0.5
professing Christians	**550**	**0.1**	**3,000**	**0.1**	**50,000**	**0.9**	**1,563**	**-3,875**	**-2,312**	**-6.02**	**45,000**	**0.8**	**26,881**	**0.4**	**45,000**	**0.3**
AFFILIATION																
unaffiliated Christians	0	0.0	0	0.0	3,975	0.1	124	-192	-68	-1.85	3,691	0.1	3,298	0.1	3,700	0.0
affiliated Christians	**600**	**0.1**	**4,210**	**0.2**	**106,025**	**1.9**	**3,314**	**-4,058**	**-744**	**-0.73**	**111,309**	**2.0**	**98,583**	**1.4**	**116,300**	**0.7**
Orthodox	0	0.0	200	0.0	100,000	1.8	3,126	-3,951	-825	-0.86	105,000	1.9	91,753	1.3	100,000	0.6
Independents	0	0.0	60	0.0	4,500	0.1	141	-41	100	2.03	5,000	0.1	5,500	0.1	14,000	0.1
Protestants	0	0.0	550	0.0	1,000	0.0	31	-21	10	0.96	1,080	0.0	1,100	0.0	2,000	0.0
Roman Catholics	600	0.1	3,300	0.2	500	0.0	16	-46	-30	-8.76	200	0.0	200	0.0	200	0.0
Anglicans	0	0.0	100	0.0	25	0.0	1	0	1	1.84	29	0.0	30	0.0	100	0.0
Trans-megabloc groupings																
Evangelicals	0	0.0	370	0.0	640	0.0	20	3	23	3.12	704	0.0	870	0.0	1,700	0.0
Pentecostals/Charismatics	0	0.0	60	0.0	4,200	0.1	131	149	280	5.24	5,108	0.1	7,000	0.1	18,700	0.1
Great Commission Christians	**600**	**0.1**	**3,700**	**0.2**	**11,000**	**0.2**	**344**	**-83**	**261**	**2.15**	**11,300**	**0.2**	**13,606**	**0.2**	**30,000**	**0.2**
Ethnoreligionists	0	0.0	0	0.0	8,200	0.2	256	-136	120	1.37	8,600	0.2	9,398	0.1	12,000	0.1
Nonreligious	0	0.0	2,500	0.1	2,900	0.1	91	-46	45	1.45	3,000	0.1	3,349	0.1	7,000	0.0
Hindus	0	0.0	500	0.0	2,400	0.0	75	-24	51	1.93	2,800	0.1	2,906	0.0	6,000	0.0
Baha'is	0	0.0	700	0.0	1,100	0.0	34	40	74	5.27	1,800	0.0	1,838	0.0	5,000	0.0
Atheists	0	0.0	1,000	0.0	1,100	0.0	34	-34	0	-0.01	1,100	0.0	1,099	0.0	2,400	0.0
World A (unevangelized persons)	594,000	99.0	2,100,523	94.2	3,708,450	67.0	115,848	-78,612	37,236	0.96	3,498,777	61.7	4,082,930	56.2	8,730,126	53.8
World B (evangelized non-Christians)	5,400	0.9	125,121	5.6	1,716,550	31.0	53,665	82,862	136,527	6.02	2,056,850	36.3	3,080,189	42.4	7,376,874	45.5
World C (Christians)	600	0.1	4,210	0.2	110,000	2.0	3,438	-4,250	-812	-0.76	115,000	2.0	101,881	1.4	120,000	0.7
Country's population	**600,000**	**100.0**	**2,229,855**	**100.0**	**5,535,000**	**100.0**	**172,951**	**0**	**172,951**	**2.76**	**5,670,628**	**100.0**	**7,265,000**	**100.0**	**16,227,000**	**100.0**

COLUMNS, ROWS.
For meanings and definitions, see Codebook (Part 3). Note that, by definition, total 'Christians' = professing + crypto-Christians, which also = affiliated + unaffiliated Christians, and also = Great Commission Christians + latent Christians. Percentages may not always total exactly, due to rounding.

CENSUSES.
The religion question has not been asked.

NOTES ON RELIGIONS
ATHEISTS. A few Marxist intellectuals. In 1976 the Somali (Communist) Socialist Revolutionary Party was formed.
BAHA'IS. Begun 1955. Growth from 1 local spiritual assembly (1964) to 5 (1973). Previously there was a large Middle Eastern presence, mainly Persians, but the last were expelled in 1975, leaving only Somali Baha'is. However, there is now a strong community of Somalis, including in 1976 one cabinet minister. By 1995 the community had collapsed in the civil war.
CRYPTO-CHRISTIANS. Unorganized individual Somalis (nationals) in the recognized churches, also isolated radio believers; in addition, Arab Christians have been sent from Lebanon as teachers.
HINDUS. Expatriate Indians, including many teachers and persons in government service; there are also a handful of Sikhs.
INDEPENDENTS. Somali crypto-Christians scattered across the country who are isolated radio believers unrelated to existing denominations.
MUSLIMS. All Sunnis (of Shafiite rite south of the Horn, with many Hanafiite north of it). There are also about 1,000 Shias (Indo-Pakistanis and other Asians). *Missionaries.* There is a large Egyptian mission sent from Al-Azhar University (Cairo). *Hajj pilgrims to Mecca.* (1970) 19; (1974) 3,767; (1975) 3,112; (1976) 7,508. Under the military regime Muslim institutions have been undercut, resulting in a revival of religion including greater attendance at Friday prayers.
NONRELIGIOUS. Italians, French, Russians and other European expatriates, with a growing number of Somali intellectuals. Most of the younger Italians entering for government service are nonreligious.
PROFESSING CHRISTIANS. The only Christians the state recognizes are expatriates (mainly Italians).
PROTESTANTS. In 1970, numerous expatriates (mostly USA missionaries); by 1976, missionaries had been expelled and Protestants were almost all Somalis. By 1995 small numbers remained, mostly clandestine.
ROMAN CATHOLICS. The rapid decline from 1970 onwards is due to emigration of Italians. The column 'Natural change' for affiliated Roman Catholics therefore includes biological increase in the Catholic community (72 persons a year), minus emigration (242 persons a year), making the nett decrease shown,–170 persons a year. The Catholic bishop was murdered in 1989.

Great Commission Instrument Panel: status of Somalia (for explanation see start of Part 4)

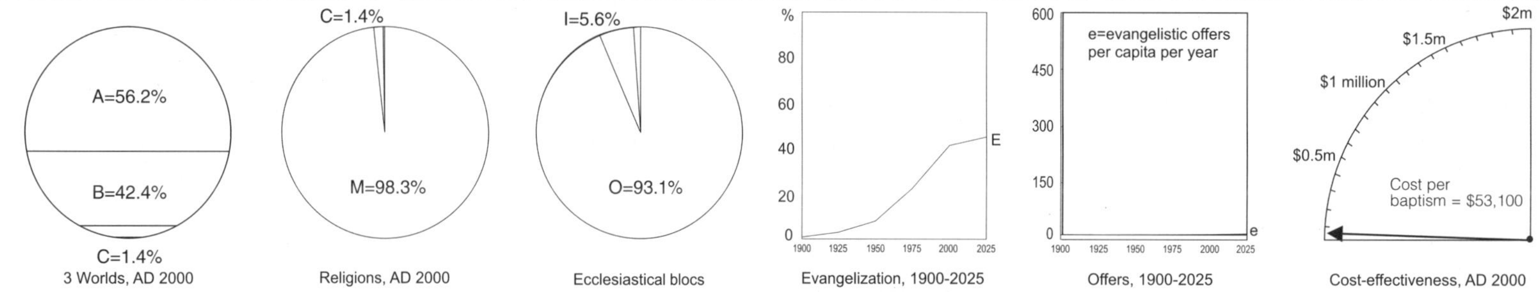

broke down many years ago, but local authorities try to maintain some semblance of court proceedings under Islamic jurisprudence. Homes are looted periodically, and there are mass evictions of civilians by opposing factions and clans. Women have suffered disproportionately in the civil war when thousands of young women were captured as spoils of war and raped. Bantu Somalis, a minority group of East African origin, are subject to severe discrimination even in refugee camps.

Human environment. A series of natural disasters since 1960 has intensified the deterioration of the fragile environment plagued by drought in 2 out of every 3 as a result of overgrazing. The country has never had a range management system. Blast fishing has destroyed coral reefs and sea grasses in coastal areas.

NON-CHRISTIAN RELIGIONS

Islam is the official religion. Somalis are virtually 100% Muslims and are all Sunnis of the Shafiite rite south of the Horn, with many of the Hanafite rite north of it. There are also about 1,000 Shias who are Indo-Pakistanis and other Asians. Despite the growing disaffection concerning religious practice among the youth in the cities, Islam continues to dominate the scene in every sphere of life. The Islamic Assembly in Mogadishu serves also as the regional office for East Africa of the World Muslim Congress, which has international headquarters in Pakistan.

Hinduism exists among the few Indians living in Mogadishu, Brava, and Kismayu, who work in technical assistance programs and others attached to the Indian diplomatic mission.

Catholic Church in Somalia. Inside burnt and vandalized cathedral, 1993.

CHRISTIANITY

CATHOLIC CHURCH. Missionaries of the Catholic Church have been in Somalia since 1881, but throughout this period, members have been predominantly foreigners with only 200 Somali Catholics by 1995. The majority are still Italians working under two-year assistance contracts, since those who resided permanently in Somalia during the colonial period have now almost all left because of the policy of Somalization in employment. Because of this predominantly expatriate character, the Catholic community has fluctuated in recent years. Deprived in its traditional missionary role by the government's prohibition of evangelistic activity, the Catholic Church has nevertheless carried on social and charitable work in service to the nation. Prior to 1972, the church was served by a bishop (who died unexpectedly in January 1973), 23 priests, 4 brothers and 85 sisters. Its 16 schools were frequented almost exclusively by Muslim pupils and contained nearly 10% of the total enrollment in the country. The church also sponsored 12 classes of lower secondary level and 6 technical schools, training young people in mechanical and electrical engineering, printing, sewing, tailoring, tanning, shoe making, secretarial work, accounting, and translation work. In addition, there were 12 Catholic dispensaries, one leprosarium, 11 orphanages, one boarding school for girls, an Association of Somali Youth in which children needing social assistance were registered, and a home for the poor which provided meals and care for the sick.

On 21 October 1972, the government passed a law nationalizing church property (schools, charitable institutions, printing presses, some churches, and other buildings), which has profoundly modified the situation of the Catholic Church. A number of priests and sisters then left the country since the institutions they worked in had been nationalized.

Country summary. **Worlds A, B, C by ethnolinguistic peoples, cities, and major civil divisions in Somalia.**

	PEOPLES							CITIES							CIVIL DIVISIONS						
World	Num	Pop 2000	C%	Christians	E%	U%	Unevangelized	Num	Pop 2000	C%	Christians	E%	U%	Unevangelized	Num	Pop 2000	C%	Christians	E%	U%	Unevangelized
A	22	1,767,623	0.21	3,712	22	78	1,383,599	3	1,457,277	2.27	33,035	48	52	761,468	13	7,264,501	1.36	98,583	44	56	4,080,365
B	1	5,398,809	0.05	2,699	50	50	2,696,705	0	0	0.00	0	0	0	0	0	0	0.00	0	0	0	0
C	6	98,070	93.98	92,171	100	0	59	0	0	0.00	0	0	0	0	0	0	0.00	0	0	0	0
Total	**29**	**7,264,502**	**1.36**	**98,582**	**44**	**56**	**4,080,363**	**3**	**1,457,277**	**2.27**	**33,035**	**48**	**52**	**761,468**	**13**	**7,264,501**	**1.36**	**98,583**	**44**	**56**	**4,080,365**

The Holy See has no diplomatic relations with Somalia in AD 2000, but has an apostolic delegate residing in Khartoum.

Catholic Church in Somalia. 1970 Cathedral in Mogadishu (right center).

ORTHODOX CHURCHES. The presence of the Orthodox church in Somalia dates back to the influx of refugees from Ethiopia in the late 1960s. In the 1980s and 1990s these numbers swelled so that by 1995 there were well over 100,000 church members, mainly of the Amhara tribe. These believers are under the patriarch of Addis Ababa, Ethiopia.

PROTESTANT CHURCHES. Protestantism in Somalia dates from the year 1898 when Swedish Lutheran missionaries began work in what is today southern Somalia. There they developed an educational, medical, and agricultural program, in addition to evangelistic outreach and the baptism of some 350 Christians by 1935. These latter were mostly Bantu-speaking former slaves, with a few Somalis among them. Italy assumed control of the area after World War I and in 1935 expelled all the Lutheran missionaries. Some indigenous Christians lapsed while others moved to Kenya, and only a few of those remaining in Somalia continued to retain a Christian commitment.

Protestantism was revived following World War II with the arrival of Mennonites in 1953 and the Sudan Interior Mission (SIM) in 1954, both having worked earlier in Ethiopia. As with the Catholics, Protestant activity has been largely confined to social service. When in 1963 the teaching of Islam was made compulsory for all schools, the SIM terminated its educational system, although it continued to operate adult English classes and a medical program consisting of 3 dispensaries and a hospital until 1972 and in 1971 produced the Somali translation of the New Testament. Following the nationalization of church property in 1972, SIM missionaries were withdrawn except for 3 who continued until 1974 to offer Bible classes on an informal person-to-person basis and to run the European Sunday school in Mogadishu.

Until 1972, the Mennonites with 35 missionaries operated 6 schools (a secondary, 2 intermediate and 3 adults schools), a community development center, a bookstore, and a hospital at Jamana including nurses' training. During 1973-76, Mennonite missionaries worked under government auspices in their former posts as well as other government institutions. In July 1975, the first Somali was ordained as a minister.

In May 1976, the Ministry of Education suddenly terminated the teaching contracts of the remaining 10 Mennonite missionaries who then had to leave the country, and no expatriate Protestant missionaries remained in Somalia. However, small groups of Somali Christians formerly associated with Mennonite and SIM work, continue to meet and worship together using Somali songs and hymns in Johar, Mahadday, Jamama, Kismayu, and several other centers, in addition to holding regular weekly services in the Catholic cathedral in Mogadishu.

ANGLICAN CHURCH. A small Anglican community, consisting mostly of expatriates, exists at Mogadishu. The church has been organized by lay persons, there being no resident clergy. Periodic chaplaincy services were until recently provided by a priest from Addis Ababa, but this is no longer possible, although Anglicans from 1976 have run the English-language Sunday school. The Anglican group, which meets in a private home, is regarded as attached to the Episcopal church in Jerusalem and the Middle East.

Indigenous missions. Very few missionaries have been sent out from Somalia.

CHURCH AND STATE

The military government in power since 21 October 1969, suspended the constitution of 1 July 1960, but government practice concerning religion has remained unchanged. The old constitution proclaimed Islam to be the state religion (Article 1, paragraph 3) and guaranteed liberty of conscience and worship (Article 29), while at the same time requiring Muslim citizens to follow the general principles of Islam (Article 30). Classes in Islam were obligatory for Muslim students in primary and secondary schools, both in public and private education (Article 35, paragraph 6), although the latter was not enforced in Christian mission schools until 1963. Freedom of education was recognized and private schools could obtain the same status as public schools although no state subsidies were available to them (Article 35, paragraphs 3-5).

The law of 21 October 1972, nationalizing church property affected all Mennonite property and most Catholic property. On 11 January 1975, the Somali government decided to revise its laws to eliminate all discrimination between men and women, which led ultra-conservative Muslims to declare the decision a 'sacrilege' and begin agitation against it. When 10 ulemas were shot on 23 January the head of state declared that Islam had come to modify and improve the society of its time and not to freeze injustices and defects. In May 1976, the last Protestant foreign missionaries were expelled.

The Ministry of Grace, Justice and Religious Affairs (Ministerio di Grazia, Ciustizia ed Affari Religiosi) deals with questions of Islamic legislation and is responsible for sanctioning mixed marriages. The churches are accepted by the government provided that they abstain from any form of proselytism meaning direct and public evangelistic activity.

BROADCASTING AND MEDIA

Somalia is a highly restrictive nation; no Christian programming is permitted to be broadcast from within its borders. Somali-language shortwave radio programs can be received from FEBA (Seychelles) and TWR (South Africa).

FUTURE TRENDS AND PROSPECTS

Civil war, famine, and economic disaster will unfortunately plague this country well into the 21st century with Christians (mainly immigrants whose status is doubtful) falling to only 0.7% by 2025.

Christianity is expected to decline as more and more Ethiopian Orthodox Christians leave the country. Christians will not likely represent more than 1% of the population over the next fifty years.

BIBLIOGRAPHY

A pastoral democracy. I. M. Lewis. London: Oxford University Press, 1961.

A religious nationalist in Somalia: a comment on modern nationalism allied with Islam as a unifying dynamic. E. A. Bayne. *Northeast Africa series*, 13, 3. New York: American Universities Field Staff, 1966. 7p.

'A study of Mennonite presence and church development in Somalia from 1950 through 1970.' D. W. Shenk. Ph.D. dissertation, New York University, 1972. 412p.

Anthropology and ethnography of the peoples of Somalia. N. Puccioni. New Haven, CT: Human Relations Area Files, 1960. 205p. (Translated from Italian).

'Conformity and contrast in Somali Islam,' I. M. Lewis, chapter 10 in *Islam in tropical Africa*, p.253–67. I. M. Lewis (ed). London: Oxford University Press, 1966.

Histoire des croyances en Somalie: religions traditionnelles et religions du Livre. M. Mohamed-Abdi. Paris: Belles Lettres, 1992. 163p.

Peoples of the Horn of Africa: Somali, Afar and Saho. I. M. Lewis. London: International African Institute, 1969.

Religion in context: cults and charisma. I. M. Lewis. Cambridge, UK: Cambridge University Press, 1986. 139p.

Somalia. M. W. DeLancey et al. *World bibliographical series*, vol. 92. Oxford, UK: CLIO Press, 1988. 222p. (See short chapter on religion, p.50-3).

Somalia: a nation in turmoil. S. S. Samatar. London: Minority Rights Group, 1991. 34p.

Somalia in word and image. K. S. Loughran et al. (eds). Washington, DC: Indiana University Press, Bloomington, 1986. 175p.

Somalia: insieme per il cammino di speranza: cinquant anni di presenza francescana in Somalia. Segretariato delle Missioni dei Frati Minori di Lombardia (ed). Milan: Edizioni Biblioteca Francescana, 1980. 293p.

Sons of Adam: stories of Somalia. O. Eby. Scottdale, PA: Herald Press, 1970.

'Spirit possession and deprivation cults,' I. M. Lewis, *Man*, 1, 3 (1966), 307–329.

'Sufi influences on Somali society.' F. Miller. M.A. thesis, Duquesne University, Pittsburgh, PA, 1973. 126p.

'The Arab factor in Somali history: the origins and the development of Arab enterprise and cultural influences in the Somali peninsula.' Ali Abdirahman Hersi. Ph.D. dissertation, University of California, Los Angeles, 1977. 345p.

The Christian Church and missions in Ethiopia (including Eritrea and the Somalilands). J. S. Trimingham. London: World Dominion Press, 1950. 74p.

Country Table 2. **Organized churches and denominations in Somalia.**

Official name (bold type = church with over 10% of all affiliated) 1	Begun 2	Type 3	Counc 4	Congs 5	Adults 6	Affiliated 1970 7	Affiliated 1995 8	G% 9	*Names, notes, and other statistics* (see Codebook, Part 3) 10
Anglican Church (D Egypt, L & N)	c1950	A-Cen	A....	1	10	100	29	-4.83	Under Episcopal Ch in Jerusalem & the Middle East. UK expatriates at Mogadishu, Hargeysa.
Catholic Church: D Mogadishu	1881	R-Lat	PxSL.	4	100	3,300	200	-10.61	*Chiesa Cattolica Romana.* Italians, Somalis. C=1+0+1. (1970) 19x,6m. (1990) 1n,1m,4w,2Yy
Ethiopian Orthodox Church	c1960	O-Eth	N....	20	70,000	200	105,000	28.47	Under P Addis Ababa. Amhara and Tulama (Shoa Golla) refugees from Ethiopian wars.
Isolated radio churches	1969	I-3rA	.....	300	3,000	60	5,000	19.35	Isolated radio believers, mostly youths ages 12-25. 4 FEBA programs weekly.
Seventh-day Adventist Church	c1970	P-Adv	x....	10	300	–	500	28.22	Mainly among Ethiopian refugees (Amhara, Tulama).
Somalia Believers Fellowship	1954	P-Non	xM...	2	20	250	30	-8.13	*SBF.* M=SIM(USA). Abandoned schools 1963. 25f (until withdrew 1974),2H,3h,3i.
Somalia Mennonite Mission	1953	P-Men	G....	3	30	300	50	-6.92	Formerly, M=EMBMC(Mennonite) (USA). 1n,30f(until 1976 expulsion),1H,3i,4r.
Other Protestant bodies	c1985	P-	.....	20	300	–	500	10.00	In some 4 missions or denominations loosely deployed or present.
Totals				**360**	**73,760**	**4,210**	**111,309**		

Churches, members, growth, 1900-2025	*Congs*	*Adults*	*Affiliated*	*G%*	*Total denominations*	*6 Megablocs:* O	R	A	P	I	m
Total churches, members, and denominations (mid-1900)	10	320	600	2.82	1	0	1	0	0	0	0
Total churches, members, and denominations (mid-1970)	40	2,225	4,210	2.82	6	1	1	1	2	1	0
Total churches, members, and denominations (mid-1990)	300	70,300	106,025	17.50	11	1	1	1	7	1	0
Total churches, members, and denominations (mid-1995)	360	73,760	111,309	0.98	11	1	1	1	7	1	0
Total churches, members, and denominations (mid-2000)	250	65,300	98,583	-2.40	11	1	1	1	7	1	0
Total churches, members, and denominations (mid-2025)	400	77,100	116,300	0.66	14	1	1	1	10	1	0

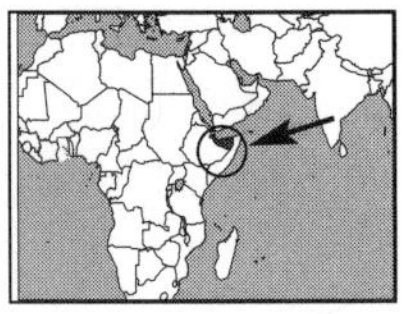

SOMALILAND

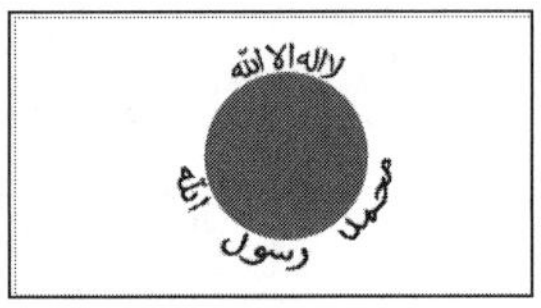

SECULAR DATA, AD 2000

STATE
Official name: The Somaliland Republic.
Short name: Somaliland. **Adjective of nationality:** of Somaliland.
Flag: That of Somalia; also the indigenous design shown.
Area: 140,000 sq. km. (54,000 sq. mi.).
Government: Provisional republic, since 1991 (1884 British protectorate, 1960 Independence, 1969 leftist military junta).
Legislature: No central government.
Official language: Somali, Arabic.
Monetary unit: 1 Somali shilling (So.Sh.) = 100 cents. **US$1=** So.Sh. 2,620.
Chief cities: Hargeyisa (Hargeisa) 102,618; Berbera 95,288.
Political divisions: 3 provinces.

DEMOGRAPHY
Population: 2,833,000.
Population density: 20.2/sq. km. (52.4/sq. mi.).
Under 15 years: 1,359,000.
Growth rate p.a.: 3.60% (births 49.94, deaths 16.71).
Mortality: Infant, per 1,000: 112.4; **Maternal per 100,000:** 1,700.0.
Life expectancy: 49 (male 47, female 51).
Household size: 5.0. **Floor area per person, sq.m:** 3.0.
Major languages: Somali, Arabic, English.
Urban dwellers: 27.49%. **Urban growth rate p.a.:** 0.00%.
Labor force: 45%.

ETHNOLINGUISTIC PEOPLES
89.7% Somali; 3.0% Somali (Ogaden); 3.0% Yemeni Arab; 2.0% Danakil (Afar); 0.8% Omani Arab.

ECONOMY
National income p.a. per person: US$154; **per family:** US$774.

EDUCATION
Adult literacy: 25% (male 35%, female 15%). **Schools:** 200.
Universities: 0. **School enrolment:** female/male: 10%/10%.

HEALTH
Access to health services: 25%. **Access to safe water:** 20%.
Hospitals: 10 (5 beds per 10,000). **Doctors:** 50.
Blind: 2,500. **Deaf:** 170,000. **Murder rate:** 2.
Lepers: 4,500.

LITERATURE
New book titles p.a.: 14 (5 p.a. per million). **Periodicals:** 0.
Newspapers: 0 dailies.

COMMUNICATION (per 1,000 people)
Phones: 1 (3% mobile). **Radios:** 20. **TV sets:** 5.
Daily newspaper circulation: <1. **Computers:** 1.

HUMAN LIFE AND LIBERTY (optimum condition=100.0%)
HDI: 28.1. **HSI:** 20.0. **HFI:** 15.0. **EFL:** 2.0.

Country Table 1. **Religious adherents in Somaliland, AD 1900-2025.**

Year	*1900*		*1970*		*mid-1990*		*Annual change, 1990-2000*				*mid-1995*		*mid-2000*		*mid-2025*	
Name	*Adherents*	*%*	*Adherents*	*%*	*Adherents*	*%*	*Natural*	*Conversion*	*Total*	*Rate*	*Adherents*	*%*	*Adherents*	*%*	*Adherents*	*%*
Muslims	164,000	100.0	1,370,230	99.9	2,228,050	99.6	59,202	38	59,240	2.39	2,518,920	99.6	2,820,452	99.6	4,962,250	99.6
Christians	**0**	**0.0**	**670**	**0.1**	**6,910**	**0.3**	**184**	**-35**	**149**	**1.97**	**7,650**	**0.3**	**8,401**	**0.3**	**14,750**	**0.3**
PROFESSION																
crypto-Christians	0	0.0	650	0.1	4,000	0.2	106	4	110	2.46	4,600	0.2	5,100	0.2	9,300	0.2
professing Christians	**0**	**0.0**	**20**	**0.0**	**2,910**	**0.1**	**77**	**-38**	**39**	**1.27**	**3,050**	**0.1**	**3,301**	**0.1**	**5,450**	**0.1**
AFFILIATION																
unaffiliated Christians	0	0.0	0	0.0	20	0.0	1	-1	0	0.00	20	0.0	20	0.0	50	0.0
affiliated Christians	**0**	**0.0**	**670**	**0.1**	**6,890**	**0.3**	**183**	**-34**	**149**	**1.98**	**7,630**	**0.3**	**8,381**	**0.3**	**14,700**	**0.3**
Orthodox	0	0.0	50	0.0	3,600	0.2	96	-16	80	2.03	4,000	0.2	4,400	0.2	7,500	0.2
Independents	0	0.0	20	0.0	2,700	0.1	72	-12	60	2.03	3,000	0.1	3,300	0.1	6,000	0.1
Protestants	0	0.0	0	0.0	280	0.0	7	-2	5	1.66	300	0.0	330	0.0	700	0.0
Anglicans	0	0.0	100	0.0	280	0.0	7	-3	4	1.34	300	0.0	320	0.0	400	0.0
Roman Catholics	0	0.0	500	0.0	30	0.0	1	-1	0	0.33	30	0.0	31	0.0	100	0.0
Trans-megabloc groupings																
Evangelicals	0	0.0	30	0.0	300	0.0	8	17	25	6.25	402	0.0	550	0.0	900	0.0
Pentecostals/Charismatics	0	0.0	20	0.0	2,460	0.1	65	57	122	4.11	3,052	0.1	3,680	0.1	8,000	0.2
Great Commission Christians	**0**	**0.0**	**600**	**0.0**	**2,240**	**0.1**	**60**	**28**	**88**	**3.37**	**2,530**	**0.1**	**3,120**	**0.1**	**6,000**	**0.1**
Hindus	0	0.0	0	0.0	1,900	0.1	51	-14	37	1.78	2,050	0.1	2,266	0.1	3,000	0.1
Nonreligious	0	0.0	0	0.0	700	0.0	19	9	28	3.45	850	0.0	983	0.0	2,500	0.1
Atheists	0	0.0	100	0.0	240	0.0	6	0	6	2.36	280	0.0	303	0.0	1,000	0.0
Baha'is	0	0.0	0	0.0	200	0.0	5	2	7	3.12	250	0.0	272	0.0	500	0.0
World A (unevangelized persons)	164,000	100.0	1,234,071	90.0	1,342,800	60.0	35,672	-13,300	22,372	1.55	1,467,400	58.0	1,566,649	55.3	2,601,648	52.2
World B (evangelized non-Christians)	0	0.0	136,449	9.9	888,290	39.7	23,611	13,335	36,946	3.54	1,054,950	41.7	1,257,950	44.4	2,367,602	47.5
World C (Christians)	0	0.0	670	0.1	6,910	0.3	184	-35	149	1.97	7,650	0.3	8,401	0.3	14,750	0.3
Country's population	**164,000**	**100.0**	**1,371,190**	**100.0**	**2,238,000**	**100.0**	**59,467**	**0**	**59,467**	**2.39**	**2,530,000**	**100.0**	**2,833,000**	**100.0**	**4,984,000**	**100.0**

COLUMNS, ROWS.
For meanings and definitions, see Codebook (Part 3). Note that, by definition, total 'Christians' = professing + crypto-Christians, which also = affiliated + unaffiliated Christians, and also = Great Commission Christians + latent Christians. Percentages may not always total exactly, due to rounding.

NOTES ON RELIGIONS
PROFESSING CHRISTIANS. Mainly French and British expatriates. Also Ethiopian refugees.
INDEPENDENTS. Isolated radio believers scattered across the country and unrelated to existing denominations.
MUSLIMS. Mostly Hanafite Sunnis.

Great Commission Instrument Panel: status of Somaliland (for explanation see start of Part 4)

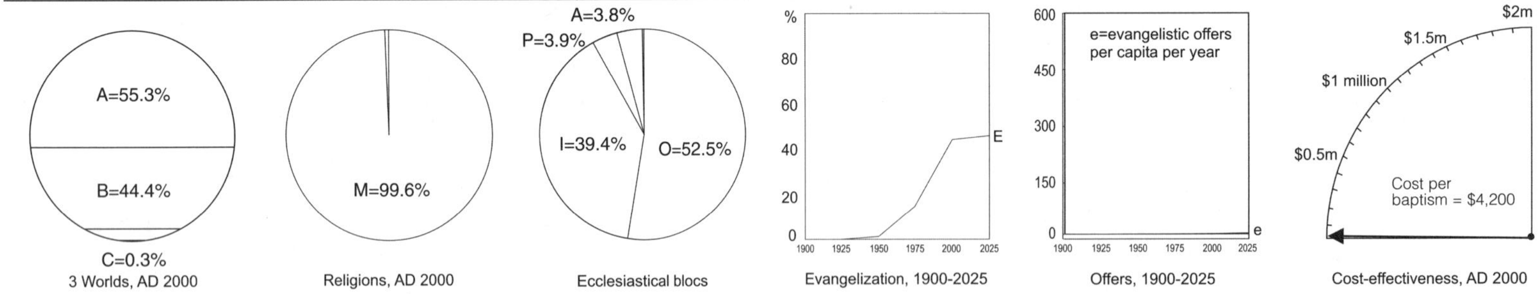

Country status. Somaliland, formerly a British overseas protectorate, is a north-eastern African country bordering the Indian Ocean near the opening of the Gulf of Suez. The population is largely engaged in nomadic stock-raising.

HUMAN LIFE AND LIBERTY

This territory suffers from most of the inadequacies of the parent republic of Somalia. Nevertheless it has escaped the terrible famines and civil wars of further south.

NON-CHRISTIAN RELIGIONS

Islam is the religion of almost the entire population.

CHRISTIANITY

Only a few Christians have been able to live and worship openly.

CATHOLIC CHURCH The Holy See has no diplomatic relations with Somaliland in AD 2000.

Indigenous missions. No missionaries have been sent out from the fledgling church in Somaliland.

FUTURE TRENDS AND PROSPECTS

Few changes are expected in the religious situation in Somaliland before 2025.

Christians will be unlikely to reach 1% of the population before the mid-century. Islam will predominate throughout the period.

BIBLIOGRAPHY

A bibliography of British Somaliland. N. M. Viney. [London: War Office], 1947. 36p. (Microfiche).
A general survey of the Somaliland Protectorate, 1944–1950. J. A. Hunt. , 1951.
Genealogies of the tribes of British Somaliland and Mijertein. Published under the authority of the Military Government, Somaliland Protectorate, 1944. 32p.
Peoples of the Horn of Africa: Somali, Afar and Saho. I. M. Lewis. London: International African Institute, 1969.
Somaliland. A. Hamilton. 1911; reprint, Westport, CT: Negro Universities Press, [1970]. 381p.
'Sufism in Somaliland: a study in tribal Islam', I. M. Lewis, *Bulletin of the School of Oriental and African Studies* (London) 17 (1955), 581-602, and 18 (1956), 145-60.
The Christian Church and missions in Ethiopia (including Eritrea and the Somalilands). J. S. Trimingham. London: World Dominion Press, 1950. 74p.
The Mad Mullah of Somaliland. D. J. Jardine. 1923; reprint, New York: Negro Universities Press, [1969]. 336p.

Country summary. **Worlds A, B, C by ethnolinguistic peoples, cities, and major civil divisions in Somaliland.**

	PEOPLES							CITIES							CIVIL DIVISIONS						
World	Num	Pop 2000	C%	Christians	E%	U%	Unevangelized	Num	Pop 2000	C%	Christians	E%	U%	Unevangelized	Num	Pop 2000	C%	Christians	E%	U%	Unevangelized
A	8	2,826,162	0.09	2,618	45	55	1,566,712	1	95,288	0.20	191	45	55	52,799	3	2,832,677	0.30	8,381	45	55	1,566,720
B	0	0	0.00	0	0	0	0	1	102,618	0.80	821	50	50	51,114	0	0	0.00	0	0	0	0
C	3	6,515	88.44	5,762	100	0	8	0	0	0.00	0	0	0	0	0	0	0.00	0	0	0	0
Total	**11**	**2,832,677**	**0.30**	**8,380**	**45**	**55**	**1,566,720**	**2**	**197,906**	**0.51**	**1,012**	**47**	**53**	**103,913**	**3**	**2,832,677**	**0.30**	**8,381**	**45**	**55**	**1,566,720**

Country Table 2. **Organized churches and denominations in Somaliland.**

Official name (bold type = church *with over 10% of all affiliated)* 1	*Begun* 2	*Type* 3	*Counc* 4	*Congs* 5	*Adults* 6	*Affiliated 1970* 7	*Affiliated 1995* 8	*G%* 9	*Names, notes, and other statistics* (see Codebook, Part 3) 10
Catholic Church (D Mogadishu)	c1900	R-Lat	P....	1	20	500	30	-10.64	Scattered believers and house churches. Many refugees. Some expatriate Europeans. M=OFM.
Episcopal Ch in Jerus & Middle East		A-Low	Aw...	5	200	100	300	0.05	*ECJME.* Mainly Arab Anglicans, also British and Americans.
Ethiopian Orthodox Church	c1960	O-Eth	N....	5	2,000	50	4,000	19.16	Under P Addis Ababa. Ethiopian refugees from recent wars.
Isolated radio churches	1969	I-3rA	.....	50	2,000	20	3,000	22.19	Isolated radio believers, mostly youths ages 12-25. R=FEBA.
Seventh-day Adventist Church	c1975	P-Adv	x....	2	200	–	300	5.00	*SDA.* Ethiopian refugees (Tulama/Shoa Golla, Amhara, Tigrai).
Totals				**63**	**4,420**	**670**	**7,630**		

Churches, members, growth, 1900-2025	*Congs*	*Adults*	*Affiliated*	*G%*	*Total denominations*	*6 Megablocs:* O	R	A	P	I	m
Total churches, members, and denominations (mid-1900)	0	0	0	0.00	1	0	1	0	0	0	0
Total churches, members, and denominations (mid-1970)	7	390	670	15.00	4	1	1	1	0	1	0
Total churches, members, and denominations (mid-1990)	40	4,000	6,890	12.36	5	1	1	1	1	1	0
Total churches, members, and denominations (mid-1995)	63	4,420	7,630	2.06	5	1	1	1	1	1	0
Total churches, members, and denominations (mid-2000)	80	4,900	8,381	1.90	5	1	1	1	1	1	0
Total churches, members, and denominations (mid-2025)	200	8,500	14,700	2.27	5	1	1	1	1	1	0

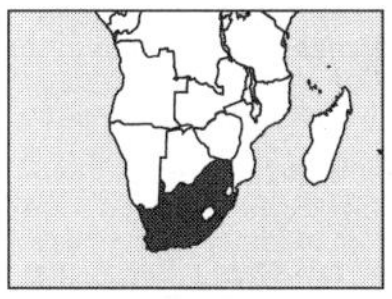

SOUTH AFRICA

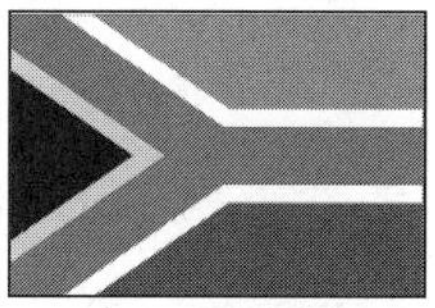

SECULAR DATA, AD 2000

STATE
Official name: The Republic of South Africa.
Short name: South Africa. **Adjective of nationality:** South African.
Flag: Orange, white, and blue stripes; in centre, replicas of Union Jack, old flag of Orange Free State, an old Transvaal Vierkleur (4-colour).
Area: 1,223,201 sq. km. (472,281 sq. mi.).
Government: Parliamentary republic, since 1961 (1652 Dutch settlement, 1814 British colony, 1910 Union of South Africa, 1934 Independence as constitutional monarchy, 1961 republic, 1993 multiracial parliament).
Legislature: National Council of Provinces, 90 members; National Assembly, 400 members.
Official language: Afrikaans and English.
Monetary unit: 1 rand (R) = 100 cents. **US$1=** R 5.83.
Chief cities: CAPE TOWN (KAAPSTAD) 3,092,000; Johannesburg 2,412,000; PRETORIA 1,558,000; Durban 1,379,000; Vereeniging 1,259,000.
Political divisions: 9 provinces.
Armed forces: 79,000.

DEMOGRAPHY
Population: 40,377,000.
Population density: 33.0/sq. km. (85.4/sq. mi.).
Under 15 years: 14,140,000.
Growth rate p.a.: 0.71% (births 25.21, deaths 18.14).
Mortality: Infant, per 1,000: 63.1; **Maternal per 100,000:** 230.0.
Life expectancy: 47 (male 45, female 49).
Household size: 4.6. **Floor area per person, sq.m:** 27.0.
Major languages: Afrikaans, English, Zulu, Xhosa, Tswana (Setswana), Pedi (Sepedi), Sotho (Sesotho), Tsonga, Swazi (siSwati), Venda, Chewa (Chichewa), Portuguese, Greek, Tamil, Hindi, Telugu, Gujarati, German, and 25 smaller languages.
Urban dwellers: 50.35%. **Urban growth rate p.a.:** 2.7%.
Labor force: 38%.

ETHNOLINGUISTIC PEOPLES
20.3% Zulu; 15.1% Xhosa; 7.2% Coloured (Eurafrican); 7.1% Pedi (Northern Sotho); 6.7% Afrikaner.

ECONOMY
National income p.a. per person: US$3,160; **per family:** US$14,536.

EDUCATION
Adult literacy: 81% (male 81%, female 81%). **Schools:** 22,447.
Universities: 32. **School enrolment:** female/male: 105%/102%.

HEALTH
Access to health services: 75%. **Access to safe water:** 70%.
Hospitals: 834 (39 beds per 10,000). **Doctors:** 25,967.
Blind: 62,000. **Deaf:** 2,775,400. **Murder rate:** 8.
Lepers: 36,000. **Underweight prevalence under 5:** 9%.

LITERATURE
New book titles p.a.: 5,850 (145 p.a. per million). **Periodicals:** 15.
Newspapers: 17 dailies.

COMMUNICATION (per 1,000 people)
Phones: 95 (25% mobile). **Radios:** 273. **TV sets:** 101.
Daily newspaper circulation: 33. **Computers:** 45.

REFUGEES
Alien refugees from other countries: 90,000.
Internal displacement: 500,000.

HUMAN LIFE AND LIBERTY (optimum condition=100.0%)
HDI: 71.6. **HSI:** 39.0. **HFI:** 7.5. **EFL:** 40.0.

Country Table 1. **Religious adherents in South Africa, AD 1900-2025.**

Year	*1900*		*1970*		*mid-1990*		*Annual change, 1990-2000*				*mid-1995*		*mid-2000*		*mid-2025*	
Name	*Adherents*	*%*	*Adherents*	*%*	*Adherents*	*%*	*Natural*	*Conversion*	*Total*	*Rate*	*Adherents*	*%*	*Adherents*	*%*	*Adherents*	*%*
Christians	**1,992,200**	**40.7**	**17,035,000**	**77.1**	**27,780,300**	**81.7**	**519,841**	**58,519**	**578,360**	**1.91**	**30,942,000**	**82.6**	**33,563,902**	**83.1**	**38,272,500**	**83.2**
PROFESSION																
professing Christians	**1,992,200**	**40.7**	**17,035,000**	**77.1**	**27,780,300**	**81.7**	**519,841**	**58,519**	**578,360**	**1.91**	**30,942,000**	**82.6**	**33,563,902**	**83.1**	**38,272,500**	**83.2**
AFFILIATION																
unaffiliated Christians	688,500	14.1	3,025,389	13.7	1,685,300	5.0	31,539	-23,758	7,781	0.45	1,727,000	4.6	1,763,113	4.4	1,022,500	2.2
affiliated Christians	**1,303,700**	**26.6**	**14,009,611**	**63.4**	**26,095,000**	**76.7**	**488,300**	**82,277**	**570,579**	**2.00**	**29,215,000**	**78.0**	**31,800,789**	**78.8**	**37,250,000**	**81.0**
Independents	15,000	0.3	4,607,156	20.9	14,965,000	44.0	280,055	73,445	353,500	2.14	16,966,992	45.3	18,500,000	45.8	23,000,000	50.0
Protestants	1,027,000	21.0	6,465,743	29.3	10,350,000	30.4	193,690	12,310	206,000	1.83	11,458,576	30.6	12,410,000	30.7	14,600,000	31.7
Roman Catholics	53,000	1.1	1,588,674	7.2	2,700,000	7.9	50,528	14,472	65,000	2.18	3,057,910	8.2	3,350,000	8.3	4,400,000	9.6
Anglicans	206,500	4.2	1,235,946	5.6	2,150,000	6.3	40,235	10,765	51,000	2.15	2,430,000	6.5	2,660,000	6.6	3,300,000	7.2
Marginal Christians	700	0.0	82,092	0.4	150,000	0.4	2,807	1,193	4,000	2.39	171,500	0.5	190,000	0.5	400,000	0.9
Orthodox	1,500	0.0	30,000	0.1	110,000	0.3	2,059	1,941	4,000	3.15	132,000	0.4	150,000	0.4	200,000	0.4
doubly-affiliated	0	0.0	0	0.0	-4,330,000	-12.7	-81,032	-31,889	-112,921	2.34	-5,001,978	-13.4	-5,459,211	-13.5	-8,650,000	-18.8
Trans-megabloc groupings																
Evangelicals	949,000	19.4	2,330,000	10.6	3,690,000	10.9	69,055	14,145	83,200	2.05	4,137,201	11.0	4,522,000	11.2	6,000,000	13.0
Pentecostals/Charismatics	805,000	16.4	4,000,000	18.1	17,330,000	51.0	324,313	62,687	387,000	2.04	19,433,547	51.9	21,200,000	52.5	25,500,000	55.4
Great Commission Christians	**490,000**	**10.0**	**4,042,000**	**18.3**	**6,395,000**	**18.8**	**119,676**	**12,534**	**132,210**	**1.90**	**7,119,000**	**19.0**	**7,717,095**	**19.1**	**9,663,000**	**21.0**
Ethnoreligionists	2,793,000	57.0	4,039,210	18.3	3,450,000	10.1	64,563	-71,985	-7,422	-0.22	3,400,000	9.1	3,375,777	8.4	3,000,000	6.5
Hindus	50,000	1.0	433,100	2.0	795,000	2.3	14,878	1,558	16,436	1.90	885,200	2.4	959,356	2.4	1,200,000	2.6
Nonreligious	2,000	0.0	150,000	0.7	700,000	2.1	13,100	12,601	25,701	3.18	830,000	2.2	957,006	2.4	1,400,000	3.0
Muslims	30,000	0.6	269,900	1.2	800,000	2.4	14,971	-256	14,715	1.70	880,000	2.4	947,148	2.4	1,100,000	2.4
Baha'is	0	0.0	15,300	0.1	200,000	0.6	3,743	1,835	5,578	2.49	230,000	0.6	255,775	0.6	500,000	1.1
Jews	30,000	0.6	119,600	0.5	150,000	0.4	2,807	-2,109	698	0.46	152,000	0.4	156,984	0.4	170,000	0.4
Atheists	0	0.0	5,000	0.0	69,000	0.2	1,291	-5	1,286	1.72	75,000	0.2	81,862	0.2	215,000	0.5
Buddhists	100	0.0	2,250	0.0	38,000	0.1	711	152	863	2.07	42,960	0.1	46,628	0.1	100,000	0.2
Sikhs	200	0.0	4,000	0.0	7,600	0.0	142	-46	96	1.20	8,800	0.0	8,560	0.0	15,000	0.0
Chinese folk-religionists	500	0.0	1,640	0.0	2,800	0.0	52	-13	39	1.31	3,000	0.0	3,190	0.0	8,000	0.0
Spiritists	1,000	0.0	2,000	0.0	2,000	0.0	37	-39	-2	-0.11	2,100	0.0	1,978	0.0	3,600	0.0
Confucianists	0	0.0	0	0.0	230	0.0	4	-3	1	0.51	240	0.0	242	0.0	500	0.0
Other religionists	1,000	0.0	10,000	0.1	17,070	0.1	319	-209	110	0.63	18,700	0.1	18,169	0.1	30,400	0.1
World A (unevangelized persons)	2,352,000	48.0	1,126,443	5.1	782,276	2.3	14,447	-13,464	983	0.13	824,345	2.2	767,163	1.9	1,150,375	2.5
World B (evangelized non-Christians)	555,800	11.3	3,925,679	17.8	5,449,424	16.0	102,171	-45,055	57,116	1.04	5,703,898	15.2	6,045,935	15.0	6,592,125	14.3
World C (Christians)	1,992,200	40.7	17,035,000	77.1	27,780,300	81.7	519,841	58,519	578,360	1.91	30,942,000	82.6	33,563,902	83.1	38,272,500	83.2
Country's population	**4,900,000**	**100.0**	**22,087,123**	**100.0**	**34,012,000**	**100.0**	**636,459**	**0**	**636,459**	**1.73**	**37,470,244**	**100.0**	**40,377,000**	**100.0**	**46,015,000**	**100.0**

COLUMNS, ROWS.
For meanings and definitions, see Codebook (Part 3). Note that, by definition, total 'Christians' = professing + crypto-Christians, which also = affiliated + unaffiliated Christians, and also = Great Commission Christians + latent Christians. Percentages may not always total exactly, due to rounding.

CENSUSES.
1911: 50.7% ethnoreligionists, 34.7% Protestants (15.0% NGK/NHK/GK, 10.0% Methodists, 3.3% Lutherans, 3.1% Congregationalists, 2.2% Presbyterians, 0.4% Moravians), 8.9%

Continued overleaf

Country Table 1–concluded

Anglicans, 1.9% Hindus, 1.5% Roman Catholics, 0.8% Jews, 0.8% Muslims, 0.7% Non-White indigenous Christians. (Total Christians in 1911, 45.7%). **1921:** 45.1% ethnoreligionists 37.5% Protestants (16.1% NGK/NHK/GK, 12.0% Methodists. 3.8% Lutherans and Moravians, 2.8% Presbyterians, 2.3% Congregationalists), 10.3% Anglicans, 2.1% Roman Catholics, 1.6% Hindus, 1.4% Non-White indigenous Christians, 0.9% Jews, 0.7% Muslims, 0.2% Buddhists, 0.2% nonreligious (Whites). (Total Christians in 1921, 51.3%). **7.V.1946:** 40.6% Protestants (16.1% NGK/NHK/GK, 11.1% Methodists, 4.1% Lutherans and Moravians, 2.3% Apostolic Faith Mission (Pentecostals), 2.2% Presbyterians, 2.0% Congregationalists), 33.5% ethnoreligionists, 9.8% Anglicans, 7.0% Non-White indigenous Christians, 4.8% Roman Catholics, 1.6% Hindus, 1.0% Muslims, 0.9% Jews, 0.3% nonreligious (Whites). (Total Christians in 1946, 62.4%). **6.IX.1960:** 39.4% Protestants (16.6% NGK/NHK/GK, 10.7% Methodists, 4.1% Lutherans, 2.0% Presbyterians, 1.8% Congregationalists, 1.2% Apostolic Faith Mission), 22.0% ethnoreligionists, 17.5% Non-White indigenous Christians, 8.8% Anglicans, 6.8% Roman Catholics, 2.1% Hindus, 1.2% Muslims, 0.8% Catholics (non-Roman), 0.7% Jews, 0.4% nonreligious (Whites), 0.1% Orthodox, 0.1% marginal Protestants. (Total Christians in 1960, 73.5%). **6.V.1970:** 39.0% Protestants (15.7% NGK/NHK/GK, 10.6% Methodists, 4.4% Lutherans, 2.7% Presbyterians, 1.8% Congregationalists, 1.0% Apostolic Faith Mission), 20.0% Non-White indigenous Christians, 18.1% ethnoreligionists, 8.7% Roman Catholics, 7.9% Anglicans, 2.0% Hindus, 1.2% Muslims, 1.1% Catholics (non-Roman), 0.7% nonreligious (Whites, Coloureds), 0.6% Jews, 0.4% marginal Protestants, 0.1% Orthodox, 0.1% other religionists. (Total Christians in 1970, 77.2%). Note: the 1970 census was incomplete in that a total of 4,349,525 Bantu were incompletely classified (No religion, no church 3,945,976; Unspecified 324,345; Other religious (non-Christian) 59,729; Object to state 19,475). It is generally agreed that whilst most of these were animists (traditional religionists), a small proportion actually belonged to indigenous churches. The 1970 percentages just given represent this modification of the census totals. Several categories, including 'pagan' have not been consistently or satisfactorily defined or employed throughout the series of censuses since 1911. **1991:** 35.8% Protestants (14.9% NGK/NHK/GK, 6.2% Methodists, 2.6% Lutherans, 1.5% Presbyterians, 1.4% Congregationalists, 1.3% Apostolic Faith Mission), 32.8% Independent Christians, 15.5% Ethnoreligionists, 7.8% Roman Catholics, 4.0% Anglicans, 1.4% Hindus, 1.1% Muslims, 1.6% nonreligious.

NOTES ON RELIGIONS

ATHEISTS. South African Communist Party (SACP) (banned 1950; pro-Soviet). There are also many humanists.

BAHA'IS. Entered before 1921. Recent growth from 28 local spiritual assemblies (1964) to 85 (1973) including 17 in Zululand. Thereafter expansion levelled off, attaining only 93 LSAs in reorganized form by 1996.

BUDDHISTS. Chinese and Bantu (Zulu and Xhosa).

ETHNORELIGIONISTS. The percentage of animists in the nation decreased from 50.7% in 1911 to 10.8% in 1995. Since 1945 there has been a resurgence of ancestor-veneration among the Bantu. Although the 1960 percentage has been acknowledged by the state department of statistics to be too low due to 11% underenumeration of Africans then (underenumeration being only 4.2% in the 1970 census), the rapid decline of animism is evident.

EVANGELICALS. The English term is used here as understood within the churches, and covers the following 4 groupings: (1) all persons affiliated to all Protestant denominations which are Conservative Evangelical in theology and emphasis, (2) Evangelicals within the non-Evangelical or conciliar Protestant denominations usually affiliated to the Ecumenical Movement, (3) a few Fundamentalists, and (4) Anglican Evangelicals.

HINDUS. In addition to Indian immigrants from India and their descendants, there are Bantu Hindus (half being Zulus), Coloured and Whites. Since 1970 there have been numerous non-Asian converts to Hindu sects including (in 1973) 5,000 adults who have 'taken knowledge' in the Divine Light Mission led by Guru Maharaj Ji. Hare Krishna (ISKCON) has 2 centers.

INDEPENDENTS. In over 3,040 African and Coloured denominations in 1995 (see Table 2). Professing adherents at the various censuses have always been considerably higher than those listed under the official classification 'Bantu separatist churches' because many have been classified under other categories. In the 1946 census for the Bantu population, in addition to 3,244,264 adherents of the main-line Western-related denominations, there were 753,891 classified under 'Native separatist churches' (9.6% of the Bantu, 6.6% of the total population and a further 52,694 under 'Various Christian sects' (0.7% of Bantu, 0.5% of total); a majority of these latter were also in indigenous churches. In the 1960 census for the Bantu population, in addition to 4,521,295 in Western-related denominations, there were 2,313,309 classified under Bantu separatist churches (21.2% of Bantu, 14.6% of total) and a further 584,048 under 'Other Christians' (5.3% of Bantu, 3.7% of total), a majority in indigenous churches. In the 1970 census for the Bantu population, in addition to 6 million in Western-related denominations, there were 2,716,019 listed under Bantu separatist or Christian churches (17.7% of Bantu, 12.7% of total), and a further 361,763 under 'Other Christian churches' (2.4% of Bantu, 1.7% of total); also, a small proportion of the 4,349,525 Bantu incompletely classified were probably in indigenous churches. In addition, in 1970 there were about 100,000 Coloureds (0.5% of population) in indigenous churches. It is probable therefore that our category of professing Non-White indigenous Christians numbered about 7.0% of the total population in 1946, about 17.5% in 1960, and in 1970 about 19.5% (Bantu) + 0.5% (Coloured) = 20.0%. *Conversions.* The Bantu and other indigenous churches are winning converts from tribal religions far more rapidly than are any other religious bodies; the total shown in the table (47,867 per year) is greater than the total for Roman Catholics, Protestants, and Anglicans combined.

JEWS. The first Jews arrived with the earliest Portuguese. A community was organized at Cape Town in 1841. By 1950 there were 200 middle-class communities, mostly in larger cities and with their own synagogues.

MUSLIMS. 49.6% Cape Coloureds (Malays, Afrikaans-speaking) 46.7% Asians (Indians and Pakistanis, speaking Gujarati and Urdu respectively, traders in Transvaal and Natal) and 3.3% Blacks of whom half were migrant laborers from Mozambique; also Whites. In 1938, Muslims numbered 111,000 (69,000 Indians, 42,000 Malays) with 100 mosques and 90 imams. Muslims are all Sunnis except for a few Shias and a mosque in Pretoria. There are also Ahmadis (Qadianis; enumerated here as Muslims although declared non-Muslim by Pakistan). Begun 1946; Qadianis (HQ Rabwah, Pakistan). There is extensive missionary propaganda among orthodox Muslims and Black Christians.

Hajj pilgrims to Mecca. (1970) 1,951; (1974) 2,015; (1975) 1,815; (1976) 1,265.

NONRELIGIOUS. 70% Whites, 30% Coloured, some Chinese.

OTHER RELIGIONISTS. Adherents of other non-Christian religions and cults. Rosicrucians (AMORC) have 6 Lodges and centers.

PENTECOSTALS/CHARISMATICS. Anglican charismatics involved (1975) around 15,000 of all races; total charismatic community including children, 30,000, increasing rapidly. In August 1977, 2,300 leaders of the charismatic renewal, from 13 denominations, held their first national conference, in Johannesburg. For Catholics, the CCR began in 1971; by 1996 it had 85 weekly prayer groups with 2,600 regular adult attenders (with 11 priests and 3 involved bishops).

Although charismatics in the non-Pentecostal denominations were strongest in the Anglican CPSA, charismatics in organized groups within non-Pentecostal Protestant denominations numbered in 1975 around 10,000 adults (total charismatic community including children, 20,000). These came mainly from English-speaking churches, Presbyterian, Methodist and others; but from 1974 onwards several hundred ministers and seminarians of the NGK, and several thousand laity, became increasingly involved. There are also numbers of young people in the Jesus Movement, mostly Whites.

By 1995 the total of all Pentecostals/Charismatics had reached 17 million, or 42.8% of the entire population and probably 65% of the entire African population.

ROMAN CATHOLICS. In 1900, 49,593 baptized (all races), about 3,000 catechumens. By 1990, annual increase was very considerable, due to (a) relatively high natural increase, (b) conversions from tribal religion, and (c) heavy immigration from Latin Europe.

SPIRITISTS. Whites. The number has remained near 2,000 since 1900.

UNAFFILIATED CHRISTIANS. In the year 1900 the 688,500 reported were unknown to the mainline mission churches and thus were categorized as 'nominal' or 'unaffiliated'. From our later perspective, however, these were early adherents of the Bantu Separatist Churches which today are reclassified as in the Independent megabloc, Neocharismatics (type I-3nA).

Great Commission Instrument Panel: status of South Africa (for explanation see start of Part 4)

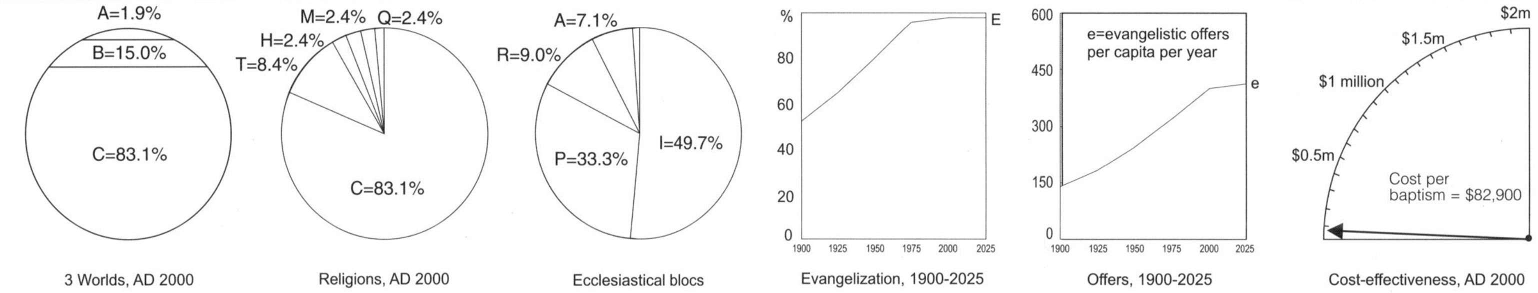

Country status. South Africa occupies the southernmost part of the African continent bordered by Namibia, Botswana, Swaziland, Mozambique, and Zimbabwe. It is the world's largest exporter of gold. Platinum, diamonds, and uranium also play an important role in the economy.

HUMAN LIFE AND LIBERTY

Human need and development. South Africa consists of 2 disparate cultures and societies, each at different stages of economic growth. The Whites for 2 centuries regarded themselves as an outpost of European culture, enjoying a living standard comparable to that in North America and Europe. They controled virtually all economic activities, and provided the capital and entrepreneurial skill and technological know-how needed to maintain their privileged status. The Blacks, on the other hand, were treated as 'hewers of wood and drawers of water' (the biblical phrase) providing largely unskilled and ill-educated manpower and subsisting on meager wages and income. On all quality of life indicators they ranked at the very bottom, but the disparities were masked in overall national statistics.

Under president Nelson Mandala from 1994, a unique, bloodless, peaceful, political revolution took place. The Black-led government now wrestles with preventable diseases, endemic malnutrition, infant mortality, and inadequate health services, all attributable to decades of neglect by White-led governments. Much of the ill health is the direct result of poor dietary habits and insanitary conditions. Black townships are overcrowded and have neither adequate water supplies nor sewage disposal systems. Blacks also lag in education, as the result of deliberate policy under the apartheid system.

Human rights and freedoms. Political and social rights are now expanding to a level comparable with that of Western democracies. Apartheid (racial segregation) was a form of enslavement and its elimination from public life is an event comparable to that of the collapse of Communism in Eastern Europe. Nevertheless the legacy of apartheid is visible in many areas where subtle forms of discrimination persist. Black-Black violence is a disturbing development that may rob South Africa of the benefits of Black-White racial harmony. But in recent years South Africa has made considerable progress toward a democratic and multiracial society. The infamous Public Safety Act and the Internal Security Act have been repealed. However, in the former Homelands, free political activities are suppressed. Certain areas are awash in violence, much of it criminally motivated. Officially sanctioned discrimination has been outlawed. The Promotion of Equality Between Men and Women Act eliminates all vestiges of the social inequality that women had suffered formerly.

Human environment. South Africa has been described as an ecological microcosm. It is home to 25,000 plant species in additions to hundreds of unique animal species. Yet much of this legacy has been squandered in the past. Destructive farming practices have promoted soil erosion in the Homelands. Air pollution problems are severe in the Eastern Transvaal Highveld region. The dry ranges of the Karoo have been moving eastward because of overgrazing by the 10 million sheep stocked there.

At the end of a1988 church conference in Soweto to plan nonviolent action against apartheid, Archbishop Desmond Tutu seizes a huge cross and processes with it.

Country summary. **Worlds A, B, C by ethnolinguistic peoples, cities, and major civil divisions in South Africa.**

	PEOPLES							CITIES							CIVIL DIVISIONS						
World	*Num*	*Pop 2000*	*C%*	*Christians*	*E%*	*U%*	*Unevangelized*	*Num*	*Pop 2000*	*C%*	*Christians*	*E%*	*U%*	*Unevangelized*	*Num*	*Pop 2000*	*C%*	*Christians*	*E%*	*U%*	*Unevangelized*
A	2	1,550	1.87	29	38	62	962	0	0	0.00	0	0	0	0	0	0	0.00	0	0	0	0
B	32	5,217,563	28.87	1,506,545	86	14	732,004	0	0	0.00	0	0	0	0	0	0	0.00	0	0	0	0
C	36	35,157,470	86.17	30,294,222	100	0	48,864	15	13,340,449	72.00	9,605,673	97	3	428,391	9	40,376,580	78.76	31,800,787	98	2	781,833
Total	**70**	**40,376,583**	**78.76**	**31,800,796**	**98**	**2**	**781,830**	**15**	**13,340,449**	**72.00**	**9,605,673**	**97**	**3**	**428,391**	**9**	**40,376,580**	**78.76**	**31,800,787**	**98**	**2**	**781,833**

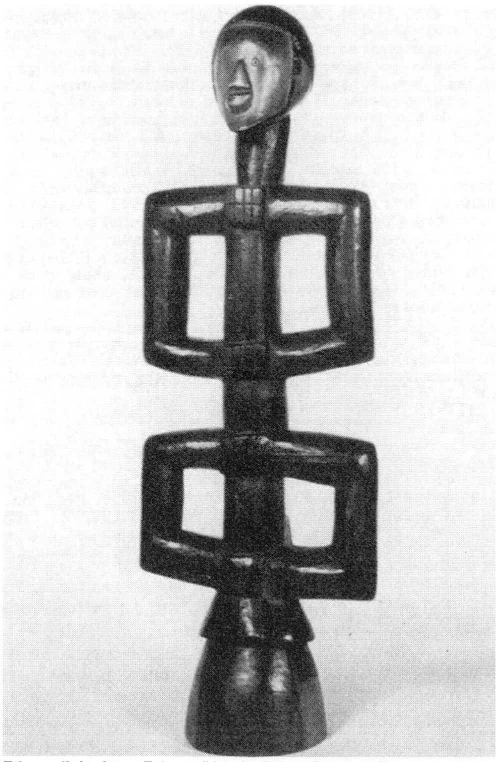

Ethnoreligionists. Zulu traditional religious figurine. The total number of adherents of tribal religions in South Africa has nearly doubled since 1990, is over 4.4 million now, and is still increasing by some 64,000 a year.

NON-CHRISTIAN RELIGIONS

Traditional religions continue to retain the allegiance of 8% of the population, the highest proportion being among the Venda who are 70% traditionalists. Traditional thought combines an emphasis on magical practices with ancestral veneration, in addition to belief in the supreme being who is known by various names: Unkulunkulu (Zulu), Thixo (Xhosa), Utixo (Hottentots), Tilo (Tsonga), Khuzwane (Lovedu), and Raluvhimba (Venda). A distinctive feature of Lovedu traditional religion is the role played by the divine queen who must be without physical weakness and who eventually commits ritual suicide by poison before the young male initiates emerge from her reign's fourth circumcision school. She is especially responsible for rain making, called to her aid her own divinity, the royal rain medicines, and the royal ancestral spirits. The supreme being is not involved. Also important is the belief in the power of medicine men (lelopo), diviners (mugome), witchcraft (vuloi), and taboo (hu-ila), as well as a female fertility cult (Vyali-Vuhwera) involving the use of 4 sacred drums (digoma). A number of spirit-possession cults have also spread to South Africa from neighboring Zimbabwe. The Molombo cult among the Venda owes its origin to the period following World War I and continues to be active. Possession is by ancestors and not by animal spirits as with the Shona or alien spirits among the Tsonga; and this is true also for the Lovedu. The older Zulu ancestral possession cult called Ukuthwasa has now given way to the Amandiki cult in which foreign spirits play a key role.

Hinduism is confined almost entirely to the Asian community. Hindus make up 2.4% of the population. Although many Hindus are being converted to Christianity, a fair number of non-Hindu Whites and other non-Asians have been converted to the Divine Light Mission.

Islam is found mostly among the Urdu- and Gujarati-speaking peoples of Indian descent, settled mainly in Natal. There is also an Afrikaans-speaking Muslim community known as Cape Malays, of Asiatic origin but now mixed with other races resulting in their being officially classed as Colored. A few African workers, immigrants from Mozambique, are also Muslims. Islam is active and has made some headway among urbanized Africans through the Islamic Bureau, based on Athlone, Cape, which promotes systematic missionary endeavor with South African. Muslims form 2.4% of the population.

Judaism is represented by a prosperous middle-class community found almost exclusively in the larger cities, in particular Cape Town and Johannesburg and to a lesser extent Durban and elsewhere. Jewish immigration dates from the end of the 19th century and has been especially large from Eastern Europe. The first synagogue was built in Cape Town in 1862, some 20 years after the establishment of the first Jewish community in the city and country (1841). The South African Jewish Board of Deputies, established in 1912, officially represents the interests of the Jewish community. Jews make up 0.4% of the population.

CHRISTIANITY

Bartholomew Diaz rounded the Cape of Good Hope in 1488, but because of the hostile attitude of the Hottentots no efforts were made to settle. The first European settlers were the Dutch in 1652, and for some years church attention centered on securing clergy for them rather than for missions to Africans. The first missionary to the Hottentots was George Schmidt, sent by Moravians in 1737.

Britain gained control of the Cape in 1795, and in 1799 the London Missionary Society founded Bethelsdorp near the southeast coast. Because of dissatisfaction with British rule and the abolition of slavery in 1833, Boer settlers trekked north to the Orange Free State, Natal, and the Transvaal between 1835 and 1848, leading to wars with the Zulus, Matabele, and other Bantu states. In 1843, Britain gained control of Natal; and after the discovery of gold and diamonds, it annexed the Orange Free State in 1871 and the Transvaal in 1877. The Boers fought to regain their independence in 1899 but lost to the British in 1902. In 1910, the 4 states became the Union of South Africa and in 1948 Dutch Afrikaners gained control of the government and began to legalize their apartheid policies, with support from the Dutch Reformed Church.

Christianity has made steady progress since the last century, and by 1995, 82.6% of the population were professing Christians. Almost all Afrikaners belong to one of the Dutch Reformed churches or the Apostolic Faith Mission. Most English-speaking Europeans are members of the Anglican, Methodist, Presbyterian or Catholic churches, living mainly in Natal and the east coast.

Dutch Reformed Church (Mother Church). Largest General Synodal Session of the Whites-only NGK ever held, with 900 Afrikaner delegates (October 1973); *above*, last session of old Cape Synod. At its October 1978 General Synod the NGK again rejected any merger or umbrella synod with its Non-White daughter churches.

PROTESTANT CHURCHES. The Dutch Reformed Church (Nederduitse Gereformeerde Kerk, NGK) began in 1652 upon the arrival of the first settlers from Holland. The needs of the indigenous peoples were largely ignored until the end of the 18th century. In 1824, a committee on missions was appointed and in 1836 the first missionary to Blacks was commissioned. In the latter half of the 19th century, several stations were built as well as a missionary training school, and the work was extended northward. Between 1853 and 1866, 5 schisms took place within the NGK. The Nederduits Hervormde Kerk (NHK) was founded in the Transvaal in 1853, separating due to their opposition to native missions and their desire for complete independence from British control. The Gereformeerde Kerk was formed in 1859 mostly over doctrinal questions, especially alleged Methodist influences in the mother church. The 3 other separations were largely regional in nature and resulted in the formation of churches in Natal, Transvaal, and the Orange Free State. In 1963, these 3 regional churches, plus a fourth which was founded later in South West Africa, reunited with the original mother church in Cape Town to form the General Synod NGK. The members of all these churches are of European descent but their missions have resulted in the creation of separate Black, Colored, and Indian churches as well. The General Synod NGK plus its mission churches are associated together in the Federal Council of the Dutch Reformed Churches. The Dutch Reformed, in all their various branches, are a principal church tradition in South Africa, with 9% of the population in 1995.

In 1806, Methodist soldiers stationed in Cape Colony built a small chapel near Table Mountain for their meetings, thus initiating the Methodist presence in South Africa. The first Methodist missionary arrived from great Britain in 1816, working in the southeast, followed by others who built a series of stations along the eastern coast. Today the Methodists have the largest Bantu membership and form the second largest Protestant church tradition in the republic with 6.7% of the population in 1995.

The next largest church tradition in South Africa is Lutheranism. The Evangelical Lutheran Church owes its origin to the work of North American, German, Swedish, and Norwegian societies during the 19th century. Lutherans numbered 4.4% of the population in 1970.

A Presbyterian church was formed in 1813 to serve Whites at the Cape, and the first Scottish Presbyterian of the Glasgow Missionary Society arrived in 1820, followed in subsequent years by several other Presbyterian societies. An outstanding product of this early influence has been the Lovedale school with its comprehensive educational and community development programs. Out of this early work has also come 2 important denominations: the Bantu Presbyterian church, which is entirely Black, and the Presbyterian church of Southern Africa, which is 65% White. Union negotiations between these 2 bodies continue. Presbyterians now account for less than 1% of the population.

The London Missionary Society entered the Cape in 1799 and produced in the early years some of Africa's best-known missionaries: Johannes Vanderkemp, Robert Moffat, John Philip, and David Livingstone. Together with 3 other missions and churches, including the work originally begun in 1835 by the American Board among the Zulus of Natal, they merged in 1967 to form the United Congregational Church of Southern Africa. Since 1970, this tradition has been declining. By 1995, only 0.3% of the population were Congregationalists.

The Apostolic Faith Mission is a Pentecostal body founded in 1908. This church and other similar but smaller denominations numbered 1.7% of the population in 1995. Its membership consists of substantial numbers of Blacks, Whites, and Coloreds. It is the only denomination outside the Dutch Reformed churches to have made extensive inroads among the Afrikaans-speaking community.

Other Protestant groups include Assemblies of God (300,000 members in 1995), Baptists, Brethren, Full Gospel Church of God, Moravians, Nazarenes, Salvation Army, Seventh-day Adventists, and a large number of smaller denominations.

Zion Christian Church. 4 million members seated on ground partake of Easter communion each year at Morija.

INDIGENOUS CHURCHES. South Africa has the greatest proliferation of separatist churches of any country in the world. Separatist movements initiated by African churchmen began near the end of the 19th century. By 1904, 3 large denominations with 25,000 followers were in existence, growing to 130 bodies in 1925, 1,300 bodies in 1946 with one million adherents, 2,000 bodies in the 1950s with 1.5 million followers, and over 4,000 bodies with nearly 13 million adherents in 1995. The first bodies were identified with the Ethiopian movement emphasizing African independence but with churches patterned after the established bodies from which they seceded. Later, the Zionist movement grew which was more pentecostal in nature, emphasizing healing and spiritual experience and drawing more freely from elements found in traditional religions. This was often accompanied by the appearance of charismatic semi-messianic figures to whom special powers were attributed. While independent churches are found throughout the continent, South Africa has been a more fertile seed bed for their growth than any other African state. Various efforts have been made to bring them together through local Bantu ministers' associations and theological correspondence courses, but more schisms than unions continue to take place each year. The largest bodies today (with 1995 statistics) are the Zion Christian Church (5,000,000), Nazarite Baptist Church (700,000), Assemblies of God (Back to God) (1,500,000), Presbyterian Church of Africa (400,000), and St John's Apostolic Faith Mission (600,000). Blacks from the USA have also played an important role on the South African scene, the most important of several Black American denominations being the African Methodist Episcopal Church (75,000).

CATHOLIC CHURCH. Catholicism was late in establishing itself in South Africa, although the first Catholic church was built by Portuguese at Mossel Bay (Natal) as early as 1501. Six Jesuits visited the Cape in 1685, but permission to celebrate mass was denied. The first priests were not allowed to settle until 1805, and regular work was not begun until 1820. A vicariate was erected in 1837 and by 1850 2 additional vicariates had been added. Also in 1850, Missionary Sisters of the Assumption built the first convent at Grahamstown. Freedom of worship for Catholics was officially guaranteed throughout the whole country in 1870, and in 1922 the Holy See appointed its first apostolic delegate to South Africa. The hierarchy was established in 1951 and the first Black bishop consecrated in 1953. There are at present 4 archdioceses, 21 dioceses and one other jurisdiction. In 1995, Catholics formed 8% of the total population.

The Holy See has diplomatic relations with South Africa and in AD 2000 is represented to government and the Catholic hierarchy by a nuncio residing in Pretoria.

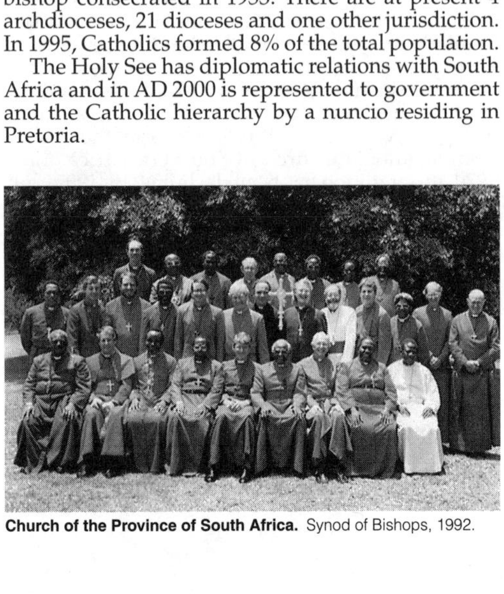

Church of the Province of South Africa. Synod of Bishops, 1992.

ANGLICAN CHURCH. Although Anglicans regularly met in a Dutch Reformed church in Cape Town after 1806, Church of England missions did not begin until the arrival of the first SPG missionary in 1821; and the most active phase followed the appointment of the first Anglican bishop in 1847. In 1870, a dissident Evangelical group separated to form the Church of England in South Africa. The main Anglican body today is the Church of the Province of Southern Africa with 11 dioceses. In 1995, Anglicans were 5.5% of the population.

Renewal movements. In the 1990s the Pentecostal/Charismatic Renewal continued to spread rapidly across most older churches, and numbered over 21,200,000 adherents (of whom 8% Pentecostals, 11% Charismatics, and 81% Independents).

Indigenous missions. From the earliest days of the establishment of Christianity in South Africa, missionaries have been sent to surrounding African countries. By the end of the 19th century, South African Christians were serving as missionaries on 6 continents. This commitment increased in the 20th century, with impetus added by the African independent churches evangelistic zeal. After 1960, South Africa's relative isolation under apartheid caused a dramatic decline in the number of missionaries working outside the country. The number began to rise again after the collapse of apartheid in 1990.

Greek Orthodox Church. Greek youngsters in Greek national dress, in Port Elizabeth Orthodox Church, 1974.

CHURCH AND STATE

The constitution of 31 May 1961, known as the Constitutional Law of the Republic of South Africa, contains no declaration of either individual or collective rights, a notable omission among 20th-century constitutions in other countries. Its preamble states: 'In humble submission to Almighty God, who controls the destinies of nations and the history of peoples, who gathered our forefathers together from many lands and gave them this land for their own, who has guided them from generation to generation, and who has wondrously delivered them from the dangers that beset them, we, who are here in Parliament assembled . . .'. The invocation of God reappears in the oaths of office taken by the president of the republic, cabinet ministers, and parliamentarians (Articles 12, 20 and 52). Article 2 affirms that 'The people of the Republic of South Africa recognize the sovereignty and help of Almighty God'.

The Dutch Reformed churches in general supported the government's policy of apartheid and frequently sought scriptural or theological justification for it. While accepting the general principles of apartheid, synodal declarations since 1948 have regularly called upon the political authorizes to respect human dignity. In 1961, the NGK withdrew from the World Council of Churches after the WCC-sponsored Cottesloe consultation following the Sharpeville massacre in 1960, which condemned apartheid. The Dutch Reformed churches defended the idea that the historic role of the Afrikaner people is to protect Christian civilization from anti-Christian forces, in particular Communism. Nevertheless, the unity of these churches was severely shaken. An ultra-conservative right wing tried to influence the government, while an active left wing grouped around the Christian Institute of South Africa broke away radically from the theory and practice of apartheid. In April 1978, the NGK severed relations with the Netherlands Reformed Church (Holland) over the latter's support of African liberation movements.

Certain Pentecostal groups adopted a strong pro-government attitude, but the English-speaking churches were for the most part officially opposed to apartheid, although their protestations were generally addressed in measured tones. In 1968, the South African Council of Churches, published a 'Message to the people of South Africa', describing the policy of apartheid as anti-Christian. It was signed by 78 South African theologians and called on the faithful also to sign it. Only 1,800 did so, of which 600 were ecclesiastics of various confessions. In 1970, when the WCC decided to allocate its firm sum of US$200,000 to 19 anti-racist organizations throughout the world for humanitarian work, the South African churches criticized the implied support thus given to terrorism. Among the beneficiaries that year was the African National Congress of South Africa and several liberation movements in Rhodesia and the Portuguese colonies. Nevertheless, no church followed the prime minister when he attempted to intimidate them into leaving the WCC under pain of sanctions. On the other hand, African clergy and laity accused the English-speaking churches of practicing an apartheid of their own.

Three other regulations from earlier periods directly affect church affairs. The Natives Urban Areas Act, Section 7, requires both municipal and government permission for the erection of churches in White residential areas if mainly for non-Whites. Only twice so far has this regulation been invoked, once against Methodists and once against Congregationalists. Second, the so-called 'church clause' of the Native Laws Amendment Act (1957) empowers the government to prohibit African church attendance in White areas which such attendance would be regarded as a nuisance, provided alternative facilities exist and municipal authorities concur. This clause has not yet been invoked. Third, the Bantu Education Act (1953) provides for the transfer of all African schools to state control. Churches may, at their own expense, maintain private church schools for Africans at the discretion of the state and provided the state syllabus is followed. Church schools for the other races are not subject to such control.

In 1993, the new government under president Mandela announced a new policy through which churches may opt to open their doors to all races without hindrance.

Churches do not have to register with government, although the mass of small indigenous churches are not recognized and so cannot be granted land for building. From 1925-65, the government had machinery for the recognition of churches, but of the 81 recognized by 1965, only 11 were indigenous churches. None of the over 2,500 Zionist denominations were ever recognized.

Ecclesiastical marriage officers must be registered, and marriages are invalid unless solemnized by a registered officer. There are no state subsidies for churches, the state subsidizes church hospitals and institutions for the handicapped in various degrees.

BROADCASTING AND MEDIA

TWR maintains a transmitter located at Johannesburg which broadcasts in Amharic, Somali, Yoruba, Fulani, Hausa, Twi, Oromo, Tigrinya, English, and reaches most of subsaharan Africa. HCJB World Radio has helped to start local stations in South Africa in cooperation with several local ministries. Shortwave radio programs from KNLS have seen some response.

Christian television programming is widespread. CBN's programs are available on a weekly basis in Ciskei & Transkei. TBN programs appear in Ciskei and Transkei on local channels, and throughout South Africa on TV1.

Over 18 million have seen the 'Jesus' Film: through television broadcasts (11 million), cinematic showings (1.3 million) and film team presentations (5.4 million). 554,000 have responded.

INTERDENOMINATIONAL ORGANIZATIONS

The South African Council of Churches (SACC) was established in 1936, building on the foundation of the South African General Missionary Conference begun in 1904.

The following 14 subregional and local councils are affiliated to the SACC and work closely with it: Bloemfontein, Bophutatswana homeland, Border, Goldfiends and Kroonstad, Kimberley, Natal, North

Natal, Northern Transvaal, Pietermaritzburg, Port Elizabeth, Transkei, Western Province, Witwatersrand, and Zululand.

Numerous attempts have been made to form associations of Black independent churches, the most important of which are the African Independent Churches Association (AICA), Federation of Non-White Pentecostal and Apostolic Missionary Churches in Africa , Reformed Independent Churches Association (RICA), Assembly of Zionist and Apostolic Churches, African Independent Churches Movement (AICM) and Association of Pentecostal Ministers of South Africa.

On the Catholic side, the South African Bishops' Conference sponsors a Commission for Ecumenism and Afrikaans Affairs.

Two commissions have been formed for dialogue between the churches. The Church Unity Commission involves the Anglican, Presbyterian, Congregational, and Methodists churches. There is also a commission responsible for official discussions between the Anglican and Catholic churches, including also a joint monthly magazine in Afrikaans and joint pastoral action in prisons.

Six ecumenical institutes and centers are in operation. The Christian Institute of Southern Africa is an unofficial radical body engaged in race relations, action against apartheid, and dialogue with African independent churches. It was established in 1963 by NGK members but has now become interdenominational and its staff includes Catholics and independents. The Ecumenical Research Unit was founded in 1970 as a joint undertaking of the Catholic Bishops' Conference, SACC and the Anglican Church and studies pastoral and missiological problems. The Edendale Lay Ecumenical Center is the only lay academy in South Africa initiated by Blacks to develop Black leadership and Black initiative. Founded in 1965 by an African pastor of the Methodist Church, it is a member of the SACC, runs an independent program and is now the base for IDAMASA, the Interdenominational African Ministers' Association of Southern Africa. Other important ecumenical institutions include the Wilgespruit Fellowship Center, which is interdenominational; Emmaus House (formerly Stellenbosch Ecumenical Center) founded in 1967, sponsored by an interdenominational committee and run by the Catholic Dominicans; and Koinonia Conference Center.

Two cooperative theological ventures are the Federal Theological Seminary at Alice and the Association of Southern African Theological Institutions.

An organization working for better relations between religions, notably Christians and Jews, is the Spiritual Unity of Nations (SUN), in Somerset West, an international association with its headquarters in South Africa.

FUTURE TRENDS AND PROSPECTS

Christian churches have grown since the end of apartheid and this is likely to continue for the next 2 decades. Christians may grow to 83.2% of the population by AD 2025 primarily due to growth among the independent churches.

With ethnoreligionists expected to continue to decline through the 21st century, it is possible that Christianity will grow to near 90% of the population. Nonetheless, non-Christians, particularly Hindus, Muslims, and the nonreligious will maintain a significant presence for the next fifty years at least.

BIBLIOGRAPHY

A bibliography of South African history, 1978–1989. B. J. Liebenberg, K. W. Smith & S. B. Spies. Pretoria: University of South Africa, 1992. 401p. (Supplements Muller's 1979 bibliography).

A Black future?: Jesus and salvation in South Africa. R. Nicolson. London: SCM Press, 1990. 281p.

A history of Christian missions in South Africa. J. Du Plessis. 1911; reprint, Cape Town: Struik, 1965. 494p.

A history of Christianity in South Africa. J. W. Hofmeyr & G. J. Pillay (eds). Pretoria: HAUM Tertiary, 1994.

A history of the church in Southern Africa: a select bibliography of published material. J. W. Hofmeyr & K. E. Cross. Pretoria, South Africa: University of South Africa, 1986. 2 vols.

A history of the New Church in Southern Africa, 1909–1991 and a tribute to the lifetime dedication of Obed S.D. Mooki. J. Evans. [1994]. 210p. (Treats New Jerusalem Church).

A select bibliography of periodical articles on Southern African church history. J. W. Hofmeyr, J. H. Rykheer & J. M. Nel (eds). *Studia composita*, 12. Pretoria: University of South Africa, 1991.

'A separatist church: Ibandla lika–Krestu,' L. Mqotsi & N. Mkele, *African studies*, 5, 2 (1946), 124ff.

Africa theology: an introduction. G. M. Setiloane. Johannesburg: Skotaville, 1986. 50p.

African traditional religion in South Africa: an annotated bibliography. D. Chidester et al. *Bibliographies and indexes in religious studies.* Westport, CT: Greenwood Press.

Afro–Christian religion at the grassroots in southern Africa. G. C. Oosthuizen & I. Hexham (eds). Lewiston, NY: E. Mellen Press, 1991. 429p.

Apartheid is a heresy. J. W. de Gruchy & C. Villa-Vicencio (eds). Cape Town: David Philip, 1983. 184p.

Bantu prophets in South Africa. B. G. M. Sundkler. Rev. ed. London: Lutterworth, 1961. 381p.

Bazalwane: African Pentecostals in South Africa. A. Anderson. *Manualia didactica*, 19. Pretoria: University of South Africa, 1992. 181p.

Bishops and prophets in a Black city: African independent churches in Soweto, Johannesburg. M. West. Cape Town: David Philip, 1975. 225p. (On 900 indigenous churches in Soweto).

Black charismatic Anglicans: the Iviyo loFakazi bakaKristu and its relations with other renewal movements. S. Hayes. *Studia specialia*, 4. Pretoria: University of South Africa, 1990. 243p.

Black Methodists and white supremacy in South Africa. D. M. Balia. Durban, South Africa: Madiba Publications, 1991. 112p.

Body of power, spirit of resistance: the culture and history of a South African people. J. Comaroff. Chicago: University of Chicago Press, 1985. 276p. (Treats Barolong boo Ratshidi people and Zion Christian Church).

Calvary now. R. A. Reeves. London: SCM Press, 1965.

Catholics in Apartheid society. A. Prior. Cape Town: David Philip, 1982. 197p.

'Chief and prophet in Zululand and Swaziland,' B. G. M. Sundkler, in *African systems of thought*, p.276–90. M. Fortes & G. Dieterlen (eds). London: Oxford University Press, 1965.

Chiefs and gods: religious and social elements in the south eastern Bantu kingship. O. Pettersson. Lund, Sweden: Gleerup, 1953. 405p.

'Christian origins and growth in South Africa: a Dutch Reformed and charismatic church case study.' J. J. Combrinck. D.Miss. thesis, Fuller Theological Seminary, Pasadena, CA, 1990. 429p.

'Christianity and black resistance to apartheid in South Africa: a comparison of Albert Lutuli, Robert Sobukwe, Steve Biko, and Desmond Tutu.' L. S. Graybill. Ph.D. dissertation, University of Virginia, Charlottesville, VA, 1991. 240p.

Christianity and democracy: a theology for a just world order. J. W. de Gruchy. *Cambridge studies in ideology and religion*, 7. New York and Cambridge, UK: Cambridge University Press, 1995. 308p.

Christianity and Xhosa tradition: belief and ritual among Xhosa–speaking Christians. B. A. Pauw. London: Oxford, 1975. 390p.

Christianity in South Africa. M. Prozesky (ed). Bergvlei, South Africa: 1989. 256p.

Christianity in South Africa: an annotated bibliography. D. Chidester, J. Tobler & D. Wratten. Westport, CT: Greenwood Press, 1997. 504p.

Christianity in the southern hemisphere: the churches in Latin America and South Africa. E. Norman. Oxford, UK: Clarendon Press, 1981.

Church and politics: a Pentecostal view of the South African situation. F. P. Möller. Braamfontein, South Africa: Gospel Publishers. 50p.

Church membership in South Africa. P. W. Brierley. *MARC monograph*, no. 13. Bromley, UK: MARC Europe, [1988]. 21p.

Church versus state in South Africa: the case of the Christian Institute. P. Walshe. London: Hurst; Maryknoll, NY: Orbis Books, 1983. 234p. (Describes the history of a multiracial Christian organization formed in 1963 in opposition to Apartheid).

Civil disobedience and beyond: law, resistance and religion in South Africa. C. Villa-Vicencio. Cape Town: David Philip, 1990. 165p.

Councils in the ecumenical movement in South Africa, 1904–1975. D. G. Thomas. Johannesburg: South Africa Council of Churches, 1979. 123p.

Eingeborenenkirchen in Sud– und Sudwestafrika: ihre Geschichte und Sozialstruktur. K. Schlosser. Kiel, Germany: W. G. Mühlau, 1958. 355p.

Ethiopia stretches out her hands unto God: aspects of Transkeian indigenous churches. H. L. Pretorius. Pretoria: Institute for Missiological Research, University of Pretoria, 1993. 131p.

Evangelical witness in South Africa: a critique of evangelical theology and practice by South African evangelicals. Concerned Evangelicals of Soweto. Grand Rapids, MI: Eerdmans, 1986. 48p.

Evangelisation in the South African context. S. C. Bate. *Inculturation*, 12. Rome: Pontifical Gregorian University, 1991. 131p.

From rags to riches: an analysis of the Faith movement and its relation to the classical Pentecostal movement. J. N. Horn. Pretoria: University of South Africa, Institute for Theological Research, 1989. 147p. (On the Word of Faith/Prosperity Gospel movement).

God in South Africa: the challenge of the gospel. A. Nolan. Cape Town: David Philip, 1988. 241p.

'Good news for the poor?: the church and community development in South Africa.' M. M. James. Ph.D. dissertation, Boston University, Boston, 1990. 285p.

Historiography and historical sources regarding African indigenous churches in South Africa: writing indigenous church history. H. L. Pretorius. Lewiston, NY: Edwin Mellen Press, 1995. 146p.

History of the church in South Africa: a document and source book. J. W. Hofmeyr, J. A. Millard & C. J. J. Froneman (eds). *Studia composita*, 11. Pretoria: University of South Africa, 1991. 453p.

History of the church in South Africa: guide to information and sources. J. W. Hofmeyr & J. A. Millard. *Studia composita*, 8. Pretoria: University of South Africa, 1990. 86p.

Index of the names of mission stations established in the Southern Africa region during the 19th and early 20th centuries. F. Frescura. Johannesburg: Transvaal Vernacular Architecture Society in conjunction with the University of the Witwatersrand, Department of Architecture, 1982. 97p.

Journal of theology for Southern Africa. Rondebosch, South Africa: University of Cape Town, Department of Religious Studies, 1972–. (Quarterly).

Living faiths in South Africa. M. Prozesky & J. de Gruchy (eds). Cape Town: David Philip; New York: St. Martin's Press; London: Hurst & Co., 1995. 247p.

Methodist Church in Africa: history of the church. L. W. M. Xozwa. *Cory Library occasional papers*, no. 2. Grahamstown, South Africa: Cory Library for Historical Research, Rhodes University, 1989. 60p.

Naught for your comfort. T. Huddleston. London: Collins, 1956. 191p.

Of revelation and revolution: Christianity, colonialism and consciousness in South Africa. J. Comaroff. Chicago: University of Chicago Press, 1991.

Pentecostal penetration into the Indian community in metropolitan Durban, South Africa. G. C. Oosthuizen. Leiden: E. J. Brill, 1975. 356p.

Recent developments in the South African mission field. G. B. A. Gerdener. Cape Town: NG Kerk-Uitgewers, 1958. 286p.

Religion alive: studies in the new movements and indigenous churches in southern Africa: a symposium. G. C. Oosthuizen (ed). Johannesburg: Hodder & Stoughton, 1986. 262p.

Religion among the Bantu in South Africa. B. L. Ellis. Johannesburg: University of the Witwatersrand Library, 1968. (Contains bibliography).

'Religion, class and culture: indigenous churches in South Africa, with special reference to Zionist–Apostolics.' G. Kruss. M.A. thesis, University of Cape Town, Cape Town, South Africa, 1985. 316p.

Religion in a Tswana chiefdom. B. A. Pauw. London: Oxford University Press for the International African Institute, 1960. 258p.

Religion, intergroup relations and social change in South Africa. G. C. Oosthuizen et al. New York: Greenwood Press, 1988. 249p.

Select bibliography of South African native life and problems. I. Schapera. London: Oxford University Press, 1941. 249p.

'Sociology and anthropology of religion in South Africa,' *Social compass*, 19, 1 (1972).

South Africa. G. V. Davis. 2nd ed. *World bibliographical series*, vol. 7. Oxford, UK: CLIO Press, 1994. 496p. (See especially section on 'Bibliographies' in chapter on 'History,' and chapter on 'Religion,' pp. 119-127).

'South Africa,' E. Higgins, in *Western religion: a country by country sociological enquiry*, p.437–58. H. Mol (ed). The Hague: Mouton, 1972.

South Africa: a Catholic perspective. N. B. Peters. Fresno, CA: Pioneer, 1991. 225p.

South Africa: sociological analyses. A. P. Hare, G. Wiendieck & M. H. von Broembsen. Cape Town: Oxford University Press, 1979. 430p.

South African Christian handbook 1993/4. M. Froise (ed). Welkom, South Africa: Christian Info, 1992. 340p. (1996/7 edition, 1996, 345p.).

South African history and historians: a bibliography. C. F. J. Muller, F. A. van Jaarsveld, T. van Wijk & M. Boucher. Pretoria: University of South Africa, 1979. 411p.

South African Jewry: a contemporary survey. M. Arkin. Cape Town: Oxford University Press, 1984. 212p.

Supplement to the Catholic directory of Southern Africa 1971–1972. Cape Town: Salesian Press, 1972.

The Bantu–speaking peoples of Southern Africa. W. D. Hammond-Tooke (ed). London: Routledge & Kegan Paul, 1974. 525p.

The birth of Christian Zionism in South Africa. G. C. Oosthuizen. KwaDlangezwa, South Africa: University of Zululand, 1987. 58p.

The Cape Malays: history, religion, traditions, folk tales: the Malay quarter. I. D. du Plessis. 3rd ed. Cape Town: Balkema, 1972. 97p.

The Catholic Church in South Africa, from its origins to the present day. E. W. Brown. London: Burns & Oates, 1960. 384p.

The Catholic Church in the Transvaal. J. B. Brain. Johannesburg: Missionary Oblates of Mary Immaculate, 1991. 454p.

The Catholic directory of southern Africa, 1971. Cape Town: Salesian Press, 1971.

'The Church of England as an international actor in Southern Africa, 1970–1980.' V. Austin. Ph.D. dissertation, University of Kent, Canterbury, UK, 1991. 302p.

The House of Phalo: a history of the Xhosa people in the days of their independence. J. B. Peires. Johannesburg: Ravan Press, 1981. 281p. (Treats Xhosa religion and response to Christianity).

The Kairos Document: challenge to the Church. A theological comment on the political crisis in South Africa. Grand Rapids, MI: Eerdmans, 1986. 58p.

The kingdom of God in South Africa: a brief survey of missions south of the Zambesi. A. Murray. 40p.

'The Lovedu of the Transvaal,' J. D. Krige & E. J. Krige, in *African worlds*, p.55–82. D. Forde (ed). London: Oxford University Press, 1954.

The planting of the churches in South Africa. J. M. Sales. Grand Rapids, MI: Eerdmans, 1971. 170p.

The production and management of therapeutic power in Zionist churches within a Zulu city. J. P. Kiernan. *Studies*

in African health and medicine, vol. 4. Lewiston, NY: E. Mellen Press, 1990. 283p.
The South African context for mission. J. J. Kritzinger. Cape Town: Lux Verbi, 1989. 148p.
The theology of a South African messiah: an analysis of the hymnal of the Church of the Nazirites. G. C. Oosthuizen. Leiden: E. J. Brill, 1967.
The Zionist Christian Church in South Africa: a case–study in oral theology. P. Naudé. Lewiston, NY: E. Mellen Press, 1995. 169p.
Theology and ministry in context and crisis: a South African perspective. J. W. de Gruchy. Grand Rapids, MI: Eerdmans, 1987. 183p.
Theses and dissertations on Southern Africa: an international bibliography. O. B. Pollak & K. Pollak. Boston: G. K. Hall, 1976. 236p. (Covers religion).
Third way theology: reconciliation, revolution, and reform in the South African church during the 1980s. A. Balcomb. Pietermaritzburg, South Africa: Cluster Publications, 1993. 291p.
Transkei for Christ: a history of the Catholic Church in the Transkeian Territories. M. Dischl. [Umtata, South Africa]: M. Dischl, 1982. 373p.
Tumelo: the faith of African Pentecostals in South Africa. A. Anderson & S. Otwang. *Studia originalia*, 17. Pretoria: University of South Africa, 1993. 181p.
Who are the independent churches? P. Makhubu. Johannesburg: Skotaville, 1988. 114p.
Women hold up half the sky: women in the church in Southern Africa. D. Ackermann, J. A. Draper & E. Mashinini (eds). Pietermaritzburg, South Africa: Cluster Publications, 1991. 416p.
Zulu Zion and some Swazi Zionists. B. Sundkler. *Oxford studies in African affairs*. Oxford, UK: Oxford University Press, 1976. 337p.

Country Table 2. **Organized churches and denominations in South Africa.**

Official name (bold type = church with over 10% of all affiliated) 1	*Begun* 2	*Type* 3	*Counc* 4	*Congs* 5	*Adults* 6	*Affiliated 1970* 7	*Affiliated 1995* 8	*G%* 9	*Names, notes, and other statistics* (see Codebook, Part 3) 10
Acts Mission Church of South Africa	c1975	I-3cA	.....	26	4,000	–	6,150	5.00	Mission church based in Cape Town. 19n
African Assemb of God (Back to God)	1943	I-3pA	x....	700	900,000	430,000	1,500,000	5.12	Rapidly-expanding Nicholas Bhengu pentecostal movement. 1959, ex AoG(USA). Xhosa, Zulu.
African Catholic Church	1947	I-Ang	....W	76	34,000	54,000	56,700	0.20	Ex CPSA. Dioceses: Vereeniging, Pretoria, Reitz OFS, Cape, Sotho, Xhosa.66n.
African Congregational Church	1917	I-Con	.....	187	9,900	70,000	16,500	-5.62	Zulu church, schism ex ABCFM. Steady growth since origin, then schisms and decline. 36n.
African Evangelical Church	1889	P-Eva	xM...	210	16,500	8,367	55,000	7.82	M=AEF (formerly SAGM). Bantu in Natal. Transvaal, Transkei. 50n,48f,1H,1h,2s.
African Gospel Church	1947	I-3fA	.....	90	40,000	50,000	100,000	2.81	Schism ex Full Gospel Ch of God. Strong in Natal. Cape: Zulu, also Xhosa. 110n.
African Methodist Episcopal Church	1892	I-Met	Vw..W	244	40,900	300,000	75,827	-5.35	Ex Wesleyan Meth Ch; 1894, affiliated to AMEC(USA), 15th Episcopal District. 182n,2f,1j,1s.
African Methodist Episcopal Zion Ch		I-Met	.....	18	1,800	9,720	5,000	0.05	M=AMEZC(USA).
African Orthodox Ch in the Rep of SA	1924	I-ARo	....W	25	7,000	10,000	14,000	1.35	*AOC.* Split ex African Ch. Link with USA Black body, severed 1960. 4 Dioceses. 50n.
Afrikaans Baptist Church		I-Bap	.....	38	8,900	5,710	14,000	0.05	Independent Baptists.
Afrikaans Protestant Church	1987	I-Ref	.....	229	25,800	–	43,000	12.50	*Afrikaanse Protestantse Kerk.* 30 ministers. Conservative Whites. Also in Namibia. 120n.
Agape Ministries International	1983	I-3cA	.....	38	3,030	–	7,030	8.33	Independent Bantu charismatics. 56n.
Alliance Church in South Africa	1901	P-Non	x....	225	7,500	19,000	15,500	-0.81	M=SAM(Sweden). Transvaal. HQ Cleveland (Joburg). Branches Swaziland, Rhodesia. 87n.
Apostle Miracle Church of South Africa	1929	I-3pA	I...I	15	1,000	2,428	1,500	-1.91	*Kereke ea MBM.* 45% Sotho, 26% Tswana, 21% Zulu. Declining. 8n,20m,30w,10Y,62z.
Apostles & Christian Brethren Ch of SA	1922	I-3pA	I...I	15	12,000	10,000	20,000	2.81	Ex AFM. Bantu pentecostals. 80% Northern Sotho. 47n,160m,240w,20Y.
Apostolic Church (Apostle Unity)	1949	I-3aX	x....	25	3,000	5,000	8,000	1.90	1949, 1957 schisms ex New Apostolic Ch. In VAC (Switzerland); 6 nations.
Apostolic Faith Mission of S Africa	1908	P-Pe2	Z....	6,204	369,000	200,000	615,000	4.60	*Apostoliese Geloof Sending.* Ex DRC. 57% Black, 33% White, 9% Coloured. 2863n.
Apostolic Holy Zion Mission of SA	1932	I-3zA	....y	30	2,500	3,200	6,000	2.55	Bantu pentecostals. Healing. 52% Zulu. 48% Sotho. Growing. 15n,7m,7w,17Y,56z.
Assemblies of God	1950	I-3pA	.....	161	8,750	2,000	19,447	9.52	Schism ex AoG(USA).
Assemblies of God Fellowship	1975	I-3pA	.....	80	8,000	–	18,000	5.00	Independent schism ex AoG. 102n.
Assemblies of God in S & Central Africa	1909	P-Pe2	ZF..E	2,000	250,000	21,676	300,000	11.08	M=AoG(UK,USA). Schisms: AoG(1950), Internat AoG(1964). 700n.
Assembly Hall Churches	c1991	I-3nC	.....	3	92	–	200	25.00	*Local Churches. Little Flock.* Chinese. Begun 1922 in China.
Association of Christian Ministries	c1975	I-3cA	.....	45	7,500	–	15,000	5.00	Independent Bantu charismatics. 40n.
Association of Vineyard Chs	c1985	I-3sW	.....	16	1,000	–	2,000	10.00	Assisted by M=AVC(USA).
Bantu Bethlehem Ch of Zion in SA		I-3zA	I...I	250	100,000	50,000	200,000	0.05	Bantu pentecostals. Healing church. Members Bantu, Coloured, Indians.
Bantu Methodist Church	1932	I-Met	.....	60	12,000	10,000	24,000	3.56	*Donkey Church* (named after church's symbol). Ex MCSA. Strong women's Manyanos.
Bantu New Christian Cath Apostolic Ch	1917	I-CCa	I...I	80	2,000	3,726	5,000	1.18	Ex Roman Catholic Ch. 54% Xhosa, 27% Sotho, 11% Zulu, 8% Coloured. 16n,200m,182Y.
Baptist Convention of Southern Africa	1927	P-Bap	T....	634	35,572	20,000	71,100	5.20	Related to BUSA. M=FMB-SBC. 105n.
Baptist International Churches	1967	I-Bap	.....	15	778	91	1,420	11.62	M=BIM(USA). 6n.
Baptist Union of Southern Africa	1820	P-Bap	T...f	489	38,175	170,000	64,000	-3.83	*BUSA. Bantu Bapt Conv*, Mahon M(SABMS). 29% English, 17% Zulu. 14% Xhosa. 500n.
Calvinist Protestant Ch of South Africa	1950	I-Ref	.....	35	5,000	6,000	10,000	2.06	Coloured schism ex DR Mission Ch. Cape Peninsula, and Namaqualand. 25n.
Catholic Church in South Africa:	1501	R-Lat	PzSSw	793	1,748,300	1,588,674	3,057,910	2.65	72% Bantu, 16% Wh, 10% Col. C=32+7+74. 1q,2s. 314n 713x 1053m 3099w 63782Yy
M Bloemfontein	1951	R-Lat	Pomi	35	57,000	51,750	94,709	2.45	94% Bantu (Sotho), 5% White, 1% Coloured. M=OMI. 5n 20x 28m 70w 404Yy
D Bethlehem	1948	R-Lat	Ps	27	40,000	41,261	73,245	2.32	Rural. 82% Sotho, 16% Zulu, 1% White. M=CSSp. 10n 17x 28m 55w 2458Yy
D Keimoes-Upington	1885	R-Lat	Posfs	21	37,000	34,642	65,879	2.60	Rural. 98% Coloured, 2% White. M=OSFS. 3n 16x 40m 44w 1325Yy
D Kimberley	1886	R-Lat	Pomi	5	64,000	53,217	110,530	2.97	Urban. 90% Tswana, 6% Coloured, 4% White. 11n 17x 29m 36w 4377Yy
D Kroonstad (Bisdom Kroonstad)	1923	R-Lat	Pop	27	59,000	56,875	113,275	2.79	Only Afrikaans-title diocese. 90% Bantu. M=OP. 3n 13x 13m 23w 2031Yy
M Cape Town (Kaapstad)	1847	R-Lat	Ps	69	126,000	101,356	245,390	3.60	54% Coloured, 40% White, 6% Bantu. 52n 64x 88m 346w 4065Yy
D Aliwal (Gariep)	1923	R-Lat	Ps	16	29,000	27,430	48,793	2.33	64% Xhosa, 28% Sotho, 6% Col, 2% White. M=SCJ. 6n 15x 17m 116w 1446Yy
D De Aar	1953	R-Lat	Pscj	8	2,700	7,404	4,748	-1.76	53% Col, 33% Xhosa, 10% Sotho, 4% White. M=SCJ. 3n 5x 5m 5w 175Yy
D Oudtshoorn	1874	R-Lat	Ps	34	9,600	11,050	17,317	1.81	Rural. 75% Coloured, 14% White, 10% Bantu. 5n 16x 27m 44w 297Yy
D Port Elizabeth	1847	R-Lat	Ps	49	52,000	59,730	89,015	1.61	41% Col, 33% White, 20% Xhosa, 2% Indian. 38n 6x 9m 201w 1801Yy
D Queenstown	1938	R-Lat	Psac	22	32,000	25,302	51,406	2.88	83% Bantu (Xhosa), 9% Coloured, 8% White. 4n 16x 19m 68w 892Yy
M Durban	1850	R-Lat	Ps	75	138,000	152,820	235,459	1.74	62% Zulu, 18% White, 13% Coloured, 6% Tamil. 24n 101x 122m 335w 5839Yy
D Dundee (Volksrust)	1958	R-Lat	Pofm	30	44,000	36,353	76,545	3.02	81% Zulu, 9% Sotho, 6% White, 2% Coloured. 6n 21x 24m 52w 2348Yy
D Eshowe (Zululand)	1921	R-Lat	Ps	29	43,000	48,829	72,952	1.62	93% Zulu, 4% White, 2% Coloured. M=OSB. 16n 22x 44m 163w 2306Yy
D Kokstad	1935	R-Lat	Pofm	14	34,000	39,399	62,370	1.85	65% Xhosa, 28% Sotho, 6% Coloured, 1% White. 0n 15x 20m 24w 1868Yy
D Mariannhill	1921	R-Lat	Pcmm	44	181,000	200,621	272,750	1.24	Rural. 98% Zulu, 1% Coloured, 1% White. M=CMM. 21n 36x 75m 421w 8340Yy
D Umtata	1930	R-Lat	Pcmm	21	40,000	44,581	70,170	1.83	Transkei. 52% Sotho, 17% Pondo, 14% Hlubi, Tembu. 9n 15x 29m 145w 1244Yy
D Umzimkulu	1954	R-Lat	Ps	15	48,000	54,343	102,461	2.57	97% Zulu, 2% White, 1% Coloured. 9n 7x 8m 35w 772Yy
M Pretoria	1948	R-Lat	Ps	53	95,000	75,904	163,668	3.12	28% Tswana, 19% Pedi, 18% White, 15% Zulu. 28n 60x 115m 251w 4405Yy
D Johannesburg (Transvaal)	1886	R-Lat	Ps	105	367,000	275,265	639,000	3.43	Industrialized. Mines, migrant labor. 37n 125x 165m 444w 5390Yy
D Klerksdorp	1965	R-Lat	Pomi	14	52,000	48,167	115,000	3.54	Urban. 89% Bantu, 8% White, 2% Coloured. M=OMI. 0n 15x 25m 5w 3510Yy
D Pietersburg	1910	R-Lat	Posb	23	77,000	49,546	120,500	3.62	67% Pedi, 16% Ndebele, 14% Tswana, 2% White. 11n 12x 28m 55w 2662Yy
D Rustenburg	1971	R-Lat	Pcssr	16	23,000	10,000	40,125	4.17	Formerly part of M Pretoria. M=CSSR. 2n 17x 22m 41w 1502Yy
D Tzaneen (Louis Trichardt-Tzaneen)	1962	R-Lat	Pmsc	15	25,000	23,794	48,145	2.86	94% Sotho/Venda/Tsonga, 5% White, Malawians. 1n 19x 25m 35w 1646Yy
D Witbank (Lydenburg-Witbank)	1923	R-Lat	Ps	21	63,000	49,200	105,000	3.08	45% Zulu, 27% Pedi, 18% Shangaan, 9% White. 10n 32x 37m 78w 2195Yy
VA Ingwavuma	1962	R-Lat	Posm	5	10,000	9,835	19,458	2.77	52% Zulu, 26% Swazi, 18% Tsonga, 2% White. 0n 11x 11m 7w 484Yy
Children of God	c1985	I-mar	.....	1	12	–	28	10.00	*The Family* Former members of Jesus Movement in USA.
Christadelphian Ecclesias	1900	m-Ade	x....	8	600	800	1,000	0.90	*Christadelphian Auxiliary Lecturing Society of SA.* 8 ecclesias (churches).
Christian Apostolic Faith Ch in Zion	1942	I-3zA	.....	100	16,000	13,000	25,000	2.65	*AmahlokoHloko.* Healing. Zulu, Sotho, Shangaan pentecostals. 20n,20m,60w,500Y.
Christian Bantu Apostolic Ch in Zion	1966	I-3zA	....J	10	3,000	2,000	4,000	2.81	*Isonto Labantu Abanga-Makrestu Asepostoli yama Zion.* 65% Zulu, 35% Sotho. 9n,343Y.
Christian Brethren	1850	P-CBr	x....	110	8,000	17,500	25,000	1.44	*SAEv&M Trust.* M=CMML(UK, USA). 52% White, 35% Zulu, 6% Xhosa. 105n.
Christian Family Church	c1975	I-3cA	.....	21	6,000	–	11,000	5.00	Independent African charismatics.
Christian Nat Apost Ch in Zion of SA	1940	I-3zA	....y	35	5,000	3,792	7,000	2.48	Very large turnover of members joining and leaving. Zulu, Sotho. 19n,10m,9w,16Y.
Church of Christ	1910	I-3pA	.....	1,500	100,000	120,000	250,000	2.98	*Ibandla lika Kristu. Bp Limba's Ch. Sigxabhayi.* Pt Elizabeth. Xhosa, all bearded.
Church of Christ Mission	1906	I-Dis	x....	346	21,000	15,000	63,000	5.91	Formerly African Christian MS. Bantu members; linked with CCCC(USA). 37n.
Church of Christ, Scientist		m-Sci	x....	27	2,500	4,500	4,000	0.05	*Christian Science.* M=CCS(USA). 79% White, 17% Bantu, 51 practitioners (7m,43w).
Church of England in South Africa	1870	I-ReA	J....	160	68,300	60,000	107,046	2.34	*Ch of Sobantu* (Colenso). Evangelical. Churches: 150 Zulu, 17 White, 2 Coloured. 100n.
Church of God in Christ		I-3pB	Z....	40	5,000	4,000	10,000	0.05	M=CoGiC(Black mission from USA). Mission across border in Botswana also; 2 bishops.
Church of God of Prophecy	1967	P-Pe3	.....	93	6,980	800	14,000	12.13	M=CGP(USA). Holiness Pentecostals.
Ch of Jesus Christ of Latter-day Saints	1853	m-LdS	x....	57	10,200	6,092	17,000	4.19	*Mormons.* M=CJCLdS(Utah, USA). Temple of Joburg. 78% White, 18% Bantu, 3% Coloured.200f
Church of the Holy Ghost/Spirit	1916	I-3zA	.....	70	7,000	10,000	15,000	1.64	*Ch of the Canaanites/Nzuza's Ch.* Zionist, exclusivist. Bus company. HQ Hammersdale.
Church of the Light	1910	I-3zA	.....	40	5,000	10,000	11,000	0.38	*Ibandla loku Kanya. Cekwane's Ch.* Zionists; colour red. HQ Himeville, Drakensberg.
Church of the Nazarene	1910	P-Hol	xF...	424	20,538	21,861	50,155	3.38	M=CoN. Fields: European, Coloured, Indian, 2 Bantu. 140n,24x,84f,2H,9h,1s(35).
Ch of the Province of Southern Africa	1806	A-Hig	AWAVW	5,000	1,200,000	1,235,946	2,430,000	2.74	*CPSA.* 16 Dioceses in SA, 6 abroad. 56% Black, 24% White. 511b,18de,18H,96h,12r,4s(81).
Churches of Christ	1900	I-Dis	x....	130	3,000	5,000	6,000	0.73	*Gemeente van Christus.* 1920, M=CCCC(Instrumental) (USA). Whites only. 46f.
Churches of Christ (Oneness)	c1980	I-3oA	.....	150	15,000	–	25,000	6.67	*Gemeente van Cristus.* Oneness pentecostals.
Churches of Christ (Non-Instrumental)	1949	I-Dis	x....	25	1,200	2,000	2,500	0.90	M=CC(Non-Instrumental) (USA). Splits ex Disciples of Christ (UCMS). 19f,2s.
Coptic Orthodox Church	1949	O-Cop	Nwa..	20	5,500	10,000	12,000	0.73	Mission under Coptic P Cairo begun 1949. Contact lost after diplomatic break.
Dutch Reformed Church in SA (NHK)	1804	P-Ref	R....	303	193,561	175,239	326,652	2.52	*Nederduitsch Hervormde Kerk van Africa.* Ex NGK. 87% White. In WCC 1948-61. 173n.
Elim Pentecostal Church	1969	P-Pe2	ZG...	24	9,000	2,800	16,400	7.33	M=Elim Foursquare Gospel Alliance (UK), Elim (Denmark). HQ Witbank, Transvaal. 34n.
Emmanuel Assemblies	1977	P-Pe2	.....	153	5,000	–	6,000	5.56	White Pentecostals. 68n.
Emmanuel Wesleyan Church	1900	P-Hol	.....	500	7,000	7,000	12,000	2.18	*Southern Africa Field.* Wesleyan doctrines. 31n,15x,2p,W=10%,531Y,188z.
Ethiopian Catholic Ch of South Africa	c1890	I-3pA	I...I	150	16,000	25,000	20,000	-0.89	Indigenous body. Recognition by president Kruger in 1896. Xhosa, Sotho members.
Evangelical Bible Churches	1889	P-Eva	xM...	168	12,100	17,000	30,300	2.34	M=TEAM(formerly Scandinavia Alliance M). 2 schools. HQ Durban. 112f,1H,3h,5s.
Evangelical Church in South Africa		P-Eva	.....	26	4,600	5,000	7,670	0.05	M=AEF.
Ev Lutheran Church in Southern Africa:		P-Lut	LW.JW	1,676	450,000	385,963	711,200	0.05	*ELCSA.* Affiliated Lutherans are under 50% of all professing Lutherans. 95% Bantu. 560n.
Evangelical Presbyterian Church in SA	1875	P-Ref	R.A.W	250	25,000	20,000	60,000	4.49	*TPC. Tsonga Presbyterian Ch.* M=Swiss Mission. A=1962. Tsonga, Ronga. 16n,9x,3h.
Evangelical Reformed Church of SA	1944	P-Ref	.....	167	9,000	7,500	20,000	4.00	White Evangelicals. 106n.
Federal Council of Dutch Ref Chs in SA:	1652	P-Ref	F....	1,943	1,474,394	2,142,000	2,768,180	1.03	*Federale Raad van Nederduitse Gereformeende Kerke. NGK.* A family of 4 racial churches. 9x.
Free Church of Scotland	1908	P-Ref	JG...	10	5,100	10,000	8,000	-0.89	M=FCSFMB(UK). HQ King William's Town. Districts: Transkei, Pirie, Burnshill, Xhosa.
Free Evangelical Lutheran Synod in SA	1890	P-Lut	...J.	10	500	3,000	1,500	-2.73	*FELS.* Schism from Hermannsburg Synod. Conservative German-speaking farmers. Declining.
Free Methodist Church in South Africa	1885	I-Hol	VF...	242	5,250	4,000	6,800	2.15	M=FMC(USA). HQ Izingolweni, Natal. 2 schools. 108N.
Free Protestant Unitarian Church of SA	1867	m-Unt	.....	2	150	300	200	-1.61	In General Assembly of Unitarian & Free Christian Chs (UK). Cape Town, Joburg. 1n.
Full Gospel Church of God	c1990	I-3fW	.....	336	90,000	–	100,000	20.00	*Irene.* Whites only. Schism ex Full Gospel Church of God in South Africa. 516N..
Full Gospel Ch of God in Southern A	1910	P-Pe3	Zq...	850	260,000	141,000	350,000	3.70	M=CoG(Cleveland). Vast Indian work. 1955, applied to WCC. c1990 schism. 1215n,10x,1j,4s.
Greater World Chr Spiritualist League		m-Spi	x....	2	100	400	300	0.05	Chr=Christian. Christian spiritist. In Foreshore and Oranjezicht (Cape Town).
Greek Orthodox Church (P Alexandria)	1907	O-Gre	Cw...	23	48,000	20,000	120,000	7.43	Dioceses: Kabe Elpis (Cape), Ioannopolis (Johannesburg). Under Cairo. Mainly Greeks.
Hanoverian Ev Luth Free Ch Mission	1890	P-Lut	.....	70	10,000	23,351	20,000	-0.62	Ex Hermannsburg after schism in German Hanover state church. Zulu, Tswana. 35f.
His People Christian Ministries	1988	I-3cW	.....	30	6,000	–	20,000	14.29	HQ Cape Town. 18 Bible schools, 20 campuses. Abroad: Europe, Namibia, Zambia, USA.

Continued opposite

Country Table 2–concluded

Official name (bold type = church with over 10% of all affiliated) 1	*Begun* 2	*Type* 3	*Counc* 4	*Congs* 5	*Adults* 6	*Affiliated 1970* 7	*Affiliated 1995* 8	*G%* 9	*Names, notes, and other statistics* (see Codebook, Part 3) 10
Holiness Union Church of South Africa	1890	P-Hol	x....	92	9,200	19,089	23,000	0.75	M=Swedish Zulu Mission. Former Swedish Holiness UM. 30n,12x,39f,1H,419Y.
Holy Apostolic Ch in Christ Mission		I-3pA	.....	10	2,500	5,000	6,000	0.05	In Pietermaritzburg (Natal). Assisted by Ev Lutheran Ch in SA. Pastors 59n.
Indian Christian Church		P-Non	xM...	25	900	1,590	1,800	0.05	M=Africa Evangelical Fellowship(formerly SAGM). Indians only; south coast.
International Assemblies of God	1964	I-3pA	Z...E	140	20,000	5,000	33,300	7.88	Left AoG in SA for closer links with AoG(USA). 160n. 30x,5s,200Y,100z.
Intern Ch of the Foursquare Gospel	1929	P-Pe2	ZF...	49	10,872	10,000	24,200	3.60	M=ICFG(Los Angeles, USA). HQ Willowvale, Transkei. 127nm,4f,1p(19),W=84%,84Y.
International Fell of Charismatic Chs	c1980	I-3cW	.....	600	400,000	–	700,000	6.67	Umbrella organization for several large independent congregations. Prosperity teaching. 900n.
International Pentecost Church	1962	I-3pA	x....	165	300,000	4,000	750,000	23.29	*IPC. International Pentecost Holiness Ch.* Split ex ZCC. HQ Silo. Prosperity teaching, polygamy.
International Pentecostal Assemblies	1964	I-3pA	.....	35	600	220	1,000	6.24	*IPA.* Schism ex Assemblies of God. Main language Northern Sotho. HQ Pietersburg. 1f.
Jehovah's Witnesses	c1895	m-Jeh	x....	1,063	48,590	50,000	139,000	4.17	*Watch Tower.* Literature begun 1907 by J. Booth. HQ Elandsfontein. (1975) 2163Y. (1995) 3985Y
Latter Rain Assemblies of SA	c1927	I-3pW	x....	40	5,000	5,000	10,000	2.81	*Spate Reën Gemeenten/Blourokkies*(Blue-clothed women). White. Huge church in Benoni.
Lutheran Church in Southern Africa	1892	P-Lut	e..J.	225	21,000	22,378	35,000	1.81	Zulu/Tswana. Related to FELS. M=MELFC(Bleckmar),LCMS. Tvl, Natal, Botswana. 66n.
Mahon Mission Chs		P-Bap	.....	300	16,227	6,560	36,227	0.05	Schism from ZCC which then called in the Mahon Mission (USA).
Members in Christ Church	1931	I-3pN	.....	160	34,000	40,000	74,000	2.49	*Christen Gemeente.* 80% Coloured. N&W Cape, Natal, also SWA. 178n.
Mennonite Church	1987	P-Men	.....	5	240	–	370	12.50	Mainline USA Mennonites.
Messianic Jewish Congregations	c1980	I-3mJ	x....	10	400	–	1,000	6.67	Jewish believers in Christ. Mainly Johannesburg. M=UMJC,IAMCS.
Methodist Church of Southern Africa	1806	P-Met	VWA.W	6,450	758,178	942,505	2,500,000	3.98	British origin. 77% Black, 17% White, 5% Coloured. 1000n,4H,1j,5r,2s(60),2400t,2u.
Moravian Ch, Eastern Cape Province	1828	P-Mor	LWAJW	160	19,000	29,073	43,000	1.58	Xhosa and Coloured members. HQ Cedarville. New Transkei work begun. 13n,3x,7f,1s.
Moravian Ch, Western Cape Province	1737	P-Mor	LWAJW	80	22,000	41,587	60,000	1.48	*Evangeliese Broederkerk.* 1737 Schmidt among Hottentots. 99% Cape Coloured. 12f,1s.
National Baptist Ch of South Africa		I-Bap	....W	110	30,000	50,000	60,000	0.05	Begun and assisted by M=NBCUSA(Black Americans). 1974 joined SAACC. 120n.
National Tembu Church	1884	I-Met	.....	6	1,000	5,000	2,000	-3.60	Founded by Nehemiah Tile, first indigenous Black theologian, ex Methodists.
Native Independent Congregational Ch	1885	I-Con	.....	10	600	1,000	1,200	0.73	Largest indigenous body out of the 19 among Tlhaping tribe. Ex LMS.
Nazarite Baptist Church	1910	I-3pA	.....	300	300,000	430,000	700,000	1.97	*Ama-Nazaretha,* founded by Isaiah Shembe. Zulus. Holy city Ekuphakameni. HQ Inanda.
New Apostolic Church	1903	I-3aX	x....	1,500	150,000	200,000	291,528	1.52	*Niuwe Apostolisch Kerk.* Begun by German immigrants. World HQ Zurich. 10500n.
New Church of Southern Africa	1912	m-Swe	x....	100	8,000	20,000	10,000	-2.73	M=Gen Conf NC(UK). 1961 merged with Ethiopian Cath Ch in Zion; declining. 5n.
New Life Ministries International	c1970	I-3oA	.....	12	2,500	–	6,000	41.62	Oneness body, member of AWCF. HQ Durban. 12n.
New World Apostolic Church in Zion	1944	I-3zA	I	10	1,200	1,269	1,700	1.18	*Niue Wereld Apostoliesie Kerk.* Bantu pentecostals. 99% Sotho. 12n,4m,7w,48Y.
Norwegian Free Evangelical Mission	1914	P-Pe2	Z....	15	2,000	2,000	3,000	1.64	M=NPY(Norway). Classical Pentecostals (2-stage). Mostly Zulus. HQ Eshowe.
Old Apostolic Church	1926	I-3aX	x....	20	3,000	5,000	5,000	0.00	White mission, split (in UK) ex Catholic Apostolic Ch. Mission in Kitwe (Zambia), also Botswana.
Pentecostal Assemblies of God	1908	P-Pe2	ZF...	250	50,000	60,000	150,000	3.73	*PAG.* 1915 M=PAoC(Canada). Co-operates with AoG (Nicholas Bhengu). 238n,14x,1s(22).
Pentecostal Holiness Ch in S Africa	1913	P-Pe3	ZF...	435	35,808	40,000	59,700	1.61	Widespread throughout Southern Africa. M=IPHC(USA). 40n,18x,900m,32f,1h,1s.
Pentecostal Protestant Church	1958	I-3pW	x....	500	88,000	12,300	135,000	10.06	*Pinkster Protestante Kerk.* HQ Germiston. 350 pastors. Work in Botswana, et alia.
People's Church of Africa	1922	I-Con	.....	19	13,500	10,000	21,216	3.05	*Volkskerk van Afrika.* Coloured schism ex Cong Union of SA, Cape Province. 9n.
Peoples Churches (Kwasizabantu)	1975	I-3cA	.....	140	80,000	–	150,000	5.00	African Independent charismatics.
Phillipian Church of South Africa		I-Lut	.....	4	1,000	5,000	3,000	0.05	In Natal based on Durban. Assisted by Ev Lutheran Ch in SA. Pastors. 69n.
Presbyterian Church of Africa	1898	I-Ref	R.A.b	9,600	426,000	300,000	927,000	4.62	*African Presbyterian Ch.* Zulu schism ex UFCSM(UK). Declining. SS=86000,8000z.
Presbyterian Church of Southern Africa	1829	P-Ref	RWA.W	220	191,000	122,000	300,000	3.66	*PCSA.* Constituted 1897. 65% White. Union talks with Bantu Presb Ch. 256n.
Reformed Apostolic Faith Mission of SA	1947	I-3aA	.....	120	7,000	1,700	12,000	8.13	*RAFMSA.* Schism ex AFMSA attempting fully to africanize Christianity.
Reformed Baptist Church	1903	P-Bap	.....	5	700	2,000	1,500	-1.14	M=Reformed Bapt M of Canada(1966, merged with Wesleyan Ch). Natal. 4n,9f,1p.
Reformed Christian Church	c1980	I-3oA	.....	1,300	112,000	–	204,000	6.67	*Oneness Pentecostal. Reformed Ch.* HQ Durban. Member of AWCF.
Reformed Church in Africa	1968	P-Ref	.....	10	1,200	600	2,400	5.70	Ties with Dutch Reformed Church, Botswana.
Reformed Church in South Africa	1859	P-Ref	J....	417	95,800	140,303	159,618	0.52	*GKSA. Gereformeerde Kerk. Doppers.* Conservative schism ex NGK. 72% White. 236n.
Reformed Covenant Church of Christ	1966	I-Ref	I	30	2,900	4,000	4,500	0.47	Indigenous body. In Bloemfontein and OFS. Xhosa, Zulu, Tswana, Sotho. 364n,300Y.
Reformed Presbyterian Ch in SA	1820	P-Ref	RWA.W	980	50,000	66,543	150,000	3.30	M=CSM(UK). A=1923. HQ Umtata. 65% Xhosa,23% Zulu, 12% Sotho, 49n,5x,12f,SS=11251.
Religious Society of Friends in SA	c1770	P-Qua	Q...W	5	200	300	400	1.16	*Quakers.* Part of Southern Africa Yearly Meeting (SA, Rhod, Bots, Zamb, Malawi) (1948).
Rhema Bible Church	1979	I-3wW	x....	130	13,000	–	18,600	6.25	Links with Rhema Bible Ch (Tulsa, USA). F=R. Macauley. Prosperity gospel. Johannesburg.
St John's Apostolic Faith Mission	c1940	I-3pA	I....	300	300,000	300,000	600,000	2.81	Begun ex AFM by person healed by Mother Mokutudu Knu. Swazi, Botswana branches.
St John's Mission	1911	I-Ang	I...I	40	25,000	30,000	40,000	1.16	Founded in Umtata, ex Anglicans. 7 bishops including 2 for Transkei and Swaziland.
St Paul's Apostolic Church of SA	1944	I-3pA	I...I	50	4,000	2,500	5,000	2.81	HQ Middleburg (Transvaal). Healing pentecostals. Expanding. 12n,50m,30w,100Y.
Salvation Army of South Africa	1883	P-Sal	xwA.W	282	19,004	50,000	27,000	-2.43	*Heilsleër. Impi yo Sindiso* (Zulu). 3 White divisions, 7 Bantu. 314n,5H,1j,2s.
Scandinavian Independent Baptist Union	1892	P-Bap	x....	35	2,000	4,000	4,000	0.00	*SIBU.* Natal Zululand. Now amalgamated with Norwegian Mission Union (1889). 32fm.
Self-Supporting Rhenish Church		I-Lut	.....	10	200	500	400	0.05	Coloured split ex Lutherans in Cape Town; links with similar Nama Hottentot bodies.
Seventh-day Adventist Church	1887	P-Adv	x....	571	63,065	50,000	145,292	4.36	*SAfrican UC* (White, Coloured), SUnion (Black). 240n,8f,1H,5h,1j,8r,538t,(36691),2046Y.
Swazi Christian Ch in Zion of SA	1962	I-3zA	Iv..I	20	7,000	10,000	12,000	0.73	Split ex mother church in Swaziland. 1966, applied to join WCC. HQ Moroka (Joburg).
Union Public Christian Apos Ch in Zion	1945	I-3zA	I...I	50	4,000	5,000	6,000	0.73	*Ensimbini.* HQ Mozodo, Johannesburg. Swazi, Zulu, Xhosa. 32n,4m,6w,70Y.
United Apostolic Faith Church	1912	I-3aA	x....	617	37,000	40,000	74,000	2.49	M=UAFC(UK). British-Israelite Pentecostals. HQ Pretoria. Mission to Malawi. 1s.
United Church of Ethiopia South Africa		I-Lut	.....	5	1,000	5,000	3,000	0.05	Zulu church based on Durban. Assisted by Ev Luth Ch in SA. 13 circuits. 24n.
United Church of the OFS Goldfields	1954	P-Uni	....W	30	3,200	3,298	5,000	1.68	Autonomous church formed by LEC (Lesotho) & UCCSA; Sotho miners. M=PEMS(France).
United Congr Ch of Southern Africa	1799	P-Con	RWA.W	2,660	244,000	210,000	382,412	2.43	*UCCSA.* 1967 union CUSA,CCA,UCMS,LMS. 50% Coloured, 40% Bantu, 10% White. 153n,1u.
United Evangelical Lutheran Ch of SA	c1850	P-Lut	L..Jw	60	8,000	24,000	20,000	-0.73	*UELCSA.* 4 German-speaking White synods (Cape, Hermannsburg, Transvaal, SWA).
United Free Church of Scotland	1931	P-Ref	Rw...	20	2,300	4,500	5,000	0.42	M=UFCSM(UK). Stations from Lovedale into Natal. Links with Bantu Presbyterian Ch.
United Methodist Church	1898	P-Met	Vwa.W	35	1,500	2,360	3,000	0.96	*SE Conference,* UMC(USA). Work among miners only, mainly Mozambicans (Tshwa). 9f.
United Pentecostal Church	1948	P-Pe1	x....	300	40,000	40,000	85,000	3.06	*Jesus Only Church.* M=UPC(USA). Indians around Durban; fast growth. 100n,4f.
Uniting Reformed Ch in Southern A	1994	P-Uni	F...W	725	518,000	940,000	1,362,000	3.00	Merger of 2 DRC Churches: NGK in Africa (Bantu Ch) and NG Sendingskerk (Coloured). 850n.
Wesleyan Church	1893	P-Hol	VF...	376	6,768	7,000	12,000	2.18	Formerly M=Pilgrim Holiness M, now WC(USA). Growing. 12 schools. 431m,30f,2h,2s.
World Missionary Association	1907	I-Eva	.....	300	96,600	120,000	151,400	0.93	Missionaries from USA, UK, Germany, Lesotho, Swaziland. 300n.
Zion Apostolic Church of South Africa	1911	I-3zA	.....	60	50,000	30,000	70,000	3.45	*ZAC.* Ex AFM. HQ Lethabong (Transvaal). Sotho, Zulu, Xhosa, Venda. 20n,15m,215Y.
Zion Apostolic in Jerusalem Church	1925	I-3zA	I...I	35	10,000	6,000	15,000	3.73	Indigenous pentecostals. Healing church. Members all Zulu. 17n,18m,18w,20Y.
Zion Christian Church	1914	I-3zA	I....	4,800	2,500,000	600,000	7,100,000	10.39	*ZCC.* Ex AFM. Colors green, yellow. Pedi. Abroad: 9 countries (Malawi to Namibia, Mozambique)
Zion Church in South Africa		I-3zA	I...I	70	30,000	40,000	70,000	0.05	Opposes Christian Institute control over AICA. Aim: a Black United Ch of SA.
Zion City Apostolic Ch of South Africa	1923	I-3zA	I...J	40	3,000	3,000	5,000	2.06	Ex Christian Apostolic Ch in Zion. 52% Venda, 20% Tsonga, 16% Xhosa. 8n,31m,200Y.
Zion Mission Church of South Africa	1922	I-3zA	.v...	1,000	11,000	20,000	35,000	2.26	Members mainly Zulu, Swazi, Xhosa. HQ Phirima, Johannesburg. 230n,15x.
Zulu Congregational Church	1896	I-Con	.....	274	80,000	100,000	150,000	1.64	Zulu schism ex ABCFM(USA). 12 circuits. Numerous schisms over the years. 304n.
Zulu Jerusalem Church in South Africa	c1970	I-3zA	.....	120	35,000	50,000	70,000	1.35	De facto merger of many Zionist bodies, paralleling political union KwaZulu.
Other Bantu indigenous churches		I-3xA	.....	4,200	950,000	850,000	1,500,000	0.05	Total around 3,000 more bodies (see below), most with under 50 adults each.
Other independent churches		I-3cA	.....	1,500	70,000	20,000	100,000	0.05	Total 500 denominations, mainly non-Bantu, including IURD/UCKG (Brazil), Durban Christian Centre.
Other Protestant denominations		P-	.....	900	150,000	200,000	300,000	0.05	Total about 100 (see list below).
Doubly-affiliated		2-aff			-2,348,216	0	-5,001,978		Evangelicals and Independents also in Catholic or Protestant churches.
Totals				**73,700**	**14,103,118**	**14,009,611**	**29,215,000**		

Churches, members, growth, 1900-2025	*Congs*	*Adults*	*Affiliated*	*G%*	*Total denominations*	*6 Megablocs:* *O*	*R*	*A*	*P*	*I*	*m*
Total churches, members, and denominations (mid-1900)	4,000	656,000	1,303,700	3.45	74	0	1	1	38	30	4
Total churches, members, and denominations (mid-1970)	41,103	7,049,491	14,009,611	3.45	1,541	2	1	1	95	1,435	7
Total churches, members, and denominations (mid-1990)	60,000	12,546,000	26,095,000	3.16	3,319	2	1	1	153	3,155	7
Total churches, members, and denominations (mid-1995)	73,700	14,103,118	29,215,000	2.28	3,328	2	1	1	153	3,164	7
Total churches, members, and denominations (mid-2000)	80,000	15,290,000	31,800,789	1.71	3,364	2	1	1	153	3,200	7
Total churches, members, and denominations (mid-2025)	100,000	17,910,000	37,250,000	0.63	5,730	8	1	1	200	5,500	20

NOTES ON TABLE ABOVE

NATIONAL COUNCILS (Column 4, 5th letter).

- b = member of AICA and also of SACC.
- E = Evangelical Alliance of South Africa (EASA)
- f = formerly a member of SACC (withdrew 1976).
- I = Africa Independent Churches Association (AICA); 478 member denominations, but mainly smaller Ethiopian ones; 1970, affiliated member organization of SACC.
- J = Federation of Non-White Pentecostal & Apostolic Missionary Churches in Africa (Federasie Pinkster Sending Kerke in SA); begun 1961, 8 branches across SA and Rhodesia, 20,000 members; now affiliated member organization of SACC.
- W = South African Council of Churches (SACC).
- w = observer member of SACC.
- y = Reformed Independent Churches Association (RICA); formed with Afrikaner help as rival to AICA; 600 member churches; member of SACC.

Other national councils. African Independent Churches' Ecumenical Movement (applied to join WCC; rejected). African Independent Churches Movement (split ex AICA in 1973; 460 small member churches). African Ministers' Independent Churches Association (begun 1934, mainly Zulu; Ethiopian and Zionist). Apostolic Ministers Association of Southern Africa (about 100 Zulu churches). Assembly of Zionist & Apostolic Churches/Apostolic and Zionist Assembly of South Africa (AZASA) (established 1965 by IDAMASA; more success than AICA in recruiting larger indigenous churches; 180 Zionist bodies in 1967, linked to SACC). Association of Evangelicals of South Africa (AESA) (Southern Africa Evangelical Council) (affiliated to WEF and AEAM). Association of Pentecostal Ministers of South Africa (Black; 20 churches; member of SACC). Bantu Independent Churches Union of South Africa (1937). Bantu United Ministers' Association (c1940; 250 independent churches). Bureau of Bantu Churches (begun 1962 in Durban, claiming 500 churches). Federation of Bantu Churches in South Africa (1943; 750 churches by 1959). Federation of Evangelical Lutheran Churches in Southern Africa (FELCSA), linking ELCSA, UELCSA, UELCSWA, Moravian Ch. Pentecostal Mission Churches Association (PMCA) (begun 1947; over 400 Zionist and Apostolic churches). South African Council of Christian Churches (SACCC) (affiliated to ICCC; no member churches in 1973). Southern African Alliance of Reformed Churches (SAARC). United Churches of Christ (1929). Zion Combination Churches in South Africa (1957; 28 Zionist churches).

Local councils. 14 regional councils are affiliated to SACC.

OTHER BANTU INDIGENOUS CHURCHES. The table above lists 40 of the better-known larger or more visible bodies. The membership of the 5 largest has been estimated from their annual sales of hymnbooks. South Africa has the greatest proliferation of separatist churches in the world. Beginning with the first secession in 1872, the total distinct denominations rose to 15 in 1906, 30 (1913), 65 (1918), 130 (1926), 293 (1932), 600 (1939), 800 (1948), 1,286 (1955), 2,100 (1958), 2,200 (1960) and to about 3,000 in 1970. For a listing, see B.G.M. Sundkler 1960: 354-374. *Membership.* The larger urban bodies are multi-tribal with members from the whole range of tribes working in the cities, but many rural and smaller bodies come from a single tribe. A number of these include in their title the name of their dominant tribe, thus: African Bavenda Ch, Lutheran Bapedi Ch of South Africa (1890), South African BaRolong Ch, Zion Apostolic Swazi Ch of South Africa (1918), Zulu Congregational Baptist Ch (2,000 members).

OTHER PROTESTANT DENOMINATIONS. These smaller bodies include: African Evangelistic Mission (1910; in mine compounds), Associated Gospel Chs, Brethren in Christ, Christian Catholic Ch (1903), Cooneyites (Go-Preachers), Ev Bible Ch (Canada, 1955), Exclusive Brethren (Raven-Taylor group), Free Baptist Ch, Igreja de Deus (Portuguese Pentecostals), Igreja Evangélica Portuguesa (serving Protestants among the 600,000 Portuguese in South Africa), Independent Assemblies of God, Metropolitan Church Association (1930), New Protestant Ch (c1958 ex DRC; Afrikaners), Protestant United Ch, Reconstituted DRC (Hervormde Nederduitse Gereformeerde Kerk, 1940; Afrikaners), Salem Mission, Swedish Free Mission, World Missions (1959). There are also a large number of Protestant groups begun by Whites among the Bantu.

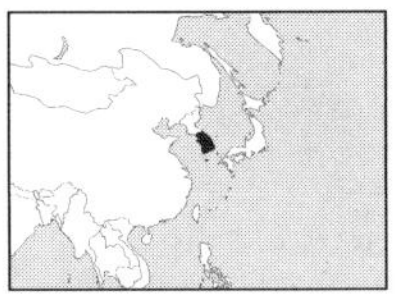

SOUTH KOREA

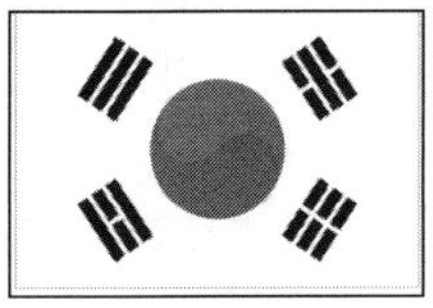

SECULAR DATA, AD 2000

STATE
Official name: Taehan Min-guk (The Republic of Korea).
Short name: South Korea. **Adjective of nationality:** of the Republic of Korea.
Flag: White field with circular emblem (red top and blue bottom); black bar design in each corner.
Area: 99,274 sq. km. (38,330 sq. mi.).
Government: Multiparty republic, since 1988 (1910 Japan possession, 1948 republic, 1961 military junta, 1972 republic under dictatorship).
Legislature: National Assembly, 299 members.
Official language: Korean (Chosenmal).
Monetary unit: 1 won (W) = 100 chon. **US$1=** W 1,386.
Chief cities: SOUL (Seoul, Kyongsong) 12,215,000; Pusan (Busan) 4,239,000; Inch'on (Incheon) 2,837,000; Taegu (Daegu, Taiku) 2,559,000; Kwangju (Kwangchu, Gwangju) 1,655,000.
Political divisions: 15 provinces.
Armed forces: 672,000.

DEMOGRAPHY
Population: 46,844,000.
Population density: 471.8/sq. km. (1,222.1/sq. mi.).
Under 15 years: 10,067,000.
Growth rate p.a.: 0.72% (births 14.11, deaths 6.55).
Mortality: Infant, per 1,000: 9.3; **Maternal per 100,000:** 130.0.
Life expectancy: 74 (male 70, female 77).
Household size: 3.8. **Floor area per person, sq.m:** 25.0.
Major languages: Korean, English, Chinese.
Urban dwellers: 86.16%. **Urban growth rate p.a.:** 1.4%.
Labor force: 45%.

ETHNOLINGUISTIC PEOPLES
97.7% South Korean; 2.0% Japanese; 0.1% USA White; 0.0% Han Chinese (Mandarin); 0.0% Eurasian.

ECONOMY
National income p.a. per person: US$9,700; **per family:** US$36,860.

EDUCATION
Adult literacy: 98% (male 99%, female 96%). **Schools:** 10,312.
Universities: 645. **School enrolment:** female/male: 98%/97%.

HEALTH
Access to health services: 100%. **Access to safe water:** 89%.
Hospitals: 600 (29 beds per 10,000). **Doctors:** 51,518.
Blind: 110,000. **Deaf:** 2,813,000. **Murder rate:** 1.
Lepers: 90,000.

LITERATURE
New book titles p.a.: 32,320 (690 p.a. per million). **Periodicals:** 126.
Newspapers: 62 dailies.

COMMUNICATION (per 1,000 people)
Phones: 415 (30% mobile). **Radios:** 928. **TV sets:** 321.
Daily newspaper circulation: 405. **Computers:** 222.

HUMAN LIFE AND LIBERTY (optimum condition=100.0%)
HDI: 71.4. **HSI:** 66.0. **HFI:** 12.5. **EFL:** 54.0.

Country Table 1. **Religious adherents in South Korea, AD 1900-2025.**

Year	1900		1970		mid-1990		Annual change, 1990-2000				mid-1995		mid-2000		mid-2025	
Name	Adherents	%	Adherents	%	Adherents	%	Natural	Conversion	Total	Rate	Adherents	%	Adherents	%	Adherents	%
Christians	**42,700**	**0.5**	**5,828,000**	**18.3**	**17,089,000**	**39.9**	**158,457**	**42,381**	**200,838**	**1.12**	**18,070,000**	**40.2**	**19,097,384**	**40.8**	**22,700,000**	**43.2**
PROFESSION																
professing Christians	**42,700**	**0.5**	**5,828,000**	**18.3**	**17,089,000**	**39.9**	**158,457**	**42,381**	**200,838**	**1.12**	**18,070,000**	**40.2**	**19,097,384**	**40.8**	**22,700,000**	**43.2**
AFFILIATION																
unaffiliated Christians	0	0.0	424,096	1.3	489,000	1.1	4,534	-11,883	-7,349	-1.62	448,000	1.0	415,508	0.9	300,000	0.6
affiliated Christians	**42,700**	**0.5**	**5,403,904**	**16.9**	**16,600,000**	**38.7**	**153,922**	**54,266**	**208,188**	**1.19**	**17,622,000**	**39.2**	**18,681,876**	**39.9**	**22,400,000**	**42.6**
Protestants	6,500	0.1	2,198,950	6.9	7,950,000	18.5	73,716	18,284	92,000	1.10	8,405,318	18.7	8,870,000	18.9	11,200,000	21.3
Independents	50	0.0	1,988,306	6.2	6,950,000	16.2	64,443	10,557	75,000	1.03	7,345,185	16.3	7,700,000	16.4	9,500,000	18.1
Roman Catholics	36,000	0.5	828,133	2.6	3,275,000	7.6	30,367	12,133	42,500	1.23	3,492,369	7.8	3,700,000	7.9	4,800,000	9.1
Marginal Christians	0	0.0	353,079	1.1	750,000	1.8	6,954	3,046	10,000	1.26	797,233	1.8	850,000	1.8	1,100,000	2.1
Anglicans	100	0.0	32,436	0.1	85,700	0.2	795	1,635	2,430	2.53	100,780	0.2	110,000	0.2	140,000	0.3
Orthodox	50	0.0	3,000	0.0	5,000	0.0	46	-46	0	0.00	5,000	0.0	5,000	0.0	7,000	0.0
doubly-affiliated	0	0.0	0	0.0	-2,415,700	-5.6	-22,399	8,657	-13,742	0.55	-2,523,885	-5.6	-2,553,124	-5.5	-4,347,000	-8.3
Trans-megabloc groupings																
Evangelicals	6,400	0.1	2,130,000	6.7	7,940,000	18.5	73,623	46,577	120,200	1.42	8,577,888	19.1	9,142,000	19.5	11,050,000	21.0
Pentecostals/Charismatics	500	0.0	250,000	0.8	6,550,000	15.3	60,734	42,266	103,000	1.47	7,088,461	15.8	7,580,000	16.2	9,455,000	18.0
Great Commission Christians	**40,000**	**0.5**	**4,790,000**	**15.0**	**11,575,000**	**27.0**	**107,328**	**68,098**	**175,426**	**1.42**	**12,500,000**	**27.8**	**13,329,255**	**28.5**	**15,760,000**	**30.0**
Ethnoreligionists	6,507,300	81.3	12,506,000	39.2	7,000,000	16.3	64,906	-32,363	32,543	0.46	7,270,000	16.2	7,325,426	15.6	8,160,000	15.5
Buddhists	800,000	10.0	5,319,000	16.7	6,700,000	15.6	62,125	-14,702	47,423	0.69	6,920,000	15.4	7,174,234	15.3	7,308,000	13.9
New-Religionists	10,000	0.1	3,380,000	10.6	6,450,000	15.1	59,807	7,294	67,101	0.99	6,817,000	15.2	7,121,012	15.2	8,070,000	15.4
Confucianists	640,000	8.0	4,758,000	14.9	4,889,000	11.4	45,333	-12,296	33,037	0.66	5,031,300	11.2	5,219,366	11.1	5,050,000	9.6
Nonreligious	0	0.0	100,000	0.3	572,000	1.3	5,304	7,371	12,675	2.02	650,000	1.5	698,754	1.5	950,000	1.8
Muslims	0	0.0	3,000	0.0	60,000	0.1	556	312	868	1.36	65,800	0.2	68,676	0.2	90,000	0.2
Atheists	0	0.0	5,000	0.0	32,000	0.1	297	1,188	1,485	3.89	40,000	0.1	46,847	0.1	75,000	0.1
Baha'is	0	0.0	14,000	0.0	24,000	0.1	223	587	810	2.95	27,300	0.1	32,096	0.1	40,000	0.1
Chinese folk-religionists	0	0.0	10,000	0.0	28,000	0.1	260	149	409	1.37	30,700	0.1	32,088	0.1	50,000	0.1
Shintoists	0	0.0	0	0.0	25,000	0.1	232	79	311	1.18	26,900	0.1	28,106	0.1	40,000	0.1
World A (unevangelized persons)	6,720,000	84.0	4,788,375	15.0	685,904	1.6	6,304	-18,222	-11,918	-1.91	629,281	1.4	562,128	1.2	577,863	1.1
World B (evangelized non-Christians)	1,237,300	15.5	21,306,125	66.7	25,094,096	58.5	232,739	-24,159	208,580	0.80	26,249,384	58.4	27,184,488	58.0	29,255,137	55.7
World C (Christians)	42,700	0.5	5,828,000	18.3	17,089,000	39.9	158,457	42,381	200,838	1.12	18,070,000	40.2	19,097,384	40.8	22,700,000	43.2
Country's population	**8,000,000**	**100.0**	**31,922,500**	**100.0**	**42,869,000**	**100.0**	**397,500**	**0**	**397,500**	**0.89**	**44,948,666**	**100.0**	**46,844,000**	**100.0**	**52,533,000**	**100.0**

COLUMNS, ROWS.
For meanings and definitions, see Codebook (Part 3). Note that, by definition, total 'Christians' = professing + crypto-Christians, which also = affiliated + unaffiliated Christians, and also = Great Commission Christians + latent Christians. Percentages may not always total exactly, due to rounding.

NOTES ON RELIGIONS
AFFILIATED CHRISTIANS. The number of annual conversions has risen markedly since 1960. From 1971-73, 150,000 soldiers in the Korean army professed conversion (75,000 a year), followed by mass baptism services, raising the proportion of Christians in the army from 12% in 1970 to 35% in 2 years. By 1977, 47% of the army were church members. In the table above, the column 'Conversion change' gives the averages for the decade 1990-2000.
ATHEISTS. No communist party is tolerated. Atheism is however prevalent in intellectual circles.
BAHA'IS. Entered first in 1921; new surge in 1950 through USA military personnel. Rapid growth from 12 local spiritual assemblies (1964) to 99 (1973); 120,000 booklets distributed but a large-scale decline then begun, resulting after reorganization in only 12 LSAs by 1996, though still with large numbers of nominal adherents.
BUDDHISTS. Mahayana. Adherents were served by 2,135 temples with 14,361 monks, priests and nuns in 1967 (in 1972, 1,912 sanctuaries and 18,629 clergy). Sects: 78% Chogye sect, 10% Pophwa sect, 5% Chingak sect; Miruk (Maitreya Buddha), Yongwhagyo and other sects.
CONFUCIANS. Adherents are 70% men, 30% women. Confucianism was introduced from China in AD 885, and remained the state religion until 1910. Although its Korean adherents are also usually involved both in Buddhism and in shamanism, the separation of the 3 into separate statistical categories by the Ministry of Culture and Information indicates that in Korea they are distinct religious systems, unlike the situation in China and among the Chinese diaspora.
COUNTRY'S POPULATION. After the Korean war (1950-53) in which about 5 million persons were killed, a further 2 million arrived after fleeing from North Korea, including several hundred thousand Protestants.
INDEPENDENTS. In over 250 denominations in 1995 (see Table 2).
MUSLIMS. First introduced in 1953 by Turkish battalion among United Nations' troops; Hanafite Sunnis.
NEW-RELIGIONISTS. Of the over 250 new non-Christian syncretistic religions (Sin Jonggyo, or Shinhung (Newly-risen) Jonggyo) in Korea, most sprang up after religious freedom was promulgated in 1945. The oldest, however, is Chondogyo (Religion of the Heavenly Way), begun in 1860 as Tonghak (Eastern Learning), syncretizing Confucianism, Buddhism, Taoism, Roman Catholicism, and Korean shamanism, with 1.3 million members in 1995 in South Korea and 2 million members underground in North Korea. Other leading New Religions are Jingsan-gyo (a system of traditionalist revitalization sects, begun 1901); Wonri (with syncretistic christology), Tangun, Ilbu, Bongnam, Kwansonggyo (with a shrine center in Kyeryongsan representing all known gods including Jesus and Buddha), Sangjegyo (a sect of Jingsan-gyo, incorporating ideas of Christian Sunday worship), Ilsimgyo (now called Yudo; HQ Namwon; with a claimed reincarnation of Jesus); the Zen (Son, in Korean) sects Bochongyo, Bohwagyo, and Samdoggyo; Ilkwando, Musul; and also Soka Gakkai from Japan since 1963 (in Korea called Ch'angga Hakhoe, Value Creation Learning Society). The Won Buddhism sect, making Buddhism more relevant to secular life, began in 1924 claimed 1.3 million members in 1995. Other sects: Daechongkyo (290,000 members), Chunrikyo (720,000), Taegukdo (300,000), Chungilhae (600,000), and International Moral Association.
NONRELIGIOUS. Mainly young Koreans and Chinese who have abandoned family religion.
PENTECOSTALS/CHARISMATICS.The Renewal consists of several distinct components.(a) **Roman Catholic Charismatics** began in 1970. Total involved adults (1974) about 300; total charismatic community including children, 1,000, increasing rapidly. Soon, numbers were doubling every 10 years. In 1990, the total Catholic Charismatic community, including children, was 350,000 (10.5% of all RCs). By 1992, 80 parishes had active prayer groups, with 5,000 weekly attenders, and 70,000 at annual rallies. By 1997, total weekly adult attenders reached 100,000, with 100 involved priests and 5 bishops. Total CCR adherents by AD2000 is expected to be 675,000. (b) **Other Charismatics.** In Protestant nonpentecostal denominations, there were over a million organized Charismatics by 1990. (c) **Pentecostals**. With 1.2 million adherents by 1990. (d) **Independents (Neocharismatics)**. In 1990, with over 2 million followers, rapidly increasing.
SHAMANISTS (here listed as Ethnoreligionists). Shamanism in Korea is a folk religion, a blend of animism, spirit-worship, geomancy, folk-healing, and fortune-telling. Rural shamans remain unorganized, but in the cities associations of shamans exist.

Country status. The Republic of Korea is the southern half of the truncated peninsula of Korea, the only country on the map still so divided, after the reunion of the 2 Germanys and the 2 Yemens in the late 1980s. Bounded by the Sea of Japan, the Yellow Sea and the Korea Strait, it has gained prominence in recent decades as one of the newly industrializing powers of Asia.

HUMAN LIFE AND LIBERTY

Human need and development. Korea emerged from World War II as a country with a shattered economy. It had lived through 20th century until 1945 as a Japanese colony, its manpower and natural resources brutally exploited and its culture suppressed by its masters. The Korean War brought further dislocations and placed further strains on the society and economy. However, within the next 40 years it made a remarkable recovery which some observers have compared to that of Japan on a minor scale. The economic resurgence was followed by a noticeable improvement in the living standards. South Koreans are better fed, better clothed and better housed than their brethren across the border in North Korea, as well as the Chinese and other mainland Asians. Its per capita income of $6,330 is higher than those of all Asian countries, except Singapore, Japan, Hong Kong, Israel, and the oil-rich emirates. Food consumption patterns reveal the greater buying power of the Korean consumers and an increased demand for processed foods and confectionaries. Sanitation problems and pollution levels are lower than those in many less industrialized Asian countries, but nevertheless remain worrisome. Until recently Seoul was considered the most polluted city in the world, with 35% of the population suffering from pollution-related respiratory problems. The population per physician has come down from 2,220 in 1970 to 1,390 in 1990. Life expectancy at 74 years is one of the highest

Great Commission Instrument Panel: status of South Korea (for explanation see start of Part 4)

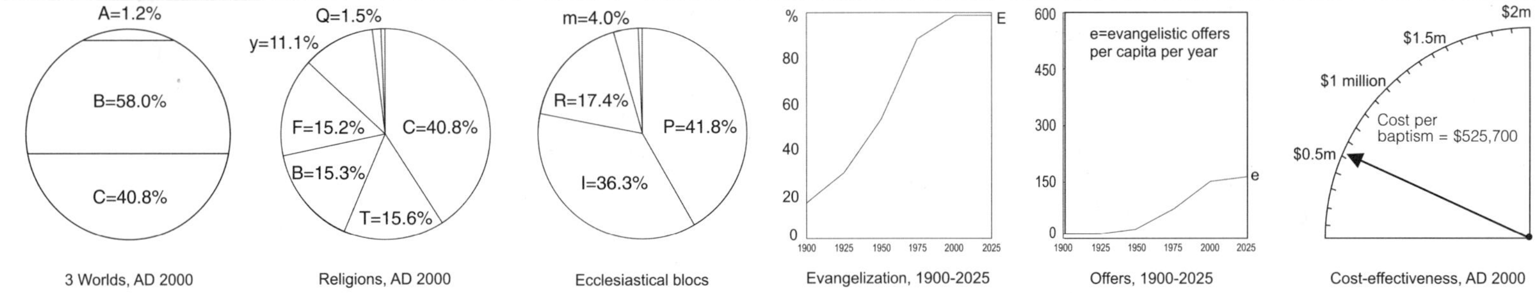

in the developing world. The concept of social welfare is relatively new and is even now limited. Traditionally, the extended family takes care of its members.

Human rights and freedoms. The Republic of Korea made its transition to democracy only in the late 1980s and had its first freely elected civilian president only in 1993. Democratic procedures have not entirely replaced the former autocratic system. A particular problem is the continued use of broad security laws originally designed to thwart subversion by North Korea. Nevertheless, there has a been a marked decrease in the number of public protests and demonstrations, as well as arbitrary arrests and detentions of political opponents. Although it is difficult to estimate the number of political prisoners, Amnesty International estimates that there are between 20 and 110 prisoners of conscience. Freedom of press is generally respected although there are limits on what is nonsubversive or permissible. As an ethnically homogeneous country with no minorities of significant size, racial discrimination has never developed. Women, however, suffer cultural, legal and economic discrimination, some of it a legacy of Confucianism. Despite an Equal Employment Opportunity Act, the average female worker earns only half of her male counterpart. Fetal sex testing and abortion of female fetuses are widely performed. The traditional preference for male children is reflected in the heavy preponderance of males in the 20-40 age group. There are also inheritance laws biased against women. A 1991 Family Law provides extensive protection for women against family violence and abuse.

Human environment. South Korea has paid an extremely high environmental price for its industrial progress during the past 3 decades. More than 200 species of animals have disappeared from the rural areas. High levels of water and air pollution make Korea one of the worst polluted countries in the Far East. The contamination level of the Han River, near one of the main intakes of the Seoul metropolitan water system, is 6 times the internationally accepted level for potable water. The extent of sulfur dioxide contamination in the Pusan area is believed to be 4 times that of New York. The extent of dust accumulations in Seoul is estimated at over 80 tons a month per square mile. Fumes from anthracite briquettes used in cooking also contribute to air pollution.

Shamanists. Korean funeral in large cemetery, incorporating shamanist, Buddhist, Catholic elements. Men wear ancient Korean costumes of white (colour of mourning). Burial of an ancestor must take place, traditionally, on a sun-warmed site.

NON-CHRISTIAN RELIGIONS

Shamanism is the traditional religion and still the most widely practiced one in Korea. It involves a strong belief in the influence of departed ancestral spirits as well as nature spirits who inhabit trees, rocks, and other natural phenomena. These in turn must be propitiated or otherwise controlled either by individuals or by priests (shamans, mudang) to ensure health, fertility, and success in life's ventures. There is a strong emphasis on exorcism and healing, with extensive use of chanting and drums. Belief in a supreme being also appears to be ancient; and this idea has been strengthened by contact with Christianity. When one realizes that Korean nature religion is carried on for the most part by private individuals, without recourse to the intermediary function of shamans, the significance of this religion becomes apparent.

Buddhists. Several thousand Buddhas at the Daehung-sa temple in Chulla-namdo.

Mahayana Buddhism continues to be active. Suppressed and eclipsed during the Yi dynasty (1392-1910) under which Confucianism was the official religion, Buddhism took on a new life at the time of the Japanese occupation. Nevertheless, it was only at the end of the Korean war in 1954 that it assumed a position of importance in Korean religious and social life. The marriage of monks, imposed by the Japanese, was forbidden from 1954, although celibacy has not yet been widely introduced except among the younger generation. The Chogye sect, which represents 78% of Buddhists in South Korea, has at its head a primate and has about 4,000 monks and 6,000 nuns. Its practices include Zen meditation and Amita pietism, both Mahayana schools, and it works vigorously for the renewal and modernization of Buddhism in close cooperation with organizations of Buddhist youth (7,000 adherents), the very active Union of Korean Students, the General Union of Buddhist Believers and the daily newspaper Korean Buddhism. It is engaged in social and charitable work as well as the renewal and spread of Buddhist doctrine. A Buddhist university, Dongguk, exists in Seoul.

Confucianism, which is a system of social ethics rather than a religion, was introduced into Korea from China in AD 885 and remained the state religion from 1392 until 1910. It still encourages the practice of ancestor veneration.

New Religions, a loose term for syncretistic religions begun in Asia over the last hundred years, are numerous, over 250 distinct non-Christian sects being known in present-day Korea. The largest is Chondogyo (Religion of the Heavenly Way), an eclectic blend of shamanistic, Buddhist, Confucian, and Christian elements which arose in the 19th century as a reaction against Western, especially Catholic, influence. The Tonghak Revolt of 1894 had its roots in Chondogyo, and it has maintained its political orientation.

Another large movement, arising out of Buddhism but completely separate from it, is popular Won Buddhism. Begun in 1924 in an attempt to purify Buddhist doctrine, it permits the marriage of monks, authorizes the religious services of women, imitates Christianity in its worship service, and stresses the importance of social work.

Atheism and ***agnosticism*** are prevalent in intellectual circles, a mood originally encouraged by the neo-Confucianist state ideology of the Yi Dynasty (1392-1910).

Islam was introduced in 1953 by Turkish troops among the United Nations occupying forces. There are at present about 68,000 believers. The Korea Muslim Federation in Seoul coordinates all Muslim work.

CHRISTIANITY

The first contacts between Christians and Korea were in 1592 when Hideyoshi, accompanied by a Catholic general and a Jesuit priest, invaded Korea from Japan. Catholic books were brought from Peking to Seoul in 1777; and a Korean baptized in China returned home in 1784 to begin the church. The first of many Catholic martyrs was recorded in 1791. Three years later, in 1794, 4,000 Christians greeted the first Chinese missionary on his arrival in Korea. A vicariate was created in 1831, but martyrdom was the principal characteristic of the church until freedom of religion was declared in the early 1880s. A Protestant missionary touched Korea briefly in 1832 and another was martyred in 1865. By 1876, Korean Protestants were being baptized in Manchuria. The doors to Christian evangelization in Korea itself were opened by the 1882 Korean treaty with the USA. The first Presbyterian missionary entered in 1884 and a Methodist soon after. Extensive missionary itineration was begun in 1887.

PROTESTANT CHURCHES. Korea remained true to its name the Hermit Kingdom until forced to capitulate to Japanese forces in 1876. When missionaries arrived in Korea during the next decade, communities of professing Christians were found waiting for further teaching, the combined result of decades of indigenous evangelization and the distribution of scriptures in China which gradually made their way into Korea as early as 1830. Korea has been the most fruitful field in Asia for Protestant missions. By 1890, Koreans were openly asking for instruction en masse. In the year 1900 alone, church membership increased by over 30%. Bible classes and the earnest simple witness of Korean Christians were primarily responsible. A third factor was the revival of 1907 which spread from Korea into Manchuria and China. The memory of this early spirit of prayer and piety has remained with Koreans over many years.

Four Presbyterian groups from northern and southern USA, Canada and Australia began work between 1884 and 1898. A central committee was set up, and in 1907, the 4 missions united to form the Presbyterian Church of Korea. Presbyterianism remains the principal church tradition of Korea up to the present time. However, many serious schisms have occurred in recent years, particularly since World War II, resulting in the division of 4 major bodies and a host of smaller groups. Two American Methodists societies from northern (1884) and southern (1896) USA, worked together closely and, in 1930, established the autonomous Korean Methodist Church, the largest single Protestant denomination in Korea. Seventh-day Adventists pioneered in 1903, followed by the Oriental Missionary Society in 1907. The latter's activity resulted in the formation of the Korea Holiness Church which has been self-governing since the 1940s. These, with more recent Pentecostal and Baptists groups, have also grown rapidly in recent years. Many Korean churches experienced internal divisions after World War II for a wide variety of reasons. Since 1945, many new missionary societies from the USA have also entered the country.

Country summary. **Worlds A, B, C by ethnolinguistic peoples, cities, and major civil divisions in South Korea.**

	PEOPLES							CITIES							CIVIL DIVISIONS						
World	Num	Pop 2000	C%	Christians	E%	U%	Unevangelized	Num	Pop 2000	C%	Christians	E%	U%	Unevangelized	Num	Pop 2000	C%	Christians	E%	U%	Unevangelized
A	1	4,684	20.00	937	49	51	2,389	0	0	0.00	0	0	0	0	0	0	0.00	0	0	0	0
B	5	46,758,265	39.82	18,619,769	99	1	558,230	54	30,871,528	41.02	12,662,859	99	1	449,253	15	46,843,989	39.88	18,681,877	99	1	560,817
C	3	81,039	75.48	61,168	100	0	198	1	350,399	69.00	241,775	100	0	280	0	0	0.00	0	0	0	0
Total	**9**	**46,843,988**	**39.88**	**18,681,874**	**99**	**1**	**560,817**	**55**	**31,221,927**	**41.33**	**12,904,634**	**99**	**1**	**449,533**	**15**	**46,843,989**	**39.88**	**18,681,877**	**99**	**1**	**560,817**

Protestantism had entered Korea in the first rush of Western technological advance and had created Korea's first modern schools both at lower and university levels. During the Japanese occupation, Protestant laymen and socialist politicians shared leadership in resistance movements against Japan, as well as in the new liberation government after World War II. In spite of Japanese Shinto persecutions during the 1930s and 1940s, followed by the Communist invasion from the north in 1950 and schisms from within during the 1950s, the Protestant community has continued to double in size every 10 years since 1940.

Protestant education in Korea pioneered an intellectual revolution. The first school was opened in 1886 by Methodists, and Protestants also pioneered in education for women. Today there are many Protestant colleges and universities, high schools, middle schools and innumerable primary schools, all legally recognized as private schools but subject to the Ministry of Education's curriculum requirements.

The first recognized Protestant medical institution in Korea was a hospital built in 1885. There are now many Protestant hospitals in operation and a great many smaller clinics, all having legal status under the Ministry of Health and Public Welfare. Protestants have also been involved in medical education. Severance Medical College of Yosei University has over the years produced a large proportion of Korea's trained doctors. Recent emphases in Christian medicine are rural medical service and family planning.

The Protestant churches have been active in land reclamation projects, slum resettlement and development, rural agricultural projects, and city planning. Protestants pioneered in literacy; but with the country now over 90% literate, this work is no longer emphasized.

Yoido Full Gospel Churches. World's largest single church (top) in Seoul with 900,000 members, 700 pastors (mostly women).

CATHOLIC CHURCH. The minor role played by the Catholic Church in the independence movement, as well as its failure to become involved earlier in education, considerably reduced its influence which had already been shaken by the 19th-century persecutions. However, this state of affairs has been largely reversed since World War II. Owing mostly to adult conversions, a huge increase occurred in the Catholic population between 1950 and 1968: the number of baptized Catholics rose from 163,471 in 1953 to 731,628 in 1967. Adult baptisms totaled 574,636 during the period 1959-70. This numerical growth was maintained throughout the Korean war of 1950-53 and the following period of national reconstructions. One of the factors contributing to this increase was the important and varied aid received by or through the Catholic Church during this period. There has also been mass immigration. Between 1946 and 1951, a total of 25,000, more than half the Catholic population of North Korea, joined with other Christians in the huge wave of refugees to the south; and after 1952, a further 2 million refugees including another 10,000 or so Catholics fled from North to South Korea. From 1970 to 1990, Catholics grew at 7.1% per annum, far outstripping the growth of the general population.

The Holy See has diplomatic relations with South Korea and in AD 2000 is represented to government and the Catholic hierarchy by a pro-nuncio residing in Seoul.

Catholic Church in Korea, Archdiocese of Kwang ju. Leprosy patients at mass in Sorokto Leprosarium.

INDIGENOUS CHURCHES. Over 100 distinct indigenous denominations existed in the 1990s. The first of many schisms from the Presbyterian Church of Korea took place in 1938, although the situation became much more serious after World War II. A conservative split appeared in 1946 which resulted in the establishment of the Koryo Presbyterian Church, followed by a much larger conservative split in 1951 which formed the Presbyterian Church in Korea (Reunited Anti-Ecumenical) and later in 1954 by a liberal split to organize the Presbyterian Church in the ROK. Methodists have also had their problems with schisms; but except for a few small groups, they were reunited by 1959.

Many Korean indigenous churches blend mysticism with reverence for the forces of nature, this being reflected in a variety of incantations, charms, omens and a preoccupation with exorcism and healing. They profess stern moral codes, which are vestiges of Confucianism and a concern for cleansing and ritual purity, drawn from Taoist, Shinto, and Buddhist practices. Resting primarily on shamanistic traditions, the most rapidly expanding of these new denominations are conspicuously influenced by Christian ideas, but the presence of strong syncretistic and non-Christian elements has led some observers to classify them as syncretistic new religions rather than (as here) as indigenous churches. The 2 largest of these movements are the Unification Church (Holy Spirit Association for the Unification of World Christianity, 1954) and the Olive Tree Church (1955). Both are strongly messianic. Sun Myung Moon, founder of the Unification Church, is widely regarded by his followers as the final messiah and the mediator between man and the powers of the spiritual world. Pak T'ae-son, founder of the Olive Tree Church, is able to cure sickness because he is filled with magical power and holy fire. He is the immortal Olive Tree (Revelation 11:4) and oracle of God. Both movements have developed widespread urban-industrial complexes and vast property holdings. At least 10 other self-proclaimed or acclaimed messiahs have appeared since the end of the Korean War in 1953.

Renewal movements. In the 1990s the Pentecostal/Charismatic Renewal continued to spread rapidly across most older churches, and numbered over 7.5 million adherents (of whom 32% Pentecostals, 27% Charismatics, and 42% Independents).

Indigenous missions. Throughout the 20th century, Koreans have been involved in missionary work, particularly in other Asian countries. Since the 1970s there has been a dramatic rise in the number of indigenous mission agencies, and correspondingly, missionaries. Though the Korean diaspora has claimed most of the attention of these missionaries in the past, more are working cross-culturally in foreign lands.

True Jesus Church, Korea Assembly. Members, mainly Chinese, in front of their church building.

CHURCH AND STATE

Religious liberty, guaranteed by Article 16 of the Yushin constitution of 27 December 1972, prohibits the government from establishing any state church and also proclaims that religion and politics shall be separated. Article 17 guarantees freedom of conscience; and Article 9, which is concerned with the equality of all citizens before the law, stipulates that no religion may practice any kind of discrimination. These articles represent no change over the constitution of 1962. However, the present constitution also states that these rights may be withdrawn by the president of the republic who has full powers, especially 'in case the national security or the public order is seriously threatened or anticipated to be threatened' (Article 53, paragraph 1 and 2).

The Religious Bodies Registration Law, included in the general registration law of December 1968 and amended in December 1969, requires religions and churches to register with the Ministry of Culture (Munhwa Kongbo-bu) before being authorized to hold public meetings or services. The Ministry of Education (Munkyo-bu) supervises the lands, buildings, and finances of religious bodies. This supervision most directly concerns the considerable properties (including many designated as national treasures) of Buddhist temples and Confucian shrines.

Religions which offend patriotism are banned until they remove their offensive features. Thus, Japanese Shinto is effectively banned because it implies loyalty to a foreign government; and Soka Gakkai from Japan was forced to omit bows towards Japan from its ritual before being allowed to register.

The government has had the power to tax religions since 1965, but it has chosen not to exercise this power and taxes neither property belonging to religions nor the incomes of their clergy.

Religions receive no direct support from government. By regulation of the Ministry of Education, religious instruction is forbidden during normal class hours, in both public and private primary and secondary schools, although schools often circumvent these rules. In May 1973, the minister of Education ordered that the law be enforced in Christian secondary schools, recommending also that teaching clergy be replaced by lay persons.

The Christians of Korea have behind them a long tradition of active resistance to the former Japanese colonial regime. Hence, after World War II, although Christians were still a small minority, many government ministers and officials were chosen from among the Christian community, mostly Protestants, including president Syngman Rhee. This explains the close collaboration between the churches and the regime and why they registered practically no reaction when Park Chong Hi became president in a military coup d'etat in 1961. The churches maintain the right to have military chaplains, and the government took the initiative in creating a corps of evangelists attached to the police who were authorized to preach to prisoners and policemen.

The first indication of Christian dissent appeared among a small group of Protestant pastors and lay persons who had been involved in an industrial mission since 1961 (extended into a wider urban mission in 1965) and who later received support from Catholic members of JOC. Opposition was first centered on the conditions faced by migrants and the misery of the masses. At the end of the 1960s, unrest grew due to new dictatorial tendencies evidenced by the regime: changes in the constitution in 1969, the state of emergency decreed in October 1971, proclamation of martial law in February 1972 and promulgation of the new Yushin ('Restoration') constitution giving to the president virtually unlimited powers. Centered in the Student Christian Movement, the opposition became increasingly public and active with as spokesmen a number of well-known Catholic and Protestant personalities including the Catholic cardinal archbishop of Seoul, Kim Soo Hwan; Catholic bishop of Wonju, Chi Hak Soon; Protestant leaders Kim Chae Hoon and Kang Won young; the president of Ewha Protestant University for Women; Catholic poet Kim Chi Ha; and others. The first collective letter of the Catholic episcopate relating to these questions, dated 18 February 1968, provided support for militant members of JOC and their chaplain, while the second letter, 'Let's defeat today's injustice' (14 November 1971), criticized more directly the endemic corruption and unjust practices of the government. Numerous Korean militants, pastors, and priests were arrested and a number of foreign missionaries were expelled.

World's largest Christian gatherings ever (up to 16 million) take place at Yoido.

BROADCASTING AND MEDIA

Virtually everyone owns a radio, though televisions are somewhat less common. FEBC maintains transmitters at Cheju-do, Inchon, Taejeon which reach China, Japan, North Korea, and much of eastern Asia. AWR's Seoul studio produces Korean-language programs. South Korea is a member of UNDA, and Catholics broadcast Sunday radio programs, including children's broadcasts, the liturgy, and special Sunday programs; and numerous daily Christian programs, including Christian Catholic News, educational programming, a reading of the catechism, an essay and hymn, a morning prayer, testimonies and stories, meditations, youth programs, and Christian music. Training in media is offered through courses at Sogang University and the Catholic Mass Communications Committee.

Some 5 million have seen the 'Jesus' Film, including 4.6 million who watched it on television. PBC, a local Catholic radio and TV station, is based in Seoul and has a regular TV program.

INTERDENOMINATIONAL ORGANIZATIONS

The Federal Council of Churches and Missions was organized in 1919, with the name changed to National Christian Council in 1924. It became the National Council of Churches in 1946. Although only 7 churches are members, the NCC represents about one-third of Korean Christians. Thirteen other churches form the National Association of Evangelicals, a fundamentalist body. Church members work together in many interdenominational groups with specialized functions, including the Christian School Association, Korean Student Movement, and Christian Broadcasting System, under the overall supervision of the NCC. Through its Justice and Peace Committee, Catholics collaborate with their Protestant counterparts in socio-economic development; and Protestant-Catholic cooperation is also maintained through the Sodepax Korea Committee and Association of Christian Hospitals, the latter founded in Seoul in 1972. Anglican and Catholic priests conduct an Institute for Ecumenical Inter-Religious Studies.

Working in close cooperation with the government, the Korean Association of Voluntary Agencies, with 36 of its 74 members church-related Protestant and Catholic groups, coordinates the distribution of relief and development aid.

FUTURE TRENDS AND PROSPECTS

Explosive church growth will most likely continue into the 21st century with church membership possibly growing to 43% by 2025. The greatest losses are expected for Shamanists (39.2% in 1970 falling to 15% by AD 2025) and Buddhists (16.7% in 1970 to less than 14% by 2025).

Christianity might continue to grow over the next century, but this may result in a percentage of Christians anywhere between 60-80% (with the most likely scenario in the middle of that range). Buddhism, Confucianism, and Shamanism could decline throughout this period.

BIBLIOGRAPHY

A comparative study between Minjung theology and Reformed theology from a missiological perspective. S. Lee. *Asian thought and culture*, vol. 22. New York: P. Lang, 1995.

A history of Christianity in Korea. S. Kim. Seoul: Presbyterian Church of Korea, 1994. 428p. (In Korean).

A history of the church in Korea. A. D. Clark. Seoul: Christian Literature Society of Korea, 1971.

'A model for leadership training in the Korean Methodist Church educational ministry.' H. B. Chung. D.Min. thesis, Garrett-Evangelical Theological Seminary, Evanston, IL, 1994. 147p.

'A project of the inner–city church growth.' Y. K. Chung. D.Min. thesis, Fuller Theological Seminary, Pasadena, CA, 1983. 228p. (Treats Seoul; text in Korean with abstract and outline in English).

'A review of the overseas mission policy of the Korean Church with special reference to Young–Nak Presbyterian Church.' Y. Lee. D.Min. thesis, Fuller Theological Seminary, Pasadena, CA, 1987. 200p. (Text in Korean with extended summary in English).

'A study of church growth through pastor's leadership: with special reference to the phenomena of Keum–Ran Methodist Church.' H. Kim. D.Min thesis, Fuller Theological Seminary, Pasadena, CA, 1987. 109p. (Text in Korean with extended summary in English).

'A study of the Korean church growth in context of the Korean national characteristics.' I. W. Kim. D.Min. thesis, Fuller Theological Seminary, Pasadena, CA, 1983.

Ancestor worship and Christianity in Korea. J. Y. Lee (ed). New York: E. Mellen Press, 1988. 94p.

Caring, growing, changing: a history of the Protestant mission in Korea. M. Huntley. New York: Friendship Press, 1984. 212p.

Catholic Korea, yesterday and now. J. C. Kim & J. J. Chung. Seoul: Catholic Korean Publishing Co., 1964.

Catholic politics in China and Korea. E. O. Hanson. *American Society of Missiology series*, no. 2. Maryknoll, NY: Orbis Books, 1980. 160p.

Caught in the web: the home cell unit system at Full Gospel Central Church, Seoul, Korea. J. W. Hurston & K. L. Hurston. [Mountain Press & Church Growth International], 1977. 95p.

Chongkyo P'yonlam (Handbook of religions). Seoul: Ministry of Culture and Information, 1969.

'Christian mission environments and strategies in Che Ju Island with special reference to mission strategies of the Sam Yang Church.' K. Han. D.Min. thesis, Fuller Theological Seminary, Pasadena, CA, 1987. 218p.

(Christian yearbook 1970). Seoul: National Council of Churches in Korea, 1970. 688p. (Korean-language only. First edition, 1957).

Christianity in modern Korea. D. N. Clark. *Asian agenda report*, 5. Lanham, MD: University Press of America, 1986. 68p.

Constructing Christian faith in Korea: the earliest Protestant mission and Ch'oe Pyong–hon. P. J. Koe. Zoetermeer, Netherlands: Boekencentrum, 1998. 288p.

'Developing a mid–life spiritual formation group in the Korean context.' Y. Bang. D.Min. thesis, Garrett-Evangelical Theological Seminary, Evanston, IL, 1994. 238p.

'Early morning prayer and church growth based on the case study of Inchon Presbyterian Church.' K. Na. D.Min. thesis, Fuller Theological Seminary, Pasadena, CA, 1987. 171p.

Fire beneath the frost: the struggles of the Korean people and the church. P. Billings et al. New York: Friendship Press, 1984.

Growing the world's largest church. K. Hurston. Springfield, MO: Chrism, 1994. 223p.

'Inculturation in the process of evangelization: with reference to the Catholic Church in Korea.' P. Y. Kim. S.T.D. thesis, Pontifica Universitas Lateranensis, Rome, 1986. 195p.

Korea and Christianity. S. J. Palmer. Seoul: Hollym Corporation, 1967.

Korea people, pastors, partners. Produced by P. Henke and M. Henke. Eau Claire Public Access Community Television Cable Channel 11: [1992]. (29 min. videocassette, treats Lutheran Church in Korea).

Korea struggles for Christ. H. S. Hong et al. (eds). Seoul: Christian Literature Society of Korea, 1966. 245p.

Korean Catholicism in the 70s. W. E. Biernotzai et al. New York: Orbis, 1975.

Korean church growth explosion. B. R. Ro & M. L. Nelson (eds). Seoul: Asia Theological Association, 1985. 374p.

Korean church history: Honam area. S. Kim & I. Hahn. Seoul: Presbyterian Church of Korea, Education Department, 1979. 434p. (Text in Korean).

Korean miracles. J. Choi. Seoul: Young San Publications, 1978. 108p.

'Liberal Protestant leaders working for social change: South Korea, 1957–1984.' Y. Yi. Ph.D. dissertation, University of Oregon, Eugene, OR, 1990. 305p.

Over mountains: the Irish St. John of God Brothers in Korea. J. McKenna. Dun Laoghaire, Ireland: Glendale Press, 1985. 120p.

Perspectives on Christianity in Korea and Japan: the Gospel and culture in East Asia. M. Mullins & R. F. Young (eds). Lewiston, NY: E. Mellen Press, 1995. 253p.

Prayer mountains. C. C. Whittaker. : Kingsway, 1989. [128]p.

'Protestant Christians and politics in Korea, 1884–1980s.' C. Park. Ph.D. dissertation, University of Washington, Seattle, WA, 1987. 498

'Receptivity of Korea and Taiwan mountain people.' E. S. Chae. Thesis, Fuller Theological Seminary, Pasadena, CA, 1973. 133p.

'Reforming lay education in the Presbyterian Church in the Republic of Korea.' H. Kim. Th.D. thesis, Boston University, Boston, 1993. 341p.

Religion in the Pacific Era. F. K. Flinn & T. Hendricks (eds). *Studies in the Pacific Era series.* New York: Paragon House, 1985. 242p. (See chapters 5, 6, and 8).

Repressive state and resisting church: the politics of CIA in South Korea. H. H. Sunoo. Fayette, MO: Korean American Cultural Association, 1976. 204p.

'Revival and church growth in Korea, 1884–1910.' H. T. Watson. M. A. thesis, Fuller Theological Seminary, Pasadena, CA, 1969.

'Teaching the basic Christian faith to new members of the Korean church.' J. G. Kim. D.Min. thesis, Westminster Theological Seminary, Chestnut Hill, PA, 1988. 2 vols.

The Christians of Korea. S. H. Moffett. New York: Friendship Press, 1962. 174p.

The history of Protestant missions in Korea, 1832–1910. I. G. Park. Seoul: Yonsei University Press, 1970.

The iconography of Korean Buddhist painting. No. 9 of section 12, *East and Central Asia*, of *Iconography of religions.* H. H. Sorensen. Leiden: E. J. Brill, 1988. 21p.

'The Korean church as a model in Asia with a missiological application to the Thai church.' Y. Lee. Th.M. thesis, Fuller Theological Seminary, Pasadena, CA, 1993. 189p.

The Korean frontier: a story of Pentecostal revival. E. D. Bernard. Hazelwood, MO: Word Aflame Press, 1989. 240p.

The new religions of Korea. S. J. Palmer (ed). 2d ed. *Transactions of the Korea Branch of the Royal Asiatic Society*, vol. 43. Seoul: Royal Asiatic Society, 1967. 124p.

'The politics of religion in South Korea, 1974–89: the Catholic church's political opposition to the authoritarian state.' N. Kim. Ph.D. dissertation, University of Washington, Seattle, WA, 1993. 400p.

'The role of Christianity in the economic modernization of South Korea.' J. Y. Kim. Ph.D. dissertation, Florida State University, Tallahassee, FL, 1984. 659p.

The Zen monastic experience: Buddhist practice in contemporary Korea. R. E. Buswell Jr. Princeton, NJ: Princeton University Press, 1994. 280p.

Wildfire: church growth in Korea. R. E. Shearer. Grand Rapids, MI: Eerdmans, 1962. 242p.

Country Table 2. **Organized churches and denominations in South Korea.**

Official name (bold type = church with over 10% of all affiliated) 1	*Begun* 2	*Type* 3	*Counc* 4	*Congs* 5	*Adults* 6	*Affiliated 1970* 7	*Affiliated 1995* 8	*G%* 9	*Names, notes, and other statistics* (see Codebook, Part 3) 10
Assembly Hall Churches	c1950	I-3nC	.....	88	9,831	1,000	25,000	13.74	*Local Churches. Little Flock.* Chinese. Begun 1922 in China.
Association of Christian Churches	1930	I-Non	.....	309	56,800	35,000	103,265	4.42	Independent Nondenominationalists.
Bible Presbyterian Church of Korea	1955	I-Fun	.TT.T	280	14,000	13,951	35,000	3.75	Schism ex Koryo Presbyterian Ch. M=IBPFM(USA). Fundamentalists. HQ Seoul. 91n.
Catholic Church in Korea:	1592	R-Lat	P.F.R	1,093	1,824,000	828,133	3,492,369	5.93	*Ch'onju Kyohwe.* C=14+2+32. 2p,2s(709),W=63%. 1603n 346x 1003m 6652w 147799Yy
M Kwang Ju	1937	R-Lat	Ps	77	124,000	67,393	238,219	5.18	*Kwangju Tae Kyogu.* Rural. Heavy emigration. 116n 27x 60m 445w 12420Yy
D Cheju	1971	R-Lat	Ps	15	20,000	11,162	39,602	4.17	Created out of M Kwang Ju. M=SSC. 16n 5x 11m 69w 2129Yy
D Jeon Ju (Chonju)	1937	R-Lat	Ps	61	71,000	54,207	133,522	3.67	*Chonju Kyogu.* Mountainous. Heavy emigration. 125n 2x 8m 248w 6122Yy
M Seoul (Soul)	1911	R-Lat	Ps	163	613,000	185,769	1,159,005	7.60	*Seoul Tae Kyogu.* Rapid urban growth. 432n 154x 404m 1786w 43295Yy
D Chun Cheon (Shunsen)	1939	R-Lat	Ps	43	29,000	33,005	52,490	1.87	Many military bases. Part in North Korea. M=SSC. 65n 4x 16m 126w 3565Yy
D Inchon	1961	R-Lat	Pmm	63	148,000	57,293	294,917	6.77	Second largest port city, many islands. M=MM. 72n 37x 59m 438w 14972Yy
D Su Won	1963	R-Lat	Ps	74	181,000	55,722	373,089	7.90	Rural, recent industry. Military bases. 139n 29x 176m 647w 18333Yy
D Tae Jeon (Taejon)	1958	R-Lat	Ps	76	86,000	65,900	161,247	3.64	Rural, and a major transportation centre. 124n 9x 33m 326w 7497Yy
D Won Ju	1965	R-Lat	Ps	31	26,000	31,420	47,497	1.67	Mountainous, rural, mining. M=MEP. 49n 0x 0m 195w 2031Yy
M Tae Gu	1911	R-Lat	Ps	96	166,000	85,309	315,067	5.36	Rural, 3 developing industrial centers. 175n 37x 127m 839w 12852Yy
D Andong	1969	R-Lat	Ps	26	22,000	28,149	40,765	1.49	Mountainous, rural, mining. 33n 7x 10m 120w 1382Yy
D Cheong Ju (Ch'ongju)	1958	R-Lat	Ps	43	52,000	45,664	102,503	3.29	Rural, agricultural industrialization. 59n 3x 26m 223w 5194Yy
D Masan	1966	R-Lat	Ps	55	64,000	30,554	121,851	5.69	Mountains, port. Least Catholic area. 79n 13x 29m 229w 4745Yy
D Pusan	1957	R-Lat	Ps	73	172,000	76,586	322,595	5.92	Urban, largest port (population 1.9 million). M=MEP. 119n 19x 44m 961w 13262Yy
OM Korea	1983	R-Lat	Ps	197	50,000	–	90,000	8.33	Military Ordinariate of Korea. 59w,3395Yy.
Central Jerusalem Church in Korea	1957	I-Non	.....	10	2,100	1,470	2,800	2.61	Indigenous group. 420 Sunday-school children. 40 deacons,5n,3m.
Chinese Christian Church	1912	I-Non	.....	3	100	582	300	-2.62	*Chung-hwa Kidokyohwei.* Chinese. Declining rapidly in numbers. HQ Seoul. 10n.
Choson Christian Church	1918	I-Non	.....	20	2,000	3,030	5,000	2.02	*Choson Kidokyo Whei* (Choson=old name for Korea). Korean Christianity. 20n.
Christian Brethren	c1895	P-CBr	x....	80	4,000	2,000	10,000	6.65	*Gospel Halls. Plymouth (Open) Brethren.* M=CMML(USA, UK). Work re-begun c1955. 20f.
Christian Church of Emmanuel	1950	I-Non	.....	40	2,600	3,441	6,000	2.25	Grouping of indigenous Korean congregations. 20n.
Christian Independent Church		I-Non	.....	15	2,000	2,300	3,500	0.05	Small group of indigenous independent congregations. 18n.
Christian Korean Pentecostal Ch of God	1964	I-3pK	.....	5	1,500	1,000	3,000	4.49	*Kidokyo Hankuk Osungol Hananim-e Kyowhei.* Korean indigenous. HQ Seoul. 3nx.
Christian Reformed Church in Korea	1967	P-Ref	.F...	901	171,000	19,015	427,943	13.26	Recent North American work. M=CRC(USA). 52n,2f.
Christian Rehabilitated Ch in Korea	1945	I-Non	.....	60	4,000	4,329	7,000	1.94	One of many splinter renewal movements. Large indigenous grouping. 12n.
Christ's Assembly	1947	I-Adv	.....	7	400	550	700	0.97	*Kurisudo Sohoe.* Small sabbatarian group. HQ Seoul. 4 evangelists, 1 minister.
Church of Christ, Scientist	1963	m-Sci	x....	1	200	200	400	2.81	*Christian Science.* M=CCS(Boston, USA). Seoul Society. Expatriate Americans.
Church of God (Cleveland)	1966	P-Pe3	ZF...	116	14,075	10,000	28,600	4.29	M=GoC(Cleveland)(USA). Holiness Pentecostals. 30 churches, 8 missions. 40n,1p.
Church of God (Seventh-day)	1962	P-Adv	x....	3	100	154	300	2.70	Related to Ch of God (Seventh-day), Adventist group in USA.
Church of God of Prophecy	1969	P-Pe3	Z....	88	94,300	5,180	123,223	13.52	M=CGP.
Ch of Jesus Christ of Latter-day Saints	1950	m-LdS	x....	146	68,000	6,329	105,133	11.90	*Malil Songdo Yesu Kristo Kyowhei. Mormons.* M=CJCLdS(USA). 116n,300f.
Constitutional Korean Presbyterian Ch	1962	I-Fun	..T.T	188	23,200	4,000	36,310	9.22	*Tae-Han Yesukyo Changno Whei (Ho-hon) (Legal).* 47n,1p,1s(23),W=75%,40Yy,300z.
Episcopal Church in Korea	1889	A-ACa	AwEAN	88	77,100	32,436	100,780	4.64	*Tae-Han Song-Kong-hwei (Korea Holy Catholic Ch).* 3 Dioceses. 3 Dioceses. 1s(11).
Evangelical Alliance Mission in Korea	1953	P-Eva	xM...	4	64	2,000	213	-8.57	*Hankuk Pokumjui Tongmaeng Sonkyo Whei.* M=TEAM(USA). HQ Seoul. 1 school. 14n,30f.
Far East Apostolic Mission	1958	P-Pe2	.....	20	2,000	3,000	4,000	1.16	M=FEAM(Texas,USA), in Korea and Japan only. 19n,4x,1p,1p(Seoul),W=70%,80Y.
Full Gospel Church	c1991	I-3kK	.....	20	90,000	–	200,000	25.00	Rapidly growing church, schism ex YFGC/FGCC (Seoul), modeled on same principles.
Full Gospel International General Mtg	1963	I-3fK	.....	54	77,500	4,100	101,233	13.68	One of many denominations stressing Full Gospel teaching.
Fundamental Presbyterian Church	1982	I-Fun	.....	216	27,900	–	69,638	7.69	FPC (Gun-bon). Fundamentalist doctrines.
Gen Assemb of Pres Chs (Bokeun)	1964	I-Ref	.....	272	15,500	3,000	34,420	10.25	Large split over doctrine.
Gen As of Pres Ch in K (BoSu) I		I-Ref	.....	1,292	589,000	–	769,343	0.05	One of larger Presbyterian bodies.
Gen As of Pr Chs (Bo-Su Hap-Tong) IV		I-Ref	.....	353	37,800	–	75,684	0.05	Smaller schism.
Gen As of Pres Chs (Hap-tong Bo-Su) II		I-Ref	.....	807	88,900	–	197,511	0.05	Large split.
Gen As of Pres Chs (Haptong Bo-Su) III		I-Ref	.....	213	74,200	–	185,431	0.05	Sizeable secession.
Gen As of Pr Chs (Haptong Chungang)	1976	I-Ref	.....	235	35,600	–	71,123	5.26	Break with parent bodies over doctrine.
Gen As of Pres Chs (Hap-tong Ho-hun)	1962	I-Ref	.....	374	19,100	4,000	42,466	9.91	Split over leadership and doctrine.
Gen As of Pres Chs (Haptong Janseen)	1955	I-Ref	.....	112	14,500	3,000	32,153	9.95	Leadership disagreements.
Gen Assemb of Pres Chs (Ho Hun)	1962	I-Ref	.....	144	16,300	4,000	36,263	9.22	Minor break off.
Gen Assemb of Pres Ch in K (Taesin)	1948	P-Ref	.....	662	54,400	10,000	120,835	10.48	One of the larger and more consequential splits.
Gospel Baptist Convention	1961	I-Bap	.....	146	33,600	5,000	67,161	10.95	Independent Baptists.
Grace and Truth Church	c1980	I-3cK	.....	5	30,000	–	57,000	6.67	Based in Anyang city. Several satellite churches.
Greek Orthodox Ch (D New Zealand)	1896	O-Gre	Cw..N	2	1,500	3,000	5,000	2.06	Under EP Constantinople; until 1970 in AD N & S America. 2n,1x,W=25%,61Yy.
Heavenly Gospel Tabernacle Church		I-mar	.....	10	1,000	5,000	2,000	0.05	1965, leader arrested for selling absolution tickets; died in police custody.
Holy Spirit Association for U of WC	1954	m-HSA	xv...	494	421,000	304,750	550,000	2.39	*T'ongil Kyohoe.* Unification Ch. Missions to USA, Japan, 120 nations. HQ Seoul. 1013n.
Independent Korean Presbyterian Ch	1949	I-Fun	..T.T	15	1,500	1,380	3,000	3.15	Split with USA fundamentalist support. Rapid growth. 11n,W=95%, 158Yy,212z.
Intern Ch of the Foursquare Gospel	1970	P-Pe2	ZF...	22	1,900	3,000	6,330	3.03	M=ICFG(USA). Classical Pentecostals. High proportion of youths. 4nm,4f,29Y.
International Pentecostal Holiness Ch	1979	P-Pe3	Z....	183	12,400	–	34,029	6.25	M=IPHC(USA). Holiness Pentecostals.
Jehovah's Witnesses	1912	m-Jeh	x....	1,055	62,193	40,000	138,000	5.08	*Wach'ui Ta-wo Songso Ch'aekja Hyop-hwei/Watchtower.*(1975) 3290Y. (1995) 4715Y.
Jesus Assembly of God of Korea	1952	P-Pe2	ZF...	1,206	1,211,000	100,000	2,000,000	12.73	*Tae-Han Kidokyo Hananim-e Song-Hwei.* M=AoG. 205n,19f,1s(300),W=77%,700Y.
Jesus End of the World Gospel Mis Soc	1963	I-Non	.....	90	23,000	9,802	30,000	4.58	Revivalist, evangelistic. Large grouping of indigenous congregations. 5n.
Jesus Korean Holiness Church	1961	I-Hol	.TT.T	819	184,443	44,525	362,346	8.75	*Yesukyo Tae-Han Songkyol-kyohwei.* HQ Seoul. 185n,1p(140),W=95%,617Y.
Jesus Korean Methodist Church	1962	I-Fun	.TT.T	306	21,600	19,960	61,663	4.62	*Yesukyo Tae-Han Kamni-Whei.* No foreign mission connections. HQ Seoul. 48n.
Jesus Presbyterian Ch, Head Presbytery	1949	I-Ref	.....	25	5,000	5,016	15,000	4.48	*Tae-Han Yesukyo Changno Whei Tok-nowhei.* HQ Seoul. 17n.
Korea Assembly of God	1945	I-3pK	.....	530	220,000	18,000	400,000	13.21	Independent pentecostals.
Korea Baptist Convention	1890	P-Bap	T....	1,800	702,000	51,613	956,840	12.39	*Hankuk Chimnehwei Yonmaeng.* East Asia Ch. 1950,M=FMB-SBC(USA). 365n,72f,1H,1s,3122Y.
Korea Bible Baptist Fellowship	1950	I-Bap	xTT.T	166	23,200	12,108	46,314	5.51	*Hankuk Songso Chimnekyo Whei.* M=BBFI(USA). Fundamentalist. HQ Seoul. 61n,20f,1s.
Korea Church of Christ (Instrumental)	1936	I-Dis	x....	194	16,500	20,000	30,000	1.64	*Hankuk Kristo-e Kyohwei (as-ki).* M=KCM(CCCCC,USA). 89n,25f,2p(202),1080Y.
Korea Ch of Christ (Non-Instrumental)	1927	I-Dis	x....	60	2,000	2,550	5,000	2.73	*Hankuk Kristo-e Kyohwei (mu-ak-ki).* M=CC(USA). USA servicemen on bases. 41nx.
Korea Church of God	c1932	P-Hol	x....	53	21,100	5,000	28,956	7.28	Linked since 1961 with M=CoG(Anderson)(USA). No missionaries now. 24n,1p,W=43%.
Korea Evangelical Church	1932	I-Ref	.....	28	10,700	4,000	13,940	5.12	Independent Reformed traditional.
Korea Holiness Evangelical Church	1907	P-Hol	xF...	2,405	301,000	577,305	901,801	1.80	*Kidokyo Tae-Han Songkyol Kyohwei.* M=OMS. 354n,14f,3s(500),W=65%,1567Y.
Korea Jesus Bible Presbyterian Church	1961	I-Ref	.TT.T	4	1,200	2,000	3,000	1.64	*Tae-Han Yesukyo Songkyong Changno-Whei.* Presbyterian schism over doctrine. Seoul.
Korea Lutheran Church	1958	P-Lut	L....	25	3,960	1,100	6,579	7.42	*Hankuk Lutokyo Sonkyobu.* M=LC Missouri Synod(USA). 6n,6x,1s,W=75%,220Yy.
Korea Peniel Church	1958	I-Hol	.....	10	2,300	1,651	3,000	2.42	Small indigenous group of churches in holiness tradition. 4n.
Korea Presbyterian Ch (Conservative)	1965	I-Ref	.....	62	1,872	851	4,000	6.39	One of Presbyterian schisms over doctrine. Expanding. HQ Seoul. 3n.
Korean Baptist Convention	c1986	I-Bap	.....	151	82,300	–	107,500	11.11	Schism of charismatic congregations from KBC related to SBC-FMB(USA).
Korea Tabernacle Temple	1965	I-Non	.....	5	1,500	1,350	2,500	2.50	Small indigenous grouping of independent congregations.
Korean Bethel Presbyterian Church	c1960	I-Fun	.....	10	500	1,005	1,200	0.71	Small fundamentalist indigenous group of Presbyterian background. 14n.
Korean Bible Presbyterian Church	c1940	I-Fun	..T.T	60	8,000	21,190	25,000	0.66	One of larger Presbyterian schisms over fundamentalism. Now anti-ICCC. 62n.
Korean Christian Pentecostal Church	c1960	I-3pK	.....	20	2,000	1,000	3,000	4.49	Small grouping of indigenous Korean pentecostals. 6n.
Korean Christian Reformed Presb Ch	c1950	I-Ref	.....	55	4,000	8,225	10,000	0.78	Presbyterian schism over doctrine and fundamentalism, with USA support. 58n.
Korean Conservative Baptist Church	c1965	I-Bap	x....	3	500	1,000	1,600	1.90	Independent Baptist churches. 4nx.
Korean Evangelical Church of Christ	1925	I-Eva	....N	106	26,900	12,000	67,161	7.13	*Kidokyo Tae-Han Pokum Kyohwei.* Founder a Korean. 20n,W=83%,400Y,4000z.
Korean Evangelical Movement	1951	I-Eva	.TT.T	5	500	1,105	1,500	1.23	Small indigenous grouping of Korean fundamentalist congregations. 1 minister.
Korean Free Methodist Church of Jesus	1961	I-Hol	.TT.T	105	14,200	8,000	23,684	4.44	*Hankuk Yesukyo Chayu Kamni-hwei.* No foreign mission. 15n,1p(25),950Y,4000z.
Korean Methodist Church	1884	P-Met	VWE.N	4,114	503,000	600,000	1,277,177	3.07	KMC. *Kidokyo Tae-Han Kamni-hwei.* M=UMC. 914n,51f,2s(375),W=89%,1850Yy,85000z.
Korean Nazarene Church	1948	P-Hol	xF...	226	27,429	20,000	44,307	3.23	*Tae-Han Kidokyo Nazaret-kyowhei.* M=CoN. 64n,3x,10f,1s,71t(9657),W=69%,320Y.
Korean United Pentecostal Church	1965	P-Pe1	x....	38	4,000	6,000	10,000	2.06	*Hankuk Yunhang Osoonch Kyohwei. Jesus Only.* M=UPC. 20n,9x,12f,4p(173),W=21%,170Y.
Meeting of Christians	1896	I-Non	.....	30	1,000	1,110	2,000	2.38	*Kristo-in-a Chip Whei-so.* Small indigenous independent groups. HQ Seoul.
New Apostolic Church		I-3aX	x....	5	3,000	1,000	5,869	0.05	*NAC.* In Canada Bezirk, NAK. Catholic Apostolic. World HQ Zurich (Switzerland).
New Jerusalem Church of Korea	1933	m-Swe	x....	5	300	800	700	-0.53	*Swedenborgians.* Had 40 congs in NKorea. Declining. 2n,2p(5),W=85%,24Y.
No-Church Movement Association of BS	1924	I-NoC	.....	5	600	300	1,000	4.93	BS=Bible Students. Influenced by Japanese Mukyokai (Non-Church). No buildings.
Olive Tree Church (Evangelical Church)	1955	I-mar	.....	200	2,100	700,520	7,000	-16.83	*Chondokwon. Preaching Tabernacle. Korean Christian Revival Society.* Vast towns. In decline.
Peniel Churches of VOCA	1946	P-Hol	x....	15	5,400	5,115	7,000	1.26	M=Voice of China AMS(USA). 50% students. 3 schools. 15n,1s(23),W=36%,562Y.
Presbyterian Church in the RoK	1954	I-Ref	RWE.N	353	37,800	218,287	75,684	-4.15	*Hankuk Kidokyo Changno-hwei.* Liberal schism. 459n,5x,23f,2s(150),W=70%,5720Yy.
Presbyterian Church of Korea (Hyuksin)	1973	I-Ref	.....	172	25,100	–	62,814	4.55	Recent schism from mainline Presbyterianism.
Presbyterian Church in Korea (Kosin)	1946	I-Ref	JTT.T	1,361	258,000	102,125	336,620	4.89	*Tae-Han Yesukyo Changno-Hwei.* (Ko Sin). Koryo Korea. M=IPM,OPM,WPM(USA). 702n.
Presb Ch of Korea (Non-Assembled)	1960	I-Ref	.....	20	4,000	7,500	12,000	1.90	Ex Koryo Presbyterian Church in long-standing fundamentalist controversy. 14n.
Presb Ch of Korea (Reformed Faith)	1954	I-Ref	.....	107	30,900	1,465	40,389	14.19	Union General Assembly of the PCK. Small Presbyterian schism over fundamentalism. 5n.
Presbyterian Ch of Korea (Restored)	1966	I-Ref	.TT.T	10	1,000	960	3,000	4.66	Small Presbyterian schism over controversy on fundamentalism. 5n.
Pr C in K (Reunited Anti-Ecumenical)	1951	I-Ref	J.T.T	4,561	772,000	550,790	2,158,597	5.62	*Tae-Han Yesukyo Changno-hwei.* (Hap Dong) *NAE.* Anti-ecumenical schism. 2096n,1s(850).
Presbyterian Ch in Korea (Tonghap)	1884	P-Ref	RWE.N	5,350	1,603,000	534,368	2,093,967	5.61	*PCK Tae-Han Yesukyo Changno-hwei.* (T'ong-hap). 1303n,109f,6H,15p,3s,16240Yy.
Presbyterian Church (Neutral)	1950	I-Ref	.....	50	3,000	7,743	10,000	1.03	One of numerous splits over fundamentalism ex Presbyterian Church of Korea. 30n.
Presbyterian Ch (Revolutionary Rehab)	1949	I-Ref	.....	5	1,000	967	2,000	2.95	*Revolutionary Rehabilitated.* Schism claiming return to Reformed origins.
Presbyterian General Assembly (Koryo)	1946	I-Ref	.....	137	14,700	10,000	32,593	4.84	Minor schism in leadership dispute.
Pure Presbyterian Church of Korea	1939	I-Ref	.....	10	1,600	4,299	2,100	-2.83	Presbyterian fundamentalist schism. Rapid decline: 6n,1p,W=80%,50Yy.
Reconstruction Presbyterian Church	1945	I-Ref	.....	114	18,000	3,449	23,569	7.99	*Tae-Han Yesukyo Changno Whei (Chae-Kon).* HQ Seoul. 35n,1s(in Dong-ku, Pusan).
Reformed Presbyterian Ch (Gaehyuk)	1955	I-Ref	.....	201	15,600	10,000	34,641	5.10	Schism due to Bible disagreement on interpretation.
Religious Society of Friends	1955	P-Qua	Q....	1	100	100	300	4.49	*Chongkyo Ch'in-u-whei (Kwei-ko). Quakers.* Small group meeting in Seoul.
Reorganized Ch of JC of Latter Day S	1960	m-LdS	x....	10	1,000	1,000	3,000	4.49	*RLDS Church.* Schism ex Mormons. HQ Seoul. World HQ Independence, MO (USA). 7nx.
Salvation Army, Korea Territory	1908	P-Sal	xwE.N	223	39,800	150,000	103,860	-1.46	*Ku-se-kun Tae-Han Pon-Yong.* 5 Divisions. 213 Officers. 16 institutions. 1s.
Seventh-day Adventist Church	1903	P-Adv	x....	727	81,300	50,000	143,058	4.29	*SDA, Korea Council.* 91n,26f,2H,1h,1j,7r,1s,W=85%,1532Y.
True Jesus Church, Korea Assembly	1944	I-3oC	x....	50	4,000	3,000	8,000	4.00	*Ch'am Yesukyo Whei Han-kuk Chongwhei.* Chinese. 21n,1sW=43%,74Y.
World Evangelical Mission of Korea		I-3cK	.....	150	5,000	5,000	15,000	0.05	Indigenous body with seminary in Seoul. 64 priests, 72 missionaries.
Worldwide Evangelization Crusade	1956	P-Non	xF...	20	3,000	4,000	6,000	1.64	Small interdenominational Evangelical body. M=WEC(UK). 16n,1f.
World-Wide Missions of Korea	1961	I-Non	x....	20	1,000	1,000	2,000	2.81	M=World-Wide Missions(USA). Evangelicals with links in Pasadena, CA (USA).
Yoido Full Gospel Churches	1958	I-3kK	Z....	100	700,000	23,000	900,000	15.80	YFGC. Adult members: (1961) 800. 100 staff, 50,000 cells. Since 1985 part of AoG.
Zion Presbyterian Church of Christ	1938	I-Ref	.....	5	300	320	600	2.55	*Sionan Yesukyo Changrohoe.* Presbyterian schism, near Kyongju. W=63%,15Yy.
Other Korean indigenous churches		I-3xK	.....	3,000	50,000	30,000	140,000	0.05	Total about 150 (see list below), including Chinese Ch of Christ.

Continued opposite

Country Table 2–concluded

Official name (bold type = church with over 10% of all affiliated) 1	*Begun* 2	*Type* 3	*Counc* 4	*Congs* 5	*Adults* 6	*Affiliated 1970* 7	*Affiliated 1995* 8	*G%* 9	*Names, notes, and other statistics* (see Codebook, Part 3) 10
Other Protestant denominations		P-	.....	1,200	35,000	40,000	70,000	0.05	Total about 80 (see below), 70 more Presbyterian denominations, USA military chaplaincies.
Other non-Korean indigenous churches		I-	.....	200	40,000	10,000	80,000	0.05	Total about 40, including JILF, 20 Chinese, Japanese, Vietnamese, Indonesian, & other bodies.
Doubly-affiliated		2-aff			-1,411,000	0	-2,523,885		Pentecostals who are also members of Catholic and other large churches.
Totals				**41,349**	**9,852,467**	**5,403,904**	**17,622,000**		

Churches, members, growth, 1900-2025	*Congs*	*Adults*	*Affiliated*	*G%*	*Total denominations*	*6 Megablocs:* *O*	*R*	*A*	*P*	*I*	*m*
Total churches, members, and denominations (mid-1900)	200	21,500	42,700	7.16	14	1	1	1	6	5	0
Total churches, members, and denominations (mid-1970)	16,589	2,720,645	5,403,904	7.16	215	1	1	1	59	147	6
Total churches, members, and denominations (mid-1990)	39,000	9,281,000	16,600,000	5.77	370	1	1	1	104	257	6
Total churches, members, and denominations (mid-1995)	41,349	9,852,467	17,622,000	1.20	375	1	1	1	104	262	6
Total churches, members, and denominations (mid-2000)	45,000	10,445,000	18,681,876	1.17	385	1	1	1	106	270	6
Total churches, members, and denominations (mid-2025)	60,000	12,524,000	22,400,000	0.73	763	1	1	1	140	600	20

NOTES ON TABLE ABOVE
NATIONAL COUNCILS (Column 4, 5th letter).
- E = Korea Evangelical Fellowship (KEF).
- N = National Council of Churches in Korea (NCCK) (Hankuk Kidokyo Yonhap-hui).
- R = Bishops' Conference of Korea (Hanguk Jukyo Hweoi).
- T = Korean Evangelical Council of Christian Churches (formerly Korea Fundamentalist Association of Churches, sometimes called National Association or Assembly of Evangelicals, NAE).

OTHER KOREAN INDIGENOUS CHURCHES. These include: Assembly of God's House, Christian Revolutionary Ch, Ch of God of Korea (member of ICCC), Jehovah's Saeil (New Work) Church, Korea Christian Ch of God, Korea Independent Lutheran Ch, Korean Christian Chs (member of ICCC), Mount Yongmun Prayer Centre, Original Jesus Ch, True Gospel Ch (pentecostal).
OTHER PROTESTANT DENOMINATIONS. These smaller bodies include: American Baptist Association, Apostolic Faith Mission (1967), Baptist Mid-Missions (1966), Ev Methodist Ch (1964), Evangelistic Faith Missions (1971), Far East Missionary Society (1968, International Gospel League (1954), Japanese Christian Ch in Korea (Seoul), Korea Christian Ch, Maranatha Baptist Mission, Mennonite Mission, Methodist Protestant Ch, Overseas Missionary Fellowship (1968), Pentecostal Holiness Ch (1979, merger with 30,000 Korean members, 142 pastors), Slavic Gospel Association, Swedish Free Mission, United World Mission (1955). There are also USA military chaplaincies among the 42,000 USA troops (1970-79).

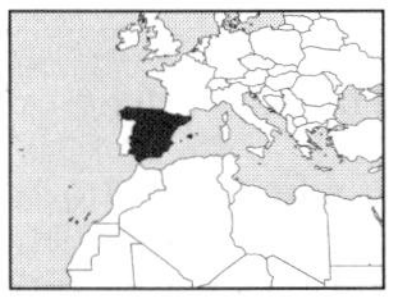

SPAIN

SECULAR DATA, AD 2000

STATE
Official name: El Reino de España (The Kingdom of Spain).
Short name: Spain. **Adjective of nationality:** Spanish, a Spaniard.
Flag: Wide yellow stripe in centre with narrow red stripes at top and bottom with coat of arms in center.
Area: 504,783 sq. km. (194,898 sq. mi.).
Government: Constitutional monarchy, since 1975 (15th century monarchy and empire, 1923 dictatorship, 1931 republic, 1938 dictatorship, 1975 monarchy).
Legislature: Senate, 257 members; Congress of Deputies, 350 members.
Official language: Spanish (Español).
Monetary unit: 1 peseta (Pta) = 100 céntimos. **US$1=** Ptas 141.88.
Chief cities: Madrid 4,198,809; MADRID 4,072,000; Barcelona 2,819,000; Bilbao (Vizcaya) 1,011,300; Valencia 754,000.
Political divisions: 17 provinces.
Armed forces: 201,000.

DEMOGRAPHY
Population: 39,630,000.
Population density: 78.5/sq. km. (203.3/sq. mi.).
Under 15 years: 5,766,000.
Growth rate p.a.: -0.08% (births 8.87, deaths 9.98).
Mortality: Infant, per 1,000: 6.1; **Maternal per 100,000:** 7.0.
Life expectancy: 79 (male 75, female 82).
Household size: 3.5. **Floor area per person, sq.m:** 25.6.
Major languages: Spanish, Catalan, Galician, Basque, Romany, Portuguese, French, English, and several others.
Urban dwellers: 77.62%. **Urban growth rate p.a.:** 0.3%.
Labor force: 39%.

ETHNOLINGUISTIC PEOPLES
44.9% Spaniard; 28.0% Catalonian; 8.1% Galician (Galega, Gallego; 5.0% Aragonese; 3.7% Basque, 1.5% Spanish Gypsy, 0.4% Black Gypsy.

ECONOMY
National income p.a. per person: US$13,579; **per family:** US$47,529.

EDUCATION
Adult literacy: 97% (male 98%, female 95%). **Schools:** 42,315.
Universities: 1,415. **School enrolment:** female/male: 114%/106%.

HEALTH
Access to health services: 90%. **Access to safe water:** 99%.
Hospitals: 813 (42 beds per 10,000). **Doctors:** 159,291.
Blind: 30,000. **Deaf:** 2,388,100. **Murder rate:** 2.
Lepers: 4,000.

LITERATURE
New book titles p.a.: 46,760 (1,180 p.a. per million). **Periodicals:** 2,797. **Newspapers:** 148 dailies.

COMMUNICATION (per 1,000 people)
Phones: 385 (30% mobile). **Radios:** 304. **TV sets:** 490.
Daily newspaper circulation: 104. **Computers:** 201.

REFUGEES
Alien refugees from other countries: 4,300.

HUMAN LIFE AND LIBERTY (optimum condition=100.0%)
HDI: 93.4. **HSI:** 89.0. **HFI:** 65.0. **EFL:** 46.0.

Country Table 1. Religious adherents in Spain, AD 1900-2025.

Year / *Name*	*1900* *Adherents*	*%*	*1970* *Adherents*	*%*	*mid-1990* *Adherents*	*%*	*Annual change, 1990-2000* *Natural*	*Conversion*	*Total*	*Rate*	*mid-1995* *Adherents*	*%*	*mid-2000* *Adherents*	*%*	*mid-2025* *Adherents*	*%*
Christians	**18,797,000**	**100.0**	**33,016,600**	**97.7**	**36,987,500**	**94.1**	**30,752**	**-18,791**	**11,961**	**0.03**	**37,161,000**	**93.9**	**37,107,109**	**93.6**	**33,712,500**	**92.0**
PROFESSION																
professing Christians	**18,797,000**	**100.0**	**33,016,600**	**97.7**	**36,987,500**	**94.1**	**30,752**	**-18,791**	**11,961**	**0.03**	**37,161,000**	**93.9**	**37,107,109**	**93.6**	**33,712,500**	**92.0**
AFFILIATION																
unaffiliated Christians	0	0.0	165,000	0.5	40,000	0.1	33	-689	-656	-1.78	36,000	0.1	33,437	0.1	22,500	0.1
affiliated Christians	**18,797,000**	**100.0**	**32,851,600**	**97.3**	**36,947,500**	**94.0**	**30,718**	**-18,101**	**12,617**	**0.03**	**37,125,000**	**93.8**	**37,073,672**	**93.6**	**33,690,000**	**91.9**
Roman Catholics	18,799,000	100.0	33,596,162	99.5	37,820,000	96.2	31,466	-5,466	26,000	0.07	38,056,562	96.2	38,080,000	96.1	34,700,000	94.7
Independents	0	0.0	37,542	0.1	295,000	0.8	245	2,255	2,500	0.82	313,568	0.8	320,000	0.8	400,000	1.1
Marginal Christians	0	0.0	40,915	0.1	170,000	0.4	141	2,859	3,000	1.64	184,080	0.5	200,000	0.5	300,000	0.8
Protestants	7,000	0.0	72,097	0.2	105,000	0.3	87	1,413	1,500	1.34	111,709	0.3	120,000	0.3	180,000	0.5
Anglicans	1,000	0.0	12,000	0.0	12,000	0.0	10	-10	0	0.00	12,000	0.0	12,000	0.0	12,000	0.0
Orthodox	0	0.0	2,000	0.0	2,150	0.0	2	8	10	0.46	2,210	0.0	2,250	0.0	3,000	0.0
doubly-affiliated	-8,000	0.0	-53,549	-0.2	-156,650	-0.4	-130	-10,263	-10,393	5.22	-205,129	-0.5	-260,578	-0.7	-205,000	-0.6
disaffiliated	-2,000	0.0	-855,567	-2.5	-1,300,000	-3.3	-1,082	-8,918	-10,000	0.74	-1,350,000	-3.4	-1,400,000	-3.5	-1,700,000	-4.6
Trans-megabloc groupings																
Evangelicals	6,500	0.0	44,000	0.1	110,000	0.3	92	908	1,000	0.87	114,295	0.3	120,000	0.3	131,000	0.4
Pentecostals/Charismatics	0	0.0	38,000	0.1	1,050,000	2.7	874	2,626	3,500	0.33	1,069,444	2.7	1,085,000	2.7	1,400,000	3.8
Great Commission Christians	**3,000,000**	**16.0**	**11,822,000**	**35.0**	**16,700,000**	**42.5**	**13,894**	**29,356**	**43,250**	**0.26**	**17,000,000**	**43.0**	**17,132,496**	**43.2**	**16,496,000**	**45.0**
Nonreligious	2,000	0.0	605,000	1.8	1,671,000	4.3	1,390	15,150	16,540	0.95	1,744,700	4.4	1,836,401	4.6	2,100,000	5.7
Atheists	0	0.0	140,000	0.4	436,200	1.1	363	136	499	0.11	440,000	1.1	441,188	1.1	532,500	1.5
Muslims	1,000	0.0	5,000	0.0	170,000	0.4	141	2,920	3,061	1.67	180,000	0.5	200,610	0.5	250,000	0.7
Buddhists	0	0.0	0	0.0	16,500	0.0	14	109	123	0.72	17,400	0.0	17,734	0.0	22,500	0.1
Baha'is	0	0.0	3,900	0.0	9,000	0.0	7	458	465	4.25	11,900	0.0	13,647	0.0	25,000	0.1
Jews	0	0.0	8,500	0.0	12,800	0.0	11	18	29	0.22	13,000	0.0	13,086	0.0	15,500	0.0
World A (unevangelized persons)	0	0.0	67,557	0.2	117,909	0.3	89	1,671	1,760	1.53	118,704	0.3	118,890	0.3	183,290	0.5
World B (evangelized non-Christians)	3,000	0.0	694,503	2.1	2,197,591	5.6	1,837	17,120	18,957	0.90	2,288,395	5.8	2,404,001	6.1	2,762,210	7.5
World C (Christians)	18,797,000	100.0	33,016,600	97.7	36,987,500	94.1	30,752	-18,791	11,961	0.03	37,161,000	93.9	37,107,109	93.6	33,712,500	92.0
Country's population	**18,800,000**	**100.0**	**33,778,661**	**100.0**	**39,303,000**	**100.0**	**32,678**	**0**	**32,678**	**0.08**	**39,568,100**	**100.0**	**39,630,000**	**100.0**	**36,658,000**	**100.0**

COLUMNS, ROWS.
For meanings and definitions, see Codebook (Part 3). Note that, by definition, total 'Christians' = professing + crypto-Christians, which also = affiliated + unaffiliated Christians, and also = Great Commission Christians + latent Christians. Percentages may not always total exactly, due to rounding.

NOTES ON RELIGIONS
AFFILIATED. By adding up diocesan totals in *Annuario Pontificio* (as is done in Table 2 below), it may be seen that (as is shown in the table above) the Roman Church in the 1990s claimed over 97% of the total population as affiliated members on the grounds that that number were, or had once been, baptized Catholics and were still on the church's rolls. However, as elaborated below, in 1995 about 714,000 were also Evangelicals or other Christians and so were doubly-affiliated, and over 1.6 million regarded themselves as having disaffiliated completely from Christianity and were now nonreligious (agnostics) or atheists. Subtracting these 2 groups from the aggregate totals claimed by the churches produces the figures on the line 'affiliated'.
AFFILIATED PROTESTANTS. Including over 20,000 expatriates (USA civilian and military, British, et alia).
ATHEISTS. Partido Comunista de Espaed on Rabwah (Pakistan) 1977; independent in Sino-Soviet dispute.
BAHA'IS. Local spiritual assemblies: 1964, 14; 1973, 26 (5 in Canary Islands). By 1996 the total had risen markedly to 78 LSAs.
COUNTRY'S POPULATION. This table for Spain excludes the population of Spanish North Africa, treated here as a separate territory, with 130,000 in AD 2000.
DISAFFILIATED. This term is used here to describe dechristianized persons who, although baptized Roman Catholics and therefore regarded by the Catholic Church as still affiliated to it (and hence enumerated in Table 2 as such), have recently disaffiliated themselves completely from Christianity and now profess (for example in polls) to be either nonreligious (agnostics) or atheists. Because their statistics represent a duplication, they are shown in the table above as a negative quantity (with a minus sign). Although in polls nonreligious persons and atheists number over 4% in urban areas, many Catholic dioceses continue to claim virtually the entire population; the archdiocese of Madrid, for instance, reported in *AP 1973* a total population of 3,965,122 within its borders, out of whom 3,952,821 (99.7%) were baptized

Continued overleaf

Country Table 1–concluded

Catholics. The table above incorporates all of these data and interpretations for 1970, 1995, and 2000.
DOUBLY-AFFILIATED. The great majority of non-Catholic Christians are also baptized Roman Catholics or are counted as affiliated by the Catholic dioceses they live in. Our term covers persons affiliated to, or claimed by, both the Catholic Church and also an Evangelical, Protestant, Anglican, Independent, Catholic (non-Roman) or Orthodox church. Because their statistics represent a duplication, they are shown in the table as a negative quantity (with a minus sign). It is in fact not uncommon for people to attend a Protestant church for some time before becoming a member, if ever.
INDEPENDENTS. In about 8 denominations from 5 countries in 1995 (see Table 2).
JEWS. Sefardic; in 7 communities. There were no Jews in Spain from their expulsion in 1492 until the 1920s in Barcelona and refugees during World War II. There are also 200,000 Marranos (Crypto-Jews, Anusim, Conversos, New Christians) whose ancestors adopted Catholicism under duress in and after 1492 and who secretly keep up the Passover and Jewish practices; in the table above, they are enumerated as Roman Catholics.
MUSLIMS. Mostly in Madrid, in 2 associations including Ahmadiya (enumerated here under Muslims although declared non-Muslim by Pakistan). Begun 1946; Qadianis, based on Rabwah (Pakistan). *Hajj pilgrims to Mecca.* (1970) 32; (1974) 196; (1975) 1; (1976) 4.
PENTECOSTALS/CHARISMATICS. Catholic Charismatics (1975): 3,000 involved adults (over 15 years old) in 50 organized prayer groups; total charismatic community including children, 5,000. The First National Conference for the Charismatic Renewal in Spain was held in Madrid in July 1977, with 1,700 attenders (including 70 priests). (1987) 275 CCR weekly prayer groups with 20,000 regular adult attenders. By 1998 the total of all involved Charismatics, Protestants and Catholics had passed 800,000.
PROTESTANTS. Protestant work began in 1835; by 1874, there were 1,840 Protestants (Evangelicals) and 360 churches.
ROMAN CATHOLICS. Including 200,000 Marranos (Crypto-Jews, Anusim, Conversos, New Christians) who are baptized and outwardly-practicing Catholics, but who also follow Jewish rites.

Great Commission Instrument Panel: status of Spain (for explanation see start of Part 4)

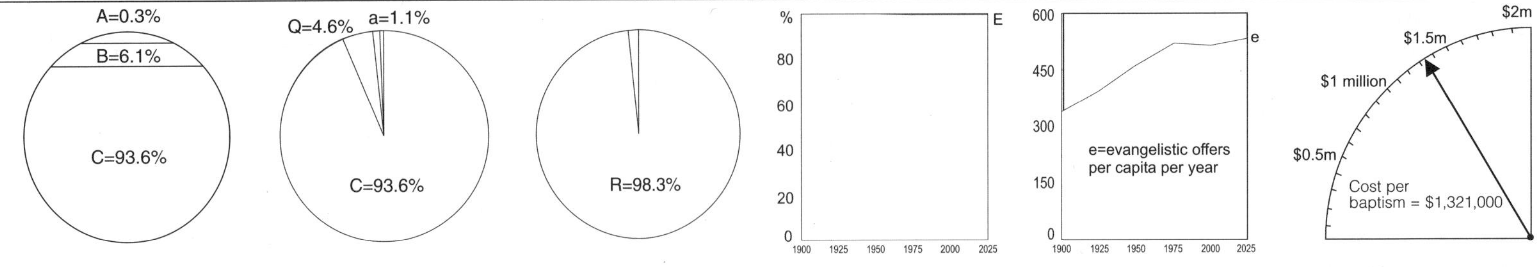

3 Worlds, AD 2000 — Religions, AD 2000 — Ecclesiastical blocs — Evangelization, 1900-2025 — Offers, 1900-2025 — Cost-effectiveness, AD 2000

Country status. Spain occupies the major part of the Iberian Peninsula on both the Atlantic Ocean and the Mediterranean Sea. It played a notable role in the exploration of the New World, and Hispanic cultural influences still dominate most of South and Central America. Major products include grains, olives, and wines.

HUMAN LIFE AND LIBERTY

Human need and development. After lagging behind most of Europe in economic development after World War and carrying the political scars of the Spanish Civil War, Spain was able to leapfrog into the modern age after joining the European Union. Political moderation and progressive governmental policies have paved the way to a rapid modernization of economic sectors. As a result standards of life have risen remarkably in the past decade, and are close to those of Western Europe. On some quality of life indicators Spain ranks fairly high even among Western countries, but in others it ranked close to the bottom. For example, it does well in physicians per capita, but badly in per capita expenditures on health. The level of infant mortality has been significantly reduced, and food consumption patterns have improved. Until the 1970s there were severe housing shortages in most parts of the country, but as a result of the national housing program, millions of new homes have been built, mostly by private enterprise. The Socialist government plans to achieve a goal of minimally acceptable dwellings for all Spaniards. All citizens have access to a comprehensive system of health insurance coverage and receive a broad range of Social Security benefits.

Human rights and freedoms. The last vestiges of the Franco era have vanished in terms of basic human rights and freedoms for all and the elimination of discrimination against certain gender or demographic groups. Continuing terrorism by the Basque separatist groups is still a challenge to the internal security forces who are often accused of exceeding the normal bounds of due process in dealing with them. The media sometimes report of mistreatment of not only Basques but also illegal aliens. The official ombudsman has denounced 'clearly racist and xenophobic attitudes' of law enforcement officials in their dealing with alien workers. The ombudsman also criticized delays in judicial proceedings. In case of petty crimes, suspects released on bail have to wait as long as 5 years before trial. The practice of warrantless searches was declared unconstitutional by the supreme court in 1993. There is no official tolerance of any type of discrimination, although prejudices survive in pockets of society. The Plan for Equality of Opportunity for Women sponsored by the official Women's Institute provides a wide range of services for women. There are sporadic incidents of violence against certain minorities, such as Gypsies and Blacks.

Human environment. Forests have fared relatively well in Spain compared to other European nations. Spain's soils are naturally poor and, combined with inefficient farming practices, tend to create conditions under which the land becomes soon depleted of nutrients. Air and water pollution are not severe but cause problems in urban areas.

NON-CHRISTIAN RELIGIONS

Judaism is adhered to by only a few thousand Jews in the country. The first synagogue constructed in Spain since the 15th century was inaugurated in Madrid in December 1968. On that occasion, the minister of Justice published a decree officially revoking the edict of 1492 with which queen Isabella had banned all Jews. By June 1973, 7 Jewish communities had been registered with the Ministry of Justice, located in Madrid, Malaga, Barcelona, Alicante, Valencia, Tenerife (Canary Islands), Palma de Majorque (Baleares); and 2 others in Ceuta and Melilla, in Spanish North Africa. There are still also some 200,000 Marranos or Crypto-Jews, baptized Catholics whose ancestors wee forcibly converted to Catholicism and who still observe the Passover and other Jewish rites.

Islam, once the ruling power in the Middle Ages, reduced to a small number of Muslims living for the most part in Madrid and other university cities. By June 1973, 4 associations had been officially registered. Two of these were in Spain proper: the Ahmadiya Mission of Islam in Spain (Mission Ahmadia del Islam en Espana) and the Muslim Association in Spain (Asociacion Musulmana en Espana), both in Madrid; 2 more are in Spanish North Africa. There is also an Islamic center at Granada, and the Egyptian government has established in Madrid an Egyptian Institute of Islamic Studies (Instituto Egipcio de Estudios Islamicos). However, more recently a large number of Muslim migrant laborers have immigrated from North Africa. By 1995, their number had swelled to over 180,000 and continues to increase every year.

Baha'i adherents were estimated in 1961 to number not more than 195, but by 1995 they had grown to 11,900 in 30 local spiritual assemblies.

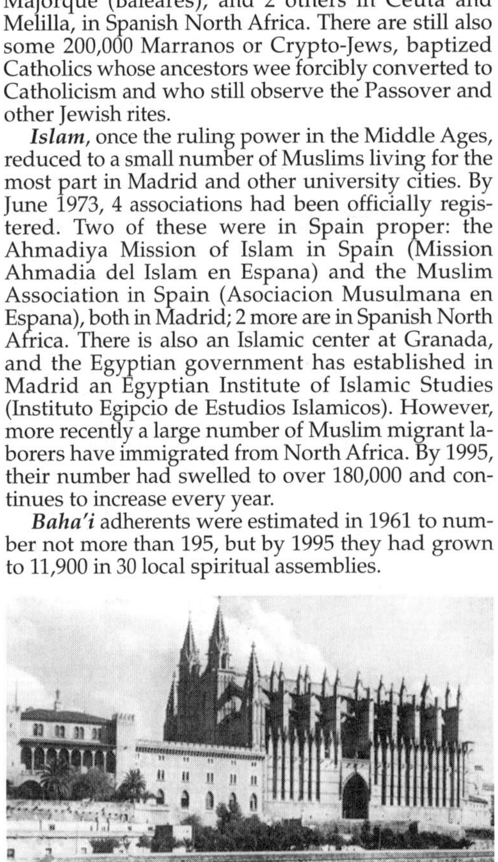

Iglesia Católica en España. Palma Cathedral and Almudaina palace, in Diocese of Mallorca (Majorca).

CHRISTIANITY

During the first century the Apostle Paul is believed to have brought Spain the Christian message. Christianity was already well-established when the invading Arian Visigoths overran the Iberian peninsula in 409. The Arians were then converted to Catholicism which was declared the state religion at Toledo in 589.

In the 8th century Spain came under the control of Muslim Berbers from North Africa, and Spanish Islam achieved its highest development in the 10th century. The gradual reconquest by Christians took on the dimensions of a crusade. In 1085 the king of Castille and Leon took the title of Ruler of All Hispania, but the last Muslim stronghold in Spain, Granada, did not fall until 1492. The allocation of large areas of land to military orders and noble families during this period resulted in the feudalistic latifundia socio-economic pattern that characterized parts of Spain during subsequent centuries. Great missionary orders began to emerge in the 12th century, and a century later religious military orders came into being as well as numerous universities. By the 16th century Spain had entered its golden age. Leading in the discovery of new lands across the world, Spain acquired a vast overseas empire and great wealth and developed the strongest army in Europe. The colonies became the arena of a new foreign missionary thrust, while the Catholic Church at home was busy with the Counter Reformation and Inquisition. The latter was intended at first to force Spanish Jews and Moors to decide either to become Christians or to leave Spain, and it effectively prevented the growth of religious or political movements outside the established church.

As Spain's power began to decline, the crown increasingly intervened in the affairs of the church. A concordat officially recognizing the system of royal patronage was concluded in 1753, and Jesuits were expelled from Spain and all Spanish territories in 1767. Most of the Spanish empire was lost during the next century.

During the 19th century, Catholic clergy came increasingly under attack from proponents of greater freedom of thought and action. In 1868 religious tolerance for non-Catholics was granted for the first time. Spanish Christians exiled to Gibraltar then returned to openly assist clandestine Protestant groups, and Protestantism began to develop gradually.

CATHOLIC CHURCH. During the past 40 years the church has experienced a significant change, from being a conventional to an optional Catholicism. The first type, also called national Catholicism, goes back to the 6th century. After a short period under the anti-clerical republic from 1931 to 1939 including the civil war of 1936-39, the Franco government renewed the tradition of national Catholicism, mingled with a new religious ideology and national mystique.

The second type of Catholicism, optional, can be traced to the 1950s when the first Catholic workers' dispute took place denouncing existing working conditions as anti-Christian. About 1956 the church began to appear as 2 distinct overlapping churches, one being traditional and politically conservative, the other progressive and opposed to the national-Catholic image. The so-called second church was given a new impetus by Vatican II and has also benefitted by the recent episcopal appointments of the Holy See. This new type of Catholicism, based more on personal faith than on the traditional cultural con-

Country summary. **Worlds A, B, C by ethnolinguistic peoples, cities, and major civil divisions in Spain.**

	PEOPLES							CITIES							CIVIL DIVISIONS						
World	Num	Pop 2000	C%	Christians	E%	U%	Unevangelized	Num	Pop 2000	C%	Christians	E%	U%	Unevangelized	Num	Pop 2000	C%	Christians	E%	U%	Unevangelized
A	3	64,994	0.10	64	47	53	34,509	0	0	0.00	0	0	0	0	0	0	0.00	0	0	0	0
B	4	157,330	4.75	7,480	58	42	66,468	0	0	0.00	0	0	0	0	0	0	0.00	0	0	0	0
C	29	39,407,454	94.06	37,066,132	100	0	24,127	69	19,293,604	93.41	18,023,104	100	0	81,238	17	39,629,773	93.55	37,073,671	100	0	125,101
Total	**36**	**39,629,778**	**93.55**	**37,073,676**	**100**	**0**	**125,104**	**69**	**19,293,604**	**93.41**	**18,023,104**	**100**	**0**	**81,238**	**17**	**39,629,773**	**93.55**	**37,073,671**	**100**	**0**	**125,101**

text of the Spanish people, began to prevail decisively in March 1972 when the conciliar bishops became a majority in the Spanish Episcopal Conference for the first time. From this constantly changing situation have emerged several new initiatives involving both clergy and laity, 2 of which will be mentioned here.

The first innovative movement consists of local communities centered on the liturgy. Their strength is in urban areas. They engage in periodical eucharistic celebrations, usually presided over by a priest, during which they jointly agree to undertake some socio-political prophetic task. The hierarchy's permission is never asked. As a general rule, the bishops do not intervene, although the meetings appear to reject the institutional church. Some bishops even give private encouragement.

Secondly, there are the New Communities. These are groups more or less structured and existing along the lines of the parish concept and rarely in conflict with it, but seeking to reshape the old anachronistic parish system. At Cordoba, the bishop decided not to create new parishes in the new suburban areas but instead left the task to priests and laity.

The Holy See has diplomatic relations with Spain and in AD 2000 is represented to government and the Catholic hierarchy by a nuncio residing in Madrid.

PROTESTANT CHURCHES. As with Islam and Judaism, following the institution of the Inquisition and 1492 Protestantism was outlawed in Spain. This remained true until 1868, when for the first time an article proclaiming religious tolerance was written into the constitution. This in turn became obsolete a century later in 1967, with the passage of the Law concerning Religious Liberty.

Attempts at Protestant activity prior to 1868 were met with severe penalties. Plymouth Brethren from England began holding house meetings in 1836, and in 1845 the Spaniard Francisco de Paula Ruet, influenced by Waldensians in Italy, began preaching in Barcelona but was exiled to Gibraltar. Others were converted in Gibraltar, and some were sent to England for theological study. From Gibraltar a clandestine evangelistic outreach was begun in Spain, the first sizable organized Protestant groups being formed in Granada and Malaga in 1863. Out of this early work and following the proclamation of religious toleration in 1868, grew the Spanish Evangelical Church, now the fourth largest Protestant church in the country. In 1880 a division took place in which the Spanish Reformed Episcopal Church was established, with special links to the Anglican Church of Ireland.

The 2 principal Protestant denominations, the Brethren and Baptist Union, also owe their origin to this period. The former is the result of the missionary activity of British Plymouth Brethren. The latter joins together work initiated by American Baptists in 1869, followed by Swedish Baptists in 1881 and Southern Baptists in 1921. In addition there are several smaller independent Baptist churches. Seventh-day Adventists appeared in 1903 and in 1928 Swedish missionaries founded the Pentecostal Church of Spain. Other Pentecostal groups followed, including the Assemblies of God in 1930 and the Church of God (Cleveland) in 1937. Since World War II a large number of small missions have flooded into the country, mostly from the USA. After 1970, Pentecostalism began to spread rapidly.

Protestants today are dispersed widely throughout the country, with their most important centers in the border areas as opposed to the interior, with the exception of urban concentrations in Barcelona and Madrid. Recruitment of members is carried on for the most part among urban marginal social strata, especially workers, small employers and newcomers from the rural areas and villages. Conversion to Protestantism in Spain can be partly explained by marginality and anomie, which also explains the pietistic and conservative spirituality of Spanish Protestants. Exceptions, however, may be found among Protestants of the second or third generation, belonging to the middle class and having experienced a certain amount of social mobility. Traditionally, Spanish Protestantism has been a social movement centered on opposition to traditional Catholicism. As a result, the renewal of Catholicism, as seen in Vatican II as well as in recent ecumenical tendencies, in addition to the passage of the Law concerning Religious Liberty in 1967, have plunged Protestantism into a profound identity crises. The institutional consequences of this have expressed themselves in the stagnation of older denominations and even a decline in memberships. This can also be observed in the increase of recently-arrived marginal groups, including Jehovah's Witnesses.

MARGINAL CHURCHES. Jehovah's Witnesses are the largest non-Catholic denomination in Spain. Their growth to over 160,000 today is all the more startling in light of the fact that they were an illegal body prior to 1967.

OTHER CHURCHES. There are about 2,000 Greek Orthodox in Spain, of whom 600 are in Madrid. The church is under the Ecumenical Patriarchate of Constantinople. In June 1973 the first Greek Orthodox church building was consecrated in Madrid. The Anglican community, of 12,000 including British residents and chaplaincies, is attached to the diocese of Gibraltar.

Iglesia Católica en España. (*From top, clockwise*). 1. Hooded laymen carry crosses in Holy Week Silence Procession, parade through streets in Seville, Archdiocese of Seville. 2. Over one million Catholics including former head of state general Franco at open-air solemn pontifical mass celebrated by papal legate cardinal Tedeschini in Plaza de Pio XII, Barcelona. 3. Madrid Junior penitents march at start of Easter weekend. 4. Javier: a million Catholics hear John Paul II.

Indigenous missions. Christians, present since the first century, have been active in missionary sending throughout Spain's history. High points occurred in the Arian invasions of the 5th century and later with limited work among Muslims and Jews. The 13th century brought the rise of the missionary orders, culminating in the founding of the Jesuits in the 16th century and a golden age of missions lasting throughout the Age of Discovery. Missions-sending from Spain continues strong throughout the 19th and 20th centuries.

Renewal movements. In the 1990s the Pentecostal/Charismatic Renewal continued to spread rapidly across most older churches, and numbered over 1,085,000 adherents (of whom 2% Pentecostals, 69% Charismatics, and 29% Independents).

CHURCH AND STATE

The relationship between church and state, especially that between the Catholic Church and the Spanish government, can best be seen by an examination of 3 fundamental legislative texts (Concordat of 1953, Organic Law of 1967, and Law concerning Religious Liberty of 1967), together with a discussion of the compromises and conflicts between the 2 powers in general and more particularly the disputes concerning the revision of the concordat.

The concordat of 1953 was completed under the pontificate of Pius XII after more than 4 years of negotiations. This replaced the concordat of 1851 which had been abrogated by the republic in 1931. Drawn up to regulate reciprocal relations 'conforming to the Law of God and to the Catholic tradition of the Spanish nation' (Introduction), the new concordat began with the following affirmation: 'The Catholic, Apostolic and Roman religion, being the only religion of the Spanish nation, enjoys rights and prerogatives which are its due conforming to Divine and Canon Law' (Article I).

Advantages to the state include the right to intervene in the alteration of ecclesiastical jurisdictions (Article IX); and the head of state's right to intervene in the naming of residential or coadjutor archbishops and bishops (Article VII, referring back to the Accord signed on 7 June 1941 between the Holy See and the Spanish government). At the time of the preliminary negotiations, the head of state, general Franco, was inclined to soften this 'privilege of presentation' of bishops. Nevertheless, at the time of signing the 2 parties accepted the stricter form agreed on in 1941. The present system is as follows. The Spanish Ministry of Foreign Affairs and the papal nuncio prepare jointly a list of 6 candidates, from among whom the pope chooses 3 listing them in order of preference. From these the head of state selects one, which is usually but not necessarily the first on the papal list; this candidate is then officially named. The Holy See retains the right to appoint, without consultation, apostolic administrators with full jurisdiction over vacant dioceses. Up to the present this right has rarely been exercised.

Advantages to the Catholic Church (36 are listed) reflect the government's recognition of its character as a 'perfect society' (Article II.I) and its juridical personality (Article IV.I). The Church receives financial advantages (Article XIX), the government giving massive annual subsidies which are however variable depending on general economic conditions. This aid includes the salaries of archbishops, bishops, vicars, generals, cathedral and college chaplains and parish clergy, as well as subsidies for seminaries, Catholic universities, the maintenance of worship, the construction and maintenance of parish churches, and religious orders, congregations and ecclesiastical institutes dedicated to missionary activities. Article XX lists 10 types of tax exemption, and Article XV states that priests and religious personnel are exempt from military service, while Article XVI prohibits their prosecution before the courts without the agreement of their bishops. Articles XXIII and XXIV provide for government recognition of the civil nature of religious marriages as well as decisions of ecclesiastical tribunals on separation and annulment. In matters of education, the teaching of the Catholic religion is obligatory in all educational institutions including universities, except when dispensation is accorded to children of non-Catholics on the request of their father or legal guardian. The church has the right to censor all educational programs (Article XXVI).

The church's own publications are however exempt from all interference by the state. Public services including radio and television are required to reserve adequate time for the exposition and defense of 'religious truth'; and priests and religious personnel are assigned to this work in agreement with the local bishop (Article XXIX).

The Organic Law of the State (Ley Organica del Estado) of January 1967 had as its purpose the modification and completion of the collection of constitutional texts of the Spanish nation. Its dispositions regarding church-state relations are in 2 categories; those concerned with the church's involvement in the institutions of highest power (head of state, government, Cortes, National Council and Council of the Realm); and those concerned with modifications in matters relating to religious liberty. The Organic Law stipulates that the head of state must 'profess the Catholic religion' (additional disposition IV, Article 9). Concerning the Cortes which until 1977 consisted of a single chamber composed of elected members as well as member appointed by the head of state, the law specifies that the head of state may appoint members of the ecclesiastical hierarchy (additional disposition III, Article 2). At the end of 1972 there were 2 prelates serving as members of the Cortes. Although theoretically they serve as individuals without involving the entire Catholic hierarchy in responsibility for their actions, public opinion generally takes it as evidence of direct co-operation between the Catholic Church, or at least certain sections of it, and the regime in power. The Council of the Realm, which includes representatives of such large bodies as the clergy, army, and university, has played an important role in the matter of succession. The clergy are to be represented on it by 'the oldest and most elevated in the hierarchical echelon among the prelate deputies to the Cortes' (additional disposition IV, Article 4). Along with the president of the Cortes and the commander of the army, this prelate also participates in the Council of Regency which exercises the powers of the head of state during an interregnum and names his successor.

With regard to religious liberty, additional disposition I of the Organic Law modifies Article 6 of the Charter of the Spaniards (Fuero de los Espanoles), the fundamental law promulgated in 1945, which is henceforth given the following wording: 'The profession and practice of the Catholic religion, which is that of the Spanish State, is officially protected. The State assumes responsibility for the protection of religious liberty which is guaranteed by an effective juridical guardianship, assuring at the same time the maintenance of morality and public order'. This modification was made following the publication of the Declaration on Religious Freedom by Vatican Council II, and its application is found in the Law regulating the Exercise of Civil Rights in Relation to Religious Liberty (ley de Regulacion del Ejercicio del Derecho Civil a la Libertad Religiosa). This law was also brought into being by external pressures from the USA. It affirms that 'The Spanish State recognizes the right of religious liberty founded on the dignity of the human person' and excludes all coercion in this regard (Article 1.1). Nevertheless, 'the exercise of the right of religious liberty' is 'conceived according to Catholic doctrine' and 'must in every case be compatible with the religion of the Spanish State as it is proclaimed in its fundamental laws' (Article 1.3). Other limitations are as follows: 'The right of religious liberty shall not have limitations other than those which stem from fidelity to the law, from respect for the Catholic religion which is the religion of the Spanish nation, and for other religious denominations; and from morality, peace and the co-existence of the legitimate rights of others as well as the demands of public order' (Article 2). It is forbidden for anyone who has been ordained in sacris or has been placed under the solemn vow of chastity in the Catholic Church to contract a marriage without having received canonical dispensation (Article 6.2). Finally, 'The legal recognition in Spain of non-Catholic religious confessions may be requested on the basis of their constitutions as confessional associations'. They may thereby obtain juridical personality by registration in a register (Article 14) held by the Ministry of Justice (Article 36). Within this Ministry, there is a Commission for Religious Liberty (Commision de Libertad Religiosa, Ministerio de Justicia). Most of the registered associations are Christian, or of Christian inspiration. Among the most important denominations, only the Spanish Evangelical Church (IEE) did not request registration. The law was poorly received by both Catholics and non-Catholics. The principal objection was the gap which exists between the spirit and letter of the conciliar texts of Vatican II, which describe religious freedom as an inalienable right of individuals and groups, and the confessional nature of the affirmations of the Spanish government.

Iglesia Evangélica Española. A congregation of the Spanish Evangelical Church ready for open-air witness.

In fact, the original draft of the law developed by the previous minister for Foreign Affairs, before consultation with other government officials, was much more liberal than the present version.

The recent profound changes in the Spanish church have had significant repercussions on its relationship with the state. Unconditional collaboration between the church and the Franco regime and its successor, that of king Juan Carlos, no longer exists, nor does the earlier interpretation of the civil war of 1936-39 as the fruit of a religious crusade against atheists and communists. With the aid of Vatican II, calls for a revision of the concordat have been increasingly heard since 1965. In the sphere of church-state relations, promises are frequently denounced and conflicts appear. Of special significance has been the rise of Opus Dei to a position of influence. This group, whose full name is Sacerdotal Society of the Holy Cross and Work of God, was founded in 1928 for the purpose of christianizing the intellectual and leadership milieux. Widespread now across the world, it is especially important in Spain where a number of its members occupy key posts in publishing universities, business, and government. In October 1969, Opus Dei members were accorded more positions in the higher echelons of the government but many of these were lost during the cabinet reshuffle of June 1973, when Opus Dei retained only a single ministry. Opposition to Opus Dei has in fact appeared not only from the extreme right but also from the conciliar wing of the church, who suspected the organization of plotting to seize political and economic control of Spanish life after Franco.

After Franco's death in November 1975, the government requested a new accord with the Holy See, and in July 1976 a revision of the concordat was signed, under which the Spanish ruler can no longer nominate or veto the nomination of Spain's bishops, and Catholic clergy are no longer immune from civil prosecution. Unrevised portions of the concordat remain in effect, with Spain therefore still officially a Catholic nation. The introduction to the 8 protocols of the new concordat taking note of a 'transformation' in Spanish society. Future revisions of the concordat are juridically within the exclusive competence of the Holy See and the Spanish government. In principle both are in agreement that any further concordat should contain no doctrinal declaration nor privileges that could be considered religiously discriminatory. Nevertheless, as the Holy See takes full control of the selection of bishops, the Spanish government will increasingly suppress all economic aid to the church. Meanwhile, a growing segment of public opinion rejects the very idea of any king of concordat.

In 1978, Parliament and a popular referendum ratified a new constitution under which Spain no longer has an official religion (Article 16). Discrimination over burial places and restrictions on the establishment of new churches were ended, and religious freedom, freedom of marriage and freedom to change ones religious beliefs are now upheld. The Roman Catholic Church still has a leading role, however: 'The public authorities will keep in mind the religious beliefs of the Spanish society and will maintain cooperation with the Catholic Church and the other confessions'.

A Christian radio station operated by Brethren Assemblies, in Seville

BROADCASTING AND MEDIA

IBRA programming can be heard via a local station in Cordoba. Shortwave radio programs from KNLS have seen some response.

Satellite TV and radio programs are received in English, Arabic, German and Italian. Spain is a member of UNDA, and Catholics produce 10 weekly national programs, 6 of which are 30 to 60 minutes in length. In addition there are 76 local Catholic radio stations. COPE is an association of local broadcasters.

Catholics also produce 77 weekly 45 minute programs, most of which are aired on Sunday. Media training courses can be taken at 6 universities.

CBN's *700 Club* and other programs can be received daily throughout the country.

INTERDENOMINATIONAL ORGANIZATIONS

Several Protestant organizations exist to promote co-operation in the Evangelical community. The Spanish Evangelical Alliance maintains an advisory committee of 20 church leaders, who meet annually to discuss matters of mutual interest. The Spanish Evangelical Council, consisting of 5 denominations, also provides opportunities for exchange of information and consideration of joint problems. Other co-operative bodies are: (1) the Spanish Evangelical Press and Publishing Association, which is dedicated to improving the quality and effectiveness of Christian journalism; (2) the Evangelical Foreign Missions Consultation Committee, which serves as an information agency on policies of missions working in Spain; and (3) the Evangelical Service of Legal Assistance, formerly the Commission of Evangelical Defense, which works towards achieving more equitable laws relating to religion and provides legal counsel and representation before the government.

Several churches have ecumenical secretariats, including the Spanish Evangelical Church and the Spanish Reformed Episcopal Church; and the National Secretariat of Ecumenism (Secretariado Nacional de Ecumenismo) of the Catholic Episcopal Conference has ecumenical commissions in 55 dioceses.

Catholics also sponsor institutes for ecumenical studies. The John XXIII Ecumenical Institute (Instituto Ecumenico Juan XXIII) at the Pontifical University of Salamanca, begun in 1962, is dedicated to study and action, oriented specifically towards spiritual, doctrinal, and pastoral ecumenism on the national and international levels. It arranges programs of studies, meetings, conferences, and seminars. The Work of Eastern Christianity and Centre for Eastern Studies (Obra del Oriente Cristiano y Centro de Estudios Orientales), begun in Madrid in 1944, offers a varied program of studies, leadership training, and conferences. It conducts scientific studies relating to problems encountered by churches in eastern Europe.

There are 2 independent interdenominational centers: the Ecumenical Centre in Barcelona, which is concerned particularly with relations between Catholics and Protestants and of which the majority of members are lay; and the Interconfessional Ecumenical Centre (Centro Ecumenico Interconfessional) in Valencia, which is devoted to spiritual and pastoral ecumenism and includes members of the Catholic, Baptist, and Reformed Episcopal Churches. In addition, 3 Catholic diocesan centers are located in Cordoba, Bilbao, and Gran Canaria. Finally, Missionaries of Unity, founded in Madrid in 1962, is a Catholic center oriented towards spirituality and ecumenical activities. It infuses ecumenical ideas among Catholics through a teaching program, correspondence courses, interdenominational meetings, dialogue, pilgrimages, and ecumenical prayers.

On the inter-religious level, Judeo-Christian Friendship (Amistad Judeo-Cristiana) in Madrid, which belongs to the Sisters of Notre Dame of Sion, maintains a documentation bureau for relations between Christians and Jews. In September 1974 Amistad Islamo-Cristiana, which has a specialized library in Madrid, organized jointly with the Hispano-Arab Institute of Culture (a state institution) Cordoba's first Islamo-Christian international congress. The Spanish government also created in Madrid in 1961 an institution for the study of Sefardic Judaism, the Instituto 'Arias Montano' de Estudios Hebraicos Sefardies y Oriente Proximo, which studies Sefardic communities in their diversity and is found in different countries. A Secretariat for Non-Believers (Secretariado para non-Creyentes) was created by the Catholic Episcopal Conference in 1974.

FUTURE TRENDS AND PROSPECTS

Roman Catholicism is expected to continue to experience steady losses after AD 2000 (from 99.5% in 1970 to 94.7% in 2025). Gains will likely be picked up by the nonreligious and internally by Evangelical Protestants.

Christianity could decline below 90% before AD 2050 with the nonreligious and atheists claiming the vast majority of the non-Christian population throughout the next several decades.

BIBLIOGRAPHY

'A critical history of Southern Baptists in Spain with implications for future ministry.' O. E. Simmons. D.Min. thesis, San Francisco Theological Seminary, San Anselmo, CA, 1982. 230p.

A history of the Inquisition of Spain. H. C. Lea. : New York, Macmillan. 4 vols.

'An evaluation of the Mennonite Brethren Missions/Services church planting ministry in Spain.' R. J. Penner. Th.M. thesis, Fuller Theological Seminary, Pasadena, CA, 1993.

Análisis sociológico del catolicismo español. R. Duocastella et al. Barcelona: Publicaciones ISPA, Editorial Nova Terra, 1967.

'Analysis of case studies of evangelism and church planting in southern Spain.' M. Mariscal. D.Min. thesis, Dallas Theological Seminary, Dallas, TX, 1994. 111p.

Anuario 1990 de la iglesia en España. E. G. Diaz & de Santiago Miguel. Madrid: Arias Montano Editores, 1990.

Anuario de la Iglesia Evangelica Española. Madrid: Iglesia Evangelica Española, 1979.

Anuario evangélico Español, 1973. Madrid: Tipografia Artistica, 1973. 272p.

Carisma e institución en la renovación carismática. T. I. J. Urresti. Barcelona: Editorial Roma, 1979.

'Christian youth ministry in Hispanic Chicago and Barcelona: an inquiry into similarities, dissimilarities, and cross-cultural themes.' M. A. Dodrill. Ed.D. thesis, Trinity Evangelical Divinity School, Deerfield, IL, 1991. 361p.

Confesiones no Católicas en España. J. A. Carro Celada. Madrid: Revista 'Eclesia', 1977.

Crisis de identidad: reflexiones sobre el momento de la Iglesia española. P. Alvarez Navarrete. Madrid: Ediciones Cristianidad, 1977. 153p.

Diccionario de Iglesias Cristianas. F. H. Cangas. Madrid: Fe Católica, 1985.

Easter in Spain. Huntsville, TX: Educational Video Network, 1992. (22 min. videocassette).

El cambio religioso en España. Barcelona: Aportación del Comité Español a la XIII Conferencia Internacional de Sociologica Religiosa, 1975.

Guia de la Iglesia en España, 1970. Madrid: Oficina General de Información y Estadística de la Iglesia, 1970.

La España Protestante. M. L. Rodriguez. Madrid: Sedmay Ediciones, 1976.

La Iglesia de Andalucía: apuesta por el futuro. R. López Pintor & M. Castillejo Gorráiz. [Córdoba]: Cajasur, 1993. 575p.

La ira sagrada: anticlericalismo, iconoclastia y antirritualismo en la España contemporánea. M. Delgado Ruiz. Barcelona: Editorial Humanidades, 1992. 176p.

La religiosidad popular. C. A. Santaló et al. Bercelona: Antropos, 1989. 3 vols.

Las confesiones no católicas. R. Saladrigas. Barcelona: Ediciones Peninsula, 1971.

Legislación eclesiástica. A. R. Bernaldez (ed). Madrid: Tecnos, 1984.

L'église et le pouvoir en Espagne. J. F. Nadinot. Paris: M. Th. Génin, 1973.

Llamamiento de Dios al pueblo Gitano. Terrassa: Adolfo Giménez, 1981.

Los Bautistas en España. J. D. Hughet. Madrid: UEBE-CBP, 1985.

Los Protestantes españoles. J. Estruch. Barcelona: Nova Terra, 1968. 230p.

'National church/missions relationships: a model for Spain.' N. F. Romero. D.Min. thesis, Columbia Biblical Seminary and Graduate School of Missions, Columbia, SC, 1995. 260p.

Passional culture: emotion, religion, and society in Southern Spain. T. Mitchell. Philadelphia: University of Pennsylvania Press, 1990. 206p.

Pluralismo religioso (confesiones Cristianas). J. G. Hernando (ed). Madrid: Atenas y Misioneras de la Unidad, 1981.

Precedentes de la Iglesia Española Reformada Episcopal. C. López Lozano. Madrid: IERE, 1991.

'Problematica de los colegios de la Iglesia en España.' R. Duocástella. Madrid: ISPA, 1969. 20p. (Duplicated).

Protestants in Modern Spain. D. G. Vought. South Pasadena, CA: William Carey Library, 1973.

Protestants in modern Spain: a struggle for religious pluralism. D. G. Vought. South Pasadena, CA: William Carey Library, 1973.

Realidades socio–religiosas de España. J. M. Vasquez. Madrid: Editorial Nacional, 1967.

Religion in the Republic of Spain. Aruajo/Grubb. London: Dominion Press, 1933.

Religión y sociedad en España. R. Díaz-Salazar & S. Giner. Madrid: Centro de Investigaciones Sociológicas, 1993.

River of light. Worcester, PA: Gateway Films. (2 videocassettes; total of 228 minutes; history of Christianity in Spain, Portugal and Mexico after the conquistadors).

'Spain,' P. Almerich, in *Western religion: a country by country sociological enquiry*, p.459–477. H. Mol (ed). The Hague: Mouton, 1972.

Spain. G. J. Shields. 2nd ed. *World bibliographical series*, vol. 60. Oxford, UK: CLIO Press, 1994. ca. 370p. (Complements first edition, focusing upon materials since 1985.).

Spain: a new day. G. Myers. : WEC Publications, [1985].

Spain, the church and the orders. E. A. Peers. London: Eyre & Spottiswoode, 1939. 218p.

'Spain: the socio–religious situation,' *Pro Mundi Vita* (Brussels), (1979), 1–55.

Spanish Catholicism: an historical overview. S. G. Payne. Madison, WI: University of Wisconsin Press, 1984. 276p.

Spanish Christian handbook: churches and missions. M. Lawson (ed). London: MARC Europe, 1991. 68p.

The Church and religion in contemporary Spain. V. Pérez Díaz. Madrid: Centro de Estudios Avanzados en Ciencias Sociales, Instituto Juan March de Estudios e Investigaciones, [1991]. 72p.

The Church Militant and Iberian expansion, 1440–1770. C. R. Boxer. *Johns Hopkins symposia in comparative history*, vol. 10. Baltimore, MD: Johns Hopkins University Press, 1978. 159p.

The oppression of Protestants in Spain. J. Delpech. London: Lutterworth Press, 1956. 114p.

The other Spanish Christ: a study in the spiritual history of Spain and South America. J. A. Mackay. 1933; reprint, Wilmington, DE: International Academic, 1979.

The road to Santiago: a pilgrimage, past and present. D. H. Armstrong. New York: P. Lang, 1995.

Un siglo de Protestantism en España. J. B. Vilar. Murcia, Spain: Universidad de Murcia, 1979.

Women of the Reformation from Spain to Scandinavia. R. H. Bainton. Minneapolis, MN: Augsburg Publishing House, 1977. 240p.

Country Table 2. **Organized churches and denominations in Spain.**

Official name (bold type = church with over 10% of all affiliated) 1	*Begun* 2	*Type* 3	*Counc* 4	*Congs* 5	*Adults* 6	*Affiliated 1970* 7	*Affiliated 1995* 8	*G%* 9	*Names, notes, and other statistics* (see Codebook, Part 3) 10
Asamblea Cristiana	1978	I-3cW	.....	9	691	–	1,540	5.88	*Christian Assembly.*
Asambleas de Dios de España	1930	P-Pe2	ZF...	160	6,927	1,500	10,000	7.88	*ADE. Assemblies of God of Spain.* M=AoG(UK, USA). Well-organized. 25n,21f,1s(7).
Asambleas de Hermanos en Cristo		P-EBr	x....	7	150	300	400	0.05	*AHC. Darbistas (Darbyites). Plymouth Brethren* (Exclusive). In Barcelona, Palma.
Asambleas Locales	c1990	I-3nC	.....	5	180	–	450	20.00	*Local Churches. Little Flock.* Chinese. Begun 1922 in China.
Asambleas Pentecostales de España	1959	I-3pW	.....	20	300	100	500	6.65	*APE. Pentecostal Assemblies of Spain.* Aid from USA. 1n,7x,1s,W=50%,13Y.
Asoc de Igl Ev Bautistas Indep de E		I-Bap	.....	6	400	500	700	0.05	*AIEBI. Assoc of Independent Baptist Chs.* Split ex UEBE. M=Strict Baptists (UK). 1s.
Asociacion Ev Bautista Española		I-Bap	.....	5	200	300	400	0.05	*Spanish Ev Baptist Association.* Small grouping of independent Baptists.
Comunión de Iglesias Misiones Ev		I-Eva	x....	41	2,004	300	3,340	0.05	*Community of Independent Chs.* M=World-Wide Missions (USA). In Torre Molinos.
Comunión Bautista Independiente	1984	I-Bap	xF...	10	400	400	600	9.09	*CBI. Indep Baptist Communion. Canary Is Gospel Mission.* Ex UEBE. M=CBFMS(USA).
Comunion Cristiana del Espiritu Santo	c1990	I-3pL	x....	15	2,000	–	5,000	20.00	*Christian Communion of the Holy Spirit.* M=IURD(Brazil, Portugal). In Madrid, 5 other big cities.
Congregaciones Ev Neotestamentarias		P-Eva	x....	6	300	400	500	0.05	*Union Misionara Neotestamentaria. New Testament Congs.* M=NTMU(UK). HQ Granada.
Fed de Igs Apost Pentecostales de E	c1960	I-3oW	.....	15	902	144	1,800	10.63	*Federation of Pentecostal Apostolic Chs of Spain.* Oneness bodies, member of AWCF. Barcelona
Federación de Iglesias Ev Indep de E	1934	I-Con	KM..C	62	4,400	4,090	11,000	4.04	*FIEIDE. Federation of Independent Ev Chs.* M=TEAM(USA). In northeast. 27n,28f,1s.
Federación de Igs Ev Pentecostales de E		P-Pe2	.....	56	2,375	1,080	4,320	0.05	*Federation of Spanish Pentecostal Chs.*
Iglesia Anglicana (D Europe)	1850	A-plu	awc..	19	10,100	12,000	12,000	0.00	*Comunidad Anglicana. Ch of England.* CCCS chaplaincies; 3 in Canary Is. 8x.
Iglesia Apostólica de España		P-PeA	Z....	3	200	200	300	0.05	*IAE. Apostolic Ch of Spain.* M=Apostolic Ch(Germany). 1 congregation in Cordoba. 1n.
Igesia Católica en España:	c 63	R-Lat	B.B.R	25,984	27,719,500	33,596,162	38,056,562	0.50	*Catholic Ch in Spain.* C=62+9+244. 114q,48s. 19054n 8970x 15922m 66322w 325401Yy
M Burgos	1075	R-Lat	Bs	998	247,000	356,360	334,630	-0.25	*Archdiócesis de Burgos.* No diocesan councils. 484n 195x 536m 1354w 2725Yy
D Bilbao	1949	R-Lat	Bs	323	738,000	1,017,245	1,000,000	-0.07	*Diócesis de Bilbao.* Basque country. D=pc(23,0.0) 489n 400x 724m 2050w 4000Yy
D Osma-Soria	c1150	R-Lat	Bs	561	64,000	110,745	87,100	-0.96	No diocesan pastoral or priests' council. 149n 40x 56m 331w 722Yy
D Palencia	c 250	R-Lat	Bs	468	134,000	205,000	182,000	-0.47	Diocesan councils: D=pc(6,6,23),PC(23,2). M=OSA. 279n 128x 257m 862w 930Yy
D Vitoria	1861	R-Lat	Bs	451	201,000	210,500	272,000	1.03	In north, in Basque country. Guerrillas active. 310n 110x 272m 891w 1837Yy
M Granada	c 250	R-Lat	Bs	314	487,000	561,645	660,222	0.65	In extreme south; Sierra Nevada. HQ Granada. 283n 189x 300m 1638w 9477Yy

Continued overleaf

Country Table 2–continued

Official name (bold type = church with over 10% of affiliated) 1	*Begun* 2	*Type* 3	*Counc* 4	*Congs* 5	*Adults* 6	*Affiliated 1970* 7	*Affiliated 1995* 8	*G%* 9	*Names, notes, and other statistics (see Codebook, Part 3)* 10
D Almería	1492	R-Lat	Bs	386	338,000	372,059	458,000	0.83	Diocesan priests' council being formed. 136n 29x 45m 497w 4963Yy
D Cartagena	c 90	R-Lat	Bs	300	738,000	830,000	1,000,000	0.75	In southeast. HQ Murcia. D=pc(0,6,20). 353n 95x 173m 1146w 12984Yy
D Guadix	c 90	R-Lat	Bs	114	88,000	140,000	119,000	-0.65	Mountainous area northeast of Granada. 70n 3x 7m 169w 1365Yy
D Jaén	c 650	R-Lat	Bs	213	480,000	667,101	650,000	-0.10	No diocesan pastoral or priests council. 256n 70x 84m 784w 8795Yy
D Málaga	c 350	R-Lat	Bs	341	866,000	740,000	1,223,203	2.03	Also 50,000 in Melilla (NAfrica). D=pc(3,2,10). 273n 132x 201m 938w 8296Yy
M Madrid	1885	R-Lat	Bs	530	2,080,000	3,787,902	2,840,872	-1.14	1972: 9 Episcopal Vicariates. D=pc(0,7,24). M=CMF. 1587n 1462x 2795m 9284w 23328Yy
D Alcola de Henares (Complutensis)	1991	R-Lat	Bs	115	446,000	–	605,000	25.00	Founded AD 450; until 1991 attached to AD Madrid. 109n 44x 175m 509w 4593Yy
D Getafe	1991	R-Lat	Bs	92	562,000	–	762,000	25.00	New diocese. Area is 72% Catholic. 102n 37x 37m 691w 9025Yy
M Merida-Badajoz (Badajoz)	1255	R-Lat	Bs	241	446,000	584,853	604,000	0.13	Southwest, bordering on Portuga. D=pc. 289n 70x 96m 920w 8433Yy
D Coria-Cáceres	1142	R-Lat	Bs	238	170,000	245,202	230,945	-0.24	On Portugal border. HQ Coria. 154n 22x 34m 325w 1828Yy
D Plasencia	1189	R-Lat	Bs	265	188,000	325,000	255,000	-0.97	Astride Sierra de Gredos. D=pc(2,2,21). 174n 34x 54m 458w 2305Yy
M Oviedo	811	R-Lat	Bs	1,286	797,000	1,045,000	1,095,000	0.08	On northwestern coastline. D=pc(0,8,19). 563n 182x 299m 1158w 6497Yy
D Astorga	747	R-Lat	Bs	713	228,000	343,655	309,000	0.08	South of Cordillera Cantabrica. D=pc(3,4,12). 368n 42x 66m 446w 2273Yy
D León	c 350	R-Lat	Bs	827	212,000	321,000	288,197	-0.43	South of Cordillera Cantabrica. 383n 131x 263m 814w 2264Yy
D Santander	1754	R-Lat	Bs	1,145	395,000	471,362	536,360	0.52	Northwest coastline, west of Bilbao. 340n 201x 305m 1120w 4034Yy
M Pamplona (& D Tudela)	c 450	R-Lat	Bs	740	386,000	455,570	523,727	0.56	Up to northwest Pyrenees. D=pc(0,4,48). M=CMF. 590n 431x 700m 2150w 2483Yy
D Calahorra y la Calzada-Logroño	c 450	R-Lat	Bs	250	191,000	240,209	259,109	0.30	South of Pamplona. HQ Calahorra. D=pc(0,7,18). 278n 113x 251m 811w 2000Yy
D Jaca	1063	R-Lat	Bs	189	29,000	48,868	40,160	-0.78	In Pyrenees area. D=pc(0,4,12). 67n 19x 28m 73w 329Yy
D San Sebastián	1949	R-Lat	Bs	239	499,000	630,000	676,000	0.28	Basque country, near France border. D=pc(10,3,16). 449n 337x 639m 2175w 4568Yy
M Santiago de Compostela	c 850	R-Lat	Bs	1,108	925,000	1,204,300	1,255,000	0.17	Extreme northwest of country. D=pc(0,6,58). 752n 220x 368m 1132w 10832Yy
D Lugo	c 150	R-Lat	Bs	1,138	225,000	320,815	304,782	-0.20	Inland diocese in northwest corner. M=OFM. 431n 34x 58m 340w 1909Yy
D Mondoñedo-Ferrol	1114	R-Lat	Bs	424	255,000	349,000	346,000	-0.03	Extreme northwestern point of Spain. D=pc(4,2,15). 219n 23x 31m 363w 1862Yy
D Orense	c 450	R-Lat	Bs	745	229,000	428,586	310,000	-1.29	Inland northwestern diocese. D=pc(6,6,28). 415n 41x 74m 386w 2527Yy
D Túi-Vigo	c 550	R-Lat	Bs	273	360,000	390,000	488,000	0.90	Coastal diocese bordering on northern Portugal. 232n 93x 158m 537w 3037Yy
M Sevilla (Seville)	c 250	R-Lat	Bs	556	1,192,000	1,729,105	1,680,000	-0.12	Southwest. D=pc,PC (with lay minority). M=OFM. 392n 281x 469m 2438w 19839Yy
D Cádiz & Ceuta	1241	R-Lat	Bs	262	465,000	500,000	630,000	0.93	Also 60,000 in Ceuta (NAfrica). D=pc(113,11). 146n 120x 180m 760w 6100Yy
D Cordoba	c 250	R-Lat	Bs	224	589,000	779,120	798,000	0.10	North of Cordillera Penibetica. D=pc(5,3,26). 265n 115x 158m 1132w 5113Yy
D Huelva	1953	R-Lat	Bs	342	328,000	405,300	445,348	0.38	Extreme southwest, bordering sea and Portugal. 122n 34x 63m 500w 5397Yy
D Islas Canarias	1406	R-Lat	Bs	327	590,000	576,700	799,894	1.32	Diocesan priests' council being formed. 180n 61x 86m 625w 9153Yy
D Jerez de la Frontera	1980	R-Lat	Bs	82	317,000	–	430,000	6.67	Recent diocese; area 90% Catholic. 82n 56x 114m 598w 5673Yy
D San Cristóbal de La Laguna	1819	R-Lat	Bs	323	512,000	555,325	694,000	0.90	Tenerife. D=pc(elected). 176n 57x 91m 552w 8528Yy
M Tarragona	c 90	R-Lat	Bs	195	264,000	250,000	358,500	1.45	Catalonia, on northeast coast. D=pc(3,3,14). 170n 54x 142m 772w 4263Yy
D Girona (Gerona)	c 90	R-Lat	Bs	403	317,000	386,400	430,000	0.43	Catalonia. D=pc(1,4,12). 273n 54x 121m 836w 4779Yy
D Lleida (Lérida)	c 450	R-Lat	Bs	255	184,000	257,931	249,620	-0.13	Catalonia. Presbyteral Commission (elected). 146n 45x 78m 338w 1973Yy
D Solsona	1593	R-Lat	Bs	163	87,000	129,290	118,200	-0.36	Catalonia. D=pc(5,7,6), PC. 123n 20x 39m 253w 883Yy
D Tortosa	c 350	R-Lat	Bs	183	172,000	227,000	233,262	0.11	Catalonia. No diocesan councils. 137n 14x 23m 402w 1366Yy
D Urgel	c 350	R-Lat	Bs	410	83,000	125,995	112,830	-0.44	Catalonia. Jurisdiction includes Andorra. D=pc. 124n 14x 52m 203w 1362Yy
D Vic (Vich)	c 450	R-Lat	Bs	250	228,000	306,600	309,000	0.03	Inland diocese in Catalonia. D=pc. 233n 36x 75m 848w 2729Yy
M Toledo	c 90	R-Lat	Bs	280	349,000	558,960	473,012	-0.67	See of primate of Spain. D=pc(10,4,29). 395n 63x 139m 1289w 6284Yy
D Albacete	1949	R-Lat	Bs	194	252,000	341,660	342,614	0.01	No diocesan pastoral or priests' council. 139n 46x 57m 493w 3707Yy
D Ciudad Real	1875	R-Lat	Bs	428	353,000	506,968	479,000	-0.23	Spanish military orders. D=pc(0,9,17),PC(5,0). 229n 52x 80m 690w 5639Yy
D Cuenca	1183	R-Lat	Bs	389	149,000	244,796	202,300	-0.76	East centre of country. 245n 14x 17m 352w 2209Yy
D Sigüenza-Guadalajara	589	R-Lat	Bs	476	110,000	159,960	150,317	0.07	HQ Sigüenza. D=pc(6,1,4). 243n 40x 66m 451w 1103Yy
M Valencia	c400	R-Lat	Bs	717	1,640,000	1,868,905	2,284,000	0.06	No diocesan pastoral or priests' council. 899n 665x 860m 3515w 14949Yy
D Ibiza	1782	R-Lat	Bs	35	61,000	51,500	83,400	1.95	Ibiza island in Balearic Islands. D=pc(0,2,11). 35n 3x 6m 55w 753Yy
D Mallorca (Majorca)	c 450	R-Lat	Bs	211	403,000	419,800	546,720	1.06	Balearic Islands. HQ Palma. D=pc. 301n 107x 224m 1029w 5234Yy
D Menorca (Minorca)	c 450	R-Lat	Bs	22	49,000	51,370	66,500	1.04	Balearic Is. HQ Ciudadela. No diocesan councils. 47n 6x 15m 88w 545Yy
D Orihuela-Alicante	1564	R-Lat	Bs	204	813,000	620,000	1,144,758	2.48	On mainland south of Valencia. D=pc(0,5,25). 286n 88x 151m 793w 7809Yy
D Segorbe-Castellón de la Plana	c 550	R-Lat	Bs	212	285,000	327,861	387,046	0.67	On mainland north of Valencia. D=pc(3,0,16). 155n 73x 99m 497w 2990Yy
M Valladolid	1595	R-Lat	Bs	327	367,000	390,000	498,000	0.98	West central Spain. D=pc(1,13,13). 306n 281x 615m 1844w 3775Yy
D Avila	c1050	R-Lat	Bs	261	125,000	206,320	170,000	-0.77	North of Sierra de Gredos. D=pc(0,5,13). 213n 48x 81m 600w 1630Yy
D Ciudad Rodrigo	c 350	R-Lat	Bs	136	35,000	65,083	48,023	-1.21	Along Portugal border. D=pc(0,0,14). 140n 0x 0m 134w 366Yy
D Salamanca	c 950	R-Lat	Bs	324	202,000	291,744	274,000	-0.25	Up to Portugal border. D=pc(5,0,3),PC(6,1). 286n 314x 615m 1009w 2636Yy
D Segovia	c 550	R-Lat	Bs	416	107,000	162,700	145,855	-0.44	North of Madrid and Sierra de Guadarama. 175n 32x 63m 459w 1478Yy
D Zamora	c 950	R-Lat	Bs	303	126,000	201,648	171,842	-0.64	Along northern Portugal border. D=pc,PC(27,15). 217n 27x 34m 565w 1382Yy
M Zaragoza	c 450	R-Lat	Bs	294	573,000	754,228	777,000	0.12	In central northeast Spain. D=pc(0,5,10),PC(14,0). 427n 327x 573m 2016w 12660Yy
D Barbastro	1100	R-Lat	Bs	153	23,000	35,365	31,118	-0.51	Among Pyrenees up to France. D=pc(1,3,10). 56n 12x 21m 72w 268Yy
D Huesca	533	R-Lat	Bs	212	59,000	84,250	80,000	0.07	Up to foothills of Pyrenees. D=pc(0,3,13). 95n 21x 41m 273w 526Yy
D Tarazona	c 450	R-Lat	Bs	140	63,000	110,532	85,982	-1.00	No diocesan pastoral or priests' council. M=SDB. 104n 11x 11m 296w 479Yy
D Teruel y Albarracín	1172	R-Lat	Bs	297	66,000	111,769	90,251	-0.85	HQ Teruel. D=pc(d,3,19),PC(26,6). 138n 14x 38m 224w 651Yy
AD Barcelona	c 350	R-Lat	bs	755	2,971,000	3,200,000	4,107,863	1.00	Includes monastery of Montserrat. D=PC(10,0). 770n 838x 1339m 4969w 20949Yy
OM España	1950	R-Lat	Bs	196	206,500	200,000	413,000	2.94	Military Ordinariate of Spain. 196 ordinaries, 72 auxiliaries, 764Yy.
Iglesia Cristiana Adventista del 7 Día	1903	P-Adv	x....	61	5,671	7,000	18,900	4.05	*SDA. Seventh-day Adventists, Spanish Ch,* SEuropean UM. 21nx,1j,1s,34t(3114),337Y.
Iglesia Cristiana Apostolica de Madrid	c1980	I-3oW	.....	10	1,000	–	3,000	6.67	*Apostolic Christian Church of Madrid.*
Iglesia Cristiana Ev de Pentecostés		I-3cW	.....	3	200	200	400	0.05	*Ev Christian Church of Pentecost.* Small charismatic group. HQ Alicante.
Iglesia de Dios de España	1937	P-Pe3	ZF...	10	400	200	600	4.49	*IDE. Ch of God.* M=CoG(Cleveland) (USA). Begun by Spanish convert from New York. 6n.
Iglesia de Dios Pentecostal	1963	I-3pW	Z....	20	1,500	2,200	3,000	1.25	*IDP. Pentecostal Ch of God.* M=PCG(Puerto Rico, USA). Madrid. 4n,2x,1p,W=25%,56Y,68z.
Iglesia de JC de los Santos de los UD		m-LdS	x....	129	11,900	815	17,000	0.05	UD=Ultimos Dias. *Ch of JC of Latter-day Saints. Mormons.* M=CJCLdS(USA). HQ Madrid.
Iglesia del Nazareno	1981	P-Hol	.....	3	186	–	256	7.14	*Church of the Nazarene.* M=CoN.
Iglesia El Buen Pastor	1960	I-3oL	.....	5	200	100	400	5.70	*Ch of the Good Shepherd.* Pentecostals from Mexico (schism ex Aaronistas).
Iglesia Española Reformada Episcopal	1880	I-Ang	UuC.C	16	10,715	1,000	19,580	12.63	*IERE. Spanish Reformed Episcopal Ch.* Ex IEE. 37% Spaniards, 63% British. 10n.
Iglesia Evangélica Comunitaria	c1965	I-3pW	...	30	900	208	1,500	8.22	*Evangelical Community Church.*
Iglesia Evangélica Elim	c1985	P-Pe2	.....	4	100	–	167	10.00	*Elim Evangelical Ch.* M=Elim Pent Ch (UK).
Iglesia Evangélica Española		P-Ref	RWC.C	35	8,400	10,000	10,000	0.05	*IEE. Spanish Ev Ch.* 1880, episcopal section (IERE) broke off. 45n,1f,1u(8).
Iglesia Evangélica Filadelfia		I-3pE	.....	363	168,000	25,000	200,000	0.05	*Philadelphia Ch. Misión Ev Gitana. Movement of Spanish Gypsies.* 21n,150m.
Iglesia Evangélica Mundial	c1985	P-Hol	.....	3	173	–	346	10.00	*World Gospel Church.* M=WGM.
Iglesia Evangélica Pentecostal de E	1928	P-Pe2	Z....	12	400	500	1,000	2.81	*Pentecostal Ch of Spain.* Oldest Pentecostal group in Spain. M=SFM(Sweden).
Iglesia Nueva Apostólica		I-3aX	x....	4	600	1,000	1,108	0.05	*New Apostolic Ch,* in Switzerland District (Bezirk Schweiz). HQ Zurich.
Iglesia Ortodoxa Griega en España	1949	O-Gre	Cwc..	3	1,550	2,000	2,210	0.40	*Spanish Greek Orthodox Ch.* Under Constantinople & D France. Greeks, Russians. 1x.
Iglesias de Cristo en España	1964	I-Dis	x....	37	1,100	1,000	2,200	3.20	*Chs of Christ.* M=CC(Non-Instrumental) (USA). USA servicemen. 12n,1k,1s,W=60%,100Y.
Iglesias del Nuevo Testamento		P-CBr	x....	20	450	500	650	0.05	*Chs of the New Testament. Plymouth Brethren.* Open, liberal (women may minister).
Iglesias Evangélicas Buenas Noticias	1976	I-3cW	.....	15	1,126	–	2,050	5.26	*Good News Evangelical Chs.*
Iglesias Evangélicas de Hermanos	1836	P-CBr	x...C	175	9,000	15,000	20,000	1.16	*IEH. Assemblies of Brethren* (Open). M=CMML(UK, USA). Extreme northwest. 120m,12f.
Iglesias Menonitas	1982	P-Men	.....	5	214	–	370	7.69	*Mennonite Churches.*
Iglesia Santidad Unión	1965	P-Hol	.....	2	60	17	100	7.35	*Holiness Union Church.* M=Holiness Union Mission (Sweden).
Misión Evangélica Española	1913	P-Eva	.G...	10	150	400	300	-1.14	*Spanish Gospel Mission.* M=SGM(UK). Valdepeñas. Declining due to emigration. 6n,30Y.
Sociedad de la Ciencia Cristiana		m-Sci	x....	3	40	100	80	0.05	*Ch of Christ, Scientist/Christian Science.* M=CCS. Madrid, Palma (Majorca). 1m,3w.
Testigos de Jehová	1919	m-Jeh	x....	1,079	84,562	39,500	166,000	5.91	*Jehovah's Witnesses.* Legalized 1967. 240 in prison. (1975) 800n,2005Y. (1995) 4151Y.
Union Evangélica Bautista Española	1869	P-Bap	T...C	63	7,405	15,000	13,500	-0.42	*UEBE. Spanish Ev Baptist Union.* 1921, M=SBC(USA). East coast. 51n,31f,1k,1s,250Y.
Other pentecostal/charismatic bodies		I-3pB	.....	50	30,000	–	50,000	0.05	Including CoGiC, Association of Vineyard Churches (2 chs), Manna Ch (Portugal).
Other Protestant denominations		P-	.....	500	15,000	20,000	30,000	0.05	Total about 210 (see list below), mostly very small groups.
Other Latin American indigenous chs		I-3gL	.....	70	3,000	1,000	5,000	0.05	From Mexico, Puerto Rico, Chile, Colombia, and other Spanish-speaking countries.
Other marginal Protestant bodies		m-	.....	20	500	500	1,000	0.05	Smaller groups and cults, including Horpenites (from Saxony, Germany).
Doubly-affiliated		2-aff			-149,000	-53,549	-205,129		Evangelicals and others who also are or were baptized Roman Catholics.
Disaffiliated		X-Aff			-981,000	-855,567	-1,350,000		Baptized Catholics who have become completely disaffiliated agnostics or atheists.
Totals				**29,183**	**26,985,531**	**32,851,600**	**37,125,000**		

Churches, members, growth, 1900-2025	*Congs*	*Adults*	*Affiliated*	*G%*	*Total denominations*	*6 Megablocs: O*	*R*	*A*	*P*	*I*	*m*
Total churches, members, and denominations (mid-1900)	10,000	13,638,000	18,797,000	0.80	7	0	1	1	4	1	0
Total churches, members, and denominations (mid-1970)	22,457	23,834,968	32,851,600	0.80	151	1	1	1	107	31	10
Total churches, members, and denominations (mid-1990)	28,000	26,856,000	36,947,500	0.59	313	1	1	1	228	64	18
Total churches, members, and denominations (mid-1995)	29,183	26,985,531	37,125,000	0.10	314	1	1	1	228	65	18
Total churches, members, and denominations (mid-2000)	30,000	26,948,000	37,073,672	-0.03	315	1	1	1	228	66	18
Total churches, members, and denominations (mid-2025)	32,000	24,488,000	33,690,000	-0.38	515	3	1	1	280	200	30

NOTES ON TABLE ABOVE

COLUMNS: for meanings and CODES (cols. 1, 3, 4, 8): see Codebook (Part 3). Column 1: **Boldface type** = church with over 10% of country's affiliated Christians.

NATIONAL COUNCILS (Column 4, 5th letter).

C = Federación Entitades Religiosas Evangelicas de España (FEREDE, 1992).

E = Alianza Evangelica Española (AEE, Spanish Evangelical Alliance, affiliated to EEA and WEF).

K Comite Espanol de Cooperacion Entre las Iglesias (CECI Spanish Committee of Cooperation between the Churches).

R = Conferencia Episcopal Española (CEE) (Spanish Episcopal Conference).

OTHER PROTESTANT DENOMINATIONS. These include about 30 denominations proper, over 50 independent congregations, about 24 foreign congregations catering for civilian expatriates from other European countries and churches (11 German-speaking, 6 Dutch-speaking, 3 Swiss Reformed, 2 English-speaking (Baptist), 1 Danish, 1 Norwegian), foreign congregations catering for USA expatriate civilians, and USA military chaplaincies among the 9,000 USA servicemen and their dependents. Denominations with some local membership include (names are given in Spanish unless better known in English): Association of Baptists for World Evangelism (1968), Baptist International Missions (1964), Bible Christian Union, Central American Mission (1971, 12 missionaries), Children of God International (Barcelona), Ejército de Salvación (Salvation Army, 1971), Federación Ev Bautista Española (Barcelona), Gospel Missionary Union (1967), Iglesia Bautista Biblica, Iglesia de la Biblia Abierta (1969; M = Open Bible Standard Chs, USA), Iglesia Ev Pentecostal de Madrid, Iglesia Ev Pentecostal Salem, Iglesia Pentecostal Unida de España, Iglesia Reformada de la Santisima Trinidad, Iglesia Reformada Presbiteriana, Oriental Missionary Society (1972), Reformed Baptista (USA), SDA Movement of Reform, Sociedad de Amigos Cuáqueros (Society of Friends, Quakers), Spanish Pioneer Mission (1930), Swedish Church Mission United World Mission (1946), West Indies Mission (1970, in Canary Islands), World Baptist Fellowship (1959), Worldwide Evangelization Crusade (1936, in Canary Islands).

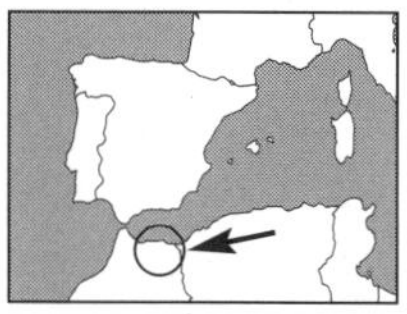

SPANISH NORTH AFRICA

SECULAR DATA, AD 2000

STATE
Official name: Africa del Norte Español (Spanish North Africa).
Short name: Spanish North Africa. **Adjective of nationality:** Spanish North African.
Flag: That of Spain.
Area: 33 sq. km. (13 sq. mi.).
Government: Overseas areas with special relationship to Spain, governed as parts of 2 provinces (1415 Portuguese possession, then Spanish: 1496 Melilla, 1580 Ceuta).
Legislature: Spanish Provincial government.
Official language: Spanish (Español).
Monetary unit: 1 peseta (Pta) = 100 céntimos. **US$1=** Ptas 141.88.
Chief cities: CEUTA 84,038; Melilla 69,690.
Political divisions: 2 provinces.

DEMOGRAPHY
Population: 130,000.
Population density: 3,939.3/sq. km. (10,000.0/sq. mi.).
Under 15 years: 42,000.
Growth rate p.a.: 1.57% (births 22.83, deaths 6.13).
Mortality: Infant, per 1,000: 41.0; **Maternal per 100,000:** 250.0.
Life expectancy: 69 (male 67, female 71).
Household size: 3.0. **Floor area per person, sq.m:** 20.0.
Major languages: Spanish, Arabic.
Urban dwellers: 90.00%. **Urban growth rate p.a.:** 1.00%.
Labor force: 40%.

ETHNOLINGUISTIC PEOPLES
84.2% Spaniard (Andalusian); 14.1% Maghrebi Arab; 1.0% Riffian (Northern Shilha); 0.5% Maghrebi Jewish.

ECONOMY
National income p.a. per person: US$8,000; **per family:** US$24,000.

EDUCATION
Adult literacy: 92% (male 94%, female 90%). **Schools:** 20.
Universities: 1. **School enrolment:** female/male: 80%/80%.

HEALTH
Access to health services: 90%. **Access to safe water:** 57%.
Hospitals: 3 (40 beds per 10,000). **Doctors:** 100.
Blind: 150. **Deaf:** 7,800. **Murder rate:** 2.
Lepers: 100.

LITERATURE
New book titles p.a.: 90 (700 p.a. per million). **Periodicals:** 0.
Newspapers: 0 dailies.

COMMUNICATION (per 1,000 people)
Phones: 350 (20% mobile). **Radios:** 250. **TV sets:** 400.
Daily newspaper circulation: 90. **Computers:** 180.

HUMAN LIFE AND LIBERTY (optimum condition=100.0%)
HDI: 91.0. **HSI:** 70.0. **HFI:** 70.0. **EFL:** 30.0.

Country Table 1. **Religious adherents in Spanish North Africa, AD 1900-2025.**

Year	1900		1970		mid-1990		Annual change, 1990-2000				mid-1995		mid-2000		mid-2025	
Name	Adherents	%	Adherents	%	Adherents	%	Natural	Conversion	Total	Rate	Adherents	%	Adherents	%	Adherents	%
Christians	**20,970**	**90.0**	**116,300**	**89.9**	**105,740**	**83.3**	**250**	**-392**	**-142**	**-0.13**	**104,060**	**81.0**	**104,324**	**80.3**	**108,000**	**77.1**
PROFESSION																
professing Christians	**20,970**	**90.0**	**116,300**	**89.9**	**105,740**	**83.3**	**250**	**-392**	**-142**	**-0.13**	**104,060**	**81.0**	**104,324**	**80.3**	**108,000**	**77.1**
AFFILIATION																
unaffiliated Christians	470	2.0	950	0.7	0	0.0	0	0	0	0.00	0	0.0	0	0.0	0	0.0
affiliated Christians	**20,500**	**88.0**	**115,350**	**89.2**	**105,740**	**83.3**	**250**	**-392**	**-142**	**-0.13**	**104,060**	**81.0**	**104,324**	**80.3**	**108,000**	**77.1**
Roman Catholics	20,500	88.0	115,000	88.9	104,640	82.4	247	-424	-177	-0.17	102,800	80.0	102,874	79.1	105,300	75.2
Independents	0	0.0	100	0.1	600	0.5	1	19	20	2.92	700	0.5	800	0.6	1,500	1.1
Protestants	0	0.0	250	0.2	500	0.4	1	14	15	2.66	560	0.4	650	0.5	1,200	0.9
Trans-megabloc groupings																
Evangelicals	0	0.0	300	0.2	260	0.2	1	3	4	1.44	260	0.2	300	0.2	500	0.4
Pentecostals/Charismatics	0	0.0	100	0.1	2,500	2.0	6	44	50	1.84	2,757	2.2	3,000	2.3	5,000	3.6
Great Commission Christians	**2,400**	**10.3**	**25,800**	**20.0**	**11,000**	**8.7**	**26**	**8**	**34**	**0.31**	**11,100**	**8.6**	**11,344**	**8.7**	**12,600**	**9.0**
Muslims	930	4.0	8,500	6.6	16,260	12.8	38	289	327	1.85	18,500	14.4	19,527	15.0	22,500	16.1
Nonreligious	0	0.0	0	0.0	3,600	2.8	9	95	104	2.57	4,000	3.1	4,642	3.6	7,000	5.0
Baha'is	0	0.0	100	0.1	600	0.5	1	27	28	3.86	740	0.6	876	0.7	1,800	1.3
Jews	1,400	6.0	4,100	3.2	800	0.6	2	-19	-17	-2.35	700	0.5	631	0.5	700	0.5
World A (unevangelized persons)	699	3.0	6,466	5.0	8,001	6.3	19	36	55	0.67	8,480	6.6	8,580	6.6	11,060	7.9
World B (evangelized non-Christians)	1,631	7.0	6,558	5.1	13,259	10.4	31	356	387	2.57	15,951	12.4	17,096	13.1	20,940	15.0
World C (Christians)	20,970	90.0	116,300	89.9	105,740	83.3	250	-392	-142	-0.13	104,060	81.0	104,324	80.3	108,000	77.1
Country's population	**23,300**	**100.0**	**129,324**	**100.0**	**127,000**	**100.0**	**300**	**0**	**300**	**0.23**	**128,491**	**100.0**	**130,000**	**100.0**	**140,000**	**100.0**

COLUMNS, ROWS.
For meanings and definitions, see Codebook (Part 3). Note that, by definition, total 'Christians' = professing + crypto-Christians, which also = affiliated + unaffiliated Christians, and also = Great Commission Christians + latent Christians. Percentages may not always total exactly, due to rounding.

NOTES ON RELIGIONS
BAHA'IS. Begun about 1955. In 1962 there were in the former Spanish Morocco 4 local spiritual assemblies and 6 groups, including an assembly in Ceuta and a group in Melilla.
JEWS. In 2 registered communities (Ceuta, Melilla). The total under the column 'Natural change' includes loss by emigration.
MUSLIMS. Arabs (Sunnis), in 2 registered associations. The total under the column 'Natural change' includes immigration. Their mosques are dependent on the Habous of Tetouan.
ROMAN CATHOLICS. In 1900, there were 12,900 Catholics in Ceuta.

Great Commission Instrument Panel: status of Spanish North Africa (for explanation see start of Part 4)

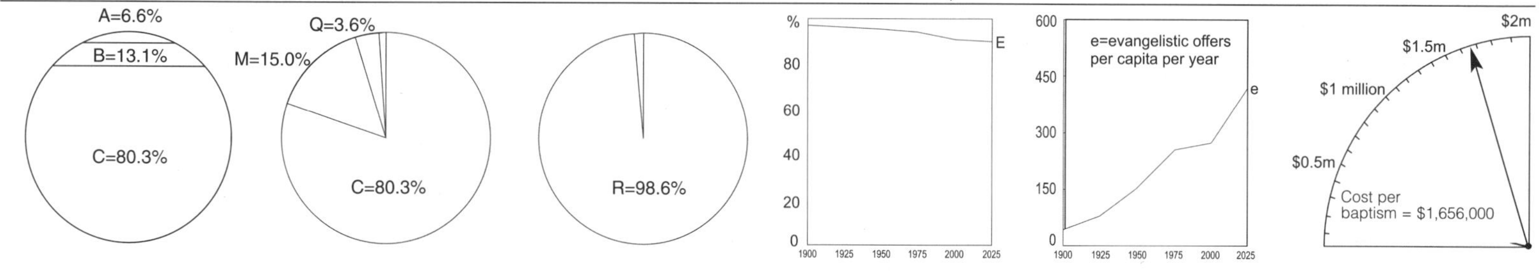

3 Worlds, AD 2000 — Religions, AD 2000 — Ecclesiastical blocs — Evangelization, 1900-2025 — Offers, 1900-2025 — Cost-effectiveness, AD 2000

Country status. Spanish North Africa consists of 2 enclaves in Morocco, Ceuta and Melilla, both on the Mediterranean Sea. Fishing and exporting iron ore are 2 important economic activities.

HUMAN LIFE AND LIBERTY

Human need and development. Leaving behind the scars of several wars, Spanish North Africa has reached economic development on par with most of Europe, as is the case with Spain. Standards of life are similar to those in Western Europe. The Socialist government has employed a national housing program and provides full access to health insurance and social security benefits to all citizens.

Human rights and freedoms. As enclaves of Spain, Spanish North Africa enjoys the same basic rights and freedoms as its mother country. Basques, illegal aliens, and minorities reportedly experience some mistreatment, though officially no type of discrimination is tolerated. The Plan for Equality of Opportunity for Women sponsored by the official Women's Institute provides a wide range of services for women.

Human environment. Naturally poor soil combined with inefficient farming practices have resulted in land depleted of nutrients. Air and water pollution are not severe in Spanish North Africa, but are somewhat of a problem.

NON-CHRISTIAN RELIGIONS

Islam is the religion of 15% of the population of the 2 cities of Ceuta and Melilla, who are Arabs. Mosques are dependent on the Habous of Tetouan. Muslim schools are staffed by Moroccan teachers from Rabat who also provide religious instruction. There are 2 officially registered bodies: the Muslim Association of Melilla (Asociacion Musulmana de Melilla), and the Zania Musulmana de Mohamadia Mahoma, in Ceuta.

CHRISTIANITY

CATHOLIC CHURCH. Arab Muslims gained control of North Africa at the end of the 7th century, and with the aid of Berbers they succeeded in conquering the Iberian peninsula itself soon afterwards. However by the end of the 15th century all Muslims had been driven out of Spain. The expansive Spanish and Portuguese Catholic regimes continued their conquest of ports along the coast of North Africa, with the sparsely-populated interior remaining in the hands of the nomadic Muslim Berbers. Ceuta was taken by the Portuguese in 1415 but passed to Spain in 1580, Melilla having already been conquered by Spain in 1496. In 1704, Our Lady of Africa church was built at Ceuta on the site of a former mosque. Although Morocco obtained its independence from France and Spain in 1956, Ceuta and Melilla have continued as possessions of Spain. Almost all the Spanish residents of the 2 cities are Catholics.

Country summary. **Worlds A, B, C by ethnolinguistic peoples, cities, and major civil divisions in Spanish North Africa.**

	PEOPLES							CITIES							CIVIL DIVISIONS						
World	Num	Pop 2000	C%	Christians	E%	U%	Unevangelized	Num	Pop 2000	C%	Christians	E%	U%	Unevangelized	Num	Pop 2000	C%	Christians	E%	U%	Unevangelized
A	2	1,950	0.15	3	35	65	1,271	0	0	0.00	0	0	0	0	0	0	0.00	0	0	0	0
B	2	18,590	0.62	115	61	39	7,224	0	0	0.00	0	0	0	0	0	0	0.00	0	0	0	0
C	1	109,460	95.20	104,206	100	0	55	2	153,728	80.55	123,823	94	6	9,659	2	130,000	80.25	104,324	93	7	8,550
Total	**5**	**130,000**	**80.25**	**104,324**	**93**	**7**	**8,550**	**2**	**153,728**	**80.55**	**123,823**	**94**	**6**	**9,659**	**2**	**130,000**	**80.25**	**104,324**	**93**	**7**	**8,550**

Ceuta is part of the Catholic diocese of Cadiz in Spain, and Melilla is in the diocese of Malaga, also in Spain. Between 1970 and 1995, Catholics declined by 12,000 members (nearly 0.5% per annum).

PROTESTANT CHURCHES. Seventh-day Adventists include Ceuta and Melilla in the sphere of influence of their Spanish Church, but there are no organized Adventist churches in either city. The Church of God has one congregation in Ceuta, whereas Spanish Baptists and the Church of Christ have concentrated their attention in Melilla. All Protestant groups are small.

Indigenous missions. Though Christians have predominated since the 15th century, there have been very few missionaries sent out from Spanish North Africa.

FUTURE TRENDS AND PROSPECTS

Except for the continued growth of Muslims and the nonreligious, few changes are expected in the religious situation in Spanish North Africa before AD 2025.

As long as Ceuta and Melilla are ruled by Spain, the Roman Catholic presence will likely predominate.

BIBLIOGRAPHY

Ceuta y Melilla en la polémica. M. Lería y Ortiz de Saracho. Madrid: Editorial San Martín, [1991]. 241p.

Fragmentos de una conversación continua sobre Alhucemas. J. Román. *Colección Zaguán de Africa*, vol. 2. Melilla, Spain: Ayuntamiento de Melilla, Fundación municipal sociocultural, Servicio de publicaciones, 1994. 311p.

Melilla y Ceuta: las ultimas colonias. E. Carabaza & M. De Santos. *Talasa ediciones*, 59. Madrid: Talasa Ediciones, 1992. 320p.

The Spanish enclaves in Morocco. R. Rézette. Paris: Nouvelles éditions latines, 1976. 192p.

Country Table 2. **Organized churches and denominations in Spanish North Africa.**

Official name (bold type = church with over 10% of all affiliated) 1	Begun 2	Type 3	Counc 4	Congs 5	Adults 6	Affiliated 1970 7	Affiliated 1995 8	G% 9	Names, notes, and other statistics (see Codebook, Part 3) 10
Iglesia Católica (D Cádiz, D Málaga)	c 400	R-Lat	B.B.r	13	90,000	115,000	102,800	-0.45	Ceuta is in D Cádiz (M=AA), Melilla in D Málaga (M=OFMCap,FSC). C=2+2+3. 24x.
Iglesia Cristiana Adventista del 7 Dia		P-Adv	x....	3	90	100	200	0.05	*SDA.* Unorganized Seventh-day Adventists, part of Spanish Church, S.European UM.
Iglesia de Cristo en Melilla	c1965	I-Dis	x....	2	80	100	100	0.00	*Ch of Christ in Melilla.* Related to CC(Non-Instrumental) in Spain and USA. 1n.
Iglesia de Dios de España		P-Pe3	Z....	1	50	50	60	0.05	*IDE. Church of God of Spain.* M=IDE(Spain). 1 church in Ceuta. 1n.
Misión Mundial de Argentina	c1992	I-3cW	.....	3	200	–	600	33.33	*World Mission of Argentina.* M=WMA(Argentina missionaries).
Unión Evangélica Bautista Española		P-Bap	T....	2	200	100	300	0.05	*UEBE. Spanish Ev Baptist Union.* M=UEBE(Spain),SBC(USA). Church in Melilla.
Totals				**24**	**90,620**	**115,350**	**104,060**		

Churches, members, growth, 1900-2025	Congs	Adults	Affiliated	G%	Total denominations	6 Megablocs: O	R	A	P	I	m
Total churches, members, and denominations (mid-1900)	10	17,800	20,500	2.50	1	0	1	0	0	0	0
Total churches, members, and denominations (mid-1970)	19	100,150	115,350	2.50	5	0	1	0	3	1	0
Total churches, members, and denominations (mid-1990)	20	92,100	105,740	-0.43	6	0	1	0	3	2	0
Total churches, members, and denominations (mid-1995)	24	90,620	104,060	-0.32	6	0	1	0	3	2	0
Total churches, members, and denominations (mid-2000)	30	90,800	104,324	0.05	6	0	1	0	3	2	0
Total churches, members, and denominations (mid-2025)	40	94,100	108,000	0.14	12	0	1	0	6	5	0

NOTES ON TABLE ABOVE
NATIONAL COUNCILS (Column 4, 5th letter).
r = Conferencia Episcopal Española (CEE) (Spanish Episcopal Conference).

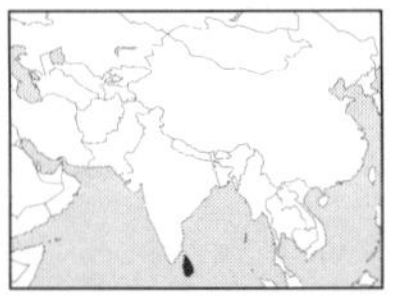

SRI LANKA

SECULAR DATA, AD 2000

STATE
Official name: Sri Lanka Prajathanthrika Samajavadi Janarajaya (The Democratic Socialist Republic of Sri Lanka).
Short name: Sri Lanka. **Adjective of nationality:** of Sri Lanka, Sri Lankan.
Flag: Yellow border around maroon rectangle with yellow finials in each corner; yellow sword-carrying lion in centre; green and orange bars at hoist.
Area: 65,610 sq. km. (25,332 sq. mi.).
Government: Parliamentary socialist republic, since 1972 (6th century BC monarchy, 1505 Portuguese settlement, c1650 Dutch, 1802 British colony, 1948 Independence as British dominion of Ceylon, 1972 socialist republic).
Legislature: National State Assembly, 225 members.
Official language: Sinhalese (Sinhala).
Monetary unit: 1 Sri Lanka rupee (SL Rs) = 100 cents. **US$1=** SL Rs 66.18.
Chief cities: COLOMBO 2,350,922; Dehiwala-Mount Lavinia 221,330; Moratuwa 190,367; Jaffna 146,789; Kotte 130,553.
Political divisions: 25 provinces.
Armed forces: 126,000.

DEMOGRAPHY
Population: 18,827,000.
Population density: 286.9/sq. km. (743.2/sq. mi.).
Under 15 years: 4,914,000.
Growth rate p.a.: 1.03% (births 17.21, deaths 5.91).
Mortality: Infant, per 1,000: 15.7; **Maternal per 100,000:** 140.0.
Life expectancy: 74 (male 72, female 76).
Household size: 5.2. **Floor area per person, sq.m:** 15.0.
Major languages: Sinhalese, English, Tamil, Punjabi, Malay, Dutch, Chinese, and others.
Urban dwellers: 23.56%. **Urban growth rate p.a.:** 2.9%.
Labor force: 41%.

ETHNOLINGUISTIC PEOPLES
72.4% Sinhalese (Singhalese); 12.6% Ceylon Tamil; 7.3% Ceylon Moor; 5.1% Indian Tamil; 0.5% Punjabi.

ECONOMY
National income p.a. per person: US$700; **per family:** US$3,640.

EDUCATION
Adult literacy: 90% (male 93%, female 87%). **Schools:** 18,654.
Universities: 8. **School enrolment:** female/male: 89%/85%.

HEALTH
Access to health services: 93%. **Access to safe water:** 46%.
Hospitals: 422 (28 beds per 10,000). **Doctors:** 3,345.
Blind: 65,000. **Deaf:** 1,129,200. **Murder rate:** 8.
Lepers: 13,000. **Underweight prevalence under 5:** 38%.

LITERATURE
New book titles p.a.: 4,710 (250 p.a. per million). **Periodicals:** 238.
Newspapers: 9 dailies.

COMMUNICATION (per 1,000 people)
Phones: 11 (25% mobile). **Radios:** 182. **TV sets:** 66.
Daily newspaper circulation: 25. **Computers:** 8.

REFUGEES
Citizen refugees in other countries: 96,000.
Internal displacement: 850,000.

HUMAN LIFE AND LIBERTY (optimum condition=100.0%)
HDI: 71.1. **HSI:** 42.0. **HFI:** 27.5. **EFL:** 47.0.

Country status. Sri Lanka is a pear-shaped tropical island in the Indian Ocean off the south-eastern coast of India. The exportation of tea, rubber, textiles, and coconuts make up the country's main economic activities.

HUMAN LIFE AND LIBERTY

Human need and development. For reasons economists have not been able to explain, Sri Lanka enjoys a higher standard of health and living conditions in general than the rest of the subcontinent. Famines have been unknown on the island, and storm and flood damage are rare. Most of the historic scourges, such as malaria, cholera, and smallpox have been eliminated. As a result of state intervention, public health, welfare, and sanitation services are reasonably adequate for the urban population. There are no serious housing shortages in the towns where most homes have running water and electricity. Rural dwellings are airy and uncrowded, and most of them have small attached gardens.

Human rights and freedoms. The ethnic conflict between the Sinhalese and the Tamils, which began in the late 1970s, is the setting for a wide range of human rights abuses by both groups. Government forces commit flagrant abuses against rebels as well as civilians, including killing those in custody and torturing prisoners openly. The Prevention of Terrorism Act and Emergency Regulations give security forces wide powers as well as immunity from prosecution. No member of the security forces has been punished or brought to trial for their participation in extrajudicial killings. Over 12,000 people are reported to have disappeared as a result of periodic security sweeps in Tamil areas. Torture and mistreatment of detainees are not only common but also standard procedures. In many cases, beatings result in broken bones. The military conducts armed attacks against civilian targets, such as public markets. In November 1993 air force jet aircraft attacked the St James Catholic Church in Jaffna killing 10. Over 150 civilians were killed in the same year in artillery attacks. There were army massacres of Tamil civilians in 1991 and 1992 and naval attacks against boats carrying unarmed civilians in the Jaffna Lagoon in 1993 killed over 100. Under former president Premadasa, opposition journalists and politicians were intimidated, harassed, and physically attacked by a group of high-ranking police officers with official encouragement. The government owns the largest newspaper chain in the country and thus has a stranglehold on the dissemination of news.

Country Table 1. **Religious adherents in Sri Lanka, AD 1900-2025.**

Name / Year	1900 Adherents	1900 %	1970 Adherents	1970 %	mid-1990 Adherents	mid-1990 %	Annual change, 1990-2000 Natural	Conversion	Total	Rate	mid-1995 Adherents	mid-1995 %	mid-2000 Adherents	mid-2000 %	mid-2025 Adherents	mid-2025 %
Buddhists	2,114,651	59.2	8,286,700	66.2	11,650,720	68.4	121,812	992	122,804	1.01	12,249,000	68.4	12,878,763	68.4	15,922,330	67.6
Hindus	828,000	23.2	2,174,000	17.4	2,000,000	11.7	20,909	-8,461	12,448	0.61	2,055,500	11.5	2,124,481	11.3	2,500,000	10.6
Christians	**378,859**	**10.6**	**1,086,000**	**8.7**	**1,575,000**	**9.2**	**16,466**	**2,394**	**18,860**	**1.14**	**1,668,000**	**9.3**	**1,763,603**	**9.4**	**2,225,000**	**9.5**
PROFESSION																
crypto-Christians	24,059	0.7	98,125	0.8	250,000	1.5	2,614	3,386	6,000	2.17	280,000	1.6	310,000	1.7	460,000	2.0
professing Christians	**354,800**	**9.9**	**987,875**	**7.9**	**1,325,000**	**7.8**	**13,852**	**-992**	**12,860**	**0.93**	**1,388,000**	**7.8**	**1,453,603**	**7.7**	**1,765,000**	**7.5**
AFFILIATION																
unaffiliated Christians	0	0.0	209	0.0	6,600	0.0	69	119	188	2.54	7,572	0.0	8,483	0.1	10,000	0.0
affiliated Christians	**378,859**	**10.6**	**1,085,791**	**8.7**	**1,568,400**	**9.2**	**16,397**	**2,275**	**18,672**	**1.13**	**1,660,428**	**9.3**	**1,755,120**	**9.3**	**2,215,000**	**9.4**
Roman Catholics	295,859	8.3	954,175	7.6	1,170,600	6.9	12,238	-3,298	8,940	0.74	1,210,211	6.8	1,260,000	6.7	1,520,000	6.5
Independents	2,000	0.1	18,936	0.2	250,000	1.5	2,614	5,498	8,112	2.85	296,013	1.7	331,120	1.8	480,000	2.0
Protestants	40,000	1.1	65,880	0.5	92,000	0.5	962	38	1,000	1.04	96,004	0.5	102,000	0.5	135,000	0.6
Anglicans	41,000	1.2	46,200	0.4	51,000	0.3	533	-133	400	0.76	53,000	0.3	55,000	0.3	67,000	0.3
Marginal Christians	0	0.0	600	0.0	4,800	0.0	50	170	220	3.85	5,200	0.0	7,000	0.0	13,000	0.1
Trans-megabloc groupings																
Evangelicals	20,000	0.6	30,000	0.2	75,000	0.4	784	366	1,150	1.44	110,744	0.6	86,500	0.5	125,000	0.5
Pentecostals/Charismatics	0	0.0	22,000	0.2	308,000	1.8	3,220	5,980	9,200	2.65	350,685	2.0	400,000	2.1	618,000	2.6
Great Commission Christians	**300,000**	**8.4**	**800,000**	**6.4**	**1,145,000**	**6.7**	**11,971**	**13,766**	**25,737**	**2.05**	**1,219,000**	**6.8**	**1,402,374**	**7.5**	**1,700,000**	**7.2**
Muslims	245,000	6.9	867,000	6.9	1,520,000	8.9	15,891	1,569	17,460	1.09	1,610,000	9.0	1,694,603	9.0	2,200,000	9.3
Nonreligious	0	0.0	50,000	0.4	280,000	1.6	2,927	3,111	6,038	1.97	315,000	1.8	340,378	1.8	633,000	2.7
Atheists	0	0.0	16,000	0.1	80,000	0.5	836	255	1,091	1.29	86,000	0.5	90,912	0.5	140,000	0.6
Sikhs	4,000	0.1	25,000	0.2	42,500	0.3	444	13	457	1.03	44,000	0.3	47,068	0.3	70,000	0.3
Baha'is	0	0.0	6,700	0.1	13,000	0.1	136	113	249	1.77	14,500	0.1	15,489	0.1	30,000	0.1
Zoroastrians	500	0.0	1,800	0.0	2,000	0.0	21	5	26	1.23	2,140	0.0	2,259	0.0	3,500	0.0
New-Religionists	0	0.0	0	0.0	800	0.0	8	4	12	1.40	850	0.0	919	0.0	1,500	0.0
Chinese folk-religionists	0	0.0	500	0.0	700	0.0	7	-2	5	0.73	720	0.0	753	0.0	1,200	0.0
Ethnoreligionists	1,990	0.1	300	0.0	160	0.0	2	-3	-1	-0.58	150	0.0	151	0.0	120	0.0
Shintoists	0	0.0	0	0.0	120	0.0	1	2	3	2.32	140	0.0	151	0.0	350	0.0
doubly-counted religionists	0	0.0	0	0.0	-120,000	-0.7	-1,255	8	-1,247	0.99	-126,000	-0.7	-132,474	-0.7	-180,000	-0.8
World A (unevangelized persons)	2,501,380	70.0	6,507,280	52.0	6,818,000	40.0	71,287	-86,028	-14,741	-0.22	6,809,593	38.0	6,664,758	35.4	7,064,100	30.0
World B (evangelized non-Christians)	693,161	19.4	4,920,720	39.3	8,652,000	50.8	90,452	83,634	174,086	1.86	9,442,389	52.7	10,398,639	55.2	14,257,900	60.5
World C (Christians)	378,859	10.6	1,086,000	8.7	1,575,000	9.2	16,466	2,394	18,860	1.14	1,668,000	9.3	1,763,603	9.4	2,225,000	9.5
Country's population	**3,573,400**	**100.0**	**12,514,000**	**100.0**	**17,045,000**	**100.0**	**178,205**	**0**	**178,205**	**1.00**	**17,919,983**	**100.0**	**18,827,000**	**100.0**	**23,547,000**	**100.0**

COLUMNS, ROWS.
For meanings and definitions, see Codebook (Part 3). Note that, by definition, total 'Christians' = professing + crypto-Christians, which also = affiliated + unaffiliated Christians, and also = Great Commission Christians + latent Christians. Percentages may not always total exactly, due to rounding.

CENSUSES.
1881: 61.5% Buddhists, 21.5% Hindus, 9.7% Christians, 7.2% Muslims. **1891:** 62.4% Buddhists, 20.5% Hindus, 10.0% Christians, 7.0% Muslims. **1901** (including 3,650 British and other foreign military personnel): 60.0% Buddhists, 23.3% Hindus, 9.9% Christians (8.1% Roman Catholics, 0.9% Anglicans, 0.8% Protestants), 6.9% Muslims. **1911:** 60.3% Buddhists, 22.9% Hindus, 10.0% Christians, 6.9% Muslims. **1921:** 61.6% Buddhists, 21.8% Hindus, 9.9% Christians, 6.7% Muslims. **1931:** 61.6% Buddhists, 22.0% Hindus, 9.8% Christians, 6.7% Muslims. **19.III.1946** (excluding 36,606 non-resident military and shipping personnel): 64.5% Buddhists, 19.8% Hindus, 9.1% Christians, 6.6% Muslims. **20.III.1953:** 64.3% Buddhists, 19.9% Hindus, 8.9% Christians (7.5% Roman Catholics, 0.6% Anglicans, 0.3% Methodists), 6.7% Muslims, 0.1% other religionists. **8.VII.1963:** 66.3% Buddhists, 18.4% Hindus, 8.3% Christians (7.2% Roman Catholics, 1.1% Protestants & Anglicans), 6.9% Muslims. **1971**: 67.4% Buddhists, 17.6% Hindus, 7.9% Christians, 7.1% Muslims. **1981**: 69.3% Buddhists, 15.5% Hindus, 7.6% Christians (6.9% Roman Catholics, 0.7% Protestants and Anglicans), 7.6% Muslims.

NOTES ON RELIGIONS
ATHEISTS. 2 parties: Communist Party of Sri Lanka (pro-Soviet), Communist Party of Sri Lanka/Marxist-Leninist (pro-Chinese), both legal. In the 1953 census, persons calling themselves freethinkers numbered 1,750 and agnostics 865.
BAHA'IS. Rapid growth from 8 local spiritual assemblies (1964) to 45 (1973).After this, involvement declines. By 1996 after reorganization there were 42 LSAs.
BUDDHISTS. Theravada (or Hinayana, Little Vehicle); Sinhalese, also about 500 Chinese. There are 6,000 temples or monasteries, 17,000 monks (bhikkus) and 14,000 novices. A number of organized full-time Buddhist missionaries are active, e.g. at Colombo airport, in various cities of India through the Maha Bodhi Society of Ceylon, and through the Buddhist Training Centre for Missionaries.
CHRISTIANS. In 1722, Protestants numbered 424,392 (21% of the population of the island) through forced conversion by the Dutch Reformed Church. In 1801 the total of all Christians was 430,000 or 18% of the total population (342,000 Protestants registered as affiliated to the Dutch Reformed Church [recognized by the British in 1802 as the established church of the country] and its schools, 85,000 Roman Catholics, a few Anglicans). By 1810 under British rule and neglect, a massive defection was under way, almost all Protestants eventually returning to Buddhism or Hinduism. Subsequently the percentage of Christians in Ceylon increased slightly up to 1911, then declined gradually with each decade up to the present, when a small number are still emigrating (especially Protestant Burhers) but considerably larger numbers are being converted back to Buddhism.
COUNTRY'S POPULATION. By agreement in 1964 between Ceylon and India, 700,000 Indian Tamils, all aliens, were to be repatriated to India over a 15-year period, with up to 300,000 to be offered Ceylonese citizenship. By 1972 only 73,000 had in fact returned, but in 1973 the rate was increased to nearly 10,000 a month.
CRYPTO-CHRISTIANS. Christians affiliated to churches, but not known as such to the state because not recorded in censuses, of 3 kinds: (a) those in recognized or legal churches, (b) members of clandestine bodies, and (c) isolated radio and correspondence course believers.
ETHNORELIGIONISTS. Animistic Veddas, Sinhalese-speaking, still retain a widely-practiced ancestral cult. The Vedda free ancestral spirits (Yakas) are controlled through emotional dances by shaman priests (*kapurala*). There has been a gradual change in Vedda population from 3,971 in 1901 (when 50% were reported as animists, 36% Hindus, 12% Buddhists, and 2% Christians) to 5,300 in 1911, to 800 in 1964, to 145 by 1995.
HINDUS. Tamils from South India, mainly resident in north and west Ceylon and in Colombo. Most are Shaivites. The proportion is rapidly declining due to the repatriation of Indian Tamils (aliens) to India, at a peak rate in 1973 of 10,000 a month. The column 'Natural' above incorporates average emigration over 1990-2000. Sects include the Ramarkrishna Order (5 centers). A neo-Hindu movement, the Theosophical Society in 1974 had 8 Lodges with 75 members.
INDEPENDENTS. In the 1901 census, 1,718 persons were reported as Independent Catholics; these belonged to the Independent Catholic Church of Ceylon, Goa and India (an 1866 schism of Latin-rite Catholics opposing Propaganda in Rome; obtained Jacobite [Antioch] succession of bishops; defunct 1950, though a few families still left in 1976). In 1995, this category was made up of about 13 denominations (see Table 2), mainly indigenous pentecostals and isolated radio believers from both the Sinhalese and Tamil language groups.
MUSLIMS. Moors (Ceylonese and Indian) and Malays of the coast; mostly Sunnis (of the Shafiite rite) with some Shias south of Colombo. There is also an Ahmadiya Mission in Colombo (Qadianis; enumerated here as Muslims though declared non-Muslim by Pakistan). Qadianis from Pakistan, begun 1951, now with 2 mosques. *Hajj pilgrims to Mecca.* (1970) 152; (1976) 126.
PENTECOSTALS/CHARISMATICS. The Catholic Charismatic Renewal began in 1971 and spread through retreats and prayer groups. In 1975, over 9,000 adults attended a charismatic rally. In early 1977, there were 70 Sinhalese-speaking and over 10 English-speaking prayer groups for adults, and over 100 for young people aged 7-12 years; and over 12,000 adults were active in the renewal, known locally as the Apostolate of Renewal, supported by the cardinal archbishop and several bishops; total charismatic community including children in 1977, 25,000. Members operate a farm to raise funds. There was in 1977 a considerable drop-out rate due to absence of follow-up and shortage of Sinhalese Bibles and literature. By 1996 there were 325 regular prayer groups with 15,000 weekly adult attenders including 50 priests and 2 bishops
PROFESSING CHRISTIANS. Professing Christians gradually rose to a peak of 10.0% by 1911, then gradually declined each subsequent decade (see censuses above). Although they are approximately 8.0% of the total population, Christians form 48.4% of the population in Chilaw, 40.2% in Mannar, 28.6% in Puttalam, and 20.7% in Colombo district; elsewhere they form a small minority.
SIKHS. Punjabis from India.
ZOROASTRIANS. Originally from India (Bombay) and Persia.

Great Commission Instrument Panel: status of Sri Lanka (for explanation see start of Part 4)

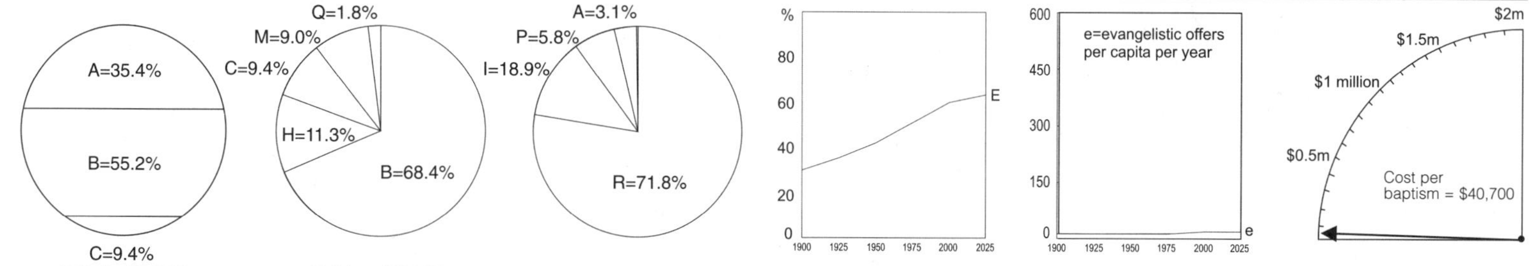

3 Worlds, AD 2000 — Religions, AD 2000 — Ecclesiastical blocs — Evangelization, 1900-2025 — Offers, 1900-2025 — Cost-effectiveness, AD 2000

Further, acts of Parliament have criminalized insults to the president and cabinet members and members of parliament and the reporting of news unfavorable to the government. In addition to the Tamils who face genocide, all non-Sinhalese minorities face some form of legal discrimination.

Human environment. Sri Lanka is generously endowed with over 700 indigenous species of wildlife, and proactive environmental programs have helped to protect many of them. However, deforestation, coastal degradation, and water pollution are beginning to affect the environment adversely.

Buddhist. Huge recumbent Buddha in Asokaramya Temple, Colombo.

NON-CHRISTIAN RELIGIONS

Theravada or ***Hinayana Buddhism*** was introduced during the 3rd century BC, and is practiced by a majority of the Sinhalese, accounting for about 70% of the population. Oppressed by Portuguese domination from 1505 on, then by the Dutch, and finally by the British up to 1948, Buddhism has for more than a century been seeking to create a modern renewal movement that will bring back its privileged and unique position of ancient times. The attempt to form a unified nationalist and social purpose is centered around 3 principal organizations: the Maha Bodhi Society of Ceylon, founded in 1891; Colombo Young

Country summary. **Worlds A, B, C by ethnolinguistic peoples, cities, and major civil divisions in Sri Lanka.**																						
	PEOPLES							*CITIES*							*CIVIL DIVISIONS*							
World	*Num*	*Pop 2000*	*C%*	*Christians*	*E%*	*U%*	*Unevangelized*	*Num*	*Pop 2000*	*C%*	*Christians*	*E%*	*U%*	*Unevangelized*	*Num*	*Pop 2000*	*C%*	*Christians*	*E%*	*U%*	*Unevangelized*
A	9	1,637,011	0.38	6,139	39	61	1,006,581	0	0	0.00	0	0	0	0	0	0	0.00	0	0	0	0
B	9	17,108,896	9.83	1,681,235	67	33	5,663,875	7	2,897,938	13.79	399,706	72	28	798,678	25	18,827,054	9.32	1,755,120	65	35	6,670,591
C	4	81,144	83.49	67,744	100	0	134	0	0	0.00	0	0	0	0	0	0	0.00	0	0	0	0
Total	**22**	**18,827,051**	**9.32**	**1,755,118**	**65**	**35**	**6,670,590**	**7**	**2,897,938**	**13.79**	**399,706**	**72**	**28**	**798,678**	**25**	**18,827,054**	**9.32**	**1,755,120**	**65**	**35**	**6,670,591**

Men's Association, founded in 1898; and the All Ceylon Buddhist Congress, founded in 1918. Displaying a certain anti-Christian bias, this movement has obtained control of a large number of public schools, formerly for the most part Christian, and has begun to provide them with Buddhist religious education.

Monasticism is well developed, with 6,000 monasteries, about 17,000 monks (bhikkus) and 14,000 novices, who apart from their religious vocation often serve as teachers. Lately there has been a decrease in religious vocations due primarily to the fact that because of existing social inequality, religious leaders have increasingly stressed the importance of social action and development, as well as modernization and scientific education. On the other hand, the missionary spirit developed by the Maha Bodhi Society and the Buddhist Training Centre for Missionaries as well as other less important missionary societies, is one of the most active and astute of Asia. Numerous missions and some of the best exegetes of the Pali Canon are sent to the West.

In rural areas, Buddhism is tainted with shamanism and Hinduism against which the struggle, aided by public authorities, progresses slowly. From a geographical standpoint, Buddhism in Sri Lanka has its strength in the center, south and west.

Hindus. Returning from the day's work. a young woman pauses to pray at Hindu shrine.

Hinduism is declining steadily and found mostly among Tamils who constitutes approximately 11% of the population. The first Tamils came from southern India to northern Ceylon about 300 BC, but other were brought as laborers by the British during the last century. They are now spread throughout the island, with their greatest concentration in the north and east, notably in Colombo and on the great tea plantations.

Islam is the religion of 9% of the population, mostly Moors and Malays of the coast, with pockets in the interior in the region of Kandy. Major Muslim organizations include the Sri Lanka Assembly of Muslim Youth in Colombo and the Islamic Study Circle of Bandarawela.

Muslims. A mosque in Kandy, where the numerous Muslim population dominates both wholesale and retail commerce.

CHRISTIANITY

According to tradition, Sri Lanka was first evangelized in the early days of the Christian era by the Apostle Thomas. In AD 537, a Nestorian Christian visitor reported the presence of many converts and churches. In more recent time, 3 different forms of Christianity have made their appearance under the 3 successive colonial powers. The Portuguese arriving in 1505 introduced Catholicism; the Dutch brought in Reformed Christianity 150 years later; and the British introduced Anglicanism during the 19th century. Most Christians live on the west coast. They make up 30% of Colombo's population and include Sinhalese, Tamils, and Burghers. The latter, who are descendants of the Dutch and Portuguese colonists are of Western culture and almost entirely Christian; but they are diminishing in numbers through emigration. Of the over 1.7 million Christians, 72% are Catholics, most being descendants of converts from Portuguese times. The second largest denomination is the Anglican Church. Conversions to the churches are almost non-existent, and they are often criticized as complacent and indifferent to mission.

CATHOLIC CHURCH. Catholicism was introduced during the Portuguese era from 1505-1656. Although many Catholics later joined the Reformed Church during the Dutch regime, most returned to Catholicism under British rule 150 years afterwards.

The Holy See has diplomatic relations with Sri Lanka and in AD 2000 is represented to government and the Catholic hierarchy by a nuncio residing in Colombo.

PROTESTANT CHURCHES. The Dutch Reformed Church, now Presbytery of Ceylon, dates back to 1642. It is made up mostly of Burghers, and at one time it numbered 20,000 families; but its membership has been vastly reduced from 424,000 in 1722 to 1,000 by 1995, and continues to decrease due to emigration.

In 1804, the London Missionary Society began its first mission in Ceylon. In 1812, through the influence of William Carey, the Baptist Missionary Society opened work. The resulting Baptist church is now autonomous but has only a small membership which continues to depend on outside financial assistance. British Methodists entered Ceylon in 1814; their church became independent in 1964. American Congregationalists, the only mission from the USA in the earlier days, in 1816 opened an educational center among the Tamils on the Jaffna peninsula; and in 1823 they founded Jaffna College, the first in Asia to offer modern higher education in English. In 1947 the Congregational Church in Ceylon became the Jaffna diocese of the Church of South India. Congregationalists, Methodists, Baptists, and Presbyterians as well as Anglicans are all involved in the negotiations leading to a united Church of Lanka. In addition, there are also a few Pentecostal churches.

Church of Ceylon, Diocese of Kurunagala. Anglican cathedral at Kurunagala (Kandy), incorporating Sinhalese and Buddhist architectural features.

ANGLICAN CHURCH. The first Anglican services were held in 1796. The Church Missionary Society sent the first group of Anglican clergy to Ceylon in 1818, 2 years after Britain had wrested the island from the Dutch. Work began at Kandy, which had just come for the first time under European control. Many Dutch Reformed Christians became Anglicans, and other centers across Ceylon were opened within the next few years. Anglicans have grown more rapidly than most Protestant churches, and until 1970 formed part of the Church of India, Pakistan, Burma, and Ceylon (CIPBC); now they form the 2 dioceses of the Church of Ceylon.

INDIGENOUS CHURCHES. There has long been a handful of dissident or independent bodies in Sri Lanka. The first was the secession from Rome in 1866 of the Independent Catholic Church of Ceylon, Goa and India, who consisted of 5,000 Latin-rite Catholics who opposed Propaganda in Rome and then obtained Syrian Orthodox (Antioch) episcopal succession; they finally submitted to Rome in 1950 and remnants were deported to India. Other bodies include pentecostal and Reformed schisms.

Indigenous missions. Although some missionaries were sent out from Sri Lanka in the early years of Christian presence there, most have been sent out in the latter part of the 20th century.

Renewal movements. In the 1990s the Pentecostal/Charismatic Renewal continued to spread rapidly across most older churches, and numbered over 400,000 adherents (of whom 13% Pentecostals, 9% Charismatics, and 78% Independents).

CHURCH AND STATE

The constitution of 23 May 1972 stipulates in chapter II, article 6, that 'In the Republic of Sri Lanka, Buddhism, the religion of the majority of the citizens, will be accorded a place appropriate to it an, in consequence, the duty of the State will be to protect the favor it, at the same time assuring all religions of the rights guaranteed in Article 18, 1d'. This latter article specifies that these rights include 'the freedom to have or to adopt the religion or belief of one's own choice as well as the freedom, individually or in groups, in public or in private, to manifest one's religion or belief by worship, observance, practice and education'. Article 16, which lists the 'principles of action of the State', affirms in section 9 that 'The State will strive to create the economic and social climate necessary for permitting people of all faiths to make their religious principles a living reality'.

Land belonging to Buddhist temples, the result of royal endowments, is exempt from taxes as well as certain properties of other religious groups in the capacity of charitable organizations.

Buddhists. Workers at wall of Dalada Maligawa temple.

During the colonial period and until 1961, Christian churches enjoyed a privileged position because of their schools, the appointment of Christians as government functionaries, and the support they provided for the United National Party, which was the conservative party in control from 1947 to 1955 and which maintained in power a Westernized group owing its origin to colonialism. After 1956, under the first Bandaranaike government, Buddhism received considerable official support although it was not raised to the rank of state religion until 1971. The Ministry of Religious and Cultural Affairs (Sanskruthika Amathyansaya), created in 1956, has become an organization catering for the revival and protection of Buddhism. In 1961 the government nationalized without compensation all private subsidized schools including the Catholic Church, 724 schools with 253,000 pupils; but it left the churches free to conduct schools without public financial aid. In 1961, in the same manner, religious personnel serving as nurses in state hospitals were dismissed. Also, in 1956, the teaching of religion was made compulsory in all schools, in each case the religion to be taught being that of the parents.

After the seizure of the schools, the Catholic Church continued to support the UNP, prohibiting the faithful from voting for other parties. This direct intervention in politics did not cease until after the elections on 1970. During the events of 1971, especially the youth revolution, the majority of Catholics did not participate, although the movement found sympathizers among Catholic youth. The church as a whole, as with the other institutions of the country, did not become involved. Nevertheless, after having pledged their moral support to the government, Protestant authorities through the National Christian Council, and Catholics through the cardinal-archbishop of Colombo, sent to the government in 1972 a memorandum requesting the revision of 2 proposed laws, 'Commissions of Criminal Justice' and the 'Amendment Bill', which were judged to be excessively repressive.

In 1966 Sunday was abolished as a day of rest and was replaced by Poya, a day of special significance to Buddhists. In 1972, however, Sunday was restored to its former position.

In late 1975, church union between Anglicans, Methodists, Presbyterians, CSI, and Baptists was finally ready, and the united Church of Lanka was to be inaugurated on 16 November 1975, the bishop having been already elected. Shortly beforehand the country's supreme court pronounced the proposed basis of union to be in conflict with the constitution of the country, enforcing abandonment of the inauguration and an indefinite delay in the creation of the new church.

BROADCASTING AND MEDIA

TWR has a transmitter in Sri Lanka which broadcasts in 15 languages primarily to the Indian subcontinent. IBRA programs in Telugu can be received from a local station, and SLBC runs programs from *Back to the Bible* and Catholic programs at Christmas and Easter. Shortwave radio broadcasts can also be received from FEBA (Seychelles) in English, Sinhala, and Tamil, and from Radio Veritas in a number of languages. AWR's studio in Colombo develops Sinhalese programs.

Sri Lanka is a member of UNDA. Catholics broadcast a magazine program called the 'Catholic Half Hour' in English, Tamil, and Sinhala. In addition, they air a daily 5-minute 'Thought for the Day' in Sinhala.

More than 3 million have seen the 'Jesus' Film, most through showings on national television. Catholics air 'Good News-Supuwatha' in Sinhala for 30 minutes once every 2 months, and a 2-minute 'Thought for the Day' every other day. Special holiday programs are also aired on television in Sinhala.

INTERDENOMINATIONAL ORGANIZATIONS

The National Christian Council of Sri Lanka was founded in 1923. Its relative lack of activities and activism tend to reflect the absence of a dynamic witness which characterizes individual churches. It maintains the Study Centre for Religion and Society founded by Methodists, but makes little use of its work or facilities. The interdenominational Christian Institute for the Study of Religion and Society founded in 1959 and related to that in Bangalore South India carries on studies of the sociological character of the churches and society, especially in the Tamil region of the island. Another co-operative organization is the Sodepax Sri Lanka Committee. Concerning interreligious dialogue, the Congress of Religions, begun in 1961 for 'service to the nation through religious harmony', gives as its goal the promotion of mutual understanding and the creation of social services with a spiritual emphasis, such as the Leprosy Association of Sri Lanka. It was also responsible for the creation of the Inter-Religions Council, composed of Buddhist, Hindu, Christian (Anglican, Presbyterian, Catholic and Methodist), Muslim, Jewish, and Zoroastrian leaders. The Council of Religions Batticaloa consists of the various religious leaders of the town of Batticaloa and is neither a regional nor a national organization. Buddhist-Christian study groups are also active at the Vidyodaya Buddhist university.

FUTURE TRENDS AND PROSPECTS

Christians are expected to increase slightly from 8.7% in 1970 to 9.5% by 2025 primarily due to church growth among Tamils (23% in 1990 up to over 25% by 2025) but also among Sinhalese (3.8% in 1990 up to near 5% by 2025). Buddhists will certainly increase and Hindus will likely decrease with a continued exodus to India.

Christianity could grow slowly over the next fifty years, perhaps even reaching 10% of the population by mid-century.

BIBLIOGRAPHY

A celebration of demons: exorcism and the aesthetics of healing in Sri Lanka. B. Kapferer. Bloomington, IN: Indiana University Press, 1983. 293p.

A history of the Diocese of Colombo. F. L. Beven (ed). Calcutta: Times of Ceylon, 1946. 426p. (Anglican).

A history of the Methodist Church in Ceylon, 1814–1964. W. J. T. Small (ed). Colombo: Wesley Press, 1971. 666p.

'A strategy for mission among the poor in Colombo.' D. R. Fernando. Th.M. thesis, Fuller Theological Seminary, Pasadena, CA, 1991. 235p.

'A study of three post–reformation renewal movements with special application to the Protestant Church in Sri Lanka.' D. J. Ephraim. D.Miss. thesis, Fuller Theological Seminary, Pasadena, CA, 1991. 320p.

A time to remember: a history of the Redemptorists in India and Sri Lanka, 1938–1972. J. C. Morgan. Bangalore, India: Redemptorist Publications, India, 1992. 287p.

Atlas of South Asia. A. K. Dutt & M. M. Geib. Boulder, CO, and London: Westview Press, 1987. 255p.

Buddhism in Ceylon and studies on religious syncretism in Buddhist countries. H. Bechert. London: E. J. Brill, 1978. 360p.

Buddhism in life: the anthropological study of religion and the Sinhalese practice of Buddhism. M. Southwald. Manchester, UK: Manchester University Press, 1983. 232p.

Buddhism transformed: religious change in Sri Lanka. R. Gombrich & G. Obeyesekere. Princeton, NJ: Princeton University Press, 1990. 500p.

'Ceylon,' *Pro Mundi Vita* (Brussels), 3 (1964).

Ceylon church history. W. L. A. Don Peter. Colombo: Catholic Press, 1963.

Christianity in Ceylon, its introduction and progress under the Portuguese, the Dutch, the British and American missions: with an historical sketch of the Brahaminical and Buddhist superstitions. J. E. Tennent. London: John Murray, 1950. 348p.

'Church growth, its dynamics and strategy: a challenge to the church in Sri Lanka today.' C. J. Daniel. M.A. project, Fuller Theological Seminary, Pasadena, CA, 1977. 128p.

'Crucified hope: beyond liberation: an appeal to the churches of Sri Lanka to guide the people of Sri Lanka to overcome the ongoing ethnic conflict.' A. Jeyakumaran. S.T.M. thesis, Andover Newton Theological School, Newton Center, MA, 1988. 165p.

'Demons and saints: possession and exorcism in Roman Catholic Sri Lanka.' M. D. Fernando. Ph.D. dissertation, Rutgers University, New Brunswick, NJ, 1988. 379p.

'Discipling in three Sri Lankan cities,' R. De Silva, *Urban mission*, 2, 4 (March 1985), 33–40.

Discipling the cities in Sri Lanka: a challenge to the church today. R. De Silva. Peradeniya, Sri Lanka: Church Growth Research Centre, 1985. 244p. (An update of the author's M.A. thesis at Fuller Theological Seminary, Pasadena, CA, 1980).

Faith of our fathers: history of the Dutch Reformed Church in Sri Lanka (Ceylon). S. D. Franciscus. Colombo: Pragna, 1983. 260p.

God's word in Serendib, 1812–1992. C. Fernando & J. P. V. Soomaratna. Ed., M. Seneviratne. Colombo: Ceylon Bible Society, 1992. 97p.

Hinduism in Ceylon. J. Cartman. Colombo: M. D. Gunasena, 1957. 188p.

Historical gleanings from Sri Lankan Church history. W. L. A. Don Peter. Colombo: W.L.A. Don Peter, 1992. 264p.

'How to develop an urban church planting movement.' T. Weerasingha. D.Min. thesis, Westminster Theological Seminary, Chestnut Hill, PA, 1992. 359p.

Kataragama: The holiest place in Ceylon. P. Wirz. Trans., D. B. Pralle. 2nd ed. Colombo: Lake House Investments, 1972. 57p.

Lament for Lanka: voices from an island in conflict. A. Wynne. Kowloon, Hong Kong: Christian Conference of Asia, International Affairs Committee, 1988. 150p.

Language, religion, and ethnic assertiveness: the growth of Sinhalese nationalism in Sri Lanka. K. N. O. Dharmadasa. Ann Arbor, MI: University of Michigan, 1993. 384p.

National Catholic directory of Sri Lanka, 1989/90. J. B. C. Anandappa (ed). Ragama: J. B. C. Anandappa, [1990]. 579p.

'Obstructions and strategizing in church planting among the Tamil Hindus in Sri Lanka.' V. Chandy. D.Miss thesis, Fuller Theological Seminary, Pasadena, CA, 1984. 276p.

Opinions and attitudes of Catholics in Ceylon. F. Houtart & G. Lemercinier. Louvain, Belgium: Centre de Recherches Socio-Religieuses, 1970. 2 vols.

Power and religiosity in a post–colonial setting: Sinhala Catholics in contemporary Sri Lanka. R. L. Stirrat. *Cambridge studies in social and cultural anthropology*, 87. Cambridge, UK: Cambridge University Press, 1992. 249p.

Two postage stamps celebrating Year of the Family with (*left*) The Three Kings arriving to worship (*right*) the baby Jesus and his parents.

Religion and ideology in Sri Lanka. F. Houtart. Bangalore, India: T.P.I., 1974.
Religious festivals in South India and Sri Lanka. G. R. Welbon & G. E. Yocum (eds). *Studies on religion in South India and Sri Lanka*, vol. 1. New Delhi: Manohar Publications, 1982. 357p.
Sidelights on Christianity in Sri Lanka. O. M. Abey'ratna. Rajagiriya: Abey'ratna, 1977. 72p.
'Sinhalese festivals, their symbolism, origins and proceedings,' C. E. Godakumbura, *Journal of the Ceylon Branch of the Royal Asiatic Society*, n.s. 14 (1970), 91–130.
'Sociology and anthropology of religion in Sri Lanka,' F. Houtart (ed), *Social Compass*, 20, 2 (1973), 99–399.
Sri Lanka. V. Samaraweera. *World bibliographical series*, vol. 20. Oxford, UK: CLIO Press, 1987. 240p. (See especially 'Religion,' p.54-62).
'Strategizing renewal in the church in Sri Lanka.' D. J. Ephraim. M.A. thesis, Fuller Theological Seminary, Pasadena, CA, 1987. 153p.
The Catholic Church in Ceylon under Dutch rule. R. Boudens. Rome: Officium Libri Catholici, 1957. 266p.
The Catholic Church in Sri Lanka: the British period. V. Perniola. Dehiwala, Sri Lanka: Tisara Prakasakayo, 1992–.
'The Christians of Ceylon and nationalist politics,' S. Arasaratnam, in *Religion in South Asia: religious conversion and revival movements in South Asia in medieval and modern times*, p.231–48. G. A. Oddie (ed). 2nd ed. Columbia, MO: South Asia Publications, 1991.
The cult of goddess Pattini. G. Obeyesekere. Chicago: University of Chicago Press, 1984. 629p.
The discipling of Muslims in Sri Lanka. V. Chandy. *Fuller Theological Seminary School of World Mission Projects*, 1981. Pasadena, CA: Fuller Theological Seminary, 1981. 163p.
The Dutch Reformed Church in Sri Lanka (Ceylon): 350th anniversary, 1642–1992. [Colombo]: The Church, [1992]. 34p.
The radical tradition: the changing shape of theological reflection in Sri Lanka. N. Abeyasingha. Colombo: The Ecumenical Institute, 1985. 238p.
Tradition and change in Theravada Buddhism: essays on Ceylon and Thailand in the 19th and 20th centuries. B. L. Smith (ed). *Contributions to Asian studies*, 4. Leiden: E. J. Brill, 1973. 195p.

Country Table 2. **Organized churches and denominations in Sri Lanka.**

Official name (bold type = church *with over 10% of all affiliated)* 1	*Begun* 2	*Type* 3	*Counc* 4	*Congs* 5	*Adults* 6	*Affiliated 1970* 7	*Affiliated 1995* 8	*G%* 9	*Names, notes, and other statistics* (see Codebook, Part 3) 10
Apostolic Church	c1960	P-PeA	.....	20	600	390	2,000	6.76	Mainline Apostolics (UK, USA, Europe).
Asia Evangelistic Fellowship	1982	P-Non	.....	2	320	–	800	7.69	M=AEF. Mobile membership due to political strife.
Assemblies of God in Sri Lanka	1925	P-Pe2	ZF..E	270	27,297	3,000	35,521	10.39	M=AOG(USA). Originated from AoG in South India. HQ Colombo 7. 32n,2s(27).
Assembly Hall Churches	c1990	I-3nC	.....	1	20	–	50	20.00	*Local Churches. Little Flock.* Chinese. Begun 1922 in China.
Calvary Church	1974	I-3cZ	.....	60	6,400	–	15,330	4.76	*Calvary International MInistries.* M=SFM. Abroad: 65 churches among Ceylonese diaspora.
Catholic Church in Sri Lanka:	1517	R-Lat	P.F.R	397	706,000	954,175	1,210,211	0.96	*Romanu Katolike Sabhava.* C=7+6+24,1p,3q,1s. 551n 258x 569m 2234w 28114Yy
M Colombo	1834	R-Lat	Ps	114	301,000	492,106	519,944	0.22	Catholics: 30% city of Colombo; & fishermen. 192n 121x 246m 1013w 13484Yy
D Anuradhapura	1975	R-Lat	Pomi	36	5,800	–	11,905	5.00	M=OMI. 13n 6x 8m 46w 230Yy
D Badulla	1972	R-Lat	Pomi	17	11,000	–	19,802	4.35	M=OMI. 27n 10x 12m 85w 412Yy
D Chilaw	1939	R-Lat	Ps	36	125,000	203,281	220,679	0.33	Catholics mainly in fishing villages. W=29%. 69n 7x 26m 208w 5892Yy
D Galle	1893	R-Lat	Ps	33	3,400	29,000	6,154	-6.01	Sinhalese fishermen; Tamil tea estate workers. 38n 8x 17m 176w 693Yy
D Jaffna	1845	R-Lat	Ps	43	93,000	135,131	163,360	0.76	Tamil fishermen, except near Anuradhapura. W=58%. 73n 54x 84m 216w 1915Yy
D Kandy	1883	R-Lat	Ps	20	42,000	58,000	72,780	0.91	Scattered tea estate Tamils; Kandy, Sinhalese. 26n 17x 107m 230w 1450Yy
D Kurunegala	1987	R-Lat	Ps	21	24,000	–	42,607	12.50	Recent new diocese; area is 2.8% Catholic. 31n 1x 4m 54w 930Yy
D Mannar	1981	R-Lat	Ps	18	39,000	–	68,586	7.14	Ex D Jaffna. Area: 35% Catholic. 25n 10x 14m 58w 1067Yy
D Ratnapura	1995	R-Lat	Ps	23	15,000	–	21,094	0.05	New diocese. Population 1.7 million. 25n 7x 9m 68w 462Yy
D Trincomalee-Batticaloa	1893	R-Lat	Ps	36	46,800	36,657	63,300	2.21	Tamil fishing villagers, Sinhalese colonists. 32n 17x 42m 80w 1579Yy
Ceylon Pentecostal Mission	1923	I-3pI	Z....	90	18,200	10,000	37,000	5.37	Communal property. M=FFFM(Finland). Tamils. 10n,1p(9),W=80%,175Y,100z. In 12 countries.
Christian Brethren		P-CBr	x....	1	35	100	70	0.05	*Plymouth Brethren, Open Brethren.* Small group meeting in Colombo 4.
Christian Fellowship Centre	1941	P-CBr	.....	2	420	750	840	0.45	Brethren background.
Church of Ceylon	1796	A-Hig	AWE.W	170	35,000	46,200	53,000	0.55	*Lanka Sabhawa.* 2 Dioceses. In 1900, 32,500 Anglicans. Until 1910 in CIPBC.
Church of Christ	1968	I-Dis	.....	2	200	124	400	4.80	Disciples. Links with USA mission.
Church of Scotland		P-Ref	Rwc.W	1	30	100	50	0.05	Single congregation in Colombo, supported by Ch of Scotland, Overseas Council.
Church of South India: D Jaffna	1816	P-Uni	.we.W	32	3,850	20,000	5,500	-5.03	Congregationalist. M=UCBWM. Tamils. HQ Vaddukoddai. 80n,2f,W=61%,24Y,85y,61z.
Evangelical Alliance Church	1955	P-Eva	.....	2	40	30	114	5.49	M=TEAM.
Fellowship of Free Churches	1948	I-3pZ	Z....	100	8,000	312	11,000	15.32	*Svenska Fria Mission.* M=SFM(Sweden). HQ Colombo 6, also Nugegoda. 10f.
Foursquare Gospel Church	1979	P-Pe2	.....	422	4,000	–	6,200	6.25	M=ICFG(USA).
Gethsemane Prayer Centre	1978	I-3cZ	.....	20	501	–	1,001	5.88	Indigenous charismatics.
Hebron Gospel Fellowship	1965	I-3cI	.....	89	22,810	500	50,000	20.23	Mainly Tamils.
Hidden Buddhist believers in Christ	c1970	I-Bud	.....	700	45,000	–	95,200	58.18	Large numbers of Sinhalese converts opting to remain in Buddhists families.
Hidden Hindu believers in Christ	c1970	I-Hin	.....	200	20,000	–	40,300	52.83	Tamils, following Jesus as Lord but remaining within Hinduism.
Isolated radio churches	1952	I-3rI	.....	200	6,000	3,600	10,000	4.17	Radio believers, mainly aged 12-25. R=4400(WEC,FEBA),T=8000(EHC,VOP,TEAM,ICI).
Jehovah's Witnesses	1910	m-Jeh	x....	40	1,298	600	5,200	9.02	*Watch Tower.* Active witnessing under way by 1926. HQ Colombo 3. (1975) 39Y. (1995) 263Y.
Lanka Christian Mission	1908	I-Non	....w	5	400	500	800	1.90	M=India Christian Mission, based in Eluru, Andhra Pradesh(India). 2f.
Living Way Church		I-3pI	....E	30	8,200	–	20,000	0.05	HQ in Colombo. Members 60% Tamils, 25% Sinhalese, Burghers.
Margaya Fellowship	1981	I-3pI	.....	18	1,475	–	3,000	7.14	*The Way Fellowship.* Home ministry to converts who are 80% Buddhists.
Methodist Church of Ceylon	1814	P-Met	VWE.W	100	15,500	25,504	26,200	0.11	Autonomous conf 1964. M=MMS(UK),VEM. 46n,6x,2r(2400),1u,W=46%,472Yy,136z.
New Apostolic Church	c1970	I-3aX	x....	30	1,300	1,000	2,199	3.20	In Canada Bezirk, NAK. World HQ Dortmund (FR Germany). Rapid growth as in India.
Pentecostal Assemblies	1982	P-Pe2	.....	12	303	–	758	7.69	M=PAoC(Canada). Trinitarian Classical Pentecostals.
Presbytery of Ceylon	1642	P-Ref	F...W	12	600	3,000	1,000	-4.30	*Dutch Ref.* 40% Burgher,30% Sinhalese,18% Tamil. Emigrating. 8n,1s,30Yy.
Presbytery of Lanka	1953	I-Ref	R...W	2	330	800	733	-0.35	Schism ex DRC (Presbytery of Ceylon). Rapidly declining. 1n,1x,W=46%,9Yy,10z.
Salvation Army	1883	P-Sal	xwF.W	183	2,000	5,000	4,000	-0.89	*Galavima Hamudava. Sri Lanka Terr.* 1 Division, 5 Districts. 100n,8x,1s.
Seventh-day Adventist Church	1920	P-Adv	x....	29	2,000	3,000	4,000	1.16	*SDA, Sri Lanka Union.* 9n,2x,89mw,12f,1H,1j,1s,25t(1303),W=75%,164Y,100z.
Sri Lanka Baptist Union	1812	P-Bap	Tv..W	20	2,027	2,460	3,000	0.80	*SL Baptist Sangamaya.* M=BMS(UK). Decline from 3,309 Baptists in 1900. 9f,1u.
Sri Lanka Lutheran Church Council	1924	P-Lut	L....	23	461	546	781	1.44	M=IELC(India),LC Missouri Synod(USA); in tea estates of Nuwara Eliya. 3f,5t(145),52Yy.
United Pentecostal Church		P-Pel	x....	31	1,090	1,000	2,170	0.05	*Jesus Only Church.* M=UPC(USA). Unitarian Pentecostals. HQ Dehiwala. 6n,5m.
Other Protestant denominations		P-	.....	30	2,000	1,000	3,000	0.05	Total about 10 (see list below).
Other indigenous churches		I-3pZ	.....	80	2,500	1,000	4,000	0.05	Total about 5, including: Zion Pentecostal Ch, and pentecostal bodies from India.
Other independent single congregations		I-sin	.....	55	2,500	1,100	5,000	0.05	In about 10 loose geographical associations or networks.
Totals				**3,481**	**948,707**	**1,085,791**	**1,660,428**		

Churches, members, growth, 1900-2025	*Congs*	*Adults*	*Affiliated*	*G%*	*Total denominations*	*6 Megablocs:* O	R	A	P	I	m
Total churches, members, and denominations (mid-1900)	400	220,000	378,859	1.52	7	0	1	1	5	0	0
Total churches, members, and denominations (mid-1970)	1,215	631,258	1,085,791	1.52	35	0	1	1	18	14	1
Total churches, members, and denominations (mid-1990)	3,000	896,000	1,568,400	1.86	60	0	1	1	27	30	1
Total churches, members, and denominations (mid-1995)	3,481	948,707	1,660,428	1.15	60	0	1	1	27	30	1
Total churches, members, and denominations (mid-2000)	3,900	1,003,000	1,755,120	1.12	61	0	1	1	27	31	1
Total churches, members, and denominations (mid-2025)	5,000	1,266,000	2,215,000	0.94	123	0	1	1	40	80	1

NOTES ON TABLE ABOVE
NATIONAL COUNCILS (Column 4, 5th letter).
E = Evangelical Alliance of Sri Lanka (EASL).
R = Bishops' Conference of Sri Lanka (BCSL) (Lanka Raja Guru Sammelanaya).
W = National Christian Council of Sri Lanka (NCCSL), 1910.
w = associated with NCCSL.
Other national councils. Evangelical Alliance of Sri Lanka (EASL) (members individuals, congregations and agencies; affiliated to WEF).
OTHER PROTESTANT DENOMINATIONS. These include: CCCI, Christian Inland Mission (Christian Enquiries), Christian Nationals Evangelism Commission (1972), Ch of Christ (Non-Instrumental), Church of God, Evangelical Alliance Mission (TEAM) (1955), World-Wide Missions (1963), Youth for Christ (a church from 1993 on), Youth With A Mission.

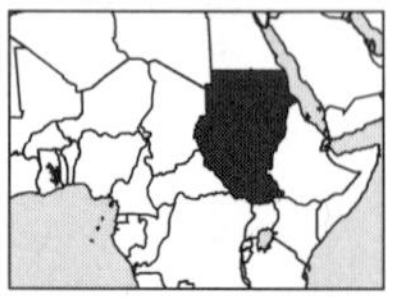

SUDAN

SECULAR DATA, AD 2000

STATE
Official name: Jamhuriyat es-Sudan (The Republic of the Sudan).
Short name: Sudan. **Adjective of nationality:** Sudanese.
Flag: Green triangle; red, white, and black stripes.
Area: 2,503,890 sq. km. (966,757 sq. mi.).
Government: Military regime, since 1989 (1820 Ottoman rule, 1885 independent theocratic Mahdist state, 1899 Anglo-Egyptian condominium, 1956 Independence as republic, 1958 military junta, 1964 civilian rule, 1969 military junta, 1971 one-party republic).
Legislature: National Assembly, 400 members.
Official language: Arabic (spoken by 51%).
Monetary unit: 1 Sudanese dinar (Sd). **US$1=** Sd 182.60.
Chief cities: AL-KHARTUM (3 Towns of Khartoum) 2,748,000; Umm Durman (Omdurman) 830,501; Al-Khartum Bahri (Khartoum North) 537,982; Bur Sudan (Port Sudan) 325,194; Wad Madani (Medoni) 228,880.
Political divisions: 9 provinces.
Armed forces: 80,000.

DEMOGRAPHY
Population: 29,490,000.
Population density: 11.7/sq. km. (30.5/sq. mi.).
Under 15 years: 11,625,000.
Growth rate p.a.: 2.10% (births 31.65, deaths 10.67).
Mortality: Infant, per 1,000: 64.6; **Maternal per 100,000:** 660.0.
Life expectancy: 57 (male 56, female 58).
Household size: 5.3. **Floor area per person, sq.m:** 5.0.
Major languages: Arabic, English, Dinka, Nuer, Bari, Shilluk, Azande, Beja, Nuba, Nubian Hausa, Fur and over 130 minor languages.
Urban dwellers: 36.12%. **Urban growth rate p.a.:** 4.6%.
Labor force: 35%.

ETHNOLINGUISTIC PEOPLES
12.1% Sudanese Arab; 6.6% Gaaliin; 3.2% Eastern Nuer(Jikany Door); 3.1% Guhayna; 3.0% Beja (Beni-Amer, Ababda).

ECONOMY
National income p.a. per person: US$800; **per family:** US$4,240.

EDUCATION
Adult literacy: 46% (male 57%, female 34%). **Schools:** 10,661.
Universities: 24. **School enrolment:** female/male: 34%/43%.

HEALTH
Access to health services: 70%. **Access to safe water:** 50%.
Hospitals: 200 (8 beds per 10,000). **Doctors:** 2,400.
Blind: 110,000. **Deaf:** 1,789,400. **Murder rate:** 4.
Lepers: 150,000. **Underweight prevalence under 5:** 34%.

LITERATURE
New book titles p.a.: 590 (20 p.a. per million). **Periodicals:** 14. **Newspapers:** 5 dailies.

COMMUNICATION (per 1,000 people)
Phones: 2 (5% mobile). **Radios:** 193. **TV sets:** 76. **Daily newspaper circulation:** 23. **Computers:** 2.

REFUGEES
Citizen refugees in other countries: 448,100.
Alien refugees from other countries: 450,000.
Internal displacement: 4,000,000.

HUMAN LIFE AND LIBERTY (optimum condition=100.0%)
HDI: 33.3. **HSI:** 11.0. **HFI:** 5.0. **EFL:** 18.0.

Country Table 1. **Religious adherents in Sudan, AD 1900-2025.**

Year	1900		1970		mid-1990		Annual change, 1990-2000				mid-1995		mid-2000		mid-2025	
Name	Adherents	%	Adherents	%	Adherents	%	Natural	Conversion	Total	Rate	Adherents	%	Adherents	%	Adherents	%
Muslims	3,390,000	62.0	9,295,450	67.1	16,620,850	69.1	374,911	36,120	411,031	2.23	18,490,730	69.5	20,731,161	70.3	32,680,400	70.6
Christians	**2,375**	**0.0**	**1,175,000**	**8.5**	**3,912,500**	**16.3**	**88,260**	**12,586**	**100,846**	**2.32**	**4,490,000**	**16.9**	**4,920,955**	**16.7**	**8,530,000**	**18.4**
PROFESSION																
crypto-Christians	1,155	0.0	270,798	2.0	500,000	2.1	11,279	2,721	14,000	2.50	560,000	2.1	640,000	2.2	1,124,400	2.4
professing Christians	**1,220**	**0.0**	**904,202**	**6.5**	**3,412,500**	**14.2**	**76,981**	**9,865**	**86,846**	**2.29**	**3,930,000**	**14.8**	**4,280,955**	**14.5**	**7,405,600**	**16.0**
AFFILIATION																
unaffiliated Christians	0	0.0	4,702	0.0	38,800	0.2	875	-99	776	1.84	40,000	0.2	46,564	0.2	38,000	0.1
affiliated Christians	**2,375**	**0.0**	**1,170,298**	**8.4**	**3,873,700**	**16.1**	**87,384**	**12,685**	**100,069**	**2.32**	**4,450,000**	**16.7**	**4,874,391**	**16.5**	**8,492,000**	**18.4**
Roman Catholics	345	0.0	687,768	5.0	2,480,000	10.3	55,945	10,914	66,859	2.42	2,780,381	10.5	3,148,593	10.7	5,500,000	11.9
Anglicans	30	0.0	300,000	2.2	1,800,000	7.5	40,605	11,395	52,000	2.57	2,100,000	7.9	2,320,000	7.9	3,600,000	7.8
Protestants	0	0.0	65,030	0.5	575,000	2.4	12,971	9,129	22,100	3.31	682,270	2.6	796,000	2.7	1,480,000	3.2
Orthodox	2,000	0.0	107,200	0.8	148,000	0.6	3,339	-2,639	700	0.46	150,180	0.6	155,000	0.5	200,000	0.4
Independents	0	0.0	10,100	0.1	90,000	0.4	2,030	3,970	6,000	5.24	134,679	0.5	150,000	0.5	400,000	0.9
Marginal Christians	0	0.0	200	0.0	700	0.0	16	4	20	2.54	767	0.0	900	0.0	2,000	0.0
doubly-affiliated	0	0.0	0	0.0	-1,220,000	-5.1	-27,521	-20,089	-47,610	3.35	-1,398,277	-5.3	-1,696,102	-5.8	-2,690,000	-5.8
Trans-megabloc groupings																
Evangelicals	30	0.0	188,000	1.4	605,000	2.5	13,648	3,952	17,600	2.59	1,346,473	5.1	781,000	2.7	1,790,000	3.9
Pentecostals/Charismatics	0	0.0	8,000	0.1	430,000	1.8	9,700	12,200	21,900	4.20	584,758	2.2	649,000	2.2	1,850,000	4.0
Great Commission Christians	**2,200**	**0.0**	**500,000**	**3.6**	**1,490,000**	**6.2**	**33,612**	**8,409**	**42,021**	**2.52**	**1,703,000**	**6.4**	**1,910,208**	**6.5**	**3,700,000**	**8.0**
Ethnoreligionists	2,077,400	38.0	3,258,000	23.5	3,275,000	13.6	73,879	-49,575	24,304	0.72	3,350,000	12.6	3,518,041	11.9	4,400,000	9.5
Nonreligious	0	0.0	100,000	0.7	220,000	0.9	4,963	1,026	5,989	2.44	250,000	0.9	279,891	1.0	588,000	1.3
Atheists	0	0.0	30,000	0.2	39,000	0.2	880	-114	766	1.81	42,200	0.2	46,658	0.2	75,000	0.2
Baha'is	125	0.0	500	0.0	1,450	0.0	33	5	38	2.34	1,650	0.0	1,828	0.0	5,000	0.0
Jews	100	0.0	50	0.0	1,200	0.0	27	-12	15	1.21	1,280	0.0	1,354	0.0	1,600	0.0
Hindus	0	0.0	0	0.0	500	0.0	11	-3	8	1.57	540	0.0	584	0.0	1,000	0.0
doubly-counted religionists	0	0.0	0	0.0	-8,500	0.0	-192	-33	-225	2.38	-9,400	0.0	-10,752	0.0	-17,000	0.0
World A (unevangelized persons)	5,251,200	96.0	10,394,250	75.0	12,271,620	51.0	276,762	-141,668	135,094	1.05	12,776,272	48.0	13,624,380	46.2	18,089,224	39.1
World B (evangelized non-Christians)	216,425	4.0	2,289,750	16.5	7,877,880	32.7	177,750	129,082	306,832	3.34	9,350,961	35.1	10,944,665	37.1	19,644,776	42.5
World C (Christians)	2,375	0.0	1,175,000	8.5	3,912,500	16.3	88,260	12,586	100,846	2.32	4,490,000	16.9	4,920,955	16.7	8,530,000	18.4
Country's population	**5,470,000**	**100.0**	**13,859,000**	**100.0**	**24,062,000**	**100.0**	**542,772**	**0**	**542,772**	**2.06**	**26,617,234**	**100.0**	**29,490,000**	**100.0**	**46,264,000**	**100.0**

COLUMNS, ROWS.
For meanings and definitions, see Codebook (Part 3). Note that, by definition, total 'Christians' = professing + crypto-Christians, which also = affiliated + unaffiliated Christians, and also = Great Commission Christians + latent Christians. Percentages may not always total exactly, due to rounding.

CENSUSES.
The religion question has never been asked.

NOTES ON RELIGIONS
ANGLICANS. Anglican growth has been extremely rapid because the CMS mission worked among the responsive Nilo-Hamitic and non-Nilotic tribes. The Azande were the first to respond the large numbers, then the Bari, Moru, Kuku and Moro (Nuba mountains).
ATHEISTS. Sudan Communist Party (SCP) (suppressed 1971); pro-Soviet): The party has changed over the years from being strongly anti-religious at its founding to formal recognition of Allah and the practice of prayer by members. Also present were 500 USSR military advisers (1973), finally evicted in 1977.
BAHA'IS. First entered the Sudan before 1892. No growth; only 4 local spiritual assemblies in both 1964 and 1973. Continual fighting disrupted new efforts for the following 25 years.
COUNTRY'S POPULATION. During the civil war of 1963-72, an estimated one million persons in the South were killed or died of starvation or attrition, over 500,000 during the 3 years 1963-66. From the mid-70s to the present another one million persons in the South were killed or died of starvation. A large proportion of these were Christians.
CRYPTO-CHRISTIANS. Christians affiliated to churches but unknown as such to the state or to society at large.
ETHNORELIGIONISTS. Animists in the South (with a few peoples in the North), especially among tribes which over the last 100 years have resisted Christianity as well as Islam. Tribes over 60% traditionalist (animist) in 1995: Didinga (90%), Ingessana (99%), Meban (96%), Murle (90%), Nuer (85%), Anuak (87%), Uduk (80%), Shilluk (62%), Krongo (95%).
INDEPENDENTS. In 4 small groupings in 1995 (see Table 2), including isolated radio believers.
MUSLIMS. Sunnis (mostly of the Malikite rite with some Shafiites). Sufi religious orders are strong in the Sudan; there are strong-based brotherhoods especially Khatimiya (Mirghaniya) with 1,000,000 followers and Ansar (Madhiya) with 3,000,000 (mostly small farmers and nomadic herdsmen, and including 200,000 armed tribesmen and 200,000 other militants), both suppressed after the Ansar revolt of 1970; other brotherhoods include Qadariya, Sammaniya, Idrisiya, Senusiya, Ismailiya, Shadhiliya and Tijaniya. The practice of Islam is widespread, Ramadan is generally observed, and many go on the hajj to Mecca. There are also about 6,000 Asians (Indo-Pakistanis and others). The spread of Islam has resulted in the islamization of tribes on the Ethiopian border, and major advances in the Darfur area among the Dadjo, Guimr, Tama, Masalit and Fur tribes, and in the Nuba mountains through the operating of schools. The Ahmadiya Mission (from Pakistan) has attempted work but is prohibited as heretical. *Missionaries.* There are a number of Egyptian missionaries sent by Al-Azhar University (Cairo), and also Egyptian and Sudanese missionaries of the Muslim Brotherhood (working in the Nuba Mountains and elsewhere). *Hajj pilgrims to Mecca.* (1968) 18,035; (1969) 20,495; (1970) 14,865; (1971) 29,004; (1972) 29,506; (1973) 33,222; (1974) 42,084; (1975) 24,209; (1976) 41,652.
PROTESTANTS. Growth has been very slow because Protestant missions have worked only among the highly-resistant nomadic Nilotic peoples (Dinka, Nuer, Shilluk, et alia).
ROMAN CATHOLICS. In the year 1910, there were 1,344 Catholics (65% Whites).

Great Commission Instrument Panel: status of Sudan (for explanation see start of Part 4)

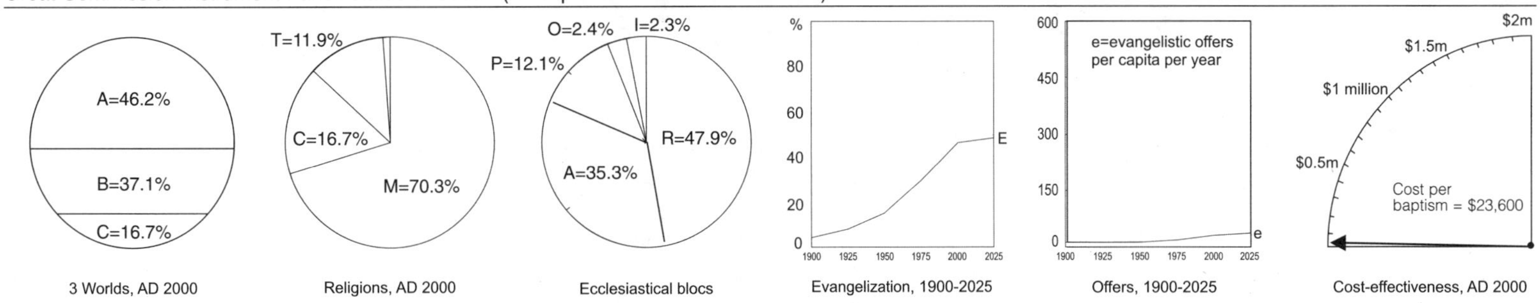

Country status. Sudan, the largest country in Africa, is a bridge between Arab North Africa and Black sub-Saharan Africa. Like Egypt, it is an entirely Nilotic region. Its chief exports are cotton, peanuts, and sorghum.

HUMAN LIFE AND LIBERTY

Human need and development. Apart from the 'Three Towns'—Khartoum, Khartoum North, and Omdurman—Sudan is mostly desert or equatorial forest. While the Muslim-dominated North has remained fairly prosperous, the Southern Region inhabited by the Nilotic tribes is one of the most destitute regions of the world. Both natural disasters and genocidal warfare by the Islamic authorities have desolated it in a manner that may not be reversed for a century. Most cultivated areas have reverted to the bush. More than 40% of the population are nomads and are on the move for at least part of a year. For example the Kababish of the northern Kordofan Province, the Beja, and the Baggara Arabs travel to wherever there is water, and when the grazing gets thinner move into other areas. The tents of the nomads are light, simple structures made of local, easily replaceable materials, and household possessions are limited to what can be carried on the backs of a few animals. Even before the civil war, Sudanese diet was generally poor, even though it varied with the seasons. But in the Southern Province, famine conditions have prevailed for years, as the government has cut off food supplies in an effort to break the will of the defiant tribes. Health conditions have deteriorated because of the incidence of such debilitating diseases as bilharziasis, a parasitic ailment that breeds primarily though the passing of human wastes into pond and river water which is then used for drinking. Ironically, settled communities are more vulnerable to water pollution and unsanitary conditions than nomads. There is no comprehensive social welfare programs, but some Arabs benefit from the Islamic charitable foundations, known as *wakfs.*

Human rights and freedoms. Over a million Sudanese have been killed by government forces in the Southern Province and over 3.5 million have been displaced, and forced to flee their homes. The air force bombed villages indiscriminately, and soldiers have engaged in stealing cattle and burning houses before putting their owners to death. Government forces have enforced conscription, and where they failed have kidnapped or enslaved the Blacks. Tens of thousands are routinely held incommunicado in prisons. The government also has unleashed an Islamization and Arabization drive withholding food and medical services until the needy can be forced to convert to Islam. The security forces have the license to act as a law unto themselves and have often undertaken mass executions of entire villages without prior notice. Torture of prisoners is commonplace. The 1991 Criminal Act based on the sharia provided 'hudood' punishments, such as amputation, stoning, and lashing for certain types of offenses. The judiciary is entirely subservient to the government, and judges suspected of not towing the official line are summarily dismissed. Warrantless searches are the norm, and are conducted at night to intimidate the suspects. Mail and telephone are subject to government scrutiny.

Country summary. **Worlds A, B, C by ethnolinguistic peoples, cities, and major civil divisions in Sudan.**

World	PEOPLES Num	Pop 2000	C%	Christians	E%	U%	Unevangelized	CITIES Num	Pop 2000	C%	Christians	E%	U%	Unevangelized	CIVIL DIVISIONS Num	Pop 2000	C%	Christians	E%	U%	Unevangelized
A	169	15,187,225	0.53	79,857	29	71	10,848,896	9	1,743,888	2.42	42,149	38	62	1,073,108	6	21,639,850	3.43	741,479	42	58	12,658,496
B	46	9,841,393	14.90	1,465,998	72	28	2,755,351	1	2,748,000	23.00	632,040	67	33	912,886	1	2,584,479	22.00	568,585	65	35	908,953
C	30	4,461,099	74.61	3,328,532	100	0	16,682	2	276,738	74.62	206,515	96	4	10,398	2	5,265,389	67.69	3,564,326	99	1	53,487
Total	**245**	**29,489,717**	**16.53**	**4,874,387**	**54**	**46**	**13,620,929**	**12**	**4,768,626**	**18.47**	**880,704**	**58**	**42**	**1,996,392**	**9**	**29,489,718**	**16.53**	**4,874,390**	**54**	**46**	**13,620,936**

All print and electronic media are government controlled, so that there is no freedom of speech or press. Foreign publications are routinely confiscated. Freedom of association is effectively curtailed under the martial law and state of emergency. The government has tried to stamp out domestic criticism of its record on human rights. It is also highly defensive about foreign criticism of its human rights violations. Under the sharia, all groups except Arab men are discriminated against. In addition to forced segregation, women suffer a number of indignities, including lashing for wearing immodest dress not covering the entire body. Non-Muslims are considered as second class citizens subject to overt discrimination, harassment, and persecution. Businesses owned by non-Muslims are denied licenses and permits. Education and public communications are entirely in Arabic as part of the Arabization policy. Non-Muslims are denied government jobs and those in service are dismissed to make room for Muslims.

Human environment. Sudan has 3 distinct environments: desert in the north and west, semitropical savannah and scrublands in the center, and tropical forests in the south. The desert is encroaching on the inhabited portion of the country at the rate of 2 to 6 miles per year. Lack of rainfall, shifting sand dunes, and overgrazing promote soil erosion and desertification. There is a consequent loss of wildlife habitats. Plant and animal pests thrive in the Nile and its tributaries and cause health problems.

NON-CHRISTIAN RELIGIONS

Islam is the professed religion of 70% of the population and has almost the complete allegiance of the peoples of the North. Muslims are Sunnis, mostly of the Malikite rite although some are Shafiites. Especially in the rural areas, Sudanese Islam is characterized by strong brotherhoods called tariqas, at the head of which are holy men (sheikhs or walis) who dictate the ritual and ascetic rules to be followed by their disciples. During the 20th century 2 tariqas have grown to national significance: the one-million-strong Khatmiya or Mirghaniya established in the 18th century and implanted to the north and east of Khartoum; and the 3-million-strong Ansar or Mahdiya, a xenophobic and eschatological movement found by Muhammed al-Mahdi Ahmed in 1881, with its strength to the south and southwest of the capital. Since 1940 these 2 brotherhoods have played a significant role in national life, each supporting its own political party. The cause of Islam is aided by the College of Arabic and Islamic studies founded at Omdurman in 1912.

Muslims. Mahdi's Tomb, Omdurman. Today the Mahdi's party (Ansar or Mahdiya) is still strong, with 3 million farmers and herdsmen as followers, despite government's crushing of 1970 Ansar revolt.

Traditional religions retain the allegiance of 12% of the population and are still a significant force in the South. Those tribes which have been especially resistant to the claims of both Islam and Christianity include the following: Anuak, Didinga, Dinka, Angessana, Krongo, Lotaka, Meban, Murle, Nuer, Shilluk, and Uduk. Unlike other Nilotic peoples, the Shilluk are distinguished by their concept of divine kingship. The king (reth) is part of the royal clan founded by Nyikang, the first Shilluk king. Shrines and priests of Nyikang, the principal cult of the Shilluk, are found in various parts of the country, and spirit possession by Nyikang is a distinctive feature of the cult. While Nyikang is believed to care for the Shilluk people as a whole, the needs of smaller groups are covered through offerings by clan heads to their own ancestral spirits. There is no cult for the direct worship of God, Juok being approached primarily though the kings and Nyikang. Names for God of other Sudanese peoples included Mboli, (among the Azande and Makaraka), Ngun (Bari, Fajulu), Tamukujen (Didinga), Nhialic (Dinka), and Kwoth (Nuer).

Ethnoreligionists. Animists number 3.5 million, still gradually increasing in numbers. *Top.* Azande witchdoctor conducts Avuré (Sorcerer's Dance). *Lower.* A traditional spirit hut.

CHRISTIANITY

Coptic Christians were in Nubia by the 4th century. The first Melkite missionaries were sent by the emperor Justinian in AD 543; but the emperor's wife, Theodora, favoring the Monophysites, also sent her representative, Julian, who succeeded in converting the king of Nobatae. Monophysitism held sway in Nubia until about AD 100 when a Nubian bishop introduced the Orthodox Melkite (Greek) tradition, provoking a split between the church in Nubia and the Copts in Egypt. Although Christianity continued to flourish up to the 14th century, Islam increasingly gained ascendancy and ultimately extinguished all Christian presence in Nubia. The modern era of Catholic missions began in 1842, with the creation of the vicariate of Central Africa at Khartoum in 1846. Franciscans took charge of the vicariate in 1861, and in 1872 it was confided to the Verona Fathers under D. Comboni, their founder. The church was virtually destroyed during the Mahdist insurrection in 1881 but was begun again in 1898. Anglicans appeared the following year (1899) followed by other Protestant and Orthodox groups at and after the turn of the century.

Destruction of Christian religion over 4-5 years: Remains of large church and congregation.

CATHOLIC CHURCH. The Catholic Church is the largest Christian body in the Sudan, having grown from 250 in 1898 to 40,000 in 1930, 78,000 in 1949, over 600,000 including catechumens by 1970 and over 2.7 million by 1995. The church is divided into 7 ecclesiastical territories, but its strength is concentrated in the South. Many southern churches and all seminaries were destroyed during the civil war of the early 1960s. Minor seminaries were opened in Wau in 1968 and a major seminary at Juba in 1971. The first ordination of Sudanese priests was in 1944 and the first Sudanese bishop was consecrated in 1955.

After 1972, following the Addis Ababa peace accord of 28 February putting an end to 17 years of civil war, and the granting of autonomy within the framework of national unity to southern Sudan (3 March), the Catholic Church was able to reorganize its work. Pope Paul VI announced on 2 December 1972 the official institution of the hierarchy in the country, there being previous to that only vicariates and prefectures. There are now 2 archdioceses, Khartoum for the north and Juba for the south. The numerical size of the church has been underestimated in the past due to the constant movement of the population and the continuing return of refugees from both the exterior and interior of the country.

However, war broke out again after 1983, and the situation once again became precarious for Catholic Christians. Thousands have died since then due primarily to the government's deliberate policy against southern Christian peoples.

The Holy See has diplomatic relations with Sudan and in AD 2000 is represented to government and the Catholic hierarchy by a pro-nuncio residing in Khartoum.

ANGLICAN CHURCH. The CMS opened the first Anglican station at Omdurman in 1899 and from there an extensive work was developed in the southern region, making Anglicanism today the second largest Christian community in the Sudan. Until 1974 the Episcopal Church in the Sudan was under the Jerusalem Archbishopric; in 1976 it became autonomous as the Province of the Episcopal Church of the Sudan, with 4 dioceses.

ORTHODOX CHURCHES. Three Oriental Orthodox churches, all Monophysite in tradition, are found in the Sudan; Copts, who are Sudanese of Egyptian origin and form the largest of the Orthodox denominations; Ethiopians, who have only been organized as a religious community since 1965; and Armenians, a small group in Khartoum without a resident priest. Eastern Orthodoxy is represented by the diocese of Nubia of the Greek Orthodox Patriarchate of Alexandria, with a resident archbishop and 14 parishes, although membership has declined significantly since 1950.These various Orthodox bodies are largely self-contained ethnic groups, existing in the north and catering for their own members, with little impact on the wider community.

Catholic Church in the Sudan. Easter communicants during mass movement in 1940. Catholics have grown phenomenally from 250 in1898 to 40,000 in 1930, to 1.0 million in 1978, to 3.1 million in AD 2000.

PROTESTANT CHURCHES. Over 10 Protestant churches are at work in Sudan, including 2 groups of Presbyterians, both of which are related to the United Presbyterian Church in the USA. The Evangelical Church in the Sudan is composed of northern Sudanese of Egyptian origin, whereas the Church of Christ in the Upper Nile consists of southern indigenous peoples. The other Protestant churches are all active in the south and are the result of the outreach of 3 faith missions: the African Inland Mission, the Sudan Interior Mission and the former Sudan United Mission. All missionaries attached to the southern churches were expelled during the 1960s but most returned after 1973, only to have to leave again in 1990.

Renewal movements. In the 1990s the Pentecostal/Charismatic Renewal continued to spread rapidly across most older churches, and numbered over 649,000 adherents (of whom 1% Pentecostals, 79% Charismatics, and 20% Independents).

Indigenous missions. Nubian and Coptic Orthodox Christians sent out missionaries to surrounding countries from the 4th to 14th centuries. In the 20th century, a number of missionaries have served in neighboring African countries.

CHURCH AND STATE

During the Anglo-Egyptian Condominium, all churches were officially recognized. In the Self Government statute of 1953, section 5(2), religious freedom was guaranteed in the following words: 'All persons shall enjoy freedom of conscience, and the right freely to profess their religion, subject only to such conditions relating to morality, public order to health as may be imposed by law'. This same section was repeated verbatim in the Sudan Transitional Constitution of 1956, and the amended Transitional Constitution of 1964. The Republic Order No. 1 issued after the coup in May 1969 suspended the constitution but made no statement regarding religious freedom; it was therefore assumed that the previous provision was still valid.

The new constitution of 12 April 1973 begins in its Preamble with these words: 'In the name of God, the Compassionate, the Merciful, the creator of peoples and grantor of freedoms'; and the Preamble terminates with a reference to 'the will of God and his favor'. Part I, Article 9 states that 'The Islamic Law and custom shall be main sources of legislation. Personal matters of non-Muslims shall be governed by their personal laws'. Part II, Chapter 1, Article 15 expresses the view that the family, which is 'the foundation of society', should be 'guided by religion, morals and citizenship'. A key section of the constitution relating to religion is Article 16: '(a) In the Democratic Republic of the Sudan Islam is the religion and the society shall be guided by Islam being the religion of the majority of its people and the State shall endeavor to express it values.

(b) Christianity is the religion (sic) in the Democratic Republic of the Sudan, being professed by a large number of its citizens who are guided by Christianity and the State shall endeavor to express its values. (c) Heavenly religions and the noble aspects of spiritual beliefs shall not be insulted or held in contempt. (d) The State shall treat followers of religions and noble spiritual beliefs without discrimination as to the rights and freedoms guaranteed to them as citizens by this Constitution. The State shall not impose any restrictions on citizens or communities on the grounds of religious faith. (e) The abuse of religious and noble spiritual beliefs for political exploitation is forbidden. Any act which is intended or is likely to promote feelings of hatred, enmity or discord among religious communities shall be contrary to this Constitution and punishable by law'. Article 22 calls for the guidance of youth 'on the basis of religion and morals'; and Article 38 affirms that Sudanese are 'equal before the courts' and 'have equal rights and duties, irrespective of origin, race, locality, sex, language or religion'. Finally, Article 47 states: 'Freedom of belief, prayer and performance of religious practices, without infringement of public order or morals, is guaranteed'.

In practice, however, Christians have in the past been severely discriminated against. Under the Missionary Societies Act of 1962, section 3, it has been illegal for any church of 'missionary society' to perform in the Sudan 'any missionary act except in accordance with the terms of the license granted by the Council of Ministers'; and although often applied for, licenses were not issued. The provisions of the Missionary Societies Act, however, were never enforced in the North and are now in disuse in all parts of the country.

Since Independence in 1956, a number of administrative measures have been felt to be restrictive of church activities. The main sources of concern have been the prohibition against increasing the number of foreign missionaries above the quota existing in 1956, the refusal to permit any expansion of the school system beyond its 1956 level, bureaucratic difficulties since 1958 in obtaining replacements for missionaries leaving the country permanently and in receiving permits to build churches and other church institutions, restrictions on the travel of all foreigners inside the country beginning in 1967, and the suspension of church-owned periodicals through the nationalization of the press in 1970. Relations between churches and government, which became very tense after the nationalization of all 295 mission schools in the South in 1957, and again after the expulsion of all foreign missionaries from the South in 1963-64, later showed a gradual improvement. These relations were indirectly affected by the fluctuating situation of the guerrilla movement in the South and also by relief and press campaigns abroad in favor of Sudanese refugees. Since 1955, accusations levelled against churches or church organizations, and fanned by the mass media, have created an atmosphere of suspicion around Christians in general and churchmen in particular.

On the other hand, there have also been numerous gestures of appreciation by the government, such as the establishment in 1966 of a Catholic minor seminary at Khartoum, the 1968 decision providing for the secondment of a number of teachers from government elementary schools to be trained for teaching Christianity in the same schools, the creation of an Office for Christian Education (Maktab Taftish deen al Maseeh) in the Ministry of Education in 1969, the establishment at the same time in Khartoum of a Catholic apostolic delegation for the Red Sea countries which was elevated to the rank of a apostolic nunciature in 1972, the granting of permission in 1971 to 5 Indian Jesuits to enter the country for the purpose of opening a new major seminary at Juba, and other personal favors to churches and churchmen. The teaching of the Christian religion to Christian pupils in government elementary schools was approved in principle in 1968, and church buildings have been exempt from taxation.

There is no government ministry dealing solely with religion, and there is no obligation that churches formally register with the government. The Ministry of the Interior is responsible for supervising the activities of churches and their foreign personnel. Minor educational matters are handled through the Office for Christian Education. The Sudan Council of Churches makes official approaches in the name of all its member Christian denominations, although questions concerning the Catholic Church are mainly dealt with between the government and the apostolic pronuncio.

BROADCASTING AND MEDIA

The Lutheran World Federation maintains a studio in Juba which produces English language programs, and Arabic-language shortwave radio broadcasts can be received from FEBA (Seychelles). Sudan is represented in UNDA, and a 30 minute program featuring church news, meditations and topical issues is broadcast each Sunday (15 minutes in Arabic, 15 minutes in English).

Around 9.5 million (28%) have seen the 'Jesus' Film: mainly through film team showings (in the south, 8 million), videocassettes (12,000) and television broadcasts (1.5 million), with 2.2 million responses.

INTERDENOMINATIONAL ORGANIZATIONS

The Sudan Council of Churches was established in 1965, being the successor to the Northern Sudan Christian Council. At present its membership includes 8 churches covering a wide Christian spectrum: Catholic, Orthodox, Anglican and Protestant, although the more conservative faith missions are not members. The council represents the churches before government, stimulates co-operation between churches, promotes observance of the Week of Christian Unity and co-ordinates the occasional diffusion of Christian programs on Radio Sudan. It has been instrumental in obtaining Catholic recognition of non-Catholic baptism, and since the 1972 Addis Ababa agreement it has begun important relief and reconstruction work in the South. The council is affiliated with the NECC and the AACC. Four offices of the various denominations are especially charged with ecumenical relations and activities; the Sudan Catholic Information Office (SCIO), secretariat of Clergy House (Anglican), Christian Literature Centre (Presbyterian), and Coptic archbishopric.

Province of the Episcopal Church of the Sudan. Kakwa-speaking Anglican Revivalists (Balokole) in their weekly after-church meeting outside Yei church. On left, a home-made megaphone. *Inset.* Anglican cathedral in Khartoum, requisitioned by government in 1971 as a security risk.

FUTURE TRENDS AND PROSPECTS

Christianity and Islam are both expected to continue to grow through 2025 with losses taken by ethnoreligionists (down from 23.5% in 1970 to less than 10% in 2025). Christians could grow to 18.4% by 2025.

The future of Christianity in Sudan is uncertain. If Islamic persecution continues throughout the 21st century, it is unlikely that Christianity will ever grow to beyond 20% of the population. If conditions change it could rapidly grow beyond 25% before AD 2050.

BIBLIOGRAPHY

A Catholic Sudan: dream, mission, reality: a study of the Roman Catholic mission to Central Africa and its protection by the Hapsburg Empire from 1846 to 1900. D. McEwan. Rome: Stabilimento Tipografico Julia, 1987. 297p.

'A contemporary account of the conversion of the Sudan to Christianity,' L. P. Kirwan, *Sudan notes and records*, 20, 2 (1937), 289–95.

'A history of the Khatmiyyah tariqa in the Sudan.' J. Voll. Ph.D. dissertation, Harvard University, Cambridge, MA, 1969. 716p.

A pilgrim church's progress. O. Allison. London: Church Missionary Society, 1966. (By the Anglican bishop).

'A study of shamanism in the Nuba mountains,' S. F. Nadel, *Journal of the Royal Anthropological Institute*, 76 (1946), 25–37.

'A study of the Evangelical Church of West Africa.' N. L. Olutimayin. S.T.M. thesis, Dallas Theological Seminary, Dallas, TX, 1976. 116p.

Across the savannas to Mecca: the overland pilgrimage route from West Africa. J. S. Birks. London: C. Hurst, 1978. 161p.

Ambassadors by the Nile. W. B. Anderson. London: USCL, 1963. 47p.

An analytical guide to the bibliographies on modern Egypt and the Sudan. C. L. Geddes. *Bibliographic series*, no. 2. Denver, CO: American Institute of Islamic Studies, 1972. 78p. (Deals with Muslim peoples in Egypt and Sudan).

Anthropology and sociology bibliography of studies in the Sudan. A. A. Amal Ayoub. Khartoum: National Council for Research, Economic and Social Research Council, 1974. 161p.

'Becoming an indigenous church: the Episcopal Church of the Sudan.' M. M. Thacker. M.A. thesis, University of Virginia, Charlottesville, VA, 1985. 125p.

Christianity in the Sudan. G. Vantini. Bologna, Italy: EMI, 1981. 302p.

Death among the Azande of the Sudan (beliefs, rites and cult). F. Gero. Trans., W. H. Paxman. *Museum Combonianum*, no. 22. Bologna, Italy: Editrice Nigrizia, 1968. 184p.

Directory of the Christian churches in the Sudan, 1967. Khartoum: Sudan Council of Churches, 1967. 45p.

Divinity and experience: the religion of the Dinka. G. Lienhardt. Oxford, UK: Clarendon, 1961. 328p.

Education, religion and politics in Southern Sudan 1899–1964. L. P. Sanderson & G. N. Sanderson. London: Khartoum University Press, 1981. 511p.

Episcopal Church of the Province of the Sudan: a description and outline history. [Juba, Sudan]: Episcopal Church of the Province of the Sudan, [1976]. 6p.

Focus on the history of the Catholic Diocese of Yei. J. M. David. Juba, Sudan: Teachers' Resources Centre, [1988]. 87p.

From mission to church: a handbook of Christianity in East Africa. Z. J. Nthamburi (ed). Nairobi: Uzima Press, 1991. 150p. (See chapter entitled 'Christianity in Sudan').

'Government and Christian missions in the Anglo–Egyptian Sudan, 1899–1914,' R. Hill, *Middle Eastern studies*, 1, 2 (1965), 113–34.

Great expectations: the civil roles of the churches in southern Sudan. Discussion paper, African rights, no. 6. London: African Rights, [1995]. 43p.

Islam in Africa. J. Kritzeck & W. H. Lewis (eds). New York: Van Nostrand-Reinhold, 1969. 339p. (Chapter 10 deals with Islam in the Sudan).

Islam in the Sudan. J. S. Trimingham. London: Oxford University Press, 1949. 280p.

Islam, nationalism and radicalism in Egypt and the Sudan. G. R. Warburg & U. M. Kupferschmidt (eds). New York: Praeger, 1983. 383p.

Islamic society in practice. C. Fluehr-Lobban. Gainesville, FL: University Press of Florida, 1994. 201p.

Juridic structure of the Christian church in the Sudan: from the origin of Christianity in Nubia before and after the diffusion of Islam. C. L. Jömbi. Rome: Pontificia Universita Lateranense, 1987. 209p.

Land beyond the Nile. M. Forsberg. New York: Harper & Brothers, 1958. 232p. (Missionary account).

Mahdism and the Egyptian Sudan: being an account of the rise and progress of Mahdiism, and of subsequent events in the Sudan to the present time. F. R. Wingate. 2nd ed. London: Cass, 1968. 657p.

Nuer religion. E. E. Evans-Pritchard. Oxford, UK: Clarendon Press, 1956. 335p.

Peoples and cultures of Ethio–Sudan borderlands. M. L. Bender (ed). *Committee on Northeast African Studies*, no. 10. East Lansing, MI: African Studies Center, Michigan State University Press, 1981. 214p.

Religion and custom in a Muslim society: the Berti of Sudan. L. Holy. *Cambridge studies in social and cultural anthropology*, 78. Cambridge, UK: Cambridge University Press, 1991. 239p.

Religion and healing in Mandari. J. Buxton. Oxford, UK: Clarendon Press, 1973. 443p.

Religion and national integration in Africa: Islam, Christianity, and politics in the Sudan and Nigeria. J. O. Hunwick. *Series in Islam and society in Africa.* Evanston, IL: Northwestern University Press, 1992. 188p.

'Some aspects of the spread of Islam in the Nuba mountains,' R. C. Stevenson, in *Islam in tropical Africa*, p.208–32. I. M. Lewis (ed). London: Oxford University Press, 1966.

Southern Sudan: regionalism and religion: selected essays. M. O. Beshir (ed). Khartoum: Graduate College, University of Khartoum, 1984. (See especially P. C. Biowel's 'The Christian Church in the southern Sudan before 1900' and S. M. Sid Ahmed's 'Christian missionary activities in Sudan').

Sudan. M. W. Daly. 2nd ed. *World bibliographical series*, vol. 40. Oxford, UK: CLIO Press, 1992. 216p. (See especially chapters on 'Peoples' and 'Religion').

The Beja tribes of the Sudan. A. Paul. Cambridge, UK: Cambridge University Press, 1954.

The black book of the Southern Sudan: on the expulsion of the missionaries from Southern Sudan: an answer. , 1964. 217p. (A governmental defense).

The divine kingship of the Shilluk of the Nilotic Sudan. E. E. Evans-Pritchard. Cambridge, UK: University Press, 1948.

The last of the Nuba. L. Riefenstahl. London: Collins, 1976. 208p. (Mostly color photographs. On the Mesakin, an unevangelized people).

The listening ebony: moral knowledge, religion, and power among the Uduk of Sudan. W. James. Oxford, UK: Clarendon Press, 1988. 391p.

The Mahdist state in the Sudan, 1881–1898. P. M. Holt. London: Oxford University Press, 1958.

The people of Kau. L. Riefenstahl. London: Collins, 1976. 224p. (Mostly color photographs. On the unevangelized Kau Nuba or South-East Nuba).

The sorrow and hope of the Egyptian Sudan: a survey of missionary conditions and methods of work in the Egyptian Sudan. C. R. Watson. Philadelphia: Board of Foreign Missions of the United Presbyterian Church of North America, 1913. 228p.

'The Sudanese 'Mahdiyya' and the Niger–Chad region,' S. Biobaku & M. al-Hajj, in *Islam in tropical Africa: studies presented and discussed at the Fifth International African Seminar, Ahmadu Bello University, Zaria, January 1964*, p.226–39. I. M. Lewis (ed). 2nd ed. Bloomington, IN: International African Institute in association with Indiana University Press, 1988.

'The unreached people of Kau,' D. B. Barrett, in *Unreached peoples 1979.* C. P. Wagner & E. R. Dayton (eds). Elgin, IL: David C. Cook, 1978.

'The Verona Fathers in Southern Sudan from 1899 to 1964: a contribution to the understanding of the historical and religious roots of the conflict between North and South in the Sudan, and the role played in it by the Verona Fathers and Brothers.' N. Lo Polito. M.A. thesis, Catholic Theological Union, Chicago, 1986. 170p.

Through fire and water: 10 critical years in the life of the Church in the Southern Sudan, 1964–1974. O. Allison. London: Church Missionary Society, 1976. 110p. (By retired Anglican bishop).

'Two Nuba religions: an essay in comparison,' S. F. Nadel, *American anthropologist*, 57 (1955), 661–79.

Country Table 2. **Organized churches and denominations in Sudan.**

Official name (bold type = church with over 10% of all affiliated) 1	*Begun* 2	*Type* 3	*Counc* 4	*Congs* 5	*Adults* 6	*Affiliated 1970* 7	*Affiliated 1995* 8	*G%* 9	*Names, notes, and other statistics* (see Codebook, Part 3) 10
Africa Inland Church	1936	P-Non	xM..C	13	40,600	1,000	70,000	18.52	M=AIM(USA). Among Madi, Lotuka, Acholi. Obliterated in civil war. By 1977, 2f.
Armenian Apostolic Church (D Egypt)	c1900	O-Arm	Ew..K	1	350	400	580	1.50	Armenian residents, in north only. Under jurisdiction of AD Cairo. No priest.
Assemblies of God	1980	P-Pe2	.....	34	4,410	–	6,410	6.67	M=AoG. Mainline Pentecostals.
Baptist International Churches	c1975	I-Bap	.....	5	183	–	458	5.00	M=BIM(USA). Fundamentalists.
Catholic Church in the Sudan:	1842	R-Lat	P.SWS	133	1,286,000	687,768	2,780,381	5.75	*Catholikiyya.* 950 Greek Catholics. C=1+2+3. 79n 98x 189m 233w 44918Yy
M Juba	1927	R-Lat	Pmcci	36	219,000	350,000	415,323	0.69	In 1960, annual growth=15%. M=MCCI. 18n 2x 31m 18w 16581Yy
D Malakal	1933	R-Lat	Ps	18	20,000	21,221	42,300	2.80	In south, from Nile to Ethiopia. Shilluk, Nuer, Anuak. 7n 3x 3m 7w 1150Yy
D Rumbek	1955	R-Lat	Pmcci	3	19,000	30,190	35,000	0.59	Extreme south. Dinka. Life totally disrupted. 2n 4x 4m 0w 267Yy
D Tombura-Yambio (Mupoi)	1949	R-Lat	Ps	12	123,000	140,694	213,204	1.68	Azande. In 1960, G=25%pa. M=FSCJ. 1230z. 5n 2x 7m 29w 1605Yy
D Torit	1983	R-Lat	Pmcci	9	206,000	–	360,000	8.33	M=MCCI. 6n 5x 5m 6w 2200Yy
D Wau	1913	R-Lat	Ps	20	294,000	82,763	620,000	8.39	50% Jur, 20% Balanda, 15% Ndogo, 5% Dinka. 11n 8x 16m 17w 3461Yy
D Yei	1986	R-Lat	Ps	5	96,000	–	167,360	11.11	Formerly part of D Rumbek. 0n 0x 0m 0w 8720Yy
M Khartoum	1846	R-Lat	Ps	21	263,000	54,250	827,194	11.51	North. Mostly southerners. M=FSCJ/MCCI,PME. 24n 64x 112m 137w 9282Yy
D El Obeid	1960	R-Lat	Pmcci	9	46,000	8,650	100,000	10.29	North, southwest of Khartoum. M=FSCJ/MCCI. 6n 10x 11m 19w 1652Yy
Church of Christ in the Upper Nile	1900	P-Ref	RuAMK	60	6,000	7,000	15,000	3.10	*Presby Ch in Sudan.* M=UPUSA, expelled 1964-73. A=1956. Shilluk,Nuer. 8n,1f,1p.
Coptic Orthodox Church in the Sudan:	c 350	O-Cop	NwaNk	28	63,000	90,000	130,000	1.48	Under P Cairo. In Northern cities and towns; 800 Blacks, 1 Black priest.
D Khartoum & the South	1947	O-Cop	Na	15	33,000	50,000	70,000	1.35	Archbishop and 14 priests. 3 churches in Khartoum, others scattered across country.
D Omdurman & the North	1947	O-Cop	Na	13	30,000	40,000	60,000	1.64	Archbishop and 12 priests. Mostly Egyptians in Omdurman and along Nile river.
Episcopal Praisers	1957	I-3cA	.....	20	450	300	1,400	6.36	*Tore (Trumpeters).* Strivers. Revivalists among Kakwa, Kuku, split ex Anglicans.
Eternal Life Church	1977	I-3pA	.....	10	950	500	2,300	5.56	Split ex Episcopal Ch over healing campaigns. M=PEFA(Kenya). HQ Juba. 2n.
Ethiopian Orthodox Ch in the Sudan	1965	O-Eth	Nwa.K	10	14,000	15,000	17,000	0.50	Eritrean and Ethiopian refugees, across North and in NE. 1 primary school. 3x.
Evangelical Revival Church	1970	I-3pA	.....	50	1,400	800	3,700	6.32	Moru revivalists. Split ex Episcopal Ch after veto on traditional Moru music.
Greek Orth P Alexandria: D Nubia	c1000	O-Ara	Cw.MK	20	1,500	1,800	2,600	1.48	*D Nubia & Ptolemais.* Greeks, Cypriots. Decline from 5,000 in 1950. Bishop,5x,1r.
Hidden Muslim believers in Christ	c1950	I-Mus	.....	70	6,000	2,500	8,500	5.02	Converted Muslims who stay within Islam as witnesses to Christ.
Isolated radio churches	c1960	I-3rA	.....	1,600	50,000	4,000	100,000	13.74	Isolated Black and Arab radio believers, mainly aged 12-25. R=400(TWR,RVOG&c),T=1000(ICI).
Jehovah's Witnesses	c1945	m-Jeh	x....	4	230	200	767	5.52	*Watch Tower.* First active witnessing 1950. No recent baptisms; underground.
New Apostolic Church	c1960	I-3aX	x....	20	1,000	2,000	1,847	-0.32	*NAC.* M=Neuapostolische Kirche. HQ Zurich (Switzerland).
Presbyterian Church in the Sudan	1900	P-Ref	...MK	286	140,000	1,500	450,000	25.63	*Injili Church.* In North. Sudanese Arabs of Egyptian origin. M=UPUSA. 6n,1k,1p,4r.
Province of the Epis Ch of the Sudan	1899	A-Eva	AWAUK	1,143	1,217,000	300,000	2,100,000	8.09	12 Dioceses. M=CMS(UK),BCMS. Bari, Azande, Moru. 91n,2x,500m,14f,1h,2r,20000Yy.
Sudan Interior Church	1937	P-Non	xM..C	135	20,000	1,500	30,000	12.73	*CECS. Ev Ch of Eastern Sudan.* M=SIM(USA, UK). Uduk, Meban, Shilluk. 2n,5m,5f,1p.
Sudanese Church of Christ	1907	P-Non	C	63	57,900	53,000	100,000	2.57	In Nuba Mountains. 1920-62, M=SUM(UK, Australia). Koalib, Moro, Otoro.
Seventh-day Adventist Church	1953	P-Adv	x....	21	1,932	30	3,860	21.44	*SDA, Sudan Station,* Middle East Division. Small expatriate group in Khartoum.
Trinity Presbyterian Ch of Sudan	1986	I-Ref	.....	310	7,266	–	16,474	11.11	*TPCOS.* Schism ex PCOS. In North Sudan and Upper Nile Province.
Other Protestant denominations		P-	.....	60	4,000	1,000	7,000	0.05	Including Baptists, Churches of Christ (CMF), and other in the South.
Doubly-affiliated		2-aff			-699,000	0	-1,398,277		Evangelicals and Pentecostals who are also baptized Catholics or Orthodox.
Totals				**4,096**	**2,225,171**	**1,170,298**	**4,450,000**		

Churches, members, growth, 1900-2025	*Congs*	*Adults*	*Affiliated*	*G%*	*Total denominations*	*6 Megablocs:* *O*	*R*	*A*	*P*	*I*	*m*
Total churches, members, and denominations (mid-1900)	20	1,200	2,375	9.26	6	3	1	1	1	0	0
Total churches, members, and denominations (mid-1970)	1,086	589,128	1,170,298	9.26	26	4	1	1	13	6	1
Total churches, members, and denominations (mid-1990)	3,600	1,937,000	3,873,700	6.17	37	4	1	1	22	8	1
Total churches, members, and denominations (mid-1995)	4,096	2,225,171	4,450,000	2.81	37	4	1	1	22	8	1
Total churches, members, and denominations (mid-2000)	4,400	2,437,000	4,874,391	1.84	37	4	1	1	22	8	1
Total churches, members, and denominations (mid-2025)	7,000	4,246,000	8,492,000	2.25	83	10	1	1	40	30	1

NOTES ON TABLE ABOVE
NATIONAL COUNCILS (Column 4, 5th letter).
C = New Sudan Council of Churches (NSCC).
E = Sudanese Evangelical Christian Association (SECA), 1973.
K = Sudan Council of Churches (SCC) (Maglis al Kanayis fi Sudan).
k = formerly full member of SCC, withdrew temporarily in 1976.
S = Sudan Episcopal Conference (SEC), also member of SCC.

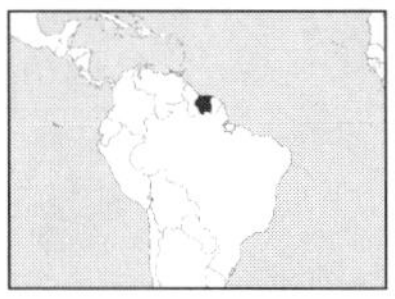

SURINAME

SECULAR DATA, AD 2000

STATE
Official name: Het Republiek Suriname/The Republic of Suriname.
Short name: Suriname. **Adjective of nationality:** Surinamese.
Flag: Stripes of green, white, red, white, and green with yellow star in centre.
Area: 163,820 sq. km. (63,251 sq. mi.).
Government: Parliamentary state, since 1975 (1651 British settlement, 1667 Dutch colony, 1815 Dutch Guiana, 1954 autonomous territory of the Netherlands, 1975 Independence, 1987 new constitution).
Legislature: National Assembly, 51 members.
Official language: Dutch (Nederlands-Vlaams).
Monetary unit: 1 Suriname guilder (Sf) = 100 cents. **US$1=** Sf 401.00.
Chief cities: PARAMARIBO 275,181; Wanica 62,800.
Political divisions: 10 provinces.
Armed forces: 1,400.

DEMOGRAPHY
Population: 417,000.
Population density: 2.5/sq. km. (6.5/sq. mi.).
Under 15 years: 127,000.
Growth rate p.a.: 0.48% (births 18.87, deaths 5.98).
Mortality: Infant, per 1,000: 25.6; **Maternal per 100,000:** 100.0.
Life expectancy: 71 (male 69, female 74).
Household size: 3.9. **Floor area per person, sq.m:** 7.0.
Major languages: Dutch, English, Sranang Tongo (Sranan) (Surinamese), Hindustani, Javanese, Chinese, Arawak, Carib, Arabic, and 10 smaller languages.
Urban dwellers: 52.25%. **Urban growth rate p.a.:** 2.1%.
Labor force: 48%.

ETHNOLINGUISTIC PEOPLES
27.8% Caribbean Hindi; 26.2% Surinamese Creole; 13.1% Guyanese; 12.7% Caribbean Javanese; 5.8% Saramaccan Bush Negro.

ECONOMY
National income p.a. per person: US$879; **per family:** US$3,431.

EDUCATION
Adult literacy: 93% (male 95%, female 91%). **Schools:** 454.
Universities: 1. **School enrolment:** female/male: 70%/70%.

HEALTH
Access to health services: 40%. **Access to safe water:** 72%.
Hospitals: 40 (47 beds per 10,000). **Doctors:** 329.
Blind: 1,300. **Deaf:** 27,100. **Murder rate:** 7.
Lepers: 3,700.

LITERATURE
New book titles p.a.: 17 (40 p.a. per million). **Periodicals:** 7.
Newspapers: 3 dailies.

COMMUNICATION (per 1,000 people)
Phones: 123 (10% mobile). **Radios:** 609. **TV sets:** 186.
Daily newspaper circulation: 103. **Computers:** 15.

HUMAN LIFE AND LIBERTY (optimum condition=100.0%)
HDI: 79.2. **HSI:** 45.0. **HFI:** 15.0. **EFL:** 22.0.

Country status. Suriname is on the tropical Atlantic coast of northern South America. Three-quarters of its exports are based on bauxite mining. Timber is also important.

HUMAN LIFE AND LIBERTY

Human need and development. Suriname is a country rich in resources, but still poor in its standard of living. Marginalized for many decades as a colony of the Netherlands, its development has been erratic, and punctuated by military interventions in politics. The flow of aid from the Netherlands, the major source of national income other than bauxite mining, has been reduced to a trickle since the last military coup in 1990. About 90% of the country is still forested, and human settlements are limited to the coast and to the capital city of Paramaribo. The Indians of the interior lead a sub-civilized life and shun contacts with the rest of the country.

Human rights and freedoms. The restoration of democracy in Suriname for the second time in the early 1990s was followed by a lull in the civil unrest that has plagued the country since independence. Incidents of new human rights abuses are few but the government has not taken any action to investigate abuses under earlier regimes. The corruption of the judiciary under the military regime has been checked by the new rulers. The court and legal systems are based on the Dutch model and afford reasonable protection against official highhandedness. Freedom of speech is respected although journalists continue to fear reprisals from the military. The Maroons and Amerindians living in the interior experience some form of discrimination and are excluded from the political process. The National Institute of Human Rights, funded by the government, is widely regarded as ineffective.

Human environment. Some 92% of the land area is forested, and the nation's forests and wildlife have suffered less depradation than those in any other country in the Americas. The rate of deforestation is the lowest in the world. The coastal swamps and mangroves are unattractive for tourists and thus have escaped development. The interior is unspoiled primeval forest with only a limited human presence and virtually no roads. The neotropical Amazonian forests contain a wide range of flora and fauna —674 species of birds, 200 species of mammals, 130 species of reptiles, and 99 species of amphibians.

NON-CHRISTIAN RELIGIONS

Islam is represented by the Surinam Muslim Association (Surinaamse Islamitisch-Vereniging), with its seat at Paramaribo. Muslims are Javanese, East Indians, and Syro-Lebanese.

Hinduism is found in 2 branches: Arya Dewaker, an orthodox group which maintains the caste system; and Sanathan Dharm, a group with modernizing tendencies under Western influence, which has abandoned the caste system.

Country Table 1. **Religious adherents in Suriname, AD 1900-2025.**

Year	1900		1970		mid-1990		Annual change, 1990-2000				mid-1995		mid-2000		mid-2025	
Name	Adherents	%	Adherents	%	Adherents	%	Natural	Conversion	Total	Rate	Adherents	%	Adherents	%	Adherents	%
Christians	**35,100**	**46.2**	**187,000**	**50.2**	**201,400**	**50.1**	**767**	**113**	**880**	**0.43**	**205,620**	**50.3**	**210,203**	**50.4**	**275,000**	**52.4**
PROFESSION																
professing Christians	**35,100**	**46.2**	**187,000**	**50.2**	**201,400**	**50.1**	**767**	**113**	**880**	**0.43**	**205,620**	**50.3**	**210,203**	**50.4**	**275,000**	**52.4**
AFFILIATION																
unaffiliated Christians	2,000	2.6	29,371	7.9	33,420	8.3	125	320	445	1.26	35,390	8.7	37,869	9.1	62,200	11.9
affiliated Christians	**33,100**	**43.6**	**157,629**	**42.3**	**167,980**	**41.8**	**611**	**-176**	**435**	**0.26**	**170,230**	**41.6**	**172,334**	**41.3**	**212,800**	**40.5**
Roman Catholics	18,000	23.7	80,000	21.5	89,400	22.2	334	26	360	0.40	91,000	22.3	93,000	22.3	120,000	22.9
Protestants	15,000	19.7	74,679	20.1	72,000	17.9	269	-336	-67	-0.09	71,935	17.6	71,334	17.1	80,000	15.2
Marginal Christians	0	0.0	1,000	0.3	3,500	0.9	13	77	90	2.31	4,000	1.0	4,400	1.1	7,000	1.3
Independents	0	0.0	950	0.3	2,250	0.6	8	47	55	2.21	2,473	0.6	2,800	0.7	5,000	1.0
Anglicans	100	0.1	1,000	0.3	830	0.2	3	-6	-3	-0.37	822	0.2	800	0.2	800	0.2
Trans-megabloc groupings																
Evangelicals	12,000	15.8	7,400	2.0	10,100	2.5	38	122	160	1.48	10,905	2.7	11,700	2.8	17,000	3.2
Pentecostals/Charismatics	0	0.0	800	0.2	9,000	2.2	34	176	210	2.12	10,033	2.5	11,100	2.7	17,000	3.2
Great Commission Christians	**4,600**	**6.1**	**41,000**	**11.0**	**66,300**	**16.5**	**247**	**218**	**465**	**0.68**	**68,700**	**16.8**	**70,952**	**17.0**	**100,000**	**19.1**
Hindus	20,100	26.5	60,000	16.1	72,700	18.1	271	-100	171	0.23	73,600	18.0	74,413	17.8	80,000	15.2
Muslims	7,600	10.0	79,000	21.2	59,130	14.7	221	-349	-128	-0.22	58,500	14.3	57,850	13.9	66,700	12.7
Nonreligious	0	0.0	3,650	1.0	18,000	4.5	67	145	212	1.12	18,800	4.6	20,117	4.8	32,250	6.1
New-Religionists	0	0.0	0	0.0	18,600	4.6	69	74	143	0.74	19,200	4.7	20,026	4.8	30,000	5.7
Spiritists	1,500	2.0	11,000	3.0	13,500	3.4	50	76	126	0.90	13,900	3.4	14,760	3.5	20,000	3.8
Ethnoreligionists	10,640	14.0	26,000	7.0	8,500	2.1	32	-75	-43	-0.52	8,300	2.0	8,070	1.9	6,000	1.1
Baha'is	0	0.0	3,000	0.8	6,000	1.5	22	20	42	0.69	6,200	1.5	6,424	1.5	9,000	1.7
Buddhists	460	0.6	1,000	0.3	2,000	0.5	7	40	47	2.13	2,300	0.6	2,470	0.6	2,500	0.5
Chinese folk-religionists	400	0.5	600	0.2	720	0.2	3	36	39	4.40	1,000	0.2	1,108	0.3	950	0.2
Jews	200	0.3	650	0.2	750	0.2	3	-1	2	0.20	760	0.2	765	0.2	1,000	0.2
Atheists	0	0.0	0	0.0	300	0.1	1	18	19	4.94	400	0.1	486	0.1	800	0.2
Other religionists	0	0.0	100	0.0	400	0.1	1	3	4	0.89	420	0.1	437	0.1	800	0.2
World A (unevangelized persons)	31,996	42.1	93,075	25.0	66,330	16.5	248	-111	137	0.20	67,082	16.4	67,554	16.2	59,850	11.4
World B (evangelized non-Christians)	8,904	11.7	92,225	24.8	134,270	33.4	499	-2	497	0.36	136,336	33.3	139,243	33.4	190,150	36.2
World C (Christians)	35,100	46.2	187,000	50.2	201,400	50.1	767	113	880	0.43	205,620	50.3	210,203	50.4	275,000	52.4
Country's population	**76,000**	**100.0**	**372,300**	**100.0**	**402,000**	**100.0**	**1,514**	**0**	**1,514**	**0.37**	**409,039**	**100.0**	**417,000**	**100.0**	**525,000**	**100.0**

COLUMNS, ROWS.
For meanings and definitions, see Codebook (Part 3). Note that, by definition, total 'Christians' = professing + crypto-Christians, which also = affiliated + unaffiliated Christians, and also = Great Commission Christians + latent Christians. Percentages may not always total exactly, due to rounding.

CENSUSES.
Percentages have fluctuated considerably from year to year due to continuous immigration and emigration. **1960:** 26.1% Protestants, 25.2% Muslims, 24.5% Hindus, 20.9% Roman Catholics, 2.2% ethnoreligionists, 0.9% Chinese folk-religionists and Buddhists, 0.2% Jews. **1961:** 25.7% Protestants, 24.7% Hindus, 24.5% Muslims, 21.6% Roman Catholics, 2.4% ethnoreligionists, 0.8% Chinese folk-religionists and Buddhists, 0.3% Jews. **1962:** 24.9% Protestants, 24.3% Hindus, 23.2% Muslims, 21.3% Roman Catholics, 5.3% ethnoreligionists, 0.8% Chinese folk-religionists and Buddhists, 0.2% Jews. **31.III.1964:** 27.0% Hindus, 25.0% Protestants, 21.9% Roman Catholics, 19.7% Muslims, 5.6% ethnoreligionists, 0.8% other religionists.

NOTES ON RELIGIONS
BAHA'IS. Rapid growth in local spiritual assemblies, from none in 1964, to 23 in 1973. Converts from Hinduism and Islam added to its appeal and by 1996 there were 45 LSAs.
BUDDHISTS. Chinese, first arriving as contract workers after 1863, then staying on as shopkeepers in rural areas.
COUNTRY'S POPULATION. Before 1960, the annual rate of growth had reached a high peak of 4.34% per year. Due to the heavy emigration to the Netherlands during 1964-75 it fell to 2.57% per year (1970-75), then after Independence in 1975 increased again with a rate of 3.45% per year for 1980-85, dropping after 1990 to 1.2% per annum.
ETHNORELIGIONISTS. Shamanism is practiced among pagan Bush Negroes (Heiden-Bosnegers, 16,875 in the 1964 census) and among many of the 7,400 lowland or jungle Amerindians, especially among the Caribs and in the interior.
HINDUS. Hindustani-speaking East Indians (mainly small farmers), with 2 branches: Arya Dewaker (orthodox), and Sanathan Dharm (modernizing). Steadily-increasing emigration (62,700 from 1964-71, and a total of 80,000 from 1965-75) culminated in an exodus of 12,000 a month in 1975 to the Netherlands before Independence, leaving only a small Hindu minority. In the column 'Natural change', this emigration is included, averaged over the decade 1990-2000.
INDEPENDENTS. In about 3 Black and Amerindian groups in 1995. (see Table 2).
JEWS. Two communities, Dutch and Portuguese, originally refugees in 1639 from persecution in Brazil.
MUSLIMS. In 3 groups: Javanese (Shafiite Sunnis) from Indonesia who form 14% of the population, mainly as small farmers; East Indians (Hindustanis); and Syro-Lebanese. There is also an Ahmadiya Mission (enumerated here although declared non-Muslim by Pakistan). Begun 1956; Qadianis (world HQ Rabwah, Pakistan).
OTHER RELIGIONISTS. Including Rosicrucians (1 AMORC center).
SPIRITISTS. Bush Negroes follow Winti and other cults derived from Ashanti religion (from Ghana). There are also many followers of Vodoun and Obeah.

Great Commission Instrument Panel: status of Suriname (for explanation see start of Part 4)

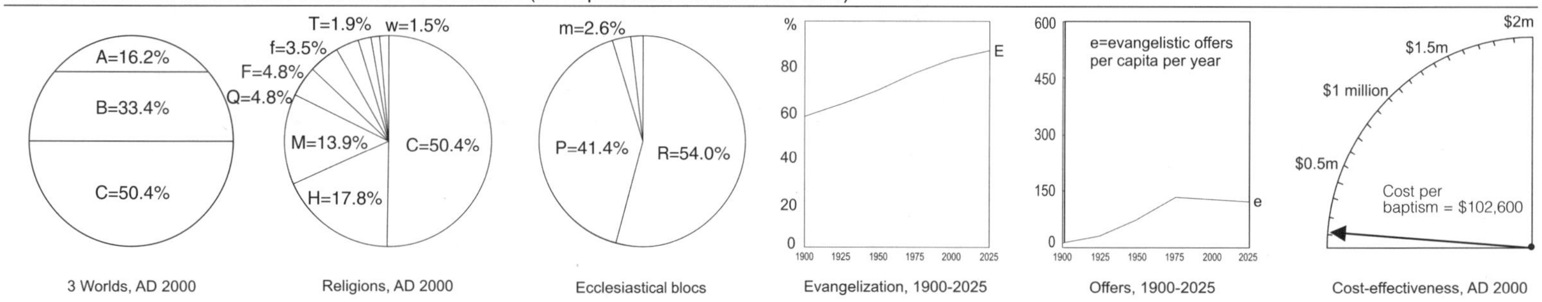

Traditional tribal religions of shamanistic type are still practiced by Bush Negroes and jungle Amerindians.

Judaism exists among 2 European groups, the Portuguese Israelite Community (Portugueese-Israelitische Gemeente) and the Dutch Israelite Community (Nederlands-Israelitische Gemeente).

CHRISTIANITY

CATHOLIC CHURCH. Although Catholic priests resided briefly in Surinam during 1682-86 and 1786-93, work of a permanent nature was not begun until 1817. At that time a prefecture was established which was elevated to vicariate in 1852. Redemptorists and Oblates (OMI) arrived in 1865 and devoted themselves to the development of schools and charitable institutions, in addition to parish activity. The diocese of Paramaribo, which covers the whole of Surinam, was erected in 1958.

The Roman Catholic Church covers most ethnic groups; 60% are of mixed race. More than 80% of Amerindians have received Catholic baptism.

The Holy See has diplomatic relations with Suriname and in AD 2000 is represented to government and the Catholic hierarchy by a nuncio residing in Port of Spain.

PROTESTANT CHURCHES. The most significant Protestant work has been carried on by Moravians who established their first congregation in 1735. The EBGS is considered by many to be the national church of Surinam, with the majority of Bush Negroes and numbers of Mestizos belonging to it. The Dutch Reformed and Lutheran churches were also formed in the 18th century. The former consists almost exclusively of Dutch settlers, while the latter counts in its membership a substantial Creole community. Twentieth-century arrivals since World War I include the Wesleyan Church, Salvation Army, Assemblies of God and Seventh-day Adventists, with several other North American missions arriving after World War II.

OTHER CHURCHES. Anglicans have been represented in Surinam since the 19th century. Surinam belongs to the diocese of Guyana of the Church of the Province of the West Indies. The African Methodist Episcopal Church also joins administratively its work in Guyana and Surinam, through a single annual conference. In addition, there is a small Old Catholic Church and an active Jehovah's Witnesses Community.

Indigenous missions. Very few missionaries have been sent out from Suriname and most of these have served in the Netherlands.

CHURCH AND STATE

Unlike the Netherlands, Surinam has no law regarding religious societies. Any group wishing to receive government subsidies must acquire juridical personality and register as such. The state gives salaries to all bishops and to Protestant pastors, as well as to teachers of religion and a certain number of Catholic priests. As far as is financially possible, public and private education are treated on equal terms, but the state does not help in the construction of private schools. Religious education can be included in the schedule of classes of a school. There is no ministry or ministerial department charged with religious affairs.

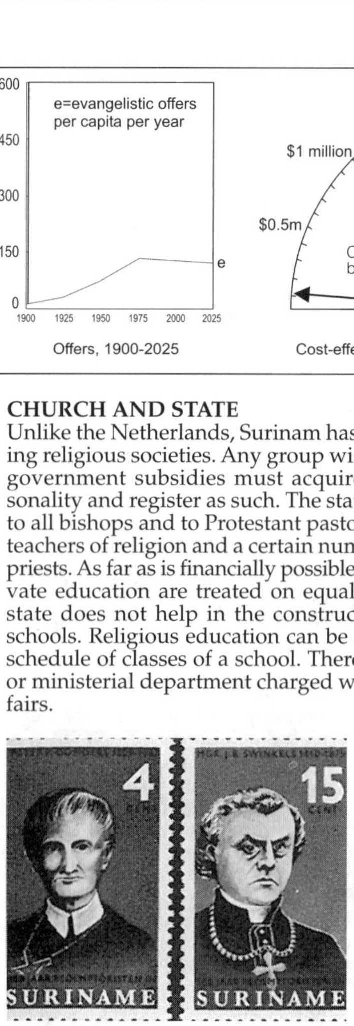

Catholic Church in Surinam. Postage stamp set commemorating Centenary of Redemptorists.

Country summary. **Worlds A, B, C by ethnolinguistic peoples, cities, and major civil divisions in Suriname.**

	PEOPLES							CITIES							CIVIL DIVISIONS						
World	*Num*	*Pop 2000*	*C%*	*Christians*	*E%*	*U%*	*Unevangelized*	*Num*	*Pop 2000*	*C%*	*Christians*	*E%*	*U%*	*Unevangelized*	*Num*	*Pop 2000*	*C%*	*Christians*	*E%*	*U%*	*Unevangelized*
A	4	2,936	8.11	238	44	56	1,654	0	0	0.00	0	0	0	0	0	0	0.00	0	0	0	0
B	9	187,826	14.36	26,975	65	35	65,234	1	275,181	55.00	151,350	94	6	15,245	10	417,130	41.31	172,334	84	16	67,699
C	15	226,368	64.11	145,124	100	0	810	0	0	0.00	0	0	0	0	0	0	0.00	0	0	0	0
Total	**28**	**417,130**	**41.31**	**172,337**	**84**	**16**	**67,698**	**1**	**275,181**	**55.00**	**151,350**	**94**	**6**	**15,245**	**10**	**417,130**	**41.31**	**172,334**	**84**	**16**	**67,699**

BROADCASTING AND MEDIA

Shortwave broadcasts from KNLS, TWR (Antilles), HCJB (Ecuador) and AWR (Costa Rica) can be received. Suriname is a member of UNDA, and Catholics broadcast 70 minutes of daily devotionals and weekly sermons on radio.

CBN's *700 Club* can be seen on Sunday in the evening throughout the country, and response is followed up from a volunteer center. Other Christian television programs can be received via satellite. Catholic World News from the Lumen 2000 program is aired on TV for 30 minutes each Sunday, and the Eucharist is aired 4 times yearly on major holidays.

Some 30,000 have seen the 'Jesus' Film as a result of film team, with. 2,100 responses.

March for Jesus proceeds through streets of Paramaribo, 1996. Flag is that of Bible Society.

INTERDENOMINATIONAL ORGANIZATIONS

The Surinam Christian Council of Churches (Comite Christelijke Kerken), founded about 1960, includes in its membership the Moravian, Catholic, Dutch Reformed, and Lutheran churches. It provides for mutual recognition of baptisms, settlement of difficulties concerning mixed marriages, exchanges of preachers, and other matters of mutual concern. The Christian Pedagogical Institute (Christelijk Peadagogisch Institut), established in 1970, is responsible for the training of Christian teachers. This institute, which is a remarkable example of ecumenical collaboration in the domain of education, is under the direction of 2 bishops (Moravian and Roman Catholic). Classes on nonreligious matters are held in common, while religious instruction is given by priests or pastors to each's own religious group.

FUTURE TRENDS AND PROSPECTS

Muslims are expected to decline to 12.7% by 2025 and Hindus to 15.2% in the same period. Christianity could grow to 52.4%.

Hinduism and Islam are expected to decline in the 21st century, perhaps as low as 20% together, allowing Christianity to grow to over 60% by AD 2050.

Evangelical Church of the West Indies. *Top.* Sunday service with translation into 3 Amerindian tribal languages. *Above.* Conference bringing together 4 Amerindian tribes.

BIBLIOGRAPHY

'About the original religion of the Creoles in Suriname.' J. Schoffelmeer. *Mededelingen van het Surinaams Museum*, no. 38 (December 1982) 6-48; no. 39 (April 1983) 4-65.

An inquiry into the animism and folklore of the Guiana Indians. W. E. Roth. 1915; reprint, New York: Johnson Reprint Corp., [1970]. 453p.

'Animism and Islam among the Javanese in Surinam,' A. De Waal Malefijt, *Anthropological quarterly*, 37, 3 (1964), 149–55.

'Bakuu: possessing spirits of witchcraft on the Tapanahony,' D. Vernon, *Nieuwe West–Indische Gids*, 54, 1 (1980), 1–38.

Bibliografie van Suriname. W. Gordijn. Amsterdam: Nederlandse Stichting voor Culturele Samenwerking met Suriname en de Nederlandse Antillen, 1972. 256p. (Section on religion).

Bonuman: een studie van zeven religieuze specialisten in Suriname. R. A. J. van Lier. Leiden: Instituut voor Culturele Antropologie en Sociologie der Niet-Westernse volken, 1983. 132p. (Discusses religious specialists' relation to Christianity).

Evolving culture: a cross–cultural study of Suriname, West Africa and the Caribbean. C. J. Wooding. Washington, DC: University Press of America, 1981. 329p. (Treats Winti cult).

Historische foto's van de R. K. Gemeente in Suriname. A. C. Schalken. Paramaribo: Leo Victor, 1983. 211p.

Indianen en kerken in Suriname: identiteit en autonomie in het binnenland. J. Vernooij. Paramaribo: Stichting Wetenschappelijke Informatie, 1989. 178p.

'Nieuwe religieuze bewegingen,' J. Vernooij, *SWI forum*, 3, 2 (1986–87), 24–46.

Onderweg van afhankelijkheid naar zelfstandigheid: 250 jaar Hernhutterzending in Suriname 1735–1985. J. Fontaine (ed). Zutphen, Netherlands: De Walburg Pers, 1985. 143p.

'Pandits, power and profit: religious organization and the construction of identity among Surinamese Hindus,' C. van der Burg & P. van der Veer, *Ethnic and racial studies*, 9, 4 (1986), 514–28.

'Perseverance of African beliefs in the religious ideas of the Bosnegers in Surinam,' B. E. Bekier, *Hemispheres*, no. 1 (1985), 93–108.

'Philosophy, initiation and myths of the Indians of Guiana and adjacent countries,' C. H. de Goeje, in *Internationales Archiv für Ethnographie*, p.1–136, vol. 44. W. D. van Nieuwenhuis et al. (eds). Leiden: E. J. Brill, 1943.

Protestantse zendingsperiodieken uit de negentiende en twintigste eeuw in Nederland, Nederlands–indie, Suriname en de Nederlandse Antillen: een bibliografische catalogus met inleiding (Protestant missionary periodicals from the nineteenth and twentieth century in the Netherlands, the Dutch East Indies and the Dutch West Indies: a bibliographical catalogue with introduction). J. A. B. Jongeneel. Leiden: Interuniversitair Instituut voor Missiologie en Oecumenica, 1990. 145p.

Secularisatie en zending in Suriname: over het secularisatie proces in verband met het zendingswerk van de Evangelische Broedergemeente in Suriname. J. van Raalte. Wageningen, Netherlands: H. Veenman, 1973. 276p.

Suriname. R. Hoefte. *World bibliographical series*, vol. 117. Oxford, UK: CLIO Press, 1990. 260p. (See especially 'Religion,' p.111–6).

Suriname, land of seven peoples: social mobility in a plural society: an ethnohistoriographical study. F. E. M. Mitrasing. Paramaribo: Mitrasing, 1979. 176p.

'The Christian churches of Surinam,' J. Vernooij, *Exchange*, 10, 29 (1981), 16–31.

The good news on the wild coast: highlights of the early efforts of the Catholic Church in Guiana, 1650's to 1850's. J. Bridges. Arima, Trinidad: St. Dominic Press. 84p.

'The Javanese in Surinam: ethnicity in an ethnically plural society.' P. Suparlan. Ph.D. dissertation, University of Illinois, Urbana–Champaign, 1976. 390p.

'The Paramacca Maroons: a study in religious acculturation.' J. D. Lenoir. Ph.D. dissertation, New School for Social Research, New York, 1973. 213p.

'The Winti cult in the Para District,' C. J. Wooding, *Caribbean studies*, 12, 1 (April 1972), 51–78.

'Witchcraft among the Tapanahoni Djuka,' W. van Wetering, in *Maroon societies: rebel slave communities in the Americas*, p.370–88. R. Price (ed). Garden City, NY: Anchor Press/Doubleday, 1973.

Country Table 2. **Organized churches and denominations in Suriname.**

Official name (bold type = church with over 10% of all affiliated) 1	*Begun* 2	*Type* 3	*Counc* 4	*Congs* 5	*Adults* 6	*Affiliated 1970* 7	*Affiliated 1995* 8	*G%* 9	*Names, notes, and other statistics* (see Codebook, Part 3) 10
African Methodist Episcopal Church		I-Met	VwM..	2	178	300	270	0.05	*Guyana-Surinam Annual Conference*, 16th Episcopal District. M=AMEC(USA). Blacks on coast.
Anglican Church (D Guyana)	c1840	A-ACa	awMR.	2	411	1,000	822	-0.78	Part of Church of the Province of the West Indies (CPWI). Mainly Black immigrants.
Assemblies of God	1958	P-Pe2	ZF...	7	480	500	700	1.35	M=AoG(USA). Classical Pentecostals (2-stage). 1n,4f.
Associated Baptist Churches	c1955	P-Bap	.....	2	370	250	617	3.68	Mainline Baptists from USA and Europe.
Catholic Church: D Paramaribo	1683	R-Lat	PzNMC	22	50,000	80,000	91,000	0.52	*Rooms-Cath Kerk.* 3,360 Chinese. C=2+1+3. 4n, 18x, 29m, 42w, 2173Yy
Christian and Missionary Alliance	1979	P-Hol	.....	2	240	–	343	6.25	M=CMA. Chinese and Hmong.
Church of God (Cleveland)	1982	P-Pe3	.....	2	100	–	182	7.69	M=CoG(Cleveland)(USA).
Church of the Nazarene	1984	P-Hol	.....	4	300	–	425	9.09	M=CoN. Nazarenes.
Dutch Reformed Church	c1750	P-Ref	C	9	3,640	10,500	6,500	-1.90	*Nederlandse Hervormde Gemeente.* Dutch officials, settlers. No inland missions. 3x.
Evangelical Church of the West Indies	1955	P-Eva	xM...	14	1,100	1,000	2,440	3.63	M=WIM(USA),IM,DTLM(USA),Surinam Interior Fellowship. Bush Negroes, Indians. 32f.
Evangelical Lutheran Ch in Surinam	1741	P-Lut	lv..C	7	2,200	4,750	4,000	-0.69	*Evangelisch-Lutherse Gemeente.* Dutch Creoles. 1967 applied to join WCC. 1x,79Yy.
Evangelical Methodist Ch in Guiana	1956	P-Hol	.T...	5	350	500	583	0.62	Bible Methodists. Fundamentalists. M=EMC(USA). HQ Paramaribo. 2x,4f.
God's Bazuin	c1965	I-3cL	.....	2	360	100	600	7.43	Latin American grassroots charismatics.
Jehovah's Witnesses	c1915	m-Jeh	x....	23	1,539	1,000	4,000	5.70	*Getuigen van Jehovah. Watch Tower.* Witnessing under way by 1929. (1975) 19Y. (1995) 118Y.
Moravian Church in Surinam	1735	P-Mor	xWM.C	55	34,900	52,180	47,745	-0.35	*EBGS. Surinam Province*/UoB. M=ZZG,DLM. 50% Bush Negroes, 30% Javanese. 53nx,3H,1s.
New Apostolic Church	c1980	I-3aX	x....	10	500	–	863	6.67	*NAC.* M=Neuapostolische Kirche. HQ Zurich (Switzerland).
Old Catholic Church		I-OCa	U....	1	20	50	40	0.05	Community of Dutch Old Catholics related to Church of Utrecht (Netherlands).
Pentecostal Mission	c1970	P-Pe2	.....	2	160	–	320	25.95	mainline Pentecostals.
Salvation Army	1926	P-Sal	xwM..	3	300	500	600	0.73	*SA, Surinam Region*, Caribbean & CAmerica Territory (HQ Kingston, Jamaica).
Seventh-day Adventist Church	1945	P-Adv	x....	11	2,097	2,000	3,000	1.64	*SDA, Surinam Mission*, Caribbean Union Conference. 2nx,27mw,12t(648),113Y.
United Baptist Church	1971	P-Bap	.....	3	123	–	410	4.17	M=FMB-SBC. Southern Baptist Convention, USA.
Wesleyan Church	c1920	P-Hol	VF...	16	700	499	1,070	3.10	*Pilgrim Holiness Ch.* M=WC(USA). Bush Negroes. 6n,1x,2f,W=24%,13Y.
Other Protestant denominations		P-	.....	30	1,500	2,000	3,000	0.05	Total about 8 (see list below).
Other indigenous churches		I-	.....	3	280	500	700	0.05	Aramawali: Waiyana prophet Ridima (1963,ex WIM) who built skyboats, airstrip; &c.

Continued overleaf

Country Table 2–concluded

Official name (bold type = church with over 10% of affiliated) 1	*Begun* 2	*Type* 3	*Counc* 4	*Congs* 5	*Adults* 6	*Affiliated 1970* 7	*Affiliated 1995* 8	*G%* 9	*Names, notes, and other statistics* (see Codebook, Part 3) 10
Totals				**237**	**101,848**	**157,629**	**170,230**		

Churches, members, growth, 1900-2025	*Congs*	*Adults*	*Affiliated*	*G%*	*Total denominations*	*6 Megablocs:* *O*	*R*	*A*	*P*	*I*	*m*
Total churches, members, and denominations (mid-1900)	50	16,000	33,100	2.25	5	0	1	1	3	0	0
Total churches, members, and denominations (mid-1970)	252	76,411	157,629	2.25	21	0	1	1	14	4	1
Total churches, members, and denominations (mid-1990)	240	101,000	167,980	0.32	33	0	1	1	23	7	1
Total churches, members, and denominations (mid-1995)	237	101,848	170,230	0.27	33	0	1	1	23	7	1
Total churches, members, and denominations (mid-2000)	250	103,000	172,334	0.25	33	0	1	1	23	7	1
Total churches, members, and denominations (mid-2025)	400	127,000	212,800	0.85	68	0	1	1	35	30	1

NOTES ON TABLE ABOVE
NATIONAL COUNCILS (Column 4, 5th letter).
C = Committee of Christian Churches in Surinam (CCCS).

SVALBARD & JAN MAYEN ISLANDS

SECULAR DATA, AD 2000

STATE
Official name: Svalbard & Jan Mayen Islands.
Short name: Svalbard & Jan Mayen Islands. **Adjective of nationality:** Svalbard & Jan Mayen Islanders.
Flag: That of Norway.
Area: 62,160 sq. km. (24,000 sq. mi.).
Government: Overseas area of Norway, since 1925 (1596 Dutch claim, 1920 Norwegian sovereignty, 1925 part of Norway).
Legislature: Norwegian provincial government.
Official language: Norwegian (Norsk).
Monetary unit: 1 Norwegian krone (NKr) = 100 øre. **US$1=** NKr 7.40.
Chief cities: LONGYEARBYEN (Longyear City) 603.
Political divisions: 1 province.

DEMOGRAPHY
Population: 4,000.
Population density: 0.3/sq. km. (0.1/sq. mi.).
Under 15 years: 1,000.
Growth rate p.a.: 0.45% (births 12.23, deaths 9.97).
Mortality: Infant, per 1,000: 4.9; **Maternal per 100,000:** 10.0.
Life expectancy: 79 (male 76, female 82).
Household size: 2.0. **Floor area per person, sq.m:** 25.0.
Major languages: Norwegian, Russian.
Urban dwellers: 80.00%. **Urban growth rate p.a.:** 0.00%.
Labor force: 45%.

ETHNOLINGUISTIC PEOPLES
57.8% Russian; 41.9% Norwegian.

ECONOMY
National income p.a. per person: US$16,050; **per family:** US$32,100.

EDUCATION
Adult literacy: 100% (male 100%, female 100%). **Schools:** 1.
Universities: 0. **School enrolment:** female/male: 90%/90%.

HEALTH
Access to health services: 85%. **Access to safe water:** 85%.
Hospitals: 1 (50 beds per 10,000). **Doctors:** 10.
Blind: 15. **Deaf:** 200. **Murder rate:** 2.
Lepers: 0.

LITERATURE
New book titles p.a.: 1 (300 p.a. per million). **Periodicals:** 0.
Newspapers: 0 dailies.

COMMUNICATION (per 1,000 people)
Phones: 100 (25% mobile). **Radios:** 1,000. **TV sets:** 150.
Daily newspaper circulation: 0. **Computers:** 1,000.

HUMAN LIFE AND LIBERTY (optimum condition=100.0%)
HDI: 80.0. **HSI:** 90.0. **HFI:** 80.0. **EFL:** 50.0.

Country Table 1. **Religious adherents in Svalbard & Jan Mayen Islands, AD 1900-2025.**

Year	*1900*		*1970*		*mid-1990*		*Annual change, 1990-2000*				*mid-1995*		*mid-2000*		*mid-2025*	
Name	*Adherents*	*%*	*Adherents*	*%*	*Adherents*	*%*	*Natural*	*Conversion*	*Total*	*Rate*	*Adherents*	*%*	*Adherents*	*%*	*Adherents*	*%*
Christians	**480**	**96.0**	**1,300**	**74.5**	**1,600**	**53.3**	**53**	**-21**	**32**	**1.85**	**1,840**	**52.6**	**1,922**	**52.3**	**2,250**	**47.9**
PROFESSION																
professing Christians	**480**	**96.0**	**1,300**	**74.5**	**1,600**	**53.3**	**53**	**-21**	**32**	**1.85**	**1,840**	**52.6**	**1,922**	**52.3**	**2,250**	**47.9**
AFFILIATION																
unaffiliated Christians	30	6.0	0	0.0	150	5.0	5	-3	2	1.44	175	5.0	173	4.7	170	3.6
affiliated Christians	**450**	**90.0**	**1,300**	**74.5**	**1,450**	**48.3**	**48**	**-18**	**30**	**1.89**	**1,665**	**47.6**	**1,749**	**47.2**	**2,080**	**44.3**
Protestants	450	90.0	1,000	57.3	850	28.3	28	-13	15	1.64	975	27.9	1,000	27.0	1,100	23.4
Orthodox	0	0.0	300	17.2	600	20.0	20	-5	15	2.24	690	19.7	749	20.2	980	20.9
Trans-megabloc groupings																
Evangelicals	200	40.0	100	5.7	140	4.7	5	-4	1	0.69	146	4.2	150	3.8	180	3.8
Pentecostals/Charismatics	0	0.0	10	0.6	65	2.2	2	1	3	3.87	85	2.4	95	2.4	200	4.3
Great Commission Christians	**40**	**8.0**	**420**	**24.1**	**850**	**28.3**	**28**	**-6**	**22**	**2.29**	**1,000**	**28.6**	**1,066**	**28.8**	**1,410**	**30.0**
Nonreligious	20	4.0	400	22.9	1,400	46.7	14	21	35	2.28	1,660	47.4	1,754	47.7	2,450	52.1
World A (unevangelized persons)	1	0.2	205	11.8	30	1.0	1	-2	-1	-2.62	24	0.7	24	0.6	20	0.4
World B (evangelized non-Christians)	19	3.8	239	13.7	1,370	45.7	13	23	36	2.50	1,635	46.7	1,730	47.1	2,430	51.7
World C (Christians)	480	96.0	1,300	74.5	1,600	53.3	53	-21	32	1.85	1,840	52.6	1,922	52.3	2,250	47.9
Country's population	**500**	**100.0**	**1,745**	**100.0**	**3,000**	**100.0**	**67**	**0**	**67**	**2.92**	**3,500**	**100.0**	**3,700**	**100.0**	**4,700**	**100.0**

COLUMNS, ROWS.
For meanings and definitions, see Codebook (Part 3). Note that, by definition, total 'Christians' = professing + crypto-Christians, which also = affiliated + unaffiliated Christians, and also = Great Commission Christians + latent Christians. Percentages may not always total exactly, due to rounding.

NOTES ON RELIGIONS
CHRISTIANS. About 1,000 Norwegian Lutherans (since 1611), and 300 Russian Orthodox (since 1715).

COUNTRY'S POPULATION. This changes seasonally; the islands are inhabited during the winter season only; during the summer months, tourist arrive.
NONRELIGIOUS. 98% Russians, 2% Norwegians.

Great Commission Instrument Panel: status of the Svalbard & Jan Mayen Islands (for explanation see start of Part 4)

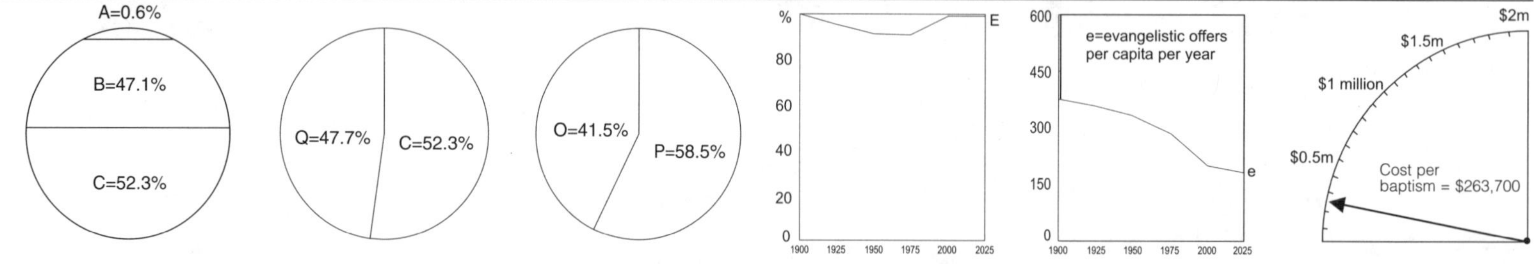

3 Worlds, AD 2000 | Religions, AD 2000 | Ecclesiastical blocs | Evangelization, 1900-2025 | Offers, 1900-2025 | Cost-effectiveness, AD 2000

Country status. Svalbard Island and Jan Mayen Island are territories of the Kingdom of Norway. Jan Mayen Island has no native inhabitants. Coal and other minerals are mined.

HUMAN LIFE AND LIBERTY.

Human rights and freedoms. Svalbard has a small population of 3,700 inhabitants of whom nearly two-thirds are Russian. There are no human rights problems on these bleak Arctic islands.

CHRISTIANITY

Formal church activities are confined to the Church of Norway. Lutheran chaplains serve a population consisting of Norwegians on temporary assignment in the islands. They are numbered among Norwegian population statistics because they belong to the municipalities in Norway in which they normally reside. The territory is theoretically also part of the Catholic vicariate of North Norway (Tromso), but there are few if any Catholics, no resident Catholic priest nor Catholic religious services.

The Holy See has no diplomatic relations with Svalbard & Jan Mayen in AD 2000.

Country summary. **Worlds A, B, C by ethnolinguistic peoples, cities, and major civil divisions in the Svalbard & Jan Mayen Islands.**

	PEOPLES							CITIES							CIVIL DIVISIONS						
World	*Num*	*Pop 2000*	*C%*	*Christians*	*E%*	*U%*	*Unevangelized*	*Num*	*Pop 2000*	*C%*	*Christians*	*E%*	*U%*	*Unevangelized*	*Num*	*Pop 2000*	*C%*	*Christians*	*E%*	*U%*	*Unevangelized*
A	0	0	0.00	0	0	0	0	0	0	0.00	0	0	0	0	0	0	0.00	0	0	0	0
B	2	2,136	35.02	748	99	1	17	1	603	47.93	289	100	0	1	1	3,676	47.58	1,749	99	1	23
C	1	1,540	65.00	1,001	100	0	5	0	0	0.00	0	0	0	0	0	0	0.00	0	0	0	0
Total	**3**	**3,676**	**47.58**	**1,749**	**99**	**1**	**22**	**1**	**603**	**47.93**	**289**	**100**	**0**	**1**	**1**	**3,676**	**47.58**	**1,749**	**99**	**1**	**23**

CHURCH AND STATE

The Svalbard archipelago and Jan Mayen Island are dependencies of Norway and are subject to the same laws regarding church and state as exist in the mother country.

FUTURE TRENDS AND PROSPECTS

Christians, 96% of the population in 1900, are likely to decline to 45% by 2025.

Christianity could continue to decline throughout the 21st century due to the influence of secularization.

BIBLIOGRAPHY

A short history of Svalbard. T. B. Arlov. *Polarhåndbok*, no. 4. Oslo: Norsk Polarinstitutt, 1989. 95p.

Svalbardlitteratur: en bibliografi. T. Sveum, P. K. Reymert & M. Hauan. [Tromsø]: Universitetsbiblioteket i Tromsø, Avd. Tromsø Museum, 1987. 54p.

Country Table 2. **Organized churches and denominations in Svalbard & Jan Mayen Islands.**

Official name (bold type = church with over 10% of all affiliated) 1	*Begun* 2	*Type* 3	*Counc* 4	*Congs* 5	*Adults* 6	*Affiliated 1970* 7	*Affiliated 1995* 8	*G%* 9	*Names, notes, and other statistics* (see Codebook, Part 3) 10
Church of Norway		P-Lut	Lwc..	1	910	1,000	975	0.05	Norske Kirke. Occasional services for temporary Norwegian staff.
Russian Orthodox Church		O-Rus	M....	1	480	300	690	0.05	Outpost of ROC Patriarchate of Moscow.
Totals				**2**	**1,390**	**1,300**	**1,665**		

Churches, members, growth, 1900-2025	*Congs*	*Adults*	*Affiliated*	*G%*	*Total denominations*	*6 Megablocs:* *O*	*R*	*A*	*P*	*I*	*m*
Total churches, members, and denominations (mid-1900)	1	330	450	1.53	0	0	0	0	0	0	0
Total churches, members, and denominations (mid-1970)	2	940	1,300	1.53	2	1	0	0	1	0	0
Total churches, members, and denominations (mid-1990)	2	1,200	1,450	0.55	2	1	0	0	1	0	0
Total churches, members, and denominations (mid-1995)	2	1,390	1,665	2.80	2	1	0	0	1	0	0
Total churches, members, and denominations (mid-2000)	2	1,500	1,749	0.99	2	1	0	0	1	0	0
Total churches, members, and denominations (mid-2025)	10	1,700	2,080	0.70	2	1	0	0	1	0	0

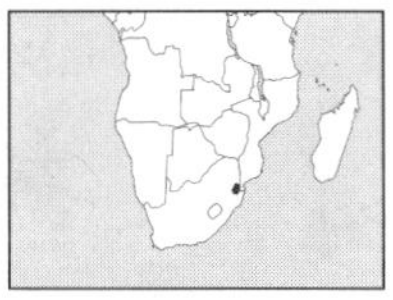

SWAZILAND

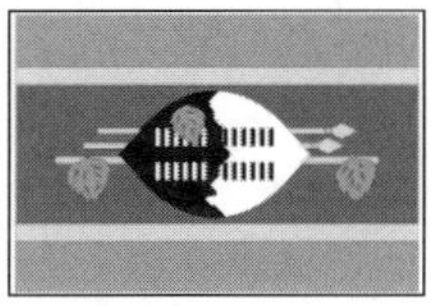

SECULAR DATA, AD 2000

STATE

Official name: Umbuso weSwatini/The Kingdom of Swaziland.
Short name: Swaziland. **Adjective of nationality:** Swazi.
Flag: Stripes of blue, yellow, red, yellow, and blue, with black and white Swazi shield of Emasotsha regiment in red stripe.
Area: 17,364 sq. km. (6,704 sq. mi.).
Government: Absolute monarchy, since 1973 (independent before 1890, 1894 South African protectorate, 1907 British protectorate, 1968 Independence as constitutional monarchy, 1973 absolute monarchy).
Legislature: Senate, 30 members; House of Assembly, 65 members.
Official language: siSwati (IsiSwathi) and English.
Monetary unit: 1 lilangeni (plural emalangeni [E]) = 100 cents. **US$1=** E 5.83.
Chief cities: MBABANE 56,223; Manzini (Bremersdorp) 44,050.
Political divisions: 4 provinces.
Armed forces: 3,000.

DEMOGRAPHY

Population: 1,008,000.
Population density: 58.0/sq. km. (150.3/sq. mi.).
Under 15 years: 433,000.
Growth rate p.a.: 2.73% (births 35.12, deaths 7.87).
Mortality: Infant, per 1,000: 55.9; **Maternal per 100,000:** 560.0.
Life expectancy: 63 (male 60, female 65).
Household size: 5.7. **Floor area per person, sq.m:** 12.0.
Major languages: Swazi (siSwati), English, Zulu, Afrikaans, Tsonga, Sotho (Sesotho), and a few others.
Urban dwellers: 35.71%. **Urban growth rate p.a.:** 4.9%.
Labor force: 40%.

ETHNOLINGUISTIC PEOPLES

82.3% Swazi (Tekeza); 9.6% Zulu; 2.3% Tsonga (Shangaan); 1.4% Afrikaner; 1.0% Coloured (Eurafrican).

ECONOMY

National income p.a. per person: US$1,169; **per family:** US$6,667.

EDUCATION

Adult literacy: 76% (male 78%, female 75%). **Schools:** 705.
Universities: 1. **School enrolment:** female/male: 92%/97%.

HEALTH

Access to health services: 45%. **Access to safe water:** 43%.
Hospitals: 24 (30 beds per 10,000). **Doctors:** 83.
Blind: 1,000. **Deaf:** 59,000. **Murder rate:** 88.
Lepers: 10,000. **Underweight prevalence under 5:** 10%.

LITERATURE

New book titles p.a.: 200 (200 p.a. per million). **Periodicals:** 28.
Newspapers: 3 dailies.

COMMUNICATION (per 1,000 people)

Phones: 21 (20% mobile). **Radios:** 550. **TV sets:** 96.
Daily newspaper circulation: 14. **Computers:** 40.

HUMAN LIFE AND LIBERTY (optimum condition=100.0%)

HDI: 58.2. **HSI:** 34.0. **HFI:** 60.0. **EFL:** 42.0.

Country Table 1. **Religious adherents in Swaziland AD 1900-2025.**

Year	*1900*		*1970*		*mid-1990*		*Annual change, 1990-2000*				*mid-1995*		*mid-2000*		*mid-2025*	
Name	*Adherents*	*%*	*Adherents*	*%*	*Adherents*	*%*	*Natural*	*Conversion*	*Total*	*Rate*	*Adherents*	*%*	*Adherents*	*%*	*Adherents*	*%*
Christians	**800**	**1.0**	**286,000**	**68.2**	**636,400**	**84.5**	**21,541**	**2,350**	**23,891**	**3.24**	**750,380**	**86.0**	**875,308**	**86.9**	**1,592,500**	**89.2**
PROFESSION																
professing Christians	**800**	**1.0**	**286,000**	**68.2**	**636,400**	**84.5**	**21,541**	**2,350**	**23,891**	**3.24**	**750,380**	**86.0**	**875,308**	**86.9**	**1,592,500**	**89.2**
AFFILIATION																
unaffiliated Christians	120	0.2	92,907	22.2	152,000	20.2	5,147	-900	4,247	2.49	170,380	19.5	194,467	19.3	351,500	19.7
affiliated Christians	**680**	**0.9**	**193,093**	**46.1**	**484,400**	**64.3**	**16,394**	**3,250**	**19,644**	**3.46**	**580,000**	**66.5**	**680,841**	**67.5**	**1,241,000**	**69.5**
Independents	100	0.1	86,000	20.5	330,000	43.8	11,175	1,825	13,000	3.38	391,572	44.9	460,000	45.6	870,000	48.7
Protestants	500	0.6	67,774	16.2	115,510	15.3	3,912	-143	3,769	2.86	133,579	15.3	153,200	15.2	255,600	14.3
Roman Catholics	0	0.0	33,984	8.1	45,500	6.0	1,541	-691	850	1.73	47,800	5.5	54,000	5.4	90,000	5.0
Anglicans	80	0.1	3,635	0.9	27,000	3.6	914	386	1,300	4.01	33,000	3.8	40,000	4.0	85,000	4.8
Marginal Christians	0	0.0	1,700	0.4	3,900	0.5	132	28	160	3.50	4,630	0.5	5,500	0.6	14,000	0.8
doubly-affiliated	0	0.0	0	0.0	-37,510	-5.0	-1,270	1,835	565	-1.62	-30,581	-3.5	-31,859	-3.2	-73,600	-4.1
Trans-megabloc groupings																
Evangelicals	400	0.5	42,200	10.1	90,300	12.0	3,058	212	3,270	3.14	105,528	12.1	123,000	12.2	235,620	13.2
Pentecostals/Charismatics	0	0.0	82,000	19.6	370,000	49.1	12,530	2,970	15,500	3.56	448,365	51.4	525,000	52.1	963,900	54.0
Great Commission Christians	**650**	**0.8**	**83,800**	**20.0**	**200,000**	**26.6**	**6,773**	**380**	**7,153**	**3.10**	**234,000**	**26.8**	**271,534**	**26.9**	**499,800**	**28.0**
Ethnoreligionists	79,200	99.0	125,700	30.0	100,000	13.3	3,386	-2,613	773	0.75	102,400	11.7	107,729	10.7	140,000	7.8
Nonreligious	0	0.0	0	0.0	7,500	1.0	254	194	448	4.79	9,500	1.1	11,975	1.2	25,000	1.4
Muslims	0	0.0	300	0.1	4,700	0.6	159	28	187	3.41	5,500	0.6	6,574	0.7	14,000	0.8
Baha'is	0	0.0	7,000	1.7	3,000	0.4	102	50	152	4.17	3,700	0.4	4,516	0.5	10,000	0.6
Hindus	0	0.0	0	0.0	1,200	0.2	41	-8	33	2.47	1,300	0.2	1,532	0.2	3,000	0.2
Atheists	0	0.0	0	0.0	200	0.0	7	-1	6	2.70	220	0.0	261	0.0	500	0.0
World A (unevangelized persons)	72,000	90.0	20,966	5.0	5,271	0.7	190	-101	89	1.49	6,107	0.7	6,048	0.6	7,140	0.4
World B (evangelized non-Christians)	7,200	9.0	112,354	26.7	111,329	14.8	3,759	-2,249	1,510	1.30	116,066	13.3	126,644	12.5	185,360	10.4
World C (Christians)	800	1.0	286,000	68.3	636,400	84.5	21,541	2,350	23,891	3.24	750,380	86.0	875,308	86.9	1,592,500	89.2
Country's population	**80,000**	**100.0**	**419,321**	**100.0**	**753,000**	**100.0**	**25,490**	**0**	**25,490**	**2.96**	**872,554**	**100.0**	**1,008,000**	**100.0**	**1,785,000**	**100.0**

COLUMNS, ROWS.
For meanings and definitions, see Codebook (Part 3). Note that, by definition, total 'Christians' = professing + crypto-Christians, which also = affiliated + unaffiliated Christians, and also = Great Commission Christians + latent Christians. Percentages may not always total exactly, due to rounding.

CENSUSES.
3.V.1921: 91.5% ethnoreligionists, 8.5% Christians (6.3% Protestants, 1.5% Anglicans, 0.3% African indigenous, 0.3% Roman Catholics). **1936:** 69.8% ethnoreligionists, 30.2% Christians (13.2% African indigenous, 11.5% Protestants (5.2% Methodists, 3.6% SDA's 1.3% Lutherans), 2.8% Anglicans, 2.7% Roman Catholics). **7.V.1946:** 62.8% ethnoreligionists, 37.2% Christians (22.8% Protestants, 8.8% African indigenous, 2.9% Roman Catholics, 2.7% Anglicans). **17.VII.1956:** this census gave 58,640 Zionists, 86,108 other Christians; altering the faulty total population figure to a correct one of 292,000, this gives 50.4% ethnoreligionists, 49.6% Christians (20.1% African indigenous). **VII.1960** (sample survey of persons of 18 years or older): 55.4% Christians (22.6% Protestants, 21.4% African indigenous, 7.2% Roman

Country Table 1–concluded

Catholics, 4.2% Anglicans), 44.6% ethnoreligionists.

NOTES ON RELIGIONS

BAHA'IS. Very rapid growth from 8 local spiritual assemblies (1964) to 57 (1973). Around 1960, one of the first Baha'i primary schools in Africa was opened in Swaziland.Thereafter, interest fell off and the recent reorganization showed a decline to 32 LSAs (1996).

ETHNORELIGIONISTS. Traditional Swazi religious beliefs and practices remain very strong, the king and his family holding that allegiance to any specific Christian denomination is incompatible with their official positions.

INDEPENDENTS. In about 54 denominations in 1995 (see Table 2). Many are called Zionists (Emazioni), others Apostolics (Emapostoli), still others have both names in their titles.

MUSLIMS. Mostly immigrants from the Comoro Islands and Mozambique-born Africans working in Swaziland. No conversions of Swazis to Islam are known to have taken place.

Great Commission Instrument Panel: status of Swaziland (for explanation see start of Part 4)

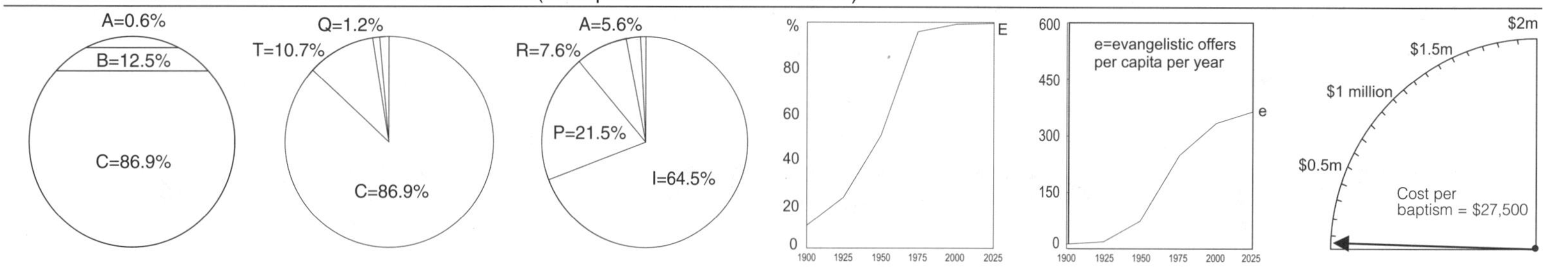

3 Worlds, AD 2000 | Religions, AD 2000 | Ecclesiastical blocs | Evangelization, 1900-2025 | Offers, 1900-2025 | Cost-effectiveness, AD 2000

Country status. Landlocked Swaziland is the smallest country in southern Africa, and it is also the only remaining monarchy in the region. Its chief exports are sugar, citrus fruit, wood pulp, and asbestos.

HUMAN LIFE AND LIBERTY

Human need and development. Although Swaziland is relatively prosperous, it has an economy in which over 70% of the people are engaged in subsistence farming. The modern sector is developing, but remains highly dependent on South Africa. South Africa accounts for 84% of Swazi imports and South African mines employ about 16% of the Swazi labor force. Most of the land is held communally, but is unproductive compared to private farms. Wealth is calculated on the basis of cattle, resulting in overstocking. Modern health and educational facilities are limited to the few towns. Only 40% of the population has access to clean water, and 60% of the deaths are attributed to lack of sanitation. The population growth rate of 3.0%, one of the highest in Africa, is likely to reduce the quality of life in the future.

Human rights and freedoms. Significant progress was achieved in human rights with the holding of parliamentary elections in 1993 and the repeal of the 60-day detention decree. Judicial powers are vested in a dual system, one modern and the other customary. The latter deals with relatively minor offenses and violations of traditional Swazi law and custom. Restraints on freedom of speech eased in 1993, but certain restrictions continue to apply to news relating to the royal family and national security. Political parties are banned. The House of Assembly has only limited powers, and the king retains ultimate legislative and executive powers. Women occupy a subordinate role in Swazi society, and the dual legal system complicates the issue of women's rights. In traditional Swazi law wives are treated as minors, but changing socioeconomic conditions are breaking down the barriers to gender equality. Physical abuse of women is common, although illegal under both modern and customary law.

Human environment. The country's cattle culture works against the environment by encouraging overstocking and overgrazing. Estimated soil erosion is estimated at 10 times the acceptable rate of 1.25 tons per acre per year. Grass fires in the dry Highveld tend to destroy all vegetation. Although the kingdom was home to vast herds of wild animals until the 20th century, wildlife is scarce outside the 2 game preserves.

NON-CHRISTIAN RELIGIONS

Traditional religion has steadily decreased the proportion of its adherents throughout the 20th century, though its influence and practice remain extremely strong. In former days the king exercised an even stronger religious function than today, and the prosperity of the nation was believed to be mystically dependent upon the strength, virility, and general well-being of the ruler. His most important role was as rain-maker, a task shared by his mother, with the royal ancestors serving as intermediaries before the First Being, Umkhulumcandi. Spirit possession by ancestors is an ancient belief among the Swazi, and around the middle of the 19th century possession by foreign and animal spirits became common. The more recent Mafefenyane possession cult (involving dancing, drumming, and speaking in tongues, but not divination) was introduced from the Pedi to the west of Swaziland. The Mandzawe cult, on the other hand, includes divination.

CHRISTIANITY

INDIGENOUS CHURCHES. Independent African churches have been an important factor in Swazi church life. Strong influences have been exerted from the proliferation of indigenous churches in neighboring South Africa, in addition to internal schism. The first secession occurred in the African Methodist Episcopal Church, itself a Black church from the USA, and the Independent Methodist Church was formed in 1906. The 1936 census listed 20 indigenous groups and a membership numbering 13% of the total population. By 1940 independents were estimated at half the Christian population. Approximately 45.6% of the population today are members of independent churches. The largest of some 40 groups at present at work are the Christian Catholic Apostolic Holy Spirit Church in Zion and the Swazi Christian Church in Zion.

PROTESTANT CHURCHES. At the invitation of the Swazi king, Methodist missionaries came from South Africa to Mahamba in the southern region as early as 1825. Today Methodists form the largest of the Swazi Protestant churches. Other early attempts to evangelize the country, by Wesleyan and Hermannsburg missionaries in 1847 and 1860, ended in failure; but German Lutherans arrived in 1887 and in 1891 the South Africa General Mission was able to plant a permanent station at Bethany on the Great Usutu river, their first mission in southern Africa. This early SAGM work is now incorporated in the Africa Evangelical Church. Indeed the major Protestant denominations in Swaziland were established prior to World War I.

The various Protestant Denominations now occupy the following areas: Methodists in southwestern, central, and eastern Swaziland; Nazarenes in the northeast; Evangelical Lutherans north of Mbabane; Africa Evangelical Church south of Mbabane; Alliance Church in Western Swaziland, south of the Great Usutu river; Emmanuel Wesleyans south of Stegi; Evangelical Church of Swaziland, Free Evangelical Assemblies, and Free Gospel Mission in the south.

CATHOLIC CHURCH. In spite of a slow beginning, considerable progress has been made by Catholics over the past 50 years. The first missionaries of the Order of the Servants of Mary (OSM) arrived in 1913. The original mission was attached to the vicariate of Natal, but within 10 years (1923) a prefecture for Swaziland was created. By 1939 this was elevated to vicariate and became a suffragan diocese of Pretoria in 1961. The major growth of the church as come since World War II.

The Holy See has diplomatic relations with Swaziland and in AD 2000 is represented to government and the Catholic hierarchy by a nuncio residing in Pretoria.

Indigenous missions. Some missionaries have been sent out but most of these work in South Africa.

Renewal movements. In the 1990s the Pentecostal/Charismatic Renewal continued to spread rapidly across most older churches, and numbered over 525,000 adherents (of whom 10% Pentecostals, 3% Charismatics, and 87% Independents).

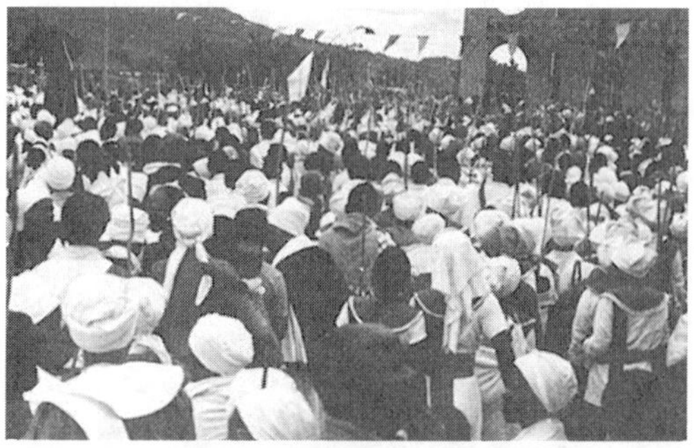

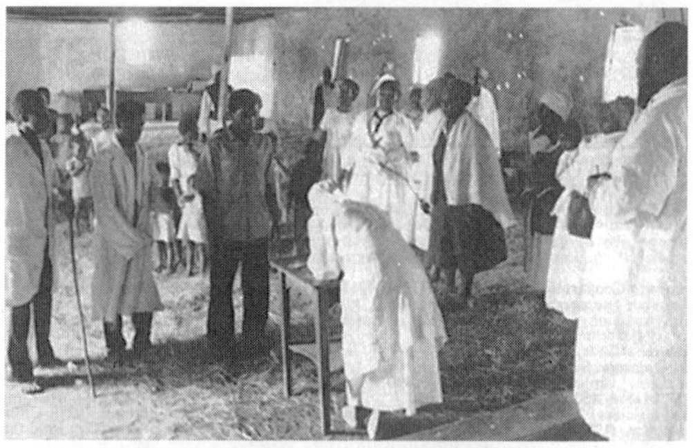

(From top). 1. National Swazi Church (building 1939-1979) is officially opened by King Sobhuza II *(left rear)* in presence of 15,000 Independents together with the Anglican and Roman Catholic bishops, and the Baha'i head, on Easter Sunday 1979. 2. **Swazi Christian Church in Zion of South Africa.** Church at Mbekelwini, with *(right)* Bishop Mncina, Vice-Chairman of League of African Churches in Swaziland. 3. **African indigenous churches.** 10,000 worshippers (League of African Churches in Swaziland) at annual 3-day Easter Festival, 1976, adjacent to Royal Kraal, Lobamba. 4. *Bottom.* 4,000 Zionists en route to Easter Sunday festival (Zionist colors: white and blue).

Country summary. **Worlds A, B, C by ethnolinguistic peoples, cities, and major civil divisions in Swaziland.**

	PEOPLES							CITIES							CIVIL DIVISIONS						
World	Num	Pop 2000	C%	Christians	E%	U%	Unevangelized	Num	Pop 2000	C%	Christians	E%	U%	Unevangelized	Num	Pop 2000	C%	Christians	E%	U%	Unevangelized
A	1	645	2.95	19	46	54	348	0	0	0.00	0	0	0	0	0	0	0.00	0	0	0	0
B	2	11,047	20.79	2,297	73	27	2,959	0	0	0.00	0	0	0	0	0	0	0.00	0	0	0	0
C	9	996,203	68.11	678,524	100	0	3,183	2	100,273	67.44	67,623	99	1	753	4	1,007,896	67.55	680,841	99	1	6,492
Total	**12**	**1,007,895**	**67.55**	**680,840**	**99**	**1**	**6,490**	**2**	**100,273**	**67.44**	**67,623**	**99**	**1**	**753**	**4**	**1,007,896**	**67.55**	**680,841**	**99**	**1**	**6,492**

CHURCH AND STATE

The constitution of February 1968, which was repealed by king Sobhuza II in April 1973, provided for a constitutional monarchy and named the Ngwanyama as chief of state. Under the 1968 constitution, the king appointed a prime minister from among members of parliament who acted as head of government; the constitution also guaranteed freedom of religion.

In 1939, king Sobhuza I attempted, with limited success, to unite the country's various small independent churches into one national Swazi church. The name of this church was changed in 1944 to the United Christian Church of Africa, and the king continues to be considered its head. Many years ago the king gave the church land near the new parliament at Lobamba to build a cathedral, but the building remained unfinished until its opening at Easter 1979 as the National Swazi Church. At Easter time members of all Swazi indigenous churches gather at the king's home at Lobamba for preaching and prayer services, the king himself traditionally attending the Easter Monday meeting.

BROADCASTING AND MEDIA

TWR operates a station in Manzini which reaches all of south and east Africa and generates over 100,000 responses per year. Shortwave radio programs from KNLS have seen some response. TBN airs programs in Mbabane.

Over 451,000 have seen the 'Jesus' Film through television (265,000) and film teams (186,000); 8,000 have responded.

INTERDENOMINATIONAL ORGANIZATIONS

The Swaziland Missionary Conference was formed in 1911. Although it went through a period of inactivity, it was revived in 1929 and continues to meet regularly. The Swaziland Conference of Churches came into existence in 1965. Its membership is one of the broadest of any African interdenominational organization, including Catholic, Adventist, and conservative Protestant representation. An association serving independent churches is the League of African Churches in Swaziland (LAC), founded in 1937. There is also an Association of Evangelicals of Swaziland. At the end of 1976, the Catholic, Anglican, Mennonite, AME, and Lutheran Church of Africa, launched an ecumenical council, the Council of Swaziland Churches (CSC).

FUTURE TRENDS AND PROSPECTS

Adherents of tribal religions are almost certain to drop dramatically, from 99% in 1900 to less than 8% by 2025. Christians could grow to 89% by AD 2025.

Tribal religions are expected to decline in fact throughout the 21st century, perhaps to as low as 1% by AD 2050. Christianity would then make up the gains by rising to 95% by AD 2050.

BIBLIOGRAPHY

'A history of Christian missions in Swaziland to 1910.' F. J. Perkins. Ph.D. dissertation, University of the Witwatersrand, Johannesburg, 1974. 507p.

A history of the church in Southern Africa: a select bibliography of published material. J. W. Hofmeyr & K. E. Cross. Pretoria, South Africa: University of South Africa, 1986. 2 vols.

A pictorial history of Manzini Nazarene Mission, 1925–1975: fifty years of service to Swaziland. Manzini, Swaziland: Nazarene Mission, 1976. 24p.

'Abakamoya: people of the spirit: a study of the Zionist movement in Swaziland with special reference to the Swazi Christian Church in Zion of South Africa and the Nazarethe Branch.' F. L. Armitage. M.L. thesis, University of Aberdeen, Aberdeen, Scotland, 1976. 445p.

An African aristocracy: rank among the Swazi. H. Kuper. London: Oxford University Press, 1947.

'Chief and prophet in Zululand and Swaziland,' B. G. M. Sundkler, in *African systems of thought*, p.276–90. M. Fortes & G. Dieterlen (eds). London: Oxford University Press, 1965.

Church co–operation in Swaziland: a test for Western church presence in Africa. G. Küsel. Berlin: Berliner Missionswerk, 1976. 127p.

Dawn in Swaziland. C. C. Watts. London: Society for the Propagation of the Gospel in Foreign Parts, 1922. 128pp.

Institutional ecumenicity: the Conference, League, and Council of Swaziland Churches. P. Kasenene. Mbabane, Swaziland: Websters, 1992. 49p.

Religion in Swaziland. A. B. T. Byaruhanga-Akiiki. Kwaluseni, Swaziland: University of Botswana, Lesotho and Swaziland, 1975. 2 vols.

Religion in Swaziland. P. Kasenene. Braamfontein, South Africa: Skotaville, 1993. 163p.

Swaziland. B. Nyeko. 2nd ed. *World bibliographical series*, vol. 24. Oxford, UK: CLIO Press, 1994. 271p.

Swaziland Christian handbook 1994. M. Froise (ed). Welkom, South Africa: Christian Info, 1994. 125p.

Swaziland Manzini mission. Kansas City, MO: Church of the Nazarene, 1988. (13 minute videocassette).

'The church as servant community in Swazi culture.' A. N. Ciccone. M.A. thesis, Catholic Theological Union, Chicago, 1975. 173p.

'The Church of Jericho, Swaziland.' A. Fogelquist. Ph.D. dissertation, University of Uppsala, Sweden, 1980.

'The effect of autonomy on the African Evangelical Church in Swaziland.' L. T. Magewu. M.A. thesis, Columbia Graduate School of Bible and Missions, Columbia, SC, 1977. 100p.

'The red–dressed Zionists: symbols of power in a Swazi independent church.' A. Fogelquist. Doctoral dissertation, University of Uppsala, Sweden, 1986. 211p.

'The royal Easter ritual and political actions in Swaziland.' H. L. Ndlovu. Ph.D. dissertation, McMaster University, Hamilton, Ontario, 1993. 337p.

The Swazi Catholic Church comes of age. P. Kasenene (ed). Mbabane, Swaziland: Websters, 1988. 77p.

'The Swazi reaction to missions,' H. Kuper, *African studies* (Johannesburg), 5, 3 (1946), 177–89.

Zulu Zion and some Swazi Zionists. B. Sundkler. *Oxford studies in African affairs.* Oxford, UK: Oxford University Press, 1976. 337p.

Country Table 2. **Organized churches and denominations in Swaziland.**

Official name (bold type = church with over 10% of all affiliated) 1	*Begun* 2	*Type* 3	*Counc* 4	*Congs* 5	*Adults* 6	*Affiliated 1970* 7	*Affiliated 1995* 8	*G%* 9	*Names, notes, and other statistics* (see Codebook, Part 3) 10
Africa Evangelical Church	1891	P-Eva	xM..E	41	3,900	1,250	7,000	7.13	M=AEF(formerly SAGM). HQ Mbabane, 3 main stations. Strong work,5nx,5lm,5f.
African Methodist Episcopal Church	1904	I-Met	Vw..W	45	1,510	5,000	2,130	-3.36	*Ikhushi.* Begun by Africans; later, M=AMEC(USA). Several schisms. 79% rural. 25n,1x.
Alliance Church of Swaziland	1915	P-Non	x...E	45	1,000	3,000	2,500	-0.73	*Iswidi.* M=Swedish Alliance Mission. In west. 85% rural. 2n,13m,5f,W=60%,40Y.
Anglican Church: D Swaziland	1881	A-ACa	AwaVW	96	16,000	3,635	33,000	9.22	*Isheshe.* 1968, diocese in CPSA. M=USPG. 500 Whites. 30n,1x.P=75%,3r,104Y,508y.
Antioch Zionist Church		I-3zA	I	30	3,000	3,500	6,000	0.05	*Antioc.* Members 83% rural (46% Highveld, 15% Middleveld, 11% Lowveld), 17% urban.
Apostolic Faith Mission of International	1981	P-Pe2	Z...E	32	2,200	2,000	3,500	7.14	M=AFM(SA). Work in south. Members 95% rural (56%in Highveld), 5% urban. 12n,1f.
Assemblies of God	c1960	P-Pe2	Z...E	140	7,505	1,000	14,000	11.13	M=Assemblies of God(USA,UK). HQ Stegi. Under Swazi leadership. Strong in north. 87n.
Bantu Swedish Free Church	1950	I-Non	....E	10	3,000	4,000	6,000	1.64	Schism ex Swedish Alliance Mission. Swazi, Zulu, Malawians. 5n,20mw,W=40%,230Y,300y.
Baptist Convention	1983	P-Bap	....E	11	368	–	580	8.33	M=FMB-SBC. Churches for Mozambique and Angolan refugees. 11f.
Catholic Church: D Manzini	1913	R-Lat	P.SSW	112	25,000	33,984	47,800	1.37	*Roma.* M=OSM. 7% White. C=2+0+4. (1970) 3n,29x,120w,1804Yy,. (1990) 6n,33x,73w,981Yy.
Christian Apostolic Ch in Zion of SA	1920	I-3zA	I	30	6,000	10,000	20,000	2.81	*Eqiniswenisweni.* Mabilitsa's Zion. Middleveld, Highveld. 82% rural. HQ Alexandra, Joburg.
Christian Cath Ap Holy Spirit Ch in Z	1913	I-3zA	I	40	16,000	21,000	32,000	1.70	Z=Zion. Nkonyane's Zion(HQ Natal). First Zionists in SAfr. 94% rural (Middleveld).
Church of God of Prophecy	1977	P-Pe3	.....	10	600	–	1,500	5.56	M=CGP(USA).
Ch of Jesus Christ of Latter-day Saints	c1985	m-LdS	.....	1	60	–	100	10.00	Mormons. M=CJCLdS(USA).
Church of the Nazarene	1910	P-Hol	xF..E	108	7,041	12,000	21,000	2.26	*Ibandla LomNazarene.* M=CoN. 88n,4x,412mw,15f,1H,15h,1s(25),149t(9954),W=78%,104Y.
Churches of Christ (Non-Instrumental)	c1970	I-Dis	.....	51	2,915	–	4,330	39.78	M=CC(USA). Independent Disciples
Damascus Church		I-Non	I	15	1,500	3,000	4,000	0.05	*Damaseko-Damascus.* Strongest in Middleveld, some in Lowveld. 90% rural.
Deeper Life Bible Church	1988	I-3pA	.....	4	840	–	1,500	14.29	Mission from vast DLBC in Lagos, Nigeria.
Dutch Reformed Church	1922	P-Ref	F...W	4	400	1,000	1,200	0.73	*NGK.* 100 Afrikaners from Transvaal synod; recently, 5 Bantu congregations begun. 1n.
Dutch Reformed Church in Africa	c1940	P-Ref	R...W	1	50	50	100	2.81	*Nederduitsch Hervormde Kerk(NHK)*; 1853 split ex NGK(SA). Afrikaners.
Emmanuel Wesleyan Church	1903	P-Hol	VF..E	28	700	1,000	1,400	1.35	M=Wesleyan Ch (USA). 1968 merged with Pilgrim Holiness Ch(USA). No growth. 33mw,5f.
Evangelical Bible Church	c1930	P-Eva	xM..E	6	500	500	1,000	2.81	Members Coloured. M=TEAM(USA, SAfrica). In Manzini, Mbabane, Mhlotsheni.
Evangelical Church of Swaziland	1892	P-Eva	xM..E	111	5,000	15,000	11,100	-1.20	Formerly Bantu Ev Ch. M=TEAM(USA, SA),Norwegian Ev M(NLM). Swazi, Zulu. 15f,2p.
Evangelical Lutheran Ch (SE Diocese)	1887	P-Lut	Lwa.W	90	1,500	3,984	3,000	-1.13	*Luthela.* Formerly, M=Berlin MS: SKM. 71% rural. 3n,5x(4 being Zulu),11m,19Y,156y.
Evangelical Lutheran Church	c1975	P-Lut	....W	11	1,000	–	2,000	5.00	*Ibandla Levangeli Lenkhululeko.* M=NLM(Norway).
Free Evangelical Assemblies Church	1909	P-Pe2	Z...E	57	2,000	3,000	4,000	1.16	M=Norwegian Pentecostal Mission(NPY). Strong in south. 25% urban. 1H,2i,1p.
Free Gospel Mission		I-3pA	....E	9	200	100	400	0.05	Schism led by Norwegian missionary ex Norwegian Ev Mission (NLM). HQ Nhlangano. 9n.
Full Gospel Ch of God in Southern A	c1950	P-Pe3	ZF..E	43	15,900	1,500	28,400	12.48	Branch of church in SA. M=Church of God (Cleveland) (USA). 5n,2f(Afrikaners).
Holiness Union Church	1930	P-Hol	....E	13	235	240	360	1.64	M=Holiness Union Miss (Sweden). 5 schools. 8n,2f.
Independent Methodist Ch of South A	1904	I-Met	.....	9	1,200	500	2,500	6.65	Schism 1906 ex African Methodist Episcopal Ch. One of oldest indigenous bodies.
Jehovah's Witnesses	c1945	m-Jeh	x....	51	1,235	1,500	3,530	3.48	*Watch Tower.* Active witnessing under way by 1949. 1976: persecution. (1975) 32Y. (1995) 169Y.
Jericho Christian Church in Zion	1951	I-3zA	I	100	3,000	5,000	7,000	1.35	*Jeliko-Jerico.* 52% Highveld, 17% Lobombo, 11% Lowveld, 10% Middleveld, 10% urban.
Methodist Church of South Africa	1825	P-Met	Vwa.W	231	10,100	20,000	18,000	-0.42	*Weseli.* Re-begun c1895. English and African circuits. 36% Highveld, 23% urban.
Metropolitan Church Association	1936	P-Hol	....E	13	2,400	200	4,300	13.06	M=MCA(USA). 2 stations. HQ Sifuntaneni Halt, Manzini. Highveld and urban. 16n,3f,1h.
New Apostolic Church	1971	I-3aX	x....	12	1,800	–	2,632	4.17	NAC/NAK. M=Neuapostolische Kirche. HQ Zurich (Switzerland).
Pentecostal Assemblies of Africa		I-3pA	....E	10	500	400	1,000	0.05	Schism ex Assemblies of God, led by African from Rhodesia. HQ Lomahasha.
Pentecostal Holiness Church	1913	P-Pe3	Z...E	3	300	50	500	9.65	M=IPHC(USA), brought in by members from South Africa. Holiness Pentecostals.
Rhema Bible Churches	c1985	I-3wW	x....	2	650	–	1,080	10.00	Word of Faith churches from USA. Prosperity Gospel teaching.
St John's Apostolic Faith Church	1951	I-3pA	x...I	50	4,000	5,500	11,000	2.81	*AbaPostoli. Ma Nku's Ch.* Sotho origin. HQ Joburg. 50% urban. Holy water ministry.
Seventh-day Adventist Church	1920	P-Adv	x...E	15	1,532	1,000	2,639	3.96	*Isabatha. Swaziland Field.* 96% Swazi,some Whites. Rural. 3n,1x,11mw,18t(800),54Y.
Swazi Christian Ch in Zion of SA	1937	I-3zA	I	150	14,000	15,000	40,000	4.00	Bp Mncina's church. One of the largest Zionist bodies. HQ Kwaluseni. 91% rural.
United Christian Church of Africa	1939	I-Ang	..A.W	50	6,000	3,000	10,000	4.93	*Ibandla lama Krestu.* National Swazi Ch, attempt by king to unite all churches. 18n.
United Pentecostal Ch of S	1982	P-Pel	.....	17	1,800	–	2,500	7.69	*UPC.* Oneness Pentecostals. M=UPC(USA). 26n,2f.
Other indigenous Zionist churches	c1917	I-3zA	I	200	134,000	10,000	240,000	13.56	Total about 40 (see list below), including many independent congregations.
Other Protestant denominations		P-	.....	30	2,000	1,000	3,000	0.05	Total about 10 (see list below).
Other marginal Protestant bodies		m-	.....	10	500	200	1,000	0.05	Including: New Church in Southern Africa.
Doubly-affiliated		2-aff			-15,600	0	-30,581		Independents and Evangelicals who are also baptized Catholics.

Continued overleaf

Country Table 2–concluded

Official name (bold type = church with over 10% of affiliated) 1	*Begun* 2	*Type* 3	*Counc* 4	*Congs* 5	*Adults* 6	*Affiliated 1970* 7	*Affiliated 1995* 8	*G%* 9	*Names, notes, and other statistics* (see Codebook, Part 3) 10
Totals				**2,147**	**295,341**	**193,093**	**580,000**		

Churches, members, growth, 1900-2025	*Congs*	*Adults*	*Affiliated*	*G%*	*Total denominations*	*6 Megablocs:* *O*	*R*	*A*	*P*	*I*	*m*
Total churches, members, and denominations (mid-1900)	12	310	680	8.40	6	0	0	1	5	0	0
Total churches, members, and denominations (mid-1970)	1,134	86,791	193,093	8.40	69	0	1	1	22	40	5
Total churches, members, and denominations (mid-1990)	1,900	247,000	484,400	4.71	103	0	1	1	32	57	12
Total churches, members, and denominations (mid-1995)	2,147	295,341	580,000	3.67	103	0	1	1	32	57	12
Total churches, members, and denominations (mid-2000)	2,400	347,000	680,841	3.26	103	0	1	1	32	57	12
Total churches, members, and denominations (mid-2025)	3,000	632,000	1,241,000	2.43	218	0	1	1	50	150	16

NOTES ON TABLE ABOVE

NATIONAL COUNCILS (Column 4, 5th letter).

- d = member of both SCC and CSC.
- E = Swaziland Conference of Churches (SCC), 1929.
- I = League of African Churches in Swaziland (LACS) or League of Swazi Independent Churches (Inhlangano yamabandla Enkolo Esizwe/Inkatsa yamabandla Enkolo ka Ngwane) (founded in 1937; mainly an Easter convention; at least 25 member churches).
- k = not a member of SCC, but its related foreign mission is a member.
- W = Council of Swaziland Churches (CSC) (set up in 1967, with members expecting to pull out of SCC within a short time).
- Z = member of LACS, SCC and CSC.

Other national councils. Association of Evangelicals of Swaziland (member of AEAM). Federation Churches in Zion/Federation of Zion Churches in Africa/League of Zionist Churches.

OTHER INDIGENOUS ZIONIST CHURCHES. These are mostly Zionist splits from Nkonyane's Zion and the Swazi Christian Church in Zion, also branches of Zulu churches from the republic of South Africa. They include: African Congregational Ch (begun 1928), African Native Baptist Ch, African Zion Ch, Apostolic Ch of Christ, Bantu Methodist Ch of SA (Donkey Church; begun 1935), Christian Apostolic Zulu Ch, Ch of Christ, Congregational Catholic Apostolic Ch (1931), Free Ev Assembly Independent Ch (Ebenezer; ex NPY), Holy Apostolic Ch in Christ (1924), Holy Spirit Apostolic Ch in Zion (EECHSACZ, or Tongo Tongo; ex Nkonyane's Zion), National Ch of Africa's Union (began 1932 ex Scandinavian Alliance Mission; member of LACS), Nazarite Baptist Ch (Shembeites) (1911), Nazirite Bible Ch (HQ South Africa), Pentecost East Star Jerusalem Ch in Sabbath, Swazi Christian Ch of the Kingdom of Swaziland in Zion (1956), United Ch of Ethiopian South Africa, Zion Apostolic Faith Mission (1912), Zion Apostolic Swazi Ch of South Africa (begun 1918 ex ZAC), Zion Christian Ch (Lekganyane) (1925), Zulu Apostolic Ch in Zion (1924 ex Nkonyane's Zion; member of LACS), Zulu Congregational Ch. Also, a USA Black mission is at work: National Baptist Convention USA (1971).

OTHER PROTESTANT DENOMINATIONS. Among these smaller bodies are the following: Gereformeerde Kerk, Mennonite Committee in Swaziland (member of 1976 council, CSC), Norwegian Mission Union, Salvation Army Swedish Zulu Mission, United Apostolic Faith Ch.

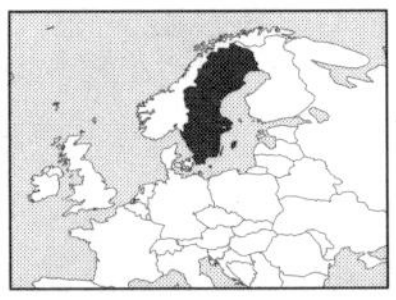

SWEDEN

SECULAR DATA, AD 2000

STATE

Official name: Det Konungariket Sverige (The Kingdom of Sweden).
Short name: Sweden. **Adjective of nationality:** Swedish, a Swede.
Flag: Light blue field with yellow cross.
Area: 449,964 sq. km. (173,732 sq. mi.).
Government: Constitutional monarchy, since 1718 (1397 united Scandinavian monarchy, 1523 independent kingdom, 1660 absolute monarchy, 1718 constitutional monarchy, 1917 parliamentary government).
Legislature: Riksdag, 350 members.
Official language: Swedish (Svensk).
Monetary unit: 1 Swedish krona (SKr) = 100 ore. **US$1=** SKr 7.88.
Chief cities: STOCKHOLM 1,582,000; Goteborg (Gothenburg) 763,000; Malmo 463,999; Uppsala 174,659; Linkoping 127,488.
Political divisions: 23 provinces.
Armed forces: 54,000.

DEMOGRAPHY

Population: 8,910,000.
Population density: 19.8/sq. km. (51.2/sq. mi.).
Under 15 years: 1,622,000.
Growth rate p.a.: 0.21% (births 9.76, deaths 11.06).
Mortality: Infant, per 1,000: 5.1; **Maternal per 100,000:** 7.0.
Life expectancy: 79 (male 77, female 82).
Household size: 2.2. **Floor area per person, sq.m:** 50.0.
Major languages: Swedish, Finnish, Greek, Serbo-Croatian, German, Norwegian, Danish, English, Dutch, Estonian, Russian, Lapp, Romany, Italian, Romanian.
Urban dwellers: 83.32%. **Urban growth rate p.a.:** 0.3%.
Labor force: 49%.

ETHNOLINGUISTIC PEOPLES

86.6% Swedish (Swede); 3.5% Finnish (Finn); 1.3% Bosniac (Muslmani); 0.6% Estonian; 0.6% German.

ECONOMY

National income p.a. per person: US$23,750; **per family:** US$52,250.

EDUCATION

Adult literacy: 100% (male 100%, female 100%). **Schools:** 5,426.
Universities: 100. **School enrolment:** female/male: 100%/100%.

HEALTH

Access to health services: 95%. **Access to safe water:** 100%.
Hospitals: 700 (52 beds per 10,000). **Doctors:** 22,200.
Blind: 15,716. **Deaf:** 533,900. **Murder rate:** 4.
Lepers: 200.

LITERATURE

New book titles p.a.: 13,450 (1,510 p.a. per million). **Periodicals:** 64.
Newspapers: 94 dailies.

COMMUNICATION (per 1,000 people)

Phones: 681 (40% mobile). **Radios:** 844. **TV sets:** 476.
Daily newspaper circulation: 515. **Computers:** 508.

REFUGEES

Alien refugees from other countries: 12,300.

HUMAN LIFE AND LIBERTY (optimum condition=100.0%)

HDI: 93.6. **HSI:** 89.0. **HFI:** 95.0. **EFL:** 49.0.

Country Table 1. **Religious adherents in Sweden, AD 1900-2025.**

Year	*1900*		*1970*		*mid-1990*		*Annual change, 1990-2000*				*mid-1995*		*mid-2000*		*mid-2025*	
Name	*Adherents*	*%*	*Adherents*	*%*	*Adherents*	*%*	*Natural*	*Conversion*	*Total*	*Rate*	*Adherents*	*%*	*Adherents*	*%*	*Adherents*	*%*
Christians	**5,077,000**	**98.9**	**6,032,000**	**75.0**	**5,875,900**	**68.7**	**24,097**	**-6,506**	**17,591**	**0.30**	**5,999,000**	**68.2**	**6,051,805**	**67.9**	**6,030,000**	**66.3**
PROFESSION																
professing Christians	**5,077,000**	**98.9**	**6,032,000**	**75.0**	**5,875,900**	**68.7**	**24,097**	**-6,506**	**17,591**	**0.30**	**5,999,000**	**68.2**	**6,051,805**	**67.9**	**6,030,000**	**66.3**
AFFILIATION																
unaffiliated Christians	0	0.0	0	0.0	40,000	0.5	164	981	1,145	2.55	47,000	0.5	51,449	0.6	30,000	0.3
affiliated Christians	**5,077,000**	**98.9**	**6,032,000**	**75.0**	**5,835,900**	**68.2**	**23,933**	**-7,487**	**16,446**	**0.28**	**5,952,000**	**67.6**	**6,000,356**	**67.3**	**6,000,000**	**66.0**
Protestants	5,404,070	105.2	8,826,511	109.7	8,175,000	95.5	33,525	-9,025	24,500	0.30	8,343,012	94.8	8,420,000	94.5	8,450,000	92.9
Roman Catholics	2,230	0.0	58,929	0.7	151,000	1.8	619	1,781	2,400	1.49	164,332	1.9	175,000	2.0	260,000	2.9
Orthodox	100	0.0	40,500	0.5	105,000	1.2	431	1,069	1,500	1.34	111,020	1.3	120,000	1.4	170,000	1.9
Independents	0	0.0	21,600	0.3	47,500	0.6	195	1,055	1,250	2.36	55,076	0.6	60,000	0.7	85,000	0.9
Marginal Christians	500	0.0	39,695	0.5	54,000	0.6	221	-21	200	0.36	55,200	0.6	56,000	0.6	60,000	0.7
Anglicans	100	0.0	3,000	0.0	2,940	0.0	12	-18	-6	-0.21	2,920	0.0	2,880	0.0	2,500	0.0
doubly-affiliated	0	0.0	-188,235	-2.3	-299,540	-3.5	-1,228	-7,170	-8,398	2.50	-349,560	-4.0	-383,524	-4.3	-477,500	-5.3
disaffiliated	-330,000	-6.4	-2,770,000	-34.4	-2,400,000	-28.0	-9,842	4,842	-5,000	0.21	-2,430,000	-27.6	-2,450,000	-27.5	-2,550,000	-28.0
Trans-megabloc groupings																
Evangelicals	3,050,000	59.4	980,000	12.2	860,000	10.1	3,527	-527	3,000	0.34	882,779	10.0	890,000	10.0	850,000	9.3
Pentecostals/Charismatics	0	0.0	295,000	3.7	565,000	6.6	2,317	3,483	5,800	0.98	605,929	6.9	623,000	7.0	750,000	8.2
Great Commission Christians	**515,000**	**10.0**	**2,372,000**	**29.5**	**2,431,000**	**28.4**	**9,969**	**-3,136**	**6,833**	**0.28**	**2,487,000**	**28.3**	**2,499,326**	**28.1**	**2,500,000**	**27.5**
Nonreligious	50,000	1.0	1,187,000	14.8	1,498,400	17.5	6,166	233	6,399	0.42	1,540,000	17.5	1,562,389	17.5	1,651,700	18.2
Atheists	5,000	0.1	799,000	9.9	1,015,000	11.9	4,162	235	4,397	0.43	1,045,000	11.9	1,058,973	11.9	1,100,000	12.1
Muslims	0	0.0	2,450	0.0	137,000	1.6	562	5,891	6,453	3.93	181,340	2.1	201,526	2.3	270,000	3.0
Jews	4,000	0.1	15,000	0.2	15,500	0.2	64	-3	61	0.39	15,890	0.2	16,110	0.2	17,500	0.2
Baha'is	0	0.0	1,500	0.0	4,300	0.1	18	57	75	1.62	4,900	0.1	5,048	0.1	6,000	0.1
Buddhists	0	0.0	300	0.0	900	0.0	4	12	16	1.66	1,000	0.0	1,061	0.0	2,000	0.0
Hindus	0	0.0	0	0.0	0	0.0	0	18	18	67.99	170	0.0	179	0.0	300	0.0
Other religionists	0	0.0	5,750	0.1	12,000	0.1	49	63	112	0.90	12,700	0.1	13,123	0.2	19,500	0.2
World A (unevangelized persons)	5,136	0.1	16,085	0.2	119,826	1.4	492	1,539	2,031	1.58	131,999	1.5	142,560	1.6	200,134	2.2
World B (evangelized non-Christians)	53,864	1.0	1,994,759	24.8	2,563,274	29.9	10,533	4,967	15,500	0.58	2,668,986	30.3	2,715,635	30.5	2,866,866	31.5
World C (Christians)	5,077,000	98.9	6,032,000	75.0	5,875,900	68.7	24,097	-6,506	17,591	0.30	5,999,000	68.2	6,051,805	67.9	6,030,000	66.3
Country's population	**5,136,000**	**100.0**	**8,042,845**	**100.0**	**8,559,000**	**100.0**	**35,122**	**0**	**35,122**	**0.40**	**8,799,986**	**100.0**	**8,910,000**	**100.0**	**9,097,000**	**100.0**

COLUMNS, ROWS.

For meanings and definitions, see Codebook (Part 3). Note that, by definition, total 'Christians' = professing + crypto-Christians, which also = affiliated + unaffiliated Christians, and also = Great Commission Christians + latent Christians. Percentages may not always total exactly, due to rounding.

CENSUSES.

Sweden's censuses of religion have obtained membership figures direct from the churches themselves, hence have measured religious affiliation and not religious preference or profession as defined in this survey.

NOTES ON RELIGIONS

AFFILIATED PROTESTANTS. The totals for the years 1900-1970 are each over 100% because many Protestants are always counted by 2 denominations at once (see DOUBLY-AFFILIATED below).

ATHEISTS. Many polls of atheists have been taken. A very conservative average estimate is that in 1995 12% of the population definitively called themselves atheists. Many of these are humanists, or are politically right-wing, but a large proportion are communist, members of the left party-communists (Vänsterpartiet Kommunisterna, VPK) (legal; split on Sino-Soviet dispute).

BAHA'IS. Local spiritual assemblies: 1964, 4; 1973, 10. A surge due partly to immigration of Middle Eastern refugees then resulted in 29 LSAs by 1996.

BUDDHISTS. In 5 groups and institutions: Uppsala, Alingsas, Strömstad, and 2 Tibetan Buddhist centers (based on Copenhagen): Stockholm and Göteburg.

DISAFFILIATED. This term is used here to describe dechristianized persons who, although mostly baptized as Lutherans in the state church and therefore regarded by that church as still affiliated to it (and hence enumerated in Table 2 as such), have recently withdrawn or disaffiliated themselves completely from Christianity and now profess to be either nonreligious (agnostics) or atheists (see polls above). Because their statistics represent a duplication, they are shown in the table above as a negative quantity (with a

Continued opposite

Country Table 1–concluded

minus sign).
DOUBLY-AFFILIATED. The term covers those affiliated to, or claimed by, both the state church and also another denomination, mostly baptized Lutherans who have recently joined another church but who retain their original membership also. Because their statistics represent a duplication, they are shown in the table as a negative quantity (with a minus sign).
JEWS. Present since 1774. In 8 congregations.
MUSLIMS. In 2 groups: earlier refugees, and more recent migrant workers (in 1995: 22,000 Turkish, 35,000 Iranians, 17,500 Levantine Arabs, 12,000 Somalis, 8,800 Syrian Arabs) including by 1995, 88,000 Bosnians. Most are Sunnis. Immigration has continued rapidly during the 1990s. There is also an Ahmadiya Mission (enumerated here under Muslims although declared non-Muslim by Pakistan).Begun 1960; HQ Goteborg. Qadianis from Pakistan (HQ Rabwah), with a few Swedish converts.
PENTECOSTALS/CHARISMATICS. (1975) The Catholic Charismatic Renewal began in 1981 and by 1997 had 15 regular prayer groups with 200 attenders (including 8 priests). There are good relations with the Church of Sweden, which had 3,000 lay charismatics and 40 clergy within the state church in 200 organized prayer groups, about 5,000 in other non-Pentecostal Protestant denominations, and about 5,000 young Jesus People within these denominations (over 100 groups of them in Stockholm), giving a total of 13,000 involved adults, and a total charismatic community including children of 26,000 by mid-1975. In 1972, 10,000 charismatics (almost all neo-pentecostals) attended the ecumenical Charisma 72 for 5 days in Stockholm.By 1996 there were over 300,000 persons in the Renewal.
ORTHODOX. In the 1990s there has been considerable immigration, including about 52,000 Serbs.
OTHER RELIGIONISTS. Adherents of other non-Christian religions and cults, including Theosophy (9 Lodges, 335 members) and Rosicrucianism (6 Lodges in AMORC, 2 centers of Lectorium Rosicrucianum).
ROMAN CATHOLICS. Only 62% of all Catholics are affiliated to parishes or known by name and address; the rest are recent immigrants unknown to the clergy. In the 1990s steady immigration has continued.

Great Commission Instrument Panel: status of Sweden (for explanation see start of Part 4)

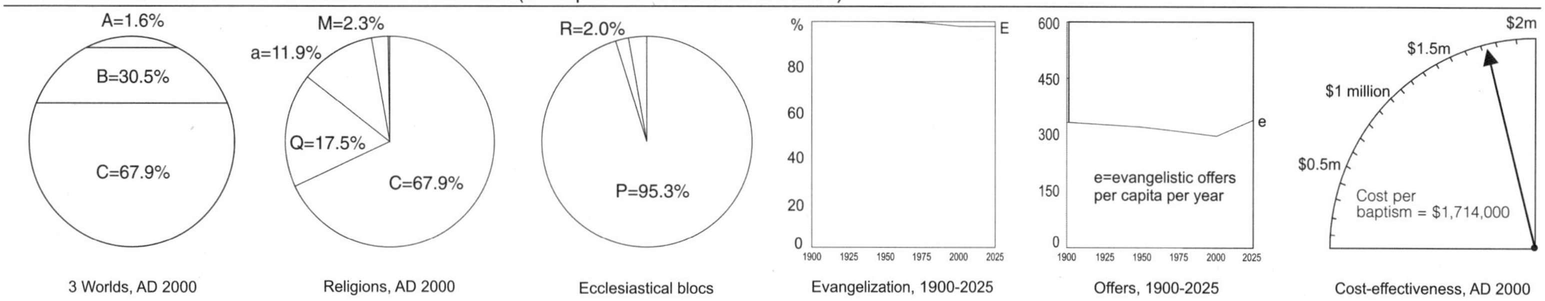

Country status. Sweden is the largest of the Scandinavian countries and is a flat tableland with forests and numerous lakes. Its main exports are wood pulp, paper products, and motor vehicles.

HUMAN LIFE AND LIBERTY

Human need and development. As the cradle of Social Democratic ideology and as a pioneering Welfare State in modern times, Sweden has an advanced political and economic system geared to meeting all the social needs of its people. It provides some of the most generous Social Security benefits in Europe, particularly to children, mothers, workers, and the elderly. With virtually full literacy, one of the highest rates of life expectancy, universal medical care, and social services of unparalleled breadth and range, Sweden has one of the highest standards of living in the world and also ranks high in social and cultural indicators.

Human rights and freedoms. Sweden has a long history of a vigorous democratic political life in which all basic human rights are not only guaranteed by the Constitution but also vigorously protected by the authorities. The ombudsman, appointed by the parliament, has the autonomy to investigate charges of alleged abuses of authority and prescribe corrective action, if required. Anti-foreigner violence has escalated in recent years, requiring strong government action as a deterrent. Women and children have separate ombudsmen responsible for their welfare. The criminal system is somewhat lenient to the defendant. Suspects may be held no longer than 12 hours without formal charges. Wiretaps are permitted in cases involving narcotics or national security, but only with court approval. There are no restrictions on freedom of speech and expression, although excessive violence in films and video is subject to censorship.

Human environment. Sweden has an ambitious environmental protection program, including water treatment for all drinking water and laws against sulfur dioxide emissions. However, its proximity to other countries with less stringent laws makes it vulnerable to third-party pollution. About 88% of all acid rain that falls on Swedish soil comes from other countries. Similarly both the North and Baltic seas have become degraded in recent years as a result of industrial effluents from bordering countries.

NON-CHRISTIAN RELIGIONS

Judaism has existed in Sweden for 2 centuries, the first Jews being authorized to settle under strict control, in 1774. Emancipated in 1870, there are now about 16,000 Jews in the country, with orthodox and liberal synagogues in Stockholm, Goteborg, and Malmo.

Islam has followers among earlier refugees and more recent migrant workers from Turkey, Morocco, Tunisia, Algeria, Syria, and Yugoslavia.

Buddhism is represented by 5 groups and institutions: Bodhi in Uppsala, Buddhistiska Institutionen in Alingsas and Sallskapet for Buddhistisk Information in Stromstad; also Tibetan Buddhist centers in Stockholm and Goteborg.

CHRISTIANITY

Anskar, a French monk, made 2 visits to Sweden in the 9th century, the second time at the invitation of king Olaf. He brought many noblemen to the faith, but Christianity lapsed until the 10th century when the first English missionaries made their appearance. During the following century Christianity spread throughout the country, the first bishop being installed at Uppsala in 1164. King Gustav Vasa was the principal leader of the Swedish Reformation, resulting in the adoption of the Lutheran Confession in 1527. Though the former ecclesiastical structures and liturgy were not radically changed, identification with the national church contributed to the growth of a national self-awareness and an independent Swedish culture, making Sweden a dominant European power in the 17th century. In the 19th century a spiritual revival took place, which placed new emphasis on the New Testament as well as on pietism and lay preaching. Out of this revival denominationalism also appeared, with the first free church emerging from it in 1878. A number of Swedes belong both to the Church of Sweden and to free churches.

Pentecostal Revival Movement of Sweden. *Above.* Annual week of tent revival meetings (Nyhemsveckan) in summer 1967, with thousands in attendance in massive tent. **Church of Sweden.** *Top.* Youth demonstration past royal castle in Stockholm (right) en route to 1968 WCC Assembly in Uppsala.

PROTESTANT CHURCHES. Anyone born a Swedish citizen is considered de facto a member of the Church of Sweden, in 1990 members being 96% of the total population. It is a folk church, closely linked to rural society, rooted in the history and tradition of the country, still tied to parochial structures inherited from the Middle Ages, and theologically inclusive of all wings of Christianity. At the international level, the Church of Sweden has long been a leader in the ecumenical and confessional movements, and played a leading role in the founding of the Lutheran World Federation in 1947. There are 4 streams of churchmanship within the contemporary church: (1) the Young Church, which places emphasis on doctrinal freedom and the folk church concept; (2) the Old Church, uniting a strong Lutheran orthodoxy with the pastoral traditions of the Pietists; (3) the Low Church, representing at one time 10% but now only 1% of the clergy, noted for new forms of spontaneous worship; and (4) the High Church, to which about one third of the clergy adhere and which is strongly influenced by Anglicanism. The latter group seeks to promote liturgical revival and rediscovery of the catholicity of the church in Sweden. A strong bond exists between the Church of England and the Church of Sweden, symbolized by their full intercommunion since 1922. Ordination of women has been permitted since 1959, and by 1963, 7 women had been ordained, although one third of the male clergy refused to co-operate with them; by 1978 this had risen to 235 women out of 3,200 active clergy (7%). At present 3% of the Swedish population attend the state church weekly, despite the fact that 80% have their children baptized and confirmed. The high proportion of church weddings among non-churchgoers indicates that church weddings serve more as a family than a religious ritual. The 96% of the population who retain official church membership assume also responsibility for the regular payment of church taxes.

The free churches in Sweden are distinguished by fervor and pietism, by their emphasis on church membership as a matter for personal decision, and by the importance they place on independence from the state. In recent years their liturgy has been slowly returning to a more traditional form not greatly different from Lutheranism. The free churches form 10% of the population, the most significant of them being the Swedish Mission Covenant Church (Svenska Missionsforbundet) which was formed in 1878. This church and the smaller Swedish Alliance Mission (Svenska Alliansmission, 1853) are strongest in rural areas, whereas the Methodist Church is urban in character. The Methodist Church is in fact the oldest of Sweden's free churches. British preachers were sent to Stockholm in 1826 to serve expatriate Methodists from the UK already there. A church was built in 1840; but because of opposition from the state church, the work came to an end in 1842. However, it was revived again by the conversion of a Swede in New York in 1850 who brought Methodism in its American connection back home with him. Another older free church is the Baptist Union of Sweden (Svenska Baptistamfundet), founded in 1848. The Salvation

Country summary. **Worlds A, B, C by ethnolinguistic peoples, cities, and major civil divisions in Sweden.**

World	PEOPLES Num	Pop 2000	C%	Christians	E%	U%	Unevangelized	CITIES Num	Pop 2000	C%	Christians	E%	U%	Unevangelized	CIVIL DIVISIONS Num	Pop 2000	C%	Christians	E%	U%	Unevangelized
A	5	82,330	0.32	263	41	59	48,983	0	0	0.00	0	0	0	0	0	0	0.00	0	0	0	0
B	7	184,709	11.69	21,600	65	35	64,531	0	0	0.00	0	0	0	0	0	0	0.00	0	0	0	0
C	39	8,643,170	69.17	5,978,489	100	0	26,796	21	4,654,704	65.31	3,040,158	98	2	88,053	23	8,910,214	67.34	6,000,355	98	2	140,311
Total	**51**	**8,910,209**	**67.34**	**6,000,352**	**98**	**2**	**140,310**	**21**	**4,654,704**	**65.31**	**3,040,158**	**98**	**2**	**88,053**	**23**	**8,910,214**	**67.34**	**6,000,355**	**98**	**2**	**140,311**

Army is divided into an English branch (1882) and a much smaller Swedish branch. All of these churches have experienced a steady decline in membership since 1930; one of the causes has been the increasing urbanization. The Pentecostal movement (Pingstrorelsen), which arose in 1907, expanded rapidly from 1930 to 1960 but since then has also experienced a decline in membership. Nevertheless, the Pentecostal Revival Movement of Sweden is now the largest Protestant denomination in the country. Other important Protestant churches are the Finnish Lutherans, Orebro Pentecostals, and a number of smaller groups. Many of these free churches since the middle of the 19th century have sent missionaries to foreign fields, in particular to Africa, India, and Japan. Pentecostals are also active in Latin America.

Protestants. Government postage stamps, 1978: (from above, clockwise) Salvation Army band, Baptist adult baptism, Pentecostal tent meeting, minister with children (Swedish Missionary Society), communion (Evangelical National Missionary Society).

CATHOLIC CHURCH. From 1604 until 1873 no Swedish citizen was permitted to be a Catholic. Even today, despite its activism the Catholic Church remains on the fringe of Swedish society. The number of Catholics has increased due to the influx of immigrant workers and political refugees, especially Poles from 1945, Hungarians in 1956, Czechs and Slovaks in 1968, also Chileans and Brazilians more recently. There were 1,390 Catholics in 1890, 4,763 in 1930, and 27,416 in 1960. By 1990 they had grown to over 150,000, largely through immigration.

In 1977 Sweden along with Scandinavia, was transferred from the jurisdiction of Propaganda (Rome) to that of the Congregation for Bishops.

The Holy See has diplomatic relations with Sweden and in AD 2000 is represented to government and the Catholic hierarchy by a nuncio residing in Denmark.

OTHER CHURCHES. As a result of the influx of refugees during World War II, Orthodox churches increased considerably in numbers of affiliated to 10,000 faithful in 1960 and over 115,000 by 1990 in 1970, including Estonians, Finns, Greeks, Romanians, Russians, Serbs, and Syrians. Jehovah's Witnesses had 39,000 adherents in 1990. English-speaking Anglican chaplaincy services are also available.

Indigenous missions. Sweden has a long history of mission-sending commencing shortly after Scandinavia was evangelized. Since the Protestant Reformation, Sweden has been a leading missionary-sending country. Swedish missionaries from all Christian traditions can be found ministering all over the world.

Renewal movements. In the 1990s the Pentecostal/Charismatic Renewal continued to spread rapidly across most older churches, and numbered over 623,000 adherents (of whom 29% Pentecostals, 61% Charismatics, and 9% Independents).

CHURCH AND STATE

Relations between church and state are governed by the Ecclesiastical Law (Kyrkolag) of 1686, the constitution of 1809, amended most recently in 1961, and the Law of Religious Freedom (Religionsfrihet-slag) of 1951. According to these, the Church of Sweden has a privileged position in relation to the state. The king, who is the supreme head of the church, names the archbishop and bishops on presentation by the Synod (Kyrkomote) of 3 candidates for each vacancy. In principle, the freedom of the church is assured by the fact that the Synod can veto parliaments proposals concerning ecclesiastical matters. Membership in the Church of Sweden is acquired automatically at birth and not by baptism; but since 1951 an individual may request to be released from membership, whether or not he wishes to join another church. The state imposes a church tax; those who do not belong to the Church of Sweden pay only 40% of this, which covers the services performed by the Church of Sweden for the civil state. The state pays the Lutheran clergy who also are responsible for keeping state registers in addition to other municipal functions. State schools provide religious instruction, which is non-denominational and objective in nature. Teachers of religion are not required to belong to a church in order to qualify. The Church of Sweden, as all other churches, provides its own denominational instruction outside of school hours.

Religious and ecclesiastical affairs are under the jurisdiction of the Office for Ecclesiastical Affairs (Byran for Kykokamerale Fragor), of the Ministry of Education (Utbildningsdepartementet). If the minister of Education does not belong to the Church of Sweden, a minister without portfolio who is a member is put in charge of ecclesiastical affairs. The Churches are not required to be registered, but clergy must receive official authorization to perform marriages recognized by the state. The opening of cloistered convents is also subject to royal authorization.

The government does not generally give subsidies to churches other than the Church of Sweden, nor to the few private schools existing in the country; but in an unusual gesture in 1971, parliament granted substantial financial aid to be shared among the Salvation Army, Baptist, Methodist, Orthodox, and Catholic churches as well as with the Jewish and Muslim communities

BROADCASTING AND MEDIA

Shortwave radio programs in European languages can be received from KNLS, AWR (Slovakia), TWR (Monaco, Albania), and HCJB (Ecuador). Christian television programming can be received via satellite. AWR's studio in Stockholm records Swedish programs.

Satellite TV and radio programs are received in English, Arabic, German and Italian. Sweden is a member of UNDA.

INTERDENOMINATIONAL ORGANIZATIONS

The Swedish churches have long been active in the ecumenical field. During World War I, archbishop Nathan Soderblom attempted to bring about a worldwide peace conference of all churches, which was later expanded to include other social and practical aspects of the Christian witness. As a result, an ecumenical conference on Life and Work took place in Stockholm in 1925, and in 1952 a Faith and Order conference in Lund. The Church of Sweden and the Swedish Mission Covenant Church joined the nascent World Council of Churches in 1939 and 1946 respectively, before its formal founding in 1948. The Swedish Ecumenical Council (Svenska Ekumeniska Namnden) was established in 1932, building on foundations laid as early as 1915; and there are now about 75 local Christian councils with others in different stages of formation. The first national conference for local ecumenical councils was held in 1971. There is also a Swedish Free Church Council and a Swedish Missionary Council (Svenska Missionsradet). The latter was originally established in 1912 following the Edinburgh Conference of 1910 and was re-organized under its present name in 1920. The Stockholm Institute for the Sociology of Religion provides regular surveys of churches and evaluation of data in the field of religion. The Nordic Ecumenical Institute is an international body created in 1940 to provide a study and information center for ecumenical and evangelistic activities in all northern European countries, including Norway, Sweden, Denmark, Finland, and Iceland. The Swedish Ecumenical Committee for Development, Justice, and Peace (SEKURF) is responsible for Sweden's Sodepax program.

FUTURE TRENDS AND PROSPECTS

The nonreligious and atheists are expected to continue to take a growing share of the population jointly reaching more than 30% by 2025 while Christianity declines to 66.3% from a high of near 100% in 1900.

The nonreligious and atheists will likely claim over 35% of Sweden's population before AD 2040 and perhaps as much as 40% by AD 2050. Christianity is expected to decline steadily throughout the next several decades.

BIBLIOGRAPHY

Catholicisme en Scandinavie. M. de Paillerets. Paris: Spes, 1967.

Gods of the North. B. Branston. London: Thames & Hudson, 1955. 318p.

Homeward to Zion: the Mormon migration from Scandinavia. W. Mulder. Minneapolis, MN: University of Minnesota Press, 1957. 375p.

'Investigating the challenge of bringing renewal to the Church of Sweden.' T. Gudina. D.Miss. thesis, Fuller Theological Seminary, Pasadena, CA, 1986. 312p.

L'Eglise Suédoise: son histoire et son organisation. R. Murray. Stockholm, 1970.

Les Scandinaves: histoire des peuples scandinaves: épanouissement de leurs civilisations des origines à la Réforme (The Scandinavians: history of the Scandinavian people: development of their civilization from its origins to the Reformation). M. Gravier. Paris: Éditions Lidis-Brepols, 1984. 686p.

Missions from the North: Nordic Missionary Council, 50 years. C. F. Hallencreutz, J. Aagard & N. E. Bloch-Hoell (eds). *Studia Missionalia Upsaliensia*, vol. 20. Oslo: Universitetsforlaget, 1974. 171p.

Northern Europe today: an introduction to culture and religion in the five Nordic countries. A. J. Kristoffersen. Ulricehamn, Sweden: The author, 1991. 91p.

Scandinavian churches: a picture of the development and life of the churches of Denmark, Finland, Iceland, Norway and Sweden. L. S. Hunter (ed). London: Faber & Faber, 1965.

Scandinavian mythology. H. R. E. Davidson. London: Paul Hamlyn, 1975. 141p.

Svensk missionsatlas. B. Sundkler & G. Sommarström. Stockholm: Svenska Institutet för Missionsforskning, 1957.

Svenska Kyrkans Arsbok, 1970. Stockholm: Verbum Kyrkliga Central-förlaget, 1970. 323p.

'Sweden,' B. Gustafsson, in *Western religion: a country by country sociological enquiry*, p.479–510. H. Mol (ed). The Hague: Mouton, 1972.

Sweden. L. B. Sather & A. Swanson. Ed., H. H. Wellisch. *World bibliographical series*, vol. 80. Oxford, UK: CLIO Press, 1987. 372p. (See especially 'Religion,' 106–13).

Swedish Christian handbook. P. W. Brierley (ed). MARC Europe, 1990. 64p.

'Technology and religion in medieval Sweden.' A. Götlind. Doctoral thesis, University of Göteborg, Sweden, 1993. 272p.

'The church and secularized society: the Scandinavian experience,' *Pro Mundi Vita* (Brussels), 29 (1969).

The church beneath the northern lights: Fenno–Scandian historical theology. A. J. Kristoffersen. [1990]. 105p.

The Church of Sweden: past and present: a book sponsored by the Swedish Bishops' Conference. R. Murray (ed). Trans., N. G. Sahlin. Malmö, Sweden: Allhem, 1960. 286p.

The English missionaries in Sweden and Finland. C. J. A. Opperman. London: Society for Promoting Christian Knowledge, 1937. 221p.

The force of tradition: a case study of women priests in Sweden. B. K. Stendahl. Philadelphia: Fortress Press, 1985. 200p.

'The reception of the Augsburg Confession in Scandinavia,' T. R. Skarsten, *Sixteenth century journal*, 11, 3 (1980), 87–98.

'The role of religion in modern Sweden,' B. Gustafsson, *American behavioral scientist*, 17, 6 (1974), 175–86.

Women of the Reformation from Spain to Scandinavia. R. H. Bainton. Minneapolis, MN: Augsburg Publishing House, 1977. 240p.

Country Table 2. **Organized churches and denominations in Sweden.**

Official name (bold type = church with over 10% of all affiliated) 1	*Begun* 2	*Type* 3	*Counc* 4	*Congs* 5	*Adults* 6	*Affiliated 1970* 7	*Affiliated 1995* 8	*G%* 9	*Names, notes, and other statistics* (see Codebook, Part 3) 10
Ancient Church of the East (P Tehran)	c1975	O-Nes	Yw...	10	2,935	1,000	5,900	5.00	*Assyrian Ch. Nestorians.* Assyrian refugees from Lebanon and Cyprus wars.
Armenian Apostolic Church	c1970	O-Arm	E....	1	1,350	–	2,248	36.17	*Gregorians.* Under C Echmiadzin (Armenia).
Association of Vineyard Churches	c1985	I-3cW	.....	7	500	–	1,000	10.00	Assisted by M=AVC(USA).
Baptist Union of Sweden	1848	P-Bap	TvX.x	359	20,796	60,000	31,554	-2.54	*Svenska Baptistsamfundet.* Decline from 1940. 266n,1p,1s,W=60%,320Y,450z.
Bulgarian Orthodox Church	c1975	O-Bul	M....	2	1,610	–	2,300	5.00	Residents from Bulgaria.
Catholic Church: D Stockholm	1783	R-Lat	bzBQW	37	120,000	58,929	164,332	4.19	*Romersk-katolska Kyrkan.* 83% aliens. C=9+0+12.(1970)8n,91x,957Yy.(1990)51n,78x,92m,242w, 1268Yy
Christian Brethren		P-CBr	x....	2	100	200	230	0.05	*Plymouth Brethren. Open Brethren. Gospel Halls.* Independent congregations.
Church of Christ, Scientist	1905	m-Sci	x....	5	2,000	4,000	3,000	-1.14	*Kristen Vetenskap. Christian Science.* M=CCS(Mother Ch,Boston, USA). 1m,8w.
Church of England (D Europe)	c1750	A-plu	awc..	6	876	3,000	2,920	-0.11	*Anglikanska Syrkan.* Anglican (English) chaplaincies for 5,000 UK citizens. 2x.
Ch of Jesus Christ of Latter-day Saints	1853	m-LdS	x....	40	4,540	5,195	7,700	1.59	*Jesu Kristi Kyrka av Sista Dagers Heliga.* Emigrating. 180f. 1Tpa,W=70%,260Yy.
Church of Norway	c1970	P-Lut	.....	11	6,000	–	11,000	45.10	Norwegian residents, members of Norway's state church.
Church of Sweden	829	P-Lut	LWX.a	2,565	3,050,000	7,941,561	7,630,000	0.09	*Svenska Kyrkan.* Begun 600 years before Reformation. 13 Dioceses. Women clergy. 3350n.
Churches of Christ	1957	I-Dis	x....	3	60	100	150	1.64	*Kristi Församling.* M=CC(Non-Instrumental)(USA). In Gothenburg, Stockholm.
Coptic Orthodox Church	c1975	O-Cop	N....	1	384	–	640	5.00	Migrant laborers from Egypt. M=COC(Egypt).
Dutch Reformed Church	c1970	P-Ref	.....	6	3,000	–	6,000	41.62	*NGK.* Members of Dutch church.
Estonian Ev Lutheran Church in Exile	1941	P-Lut	LWC..	64	15,250	55,000	20,000	-3.97	*Eesti Evangeeliumi Luteri Usu Kirik.* Estonian refugees. World HQ Stockholm.
Estonian Orthodox Church in Exile	c1945	O-Est	C...w	1	1,070	4,000	1,430	-4.03	Estonian refugees from USSR. Bishop and one large congregation in Stockholm.
Ethiopian Orthodox Church	c1980	O-Eth	N....	1	683	–	1,050	6.67	Laborers from Ethiopia.
Evangelical Church of Germany	c1970	P-LuR	.....	9	4,000	–	9,000	43.94	*EKD.* German church members.
Evangelical Lutheran Ch of Finland	c1950	P-Lut	Lwc..	100	120,000	45,000	150,000	4.93	*Finsksprakigt Lutherskt Församlingsarbete.* Serves 350,000 Finnish migrant workers.
Free Baptist Union	1872	I-Bap	x...C	12	905	3,200	1,241	-3.72	*Fribaptistsämfundet. Scandinavian Independent Baptist Union.* In south. 20n.
Free Pentecostal Mission	1930	I-3pW	.....	5	500	500	1,000	2.81	*Fria Pingstforsamlingen.* Schism from Filadelfia, Stockholm Ch (SFM).
Gypsy Evangelical Movement	c1970	I-3pE	.....	40	1,000	–	3,000	37.75	M=GGMS. Gypsies in registered church.
Hungarian Protestant Congregations	1957	P-LuR	.....	5	3,600	3,000	4,483	1.62	*Ungerska Protestantiska Forsämlingen.* Hungarian refugees, Reformed and Lutheran.
Jehovah's Witnesses	1899	m-Jeh	x....	338	22,742	27,000	39,200	1.50	*Jehovas Vittnen. Watch Tower.* Active witnessing by 1926. HQ Jakobsberg. 826Y.
Latvian Ev Lutheran Church in Exile	1945	P-Lut	Lwc..	6	752	4,500	2,149	-2.91	*Lettiska Evangelisk-Lutherska Kyrkan.* Latvian refugees. 7n,W=36%,5Yy.
Liberal Catholic Church	1925	I-Lib	xv...	2	50	300	100	-4.30	*Liberala katolska Kyrkan.* M=LCC(UK), HQ Lindingo. 1968, applied to join WCC.
Macedonian Orthodox Church	c1965	O-Mac	c....	4	6,400	500	7,855	11.65	Split from Serbian Orthodox Church in 1975.
Maranatha Revival Church	1959	I-3pW	x....	30	15,000	15,000	20,000	1.16	*Maranataväckelsen.* Radical schism ex Filadelfia Church. 3 factions. HQ Bromma.
Methodist Church in Sweden	1826	P-Met	VwX.z	84	4,183	25,000	9,328	-3.87	*Metodistkyrkan. Swedish Annual Conf,* NEurope CC, UMC(USA). 123n,1s,71Yy.
National Church of Denmark	c1970	P-Lut	.....	5	2,000	–	5,000	40.59	Danish members of state church of Denmark.
New Apostolic Church	1898	I-3aX	x....	10	250	1,000	366	-3.94	*Nypostoliska Kyrkan.* In Hamburg Bezirk; world HQ Zurich. Germans.
New Church	1887	m-Swe	x....	2	50	200	100	-2.73	*Nya Kyrkan. Swedenborgians. Stockholm Society,* and *Jönköping Circle.*
Örebro Mission Church	1892	P-Pe2	Z.D.x	362	20,272	44,650	33,233	-1.17	*Örebro Missionsforening.* 1937 ex BUS. HQ Örebro. 165n,140m,2j,1s,W=33%,370Y.
Orthodox Church in Sweden: D Swedia	1960	O-Gre	Cwc.w	13	11,600	20,000	37,500	2.55	*Grekisk-Ortodoxa Kyrkan. D Swedia & All Scandinavia,* & E Northern Lands. Greeks. 2x.
Orthodox Church of Finland	1958	O-Fin	Cwc.w	10	3,000	4,000	5,980	1.62	*Routsin Suomalainen Ortodoksinen Seurakunta.* Finns. Use Swedish churches. 1n,6Yy.
Pentecostal Revival Movement of S	1907	P-Pe2	Z.D.a	2,115	97,282	230,000	155,778	-1.55	*Pingstväckelsen i Sverige/Pingströrelsen/Filadelfia Ch.* SFM. 1200n,1j,1s,1300Y.
Religious Society of Friends	c1916	P-Qua	Q....	9	420	500	516	0.13	*Vännernas Samfund i Sverige. Sweden Yearly Meeting* (1935). *Quakers.* HQ Stockholm.
Romanian Orthodox Church	c1970	O-Rum	Cwc.w	5	2,710	1,000	4,168	5.88	In Stockholm. Under jurisdiction of P Bucharest. Romanians. Migrant laborers.
Russian Orth Ch: D Western Europe	1617	I-Rus	x...w	1	626	1,000	1,251	0.90	In Russian Orthodox Ch Outside Russia (Paris). Bishop in Sweden. Conservative.
Salvation Army	1882	P-Sal	xwx.a	470	9,984	90,000	29,511	-4.36	*Frälsningsarmén. Sweden Territory.* Declining. 101 institutions,650n,1s.
Serbian Orthodox Church	1972	O-Ser	Cwc.w	4	14,400	9,000	28,833	4.35	Under P Belgrade; bishop in England. Many Serbian migrant laborers. In Vasteras.
Seventh-day Adventist Church	1880	P-Adv	x....	46	3,285	7,200	4,574	-1.80	*Swed UC* (excl Finland Swedish Conf,Finland). 33n,2H,1j,1p,1s(8),W=71%,111Y.
Swedish Alliance Mission	1853	P-Non	x.D.x	279	11,712	33,900	23,739	-1.42	*Svenska Alliansmissionen.* Only 23 churches have over 100 members. 170n.
Swedish Evangelical Mission	1856	P-Lut	.....	288	23,006	48,000	46,301	-0.14	*Evangeliska Fosterlands-Stiftelsen.*
Swedish Holiness Union	1886	P-Hol	x.D.x	418	5,021	15,000	8,986	-2.03	*Helgelseförbundet/Covenant of Sanctification.* USA links. 163n,1p,W=71%.
Swedish Mission Covenant Church	1878	P-Con	xWX.z	1,056	77,058	213,000	154,400	-1.28	*SMF. Svenska Missionsförbundet.* Revival ex state church. 623n,150m,31w,1s(107).
Swedish Orthodox Church		O-Rus	.....	3	1,250	–	1,844	0.05	Russian-speaking parish and clergy.
Swedish Religious Reform Society		m-Unt	.....	1	100	300	200	0.05	*Sveriges Religiosa Reförmforbund.* Unitarians. Links with UUA(USA). HQ Skepptuna.
Swedish Salvation Army	1905	P-Sal	x.D.x	17	1,787	5,000	2,230	-3.18	*Svenska Frälsningsarmén.* 1905, rejected authority of international HQ, London. 25n.
Syrian Orthodox Church	1970	O-Syr	Dw.Nw	17	7,100	1,000	11,272	10.17	Under P Antioch (Damascus). Mainly Western Syriac (Turyoyo), also Arabs. Migrant laborers.
True Friends of the Bible	c1950	I-Lut	.....	33	2,663	300	4,768	11.70	*Bibeltrogna Vanner.* Lutheran foreign mission agency.
Word of Life	c1975	I-3cW	.....	100	6,000	–	20,000	5.00	*Livets Ord. Faith Movement (Uppsala).* M=IFM,Rhema BC(Tulsa, USA). Also in Russia.
Other pentecostal denominations		I-3pB	x....	15	1,000	–	2,000	0.05	Including Ch of God in Christ (USA), Assembly Hall Churches (1 ch).
Other Protestant denominations		P-	.....	20	2,000	5,000	5,000	0.05	Total about 30 (see list below), including GKN, GKV, Swiss Reformed Chs, PCK-T(Koreans).
Other marginal Protestant bodies		m-	.....	50	2,000	3,000	5,000	0.05	Total over 30 smaller marginal sects and cults, including Children of God, Christadelphians.
Other independent Catholic churches		I-CCa	.....	20	100	200	200	0.05	Small bodies including Cath Apost Ch (Katolsk-apostoliska Kyrkan), Apostolic Episcopal Ch.
Doubly-affiliated		2-aff			-149,000	-188,235	-349,560		90% of all free church members including Pentecostals remain in state church.
Disaffiliated		X-Aff			-1,034,000	-2,770,000	-2,430,000		Baptized Lutherans who have become completely disaffiliated agnostics or atheists.
Totals				**9,125**	**2,533,962**	**6,032,000**	**5,952,000**		

Churches, members, growth, 1900-2025	*Congs*	*Adults*	*Affiliated*	*G%*	*Total denominations*	*6 Megablocs:* O	R	A	P	I	m
Total churches, members, and denominations (mid-1900)	7,000	2,041,000	5,077,000	0.25	19	0	1	1	10	3	4
Total churches, members, and denominations (mid-1970)	11,258	2,424,600	6,032,000	0.25	75	8	1	1	31	13	21
Total churches, members, and denominations (mid-1990)	10,000	2,484,000	5,835,900	-0.17	156	13	1	1	52	48	41
Total churches, members, and denominations (mid-1995)	9,125	2,533,962	5,952,000	0.39	156	13	1	1	52	48.	41
Total churches, members, and denominations (mid-2000)	9,500	2,554,000	6,000,356	0.16	156	13	1	1	52	48	41
Total churches, members, and denominations (mid-2025)	10,000	2,554,000	6,000,000	0.00	247	20	1	1	70	100	55

NOTES ON TABLE ABOVE

NATIONAL COUNCILS (Column 4, 5th letter).

a = member of both SEC and SEA.

C = Swedish Free Church Council (SFCC) (Sveriges Frikyrkorad).

d = member of both SFCC and SEC.

E = Swedish Evangelical Alliance (SEA) (Evangeliska Alliansens Svenska Avdelning)

W = Swedish Ecumenical Council (SEC) (Svenska Ekumeniska Nämnden).

w = associate member of SEC.

x = member of both SFCC and SEA.

z = member of both SFCC, SEC, and SEA.

Local councils. About 75.

OTHER PROTESTANT DENOMINATIONS. There are about 30 additional smaller denominations, including: Apostolic Faith (Apostoliska Trons Mission), Christian Society, Ch of God (Anderson) (1 church), Ch of the Nazarene, Exclusive Brethren (Raven-Taylor), French Reformed Ch (Eglise Réformée de France: Fransk-Reformerta Församlingen), International Ch, Moravian Ch (Evangeliska Brödrförsamlingen), Worldwide Evangelization Crusade.

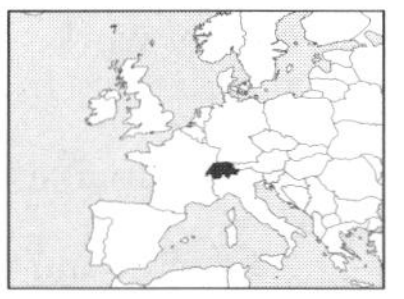

SWITZERLAND

SECULAR DATA, AD 2000

STATE
Official name: Die Schweizerische Eidtgenossenschaft/La Confédération Suisse (The Swiss Confederation).
Short name: Switzerland. **Adjective of nationality:** Swiss.
Flag: White cross on red field.
Area: 41,284 sq. km. (15,940 sq. mi.).
Government: Federal Republic, since 1848 (1291 Swiss confederation, 1499 independent, 1798 Helvetic Republic).
Legislature: Parliament: Council of States (Stränderat), 46 members; National Council (Nationalrat), 200 members.
Official language: German (Deutsch), French (Français), Italian, Romansch.
Monetary unit: 1 Swiss Franc (Sw F) = 100 centimes. **US$1=** Sw F 1.38.
Chief cities: Zurich 984,000; Basel (Basle, Bale) 630,508; Geneve (Genf, Geneva) 515,371; BERN (Berne) 327,165; Lausanne 288,873.
Political divisions: 26 provinces.
Armed forces: 20,000.

DEMOGRAPHY
Population: 7,386,000.
Population density: 178.9/sq. km. (463.3/sq. mi.).
Under 15 years: 1,288,000.
Growth rate p.a.: 0.40% (births 10.07, deaths 8.90).
Mortality: Infant, per 1,000: 5.5; **Maternal per 100,000:** 6.0.
Life expectancy: 79 (male 76, female 82).
Household size: 2.2. **Floor area per person, sq.m:** 50.0.
Major languages: 64.9% German, 18.1% French, 11.9% Italian, 0.8% Romansh, Spanish, English, Turkish, Hungarian, Dutch, Czech, Greek.
Urban dwellers: 62.58%. **Urban growth rate p.a.:** 1.0%.
Labor force: 51%.

ETHNOLINGUISTIC PEOPLES
55.2% German Swiss (Alemannic); 16.8% Franco-Swiss; 11.0% Italo-Swiss (Ticanese); 2.1% French (Vaudois); 2.0% Spaniard.

ECONOMY
National income p.a. per person: US$40,629; **per family:** US$89,385.

EDUCATION
Adult literacy: 100% (male 100%, female 100%). **Schools:** 3,000.
Universities: 12. **School enrolment:** female/male: 95%/96%.

HEALTH
Access to health services: 95%. **Access to safe water:** 100%.
Hospitals: 500 (78 beds per 10,000). **Doctors:** 23,000.
Blind: 9,000. **Deaf:** 444,700. **Murder rate:** 2.
Lepers: 300.

LITERATURE
New book titles p.a.: 15,880 (2,150 p.a. per million). **Periodicals:** 4,311. **Newspapers:** 80 dailies.

COMMUNICATION (per 1,000 people)
Phones: 613 (26% mobile). **Radios:** 791. **TV sets:** 370.
Daily newspaper circulation: 415. **Computers:** 443.

REFUGEES
Alien refugees from other countries: 29,000.

HUMAN LIFE AND LIBERTY (optimum condition=100.0%)
HDI: 93.0. **HSI:** 97.0. **HFI:** 85.0. **EFL:** 64.0.

Country Table 1. Religious adherents in Switzerland, AD 1900-2025.

Year	*1900*		*1970*		*mid-1990*		*Annual change, 1990-2000*				*mid-1995*		*mid-2000*		*mid-2025*	
Name	*Adherents*	*%*	*Adherents*	*%*	*Adherents*	*%*	*Natural*	*Conversion*	*Total*	*Rate*	*Adherents*	*%*	*Adherents*	*%*	*Adherents*	*%*
Christians	**3,294,600**	**99.4**	**6,074,000**	**98.2**	**6,136,420**	**89.8**	**49,535**	**-10,446**	**39,089**	**0.62**	**6,369,600**	**89.2**	**6,527,305**	**88.4**	**6,595,200**	**86.9**
PROFESSION																
professing Christians	**3,294,600**	**99.4**	**6,074,000**	**98.2**	**6,136,420**	**89.8**	**49,535**	**-10,446**	**39,089**	**0.62**	**6,369,600**	**89.2**	**6,527,305**	**88.4**	**6,595,200**	**86.9**
AFFILIATION																
unaffiliated Christians	65,600	2.0	174,000	2.8	86,420	1.3	698	-1,164	-466	-0.55	84,400	1.2	81,757	1.1	125,000	1.7
affiliated Christians	**3,229,000**	**97.4**	**5,900,000**	**95.4**	**6,050,000**	**88.5**	**48,837**	**-9,282**	**39,555**	**0.64**	**6,285,200**	**88.0**	**6,445,548**	**87.3**	**6,470,200**	**85.3**
Roman Catholics	1,321,900	39.9	2,860,611	46.2	3,120,000	45.7	25,201	-11,201	14,000	0.44	3,197,567	44.8	3,260,000	44.1	3,200,000	42.2
Protestants	1,864,600	56.2	2,808,031	45.4	2,900,000	42.4	23,424	-9,424	14,000	0.47	2,957,314	41.4	3,040,000	41.2	3,000,000	39.5
Independents	40,000	1.2	97,804	1.6	135,000	2.0	1,090	1,410	2,500	1.71	151,942	2.1	160,000	2.2	240,000	3.2
Marginal Christians	1,000	0.0	134,702	2.2	127,000	1.9	1,026	-1,526	-500	-0.40	125,940	1.8	122,000	1.7	110,000	1.5
Orthodox	1,000	0.0	19,000	0.3	23,000	0.3	186	114	300	1.23	24,700	0.4	26,000	0.4	38,000	0.5
Anglicans	500	0.0	10,000	0.2	11,800	0.2	95	55	150	1.20	13,000	0.2	13,300	0.2	14,000	0.2
doubly-affiliated	0	0.0	-30,148	-0.5	-266,800	-3.9	-2,155	11,260	9,105	-4.09	-185,263	-2.6	-175,752	-2.4	-131,800	-1.7
Trans-megabloc groupings																
Evangelicals	470,000	14.2	257,000	4.2	277,000	4.1	2,237	-87	2,150	0.75	290,330	4.1	298,500	4.0	303,000	4.0
Pentecostals/Charismatics	0	0.0	75,000	1.2	407,000	6.0	3,287	3,263	6,550	1.50	442,628	6.2	472,500	6.4	569,000	7.5
Great Commission Christians	**500,000**	**15.1**	**1,545,000**	**25.0**	**2,290,000**	**33.5**	**18,497**	**6,619**	**25,116**	**1.05**	**2,428,000**	**34.0**	**2,541,157**	**34.4**	**2,731,000**	**36.0**
Nonreligious	5,700	0.2	46,800	0.8	425,000	6.2	3,433	6,265	9,698	2.08	464,920	6.5	521,979	7.1	621,500	8.2
Muslims	400	0.0	16,400	0.3	158,000	2.3	1,276	3,111	4,387	2.48	180,000	2.5	201,870	2.7	235,000	3.1
Atheists	1,000	0.0	20,000	0.3	70,000	1.0	565	418	983	1.32	76,000	1.1	79,834	1.1	105,000	1.4
Hindus	0	0.0	2,000	0.0	15,800	0.2	128	567	695	3.71	21,000	0.3	22,754	0.3	4,600	0.1
Jews	13,000	0.4	20,700	0.3	17,400	0.3	141	-110	31	0.18	17,600	0.3	17,711	0.2	15,000	0.2
Buddhists	0	0.0	2,000	0.0	5,030	0.1	41	242	283	4.57	7,500	0.1	7,863	0.1	2,200	0.0
Baha'is	0	0.0	3,100	0.1	3,700	0.1	30	-27	3	0.08	3,720	0.1	3,728	0.1	4,500	0.1
Other religionists	300	0.0	2,000	0.0	2,650	0.0	21	-20	1	0.05	2,660	0.0	2,663	0.0	4,000	0.1
World A (unevangelized persons)	3,315	0.1	6,186	0.1	109,344	1.6	888	1,168	2,056	1.73	121,429	1.7	132,948	1.8	189,675	2.5
World B (evangelized non-Christians)	17,484	0.5	106,463	1.7	588,236	8.6	4,747	9,278	14,025	2.12	651,874	9.1	725,747	9.8	802,125	10.6
World C (Christians)	3,294,600	99.4	6,074,000	98.2	6,136,420	89.8	49,535	-10,446	39,089	0.62	6,369,600	89.2	6,527,305	88.4	6,595,200	86.9
Country's population	**3,315,400**	**100.0**	**6,186,650**	**100.0**	**6,834,000**	**100.0**	**55,170**	**0**	**55,170**	**0.78**	**7,142,904**	**100.0**	**7,386,000**	**100.0**	**7,587,000**	**100.0**

COLUMNS, ROWS.
For meanings and definitions, see Codebook (Part 3). Note that, by definition, total 'Christians' = professing + crypto-Christians, which also = affiliated + unaffiliated Christians, and also = Great Commission Christians + latent Christians. Percentages may not always total exactly, due to rounding.

CENSUSES.
(Held every 10 years since 1860). **1860:** 58.9% Protestants, 40.7% Roman Catholics, 0.2% Jews, 0.2% nonreligious and other religionists. **1900:** 57.8% Protestants 40.6% Roman Catholics, 1.0% Old Catholics (non-Roman), 0.4% Jews, 0.2% nonreligious and other religionists. **1910:** 56.1% Protestants, 41.5% Roman Catholics, 1.0% Old Catholics, 0.9% nonreligious and other religionists, 0.5% Jews. **1920:** 57.5% Protestants, 39.9% Roman Catholics, 1.1% nonreligious and other religionists, 1.0% Old Catholics, 0.5% Jews. **1930:** 57.3% Protestants, 40.1% Roman Catholics, 1.3% nonreligious and other religionists, 0.9% Old Catholics, 0.4% Jews. **1941:** 57.6% Protestants, 40.4% Roman Catholics, 0.8% nonreligious and other religionists, 0.7% Old Catholics, 0.5% Jews. **1.XII.1950** (de jure): 56.3% Protestants, 41.6% Roman Catholics, 1.1% nonreligious and atheists and other religionists, 0.6% Old Catholics (non-Roman), 0.4% Jews. **1.XII.1960** (de jure): 52.7% Protestants, 45.4% Roman Catholics, 0.8% nonreligious and atheists and other religionists, 0.5% Old Catholics, 0.4% Jews, 0.1% Orthodox. **1.XII.1970:** 49.6% Roman Catholics, 47.0% Protestants, 1.1% nonreligious and atheists, 0.8% Catholics (non-Roman) (0.5% New Apostolics, 0.3% Old Catholics), 0.3% Orthodox, 0.3% marginal Protestants, 0.3% Jews, 0.3% Muslims, 0.2% Anglicans, 0.1% other religionists. **1980**: 48.1% Roman Catholics, 44.8% Protestants, 3.8% nonreligious, 1.0% other Christians, 0.9% Muslims, 0.6% Orthodox, 0.3% Old Catholics, 0.3% Jews, 0.2% other religionists. **1990**: 47.0% Roman Catholics, 40.6% Protestants, 7.4% nonreligious, 2.2% Muslims, 1.0% Orthodox, 0.9% other Christians, 0.4% other religionists, 0.3% Jews, 0.2% Old Catholics.

NOTES ON RELIGIONS
ATHEISTS. Parti Suisse du Travail (PST), and 2 extreme leftist factions: Partie Populaire Suisse (PPS), Organisation des Communistes de Suisse (OCS/ML). 71% of all communists, and of Communist voters, are from French-speaking cantons.
BAHA'IS. Entered before 1921. Local spiritual assemblies: 1964, 12; 1973, 16. HQ Bern. By 1996, organized bodies had grown to 26 LSAs.
BUDDHISTS. Initially, 500 refugees from Tibet after the 1950 occupation by China; and also about 1,400 Chinese. There are several important centers of Buddhist studies.
COUNTRY'S POPULATION. There has been substantial immigration of foreign workers since 1930, mainly Roman Catholics from Mediterranean countries. In 1990-2000 most of the annual natural increase was due to immigration. The column 'Natural change' above incorporates both immigration and biological increase figures, and shows the division of the total among the various religions and blocs.
HINDUS. Ramakrishna Mission, and numerous young Swiss converts to the Divine Light Mission, ISKCON (Hare Krishna), Ananda Marga, and a few other groups, including a neo-Hindu movement, the Theosophical Society.
JEWS. 42% expatriates; urban, in over 22 cities. Co-ordinated through the Union of Swiss Jewish Communities (Zürich).
MUSLIMS. 2 distinct groups: Turkish migrant workers since 1960 (57,300 in 1995), and later immigrants including 103,000 Bosnians, 35,000 Kurds, and 2,600 Arabs, all being Sunnis; and since 1948 the Ahmadiya Mission (Qadianis) (enumerated here under Muslims, though declared non-Muslim by Pakistan) based on Zürich. Qadianis, based on Rabwah (Pakistan), with mostly Swiss converts; mosque in Zürich, opened in 1963.
OTHER RELIGIONISTS. Adherents of numerous smaller religions and cults, including Rosicrucians (10 AMORC centers).
PENTECOSTALS/CHARISMATICS. (1974). Charismatics within the non-Pentecostal Protestant denominations, in the French-speaking Reformed churches (12 pastors involved) and German-speaking (3 pastors). There are also a number of youths in the Jesus Movement. The Catholic Charismatic Renewal began in 1972; by 1996 there were 90 French-speaking regular prayer groups, 110 German-speaking, and 12 Italian-speaking. Weekly attenders numbered 5,400 including 44 priests and 9 bishops.
ROMAN CATHOLICS. The increase in proportion over the decades has been due to (1) higher Roman Catholic fertility than Protestant fertility and (2) the much larger influx of Roman Catholic foreign workers. Expatriate Roman Catholics increased from 202,445 professing in the census of 1950, to 464,553 in 1960, to 864,666 in 1970, and to 1,877,800 in 1990.

Great Commission Instrument Panel: status of Switzerland (for explanation see start of Part 4)

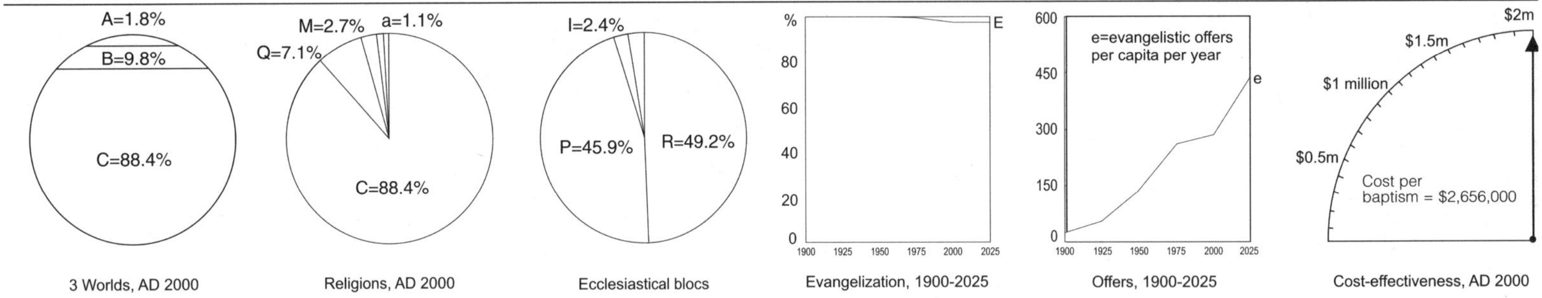

Country status. Switzerland is a landlocked mountainous country in the heart of Europe, unique for its strong tradition of political neutrality as well as economic prosperity. International finance and tourism are 2 of its main economic activities.

HUMAN LIFE AND LIBERTY

Human need and development. Switzerland is one of the most advanced countries in the world with a per capita income that surpasses the United States. Its closely knit social and political organization and its historic status as a safe haven for the persecuted have been important elements in its success. The recent influx of alien immigrants has introduced some discord in a system that has known no conflict for centuries. These immigrants live substandard lives and are excluded from the mainline economic and social activities. However, they also enjoy all the social welfare benefits as the Swiss nationals.

Human rights and freedoms. All basic human rights are guaranteed and respected in the country. To deter attacks on foreigners, a new antiracism law was passed by the Federal Assembly.

Human environment. Despite its pristine appearance Switzerland suffers from environmental problems generally associated with larger countries. These include water pollution (despite extensive waste-water treatment), acid rain from incinerators, and loss of biodiversity in the Alpine region whose fragile ecology is being increasingly affected by human activity.

NON-CHRISTIAN RELIGIONS

Judaism decreased slightly in numbers from 1930 to 1995 (17,973 to 17,600, but the proportion of Jews in the total population decreased over the same period from 0.4% to 0.3%. Jews are strongest in urban centers: Geneva (1.3% of the population). Basel (0.9%), Zurich (0.6%), Vaud (0.5%) and Bern (0.1%). The Union of Swiss Jewish Communities, in Zurich, included in 1970 groups in over 22 cities. Switzerland is the headquarters of the very important World Jewish Congress, founded in Geneva in 1936, whose purposes are to assure the survival of the Jewish people, to reinforce their unity and to co-ordinate the work of the European offices of the American Jewish Joint Distribution Committee.

Islam is represented by Turkish migrant workers by recent Kurdish and Bosnian refugees, and by the Ahmadiya Mission of Islam in Zurich.

Baha'i has followers in over 16 local spiritual assemblies, with headquarters in Bern.

Hinduism is represented by the Krishnamurti Friends of Switzerland (Krishnamurti-Freunde der Schweiz) in Novaggio; the Vedantic Centre (Centre Vedantique) in Geneva, which disseminates the thought of Sri Ramakrishna and commentaries of the Gita; and a recent sect, the Divine Light Centre (Divine Light Zentrum) in Winterthur.

Buddhism has about 7,800 followers in the country, including 500 Tibetan refugees after the annexation of their country by China in 1950. Nevertheless, Switzerland plays an important role in Buddhist studies though its universities, the review *Cahiers Bouddhistes* and the Zurich Buddhist library. It is also in Switzerland that several important Buddhist centers serving Europe are found: (1) the Tibet Institute of Rikon, near Zurich, where the Dalai Lama has assigned many Gelukpa and Sakyapa lamas and which maintains an important specialized library, a center for oral instruction, a periodical *Opuscula Tibetana*

Country summary. **Worlds A, B, C by ethnolinguistic peoples, cities, and major civil divisions in Switzerland.**

World	PEOPLES Num	Pop 2000	C%	Christians	E%	U%	Unevangelized	CITIES Num	Pop 2000	C%	Christians	E%	U%	Unevangelized	CIVIL DIVISIONS Num	Pop 2000	C%	Christians	E%	U%	Unevangelized
A	4	44,314	0.25	109	39	61	26,848	0	0	0.00	0	0	0	0	0	0	0.00	0	0	0	0
B	7	235,383	4.82	11,339	59	41	96,488	0	0	0.00	0	0	0	0	0	0	0.00	0	0	0	0
C	28	7,106,010	90.54	6,434,099	100	0	7,220	19	3,997,647	86.01	3,438,497	98	2	80,566	26	7,385,708	87.27	6,445,548	98	2	130,557
Total	**39**	**7,385,707**	**87.27**	**6,445,547**	**98**	**2**	**130,556**	**19**	**3,997,647**	**86.01**	**3,438,497**	**98**	**2**	**80,566**	**26**	**7,385,708**	**87.27**	**6,445,548**	**98**	**2**	**130,557**

and relations with the universities of Zurich, Gotingen, and Giessen; and (2) the European Institute for Buddhist Studies, in Geneva, which emphasizes (though not exclusively) Japanese Jodo-Shinshu and facilitates its spread to francophone countries. There exist also numerous local Buddhist groups which are attempting to federate into a Buddhist Community of Switzerland. This in turn is expected to be a member of Buddhist Community of Europe, which is also still in the process of formation.

Eglises Réformées. International Monument to the Reformation, Geneva: from left, Farel, Calvin, Beza, Knox.

CHRISTIANITY

The Christian faith was originally brought to Switzerland from Gaul and Italy by merchants, soldiers, and slaves who passed along the imperial highway of Helvetia. The abbey of St Maurice was built in 300, followed by the abbey of Romainmotiers in 400. From Ireland, Colomban's mission profoundly influenced the Christianization of the country through the foundation of the abbey of St Gall in 613. In the 12th century more monasteries were added through the Cistercian reform, including at Einsiedeln, while a mystic movement centered in mendicant orders came into being 100 years later.

Katholische Kirche in der Schweiz, Abtei Nullius Maria Einsiedein. The Abbey Church, built in 1719-35, is a major pilgrimage centre. *Top.* Baroque interior of Abbey Church. *Above.* 3-dimensional tableau in circular Panorama of the Crucifixion.

In 1519 Zwingli began to preach the 'pure Gospel' at Zurich, but soon found himself in conflict with Anabaptists as well as Catholics. Efforts to establish the Catholics by force were successful at Baden in 1526, but the Reform movement continued to spread at St Gall, Bern, Basel, and Schaffhouse. Fighting broke out between the Defensive Alliance consisting of the Reformed cantons, and the Christian Union consisting of the Catholic cantons under Ferdinand of Austria; and Zwingli himself was killed in the second battle of Kappel. Catholics were victorious again in 1531; but the Reform movement aided by Bern freed itself from the Catholic dukes of Savoy. In 1536 Calvin established a Christian community in Geneva. Fribourg became the pivot of Catholicism in the western part of the country, and the Counter Reformation emerged under the influence of Charles Borromeo and Francis de Sales.

Catholic-Protestant rivalry contained to characterize Swiss political and religious life during succeeding centuries. It is only in relatively recent years that an ecumenical spirit has begun to manifest itself.

Catholicism has since 1970 become the majority religion of Switzerland. In 1930 there were 2,330,303 Protestants, forming 57.3% of the population, compared with 1,629,043 Catholics (40.1%). Between 1930 and 1970 Protestants continued to increase in absolute numbers to 2,991,694, but proportionally they decreased to 47.0% of the population. During the same period Catholics grew to 3,096,654, or 49.6% of the population. This rapid growth is due in part to immigration patterns, especially the large influx of expatriate workers from the Roman Catholic Mediterranean countries. The Swiss citizen population remains in majority Protestant (55%, as against 43% for Catholics), whereas the expatriate population is overwhelmingly Catholic (80%, as against 12.7% for Protestants). By 1995, the gap between Catholics and Protestants had further widened with Catholics representing 46.9% of the population and Protestants 43.9%.

These population movements have resulted in an increasing mixture of the Protestant and Catholic communities. Hence the traditionally Protestant cities of Bern, Vaud, Zurich, and Basel are becoming increasingly Catholic, and the traditionally Catholic cities of Valais, Tessin, and Fribourg increasingly Protestant. This is also true of the cantons themselves.

CATHOLIC CHURCH. In Switzerland each Catholic diocese is directly dependent on the Holy See in Rome, there being no metropolitan archbishopric and no ecclesiastical province. Vatican II has been the source of a much greater collaboration between the dioceses, which is especially apparent in the Episcopal Conference. It is still time to say, however, that the secretariat of this conference is very limited in its organization and function.

Although there are no worker priests in Switzerland in the strict sense of the word, there exist different types of experimental ministries: Workers' Soul Care (Arbeiterseelsorger) in Ennetbaden, founded about 1940, with 12 'pastors to workers'; Church and Industry Swiss Catholic Work Team (Schweizerische Katholishe Arbetsgemeinschaft 'Kirche und Industrie'), begun in 1969, with 12 priests and laymen who study the problems of workers in industry and provide interconfessional training for pastors already at work with local groups; and Industrial Seminar with Workshop Experience for Theological Students (Industrieseminar mit Betribspraktikum fur Theologiestudenten), formed in 1970.

The Holy See has diplomatic relations with Switzerland and in AD 2000 is represented to government and the Catholic hierarchy by a nuncio residing in Bern.

PROTESTANT CHURCHES. The principal body is the Federation of the Protestant Churches of Switzerland, which consists of 18 cantonal Reformed churches, with the Free Church of Geneva and the Evangelical Methodist Church. Each cantonal church is autonomous, there being no single or unified Swiss Reformed Church. Their legal status varies. Some have concordat relationships with the state, some are state churches, while others are entirely independent. They also display a surprising diversity in liturgy and constitution. However, most maintain synods and synodal councils which exercise legislative and executive functions for their member congregations. Zwinglian influences have been predominant in the German-speaking region, whereas Calvinism has been more important in the French areas. However, spiritual unity is maintained through the acceptance by most cantonal churches of the Helvetic Confession of 1566. The first attempt to unite the cantonal churches was made through the formation of the Conference of Swiss Churches in 1858, and in 1920 the present Federation was established, consisting at first only of Reformed churches until the Free and Methodist churches were added. There is some question as to whether this is a church or a federation of churches as its name seems to imply. It is in fact both in the sense that its constituent bodies maintain their independence but delegate part of their authority to the federation and its council. It is through the Federation, and not as individual churches, that representation in supranational or ecumenical bodies is usually carried on, including membership in the WCC and WARC.

The Salvation Army, Lutherans, Adventists, Mennonites and a host of smaller denominations are also active. Pentecostalism has not been very successful in Switzerland, although some 25 distinct bodies have been identified. The largest is the Swiss Pentecostal Mission.

MARGINAL CHURCHES. The Friends of Man is a group founded in 1919 by Alexandre Freytag, who was baptized in a Reformed church but later was converted to Adventism and then to Jehovah's Witnesses in 1898. A schism in 1947 by Bernand Sayerce, formerly a Catholic, produced the Sayerce branch of the Friends of Man.

Jehovah's Witnesses have been in Switzerland since the end of the last century, early on many faithful were lost to the Friends of Man. In more recent years Jehovah Witnesses have grown 6 times faster than the Friends of Man. Small groups of Christian Scientists and Mormons also exist, the latter having one of their 15 world temples in Switzerland.

Eglises Réformées. Bern Cathedral, with 'Last Judgement' over main doors.

INDEPENDENT CHURCHES. Several movements out of the church of Rome have been active in Switzerland since the last century. Until recently the most important was the Christian Catholic Church, a schism from Catholicism in Bern in 1872 resulting from the papal infallibility dogma of Vatican I. Membership has declined from 37,307 (0.9% of the population) in 1930 to 19,900 (0.3%) in 1995.

Schismatic Catholic archbishop Marcal Lefebvre ordains (*lower*) new priests and consecrates (*upper*) 4 bishops in 1988 at his seminary in Econe.

In the 1980s a spectacular schism from the Church of Rome took place when a former archbishop of Dakar (Senegal), M. Lefebvre defied pope Paul VI by consecrating ultra-conservative bishops and clergy, for which he was excommunicated. Although polls showed that 24% of all Catholics in Europe took his side, he died soon after and the schism petered out.

The Catholic Apostolic Church spread from England to Switzerland about 1850, but is has been rapidly losing members in recent years. On the other hand, a schism from the above, the New Apostolic Church, is growing rapidly and has now twice as many members as the Christian Catholic Church.

Indigenous missions. Missionaries were sent out from Switzerland in the early Christian centuries, especially through the influence of the monastic movement. Though many more were sent out during the Protestant Reformation, most of these worked in heavily-Christian countries. At the beginning of the 18th century, Swiss missionaries began to cross the oceans and have made a stellar contribution to world missions since then.

Renewal movements. In the 1990s the Pentecostal/Charismatic Renewal continued to spread rapidly across most older churches, and numbered over 472,000 adherents (of whom 9% Pentecostals, 66% Charismatics, and 25% Independents).

CHURCH AND STATE

Switzerland being a confederation, it is the responsibility of the federal government to assure religious liberty and peace between the religions, and to legislate for each of its 25 cantons or semi-cantons on matters concerning relations with the churches.

The federal constitution, established 29 May 1874 but often modified subsequently, begins with a religious affirmation; 'In the name of Almighty God, the Swiss Confederation...has adopted the following Federal Constitution.' It then guarantees freedom of conscience and belief (Article 49.1) as well as freedom of worship (Article 50.1). Additional provisos are included concerning the exercise of religious freedom (Article 49.2-6), such as the fixing of 16 years of age as the limit of parental authority for the religious education of children (Article 49.3). Religious conflicts of the past were responsible for the article stipulating that 'The cantons and the confederation may take necessary measures to maintain public order and peace between members of different religious communities' (Article 50.2). Recourse to the government is possible in cases of disputes concerning the creation of or divisions between religious communities (Article 50.3). Originally the establishment or modification of bishoprics was submitted for approval to the confederation (Article 50.4); but in June 1972, the Council of States (the federal legislative assembly elected by the cantonal assemblies) accepted a motion from the National Council (the federal legislative assembly elected by direct popular suffrage) tending to abrogate this article. Article 51 on the suppression of the Jesuits, and Article 51 prohibiting the reestablishment of convents and suppressed religious orders, were abrogated on 20 May 1973 by a referendum, with 790,799 voting for and 648,959 against. Introduced into the constitution following the war of Sonderbund in the middle of the 19th century in which Catholics and Protestants opposed each other, these articles had already fallen into disuse before the voting of May 1973. In fact there were about 80 Jesuits openly living in Switzerland at the time. Nevertheless, their official abrogation permitted the Helvetic Confederation to ratify the European Declaration of the Rights of Man. In addition, 2 other restrictive constitutional provisions are still being discussed: Article 75 declaring church officials ineligible for the National Council, and Article 25 forbidding the ritual slaughter of animals by orthodox Jews.

According to the federal constitution, cantons may freely determine their own relationships with the churches. Separation of church and state is followed by Geneva and Neuchatel, although in an incomplete manner (Cantonal Constitution of Geneva Article 166, and Neuchatel Article 71). Any religious community may establish itself, under federal civil law, without having to be registered. In addition, there is a system of public ecclesiastical sovereignty. The Catholic and Reformed churches are officially recognized by the constitution or legislation of all cantons, with the exception of Basel-City (Reformed Church only) and Tessin (Catholic Church only). Previously the Catholic

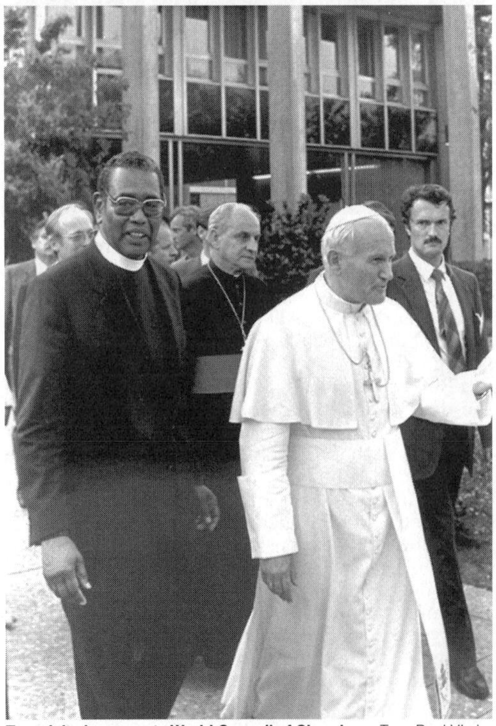

Two visits by popes to World Council of Churches. *Top.* Paul VI visits in June 1969. *Bottom.* John Paul II on 3-hour visit 15 years later.

Church was also the state church in Valais, but this was abolished by a referendum held on 17 March 1974. The Christian Catholic Church is juridically recognized in the cantons of Zurich, Bern, Luzern, Soleure Bale, St. Gall, and Argovic. Public ecclesiastical sovereignty varies from full religious liberty existing in certain cantons to the establishment of national churches in others. The financial situation also varies according to different juridical situations, cantons with a strong Reformed tradition commonly making state funds available to the churches. Religious education is generally included in the curriculum of schools; and if not, the school building may be used by churches for religious instruction.

State departments of religion exist in a few cantons. More generally the cantonal department of the Interior or of Justice handles ecclesiastical matters when they arise. Where federal regulations are involved, matters are then dealt with by the federal Department of Justice and the police.

BROADCASTING AND MEDIA

Shortwave radio programs in European languages can be received from KNLS, AWR (Slovakia), TWR (Monaco, Albania) and HCJB (Ecuador). ERF programs are aired on local radio stations. Satellite TV and radio programs are received in English, Arabic, German and Italian. Catholics air a 60-minute program 'Messe' each Sunday morning and a 15-minute magazine-format 'Racines' each Sunday evening.

Switzerland is a member of UNDA. There are 2 hour-day radio programs each week. Radio Cite is a Catholic-operated station.

INTERDENOMINATIONAL ORGANIZATIONS

The headquarters of many international interconfessional bodies are in Switzerland, as well as those of several national interdenominational bodies. A few of the major ones are described below.

WORLD COUNCIL OF CHURCHES. The WCC has its secretariat in Geneva. It was inaugurated in 1948, based on a decision made in 1938 to combine the 2 movements Faith and Order, and Life and Work, to facilitate the co-operative work of churches throughout the world. In 1961 the International Missionary Council was also amalgamated with the WCC. The WCC's principal policy-making bodies are the General Assembly, which has met 5 times since its foundation (Amsterdam 1948, Evanston 1954, New Delhi 1961, Uppsala 1968, and Nairobi 1975), and the Central Committee, which meets yearly. WCC membership is open to those churches which 'confess the Lord Jesus Christ as God and Saviour according to the Scriptures and therefore seek to fulfill together their common calling to the glory of the one God, Father, Son and Holy Spirit'. Other criteria such as size and stability are taken into consideration in assessing membership qualifications. In mid-1974 there were 260 Protestant, Orthodox, Anglican, Old Catholic, and Independent member churches in 90 countries. Most of the historical Orthodox churches are now members, and at the Uppsala Assembly nearly twice as many Third-World churches were represented as at Amsterdam. The World Council was reorganized in 1971 into 3 Programme Units: Faith and Witness, Justice and Service, Education and Communication. Included in Faith and Witness are 2 commissions (Commission on Faith and Order, Commission on World Mission and Evangelism, CWME) and several agencies: Department on Church and Society, Dialogue with Men of Living Faiths and Ideologies, Christian Medical Missions, Agency for Christian Literature Development, and Theological Education Fund (TEF). Justice and Service is divided into 6 branches; Commission on Inter-Church Aid, Refugee and World Service, Ecumenical Church Loan Fund (ECLoF), Commission of the Churches on International Affairs (CCIA), Commission on the Churches' Participation in Development, Advisory Committee on Technical Services, and Ecumenical Programme to Combat Racism. Education and Communication carries on its work through 3 Staff Working Groups (Renewal, Education, Communication) and an office for Relations with Regional and National Councils. In addition, there are sections dealing with Finance and Central Services and Periodicals. The Ecumenical Institute of Bossey and Special Study Portfolios are under the direct supervision of the General Secretariat; the former was founded by the WCC in 1946 as a center for study and research as well as being a place of encounter between Christianity and the modern world. Courses are also offered for students at the nearby University of Geneva leading to academic certificates.

SODEPAX. The Committee for the Study of the Problems of Society, Development and Peace, commonly known as SODEPAX, was founded in Geneva in 1968. This is a joint organization of the WCC and the Justice and Peace Pontifical Commission of the Vatican, with the general secretary a Catholic and the associate general secretary a Protestant. Between 1968 and 1970, SODEPAX organized a series of conferences, including 2 on World Cooperation for Development at Beirut in 1968 and Montreal in 1969 and the interreligious conference on peace at Kyoto (Japan) in 1970, as well as consultations at Driebergen (Netherlands) in 1970 on Church, Communications, and Development, and at Baden (Austria) on Christian Preoccupation for Peace. In 1970 conferences were also organized on the interest of under-developed countries and on international monetary reform, as well as ones dealing with the second decade of development. Altogether these meetings have produced a large number of reports, as well as contributing to the creation of co-operative ecumenical organizations dedicated to development and peace in several countries; including among others Australia, Canada, Hong Kong, Indonesia, Japan, Lesotho, Malawi, Papua New Guinea, South Korea, Sri Lanka, Sweden, Switzerland, and Uruguay. In 1971, the 2 promoting organizations decided to limit the activities of SODEPAX which, with a reduced secretariat, has been devoting its attention to the promotion of education. In 1975 SODEPAX was given a new mandate by the WCC and the Vatican, for an additional 3-year period, until the end of 1978.

YMCA. The interconfessional World Alliance of Young Men's Christian Associations (YMCA) was founded in 1855 and has its headquarters in Geneva.

INTERNATIONAL CHRISTIAN YOUTH EXCHANGE. This was begun in Geneva in 1946 as an independent movement which however works closely with the WCC and national and regional youth movements. Its purpose is to promote exchange visits between youth of different denominations and countries as a means of training them for undertaking Christian action concerning justice and peace in the world.

25th International Congress of Old Catholics, August 1990 in Geneva, with 600 attendees, proclaims 'New Life in Jesus Christ'.

CHRISTIAN COUNCILS. The Working Community of the Christian Churches in Switzerland is an official organization begun in 1971, consisting of the Reformed, Catholic, Old Catholic, Methodist, and Baptist churches, as well as the Salvation Army. Its purposes are to foster ecumenical dialogue and collaboration and to promote common interests in public life. The Swiss Missionary Council (Schweizerischer Evangleischer Missionsrat/Conseil Suisse des Missions Evangeliques), founded in 1944, provides opportunities for interdenominational contacts between the various Protestant groups, and there are also co-operative unions of missionary societies serving respectively the German-speaking and French-speaking churches. Swiss Protestant Interchurch (Entraide Protestante Suisse aux Eglises de l'Etranger et aux Refugies, EPER) is similarly involved in joint relief and development projects. Catholic ecumenical concerns are co-ordinated by the Commission for Ecumenism of the Catholic Episcopal Conference.

OTHER ORGANIZATIONS. The Commission for Dialogue between the Reformed Churches and the Roman Catholic Church was formed in 1966 by the Federation of Swiss Protestant Churches and the Catholic Bishops' Conference. Its Secretariat is located at the Institute of Ecumenical Studies of the University of Fribourg. The Commission of Dialogue between the Roman Catholic Church and Christian Catholic Church was begun in 1966 by the Synodal Council of the latter and the Catholic Bishops' Conference. It provides for mutual aid in liturgical and pastoral matters.

The Swiss Evangelical Alliance (Schweizerische Evangelische Allianz) is not an association of churches but of individuals dedicated to the promotion of evangelization, prayer, Bible study, and Christian fellowship.

Switzerland and the Third World is a commission of the Swiss churches begun in 1970. Its purpose is to stimulate public conscientization concerning development and peace in conformity with the WCC's Church and Society stance and the Catholic encyclical 'Populorum progressio'. It functions as a Swiss SODEPAX committee.

There is also a joint Commission for Pastoral Work among Mixed Families.

Seven WCC Presidents. At Ecumenical Center, Geneva, in 1991: *left to right*, Bishop Leslie Boseto, Rev. Eunice Santana, H.H. Pope Shenouda, Ms. Priyanka Mendis, Dr. Aaron Tolen, Pfof. Dr. Anna Marie Aagaard, Bishop Vinton Anderson.

The Orthodox Centre of the Ecumenical Patriarchate, in Chambesy promotes contact and collaboration between autocephalous Orthodox churches, the organization of inter-Orthodox and ecumenical consultations, the collection of information on the life and activity of Orthodox churches throughout the world, and the establishment of a secretariat for a future Pan-Orthodox world meeting provisionally called the Great and Holy Council.

The Institute of Ecumenical Studies of the University of Fribourg, founded in 1964, is a research center attached to the Faculty of Theology. It studies the common origins of diverse Christian peoples, analyzes the causes of divergences and carries out research on ways of promoting reconciliation. Its archives include files on ecumenical theology, church life, and hermeneutics. It conducts conferences, seminars, special courses and has a library that specializes in ecumenical literature, both Protestant and Orthodox, particularly of the 16th, 19th, and 20th centuries.

The Protestant Study Centre, in Geneva, was founded in 1954 by the National Protestant Church of Geneva. It is concerned with the training of Christians, dialogue with the modern world and research required by the churches. It also conducts work projects, courses, and conferences.

The John Knox Centre was founded in Geneva in 1953 by the Presbyterian Church of the USA and the National Protestant Church of the USA and the National Protestant Church of Geneva. It serves as an international meeting-place for students and for conferences. Attached to it is an agency for the study of relations between the Third World and Europe.

Das Schweizerisch Ostkirchenwerk Catholica Unio, founded in Luzern in 1958, is a center for Catholic action. The Catholica Unio movement in reality was begun in 1923, its purpose being to study and develop contacts between Catholics and Orthodox, without however today seeking for the return of the Orthodox to the Catholic Church. Approved by the Congregation for the Oriental Churches in Rome, the movement exists also in Austria, Germany, and Brazil.

Two organizations are dedicated to Jewish-Christian dialogue; The Church and the Jewish People, sponsored by the WCC in Geneva, and the Christlich-Judische Arbeitsgemeinschaft in der Schweiz/Amitie Judeo-Chretienne en Suisse/Amicitia. With other religions there are as yet no formalized institutions, but such an organization is under study at the Faculty of Theology at the University of Fribourg.

FUTURE TRENDS AND PROSPECTS

Christians are most likely to decrease from 98.2% in 1970 to less than 87% by AD 2025. The nonreligious are expected to grow to 8% by the same date.

The nonreligious and atheists are expected to jointly grow beyond 15% of the population by mid-21st century. With immigrant non-Christian religions also expected to grow, Christianity will probably decline below 80% before AD 2050.

BIBLIOGRAPHY

Agenda pastoral des églises protestantes de Suisse, 1970. Basel: Verlag Friedrich Reinhardt, 1970. 332p.

Anglicans in Switzerland: a history of Anglican chaplaincies in Switzerland. P. W. Schniewind. *Texte der Evangelischen Arbeitsstelle Oekumene Schweiz*, 17. Bern: Evangelische Arbeitsstelle Oekumene Schweiz, 1992. 167p.

Calvin and the Reformation. J. Mackinnon. New York: Russell & Russell, 1962. 302p.

Chronik der Evangelisch–Lutherischen Kirche Zürich, Nordost– und Zentralschweiz, 1891–1991: herausgegeben zum 100 jährigen Jubiläum. E. H. Newman (ed). Zurich: Die Kirche, [1991]. 83p.

'Church growth perspectives with special reference to the church in Switzerland.' W. W. Sidler-Klaus. Project, Fuller Theological Seminary, Pasadena, CA, 1978. 228p.

Conrad Grebel, c.1498–1526: the founder of the Swiss Brethren, sometimes called Anabaptists. H. S. Bender. Goshen, IN: Mennonite Historical Society, 1950. 326p.

'Contemporary Swiss worldview in the light of its historical development.' M. Krüsi. M.A. thesis, Fuller Theological Seminary, Pasadena, CA, 1991. 208p.

'Contextualization into the contemporary Swiss–German youth worldview in French–speaking Neuchatel regarding God, person, music, and time.' S. Schmid. M.A. thesis, Trinity Evangelical Divinity School, Deerfield, IL, 1993. 140p.

Des Actes de l'église: le christianisme en suisse romande. J. Berthoud. Lausanne: L'Age d'homme, 1993. 170p.

Die Orthodoxen Kirchen in der Schweiz: eine Uebersicht. Texte der Evangelischen Arbeitsstelle Oekumene Schweiz, no. 2. Bern: Evangelische Arbeitsstelle Oekumene Schweiz, 1983. 40p.

Evangelical Lutheran Church of Geneva, 1707–1991, profile of its congregations, and 1989–1991, renovation of its home. Geneva: Eglise Évangélique–Luthérienne de Genève, 1991. 242p.

Geschichte der Juden in der Schweiz. Vom 16. Jahrhundert bis nach der Emanzipation. A. Weldler-Steinberg & F. Guggenheim-Grünberg. Zurich: Schweizerischer Israelitischer Gemeindebund, 1966–70. 2 vols.

Handbuch der reformierten Schweiz. Schweizerischer Protestantischer Volksbund. Zurich: EVZ, 1962. 573p.

Handbuch die Kirchen, sonder Gruppen und religiosen Vereinigungen. O. Eggenberger. Zürich: Evangelische Verlag, 1965.

Helvetia Sacra. Kuratorium of Helvetia Sacra. Bern: Francke, 1972–.

History of the Anabaptists in Switzerland. H. S. Burrage. Philadelphia: American Baptist Publication Society, 1882. 231p.

Hundert Jahre Christkatholische Kirchgemeinde Bern: 1875–1975. Bern, [1975]. 33p.

'Is religious freedom compatible with the establishment of churches under the Swiss constitution?: The case of the Protestant territorial churches.' T. C. Bolliger. LL.M. thesis, Harvard Law School, Cambridge, MA, 1985. 62p.

Juden in der Schweiz: Glaube, Geschichte, Gegenwart. F. Guggenheim-Grünberg, R. Weingarten, R. Guggenheim & J. Teichmann. 2nd ed. Küsnacht, Switzerland: Edition Kürz, 1983. 160p.

Katholische Kirche Schweiz: der schwierige Weg in die Zukunft. L. Karrer. Freiburg: Universitätsverlag Paulusverlag, 1991. 503p.

Kirche und Staat in der Schweiz: Darstellung ihrer rechtlichen Verhältnisse. U. Lampert. Freiburg: Hess, 1937. 2 vols.

Kirchengeschichte der Schweiz. R. Pfister. Zurich: Zwingli Verlag, 1964–84. 3 vols.

Le Christianisme en Suisse Romande. P. W. Brierley. *MARC monograph*, no. 13. : MARC Europe, 1990. 32p.

Les Eglises protestantes de la Suisse au siècle de l'oecuménisme et de l'entraide: 50 ans de Fédération 1920–1970. A. Mobbs. Bern: Fédération des Eglises Protestantes de la Suisse, 1970. 117p.

Les nouvelles voies spirituelles: enquête sur la religiosité parallèle en Suisse. J. Mayer. Lausanne: L'Age d'Homme, 1993.

New move forward in Europe: growth patterns of German speaking Baptists in Europe. W. L. Wagner. South Pasadena, CA: William Carey Library, 1978. 362p.

Schweizer Katholizismus, Eine Geschichte der Jahre 1925–1975: Zwischen Ghetto und konziliarer Öffnung. A. Stoecklin. Zurich: Benziger, 1978. 359p.

'Swiss churches in the twentieth century,' F. Büsser, in *Modern Switzerland*, p.381–402. J. M. Luck (ed). Palo Alto, CA: Society for the Promotion of Science and

Scholarship, 1978.
'Switzerland,' R. J. Campiche, in *Western religion: a country by country sociological enquiry*, p.511–28. H. Mol (ed). The Hague: Mouton, 1972.
Switzerland. H. K. Meier & R. A. Meier. *World bibliographical series*, vol. 114. Oxford, UK: CLIO Press, 1990. 430p. (See especially 'Religion,' pp. 120-32).
'The Catholic Church in Switzerland,' *Pro Mundi Vita*, (1982), 1–35.
The Radical Reformation. G. H. Williams. London: Weidenfeld and Nicolson, 1962. 924p.
The Reformation in Germany and Switzerland. P. Johnston & R. W. Scribner. Cambridge, UK: Cambridge University Press, 1993. 160p.

Country Table 2. **Organized churches and denominations in Switzerland.**

Official name (bold type = church with over 10% of all affiliated) 1	*Begun* 2	*Type* 3	*Counc* 4	*Congs* 5	*Adults* 6	*Affiliated 1970* 7	*Affiliated 1995* 8	*G%* 9	*Names, notes, and other statistics* (see Codebook, Part 3) 10
Amis de l'Homme (Freytag)	1919	m-Jeh	x....	60	30,000	90,000	70,000	-1.00	*Friends of Man.* Schism ex Jehovah's Witnesses by A.Freytag.
Amis de l'Homme (Sayerce)	1947	m-Jeh	x....	7	4,000	10,000	7,000	-1.42	*Friends of Man/Kingdom of God Ch.* Split ex Freytag by former Catholic B. Sayerce.
Assemblées de Dieu	1967	P-Pe2	ZF...	400	20,000	300	25,000	19.35	*Assemblies of God.* Links with M=AoG(USA). Classical Pentecostals (2-stage).2n,2f.
Assemblées des Frères Darbystes	1838	P-EBr	x....	225	9,000	5,000	20,000	5.70	*Brethren* (Closed, some Open). Schisms ex Eglise Libre after visits by JNDarby. 2f.
Assemblées Ev de Suisse Romande		P-Eva	.....	39	1,750	2,000	2,500	0.05	*Evangelical Assemblies of French-speaking Switzerland.*
Assemblées Locales	c1980	I-3mC	.....	2	68	–	150	6.67	*Local Churches. Little Flock.* Chinese. Begun 1922 in China.
Biblische Glaubensgemeinde	1951	I-3pW	.....	10	400	400	1,000	3.73	*Bible-Believing Congregations.* HQ Bern. Ex Volksmission Entschiedener Christen.
Brüdergemeine im Schweiz		P-Mor	xwc..	14	350	500	600	0.05	European Continental Conf, Unity of Brethren. Moravians. In cities. HQ Birsfelden.
Bund der Baptistengemeinden in der S	1849	P-Bap	T.C.d	15	1,382	3,000	2,300	-1.06	*Baptist Union of Switzerland.* HQ Ruschlikon-Zurich. 1948, M=SBC(USA). 21f.1s.
Bund Evangelische Gemeinden	1970	I-3cW	.....	10	1,000	–	1,430	33.73	*New Life.* White-led Postdenominationalist charismatics.
Bund Freier Ev Gemeinden der Schweiz	1824	P-Con	K...C	101	5,800	5,000	9,000	2.38	*Federation of Free Evangelical Congregations in Switzerland.* HQ Steffisburg. 20n.
Bund Pfingstlicher Freikirchen	1961	I-3pW	.....	400	15,000	14,600	29,000	2.78	*Fellowship of Pent Free Chs. Fed d'Egs Libres Pentecôtistes.*
Chiese Evangeliche di lingua Italiana		P-Ref	.....	5	550	1,000	1,000	0.05	*ACELIS. Italian-speaking Ev Chs.* In Basel, Geneva, Chaux-de-Fonds,Renens, Zurich.
Christadelphianer		m-Ade	x....	1	30	50	40	0.05	*Christadelphian Bible Mission.* 1 ecclesia (church) in Leysin (Vaud). Pacifist.
Christengemeinschaft	1911	m-Gno	x....	1	400	1,000	600	-2.02	*Sonnenwesen/Sun-Being. General Anthroposophical Society.* HQ Dornach (Basel).
Christkatholische Kirche der Schweiz	1872	I-OCa	UW..K	49	13,900	20,268	19,900	-0.07	*Christian Cath Ch, D Bern.* Schism ex Ch of Rome. Declining 5%pa. 45n,2x,1s,200Yy.
Deutsche Spätregenmission		I-3pW	x....	5	200	200	400	0.05	*Latter Rain Mission*, from South Africa and Germany. Revivalist Pentecostals.
Eglise Adventiste du Septième Jour	1870	P-Adv	x....	57	4,067	8,000	8,130	0.06	*Seventh-day Adv, German* (55%), *& French*, (45%) *Swiss Confs.* 31nx,93m,1H,1j,2r,133Y.
Eglise Anglicane au Suisse	1552	A-plu	awc..	7	6,000	10,000	13,000	1.05	*Ch of England, D Europe.* Chaplaincies (19 seasonal). 11x.
Eglises Apostoliques Suisses	c1980	I-3aW	.....	20	1,000	–	2,000	6.67	*EAS. Swiss Apostolic Churches.*
Eglise Catholique Apostolique	c1850	I-3aX	x....	5	50	300	100	-4.30	*Catholic Apostolic Ch. Irvingites.* Rapidly dwindling since death of last clergy.
Eglise de Dieu (Anderson)		P-Hol	x....	5	80	100	150	0.05	*Ch of God (Anderson).* M=CoG(Anderson) (USA). Holiness denomination. 2n.
E de JC des Saints des Derniers Jours	1850	m-LdS	x....	32	4,340	5,652	6,200	0.37	*Latter-day Saints.* Zollikofen: Mormon temple (only 15 in world). 70f.
Eglise du Christ Scientiste		m-Sci	x....	20	700	2,000	1,500	0.05	*Ch of Christ, Scientist/Christliche Wissenschaft/Christian Science.* M=CCS. 8m,42w.
Eglise du Nazarène	1978	P-Hol	.....	2	89	–	179	5.88	*Church of the Nazarene.* M=CoN.
Eglise du Seigneur Vivant		I-3oW	.....	5	400	–	1,000	0.05	*Church of the Living Saviour.* Network with Oneness theology.
Eglise d'Ecosse	1566	P-Ref	Rwc..	3	200	500	400	-0.89	*Ch of Scotland.* Scots in Geneva et alia. HQ Grand-Saconnex. 1x,W=52%,11Yy,2z.
Eglise Evangélique du Réveil	1933	I-3pW	Z...H	10	1,400	2,000	3,000	1.64	*Evangelische Kirke der Erweckung. Ev Ch of Revival.* HQ Geneva. M=AdD(France). 1s. In CAR.
Eglise Ev Libre du Canton de Vaud	1847	I-3cW	....K	15	1,500	3,000	3,500	0.62	*Ev Free Ch of Vaud Canton.* Renewal movement ex Eglise Réformée Vaudoise.
Eglise Luthérienne Charismatique	1980	I-3cW	.....	30	2,000	–	3,000	6.67	*ELC. Charismatic Lutheran Church.* Missionaries in Africa (CAR).
Eglise Orthodoxe Romaine		O-Rum	Cwc..	4	4,000	5,000	6,000	0.05	*Biserica Ortodoxa Romana.* Under P Bucharest. Geneva, Bern, Zurich. Romanians. 4x.
Eglise Orthodoxe Russe		O-Rus	Mwc..	5	1,500	3,000	3,200	0.05	*Russian Orthodox Ch.* In jurisdiction of Moscow Patriarchate, and bishop of Zürich.
Eglise Orthodoxe Russe de Genève		I-Rus	x....	15	600	2,000	1,600	0.05	*D Western Europe, Russian OC Outside of Russia* (HQ, USA). Bishop in Netherlands.
Egls Ev Espagnoles en Suisse		P-Ref	....	4	200	300	500	0.05	*Spanish-speaking Ev Churches in S.* Basel, Geneva. Linked with cantonal churches.
Enfants du Dieu	c1980	I-mar	x....	1	46	–	130	6.67	*Children of God*, also known as The Family.
Ev Gesellschaft des Kantons Bern	1931	I-3cW	C	22	4,200	4,000	6,000	1.64	Renewal movement in Bern cantonal church; virtually a free church.
Ev-Lutherische Kirche im Schweiz & L	1891	P-Lut	l....	16	9,380	11,000	13,401	0.79	*Assoc of Ev Luth Chs in S & Liechtenstein.* Includes ELC of Basel & NWSwitzerland.
Fédération des Eglises Ev Libres		I-Con	.....	6	500	615	769	0.05	*Federation of Free Evangelical Chs* (French).
Fédérat des Egls Prot de la Suisse:	1920	P-Ref	RWC.K	1,500	2,100,000	2,714,331	2,836,167	0.18	*FEPS. Schweizerischer Ev Kirchenbund (Swiss Federation of Prot Chs).* 1697n.
Eglise Evangélique Libre de Genève	1849	P-Ref	R...K	5	600	1,000	1,000	0.00	*Evangelical Free Ch of Geneva.* Geneva, Neuchatel.
Eglises Réformées Cantonales	c1520	P-Ref	Rwc.K	1,242	2,089,100	2,692,500	2,813,767	0.18	18 independent cantonal churches. French=Calvinist, German-Zwinglian.
Evangelisch-Methodistische Kirche	c1830	P-Met	VwC.d	253	10,300	20,831	21,400	0.11	*Methodist Ch* (including EUB). In C&S Europe CC, UMC(USA).
Fraternité Chrétienne	c1950	I-3pW	.....	6	200	300	600	2.81	*Christian Brotherhood.* HQ Yverdon. Healing ministry to the handicapped and sick.
Free Christengemeinden der Schweiz	1920	I-3pW	....H	30	800	2,000	2,600	1.05	*Free Christian Assemblies.* HQ Kappel. 1962, split in 3 groups. Africa mission. 10n.
Free Pfingstgemeinde		I-3pW	.....	5	300	200	650	0.05	*Free Pentecostal Assemblies.* HQ Neuhausen. Split ex Swiss Pentecostal Mission.
Gemeinde Christi	1955	I-Dis	x....	1	200	300	500	2.06	*Churches of Christ.* M=CC(Non-Instrumental) (USA). In all largest cities. 9f.
Gemeinde Entschiedener Christen		I-3pW	....H	5	150	300	450	0.05	*Community of Definite Christians.* 2-stage Pentecostals. In Basel, Zürich.
Gemeinde für Urchristentum	1919	P-PeA	Z...H	90	1,600	2,000	2,200	0.38	*Apostolic Ch.* Works with Apostolic European Council. Hierarchical. 18n,2x,1j,1p.
Gemeinde Gottes (Cleveland)		P-Pe3	ZF...	5	150	300	400	0.05	*Ch of God.* M=CoG(Cleveland)(USA). HQ Rorschach/SG. 5n,8f,1p.
Gemeinschaft Evangelisch-Taufgesinnter	1832	P-Hol	x....	37	1,300	2,000	2,100	0.20	*Apostolic Christian Church (Nazarean).* Spread 1847 to USA; also 16 nations.
Griechisch-Orth Kirche (D Österreich)		O-Gre	Cwc..	5	8,000	10,000	11,500	0.05	*Greek Orthodox Ch.* Part of D Austria, under EP Constantinople. Greeks.
Heilsarmee (Armée du Salut)	1882	P-Sal	xwc.d	91	6,100	30,000	9,390	-4.54	*Salvation Army, S & Austria Territory.* 300 officers, 39 institution. HQ Bern. 1s.
Katholische Kirche in der Schweiz:	c 200	R-Lat	b.B.S	1,946	2,429,560	2,860,611	3,197,567	0.45	*Eglise Catholique. Catholic Ch.* C=27+2+50. 2037n 1402x 1836m 8442w 34124Yy
D Basel (Bâle)	740	R-Lat	bs	680	848,000	1,100,000	1,115,775	0.08	*Bistum Basel.* 6 Pastoral Regions (1 French). 1s. 677n 335x 395m 2740w 12660Yy
D Chur (Coira, Cuera)	451	R-Lat	bs	398	515,000	555,360	678,393	0.06	*Uestgiu da Cuera.* 16 Deaneries (1 Italian). 1s. 414n 266x 358m 2632w 6610Yy
D Lausanne, Genève & Fribourg	c 550	R-Lat	bs	292	502,000	542,000	660,000	0.79	*Diocèse de LGF.* In west. HQ Fribourg. 2s. 375n 312x 436m 1462w 6154Yy
D Lugano	1888	R-Lat	bs	256	179,000	220,313	235,669	0.27	*Diocesi di Lugano.* In south, adjoining Italy. 213n 98x 120m 777w 2197Yy
D Sankt Gallen (Saint-Gall)	1823	R-Lat	bs	140	210,000	234,497	276,100	0.66	*Bistum SG.* Northeast of country, adjoining Bodensee. 170n 122x 134m 122w 3468Yy
D Sion (Sitten)	381	R-Lat	bs	173	171,000	204,000	225,562	0.06	*Diocèse de Sion (Bistum Sitten).* Illegal seminary. 188n 144x 217m 632w 2955Yy
AN Maria Einsiedeln	934	R-Lat	bosb	1	160	455	187	0.09	*Abtei Nullius Unserer Lieben Frau.* Pilgrimages. 0n 52x 94m 1w 0Yy
AN Saint-Maurice	515	R-Lat	bs	6	4,400	3,986	5,881	0.07	*Abbaye St-Maurice d'Aganne.* Valais.Under Holy See. 0n 73x 82m 76w 80Yy
Kirche Schwedens (AD Uppsala)	c1962	P-Lut	Lwc..	5	900	2,000	1,400	-1.42	*Ch of Sweden (Overseas).* Swedes in Bern, Geneva, Lausanne, Lugano, Zürich.
Konferenz der Mennoniten der Schweiz	1614	P-Men	G...C	15	3,000	5,000	4,290	-0.61	*Mennonite Conference of Switzerland.* First begun 1614 in Zurich. HQ Emmental, Kanton Bern.
Mouvement Evangélique Tsigane	1913	I-3pE	x....	100	3,000	4,000	5,000	0.90	*Gypsy Evangelical Movement. GGMS.* Work abroad in 15 European countries, also USA, India.
Neuapostolische Kirche	c1870	I-3aX	x....	250	25,000	32,000	37,003	0.58	*New Apostolic Ch.* 1954, 2 Swiss Apostles deposed by Chief Apostle in Germany. HQ Zurich.
Pilgermission St-Chrischona	1840	I-Non	x...C	216	5,300	5,000	17,200	5.07	Based on St-Chrischona, near Basel. Communities in Alsace, Germany, Ethiopia.
Religiöse Gesellschaft der Freunde	1934	P-Qua	Q....	6	100	200	167	-0.72	*Société Religieuse des Amis/Switzerland Yearly Meeting/RS Friends.*W=66%.
Schweizerische Pfingstmission	1920	P-Pe2	Z...H	110	3,300	6,000	6,600	0.38	*SPM. Swiss Pentecostal Mission.* HQ Zurich. Foreign missions: 5 fields. 25n,366Y. In CAR.
Schweizerischer Verein für Freies C		m-Unt	.....	45	1,800	5,000	4,000	0.05	*C=Christentum. Free Christian Union.* Unitarians. M=UUA(USA). Zurich, St-Gall.
Strome der Kraft		I-3pW	.....	20	400	500	700	0.05	*Rivers of Power.* Ben Hoekendijk Evangelistic Campaigns (Holland). HQ Schaffhausen.
Tamil Christian Churches		I-Ref	.....	20	540	–	1,000	0.05	Ceylonese Tamils, who are refugees or migrant laborers from Sri Lanka.
Témoins de Jéhovah	1891	m-Jeh	x....	297	16,552	15,000	29,600	2.76	*Zeugen Jehovas. Jehovah's Witnesses.* Activity begun 1927. (1975) 673Y. (1995) 770Y.
Union Ev d'Egls Bap de Suisse Romande	1890	P-Bap	TT...	15	560	1,500	1,440	-0.16	Ex FEEBF(France). 2n,4x,W=33%,10Y.
Vereinigung Apostolischer Christen	1954	I-3aX	x....	26	1,100	2,000	2,100	0.20	*VAC. Union of Apostolic Christians.* Union of splits ex New Apost Ch. In 6 nations.
Vereinigung Freier Missionsgemeinden	1967	I-Non	.....	71	3,200	321	4,560	11.20	*Union of Free Mission Congregations.*
Volksmission Entschiedener Christen	1934	I-3pW	x...H	13	300	500	700	1.35	*People's Mission of Definite Christians.* 2-stage Pentecostals. HQ Aarburg. 1j.
Other Protestant denominations		P-	.....	100	5,000	8,000	10,000	0.05	Total about 40 (see list below), including Hungarian Reformed Congregations, CCINE.
Other marginal Protestant bodies		m-	.....	45	3,000	6,000	7,000	0.05	Total over 20 (see list below).
Other Orthodox churches		O-	.....	10	2,000	1,000	4,000	0.05	Armenian Apost Ch, Syrian OC (100 Arab families), Ukrainian OC (Sobornopravna), Coptic OC.
Other independent Catholic chs		I-CCa	.....	30	400	500	600	0.05	Total about 10 (see list below), including 20 churches under bishops-at-large.
Other independent bodies		I-	.....	30	3,000	2,500	5,300	0.05	Total 20, incl Assoc of Vineyard Chs, Japan Gospel Christian Ch, Manna Ch (Portugal).
Doubly-affiliated		2-aff			-137,000	-30,148	-185,263		Evangelicals and Pentecostals who are also baptized Catholics or Reformed.
Totals				**6,773**	**4,635,894**	**5,900,000**	**6,285,200**		

Churches, members, growth, 1900-2025	*Congs*	*Adults*	*Affiliated*	*G%*	*Total denominations*	*6 Megablocs:* O	*R*	*A*	*P*	*I*	*m*
Total churches, members, and denominations (mid-1900)	3,000	2,410,000	3,229,000	0.86	20	0	1	1	11	5	2
Total churches, members, and denominations (mid-1970)	6,712	4,403,967	5,900,000	0.86	109	10	1	1	40	38	19
Total churches, members, and denominations (mid-1990)	6,700	4,463,000	6,050,000	0.13	182	18	1	1	63	66	33
Total churches, members, and denominations (mid-1995)	6,773	4,635,894	6,285,200	0.77	182	18	1	1	63	66	33
Total churches, members, and denominations (mid-2000)	6,900	4,755,000	6,445,548	0.51	182	18	1	1	63	66	33
Total churches, members, and denominations (mid-2025)	7,300	4,773,000	6,470,200	0.02	421	30	1	1	100	250	39

NOTES ON TABLE ABOVE

Language. Names in column 1 are given in either German, French, or Italian, depending on which is the major usage.

NATIONAL COUNCILS (Column 4, 5th letter).

- C = Verband Unabhängiger Evangelischer Kirchen und Korperschaften der Schweiz (Aarauer Verband).
- d = member of both ACKS and Aarauer Verband.
- E = Schweizerische Evangelische Allianz (SEA).
- H = Bund Pfingstlicher Gemeinder (Federation of Pentecostal Churches), begun 1961.
- K = Arbeitsgemeinschaft Christlicher Kirchen in der Schweiz (ACKS)/Commission de Travail des Eglises Chrétiennes en Suisse (Working Community of the Christian Churches in Switzerland).
- S = Conférence des Evêques Suisses/Schwiezerische Bischofskonferenz/Conferenza die Vescovi Svizzeri (Conference of Swiss Bishops), also member of AKCS.

OTHER PROTESTANT DENOMINATIONS. Among the large number of other smaller denominations are the following: Amis du Réveil, Bible Christian Union (1954), Children of God International, Christian Ch of North America (Italian Christian Churches of North Europe, CCINE; Pentecostal), Ch of the Kingdom of God (Geneva 1920), Communauté Chrétiens, Dutch Reformed Congregations, Eglises Vaudoises d'Italie en Suisse, Elim Missionary Assemblies (USA, 1956), Evangelical Lutheran Ch of Geneva (founded 1707), Ev Lutheran Ch in Bern, Fribourg & Neuchâtel (1,700 members; begun 1951), Exclusive Brethren (Raven-Taylor, and Kelly-Continental) (nicknamed Mômires, Bigots), Gemeinde der Christen Ecclesia (Zürich), Glaubensheim Bethel, Gospel Missionary Union (USA, 1962), Gypsy Gospel Mission of Switzerland (1913), Hungarian Reformed Congregations, International Protestant Ch of Zürich, Mission de l'Evangile, Mission Populaire Ev de France, Pentecôtistes Libres, Presbyterian Ch (Lausanne), World-Wide Missions (USA), 1969; also several other independent Lutheran groups.

OTHER MARGINAL PROTESTANT BODIES. There is a large number of small cults and sects, including: Eglise Chrétienne Universelle (Témoins du Christ Revenu), Gralsbewegung (HQ Vomperberg, Tyrol), New Church (Swedenborgians) (3 churches, 107 members), Temple de l'Arc-en-Ciel (British-Israelite) (Lausanne).

OTHER CATHOLIC (NON-ROMAN) CHURCHES. These include: Antoinists (from Belgium and France), Eglise Apostolique Primitive, Eglise Catholique Apostolique des Frères Philadelphie, Eglise Catholique Libérale, Eglise Mariavite; and about 20 minuscule episcopal churches under bishops-at-large (episcopi vagantes) (see names in table at end of Part 6).

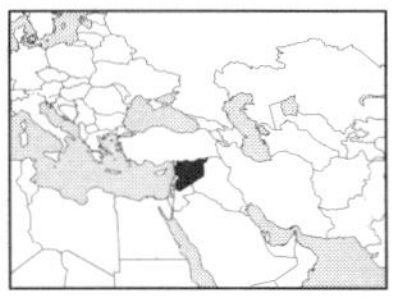

SYRIA

SECULAR DATA, AD 2000

STATE
Official name: Al-Jumhuriya al-Arabya as-Suriya (The Syrian Arab Republic).
Short name: Syria. **Adjective of nationality:** Syrian.
Flag: Red, white and black stripes, with hawk in centre stripe.
Area: 185,180 sq. km. (71,498 sq. mi.).
Government: Socialist republic, since 1973 (1516 under Ottoman empire, 1920 French mandated territory, 1946 Independence as republic, 1958-61 in United Arab Republic (with Egypt), 1968, military junta).
Legislature: People's Council, 250 members.
Official language: Arabic.
Monetary unit: 1 Syrian pound (LS) = 100 piastres. **US$1=** LS c. 52.
Chief cities: DIMASHQ (Damas, Damascus) 2,335,000; Halab (Alep, Aleppo) 2,173,000; Hims (Homs) 673,030; Al-Ladhiqiyar (Latakia) 374,909; Hamar (Hama, Hamah) 334,256.
Political divisions: 14 provinces.
Armed forces: 320,000.

DEMOGRAPHY
Population: 16,125,000.
Population density: 87.0/sq. km. (225.5/sq. mi.).
Under 15 years: 6,577,000.
Growth rate p.a.: 2.46% (births 29.16, deaths 4.51).
Mortality: Infant, per 1,000: 28.0; **Maternal per 100,000:** 180.0.
Life expectancy: 70 (male 68, female 73).
Household size: 6.2. **Floor area per person, sq.m:** 30.0.
Major languages: Arabic, Kurdish, French, Armenian, Turkoman, Circassian, Chaldean (Aramaic), others.
Urban dwellers: 54.47%. **Urban growth rate p.a.:** 3.3%.
Labor force: 28%.

ETHNOLINGUISTIC PEOPLES
74.9% Syrian Arab; 7.4% Bedouin Arab; 7.3% Western Kurd (Kermanji); 3.9% Palestinian Arab; 2.7% Armenian.

ECONOMY
National income p.a. per person: US$1,120; **per family:** US$6,944.

EDUCATION
Adult literacy: 70% (male 85%, female 55%). **Schools:** 10,219.
Universities: 47. **School enrolment:** female/male: 72%/82%.

HEALTH
Access to health services: 90%. **Access to safe water:** 85%.
Hospitals: 213 (12 beds per 10,000). **Doctors:** 11,808.
Blind: 12,000. **Deaf:** 967,600. **Murder rate:** 1.
Lepers: 6,500. **Underweight prevalence under 5:** 12%.

LITERATURE
New book titles p.a.: 970 (60 p.a. per million). **Periodicals:** 42.
Newspapers: 8 dailies.

COMMUNICATION (per 1,000 people)
Phones: 63 (25% mobile). **Radios:** 207. **TV sets:** 89.
Daily newspaper circulation: 18. **Computers:** 70.

REFUGEES
Alien refugees from other countries: 342,300.
Internal displacement: 300,000.

HUMAN LIFE AND LIBERTY (optimum condition=100.0%)
HDI: 75.5. **HSI:** 36.0. **HFI:** 12.5. **EFL:** 16.0.

Country Table 1. **Religious adherents in Syria, AD 1900-2025.**

Year	1900		1970		mid-1990		Annual change, 1990-2000				mid-1995		mid-2000		mid-2025	
Name	Adherents	%	Adherents	%	Adherents	%	Natural	Conversion	Total	Rate	Adherents	%	Adherents	%	Adherents	%
Muslims	1,453,900	83.1	5,570,744	89.0	11,003,965	88.8	332,142	6,971	339,113	2.72	12,646,360	89.1	14,395,091	89.3	23,215,760	88.3
Christians	**274,000**	**15.7**	**621,156**	**9.9**	**1,036,900**	**8.4**	**31,301**	**-8,719**	**22,582**	**1.99**	**1,145,200**	**8.1**	**1,262,719**	**7.8**	**2,033,000**	**7.7**
PROFESSION																
crypto-Christians	94,000	5.4	246,156	3.9	410,000	3.3	12,377	-1,377	11,000	2.41	460,000	3.2	520,000	3.2	700,000	2.7
professing Christians	**180,000**	**10.3**	**375,000**	**6.0**	**626,900**	**5.1**	**18,924**	**-7,342**	**11,582**	**1.71**	**685,200**	**4.8**	**742,719**	**4.6**	**1,333,000**	**5.1**
AFFILIATION																
unaffiliated Christians	0	0.0	0	0.0	3,000	0.0	91	110	201	5.26	4,012	0.0	5,010	0.0	5,600	0.0
affiliated Christians	**274,000**	**15.7**	**621,156**	**9.9**	**1,033,900**	**8.4**	**31,211**	**-8,830**	**22,381**	**1.98**	**1,141,188**	**8.0**	**1,257,709**	**7.8**	**2,027,400**	**7.7**
Orthodox	218,000	12.5	412,648	6.6	670,000	5.4	20,225	-7,398	12,827	1.77	732,000	5.2	798,269	5.0	1,250,000	4.8
Roman Catholics	55,000	3.1	179,468	2.9	265,000	2.1	8,000	-2,000	6,000	2.06	293,677	2.1	325,000	2.0	530,000	2.0
Independents	0	0.0	7,500	0.1	68,000	0.6	2,053	1,147	3,200	3.93	82,400	0.6	100,000	0.6	200,000	0.8
Protestants	1,000	0.1	20,990	0.3	27,500	0.2	830	-576	254	0.89	29,111	0.2	30,040	0.2	42,000	0.2
Anglicans	0	0.0	50	0.0	3,000	0.0	91	9	100	2.92	3,600	0.0	4,000	0.0	5,000	0.0
Marginal Christians	0	0.0	600	0.0	400	0.0	12	-12	0	0.00	400	0.0	400	0.0	400	0.0
doubly-affiliated	0	0.0	-100	0.0	0	0.0	0	0	0	0.00	0	0.0	0	0.0	0	0.0
Trans-megabloc groupings																
Evangelicals	800	0.1	10,300	0.2	28,500	0.2	860	320	1,180	3.53	34,381	0.2	40,300	0.3	79,000	0.3
Pentecostals/Charismatics	0	0.0	6,000	0.1	79,000	0.6	2,385	715	3,100	3.37	94,334	0.7	110,000	0.7	210,000	0.8
Great Commission Christians	**175,000**	**10.0**	**380,000**	**6.1**	**600,000**	**4.8**	**18,112**	**1,039**	**19,151**	**2.81**	**688,700**	**4.9**	**791,510**	**4.9**	**1,314,600**	**5.0**
Nonreligious	0	0.0	50,000	0.8	325,000	2.6	9,811	1,759	11,570	3.09	385,000	2.7	440,698	2.7	1,000,000	3.8
Atheists	0	0.0	12,000	0.2	26,000	0.2	785	5	790	2.69	30,000	0.2	33,904	0.2	60,000	0.2
Jews	22,000	1.3	4,000	0.1	4,000	0.0	121	-108	13	0.32	4,000	0.0	4,128	0.0	3,000	0.0
Baha'is	100	0.0	100	0.0	105	0.0	3	-1	2	1.59	110	0.0	123	0.0	200	0.0
Zoroastrians	0	0.0	0	0.0	30	0.0	1	-1	0	0.65	30	0.0	32	0.0	40	0.0
doubly-counted religionists	0	0.0	0	0.0	-10,000	-0.1	-302	94	-208	1.91	-10,700	-0.1	-12,078	-0.1	-20,000	-0.1
World A (unevangelized persons)	1,100,750	62.9	3,379,320	54.0	5,276,436	42.6	159,049	-76,752	82,297	1.46	5,679,944	40.0	6,095,250	37.8	8,203,104	31.2
World B (evangelized non-Christians)	375,250	21.4	2,257,524	36.1	6,072,664	49.0	183,512	85,471	268,983	3.74	7,374,716	51.9	8,767,031	54.4	16,055,896	61.1
World C (Christians)	274,000	15.7	621,156	9.9	1,036,900	8.4	31,301	-8,719	22,582	1.99	1,145,200	8.1	1,262,719	7.8	2,033,000	7.7
Country's population	**1,750,000**	**100.0**	**6,258,000**	**100.0**	**12,386,000**	**100.0**	**373,862**	**0**	**373,862**	**2.67**	**14,199,860**	**100.0**	**16,125,000**	**100.0**	**26,292,000**	**100.0**

COLUMNS, ROWS.
For meanings and definitions, see Codebook (Part 3). Note that, by definition, total 'Christians' = professing + crypto-Christians, which also = affiliated + unaffiliated Christians, and also = Great Commission Christians + latent Christians. Percentages may not always total exactly, due to rounding.

CENSUSES.
1944 (government estimate): 81.7% Muslims, 10.1% Orthodox (4.8% Greek, 3.6% Armenian, 1.4% Syrian, 0.3% Nestorian), 3.6% Roman Catholics, 3.0% Druzes, 1.0% Jews, 0.4% Protestants. **1949** (estimate): 81.8% Muslims, 9.9% Orthodox (4.8% Greek, 3.4% Armenian, 1.4% Syrian, 0.3% Nestorian), 3.6% Roman Catholics, 3.0% Druzes, 1.0% Jews, 0.4% Protestants. **20.IX.1960:** 91.6% Muslims, 8.3% Christians (361,064 persons), 0.1% Jews (5,067 persons).

NOTES ON RELIGIONS
ATHEISTS. Communist Party of Syria (CPS) (proscribed; split over Sino-Soviet dispute). Also present were 1,100 USSR military advisers (1973).
BAHA'IS. First entered Syria before 1892. Ever since, Baha'is have been subjected to severe persecution by Muslim and government authorities, rendering organized development impossible.
INDEPENDENTS. Isolated Arab radio and correspondence course believers, also one Assyrian schism (see Table 2).
JEWS. Arabic-speaking Sefardis. Decline from 1.0% of the population in 1944 by emigration to Israel.
MUSLIMS. Orthodox Muslims are 85% Sunnis, 13% Alawites or Nusayris (Shias, Latakia province), 1.2% Ismailis, and other Shia sects (0.5%). There are also the heterodox or syncretistic (1) Druzes, an 11th-century Muslim Shia Ismaili schism with Christian and Jewish elements, found mainly in the south in Djebel Druze; and (2) Yazidis, or Devil Worshippers are a 12th-century Muslim syncretistic religion centered around Taziral, Aleppo, and in the extreme northeast in Djebel Sinjar; and (3) a small Ahmadiya community in Damascus (begun 1924), all of which are enumerated here under Muslims. Hajj pilgrims to Mecca. (1968) 14,521; (1969) 22,383;(1970) 42,339; (1971) 27,045; (1972) 31,777; (1973) 10,448; (1974) 31,583; (1975) 31,209; (1976) 24,446.
ORTHODOX. The majority are Greek Orthodox and Syrian Orthodox. In 1905, there were about 15,000 Armenian Apostolics (2,000 in the diocese of Damascus or Sham); after 1915, vast numbers immigrated as refugees from Turkey, but subsequently about 100,000 Orthodox have emigrated from Syria to Lebanon in recent years.
PROFESSING CHRISTIANS. There has been very considerable and continuous emigration after 1944 (when Christians were 14.1% of the population) to 1949 (13.9%), 1960 (8.3%), 1970 (6.0%), and 1990 (5.1%).

Great Commission Instrument Panel: status of Syria (for explanation see start of Part 4)

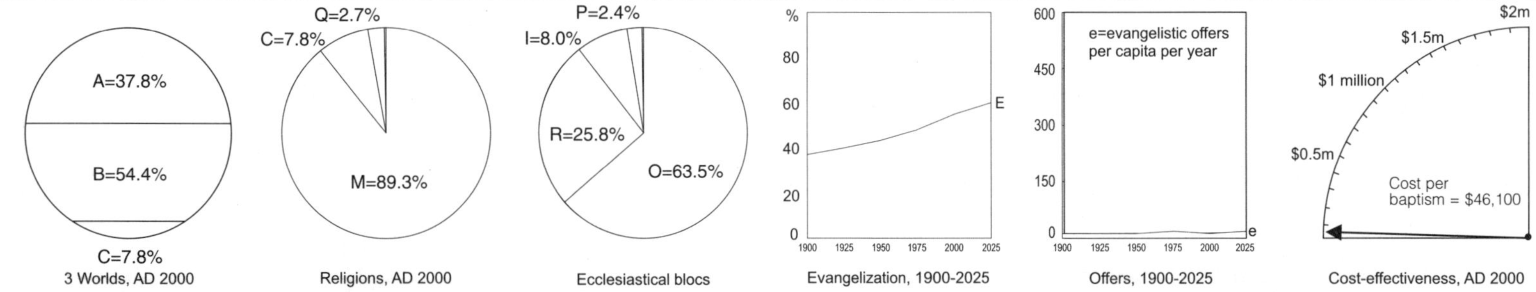

Country status. Syria is a country in south-west Asia on the Mediterranean Sea, bordered by Jordan, Turkey, Iraq, Lebanon, and Israel. Agriculture is widespread but oil revenues provide the bulk of Syria's income.

HUMAN LIFE AND LIBERTY.

Human need and development. Although endowed with very little natural wealth, unlike its Arab neighbors to the east, Syria is economically more advanced than most of them. Syrians are noted for their hard work and business acumen, and both qualities have served them in good stead at home as well as abroad. However, the long period of instability after independence and the particularly harsh regime of Assad have depressed living conditions and provided little

Country summary. Worlds A, B, C by ethnolinguistic peoples, cities, and major civil divisions in Syria.

	PEOPLES							CITIES							CIVIL DIVISIONS						
World	Num	Pop 2000	C%	Christians	E%	U%	Unevangelized	Num	Pop 2000	C%	Christians	E%	U%	Unevangelized	Num	Pop 2000	C%	Christians	E%	U%	Unevangelized
A	8	2,620,896	0.29	7,577	32	68	1,781,404	3	332,461	0.50	1,662	50	50	166,530	4	2,299,190	0.99	22,730	40	60	1,372,970
B	9	12,966,288	5.97	773,627	67	33	4,310,954	12	6,754,059	12.03	812,689	70	30	2,035,650	10	13,825,428	8.93	1,234,979	66	34	4,719,996
C	11	537,431	88.66	476,502	100	0	609	0	0	0.00	0	0	0	0	0	0	0.00	0	0	0	0
Total	**28**	**16,124,615**	**7.80**	**1,257,706**	**62**	**38**	**6,092,967**	**15**	**7,086,520**	**11.49**	**814,351**	**69**	**31**	**2,202,180**	**14**	**16,124,618**	**7.80**	**1,257,709**	**62**	**38**	**6,092,966**

incentive to mass participation in the development of the country. Its per capita GNP of $1,120 is only slightly above that of Jordan. Nearly one-third of its citizens are still illiterate. Significant progress has been made in some sectors such as education and health, mostly as a result of private initiatives. The public sector is quite inefficient, burdened with an unwieldy and corrupt bureaucracy. Since the eastern part of the country is mostly desert, the coastal areas and Damascus have a heavy concentration of both people and resources.

Human rights and freedoms. Except for a hiatus in 1973-74, Syria has been under martial law since 1963. The martial law is justified on the grounds of the state of war with Israel and continuing threats of terrorist groups. The suppression of all opposition for so long a period has been very effective, and antiregime manifestations have become very rare. The government maintains an extensive security apparatus system outside the legal system. It is responsible for severe human rights violations. Several thousands remain in prison without trial. All basic human rights are tightly restricted, as they have been for the past 30 years. Because the government does not permit outside monitoring, the actual extent of human rights abuses is not known. Many political prisoners have been held indefinitely and eventually died in custody. Numbers of detainees have been subjected to continuous physical abuse and torture. While civil courts generally provide for due process, the security courts do not. Under the State of Emergency Law, government may arrest persons secretly without warrant and hold them indefinitely without charge or trial. Detainees have no legal redress and may not be contacted by family or friends. The security agency maintains an extensive surveillance network, and their presence is pervasive in all major cities. Security checkpoints are set up on important roads. Telephone and fax communications are subject to interception and mail is censored. A free press does not exist, and the government and the ruling Ba'ath Party own all print and electronic media. Both foreign and domestic news are censored and subjects deemed by the government to be contrary to its interests are not permitted to be discussed. Public meetings, assemblies, and demonstrations may be held only with prior official approval, which is never granted except to the Ba'ath Party. The government also controls professional organizations and their meetings. Because of the Ba'ath Party's secular ideology, there is no overt discrimination in society against religious minorities; nevertheless, there are pockets of informal discrimination in matters relating to law, education, and public service.

Human environment. Syria's principal environmental problems are water and coastal pollution and land degradation. Water is generally unsafe for drinking because of the dumping of sewage and industrial wastes into the rivers or in riverine areas. Irrigated land is affected by waterlogging. Overgrazing is contributing to desertification.

NON-CHRISTIAN RELIGIONS

Islam is the main religion of Syria and makes up 89% of the population. Muslims conquered the country in AD 636, and between 660 and 750 Damascus was the center of the vast Umayyad empire. In later centuries Syria was ruled by Egyptian Mamelukes, Asian Mongols, and Ottoman Turks. Most Muslims today are Sunnis, although there are also Alawites, Ismailis, and several other smaller Shia sects. Alawites form at least 11% of the population and are centered in the province of Latakia. Ismailis, 1% of the population, have their strength in the Salamiya district.

Druzes are a sect begun in the 11th century when their founder, Darasi, identified Egyptian caliph al-Hakim as the incarnation of Allah. They represent a mixture of Jewish, Christian and Muslim elements. Their community exceeds 380,000 found mostly in the southern area of Djebel Druze.

Muslims. Omayad Mosque in Damascus, built in AD 715, traditional repository of the head of John the Baptist (revered as an Islamic prophet).

Yazidi religion is a complex mixture of ideas taken from many religious (Islam, Judaism, Manachaeism, Zoroastrianism, Nestorianism), although Muslim thought is predominant. It was founded in the 12th century by Shaikh Adi, who was regarded as the incarnation of the fallen angel Malak Ta'us. Yezidis consist of some 19,000 living at Aleppo in the northern part of Djebel Sinjar.

Judaism has suffered from emigration to Israel since World War II, but a small Arabic speaking Sefardic community remains.

CHRISTIANITY

In Syria, Christianity antedates the Apostle Paul who was converted on his way to Damascus; and after the fall of Jerusalem in AD 70, Antioch became the Christian center of the eastern half of the Roman empire. Antioch's theologians played a leading role in the controversies concerning the nature of Christ in the early centuries, with Nestorians and Jacobites becoming increasingly separated from the rest of the church following the Council of Chalcedon in 451. Catholic Uniate churches began to emerge as early as 1181, the Maronites coming fully under the authority of Rome in 1516. Periodic movements among branches of Eastern-rite churches from the 16th to the 18th centuries resulted in the creation of more Uniate churches, including the Chaldean, Armenian, Greek Melkite, and Syrian Catholic churches, although the Greek Orthodox church has remained the largest Christian denomination in the country. Christians increased in number when Armenians fled into Syria from massacres in Turkey and Iraq, but in recent years Christians have been migrating to other parts of the world.

Protestant missionaries began exploratory missions in the 19th century, seeking Jewish and Muslim converts, but most of their members have in fact come from other Christian churches. This has made them suspect to both Muslims and Eastern-rite Christians, as well as to the government which has been apprehensive of any kind of European intervention.

Until recent years, Syrian Christian communities were composed mostly of peasants. In the urban milieux they formed part of the commercial and industrial bourgeoisie and the liberal professions, in addition to being artisans and skilled workers. Whether rural or urban, they remained attached to their ancient religious traditions, fervent but with-drawn from society in closed and close-knit communities.

Independence in 1943 and the evolution of Syrian society since 1963 have changed this situation. The majority of the socio-professional categories continue, but the old bourgeoisie has been partially broken up or has emigrated, many going to Lebanon; and a new class of young adults from the peasant, artisan and semi-proletarian classes are coming to the fore. Many of these have technical or university training, while the army and government include important and often influential numbers of Christians. The result is that today Christians are integrating themselves more into the main stream of society, whose tendency is in the general direction of secularization. The rural exodus is helping to create a new social mixture and a socio-cultural development which may well contribute to the wider introduction of Christianity into Syrian life.

The recovery by Syria of a part of the Golan Heights, following the signing of the disengagement agreement by Syrian and Israeli armed forces on 31 May 1974, has had no effect on the size of the Christian community since the Syrian population of the area had taken refuge in the interior of the country. Before leaving, Israelis completely destroyed the city of Kuneitra, pillaging churches and mosques, including the Orthodox cathedral. Only the Catholic church remained intact, due undoubtedly to the international political position of the Holy See.

In summary, it can be stated that the influence of Western Christianity, especially Latin and European, has been strongly felt since 1890 especially due to the large part its schools have played in training an intellectual elite. At present the Christian minority is characterized by: (1) the traditionalism and conservatism of its past ecclesiastical structures mixed with a practical ecumenism which seeks to break down the rigid barriers between Catholics and Orthodox; (2) a new approach to the reformist wing of the Muslim community which is more liberal and tolerant; and (3) a movement towards social and political awareness which has introduced a quality of dynamism and modernism into Christian institutions.

ORTHODOX CHURCHES. The Greek Orthodox form the most deeply-rooted Christian community in the country, and the best-adapted to its recent evolution. It is Greek only in its Byzantine traditions, since its liturgy is in Arabic and its membership and leaders are Arabs. It is historically the mother church of the Jacobites, who broke away in the 6th century, and the Greek Catholics (Melkites) who separated in the 16th century. There are 2 monasteries (Our Lady of Saidnaya near Damascus, and St Georges, in the valley of the Christians between Homs and Latakia) which are places of pilgrimage visited by many since medieval times. The patriarch lives in Damascus and is assisted in the governing of the church by the synod of bishops and a mixed commission of laymen and clergy. The lay element has often had a decisive influence in episcopal elections and especially in the administration of church property (Wakfs). The church maintains good relations with the other autocephalous Orthodox churches, particularly with the Moscow Patriarchate. The latter gave its support in 1898 to the proposal that the patriarch of Antioch should be a native Syrian rather than a Greek. The church's strength is in the western half of the country near Aleppo, Homs, and Latakia. The Movement of Orthodox Youth is especially active, as in Lebanon.

The Armenian Orthodox are the third largest Christian community in Syria, after the Greek Orthodox and Catholic churches. Monophysite in tradition, they are administratively related to the catholicate of Cilicia (Sis) at Antelias in Lebanon. Nearly half their membership is found in the city of Aleppo where they form the largest Christian community.

Syrian Orthodox Patriarchate of Antioch. Church of Qalb Lozah.

The Syrian Orthodox or Jacobites are also of the Monophysite tradition. Most are found in the extreme northeast in the Qamishli area across the Turkish border from Tour Abdin where their ancient monastic institutions are located, Deir-el-Zeferan and Deir Gabriel. There is also a large membership at Aleppo and Homs. The patriarchal see, which has jurisdiction over such foreign communities as the Syrian Malankaras in Kerala, India, and the Syrian Orthodox in America, was moved from Homs to Damascus in 1954. A new faculty of theology is being planned for Bikfaia, Lebanon.

The Assyrian Church of the East consists of a small community found in eastern Syria. Assyrians are stronger in Iraq and Iran than in Syria.

Syrian Orthodox Church. Priest expounding the gospel to huge parish congregation in Fuhaila.

CATHOLIC CHURCH. Six different Catholic rites exist in Syria, in order of size: Greek Catholic (Melkite), Armenian, Syrian, Maronite, Latin, and Chaldean.

Melkites are the predominant Catholic group in the country due to their leadership, tradition, and institutions. The Melkite patriarch has his residence at Damascus, but his jurisdiction goes beyond the limits of the patriarchate of Antioch since he has held also for more than a century the titles and jurisdiction of the patriarchs of Jerusalem and Alexandria. He also has jurisdiction over Melkite districts erected in 1971-72 in America and in other parts of the diaspora. On the whole the Melkite clergy observe the Byzantine tradition. Married clergy are in charge of rural parishes, while diocesan clergy are celibate. The latter and also religious personnel are generally well-educated, including some highly-trained elites, and concerned to meet the needs of Melkite society which is considered conservative in the domain of religion. Their major strength is in Aleppo. The establishment of a Melkite major seminary in Syria is seen as a priority.

Armenians form a strong ethnic minority who fled to Syria during the Turkish massacres of 1894-96 and 1917-21. They are the strongest Catholic community in Aleppo.

Syrian Catholics are found mostly in Djezire in the extreme northeast, as well as in Aleppo, Homs, and Damascus, the latter with no more than 200 families. An active lay movement, Institut Jesus Ouvrier, is centered in Aleppo.

Maronites are concentrated in the west. Their principal center is Aleppo which lies near the traditional home of St Maron from whom they derive their name. However, Maronites are few in Syria as compared with neighboring Lebanon.

Latin Catholics live in western Syria with nearly half their membership in Aleppo where the vicar apostolic has his residence. Aleppo has been a center of Latin influence since the 13th century when it played an important role in the Crusades.

Chaldeans are strongest in eastern Syria, in addition to some 1,500 in Aleppo and 500 in Damascus.

Co-ordination and collaboration between these 6 rites exist at both the national and local levels in such cities as Damascus and Aleppo where Catholic bishops of different rites meet together regularly. Specialized Catholic Action youth movements have not been successful, possibly because of their Western origin. It is to be noted also that youth groups were suppressed in 1964 after the Baathist regime came to power. Some of the most important existing inter-rite organizations are those concerned with catechetics. These have taken on a special significance since the seizure and closing of Catholic schools when they did not conform to government edicts in 1967. At Damascus there exists a center for advanced religious training, run by Lazarists and called the St Paul Centre. Numerous other centers are active where laymen, especially youth, collaborate with clergy and religious personnel in teaching the catechism to children of different school levels. Such centers attached to the Catechism Society are found in Damascus, Homs, Latakia, and especially at Aleppo. Another group at Damascus and Aleppo called 'The Flame' mobilizes the generosity of city Christians to help poor rural parishes.

The Holy See has diplomatic relations with Syria and in AD 2000 is represented to government and the Catholic hierarchy by a nuncio residing in Damascus.

PROTESTANT CHURCHES. The first Protestant to explore mission work in Syria was a member of the London Jews' Society in 1822. The American Board (ABCFM) began work in Beirut in 1823, moving to Syria in 1848. In 1879, it transferred its work to the Presbyterian Church in the USA. Other early groups were the North American Reformed Presbyterian Mission and the Danish Mission to the Orient. During the 1940s these 3 joined together to form the autonomous National Evangelical Synod of Syria and Lebanon, which is Presbyterian in Polity. It is now declining rapidly by emigration.

The Union of Armenian Evangelical Churches is strong in the north where Armenian refugees from Turkey fled after World War I. The Armenian Union and National Evangelical Synod together form the bulk of the Protestant population which is about 36,000.

The CMA from the USA arrived in 1921, followed by Nazarene missionaries and number of other groups later. All foreign missionaries were expelled in 1963, but small churches continue under Syrian leadership. Two CMA congregations are known to exist in Homs and Damascus. Several expelled mission groups maintain contact with Syria from Beirut, which has long been the central headquarters of the Christian churches in the Middle East.

Protestants. American church in Aleppo.

Indigenous missions. Early Christian missionary bands were sent out into the Mediterranean region in the first few centuries of the church. Orthodox Christian churches later sent missionaries to the East. This tradition has continued to the present day but has been set back by the diminishing presence of the church in Syria.

Renewal movements. In the 1990s the Pentecostal/Charismatic Renewal continued to spread rapidly across most older churches, and numbered over 110,000 adherents (of whom <1% Pentecostals, 16% Charismatics, and 84% Independents).

CHURCH AND STATE

Until the beginning of 1973, Syria was officially a Muslim state, but the new regime then inaugurated instituted by general Hafez El-Assad in November 1970 has sought to divorce the state from any religious commitment. In fact the new constitution of March 1973, envisages Islam as the religion of the head of state only, and no longer the religion of the state itself. This resulted in religious riots in some towns in February and April 1973, just before a referendum to ratify the constitution. Since the end of the French mandate (1920-45), Christians have always advocated just such a constitutional change which would recognize Islam as the religion of the majority of the population but not the official religion of the state. Christian churches and socio-religious communities are legally recognized and designated by the state as juridical personalities with definite rights and privileges. The Ministry of Religious Foundations (Wizarat Al-Awkaf) is nominally occupied with the management of religious properties, but in actuality is involved in all that relates to religious personnel, worship, and Muslim politics in the country.

Freedom of religion, sanctioned by law, does in fact exist. Solemn processions are authorized during the course of the year, and the construction of new religious buildings encounters no legal obstacle.

Private religious schools which had been placed under the direct control of the Ministry of National Education in 1967, were restored to their owners following a decision of the supreme administrative court in December 1974. Except for Catholics, the different religious communities, Christian and Muslim, had accepted the 1967 decision as final. It was thus a Catholic appeal which produced the definitive court decision of 1974, recognizing the private character of all religious schools. From November 1970 on, the government attempted to soften its position by extending to all Syrian citizens the right to establish private schools, a measure which was used by Catholics to open a certain number of allegedly new schools.

Another mark of the liberalism of the state and Islam in Syria is the law, especially evident in the proceedings of the Court of Appeal, which allows minor children when they come of age to change their religion if they were only considered Muslim because of the conversion of their fathers. Normally Islamic law prohibits converts and their minor children, who are automatically considered Muslims, from changing their religion, and minor children continue to be considered Muslims after they come of age.

The churches themselves are not subsidized, nor do they receive any material assistance from the state. Nevertheless, church communities do have certain administrative and jurisdictional rights, since Islam recognizes them as 'civil and religious nations' within the larger Muslim society. Thus, churches may keep registers of baptisms and marriages, and their official certificates have public recognition. The state accepts as valid only those marriages formally solemnized by a church according to its established procedures. Church tribunals in each community have competence in that which relates to the religious aspects of matrimonial contracts and mixed marriages, such as the care of children. Real estate (Wakfs) belonging to places of worship or to patriarchates has the same exemptions and privileges as that of Muslim communities.

No church enjoys privileges at the expense of others, but those which are the most deeply-rooted in the country and which have broken their ties with former colonial regimes are in fact favored; and their missionary, social, and cultural activities are not hindered. In actuality, Christians are well represented at all levels of public life, such as in administration, army, and liberal professions. Greek Orthodox political thinkers, intelligentsia, and middle classes have often been a determining factor in decisions concerning the destiny of the country. Between 1925 and 1945, the thought of Antoun Saadeh, founder of the Syrian Popular Party (PPS), and since 1950 that of another Orthodox, Michel Aflak, ideological pioneer of the Baathist party, have played an important role in the political and national evolution of Syria and Lebanon as well as that of other Arab countries in the Middle East.

BROADCASTING AND MEDIA

Shortwave radio programs in Arabic can be received from FEBA (Seychelles), TWR (Monaco, Albania) and HCJB (Ecuador). Syria is a member of UNDA.

Satellite TV programs are received mainly in Arabic. Christian television programming can be received from CTV and SAT-7.

Around 583,000 have seen the 'Jesus' Film: through broadcasts on national television (416,000) and radio versions (166,000).

INTERDENOMINATIONAL ORGANIZATIONS

The Middle East Council of Churches, founded in Beirut in 1927, includes 6 Syrian churches in its membership. Since 1948 the council has been active in Palestinian refugee work and has received considerable assistance from the WCC and CWS.

The Greek Orthodox and Greek Catholic patriarchates each have an ecumenical commission. The Catholic Commission founded in 1968 is under the annual Melkite synod. Although no permanent organizations for ecumenical co-ordination or collaboration exist, in 1967 experts named by all the hierarchies at government request prepared a single manual of Christian religious education consisting of several volumes, which was accepted by the Ministry of Education for examinations in government schools. In 1972, a liturgical congress took place between Greek Catholics and Greek Orthodox, as an experiment and without publicity. The visit of the Syrian Orthodox patriarch Jacob III to pope Paul VI in Rome in 1971, followed by visit by cardinal Willebrands as papal representative to Damascus in 1972, has had a profound effect in Syria. The Rome meeting resulted in the joint signing of a Declaration of Doctrinal Order.

FUTURE TRENDS AND PROSPECTS

Islam will likely continue to claim about 88% of the population while Christianity is expected to remain at under 8% by AD 2025. The nonreligious would grow to near 4% by 2025.

Christianity is thought likely to decline in Syria throughout the 21st century, dropping as low as 7% by AD 2050. Islam would then continue to remain the same in the same period.

BIBLIOGRAPHY

A history of the monks of Syria. Theodoret of Cyrrhus. Trans., R. M. Price. *Cistercian studies series*, no. 88. Kalamazoo, MI: Cistercian Publications, 1985. 260p.

American interests in Syria, 1800–1901: a study of educational, literary, and religious work. A. L. Tibawi. Oxford, UK: Clarendon Press, 1966. 333p.

'American missions and Arab nationalism in 19th century Syria.' A. M. Abu-Ghazaleh. Paper, Middle East Studies Association annual meeting, Salt Lake City, UT, 1979. 23p.

American missions in Syria: a study of American missionary contribution to Arab nationalism in 19th century Syria. A. Abu-Ghazaleh. Brattleboro, VT: Amana Books, 1990. 95p.

Die syrisch–orthodoxe Kirche von Antiochien: ein geschichtlicher Überblick. H. Aydin. Losser, Holland: Bar Hebräus, 1990. 193p.

Eglises de village de la Syrie du nord. G. Tchalenko & E. Baccache. Paris: Librairie Orientaliste P. Geuthner, 1979–1980. 2 vols.

'English and Irish reaction to the massacres in Lebanon and Syria, 1860,' A. P. Saab, *Muslim world*, 74, 1 (1984), 12–25.

(History of the Syrian church of Antioch). S. J. Tuma (Patriarch of Antioch). Beirut, 1953–57. 2 parts. (In Arabic).

'Jews in late Ottoman Syria: community, family and religion,' W. P. Zenner, in *Jewish societies in the Middle East: community, culture and authority*, p.187–209. S. Deshen & W. P. Zenner (ed). Washington, DC: University Press of America, 1982.

'Le statut personnel des communautés chrétiennes en Syrie et au Liban,' P. Mazas, *En Terre d'Islam* (France), 21 (1937), 133–45.

L'église d'Arabie: essai historique et juridique dès l'origine jusqu'à l'avènement de l'Islam: la conversion des arabes de la province romaine d'Arabie, Transjordanie et Syrie, de Petra à Damas. J. Hijazin. Rome: Pontificia Universitas Lateranensis, 1979. 78p.

Les confessions d'un Arabe catholique. F. Abou Mokh. Ed., J. Chabert & F. Mourvillier. Paris: Centurion, 1991. 264p.

Muslim–Christian relations and inter–Christian rivalries in the Middle East: the case of the Jacobites in an age of transition. J. Joseph. Albany, NY: State University of New York Press, 1983. 240p.

'Presbyterian missionaries in the Middle East.' D. Dawson. S.T.M. thesis, Yale Divinity School, New Haven, CT, 1987. 109p.

'Religion,' chapter 11 in *US Army area handbook for Syria*, p.123–141. Washington, DC: US Government Printing Office, 1965.

'Religion and state in Syria,' A. R. Kelidar, *Asian affairs*, 61, 1 (1974), 16–22.

'Shia movements in Lebanon: their formation, ideology, social basis, and links with Iran and Syria,' M. Deeb, *Third world quarterly*, 10, 2 (1988), 683–98.

Studies in Syriac Christianity: history, literature, and theology. S. P. Brock. Hampshire, UK: Variorum, 1992.

Syria. I. J. Seccombe. *World bibliographical series*, vol. 73. Oxford, UK: CLIO Press, 1987. 376p. (See sections on 'Minorities.' No separate chapter on religion).

Syrian Christians in Muslim society: an interpretation. R. M. Haddad. *Princeton studies on the Near East.* Princeton, NJ: Princeton University Press, 1970. 126p.

'Syria's patterns of population distribution,' J. C. Dewdney, in *Population of the Middle East and North Africa: a geographical approach*, p.130–42. J. I. Clarke & W. B. Fisher (eds). London: University of London Press, 1972.

'The Alawi community of Syria: a new dominant political force,' M. A. Faksh, *Middle Eastern studies*, 20, 2 (1984), 133–53.

The Armenian communities in Syria under Ottoman dominion. A. K. Sanjian. *Harvard Middle East studies*, no. 10. Cambridge, MA: Harvard University Press, 1965. 390p.

The Druzes: a new study of their history, faith and society. N. M. Abu-Izzeddin. Leiden: E. J. Brill, 1984. 259p.

The Eastern Christian churches: a brief survey. R. G. Roberson. 3rd ed. Rome: Pontificum Studiorum Orientalium, 1990. 129p.

'The Islamic revolution of Syria (1979–1982): class relations, sectarianism, and socio–political culture in a national progressive state.' S. A. Badaro. M.A. thesis, Ohio State University, Columbus, OH, 1987. 285p.

The Islamic struggle in Syria. U. F. Adb-Allah. Berkeley, CA: Mizan Press, 1983. 300p.

The legal status of non–Moslem communities in the Near East, and especially in Syria and Lebanon. I. A. Khairallah. Beirut: American University of Beirut, 1965. 187p.

The religions of modern Syria and Palestine. F. J. Bliss. New York: Scribner, 1912. 368p.

Country Table 2. **Organized churches and denominations in Syria.**

Official name (bold type = church with over 10% of all affiliated) 1	*Begun* 2	*Type* 3	*Counc* 4	*Congs* 5	*Adults* 6	*Affiliated 1970* 7	*Affiliated 1995* 8	*G%* 9	*Names, notes, and other statistics* (see Codebook, Part 3) 10
Ancient Church of the East: D Hassaké	1933	O-Nes	Yw...	22	22,000	20,000	40,000	2.81	*Assyrian Ch. Nestorians.* 1933 mass refugees from Iraq; in Khabur Valley. 5nx.
Armenian Apostolic Ch (C Cilicia):	c1440	O-Arm	Sw.N.	60	200,000	111,648	300,000	4.03	*Gregorians.* Under jurisdiction of C Sis (Lebanon). Half members in Aleppo.
AD Dimashq (Damascus)		O-Arm	Sa	28	101,000	56,000	160,000	0.05	Armenians are the main non-Arab Christian community in the capital.
AD Halab (Aleppo)		O-Arm	Sa	32	99,000	55,648	140,000	0.05	Northern Syria. Largest Christian community in city of Aleppo.
Armenian Ev Spiritual Brethren	1920	I-CBr	x....	1	100	200	300	1.64	*Holiness Brethren.* Ex other Armenian churches. 25 Armenian families in Aleppo.
Assemblies of God		P-Pe2	Z....	2	60	100	200	0.05	M=AoG(USA). Small mission in Classical Pentecostal (2-stage) tradition.
Bible Preaching Church	1962	I-Non	x....	3	500	800	1,000	0.90	M=World-Wide Missions(USA). Evangelicals, with links in Pasadena, CA (USA).
Catholic Church in Syria:	295	R-LEr	O...R	226	158,600	179,468	293,677	0.06	*Al-Kanissa al-Kathoulikiah.* Six rites. C=7+1+18. 3q. 151n 76x 107m 403w 2194Yy
EP Syria (P Cilicia) *(Armenian)*	1742	R-Arm	Os	1	1,900	2,600	3,200	0.83	*Patriarchal Exarchate.* Damascus patriarch in Beirut. 0n 1x 1m 3w 29Yy
AD Halab (Aleppo) *(Armenian)*	1710	R-Arm	Os	8	8,400	16,000	17,000	0.24	*Al-'rman al-Kathoulik.* Under P Cilicia (Lebanon). 8n 5x 5m 10w 135Yy
D Al Qamischli (Kamichlie) *(Armenian)*	1954	R-Arm	Os	4	3,500	2,900	5,000	2.20	Qameshliyeh. In northeast, on Turkish frontier. 2n 2x 2m 3w 29Yy
D Halab *(Chaldean)*	1957	R-Cha	Os	9	8,400	9,000	15,000	2.06	*Al-Kaldan.* Under P Babilonia. From Iraq. M=SJ. 3n 3x 3m 2w 75Yy
M Bostra & Hauran *(Melkite)*	c 250	R-Mel	Os	45	15,000	16,800	27,000	1.92	*Al Rounn al-Malakioun al-Kathoulik.* Growing. 16n 0x 0m 9w 357Yy
M Dimashq (Damascus)*(Melkite)*	c 260	R-Mel	Os	19	53,000	35,000	95,000	4.07	*Patriarchal diocese, P Antioch & All the East.* 31n 9x 9m 43w 290Yy
M Halab (Aleppo)*(Melkite)*	c 350	R-Mel	Os	8	7,200	15,000	18,000	0.73	Numerical decline. 7 schools until 1967. M=BA. 16n 2x 2m 37w 167Yy
M Hims (Homs, Emesa)*(Melkite)*	c 250	R-Mel	Os	17	14,000	15,600	25,000	1.90	Restored 1849. M Homs, Hama & Jabrud. M=BC. 6n 3x 4m 22w 281Yy
AD Al Ladhiqiyah (Latakia)*(Melkite)*	1961	R-Mel	Os	16	3,600	12,000	10,000	-0.73	*AD Laodicea of Syria.* Numerical decline. 13n 4x 4m 11w 44Yy
VA Halab *(Latin)*	1762	R-Lat	Os	30	5,800	12,000	9,800	-0.81	*Al-Latinn.* Half in Aleppo, growing. M=OFM,SDB. 0n 36x 63m 207w 115Yy
AD Dimashq (Damascus)*(Maronite)*	1527	R-Mar	Os	1	4,400	2,002	8,000	5.70	*Al-Mawarinah.* In P Antioch (Lebanon). 1n 3x 3m 2w 33Yy
AD Halab *(Maronite)*	c1650	R-Mar	Os	5	2,000	3,420	3,700	0.32	D Beroea. 2 schools closed 1967. 7n 3x 3m 0w 36Yy
D Al Ladhiqiyah *(Maronite)*	1954	R-Mar	Os	32	15,000	15,700	27,000	2.19	Laodicea of Syria. Parishes of D Tripoli (Lebanon). 16n 3x 3m 36w 285Yy
M Dimashq (Damascus)*(Syrian)*	1633	R-Syr	Os	4	3,100	3,350	6,000	2.36	*Al-Sourian al-Kathoulik.* Under P Antioch (Lebanon). 6n 0x 0m 6w 51Yy
M Hims (Homs, Emesa)*(Syrian)*	1678	R-Syr	Os	18	5,600	6,000	10,100	2.10	*M Homs-Emesa, Hama & Nabk.* 6 schools until 1967. 11n 0x 2m 0w 130Yy
AD Al Hasakah *(Syrian)*	1957	R-Syr	Os	7	2,800	3,596	5,077	1.39	In northeast. 5 schools until 1967. Declining. 4n 1x 2m 7w 67Yy
AD Halab (Aleppo)*(Syrian)*	1659	R-Syr	Os	2	4,900	8,500	8,800	0.14	Gradual numerical growth. 4 schools until 1967. 11n 1x 1m 5w 70Yy
Church of God (Anderson)		P-Hol	x...C	3	200	500	500	0.05	M=CoG(Anderson)(USA). Holiness denomination.
Church of God (Cleveland)		P-Pe3	ZF...	1	60	100	120	0.05	M=CoG(Cleveland)(USA). Small Holiness Pentecostal (3-stage) body.
Church of the East		I-Nes	.....	2	600	1,000	1,100	0.05	Assyrian schism (anti-party) from patriarchate in Iraq. Refugees. 2x.
Episcopal Ch in Jer & ME(D Jerusalem)		A-Low	aw.NC	2	1,500	50	3,600	0.05	Formerly in Jerusalem Archbishopric. Palestinian Arabs, with Arab bishop in Jerusalem.
Evangelical Church in Damascus		P-Ref	.....	2	300	500	700	0.05	Congregation in Damascus; 1950s, refused to join National Evangelical Synod.
Evangelical Church of the Nazarene	1920	P-Hol	xF..C	5	210	640	284	-3.20	*Kniset Innasari Il Injiliyeh.* M=CoN(USA). Declining in numbers. 13m,11t(500).
Greek Orth Patriarchate of Antioch:	33	O-Ara	CW.N.	150	135,000	200,000	242,000	0.05	Members Arabs, liturgy Arabic. Strongest in the west. 34 bishops.
AD Dimashq (Damascus)		O-Ara	Cp	45	40,200	60,000	72,000	0.05	P Antioch is main bastion of Greek Orthodox in Middle East. 50n,5d(75 monks).
D Al Ladhiqiyah (Latakia)		O-Ara	Cm	30	26,800	40,000	48,000	0.05	North coast. Most deeply-embedded of all Christian communities in Syria.
D Halab (Aleppo)(Beroa)		O-Ara	cm	15	13,400	20,000	24,000	0.05	*Diocese of Beroa & Alexandretta* (Iskendarun, Turkey). In northwest.
D Hamah (Epiphania)		O-Ara	Cm	22	20,100	30,000	36,000	0.05	North central Syria. HQ Hamah, 50 km north of Hims. 18 parish priests.
D Hims (Homs, Emessa)		O-Ara	Cm	22	20,500	30,000	37,000	0.05	Central Syria. HQ Archevêché Grec-Orthodoxe, Hims. 16 parish priests.
D Vostro (Bostra, Soueida)		O-Ara	Cm	16	14,000	20,000	25,000	0.05	South, HQ Archevêché Grec-Orthodoxe, Soueida (As-Suwayda). 9 parish priests.
Hidden Muslim believers in Christ	c1970	I-Mus	.....	200	6,000	–	10,000	44.54	Converted Muslims who choose to stay in Islam to witness to Christ.
Isolated radio churches	c1950	I-3rS	.....	2,000	40,000	5,500	70,000	10.71	Arab radio believers, mainly aged 12-25. R=500(TWR,RVOG,&c),T=30000(ICI,GMU).
Jehovah's Witnesses	c1920	m-Jeh	x....	6	240	600	400	-1.61	*Témoins de Jéhovah. Watch Tower.* Active witnessing under way by 1926. Badly persecuted. 2Y.
National Ev Christian Alliance Church	1921	P-Hol	x...C	19	807	2,000	1,107	-2.34	M=CMA(USA). A=1956. Damascus, Homs, other towns. Growing 8%pa. 3n,W=50%,8Y,15z.
National Ev Synod of Syria & Lebanon	1823	P-Ref	RW.NC	38	4,800	10,000	7,600	-1.09	Scattered. Decline by emigration. M=ABCFM/UCBWM. 8n,1H,W=57%,47Yy,66z.
Seventh-day Adventist Church	1890	P-Adv	x...C	1	100	50	200	5.70	*SDA, Syria Station,* East Mediterranean Field, Middle East Union. In Damascus.
Syria Baptist Convention		P-Bap	T....	5	160	100	400	0.05	Mainline Baptists.
Syrian Orth Patriarchate of Antioch:	33	O-Syr	DW.N.	130	60,000	81,000	150,000	0.05	*Jacobites.* Members mainly in northeast. HQ Damascus. 12 Dioceses, 40 bishops.
AD Dimashq (Damascus)		O-Syr	Dp	39	18,000	26,000	45,000	0.05	Patriarchal diocese. 1919-57, patriarch resided at Homs. Heavy emigration.
D Al Hasakah (Hassaké)		O-Syr	Dm	71	33,000	45,000	82,000	0.05	Strongest concentration of members in Qamishli area, in extreme northeast corner.
D Halab (Aleppo)		O-Syr	Dm	9	4,000	5,000	10,000	0.05	Northwest Syria. Contacts with, and support for, Syrian Orthodox in Turkey.
D Hims (Homs)		O-Syr	Dm	11	5,000	5,000	13,000	0.05	Formerly patriarchal seat until 1957. Central Syria, north of Damascus.
Union of Armenian Ev Chs in Near East	1918	P-Con	Rw.NC	29	7,150	6,000	13,000	3.14	Armenian refugees from 1914-18 Turkey massacres. World HQ Beirut. 9 schools,1H.
Other Protestant denominations		P-	.....	40	3,000	1,000	5,000	0.05	Total about 7 (see list below).
Doubly-affiliated		2-aff			0	-100	0		Evangelicals and Independents who are also baptized Catholics or Orthodox.
Totals				**2,947**	**641,387**	**621,156**	**1,141,188**		

Churches, members, growth, 1900-2025	*Congs*	*Adults*	*Affiliated*	*G%*	*Total denominations*	*6 Megablocs:* *O*	*R*	*A*	*P*	*I*	*m*
Total churches, members, and denominations (mid-1900)	200	152,000	274,000	1.18	7	3	1	0	2	1	0
Total churches, members, and denominations (mid-1970)	692	345,612	621,156	1.18	24	4	1	1	13	4	1
Total churches, members, and denominations (mid-1990)	2,000	581,000	1,033,900	2.58	29	4	1	1	17	5	1
Total churches, members, and denominations (mid-1995)	2,947	641,387	1,141,188	1.99	29	4	1	1	17	5	1
Total churches, members, and denominations (mid-2000)	3,800	707,000	1,257,709	1.96	29	4	1	1	17	5	1
Total churches, members, and denominations (mid-2025)	6,000	1,139,000	2,027,400	1.93	65	12	1	1	30	20	1

NOTES ON TABLE ABOVE

NATIONAL COUNCILS (Column 4, 5th letter).

C = Conseil Supérieur des Eglises Evangéliques de Syrie et du Liban (Supreme Council of Evangelical Churches of Syria and Lebanon).

R = Assemblée de la Hiérarchie Catholique en Syrie (Assembly of Bishops in the Syrian Arab Republic); inter-rite.

OTHER PROTESTANT DENOMINATIONS. These small bodies include: Chs of Christ (Christian Chs), Ev Baptist Missions (1957), Mennonite Ch (1923), Religious Society of Friends (1869), World-Wide Missions (1962).

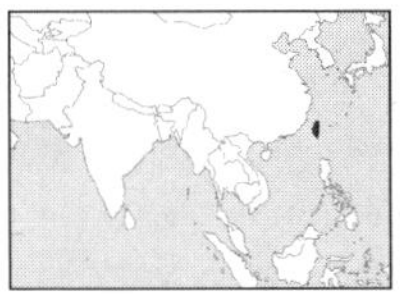

TAIWAN

SECULAR DATA, AD 2000

STATE
Official name: Chung-hua Min-kuo (The Republic of China).
Short name: Taiwan. **Adjective of nationality:** Taiwanese.
Flag: Red field bearing blue rectangle, upper left, containing 12-point white sun.
Area: 36,179 sq. km. (13,969 sq. mi.).
Government: Multiparty republic, since 1992 (1895 part of Japan, 1945 return to China, 1949 Independence, 1949 one-party parliamentary republic).
Legislature: National Assembly, 334 members; Legislative Yuan, 164 members.
Official language: Chinese (Peking dialect).
Monetary unit: 1 New Taiwan dollar (NT$) = 100 cents. **US$1=** NT$34.55.
Chief cities: TAIPEI (Taibei, Tai-Pei, T'aipei) 2,880,000; Kaohsiung (Gaoxiong, Dagon) 1,534,000; Taizhong (Taichung, Tai-chung) 846,367; Tainan (Tai-nan) 746,048; Banqiao (Panchiao, Taipei-hsien) 588,306.
Political divisions: 23 provinces.
Armed forces: 425,000.

DEMOGRAPHY
Population: 22,401,000.
Population density: 619.1/sq. km. (1,603.6/sq. mi.).
Under 15 years: 5,562,000.
Growth rate p.a.: 0.75% (births 14.60, deaths 6.97).
Mortality: Infant, per 1,000: 36.0; **Maternal per 100,000:** 50.0.
Life expectancy: 71 (male 69, female 74).
Household size: 3.8. **Floor area per person, sq.m:** 25.0.
Major languages: Mandarin Chinese, Taiwanese, Hokkien, Hakka, English, Kaoshan, with over 20 smaller languages.
Urban dwellers: 76.00%. **Urban growth rate p.a.:** 1.00%.
Labor force: 43%.

ETHNOLINGUISTIC PEOPLES
71.2% Taiwanese (Hoklo); 15.8% Han Chinese (Mandarin); 10.1% Han Chinese (Hakka); 0.6% Ami (Amis, Pangtsah); 0.3% Filipino.

ECONOMY
National income p.a. per person: US$12,399; **per family:** US$47,119.

EDUCATION
Adult literacy: 94% (male 97%, female 90%). **Schools:** 3,654.
Universities: 125. **School enrolment:** female/male: 90%/90%.

HEALTH
Access to health services: 75%. **Access to safe water:** 80%.
Hospitals: 810 (48 beds per 10,000). **Doctors:** 27,288.
Blind: 18,510. **Deaf:** 1,344,100. **Murder rate:** 8.
Lepers: 55,000.

LITERATURE
New book titles p.a.: 22,850 (1,020 p.a. per million). **Periodicals:** 5,788. **Newspapers:** 50 dailies.

COMMUNICATION (per 1,000 people)
Phones: 467 (12% mobile). **Radios:** 402. **TV sets:** 327.
Daily newspaper circulation: 188. **Computers:** 232.

HUMAN LIFE AND LIBERTY (optimum condition=100.0%)
HDI: 90.0. **HSI:** 75.0. **HFI:** 55.0. **EFL:** 61.0.

Country Table 1. **Religious adherents in Taiwan, AD 1900-2025.**

Year	1900		1970		mid-1990		Annual change, 1990-2000				mid-1995		mid-2000		mid-2025	
Name	Adherents	%	Adherents	%	Adherents	%	Natural	Conversion	Total	Rate	Adherents	%	Adherents	%	Adherents	%
Chinese folk-religionists	2,193,000	68.6	7,400,900	50.4	10,279,700	50.7	108,520	-922	107,598	1.00	10,936,630	50.7	11,355,677	50.7	12,896,500	50.1
Buddhists	580,000	18.1	3,679,000	25.1	4,280,000	21.1	45,183	-4,621	40,562	0.91	4,535,000	21.0	4,685,620	20.9	5,040,250	19.6
Taoists	300,000	9.4	1,534,000	10.5	2,066,000	10.2	21,810	-216	21,594	1.00	2,200,000	10.2	2,281,940	10.2	2,550,000	9.9
New-Religionists	0	0.0	926,000	6.3	1,358,000	6.7	14,336	1,885	16,221	1.13	1,460,000	6.8	1,520,208	6.8	1,900,000	7.4
Christians	**9,000**	**0.3**	**1,003,000**	**6.8**	**1,300,000**	**6.4**	**13,724**	**-2,693**	**11,031**	**0.82**	**1,360,000**	**6.3**	**1,410,310**	**6.3**	**1,700,000**	**6.6**
PROFESSION																
professing Christians	**9,000**	**0.3**	**1,003,000**	**6.8**	**1,300,000**	**6.4**	**13,724**	**-2,693**	**11,031**	**0.82**	**1,360,000**	**6.3**	**1,410,310**	**6.3**	**1,700,000**	**6.6**
AFFILIATION																
unaffiliated Christians	1,850	0.1	181,253	1.2	218,300	1.1	2,305	-1,078	1,227	0.55	232,300	1.1	230,567	1.0	263,500	1.0
affiliated Christians	**7,150**	**0.2**	**821,747**	**5.6**	**1,081,700**	**5.3**	**11,419**	**-1,615**	**9,804**	**0.87**	**1,127,700**	**5.2**	**1,179,743**	**5.3**	**1,436,500**	**5.6**
Independents	0	0.0	231,389	1.6	390,000	1.9	4,117	1,992	6,109	1.47	413,034	1.9	451,093	2.0	665,000	2.6
Protestants	4,500	0.1	274,793	1.9	370,000	1.8	3,906	-906	3,000	0.78	389,817	1.8	400,000	1.8	425,000	1.7
Roman Catholics	2,650	0.1	304,877	2.1	300,000	1.5	3,167	-3,167	0	0.00	300,169	1.4	300,000	1.3	300,000	1.2
Marginal Christians	0	0.0	8,623	0.1	20,000	0.1	211	489	700	3.05	23,000	0.1	27,000	0.1	45,000	0.2
Anglicans	0	0.0	2,065	0.0	1,700	0.0	18	-23	-5	-0.30	1,680	0.0	1,650	0.0	1,500	0.0
Trans-megabloc groupings																
Evangelicals	4,200	0.1	136,000	0.9	190,000	0.9	2,006	494	2,500	1.24	207,748	1.0	215,000	1.0	247,000	1.0
Pentecostals/Charismatics	0	0.0	165,000	1.1	303,000	1.5	3,199	2,401	5,600	1.71	337,400	1.6	359,000	1.6	488,800	1.9
Great Commission Christians	**7,000**	**0.2**	**440,000**	**3.0**	**715,000**	**3.5**	**7,548**	**3,027**	**10,575**	**1.39**	**770,000**	**3.6**	**820,752**	**3.7**	**1,000,000**	**3.9**
Nonreligious	0	0.0	20,000	0.1	803,000	4.0	8,477	5,742	14,219	1.64	879,000	4.1	945,189	4.2	1,400,000	5.4
Muslims	6,000	0.2	60,000	0.4	80,000	0.4	845	-156	689	0.83	83,500	0.4	86,889	0.4	90,000	0.4
Ethnoreligionists	110,000	3.4	40,000	0.3	51,140	0.3	540	375	915	1.66	56,000	0.3	60,291	0.3	65,000	0.3
Atheists	0	0.0	10,000	0.1	35,000	0.2	369	345	714	1.87	40,000	0.2	42,139	0.2	68,000	0.3
Baha'is	0	0.0	3,000	0.0	9,000	0.0	95	261	356	3.38	10,700	0.1	12,555	0.1	20,000	0.1
Jews	0	0.0	100	0.0	160	0.0	2	0	2	1.24	170	0.0	181	0.0	250	0.0
World A (unevangelized persons)	2,801,448	87.6	8,805,600	60.0	7,091,700	35.0	74,858	-86,186	-11,328	-0.16	7,115,130	33.0	6,989,112	31.2	5,995,090	23.3
World B (evangelized non-Christians)	387,552	12.1	4,867,400	33.2	11,870,300	58.6	125,319	88,879	214,198	1.67	13,085,870	60.7	14,001,578	62.5	18,034,910	70.1
World C (Christians)	9,000	0.3	1,003,000	6.8	1,300,000	6.4	13,724	-2,693	11,031	0.82	1,360,000	6.3	1,410,310	6.3	1,700,000	6.6
Country's population	**3,198,000**	**100.0**	**14,676,000**	**100.0**	**20,262,000**	**100.0**	**213,901**	**0**	**213,901**	**1.01**	**21,561,000**	**100.0**	**22,401,000**	**100.0**	**25,730,000**	**100.0**

COLUMNS, ROWS.
For meanings and definitions, see Codebook (Part 3). Note that, by definition, total 'Christians' = professing + crypto-Christians, which also = affiliated + unaffiliated Christians, and also = Great Commission Christians + latent Christians. Percentages may not always total exactly, due to rounding.

CENSUSES.
The religion question has not been asked in government censuses.

NOTES ON RELIGIONS.
ATHEISTS. No communists or Communist party are tolerated, but there are underground groups, also non-communist humanists.
BAHA'IS. Rapid growth from 2 local spiritual assemblies (1964) to 17 (1973), and then continuously expanding to 62 LSAs by 1996.
BUDDHISTS. Mostly of the Pure Land school, with the Contemplative school influential among intellectuals. In 1959 there were 354 monks and 482 nuns in 881 monasteries and nunneries; in 1964, 865 monks and 1,355 nuns; but by 1976 these had risen to 7,750 religious personnel in 2,250 temples and monasteries. Only around 3 million are in any way active Buddhists. There are also a few Mongolian and Tibetan Lamaists, with a worship center in Taipei.
CHINESE FOLK-RELIGIONISTS. Mainly followers of Taiwanese popular religion (with some mainland Chinese), which is an amalgam of Buddhism, Taoism, Confucianism, animism, and local elements; including 21,000 orthodox Taoist devotees with 2,800 Taoist temples, and 100,000 prohibited but underground Taoists in the powerful I-Kuan-Tao sect. There are also other underground sects.
ETHNORELIGIONISTS. Aboriginal tribes in the mountains; animists.
INDEPENDENTS. In over 65 denominations in 1995 (see Table 2); Chinese, with a few Korean indigenous Christians.
MUSLIMS. 50% are refugees from mainland China since 1950 (Sunnis of the Hanafite rite). Since 1960, Muslim missionaries from Saudi Arabia have been at work and now claim 40,000 as their converts. *Hajj pilgrims to Mecca.* (1976) 100.
NONRELIGIOUS. Mainly young Chinese abandoning their family religions.
PENTECOSTALS/CHARISMATICS. Totals (January 1974): 300 involved adults (over 15 years old) in 20 organized prayer groups; total charismatic community including children, 600. Though small in numbers, the Catholic Charismatic Renewal has a significant presence. Begun in 1969, by 1997 it had 20 weekly prayer groups with 800 attenders including a high number of priests (90) and 5 bishops.

Great Commission Instrument Panel: status of Taiwan (for explanation see start of Part 4)

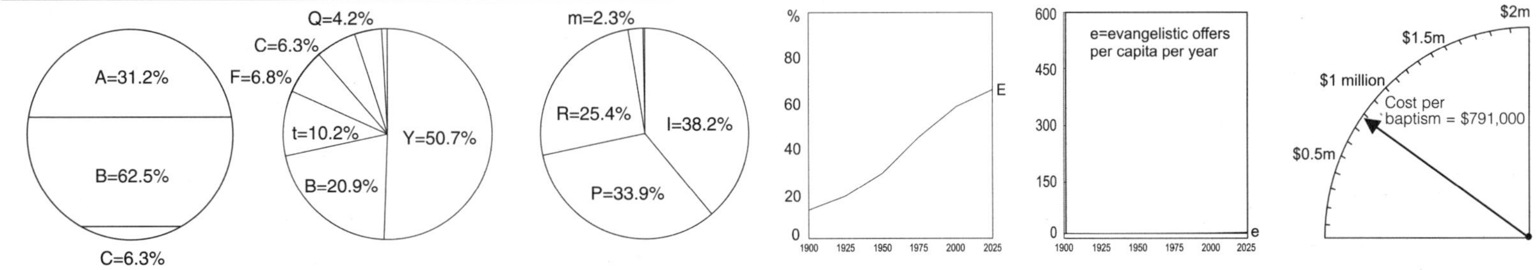

3 Worlds, AD 2000 — Religions, AD 2000 — Ecclesiastical blocs — Evangelization, 1900-2025 — Offers, 1900-2025 — Cost-effectiveness, AD 2000

Country status. Taiwan is a mountainous island in the Pacific Ocean off the south-east coast of China. It is a leading exporter of electronics, textiles, and consumer goods.

HUMAN LIFE AND LIBERTY

Human rights and freedoms. After military rule and other nondemocratic regimes, Taiwan has taken care to develop human rights to a significant degree.

NON-CHRISTIAN RELIGIONS

Chinese folk religion, known here as Taiwanese popular religion, is practiced by the Taiwanese who were immigrants from China in the 6th and 7th centuries AD. It consists of a combination of magic, an-

Country summary. **Worlds A, B, C by ethnolinguistic peoples, cities, and major civil divisions in Taiwan.**

	PEOPLES							CITIES							CIVIL DIVISIONS						
World	Num	Pop 2000	C%	Christians	E%	U%	Unevangelized	Num	Pop 2000	C%	Christians	E%	U%	Unevangelized	Num	Pop 2000	C%	Christians	E%	U%	Unevangelized
A	6	118,927	3.78	4,495	38	62	74,226	0	0	0.00	0	0	0	0	0	0	0.00	0	0	0	0
B	6	21,801,090	3.54	772,352	68	32	6,902,707	28	10,658,026	5.12	545,190	71	29	3,115,764	23	22,400,998	5.27	1,179,744	69	31	6,977,714
C	18	480,983	83.76	402,895	100	0	781	0	0	0.00	0	0	0	0	0	0	0.00	0	0	0	0
Total	**30**	**22,401,000**	**5.27**	**1,179,742**	**69**	**31**	**6,977,714**	**28**	**10,658,026**	**5.12**	**545,190**	**71**	**29**	**3,115,764**	**23**	**22,400,998**	**5.27**	**1,179,744**	**69**	**31**	**6,977,714**

cestor-veneration and devotion to divinities, with influences from Taoism, Buddhism, and Confucianism as well as traditional animistic beliefs and practices. The proportion of each varies between different localities depending upon the socio-religious group which constitutes it. Among the divinities worshiped in Taiwan are Kuan-yin, goddess of mercy and Thi-Kong, Jade Emperor and Supreme Ruler of Heaven who is generally believed to be superior to Buddhist and Taoist deities. Popular religion is still influential in rural areas and small towns, where new temples continue to be built. However, in large cities, apart from religious festivals and processions it is confined to observances in the home. Young educated people do not normally participate in temple ceremonies, but they are expected to take part in practices related to ancestor-veneration. In 1995, less than 1% of college youths claimed to hold these beliefs.

Buddhists. Mammoth statue of the Buddha at Changh.

Buddhism is a strong force in Taiwan, but those who practice it strictly are few. The majority of Taiwan's Buddhists belong to the Pure Land school, although the Contemplative school is more influential among intellectuals.

Several Buddhist groups are collectively known as Vegetarians (Chai-chiao), having adopted elements from Confucianism and Taoism. They are treated by orthodox Buddhists are heretics on account of their alleged syncretism.

Buddhism shows evidence of revival, with a number of new temples being built recently and new magazines published. Especially among youth there is a concern that Buddhism be purified from superstitious influences and become involved in social action. There are over 10.5 million Buddhists in Taiwan. In 1959, there were 354 monks and 482 nuns, rapidly rising by 1976 to 7,750 religious personnel.

Islam is primarily confined to the Chinese community, one-half of all Muslims being refugees from the mainland since 1950. In 1964, there were 6 mosques in Taiwan, 2 more than existed in 1963. There are 2 important Muslim organizations: (1) the Chinese Muslim Association, founded in 1937 on the mainland, with the entire Muslim population of 60,000 counted as members in 1969, which is active in promoting friendship and cultural exchange with Muslim countries; and (2) the Chinese Muslim Youth League, with 500 members, whose purpose is to study Islamic culture and to promote conversions to Islam.

Taoism exists in 2 forms: as a formal orthodox organization and as part of the syncretistic popular religion which has wide currency in Taiwan.

Orthodox Taoism concentrates on a higher level of worship, the Tao itself, and is represented by the National Taoist Association of the Republic of China. There is also a powerful sect of Taoism operating underground called I-Kuan-Tao, which has strict rules.

Tribal religions are still practiced by remnants of the 10 Aboriginal tribes in the mountains, who until recently were all head-hunting animists. Since 1945, they have experienced mass conversion to Christianity.

Catholic Church in Taiwan. Enthusiastic welcome for new archbishop of Taipei.

CHRISTIANITY

CATHOLIC CHURCH. Dominicans from the Philippines began work on Taiwan in 1621, but their work was not sustained after the Dutch gained control during 1624-62. Taiwan was later administered as part of China with ports closed until 1858. Catholics then returned the following year. Japan gained possession of the island from 1895 to 1945. Taiwan became a Catholic prefecture in 1913 when there were over 3,000 Catholics, with the number increasing to 8,000 in 1945. Refugees from mainland China and work among the Aborigines raised the total to 48,400 by 1955 more than 300,000 by 1970, with a slight decline by 1990.

As with the total Christian population, Catholics in Taiwan are divided into 3 more or less equal groups: about 100,000 Aborigines, 100,000 Taiwan islanders, and 100,000 China mainlanders. The fast-developing industrialization of the country, with its rapid shifts in population, has had detrimental effects on church growth. However, steps are now being taken to identify and aid rural parishioners when they migrate to Taiwan's cities.

Lay cell groups are increasingly effective in providing informal meeting places for fostering spiritual nurture. The Legion of Mary is also active in missionary outreach.

The Holy See has diplomatic relations with Taiwan and in AD 2000 is represented to government and the Catholic hierarchy by a nuncio residing in Taipei.

PROTESTANT CHURCHES. During the Dutch occupation from 1624-62, about 6,000 conversions among the tribal peoples were recorded by the Dutch Reformed Church, but all missionaries and Christians were killed when a Chinese pirate later took control of the island. The first Protestant missionaries of the present era were English Presbyterians who arrived in the south in 1865.

Canadian Presbyterians followed 7 years later in the north. When the Japanese occupied Taiwan in 1895 and attempted to suppress Christianity, membership increased two-fold during the first 10 years. Forty years later, a similar resistance to Japan's anti-Christian campaign became evident when hundreds were brought to Christ during World War II through the instrumentality of Chi-oang, a Sediq (Atayal) tribeswoman. Missionaries returned after the war to find 4,000 Atayals meeting in churches which they had built themselves. A Presbyterian Double-the-Church movement succeeded in more than doubling the number of churches and members during the decade 1955-65. Today, all 10 mountain tribes are heavily Christian.

Five Presbyterian missions cooperate with the Presbyterian Church in Taiwan, the largest Protestant denomination.

When mainland China was evacuated by missionaries in 1949, many followed the Nationalist Chinese to Taiwan. These and new groups attracted to the island at that time have resulted in a vast increase in the number of Protestant missions, the majority being from North America. The most successful of these new missions has been the Southern Baptist Convention, USA. Christianity has achieved some prestige due to the fact that the former president, Chiang Kai-chek, was a practicing Christian. Churches are becoming self-supporting, but church growth is beginning to decline.

INDIGENOUS CHURCHES. The Little Flock, or Assembly Hall Churches, the third largest church in Taiwan (after Catholics and Presbyterians), was begun on the mainland in 1926 under the notable leadership of Watchman Nee. Similar in the looseness of its structure to the Plymouth Brethren, but denying any relationship to Protestant churches, it was brought to Taiwan in 1948, growing to 40,000 adult members and a Christian community of 80,000 by 1970. Stress is placed on small house churches and personal evangelism as well as prayer, preaching, tract distribution, parades, and home visitation.

Since 1970, however, church membership has declined, falling to 68,100 by 1995.

True Jesus Christ Church in Taiwan. Many of the TJC churches in Taiwan have packed congregations (as at *top*); *lower*, many have outstanding architecture (Dounan in Huwei county).

The True Jesus Church, fourth in size, is a Pentecostal group founded by Paul Wei in Peking in 1917. Spreading to Taiwan in 1926, it grew to 5,000 adherents by the end of World War II and has since multiplied to embrace a Christian community of 42,000. In contrast to the Assembly Hall Churches, it has a sophisticated organization which, without diminishing the importance of the local congregation, involves one national and 5 regional councils. Most of its new members are tribal converts. Both of these indigenous denominations stress church planting and also lay training. A number of other small independent churches have been formed since 1950.

Indigenous missions. Chinese Christians, unable to leave their homeland, have begun to express their missions commitment by reaching out to less reached ethnic groups in China. Whether this means Lisu evangelists among the peoples of the South or Han businessmen in the Northwest frontier, new mission initiatives are resulting in the penetration of previously unreached peoples.

Renewal movements. In the 1990s the Pentecostal/Charismatic Renewal continued to spread rapidly across most older churches, and numbered over 359,000 adherents (of whom 7% Pentecostals, 18% Charismatics, and 74% Independents).

Tunghai University chapel in Taichung shows the modern trend of architecture.

CHURCH AND STATE

The constitution of 1947 guarantees freedom of religious belief (Article 13) and of assembly and association (Article 14). This freedom is not to be restricted by law 'except by such as may be necessary to prevent infringement upon the freedom of other persons, to avert imminent crisis, to maintain social order or to advance public welfare' (Article 23).

Churches and adjacent buildings are legally considered as being available for service to the public, although churches are not obliged to register officially. The Bureau of Social Affairs of the Ministry of the Interior is in charge of religious matters.

BROADCASTING AND MEDIA

Programs from KNLS, TWR (Guam), FEBC (Philippines), VERITAS and other international broadcasters cover the island. Taiwan is a member of UNDA, and Catholic programs saturate the radio channels. Weekdays, a daily 20-minute short story with Scripture is aired in the afternoon, and a 60-second radio advertisement for a Doctrine Correspondence Course is aired every 30 minutes. On Sundays there are 17 30-minute radio programs blanketing the morning and evening hours with music, Scripture readings and sermons. Training programs are offered by the Kuangchi Program Service and Fu Jen University. Yih-Syh broadcast station and Chung Sheng Broadcast Station air programs in Mandarin and Taiwanese.

CBN's *International 700 Club* can be seen each Tuesday in the afternoon, and a ministry center located in Taiwan does follow up. Television has aired the 'Jesus' Film to 3 million. TBN programs have aired in Taipei on local channels. Additional programs are available via satellite.

INTERDENOMINATIONAL ORGANIZATIONS

There is no ecumenical council of churches in Taiwan, but several organizations coordinate Protestant activities. In 1966, the Association of Christian Churches of the Republic of China was organized with membership open to all denominations, local churches, and individuals. Its organization is loose, serving primarily as a link between the Christian community and government. The Catholic Church has formed a Committee for Christian Unity within its Episcopal Commission for Social Action and the Lay Apostolate. Another body, the Taiwan Missionary Fellowship, has more than 800 foreign missionaries as members from 78 societies and agencies. An Ecumenical Cooperative Committee has also come into existence composed of 8 churches and Christian organizations.

Taiwan Christian Service coordinates relief activities sponsored by Church World Service and Lutheran World Relief, and for Catholics, the Taiwan Ecumenical Industrial Ministry (TEIM) works in close cooperation with other churches.

The Association of Friends for the Study of Chinese Culture is a small group composed of Taoists, Buddhists, Muslims, Catholics, and Protestants who meet regularly for dialogue and discussion concerning beliefs and practices of the various religions in Taiwan.

Chinese folk-religionists. The Confucius Temple in Taipei. Taiwanese folk religion worships 250 deities.

FUTURE TRENDS AND PROSPECTS

Christianity seems set to grow to about 6.6% of the population by AD 2025.

Christianity could then grow beyond 7% by AD 2050. Buddhists and Chinese folk-religionists are both likely to decline with increasing secularization among the youth.

BIBLIOGRAPHY

'A religious ethnography of a Chinese village in Taiwan: an analysis of four rituals.' Y. H. T. Tsu. Ph.D. dissertation, Princeton University, Princeton, NJ, 1991. 291p.

'American evangelicalism in Chinese environment: Southern Baptist Convention missionaries in Taiwan, 1949–1981,' M. A. Rubinstein, *American Baptist quarterly*, 2, 3 (1983), 269–89.

'An analysis of the church planting grid for the Baptist churches in Taiwan.' R. E. West. M.A.M. thesis, Southwestern Baptist Theological Seminary, Fort Worth, TX, 1993. 105p.

An introduction to Taiwanese folk religions. G. P. Kramer & G. Wu. Taipei, 1970. 89p.

'Aspects of ancestor worship in northern Taiwan,' A. P. Wolf, in *Ancestors*, p.339–64. W. H. Newell (ed). The Hague: Mouton, 1976.

Catholic politics in China and Korea. E. O. Hanson. *American Society of Missiology series*, no. 2. Maryknoll, NY: Orbis Books, 1980. 160p.

Chinese creeds and customs. V. R. Burkhardt. Hong Kong: South China Morning Post, 1953–58. 3 vols.

Christianity and animism in Taiwan. A. F. Gates. San Francisco: Chinese Materials Center, 1979. 262p.

Christianity in Taiwan: a history. H. K. Tong. Taipei, Taiwan: China Post, 1961. 249p.

Christianity in Taiwan: a profile. Church Growth Society of Taiwan. Taipei, Taiwan: Overseas Crusades, 1974. 34p.

'Christianity in Taiwan under Japanese rule, 1895–1945.' W. J. Richardson. Ph.D. dissertation, St. John's University, Jamaica, NY, 1972. 231p.

Church directory of the Republic of China, 1969. Taipei, Taiwan: China Evangelical Fellowship, 1969. 94p. (In Chinese).

Faith that moves mountains: a study of the Tribal Church in Taiwan. G. Vicedom. Taipei, Taiwan: China Post, 1967. 145p.

Gods, ghosts, and ancestors: the folk religion of a Taiwanese village. D. K. Jordan. Berkeley, CA: University of California Press, 1972. 197p.

'Historical aspects of leadership emergence and development and their relationship to church growth among the Friends churches of Taiwan.' J. R. Elwood. D.Miss. thesis, Biola University, La Mirada, CA, 1989. 168p.

I will build my church: ten case studies of church growth in Taiwan. A. J. Swanson (ed). Taichung, Taiwan: Taiwan Church Growth Society, 1977. 173p.

'Introducing Christianity to non–Christian Taiwan: a booklet and commentary.' C. C. Chen. D.Min. thesis, University of the South, Sewanee, TN, 1993. 235p.

Joint action for mission in Formosa: a call for advance into a new era. C. H. Hwang. New York: CWME & Friendship Press, 1967. 127p.

Mending the nets: Taiwan church growth and loss in the 1980s'. A. J. Swanson. Pasadena, CA: William Carey Library, 1986. 283p.

'Modes of belief in Chinese folk religion,' S. Harrell, *Journal for the scientific study of religion*, 16, 1 (1977), 55–65.

'Neighborhood cult associations in traditional Taiwan,' K. M. Schipper, in *The city in late imperial China*, p.651–76. G. W. Skinner (ed). Stanford, CA: Stanford University Press, 1977.

'Pentecostalism becomes Chinese: the True Jesus Church, 1917–1984.' M. A. Rubinstein. Typescript, 1984. 82p.

Protestantism in changing Taiwan: a call to creative response. D. A. Raber. South Pasadena, CA: William Carey Library, 1978. 363p.

'Receptivity of Korea and Taiwan mountain people.' E. S. Chae. Thesis, Fuller Theological Seminary, Pasadena, CA, 1973. 133p.

Religions of China: the world as a living system. D. L. Overmyer. San Francisco: Harper & Row, 1986. 125p.

Taiwan. W. Lee. *World bibliographical series*, vol. 113. Oxford, UK: CLIO Press, 1990. 284p. (See especially 'Religion,' p.34-42).

Taiwan: a comprehensive bibliography of English–language publications. J. B. Jacobs, J. Hagger & A. Sedgley. *Occasional papers of the East Asia Institute.* Bundoora, Australia: Borchardt Library, La Trobe University, 1984. 214p.

Taiwan Catholic directory 1970. Taipei, Taiwan: Catholic Central Bureau, 1970.

Taiwan Christian yearbook 1968: a survey of the Christian movement in Taiwan, 1965–1968. Taipei, Taiwan: Taiwan Missionary Fellowship, 1968. 198p.

Taiwan: mainline versus independent church growth: a study in contrasts. A. J. Swanson. South Pasadena, CA: William Carey Library, 1970. 299p.

Taiwan Missionary Fellowship directory 1972. Taipei, Taiwan: Dixon Press, 1972. 159p.

'Taiwan's Churches of the Holy Spirit,' M. A. Rubinstein, *The American Asian review*, 6, 3 (1988), 23–58.

'The Chinese church and its relationship to ancestor practices, particularly within the Taiwanese context.' S. J. Wagner. M.A. thesis, Anderson College, Anderson, SC, 1987. 138p.

'The Chinese of the diaspora in South East Asia,' *Pro Mundi Vita* (Brussels), 23 (1968).

'The church growth of the Presbyterian Church in Taiwan.' J. Lin. D.Min. thesis, Fuller Theological Seminary, Pasadena, CA, 1988. 281p.

The church in Taiwan, profile 1980: a review of the past, a projection for the future. A. J. Swanson. Pasadena, CA: William Carey Library, 1981. 465p.

The description of the True Jesus Church. Taipei, Taiwan: General Assembly of the True Jesus Church in Taiwan, 1967. 41p.

'The development of Taiwanese folk religion, 1683–1945.' H. Chen. Ph.D. dissertation, University of Washington, Seattle, WA, 1995. 217p.

'The evangelization of the urban industrial workers in Taiwan in missiological perspectives.' K. Tsai. D.Miss. thesis, Fuller Theological Seminary, Pasadena, CA, 1985. 362p.

The flying phoenix: aspects of Chinese sectarianism in Taiwan. D. K. Jordan & D. L. Overmyer. Princeton, NJ: Princeton University Press, 1986. 329p.

The imperial metaphor: popular religion in China. S. Feuchtwang. London: Routledge, 1992. 223p.

The mountains sing: God's love revealed to Taiwan tribes. R. Winslow. Winona Lake, IN: Light and Life Press, 1984. 168p.

The Protestant community of modern Taiwan: mission, seminary, and church. M. A. Rubinstein (ed). N.p.: M.E. Sharpe, 1990. 250p.

'Turning to God in Taiwan: a study of conversion.' D. T. H. Chee. D.Min. thesis, Pacific School of Religion, Berkeley, CA, 1983. 153p.

Unities and diversities in Chinese religion. R. P. Weller. Seattle, WA: University of Washington Press, 1987. 215p.

Wine for the gods: an account of the religious traditions and beliefs of Taiwan. H. Y. Wei & S. Coutanceau. Taipei, Taiwan: Cheng-wen, 1976. 234p.

Country Table 2. **Organized churches and denominations in Taiwan.**

Official name (bold type = church with over 10% of all affiliated) 1	*Begun* 2	*Type* 3	*Counc* 4	*Congs* 5	*Adults* 6	*Affiliated 1970* 7	*Affiliated 1995* 8	*G%* 9	*Names, notes, and other statistics* (see Codebook, Part 3) 10
Assembly Hall Churches	1948	I-3nC	x....	228	37,440	80,000	68,100	-0.64	*Chu Hui So. Little Flock. Local Church.* F=Watchman Nee. Mandarin. 70n. In 50 countries.
Baptist Bible Fellowship	1950	I-Bap	x....	15	1,200	3,000	3,000	0.00	M=BBFI(USA). Fundamentalists. HQ Taichung. 6n,5m,11f,14t(950).
Catholic Church in Taiwan:	1621	R-Lat	P.FZK	469	164,800	304,877	300,169	-0.06	*T'ien Chu Chiao.* C=16+2+50. Declining. 227n 464x 633m 1146w 44Yy
M Taipeh (T'aipe)	1949	R-Lat	Ps	124	43,000	51,586	79,444	1.74	*Taipei Tsung Chiao-ch'u.* Trilingual. M=OFM. 70n 192x 304m 428w 813Yy
D Kiayi (Chiai)	1952	R-Lat	Ps	60	10,000	20,562	18,647	-0.39	*Chiayi Chiao-ch'u.* Rural. 80% Minnan. 40n 27x 31m 75w 193Yy
D Hsinchu	1961	R-Lat	Ps	82	28,000	62,484	50,615	-0.84	Rural, industry in north. Quadrilingual. 29n 61x 65m 161w 252Yy
D Hwalien (Hualien)	1952	R-Lat	Pmep	48	32,000	60,166	58,018	-0.15	Multilingual. 70% Amis (Aborigines). M=SMB,MEP. 20n 28x 31m 116w 892Yy
D Kaohsiung	1949	R-Lat	Ps	58	25,000	50,058	44,849	-0.44	Multilingual. Rapid industrialization. M=SJ,OP,CM. 17n 71x 79m 152w 502Yy
D Taichung	1950	R-Lat	Pmm	44	18,000	40,018	32,306	-0.85	44% Taiwanese, 39% Mainlander, 17% Abor. M=MM. 21n 53x 79m 137w 534Yy
D Tainan	1961	R-Lat	Ps	53	8,800	20,003	16,290	-0.82	90% Minnan. Also Pescadores Islands. 30n 32x 44m 77w 158Yy
Central Taiwan Lutheran Church		P-Lut	.....	20	400	400	1,000	0.05	M=Norwegian Evangelical Lutheran Free Church Mission. 2n,5m,13f,9t(395),1u.
China Assemblies of God	1948	P-Pe2	ZF...	49	1,942	6,000	3,840	-1.77	*Taiwan District.* M=AoG(USA). 7,052 in mail courses. 54n,17f,1s(59),50t(587),W=64%.
China Church of God (Cleveland)	1982	P-Pe3	.....	1	153	–	255	7.69	M=CoG(Cleveland).
China Evangelical Lutheran Church	1951	P-Lut	e....	32	2,290	3,000	4,160	1.32	Western cities. M=LC Missouri Synod (USA). 18n,4x,24f,1s,25t(1344),109Yy.
China Free Methodist Church	1952	I-Hol	VF...	53	4,898	3,000	7,540	3.76	M=FMC(USA). In southwest and Taipei. 35n,10f,
China Holiness Church	1953	P-Hol	x....	18	1,600	2,000	2,170	0.33	M=Swedish Holiness Mission. Northwest. 2n,4x,7m,8f,15f(750),W=33%,15Y,20z.
China Lutheran Gospel Church		I-Lut	.....	9	662	700	1,100	0.05	Independent Lutherans.
China Peniel Church	1946	P-Hol	x....	3	343	500	858	2.18	M=VOCA(Voice of China & Asia MS). HQ Mushan, Taipei. 7n,2m,2f,7t(435).
China Presbyterian Church of Christ	1934	I-Ref	.TT.T	2	1,347	400	2,450	7.52	M=IBPFM(USA). Mandarin, some Taiwanese. 1966, 40% secede. 6n,5m,3f,5t(200).
Chinese Baptist Convention	1948	P-Bap	T...K	152	18,514	25,000	37,000	1.58	M=SBC. Mandarin; few Taiwanese. 49n,71f,1s(23),95t(7420).W=50%,696Y,1500z.
Chinese Lutheran Church	1951	P-Lut	l....	17	1,008	2,000	2,100	0.20	*Chung-Hua.* M=CLB. In Taiwan Lutheran Ch till 1957. 7n,4x,7f,G=-1.0%pa,23t,1u,57Yy.
Christian & Missionary Alliance	1952	P-Hol	xF..E	21	1,393	1,000	2,090	2.99	*Union of Taiwan.* M=CMA(USA). Mandarin. 5n,15f,10t(625),W=60%,42Y,58z.
Christian Assemblies		P-CBr	x....	12	1,200	3,000	1,710	0.05	*Christian (Plymouth, Open) Brethren.* M=CMML(USA, Australia, UK). 18m,14f,14t(800).
Christian Church of Salvation	1958	I-Non	.TT.T	6	700	2,000	2,100	0.20	Formerly Shou Shan Christian Ch. Independent of foreign missions. 2n,8m,6t(200).
Christian Lutheran Evangelical Ch		I-Lut	.....	8	164	80	328	0.05	Independent Lutherans.
Chr Nationals Evangelism Commission	1959	I-Non	xF...	4	200	500	400	-0.89	*CNEC.* Begun China 1942, Mission now based on San Jose, CA (USA). 5n,4t(300).
Christian Revival Fellowship	1953	I-3pC	Z....	10	500	500	1,500	4.49	M=Independent AoG(USA). M=Scandinavian Pentecostals. 4n,4f,5t(160).
Christianity Bible Church	1956	I-Non	.....	5	200	200	300	1.64	Small indigenous body begun by Chinese. 1n,3m.
Ch of Jesus Christ of Latter-day Saints	1950	m-LdS	x....	47	11,100	4,623	17,000	5.35	*Mormons.* M=CJCLdS(Utah, USA). Many USA expatriates and military. 120f.
Church of the Nazarene	1956	P-Hol	xF...	30	1,737	3,000	2,550	-0.65	M=CoN. Mandarin, Taiwanese, Paiwanese. 6n,5x,23m,10f,1s(24),25t,W=65%,150Y.
Churches of Christ	1960	I-Dis	x....	10	120	600	300	-2.73	M=CCCC(instrumental)(USA). Taichung. Taipei. Many USA personnel. 11f.
Conservative Baptist Association	1952	I-Bap	xF...	25	1,672	2,000	4,780	3.55	M=CBFMS(USA). Mandarin. 6n,5x,8m,41f,1k,1s(21),21t(900),W=45%,45Y,243z.
Elim Foursquare Gospel Alliance	1963	P-Pe2	ZF...	18	2,400	5,000	5,330	0.26	M=Elim FGA(UK), PAoC(Canada). HQ Taipei. 15n,6f.
Evangelical Alliance Mission	1951	P-Eva	xM...	33	1,523	3,000	3,810	0.96	M=TEAM,FEGC(USA). Began in Hualien area. Radio work. 18m,81f,1H,2h,31t(1500).
Evangelize China Fellowship	1947	I-Non	x....	6	2,000	4,000	4,400	0.38	Begun in China by a Chinese. M=ECF(HQ,USA). Some Aborigines, 12n,10m,7t(500).
Fellowship of Chinese Covenant Chs	1952	P-Con	K....	27	2,346	2,000	3,910	2.72	M=Free Mission Covenant Ch (Finland), ECCA(USA). Mostly Mandarin. 9m,10f,12t(500).
Fellowship of Mennonite Chs in Taiwan	1948	P-Men	G...K	20	1,493	1,600	4,500	4.22	M=General Conference MC(USA). 11n,7m,34f.G=6.6%pa,1H,1p(5).11t(394),W=49%,87Y,80z.
Formosa Christian Mission	1955	I-Non	.....	15	400	1,000	1,100	0.38	Indigenous, entirely Chinese, 2n,16m,5t(114),450z.
Full Gospel Assemblies	1953	P-Pe2	Z....	75	3,000	3,000	7,500	3.73	M=FFFM(Finland). Countries: Miaoli, Taichung, Hualien. 8n,11m,14f,32t(1000).
Glad Tidings Church	1952	I-3pC	x....	10	802	600	1,100	2.45	M=Glad Tidings Missionary Soc (Canada). HQ Taichung. 8n,8m,13f,1p(120),13t(600).
Gospel Baptist Church	1953	I-Bap	x....	6	320	800	533	-1.61	M=Baptist Missionary Association of America. 3n,2f,6t(150).
Gospel Quakers		I-Qua	.....	3	164	140	328	0.05	Independent Quakers (Society of Friends).
Gospelaires Missionary Church	1955	I-Non	.TT.T	3	700	2,000	1,900	-0.20	M=Gospelaires Missionary Association. HQ Taipei. 3n,8m,3t(200).
Home of Christ Church		I-3cC	.....	4	575	500	958	0.05	Chinese Independent charismatics.
Independent Mandarin churches	1952	I-Non	xM...	50	4,000	7,000	11,000	1.82	M=Overseas Missionary Fellowship (former CIM, Nei Ti Hui). 44f,1j.
Internat Ch of the Foursquare Gospel	1988	P-Pe2	ZF...	4	320	500	800	14.29	M=ICFG(USA). Classical Pentecostals: world HQ Los Angeles, USA, HQ Taipei.
International Gospel League	1958	I-Non	..T.T	2	30	200	100	-2.73	*Jesus Christ's Gospel Hall*, et al. M=IGL(USA). Declining. 4n,3t(40).
Isolated radio churches		I-3rC	.....	300	10,000	3,000	15,000	0.05	Isolated believers linked by Christian radio programs.
Jehovah's Witnesses	1928	m-Jeh	x....	35	1,690	4,000	6,000	1.64	*Watch Tower.* First lectures 1928, witnessing 1932. Many Ami tribals. (1975) 63Y. (1995) 366Y.
Korean Church in Taiwan	1949	I-Ref	.....	20	500	215	1,000	6.34	Migrant Presbyterians from Korea, maintaining own separate organization. 1n,5m.
Liebenzelle Church	1953	P-Non	xM...	10	200	200	300	1.64	M=LM(USA), from Bad Liebenzell (Germany). HQ Puli (Nantou). 7f,4t(80).
Living Way Presbyterian Church		I-Ref	.TT.T	5	290	400	400	0.05	Formerly Tao-Seng Mission. Split ex China Presb Ch of Christ. 5n,10m,5t(188),105z.
Local Mandarin-speaking Churches		I-Non	.....	20	3,000	7,000	8,000	0.05	Indigenous independent congregations loosely related to preacher Wu Yung. 15n.
Lutheran Church of Republic of China	1956	P-Lut	.....	15	562	1,000	937	-0.26	M=Finnish Missionary Society. Hengchun (extreme south). 2n,24f,1h,50t(2300),1u.
Methodist Ch of the Republic of China	1952	P-Met	VwE.K	20	2,543	10,000	5,090	-2.67	*Taiwan Annual Conference*, UMC(USA); A=1972. 13n,16f,2H,2s,21t(1683),1u,1v,554z.
New Apostolic Church	c1980	I-3aX	x....	3	100	–	135	6.67	M=NAC/NAK. HQ Zurich (Switzerland).
Norwegian Missionary Alliance	1945	P-Non	.....	10	200	300	500	2.06	M=NMA(Norske Misjonsalianse), begun China 1901. HQ Puli. 1n,6m,17f,2H,10t(310).
Norwegian Pentecostal Mission	c1960	P-Pe2	Z....	15	4,000	5,000	6,000	0.73	M=Norske Pinsevenners Ytremisjon. Begun unintentionally by itinerant Chinese.
Pentecostal Assemblies	1963	P-Pe2	ZF...	9	503	2,000	838	-3.42	Classical (2-stage) Pentecostals. M=PAoC(Canada). 3n,12m,3F.30t(3000).
Presbyterian Church in Taiwan	1865	P-Ref	R.E.K	1,126	87,500	154,680	222,263	1.46	70% Taiwanese, 30% Aborigine. 373n,12x,76f,2H,4s(548),929t(58221),W=35%,8697Yy.
Quemoy Christian Church of Christ		I-Fun	.TT.T	2	100	1,000	200	0.05	*Quemoy Huo Pu Christian Ch.* Fundamentalists on island 5 miles from mainland China.
Republic of Taiwan Lutheran Church	1953	P-Lut	.....	22	1,484	2,000	2,120	0.23	Former China (Chung-Kuo) Luth Ch. M=Norwegian Lutheran Mission. 3n,8m,10f,12t(570),1u.
Salvation Army	1928	P-Sal	xwE.E	5	121	400	173	-3.30	*Kuei Sai Kuen. SA, Taiwan Region.* Pioneers Japanese. 10n,4x,1s,4t(270),W=88%,50z.
Seventh-day Adventist Church	1912	P-Adv	x....	41	5,983	15,000	15,000	0.00	*SChina Island UM.* Mountain tribes. 32n,122m,33f,1H,1j,1r,2s(82),113t(8342),151Y.
Spiritual Food Church	c1965	I-Non	x....	8	6,140	700	15,400	13.16	*Ling Liang Worldwide Evangelistic Mission* (from Hong Kong). 1n,1t(80),50z.
Taipei Truth Church		I-3pC	.....	1	1,540	154	2,370	0.05	Independent Chinese pentecostals.
Taiwan Assembly of God	1953	I-3pC	.....	30	2,000	3,000	3,500	0.62	Indigenous local assemblies begun by Chinese. 5n,33m.
Taiwan Church of God (Anderson)	1981	P-Hol	.....	4	320	–	533	7.14	M=CoG(Anderson).
Taiwan Congregational Association		I-Con	.TT.T	8	100	200	250	0.05	M=Congregational Christian Churches (USA). Fundamentalists. 2n,7t(350).
Taiwan Episcopal Church: D Taiwan	c1940	A-Hig	awEAK	17	921	2,065	1,680	-0.82	1960 missionary Diocese of ECUSA, Province VIII. Static. 16n,2x,9f,2h,1r,7t(321),1u,4Y,30y.
Taiwan Fellowship Deaconry Mission	1952	P-Non	.....	10	200	500	600	0.73	M=Marburger Mission (Germany). Former Yunnan Mission in China. 3n,11m,11m,13f,6t(500).
Taiwan Friends Church	1953	P-Qua	QF...	35	3,183	3,000	7,960	3.98	M=Taiwan Friends Mission (Ohio, USA). Mostly in Chiayi. 13n,10f,1s,26t(1000).
Taiwan Gospel Church		I-Non	.....	4	300	1,000	700	0.05	M=Taiwan Gospel Mission. Independent congregations. Declining. 4n,4t(200).
Taiwan Holiness Church	1928	P-Hol	xF...	83	10,700	5,000	19,400	5.57	Begun 1929 by Japanese. 1951, M=OMS(USA). 55n,16f,1s(38),53t(2911),201Y,1103z.
Taiwan Lutheran Church	1951	P-Lut	L...K	46	3,911	5,913	7,820	1.12	Begun by mainland refugees. 8 missions. Declining in influence. 23n,23f,1H,1s,44t(2280).
Taiwan Reformed Presbyterian Church	1950	P-Ref	xF...	15	400	800	700	-0.53	M=CRC,OPC,EPC(all USA),RC(New Zealand). 5n,11m,18f,1s,18t(785),256z.
Taiwan (Tao Seng) Presbyterian Ch	1952	I-Ref	.....	7	381	500	762	1.70	Split from China Presbyterian Church of Christ. 4n,7t(220),259z.
True Jesus Church in Taiwan	1926	I-3oC	x...K	242	29,400	50,000	42,000	-0.69	*Chen Ye-su Chiao Hui.* Rapid growth. Taiwanese. 43n,43m,1s(12),132t((9352),1000Yy.
United Pentecostal Church	1978	P-Pe1	.....	5	400	–	1,000	5.88	*UPC.* Oneness Pentecostals. *Jesus Only Church.* 4f.
Other indigenous single congs	c1960	I-sin	.....	400	60,000	50,000	200,000	5.70	In over 30 groupings. Mostly single congregations unrelated to others. 200nm.
Other Protestant denominations		P-	.....	40	11,000	8,000	15,000	0.05	About 25 bodies (see list below), including USA military chaplaincies.
Other indigenous charismatic chs		I-3cC	.....	60	3,000	5,000	10,000	0.05	15 bodies (see below), including Jesus is Lord Fellowship (Philippines), New Testament Ch.
Totals				**4,195**	**528,328**	**821,747**	**1,127,700**		

Churches, members, growth, 1900-2025	*Congs*	*Adults*	*Affiliated*	*G%*	*Total denominations*	*6 Megablocs:* *O*	*R*	*A*	*P*	*I*	*m*
Total churches, members, and denominations (mid-1900)	100	3,400	7,150	7.01	2	0	1	0	1	0	0
Total churches, members, and denominations (mid-1970)	3,014	396,134	821,747	7.01	97	0	1	1	42	51	2
Total churches, members, and denominations (mid-1990)	4,000	507,000	1,081,700	1.38	151	0	1	1	58	89	2
Total churches, members, and denominations (mid-1995)	4,195	528,328	1,127,700	0.84	152	0	1	1	59	89	2
Total churches, members, and denominations (mid-2000)	4,200	553,000	1,179,743	0.91	153	0	1	1	60	89	2
Total churches, members, and denominations (mid-2025)	5,000	673,000	1,436,500	0.79	247	0	1	1	80	160	5

NOTES ON TABLE ABOVE

COLUMNS: for meanings and CODES (cols. 1, 3, 4, 8): see Codebook (Part 3). Column 1: **Boldface type** = church with over 10% of country's affiliated Christians.

NATIONAL COUNCILS (Column 4, 5th letter).

E = Evangelical Fellowship of Taiwan (begun 1952 as China Evangelical Fellowship CEF; mostly individuals).

K = National Council of Churches in Taiwan (NCCT; formerly Ecumenical Co-operative Committee.

T = Republic of China Council of Christian Churches.

Other national councils. Taiwan Missionary Fellowship (composed of all Protestant missionaries). Association of Christian Churches of the Republic of China (for all Protestant groups to obtain representation before government). Taiwan Christian Service (co-operating with almost all Christian bodies except Little Flock, Mormons, Jehovah's Witnesses).

OTHER PROTESTANT DENOMINATIONS. About 15 smaller bodies, including: Apostolic Church of Pentecost (Canada), Baptist Mid-Missions (1972), Ch of Christ, Emmanuel Baptist Mission, Ev Wesleyan Mission, Go-Ye Fellowship, Hundred Nations Crusade (member of ICCC), International Missions (1946), Swedish Free Mission, Taiwan Ev Presbyterian Church, Wesleyan Ch, Worldwide Evangelization Crusade, World-Wide Missions (1961). There are also USA military chaplaincies among the 9,000 USA troops.

OTHER INDIGENOUS CHURCHES. These include: Cina Ch of Christ (member of ICCC), Conservative Congregational Ch (member of ICCC), Holy Spirit Association for Unification of World Christianity (from Korea), Taipei Chunking Christian Ch (member of ICCC).

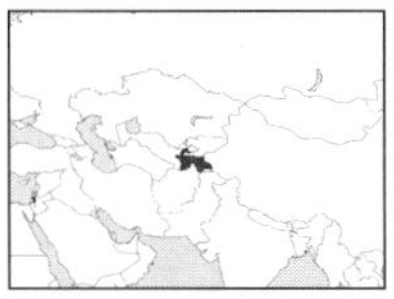

TAJIKISTAN

SECULAR DATA, AD 2000

STATE
Official name: Jumkhurii Tojikistan (The Republic of Tajikistan).
Short name: Tajikistan. **Adjective of nationality:** Tajik.
Flag: Red, white, and green stripes with coat of arms in center.
Area: 143,100 sq. km. (55,300 sq. mi.).
Government: Republic with one legislative house, since 1990 (1929 Soviet rule).
Legislature: Supreme Council, 181 members.
Official language: Tajik.
Monetary unit: 1 Tajik ruble. **US$1=** 754 Tajik ruble.
Chief cities: DUSANBE (Dushanbe, Stalinabad) 745,895; Khudzhand (Leninabad, Khojend) 210,679; Kul'ab 101,561; Kurgan-T'ube 74,794.
Political divisions: 6 provinces.
Armed forces: 7,000.

DEMOGRAPHY
Population: 6,188,000.
Population density: 43.2/sq. km. (111.9/sq. mi.).
Under 15 years: 2,496,000.
Growth rate p.a.: 1.28% (births 28.66, deaths 6.31).
Mortality: Infant, per 1,000: 51.1; **Maternal per 100,000:** 130.0.
Life expectancy: 69 (male 66, female 71).
Household size: 6.1. **Floor area per person, sq.m:** 20.0.
Major languages: Tajik, Uzbek, Russian, Kirghiz, Farsi, Tatar.
Urban dwellers: 32.86%. **Urban growth rate p.a.:** 2.8%.
Labor force: 37%.

ETHNOLINGUISTIC PEOPLES
66.1% Tajik (Tadzhik); 23.5% Northern Uzbek; 2.2% Russian; 1.4% Tatar; 1.2% Kirghiz.

ECONOMY
National income p.a. per person: US$340; **per family:** US$2,074.

EDUCATION
Adult literacy: 97% (male 98%, female 96%). **Schools:** 3,350.
Universities: 22. **School enrolment:** female/male: 80%/86%.

HEALTH
Access to health services: 60%. **Access to safe water:** 50%.
Hospitals: 449 (88 beds per 10,000). **Doctors:** 13,084.
Blind: 6,000. **Deaf:** 383,900. **Murder rate:** 2.
Lepers: 1,500.

LITERATURE
New book titles p.a.: 210 (34 p.a. per million). **Periodicals:** 36.
Newspapers: 2 dailies.

COMMUNICATION (per 1,000 people)
Phones: 45 (0% mobile). **Radios:** 100. **TV sets:** 258.
Daily newspaper circulation: 13. **Computers:** 20.

REFUGEES
Citizen refugees in other countries: 170,400.

HUMAN LIFE AND LIBERTY (optimum condition=100.0%)
HDI: 58.0. **HSI:** 10.0. **HFI:** 5.0. **EFL:** 20.0.

Country Table 1. **Religious adherents in Tajikistan, AD 1900-2025.**

Year	*1900*		*1970*		*mid-1990*		*Annual change, 1990-2000*				*mid-1995*		*mid-2000*		*mid-2025*	
Name	*Adherents*	*%*	*Adherents*	*%*	*Adherents*	*%*	*Natural*	*Conversion*	*Total*	*Rate*	*Adherents*	*%*	*Adherents*	*%*	*Adherents*	*%*
Muslims	475,000	98.3	1,858,500	63.2	4,233,000	79.8	70,643	23,201	93,844	2.02	4,719,300	82.1	5,171,439	83.6	8,000,000	90.3
Nonreligious	1,000	0.2	570,000	19.4	700,000	13.2	11,682	-7,640	4,042	0.56	725,000	12.6	740,415	12.0	600,000	6.8
Christians	**5,000**	**1.0**	**83,500**	**2.8**	**146,500**	**2.8**	**2,467**	**-4,058**	**-1,591**	**-1.14**	**140,000**	**2.4**	**130,594**	**2.1**	**125,000**	**1.4**
PROFESSION																
crypto-Christians	0	0.0	60,000	2.0	100,000	1.9	1,691	-691	1,000	0.96	110,000	1.9	110,000	1.8	90,000	1.0
professing Christians	**5,000**	**1.0**	**23,500**	**0.8**	**46,500**	**0.9**	**776**	**-3,367**	**-2,591**	**-7.82**	**30,000**	**0.5**	**20,594**	**0.3**	**35,000**	**0.4**
AFFILIATION																
unaffiliated Christians	0	0.0	0	0.0	1,500	0.0	25	-77	-52	-4.15	1,325	0.0	982	0.0	700	0.0
affiliated Christians	**5,000**	**1.0**	**83,500**	**2.8**	**145,000**	**2.7**	**2,442**	**-3,981**	**-1,539**	**-1.12**	**138,675**	**2.4**	**129,612**	**2.1**	**124,300**	**1.4**
Orthodox	4,000	0.8	61,000	2.1	108,500	2.1	1,811	-3,361	-1,550	-1.53	100,500	1.8	93,000	1.5	85,000	1.0
Protestants	0	0.0	20,300	0.7	19,300	0.4	322	-552	-230	-1.26	18,875	0.3	17,000	0.3	15,000	0.2
Independents	0	0.0	1,200	0.0	12,000	0.2	200	100	300	2.26	14,100	0.3	15,000	0.2	20,000	0.2
Roman Catholics	1,000	0.2	1,000	0.0	5,000	0.1	83	-142	-59	-1.24	5,000	0.1	4,412	0.1	4,000	0.1
Marginal Christians	0	0.0	0	0.0	200	0.0	3	-3	0	0.00	200	0.0	200	0.0	300	0.0
Trans-megabloc groupings																
Evangelicals	0	0.0	300	0.0	1,500	0.0	25	15	40	2.39	2,038	0.0	1,900	0.0	2,000	0.0
Pentecostals/Charismatics	0	0.0	100	0.0	2,800	0.1	47	-7	40	1.34	3,089	0.1	3,200	0.1	6,800	0.1
Great Commission Christians	**4,500**	**0.9**	**40,800**	**1.4**	**65,000**	**1.2**	**1,085**	**-2,514**	**-1,429**	**-2.45**	**62,000**	**1.1**	**50,711**	**0.8**	**55,000**	**0.6**
Atheists	0	0.0	421,000	14.3	200,000	3.8	3,338	-11,459	-8,121	-5.08	140,000	2.4	118,788	1.9	80,000	0.9
Jews	2,000	0.4	9,000	0.3	8,400	0.2	140	-92	48	0.55	8,800	0.2	8,875	0.1	11,000	0.1
Zoroastrians	0	0.0	0	0.0	6,000	0.1	100	43	143	2.16	7,000	0.1	7,426	0.1	21,000	0.2
Ethnoreligionists	0	0.0	0	0.0	5,000	0.1	83	9	92	1.71	5,500	0.1	5,922	0.1	10,000	0.1
Buddhists	0	0.0	0	0.0	3,500	0.1	58	-8	50	1.34	3,700	0.1	3,999	0.1	8,000	0.1
Baha'is	0	0.0	0	0.0	600	0.0	10	4	14	2.16	700	0.0	743	0.0	2,000	0.0
World A (unevangelized persons)	473,340	98.0	2,250,247	76.5	3,234,830	61.0	53,988	-31,711	22,277	0.67	3,335,288	58.0	3,459,092	55.9	4,499,356	50.8
World B (evangelized non-Christians)	4,660	1.0	607,752	20.7	1,921,670	36.2	32,066	35,769	67,835	3.06	2,275,208	39.6	2,598,314	42.0	4,232,644	47.8
World C (Christians)	5,000	1.0	83,500	2.8	146,500	2.8	2,467	-4,058	-1,591	-1.14	140,000	2.4	130,594	2.1	125,000	1.4
Country's population	**483,000**	**100.0**	**2,941,500**	**100.0**	**5,303,000**	**100.0**	**88,521**	**0**	**88,521**	**1.56**	**5,750,497**	**100.0**	**6,188,000**	**100.0**	**8,857,000**	**100.0**

COLUMNS, ROWS.
For meanings and definitions, see Codebook (Part 3). Note that, by definition, total 'Christians' = professing + crypto-Christians, which also = affiliated + unaffiliated Christians, and also = Great Commission Christians + latent Christians. Percentages may not always total exactly, due to rounding.

NOTES ON RELIGIONS.
BAHA'IS. After years of Soviet repression, by 1996 Baha'is had organized themselves into 16 local spiritual assemblies.
ETHORELIGIONISTS. Shamanists among Koreans, Kirghiz, Mari, and Udmurt.
JEWS. 60% are Central Asian or Bokharan Jews.
NONRELIGIOUS. Rapid decline after 1989 due to collapse of Communism and emigration of Russians and Ukranians.
ORTHODOX. Declining due to Russian and Ukranian emigration.

Great Commission Instrument Panel: status of Tajikistan (for explanation see start of Part 4)

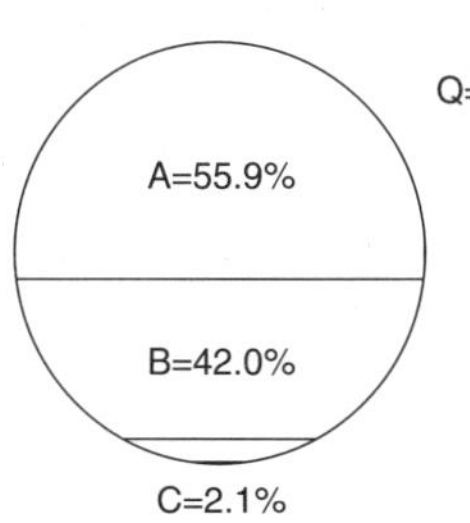

3 Worlds, AD 2000

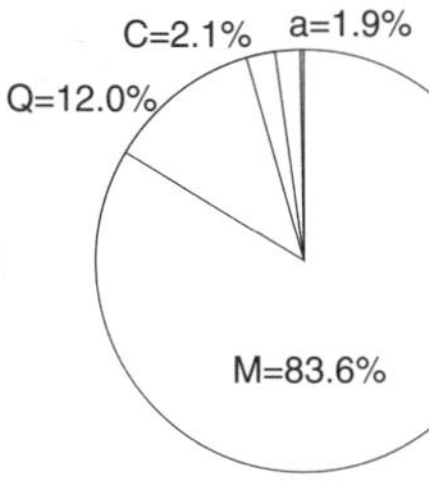

Religions, AD 2000

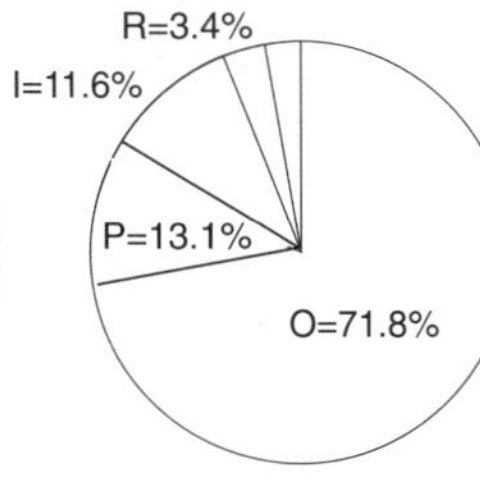

Ecclesiastical blocs

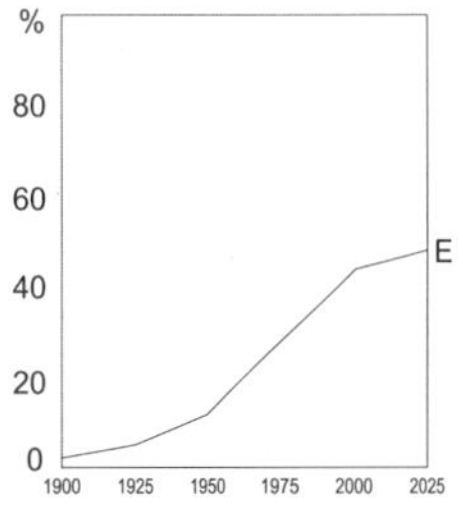

Evangelization, 1900-2025

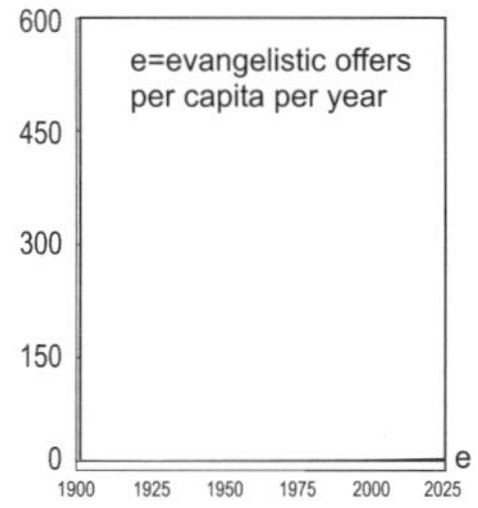

Offers, 1900-2025

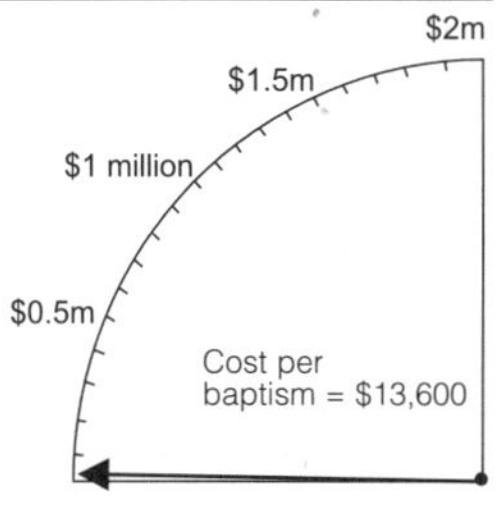

Cost-effectiveness, AD 2000

Country status. Tajikistan, a former republic of the Soviet Union, is a mountainous country in Central Asia bordered by Uzbekistan, Afghanistan, Kirghizia, and China. It is rich in minerals, including coal, oil, lead, and zinc.

HUMAN LIFE AND LIBERTY

Human need and development. Tajikistan was the least economically developed republic of the former Soviet Union when it disbanded in 1991. The difficult transition to a market economy caused rampant crisis within the newly formed government and led to a savage civil war that caused severe damage to every facet of society and culture. Hospitals, homes, schools, communications, and the agricultural infrastructure were destroyed. The repercussions of this war will likely be felt for some time. It is estimated that 80-90% of the population have incomes which fall well below any of the various measures of economic well being. Nearly 10% of the population receives pensions. The number of those receiving social assistance has increased by 17% since 1990 and social service agencies have increased by 20%. During the civil war 300,000 persons were rendered homeless.

Universal free health care is provided in the Constitution but to maintain standards of excellent care has proved difficult. Inadequate funds exacerbate the government's inability to pay medical personnel, furnish medicines and medical supplies, update equipment, facilities, and infrastructure.

In the education realm, the current textbooks are those used before independence, and basic school supplies such as notebooks, paper, and writing utensils are either non-existent or in very short supply. Teacher population has also declined. At the beginning of the '95 school year, 12,000 teachers did not return to work

Human rights and freedoms. Soon after it declared its independence from the Soviet Union in 1991, Tajikistan was wracked by a civil war. The losing side in this civil war comprised a loose grouping of Islamic fundamentalists supported by mujahedin

Country summary. **Worlds A, B, C by ethnolinguistic peoples, cities, and major civil divisions in Tajikistan.**

	PEOPLES							CITIES							CIVIL DIVISIONS						
World	*Num*	*Pop 2000*	*C%*	*Christians*	*E%*	*U%*	*Unevangelized*	*Num*	*Pop 2000*	*C%*	*Christians*	*E%*	*U%*	*Unevangelized*	*Num*	*Pop 2000*	*C%*	*Christians*	*E%*	*U%*	*Unevangelized*
A	23	5,967,988	0.07	4,207	42	58	3,448,041	4	1,132,929	2.27	25,714	45	55	622,093	6	6,188,202	2.09	129,612	44	56	3,457,771
B	6	39,172	25.70	10,067	77	23	9,073	0	0	0.00	0	0	0	0	0	0	0.00	0	0	0	0
C	12	181,042	63.71	115,338	100	0	658	0	0	0.00	0	0	0	0	0	0	0.00	0	0	0	0
Total	**41**	**6,188,202**	**2.09**	**129,612**	**44**	**56**	**3,457,772**	**4**	**1,132,929**	**2.27**	**25,714**	**45**	**55**	**622,093**	**6**	**6,188,202**	**2.09**	**129,612**	**44**	**56**	**3,457,771**

from Afghanistan. Opposition forces continue to pose a threat to the government by staging frequent raids across the Afghan border. Because of the civil war and its aftermath, human rights have made only slow progress in Tajikistan and are frequently observed in their breach. The progovernment People's Front Militia as well as internal security forces commit numerous human rights abuses. Detainees are beaten and tortured. While the total death toll in the civil war is estimated at over 20,000, more deaths occurred after the victory of the government forces when a pogrom was unleashed against Pamiri and Garm-origin males. There are also reports of disappearances of hundreds of opposition fighters. The Criminal Code has not been significantly amended since independence and the old abuses continue. The system allows for lengthy pretrial detention and provides few checks on the power of prosecutors and police to arrest individuals and to hold prisoners incommunicado for long periods. The judiciary is subject to interference not only from the government but also from paramilitary groups. Many verdicts are decided at the point of a kalashnikov. In some cases judges have been killed when they did not obey orders from the paramilitary groups. The government muzzles the press through various means: errant journalists are dismissed from the state-owned media or subjected to criminal prosecution, opposition newspapers are intimidated and harassed by the paramilitary groups, government subsidies and newsprint are denied to critical journals, and printing press facilities are denied to papers that flout government directives. Soviet-era restrictions on criticism of government leaders still apply. Church and state are separate. However, almost all the senior Islamic clerics who had supported the rebels were either demoted, arrested or replaced. Following the civil war about 90,000 Pamiri and Garm-origin nationals fled to Afghanistan (which has its own political problems) and about 40,000 still remain in that country. Another 30,000 live as transients in the Gorno-Badakshan region. Of the 600,000 ethnic Russians in the country before the civil war, more than 350,000 have left. The civil war also has resulted in the hardening of the old authoritarian regime. Opposition political parties are banned and opposition leaders have been arrested, jailed or driven into exile. No parliamentary elections have been held since independence. There are no active human rights monitoring organizations in the country.

Human environment. Environmental problems stem from the result of agricultural policies imposed during th Soviet Union's existence. Heavy use of menial fertilizers and agricultural chemicals was a major cause of pollution. These chemicals contaminated not only the land, air, and water but also cottonseeds, whose oil is used for cooking. These toxic sources are believed to contribute to the high incidence of maternal and child mortality and birth defects.

Between 1964 and 1996 the Soviet and post-Soviet agricultural planners mandated a 50% increase in cotton cultivation thereby overtaxing the regional water supplies. Poorly designed irrigation networks led to massive runoff, which increased soil salinity and carried toxic agricultural chemicals downstream to populated areas, other streams and the Aral sea.

Pollution problems are furthered by industrial production, especially in the area of nonferrous metal. Large amounts of toxic waste gases emitted from such industries have been blamed for birth defects among people who live within range of its emissions.

Activities such as construction, road building, and irrigation have often aggravated the geologic processes prone to this area such as earthquakes, landslides, and mudslides.

Forced relocation has resulted in 90% of the population concentrated on less than 7% of the land. In addition, virtually all industrial agricultural activity is confined to these areas which further contribute to the depletion and contamination of natural resources and the surrounding environment.

Ironically, war and economic decline may have had somewhat of a positive effect on the environment. The use of agricultural chemicals has substantially declined, and the use of fertilizers and insecticides is non-existent in some places, resulting in the disappearance of these chemicals in the food chain and diminishing amounts of soil and water concentrations.

NON-CHRISTIAN RELIGIONS

Islam. Most of the population of Tajikistan belongs, however loosely, to the Hanafi branch of Sunni Islam. There are some Shia communities, mainly amongst the mountain Tajiks. The number of mosques in the country grew from 18 in 1990 to more than 2500 in 1992.

Other religious groups include ***Buddhists, Baha'is*** (who first came around 1989), ***Jews***, and ***atheists***.

Independents. Flourishing Tajik house church. Many young people attend.

CHRISTIANITY

Christianity appeared in Central Asia around AD 250 via Christian travelers who used the Silk route that connected the regions between China and the West. Christianity was strongly opposed but by the year 410, one fourth of the population of this region was reported to be Christian. Traces remained through the centuries but with the Islamic revolution that began in the 8th century, Christianity gradually disappeared only resurfacing in recent years.

ORTHODOX CHURCH. There are 20 Russian Orthodox congregations in Tajikistan. In November of 1996 the Orthodox Christian Temples celebrated 125 years of establishment in the region. There are 7 temples in the in the territory of the republic. Two are found in Dushanbe and others are in Khojand, Chkalovsk, Kurgon-Teppa, and Tursunzoda

CATHOLIC CHURCH. The Holy See has no diplomatic relations with Tajikistan in AD 2000.

Indigenous missions. There have been very few Christians sent out as missionaries from Tajikistan.

CHURCH AND STATE

Article 26 of the Constitution provides for freedom of religion. State and religion are separate and there are no restrictions on religious worship imposed by law or government. However according to the law on Freedom of Faith, the Committee on Religious Affairs, headed by the council of Ministers, registers religious communities and monitors the activities of the various religious establishments. While the official reason given is to ensure that they are acting in accordance with the law, the practical purpose is to ensure that they do not become overtly political.

BROADCASTING AND MEDIA

Programming in central Asian languages (Kazakh, Tajik, Uzbek, Kyrgyz) can be received from TWR (Guam), FEBC (Saipan), and HCJB (Ecuador), and in Turkish from TWR (Albania) and TWR (Monaco). IBRA-produced programs in Turkish, Arabic, Azeri, and Farsi can be received from the ultra-powerful Radio Moscow stations in Krasnodar, St Petersburg, and Samara.

Over 2.4 million have seen the 'Jesus' Film, mainly on a television broadcast of the film.

FUTURE TRENDS AND PROSPECTS

The nonreligious and atheists represented over 30% of the population in 1970 but in the post-Soviet era these will likely decline to less than 8% by AD 2025. Islam will make the major gains, likely growing to over 90% in the same period. Christians are expected to decline below 2% by AD 2025.

With non-Muslims expected to continue emigration throughout the 21st century, the numbers of Christians, atheists, and the nonreligious could jointly represent less than 5% of the population by AD 2100.

BIBLIOGRAPHY

Country profile, Tajikistan. London: International Institute for the Study of Islam and Christianity, 1994. 104p.

Drevnie obrazy mifologii u tadzhikov doliny Zerzvshana. O. Murodov. Dushanbe, Tajikistan: Donish, 1979. 116p.

Major ethnic groups in Tajikistan. [Washington, DC: Central Intelligence Agency, 1993]. (Map).

'Muslim resurgence in Soviet Central Asia,' H. Malik, *Occasional papers on religion in Eastern Europe*, 11 (March 1991), 1–11. (Focuses on Uzbekistan and Tajikistan).

Tadjikistan: nationalism, religion, and political change. M. Atkin. Washington, DC: National Council for Soviet and East European Research, 1992. 36p.

'Tajikistan and the Islamic revival.' T. B. Samuels. M.A. thesis, University of Virginia, Charlottesville, VA, 1987. 85p.

The subtlest battle: Islam in Soviet Tajikistan. A. Muriel. Philadelphia: Foreign Policy Research Institute, 1989.

Country Table 2. **Organized churches and denominations in Tajikistan.**

Official name (bold type = church with over 10% of all affiliated) 1	*Begun* 2	*Type* 3	*Counc* 4	*Congs* 5	*Adults* 6	*Affiliated 1970* 7	*Affiliated 1995* 8	*G%* 9	*Names, notes, and other statistics* (see Codebook, Part 3) 10
Armenian Apostolic Church		O-Arm	E....	3	2,000	500	3,200	0.05	Gregorians, under C Echmiadzin.
Baptist Churches in Tajikistan		P-Bap	T....	7	375	500	500	0.05	*Union of Ev Christians-Baptists of Middle Asia.* Former AUCECB. Russians,Ukrainians,Germans
Bulgarian Orthodox Church		O-Bul	C....	1	500	200	800	0.05	Bulgarians, under P Sofia.
Catholic Church in Tajikistan		R-LEr	B....	2	3,000	1,000	5,000	0.05	Ukrainians, Byelorussians, Lithuanians, Poles.
German Ev Lutheran Church		P-Lut	L....	10	8,600	19,000	15,000	0.05	Germans. Rapid emigration after 1990.
Isolated radio believers	c1970	I-3rZ	.....	40	400	–	500	28.22	Believers linked by Christian radio programs.
Jehovah's Witnesses		m-Jeh	x....	1	60	–	200	0.05	*Watch Tower.* IBSA.
Korean Methodist Church		P-Met	V....	2	1,000	200	2,000	0.05	Koreans retaining their original Methodist background.
Korean Pentecostal Church		I-3pK	.....	1	350	–	600	0.05	Korean Pentecostals.
Pentecostal Churches		P-Pe2	.....	3	150	–	375	0.05	Mainline Pentecostals, mainly Russians and Ukrainians.
Russian Orthodox Ch (D Tashkent)		O-Rus	M....	20	70,000	60,000	95,000	0.05	*Diocese of Tashkent & Central Asia.* Russians: 1992 emigration; many atheists converted.
Old Ritualist Church		I-OBe	x....	1	1,000	200	2,000	0.05	Old Believers. Russians, Byelorussians. Conversions of many former atheists.
Ukrainian Orthodox Ch (P Kiev)		I-Ukr	M....	10	8,000	1,000	11,000	0.05	1992 emigration to Ukraine, but also conversion of many atheists.
Other Orthodox churches		O-	.....	5	1,000	300	1,500	0.05	Total 5, including Georgian OC (C Tiflis), Greek OC, Moldavian OC, Ukrainian AOC, ROCOR.

Continued opposite

Country Table 2–concluded

Official name (bold type = church with over 10% of affiliated) 1	*Begun* 2	*Type* 3	*Counc* 4	*Congs* 5	*Adults* 6	*Affiliated 1970* 7	*Affiliated 1995* 8	*G%* 9	*Names, notes, and other statistics* (see Codebook, Part 3) 10
Other Protestant bodies		P-	.....	10	700	600	1,000	0.05	Total 8, including Old Mennonites (Germans), SDA, CEF, CCECB, IPKh.
Totals				**116**	**97,135**	**83,500**	**138,675**		

Churches, members, growth, 1900-2025	*Congs*	*Adults*	*Affiliated*	*G%*	*Total denominations*	*6 Megablocs:*	*O*	*R*	*A*	*P*	*I*	*m*
Total churches, members, and denominations (mid-1900)	10	3,100	5,000	4.10	1	....	1	0	0	0	0	0
Total churches, members, and denominations (mid-1970)	47	52,550	83,500	4.10	15	....	5	1	0	7	2	0
Total churches, members, and denominations (mid-1990)	90	102,000	145,000	2.80	26	....	8	1	0	12	4	1
Total churches, members, and denominations (mid-1995)	116	97,135	138,675	-0.89	26	....	8	1	0	12	4	1
Total churches, members, and denominations (mid-2000)	100	90,800	129,612	-1.34	26	....	8	1	0	12	4	1
Total churches, members, and denominations (mid-2025)	100	87,100	124,300	-0.17	52	....	10	1	0	20	20	1

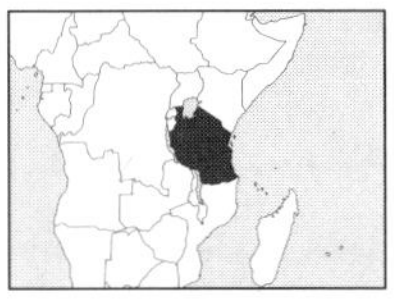

TANZANIA

SECULAR DATA, AD 2000

STATE
Official name: Jamhuri ya Muungano wa Tanzania/The United Republic of Tanzania.
Short name: Tanzania. **Adjective of nationality:** Tanzanian.
Flag: Green triangle (upper left) and blue triangle (lower right) separated by diagonal gold-bordered black stripe.
Area: 942,799 sq. km. (364,017 sq. mi.).
Government: Multiparty republic, since 1992 (1890 British protectorate (Zanzibar) and German protectorate (Tanganyika), 1918 British mandated territory, 1961 Independence, 1964 Tanganyika and Zanzibar united).
Legislature: National Assembly, 232 members.
Official language: Swahili (Kiswahili), English.
Monetary unit: 1 Tanzania shilling (T Sh) = 100 cents. **US$1=** T Sh 659.65.
Chief cities: DAR ES SALAAM (Dar as-salam) 2,051,000; Tabora (Kazeh) 1,488,000; Mwanza 216,028; Zanzibar 207,907; Tanga 195,357.
Political divisions: 25 provinces.
Armed forces: 35,000.

DEMOGRAPHY
Population: 33,517,000.
Population density: 35.5/sq. km. (92.0/sq. mi.).
Under 15 years: 15,227,000.
Growth rate p.a.: 2.32% (births 38.97, deaths 14.99).
Mortality: Infant, per 1,000: 74.9; **Maternal per 100,000:** 770.0.
Life expectancy: 48 (male 47, female 49).
Household size: 5.1. **Floor area per person, sq.m:** 17.0.
Major languages: Swahili, English, Sukuma, Nyamwezi, Hehe, Makonde, Chagga, Haya, Ha, Gogo, Nyakyusa, Sambaa, Arabic, Luguru, Chinese, and over 110 other tribal languages.
Urban dwellers: 27.83%. **Urban growth rate p.a.:** 5.2%.
Labor force: 46%.

ETHNOLINGUISTIC PEOPLES
9.4% Sukuma; 4.4% Gogo; 4.2% Haya (Ziba, Bumbira); 3.5% Nyamwezi (Nyanyembe); 3.3% Makonde (Matambwe).

ECONOMY
National income p.a. per person: US$120; **per family:** US$611.

EDUCATION
Adult literacy: 67% (male 79%, female 56%). **Schools:** 10,892.
Universities: 4. **School enrolment:** female/male: 43%/45%.

HEALTH
Access to health services: 80%. **Access to safe water:** 49%.
Hospitals: 170 (11 beds per 10,000). **Doctors:** 1,065.
Blind: 40,000. **Deaf:** 2,021,200. **Murder rate:** 6.
Lepers: 200,000. **Underweight prevalence under 5:** 29%.

LITERATURE
New book titles p.a.: 270 (8 p.a. per million). **Periodicals:** 84.
Newspapers: 3 dailies.

COMMUNICATION (per 1,000 people)
Phones: 3 (19% mobile). **Radios:** 123. **TV sets:** 16.
Daily newspaper circulation: 8. **Computers:** 10.

REFUGEES
Alien refugees from other countries: 703,000.

HUMAN LIFE AND LIBERTY (optimum condition=100.0%)
HDI: 35.7. **HSI:** 29.0. **HFI:** 25.0. **EFL:** 31.0.

Country Table 1. **Religious adherents in Tanzania, AD 1900-2025.**

Year	*1900*		*1970*		*mid-1990*		*Annual change, 1990-2000*				*mid-1995*		*mid-2000*		*mid-2025*	
Name	*Adherents*	*%*	*Adherents*	*%*	*Adherents*	*%*	*Natural*	*Conversion*	*Total*	*Rate*	*Adherents*	*%*	*Adherents*	*%*	*Adherents*	*%*
Christians	**92,000**	**2.4**	**4,937,000**	**36.1**	**12,286,200**	**48.2**	**388,171**	**71,465**	**459,636**	**3.23**	**14,840,500**	**49.6**	**16,882,561**	**50.4**	**32,500,000**	**56.1**
PROFESSION																
professing Christians	**92,000**	**2.4**	**4,937,000**	**36.1**	**12,286,200**	**48.2**	**388,171**	**71,465**	**459,636**	**3.23**	**14,840,500**	**49.6**	**16,882,561**	**50.4**	**32,500,000**	**56.1**
AFFILIATION																
unaffiliated Christians	14,600	0.4	612,375	4.5	936,200	3.7	29,578	-7,220	22,358	2.16	1,075,000	3.6	1,159,783	3.5	1,500,000	2.6
affiliated Christians	**77,400**	**2.0**	**4,324,625**	**31.6**	**11,350,000**	**44.6**	**358,592**	**78,686**	**437,278**	**3.31**	**13,765,500**	**46.0**	**15,722,778**	**46.9**	**31,000,000**	**53.5**
Roman Catholics	62,400	1.6	2,806,662	20.5	6,215,000	24.4	196,357	10,443	206,800	2.91	7,354,860	24.6	8,283,000	24.7	16,000,000	27.6
Protestants	10,000	0.3	1,068,428	7.8	3,998,000	15.7	126,313	26,887	153,200	3.30	4,816,870	16.1	5,530,000	16.5	10,425,000	18.0
Anglicans	5,000	0.1	386,095	2.8	1,900,000	7.5	60,029	14,971	75,000	3.38	2,300,000	7.7	2,650,000	7.9	5,300,000	9.2
Independents	0	0.0	50,440	0.4	440,000	1.7	13,901	5,899	19,800	3.79	541,067	1.8	638,000	1.9	1,700,000	2.9
Marginal Christians	0	0.0	4,000	0.0	11,000	0.0	348	352	700	5.05	14,100	0.1	18,000	0.1	40,000	0.1
Orthodox	0	0.0	9,000	0.1	11,200	0.0	354	-224	130	1.10	11,700	0.0	12,500	0.0	22,500	0.0
doubly-affiliated	0	0.0	0	0.0	-1,225,200	-4.8	-38,709	20,357	-18,352	1.41	-1,273,097	-4.3	-1,408,722	-4.2	-2,487,500	-4.3
Trans-megabloc groupings																
Evangelicals	9,500	0.3	716,000	5.2	3,385,000	13.3	106,946	40,554	147,500	3.68	4,176,567	14.0	4,860,000	14.5	9,275,000	16.0
Pentecostals/Charismatics	0	0.0	150,000	1.1	2,180,000	8.6	68,875	55,625	124,500	4.62	2,819,341	9.4	3,425,000	10.2	8,687,700	15.0
Great Commission Christians	**75,000**	**2.0**	**1,730,000**	**12.6**	**4,202,000**	**16.5**	**132,758**	**9,783**	**142,541**	**2.96**	**4,967,000**	**16.6**	**5,627,411**	**16.8**	**10,425,000**	**18.0**
Muslims	266,000	7.0	4,311,000	31.5	8,050,000	31.6	254,333	5,070	259,403	2.83	9,480,000	31.7	10,644,033	31.8	19,000,000	32.8
Ethnoreligionists	3,439,900	90.5	4,359,000	31.8	4,697,230	18.4	148,404	-78,853	69,551	1.39	5,080,400	17.0	5,392,739	16.1	5,170,000	8.9
Hindus	2,000	0.1	21,000	0.2	210,000	0.8	6,635	1,310	7,945	3.26	250,000	0.8	289,454	0.9	600,000	1.0
Baha'is	0	0.0	41,000	0.3	102,000	0.4	3,223	636	3,859	3.26	124,000	0.4	140,593	0.4	250,000	0.4
Nonreligious	0	0.0	18,000	0.1	60,000	0.2	1,896	576	2,472	3.51	75,900	0.3	84,723	0.3	214,350	0.4
Buddhists	0	0.0	0	0.0	36,000	0.1	1,137	-182	955	2.38	40,800	0.1	45,550	0.1	90,000	0.2
Atheists	0	0.0	3,000	0.0	14,000	0.1	442	70	512	3.16	17,000	0.1	19,117	0.1	50,000	0.1
Sikhs	0	0.0	3,000	0.0	8,100	0.0	256	-60	196	2.19	9,000	0.0	10,055	0.0	25,000	0.0
Jains	100	0.0	800	0.0	6,200	0.0	196	-32	164	2.38	7,100	0.0	7,841	0.0	18,000	0.0
Jews	0	0.0	100	0.0	170	0.0	5	0	5	2.57	190	0.0	219	0.0	400	0.0
Zoroastrians	0	0.0	100	0.0	100	0.0	3	0	3	2.66	110	0.0	130	0.0	250	0.0
World A (unevangelized persons)	3,100,800	81.6	5,477,560	40.0	6,010,920	23.6	189,565	-166,783	22,782	0.37	6,134,707	20.5	6,234,162	18.6	7,529,340	13.0
World B (evangelized non-Christians)	607,200	16.0	3,279,340	23.9	7,172,880	28.2	226,965	95,318	322,283	3.79	8,950,196	29.9	10,400,277	31.0	17,888,660	30.9
World C (Christians)	92,000	2.4	4,937,000	36.1	12,286,200	48.2	388,171	71,465	459,636	3.23	14,840,500	49.6	16,882,561	50.4	32,500,000	56.1
Country's population	**3,800,000**	**100.0**	**13,693,900**	**100.0**	**25,470,000**	**100.0**	**804,701**	**0**	**804,701**	**2.78**	**29,925,404**	**100.0**	**33,517,000**	**100.0**	**57,918,000**	**100.0**

COLUMNS, ROWS.
For meanings and definitions, see Codebook (Part 3). Note that, by definition, total 'Christians' = professing + crypto-Christians, which also = affiliated + unaffiliated Christians, and also = Great Commission Christians + latent Christians. Percentages may not always total exactly, due to rounding.

CENSUSES.
1931 (Tanganyika; non-Africans): 52.5% Muslims, 24.3% Christians, 19.0% Hindus, 1.9% Sikhs, 0.1% Jains, 0.1% Parsis. **1931** (Zanzibar): 95.2% Muslims (83.4% Sunnis, 8.5% Ibadis, 1.4% Ismailis, 0.9% Ithna-Asharis, 0.8% Boharas, 0.2% other Shias), 1.5% Hindus, 1.4% ethnoreligionists, 1.1% Roman Catholics, 0.7% Protestants, 0.1% Parsis. **25.II.1948** (Tanganyika; Africans): 57.5% ethnoreligionists, 24.9% Muslims, 17.6% Christians. **1948** (Tanganyika; non-Africans): 54.5% Muslims (22.1% Ismailis, 8.3% Sunnis, 6.0% Ibadis, 5.7% Ithna-Asharis, 5.6% Hanafies), 22.3% Hindus, 19.3% Christians (7.4% Roman Catholics, 6.2% Anglicans), 2.5% Sikhs, 0.6% Jains, 0.1% Parsis. **1948** (Zanzibar): 94.8% Muslims, 2.1% Christians, 1.6% Hindus, 1.3% ethnoreligionists, 0.1% Jains, 0.1% Parsis. **1957** (Tanganyika; Africans): 44.2% ethnoreligionists, 30.9% Muslims, 24.9% Christians (17.1% Roman Catholics, 7.8% Protestants and Anglicans). **1957** (Tanganyika; non-Africans): 49.2% Muslims, 23.7% Hindus, 22.4% Christians, 3.5% Sikhs, 0.7% Jains, 0.1% Parsis. **1957** (Tanganyika; all races): 43.6% ethnoreligionists, 31.1% Muslims, 24.9% Christians, 0.3% Hindus. **20.II.1957** (Tanganyika and Zanzibar; all races): 42.2% ethnoreligionists, 33.2% Muslims, 24.2% Christians, 0.4% Hindus. **27.VIII.1967** (heads of households only): 36.2% ethnoreligionists ('local belief'), 31.6% Christians, 31.4% Muslims, 0.8% Hindus, Baha'is and other religionists. **27.VIII.1967** (mainland only): 37.3% ethnoreligionists, 32.4% Christians, 29.5% Muslims, 0.8% Hindus and other religionists. **27.VIII.1967** (Zanzibar): 95.5% Muslims, 2.9% Christians (9,877 persons), 1.0% Hindus and other world-religionists, 0.6% ethnoreligionists. Since pagan heads of households are one generation older than their children, and since the % Christian is higher among children due to education in Christian schools, adjusted figures for the whole population in 1967 are: 34.3% ethnoreligionists, 33.5% Christians, 31.4% Muslims, 0.8% Hindus and other religionists.

NOTES ON RELIGIONS
ATHEISTS. Mainly intellectuals, gradually increasing in numbers in the 1990s; also a large number of expatriate technicians from the People's Republic of China.
BAHA'IS. Growth from 66 local spiritual assemblies (1964) to 211 (1973). As with Uganda and Kenya, the work had been deeply entrenched in certain African tribes. By 1996, however, interest had fallen off to the point where reorganization resulted in a decline to 90 LSAs.
ETHNORELIGIONISTS. Animists. Tribes with over 60% traditionalists in 1995; Dorobo (98% animist), Barabaig (97%), Safwa (78%), Maasai (86%), Sonjo (90%), Iraqw (72%).
INDEPENDENTS. In 41 denominations in 1995 (see Table 2).
MUSLIMS. Conversions to Islam on a large scale began around 1880 and were especially numerous from 1910-30. The most important wave of mass conversions followed the collapse of German rule in 1917. *Regions.* Zanzibar is 95.0% Muslim, Tanganyika (mainland) 21.0% Muslim. *Communities.* Africans are Shafiite Sunnis, and there are also 12,000 Shias, about 200,000 Arabs, other Sunnis and 6,000 Ibadis on Zanzibar. Indians and Pakistanis are mainly Shias (30,000), Ismailis (90% Tanzania citizens), Ithna-Asharis, 7,000 Boharas, also Sunnis). There is also an Ahmadiya Mission (enumerated here under Muslims though declared non-Muslim by Pakistan). Begun 1934; Qadianis, with work in Dar es Salaam, Rufiji (Utete), Lindi and Tabora, and about 40 other branches. Most Asian followers emigrated after 1963, leaving mainly African followers. *Missionaries.* There are numerous Egyptian doctors and others sent by Al-Azhar University (Cairo), with many clinics in Tanzania. *Hajj pilgrims to Mecca.* (1970) under 50; (1974) 645; (1975) 580; (1976) 591. *Conversions to Islam.*

Continued overleaf

Country Table 1–concluded

Islamization is still proceeding among several tribes, although the rate of conversion has slowed appreciably since Independence in 1961. Today many pagan schoolchildren leave school as Muslims. The Shia Ithna-Ashari community operate the Bilal Muslim Mission in Arusha, Dar es Salaam and elsewhere, and claim several hundred converts from Christianity. *Islamized tribes.* The Makonde (990,000 in Tanzania and 320,000 in Mozambique) are typical of the numerous islamized tribes; they have been 90% Muslims since their mass conversion in 1910-20 but still retain intact most of their traditional animism, with a bare minimum of Muslim customs. Similarly, the Zaramo (296,000) are 95% Muslim but are still strong animists in practice. Other largely Muslim tribes: Mwera (70%), Rangi (70%), Sambaa (54%), Zigula (89%).
NONRELIGIOUS. Chinese technicians from People's Republic of China.
PENTECOSTALS/CHARISMATICS. Total involved, over 1 million (1996). The Catholic Charismatic Renewal began in 1981. By 1996 there were 3 weekly prayer groups and 2 covenant communities, with 3,170 regular adult attenders, including 26 priests.
ROMAN CATHOLICS. In the year 1900, there were 29,400 indigenous baptized Catholics, and 33,000 catechumens.

Great Commission Instrument Panel: status of Tanzania (for explanation see start of Part 4)

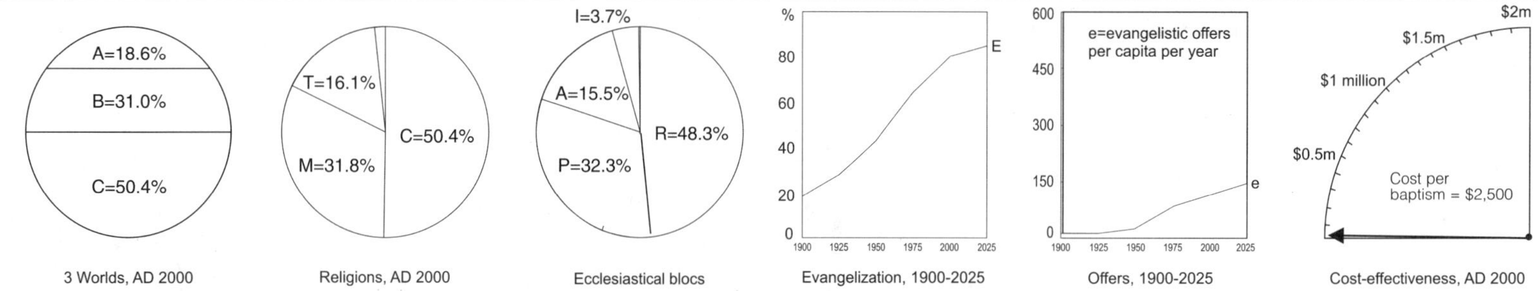

Country status. Tanzania is in East Africa on the Indian Ocean, south of the equator, and includes the islands of Mafia, Pemba, and Zanzibar. Its economy is based in agriculture and it exports sisal, cloves, cotton, and coffee.

HUMAN LIFE AND LIBERTY

Human need and development. Despite some bold social and economic experiments initiated by Julius Nyerere, Tanzania remains stunted in its growth. Next to Mozambique it is the poorest country in the world, according to the World Bank with an average life expectancy of 48, a per capita GNP of $120, an illiteracy rate of 33%, and an infant mortality rate of 75 per 1,000 births. It also has the highest birth rate in the world of 3.9%. Outside Dar es Salaam, the former capital, there is stark poverty with very few or no efforts at providing relief.

Human rights and freedoms. Tanzania was one of the independent nations in Africa to adopt a one-party style of autocratic government. Some of the worst features of such a government were shed upon the retirement of Julius Nyerere as president, but the political system itself remains cast in an authoritarian mould. Further, with the election of a Muslim to the presidency, new religious tensions have been introduced which do not augur well for the country. Under the guise of citizen's anti-crime vigilante squads, groups known as sungusungu in urban areas and wasalama in rural areas (affiliated with the ruling Chama Cha Mapinduzi party) have been empowered to terrorize citizens. Spontaneous mob justice for suspected criminals remains common throughout the country. Under the preventive Detention Act, the president may order the arrest and indefinite detention of any person considered dangerous to public order and national security. Arbitrary arrests occur in criminal cases where police arrest innocent relatives of criminal suspects , holding them in custody without charge for several years in order to force suspects to turn themselves in. The government uses its legal powers to harass and intimidate political opponents, using such vague charges as disturbing public tranquillity and use of abusive language in public. Freedom of the press and speech, firmly established under British rule, continues to be observed, although the electronic media are under state control. Freedom of assembly and association is restricted by the requirement of a government permit for any public meeting and for the establishment of any political party. The Constitution prohibits discrimination against women. However, as in other traditional societies, gender discrimination exists in every sector of society, more in rural areas than in the towns. Women have less access to educational and employment opportunities. Violence against women is common. Legal remedies exist, but in practice are difficult to obtain.

Human environment. Tanzania's underdevelopment has not shielded it from the kind of ecological deterioration caused by poor farming practices, lack of proper sewage, water misuse, and deforestation. Yet, the damage has not been severe except in naturally arid areas.

Ethnoreligionists. Kutimbana (private prayer to ancestors): a pagan chief of the Kimbu (who are 25% pagan), wearing white cloth and hat, spits offering of *impemba* (white maize flour and water) from gourd before empty *ichanga* (ancestor spirit hut), makes petition, ends with formula 'Ilyuva liwine' (God has seen it).

NON-CHRISTIAN RELIGIONS

Traditional religions, usually based on animism, were followed by 17% of the population in 1995, declining by just under 1% per year. The greatest number is found among the Sukuma whose 1.8 million members remain 80% traditionalist. Other large ethnic groups with a high proportion of traditionalists are the Nyamwezi (total population 590,000 in 1972; 60% traditionalist), Gogo (480,000; 70%), Nyakyusa 83%), Arusha (110,000; 88%), Safwa (102,000; 97%), and Maasai (100,000; 95%). The Zinza, Barabaig, Burungi, Sonjo, and Dorobo are smaller tribes over 75% traditionalist. The idea that natural phenomena are manifestations of God is a common idea, resulting in the use of the same word for God and the sun among several Tanzanian peoples: Ruva (Chagga), Iruva (Meru), Nguruvi (Safw), and Riob (Sonjo). For the Maasai, En-Kai means rain and sky as well as God, and the word Engai for God is also found among the Arusha. Mulungu, Mlungu and Murungu are common names for the supreme being found among the Bena, Bondei, Luguru, Sukuma, and Turu; while other names include Kyala (among the Nyakyusa), Kyumbi (Pare), Ishwanga (Haya), and Isewahanga (Zinza). In addition to belief in a supreme being, there is still considerable emphasis on the veneration of ancestor spirits (Masamva among the Sukuma), amulets (mnigi), diviners (vafumo), as well as the evil activities of the sorcerer (nogi). The ancient Shetani spirit-possession cults, which owe their origin to the Muslim coastal towns, have made an impact on the Zaramo, Kaguru, Nguu, and Pare peoples. Among the Zaramo, the alien Shetani spirits have been absorbed into the traditional cult of the departed, a common belief being that they are no longer independent but are now under the control of the ancestors. This is also happening with the Hini, a new group of coastal spirits.

Islam is the professed religion of 32% of the population. Islam is strongest on the coast and along the traditional caravan route through Tabora to Ujiji on Lake Tanganyika. The Zaramo (95%), Makonde (90 %) and Yao (85%) are overwhelmingly among the Shambala (65%), Matumbi (50%), Kwere (33%), and Nyamwezi (25%). Muslims are mainly Sunnis of the Shafiite rite, although there are some Ismailis, Ahmadis, and Ibadites. A major Islamic coordinating agency with government recognition is the National Muslim Council of Tanzania (Bakwata).

Baha'i and ***Hinduism*** both have sizeable followings.

Muslims (Ahmadis). Village in Pangale, Unyanyembe, of African converts to Ahmadiya with Pakistani missionary (*center*, with white turban), 1958.

CHRISTIANITY

CATHOLIC CHURCH. Although Portuguese Catholic priests attempted to found a church in Tanganyika in the 16th century, Christian influence was never significant and the eclipse of Portugal as a maritime power resulted in the disintegration of the church by the end of the 17th century. A new beginning was made in 1860 when 3 secular priests moved to Zanzibar from the island of Reunion. They were joined in 1863 by Holy Ghost priests who founded Bagamoyo on the mainland in 1868. Originally a freed-slave settlement, Bagamoyo became the base for evangelistic activity in the interior including the thrust of White Fathers towards Uganda in 1878. Benedictines of St Ottilien of Bavaria appeared in 1887 after Tanganyika had become a German colony. These were followed after World War I by Consolata priests (1920), Capuchins (1921), Passionists (1933), Pallotines (1940), Rosminians (1945), Maryknoll priests (1946), Salvatorians (1955), and more recently Camillian priests, Priests of the Precious Blood and Jesuits. Missionary sisters, brothers, and laymen have also made significant contributions. Even more important has been the role of Tanzanian priests, brothers, sisters, and catechists. Tanzanian sisters now greatly outnumber missionary sisters. The church is organized into 2 provinces under national leadership.

The Seminar Study Year (SSY) of 1969 proved to be a milestone in the Tanzanization of the Catholic Church. Parish discussions on the state of the church were followed in December 1969 by a general meeting, called unofficially a pastoral council. Although council members were only one-third Africans, with little lay representation, the African voice dominated the discussions, contributing to a new understanding of the problems of ecclesiastical life. Subsequent to the Arusha Declaration of 1967, Catholics have played leading roles in church renewal and development.

The Holy See has diplomatic relations with Tanzania and in AD 2000 is represented to government and the Catholic hierarchy by a nuncio residing in Dar-es-Salaam.

Country summary. **Worlds A, B, C by ethnolinguistic peoples, cities, and major civil divisions in Tanzania.**																						
	PEOPLES							***CITIES***							***CIVIL DIVISIONS***							
World	*Num*	*Pop 2000*	*C%*	*Christians*	*E%*	*U%*	*Unevangelized*	*Num*	*Pop 2000*	*C%*	*Christians*	*E%*	*U%*	*Unevangelized*	*Num*	*Pop 2000*	*C%*	*Christians*	*E%*	*U%*	*Unevangelized*
A	38	4,573,437	2.73	124,969	41	59	2,702,591	2	302,649	5.60	16,959	40	60	181,246	4	1,829,616	8.05	147,358	43	57	1,050,857
B	56	15,555,713	31.23	4,857,406	78	22	3,492,779	6	4,108,927	39.39	1,618,708	74	26	1,072,229	15	20,250,817	39.33	7,963,730	75	25	4,990,607
C	69	13,387,859	80.22	10,740,402	100	0	32,449	5	612,452	66.85	409,432	97	3	18,795	6	11,436,579	66.56	7,611,689	98	2	186,353
Total	**163**	**33,517,009**	**46.91**	**15,722,777**	**81**	**19**	**6,227,819**	**13**	**5,024,028**	**40.71**	**2,045,099**	**75**	**25**	**1,272,270**	**25**	**33,517,012**	**46.91**	**15,722,777**	**81**	**19**	**6,227,817**

Catholic Church in Tanzania. Striking architecture in (*top*) Diocese of Moshi; and (*lower*) new cathedral for Diocese of Bukoba.

PROTESTANT CHURCHES. The Evangelical Lutheran Church in Tanzania, the largest Protestant church in the country, was created in 1963 through the union of 7 dioceses and synods originally initiated by several distinct German, American, and Scandinavian societies beginning at the end of the 19th century. German missions entered soon after Germany assumed control of the country. The first was Berlin Mission III which arrived in Zanzibar in 1886 and moved to the mainland the following year. Next were the Bethel and Leipzig Missions in 1889 and 1893, and Berlin Mission I in 1901. German missionaries were forced out during World War I, and American Lutherans were asked to provide support. The Augustana Lutheran Church of America responded by sending personnel in 1922, followed by Swedish Lutherans in 1939. The National Lutheran Council of America assumed responsibility for the work following the exodus of German missionaries once again during World War II, and after the war, aid was also received from the Lutheran churches of Finland, Denmark, and Norway.

In 1891, German Moravians took over the work pioneered by the LMS in 1879. The United Free Church of Scotland provided interim assistance at the time of World War I until 1926 when the German Moravian missionaries were able to return. In World War II German Moravian missionaries were replaced by British Moravians. Today Tanzania's Moravians, who are concentrated in the west and southwest, form the largest Moravian provinces in the world. The Moravians sponsor 4 hospitals and 5 dispensaries.

The area east of Lake Victoria is served by the Adventist, Mennonite, and Africa Inland churches. German Adventists first appeared in 1903 followed by the Africa Inland Mission in 1908 and American Mennonites in 1934. The Africa Inland Churches have experienced phenomenal growth from 80,000 members in 1970 to 600,000 by 1995.

Pentecostals from Sweden, Canada, and the USA have been at work since the 1930s and have built up a sizeable Pentecostal community. Other groups include the Baptist Convention of Tanzania, Salvation Army, Church of God, and Churches of Christ.

ANGLICAN CHURCH. Anglicans form the third largest church in Tanzania, following Catholics and Lutherans. Four different foreign missionary societies have been active. The UMCA was the first Anglican society beginning on Zanzibar in 1864 and moving to the mainland in 1875. The High Church UMCA and SPG joined together in 1965 to form the USPG. Evangelical Anglicans arrived to work among the Gogo in 1878 through the CMS from Britain, Australia, and later New Zealand, followed still later by the Low-church BCMS. In 1970, the Church of the Province of East Africa was divided into separate jurisdictions for Kenya and Tanzania. The present Church of the Province of Tanzania has 9 dioceses in 1977. In 1969, there were 17 hospitals, 22 dispensaries and one leprosarium. The church's 101 primary schools, 5 secondary schools and3 teaching training colleges were taken over by government in 1969.

Church of the Province of Tanzania. Bishops, clergy and laity celebrate launch of Gogo New Testament, 1992 at Anglican cathedral, Dodoma.

INDIGENOUS CHURCHES. Tanzania is characterized by the relative absence of independent churches. Indeed the most important indigenous groups, such as Mario Legio, Nomiya Luo and the Church of Christ in Africa, have spread into Tanzania from nearby Kenya. The largest body indigenous to Tanzania itself has been the Church of the Holy Spirit which was the result of a schism among the Haya in 1953. Most of its members subsequently returned to the Lutheran church. In 1956, 2 Gogo Anglican clergy seceded to form the Tanzania African Church. Reduced from 40 congregations at its height to 14 in 1970 (and to only 5 by 1990), it applied for membership in the AACC in 1966 as the Tanzania African Church. Several small schisms have taken place among the Nyakyusa of southwestern Tanzania following World War I, but none has become significant.

Indigenous missions. At the end of the 19th century Tanzania was a base for outreach into the interior of Africa resulting in many indigenous Christians becoming foreign missionaries. In the 20th century most of the missionaries have served in surrounding African countries and in Germany.

Renewal movements. In the 1990s the Pentecostal/Charismatic Renewal continued to spread rapidly across most older churches, and numbered over 3.4 million adherents (of whom 43% Pentecostals, 39% Charismatics, and 18% Independents).

CHURCH AND STATE

The interim constitution of July 1965 is devoted entirely to the constitutional arrangements resulting from the unification of Tanganyika with Zanzibar. Annexed to it, under the title 'First Schedule', is the constitution of the Tanganyika African National Union (TANU), Tanganyika's only political party (renamed in 1976 CCM, Chama cha Mapinduzi/Party of the Revolution), which includes among its principal aims the following: 'To safeguard the inherent dignity of the individual in accordance with the Universal Declaration of Human Rights', and 'to see that the Government gives equal opportunity to all men and women irrespective of race, religion or status'. (Article 2, Preamble). This text is also reproduced without change in the Arusha Declaration of 1967 which serves as the charter for Tanzania socialism. Church and state are separate in Tanzania, the churches being considered as voluntary agencies invited by the state to collaborate in the development of the country. The position was clearly stated by president Nyerere in December 1973; 'Tanzania has no religion, the Party has no religion, the Government has no religion, but most Tanzanians are religious people and the Party and the Government guarantee to each citizen the freedom to choose his own religion'. Since the Christian churches have exercised an important historical responsibility in education and medical service, problems in church-state relations are situated primarily in these areas. Except for about 10 free schools mostly serving foreigners, all private schools were nationalized in 1969, although their administration has remained for the most part unchanged, since previously also they had been subsidized by government. In the realm of medical service, conflicts have arisen over the subsidizing of salaries of personnel in church medical institutions.

The CCM requires the churches to become more involved in the formation and organizations of ujamaa (brotherhood) villages, communal villages which are the basis of Tanzanian socialism. A part of the clergy has been reticent, because of the resistance of local populations in some areas and from fear of being used for political purposes; whereas others, including bishops, have collaborated in these initiatives. Numerous seminars have been organized between leaders of CCM and the churches.

In August 1975, 2 Muslim sects were banned by government, the Sunni Jamat and United Cutchi Sunni Muslim Jamat, in an apparent attempt to avoid conflict between them and the National Muslim Council of Tanzania (Bakwata) which has government support. At the same time, 2 other Muslim groups in the West Lake Region, the Shaffi 'R.A'. Ijumaa and Adhuhuri, were ordered to desist from all activities for failure to fulfill official registration requirements.

Publication of new Sukuma Gospel of Mark: *top*, arrival by MAF aircraft; *bottom*, dedication service, Mwanza, 1995.

BROADCASTING AND MEDIA

Most families have radios, but televisions are rare. IBRA-language programs can be heard on local radio channels. Swahili and Yao-language shortwave radio broadcasts can be received from FEBA (Seychelles). The Lutheran World Federation maintains a studio in the country which produces Swahili-language programs. Through UNDA, Catholics broadcast 6 programs each Sunday (2 hours) and 2 short 5-minute programs daily.

INTERDENOMINATIONAL ORGANIZATIONS

The Tanganyika Missionary Council, formed in 1936, was the predecessor of the present Christian Council of Tanzania (CCT). Full members include Lutherans, Anglicans, Moravians, Baptists, Mennonites, AIC, Salvation Army and Friends, while Adventists and Assemblies of God are consultative members. Tanganyika Christian Refugee Service is separately organized, operated by the Lutheran World Federation in consultation with the CCT. Two conservative missions joined the Evangelical Fellowship of East Africa, reorganized later as the Tanzania Evangelical Fellowship. During the 1960s, church discussions were carried on between Lutherans, Anglicans, Moravians, Presbyterians and Methodists of Tanzania and Kenya; but these broke down in 1968.

The Catholic Church sponsors an Episcopal Commission for Ecumenism, and relations between Catholics and Protestants are cordial. The Dar es Salaam Committee of Churches includes Catholics; the education secretaries of the various churches meet regularly; the Tanzania Christian Medical Association is completely ecumenical; religious broadcasting over Radio Tanzania is regulated by a joint committee; and Bible distribution is carried on cooperatively. In addition, joint worship services are widely held at Christmas and Easter and during the Week of Prayer for Christian Unity.

FUTURE TRENDS AND PROSPECTS

Ethnoreligionists, over 90% of the population in 1900, could fall below 9% by 2025 while Christians rise to 56.1%. Muslims are expected to grow to about 33% in the same period.

With the expected decline of tribal religions in the 21st century, Christianity and Islam are both expected to grow, perhaps reaching a 65/35 symbiosis by AD 2050.

BIBLIOGRAPHY

'A Christian response to Islam in Tanzania.' V. L. Mokiwa. M.T.S. thesis, Virginia Theological Seminary, Alexandria, VA, 66p.

A history of the Catholic Church in Tanzania. L. Malishi. N.p.: Tanzania Episcopal Conference, 1990. 55p.

'Case study: urban missions in Tanzania, East Africa,' S. Mwantila, *Urban mission*, 2, 4 (March 1985), 44–47.

Catholic directory of Eastern Africa, 1977–79. Tabora, Tanzania: TMP Book Department, 1977. 258p. (Earlier editions: 1959, 1965, 1968, 1971, 1974–76, then irregularly to the present).

Christian Council of Tanzania directory, 1972. Dar es Salaam, Tanzania: Christian Council, 1972. 31p.

Christian–Muslim relations in Africa: the cases of northern Nigeria and Tanzania compared. L. Rasmussen. London: British Academic Press, 1993. 143p.

Church, clan and the world. J. M. Kibira. *Studia Missionalia Upsaliensia*, 21. Uppsala, Sweden: Almqvist & Wiksell, 1974. 128p. (By Lutheran bishop of NW Tanganyika).

'Church, mission and state relations in pre– and post–independent Tanzania.' L. W. Swartz. Occasional Paper 19, Syracuse University Program of Eastern African Studies, Syracuse, NY, 1967.

Communal rituals of the Nyakyusa. M. Wilson. London: Oxford University Press, 1959. 228p.

'Contextualization of the Gospel in the Kinga culture.' S. Manyiewa. S.T.M. thesis, Wartburg Theological Seminary, Dubuque, IA, 1987. 199p.

Development and religion in Tanzania: sociological soundings on Christian participation in rural transformation. J. P. van Bergen. Madras: Christian Literature Society, 1981. 352p.

Doing theology with the Maasai. D. Priest Jr. Pasadena, CA: William Carey Library, 1990. 248p.

'Effective pastoral leadership in the Evangelical Lutheran Church in Tanzania with reference to the Northern Diocese.' P. I. Akyoo. S.T.M. thesis, Wartburg Theological Seminary, Dubuque, IA, 1987. 265p.

Eglise et socialisme en Tanzanie. B. Joinet. Paris: Centre Lebret, 1976. Nos. 39-40.

From Krapf to Rugambwa—a church history of Tanzania. C. Sahlberg. 2nd ed. Nairobi, Kenya: Evangel, 1986. 206p.

Gemeinsam auf eigenen Wegen: Evangelisch–Lutherische Kirche in Tanzania nach hundert Jahren: ein Handbuch. J. Ngeiyamu & J. Triebel (eds). *Erlanger Taschenbücher*, vol. 99. Erlangen, Germany: Verlag der Ev.-Luth. Mission, 1994. 357p.

German missionaries in Tanganyika, 1891–1941. M. Wright. Oxford, UK: Clarendon, 1971. 249p.

Islam and politics in East Africa: the Sufi order in Tanzania. A. H. Nimtz Jr. Minneapolis, MN: University of Minnesota Press, 1980. 234p.

Islam in Tanzania. S. von Sicard. *CSIC papers—Africa*, no. 5. Birmingham, UK: Centre for the Study of Islam and Christian-Muslim Relations, 1991. 17p.

'Kamcape: an anti–sorcery movement in southwest Tanzania,' *Africa*, 38, 1 (1968), 1–15.

'Leadership in the small Christian communities of Rosana Parish, Musoma Diocese, Tanzania: a pastoral perspective.' M. A. Rutatinisibwa. Thesis, Maryknoll School of Theology, Maryknoll, NY, 1991. 84p.

Lutherische Kirche Tanzania: Ein Handbuch. G. Mellinghoff & J. Kiwovele (eds). *Erlanger Taschenbücher*, Band 39. Erlangen, Germany: Ev-Lutherische Mission, 1976. 393p.

'Missionary adaptations of African religious institutions: the Masasi case,' T. O. Ranger, in *The historical study of African religion*, p.221–51. T. O. Ranger & I. N. Kimambo (eds). Berkeley, CA and Los Angeles: University of California Press, 1972.

Missionary work in the church of Tanzania in the past and present. J. A. Stefano. *World mission scripts*, 1. Erlangen, Germany: Evangelical Lutheran Mission Pub. House, 1990. 177p.

Missions on a colonial frontier west of Lake Victoria: evangelical missions in north–west Tanganyika to 1932. C. J. Hellberg. Lund, Sweden: Gleerup, 1965. 256p.

'Seminar study year 1969: the Church in Tanzania today,' *Pro Mundi Vita* (Brussels), Special notes, 13 (1970).

'Significance of the Arusha Declaration as seen in teachings and practices of the Christian Church in Tanzania today.' Z. Gunda. Thesis, Lutheran School of Theology, Chicago, 1971.

Socialisme et église en Tanzanie. S. Urfer. Paris: IDOC-France, 1975.

'Sociological factors in the contact of the Gogo of central Tanzania with Islam,' P. J. A. Rigby, in *Islam in Tropical Africa*, p.268–95. I. M. Lewis (ed). London: Oxford University Press, 1966.

Tanzania. C. Darch. *World bibliographical series*, vol. 54. Oxford, UK: CLIO Press, 1985. 344p. (See especially 'Religion,' p.64-74).

The African churches of Tanzania. T. O. Ranger. *Historical Association of Tanzania*, paper no. 5. Nairobi, Kenya: East African Publishing House, 1972. 29p.

The Catholic Church in Tanzania. S. Rweyemamu & T. Msambure. Peramiho, Tanzania: Benedictine Publications Ndanda, 1989. 60p.

'The growth of Tanzanian churches: a study of the helps and hindrances of external aid.' R. J. Taylor. Th.D. thesis, Australian College of Theology, Sydney, Australia, 1980. 424p.

The Lutheran Church on the coast of Tanzania, 1887–1914, with special reference to the ELCT Synod of Uzaramo–Uluguru. S. von Sicard. London: E. J. Brill, 1970. 260p.

The missionary factor in East Africa. R. Oliver. 2nd ed. London: Longman, 1965. 302p.

The missionary vocation of the eastern African Christian family: focus on small Christian communities. L. Mahogha. Rome: Pontificia Universitas Urbaniana, Facultas Missiologiae, 1991. 202p.

The pilgrimage of faith of Tanzania Mennonite Church, 1934–83. M. M. Hess. Musoma, Tanzania: Eastern Mennonite Board of Missions and Charities, 1985. 175p.

The prophetic role of the church in Tanzania today: symposium of five papers. L. Magesa (ed). Eldoret, Kenya: AME-CEA Gaba Publications, 1991. 94p.

'The spirit possession cults and their social setting in a Zaramo coastal community,' M. L. Swartz, in *Proceedings of Social Science Conference.* Dar es Salaam, Tanzania: 1968, 3

'"There is only one God": a social–scientific and theological study of popular religion and evangelization in Sukumaland, Northwest Tanzania.' F. J. S. Wijsen. Ph.D. dissertation, Katholieke Universiteit Nijmegen, Kampen, 1993. 338p.

Thunder in the valley: the amazing spiritual harvest in Tanzania. D. Knapp, E. Knapp & R. O'Brien. Nashville, TN: Broadman Press, 1986. 240p.

Toward an African Christianity: inculturation applied. E. Hillman. New York: Paulist Press, 1993. 106p.

Transition in African beliefs, traditional religion and Christian change: a study in Sukumaland, Tanzania, East Africa. R. E. S. Tanner. Maryknoll, NY: Maryknoll Publications, 1967.

Country Table 2. **Organized churches and denominations in Tanzania.**

Official name (bold type = church with over 10% of all affiliated) 1	*Begun* 2	*Type* 3	*Counc* 4	*Congs* 5	*Adults* 6	*Affiliated 1970* 7	*Affiliated 1995* 8	*G%* 9	*Names, notes, and other statistics* (see Codebook, Part 3) 10
Africa Inland Church	1908	P-Non	xM..K	700	300,000	80,000	600,000	8.39	*AIC.* 1887 M=CMS; 1908 AIM, AMB. 80% Sukuma, 15% Jita. 60n,25x,73f,1H,10h,1j,8k,2p.
African Apostolic Ch of Johane Masowe	1964	I-3aA	x....	10	2,000	1,500	3,000	2.81	*Gospel of God Ch. Vapostori (Apostles).* Shona body from Rhodesia. In Dar, Arusha.
African Brotherhood Church	1960	I-Non	Iva.K	5	400	340	600	2.30	M=ABC(Kenya). Kamba migrants from Kenya; HQ Kibauni. In 1960: 178 Christians.
African Greek Orth Ch (D Eirenopolis)		O-Gre	Cw...	9	7,000	9,000	11,700	0.05	Under Greek P Alexandria. HQ Nairobi. Kikuyu, Greeks, Cypriot farmers. 1h,1000z.
African Israel Church Nineveh	c1960	I-3pA	Iw...	30	7,000	8,000	15,000	2.55	M=AICN(Kenya). Luo migrants from Kenya (HQ Nineveh, Kisumu); also Luhya members.
African Methodist Episcopal Church	1933	I-Met	Vw...	6	600	1,000	1,400	1.35	*AMEC.* Begun in Ufipa by Zambians. 1945, branches opened in Mbeya, Tukuyu, Kyela.
African National/International Church	1932	I-Ref	.....	3	600	1,000	1,300	1.05	*ANC.* Schism in Nyasaland ex CCAP. 90% Nyakyusa. Polygamists. HQ Rungwe.
Baptist Convention of Tanzania	1956	P-Bap	T...K	1,400	96,258	20,000	167,000	8.86	M=BMEA(SBC, USA). 50% Nyakyusa. 1 school. 2n,21x,58f,1H,4h,1p,1s2000Y.
Bible Church	1957	P-CBr	x....	110	700	1,000	2,000	2.81	M=CMML(Germany). 50% Ngoni, 25% Makua, 20% Makonde. 3n,10x,22f,1H,3h,1p,48Y.
Catholic Church in Tanzania:	1449	R-Lat	P.SER	848	3,648,000	2,806,662	7,354,860	3.93	*Kanisa Katoliki.* C=13+4=39. 12p,4s(389). 1161n 622x 1287m 6458w 276804Yy
M Dar es Salaam	1887	R-Lat	Ps	21	250,000	71,287	500,000	8.10	*Jimbo Kuu la D.* Catholics up-country tribes. 14n 46x 59m 188w 8481Yy
D Arusha	1963	R-Lat	Ps	25	50,000	19,770	114,726	7.29	72% Chagga, 11% Kikuyu, 4% Sonjo. M=CSSp. 36n 47x 130m 99w 7874Yy
D Dodoma	1935	R-Lat	Ps	36	123,000	123,630	236,149	2.62	24% Sandawe, 16% Gogo, 15% Hehe, Rangi. M=CP. 35n 45x 86m 362w 6744Yy
D Mahenge	1964	R-Lat	Ps	32	111,000	91,072	213,428	3.47	56% Pogoro, 17% Bena, 14% Ndamba, Mbunga. 44n 10x 28m 227w 10181Yy
D Mbulu	1943	R-Lat	Ps	30	97,000	66,452	197,008	4.44	40% Turu, 30% Iraqw, 10% Goroa, Mbugwe. M=SAC. 28n 22x 25m 72w 9831Yy
D Morogoro	1906	R-Lat	Ps	79	191,000	190,201	450,973	3.51	62% Luguru, 23% Sagara, 10% Nguru, 5% Kwere. 64n 24x 32m 536w 10030Yy
D Moshi	1910	R-Lat	Ps	39	370,000	318,024	685,420	3.12	90% Chagga, 2% Pare, Haya, Luo. 1s. 172n 28x 68m 977w 16510Yy
D Same	1963	R-Lat	Ps	91	23,000	17,603	43,253	3.66	99% Pare. Many missions; no pagans left. M=CSSp. 24n 9x 13m 34w 647Yy
D Tanga	1950	R-Lat	Ps	48	63,000	52,952	160,705	4.54	*Jimbo la Tanga.* Shambaa, Bondei, Ngoni, 1p. 37n 24x 40m 401w 5756Yy
D Zanzibar & Pemba	1964	R-Lat	pzs	7	6,000	3,000	12,257	5.79	2 islands. First mission 1449. Formerly M=CSSp. 8n 0x 0m 28w 272Yy
M Mwanza	1929	R-Lat	Ps	23	95,000	146,312	179,000	0.81	66% Sukuma, 29% Kerewe, 3% Zinza, 2% Kara. 38n 26x 62m 132w 7814Yy
D Bukoba (Rutabo)	1951	R-Lat	Ps	25	281,000	222,500	522,664	3.48	85% Haya, 5% Subi, 5% Ruanda, Ganda. M=OSB. 94n 5x 5m 475w 56729Yy
D Geita	1984	R-Lat	Ps	9	49,000	–	118,059	9.09	Formerly in D Mwarza. 9n 9x 11m 42w 3024Yy
D Musoma	1950	R-Lat	Ps	23	101,000	107,501	193,800	2.39	36% Luo, 21% Kwaya, 13% Kuria, 6% Jita. M=MM. 29n 18x 25m 152w 9100Yy
D Rulenge	1960	R-Lat	Ps	19	279,000	126,667	486,992	5.53	49% Haya, 24% Zinza, 22% Hangaza. 45n 8x 19m 227w 7656Yy
D Shinyanga	1950	R-Lat	Ps	25	82,000	52,198	162,779	4.65	98% Sukuma. Workers in Mwadui mine. M=MM. 20n 29x 32m 46w 5930Yy
D Songea (Peramiho)	1927	R-Lat	Ps	24	121,000	223,058	226,340	0.06	Until 1969, AN Peramiho. M=OSB. 1p,1s. 63n 35x 220m 391w 6947Yy
D Iringa	1922	R-Lat	Ps	30	235,000	207,554	465,035	3.28	70% Hehe, 16% Bena, 8% Kinga, 6% Sangu. M=IMC. 35n 50x 129m 388w 35354Yy
D Lindi (Nachingwea)	1963	R-Lat	Ps	26	58,000	37,983	110,332	4.36	52% Makua, 25% Yao, 18th Mwera, Ndonde. M=SDS. 37n 11x 12m 56w 3576Yy
D Mbeya	1932	R-Lat	Ps	22	98,000	70,483	190,688	4.06	40% Safwa, 22% Nyakyusa, 17% Lambya. 1p. 36n 20x 23m 144w 9453Yy
D Mbinga	1986	R-Lat	Ps	19	139,000	–	267,715	11.11	Formerly in D Songea. 55n 8x 11m 146w 5844Yy
D Mtwara (Ndanda)	1931	R-Lat	Ps	15	30,000	69,206	55,940	-0.85	Formerly AN Ndanda (OSB). 58% Mwera. Makonde. 21n 19x 42m 127w 2283Yy
D Njombe	1968	R-Lat	Ps	81	118,000	116,605	255,769	3.19	28% Ngoni, 27% Matengo, 12% Bena, Pangwa. OSB. 52n 23x 29m 379w 6334Yy
D Tundura-Masasi	1986	R-Lat	Ps	15	34,000	–	67,585	11.11	Formerly part of D Nachingwea (Lindi). 18n 17x 54m 59w 1338Yy
M Tabora (Unyanyembe)	1887	R-Lat	Ps	18	150,000	84,589	298,716	5.18	84% Nyamwezi, 8% Fipa, 5% Sumbwa, 2% Ha. 1s. 27n 29x 51m 294w 3643Yy
D Kahama	1983	R-Lat	Ps	7	40,000	–	78,128	8.33	Formerly part of M Tabora. 15n 6x 6m 24w 3490Yy
D Kigoma	1887	R-Lat	Ps	15	106,000	86,065	213,000	3.69	95% Ha, 5% Congolese. 1p. 20n 23x 26m 67w 8292Yy
M Singida	1972	R-Lat	Ps	18	54,000	68,094	107,599	4.35	*Jimbo la Singida.* 50% Turu, 30% Iramba. M=SAC. 19n 22x 22m 116w 4233Yy
D Sumbawanga (Karema)	1946	R-Lat	Ps	26	294,000	233,856	740,800	4.72	65% Fipa, 4% Bende, 1% Lungu. 2p. 66n 9x 27m 269w 19438Yy
Christian Brethren	1951	P-CBr	x....	70	35,500	500	66,000	21.57	M=CMML(UK), Works with Bible Church. In towns. HQ Dar es Salaam. 18f,1H.
Christian Missionary Fellowship	1990	I-Dis	.....	1	11	–	35	20.00	M=CMF(USA).
Christian Revival Ch Meeting Group	c1968	I-Ang	IT.T.	30	3,000	3,000	6,000	2.81	*Revivalist Churches.* Group of revivalists. Many ex Anglicans. HQ Mwanza. 3n.
Christian Witness Church	c1968	I-Ang	.....	8	250	300	600	2.81	*Mashaidi wa Ukristo.* Schism ex Anglicans. Geita. 30% Sukuma. 1n,3m,W=50%,17Y,28y.
Church of Christ in Africa	1957	I-Ang	IT.T.	30	3,000	3,000	9,000	4.49	*Area Diocese of Musoma. JoHera (People of Love).* M=CCA(Kenya), Luo schism ex CMS.

Continued opposite

Country Table 2–concluded

Official name (bold type = church with over 10% of affiliated) 1	*Begun* 2	*Type* 3	*Counc* 4	*Congs* 5	*Adults* 6	*Affiliated 1970* 7	*Affiliated 1995* 8	*G%* 9	*Names, notes, and other statistics* (see Codebook, Part 3) 10
Church of God	1951	P-Pe3	ZF...	57	113,000	600	210,000	26.40	M=Ch of God (Cleveland) (USA). Begun by immigrants from Zambia, Malawi. 1n.
Church of God in East Africa	1958	P-Hol	x....	50	4,000	5,000	7,000	1.35	*CGEA.* M=CoG(Anderson) (USA). Migrants from large Kenya CoG church. 29n,4f,1s,W=50%.
Church of God of Prophecy	1978	P-Pe3	Z....	17	900	–	1,450	5.88	M=CGP(USA).
Church of the Foursquare Gospel		P-Pe2	Z....	12	690	–	1,276	0.05	M=ICFG(USA).
Church of the Nazarene	1990	P-Hol	.....	20	2,010	–	3,490	20.00	M=CoN. Holiness body. (Nazarenes).
Church of JC the Light of the World	1967	I-Ang	.....	20	2,000	2,000	4,000	2.81	*Kujitawala (Independence). Neukirchner Uhuru Ch.* Ha schism ex Anglicans in west.
Church of the Holy Spirit	1953	I-Lut	.T...	2	500	2,000	1,000	-2.73	Balokole (Revival) split ex ELCT(NW Diocese), Bukoba. 99% Haya. 1962, 50% returned.
Church of the Province of Tanzania	1864	A-plu	AWAVK	7,000	1,100,000	386,095	2,300,000	7.40	*CPT. Kanisa la Jimbo la Tanzania (KJT).* 16 Dioceses. 160f,3s(55),305n,43x,8629Y,16200y.
Church of the Watch Tower	1919	I-Jeh	x....	5	500	1,000	1,100	0.38	Ex Jehovah's Witnesses. Entered Ufipa from NRhodesia. Anti-state. Declining.
Churches of Christ		I-Dis	x....	100	3,000	4,000	7,000	0.05	M=CC(Non-Instrumental)(USA). Independents. Southern Highlands.
Evangelical Lutheran Ch in Tanzania	1886	P-Lut	LWA.K	4,500	1,050,000	592,342	2,200,000	5.39	*ELCT. KKKT*(Swahili). A=1963. 10 Dioceses and Synods. M=TAC. 1641m,1s(126),W=75%.
Full Gospel Bible Fellowship	1987	I-3fA	.....	20	12,000	–	30,000	12.50	*FGBF.* Begun by Deeper Life BC (Nigeria). Fastest growing church in Tanzania.
Gospel Furthering Fellowship	1935	I-Non	.M...	1	50	300	100	-4.30	M=GFF(USA). Schism ex AIM by missionaries. Mbugwe, Fiome.
Jehovah's Witnesses	1919	m-Jeh	x....	120	3,619	4,000	14,100	5.17	First apostles entered Ufipa in 1919 from Zambia. Banned from 1966. 721Y.
Last Church of God & His Christ	1929	I-Ref	I....	3	1,000	5,000	2,000	-3.60	*BaNgemela (Ngemela's Ch).* Nyakyusa. Polygamy, communal life. HQ Rungwe.
Living Waters Churches	c1990	I-3cA	x....	2	1,000	–	3,000	20.00	Rapidly-growing charismatic body originating in Blantyre (Malawi).
Manchira Monthly Meeting		P-Qua	Q...K	12	500	500	1,000	0.05	Musoma area. Friends (Quakers). Immigrant Luhya from Nyanza (Kenya). 1n.
Maria Legio of Africa	1963	I-3sA	x....	30	15,000	3,000	25,000	8.85	M=MLA(Kenya). Luo immigrants from Kenya schism ex Roman Catholic Church, D Kisii.
Moravian Church in Tanzania	1879	P-Mor	xvA.K	177	115,000	99,500	230,000	3.41	2 Provinces: *Western* (Nyamwezi), *Southern* (Nyakyusa). M=MBG. 72n,5x,21f,4H,5h,1s.
New Apostolic Church	c1985	I-3aX	x....	1,200	210,000	–	375,432	10.00	*NAC.* M=NAK(Germany). Polygamy, alcohol allowed for excommunicated Moravians.
Nomiya Luo Church	1929	I-Ang	I....	20	2,500	2,000	4,000	2.81	Nomiya=God gave me His Word. M=NLC(Kenya). Luo immigrants in Musoma area.
Pemba Yearly Meeting of Friends	1897	P-Qua	Q....	3	200	400	400	0.00	On Pemba Island. 1897 Industrial Mission (UK); 1916, Yearly Meeting. 1n,4m,1p.
Pentecostal Assemblies of God	1944	P-Pe2	ZF...	750	24,200	15,000	44,900	4.48	*PAG.* M=PAoC(Canada). Lake Victoria area. Members. Mbugwe, Fiome. 80n,8x,8f.
Pentecostal Churches in Tanzania	1932	P-Pe2	Z....	2,700	270,000	40,000	460,000	10.26	*PCAT, UMPT.* M=SFM,NPY,FFFM. 50% Ha,40% Nyamwezi. 1800n,90f,2679Y.
Pente Evangelistic Fellowship of Africa	1946	P-Pe2	ZG...	190	4,859	20,000	12,720	-1.79	*PEFA.* M=Elim FGA(UK),IPA(USA). North. 20 churches closed 1973 in ujamaa resettling.
Pente Holiness Association Mission	c1938	P-Pe3	Z....	95	28,000	35,000	66,300	2.59	M=PHC(Zambia). Until 1945 M=PHC(USA). Southern Highlands. Nyakyusa. 33n,25m.
Presbyterian Church of East Africa		P-Ref	Rwa.K	20	3,000	450	5,000	0.05	*PCEA*(Kenya). Main church in Dar es Salaam. 70% Malawians; some Whites. 1n,1x.
Salvation Army	1933	P-Sal	xwa.K	78	7,000	8,682	11,700	1.20	*Jeshi la Wokova. Tanzania Division.* HQ Dar es Salaam. 25n,5x,20m.
Seventh-day Adventist Church	1903	P-Adv	x...k	505	106,000	105,000	265,000	3.77	*Tanzania Union.* 3 aircraft. 81n,6x,12f,1H,21h,3j,1r,1s,571t(44416),W=88%,1418Y.
Tanganyika Mennonite Church	1934	P-Men	G...K	196	20,078	24,454	46,634	2.62	*TMC.* M=EMBMC. 35% Luo,30% Jita,30% Kuria. 24n,1x,22f,1H,5h,1j,1p,1r,1s,W=75%,650Y.
Tanzania African Church	1956	I-Ang	.T.T.	5	300	3,000	1,000	-4.30	*TAC.* Schism ex Anglican DCT. 70% Gogo, 30% Nyamwezi. 1966, tried to join AACC.
Tanzania Assemblies of God	1930	P-Pe2	ZF..k	980	244,200	15,000	400,000	14.04	*TAG.* M=AoG(USA). Classical Pentecostals. Arusha, Moshi, Mbeya. 114n,17f,2s(76).
Yoido Full Gospel Ch of Korea	c1990	I-3fA	.....	3	200	–	500	20.00	Mission from Seoul (Korea). Work in Moshi.
Other African indigenous churches		I-3pA	.....	100	30,000	10,000	50,000	0.05	Total about 25 (see list below), especially from Kenya, Malawi, Zaire, Zambia.
Other Protestant denominations		P-	.....	40	5,000	5,000	15,000	0.05	Total about 20 (see list below).
Doubly-affiliated		2-aff			-634,000	0	-1,273,097		Evangelicals and Pentecostals who are also baptized Roman Catholics.
Totals				**22,293**	**6,850,625**	**4,324,625**	**13,765,500**		

Churches, members, growth, 1900-2025	*Congs*	*Adults*	*Affiliated*	*G%*	*Total denominations*	*6 Megablocs:* O	*R*	*A*	*P*	*I*	*m*
Total churches, members, and denominations (mid-1900)	100	41,000	77,400	5.92	5	0	1	1	3	0	0
Total churches, members, and denominations (mid-1970)	8,769	2,289,104	4,324,625	5.92	54	1	1	1	22	28	1
Total churches, members, and denominations (mid-1990)	19,000	5,649,000	11,350,000	4.94	80	1	1	1	29	47	1
Total churches, members, and denominations (mid-1995)	22,293	6,850,625	13,765,500	3.93	80	1	1	1	29	47	1
Total churches, members, and denominations (mid-2000)	24,000	7,825,000	15,722,778	2.69	81	1	1	1	30	47	1
Total churches, members, and denominations (mid-2025)	40,000	15,429,000	31,000,000	2.75	175	2	1	1	50	120	1

NOTES ON TABLE ABOVE

NATIONAL COUNCILS (Column 4, 5th letter).
- E = Tanzania Evangelical Fellowship (TEF).
- K = Christian Council of Tanzania (CCT) (Jumuiya ya Makanisa ya Tanzania).
- k = consultative member of CCT.
- R = Tanzania Episcopal Conference (TEC).

Other national councils. Tanzania Evangelical Fellowship (in process of formation in 1976; to be affiliated to AEAM).

OTHER AFRICAN INDIGENOUS CHURCHES. Although there are very few Tanzanian-founded bodies, numerous bodies from Kenya, Malawi, Rhodesia, Zaire and Zambia have churches in Tanzania. The total includes: African Catholic Ch, Chief Mayuta's Ch, Christ the Light of the Universe (Kristo Mwanga wa Ulimwengu; ex Anglicans, HQ Kasulu; banned in 1977), Ch of Jesus Christ (HQ Sumbawanga; Fipa tribe; member of ICCC), Deliverance Ch (Kenya), Dini ya Bapali (Polygamous Ch, or Malakite Ch; from Uganda 1924), Eglise Kimbanguiste (EJCSK, Zaire), Episcopal Ch of Africa (Luos from Kenya), Evangelical Assemblies of God, Holy Ghost Ch of the Cross, Lyimo's Ch, Nomiya Luo Sabbath (from Kenya), Revival Assemblies of God. In 1975, a Korean movement, Holy Spirit Association for the Unification of World Christianity, sent 3 evangelists (a German, a Japanese and one English) but they were imprisoned and deported.

OTHER PROTESTANT DENOMINATIONS. These include: Christian Ch in East Africa, Independent Assemblies of God, Swedish Holiness Union Mission (2 congregations), World-Wide Missions (1965).

OTHER MARGINAL PROTESTANT BODIES. Branhamites (Local Believers, End Time Believers) from USA.

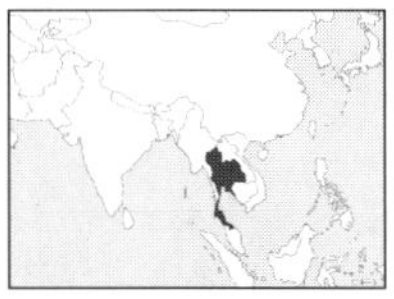

THAILAND

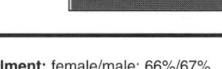

SECULAR DATA, AD 2000

STATE
Official name: Prathet Thai/Muang-Thai (The Kingdom of Thailand).
Short name: Thailand. **Adjective of nationality:** Thai.
Flag: Red, white, blue (double width), white, and red stripes.
Area: 513,115 sq. km. (198,115 sq. mi.).
Government: Constitutional monarchy controlled by military junta, since 1957 (13th century kingdom, 1939 name changed from Siam to Thailand, 1957 military junta, 1974 democratic constitution, 1976 military junta).
Legislature: Senate, 260 members; House of Representatives, 393 members.
Official language: Thai.
Monetary unit: 1 Thai baht (B) = 100 stangs. **US$1=** B 38.85.
Chief cities: KRUNG THEP (Bangkok-Thonburi) 7,221,000; Thon Buri (Thonburi) 979,068; Nonthaburi 250,837; Nakhon Ratchasima (Khorat) 235,476; Chiang Mai (Chiengmai) 188,432.
Political divisions: 7 provinces.
Armed forces: 266,000.

DEMOGRAPHY
Population: 61,399,000.
Population density: 119.6/sq. km. (309.9/sq. mi.).
Under 15 years: 15,491,000.
Growth rate p.a.: 0.83% (births 15.78, deaths 7.19).
Mortality: Infant, per 1,000: 24.0; **Maternal per 100,000:** 200.0.
Life expectancy: 69 (male 66, female 73).
Household size: 5.3. **Floor area per person, sq.m:** 15.0.
Major languages: Thai, English, Lao, Chinese, Malay, Khmer, Vietnamese, and 40 smaller languages.
Urban dwellers: 21.58%. **Urban growth rate p.a.:** 2.5%.
Labor force: 54%.

ETHNOLINGUISTIC PEOPLES
34.9% Central Thai (Siamese); 26.4% Northeastern Tai (Isan); 10.5% Northern Tai (Yuan, Phyap; 8.2% Han Chinese; 7.8% Southern Tai (Pak Thai).

ECONOMY
National income p.a. per person: US$2,740; **per family:** US$14,522.

EDUCATION
Adult literacy: 93% (male 96%, female 91%). **Schools:** 37,409.
Universities: 84. **School enrolment:** female/male: 66%/67%.

HEALTH
Access to health services: 90%. **Access to safe water:** 81%.
Hospitals: 1,097 (17 beds per 10,000). **Doctors:** 13,398.
Blind: 210,000. **Deaf:** 3,629,700. **Murder rate:** 7.
Lepers: 500,000. **Underweight prevalence under 5:** 25%.

LITERATURE
New book titles p.a.: 8,290 (135 p.a. per million). **Periodicals:** 1,810.
Newspapers: 35 dailies.

COMMUNICATION (per 1,000 people)
Phones: 59 (29% mobile). **Radios:** 167. **TV sets:** 227.
Daily newspaper circulation: 47. **Computers:** 51.

REFUGEES
Alien refugees from other countries: 98,200.

HUMAN LIFE AND LIBERTY (optimum condition=100.0%)
HDI: 83.3. **HSI:** 46.0. **HFI:** 35.0. **EFL:** 54.0.

Country status. Thailand is a large country in Southeast Asia on the Gulf of Thailand. It is one of the world's leading exporters of rice. Sugar, tapioca, tin, and tungsten are also important.

HUMAN LIFE AND LIBERTY

Human need and development. Thailand is now considered as one of the 'Asian Tigers', a name it shares with other industrializing countries, such as Singapore, Hong Kong, Korea, and Taiwan. However, industrialization has not led to an improvement in the standard of living for the average Thai. Social indicators have been rising for the past 2 decades, and there has been marked and measurable progress in health, education, and nutrition. Life expectancy is 69, literacy 93%, and the per capita GNP $2,740. Much of the apparent progress is limited to Bangkok, and it has not trickled down to the countryside. Even in Bangkok, the poor remain trapped in poverty, prostitution is flourishing on a scale unparalleled in any modern nation, and housing is unaffordable for the majority of the residents. Many aspects of public health remain bleak, one of the most critical being water supply. Medical facilities and doctors also are concentrated in Bangkok.

Human rights and freedoms. After the fall of the military regime and the holding of free and fair elections in 1992, all areas of human rights have expanded and human rights abuses have become rare. The Criminal and Penal Codes are based largely on Western European models. Generally, arrest warrants are required, and specific charges must be brought against detainees within 48 hours. There is a functioning bail system and defendants have access to courts or administrative tribunals for redress of grievances. Search warrants are required for entry into homes, but they are not subject to prior judicial review. Thai citizens enjoy a substantial degree of freedom of speech, barring criticisms of the royal family or other sensitive issues involving national security. Censorship is exercised over certain topics, such as misconduct of the Buddhist clergy, pornography, police corruption, and Thai military matters. Women have equal legal rights, but suffer social disabilities in a number of areas. Prostitution is acknowledged as

Country Table 1. **Religious adherents in Thailand, AD 1900-2025.**

Year	1900		1970		mid-1990		Annual change, 1990-2000				mid-1995		mid-2000		mid-2025	
Name	Adherents	%	Adherents	%	Adherents	%	Natural	Conversion	Total	Rate	Adherents	%	Adherents	%	Adherents	%
Buddhists	5,487,850	90.9	32,931,170	92.1	47,639,100	85.7	497,370	-23,026	474,344	0.95	50,081,480	85.5	52,382,535	85.3	61,330,200	84.3
Muslims	90,000	1.5	1,395,000	3.9	3,700,000	6.7	38,627	8,675	47,302	1.21	3,930,000	6.7	4,173,015	6.8	5,000,000	6.9
Christians	**35,150**	**0.6**	**340,700**	**1.0**	**1,183,000**	**2.1**	**12,350**	**5,529**	**17,879**	**1.42**	**1,294,000**	**2.2**	**1,361,788**	**2.2**	**1,766,000**	**2.4**
PROFESSION																
crypto-Christians	12,150	0.2	136,000	0.4	475,000	0.9	4,959	4,541	9,500	1.84	520,000	0.9	570,000	0.9	900,000	1.2
professing Christians	**23,000**	**0.4**	**204,700**	**0.6**	**708,000**	**1.3**	**7,391**	**988**	**8,379**	**1.12**	**774,000**	**1.3**	**791,788**	**1.3**	**866,000**	**1.2**
AFFILIATION																
unaffiliated Christians	0	0.0	18	0.0	15,770	0.0	165	-80	85	0.53	15,758	0.0	16,621	0.0	19,500	0.0
affiliated Christians	**35,150**	**0.6**	**340,682**	**1.0**	**1,167,230**	**2.1**	**12,186**	**5,608**	**17,794**	**1.43**	**1,278,242**	**2.2**	**1,345,167**	**2.2**	**1,746,500**	**2.4**
Independents	0	0.0	90,820	0.3	665,000	1.2	6,942	4,430	11,372	1.59	735,801	1.3	778,717	1.3	1,000,000	1.4
Protestants	5,000	0.1	93,653	0.3	255,000	0.5	2,662	2,138	4,800	1.74	287,260	0.5	303,000	0.5	450,000	0.6
Roman Catholics	30,000	0.5	153,831	0.4	240,000	0.4	2,506	-1,006	1,500	0.61	247,346	0.4	255,000	0.4	280,000	0.4
Marginal Christians	50	0.0	1,678	0.0	6,750	0.0	70	55	125	1.71	7,370	0.0	8,000	0.0	16,000	0.0
Anglicans	100	0.0	700	0.0	480	0.0	5	-8	-3	-0.64	465	0.0	450	0.0	500	0.0
Trans-megabloc groupings																
Evangelicals	4,300	0.1	60,000	0.2	167,000	0.3	1,743	957	2,700	1.51	189,510	0.3	194,000	0.3	263,000	0.4
Pentecostals/Charismatics	0	0.0	105,000	0.3	684,000	1.2	7,141	7,349	14,490	1.94	755,728	1.3	828,900	1.4	1,200,000	1.7
Great Commission Christians	**30,000**	**0.5**	**272,000**	**0.8**	**950,000**	**1.7**	**9,918**	**13,874**	**23,792**	**2.26**	**1,022,000**	**1.7**	**1,187,923**	**1.9**	**1,660,000**	**2.3**
Ethnoreligionists	180,000	3.0	250,000	0.7	1,180,000	2.1	12,319	1,336	13,655	1.10	1,240,000	2.1	1,316,549	2.1	1,450,000	2.0
Nonreligious	0	0.0	80,000	0.2	1,000,000	1.8	10,440	12,156	22,596	2.06	1,150,000	2.0	1,225,959	2.0	1,800,000	2.5
Chinese folk-religionists	240,000	4.0	640,000	1.8	540,000	1.0	5,637	-6,633	-996	-0.19	530,000	0.9	530,043	0.9	500,000	0.7
Confucianists	0	0.0	0	0.0	198,500	0.4	2,072	230	2,302	1.10	210,000	0.4	221,523	0.4	300,000	0.4
Hindus	6,000	0.1	60,000	0.2	180,000	0.3	1,879	1,482	3,361	1.73	200,000	0.3	213,614	0.4	360,000	0.5
Baha'is	0	0.0	6,460	0.0	130,000	0.2	1,357	67	1,424	1.05	136,800	0.2	144,243	0.2	240,000	0.3
Atheists	0	0.0	30,000	0.1	80,000	0.1	835	35	870	1.04	84,000	0.1	88,695	0.1	250,000	0.3
Sikhs	1,000	0.0	10,000	0.0	17,000	0.0	177	18	195	1.09	17,900	0.0	18,954	0.0	35,000	0.1
New-Religionists	0	0.0	1,600	0.0	12,000	0.0	125	136	261	1.99	13,400	0.0	14,613	0.0	35,000	0.1
Shintoists	0	0.0	0	0.0	320	0.0	3	2	5	1.41	340	0.0	368	0.0	700	0.0
Jews	0	0.0	70	0.0	80	0.0	1	-1	0	0.37	80	0.0	83	0.0	100	0.0
doubly-counted religionists	0	0.0	0	0.0	-265,000	-0.5	-2,767	-6	-2,773	1.00	-278,000	-0.5	-292,732	-0.5	-350,000	-0.5
World A (unevangelized persons)	5,200,440	86.1	23,234,321	65.0	26,796,790	48.2	279,814	-308,896	-29,082	-0.11	26,667,693	45.5	26,524,368	43.2	25,014,648	34.4
World B (evangelized non-Christians)	804,410	13.3	12,170,088	34.0	27,615,210	49.7	288,261	303,367	591,628	1.95	30,648,621	52.3	33,512,844	54.6	45,936,352	63.2
World C (Christians)	35,150	0.6	340,700	1.0	1,183,000	2.1	12,350	5,529	17,879	1.42	1,294,000	2.2	1,361,788	2.2	1,766,000	2.4
Country's population	**6,040,000**	**100.0**	**35,745,110**	**100.0**	**55,595,000**	**100.0**	**580,425**	**0**	**580,425**	**1.00**	**58,610,315**	**100.0**	**61,399,000**	**100.0**	**72,717,000**	**100.0**

COLUMNS, ROWS.
For meanings and definitions, see Codebook (Part 3). Note that, by definition, total 'Christians' = professing + crypto-Christians, which also = affiliated + unaffiliated Christians, and also = Great Commission Christians + latent Christians. Percentages may not always total exactly, due to rounding.

CENSUSES.
1937 (Thai year 2480): 95.1% Buddhists and Chinese folk-religionists, 4.3% Muslims, 0.5% Christians, 0.1% others. **23.V.1947** (Thai year 2490): 94.1% Buddhists, 3.8% Muslims, 1.6% Chinese folk-religionists, 0.5% Christians. **25.IV.1960:** 93.6% Buddhists, 3.9% Muslims, 1.8% Chinese folk-religionists, 0.6% Christians, 0.1% ethnoreligionists. **1966:** 93.6% Buddhists. **1.IV.1970** (excluding unenumerated hill peoples): 93.6% Buddhists, 3.9% Muslims, 1.8% Chinese folk-religionists, 0.6% Christians (195,300 persons), 0.2% Hindus and Sikhs. **1990**: 95.1% Buddhists, 4.1% Muslims, 0.53% Christians (289,733 persons), 0.04% Hindus, 0.23% other religionists and nonreligious.

NOTES ON RELIGIONS
AFFILIATED PROTESTANTS. Among recent conversions to Thai churches have been several hundred Buddhists, including monks and nuns through the ministry of CCCI.
ATHEISTS. Communist Party of Thailand (CPT) (prohibited since 1952; clandestine; pro-Chinese).
BAHA'IS. Growth from 22 local spiritual assemblies (1964) to 43 (1973). Tribal converts include Yao, Manser, Yaw, Khon Muang. By 1996, involvement had grown slightly to 51 LSAs.
BUDDHISTS. Theravada (or Hinayana, Lesser Vehicle), in 2 religious orders: Thommayutt and Mohanikay. Peoples: Thai, Chinese, Vietnamese, Khmer.
CRYPTO-CHRISTIANS. Christians affiliated to churches but not known as such to the state or society, or in censuses, of 2 kinds: (1) secret believers in the known churches, and (2) isolated radio and Bible correspondence course believers.
ETHNORELIGIONISTS. Animists among the Montagnards and other tribes: Akha, Kui, Lisu, Lu, Meo, Pwo Karen, Sgaw Karen, Tin, Yao.
HINDUS. Of 3 kinds: (1) 4,000 Brahmin families, astrologers, who almost always direct and perform royal and official ceremonies, blending their rites with those of Buddhism; (2) large numbers of Indian merchants and traders, speaking various languages of India, concentrated in the central region chiefly around Bangkok; and (3) adherents of newer Hindu sects including Ananda Marga.
INDEPENDENTS. Chinese and Thai indigenous churches, in about 11 denominations in 1995, the vast majority being isolated radio and Bible correspondence course believers (see Table 2).
MUSLIMS. Sunnis (of the Shafiite rite); Malays (islamized here since the 14th century) and others in the extreme south. Muslims form about 85% of the 2 million inhabitants of the southern peninsula. There are 1,400 mosques. *Hajj pilgrims to Mecca.* (1970) 4,981; (1975) 654; (1976) 192.
NEW-RELIGIONISTS. Adherents of Soka Gakkai (Japan), Cao Dai (Viet-Nam), and Chinese syncretistic New Religions.
NONRELIGIOUS. Including many foreigners (especially European, Chinese, USA military), Thai communist sympathizers, et alii.
ROMAN CATHOLICS. In the year 1900, 22,480 baptized Catholics, and 44 schools with 3,020 children.
SIKHS. In central region, mainly in and around Bangkok; Punjabis from India.

Great Commission Instrument Panel: status of Thailand (for explanation see start of Part 4)

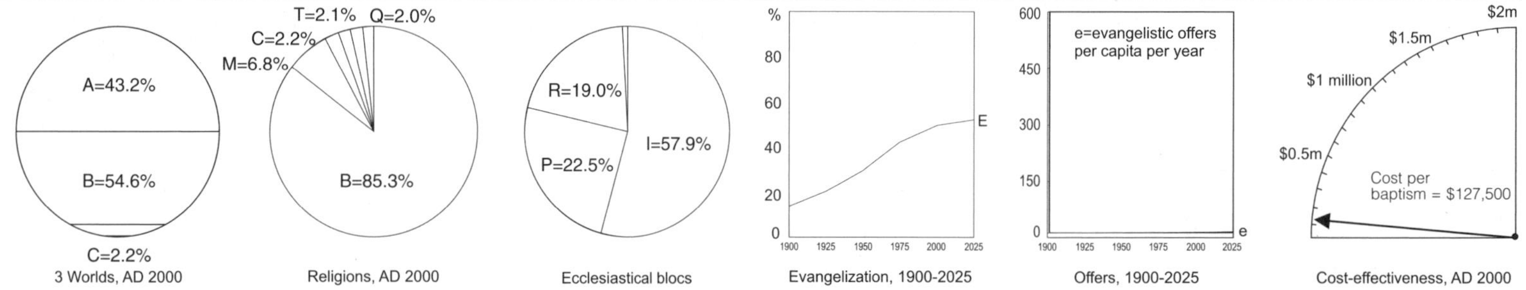

the country's most pervasive and troubling problem. The number of prostitutes in Bangkok is estimated at between half a million and one million.

Human environment. Like other tropical countries, Thailand is richly endowed with flora and fauna, including 15,000 species of flowering plants, 900 species of birds, and 265 species of mammals. However, indiscriminate logging, which was officially banned in 1989, has caused considerable environmental damage. The destruction of the forested watersheds, flooding and inadequate water control have led to deterioration in water quality as well as shortage of water in some areas. Bangkok suffers from the usual problems associated with industrial and air pollution.

NON-CHRISTIAN RELIGIONS

Theravada Buddhism (also called Hinayana or Lesser Vehicle) is the official religion of Thailand and the religion of the great majority of the population, with more than 24,000 temples and 200,000 monks. The number of persons in monasteries fluctuates because of the traditional requirement that each adolescent should sometime spend 6 months to 2 years in residence in a monastery. It is in Thailand that the movement for the renewal of Buddhism is most accepted. This movement is part of the program of the great universities of Mahâmakuta and Mahâchulalongkorn which steer monks towards social service to the lay community and prepare students for teaching posts in the provinces. Monks in the provinces are supposed to follow where possible a social education course at the Phra Kiihiwuttho Centre in Chonburi, a suburb of Bangkok. Of importance also is the movement towards a deep renewal of monastic and religious life under the influence of Bhikkhu (monk) Buddhadâsa, the head of the Wat Mahadhatu monastery in Chaiya, south Thailand, who has attempted to create a degree of uniformity in Buddhist doctrine by mixing traditional Theravada with aspects from Mahayana. His disciple, Khun Sunya Dhammasakti, president of the most important lay group, spreads his doctrine among the populace.

Bangkok is the central headquarters of the World Fellowship of Buddhists (WFB), founded in Sri Lanka in 1950, which works for peace and the well-being of peoples through following Buddha's teaching principles, and which has regional centers in 34 countries of Asia, America, Europe, and Oceania. Thailand also serves as the center for Theravada in its mission of conciliation between the various orientations of Buddhism.

Buddhists. Monks at daily prayers in temple.

Islam is Thailand's second largest religion. Mostly Sunnis of the Shafiite rite, Muslims are found in the south where they are the predominant group, and include almost the entire Malay population as well as others. The region of Bangkok-Thonburi has about 100 of the country's 1,400 mosques. A National Council of Muslims in Thailand was established in

Country summary. **Worlds A, B, C by ethnolinguistic peoples, cities, and major civil divisions in Thailand.**

	PEOPLES							*CITIES*							*CIVIL DIVISIONS*						
World	*Num*	*Pop 2000*	*C%*	*Christians*	*E%*	*U%*	*Unevangelized*	*Num*	*Pop 2000*	*C%*	*Christians*	*E%*	*U%*	*Unevangelized*	*Num*	*Pop 2000*	*C%*	*Christians*	*E%*	*U%*	*Unevangelized*
A	52	9,272,557	0.82	75,824	43	57	5,261,545	0	0	0.00	0	0	0	0	0	0	0.00	0	0	0	0
B	36	52,079,187	2.37	1,236,061	59	41	21,247,493	19	9,036,006	2.65	239,811	61	39	3,495,008	7	61,399,248	2.19	1,345,164	57	43	26,509,176
C	7	47,505	70.07	33,285	100	0	142	0	0	0.00	0	0	0	0	0	0	0.00	0	0	0	0
Total	**95**	**61,399,249**	**2.19**	**1,345,170**	**57**	**43**	**26,509,180**	**19**	**9,036,006**	**2.65**	**239,811**	**61**	**39**	**3,495,008**	**7**	**61,399,248**	**2.19**	**1,345,164**	**57**	**43**	**26,509,176**

1945, and provincial councils exist in areas of heavy Muslim population. Quranic schools (*pondoks*) are also numerous.

Confucianism maintains its importance among the Chinese, who place special emphasis on the ancestor cult. Usually termed Chinese folk-religionists, Confucianists are usually also adherents of Mahayana Buddhism (Great Vehicle).

Hinduism and ***Sikhism*** are religions professed by immigrants from India, the majority of whom are artisans and merchants in the larger cities.

Traditional tribal religions still exist among the Montagnard peoples, the Karen, Meo, Tin and Yao. The supreme being among the Karen is called Y'wa; although they have been strongly influenced by Christianity, many remain animists.

CHRISTIANITY

Although citizens, Thailand's Christians are often considered foreigners due to their ethnic origin. Most Catholics are Vietnamese and Chinese with a growing number of Montagnards. Protestantism is strongest among Chinese and has also made recent gains among Montagnards. Christianity's inability to penetrate the Hinayana Buddhist world contributes to the conviction that a Thai cannot become a Christian without abandoning the Thai community. On the other hand, its success with Montagnard peoples shows that it appeals to animists. Numerous Christians are found among North Vietnamese refugees, but it has not been easy to integrate them into local communities. Recently significant inroads have been made into the central Thai community, particularly through radio ministries.

Catholic Church in Thailand. *Top.* Holy Redeemer Church, Bangkok follows temple style. *Bottom.* Cambodian Catholics enter church in guerrilla-controlled refugee camp.

CATHOLIC CHURCH. In 1554, 2 Dominican priests took up positions as chaplains to Portuguese soldiers attached to the king of Siam and were instrumental in the conversion of some 1,500 Thais. Franciscans entered in 1583 followed by Jesuits in 1606, and the vicariate of Siam was erected in 1673. The 18th century was characterized by a series of violent persecutions which left only a few Christians, but more progress has been made subsequently. The first Thai bishop was consecrated in 1945.

Catholics are found in all parts of the country but their greatest concentration is in the central and northeastern areas. Catholic rural communities are often regrouped in so-called Christian villages. Socially and economically the Catholic milieu is humble, even poor, especially in the countryside. At Bangkok, on the other hand, all social levels are represented, with a majority in the merchant classes.

The first Catholic monastery in Thailand was founded in 1970 at Nongri. It attempts to be typically Thai in mentality and customs and has sought contacts with Buddhist monasteries.

The Holy See has diplomatic relations with Thailand and in AD 2000 is represented to government and the Catholic hierarchy by a nuncio residing in Bangkok.

PROTESTANT CHURCHES. Missionaries of the Netherlands and London societies (NZG and LMS) arrived in 1828, followed by representatives of the American Board in 1831, American Baptists who opened work among the Chinese in 1833 and American Presbyterians in 1840, the latter being the principal force at work among the Thai. In 1934 the Presbyterians united with the Baptists, Disciples of Christ, and Lutherans of the Marburger Mission (the latter 2 having begun work later) to form the Church of Christ in Thailand (CCT). This is now the largest Protestant church in the country and is composed of Thai, Chinese, and Karen congregations. In 1957 all missions were integrated into the church and missionaries have since been received from India, Japan, Korea, Indonesia, and the Philippines, as well as Europe and North America. In addition to its theological seminary at Chieng Mai, the church sponsors 37 primary and 5 secondary schools, 5 hospitals, 32 dispensaries, a mobile clinic, a rehabilitation institute, an agricultural farm, and an adult literacy department.

Numerous other Protestant denominations are now active including Seventh-day Adventists, who have a large hospital in Bangkok and a smaller one at Haadyai; Evangelical Gospel Church related to the CMA; and the Karen Baptists who originally came from Burma.

INDIGENOUS CHURCHES. A number of these exist; some are growing very fast, particularly Hope of Thailand International.

Indigenous missions. Only a few missionaries have been sent out from the Christian churches in Thailand.

Renewal movements. In the 1990s the Pentecostal/Charismatic Renewal continued to spread rapidly across most older churches, and numbered over 828,000 adherents (of whom 4% Pentecostals, 6% Charismatics, and 90% Independents).

CHURCH AND STATE

According to the 1968 constitution, Buddhism is the state religion; the king must profess and defend the Buddhist faith (Chapter II, section 6); 'Everyone, notwithstanding his birth and religion, has an equal right to the protection of the Constitution' (Chapter III, section 24); there is full liberty to profess 'every religion, sect and religious belief' and to participate in the worship which is related to it; and protection is assumed against any act of the state which would violate the exercise of this freedom (Chapter III, section 26).

Buddhist influence is often utilized by the political rulers to reinforce national unity and to thai-ize the non-Thai peoples. The state legislates on questions of religious organization by passing laws for the Buddhist community such as those of 1902, 1941 and 1962. The latter, promulgated in October 1962, strengthened considerably the central direction of the Buddhist organization (known as the Buddhist Church), placing full power of decision in the hands of the supreme partriarch, (then Somdet Phrasangkharaat) who appoints the members of his council (the Council of Elders, or Mahaatheera-samaakom).

Religious matters come within the jurisdiction of the Department of Religious Affairs (Kromkarn Satsana), which forms part of the Ministry of Education. Its director-general is also secretary-general, ex-officio, of the Council of Elders of the Buddhist Church. This department organizes every year, in consultation with the churches, a 'National Day of the Religions', when by means of posters, conferences, displays, and films, all religions have the opportunity of publicizing their aims and activities. Religious toleration is a reality in Thailand. Although more symbolic than real, the Department of Religious Affairs provides subsidies to the different religious groups based on size of membership. Moreover, the state exempts churches from direct taxation except for property tax. Private confessional schools which receive less than 100 bahts per student per term or trimester may request financial aid from the Ministry of Education for their teachers' salaries.

Buddhists. *Above.* 70-foot Standing Buddha. *Right.* Temple of Dawn (Wat Aroon), Bangkok.

State and private schools are subject to similar control. Religious instruction is authorized in schools, but it must be given outside regular school hours, even in confessional schools.

Special Islamic judges (Dato Yuttitham, or kadis) are provided for the administration of justice in predominantly Muslim areas, namely the south. A *kadi* sits with 2 trial judges in order to administer Islamic laws in civil cases involving questions of family or inheritance where all parties concerned are Muslims. In such cases the *kadi's* interpretation is final.

BROADCASTING AND MEDIA

IBRA programs can be received over 17 radio and 6 television stations for a total of 33 hours weekly. Programs in Akha, Hmong, Lahu, and Wa can be received via shortwave radio from FEBC (Philippines). Shortwave radio programs from KNLS have seen some response. Thailand is a member of UNDA. Catholics offer 7 30-minute evangelistic programs on weekends, and a 30-minute sermon each day at noon.

Over 5.5 million (9%) have seen the 'Jesus' Film, most through presentations by film teams.

Independents. Hope of Bangkok Church in renovated movie theater.

INTERDENOMINATIONAL ORGANIZATIONS

The Church of Christ in Thailand was formed in 1934 as the Thai United Church, a union of members of the Siam National Christian Council begun in 1930. Protestant ecumenical contacts are now centered in the supra-national Christian Conference of Asia (CCA). Catholic-Protestant co-operation is evident in the Asian Ecumenical Conference on Health. The Evangelical Fellowship of Thailand has a membership of 27 foreign missions, 11 Thai bodies, and 100 individual congregations.

With regard to interreligious relations, 2 organizations are active. (1) The Asian Religious and Cultural Forum on Development (ARCFOD), founded in 1972, unites the representatives of 5 religions (Christianity, Buddhism, Shinto, Islam, and Hinduism) in 6 Asian countries: Japan, Philippines, Malaysia, Sri Lanka, India, and Thailand. National committees exist in each of these countries, with a central organization in Bangkok. The principal purpose is to provide an interreligious forum to discuss problems of development and to decide what type of cooperative action the religions can take in a given country. (2) The National Interreligious Committee to Promote Sane Morals, which includes representatives of all the major religions of Thailand, was created through the initiative of the Council for Social Works of Thailand, with the king as patron. Its aim is to sensitize the conscience of the population concerning moral values.

FUTURE TRENDS AND PROSPECTS

Christians will probably grow very slowly into the 21st century up to only 2.4% by 2025 with most growth among ethnoreligionists and the Central Thai near Bangkok. Buddhists are expected to decline to 84.3% in the same period.

If there is significant penetration of ethnic Thais by Christianity in the 21st century, Christianity could grow past 3% before AD 2050. The nonreligious are also expected to grow beyond 5% in the same period. Buddhism will likely continue to decline as a percentage of the population but remain strong in religious, social, and political life.

BIBLIOGRAPHY

1972 Mission directory of Thailand, Cambodia and Laos. B. Bray (ed). Bangkok: Newsasia, 1972.
1978 Thailand Christian directory. Bangkok: S. Chaviwan, 1978. 82p.
'A history of Baptist missions in Thailand.' A. G. Smith. Paper, Western Evangelical Seminary, Portland, OR, 1980. 99p.
'A history of church growth in Thailand: an interpretive analysis, 1816–1980.' A. G. Smith. D.Miss. thesis, Fuller Theological Seminary, Pasadena, CA, 1980. 580p.
A look at Christianity in Bangkok. M. Bowditch. Fresno, CA: Emmanuel Lutheran Church, 1991. (35 minute videocassette).
Allons faire le tour du ciel et de la terre: le chamanisme des Hmong vu dans les textes. J. Mottin. Bangkok: White Lotus, 1982. 559p.
Annual report of religious activities for 1967. Bangkok: Ministry of Education, 1967.
Buddhism and the spirit cults in northeast Thailand. S. J. Tambiah. Cambridge, UK: Cambridge University Press, 1970. 338p.
Buddhism in transition. D. K. Swearer. Philadelphia: Westminster Press, 1970.
Catholic directory of Thailand, 1967. Bangkok: Xavier Hall, 1967.
Chinese churches in Thailand. C. E. Blanford. Bangkok: Suribayan Publishers, 1975. 272p.
Christian directory to Thailand, Vietnam, Laos, Khmer Republic and Malaysia, 1974. Bangkok, 1974.
'Christianizing the Karen.' K. M. Dettmer. M.A. thesis, Arizona State University, Tempe, AZ, 1987. 113p.
Description du royaume Thai ou Siam. J. B. Pallegoix. N.p.: Au profit de la mission Siam, 1854. 2 vols.
Divination in Thailand: the hopes and fears of a Southeast Asian people. H. G. Q. Wales. London: Curzon Press, 1982. 145p.
'Dynamic Biblical Christianity in the Buddhist/Marxist context: Northeast Thailand.' T. N. Wisley. Th.D. thesis, Fuller Theological Seminary, Pasadena, CA, 1984. 485p.
'Evaluation of Campus Crusade for Christ's strategy for planting churches in rural Thailand.' R. S. Rosedale. D.Miss. thesis, Fuller Theological Seminary, Pasadena, CA, 1991. 353p.
Folk stories of the Hmong: peoples of Laos, Thailand, and Vietnam. N. J. Livo & D. Cha. Englewood, CO: Libraries Unlimited, 1991. 147p.
'Growth study in North Thailand.' J. E. Hudspith. Thesis, Fuller Theological Seminary, Pasadena, CA, 1969. 363p. (Among 9 tribes).
Guide to Christian work in Thailand. Bangkok: Church of Christ in Thailand. 29p.
History of Protestant work in Thailand, 1828–1958. K. E. Wells. Bangkok: Church of Christ in Thailand, 1958. 213p.
'Hope of Bangkok: a visionary model of church growth and church planting,' K. Chareonwongska, *Urban mission*, 7, 3 (January 1990), 25–35.
'In search of the Karen king: a study in Karen identity with special reference to 19th century Karen evangelism in Northern Thailand.' A. P. Hovemyr. Doctoral dissertation, University of Uppsala, Uppsala, Sweden, 1989. 207p.
Khrischak muang nua: a study in northern Thai church history. H. R. Swanson. Bangkok: Chuan Printing Press, 1984. 209p.
Les cetiya de sable au Laos et en Thailande: les textes. L. Gabaude. *Publications de l'École Française d'Extrême-Orient*, vol. 118. Paris: École Française d'Extrême-Orient, 1979. 338p.
'Men of the sea: coastal tribes of southern Thailand's west coast,' D. W. Hogan, *Journal of the Siam society*, 60, pt. 1 (1972), 205–234.
Monks and magic: an analysis of religious ceremonies in central Thailand. B. J. Terwiel. 2nd ed. *Scandinavian Institute of Asian Studies monograph*, no. 24. London: Curzon Press, 1979. 296p.
Peoples of the Golden Triangle: six tribes in Thailand. P. W. Lewis & E. Lewis. London: Thames and Hudson, 1984. 300p. (Deals with Karen, Hmong, Mien, Akha, Lahu, and Lisu).
Please leave your shoes at the door. C. Sahlberg. *The Jaffray collection of missionary portraits*, 5. Camp Hill, PA: Christian Publications, 1992. 191p.
Principles of church planting as illustrated in Thai Theravada Buddhist context. H. Shin. Bangkok: OMF, 1989. 263p.
Religion and legitimation of power in Thailand, Laos and Burma. B. L. Smith. Chambersburg, PA: Anima, 1978.
'Strategizing leadership training in Thailand.' T. Jeng. D.Miss. thesis, Fuller Theological Seminary, Pasadena, CA, 1983. 374p. (In Thai with English summaries).
Strategy to multiply rural churches: a Central Thailand case study. A. G. Smith. Bangkok: OMF, 1977. 272p.
'Syncretistic rural Thai Buddhism.' J. W. Gustafson. M.A. thesis, Fuller Theological Seminary, Pasadena, CA, 1970. 279p.
Thai Buddhism: its rites and activities. K. E. Wells. Bangkok: Bangkok Times Press, 1939; reprint, Bangkok: Bangkok Christian Bookstore, 1960. 320p.
Thai culture, values and religion: an annotated bibliography of English–language materials. P. J. Hughes. Chiang Mai, Thailand: P. J. Hughes, 1982. 56p.
Thailand. M. Watts. *World bibliographical series*, vol. 65. Oxford, UK: CLIO Press, 1986. 275p. (See especially 'Religion and spirit beliefs,' p.109–18).
Thailand: an annotated bibliography of bibliographies. D. V. Hart. *Center for Southeast Asia Studies occasional paper*, no. 5. De Kalb, IL: Northern Illinois University, 1977. 96p.
'Thailand in transition: the church in a Buddhist country,' *Pro Mundi Vita* (Brússels), 48 (1973).
'The folk religion of Ban Nai: a hamlet in central Thailand.' K. Attagara. Ph.D. dissertation, Indiana University, Bloomington, IN, 1967. 596p.
'The history and growth of the Church of Christ in Thailand: an evangelistic perspective.' V. Koydul. Th.M. thesis, Fuller Theological Seminary, Pasadena, CA, 1990. 226p.
The Indianized states of Southeast Asia. G. Coedès. Honolulu, HI: East-West Center Press, 1968. 403p.
'The issues of church management in the Thai church.' B. Boayen. D.Min. thesis, School of Theology at Claremont, Claremont, CA, 1982. 117p.
'The Korean church as a model in Asia with a missiological application to the Thai church.' Y. Lee. Th.M. thesis, Fuller Theological Seminary, Pasadena, CA, 1993. 189p.
'The relationship between cognitive styles, leadership styles, preaching styles, and the rate of growth in Thai churches.' W. Jariyaphruttipong. M.A. thesis, Wheaton College, Wheaton, IL, 1986. 128p.
The role of Thailand in world Buddhism. R. A. Gard. Bangkok: World Fellowship of Buddhists, 1971.
'The unfinished mission in Thailand.' S. Kim. Ph.D. dissertation, Fuller Theological Seminary, Pasadena, CA, 1974.
'The way of the monk and the way of the world: Buddhism in Thailand, Laos and Cambodia,' J. Bunnag, in *The world of Buddhism: Buddhist monks and nuns in society and culture*, p.159–70. H. Bechert & R. Gombrich (eds). London: Thames & Hudson, 1984.
To what extent?: incarnation and the Thai context. H. R. Swanson (ed). N.p.: Manuscript Division, Payap College, 1982. 53p.
Towards a clean church: a case study in nineteenth–century Thai church history. H. R. Swanson. N.p.: Office of History, Church of Christ in Thailand, 1991. 80p.
Tradition and change in Theravada Buddhism: essays on Ceylon and Thailand in the 19th and 20th centuries. B. L. Smith (ed). *Contributions to Asian studies*, 4. Leiden: E. J. Brill, 1973. 195p.
Tribal communities: issues, analysis and organization: a resource book based on the tribal organizers training programme in Southeast Asia, April–May 1987. Kowloon, Hong Kong: Christian Conference of Asia, 1988. 103p.
Understanding a state and its minorities from a religious and cultural perspective: the case of Siam and Burma. Sulak Sivaraksa. [Bangkok]: Sathoaban Santi Prachoatham, [1988]. 20p.
Understanding Thai Buddhism. M. L. M. Jumsai. Bangkok: Chalermnit Press, 1973. 124p.
World conqueror and world renouncer: a study in Buddhism and polity in Thailand against a historical background. S. J. Tambiah. Cambridge, UK: Cambridge University Press, 1976. 557p.
'Worldview evangelism: a case study of the Karen Baptist Church in Thailand.' J. E. Conklin. D.Miss. thesis, Fuller Theological Seminary, Pasadena, CA, 1984. 315p.
'Yao religion and society,' J. Lemoine, in *Highlanders of Thailand*, p.195–211. J. McKinnon & W. Bhruksasri (eds). Kuala Lumpur, Malaysia: Oxford University Press, 1983.

Country Table 2. **Organized churches and denominations in Thailand.**

Official name (bold type = church with over 10% of all affiliated) 1	*Begun* 2	*Type* 3	*Counc* 4	*Congs* 5	*Adults* 6	*Affiliated 1970* 7	*Affiliated 1995* 8	*G%* 9	*Names, notes, and other statistics* (see Codebook, Part 3) 10
Anglican Church (D Singapore)	1894	A-Cen	aweAE	4	200	700	465	-1.62	*Christ Church.* Bangkok. 1903, M=SPG(UK). 99% expatriates (UK, USA). W=40%.
Assembly Hall Churches	1963	I-3nC	x....	31	1,026	200	3,340	11.92	*Local Churches. Little Flock.* Begun mainland China 1922. In south. Chinese.
Bonds of Fellowship	1947	P-Non	xF..E	60	1,200	800	3,000	5.43	M=WEC(UK, USA, Germany). North. HQ Tak (Raheng). 20x,45f,6h,W=75%,75Y.
Baptist International Missions	1979	I-Bap	.....	3	150	–	250	6.25	M=BIM(USA). Fundamentalist Baptists.
Catholic Church in Thailand:	1554	R-Lat	P.F.R	364	132,600	153,831	247,346	1.92	*Phrasatsanachakr Roman Khatholik.* C=9+2+20. 335n 212x 440m 1327w 6469Yy
M Bangkok	1841	R-Lat	Ps	59	41,000	46,915	73,384	1.81	Rapid industrializing. Most RCs Chinese. 99n 79x 236m 482w 1898Yy
D Chanthaburi	1944	R-Lat	Ps	38	16,000	22,522	29,175	1.04	Vietnamese(inSE), Thai-Lao(NE),Chinese. 57n 10x 33m 187w 574Yy
D Chiang Mai	1959	R-Lat	Ps	21	13,000	6,144	26,147	5.96	Rural. RCs Karien elephant breeders. M=SCJ. 15n 23x 34m 59w 1211Yy
D Nakhon Sawan	1967	R-Lat	Ps	20	4,500	4,732	8,926	2.57	Rural plains, mountains. Non-Thai tribes. M=MEP. 19n 8x 12m 23w 328Yy
D Ratchaburi	1930	R-Lat	Ps	30	6,300	14,061	14,329	0.08	All rural; rice, plantations. RCs Chinese. 43n 20x 25m 110w 375Yy
D Surat Thani	1969	R-Lat	Psdb	38	3,200	4,341	6,426	1.58	Muslims (Malays) strong. RCs Chinese. M=SDB. 3n 38x 43m 110w 170Yy
M Tharé & Nonseng	1950	R-Lat	Ps	33	25,600	27,432	46,629	2.14	RCs Thai-Lao; 2, 100 Vietnamese refugees. 47n 0x 0m 99w 829Yy

Continued opposite

Country Table 2–concluded

Official name (bold type = church with over 10% of affiliated) 1	*Begun* 2	*Type* 3	*Counc* 4	*Congs* 5	*Adults* 6	*Affiliated 1970* 7	*Affiliated 1995* 8	*G%* 9	*Names, notes, and other statistics* (see Codebook, Part 3) 10
D Nakhon Ratchasima	1965	R-Lat	Ps	38	2,700	3,369	5,105	1.68	Many migrants to Bangkok. RCs Thai-Lao. M=MEP. 21n 0x 3m 33w 97Yy
D Ubon Ratchathani	1953	R-Lat	Ps	25	11,900	14,265	22,304	1.80	Rural. RCs Thai-Lao. 310 aliens. M=MEP. 21n 12x 22m 121w 610Yy
D Udon Thani	1953	R-Lat	Pcssr	62	8,400	10,050	14,921	1.59	Impoverished. Most RCs Vietnamese. M=CSSR. 10n 22x 32m 103w 377Yy
Children of God	c1985	I-mar	x....	1	71	–	99	10.00	The Family. Former members of Jesus Movement in USA.
China Evangelical Mission	c1975	I-Eva	.....	6	300	–	500	5.00	Independent Evangelicals.
Christian Brethren	c1885	P-CBr	x...E	12	196	600	327	-2.40	M=CMML(UK,Australia,Z). Pentecostal. Chinese. Work in south, Sea Gypsies. 19f.
Christian Churches/Churches of Christ	1949	I-Dis	x....	90	1,000	400	2,000	6.65	M=CCCC(USA). Mountain tribes (Yao); USA military personnel. 16f,1h,W=75%,20Y.
Chr Nationals Evangelism Commission	1955	I-Non	.F..E	10	130	190	200	0.21	*CNEC. Chung Hui Chuan Do Hwei.* Begun China 1942. 2 schools. W=60%.
Church of Christ in Thailand	1828	P-Uni	RWE.N	620	45,308	40,000	82,400	2.93	*CCT.* 65% Thai, 25% Chinese, 5% Karen. 48n,16x,150f,6H,33h,3k,2p,5r,2s,2089Yy.
Church of Christ, Scientist		m-Sci	x....	1	110	100	150	0.05	*Christian Science.* M=CCS(Boston, USA). Bangkok Society. Many Americans.
Church of God (Anderson)	1968	P-Hol	.....	25	535	33	892	14.10	M=CoG(Anderson).
Church of God (Cleveland)	1977	P-Pe3	.....	4	179	–	325	5.56	M=CoG(Cleveland).
Church of God of Prophecy	1968	P-Pe3	.....	22	250	55	455	8.82	M=CGP. Holiness Pentecostals.
Ch of Jesus Christ of Latter-day Saints	1854	m-LdS	x....	18	2,210	578	4,100	8.15	*Mormons.* M=CJCLdS(Utah, USA). Mainly USA Military. Missionaries imprisoned 1972.
Church of the Nazarene	1969	P-Hol	.....	1	50	40	89	3.25	M=CoN. Nazarenes.
Churches of Christ (Non-Instrumental)	1957	I-Dis	x....	70	1,000	2,000	2,000	0.00	M=CC(Non-Instrumental) (USA). Mainly USA military personnel. 1 school. 19f.
Evangelical Covenant Church	1971	P-Con	.....	74	3,000	–	5,000	4.17	M=ECCA(USA).
Evangelical Gospel Church of Thailand	1929	P-Hol	xF..E	107	3,153	6,000	5,148	-0.61	M=CMA. Thais, 160 aliens. Losses to UPC. 11n,70f,1h,2p(63),W=86%,131Y.
Finnish Free Mission Churches	1948	P-Pe2	.....	58	3,500	6,750	8,750	1.04	M=FFFM.
Full Gospel Church Foundation	1951	P-Pe2	.....	21	2,846	1,800	5,690	4.71	M=SFM(Sweden).
Fundamental Baptist Church	1964	I-Fun	xT..E	11	200	100	333	4.93	M=Philippine ABWE(Filipinos). Thai, Chinese. Expanding. 1x,5f,W=90%,7Y,3z.
Hidden Buddhist believers in Christ	c1970	I-Bud	.....	1,500	140,000	–	195,100	62.78	Converted Buddhists who stay within Buddhism as witnesses for Christ.
Hope of God International	1980	I-3kZ	.....	800	15,000	–	36,000	6.67	*Hope of Bangkok/Thailand.* Converted Buddhists. Abroad: 40 chs in 19 countries (Asia, Europe).
Intern Ch of the Foursquare Gospel	c1980	P-Pe2	.....	4	34	–	57	6.67	M=ICFG(USA).
Isolated radio churches	1952	I-3rZ	.....	5,000	200,000	86,000	300,000	5.12	Isolated Thais and Chinese, mainly aged 12-25. R=16000 (FEBC),T=166000 (FEBC,ICI,&c).
Jehovah's Witnesses	1936	m-Jeh	x....	37	1,310	1,000	3,120	4.66	*Watch Tower. IBSA.* First pioneer 1936. HQ Bangkok 11. (1975) 29Y. (1995) 111Y.
Karen Baptist Convention of Thailand	1880	P-Bap	Twe.N	182	15,050	4,000	19,000	6.43	Begun by M=BBC(Burma); 1952, ABFMS(US). Karen, Mon. Loose affiliation in CCT.
Korean Presbyterian Chs	1970	I-Ref	.....	25	1,000	–	2,000	35.53	M=KIM.
Lahu Baptist Convention of Thailand		I-Bap	T....	120	7,500	1,130	15,000	0.05	Chinese Baptists.
Lutheran Church in Thailand	1986	P-Lut	....E	13	334	100	667	11.11	*Lutheran Church Center.* Bangkok. M=Lutheran Council in USA. Mainly expatriates.
New Apostolic Church		I-3aX	x....	200	30,000	–	52,979	0.05	*NAC/NAK.* M=Neuapostolische Kirche. HQ Zurich (Switzerland).
New Tribes Mission	1951	P-Fun	x...E	15	1,421	475	2,060	6.04	M=NTM(USA). HQ Kanchanaburi. Lawa & other tribes. 1 school,12n,20f,1h,W=60%,60Y.
Northern Christian Mission	1971	I-Non	.....	24	3,600	–	5,000	4.17	Independent Nondenominationalists.
Overseas Missionary Fellowship	1951	P-Non	xM..E	186	6,200	2,000	12,400	7.57	M=OMF. Lisu, Thai, Malay. Believers 50% lepers. 20x,227f,3H,2p,W=50%,105Y.
Seventh-day Adventist Church	1918	P-Adv	x....	33	8,740	4,000	16,800	5.91	*Thailand M,* SE Asia UM. 4n,5x,62f,3H,3h,1j,6p,1s,17t(1586),W=59%,174Y.
Thai Ezra Churches	c1980	I-3nZ	x....	15,000	75,000	–	110,000	6.67	*New Life Chs.* Begun in northeast Thailand after screenings of 'Jesus' Film. M=CCCI-JFP.
Thai Full Gospel Fellowship Church	1948	P-Pe2	ZF..E	83	4,370	3,000	14,080	6.38	*Assemblies of God.* M=FFFM,SFM(Sweden),PAoC. 13n,9x,50f,1s(12),W=65%,50Y.
Thailand Baptist Churches Association	1949	P-Bap	T...E	39	3,203	2,000	7,120	5.21	M=SBC(USA). 25% Thai, 10% Chinese. 16n,2x,69f,1H,8h,1s,W=40%,96Y,146z.
True Jesus Church	1956	I-3oC	x....	10	1,000	200	1,500	8.39	*Chen Ye-su Chiao Hui.* Chinese body begun on mainland China in 1917.
United Pentecostal Church of Thailand	c1945	P-Pe1	x....	6	1,600	2,000	3,000	1.64	*Jesus Only Church.* M=UPC(USA). Many ex Gospel Church of T(CMA). 95n,45m,5000Y.
World-Wide Missions of Thailand	1965	I-Non	x....	3	300	300	500	2.06	M=World-Wide Missions (USA). Evangelicals with base in Pasadena, CA (USA).
Other Protestant denominations		P-	.....	100	40,000	20,000	100,000	0.05	Total about 12 (see list below).
Other indigenous churches		I-	.....	80	4,000	300	9,000	0.05	Total about 3, Chinese and Thai, including: Evangelize China Fellowship (1958).
Totals				**25,073**	**758,876**	**340,682**	**1,278,242**		

Churches, members, growth, 1900-2025	*Congs*	*Adults*	*Affiliated*	*G%*	*Total denominations*	*6 Megablocs:* O	*R*	*A*	*P*	*I*	*m*
Total churches, members, and denominations (mid-1900)	400	18,200	35,150	3.30	7	0	1	1	4	0	1
Total churches, members, and denominations (mid-1970)	3,049	176,145	340,682	3.30	37	0	1	1	22	10	3
Total churches, members, and denominations (mid-1990)	20,000	693,000	1,167,230	6.35	58	0	1	1	32	21	3
Total churches, members, and denominations (mid-1995)	25,073	758,876	1,278,242	1.83	58	0	1	1	32	21	3
Total churches, members, and denominations (mid-2000)	30,000	799,000	1,345,167	1.03	58	0	1	1	32	21	3
Total churches, members, and denominations (mid-2025)	40,000	1,037,000	1,746,500	1.05	157	0	1	1	50	100	5

NOTES ON TABLE ABOVE

NATIONAL COUNCILS (Column 4, 5th letter).

E = Evangelical Fellowship of Thailand (EFT) (United Christian Fellowship), 1969.

N = Council of the Church of Christ and Affiliated Missions in Thailand (CCT) (formerly National Council of Churches in Thailand).

R = Episcopal Conference of Thailand (ECT) (Sapa Sangkharat Heng Prathet Thai).

OTHER PROTESTANT DENOMINATIONS. These include: Children of God International (USA), General Conference Mennonite Ch (1967); also USA military chaplaincies among the 45,000 USA servicemen present until 1976.

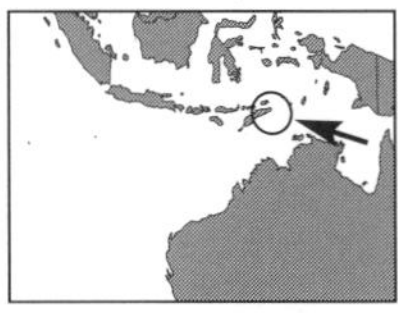

TIMOR

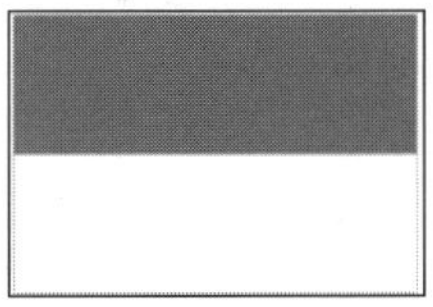

SECULAR DATA, AD 2000

STATE

Official name: Timor.
Short name: Timor. **Adjective of nationality:** Timorese.
Flag: That of Indonesia (temporarily).
Area: 14,874 sq. km. (5,743 sq. mi.).
Government: Independent territory annexed by Indonesia, since 1976 (1586 Portuguese colony, 1896 Portuguese province, 1975 civil war and Independence declared, 1976 annexed by Indonesia as its 27th province). 1999 Independence won after UN plebiscite.
Legislature: In formation.
Official language: Portuguese (Português), Indonesian.
Monetary unit: 1 Indonesian rupiah (Rp) = 100 sen.
US$1= Rp 10,850.
Chief cities: OEKUSI (Dili, Dilly, Dilli) 147,479.
Political divisions: 1 province.

DEMOGRAPHY

Population: 885,000.
Population density: 59.4/sq. km. (154.0/sq. mi.).
Under 15 years: 344,000.
Growth rate p.a.: 1.42% (births 27.60, deaths 13.46).
Mortality: Infant, per 1,000: 120.9; **Maternal per 100,000:** 1,000.0.
Life expectancy: 50 (male 49, female 51).
Household size: 4.0. **Floor area per person, sq.m:** 10.0.
Major languages: Timorese, Indonesian, Portuguese, Chinese, and 15 smaller languages.
Urban dwellers: 7.49%. **Urban growth rate p.a.:** 2.2%.
Labor force: 30%.

ETHNOLINGUISTIC PEOPLES

44.8% Eastern Tetum (Belu); 10.9% Mambai (Damata); 7.0% Timorese (Vaikino); 6.8% Galoli (Edi, Baba); 6.8% Tokode (Tukudede).

ECONOMY

National income p.a. per person: US$644; **per family:** US$2,577.

EDUCATION

Adult literacy: 90% (male 94%, female 86%). **Schools:** 750.
Universities: 5. **School enrolment:** female/male: 75%/75%.

HEALTH

Access to health services: 40%. **Access to safe water:** 60%.
Hospitals: 5 (5 beds per 10,000). **Doctors:** 100.
Blind: 800. **Deaf:** 53,000. **Murder rate:** 5. **Lepers:** 1,000.

LITERATURE

New book titles p.a.: 9 (10 p.a. per million). **Periodicals:** 3.
Newspapers: 1 daily.

COMMUNICATION (per 1,000 people)

Phones: 15 (10% mobile). **Radios:** 100. **TV sets:** 100.
Daily newspaper circulation: 15. **Computers:** 5.

HUMAN LIFE AND LIBERTY (optimum condition=100.0%)

HDI: 52.0. **HSI:** 20.0. **HFI:** 10.0. **EFL:** 30.0.

Country status. Timor is the largest of the Lesser Sunda Islands in the southern Malay Archipelago and has been struggling for independence from Indonesia for 2 decades.

HUMAN LIFE AND LIBERTY

Human rights and freedoms. Timor, formerly East Timor, was de facto part of Indonesia, having been seized by it in defiance of the United Nations. In order to suppress local resistance movements, the government of Indonesia maintained a strong police and military presence in the area. These security forces were guilty of widespread violations of human rights, including torture, extrajudicial murder, and detention. In order to intimidate the civilian population, the military authorities detained people without charges for short periods and then required them to report daily or weekly to the police after their release. The Timorean resistance leader, Jose Xanana Gusmao, was tried and sentenced to Cipinang Prison in Jakarta. But in 1999 Timor voted overwhelmingly for independence, and Indonesia's parliament consented.

NON-CHRISTIAN RELIGIONS

Traditional tribal religions centered in ancestor veneration until recently were the main religions of the largely illiterate interior tribes: the Tetum, Mambai, Macassai, Bunaque, Dagadá, Tocodé, Galoli, Quemaque, Vaiqueno, and others. Today most are heavily Christian.

Islam has won a few converts among the coastal peoples, having been introduced by Indonesian traders. Most Muslims are Indonesians.

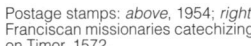

Postage stamps: *above,* 1954; *right,* Franciscan missionaries catechizing on Timor, 1572.

Country Table 1. **Religious adherents in Timor, AD 1900-2025.**

Year	*1900*		*1970*		*mid-1990*		*Annual change, 1990-2000*				*mid-1995*		*mid-2000*		*mid-2025*	
Name	*Adherents*	*%*	*Adherents*	*%*	*Adherents*	*%*	*Natural*	*Conversion*	*Total*	*Rate*	*Adherents*	*%*	*Adherents*	*%*	*Adherents*	*%*
Christians	**45,000**	**12.2**	**211,000**	**34.9**	**676,500**	**91.4**	**13,208**	**733**	**13,946**	**1.89**	**749,000**	**92.0**	**815,959**	**92.2**	**1,128,300**	**95.2**
PROFESSION																
crypto-Christians	5,000	1.4	43,806	7.3	87,500	11.8	1,715	535	2,250	2.31	100,000	12.3	110,000	12.4	160,000	13.5
professing Christians	**40,000**	**10.8**	**167,194**	**27.7**	**589,000**	**79.6**	**11,493**	**203**	**11,696**	**1.83**	**649,000**	**79.7**	**705,959**	**79.8**	**968,300**	**81.7**
AFFILIATION																
unaffiliated Christians	0	0.0	294	0.1	500	0.1	10	-3	7	1.28	500	0.1	568	0.1	1,000	0.1
affiliated Christians	**45,000**	**12.2**	**210,706**	**34.9**	**676,000**	**91.4**	**13,198**	**741**	**13,939**	**1.89**	**748,500**	**92.0**	**815,391**	**92.1**	**1,127,300**	**95.1**
Roman Catholics	45,000	12.2	206,706	34.2	660,000	89.2	12,884	716	13,600	1.89	732,017	89.9	796,000	89.9	1,080,000	91.1
Protestants	0	0.0	4,000	0.7	36,000	4.9	705	395	1,100	2.70	42,125	5.2	47,000	5.3	73,500	6.2
doubly-affiliated	0	0.0	0	0.0	-20,000	-2.7	-392	-369	-761	3.28	-25,642	-3.2	-27,609	-3.1	-26,200	-2.2
Trans-megabloc groupings																
Evangelicals	0	0.0	2,400	0.4	3,800	0.5	74	26	100	2.36	4,300	0.5	4,800	0.5	7,200	0.6
Pentecostals/Charismatics	0	0.0	2,100	0.4	33,600	4.5	658	602	1,260	3.24	40,111	4.9	46,200	5.2	94,800	8.0
Great Commission Christians	**18,500**	**5.0**	**36,270**	**6.0**	**33,670**	**4.6**	**660**	**-83**	**577**	**1.59**	**36,630**	**4.5**	**39,435**	**4.5**	**50,000**	**4.2**
Muslims	800	0.2	1,000	0.2	20,000	2.7	392	442	834	3.55	24,800	3.1	28,339	3.2	30,000	2.5
Ethnoreligionists	324,200	87.6	383,800	63.5	30,750	4.2	603	-1,035	-432	-1.50	27,000	3.3	26,435	3.0	10,000	0.8
New-Religionists	0	0.0	0	0.0	4,800	0.7	94	-70	24	0.49	4,800	0.6	5,042	0.6	6,500	0.6
Nonreligious	0	0.0	0	0.0	2,800	0.4	55	7	62	2.01	3,200	0.4	3,418	0.4	5,000	0.4
Buddhists	0	0.0	6,000	1.0	1,800	0.2	35	-47	-12	-0.68	1,700	0.2	1,681	0.2	900	0.1
Chinese folk-religionists	0	0.0	3,000	0.5	1,500	0.2	29	-38	-9	-0.58	1,450	0.2	1,415	0.2	800	0.1
Baha'is	0	0.0	200	0.0	950	0.1	19	5	24	2.28	1,050	0.1	1,190	0.1	1,700	0.1
Hindus	0	0.0	0	0.0	900	0.1	18	-2	16	1.66	1,000	0.1	1,061	0.1	1,800	0.2
World A (unevangelized persons)	293,040	79.2	350,610	58.0	14,800	2.0	290	-701	-411	-3.20	13,022	1.6	10,620	1.2	10,665	0.9
World B (evangelized non-Christians)	31,960	8.6	42,890	7.1	48,700	6.6	955	-37	918	1.84	51,883	6.4	58,421	6.6	46,035	3.9
World C (Christians)	45,000	12.2	211,000	34.9	676,500	91.4	13,208	738	13,946	1.89	749,000	92.0	815,959	92.2	1,128,300	95.2
Country's population	**370,000**	**100.0**	**604,500**	**100.0**	**740,000**	**100.0**	**14,453**	**0**	**14,453**	**1.81**	**813,906**	**100.0**	**885,000**	**100.0**	**1,185,000**	**100.0**

COLUMNS, ROWS.
For meanings and definitions, see Codebook (Part 3). Note that, by definition, total 'Christians' = professing + crypto-Christians, which also = affiliated + unaffiliated Christians, and also = Great Commission Christians + latent Christians. Percentages may not always total exactly, due to rounding.

CENSUSES.
15.XII.1970: 74.2% ethnoreligionists, 25.1% Roman Catholics, 0.5% Protestants, 0.1% Muslims.

NOTES ON RELIGIONS
BAHA'IS. Begun 1958. Growth from 1 local spiritual assembly (1964) to 3 (1973), assisted by Australian Baha'is missionaries. Expansion thereafter had been hampered by civil war.
BUDDHISTS. Chinese.
COUNTRY'S POPULATION. During the fighting of 1975-76 before annexation by Indonesia, about 60,000 East Timorese were killed and 100,000 imprisoned.
CRYPTO-CHRISTIANS. Persons affiliated to the churches are considerably more numerous than those professing to be Christians in censuses. These crypto-Christians are mostly interior tribesmen and others from societies hostile or opposed to conversion to Christianity.
ETHNORELIGIONISTS. Animists and ancestor-venerators among interior tribes, especially the Akit, Batin, Benua, Bunaque, Dagadá, Gololi, Kubu, Lubu, Macassai, Mambai, Quemaque, Tetum, Tocodé, Utan, and Vaiqueno.
MUSLIMS. Indonesian traders among coastal peoples, and subsequent converts; Sunnis (of the Shafiite rite). Muslims are few also in western (Indonesian) Timor (East Nusa Tenggara Timur). After the 1976 takeover of Timor by Indonesia, the number of Muslims increased rapidly by immigration as well as by conversions from among pagans. The column above, 'Natural change', incorporates this immigration.

Great Commission Instrument Panel: status of Timor (for explanation see start of Part 4)

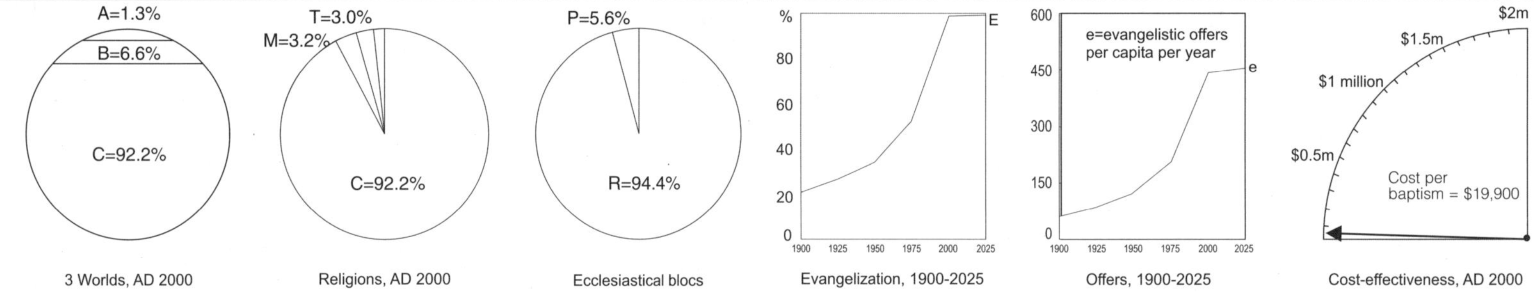

Ethnoreligionists. *Left.* A typical country dwelling in Lospalos, with spirit and ancestor worship accoutrements. *Above.* A Timorese native chief, long with traditional religious powers.

CHRISTIANITY

CATHOLIC CHURCH. Portugal and Christianity first made contact with Timor in 1511, and by 1561 the principal ruler of the island had been converted to Christianity. Early missionary activity was carried on by Dominicans, but their work was decimated by the Dutch in 1754. A new beginning was made after the arrival of priests of the Oblates of Mary Immaculate in 1816, and in 1881 the Catholic population numbered 40,000. Originally part of the diocese of Macao, Dili was made a suffragan diocese of Goa in 1940. Growth has been especially rapid since the mid-1950s, as revealed by the following figures of baptized Catholics: 66,790 in 1956, 91,332 in 1961 and 179,911 in 1970, and over 700,000 by 1995.

The Holy See has no diplomatic relations with Timor in AD 2000.

PROTESTANT CHURCHES. There were no large-scale organized Protestant churches in Portuguese Timor. There is a small work of the Assemblies of God, and also work carried on by members of the strong Protestant churches in west Timor and adjacent islands. The Worldwide Evangelization Crusade has been attempting unsuccessfully to enter Timor since 1961.

Indigenous missions. Very few missionaries have been sent out from Timor.

CHURCH AND STATE

Until 1975 church-state relations were covered by Portugal's concordat of 1940 with the Vatican, which applied to Timor as to all other overseas Portuguese territories as long as Portugal was in control. However, during 1976 Indonesia formally announced its takeover of Timor, after which the church-state relations existent in Indonesia began to be applied.

Country summary. **Worlds A, B, C by ethnolinguistic peoples, cities, and major civil divisions in Timor.**

World	PEOPLES Num	Pop 2000	C%	Christians	E%	U%	Unevangelized	CITIES Num	Pop 2000	C%	Christians	E%	U%	Unevangelized	CIVIL DIVISIONS Num	Pop 2000	C%	Christians	E%	U%	Unevangelized
A	1	61	19.67	12	43	57	35	0	0	0.00	0	0	0	0	0	0	0.00	0	0	0	0
B	4	41,017	15.32	6,284	77	23	9,264	0	0	0.00	0	0	0	0	0	0	0.00	0	0	0	0
C	17	843,465	95.93	809,095	100	0	1,391	1	147,479	85.00	125,357	94	6	9,424	1	884,541	92.18	815,391	99	1	10,692
Total	**22**	**884,543**	**92.18**	**815,391**	**99**	**1**	**10,690**	**1**	**147,479**	**85.00**	**125,357**	**94**	**6**	**9,424**	**1**	**884,541**	**92.18**	**815,391**	**99**	**1**	**10,692**

Igreja Católica do Timur. Diocese of Dili. St. Anthony's Church, Dili.

FUTURE TRENDS AND PROSPECTS

With the expected precipitous decline of ethnoreligionists (87% in 1900 to less than 1% by 2025) Christianity is likely to grow to over 95% of the population in the same period.

With the disappearance of these tribal religions by the middle of the 21st century, Christians and Muslims will probably share the population in a 96/4 proportion after these few decades.

BIBLIOGRAPHY

A bibliography of Timor. K. Sherlock. *Aids to research series*, no. A/4. Canberra, Australia: Australian National University, Research School of Pacific Studies, 1980. 292p.

A maternal religion: the rôle of women in Tetum myth and ritual. D. Hicks. *Monograph series on Southeast Asia, Special Report*, no. 22. De Kalb, IL: Northern Illinois University, Center for Southeast Asian Studies, 1984. 141p.

'A ordem de Sao Domingos e as origens de Timor,' J. D. A. Branco, *Independência*, no. 5 (1987), 35–47.

'Adam and Eve on the island of Roti,' J. J. Fox, *Indonesia*, 36 (October 1983), 15–23.

'Adat and Christianity in Nusa Tenggara Timur: reaction and countereaction,' R. A. F. Webb, *Philippine quarterly of culture and society*, 14, 4 (1986), 339–65.

'Art and religion in Timor,' D. Hicks, In *Islands and ancestors: indigenous styles of Southeast Asia*, p.138–51. J. P. Barbier & D. Newton (eds). Munich: Prestel, 1988.

Bibliography of Indonesian peoples and cultures. R. Kennedy. 3rd ed. *Yale anthropological series*, no. 4. New Haven, CT: Yale University Press, 1974. 207p.

Cosmology and social life: ritual exchange among the Mambai of East Timor. E. G. Traube. Chicago: University of Chicago Press, 1986. 273p.

Curse, retribution, enmity as data in natural religion, especially in Timor, confronted with scripture. P. Middlekoop. Amsterdam: Jacob van Campen, 1960. 168p.

Der missionarische Einsatz der Schwestern auf den Inseln Flores und Timor (Südost–Indonesien). O. Stegmaier. St. Augustin: Steyler, 1974. 118p.

East Timor: a Christian reflection/Timor Oriental: une reflexion Chrétienne. London: Catholic Institute for International Relations, 1987. 21p. (In English and French).

'East Timor: church is the next target,' M. Ferreira, in *Out of control*, p.98–102. C. Tremewan (ed). Singapore: Christian Conference of Asia Youth, 1985.

East Timor: just a political question? G. S. Hull. North Sydney: Australian Catholic Social Justice Council, [1992]. 19p. (Religion in Timor).

Indonesian revival: focus on Timor. G. W. Peters. Grand Rapids, MI: Zondervan, 1974. 117p.

Liturgische vormen en patronen in de Evangelische Kerk op Timor. J. L. C. Abineno. [The Hague, 1956]. 154p.

'Nári,' F. Z. Gomes, *Geographica*, 8, 31 (1972), 64–74.

Palms and the cross: socio–economic development in Nusatenggara, 1930–1975. R. A. F. Webb. *Centre for Southeast Asian Studies monograph*, no. 15. Townsville, Australia: James Cook University of North Queensland, 1986. 284p.

'Space, motion and symbol in Tetum,' D. Hicks, In *Indonesian religions in transition*, p.35–47. R. S. Kipp & S. Rodgers (ed). Tucson, AZ: University of Arizona Press, 1987.

'Spirit movements on Timor,' G. Brookes, in *Cargo cults and millenarian movements*, p.263–91. G. Trompf (ed). *Religion and society*, 29. Berlin: de Gruyter, 1990.

Survey of the Christian Evangelical Church of Timor. F. L. Cooley (ed). Jakarta: DGI, 1976. 413p.

The church and the sandalwood islands: Protestants and Catholics in Sumba and Timor, 1960–1980. R. A. F. Webb. *Southeast Asian Studies Committee occasional paper*, no. 4. Townsville, Australia: James Cook University of North Queensland, 1980. 29p.

The gentle breeze of Jesus. M. Tari & N. Tari. London: Coverdale House, 1974. 160p.

'The "movement of the spirit" in the Timor area: Christian traditions and ethnic identities,' J. J. Fox, in *Indonesia: Australian perspectives; Indonesia: the making of a culture*, p.235–46. J. J. Fox (ed). Canberra, Australia: Australian National University Research School of Pacific Studies, 1980.

'The people and languages of Timor.' A. Capell. *Oceania*, 14, 3 (1944), 191-219; 14, 4 (1944), 311-37; 15, 1 (1944), 19-48.

'The people of the Book: Christians and Muslims in Indonesia: a brief survey of Nusa Tenggara Timur,' R. A. F. Webb, *Indonesia circle*, 35 (1984), 59–69.

'The revival in Timor,' F. L. Cooley, in *Gospel and frontier peoples: a report of a consultation, December 1972*, p.205–30. R. P. Beaver (ed). South Pasadena, CA: William Carey Library, 1973. (See also *South East Asia journal of theology* 14, 2 [1973] 78-93).

Timor. I. Rowland. *World bibliographical series*, vol. 142. Oxford, UK: CLIO Press, 1992. 160p. (See especially 'Religion,' p.53-7).

Country Table 2. **Organized churches and denominations in Timor.**

Official name (bold type = church with over 10% of all affiliated) 1	Begun 2	Type 3	Counc 4	Congs 5	Adults 6	Affiliated 1970 7	Affiliated 1995 8	G% 9	Names, notes, and other statistics (see Codebook, Part 3) 10
Assembléias de Deus		P-Pe2	.....	35	2,500	2,000	3,500	0.05	*Assemblies of God.* Considerable expansion. Links with AoG (Portugal, Indonesia).
Igreja Católica do Timur:	1511	R-Lat	Pz...	200	400,000	206,706	732,017	5.19	*Catholic Ch.* Suffragan of P Goa. C=2+0+2. 36n,57x,188m,199w,35000Yy.
D Baucau	1996	R-Lat	P....	90	100,000	–	222,313	0.05	1996 erected out of D Dili. (1995) 9n,14x,14m,16w,10000Yy
D Dili	1940	R-Lat	P....	50	300,000	194,206	509,704	0.05	*Catholic Ch*, Diocese of Dili. M=SDB. 27n,43x,174m,183w,25170Yy.
Igreja Cristiana do Timur	1570	P-Ref	.W...	0	20,000	–	34,625	51.91	*GKTT. Christian Ch of East Timor.* Organized by Indonesia Protestant bodies. HQ Dili. 20n.
Other Protestant denominations		P-	.....	100	2,800	2,000	4,000	0.05	Mostly Indonesian nationals from western Timor, including from M=GMIT.
Doubly-affiliated		2-aff			-14,100	0	-25,642		Evangelicals and Pentecostals who are also baptized Roman Catholics.
Totals				**475**	**411,200**	**210,706**	**748,500**		

Churches, members, growth, 1900-2025	*Congs*	*Adults*	*Affiliated*	*G%*	*Total denominations*	*O*	*R*	*A*	*P*	*I*	*m*
Total churches, members, and denominations (mid-1900)	40	26,100	45,000	2.23	2	0	1	0	1	0	0
Total churches, members, and denominations (mid-1970)	123	122,200	210,706	2.23	5	0	1	0	4	0	0
Total churches, members, and denominations (mid-1990)	100	371,000	676,000	6.00	9	0	1	0	8	0	0
Total churches, members, and denominations (mid-1995)	475	411,200	748,500	2.06	10	0	1	0	9	0	0
Total churches, members, and denominations (mid-2000)	200	448,000	815,391	1.73	10	0	1	0	9	0	0
Total churches, members, and denominations (mid-2025)	300	619,000	1,127,300	1.30	52	0	1	0	30	20	1

(6 Megablocs: O R A P I m)

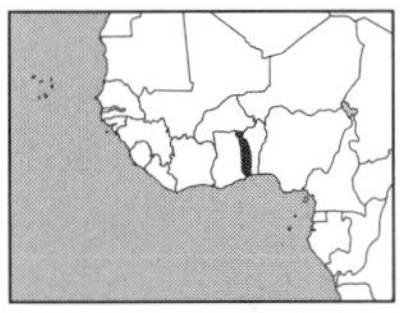

TOGO

SECULAR DATA, AD 2000

STATE

Official name: La République Togolaise (The Togolese Republic).
Short name: Togo. **Adjective of nationality:** Togolese.
Flag: Green and yellow stripes, with white star centered in red square at upper hoist corner.
Area: 56,785 sq. km. (21,925 sq. mi.).
Government: Multiparty republic, since 1992 (1885 German colony, 1922 French mandated territory, 1946 UN trusteeship, 1960 Independence, 1963 military junta, 1967 military dictatorship).
Legislature: National Assembly, 81 members.
Official language: French (Français).
Monetary unit: 1 CFA franc (CFAF) = 100 centimes. **US$1=** CFAF 560.38.
Chief cities: LOME 748,828; Sokode 82,371.
Political divisions: 5 provinces.
Armed forces: 7,000.

DEMOGRAPHY

Population: 4,629,000.
Population density: 81.5/sq. km. (211.1/sq. mi.).
Under 15 years: 2,122,000.
Growth rate p.a.: 2.52% (births 39.47, deaths 14.34).
Mortality: Infant, per 1,000: 76.3; **Maternal per 100,000:** 640.0.
Life expectancy: 50 (male 49, female 51).
Household size: 5.6. **Floor area per person, sq.m:** 8.0.
Major languages: French, Ewe, Fon, Kabre, Moba, Tem, Akposo, Gurma, Yoruba, Hausa, Twi, and over 30 other tribal languages.
Urban dwellers: 33.27%. **Urban growth rate p.a.:** 4.3%.
Labor force: 40%.

ETHNOLINGUISTIC PEOPLES

22.2% Ewe (Ahoulan, Ehve); 13.4% Kabre (Cabrai, Kabure); 10.0% Wachi (Watyi); 5.6% Mina (Ge, Popo, Guin); 5.6% Kotokoli (Tim, Temba).

ECONOMY

National income p.a. per person: US$309; **per family:** US$1,735.

EDUCATION

Adult literacy: 51% (male 67%, female 37%). **Schools:** 2,594.
Universities: 1. **School enrolment:** female/male: 48%/80%.

HEALTH
Access to health services: 61%. **Access to safe water:** 63%.
Hospitals: 30 (16 beds per 10,000). **Doctors:** 319.
Blind: 9,000. **Deaf:** 280,600. **Murder rate:** 7.
Lepers: 80,000. **Underweight prevalence under 5:** 24%.

LITERATURE
New book titles p.a.: 690 (150 p.a. per million). **Periodicals:** 14.
Newspapers: 1 daily.

COMMUNICATION (per 1,000 people)
Phones: 5 (19% mobile). **Radios:** 170. **TV sets:** 12.
Daily newspaper circulation: 2. **Computers:** 8.

REFUGEES
Citizen refugees in other countries: 95,000.
Alien refugees from other countries: 10,000.

HUMAN LIFE AND LIBERTY (optimum condition=100.0%)
HDI: 36.5. **HSI:** 29.0. **HFI:** 20.0. **EFL:** 22.0.

Country Table 1. **Religious adherents in Togo, AD 1900-2025.**

Year	*1900*		*1970*		*mid-1990*		*Annual change, 1990-2000*				*mid-1995*		*mid-2000*		*mid-2025*	
Name	*Adherents*	*%*	*Adherents*	*%*	*Adherents*	*%*	*Natural*	*Conversion*	*Total*	*Rate*	*Adherents*	*%*	*Adherents*	*%*	*Adherents*	*%*
Christians	**4,000**	**0.9**	**595,840**	**29.5**	**1,467,000**	**41.8**	**46,658**	**3,803**	**50,461**	**3.00**	**1,710,000**	**42.1**	**1,971,610**	**42.6**	**4,150,000**	**48.9**
PROFESSION																
professing Christians	**4,000**	**0.9**	**595,840**	**29.5**	**1,467,000**	**41.8**	**46,658**	**3,803**	**50,461**	**3.00**	**1,710,000**	**42.1**	**1,971,610**	**42.6**	**4,150,000**	**48.9**
AFFILIATION																
unaffiliated Christians	670	0.1	80,282	4.0	207,000	5.9	6,584	-5,032	1,552	0.73	225,188	5.6	222,515	4.8	100,000	1.2
affiliated Christians	**3,330**	**0.7**	**515,558**	**25.5**	**1,260,000**	**35.9**	**40,075**	**8,835**	**48,910**	**3.33**	**1,484,812**	**36.6**	**1,749,095**	**37.8**	**4,050,000**	**47.8**
Roman Catholics	2,130	0.5	427,594	21.2	822,000	23.4	26,144	3,956	30,100	3.17	956,205	23.6	1,122,995	24.3	2,450,000	28.9
Protestants	1,200	0.3	66,700	3.3	342,000	9.7	10,877	2,923	13,800	3.45	408,136	10.1	480,000	10.4	1,200,000	14.2
Independents	0	0.0	18,264	0.9	71,000	2.0	2,258	1,642	3,900	4.48	90,171	2.2	110,000	2.4	300,000	3.5
Marginal Christians	0	0.0	3,000	0.2	25,000	0.7	795	315	1,110	3.74	30,300	0.8	36,100	0.8	100,000	1.2
Trans-megabloc groupings																
Evangelicals	1,000	0.2	13,800	0.7	87,800	2.5	2,793	2,327	5,120	4.70	112,454	2.8	139,000	3.0	400,000	4.7
Pentecostals/Charismatics	0	0.0	24,000	1.2	250,000	7.1	7,951	4,549	12,500	4.14	308,958	7.6	375,000	8.1	965,000	11.4
Great Commission Christians	**3,300**	**0.7**	**282,800**	**14.0**	**576,000**	**16.4**	**18,320**	**15,859**	**34,179**	**4.77**	**690,000**	**17.0**	**917,794**	**19.8**	**1,615,000**	**19.0**
Ethnoreligionists	447,000	95.1	1,162,260	57.5	1,366,700	38.9	43,492	-5,603	37,841	2.47	1,554,050	38.3	1,745,105	37.7	2,528,000	29.8
Muslims	19,000	4.0	258,700	12.8	650,000	18.5	20,673	1,602	22,275	2.99	762,000	18.8	872,749	18.9	1,700,000	20.0
Baha'is	0	0.0	2,100	0.1	18,000	0.5	572	168	740	3.50	22,000	0.5	25,395	0.6	55,000	0.7
Nonreligious	0	0.0	500	0.0	7,200	0.2	229	98	327	3.82	8,500	0.2	10,470	0.2	40,000	0.5
Atheists	0	0.0	0	0.0	1,000	0.0	32	-1	31	2.71	1,150	0.0	1,306	0.0	4,000	0.1
Other religionists	0	0.0	600	0.0	2,100	0.1	67	-19	48	2.09	2,300	0.1	2,583	0.1	5,000	0.1
World A (unevangelized persons)	424,880	90.4	888,800	44.0	990,384	28.2	31,487	-18,658	12,829	1.23	1,059,549	26.1	1,120,218	24.2	1,603,098	18.9
World B (evangelized non-Christians)	41,120	8.7	535,360	26.5	1,054,616	30.0	33,578	14,855	48,433	3.84	1,290,025	31.8	1,537,172	33.2	2,728,902	32.2
World C (Christians)	4,000	0.9	595,840	29.5	1,467,000	41.8	46,658	3,803	50,461	3.00	1,710,000	42.1	1,971,610	42.6	4,150,000	48.9
Country's population	**470,000**	**100.0**	**2,020,000**	**100.0**	**3,512,000**	**100.0**	**111,723**	**0**	**111,723**	**2.80**	**4,059,575**	**100.0**	**4,629,000**	**100.0**	**8,482,000**	**100.0**

COLUMNS, ROWS.
For meanings and definitions, see Codebook (Part 3). Note that, by definition, total 'Christians' = professing + crypto-Christians, which also = affiliated + unaffiliated Christians, and also = Great Commission Christians + latent Christians. Percentages may not always total exactly, due to rounding.

CENSUSES.
XI.1958-XII.1960: 67.0% ethnoreligionists, 24.2% Christians (17.7% Roman Catholics, 6.5% Protestants), 8.8% Muslims. **1.III-30.IV.1970:** 56.3% ethnoreligionists, 30.4% Christians (23.5% Roman Catholics, 6.9% Protestants, African indigenous and marginal Protestants), 13.2% Muslims. This latter census uses the term 'traditionalists' to cover ethnoreligionists. **1981**: 58.9% Ethnoreligionists, 28.3% Christians (21.5% Roman Catholics, 6.8% Protestants, Independents, and Marginal Christians), 12.1% Muslims, 0.7% other religionists.

NOTES ON RELIGIONS
BAHA'IS. Begun 1955. Growth to 11 local spiritual assemblies by 1973. This was then followed by a period of phenomenal expansion resulting by 1996 in 139 LSAs.
ETHNORELIGIONISTS. Animists. Tribal religion is still extremely strong. Tribes with over 60% traditionalists in 1995: N'Gangan (94%), Moba (70%), Wachi (61%), Kabre (61%), Kpessi (84%), Bassari (70%), Adele (79%), Kebu (67%). There are several fetishist initiation convents, but the ones which still draw the biggest numbers of Togolese are those in Benin and Ghana.
INDEPENDENTS. In about 28 denominations in 1995 (see Table 2).
MUSLIMS. All Sunnis (of the Malikite rite); in the north, especially among the Chakossi (48%), Chamba (95%), Fulani (Fula, Peulh, 84%), Hausa, Mande, Mossi (59%), Nago (Egba, Yoruba; 72%), Tamberma (60%) and Tem (Kotokoli; 74%). There is a small Ahmadiya Mission (enumerated here although declared non-Muslim by Pakistan). Begun 1960; Qadianis (HQ Rabwah, Pakistan). Many Ghanaians, also Yoruba. *Hajj pilgrims to Mecca.* (1970) 111; (1976) 95. Conversions. Islam has spread rapidly among pagan peoples in the north, the proportion of Muslims in the country rising from 8.8% in 1960 to 13.2% in 1970. There are numerous schools staffed by Arab teachers.
OTHER RELIGIONISTS. Including Rosicrucians (11 AMORC centers).
PROTESTANTS. The 1900 statistics refer to the situation only in the territory which forms present-day Togo. At that time the main Protestant work (the Bremen Mission) was in western German Togoland (Ho) which is now in Ghana.
ROMAN CATHOLICS. In 1900, there were 1,331 baptized Catholics and 800 catechumens.

Great Commission Instrument Panel: status of Togo (for explanation see start of Part 4)

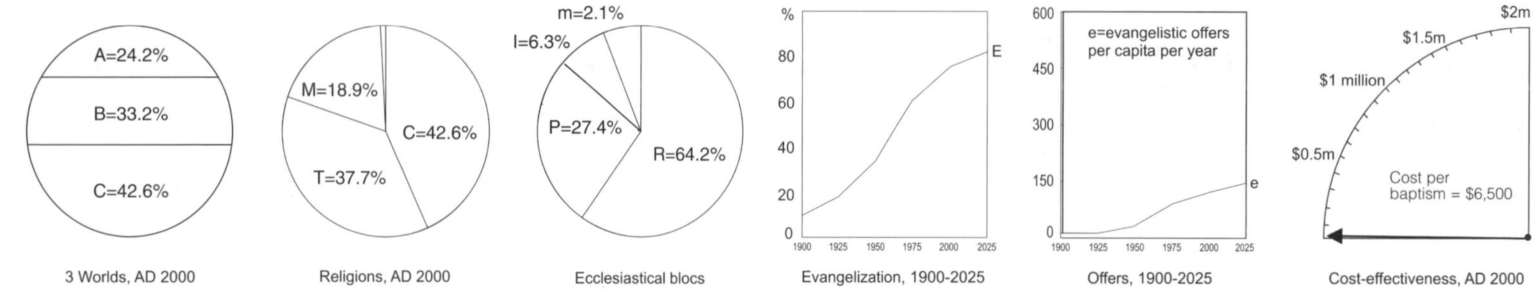

Country status. Togo is a small, elongated country in West Africa with a short coastline on the Gulf of Guinea. Its chief exports are cocoa, coffee, and cotton.

HUMAN LIFE AND LIBERTY

***Human need and development*.** Togo is one of the low-income countries of Africa with a per capita GNP of $309, a literacy rate of 51% and a life expectancy of 50. About 80% of its 3.5 million people are engaged in subsistence agriculture. The economy has deteriorated in recent years as a result of civil strife. The south is relatively more prosperous than the north. About one in 6 Togolese children suffer from malnutrition. Health facilities and personnel are limited to the capital and a few large towns. There are few sanitation programs and virtually no sewage or water treatment facilities.

Human rights and freedoms. The human rights situation has deteriorated significantly since 1993 when Togo's progress toward full democracy was halted and president Gnassingbe Eyadema unleashed a counteroffensive against his opponents with the help of the army. The security forces have engaged in massive abuses, including killings and torture of enemies. The judicial system is subject to interference by the executive. The court system is overburdened and understaffed. Confessions are coerced from political detainees. Searches of private residences need no prior judicial authorization in political and national security cases. Telephones are tapped and correspondence is monitored by the intelligence services. Death threats and surveillance against opposition leaders are common. Constitutional provisions on freedom of speech and press are ignored. Offices of newspapers opposed to the president are sometimes bombed by the security forces and editors are harassed, imprisoned and threatened for publishing defamatory articles. Elections are flawed by serious irregularities, such as inflated electoral rolls, double voting, intimidation of voters, and disqualification of opposition candidates. Despite constitutional protections, women suffer de facto discrimination under traditional law. Generally, southern Togolese are discriminated by the Eyadema regime, which is based on northern support.

Ethnoreligionists. *Left.* Traditionalist funeral and burial among the 100,000 Bassari animists, who are still 80% pagan. Note corpse and bearers sprinkled with whitewash; and gun at right. *Above.* Spirit offerings made by Bassari animists.

Country summary. Worlds A, B, C by ethnolinguistic peoples, cities, and major civil divisions in Togo.

World	PEOPLES Num	Pop 2000	C%	Christians	E%	U%	Unevangelized	CITIES Num	Pop 2000	C%	Christians	E%	U%	Unevangelized	CIVIL DIVISIONS Num	Pop 2000	C%	Christians	E%	U%	Unevangelized
A	11	435,169	6.10	26,525	40	60	259,421	0	0	0.00	0	0	0	0	0	0	0.00	0	0	0	0
B	29	2,725,364	22.71	618,863	69	31	855,211	2	831,199	44.41	369,172	86	14	115,719	5	4,629,218	37.78	1,749,094	76	24	1,118,285
C	13	1,468,681	75.15	1,103,710	100	0	3,657	0	0	0.00	0	0	0	0	0	0	0.00	0	0	0	0
Total	**53**	**4,629,214**	**37.78**	**1,749,098**	**76**	**24**	**1,118,289**	**2**	**831,199**	**44.41**	**369,172**	**86**	**14**	**115,719**	**5**	**4,629,218**	**37.78**	**1,749,094**	**76**	**24**	**1,118,285**

Human environment. Environmental degradation is due more to lack of sewage, improper farming practices and lack of conservation efforts than to industrial or air pollution. The impact of the virtual civil war since 1993 is also felt on the ecology of the land where much of the productive land has been left untended.

NON-CHRISTIAN RELIGIONS

Traditional religions still retain the allegiance of over a million people in Togo, displaying considerable resistance to both Islam and Christianity. Togo in 1995 was 38% traditionalist, with a number of peoples still over 70%: Adele, Bassari, Gurma, Kabre, Kebu, Konkomba, Kpessi, Lamba, Moba, Naudeba (Losso), and Wachi. Togo's largest tribe, the Ewe, has been strongly influenced by Christianity, but a minority continue to make sacrifices to the traditional voodoo (vudi) divinities such as Sakpata (smallpox) and So (thunder). The Ewe Supreme Being, Mawu, is regarded as mother, creator, judge and law giver. Among some Ewe peoples, Mawu has priests and temples, and receives regular sacrifices; for others including the Ge and Adja sub-tribes, Mawu is not directly worshiped.

Islam was introduced in the 18th century by the warrior Chakossi tribe, and its expansion was aided by German colonial policy. Sokode can be considered the historic capital of Islam in Togo, the first mosque being built there in 1820. All Togolese Muslims are Sunnis of the Malikite rite. Although generally localized in the north, they are also numerous in the southern cities. Islam has the allegiance of a majority of the Chamba, Mossi, Nagot, Fulani, Tamberma and Tem (Kotokoli). The Muslim Union of Togo (Union Musulmane du Togo) was formed in late 1973 and is involved especially in a struggle against deviant marabouts and unorthodox brotherhoods. Mosques of permanent construction are at present being built throughout the country, as are Quranic schools staffed by Arab teachers.

CHRISTIANITY

CATHOLIC CHURCH. The area was visited by Roman Catholic priests considerably earlier than the first mission stations were established, in 1871 at Agoue and 1886 by the Society of African Missions, from Lyons, France. Togo was declared a prefecture in 1892 and a vicariate in 1914 under SVD priests; but Lyons Fathers returned in 1918 after German missionaries were forced to leave the country. They are still the principal foreign religious society. The first Togolese priest was ordained in 1930 and by 1962 Togo had an African archbishop. The church is strongest in the south, since up-country missions were not authorized by German authorities until 1913.

The Holy See has diplomatic relations with Togo and in AD 2000 is represented to government and the Catholic hierarchy by a nuncio residing in Accra, Ghana.

PROTESTANT CHURCHES. The earliest Protestants in what is now Togo were immigrants or local men trained in Christian schools on the Gold Coast. In Anecho by 1870, the ruling Lawson clan were strong Methodists. A Methodist catechist, an African from Lagos, was appointed to Anecho in 1876, and the first Methodist European missionary in 1880. In 1893 the Bremen Mission opened their Lome station. At the beginning of World War I all German missionaries were expelled from the area, which helped to create self-reliance among indigenous Christians, a sense which was not lost when aid was later received from the Paris Mission and the UCBWM. The autonomous Evangelical Church of Togo (EET) is the largest Protestant body in the country and carries on extensive educational and social work as well: primary and secondary schools, a hospital and clinics, social and literacy centers, hostels, a professional training program and agricultural centers.

The Methodist Church, related to British Methodism, is still confined largely to the coastal area around Anecho. The third largest Protestant denomination today is the Assemblies of God who entered Togo in 1937 and opened the first Protestant stations in the north in 1940. Other groups making their appearance more recently are Seventh-day Adventists and Southern Baptists. The latter came to Lome at the request of indigenous Baptists who were first evangelized by Nigerian traders. Methodists have one secondary and 7 primary schools, and Adventists and Assemblies of God each have 2 schools.

Calvary Temple, a new Pentecostal church under construction in Lomé.

INDIGENOUS CHURCHES. The Apostles Revelation Society began in Ghana in 1939 as a schism from the Ewe (now Evangelical) Presbyterian Church led by prophet Wovenu; it then entered Togo the following year. In 1951, the Apostolic Church of Togo was founded and has spread to Benin, although a split during the mid 1950s resulted in the creation of a new body, the Pentecostal Apostolic Church. Other indigenous bodies include the White Cross Society, Heavenly Christianity Church Sacred Order of Deliverance, Cherubim and Seraphim, and Church of the Lord (Aladura). The latter 2 are also widely dispersed across other countries of West Africa.

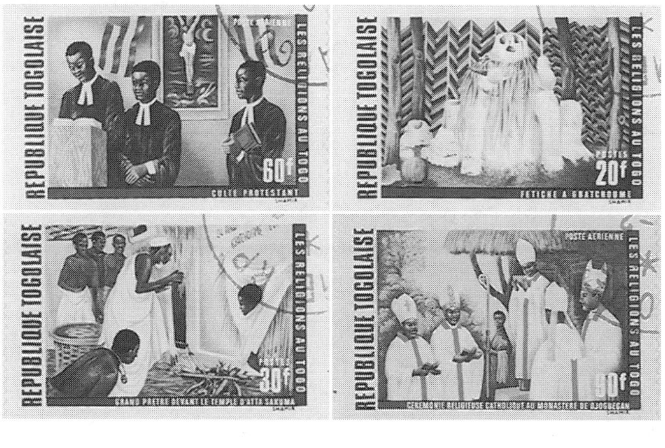

Religions of Togo on stamps: *Top left, clockwise:* Presbyterian clergy; Great Fetish of Gbatchoume; Catholic bishops; chief priest in front of Atta Sakuma temple.

Indigenous missions. Some Christians from Togo have served as foreign missionaries, though nearly all of these have served in surrounding African countries.

Renewal movements. In the 1990s the Pentecostal/Charismatic Renewal continued to spread rapidly across most older churches, and numbered over 375,000 adherents (of whom 23% Pentecostals, 47% Charismatics, and 29% Independents).

CHURCH AND STATE

The military regime which came to power in 1967 suspended the constitution of May 1963, although its general principles relative to the government attitude towards religion continue to be respected. According to that constitution, the Togolese republic is described as secular. The state 'respects all creeds' (Article 1) and assures all citizens of equality before the law without distinction of religion. Freedom of conscience and religion are guaranteed to all (Article 17). Religious institutions and communities 'have the right to develop without impediment in conformity with current laws and regulations' (Article 17), for their educational role is fully recognized (Article 16). 'Private and confessional schools may be opened with the authorization of and under the control of the State' (Article 16). Substantial financial grants in aid to Catholic and Protestant confessional schools were authorized in October 1970.

In 1978, the People's Party of Togo (RPT) banned 20 religious bodies including Jehovah's Witnesses and various indigenous pentecostal churches, on the grounds that sects were proliferating alarmingly. The only bodies permitted to continue were the Roman Catholic and Protestant churches, Assemblies of God, Seventh-day Adventists, and the Baptist Church of Togo; and also Islam.

Eglise Evagélique du Togo. The Cassette Club using 'Faith Comes By Hearing' material.

BROADCASTING AND MEDIA

One person in 5 owns a radio. Television sets are very limited. HCJB World Radio has helped to start local stations in Togo in cooperation with International Media Ministries. Shortwave radio programs from KNLS have seen some response. Togo is represented in UNDA.

Most of the country has seen the 'Jesus' Film, chiefly through television broadcasts (4.5 million) and film team presentations (1.2 million).

INTERDENOMINATIONAL ORGANIZATIONS

There is no ecumenical Christian council in Togo. In the field of ecumenical studies, both Catholic and Protestant clergy and laity (especially OSB priests) cooperate in the South Togo Cultural and Religious Research Group (Groupe de Recherches Culturelles et Religieuses dans le Sud Togo, or GREST), with headquarters at the monastery of Dzoghegan near Palime, which began its activities in 1967 with a study of the ancestor cult and is now engaged on cultural and ecumenical research.

FUTURE TRENDS AND PROSPECTS

Ethnoreligionists are expected to drop precipitously through 2025 with most gains being made by Christians (29.5% in 1970 to 48.9% by 2025). Ethnoreligionists will likely fall below 30% by 2025 from 57.5% in 1970.

As traditional religionists decline throughout the 21st century, Christians and Muslims could share the population in a 70/30 ratio after AD 2050.

BIBLIOGRAPHY

150 years of North German mission, 1836–1986. E. Schöck-Quinteros & D. Lenz (eds). Bremen, 1989. 83p. (Deals with work of North German missions in Togo, Ghana, and Japan).

A church between colonial powers: a study of the Church in Togo. H. W. Debrunner. *World studies of churches in mission.* London: Lutterworth Press, [1965]. 379p. (On the Evangelical Church of Togo).

A travers les missions du Togo et du Dahomey. A. Boucher. Paris: Librairie P. Téqui, 1926. 164p.

Geschichte der katholischen Kirche in Togo. K. Müller. Kaldenkirchen: Steyler, 1958. 573p.

Heviesso et le bon ordre du monde: approche d'une religion africaine. B. Gilli. *Studium combonianum*, 40. Lomé, Togo: Editions HAHO, [1987]. 230p.

La structure socio–politique et son articulation avec la pensée religieuse chez les Aja–Tado du Sud–est Togo. K. E. Kossi. *Arbeiten aus dem Seminar für Völkerkunde der Johann Wolfgang Goethe-Universität Frankfurt am Main*, vol. 21. Stuttgart: F. Steiner, 1990. 325p.

Le système religieux des Evhé. A. de Surgy. Paris: L'Harmattan, 1988. 343p.

Le vodu en Afrique de l'Ouest: rites et traditions: le cas des sociétés Guen–Mina (Sud–Togo). I. de La Torre. *Collection anthropologie—Connaissance des hommes.* Paris: L'Harmattan, 1991. 179p.

Les ancêtres et nous: analyse de la pensée religieuse des Bê de la commune de Lomé. K. Agbetiafa. Dakar, Senegal: Nouvelles Editions Africaines, 1985. 95p.

Les musulmans au Togo. R. Delval. *Centre de hautes études sur l'Afrique et l'Asie modernes collection.* Paris: Publications Orientalistes de France, 1980. 376p.

Muslims in Mango (Northern Togo). E. A. van Rouveroy van Nieuwaal. Leiden: African Studies Centre, 1986. 66p.

Nature et fonction des fétiches en Afrique noire: le cas du Sud–Togo. A. de Surgy. *Collection anthropologie—Connaissance des hommes.* Paris: L'Harmattan, 1994. 462p.

Panorama sociologique des sectes religieuses au Togo: étude et documents. K. Sossah. Lomé, Togo: Institut National de la Recherche Scientifique, 1976. 233p.

'Personhood, possession and the law in Ewe gorovodu culture.' J. V. Rosenthal. Ph.D. dissertation, Cornell University, Ithaca, NY, 1993. 389p.

Pratique de la tradition religieuse et reproduction sociale chez les Guen/Mina du Sud–est du Togo. E. Adjakly. Geneva: Institut Universitaire d'Études du Développement, 1985. 150p.

Religieuses au Togo. Togo: Archevêché de Lomè, 1991. 29p.

'The Evangelical Presbyterian Church (Ghana and Togo), 1914–1946: a study in European mission relations affecting the beginning of an indigenous church.' E. E. Grau. Ph.D. dissertation, Hartford Seminary Foundation, Hartford, CT, 1964. 262p.

The Guardian of the forces. A.–L. F. Reimann. London: Royal Anthropological Institute, 1992. (55 minute videorecording)

The Lutheran Church in Togo. W. L. DeMoss & R. L. Buck. 1984-1988 (4 videocassettes).

Togo. S. Decalo. *World bibliographical series*, vol. 178. Oxford, UK: CLIO Press, 1995. 222p.

Togo singt ein neues Lied Equipen im Mono–Gebiet. E. Viering. *Erlanger Taschenbücher*, vol. 10. Erlangen: Verlag der Evangelisch-Lutherischen Mission, [1969]. 269p.

'Training leaders concerning spiritual issues for the growth of the church in Togo, West Africa.' G. L. Jones. D.Min. thesis, Fuller Theological Seminary, Pasadena, CA, 1993. 253p.

Country Table 2. **Organized churches and denominations in Togo.**

Official name (bold type = church with over 10% of all affiliated) 1	*Begun* 2	*Type* 3	*Counc* 4	*Congs* 5	*Adults* 6	*Affiliated 1970* 7	*Affiliated 1995* 8	*G%* 9	*Names, notes, and other statistics* (see Codebook, Part 3) 10
Assemblées de Dieu	1921	P-Pe2	ZF...	414	55,908	5,000	70,000	11.13	*Assemblies of God.* M=AoG(USA). North:Bassari, Moba. 2 schools. 26n,14f,1p,1s(30).
Chérubin et Séraphin du Mont Zion du T	1964	I-3aA	x...I	30	3,000	364	4,000	10.06	*Ordre Sacré des C&S.* Mt Zion(Nigeria). 83% Ewe; Mina. 1n,7m,9w,W=70%,38Y,12y.
Convention Baptiste Togolaise	c1950	P-Bap	T....	225	12,447	1,500	21,100	11.15	*Togo Baptist Assoc.* Begun by Nigerian traders. M=NBC,FMB-SBC. HQ Lome. 2n,11f,1p,80Y.
Eglise Adventiste du Septième Jour	1964	P-Adv	x....	5	622	200	1,036	6.80	*Seventh-day Adventists, Togo-Dahomey Mission*, WAfrican UM. Lome. 1nx,2f,5t,20Y.
Eglise Apostolique du Togo et Bénin	1951	I-3aA	x.I.I	30	6,000	5,000	10,000	2.81	*Apostolic Ch Divine Healers Temple. Praisers.* Ewe. Across south, and Benin. Banned 1978.
Eglise Catholique au Togo:	1871	R-Lat	P.SFR	633	498,100	427,594	956,205	3.27	C=4+5+15. (1970) 87n,53x,257w,15509Yy,2p.(1990) 258n 141x 352m 723w 38900Yy
M Lomé	1892	R-Lat	Ps	47	177,000	291,060	327,128	0.47	Capital. Coastal area, plateau. Ewe, Mina, Popo. 89n 53x 157m 284w 14639Yy
D Aneho	1994	R-Lat	Ps	10	57,000	–	106,664	10.00	Population is 20% Catholic. 25n 16x 45m 52w 3000Yy
D Atakpamé	1964	R-Lat	Ps	512	95,000	78,605	143,270	2.43	Plateau region. 443 alien RCs. Akposo, Egba. 33n 6x 19m 80w 8260Yy
D Dapaong (Dapango)	1960	R-Lat	Ps	12	16,000	7,300	25,903	5.20	35% Moba, 35% Gurma, 28% Kabre. M=OFM,IEME. 20n 26x 44m 44w 2106Yy
D Kara	1994	R-Lat	Ps	14	27,500	–	88,630	10.00	Formerly in D Sokode. 30n 9x 19m 68w 1400Yy
D Kpalime	1994	R-Lat	Ps	14	95,000	–	207,910	10.00	Formerly in M Lome. 30n 4x 21m 54w 4000Yy
D Sokodé	1937	R-Lat	Ps	24	30,600	50,629	56,700	0.45	Central and La Kara regions. Kabre, Bassari. 1p. 31n 27x 47m 141w 5495Yy
Eglise de la Guérison Divine du Togo	c1960	I-3pA	x.I..	20	1,500	1,000	3,000	4.49	*Togo Mawu me Doyo Ha. Divine Healer's Ch of Togo.The Lord is There Temple.*M=DHC(Ghana)
Eglise de Pentecôte Apostolique	c1955	I-3aA	I	5	700	300	1,000	4.93	*Pentecostal Apostolic Ch.* Ex Eglise Apostolique opposing TLOsborn (USA) aid. Ewe.
Eglise du Christ	1962	I-3pA	I	6	600	500	800	1.90	*Church of Christ.* Begun in Lomé by an Ewe pastor. Work in Ghana also. Ewe, Mina.
Eglise du Christanisme Céleste	1963	I-3aA	x.I.I	15	2,000	1,000	3,000	4.49	*Celestial Ch of Christ. Heavenly Christianity.* HQ Porto Novo(Benin). Mina, Ewe, Yoruba, Gun.
Eglise du Pentecôte du Togo	c1950	I-3oA	.G...	225	4,500	5,000	11,300	3.32	*Ch of Pentecost in Togo.* M=CoP(Ghana),EMS(UK). Banned 1978, doors cemented up.
Eglise du Seigneur (Aladura)	1960	I-3pA	xwI.I	20	1,000	500	2,000	5.70	*Church of the Lord (Aladura) (Praying).* M=CLA(Nigeria). HQ Lome. Ewe, Mina, Yoruba.
Eglise Evangélique Baptiste	1978	P-Bap	.....	22	1,750	–	3,500	5.88	*Evangelical Baptist Church.*
Eglise Evangélique du Togo	1893	P-Ref	xWA.C	516	117,525	56,000	300,000	6.94	*EET. Ev Ch of Togo.* 1893, M=NBM; PEMS,UCC,UCBWM. 57% Ewe. 37n,5x,36f,1H,2h,1p,2r.
Eglise Luthérienne au Togo	c1975	P-Lut	e....	31	2,000	–	4,000	5.00	*Lutheran Church in Togo.* M=LCMS(USA).
Eglise Neo-Apostolique	c1975	I-3aX	x....	100	15,000	–	25,671	5.00	*NAC/NAK.* M=Neuapostolische Kirche. HQ Zurich (Switzerland).
Eglise pour la Victoire	c1980	I-3vA	x....	10	3,000	–	7,000	6.67	*Ch for the Advancement of Victory.* Deliverance pentecostal. Lomé. M=Victory Outreach (USA).
Eglise Prot Méthodiste au Togo	c1860	P-Met	VWA.C	25	3,750	4,000	7,500	2.55	*Meth Ch.* M=MMS(UK). 95% Mina. Many Togolese elite. 2n,1x,1p,1r,1s,41Y,202y,157z.
Mission Evangélique de la Foi		I-3nA	.....	10	400	–	1,000	0.05	*Gospel Faith Mission.* Work among Ewe, Mina.
Ordre Sacré de Déliverance	1968	I-3pA	I	2	200	100	400	5.70	*Sacred Order of Deliverance.* Founded locally by an Ewe. HQ Lome. Ewe, Mina.
Société de la Croix Blanche		I-3pA	.....	10	2,000	2,000	3,000	0.05	*White Cross Society. Atitso Gaxie Habobo. EP Healing Group.* Ex EPC(Ghana)..Ewe.
Société Révélation Apostolique	1940	I-3aA	x...I	10	1,000	500	2,000	5.70	*Apostolowo Fe Dedefia Habobo.* M=Apostles Revelation Society (Ghana). Ewe. Banned 1978.
Témoins de Jéhovah	c1945	m-Jeh	x....	120	15,318	3,000	30,300	9.69	*Jehovah's Witnesses.* Witnessing by 1949. Akposo et al. Banned 1978. (1975)248Y.(1995)1147Y.
Other African indigenous churches		I-3pA	.....	100	10,000	2,000	16,000	0.05	Total about 18 (see list below): Ghanaians, Nigerians, Harrist Ch (from Ivory Coast).
Other Protestant churches	c1975	P-	.....	15	500	–	1,000	5.00	In 3 recently-arrived missions or denominations.
Totals				**2,599**	**758,820**	**515,558**	**1,484,812**		

Churches, members, growth, 1900-2025	*Congs*	*Adults*	*Affiliated*	*G%*	*Total denominations*	*O*	*R*	*A*	*P*	*I*	*m*
Total churches, members, and denominations (mid-1900)	10	1,800	3,330	7.47	3	0	1	0	2	0	0
Total churches, members, and denominations (mid-1970)	745	284,832	515,558	7.47	26	0	1	0	5	19	1
Total churches, members, and denominations (mid-1990)	1,300	644,000	1,260,000	4.57	44	0	1	0	10	32	1
Total churches, members, and denominations (mid-1995)	2,599	758,820	1,484,812	3.34	44	0	1	0	10	32	1
Total churches, members, and denominations (mid-2000)	3,200	894,000	1,749,095	3.33	45	0	1	0	10	33	1
Total churches, members, and denominations (mid-2025)	6,000	2,070,000	4,050,000	3.42	113	0	1	0	30	80	2

(*6 Megablocs:* O, R, A, P, I, m)

NOTES ON TABLE ABOVE
NATIONAL COUNCILS (Column 4, 5th letter).
C = Christian Council of Togo (CCT), 1980.
I = Association des Eglises Chrétiennes (AEC) (Association of Christian Churches).
R = Conférence Episcopale du Togo (CET) (Episcopal Conference of Togo).

OTHER AFRICAN INDIGENOUS CHURCHES. A number of other Ghanaian and Nigerian bodies have followers in Togo. Among the total are: African Faith Tabernacle Ch, Army of the Cross of Christ Ch (MDCC) (from Ghana, among the Fante; 94 members), Bethlehem Revival Ch, Eglise du Christ Apostolique (Christ Apostolic Church from Nigeria).

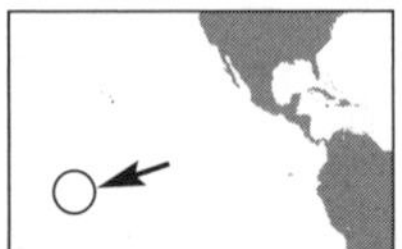

TOKELAU ISLANDS

SECULAR DATA, AD 2000

STATE
Official name: The Territory Overseas of the Tokelau Islands.
Short name: Tokelau Islands. **Adjective of nationality:** Tokelau Islanders.
Flag: That of New Zealand.
Area: 10 sq. km. (4 sq. mi.).
Government: Territory overseas of New Zealand, since 1949 (1925 New Zealand possession).
Legislature: Parliament and Council of Elders, 195 members.
Official language: English.
Monetary unit: 1 New Zealand dollar ($NZ) = 100 cents. **US$1=** $NZ 2.02.
Chief cities: Nukunonu 370.
Political divisions: 1 province.

DEMOGRAPHY
Population: 2,000.
Population density: 150.0/sq. km. (375.0/sq. mi.).
Under 15 years: 1,000.
Growth rate p.a.: 1.85% (births 27.33, deaths 4.64).
Mortality: Infant, per 1,000: 19.3; **Maternal per 100,000:** 50.0.
Life expectancy: 73 (male 71, female 75).
Household size: 5.0. **Floor area per person, sq.m:** 15.0.
Major languages: English, Tokelauan, Samoan.
Urban dwellers: 0.0%. **Urban growth rate p.a.:** 0.0%.
Labor force: 35%.

ETHNOLINGUISTIC PEOPLES
97.0% Tokelauan; 1.0% Samoan.

ECONOMY
National income p.a. per person: US$3,333; **per family:** US$16,666.

EDUCATION
Adult literacy: 99% (male 99%, female 99%). **Schools:** 1.
Universities: 0. **School enrolment:** female/male: 70%/70%.

HEALTH
Access to health services: 65%. **Access to safe water:** 70%.
Hospitals: 1 (20 beds per 10,000). **Doctors:** 5.
Blind: 15. **Deaf:** 100. **Murder rate:** 6.
Lepers: 0.

LITERATURE
New book titles p.a.: 1 (400 p.a. per million). **Periodicals:** 1.
Newspapers: 0 dailies.

COMMUNICATION (per 1,000 people)
Phones: 70 (20% mobile). **Radios:** 700. **TV sets:** 100.
Daily newspaper circulation: <1. **Computers:** 200.

HUMAN LIFE AND LIBERTY (optimum condition=100.0%)
HDI: 70.0. **HSI:** 75.0. **HFI:** 75.0. **EFL:** 35.0.

Country Table 1. **Religious adherents in the Tokelau Islands, AD 1900-2025.**

Year / Name	1900 Adherents	1900 %	1970 Adherents	1970 %	mid-1990 Adherents	mid-1990 %	Annual change, 1990-2000 Natural	Conversion	Total	Rate	mid-1995 Adherents	mid-1995 %	mid-2000 Adherents	mid-2000 %	mid-2025 Adherents	mid-2025 %
Christians	**900**	**100.0**	**1,640**	**96.8**	**1,540**	**96.3**	**-11**	**0**	**-11**	**-0.70**	**1,435**	**95.7**	**1,435**	**95.7**	**1,400**	**93.3**
PROFESSION																
professing Christians	**900**	**100.0**	**1,640**	**96.8**	**1,540**	**96.3**	**-11**	**0**	**-11**	**-0.70**	**1,435**	**95.7**	**1,435**	**95.7**	**1,400**	**93.3**
AFFILIATION																
unaffiliated Christians	0	0.0	240	14.2	80	5.0	-1	0	-1	-1.76	75	5.0	67	4.8	50	3.3
affiliated Christians	**900**	**100.0**	**1,400**	**82.6**	**1,460**	**81.3**	**-9**	**0**	**-9**	**-0.65**	**1,360**	**90.7**	**1,368**	**81.2**	**1,350**	**90.0**
Protestants	900	100.0	1,000	59.0	1,000	62.5	0	0	0	0.00	1,000	66.7	1,000	66.7	1,000	66.7
Roman Catholics	0	0.0	400	23.6	540	33.8	1	1	2	0.36	550	36.7	560	37.3	600	40.0
Marginal Christians	0	0.0	0	0.0	30	1.9	0	0	0	0.00	30	2.0	30	2.0	50	3.3
doubly-affiliated	0	0.0	0	0.0	-110	-6.9	-10	-1	-11	7.27	-220	-14.7	-222	-14.8	-300	-20.0
Trans-megabloc groupings																
Evangelicals	0	0.0	50	3.0	80	5.0	0	1	1	1.18	85	5.7	90	6.0	120	8.0
Pentecostals/Charismatics	0	0.0	20	1.2	70	4.4	0	1	1	0.69	71	4.7	75	5.0	90	6.0
Great Commission Christians	**60**	**6.7**	**200**	**11.8**	**290**	**18.1**	**0**	**-1**	**-1**	**-0.24**	**280**	**18.7**	**283**	**18.9**	**320**	**21.3**
Baha'is	0	0.0	60	3.5	60	3.8	0	1	1	0.80	65	4.3	65	4.3	100	6.7
World A (unevangelized persons)	0	0.0	3	0.2	2	0.1	0	0	0	0.00	1	0.1	2	0.1	2	0.1
World B (evangelized non-Christians)	0	0.0	50	3.0	58	3.6	0	1	1	2.09	63	4.2	63	4.2	98	6.6
World C (Christians)	900	100.0	1,640	96.8	1,540	96.3	-10	-1	-11	-0.70	1,435	95.7	1,435	95.7	1,400	93.3
Country's population	**900**	**100.0**	**1,694**	**100.0**	**1,600**	**100.0**	**-10**	**0**	**-10**	**0.00**	**1,500**	**100.0**	**1,500**	**100.0**	**1,500**	**100.0**

COLUMNS, ROWS.
For meanings and definitions, see Codebook (Part 3). Note that, by definition, total 'Christians' = professing + crypto-Christians, which also = affiliated + unaffiliated Christians, and also = Great Commission Christians + latent Christians. Percentages may not always total exactly, due to rounding.

CENSUSES.
25.IX.1945: 66.9% Protestants, 33.1% Roman Catholics. **25.IX.1951** (indigenous population only): 63.2% Protestants, 36.3% Roman Catholics, 0.4% other religionists. **25.IX.1961**: 62.9% Protestants (LMS), 37.0% Roman Catholics. **21.II.1972**: 70.2% Protestants (LMS), 28.3% Roman Catholics, 1.4% other religionists.

NOTES ON RELIGIONS
BAHA'IS. With at present no organized local spiritual assembly.
COUNTRY'S POPULATION. After 1960, the population fell from 1,870 (1961) to 1,700 (1970), and to 1,600 in 1980, due to 700 Tokelauans being encouraged to emigrate for resettlement in the North Island of New Zealand; in 1990 emigration was continuing at the rate of 100 persons a year, considerably larger than the natural (biological) population increase. The column 'Natural change' above shows the average annual natural increase (biological plus migration) from 1990-2000.
ROMAN CATHOLICS. Though Catholics were present in numbers as immigrants long before 1946, mission work was not organized until that year.

Great Commission Instrument Panel: status of the Tokelau Islands (for explanation see start of Part 4)

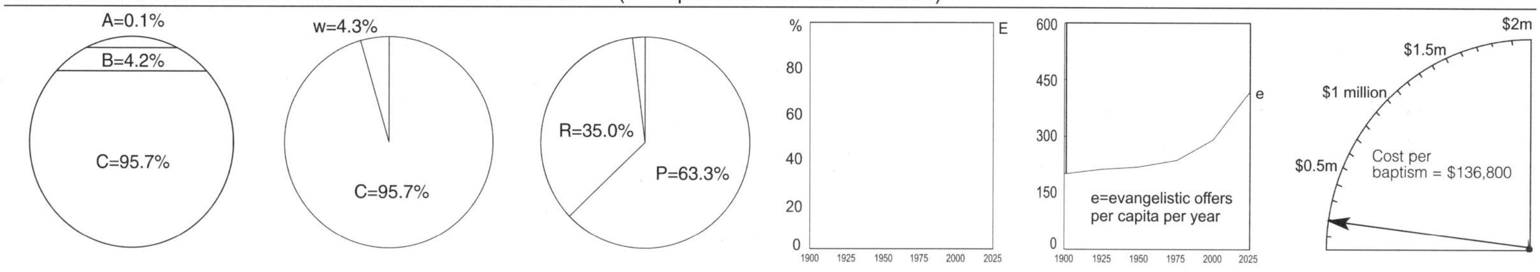

3 Worlds, AD 2000 — Religions, AD 2000 — Ecclesiastical blocs — Evangelization, 1900-2025 — Offers, 1900-2025 — Cost-effectiveness, AD 2000

Country summary. **Worlds A, B, C by ethnolinguistic peoples, cities, and major civil divisions in the Tokelau Islands.**

World	PEOPLES Num	Pop 2000	C%	Christians	E%	U%	Unevangelized	CITIES Num	Pop 2000	C%	Christians	E%	U%	Unevangelized	CIVIL DIVISIONS Num	Pop 2000	C%	Christians	E%	U%	Unevangelized
A	0	0	0.00	0	0	0	0	0	0	0.00	0	0	0	0	0	0	0.00	0	0	0	0
B	0	0	0.00	0	0	0	0	0	0	0.00	0	0	0	0	0	0	0.00	0	0	0	0
C	3	1,500	91.20	1,368	100	0	1	1	370	91.35	338	100	0	1	1	1,500	91.20	1,368	100	0	1
Total	**3**	**1,500**	**91.20**	**1,368**	**100**	**0**	**1**	**1**	**370**	**91.35**	**338**	**100**	**0**	**1**	**1**	**1,500**	**91.20**	**1,368**	**100**	**0**	**1**

Country status. Tokelau Islands is a group of islands in the western Pacific Ocean between Kiribati and Samoa.

HUMAN LIFE AND LIBERTY

Human rights and freedoms. Tokelau Islands is a territory of New Zealand where New Zealand laws protecting human rights apply.

NON-CHRISTIAN RELIGIONS

Baha'i has a small work in the islands. No other religions exist, the original traditional Polynesian religions having disappeared over the past 2 centuries.

CHRISTIANITY

Only 2 churches exist in the islands, the Church in Tokelau and the Catholic Church. The former is congregationalist in polity and owes its origin to the evangelistic outreach of the London Missionary Society from 1861. Congregationalists in 1995 made up 63% of the population, and Catholics 37%. The inhabitants of Atafu Island are Protestants while Nukunono Island is entirely Catholic. Both denominations are present on Fakaofo Island. Catholic administration places the Tokelau Islands in the diocese of Apia in Western Samoa. There are 2 Catholic parishes, the one on Nukunono Island being administered by a priest, while the other on Fakaofo Island is served by a full-time catechist with the faculties of a deacon.

The Holy See has no diplomatic relations with Tokelau Islands in AD 2000 but has an apostolic delegate for the Pacific Ocean residing in Wellington, New Zealand.

Indigenous missions. A few Christians have served as foreign missionaries, primarily in other islands in the Pacific.

CHURCH AND STATE

Atafu Island was first sighted by British seamen in 1765, followed by Nukunono in 1791 and Fakaofo in 1835. A British protectorate was proclaimed over the 3 atolls in 1877, and in 1925 the islands became territories of New Zealand. Freedom of religion has never been an issue and since 1926 has been guaranteed by New Zealand's constitution.

Two of the numerous postage stamps with Christian themes: Nativity in 1969 and 1970.

FUTURE TRENDS AND PROSPECTS

Baha'is are expected to grow to over 6% of the population before 2025.

Nonetheless, the Tokelau Islands will likely remain predominately Christian for the next fifty years.

BIBLIOGRAPHY

Archives of the Catholic Diocese of Samoa and Tokelau. : Catholic Church Diocese of Samoa and Tokelau, 1985. (49 reels of microfilm).
Bibliographies of the Kermadec Islands, Niue, Swains Island and the Tokelau Islands. W. G. Coppell. Honolulu, HI: Pacific Islands Studies Program, University of Hawaii, 1975. 102p.
Matagi Tokelau: history and traditions of Tokelau. Trans., A. Hooper & J. Huntsman. Apia, Western Samoa: Office for Tokelau Affairs, Institute of Pacific Studies, University of the South Pacific, 1991. 284p.
'Religion as a factor in the adjustment of immigrants: Tokelau Island community in the Wellingston area,' D. W. Boardman, *Social compass*, 26, 1 (1979), 73–85.
Report on survey of music in Tokelau, Western Polynesia. A. Thomas. *Working papers in anthropology, archaeology, linguistics, Maori studies*, no. 79. Auckland, New Zealand: Dept of Anthropology, University of Auckland, [1988]. 20p.
Songs and stories of Tokelau: an introduction to the cultural heritage. A. Thomas, I. Tuia & J. Huntsman (eds). Wellington, New Zealand: Victoria University Press, 1990. 88p.
Tokelau national bibliography (= Fakamaumauga o na Tuhituhiga o Tokelau), (1992–). (Cumulative, published irregularly).

Country Table 2. **Organized churches and denominations in the Tokelau Islands.**

Official name (bold type = church with over 10% of all affiliated) 1	*Begun* 2	*Type* 3	*Counc* 4	*Congs* 5	*Adults* 6	*Affiliated 1970* 7	*Affiliated 1995* 8	*G%* 9	*Names, notes, and other statistics* (see Codebook, Part 3) 10
Catholic Church: m Tokelau	1946	R-Lat	P.PY.	2	250	400	550	1.28	*Mission Sui Juris of Tokelau.* All Nukunono, part Fakaofo, M=SM2. School. 1n,1m,2w,25Yy
Congregational Christian Ch in Samoa	1861	P-Con	Rwp..	6	420	1,000	900	-0.42	*Church in Tokelau.* M=LMS(UK),CCCS(Samoa). Atafu, part Fakaofo. 40mw,W=95%,24y.
Jehovah's Witnesses	1985	m-Jeh	x....	1	8	–	30	10.00	*Watch Tower. IBSA.*
Other Protestant churches	c1980	P-	.....	3	50	–	100	6.67	Other visiting Protestant bodies, including Seventh-day Adventists (15 members).
Doubly-affiliated		2-aff			-100	0	-220		Evangelicals who are also baptized Roman Catholics.
Totals				**12**	**628**	**1,400**	**1,360**		

Churches, members, growth, 1900-2025	*Congs*	*Adults*	*Affiliated*	*G%*	*Total denominations*	*6 Megablocs:* O	R	A	P	I	m
Total churches, members, and denominations (mid-1900)	4	390	900	0.63	1	0	0	0	1	0	0
Total churches, members, and denominations (mid-1970)	7	600	1,400	0.63	2	0	1	0	1	0	0
Total churches, members, and denominations (mid-1990)	10	670	1,460	0.21	6	0	1	0	4	0	1
Total churches, members, and denominations (mid-1995)	12	628	1,360	-1.41	6	0	1	0	4	0	1
Total churches, members, and denominations (mid-2000)	20	630	1,368	0.12	6	0	1	0	4	0	1
Total churches, members, and denominations (mid-2025)	30	620	1,350	-0.05	20	0	1	0	8	10	1

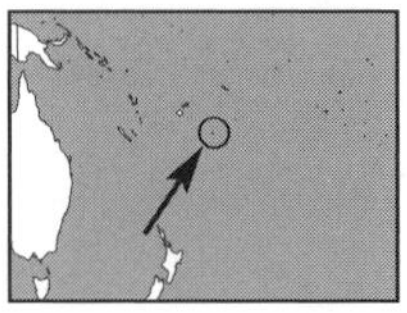

TONGA

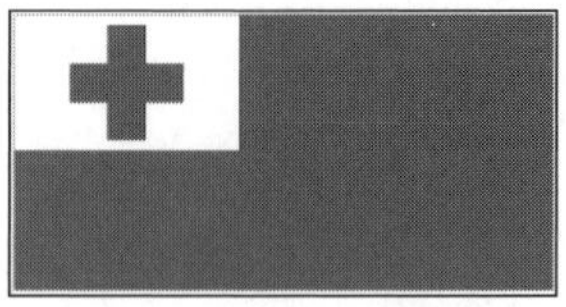

SECULAR DATA, AD 2000

STATE
Official name: Pule'anga Fakatu'i 'o Tonga/The Kingdom of Tonga.
Short name: Tonga. **Adjective of nationality:** Tongan.
Flag: Red field with red cross on white square in upper hoist corner.
Area: 750 sq. km. (290 sq. mi.).
Government: Constitutional monarchy, since 1862 (c1000 absolute monarchy, 1862 constitutional monarchy, 1900 British protectorate, 1970 Independence).
Legislature: Legislative Assembly, 30 members.
Official language: Tongan, English.
Monetary unit: 1 pa'anga (T$) = 100 ceniti. **US$1=** T$1.70.
Chief cities: NUKU'ALOFA 23,605.
Political divisions: 5 provinces.
Armed forces: 300.

DEMOGRAPHY
Population: 99,000.
Population density: 131.3/sq. km. (339.8/sq. mi.).
Under 15 years: 38,000.
Growth rate p.a.: 1.85% (births 27.33, deaths 4.64).
Mortality: Infant, per 1,000: 19.3; **Maternal per 100,000:** 60.0.
Life expectancy: 73 (male 71, female 75).
Household size: 6.1. **Floor area per person, sq.m:** 13.0.
Major languages: Tongan, English.
Urban dwellers: 46.37%. **Urban growth rate p.a.:** 2.3%.
Labor force: 34%.

ETHNOLINGUISTIC PEOPLES
95.1% Tongan; 1.6% Niuatoputapu; 0.7% Euronesian (Eurasian); 0.6% Niuafoou; 0.3% Anglo-Australian.

ECONOMY
National income p.a. per person: US$1,633; **per family:** US$9,965.

EDUCATION
Adult literacy: 92% (male 92%, female 92%). **Schools:** 163.
Universities: 1. **School enrolment:** female/male: 90%/90%.

HEALTH
Access to health services: 80%. **Access to safe water:** 100%.
Hospitals: 4 (31 beds per 10,000). **Doctors:** 46.
Blind: 80. **Deaf:** 6,000. **Murder rate:** 3. **Lepers:** 200.

LITERATURE
New book titles p.a.: 30 (300 p.a. per million). **Periodicals:** 11.
Newspapers: 1 daily.

COMMUNICATION (per 1,000 people)
Phones: 67 **(20% mobile). Radios:** 400. **TV sets:** 20.
Daily newspaper circulation: 73. **Computers:** 30.

HUMAN LIFE AND LIBERTY (optimum condition=100.0%)
HDI: 62.9. **HSI:** 70.0. **HFI:** 65.0. **EFL:** 35.0.

Country Table 1. **Religious adherents in Tonga, AD 1900-2025.**

Year	*1900*		*1970*		*mid-1990*		*Annual change, 1990-2000*				*mid-1995*		*mid-2000*		*mid-2025*	
Name	*Adherents*	*%*	*Adherents*	*%*	*Adherents*	*%*	*Natural*	*Conversion*	*Total*	*Rate*	*Adherents*	*%*	*Adherents*	*%*	*Adherents*	*%*
Christians	**20,000**	**100.0**	**80,670**	**98.7**	**90,700**	**94.7**	**261**	**-172**	**89**	**0.10**	**90,850**	**93.5**	**91,588**	**92.9**	**95,360**	**90.8**
PROFESSION																
professing Christians	**20,000**	**100.0**	**80,670**	**98.7**	**90,700**	**94.7**	**261**	**-172**	**89**	**0.10**	**90,850**	**93.5**	**91,588**	**92.9**	**95,360**	**90.8**
AFFILIATION																
unaffiliated Christians	80	0.4	545	0.7	1,680	1.8	5	17	22	1.24	1,805	1.9	1,900	1.9	1,360	1.3
affiliated Christians	**19,920**	**99.6**	**80,125**	**98.0**	**89,020**	**92.4**	**256**	**-189**	**67**	**0.07**	**89,045**	**91.7**	**89,688**	**90.9**	**94,000**	**89.5**
Protestants	3,080	15.4	38,691	47.3	41,900	43.8	109	-67	42	0.10	41,905	43.1	42,320	42.9	43,000	41.0
Independents	16,360	81.8	14,300	17.5	19,700	20.5	62	48	110	0.54	20,358	21.0	20,798	21.0	27,000	25.7
Marginal Christians	0	0.0	15,992	19.6	14,500	15.1	45	-60	-15	-0.10	14,391	14.8	14,350	14.5	13,800	13.1
Roman Catholics	480	2.4	14,342	17.5	13,750	14.3	43	-28	15	0.11	13,824	14.2	13,900	14.0	14,200	13.5
Anglicans	0	0.0	800	1.0	670	0.7	2	-3	-1	-0.15	667	0.7	660	0.7	600	0.6
doubly-affiliated	0	0.0	-4,000	-4.9	-1,500	-1.6	-5	-79	-84	4.55	-2,100	-2.2	-2,340	-2.4	-4,600	-4.4
Trans-megabloc groupings																
Evangelicals	2,600	13.0	6,400	7.8	7,200	7.5	23	-8	15	0.21	7,276	7.5	7,350	7.4	8,000	7.6
Pentecostals/Charismatics	0	0.0	1,300	1.6	11,200	11.7	35	75	110	0.94	11,843	12.2	12,300	12.4	15,000	14.3
Great Commission Christians	**1,400**	**7.0**	**14,720**	**18.0**	**26,580**	**27.8**	**83**	**52**	**135**	**0.50**	**27,470**	**28.3**	**27,926**	**28.4**	**33,000**	**31.4**
Baha'is	0	0.0	1,100	1.4	4,875	5.1	15	156	171	3.05	6,045	6.2	6,582	6.7	9,000	8.6
Nonreligious	0	0.0	0	0.0	100	0.1	0	6	6	4.48	130	0.1	155	0.2	400	0.4
Buddhists	0	0.0	0	0.0	90	0.1	0	3	3	2.75	100	0.1	118	0.1	180	0.2
Hindus	0	0.0	30	0.0	30	0.0	0	7	7	12.68	70	0.1	99	0.1	50	0.1
Ethnoreligionists	0	0.0	0	0.0	5	0.0	0	0	0	0.00	5	0.0	5	0.0	10	0.0
World A (unevangelized persons)	0	0.0	0	0.0	96	0.1	0	3	3	4.25	97	0.1	99	0.1	105	0.1
World B (evangelized non-Christians)	0	0.0	1,080	1.3	5,204	5.2	15	169	184	3.46	6,214	6.4	7,313	7.0	9,535	9.1
World C (Christians)	20,000	100.0	80,670	98.7	90,700	94.7	261	-172	89	0.10	90,850	93.5	91,588	92.9	95,360	90.8
Country's population	**20,000**	**100.0**	**81,750**	**100.0**	**96,000**	**100.0**	**276**	**0**	**276**	**0.31**	**97,162**	**100.0**	**99,000**	**100.0**	**105,000**	**100.0**

COLUMNS, ROWS.
For meanings and definitions, see Codebook (Part 3). Note that, by definition, total 'Christians' = professing + crypto-Christians, which also = affiliated + unaffiliated Christians, and also = Great Commission Christians + latent Christians. Percentages may not always total exactly, due to rounding.

CENSUSES.
26-27.IX.1956: 51.1% Protestants (49.6% Free Wesleyans, 1.5% SD Adventists), 27.7% Polynesian indigenous (17.6% Free Ch of Tonga, 9.9% Ch of Tonga), 14.8% Roman Catholics, 5.2% marginal Protestants (Mormons), 0.9% Anglicans, 0.3% other religionists.
30.XI.1966: 52.0% Protestants (49.9% Free Wesleyans, 1.8% SD Adventists), 23.4% Polynesian indigenous (14.3% Free Ch of Tonga, 9.0% Ch of Tonga), 16.0% Roman Catholics, 7.3% marginal Protestants (Mormons), 1.0% Anglicans, 0.3% Baha'is.

NOTES ON RELIGIONS
BAHA'IS. Growth from 6 local spiritual assemblies (1964) to 13 (1973), followed by a vast surge of interest resulting by 1995 in 70 LSAs.
HINDUS. Indians.
INDEPENDENTS. In 4 denominations in 1995 (see Table 2), the first dating from the year 1885.
MARGINAL CHRISTIANS. Professing Mormons grew from 2,925 (5.2% of the population) in the 1956 census to 5,519 (7.3%) in the 1966 census. However, affiliated Mormons known to the church itself have been far more numerous: in 1930, 1,185; (1940) 1,777; (1950) 2,820; (1960) 5,160; (1965) 8,560; (1967) 10,835; (1970) 14,355; (1971) 15,842. This has been due to a vast and continuing influx of persons professing in censuses to be Methodists into the new Mormon churches and schools. Although the growth rate of affiliated Mormons rose as high as 10% per year in 1970, it then rapidly fell to its average of 3.4% per year for the 2 decades 1970-90.

Country status. The Kingdom of Tonga, formerly a British protected state and now an independent member of the Commonwealth, comprises 169 islands in the South Pacific. Its chief exports are copra, coconut products, and fish.

HUMAN LIFE AND LIBERTY

Human rights and freedoms. Although Tonga is a constitutional monarchy, tradition gives the king wide powers and a small group of nobles dominate political life. The nobles own much of the land and also control the Legislative Assembly.

NON-CHRISTIAN RELIGIONS

Baha'i has a growing community of followers who have experienced phenomenal growth for 20 years or more.

CHRISTIANITY

PROTESTANT CHURCHES. Pioneers of the London Missionary Society reached Tonga as early as 1797, but local opposition forced their withdrawal after 3 missionaries were massacred in 1799. A further unsuccessful attempt was made in 1822 by Wesleyan missionaries, but after 1825 a permanent work resulted. Evangelization centered on the conversion of chiefs who in turn led their peoples into the church. When Taufa'ahau (later George Tupou I) became king of Tonga in 1845, Christianity became the dominant religion, and by 1853 all Tongans were Christians, at

Great Commission Instrument Panel: status of Tonga (for explanation see start of Part 4)

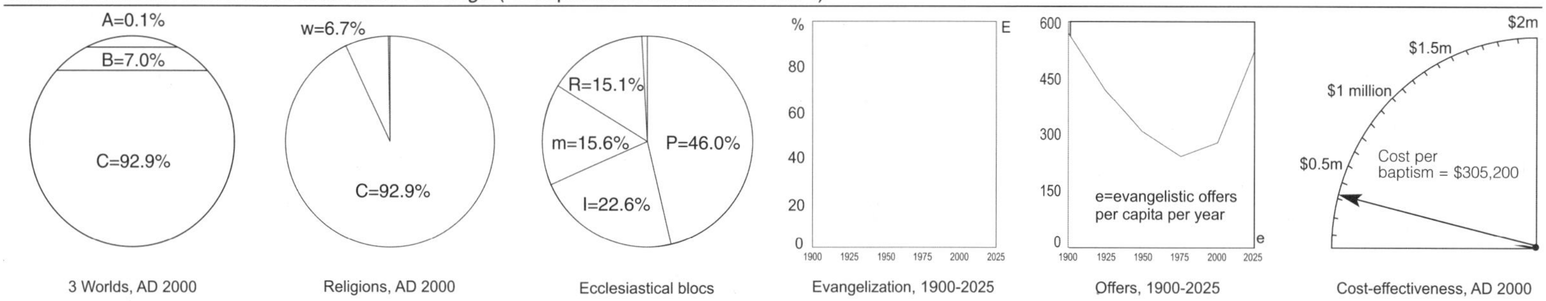

Country summary. **Worlds A, B, C by ethnolinguistic peoples, cities, and major civil divisions in Tonga.**

	PEOPLES							*CITIES*							*CIVIL DIVISIONS*						
World	*Num*	*Pop 2000*	*C%*	*Christians*	*E%*	*U%*	*Unevangelized*	*Num*	*Pop 2000*	*C%*	*Christians*	*E%*	*U%*	*Unevangelized*	*Num*	*Pop 2000*	*C%*	*Christians*	*E%*	*U%*	*Unevangelized*
A	0	0	0.00	0	0	0	0	0	0	0.00	0	0	0	0	0	0	0.00	0	0	0	0
B	1	197	29.95	59	99	1	1	0	0	0.00	0	0	0	0	0	0	0.00	0	0	0	0
C	9	98,349	91.13	89,630	100	0	89	1	23,605	90.00	21,245	100	0	45	5	98,547	91.01	89,688	100	0	92
Total	**10**	**98,546**	**91.01**	**89,689**	**100**	**0**	**90**	**1**	**23,605**	**90.00**	**21,245**	**100**	**0**	**45**	**5**	**98,547**	**91.01**	**89,688**	**100**	**0**	**92**

least in name. Methodists today are divided into 4 denominations. The main body is the Free Wesleyan Church, the original mission-controlled parent body. In 1885, however, in a desire for local autonomy led by the king and his prime minister (previously a Methodist missionary), an independent body, the Wesleyan Free Church, was founded by the king in opposition to the original church and mission and all Christians were ordered to join it on pain of persecution.

Methodists. Worship in Methodist church on outskirts of Nuku' Alofa.

INDIGENOUS CHURCHES. For 4 decades the 2 churches were bitter rivals. An attempt by the monarch to unite the 2 groups in 1924 brought together 4,000 old Wesleyans with 12,000 Free Wesleyans while another 6,000 Free Wesleyans refused, preferring to continue as the separate body, renamed the Free Church of Tonga. This latter church has been declining rapidly in influence since then, especially since the 1950s, and has experienced 2 further schisms: the Church of Tonga in 1929, and the much smaller Church of the Red Coats in 1962. Tonga is still predominantly Methodist, although Methodists are tending to lose their proportionate place in the population to the rapidly-growing Assemblies of God, Adventists, and Mormons.

Church of Jesus Christ of Latter-day Saints. Mormon Temple in Nuku' Alofa.

CATHOLIC CHURCH. A Catholic missionary tried unsuccessfully to enter Tonga in 1837. Marist Fathers also suffered persecution after their arrival in 1842, but religious freedom was proclaimed in a treaty between Tonga and France in 1855. The first Tongan priest was ordained in 1933. The vicariate of Tonga was erected in 1937 and became a diocese in 1966. The Catholic population continues to grow.

The Holy See has diplomatic relations with Tonga and in AD 2000 is represented to government and the Catholic hierarchy by a nuncio residing in Wellington, New Zealand.

MARGINAL CHURCHES. Mormons have recently become the fastest-growing denomination in Tonga, mostly at the expense of Methodists. With a very large number of Mormon missionaries from the USA, they have launched an aggressive program of building 40 new churches a year and are attracting large numbers through their extensive school system. A small Jehovah's Witnesses community exists also.

Indigenous missions. Since 1829, many Tongans have served as missionaries, particularly in the South Pacific. In recent times, many have served in Asia and other parts of the world.

Free Wesleyan Church of Tonga. Speech from the Throne by king Tanfa'ahai Tupou IV after 1967 Coronation by Methodist clergy.

CHURCH AND STATE

The Tongan state specifies its religious conviction in its constitution of 1 January 1967, Part I, Declaration of Rights, Article 1: 'Since it appears to be the will of God that man should be free as He has made all men of one blood...'. Constitutionally, the Tongan monarch is the head of the Free Wesleyan Church of Tonga and ratifies the annual appointment of the church's elected president. The Free Wesleyan Church enjoys a special position because of its majority status and the prominence given to the royal family within its membership. From earliest days the monarchs have played an active role. The 19th-century kings were the principal forces contributing to the christianization of the islands. In 1885 king Tupou I was a prime mover in the separation of the Free Church from its parent body, the Wesleyan Church; and in 1924, the queen, recognized as the 'chief member' of the Free Church, was involved in the attempt to heal the breach between the 2 churches.

Tonga is one of the few countries of the world where the observance of Sunday as a day of rest receives special mention in the constitution: 'The Sabbath Day shall be sacred in Tonga for ever and it shall not be lawful to do work or play games or trade on the Sabbath. And any agreement made or documents witnessed on this day shall be counted void and not recognized by the Government' (Article 6).

BROADCASTING AND MEDIA

CBN's *International 700 Club* and *Another Life* can be viewed on local channels 3 days a week. TBN programs appear in Nuku-Alofa on local channel 7. Some 30% have seen the 'Jesus' film.

Tonga is a member of UNDA.

INTERDENOMINATIONAL ORGANIZATIONS

The Tonga Council of Churches has functioned effectively since its formation in 1973.

FUTURE TRENDS AND PROSPECTS

Baha'is are expected to grow from 1.4% in 1970 to 8.6% by AD 2025 with corresponding losses among Christians.

Christianity is therefore likely to decline slowly but steadily over the next fifty years due to the growth of Baha'is and the nonreligious.

BIBLIOGRAPHY

A bibliography of the Church of Jesus Christ of Latter–day Saints in Tonga. F. A. Bruno & C. Cox. Laie, HI, 1989. 17p.

'A study in authority and power in the Free Wesleyan Church of Tonga, 1977–82.' J. M. Connan. Th.M. thesis, Fuller Theological Seminary, Pasadena, CA, 1985. 144p.

'A study in the nature of the church as seen in the Anglican Church in Tonga.' V. T. Tohi. B.D. thesis, Pacific Theological College, Suva, Fiji, 1972. 122p.

'Adult Christian education for the Free Wesleyan Church in Tonga.' A. M. Mone. D.Min. thesis, School of Theology at Claremont, Claremont, CA, 1979. 104p.

Archives of the Catholic Diocese of Tonga. Catholic Church Diocese of Tonga. Nukualofa, Tonga: Bishop's House, Havelu-loto, 1985. 25 reels in microform.

'Church and politics in Tonga: an attempt to analyze the political system and to see the roles of the church in the distribution of political power.' M. K. Tafea. B.D. thesis, Pacific Theological College, Suva, Fiji, 1978. 85p.

'Church and state in Tonga: the influence of the Wesleyan Methodist missionaries on the political development of Tonga, 1826–1875.' S. Loatoukefu. Ph.D. dissertation, Australian National University, Canberra, Australia, 1967. 637p.

'Family life in the village of Tongoleleka (Haapai): a concern for Christian pastoral care.' S. V. Taufatofua. B.D. thesis, Pacific Theological College, Suva, Fiji, 1986. 94p.

In the eye of the storm. J. H. Groberg. Salt Lake City, UT: Bookcraft, 1993. 315p. (On Mormon missionaries to Tonga).

'Inventing Mormon identity in Tonga.' T. G. Gordon. Ph.D. dissertation, University of California, Berkeley, CA, 1988. 240p.

'Marriage and family life in Tonga: strategies to strengthen marriages and family life in Tongan villages through the Free Wesleyan Church of Tonga.' S. T. Finau. D.Min. thesis, School of Theology at Claremont, Claremont, CA, 1979. 177p.

'Methodist missionary influence on native education in Tonga, Fiji and Papua–New Guinea with special reference to government–mission relationships since 1942.' R. C. Wilkinson. M.Ed. thesis, University of Sydney, Sydney, Australia, 1959. 372p.

'Missionaries in the last kingdom.' D. P. Harris. B.A. thesis, Harvard University, Cambridge, MA, 1989. 89p.

Overseas missions of the Australian Methodist Church. A. H. Wood. Melbourne: Aldersgate Press, [1975–78]. 3 vols.

'Pastoral visiting (an aspect of pastoral care): a critical assessment of pastoral visiting in Tongan Free Wesleyan village churches.' S. T. Finau. B.D. project, Pacific Theological College, Suva, Fiji, 1975. 106p.

People movements in Southern Polynesia: studies in the dynamics of church–planting and growth in Tahiti, New Zealand, Tonga, and Samoa. A. R. Tippett. Chicago: Moody Press, 1971. 288p.

Seeds of the word: Tongan culture and Christian faith: report of Tonga Workshop, June 20 – July 3, 1979. C. Wright (ed). Vila, New Hebrides: Pacific Churches Research Centre, 1979. 43p.

'Sunday school in the Church of Tonga.' T. F. Mafi. Project, Pacific Theological College, Suva, Fiji, 1978. 126p.
'The emergence of the Maamaf'ou movement from the Free Wesleyan Church of Tonga: a project.' M. Finau. B.D. thesis, Pacific Theological College, Suva, Fiji, 1986. 121p.
Tongan prayers and sermons. K. Lofstrom (ed). N.p., 1984. (Primarily Methodist, in Tongan).
Tongan saints: legacy of faith. E. B. Shumway (ed). Laie, HI: Institute for Polynesian Studies, 1991. 369p. (Mormon history).
'Toward contextualization: an attempt at contextualizing theology for the Tongan church.' T. T. M. Puloka. D.Min. thesis, School of Theology at Claremont, Claremont, CA, 1979. 170p.

Country Table 2. **Organized churches and denominations in Tonga.**

Official name (bold type = church with over 10% of all affiliated) 1	*Begun* 2	*Type* 3	*Councl* 4	*Congs* 5	*Adults* 6	*Affiliated 1970* 7	*Affiliated 1995* 8	*G%* 9	*Names, notes, and other statistics* (see Codebook, Part 3) 10
Anglican Church (D Polynesia)	1902	A-Hig	awpKK	7	400	800	667	-0.72	*CPNZ.* In Ch of the Province of New Zealand. 80% Tongan. 3n,W=21%,3Y,31y.
Assemblies of God of Tonga	c1930	P-Pe2	ZF...	21	1,018	1,250	1,325	0.23	1965, M=AoG(USA). Rapid growth. Many nominal Methodists. 65n,2x,2f,W=75%,100Y.
Catholic Church: D Tonga	1837	R-Lat	pzPYK	13	7,000	14,342	13,824	-0.15	C=1+0+1. (1970) 8n,10x,2m,75w,914Yy. (1990) , 15n, 6x, 27m, 55w, 429Yy
Christian Brethren	c1960	P-CBr	x....	2	150	100	300	4.49	*Plymouth Brethren. Open Brethren. Gospel Hall.* Independent congregation.
Church of Christ (Nashville)		I-3oW	x....	1	40	–	60	0.05	Oneness pentecostal mission from USA.
Church of God & the People of Tonga	1962	I-Met	.....	2	30	100	60	-2.02	*Church of the Red Coats.* Indigenous schism ex Free Church of Tonga.
Ch of Jesus C of Latter-day Saints	1916	m-LdS	x....	117	11,483	15,842	14,200	-0.44	*Mormons* (USA). Many new churches each year, also schools. 250f,1r(1200).
Church of Tonga	1929	I-Met	..P.K	41	4,140	6,000	6,222	0.15	Large indigenous schism ex Free Church of Tonga. Methodist polity.
Churches of Christ	c1955	I-Dis	x....	2	75	200	150	-1.14	M=Churches of Christ(Non-Instrumental) (USA). In Nuku'alofa. Independents. 1f.
Free Church of Tonga	1885	I-Met	....k	81	7,320	8,000	9,286	0.60	Schism of 82% ex Wesleyan Ch, led by king. 1967, prophetess movement. Declining.
Free Constitutional Church	c1980	I-Met	.....	15	900	–	1,200	6.67	Independent Methodists.
Free Wesleyan Church of Tonga	1822	P-Met	VWP.K	190	11,400	35,641	34,000	-0.19	*FWCT. Siasi Vesiliana Tauataina o Tonga.* 114n,3x,92mw,8r,1s,W=55%,870Yy.
Jehovah's Witnesses	c1937	m-Jeh	x....	3	63	150	191	0.97	*Watch Tower. IBSA.* Active witnessing in 1937, reported from 1963 on. (1975) 2y. (1995) 7Y
New Apostolic Church	c1992	I-3aX	x....	2	80	–	121	33.33	*NAC.* M=Neuapostolische Kirche. HQ Zurich (Switzerland).
Salvation Army		P-Sal	.....	6	110	–	150	0.05	M=Salvation Army(UK,NZ).
Seventh-day Adventist Church	1895	P-Adv	x...k	15	2,190	1,700	5,130	4.52	*Tonga Mission*, Central Pacific UM. Organized 1921. 10nx,25mw,1s,25t(1200),28Y.
Tokaikolo Christian Fellowship	1978	I-3cP	.....	10	1,530	–	3,059	5.88	*TCF.* Ex Free Wesleyan Ch of Tonga. 20n,60 deacons. Abroad: NZ, USA, Australia.
Tongan Fellowship for Revival	c1980	I-3cP	.....	4	70	–	200	6.67	Tongan indigenous charismatics.
Other Protestant bodies	c1975	P-	.....	10	600	–	1,000	5.00	Total about 8 recent missions.
Doubly-affiliated		2-aff			-1,100	-4,000	-2,100		Pentecostals and Evangelicals who are also baptized Catholics or Methodists.
Totals				**542**	**47,499**	**80,125**	**89,045**		

Churches, members, growth, 1900-2025	*Congs*	*Adults*	*Affiliated*	*G%*	*Total denominations*	*6 Megablocs:* O	R	A	P	I	m
Total churches, members, and denominations (mid-1900)	100	11,000	19,920	2.01	4	0	1	0	2	1	0
Total churches, members, and denominations (mid-1970)	470	44,234	80,125	2.01	12	0	1	1	4	4	2
Total churches, members, and denominations (mid-1990)	500	47,500	89,020	0.53	26	0	1	1	13	9	2
Total churches, members, and denominations (mid-1995)	542	47,499	89,045	0.01	26	0	1	1	13	9	2
Total churches, members, and denominations (mid-2000)	600	47,800	89,688	0.14	26	0	1	1	13	9	2
Total churches, members, and denominations (mid-2025)	1,000	50,100	94,000	0.19	60	0	1	1	25	30	3

NOTES ON TABLE ABOVE
NATIONAL COUNCILS (Column 4, 5th letter).
E = Tonga Evangelical Union (TEU).
K = Tonga Council of Churches (TCC) (1973; formerly Inter-Church Committee, formed 1968).
k = fraternal member of TCC.

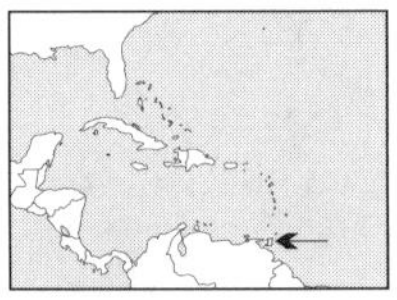

TRINIDAD & TOBAGO

SECULAR DATA, AD 2000

STATE
Official name: The Republic of Trinidad and Tobago.
Short name: Trinidad & Tobago. **Adjective of nationality:** of Trinidad and Tobago.
Flag: Red field crossed diagonally by white-bordered black stripe.
Area: 5,128 sq. km. (1,980 sq. mi.).
Government: Parliamentary republic, since 1976 (1498 Spanish possession, 1802 British crown colony of Trinidad, 1889 colony with Tobago, 1958-61 in West Indies Federation, 1962 Independence as parliamentary constitutional monarchy, 1976 republic).
Legislature: Parliament: Senate, 21 members; House of Representatives, 36 members.
Official language: English.
Monetary unit: 1 Trinidad and Tobago dollar (TT$) = 100 cents.
US$1= TT$6.24.
Chief cities: PORT OF SPAIN 434,022; San Fernando 83,683.
Political divisions: 12 provinces.
Armed forces: 2,100.

DEMOGRAPHY
Population: 1,295,000.
Population density: 252.5/sq. km. (654.0/sq. mi.).
Under 15 years: 324,000.
Growth rate p.a.: 0.53% (births 13.72, deaths 6.01).
Mortality: Infant, per 1,000: 12.8; **Maternal per 100,000:** 90.0.
Life expectancy: 75 (male 73, female 77).
Household size: 4.1. **Floor area per person, sq.m:** 14.0.
Major languages: English, Spanish, Hindi, Chinese, Portuguese, Arabic, Arawak.
Urban dwellers: 74.08%. **Urban growth rate p.a.:** 1.5%.
Labor force: 41%.

ETHNOLINGUISTIC PEOPLES
39.2% Trinidad Black; 34.9% East Indian; 16.3% Trinidad Mulatto; 3.7% Caribbean Hindi (Awadhi); 1.6% Han Chinese (Hakka).

ECONOMY
National income p.a. per person: US$3,770; **per family:** US$15,457.

EDUCATION
Adult literacy: 97% (male 98%, female 97%). **Schools:** 576.
Universities: 1. **School enrolment:** female/male: 88%/86%.

HEALTH
Access to health services: 100%. **Access to safe water:** 82%.
Hospitals: 31 (33 beds per 10,000). **Doctors:** 1,051.
Blind: 1,300. **Deaf:** 80,400. **Murder rate:** 11.
Lepers: 3,000. **Underweight prevalence under 5:** 7%.

LITERATURE
New book titles p.a.: 50 (40 p.a. per million). **Periodicals:** 28.
Newspapers: 4 dailies.

COMMUNICATION (per 1,000 people)
Phones: 166 (8% mobile). **Radios:** 433. **TV sets:** 328.
Daily newspaper circulation: 135. **Computers:** 50.

HUMAN LIFE AND LIBERTY (optimum condition=100.0%)
HDI: 88.0. **HSI:** 71.0. **HFI:** 62.5. **EFL:** 50.0.

Country status. Trinidad and Tobago is the southernmost island country of the Lesser Antilles in the Caribbean, near the coast of Venezuela. It has an unusual racial composition comprising East Indians and Blacks. Its main economic activity is the production of petroleum products.

HUMAN LIFE AND LIBERTY

Human need and development. Despite the economic reverses of the late 1980s, Trinidad has a relatively high standard of living and also high level of human services, including health and education. The income is fairly evenly distributed and the entire population participates in the market economy. Extreme poverty is rare. One factor contributing to this absence of destitution is the extended family system which makes it possible for impoverished members to be supported by the more affluent ones. There is also a wide range of public services covering medical and child care, housing, nutritional assistance for children, and pensions for the elderly. The average diet is adequate or very close to adequate in numbers of calories and proteins. There is a fairly serious housing shortage , particularly in urban areas, despite an extensive public housing program. Health conditions are good. The mortality rate is low, the incidence of most diseases is declining and hospital and outpatient facilities are well distributed. The water supply in urban areas is pure and can be drunk without treatment. Sewage is less satisfactory. The larger towns have municipal sewage disposal systems. Nearly all urban homes as well as most rural homes have electricity.

Human rights and freedoms. Trinidad and Tobago is a parliamentary democracy on the Westminster model, and all political and civil rights are guaranteed by the Constitution and respected in practice. Human rights violations are sporadic in nature, resulting from police brutality. The administration of justice suffers from corruption, favoritism, and prolonged delays. Freedom of speech and press is enjoyed by the media. However, the threat of libel suits limits the scope of investigative reporting and encourages self-censorship. Discrimination based on race, gender, language or social status is prohibited by law, but social prejudices continue to mar inter-ethnic relations.

Human environment. Despite its small area and population, Trinidad and Tobago suffers from air, land, and water pollution comparable to those of larger and more industrialized countries. The oil industry is responsible for much of this pollution with tourism ranking second as a polluter.

Hindus. New Hindu temple in Port of Spain. Hindus in Trinidad are mostly East Indians and are 69% Sanatanists (idol-worshippers).

NON-CHRISTIAN RELIGIONS

Hinduism is the principal non-Christian religion in Trinidad and Tobago, followed by 22.8% of the population. Most Hindus belong to the Sanatan Dharma

Country Table 1. Religious adherents in Trinidad & Tobago, AD 1900-2025.

Year	1900		1970		mid-1990		Annual change, 1990-2000				mid-1995		mid-2000		mid-2025	
Name	Adherents	%	Adherents	%	Adherents	%	Natural	Conversion	Total	Rate	Adherents	%	Adherents	%	Adherents	%
Christians	**193,500**	**70.7**	**671,600**	**69.2**	**801,000**	**65.9**	**5,268**	**-1,669**	**3,599**	**0.44**	**826,000**	**65.4**	**836,991**	**64.6**	**896,000**	**60.0**
PROFESSION																
professing Christians	**193,500**	**70.7**	**671,600**	**69.2**	**801,000**	**65.9**	**5,268**	**-1,669**	**3,599**	**0.44**	**826,000**	**65.4**	**836,991**	**64.6**	**896,000**	**60.0**
AFFILIATION																
unaffiliated Christians	2,900	1.1	10,079	1.0	37,900	3.1	250	73	323	0.82	39,171	3.1	41,126	3.2	51,000	3.4
affiliated Christians	**190,600**	**69.6**	**661,521**	**68.1**	**763,100**	**62.8**	**5,019**	**-1,742**	**3,277**	**0.42**	**786,829**	**62.3**	**795,865**	**61.5**	**845,000**	**56.6**
Roman Catholics	88,700	32.4	363,000	37.4	395,000	32.5	2,601	-2,314	287	0.07	395,000	31.3	397,865	30.7	390,000	26.1
Protestants	27,400	10.0	118,921	12.3	163,000	13.4	1,073	527	1,600	0.94	170,238	13.5	179,000	13.8	220,000	14.7
Anglicans	73,100	26.7	150,000	15.5	152,500	12.6	1,004	-854	150	0.10	162,000	12.8	154,000	11.9	170,000	11.4
Independents	1,400	0.5	20,200	2.1	33,500	2.8	221	629	850	2.29	38,931	3.1	42,000	3.2	70,000	4.7
Marginal Christians	0	0.0	5,300	0.6	12,000	1.0	79	171	250	1.91	13,100	1.0	14,500	1.1	25,000	1.7
Orthodox	0	0.0	4,100	0.4	7,100	0.6	47	93	140	1.82	7,560	0.6	8,500	0.7	15,000	1.0
Trans-megabloc groupings																
Evangelicals	25,000	9.1	95,000	9.8	149,500	12.3	984	466	1,450	0.93	157,155	12.5	164,000	12.7	200,000	13.4
Pentecostals/Charismatics	10,000	3.7	50,000	5.2	115,400	9.5	760	1,400	2,160	1.73	129,131	10.2	137,000	10.6	185,000	12.4
Great Commission Christians	**13,700**	**5.0**	**126,200**	**13.0**	**243,000**	**20.0**	**1,600**	**2,883**	**4,483**	**1.71**	**265,000**	**21.0**	**287,827**	**22.2**	**373,000**	**25.0**
Hindus	68,900	25.2	220,900	22.8	274,000	22.6	1,804	291	2,095	0.74	281,000	22.3	294,949	22.8	355,100	23.8
Muslims	10,450	3.8	60,200	6.2	81,500	6.7	537	164	701	0.83	86,000	6.8	88,513	6.8	120,700	8.1
Nonreligious	0	0.0	1,000	0.1	20,500	1.7	135	613	748	3.16	25,000	2.0	27,980	2.2	50,000	3.4
Spiritists	770	0.3	4,000	0.4	13,460	1.1	89	491	580	3.65	17,745	1.4	19,264	1.5	26,000	1.7
Baha'is	0	0.0	6,000	0.6	13,500	1.1	89	124	213	1.47	14,800	1.2	15,627	1.2	28,000	1.9
Chinese folk-religionists	200	0.1	4,000	0.4	5,000	0.4	33	-25	8	0.15	5,100	0.4	5,078	0.4	7,500	0.5
Buddhists	180	0.1	2,000	0.2	3,900	0.3	26	-13	13	0.33	4,000	0.3	4,032	0.3	6,500	0.4
Jews	0	0.0	300	0.0	600	0.1	4	-3	1	0.08	610	0.1	605	0.1	700	0.1
Atheists	0	0.0	0	0.0	240	0.0	2	-2	0	0.00	245	0.0	240	0.0	500	0.0
Other religionists	0	0.0	1,000	0.1	1,300	0.1	9	29	38	2.59	1,500	0.1	1,679	0.1	2,000	0.1
World A (unevangelized persons)	27,380	10.0	174,755	18.0	130,005	10.7	857	-2,925	-2,068	-1.72	119,935	9.5	110,075	8.5	100,031	6.7
World B (evangelized non-Christians)	52,920	19.4	124,509	12.8	283,995	23.4	1,871	4,594	6,465	2.05	316,538	25.1	347,934	26.9	496,969	33.3
World C (Christians)	193,500	70.6	671,600	69.2	801,000	65.9	5,268	-1,669	3,599	0.44	826,000	65.4	836,991	64.6	896,000	60.0
Country's population	**273,800**	**100.0**	**970,865**	**100.0**	**1,215,000**	**100.0**	**7,996**	**0**	**7,996**	**0.64**	**1,262,474**	**100.0**	**1,295,000**	**100.0**	**1,493,000**	**100.0**

COLUMNS, ROWS.
For meanings and definitions, see Codebook (Part 3). Note that, by definition, total 'Christians' = professing + crypto-Christians, which also = affiliated + unaffiliated Christians, and also = Great Commission Christians + latent Christians. Percentages may not always total exactly, due to rounding.

CENSUSES.
First census, **1851** (Trinidad only, population 68,600): 63.6% Roman Catholics, 23.7% Anglicans, 6.1% Protestants, 3.9% Hindus, 1.5% Muslims, 1.2% other non-Christians. **1891** (Trinidad & Tobago): 33.8% Roman Catholics, 25.5% Hindus, 25.5% Anglicans, 10.9% Protestants, 4.0% Muslims, 0.2% Buddhists. **21.IV.1901:** 32.6% Roman Catholics, 27.4% Anglicans, 25.2% Hindus, 10.7% Protestants, 3.8% Muslims, 0.2% nonreligious, 0.1% Buddhists. **9.IV.1946:** 34.5% Roman Catholics, 24.3% Anglicans, 22.7% Hindus, 11.9% Protestants (3.6% Presbyterians, 2.5% Wesleyan Methodists, 2.2% Baptists, 1.3% Moravians, 1.2% SDAs), 5.8% Muslims, 0.5% nonreligious, 0.1% marginal Protestants, 0.1% Jews, 0.1% other religionists. **7.IV.1960:** 36.2% Roman Catholics, 23.0% Hindus (15.8% Sanatanists, 0.1% Arya Samajists), 21.1% Anglicans, 12.6% Protestants (3.9% Presbyterians, 2.3% Methodists, 1.5% SDAs, 1.4% Baptists, 0.9% Moravians), 6.0% Muslims, 0.5% marginal Protestants, 0.5% nonreligious, 0.4% Black indigenous (3,644 Spiritual Baptists), 0.1% Orthodox. **7.IV.1970:** 35.6% Roman Catholics, 24.7% Hindus, 18.1% Anglicans, 12.3% Protestants (4.2% Presbyterians, 1.8% SDAs, 1.7% Methodists, 0.7% Moravians), 6.3% Muslims, 3.0% others. In censuses, Baha'is are usually enumerated as Muslims or Hindus, or 'Others'. **1980:** 33.5% Roman Catholics, 25.5% Hindus, 15.5% Anglicans, 13.6% Protestants (3.8% Presbyterians, 3.5% Pentecostals, 2.5% SDAs, 2.4% Baptists, 1.4% Methodists), 6.0% Muslims, 4.1% other religionists, 1.0% nonreligious, 0.8% marginal Christians (Jehovah's Witnesses). **1990:** 31.4% Roman Catholics, 24.7% Hindus, 18.8% Protestants (7.5% Pentecostals, 3.7% SDAs, 3.4% Presbyterians, 3.0% Baptists, 1.2% Methodists), 11.9% Anglicans, 5.9% Muslims, 4.8% other religionists, 1.3% marginal Christians (Jehovah's Witnesses), 1.2% nonreligious.

NOTES ON RELIGIONS
BAHA'IS. Rapid growth from 1 local spiritual assembly (1964) to 60 (1973), followed by 25 years of precipitous decline to 25 LSAs in 1995. Many are East Indians, formerly Hindus or Muslims. From 1971 weekly radio programs have been broadcast.
BUDDHISTS. Chinese.
DOUBLY-AFFILIATED. The term covers those affiliated to, or claimed by, both the Roman Catholic Church and also the Anglican Church or a Protestant, marginal Christian or Independent church, i.e. persons who have recently changed their denominational allegiance without withdrawing from their original churches. Because their statistics represent a duplication, they are shown in the table as a negative quantity (with a minus sign).
HINDUS. Mostly Indians who are 69% Sanatanists (idol-worshippers) and 0.6% Arya Samajists. The Divine Light Mission is also at work; and 1 center of ISKCON (Hare Krishna).
INDEPENDENTS. In about 28 denominations in 1995 (see Table 2).
MUSLIMS. Indo-Pakistanis, with some Syro-Lebanese Arabs. There is also an Ahmadiya Mission (Qadianis; enumerated here under Muslims although declared non-Muslim by Pakistan). Begun 1950; Qadianis (world HQ Rabwah, Pakistan) Mission in Calcutta Settlement. *Mosques.* Over 60.
NONRELIGIOUS. Mainly Chinese youth who have abandoned their family religion.
OTHER RELIGIONISTS. Adherents of smaller religions and cults, including Rosicrucians (1, AMORC center).
PENTECOSTALS/CHARISMATICS. The Catholic Charismatic Renewal was begun in 1971 by 2 nuns. Totals (mid-1975); 4,000 involved adults (over 15 years old) in 55 prayer groups; total charismatic community including children, 8,000; (January 1977) over 4,000 adults in 120 prayer groups; over 7,000 attenders at second National Rally, Port of Spain; then mushrooming to over 40,000 by 1996. On 5 January 1997 the CCR organized a second annual March for Jesus in heavy rain with 50,000 participants from Trinidad, St Lucia, Dominica, Grenada, and Guyana; also with many Anglicans and Protestants.
ROMAN CATHOLICS. Many Roman Catholics are involved in organized spiritism and spirit-possession cults (Shango, Obeah, et alia).
SPIRITISTS. Non-Christian adherents of Afro-Caribbean cults. There are numerous centers of Shango (Yoruba syncretism), led in the main by men only; also Obeah and other spirit-possession cults. In addition, there are numerous Rastafarians (from Jamaica), and young Blacks especially are joining.

Great Commission Instrument Panel: status of Trinidad & Tobago (for explanation see start of Part 4)

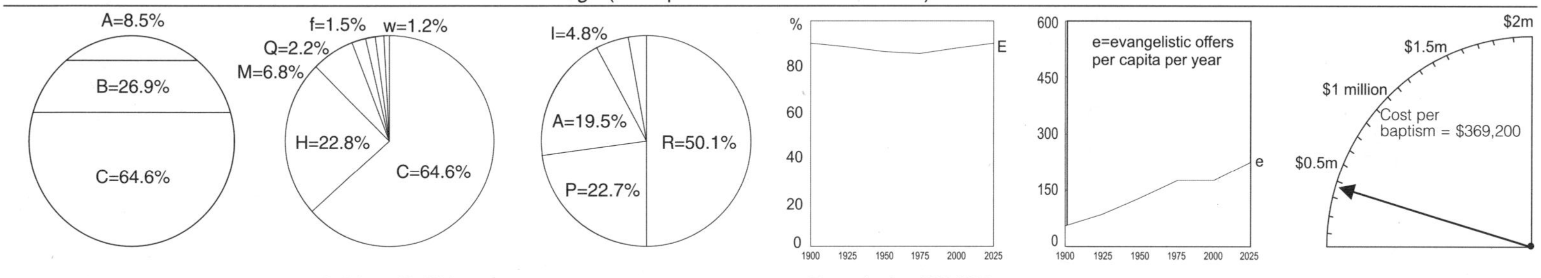

Maha-Sabha, other organizations being the Vighna Hindu Parishad, Kabir Panthi, Divine Life Society, and Arya Prithindi Sabha.

Muslims. Mosque on outskirts of Port of Spain. Muslims in Trinidad are Indo-Pakistanis and Arabs, who are Sunnis with some Ahmadis.

Islam is the religion of 7% of the population. As with Hindus, Muslims are Indo-Pakistanis who came to work on the islands' plantations between 1845 and 1917. Four important Muslim organizations are the Anjuman Sunnatul Jamat Association, a Sunni group in San Fernando; the Islamic Missionaries Guild of the Caribbean and South America, in Port of Spain; Tackveeyatul Islamic Association; and the Trinidad Muslim League.

Afro-American spiritism is composed of several syncretistic religions based on African cults including the Yoruba cult of Shango and has been evolved over the last 2 centuries.

CHRISTIANITY

CATHOLIC CHURCH. The islands were discovered by Columbus in 1498. The first 2 Dominican missionaries, who arrived in Trinidad in 1513, were subsequently killed; but Carmelites, Capuchins, and Jesuits soon followed, nominally under the jurisdiction of the vicariate of London. Spain offered free land grants in 1783 which attracted many non-Spanish settlers, especially French. Britain took over Trinidad in 1797, but the status of the church was little changed, and the government continued to subsidize clergy. In 1818, a vicariate was established at Trinidad which included British Guiana and the Antilles as far as Puerto Rico. In 1850, Port of Spain became an archdiocese, composed of the islands of Dominica, St Lucia, St Vincent, Barbados, Trinidad and Tobago, Grenada, and the Grenadines. In 1968, a Trinidadian was first appointed archbishop. Most of the clergy are members of European religious orders, especially from Ireland, with others from England and France. Catholicism is strongest in urban areas and among the Negro, White, and mixed races; it has had little success among East Indians. The church has an overseas interest: some Trinidadian Holy Ghost priests are involved in missionary activity in the diocese of Concepcion, Paraguay.

The Holy See has diplomatic relations with Trinidad & Tobago and in AD 2000 is represented to government and the Catholic hierarchy by a pronuncio residing in Port of Spain.

Secular Data–concluded

Country summary. **Worlds A, B, C by ethnolinguistic peoples, cities, and major civil divisions in Trinidad & Tobago.**

	PEOPLES							CITIES							CIVIL DIVISIONS						
World	Num	Pop 2000	C%	Christians	E%	U%	Unevangelized	Num	Pop 2000	C%	Christians	E%	U%	Unevangelized	Num	Pop 2000	C%	Christians	E%	U%	Unevangelized
A	1	609	0.66	4	40	60	368	0	0	0.00	0	0	0	0	0	0	0.00	0	0	0	0
B	3	501,654	22.19	111,296	78	22	107,976	0	0	0.00	0	0	0	0	1	467,486	59.08	276,172	89	11	50,631
C	12	792,697	86.36	684,568	100	0	1,079	2	517,705	60.81	314,807	91	9	47,121	11	827,471	62.80	519,693	93	7	58,791
Total	**16**	**1,294,960**	**61.46**	**795,868**	**92**	**8**	**109,423**	**2**	**517,705**	**60.81**	**314,807**	**91**	**9**	**47,121**	**12**	**1,294,957**	**61.46**	**795,865**	**92**	**8**	**109,422**

ANGLICAN CHURCH. Although the Anglican Church had become well established in the West Indies during the 18th century, by 1836 there was still only one clergyman in Trinidad. Missionaries of the SPG arrived that year, followed soon after by members of the CMS. Special attention was given to educational work among Negro freed slaves, and similar educational efforts were initiated for indentured workers arriving from India. In 1845, the colonial government divided Trinidad into 17 Anglican parishes and also began subsidizing Anglican clergy. When the Church of England was disestablished in the West Indies, Trinidad became an independent diocese, and it now belongs to the Church of the Province of the West Indies.

PROTESTANT CHURCHES. Moravian missionaries arrived in the islands in 1783, but the church has remained small in membership. British Methodists entered in 1795, devoting their attention primarily to the large Negro population. The 2 most important Protestant denominations today trace their history to Canadian missionary outreach. The Presbyterian Church in Trinidad and Grenada owes its origin principally to the initiative in 1868 of a Nova Scotian clergyman of the Canadian Presbyterian Church, who was concerned about conditions among the newly arriving indentured workers from India. Schools were organized with financial help from plantation owners and later from government. This church, which is 95% East Indians, maintains a continuing close relationship with the United Church of Canada. The other important Canadian influence has been Pentecostal and has resulted in the establishment of the Pentecostal Assemblies of the West Indies. Seventh-day Adventists and New Testament Church of God also have a strong work in the islands. The latter was begun by the Baptist Missionary Society from Great Britain in 1815 and is now supported by Southern Baptists from the USA.

Christian Brethren, Nazarenes, The Baptist Union, Open Bible Standard Churches, and a number of smaller Protestant groups are also active.

National Evangelical Spiritual Baptist Church. *Top.* New church in Gonzales. *Below.* 'Dancing, trumping and laboring for the Holy Ghost' counter-clockwise around center post (center of the world 'axis to heaven').

INDIGENOUS CHURCHES. The main Black independent churches are several different bodies of Spiritual Baptists, who came into existence around 1860. The influence of Blacks from the USA has also been strong and has resulted in the establishment of the African Methodist Episcopal Church, Church of God in Christ, and the United Holy Church of America.

ORTHODOX CHURCHES. Orthodoxy is represented by the Greek and Ethiopian Orthodox churches, the latter with 24 congregations in 1990.

Indigenous missions. Missionaries from the churches in Trinidad and Tobago have served in many countries around the world.

Renewal movements. In the 1990s the Pentecostal/Charismatic Renewal continued to spread rapidly across most older churches, and numbered over 137,000 adherents (of whom 39% Pentecostals, 35% Charismatics, and 26% Independents).

CHURCH AND STATE

Section 3 of the 1962 constitution identifies the state as religious: 'The People of Trinidad and Tobago have affirmed that the nation is founded on principles that acknowledge the supremacy of God, faith . . . endowed by their Creator'.

There has not always been religious freedom for all churches, however. In 1917, the colony's Legislative Council passed the Shouters Prohibition Ordinance, an attempt to end charismatic practices, prohibiting the Spiritual Baptists from holding worship services or funerals, or having buildings. In fact, this body of Christians merely went underground until they successfully forced the repeal of the legislation in 1949.

Article 1 of the constitution of 22 January 1974, now guarantees 'freedom of conscience, of expression and of assembly and association', and these guarantees are made even more explicit as related to freedom of religion in Article 9, including the freedom to change one's religion and to propagate it. Article 9 also makes provision for the establishment of confessional schools and the teaching of religion in them, provided that no one is required to receive such instruction against his will.

Several churches, specifically Catholics and Anglicans, receive subsidies from the government, an apparent relic of the Spanish days when clergy were paid by the state. As stated in the constitution, churches are allowed to operate private schools, provided these schools meet the physical and educational requirements of the government and are registered with the Ministry of Education. Religious instruction is permitted in both government and private schools. Buildings for churches and schools are exempt from taxation, but the property on which churches and schools are constructed is taxed. Churches are not required to register with the government; but if they wish to own property in the name of the church or denomination, they must be incorporated and consequently registered. There is no ministry in charge of religious affairs, although priests and ministers must receive permission from the Ministry of Home Affairs in order to perform marriages.

BROADCASTING AND MEDIA

Shortwave broadcasts from KNLS, TWR (Antilles), HCJB (Ecuador), and AWR (Costa Rica) can be received. An hour of Catholic programming in a magazine format is broadcast each Sunday on radio. Trinidad is a member of UNDA.

Christian television programming can be seen on local channels. CBN's programs can be seen each weekday. LeSEA programming can be viewed on the World Harvest Satellite network. Some 70,000 have seen the 'Jesus' Film via film team presentations; 8,400 (11%) have responded.

INTERDENOMINATIONAL ORGANIZATIONS

The Christian Council of Trinidad and Tobago (CCTT) was formed in 1966, including the large Roman Catholic and Anglican churches, as well as 9 other members and associated bodies. A Federal Council of Evangelical Churches of Trinidad and Tobago also exists, begun about 1940, now named the Trinidad and Tobago Council of Evangelical Churches. Indigenous bodies are united in the National Spiritual Baptist Council of Churches.

St Andrew's Theological College, formerly training Indians for the Presbyterian ministry, now offers interdenominational training for lay leadership, with several confessions represented on its staff. An ecumenically sponsored program is offered at Christ College to provide vocational training to boys in the area, and an Institute for Social and Religious Action is being set up in the Ecumenical Center at the University of Trinidad.

Concerning relations between the various religions, the Inter-Religious Organizations of Trinidad and Tobago (IRO) was formed in 1970 and held its first elections in 1972. Full members are 10 Christian denominations (AMEC, Anglican, Catholic, Methodist, Salvation Army, Ethiopian Orthodox and 4 indigenous groups: West Indies Spiritual Baptist Churches, Mount Horeb Pentecostal Church, Unity Faith Healing Church, and National Spiritual Baptist Council of Churches), 5 Hindu bodies (Arya Prithindi Sabha, Divine Light Society, Kabir Panthi, Sanatan Dharma Maha-Sabha, Vishna Hindu Parishad), and 4 Muslim bodies (Anjuman Sunnar-ul-Jamaat Association, Islamic Missionary League, Tackveeyatul Islamic Association, Trinidad Muslim League).

FUTURE TRENDS AND PROSPECTS

Christians will likely lose adherents while Hindus and Muslims remain about the same through 2025.

Christianity might in fact decline to less than 55% of the population by mid-century. Muslims and Hindus could then represent close to 40% of the population.

BIBLIOGRAPHY

'A history of the Church of the Nazarene in Trinidad and Tobago.' R. O. Saxon. B.D. thesis, Nazarene Theological Seminary, Kansas City, MO, 1967. 192p.

A history of the Presbyterian church in Trinidad, 1868–1968: the struggles of a church in colonial captivity. I. Hamid. San Fernando, Trinidad: St. Andrew's Theological College, 1980. 274p.

A history of the Shouter Baptists in Trinidad and Tobago. E. Thomas. Ithaca, NY: Calaloux Publications, 1987. 75p.

'A proposed strategy for evangelizing the Hindus of the Republic of Trinidad and Tobago.' W. F. Kerr. D.Min. report, Andrews University, Barrien Springs, MI, 1989. 330p.

A short history of the early Presbyterian Church and the Indian immigrant in Trinidad, 1845–1945. S. Doodnath. N.p., 1983. 114p.

'African feasts in Trinidad,' M. Warner, *Bulletin of the African Studies Association of the West Indies*, 4 (December 1971), 85–94.

Black religions in the New World. G. E. Simpson. New York: Columbia University Press, 1978. 429p.

Called to serve: a history of the Dominican sisters in Trinidad & Tobago, 1868–1988: Congregation of Saint Catherine of Siena O.P., Etrépagny, France. M. T. Rétout. Newtown, Trinidad: Paria, 1988. 193p.

Catholic church in Trinidad, 1797–1820. V. Leahy. *West Indian Church History*, 1. Arima, Trinidad and Tobago: St. Dominic Press, 1980. 218p.

Cult music of Trinidad, G. E. Simpson (recorder), New York: Folkways Record and Service Corporation, 1961. Phonodisc.

'East Indian festivals in Trinidad life,' D. J. Crowley, *Caribbean Commission monthly information bulletin*, 7, 9 (1954), 202–208.

'Education for leadership: an historical study of major problems of the provision of theological training by evangelical churches in Trinidad and Tobago, 1946–1975.' F. D. Drakes. M.A. thesis, University of the West Indies, Mandeville, Jamaica, 1986. 89p.

'Faith healing and medical practice in the southern Caribbean,' F. Mischel, *Southwestern journal of anthropology*, 15, 4 (1959), 407–417.

Flares in the night: the story of Nazarene missions in Trinidad and Tobago. R. O. Saxon. Kansas City, MO: Nazarene Publishing House, 1970. 86p.

'Folk medicine in Trinidad,' G. E. Simpson, *Journal of American folklore*, 75, 298 (1962), 326–40.

'Leadership roles, church organization, and ritual change among the Spiritual Baptists of Trinidad.' S. D. Glazier. Ph.D. dissertation, University of Connecticut, Storrs, CT, 1981. 168p.

'Leadership training in Trinidad and Tobago: analysis of five leadership training programs.' H. E. Lehmann. D.Miss. thesis, Biola University, La Mirada, CA, 1992. 171p.

'Listening to the church: the perceptions of Trinidad church leaders regarding the educational needs of their churches.' D. Broucek. D.Miss. thesis, Trinity Evangelical Divinity School, Deerfield, IL, 1990. 249p.

Marchin' the pilgrims home: leadership and decision. S. D. Glazier. *Contributions to the study of religions series*, 10. Westport, CT: Greenwood Press, 1983. 165p. (Study of Spiritual Baptists of Trinidad).

'Mermaids and fairymaids or water gods and goddesses of Tobago,' H. B. Meikle, *Caribbean quarterly*, 5, 2 (1958), 103–108.

Out of the depths: papers presented at four missiology conferences held in Antigua, Guyana, Jamaica and Trinidad, 1975. I. Hamid (ed.). San Fernando, Trinidad: St. Andrew's Theological College, 1977. 261pp.

Perspectives on Pentecostalism: case studies from the Caribbean and Latin America. S. D. Glazier (ed). Washington, DC: University Press of America, 1980. 197p.

Presbyterian missions to Trinidad and Puerto Rico. G. S. Mount. Hantsport, Canada: Lancelot Press, 1983. 356p.

'Religion and reconciliation in the multi–ethnic states of the Third World: Fiji, Trinidad, and Guyana.' R. R. Premdas. Ph.D. dissertation, McGill University, Montreal, Canada, 1991. 290p.

Religious cults of the Caribbean: Trinidad, Jamaica and Haiti. G. E. Simpson. 3rd ed. *Caribbean Monograph Series*, No. 15. Río Piedras, Puerto Rico: Institute of Caribbean Studies, University of Puerto Rico, 1980. 347p.

'Shango–Cult und Shouter–Kirche auf Trinidad und Grenada,' A. Pollak-Eltz, *Anthropos*, 65, 5-6 (1970), 814–32.

Spirits, blood, and drums: the Orisha religion in Trinidad. J. T. Houk. Philadelphia: Temple University Press, 1995. 238p.

Spiritual Baptist music of Trinidad, S. D. Glazier (recorder), New York: Folkways Record and Service Corporation, 1980. Phonodisc.

'The acculturative process in Trinidadian Shango,' G. E. Simpson, *Anthropological quarterly*, 37 (1964), 16–27.

'The Baptist churches of South Trinidad and their missionaries, 1815–1892.' P. D. Brewer. M.Th. thesis, University of Glasgow, Glasgow, Scotland, 1988. 182p.

The Baptist denomination: a concise history commemorating one hundred and seventy five years (1816–1991) of the establishment of the 'company villages' and the Baptist faith in Trinidad and Tobago. J. M. Hackshaw. Diego Martin, Trinidad and Tobago: Amphy and Bashana Jackson Memorial Society, 1992. 152p.

'The Canadian mission in Trinidad, 1868–1939: studies in a colonial church.' G. D. Johnston. Th.D. thesis, Knox College, Toronto School of Theology, Toronto, Canada, 1976. 335p.

The Catholic Church in Trinidad, 1498–1852. J. T. Harricharan. Port of Spain, Trinidad: Imprint Caribbean, 1983.

'The Hindu sacraments (*rites de passage*) in Trinidad and Tobago,' J. C. Jha, *Caribbean quarterly*, 22, 1 (1976), 40–52.

The history of our church women of Trinidad, 1868–1983. M. Brandow. Regina, Canada: M. Brandow, 1983. 132p.

'The Shango cult in Nigeria and in Trinidad,' G. E. Simpson, *American anthropologist*, 64, 2 (1963), 1204–19.

The work of the Christian churches among the East Indians in Trinidad during the period of indentureship, 1845–1917. J. T. Harricharan. Port-of-Spain, Trinidad: Harricharan, [1975]. 38p.

Trinidad and Tobago. F. Chambers. *World bibliographical series*, vol. 74. Oxford, UK: CLIO Press, 1986. 214p. (See especially 'Religion,' p.70f).

'Yoruba religion in Trinidad: transfer and reinterpretation,' M. W. Lewis, *Caribbean quarterly*, 24, 3–4 (1978), 18–32.

Country Table 2. **Organized churches and denominations in Trinidad & Tobago.**

Official name (bold type = church *with over 10% of all affiliated*) 1	*Begun* 2	*Type* 3	*Counc* 4	*Congs* 5	*Adults* 6	*Affiliated 1970* 7	*Affiliated 1995* 8	*G%* 9	*Names, notes, and other statistics* (see Codebook, Part 3) 10
African Methodist Episcopal Church		I-Met	VwM.a	16	1,300	1,000	3,250	0.05	Windward Is Annual Conference, 16th Episcopal District. M=AMEC(USA Blacks).
Anglican Ch: D Trinidad & Tobago	1797	A-Hig	AwMRN	83	113,000	150,000	162,000	0.31	In CPWI. 80% Black, 10% White, 5% Indian (Asian). 27n,11x,P=61%,5r,3800Yy.
Assembly of God	1946	I-3pU	.....	8	1,300	1,000	1,700	2.15	Indigenous pentecostal group begun by taxi driver at Piarco Village, Trinidad.
Association of Evangelical Baptists	1978	P-Eva	.....	14	1,013	–	2,410	5.88	M=TEAM. Fundamentalist Evangelicals from USA.
Baptist Union of Trinidad & Tobago	1815	P-Bap	T.H.a	22	3,300	10,000	6,600	-1.65	Begun by military settlers. 1962, M=SBC; BMS. 13n,6x,10f,W=39Y,37%,250z.
Catholic Church: M Port of Spain	1513	R-Lat	PzMMN	69	220,000	363,000	395,000	0.34	M=CSSp. C=3+1+6. (1970) 38n,100x,9923Yy. (1990) , 39n, 74x, 95m, 163w, 5723Yy
Christadelphian Ecclesias		m-Ade	x....	3	50	100	100	0.05	*Christadelphian Bible Mission (CBM).* 3 ecclesias (churches) HQ Birmingham (UK).
Christian Brethren	c1915	P-CBr	x....	37	2,000	2,600	4,000	1.74	*Plymouth Brethren, Gospel Halls, Open Brethren.* M=CMML(UK). 6f.
Christian Brethren (Exclusive)		P-EBr	x....	10	600	1,200	1,100	0.05	*Exclusive* (Closed) *Plymouth Brethren.* Groups: Ames, Kelly-Continental.
Church of Christ, Scientist		m-Sci	x....	2	150	200	200	0.05	*Christian Science.* M=CCS(Boston, USA). Port of Spain. 1m.
Church of God in Christ		I-3pB	Z....	2	300	200	500	0.05	M=CoGiC(USA Black Pentecostals). Small body loosely supported from Memphis (USA).
Church of God of Prophecy	1954	P-Pe3	Z....	20	500	1,000	1,430	1.44	M=CGP(USA). Split in USA ex CoG (Cleveland). Holiness Pentecostals.
Church of God (Anderson)	1906	P-Hol	x.H.L	53	1,600	1,500	4,000	4.00	*General Assembly of the CoG (T&T).* M=CoG(Anderson) (USA). 12n,2f,1s,W6=2%.
Church of Scotland		P-Ref	Rwc.a	2	60	100	120	0.05	M=CSM(UK), continuing separate from Presbyterian Ch in Trinidad & Grenada.
Church of the Nazarene	1926	P-Hol	xFH.L	26	2,489	3,500	4,133	0.67	M=CoN(USA). HQ Port of Spain. 9n,6x,12m,17f. 2Tpa,1s(8),35t(3350),W=80%,88Y,56z.
Churches of Christ		I-Dis	x....	12	1,000	1,000	2,000	0.05	M=CC(Non-Instrumental) (USA). In San Fernando, Papira. Rapidly growing.
Episcopal Orth Ch (Greek Communion)	c1920	I-Lib	x....	3	800	1,000	1,500	1.64	Black. Schism ex AOC(USA). HQ Bridgetown (Barbados), but founded first in Trinidad.
Ethiopian Orthodox Church: D Trinidad	c1970	O-Eth	Nwa.n	24	4,800	4,000	6,860	2.18	*EOC.* Under P Addis Ababa (Ethiopia). Blacks. Parallel missions in Jamaica, Guyana.
Evangelical Church of the West Indies	1951	P-Eva	xM...	38	750	1,000	1,880	2.56	M=TEAM,WIM(USA). Radio station. Work began at Blanchisseuse (north coast). 22f,1s.
Greek Orthodox Church		O-Gre	Cw...	1	100	100	200	0.05	Congregation under Greek Orthodox AD North & South America (USA). Mostly Arabs
Intern Ch of the Foursquare Gospel	c1960	P-Pe2	.....	15	2,140	1,000	4,675	6.36	M=ICFG. Mainline Pentecostals from USA.
Jehovah's Witnesses	1912	m-Jeh	x....	61	5,749	5,000	12,800	3.83	Branch 1921. Witnessing by 1926; 1932 to Tobago (now 2 churches). (1975) 231Y. (1995) 472Y.
Lutheran Church in America	1964	P-Lut	LwM.N	2	100	150	200	1.16	Caribbean Synod. M=LCA(USA). 1964 arrival despite FCEC disapproval. 1m,2f.
Mennonite Ch of Trinidad & Tobago	1974	P-Men	.....	2	110	–	130	4.76	M=EMC. Mainline Mennonites from USA.
Methodist Ch in Caribbean & Americas	1795	P-Met	VwM.a	28	4,400	9,000	11,000	0.81	In MCCA, South Caribbean District. 3 Circuits. M=MMS(UK). 7n,1x,1Y,239y.
Moravian Church	1783	P-Mor	xwM.a	8	1,200	4,985	2,260	-3.11	Eastern WI Province. Decline from 6,320 in 1900, 7,152 in 1946. 2f,1u,W=46%,119Yy.
National Ev Spiritual Baptist Ch	c1860	I-3sU	I	30	2,600	3,000	5,000	2.06	*Shouters.* Banned 1917-51. Cathedral in Gonzales. Many former RCs and Anglicans.
New Apostolic Church	c1990	I-3aX	x....	7	250	–	381	20.00	*NAC/NAK.* M=Neuapostolische Kirche. HQ Zurich (Switzerland).
New Testament Church of God	1940	P-Pe3	ZF...	51	5,780	3,000	14,500	6.50	M=CoG(Cleveland) (USA). 1956 joined by Christian General Assembly (1950). 28n,2f,1s.
Open Bible Standard Churches	1953	I-3pW	ZF...	52	5,000	7,000	10,000	1.44	M=NPY(Norway). Mainly Tobago. Radio station. 14n,5x,7f,1k,2p,1s,400Y,75z.
Orthodox Baptist Churches		I-Bap	.....	12	2,000	2,000	2,500	0.05	Independent Baptist congregation. Also in St. Lucia. Mainly Blacks.
Pentecostal Assemblies of the W Indies	1926	P-Pe2	ZF...	300	15,000	30,000	30,000	0.00	M=PAoC(Canada). A=1953. Mainly Trinidad. 49n,3x,3f,1s,W=60%,625Y,200z.
Presbyterian Ch in Trinidad & Grenada	1968	P-Ref	RWM.a	115	14,000	30,000	40,000	1.16	M=PCC(Canada). 95% Hindi-speaking East Indians. San Fernando. 15n,4x,7w,7r,1u(6).
Salvation Army	1901	P-Sal	xwM.a	5	300	400	800	2.81	*SA, Trinidad Division*, Caribbean & CAmerica Terr (HQ Kingston). HQ Port of Spain.
Seventh-day Adventist Church	1893	P-Adv	x....	78	14,000	13,000	31,000	3.54	*SDA*, South Caribbean Conference, Caribbean Union Conference, 1 plane,1H,3h,5r,1s.
Syrian Orthodox Church	c1970	O-Syr	D....	1	300	–	500	28.22	Syrian Arab immigrants, under P Damascus.
United Holy Church of America	c1960	I-3pB	x.H.L	10	900	1,000	1,500	1.64	M=UHCA(USA). Black pentecostals. Spread from Barbados. HQ Laventille. One bishop.
Wesleyan Church	1911	P-Hol	VFH.L	26	1,800	1,486	3,000	2.85	M=Pilgrim Holiness Ch, now WC(USA). HQ St. Joseph. 10n,W=35%,61Y,23z.
West Indies Inland Missions		I-3oU	.....	30	2,300	–	3,600	0.05	Independent Afro-Caribbean pentecostals stressing signs and wonders.
West Indies Spiritual Baptist Churches	c1860	I-3sU	I	20	2,000	2,000	4,000	2.81	*Shouters, Shakers.* Banned 1917-51. White robes, vestments, RC ritual, Obeah; bishop.
Other Protestant denominations		P-	.....	40	3,000	5,000	7,000	0.05	Total about 35 (see list below).
Other Black indigenous churches		I-	.....	30	2,000	1,000	3,000	0.05	Total about 20 (see list below).
Totals				**1,368**	**440,041**	**661,521**	**786,829**		

Churches, members, growth, 1900-2025	*Congs*	*Adults*	*Affiliated*	*G%*	*Total denominations*	*6 Megablocs:* *O*	*R*	*A*	*P*	*I*	*m*
Total churches, members, and denominations (mid-1900)	200	107,000	190,600	1.79	10	0	1	1	5	3	0
Total churches, members, and denominations (mid-1970)	900	359,399	661,521	1.79	60	2	1	1	34	19	3
Total churches, members, and denominations (mid-1990)	1,300	427,000	763,100	0.72	93	3	1	1	54	31	3
Total churches, members, and denominations (mid-1995)	1,368	440,041	786,829	0.61	95	3	1	1	55	32	3
Total churches, members, and denominations (mid-2000)	1,400	445,000	795,865	0.23	97	3	1	1	56	33	3
Total churches, members, and denominations (mid-2025)	1,700	473,000	845,000	0.24	197	10	1	1	80	100	5

NOTES ON TABLE ABOVE

NATIONAL COUNCILS (Column 4, 5th letter).

a = full or associate member of both CCTT and TTCEC.
E = Trinidad and Tobago Council of Evangelical Churches (TTCEC).
I = National Spiritual Baptist Council of Churches.
N = full member of Christian Council of Trinidad and Tobago (CCTT).
n = associate member of CCTT.

Other national councils. Ecumenical Commission of Tobago (Catholic Church, Salvation Army, et alia). Inter-Religious Organisation of Trinidad and Tobago (IRO) (members: 10 Christian denominations, 5 Hindu bodies, 4 Muslim bodies).

Local councils. Commission for Tobago Affairs (Anglican, Methodist, Moravian, RC, Salvation Army).

OTHER PROTESTANT DENOMINATIONS. Other smaller bodies include: Assemblies of God, Bethany Fellowship Missions (1970), Evangelical Orthodox Assembly of the Western Hemisphere, International Pentecostal Assemblies, Pentecostal Ch of God in Trinidad (PCG of American), Streams of Power, Trinidad Mennonite Mission (1971), United Ch of Canada Mission (1868), World-Wide Missions (1968).

OTHER BLACK INDIGENOUS CHURCHES. These include several other Different varieties of Spiritual Baptists, also Mount Horeb Pentecostal Ch, Unity Faith Healing Ch, and others; the Ch of the Lord (Aladura) from Nigeria; and a few churches of 2 USA Black bodies: the American Catholic Ch, Archdiocese of New York; and Bible Way Churches of Our Lord Jesus Christ World Wide.

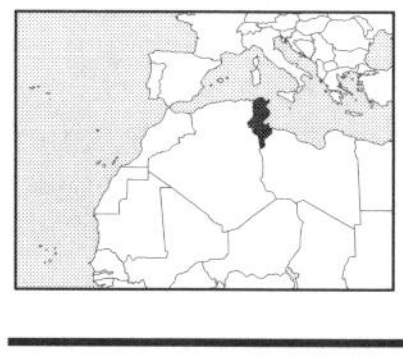

TUNISIA

SECULAR DATA, AD 2000

STATE

Official name: Al-Jumhuriya at-Tunisiya (The Republic of Tunisia).
Short name: Tunisia. **Adjective of nationality:** Tunisian.
Flag: Red field with white circle containing red crescent and star.
Area: 164,150 sq. km. (63,378 sq. mi.).
Government: Multiparty republic, since 1957 (1574 Turkish province, 1883 French protectorate, 1956 Independence as monarchy, 1957 republic).
Legislature: Chamber of Deputies, 163 members.
Official language: Arabic.
Monetary unit: 1 dinar (D) = 1,000 millimes. **US$1=** D 1.09.
Chief cities: TUNIS (Tunus) 1,905,000; Sfax (Safaqis) 423,975; Susah (Sousse) 218,826; Aryanah (Ariana) 134,926; Bizerte (Bizerta, Banzart) 129,256.
Political divisions: 23 provinces.
Armed forces: 35,000.

DEMOGRAPHY

Population: 9,586,000.
Population density: 58.4/sq. km. (151.2/sq. mi.).
Under 15 years: 2,907,000.
Growth rate p.a.: 1.34% (births 19.72, deaths 6.35).
Mortality: Infant, per 1,000: 25.5; **Maternal per 100,000:** 170.0.
Life expectancy: 71 (male 70, female 72).
Household size: 5.1. **Floor area per person, sq.m:** 12.0.
Major languages: Arabic, French, Berber (Tmagourt-Sened-Jerba),

Italian, Maltese.
Urban dwellers: 65.52%. **Urban growth rate p.a.:** 2.5%.
Labor force: 30%.

ETHNOLINGUISTIC PEOPLES
67.1% Tunisian Arab; 21.4% Sahel Bedouin; 3.5% Hamama Bedouin; 2.4% Algerian Arab; 2.0% Levantine Arab.

ECONOMY
National income p.a. per person: US$1,820; **per family:** US$9,282.

EDUCATION
Adult literacy: 66% (male 78%, female 54%). **Schools:** 4,998.
Universities: 0. **School enrolment:** female/male: 82%/89%.

HEALTH
Access to health services: 90%. **Access to safe water:** 99%.
Hospitals: 138 (20 beds per 10,000). **Doctors:** 4,670.
Blind: 25,000. **Deaf:** 590,200. **Murder rate:** 2.
Lepers: 10,000. **Underweight prevalence under 5:** 9%.

LITERATURE
New book titles p.a.: 620 (65 p.a. per million). **Periodicals:** 1.
Newspapers: 7 dailies.

COMMUNICATION (per 1,000 people)
Phones: 58 (1% mobile). **Radios:** 193. **TV sets:** 156.
Daily newspaper circulation: 46. **Computers:** 10.

REFUGEES
Alien refugees from other countries: 500.

HUMAN LIFE AND LIBERTY (optimum condition=100.0%)
HDI: 74.8. **HSI:** 47.0. **HFI:** 27.5. **EFL:** 47.0.

Country Table 1. **Religious adherents in Tunisia, AD 1900-2025.**

Year	*1900*		*1970*		*mid-1990*		*Annual change, 1990-2000*				*mid-1995*		*mid-2000*		*mid-2025*	
Name	*Adherents*	*%*	*Adherents*	*%*	*Adherents*	*%*	*Natural*	*Conversion*	*Total*	*Rate*	*Adherents*	*%*	*Adherents*	*%*	*Adherents*	*%*
Muslims	1,399,900	87.5	5,077,200	99.0	8,070,750	99.0	141,467	-62	141,405	1.63	8,847,050	98.9	9,484,802	98.9	12,659,000	98.6
Christians	**120,100**	**7.5**	**33,400**	**0.7**	**46,350**	**0.6**	**813**	**-291**	**522**	**1.07**	**50,000**	**0.6**	**51,566**	**0.5**	**80,000**	**0.6**
PROFESSION																
crypto-Christians	1,100	0.1	15,280	0.3	30,000	0.4	526	214	740	2.23	34,500	0.4	37,400	0.4	64,000	0.5
professing Christians	**119,000**	**7.4**	**18,120**	**0.4**	**16,350**	**0.2**	**287**	**-505**	**-218**	**-1.42**	**15,500**	**0.2**	**14,166**	**0.2**	**16,000**	**0.1**
AFFILIATION																
unaffiliated Christians	0	0.0	87	0.0	770	0.0	14	15	29	3.28	806	0.0	1,063	0.0	1,540	0.0
affiliated Christians	**120,100**	**7.5**	**33,313**	**0.7**	**45,580**	**0.6**	**799**	**-307**	**492**	**1.03**	**49,194**	**0.6**	**50,503**	**0.5**	**78,460**	**0.6**
Independents	0	0.0	7,133	0.1	24,000	0.3	421	220	641	2.40	28,115	0.3	30,413	0.3	60,000	0.5
Roman Catholics	120,000	7.5	25,000	0.5	20,500	0.3	359	-509	-150	-0.76	20,000	0.2	19,000	0.2	17,000	0.1
Protestants	50	0.0	630	0.0	650	0.0	11	-9	2	0.30	656	0.0	670	0.0	900	0.0
Orthodox	0	0.0	250	0.0	270	0.0	5	-5	0	0.00	270	0.0	270	0.0	400	0.0
Anglicans	50	0.0	150	0.0	100	0.0	2	-2	0	0.00	100	0.0	100	0.0	100	0.0
Marginal Christians	0	0.0	150	0.0	60	0.0	1	-2	-1	-1.81	53	0.0	50	0.0	60	0.0
Trans-megabloc groupings																
Evangelicals	20	0.0	1,700	0.0	5,000	0.1	88	112	200	3.42	5,956	0.1	7,000	0.1	12,000	0.1
Pentecostals/Charismatics	0	0.0	200	0.0	12,300	0.2	216	184	400	2.86	14,822	0.2	16,300	0.2	24,300	0.2
Great Commission Christians	**88,000**	**5.5**	**23,700**	**0.5**	**33,200**	**0.4**	**582**	**-252**	**330**	**0.95**	**35,700**	**0.4**	**36,504**	**0.4**	**58,500**	**0.5**
Nonreligious	0	0.0	3,000	0.1	31,000	0.4	544	336	880	2.53	37,000	0.4	39,801	0.4	89,000	0.7
Jews	80,000	5.0	12,000	0.2	3,600	0.0	63	-43	20	0.53	3,750	0.0	3,796	0.0	3,000	0.0
Atheists	0	0.0	1,000	0.0	2,800	0.0	49	44	93	2.91	3,400	0.0	3,729	0.0	8,000	0.1
Baha'is	0	0.0	400	0.0	1,500	0.0	26	16	42	2.48	1,800	0.0	1,917	0.0	4,000	0.0
World A (unevangelized persons)	1,312,000	82.0	3,845,250	75.0	4,599,984	56.4	80,614	-50,888	29,728	0.63	4,739,816	53.0	4,898,446	51.1	5,702,292	44.4
World B (evangelized non-Christians)	167,900	10.5	1,248,350	24.3	3,509,666	43.0	61,535	51,177	112,712	2.82	4,153,233	46.4	4,635,988	48.4	7,060,708	55.0
World C (Christians)	120,100	7.5	33,400	0.7	46,350	0.6	813	-291	522	1.07	50,000	0.6	51,566	0.5	80,000	0.6
Country's population	**1,600,000**	**100.0**	**5,127,000**	**100.0**	**8,156,000**	**100.0**	**142,962**	**0**	**142,962**	**1.63**	**8,943,050**	**100.0**	**9,586,000**	**100.0**	**12,843,000**	**100.0**

COLUMNS, ROWS.
For meanings and definitions, see Codebook (Part 3). Note that, by definition, total 'Christians' = professing + crypto-Christians, which also = affiliated + unaffiliated Christians, and also = Great Commission Christians + latent Christians. Percentages may not always total exactly, due to rounding.

CENSUSES.
1.XI.1946: 90.4% Muslims, 7.4% Christians & others, 2.2% Jews.
1.II.1956: 92.1% Muslims, 6.4% Christians (250,000), 1.5% Jews (57,792 persons).

NOTES ON RELIGIONS
ATHEISTS. Tunisian Communist Party (TCP) (banned 1963; pro-Soviet). Also, up to 1,000 communist technicians from Communist nations including China are at work in Tunisia. There have been in addition numerous atheists among the French and Italian communities.
BAHA'IS. Growth from 1 local spiritual assembly (1964) to 3 (1973); little subsequent development.
CHRISTIANS. Declining annually by emigration of Catholics, also of individuals and families from most other Christian bodies.
CRYPTO-CHRISTIANS. Christians unrecognized by the state and society, mainly Arabs (Tunisian and expatriate church members, and Tunisian isolated radio believers).
INDEPENDENTS. Mostly isolated radio believers (see Table 2).
JEWS. Maghreb Jews, declining rapidly due to emigration to Israel and France. In 1956, there were 57,840 Tunisian Jews; from 1956-70, some 100,000 Jews (French, Italian and others as well as Tunisian) left Tunisia, with only 10% remaining.
MUSLIMS. Mainly Sunnis (of the Malikite rite), with an Ibadi (Kharijite) minority of 40,000 on Djerba island; Arabs (Tunisian and expatriate), also Berbers. *Hajj pilgrims to Mecca.* (1970) 4,407; (1974) 10,785; (1975) 7,673; (1976) 7,538. *Missionaries.* There are a number of Egyptians sent by Al-Azhar University (Cairo).
NONRELIGIOUS. French.
ROMAN CATHOLICS. In the year 1900, all Italians and other Europeans, except 350 indigenous Tunisian (Arab) Catholics. In 1990, French, Italians, Maltese. Baptized Catholics have declined drastically by emigration recently, from 280,000 (1954) to 70,000 (1959), 25,000 (1970), and to 14,000 (1990).

Great Commission Instrument Panel: status of Tunisia (for explanation see start of Part 4)

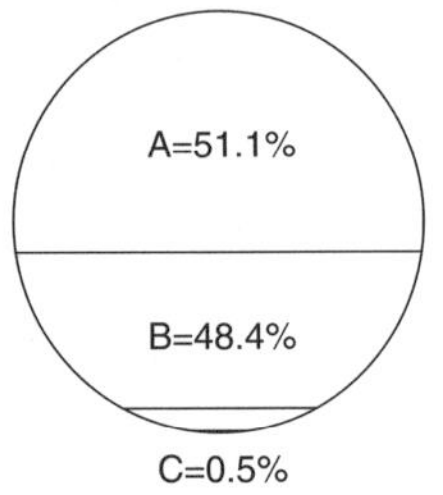

3 Worlds, AD 2000

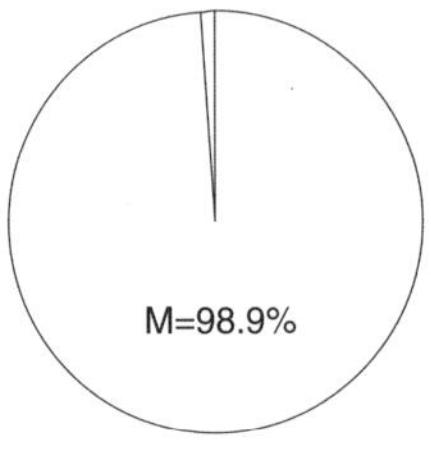

Religions, AD 2000

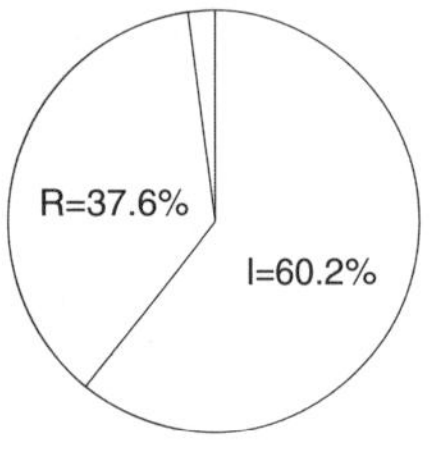

Ecclesiastical blocs

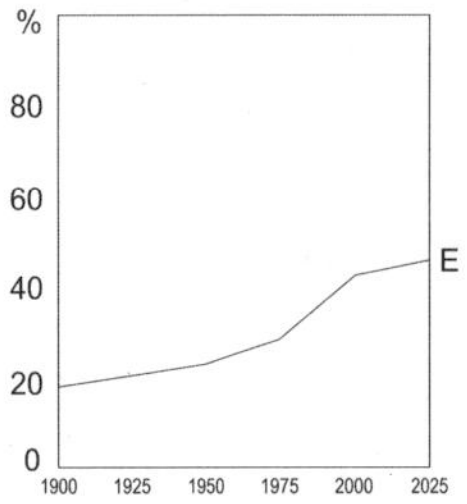

Evangelization, 1900-2025

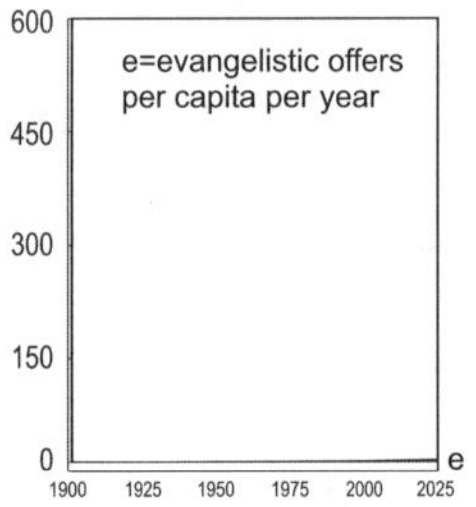

Offers, 1900-2025

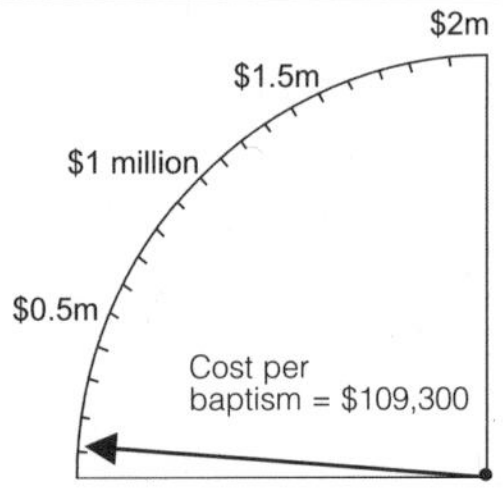

Cost-effectiveness, AD 2000

Country status. Tunisia is one of the Northern African Islamic countries on the Mediterranean Sea forming part of the region known in Arabic as the Maghreb. The economy is based almost entirely on oil and mining.

HUMAN LIFE AND LIBERTY

Human need and development. Although not a rich country by the standards of the oil producers of the Middle East, Tunisia is a moderately affluent country where living conditions are adequate. Food intake falls below accepted minimum standards for only about one-tenth of the population. Housing is not sufficient to meet demand in some areas, although the rich and middle classes have comfortable homes, many of them left behind by the departing Europeans when Tunisia became independent. The poorer migrants to the cities live in *gourbis,* or mud huts, in sections known as *gourbivilles.* Medical progress during the past 2 decades has been impressive, but limited to towns. Public sanitation is poor or lacking, except in Tunis and a few other urban centers.

Human rights and freedoms. Although a parliamentary democracy on paper, Tunisia is a one-party state where the president is all-powerful. As in Egypt, Algeria, and other countries, the threat of Islamic fundamentalism places the government on the defensive, and fearful of the consequences of loosening strict controls on society and the media. A number of reforms were enacted in 1993, but had no effect on the government's continued campaign against its Islamic and Communist opponents, many of whom were arrested and jailed without due process. Confessions are extracted through torture and detainees are beaten and mistreated. During pre-arraignment detention detainees do not have the right to a lawyer. Bail is granted rarely. Freedom of press is limited both by restrictive laws and practices and by self-censorship arising from a fear of government sanctions. The Press Code prohibits defamation of government officials. The government exerts considerable control over the editorial content of newspapers, providing extensive advance guidance on important issues and reprimanding editors when guidelines are crossed. Prepublication censorship under the 1988 Press Code requires printers to deposit all copies of their publications with the government prior to release. Tunisia is one of the more progressive Muslim countries with regard to the rights of women. Nevertheless, nearly one-half of the women are illiterate compared to one-fourth of the men.

Human environment. The depletion of vegetation is common to much of the land close to the desert. Extensive soil erosion also helps desertification. Water is scarce and drought is common. Untreated sewage contaminates existing water supplies and leads to the overfertilization of the sea. Waste sites are poorly designed and often leak toxic materials.

NON-CHRISTIAN RELIGIONS

Islam is the official and preponderant religion of the country. Muslims are principally Sunnis of the Malikite rite. A Kharijite minority is found on the island of Djerba. Kairouan, a holy city and place of pilgrimage, is famous as an Islamic center.

Judaism has declined massively in numbers over the past 15 years. Between 1965 and 1968, more than 50,000 Tunisian Jews departed from the country, leaving only a small Jewish remnant.

CHRISTIANITY

CATHOLIC CHURCH. Christianity was implanted near the end of the 1st century and suffered the first of many persecutions in AD 180. In the 4th century, the church was rented by the Donatist schism, and 3 centuries later Islam swept across North Africa. Nevertheless, although the loss of Christians

Country summary. **Worlds A, B, C by ethnolinguistic peoples, cities, and major civil divisions in Tunisia.**

	PEOPLES							CITIES							CIVIL DIVISIONS						
World	*Num*	*Pop 2000*	*C%*	*Christians*	*E%*	*U%*	*Unevangelized*	*Num*	*Pop 2000*	*C%*	*Christians*	*E%*	*U%*	*Unevangelized*	*Num*	*Pop 2000*	*C%*	*Christians*	*E%*	*U%*	*Unevangelized*
A	15	2,703,209	0.05	1,250	29	71	1,921,161	9	985,163	0.23	2,235	49	51	506,308	19	6,554,754	0.31	20,148	47	53	3,472,281
B	3	6,858,696	0.43	29,473	57	43	2,976,083	2	2,328,975	0.86	20,113	53	47	1,093,185	4	3,030,855	1.00	30,355	53	47	1,424,999
C	7	23,707	83.44	19,781	100	0	39	0	0	0.00	0	0	0	0	0	0	0.00	0	0	0	0
Total	**25**	**9,585,612**	**0.53**	**50,504**	**49**	**51**	**4,897,283**	**11**	**3,314,138**	**0.67**	**22,348**	**52**	**48**	**1,599,493**	**23**	**9,585,609**	**0.53**	**50,503**	**49**	**51**	**4,897,280**

to Islam and by emigration to Europe was enormous, the church continued to exist for another 300 years. The last contacts between the Roman pope and a bishop of Carthage took place in 1076. A new venture was launched by Franciscans and Dominicans in Tunis in the early part of the 13th century and by Capuchins and Lazarists in the 17th century. A prefecture was erected in 1650 which became a vicariate in 1843, Catholic membership consisting almost entirely of foreigners. The archbishop of Carthage was reestablished in 1884 under cardinal Lavigerie, served by White Fathers, but Independence in 1957 brought about a mass exodus of Europeans (from 280,000 in 1954 to 25,000 in 1970) and consequent diminution of Catholic influence.

Catholics are an ethnically or socially heterogeneous community, consisting mostly of French expatriates.

The Holy See has diplomatic relations with Tunisia and in AD 2000 is represented to government and the Catholic hierarchy by a pro-nuncio residing in Algiers.

Eglise Méthodiste en Afrique du Nord. Arab girl in Tunis explains Bible verse on blackboard.

OTHER CHURCHES. Through the Church's Ministry among the Jews, Anglicans began work in Tunis as early as 1829; but the first Protestants, the North Africa Mission, did not arrive until 1881. The latter began an extensive and popular Bible correspondence course in 1962 which reached 20,000 Muslims before being banned by government. The course office has now been transferred to Marseilles, France; but the NAM continues to work in Tunisia as well.

Three North American missions entered prior to World War I, namely Adventists, Methodists and Pentecostals; and French Reformed and Brethren congregations have also been formed to serve the expatriate community.

Methodists carry on some kindergarten and youth camp activities; but the Protestant churches all remain small, having a limited influence both in numbers and in social work. Greek and Russian Orthodox also have organized congregations in Tunisia.

Indigenous missions. Christian missionaries were sent out by the hundreds from Tunisia but this was all before the Muslim conquest in the 7th century. Since then, virtually no missionaries have been sent out from this predominantly Muslim country.

CHURCH AND STATE

The constitution of the Tunisian republic (June 1, 1959) proclaims that Islam is the state religion (Article 1), stipulates that the chief of state must be a Muslim (Article 37), guarantees freedom of conscience and protects the free exercise of worship.

Since national Independence, modernizing tendencies at the heart of Tunisian Islam as represented by the intelligentsia and the Neo-Dastur party are gaining ground over traditional groups associated with the mosques and the Al-Zituna University. The Code of Personal Status, proclaimed by government on 13 August 1956, contributes to the improvement of the status of women by guaranteeing the juridical equality of both spouses, although this new interpretation of Islamic law has not been accepted by certain Islamic religious groups. The educational measures of 1958 integrated all secondary schools and post-secondary studies at Al-Zituna into a single system of state education.

The juridical situation of the Catholic Church, the principal Christian confession in Tunisia, is regulated by the modus vivendi concluded on 10 July 1964, between the Tunisian government and the Holy See. According to the terms of this agreement, the Catholic Church is given juridical personality, and a Catholic pro-nuncio is nominated by the Holy See after secret consultation with the Tunisian government. The church ceded to the government, without request for compensation, all but 5 of its places of worship and all but one of its landed properties. Educational and medical institutions belonging to the various religious associations or societies are authorized to exercise their activities. Established chapels in these institutions and certain private homes (if they have received authorization), may serve as places of worship. In case of need, the government may also assign other places for Catholic worship.

Since this agreement, the government interprets it in a liberal way. It also shows an attitude of tolerant neutrality with regard to other Christian confessions in the country. The Ministry of Foreign Affairs (Wizarat al-Umuri al-Kharjiya) is responsible for all questions relating to Christianity.

BROADCASTING AND MEDIA

Radios are common. Shortwave radio programs in Arabic can be received from FEBA (Seychelles) and HCJB (Ecuador). Satellite TV and radio programs are received in English, Arabic, German and Italian. Tunisia is a member of UNDA. Over 166,000 have heard the 'Jesus' Film in radio broadcasts.

Muslims. Great Mosque in Kairouan, a renowned holy city and pilgrimage centre.

INTERDENOMINATIONAL ORGANIZATIONS

An Inter-Church Council composed of Anglican, Greek Orthodox, Russian Orthodox, Methodist and Reformed Churches was organized in 1964. A Catholic priest participates in its program of social service and aid to refugees. In similar vein, a Protestant pastor serves on the Catholic Pastoral Council. The Service Oecumenique en Tunisie operates the Association pour le Developpement et l'Animation Rurale (ASDEAR) based in Tunis.

With regard to interreligious relations, an important Islamic-Christian colloquium was held in Tunisia in November 1974 on the initiative of the Center for Studies and Economic and Social Research (Centre d'Etudes et de Recherches Economiques et Sociales) of the University of Tunisia and the Hammamet International Cultural Center (Centre Culturel International de Hammamet).

FUTURE TRENDS AND PROSPECTS

The religious situation in Tunisia is not expected to change significantly before AD 2025.

Christianity could reach 1% by AD 2050 but only with an influx of Christian immigrants or with significant penetration of the indigenous peoples. In any case, Islam is likely to claim the vast majority of the population for the next half-century.

BIBLIOGRAPHY

'An Islamic movement in a modernizing context: the Islamic Tendency Movement in Tunisia.' J. P. Cavano. M.A. thesis, University of Utah, Salt Lake City, UT, 1990. 194p.

Baal, Christ and Mohammed: religion and revolution in North Africa. J. K. Cooley. New York: Holt, Rinehart & Winston, 1965. 369p.

Bibliographie ethno–sociologique de la Tunisie. A. Louis. *Publications de l'Institut des belles lettres arabes*, 31. Tunis: N. Bascone, 1977. 448p.

Ethnography, North Africa (Tunisia, Algeria). R. Herzog. Berlin: Gebrüder Borntraeger, 1981. 46p. (Summaries in English and French).

Européens de Tunisie et questions religieuses (1892–1901): étude d'une opinion publique. P. Soumille. Aix-Marseille: Editions du Centre National de la Recherche Scientifique, 1975. 264p.

Géographie de l'Afrique chrétienne Proconsulaire. J. A. Toulotte. Rennes-Paris: Oberthur, 1892. 408p.

'Islamic reform in contemporary Tunisia: a comparative ethnographic study.' D. K. Magnuson. Ph.D. dissertation, Brown University, Providence, RI, 1986. 364p.

Islamic society in practice. C. Fluehr-Lobban. Gainesville, FL: University Press of Florida, 1994. 201p.

J'ai recontré l'Islam. M. Lelong. Paris: Éditions du Cerf, 1976. 172p.

La situation des cultes en Tunisie. R. Darmon. 2d ed. Paris: A. Rousseau, 1930. 168p.

La Tunisie chrétienne. J. de Sainte-Marie. Lyon: Bureaux des Missions Catholiques, 1878. 164p.

Lavigerie in Tunisia: the interplay of imperialist and missionary. J. D. O'Donnell. Athens, GA: University of Georgia Press, 1979. 318p.

Les iles Kerkena, Tunisie: étude d'ethnographie tunisienne et de geographie humaine. A. Louis. Tunis: Bascone & Muscat, 1961–63. 3 vols.

Les Khroumirs: changements politiques et religieux dans la période 1850–1987. B. Venema. Amsterdam: VU University Press, 1990. 152p.

L'Islam dans les cinq pays du maghreb arabe. L. Pruvost. *Dossiers de la C.R.R.M*, no. 6. : Commission pour les Relations Religieuses avec les Musulmans, Conseil Pontifical pour le Dialogue Interreligieux, 1993. 18p.

Missions des Pères Blancs en Tunisie, Algérie, Kabylie, Sahara. A. Philippe. Paris: Dillen, 1931. 146p.

Ordo et annuaire de la prélature de Tunis pour l'année 1970. Tunis: Prelature, 1970.

Pistes de réponses aux questions qu'on nous pose. Collection 'Studi arabo-islamici del PISAI', no 2. Rome: Pontificio Istituto di Studi Arabi e d'Islamistica (PISAI), 1987. 113p.

'Political attitudes and activities of the ulama in the liberal age: Tunisia as an exceptional case,' A. H. Green, *International journal of Middle Eastern studies*, 7 (1976), 209–241.

'Political change and the Islamic revival in Tunisia,' M. A. Tessler, *Maghreb review*, 5, 1 (1980), 8–19.

Renaissance or radicalism?: political Islam: the case of Tunisia's al–Nahda. M. C. Dunn. Washington, DC: International Estimate, 1992. 121p.

'Situation actuelle de l'Islam maghrébin,' *Maghreb*, 47 (September–October 1971), 30–46.

Symbolique de l'espace et habitat chez les Beni–Aïssa du Sud–Tunisien. G. Libaud. *Les Cahiers du C.R.E.S.M*, 17. Paris: Editions du Centre National de la Recherche Scientifique, 1986. 220p.

'The resilience of religious institutions and the making of protest movements: a comparative study of Tunisia and Iran.' K. Ghozzi. Ph.D. dissertation, University of Pennsylvania, Philadelphia, 1994. 265p.

'The restitution of Islam: a comparative study of the Islamic movements in contemporary Tunisia and Morocco.' E. E. A. Shahin. Ph.D. dissertation, Johns Hopkins University,

Baltimore, MD, 1990. 314p.
Tunisia. A. M. Findlay, A. M. Findlay & R. I. Lawless. *World bibliographical series*, vol. 33. Oxford, UK: CLIO Press, 1982. 280p. (See especially 'Religion,' p.80-3).
Tunisie, terre d'Islam. Tunisia Secretariat of State for Information. Tunis: Cérès Productions, 1977. 93p.

Country Table 2. **Organized churches and denominations in Tunisia.**

Official name (bold type = church with over 10% of all affiliated) 1	*Begun* 2	*Type* 3	*Counc* 4	*Congs* 5	*Adults* 6	*Affiliated 1970* 7	*Affiliated 1995* 8	*G%* 9	*Names, notes, and other statistics* (see Codebook, Part 3) 10
Eglise Anglicane (D Egypt)	1829	A-Cen	aw.UC	1	33	150	100	-1.61	In Episcopal Ch in Jerusalem & Middle East. St George's Ch, Tunis. M=CMJ(UK). 1x.
Eglise Catholique: D Tunis	1219	R-Lat	bxSH.	15	0	25,000	20,000	-0.89	M=WF. C=4+1+15. (1970) 83x,350w,162Yy. (1990) , 18n, 25x, 34m, 169w, 24Yy
Eglise Méthodiste en Afrique du Nord	1908	P-Met	Vw.NC	1	7	30	10	-4.30	*Methodist Ch in North Africa.* In NA Annual Conference, related to UMC(USA). 4f.
Eglise Orthodoxe Grecque: D Carthage		O-Ara	Cw.NC	1	100	200	200	0.05	*St George*, Tunis. Under P Alexandria. Decline from 10,000 Greeks before 1959.
Eglise Orthodoxe Russe	1917	O-Rus	C	1	35	50	70	1.35	*Ch of the Resurrection*, Tunis. White Russian exiles, independent of P Moscow.
Eglise Pentecôtiste	1911	P-Pe3	Z....	1	15	100	21	-6.05	1947, M=CoG(Cleveland) (USA). Formerly, Assemblea di Dio (Italian Tunisians).
Eglise Réformée en Tunisie		P-Ref	C	1	45	200	75	0.05	*Reformed Ch in Tunisia.* Serves French Protestants in Tunis, Bizerta, Sfax. 1x.
Eglises radiophoniques isolées		I-rad	.....	300	20,000	6,900	28,000	0.05	Isolated Arab believers, mostly aged 12-25. R=420,T=52000(NAM,ICI,GMU,&c).
Frères Larges		I-CBr	x....	1	15	200	30	0.05	*Christian (Plymouth, Open) Brethren.* Fluctuating small indigenous fellowship.
Mission Adventiste du Septième Jour	1905	P-Adv	x....	1	35	100	50	-2.73	*SDA. Seventh-day Adventists*, in North African Mission, Euro-Africa Division.
Mission d'Afrique du Nord	1881	P-Non	xMg..	3	100	100	200	2.81	*NAM.* M=Arab World Ministries. First Protestants. Mail courses; banned 1963. 2x,11f,1j.
Témoins de Jéhovah	c1950	m-Jeh	x....	1	37	150	53	-4.08	*Jehovah's Witnesses.* Active witnessing under way by 1950. No baptisms in 1971.
Other Protestant denominations		P-	.....	10	100	100	300	0.05	Including Children of God International (USA, Europe: drug addict ministry).
Other indigenous congregations	c1965	I-3cS	.....	2	50	33	85	3.86	A handful of private house churches.
Totals				**339**	**34,506**	**33,313**	**49,194**		

Churches, members, growth, 1900-2025	*Congs*	*Adults*	*Affiliated*	*G%*	*Total denominations*	*6 Megablocs:* O	R	A	P	I	m
Total churches, members, and denominations (mid-1900)	500	65,200	120,100	-1.82	3	0	1	1	1	0	0
Total churches, members, and denominations (mid-1970)	206	18,077	33,313	-1.82	15	2	1	1	7	3	1
Total churches, members, and denominations (mid-1990)	300	32,000	45,580	1.58	20	2	1	1	10	5	1
Total churches, members, and denominations (mid-1995)	339	34,506	49,194	1.54	20	2	1	1	10	5	1
Total churches, members, and denominations (mid-2000)	360	35,400	50,503	0.53	20	2	1	1	10	5	1
Total churches, members, and denominations (mid-2025)	600	55,000	78,460	1.78	45	5	1	1	20	15	3

NOTES ON TABLE ABOVE
NATIONAL COUNCILS (Column 4, 5th letter).
C = Inter-Church Council of Tunisia.

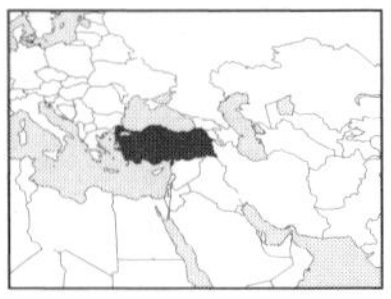

TURKEY

SECULAR DATA, AD 2000

STATE
Official name: Türkiye Çumhuriyeti (The Republic of Turkey).
Short name: Turkey. **Adjective of nationality:** Turkish, a Turk.
Flag: Red field with white crescent and star.
Area: 779,452 sq. km. (300,948 sq. mi.).
Government: Multiparty republic with one legislative house, since 1982 (1453 Turkish Ottoman Empire, 1923 republic, 1960 military junta, 1961 republic, 1980 military junta).
Legislature: Turkish Grand National Assembly, 550 members.
Official language: Turkish.
Monetary unit: 1 Turkish lira (LT) = 100 kurush. **US$1=** LT 276,485.
Chief cities: Istanbul (Stambul, Constantinople) 9,413,000; ANKARA (Ancyra, Angora) 3,190,000; Izmir (Smyrna) 2,399,000; Bursa (Brusa) 1,299,000; Adana (Ataniya, Seyhan) 1,289,000.
Political divisions: 8 provinces.
Armed forces: 639,000.

DEMOGRAPHY
Population: 66,591,000.
Population density: 85.4/sq. km. (221.2/sq. mi.).
Under 15 years: 18,845,000.
Growth rate p.a.: 1.43% (births 19.75, deaths 6.25).
Mortality: Infant, per 1,000: 38.2; **Maternal per 100,000:** 180.0.
Life expectancy: 71 (male 68, female 73).
Household size: 4.5. **Floor area per person, sq.m:** 18.2.
Major languages: Turkish (spoken by 98%; Osmanli), Kurdish, Arabic, French, German, English, Turkoman, Circassian, Armenian, Greek, Georgian, Ladino, Chinese, Chaldean, Abkhazi, Laze and numerous others.
Urban dwellers: 75.33%. **Urban growth rate p.a.:** 2.5%.
Labor force: 35%.

ETHNOLINGUISTIC PEOPLES
64.5% Turk; 8.9% Northern Kurd (Kermanji); 8.0% Turkish Kurd; 7.0% Crimean Tatar; 1.8% Levantine Arab.

ECONOMY
National income p.a. per person: US$2,780; **per family:** US$12,510.

EDUCATION
Adult literacy: 82% (male 91%, female 72%). **Schools:** 50,701.
Universities: 424. **School enrolment:** female/male: 71%/88%.

HEALTH
Access to health services: 75%. **Access to safe water:** 92%.
Hospitals: 857 (24 beds per 10,000). **Doctors:** 50,639.
Blind: 38,178. **Deaf:** 3,943,900. **Murder rate:** 3.
Lepers: 50,000. **Underweight prevalence under 5:** 10%.

LITERATURE
New book titles p.a.: 7,990 (120 p.a. per million). **Periodicals:** 1,855.
Newspapers: 57 dailies.

COMMUNICATION (per 1,000 people)
Phones: 215 **(17% mobile). Radios:** 141. **TV sets:** 240.
Daily newspaper circulation: 44. **Computers:** 27.

REFUGEES
Citizen refugees in other countries: 15,000.
Alien refugees from other countries: 21,150.
Internal displacement: 2,000,000.

HUMAN LIFE AND LIBERTY (optimum condition=100.0%)
HDI: 77.2. **HSI:** 47.0. **HFI:** 17.5. **EFL:** 40.0.

Country Table 1. **Religious adherents in Turkey, AD 1900-2025.**

Year	*1900*		*1970*		*mid-1990*		*Annual change, 1990-2000*				*mid-1995*		*mid-2000*		*mid-2025*	
Name	*Adherents*	*%*	*Adherents*	*%*	*Adherents*	*%*	*Natural*	*Conversion*	*Total*	*Rate*	*Adherents*	*%*	*Adherents*	*%*	*Adherents*	*%*
Muslims	10,978,370	77.3	34,925,300	98.9	54,501,400	97.2	1,019,431	1,812	1,021,243	1.73	59,545,300	97.2	64,713,833	97.2	84,924,000	96.7
Nonreligious	0	0.0	30,000	0.1	1,110,000	2.0	20,762	3,101	23,863	1.97	1,225,000	2.0	1,348,632	2.0	2,300,000	2.6
Christians	**3,091,530**	**21.8**	**290,000**	**0.8**	**365,000**	**0.7**	**6,827**	**-4,451**	**2,376**	**0.63**	**375,700**	**0.6**	**388,757**	**0.6**	**450,000**	**0.5**
PROFESSION																
crypto-Christians	476,530	3.4	65,585	0.2	138,000	0.3	2,581	709	3,290	2.16	150,000	0.2	170,900	0.3	240,000	0.3
professing Christians	**2,615,000**	**18.4**	**224,415**	**0.6**	**227,000**	**0.4**	**4,246**	**-5,160**	**-914**	**-0.41**	**225,700**	**0.4**	**217,857**	**0.3**	**210,000**	**0.2**
AFFILIATION																
unaffiliated Christians	1,000	0.0	8,735	0.0	13,300	0.0	249	-19	230	1.61	13,819	0.0	15,602	0.0	45,200	0.1
affiliated Christians	**3,090,530**	**21.8**	**281,265**	**0.8**	**351,700**	**0.6**	**6,578**	**-4,432**	**2,146**	**0.59**	**361,881**	**0.6**	**373,155**	**0.6**	**404,800**	**0.5**
Orthodox	2,950,000	20.8	221,500	0.6	224,000	0.4	4,190	-3,824	366	0.16	227,000	0.4	227,655	0.3	200,000	0.2
Independents	0	0.0	5,800	0.0	65,000	0.1	1,216	84	1,300	1.84	70,690	0.1	78,000	0.1	120,000	0.1
Protestants	60,000	0.4	24,370	0.1	29,500	0.1	552	-252	300	0.97	30,214	0.1	32,500	0.1	40,000	0.1
Roman Catholics	74,500	0.5	26,487	0.1	29,200	0.1	546	-416	130	0.44	29,787	0.1	30,500	0.1	38,000	0.0
Marginal Christians	30	0.0	1,108	0.0	1,900	0.0	36	14	50	2.36	2,090	0.0	2,400	0.0	4,500	0.0
Anglicans	6,000	0.0	2,000	0.0	2,100	0.0	39	-39	0	0.00	2,100	0.0	2,100	0.0	2,300	0.0
Trans-megabloc groupings																
Evangelicals	45,000	0.3	6,200	0.0	12,300	0.0	230	-110	120	0.94	12,908	0.0	13,500	0.0	18,000	0.0
Pentecostals/Charismatics	0	0.0	1,500	0.0	45,000	0.1	842	1,158	2,000	3.75	61,121	0.1	65,000	0.1	98,000	0.1
Great Commission Christians	**2,130,000**	**15.0**	**168,000**	**0.5**	**186,000**	**0.3**	**3,479**	**-2,274**	**1,205**	**0.63**	**190,000**	**0.3**	**198,054**	**0.3**	**242,000**	**0.3**
Atheists	0	0.0	10,000	0.0	57,000	0.1	1,066	44	1,110	1.80	62,000	0.1	68,099	0.1	100,000	0.1
Buddhists	0	0.0	5,000	0.0	30,000	0.1	561	266	827	2.46	34,500	0.1	38,267	0.1	60,000	0.1
Jews	80,000	0.6	37,000	0.1	22,000	0.0	412	-453	-41	-0.19	22,000	0.0	21,595	0.0	15,000	0.0
Baha'is	100	0.0	3,700	0.0	14,600	0.0	273	229	502	3.00	17,900	0.0	19,618	0.0	35,000	0.0
Chinese folk-religionists	0	0.0	5,000	0.0	13,500	0.0	253	-15	238	1.64	14,500	0.0	15,877	0.0	22,000	0.0
Ethnoreligionists	50,000	0.4	15,000	0.0	10,500	0.0	196	-180	16	0.15	10,500	0.0	10,655	0.0	8,000	0.0
doubly-counted religionists	0	0.0	0	0.0	-26,000	-0.1	-486	-353	-839	2.84	-31,400	-0.1	-34,394	-0.1	-45,000	-0.1
World A (unevangelized persons)	7,653,800	53.9	28,256,800	80.0	33,097,820	59.0	619,123	-504,769	114,354	0.34	33,211,377	54.2	34,227,774	51.4	40,244,002	45.8
World B (evangelized non-Christians)	3,454,670	24.3	6,774,200	19.2	22,635,180	40.3	423,345	509,220	932,565	3.51	27,688,527	45.2	31,974,469	48.0	47,174,998	53.7
World C (Christians)	3,091,530	21.8	290,000	0.8	365,000	0.7	6,827	-4,451	2,376	0.63	375,700	0.6	388,757	0.6	450,000	0.5
Country's population	**14,200,000**	**100.0**	**35,321,000**	**100.0**	**56,098,000**	**100.0**	**1,049,295**	**0**	**1,049,295**	**1.73**	**61,275,605**	**100.0**	**66,591,000**	**100.0**	**87,869,000**	**100.0**

COLUMNS, ROWS.
For meanings and definitions, see Codebook (Part 3). Note that, by definition, total 'Christians' = professing + crypto-Christians, which also = affiliated + unaffiliated Christians, and also = Great Commission Christians + latent Christians. Percentages may not always total exactly, due to rounding.

Continued opposite

Country Table 1–concluded

CENSUSES.
21.X.1945: 98.4% Muslims, 1.1% Christians (0.9% Orthodox, 0.1% Roman Catholics), 0.4% Jews, 0.1% other religionists. **23.X.1955:** 98.9% Muslims, 0.9% Christians, 0.2% Jews. **23.X.1960:** 99.0% Muslims, 0.79% Christians (0.64% Orthodox, 0.09% Roman Catholics, 0.06% Protestants), 0.16% Jews. **24.X.1965:** 99.2% Muslims, 0.68% Christians (0.5% Orthodox, 0.09% Roman Catholics, 0.07% Protestants), 0.12% Jews. These censuses have all included expatriates, both civilians and USA military personnel.

NOTES ON RELIGIONS
AFFILIATED PROTESTANTS. Mainly expatriate civilians and USA military. Protestants who are also Turkish citizens are found mainly in Istanbul, but with small communities of Syriac origin in Kurdish country in southeast Anatolia, and a few families in Iskenderun.
ANGLICANS. In 1865, an Armenian Apostolic archbishop at Gaziantep and congregations in 7 cities seceded to Anglicanism (Jerusalem Archbishopric). They were dispersed in the Armenian massacres of World War I, and today Anglicans are only expatriate UK and USA personnel.
ATHEISTS. Communist Party of Turkey (Türkiye Komünist Partisi, TKP) (illegal since 1925; pro-Soviet), also a Marxist group, the Turkish Workers' Party (TIS).
BAHA'IS. First entered Turkey before 1892. Recent growth from 12 local spiritual assemblies (1964) to 25 (1973); followed by massive expansion to 82 LSAs (1996).
CRYPTO-CHRISTIANS. Turkish subjects who prefer not to reveal their Christian affiliation in government censuses.
ETHNORELIGIONISTS. (Shamanists). Traditional religions are still practiced by a number of peoples resistant to Islam and Christianity.
INDEPENDENTS. In 5 denominations or groupings in 1995 (see Table 2). Only the Turkish Orthodox Church is recognized or acknowledged by the state.
JEWS. Turkish Jews are almost all Sefardis, declining by emigration to Israel since 1948.
MUSLIMS. Almost all Sunnis (of the Hanafite rite), with a 15% Shia minority (including Alevis or Alawites in Cilicia) among the Kurds and in Izmir, Taurus, northeast and east; also some Yazidis around Diyarbakir, and several semi-Muslim shamanistic sects (Tahtacis, Ahl-el Hak) (here enumerated also with Muslims). *Mosques.* 43,000. *Hajj pilgrims to Mecca.* (1968) 41,998; (1969) 56,578; (1970) 13,269; (1971) 23,922; (1972) 27,235; (1973) 36,258; (1974) 106,045; (1975) 136,115; (1976) 137,291.
NONRELIGIOUS. Europeans and many of the 41,000 Chinese (in 1995), but also including a growing number of Turkish intellectuals and others.
ORTHODOX. In 1900, there were 1,350,000 Greek Orthodox and 1,600,000 Armenian Apostolics. In 1915, the Turkish state attempted to deport the 1,750,000 Armenians; at least 600,000 were massacred and 600,000 deported, leaving 550,000 in Turkey, of whom the vast majority have subsequently emigrated. In 1923, 1,500,000 Greek Orthodox resident in Turkey (Anatolia and Thrace) including the 50,000 Karamanlis (Turkish-language Orthodox) were forcibly repatriated to Greece in exchange for 400,000 Muslim Turks resident in Greece. In 1970, steady and rapid emigration of Armenians, Syrians, and (more rapidly) of Greeks took place each year, at an average rate (for affiliated Orthodox) of 7,570 emigrants a year.
PROFESSING CHRISTIANS. The total relative to the population has declined by emigration from 1.1% in 1945 to 0.4% in 1990.
ROMAN CATHOLICS. In 1990, largely expatriate Italians, French, Germans, et alia. In 1905 there were 58,500 Armenian Catholics alone, apart from Latin and other Eastern-rite Catholics.
UNAFFILIATED CHRISTIANS. Expatriate Catholics (from Italy, France) and Protestants (USA) who profess to be Christians in censuses but have not affiliated themselves to any church.

Great Commission Instrument Panel: status of Turkey (for explanation see start of Part 4)

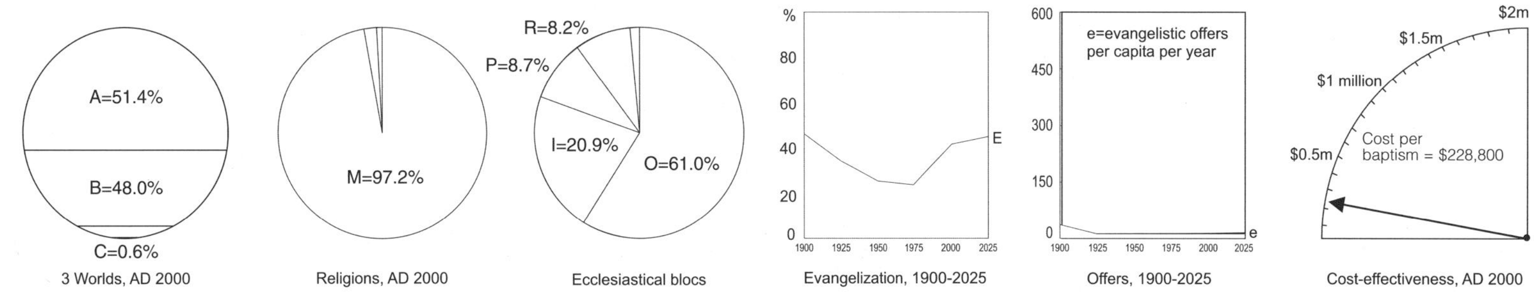

Country status. Turkey straddles Asia and Europe. It includes a roughly rectangular peninsula often known as Anatolia, a mountainous region to its east, and the small tip of the south-eastern Balkans in Europe to the west. Agriculture, industry, and tourism all play significant roles in the growing economy.

HUMAN LIFE AND LIBERTY

Human need and development. Neither developed nor underdeveloped, Turkey exists in 2 economic worlds. There are large pockets in Anatolian rural areas where the conditions of life are primitive. Istanbul and a few other cities present a different picture, but even here the dichotomy exists between a modern economy and a traditional one. On the major indicators, Turkey fares reasonably well on some and poorly on others. For example, the illiteracy rate is still a high 18% and the per capita GNP is lower than all nations in the Balkans except Romania. Cities have adequate housing, medical facilities, and educational services. Unemployment is severe in all parts of the country, and restrictions on emigration to Western Europe have exacerbated the problem.

Human rights and freedoms. Although a secular and constitutional democracy in name, Turkey is beset with internal strife and terrorism to the extent that it has ceased to be secular or democratic. A state of emergency was declared in 1987 in the 10 southeastern provinces affected by the separatist Kurdish insurgency. In its efforts to suppress threats from minorities, the government has reverted to the brutality of Ottoman times. Killings and disappearances, and abuse and torture of prisoners is routine. In 1992 the European Committee for the Prevention of Torture publicly condemned Turkey as did the United Nations Committee on Torture. More than 100 deaths are attributed annually to extrajudicial killings by the police. Whole villages are burned or forcible evacuated by security forces in areas suspected to be sympathetic to the Kurds. According to human rights organizations, more than 8,000 political prisoners are in custody without trial under the Anti-Terror Law. The security forces also act against Christians, even when they do not pose any threat to the state. In 1993, 200 Syriac Christians were driven from their homes in Hassana in Mardin Province. Christians are tortured by having crosses burnt into their chests with molten plastic. Certain towns are subject to food embargo in order to coerce its citizens. Freedom of speech and the press has become a dead letter because the Anti-Terror Law and the Penal Code make it a crime to insult Ataturk, secularism, Islam, the security forces, and the president. The offices of a daily that published excerpts from Salman Rushdie's Satanic Verses were attacked and trashed, and its editor was jailed. Increasing number of journalists are murdered in mysterious circumstances. The Anti-Terror Law is used to intimidate writers, artists, and musicians as well as journalists. Books may be banned if the Education Ministry declares them to be without utility. Ethnic minorities face various forms of societal discrimination as well actual violence from the security forces. The Kurds have been subjected to near-genocidal pogroms which may soon obliterate their existence as a separate community.

Human environment. Air and water pollution has kept pace with the country's growing urbanization and industrialization. High levels of sulfur dioxide and lead pollution are found in Istanbul's air, and mercury pollution in the nearby Sea of Marmara. Deforestation is threatening the ancient forests in eastern Turkey.

NON-CHRISTIAN RELIGIONS

Islam came to Turkey at the end of the 10th century, and today Muslims form 97% of the entire population. The great majority are Sunnis of the Hanafite rite, as is also the official organization of Islam in Turkey. A minority of Shias (Alevis), especially among the Kurds, are dispersed in different regions of the country, but they are unorganized and, because government censuses do not count members of this rite, there are no accurate statistics. A few small sects such as the Tahtacis and Ahl-el Hak are separatists (semi-Muslim, semi-shamanistic), but it is difficult to determine their number, for officially they pass as Muslim. The efforts of Mustafa Kemal Ataturk to modernize Turkey after the fall of the Ottoman Empire led him to challenge the control exerted by Muslim religious leaders over political and public life in the country. Nevertheless, the reforms of those days seem to have had only a limited effect, particularly in rural areas. The rigid divorce of religion from the state began to ease after the death of Ataturk in 1938. Especially since 1950, the state has taken measures to relax its militant secularization, without renouncing its principle of the separation of civil and religious powers. Measures favorable to Islam, including multiplication of mosques, establishment of a more structured Islamic organization, re-introduction of Islamic education in primary schools in 1949 and in secondary schools in 1956 after being suppressed since before World War II, have all been inspired in part by the desire to provide a strong front in the face of atheistic Communism, in addition to the conviction that lack of religious education has favored multiplication of sects and increase of superstitious practices. These measures have, however, not been considered adequate by some Islamic preachers of the extreme right. Education for Islamic teachers and imams has been undertaken by the Ankara Faculty of Theology (Ilahiyat Fakultesi) and 5 higher institutes of Islamic studies (Yuksek Islam Enstitusu), particularly at Istanbul since 1959 and Konya since 1962, as well as by 114 schools for imams and preachers. Eight primary schools for imams were opened in 1949. All these establishments are under the Ministry of Education rather than the Presidency of Religious Affairs.

Muslims. Istanbul is renowned for its mosques. *Top.* Blue Mosque (Mosque of Ahmed I, AD 1616, with 6 minarets in place of customary 4). *Bottom.* Hagia/Santa Sophia (left, built AD 531-7, now a museum).

Early Christian history on postage stamps: *left*, Santa Claus Kilisesi, Demre (St. Nicholas Church); *right*, remains at Ephesus.

Country summary. **Worlds A, B, C by ethnolinguistic peoples, cities, and major civil divisions in Turkey.**

	PEOPLES							CITIES							CIVIL DIVISIONS						
World	*Num*	*Pop 2000*	*C%*	*Christians*	*E%*	*U%*	*Unevangelized*	*Num*	*Pop 2000*	*C%*	*Christians*	*E%*	*U%*	*Unevangelized*	*Num*	*Pop 2000*	*C%*	*Christians*	*E%*	*U%*	*Unevangelized*
A	36	21,522,251	0.11	23,996	36	64	13,823,655	98	20,026,413	0.17	34,899	48	52	10,374,835	6	48,239,570	0.12	56,254	46	54	26,240,927
B	7	44,724,400	0.22	98,280	54	46	20,418,945	4	12,395,897	1.47	182,678	52	48	5,890,069	2	18,351,371	1.73	316,900	56	44	8,002,610
C	14	344,288	72.87	250,880	100	0	932	0	0	0.00	0	0	0	0	0	0	0.00	0	0	0	0
Total	**57**	**66,590,939**	**0.56**	**373,156**	**49**	**51**	**34,243,532**	**102**	**32,422,310**	**0.67**	**217,577**	**50**	**50**	**16,264,904**	**8**	**66,590,941**	**0.56**	**373,154**	**49**	**51**	**34,243,537**

Judaism was already present at the beginning of the Christian era, as indicated by the communities in Asia Minor visited by the Apostle Paul. A new influx came from Spain following the anti-Jewish edict of 1492. Turkish Jews are almost all Sefardis, consisting of a community of 22,000 in 1995, whose number is diminishing because of emigration to Israel. All Jews are under the jurisdiction of the Great Rabbi who resides at Istanbul.

Shamanism still prevails among a number of Turkish peoples who have been resistant to Islam and Christianity. In addition to ancestor veneration, emphasis is placed on an extensive pantheon of divinities headed by Yulgen (formerly called Tengri) who resides in the sky. Evil is centered in the figure of Erlik, Yulgen's arch-opponent.

CHRISTIANITY

In the first century, the Apostle Paul brought the gospel to Asia Minor, transforming it into a center for the establishment and dissemination of the Christian faith. According to tradition, the Apostle Andrew preached in Byzantium in AD 38 and ordained Stachys as bishop there. Many of the early ecumenical councils important in the shaping of doctrine were held in present-day Turkey. When Constantine moved the capital of the Roman empire to Constantinople in AD 330, its patriarch achieved a new status; but the split between the western and eastern churches began to widen, resulting ultimately in the Great Schism of 1054. Muslim invasions weakened the Orthodox hold over the people, and the Crusades did more harm than good to the Christian cause in Asia Minor. Islam's influence continued to grow during the period of the Ottoman empire.

At the beginning of World War I, Christians still made up a sizeable force of over 20% of the country. In 1914, Roman Catholics had 4 archdioceses, 16 dioceses, 2 vicariates and 2 missions sui juris. Between 1915 and 1917, however, over 600,000 Armenians and many Chaldeans were massacred by Turks, and over 600,000 more Armenians were deported. The subsequent massive exodus of the survivors and their emigration to other countries, followed in 1923 after the treaty of Lausanne by the forced exchange of 1.5 million Greek Orthodox from Anatolia in Turkey for Turkish Muslims in Greece, and later by slow but steady emigration, have reduced the number of Christians to a small minority. Today what remains of Christianity is found in only a few centers, divided among numerous denominations and rites, the majority being Oriental Orthodox. The 2 principal centers for Christianity are Istanbul and the southeastern part of the country (Upper Mesopotamia), other islands of relative importance being Ankara and Izmir. In addition, there are small dispersed and isolated groups, often with neither priest nor church; but their members tend to migrate to the cities, especially Istanbul.

A main reason for the diminution of Christians in recent years has been their emigration to Syria and Lebanon and as laborers to European countries, particularly West Germany. This exodus is not a uniquely Christian phenomenon, but their small numbers make it most strongly felt among Christians. Conversions to Islam are rare, more rare than in such countries as Egypt, but the children of mixed marriages invariably become Muslim.

Christians are generally considered aliens in the country, even if this is an unconscious feeling and their families have lived in Turkey for centuries. This is especially true for Latin Catholics, the majority of whom are descendants of immigrant families. Oriental Christians resent the fact that national life is based on the Muslim community and is frequently identified with it. This discrimination, although a reality in daily life, does not exist as far as legislation is concerned, since the state is secular and does not judge its citizens by their beliefs.

Orthodox. Summit of the Primates of the Orthodox Churches, at the Phanar, Istanbul, March 1992; in Liturgy celebrating 'The Triumph of Orthodoxy'.

ORTHODOX CHURCHES. Orthodoxy is represented by a wide variety of traditions in Turkey. The ecumenical patriarch of Constantinople, who has a unique position of honor in Eastern Orthodoxy although without power to interfere in the affairs of other churches, has his see in Istanbul. In AD 1000 the patriarchate had under it some 624 dioceses, but its jurisdiction has been radically reduced since then, especially since the Greco-Turkish war of 1922 and the more recent anti-Greek riot of September 1955, when 60 of the patriarchate's 80 churches in Istanbul were sacked. Today the patriarch has oversight in Turkey, Crete, Mount Athos, Finland, and over Greeks of the dispersion, mostly in North America. In Turkey itself there exist the Holy Synod, and 4 metropolitans with 80 clergy. The overwhelming majority of the faithful are found in Istanbul.

Ecumenical Patriarchate of Constantinople. Meetings of Holy Synod in Cathedral of St. George: *top*, 1967; *lower*, 1992.

Other Eastern Orthodox, not directly under the ecumenical patriarch, are Greek Orthodox Arabs related to the patriarchate of Antioch, with 5 congregations in southern Turkey; Bulgarian Orthodox, with 2 churches and an exarch at Istanbul, and a parish at Edirne; Russian Orthodox with a church in Istanbul; and Serbian Orthodox under the patriarchate of Belgrade.

Non-Chalcedonian Oriental Orthodox are divided into Armenian and Syro-Jacobite communities, and form the largest single Christian tradition in Turkey. The Armenian patriarchate of Constantinople, with its see at Istanbul, is dependent on the Catholicate of Echmiadzin in Soviet Armenia. The faithful are concentrated in Istanbul, where 35 of the patriarchate's 44 parishes are located, although there are also churches in Ankara, Kastamonu, Kayseri, Malatya, Sivas, Diyarbakir, and Iskenderum. Educational and social service institutions include 2 orphanages in Istanbul. Syrian Orthodox are found mostly in the southeast, their 2 dioceses of Mardin and Midyat stretching along the Syrian border; there are also groups at Istanbul and Ankara which are growing at present due to migration from the rural southeast. These are administratively related to the diocese of Mardin, the latter having jurisdiction over the entire country with the exception of Midyat. The Syrians are dependent on the patriarchate of Antioch with its see in Damascus.

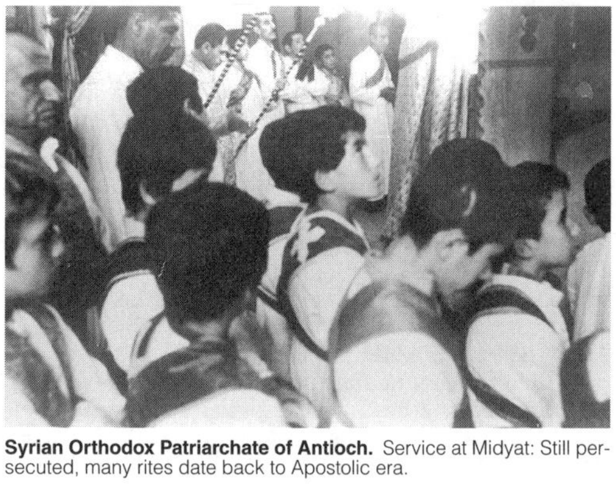

Syrian Orthodox Patriarchate of Antioch. Service at Midyat: Still persecuted, many rites date back to Apostolic era.

In 1922, an attempt was made by Turkish nationals under the ecumenical patriarch to establish an autocephalous Turkish Orthodox Church, with the strong support of Mustafa Kemal and the government of Turkey. The expectation that it would be joined by the 50,000 Karamanlis (Turkish-language Orthodox) was frustrated when the latter were all deported to Greece in 1923. The resulting schism has continued ever since, but with decreasing support and numbers, though a large following is claimed among emigres in the USA.

CATHOLIC CHURCH. Catholics are divided among several rites: Latin, Armenian, Chaldean, Syrian, and Byzantine. Most Latin Catholics live in Istanbul, Ankara, Izmir, and their suburbs. There is also a parish at Mersin and another at Iskenderun, both within the vicariate of Istanbul, in addition to the parishes of Trabzon (Trebizonde) and Sumsun, in the mission sui juris of the Black Sea, and a few isolated groups scattered in other parts of the country. The faithful in Istanbul are largely descendants of families who immigrated from the west in the distant past and are all Turkish citizens. Those at Ankara are for the most part foreigners who reside there temporarily as civil servants, technicians or professionals. The same holds true for a number of other Catholics scattered about the country isolated from the services of a priest. Several languages are used in the liturgy: Latin, French, Italian, German, English, and Turkish.

Armenian Catholics are concentrated in Istanbul and its suburbs, with some living in Ankara, Malatya, Sivas, Diyarbakir, and in small groups or isolated families throughout the country. All clergy are centered in Istanbul.

Most of the Chaldeans live in the southeast near the Iraqi border, although there is also a sizeable Chaldean Catholic community in Istanbul.

Syrian Catholics are found in both Istanbul and the southeast at Mardin or in neighboring villages.

Their small numbers notwithstanding, Catholics of the Byzantine rite are divided between the apostolic exarchate of Istanbul, which includes Greek Catholics directly under Rome, and the patriarchal vicariate of Istanbul, which includes Melkites, some in Istanbul and others in the southeast. The latter are directly under the Greek-Melkite patriarch of Antioch.

There are also a few Maronites, mostly in the south together with some Bulgarians and Georgians. They have no local hierarchy, clergy or places of worship, but usually attend churches of other Catholic rites.

The Holy See has diplomatic relations with Turkey and in AD 2000 is represented to government and the Catholic hierarchy by a nuncio residing in Ankara.

OTHER CHURCHES. British Anglicans and German Lutherans each have parishes at Istanbul, Ankara, and Izmir which cater exclusively for their expatriate communities; while the large numbers of USA military personnel are served by North American military chaplaincies, as well as through the Churches of Christ and the Union Church of Istanbul. Other ethnic minority denominations are the Bulgarian Congregational and Greek Evangelical churches. A number of North American bodies (Seventh-day Adventists, Southern Baptists, World-Wide Missions, Mormons, Jehovah's Witnesses) have been active but with indifferent success.

Indigenous missions. Some of the earliest Christian missionaries were sent out from the first century churches in Turkey. Since the Muslim conquest of Constantinople (1453) little mission activity has been evident.

Bible bookshop in main shopping street of Izmit, with bold text 'In the beginning the Word already existed' (John 1:1).

CHURCH AND STATE

In contrast to almost all other Islamic countries, Turkey, although having a Muslim population of 99%, is officially a secular state (Article 2 of the constitution of 1961). After proclaiming a republic in 1923, Ataturk abolished Islam as the state religion 5 years later, replaced Islamic law with European law, and introduced secularization in 1928 and had it legalized in the constitution in 1937.

Article 12 of the constitution of 1961, which was revised in 1971, states that all citizens are 'equal before the law, without distinction of language, race, sex, political opinion, philosophical belief, religion or worship'. Article 19 states that 'Everyone has freedom of conscience and opinion and religious faith. Religious prayers, rites, and ceremonies may be freely practiced as long as they are not incompatible with public order or public morals or with laws promulgated to this effect. No one may be restrained from taking part in religious prayers, rites, and ceremonies nor from declaring his religious beliefs and opinions. No one may be criticized for his religious beliefs and opinions. Religious education is dependent on the desire of each person or legal representative in the case of minors. No one may exploit religion or religious sentiments or those things considered sacred by a religion, or abuse them in such a manner that they are used to exert personal or political influence on the social, economic, political or juridical order of the state. Those who contravene this interdiction or incite others to do so are liable to punishment before the law'. Finally, Article 20 guarantees freedom of thought and conviction, and freedom of 'diffusing them by written or spoken word, by pictures or other means'. Nevertheless, 163 of the Turkish criminal code states that proselytism is prohibited.

Despite the secular character of the Turkish state and the unstructured nature of Islam (which usually has no hierarchy nor organization comparable to that of Christian churches), supreme authority for Islam in Turkey has, since the abolition of the Caliphate on 3 March 1924, been vested in the presidency or office of religious affairs (Diyanet Isleri Baskanligi), which is attached directly to the Presidency of the Council with its seat at Ankara. Law 633 of 22 June 1965, which constitutes the latest reorganization of this body, lists its purposes as follows: 'To direct the affairs pertaining to the beliefs of the Muslim religion and to the foundations of worship and morals: to enlighten the population on the subject of religion and to administer places of worship' (Article 1). The supreme authority is the president of religious affairs (Diyanet Isleri Boskani) who is named and removed from office by the president of the Republic. Under him in each province or department (vilayet) is a mufti; these now number 67. At a still lower level, each ward (ilce) has a mufti of second rank (now numbering 572), under whom are imams for each locality in the district. The Presidency of Religious Affairs publishes numerous religious works, including 2 journals (a monthly and a weekly) both of which are called Divanet. It also sends delegations of imams and teachers to other countries, especially Germany, to provide for the care of Turkish migrant workers. The salaries of such Muslim functionaries as muftis and imams are paid from the state budget.

Non-Muslim religious communities are not subject to the Presidency of Religious Affairs. Thus deprived of public or private juridical personality, they are reduced to 'juridically amorphous gatherings of individuals' with the old Ottoman millet system having been abolished for these communities, although not completely so for Muslims. Concerning Christian communities, a distinction is made between the churches of 'minorities', those consisting of Turkish citizens, and those falling under special conditions given to certain foreign institutions as defined in the 1923 Treaty of Lausanne, which paved the way for the independence of Turkey and abolished the so-called Capitulations. Freedom of action for the first group is guaranteed by Articles 38-44 of the Treaty of Lausanne. Local churches of minorities are subject in every way to the legislation of the country, and their clergy must be of Turkish nationality. In the eyes of the Turkish state, the most important of these minority churches, the Ecumenical Patriarchate of Constantinople (called by the Turkish Republic the 'Patriarchate of Istanbul'), is no more than a Turkish national institution whose jurisdiction extends over all Turkish citizens of the Greek Orthodox religion. It is subject to legal control and must limit itself to purely religious activities. For this reason its publishing house was suppressed in 1964, and the finances of the properties of the Monastery of St George (the patriarchate) are audited. The paradox of this sociologically Greek but legally Turkish patriarchate, whose patriarch and clergy are of Turkish nationality, is evident when one compares the attitude of both Turkey and Greece towards it. Turkey recognizes it only as having an exclusively religious character, uniquely at the national level, while a foreign power, Greece, refers to the same body in its own constitution.

As far as French, Italian, and English religious, educational, and medical institutions are concerned, their existence in Turkey in 1914 was officially recognized in letters annexed to the Treaty of Lausanne. Thus, they may continue their work as at that time, although in actuality a large number no longer exist. Nevertheless, it is legal for those still active to have foreign priests, superiors, and teachers.

Christian clergy are not paid by the state. They are usually provided for by their respective communities through the *vakif* or foundations administered by a committee of laymen of the community, under the supervision (sometimes interference) of the civil authorities. It is for this reason that clergy or pastors of Christian communities are not considered to be the heads of their communities by the civil authorities, who recognize instead the presidents of these committees of laymen.

According to Law 1778 of 25 March 1931, no foreigner may teach Turkish citizens in primary schools. Since that time all foreign schools (except those catering entirely for foreign students), including religious schools run by Western religious congregations, have been only at the college or secondary level.

BROADCASTING AND MEDIA

Shortwave radio programs in Arabic can be received from FEBA (Seychelles) and HCJB (Ecuador), and in Turkish from TWR (Albania) and TWR (Monaco). Shortwave radio programs from KNLS have seen some response. Satellite TV programs are received mainly in Arabic. Turkey is a member of UNDA. The 'Jesus' Film has been shown to 673,000: chiefly through film team showings (524,000) and videocassettes (150,000), with 56,000 responding.

INTERDENOMINATIONAL ORGANIZATIONS

No organization or structured group dedicated to ecumenical matters exists, with the exception of the Commission for Ecumenical Affairs of the Latin vicariate of Istanbul, which is official but largely inactive. A Library for Ecumenical Questions was created in 1969 by the Greek Catholic exarchate of Istanbul but was forced to close in 1973. An unofficial Protestant union of congregations also exists.

FUTURE TRENDS AND PROSPECTS

Greeks, Armenians, and Americans probably will continue to represent the bulk of Christianity in Turkey through 2025, while the Christian percentage remains at 0.6% throughout the period. Muslims will dominate the majority of the peoples at over 95% through 2025.

Christianity is not expected to grow to even 1% of Turkey's population, even after AD 2050. Islam will likely predominate throughout the next fifty years at least.

BIBLIOGRAPHY

A brief history of American Board schools in Turkey. E. W. Putney. Istanbul: Nesriyat Dairesi, 1964. 11p.

'An autocephalous Turkish Orthodox Church,' X. Jacob, *Eastern churches review*, 3, 1 (1970), 59–71.

Aspects of religion in secular Turkey. J. M. Wagstaff (ed). Durham, UK: Centre for Middle Eastern and Islamic Studies, University of Durham, 1990. 38p.

Byzantine Constantinople: the churches. J. Phillips & T. A. Roe. *Architecture series—bibliography*, A-870. Monticello, IL: Vance Bibliographies, 1982. 37p.

Catholics and sultans: the church and the Ottoman Empire, 1453–1923. C. A. Frazee. London: Cambridge University Press, 1983. 395p.

Christianity and Islam under the sultans. F. W. Hasluck. Ed., M. M. Hasluck . New York: Octagon Books, 1973. 2 vols.

Christians and Jews in the Ottoman empire: the functioning of a plural society. B. Braude & B. Lewis (eds). New York: Holmes & Meier, 1982. 2 vols.

Christliche Stätten in der Türkei: Info. P. Guntermann & H. Hammer. Turkey, 1988. 65p.

De Syrisch Orthodoxen in Istanbul: een volk, uit een ver verleden overgebleven. J. Roldanus. Kampen: Kok, 1984. 163p.

Folk religion of the Kurds. A. Rahman. Altadena, CA: Friends of the Kurds, Zwemer Institute, 1988. 60p.

From Istanbul to Aghtamar: an Armenian pilgrimage. H. J. Nersoyan. New York: Ashod Press, 1990. 98p.

Imperialism, evangelism, and the Ottoman Armenians, 1878–1896. J. Salt. London: Frank Cass and Co., 1993. 198p.

Islam in modern Turkey: religion, politics, and literature in a secular state. R. Tapper (ed). London: St. Martin's Press, 1994. 319p.

'Islamic resurgence in Turkey?: an analysis of political and social elements.' R. Miranda. M.S. thesis, Naval Postgraduate School, Monterey, CA, 1993. 137p.

'Le giurisdizioni delle chiese cristiane sul territorio della Republica Turca,' L. A. Missir, *Il diritto ecclesiastico*, 78, 3-4 (1967), 346–52.

'Lo statuto dei beni ecclesiastici in Turchia.' L. A. Missir. Contribution à la XXXIX Semaine de Missiologie de Louvain, Namur, 24-28 août 1969, Louvain, Belgium, 1969. P.31–51.

Musulmanes et modernes: voile et civilisation en Turquie. N. Göle. Trans., J. Riegel. *Textes à l'appui Série Sociologie.* Paris: Editions La Découverte, 1993. 167p.

Mysticism and magic in Turkey: an account of the religious doctrines, monastic organisation, and ecstatic powers of the dervish orders. L. M. J. Garnett. New York: Scribner's Sons, 1912. 202p.

New martyrs of the Turkish yoke. Seattle, WA: St. Nectarios Press, 1985. 409p.

Ottomans, Turks and the Jewish polity: a history of the Jews of Turkey. W. F. Weiker. Lanham, MD: University Press of America, 1992. 386p.

'Religion and culture,' chapter XII in *The emergence of modern Turkey*, p.395–418f. B. Lewis (ed). London: Oxford University Press, 1961.

Religion in the Middle East: three religions in concord and conflict. A. J. Arberry. Cambridge, UK: Cambridge University Press, 1969. 2 vols. (Vol. 1: *Judaism and Christianity*; vol. 2: *Islam*, and *Concord and Conflict*).

'Religious changes in republican Turkey,' P. Stirling, *Middle East journal*, 12, 4 (1958), 395–408.

Studies and documents relating to the history of the Greek Church and people under Turkish domination. T. Papadopoullos. 2nd ed. 1952; reprint, Aldershot, UK: Variorum Gower, 1990. 458p.

Temples, churches, and mosques of Turkey. J. Steele & E. Alok. London: K. Paul International, 1991.

The Armenians in history and the Armenian question. E. Uras. Istanbul: Documentary Publications, 1988. 1064p.

'The celebration of worship in the Air Force Remote Site Ministry.' R. S. Leeds. Thesis, San Francisco Theological Seminary, San Anselmo, CA, 1979. 126p. (Examines military chaplaincy at the Pirinclik Common Defense

Installation, Diyarbakir, Turkey).
'The crypto–Christians of Turkey,' R. M. Dawkins, *Byzantion*, 8 (1933), 247–275.
The development of secularism in Turkey. N. Berkes. Montreal, Canada: McGill University Press, 1964. 550p.
The Great Church in captivity: a study of the patriarchate of Constantinople from the eve of the Turkish conquest to the Greek War of Independence. S. Runciman. Cambridge, UK: Cambridge University Press, 1968. 455p. *The Jews of the Ottoman Empire and the Turkish Republic*. S. J. Shaw. New York: New York University Press, 1991. 393p.
The Kurds: a concise history and fact book. M. Izady. Washington, DC: Crane Russak, 1991. 285p.
The Union Church of Istanbul: a history. A. G. Edmonds. Istanbul: Union Church of Istanbul, 1986. 57p.
'Toward a culturally relevant and practical church planting strategy for use in Istanbul, Turkey.' J. G. Romaine. D.Min. thesis, Columbia Biblical Seminary and Graduate School of Missions, Columbia, SC, 1993. 409p.
Turkey, ecumenical pilgrimage. Pope John Paul II. Boston: St. Paul Editions, 1980. 113p.
Turkey in Europe. C. Eliot. London: Cass, 1965. 459p.
Turkish life in town and country. L. M. J. Garnett. New York: G. P. Putnam's Sons, 1905. 336p.

Country Table 2. **Organized churches and denominations in Turkey.**

Official name (bold type = church with over 10% of all affiliated) 1	*Begun* 2	*Type* 3	*Counc* 4	*Congs* 5	*Adults* 6	*Affiliated 1970* 7	*Affiliated 1995* 8	*G%* 9	*Names, notes, and other statistics* (see Codebook, Part 3) 10
Ancient Church of the East (P Tehran)	500	O-Nes	Yw...	20	17,200	18,000	25,000	0.07	*Nestorians*. Assyrian massacre remnants. Scattered families in southeast. No clergy.
Armenian Apostolic P Constantinople	c 400	O-Arm	EW...	40	48,000	80,000	82,000	0.10	*Armeni Patrikhanesi*. 45 dioceses till 1915 massacres. 1997, 75% in Istanbul. 3 bps,41n,900Yy.
Baptist Church		P-Bap	T....	1	100	100	150	0.05	*Galatian Baptist Church*, Ankara. English-language. Expatriates, USA workers. 1x.
Broadsheet Readers' Clubs	c1990	I-3pZ	.....	2	100	–	300	20.00	Readers of Gospel Broadsheets produced by GEM, Richmond, VA.
Bulgarian Congregational Church	c1900	P-Con	.....	5	600	1,000	1,100	0.38	*Soborna Congrezanska Crkva*. Bulgarians, now citizens, in west. Aid, M=CCCI(USA).
Bulgarian Orthodox Church: E Turkey	1870	O-Bul	Mwc..	10	11,000	2,200	23,000	9.84	*Bulgar Eksarhanesi*. Under P Sofia. Bulgarians in west, also many Pomak converts. 1n.
Catholic Church in Turkey:	1198	R-LEr	O...R	50	16,980	26,487	29,787	0.47	*Katolik Kilisesi*. C=9+1+8. (1970) 25n,51x. (1990) 21n 42x 56m 113w 122Yy
M Izmir (Smyrna) *(Latin)*	1322	R-Lat	Os	8	750	2,650	1,257	-2.94	Latin metropolitan see 1322, 1818. 3 schools. 1H. 0n 7x 10m 11w 14Yy
AD Diarbekir (Amida) *(Chaldean)*	1553	R-Cha	Os	6	1,900	8,000	2,700	-4.25	Under P Babylon. Destroyed 1918, restored 1966. 6n 0x 0m 0w 27Yy
AD Istanbul *(Armenian)*	1830	R-Arm	Os	10	2,100	8,300	3,680	-3.20	Under P Cilicia. 14 dioceses destroyed 1915. 2n 0x 0m 7w 27Yy
EP Turkey *(Syrian)*	1888	R-Syr	Os	3	1,200	1,300	2,100	1.94	*Patriarchal Exarchate*, P Antioch. 1972 D Mardin. 3n 1x 1m 0w 10Yy
EA Istanbul *(Greek)*	1911	R-Gre	Os	1	30	82	50	-1.96	Byzantine-rite Catholics across Turkey. Rapid decline. 1n 0x 0m 0w 0Yy
VA Istanbul *(Latin)*	1742	R-Lat	Os	15	8,800	6,000	15,000	3.73	All aliens. 10,900 in 1955. 17 schools. M=AA,OP. 6n 27x 38m 91w 39Yy
VA Anatolia (Trabzon) *(Latin)*	c1650	R-Lat	Os	7	2,200	155	5,000	14.91	*Latin Katolik Kilisesi*. PA until 1896. M=OFMCap. 3n 7x 7m 4w 5Yy
Christian Brethren	1900	P-CBr	x...	2	100	200	200	0.00	*Plymouth Brethren. Open Brethren.* Initial work among Armenians. M=CMML(UK, USA). 4f.
Church of England (D Europe)	1598	A-plu	awc..	6	1,400	2,000	2,100	0.20	1865 Armenian Apostolic schism to Anglicanism. Now UK, USA, other anglophones. 2x.
Ch of Jesus Christ of Latter-day Saints	1884	m-LdS	x....	2	200	308	400	1.05	*Mormons*. M=CJCLdS(Utah, USA). Former Armenian work; now mainly USA expatriates.
Churches of Christ		I-Dis	x....	10	700	3,000	2,000	0.05	M=CC(Non-Instrumental) (USA). USA personnel on military and air force bases.
Ecumenical Patriarchate of Constantinople:	38	O-Gre	CWC..	103	9,900	65,000	20,000	0.05	*Rum Ortodoks Patrikhanesi*. 70% citizen Greeks; emigration 9%pa. (1970) 89n. (1995) 110 bps.
AD Constantinople		O-Gre	Cp	67	4,600	30,000	9,200	0.05	Mostly Greeks. 8 auxiliary bishops, 35 pilgrimage centers. 58n,8d,6r.
D Chalcedon		O-Gre	Cm	12	1,400	9,000	2,800	0.05	Greeks. 1 auxiliary bishop. HQ Kadiköy. 7 schools, 6 welfare associations. 10n.
D Derkos		O-Gre	Cz	6	900	6,000	2,000	0.05	Bogaziçi. Bosphorus. Greeks. 2 welfare associations, 3 educational unions. 5n.
D Imbross & Tenedos (Bozcaada)		O-Gre	Cm	13	2,100	14,000	4,200	0.05	*Rum Ortodoks Imroz Metropoliti*. 2 islands in Dardanelles. HQ Imroz Adasi. 11n.
D Prinkipos (Prinkiponnisa)		O-Gre	Cm	5	900	6,000	1,800	0.05	*Rum Ortodoks Adalar Metropoliti*. HQ Büyükada, Istanbul. 2 welfare bodies. 5n.
Evangelical Alliance Church	c1960	P-Eva	.....	1	10	30	14	-3.00	M=TEAM. Fundamentalist Evangelicals from USA.
Followers of Jesus		I-3nZ	.....	70	3,000	1,000	5,000	0.05	*Jesusists*. Muslims who accept Jesus but reject name Christian. Around Gaziantep.
Georgian Orthodox Church		O-Geo	M....	5	3,000	3,000	4,000	0.05	Western Georgians bilingual in Turkish. Small remnant under Georgian Orthodox C Tiflis.
German Protestant Church	1843	P-Lut	.....	5	2,000	1,500	3,500	3.45	*Deutsch Ev Gemeinde in der Turkei*. Germans in Istanbul, Izmir, Ankara. 1x,1H,8y.
Greek Evangelical Church	1888	P-Ref	Rwc.C	2	300	200	600	4.49	Greek Protestants, related to main body in Greece. In Istanbul. 1n,W=40%,3y,4z.
Greek Orth P Antioch: D Tarsus-Adana	c 33	O-Ara	Cw.N.	10	3,000	2,000	5,000	3.73	Arabic churches in southern Turkey: HQ Mersin; Antioch, Alexandretta. Half Arabs, half Greeks.
Hidden Muslim believers in Christ	c1970	I-Mus	.....	200	17,000	–	34,600	51.90	Converted Muslims who choose to stay in Islam as witnesses to Christ.
Isolated radio churches	c1960	I-rad	.....	600	15,000	200	20,000	20.23	Isolated radio believers, mostly aged 12-25, scattered over country. T=1000 (ICI).
Jehovah's Witnesses	1933	m-Jeh	x....	14	1,013	800	1,690	3.04	Turkish converts from Islam. Istanbul, Ankara, southeast. Persecution. 142Y.
New Apostolic Church		I-3aX	x....	4	170	–	240	0.05	*NAC/NAK. M=Neuapostolische Kirche. HQ Zurich (Switzerland).*
New Life for Turks	1982	I-3cZ	.....	25	2,000	–	3,000	7.69	Indigenous Turkish movement; charismatics.
Operation Mobilisation	1963	P-	x....	10	200	100	300	4.49	M=OM(UK). Literature evangelism, small churches in Ankara et alia. Ship MV Logos.
Pentecostal Churches		I-3pZ	.....	30	1,500	300	3,000	0.05	*Pentakostçu*. Turkish indigenous pentecostals. Underground.
Protestant Church		I-Ref	.....	3	510	500	850	0.05	Immigrants in Tarsus-Antakya region. Origins with M=UPUSA and other missions.
Religious Society of Friends	1957	P-Qua	Q....	1	30	40	50	0.90	Small Quaker meeting in Istanbul. Little connection with Quakers abroad.
Romanian Orthodox Church		O-Rum	.....	5	9,000	8,000	14,000	0.05	Migrants from Romania. Under P Bucharest.
Russian Orthodox Church		O-Rus	Mwc..	10	2,000	300	4,000	0.05	*Russkaya Pravoslavnaya Tserkov*. Russian emigres, Ossetians, other ethnic peoples. 1x.
Serbian Orthodox Church		O-Ser	Cwc..	20	14,000	3,000	21,000	0.05	Under P Belgrade. Serbian immigrants and transients from Yugoslavia.
Seventh-day Adventist Church	1889	P-Adv	x....	10	500	200	1,000	6.65	*SDA, Turkey Station*, East Mediterranean Field, Middle East Union. In Istanbul.
Syrian Orth Patriarchate of Antioch	c 33	O-Syr	Dw.N.	34	16,000	30,000	25,000	-0.73	*Süryani Kadim Kilisesi*. D Mardin, D Midyat. 65n,5d,1e(8),1900Yy.
Turkish Orthodox Church: P Istanbul	1922	I-ReO	xv...	5	500	300	1,000	4.93	*Müstakil Türk Ortodoks Kilisesi*. State-aided schism. 1954 applied to WCC. In USA.
Union Church of Istanbul		P-com	C	1	100	200	300	0.05	Dutch chapel (in Netherlands embassy). English-speaking, interdenominational.
Union of Armenian Ev Chs in Near East	1819	P-Con	Rw.NC	4	400	800	1,000	0.90	M=UCBWM. 1914, 60,000; 50% massacred. Emigration. 63f,1H,1h,1j,3r,3s,W=80%.
World-Wide Missions	1961	I-Non	x....	3	300	500	700	1.35	M=World-Wide Missions(USA). Evangelicals with links in Pasadena, CA(USA).
Other Protestant denominations		P-	.....	30	15,200	20,000	22,000	0.05	Expatriates (USA, UK, German, Dutch), NATO and USA military chaplaincies; Korean churches.
Other Orthodox churches		O-	.....	6	3,000	10,000	4,000	0.05	Total about 5, including Albanian OC, Ukrainian OC, ROCOR.
Totals				**1,359**	**216,013**	**281,265**	**361,881**		

Churches, members, growth, 1900-2025	*Congs*	*Adults*	*Affiliated*	*G%*	*Total denominations*	*6 Megablocs:* *O*	*R*	*A*	*P*	*I*	*m*
Total churches, members, and denominations (mid-1900)	1,500	1,822,000	3,090,530	-3.37	19	11	1	1	5	0	1
Total churches, members, and denominations (mid-1970)	419	165,805	281,265	-3.37	41	12	1	1	18	7	2
Total churches, members, and denominations (mid-1990)	1,240	210,000	351,700	1.12	56	15	1	1	26	11	2
Total churches, members, and denominations (mid-1995)	1,359	216,013	361,881	0.57	56	15	1	1	26	11	2
Total churches, members, and denominations (mid-2000)	1,370	223,000	373,155	0.62	56	15	1	1	26	11	2
Total churches, members, and denominations (mid-2025)	1,800	242,000	404,800	0.33	101	25	1	1	40	30	4

NOTES ON TABLE ABOVE

NATIONAL COUNCILS (Column 4, 5th letter).
C = Union of Evangelical Churches (UEC) (unofficial groupings of congregations and UCBWM in Istanbul; begun 1965).
R = Episcopal Conference of Turkey (begun 1978).

SUPPRESSED DIOCESES. During 1915-18, of the 1,750,000 Turkish Armenians, 600,000 were massacred and 600,000 deported, resulting in the destruction of 45 Armenian Apostolic dioceses and 14 Armenian Catholic ones. The Chaldean Catholic dioceses of Mardin and Siirt were also destroyed at the same time.

OTHER CATHOLIC (NON-ROMAN) CHURCHES. The New Apostolic Ch (Germany) maintains a small work, under the Wiesbaden Bezirk (District).

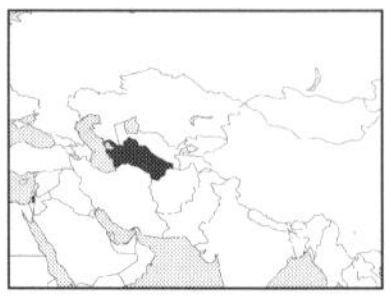

TURKMENISTAN

SECULAR DATA, AD 2000

STATE
Official name: Turkmenostan Respublikasy (The Republic of Turkmenistan).
Short name: Turkmenistan. **Adjective of nationality:** Turkmen.
Flag: Green field with small crescent and stars; red pattern on left.
Area: 488,100 sq. km. (188,500 sq. mi.).
Government: Unitary republic with one legislative body, since 1991 (1881 Russian empire, 1924-25 Soviet rule).
Legislature: Majlis (Parliament), 50 members.
Official language: Turkmen.
Monetary unit: manat. **US$1=** 5,200 manat.
Chief cities: ASCHABAD (Ashkhabad) 500,892; Cardzou (Chardzhou, Charjui) 202,203; Tasauz (Tashauz) 142,174; Mary 115,319; Nebit-Dag 108,271.
Political divisions: 6 provinces.
Armed forces: 21,000.

DEMOGRAPHY
Population: 4,459,000.
Population density: 9.1/sq. km. (23.6/sq. mi.).
Under 15 years: 1,679,000.
Growth rate p.a.: 1.62% (births 25.31, deaths 6.53).
Mortality: Infant, per 1,000: 49.0; **Maternal per 100,000:** 55.0.
Life expectancy: 67 (male 64, female 70).
Household size: 5.6. **Floor area per person, sq.m:** 10.0.
Major languages: Turkmen, Uzbek, Russian, Kazakh.
Urban dwellers: 45.51%. **Urban growth rate p.a.:** 2.5%.
Labor force: 41%.

ETHNOLINGUISTIC PEOPLES
79.2% Turkmen (Trukhmeny); 9.0% Uzbek; 3.0% Russian; 2.5% Kazakh; 1.1% Tatar.

ECONOMY
National income p.a. per person: US$920; **per family:** US$5,152.

EDUCATION
Adult literacy: 97% (male 98%, female 96%). **Schools:** 1,832.
Universities: 9. **School enrolment:** female/male: 60%/60%.

HEALTH
Access to health services: 70%. **Access to safe water:** 85%.
Hospitals: 368 (115 beds per 10,000). **Doctors:** 14,000.
Blind: 4,000. **Deaf:** 268,800. **Murder rate:** 5.
Lepers: 500.

LITERATURE
New book titles p.a.: 580 (130 p.a. per million). **Periodicals:** 46.
Newspapers: 2 dailies.

COMMUNICATION (per 1,000 people)
Phones: 71 (0% mobile). **Radios:** 189. **TV sets:** 189.
Daily newspaper circulation: 250. **Computers:** 8.

HUMAN LIFE AND LIBERTY (optimum condition=100.0%)
HDI: 72.3. **HSI:** 10.0. **HFI:** 5.0. **EFL:** 15.0.

Country Table 1. **Religious adherents in Turkmenistan, AD 1900-2025.**

Year	1900		1970		mid-1990		Annual change, 1990-2000				mid-1995		mid-2000		mid-2025	
Name	*Adherents*	*%*	*Adherents*	*%*	*Adherents*	*%*	*Natural*	*Conversion*	*Total*	*Rate*	*Adherents*	*%*	*Adherents*	*%*	*Adherents*	*%*
Muslims	482,000	98.4	1,301,500	59.5	3,037,940	82.8	65,543	19,425	84,968	2.50	3,488,260	85.5	3,887,617	87.2	5,918,100	94.1
Nonreligious	500	0.1	444,000	20.3	415,000	11.3	8,949	-10,359	-1,410	-0.35	405,900	10.0	400,896	9.0	250,000	4.0
Christians	**4,500**	**0.9**	**120,000**	**5.5**	**120,500**	**3.3**	**2,599**	**-4,484**	**-1,885**	**-1.69**	**109,000**	**2.7**	**101,648**	**2.3**	**93,000**	**1.5**
PROFESSION																
crypto-Christians	0	0.0	30,000	1.4	80,000	2.2	1,725	-3,225	-1,500	-2.05	75,000	1.8	65,000	1.5	50,000	0.8
professing Christians	**4,500**	**0.9**	**90,000**	**4.1**	**40,500**	**1.1**	**873**	**-1,258**	**-385**	**-0.99**	**34,000**	**0.8**	**36,648**	**0.8**	**43,000**	**0.7**
AFFILIATION																
unaffiliated Christians	0	0.0	7,000	0.3	3,970	0.1	86	-207	-121	-3.55	3,520	0.1	2,765	0.1	2,200	0.0
affiliated Christians	**4,500**	**0.9**	**113,000**	**5.2**	**116,530**	**3.2**	**2,513**	**-4,278**	**-1,765**	**-1.63**	**105,480**	**2.6**	**98,883**	**2.2**	**90,800**	**1.4**
Orthodox	4,000	0.8	108,200	4.9	98,100	2.7	2,116	-4,468	-2,352	-2.70	84,100	2.1	74,583	1.7	70,000	1.1
Independents	0	0.0	3,000	0.1	13,500	0.4	291	259	550	3.48	16,350	0.4	19,000	0.4	12,000	0.2
Protestants	0	0.0	1,600	0.1	2,800	0.1	60	-60	0	0.00	2,800	0.1	2,800	0.1	5,000	0.1
Roman Catholics	500	0.1	200	0.0	1,900	0.1	41	-21	20	1.01	2,000	0.1	2,100	0.1	3,000	0.1
Marginal Christians	0	0.0	0	0.0	230	0.0	5	12	17	5.69	230	0.0	400	0.0	800	0.0
Trans-megabloc groupings																
Evangelicals	0	0.0	300	0.0	730	0.0	16	1	17	2.12	883	0.0	900	0.0	1,300	0.0
Pentecostals/Charismatics	0	0.0	100	0.0	7,400	0.2	160	175	335	3.80	9,050	0.2	10,750	0.2	20,700	0.3
Great Commission Christians	**3,900**	**0.8**	**60,000**	**2.7**	**64,000**	**1.7**	**1,380**	**-2,980**	**-1,600**	**-2.84**	**58,000**	**1.4**	**48,002**	**1.1**	**54,500**	**0.9**
Atheists	0	0.0	320,500	14.6	90,000	2.5	1,941	-4,540	-2,599	-3.35	70,000	1.7	64,007	1.4	20,000	0.3
Jews	3,000	0.6	3,000	0.1	2,600	0.1	56	-37	19	0.71	2,700	0.1	2,790	0.1	2,000	0.0
Baha'is	0	0.0	0	0.0	800	0.0	17	-1	16	1.88	880	0.0	964	0.0	2,000	0.0
Ethnoreligionists	0	0.0	0	0.0	640	0.0	14	-4	10	1.46	680	0.0	740	0.0	1,000	0.0
Buddhists	0	0.0	0	0.0	520	0.0	11	0	11	1.94	580	0.0	630	0.0	900	0.0
World A (unevangelized persons)	460,110	93.9	1,750,800	80.0	2,600,612	70.9	56,099	-24,209	31,890	1.16	2,736,240	67.1	2,920,645	65.5	3,797,348	60.4
World B (evangelized non-Christians)	25,390	5.2	317,700	14.5	946,888	25.8	20,432	28,693	49,125	4.26	1,232,614	30.2	1,436,707	32.2	2,396,652	38.1
World C (Christians)	4,500	0.9	120,000	5.5	120,500	3.3	2,599	-4,484	-1,885	-1.69	109,000	2.7	101,648	2.3	93,000	1.5
Country's population	**490,000**	**100.0**	**2,188,500**	**100.0**	**3,668,000**	**100.0**	**79,130**	**0**	**79,130**	**1.97**	**4,077,855**	**100.0**	**4,459,000**	**100.0**	**6,287,000**	**100.0**

COLUMNS, ROWS.
For meanings and definitions, see Codebook (Part 3). Note that, by definition, total 'Christians' = professing + crypto-Christians, which also = affiliated + unaffiliated Christians, and also = Great Commission Christians + latent Christians. Percentages may not always total exactly, due to rounding.

NOTES ON RELIGIONS
BAHA'IS. Rapid expansion after 1991 independence, to 10 local spiritual assemblies (1996).
INDEPENDENTS. Isolated radio believers and the small Pentecostal Church (see Table 2).
ORTHODOX. Declining due to emigration of ethnic Russians and Ukrainians.

Great Commission Instrument Panel: status of Turkmenistan (for explanation see start of Part 4)

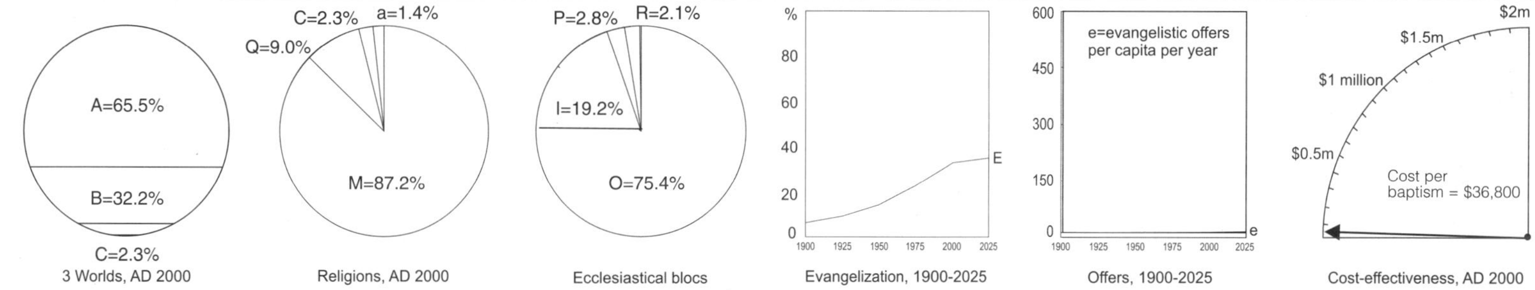

Country summary. **Worlds A, B, C by ethnolinguistic peoples, cities, and major civil divisions in Turkmenistan.**

	PEOPLES							CITIES							CIVIL DIVISIONS						
World	*Num*	*Pop 2000*	*C%*	*Christians*	*E%*	*U%*	*Unevangelized*	*Num*	*Pop 2000*	*C%*	*Christians*	*E%*	*U%*	*Unevangelized*	*Num*	*Pop 2000*	*C%*	*Christians*	*E%*	*U%*	*Unevangelized*
A	21	4,234,074	0.05	1,966	31	69	2,911,141	7	1,208,613	2.58	31,169	36	64	768,561	6	4,459,293	2.22	98,883	35	65	2,918,902
B	5	144,484	28.21	40,754	95	5	7,515	0	0	0.00	0	0	0	0	0	0	0.00	0	0	0	0
C	12	80,736	69.56	56,161	100	0	245	0	0	0.00	0	0	0	0	0	0	0.00	0	0	0	0
Total	**38**	**4,459,294**	**2.22**	**98,881**	**35**	**65**	**2,918,901**	**7**	**1,208,613**	**2.58**	**31,169**	**36**	**64**	**768,561**	**6**	**4,459,293**	**2.22**	**98,883**	**35**	**65**	**2,918,902**

Country status. Turkmenistan, a former republic of the Soviet Union, is a landlocked country dominated by desert in Central Asia to the east of the Caspian Sea. The economy is dependent on its rich mineral resources including oil, gas, coal, and sulphur.

HUMAN LIFE AND LIBERTY

Human rights and freedoms. Even though Turkmenistan achieved independence in 1991 with the promise of a transformation into a democratic state, it has made very little progress in this direction. It remains a one-party state dominated by the president and his clique of advisers. As a result, political and civil liberties remain severely restricted. Opposition political organizations are not permitted. The media function under state yoke with little or no criticism of the government. Opposition leaders are routinely detained. The security officials use physical surveillance, telephone tapping, and informers. Although a secular state, the government has encouraged some aspects of Muslim culture and it gives financial and other support to Islamic groups. There are no local human rights monitoring groups.

NON-CHRISTIAN RELIGIONS

Islam. After decades of suppression of religion under the Soviet government a renewed interest in Islam has arisen in Turkmenistan. Sunni Muslims of the Hanafi school make up 88.5% of the population, which is an increase of almost 30% since 1970. They come under the jurisdiction of the Spiritual Directorate for Central Asia and Kazakhstan. President Niyazov, who was originally put in office by Moscow with one of his responsibilities being to contain and curtail Islam, has sponsored numerous mosques and has made a pilgrimage to Mecca.

The influence of Sufi sects, especially the Naqshbandiyya, is strong among the Turkmen.

Atheism. After the fall of the Soviet empire, atheism decreased markedly in Turkmenistan.

CHRISTIANITY

CATHOLIC CHURCH. The Holy See has no diplomatic relations with Turkmenistan in AD 2000.

ORTHODOX CHURCH. The Russian Orthodox church is the largest Christian denomination in Turkmenistan, although it remains a small minority at 2%.

BROADCASTING AND MEDIA

Programming in central Asian languages (Kazakh, Tajik, Uzbek, Kyrgyz) can be received from TWR (Guam), FEBC (Saipan), and HCJB (Ecuador). IBRA-produced programs in Turkish, Arabic, Azeri, and Farsi can be received from the ultra-powerful Radio Moscow stations in Krasnodar, St Petersburg, and Samara. Additional Turkish-language program can be received from TWR's stations in Albania and Monaco.

Over 1.3 million have seen the 'Jesus' film, mainly on television.

FUTURE TRENDS AND PROSPECTS

In the post-Soviet period, Christians are likely to decline through emigration, while the nonreligious and atheists of the Soviet era steadily convert to Islam. Christianity, atheism, and the nonreligious are all expected to decline. Islam will probably pass the 95% mark before AD 2050. This will remain the case at mid-century at least.

BIBLIOGRAPHY

'A history of the Turkman people,' V. V. Barthold, in *Four studies of the history of Central Asia*. Leiden: E. J. Brill, 1962.
Country profile, Turkmenistan. London: International Institute for the Study of Islam and Christianity, 1994. 82p.
Documents: Soviet Russia's anti–Islam–policy in Turkestan. B. Hayit. Düsseldorf: Gerhard von Mende, 1958–59. 2 vols.
Islam and Turkestan under Russian rule. B. Hayit. Istanbul: B. Hayit, 1987. 560p.
Istoriia religioznykh verovanii narodov turkmenistana. S. M. Demidov. Ashkhabad: Ylym, 1990. 143p.
'Keramatly erler' khakynda khakykat. S. Jumadurdyev (ed). Ashgabat: Ylym, 1986. 96p.
Religioznye perezhitki i puti ikh preodoleniia v Turkmenistane. N. Bairamsakhatov, K. Akmuradov & S. Demidov. Ashkhabad: Ylym, 1977. 183p.
Semia i formirovanie lichnosti: analiz aspektov ateisticheskogo i religioznogo vospitaniia. M. Annanurov. Ashkhabad: Ylym, 1991. 101p.
Soviet Asia: bibliographies (a compilation of social science and humanities sources on the Iranian, Mongolian and Turkic nationalities, with an essay on the Soviet–Asia controversy). E. Allworth. New York: Praeger, 1975.
Soviet empire: the Turks of Central Asia and Stalinism. O. K. Caroe. New York: St. Martin's Press, 1953.
The challenge of Central Asia: a brief survey of Tibet and its borderlands, Mongolia, NW Kansu, Chinese Turkestan and Russian Central Asia. M. Cable et al. London: World Dominion Press, 1932. 141p.
The steep ascent: the story of the Christian church in Turkestan. R. Wingate. London: British and Foreign Bible Society.

'The Turkmen in the age of imperialism: a study of the Turkmen people and their incorporation into the Russian Empire.' M. Saray. University Society Printing House, 1989.
'Turkmen,' W. G. Irons, in *Muslim peoples: a world ethnographic survey*. 2nd ed. Westport, CT: Greenwood Press, 1984. Ed. R. V. Weekes.

Country Table 2. **Organized churches and denominations in Turkmenistan.**

Official name (bold type = church with over 10% of all affiliated) 1	*Begun* 2	*Type* 3	*Counc* 4	*Congs* 5	*Adults* 6	*Affiliated 1970* 7	*Affiliated 1995* 8	*G%* 9	*Names, notes, and other statistics* (see Codebook, Part 3) 10
Armenian Apostolic Church		O-Arm	E....	13	13,900	18,000	22,000	0.05	Gregorians, under C Echmiadzin.
Baptist Church in Turkmenistan		P-Bap	T....	3	80	200	200	0.05	Formerly AUCECB. Ukrainians, Russians, a few Westerners. Emigration.
Catholic Ch in Turkmenistan		R-LEr	B....	4	1,000	200	2,000	0.05	Residents, migrant workers. Ukrainians, Byelorussians, Lithuanians, Poles.
Full Gospel Christian Church	c1992	I-3fZ	.....	3	1,000	–	3,000	33.33	Main churches in Tashkent, Ashkhabad. State harassment. Uzbeks, Turkmen, Russians.
German Ev Lutheran Church		P-Lut	L....	8	1,500	1,000	2,000	0.05	Longtime German residents; many former members have emigrated to Germany.
Isolated radio believers		I-3rZ	.....	9	90	–	100	0.05	Many young Turkmen believers, especially school pupils.
Jehovah's Witnesses		m-Jeh	x....	1	69	–	230	0.05	Watch Tower. *IBSA*.
Korean Methodist Church		P-Met	V....	2	200	100	400	0.05	Koreans who immigrated and retained Methodism.
Moldavian Orthodox Ch	c1975	O-Mol	M....	1	500	–	1,000	5.00	Moldavians.
Pentecostal Churches	c1990	I-3pZ	.....	10	2,100	–	5,250	20.00	Ex Ev Christians/Baptists.
Russian Orthodox Ch (D Tashkent)		O-Rus	M....	10	40,000	90,000	60,000	0.05	Diocese of Tashkent and Central Asia.
Ukrainian Orthodox Ch (P Kiev)		I-Ukr	.....	6	7,000	3,000	8,000	0.05	Ukrainians from dissident Patriarchate of Kiev.
Other Orthodox churches		O-	.....	10	600	200	1,100	0.05	Total 8, including Bulgarian OC, Georgian OC, Greek OC, UAOC, ROCOR, Old Believers.
Other Protestant groups		P-	.....	6	100	300	200	0.05	Total 3 millions, including ELCL, RCL.
Totals				**86**	**68,139**	**113,000**	**105,480**		

Churches, members, growth, 1900-2025	*Congs*	*Adults*	*Affiliated*	*G%*	*Total denominations*	*6 Megablocs:* *O*	*R*	*A*	*P*	*I*	*m*
Total churches, members, and denominations (mid-1900)	3	3,100	4,500	4.71	3	3	0	0	0	0	0
Total churches, members, and denominations (mid-1970)	27	78,850	113,000	4.71	12	6	1	0	4	1	0
Total churches, members, and denominations (mid-1990)	40	75,300	116,530	0.15	23	11	1	0	6	4	1
Total churches, members, and denominations (mid-1995)	86	68,139	105,480	-1.97	23	11	1	0	6	4	1
Total churches, members, and denominations (mid-2000)	100	63,900	98,883	-1.28	23	11	1	0	6	4	1
Total churches, members, and denominations (mid-2025)	200	58,700	90,800	-0.34	53	16	1	0	15	20	1

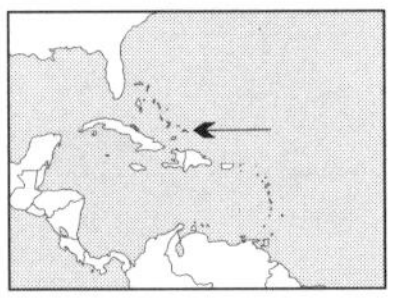

TURKS & CAICOS ISLANDS

SECULAR DATA, AD 2000

STATE
Official name: The Crown Colony of the Turks & Caicos Islands.
Short name: Turks & Caicos Islands. **Adjective of nationality:** Turks & Caicos Islander.
Flag: British Blue Ensign with shield of the Colony in the fly.
Area: 497 sq. km. (192 sq. mi.).
Government: Crown colony of the United Kingdom, since 1962 (1678 under Bermuda and Jamaica, 1988 new constitution).
Legislature: Legislative Council, 19 members.
Official language: English.
Monetary unit: 1 dollar (U.S.$) = 100 cents. **US$1=** 1.00.
Chief cities: GRAND TURK (Cockburn Town) 5,294.
Political divisions: 1 province.

DEMOGRAPHY
Population: 16,760.
Population density: 33.7/sq. km. (87.2/sq. mi.).
Under 15 years: 4,000.
Growth rate p.a.: 1.19% (births 15.26, deaths 5.77).
Mortality: Infant, per 1,000: 7.8; **Maternal per 100,000:** 40.0.
Life expectancy: 78 (male 75, female 82).
Household size: 3.0. **Floor area per person, sq.m:** 15.0.
Major languages: English.
Urban dwellers: 45.19%. **Urban growth rate p.a.:** 3.8%.
Labor force: 40%.

ETHNOLINGUISTIC PEOPLES
77.0% Black; 17.3% Mulatto; 4.3% USA White; 1.2% British; .

ECONOMY
National income p.a. per person: US$2,147; **per family:** US$6,443.

EDUCATION
Adult literacy: 93% (male 95%, female 91%). **Schools:** 20.
Universities: 0. **School enrolment:** female/male: 90%/90%.

HEALTH
Access to health services: 65%. **Access to safe water:** 90%.
Hospitals: 1 (20 beds per 10,000). **Doctors:** 7.
Blind: 10. **Deaf:** 1,000. **Murder rate:** 4.
Lepers: 0.

LITERATURE
New book titles p.a.: 4 (250 p.a. per million). **Periodicals:** 3.
Newspapers: 0 dailies.

COMMUNICATION (per 1,000 people)
Phones: 127 **(25% mobile). Radios:** 190. **TV sets:** 150.
Daily newspaper circulation: 80. **Computers:** 25.

HUMAN LIFE AND LIBERTY (optimum condition=100.0%)
HDI: 66.6. **HSI:** 70.0. **HFI:** 65.0. **EFL:** 45.0.

Country Table 1. **Religious adherents in the Turks & Caicos Islands, AD 1900-2025.**

Year / *Name*	*1900* *Adherents*	*%*	*1970* *Adherents*	*%*	*mid-1990* *Adherents*	*%*	*Annual change, 1990-2000* *Natural*	*Conversion*	*Total*	*Rate*	*mid-1995* *Adherents*	*%*	*mid-2000* *Adherents*	*%*	*mid-2025* *Adherents*	*%*
Christians	**5,100**	**100.0**	**5,570**	**99.5**	**10,720**	**92.4**	**479**	**-16**	**463**	**3.65**	**12,900**	**92.1**	**15,349**	**91.6**	**30,640**	**90.7**
PROFESSION																
professing Christians	**5,100**	**100.0**	**5,570**	**99.5**	**10,720**	**92.4**	**479**	**-16**	**463**	**3.65**	**12,900**	**92.1**	**15,349**	**91.6**	**30,640**	**90.7**
AFFILIATION																
unaffiliated Christians	100	2.0	190	3.4	1,100	9.5	46	53	99	6.61	1,688	12.1	2,087	12.5	2,940	8.7
affiliated Christians	**5,000**	**98.0**	**5,380**	**96.5**	**9,620**	**82.9**	**433**	**-69**	**364**	**3.26**	**11,212**	**80.0**	**13,262**	**79.1**	**27,700**	**82.0**
Protestants	2,250	44.1	3,800	68.2	6,000	51.7	250	-39	211	3.06	6,897	49.2	8,112	48.4	16,300	48.2
Anglicans	2,750	53.9	1,000	17.9	1,600	13.8	67	-27	40	2.26	1,800	12.9	2,000	11.9	3,500	10.4
Independents	0	0.0	450	8.1	1,320	11.3	55	13	68	4.24	1,610	11.5	2,000	11.9	5,000	14.8
Roman Catholics	0	0.0	100	1.8	480	4.1	20	7	27	4.56	605	4.3	750	4.5	1,700	5.0
Marginal Christians	0	0.0	30	0.5	220	1.9	9	9	18	6.16	300	2.1	400	2.4	1,200	3.5
Trans-megabloc groupings																
Evangelicals	2,000	39.2	1,560	28.0	2,600	22.4	108	-68	40	1.44	2,673	19.1	3,000	17.9	5,000	14.8
Pentecostals/Charismatics	0	0.0	1,000	17.9	2,900	25.0	121	19	140	4.02	3,575	25.5	4,300	25.7	9,100	26.9
Great Commission Christians	**500**	**9.8**	**1,000**	**17.9**	**2,380**	**20.5**	**99**	**14**	**113**	**3.97**	**2,900**	**20.7**	**3,513**	**21.0**	**7,500**	**22.2**
Nonreligious	0	0.0	0	0.0	500	4.3	21	12	33	5.24	640	4.6	833	5.0	2,100	6.2
Spiritists	0	0.0	0	0.0	280	2.4	12	3	15	4.43	335	2.4	432	2.6	750	2.2
Baha'is	0	0.0	30	0.5	90	0.9	4	0	4	3.67	110	0.8	129	0.8	250	0.7
Atheists	0	0.0	0	0.0	10	0.1	0	1	1	5.45	15	0.1	17	0.1	60	0.2
World A (unevangelized persons)	0	0.0	0	0.0	36	0.3	1	0	1	1.55	28	0.2	34	0.2	68	0.2
World B (evangelized non-Christians)	0	0.0	30	0.5	844	7.3	36	16	52	2.66	1,079	7.7	1,417	8.2	3,292	9.1
World C (Christians)	5,100	100.0	5,570	99.5	10,720	92.4	479	-16	463	3.65	12,900	92.1	15,349	91.6	30,640	90.7
Country's population	**5,100**	**100.0**	**5,600**	**100.0**	**11,600**	**100.0**	**516**	**0**	**516**	**3.54**	**14,008**	**100.0**	**16,800**	**100.0**	**33,800**	**100.0**

COLUMNS, ROWS.
For meanings and definitions, see Codebook (Part 3). Note that, by definition, total 'Christians' = professing + crypto-Christians, which also = affiliated + unaffiliated Christians, and also = Great Commission Christians + latent Christians. Percentages may not always total exactly, due to rounding.

CENSUSES.
7.IV.1960 (de jure): 79.1% Protestants (44.2% Baptists, 25.1% Methodists, 6.5% Ch of God), 20.5% Anglicans, 0.4% Roman Catholics (25 persons). **29.X.1970:** 76.7% Protestants (42.4% Baptists, 22.7% Methodists), 20.9% Anglicans, 1.9% Roman Catholics (106 persons), 0.5% other religionists. **1990:** 76.7% Protestants (40.2% Baptists, 15.8% Methodists, 10.9% Church of God, 1.7% SDAs), 18.7% Anglicans, 1.7% Roman Catholics, 1.5% other religionists, 1.4% nonreligious.

NOTES ON RELIGIONS
BAHA'IS. With one single local spiritual assembly (1996).
INDEPENDENTS. In about 4 small groupings in 1995 (see Table 2).
MIGRATION. All figures in the column 'Natural change' represent nett immigration (plus) or emigration (minus).

Country status. The Turks & Caicos Islands are a group of 30 subtropical islands in the Caribbean Sea. Fishing, tourism, and offshore finance are the main economic activities.

HUMAN LIFE AND LIBERTY

Human rights and freedoms. The Turks & Caicos Islands are a dependent territory of the United Kingdom. The UK-based legal system guarantees and protects all human rights.

CHRISTIANITY

PROTESTANT CHURCH. Baptists are the principal denomination on the island, as in the nearby Bahamas. Most are related to the Jamaica Baptist Union, dating from the middle of the last century, al-

Great Commission Instrument Panel: status of the Turks & Caicos Islands (for explanation see start of Part 4)

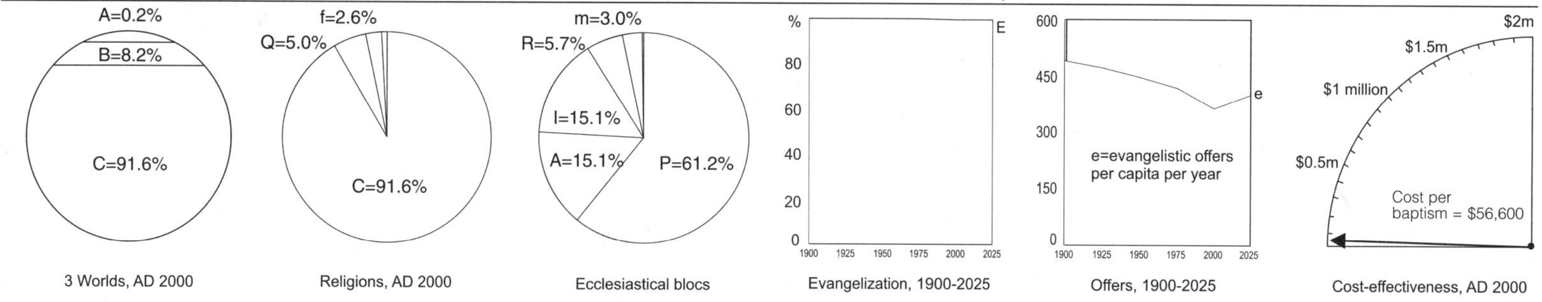

Country summary. **Worlds A, B, C by ethnolinguistic peoples, cities, and major civil divisions in the Turks & Caicos Islands.**

World	PEOPLES Num	Pop 2000	C%	Christians	E%	U%	Unevangelized	CITIES Num	Pop 2000	C%	Christians	E%	U%	Unevangelized	CIVIL DIVISIONS Num	Pop 2000	C%	Christians	E%	U%	Unevangelized
A	0	0	0.00	0	0	0	0	0	0	0.00	0	0	0	0	0	0	0.00	0	0	0	0
B	0	0	0.00	0	0	0	0	0	0	0.00	0	0	0	0	0	0	0.00	0	0	0	0
C	5	16,760	79.13	13,263	100	0	35	1	5,294	74.01	3,918	100	0	23	1	16,760	79.13	13,262	100	0	35
Total	**5**	**16,760**	**79.13**	**13,263**	**100**	**0**	**35**	**1**	**5,294**	**74.01**	**3,918**	**100**	**0**	**23**	**1**	**16,760**	**79.13**	**13,262**	**100**	**0**	**35**

though there is also a small Baptist Bible Church.

Methodist have maintained their position as the second largest denomination, although their proportion of the population decreased during the decades 1970-90. Methodist work began in the nearby Bahamas and spread to Turks and Caicos about the turn of the century.

Two American Pentecostal missions are active, the Church of God of Prophecy which has work at Grand Turk, Bottle Creek, Salt Cay, Kew, and Blue Hills; and the Church of God (Cleveland) with a congregation on Grand Turk known as the New Testament Church of God. Small Christian Brethren and Adventist communities also exist.

ANGLICAN CHURCH. Anglicans opened work in the islands during the 18th century and represent the third largest denomination, with 6% of the population. The church belongs to the diocese of Nassau and the Bahamas, in the Church of the Province of the West Indies.

CATHOLIC CHURCH. Although still a very small minority, the Catholic community has been growing due to immigration, from 25 people in the census of 1960 to 106 in 1970, and to 605 baptized Catholics in 1995. The Turks and Caicos islands belong to the diocese of Nassau and are served by an OCD priest who resides on Grand Turk.

The Holy See has no diplomatic relations with Turks & Caicos Islands in AD 2000.

Indigenous missions. Very few missionaries have been sent out from the islands.

CHURCH AND STATE

The islands were uninhabited when discovered by Ponce de León in 1512 and remained so until 1678 when salt was first extracted for use in Bermuda. Administered from Jamaica until 1962. Turks and Caicos are now governed by an administrator appointed by the British sovereign. There are no church-operated schools or medical institutions in the islands. Freedom of religion is guaranteed, but there is no established church.

BROADCASTING AND MEDIA

Shortwave broadcasts from TWR (Antilles), HCJB (Ecuador), and AWR (Costa Rica) can be received. Christian television programming can be received via satellite.

INTERDENOMINATIONAL ORGANIZATIONS

On the initiative of the Anglican vicar on Grand Turk, informal discussions have begun regarding the formation of a Christian council.

FUTURE TRENDS AND PROSPECTS

All non-Christian traditions are expected to grow slightly over the next 30 years with corresponding losses to Christianity.

Christianity is likely to predominate in the 21st century, although it may fall below 80% before AD 2050.

BIBLIOGRAPHY

A history of Turks and Caicos Islands. H. Smith. Hamilton, Bermuda, 1968. 77p.

Turks and Caicos Islands. P. G. Boultbee. *World bibliographical series*, vol. 137. Oxford, UK: CLIO Press, 1991. 100p. (No section on religion, but some books of interest scattered throughout).

Christian themes occur on numerous postage stamps: here (Easter 1970), a series on the Crucifixion by Dürer (AD 1400).

Country Table 2. **Organized churches and denominations in the Turks & Caicos Islands.**

Official name (bold type = church with over 10% of all affiliated) 1	*Begun* 2	*Type* 3	*Counc* 4	*Congs* 5	*Adults* 6	*Affiliated 1970* 7	*Affiliated 1995* 8	*G%* 9	*Names, notes, and other statistics* (see Codebook, Part 3) 10
Anglican Church (D Nassau & B)	c1750	A-ACa	awMRC	3	1,300	1,000	1,800	2.38	In Ch of the Province of the West Indies, D Nassau and the Bahamas. On Grand Turk.
Baptist Bible Church		I-Bap	x....	1	30	50	60	0.05	Related to BBFI (USA). Small congregation on Grand Turk. Fundamentalists.
Catholic Ch: m Turks & Caicos		R-Lat	PxNMC	2	450	100	605	0.05	*Mission Sui Juris* of Turks & Caicos. One priest, residing on Grand Turk. M=OCD,SJ.
Christian Brethren		P-EBr	x....	1	50	100	100	0.05	*Exclusive* (Closed) *Brethren. Plymouth Brethren.* Group: Kelly-Continental.
Church of God in Christ		I-3pB	Z....	1	150	100	250	0.05	M=CoGiC(Black mission from USA) on Grand Turk. Based in neighboring Jamaica.
Church of God of Prophecy	1932	P-Pe3	Z....	6	250	300	600	2.81	CGP(USA). Holiness Pentecostals. Split in USA ex CoG(Cleveland).
Jamaica Baptist Union	c1849	P-Bap	T.M.C	13	2,700	2,000	3,600	2.38	Part of Jamaica Baptist Union, M=SBC(USA). On Grand Turk.
Jehovah's Witnesses	c1958	m-Jeh	x....	3	72	30	300	9.65	*Watch Tower. International Bible Students Association.* Witnessing since 1959. 18Y.
Meth Ch in Caribbean & Americas	c1800	P-Met	VwM.C	4	1,500	1,000	2,000	2.81	Part of Bahamas District, MCCA. On Grand Turk. 1n.
New Testament Church of God	1922	P-Pe3	ZF...	2	153	300	380	0.95	M=CoG(Cleveland) (USA). Holiness Pentecostals. Congregation on Grand Turk. 1n.
Seventh-day Adventist Church	1964	P-Adv	x....	3	130	100	217	3.15	*SDA, T&CI Mission*, WIndies Union Conference. HQ Grand Turk. 1nx,6mw,1r,3t(179),5Y.
Spiritual Baptist Churches		I-3sU	.....	2	200	100	300	0.05	*SBC. Shouters, Shakers.* White robes, vestments, RC ritual.
Other Black indigenous churches		I-3nU	.....	10	600	200	1,000	0.05	Small groupings, including Blacks from North and South America.
Totals				**51**	**7,585**	**5,380**	**11,212**		

Churches, members, growth, 1900-2025	*Congs*	*Adults*	*Affiliated*	*G%*	*Total denominations*	*6 Megablocs:* O	R	A	P	I	m
Total churches, members, and denominations (mid-1900)	20	2,500	5,000	0.10	3	0	0	1	2	0	0
Total churches, members, and denominations (mid-1970)	39	2,677	5,380	0.10	14	0	1	1	6	5	1
Total churches, members, and denominations (mid-1990)	50	6,500	9,620	2.95	17	0	1	1	6	8	1
Total churches, members, and denominations (mid-1995)	51	7,585	11,212	3.11	17	0	1	1	6	8	1
Total churches, members, and denominations (mid-2000)	50	9,000	13,262	3.42	17	0	1	1	6	8	1
Total churches, members, and denominations (mid-2025)	300	18,700	27,700	2.99	38	0	1	1	15	20	1

NOTES ON TABLE ABOVE

NATIONAL COUNCILS (Column 4, 5th letter).

C = Turks & Caicos Inter-Church Committee (TCICC).

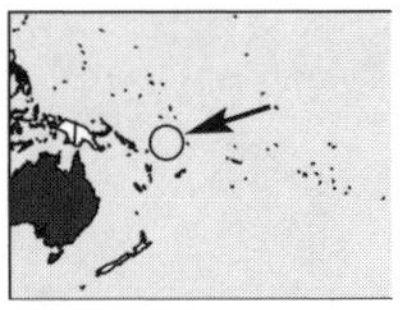

TUVALU

SECULAR DATA, AD 2000

STATE
Official name: The State of Tuvalu.
Short name: Tuvalu. **Adjective of nationality:** Tuvaluan.
Flag: Blue with British Union Jack at upper hoist corner; nine golden stars placed in the same relation as the nine principal islands of Tuvalu.
Area: 24 sq. km. (9 sq. mi.).
Government: Parliamentary state, since 1978 (1892 British protectorate of Ellice Islands with Gilbert Islands, 1916 British crown colony of Gilbert & Ellice Islands, 1976 secession as separate colony, 1978 Independence).
Legislature: Parliament, 12 members.
Official language: English.
Monetary unit: 1 Tuvalu dollar = 100 Tuvalu and Australian cents.
US$1= $A 1.70.
Chief cities: FONGAFELA-Funafuti 3,255.
Political divisions: 9 provinces.
Armed forces: 50.

DEMOGRAPHY
Population: 12,000.
Population density: 488.2/sq. km. (1,302.1/sq. mi.).
Under 15 years: 4,000.
Growth rate p.a.: 1.85% (births 27.33, deaths 4.64).
Mortality: Infant, per 1,000: 19.3; **Maternal per 100,000:** 200.0.
Life expectancy: 73 (male 71, female 75).
Household size: 6.4. **Floor area per person, sq.m:** 12.0.
Major languages: English, Tuvaluan (Ellice, Samoan), Gilbertese.
Urban dwellers: 52.21%. **Urban growth rate p.a.:** 3.0%.
Labor force: 65%.

ETHNOLINGUISTIC PEOPLES
96.3% Tuvaluan (Ellice Islander; 1.0% Euronesian; 1.0% Kiribertese (Gilbertese); 0.5% British; 0.4% Han Chinese.

ECONOMY
National income p.a. per person: US$767; **per family:** US$4,915.

EDUCATION
Adult literacy: 95% (male 96%, female 95%). **Schools:** 11.
Universities: 0. **School enrolment:** female/male: 85%/85%.

HEALTH
Access to health services: 70%. **Access to safe water:** 100%.
Hospitals: 8 (36 beds per 10,000). **Doctors:** 8.
Blind: 10. **Deaf:** 600. **Murder rate:** 3.
Lepers: 50.

LITERATURE
New book titles p.a.: 2 (200 p.a. per million). **Periodicals:** 3.
Newspapers: 0 dailies.

COMMUNICATION (per 1,000 people)
Phones: 165 (2% mobile). **Radios:** 320. **TV sets:** 200.
Daily newspaper circulation: 60. **Computers:** 20.

HUMAN LIFE AND LIBERTY (optimum condition=100.0%)
HDI: 56.7. **HSI:** 70.0. **HFI:** 70.0. **EFL:** 30.0.

Country Table 1. **Religious adherents in Tuvalu, AD 1900-2025.**

Year	1900		1970		mid-1990		Annual change, 1990-2000				mid-1995		mid-2000		mid-2025	
Name	Adherents	%	Adherents	%	Adherents	%	Natural	Conversion	Total	Rate	Adherents	%	Adherents	%	Adherents	%
Christians	**2,500**	**100.0**	**5,700**	**98.3**	**8,045**	**90.4**	**255**	**-13**	**242**	**2.66**	**9,160**	**89.4**	**10,461**	**89.3**	**18,000**	**87.0**
PROFESSION																
professing Christians	**2,500**	**100.0**	**5,700**	**98.3**	**8,045**	**90.4**	**255**	**-13**	**242**	**2.66**	**9,160**	**89.4**	**10,461**	**89.3**	**18,000**	**87.0**
AFFILIATION																
unaffiliated Christians	0	0.0	0	0.0	520	5.8	17	3	20	3.25	620	6.1	716	6.0	1,300	6.3
affiliated Christians	**2,500**	**100.0**	**5,700**	**98.3**	**7,525**	**84.6**	**238**	**-16**	**222**	**2.62**	**8,540**	**83.4**	**9,745**	**83.3**	**16,700**	**80.7**
Protestants	2,500	100.0	5,576	96.1	9,080	102.0	293	2	292	2.83	10,440	101.9	12,000	102.6	20,500	99.0
Marginal Christians	0	0.0	24	0.4	200	2.2	7	2	9	3.79	240	2.3	290	2.5	600	2.9
Independents	0	0.0	0	0.0	150	1.7	5	5	10	5.24	200	2.0	250	2.2	500	2.4
Roman Catholics	0	0.0	100	1.7	100	1.1	3	-4	-1	-0.51	97	1.0	95	0.8	150	0.7
doubly-affiliated	0	0.0	0	0.0	-2,005	-22.5	-67	-22	-89	3.72	-2,437	-23.8	-2,890	-24.7	-5,050	-24.4
Trans-megabloc groupings																
Evangelicals	600	24.0	230	4.0	350	3.9	12	9	21	4.81	449	4.4	560	4.7	1,240	5.9
Pentecostals/Charismatics	0	0.0	50	0.9	1,420	15.9	47	21	68	3.99	1,729	16.9	2,100	17.6	4,350	21.0
Great Commission Christians	**150**	**6.0**	**700**	**12.1**	**1,650**	**18.4**	**55**	**4**	**59**	**3.10**	**1,920**	**18.8**	**2,240**	**18.8**	**4,400**	**21.3**
Nonreligious	0	0.0	0	0.0	400	4.4	13	7	20	4.07	490	4.8	596	5.1	1,200	5.8
Baha'is	0	0.0	100	1.7	400	4.4	13	5	18	3.79	480	4.7	580	5.0	1,400	6.8
Atheists	0	0.0	0	0.0	50	0.6	2	0	2	3.27	60	0.6	69	0.6	80	0.4
Buddhists	0	0.0	0	0.0	5	0.1	0	1	1	10.84	10	0.1	14	0.1	20	0.1
World A (unevangelized persons)	0	0.0	0	0.0	9	0.1	0	1	1	7.18	20	0.2	24	0.2	21	0.1
World B (evangelized non-Christians)	0	0.0	100	1.7	846	9.5	28	12	40	4.82	1,061	10.4	1,215	10.5	2,679	12.9
World C (Christians)	2,500	100.0	5,700	98.3	8,045	90.4	255	-13	242	2.66	9,160	89.4	10,461	89.3	18,000	87.0
Country's population	**2,500**	**100.0**	**5,800**	**100.0**	**8,900**	**100.0**	**283**	**0**	**283**	**2.92**	**10,242**	**100.0**	**11,700**	**100.0**	**20,700**	**100.0**

COLUMNS, ROWS.
For meanings and definitions, see Codebook (Part 3). Note that, by definition, total 'Christians' = professing + crypto-Christians, which also = affiliated + unaffiliated Christians, and also = Great Commission Christians + latent Christians. Percentages may not always total exactly, due to rounding.

CENSUSES.
In the 1963 and 1968 censuses, the question on religion was asked. Combined results are given under Table 1 for Kiribati.

NOTES ON RELIGIONS
BAHA'IS. In 1969 a small section of land was leased by Baha'is on Funafuti, an atoll of 30 islets. Converts are former Congregationalists. By 1996, 5 local spiritual assemblies had been organized.

Great Commission Instrument Panel: status of Tuvalu (for explanation see start of Part 4)

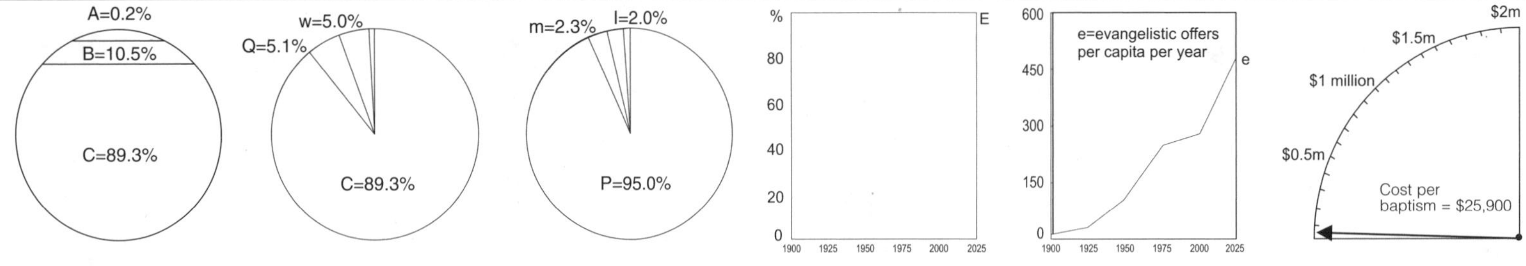

3 Worlds, AD 2000 | Religions, AD 2000 | Ecclesiastical blocs | Evangelization, 1900-2025 | Offers, 1900-2025 | Cost-effectiveness, AD 2000

Country status. Tuvalu, one of the world's smallest nations, consists of 9 islands in the southwest Pacific Ocean. Its chief product is coconuts.

HUMAN LIFE AND LIBERTY

Human rights and freedoms. Tuvalu is a member of the Commonwealth. Its 32-member constabulary has no problem in keeping law and order among the peace-loving Tuvaluans. Social behavior is determined more by custom and tradition than by law and is enforced by village elders.

NON-CHRISTIAN RELIGIONS

Baha'i has had significant numbers of converts in Tuvalu from among Congregationalists.

CHRISTIANITY

PROTESTANT CHURCHES. In 1861 Congregationalist pastors from Samoa began preaching in the Ellice Islands, aided after 1870 by J. S. White of the London Missionary Society. By the year 1900 the whole population was Congregationalist. For many years the LMS served a united church of the Gilbert and Ellice Islands, but as a result of ethnic tensions separate churches for the 2 groups were formed in 1968. Adventists have had a small work for over 40 years.

CATHOLIC CHURCH. There is only a small Catholic community.

The Holy See has no diplomatic relations with Tuvalu in AD 2000, but has an apostolic delegate for the Pacific Ocean residing in Wellington, New Zealand.

Indigenous missions. A few missionaries have been sent out from Tuvalu, sent by the Tuvalu Church.

CHURCH AND STATE

Until 1964, Catholics were unable to open work in the Ellice Islands, these having been declared until then a 'closed district' in which only Protestants were allowed to work. Although Catholics are now legally permitted in Tuvalu, local anti-Catholic sentiment prevents the building of Catholic churches on most islands.

FUTURE TRENDS AND PROSPECTS

All non-Christian traditions are expected to grow slightly over the next 30 years with corresponding losses to Christianity.

Christianity will likely decline below 80% by AD 2100 with Baha'is and the nonreligious growing in their place.

Country summary. **Worlds A, B, C by ethnolinguistic peoples, cities, and major civil divisions in Tuvalu.**

World	PEOPLES Num	Pop 2000	C%	Christians	E%	U%	Unevangelized
A	0	0	0.00	0	0	0	0
B	0	0	0.00	0	0	0	0
C	7	11,719	83.16	9,746	100	0	19
Total	**7**	**11,719**	**83.16**	**9,746**	**100**	**0**	**19**

World	CITIES Num	Pop 2000	C%	Christians	E%	U%	Unevangelized
A	0	0	0.00	0	0	0	0
B	0	0	0.00	0	0	0	0
C	1	3,255	76.99	2,506	100	0	7
Total	**1**	**3,255**	**76.99**	**2,506**	**100**	**0**	**7**

World	CIVIL DIVISIONS Num	Pop 2000	C%	Christians	E%	U%	Unevangelized
A	0	0	0.00	0	0	0	0
B	0	0	0.00	0	0	0	0
C	9	11,719	83.16	9,745	100	0	20
Total	**9**	**11,719**	**83.16**	**9,745**	**100**	**0**	**20**

Postage stamps illustrating (left) New Testament translation and (right) the largest church buildings.

Tuvalu Church. Formerly Ellice Islands Church. *Above.* Church at Funafuti. *Right.* Baptism of an infant.

BIBLIOGRAPHY

A pattern of islands. A. F. Grimble. 1952; reprint, Harmondsworth: Penguin, 1981. 264p.
Bibliography of the Ellice Islands, Western Pacific. N. L. H. Krauss. Honolulu, HI, 1969. 13p.
Gaaluega e fai ite Lukinga Faka te Anganga i Fakakai (LSA). Bikenibu, Tarawa: National Spiritual Assembly of the Baha'is of the Gilbert Islands and Tuvalu, 1978. 7p.
'Heirs of Tefolaha: tradition and social organization in Nanumea, a Polynesian atoll community.' K. S. Chambers. Ph.D. dissertation, University of California, Berkeley, CA, 1984. 351p.
'Illness and healing in Nanumea, Tuvalu,' A. Chambers & K. S. Chambers, in *Healing practices in the South Pacific,* p.16–50. C. D. F. Parsons (ed). Honolulu, HI: Institute for Polynesian studies, 1985.
'Land tenure, kinship and community structure: strategies for living in the Ellice Islands of western Polynesia.' I. A. Brady. Ph.D. dissertation, University of Oregon, Eugene, OR, 1970. 275p.
'The Tuvalu Church: a socio–historical survey of its development towards an indigenous church.' L. Kofe. B.D. project, Pacific Theological College, Suva, Fiji, 1976. 96p.
Tuvalu, a celebration in photos of ten years independence. P. McQuarrie. Funafuti: Government of Tuvalu, 1988. 104p.
Tuvalu, a history. H. Laracy (ed). Suva, Fiji: Institute of Pacific Studies and Extension Services, University of the South Pacific and the Ministry of Social Services, Government of Tuvalu, 1983. 228p.

Country Table 2. **Organized churches and denominations in Tuvalu.**

Official name (bold type = church with over 10% of all affiliated) 1	*Begun* 2	*Type* 3	*Counc* 4	*Congs* 5	*Adults* 6	*Affiliated 1970* 7	*Affiliated 1995* 8	*G%* 9	*Names, notes, and other statistics* (see Codebook, Part 3) 10
Catholic Church: m Funafuti	1964	R-Lat	P.PY.	2	50	100	97	-0.12	*Mission Sui Juris of Funafuti.* Closed to RC missions until 1964. M=SM. 1x,3Yy.
Jehovah's Witnesses	c1965	m-Jeh	x....	3	50	24	240	9.65	*Watch Tower.* 1Y.
Kiribati Protestant Church	c1900	P-Con	.....	1	40	40	50	0.90	*Gilbert Islands Protestant Ch (GIPC).* Kiribertese immigrants, residents, migrant workers.
Pentecostal Churches	c1975	I-3pP	.....	3	65	–	200	5.00	Indigenous pentecostal bodies.
Seventh-day Adventist Church	1955	P-Adv	x....	1	192	70	320	6.27	*SDA, G&EI Mission.* Central Pacific Union Mission. Begun from Abemama (Gilbert Is).
Tuvalu Church	1861	P-Con	..P..	15	3,270	5,436	10,000	2.47	*Ekalesia Kelisiano Tuvalu. Ekalesia Elise.* M=LMS, now CWM(UK). A=1968. 12n,7m,4w,1f,110y.
Other Protestant churches		P-	.....	3	50	30	70	0.05	Total 3, including CCCS (Samoa).
Doubly-affiliated		2-aff			-830	0	-2,437		Persons who are members of 2 or 3 other churches also.
Totals				**28**	**2,887**	**5,700**	**8,540**		

Churches, members, growth, 1900-2025	*Congs*	*Adults*	*Affiliated*	*G%*	*Total denominations*	*6 Megablocs:* O	R	A	P	I	m
Total churches, members, and denominations (mid-1900)	10	1,200	2,500	1.18	2	0	0	0	2	0	0
Total churches, members, and denominations (mid-1970)	19	2,728	5,700	1.18	6	0	1	0	4	0	1
Total churches, members, and denominations (mid-1990)	20	2,500	7,525	1.40	9	0	1	0	6	1	1
Total churches, members, and denominations (mid-1995)	28	2,887	8,540	2.56	9	0	1	0	6	1	1
Total churches, members, and denominations (mid-2000)	30	3,300	9,745	2.68	9	0	1	0	6	1	1
Total churches, members, and denominations (mid-2025)	60	5,700	16,700	2.18	22	0	1	0	10	10	1

NOTES ON TABLE ABOVE
NATIONAL COUNCILS (Column 4, 5th letter).
C = Protestant Churches in Tuvalu & Kiribati.

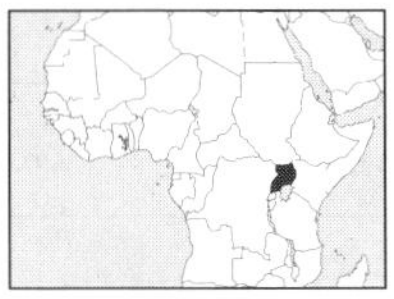

UGANDA

SECULAR DATA, AD 2000

STATE
Official name: The Republic of Uganda.
Short name: Uganda. **Adjective of nationality:** Ugandan.
Flag: Black, yellow, and red stripes, with crested crane on white circle in centre.
Area: 241,040 sq. km. (93,070 sq. mi.).
Government: Parliamentary democracy, since 1979 (c1500 several kingdoms, 1894 British protectorate, 1962 Independence as federal state, 1966 one-party republic, 1971 military dictatorship).
Legislature: National Assembly, 279 members.
Official language: English.
Monetary unit: 1 Uganda shilling (U Sh) = 100 cents. **US$1=** U Sh 1,275.
Chief cities: KAMPALA 1,207,000; Jinja 80,733; Mbale 71,008; Masaka 64,966.
Political divisions: 38 provinces.
Armed forces: 50,000.

DEMOGRAPHY
Population: 21,778,000.
Population density: 90.3/sq. km. (234.0/sq. mi.).
Under 15 years: 10,902,000.
Growth rate p.a.: 3.21% (births 49.23, deaths 17.23).
Mortality: Infant, per 1,000: 94.1; **Maternal per 100,000:** 1,200.0.
Life expectancy: 45 (male 44, female 46).
Household size: 4.8. **Floor area per person, sq.m:** 10.0.
Major languages: English, Ganda (Luganda), Swahili, Nkole, Teso, Soga, Kiga (Ruchiga), Ruanda, Lango, Acholi, Gisu, Lugbara, Toro, Nyoro, Arabic, and over 45 other tribal languages.
Urban dwellers: 14.16%. **Urban growth rate p.a.:** 5.5%.
Labor force: 44%.

ETHNOLINGUISTIC PEOPLES
13.8% Ganda; 8.8% Nkole (Nkore); 7.4% Chiga (Kiga); 7.3% Soga (Kenyi); 5.4% Rwandese Hutu.

ECONOMY
National income p.a. per person: US$240; **per family:** US$1,152.

EDUCATION
Adult literacy: 61% (male 73%, female 50%). **Schools:** 8,815.
Universities: 9. **School enrolment:** female/male: 41%/53%.

HEALTH
Access to health services: 49%. **Access to safe water:** 34%.
Hospitals: 89 (12 beds per 10,000). **Doctors:** 774.

Blind: 209,000. **Deaf:** 1,347,500. **Murder rate:** 9.
Lepers: 200,000. **Underweight prevalence under 5:** 27%.

LITERATURE
New book titles p.a.: 1,960 (90 p.a. per million). **Periodicals:** 36.
Newspapers: 2 dailies.

COMMUNICATION (per 1,000 people)
Phones: 2 (35% mobile). **Radios:** 507. **TV sets:** 26.
Daily newspaper circulation: 2. **Computers:** 10.

REFUGEES
Alien refugees from other countries: 230,000.

HUMAN LIFE AND LIBERTY (optimum condition=100.0%)
HDI: 32.8. **HSI:** 15.0. **HFI:** 30.0. **EFL:** 43.4.

Country Table 1. **Religious adherents in Uganda, AD 1900-2025.**

Year	1900		1970		mid-1990		Annual change, 1990-2000				mid-1995		mid-2000		mid-2025	
Name	Adherents	%	Adherents	%	Adherents	%	Natural	Conversion	Total	Rate	Adherents	%	Adherents	%	Adherents	%
Christians	**180,000**	**6.8**	**6,766,000**	**69.0**	**14,368,000**	**87.3**	**464,557**	**30,754**	**495,311**	**3.01**	**16,724,000**	**88.3**	**19,321,113**	**88.7**	**40,900,000**	**92.0**
PROFESSION																
professing Christians	**180,000**	**6.8**	**6,766,000**	**69.0**	**14,368,000**	**87.3**	**464,557**	**30,754**	**495,311**	**3.01**	**16,724,000**	**88.3**	**19,321,113**	**88.7**	**40,900,000**	**92.0**
AFFILIATION																
unaffiliated Christians	50,000	1.9	1,860,195	19.0	368,000	2.2	11,898	-11,004	894	0.24	337,230	1.8	376,940	1.7	300,000	0.7
affiliated Christians	**130,000**	**4.9**	**4,905,805**	**50.0**	**14,000,000**	**85.1**	**452,658**	**41,759**	**494,417**	**3.07**	**16,386,770**	**86.5**	**18,944,173**	**87.0**	**40,600,000**	**91.4**
Roman Catholics	70,000	2.6	3,394,988	34.6	6,800,000	41.3	219,863	13,137	233,000	2.99	7,932,782	41.9	9,130,000	41.9	19,000,000	42.8
Anglicans	60,000	2.3	1,291,000	13.2	6,380,000	38.8	206,283	13,717	220,000	3.01	7,440,000	39.3	8,580,000	39.4	18,400,000	41.4
Independents	0	0.0	97,500	1.0	527,000	3.2	17,039	11,761	28,800	4.46	678,745	3.6	815,000	3.7	2,100,000	4.7
Protestants	0	0.0	112,017	1.1	410,000	2.5	13,256	5,344	18,600	3.81	497,719	2.6	596,000	2.7	1,600,000	3.6
Orthodox	0	0.0	10,000	0.1	20,000	0.1	647	553	1,200	4.81	25,000	0.1	32,000	0.2	70,000	0.2
Marginal Christians	0	0.0	300	0.0	3,000	0.0	97	203	300	7.18	4,000	0.0	6,000	0.0	24,000	0.1
doubly-affiliated	0	0.0	0	0.0	-140,000	-0.9	-4,527	-2,956	-7,483	4.37	-191,476	-1.0	-214,827	-1.0	-594,000	-1.3
Trans-megabloc groupings																
Evangelicals	60,000	2.3	609,000	6.2	2,850,000	17.3	92,148	11,852	104,000	3.16	3,334,322	17.6	3,890,000	17.9	8,647,000	19.5
Pentecostals/Charismatics	0	0.0	175,000	1.8	3,470,000	21.1	112,195	41,805	154,000	3.74	4,210,188	22.2	5,010,000	23.0	12,445,000	28.0
Great Commission Christians	**100,000**	**3.8**	**1,078,000**	**11.0**	**2,172,000**	**13.2**	**70,227**	**14,571**	**84,798**	**3.35**	**2,575,000**	**13.6**	**3,019,984**	**13.9**	**6,665,000**	**15.0**
Muslims	53,000	2.0	588,400	6.0	904,150	5.5	29,278	-5,952	23,326	2.32	1,013,900	5.4	1,137,405	5.2	2,075,800	4.7
Ethnoreligionists	2,416,700	91.2	2,152,300	22.0	840,000	5.1	27,160	-15,804	11,356	1.28	855,000	4.5	953,557	4.4	700,000	1.6
Hindus	300	0.0	65,000	0.7	132,000	0.8	4,268	-31	4,237	2.82	157,600	0.8	174,373	0.8	365,000	0.8
Nonreligious	0	0.0	1,000	0.0	80,000	0.5	2,587	393	2,980	3.22	95,000	0.5	109,796	0.5	300,000	0.7
Baha'is	0	0.0	226,000	2.3	120,000	0.7	3,880	-9,225	-5,345	-5.73	75,000	0.4	66,546	0.3	60,000	0.1
Atheists	0	0.0	0	0.0	8,000	0.1	259	-35	224	2.50	9,300	0.1	10,243	0.1	25,000	0.1
Jews	0	0.0	500	0.0	2,000	0.0	65	-37	28	1.32	2,200	0.0	2,280	0.0	3,200	0.0
Jains	0	0.0	1,000	0.0	1,650	0.0	53	-18	35	1.93	1,800	0.0	1,997	0.0	5,000	0.0
Sikhs	0	0.0	5,700	0.1	1,200	0.0	39	-45	-6	-0.51	1,200	0.0	1,140	0.0	1,000	0.0
Zoroastrians	0	0.0	100	0.0	0	0.0	0	0	0	0.00	0	0.0	0	0.0	0	0.0
World A (unevangelized persons)	2,019,300	76.2	784,512	8.0	246,855	1.5	7,760	-12,210	-4,450	-2.03	246,153	1.3	196,002	0.9	266,610	0.6
World B (evangelized non-Christians)	450,700	17.0	2,255,888	23.0	1,842,145	11.2	59,829	-18,544	41,285	2.07	1,964,742	10.4	2,260,885	10.4	3,268,390	7.4
World C (Christians)	180,000	6.8	6,766,000	69.0	14,368,000	87.3	464,557	30,754	495,311	3.01	16,724,000	88.3	19,321,113	88.7	40,900,000	92.0
Country's population	**2,650,000**	**100.0**	**9,806,400**	**100.0**	**16,457,000**	**100.0**	**532,146**	**0**	**532,146**	**2.84**	**18,934,896**	**100.0**	**21,778,000**	**100.0**	**44,435,000**	**100.0**

COLUMNS, ROWS.
For meanings and definitions, see Codebook (Part 3). Note that, by definition, total 'Christians' = professing + crypto-Christians, which also = affiliated + unaffiliated Christians, and also = Great Commission Christians + latent Christians. Percentages may not always total exactly, due to rounding.

CENSUSES.
1911: 82.2% ethnoreligionists, 8.1% Roman Catholics, 7.1% Anglicans, 2.6% Muslims. Buganda: 42.7% Christians (23.5% Roman Catholics, 19.2% Anglicans). **1921** (Africans only): 76.8% ethnoreligionists, 8.7% Anglicans, 8.3% Roman Catholics, 3.2% Muslims, 3.0% African indigenous (KOAB Malakites). **1931** (all races): 71.9% ethnoreligionists, 11.5% Roman Catholics, 11.1% Anglicans, 3.6% Muslims, 1.6% African indigenous (KOAB), 0.2% Hindus. **18-19.VIII.1959.** (all races): 36.9% ethnoreligionists, 32.2% Roman Catholics, 24.6% Anglicans, 5.4% Muslims, 0.7% Hindus, 0.1% Sikhs. The religion question was not asked in subsequent censuses.

NOTES ON RELIGIONS
ANGLICANS. In the year 1896, there were 6,905 baptized Anglicans, and 2,591 catechumens, with 57,380 readers or enquirers; in 1902, 35,897 baptized; by 1912, 83,200. At this early period, readers (still mostly pagans) and enquirers were over twice as numerous as baptized Anglicans.
BAHA'IS. Mostly Africans, especially around Mount Elgon; all Asian Baha'is were expelled 1972. In 1955, there were 900 believers in 100 centers, then rapid growth took place from 671 local spiritual assemblies (1964) to 1,507 (1973). One of the world's 7 Baha'i temples is in Kampala. In September 1977, Baha'i was banned by the government, and the subsequent civil war dealt the earlier mushrooming expansion a lethal blow. After reorganization in the 1990s Baha'i remained with only 93 LSAs (1996).
COUNTRY'S POPULATION. From 1971-78 over 300,000 Ugandans (mostly Christians) were killed by the Amin regime, including 20,000 soldiers and several thousand police, and over 250,000 others fled to exile in Kenya and elsewhere (including, in 1972, the 50,000 Asians expelled).
ETHNORELIGIONISTS. Animists, mainly among the Pokot (Suk) (51%), Amba (55%), Twa (95%), Mening (80%), and Nyangiya (80%).
HINDUS. Indians, almost all expelled in 1972, but returning in the 1980s.
INDEPENDENTS. In 1995 there were about 37 indigenous denominations (see Table 2). The first movement, the KOAB (Katonda Omu Zinza Byona: Society of the One Almighty God) or Bamalaki (People of Malaki, Malakite Church), began in 1914 and had 91,740 Ganda adherents in 1921, 56,952 in 1930 and declined to 1,000 by 1970 and to only 100 by 1990.
JEWS. A congregation of African Jews (Bayudaya) with a synagogue exists in Mbale, begun in 1926 by a Muganda (a former Anglican and Malakite) without external Jewish influence. From a peak of 2,000 followers in 1928, numbers subsequently declined to 350 in 1962, rising to 500 by 1968 when the state of Israel was in favor with the Obote regime. In September 1977, they were declared banned by the Amin regime, but in the 1980s the community flourished.
MUSLIMS. Islam was introduced to Buganda from 1844 onwards. African Muslims are all Sunnis (of the Shafiite rite, with Sudanese (Nubians) of the Malikite rite in Arua and West Nile). The main Muslim areas are Madi (36% Muslim in 1959), Busoga (13%), and West Nile (9%). Before their mass expulsion in 1972 Asian Muslims numbered 11,000 Ismailis, 4,000 Ithna-Asharis, also Bohoras and Memons (all with no African members). There is also an Ahmadiya Mission (enumerated here as Muslims, though declared non-Muslim by Pakistan). Introduced around 1946, organized in 1956, by Qadianis from Pakistan, with HQ in Jinja and a mosque built there in 1959 by Pakistani missionaries. Most Asian followers emigrated after 1963 or were expelled in 1972, leaving only African followers (including many Soga and Ganda formerly nominal Christians or Muslims). Islamization still proceeds among Bantu tribes in several areas, including Toro, but only slowly. At the same time, steady numbers of Muslims are being converted to the Catholic and Anglican churches. Missionaries. By 1977, there were numerous Egyptian missionaries at work sent by Al-Azhar University (Cairo). *Hajj Pilgrims to Mecca.* (1970) 940; (1974) 3,107; (1975) 3,031; (1976) 2,491.
NONRELIGIOUS. Mainly European expatriates.
PENTECOSTALS/CHARISMATICS. The Catholic Charismatic Renewal was begun in 1973. Totals (mid-1975): about 1,000 adults, or 2,000 total charismatic community including children. By 1992 these had increased to 40,000 regular adult attenders in 400 weekly prayer groups, with 150 priests involved, also 300 religious personnel, and 2 bishops. (1997) After years of civil war and unrest, 16 dioceses out of 17 had CCR prayer groups, with from 20 to 4,000 attenders (including children) per group.
ROMAN CATHOLICS. In the year 1903, there were 106,234 indigenous baptized Catholics (60,000 in Buganda) in the 2 vicariates of North Nyanza (White Fathers) and Upper Nile (Mill Hill Mission), covering the present-day territory of Uganda. At this period, enquirers, interested persons (still pagans) and catechumens were nearly twice as numerous as baptized Catholics.
SIKHS. Indians, all expelled in 1972, returning in smaller numbers after 1985.

Great Commission Instrument Panel: status of Uganda (for explanation see start of Part 4)

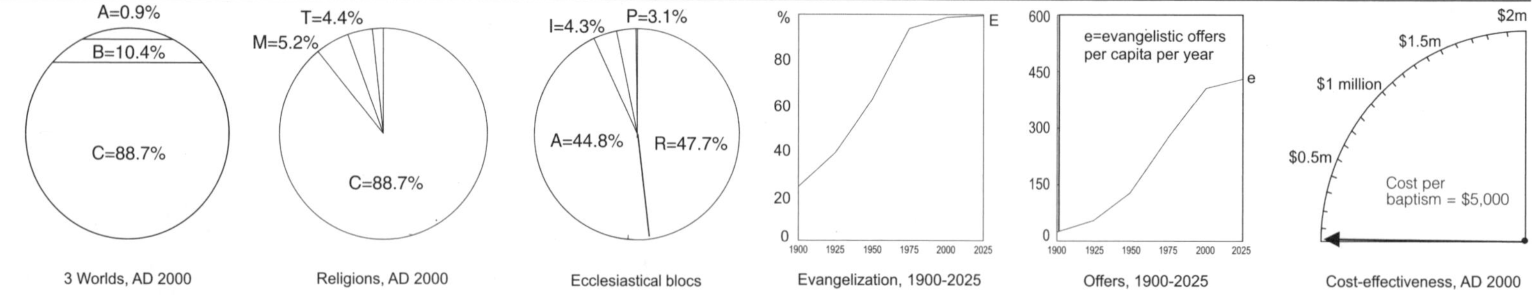

Country status. Uganda is a small, landlocked country in East Africa, bounded by Sudan, Kenya, Tanzania, Rwanda, and Zaire. Its chief exports include coffee, tea, tobacco, and cotton.

HUMAN LIFE AND LIBERTY

Human need and development. Over 95% of the people are engaged in agriculture. Living conditions vary according to the climate. Differences in diet and culture are greatest between the pastoral peoples of the northeast and cultivators elsewhere and also between urban and rural residents. The tropical climate fosters epidemic diseases. Rural families are largely self-sufficient. Most rural houses are built of locally available materials, such as wattle and daub, and the floor is made of hardened mud. Ventilation is poor and interiors are blackened from the smoke of cooking fires. In urban areas there is a dire shortage of housing, and many people live in makeshift accommodations. Safe water is available only in few areas and there are seasonal water shortages. The country as a whole is self-sufficient in food, and droughts and crop failures are rare. However, people do not enjoy good health as the many tropical infectious and parasitic diseases take their toll. Social welfare is traditionally a function of the lineage or extended family.

Muslims. Kibuli Mosque (Sunni), Kampala.

Country summary. **Worlds A, B, C by ethnolinguistic peoples, cities, and major civil divisions in Uganda.**

	PEOPLES							CITIES							CIVIL DIVISIONS						
World	*Num*	*Pop 2000*	*C%*	*Christians*	*E%*	*U%*	*Unevangelized*	*Num*	*Pop 2000*	*C%*	*Christians*	*E%*	*U%*	*Unevangelized*	*Num*	*Pop 2000*	*C%*	*Christians*	*E%*	*U%*	*Unevangelized*
A	5	228,644	0.44	1,017	43	57	130,110	0	0	0.00	0	0	0	0	0	0	0.00	0	0	0	0
B	7	199,861	44.02	87,969	84	16	32,549	0	0	0.00	0	0	0	0	0	0	0.00	0	0	0	0
C	51	21,349,945	88.31	18,855,187	100	0	32,840	4	1,423,707	80.31	1,143,333	99	1	16,721	38	21,778,450	86.99	18,944,173	99	1	195,502
Total	**63**	**21,778,450**	**86.99**	**18,944,173**	**99**	**1**	**195,499**	**4**	**1,423,707**	**80.31**	**1,143,333**	**99**	**1**	**16,721**	**38**	**21,778,450**	**86.99**	**18,944,173**	**99**	**1**	**195,502**

Human rights and freedoms. With the apparent end of major armed insurgencies, the human rights situation in Uganda has stabilized. The government has released all political prisoners. Some vestiges of the former civil strife, such as arrests of journalists on sedition charges and incidents of beatings and torture of prisoners are reported occasionally. Uganda has one of the world's highest death rates among prisoners, primarily as a result of AIDS, which has assumed epidemic proportions in the country. Although there is no formal censorship, the enabling laws remain on the statute books, and are invoked periodically against journalists. Women suffer a number of traditional and legal disabilities. Women may not own or inherit property or have custody of children under customary law. Domestic violence and rape are common and wife beating is considered as a male prerogative.

Human environment. With the loss of forests to farmers and developers, Uganda's once rich wild life is almost extinct. The lantana bushes where the tsetse flies breed, have been growing since the time of the civil war. The wetlands are disappearing as they are drained for agriculture.

NON-CHRISTIAN RELIGIONS

Traditional religions are followed by a rapidly-decreasing minority of most of Uganda's peoples. The Ganda, Uganda's largest tribe, still have numerous traditionalists who revere a complex pantheon of more than 40 divinities (Balubaale) who act as intermediaries between the supreme being Katonda and his people. Katonda's wife is Nalwanga and his chief minister Mukasa. The oldest of the divinities is Wanga, Mukasa's grandfather; while his brother, Kibuka, and father, Mususi, are appealed to respectively in time of war and earthquake. Other divinities are responsible for such matters as childbirth, plague, hunting, agriculture, and death. A less-developed system is found among the Bahima and Bunyoro. Both identify God as Ruhanga (Creator). Among the Bahima, Ruhanga's son Rugaba distributes good and evil and his son Kazoba is responsible for providence. The same functions are performed in Bunyoro by Ruhanga's brothers, Nkya and Kakya. Spirit-possession cults in Uganda include the Cwezi and Embandwa in Bunyoro and the Yakan cult of the Alur and Lugbara.

Islam was first brought to Uganda in the mid-19th century by Arab traders from the coast. They achieved considerable influence at the court of the Kabaka of Buganda, particularly under Mutesa I, and a good number of the Ganda became Muslims. One factor in the spread of Islam throughout Uganda was the use made by the British colonial power of Muslims as low-ranking officials and interpreters. Islam was also brought into Uganda from the north by Sudanese troops who came with Emin Pasha and were then allowed to settle in the country. These Sudanese (known, incorrectly, as Nubians) are numerous in West Nile although pockets of them also survive in Bombo, Jinja, and Entebbe. African Muslims are all Sunnis. Previous to the expulsion and flight of Asians in 1972 there were 11,000 Ismailis, 4,000 Ithna-Asharis, and smaller numbers of Bohoras and Memons. These sects had hardly any African members. Ahmadiya, whose first missionary came to Uganda in 1946, claim to number about 10,000 today. African Muslims divided on the death of their leader Mbogo in 1921, one group following Badru Kakungulu, while the other group refused to recognize him. A third sect was formed in 1947. The National Association for the Advancement of Muslims (NAAM) has been formed to bring all these groups together and produced a constitution in 1970 which purports to be for all Muslims in Uganda.

Baha'is. First Baha'i House of Worship (Temple) in Africa, on a hill in Kampala. Baha'i has, in Uganda, one of its strongest mission fields.

Baha'i had in Uganda one of its strongest mission fields, with in 1973 over 1,500 local spiritual assemblies and one of the world's 7 Baha'i temples in Kampala. In 1977, it was declared banned by the Amin regime. This, followed by 20 years of civil war and unrest, destroyed its organizational aspect. By 1996 there were only 93 local spiritual assemblies functioning.

Hinduism, which has temples in Kampala and many towns, has continued to grow.

CHRISTIANITY

One of the most vigorous examples of Christianity existing anywhere in Africa is found in Uganda, Christian witness there being largely concentrated in 2 churches, Catholic and Anglican. The pioneers were Anglicans who responded to Stanley's call for missionaries after visiting Kabaka Mutesa in 1875. The first resident evangelist was an African, Dallington Maftaa, a UMCA Anglican freed slave from Nyasaland, whom Stanley left behind to teach the Bible to the Kabaka. This he did for 2 years until the arrival of the first CMS missionaries in 1877. They were followed some months later by the first Catholic missionaries. The early history of Uganda involves a complex interaction of political and religious forces, with Catholics, Anglicans, and Muslims all playing a role. One of the results was the martyrdom of between 200 and 300 Catholic and Anglican African Christians at Namugongo during 1885-86.

CATHOLIC CHURCH. Catholicism was introduced into Uganda in 1879 when White Fathers reached the court of Kabaka Mutesa. They were joined in 1895 by Mill Hill priests, who assumed responsibility for eastern Uganda, and by Mill Hill sisters in 1902. These efforts proved successful from the beginning, and by 1912 there were 136,204 baptized Catholics in the 2 vicariates. In 1936 Catholic membership had grown to 477,000, 13% of the total population. Today the church has over 7 million baptized members and over 36% of the population profess to be Catholics. Impulses towards the early development of an indigenous clergy were also evident. The first Ugandan priests were ordained in 1913; the first East African bishop was consecrated in 1939. A local sisterhood, the novitiate for the Bannabikira, was opened in 1908, and today there are numerous indigenous congregations of priests, brothers, and sisters.

The visit of Pope Paul VI to Uganda in 1969, at which time he canonized 22 of the Catholic Namugongo martyrs, was an event of great significance and a sign of the importance which the Vatican attaches to this church.

The Holy See has diplomatic relations with Uganda and in AD 2000 is represented to government and the Catholic hierarchy by a pro-nuncio residing in Kampala.

Catholic Church in Uganda. Visit of pope Paul VI in 1969. Top. Concelebrated mass on Kololo Hill with consecration of 12 African bishops in presence of 20,000 Catholics. Lower. Paul VI prays with Anglican archbishop Sabiti at Anglican Martyrs shrine Namugongo.

ANGLICAN CHURCH. The Anglican Church accounts for over 25% of Uganda's population. As with Catholics, growth has been rapid and there has been sustained momentum through the years. By 1914 baptized members numbered 98,477, increasing threefold over the next 2 decades to 301,000 in 1936.

Today there are 5 million baptized Anglicans, with many new converts every year. The first Ugandan clergy were ordained in 1893, and the first African bishop and archbishop were appointed respectively in 1947 and 1966. The CMS has since 1877 been the principal foreign missionary society, augmented since 1918 by the African Inland Mission in the diocese of Madi and West Nile, and since 1929 by the BCMS among the Karamojong. The Ugandan church also has produced missionaries, the most famous being Apolo Kivebulaya, who pioneered among the pygmies of Congo's Ituri forest as early as 1897. In 1961 the Church of Uganda, Rwanda, and Burundi became an independent province in the Anglican Communion. A great stimulus to Anglican growth has come from the East African Revival (Balokole, Saved Ones) which began in Ruanda in 1927 and continues to make its influence widely felt.

History on Stamps. *From left.* First Anglican Cathedral; present Namiremte Cathedral (Anglican); early CMS pioneers; Apolo Kivebulaya, pioneer missionary to Pygmies; first African Catholic Bishop Joseph Kiwanuka.

PROTESTANT CHURCH. Seventh-day Adventists began work in 1926, the Salvation Army in 1931, and the Pentecostal Assemblies of Canada in 1935. By 1990 another 20 denominations had entered and begun work.

INDIGENOUS CHURCHES. In 1914 a sizeable schism occurred among the Ganda members of the Anglican Church, the KOAB or Society of the One Almighty God. By 1921 membership had grown to one-third of the whole Anglican Church; but after 1940 the movement collapsed. The East African Revival has been responsible for 2 schisms: one from the AIM in 1955, known among local Kakwa and Okefu tribesmen as Trumpeters or Praisers; and the other from the Anglicans in 1967 among the Acholi, called the Chosen Evangelical Revival. At least 14 independent churches have spread to Uganda from neighboring Kenya, including the African Israel Church Nineveh, Church of Christ in Africa, and Maria Legio of Africa.

African Greek Orthodox Church. *Top.* Cathedral, with a Soga priest. *Above.* Founder, and eventually bishop, Reuben S.M.M. Spartas.

ORTHODOX CHURCH. The African Greek Orthodox Church began as an indigenous split from the Anglicans (CMS) in 1929, but succeeded in gaining admittance to the Greek Orthodox communion in 1946. Dissatisfaction with inadequacies of Greek Orthodox assistance provoked a further split in 1957, and later in 1966 the formation of the African Orthodox Autonomous Church South of the Sahara.

Indigenous missions. Ugandan Christians have served as missionaries in surrounding countries since the introduction of Christianity in the region in the 19th century. In the 20th century, missionaries were sent to Europe and North America. There is also a significant home missionary movement with over 1,000 Christians serving in this capacity.

Renewal movements. In the 1990s the Pentecostal/Charismatic Renewal continued to spread rapidly across most older churches, and numbered over 5 million adherents (of whom 7% Pentecostals, 77% Charismatics, and 15% Independents).

CHURCH AND STATE

The constitution of 8 September 1967 establishes, in Articles 16 and 20, freedom of conscience and religion, the right to manifest and propagate one's religion, as well as the unconstitutionality of all discriminatory acts, including those for religious reasons. After general Idi Amin, a Muslim Nubian of the Kakwa tribe seized power, a wave of killings began. A Department of Religious Affairs within the office of the president was created in 1971 to facilitate surveillance of the churches. In early 1972 Amin intervened in a leadership dispute which threatened to divide the Anglican Church, refusing to allow the dioceses of West Buganda and Namirembe to secede from the rest of the church. In late 1972, Amin expelled 58 millionaires from the country, 55 of whom were Catholics. The break in relations with Israel in 1972, followed by Uganda's increasingly friendly contacts with the Muslim countries of North Africa and the Middle East, particularly Libya, resulted in a growing aggressiveness on the part of Muslims.

In June 1973 Amin accused 28 Christian denominations and organizations of subversive activities and later banned them from the country. As a result, some groups were brought under the wing of the Anglican Church, while others went underground.

By 1976, the Amin government had been widely recognized internationally as a lawless regime. Killings were continuing to such an extent that around 400,000 Christians had either been killed by the regime's death squads since 1971, had disappeared without trace, or had fled the country. In August 1976, therefore, Catholic and Muslim leaders sent a joint memorandum documenting these to Amin demanding an end to the killings. In February 1977 the Anglican bishops sent a further demand. Whereupon the Anglican archbishop Janani Luwum, was summoned to the president's office and was murdered apparently by Amin himself. Five further Anglican bishops on the death list managed to flee the country, and the missionary bishop of Karamoja was deported. Other victims included the Muslim chief Kadhi of Uganda. Documents then became available indicating that the regime intended to murder all leading Anglicans in government or positions of influence, and also every male in the Acholi and Lango tribes. A number of Pentecostal pastors in these 2 tribes were killed, and the 2 Anglican dioceses of Northern Uganda and Lango ceased to have any overt administration and went underground. Meanwhile, widespread charismatic revival among youth gathered momentum across Northern Uganda' and international outrage over Luwum's death became massive.

In September 1977, the regime announced the banning of 27 religious organizations for alleged subversion, including Baha'i, Salvation Army, Seventh-day Adventists, Southern Baptists, and a number of indigenous churches. Three months later, Friday was decreed a national day of rest in addition to Sunday.

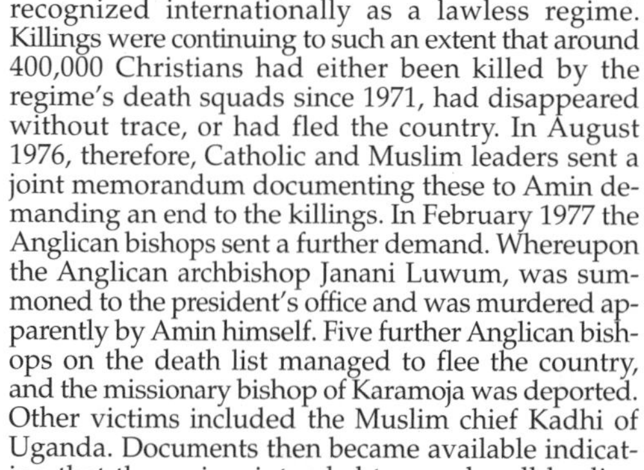

Religious TV: Sisters Scholastica from Diocese of Jinja with traditional musical instruments (rattles, harps, etc.), 1969.

BROADCASTING AND MEDIA

Radios are common. Shortwave broadcasts from FEBA (Seychelles) in Swahili can be received. Shortwave radio programs from KNLS have seen some response. Uganda is a member of UNDA, and Catholics broadcast 5 15-minute programs each Sunday (covering English, Luo, and Lugbara). Though Christian television programming can be received via satellite, the few television sets makes this a less effective way of reaching the populace. Catholics broadcast a half hour program twice a month on Sunday over television, addressing various religious topics selected according to the season and the holidays.

INTERDENOMINATIONAL ORGANIZATIONS

The Uganda Joint Christian Council with Anglican, Catholic, and Orthodox membership, was founded in 1963 to provide for joint participation in education, social and medical work, press, radio and television, and to further ecumenical relations in the country. There is also the Uganda Association of Evangelicals, linking 4 denominations.

FUTURE TRENDS AND PROSPECTS

Christians will most likely grow to over 90% by 2025 with corresponding losses among Muslims and ethnoreligionists.

By AD 2050 it is possible that Christianity will grow to about 93% of the population, while Baha'is, the nonreligious, and Muslims will make up the majority of the remaining 7%.

BIBLIOGRAPHY

A century of Christianity in Uganda, 1877–1977: a historical appraisal of the development of the Uganda Church over the last one hundred years. A. D. T. Tuma & P. Mitibwa. Nairobi: Uzima Press, 1978. 212p. (History of the Anglican Church).

'A congregation of African Jews in the heart of Uganda,' A. Oded, *Dini na mila*, 3, 1 (1968), 7–11.

A dictionary of Christianity in Uganda. M. L. Pirouet (ed). Kampala, Uganda: Makerere University College, 1969. 86p. (Mimeographed).

A distant grief. F. K. Sempangi & B. R. Thompson. Glendale, CA: Regal Books, 1979. 192p.

'A history of the church of Uganda, 1800–1980: the impact of Christianity on the political, social, economic, and religious life of the people of Uganda.' S. C. Kamya. M.T.S. thesis, Virginia Theological Seminary, Alexandria, VA, 1990. 129p.

A short history of the Vicariate of the Upper Nile, Uganda. J. Biermans. London: St. Joseph's Society for Foreign Missions, 1920. 39p. (By one of the first Catholic bishops).

'A survey and directory of mission agencies in Uganda.' E. N. Tumusiime. M.A. thesis, Daystar University College and Wheaton College, Wheaton, IL and Nairobi, Kenya, 1994. 361p.

'Abamalaki in Buganda, 1914–1919,' F. B. Welbourn, *Uganda journal* (Kampala, Uganda), 21, 2 (1957), 150–61.

'An approach to a holistic ministry in a Seventh–day Adventist urban church in Uganda.' N. M. Walemba. D.Min. thesis, Andrews University, Seventh-day Adventist Theological Seminary, Barrien Springs, MI, 1988. 317p.

Bantu philosophy of life in the light of the Christian message: a basis for an African vitalistic theology. D. R. K. Nkurunziza. Frankfurt: Lang, 1989. 307p.

Black evangelists: the spread of Christianity in Uganda, 1891–1914. M. L. Pirouet. London: Rex Collings, 1978. 269p.

Building a Ugandan church: African participation in church growth and expansion in Busoga, 1891–1940. A. D. T. Tuma. Nairobi: East African Literature Bureau, 1980. 239p.

Catholic directory of Eastern Africa, 1977–79. Tabora, Tanzania: TMP Book Department, 1977. 258p. (Earlier editions: 1959, 1965, 1968, 1971, 1974–76, then irregularly to the present).

Christian response to change in East African traditional societies. G. G. Brown. *Woodbrooke occasional papers*, 4. London: Friends Home Service Committee for Woodbrooke College, 1973. 55p.

Christianity in contemporary Africa: Uganda. W. B. Anderson (ed). Kampala, Uganda: Department of Religious Studies and Philosophy, Makerere University, 1973. 250p.

Church planting in Uganda: a comparative study. G. Van Rheenen. South Pasadena, CA: William Carey Library, 1976. 168p.

East African rebels: a study of some independent churches. F. B. Welbourn. London: SCM, 1961.

Ecclesiological meaning of small Christian communities in Uganda today. S. Twinomugisha. Rome: Pontificia Universitas Urbaniana, 1991. 124p.

'Ethnicity, Christianity, and the development of social stratification in colonial Ankole, Uganda,' M. R. Doornbos, *International journal of African historical studies*, 9, 4 (1976), 555–75.

From mission to church: a handbook of Christianity in East Africa. Z. J. Nthamburi (ed). Nairobi: Uzima Press, 1991. 150p. (Chapters by Kevin Ward entitled 'A history of Christianity in Uganda' and '"Tukutendereza Yesu": the Balokole revival movement in Uganda').

Incarnating Christianity in Uganda. J. M. Waliggo & D. M. Byabazaire (eds). , 1983. 342p.
Islam and the confluence of religions in Uganda, 1840–1966. N. Q. King, A. Kasozi & A. Oded. *Studies in religion*. Tallahassee, FL: American Academy of Religion, 1973. 69p.
La fontana dalle molte sorgenti: cento anni di cristianesimo in Uganda. D. Bosa. Bologna: Editrice Missionaria Italiana, 1979. 223p.
'Liturgical inculturation: Ugandan dialogue with the eucharistic rite.' L. Sullivan. M.A. thesis, Santa Clara University, Santa Clara, CA, 1994. 123p.
Lugbara religion: ritual and authority among an East African people. J. Middleton. London: Oxford University Press, 1960. 276p.
Magic and witchcraft in southern Uganda. J. O'Donohue. Kampala: Pastoral Institute of Eastern Africa, 1975. 50p.
Men of God: twelve short biographies of Baptist leaders in Uganda. R. K. Hesch. Kampala, Uganda: Baptist Literature Department, 1994. 75p.
Men without God?: a study of the impact of the Christian message in the North of Uganda. J. K. Russell. London: Highway Press, 1966. 96p. (By the Anglican bishop in the North).
Mission, church, and state in a colonial setting: Uganda, 1890–1925. H. B. Hansen. New York: St. Martin's Press, 1984. 668p.
'Overview of "A communication agenda for Christian discipleship in Uganda": a video production related to discipleship strategies in the church in Uganda.' M. K. Ntende. Communications graduate project, Wheaton College, Wheaton, IL, 1989. (24 min. videocassette plus 45p).
'Polygamy or monogamy: challenges and ramifications for Christian marriage in the Anglican Church of Uganda today.' E. K. Sserunjogi-Salongo. M.S.T. thesis, Trinity Lutheran Seminary, Columbus, OH, 1992. 255p.
Religions in Uganda, 1960–1990. E. G. Rutiba. Kampala, Uganda: Department of Religious Studies, Faculty of Arts, Makerere University, 1993. 25p.
Revival: an enquiry. M. A. C. Warren. London: SCM Press, 1954. 123p. (On the Balokole or East African Revival).
So abundant a harvest: the Catholic Church in Uganda, 1879–1979. Y. Tourigny. London: Darton, Longman and Todd, 1979. 228p. (Centenary volume for Catholic Church in Uganda).
The autobiography of Sir Henry Morton Stanley. S. H. M. Stanley. Ed., D. Stanley. London: Sampson Low, 1909. 568p.
The bruised pearl of Africa: Uganda past and present. M. L. Prentice. Richmond, Australia: Spectrum, 1990. 109p.
'The changing role of women in the Anglican and Baptist church of Busoga province in Uganda.' E. B. Baleke. Communications graduate project, Wheaton College, Wheaton, IL, 1991. 124p.
The Church of Uganda, Rwanda and Burundi: survey on administration and finance of the Church in Uganda. J. Bikangaga. Kampala, Uganda: Uganda Bookshop, 1969. 74p.
The contribution of the Christian churches to the development of Western Uganda, 1894–1974. D. M. Byabazaire. Frankfurt: Lang, 1979. 198p.
'"The fellowship of suffering": a theological interpretation of Christian suffering under Idi Amin.' E. B. Muhima. Ph.D. dissertation, Northwestern University, Evanston, IL, 1981. 185p.
'The ghost cult in Bunyoro,' J. H. M. Beattie, *Ethnology*, 3, 2 (1964), 127–151.
The growth of the church in Buganda. J. V. Taylor. London: SCM Press, 1958. 288p.
'The introduction and growth of Christianity in Busoga, 1891–1940, with particular reference to the roles of the Basoga clergymen, catechists and chiefs.' T. Tuma. Ph.D. dissertation, University of London (SOAS), 1973. 392p.
'The political crisis of church institutions in Uganda,' A. B. Mujaju, *African affairs*, 75, 298 (1976), 67–85.
The role of religious organisations in development of Uganda. S. A. H. Abidi (ed). *African development series*, no. 5. Kampala, Uganda: Foundation for African Development, 1991. 217p.
'The Yakan or Allah water cult among the Lugbara,' J. Middleton, *Journal of the Royal Anthropological Institute*, 93, 1 (1963), 80–108.
'Tukutendereza: a study of social change and sectarian withdrawal in the Balokole Revival of Uganda.' C. E. Robins. Ph.D. dissertation, Columbia University, New York, 1975. 462p.
Uganda. R. L. Collison. *World bibliographical series*, vol. 11. Oxford, UK: CLIO Press, 1981. 159p. (See especially 'Religions,' p.54-8).
Uganda and the Mill Hill Fathers. H. P. Gale. London: Macmillan, 1959.
Uganda holocaust. D. Wooding & R. Barnett. London: Pickering & Inglis, 1980. 254p.
'Witchcraft and sorcery in Lugbara,' in *Witchcraft and sorcery in East Africa*, p.257–75. J. Middleton & E. H. Winter (eds). London: Routledge & Kegan Paul, 1963.

Country Table 2. **Organized churches and denominations in Uganda.**

Official name (bold type = church with over 10% of all affiliated) 1	*Begun* 2	*Type* 3	*Counc* 4	*Congs* 5	*Adults* 6	*Affiliated 1970* 7	*Affiliated 1995* 8	*G%* 9	*Names, notes, and other statistics* (see Codebook, Part 3) 10
African Brotherhood Church	c1960	I-Non	xva..	3	1,000	1,000	2,000	2.81	*ABC, Uganda Pastorate*. M=ABC(Kenya). Kamba immigrants, et alii.
African Greek Orth Ch (D Eirenopolis)	1929	O-Gre	Cw..K	58	15,000	10,000	25,000	3.73	*AGOC*. Under Greek P Alexandria. Schism ex CMS over paternalism. Ganda, Langi. 2x.
African Israel Church Nineveh	c1960	I-3pA	Iw...	70	40,000	32,000	60,000	2.55	M=AICN(Kenya). Brought by workers of Mowlem contractors. Luo, Luhya. Banned 1977.
African Orthodox Autonomous Ch SS	1966	I-ReO	.....	2	200	1,000	500	-2.73	SS=South of the Sahara. Schism ex AGOC protesting Greek paternalism. Banned 1977.
Assemblies of God	1980	P-Pe2	Z....	35	1,900	1,400	3,250	6.67	M=AoG(USA). Missionary (USA) no longer present.
Assembly Hall Churches	c1991	I-3nC	.....	3	22	–	50	25.00	*Local Churches. Little Flock*. Chinese. Begun 1922 in China.
Association of Baptist Churches	1961	I-Bap	xFG.G	60	2,500	2,000	5,000	3.73	M=CBFMS(USA). Ganda. 12f; missionaries expelled 1973. HQ Masaka.
Back to the Bible Truth	1981	I-3pA	.....	18	1,350	–	3,000	7.14	Work mainly among Bakonjo, some Acholi and Lugbara.
Baptist Union of Uganda	1962	P-Bap	T....	512	16,896	7,000	22,000	4.69	M=Baptist Mission of EAfrica(FMB-SBC, USA). Banned 1977. 80n,24f,6p,1s,1711Y.
Broadsheet Readers' Clubs	c1980	I-3nA	.....	52	900	–	3,000	6.67	Readers of Gospel Broadsheets produced by M=WEC(UK).
Catholic Church in Uganda:	1879	R-Lat	P.SES	432	4,475,500	3,394,988	7,932,782	3.45	*Eklezia Enkatoliki*. C=6+3+17. 11p,4s(254). 929n 301x 1061m 2657w 288323Yy
M Kampala (Rubaga)	1894	R-Lat	Ps	59	323,000	648,070	600,773	-0.30	70% Ganda, 5% Ruanda, 5% Rundi, Goans. 1s. 219n 67x 196m 713w 39696Yy
D Arua	1958	R-Lat	Ps	34	463,000	386,680	545,000	1.38	42% Lugbara, 38% Alur, 18% Madi, Kakwa. M=FSCJ. 69n 33x 65m 143w 33808Yy
D Fort Portal	1961	R-Lat	Ps	14	274,000	182,300	511,600	4.21	68% Toro, 13% Konjo, 8% Amba, 6% Kiga. M=CSC. 56n 8x 36m 163w 16764Yy
D Gulu (Equatorial Nile)	1923	R-Lat	Ps	22	186,000	227,489	477,487	3.01	90% Acholi. 17,000 Sudanese (1972). 1p. 32n 27x 39m 293w 10230Yy
D Hoima	1965	R-Lat	Ps	18	238,000	140,600	450,052	4.76	98% Nyoro (only tribe living in diocese). 45n 9x 16m 119w 15404Yy
D Jinja	1966	R-Lat	Pmhm	19	253,000	157,198	468,073	4.46	In east. 98% Soga, 2% Samia (Luhya). M=MHM. 1p. 35n 30x 113m 89w 18583Yy
D Kabale	1966	R-Lat	Pwf	25	240,000	239,424	417,400	2.25	In extreme west. 85% Kiga, 15% Ruanda. M=WF. 1p. 65n 12x 15m 123w 21041Yy
D Kasana-Luweero	1996	R-Lat	Ps	9	76,400	–	153,000	0.05	1996. Formed out of M Kampala. 18n 8x 8m
D Kasese	1989	R-Lat	Ps	6	76,000	–	132,324	16.67	Formerly in D Fort Portal. M=CSC. 15n 6x 9m 26w 5942Yy
D Kiyinda-Mityana	1981	R-Lat	Ps	18	200,000	–	457,000	7.14	Formerly in M Kampala. 55n 7x 17m 126w 17226Yy
D Kotido	1991	R-Lat	Ps	8	49,000	–	86,764	25.00	Formerly in D Moroto. M=MCCI. 5n 12x 16m 24w 1069Yy
D Lira	1968	R-Lat	Ps	16	248,000	181,470	451,335	3.71	90% Lango. First parish 1930. 1p. 23n 29x 35m 132w 19389Yy
D Lugazi	1996	R-Lat	Ps	16	0	–	332,600	0.05	1996. Formed out of M Kampala 34m 6x 6m
D Masaka	1939	R-Lat	Ps	38	495,000	347,821	870,620	3.74	80% Ganda, 10% Haya, 10% Ruanda. 1p,1s. 158n 10x 122m 498w 31160Yy
D Mbarara (Ruwenzori)	1934	R-Lat	Ps	24	375,000	233,304	681,836	4.38	78% Nkole, 8% Kiga, 8% Ruanda. M=WF. 1p. 64n 14x 21m 281w 29396Yy
D Moroto	1965	R-Lat	Ps	9	82,000	98,288	104,099	0.23	55% Karamojong, 20% Jie, 10% Topotha. M=FSCJ. 13n 20x 31m 52w 3453Yy
D Nebbi	1996	R-Lat	Ps	13	225,000	–	291,353	0.05	1996. Formed out of D Arua. 26n 9x 15m 42w
D Soroti	1980	R-Lat	Ps	18	247,000	–	403,000	6.67	Formed out of D Tororo. 20n 11x 12m 58w 6100Yy
D Tororo (Upper Nile)	1894	R-Lat	Ps	36	229,000	542,344	458,466	-0.67	60% Teso, 15% Gisu, 10% Sabei, 10% Luo. 1p. 55n 6x 25m 110w 19062Yy
OM Uganda	1964	R-Lat	Ps	30	30,000	10,000	40,000	5.70	Military Ordinariate of Uganda.
Charismatic Church of Uganda	1996	I-3cW	x....	210	40,600	–	101,000	50.00	Massive growth due to M=ICCEC (USA), at expense of Church of Uganda.
Chosen Evangelical Revival	1949	I-Ang	I....	5	700	1,000	1,500	1.64	*CER. Lwak Ayera (Chosen Ones): Trumpeters*. Revival schism ex CURBZ. Acholi, Alur.
Christian Reformed Ch in Eastern Africa	1992	I-Ref	.....	100	3,000	–	4,000	33.33	Begun 1992 in Kenya ex Reformed Ch of East Africa.
Christ's Disciples Church	c1980	I-3pA	I....	40	4,000	–	7,000	6.67	Indigenous Ugandan pentecostals. Active in OAIC.
Church of Christ in Africa	c1960	I-Ang	IT.T.	20	11,000	5,000	15,000	4.49	*Area Diocese of Tororo*. One of 8 Dioceses of M=CCA(Kenya). 80% Luo. Banned 1977.
Church of God (Cleveland)	1982	P-Pe3	Z....	17	1,762	–	3,440	7.69	M=CoG(Cleveland).
Church of God in East Africa	1969	P-Hol	x....	262	12,000	4,000	30,000	8.39	Luhya from M=CGEA(Kenya), aided by M=CoG(Anderson) (USA). Kampala, rural areas. 2f.
Church of God of Prophecy	1981	P-Pe3	.....	20	850	–	1,670	7.14	M=CGP. (USA). Holiness Pentecostals.
Church of the Nazarene	1988	P-Hol	.....	3	153	–	200	14.29	M=CoN. Nazarenes, from USA.
Church of the Redeemed	c1960	I-3cA	.....	400	40,000	28,000	80,000	4.29	An early Revival breakoff by charismatics.
Church of Uganda	1875	A-Eva	AWAVK	13,000	3,747,000	1,281,000	7,400,000	7.27	27 Dioceses. Balokole Revival. Schisms to new AICs. M=CMS,RCMS,AIM(UK). 142f,8H.
Deeper Life Christian Church	c1985	I-3pA	.....	1	225	–	400	10.00	*Deeper Life Bible Church*. M=DLBC(Nigeria).
Deliverance Church	1962	I-3pA	x....	120	18,000	1,000	36,000	15.41	Split ex PAG. 1969 spread to Kenya (YCAF). Kampala. Youths. Banned 1977.
Eastern Orthodox Church	1957	I-ReO	.....	2	200	200	500	3.73	Schism ex AGOC by disaffected African Orthodox priest. Ganda.
Elim Foursquare Gospel Alliance	1996	P-Pe2	.....	49	3,500	–	5,000	40.00	*EFGA*. Mainline Pentecostals.
Elim Pentecostal Fellowship of Uganda	1962	P-Pe2	ZGG.G	1,125	45,000	30,000	98,000	4.85	*PEFA*. 1962, M=EMA,IPA(USA). Widespread. Kampala, in north. Banned 1973. 12f,1s.
Episcopal Church in the Sudan	1964	A-Low	aw...	30	20,000	10,000	40,000	5.70	1966: 120,000 refugees, 2 bishops, 30 priests from Sudan. Most returned by 1974.
Evangelical Free Ch of Uganda	1986	I-Ref	.....	15	12,000	–	20,000	11.11	Formed ex Presbyterian Ch of East Africa. HQ Muyenga, Kampala.
Full Gospel Churches of Uganda	1959	P-Pe2	x.G.G	200	7,000	6,000	20,000	4.93	*Mungu Mwema (God is Good)*. M=Glad Tidings Miss Soc (Canada). Banned 1977,16f,1p.
Israel Anglican Church	1948	I-mar	.....	15	1,600	2,000	3,000	1.64	*Dini ya Msambwa (Religion of the Ancestral Spirits)*. 1967, Gisu resurgence.
Jehovah's Witnesses	1935	m-Jeh	x....	19	999	300	4,000	10.92	*IBSA*. 1935, literature distributed by missionaries. Banned 1973. (1975) 17f,18Y. (1995) 265Y.
Maria Legio of Africa	c1968	I-3sA	.....	20	9,000	5,000	25,000	6.65	M=MLA(Kenya), large schism ex Roman Catholic Church. 90% Luo. Banned 1973.
New Apostolic Church		I-3aX	x....	200	110,000	–	228,595	0.05	*NAC*. M=Neuapostolische Kirche (HQ Zurich, Switzerland).
New Life Presbyterian Church	1986	I-Ref	.....	27	500	–	1,000	11.11	Begun by M=World Harvest Mission(USA). Fort Portal area.
Open Bible Standard Church	1983	I-3pW	.....	73	4,200	–	8,250	8.33	M=OBSC(USA). Independent pentecostals.
Pentecostal Assemblies of God	1935	P-Pe2	ZFG.G	2,200	62,000	40,000	154,000	5.54	*PAG*. M=PAoC. 40% Teso, 15% Gisu, 15% Luhya. Banned 1973. 117n,9x,11f,1s(100),685Y.
Pentecostal Churches of Uganda	1963	P-Pe2	.....	355	18,000	1,000	25,000	13.74	*PCU*. M=NPY, FFFM. Begun from Kenya.
Pentecostal Holiness Church	c1985	P-Pe3	.....	5	1,120	–	2,618	10.00	M=IPHC(USA). Holiness Pentecostals.
Presbyterian Church of Uganda	c1950	P-Ref	Rwa..	27	3,379	1,000	4,101	5.81	*PCEA*(Kenya). Chaplaincy to expatriates (Kikuyu, Scottish) in Kampala. Banned 1977.
Reformed Presbyterian Ch in Uganda	1990	I-Ref	.....	23	3,000	–	5,000	20.00	Schism ex PCEA over church discipline.
Religious Society of Friends	1955	P-Qua	Q....	73	2,900	600	6,440	9.96	East Africa Yearly Meeting. 30% Luhya from EAYM(Kenya). Banned 1973-1979. W=85%.
Salvation Army	1931	P-Sal	xwa..	20	3,000	2,017	5,000	3.70	*Jeshi la Wokovu. Uganda Div*. 40% Gisu, 20% Kenyans, 15% Soga, 10% Bakedi. Banned 1977.
Seventh-day Adventist Church	1926	P-Adv	x....	399	65,000	18,000	110,000	7.51	50% Ganda, 21% Konjo. Banned 1977. 31n,1x,26f,1H,3h,1s,393t(15785),W=75%,1313Y.
Society of the One Almighty God	1914	I-Ang	.....	1	50	1,000	100	-8.80	*KOAB. Bamalaki. Malakite Ch*. 1914, schism of 92,000 ex CMS. Almost extinct.
United Pentecostal Church	1969	I-3pA	.....	80	2,700	2,000	7,850	5.62	Split ex PEFA (Elim) among Toro, supported by Swedish and Finnish Pentecostals.
World-Wide Missions	1962	I-Non	x....	2	700	300	1,000	4.93	M=World-Wide Missions (USA). Evangelicals linked with Pasadena, CA (USA).
Other African indigenous churches		I-3cA	.....	300	30,000	16,000	60,000	0.05	Total 24 (see below),including 15 immigrant bodies from Kenya & Zaire, also new charismatics.
Other Protestant denominations		P-	.....	30	4,000	1,000	7,000	0.05	Total about 5 (see list below).
Doubly-affiliated		2-aff			-102,000	0	-191,476		Evangelicals and Pentecostals who are also baptized Roman Catholics.
Totals				**20,733**	**8,742,406**	**4,905,805**	**16,386,770**		

Churches, members, growth, 1900-2025	*Congs*	*Adults*	*Affiliated*	*G%*	*Total denominations*	*6 Megablocs:* *O*	*R*	*A*	*P*	*I*	*m*
Total churches, members, and denominations (mid-1900)	60	73,000	130,000	5.32	2	0	1	1	0	0	0
Total churches, members, and denominations (mid-1970)	8,679	2,754,504	4,905,805	5.32	43	1	1	2	13	25	1
Total churches, members, and denominations (mid-1990)	15,000	7,469,000	14,000,000	5.38	74	1	1	2	20	49	1
Total churches, members, and denominations (mid-1995)	20,733	8,742,406	16,386,770	3.20	76	1	1	2	21	50	1
Total churches, members, and denominations (mid-2000)	25,000	10,107,000	18,944,173	2.94	78	1	1	2	22	51	1
Total churches, members, and denominations (mid-2025)	40,000	21,660,000	40,600,000	3.10	147	3	1	2	40	100	1

Continued overleaf

Country Table 2–concluded

NOTES ON TABLE ABOVE
NATIONAL COUNCILS (Column 4, 5th letter).
E = Evangelical Fellowship of Uganda (EFU).
G = Uganda Association of Evangelicals (formerly, Evangelical Fellowship of Uganda).
K = Uganda Joint Christian Council (UJCC).
S = Uganda Episcopal Conference (UEC), also member of UJCC.
OTHER AFRICAN INDIGENOUS CHURCHES. Immigrant bodies from Kenya, in addition to those in table, are about 13, including: African Ch of the Holy Spirit, African Divine Ch (banned 1977), Apostolic Faith of Africa, Calvary Reformed Church (1994), Evangelical Presbyterian Ch in Uganda (1987), Holy Ch of Kenya/Uganda, Holy Ghost Ch of East Africa (banned 1977), Lost Israelites of Kenya, Miracle Revival Fellowship Pentecostal Ch (claiming 15,000 adherents in Uganda), Nomiya Luo Ch. In addition, there are about 12 other groups, including: Apostolic Ch of Christ, Apostolic Ch of East Africa, Church of Christ in the World (Ugandan pentecostal), Church of Jesus the Messiah (in Luganda: Kanisa ya Isa Mesia; banned 1977), Eglise Kimbanguiste (EJCSK) from Zaire, Gospel of God (Vapostori, Apostles, from Rhodesia), Redeemed Ch of Uganda (leader from Ghana; banned 1977), Wide World Miracle Ch (banned 1977).
OTHER PROTESTANT DENOMINATIONS. These smaller groups include: Reformed Episcopal Ch (USA; 1956; working with AIM and CURBZ), Uganda Ch of Christ (Non-Instrumental) (banned 1973), United Pentecostal Ch (banned 1973).
OTHER MARGINAL PROTESTANT BODIES. Branhamites (Local Believers, End Time Believers) from USA.

UKRAINE

SECULAR DATA, AD 2000

STATE
Official name: Ukrayina (Ukraine).
Short name: Ukraine. **Adjective of nationality:** Ukrainian.
Flag: Blue and yellow stripes.
Area: 603,700 sq. km. (233,100 sq. mi.).
Government: Unitary multiparty republic with a single legislative body, since 1991 (1922 Soviet rule).
Legislature: Supreme Council, 450 members.
Official language: Ukranian.
Monetary unit: hryvnia (pl. hryvny), no decimal unit. **US$1=** 3,80 hryvny.
Chief cities: KIJEV (Kiyev, Kiev) 2,897,000; Char'kov (Kharkov, Kharkiv) 1,701,000; Dnepropetrovsk (Ekaterinoslav) 1,244,000; Doneck (Donetsk, Stalino) 1,158,000; Odessa 1,123,000.
Political divisions: 25 provinces.
Armed forces: 387,000.

DEMOGRAPHY
Population: 50,456,000.
Population density: 83.5/sq. km. (216.4/sq. mi.).
Under 15 years: 8,966,000.
Growth rate p.a.: -0.37% (births 9.71, deaths 13.82).
Mortality: Infant, per 1,000: 15.3; **Maternal per 100,000:** 50.0.
Life expectancy: 70 (male 66, female 75).
Household size: 3.2. **Floor area per person, sq.m:** 21.0.
Major languages: Ukrainian, Russian, Polish, Romani, Belorussian.
Urban dwellers: 72.51%. **Urban growth rate p.a.:** 0.15%.
Labor force: 46%.

ETHNOLINGUISTIC PEOPLES
70.4% Ukrainian; 20.0% Russian; 2.3% Polish (Pole); 1.3% Balkan Gypsy; 1.1% Ruthene (Ruthenian), many smaller immigrant peoples.

ECONOMY
National income p.a. per person: US$1,630; **per family:** US$5,215.

EDUCATION
Adult literacy: 98% (male 99%, female 97%). **Schools:** 22,448.
Universities: 159. **School enrolment:** female/male: 92%/88%.

HEALTH
Access to health services: 75%. **Access to safe water:** 97%.
Hospitals: 3,900 (130 beds per 10,000). **Doctors:** 230,000.
Blind: 43,000. **Deaf:** 3,048,100. **Murder rate:** 8.
Lepers: 1,000.

LITERATURE
New book titles p.a.: 5,550 (110 p.a. per million). **Periodicals:** 449.
Newspapers: 90 dailies.

COMMUNICATION (per 1,000 people)
Phones: 161 **(0% mobile). Radios:** 346. **TV sets:** 233.
Daily newspaper circulation: 118. **Computers:** 45.

REFUGEES
Alien refugees from other countries: 6,000.

HUMAN LIFE AND LIBERTY (optimum condition=100.0%)
HDI: 68.9. **HSI:** 55.0. **HFI:** 35.0. **EFL:** 20.0.

Country Table 1. **Religious adherents in Ukraine, AD 1900-2025.**

Year	*1900*		*1970*		*mid-1990*		*Annual change, 1990-2000*				*mid-1995*		*mid-2000*		*mid-2025*	
Name	*Adherents*	*%*	*Adherents*	*%*	*Adherents*	*%*	*Natural*	*Conversion*	*Total*	*Rate*	*Adherents*	*%*	*Adherents*	*%*	*Adherents*	*%*
Christians	**28,501,000**	**97.2**	**28,400,000**	**60.0**	**41,800,000**	**80.6**	**-115,594**	**122,439**	**6,845**	**0.02**	**42,000,000**	**81.7**	**41,868,446**	**83.0**	**40,000,000**	**87.6**
PROFESSION																
crypto-Christians	0	0.0	5,930,000	12.5	0	0.0	0	0	0	0.00	0	0.0	0	0.0	0	0.0
professing Christians	**28,501,000**	**97.2**	**22,470,000**	**47.5**	**41,800,000**	**80.6**	**-115,594**	**122,439**	**6,845**	**0.02**	**42,000,000**	**81.7**	**41,868,446**	**83.0**	**40,000,000**	**87.6**
AFFILIATION																
unaffiliated Christians	2,000,000	6.8	1,220,900	2.6	240,000	0.5	-664	-3,401	-4,065	-1.84	207,106	0.4	199,349	0.4	100,000	0.2
affiliated Christians	**26,501,000**	**90.4**	**27,179,100**	**57.4**	**41,560,000**	**80.1**	**-114,931**	**125,841**	**10,910**	**0.03**	**41,792,894**	**81.3**	**41,669,097**	**82.6**	**39,900,000**	**87.3**
Orthodox	20,781,000	70.9	24,546,000	51.9	27,200,000	52.4	-75,219	95,219	20,000	0.07	27,275,000	53.0	27,400,000	54.3	27,000,000	59.1
Independents	0	0.0	1,734,300	3.7	7,800,000	15.0	-21,570	91,570	70,000	0.86	8,264,723	16.1	8,500,000	16.9	9,000,000	19.7
Roman Catholics	5,220,000	17.8	1,667,000	3.5	5,540,000	10.7	-15,320	19,210	3,890	0.07	5,564,671	10.8	5,578,901	11.1	5,700,000	12.5
Protestants	500,000	1.7	772,000	1.6	1,300,000	2.5	-3,595	7,595	4,000	0.30	1,317,000	2.6	1,340,000	2.7	1,380,000	3.0
Marginal Christians	0	0.0	10,000	0.0	120,000	0.2	-332	1,832	1,500	1.18	130,000	0.3	135,000	0.3	140,000	0.3
doubly-affiliated	0	0.0	-1,550,200	-3.3	-400,000	-0.8	1,106	-89,586	-88,480	12.38	-758,500	-1.5	-1,284,804	-2.6	-3,320,000	-7.3
Trans-megabloc groupings																
Evangelicals	460,000	1.6	530,000	1.1	986,000	1.9	-2,727	5,727	3,000	0.30	1,049,350	2.0	1,016,000	2.0	1,379,000	3.0
Pentecostals/Charismatics	0	0.0	1,220,000	2.6	3,645,000	7.0	-10,080	49,080	39,000	1.02	3,940,180	7.7	4,035,000	8.0	4,568,000	10.0
Great Commission Christians	**2,350,000**	**8.0**	**7,570,000**	**16.0**	**6,071,000**	**11.7**	**-16,789**	**20,748**	**3,959**	**0.07**	**6,171,000**	**12.0**	**6,110,588**	**12.1**	**5,939,000**	**13.0**
Nonreligious	60,000	0.2	10,559,000	22.3	6,456,470	12.4	-17,857	-79,757	-97,614	-1.63	6,040,250	11.7	5,480,329	10.9	3,750,000	8.2
Atheists	2,000	0.0	7,536,000	15.9	2,553,100	4.9	-7,060	-47,013	-54,073	-2.35	2,300,000	4.5	2,012,368	4.0	893,000	2.0
Muslims	50,000	0.2	250,000	0.5	820,000	1.6	-2,268	6,530	4,262	0.51	845,000	1.6	862,621	1.7	880,000	1.9
Jews	720,000	2.5	572,000	1.2	250,000	0.5	-691	-2,274	-2,965	-1.25	235,000	0.5	220,353	0.4	150,000	0.3
Ethnoreligionists	0	0.0	0	0.0	9,000	0.0	-25	38	13	0.15	9,100	0.0	9,132	0.0	10,000	0.0
Buddhists	0	0.0	0	0.0	2,400	0.0	-7	15	8	0.32	2,450	0.0	2,479	0.0	4,000	0.0
Baha'is	0	0.0	0	0.0	30	0.0	0	22	22	23.72	200	0.0	252	0.0	1,000	0.0
World A (unevangelized persons)	58,666	0.2	4,731,650	10.0	1,037,820	2.0	-2,868	-25,548	-28,416	-3.15	925,767	1.8	756,840	1.5	548,256	1.2
World B (evangelized non-Christians)	773,334	2.6	14,184,850	30.0	9,053,180	17.4	-25,040	-96,891	-121,931	-1.44	8,505,778	16.5	7,830,714	15.5	5,139,744	11.2
World C (Christians)	28,501,000	97.2	28,400,000	60.0	41,800,000	80.6	-115,594	122,439	6,845	0.02	42,000,000	81.7	41,868,446	83.0	40,000,000	87.6
Country's population	**29,333,000**	**100.0**	**47,316,500**	**100.0**	**51,891,000**	**100.0**	**-143,502**	**0**	**-143,502**	**-0.28**	**51,431,546**	**100.0**	**50,456,000**	**100.0**	**45,688,000**	**100.0**

COLUMNS, ROWS.
For meanings and definitions, see Codebook (Part 3). Note that, by definition, total 'Christians' = professing + crypto-Christians, which also = affiliated + unaffiliated Christians, and also = Great Commission Christians + latent Christians. Percentages may not always total exactly, due to rounding.

NOTES ON RELIGIONS
BAHA'IS. After Independence in 1991, Baha'i experienced widespread interest. By 1997 there were 300 Baha'is and 18 local spiritual assemblies.
ETHNORELIGIONISTS. Shamanists among the Komi, Mari, Buryat, Udmurt, and Yakut. Also Koreans.
JEWS. Declining due to emigration to Israel.
MUSLIMS. Mainly Balkan Gypsies, Turks, and Tatars.

Great Commission Instrument Panel: status of Ukraine (for explanation see start of Part 4)

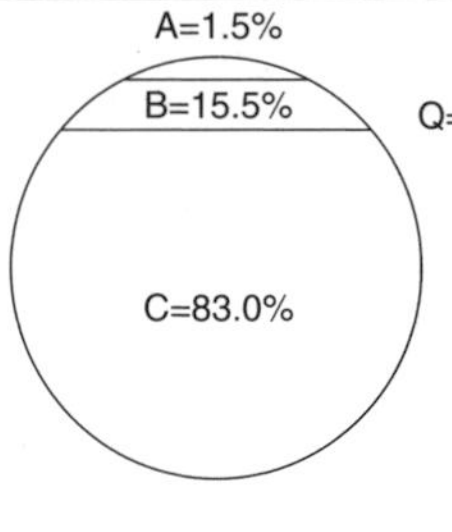

3 Worlds, AD 2000

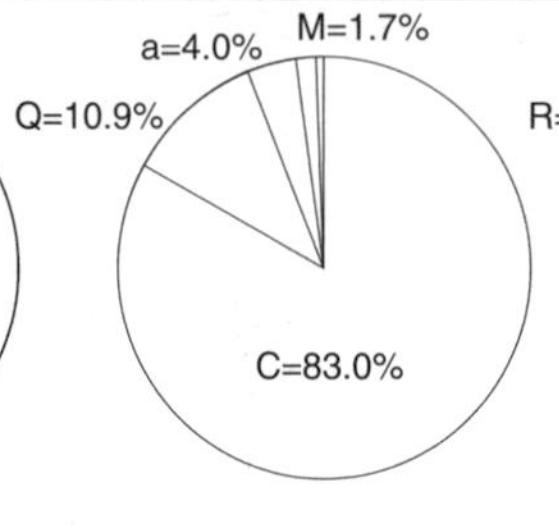

Religions, AD 2000

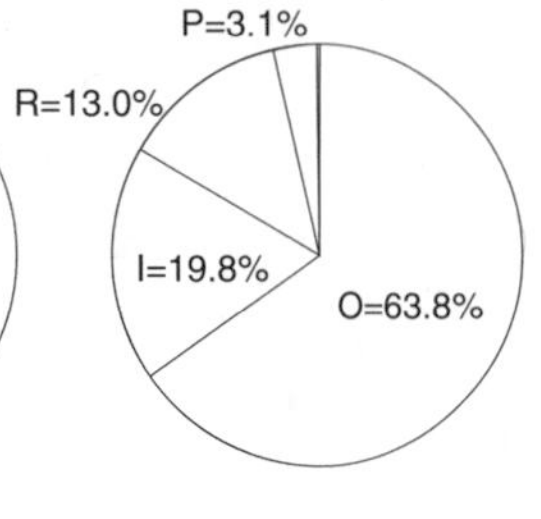

Ecclesiastical blocs

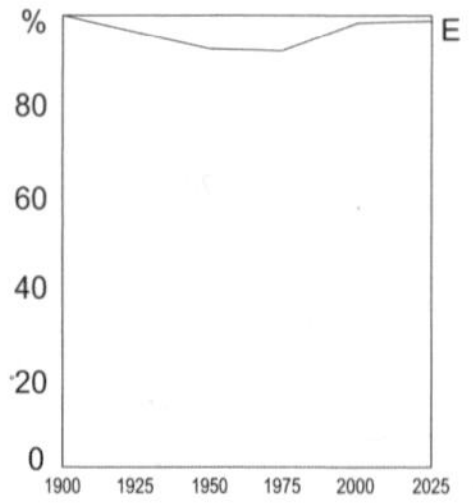

Evangelization, 1900-2025

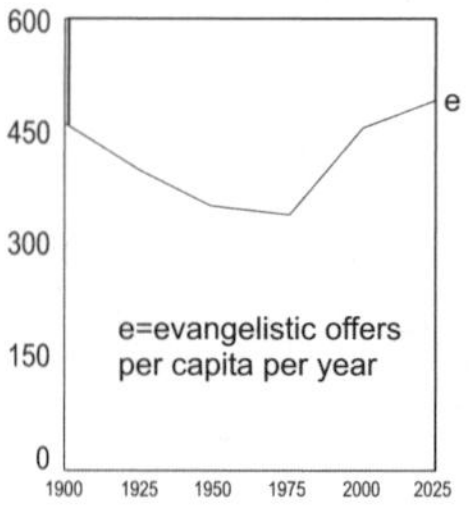

Offers, 1900-2025

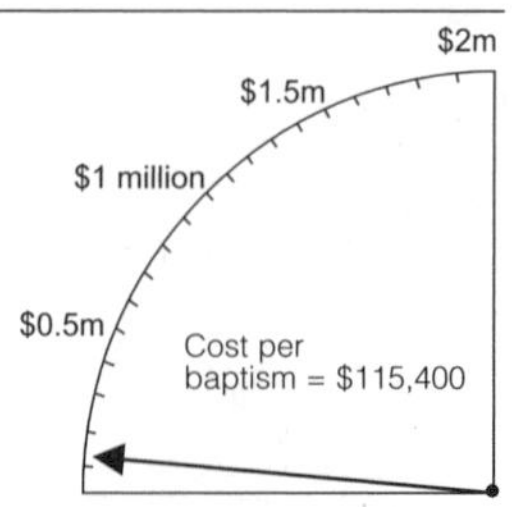

Cost-effectiveness, AD 2000

Country status. Ukraine, a former republic of the Soviet Union, is a large country, mainly steppeland, in Eastern Europe north of the Black Sea. Its chief economic activities are heavy industry and the production of oil and gas.

HUMAN LIFE AND LIBERTY

Human need and development. Since declaring independence in 1991, many basic changes have been accomplished in Ukraine. The institutions of central planning have been dissolved, the deregulation of pricing and the process of charging for many hitherto free services has been initiated. As with other nations, the transition from centralized planning to a market economy has had drastic economic impacts. The greatest burden directly falls upon the populace

Country summary. **Worlds A, B, C by ethnolinguistic peoples, cities, and major civil divisions in Ukraine.**

	PEOPLES							CITIES							CIVIL DIVISIONS						
World	*Num*	*Pop 2000*	*C%*	*Christians*	*E%*	*U%*	*Unevangelized*	*Num*	*Pop 2000*	*C%*	*Christians*	*E%*	*U%*	*Unevangelized*	*Num*	*Pop 2000*	*C%*	*Christians*	*E%*	*U%*	*Unevangelized*
A	23	582,080	0.33	1,899	41	59	341,260	0	0	0.00	0	0	0	0	0	0	0.00	0	0	0	0
B	15	824,326	14.77	121,737	59	41	337,950	0	0	0.00	0	0	0	0	0	0	0.00	0	0	0	0
C	28	49,049,573	84.70	41,545,463	100	0	73,631	87	24,947,967	79.59	19,857,245	98	2	444,084	25	50,455,979	82.59	41,669,097	99	1	752,836
Total	**66**	**50,455,979**	**82.59**	**41,669,099**	**99**	**1**	**752,841**	**87**	**24,947,967**	**79.59**	**19,857,245**	**98**	**2**	**444,084**	**25**	**50,455,979**	**82.59**	**41,669,097**	**99**	**1**	**752,836**

which have depended on the government for so many of their basic needs. With the implementation of a market economy these basic needs are now solely the responsibility of the individual. President Leonid Kuchma came to power in 1994 and his commitment to relieve some of this burden has been aimed at privatization. The National Bank of Ukraine issued one free certificate of privatization to each citizen. By the end of 1995, 28 million citizens had received certificates and 5 million had become owners of shares, entitlements, or portions of private property. At the beginning of 1996, approximately 26,000 enterprises had been privatized. While helping somewhat, real incomes in the Ukraine have clearly fallen below the threshold levels at which households are able to satisfy their range of basic needs. The housing situation, which is drastically overcrowded and in disrepair, often lacking in basic utilities such as heat and waste treatment, has also been worsened by the need to resettle peoples from the regions contaminated by the Chernobyl accident, by returning groups of Ukraine's indigenous populations, and by deportees from other former Soviet countries.

In October 1995, the Ministry of Statistics conducted a survey to obtain an assessment of unemployment and underemployment. The unemployment rate among the active population was 4.7%. In early 1996 it was estimated that 3.8% of the active population were only employed part-time and in 1995 an additional 11.9% or 2.7 million people were estimated to be on administrative leave with either no pay or partial pay. While official unemployment has remained low, it is now recognized that the use of administrative leave has concealed the real unemployment rate and inflated the level of underemployment. Currently the law requires enterprises to pay 3 months severance pay. But with companies facing declining output and demand, this is often impossible and they resort to administrative and maternity leave. Worker's prefer this to being officially unemployed because of low unemployment wages and the hope of being recalled. In addition they still have access to health clinics, sports clubs, and other corporate amenities. Unpaid back wages further exacerbate the unemployment condition, and in March 1996 it was reported that the sum of wage arrears had risen to 98 trillion karbovanets($500 million) or half the total monthly wage bill. Initial results of the Poverty Assessment conducted by the World Bank estimate that 29.5% of households and 31.7% of individuals are just below the poverty line. Ukraine had the highest percentage of pensioners of all former Soviet countries.

The average family spends 65% of its income on food while low income families spend more than 90%, but in spite of such large spending the diet and nutrition of most Ukrainians is inadequate. Poor nutrition is one of the factors which has led to poor health in Ukraine. The rate of tuberculosis is reported at 36.7 per 10,000 but is believed to be much higher because of unreported cases and lack of medicine in local clinics. Due to sanitary degradation and hygiene standards, water borne and parasitic diseases, diphtheria, measles, and cholera increases have caused alarm among the medical profession. Vaccinations and preventive health check-ups have been mandatory but a WHO/UNICEF team discovered in 1993 that only 3/4 of children had received necessary vaccinations. Environmental, medical, social, food processing/distribution, and morale are all areas heavily influenced by the Chernobyl disaster as well as such factors as ignorance, poverty, and poor production.

Human rights and freedoms. Ukraine, which declared its independence in 1991, is still governed by its 1978 Constitution drawn up when it was a unit of the Soviet Union. Its new Constitution is expected to enhance the powers of both the Rada (parliament) and the presidency. The human rights picture is mixed. While there are few significant violations, neither is there progress toward a clearer definition of civil liberties. Ukraine, unlike other former Soviet republics, has been remarkably free of inter-ethnic antagonisms. The 1992 law on national minorities grants ethnic groups specific rights, such as the right to maintain their own schools and cultural facilities. Many of the flagrant abuses under the old Soviet system have been done away with. For example, political prisoners are not subject to harsh psychiatric treatment. The Soviet-era law on detentions has only been slightly amended but is being applied more humanely. As defendants become more aware of their rights, they are taking advantage of changes in legal procedure. Despite a law protecting freedom of speech and press, serious impediments plague the media. Government has categorized newsprint as a strategic material in order to control its distribution to newspapers. Another threat to free and open discussion comes from organized crime which has grown enormously in power since independence. Journalists now fear criminal rowdies more than the state. Most newspapers receive state subsidies and some kind of patron-client relationship persists between the media and the government. There are reports of violence against women, mostly involving alcoholic husbands. Women have made little progress against economic and job discrimination and account for 90% of the unemployed. There are scattered reports of anti-Semitism, especially associated with extremist ultranationalists.

Human environment. Industrial production has fallen by two thirds since 1991, greatly reducing the hazards that permeated the air and water, but the overall levels of pollutants remain extremely high.

In 1994, 8.3 million tons of air pollutants were emitted from stationary and mobile sources. For instance, Donetsk Oblast, a major industrial center, contributes 26.7% of the nations industrial output, and oxygen levels in downtown areas are on average 42% lower than in suburban areas. This activity has created a heat cupola from 200-500 meters in height above most cities, reducing aeration and illumination. As a result, precipitation is most often caused by the steam of thermal power plants rather than natural rain. With 86 people per square mile, Ukraine ranks 12th highest among European countries for population density. With such high density, two-thirds of Ukraines population is exposed to unhealthy atmosphere.

Drinking water is scarce in many areas, especially in the steppe regions of Crimea where a drought in 1994 rendered the area chronic. The infrastructure is in urgent need of updating purification equipment and chlorine and aluminum sulphate additives have had to be increased because of the poor quality of existing machinery and filtering systems. Only one fifth of the rural population, which comprises some 28,864 villages, is provided with treated drinking water.

Garbage is another contaminant of the Ukrainian environment. Four out of 5 of the open air dumps have no facilities to protect the underground water or the air from contamination and are resultant toxic areas. Agricultural lands around these areas suffer low productivity due to the soil's pollution and destruction of natural micro organisms. In addition to these environmental burdens, there is still the pervading confusion concerning the effects of Chernobyl and non-Chernobyl radiation contamination.

NON-CHRISTIAN RELIGIONS

Atheism and ***nonreligion*** (agnosticism) remain a major force, but, with greatly reduced influence and numbers in comparison to Soviet days.

CHRISTIANITY

Legend attributes that the Apostle Andrew came up through the Black Sea and landed on the Crimean peninsula and preached in the city of Chersonesus,present day Sevastopol. He later sailed up the Dneiper river and preached to the tribesman who lived along its banks predicting that one day a powerful holy city would be built there. Chersonesus is also the site where prince Vladimir's baptism took place-inaugurating the official acceptance of Christianity to the region. In 988, he adopted Christianity as the religion of his territory and had the inhabitants of Kiev baptized. Byzantine Christianity was established and quickly permeated the culture . A church hierarchy was founded, headed by the metropolitan of Kiev, who was appointed by the Patriarch of Constantinople. Along with Christianity came new forms of architecture, art, music, and a written language (Church Slavonic). Vladimir's son Yaroslav continued in his father's footsteps developing the first Slavic code of laws, establishing churches, translating Greek religious works into Slavic, and building the Cathedral of Saint Sophia.

Ukrainian Orthodox Church, under Patriarchate of Moscow. Church in city of Kiev.

ORTHODOX CHURCHES. The Orthodox Church has a history of a thousand years starting from the first baptisms in Kiev. Over 50% of the population are members of 3 major rival bodies—the Russian Orthodox Church still claiming jurisdiction, and 2 nationalist bodies: the Ukrainian Orthodox Church claiming to be a patriarchate under Kiev, and the long-standing Ukrainian Autocephalous Church.

The Orthodox church was inaugurated upon the acceptance of Christianity by prince Vladimir, and this adherence brought the political relationship with the Byzantine empire. Such a relationship facilitated the marriage of Vladimir and the sister of the basileus of Byzantium Constantinople. Vladimir's marriage and conversion were sincere and enthusiastic as pagan idols and temples to Slav gods were destroyed and paganism outlawed. Taking the role of a shepherd, Vladimir saw to it that the people had genuine conversions as well by having priests come and teach the peoples and calling for the construction of churches throughout the region. His son and subsequent leaders followed his steps and during the 11th century a strong church emerged, bishops were appointed, and monastic communities were established.

In the 12th and 13th centuries a series of Mongol invasions disintegrated the Kievan state into a number of smaller principalities and the center of political activity shifted away from Kiev to the Northeast. Eventually, most of present day Ukraine fell under the rule of the Grand Duchy of Lithuania, which had lasting impact upon the Orthodox church. In 1299 the metropolitan of Kiev moved North and settled in Moscow. Claiming the title, 'Metropolitan of Kiev and all Rus' caused great dispute amongst the Lithuania rulers and the appointment for a separate Metropolitan to reside in Kiev was initiated. This conflict resulted in a split after 1448. This group headed by the Moscow Metropolitan declared its independence from Constantinople and a separate Russian Orthodox Church was foundationalized and brought to finality 150 years later in 1598 with the establishment of the patriarchate of Moscow.

At present there are divisions of the once prevalent Orthodox Church. The Ukrainian Orthodox Church (Moscow Patriarchate) is headed by metropolitan Vladimir of Kiev and all Ukraine. This group comprises the majority of Orthodox believers in Ukraine, but it tends to be seen as an 'instrument of Russian

Imperialism' and has no support from state officials. The Ukrainian Orthodox Church (Kiev Patriarchate) is headed by patriarch Filaret of Kiev and all Ukraine. This group came into being in 1992 when then metropolitan Filaret was expelled by the Moscow Patriarchate. He was also defrocked by the Bishops council for cooperation with the Soviet State. After gaining much support from church officials who disagreed with the council's decision, a schism occurred separating the groups into the aforementioned units with both still claiming to be the rightful church.

The Ukrainian Autocephalous Orthodox Church has its roots in the Ukrainian Autocephalist Orthodox Church, which was formed out of the Ukraine Church movement in 1921, and the Ukrainian Autocephalous Orthodox Church,which was established in 1942 during the German occupation of Ukraine. It has roughly 1200 parishes and is headed by patriarch Dimitry of Kiev and all Ukraine.

Catholic Church in the Ukraine. Still underground and persecuted in 1989, the 4 million Ukrainian-rite Catholics finally forced the return of their church buildings as a result of (*top*) massed processions of 100,000 Catholics in the city of Lvov, and (*bottom*) continual demands at all centers of influence.

CATHOLIC CHURCH. At the Council of Brest in 1596, the Ruthenian Church(Orthodox), officially united with the Roman Church and accepted the primacy of the Roman Pontiff as well as Catholic creedal and doctrinal stances. The church was allowed to retain its Byzantine heritage, its Church Slavonic liturgical language, etc. and full autonomy as a 'particular' church was guaranteed.

The partitions of Poland (1772-1795) allowed the Russian territory to advance the cause of Orthodoxy, leading to great restrictions upon Uniate (catholic) territory. This period of persecution elicited an imperial decree in 1839 which called for complete elimination of the Catholic Church, forcing it underground while continuing to thrive in western regions which were now part of the Austrian empire. An act of State in 1946 rejected the validity of Ukrainian Catholicism and was translated into a law that deprived Eastern Catholics of all civil rights, no spiritual legitimacy, and no legal legitimacy. In spite of this massive persecution that continued after the Second World War, 'The Church of the Catacombs' as it came to be known, survived in this capacity for nearly 5 decades.

Immediately after Independence in 1991, the 3.5 million Ukrainian-rite Catholics brutally persecuted under Stalin seized many of their church buildings back and were reorganized by the Vatican into the 13 new jurisdictions shown in Country Table 2. This perpetuated yet another period of hostile relations between Rome, Moscow, and Kiev.

The Holy See has diplomatic relations with Ukraine and in AD 2000 is represented to government and the Catholic hierarchy by a nuncio residing in Kiev.

Seventh-day Adventist Church. Packed evangelistic service at the Kiev church.

Seventh-day Adventist Church.. Packed evangelistic service at the Kiev church.

OTHER CHURCHES. Large numbers of other churches began in the post-Independence climate of freedom of religion.

Indigenous missions. Ukrainian Christians sent missionaries to surrounding countries beginning shortly after the introduction of Christianity to the region in the 10th century. This continued throughout the centuries but was interrupted by Communist rule in the 20th century. After the collapse of Communism, Christians are again sending missionaries outside of the country.

Renewal movements. In the 1990s the Pentecostal/Charismatic Renewal continued to spread rapidly across most older churches, and numbered over 4 million adherents (of whom 10% Pentecostals, 15% Charismatics, and 76% Independents).

CHURCH AND STATE

The Constitution provides for freedom of religion and the separation of Church and state. The 1991 law on freedom of conscience and religion permits religious organizations to establish places of worship and to train clergy. No religious organization may be denied such registration, but at the local level there are long delays. Churches are permitted to maintain links with coreligionists in other countries. Religious publications are freely allowed. Easter and Christmas are official holidays. There are no restrictions on proselytization and distribution of Bibles. There is a strong effort by the Orthodox Church to limit the activities of foreign Protestant groups. Religious organization are required to register with local authorities and with the Government's committee for religious affairs; plus a 1993 amendment restricts the activities of nonnative religious organizations. It narrowly defines the active parameters that clergy, preachers, teachers, and other foreign citizen representatives must abide by. They may preach, administer religious ordinances, or practice other canonical activities 'only in those religious organizations which invited them to Ukraine and with official approval of the governmental body that registered the statutes and the articles of the pertinent religious organizations.' The government has acted to reduce rental payments and utility fees for places of worship, bring exemption from land tax, expedite allotment of land plots for construction of new ones and the returning of religious buildings to the former owners.

BROADCASTING AND MEDIA

The Ukraine is heavily saturated with Christian broadcasts. On shortwave radio, programs may be received from KNLS, FEBC (Saipan), TWR (Monaco, Albania), HCJB (Ecuador), AWR (Slovakia), and FEBC (Philippines). Radio Voskresinnia ('Radio Resurrection') has a daily 30 minute radio programs for the Ukrainian Greek-Catholic Church and the Ukrainian Orthodox Church, and copies of their radio programs are sent to Radio Veritas (Philippines) and Radio Monte Carlo. HCJB is cooperating with several other ministries to plant local radio stations in Ukraine.

Independents. Baptism of 130 new believers by Good Samaritan Mission.

A number of television programs are also available. Satellite TV programs are received mainly in Arabic. CBN's *700 Club*, animated specials and *Answers* program are available in virtually every viewing region on at least a weekly, and in some places a daily, basis. Some 24 million have seen the 'Jesus' Film on television, joined by 880,000 who have seen it in a theater, and 820,000 who watched a presentation by a film team. Good Samaritan Mission airs a TV program every other week (7 million viewed) and a weekly evangelistic program on radio (10 million).

The Communist government built a radio into each home, preset to receive only the official government channel. Ukraine officials have offered opportunities to broadcast on that channel—which also enters virtually all former Communist countries.

FUTURE TRENDS AND PROSPECTS

In the post-Soviet period, Christianity is projected to grow as the nonreligious and atheists decline. The nonreligious and atheists in 1970 represented more than 38% of the population but are now expected to decline to less than 11% by 2025.

Christianity could grow beyond 90% before AD 2050 with atheists and the nonreligious jointly falling below 10% long before then.

BIBLIOGRAPHY

A history of the church in Ukraine. S. Senyk. *Orientalia Christiana analecta*, 243. Rome: Pontificio Istituto Orientale, 1993–.

A millennium of Christian culture in Ukraine. A. Sorokowski (ed). London: Ukrainian Millennium Committee in Great Britain, 1988. 197p.

A thousand years of Christianity in Ukraine: an encyclopedic chronology. O. Zinkewych & A. Sorokowski (eds). New York: Smoloskyp Publishers and the National Committee to Commemorate the Millennium in Ukraine, 1988. 312p.

'Antireligious activity in Ukraine,' R. P. Moroziuk, *Ukrainian quarterly*, 36, 1 (1980), 48–64.

'Bolshevik persecution of the Orthodox Church in the Ukraine,' M. Miller, *Ukrainian review* (Munich), 7 (1959), 10–21.

Church, nation and state in Russia and Ukraine. G. A. Hosking (ed). New York: St. Martin's Press, 1991. 372p.

Die Orthodoxe Kirche in der Ukraine von 1917 bis 1945. F. Heyer. Cologne: Ost-Europa und der deutsche Osten, 1953. 259p.

Encyclopedia of Ukraine. V. Kubijovyc (ed). Toronto: University of Toronto Press, 1993. 5 vols.

First victims of Communism: white book of the religious persecution in Ukraine. Rome: Analecta O.S.B.M., 1953. 114p.

Istoriia khrystiianstva na Rusi–Ukraini (History of Christianity in Rus'–Ukraine). M. Chubaty. Rome: Ukrainian Catholic University Press, 1965. 816p.

Ukrainian Catholic Church, vol. 1 of *Martyrology of Ukrainian churches.* O. Zinkewych and T. Lonchyna. Baltimore, MD: Smoloskyp, 1985. 839p.

Millennium of Christianity in Ukraine: a symposium. Ottawa, Ontario: Saint Paul University, 1987. 303p. (In English and French).

Millennium of Christianity in Ukraine, 988–1988. O. W. Gerus & A. Baran. Winnipeg, Canada: Ukrainian Academy of Arts and Sciences in Canada, 1989. 314p.

One thousand years of Christianity in Ukraine: papers from a Symposium at the Australian National University, Canberra, 15 August 1987. M. Pavlyshyn (ed). Melbourne, Australia: Dept. of Slavic Languages, Monash University, 1988. 72p.

Outline history of the Ukrainian Orthodox Church. I. Wlasowsky. 2nd ed. New York: Ukrainian Orthodox Church of USA, 1974–79. 2 vols.

Passion and resurrection: the Greek Catholic Church in Soviet Ukraine, 1939–1989. S. Keleher. Lvov, Ukraine: Stauropegion, 1993. 299p.

Persecution and destruction of the Ukrainian Church by the Russian Bolsheviks. G. Luznycky. New York: Ukrainian Congress Committee, 1960. 64p.
Persécution soviétique de l'Eglise en Ukraine. Congrès mondial des Ukrainiens libres. Paris: Éditions P.I.U.F, 1978. 66p.
Proceedings of the International Congress commemorating the millennium of Christianity in Rus'–Ukraine. O. Pritsak & I. Sevcenko (eds). Cambridge, MA: Ukrainian Research Institute, Harvard University, 1990. 894p.
Religion and culture in early modern Russia and Ukraine. S. H. Baron & N. S. Kollmann (eds). DeKalb, IL: Northern Illinois University Press, 1998. 224p.
'Religion and nationalism in Ukraine,' V. Markus, in *Religion and nationalism in Soviet and East European politics*, p.138–170. P. Ramet (ed). 2nd ed. Durham, NC: Duke University Press, 1989.
'Religion and nationality: the Uniates of the Ukraine,' V. Markus, in *Religion and atheism in the U.S.S.R. and Eastern Europe*, p.101–122. B. R. Bociurkiw & J. Strong (eds). London: Macmillan, 1975.
'Religion in the Soviet Ukraine: a political problem of modernizing society,' V. Markus, in *Nationalism and human rights*, p.155–67. I. Kamenetsky (ed). Littleton, CO: Libraries Unlimited, 1977.
'Religious situation in Soviet Ukraine,' B. R. Bociurkiw, in *Ukraine in the changing world.* W. Dushnyck (ed). New York: Ukrainian Congress Committee of America, 1977. 173-94.
Russian resurrection: strength in suffering: a history of Russia's evangelical church. M. Rowe. London: Marshall Pickering, 1994. 263p.
Seeking God: the recovery of religious identity in Orthodox Russia, Ukraine, and Georgia. S. K. Batalden (ed). DeKalb, IL: Northern Illinois University Press, 1993. 299p.
'Soviet church policy in the Ukraine, 1919–1939.' B. Bociurkiw. Ph.D. dissertation, University of Chicago, 1961. 566p.
Soviet persecution of religion in Ukraine. Toronto: World Congress of Free Ukrainians, 1976. 54p.
'The catacomb church: Ukrainian Greek Catholics in the USSR,' B. R. Bociurkiw, *Religion in Communist lands*, 5, 1 (Spring 1977), 26–34.
The catacomb Ukrainian Catholic Church and Pope John Paul II. I. Hvat. *The Millennium series.* Cambridge, MA: Ukrainian Studies Fund, Harvard University, 1984. 30p.
'The distinguishing characteristics of the Ukrainian church,' N. Polonska-Vasylenko, *Ukrainian review* (Munich), 8 (1959), 78–94.
The millennium: Christianity and Russia, A.D. 988–1988. A. Leong (ed). Crestwood, NY: St. Vladimir's Seminary Press, 1990.
The Millennium of Ukrainian Christianity. N. L. Fr.-Chirovsky (ed). New York: Philosophical Library, 1988. 617p.
The quest for an Ukrainian Catholic patriarchate. J. V. Pospishil & H. M. Luzhnycky. Philadelphia: Ukrainian Publications, 1971. 75p.
'The struggle of the church union in Carpatho–Ukraine.' B. Boysak. Ph.D. dissertation, University of Montreal, 1961. 290p.
'The suppressed church: Ukrainian Catholics in the Soviet Union,' V. Markus, in *Marxism and religion in Eastern Europe.* R. T. De George & J. P. Scanlan (eds). Boston: D. Reidel Publishing, 1976.
The Ukrainian Catholic Church 1945–1975. M. Labunka & L. Rudnytsky (eds). Philadelphia: St. Sophia Religious Association, 1976. 162p. (With 18–page bibliography, also chronology from 1945–75).
Ucrainica: a selected bibliography on Ukraine in Western European languages. E. J. Pelenskyi. *Memoirs of the Shevchenko Scientific Society*, vol. 158. Munich: Bystrycia, 1948. 111p. (2,600 titles).
Ukraine: a bibliographic guide to English–language publications. B. S. Wynar. Englewood, CO: Libraries Unlimited, Ukrainian Academic Press, 1990. 406p. (See especially chapter 13, 'Religion,' 345f).
Ukraine: a concise encyclopaedia. V. Kubijovyc (ed). Toronto: University of Toronto Press, 1963–71. 2 vols.
Ukraine: the legacy of intolerance. D. Little. *Series on religion, nationalism, and intolerance.* Washington, DC: United States Institute of Peace, 1991. 133p.
Ukrainian churches under Soviet rule: two case studies. B. R. Bociurkiw. *Millennium series.* Cambridge, MA: Ukrainian Studies Fund, Harvard University, 1984. 60p.
Women's monasteries in Ukraine and Belorussia to the period of suppressions. S. Senyk. *Orentalia Christiana Analecta*, no. 222. Rome: Pont. Institutum Studiorum Orientalium, 1983. 235p.

Country Table 2. **Organized churches and denominations in Ukraine.**

Official name (bold type = church with over 10% of all affiliated) 1	*Begun* 2	*Type* 3	*Counc* 4	*Congs* 5	*Adults* 6	*Affiliated 1970* 7	*Affiliated 1995* 8	*G%* 9	*Names, notes, and other statistics* (see Codebook, Part 3) 10
All-Ukrainian Union of Assocs of ECBs		P-Bap	T....	1,437	162,000	300,000	492,000	0.05	*ECBs*=Evangelical Christians-Baptists. *Former AUCECB, after Pentecostals left in 1992.*
Apocalyptic Orthodox Church		I-Apo	.....	2	400	–	800	0.05	One of several sub-Orthodox sects.
Apocalyptists	1923	I-Apo	.....	90	1,500	1,000	2,500	3.73	*Apokalipsisty.* Begun Vinnitsa by Catholic priest, spread to Far East; underground.
Armenian Apostolic Church		O-Arm	E....	3	26,000	23,000	36,000	0.05	*Gregorians.* M=AAC (Armenian).
Assembly Hall Churches	c1975	I-3nC	.....	7	267	–	500	5.00	*Local Churches. Little Flock.* Chinese. Begun 1922 in China.
Basic Link of Christ	1957	I-Tru	.....	120	2,000	3,000	4,000	1.16	*Osnovnoe Zveno Khrista.* True Orthodox Christians in Crimea & Ukraine. Underground.
Brethren of Christ	1765	I-Ose	.....	50	10,000	50,000	30,000	-2.02	*Skoptsy (Castrated Ones). White Lambs,* Spiritual Christians. Danube delta.
Bulgarian Orthodox Church		O-Bul	Mwc.u	30	70,000	20,000	160,000	0.05	*Balgarskata Prayoslavna Crkya.* Bulgarians in Moscow; resident bishop of Kropunich.
Catholic Church in the Ukraine:	1084	R-LEr	B...u	3,282	3,456,500	1,667,000	5,564,671	4.94	*Rimsko-Katolicheskaya Tserkov.* Survived, 1944-91. 1200n 357x 840m 931w 55509Yy
MM Lviv of the Ukrainians (Lvov)	1540	R-Ukr	Os	829	1,000,000	1,300,000	1,607,008	0.85	MM=Great/Major Archdiocese(1 of only 2 in world). 291n 132x 527m 526w 18746Yy
D Ivan-Frankivsk (Stanislaviv)	1885	R-Ukr	Os	203	398,000	150,000	640,300	5.98	M=OSBM, CSSR, SVD. 143n 7x 9m 71w 7969Yy
D Kolomjia-Chernivci	1993	R-Ukr	Os	318	362,000	–	583,892	50.00	Restored diocese where once severe persecution. 132n 4x 10m 7w 6845Yy
D Sambir-Drohobych	1993	R-Ukr	Os	370	290,000	–	466,892	50.00	M=MSU. 146n 30x 36m 18w 3646Yy
D Ternopil	1993	R-Ukr	Os	430	361,000	–	580,300	50.00	M=CSSR. 186n 11x 13m 56w 4090Yy
D Zboriv	1993	R-Ukr	Os	381	257,000	–	414,279	50.00	M=CSSR. 96n 34x 73m 26w 5980Yy
M Lviv of the Latins (Lvov)	1412	R-Lat	Bs	155	112,000	10,000	180,000	12.26	Southwest. In 1935, 1,015,000 RCs. M=OFMConv. 22n 36x 53m 50w 930Yy
D Kamyanets-Podilsky	c1350	R-Lat	Bs	109	242,000	100,000	390,000	5.59	M=MIC,OFM. 50n 51x 56m 75w 1210Yy
D Luck (Lutsk)	c1250	R-Lat	Bs	31	18,000	5,000	30,000	7.43	Formerly Polish territory. 1935: 260,000 Catholics. 10n 8x 8m 0w 300Yy
D Zhytomir (Zhitomir)	1321	R-Lat	Bs	164	186,000	100,000	300,000	4.49	Volhynia. In 1910, diocese had 489,924 Catholics. 9n 31x 42m 55w 783Yy
AD Lviv of the Armenians (Lvov)	c1350	R-Arm	Os	1	1,500	200	2,000	9.65	Lviv=one of only 2 Major Archdioceses in world (other, Ernakulam in India.)
D Mukachevo	1771	R-Rut	Os	221	186,000	1,800	300,000	22.71	Ruthenians. 1949, forced into Orth D Mukachevo. 104n 5x 5m 23w 4200Yy
AA Zakarpatia	1993	R-Lat	Bs	70	43,000	–	70,000	50.00	Reordering of persecuted churches in south. 11n 8x 8m 24w 810Yy
Christ Groups	c1992	I-3hW	.....	9	300	–	1,000	33.33	House churches for isolated believers after EHC (Every Home for Christ) campaign in Ukraine.
Christian Charismatic Church	1985	I-3cW	.....	30	5,000	–	8,330	10.00	Recent growth, charismatic by preference to pentecostal.
Christians of Evangelical Faith	1921	P-Pe2	.....	800	320,000	220,000	400,000	2.42	*CEF. Khristiane Evangel'skoy Very.* Underground. 65% of all CEF; rest are in AUCECB.
Christians of Zion	c1935	I-3pW	.....	60	6,000	5,000	15,000	4.49	*Khristiane Siona. Murashkovtsy* (founder Murashko). Polish Ukraine; across USSR.
Ch of Jesus Christ of Latter-day Saints	1989	m-LdS	.....	30	6,000	–	10,000	16.67	*Mormons.* Small beginnings.
Council of Churches of Ev Chr-Baptists	1961	I-Bap	.....	1,200	70,000	100,000	150,000	1.64	*STEKhB/CCECB/Initsiativniki.* Anti-state schism ex AUCECB. Viciously harassed. 1j.
Ev Christian Pentecostal Zionists	c1920	I-3pW	.....	150	20,000	20,000	40,000	2.81	*Evangel'skie Khristiane Pyatidesyatniki-Sionisty.* Ukraine; split ex CEF. 7th-day.
Followers of John	c1883	I-Ose	.....	150	900	2,000	1,500	-1.14	*Ioannitsy.* Founder John Kronshtadtsky. Still active Ukraine, Voronezh, Krasnodar.
Full Gospel Church of Lutsk	1989	I-3fW	.....	30	5,000	–	12,000	16.67	Large Ukrainian church of Full Gospel theology. 24 bishops.
Georgian Orthodox Church	c1100	O-Geo	Mw...	5	2,000	1,000	5,000	6.65	*Catholicate of Mtskheta & Tiflis.*
German Evangelical Lutheran Church		P-LuR	.....	30	10,000	2,000	25,000	0.05	Among 150,000 German-speaking farmers: Altai, Kirgizia, Kazakhstan. Unregistered.
Global Strategy Christian Assoc	1991	I-3cW	x....	6	1,000	–	2,000	25.00	*GSCA.* M=Global Strategy Missions Association (GSMA, Louisiana, USA). Cell churches.
Greek Orthodox Church		O-Gre	C....	12	30,000	15,000	60,000	0.05	Among Greek residents and transients.
Isolated radio churches	1939	I-3rW	.....	30,000	1,200,000	790,000	2,000,000	3.79	Isolated radio believers. R=6000 (2800 SGA,415 HCJB,300 FEBC,60 TWR,RVatican,BBC,&c).
Jehovah's Witnesses	c1920	m-Jeh	x....	350	30,000	10,000	120,000	10.45	*Svideteli Iegovi.* Deportations 1948-51 Siberia, Arctic. In USSR, strongest in Ukraine. 13089Y
Mennonite Brethren (New Mennonites)	c1750	I-Men	.....	120	25,000	40,000	55,000	1.28	AUCECB 1963. German-speaking. Siberia, Frunze, Karaganda; rapid growth in Ukraine.
Messianic Congs & Synagogues	c1975	I-3mJ	x....	30	1,500	–	4,000	5.00	*Messianic Jews.* Main work centers on Odessa. M=JFJ(19f),UMJC,IAMCS. et alia.
New Apostolic Church	c1970	I-3aX	x....	10	700	–	1,093	32.30	Recent arrival. Small but fast-growing. M=NAK (Germany).
Old Ritualist Ch Belokrinitsa Concord	1666	I-OBe	x...u	1,200	260,000	290,000	350,000	0.76	*AD Moscow. Raskolniki (Schismatics), Popovtsy (Priestists).* 5 Dioceses. 200n.
Pentecostal Union		I-3pW	.....	900	100,000	33,300	333,000	0.05	24 bishops. Church in Kiev has 1,000 member.
Reformed Church in Carpatho-Ukraine	1945	P-Ref	Rv..u	120	70,000	120,000	160,000	1.16	Until 1918 in Ref Ch of Hungary, till 1945 Ref Ch of Slovakia. Hungarians. 70n.
Russian Orthodox Ch in Exile	c1990	I-Rus	x....	200	400,000	–	600,000	20.00	*Russian Orthodox Church Outside of Russia.* M=ROCOR(until 1990, in exile in USA).
Seventh-day Adventist Church	1883	P-Adv	x...u	1,250	90,000	100,000	200,000	2.81	*SDA.* Organized 1920. Strong in Ukraine, Siberia, Central Asia. 834t(46814),W=60%.
Ukrainian Autocephalous Orthodox Ch	1918	I-Ukr	.....	1,200	360,000	300,000	554,000	2.48	1917-35, 1941-42 UAOC. 3 million former RC Uniates. 1991 large influx from UOC.
Ukrainian Orthodox Ch: P Kiev	1991	I-Ukr	.....	1,332	1,800,000	–	3,800,000	25.00	Anti-Russian schism, forming own Patriarchate. Huge start, then decline. 36 bps.
Ukrainian Orthodox Ch (P Moscow):	991	O-Ukr	M....	2,917	18,623,000	24,480,000	26,994,000	0.10	*Russian Orthodox Church, Exarchate of the Ukraine*, under P Moscow. 37 bishops.
M Kiyev (Kiev) & Galitsiya	991	O-Ukr	Me...	240	1,897,000	2,500,000	2,757,000	0.10	Diocese of exarch. 57% urban. 1959, 680 churches open; 1971, 220. 2 convents open.
D Chernigov & Nezhin	992	O-Ukr	Mb...	120	595,000	780,000	860,000	0.10	35% urban. 1961 bishop given 8 years prison. 1973 cathedral closed, bishop removed.
D Chernovtsy & Bukovina	1945	O-Ukr	Mb...	35	320,000	420,000	463,000	0.39	Traditionally 95% Orthodox. Romanian Orth until forced into ROC 1945. 35% urban.
D Dnepropetrovsk & Zaporozhye	1775	O-Ukr	Mb...	110	1,952,000	2,560,000	2,823,000	0.39	73% urban. Vacant since 1965, administered as part of D Simferopol & Crimea.
D Ivano-Frankovsk & Kolomyya	1946	O-Ukr	Ma...	115	474,000	630,000	695,000	0.39	Traditionally Orthodox. Uniate D Stanislav till 1946 forced into ROC. 31% urban.
D Kharkov & Bogodukhov	1799	O-Ukr	Ma...	110	1,070,000	1,410,000	1,555,000	0.39	1833 named Kharkov. 69% urban. Many illegal beatings-up and trials of believers.
D Khmelnitskiy & Kemenets-P	1795	O-Ukr	Mb...	66	618,000	810,000	893,000	0.39	Kemenets-Podolskiy. 27% urban. Since 1966 administered as part of D Vinnitsa.
D Kirovograd & Nikolayev	1837	O-Ukr	Mb...	100	915,000	1,200,000	1,323,000	0.39	48% urban. Many former and present Uniate Roman Catholics in area.
D Lugansk & Donetsk	1943	O-Ukr	Mb...	44	2,900,000	3,820,000	4,213,000	0.39	80% workers, 86% urban. Vacant 1965; under D Odessa. 1,500 parishes, only 40 open.
D Lvov & Ternopol	1946	O-Ukr	Ma...	1,040	1,742,000	2,290,000	2,525,000	0.39	Uniate D Lvov till 1946. Includes D Drogobych & Sambor. 1959, 1,300 churches open.
D Mukachevo & Uzhgorod	1945	O-Ukr	Ma...	440	397,000	530,000	584,000	0.39	Zakarpat. RC Greek-Ruthenian diocese till forced into ROC in 1946. 30% urban. 1d.
D Odessa & Kherson	1837	O-Ukr	Ma...	100	1,301,000	1,710,000	1,886,000	0.39	1959, 400 churches open. Still open: Rozhdestvensky convent, Uspensky monastery.
D Poltava & Kremenchug	1775	O-Ukr	Mb...	65	650,000	850,000	937,000	0.39	40% urban. Theological materials circulate in typewritten samizdat form.
D Simferopol & Crimea	1859	O-Ukr	Mb...	13	694,000	910,000	1,003,000	0.39	First Christian settlements AD 250. Now 63% urban. Cathedral re-opened 1965.
D Sumy & Akhtyrka	1860	O-Ukr	Mb...	55	573,000	750,000	827,000	0.39	44% urban. Vacant since 1959; 1964, under D Chernigov; 1973 bishop appointed.
D Vinnitsa & Bratslav	1912	O-Ukr	Ma...	88	816,000	1,070,000	1,180,000	0.39	25% urban. Many Protestants in area, also Uniates; systematic beatings-up reported.
D Volhynia & Rovno	992	O-Ukr	Ma...	110	1,092,000	1,430,000	1,577,000	0.10	Lutsk. Traditionally 95% Orthodox. 30% urban. Strong religious life. 1e(Pochaev).
D Zhitomir & Ovruch	1795	O-Ukr	Ma...	66	617,000	810,000	893,000	0.39	35% urban. 1961 Ovruch Convent closed at gun-point. 1973 lay protests at closures.
Other pentecostal bodies		I-3pW	.....	1,100	180,000	100,000	300,000	0.05	Total over 40 underground bodies, including Ev Christians in the Apostles' Faith.
Other Protestant denominations		P-	.....	350	30,000	30,000	40,000	0.05	Total about 30, all unregistered and mostly underground.
Other Orthodox churches		O-	....u	20	6,000	7,000	20,000	0.05	Small congregations of immigrants from Eastern European countries.
Doubly-affiliated		2-aff			-488,000	-1,550,200	-758,500		Pentecostals and Evangelicals who are also baptized Orthodox or Catholics.
Totals				**48,632**	**26,893,067**	**27,179,100**	**41,792,894**		

Churches, members, growth, 1900-2025	*Congs*	*Adults*	*Affiliated*	*G%*	*Total denominations*	*O*	*R*	*A*	*P*	*I*	*m*
Total churches, members, and denominations (mid-1900)	20,000	18,009,000	26,501,000	0.04	13	6	1	0	2	4	0
Total churches, members, and denominations (mid-1970)	30,078	18,470,700	27,179,100	0.04	62	8	1	0	18	34	1
Total churches, members, and denominations (mid-1990)	45,000	26,743,000	41,560,000	2.15	120	12	1	0	35	70	2
Total churches, members, and denominations (mid-1995)	48,632	26,893,067	41,792,894	0.11	122	12	1	0	35	72	2
Total churches, members, and denominations (mid-2000)	51,000	26,813,000	41,669,097	-0.06	124	12	1	0	35	74	2
Total churches, members, and denominations (mid-2025)	70,000	25,675,000	39,900,000	-0.17	289	20	1	0	60	200	8

6 Megablocs: O R A P I m

NOTES ON TABLE ABOVE
NATIONAL COUNCILS (Column 4, 5th letter).
C = Hungarian Consultative Synod.

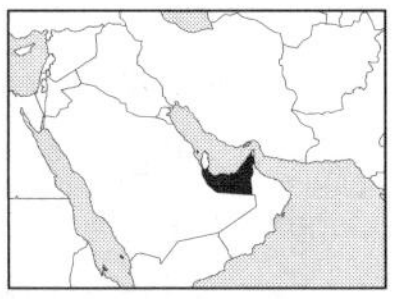

UNITED ARAB EMIRATES

SECULAR DATA, AD 2000

STATE
Official name: Al-Imarat al-Arabiya al-Muttahida (The United Arab Emirates).
Short name: United Arab Emirates. **Adjective of nationality:** of the United Arab Emirates.
Flag: Red bar at Hoist; stripes of green, white, and black.
Area: 83,600 sq. km. (32,280 sq. mi.).
Government: Confederation of monarchies, since 1971 (c1500 Portuguese rule, 1853 British protectorate of the Trucial States, 1971 Independence).
Legislature: Federal National Council, 40 members.
Official language: Arabic.
Monetary unit: 1 U.A.E. dirham (Dh) = 100 fils. **US$1=** Dh 3.67.
Chief cities: ABU ZABY (Abu Dhabi) 928,000; Dubayy (Dubai) 551,493; Ash-Shariqah (Sharjah) 259,760; Al'Ayn (Ap-Ain, Al Ain) 211,012; Ra's al-Khaymah 87,175.
Political divisions: 7 provinces.
Armed forces: 60,000.

DEMOGRAPHY
Population: 2,441,000.
Population density: 29.2/sq. km. (75.6/sq. mi.).
Under 15 years: 684,000.
Growth rate p.a.: 1.65% (births 17.88, deaths 3.32).
Mortality: Infant, per 1,000: 13.4; **Maternal per 100,000:** 26.0.
Life expectancy: 76 (male 75, female 78).
Household size: 6.8. **Floor area per person, sq.m:** 18.0.
Major languages: Arabic, Persian, English, Hindi, Baluchi, Urdu, Shihuh, and others.
Urban dwellers: 85.89%. **Urban growth rate p.a.:** 2.0%.
Labor force: 47%.

ETHNOLINGUISTIC PEOPLES
12.2% Gulf Arab (Emirian); 9.4% Gulf Bedouin; 7.1% Southern Baluch; 7.0% Malayali; 6.2% Egyptian Arab.

ECONOMY
National income p.a. per person: US$17,400; **per family:** US$118,320.

EDUCATION
Adult literacy: 79% (male 78%, female 79%). **Schools:** 363.
Universities: 1. **School enrolment:** female/male: 104%/102%.

HEALTH
Access to health services: 99%. **Access to safe water:** 98%.
Hospitals: 35 (21 beds per 10,000). **Doctors:** 3,090.
Blind: 400. **Deaf:** 146,600. **Murder rate:** 1. **Lepers:** 50.

LITERATURE
New book titles p.a.: 340 (140 p.a. per million). **Periodicals:** 112.
Newspapers: 8 dailies.

COMMUNICATION (per 1,000 people)
Phones: 283 (35% mobile). **Radios:** 206. **TV sets:** 26.
Daily newspaper circulation: 126. **Computers:** 100.

REFUGEES
Alien refugees from other countries: 400.

HUMAN LIFE AND LIBERTY (optimum condition=100.0%)
HDI: 86.6. **HSI:** 66.0. **HFI:** 15.0. **EFL:** 58.0.

Country Table 1. **Religious adherents in the United Arab Emirates, AD 1900-2025.**

Year / *Name*	*1900* Adherents	%	*1970* Adherents	%	*mid-1990* Adherents	%	*Annual change, 1990-2000* Natural	Conversion	Total	Rate	*mid-1995* Adherents	%	*mid-2000* Adherents	%	*mid-2025* Adherents	%
Muslims	49,950	99.9	205,900	92.4	1,495,350	77.8	40,522	-5,451	35,071	2.13	1,683,100	76.2	1,846,055	75.6	2,483,000	75.6
Christians	**50**	**0.1**	**13,600**	**6.1**	**201,400**	**10.5**	**5,452**	**1,432**	**6,884**	**2.98**	**237,300**	**10.7**	**270,244**	**11.1**	**390,000**	**11.9**
PROFESSION																
crypto-Christians	50	0.1	6,370	2.9	95,000	5.0	2,572	428	3,000	2.78	110,000	5.0	125,000	5.1	180,000	5.5
professing Christians	**0**	**0.0**	**7,230**	**3.2**	**106,400**	**5.5**	**2,880**	**1,004**	**3,884**	**3.16**	**127,300**	**5.8**	**145,244**	**6.0**	**210,000**	**6.4**
AFFILIATION																
unaffiliated Christians	0	0.0	80	0.0	5,000	0.3	135	115	250	4.14	5,406	0.2	7,499	0.3	10,000	0.3
affiliated Christians	**50**	**0.1**	**13,520**	**6.1**	**196,400**	**10.2**	**5,316**	**1,319**	**6,635**	**2.95**	**231,894**	**10.5**	**262,745**	**10.8**	**380,000**	**11.6**
Roman Catholics	30	0.1	2,400	1.1	93,000	4.8	2,517	618	3,135	2.95	110,000	5.0	124,345	5.1	175,000	5.3
Orthodox	0	0.0	5,500	2.5	50,000	2.6	1,353	647	2,000	3.42	61,000	2.8	70,000	2.9	100,000	3.1
Independents	0	0.0	720	0.3	34,000	1.8	920	380	1,300	3.29	40,430	1.8	47,000	1.9	80,000	2.4
Protestants	0	0.0	3,200	1.4	11,000	0.6	298	-118	180	1.53	11,964	0.5	12,800	0.5	16,000	0.5
Anglicans	20	0.0	1,700	0.8	8,400	0.4	227	-207	20	0.24	8,500	0.4	8,600	0.4	9,000	0.3
Trans-megabloc groupings																
Evangelicals	0	0.0	1,700	0.8	10,200	0.5	276	54	330	2.84	12,014	0.5	13,500	0.6	23,000	0.7
Pentecostals/Charismatics	0	0.0	600	0.3	38,500	2.0	1,042	508	1,550	3.44	48,335	2.2	54,000	2.2	100,000	3.1
Great Commission Christians	**50**	**0.1**	**8,500**	**3.8**	**105,000**	**5.5**	**2,842**	**384**	**3,226**	**2.72**	**122,000**	**5.5**	**137,255**	**5.6**	**228,000**	**6.9**
Hindus	0	0.0	1,000	0.5	125,000	6.5	3,384	2,774	6,158	4.09	166,000	7.5	186,576	7.6	200,000	6.1
Baha'is	0	0.0	1,000	0.5	40,000	2.1	1,083	438	1,521	3.28	50,000	2.3	55,214	2.3	85,000	2.6
Buddhists	0	0.0	0	0.0	36,000	1.9	974	283	1,257	3.04	43,000	2.0	48,573	2.0	75,000	2.3
Nonreligious	0	0.0	1,500	0.7	16,000	0.8	433	365	798	4.13	21,000	1.0	23,979	1.0	35,000	1.1
Sikhs	0	0.0	0	0.0	4,000	0.2	108	78	186	3.89	5,300	0.2	5,859	0.2	9,000	0.3
Atheists	0	0.0	0	0.0	2,400	0.1	65	67	132	4.47	3,200	0.1	3,715	0.2	5,000	0.2
New-Religionists	0	0.0	0	0.0	850	0.0	23	14	37	3.69	1,100	0.1	1,221	0.1	2,000	0.1
World A (unevangelized persons)	49,500	99.0	167,798	75.3	950,895	49.5	25,716	-17,874	7,842	0.80	1,001,008	45.3	1,027,661	42.1	1,198,660	36.5
World B (evangelized non-Christians)	450	0.9	41,441	18.6	768,705	40.0	20,876	16,442	37,318	4.05	971,422	44.0	1,143,095	46.8	1,695,340	51.6
World C (Christians)	50	0.1	13,600	6.1	201,400	10.5	5,452	1,432	6,884	2.98	237,300	10.7	270,244	11.1	390,000	11.9
Country's population	**50,000**	**100.0**	**222,840**	**100.0**	**1,921,000**	**100.0**	**52,044**	**0**	**52,044**	**2.42**	**2,209,731**	**100.0**	**2,441,000**	**100.0**	**3,284,000**	**100.0**

COLUMNS, ROWS.
For meanings and definitions, see Codebook (Part 3). Note that, by definition, total 'Christians' = professing + crypto-Christians, which also = affiliated + unaffiliated Christians, and also = Great Commission Christians + latent Christians. Percentages may not always total exactly, due to rounding.

CENSUSES.
15.III-16.IV.1968 (home population excluding foreign workers): 96.0% Muslims, 2.1% Christians, 1.9% other religionists.

NOTES ON RELIGIONS
INDEPENDENTS. South Indian and Arab indigenous congregations, in 19 groupings in 1995 (see Table 2).
BAHA'IS. Growth from 6 local spiritual assemblies (1964) to 10 (1973), with some development thereafter. Many Baha'is are aliens or refugees whose religious motivations are held suspect by government authorities.
COUNTRY'S POPULATION. 80% expatriates (from India, Pakistan, Iran, Syria, Lebanon, Jordan, Egypt, Europe, USA). About 10% of nationals are nomads. The figures in the last row of the table include all categories of resident immigrant worker.
CRYPTO-CHRISTIANS. Many Arabs are known to the churches as believers though regarded as Muslims by the state or in censuses. During the 1990s the state tended to ignore the large number of expatriate Arab Christians who were entering as immigrant workers, and regarded them also as Muslims. There is also a growing number of isolated radio believers. The column 'Natural change' above includes nett immigration for all rows.
HINDUS. Expatriate Indians.
MUSLIMS. Nationals are mostly Sunnis of various rites, with a small Shia minority. There are also expatriate Muslims from all schools and sects. *Hajj pilgrims to Mecca.* (1970) 2,164; (1976) 4,196.
NONRELIGIOUS. Europeans, Japanese and other expatriates.

Great Commission Instrument Panel: status of the United Arab Emirates (for explanation see start of Part 4)

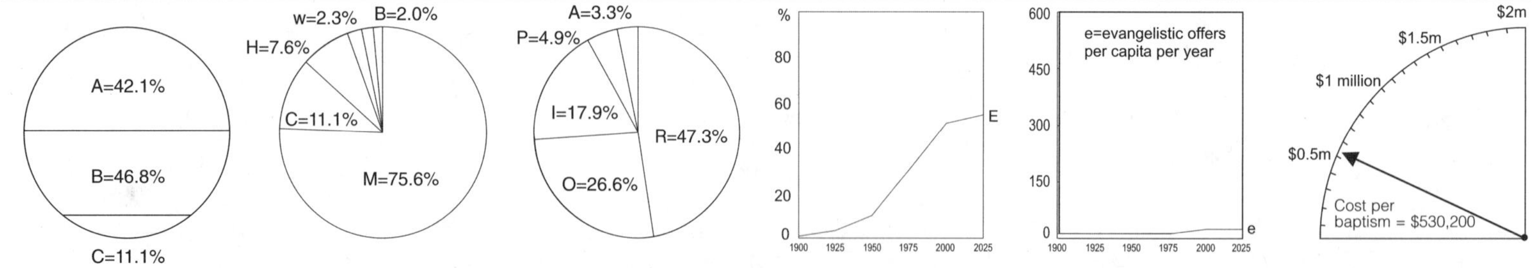

3 Worlds, AD 2000 — Religions, AD 2000 — Ecclesiastical blocs — Evangelization, 1900-2025 — Offers, 1900-2025 — Cost-effectiveness, AD 2000

Country status. The United Arab Emirates is a western Asian country on the Persian Gulf formed by the union of 7 sheikdoms in 1971. The economy is based on the production of oil and gas.

HUMAN LIFE AND LIBERTY

Human rights and freedoms. These are taken considerably more seriously in the UAE and other Gulf states than in Saudi Arabia. Muslims dominate and received favored treatment, but other religions and their rights are also respected.

NON-CHRISTIAN RELIGIONS

Islam is the majority religion, most Muslims (nationals and expatriates) being Sunnis belonging to various rites. A small Shia minority also exists.

Hinduism is the religion of many expatriate Indians working in the oilfields.

Christian events are often on postage stamps: here, US president Eisenhower and wife visit pope John XXIII in Vatican.

Country summary. **Worlds A, B, C by ethnolinguistic peoples, cities, and major civil divisions in the United Arab Emirates.**

	PEOPLES							CITIES							CIVIL DIVISIONS						
World	Num	Pop 2000	C%	Christians	E%	U%	Unevangelized	Num	Pop 2000	C%	Christians	E%	U%	Unevangelized	Num	Pop 2000	C%	Christians	E%	U%	Unevangelized
A	18	1,145,132	0.43	4,962	37	63	717,645	1	87,175	4.00	3,487	49	51	44,355	3	222,674	1.63	3,635	40	60	133,567
B	15	1,154,897	12.24	141,321	73	27	310,522	4	1,950,265	12.36	241,077	62	38	734,944	4	2,218,763	11.68	259,110	60	40	894,849
C	6	141,407	82.36	116,463	100	0	249	0	0	0.00	0	0	0	0	0	0	0.00	0	0	0	0
Total	**39**	**2,441,436**	**10.76**	**262,746**	**58**	**42**	**1,028,416**	**5**	**2,037,440**	**12.00**	**244,564**	**62**	**38**	**779,299**	**7**	**2,441,437**	**10.76**	**262,745**	**58**	**42**	**1,028,416**

CHRISTIANITY

CATHOLIC CHURCH. The vicariate of Arabia was erected in Aden in 1889, building on work begun by a Servite priest as early as 1841. After its expulsion from South Yemen in 1974, the vicariate's headquarters were transferred to Abu Dhabi. In recent years, the vicariate has shown steady growth due to the increase in foreign Christians in the various Gulf countries. In 1995 the vicariate included 110,000 faithful.

The Holy See has no diplomatic relations with United Arab Emirates in AD 2000, but has an apostolic delegate residing in Lebanon.

Anglicans. Holy Trinity Church, Abu Dubai.

OTHER CHURCHES. St Andrew's Church in Abu Dhabi is the center for the Anglican chaplaincy of Qatar, Muscat, and Oman and the United Arab Emirates, in the Anglican diocese of Cyprus and the Gulf. Another Anglican priest has recently been installed at Dubai to cover the northern Emirates and Muscat.

Syrian Orthodox clergy have been present in the Emirates for a number of years serving the expatriate Arab and Indian Syrian community.

Protestant groups include the Reformed Presbyterian Church Evangelical Synod, Plymouth Brethren, Independent Presbyterians, and the Evangelical Alliance Mission (TEAM). At the request of the ruler, the latter mission opened a hospital in 1960 at the Buraimi oasis in the southeastern part of the country. Permission was given at the same time to preach and teach the Bible, but this is no longer possible.

Indigenous missions. There have been few missionaries sent out from the United Arab Emirates.

CHURCH AND STATE

According to the provisional constitution of the United Arab Emirates, 'Islam shall be the official religion of the Union', the Islamic Sharia (Law) is the main source of legislation and Arabic is the official language of the union (Article 7). The union is an Islamic and Arab society...the Supreme and Omnipotent Creator...may Allah, our best Protector and Defender, grant us success'. All persons are equal before the law, without distinction due to race, religious belief or social status (Article 25). Freedom to exercise religious worship is guaranteed in accordance with established customs, or public morals (Article 32).

Prior to April 1975, there was little anti-Christian sentiment in the United Arab Emirates. The various rulers not only permitted the building of churches but also provided land for them, and in some cases were present at their opening ceremonies and provided free electrical power for their air-conditioning as is done with mosques. The rulers welcomed personal visits by Anglican, Syrian Orthodox and Catholic priests as well as the various North American missionaries resident in the country. Christians were able to work openly and freely.

In April 1975, however, the sheikdoms comprising the federation agreed to forbid in their territories all missionary or proselytizing activities by non-Muslims. The Abu Dhabi Ministry of Justice now fines or imprisons anyone found contravening the new ruling. This hardening of attitude towards Christians is similar to that experienced in other Arab states.

Muslims. Almost all the rulers are Sunni Muslims, here in legislative session.

BROADCASTING AND MEDIA

Shortwave radio programs in Arabic can be received from FEBA (Seychelles) and HCJB (Ecuador).

FUTURE TRENDS AND PROSPECTS

Immigrant workers will continue to dictate the strength of Christianity into the 21st century with the total Christian community reaching 11.9% by 2025. Lebanese Arabs account for over half of the Christian population and almost 2% of the UAE by 2025.

Christianity will potentially hover between 10-14% for the next half-century depending on how many foreign Christian workers reside in the country. Islam will predominate.

BIBLIOGRAPHY

'Aesthetics and ritual in the United Arab Emirates.' A. S. Kanafani. Ph.D. dissertation, University of Texas, Austin, TX, 1979. 384p.

Analytical guide to the bibliographies on the Arabian Peninsula. C. L. Geddes. *Bibliographic series*, 4. Denver, CO: American Institute of Islamic Studies, 1974.

Egalität und Klassengesellschaft in Südarabien: anthropologische Untersuchungen zur sozialen Evolution. W. Dostal. *Wiener Beiträge zur Kulturgeschichte und Linguistik*, Bd. 20. Horn, Austria: F. Berger & Söhne, 1985. 484p.

From trucial states to United Arab Emirates: a society in transition. F. Heard-Bey. London: Longman, 1982. 548p.

'Imperialism, tribal structure, and the development of ruling elites: a socio–economic history of the Trucial States between 1892 and 1939.' O. A. Butti. Ph.D. dissertation, Georgetown University, Washington, DC, 1992. 289p.

Mother without a mask: a Westerner's story of her Arab family. P. Holton. London: Kyle Cathie, 1991. 278p.

Persian Gulf states: country studies. H. C. Metz (ed). 3rd ed. *Area handbook series.* Lanham, MD: Bernan, 1994. 501p.

'Present–day Christianity in the Gulf States of the Arabian Peninsula,' N. A. Horner, *Occasional bulletin of missionary research*, 2 (April 1978), 53–63.

Source book on Arabian Gulf States, Arabian Gulf in general, Kuwait, Bahrain, Qatar and Oman. S. Kabeel. Kuwait: Kuwait University, Libraries Department, 1975. 427p. (With over 3,000 item bibliography).

The seven shaikhdoms: life in the Trucial States before the federation of the United Arab Emirates. R. Codrai. London: Stacey International, 1990. 174p.

The United Arab Emirates 1993. Abu Dhabi, UAE: Ministry of Information and Culture, 1993. 177p.

The United Arab Emirates: an economic and social survey. K. G. Fenelon. 2nd ed. London: Longman, 1976. 164p.

The women of the United Arab Emirates. L. U. Soffan. London: Croom Helm, 1980. 127p.

United Arab Emirates. F. A. Clements. *World bibliographical series*, vol. 43. Oxford, UK: CLIO Press, 1983. 164p. (See especially 'Religion,' p.58-9).

United Arab Emirates: profile of a country's heritage and modern development. P. Vine & P. Casey. London: Immel, 1992. 160p.

Many postage stamps, especially those issued by individual emirates before 1972, have carried Christian themes; here, the 14 Stations of the Cross, with the Ascension added.

Country Table 2. **Organized churches and denominations in the United Arab Emirates.**

Official name (bold type = church with over 10% of all affiliated) 1	Begun 2	Type 3	Counc 4	Congs 5	Adults 6	Affiliated 1970 7	Affiliated 1995 8	G% 9	Names, notes, and other statistics (see Codebook, Part 3) 10
Anglican Church (D Cyprus & the Gulf)		A-plu	aw...	17	4,050	1,700	8,500	0.05	Chaplaincy, in Episcopal Ch in Jerusalem & ME. Abu Dhabi, Dubai. British, Americans. 2x.
Armenian Apostolic Church	c1960	O-Arm	E....	2	3,000	2,000	5,000	3.73	Armenian workers, under C Echmiadzin and/or C Cilicia.
Catholic Church (VA Arabia)	1964	R-Lat	P..L.	13	80,000	2,400	110,000	16.53	Expatriates. Filipinos, Arabs including Maronites. 2x,2b(Abu Dhabi, Dubai), 1r(580).
Christian Brethren		P-CBr	x....	4	700	200	1,000	0.05	*Plymouth (Open) Brethren. Gospel Halls.* Indians, few Arabs; in Abu Dhabi, Dubai.

Continued overleaf

Country Table 2–concluded

Official name (bold type = church with over 10% of affiliated) 1	*Begun* 2	*Type* 3	*Counc* 4	*Congs* 5	*Adults* 6	*Affiliated 1970* 7	*Affiliated 1995* 8	*G%* 9	*Names, notes, and other statistics* (see Codebook, Part 3) 10
Coptic Evangelical Church	c1975	P-Ref	RWANK	3	1,000	–	2,000	5.00	Egyptian workers. M=CEC(Egypt).
Coptic Orthodox Ch (P Alexandria)	c1970	O-Cop	N....	10	11,000	–	21,000	48.90	Egyptian migrant workers, under Coptic P Alexandria.
Evangelical Alliance Church	1960	P-Eva	xM...	12	675	1,000	964	-0.15	EAC/EAM. M=TEAM(USA),MECO(MEGM/USA). Clinic in Al-Buraymi oasis. 22f,1H,1h,1k.
Greek Orthodox Ch (P Antioch)		O-Ara	C....	10	12,000	1,000	21,000	0.05	Mostly Arabs under P Antioch; also others under P Jerusalem, P Alexandria.
India Pentecostal Church of God	c1971	I-3pI	x....	40	5,000	–	8,000	4.17	South Indians from large India denomination IPCOG.
Isolated radio churches	c1950	I-3rS	....	1,500	15,000	270	25,000	19.86	Isolated Arab radio believers: pupils and students aged 12-25. T=2000(ICI,&c).
Mar Thoma Syrian Ch (D Bahya Kerala)		I-ReO	xwe..	2	600	200	1,000	0.05	MTSC. In Diocese of Outside Kerala. South Indian Malayalis in Abu Dhabi, Dubai. 2x.
Orthodox Syrian Church of the East		O-SyM	Dw...	4	1,000	500	2,000	0.05	OSCE. In D Bahya Kerala. South Indians from Kerala, under Catholicate of the East.
Syrian Orthodox Ch (P Antioch)	c1975	O-Syr	D....	1	500	–	1,000	5.00	Syrian Arab workers, under P Antioch in Damascus.
Tree of Life Churches	c1980	I-3aS	x....	17	1,000	–	3,000	6.67	M=Network International(HQ TX, USA). Social and evangelistic ministries.
Other indigenous charismatic chs	c1965	I-3cW	.....	2	172	250	430	2.19	Including New Apostolic Church.
Other Asian indigenous churches	c1980	I-	.....	20	2,000	–	3,000	6.67	Total about 15, including INC, PIC, and other Filipino bodies.
Other Orthodox churches	c1965	O-	.....	15	5,000	2,000	11,000	7.06	Small numbers of members from a variety of ethnic Orthodox chs abroad, in house meetings.
Other Protestant denominations		P-	.....	20	4,000	2,000	8,000	0.05	IBPM and other USA bodies, UCCP (Filipinos), CSI (Indians), Pakistanis, Koreans, et al.
Totals				**1,692**	**146,697**	**13,520**	**231,894**		

Churches, members, growth, 1900-2025	*Congs*	*Adults*	*Affiliated*	*G%*	*Total denominations*	*6 Megablocs:* *O*	*R*	*A*	*P*	*I*	*m*
Total churches, members, and denominations (mid-1900)	1	29	50	8.33	0	0	0	0	0	0	0
Total churches, members, and denominations (mid-1970)	33	7,900	13,520	8.33	22	5	1	1	11	4	0
Total churches, members, and denominations (mid-1990)	1,500	124,000	196,400	14.32	70	15	1	1	23	30	0
Total churches, members, and denominations (mid-1995)	1,692	146,697	231,894	3.38	71	15	1	1	23	31	0
Total churches, members, and denominations (mid-2000)	1,800	166,000	262,745	2.53	72	15	1	1	23	32	0
Total churches, members, and denominations (mid-2025)	3,000	240,000	380,000	1.49	123	20	1	1	40	60	1

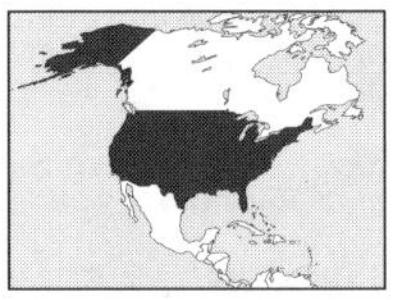

UNITED STATES OF AMERICA

SECULAR DATA, AD 2000

STATE
Official name: The United States of America.
Short name: United States of America. **Adjective of nationality:** of the United States of America, American.
Flag: Seven red and 6 white alternating stripes; blue canton with 50 white 5-pointed stars, one for each state.
Area: 9,529,063 sq. km. (3,679,192 sq. mi.).
Government: Federal republic, since 1776 (1620 settlement followed by British, Spanish, French, Dutch and Swedish colonies) 1763 British colony dominant; 1776 Independence).
Legislature: Congress: Senate, 100 members; House of Representatives, 435 members.
Official language: English.
Monetary unit: 1 dollar (U.S.$) = 100 cents. **US$1=** 1.00.
Chief cities: New York-N.New Jersey-Long Island, NY 16,626,000; Los Angeles-Anaheim-Riverside, CA 13,129,000; Los Angeles-Long Beach, CA 9,756,479; New York, NY (PMSA) 9,408,623; Chicago, IL (PMSA) 8,158,103.
Political divisions: 51 provinces (50 States, 1 District).
Armed forces: 1,650,000.

DEMOGRAPHY
Population: 278,357,000.
Population density: 29.2/sq. km. (75.6/sq. mi.).
Under 15 years: 59,763,000.
Growth rate p.a.: 0.71% (births 12.98, deaths 8.59).
Mortality: Infant, per 1,000: 6.7; **Maternal per 100,000:** 12.0.
Life expectancy: 77 (male 74, female 81).
Household size: 2.6. **Floor area per person, sq.m:** 50.0.
Major languages: English, Spanish, German, Italian, Polish, Irish, French, Yiddish, Navajo, Cherokee, Sioux, Hindi, Swedish, Japanese, Norwegian, Hungarian, Chinese, Dutch, Czech, Slovak, Russian, Greek, Portuguese, Filipino, Korean, Vietnamese.
Urban dwellers: 77.21%. **Urban growth rate p.a.:** 1.0%.
Labor force: 50%.

ETHNOLINGUISTIC PEOPLES
41.4% USA White; 8.7% USA Black (Afro-American); 3.5% American Part-Indian; 3.4% Mexican Mestizo; 3.3% USA Mestizo (Chicano).

ECONOMY
National income p.a. per person: US$26,980; **per family:** US$70,148.

EDUCATION
Adult literacy: 95% (male 95%, female 95%). **Schools:** 85,393.
Universities: 5,758. **School enrolment:** female/male: 102%/103%.

HEALTH
Access to health services: 85%. **Access to safe water:** 90%.
Hospitals: 6,580 (46 beds per 10,000). **Doctors:** 670,300.
Blind: 482,850. **Deaf:** 16,669,300. **Murder rate:** 9.
Lepers: 1,000.

LITERATURE
New book titles p.a.: 77,940 (280 p.a. per million). **Periodicals:** 16,230. **Newspapers:** 1,548 dailies.

COMMUNICATION (per 1,000 people)
Phones: 626 (28% mobile). **Radios:** 1,976. **TV sets:** 780.
Daily newspaper circulation: 228. **Computers:** 580.

REFUGEES
Alien refugees from other countries: 152,200.

HUMAN LIFE AND LIBERTY (optimum condition=100.0%)
HDI: 94.2. **HSI:** 95.0. **HFI:** 82.5. **EFL:** 62.0.

Country Table 1. **Religious adherents in the United States of America, AD 1900-2025.**

Year	*1900*		*1970*		*mid-1990*		*Annual change, 1990-2000*				*mid-1995*		*mid-2000*		*mid-2025*	
Name	*Adherents*	*%*	*Adherents*	*%*	*Adherents*	*%*	*Natural*	*Conversion*	*Total*	*Rate*	*Adherents*	*%*	*Adherents*	*%*	*Adherents*	*%*
Christians	**73,270,200**	**96.4**	**191,182,000**	**91.0**	**217,718,600**	**85.7**	**2,080,647**	**-278,342**	**1,802,305**	**0.80**	**227,585,870**	**85.2**	**235,741,652**	**84.7**	**261,348,500**	**80.3**
PROFESSION																
professing Christians	**73,270,200**	**96.4**	**191,182,000**	**91.0**	**217,718,600**	**85.7**	**2,080,647**	**-278,342**	**1,802,305**	**0.80**	**227,585,870**	**85.2**	**235,741,652**	**84.7**	**261,348,500**	**80.3**
AFFILIATION																
unaffiliated Christians	18,845,200	24.8	37,882,748	18.0	41,898,600	16.5	400,408	-198,865	201,543	0.47	43,342,070	16.2	43,914,025	15.8	50,348,500	15.5
affiliated Christians	**54,425,000**	**71.6**	**153,299,252**	**73.0**	**175,820,000**	**69.2**	**1,680,240**	**-79,477**	**1,600,763**	**0.88**	**184,243,800**	**69.0**	**191,827,627**	**68.9**	**211,000,000**	**64.8**
Independents	5,850,000	7.7	35,644,624	17.0	66,900,000	26.3	639,336	525,664	1,165,000	1.62	72,943,155	27.3	78,550,000	28.2	100,000,000	30.7
Protestants	35,000,000	46.1	58,567,984	27.9	60,216,000	23.7	575,460	-140,060	435,400	0.70	62,525,488	23.4	64,570,000	23.2	69,000,000	21.2
Roman Catholics	10,775,000	14.2	48,305,318	23.0	56,500,000	22.2	539,947	-389,947	150,000	0.26	56,715,013	21.2	58,000,000	20.8	65,000,000	20.0
Marginal Christians	800,000	1.1	6,125,815	2.9	8,940,000	3.5	85,436	28,564	114,000	1.21	9,502,253	3.6	10,080,000	3.6	17,000,000	5.2
Orthodox	400,000	0.5	4,163,050	2.0	5,150,000	2.0	49,216	11,984	61,200	1.13	5,472,153	2.1	5,762,000	2.1	7,162,000	2.2
Anglicans	1,600,000	2.1	3,196,277	1.5	2,450,000	1.0	23,414	-28,414	-5,000	-0.21	2,445,286	0.9	2,400,000	0.9	2,100,000	0.7
doubly-affiliated	0	0.0	-2,703,816	-1.3	-24,336,000	-9.6	-232,569	-87,268	-319,837	1.24	-25,359,548	-9.5	-27,534,373	-9.9	-49,262,000	-15.1
Trans-megabloc groupings																
Evangelicals	32,068,000	42.2	31,516,000	15.0	37,349,000	14.7	356,929	-27,829	329,100	0.85	39,313,787	14.7	40,640,000	14.6	47,208,000	14.5
Pentecostals/Charismatics	46,100	0.1	22,510,000	10.7	63,519,000	25.0	607,025	556,675	1,163,700	1.70	69,868,562	26.2	75,156,000	27.0	104,180,000	32.0
Great Commission Christians	**11,000,000**	**14.5**	**45,500,000**	**21.7**	**87,656,000**	**34.5**	**837,692**	**262,916**	**1,100,608**	**1.19**	**93,457,000**	**35.0**	**98,662,079**	**35.4**	**120,462,000**	**37.0**
Nonreligious	1,000,000	1.3	10,070,000	4.8	21,414,000	8.4	204,659	161,725	366,384	1.59	23,150,000	8.7	25,077,844	9.0	40,000,000	12.3
Jews	1,500,000	2.0	6,700,000	3.2	5,535,000	2.2	52,896	-44,262	8,634	0.15	5,600,000	2.1	5,621,339	2.0	6,100,000	1.9
Muslims	10,000	0.0	800,000	0.4	3,560,000	1.4	34,021	23,170	57,191	1.50	3,825,000	1.4	4,131,910	1.5	5,920,000	1.8
Buddhists	30,000	0.0	200,000	0.1	1,880,000	0.7	17,966	38,991	56,957	2.68	2,150,000	0.8	2,449,570	0.9	5,000,000	1.5
Atheists	1,000	0.0	200,000	0.1	770,000	0.3	7,359	30,590	37,949	4.09	950,000	0.4	1,149,486	0.4	1,600,000	0.5
Hindus	1,000	0.0	100,000	0.1	750,000	0.3	7,167	21,001	28,168	3.24	930,000	0.4	1,031,677	0.4	1,500,000	0.5
New-Religionists	0	0.0	110,000	0.1	575,000	0.2	5,495	18,091	23,586	3.50	690,000	0.3	810,859	0.3	930,000	0.3
Baha'is	2,800	0.0	138,000	0.1	600,000	0.2	5,734	9,608	15,342	2.30	682,000	0.3	753,423	0.3	1,150,000	0.4
Ethnoreligionists	100,000	0.1	70,000	0.0	280,000	0.1	2,676	12,809	15,485	4.50	387,000	0.1	434,851	0.2	500,000	0.2
Sikhs	0	0.0	1,000	0.0	160,000	0.1	1,529	5,853	7,382	3.87	192,300	0.1	233,820	0.1	310,000	0.1
Spiritists	0	0.0	0	0.0	120,000	0.1	1,147	694	1,841	1.44	132,800	0.1	138,412	0.1	175,000	0.1
Chinese folk-religionists	70,000	0.1	90,000	0.0	76,000	0.0	726	-476	250	0.32	77,000	0.0	78,497	0.0	65,000	0.0
Shintoists	0	0.0	0	0.0	50,000	0.0	478	144	622	1.18	53,900	0.0	56,220	0.0	70,000	0.0
Zoroastrians	0	0.0	0	0.0	42,400	0.0	405	627	1,032	2.20	47,530	0.0	52,721	0.0	84,000	0.0
Taoists	0	0.0	0	0.0	10,000	0.0	96	17	113	1.08	10,600	0.0	11,134	0.0	13,500	0.0
Jains	0	0.0	0	0.0	5,000	0.0	48	148	196	3.36	6,000	0.0	6,959	0.0	7,000	0.0
Other religionists	10,000	0.0	450,000	0.2	530,000	0.2	5,065	-388	4,677	0.85	550,000	0.2	576,767	0.2	800,000	0.3
World A (unevangelized persons)	75,995	0.1	1,050,555	0.5	3,557,064	1.4	33,926	19,511	53,437	1.41	3,738,277	1.4	4,175,355	1.5	7,162,606	2.2
World B (evangelized non-Christians)	2,648,805	3.5	17,878,539	8.5	32,800,336	12.9	313,541	258,831	572,372	1.60	35,695,697	13.4	38,439,993	13.8	57,061,894	17.5
World C (Christians)	73,270,200	96.4	191,182,000	91.0	217,718,600	85.7	2,080,647	-278,342	1,802,305	0.80	227,585,870	85.2	235,741,652	84.7	261,348,500	80.3
Country's population	**75,995,000**	**100.0**	**210,111,095**	**100.0**	**254,076,000**	**100.0**	**2,428,114**	**0**	**2,428,114**	**0.92**	**267,019,845**	**100.0**	**278,357,000**	**100.0**	**325,573,000**	**100.0**

Continued opposite

Country Table 1–continued

COLUMNS, ROWS.
For meanings and definitions, see Codebook (Part 3). Note that, by definition, total 'Christians' = professing + crypto-Christians, which also = affiliated + nominal Christians. Percentages may not always total exactly, due to rounding. *Natural change.* The column of this name above includes both biological increase (with certain groups including Roman Catholics and Blacks having higher fertility than the national average) and also net immigration increase (with certain non-Christian religions in particular having higher immigration rates than the national average.

CENSUSES.
No question on religious adherence (profession) has ever been included in the decennial US censuses. However, enumerators collected statistics direct from churches during the censuses of 1850, 1860, 1870, 1880 and 1890; and in 1906, 1916, 1926 and 1936, the US Bureau of the Census conducted a Census of Religious Bodies; since the membership statistics thus obtained came direct from church bodies themselves they therefore measured not what we here term professing Christians but what we term affiliated Christians. *Statistics for 1900.* Our estimates for the year 1900 in the table above are based on the government enumerations of 1890 and 1906, modified by the methodology evolved in this survey.

NOTES ON RELIGIONS
ATHEISTS. Communist Party of the USA (CPUSA) (legal, pro-Soviet): about 7 splinter groups including pro-Chinese Progressive Labour Party (PLP), WWP, MLCP, SWP, ACFI.
BAHA'IS. Entered USA soon after 1892. Rapid growth from 350 local spiritual assemblies (1964) to 928 (1973) to 1,312 (1996); many young White adherents. One of the world's 7 Baha'i Houses of Worship (temples) is at Wilmette, Chicago. From 1970-72 in South Carolina, nearly 20,000 rural Blacks were claimed to have joined as converts. In 1970 there were 23,879 regularly-active adult Baha'is in the USA excluding Alaska and Hawaii, with an annual increase of 3,219 members. The statistics on this line in the table refer to total adherents including children, and also include the largest of several minor schisms from Baha'i, the Orthodox Abha World Faith begun in 1960 by an American, Charles Mason Remey, who claimed to be the Second Guardian of the Faith. It also has a handful of followers in Pakistan and elsewhere.
BLACK MUSLIMS. Officially termed the World Community of Al-Islam in the West (America), or (before 1977) the Nation of Islam; also called Bilalians. Begun 1913 as Moorish Science Temples; 1930 Temple of Islam; 1959, 30,000; 1961, 69 USA temples and 100,000 followers; 1975, claimed a total community of 500,000 US Blacks, 300,000 being militants, in 80 temples, with 50,000 new converts a year mostly nominally-Christian Blacks. By the end of 1976 over 235 mosques had been set up, daily radio broadcasts of Quranic verses and teachings were under way, and the movement was being realigned with orthodox Quranic Islam.
BLACK/NON-WHITE INDIGENOUS or (more fully) BLACK/NON-WHITE/THIRD-WORLD INDIGENOUS CHRISTIANS, i.e. persons in churches indigenous to the Black/Non-White population or to the Third World (see extended definition and discussion in Part 3). *Statistics for 1900.* These are based on those reported for the year 1906 by the US Bureau of the Census, when those reporting numbered 29,547 all-Negro congregations (18,359 Baptist, 11,188 Methodist) with 3,166,393 communicant members (2,296,683 Baptists, 869,710 Methodists); the total community of Negro independent churches then was about 6 million including children, infants and adherents. Since in the year 1900 the USA had a Negro population of 8,834,000 (11.6% of the total population), this indicates that persons affiliated to Negro independent churches in 1900 numbered around 5,650,000 or 64% of all Negroes. Another type of indigenous church at that period was the Native American Church with around 100,000 Indians (about 40% of the 237,200 American Indians then). In sum, as Table 2 below indicates, there were in the year 1900 about 20 Black independent denominations in existence (7 Methodist, 7 pentecostal, 3 Baptist, 1 Reformed) and 6 American Indian denominations. *Statistics for 1970.* In the year 1970, this bloc's 19,678,819 affiliated adherents in the USA consisted of over 200 distinct and separate denominations (as detailed in Table 2 below) in 4 distinct groups: (1) 18,929,019 in US Black churches (including 2,753,090 Black pentecostals), (2) 482,000 in American Indian churches, (3) 184,000 in Hispanic (Spanish-speaking; Spanish American and Latin American) churches, and (4) 83,800 in other immigrant Third-World indigenous churches.
BUDDHISTS. This category here covers only orthodox Buddhism, excluding the Japanese New Religions (Soka Gakkai et alia, listed here under NEW-RELIGIONISTS). Buddhists are Japanese and Chinese, with White converts. There are also several Lamaist temples, built with government grants from China (Taiwan), for Mongolians resident in the USA; and adherents of over 40 other Buddhist sects. In the year 1900, Buddhists included most of the 24,326 Japanese in the USA and some of the 89,863 Chinese. From 1960 onwards, large numbers of Buddhists began to be converted to the Japanese New Religions, especially to Nichiren Shoshu (Soka Gakkai). In particular, the organized Buddhist Churches of America (founded 1899; representing the Jodo Shinshu sect of Buddhism in the USA) reported a rapid decline in membership over the period 1970-74, from 100,000 with 101 priests in 1970, to 60,000 with 86 priests in 1974.
CHINESE FOLK-RELIGIONISTS. Chinese in the USA increased from 34,933 in 1860, to 89,863 in 1900, to 435,062 in 1970 to 1,575,000 in 1995. Initially the majority practiced Chinese folk religion, with some Buddhists; now only a decreasing minority practice either.
COUNTRY'S POPULATION. The column 'Natural increase' includes both biological increase (births minus deaths each year) and also migration increase.
ETHNORELIGIONISTS. American Indians in the USA declined in numbers from 850,000 in the 16th century to 237,196 in 1900, at which time nearly half still followed Indian traditional or shamanistic religion. In 1995, they had increased again to 312,000 in 150 tribes, of whom about 9% professed to be traditionalists and 91% Christians.
EVANGELICALS. In the table above, there are 3 separate rows termed Evangelicals, indicating that in the USA the term is used to cover 3 groupings, Protestant Evangelicals, Black Evangelicals and Anglican (Episcopalian) Evangelicals. There is a history of polls on this subject. In a 1955 poll (Opinion Research Corporation) of Protestant and Episcopalian clergymen, 35% stated that they were Fundamentalist, 39% Conservative or Conservative Evangelical and 26% Neo-orthodox or Liberal. A 1970 poll found that about 42 million adults in the USA (30%) said they were Evangelicals, found primarily in the Protestant and Black denominations. A 1976 poll (AIPO) gave the following percentages for evangelicals (with a small 'e') in various church traditions: 42% of all Baptists, 39% of Lutherans, 28% of Methodists, 22% of Presbyterians, 25% of Episcopalians, and 60% of all Black Christians. AIPO's definition included Roman Catholics who term themselves evangelicals, whereas our definition of Evangelicals here refers (more correctly) only to Protestants, Anglicans and Non-White indigenous Christians.

In 1970 our table above indicates that in all denominations these together totalled 64,724,600 Evangelicals (31.6% of the total population), increasing by 1975 to 69,393,900 (32.4%). The 3 groupings we use in our table are defined, and may be further subdivided, as follows (with 1970 statistics added). (1) Protestant Evangelicals (50.7 million or 24.7% in 1970) from a movement within the Protestant churches, and consist of 3 major subdivisions: (a) Conservative Evangelicals (26 million in 1970), sometimes also called non-Conciliar Evangelicals, or Neo-Evangelicals, or Neo-Fundamentalists, enumerated here in 2 groups: (i) the total communities, including children, affiliated to institutionalized Conservative Evangelicalism, i.e. to the NAE (4.1 million) or the WEF (6.1 million in the USA), and (ii) the total communities affiliated to all other Conservative Evangelical denominations which are not aligned with the NAE or WEF (19 million in the USA), of which the largest are the Southern Baptist Convention (14.2 million in 1970; approximately 95% Evangelical, 5% Liberal), Churches of Christ (Non-Instrumental) (4.0 million), and Lutheran Church—Missouri Synod (3.0 million), together with a mass of smaller denominations and isolated congregations; (b) Conciliar Evangelicals (19 million in 1970), sometimes called ecumenical Evangelicals but who usually call themselves simply Evangelicals, who remain within and are affiliated to Protestant denominations not regarded as entirely Conservative Evangelical but which are instead within the Ecumenical Movement affiliated to the NCC-CUSA and/or the WCC (e.g. American Baptist Churches in the USA, who are about 50% Evangelicals); and (c) Fundamentalists (20 million in 1970), moderate or extreme, enumerated here as the total communities of Protestant denomination of fundamentalist doctrine and emphasis, in several cases affiliated to the ACCC, ACAC or ICCC. Secondly, (2) Black Evangelicals (13.6 million or 6.6% in 1970) are affiliated members of Black denominations in the USA who regard themselves as Evangelicals or part of the Conservative Evangelical movement; the largest denominational group is that in the NBCUSA (itself 6.4 million) which is the most conservative of the 3 largest Black Baptist denominations. Thirdly, (3) Anglican Evangelicals (485,000 in 1970) are those within the Episcopal Church in the USA, together with members of several Anglican Evangelical bodies, shown in Table 2 below, which have split from ECUSA. Experience of new birth. Traditionally this emphasis, together with literal belief in the Bible and personal evangelism, have been regarded as the hallmarks of Evangelicalism, but by 1976 they were also characterizing large sections of non-Evangelical and non-Protestant denominations. In a 1976 Gallup poll, 34% of all Americans (nearly 50 million over age 18; 48% of all Protestants, 18% of all Catholics) said they had had a 'born-again' experience, a turning-point where they committed themselves to Jesus Christ; 38% of Americans are biblical fundamentalists, believing the Bible 'literally, word for word'; and 47% of the population (58% of all Protestants) said they had done personal witnessing (encouraging others to believe in Christ or to accept him as Saviour). A large number of all these persons are not Evangelicals nor Protestants but are Episcopalians or Roman Catholics, especially Catholic pentecostals and other charismatics.
HINDUS. These include (1995) about one million Hindu immigrants from India, and also large numbers of American devotees of about 60 neo-Hindu or new Hindu sects: 50,000 adult Americans who have 'taken knowledge' in the Divine Light Mission (DLM) led by Guru Maharaj Ji since its introduction in 1971; about 10,000 followers of ISKCON (International Society for Krishna Consciousness, or the Hare Krishna Movement) introduced in 1965, with 28 centers and 6 farms by 1975; about 2,000 adherents (with 500 committed disciples) of the Bengali movement Sri Chinmoy Center; 7,000 followers of messiah Meher Baha; 67 centers of the Self-Realization Fellowship (150 centers worldwide); 20 satsang societies of Eckankar (500,000 followers worldwide); 11 Sri Aurobindo Society centers; 2,000 in the Ramakrishna Mission; Ananda Marga (Path of Bliss); the neo-Hindu movement the Theosophical Society in America, et alia. There is also a movement with Hindu origins which claims to be a philosophy but not a religion: the Science of Creative Intelligence (SCI) with about 80,000 adult meditators (with 500,000 followers in other religions also) following Transcendental Meditation (TM, introduced about 1963), with over 4,000 teachers; on the world scene it has 1.3 million meditators and 10,000 teachers, mainly in the USA, UK, Germany and Switzerland.
JEWS. Growth: beginning in 1654 with 23 Portuguese Sefardi Jews in New Amsterdam; 3,000 in 1776, 15,000 (1840); then waves of Ashkenazi immigration from Germany in the 1840s and 1850s; 200,000 (1858), 1,500,000 (1900), 4,200,000 (1928), 3,868,000 professing Jews of 14 years and over (3.27% of the entire population) in 1957 survey (US Bureau of the Census); 5,500,000 affiliated to 3,990 synagogues and congregations in 1964, 6,115,000 affiliated to 5,000 congregations in 1972, with 6,400 rabbis (5,100 in charge of congregations). The statistics on this line in the table refer to professing Jews (including both those affiliated to synagogues and those not affiliated). *Division.* 28% Orthodox (in congregations with 1 million active members), 42% Conservative (1.5 million), 30% Reform (1.1 million). *Race.* The great majority of USA Jews are White, but about 250,000 are Black, of 5 kinds: (1) Blacks in White Jewish synagogues; (2) Black Jews: 38,000 in the Church of God and Saints of Christ (classified in this Encyclopedia as a Christian rather than a Jewish body), and Church of God (Black Jews); (3) 150,000 Black Hebrews, followers of conservative Orthodox Judaism; (4) Falashas (Black Jews) from Ethiopia; and (5) many thousands of Black Israelites (Original Hebrew Israelite Nation), many of whom have emigrated to Israel. *Organizations.* There are over 220 national Jewish organizations in the USA. *Periodicals.* There are over 210 Jewish periodicals and newspapers in 43 states. *Conversions from Judaism.* Since 1965 an estimated 30,000 American Jews have become Christians (survey by Jews for Jesus Organization); by 1972, about 6,500 young Jews were converting to Christianity each year. There are about 10,000 in Hebrew-Christian bodies, 100,000 Jews (including children and infants) belong to the main USA Protestant denominations, and a further large number prefer to remain as witnesses to Jesus within their own synagogues and communities. In addition to conversions to Christianity, there is a small number of Jews each year who abandon religion and regard themselves as nonreligious.
MARGINAL CHRISTIANS. In about 330 denominations in 1995 (see Table 2). Many have grown very rapidly since 1900; e.g. Mormons from 268,331 (1900) to 393,437 (1910), 526,032 (437,500 in the USA) (1920), 672,488 (541,900 in the USA) (1930), 862,664 (670,500 in the USA) (1940), 1,111,314 (926,700 in the USA) (1950), 1,693,180 (1,422,700 in the USA) (1960), 2,930,810 (2,016,800 in the USA) (1970), to 3,321,556 in 1973 and to 7,401,770 (4,430,000 in the USA). In 1906 also there were 70,542 adult Unitarians, 64,158 Universalists, and 85,717 Christian Scientists (the latter rising to 268,915 in 1936). The annual growth rates for 1970-1995 are given in Table 2, column 8. Unitarian Universalists are declining; Mormons, Jehovah's witnesses, Worldwide Church of God and other newer bodies are increasing rapidly.
MUSLIMS. There are 3 groupings. (1) Orthodox (mainly Sunni) Muslims: their number has increased greatly since 1900 with the immigration of Middle East Arabs (300,000 by 1970), Turks (24,000), Persians (24,000), Albanians (8,000), Malays (6,000), and other Muslim peoples, making a total of over 800,000 by 1975; (2) the World Community of Islam in the West (America) (before 1977 called the Nation of Islam), or Black Muslims, or Bilalians; and (3) Ahmadiya. These last 2 are enumerated here under Muslims although Black Muslims are regarded as heretical by the bulk of Islam, and Ahmadis have been declared non-Muslim by Pakistan. Ahmadiya (Qadianis, from Pakistan) has had its USA HQ in Washington since its beginning in 1921. Followers are US Blacks with some Pakistani immigrants. From 1975, there have been 5 Pakistani missionaries in the USA. *Hajj pilgrims to Mecca.* (1970) 84; (1974) 136; (1975) 354; (1976) 80.
NEW-RELIGIONISTS. Several of the Japanese syncretistic New Religions (or, new religious movements) have branches in the USA; of these the largest is Nichiern Shoshu of America (NSA) (True Church of Nichiren), known in Japan as Soka Gakkai (Value Creation Society). Begun in Los Angeles in 1960 with 300 Japanese members, the USA branch had 30,000 by 1967; and in 1972, NSA claimed 100,000 households, with 300,000 members (70% non-Asians; including 28,800 in Hawaii) and 60,000 Americans (mostly young Whites) were undergoing *shakubuku* (aggressive-conversion process) each year. Among the smaller Japanese bodies are the Sect of the Dancing Goddess (Tensho Kotai Jingu Kyo) in Hawaii, and the Church of Perfect Liberty (PL Kyodan) with 5,000 US adherents mainly in southern California (50% Japanese, 25% White, 15% Black, 10% Spanish-American; 6 churches, 15 missions); also Tenrikyo (2,000 members, 99% Japanese, in 60 churches and missions in the USA), Seicho no Iye (7,000 in the USA, 98% Japanese), and Sekai Kyusei Kyo (Church of World Messianity; 3,500 in USA, half in Hawaii; 35% Japanese). By 1975, there were other New Religions also from Korea, Viet Nam, Indonesia (including 2,000 followers in 70 cities of Subud, founded 1925 in Indonesia) and the Chinese diaspora.
NONRELIGIOUS. Persons professing no religion, or agnostics, have increased gradually over recent years. In the 1950s, persons who were not Protestant, Catholic or Jew but who had another religion or no religion averaged under 3% in all polls. In the 1957 survey (US Bureau of the Census), those with no religion numbered 2.7%. In the 1960s, those with no religion averaged 3-4%. From 1970-75, those with no formal religion or religious preference rose from 5% to 6%, of whom at least 3% regarded themselves as definitely non-believers, the rest being indifferent to religion (*Religion in America 1975,* Gallup).
OTHER RELIGIONISTS. This term covers only committed non-Christian members of a large number of smaller bodies, including the following: (1) a host of non-Christian or part-Christian or syncretistic movements begun in the USA, including non-Christian Spiritism, Rosicrucianism (AMORC, begun 1915 and now with 91 Lodges; 2 centers of Lectorium Rosicrucianum; and over 8 other bodies), Neo-Paganism, Druidism, Psychiana, Mighty I Am (at one time claiming 350,000), Church Universal and Triumphant (summit International; 1958 split from I Am; 80 centers, also 6 overseas countries especially Ghana), Arcane School, Astara Foundation, Satanic Church (15,000), First Church of Voodoo (Tennessee) and other occult, psychical and magical bodies, together with a large number of persons experimenting with Eastern mysticism; (2) immigrant Asian religions including 43,500 Shintoists in Hawaii, Parsis, 5,000 Indian Sikhs and several thousand White Americans in the quasi-Sikh Healthy-Happy-Holy Organization (3HO) (110 ashrams in the USA, Canada and overseas in 1977), et alia (in 1970 new immigrants from Asia numbered 91,059; in 1972, 115,978); and (3) immigrant religions from elsewhere, including Afro-American spiritists (Santeria from Cuba, with centers in Miami and many northern cities among immigrant Cubans with some US Black followers; Vodoun; over 7,000 Rastafarians (from Jamaica and West Indies islands) in New York, many allegedly with criminal records; et alii). In addition to these committed non-Christian members, it is estimated that some 10 million Americans dabble in the occult arts (witchcraft, black masses, orgies), of whom at least 6 million are devotees or part-time adherents of some sect or cult; and a further 15 million (mostly unaffiliated Christians) are sympathetic and interested onlookers. The 10,000 registered astrologers in the USA claim 40 million customers a year. Another quasi-religious movement is Freemasonry, an international male brotherhood which is the largest worldwide secret society and which affirms belief in the Supreme Being and reveres the Bible as the Volume of the Sacred Law. Of the USA's 4 million Freemasons, some practice it as a non-Christian religion, although most are either professing or unaffiliated Protestants, or nonreligious.
PENTECOSTALS/CHARISMATICS. *Anglican Charismatics.* The Pentecostal or Charismatic renewal within the non-Pentecostal denominations in the USA began in 1960 within the Protestant Episcopal Church. By 1973 it involved 30,000 adults (60,000 total community) in 1,500 prayer groups, including over 1,100 clergy and several bishops, the totals increasing rapidly (to 3,200 clergy by 1977). These figures include Episcopalian youth involved in the Jesus Movement (Jesus People). *Catholic Charismatics.* Since its beginning at Duquesne University in 1967, the Catholic Charismatic Renewal (CCR) in the USA grew rapidly to involve 200,000 charismatic or neo-pentecostal adult Catholics by 1972, and 500,000 (these being adults over 15 with a definite commitment to Christ) by 1974, rising to around 670,000 by mid-1976, and including a score of bishops and 3 cardinals, in 1,800 prayer groups. Most members are 20-40 years old. These statistics do not include children or infants; if the children of members are included the totals should be at least doubled, giving in 1974 a Catholic charismatic community of 1 million in the USA, rising to 1.2 million in 1975. All these totals include Catholic youth involved in the Jesus Movement (Jesus People). In addition to these committed members shown in the table, there were in 1977 a further one million or more sympathizing Catholics involved or less involved than those with full commitment. By 1980, 8 million adult Catholics were identifying themselves as charismatics, though not all actively involved. In 1985, 50% of all USA Catholics were said to be attenders at 6,500 weekly prayer meetings.

In 1992, it was estimated that 1 million USA Catholics were regular attenders at 5,500 weekly prayer groups, with a total Catholic Charismatic community of 10 million. By 1998 these numbers had fallen slightly to 500,000 regularly involved either in 4,800 weekly prayer groups (many now being ethnic, with 900,000 Hispanics, 10,000 Haitians, 9,000 Vietnamese, Chinese, et alia), or in 100 covenant communities (5,000 members), or in cells, home meetings, sharing groups or other nondiocesan activities, with some 2,000 involved priests; with a total Charismatic community, including children, of 9 million. 70 dioceses have active renewal conferences, and 50% of all USA bishops support the Renewal. The future numerical expansion of the movement shown in the table above is one possible projection based on current trends.

Charismatics active in the organized charismatic renewal who remain within non-Pentecostal Protestant denominations numbered in 1973 around 305,000 adults (or total charismatic community including children, 610,000) in around 5,000 prayer groups, the adults being distributed approximately as follows: 30,000 Baptists (including 10,000 Southern Baptists), 110,000 Lutherans, 45,000 Methodists, 40,000 Presbyterians and Reformed, and at least 80,000 in other Protestant denominations including 1,000 SDAs; and these totals were rapidly growing. In addition, youth in these denominations who were involved in the Jesus Movement (Jesus

Continued overleaf

Country Table 1–concluded

People) were estimated in 1972 at considerably over 200,000 in over 5,000 communes and communities. Allowing for overlapping involvements, this makes a total Neo-pentecostal community of about 800,000 in 1973 rising to around one million by 1975. By 1977, most large denominations had sizeable charismatic followings (e.g. American Baptist Churches in the USA, with over 100,000), and most had each its own denominational charismatic organization for fellowship and services. The number of priests and clergy involved averages 10-15% of all clergy in each denomination. By 1977 the renewal was still largely White, on non-Black, with very few participants from the Black churches (AMEC, AMEZC, NBCA, NBCUSA, et alia) and little contact with the Black pentecostal churches in the USA. In 1980, some 6 million more called themselves charismatics though not actively involved.

Orthodox Charismatics. The charismatic renewal within the Orthodox churches began in 1968 in the Greek Orthodox Archdiocese. By 1973 it involved over 30 Greek parishes with 12 priests and 2,000 lay adults, also 2 Antiochian priest, some in the OCA, some Ukrainian Orthodox, and 3 priests in ROCOR. The movement was in 1975 encountering considerable church opposition, in contrast to its Catholic, Protestant, and Episcopalian counterparts.

Active charismatics (more traditionally, 'sanctified' Black/Negro/Colored persons) in the non-pentecostal Black denominations (NBCUSA, NBCA, AMEC, AMEZC, CMEC, PBC, et alia). About 6 million others call themselves charismatics but are not actively involved.

PROTESTANTS. This term in almost all polls, and to the US Bureau of the Census (1957 et alia), includes also Episcopalians (Anglicans), marginal Christians, and members of Black and Third-World indigenous churches. In our present survey, we exclude these latter 3 blocs from our definition of Protestants. *Losses and gains.* The column in the table 'Total annual change' indicates a net loss by conversion of 288,560 affiliated Protestants every year during the period 1990-2000, offset and hidden by a larger natural (biological and immigration) increase. This net loss itself masks great variations among denominations: Methodists, Presbyterians, and Lutherans are losing vast numbers of members each year, whilst other traditions, mainly Pentecostals, are gaining them. The exact annual growth or decline figures for 1970-1990 are given for many denominations in Table 2, column 8.

ROMAN CATHOLICS. The proportions of professing and affiliated Catholics in the USA have increased since 1900, and are still increasing, due to both immigration (especially of Puerto Ricans, whose immigration is restricted by no quota) and higher natural fertility of Catholic families. Conversions, which have declined in number recently, are mostly due to mixed marriages. *Growth.* By 1995 Catholics had increased to 56,715,013, with an annual increase of 150,000 projected for 1990-2000.

UNAFFILIATED CHRISTIANS. Defined in this Encyclopedia as: Persons professing in polls to be Christians, but not affiliated to churches, i.e. not church members; unaffiliated or unchurched; Christians not, or no longer, attached to organized Christianity, or who have rejected the institutional churches whilst retaining Christian beliefs and values. In the USA, these nominal Christians are mainly Protestants (chiefly Methodists, Baptists, Presbyterians, Lutherans). In the early days of the USA republic, up to as late as 1900, large numbers of professing Christians, especially recent immigrants, remained uncontacted by, and hence unaffiliated to, the various denominations. By the 1990s, large numbers of nominal Christians were involved in occult religions (see note on OTHER RELIGIONISTS above).

Great Commission Instrument Panel: status of the United States of America (for explanation see start of Part 4)

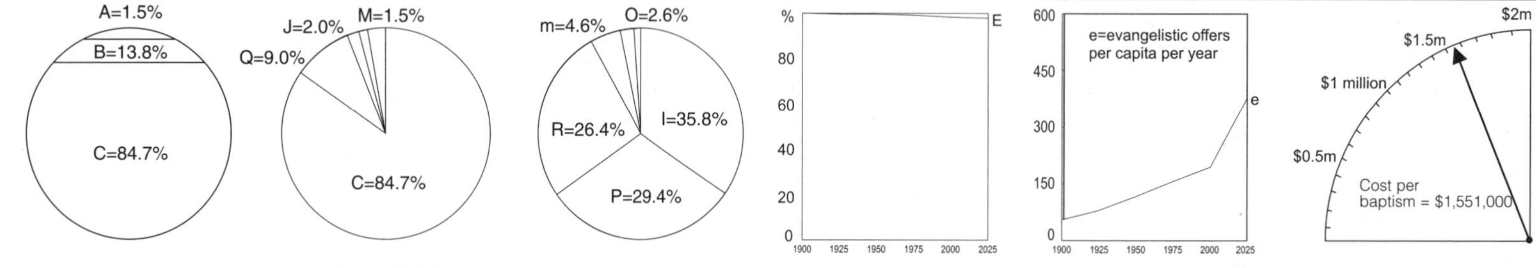

3 Worlds, AD 2000 | Religions, AD 2000 | Ecclesiastical blocs | Evangelization, 1900-2025 | Offers, 1900-2025 | Cost-effectiveness, AD 2000

Country status. United States of America is a large, diverse country in North America bordered by both the Atlantic and Pacific oceans. The USA is a leading exporter of machinery, motor vehicles, cereals, and chemicals.

HUMAN LIFE AND LIBERTY

Human need and development. United States is a developed country and the bellwether in almost all major international economic indicators. Although a wealthy country in natural resources and productivity, the wealth is unevenly distributed and there are numerous pockets of poverty in every state. Serious social problems, like crime, homelessness, and lack of universal healthcare have been allowed to fester for so long that they have become a complex malaise defying political solution. A significant segment of African-Americans and the poorer Hispanics are living below the poverty level. Welfare has become a condition of life for the deprived classes, both black and white, and among them there are shocking rates of illegitimacy and teen age pregnancies unparalleled in the Western world. Among African-Americans, nearly one-third of all young males have a criminal record, imposing a heavy burden on the criminal justice system. The ratio of prisoners to the general population is exceeded only in Russia. Despite efforts to control the sale of guns, there is more violence on American streets than in any comparable advanced nation.

Human rights and freedoms. The Constitution grants U S citizens extraordinarily broad rights and these freedoms are among those most cherished by Americans. Moreover, these rights have expanded in scope over the years particularly through judicial review, legislative activity and, more recently, media scrutiny. Scores of human rights organizations and advocacy groups serve as watchdogs of every sector of human rights ready to leverage the judicial system to correct real or apparent wrongs. The Civil Rights Act, the most important post-World War II legislation, removed from the political system all vestiges of racism, a potent source of human rights violations in earlier times. Gender, race, age, religious and other types of human rights abuses have been effectively criminalized. The United States also works hard through its foreign economic programs to promote human rights around the world.

Human environment. Within the space of some 2 decades, the United States has made enormous strides toward cleaning up its environment, air, land, and water. Although many urban areas still do not meet national standards, air quality has improved overall. Controls on municipal and industrial effluents have helped to improve water quality dramatically, making many of the major rivers once again safe for fish. Despite these achievements, the United States still lags behind in its efforts to reduce emission of greenhouse gases (mostly from automobiles). Toxic dumping also poses problems in many states.

NON-CHRISTIAN RELIGIONS

Judaism is a major force in American life. The Jewish community, numbering over 5.6 million, constitutes the largest concentration of Jews in the world, twice the number of Jews in Israel and also in the USSR, and accounts for nearly half of world Jewry. Despite their small numbers relative to the general population, Jews hold generally high status as one of the so-called 3 major religions in the USA, namely Protestant, Catholic, Jew, these being regarded as the 'triple melting pot' through which the American identity is realized. Even though the Jewish community is only 2% of the total population, both as a group and individually it plays significant roles in such spheres of American life as religion, education, cultural activities, and national urban politics.

The Jews have their greatest numerical population strength in the metropolitan centers of the USA (over 3 million in 10 cities), although since World War II there has been a pronounced move to the suburbs. In recent years, there has been a gradual decline in numbers owing to a low fertility rate (2.1%), and a rise in intermarriage, estimated nationally at 40%.

The American Synagogue includes 3 major branches: Orthodox (28% of all Jews), Conservative (42%), and Reform (30%). Each of these Jewish denominations has its own national rabbinic body and lay congregational group. The Orthodox groups are the Rabbinical Council of America and the Union of Orthodox Jewish Congregations; the Conservative are the Rabbinical Assembly and the United synagogue of America; and the Reform are the Central Conference of American Rabbis and the Union of American Hebrew Congregations (750 temples). These groups are member agencies of the Synagogue Council of America, founded in New York City in 1926, which co-ordinates common activity in social, interreligious, and international affairs. There are other Jewish religious bodies which are not members of the Synagogue Council, including the Union of Orthodox Rabbis, the Agudas Israel, and Young Israel. In most local Jewish communities there exist also interdenominational rabbinic associations.

Orthodox Jews observe Jewish religious traditions based on the commandments (*mitzwot*) contained in the Torah, the Five Books of Moses, in accordance with the interpretations of the rabbinic codes which guide the religious practices and ethical behavior of Jews in their daily conduct. Reform Jews are so called because they have reformed many of the traditional rituals and ceremonies, believing that the forms of religion which reflect particular historic or cultural situations should change as life itself changes. Conservative Jews are the center movement in American Judaism, appearing sometime to lean closer to the Orthodox; at other times, they resemble Reform Jews. Within Conservative Judaism there exists the Reconstructionist schools of thought which have sought to rebuild Judaism as a natural religion in order to make it relevant to contemporary rational and scientific thought. Almost 3,000 of the 4,000 American synagogues are identifiable as Orthodox, although no more than 720 are formally affiliated with the national body, the Union of Orthodox Jewish Congregations. Affiliated with Conservative Judaism are over 800 congregations. Reform or Liberal Judaism reports around 700 synagogues or temples.

The 3 branches of Judaism maintain their own seminaries for the training of rabbis. The major Orthodox seminary is at Yeshiva University in New York City. Conservative Judaism's seminary is the Jewish Theological Seminary, also in New York. The Reform Seminary has 2 branches: the Jewish Institute of Religion in New York City, and Hebrew Union College in Cincinnati. Each group also has west coast branches in Los Angeles. The Reconstructionist movement has a rabbinical school in Philadelphia. There are a number of less prominent Orthodox talmudic schools (*yeshivas*) in various parts of the USA. The Lubavitcher Hasidic movement has demonstrated a remarkable vitality in its religious outreach to American Jewry through its headquarters in the Williamsburgh section of New York.

The most impressive evidence of the expansion of religious life among the Jews of America is to be seen in increased enrolment in every type of synagogue school. There are an estimated 500,000 children attending some 2,700 Jewish schools of various types in which they receive some form of Jewish education.

Another recent development is the growth of Jewish study programs on secular colleges and university campuses which now number some 200 chairs of Jewish studies or lecture courses in Judaica. This is in part due to the large number of Jewish students on the university scene, estimated to be about 400,000 or 80% of all Jews of college age.

In contrast to Christian church-centered groups, the Jewish community carries out much of its work in social welfare, education, and community relations through specialized agencies which are not under the auspices of synagogues. Among the more important of these may be mentioned the following: Council of Jewish Federations and Welfare funds, National Jewish Welfare Board, American Association for Jewish Education, Jewish Publican Society, American Jewish Committee, American Jewish Congress, National Jewish Community Relations Advisory Council, National Council of Jewish Women, and B'nai B'rith (including its Hillel Foundation and Anti-Defamation League).

Country summary. **Worlds A, B, C by ethnolinguistic peoples, cities, and major civil divisions in the United States of America.**

World	PEOPLES Num	Pop 2000	C%	Christians	E%	U%	Unevangelized	CITIES Num	Pop 2000	C%	Christians	E%	U%	Unevangelized	CIVIL DIVISIONS Num	Pop 2000	C%	Christians	E%	U%	Unevangelized
A	22	170,552	2.38	4,055	44	56	95,731	0	0	0.00	0	0	0	0	0	0	0.00	0	0	0	0
B	42	14,578,619	12.75	1,859,113	78	22	3,246,421	2	1,262,441	56.43	712,413	94	6	77,193	0	0	0.00	0	0	0	0
C	243	263,607,978	72.06	189,964,474	100	0	742,222	342	186,968,810	67.29	125,813,999	98	2	3,727,173	51	278,357,145	68.91	191,827,626	99	1	4,084,371
Total	**307**	**278,357,149**	**68.91**	**191,827,642**	**99**	**1**	**4,084,374**	**344**	**188,231,251**	**67.22**	**126,526,412**	**98**	**2**	**3,804,366**	**51**	**278,357,145**	**68.91**	**191,827,626**	**99**	**1**	**4,084,371**

Black Muslims. African American women of the World Community of Al-Islam in the West/America listen to former leader Elijah Muhammad.

Islam has grown appreciably since large numbers of Muslims began arriving in the USA in the 1860s. Although no US Bureau of the Census growth statistics are available, Muslim officials estimated that in 1995 approximately 3,000,000 orthodox Sunni Muslims resided in North America, mostly in the USA. Immigrants have come from all over the world. At present, most new immigrants are of Asian heritage, though the majority of the total immigrant population is Middle Eastern in origin.

Islam is of special significance for Black Americans. As they relate to Islam, Blacks fall into 2 categories: those who follow historical Islam, associate with Tolamic mosques, and openly protest the use of the name Muslim by the Nation of Islam; and secondly, the followers of the Nation of Islam itself, known as Black Muslims or Bilalians, who are regarded as heretical by Sunnis.

Several important Islamic organizations are active. The Federation of Islamic Associations of the United States and Canada (FIA), was founded in Cohasset (MA) in 1952, and received support from Al-Azhar, Egypt's religious university. The Muslim Students Association of the United States and Canada (MSA), in Gary (IN), has a membership of several thousand students from foreign countries studying at 300 colleges and universities in North America. The Islamic Center and Mosque, founded in Washington, DC, in 1952, sponsors public lectures and publishes material on Islam.

Buddhism as a movement in the USA is as rich as it is scattered over the country. In the past its greatest success has been in Hawaii and in California among the large number of residents there of Japanese ancestry. More recently, a large influx of Vietnamese, Cambodians, Thais and other Asian Buddhists has greatly swelled Buddhist numbers. Its major organization which has recently celebrated its 100th anniversary is the Buddhist Churches of America, with headquarters in San Francisco, which is predominantly Jôdo-shinshû but seeks unity among the various schools of Buddhism in the USA. Three major institutions have an international reputation. (1) The College of Oriental Studies, in Los Angeles, is devoted to the study of Buddhist philosophy (Indian, Tibetan, Chinese and Japanese traditions), Zen and its origins and comparative religions, and arranges exchanges of staff and students with several Far Eastern counterparts. Affiliated with the college is the Buddhist Meditation Center which promotes Tibetan, Sesshins Zen, Yoga, and Tai-chi-shuan meditation. (2) The Institute of Buddhist Studies, established in Berkeley, California by the Japanese community in the USA, is dedicated to the task of teaching Buddhism both academically and practically through an emphasis on intensive meditation. Served by a predominantly Japanese faculty, comparative studies are made of other religions and Buddhism's various schools, with special stress on Jôdo-shinshû Amidism. (3) A number of centers of Zen have been opened including the Zen Center, founded in San Francisco in 1959; and the Zen Mountain Center, Zenshinji Monastery, in Carmel Valley, Tassajara, California, founded in 1967. In addition to these there are several centers of Tibetan Lamaism, including Vajra Datu Karma Dzong, in Boulder, Colorado, which has 33 branches; Lamaist Buddhist Monastery, in Farmington, New Jersey; and Tail of the Tiger Buddhist Community in Barnet, Vermont.

Other religions found in the USA number over 600. Among the more significant are Baha'i, Hinduism, American Indian tribal religions and a wide variety of small groups representing most of the world's religious traditions.

US postal stamps now have increasing references to God and religion. *Left.* Flushing Remonstrance, 1657-1957.

CHRISTIANITY

PROTESTANT CHURCHES. Protestantism continues to constitute the Christian majority in the USA, although its proportional place in the population has steadily diminished during the present century, from 65% in 1900 to about 44% in 1995, due primarily to the growth of Catholicism by immigration.

Baptists form the principal Protestant tradition at the present time, a position held by Methodists in 1900. The American Baptist Churches in the USA, the largest of the northern Baptist denominations, look to Roger Williams as the founder of the country's first Baptist church, in Providence, Rhode Island in 1639. For a century and a half work was confined entirely to local communities, and after the Revolutionary War, associations were formed in several states; but the first national body (the Northern Baptist Convention) was not created until 1907. The name was changed to the American Baptist Convention in 1950 and to its present name in 1972.

The largest Baptist church in America is the Southern Baptist Convention, which came into being in 1845 in reaction to the refusal of the American Baptist Foreign Mission Society, with headquarters in Boston, to accept slave-owners as missionaries. Southern Baptists immediately established a strong central administration, a factor which has contributed to their extraordinary growth over the past century. Conventions now exist in 35 states, and there are a large number of denominational organizations. Of special note are their impressive Sunday school program in the USA and extensive overseas missionary work, the latter with 4,000 workers in over 120 countries in 1995. Unlike many large Protestant denominations, Southern Baptist numerical growth has shown few signs of decreasing in recent years.

Schisms and the creation of new Baptist denominations have taken place almost since the beginning, these including the National Association of Free Will Baptists in 1701, General Association of General Baptists in 1714, Primitive Baptists about 1830 and Baptist General Conference in 1852; and the present century has witnessed the formation of several large fundamentalist groups: the American Baptist Association in 1905, Conservative Baptist Association of America in 1947, Baptist Missionary Association of America in 1950, and Baptist Bible Fellowship International also in 1950. In addition to these larger bodies, all with communities over 100,000, there are many small Baptist denominations and independent congregations.

Methodists constitute the second largest Protestant tradition in the USA; but unlike the Baptists, the overwhelming majority are found in one denomination, the United Methodist Church. A number of other Methodist groups exist but they are for the most part small. Although John and Charles Wesley worked in Georgia as early as 1736, the first Methodist society in the New World was not formed until 1766, with the Methodist Episcopal Church itself being organized in 1784. During the 19th century schisms took their toll, the Methodist Protestant Church seceding in 1830 over the question of episcopal authority and the whole southern branch of the church in 1845 over slavery. Nevertheless these 3 bodies united once again in 1939 to form The Methodist Church, and a further merger with the Evangelical United Brethren Church in 1968 has produced the present United Methodist Church. The Church is organized into 5 jurisdictional and 81 annual conferences (including Puerto Rico) and 45 episcopal areas. The United Methodist Church is about half the size of the Southern Baptist Convention, the difference being that the former has experienced annual decreases in adherents in recent years, while the latter has continued to grow in membership.

Other Methodist denominations exist which have broken with the main denomination in order to re-emphasize the Wesleyan doctrine of sanctification, and which now form part of the 2-million strong American holiness movement, including the Wesleyan Church and the Free Methodist Church, founded respectively in 1843 and 1860.

Other important bodies in the holiness movement include the Church of God (Anderson), Christian and Missionary Alliance, and Church of the Nazarene.

Lutherans from Germany first came to New York in 1623 and were known to have organized a congregation there by 1649. Other European immigrants followed; but the first synod, called the Ministerium of Pennsylvania, was not assembled until 1748. A general synod was held in 1820.

Most of these early synods remained independent until 1918 when they merged to form the United Lutheran Church. In 1962 the Lutheran Church of America was created by a merger of the United Lutheran Church with the Swedish-speaking Augustana Lutheran Church (founded in 1860), Finnish Evangelical Lutheran Church (1890) and the American Evangelical Lutheran Church (1872), the latter working particularly among Danish immigrants. In 1987, the Lutheran Church in America and the American Lutheran Church merged to form the Evangelical Lutheran Church in America, by far the largest Lutheran denomination in the USA.

About half the size of the above is the Lutheran Church—Missouri Synod which was founded in Missouri by German immigrants from Saxony who joined with others in 1847 to form the German Evangelical Lutheran Synod of Missouri, Ohio and Other States. This church has been noted for its doctrinal conservatism but has in recent years been rent by division over alleged liberalism in its principal theological school, Concordia Seminary.

The American Lutheran Church came into being in 1960 through the union of 3 denominations: a church of the same name (American Lutheran Church), which was German in background and traced its history to 1818; the United Evangelical Lutheran Church, founded by Danes in 1896; and the Evangelical Lutheran Church, which consisted mostly of Norwegians. A further merger in 1963 also brought in the Lutheran Free Church, another Norwegian body.

Among a number of other smaller Lutheran denominations, the most important is the Wisconsin Evangelical Lutheran Synod.

Disciples of Christ form a relatively recent tradition in American Protestantism. In the early part of the 19th century, 2 separate groups concerned for Christian unity arose among Presbyterians in Kentucky and Pennsylvania. The Kentucky group called themselves 'Disciples' while the Pennsylvania group were identified simply as 'Christians'. In 1832 they joined together to form the Christian Church (Disciples of Christ). This church, whose supreme body at the national level is a general assembly, is divided into 40 regions.

Two massive schisms have taken place among the Disciples since the founding of their church. The first was a conservative split which took place about 1870 and resulted in the creation of the Churches of Christ, a denomination which is commonly described by the adjective Non-Instrumental for its refusal to allow the use of organs or musical instruments during worship services. This body is completely congregational in structure, with no hierarchical or centralized organization, and maintains an extensive missionary work throughout the world. It is also one of the fastest-growing denominations in the USA at the present time.

The second major schism came about 1935 and produced the Christian Churches and Churches of Christ, which is usually described as Instrumental because it permits musical instruments in worship.

Striking architectural innovations characterize many US churches. *Above.* Crystal Cathedral (Reformed Church in America), California.

Presbyterians and *Reformed* constitute another major tradition, the former being the term for those of British origin (Scots and Irish), and the latter for those of Continental origin, mainly Dutch. In North America the Presbyterian wing is by far the most significant.

The United Presbyterian Church in the USA, the largest of all these groups, was formed in 1958 from a union of the Presbyterian Church in the USA and the United Presbyterian Church of North America. The former was first organized in 1706, whereas the latter was itself the result of a merger of the Associate Presbyterian Church and the Associate Reformed Presbyterian Church in 1858. The church is today organized into congregations, presbyteries and synods, questions of national significance being handled by the annual general assembly, the general council and the judicial commission.

Presbyterianism, as was true of many American denominations, suffered from the North-South conflict over slavery which ended finally in the Civil War of 1861-65. Out of this period came 2 splits of southern synods and presbyteries within the Presbyterian Church in the USA, the first in 1857 and the second in 1861. These 2 southern groups in turn united in 1865 to form the Presbyterian Church in the US.

The 2 principal Reformed denominations are the Reformed Church in America, founded by Dutch settlers to New York in 1628, and the Christian Reformed Church, a schism from the former which took place in Michigan in 1837 over questions of discipline and doctrine.

Pentecostals in the USA form a dynamic tradition which grew out of the 19th-century American holiness movement, adding to its teaching an emphasis on the baptism of the Holy Spirit, faith healing, and the exercise of charismatic gifts. Several bodies including the Pentecostal Holiness Church, founded in 1898, continue to retain both emphases in their titles or in their teaching, and the first Pentecostal body in the USA, the Church of God (Cleveland), was at one point actually the Holiness Church. The latter began as a study and fellowship group in Cleveland, Tennessee in 1886, and a key event in its development took place in 1903 when A. J. Tomlinson, who had previously worked for the American Bible Society, joined its ranks, becoming moderator in 1909. The church has shown great vitality in its growth during the present century. In 1923 Tomlinson was removed from office and withdrew to form a separate Pentecostal body which adopted the name Church of God of Prophecy in 1953.

The largest Pentecostal body in the USA with mainly White members at the present time is the Assemblies of God, which dates its beginnings to 1906, although its founding meeting did not take place until 1914. Its churches, although entirely self-governing, are organized into 47 districts and include every state.

One of the most notable of America's Pentecostal denominations is the International Church of the Foursquare Gospel, which grew out of the revival meetings of Aimée Semple McPherson in Los Angeles, beginning in 1918.

Other important bodies include the United Pentecostal Church (1914) and the Pentecostal Church of God of America (1919).

Congregationalists have had a variegated history. They first came to the USA with the pilgrims in 1620 and have always had their strength in New England. In 1959 they entered on a major merger with the Evangelical and Reformed Church, a German Calvinistic body, which was itself the result of a union in 1934 of the Evangelical Synod of North America dating back to 1840, and the Reformed Church in the US begun by Germans in Pennsylvania as early as 1730. The resulting United Church of Christ, which at union was 64% Congregationalists and 36% E & R, represents an attempt to blend Congregationalism and Presbyterianism. Although local churches have full autonomy, there are area associations, regional conferences and the general synod at the national level which play an important role.

A still more ambitious union scheme is the Consultation on Church Union which was begun in 1962 and proposes to unite in one church 9 churches: Disciples, Episcopalian, Methodist (4 groups, including 3 Black Methodist denominations), Presbyterian (2) and the United Church of Christ.

Other Protestants exist in a great variety of traditions, many of them with very significant constituencies. Among the more important of these are the Seventh-day Adventist Church, founded in 1844, with 9 unions in the USA; the Salvation Army, which entered in 1880 and now has 38 USA divisions; several Brethren (German Baptist or Dunker) groups; 5 Quaker bodies, the earliest going back to 1656; and a large number of Mennonite groups from as early as 1683.

Lastly, there are over 2,500 single independent congregations unaffiliated with any particular Protestant tradition, some of which have up to 8,000 members each. Altogether they total around 1.3 million adherents.

CATHOLIC CHURCH. Catholic history in the USA dates from the first Spanish missions to Indians in 1526, and the year 1565 when the first permanent Catholic community was established at St Augustine, Florida. Maryland became a Catholic colony in 1634, but it was not until the adoption of the American constitution in 1787 that Catholics received full religious liberty. The first Catholic diocese was erected in Baltimore in 1789, becoming an archdiocese in 1808. The USA had its first cardinal appointed from Rome in 1875. By 1990, there were over 56 million Catholics in 32 archdioceses and 134 dioceses in the USA. Jurisdictions with over 2 million Catholics each include Chicago and Boston, joined in 1975 by Los Angeles; and 6 others had over a million each in 1990.

In addition to English-speaking White Americans, the 2 major ethnic groups within the US Catholic Church are over 10 million Spanish-speaking Catholics and one million Black Catholics, in 1990. These 2 latter groups are beginning to come into their own evidenced by the appointment of a 40-year-old Mexican-American priest as archbishop of Santa Fé, New Mexico, and the continued growth and vitality of the National Office for Black Catholics (NOBC), founded in 1970. The NOBC maintains close ties with the National Conference of Catholic Bishops and is funded by annual collections sponsored by the bishops in their dioceses. The NOBC has sponsored studies and seminars to improve the work of the church among Black Catholics, foster pride in their heritage, promote vocations among Blacks, and to assist those of all races and backgrounds to relate more effectively to the Black community. For the Spanish-speaking community, a similar function is performed by the Mexican American Cultural Centre in San Antonio, Texas. In 1974, the USCC Division for the Spanish-speaking, which was formerly a part of the Department of Social Development and World Peace, was upgraded to the status of a secretariat within the USCC.

Historically, the Catholic community in the USA has lived until recent years in a certain isolation from attitudes and values prevailing in the larger American society. It remained separate and homogeneous so that in a host of different ways, from the trivial to the essential, the distinctiveness of Catholic beliefs, values and practices was affirmed and reinforced.

This state of affairs has changed markedly and with increasing rapidity since the end of Vatican Council II. An important question now is whether Catholics in the USA are more influenced by the church or by secular society. Many would say that for a large number of Catholics, the influence of secular society, for good as well as ill, counts more heavily than the influence of the church.

As a result, the Catholic Church in the USA has many of the same problems as the rest of organized religion. Polarization and ferment are widespread in the church, not least in religious life. The shortage of vocations to the priesthood and religious life remains a serious problem.

On the other hand, there are now many signs that a profound spiritual renewal is taking place among American Catholics. Centers and movements for the study and practice of spirituality among priests, religious and laity are springing up in many places. Over 4 million adult Catholics including large numbers of religious personnel and several bishops are involved and active in the pentecostal Catholic Charismatic Renewal. Spiritually-oriented movements for married couples are attracting increasing numbers. After a period of transition, liturgical reforms are now widely accepted and working well. Parish and diocesan councils have spread extensively and involved more people than ever before in the exercise of shared responsibility. Many priests and religious, after a period of uncertainty and confusion, manifest renewed dedication to the mission of the church.

The Holy See has diplomatic relations with United States of America and in AD 2000 is represented to government and the Catholic hierarchy by a pronuncio residing in Washington, D.C.

BLACK/INDIAN/THIRD-WORLD CHURCHES. Some 34.8 million US Blacks, American Indians, Spanish-Americans and immigrants from Third-World countries belong to churches indigenous to their own communities, separate from, unsupported by and uncontrolled by White denominations.

Black churches. Although Blacks are found in most of the major USA denominations, with the largest numbers in the Roman Catholic Church (1,000,000) and the United Methodist Church (400,000), the majority of all USA Blacks are members of over 140 separate Blacks denominations which have split either from predominantly White or White-controlled denominations or from other Black groups over the past 2 centuries.

The majority of American Blacks are Baptists. The first independent Black Baptist congregation was formed in 1773, at Silver Bluff near Augusta, Georgia, although it was not until 1836 that an association of Black Baptists was organized, the Providence Baptist Association of Ohio. The first national body established was in 1880, called the Foreign Mission Baptist Convention. Others followed: the American National Baptist Convention in 1886 and the Baptist National Educational Convention in 1893, both of which joined the Foreign Mission Baptist Convention to form the National Baptist Convention of America in 1895. In 1915 a major dissension occurred from which emerged 2 churches, the National Baptist Convention USA, and the National Baptist Convention of

America. These remain the largest Black denominations in the USA. A further schism from the NBCUSA produced the Progressive National Baptist Convention in 1961. Another very large denomination is the National Primitive Baptist Convention. In addition, there are many small Black Baptist denominations and independent congregations.

The second largest church tradition claiming the allegiance of Blacks is Methodism. A first group of Black dissidents appeared in Philadelphia in 1787 and in 1816 officially organized the African Methodist Episcopal Church. Another group began in New York City in 1796 and eventually grew to be known as the African Methodist Episcopal Zion Church. A third important body, the Colored (now Christian) Methodist Episcopal Church, was formed in 1870 as a schism from the Methodist Episcopal Church South. The AME, AME Zion and CME churches are all now involved in church union negotiations among themselves, as well as being members of COCU, the Consultation on Church Union. Many small Black Methodist churches are also active.

Church of God in Christ. Black pentecostals (in USA denominations) totalled 3.2 million by 1978. Largest of all USA pentecostal churches is the Church of God in Christ, whose Bishop B.R. Stewart (*above*) is seen celebrating a Black rock star's marriage in New York's Madison Square before 23,000 fans.

Pentecostalism has had a wide appeal among Blacks. The largest body is the Church of God in Christ, which was begun in 1895 through a Baptist interested in 'the doctrine of entire sanctification through the outpourings of the Holy Spirit'. A major schism from this body in 1969 produced the Church of God in Christ International. Other important Black pentecostal denominations are the Pentecostal Assemblies of the World (1914), United Holy Church of America (1886) and a host of smaller churches and individual congregations.

Native American Church of North America. Contemporary Navajo peyote ritual session, declared legal by US Supreme Court in 1961 because 'The NAC is a legitimate church entitled to the protection of the 1st Amendment'. Drummer (*left*) accompanies chanter (*center*), while Road Chief (officiating priest, *right*) guides ceremony. The NAC has 23 Chapters and over 400,000 members.

American Indian churches. A small number of churches begun by, and indigenous to, American Indians have come into being during the past century, some 20 separate groups being in existence in 1990. The largest is the Native American Church of North America, dating from 1870, which is now found among almost all American Indian tribes. Because of its incorporation of Indian traditional religious concepts and practices including use of the drug peyote, it is regarded by most other American churches as only marginally Christian. The Navajo Native American Church, formed around the turn of the century has an estimated 60% of all Navajos in the USA. The oldest independent Indian group is the Narraganset Indian Church organized in Charlestown, Rhode Island, in 1741. Another early group was the Yaqui Church which, although now very small, traces its origin to Jesuit work in Arizona during the later half of the 18th century.

Hispanic churches. In addition to USA Black and American Indian churches, there are several churches, begun in the USA by, and indigenous to, the Spanish-speaking community of USA nationality, especially among those of Puerto Rican and Mexican origin.

Third-World indigenous churches. All of the above bodies are indigenous to the USA. Over and above them, however, there are a large and growing number of Third-World indigenous bodies, i.e. originating in the Third World among Non-White peoples, which have been introduced into the USA by immigrant adherents from Africa, Asia, the Caribbean, Latin America and Oceania. The greatest impact thus far has been made by Spanish-speaking groups from Latin America, and Puerto Rico, the largest of these being the Spanish wing of the Assemblies of God and the Apostolic Assembly, both of which have entered the USA from Mexico. New denominations introduced from Africa include the African Apostolic Church of Johane Maranke from Zimbabwe, the Kimbanguist Church from Zaire and the Church of the Lord (Aladura) from West Africa. The Church of the First-Born and the International City have both come from Jamaica, while the True Jesus Church and the Church of Christ (Iglesia ni Cristo) owe their beginnings respectively to China and the Philippines. More than 60 such churches existed in the USA in 1990; and although most are still small, they will undoubtedly grow in numbers over the next decade or two.

Orthodox Church in America. Metropolitan Ireney (third bishop from left), head of Russian-origin million-member OCA, concelebrates with Bishop Elias of Patriarchate of Antioch (second bishop from left) and 2 other hierarchs during 1974 Orthodox Education Day at St. Vladimir's Seminary.

ORTHODOX CHURCHES. *Eastern Orthodoxy* in the USA represents a phenomenon of great variety and complexity. Churches of the Byzantine and Slavic traditions consist of more than 20 separate churches, the largest single denomination being the Greek Orthodox Archdiocese of North and South America. Although a Greek community was founded in New Smyrna, Florida as early as 1767, the first church in New Orleans, was not organized until 1864. The archdiocese itself was established in 1921 with headquarters in New York City. This church, which is part of the Ecumenical Patriarchate of Constantinople, suffered 3 or 4 minor schisms by Old Calendrist bodies following the acceptance of the new Gregorian calendar in 1924.

In 1792, 8 Russian Orthodox missionary monks arrived in Kodiak, Alaska, where they built their base and first church; and by 1794 they had baptized 25,000 Eskimos. Alaska remained part of Russia until 1867. Russian Orthodoxy at present is represented by 3 bodies in the USA, of which the Orthodox Church in America (OCA) has the longest history (1792) and the greatest number of adherents. Originally known as the Russian Orthodox Greek Catholic Church of America, it was granted autocephalous status by the Moscow Patriarchate in 1970 and adopted its new name in the same year. The Romanian Orthodox Episcopate and the Albanian Orthodox Archdiocese, founded respectively in 1904 and 1908, are at present under the canonical jurisdiction of the OCA. Two other smaller denominations which have entered the USA in the present century are the Russian Orthodox Church in the Americas, an exarchate of the Moscow Patriarchate, and the Russian Orthodox Church Outside of Russia. The latter is strongly opposed to the Moscow Patriarchate because of its collaboration with the Soviet communist regime.

A large number of Orthodox bodies have been formed by other ethnic immigrant groups from Eastern Europe, and these are today often divided into 2 distinct rival bodies (as are each the Albanian, Bulgarian, Romanian, and Serbian) or even 3 (as is the Ukrainian). In addition there are Belorussian, Estonian, Finnish, Hungarian, Macedonian, and Carpatho-Russian bodies. Two rival groups related to the Patriarchate of Antioch in Syria are also active. An attempt in 1932 to unite all Eastern Orthodox in America into one church produced yet another denomination, the American Holy Orthodox Catholic Eastern Church.

The most important organization providing for contacts between the various Eastern Orthodox groups is the Standing Conference of Canonical Orthodox Bishops in the Americas, with 11 member churches.

Oriental Orthodoxy has a following of over 700,000. Of the 5 non-Chalcedonian churches in the USA, the largest are the Armenian Church of North America, and the Armenian Apostolic Church of America. The former, begun in 1889, owes allegiance to the Catholicate of Echmiadzin in Soviet Armenia, while the latter, which split from it in 1933, is now related to the Catholicate of Cilicia (sis) at Antelias in Lebanon.

The Syrian Orthodox Church (Jacobite) was introduced into North America in 1895. Forming part of the Patriarchate of Antioch with headquarters in Damascus, Syria, the archdiocese of the USA and Canada is based in Hackensack, New Jersey. Two other small Monophysite groups are the Ethiopian and Coptic Orthodox churches which entered the USA with immigrants in 1959 and 1960.

Nestorians. The Nestorian branch of Christianity, the Ancient Church of the East, has been present in the USA since 1907, and has the name Holy Apostolic and Catholic Church of the East. Its patriarchate was moved from Iraq to San Francisco in 1940; there are 35,000 faithful.

MARGINAL CHURCHES. Several large churches exist on the periphery of American Protestantism which are not properly termed Protestant because they do not accept mainline Protestant christocentric orthodoxy. In this survey they are called, for want of a better term, marginal Protestant bodies.

Church of Jesus Christ of Latter-day Saints. Mormon Temple and headquarters, Salt Lake City.

Mormons. The Church of Jesus Christ of Latterday Saints, better known as Mormonism, traces its history to visions of its founder, Joseph Smith, at Fayette, New York in 1830. Severely persecuted everywhere, the Mormons ultimately settled in Utah where they built up a large religious community under the leadership of Brigham Young. Mormonism has 2 orders of priests, the higher priesthood of Melchizedek and the lesser priesthood of Aaron. Church organization is highly centralized, including the First Presidency, which is the supreme executive and legislative body of the church, and the Council of the Twelve Apostles, which carries out the directives of the First Presidency and ordains ministers. The geographical districts of the church are called stakes and local congregations, wards. Mormons are responsible for an extensive educational and social service program and are heavily involved in missionary work. In addition to full-time missionaries, some 5,000 youth are sent out yearly in pairs to spend a 2-year short-term service in propagating Mormonism throughout the world. The result has been vast expansion on all other continents except Africa, due to, until recently, the Mormon refusal to open its priesthood to Blacks, a problem which has also hindered Mormon work among Blacks in the USA.

Since 1831 at least 89 schismatic offshoots have split from the mother LDS church, while retaining essential Mormon beliefs and practices. The largest is the Reorganized Church of Jesus Christ of Latter-day Saints; others are known as Temple Lot, Bickertonites and Strangites.

Jehovah's Witnesses came into being through the work of Charles Taze Russell, a Congregationalist who was influenced by Adventism in 1870. Russell organized his first congregation in Pittsburgh in 1872 and registered his first incorporated society in 1884. Until the name Jehovah's Witnesses was adopted in 1931, adherents were known as Russellites, Millenial Dawnists, and International Bible Students. At present the organization is based on 3 USA corporations, the Watch Tower Bible and Tract Society of Pennsylvania, Watchtower Bible and Tract Society of New York, and the International Bible Students Association. Congregations meet in kingdom halls and are grouped into circuits and districts, there being 31 districts in the USA. There is no separate clergy; all members are ministers and are expected to give personal witness and distribute literature from door to door, resulting in a massive voluntary missionary enterprise technically known as publishing, with members being called publishers. As with the Mormons, a sizeable number of schisms have broken from Jehovah's Witnesses through the years, several in a mainline Protestant direction, including the Laymen's Home Missionary Movement (1918), Churches of the Kingdom of God, Greek Bible Students, and Converted Jehovah's Witnesses.

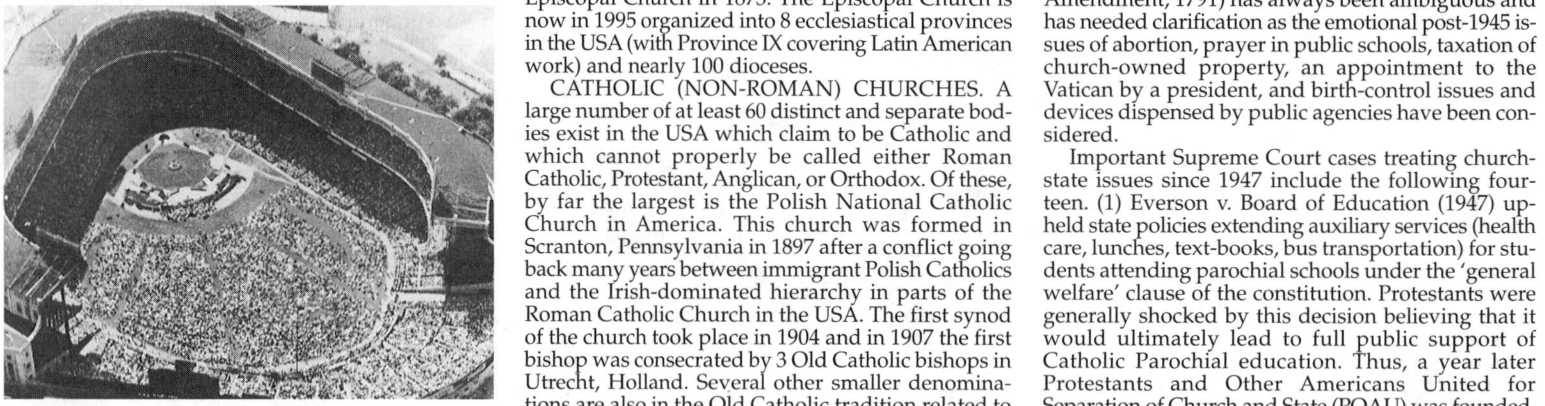

Jehovah's Witnesses. One of a series of huge international conventions: 1953 New World Society Assembly, New York.

Christian Science. The Church of Christ, Scientist was founded at Boston in 1879, by Mary Baker Eddy, whose own personal experience of healing in 1866 led to the founding of a worldwide movement centered on spiritual healing. The denomination retains its headquarters in Boston, where the First Church of Christ, Scientist is still universally regarded as the Mother Church. The Christian Science Board of Directors in Boston is the supreme administrative body of the church. In addition to Sunday and weekday services, local churches maintain reading rooms and an extensive literature distribution program. Key congregational leaders are known as readers, teachers, and practitioners, the latter bearing special responsibility for healing.

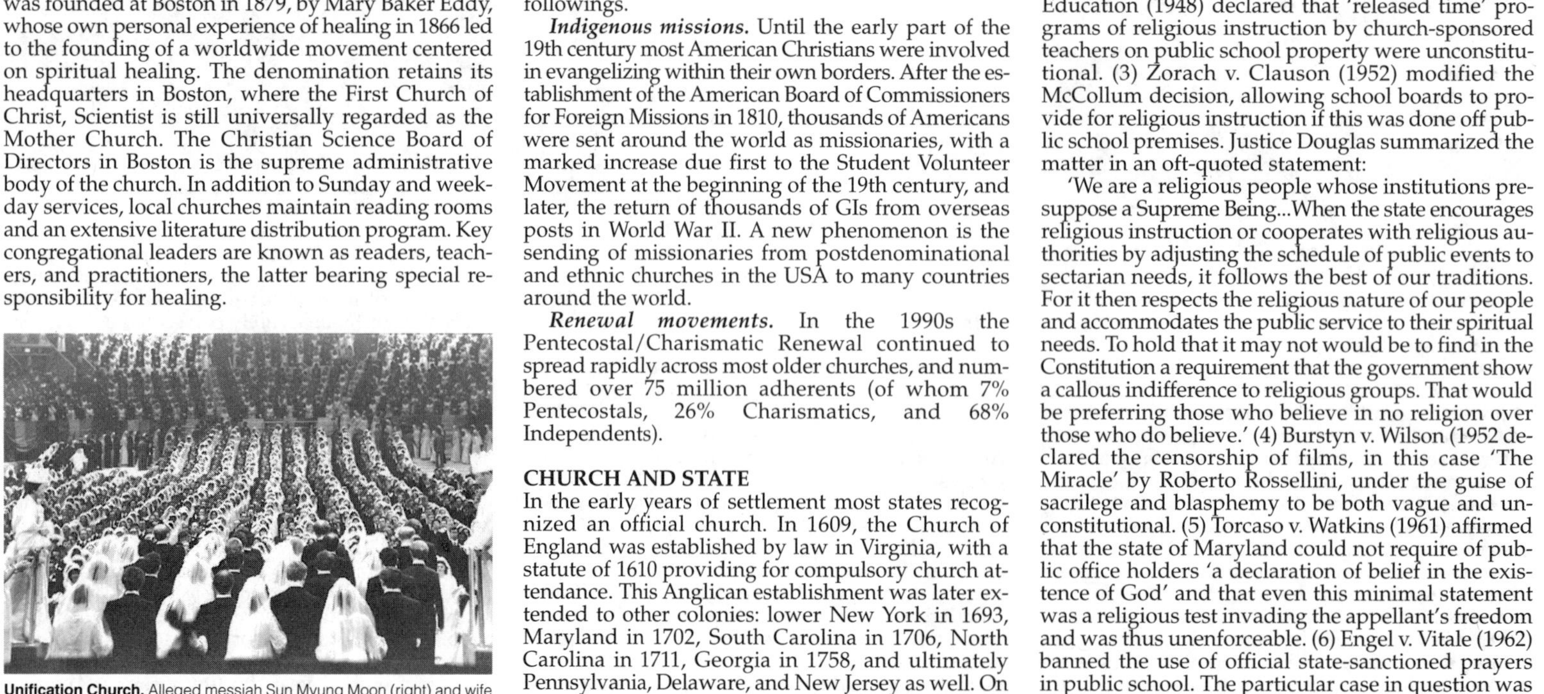

Unification Church. Alleged messiah Sun Myung Moon (right) and wife (left) performed mass wedding of 2,200 couples, New York 1982.

Unitarianism. Universalists organized their first church in 1778, and Unitarians in 1796. In 1961 they joined to form the Unitarian Universalist Association. The strength of the movement has been in New England and Boston remains the national headquarters, but membership is declining.

Spiritism or Spiritualism has a wide appeal in the USA and is organized into many separate groups, the largest being the International General Assembly of Spiritualists formed in 1936.

A host of over 300 smaller marginal Protestant bodies of all kinds are also active in the USA. Many of them have expanded overseas during the 20th century.

Schisms in a Protestant, or mainline Christian, direction have taken place over the years from most other major bodies as well as from Mormons and Jehovah's Witnesses. In 1973, the largest USA congregation of Unity School of Christianity (in Los Angeles, with 5,000 members) became pentecostal and broke from Unity; and there have been numerous other such cases.

ANGLICAN CHURCH. Sir Francis Drake touched the shores of California in 1578, claiming the New World for the British queen and the Church of England, but it was not until the foundation of the Virginia colony in 1607 that Anglicans began evangelistic work in America. Anglicanism nearly came to an end at the time of the Revolutionary War, with many of its clergy fleeing to England or Canada. Nevertheless, the period after 1783 was a time of rebuilding, and the constitution of the newly-created Protestant Episcopal Church in the USA was adopted in 1789. Although the church was spared the divisions which rent many Protestant denominations at the time of the Civil War, it has experienced several minor schisms since the formation of the Reformed Episcopal Church in 1873. The Episcopal Church is now in 1995 organized into 8 ecclesiastical provinces in the USA (with Province IX covering Latin American work) and nearly 100 dioceses.

CATHOLIC (NON-ROMAN) CHURCHES. A large number of at least 60 distinct and separate bodies exist in the USA which claim to be Catholic and which cannot properly be called either Roman Catholic, Protestant, Anglican, or Orthodox. Of these, by far the largest is the Polish National Catholic Church in America. This church was formed in Scranton, Pennsylvania in 1897 after a conflict going back many years between immigrant Polish Catholics and the Irish-dominated hierarchy in parts of the Roman Catholic Church in the USA. The first synod of the church took place in 1904 and in 1907 the first bishop was consecrated by 3 Old Catholic bishops in Utrecht, Holland. Several other smaller denominations are also in the Old Catholic tradition related to Utrecht, but most of the others are not recognized by Utrecht. About 30 of these bodies are miniscule episcopal churches under bishops-at-large with very small followings.

Indigenous missions. Until the early part of the 19th century most American Christians were involved in evangelizing within their own borders. After the establishment of the American Board of Commissioners for Foreign Missions in 1810, thousands of Americans were sent around the world as missionaries, with a marked increase due first to the Student Volunteer Movement at the beginning of the 19th century, and later, the return of thousands of GIs from overseas posts in World War II. A new phenomenon is the sending of missionaries from postdenominational and ethnic churches in the USA to many countries around the world.

Renewal movements. In the 1990s the Pentecostal/Charismatic Renewal continued to spread rapidly across most older churches, and numbered over 75 million adherents (of whom 7% Pentecostals, 26% Charismatics, and 68% Independents).

CHURCH AND STATE

In the early years of settlement most states recognized an official church. In 1609, the Church of England was established by law in Virginia, with a statute of 1610 providing for compulsory church attendance. This Anglican establishment was later extended to other colonies: lower New York in 1693, Maryland in 1702, South Carolina in 1706, North Carolina in 1711, Georgia in 1758, and ultimately Pennsylvania, Delaware, and New Jersey as well. On the other hand strong anti-Anglican feelings in New England brought by the Pilgrims contributed to the establishment of the Congregational Church as the official religion in Massachusetts and Connecticut. In 1632 Maryland was created as a home for Catholics, and many of the first Catholic immigrants settled there. However, after 1689 Protestants were in control and succeeded in passing laws discriminating against Catholics. Indeed in this early period a strong anti-Catholic bias existed everywhere except in Rhode Island and Pennsylvania.

The desire for religious freedom, accompanied by resentment against Anglicanism because of its ties to Great Britain, was a dominant factor in the religious situation during 1776-89 and resulted in the disestablishment of the Church of England in the southern and middle colonies from 1776-90 and also of Congregationalism in New England (1818 in Connecticut, 1833 in Massachusetts). An important impulse towards that end came from the first federal constitution of 1789 which gave clear expression to the idea of the separation of church and state which had been growing since before the Revolutionary War. Since the formulation of the US constitution in 1787, therefore, the United States has been clearly defined as a secular state in which church and state are legally separated. The constitution makes no reference to God (except for George Washington's signature 'In the Year of our Lord 1787'), nor to the state as believing in God, although in 1954 Congress added the words 'under God' to the Pledge of Allegiance.

From a legal standpoint the past 50 years have seen a number of important Supreme Court decisions that have further clarified the nature of the separation of church and state in America. The intent of the 16-word constitutional requirement 'Congress shall make no law respecting an establishment of religion or prohibiting the free exercise thereof' (First Amendment, 1791) has always been ambiguous and has needed clarification as the emotional post-1945 issues of abortion, prayer in public schools, taxation of church-owned property, an appointment to the Vatican by a president, and birth-control issues and devices dispensed by public agencies have been considered.

Important Supreme Court cases treating church-state issues since 1947 include the following fourteen. (1) Everson v. Board of Education (1947) upheld state policies extending auxiliary services (health care, lunches, text-books, bus transportation) for students attending parochial schools under the 'general welfare' clause of the constitution. Protestants were generally shocked by this decision believing that it would ultimately lead to full public support of Catholic Parochial education. Thus, a year later Protestants and Other Americans United for Separation of Church and State (POAU) was founded, supported mainly by Baptist, Unitarian, and independent Protestant groups, to protect the separation of church and state. (2) McCollum v. Board of Education (1948) declared that 'released time' programs of religious instruction by church-sponsored teachers on public school property were unconstitutional. (3) Zorach v. Clauson (1952) modified the McCollum decision, allowing school boards to provide for religious instruction if this was done off public school premises. Justice Douglas summarized the matter in an oft-quoted statement:

'We are a religious people whose institutions presuppose a Supreme Being...When the state encourages religious instruction or cooperates with religious authorities by adjusting the schedule of public events to sectarian needs, it follows the best of our traditions. For it then respects the religious nature of our people and accommodates the public service to their spiritual needs. To hold that it may not would be to find in the Constitution a requirement that the government show a callous indifference to religious groups. That would be preferring those who believe in no religion over those who do believe.' (4) Burstyn v. Wilson (1952 declared the censorship of films, in this case 'The Miracle' by Roberto Rossellini, under the guise of sacrilege and blasphemy to be both vague and unconstitutional. (5) Torcaso v. Watkins (1961) affirmed that the state of Maryland could not require of public office holders 'a declaration of belief in the existence of God' and that even this minimal statement was a religious test invading the appellant's freedom and was thus unenforceable. (6) Engel v. Vitale (1962) banned the use of official state-sanctioned prayers in public school. The particular case in question was that of the New York State Board of Regent's prayer:

'Almighty God, we acknowledge our dependence upon Thee, and we beg Thy blessings upon us, our parents, our teachers and our country.' A storm of protest followed this decision, and there is sentiment in both Houses of Congress for a constitutional amendment which would allow prayer in school. (7) Pennsylvania v. Schempp (1963) held that the reading of Bible verses without comment or interpretation was unconstitutional, because for some the exercise had a devotional and religious character. (8) McGowan v. Maryland (1961) invalidated a state's co-called 'blue laws' relating to required closure of certain businesses on Sundays. Other decisions during the past decade have extended civil and religious freedom. Black Muslim prisoners have been given access to religious literature, services and pastoral visitation; Seventh-day Adventists and Orthodox Jews have had their job security protected when they abstain from Saturday work; and Jehovah's Witnesses have been exempted from securing licenses to sell their literature and may restrain from the public school flag-salute and Pledge of Allegiance. In the latter case (West Virginia School Board of Education v. Barnette, 1943), justice Jackson stated in a widely-quoted passage: 'To believe that patriotism will not flourish if patriotic ceremonies are voluntary and spontaneous instead of a compulsory routine is to make an unflattering estimate of the appeal of our institutions to free minds. We can have intellectual individualism and the rich cultural diversities that we owe to exceptional minds only at the price of occasional eccentricity and abnormal attitudes...If there is any fixed star in our constitutional constellation, it is that no official, high or petty, can prescribe what shall be orthodox in politics, nationalism, religion, or other matters of opinion or force citizens to confess by word or act their faith therein.' (9) Welsh v. United States (1970) liberalized and legalized a new basis for conscientious objection to war and exemption from military service. Hitherto, belief in a supreme being was necessary. Afterwards, a deeply-held and morally-consistent repugnance to war and the taking of life was deemed acceptable. (10) Walz v. Tax Commission of New York (1970) denied that the tax-exempt status of church property constituted an 'establishment of religion' and continued such exemption as long as such property was for religious use exclusively. Noting that many municipal governments are hard-pressed for revenue, some churches have recently made token gifts for such public services as police and fire protection. (11) Sloan v. Lemon (1973) and Committee for Public Education and Religious Liberty v. Nyquist (1973) were 2 significant decisions in the long and continuing controversy over providing significant state aid to parochial schools. In the former judgement, a Pennsylvania statute providing for reimbursement of tuition paid by parents who send their children to non-public schools was declared unconstitutional under the establishment clause. In the latter, a New York case, repair grants and highly-complicated tuition reimbursement arrangements to parents of students in parochial schools in low-income areas were judged contrary to the First Amendment. (12) Miller v. California (1973) in a close 5-4 decision allowed states and/or their local communities to take punitive action against those who produce, sell, exhibit or display works 'which appeal to the prurient interest in sex, which portray sexual conduct in a patently offensive way and which taken as a whole, do not have serious literary, artistic, political or scientific value'. Chief justice Warren Burger wrote: 'It is neither realistic nor constitutionally sound to read the First Amendment as requiring that the people of Maine or Mississippi accept the public depiction of conduct found tolerable in Las Vegas or New York City'. The minority opinion claimed that the decision would not relieve the court of 'the awesome task' of making case-by-case decisions and thus would be unworkable. Their position seemed to be substantiated in the first test case of the above Miller decision, Jenkins v. Georgia (1974), when the court overturned a state's decision that the film 'Carnal Knowledge' was pornographic and obscene. (13) Wheeler v. Barrera (1974) decided that educationally-deprived non-public-school children should have equitable treatment regarding the distribution of federal funds in aid of special programs for the disadvantaged. The court affirmed that the federal statute (Title I) did not obligate the state to provide on-the-premises instruction in non-public schools (as prohibited by the Missouri Constitution) and that state and local officials had various other options available in order to comply with the requirement of comparable services to all schools. (14) Roe v. Wade (1973), perhaps the most important decision of the past several decades, found the court in a 7-2 decision drafting national guide lines that broadly liberalized abortion laws. Only during the last 10 weeks of pregnancy, the period during which the fetus is judged to be capable of surviving if born, can a state prohibit abortion. The majority decision rejected the view that a fetus becomes a 'person' upon conception, while the dissenting opinion called the decision 'an exercise of raw judicial power' that values 'the convenience of the pregnant mother more than the continued existence and development of the life or potential life which she carries'. The Catholic hierarchy together with some conservative Protestant churches bitterly attacked the decision and have been instrumental in founding politically-powerful Right to Life groups whose aim is the defeat of abortion-on-demand politicians and the passage of a constitutional amendment prohibiting abortion. The issue is a divisive one that will traumatize the body politic for some time into the future and will probably retard the ecumenical movement.

In terms of common practice and general trends regarding the future, there is no governmental ministry of religious affairs, nor are churches obligated to register with the government, nor is this situation likely to change.

The post-World War II trend of American Protestantism may be described as transformationist with regard to church-state relations. This position applies a theocentric principle (the sovereignty of God) to church-state theory and practice, and is committed to a prophetic church, a strong social ethic and a realistic view of sin. Transformationism neither advocates a unity of church and state nor their complete separation, but an intermediate position. It avoids a negative separationism that leads to increased secularization of culture and irresponsibility in politics; yet it guards against preferential privilege for any one church whereby the independent stance necessary for prophetic criticism of the state is lost and injustice is done to non-preferred religious bodies. Thus what is being sought is a new kind of 'creative co-operation' or 'benevolent neutrality' between church and state.

March for Jesus: 40,000 in 1995 Nashville, TN. From 1990-2000 annual totals skyrocketed worldwide.

BROADCASTING AND MEDIA

The United States is blanketed with Christian radio, television and satellite programming. Hundreds of local stations broadcast Christian evangelistic and discipleship programs.

Aside from English, there are several stations devoted to broadcasting Christian programs in other languages (i.e. Spanish).

From Christian broadcasting's humble beginnings in 1921 in Pittsburgh, when KDKA aired the first religious broadcast, it has exploded into one of the most powerful evangelistic forces in the United States today. Many innovations have continued to make it easier to reach ever larger audiences.

Virtually every media outlet in the country carries at least one Christian program each year—typically a holiday special. Many local stations carry weekly Sunday morning devotionals. There are more than 1,200 exclusively Christian radio and television stations. Many of these belong to one of 20 religious networks. LeSEA and TBN are among the largest of these. LeSEA, founded in 1968 by Dr. Lester Sumrall, reaches 8 million households through a network of low-power repeaters, 11 television stations, cable stations and the World Harvest Satellite network on Galaxy-4. Its shortwave service, started in 1985, covers Asia, Latin America, Europe, Russia and Africa with programs in English, Spanish, Russian, Mandarin, and Japanese. Its satellite network covers all the United States, half of Canada, and most of Central America. One of its affiliates, WHMB, is the longest continually operated Christian station in the United States; another, WHME, is the top-rated Christian station in the nation. LeSEA's Hawaii station, KWHE, also operates a shortwave transmitter which broadcasts programming worldwide, most specifically aimed at East Asia. Programs are in English, Spanish, Russian, Mandarin, and Japanese. Trinity Broadcast Network, founded by Paul Crouch, has cable, satellite and television outlets, reaching several million households. Other networks include the Catholics Eternal Word Television Network and Life Broadcasting Network. CBN's television programs are aired across the United States on cable (the Family Channel) and several local Christian television stations, as well as occasionally on LeSEA and TBN's networks.

The USA is a member of UNDA. Some 38 organizations produce Catholic media, including radio and TV programs as well as videos. There are 40 Catholic radio stations. The Catholic Television Network is based out of Washington D.C. and has offices in 11 states.

Many of these stations receive their programs from other organizations. There are 380 such agencies. Programs from *Back to the Bible* air on 850 stations. Promise Keeper's short 'Highlights' airs on over 1,200 radio stations. Mission Network News and the Mission Vision Network provides short mission-oriented radio spots to more that a thousand stations. CBN airs its '700 Club' on cable (the Family channel) and on numerous local Christian television stations.

All of the international broadcasters have offices in the USA. AWR has studios in California and Michigan. KNLS, WORHAR, and WYFR have transmitters based in America that cover most of the world.

These broadcasters associate together through several national organizations. The National Religious Broadcasters is an association of 800 broadcasters, including networks and stations, its annual convention is one of the most important for anyone involved in media. The Hispanic Religious Broadcasters is a spinoff association of UNDA and serves a similar function for Catholic broadcasters.

In addition to television and radio, several media outlets are seeking out a new technology: broadcasting their shows via Real Audio and Real Video servers on the Internet. Through this medium, anyone in the world with the necessary equipment can listen to the broadcasts. Nearly all are in English. There are currently more than 40 Christian broadcasters on the Internet. CIRnet is a live 24-hour Christian Internet-only radio network. Churches.NET is the home of CINN, the Christian Internet News Network. Many churches offer online sermons. LeSEA broadcasts its shortwave programs simultaneously on Real Audio sermons. The Bible Broadcasting Network is a national broadcaster headquartered in South Carolina that also provides its programs on the Internet. The Jesus Fellowship Internet Radio Station is a church-sponsored Internet broadcaster. The listening Room features a library of 7,000 recorded sermons and books. The American Christian Network airs well known Bible teachers live 24 hours a day.

AWR operates 2 studios: California (English, Vietnamese) and Michigan (English). Several stations based in the United States use shortwave to reach other world regions: KNLS (Alaska), WORHAR, and WYFR.

INTERDENOMINATIONAL ORGANIZATIONS

National and local councils of churches. The major national co-ordinating body is the National Council of the Churches of Christ in the USA (NCCCUSA), founded in New York City in 1950, growing out of the earlier Federal Council of the Churches of Christ in North America (1908). Member denominations number 32, including most of America's largest Protestant, Orthodox, and Black churches. Notable by their absence are the Roman Catholic Church and the Southern Baptist Convention. However, Catholic interest in ecumenism, which is co-ordinated by the Bishop's Committee for Ecumenical and Interreligious Affairs of the NCCB, is strong. In 1969 a joint Catholic—NCCC commission was appointed to investigate the possibility of eventual Catholic membership in the council. The work of the NCCC is carried out through 3 divisions (Church and Society, Education and Ministry, Overseas Ministry), 4 commissions, and 3 offices.

With the exception of Alabama and Mississippi, every state in the USA has its own council or conference of churches, interchurch or interfaith association or agency; and several states have more than one. In addition there are a vast number of city-wide councils. The Catholic Church holds membership in 15 state councils of churches and more than 50 metropolitan ecumenical agencies.

Other national inter-denominational co-ordinating bodies include the National Association of Evangelicals (NAE), National Black (formerly Negro) Evangelical Association (NBEA, NNEA), Associated Gospel Churches (representing fundamentalist denominations with over 4 million members), Pan-Indian Ecumenical Association, American Council of Christian Churches, Christian Holiness Association, Council of Japanese American Christian Churches in North America and National Fraternal Council of Churches.

Intervarsity Urbana Missions convention held every three years in Urbana, Illinois.

International bodies with headquarters in the USA include: International Association of Women Ministers; International Christian Youth Exchange; International Ministerial Federation; and World's Christian Endeavor Union.

International ecumenical organizations with branches in the USA include: Ecumenical Satellite Commission (which is concerned for press, cinema, radio and TV), United States Conference for the World Council of Churches, North American Office of the World Student Christian Federation.

National service agencies include the American Bible Society, American Tract Society, Associated Church Press, Christian Ministry in the National Parks, Church Women United, Evangelical Press Association, General Commission on Chaplains and Armed Forces Personnel, National Association of Christian Schools, National Association of Ecumenical Staff, National Council of YMCAs, National Interreligious Service Board for Conscientious Objectors, North American Academy of Ecumenists, Religion in American Life (which attempts to reach the American public through advertising), Religion Newswriters Association, Religious Public Relations Council, and YWCA of the USA.

Confessional councils. National and international confessional councils and federations with their world headquarters in the USA, serving one ecclesiastical confession, include the Baptist World Alliance, Lutheran Council in the USA; Mennonite World Conference, North American Baptist Fellowship, Pentecostal Fellowship of North America, Standing Conference of the Canonical Orthodox Bishops in the Americas, World Convention of Churches of Christ (Disciples) and World Methodist Council.

Other international bodies with branches but not world headquarters in the USA include: Friends World Committee for Consultation, Lutheran World Federation, Pentecostal World Conference and World Alliance of Reformed Churches, the latter serving Presbyterians and Congregationalists.

Dialogue consultation. A significant number of other conversations are in progress sponsored by churches and confessional families nationally. These include joint dialogue between Lutherans and Anglicans, Anglicans and Orthodox, Lutherans and Orthodox, and 8 consultations in which Catholics are involved. Concerning these latter, joint dialogue is being carried on between the Catholic episcopal conference (Bishops' Committee for Ecumenical and Interreligious Affairs) and the following: American Baptist Convention (Division of Cooperative Christianity; first meeting held in April, 1967); Christian Church (Disciples of Christ) (Council of Christian Unity; March, 1967); Episcopal Church (Joint Commission on Ecumenical Relations; begun June, 1965); Lutheran churches (USA National Committee of the Lutheran World Federation; March, 1965); United Methodist Church; June, 1966; Orthodox churches (Standing Conference of Canonical Orthodox Bishops of America; September, 1969); Presbyterian-Reformed churches (North American Council of the World Alliance of Reformed churches; July, 1965); and Southern Baptists (Department of Interfaith Witness; May 1969). These continuing consultations aim through dialogue to investigate points at issue which have been factors in the separation of churches, with the hope of achieving a deeper and broader agreement among Christians.

Theological education. A major future of the current North American ecumenical scene is the growth of clusters and consortia of theological schools, involving Protestant, Catholic, Orthodox, and Anglican institutions. The most important are the Chicago Cluster of Theological Schools, California Graduate Theological Union, Washington Theological Consortium, and Boston Theological Institute. These co-operative enterprises differ greatly in emphasis but involve cross-registration, joint planning, and the development of a common network of library facilities. Some follow a practice of exchanging teaching staff and others conduct joint research programs.

Study and research. Many societies and associations dedicated to the scientific study of religion on an ecumenical basis have been formed, the most important of which belong to the Council on the Study of Religion. Members of the council include the following: American Academy of Religion, American Society of Christian Ethics, American Society of Church History, American Society of Missiology, American Theological Library Association, Catholic Biblical Association, Catholic Theological Society of America, College Theological Society, Society of Biblical Literature, Society for the Scientific Study of Religions, and Religious Education Association.

Other academic institutions giving special attention to ecumenical study and research are: (1) the Ecumenical Continuing Education Centre, founded at Yale University in 1967, which links the Yale Religious Ministry, United Ministries in Higher Education at Yale, New Haven and Connecticut Councils of Churches, includes on its board of directors Protestants, Catholics, and Orthodox, and provides opportunities for pastors and lay persons to engage in study programs in a university setting; (2) the Ecumenical Institute, founded in Chicago in 1954, which is a Division of the Church Federation of Greater Chicago and provides a research, study and training center for religious renewal on an ecumenical basis focusing on the needs of the local congregation; (3) the Ecumenical Institute of Religious Studies, founded in Worcester, Massachusetts in 1967, which is run by Catholic Assumptionists; (4) Graymoor Ecumenical Institute, founded in Garrison, New York in 1967, which is operated by Catholic Friars of the Atonement under an interdenominational board, with its research, study and action center dedicated to the search for a Christian response to social and religious issues facing American life; and to ecumenical and interreligious dialogue; (5) the Institute for Advanced Religious Studies, founded at the University of Notre Dame in Indiana in 1966, which explores the conveyance of religion with other fields of study and concentrates on the relationship of Christianity to the non-Christian world; (6) the Institute for Ecumenical and Cultural Research, founded at St John's University in Collegeville, Minnesota in 1967, which though centered in a Catholic university is independently incorporated, having a predominantly Protestant board of directors, and which offers research facilities to individual scholars studying the problems of ecumenism broadly conceived; (7) John XXIII Institute for Eastern Christian Studies, founded at Fordham University in New York City in 1971, which is a Catholic institute emphasizing Orthodox-Catholic relations and the study of the Eastern tradition of Christianity; and (8) Institute for Thomistic and Ecumenical Studies, founded by the Dominican Province of the Holy Name in Berkeley, California in 1966, which provides facilities for competent scholars to pursue post-doctoral studies related to ecumenism.

Ecumenical action. Centers and agencies for ecumenical action include: (1) Berkeley Center for Human Interaction, founded in Berkeley, California in 1966, which sponsors intensive small-group conferences and programs; (2) Christians Associated for Relationships with Eastern Europe (CAREE), in Elgin, Illinois, which aims to foster good relations with Christians in Eastern Europe especially through the Christian Peace Conference, to promote Christian-Marxist dialogue and to work for international peace and justice; (3) Cooperation in Development (CODEL), founded in New York City in 1969, an inter-faith consortium which co-ordinates the work of member Christian service and mission groups in the areas of hunger, health, and housing; (4) the Ecumenical Institute, founded at Wake Forest University in Winston Salem, NC, in 1968, which is a Southern Baptist center offering resources for conferences, study, and dialogue; (5) the Ecumenical Institute, founded in Merrimac, Massachusetts in 1964, which emphasizes the renewal of the local congregation; (6) the Gustav Weigel Society, founded at Wesley Theological Seminary in Washington, DC in 1966, which promotes spiritual ecumenism through retreats for pastors and lay persons; (7) John XXIII Ecumenical Center, founded in Paoli, Pennsylvania in 1969, which is an independent and interdenominational institution seeking to enlist all men in the common worship of God and service of their neighbor; (8) John LaFarge Institute, founded by Jesuits in New York City in 1964, which promotes ecumenical and interracial activities and holds conferences; (9) LAOS, in Washington, DC, which is an ecumenical agency for training and recruiting volunteers with professional skills for work in developing countries and in areas of need in the USA; (10) Laymen's Academy for Ecumenical Studies, founded in Amherst, Massachusetts in 1961, which emphasizes Catholic-Protestant and Black-White relations, in addition to lay theological education; (11) Packard Manse Ecumenical Center, founded in Stoughton in Massachusetts, 1947, which is dedicated to social ecumenism at the local level; and (12) the World Center for Liturgical Studies, founded in Boyton Beach, Florida in 1965, which sponsors conferences and provides study facilities for the continuing education of church leaders with special emphasis on pastoral and liturgical areas of the ministry.

Jewish-Christian relations. The major concern of inter-religious dialogue in the USA is Jewish-Christian relations, and a number of Christian, Jewish, and joint organizations have been formed to improve contacts between Christians and Jews.

Joint organizations include: (1) Interreligious Committee of General Secretaries, founded in 1968, which enables the executive officers of the NCC-CUSA, USCC, and the Synagogue Council of America to collaborate in matters of mutual interest; (2) National Conference of Christians and Jews (NCCJ), founded in New York City in 1928, which is a member of the international Council of Christians and Jews in London, and seeks to combat religious and social prejudice through its 70 regional offices, its sponsorship of Religious News Service (RNS), and its promotion of an annual Brotherhood Commitment Week; (3) World Conference of Religion for Peace (WCRP), established as a permanent interreligious body in 1971 following the first world conference on religion and peace in Kyoto, Japan in 1970, which includes members of all the principal world faiths in sharing insights and promoting common action for peace, justice and mutual understanding; (4) US Interreligious Committee on Peace (USICOP), founded in Washington, DC in 1964, which works in close co-operation with WCRP in promoting peace issues and action among the entire spectrum of religious groups in the USA; and (5) Inter-met (Interfaith Association in Metropolitan Theological Education), founded in Washington, DC in 1969, which is an interfaith (Protestant, Catholic, Jewish) organization seeking to develop a metropolitan-wide system of theological training for continuing education and to effect a better structure of education for congregational ministries.

Specifically-Christian institutions and organizations include: (1) Office for Jewish-Christian Relations of the NCCCUSA, organized in New York City in 1974, which disseminates information and encourages meetings and action programs involving the 2 communities; (2) Ecumenical and Interreligious Affairs Committee of the NCCB, founded in Washington, DC in 1964, which is concerned for relations among Christians and Christianity and secularism, as well as inter-faith dialogue through its separate Secretariat for Catholic-Jewish Relations; (3) Saint-Meinrad School of Theology, in St Meinrad, Indiana, which stresses Jewish studies and is engaged in co-operative ventures with several Jewish agencies; (4) Boston College, which offers courses in Jewish-Christian relations; (5) Institute of Judeo-Christian Studies, a Catholic institute founded at Seton Hall University, New Jersey, in 1951; (6) Centre for Judaic Studies, founded by the Graduate Theological Union in Berkeley, California; (7) Philo Institute, founded at McCormick Theological Seminary in Chicago in 1971, which studies Judaism's influence on early Christianity and publishes *Studia Philonica;* (8) Israel Study Group, attached to the NCCCUSA in New York City; and (9) Christians Concerned about Israel, in Philadelphia.

Jewish institutions and organizations include: (1) Synagogue Council of America, in New York City, which relates mainly to the executives of the NCCCUSA and USCC and has little substantive programming; (2) Jewish Institute of Religion at Hebrew Union College, in Cincinnati, Ohio, which offers doctoral studies in Rabbinic Judaism to Christian ministers; (3) Dropsie University, in Philadelphia, which also provides advanced Jewish studies by Christians; (4) Jewish Theological Seminary, in New York City, which conducts institutes on social studies for Christian and Jewish clergy, seminary students, and academicians; (5) Interreligious Affairs Department of the American Jewish Committee, in New York City, which conducts colloquia, institutes, seminars, and dialogues with Catholic, Protestant, Orthodox, Evangelical, and Black groups in the USA; (6) Anti-Defamation League of B'nai B'rith in New York City, which specializes in studies and programs combatting anti-Semitism, conducts conferences with Christian leaders and publishes materials on Jewish-Christian relations; (7) Jewish Chautauqua Studies of the Union of American Hebrew Congregations, in New York City, which produces films and audio-visual aids and provides Jewish lectures to seminaries and college campuses; and (8) Centre of Interreligious Research, in Chicago, which is a small group of university and seminary staff seeking to organize systematic research on an interreligious basis.

FUTURE TRENDS AND PROSPECTS

Church affiliation is projected to decline to 64.8% by 2025. The nonreligious and atheists will likely jointly top 12% by 2025 while most of the other world religions are expected to grow due to immigration.

Christianity is expected to decline steadily throughout the next fifty years, perhaps dropping below 75% by AD 2050. This decline will primarily be the result of the growth of non-Christian immigrant religions, such as Islam and Buddhism, as well as the steady rise of the nonreligious.

BIBLIOGRAPHY

1988 Higher education directory. M. P. Rodenhouse (ed). Falls Church, VA: Higher Education Publications, 1998. 686p. (Colleges, universities, professional, and technical schools in the USA and US territories. Lists basic data, including administrative and academic officers).

1993–94 Accredited institutions of postsecondary education: a directory of accredited institutions, professionally accredited institutions, and candidates for accreditation. W. A. Wade (ed). Washington, DC: American Council on Education, for the Commission on Recognition of Postsecondary Accreditation, 1994.

A bibliography of Black Methodism. J. G. Melton. Evanston, IL: Institute for the Study of American Religion, 1970. 45p.

A directory of religious bodies in the United States. J. G. Melton. New York: Garland, 1977. 305p. (1,200 Christian denominations and non-Christian groups).

A directory of religious organizations in the United States. J. G. Melton. London: E. J. Brill, 1977. 553p.

A documentary history of religion in America. E. S. Gaustad. Grand Rapids, MI: Eerdmans, 1982–83. 2 vols.

A history of Christianity in the United States and Canada. M. A. Noll. Grand Rapids, MI: Eerdmans, 1992. 592p.

A history of the Catholic Church in the United States. T. T. McAvoy. South Bend, IN: University of Notre Dame Press, 1969. 504p.

A history of the churches in the United States and Canada. R. T. Handy. *Oxford history of the Christian Church.* Oxford, UK: Oxford University Press, 1977. 486p.

A religious history of the American people. S. E. Ahlstrom. New Haven, CT: Yale University Press, 1972. 1,174p. (A classic text on the history of Christianity and other religions in the United States).

A survey of 20th–century revival movements in North America. R. M. Riss. Peabody, MA: Hendrickson, 1988. 202p.

Active faith: how Christians are changing the face of American politics. R. Reed. New York: Free Press, 1996. 304p. (By former executive director of the Christian Coalition).

African–American religion in the twentieth century: varieties of protest and accommodation. H. A. Baer & M. Singer. Knoxville, TN: University of Tennessee Press, 1992. 288p.

Amazing grace: Evangelicalism in Australia, Britain, Canada, and the United States. G. A. Rawlyk & M. A. Noll (eds). Grand Rapids, MI: Baker Books, 1993. 429p.

American Christianity: an historical interpretation with representative documents. H. S. Smith, R. T. Handy & L. A. Loetscher. New York: Scribner, 1960–63. 2 vols.

American evangelicalism: an annotated bibliography. N. A. Magnuson & W. G. Travis. West Cornwall, CT: Locust Hill Press, 1990. 514p.

American mosaic: social patterns of religion in the United States. P. E. Hammond & B. Johnson (eds). New York: Random House, 1970. 354p.

American religious creeds: an essential compendium of more than 450 statements of belief and doctrine. J. G. Melton (ed). 1988; New York: Triumph Books, 1991. 3 vols. (Texts of doctrinal documents of a wide variety of Christian and non–Christian religious groups in the U.S.).

American universities and colleges. 14th ed. New York: Walter de Gruyter, 1992. 2,011p.

America's alternative religions. T. Miller (ed). *SUNY series in religious studies.* Albany, NY: State University of New York Press, 1995. 484p. (Includes some Christian denominations and sects).

An encyclopedia of religious groups in the United States. J. G. Melton. Wilmington, NC: Consortium Books, 1977. 4 vols. (Describes 1,200 denominations/primary religious groups, including non-Christian ones).

Aspects sociologiques du Catholicisme américain: vie urbaine et institutions religieuses. F. Houtart. Paris: Editions Ouvrières, 1957. 340p.

'Black Pentecostal Concept: interpretations and variations,' W. J. Hollenweger, *Concept* (Geneva), 30 (June 1970), 1–68. (Documentation on 33 USA Black pentecostal churches).

Christian Indians and Indian nationalism, 1885–1950: an interpretation in historical and theological perspectives. G. Thomas. Frankfurt: Lang, 1979. 271p.

Christian voluntarism in Britain and North America: a bibliography and critical assessment. W. H. Brackney. *Bibliographies and indexes in religious studies,* no. 35. Westport, CT: Greenwood Press, 1995. 320p.

Christianity in the 21st century: reflections on the challenges ahead. R. Wuthnow. Oxford, UK: Oxford University Press, 1993. 256p.

Church and State in the United States. A. P. Stokes. New York: Harper & Brothers, 1964. 3 vols.

Churches & church membership in the United States: an enumeration by region, state and county. D. W. Johnson, P. R. Picard & B. Quinn (eds). Washington, DC: Glenmary Research Center, 1971. 247p.

Contemporary Catholicism in the United States. P. Gleason (ed). South Bend, IN: University of Notre Dame Press, 1969.

Crime in the United States: uniform crime reports. Washington, DC: US Department of Justice, Federal Bureau of Investigation, Annual. (Includes ecclesiastical crime).

Dictionary of American religious biography. H. W. Bowden. 2nd ed. Westport, CT: Greenwood Press, 1993. 698p.

Dictionary of Christianity in America: a comprehensive resource on the religious impulse that shaped a continent. D. G. Reid et al. (eds). Downer's Grove, IL: InterVarsity Press, 1990. 1335p.

Dictionary of pentecostal and charismatic movements. S. M. Burgess & G. B. McGee (eds). Grand Rapids, MI: Zondervan, 1988. 927p. (A new edition, *The new international dictionary of Pentecostal and Charismatic movements,* Stanley Burgess, ed., will appear in 1999).

Die religionen Nordeurasiens und der amerikanischen Arktis. I. Paulson, Å. Hultkrantz & K. Jettmar. *Die Religionen der Menschheit,* vol. 3. Stuttgart: W. Kohlhammer, 1962. 425p.

Directory of departments and programs of religious studies in North America. D. G. Truemper (ed). Valparaiso, IN: Council of Societies for the Study of Religion, 1994. 545p.

Elements of Southeastern Indian religion. No. 1 of section 10, *North America,* of *Iconography of religions.* C. Hudson. Leiden: E. J. Brill, 1984. 36p.

Encyclopedia of African American religions. L. G. Murphy, J. G. Melton & G. L. Ward (eds). New York: Garland, 1993. 1,002p.

Encyclopedia of American biographies. J. Garraty & J. L. Sternstein. 2nd ed. N.p.: HarperCollins, forthcoming. 1,280p.

Encyclopedia of American religions. J. G. Melton. 5th ed. Detroit, MI: Gale Research, 1996.

Encyclopedia of associations: a guide to more than 22,000 national and international organizations. C. A. Schwartz & R. A. Turner (eds). 29th ed. Detroit, MI: Gale Research, 1995. 3 vols. (Part 2, section 11 provides a list of religious organizations).

Encyclopedia of religions in the United States: 100 religious groups speak for themselves. W. B. Williamson (ed). New York: Crossroad Publishing, 1991. 371p.

Encyclopedia of religious fundamentalism and modernism in America. , 1996.

Encyclopedia of Southern Baptists. Nashville, TN: Broadman, 1958. 2 vols. (Includes all Baptist denominations and movements).

Encyclopedia of the American religious experience. C. H. Lippy & P. W. Williams (eds). New York: Scribner, 1987. 1,888p. in 3 vols.

Encyclopedic handbook of cults in America. J. G. Melton (ed). 2d ed. New York and London: Garland Publishing, 1992. 422p.

Ethnographic bibliography of North America. G. P. Murdock. 3rd ed. New Haven, CT: Human Relations Area Files, 1960. 393p.

Ethnographic bibliography of North America, 4th edition. Supplement 1973–1987. M. M. Martin & T. J. O'Leary. New Haven, CT: Human Relations Area Files Press, 1990. 3 vols. (Previously published as *Ethnographic bibliography of North America.* G. P. Murdock, 1960, 1975.).

Guide to schools and departments of religion and seminaries in the United States and Canada: degree programs in religious studies. New York: Macmillan, 1987. 623p.

Handbook of American Orthodoxy, 1972. New York: Forward Movement Publications, 1972. 191p.

Handbook of denominations in America. F. S. Mead & S. S. Hill. 10th ed. Nashville, TN: Abingdon, 1995. 352p.

Handbook of the National Council of the Churches of Christ in the USA. New York: NCCCUSA, 1967, 1968, 1969.

Harvard encyclopedia of American ethnic groups. S. Thernstrom (ed). Cambridge, MA: Harvard University Press, 1980.

Historical atlas of religion in America. E. S. Gaustad. New York: Harper & Row, 1962.

Hopi Indian altar iconography. No. 5 of section 10, *North America,* of *Iconography of religions.* A. W. Geertz. Leiden: E. J. Brill, 1987. 39p.

Indians of Northeastern North America. No. 7 of section 10, *North America,* of *Iconography of religions.* A. W. Geertz. Leiden: E. J. Brill, 1986. 50p.

Islam in North America: a sourcebook. M. A. Köszegi & J. G. Melton (eds). New York: Garland, 1992. 392p.

Mission handbook: North American Protestant ministries overseas. E. R. Dayton (ed). Monrovia, CA: MARC, 1973. 645p. (Triennial).

Modern American religion. M. E. Marty. Chicago: University of Chicago Press, 1986–1996. 3 vols.

Money matters: personal giving in American churches. D. R. Hoge et al. Louisville, KY: Westminster John Knox Press, 1996. 260p.

Muslims in America. Y. Y. Haddad (ed). Oxford, UK: Oxford University Press, 1991. 272p. (Includes both Canada and the U.S.A.).

Native American religions: a geographical survey. J. J. Collins. Lewiston, NY: E. Mellen Press, 1991. 411p.

Native and Christian: indigenous voices on religious identity in the United States and Canada. J. Treat (ed). New York: Routledge, 1996. 256p.

New religious movements in the United States and Canada: a critical assessment and annotated bibliography. D. Choquette. *Bibliographies and indexes in religious studies,* 5. Westport, CT: Greenwood, 1985. 235p.

'New religious movements in the USA,' *Social compass* (Louvain), 21, 3 (1974), 223–360. (10 essays).

Official Catholic directory. New York: P. J. Kennedy & Sons, 1978. 1,608p. (Annual; first issue 1817; 63 categories of current statistics).

Official guide to Catholic educational institutions and religious communities in the US, 1972–73. D. B. Gray (ed). Washington, DC: US Catholic Conference, 1972.

'Old and new religions among North American Indians: missiological impressions and reflections,' H. W. Turner, *Missiology* (South Pasadena, CA), 1, 2 (1973), 47–66.

One nation under God: religion in contemporary American society. B. A. Kosmin & S. P. Lachman. New York: Harmony Books, 1993. 312p.

Parishes and clergy of the Orthodox and other Eastern Churches in North and South America, together with the parishes and clergy of the Polish National Catholic Church, 1970–71. New York: Episcopal Church in the USA, 1971. 208p. (Illustrated).

Popular religion: inspirational books in America. L. Schneider & S. M. Dornbusch. Chicago: University of Chicago Press, 1958. 186p.

Prairie and plains Indians. No. 2 of section 10, *North America,* of *Iconography of religions.* Å. Hultkrantz. Leiden: E. J. Brill, 1973. 46p.

Profiles in belief: the religious bodies of the United States and Canada. A. C. Piepkorn. New York: Harper & Row, 1977–79. 4 vols in 3.

Pueblo cultures. No. 4 of section 10, *North America,* of *Iconography of religions.* B. Wright. Leiden: E. J. Brill, 1986. 29p.

Religion and American culture. G. M. Marsden. Chicago: Harcourt Brace Jovanovich, 1990. 320p.

Religion, culture, and values: a cross–cultural analysis of motivational factors in native Irish and American Irish Catholicism. B. F. Biever. *The Irish–Americans.* New York: Arno Press, 1976. 869p.

Religion in America: an historical account of the development of American religious life. W. S. Hudson. 3d ed. 1965; New York: Charles Scribner's Sons, 1981. 502p.

Religion in America: the Gallup Opinion Index, 1977–78. Report No. 145. Princeton, NJ: Gallup International, 1977. 119p. (Also 1975, 1973, 1971 and earlier editions, then up to 1998).

Religion in native North America. C. Vecsey (ed). Moscow, ID: University of Idaho Press, 1990. 208p.

Religion in the United States: a concise introduction to 53 denominations and groups. B. Y. Landis. New York: Barnes & Noble, 1965. 120p.

'Religion reported by the civilian population of the United States: March 1957', US Bureau of the Census, Current population reports, 2 February 1958, Series p-20, No. 79. (A sample survey of 100,000 persons).

Religions of the circumpolar north. R. Minion. *BINS bibliographic series*, no. 15. Edmonton, Alberta: University of Alberta, Boreal Institute for Northern Studies, 1985. 92p.

Religious and spiritual groups in modern America. R. S. Ellwood Jr. Englewood Cliffs, NJ: Prentice-Hall, 1973. 334p. (Contemporary sects and cults).

Religious leaders of America: a biographical guide to founders and leaders of religious bodies, churches, and spiritual groups in North America. J. G. Melton. Detroit, MI: Gale Research, 1991. 625p.

Religious movements in contemporary America. I. I. Zaretsky & M. P. Leone (eds). Princeton, NJ: Princeton University Press, 1974. 837p. (On marginal religious movements. Bibliography of 1,100 items).

Researching modern evangelicalism: a guide to the holdings of the Billy Graham Center, with information on other collections. R. D. Shuster, J. Stambaugh & F. Weiner. Westport, CT: Greenwood Press, 1990. 353p.

Revive us again: the reawakening of American fundamentalism. J. A. Carpenter. New York: Oxford University Press, 1997. 335p.

Seasons of refreshing: evangelism and revivals in America. K. J. Hardman. Grand Rapids, MI: Baker, 1994. 304p.

Songs of life: an introduction to Navajo religious culture. No. 3 of section 10, *North America*, of *Iconography of religions*. S. D. Gill. Leiden: E. J. Brill, 1979. 31p.

South Asian religions in the Americas: an annotated bibliography of immigrant religious traditions. J. Y. Fenton. *Bibliographies and indexes in religious studies*. Westport, CT: Greenwood.

The American Holiness movement: a bibliographic introduction. D. W. Dayton. Wilmore, KY: B. L. Fisher Library (Asbury Theological Seminary), 1971.

The American Pentecostal movement: a bibliographical essay. D. W. Faupel. Wilmore, KY: B. L. Fisher Library (Asbury Theological Seminary), 1972. 56p.

The Black church in the African American experience. C. E. Lincoln & L. H. Mamiya. Durham, NC: Duke University Press, 1990. 519p.

The Black Muslims in America. C. E. Lincoln. Boston: Beacon Press, 1961. 276p.

The churching of America, 1776–1990: winners and losers in our religious economy. R. Finke & R. Stark. New Brunswick, NJ: Rutgers University Press, 1992. 344p.

The churching of America 1776–1990: winners and losers in our religious economy. R. Finke & R. Stark. New Brunswick, NJ: Rutgers University Press, 1992. 342p.

The democratization of American Christianity. N. O. Hatch. New Haven, CT: Yale University Press, 1989. 326p.

The encyclopedia of native American religion: an introduction. A. Hirschfelder & P. Molin (eds). New York and Oxford, UK: Facts on File, 1992. 379p.

The history and philosophy of the metaphysical movements in America. J. S. Judah. Philadelphia: Westminster Press, 1967. 317p.

'The history of the 'Black Muslim' movement in America,' I. Crichton, *Urban mission*, 1 (May 1984), 5–15.

The Holiness Pentecostal movement in the United States. H. V. Synan. Rev. ed. Grand Rapids, MI: Eerdmans, 1997. 239p.

The Howard University bibliography of African and Afro–American religious studies: with locations in American libraries. E. L. Williams & C. F. Brown. Wilmington, DE, 1977. 547p.

The Jews in America: four centuries of an uneasy encounter: a history. A. Hertzberg. New York: Simon and Schuster, 1989. 428p.

The Latter–day Saints: the Mormons yesterday and today. R. Mullen. Garden City, NY: Doubleday, 1966. 316p.

The Native American Christian community: a directory of Indian, Aleut and Eskimo churches. R. P. Beaver. Monrovia, CA: MARC, 1979. 395p.

The Negro Church in America. E. F. Frazier. New York: Schocken Books, 1964. 92p.

The New Age movement in American culture. R. Kyle. Lanham, MD: University Press of America, 1995. 289p.

The people's religion: American faith in the 90's. G. Gallup Jr. & J. Castelli. New York: Macmillan; London: Collier Macmillan, 1989. 298p.

The Peyote religion. J. S. Slotkin. Glencoe, IL: Free Press, 1956.

The Protestant Churches of America. J. A. Hardon. New York: Doubleday, 1969. 439p.

The religious dimension in Hispanic Los Angeles: a Protestant case study. C. L. Holland. South Pasadena, CA: William Carey Library, 1974. 541p. (Churches among 3.5 million Spanish-speaking Mexican Americans in California).

The restructuring of American religion: society and faith since World War II. R. Wuthnow. *Studies in church and state*. Princeton, NJ: Princeton University Press, 1988. 388p.

The small sects in America. E. T. Clark. New York: Abingdon Press, 1937, 1949. 256p. (Study of 300 sects).

The state of the churches in the U.S.A. and Canada, 1985, as shown in their own official yearbooks and other reports: a study resource. Sun City, AZ: Ecumenism Research Agency, 1985. 15 microfilm reels. (Listing of USA denominational yearbooks, minutes, and reports).

Twentieth–century evangelicalism: a guide to the sources. E. L. Blumhofer & J. A. Carpenter. New York: Garland, 1990. 384p.

Twentieth–century shapers of American popular religion. C. H. Lippy (ed). New York: Greenwood Press, 1989. 519p.

Two worlds of Judaism: the Israeli and American experiences. C. S. Liebman & S. M. Cohen. New Haven, CT: Yale University Press, 1990. 183p.

Why Conservative churches are growing: a study in sociology of religion. D. M. Kelley. 2nd ed. New York: Harper & Row, 1972. 184p.

World religions in America: an introduction. J. Neusner (ed). Louisville, KY: Westminster John Knox Press, 1994. 318p.

Yearbook of American and Canadian churches, 1998. K. B. Bedell (ed). Nashville, TN: Abingdon Press, for the Communication Division of the National Council of Churches of Christ in the U.S.A., 1998. 300p. (Annual publication. 1998 edition is the 66th issue).

Country Table 2. **Organized churches and denominations in the United States of America.**

Official name (bold type = church with over 10% of all affiliated) 1	*Begun* 2	*Type* 3	*Counc* 4	*Congs* 5	*Adults* 6	*Affiliated 1970* 7	*Affiliated 1995* 8	*G%* 9	*Names, notes, and other statistics* (see Codebook, Part 3) 10
Abbott Loop Fell of Community Chs	1959	I-3fW	.....	54	15,000	2,000	25,000	10.63	HQ Anchorage. Abroad: Mexico, Canada, Philippines, Ireland, UK, Swaziland.
Advent Christian Church	1854	P-Adv	xF...	329	19,099	40,000	27,700	-1.46	*General Conf of America*. 31 Confs. 493n,2j,2s(70),360t(24481),W=68%.
African Methodist Episcopal Church	1787	I-Met	VW..b	10,789	2,050,000	1,529,000	3,300,000	3.13	*AMEC*. Black. 13 Districts in USA. 20 bps. Many new megachurches. Africa, West Indies. 7089n.
African Methodist Episcopal Zion Ch	1796	I-Met	VW..b	3,000	942,857	1,307,000	1,142,016	-0.54	*AMEZC*. Black. 10 bishops in Americas, Europe, 2 in Africa. 5500n,1j,6r.
African Orthodox Church	1919	I-ARo	x...J	17	2,000	6,000	5,100	-0.65	*AOC*. Schism ex PECUSA. West Indian Blacks. HQ New York. Many overseas fields. 50n.
African Union First Colored MP Ch	1866	I-Met	.....	30	1,500	5,000	2,000	-3.60	*MP=Methodist Protestant*. Black members. Schism ex Methodist Episcopal Ch. 48n.
Albanian Orth Archdiocese in America	1908	O-Alb	M.o..	13	20,000	62,000	27,000	-3.27	Albanian refugees. Linked to Orthodox Ch in America. 23n,13t(1375),W=66%.
Albanian Orth Diocese of America	1950	O-Alb	C.O..	2	1,500	5,150	1,873	-3.97	Albanian refugees. Rapid growth through mixed marriages. 4n,W=57%,25Yy.
Allegheny Wesleyan Meth Connection	1843	P-Hol	.....	120	2,037	9,089	2,526	-4.99	Original Wesleyan conference in area. Mostly in eastern USA. 150n,W=68%.
Alliance for Renewal Churches	1980	I-3cW	.....	10	1,000	–	1,500	6.67	*ARC*. 1979 called Crossroads. Also in Britain.
Alliance of Christian Churches	1986	I-3cW	.....	35	1,600	–	2,000	11.11	*ACC*. Until 1996, Advance Christian Ministries. Homosexual-affirming Evangelicals.
Amana Church Society	1842	m-Gno	.....	1	400	1,500	600	-3.60	1714, Community of True Inspiration (Germany), Amana (Faithfulness), Iowa. One single church.
American Anglican Catholic Church	c1970	I-3cW	.....	30	3,000	–	4,000	39.34	*AACC*. Charismatics ex Anglican Communion.
American Association of Lutheran Chs	1987	I-Lut	.....	78	10,000	–	15,150	12.50	*AALC*. Schism ex ALCA holding infallibility of Bible. HQ Minneapolis. Churches across USA.
American Baptist Association	1905	I-Bap	xT...	1,849	270,000	869,000	900,000	0.14	*ABA. Landmarkers*. Regular Baptists. Mainly south. 3368n,2s,3336t(450000). (1993) 1760n.
American Baptist Chs in the USA	1639	P-Bap	TW..W	5,801	1,504,573	2,100,000	2,280,000	0.33	Formerly American Baptist Convention. 8222n,9s(1090),W=34%,3456Y.
American Carpatho-Russian OGC Ch	1891	O-Ukr	C.O..	69	14,610	106,900	25,000	-5.65	*OGC=Orthodox Greek Cath*. Former Uniates from USSR. 67n,1s(19),56t(5098).
American Cath Ch (Syro-Antiochian)	1915	I-CCa	.....	6	1,190	1,500	1,750	0.62	*Assyrian Jacobite Apost Ch*. Monophysite. Orders from Syrian P Antioch. 9n,1t(37).
American Catholic Ch, AD New York	1927	I-ARo	.....	18	2,840	4,369	3,600	-0.77	Black, Schism ex AOC. Old Catholic; Jacobite orders through Vilatte. 16t(450).
American Episcopal Church	1968	I-ReA	.....	10	500	1,000	800	-0.89	Schism ex PECUSA. Eastern and southern USA. Whites. 7n,1s(2),W=70%.
American Ev Christian Churches	1944	I-Eva	.....	123	19,000	20,000	29,700	1.59	*AECC. Community Churches. American Bible Chs*. HQ Chicago. (1970) 164n, (1994) 200n.197n
American Evangelistic Association	1954	I-3pW	.....	2,000	200,000	25,000	500,000	12.73	*AEA*. Latter Rain. Ministers 2,057 (1968), and 1,000 abroad. HQ Lake City, Florida.
American Holy Orth Cath Apost E Ch	1932	I-ARo	.....	20	2,000	5,000	3,000	-2.02	*E=Eastern*. Schism ex AOC (Black). Greek rite. Attempt to unite all Orthodox. 35n.
American Orthodox Catholic Church	1961	I-ReO	.v...	3	700	2,000	1,500	-1.14	*AOCC*. Rival groups, White (Russian) and Black. Continual mergers, fresh schism.
American Orth Cath Ch (AD N&S Am)	1964	I-ReO	xv...	34	9,100	14,000	13,000	-0.30	Ex Ukrainian Orth Ch of USA. 8 bishops. US Virgin Islands France, Zaire, Nigeria.
American Rescue Workers	1896	I-Non	.....	20	2,600	10,000	4,330	-3.29	Home missionary society, military organization. HQ Philadelphia. 53n,36t(9226).
Anchor Bay Evangelistic Association	1940	I-3pW	.....	100	6,000	1,000	10,000	9.65	Independent pentecostals.
Anglican Cath Ch in North America	1977	I-ReA	x....	160	3,000	–	8,000	5.56	*ACC*, previously *ACNA*. Schism ex ECUSA protesting ordination of women. 4 Dioceses.Declining
Anglican Orth Ch of North America	1963	I-ReA	xT...	45	4,500	4,000	6,920	2.22	Split ex PECUSA in NCarolina. Anglican Orthodox Communion in 10 nations. 19n,35t.
Antioch Network of Chs & Ministries	1980	I-3aW	.....	110	27,000	–	40,000	6.67	*ACM*. 45n,10 apostles. Abroad: 62 networks in 42 countries, 4100 chs.
Antiochian Orth Christian AD NAm	c1920	O-Ara	CWO.W	190	180,000	140,000	350,000	3.73	Formerly Syrian Antiochian Orth AD NY & NA. In Greek P Antioch. 95% Arab.1975 merger.110n.
Apostolic Assemblies of Christ Int	1970	I-3aO	.....	200	21,800	–	30,000	51.04	*AACI*. Oneness pentecostals.
Apostolic Assembly of the Faith in JC	1911	I-3oL	.....	475	40,000	50,000	75,000	1.64	*Asamblea Apostólica de la Fe en CJ*. M=Iglesia AFCJ(Mexico). In 6 states. Mission to Mexico.
Apostolic Brethren	1960	I-3oW	.....	30	2,700	2,000	6,000	4.49	White Oneness Pentecostals. 3 overseas churches.
Apostolic Christian Chs International	1845	I-3oW	.....	10	3,124	3,000	5,000	2.06	*ACCI*. White Oneness Pentecostals. Churches in 15 countries: Bermuda, Jamaica, Grenada, etc
Apostolic Christian Ch (Nazarean)	1907	I-Hol	x....	48	2,821	4,000	3,516	-0.51	Split ex ACCA protesting use of German. In IL, OH, 17 nations. 147n,39t(1575).
Apostolic Christian Ch of America	1847	P-Hol	x....	79	11,189	15,000	19,509	1.06	*ACCA*. Swiss origin. Pacifist (a peace church), holiness emphasis. 273n,77t(8950).
Ap Commission of Christ Ch Ministries	1989	I-3aA	.....	200	25,000	–	58,000	16.67	*ACCCM*. Begun in Nigeria 1976 by F=A. Ofili, Christ Chosen Ch of God of Nigeria.
Apostolic Episcopal Church	1925	I-ARo	x....	25	1,200	3,000	3,500	0.62	*Holy Eastern Cath & Apostolic Orth Ch*. Ex PECUSA. Chaldean rite. In 5 nations.
Apostolic Faith Church	1923	I-3oW	.....	10	1,000	1,000	2,000	2.81	*Jesus Coming Soon Church*. Holiness Pentecostals (3-stage). 4n,W=50%,120Y.
Apostolic Faith Mission	1900	P-Pe3	x....	45	4,100	7,000	5,940	-0.65	*AFM Portland*, Oregon. 65% White, 35% Black. 75n,120Y. Abroad: 20,000 members,1,000 chs.
Apostolic Faith Mission Ch of God	1906	I-3pB	.....	53	6,000	13,000	14,000	0.30	HQ Cantonment, Florida.
Apostolic Lutheran Ch of America	1872	P-Lut	xv...	53	3,005	16,000	7,812	-2.83	*ALCA. Church of Laestadius*. Finnish-speaking; in Midwest. White. In 4 nations. 65n.
Apos Ministers Conf of Philadelphia	1970	I-3aO	.....	300	80,000	20,000	100,000	6.65	*AMCP*. Black Oneness pentecostals.
Apostolic Overcoming Holy Ch of God	1916	I-3oO	.....	177	12,479	75,000	31,200	-3.45	Black pentecostals. Ex Methodists. Foot-washing, liturgical dance. 350n,1j.
Armenian Apostolic Ch of America	1933	O-Arm	Sw.N.	30	140,000	150,000	180,000	0.73	*Gregorians*. 1933 split ex Echmiadzin; 1957, under C Cilicia. 28nx,500Yy.
Armenian Church of North America	1889	O-Arm	Ewc.W	68	270,000	372,000	450,000	0.76	*D California, D NAmerica*. Under C Echmiadzin. 60% all US Armenians. 71n,90t(8000).
Armenian Ev Spiritual Brethren	c1925	I-CBr	x....	6	1,500	2,000	3,000	1.64	Schism ex Armenian Evangelical Union. Plymouth Brethren and Holiness doctrines.
Armenian Ev Union of Churches	c1920	P-Con	Rw...	50	17,000	20,000	35,000	2.26	Eastern US, California. Armenian refugees after 1915; also in Middle East.
Ascension Fellowships International	1982	I-3aW	.....	16	1,500	–	2,200	7.69	*AFI*. White. Related to Apostolic Ch (Wales). 500 members abroad in 2 chs (Canada, Mexico).
Assemblies of God	1906	P-Pe2	ZF.XE	11,149	1,280,760	1,500,000	2,161,610	1.47	*General Conference*. 95% White. 12037n,1j,4r,13s9200t(1078332),20864Y.
Assemblies of God (Spanish)	c1915	I-3pL	.....	500	90,000	70,000	200,000	4.29	*Asambleas de Dios*. Spanish-speaking pentecostals (California Mexicans, et al).
Assemblies of God Fellowship Int	1911	I-3pW	.....	700	550,000	500,000	700,000	1.35	*AGFI*. Scandinavian origins; claims all AoG churches worldwide. 2000n.
Assemblies of the Lord Jesus Christ	1952	I-3oW	.....	500	40,000	60,000	130,000	3.14	Mainly in MS, GA, TN. 27 Districts; abroad, 216 chs, 7,000 members in Chile, 4 others. 300n.
Assembly Hall Churches	1954	I-3nC	x....	229	19,635	4,000	27,100	7.95	*The Local Ch. Little Flock*. Begun China 1922 by Watchman Nee. 60% White, 33% Chinese.
Assembly of Christian Churches	1939	I-3pL	x....	120	6,000	10,000	20,000	2.81	*Asamblea de Igl Cristianas*. Split ex LACCC. Mostly Puerto Ricans. HQ Brooklyn (NY).
Associate Reformed Presbyterian Ch	1782	P-Ref	F....	187	32,787	34,625	37,988	0.37	*ARPC, Gen Synod. Covenanters*. SE USA. 142n,1s,141t(17109),W=50%,553Yy.
Associated Brotherhood of Christians	1915	I-3oW	x....	110	4,000	6,000	9,000	1.64	Jesus Only schism ex Assemblies of God. White Oneness pacifists. HQ Hot Springs (AR).
Associated Churches of God	1974	I-BrI	.....	50	5,500	–	12,000	4.76	Schism ex Worldwide Ch of God rejecting multiple tithing. HQ Washington DC. 40n.
Associated Gospel Churches	1939	I-Met	.t..t	40	2,000	3,000	5,000	2.06	Formerly ABFA, ex Meth Prot Ch. Also agency serving 3 million fundamentalists.
Association of American Lutheran Chs	1987	I-3cW	.....	70	10,000	–	20,000	12.50	*AALC*. Split ex ELCA, allowing charismatic gifts. Missions in Africa, Asia, Europe.
Association of Ev Congs & Ministries	1964	I-3cW	.....	50	20,000	10,000	25,000	3.73	*AECM*. Ex Lutheran Charismatics. Church planting. Abroad: 50 chs. 3,000 members.
Association of Ev Gospel Assemblies	1976	I-3fW	.....	90	7,000	–	10,000	5.26	*AEGA*. White Charismatics, Full Gospel theology. Africa: 195,000 members in 75 churches.
Association of Ev Lutheran Chs	1976	I-Lut	Lv...	320	120,000	–	180,000	5.26	*AELC*. Liberal schism ex LCMS (Missouri). 5 Regional Synods. ELIM,1s. HQ St Louis.
Association of Faith Chs & Ministries	1978	I-3wW	.....	800	126,868	–	145,000	5.88	*AFCM, Word Churches*. HQ Tulsa, OK. Abroad: 10,510 members, 80 churches.
Assoc of Free Lutheran Congs	1897	I-Lut	.....	225	20,945	10,000	28,469	4.27	Lutheran Free Ch rejecting 1963 ALC merger. Norwegian origin. In 26 US states. 78n,1p(20),1s.
Assoc of Independent Methodists	c1965	I-Met	.....	40	4,000	5,000	7,000	1.35	Conservative schism ex United Methodist Church. In Alabama, Mississippi, Tennessee.
Assoc of Intern Gospel Assemblies	1962	I-3fW	.....	458	210,000	250,000	260,000	0.16	*AIGA*. F=Granville Rayl. HQ Desoto. Abroad: 1,500 chs, 5,000 ministers in 33 countries.

Continued opposite

Country Table 2–continued

Official name (bold type = church with over 10% of affiliated) 1	*Begun* 2	*Type* 3	*Counc* 4	*Congs* 5	*Adults* 6	*Affiliated 1970* 7	*Affiliated 1995* 8	*G%* 9	*Names, notes, and other statistics* (see Codebook, Part 3) 10
Association of Vineyard Churches	1978	I-3cW	.....	505	115,000	–	165,000	5.88	Integrated Charismatics. M=VMI. 29% of new churches are Adopts, 71% Plants.
Assyrian Ch of the East (P Tehran)	1907	O-Nes	YW...	30	20,000	10,000	35,000	5.14	*Holy Apostolic & Cath Ch of the East.* From Iran, Iraq, Lebanon. World HQ: IL. 14 bps,40n.
Autocephalous Greek Orthodox Ch	c1924	I-OCd	c....	5	1,500	2,000	2,500	0.90	Split ex GOC rejecting New (Gregorian) Calendar. Parishes: Newark, Memphis (TN).
Azuza Fellowship		I-3cD	.....	100	60,000	60,000	90,000	0.05	Black Charismatics.
Baptist Bible Fellowship International	1950	I-Bap	x....	3,500	900,000	1,200,000	1,500,000	0.90	*BBFI.* Ex SBC et alia. 1.7 million by 1976. Whites. In 48 countries. 1s.
Baptist General Conference	1852	P-Bap	TF..E	849	132,994	130,000	167,874	1.03	Early Swedes, most now non-Swedish. 1032n,1p,1s,681t(119192),W=80%,4182Y.
Baptist Missionary Assoc of America	1950	I-Bap	x....	1,374	228,287	230,000	289,969	0.93	NA Bapt Assoc to 1968. Regular Baptist. 3000n,5p,3s,1408t(107406),W=60%,9431Y.
Beachy Amish Mennonite Church	1927	I-Men	G....	91	6,525	8,000	8,243	0.12	Ex Old Order Amish MC. Amish Mennonite Aid. 103n (& 35 bishops, 25 deacons).
Berean Fundamental Churches	1932	I-Fun	.....	64	5,389	4,500	8,000	2.33	Conservative theology. Most midwest, Colorado. HQ Nebraska. 45n,50t(4466).
Bethel Baptist Assembly	1934	I-Bap	.....	30	5,000	6,000	8,000	1.16	*Bethel Ministerial Association.* Mainly Indiana (begun Evansville). 105n,25t(5500).
Bethesda Missionary Temple	1934	I-Non	.....	10	3,000	3,000	4,000	1.16	Independent churches. National radio ministry. 8n,W=83%,300Y,425z.
Bible Fellowship Churches	1858	I-Eva	.....	57	2,000	1,000	3,000	4.49	From Mennonites in Canada and Pennsylvania.
Bible Methodist Church	1929	I-Hol	.....	20	1,100	2,000	2,200	0.38	*Bible Methodist Connection of Tennessee.* HQ Knoxville. 37n,5p,W=60%,50Yy.
Bible Presbyterian Church	1938	I-Ref	xT..T	70	5,100	8,000	8,200	0.10	Fundamentalist schism ex Orthodox Presbyterian Ch. ICCC base. HQ: NJ. In 11 countries.
Bible Way Chs of Our Lord JC WW	1951	I-3oO	x...J	1,000	412,000	42,000	600,600	11.23	*WW=World Wide.* Black Oneness pentecostals. Ex COLJCAF. 360n,4p,W=95%,1000Y.
Bible Way Association	1958	I-3fL	.....	150	12,650	10,000	17,000	2.15	*BWA.* Abroad: 6,000 members, 300 churches in Mexico, Guatemala, Central America.
Brazil for Christ Pentecostal Ch	c1970	I-3pY	.....	10	2,000	–	3,000	37.75	*Igreja Ev Pentecostal 'O Brasil para Cristo'.* Brazilians, from Brazil.
Brethren Church	1883	P-Dun	x....	100	13,322	9,000	16,000	2.33	Dunkers or Tunkers.
Brethren Church (Ashland, Ohio)	1881	P-Dun	xF..E	124	13,060	35,000	18,700	-2.48	Ex CoBrethren; 1939, NFBC (Grace) secedes. 130n,1s,119t(12377),W=58%.
Brethren in Christ Church	1778	P-Men	GF..E	184	16,697	19,000	40,642	3.09	Known as River Brethren until 1863. In Ohio, PA, WV, MD. 325n,155t(17729).
Bulgarian Eastern Orthodox Church	1907	O-Bul	MwO..	9	20,000	86,000	40,000	-3.02	*D N&S America & Australia.* Under P Sofia. Dioceses: New York, Akron, Detroit. 13nx.
Byelorussian Autocephalic Orth Ch	1948	O-Bye	x....	5	8,000	20,000	15,000	-1.14	Refugees from White Russian church begun in AD 1291. 4 bishops (1 in Canada).
Byzantine Catholic Church	1984	I-Byz	.....	30	3,000	–	6,000	9.09	Independent Catholics. Membership abroad: 250,000 in Europe, Africa, Latin America.
Calvary Chapels International	1965	I-3cW	.....	750	275,000	5,000	400,000	19.16	Major successor to the Jesus Movement. HQ Santa Ana, CA. 400 Romanian members.
Calvary Grace Churches of Faith	1954	I-Non	.....	70	8,000	20,000	15,000	-1.14	Independent White group, one of many similar loosely-structured mail-order denominations.120n.
Calvary Pentecostal Church	1931	P-Pe2	.....	25	9,000	15,000	19,000	0.95	White. Begun in Olympia (WA) by group of ministers. Missions in Brazil, India.
Calvary Temple	1950	I-3oW	.....	3,000	200,000	10,000	300,000	14.57	Mostly White Charismatics. 1971, assisted by M=CMI (Calvary Ministries International).
Cathedral of Tomorrow	1952	I-3pW	.....	3	5,000	20,000	10,000	-2.73	In Akron. On 534 TV stations to 20 million in 15 countries. Staff 150. Pentecostal.
Catholic Apostolic Church	1851	I-3aX	x....	2	600	2,500	1,000	-3.60	*Irvingites,* from UK. Millenarian, 12-fold apostleship. No clergy alive now, so rapid decline.
Catholic Church in the USA:	1526	R-LEr	B...R	21,873	38,950,100	48,305,318	56,715,013	0.64	*Below.* State, Region. Totals: 31821n 16775x 25787m 91875w 1090535Yy
M Anchorage	1966	R-Lat	Bs	23	18,300	30,588	26,612	-0.56	AK XII 17n 12x 15m 55w 771Yy
D Fairbanks	1894	R-Lat	Psj	41	11,900	13,241	17,356	1.09	AK XII 6n 27x 31m 22w 509Yy
D Juneau	1951	R-Lat	Bs	13	3,400	3,707	5,009	1.21	AK XII 6n 4x 4m 7w 176Yy
M Atlanta	1956	R-Lat	Bs	72	136,000	59,452	197,386	4.92	GA IV. M=SSJ. 101n 115x 127m 138w 4371Yy
D Charleston	1820	R-Lat	Bs	121	67,000	46,752	97,501	2.98	SC IV 90n 49x 71m 176w 2752Yy
D Charlotte	1971	R-Lat	Bs	89	66,000	–	95,606	4.17	NC IV 63n 67x 71m 156w 3644Yy
D Raleigh	1924	R-Lat	Bs	72	66,000	35,220	95,605	4.08	NC IV 70n 47x 57m 90w 2386Yy
D Savannah	1850	R-Lat	Bs	80	45,500	35,850	66,295	2.49	GA IV 60n 28x 46m 158w 1923Yy
M Baltimore	1789	R-Lat	Bs	164	318,500	416,622	461,739	0.41	MD IV 268n 229x 324m 1421w 9703Yy
D Arlington	1974	R-Lat	Bs	60	186,700	–	270,650	4.76	VA IV 129n 78x 101m 225w 6631Yy
D Richmond	1820	R-Lat	Bs	142	118,600	249,453	172,311	-1.47	VA IV 161n 39x 50m 325w 3397Yy
D Wheeling-Charleston	1850	R-Lat	Bs	178	74,400	96,621	107,899	0.44	WV IV 125n 69x 75m 321w 2039Yy
D Wilmington	1868	R-Lat	Bs	76	106,900	115,036	155,003	1.20	DE IV 125n 86x 121m 315w 3393Yy
M Boston	1808	R-Lat	Bs	415	1,375,200	2,018,034	1,993,126	-0.05	MA I 955n 740x 1029m 3384w 30345Yy
D Burlington	1853	R-Lat	Bs	97	100,400	144,239	145,532	0.04	VT I 145n 51x 73m 237w 1427Yy
D Fall River	1904	R-Lat	Bs	112	251,800	305,000	365,000	0.72	MA I. M=OFMCap. 183n 125x 153m 474w 5944Yy
D Manchester	1884	R-Lat	Bs	131	219,400	263,233	318,003	0.76	NH I 247n 115x 172m 873w 6380Yy
D Portland	1853	R-Lat	Bs	143	176,600	271,428	256,036	-0.23	ME I. M=OSB. 187n 64x 93m 585w 4431Yy
D Springfield in Massachusetts	1870	R-Lat	Bs	187	220,700	383,052	319,872	-0.72	MA I 217n 76x 101m 715w 5114Yy
D Worcester	1950	R-Lat	Bs	129	233,200	343,585	338,000	-0.07	MA I 279n 111x 213m 580w 5402Yy
M Chicago	1843	R-Lat	Bs	389	1,591,000	2,496,300	2,306,000	-0.32	IL VII 1008n 898x 1442m 3947w 40789Yy
D Belleville	1887	R-Lat	Bs	143	84,900	115,250	123,079	0.26	IL VII 145n 38x 50m 250w 2248Yy
D Joliet in Illinois	1948	R-Lat	Bs	147	329,500	322,000	477,624	1.59	IL VII 192n 124x 219m 836w 10529Yy
D Peoria	1875	R-Lat	Bs	172	160,300	214,968	232,457	0.31	IL VII 222n 61x 68m 414w 3776Yy
D Rockford	1908	R-Lat	Bs	154	164,100	205,609	237,947	0.59	IL VII 157n 61x 76m 450w 5768Yy
D Springfield in Illinois	1853	R-Lat	Bs	170	124,000	182,674	179,731	-0.06	IL VII 143n 72x 102m 751w 2880Yy
M Cincinnati	1821	R-Lat	Bs	242	375,400	529,220	544,100	0.11	OH VI 371n 282x 463m 1544w 10913Yy
D Cleveland	1847	R-Lat	Bs	240	562,700	879,771	815,608	-0.30	OH VI 539n 163x 254m 1803w 13680Yy
D Columbus	1868	R-Lat	Bs	119	149,500	178,000	216,742	0.79	OH VI 182n 78x 88m 433w 4900Yy
D Steubenville	1944	R-Lat	Bs	82	32,100	55,600	46,476	-0.71	OH VI 91n 16x 21m 90w 1158Yy
D Toledo	1910	R-Lat	Bs	163	223,800	328,977	324,393	-0.06	OH VI 204n 57x 62m 914w 6024Yy
D Youngstown	1943	R-Lat	Bs	185	190,700	312,708	276,395	-0.49	OH VI 187n 33x 60m 305w 4816Yy
M Denver	1887	R-Lat	Bs	111	229,000	298,784	332,000	0.42	CO VIII 164n 139x 212m 531w 9985Yy
D Cheyenne	1887	R-Lat	Bs	70	32,800	45,000	47,600	0.22	WY VIII 43n 9x 12m 48w 1335Yy
D Colorado Springs	1983	R-Lat	Bs	29	45,900	–	66,482	8.33	CO VIII 35n 17x 27m 165w 1575Yy
D Pueblo	1941	R-Lat	Bs	56	66,700	105,197	96,602	-0.34	CO VIII 74n 41x 49m 111w 2417Yy
M Detroit	1833	R-Lat	Bs	316	1,021,200	1,619,081	1,480,116	-0.36	MI VI. M=SSE. 545n 242x 345m 1942w 20269Yy
D Gaylord	1970	R-Lat	Bs	82	58,800	66,000	85,349	1.03	MI VI 69n 17x 20m 91w 1702Yy
D Grand Rapids	1882	R-Lat	Bs	102	102,500	147,672	148,584	0.02	MI VI 122n 28x 31m 338w 2992Yy
D Kalamazoo	1970	R-Lat	Bs	60	71,100	83,416	103,030	0.85	MI VI 56n 21x 26m 269w 1751Yy
D Lansing	1937	R-Lat	Bs	93	154,000	184,309	223,170	0.77	MI VI 142n 39x 48m 435w 4886Yy
D Marquette	1857	R-Lat	Bs	91	53,700	100,359	77,805	-1.01	MI VI 117n 7x 7m 88w 1273Yy
D Saginaw	1938	R-Lat	Bs	110	102,800	157,560	149,009	-0.22	MI VI 111n 14x 16m 157w 2827Yy
M Dubuque	1837	R-Lat	Bs	215	154,400	230,215	223,768	-0.11	IA IX. M=OSB. 261n 32x 75m 1031w 4453Yy
D Davenport	1881	R-Lat	Bs	109	72,900	108,365	105,623	-0.10	IA IX 148n 10x 11m 312w 2460Yy
D Des Moines	1911	R-Lat	Bs	93	63,500	80,786	92,061	0.52	IA IX 115n 4x 9m 130w 2049Yy
D Sioux City	1902	R-Lat	Bs	117	69,600	106,378	100,948	-0.21	IA IX 172n 2x 3m 131w 1931Yy
M Hartford	1843	R-Lat	Bs	223	553,800	806,902	802,688	-0.02	CT I 372n 136x 343m 1093w 13883Yy
D Bridgeport	1953	R-Lat	Bs	88	239,300	322,500	346,915	0.29	CT I 219n 82x 90m 551w 6252Yy
D Norwich	1953	R-Lat	Bs	101	151,300	196,384	219,359	0.44	CT I 124n 77x 217m 310w 3347Yy
D Providence	1872	R-Lat	Bs	173	445,400	600,595	645,653	0.29	RI I 308n 136x 268m 864w 7619Yy
M Indianapolis	1834	R-Lat	Bs	139	142,300	209,412	206,314	-0.06	IN VII. M=OSB. 177n 121x 194m 866w 5638Yy
D Evansville	1944	R-Lat	Bs	80	60,500	85,074	87,707	0.12	IN VII 102n 8x 10m 321w 1753Yy
D Fort Wayne-South Bend	1857	R-Lat	Bs	91	105,900	155,624	153,491	-0.06	IN VII. M=SJ. 112n 181x 299m 720w 3419Yy
D Gary	1956	R-Lat	Bs	94	126,700	184,876	183,629	-0.03	IN VII 129n 57x 80m 162w 2666Yy
D Lafayette in Indiana	1944	R-Lat	Bs	63	58,000	83,383	84,146	0.04	IN VII 104n 28x 34m 92w 1977Yy
M Kansas City in Kansas	1877	R-Lat	Bs	119	123,000	138,350	178,290	1.02	KS IX 96n 65x 85m 865w 3506Yy
D Dodge City	1951	R-Lat	Bs	57	27,200	33,408	39,363	0.66	KS IX 45n 4x 4m 124w 1035Yy
D Salina	1887	R-Lat	Bs	93	39,000	55,776	56,474	0.05	KS IX 64n 24x 24m 275w 1230Yy
D Wichita	1887	R-Lat	Bs	111	72,100	88,202	104,474	0.68	KS IX 120n 12x 12m 451w 2561Yy
M Los Angeles	1922	R-Lat	Bs	285	2,456,200	1,791,932	3,559,816	2.78	CA XI 681n 686x 1017m 2116w 92940Yy
D Fresno	1967	R-Lat	Bs	86	243,800	268,145	353,400	1.11	CA XI 116n 43x 58m 141w 17719Yy
D Monterey	1840	R-Lat	Bs	45	115,800	95,000	167,850	2.30	CA XI 98n 35x 59m 122w 4973Yy
D Orange	1976	R-Lat	Bs	57	413,100	–	598,663	5.26	CA XI 176n 80x 110m 386w 18836Yy
D San Bernardino	1978	R-Lat	Bs	100	393,000	–	570,040	5.88	CA XI 185n 63x 77m 159w 10520Yy
D San Diego	1936	R-Lat	Bs	99	446,500	512,412	647,094	0.94	CA XI 302n 89x 108m 370w 13350Yy
M Louisville	1808	R-Lat	Bs	121	129,700	192,861	188,022	-0.10	KY V. M=OP. 195n 70x 164m 1177w 3475Yy
D Covington	1853	R-Lat	Bs	51	57,700	103,500	83,583	-0.85	KY V 108n 2x 8m 539w 1642Yy
D Knoxville	1988	R-Lat	Bs	38	24,700	–	35,805	14.29	KY V 40n 20x 32m 55w 781Yy
D Lexington	1988	R-Lat	Bs	48	28,800	–	41,803	14.29	KY V 53n 20x 23m 193w 952Yy
D Memphis	1970	R-Lat	Bs	49	39,200	39,006	56,786	1.51	TN V. M=SVD. 83n 10x 47m 106w 1126Yy
D Nashville	1837	R-Lat	Bs	50	37,600	53,558	54,484	0.07	TN V 46n 21x 23m 161w 1371Yy
D Owensboro	1937	R-Lat	Bs	80	34,200	48,412	49,631	0.10	KY V 70n 14x 20m 257w 1278Yy
M Miami	1958	R-Lat	Bs	208	479,200	569,543	694,558	0.80	FL IV 318n 123x 181m 402w 17041Yy
D Orlando	1968	R-Lat	Bs	70	185,700	136,957	269,249	2.74	FL IV. M=CP. 127n 52x 59m 130w 5691Yy
D Palm Beach	1984	R-Lat	Bs	50	133,000	–	192,673	9.09	FL IV 98n 40x 43m 192w 4504Yy
D Pensacola-Tallahassee	1975	R-Lat	Bs	60	41,300	–	59,768	5.00	FL IV 83n 14x 14m 58w 1332Yy
D Saint Augustine	1870	R-Lat	Bs	50	73,100	76,828	105,960	1.29	FL IV 94n 21x 22m 125w 2209Yy
D Saint Petersburg	1968	R-Lat	Bs	73	231,500	154,628	335,637	3.15	FL IV 180n 140x 187m 353w 5209Yy
D Venice	1984	R-Lat	Bs	62	118,100	–	171,254	9.09	FL IV 137n 53x 75m 147w 3430Yy
M Milwaukee	1843	R-Lat	Bs	296	425,200	696,090	616,276	-0.49	WI VII. M=OSB. 493n 379x 493m 2494w 11334Yy
D Green Bay	1868	R-Lat	Bs	232	260,000	317,102	376,847	0.69	WI VII 238n 147x 202m 766w 6293Yy
D La Crosse	1868	R-Lat	Bs	192	151,400	200,023	219,365	0.37	WI VII 185n 26x 31m 602w 4367Yy
D Madison	1945	R-Lat	Bs	137	172,600	195,132	250,167	1.00	WI VII 171n 22x 34m 426w 3683Yy
D Superior	1905	R-Lat	Bs	116	59,300	84,272	85,977	0.08	WI VII 79n 20x 20m 125w 1560Yy
M Mobile	1829	R-Lat	Bs	97	45,700	45,016	66,257	1.56	AL V 90n 52x 66m 234w 1651Yy
D Biloxi	1977	R-Lat	Bs	58	43,000	–	62,273	5.56	AL V 65n 31x 69m 71w 1370Yy
D Birmingham, USA	1829	R-Lat	Bs	74	45,500	41,202	65,924	1.90	AL V 56n 22x 38m 148w 1295Yy
D Jackson (Natchez-Jackson)	1837	R-Lat	Bs	78	30,500	84,554	44,340	-2.55	MS V 48n 26x 39m 285w 911Yy
M Newark	1853	R-Lat	Bs	410	906,600	1,703,356	1,314,000	-1.03	NJ III. M=SVD,OAR. 771n 341x 454m 1657w 20815Yy
D Camden	1937	R-Lat	Bs	157	279,300	319,984	404,860	0.95	NJ III 315n 44x 59m 404w 9501Yy
D Metuchen	1981	R-Lat	Bs	108	330,600	–	479,200	7.14	NJ III 240n 47x 83m 488w 7623Yy
D Paterson	1937	R-Lat	Bs	116	251,800	308,042	365,000	0.68	NJ III 230n 181x 229m 1033w 9058Yy

Continued overleaf

Country Table 2–continued

Official name (bold type = church with over 10% of all affiliated) 1	*Begun* 2	*Type* 3	*Counc* 4	*Congs* 5	*Adults* 6	*Affiliated 1970* 7	*Affiliated 1995* 8	*G%* 9	*Names, notes, and other statistics (see Codebook, Part 3)* 10
D Trenton	1881	R-Lat	Bs	124	484,300	729,727	701,987	-0.15	NJ III 224n 117x 179m 607w 10958Yy
M New Orleans	1793	R-Lat	Bs	144	333,200	666,702	482,868	-1.28	LA V 238n 251x 434m 973w 8417Yy
D Alexandria	1853	R-Lat	Bs	53	35,900	73,451	52,000	-1.37	LA V 54n 12x 17m 62w 812Yy
D Baton Rouge	1961	R-Lat	Bs	71	165,400	145,529	239,835	2.02	LA V 95n 52x 66m 124w 3399Yy
D Houma-Thibodaux	1977	R-Lat	Bs	46	81,300	–	117,842	5.56	LA V 53n 7x 17m 41w 2079Yy
D Lafayette	1918	R-Lat	Bs	121	229,200	395,035	332,207	-0.69	LA V 147n 61x 116m 181w 6653Yy
D Lake Charles	1980	R-Lat	Bs	37	54,700	–	79,260	6.67	LA V 51n 21x 27m 23w 1911Yy
D Shreveport	1986	R-Lat	Bs	54	25,700	–	37,189	11.11	LA V 13n 11x 12m 65w 831Yy
M New York	1808	R-Lat	Bs	415	1,577,400	1,800,000	2,286,187	0.96	NY II 1100n 1070x 1657m 4274w 38509Yy
D Albany	1847	R-Lat	Bs	260	278,300	424,219	403,414	-0.20	NY II 315n 133x 207m 1061w 7062Yy
D Brooklyn	1853	R-Lat	Bs	226	1,124,600	1,487,360	1,630,013	0.37	NY II 773n 180x 389m 1710w 27123Yy
D Buffalo	1847	R-Lat	Bs	280	523,200	931,623	758,313	-0.82	NY II 481n 210x 277m 1598w 10259Yy
D Ogdensburg	1872	R-Lat	Bs	151	122,800	171,536	178,000	0.15	NY II 166n 22x 39m 231w 2739Yy
D Rochester	1868	R-Lat	Bs	162	235,500	316,790	341,380	0.30	NY II 298n 85x 137m 837w 7511Yy
D Rockville Center	1957	R-Lat	Bs	133	921,900	969,611	1,336,197	1.29	NY II 491n 86x 198m 1583w 22734Yy
D Syracuse	1886	R-Lat	Bs	172	252,000	411,523	365,252	-0.48	NY II 317n 75x 109m 584w 7377Yy
M Oklahoma City	1905	R-Lat	Bs	77	62,600	65,715	90,841	1.30	OK X 110n 34x 48m 163w 2009Yy
D Little Rock	1843	R-Lat	Bs	104	55,500	55,025	80,386	1.53	AR V 116n 59x 106m 364w 2438Yy
D Tulsa	1972	R-Lat	Bs	90	35,400	–	51,268	4.35	OK X 77n 22x 30m 157w 1645Yy
M Omaha	1885	R-Lat	Bs	166	142,300	199,045	206,186	0.14	NE IX 208n 122x 161m 467w 5022Yy
D Grand Island	1912	R-Lat	Bs	86	35,900	51,169	52,005	0.06	NE IX 76n 0x 0m 103w 1248Yy
D Lincoln	1887	R-Lat	Bs	134	57,200	59,956	82,931	1.31	NE IX 123n 14x 25m 104w 1523Yy
M Philadelphia	1808	R-Lat	Bs	304	985,500	1,359,012	1,428,395	0.20	PA III 832n 452x 642m 4316w 22830Yy
D Allentown	1961	R-Lat	Bs	181	179,000	256,443	259,379	0.05	PA III 274n 83x 108m 665w 4438Yy
D Altoona-Johnstown	1901	R-Lat	Bs	126	84,400	147,069	122,338	-0.73	PA III 161n 70x 81m 190w 1994Yy
D Erie	1853	R-Lat	Bs	127	176,500	213,286	255,882	0.73	PA III 246n 17x 17m 603w 3576Yy
D Greensburg	1951	R-Lat	Bs	112	139,600	220,043	202,267	-0.34	PA III 152n 98x 140m 333w 2728Yy
D Harrisburg	1868	R-Lat	Bs	118	157,000	190,252	227,567	0.72	PA III 169n 56x 59m 608w 3112Yy
D Pittsburgh	1843	R-Lat	Bs	249	546,600	921,148	792,178	-0.60	PA III 568n 158x 214m 2063w 11053Yy
D Scranton	1868	R-Lat	Bs	221	248,400	356,056	359,992	0.04	PA III 368n 97x 102m 945w 6026Yy
M Philadelphia *(Ukrainian)*	1913	R-Ukr	Os	82	53,100	167,085	77,000	-3.05	PA III Ukrainian-rite dioceses. 69n 14x 17m 113w 607Yy
D St Josaphat in Parma *(Ukrainian)*	1983	R-Ukr	Os	37	8,100	–	11,727	8.33	OH 39n 0x 0m 11w 129Yy
D St Nicholas of Chicago *(Ukrainian)*	1961	R-Ukr	Os	38	12,400	29,893	18,000	-2.01	IL VII. M=CSSR,OSBM. 33n 13x 18m 9w 212Yy
D Stamford *(Ukrainian)*	1956	R-Ukr	Os	53	24,000	87,700	34,822	-3.63	CT I. M=OSBM. 53n 19x 21m 43w 252Yy
M Pittsburgh (Munhall, *Byzantine*)	1924	R-Byz	Os	85	69,700	150,000	101,122	-1.56	PA III. Formerly Ruthenian-rite. 64n 7x 18m 114w 716Yy
D Parma *(Ruthenian)*	1969	R-Rut	Os	43	10,800	27,847	15,650	-2.28	OH VI 36n 1x 1m 5w 216Yy
D Passaic *(Ruthenian)*	1963	R-Rut	Os	108	50,000	99,968	72,500	-1.28	NJ III 85n 22x 23m 25w 426Yy
D Van Nuys *(Ruthenian)*	1981	R-Rut	Os	20	2,200	–	3,265	7.14	20n 3x 5m 2w 117Yy
M Portland in Oregon (Oregon City)	1846	R-Lat	Bs	127	186,100	188,061	269,774	1.45	OR XII 161n 209x 291m 497w 5131Yy
D Baker	1903	R-Lat	Bs	36	19,500	23,818	28,325	0.70	OR XII 33n 7x 7m 35w 930Yy
D Boise City	1893	R-Lat	Bs	73	73,700	59,117	106,875	2.40	ID XII 92n 18x 27m 112w 2856Yy
D Great Falls-Billings	1904	R-Lat	Bs	130	42,900	67,916	62,160	-0.35	MT XII. M=OFMCap. 65n 22x 23m 101w 1266Yy
D Helena	1884	R-Lat	Bs	111	45,700	70,500	66,313	-0.24	MT XII 88n 9x 9m 68w 1380Yy
M Saint Louis	1826	R-Lat	Bs	256	387,100	517,870	561,000	0.32	MO IX 493n 421x 661m 2565w 8520Yy
D Jefferson City	1956	R-Lat	Bs	97	55,200	66,000	80,143	0.78	MO IX 100n 11x 14m 106w 1617Yy
D Kansas City-Saint Joseph	1868	R-Lat	Bs	102	100,600	126,695	145,831	0.56	MO IX 122n 112x 181m 346w 2820Yy
D Springfield-Cape Girardeau	1956	R-Lat	Bs	87	35,800	40,462	51,920	1.00	MO IX 72n 62x 143m 185w 1404Yy
M Saint Paul & Minneapolis	1850	R-Lat	Bs	227	476,900	541,958	691,180	0.98	MN VIII 359n 175x 255m 1503w 12683Yy
D Bismarck	1909	R-Lat	Bs	111	47,400	72,968	68,740	-0.24	ND VIII 69n 34x 60m 182w 1382Yy
D Crookston	1909	R-Lat	Bs	80	30,200	38,591	43,825	0.51	MN VIII 41n 10x 11m 218w 837Yy
D Duluth	1889	R-Lat	Bs	101	59,000	99,318	85,500	-0.60	MN VIII. M=OMI. 76n 18x 19m 180w 1151Yy
D Fargo	1889	R-Lat	Bs	162	67,900	98,858	98,413	-0.02	ND VIII 132n 16x 17m 249w 1706Yy
D New Ulm	1957	R-Lat	Bs	84	48,500	69,673	70,259	0.03	MN VIII 67n 1x 1m 101w 1561Yy
D Rapid City (Lead)	1902	R-Lat	Bs	112	26,900	36,000	38,951	0.32	SD VIII. M=OFMCap. 38n 33x 47m 80w 1002Yy
D Saint Cloud	1889	R-Lat	Bs	143	103,100	145,347	149,427	0.11	MN VIII 142n 138x 212m 619w 2670Yy
D Sioux Falls	1889	R-Lat	Bs	157	79,500	99,673	115,200	0.58	SD VIII 113n 43x 57m 476w 2399Yy
D Winona	1889	R-Lat	Bs	123	87,300	118,393	126,643	0.27	MN VIII 122n 13x 34m 549w 2320Yy
M San Antonio	1874	R-Lat	Bs	142	433,800	533,382	628,776	0.66	TX X 141n 238x 367m 1082w 14238Yy
D Amarillo	1926	R-Lat	Bs	37	25,400	64,571	36,795	-2.22	TX X 47n 8x 8m 154w 1239Yy
D Austin	1947	R-Lat	Bs	88	165,600	138,221	240,000	2.23	TX X 105n 60x 107m 111w 6336Yy
D Beaumont	1966	R-Lat	Bs	55	59,700	91,200	86,640	-0.20	TX X 53n 17x 21m 63w 1951Yy
D Brownsville	1965	R-Lat	Bs	61	450,000	264,186	652,214	3.68	TX X 48n 63x 74m 138w 8781Yy
D Corpus Christi	1912	R-Lat	Bs	93	241,100	180,060	349,500	2.69	TX X 104n 70x 95m 311w 7256Yy
D Dallas	1890	R-Lat	Bs	69	198,600	111,984	287,826	3.85	TX X 110n 85x 102m 180w 8842Yy
D El Paso	1914	R-Lat	Bs	58	344,600	200,664	499,376	3.71	TX X 80n 46x 92m 240w 6787Yy
D Fort Worth	1969	R-Lat	Bs	84	120,800	67,076	175,087	3.91	TX X 55n 63x 77m 108w 4720Yy
D Galveston-Houston	1847	R-Lat	Bs	171	516,600	320,300	748,781	3.46	TX X 194n 224x 254m 570w 18047Yy
D Lubbock	1983	R-Lat	Bs	63	30,600	–	44,338	8.33	TX X 35n 12x 12m 33w 1936Yy
D San Angelo	1961	R-Lat	Bs	50	55,600	62,340	80,600	1.03	TX X. M=OMI. 38n 22x 22m 44w 2456Yy
D Tyler	1986	R-Lat	Bs	43	24,500	–	35,581	11.11	TX X 24n 22x 23m 73w 1235Yy
D Victoria in Texas	1982	R-Lat	Bs	72	75,200	–	109,000	7.69	TX X 53n 16x 17m 143w 1844Yy
M San Francisco	1853	R-Lat	Bs	106	234,900	827,950	340,416	-3.49	CA XI 260n 254x 306m 1028w 9581Yy
D Honolulu (Hawaii)	1844	R-Lat	Bs	69	147,500	216,500	213,767	-0.05	HA XI 72n 90x 184m 277w 5058Yy
D Oakland	1962	R-Lat	Bs	99	328,400	331,700	476,023	1.46	CA XI 189n 286x 448m 204w 9499Yy
D Reno-Las Vegas	1931	R-Lat	Bs	50	133,400	87,000	193,346	3.25	NV XI 50n 27x 34m 110w 4208Yy
D Sacramento	1886	R-Lat	Bs	142	249,300	226,028	361,389	1.89	CA XI 171n 65x 98m 259w 9527Yy
D Salt Lake City (Salt-Lake)	1891	R-Lat	Bs	43	51,800	50,581	75,102	1.59	UT XI 59n 37x 57m 86w 2128Yy
D San Jose in California	1981	R-Lat	Bs	48	260,800	–	378,000	7.14	CA XI 120n 217x 296m 445w 7405Yy
D Santa Rosa	1962	R-Lat	Bs	53	78,000	64,169	113,000	2.29	CA XI 95n 20x 62m 119w 3261Yy
D Stockton	1962	R-Lat	Bs	34	128,300	92,964	185,957	2.81	CA XI 68n 24x 28m 60w 5288Yy
M Santa Fe	1850	R-Lat	Bs	97	189,400	267,231	274,485	0.11	NM X 151n 93x 183m 316w 7270Yy
D Gallup	1939	R-Lat	Bs	92	27,700	68,481	40,166	-2.11	MN X. M=SSS. 40n 29x 41m 172w 1267Yy
D Las Cruces	1982	R-Lat	Bs	47	86,000	–	124,600	7.69	M=CSB. 32n 44x 48m 84w 3158Yy
D Phoenix	1969	R-Lat	Bs	115	245,000	211,131	355,052	2.10	AZ X 164n 116x 132m 233w 9741Yy
D Tucson	1897	R-Lat	Bs	65	244,100	174,757	353,809	2.86	AZ X 152n 71x 84m 318w 7528Yy
M Seattle (Nesqually)	1850	R-Lat	Bs	147	240,400	336,475	348,500	0.14	WA XII 207n 143x 171m 650w 7527Yy
D Spokane	1913	R-Lat	Bs	81	54,900	71,967	79,623	0.41	WA XII 73n 96x 127m 361w 1773Yy
D Yakima	1951	R-Lat	Bs	48	41,000	50,384	59,400	0.66	WA XII. M=OMI. 50n 10x 11m 50w 2442Yy
M Washington DC	1939	R-Lat	Bs	139	372,600	387,220	540,000	1.34	DC IV. M=SJ,SVD. 394n 447x 821m 980w 8829Yy
D St Maron of Brooklyn *(Maronite)*	1966	R-Mar	os	61	38,300	152,407	55,485	-3.96	US. Maronite rite. 84n 5x 21m 11w 664Yy
D Newton *(Melkite)*	1966	R-Mel	os	42	17,400	20,000	25,200	0.93	US - M=BS. Melkite rite. 48n 21x 29m 3w 464Yy
EA USA & Canada *(Armenian)*	1981	R-Arm	Os	8	25,800	–	37,500	7.14	US Armenian rite. 8n 3x 3m 11w 92Yy
D Our Lady of Lebanon *(Maronite)*	1994	R-Mar	os	10	34,500	–	50,000	10.00	Maronite rite.
D St George's in Canton *(Rumanian)*	1982	R-Rum	os	17	3,600	–	5,250	7.69	Rumanian rite. 21n 0x 0m 0w 48Yy
D St Thomas of Detroit *(Chaldean)*	1982	R-Cha	os	11	41,400	–	60,000	7.69	Chaldean rite. 16n 0x 0m 10w 933Yy
OM United States of America	1957	R-LEr	Bs	444	467,000	1,990,000	934,000	-2.98	*Military Ordinariate for USA. AD for Military Services.* 547 ordinaries, 757 auxiliaries. 10836Yy.
Celestial Church of Christ	c1970	I-3pA	.....	40	2,000	–	4,000	39.34	*CCC.* Large apostolic church in Benin, Nigeria, and West Africa: Yoruba elites and professionals.
Centers of Christian Love	c1980	I-3cL	x....	30	2,000	–	5,000	6.67	*Centros Amistad Cristiana.* Mexican immigrants from large network of house churches.
Central Baptist Association	1956	I-Bap	.....	37	4,000	2,500	5,000	2.81	Primitive Baptists. In VA, KY, TN, IN, SC. HQ Jasper (VA).
Charismatic Episcopal Church of NA	1992	I-3cW	.....	180	12,500	–	25,000	33.33	*ICCEC (International Communion of CEC).* Ex ECUSA. Abroad: 50,000 in 200 chs, 42 countries.
Children of God International	1965	I-mar	xv...	20	600	5,000	1,000	-6.23	*Teens for Christ. Family of Love.* 12,000 in 800 Colonies, 80 countries. 267 million letters sent.
Chinese Full Gospel Fell International	1982	I-3fC	.....	100	7,000	–	15,000	7.69	*CFGFI.* HQ Houston, TX. Abroad (HQ Kowloon, Hong Kong): 100 chs, 200 ministers.
Christ Apostolic Church	c1985	I-3pA	I....	15	2,500	–	4,000	10.00	*CAC.* Africans from large Apostolic body in Nigeria. US churches across entire nation.
Christ Cath Ch of America & Europe	1965	I-OCa	.....	12	1,301	1,000	1,558	1.79	*D Boston.* Old Catholic. Aims at total comprehensiveness. 5n,2t(75),W=42%,92Yy.
Christ for the Nations		I-3fW	.....	600	20,000	–	40,000	0.05	*CFTN.* Large evangelistic agency based in Dallas, TX, Full Gospel theology.
Christ Gospel Churches International	1963	I-3oW	.....	3	10,000	9,000	13,000	1.48	*Branhamites.*Organized around ministry of W. M. Branham.
Christ Orth Cath Ex of Americas	1959	I-CCa	.....	10	2,000	5,513	3,000	-2.40	Ex=Exarchate. Byelorussian origins. 1959 merger Old Catholic and Orthodox. 21n,3x.
Christ's Church Fellowship	1988	I-3cW	.....	27	3,200	–	7,000	14.29	*CCF.* Abroad, 15,000 in 145 chs. Church planting mainly in Ethiopia, Russia, Ukraine, Nigeria.
Christadelphian Ecclesias	1844	m-Ade	x....	600	11,000	22,000	15,000	-1.52	*Brothers of Christ.* No central organization or clergy. Pacifist, adventist.
Christian & Missionary Alliance	1881	P-Hol	xF..E	1,923	289,391	150,000	371,865	3.70	*CMA.* 18 districts in USA. Work in 42 countries. 1340n,5p(85),3s,1085t(141924),W=66%,5133Y.
Christian Believers United	1974	I-3cW	.....	60	9,000	–	12,000	4.76	*CBU.* Conferences, church planting, mission.
Christian Brethren (Exclusive)	1870	P-EBr	x....	250	6,000	20,000	17,000	-0.65	*Assemblies. Plymouth Brethren* I/II/IV/V/VI/VII/VIII (separate groups). White.
Christian Brethren (Open)	c1880	P-CBr	x....	820	52,740	80,000	98,000	0.82	*Plymouth Brethren II. Brethren Assemblies.* 2p,1s,700t(33000),W=90%.
Christian Catholic Church	1896	P-Con	x....	5	1,100	3,000	2,000	-1.61	In church-planned Zion City (IL). Healing. 2 Navajo Indian churches. In 7 nations.
Christian Church of North America	1904	I-3pW	xF..K	108	19,490	11,800	24,600	2.98	*CCNA.* 1948 merger. 134n. Abroad: 3,600 chs, 1.8 million members.
Christian Church (Disciples of Christ)	1809	P-Dis	xW..W	4,035	677,223	1,641,628	1,037,757	-1.82	Liberal wing, Restoration Movement. Schisms, 6886n,4s(348),W=39%,24481Y.
Christian Churches & Chs of Christ	c1935	I-Dis	x....	5,238	966,976	1,500,000	1,213,188	-0.85	*Church of Christ (Instrumental).* Schism ex Disciples. 7312n,40s,6012t(1243445).
Christian Churches of the Word	c1970	I-3gL	.....	60	10,000	–	25,000	49.94	*Iglesia Cristiana del Verbo. Gospel Outreach.* In Guatemala, Nicaragua, UK, Germany.
Christian Congregation	1887	P-Hol	.....	1,454	110,900	100,000	130,000	1.05	Non-credal body in rural, mountainous and neglected areas in NC. 265n,252t(33355).
Christian Evangelistic Assemblies	1934	I-3fW	.....	82	92,158	60,000	120,000	2.81	*CEA.* F=O.C. Harms. Church planting. Integrated Charismatics, Full Gospel theology.
Christian Fellowship International	1992	I-3fW	.....	800	40,000	–	80,000	33.33	*CFI.* HQ Safety Harbor, FL. Abroad: 90,000 members in 300 chs in India, Haiti, Africa.
Christian Growth Ministries	1970	I-3cW	x....	3,000	150,000	100,000	300,000	4.49	*CGM.* Charismatic paradenomination, stressing authority, shepherding. HQ Florida.
Christian International Network of Chs	1967	I-3aW	.....	200	15,000	10,000	25,000	3.73	*CINC. Int Ministries.*Agencies: CIBN,CIPC,CIST,CILN,CIFC,CI-ITC. Abroad: 25,000, 175 chs.

Continued opposite

Country Table 2–continued

Official name (bold type = church with over 10% of all affiliated) 1	*Begun* 2	*Type* 3	*Counc* 4	*Congs* 5	*Adults* 6	*Affiliated 1970* 7	*Affiliated 1995* 8	*G%* 9	*Names, notes, and other statistics (see Codebook, Part 3)* 10
Christian Methodist Episcopal Church	1870	I-Met	VW..b	3,000	438,000	600,000	800,000	1.16	Black members ex Methodist Episcopal Ch South; Colored MEC until 1956. 2259n,5s.
Christian Nation Church, USA	1895	P-Hol	.....	5	780	5,000	1,000	-6.23	Begun by independent 'equality evangelists' in Indiana. Declining. 29n, 11t(2000).
Christian Outreach Centers	c1996	I-3cW	x....	12	1,200	–	2,000	50.00	*COC.* Part of overseas work of COC (Australia, HQ Brisbane, 70,000 members, 700 chs).
Christian Reformed Ch in N America	1837	P-Ref	JF...	716	146,402	285,628	226,163	-0.93	Ex RCA. Some Dutch churches. 6-year decline. 999n,1p,1s(183),601t(69240),5733Yy.
Christian Union of America	1864	P-Con	....E	114	6,050	11,000	10,100	-0.34	Origins in revivals of 1860s. Central USA. 96n,1p,108t(10055),W=69%.
Christ's Sanctified Holy Church	1892	I-3pB	.....	35	1,000	2,000	3,000	1.64	Black pentecostals. Schism ex CME Church. East, southeast USA. 30n,W=62%,200z.
Church of Christ (Manalista)	1968	I-3nF	x....	50	6,000	1,000	10,000	9.65	*INC. Iglesia ni Cristo* (Manalista) (HQ Manila). Filipinos in Hawaii, California, Virginia.
Ch of Christ Conf on Spiritual Renewal	1992	I-3cW	.....	400	10,000	–	15,000	33.33	1992 schism ex Disciples of Christ/Christian Churches. Charismatics.
Church of Christ (Holiness) USA	1894	I-3pB	.....	224	13,000	20,000	26,000	1.05	Black pentecostals. Foot-washing, episcopal church order. 76n,1j,1s.
Church of Christ (Temple Lot)	1852	m-LdS	.....	30	2,400	3,000	3,100	0.13	Schism ex LdS(Utah). Some Maya Indian members, Yucatan, Mexico. 5 splits. 188n.
Church of Christ, Scientist	1879	m-Sci	x....	2,300	400,000	1,000,000	900,000	-0.42	*Christian Science.* Healing ministry. HQ Mother Church, Boston. Decline 2%pa. 5848n.
Church of God & Saints of Christ	1896	I-Jew	x....	200	20,000	50,000	30,000	-2.02	*Black Jews* (Jewish observances). Black members. Also Africa, West Indies.
Church of God by Faith	1914	I-3pW	.....	167	6,819	10,000	8,235	-0.77	In eastern and southeastern USA (FL, GA, AL, SC, MD, NJ, NY). One bishop. 155n.
Ch of God Founded by Jesus Christ	c1950	I-3pB	.....	40	1,100	2,000	2,200	0.38	Black pentecostals. HQ Salisbury (North Carolina).
Church of God in Christ	1895	I-3pB	Z...J	15,300	4,281,000	1,600,000	5,499,875	5.06	Black. Largest pentecostal church in USA. HQ Memphis (TN). (1970) 5000n. (1990) 33593n.
Church of God in Christ International	1969	I-3pB	x....	40	5,000	501,000	12,000	-13.87	Black. Schism ex Ch of God in Christ by 14 bishops. 18 US dioceses. Huge losses. 1465n,948t.
Church of God in Christ, Mennonite	1859	P-Men	G....	111	9,665	10,000	12,535	0.91	Schism ex Mennonite Ch, Ohio. Also Canada, Mexico, Nigeria, Haiti, Brazil. 86n
Church of God in Christ United	1968	I-3pB	.....	50	10,000	900	15,000	11.91	*CoGiCU.* Schism ex CoGiC. Abroad: 331 chs (200 in South Africa, 52 Puerto Rico, 50 Jamaica).
Church of God, International	1978	I-Eva	x....	50	5,000	–	7,000	5.88	Schism by son of founder. Ex Worldwide Church of God. HQ Tyler, TX.
Church of God of Prophecy	1923	P-Pe3	Z....	2,101	73,224	120,000	146,000	0.79	*All Nations Flag Ch.* Ex CoG(Cleveland). 1487n,35x,1j,18p,1s,12436Y.
Church of God of the Apostolic Faith	1913	I-3pW	.....	30	1,100	1,600	1,900	0.69	HQ Pharr (Texas). Mission and seminary in Mexico. White Pentecostals. 50n.
Church of God General Conf	1800	m-Ade	x....	89	5,526	11,500	8,000	-1.44	*CoG(Abrahamic Faith.* Formerly Chs of God in Christ Jesus. 110n,1s.
Church of God (Anderson)	1880	P-Hol	x....	2,336	182,419	390,000	232,876	-2.04	Movement calling all to church union. In 83 countries. 2793n,1j,1p,4s,2000t(238692),W=80%.
Church of God (Apostolic)	1897	I-3aO	.....	50	10,500	1,500	14,000	9.35	*CGA.* Black Oneness pentecostals.
Church of God (Charleston, TN)	1993	I-3pW	.....	136	8,262	–	10,000	50.00	Schism ex CGP. Abroad: 12,400 members in 203 churches.
Church of God (Cleveland)	1886	P-Pe3	ZF.XE	5,776	672,008	600,000	855,000	1.43	First US Pentecostal body. 95% White. In 107 countries. 7359n,1j,30,1s,5266t(478984).
Church of God (Holiness)	1882	I-Hol	.....	120	1,500	1,600	3,000	2.55	Small rural denomination.
Church of God (Huntsville)	1943	I-3pW	x....	2,027	75,000	105,000	103,000	-0.08	Ex CoG(Cleveland); HA Tomlinson visits worldwide as King of Nations. 1968, HQ Huntsville (AL).
Church of God (Jerusalem Acres)	1957	I-3pW	.....	10	8,000	6,000	10,000	2.06	Teaching, equipping, church planting, mission. White 7th-day Pentecostals.
Church of God (Mountain Assembly)	1895	I-3fW	...x.	111	6,000	10,000	15,000	1.64	Schism ex Baptists. HQ Jellico (TN). 136n,160Y. Abroad: 350 chs in 17 countries, mainly African.
Church of God (Seventh-day)	1865	P-Adv	.....	5	1,500	5,000	3,000	-2.02	HQ Salem (West Virginia). Reorganized 1933. Schism: Radio Church of God. 9n.
Church of God (Seventh-day) (Denver)	1858	P-Adv	x....	153	5,491	10,000	7,511	-1.14	A faction maintains CoG (Seventh-day) World HQ, in Jerusalem (Israel). 76n,1j.
Church of Illumination	1908	m-Gno	.....	10	1,200	12,500	1,700	-7.67	Attempt to harmonize all philosophy and religion. By correspondence. (1970) 60n. (1990) 18n.
Church of Jesus Christ	1927	I-3pW	.....	500	100,000	50,000	120,000	3.56	Divine healing. Missions in Africa, India, Australia, Israel, Mexico. HQ Cleveland (TN).
Ch of Jesus Christ of Latter-day Saints	1830	m-LdS	x....	9,654	2,920,000	2,185,810	4,430,000	2.87	*Mormons.* HQ Utah. Also 700,000 overseas. (1970) 17272n,91237Y. (1990) 28962n.
Ch of Our Lord JC of Apostolic Faith	1919	I-3aO	x...J	160	41,000	60,000	70,000	0.62	*COLJCAF.* Black pentecostals. 5 Apostles, 32 bps. 320n,2362Y. WAfrica, WIndies, Philippines.
Church of Our Lord JC (Bickertonites)	1862	m-LdS	x....	63	2,707	4,200	4,500	0.28	*Bickerton Organization.* Ex CJCLdS (Mormons). In 5 nations. 215n,50t(4125).
Church of the Brethren	1719	P-Dun	xW..W	1,121	149,951	252,000	208,000	-0.76	1708, German pietist origins. Declining. 2011n,1s,1034t(82079),W=51%,4784Y.
Church of the Christian Crusade	1948	I-Fun	.....	40	5,000	25,000	10,000	-3.60	*Christian Echoes Ministry.* HQ Tulsa. Fundamentalist, anti-Communist, White.
Church of the Living God	1889	I-3pB	.....	170	12,600	150,000	42,000	-4.96	*CWFF. Christian Workers for Fellowship.* Black. Freemasonry doctrine. 165n.
Church of the Living Waters	c1987	I-3cW	.....	1	500	–	800	12.50	*CLW.* Overseas: 6 churches in Kenya, 1 in Uganda. Schism within Anglicanism in USA.
Church of the Living Word	1951	I-3pW	.....	40	4,000	8,000	5,000	-1.86	Independent pentecostal body with network of churches.
Ch of the Living God (Pillar & G of T)	1925	I-3pB	.....	100	2,000	5,000	4,000	-0.89	*GofT=Ground of Truth.* Black pentecostals, split ex Ch of the Living God.
Ch of the Lutheran Brethren of Amer	1900	P-Lut	x....	109	7,487	10,000	17,793	2.33	Members formerly United Norwegians. Upper Midwest. 70n,1p,1s(20),W=89%.
Church of the Lutheran Confession	1959	I-Lut	x....	69	6,397	9,449	8,753	-0.31	*CLC.* Schism ex Synodical Conference over practice. 60n,1p,1s(8),280Yy.
Church of the Nazarene	1907	P-Hol	xF...	5,158	561,253	885,038	864,703	-0.09	*International Ch of the Nazarene.* 6976n,1j,72,48065(868911),W=49%,25644Y.
Church of the Universal Truth	1969	m-The	.....	12	700	1,210	1,000	-0.76	Small marginal Christian body with metaphysical dogmas. 5n,W=68%,96Yy.
Churches of Christ in Christian Union	1909	P-Hol	xF..E	250	9,674	20,000	19,300	-0.14	Wesleyan doctrine. East, southwest. 362n,1j,10,1s,231t(16623).
Chs of Christ (Non-Instrumental)	c1870	I-Dis	x....	13,097	1,280,000	4,000,000	1,681,013	-3.41	Conservative anti-organ split ex Disciples. 10% Black. 10000n,22s,130000Y.
Chs of God General Conference	1830	P-Ref	x...t	350	33,909	50,000	46,500	-0.29	*General Eldership.* 1975 name change. Begun in 19th-century revival. 353n,1s.
Churches of God (Holiness)	1890	I-3pB	x....	30	25,000	35,000	30,000	-0.61	Black pentecostals. Missions in Caribbean. Footwashing practiced. HQ Atlanta. 29n.
Churches on the Rock International	1950	I-3cW	.....	115	40,500	4,000	120,000	14.57	*COTRI.* M= Calvary Ministries. Ex Bapt. Abroad: 400,000, 3,000 chs (200 in India), 6 countries.
Citadel Ministries International	1995	I-3fW	.....	35	3,000	–	5,000	46.57	*CMI.* Restorationist Charismatics. Abroad: 30 churches in Brazil, Italy, Switzerland, India.
Communion of Ev Episcopal Chs	1993	I-3fW	.....	210	12,000	–	25,000	50.00	*CEEC.* Historic episcopacy. Churches abroad: India 125, Philippines 3,400; 138,200 members.
Conference of Fundamental Chs		I-Fun	....T	20	3,000	6,000	4,000	0.05	Grouping of independent fundamentalist congregations. White.
Congregational Bible Churches	1922	I-3pW	.....	450	80,000	60,000	100,000	2.06	1977 merger of Light of the Way Open Door Ch, with Independent Holiness Ch. In 10 countries.
Congregational Christian Churches	1955	I-Con	.....	399	79,255	150,000	139,999	-0.28	*National Assoc of CCC.* North-central, NE USA. 35% Black. 391n,326t(30000),W=33%.
Congregational Holiness Church	1921	I-3pW	x..X.	176	7,116	7,377	10,000	1.22	Schism ex Pentecostal Holiness Ch. Southern states. 302n,1j,W=54%,378Y.
Congregational Methodist Church	1852	I-Hol	.T..T	187	11,000	25,000	14,738	-2.09	Schism ex Methodist Episcopal Church, HQ Dallas, College in Tehuacana, TX. 1p.
Conservative Bapt Assoc of America	1947	I-Bap	xF...	1,121	204,496	450,000	292,000	-1.72	Official name: *CB America.* No central organization. HQ Wheaton, IL.Missions: CBI. 2s,5253Y.
Conservative Congr Christian Conf	1935	I-Con	.E..E	224	39,069	30,000	43,600	1.51	*CCCC.* Schism ex Congr Christian Chs. 196n. Abroad: in Micronesia, Brazil, Canada.
Conservative Lutheran Association	1965	I-Lut	.....	12	1,000	500	1,530	4.58	*CLA.* Founded in Cedar Rapids (Iowa) by 10 inerrantist pastors and laymen. HQ Anaheim (CA).
Conservative Mennonite Conference	1910	P-Men	G....	100	8,856	10,000	10,100	0.04	Accepts Dortrecht Confession of faith. 121n (and 43 bishops),1p,W=90%.
Converted Jehovah's Witnesses		I-Jeh	.....	35	6,000	10,000	12,000	0.05	One of the many schisms ex Jehovah's Witnesses in a Protestant direction.
Cooneyites (Tramp-Preachers)	c1910	I-Fun	x....	200	130,000	100,000	270,000	4.05	*Go-Preachers.* Irish itinerants. Europe, Australia. Fundamentalists. House churches 50 states.
Coptic Orthodox Ch (P Alexandria)	1964	O-Cop	NwaNW	85	150,000	43,000	180,000	5.89	Egyptian immigrants. 1977: 50,000 across USA; visit by Cairo pope. (1970) 5n,14x. (1990) 68n.
Covenant Ministries International	1988	I-3fW	.....	6	50,000	–	70,000	14.29	Faith Fellowship Ministries. Church planting. Integrated Charismatics (Full Gospel).
Creek Independent Indian Bapt Chs	c1910	I-Bap	I	50	1,500	5,000	4,000	-0.89	Creek Indians. Chain of 54 churches in Oklahoma. Annual Bible school.
Crenshaw Christian Center	1970	I-3cD	.....	20	15,000	–	21,000	48.90	An influential megachurch in Los Angeles. HQ Los Angeles
Crusaders Church	1976	I-3vW	.....	50	5,000	–	10,000	5.26	*IMPAC. Internat Ministries of Prophetic & Apostolic Chs.* HQ Chicago. In 21 nations.
Cumberland Presbyterian Church	1810	P-Ref	R....	737	85,027	92,025	91,040	-0.04	*CPC.* White (Blacks belong to Second Cumberland PC). 717n,1s,880t(57726).
Czechoslovak Bapt Conv of USA/Can	c1989	P-Bap	T....	7	1,500	–	2,000	16.67	Refugees from Czechoslovakia.
Czechoslovak Hussite Church	c1950	I-ReC	.wc..	20	20,000	1,000	50,000	16.94	*Ceskoslovenska Cirkev.*1920 schism ex Ch of Rome in Prague. (1970) 500. Massive immigration
Damascus Christian Church	1939	I-3pL	x....	30	3,000	2,000	7,000	5.14	Spanish-speaking churches in New York City (HQ Bronx). Puerto Ricans.
Deeper Life Bible Church	c1980	I-3pA	.....	20	3,000	–	5,000	6.67	*DLBC/DLB Fellowship.* Mission from huge African denomination based on Lagos, Nigeria.
Defenders of the Christian Faith	1925	I-3pL	.....	50	15,000	3,000	22,000	8.30	Hispanic Pentecostals. 6,000 in Puerto Rico, others Mexico, Cuba, Dominican Republic.
Deliverance Evangelistic Church	1960	I-3vB	.....	32	83,000	25,000	100,000	5.70	Black Americans stressing deliverance ministry.
Divine Science Federation Int	1888	m-Sci	i....	40	4,000	10,000	8,000	-0.89	Metaphysical (New Thought). In INTA. Christ Method of Healing. HQ Denver. 30mw, 1s.
Door of Faith Churches of Hawaii	1940	I-3wP	x....	50	3,500	2,000	4,000	2.81	A network of cell-based churches, most in Pennsylvania.
Dove Christian Fellowship Int	1971	I-3kW	.....	15	2,000	–	3,000	4.17	*DCFI.* Cell-based ministries. Abroad: 600 members, 5 chs in UK, NZ, Brazil, Kenya.
Duck River & Kindred As of Baptists	1825	P-Bap	.....	102	10,672	13,000	16,400	0.93	Calvinistic schism. 5 associations, in 4 southern states. White. 128n.
Eagle's Nest Ministries	1978	I-3aW	.....	13	1,000	–	1,300	5.88	Prophetic ministries. Financial problems.
Ecclesiastical Soc of Gospel Outreach	1970	I-3cL	.....	23	1,420	–	2,000	35.53	*ESGO.* HQ Eureka, CA. Abroad: 15,000 members in 120 chs in Latin America.
Elim Assemblies	1924	P-Pe2	Z..XE	180	20,000	10,000	29,000	4.35	*EMA. Elim Missionary Assemblies, Elim Ministerial Fellowship.* (1970) 200n,1s,70t. (1990) 322n.
Embassy Christian Churches	1983	I-3aW	.....	35	3,000	–	6,000	8.33	M=SLBC,RLM,LMA. HQ Irvine, CA. Abroad: 10 chs, mission teams.
Emmanuel Holiness Church	1953	I-3pW	...X.	40	3,900	6,000	5,000	-0.73	Schism ex Pentecostal Fire Baptised Holiness Ch. Southern US. Mission in Mexico.
Episcopal Church in the USA	1578	A-plu	AW.RW	7,333	1,695,878	3,196,277	2,445,286	-1.07	*ECUSA.* (1970) 8 US Provinces, 109 Dioceses. 11272n,14s,6370Y,62814y. (1990) 14878n.
Estonian Evangelical Lutheran Ch	1941	P-Lut	LWC..	25	4,057	12,000	7,298	-1.97	*Eesti Evangeeliumi Luteri Usu Kirik.* Refugees ex USSR. HQ Stockholm. (1970) 27n. (1990) 19n.
Estonian Orthodox Church in Exile	c1940	O-Est	C....	3	600	1,000	900	-0.42	Refugees from USSR, Parishes: Los Angeles (HQ), San Francisco, Chicago, NY, Canada.
Ethiopian Orthodox Ch in the USA	1959	O-Eth	Nwa..	10	1,500	2,000	3,000	1.64	Under P Addis Ababa (Ethiopia). Mostly US Blacks, 1n(Black),2x(Ethiopians).
Evangel Christian Alliance	1955	I-3cD	.....	4	2,500	1,000	4,000	5.70	Pioneering charismatic ministry in areas of worship, spirituality, outreach.
Evangel Fell of Ministers & Chs Int	1984	I-3fW	.....	180	16,950	–	50,000	9.09	Mostly White. Abroad: 80,000 members in 175 chs in 11 countries, especially in Russia.
Evangelical Baptist Churches	1935	I-3pW	.....	40	2,500	3,000	3,500	0.62	*General Conference.* Formerly Ch of the Full Gospel, ex Free Will Baptists. 37n,1s.
Evangelical Christian Churches	1966	I-Eva	.....	70	10,000	20,000	15,000	-1.14	Grouping of independent congregations, based on Fontana (California). 164n.
Evangelical Church of North America	1968	I-Hol	....E	150	8,000	14,500	10,000	-1.48	EUB chs rejecting 1968 merger with UMC. Wesleyan/Arminian. 88n. Sends 150 missionaries.
Evangelical Congregational Church	1922	I-Hol	xF..E	159	24,619	40,000	33,166	-0.75	Former East Pennsylvania Conf. East USA. HQ Myerstown (PA). 210n,1s,159t(28311).657Y.
Evangelical Covenant Ch of America	1885	P-Con	K....	617	89,648	100,000	132,000	1.12	*ECCA.* 19th-century pietist revivals (Sweden). (1970) 669n, 2761Y. (1990) 1028n.
Evangelical Free Church of America	1884	P-Con	KF..E	1,173	117,027	100,000	214,186	3.09	*EFCA.* Swedish immigrants, later Norwegian, Danish denominations. Rapid growth. (1990)1817n
Evangelical Friends International	1965	I-Qua	QF..E	217	21,435	40,000	37,000	-0.31	Until 1968: Ev Friends Alliance. 4 YMs: Ev Friends Ch, Kansas, Rocky M, Northwest.
Ev Luth Ch in America (Eielsen Synod)	1846	P-Lut	.....	2	700	1,500	1,000	-1.61	Norwegians (first synod in USA). Declining. Mostly Minnesota and Wisconsin. 1n.
Evangelical Lutheran Ch in America	1623	P-Lut	.....	10,912	3,889,462	5,772,232	5,226,798	-0.40	1987 Union of American Lutheran Ch and Lutheran Church in America. (1990) 17416n.
Evangelical Lutheran Synod	1917	I-Lut	.....	126	16,173	15,663	21,523	1.28	Norwegian groups rejecting 1917 merger. Decline. Upper Midwest. 81n,1s,79t(4381).
Evangelical Mennonite Church	1865	P-Men	GF..E	27	3,470	5,200	4,600	-0.49	Formerly, Defenseless Mennonite Ch. Ex Amish. 67n,W=80%,115Y.
Evangelical Methodist Ch in America	1946	I-Hol	xF..E	132	8,860	17,000	14,300	-0.69	Protest against theological liberalism. HQ Altoona (PA). 257n,W=63%,577Yy.
Evangelical Presbyterian Church	1981	I-Ref	RF..E	174	51,423	–	60,000	7.14	*EPC.* Conservative denomination with 9 geographical presbyteries (8 USA, 1 Argentina).2n.382n
Evangelistic Messengers Association		I-3cW	.....	400	70,000	–	100,000	0.05	Integrated Charismatics. HQ Cleveland, TN.
Evangelistic Ministries Ch Intern	1995	I-3fB	.....	16	7,800	–	10,000	98.11	*EMCI.* Full Gospel theology. Schism ex CoGiC. HQ Arkansas. Abroad: 700 in 1 church in Japan.
Evangelistic Missionary Fellowship	1928	I-3fW	.....	20	2,500	2,000	3,000	1.64	Evangelism, missions, church planting. White Charismatics, with Full Gospel theology.
Faith Christian Fellowship Intern	1977	I-3cW	.....	272	89,500	–	200,000	5.56	*FCFI.* Integrated nondenominational Charismatics. HQ Tulsa (OK). Abroad: 245,700 in 818 chs.
Faith Ministries Christian Church	1972	I-3fW	.....	12	3,000	–	4,000	4.35	F=P.E. Paino. *Calvary Temple.* 7 overseas mission fields.
Faith Tabernacle Council of Churches	1962	I-3aO	.....	50	20,000	8,000	23,000	4.31	*FTCC.* Black Oneness pentecostals.
Father Divine Peace Mission	1919	I-mar	x....	1	500	10,000	1,000	-8.80	Formerly 1 million followers. 1965 death of founder. 95% Black. In 13 nations.
Fell of Charismatic Chs & Ministries	c1975	I-3cW	.....	100	20,000	–	30,000	5.00	*FCCM.* F=William Ligon.
Fellowship of Christian Assemblies	1922	I-3pW	.....	140	30,240	30,000	50,000	2.06	Latter Rain doctrines. Whites. Abroad: 20,400 in 85 chs in Canada; also 46 other countries.
Fellowship of Christians & Chs United	1993	I-3cW	.....	10	6,200	–	9,000	50.00	*FOCCUS.* S=Service. Network of Bible schools and churches. No foreign work.
Fellowship of Chs and Ministers Int	1986	I-3cW	.....	30	4,325	–	5,000	11.11	*FCMI.* Whites, Full Gospel theology. Some work abroad.
Fellowship of Connected Churches	1996	I-3dW	.....	20	10,000	–	15,000	20.00	Group of Southern Baptist charismatic congregations. Based Forth Worth, TX. No work abroad
Fellowship of Ev Bible Churches	1889	P-Men	G...E	37	4,400	6,500	5,200	-0.89	Formerly Evangelical Mennonite Brethren. Russian immigrants. 37n. 156 missionaries abroad.
Fellowship of Fundamental Bible Chs	1939	I-Fun	xT..T	25	1,436	3,186	2,090	-1.67	*FFBC.* Schism ex Methodist Protestant Ch as Bible Protestant Ch. HQ Glassboro, NJ. 60n.
Fellowship of Grace Brethren Chs	1939	I-Dun	.....	322	39,237	12,000	45,000	5.43	Calvinistic schism ex Ch of the Brethren. 1969 Statement of Faith. HQ Winona Lake (IN).
Fellowship of International Chs	1993	I-3aB	.....	30	4,000	–	8,000	50.00	*FOIC.* Ex AMEZC. Initially, Black, HQ Duluth, GA.
Fellowship of Messianic Congs		I-3mJ	.....	20	2,000	–	4,000	0.05	*FMC.* 10% are Messianic Jewish believers in Christ, 90% are Gentiles.
Fellowship of Vineyard Harvester Chs	1989	I-3pW	.....	40	6,000	–	9,000	16.67	Mostly White. HQ Cedartown, GA. Member in International Communion of Charismatic Chs.

Continued overleaf

Country Table 2–continued

Official name (bold type = church with over 10% of all affiliated) 1	Begun 2	Type 3	Counc 4	Congs 5	Adults 6	Affiliated 1970 7	Affiliated 1995 8	G% 9	Names, notes, and other statistics (see Codebook, Part 3) 10
Filipino Assemblies of the Firstborn	1933	I-3pF	.....	50	5,000	5,000	8,000	1.90	Largely immigrant Filipino pentecostals.
Fire-Baptized Holiness Ch (Wesleyan)	1904	P-Hol	.F..E	49	692	1,000	900	-0.42	Very small denomination, but a member of NAE.
First Church of Jesus Christ	1962	I-3pW	.....	50	3,000	3,000	4,000	1.16	Schism ex Church of Jesus Christ. 43 clergy.
First Ch of Jesus Christ Apostolic	1965	I-3aU	.....	60	10,000	1,000	15,000	11.44	*FCJCA.* Mainly Haitians (with some Jamaicans). Abroad: 27 chs (Haiti 20, Jamaica 4).
First Congregational Methodist Ch	1852	I-Hol	.....	70	4,000	10,000	7,000	-1.42	Schism ex Methodist Episcopal Ch South. In southern states. 50n,657Yy.
First Glorious Temple Apostolic	c1980	I-3aO	.....	20	2,000	–	3,000	6.67	Black Apostolic (Oneness) denomination.
Foundation of Praise	1970	I-3cW	.....	300	35,000	–	45,000	53.51	Literature distribution. White Charismatics.
Free Christian Zion Church of Christ	1905	I-3pB	.....	667	20,000	30,000	27,400	-0.36	Black pentecostals. Split ex AMEZC & Nat Bapt Conv USA. Relief programs. 340n.
Free Church of God	1935	I-3pW	.....	100	5,000	2,000	10,000	6.65	*FCG.* Schism ex CoG of Prophecy. Archbishop, 5 bishops, 200 ministers. HQ Michigan.
Free Gospel Church	1916	I-3pW	...X.	20	2,000	2,000	3,100	1.77	*FGC.* 1916, ex CMA. Small pentecostal denomination. Rigid membership standards. 20n,1s.
Free Methodist Ch of North America	1860	I-Hol	VF..E	1,038	57,696	225,000	82,766	-3.92	3 *General Conferences: NAmerica, Egypt, Japan.* In 30 countries. 700n,1j,1s(59),W=58%.
Friends General Conference	1656	P-Qua	QW...	520	17,442	50,000	31,700	-1.81	*FGC.* Organized 1900. 9 YMs in USA (4 also in FUM), including Philadelphia, NY.
Friends United Meeting	1902	P-Qua	QW..W	535	55,000	100,000	80,000	-0.89	*FUM. Five Years Meeting.* 26% all world's Quakers. 11 YMs in USA. 548n,412t(36299).
Friends Yearly Meetings (unaffiliated)		P-Qua	Q....	118	6,724	8,000	9,610	0.05	6 *YMs. Alaska, Central, Missouri Valley, Oregon, Pacific, Southern Appalachian.*
Full Counsel Christian Fell of Chs	1984	I-3wW	.....	7	2,500	–	3,000	9.09	*FCCFC.* Word of Faith. Ch planting, training, development. One church abroad (700 members).
Full Faith Church of Love	1966	I-3cW	.....	3	9,300	500	12,000	13.56	Integrated, mostly White Charismatics.
Full Gospel Assemblies International	1947	I-3fW	.....	274	13,700	6,000	17,140	4.29	From the Full Gospel Bible Institute, HQ Coatesville, PA. Integrated, mostly White Charismatics.
Full Gospel Baptist Church Fellowship	1993	I-3fD	.....	5,000	500,000	–	1,100,000	50.00	*FGBCF.* F=bp Paul Morton. Black. Ex NBCA, NBCUSA. Missions: Bahamas, S Africa, Russia.
Full Gospel Catholic Church	c1985	I-3fB	.....	10	1,000	–	2,000	10.00	Schism ex RCC(M-Washington DC) by Black priests and congregations.
Full Gospel Church Association	1952	I-3fW	.....	80	2,300	3,000	3,500	0.62	One of several small Full Gospel networks.
Full Gospel Church in Christ	1960	I-3fW	.....	25	10,000	2,000	15,000	8.39	*FGCC.* Evangelism, church-planting, missions. Mostly White Charismatics.
Full Gospel Chs International	1974	I-3fW	.....	125	6,250	–	8,000	4.76	*FGCI.* Full Gospel theology. HQ Cahokia, IL. Abroad: 3,000 members in 24 chs.
Full Gospel Evangelistic Association	1982	I-3fW	.....	50	5,500	–	8,000	7.69	*FGEA.* White Pentecostals. HQ Lafayette, LA. No work abroad.
Full Gospel Fell of Chs & Ministries	1962	I-3fW	.....	650	195,000	3,000	320,000	20.54	Deliverance movement. Mostly Whites. HQ Dallas(TX). Abroad: 300,000 in 590 churches.
Full Gospel Ministers Association	1967	I-3fW	.....	76	12,000	–	13,000	46.07	White Pentecostals. HQ Paducah, KY. Abroad: 20,000 in 224 churches.
Full Gospel Mission in Hawaii	1936	I-3fF	.....	25	2,000	2,000	4,000	2.81	1936 founded in Hawaii, linked with M=ICFG(Los Angeles). All Filipinos. 1s.
Fullness/Praise Network of Churches	1978	I-3cW	.....	6,000	1,800,000	–	3,300,000	5.88	Network of Southern Baptist charismatic churches, many expelled from SBC.
Fundamental Methodist Church	c1970	I-Fun	.....	12	675	–	1,075	32.21	White Fundamentalists.
Gate Fellowship of Churches	c1980	I-3cW	.....	5	6,200	–	8,000	6.67	*GFC.* Network with mostly White Charismatics.
General Assoc of General Baptists	1714	P-Bap	TF...	1,187	94,451	100,000	115,000	0.56	Organized 1870. Mid-central, SW USA. 1115n,1j,1s,854t(80500),W=80%,500Y.
General Assoc of Regular Baptist Chs	1932	I-Bap	xt..t	1,582	216,408	360,000	333,000	-0.31	*GARBC.* Anti-modernist, ex Amer Bapt Conv. 1976: 1,528 churches. 6s,10445Y.
General Church of the New Jerusalem	1897	m-Swe	x....	34	3,049	1,940	5,424	4.20	*New Ch.* Swedenborgian Ch. Schism ex General Conv of NJ. 31n,7s,W=25%,120Yy.
Gen Conf Mennonite Brethren Chs	1876	P-Men	GF..E	134	50,915	20,000	82,130	5.81	1860 schism in Ukraine. 1960, joined by Krimmer MBC. 173n,1s.
General Conf Ch of God (7th-day)	1860	P-Adv	.....	153	5,700	8,000	7,000	-0.53	1860 separated from Adventist movement; name chosen in 1884.
General Conference Mennonite Ch	1860	P-Men	G....	227	33,812	49,105	43,162	-0.51	*GCMC.* Large membership in Canada and South America. 314n,1s. 1995 merged with MC.
Global Network of Christian Ministries	1957	I-3oW	.....	350	35,000	2,500	45,000	12.26	Merger Global Christian Min, Int Network of Ministries. Ex UPC. 500n. Abroad: 20,000 in 50 chs.
Glorious Ch of God in Christ Apostolic	1921	I-3aO	.....	20	2,000	2,700	2,300	-0.64	Major split as Original GCoGiC secedes in 1952, over divorce. Black Oneness. Declining.
God's Missionary Church	1935	I-Met	.....	40	1,700	2,000	2,200	0.38	High membership standards. Eastern, southern USA. 41n,1p,W=98%,1483z.
Gospel Crusade Ministerial Fellowship	1953	I-3cW	.....	175	35,000	2,000	90,000	16.45	Begun by disfellowshiped Mennonites. 44 overseas mission fields: 6,600 members in 33 chs.
Gospel Harvester Churches	1961	I-3pW	.....	20	8,000	10,000	11,000	0.38	F=Earl P. Paulk, Jr. M=GHEA. Ex CoG(Cleveland).
Gospel Ministers & Churches Intern	1982	I-3fW	.....	40	8,130	–	10,000	7.69	*GMCI.* Full Gospel theology and teaching.
Grace Gospel Fellowship	1939	I-Non	.F...	128	45,000	10,000	60,000	7.43	Ultra-dispensationalist. Teaches Holy Spirit baptism. HQ Grand Rapids. (1970) 62n. (1990) 196n.
Grace Gospel Fell (Network of Ministers)	1938	I-3aW	.....	25	24,900	9,000	32,000	5.20	*GGF (Network of Ministries).* 5-fold ministry. Waco (TX). Abroad: 50,000 members in 500 chs.
Grace Korean Ch & Missions	1982	I-3aK	.....	15	4,000	–	7,000	7.69	154 missionaries in 38 countries: Russia 670 chs, China 600 chs, Viet Nam 280 chs.
Grace Presbytery	1982	I-3aW	.....	20	3,000	–	6,000	7.69	M=GPSM,GM,ARC Ministries. Abroad: Romania and 21 countries.
Greater Emmanuel Int Fell of Chs & Min	1961	I-3aO	.....	40	31,100	7,000	40,000	7.22	1991 name changed from GE Apostolic Faith Tabernacle. Abroad: 47 chs. Black Oneness.
Greek Evangelical Church	c1960	P-Ref	Rwc..	30	3,000	1,000	4,000	5.70	*Hellenike Evangelike Ekklesia.* Immigrants from GEC (Greece). HQ Boston.
Greek Orthodox AD of N & S America	1864	O-Gre	CwO.W	579	1,400,000	1,900,000	1,950,000	0.10	AD, 1922. In EP Constantinople. 15 bishops. 585n,14r,1s(120),709t(64471),W=30%,12650Yy.
Gulf States Pastors & Chs Fellowship	1977	I-3cW	.....	270	10,000	–	20,000	5.56	In Louisiana, Mississippi. Gulf States Missions Agency (GSMA). 1,400 linked USA churches.
Handsome Lake Long House Religion	1800	I-mar	.....	10	1,000	4,000	3,000	-1.14	Seneca Iroquois Indians, NY. Oldest continuing prophet movement in world.
Harvest Christian Fellowship	c1980	I-3cW	.....	10	12,000	–	20,000	6.67	*HCF.* In Riverside, CA. One million have attended annual crusades in Anaheim since 1989.
Harvest International Ministries	1995	I-3cW	.....	100	6,000	–	10,000	98.11	*HIM.* HQ Pasadena, CA. No work abroad.
Hebrew-Christian communities	1894	I-3mJ	x....	50	10,000	10,000	20,000	2.81	M=American Board of Missions to Jews. 100,000 converts in other denominations also.
Hellenic Orthodox Church of America	1924	I-OCd	c....	4	1,000	1,000	2,000	2.81	Schism ex Greek Orthodox AD rejecting New (Gregorian) Calendar. Astoria (LI).
Higher Dimensions Chs Network	c1980	I-3cD	.....	1	3,000	–	4,000	6.67	*HDCN.* Black leadership for large charismatic network with TV ministry.
Highland Park Baptist Chs	1939	I-Bap	.....	71	57,000	50,000	80,000	1.90	*HPBC.* Independent Baptists. HQ Chattanooga, TN. 70 satellite congregations.
Highway Christian Ch of Christ	1929	I-3aO	.....	13	3,000	3,100	4,000	1.02	*HCCC.* Conservative Oneness pentecostals. Black.
Holiness Christian Church	1882	I-Hol	.....	50	5,400	5,900	7,000	0.69	White. Rigid membership requirements. In mid-Atlantic states. 44n,W=36%.
Holiness Methodist Churches	1900	P-Hol	x....	20	1,600	3,000	2,500	-0.73	Two bodies: N Carolina, N Dakota. Grew out of Northwestern Holiness Assoc. 1s.
Holy Temple Church of Christ	1969	I-3aO	.....	10	2,000	1,000	3,000	4.49	*HTCC.* Black Oneness pentecostals.
Holy Ukrainian Autocephalic OC Exile	1951	I-Ukr	C.O..	17	3,800	4,800	5,500	0.55	*OC=Orthodox Ch in.* Schism ex Ukrainian Orth Ch in the USA. 1 bishop,24n.
Hopi Independent Indian Churches	1946	I-Non	I	8	400	1,000	1,000	0.00	Several Hopi churches in Arizona. Ex Mennonites. One centre in Hotevilla.
Hosanna Christian Fellowship		I-3aW	.....	0	0	–	0	0.05	*HCF.* White Apostolics.
House of God, Ch of the Living God	1889	I-3pB	.....	100	2,600	3,000	3,100	0.13	*Pillar & Ground of the Truth.* Black pentecostals. Freemason origin. 200n,1p,24Y.
House of God, Ground of Truth	1919	I-3pB	.....	64	2,000	4,000	3,100	-1.01	*Saints in Christ.* Black pentecostals. Holiness living. Declining.
Hungarian Reformed Ch in America	1891	P-Ref	RW..W	27	7,280	11,250	9,780	-0.56	Immigrants from Reformed Ch of Hungary, 1924 refusal to join E & RC (now UCC). 34n.
Hutterian Brethren	1874	P-Men	x....	95	36,700	8,800	42,800	6.53	Origin from Jacob Hutter (c1550). Mid-west. Majority in Canada. White. 20h.
Independent AME Church	1907	I-Met	.....	10	900	2,000	1,800	-0.42	Schism ex African Methodist Episcopal Church in Jacksonville (Florida). Black.
Independent Assemblies Fellowship	1955	I-3fW	.....	300	45,000	2,000	60,000	14.57	Full Gospel. HQ Avant, OK. Abroad: 500,000 in 500 chs: Africa, Philippines, Australia, Mexico.
Independent Assemblies of God	1911	I-3pW	.....	476	9,000	20,000	25,000	0.90	*Philadelphia Chs.* Scandinavians: Swedish Pentecostals. (M=SFM). 367n. Abroad: 600 chs.
Independent Assemblies of God Intern	1918	I-3pW	.....	800	100,000	80,000	170,000	3.06	In 17 countries (500,000 in Brazil), 200 missionaries. 1947, Latter Rain controversy. 1800n,12s.
Independent Bible Baptist Missions	1949	I-Fun	xT..T	20	15,000	30,000	35,000	0.62	Independent fundamentalist Baptist churches with strong overseas missions. 1s.
Independent Catholic Ch Intern	c1800	I-CCa	.....	10	1,800	2,000	3,000	1.64	Early schism from Roman Catholic Ch. In 1990s, aggressive electronic evangelism via Internet.
Independent Christian Chs Intern	1984	I-Fun	.....	110	12,000	–	15,000	9.09	*ICCI.* HQ Texas. 147 ministers. Overseas work is same size as in USA.
Indep Chs of the Latter Rain Revival	1948	I-3pW	.....	400	30,000	10,000	40,000	5.70	Tabernacle David; Portland Bible College.
Independent Faith Movement	1975	I-3wW	.....	600	10,000	–	20,000	5.00	RMAI. Rhema Bible Chs. Prosperity teaching. HQ Tulsa, OK. 50% ex-mainline Charismatics.
Indep Fundamental Chs of America	1922	I-Fun	.t..t	698	82,400	210,000	127,000	-1.99	Organized to safeguard fundamentalist doctrine.2131n,10,4s,904t(203812).(1993)1,366 workers.
Independent Spiritualist Association	1924	m-Spi	.....	80	4,000	10,000	7,000	-1.42	*ISA.* Schism ex NSA. Rapid growth, now schisms. 700 mediums, healers, missioners.
Indian Pentecostal Ch of America	c1975	I-3pI	.....	300	80,000	–	190,000	5.00	*IPCA.* Large independent church from India. Abroad: 950,000 members in 20 countries.
Indian Shaker Church	1883	I-mar	I	15	1,500	5,000	4,000	-0.89	Yakima Reservation. Shuffle dance. 1960s upsurge among young Indians, NCalifornia.
Indonesian Full Gospel Fellowship	1980	I-3fG	.....	25	2,000	–	3,000	6.67	Begun by Indonesia students. Abroad: 60 chs, 10,000 members Singapore,Taiwan,Malaysia et al
Integrity Leadership Ministries	1990	I-3cW	.....	60	60,000	–	100,000	20.00	High-visibility White charismatics, based on mother church of 15,000 in Dallas, TX.
Int Assoc of Messianic Congs & Syna	1967	I-3mJ	x....	360	10,000	2,000	16,000	8.67	*IAMCS. S=Synagogues.* Branches in UK, Russia. Members are mostly Gentiles.
Interdenominational Ministries Intern		I-3cW	.....	100	20,000	–	30,000	0.05	Integrated Charismatics. HQ Vista, CA.
Intern Alliance of Chs of the Truth	1987	m-Div	.....	20	500	–	1,000	12.50	*Divine Science.* Metaphysical, New Thought. Aggressive ch-planting in CA, ID, BC (Canada).
International Apostolic Fellowship	1969	I-3oW	.....	100	15,000	1,000	20,000	12.73	White Oneness Pentecostals.
Int Assoc of Religious Science Chs	1948	m-Sci	x....	30	3,000	10,000	7,000	-1.42	*IARSC.* Schism ex Ch of Religious Science, rejecting authority of mother church.
Intern Ch of the Foursquare Gospel	1918	P-Pe2	ZF.XE	1,832	231,522	200,000	367,000	2.46	*ICFG.* HQ Angelus Temple, Los Angeles. 90% White. 2690n,11603Y. Missions in 78 countries.
Intern Council of Community Chs	1946	P-Con	.W..W	517	195,000	200,000	250,000	0.90	Formerly National Council of CCs (White) & Biennial Council of CCs (Black). 1974 joined WCC.
Int Christian Ch & Ministerial Assoc	1966	I-3fW	.....	141	20,236	3,000	30,000	9.65	*ICCMA.* Oneness Charismatics, some Trinitarians, ex UPC. Sunday attenders 9,115.
International Christian Churches	1943	I-3pP	.....	2	600	1,000	1,100	0.38	*ICC.* Schism ex Disciples of Christ in the Philippines, Mainly in Hawaii.
International Churches of Christ	1979	I-3cW	.....	124	110,000	–	152,600	6.25	1979 Crossroads, then Boston Ch of Christ. Britain, 113 countries. Shepherding controversy
Intern Conf of Charismatic Chs	c1965	I-3cW	.....	3,000	100,000	20,000	150,000	8.39	*ICCC.* Attempt to create a global communion.F=Meares,Paulk,Idahosa(Nigeria),McAllister(Brazil)
Intern Conference of Word Ministries	1979	I-3wW	.....	40	5,500	–	7,000	6.25	*ICWM.* Integrated Charismatics.
Int Convention of Faith Chs & Minis	1978	I-3wW	.....	1,000	172,864	–	190,000	5.88	*ICFCM.* Word of Faith tradition. HQ Tulsa. Abroad (Philippines, 20 countries), 325,500 members.
International Deliverance Churches	1962	I-3pW	.....	20	1,000	10,000	2,000	-6.23	Related to Branhamites. HQ Dallas. Conventions, conferences, ordinations.
International Evangelical Churches	1964	I-3cB	.....	70	360,000	80,000	500,000	7.61	*IEC.* Churches: Africa 430, USA 70, South America 50, Italy 20, Jamaica 1.
International Evangelism Church	1959	I-Non	.....	100	4,700	8,000	7,000	-0.53	*IEC.* Independent White grouping. Autonomous congregations. 150n,1p,1s,W=80%,100Y.
International Evangelism Crusaders	1959	I-3fW	.....	50	175,000	30,000	240,000	8.67	'Harmony of Space, Science & True Christianity'. HQ Van Nuys (CA). Abroad: 430,000; 325 chs.
International Fellowship		I-3pW	.....	50	10,000	–	13,000	0.05	Small pentecostal body.
Intern Fellowship of Faith Ministries	c1970	I-3wW	.....	2,000	150,000	–	200,000	62.95	*IFFM.* Attempt to form overall communion. F=K. Hagin, K. Copeland, O. Roberts.
International Full Gospel Fellowship	1947	I-3fW	.....	105	2,800	3,600	4,000	0.42	Mainly in southeastern Pennsylvania.
Intern Gen Assembly of Spiritualists	1936	m-Spi	.....	35	2,668	164,072	4,000	-13.81	Overall organization to sponsor new spiritualist churches. 221n. Drastic decline.
International Gospel Assemblies	1962	I-3pW	.....	500	300,000	10,000	400,000	15.90	Large agglomeration of White-led pentecostal congregations.
International Ministerial Fellowship	1958	I-3cW	.....	110	58,690	40,000	182,500	6.26	Credentializing, support, missions-sending. Liturgical. Abroad: 20 chs, 5,000 members.
International Ministers Forum	1950	I-3fW	.....	400	99,750	25,000	140,000	7.13	*IMF.* Full Gospel. F=Louise Copeland. Integrated. High % women pastors.
International Pentecostal Ch of Christ	1914	I-3pW	x..XE	78	2,612	3,500	5,102	1.52	White Pacifists. 1976 merger of IPA, PCC. 11 states. 13 countries, 1,900 chs, 150,000 members.
International Pentecostal Holiness Ch	1898	P-Pe3	ZF.XE	1,582	137,313	250,000	262,000	0.19	*IPHC.* White. 3-body merger. Worldwide. 41 periodicals. 2422n,1j,4p,2s,W=60%.
International Revival Network	1994	I-3fW	.....	50	7,000	–	20,000	100.00	*IRN.* Toronto Blessing congregations ex Vineyard and other denominations. In 70 countries.
Jehovah's Witnesses	1872	m-Jeh	x....	9,890	914,079	1,000,000	2,260,000	3.32	*Watch Tower.* World HQ Brooklyn. In USA, 22% Blacks (1975) 25740n,40814Y. (1995) 43663Y.
Jesus is Lord Fellowship/Ministries	c1985	I-3pF	x....	150	15,000	–	25,000	10.00	*JILF.* F=E. Villanueva. Movement in Philippines, among youth, students. Multiple ministries.
Kingsway Fellowship International	1966	I-3fW	.....	170	17,314	10,000	20,000	2.81	*KFI.* Full Gospel. F=D.L. Browning. HQ Des Moines, Iowa. Abroad: 449 chs, 62,250 members.
Kodesh Church of Immanuel	1929	I-Hol	.....	10	600	800	1,000	0.90	Black Holiness body, ex AMEC.
Korean American Presbyterian Ch	1976	P-Ref	.....	500	26,988	–	52,000	5.26	*KAPC.* M=KPC(Hap Tong) from Korea. Missionaries to Kazakhstan et alia. 1s(120).
Korean Baptist Convention	c1970	P-Bap	T....	800	90,000	–	210,000	63.26	*KBC.* Korean immigrants and transients; related to SBC, BWA.
Korean Full Gospel Chs of America	c1980	I-3fK	.....	600	100,000	–	200,000	6.67	*KFGCA.* M=FGC of Seoul, Korea. Many independent Korean churches in USA.
Korean Presbyterian Church	c1930	P-Ref	RWE..	1,560	200,000	250,000	510,000	2.89	*KPC.* M=KPC(Tong Hap) from Korea. Koreans.
Korean Presbyterian Ch in America	c1980	P-Ref	R....	203	21,788	–	26,988	6.67	*KPCA.* Korean immigrants.
Latin Ameri Council of Christian Chs	1923	I-3pL	.....	130	54,500	20,000	70,000	5.14	*LACCC. Concilio Latino-Americano de Igls Cr.* Begun by Mexicans, ex AoG. 50% in Texas.
Latvian Ev Lutheran Ch in America	1946	P-Lut	Lw...	56	13,004	20,000	16,900	-0.67	*Latvijas Ev Lut Baznica.* Latvian refugees from USSR. 84n,W=30%,197Yy.
LeSEA Ministries Network	1957	I-3wW	.....	200	5,500	1,000	8,000	8.67	Integrated, mostly White. Lester Sumrall Evangelistic Assoc Ex AoG. Sizable work overseas.
Liberal Catholic Church	1947	I-Lib	.....	34	2,500	4,000	6,800	2.15	LCC(California). Split ex LCC in Christian direction. 5 bishops,62n,W=35%,110Yy.
Liberal Cath Ch, Order of St Germain	1969	I-Lib	.....	4	1,000	3,000	1,400	-3.00	In Texas, Colorado, Oklahoma, California. 22n,5p(58),W=50%,79Yy.

Continued opposite

Country Table 2–continued

Official name (bold type = church with over 10% of all affiliated) 1	*Begun* 2	*Type* 3	*Counc* 4	*Congs* 5	*Adults* 6	*Affiliated 1970* 7	*Affiliated 1995* 8	*G%* 9	*Names, notes, and other statistics (see Codebook, Part 3)* 10
Liberty Baptist Churches	1956	I-Fun	.....	510	200,000	30,000	250,000	8.85	Independent Baptists. HQ Lynchburg, VA. College, seminary, TV ministry. 1500n. 110n
Liberty Fellowship of Chs & Ministers	1974	I-3cW	.....	200	22,500	–	30,483	4.76	White. HQ Birmingham (AL), Pensacola (FL). Agency: Global Missionary Evangelism.
Life Links International Fellowship	1986	I-3cW	.....	21	1,950	–	3,000	11.11	*LLIF.* Related to UK's New Churches (Cornerstone). Abroad: 3,750 in 30 chs.
Life Ministerial Fellowship Intern	1981	I-3cW	.....	10	4,000	–	5,100	7.14	*LMFI.* White Charismatics. Abroad: 7,000 members in 26 churches, in Philippines, Myanmar, &c.
Light of the World Ch (Aaronistas)	c1950	I-3oL	x....	50	3,000	2,000	5,000	3.73	*Iglesia La Luz del Mundo (Aaronistas).* Pentecostals from Mexico; in California.
Lighthouse Gospel Fellowship	1958	I-3pW	.....	300	27,500	3,000	35,000	10.33	*LGF.* F=H.A. Chaney.
Lithuanian National Cath Ch in Ameri	1914	I-OCa	U....	3	1,200	4,000	2,000	-2.73	Old Catholics from USSR. Under jurisdiction of Polish NCC of America. 4n.
Living Faith Christian Centers	1987	I-3cF	.....	297	15,000	–	30,000	12.50	*LFCC. Living Faith Ministries.* Filipinos. HQ Duluth, MN. Abroad: 37 chs in 16 countries.
Living Witness of the Apostolic Faith	c1965	I-3aO	.....	30	2,000	1,000	2,500	3.73	*LWAF.* Oneness Pentecostals. Black.
Lutheran Church-Missouri Synod	1847	P-Lut	x....	5,964	1,955,008	2,895,668	2,600,846	-0.43	*LCMS.* German origin. 1976 schism: AELC. 7041n,16s(1041),5552t(815522),W=45%,94363Yy.
Lutheran Chs of the Reformation	1964	I-Lut	.....	25	4,500	6,273	5,000	-0.90	Split ex LCMS to establish confessional Lutheranism. HQ Detroit. 31n,31t(1950).
Malankara Orthodox Syrian Ch	1968	O-SyM	DWE..	65	20,000	1,000	30,000	14.57	*Orthodox Syrian Ch of the East. SOC of Malabar.* Diocese under Catholicate rejecting P Antioch.
Manna Church	c1990	I-3cW	.....	10	2,000	–	3,000	20.00	*Mana-Igreja Crista.* Large Charismatic movement from Portugal (begun 1980 there, now huge).
Mar Thoma Syrian Church of Malabar	c1940	I-ReO	xWE..	2	2,000	2,000	4,000	2.81	Immigrant Malayalam-speaking Syrians from South India, with own clergy.
Maranatha Christian Churches	1972	I-3cW	.....	150	5,000	–	8,000	4.35	Ex AoG. Begun as a campus ministry. Work in 17 foreign countries. Founder withdrew 1988.
Mariavite Old Catholic Church	1930	I-OCa	U....	200	220,000	200,000	358,176	2.36	Immigrants from Poland, where church began in 1893. 1 archbishop, 2 bishops, 48n,30w,10 m.
Melodyland Christian Center	1961	I-3cW	.....	5	1,000	5,000	3,000	-2.02	Famed during 1970s (15,000 Sunday attenders); 1985, crisis, financial trouble.
Mennonite Church General Assembly	1683	P-Men	G....	1,055	102,276	120,000	159,165	1.14	German. Regions II-IV(I in Canada). 2236n,1p,3s,967t(110475),W=80%,2845Y.
Mennonites (unaffiliated)	c1800	I-Men	.....	353	17,200	8,000	21,000	3.94	Scattered Amish and other groups unrelated to any Mennonite denomination.
Metropolitan Church Association	1894	P-Hol	x....	20	600	1,000	2,000	2.81	Formed 1894 as Metropolitan Holiness Ch, ex Methodist Episcopal Ch. Many foreign fields.
Metropolitan Spiritual Chs of Christ	1925	I-3aB	.....	100	12,000	15,000	20,000	1.16	Black Trinitarian Apostolics. Eastern USA, HQ Baltimore, MD. Overseas work in Ghana, Liberia.
Midwest Cong Christian Fellowship	1958	I-Con	....E	30	4,000	8,000	7,000	-0.53	Grouping of independent White congregations. HQ Union City (Indiana).
Ministerial Fellowship of USA	1947	I-3fW	.....	110	1,500	1,000	2,000	2.81	Full Gospel network. F=John G. Lake.
Ministers Fellowship International	1987	I-3cW	.....	600	34,500	–	50,000	12.50	*MFI.* HQ Bible Temple, Portland, OR. Covering for 1,000 pastors and elders worldwide.
Miracle Life Fellowship	1951	I-3fW	.....	200	13,000	10,000	20,000	2.81	*MRF.* 1970, Miracle Revival Fellowship (M=A.A. Allen Revivals).
Missionary Church	1889	P-Hol	xF..E	303	26,910	38,000	39,948	0.20	1969 union Missionary Ch Assoc, United Miss Ch. 10 Districts. 489n,1j,1s,W=66%,1333Y.
Missionary Gospel Ch International	1972	I-3pW	.....	500	22,500	–	30,000	4.35	Integrated White Charismatics. HQ South Carolina. Abroad: 50 churches.
Missionary Methodist Ch of America	1913	I-Hol	.....	15	900	1,330	1,100	-0.76	Schism ex Wesleyan Methodist Church. Mainly North Carolina. 29n,W=24%,38Yy.
Missionary Revival Crusade	1959	I-3cW	.....	20	1,500	2,000	3,000	1.64	Based in Laredo, TX. 52 workers. Work abroad in Mexico, Colombia.
Morning Star International	1994	I-3vW	.....	73	6,000	–	8,000	100.00	Whites, Filipinos. In CA, NV. Churches abroad in 15 countries: Philippines 30, China, Indonesia.
Moravian Church in America	1734	P-Mor	xW..W	153	43,524	100,000	57,857	-2.17	3 *Provinces (Northern, Southern, Alaska), Unity of Brethren.* 136n,4r,1s(14).
Mount Tabor As of Regular Baptists	1890	P-Fun	x....	6	800	1,200	1,000	-0.73	Independent fundamentalist grouping. In Indiana and Illinois. White. W=50%,30Y.
Mt Sinai Holy Ch of North America	1924	I-3pB	.....	300	35,000	10,000	50,000	6.65	Black pentecostals.
Narraganset Indian Church	1741	I-Non	I	1	400	1,000	800	-0.89	In RI. Oldest Indian independent ch in USA. Focus for large Indian annual meetings.
National Assoc of Free Will Baptists	1701	P-Bap	xF...	2,461	234,508	280,000	345,000	0.84	Ex ABC. Whites. 1972, left NAE. 3669n,3s(250),2200t(181000),W=60%,3500Y.
National Baptist Conv of America	1880	I-Bap	TW..W	19,744	3,500,000	3,300,000	4,270,000	1.04	*NBC.* Part of first major Black Baptist body; NBCUSA split off in 1915. 28574n,1s.
National Baptist Convention, USA	1773	I-Bap	TW..b	44,444	8,200,000	6,426,000	9,410,000	1.54	*NBC.* 1915 split from NBC America. Black. HQ Nashville. (1970) 27500n,1s. (1990) 32832n.
National Baptist Ev LSS Assembly	1937	I-Bap	.....	270	60,000	70,000	80,000	0.54	*LSS=Life & Soul Saving.* Black. Begun 1921, under NBC until 1937 split. 137n.
National Conservative Christian Ch	1993	I-Eva	.....	20	2,285	–	6,000	50.00	*NCCC.* White. HQ Sarasota. Abroad: 2,100; 13 chs: Saudi Arabia, Bonaire, Brazil, Turkey, India.
Nat David Spiritual Temple of Christ	1932	I-3pB	.....	70	45,000	60,000	65,000	0.32	Black. Ex Baptist Missionary Ch; founder archbishop David Short. 1j,1s.
National Fellowship of Brethren Chs	1939	I-Dun	xF...	240	35,000	50,000	60,000	0.73	*NFBC (Winona Lake).* Grace Brethren. Ex Ashland. 404n,1s,226t(40326),W=86%,2275Y.
National Missionary Baptist Conv of A	1988	I-Bap	T....	1,000	2,500,000	–	3,000,000	14.29	*NMBCA.* Split ex NBCA over control of publishing; claims 89% of all members. HQ Nashville.
National Primitive Baptist Convention	1865	I-Bap	.....	1,530	1,000,000	2,007,000	1,300,000	-1.72	Black. Formerly Colored Primitive Baptists. HQ Tallahassee (FL). 597n,2150t(32200).
National Spiritual Alliance of the USA	1913	m-Spi	.....	30	2,000	5,000	3,000	-2.02	Schism ex NSA. Social, literary, educational, music activity. 56n.
National Spiritualist Assoc of Chs	1893	m-Spi	x....	120	3,406	8,000	4,670	-2.13	*NSA.* Main orthodox spiritualist body. Provides spiritism's literature. 163n,1s.
Native American Ch of North America	1870	I-mar	x...I	450	110,000	400,000	300,000	-1.14	*NAC.* 23 Chapters. Among all US Indian tribes. Strict ethics; peyote eating.
Navajo Native American Church	c1900	I-mar	I	40	15,000	60,000	40,000	-1.61	60% of all Navajo Indians. Linked with NAC. One of many Navajo indigenous bodies.
Neo-American Church	1903	I-Non	.....	20	2,000	10,000	6,000	-2.02	Begun by plains settlers in Oklahoma. Declining. 73n,1p,1s(18),W=25%.
Neo-American Church of California	c1960	m-Gno	.v...	3	1,000	8,000	2,000	-5.39	Syncretistic body mainly in California, with chief priest. Hippies et alii.
Netherlands Reformed Congregations	1865	P-Ref	.....	23	4,218	7,319	8,753	0.72	Immigrants from Holland. HQ Grand Rapids (Michigan). 4n,120Yy.
Network International	1987	I-3aW	x....	31	3,500	–	6,000	12.50	*Tree of Life Church.* HQ San Angelo, TX. Mainly White. 100 churches in 18 countries.
Network of Christian Ministries	1985	I-3aW	.....	200	10,000	–	20,000	10.00	*NCM.* F=Charles Green. Attempt to unite or represent all Neocharismatic networks; collapsed.
Network of Kingdom Churches	1960	I-3pW	.....	900	200,000	70,000	230,000	4.87	*NKC.* Integrated Pentecostals. F=Don Paulk, ex Ch of God. HQ Decatur, GA.
Network of Restoration Churches	1963	I-3cW	.....	100	20,000	1,200	25,000	12.91	*NRC.* Formerly, Revival Fellowship Group. Full Gospel theology. HQ Brea, CA.
New Apostolic Ch of North America	1863	I-3aX	x....	549	25,201	30,000	41,263	1.28	World organization based on Chief Apostle in Zurich (Switzerland). (1970) 383n. (1990) 925n.
New Beginnings Fellowship	c1965	I-3pW	.....	30	2,000	1,000	3,000	4.49	Split from *New Wine* teaching. *Holy Spirit Teaching Ministry.* British Israelite. In USA, Europe.
New Covenant Churches of Maryland	c1975	I-3aW	.....	25	2,500	–	3,000	5.00	*NCCM.* F=Robert Wright.
New Life Christian Fellowship	1988	I-3pW	.....	25	2,500	–	3,000	14.29	*NLCF.* HQ Missouri. Abroad: 300 members in 11 churches (Philippines, Korea).
New Testament Christian Church	1969	I-3pW	.....	70	7,000	1,500	10,000	7.88	1969-86 named New Testament Ch of God. Strict rules.Canada,Costa Rica,Dominican Republic.
New Testament Church of God	1942	I-Hol	.....	850	9,000	15,000	17,000	0.50	*NTCOG.* Schism ex CoG(Anderson). Foreign missions in 8 countries: Latin America, Asia, Africa
New Testament Holiness Church	1966	I-3pW	.....	20	1,000	200	2,000	9.65	Mainly in southeastern US states. HQ Dallas, TX. Emphasis on End-time prophecy.
North American Baptist General Conf	1840	P-Bap	TF...	388	61,000	60,000	90,700	1.67	German Baptist immigrants in 19th century. 423n,1s,332t(55815),1910Y.
North American Catholic Church	1958	I-CCa	.....	15	600	1,290	900	-1.43	Ex original NAORCC. Declining. HQ Brooklyn. Under bishops-at-large.
North American Old Roman Cath Ch	1912	I-CCa	.....	133	41,300	60,098	62,611	0.16	*NAORCC.* Ex RCC. Italians, Poles, Lithuanians. 11n,3s(53),33t,230Yy.
Northwest Yearly Meeting of Friends	1893	P-Qua	.....	53	4,813	8,000	7,422	-0.30	Formerly Oregon Yearly Meeting of Friends. Abroad: work in 6 countries.
Old Calendar Greek Orthodox Church	1924	I-OCd	c....	15	2,500	3,000	3,500	0.62	*Authentic Orth Ch* (200,000 in Greece). Schism rejecting New (Gregorian) Calendar.
Old German Baptist Brethren	1881	I-Dun	.....	55	5,435	8,000	9,880	0.85	*Old Order Dunkers.* Schism ex Church of the Brethren. Ultra-conservative Whites. 130n.
Old Order & Wisler Mennonite Church	1872	P-Men	G....	49	10,000	10,000	18,200	2.42	*Pleasant View Mennonite Ch.* Indiana, OH, PA, VA. 19 bishops. Also in Canada. 101n,125Y.
Old Order Amish Mennonite Church	1720	P-Men	G....	784	56,200	32,000	127,800	5.70	Amish immigrants 1720-40. Iowa. Not centralized. Worship in homes. 1497n,1j.
Old Ritualist Church (Priestless)	1952	I-OBe	.....	15	2,000	1,000	4,000	5.70	*Old Believers. Bespopovsty.* Ex Russian OC, refugees from Turkey, 1952. 1n,1j.
Old Roman Catholic Apostolic Ch	c1965	I-CCa	.....	2	1,000	2,500	2,000	-0.89	Italians, ex Ch of Rome. New York state. Bishop consecrated in Vilatte succession.
Old Roman Catholic Ch (English Rite)	1963	I-CCa	.....	100	15,000	65,128	30,000	-3.05	*Veteris Romanae Catholicae Ecclesiae, US Province.* Declining. 214n,1s(14),W=60%.
Oneness Ministries Network Intern		I-3oW	.....	100	7,000	–	12,000	0.05	*OMNI.* A White-led attempt to organize 'Jesus Only' denominations.
Open Bible Standard Churches	1919	I-3pW	ZF.XE	368	42,000	35,000	52,500	1.64	1932 schism ex ICFG against founder. 725n,1j,3s(250). Missions in 30 countries.
Original Church of God	1886	I-3pW	.....	70	12,000	30,000	20,000	-1.61	Schism ex CoG (Cleveland). White. Mainly east, south-central USA. 150n,40t(129).
Original Glorious Chs of God in Christ	1952	I-3aO	.....	50	4,050	3,000	5,000	2.06	Black Oneness Pentecostals.
Original United Holy Ch, International	1977	I-3aO	.....	220	16,000	–	25,000	5.56	*OUHCI.* Ex UHCA. Black Oneness pentecostals. Abroad: 400 members in 6 chs.
Orthodox Church in America	1792	O-Rus	MWO.W	1,000	616,000	960,000	2,030,000	3.04	*OCA.* Formerly Russian Orth Gk-Cath Ch. A=1970. 7 US dioceses, 15 bps. 440n,33x,2s(150).
Orthodox Presbyterian Church	1932	I-Ref	Jt..t	188	12,600	14,300	19,094	1.16	Anti-modernism schism by 100 ministers ex Presbyterian Ch in USA. 190n.
Overcoming Faith Fellowship Intern	1992	I-3fW	.....	100	9,000	–	12,500	33.33	M=Jerry Savelle Ministries. Abroad: Overcoming Faith Chs of Kenya,Ghana, Nigeria, Philippines
Pentecostal Assemblies of the AF	1984	I-3pW	.....	47	28,000	–	35,000	9.09	*PAAF.* (AF=Apostolic Faith). HQ Carrollton (GA). Abroad: 6 chs (Haiti, Israel, Philippines).
Pentecostal Assemblies of the World	1906	I-3aO	x....	1,600	950,000	60,000	1,270,000	12.99	*PAOW.* Black pentecostals.600n,1s.Missions in Caribbean, India, Israel, Nigeria; over 1,000 chs.
Pentecostal Assembly of Chs of JC	1954	I-3aB	.....	30	2,500	500	3,000	7.43	*PACJC.* HQ Elkton (MD). 55% Black. Half of pastors are female. No foreign work.
Pentecostal Chs of the Apostolic Faith	1957	I-3aO	.....	170	46,000	30,000	60,000	2.81	Black Oneness Pentecostals. 380 ministers.
Pentecostal Church of God	1919	P-Pe2	Z...E	1,171	39,673	180,000	101,786	-2.25	White. HQ Joplin (MO). 1325n,1j,2p,2r. 46 missionaries in 32 countries.
Pentecostal Churches of Christ	1930	I-3pW	.....	50	2,000	2,000	2,500	0.90	Schism ex Pentecostal Ch of Christ (Ohio). Holiness Pentecostals.
Pentecostal Fire-Baptized Holiness Ch	1918	I-3pW	....E	27	200	1,000	400	-3.60	*PFBHC.* Independent pentecostals.
Pentecostal Free Will Baptist Church	1919	I-3pW	...X.	141	11,757	20,000	18,100	-0.40	Schism ex Free Will Baptists. Mostly east coast. 221n,2p,1s(75),W=60%. Decline.
Pentecostal Ministerial Association	1958	I-3pW	.....	125	9,000	1,500	12,000	8.67	*PMA.* Old style Holiness Pentecostal grouping. Conservative. Abroad: 15 churches.
People of Destiny International	1978	I-3aW	.....	100	5,000	–	7,000	5.88	*PDI.* Founded by former RC Charismatics (L. Tomczak). HQ Washington, DC.
Philippine Independent Church	1959	I-ReC	Uwe..	50	7,000	2,000	15,000	8.39	*PIC. Iglesia Filipina Independiente* (HQ Manila). Filipinos in Hawaii. M=PECUSA,ECUSA. 3x.
Pillar of Fire	1901	I-Hol	x....	20	1,500	7,000	2,000	-4.89	Ex Methodists. Until 1917, Pentecostal Union. Missions: Liberia, UK, 8 others. 2 radio stations.
Polish National Catholic Ch of America	1897	I-OCa	UW..W	260	210,000	272,082	350,000	1.01	*PNCC.* Poles, ex Irish-dominated USA RC dioceses. 4 Dioceses, plus one in Canada. 151n,1s.
Potter's Wheel	c1992	I-3pB	.....	3	20,000	–	25,000	33.33	In Dallas; fastest growing local church. F=T.D. Jakes, ex PAOW. Trinitarian.
Presbyterian Church in America	1970	I-Ref	xF...	1,161	183,090	75,000	221,392	4.42	*PCA.* Organized in 1973 as National Presb Ch. Conservative schism ex PCUS. White. 260n.
Presbyterian Church (USA)	1706	P-Ref	RW..W	11,433	2,847,329	4,766,941	3,553,335	-1.17	*PCUSA.* 1983 merger of UPUSA, PCUS. 1973, 8% lost in schism. 4595n,4s. Missions: 9 nations
Primitive Advent Christian Church	c1930	I-Adv	.....	10	340	1,000	700	-1.42	Schism ex Advent CC. HQ Sissonville (West Virginia). 15n,W=50%,25Y.
Primitive Baptists	c1830	I-Bap	.....	2,647	90,000	100,000	125,000	0.90	*Old School Baptists.* 4 factions: Absolute, Absoluter, Conditionalist, Progressive.
Primitive Methodist Church, USA	1829	P-Hol	VF..E	81	5,626	20,000	7,937	-3.63	Missions in Guatemala and other countries. 59n,W=61%.
Process Ch of the Final Judgement	1966	m-Apo	xv...	1	500	10,000	1,000	-8.80	Begun 1960 in UK. Chicago, New Orleans, Cambridge, NY. 1972, applied to WCC. Collapsed
Progressive National Baptist Conv	1961	I-Bap	TW..W	1,800	2,500,000	636,000	3,000,000	6.40	*PNBC.* Black. Schism ex NBCUSA, over elections. 863n. Share NBC seminary.
Progressive Spiritual Church	1907	m-Spi	.....	15	6,000	20,000	15,000	-1.14	Spiritualist body with benevolent, social, literary and psychical activities.
Protestant Conference (Lutheran)	1926	I-Lut	.....	7	870	2,600	1,095	-3.40	Begun by 45 pastors suspended from Wisconsin ELS. 15n,7t(600),W=40%,50Yy.
Protestant Reformed Chs in America	1926	I-Ref	.....	35	3,180	3,187	6,000	2.56	Schism ex Christian Reformed Church. Mainly Mid-West. HQ Oak Lawn (IL). 17n,1s.
Rancho Christian Center Churches	1977	I-3cW	.....	4	700	–	1,400	5.56	*RCCC.* HQ Rancho Cucamonga, CA. Abroad: over 400 chs in UK, Latvia, 6 African countries.
Reconciliation Network of Churches		I-3cW	.....	75	2,500	–	4,000	0.05	An independent charismatic paradenomination.
Redeemed Christian Church of God	c1990	I-3fA	.....	18	1,800	–	3,000	20.00	*RCCG.* Mainly Africans from denomination in Nigeria. Main US church in Tallahassee, FL.
Reformed Baptist Churches	c1680	I-Bap	.....	350	13,500	20,000	27,000	1.21	*Particular Baptists.* Strict 5-point Calvinism (Philadelphia Confession).No HQ. 43n.In 5 countries.
Ref Cath Ch (Utrecht Confession)	c1950	I-ARo	x....	15	800	2,200	1,500	-1.52	Schism in UK ex Old Cath Ev Ch of God. HQ Los Angeles. Bishops in UK, France, FRG.
Reformed Church in America	1628	P-Ref	RW..W	917	196,953	367,606	362,932	-0.05	*RCA.* Begun by Dutch settlers. 1307n,2s(170),905t(127359),W=80%,7071Yy.
Reformed Church in the United States	1934	I-Ref	.....	37	2,881	4,038	4,178	0.14	Churches rejecting 1934 merger. North central. (1970) 25n,24t(807),W=90%,76Yy. (1993) 39n.
Reformed Episcopal Church	1873	I-ReA	xv...	102	5,889	11,000	9,200	-0.71	Ex PECUSA led by asst bishop of Kentucky. 54% Black. 95n,1p,1s(10),W=75%,240Yy.
Reformed Mennonite Church	1812	I-Men	G....	10	500	1,000	900	-0.42	Pacifist. White. In Pennsylvania. Members also in Canada. 21n.
Ref Methodist Union Episcopal Ch	1885	I-Met	.....	17	3,500	8,000	5,560	-1.44	Black. Schism ex AME Church. HQ Charleston (NC). Bishops since 1899. 21n.
Reformed Presbyterian Ch of North A	1743	I-Ref	JF..E	68	3,737	7,500	5,174	-1.47	*Covenanters.* Synod 1798. 7 Presbyteries. 91n,1r,1s(12),W=67%,174Yy.
Reformed Presbyterian Ch, Ev Synod	1774	I-Ref	x...t	110	13,000	17,400	16,000	-0.33	1965 union Ev Presb Ch, RPC in NA. Scots. 310n,10x,1s(50),W=75%,351Yy.
Reformed Zion Union Apostolic Ch	1869	I-Met	.....	40	8,000	16,000	15,000	-0.26	Black. Schism ex AME Zion Church. HQ South Hill (Virginia). 23n.
Regional Brothers Fellowship	1977	I-3cW	.....	8	830	–	1,410	5.56	*RBF.* HQ West Lafayette, IN. Abroad: missionaries in 21 countries.
Religious S of Friends (Conservative)	c1845	P-Qua	Q....	28	2,052	3,000	3,095	0.12	*S=Society.* Wilburites. 3 Yearly Meetings: Iowa, North Carolina, Ohio. White.
Reorganized Ch of JC of LD Saints	1860	m-LdS	xv...	1,137	190,950	202,675	258,000	0.97	*LD=Latter Day.* Ex Mormons, over legal succession. In 28 nations. 13720n,1H,1s,4871Yy.
Resurrection Churches & Ministries	1983	I-3aW	.....	50	20,000	–	26,000	8.33	*RCM.* Living Waters Fellowship, Living Faith Ch, Revival Fellowship Group. Missions.
Revival Tabernacle	1971	I-3pW	.....	5	2,500	–	4,000	4.17	White Pentecostals, based in Stanley, NC. Abroad: 2,800 members in 7 churches.
Rhema Bible Churches	1960	I-3wW	.....	1,500	272,456	100,000	500,000	6.65	*RBC. RMAI. Rhema Ministerial Association International* . F=K. Hagin. Abroad: 82 chs.

Continued overleaf

Country Table 2–continued

Official name 1	Begun 2	Type 3	Counc 4	Congs 5	Adults 6	Affiliated 1970 7	Affiliated 1995 8	G% 9	Names, notes, and other statistics (see Codebook, Part 3) 10
Rock Church & Ministerial Fellowship	1968	I-3cW	.....	200	5,000	2,000	6,000	4.49	*RCMF.* Independent charismatics.
Romanian Orth Episcopate of America	1904	I-Rum	MW...	43	65,000	50,000	92,900	2.51	Schism rejecting P Bucharest. Now under Orth Ch in America. 50n,39t(1693).
Romanian Orth Missionary Episcopate	1929	O-Rum	Cwo..	10	4,000	5,000	8,000	1.90	Bishop of N and S America & Canada; in communion with P Bucharest (Romania).
Russian Orth Ch in the Americas, PE	c1950	O-Rus	MwO.W	38	9,000	50,000	15,000	-4.70	*Patriarchal Exarchate* of P Moscow. Parishes joining Orthodox Ch in A. (1970) 65nx. (1990) 45n.
Russian Orthodox Ch Outside Russia	1920	I-Rus	x....	122	36,500	55,000	50,000	-0.38	*ROCOR.* 1950 world HQ moved to New York. 5 Dioceses. Ultra-conservative. 168n,1d,1s.
Russia/Ukraine Ev Baptist Union	1901	P-Bap	T....	24	1,055	4,000	2,000	-2.73	Baptists from Russia migrating in 1901 to North Dakota. Abroad: 21 missionaries.
St Joseph's Indian Reform Church		I-Non	I	2	600	1,000	1,100	0.05	Apache Reservation, Mescalero (NM). Linked to Apache ceremonial grounds, dances.
St Peter's World Outreach Center	1928	I-3jW	.....	5	1,000	2,500	2,800	0.45	Healing ministry by White Charismatics.
Salvation Army	1880	P-Sal	xw...	1,122	347,000	392,299	445,566	0.51	*Territories: Central, Eastern, Southern, Western.* 38 Divisions. 3735n,33H,4s. In 93 countries.
Schwenkfelder Church in the USA	1782	P-Lut	.....	5	1,100	2,250	2,475	0.38	German Silesian immigrants. In Philadelphia only; disappeared in Europe. 9n,1r.
Second Cumberland Presbyterian Ch	1869	I-Ref	R....	147	6,300	15,000	15,500	0.13	Black. Formerly Colored Cumberland PC; related to Cumberland PC (Whites). 125n.
Seminole Independent Indian Church	c1950	I-Bap	I	4	400	1,000	1,000	0.00	Seminole Indians, split ex Southern Baptists, Florida. No ministers.
Separate Baptists in Christ	1695	I-Bap	.....	101	10,000	11,000	14,900	1.22	Early refugees from England. Completely independent, rejecting mergers. 106n. (1988) 175n.
Serbian Orth Ch in the USA & Canada	1894	O-Ser	CwO.W	68	67,000	150,000	83,800	-2.30	3 *Dioceses* under P Belgrade: *Mid-West, Western, Eastern America & Canada.* 64nx.
Serbian Orthodox Ch: D Libertyville	1963	I-Ser	.....	5	3,000	3,000	4,000	1.16	Schismatic diocese, HQ Libertyville, led by bishop Dionysie, opposing P Belgrade.
Seventh Day Baptist General Conf	1671	P-Bap	TW..f	90	5,145	8,000	7,680	-0.16	Immigrants from England. 1973, left NCCC. 81n,1s,47t(2837),W=56%,79Y.
Seventh-day Adventist Church	1844	P-Adv	x....	4,214	717,443	700,000	957,000	1.26	*SDA. 9 Unions.* 18% Black. 3365n, 42H,5j,88r,3s,3315t(375031),W=88%,24575Y.
Shield of Faith Fellowship	1991	I-3cW	.....	9	1,000	–	3,000	25.00	Schism ex Southern Baptist Convention, Texas. Abroad: 2,000 members in 7 chs in Ghana.
Shiloh Apostolic Temple	1953	I-3aO	.....	23	4,500	2,500	5,000	2.81	Black Apostolic charismatics.
Slovak National Cath Ch in America		I-OCa	U....	5	3,000	3,000	5,000	0.05	Old Catholics from Slovakia. Under jurisdiction of Polish NCC of America.
Social Brethren	1867	P-Non	.....	30	1,200	3,000	2,000	-1.61	Group in Illinois with Baptist and Methodist customs. 42n,30t.
Southern Baptist Convention	1845	P-Bap	T....	39,910	15,404,621	14,200,000	21,500,000	1.67	*SBC.* 1845 ex North. 99% White. (1970) 31000n,2H,6s,W=39%,409659Y. (1990) 63352n.
Southern Methodist Church	1939	I-Met	.T..T	137	7,572	20,000	15,100	-1.12	White. Ex Meth Epis Ch South rejecting 1939 merger. HQ Orangeburg. 63n,150t(9630).
Sovereign Grace Baptists	1954	I-Bap	.....	300	6,700	4,000	8,670	3.14	Calvinist. HQ St Croix Falls, WI.
Spanish Christian Churches		I-3pL	.....	300	40,000	30,000	70,000	0.05	Linked, Latin American Council of Chs. Spanish-speaking Puerto Ricans, Mexicans.
Spiritual Life Concepts	1977	I-3cW	.....	300	10,000	–	15,000	5.56	*SLC.* HQ Largo, FL. Abroad: 300 chs in 13 countries: Uganda, Nigeria, India, Nepal, Philippines
Spiritual Science Church	1923	m-Spi	.....	40	15,000	50,000	30,000	-2.02	*Ecclesiastical Council.* Spiritualists ex Christian Science. Mainly NY state. 40n.
Spiritualist Episcopal Church	1941	m-Spi	.....	30	2,000	5,000	3,000	-2.02	Schism ex ISA. Liturgical services, healing. 1956, serious schism.
Strategic Christian Services	1979	I-3aW	.....	30	6,000	–	7,000	6.25	Apostolic ministry and discipling.
Swedenborgian Church, General Conv	1792	m-Swe	x...W	50	2,423	10,000	6,060	-1.98	*New Church.* 1817, General Convention of the New Jerusalem. 66n,1s(5).
Synod of Evangelical Lutheran Chs	1902	P-Lut	.....	70	11,000	21,500	24,000	0.44	Slovak Lutherans, conservative theology. Since 1971 under LC Missouri Synod. White.
Syrian Orth P Antioch: AD USA /Canada	1895	O-Syr	Dw..W	29	15,000	50,000	33,000	-1.65	Under Syrian Orthodox P Antioch. HQ Hackensack (NJ). Syrians. (1970) 14nx. (1990)18n.
Team Networks International	1994	I-3aW	.....	50	5,000	–	10,000	100.00	*TNI.* Work with Chinese, Filipinos, Afro-Americans.
The Way International	1953	I-3pW	.....	10	5,000	30,000	10,000	-4.30	Ex Jesus Revolution. HQ New Knoxville. 3000 WOW (Word over World) workers. 50n,1s.
Tioga River Christian Conference	1931	I-Con	.T..T	2	1,000	3,000	2,000	-1.61	Group rejecting Congregational-Christian merger of 1931. White. New York state.
Trinity Church Network		I-3cW	.....	15	70,000	–	100,000	0.05	*TCN.* Local network (ex AoG) in Houston, Dallas, west Texas.
Trinity Fellowship Association of Chs		I-3aW	.....	28	1,000	–	2,000	0.05	*TFAC.* White Apostolics.
Triumph the Church & KoG in Christ	1902	I-3pB	.....	500	45,000	55,090	56,300	0.09	*KoG=Kingdom of God.* Black pentecostals. Pacifists. 1375n. Work in Liberia, Philippines.
True Orthodox Ch of Greece: E Ameri	1933	I-OCd	.....	9	1,000	500	1,500	4.49	*American Exarchate, Synod of Metro Cyprian. Old Calendarists.* M=True Orth Ch of Greece. 23n
True Vine Pentecostal Chs of Jesus	1961	I-3aO	.....	10	900	1,500	1,700	0.50	Black Oneness pentecostals.
Turkish Orthodox Church in America	1924	I-ReO	xv...	15	9,000	14,800	12,000	-0.84	1922 schism in Turkey ex EP Constantinople; under own P Istanbul. In USA,Black members.26n
Ukrainian Ev Baptist Convention	1945	P-Bap	.T..T	25	2,900	4,500	5,000	0.42	USSR refugees. 6 radio programs (2 to USSR). HQ Chester (PA). 20n,1p,W=80%,50Y.
Ukrainian Orthodox Ch of America	1924	O-Ukr	C.O.W	23	5,000	45,000	7,580	-6.88	*UOCA (Ecumenical Patriarchate).* Canonical, recognized by Constantinople. 52n.
Ukrainian Orthodox Ch of the USA	1919	I-Ukr	X....	95	18,000	87,475	26,100	-4.72	Disputed succession. Dioceses: 3 USA; 3 Canada; Brazil; Germany; Australia. 131n.
Ukrainian Orth Ch (Sobornopravna)	1947	I-Ukr	X....	3	600	2,000	1,200	-2.02	*UOC (Democratic).* Ukrainians. HQ Chicago; also a bishop for Europe (Geneva). 12n.
Unification Church of America	c1956	m-HSA	xv...	90	9,000	30,000	20,000	-1.61	M=HSAUWC(Korea). Many Whites. 1973 applied to WCC. 1976, 700 deported (Asians).
Unified Pentecostal Local Chs	c1935	I-3pL	.....	200	8,000	3,000	12,000	5.70	*UPLC.* Hispanic Trinitarians. HQ Denver (CO). Church abroad also.
Union American Meth Episcopal Ch	1805	I-Met	.....	210	11,000	27,560	20,000	-1.27	Black. One of first Negro independent Methodist chs. On East Coast, also Canada. 276n.Decline
Union of Latvian Baptists in America	c1990	I-Bap	T....	8	390	–	1,000	20.00	Refugees from Latvia. Mainline Baptists.
Union of Messianic Jewish Congs	1979	I-3mJ	x....	105	12,000	–	15,000	6.25	Members 90% Gentiles, 10% Messianic Jews. Branches Canada, UK, Israel, Russia. M=JFJ.
Unitarian Universalist Association	1778	m-Unt	.....	1,010	141,330	265,408	190,199	-1.32	1961 merger of Unitarian Ch, Universalist Chs. Declining. 886n,2s(150).
United Baptist Church	1787	I-Bap	.....	450	50,000	100,000	70,000	-1.42	Merger of Separate & Regular Baptists. White. In southeast USA. 1100n.
United Brethren in Christ	1767	P-Hol	xF..E	251	24,014	40,000	40,000	0.00	Arose from 1760s revival in Pennsylvania & Maryland. HQ Huntington (IN). 197n,1s.
United Christian Ch & Minist Assoc	1956	I-3cW	.....	125	12,500	3,000	15,000	6.65	Mostly White Charismatics. F=H. Richard Hall. Abroad: 40,000 members in 50 churches.
United Church of Christ	1620	P-Uni	RW..W	6,260	1,599,539	2,680,000	1,993,459	-1.18	*UCC.* 1957 union. 1% Black. Missions in 8 Caribbean, West African countries. 9478n,13s.
United Church of God	1995	I-BrI	.....	70	3,000	–	5,000	46.57	Conservative schism of 100 pastors (out of 350) ex Worldwide Church of God.
United Ch of Jesus Christ (Apostolic)	1945	I-3aO	.....	80	50,000	60,000	100,000	2.06	*UCJC.* Black Oneness. 150 ministers in North America. Missions in Africa, West Indies, England.
United Church of Religious Science	1917	m-Sci	i....	80	6,000	20,000	10,000	-2.73	Metaphysical (New Thought, mental science). Healing crusades, literature. 156mw.
United Churches of Jesus (Apostolic)	1970	I-3aO	.....	39	2,200	–	3,000	37.75	Black Oneness pentecostals. Schism ex Apostolic Ch of Christ of God. 30n,6 bps.
United Crusade Fellowship Conf		I-3pW	.....	6	1,000	–	2,000	0.05	*UCFC.* Black. Member of Federated Pentecostal Church International.
United Evangelical Churches	1958	I-3cW	.....	200	20,000	14,000	57,016	5.78	Whites ex mainline denominations. In 24 states. Abroad: 22,000 members, 247 chs; 70 nations.
United Free Will Baptist Church	1901	I-3pB	.....	750	90,000	122,000	110,000	-0.41	*UFWBC (Colored).* Black members, in NC, GA, FL, MS, LA, TX. HQ Kingston (NC). 915n.
United Full Gospel Churches	1951	I-3fW	.....	80	19,000	70,000	30,000	-3.33	*United Full Gospel Ministries Association.* Integrated, mostly White Charismatics. Declining.
United Fundamentalist Church	1939	I-3pW	.....	310	15,000	20,000	25,000	0.90	*UFC.* White Pentecostals (2-stage type). HQ Flagstaff (Arizona). Prophecies, healings.
United Gospel Fell Covenant Ministries	1980	I-3fW	.....	10	6,000	–	10,000	6.67	*UGFCM.* Ministry directed mainly at military bases in the USA.
United Holy Church of America	1886	I-3aO	x....	88	9,000	50,000	14,000	-4.96	*UHCA.* 1976, 50% exit to Original United Holy Ch. Missions: Liberia, SAfrica, Trinidad, UK. 400n
United House of Prayer for All People	1919	I-3pB	.....	120	25,000	50,000	39,000	-0.99	Black pentecostals. Founder Bishop (Daddy) Grace, died 1960. 1998:2,000 baptized by fire hose
United Liberal Catholic Ch of the USA	1917	I-Lib	xv...	20	900	2,000	1,200	-2.02	UK origin ex Old Roman Cath Ch. Theosophical. HQ London (UK). 84n,W=30%,100Yy.
United Methodist Church	1766	P-Met	VW..W	37,238	8,849,803	14,353,000	11,091,032	-1.03	*UMC.* 1968, EUB merger. 96% White, 4% Black. 81 Confs. 34974n,13s,W=36%.
United Network of Christian Min & Chs	1985	I-3cW	.....	40	15,000	–	26,500	10.00	*UNCMC.* Schism ex LCMS based on Blaine, MN. Abroad: 8,000 members, 12 chs.
United Old Catholic Church	1964	I-OCa	.....	25	800	3,000	1,000	-4.30	Attempt to unite all Old Catholic factions. 1 monastery. 28n,2s(8),W=73%,73Yy.
United Pentecostal Church International	1914	P-Pel	x....	3,728	550,000	450,000	833,000	2.49	1945 union PAJC, PC. White. (1970) 4800n. (1990) 7512n.Missions in 74 countries. (83n).7483n
United States (USA) Episcopal Church	1970	I-ReA	.....	40	4,000	10,000	7,000	-1.42	Schism ex PECUSA protesting ordination of women priests. Formerly Anglicans United.
United Way of the Cross Chs of Christ	1974	I-3aO	.....	18	3,100	–	4,400	4.76	*UWCCC.* Oneness. 30 ministers and 4 bishops. Abroad: 3,000 members, 58 chs in Haiti.
United Zion Church	1855	I-Men	.....	13	850	1,500	1,400	-0.28	Mainly in Pennsylvania. Veiling of women. Schism ex BiCC. 22n,13t(1327),W=86%,35Y.
Unity of the Brethren	c1880	P-Mor	x....	26	2,674	10,000	4,336	-3.29	*Unitas Fratrum.* Until 1962, Ev Unity of Czech-Moravian Brethren. In Texas. White.
Unity School of Christianity	1887	m-Sci	i....	600	40,000	50,000	100,000	2.81	Ex Christian Science. 1.5 million world subscribers, 75 million booklets annually. 700 workers.
Universal Christian Spiritual Faith	1952	I-3aO	.....	20	5,000	40,816	10,000	-5.47	*UCSF.* Black Oneness pentecostals. Declining rapidly.
Universal Church of Christ	1972	I-3aO	.....	20	400	–	1,000	4.35	Apostolic. In northeast USA. A few congregations also in the West Indies.
Universal Fellowship of MCCs	1968	I-Gay	x....	300	119,000	30,000	152,296	6.71	*UFMCC. MCCs=Metropolitan Community Chs.* Gays and lesbians. In 17 nations. 500n,W=69%.
Universal Spiritualist Association	1956	m-Spi	.....	15	1,000	4,000	3,000	-1.14	Schism ex Spiritualist Episcopal Church by its founder. In 10 US states.
Victory Fellowship of Ministries	c1960	I-3vW	.....	400	95,300	100,000	140,000	1.35	*VFM.* HQ Tulsa, OK. Members abroad: 15,000 in 8 churches in Russia, 45 countries.
Voice of the Nazarene Assoc of ICs	1955	I-Fun	.T...	12	1,000	4,000	2,000	-2.73	*ICs=Independent Churches.* Grouping of fundamentalist holiness congregations. 45Y.
Volunteers of America	1896	P-Sal	x....	277	25,200	32,760	40,000	0.80	Social welfare agency run on military lines. Extensive ministry in prisons. 432n.
Way of the Cross Church of Christ	1927	I-3aO	.....	48	50,000	55,000	60,000	0.35	Oneness. Ex COLJCAF. F=Henry C. Brooks.
Wesleyan Church	1843	P-Hol	VF..E	1,657	102,726	120,000	259,740	3.14	1968 union Pilgrim Holiness, Wesleyan Meth Chs. In 30 nations. 2925n,2s.
Wesleyan Holiness Assoc of Chs	1960	I-Hol	.....	60	1,800	4,000	3,500	-0.53	Association stressing sanctification and rejecting Wesleyan mergers. 112n,67t.
Willow Creek Association of Chs	1975	I-Eva	.....	2,700	200,000	–	500,000	5.00	*Seeker Churches.* F=Bill Hybels. Abroad: 1,500 chs, 70 denominations, 24 countries.
Wisconsin Ev Lutheran Synod	1850	P-Lut	x....	1,228	316,745	381,321	419,928	0.39	*WELS.* Prussian origin. In Luth Synodical Conf. 957n,25x,1s(225),8018Yy.
Word Fellowship of Ministers	1953	I-3wW	.....	100	3,000	1,000	4,000	5.70	*WFOM.* Evangelism, church planting, Bible colleges. F=Charles Green.
Word of Faith Fellowship/Ministries	1969	I-3kB	.....	10	17,500	200	23,500	21.00	*WFFM.* Cell-based churches. Abroad: 5,000 members in 74 chs (Africa 58, Pakistan 16).
World Baptist Fellowship	1928	I-Fun	xT..T	8	2,000	5,000	5,500	0.38	*WBF.* Fundamentalist mission body (20 nations) with affiliated churches in USA. 1s.
World Bible Way Fellowship	1943	I-3fW	.....	400	40,000	20,000	55,000	4.13	*WBWF.* Full Gospel theology. Abroad: 50,000 members, 250 chs.
World Council of Indep Christian Chs	1992	I-3cW	.....	200	15,000	–	35,000	33.33	*WCICC.* White Charismatics. HQ Maple Shade, NJ. Abroad: 385,000 in 74 countries.
World Evangelism Fellowship	1961	I-3pW	.....	30	4,700	2,000	6,000	4.49	*WEF.* HQ Baton Rouge(LA). M=J. Swaggart Ministries. Major worldwide collapse in 1988.
World Gospel Mission	c1985	I-Hol	.....	1	110	–	143	10.00	M=WGM. American Indians.
World Harvest Church Min Assoc	1997	I-3fW	.....	100	20,000	–	35,000	-50.00	*WHC Ministers Association.* F=Rod Parsley. HQ Columbus, OH. Abroad: 1,000 in 4 chs.
World Harvest Ministerial Association	1957	I-3fW	.....	40	5,500	1,000	7,000	8.09	*WHMA.* HQ South Bend, IN. M=LSEA.
World Ministries Fellowship	1963	I-3cW	.....	200	41,000	10,000	60,000	7.43	*WMF.* Mostly White Charismatics. HQ Plano, TX. Abroad: 65,000 members, 500 ministers.
World Missionary Church	c1970	I-3pW	.....	100	15,000	–	25,000	49.94	*WMC. International Gospel Crusade.* F=T.L.O. Osborn. Feminist-oriented worldwide campaigns.
World Outreach Fellowship	c1980	I-3cW	.....	25	20,000	–	30,000	6.67	*WOF.* White charismatics.
World Salt	c1990	I-3cW	.....	50	30,000	–	35,000	20.00	F=Steven Satow. HQ Knoxville, TN.
Worldwide Church of God	1930	I-BrI	x...E	200	40,000	200,000	70,000	-4.11	*Radio Ch of God.* Ex CoG(SD). Doctrinal realignments. Schisms 1974. In 124 countries. 400n.
Worldwide Churches of Deliverance	1978	I-3fB	.....	3	2,000	–	3,000	5.88	*WCD.* Healing, deliverances, Full Gospel theology. HQ Fayetteville, NC. Abroad: 400 members.
Worldwide Missionary Evangelism	1971	I-3fW	.....	100	20,000	–	30,000	4.17	*WME.* Full Gospel teaching. Integrated Charismatics. Linked with IAGI.
Worldwide/Last Churches	1948	I-3jW	.....	250	150,000	300,000	200,000	-1.61	Branhamites. Voice of God Recordings. 300,000 worldwide.
Yaqui Church	1769	I-mar	.....	10	1,400	2,000	1,800	-0.42	Yaqui Indians in Arizona. 1760, abandoned by Jesuits in NW Mexico. Easter dramas.
Zion Evangelistic Fellowship	c1950	I-3pW	.....	120	15,000	20,000	30,000	1.64	Grouping of Pentecostals; little contact with other Pentecostals.
Other Full Gospel single congs	1980	I-3fW	.....	2,500	400,000	–	600,000	6.67	Including 1,500 unattached congregations participating in Chaplaincy of Full Gospel Churches.
Other independent charismatic chs	1975	I-3cW	.....	50,000	3,000,000	–	5,000,000	5.00	Including 1,500 smaller networks & 20,000 autonomous single congregations. (El Shaddai, et al)
Other independent pentecostal chs	c1970	I-3pW	.....	3,000	100,000	–	300,000	65.61	Smaller autonomous bodies affirming initial evidence and Pentecostal theology.
Other nondenominational single chs	c1950	I-sin	.....	2,500	700,000	1,000,000	1,300,000	1.05	In over 100 noncharismatic single congregations (Moody Bible Institute 8,000 members).
Other marginal Protestant bodies	1930	m-	.....	4,000	800,000	1,000,000	1,200,000	0.73	Total about 300.
Other megachurches or networks	1960	I-3cW	.....	30,000	2,000,000	300,000	3,000,000	9.65	Including 300 unattached charismatic megachurches in 300 cities.
Other Protestant denominations	c1940	P-	.....	2,900	160,000	274,000	400,000	1.52	Total about 500, including over 40 White Pentecostal bodies.
Other Black indigenous churches	c1950	I-	.....	1,400	100,000	98,000	200,000	2.89	Total over 200, and also many independent congregations.
Other Black Oneness bodies	c1930	I-3oO	.....	200	20,000	20,000	50,000	3.73	Total over 100.
Other Third-World indigenous chs	1970	I-	.....	600	20,000	28,000	40,000	1.44	Total over 30, especially African Independent Churches.
Other independent Catholic chs	c1900	I-CCa	.....	60	4,000	5,000	8,000	1.90	Total about 40, including 30 small churches under bishops-at-large.
Other Ibero-Hispanic churches	c1970	I-3pY	.....	3,000	250,000	–	400,000	67.53	50 denominations from abroad, including Igreja de Nova Vida, IURD(Brazil).
Other Orthodox churches	1905	O-	.....	40	3,000	4,000	7,000	2.26	Total about 20 smaller bodies.
Other Amerindian indigenous chs	c1960	I-	.....	150	1,300	2,000	2,500	0.90	Total about 110, among North American Indians, mostly Navajo; few neocharismatics.
Other Anglican denominations	1962	I-Ang	.....	20	1,200	2,000	2,300	0.56	Total 20, including Anglican Rite Jurisdiction (1991).

Continued opposite

Country Table 2–concluded

Official name 1	Begun 2	Type 3	Counc 4	Congs 5	Adults 6	Affiliated 1970 7	Affiliated 1995 8	G% 9	Names, notes, and other statistics (see Codebook, Part 3) 10
Other White Oneness pentecostals	c1970	I-3oW	.....	730	32,000	–	64,000	55.69	Total over 60, following Apostolic and Jesus Only guidelines.
Doubly-affiliated		2-aff			-17,598,000	-2,703,816	-25,359,548		Persons holding membership in 2, 3 or more denominations.
Totals				**567,571**	**127,851,486**	**153,299,252**	**184,243,800**		

Churches, members, growth, 1900-2025	*Congs*	*Adults*	*Affiliated*	*G%*	*Total denominations*	*6 Megablocs:*	*O*	*R*	*A*	*P*	*I*	*m*
Total churches, members, and denominations (mid-1900)	60,000	37,679,000	54,425,000	1.49	175		8	1	1	85	60	20
Total churches, members, and denominations (mid-1970)	373,899	106,131,217	153,299,252	1.49	1,303		34	1	1	369	684	214
Total churches, members, and denominations (mid-1990)	540,000	122,006,000	175,820,000	0.69	4,270		40	1	1	598	3.300	330
Total churches, members, and denominations (mid-1995)	567,571	127,851,486	184,243,800	0.94	4,446		40	1	1	600	3,474	330
Total churches, members, and denominations (mid-2000)	600,000	133,114,000	191,827,627	0.81	4,684		40	1	1	610	3,700	332
Total churches, members, and denominations (mid-2025)	690,000	146,419,000	211,000,000	0.38	6,222		60	1	1	660	5,100	400

NOTES ON TABLE ABOVE

NATIONAL COUNCILS (Column 4, 5th letter).

- b = member of both NCCCUSA and NFCC.
- E = National Association of Evangelicals (NAE) (and linked body, National Black (formerly Negro) Evangelical Association, NBEA).
- I = Pan-Indian Ecumenical Association of the USA and Canada (annual conferences: 1970 Cree Reservation, Montana, 1971 Stony Reserve, Alberta).
- J = National Fraternal Council of Churches (NFCC) (Black: began 1929).
- R = National Conference of Catholic Bishops (NCCB).
- T = American Christian Action Council (ACAC) (affiliated to ICCC).
- t = American Council of Christian Churches (ACCC) (affiliated to ICCC until withdrawal in 1968), including 6 bodies formerly in ACCC, now withdrawn; in addition, ACCC has as members 8 of the 12 bodies still in ICCC, ACAC.
- W = National Council of the Churches of Christ in the USA (NCCCUSA) (constituent bodies), 1908.

Other national councils. Anglican Episcopal Council of Churches (formed 1975). Associated Gospel Churches (service agency for 3-million strong fundamentalist denominations). Christian Holiness Association (CHA) (Wesleyan-Armenian bodies; before 1971, National Holiness Association, NHA). Christian Hope Indian Eskimo Fellowship (CHIEF) (for native Amerindian groups in North and South America). Council of Japanese American Christian Churches in North America. Inter-church Holiness Convention (IHC). Lutheran Council in the USA (members ALC, LCA, LCMS). National Conference of Independent Catholic and Orthodox Jurisdictions. National Federation of Pentecostal Churches (Black). North American Baptist Fellowship. North American Presbyterian and Reformed Council (NAPARC) (begun 1975 with 6 member denominations: CRC, OPC, RPCES, RPCNA, PCA, ARPC).

Local councils. Over 50 state councils of churches linked with NCCCUSA, also many hundreds of metropolitan and city councils.

OTHER MARGINAL CHRISTIAN BODIES. The table includes all known larger marginal Protestant bodies. In addition, there is a vast proliferation of smaller bodies, many being schisms, in a more orthodox or christocentric direction, out of the 3 major bodies (Church of Christ Scientist, Jehovah's Witnesses, Mormons). Among these are the following better-known bodies: American Prophetic League, Anthroposophical Society in America (Christian Community Ch), Aquarian Brotherhood of Christ, Assembly of Yahvah, Associated Bible Students, Believerism (Balanced Life), Branhamites (Local Church, End Time Local Believers, Spoken Word Believers; HQ Jeffersonville, IN), Brotherhood of the Followers of the Present Jesus, Christ Temple Ch of Personal Experience, Christ Truth League (member of INTA), Christ Unity Science Ch, Christ's True Ch & School of Wisdom, Ch of God International (1978 schism ex Worldwide Ch of God by founder's son), Ch of Jesus Christ (Cutlerites), Ch of Jesus Christ of Latter-day Saints (Strangites) (300), Ch of Light, Ch of the Awakening (1958; pharmacological (peyote, mescaline); 400 Whites; now illegal), Ch of the Firstborn of the Fulness of Times (ex Mormons' polygamous fundamentalists), Ch of the Healing Christ, Ch of the Lord Jesus Christ (Ishi Temple), Ch of the One, Ch of the Truth (member of INTA), Cosmopolitan Churches of Prayer (Spiritual), Dawn Bible Students Association (ex JWs), Ev Ch of Christ Scientist, Fellowship of the Order of Christian Mystics, First Christian (Essene) Ch, Good Samaritan Ch of Truth, Greek Bible Students, Home of Truth (member of INTA), Institute of Religious Science and Philosophy, ISMAS (a Christian psychic group in California), Laymen's Home Missionary Movement (1918 split ex Jehovah's Witnesses), New Age Bible Centre, Order of the Cross (3 centers), Philanthropic Assembly (Chs of the Kingdom of God; in Europe, Amis de l'Homme; split ex Jehovah's witnesses), Primitive Ch of Christ Scientist, Purgatorial Society, Servants of Yah (ex Jehovah's Witnesses), Spiritual Frontiers Fellowship, Stand Fast Bible Students, Twentieth Century Ch of God (ex Worldwide Ch of God), United Society of Believers in Christ's Second Appearing (Shakers), Universal Life Ch (claims 2 million mail-order followers in USA; inquiry re membership made to WCC), Warriors for Faith & Truth (Horpenites; from Saxony, Germany). In addition to these organized denominations, there are large numbers of independent congregations including 130 metaphysical groupings affiliated to INTA.

OTHER PROTESTANT DENOMINATIONS. The table includes known denominations with 1,000 adherents or more. There is however a vast number of smaller Protestant denominations down to bodies with only a handful of members and congregations. Now US-founded bodies come into existence every year; also, many large churches elsewhere in the world start congregations in the USA as their members immigrate (e.g. in 1976 the Korean Presbyterian Ch in the USA was organized). The following list gives 91 of the 500 or more smaller Protestant (White) denominations in 1973, with in parentheses date of origin, total affiliated, etc: Albigensian Ch, American World Patriarchates (1961), Anchor Bay Evangelistic Association, Apostolic Ch, Apostolic Christian Ch of Jesus Christ, Apostolic Methodist Ch, Associate Presbyterian Ch of North America, Back to the Bible Way, Berean Fellowship International, Bethel Pentecostal Temple (Seattle), Bible Fellowship Ch (Mennonite), Bible Missionary Chs, Carolina Evangelistic Association, Ch of Christian Liberty (begun 1969; 400), Ch of Eternal Life, Ch of God as Organized by Christ, Ch of God (Apostolic) (600), Ch of God (Bishop Poteat), Ch of God (Greenville), Ch of God Holiness (HQ Overland Park, Kansas), Ch of God (New Dunkards), Ch of Jesus Christ, Ch of Liberty, Ch of the Awakening, Ch of the Blessed Hope, Ch of the Full Gospel (300), Ch of the Gospel (100), Ch of the New Birth, Ch of the Revelation (750), Ch Which is Christ's Body, Christian Believers Conference, Churches of God in the British Isles & Overseas (5 churches), Concordia Lutheran Conference (1945 split ex LCMS; 6 churches), Cumberland Methodist Ch, Eglise Ev Française, Ev Ch of Christ, Followers of Jesus (ex Roman Catholic Ch; 600 members in 1969), Free Pentecostal Ch, Free Reformed Ch of North America (2 churches, 575 members), Free Will Baptist Ch of the Pentecostal Faith, Full Gospel Grace Fellowship (1954), Fundamental Conference of America, General Six-Principle Baptists, Gospel Lighthouse Ch (Dallas, Texas), Gospel Mission Corps, Gypsy Ev Movement (France), House of David (900), Independent Baptist Bible Mission, Independent Baptist Ch of America, Independent Pentecostal Assemblies, International Conference of Calvary Tabernacles (member of ICCC), International Deliverance Chs (Pentecostal), International Evangelical Ch (Pentecostal; member of WCC), Israel Gospel Ch, Jesus Ch, Justified Ch of God, Latter Rain Movement, Lithuanian Reformed Ch in Exile (1968 applied to join WCC), Methodist Protestant Ch (member of ICCC), Militant Fundamental Bible Chs, Miracle Revival Fellowship (1951), Mount Calvary Holy Ch of America, New Bethel Ch of God in Christ Pentecostal, New Congregational Methodist Ch, New Covenant Apostolic Order (NCAO, begun 1970; led by former Campus Crusade (CCCI) leaders named apostles stressing authority and congregational discipline; 2,000 members, all Whites, no pastors; 1978, 25% secede), New Testament Association of Independent Baptist Chs, Orthodox Baptists, Orthodox Lutheran Conference (1955), Pentecostal Ev Ch of God, People's Christian Ch, People's Methodist Chs, People's Mission Ch, People's Temple (founded 1956; de facto ex Disciples of Christ; 90% USA Black; 1974 exodus to Jonestown in Guyana jungle; 1978 mass suicide-murder there of 912 followers), Reformed Cumberland Presbyterian Ch, Reformed New Congregational Methodist Ch, Remnant Ch, Seventh Day Baptists (German), Stauffer Mennonite Ch, True Ch of Jesus Christ (mail-order body), True Dutch Reformed Ch, Two-Seed-in-the-Spirit Predestinarian Baptists, United Christian Ch (400; member of ICCC), United Ev Chs (1961), United Indian Missions, United Seventh-day Brethren, United Wesleyan Methodist Ch of America (550), Universal World Ch, Waldensian Ch in America, Weaver Mennonite Ch, Welsh Calvinistic Methodist Ch.

OTHER BLACK INDIGENOUS CHURCHES. In addition to the US Black bodies listed in the table, there are a very large number of independent single congregations; and also around 100 smaller Black denominations, including: African Orthodox Ch of New York & Massachusetts (1938 schism ex AOC), African Universal Ch (begun 1927; pentecostal; missionaries to Ghana), Apostolic Ch of Jesus Christ (Jesus Only pentecostals), Black Christian Nationalist Ch (1972, ex United Ch of Christ), Black Unitarian Universalist Ch (Black Humanist Fellowship; not yet separate from UUA), Ch of God (Mother Horn), Fire-Baptized Holiness Ch (998), Free Ch of God in Christ, Fundamental Baptist Fellowship Association ((1962), Glorified Ch of God, Holiness Ch of God (begun 1920), Holsteen Ch of God, House of Faith, House of the Lord, Kodesh Ch of Immanuel (582), Latter House of the Lord for All People, Mount Carmel Holy Ch of the Lord Jesus (HQ Camden, NJ), Mount Sinai Holy Ch of America (begun 1924; in 18 states, 3 nations; women bishops), Pentecostal Fire-Baptized Ch of the Americas, Pentecostal Fire-Baptized Holiness Ch, School of the Prophets (a Father-Only organization), Sought-out Ch of God in Christ, United Christian Evangelistic Association (formerly United Ch of Jesus Christ for All People; ex Bible Way Ch; 'Science of Living', 'Mind Science'; daily radio program over 270 stations, also TV, from United Palace and Science of Living Institute, New York City; claims one million Blacks), Victory Way Free Ch of God True Holiness USA (in 6 Mid-West states). There are also several miniscule episcopal churches under bishops-at-large (episcopi vagantes).

OTHER THIRD-WORLD INDIGENOUS CHURCHES. There are an increasing number of immigrant indigenous churches from Africa, Asia, Latin America, and the Caribbean, usually established in the USA by their immigrant followers. In addition to the 12 listed in the table, the over 30 others include: African Apostolic Ch of Johane Maranke (from Rhodesia), Ceylon Pentecostal Mission, Ch of the First-Born (from Jamaica), Ch of the Gospel of Jesus Christ (in Hawaii), Ch of the Lord (Aladura) (1968, from Nigeria), Defenders of the Faith (Puerto Rico; 1923), Filipino Assemblies of the First Born (1933), Gideon's Evangelistic Band (Mexico), Iglesia Ev Pentecostal de Chile (1 church in New York), International City Mission (Jamaica), Kimbanguist Ch (EJCSK, from Zaire; US Blacks), Prince of Peace (Kealiiokamalu; in Hawaii), True Jesus Ch (Chinese, begun 1930 in Honolulu; 148 baptized in 3 churches and 1 preaching hall, in California and Hawaii), True Jesus Mission of the Latter Rain (in Hawaii). There is also a Nestorian schism from Iraq, the American Assyrian Apostolic Ch (c1950 schism ex Ancient Ch of the East; HQ Chicago).

OTHER CATHOLIC (NON-ROMAN) CHURCHES. The total includes around 30 miniscule unrecognized episcopal churches under bishops-at-large (episcopi vagantes) (for names, see part 9); this total excludes numerous other such bodies in existence earlier but now defunct. Among other autocephalous Catholic churches with larger followings are: American Orthodox Missionary Ch, Byzantine American Ch, Free Protestant Episcopal Ch (Ecumenical Church Foundation) (12 congregations, several bishops), Holy Orthodox Ch in America (Eastern Catholic & Apostolic), Independent Episcopal Ch of the USA and Canada, International Liberal Catholic Ch, Old Catholic Ch in America, Polish Mariavite Ch. For details of all these bodies see table at end of part 9. There are also several cults stemming from Roman Catholicism, including Antoinists (from France and Belgium).

OTHER ORTHODOX CHURCHES. There are several smaller bodies, including: Alexandrian Orthodox Ch in America (Russians, Ukrainians; Blacks), Assyrian Ch of the East (Mar Addai's faction), Autocephalous Slavonic Orthodox Ch in Exile, Bulgarian Orthodox Diocese of America (under ROCOR), Finnish Orthodox Ch (1955), Hungarian Orthodox Greek Catholic Ch, Macedonian Orthodox Ch (1961), Molokan Christian Ch (1905; Russians), 2 Romanian Orthodox independent parishes.

OTHER AMERINDIAN INDIGENOUS CHURCHES. Since their first contact with Whites in North America, American Indians have produced over 100 distinguishable new religious movements (1740-1975); among them many have had distinctively Christian elements, and of these some 20 still existed in 1975. In addition to the 10 American Indian churches listed in the table, there are about 100 other small Indian bodies or single Indian congregations, including: American Indian Ch Independent (Chicago), American Indian Ev Ch (1956; pentecostal), Apache Pentecostal Ch (San Carlos Reservation), First Born Ch of Christ (begun 1914 at Redrock, Oklahoma), Miccosukee Independent Indian Ch (Florida, ex Southern Baptist Mission), Mohave Mission Ch, Pima Independent Ch, San Carlos Apache Independent Ch. Several of these bodies support the Southwest Indian Bible Conference, with its grounds in Prescott, Arizona. The majority however are found in Navajoland.

OTHER ANGLICAN DENOMINATIONS. There are a number of other secessions from the Episcopal Church in the USA (PECUSA), which still regard themselves as authentically Anglican in tradition. These include: Anglican Ch of America (1968), Anglican Episcopal Ch of North America (c1972), Episcopal Ch (Evangelical), United Episcopal Ch (1973), these 4 belonging to the Anglican Episcopal Council of Churches (1975); also Old Episcopal Ch (c1960), Southern Episcopal Ch (1953). In addition, there are numerous other formerly Anglican (Episcopalian) schisms which regard themselves as no longer Anglican but now belonging to another tradition, either Catholic (non-Roman), Orthodox or Protestant.

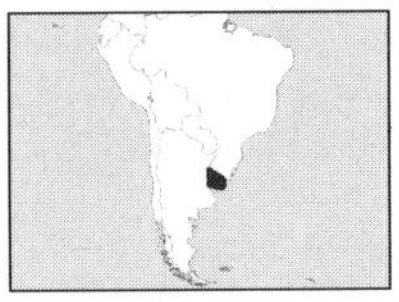

URUGUAY

SECULAR DATA, AD 2000

STATE
Official name: República Oriental del Uruguay (The Eastern Republic of Uruguay).
Short name: Uruguay. **Adjective of nationality:** Uruguayan.
Flag: Blue stripes on white field, with golden sun in upper hoist corner.
Area: 176,215 sq. km. (68,037 sq. mi.).
Government: Republic, since 1985 (1624 Spanish settlement, 1820 part of Brazil, 1825 Independence as republic, 1973 military rule).
Legislature: Senate, 31 members; Chambers of Representatives, 99 members.
Official language: Spanish (Español/Castella).
Monetary unit: 1 peso uruguayo (Uruguayan peso). **US$1=** Ur$10.87.
Chief cities: MONTEVIDEO 1,361,000; Salto 87,975; Paysandu 82,933; Las Piedras 63,445; Rivera 62,387.
Political divisions: 19 provinces.
Armed forces: 26,000.

DEMOGRAPHY
Population: 3,337,000.
Population density: 18.9/sq. km. (49.0/sq. mi.).
Under 15 years: 827,000.
Growth rate p.a.: 0.70% (births 16.86, deaths 9.32).
Mortality: Infant, per 1,000: 13.1; **Maternal per 100,000:** 85.0.
Life expectancy: 75 (male 72, female 79).
Household size: 3.3. **Floor area per person, sq.m:** 22.0.
Major languages: Spanish, Italian, Galician, German, Portuguese, Russian, Greek, and others.
Urban dwellers: 91.33%. **Urban growth rate p.a.:** 0.7%.
Labor force: 45%.

ETHNOLINGUISTIC PEOPLES
82.8% Uruguayan White; 3.0% Uruguayan Mestizo; 2.6% Italian; 1.7% Jewish; 1.7% Mulatto.

ECONOMY
National income p.a. per person: US$5,170; **per family:** US$17,061.

EDUCATION
Adult literacy: 97% (male 96%, female 97%). **Schools:** 2,862.
Universities: 2. **School enrolment:** female/male: 98%/92%.

HEALTH
Access to health services: 82%. **Access to safe water:** 34%.
Hospitals: 112 (45 beds per 10,000). **Doctors:** 11,201.
Blind: 3,000. **Deaf:** 196,500. **Murder rate:** 4.
Lepers: 2,000. **Underweight prevalence under 5:** 4%.

LITERATURE
New book titles p.a.: 1,330 (400 p.a. per million). **Periodicals:** 651.
Newspapers: 32 dailies.

COMMUNICATION (per 1,000 people)
Phones: 199 **(19% mobile). Radios:** 591. **TV sets:** 310.
Daily newspaper circulation: 237. **Computers:** 30.

HUMAN LIFE AND LIBERTY (optimum condition=100.0%)
HDI: 88.3. **HSI:** 63.0. **HFI:** 20.0. **EFL:** 44.0.

Country Table 1. **Religious adherents in Uruguay, AD 1900-2025.**

Year	1900		1970		mid-1990		Annual change, 1990-2000				mid-1995		mid-2000		mid-2025	
Name	Adherents	%	Adherents	%	Adherents	%	Natural	Conversion	Total	Rate	Adherents	%	Adherents	%	Adherents	%
Christians	**574,700**	**62.8**	**1,902,600**	**67.8**	**2,037,900**	**65.6**	**15,156**	**-1,106**	**14,050**	**0.67**	**2,105,000**	**65.4**	**2,178,396**	**65.3**	**2,520,000**	**64.5**
PROFESSION																
professing Christians	**574,700**	**62.8**	**1,902,600**	**67.8**	**2,037,900**	**65.6**	**15,156**	**-1,106**	**14,050**	**0.67**	**2,105,000**	**65.4**	**2,178,396**	**65.3**	**2,520,000**	**64.5**
AFFILIATION																
unaffiliated Christians	0	0.0	0	0.0	12,500	0.4	93	324	417	2.92	14,800	0.5	16,667	0.5	20,000	0.5
affiliated Christians	**574,700**	**62.8**	**1,902,600**	**67.8**	**2,025,400**	**65.2**	**15,063**	**-1,430**	**13,633**	**0.65**	**2,090,200**	**65.0**	**2,161,729**	**64.8**	**2,500,000**	**64.0**
Roman Catholics	637,000	69.6	2,115,337	75.3	2,425,000	78.1	18,035	265	18,300	0.73	2,513,100	78.1	2,608,000	78.2	3,100,000	79.3
Protestants	14,600	1.6	57,053	2.0	96,000	3.1	714	686	1,400	1.37	104,552	3.3	110,000	3.3	150,000	3.8
Marginal Christians	0	0.0	24,553	0.9	75,000	2.4	558	1,442	2,000	2.39	83,800	2.6	95,000	2.9	170,000	4.4
Independents	0	0.0	28,200	1.0	46,500	1.5	346	254	600	1.22	49,921	1.6	52,500	1.6	75,000	1.9
Orthodox	100	0.0	18,500	0.7	24,000	0.8	178	72	250	1.00	25,150	0.8	26,500	0.8	40,000	1.0
Anglicans	0	0.0	1,000	0.0	1,200	0.0	9	-9	0	0.00	1,200	0.0	1,200	0.0	1,600	0.0
doubly-affiliated	0	0.0	-53,000	-1.9	-104,800	-3.4	-779	-1,888	-2,667	2.29	-120,523	-3.8	-131,471	-3.9	-135,300	-3.5
disaffiliated	-77,000	-8.4	-289,043	-10.3	-537,500	-17.3	-3,998	-2,252	-6,250	1.11	-567,000	-17.6	-600,000	-18.0	-901,300	-23.1
Trans-megabloc groupings																
Evangelicals	6,000	0.7	27,700	1.0	58,800	1.9	437	163	600	0.98	61,774	1.9	64,800	1.9	110,000	2.8
Pentecostals/Charismatics	0	0.0	44,000	1.6	270,000	8.7	2,008	1,392	3,400	1.19	288,907	9.0	304,000	9.1	470,000	12.0
Great Commission Christians	**46,000**	**5.0**	**280,800**	**10.0**	**760,000**	**24.5**	**5,652**	**7,496**	**13,148**	**1.61**	**820,000**	**25.5**	**891,482**	**26.7**	**1,133,000**	**29.0**
Nonreligious	340,180	37.2	790,700	28.2	839,000	27.0	6,248	-705	5,543	0.64	865,710	26.9	894,425	26.8	1,084,300	27.8
Atheists	1,000	0.1	57,000	2.0	177,000	5.7	1,316	1,867	3,183	1.67	194,000	6.0	208,831	6.3	250,000	6.4
Jews	60	0.0	52,000	1.9	40,500	1.3	301	-263	38	0.09	40,300	1.3	40,879	1.2	34,000	0.9
Baha'is	0	0.0	3,400	0.1	5,500	0.2	41	145	186	2.95	6,300	0.2	7,356	0.2	9,200	0.2
Spiritists	0	0.0	1,500	0.1	4,090	0.1	30	28	58	1.34	4,460	0.1	4,672	0.1	5,500	0.1
Muslims	60	0.0	300	0.0	450	0.0	3	2	5	1.08	470	0.0	501	0.0	900	0.0
Buddhists	0	0.0	0	0.0	60	0.0	0	0	0	0.65	60	0.0	64	0.0	100	0.0
Other religionists	0	0.0	500	0.0	1,500	0.1	11	32	43	2.57	1,700	0.1	1,934	0.1	3,000	0.1
World A (unevangelized persons)	99,811	10.9	140,421	5.0	49,696	1.6	368	-1,009	-641	-1.38	45,054	1.4	43,381	1.3	39,070	1.0
World B (evangelized non-Christians)	241,188	26.4	765,411	27.2	1,018,404	32.8	7,582	2,115	9,697	0.91	1,068,132	33.2	1,115,223	33.4	1,347,930	34.5
World C (Christians)	574,700	62.7	1,902,600	67.8	2,037,900	65.6	15,156	-1,106	14,050	0.67	2,105,000	65.4	2,178,396	65.3	2,520,000	64.5
Country's population	**915,700**	**100.0**	**2,808,433**	**100.0**	**3,106,000**	**100.0**	**23,106**	**0**	**23,106**	**0.72**	**3,218,187**	**100.0**	**3,337,000**	**100.0**	**3,907,000**	**100.0**

COLUMNS, ROWS.
For meanings and definitions, see Codebook (Part 3). Note that, by definition, total 'Christians' = professing + crypto-Christians, which also = affiliated + unaffiliated Christians, and also = Great Commission Christians + latent Christians. Percentages may not always total exactly, due to rounding.

CENSUSES.
1908 (all ages): 61.2% Roman Catholics, 37.1% nonreligious (22.7% of no religion, 14.4% freethinkers), 1.6% Evangelicals (16,498 persons), 0.1% atheists. **1908** (adults only, over 14 years old): 70.0% Roman Catholics, 27.9% nonreligious (20.6% freethinkers (126,425 adults)), 2.0% Evangelicals (12,232 adults), 0.1% atheists. **1963:** 62% Roman Catholics.

NOTES ON RELIGIONS
ATHEISTS. Uruguayan Communist Party (PCU) (legal; pro-Soviet). Leftist terrorist groups (National Liberation Movement (MLN), Tupamaros) are numerous also.
BAHA'IS. Rapid growth from 3 local spiritual assemblies (1964) to 23 (1973), then to 42 (1996).
DISAFFILIATED. This term is used here to describe persons who, although baptized Roman Catholics and therefore regarded by the Catholic Church as still affiliated to it (and hence enumerated as such), have recently disaffiliated themselves completely from Christianity and now profess in polls to be either nonreligious (agnostics) or atheists. Because their statistics represent a duplication, they are shown in the table above as a negative quantity (with a minus sign).
DOUBLY-AFFILIATED. The term covers those affiliated to, or claimed by, both the Catholic Church and also a church termed Evangélica by the state (Protestant, marginal Christian, Anglican, or Independents) or other churches, i.e. baptized Catholics who have recently become Evangelicals or others. Because their statistics represent a duplication, they are shown in the table as a negative quantity (with a minus sign).
INDEPENDENTS. In about 8 denominations in 1995 (see Table 2).
JEWS. In 6 synagogues. Jews immigrated in 3 major waves from Russia, Germany, Eastern Europe, and the Middle East.
NONRELIGIOUS. There has been a longer history of large-scale non-religion in Uruguay than in any other Latin American nation, or than in most European nations. In the 1908 census, 37.2% professed to be *liberales*, i.e. nonreligious (14.4% calling themselves freethinkers, the rest agnostics, pantheists, materialists, theosophists, evolutionists, and several other categories); in 1970, 34% called themselves nonreligious or atheists. Among the numerous causative factors are a history of 19th-century anti-clericalism, steady influx of nonreligious Spaniards, Italians and French from Europe, early separation of church and state, diffusion of liberal and agnostic philosophies from Europe, and the presence of thousands of short-term residents from Argentina awaiting divorces under Uruguay's liberal laws.
OTHER RELIGIONISTS. Adherents of smaller religions and cults, including Rosicrucians (1 AMORC center).
PRACTICING CHRISTIANS. *Church attendance.* 1965: (Catholics) 10.4% weekly in all churches in Salto, Colonia, and Canelones. 1968: weekly church attenders (in cities only) 24% of whole population. November 1970: 18% attended church in previous 7 days.
SPIRITISTS. Afro-American non-Christian low spiritism among the 10,000 Blacks and 50,000 Mulattoes remained relatively unorganized and ineffective until 1973 when Umbanda was introduced from Brazil and began winning converts from among the lowest classes in the larger cities.

Great Commission Instrument Panel: status of Uruguay (for explanation see start of Part 4)

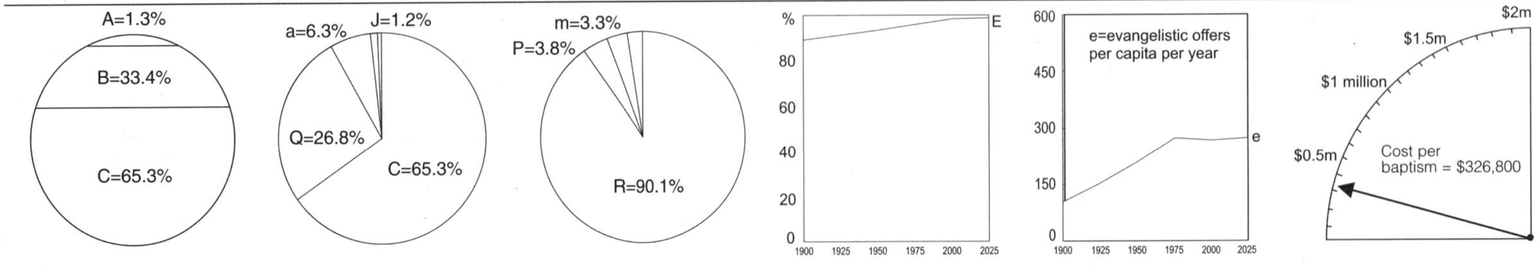

3 Worlds, AD 2000 — Religions, AD 2000 — Ecclesiastical blocs — Evangelization, 1900-2025 — Offers, 1900-2025 — Cost-effectiveness, AD 2000

Country status. Uruguay is a country in South America on the Atlantic Ocean south of Brazil. Its chief exports are meat, wool, hides, and fish.

HUMAN LIFE AND LIBERTY.

Human need and development. Uruguay is one of the most prosperous countries in the continent. About half of the population live in the capital city of Montevideo which enjoys the best medical, educational, and commercial services. Towns in the interior have fewer amenities. With an economy based primarily on stockraising and agriculture, there is an

Country summary. **Worlds A, B, C by ethnolinguistic peoples, cities, and major civil divisions in Uruguay.**																					
	PEOPLES							*CITIES*							*CIVIL DIVISIONS*						
World	*Num*	*Pop 2000*	*C%*	*Christians*	*E%*	*U%*	*Unevangelized*	*Num*	*Pop 2000*	*C%*	*Christians*	*E%*	*U%*	*Unevangelized*	*Num*	*Pop 2000*	*C%*	*Christians*	*E%*	*U%*	*Unevangelized*
A	1	58,399	0.10	58	46	54	31,477	0	0	0.00	0	0	0	0	0	0	0.00	0	0	0	0
B	2	3,497	50.01	1,749	83	17	602	0	0	0.00	0	0	0	0	0	0	0.00	0	0	0	0
C	29	3,275,164	65.95	2,159,923	100	0	11,014	7	1,718,358	64.10	1,101,440	99	1	24,352	19	3,337,053	64.78	2,161,729	99	1	43,088
Total	**32**	**3,337,060**	**64.78**	**2,161,730**	**99**	**1**	**43,093**	**7**	**1,718,358**	**64.10**	**1,101,440**	**99**	**1**	**24,352**	**19**	**3,337,053**	**64.78**	**2,161,729**	**99**	**1**	**43,088**

ample supply of food for all classes of people. Good medical care, generous social welfare services, and satisfactory environmental sanitation have resulted in Uruguay having one of the highest life expectancy rates in the world. The pace of life is leisurely, the working hours are short and the number of national holidays is high. As a result recreation occupies the time of the average Uruguayan more than it does elsewhere.

Human rights and freedoms. While Uruguayans have historically enjoyed all basic freedoms even when the rest of the continent was characterized by their absence, there are a few black spots on the record. Police abuse of detainees is considered normal and prison conditions are substandard.

Human environment. As a small country, Uruguay has escaped many of the environmental ravages suffered by its neighbors. Pollution is limited to Montevideo.

NON-CHRISTIAN RELIGIONS

Non-religion and ***atheism*** have had a longer history, and are numerically far stronger, in Uruguay than in any other South American nation. About 94% of Uruguay's population are Europeans or of European origin mostly coming originally from Spain, Italy, and France, who brought with them those countries' anti-clericalism and opposition to state-related Catholicism. There were only small numbers of Indian inhabitants when Spanish settlement was begun, and the last were exterminated in 1832. The high literacy rate, large urban middle class and early separation of church and state (formalized in 1916) all contributed to a further reduction in Catholic influence and to the creation of a substantial group by the year 1900 claiming to be freethinkers, agnostics or atheists; and this situation has continued relatively unchanged to the present day. Uruguay is in fact the least Catholic and least Christian of any Latin American Spanish- or Portuguese-speaking country.

Judaism has 40,000 adherents today.

Baha'i has grown rapidly since 1970, from 3,400 adherents to over 6,200 by 1995.

Umbanda, a syncretistic Afro-Brazilian religion, was introduced from Brazil during 1973-74 and has already begun to make inroads among the lower classes of the large cities. At the end of 1974 a survey in Montevideo showed the existence of some 40 *terreiros* (cult centers). The sudden appearance and vogue of Umbanda are undoubtedly a reaction to Uruguay's desperate political and economic situation. in the mid-1970s. Umbanda's ceremonies are conducted in Portuguese.

CHRISTIANITY

CATHOLIC CHURCH. Franciscan and Jesuit missionaries arrived in 1616, and the Jesuits were soon involved in developing communal villages among the Indians. These were later destroyed following the expulsion of Jesuits from Uruguay in 1767. In 1726 Montevideo became a Catholic parish under the see of Buenos Aires. A diocese was established in 1878 which became an archdiocese in 1897.

A large number of Uruguay's postal stamps over the last 100 years have carried Christian themes, events, personalities: here, 1967 stamp commemorating October 1966 visit of Archbishop Makarios of Cyprus.

In contrast with its early preoccupation with evangelization only, the church has in recent years turned its attention towards problems of development in urban ghettos. This change, begun in 1957 at the time of the restructuring of Catholic Action into specialized movements, was carried further due to the influence of Medellín and the papal encyclical 'Populorum progressio', which focused attention on the needs of society and contributed to the polarization of leftist and rightist wings in the church. The hierarchy itself is deeply divided, but the progressivist wing prevails, as seen in the collective pastoral letter on social problems of 1967, and various pastoral letters by the archbishop of Montevideo on the state of the country (1968), and the church and politics (1970). At the level of internal church organization, new initiatives have been taken towards increasing the role of the laity in certain dioceses, through lay and parish groups.

The Holy See has diplomatic relations with Uruguay and in AD 2000 is represented to government and the Catholic hierarchy by a nuncio residing in Montevideo.

1895 postal stamp showing Montevideo Catholic Cathedral.

PROTESTANT CHURCHES. North American Methodists were the first to assign a missionary to Uruguay, in 1838. Due to continued civil war and revolutions the mission was closed, but re-opened again in 1878. Methodism has produced some of the most able leaders in Uruguay and also in all Latin America, but the church itself remains small.

The Waldensian Church began with the arrival of Italians in 1856, the first pastor being appointed in 1877. It is the second largest Protestant church, and many of its congregations are under the pastoral care of laymen. Other important groups which became established during the last century are German Lutherans, Salvation Army, and Seventh-day Adventists.

Southern Baptists entered Montevideo from Argentina in 1911. With few missionaries in the early days, progress was slow until recently. Seven Pentecostal churches are at work and have made an important impact on the country. The largest numerical increases have been recorded by the Assemblies of God. A number of smaller denominations are also present.

OTHER CHURCHES. The largest denomination outside Catholicism is the Jehovah's Witnesses, found mainly among recent German immigrants. Other groups of importance are Mormons, Greek and Russian Orthodox, and New Apostolic Church. Anglicans also have a small community with 4 urban congregations.

Indigenous missions. Christians from Uruguay have been active as missionaries outside of the country but their service has been mainly in surrounding South American countries such as Argentina, Bolivia, Brazil, etc. New agencies have sprung up among Protestants since 1980 focused on North Africa and other parts of the world.

Renewal movements. In the 1990s the Pentecostal/Charismatic Renewal continued to spread rapidly across most older churches, and numbered over 304,000 adherents (of whom 13% Pentecostals, 71% Charismatics, and 16% Independents).

Luis Palau Team Uruguay Campaign, 1978; 101,000 persons attended in 6 cities, with 8,000 decisions for Christ recorded.

CHURCH AND STATE

The juridical status of the Catholic Church has not been modified since 1916, when the church was formally separated from the state. Since then the church has been free to name its own bishops. The constitution of 15 February 1967 stipulates in Chapter III, Article 5: 'All religions are authorized in Uruguay. The State supports no religion whatever. It recognizes the right of the Catholic Church to ownership of all temples'. The same article regulates, to the advantage of the Catholic Church, the question of ownership of religious buildings built with government funds. Also, 'buildings dedicated for worship by the diverse religions' are declared exempt from all taxes.

During the first part of the 20th century, progressive ideas exemplified by the statesman José Batlle y Ordoñez were translated into a campaign against alleged obscurantism in the church, resulting in anticlerical laws and, in 1909, prohibition of religious instruction in public schools. The Catholic Church then went on the defensive, developing a network of organizations parallel to those of the state: schools, agricultural unions, savings and loan centers, banks and other economic and social institutions. Of this whole network only the Catholic schools remain today, and they now collaborate with the state.

After a short period of peaceful co-existence between church and state, tension arose again, this time between a church critical of the capitalist system (especially after Medellín and 'Populorum progressio') and a government becoming increasingly conservative. The new conflict between church and state has manifested itself in different ways: episcopal declarations on social and economic matters, arrests of priests suspected of encouraging revolutionary movements, and police searches of churches and convents. During this period, the episcopate was more involved than in merely making public declarations.

After the fascist military coup of 27 June 1973, the Catholic episcopate and the Federation of Evangelical Churches published separate protests. As in other parts of South Ameirca, the repression of alleged subversive activities has affected both non-Catholics and Catholics, including priests, sisters, and lay militants. Pastor Emilio Castro, of the CWME/WCC, and msgr Mendiharat bishop of Salto, went into exile. Among others, the government suspended at the end of 1974 the official organ of the Waldensian Church, *Mensajero Valdense*, which provoked a conflict between the WCC and government, the latter claiming that the former 'invariably favors Marxist subversion on the 5 continents'. Ironically the Waldensian Church in the River Plate is not a member of the WCC.

A more direct conflict with the Catholic Church has been provoked by the government's decision to restrict the autonomy of confessional teaching centers, accused of fomenting 'Marxist conscientization'. The Catholic episcopate, though divided into conservative and progressivist factions, has unanimously opposed the government plan which it insists is unconstitutional.

BROADCASTING AND MEDIA

IBRA programs can be received on a daily basis from 18 local stations. In addition, shortwave radio programs can be received from KNLS, HCJB (Ecuador), TWR (Antilles), and AWR (Costa Rica). Uruguay is a member of UNDA.

Some 190,000 have seen the 'Jesus' Film, mainly through TV broadcasts and film team presentations, with 9,000 responders.

INTERDENOMINATIONAL ORGANIZATIONS

The Federation of Evangelical Churches of Uruguay (Federación de Iglesias Evangélicas del Uruguay, FIEU) has 8 full members and 2 associate members. It was founded in 1956 as the successor to the Uruguay Committee of the Confederation of Evangelical Churches of the River Plate, which held its first meeting in 1939. The council is affiliated to the Commission on World Mission and Evangelism, World Council of Churches, and also to 2 regional organizations: the Latin American Christian Education Council (Comisión Evangélica Latinoamericana de Educación Cristiana, CELADEC), and UNELAM (Movimiento pro Unidad Evangélica Latino-americana). The latter body has its headquarters in Montevideo. The Evangelical Institute of Montevideo was opened by Lutherans in 1966 and includes on its staff Catholic as well as Protestant theologians. A Sodepax-type organization is also active.

Concerning interreligious relations, the Judeo-Christian Brotherhood (Confraternidad Judeo-Cristiana) was formed in 1964 and devotes itself to cultural initiatives and the organization of theological symposia concerning problems of common interest.

FUTURE TRENDS AND PROSPECTS

Christians are projected to continue to experience steady but minor losses with the percentage of Christians falling to 64% by 2025. The nonreligious and atheists make up most of the rest buttressed by European anti-clericalism. Uruguay will likely remain the least Catholic and least Christian of any Latin American Spanish- or Portuguese-speaking country.

Christianity could decline below 63% by AD 2050 as atheism and the nonreligious continue to grow slowly and steadily, jointly reaching over 35% of the population by AD 2050.

BIBLIOGRAPHY

'A history of Uruguayan Baptists with particular reference to church growth.' J. W. Bartley. Th.D. thesis, Southwestern Baptist Theological Seminary, Fort Worth, TX, 1972. 323p.

Aspectos religiosos de la sociedad uruguaya. Montevideo: Centro de Estudios Cristianos, 1965. 143p.

Breve visión de la historia de la Iglesia en el Uruguay. D. Bazzano. Montevideo: OBSUR Librería San Pablo, 1993. 146p.

Católicos, en Uruguay. J. Fuentes. Montevideo, 1985. 201p.

Guía de la Iglesia Católica Uruguaya. Montevideo: Departamento de Comunicación Social, Conferencia Episcopal Uruguaya, 1990. 199p.

Guia de la Iglesia Uruguaya. Montevideo: Curia Eclesiástica de Montevideo, 1971.

Historia de la Iglesia en el Uruguay en cifras: V centenario de la evangelización de América. J. Villegas. Montevideo: Universidad Católica del Uruguay, 1987. 100p.

Huellas de una iglesia: la Iglesia Evangélica y su desarrollo en Uruguay. P. Lapadjián. Montevideo: Ediciones Trilce, 1994. 136p.

Iglesia Católica y comunicación en el Uruguay: año 1992. M. L. Recarey & T. Iglesias. Montevideo: Observatorio del Sur, 1993. 44p.

La Iglesia en el Uruguay: libro conmenorativo en el primer centenario de la erección del obispado de Montevideo. Primero en el Uruguay, 1878–1978. Montevideo: Instituto Teológico del Uruguay, 1978. 356p.

La otra cara: de la Iglesia católica en el Uruguay. M. Porras de Hugues. Montevideo: Talleres Don Bosco, 1988. 110p.

La religión en Uruguay. C. M. Rama. Montevideo: Nuestro Tiempo, 1964.

Los dominicos y la evangelización del Uruguay. A. Esponera Cerdán. *Los Dominicos y América*, 8. Salamanca: Editorial San Esteban, 1992. 375p.

'Nationalism and religion in Argentina and Uruguay,' A. P. Whitaker, in *Religion, revolution, and reform: new forces for change in Latin America*, p.73–90. W. V. D'Antonio & F. B. Pike (eds). London: Burns and Oates, 1964.

'Patterns of church growth within the Seventh–day Adventist Church in the River Platte Republics.' J. C. Viera-Rossano. M.A. thesis, Fuller Theological Seminary, Pasadena, CA, 1988. 165p. (Text in Spanish with extended summary in English).

Presencia cristiana en las experiencias de promoción popular. J. Ferrando & M. Bonino. Montevideo: OBSUR, 1994. 140p.

'Separation in Uruguay,' J. L. Mecham, in *Church and state in Latin America: a history of politico–ecclesiastical relations*, p.252–60. 2nd ed. Chapel Hill, NC: University of North Carolina Press, 1966.

The evangelical church in the River Plate republics: a study of the economic and social basis of the evangelical church in Argentina and Uruguay. J. M. Davis. New York: International Missionary Council, 1943. 119p.

The River Plate republics: a survey of the religious, economic and social conditions in Argentina, Paraguay and Uruguay. W. E. Browning. London: World Dominion Press, 1928. 139p.

The Waldenses in the New World. G. B. Watts. Durham, NC: Duke University Press, 1941. 309p.

Ubicación del Metodismo en el Río de la Plata. D. P. Monti. Buenos Aires: Editorial La Aurora, 1976. 270p.

Uruguay. H. Finch & A. C. de Barrán. *World bibliographical series*, vol. 102. Oxford, UK: CLIO Press, 1989. 334p. (See especially 'Religion,' p.64-6).

Country Table 2. **Organized churches and denominations in Uruguay.**

Official name (bold type = church with over 10% of all affiliated) 1	*Begun* 2	*Type* 3	*Counc* 4	*Congs* 5	*Adults* 6	*Affiliated 1970* 7	*Affiliated 1995* 8	*G%* 9	*Names, notes, and other statistics* (see Codebook, Part 3) 10
Alianza Cristiana y Misionera del U	1960	P-Hol	x....	15	9,000	900	12,000	10.92	M=Christian & Missionary Alliance (USA), begun from Argentina. 2x,W=74%,75Y.
Asambleas de Dios (Sueca)	1938	P-Pe2	Z...	36	4,000	3,000	10,000	4.93	*Assemblies of God (Swedish).* M=SFM(Sweden), FFFM(Finland). Classical Pentecostals.
Asambleas de Dios (USA)	1944	P-Pe2	ZF...	478	10,630	10,000	17,527	2.27	*Assemblies of God.* M=AoG(USA). Classical Pentecostals (2-stage). 75n,8f,1s(28).
Asambleas Locales	c1990	I-3nC	.....	3	150	–	200	20.00	*Local Churches. Little Flock.* Chinese. Begun 1922 in China.
Congregación Ev Luterana (Misurí)	1935	P-Lut	x....	2	150	142	200	1.38	*San Pablo* (Montevideo). 1942, M=LC Missouri Synod (USA). Montevideo, Paysandu.
Consejo de Congs Hermanos Menonitas	1966	P-Men	GFu.N	6	160	306	200	-1.69	Council of Mennonite Brethren Congregations. M=MBCNA(USA). 2n,1x,4f,2p,W=21%,19Y.
Convención Evangélica Bautista del U	1911	P-Bap	T....	46	3,836	3,500	9,590	4.11	*Ev Baptist Convention.* M=SBC(USA). 27n,4x,22f,G=4.1%pa,4h,1s(12),W=38%,294Y,185z.
Ejército de Salvación	1890	P-Sal	xwu.N	6	700	2,000	1,400	-1.42	*Salvation Army, Uruguay & Argentina Littoral District*, SAmerica East Territory.
Iglesia Adventista del Séptimo Día	1895	P-Adv	x....	36	6,013	6,000	12,000	2.81	*Seventh-day Adventists, Uruguay M*, Austral UC. 8n,1x,50mw,26f,G=4.4%pa,1r,267Y.
Iglesia Anglicana (D Argentina & ESA)		A-Eva	aw.C.	4	900	1,000	1,200	0.05	*Anglican Ch in ACSCA.* ESA=Eastern South America. Urban. Uruguayans of UK origin. 1x.
Iglesia Apostólica Armenia: D Uruguay		O-Arm	Ewc..	1	270	500	650	0.05	*Armenian Apostolic Ch. Gregorians.* Under jurisdiction of C Echmiadzin (USSR). 2nx.
Iglesia Bautista Libre	1962	I-Bap	xF...	5	100	500	200	-3.60	*Free Will Baptist Ch.* M=NAFWB(USA). HQ Rivera (Brazil border). 1n,5f.
Iglesia Bautista Nacional	1965	I-Bap	Tw...	2	150	200	300	1.64	M=National Baptist Convention USA. Blacks, assisting Uruguayan Baptists.
Iglesia Católica en el Uruguay:	1616	R-Lat	BzL.R	822	1,841,000	2,115,337	2,513,100	0.69	*Catholic Ch in Uruguay.* C=34+1+51. 1s,W=18%. 248n 322x 477m 1582w 37459Yy
M Montevideo	1878	R-Lat	Bs	121	671,000	910,000	850,000	-0.27	1968: 10,000 laity mobilized in parish groups. M=SDB. 1s. 93n 220x 338m 974w 12709Yy
D Canelones	1961	R-Lat	Bs	148	265,000	245,565	371,000	1.66	Northeast of capital. Low religious practice: M=SDB. 24n 30x 40m 212w 5076Yy
D Florida	1897	R-Lat	Bs	95	56,000	100,000	81,000	-0.84	Central area of Uruguay: hilly, lakes. 11n 14x 21m 47w 2104Yy
D Maldonado-Punta del Este	1966	R-Lat	Bs	95	131,000	90,100	175,000	2.69	Southeast coastal area. HQ Maldonado. 11n 8x 11m 30w 2318Yy
D Melo	1897	R-Lat	Bs	71	75,000	80,000	109,000	1.24	Northeast part of country, bordering on Brazil. 12n 9x 11m 57w 1223Yy
D Mercedes	1960	R-Lat	Bs	82	127,000	137,572	170,000	0.85	Same name as Argentina diocese across. M=SDB. 21n 9x 11m 53w 2452Yy
D Minas	1960	R-Lat	Bs	12	58,000	69,000	94,000	1.24	Inland southeastern area of country. 18n 1x 7m 34w 2670Yy
D Salto	1897	R-Lat	Bs	16	277,000	238,000	401,000	2.11	Scattered. Numerous wealthy landowners. M=SJ. 24n 16x 19m 75w 4900Yy
D San José de Mayo	1955	R-Lat	Bs	77	63,000	105,100	90,100	-0.61	Coast area west of Montevideo. 14n 3x 7m 33w 1666Yy
D Tacuarembó	1960	R-Lat	Bs	105	118,000	140,000	172,000	0.83	Centre north of country, adjoining Brazil. 10n 12x 12m 67w 2428Yy
Iglesia de Dios de la Profecía	1957	P-Pe3	Z....	11	800	300	1,070	5.22	*Ch of God of Prophecy.* M=CGP(USA). Holiness Pentecostals; ex CoG(Cleveland). 2f.
Iglesia de Dios (Cleveland)	1940	P-Pe3	ZF...	44	2,151	4,500	5,380	0.72	*Ch of God.* M=CoG(Cleveland) (USA). Begun by laymen from Argentina. 22n,1p.
Iglesia de JC de los Santos de los UD	c1942	m-LdS	x....	118	42,000	16,053	56,000	5.12	*Ch of JC of Latter-day Saints. Mormons.* M=CJCLdS(USA). 300f.
Iglesia del Evangelio Cuadrangular		P-Pe2	ZF...	5	225	300	450	0.05	*International Ch of the Foursquare Gospel.* M=ICGF(USA). 1962, mission withdrew.
Iglesia del Nazareno	1949	P-Hol	xF..n	20	1,209	1,000	2,444	3.64	*Nazarenes.* M=CoN(USA). 4n,3x,7m,6f,1s(12),14t,(878),W=90%,42Y,62z.
Iglesia Evangélica Armenia	1930	P-Con	..u.N	2	300	300	500	2.06	*Armenian Ev Ch.* 1965, M=Armenian Missionary Association of America. Refugees.
Iglesia Evangélica del Río de la Plata	1860	P-LuR	.wu.N	13	2,000	4,400	5,000	0.51	*La Plata Ev Ch. Igl Ev Alemana.* 1899 union German diaspora congs (10% Reformed).
Iglesia Evangélica Metodista en el U	1838	P-Met	Vuu.N	17	3,000	6,000	4,000	-1.61	*Ev Methodist Ch of U.* A=1968. M=UMC(USA).12n,2x,2f,2r,2s,20t,W=20%.
Iglesia Ev Pentecostal de Chile	c1950	I-3pL	x....	7	1,300	1,500	3,250	3.14	*Ev Pentecostal Ch of Chile.* Indigenous mission from Chile. Chilean Mestizos.
Igl Ev Valdense del Río de la Plata	1856	P-Wal	R.u.N	15	9,000	7,945	12,000	1.66	*Waldensian Ch in River Plate.* Italian immigrants. Strong youth movement. 17n,1u.
Iglesia Menonita	1956	P-Men	G...n	10	717	1,300	1,091	-0.70	M=GCMC(USA). Germans, Poles, Russians; re-emigrating. 22n,4x,1s,W=15%,28Y.
Iglesia Nueva Apostólica		I-3aX	x....	115	17,300	20,000	28,246	0.05	*NAC. New Apostolic Ch.* Many German immigrants. World HQ Zurich (Switzerland).
Iglesia Ortodoxa Griega		O-Gre	Cwo..	6	9,500	10,000	13,500	0.05	Part of 10th Archidiocesan District, Greek Orthodox AD of N&SAmerica. Greeks.
Iglesia Ortodoxa Russa (D Argentina)		I-Rus	x....	1	650	1,000	1,300	0.05	Russian Orth Ch Outside of Russia. M=ROCOR(New York, USA). Conservative Russians.
Iglesia Ortodoxa Russa (P Moscú)		O-Rus	Mwo..	4	6,000	8,000	11,000	0.05	*Russian Orthodox Church.* Under P Moscow. Russian emigres after 2 World Wars.
Iglesia Ortodoxa Ucrania		I-Ukr	X....	2	700	1,000	1,400	0.05	*Ukrainian Autocephalous Orthodox Ch.* M=UOCUSA. Ukrainian refugees from USSR.
Iglesia Pentecostal Unida	1956	P-Pe1	x....	10	500	500	1,000	2.81	*United Pentecostal Ch. Jesus Only Church.* M=UPC(USA). Oneness theology. 2n,4f,2p(70).
Iglesia Reformada Ungara del Uruguay	c1956	P-Ref	..u.N	1	400	500	600	0.73	*Hungarian Reformed Ch of Uruguay.* Refugees from Hungary from 1956 and later.
Iglesias Biblicas	c1980	I-3pW	.....	3	245	–	445	6.67	Bible churches. M=OBSC(USA).
Iglesia Unificación		m-HSA	x....	12	1,100	1,000	1,400	0.05	*HSAUWC.* In Montevideo, owns luxury hotel, newspaper, large financial institution.
Iglesias Cristianas	c1975	I-Dis	.....	8	112	–	280	5.00	*Christian Churches & Churches of Christ. CCCC.*
Iglesias Cristianas Evangélicas		P-CBr	x....	30	900	1,500	2,000	0.05	*Ev Christian Churches. Plymouth (Open) Brethren.* M=CMML(NA, UK, USA). 9f.
Misión de la Igl Luterana en América	1948	P-Lut	l.u.N	2	200	160	300	2.55	1952, M=Lutheran Church in America(USA). In Rivera. Begun from Argentina. 2f.
Nuevos Israelitas		I-Ose	.....	5	650	1,000	1,300	0.05	*New Israelites. Novy Izrail.* Russian Spiritual Christians from Rostov region, USSR.
Sociedad de la Ciencia Cristiana		m-Sci	x....	3	200	500	500	0.05	*Ch of Christ, Scientist. Christian Science.* M=CCS(Boston, USA). Montevideo. 6w.
Testigos de Jehovà	1923	m-Jeh	x....	106	7,755	7,000	25,900	5.37	*Jehovah's Witnesses.* Active witnessing under way by 1940. (1975) 405Y. (1995) 741Y.
Unión Misionera Neotestamentaria		P-Non	x....	3	400	500	800	0.05	M=New Testament Missionary Union(UK, USA). Strong in Paraguay, Argentina, Brazil. 2f.
Other pentecostal churches		I-3pL	.....	50	5,000	2,000	10,000	0.05	Total 70 bodies.

Continued opposite

Country Table 2–concluded

Official name (bold type = church with over 10% of affiliated) 1	*Begun* 2	*Type* 3	*Counc* 4	*Congs* 5	*Adults* 6	*Affiliated 1970* 7	*Affiliated 1995* 8	*G%* 9	*Names, notes, and other statistics* (see Codebook, Part 3) 10
Other Protestant denominations		P-	.....	40	2,000	2,000	5,000	0.05	Total about 15 (see list below).
Other Non-White indigenous churches		I-3nN	.....	30	2,000	1,000	3,000	0.05	Total about 5 (see list below).
Doubly-affiliated		2-aff			-86,600	-53,000	-120,523		Evangelicals who also are or were baptized Roman Catholics.
Disaffiliated		X-Aff			-407,000	-289,043	-567,000		Baptized Catholics who have become completely disaffiliated agnostics or atheists.
Totals				**2,155**	**1,501,773**	**1,902,600**	**2,090,200**		

Churches, members, growth, 1900-2025	*Congs*	*Adults*	*Affiliated*	*G%*	*Total denominations*	*6 Megablocs:* O	R	A	P	I	m
Total churches, members, and denominations (mid-1900)	200	410,000	574,700	1.72	7	0	1	0	6	0	0
Total churches, members, and denominations (mid-1970)	959	1,357,554	1,902,600	1.72	78	3	1	1	29	40	4
Total churches, members, and denominations (mid-1990)	2,100	1,455,000	2,025,400	0.31	130	3	1	1	37	84	4
Total churches, members, and denominations (mid-1995)	2,155	1,501,773	2,090,200	0.63	131	3	1	1	37	85	4
Total churches, members, and denominations (mid-2000)	2,200	1,553,000	2,161,729	0.68	132	3	1	1	37	86	4
Total churches, members, and denominations (mid-2025)	2,700	1,796,000	2,500,000	0.58	210	10	1	1	50	140	8

NOTES ON TABLE ABOVE
NATIONAL COUNCILS (Column 4, 5th letter).
- E = Asociacion Cristiana de Iglesias Evangelicas de la Republica de Uruguay (ACIERU)
- N = Federación de Iglesias Evangélicas del Uruguay (FIEU) (Federation of Evangelical Churches of Uruguay).
- n = affiliate members of FIEU.
- R = Conferencia Episcopal del Uruguay (CEU) (Uruguay Episcopal Conference).

OTHER PROTESTANT DENOMINATIONS. These include: Apostolic Christian Ch (Nazarean), Baptist Bible Fellowship International (1959), Baptist Missionary Association of America (1965), Baptist World Mission (1964), Christian Ch of North America, Ch of God (Seventh-day), Ch of Scotland, Chs of Christ (Non-Instrumental), Ev Mission to Uruguay (Baptist), Gospel Mission of South America (1971), Independent Bible Baptist Missions (1950), Slavic Gospel Association, Uruguayan Evangelistic Mission Worldwide Evangelization Crusade.

OTHER NON-WHITE INDIGENOUS CHURCHES. These consist of small groups from the strong indigenous pentecostal bodies in Brazil, Argentina and Chile. They include: Iglesia Pentecostal Independiente, Misión Iglesia Pentecostal (from Chile).

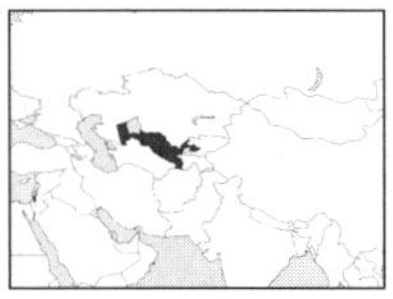

UZBEKISTAN

SECULAR DATA, AD 2000

STATE
Official name: Ozbekiston Respublikasy (The Republic of Uzbekistan).
Short name: Uzbekistan. **Adjective of nationality:** Uzbek.
Flag: Blue, red, white, red, and green stripes with white crescent and 12 stars.
Area: 447,400 sq. km. (172,700 sq. mi.).
Government: Multiparty republic with a single legislative body, since 1991 (1924 Soviet rule).
Legislature: Supreme Assembly, 250 members.
Official language: Uzbek.
Monetary unit: sum (plural sumy). **US$1=** 300,000 sumy.
Chief cities: TASKENT (Tashkent) 2,495,000; Samarkand 450,068; Namangan 387,751; Andizan (Andizhan) 362,362; Buchara (Bukhara, Bokhara) 303,203.
Political divisions: 13 provinces.
Armed forces: 49,000.

DEMOGRAPHY
Population: 24,318,000.
Population density: 54.3/sq. km. (140.8/sq. mi.).
Under 15 years: 9,107,000.
Growth rate p.a.: 1.56% (births 25.72, deaths 6.15).
Mortality: Infant, per 1,000: 39.0; **Maternal per 100,000:** 55.0.
Life expectancy: 69 (male 66, female 72).
Household size: 5.5. **Floor area per person, sq.m:** 20.0.
Major languages: Uzbek, Kazakh, Tajik, Russian, Tatar, Kirghiz.
Urban dwellers: 42.39%. **Urban growth rate p.a.:** 2.7%.
Labor force: 39%.

ETHNOLINGUISTIC PEOPLES
78.2% Northern Uzbek; 4.7% Tajik (Tadzhik); 4.0% Kazakh; 2.5% Russian; 2.3% Tatar.

ECONOMY
National income p.a. per person: US$969; **per family:** US$5,334.

EDUCATION
Adult literacy: 97% (male 98%, female 96%). **Schools:** 9,347.
Universities: 52. **School enrolment:** female/male: 83%/90%.

HEALTH
Access to health services: 75%. **Access to safe water:** 90%.
Hospitals: 1,388 (85 beds per 10,000). **Doctors:** 79,000.
Blind: 22,000. **Deaf:** 1,501,100. **Murder rate:** 5.
Lepers: 1,000.

LITERATURE
New book titles p.a.: 1,580 (65 p.a. per million). **Periodicals:** 85.
Newspapers: 4 dailies.

COMMUNICATION (per 1,000 people)
Phones: 76 (1% mobile). **Radios:** 250. **TV sets:** 176.
Daily newspaper circulation: 264. **Computers:** 35.

REFUGEES
Citizen refugees in other countries: 48,000.

HUMAN LIFE AND LIBERTY (optimum condition=100.0%)
HDI: 66.2. **HSI:** 45.0. **HFI:** 10.0. **EFL:** 25.0.

Country Table 1. **Religious adherents in Uzbekistan, AD 1900-2025.**

Year / *Name*	*1900* Adherents	%	*1970* Adherents	%	*mid-1990* Adherents	%	*Annual change, 1990-2000* Natural	Conversion	Total	Rate	*mid-1995* Adherents	%	*mid-2000* Adherents	%	*mid-2025* Adherents	%
Muslims	2,215,000	98.4	6,000,000	50.1	14,672,950	71.5	272,002	112,519	384,521	2.35	16,842,230	74.9	18,518,161	76.2	28,000,000	84.0
Nonreligious	1,000	0.0	3,000,000	25.1	3,900,000	19.0	72,282	-21,802	50,480	1.22	4,147,500	18.5	4,404,803	18.1	4,388,000	13.2
Atheists	0	0.0	2,022,000	16.9	1,000,000	4.9	18,538	-32,530	-13,992	-1.50	850,000	3.8	860,079	3.5	450,000	1.4
Christians	**20,000**	**0.9**	**875,000**	**7.3**	**812,500**	**4.0**	**15,062**	**-56,198**	**-41,136**	**-6.81**	**508,000**	**2.3**	**401,143**	**1.7**	**380,000**	**1.1**
PROFESSION																
crypto-Christians	0	0.0	170,000	1.4	260,000	1.3	4,820	-9,820	-5,000	-2.11	225,000	1.0	210,000	0.9	223,000	0.7
professing Christians	**20,000**	**0.9**	**705,000**	**5.9**	**552,500**	**2.7**	**10,242**	**-46,378**	**-36,136**	**-10.07**	**283,000**	**1.3**	**191,143**	**0.8**	**157,000**	**0.5**
AFFILIATION																
unaffiliated Christians	500	0.0	5,500	0.1	9,130	0.0	169	-401	-232	-2.89	6,380	0.0	6,809	0.0	8,000	0.0
affiliated Christians	**19,500**	**0.9**	**869,500**	**7.3**	**803,370**	**3.9**	**14,893**	**-55,797**	**-40,904**	**-6.87**	**501,620**	**2.2**	**394,334**	**1.6**	**372,000**	**1.1**
Orthodox	16,500	0.7	827,900	6.9	572,170	2.8	10,607	-48,931	-38,324	-10.49	251,000	1.1	188,934	0.8	150,000	0.5
Independents	0	0.0	31,500	0.3	140,000	0.7	2,595	-4,595	-2,000	-1.53	159,070	0.7	120,000	0.5	145,000	0.4
Protestants	1,000	0.0	7,000	0.1	44,000	0.2	816	-816	0	0.00	45,250	0.2	44,000	0.2	40,000	0.1
Roman Catholics	2,000	0.1	3,000	0.0	46,000	0.2	853	-1,453	-600	-1.39	45,000	0.2	40,000	0.2	35,000	0.1
Marginal Christians	0	0.0	100	0.0	1,200	0.0	22	-2	20	1.55	1,300	0.0	1,400	0.0	2,000	0.0
Trans-megabloc groupings																
Evangelicals	800	0.0	1,600	0.0	8,200	0.0	152	278	430	4.31	8,596	0.0	12,500	0.1	29,000	0.1
Pentecostals/Charismatics	0	0.0	7,000	0.1	121,000	0.6	2,243	657	2,900	2.17	139,525	0.6	150,000	0.6	200,000	0.6
Great Commission Christians	**18,000**	**0.8**	**185,000**	**1.6**	**520,000**	**2.5**	**9,640**	**-37,201**	**-27,561**	**-7.27**	**320,000**	**1.4**	**244,386**	**1.0**	**260,000**	**0.8**
Jews	8,000	0.4	66,000	0.6	60,000	0.3	1,112	-1,705	-593	-1.03	57,000	0.3	54,075	0.2	35,000	0.1
Ethnoreligionists	0	0.0	0	0.0	45,000	0.2	834	-395	439	0.94	47,500	0.2	49,391	0.2	50,000	0.2
Buddhists	8,000	0.4	10,000	0.1	30,000	0.2	556	-25	531	1.64	33,000	0.2	35,312	0.2	60,000	0.2
Zoroastrians	0	0.0	0	0.0	2,000	0.0	37	67	104	4.28	2,500	0.0	3,042	0.0	6,000	0.0
Baha'is	0	0.0	0	0.0	500	0.0	9	12	21	3.54	660	0.0	708	0.0	2,000	0.0
Hindus	0	0.0	0	0.0	550	0.0	10	0	10	1.68	610	0.0	650	0.0	1,000	0.0
doubly-counted religionists	0	0.0	0	0.0	-8,500	0.0	-158	57	-101	1.13	-9,000	0.0	-9,512	0.0	-17,000	-0.1
World A (unevangelized persons)	2,101,116	93.3	9,578,400	80.0	12,719,300	62.0	235,784	-251,916	-16,132	-0.13	12,588,960	56.0	12,548,088	51.6	15,343,300	46.0
World B (evangelized non-Christians)	130,884	5.8	1,519,600	12.7	6,983,200	34.0	129,438	308,114	437,552	4.99	9,383,325	41.7	11,368,769	46.7	17,631,700	52.9
World C (Christians)	20,000	0.9	875,000	7.3	812,500	4.0	15,062	-56,198	-41,136	-6.81	508,000	2.3	401,143	1.7	380,000	1.1
Country's population	**2,252,000**	**100.0**	**11,973,000**	**100.0**	**20,515,000**	**100.0**	**380,284**	**0**	**380,284**	**1.72**	**22,480,286**	**100.0**	**24,318,000**	**100.0**	**33,355,000**	**100.0**

COLUMNS, ROWS.
For meanings and definitions, see Codebook (Part 3). Note that, by definition, total 'Christians' = professing + crypto-Christians, which also = affiliated + unaffiliated Christians, and also = Great Commission Christians + latent Christians. Percentages may not always total exactly, due to rounding.

NOTES ON RELIGIONS.
BAHA'IS. After 1991 there was considerable expansion, and by 1996 there were 18 local spiritual assemblies.

ORTHODOX. Massive decline after 1980 due to emigration of ethnic Russians and Ukrainians.

Country status. Uzbekistan, a former republic of the Soviet Union, is a landlocked country in Central Asia. Its chief products include cotton, textiles, machinery, and heavy equipment.

HUMAN LIFE AND LIBERTY

Human need and development. In 1994, average monthly wages were less than US$50, making Uzbekistan one of the poorest developed countries in the world. Ironically, expansive natural resources suggest the possibility of it becoming one of the most prosperous countries in Central Asia. As with the other former Soviet states, the claim of Independence

Great Commission Instrument Panel: status of Uzbekistan (for explanation see start of Part 4)

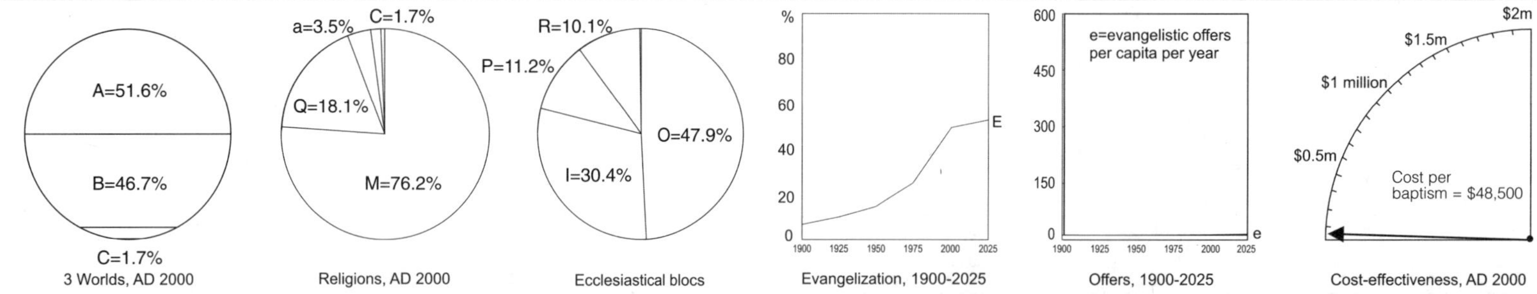

has brought its share of woes. The 1991 Law of Privatization transformed Uzbekistan from a centralized economy to a market economy, placing the burden upon the individual. Businesses, homes, land, and agricultural privatization have been underway since establishing a state agency in 1992. In mid-1995, 69% of enterprises had been privatized although all heavy industry remained in state ownership. The completion of privatization is not expected until well after AD 2000.

In the realm of health, frequent Uzbek press releases report increases in typhoid, paratyphoid and hepatitis from contaminated drinking water; increase in cancer and intestinal diseases; plus cases of anemia, dystrophy, cholera, dysentery, and a host of other illnesses. One health official has declared that 69 in every 100 adults living in the Aral Sea region are deemed incurably ill. The average life expectancy is 66 for males and 72 for females, but some villages in the Aral Sea region estimate life expectancy at 38 years.

Health care facilities are inadequate due to poorly trained medical staff. Medicine and vaccinations are in extremely short supply or non-existent and often corruption within the medical profession exacerbates existing shortages.

Development is slower than in most developed nations, but a brighter educational future and a strengthening economy forecast marked improvement in all realms of human need.

Human rights and freedoms. Uzbekistan, which became independent in 1991, has made little progress toward pluralistic democracy. The old Communist Party (now renamed National Democratic Party) is still dominant and its monopoly of power is scarcely touched by the liberalization movement in other former Soviet republics. The government justifies its repressive policies by invoking the specter of Islamic fundamentalism and the civil strife that has plagued neighboring Tajikstan. Security forces under the Ministry of Interior routinely detain, beat up, and arrest opposition leaders. Two political dissidents were convicted of insulting the president's honor. By requiring that all political parties must be registered and by denying registration to all of them, the government has successfully maintained its virtual monopoly of power. There have been assassination attempts against the president's political rivals. The legal provision permitting detention without filing of charges is used extensively to harass the opposition. Freedom of the press is severely limited. The majority of the daily press is government owned and so are television and radio. The government censors foreign publications, including those from the former Soviet Union. There are no private publishing houses. Freedom of religion is legally guaranteed.

There are no human rights watchdog agencies and the government has refused entry to or expelled several international human rights monitoring delegations. Human rights activists are arrested or deported.

Human environment. Comprising an area of 447,400 square kilometers(approximately the size of France), nearly 80% of the country's topography is desert. Environmentally, Uzbekistan is riddled with devastation that has impacted nearly every facet of ecology and natural surroundings. Because of very little rainfall, heavy irrigation is needed for crop production. The Aral sea is the main source for this irrigation but it has shrunk from the world's fourth largest inland sea to less than half its 1960 geographical size. What was once the sea's bottom is now an exposed multilayer of salt and dust that frequently becomes fuel for storm. These salt and dust storms wreak havoc on the agriculture ecosystems and the population's health. Each year tons of salt are carried as far as 800km in distance.

Largescale use of chemicals for cotton cultivation, inefficient irrigation systems, and poor drainage systems have led to high filtration of salinized and contaminated water back into the soil. In addition to agro-chemical contamination, industrial and chemical waste have polluted virtually all of the large underground fresh water supplies. Estimates show that half of the population live in regions with contaminated water.

High levels of heavy metals such as mercury, manganese, copper, lead, nickel, and zinc have been found in the air—mainly from fossil fuel burning, waste material burning, and ferrous and nonferrous metallurgy burnings. Fewer than half of factory smokestacks have filtration equipment and none can filter gaseous emissions.

Muslims. A man teaches Arab children in one of Jeinar's mosques.

NON-CHRISTIAN RELIGIONS

Islam in Uzbekistan has always been the majority religion, even when violently persecuted under Stalinism. Most Muslims are Sunnis of the Hanafite school. Independent Sufi sects, often armed and operating underground, have long been widespread.

During the Soviet period, Uzbekistan had as many as 3000 active Mullahs and other clerics, plus 65 registered mosques. It was during this time that the government was promoting Islam on one hand, while trying to eradicate it with the other. Since independence, a search to recapture the history and culture of Islam has been increasing. In the late 1990s, Islam has been experiencing a significant revival. While before independence there were only 100 mosques in the country, there are now over 5,000. Quranic education has become popular, although it is not included in state schools.

Judaism Approximately 55,000 Jews are present in Uzbekistan and synagogues function freely. Hebrew education, Jewish cultural events, and publication of a community paper occur undisturbed.

Buddhists, Hindu, and Bahai's are all found in small communities scattered throughout.

Korean Baptist Church. Protestant connections support ministry to Korean community in Fergana, Uzbekistan.

CHRISTIANITY

The Christian faith appeared in Central Asia around AD 250 via Christian travelers who used the Silk Route that connected the regions between China and the West. Christianity was strongly opposed even though one fourth of the population was Christian by the year AD 410. Traces have remained through the years, but with the Islamic revolution that began in the 8th century, Christianity virtually disappeared until the modern period.

CATHOLIC CHURCH. The Holy See has diplomatic relations with Uzbekistan and in AD 2000 is represented to government and the Catholic hierarchy by a nuncio residing in Almaty.

Renewal movements. In the 1990s the Pentecostal/Charismatic Renewal continued to spread rapidly across most older churches, and numbered over 150,000 adherents (of whom none are Pentecostals, 9% Charismatics, and 91% Independents).

CHURCH AND STATE

The Constitution provides for freedom of religion and the principle of Church and State separation as stated in Articles 31 & 61 respectively. Fearing the destabilizing influence of Islamic fundamentalism, the government has tended to temper the extent of the Islamic revival by controlling the Muslim hierarchy and ousting anti-government muftis from their positions. By contrast, Christian and Jewish communities have freedom to build churches and to worship without let or hindrance. However, despite this fact of freedom, the government suppresses some religious groups that defy the authority of state-appointed religious authorities, particularly Islamic dissidents. Distribution of religious literature is legal, but missionary activity and proselytizing are not. The gov-

Country summary. **Worlds A, B, C by ethnolinguistic peoples, cities, and major civil divisions in Uzbekistan.**

	PEOPLES							CITIES							CIVIL DIVISIONS						
World	Num	Pop 2000	C%	Christians	E%	U%	Unevangelized	Num	Pop 2000	C%	Christians	E%	U%	Unevangelized	Num	Pop 2000	C%	Christians	E%	U%	Unevangelized
A	35	23,257,259	0.13	30,493	46	54	12,511,739	23	3,976,624	1.40	55,520	47	53	2,125,123	12	19,435,899	1.26	245,601	47	53	10,246,634
B	15	943,544	29.22	275,682	95	5	46,651	1	2,495,000	3.00	74,850	54	46	1,154,187	1	4,881,954	3.05	148,734	53	47	2,312,050
C	14	117,052	75.32	88,159	100	0	290	0	0	0.00	0	0	0	0	0	0	0.00	0	0	0	0
Total	**64**	**24,317,855**	**1.62**	**394,334**	**48**	**52**	**12,558,680**	**24**	**6,471,624**	**2.01**	**130,370**	**49**	**51**	**3,279,310**	**13**	**24,317,853**	**1.62**	**394,335**	**48**	**52**	**12,558,684**

ernment keeps a close watch on indigenous and foreign Christians. They are frequently interrogated and intimidated by authorities. Uzbeki pastors have been jailed on specious charges. A new law passed in 1996 imposed a 40% tax on the income of foreign Christian workers. Amendments to the 1991 law, passed in 1998, required all religious organizations to register or be prosecuted for breaking the law. A previous clause, permitting religious meetings to be held in homes was deleted.

BROADCASTING AND MEDIA

Programming in central Asian languages (Kazakh, Tajik, Uzbek, Kyrgyz) can be received from TWR (Guam), FEBC (Saipan), and HCJB (Ecuador). IBRA-produced programs in Turkish, Arabic, Azeri, and Farsi can be received from the ultra-powerful Radio Moscow stations in Krasnodar, St Petersburg and Samara, and additional Turkish language programming can be received from TWR's transmissions in Albania and Monaco. HCJB and TWR are together planting a local radio ministry in Uzbekistan.

Over 7.7 million have seen the 'Jesus' Film, mostly through television broadcasts.

FUTURE TRENDS AND PROSPECTS

In the post Soviet period, Christians are continuing to decline through emigration, while the nonreligious and atheists of the Soviet era steadily convert to Islam.

Christianity, atheism, and the nonreligious are all expected to decline with Islam passing the 90% mark before AD 2050. This will likely remain the case at mid-century.

Independents. There are a large number of Uzbek pentecostal and charismatic networks, including Uzbekistan Christian Fellowship (showing overflow meeting of 3,000 members, Tashkent).

BIBLIOGRAPHY

Drevnie obrazy mifologii u tadzhikov doliny Zerzvshana. O. Murodov. Dushanbe, Tajikistan: Donish, 1979. 116p.

Islam, ethnic identity, and public opinion in Uzbekistan. R. B. Dobson. Washington, DC: Office of Research, US Information Agency, 1992. 13p.

Islam v Uzbekistane. O. A. Sukhareva. Tashkent, Uzbekistan: Izd-vo Akademii nauk Uzbekskoi SSR, 1960. 84p.

K kharakteristike religioznoi situatsii v Shakhimardane (Uzbekistan). A. N. Satvaldyev. *Issledovaniia po prikladnoi i neotlozhnoi etnologii. Seriia A, Mezhnatsionalnye otnosheniia v sovremennom mire*, no. 31. Moscow: In-t etnologii i antropologii RAN, 1992. 18p.

'Muslim resurgence in Soviet Central Asia,' H. Malik, *Occasional papers on religion in Eastern Europe*, 11 (March 1991), 1–11. (Focuses on Uzbekistan and Tajikistan).

Nationalism in Uzbekistan: a Soviet republic's road to sovereignty. J. Critchlow. San Francisco, CA: Westview Press, 1991.

'Pan–Turkism and Pan–Islam among the Uzbeks: its history and status in the Gorbachev era.' J. R. Sharp. M.A.I.S. thesis, University of Washington, Seattle, WA, 1990. 89p.

'Process of departure of the Uzbek population from religion,' S. M. Mirhasilov, in *Secularization in multi–religious societies: Indo–Soviet perspectives: papers presented at the Indo–Soviet Symposium on Problems of Secularization in Multi–Religious Societies, Tashkent, 1978*, p.241–57. S. C. Dube & V. N. Basilov (ed). New Delhi: Indian Council of Social Science Research, 1983.

Secularisation in the USSR: a study of Soviet cultural policy in Uzbekistan. Shams-us-din. New Delhi: Vikas, 1982. 266p.

The Islamization of Central Asia: a case study of Uzbekistan. D. Ibrahim. Markfield, UK: The Islamic Foundation, 1993.

The modern Uzbeks: from the fourteenth century to the present: a cultural history. E. A. Allworth. Stanford, CA: Hoover Institution Press, 1990. 424p.

'The Uzbeks and their ideas of ultimate reality and meaning,' H. R. Battersby, *Ultimate reality and meaning*, 8, 3 (1985), 172–95.

Uzbekistan. F. Wilkins. New York: Chelsea House, 1988.

'Uzbeks,' *The Commission* (Southern Baptist Convention, Foreign Mission Board, Richmond, VA), (April 1991), 16–31, 69.

Country Table 2. **Organized churches and denominations in Uzbekistan.**

Official name (bold type = church with over 10% of all affiliated) 1	*Begun* 2	*Type* 3	*Counc* 4	*Congs* 5	*Adults* 6	*Affiliated 1970* 7	*Affiliated 1995* 8	*G%* 9	*Names, notes, and other statistics* (see Codebook, Part 3) 10
Armenian Apostolic Church		O-Arm	E....	10	25,000	3,000	30,000	0.05	Gregorians. Armenians, under C Echmiadzin.
Baptist Union in Uzbekistan		P-Bap	T....	10	2,000	4,000	6,000	0.05	*Union of Ev Chr Baptists of Middle Asia.* AUCECB. Uzbeks 5%, some all-Uzbek congregations.
Bulgarian Orthodox Church		O-Bul	M....	1	600	400	1,200	0.05	Bulgarian residents.
Catholic Church in Uzbekistan		R-LEr	P....	20	30,000	3,000	45,000	0.05	Ukrainians, Poles, Lithuanians, Hungarians, Byelorussians.
Full Gospel Christian Church	c1990	I-3fZ	.....	10	5,000	–	8,000	20.00	HQ church in Tashkent. Interference and harassment by state bureaucrats.
Georgian Orthodox Church		O-Geo	M....	1	400	500	800	0.05	Georgians, members of Georgia Church.
German Evangelical Lutheran Ch		P-Lut	.....	12	8,000	2,000	12,000	0.05	Germans remaining despite heavy emigration to Germany from 1987 on. Uzbeks 1%.
Greek Orthodox Church		O-Gre	C....	1	2,000	1,000	5,000	0.05	Greeks and others preferring Greek worship.
Hidden Muslim believers in Christ	c1970	I-Mus	....	100	4,000	–	11,400	45.30	Converted Muslims who opt to remain in Islam to witness to Christ.
Isolated radio churches	c1970	I-3rZ	.....	900	14,000	–	20,000	48.61	Uzbeks 20%.
Jehovah's Witnesses		m-Jeh	x....	10	520	100	1,300	0.05	*IBSA.* Spreading rapidly.
Karakalpak Full Gospel Chr Ch	c1992	I-3fZ	.....	4	2,000	–	4,000	33.33	Main church in Nukus. Harassment by city bureaucrats, pastor imprisoned.
Korean Baptist Churches	c1980	P-Bap	.....	15	1,500	–	3,000	6.67	Korean immigrants bringing their Baptist background also.
Korean Methodist Church		P-Met	.....	10	2,000	1,000	3,000	0.05	Korean Methodists with Methodist background.
Korean Pentecostal Churches	c1975	I-3pK	.....	20	3,000	–	6,000	5.00	Links with organized Pentecostalism in South Korea.
Korean Presbyterian Church	c1970	P-Ref	.....	20	2,500	–	6,250	41.85	Vast Presbyterian influence from Korea.
Old Ritualist Church		I-OBe	.....	1	2,000	2,500	3,000	0.05	*Old Believers.* Russians, Byelorussians.
Pentecostal Churches		I-3pZ	.....	15	1,500	2,000	5,000	0.05	Russians, Koreans, others; Uzbeks 10% including independent Uzbek congregations.
Pentecostal Union		I-3pW	.....	3	4,000	4,000	6,670	0.05	Formerly in AUCECB. Russians, Ukrainians, also Uzbeks 11% & Tatars 2%;many all-Uzbek chs.
Romanian Orthodox Church		O-Rum	.....	2	2,000	2,000	4,000	0.05	Romanians, in their own Orthodox Church.
Russian Orth Ch: D Tashkent	1871	O-Rus	.....	15	163,000	810,000	200,000	-5.44	Russians, Tatars 3%, Bashkirs 2%, Chuvash 1.5%, Mari 1%, Uzbeks 1%,Ossetians 1%,Udmurts
Ukrainian Orthodox Ch (P Kiev)		I-Ukr	.....	15	12,000	3,000	20,000	0.05	Falling by emigration to 25,000 Ukrainians by 1995.
Other independent bodies	1965	I-	.....	50	5,000	20,000	10,000	-2.73	About 10 indigenous Russian groupings: True Orthodox Ch (IPKh), CCECB.
Other independent charismatic chs	c1990	I-3cZ	.....	15	39,100	–	65,000	20.00	Including Word of Life Movement.
Other Orthodox churches		O-	.....	10	7,150	11,000	10,000	0.05	Total, including Moldavian OC, Ukrainian AOC.
Other Protestant bodies	c1986	P-	.....	60	10,000	–	15,000	11.11	Total 30, ELCE, MCE, ELCL, RCL, ERCL, Old Mennonites, RCCU, CEF, SDA, CWE.
Totals				**1,330**	**348,270**	**869,500**	**501,620**		

Churches, members, growth, 1900-2025	*Congs*	*Adults*	*Affiliated*	*G%*	*Total denominations*	*6 Megablocs:* O	*R*	*A*	*P*	*I*	*m*
Total churches, members, and denominations (mid-1900)	10	13,200	19,500	5.57	5	5	0	0	0	0	0
Total churches, members, and denominations (mid-1970)	266	590,240	869,500	5.57	19	9	1	0	3	5	1
Total churches, members, and denominations (mid-1990)	1,000	558,000	803,370	-0.39	68	12	1	0	40	14	1
Total churches, members, and denominations (mid-1995)	1,330	348,270	501,620	-8.99	74	12	1	0	45	15	1
Total churches, members, and denominations (mid-2000)	1,000	274,000	394,334	-4.70	80	12	1	0	50	16	1
Total churches, members, and denominations (mid-2025)	1,500	258,000	372,000	-0.23	202	20	1	0	80	100	1

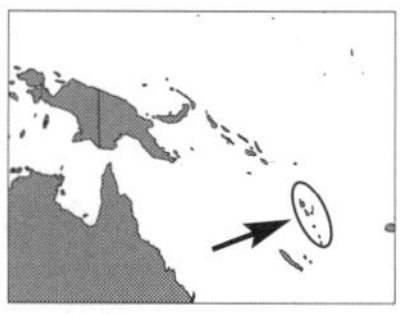

VANUATU

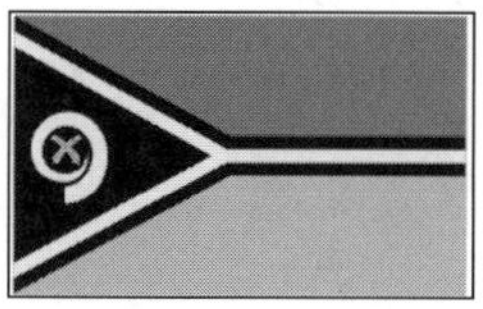

SECULAR DATA, AD 2000

STATE
Official name: Ripablik blong Vanuatu/The Republic of Vanuatu.
Short name: Vanuatu. **Adjective of nationality:** of Vanuatu.
Flag: British Union flag, and French tri-colour, until 1980; thereafter, national flag as shown.
Area: 12,190 sq. km. (4,707 sq. mi.).
Government: State, formerly Anglo-French condominium, since 1906 (1887 joint Franco-British commission, 1980 Independence).
Legislature: Parliament, 50 members.
Official language: .
Monetary unit: vatu (VT). **US$1=** VT 131.87.
Chief cities: PORT VILA (Vila) 30,239.
Political divisions: 11 provinces.
Armed forces: 300.

DEMOGRAPHY
Population: 190,000.
Population density: 15.6/sq. km. (40.4/sq. mi.).
Under 15 years: 79,000.
Growth rate p.a.: 2.35% (births 29.98, deaths 5.34).
Mortality: Infant, per 1,000: 31.7; **Maternal per 100,000:** 280.0.
Life expectancy: 69 (male 67, female 71).
Household size: 5.1. **Floor area per person, sq.m:** 18.0.
Major languages: French, English, Bislama (Pidgin English), Melanesian, Uvean, Vietnamese, Gilbertese, and about 110 other languages.
Urban dwellers: 20.05%. **Urban growth rate p.a.:** 4.1%.
Labor force: 47%.

ETHNOLINGUISTIC PEOPLES
15.9% Detribalized Vanuatuan; 4.3% Lenakel Tannese; 4.2% North Raga (Lamalanga); 4.0% Uripiv (Uri, Tautu); 3.9% Paama (Pauma).

ECONOMY
National income p.a. per person: US$1,202; **per family:** US$6,133.

EDUCATION
Adult literacy: 52% (male 57%, female 47%). **Schools:** 272.
Universities: 1. **School enrolment:** female/male: 65%/67%.

HEALTH
Access to health services: 70%. **Access to safe water:** 72%.
Hospitals: 90 (22 beds per 10,000). **Doctors:** 12.
Blind: 200. **Deaf:** 11,500. **Murder rate:** 4.
Lepers: 400. **Underweight prevalence under 5:** 20%.

LITERATURE
New book titles p.a.: 34 (180 p.a. per million). **Periodicals:** 8.
Newspapers: 0 dailies.

COMMUNICATION (per 1,000 people)
Phones: 250 (4% mobile). **Radios:** 327. **TV sets:** 12.
Daily newspaper circulation: 70. **Computers:** 15.

HUMAN LIFE AND LIBERTY (optimum condition=100.0%)
HDI: 54.7. **HSI:** 55.0. **HFI:** 55.0. **EFL:** 35.0.

Country Table 1. **Religious adherents in Vanuatu, AD 1900-2025.**

Year	1900		1970		mid-1990		Annual change, 1990-2000				mid-1995		mid-2000		mid-2025	
Name	Adherents	%	Adherents	%	Adherents	%	Natural	Conversion	Total	Rate	Adherents	%	Adherents	%	Adherents	%
Christians	**14,500**	**32.2**	**80,000**	**91.6**	**137,160**	**92.1**	**3,815**	**181**	**3,996**	**2.59**	**156,200**	**92.5**	**177,122**	**93.0**	**301,900**	**94.6**
PROFESSION																
professing Christians	**14,500**	**32.2**	**80,000**	**91.6**	**137,160**	**92.1**	**3,815**	**181**	**3,996**	**2.59**	**156,200**	**92.5**	**177,122**	**93.0**	**301,900**	**94.6**
AFFILIATION																
unaffiliated Christians	1,700	3.8	8,291	9.5	6,360	4.3	175	-104	71	1.06	6,651	3.9	7,068	3.7	1,900	0.6
affiliated Christians	**12,800**	**28.4**	**71,709**	**82.1**	**130,800**	**87.8**	**3,640**	**285**	**3,925**	**2.66**	**149,549**	**88.6**	**170,054**	**89.3**	**300,000**	**94.0**
Protestants	7,000	15.5	37,000	42.4	77,500	52.0	2,133	342	2,475	2.81	90,280	53.5	102,254	53.7	175,000	54.9
Anglicans	1,800	4.0	10,000	11.5	26,000	17.5	715	135	850	2.87	30,100	17.8	34,500	18.2	60,000	18.8
Roman Catholics	4,000	8.9	13,169	15.1	22,800	15.3	627	33	660	2.57	25,920	15.4	29,400	15.5	54,000	16.9
Independents	0	0.0	11,500	13.2	14,500	9.7	399	-199	200	1.30	15,077	8.9	16,500	8.7	27,000	8.5
Marginal Christians	0	0.0	40	0.1	1,000	0.7	28	12	40	3.42	1,172	0.7	1,400	0.7	4,000	1.3
doubly-affiliated	0	0.0	0	0.0	-11,000	-7.4	-303	3	-300	2.44	-13,000	-7.7	-14,000	-7.4	-20,000	-6.3
Trans-megabloc groupings																
Evangelicals	6,500	14.4	13,000	14.9	38,700	26.0	1,065	395	1,460	3.25	45,845	27.2	53,300	28.1	95,700	30.0
Pentecostals/Charismatics	0	0.0	1,800	2.1	34,000	22.8	936	384	1,320	3.33	40,061	23.7	47,200	24.8	89,300	28.0
Great Commission Christians	**2,300**	**5.1**	**6,100**	**7.0**	**21,600**	**14.5**	**594**	**128**	**722**	**2.93**	**25,300**	**15.0**	**28,820**	**15.2**	**55,000**	**17.2**
Ethnoreligionists	30,600	67.9	7,030	8.1	7,350	4.9	202	-280	-78	-1.11	6,900	4.1	6,573	3.5	4,000	1.3
Baha'is	0	0.0	100	0.1	3,600	2.4	99	83	182	4.17	4,740	2.8	5,418	2.9	10,800	3.4
Nonreligious	0	0.0	200	0.2	550	0.4	15	6	21	3.33	670	0.4	763	0.4	1,500	0.5
Buddhists	0	0.0	70	0.1	200	0.1	6	11	17	6.46	330	0.2	374	0.2	600	0.2
New-Religionists	0	0.0	0	0.0	60	0.0	2	1	3	3.79	80	0.1	87	0.1	100	0.0
Atheists	0	0.0	0	0.0	80	0.1	2	-2	0	0.00	80	0.1	80	0.0	100	0.0
World A (unevangelized persons)	27,511	61.0	5,242	6.0	1,490	1.0	41	-60	-19	-1.32	1,350	0.8	1,330	0.7	1,914	0.6
World B (evangelized non-Christians)	3,089	6.8	2,158	2.4	10,350	6.9	285	-121	164	1.10	11,284	6.7	11,948	6.3	15,186	4.8
World C (Christians)	14,500	32.2	80,000	91.6	137,160	92.1	3,815	181	3,996	2.59	156,200	92.5	177,122	93.0	301,900	94.6
Country's population	**45,100**	**100.0**	**87,400**	**100.0**	**149,000**	**100.0**	**4,141**	**0**	**4,141**	**2.46**	**168,835**	**100.0**	**190,400**	**100.0**	**319,000**	**100.0**

COLUMNS, ROWS.
For meanings and definitions, see Codebook (Part 3). Note that, by definition, total 'Christians' = professing + crypto-Christians, which also = affiliated + unaffiliated Christians, and also = Great Commission Christians + latent Christians. Percentages may not always total exactly, due to rounding.

CENSUSES.
28.V.1967: 52.2% Protestants (40.0% Presbyterians, 5.7% SD Adventists, 5.1% Churches of Christ), 16.1% Roman Catholics, 14.3% Anglicans, 8.8% Melanesian indigenous (6.0% John Frum cults, 1.6% French Protestant), 8.5% ethnoreligionists, 0.1% other religionists.**1979**: 49.6% Protestants (39.7% Presbyterians, 6.1% SDAs, 3.8% Churches of Christ), 15.9% Anglicans, 15.6% Roman Catholics, 10.0% Independents, 7.6% Ethnoreligionists, 1.1% nonreligious, 0.2% other religionists. **1989**: 51.2% Protestants (38.3% Presbyterians, 8.2% SDAs, 4.7% Churches of Christ), 15.0% Roman Catholics, 14.5% Anglicans, 12.7% Independents, 4.5% Ethnoreligionists, 1.7% nonreligious, 0.4% other religionists.

NOTES ON RELIGIONS
BAHA'IS. Begun 1953. Growth from 1 local spiritual assembly (1964) to 4 (1973), followed by mushrooming expansion to 35 LSAs (1996).
BUDDHISTS. North Vietnamese (Tonkinese), and a few Chinese.
ETHNORELIGIONISTS. Animists (termed followers of Custom) are still numerous on Aniwa, and are significant minorities on Santo and Vao. Many have been non-Christian adherents of cargo cults.
INDEPENDENTS. Two distinct groupings: (a) indigenous churches of main-line Christian type (Eglise Libre, and other congregations), and (b) those cargo cults, particularly the 3 John Frum factions, of anti-mission type which have broken off from Western mission-related churches. Although rejecting much of Christianity, these latter protest movements retain enough Christian elements for them to be classified as here, as part of the worldwide complex of anti-Western indigenous churches and movements.
NONRELIGIOUS. Mainly French.
ROMAN CATHOLICS. In 1900, 1,000 baptized Catholics, 3,000 catechumens.

Great Commission Instrument Panel: status of Vanuatu (for explanation see start of Part 4)

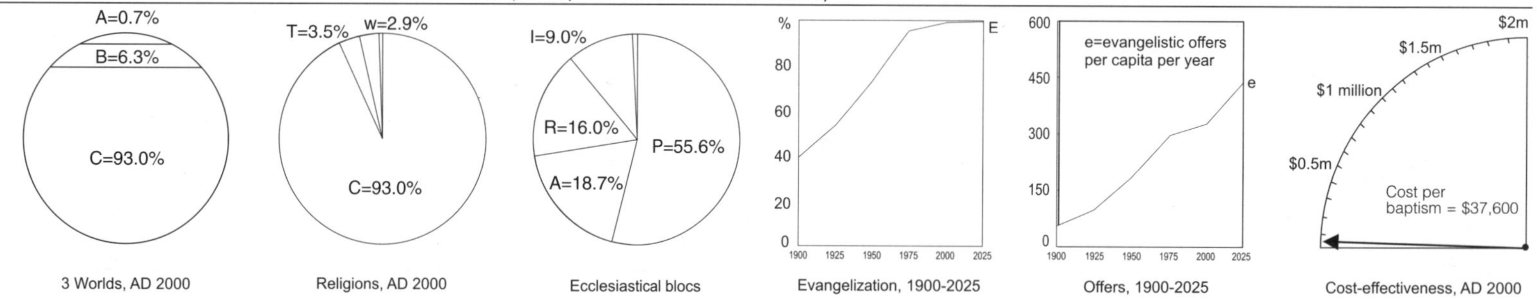

Country status. Vanuatu is an island chain in the southwest Pacific Ocean. Its chief exports are fish, manganese, copra, coffee, and cocoa.

HUMAN LIFE AND LIBERTY

Human rights and freedoms. Vanuatu's Anglo-French colonial legacies include a respect for parliamentary government and for human rights. However, the government controls both print and electronic media and show little inclination to give up its monopoly. While women have equal rights under law, traditional cultural norms force them to adopt a subordinate role both within the family and in public life. There are no women serving in positions of leadership in the government or in the private sector. Domestic violence against women is common and is often condoned in the courts.

NON-CHRISTIAN RELIGIONS

Traditional religion, popularly known in Vanuatu as Custom, was the professed faith of 4.1% of the population in 1995. Followers of Custom are predominant on Tanna and Aniwa while significant minorities are also found on Santo and Vao. Over 8 distinct cargo cults have arisen in Vanuatu.

Baha'i has had mushrooming growth since 1975.

CHRISTIANITY

PROTESTANT CHURCHES. The first missionary to the New Hebrides was John Williams of the London Missionary Society, who was martyred on the island of Eromanga in 1839. Presbyterians from Nova Scotia in Canada arrived in 1848 and were later fol-

Country summary. **Worlds A, B, C by ethnolinguistic peoples, cities, and major civil divisions in Vanuatu.**																					
	PEOPLES							*CITIES*							*CIVIL DIVISIONS*						
World	*Num*	*Pop 2000*	*C%*	*Christians*	*E%*	*U%*	*Unevangelized*	*Num*	*Pop 2000*	*C%*	*Christians*	*E%*	*U%*	*Unevangelized*	*Num*	*Pop 2000*	*C%*	*Christians*	*E%*	*U%*	*Unevangelized*
A	1	2	0.00	0	50	50	1	0	0	0.00	0	0	0	0	0	0	0.00	0	0	0	0
B	12	3,480	42.18	1,468	73	27	943	0	0	0.00	0	0	0	0	0	0	0.00	0	0	0	0
C	110	186,931	90.18	168,583	100	0	356	1	30,239	83.00	25,098	99	1	451	11	190,416	89.31	170,054	99	1	1,303
Total	**123**	**190,413**	**89.31**	**170,051**	**99**	**1**	**1,300**	**1**	**30,239**	**83.00**	**25,098**	**99**	**1**	**451**	**11**	**190,416**	**89.31**	**170,054**	**99**	**1**	**1,303**

lowed by others from Scotland, Australia, and New Zealand. The Presbyterian Church is the principal denomination of the islands, and has been autonomous since 1948. Presbyterians are almost entirely absent from the Torres and Banks Islands of the north, but they form the majority on most of the other islands with the exception of Tanna (Tana) and Aniwa (where Custom predominates) and the Malekula offshore islands of Vao, Atchin, and Wala.

Adventists (5.5% of the population in 1995) have been active since 1912. They are scattered throughout the islands and form about half the population of Aore, Atchin and Buninga. They are also well represented in Vao and Wala. The Churches of Christ (3.4% in 1995) are assisted by the Australian Churches of Christ Mission. They are strong in Aoba, Maewo, and Pentecost as well as on some of the Santo offshore islands including Tutuba and Malo. The Apostolic Church came to the New Hebrides from Australia in 1945. Apostolics are largely restricted to Aoba where they account for over 10% of the population. The Assemblies of God, who experienced rapid growth 1970-1990, have been represented at Vila on Efate Island by a Fijian pastor since 1967, and the small Independent Presbytery Mission from Australia has 3 congregations.

Presbyterian Church of New Hebrides. A congregation on Tanna leaves church on Sunday. Presbyterians on Tanna numbered 90% of the population until mass defections from 1940-45 to the John Frum cult; now they number only 15%.

CATHOLIC CHURCH. Although the first Catholic missionaries arrived in Eromanga as early as 1839, systematic evangelization did not begin until 1887. A prefecture was established in 1901, becoming a vicariate in 1904. The first national priest was ordained in 1955. Catholics are predominant on the islands of Vao, Atchin, and Wala. Catholics were 15% of the population in 1995.

The Holy See has diplomatic relations with Vanuatu and in AD 2000 is represented to government and the Catholic hierarchy by a nuncio residing in Wellington, New Zealand.

ANGLICAN CHURCH. Anglican missionaries arrived from New Zealand in 1848 and concentrated their attention on the northern islands. The Banks and Torres islanders are today almost exclusively Anglican, and in Aoba, Maewo, and Pentecost about half the combined populations also are Anglicans. Elsewhere their numbers are negligible. The Diocese of New Hebrides is part of the Church of the Province of Melanesia, formed in 1975 and based on Honiara, Solomon Islands.

INDIGENOUS CHURCHES. The John Frum cargo cults, of which there are 3 distinct factions, began in 1935 and still have followers. The movement was begun on Tanna Island among large numbers of Presbyterians and grew in strength after the arrival of North American military personnel with their extensive material possessions during World War II. As with other cargo cults, the principal belief of the faithful concerns the predicted arrival of mythical figure John Frum (Frum=Broom), whom would sweep away all Whites and would bring great wealth to the local population. Although many members have been former Presbyterians, the movement has adopted a number of nativistic elements and has often taken an anti-missionary, anti-government stance.

The Free Church was founded through the missionary activity of an indigenous group from New Caledonia which split from the Evangelical Church of New Caledonia and the Loyalty Islands. Although their official title is the Free Church, they are locally known as the French Protestant Church. They are found mainly on Atchin and Wala, although there are small groups on Santo and Malekula as well. Another body, the Voice of Daniel, was formed in 1932 as the result of a schism from the Anglican Church on Pentecost Island.

Indigenous missions. A few missionaries have been sent out to neighboring islands and Australia.

CHURCH AND STATE

The first European to set eyes on the islands was a Spanish navigator in 1606, with Captain James Cook making a more thorough exploration in 1774. Sandalwood was discovered at Port Resolution in 1825 which stimulated European trade and settlement, mostly French and British. A decline in the supply of sandalwood prompted some traders to turn to labour recruitment (popularly called blackbirding) for the cotton plantations of Fiji and the cotton and sugar plantations of Queensland. Missionary protest at the abuses of blackbirding forced the passage of the Pacific Islanders Protection Bill by the British parliament in 1872. A joint French-British condominium was declared in 1906, with full guarantees for the free practice of religion.

Until 1980, the territory was secular in its attitude to religion. In 1979 in preparation for Independence, however, the new constitution affirmed the Christian faith: 'We the people of the New Hebrides proclaim the establishment of the United and Free Republic of the New Hebrides, founded on traditional Melanesian values, faith in God and Christian principles'.

Top. **Church of Melanesia, Diocese of Vanuatu.** An Anglican priest vested for the Eucharist. *Lower.* **John Frum cargo cults.** At Sulphur Bay, cargo cult centre on Tanna island, an adherent ('missionary') performs cultus in front of red-painted image of mythical cult founder John Frum, red-painted crosses, and red-painted aircraft, which symbolizes imminent arrival of cargo (cars, machines, clothes, utensils, etc.). Adherents number 79% of Tanna's population.

INTERDENOMINATIONAL ORGANIZATIONS

The New Hebrides Christian Council was founded in 1967 and includes as full members Anglican, Catholic, and Presbyterian churches, and the Churches of Christ. The Adventist and Apostolic churches are observer members. The council co-ordinates joint activities in literature translation, religious broadcasting, and an interdenominational chapel in the new central hospital

FUTURE TRENDS AND PROSPECTS

With conversions from indigenous religions to Christianity expected to continue, Christianity could claim 94.6% of the population by AD 2025.

Christianity could then grow as high as 98% by AD 2050, with remaining ethnoreligionists becoming Christian in the 21st century.

BIBLIOGRAPHY

'Church change and economic development: with special reference to the New Hebrides.' H. K. Blessing. B.D. thesis, Pacific Theological College, Suva, Fiji, 1974. 90p.

'Culture contact and the John Frum movements on Tanna, New Hebrides,' J. Guiart, *Southwestern journal of anthropology*, 12 (1956), 105–16. (Review from 1774 to 1955).

'Forerunners of Melanesian nationalism,' J. Guiart, *Oceania*, 22, 2 (1951), 81–90. (Cargo cults in New Hebrides and New Caledonia).

God, ghosts and men in Melanesia: some religions of Australian New Guinea and the New Hebrides. P. Lawrence & M. J. Meggitt (eds). London: Oxford University Press, 1965.

'Independens long Vanuatu: the churches and politics in a Melanesian nation.' M. D. Myers. Ph.D. dissertation, University of Auckland, Auckland, Australia, 1984. 509p.

'John Frum movement in Tanna,' J. Guiart, *Oceania*, 22 (1951), 165–75.

John G. Paton: missionary to the New Hebrides: an autobiography. J. G. Paton. 12th ed. Reprint, Edinburgh: Banner of Truth Trust, 1994. 533p.

'Les missions dans la Pacifique,' *Journal de la Société des Océanistes*, 25, 25 (1969).

'Les mouvements de John Frum et de Tieka: deux faits sociaux totaux aux Nouvelles–Hébrides,' P. Martin, *Le monde nonchrétien*, 43/44 (July–December 1957), 225–65.

Light in dark isles: a jubilee record and study of the New Hebrides mission of the Presbyterian Church of New Zealand. A. Don. Dunedin: Foreign Missions Committee, PCNZ, 1918. 200p.

Live: a history of church planting in the New Hebrides to 1880. J. G. Miller. Sydney, Australia: Committees on Christian Education and Overseas Missions, General Assembly of the Presbyterian Church of Australia, 1978. (See related volumes in series).

Misi Gete: John Geddie, pioneer missionary to the New Hebrides. R. S. Miller (ed). Launceston, Australia: Presbyterian Church of Tasmania, 1975.

'Mission imperatives for Churches of Christ in the New Hebrides.' J. Liu. B.D. thesis, Pacific Theological College, Suva, Fiji, 1976. 118p.

'Naked cult in central west Santo,' J. G. Miller, *Journal of the Polynesian Society*, 57, 4 (1948), 330–41.

New Hebridean culture and Christian faith: report of education workshop, Aulua, New Hebrides, April 19–May 3, 1979. C. Wright. Vila, New Hebrides: Pacific Churches Research Center, 1979. 35p.

One hundred years of mission: the Catholic Church in New Hebrides, Vanuatu, 1887–1987. P. Monnier (ed). Port-Vila, Vanuatu: Diocese of Port-Vila, 1987. 147p. (Also in French).

'The early history of the Churches of Christ in the New Hebrides.' S. Vusi. B.D. thesis, Pacific Theological College, Suva, Fiji, 1988. 121p.

The gospel in the southern New Hebrides, 1839–1958. G. S. Parsonson. Dunedin, New Zealand: Presbyterian Historical Society of New Zealand, 1985. 16p.

'The movements in the New Hebrides,' in *The trumpet shall sound: a study of cargo cults in Melanesia*, p.146–69. P. Worsley. New York: Schocken, 1968.

'The Presbyterian Church in the New Hebrides: the Tangoa Training Institute: a case study of missionary activity.' P. R. Smith. M.A. thesis, University of Auckland, Auckland, New Zealand, 1976. 56p.

Vanuatu victory: four generations of sharing Christian faith in the Pacific. H. R. Gillan. Richmond, Australia: Spectrum Publications, 1988. 359p.

Won by blood: the story of Erromanga, the martyr isle. A. K. Langridge. 1922; reprint, Strathpine North, Queensland: Covenanter Press, 1978. 135p.

Country Table 2. Organized churches and denominations in Vanuatu.

Official name (bold type = church with over 10% of all affiliated) 1	*Begun* 2	*Type* 3	*Counc* 4	*Congs* 5	*Adults* 6	*Affiliated 1970* 7	*Affiliated 1995* 8	*G%* 9	*Names, notes, and other statistics* (see Codebook, Part 3) 10
Apostolic Church	1945	P-PeA	Z...k	14	850	800	1,700	3.06	M=Apostolic Ch of Australia & NZ. M=ACMM(UK). On Aoba, with a few on Santo and Malo.
Assemblies of God	1968	P-Pe2	ZF...	265	10,500	1,000	21,100	12.97	M=AoG(USA). Classical Pentecostals (2-stage). Fijian pastor in Vila from 1967. 110n.
Catholic Church: D Port Vila	1839	R-Lat	P.PYK	45	11,000	13,169	25,920	2.75	C=1+1+2. M=SM2 (1970) 3n,23x,89w,402Yy. (1990) 8n, 16x, 32m, 68w, 1570Yy
Christ Groups	c1980	I-3hP	x....	27	400	–	1,000	6.67	Home churches for converts after nationwide EHC campaign.
Christian Fellowship of CMA	c1975	P-Hol	.....	8	45	–	60	5.00	CMA=Christian & Missionary Alliance. M=CMA.
Ch of Jesus Christ of Latter-day Saints	c1980	m-LdS	.....	1	140	–	227	6.67	*Mormons.* M=CJCLdS.
Church of Melanesia: D Vanuatu	1848	A-ACa	AwpKK	167	17,500	10,000	30,100	4.51	HQ Honiara. Formerly in CPNZ. Includes New Caledonia. 20m,10w,W=75%,20Y,500y.
Churches of Christ in Vanuatu	1903	I-Dis	x.P.K	49	2,450	3,900	5,800	1.60	Begun by deported Kanakas. M=Australian Churches of Christ Mission. On Aoba. 16f.
Free Evangelical Church		I-Ref	.....	21	1,250	1,200	1,700	0.05	*Eglise Libre. French Protestant Church.* Mission of schism ex EENC(New Caledonia).
Independent Presbytery Mission	c1968	I-Ref	.....	3	225	200	450	3.30	Centre on Malekula. Schism in Australia ex Presbyterian Ch of Australia. 1f.
Jehovah's Witnesses	1933	m-Jeh	x....	2	189	40	945	13.48	*Watch Tower, IBSA.* Placed under Australian branch 1933. 8Y.
John Frum cargo cults	c1935	I-mar	.....	10	700	4,000	1,000	-5.39	Frum=Broom. 3 cults on Tanna, ex Presbyterian. Red crosses, flags. HQ Sulphur Bay.
Nagriamel (Palm Tree) Church of Christ	1967	I-mar	.....	1	300	1,000	800	-0.89	Linked to land reappropriation movement. Ex Chs of Christ. HQ Fanafo, SW Santo. 2n.
New Apostolic Church	c1980	I-3aX	x....	15	600	–	1,027	6.67	*NAC/NAK.* M=Neuapostolische Kirche. HQ Zurich (Switzerland).
Presbyterian Ch of Vanuatu	1848	P-Ref	RWP.K	304	31,600	30,000	56,000	2.53	M=PCs of Australia, NZ, Canada; FCS(UK). A=1948. 33n,9x,2H,1p(6),822Yy.
Seventh-day Adventist Church	1912	P-Adv	x...k	41	6,878	4,300	9,300	3.13	*SDA, NH Mission*, Central Pacific Union Mission. 7nx,91mw,1H,1s53t(3100),131Y.
United Pentecostal Church	c1985	P-Pel	.....	2	80	–	120	10.00	M=UPC(USA). Oneness Pentecostals.
Voice of Daniel	1932	I-Ang	.....	1	100	200	300	1.64	*Silon Daniel.* Vision by Anglican lay reader Daniel Tambe. In Raga, Pentecost.
Other Melanesian indigenous churches		I-mar	.....	20	1,500	1,000	3,000	0.05	Several of the 8 cargo cults have produced christianized congregations.
Other Protestant churches		P-	.....	15	1,000	900	2,000	0.05	About 5 other British, French, and Australian missions.
Doubly-affiliated		2-aff			-7,000	0	-13,000		Persons who are baptized members of 2, 3 or more denominations.
Totals				**1,011**	**80,307**	**71,709**	**149,549**		

Churches, members, growth, 1900-2025	*Congs*	*Adults*	*Affiliated*	*G%*	*Total denominations*	*6 Megablocs: O*	*R*	*A*	*P*	*I*	*m*
Total churches, members, and denominations (mid-1900)	90	7,200	12,800	2.49	3	0	1	1	1	0	0
Total churches, members, and denominations (mid-1970)	476	40,347	71,709	2.49	17	0	1	1	6	8	1
Total churches, members, and denominations (mid-1990)	890	70,300	130,800	3.05	25	0	1	1	10	11	2
Total churches, members, and denominations (mid-1995)	1,011	80,307	149,549	2.72	27	0	1	1	11	12	2
Total churches, members, and denominations (mid-2000)	1,150	91,300	170,054	2.60	29	0	1	1	12	13	2
Total churches, members, and denominations (mid-2025)	2,030	161,000	300,000	2.30	72	0	1	1	25	40	5

NOTES ON TABLE ABOVE
NATIONAL COUNCILS (Column 4, 5th letter).
K = Vanuatu Christian Council (VCC).
k = observer member of VCC.
Local councils. Santo Community Project Committee.

VENEZUELA

SECULAR DATA, AD 2000

STATE
Official name: La República de Venezuela (The Republic of Venezuela).
Short name: Venezuela. **Adjective of nationality:** Venezuelan.
Flag: Yellow, blue, and red stripes, with 7 white stars in semicircle in centre, national coat of arms in upper hoist corner.
Area: 912,050 sq. km. (352,144 sq. mi.).
Government: Republic, since 1958 (1567 Spanish rule, 1811 Independence declared, several dictatorships, 1935 military junta, 1945 republic, 1948 military junta, 1958 republic).
Legislature: Congress: Senate, 52 members; Chamber of Deputies, 199 members.
Official language: Spanish (Español/Castella).
Monetary unit: 1 bolívar (B, plural Bs) = 100 céntimos. **US$1=** BS 580.25.
Chief cities: CARACAS 3,153,000; Maracaibo 1,857,000; Valencia 1,817,000; Maracay 1,077,000; Barquisimeto 914,000.
Political divisions: 23 provinces.
Armed forces: 79,000.

DEMOGRAPHY
Population: 24,170,000.
Population density: 26.5/sq. km. (68.6/sq. mi.).
Under 15 years: 8,227,000.
Growth rate p.a.: 1.82% (births 22.84, deaths 4.68).
Mortality: Infant, per 1,000: 18.9; **Maternal per 100,000:** 120.0.
Life expectancy: 73 (male 71, female 77).
Household size: 5.3. **Floor area per person, sq.m:** 15.0.
Major languages: Spanish, Italian, English, Portuguese, Arawak, Carib, Guajiro, Chinese, and 30 smaller languages.
Urban dwellers: 87.35%. **Urban growth rate p.a.:** 2.1%.
Labor force: 36%.

ETHNOLINGUISTIC PEOPLES
63.6% Venezuelan Mestizo; 20.0% Venezuelan White; 10.0% Venezuelan Black; 1.3% Italian; 0.7% Guajiro (Arahuaco).

ECONOMY
National income p.a. per person: US$3,020; **per family:** US$16,006.

EDUCATION
Adult literacy: 91% (male 91%, female 90%). **Schools:** 17,421.
Universities: 99. **School enrolment:** female/male: 87%/83%.

HEALTH
Access to health services: 60%. **Access to safe water:** 79%.
Hospitals: 610 (26 beds per 10,000). **Doctors:** 32,616.
Blind: 18,000. **Deaf:** 1,450,200. **Murder rate:** 22.
Lepers: 40,000. **Underweight prevalence under 5:** 5%.

LITERATURE
New book titles p.a.: 3,630 (150 p.a. per million). **Periodicals:** 63.
Newspapers: 89 dailies.

COMMUNICATION (per 1,000 people)
Phones: 111 (42% mobile). **Radios:** 372. **TV sets:** 183.
Daily newspaper circulation: 215. **Computers:** 61.

REFUGEES
Alien refugees from other countries: 700.

HUMAN LIFE AND LIBERTY (optimum condition=100.0%)
HDI: 86.1. **HSI:** 49.0. **HFI:** 72.5. **EFL:** 30.0.

Country Table 1. Religious adherents in Venezuela, AD 1900-2025.

Year	1900		1970		mid-1990		Annual change, 1990-2000				mid-1995		mid-2000		mid-2025	
Name	*Adherents*	*%*	*Adherents*	*%*	*Adherents*	*%*	*Natural*	*Conversion*	*Total*	*Rate*	*Adherents*	*%*	*Adherents*	*%*	*Adherents*	*%*
Christians	**2,297,700**	**93.0**	**10,317,100**	**96.2**	**18,548,700**	**95.1**	**443,982**	**-7,842**	**436,140**	**2.13**	**20,750,000**	**95.0**	**22,910,095**	**94.8**	**32,677,500**	**94.0**
PROFESSION																
professing Christians	**2,297,700**	**93.0**	**10,317,100**	**96.2**	**18,548,700**	**95.1**	**443,982**	**-7,842**	**436,140**	**2.13**	**20,750,000**	**95.0**	**22,910,095**	**94.8**	**32,677,500**	**94.0**
AFFILIATION																
unaffiliated Christians	50,000	2.0	255,237	2.4	208,700	1.1	4,995	-8,439	-3,444	-1.79	200,000	0.9	174,261	0.7	100,500	0.3
affiliated Christians	**2,247,700**	**91.0**	**10,061,863**	**93.9**	**18,340,000**	**94.0**	**438,986**	**597**	**439,583**	**2.17**	**20,550,000**	**94.1**	**22,735,834**	**94.1**	**32,577,000**	**93.7**
Roman Catholics	2,247,100	91.0	9,775,054	91.2	18,331,880	94.0	438,792	9,620	448,412	2.21	20,656,866	94.6	22,816,000	94.4	31,800,000	91.5
Protestants	5,000	0.2	143,187	1.3	380,000	2.0	9,096	2,904	12,000	2.78	431,634	2.0	500,000	2.1	950,000	2.7
Independents	500	0.0	109,015	1.0	270,000	1.4	6,463	1,537	8,000	2.63	311,441	1.4	350,000	1.5	600,000	1.7
Marginal Christians	0	0.0	21,667	0.2	230,000	1.2	5,505	1,495	7,000	2.69	263,300	1.2	300,000	1.2	550,000	1.6
Orthodox	0	0.0	11,800	0.1	22,000	0.1	527	-27	500	2.07	23,600	0.1	27,000	0.1	38,000	0.1
Anglicans	100	0.0	1,140	0.0	600	0.0	14	-14	0	0.00	600	0.0	600	0.0	600	0.0
doubly-affiliated	-5,000	-0.2	0	0.0	-894,480	-4.6	-21,410	-14,919	-36,329	3.47	-1,137,441	-5.2	-1,257,766	-5.2	-1,361,600	-3.9
Trans-megabloc groupings																
Evangelicals	4,500	0.2	90,000	0.8	234,000	1.2	5,601	1,199	6,800	2.58	268,434	1.2	302,000	1.3	556,000	1.6
Pentecostals/Charismatics	0	0.0	210,000	2.0	2,850,000	14.6	68,218	13,782	82,000	2.56	3,317,122	15.2	3,670,000	15.2	5,920,000	17.0
Great Commission Christians	**100,000**	**4.1**	**643,000**	**6.0**	**1,443,000**	**7.4**	**34,540**	**7,333**	**41,873**	**2.58**	**1,638,000**	**7.5**	**1,861,728**	**7.7**	**3,129,000**	**9.0**
Nonreligious	0	0.0	49,000	0.5	347,000	1.8	8,306	6,412	14,718	3.60	403,400	1.9	494,180	2.0	947,000	2.7
Spiritists	49,000	2.0	100,000	0.9	200,000	1.0	4,759	704	5,463	2.44	229,100	1.1	254,628	1.1	400,000	1.2
Ethnoreligionists	123,000	5.0	200,000	1.9	145,000	0.7	3,471	-1,829	1,642	1.08	152,000	0.7	161,417	0.7	100,000	0.3
Baha'is	0	0.0	24,900	0.2	95,000	0.5	2,274	2,333	4,607	4.03	122,000	0.6	141,072	0.6	250,000	0.7
Muslims	0	0.0	500	0.0	62,000	0.3	1,484	268	1,752	2.52	71,700	0.3	79,518	0.3	180,000	0.5
Jews	300	0.0	12,000	0.1	39,000	0.2	934	-93	841	1.97	42,800	0.2	47,413	0.2	75,000	0.2
Atheists	0	0.0	10,000	0.1	36,000	0.2	862	115	977	2.43	40,600	0.2	45,772	0.2	90,000	0.3
Buddhists	0	0.0	2,000	0.0	23,700	0.1	567	17	584	2.23	26,600	0.1	29,535	0.1	50,000	0.1
Chinese folk-religionists	0	0.0	5,000	0.1	4,750	0.0	114	-77	37	0.76	4,900	0.0	5,124	0.0	4,000	0.0
Other religionists	0	0.0	500	0.0	850	0.0	20	-8	12	1.30	900	0.0	967	0.0	1,500	0.0
World A (unevangelized persons)	71,630	2.9	107,210	1.0	136,514	0.7	3,267	-1,969	1,298	0.91	152,911	0.7	145,020	0.6	173,875	0.5
World B (evangelized non-Christians)	100,670	4.1	296,771	2.8	816,786	4.2	19,524	9,811	29,335	3.16	941,569	4.3	1,114,885	4.6	1,923,625	5.5
World C (Christians)	2,297,700	93.0	10,317,100	96.2	18,548,700	95.1	443,982	-7,842	436,140	2.13	20,750,000	95.0	22,910,095	94.8	32,677,500	94.0
Country's population	**2,470,000**	**100.0**	**10,721,082**	**100.0**	**19,502,000**	**100.0**	**466,773**	**0**	**466,773**	**2.17**	**21,844,481**	**100.0**	**24,170,000**	**100.0**	**34,775,000**	**100.0**

Continued opposite

Country Table 1–concluded

COLUMNS, ROWS.
For meanings and definitions, see Codebook (Part 3). Note that, by definition, total 'Christians' = professing + crypto-Christians, which also = affiliated + unaffiliated Christians, and also = Great Commission Christians + latent Christians. Percentages may not always total exactly, due to rounding.

CENSUSES.
1891 (excluding jungle Indians): 95.6% Roman Catholics, 0.1% Protestants (3,361 persons), 4.3% other religionists (including 247 Jews). The religion question has not been asked subsequently.

NOTES ON RELIGIONS
ATHEISTS. Parties: Communist Party of Venezuela (PCV; pro-Soviet), Movement of the Revolutionary Left (MIR), Union for Advancement (UPA), Movement to Socialism (MAS) (all legal).
BAHA'IS. Rapid growth from 6 local spiritual assemblies (1964) to 166 (1973), especially among coastal Blacks and Guajiro Indians; over 1,000 Guajiro were enrolled as converts in May 1970 alone. By 1996, numbers were still holding, with 193 LSAs, though there has been little expansion in recent years.
BUDDHISTS. Chinese.
DOUBLY-AFFILIATED. The term covers those affiliated to, or claimed by, the Catholic Church and also a church termed Evangélica by the state (Protestant, Independent, Anglican, or marginal Christian) or other church, i.e. baptized Catholics who have recently become Evangelicals or others. Because their statistics represent a duplication, they are shown in the table as a negative quantity (with a minus sign).
ETHNORELIGIONISTS. Of the over 300,000 pure tribal lowland or jungle Amerindians (including 170,000 Guajiros) in 1995, a high proportion are still animists and shamanists, including among the Chibcha, Arawak and Carib families.
JEWS. There are 2 groups. The Sefardis (originally from Spain) are the oldest, located mainly in the west (Coro area) and east. The Ashkenazis (originally from Eastern Europe) arrived after World War II from 1945 onwards.
OTHER RELIGIONISTS. Adherents of other non-Christian religions and syncretistic cults, including Rosicrucians (AMORC, 17 Lodges and centers).
PENTECOSTALS/CHARISMATICS. The Catholic Charismatic Renewal began in 1973. Totals (January 1974): 1,000 involved adults (over 15 years old) including many priests, nuns and a bishop in 30 prayer groups, rising by 1975 to 6,000 in 190 groups; total charismatic community including children (1975), 20,000. In January 1976, over 25,000 persons attended the First National Charismatic Encounter in Barquisimeto, led by the Catholic archbishop (a charismatic) and 3 other bishops. In January 1977, ECCLA V was held in Caracas; at its conclusion, 30,000 attended a charismatic National Day of Prayer. By 1997 there were 3,000 weekly prayer groups attended by 60,000 regular adult attenders; and 300 covenant communities.
ROMAN CATHOLICS. Many Roman Catholics are involved regularly with the Aboriginal Cult of Maria Lionza, and other non-Christian cults.
SPIRITISTS. The term describes non-Catholic and non-Christian adherents of the Culto Aborigen de Maria Lionza (Aboriginal Cult of Maria Lionza), which syncretizes African Caribbean, Amerindian and Catholic religious elements. Each year in Holy Week, 30,000 make the pilgrimage to pray to the goddess Maria Lionza. There are also other cults including Shango (a Yoruba survival), and some Rastafarians (from Jamaica).
VENEZUELAN INDIGENOUS. In about 41 denominations in 1995 (see Table 2).

Great Commission Instrument Panel: status of Venezuela (for explanation see start of Part 4)

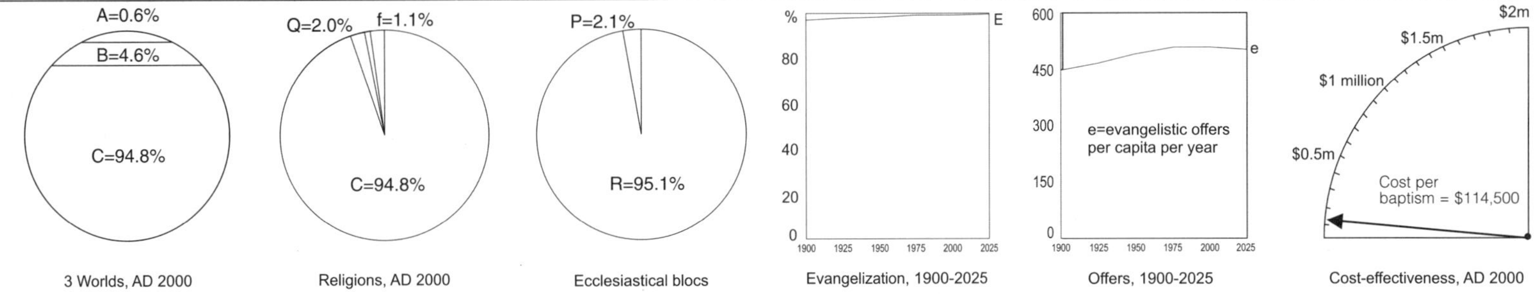

Country status. Venezuela is a country in northern South America on the Atlantic Ocean and Caribbean Sea. Its chief exports are oil, iron ore, aluminum, steel, and coffee.

HUMAN LIFE AND LIBERTY

Human need and development. Oil wealth has transformed Venezuela into a major economic power in the continent and caused its living standards to rise faster than its neighboring countries. As a result, Venezuela, which was one of the poorest of the Spanish colonies, has become an equal with Argentina, Uruguay, Mexico, and Brazil. However, living conditions of the urban and rural poor have changed little in this century. *Barrios*, or slums, are found near or in major towns and cities, and they are populated by workers and unemployed people close to destitution. Government social welfare programs, financed by oil wealth, have helped Venezuela to make rapid strides in provision of educational and medical services to most of its citizens. In literacy, longevity, and other quality of life indicators, Venezuela ranks high in the region.

Human rights and freedoms. Despite the turbulent history of the country, Venezuelans have traditionally enjoyed, especially after the death of dictator Gomez in 1935, a wider range of freedoms than their fellow Latin Americans. Nevertheless, serious human rights abuses occur, although not on a systematic scale. These include arbitrary and excessively lengthy detentions, abuse of detainees, extrajudicial killings by police and military, corruption and inefficiency in the judicial and law enforcement systems, deplorable prison conditions and lack of respect for the rights of indigenous peoples. According to Amnesty International, torture continues in Venezuela, primarily because the government rarely investigates complaints or brings those responsible to justice. Numerous prison riots occur. More than 600 prisoners are reported killed annually as a result of such riots. Arbitrary arrests and arrests without warrants are common. The Vagrancy Law permits detention for up to 5 years, without warrant, trial or judicial appeal, of people deemed by the police to be a danger to society, even though there is no evidence against them of a punishable crime. The legal system is overburdened, slow, corrupt and vulnerable to political influence. Venezuela has a free and lively press, despite occasional government attempts to curb journalistic privileges. Women's rights are fully established in law, but, nevertheless, women are not generally aware of and have little access to many of these rights. The plight of children in the country has been documented by UNICEF which reported in 1993 that 206,000 children under the age of 18 loiter in the streets and another 176,000 beg for money.

Human environment. Since most of the population is concentrated on the Caribbean coast, industrial pollution is severe in this region. Deforestation is a major problem in the interior where over 1,000 square miles of forests were lost every year in the 1980s. The country has 2 major lakes—Valencia and Maracaibo—both of which are polluted, the former from sewage and the latter from oil industry operations.

NON-CHRISTIAN RELIGIONS

Traditional Indian religions remain influential among peoples of the Chibcha, Arawak, and Carib families found mostly in the southern part of country. The Yanamamö ('the fierce people'), saddling the Venezuela-Brazil border, have a population of 15,000 living in 125 villages. A violent, aggressive people living in a chronic state of warfare, they are one of the least-acculturated tribes left in all of South America. Their cosmology includes belief in the powers of medicine men or shamans (*shabori*), spirits (Yai), and a divinity called Wadawadariwa (Son of Thunder).

Afro-American spiritists. Folkloric event each May in town in Venezuelan Andes, combining elements of Catholicism, town saint's day, spiritism, and the Aboriginal Cult of Maria Lionza goddess of water and vegetation.

Afro-American spiritism is evident in the Maria Lionza cult which is a syncretistic movement composed of diverse African, Caribbean, Amerindian, and Catholic elements. Central to its worship is the veneration of Maria Lionza, goddess of water and vegetation, who is associated by the populace with the Virgin Mary and popular Catholic saints, as well as with the Cacique Indians who resisted Spanish penetration at the Conquest, historical personages such as Negro Miguel (instigator of an uprising among the slaves) and even the nation's founding father Simon Bolivar. Maria Lionza is particularly venerated in the mountains of Sorte in Yaracuy state in the northwest, and also in rural and urban chapels and sanctuaries. Followers are drawn from all social classes, and include many nominal Catholics. The cult requires mediums or *bancos* who also supervise services and rituals. An attempt at unification of the various Maria Lionza groups was made in 1968 when the society was legalized under the name Aboriginal Cult of Maria Lionza (Culto Aborigen de Maria Lionza) with headquarters in Caracas.

Baha'i has grown phenomenally since 1970, from 24,900 then to 122,000 by 1995. Coastal Blacks and Guajiro Indians have been most responsive.

Judaism is represented by 2 groups. Sefardi Jews originated in Spain and are the oldest Jewish community in Venezuela. They are most prevalent in the west and east. At Coro is located the oldest Jewish cemetery in Latin America. The second group are Ashkenazi Jews who came from central and eastern Europe at the end of World War II.

Iglesia Católica en Venezuela. 'I am the Way, the Truth and the Life.' Massive statue of Christ in town of San Juan de los Morros, southwest of Caracas.

CHRISTIANITY

CATHOLIC CHURCH. Dominican and Franciscan priests arrived in the northeastern part of the country in 1513 and opened cocoa, coffee,and sugar plantations as well as training the Indian population in stock-raising. Between 1658 and 1758, Capuchins founded 100 stations in the plains around Caracas, while Jesuits were opening missions along the

Country summary. **Worlds A, B, C by ethnolinguistic peoples, cities, and major civil divisions in Venezuela.**

	PEOPLES							CITIES							CIVIL DIVISIONS						
World	*Num*	*Pop 2000*	*C%*	*Christians*	*E%*	*U%*	*Unevangelized*	*Num*	*Pop 2000*	*C%*	*Christians*	*E%*	*U%*	*Unevangelized*	*Num*	*Pop 2000*	*C%*	*Christians*	*E%*	*U%*	*Unevangelized*
A	5	76,860	0.58	445	40	60	46,220	0	0	0.00	0	0	0	0	0	0	0.00	0	0	0	0
B	21	488,988	34.08	166,642	83	17	85,160	0	0	0.00	0	0	0	0	0	0	0.00	0	0	0	0
C	44	23,603,877	95.61	22,568,755	100	0	18,093	40	13,955,883	93.31	13,021,964	99	1	119,681	23	24,169,722	94.07	22,735,834	99	1	149,477
Total	**70**	**24,169,725**	**94.07**	**22,735,842**	**99**	**1**	**149,473**	**40**	**13,955,883**	**93.31**	**13,021,964**	**99**	**1**	**119,681**	**23**	**24,169,722**	**94.07**	**22,735,834**	**99**	**1**	**149,477**

Orinoco river. Much of this work was later destroyed before and during the wars of independence. A diocese of Caracas was established in 1637, becoming a metropolitan see in 1803.

The Holy See has diplomatic relations with Venezuela and in AD 2000 is represented to government and the Catholic hierarchy by a nuncio residing in Caracas.

PROTESTANT CHURCHES. Although agents of the British and Foreign Bible Society visited Caracas in 1819, it was not until 1883 that the Brethren were able to organize a permanent congregation. The main thrust of Brethren activity came after 1910, and this is now one of the major Protestant denominations of Venezuela. Presbyterian missionaries from the USA arrived in 1897, but despite their extensive involvement in the development of institutions, the growth of the Iglesia Presbyteriana itself has been slow.

In 1898 an independent missionary couple opened work which was taken over in 1920 by the Evangelical Free Church Association (EFCA) and is now organized under the name Iglesias Evangélicas Libres de Venezuela. This church works closely with the Organización Venezolana de Iglesias Cristianas Evangélicas (OVICE), which was established through the missionary outreach of the Evangelical Alliance Mission (TEAM) in 1906. These 2 groups jointly founded the United Evangelical Seminary in 1969. TEAM built a press in 1907 and began publishing an evangelical newspaper, *La Estrella de la Mañana* (Morning Star), which reaches every Latin American country.

Seventh-day Adventists appeared in 1910, and 8 years later the Orinoco River Mission entered eastern Venezuela, the latter work at present being included in the Asociación de Iglesias Evangélicas del Oriente. They are today the largest Protestant denomination.

The Assemblies of God, the first Pentecostal church to arrive and the country's largest Protestant denomination, came to Venezuela in 1916. They have experienced rapid growth in recent years aided by a network of Bible institutes, and recent evangelistic activity among the Guajiro Indians has produced many new members. The United Pentecostal Church and the International Church of the Foursquare Gospel have also built up important constituencies since the early 1950s.

Two Baptist denominations, related to Southern Baptists and Baptist Mid-Missions, are active; and the New Tribes Mission has created Christian communities among the Guaica, Maquiritare, and Piaroa Indians. A host of other small mostly USA-based groups are also present.

INDIGENOUS CHURCHES. Venezuela has a significant number of churches begun solely by nationals. The earliest is the Alleluia Church, dating back over 100 years. The largest, although it has suffered losses from recent schisms, is the Iglesias Nativas Venezolanas de Apure, commonly known as Bethel Church.

Most of Venezuela's indigenous churches are pentecostal in theology and worship. Some such as the Iglesia Ebenezer and the Unión Evangélica Pentecostal Venezolana, both formed during the latter 1950s, rival the larger Protestant churches in membership while many others are small denominations or independent single congregations.

OTHER CHURCHES. The first non-Catholic group to work in Venezuela were Anglicans, who began chaplaincy service for British nationals as early as 1832. The small Iglesia Anglicana de Venezuela was for long part of the diocese of Trinidad and Tobago of the Church of the Province of the West Indies, and in 1976 became a separate diocese. Six Orthodox churches are present, the largest being the Greek and Ukrainian churches. All are related to Orthodox bodies in the USA.

Jehovah's Witnesses, with a community of 201,000, have been in Venezuela since 1936, and are the largest non-Catholic denomination in Venezuela.

Indigenous missions. Throughout the history of the church in Venezuela, large numbers of missionaries, nearly all Roman Catholic, have been sent out, many outside the borders of South America. In recent times, Protestant churches have begun sending foreign missionaries.

Renewal movements. In the 1990s the Pentecostal/Charismatic Renewal continued to spread rapidly across most older churches, and numbered over 3,670,000 adherents (of whom 4% Pentecostals, 87% Charismatics, and 8% Independents).

CHURCH AND STATE

The constitution of 23 January 1961 invokes in its Preamble 'the protection of God Almighty', and then prohibits all discrimination based on religious belief (Article 16) and guarantees freedom of conscience and religion, specifying that 'Religious belief and practice may not be invoked either to avoid obeying the law or to prevent anyone from exercising his rights' (Article 65). Relations between the state and the Catholic Church, which have in the past been severely strained, are now regulated by a Bilateral Agreement drawn up in March 1964 between the Holy See and the government of Venezuela. It replaces the law of patronage (Ley de Patronato), voted in 1824 and ratified in 1830 at the time of the separation of Venezuela from Colombia. This law extended to the republican regime privileges originally granted to the Spanish crown, but in recent times these have had only limited significance. According to the 1964 Agreement, the government recognizes that the Holy See and the Catholic Church have legal status and guarantees their right to undertake work. The church informs the government in confidence of the names of candidates to fill episcopal vacancies prior to publication, in order that any 'objections of a general political character' may be discussed before the appointments are made public. Candidates for the episcopacy must be Venezuelan nationals, with the exception of nominees for missionary jurisdictions dependent on the Congregation for the Evangelization of Peoples in Rome. The state for its part pledges financial assistance to bishops, vicars general, and cathedral canons, as well as aid towards the construction and maintenance of churches and seminaries. The rights of Catholic lay associations are also recognized, and bishops may request entry visas for foreign ecclesiastical personnel. Successive governments up to the present have accorded appreciable economic aid to churches and denominations in the country. Religious personnel receive no remuneration from the state, with the exception of dignitaries as noted above; and there is no general plan of subsidies agreed to by either state or church. Those grants which the state does make are given for specific projects or causes in special circumstances. Thus Catholic education recently received a subsidy to provide salary increases for lay teachers.

Ecclesiastical matters are the concern of the Department of Religion and Indian Affairs (Dirección de Cultos y Asuntos Indígenas) under the Ministry of Justice. This department is administratively responsible for keeping an up-to-date ecclesiastical catalogue (Nomenclador Eclesiástico) of buildings and religious personnel of the different churches and denominations. In addition, the department co-ordinates the state's activities concerning the Indian population with those of other involved agencies, particularly Catholic organizations to which the state is bound by the Law Concerning Missions (Ley de Misiones) of 1915. This law has only 8 clauses and refers to the Indian population from a strictly civil point of view, with the aim of incorporating them more fully into settled existence and into national life. Its application is entrusted to missionaries, in that the law permits the government to make contracts with religious orders concerning territories placed in their care. The Law Concerning Missions has not been reviewed since its promulgation, but recent legislation such as that on agrarian reform, which affects Indians as well as others, trends to reflect a new spirit. Thus Indians are no longer considered as second-class citizens, and there are no longer special privileges for missionaries.

The Catholic Church is not formally linked to the state. However, the church often justifies its decisions and warnings on social matters by reference to the need to strengthen the functioning of democratic institutions which did not exist prior to 1958. The government, for its part, proclaims the importance of these institutions, while calling to mind from time to time the memory of recent dictatorships as an argument for them, in the same way that the church does. The Christian Socialist Party (COPEI) founded in 1946 and a Christian trade union (CODESA) begun in 1958 both owe their existence to Catholic initiative. These organizations, officially and through individual members, try to maintain their own identity as separate institutions, but they are not always successful. The political sympathies of the clergy are divided, and there is little to distinguish them at the popular level where church, state and Catholic political party tend to be seen as one.

BROADCASTING AND MEDIA

Shortwave broadcasts from KNLS, TWR (Antilles), HCJB (Ecuador), and AWR (Costa Rica) can be received. Venezuela is a member of UNDA; broadcasts are aired 24 hours a day via 9 local Catholic radio stations.

CBN's *700 Club* and children's specials can be seen on several channels at least one day a week in every region of the country, and response is followed-up with discipleship courses on Saturdays. TBN can be seen in Caracas on cable. There are 6 Catholic television stations.

Some 4.6 million have seen the 'Jesus' Film, mainly on TV (4.2 million) and through film team presentations (412,000), with 54,400 responding.

INTERDENOMINATIONAL ORGANIZATIONS

The Venezuela Council of Churches (Consejo Evangélico de Venezuela) was organized in 1967, uniting most Protestant churches and missions in the country. It has no wider external affiliations. There is also a small English-speaking group, Ministerium, begun in 1965 and bringing together some 30 clergy and pastors of the main churches, as well as one Jewish rabbi, for monthly study meetings and social action projects. Catholic organizations responsible for ecumenism are the Secretariat for the Faith (Secretariado de la Fe), the executive arm of the Episcopal Conference's Commission on Faith, Morals, and Ecumenism; and in Caracas, there is an Archdiocesan Commission on Ecumenism (Comisión Arquidiocesana de Ecumenismo).

FUTURE TRENDS AND PROSPECTS

Expected losses among ethnoreligionists (down from 1.9% in 1970 to 0.3% in 2025) would result in gains among Christians. However, because of the expected growth of the nonreligious, Christians could decline to 94% by 2025 (from 96% in 1970).

Christianity is expected to decline below 92% in the 21st century with the nonreligious and Baha'is growing to over 5% jointly before AD 2050.

BIBLIOGRAPHY

A history of the Church in Venezuela, 1810–1930. M. Watters. Chapel Hill, NC: University of North Carolina Press, 1933; reprint, New York: AMS, 1971. 260p.

A history of the Presbyterian Church in Venezuela. C. A. Philipps. Caracas, Venezuela: Presbyterian Mission Press, 1958. 80p.

'A question of evangelism of Latin Americans in Venezuela: anthropological and theological understanding.' R. L. Schuller. M.Div. thesis, Concordia Theological Seminary, Fort Wayne, IN, 1982. 72p.

Cuarenta años entre las pemones. E. de Villarrín. *Colección Evangelizadores de América*, 24. Caracas, Venezuela: Tripode, 1992. 159p.

Del ayer al hoy de la evangelización. B. E. Porras Cardozo. *Colección Evangelizadores de América*, 22. Caracas, Venezuela: Tripode, 1991. 118p.

Die Geister steigen herab: die María–Lionza–Religion in Venezuela. R. Mahlke. Berlin: D. Reimer Verlag, 1992. 279p.

Directorio de la iglesia católica en Venezuela. Centro de Investigaciones en Ciencias Sociales. Caracas, Venezuela: Secretariado Permanente del Episcopado, 1975.

El patronato, el concordato, el convenio con la Santa Sede: relaciones entre la Iglesia y el Estado en Venezuela. R. Oliva Sala. Caracas, Venezuela: Ediciones Tripode, 1989. 126p.

Evangelizar hoy a Venezuela. J. C. Ayestarán & C. Pastore (eds). *Colección Estudios teológicos,* 1. Caracas, Venezuela: Publicaciones ITER, 1985. 157p.

Iglesia y crisis de fe: el caso venezolano. Caracas, Venezuela: SEDECO, 1985. 120p.

La Iglesia en Venezuela y Ecuador. I. Alonso et al. Fribourg, Switzerland: FERES, 1962.

La Iglesia venezolana en marcha con el Concilio: a los 20 años del Vaticano II. J. C. Ayestarán & C. Pastore (eds). *Colección estudios teológicos,* 2. Caracas, Venezuela: ITER, 1987. 443p.

La iglesia—institución de dominación o liberación?: caso Venezuela: ensayo exploratorio hacia una teoría crítica del control social. E. Arreaza Camero. Maracaibo, Venezuela: La Universidad del Zulia, Instituto de Criminología, Consejo de Desarrollo Científico y Humanístico, 1993. 288p.

La tierra de Venezuela y los cielos de sus santos. A. Armas Alfonzo. *Serie Venezuela.* Caracas, Venezuela: E. Armitano, 1977. 271p.

Las animas miligrosas en Venezuela. A. Pollak–Eltz. *Colección País adentro,* 1. Caracas, Venezuela: Fundación Bigott, 1989. 71p.

Los protestantes en Venezuela: quiénes son, qué hacen. J. Ayerra. *Iglesia y sociedad,* 14. Caracas, Venezuela: Ediciones Trípode, 1980. 299p.

Maria Lionza, mito y culto venezolano. A. Pollack–Eltz. Caracas, Venezuela: Instituto de Investigaciones Historicas, 1972.

Milagreros del camino. M. Díaz. Caracas, Venezuela: Fundación Bigott, 1989. 181p.

Misionero en la Gran Sabana. N. de Cármenes. *Colección evangelizadores de América,* 20. Caracas, Venezuela: Tripode, 1991. 160p.

Popular voices in Latin American Catholicism. D. H. Levine. *Studies in church and state.* Princeton, NJ: Princeton University Press, 1992. 425p.

Religion and politics in Latin America: the Catholic Church in Venezuela and Colombia. D. H. Levine. Princeton, NJ: Princeton University Press, 1981. 342p.

'Religion and social transformation in Venezuela: grassroots religious organizations in contemporary Caracas.' B. T. Froehle. Ph.D. dissertation, University of Michigan, Ann Arbor, MI, 1993. 614p.

Religiosidad popular en Venezuela: estudio preliminar. Caracas, Venezuela: Centro de Investigaciones en Ciencias Sociales, 1970. 263p.

'Seeking a strategy to evangelize high–rise dwellers in Caracas, Venezuela.' T. L. Watson. D.Min. thesis, Southwestern Baptist Theological Seminary, Fort Worth, TX, 1984. 255p.

'Self–expression as integral to indigeneity with special reference to the Venezuelan Baptist Convention.' T. M. Collins. Ph.D. dissertation, Southern Baptist Theological Seminary, Louisville, KY, 1990. 337p.

Sin temor al futuro. N. Garcia Robayna. , 1990. 135p.

Strategy statement for the mission in Venezuela of the Lutheran Church–Missouri Synod, Board for Mission Services. St. Louis: The Board, 1984. 78p.

'Venezuela,' *Pro Mundi Vita* (Brussels), 14 (1966).

Venezuela. D. A. G. Waddell. *World bibliographical series,* vol. 110. Oxford, UK: CLIO Press, 1990. 207p. (See especially 'Religion,' p.103f).

Venezuela: a new face for missions. V. R. Lozuk. Nashville, TN: Convention Press, 1991. 47p.

Venezuela, su Iglesia y sus gobiernos. C. Maradei Donato. *Iglesia y sociedad,* 4. Caracas, Venezuela: Trípode, 1978. 223p.

Venezuela survey report: potential for revolutionary church growth. A. E. Johnson. Fort Washington, PA: Worldwide Evangelization Crusade, 1967. 60p.

Walk about the land: God's time for Venezuela. C. W. Porter & J. Porter. Kansas City, MO: Nazarene Publishing House, 1986. 117p.

'While the sun is high': the story of Evangelical Free Church missions in South America. B. A. Palmer & M. Palmer. Minneapolis, MN: Free Church Publications, 1984. 493p.

Country Table 2. **Organized churches and denominations in Venezuela.**

Official name (bold type = church with over 10% of all affiliated) 1	*Begun* 2	*Type* 3	*Counc* 4	*Congs* 5	*Adults* 6	*Affiliated 1970* 7	*Affiliated 1995* 8	*G%* 9	*Names, notes, and other statistics (see Codebook, Part 3)* 10
Asambleas de Dios en Venezuela	1916	P-Pe2	ZF...	711	62,965	25,000	90,000	5.26	*Assemblies of God.* M=AoG(USA). Losses to schism in 1957. 147n,13f,1s(27).
Asambleas Locales	c1980	I-3nC	.....	12	327	–	600	6.67	*Local Churches. Little Flock.* Chinese. Begun 1922 in China.
Asoc de Iglesias Bautistas Biblicas	1958	I-Bap	x....	6	550	200	1,380	8.03	*Association of Baptist Bible Churches.* M=BBFI(USA). HQ Maracay, Aragua. 8f.
Asoc de Iglesias Evangélicas de V		I-Eva	.....	12	500	400	1,000	0.05	*Association of Evangelical Churches of Venezuela.* HQ Puerto Ordaz, Edo Bolivar.
Asoc de Iglesias Ev del Oriente	1918	P-Eva	.M..C	84	6,720	13,000	15,000	0.57	*ASIGEO. Chs of East.* M=Orinoco River M. 5n,25x,47f,1k,1s(20),W=61%,450Y.
Asoc de Iglesias Pentecostales Peniel		I-3pL	.....	25	6,050	5,000	11,000	0.05	*AIPP. Peniel Pentecostal Association.* Indigenous. HQ Caripito, Monagas.
Asociación de Igls Pente Peniel Libre		I-3pL	.....	10	1,300	5,000	3,250	0.05	*Free Peniel Pentecostal Association.* Schism ex AIPP. HQ San Juan de los Morros. Declining.
Asoc Evangelistica Peniel El que Vive		I-3pL	.....	5	300	200	600	0.05	*Peniel Pentecost Association 'He who lives'.* Indigenous pentecostals. HQ Caracas.
Centro Evangélico Pentecostal	1964	I-3pU	Z....	5	600	215	1,000	6.34	*Pente Ev Centre.* Members Trinidad Blacks, Italians. Rapid growth. 1x,W=90%,2Y.
Conf de Igls Bautistas de D, M y G	1924	I-Bap	x...C	25	4,100	3,000	6,500	3.14	D, M y G=Delta, Mohagas y Guayana. *Conf of Baptist Chs in D, M, G.* M=BMM(USA). 1n,5x,13f.
Congregación Cristiana	c1950	I-3pY	.....	63	7,500	2,000	25,000	10.63	*Christian Congregation.* Brazilian pentecostals.
Consejo Luterano de Venezuela	1949	P-Lut	L...C	19	2,810	3,000	4,016	1.17	*Lutheran Council.* Begun by LWF for large German influx. 3n,4x,6f,W=10%,54Yy.
Convención Nacional Bautista de V	1945	P-Bap	T...C	212	20,000	6,000	45,100	8.40	*National Baptist Convention of V.* M=SBC(USA). 80n,4x,33f,1k,1s(17),W=33%,209Y.
Cristo Viene	c1965	I-3gL	.....	23	7,700	1,000	12,000	10.45	*Christ is Coming.* Latin American grassroots charismatics.
Discipulos de Cristo	1963	I-Dis	.....	15	1,000	200	2,000	9.65	*Disciples of Christ.* Independent Disciples from USA.
Hermanos in Cristo	1982	P-Men	.....	3	110	–	250	7.69	*Brethren in Christ. M=BiCC(USA).*
Hermanos Unidos	1883	P-CBr	x....	78	7,800	20,000	19,500	-0.10	*United Brethren.* Formerly M=Canadian Brethren. CMML,UB(Scotland). 5n,20x,57m,1j.
Iglesia Adventista de Séptimo Día	1910	P-Adv	x....	175	47,000	20,000	118,000	7.36	*Seventh-day Adventists, E&W Venez Missions.* Very rapid growth. 24nx,145mw,6f,697Y.
Iglesia Alianza Cristiana y Missioners	1972	P-Hol	.....	5	320	–	718	4.35	*Christian & Missionary Alliance Church.* M=CMA.
Iglesia Alleluia	c1870	I-3pR	.....	10	800	1,000	1,500	1.64	*Hallelujah Church,* based in Guyana. Macushi and other tribes straddling border.
Iglesia Anglicana de Venezuela	1832	A-Hig	aw.J.	5	180	1,140	600	-2.53	1976, Anglican *D Venezuela,* Ch of Province of the West Indies. 1n,3x,3f,W=80%,18Yy.
Igl Apostólica Venezolana y Misionera		I-3aL	.....	12	800	1,000	2,000	0.05	*Venezuela Apostolic Missionary Ch.* HQ Instituto de Hebron, Caracas.
Iglesia Armenia de Venezuela	1910	O-Arm	Ew...	10	400	300	600	2.81	*Armenian Apostolic Ch of V. Gregorians.* Armenian immigrants since 1910.
Iglesia Biblica Misionera	1984	P-Hol	.....	2	200	–	320	9.09	*Bible Missionary Church.* M=BMC(USA).
Iglesia Católica Apostólica Venezolana	1946	I-CCa	.....	30	2,000	2,000	4,000	2.81	Schism ex Rome by 33 RC priests. M=ICAB(Brazil),Free Cath Ch in Germany. Caracas.
Iglesia Católica en Venezuela:	1513	R-Lat	B.L.R	2,340	11,193,200	9,775,054	20,656,866	3.04	*Catholic Church.* C=31+3+78. 1q,5s(101),W=10%. 997n 1082x 1659m 4407w 372890Yy
M Barquisimeto	1863	R-Lat	Bs	83	572,000	585,000	1,086,000	2.51	Area=Lara state. Both bishops are charismatics. 90n 66x 97m 258w 22000Yy
D Carora	1992	R-Lat	Bs	23	106,000	–	206,382	33.33	In Edo. Lara. Area is 95% Catholic. 16n 8x 9m 38w 3986Yy
D Guanare	1954	R-Lat	Bs	186	307,000	293,500	629,765	3.10	Area=Portuguesa state, in west. 23n 10x 10m 56w 13758Yy
D San Felipe	1966	R-Lat	Bs	166	219,000	234,740	415,000	2.31	Area=Yaracuy state, in northwest. 21n 3x 4m 64w 9600Yy
M Calabozo	1863	R-Lat	Bs	23	148,000	355,500	268,000	-1.12	In Guárico state south of Caracas. 10n 4x 25m 25w 7945Yy
D San Fernando de Apure	1954	R-Lat	Bop	13	159,000	160,000	298,000	2.52	Apure state. M=OP(Indian work). 1974, Diocese. 9n 10x 11m 32w 5286Yy
D Valle de la Pascua	1992	R-Lat	Bs	22	178,000	–	339,000	33.33	In Edo. Guarico. Area is 99% Catholic. 11n 4x 4m 35w 5357Yy
M Caracas (Santiago de Venezuela)	1637	R-Lat	Bs	121	1,963,000	1,800,000	3,570,000	2.78	Huge urban area (2.2 million population). W=13%. 119n 502x 823m 1585w 36826Yy
D Guarenas	1996	R-Lat	Bs	22	310,600	–	470,923	0.05	Suffragan diocese of M Caracas. 15n 17x 17m 56w 7000Yy
D La Guaira	1970	R-Lat	Bs	34	214,000	181,200	392,000	3.13	Coastal area of federal district. 35n 10x 10m 94w 6590Yy
D Los Teques	1965	R-Lat	Bs	50	334,000	350,025	529,000	1.67	Covers most of Miranda state. M=SJ. 41n 39x 66m 288w 19609Yy
M Ciudad Bolívar	1790	R-Lat	Bs	103	184,000	310,000	384,000	0.86	Vast area across Venezuela (Guyana to Colombia). 17n 8x 9m 71w 6902Yy
D Ciudad Guayana	1979	R-Lat	Bs	61	438,000	–	782,000	6.25	In Edo. Bolivar. Area is 91% Catholic. 17n 22x 29m 63w 11027Yy
D Maturín	1958	R-Lat	Bs	32	213,000	304,000	387,000	0.97	Area=Monagas state. W=16%. 23n 5x 5m 40w 4500Yy
M Cumaná	1922	R-Lat	Bs	61	376,000	480,000	693,000	1.48	Area=Sucre state in northeast, with islands. 42n 9x 10m 73w 17791Yy
D Barcelona	1954	R-Lat	Bs	56	430,000	377,000	815,000	3.13	Area=Anzoátegui state, to river Orinoco. M=SDB. 42n 22x 22m 75w 16348Yy
D Margarita	1969	R-Lat	Bs	107	105,000	125,000	310,000	3.70	Recently-formed diocese. HQ La Asunción. 22n 4x 9m 34w 6555Yy
M Maracaibo (Zulia)	1897	R-Lat	Bs	56	885,000	800,000	1,530,000	2.63	Major oil-producing area, with Maracaibo. 52n 42x 54m 300w 28500Yy
D Cabimas	1965	R-Lat	Bs	28	302,000	360,000	625,000	2.23	Bishop a leader in ECCLA (Charismatic Renewal). 29n 12x 13m 12w 15000Yy
D Coro	1531	R-Lat	Bs	46	348,000	436,982	652,890	1.62	First founded 1531. Covers Falcon state. M=SDB. 28n 17x 23m 91w 8794Yy
D El Vigia-San Carlos del Zulia	1994	R-Lat	Bs	96	171,000	–	390,000	2.00	In Edo. Merida. Area is 97% Catholic. 13n 3x 3m 38w 5000Yy
M Mérida	1778	R-Lat	Bs	65	353,000	340,136	642,000	2.57	Area=Mérida state, in west. M=CIM(Eudists). W=41%. 62n 45x 63m 243w 16072Yy
D Barinas	1965	R-Lat	Bs	70	205,000	242,500	381,000	1.82	Area=Barinas state, north of river Apure. 32n 11x 17m 41w 4500Yy
D San Cristóbal de Venezuela	1922	R-Lat	Bs	466	437,000	514,000	803,000	1.80	Area=Tachira state, in extreme southwest. 92n 39x 86m 295w 19132Yy
D Trujillo	1957	R-Lat	Bs	62	282,000	386,000	539,000	1.34	Small diocese in area, east of Lago de Maracaibo 39n 17x 19m 88w 13851Yy
M Valencia en Venezuela	1922	R-Lat	Bs	64	880,000	590,000	1,410,000	3.55	1974, elevated as M Valencia en Venezuela. 52n 67x 90m 175w 24468Yy
D Maracay	1958	R-Lat	Bs	47	826,000	396,641	1,599,808	5.74	City of Maracay (193,000), big rural area. M=SDB. 36n 24x 37m 120w 20230Yy
D Puerto Cabello	1994	R-Lat	Bs	42	133,000	–	270,000	2.00	90% Catholics in area, few clergy or nuns. 7n 7x 12m 16w 4000Yy
D San Carlos de Venezuela	1972	R-Lat	Bs	68	114,000	–	205,316	4.35	In Edo. Cojedes. 13n 5x 5m 20w 4559Yy
EA Venezuela (Melkite)	1990	R-Mel	Os	7	26,000	–	48,000	20.00	For Greek Melkite-rite in USA. 0n 6x 6m 0w 300Yy
VA Caroní	1922	R-Lat	Pofmc	5	19,000	12,150	31,200	3.84	In SE. Indians: Pemone, Taurepane, Arekuna. 2n 10x 12m 20w 718Yy
VA Machiques	1943	R-Lat	Pofmc	17	116,000	90,000	233,000	3.88	30 tribes: Motilone, Goajiro, Paraujano. M=OFMCap. 2n 21x 27m 38w 7526Yy
VA Puerto Ayacucho	1932	R-Lat	Psdb	12	29,000	15,000	70,000	6.36	Indians: Maco, Piaroa, Waica, Maquiritare. M=SDB. 0n 24x 34m 59w 3660Yy
VA Tucupita	1954	R-Lat	Pofmc	6	50,000	35,680	95,600	4.02	Area=Delta Amacuro. Guarauno Indians. M=OFMCap. 0n 6x 15m 20w 2500Yy
OM Venezuela	1995	R-Lat	B....	20	6,600	–	10,000	0.05	Organized very recently, for Armed Services.
Doubly-counted Catholics		R-Lat		0	-246,000	–	-454,018		Catholics counted in a new diocese but also in older parent diocese.
Iglesia Católica Liberal		I-Lib	xv...	1	100	200	200	0.05	*Liberal Catholic Ch.* St Martin. Caracas. HQ London (UK). 1965 applied to join WCC.
Iglesia de Cristo	c1970	I-Dis	.....	13	400	–	1,000	31.83	*Church of Christ.* Independent Disciples.
Iglesia de Cristo, Scientista		m-Sci	x....	3	150	200	300	0.05	*Ch of Christ, Scientist. Christian Science.* M=CCS(Boston, USA). Caracas. 1w.
Iglesia de Dios (Cleveland)	1951	P-Pe3	.....	24	955	667	3,180	6.45	*Church of God.* M=CoG(Cleveland).
Iglesia de Dios de la Profecía		P-Pe3	.....	33	957	700	3,190	0.05	*Church of God of Prophecy.* M=CGP.
Iglesia de Dios Pentecostal		P-Pe2	Z....	28	2,800	1,000	9,000	0.05	*Pentecostal Ch of God.* M=PCG(Puerto Rico, USA). Classical Pentecostals. HQ Caracas.
Iglesia de Jesucristo de los SUD	1966	m-LdS	x....	135	31,000	1,467	62,000	16.16	*Ch of Jesus of Latter-day Saints, Mormons.* M=CJCLdS(USA).
Iglesia de La Cruz	c1970	I-3pL	.....	12	2,400	–	8,000	43.26	*Church of the Cross.*
Iglesia del Evangelio Cuadrangular	1952	P-Pe2	ZF...	46	4,235	5,000	6,520	1.07	*Int Ch of Foursquare Gospel.* M=ICFG(USA). In Tachira. 21nm,2f,1p(18),W=77%,146Y.
Iglesia del Nazareno	1982	P-Hol	.....	63	2,510	–	4,410	7.69	*Church of the Nazarene.* M=CoN(USA).
Iglesia Ebenezer y Maranatha	1958	I-3pL	.....	71	8,500	20,000	25,800	1.02	*Ebenezer Church.* 1958 A. A. Allen faith-healing campaigns. 1,000 lost in schism. 1s.
Iglesia Evangélica Emmanuel		I-3pL	.....	15	1,800	2,000	6,000	0.05	Emmanuel Evangelical Church. Indigenous Venezuelan pentecostals.
Iglesia Evangelica Menonita	1980	P-Men	.....	2	60	–	140	6.67	*Evangelical Mennonite Church. M=EMC.*
Iglesia Ev Pentecostal de Las Acacias	1954	I-3pL	.....	31	3,500	700	10,000	11.22	*Pentecostal Ev Ch of Las Acacias.* Indigenous. Drug ministry. 1x,W=28%,30Y,15z.
Iglesia Independiente de Venezuela		I-Non	.....	10	700	1,000	1,500	0.05	*Independent Church of Venezuela.* Indigenous Venezuelans in independent groups.
Iglesia La Luz del Mundo	c1970	I-3oL	.....	300	35,000	–	60,000	55.28	*Light of the World Church. Aaronistas.* Large indigenous mission from Mexico.
Iglesia Metodista Libre	c1975	I-Hol	.....	5	180	–	287	5.00	*Free Methodist Church.* M=FMC.
Iglesia Nueva Apostólica		I-3aX	x....	10	4,000	1,000	7,755	0.05	*New Apostolic Ch.* In Canada Bezirk. Germans. World HQ Zurich (Switzerland).
Iglesia Ortodoxa Griega		O-Gre	Cwo..	5	6,000	6,000	12,000	0.05	In 12th Archdiocesan District, Greek Orthodox AD of N&S America. Greeks, Arabs.

Continued overleaf

Country Table 2–concluded

Official name 1	Begun 2	Type 3	Counc 4	Congs 5	Adults 6	Affiliated 1970 7	Affiliated 1995 8	G% 9	Names, notes, and other statistics (see Codebook, Part 3) 10
Iglesia Ortodoxa Romana		O-Rum	Cwo..	2	600	500	1,000	0.05	*Romanian Orthodox Ch*, SS Constantine & Helen, Caracas. In RO Miss Epis (USA). 1x.
Iglesia Ortodoxa Russa		O-Rus	Mwo..	6	1,000	1,000	2,000	0.05	*Russian Orthodox Ch.* In D SAmerica, Orthodox Ch in America (USA). Russians. 1x.
Ig Ortodoxa Russa: D Caracas & V		I-Rus	x....	14	600	500	1,000	0.05	*Russian Orthodox Ch Outside of Russia.* M=ROCOR(USA). Ultra-conservative Russians.
Iglesia Ortodoxa Ucrania		O-Ukr	X....	5	5,000	4,000	8,000	0.05	Branch of Ukrainian Orthodox Ch in the USA. Ukrainian refugees from USSR.
Iglesia Pentecostal Santidad		P-Pe3	.....	18	705	–	2,010	0.05	*Pentecostal Holiness Church.* M=IPHC.
Iglesia Pentecostal Unida de V	1954	P-Pe1	x....	172	13,800	10,000	25,000	3.73	*Jesus Only Ch.* M=UPC(USA). In 14 states. 42n,4x,6f,1p(5),W=99%,800Yy.
Iglesia Presbiteriana de Venezuela	1897	P-Ref	RvU.C	12	650	5,000	1,500	-4.70	*Presb Ch.* M=UPUSA. Widespread institutions. 8n,3x, 6f,W=36%,87Yy,134z.
Iglesias Bautistas Conservadores	1986	I-Bap	.....	1	87	–	249	11.11	*Conservative Baptist Churches.* M=CBI(USA).
Iglesias Cristianas	c1980	I-Dis	.....	3	130	–	300	6.67	*Christian Churches/Churches of Christ.* Disciples (USA).
Iglesias de La Cruzada Mundial Ev	1954	P-Non	xF...	25	2,300	750	3,600	6.48	*Worldwide Ev C.* M=WEC(USA, UK). Many lost in split. 1x,6f,2k,1p,W=47%,45Y.
Iglesias de la Misión Mundo Unido	1924	P-Non	xF...	21	3,000	1,200	10,000	8.85	*Asoc Ev de IMMU.* Since 1947, M=UWM(USA). 4n,3x,8f,1s(4),W=70%,26Y.
Iglesias Ev Indep y Nacionales de V		I-Eva	C	40	2,000	3,000	6,000	0.05	*Organización Venezolana de IEINV. National & Independent Chs of V.* HQ Maturín.
Iglesias Ev Libres de Venezuela	1898	P-Con	xF..C	69	2,480	3,620	5,480	1.67	*Asoc de IELV.* 1920, M=EFCA; also VIM till 1949. 8n,10x,61f,1p,1s,234Y.
Iglesias Luteranas en Venezuela	1951	P-Lut	x...C	53	2,400	1,250	4,000	4.76	*Conf of LCs.* M=LC Missouri S (USA). 2n,5x,3m,1s(7),10t(705),W=30%,17Yy.
Iglesias Menonitas	1979	P-Men	.....	5	120	–	400	6.25	*Mennonite churches.*
Iglesias Nativas Venezolanas de Apure	1925	I-Non	.....	100	10,000	30,000	13,000	-3.29	*Native Chs in Apure State. Bethel Ch.* Lay founder Aristides Diaz. Many losses.
Iglesias Pente El Buen Samaritano		I-3pL	.....	15	1,500	1,000	4,550	0.05	*Good Samaritan Pentecostal Association.* Indigenous pentecostals. HQ Caracas.
Iglesias Pentecostales Emmaus		I-3pL	.....	20	3,000	1,000	8,570	0.05	*Emmaus Pentecostal Chs.* Venezuelan indigenous pentecostals. HQ Antimano, Caracas. 1p.
Iglesias Pentecostales Juan 3,16		I-3pL	.....	10	500	400	1,000	0.05	*John 3.16 Pentecostal Churches.* Indigenous. HQ Barquisimeto.
Iglesias radiofónicas solitarias	1959	I-rad	.....	700	15,000	1,500	30,000	12.73	Isolated radio believers in jungles, mainly youths. R=6500. BCCs: WEC,TEAM,&c.
Iglesias Unidas Hebrón		I-Non	.....	10	200	200	400	0.05	*Hebron United Churches.* Indigenous groups around San Fernando de Apure.
Igreja Presbiteriana do Brasil		P-Ref	R.u..	10	2,000	2,000	3,000	0.05	*Presbyterian Ch of Brazil.* Immigrant Brazilians from large church in Brazil.
Misión Evangélica Venezuela	1965	I-3pL	.....	12	1,000	1,200	2,000	2.06	*Venezuela Evangelical Mission.* Mainly in Bolivar state. 10n,W=76%,70Y,60z.
Misión Nuevas Tribus de Venezuela	1946	P-Fun	x....	74	6,900	7,000	10,800	1.75	M=NTM(USA). Indians: Maquiritare, Piaroa, Guaica. 61f,1h,1j,W=80%,400Y.
Niños de Dios	c1980	I-mar	.....	5	156	–	400	6.67	*Children of God.*
Organización Venezolana de Igls Cri Ev	1906	P-Fun	xM..C	665	21,320	10,000	35,500	5.20	*OVICE. Organiz of Ev Chr Chs of V.* M=TEAM(USA). Many schisms. 7n,16x,95f,1j,2s.
Testigos de Jehová	1936	m-Jeh	x....	850	60,444	20,000	201,000	9.67	*Jehovah's Witnesses.* Active witnessing under way by 1940. (1975) 979Y. (1995) 6898Y.
Unión Cristiana Libre	1964	I-3pL	C	12	600	300	1,000	4.93	*Free Christian Union.* Indigenous. HQ Barquisimeto. 1n.G=14.9%pa,W=45%,18Y,16z.
Unión Evangelistica Mundial		I-3pL	.....	10	900	800	1,600	0.05	*World Evangelistic Union.* Indigenous pentecostals. HQ Puerto La Cruz. Anzoategui.
Unión Ev Pentecostal Venezolana	1957	I-3pL	..U.C	80	7,000	10,000	14,000	1.35	*Venezuela Ev Pentecostal Union.* Schism ex AoG. 6n,4f (from Puerto Rico). 1p.
Unión Misionera Evangélica	1967	I-Eva	.....	100	6,000	7,000	15,000	3.10	*Evangelical Missionary Union.* Indigenous grouping. 5n,W=90%,60Y,200z.
Other indigenous pentecostal chs		I-3pL	.....	300	10,000	6,000	20,000	0.05	Total about 10 groupings begun by Venezuelans (Mestizos, Blacks), also IURD(Brazil).
Other English-language congregations		P-com	.....	14	2,700	3,000	4,000	0.05	Union Ch of Eastern V, United Christian Ch of Caracas, et al. USA expatriates.
Other Protestant denominations		P-	.....	120	3,000	5,000	7,000	0.05	Total about 15 (see list below). Many independent congregations.
Doubly-affiliated		2-aff			-612,000	0	-1,137,441		Evangelicals who also are or were baptized Roman Catholics.
Totals				**8,257**	**11,055,571**	**10,061,863**	**20,550,000**		

Churches, members, growth, 1900-2025	*Congs*	*Adults*	*Affiliated*	*G%*	*Total denominations*	*6 Megablocs:* O	R	A	P	I	m
Total churches, members, and denominations (mid-1900)	500	1,229,000	2,247,700	2.16	6	0	1	1	3	1	0
Total churches, members, and denominations (mid-1970)	3,123	5,503,029	10,061,863	2.16	74	5	1	1	28	36	3
Total churches, members, and denominations (mid-1990)	6,000	9,867,000	18,340,000	3.05	102	5	1	1	44	48	3
Total churches, members, and denominations (mid-1995)	8,257	11,055,571	20,550,000	2.30	106	5	1	1	46	50	3
Total churches, members, and denominations (mid-2000)	9,500	12,232,000	22,735,834	2.04	110	5	1	1	48	52	3
Total churches, members, and denominations (mid-2025)	11,000	17,526,000	32,577,000	1.45	237	10	1	1	70	150	5

NOTES ON TABLE ABOVE
NATIONAL COUNCILS (Column 4, 5th letter).
C = Consejo Evangélico de Venezuela (CEV, Venezuelan Evangelical Council), 1958.
R = Conferencia Episcopal Venezolana (CEV) (Venezuela Episcopal Conference).

Other national councils. Alianza de Evangélicos (Alliance of Evangelicals).

OTHER PROTESTANT DENOMINATIONS. These include: Children of God International (in Caracas), Christian Ch of North America (Italian), Chs of Christ (Instrumental) (1970), Chs of Christ (Non-Instrumental), South America Mission (1972), World-Wide Missions (1964).

VIET NAM

SECULAR DATA, AD 2000

STATE
Official name: Công Hòa Xã Hôi Chu Nghïa Viêt Nam (The Socialist Republic of Viet Nam).
Short name: Viet Nam. **Adjective of nationality:** Vietnamese.
Flag: Gold star centered on red field (North Viet-Nam's flag before 1976).
Area: 331,041 sq. km. (127,816 sq. mi.).
Government: One-party Communist state, since 1976 (Chinese rule until 939, 1471 unified empire, 1859 French conquest, 1867 South a colony, 1884 French protectorate over North and South, 1945 Independence declared by Ho Chi Minh, 1965 USA military involvement, 1975 South conquered by North.
Legislature: National Assembly, 450 members.
Official language: Vietnamese.
Monetary unit: 1 dong (D) = 10 hao = 100 xu. **US$1=** D 13,904.
Chief cities: Thanh-Pho Ho Chi Minh (Saigon) 3,678,000; Hai-phong 1,833,594; HANOI 1,312,000; Da-nang (Da-Nhang) 468,346; Bien Hoa 346,925.
Political divisions: 7 provinces.
Armed forces: 572,000.

DEMOGRAPHY
Population: 79,832,000.
Population density: 241.1/sq. km. (624.5/sq. mi.).
Under 15 years: 26,512,000.
Growth rate p.a.: 1.32% (births 19.51, deaths 6.26).
Mortality: Infant, per 1,000: 31.9; **Maternal per 100,000:** 160.0.
Life expectancy: 69 (male 67, female 72).
Household size: 4.8. **Floor area per person, sq.m:** 12.0.
Major languages: Vietnamese, French, Chinese, Thai, Muong, Khmer, Montagnard, English, and 60 others.
Urban dwellers: 19.73%. **Urban growth rate p.a.:** 2.4%.
Labor force: 47%.

ETHNOLINGUISTIC PEOPLES
85.0% Vietnamese (Kinh); 1.6% Han Chinese; 1.4% Tho (Tai Tho, Tay); 1.4% Muong (Thang, Wang); 1.2% Center Khmer (Cambodian).

ECONOMY
National income p.a. per person: US$240; **per family:** US$1,152.

EDUCATION
Adult literacy: 93% (male 96%, female 91%). **Schools:** 19,841.
Universities: 104. **School enrolment:** female/male: 73%/36%.

HEALTH
Access to health services: 90%. **Access to safe water:** 38%.
Hospitals: 12,500 (27 beds per 10,000). **Doctors:** 28,500.
Blind: 200,000. **Deaf:** 4,832,900. **Murder rate:** 6.
Lepers: 240,000. **Underweight prevalence under 5:** 45%.

LITERATURE
New book titles p.a.: 6,150 (77 p.a. per million). **Periodicals:** 42.
Newspapers: 4 dailies.

COMMUNICATION (per 1,000 people)
Phones: 11 **(7% mobile). Radios:** 95. **TV sets:** 163.
Daily newspaper circulation: 8. **Computers:** 12.

REFUGEES
Citizen refugees in other countries: 294,850.
Alien refugees from other countries: 25,000.

HUMAN LIFE AND LIBERTY (optimum condition=100.0%)
HDI: 55.7. **HSI:** 24.0. **HFI:** 12.5. **EFL:** 6.0.

Country status. Viet Nam is a country in Southeast Asia on the South China Sea bordered by China, Laos, and Cambodia. It is a major world producer of rice.

HUMAN LIFE AND LIBERTY

Human need and development. The scene of one of the bloodiest conflicts in post-World War II history, Viet Nam still bears the physical scars of this tragic period. Economically, the country is burdened not only by the legacies of the war, but also the fallout from the collapse of Communism. Its peoples are recognized to have survived one of the most repressive regimes in the world. Because of the isolation from the rest of the world and a virtual trade embargo by the United States and other Western nations, consumer goods are scarce and, where available, prohibitively expensive. A large proportion of the population is debilitated by chronic ailments, and are treated by practitioners of Oriental medicine. Many towns have polluted water supplies that breed waterborne diseases. Sewage and waste disposal methods are rudimentary. Hoarding and blackmarketing, legacies of the war, are widespread. As in most communist countries, there is an array of social welfare services which render the otherwise bleak living conditions somewhat tolerable.

Human rights and freedoms. The lessons of the fall of Communism in Europe have not been lost on the Vietnamese government, which has, over the past five years, initiated some major economic and political reforms.While these reforms have helped to modernize the economy, they have left untouched the area of human rights. The government continues to suppress all forms of dissent, and to limit severely the civil rights and freedoms of the average Vietnamese. On frequent occasions, opponents of the regime have been arrested arbitrarily and held incommunicado for long periods of time without formal charges. Under the Vietnamese legal systems certain forms of peaceful expression, such as anti-Socialist propaganda, are criminalized and offenders are sent to re-education camps, after which victims have been barred from public employment, housing, and admission to educational institutions. There has long been a pervasive network of informants designed to chill free speech. However, restrictions on travel have eased and contacts with foreigners are more widely tolerated.

Human environment. Forests once covered two-thirds of Viet Nam, but the use of the defoliant Agent Orange by US military forces led to the destruction of most of them. Nothing is expected to grow in these areas for many decades, if ever. Illegal cutting of firewood also contributes to the loss of forests. The distribution of water resources is highly uneven. In the dry season there are severe shortages followed by floods in the rainy season. The destruction of mangrove swamps during the war has reduced land available to wildlife.

Country Table 1. **Religious adherents in Viet Nam, AD 1900-2025.**

Year / *Name*	*1900* *Adherents*	*%*	*1970* *Adherents*	*%*	*mid-1990* *Adherents*	*%*	*Annual change, 1990-2000* *Natural*	*Conversion*	*Total*	*Rate*	*mid-1995* *Adherents*	*%*	*mid-2000* *Adherents*	*%*	*mid-2025* *Adherents*	*%*
Buddhists	7,623,000	69.3	26,235,000	61.4	33,501,740	50.2	660,215	-56,998	603,217	1.67	36,797,000	49.8	39,533,909	49.5	49,431,200	45.8
Nonreligious	0	0.0	4,200,000	9.8	9,000,000	13.5	177,371	3,535	180,906	1.85	9,980,000	13.5	10,809,059	13.5	16,000,000	14.8
New-Religionists	0	0.0	4,500,000	10.5	7,392,000	11.1	145,681	17,865	163,546	2.02	8,320,000	11.3	9,027,461	11.3	12,500,000	11.6
Ethnoreligionists	2,200,000	20.0	1,960,000	4.6	5,600,000	8.4	110,364	8,945	119,309	1.95	6,250,000	8.5	6,793,086	8.5	9,000,000	8.3
Christians	**900,000**	**8.2**	**3,264,000**	**7.6**	**5,212,000**	**7.8**	**102,718**	**34,715**	**137,433**	**2.37**	**5,935,000**	**8.0**	**6,586,329**	**8.3**	**11,345,000**	**10.5**
PROFESSION																
crypto-Christians	300,000	2.7	1,118,577	2.6	1,700,000	2.6	33,503	-3,503	30,000	1.64	1,855,000	2.5	2,000,000	2.5	2,500,000	2.3
professing Christians	**600,000**	**5.5**	**2,145,423**	**5.0**	**3,512,000**	**5.3**	**69,214**	**38,219**	**107,433**	**2.70**	**4,080,000**	**5.5**	**4,586,329**	**5.7**	**8,845,000**	**8.2**
AFFILIATION																
unaffiliated Christians	0	0.0	156,423	0.4	21,100	0.0	416	-685	-269	-1.36	19,641	0.0	18,407	0.0	16,000	0.0
affiliated Christians	**900,000**	**8.2**	**3,107,577**	**7.3**	**5,190,900**	**7.8**	**102,302**	**35,400**	**137,702**	**2.38**	**5,915,359**	**8.0**	**6,567,922**	**8.2**	**11,329,000**	**10.5**
Roman Catholics	900,000	8.2	2,899,354	6.8	4,220,000	6.3	83,167	26,915	110,082	2.34	4,771,483	6.5	5,320,822	6.7	9,050,000	8.4
Independents	0	0.0	37,691	0.1	490,000	0.7	9,657	5,343	15,000	2.71	578,583	0.8	640,000	0.8	1,235,000	1.1
Protestants	0	0.0	161,005	0.4	460,000	0.7	9,066	2,934	12,000	2.35	527,010	0.7	580,000	0.7	1,000,000	0.9
Marginal Christians	0	0.0	7,327	0.0	18,000	0.0	355	245	600	2.92	35,283	0.1	24,000	0.0	40,000	0.0
Anglicans	0	0.0	2,200	0.0	2,900	0.0	57	-37	20	0.67	3,000	0.0	3,100	0.0	4,000	0.0
Trans-megabloc groupings																
Evangelicals	0	0.0	167,000	0.4	493,000	0.7	9,716	3,784	13,500	2.45	559,443	0.8	628,000	0.8	1,101,000	1.0
Pentecostals/Charismatics	0	0.0	30,000	0.1	553,000	0.8	10,898	13,602	24,500	3.74	688,867	0.9	798,000	1.0	1,400,000	1.3
Great Commission Christians	**781,000**	**7.1**	**2,500,000**	**5.9**	**4,400,000**	**6.6**	**86,715**	**32,997**	**119,712**	**2.44**	**4,950,000**	**6.7**	**5,597,118**	**7.0**	**9,750,000**	**9.0**
Atheists	0	0.0	1,080,000	2.5	4,600,000	6.9	90,656	9,635	100,291	1.99	5,150,000	7.0	5,602,910	7.0	8,000,000	7.4
Chinese folk-religionists	200,000	1.8	900,000	2.1	800,000	1.2	15,766	-15,934	-168	-0.02	802,000	1.1	798,317	1.0	800,000	0.7
Muslims	77,000	0.7	390,000	0.9	520,000	0.8	10,248	-4,877	5,371	0.99	544,000	0.7	573,711	0.7	750,000	0.7
Baha'is	0	0.0	200,000	0.5	275,000	0.4	5,420	2,693	8,113	2.62	320,000	0.4	356,133	0.5	540,000	0.5
Hindus	0	0.0	0	0.0	27,980	0.0	551	194	745	2.39	32,700	0.0	35,426	0.0	70,000	0.1
Shintoists	0	0.0	0	0.0	140	0.0	3	-1	2	1.34	150	0.0	160	0.0	400	0.0
Taoists	0	0.0	0	0.0	140	0.0	3	-1	2	1.28	150	0.0	159	0.0	400	0.0
doubly-counted religionists	0	0.0	0	0.0	-240,000	-0.4	-4,730	229	-4,501	1.73	-265,000	-0.4	-285,009	-0.4	-400,000	-0.4
World A (unevangelized persons)	8,052,000	73.2	20,510,005	48.0	26,675,600	40.0	525,720	-541,665	-15,945	-0.06	27,330,314	37.0	26,504,224	33.2	27,225,324	25.2
World B (evangelized non-Christians)	2,048,000	18.6	18,955,172	44.4	34,801,400	52.2	685,828	506,950	1,192,778	2.99	40,600,401	55.0	46,741,447	58.5	69,466,676	64.3
World C (Christians)	900,000	8.2	3,264,000	7.6	5,212,000	7.8	102,718	34,715	137,433	2.37	5,935,000	8.0	6,586,329	8.3	11,345,000	10.5
Country's population	**11,000,000**	**100.0**	**42,729,178**	**100.0**	**66,689,000**	**100.0**	**1,314,266**	**0**	**1,314,266**	**1.82**	**73,865,716**	**100.0**	**79,832,000**	**100.0**	**108,037,000**	**100.0**

COLUMNS, ROWS.
For meanings and definitions, see Codebook (Part 3). Note that, by definition, total 'Christians' = professing + crypto-Christians, which also = affiliated + unaffiliated Christians, and also = Great Commission Christians + latent Christians. Percentages may not always total exactly, due to rounding.

CENSUSES.
The religion question has not been asked in the major official censuses, but occasional surveys have been made. **1958** (urban survey of South Viet-Nam only, covering Saigon, Cantho, Dalat, Giadinh, Hue, Nhatrang): 52.4% Buddhists, 31.6% ethnoreligionists and nonreligious, 14.2% Roman Catholics, 1.7% other religionists. **1962** (Saigon city): 73.7% Buddhists, 13.6% ethnoreligionists and nonreligious, 11.1% Roman Catholics, 1.6% other religionists.

NOTES ON RELIGIONS
ATHEISTS. (a) *North*. Vietnam Lao Dong (Workers') Party (in power; neutral over Sino-Soviet dispute): Of Communist party members, around 20% are estimated to be committed atheists, the rest being nonreligious with a considerable minority of professing religionists (Buddhists, some Christians). (b) *South*. The Communist party based in Hanoi was outlawed in the South from 1955 and had only unorganized members until 1975.
BAHA'IS. Begun 1954 almost entirely in the South; very rapid growth to 3,000 Baha'is by 1962, then to 195 local spiritual assemblies (1964), 602 (1971) with 116,088 adult members, and 659 (1973) with 972 other isolated centers or groups. Since 1975, however, Baha'is have barely been tolerated by the Communist regime and have been repeatedly harassed and persecuted. There still remains, however, a large body of adherents.
BUDDHISTS. Although most Vietnamese are regarded as Buddhists, Vietnamese religion is in reality a folk religion merging local folklore, animism, the ancestor cult and multiple village spirit cults and rites, together with Mahayana Buddhism, Confucianism and Taoism (in Viet Nam, the latter is a system of magic with a cult of sorcerers, practitioners, and diviners). Buddhism in Viet Nam is divided into 16 sects. Active Buddhists in the South numbered about 4.3 million Vietnamese in 1995 (mainly Mahayana, with some Hinayana influence from Laos and Cambodia), 900,000 Cambodians (Hinayana; arrived 1880; in 10 delta provinces; 20,000 monks, no nuns), and about 800,000 Chinese (Mahayana, with priests and temples separate from the Vietnamese). In 1963, Northern and Southern Buddhists united to form a body unique in world Buddhism, the Unified Buddhist Church (HQ Vietnam Quoc Tu/National Pagoda of Vietnam). The most important sect is Thien (Japanese, Zen) Buddhism, which in 1975 had 12,000 monks and 4,000 temples in Viet Nam. Another sect very popular with the masses is Amidism or the Pure Land School.
CHRISTIANS. In the South, before 1965, and after 1974, almost all were Vietnamese nationals; between these dates the totals include members of the USA armed forces (which built up to a peak of 541,500 in March 1969, fell to 343,700 by 1970, then to zero by 1972), also Korean, Filipino and other military, and USA civilians. *Emigration.*
COUNTRY'S POPULATION. The table includes the 343,700 USA troops in the country in 1970, this total then falling to zero by 1975. During the war of 1961-75, an estimated 250,000 South Vietnamese soldiers were killed and 1,400,000 civilians suffered casualties.
CRYPTO-CHRISTIANS. Christians affiliated to churches but unknown as such to either state, society or Buddhist authorities; including from 1952 many thousands of isolated radio believers in both North and South. Before 1975 in the North, and after 1975 in the South increasingly, many were Vietnamese unwilling to acknowledge their faith publicly before the Communist regime.
ETHNORELIGIONISTS. Animists properly so called, particularly among the Montagnard tribes mainly in the South, including Chrau (population 16,000), Bahnar, Loven, Mnong, Sedang, Jarai, Raglai, Rhade. In addition, many ethnic Vietnamese have been, and still are, more correctly described as animists than as Buddhists.
INDEPENDENTS. In 1995, in 2 groupings in the North and 8 denominations in the South (see Table 2); Vietnamese and Chinese.
MUSLIMS. Sunnis; especially found among the Cham (Cham-Malay) minority, along the Mekong river. Organized by the Cham and Vietnam Muslim Association, Saigon. *Hajj pilgrims to Mecca.* In 1970, 71 Muslims from South Viet-Nam performed the hajj.
NEW-RELIGIONISTS. There are 2 major religio-political millenarian sects, both located mainly in Mekong delta: (1) Cao Dai, or the Cao Daist Missionary Church (Dai Dao Tam Ky Pho Do/Doctrine of the Third Revelation of God, or Third Amnesty for Sins) which was begun in 1919 to create an acceptable syncretism of the First Revelation (ancestor-worship, Taoism, Judaism, Buddhism), and the Second Revelation (Confucianism, Christianity, Islam), with Vietnamese culture, values and spiritism; its HQ is at Tay Ninh, 70 miles northwest of Saigon; there are 8 Cao Dai sub-divisions, sects or denominations, with a total of around 2.8 million adherents, ruled by a pope, 6 cardinals, 36 archbishops, 72 bishops, 3,000 priests, and monks and nuns; (2) Hoa Hao, a reformist variant of Hinayana Buddhism founded in 1936 to seek a purer Buddhism, which claims 1.5 million followers. Other sects include Binh Xuyen, Tien Thien, and Coconut Palm Religion (5,000 members, syncretizing Buddhism and Christianity).
NONRELIGIOUS. Mostly secularized former Buddhists and Vietnamese folk-religionists in the North since 1945.
ROMAN CATHOLICS. Baptized Catholics have grown from 130,000 in 1639 (80,000 in North, 50,000 in South) to 270,000 in 1658, 320,000 in 1802, 420,000 in 1840, 600,000 in 1885, and 708,000 in 1890, with 70,000 converts recorded in the year 1890. In the last decade, Catholics were almost all Vietnamese nationals.

Great Commission Instrument Panel: status of Viet Nam (for explanation see start of Part 4)

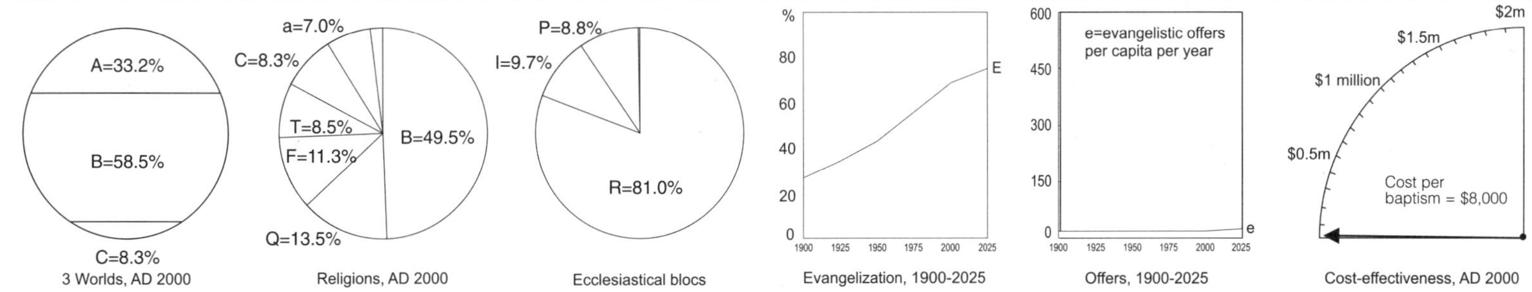

NON-CHRISTIAN RELIGIONS

Buddhism has long been the religion of the majority. Introduced in the 2nd century AD, principally in the North, Mahayana (Great Vehicle) grew significantly between the 11th and 16th centuries, after which it experienced decline. In 1930 a Buddhist assembly met in Hué for the purpose of integrating the 2 streams (Great Vehicle and Small Vehicle) and forming a renewed Buddhism, which in 1963 became formalized as the Unified Buddhist Church. At the summit of leadership was the supreme patriarchate (Tang Thong) and below it 2 assemblies, one of which was the Committee of the Supreme Patriarchate (Thuong Hoa) handling doctrinal questions while the other (Vien Hoa Dao) was more administrative.

Following the division of the country, Buddhists became more active politically, especially in their opposition to Catholic dominance. In the North, prior to 1954 the majority of the population had regarded itself as Buddhist, although many did not attend pagoda services and most continued to observe Confucian ancestral rites. Subsequently, the Communist government radio on occasion gave publicity to Buddhist celebrations in Hanoi. Nevertheless, subtle pressures were often used against those who engaged in religious activity, and many pagodas and temples were destroyed or taken over for secular uses. The Unified Buddhist Association of Viet Nam expressed its sympathy for and worked in co-operation with the Communist regime.

Buddhists. Two nuns (right) assaulted by stick-wielding plainclothes police in Saigon during January 1975 anti-government demonstrations.

Country Table 1–concluded

Country summary. **Worlds A, B, C by ethnolinguistic peoples, cities, and major civil divisions in Viet Nam.**

World	*PEOPLES* Num	Pop 2000	C%	Christians	E%	U%	Unevangelized
A	52	5,345,009	3.38	180,515	33	67	3,566,504
B	41	73,375,297	7.47	5,482,925	69	31	22,947,583
C	7	1,111,344	81.39	904,486	100	0	2,069
Total	**100**	**79,831,650**	**8.23**	**6,567,926**	**67**	**33**	**26,516,156**

World	*CITIES* Num	Pop 2000	C%	Christians	E%	U%	Unevangelized
A	0	0	0.00	0	0	0	0
B	43	12,710,168	12.02	1,527,947	71	29	3,736,192
C	0	0	0.00	0	0	0	0
Total	**43**	**12,710,168**	**12.02**	**1,527,947**	**71**	**29**	**3,736,192**

World	*CIVIL DIVISIONS* Num	Pop 2000	C%	Christians	E%	U%	Unevangelized
A	0	0	0.00	0	0	0	0
B	7	79,831,649	8.23	6,567,921	67	33	26,516,152
C	0	0	0.00	0	0	0	0
Total	**7**	**79,831,649**	**8.23**	**6,567,921**	**67**	**33**	**26,516,152**

In the South, in 1958 Buddhists experienced difficulties with the Diem regime and openly protested against privileges being accorded to Catholics. Government harassment of them in turn created more conflicts, provoking the self-immolation of monks. Among Buddhists, 2 opposing tendencies emerged, a minority movement in favor of the government and represented by an anti-communist group of Buddhist refugees from the North (about 200,000 in 1954) led by Thich Tam Chau, and the majority who were opposed to the government and led by Thich Tri Quang of the An Quang pagoda. In 1966 a Buddhist attempt to overthrow the Thieu-Ky government in favor of free elections and a representative government was followed by severe repression. While opposing direct political intervention, Tri Quang presented Buddhism as the political conscience of the nation. During the latter years of the war, Buddhism represented the anti-American and anti-communist lower middle class. After the Paris Agreement, they became more active, proposing that Buddhism could serve as a mediating force for reconciliation in the country.

Vietnamese popular and folk religion continues to exert an important influence on the life of the people, although its communal aspects are much less significant than previously. It is a syncretistic mixture of Buddhism, Confucianism, and Taoism combined with magic, fortune-telling, astrology, geomancy, and ancestral veneration, although the majority of its adherents are regarded simply as Buddhists. Diviners, medicine men, and other occult specialists retain their importance. Many families have had their own temples, with altars for the ancestors, sometimes with other altars dedicated to the Buddha and such lesser divinities as the god of the hearth. Communal worship has traditionally been centered around the village temple (*dinh*) where offerings are made especially during the planting and harvesting seasons to the guardian spirit of the village and the divinity of the soil. Many of these temples have now been destroyed, but house altars are still used, not uncommonly with the photograph of Ho Chi Minh found displayed around those of the family ancestors.

New Religions syncretizing Buddhism and other world religions, which are in reality religio-political millenarian sects, have sizeable followings in the South. The largest is the Cao Daist Missionary Church (Doctrine of the Third Revelation of God), founded in the South in 1919 by Le Van Trung. It is a syncretistic faith involving a mixture of popular Buddhism, Confucian ethics, the ancestral cult, and a Catholic-type organization. It is mostly found in the Mekong Delta along the Cambodian frontier. The second pope, Pham Long Tac, allied himself with the Japanese against the French during World War II and continued to support the emperor Bao Dai. The hostility of the Diem regime resulted in the exile of Pham Long Tac to Phnom Penh, where he died in 1956 and many Cao Dai followers were massacred in Cambodia under the Lon Nol regime. Cao Dai has its Holy See at Tay Ninh. Another religio-political sect, Hoa Hao, is a reformist Buddhist sect founded in 1939 at Hoa Hao, dedicated to the attainment of a better life with the end of foreign domination. It is mostly found in the Mekong Delta. The Diem regime persecuted them viciously and at the end of the Thieu period military operations were being mounted against their militia. Their headquarters are at Cai San, in An-giang Province. Another recent syncretistic sect is the Coconut Palm Religion (Religion du Cocotier) founded on Mekong island during the 1950s by Nguyen Thanh Nam, an engineer, as a reaction against modernization. The founder was arrested several times by Ngo Dinh Diem. The movement still has several thousand followers. And there are several other such sects.

Animism, with its emphasis on the ancestral cult and protection against evil spirits, forms a foundation for the practical religious life of much of the population and is the basic religion of the ethnic minorities of the high plateaus, who number about 6 million.

Confucianism was introduced from China in the 11th century by the upper class and continues to coexist with popular Buddhism.

Taoism, also coming from China, is mixed with popular animistic religion as well as Buddhism. The 2 together compose Chinese folk religion, followed by a majority of Chinese in Viet Nam.

Islam exists among the Cham minority and is represented by the Cham and Viet Nam Muslim Association in Saigon.

Baha'i has grown to be a large minority from a wide range of ethnic backgrounds.

Hindus. *Above.* Saigon temple, serving Tamils, other Indians, and Cham followers. *Right.* Image inside temple.

Hinduism remains both among Tamil and other remnants of earlier Indian presence and also among the Cham peoples.

New-Religionists: Cao Daist Missionary Church. *Top.* Entrance to Holy City at Tay Ninh near Cambodian border, with above gate 'The Doctrine of the Third Revelation of God.' *Center left.* A family in front of twin-towered Holy See Great Divine Temple, built 1933-41. Centre right. Cao Daist priests on steps of Temple. *Bottom.* celebrants of Cao Daist mass inside temple facing altar and Divine Eye (women on left, men on right, as always).

CHRISTIANITY

The first missionaries were Franciscans from the Philippines in 1580, followed by Jesuits in 1615. Two Jesuits, Francesco Busomi and Álexandre de Rhodes, advocated a policy of adaptation to traditional culture, and the latter with the help of Vietnamese catechists invented the present alphabet. By 1639 there were 80,000 Catholics in the North and 50,000 in the South; and the viceroy of Kuang-Si, a convert, protected Catholicism. Christianity suffered its first persecution in 1645. In 1659 Propaganda in Rome, in opposition to the Patroado, created 2 vicariates (North and South), but without fixed residence because of persecution by the Confucian emperors. The year 1668 saw the ordination of 4 Vietnamese priests and the following year the formation of an indigenous female congregation: Lovers of the Cross. In 1678 msgr Pallu, founder of the Missions Etrangères de Paris, called for the consecration of 6 Vietnamese bishops, but this was rejected by Rome. In 1679 Spanish Dominicans of the Province of Manila were made responsible for the Red River Delta of the North, while the South, Laos, and Cambodia were given to the MEP. New persecutions appeared in 1698, and in 1789 msgr Pierre Pigneaux de Behaine requested the intervention of French troops. In 1825 the emperor Minh Mang prohibited the entry of foreign missionaries. French interventions for the liberation of missionaries took place in 1843 and 1847, resulting in strong reaction against the Catholic minority. The Edict of Tu Du in 1851 resulted in the death of 115 priests and 90,000 faithful. The French imposed religious liberty in 1882 and 2 years later declared a protectorate over the territory. Thus the religious argument served as the pretext for colonial domination. The first Vietnamese Catholic bishop was consecrated at Phat Diem in the North in 1933. Catholic Christianity has experienced numerous persecutions, with a total of 130,000 martyrs across the years.

Catholic Church in Viet Nam. Hierarchy of 12 Vietnamese bishops and cardinal visit Propaganda Fide, Vatican.

CATHOLIC CHURCH. The Catholic Church of North Viet Nam has managed to maintain its relationship with Rome intact from 1954-75, for unlike the situation in China the government did not succeed in creating an autonomous Catholic Church opposed to Rome, except for a handful of 15 priests who in 1955 and 1963 at government instigation renounced the Vatican and formed a Patriotic Catholic Church, of which little has subsequently been heard. A high proportion of the faithful, around 85%, attend Sunday mass each week, and those Sundays when a priest is unable to come, parishioners meet for prayer. There is extensive use of traditional conservative Catholic devotions: rosary, perpetual adoration, invocation of saints and Our Lady of Fatima (the latter serving also as an expression of opposition to Communism), processions, and pilgrimages. Catechetical sessions are held before and after mass in the churches as well as in homes. There is a catechist in every parish who organizes public prayers. The liturgy is celebrated in Vietnamese, but European chants are also used; during mass the priest keeps his back to the people. The theology of Vietnamese Catholicism remains traditionalist, based on old manuals with little influence from the perspectives of Vatican II.

After the unification of Viet Nam in 1976, the church began to face the vast problems involved in unifying itself also.

The Holy See has no diplomatic relations with Viet Nam in AD 2000, but has an apostolic delegate residing in Bangkok.

Catholic Church in Viet Nam. Saigon Cathedral.

PROTESTANT CHURCHES. The first and by far the largest Protestant church has been the Evangelical Church of Viet Nam. Although 2 CMA missionaries visited the North from China in 1895, it was not until 1911 that permission was granted by the French authorities to begin a mission at Da Nang. Success was almost immediate and included influential members of the community. In 1927 the CMA granted the church autonomy, and 2 years later governmental restrictions on the expansion of the church were withdrawn. Work among tribal peoples (especially the Raday and Koho) of the south-central highlands was initiated in 1934. Theological training has been provided by the Bible and Theological Institute in Nhatrang which offered a degree program after 1969; and Bible institutes have also been active at Dalat and Ban Me Thout.

Although Seventh-day Adventists began work in 1929, no new Protestant group appeared prior to the fall of Dien Bien Phu in 1954.

In the North, there has been only one active Protestant denomination, and the Evangelical Church of North VietNam (begun by the CMA).

As a result of the fall of the Thieu regime in 1975, organized Protestant churches and agencies were largely dispersed and many Protestants were evacuated as refugees out of Viet Nam. Several hundred pastors of the Evangelical Church (CMA) left in this way. By 1997 however it had reverted to its earlier strength.

Evangelical Church of Viet-Nam. Believers emerging from worship service in Hanoi.

Evangelical Church of Viet-Nam. Da Nang children's choir, 1993.

INDIGENOUS CHURCHES. A total of 10 small indigenous groupings have been begun by Vietnamese Christians independently of Western foreign missions. Three small independent denominations formed during the 1960s were the Church of Christ (which consisted entirely of Filipinos), Church of God, and Viet Nam Christ's Church, the latter being a schism from the Evangelical Church in 1964. In the 1990s, several large networks of unregistered house churches came into prominence due to unsuccessful government attempts to suppress them. Followers approach 100,000.

Indigenous missions. Large numbers of Roman Catholics served overseas in the middle of the 20th century but this was curtailed in the middle 1970s. Today, very few missionaries are sent out of the country.

Renewal movements. In the 1990s the Pentecostal/Charismatic Renewal continued to spread rapidly across most older churches, and numbered over 798,000 adherents (of whom 7% Pentecostals, 20% Charismatics, and 74% Independents).

CHURCH AND STATE

Relations between church and state in Viet Nam have been mixed since unification in 1976.

After the collapse of the Thieu regime on 30 April 1975, the Catholic hierarchy made no move to evacuate Catholics and all bishops remained in their dioceses, a policy agreed on by the Episcopal Conference in January 1975. This represented a radically different position from that of 1954. In 1975, the bishops of Hué and Kontum, absent from their dioceses at the time of the revolutionary offensive, returned immediately to their posts. A new bishop was consecrated at Ban Me Thuot following the arrival of revolutionary forces in that city. The archbishop of Hué published a pastoral letter to all the faithful of central Viet Nam, in which he expressed his joy at the recovery of peace and his willingness to co-operate loyally with the PRG. A few weeks after the end of hostilities and soon after the expulsion of the apostolic delegate, the archbishop of Saigon affirmed that Catholics had not been interfered with and that North Vietnamese soldiers were attending church services. During this period, the new regime disseminated widely their instructions of 18 July 1973 relative to religions and religious belief. Some foreign missionaries left voluntarily, while others were asked to leave; still others were provisionally permitted to remain.

Subsequently both sides, regime and churches, have alternated between hardline position-taking and periods of negotiation and coexistence. Although scores of clergy and pastors were murdered and tens of thousands of lay Christians were killed, massacred, or died in prison, by the 1990s a modus vivendi had been worked out which compromised neither the essentials of Christian life and mission nor the government's responsibilities.

BROADCASTING AND MEDIA

Shortwave radio programs can be received from FEBC (Philippines) in Bahnar, Black Tai, Bru, Chrau, Chru, Eastern Cham, Hre, Jeh, Jarai, Katu, Koho, Mnong, Muong, Nung, Rade, Rengao, Roglai, Sedang, Stieng, Tho, White Tai, Vietnamese, Mien, and from FEBC (Saipan) in Jarai, Koho, Vietnamese. Vietnamese-language radio programs can also be received from TWR (Guam). Vietnam is a member of UNDA.

Over 173,00 have seen the 'Jesus' Film through film team presentations; 7,500 have responded.

INTERDENOMINATIONAL ORGANIZATIONS

Relief and rehabilitation have been the focus of co-operative work in Viet Nam since World War II, the most significant agency being Viet-Nam Christian Service, created in 1966 as a joint venture of the Mennonite Central Committee, Church World Service, and the Lutheran World Federation. For Conservative Evangelical bodies, the World Relief Commission of the USA-based National Association of Evangelicals has been active. The Evangelical Fellowship of Viet Nam was also active up to 1975.

Inter-religious dialogue has been sponsored by the Council of Religions in Saigon, which serves as an organ of contact between Buddhism, Cao Dai, Hoa Hao, Catholicism, and Protestantism.

FUTURE TRENDS AND PROSPECTS

After AD 2000, Buddhism could fall below 46% for the first time in centuries while gains are made by the nonreligious (1970, 9.8% to 2025, 14.8%) and Christians (1970, 7.6% to 2025, 10.5%).

By 2050, Viet Nam could have a radically different religious profile. Christianity and the nonreligious would both be above 12%, Buddhism under 40%, and New-Religionists over 12%.

BIBLIOGRAPHY

'A short history of the Evangelical Church of Vietnam.' L. H. Phu. Ph.D. dissertation, New York University, New York, 1972.

By life and death. J. C. Hefley. Grand Rapids, MI: Zondervan, 1969.

Cao Dai spiritism: a study of religion in Vietnamese society. V. L. Oliver. *Studies in the history of religions*, 34. Leiden: E. J. 3Brill, 1976. 145p.

Catholiques et Bouddhistes au Vietnam. P. Gheddo. Paris: Alsatia, 1969. 422p.

Croyances et pratiques religieuses des Viêtnamiens. L. M. Cadière. 3 vols. Vol. 1, Saigon: Imprimerie Nouvelle d'Extrême-Orient, 1958 (Publications de la Société des Études Indochinoises); Vols. 2 and 3, Saigon: École Française d'Extrême-Orient, 1955 and 1957 (Publications hors série de l'École Française d'Extrême-Orient).

Dieu et César: les catholiques dans l'histoire du Vietnam. T. T. Tinh. Paris: Sudestasie, 1978. 240p.

Documents on the present situation of the Catholic church in Vietnam. Mainz, Germany: Association of Vietnamese Catholics in Germany, 1986. 28p.

'Eglise Catholique au Vietnam: des chrétiens du Viet Nam relisent l'histoire de leur Eglise,' T. T. Tinh, *Foi et développement* (Paris), 31 (November 1975), 1–4.

Ethnic groups of French Indochina. L. Malleret. Washington, DC: US Joint Publications Research Service, 1962. 110p. (Translation of 1937 French edition).

Ethnic minorities in Vietnam. D. N. Van, C. T. Son & L. Hung. Hanoi: Foreign Languages Publishing House, 1984. 305p.

'Evangelization of Vietnamese Buddhist refugees.' S. X. Nguyen. D.Min. thesis, School of Theology at Claremont, Claremont, CA, 1985. 101p.

Folk stories of the Hmong: peoples of Laos, Thailand, and Vietnam. N. J. Livo & D. Cha. Englewood, CO: Libraries Unlimited, 1991. 147p.

History and philosophy of Caodaism: reformed Buddhism, Vietnamese spiritism, new religion in Eurasia. G. Gobron. Saigon: Lè-Van-Tân, 1950. 189p. (Also in French).

History of Buddhism in Vietnam. N. T. Thu (ed). Hanoi: Social Sciences Publishing House, 1992. 472p.

La tradition religieuse, spirituelle et sociale au Vietnam: sa confrontation avec le christianisme. J. H. L. Nguyen. Paris: Beauchesne, 1981. 525p.

'Les Catholiques au Vietnam–Nord,' J. Vogel, *Information catholique internationel* (Paris), 422 (December 1972), 12–16, 25–27.

Minority groups in the Republic of Vietnam. J. L. Schrock et al. Washington, DC: Department of the Army, Pamphlet, no. 550–105, 1966. 1,163p.

Peasant politics and religious sectarianism: peasant and priest in the Cao Dai in Viet Nam. J. S. Werner. *Monograph series*, no. 23. New Haven, CT: Yale University Southeast Asia Studies, 1981. 123p.

Protestant directory of churches, missions and organizations in South Vietnam. R. E. Reimer (ed). Saigon: Office of Missionary Information, 1973. 50p.

Technique et panthéon des médiums viêtnamiens (dong). M. Durand. *Publications de l'École Française d'Extrême-Orient*, vol. 45. Paris: École Française d'Extrême-Orient, 1959. 333p.

The bamboo cross. H. E. Dowdy. New York: Harper and Row, 1964.

'The Catholics and the national movement,' T. Hung et al., *Vietnamese studies* (Hanoi), 53 (1978), 1–211. (Marxist viewpoint).

The cross and the bo–tree. P. Gheddo. New York: Sheed and Ward, 1970.

'The Evangelical Church of Viet Nam during the Second World War and the War of Independence.' P. H. Le. M.A. thesis, Wheaton College, Wheaton, IL, 1967. 141p.

'The growth of certain Protestant churches in Saigon under the Vietnamese Communist government from 1975.' C. H. Nguyen. D.Min. thesis, San Francisco Theological Seminary, San Anselmo, CA, 187p.

'The influence of the Vietnamese trauma on the Vietnamese Christian theology.' D. N. Pham. M.Th. thesis, Bethany Theological Seminary, Richmond, IN, 1983. 110p.

'The political–religious sects of Vietnam,' B. B. Fall, *Pacific affairs*, 28, 3 (1955), 235–53.
'The Protestant movement in Vietnam: church growth in peace and war among the ethnic Vietnamese.' R. E. Reimer. M. A. thesis, Fuller Theological Seminary, Pasadena, CA, 1972. 336p.
The religions of South Vietnam in faith and fact. Washington, DC: Department of the Navy, 1967.
Two cities: Hanoi and Saigon today. N. Sheehan. London: Cape, 1992. 131p.
Vietnam. D. G. Marr. *World bibliographical series*, vol. 147. Oxford, UK: CLIO Press, 1992. 472p. (See especially 'Minorities and nationalities,' p.168f, and 'Religion,' p.192–8).
Viêt–Nam Công–Giáo Niên–Giám, 1964/Annuaire catholique du Vietnam. Saigon: Tu sách Sacerdos, 1963. 527p.
Vietnam: the Christian, the gospel, the church. Philadelphia: United Presbyterian Church in the USA, 1967.
'Vietnam: the long road to religious oppression,' P. O'Connor, *Religion and Communism*, (October 1976), 4.
Vietnam: the lotus in the sea of fire. T. N. Hanh. London: SCM, 1967. 128p.

Country Table 2. **Organized churches and denominations in Viet Nam.**

Official name (bold type = church with over 10% of all affiliated) 1	*Begun* 2	*Type* 3	*Counc* 4	*Congs* 5	*Adults* 6	*Affiliated 1970* 7	*Affiliated 1995* 8	*G%* 9	*Names, notes, and other statistics (see Codebook, Part 3)* 10
Anglican Church (D Singapore)		A-Cen	aweA.	4	2,000	2,200	3,000	0.05	*Mekong Missionary District.* 60% USA including military, 40% British. W=27%.
Assemblies of God in Viet Nam	1972	P-Pe2	ZF...	165	16,100	200	33,000	4.35	M=AoG(USA). 6f. Regarded as unofficial. 1994 denied registration; harsh persecution.
Assembly Hall Churches	c1970	I-3nC	.....	28	1,124	–	2,000	35.53	*Local Churches. Little Flock.* Chinese. Begun 1922 in China.
Catholic Church in Viet Nam:	c1530	R-Lat	P.F.R	3,631	3,011,600	2,899,354	4,771,483	2.01	*Cong Giao.* C=11+10+12. (1970) 84781Yy. (1990) 1615n 293x 1056m 6375w 137323Yy
M Ha Noi (Hanoi)	1678	R-Lat	Ps	120	258,000	204,300	400,000	2.72	Severe losses in bombings. Urban. 6% RC. 1s. 27n 1x 3m 120w 10000Yy
D Bac Ninh	1883	R-Lat	Ps	46	61,000	47,400	95,000	2.82	Industrial complex of Thai Nguyen. 1.7% RC. 2n 0x 0m 22w 2375Yy
D Bui Chu	1848	R-Lat	Ps	117	226,000	217,500	358,000	2.01	Red river delta. 1954, 34% RC; 1955,19%. 30n 0x 1m 90w 1000Yy
D Hai Phong (Haiphong)	1678	R-Lat	Ps	63	103,000	72,500	160,000	3.22	Port, coastal, mining. 3.6% RC. Few clergy. 18n 0x 0m 50w 120Yy
D Hung Hoa	1895	R-Lat	Ps	305	111,000	92,300	172,450	2.53	Plateaus, China-Laos; Diem Bien Phu area. 4% RC. 17n 0x 0m 65w 750Yy
D Lang Son & Cao Bang	1913	R-Lat	Ps	11	1,600	3,300	3,400	0.12	On China frontier. Scattered population, 0.7% RC. 4n 0x 0m 7w 0Yy
D Phat Diem	1901	R-Lat	Ps	240	86,000	77,800	135,036	2.23	Delta. 1950s, anti-communist RC militias. 13% RC. 22n 1x 1m 24w 3687Yy
D Thai Binh	1936	R-Lat	Ps	64	77,000	116,000	120,000	0.14	Red river delta. 1954, 10% RC; 1955,5%. 31n 0x 0m 65w 10200Yy
D Thanh Hoa	1932	R-Lat	Ps	262	77,000	62,000	111,522	2.38	1950s, scene of heavy RC/Communist battles. 25n 0x 0m 52w 1000Yy
D Vinh	1846	R-Lat	Ps	780	249,000	206,900	387,153	2.54	Mountainous, poor. Worst-bombed diocese. 8% RC. 95n 0x 74m 200w 14513Yy
M Hué	1850	R-Lat	Ps	189	26,000	83,988	49,560	-2.09	Northern Coast. Ancient imperial capital. 72n 6x 25m 365w 2000Yy
D Ban Mê Thuôt	1967	R-Lat	Ps	75	97,000	46,338	150,000	4.81	High plateau. Tribes. RCs all from North. 43n 0x 0m 120w 2130Yy
D Da Nang	1963	R-Lat	Ps	38	32,000	111,216	52,000	-3.00	Coastal area, heavily damaged during war. 54n 0x 1m 286w 2224Yy
D Kontum	1932	R-Lat	Ps	45	77,000	78,772	120,000	1.70	Many tribes. 620,000 animists. M=MEP. 28n 4x 4m 173w 1000Yy
D Nha Trang	1957	R-Lat	Ps	60	96,000	136,000	155,207	0.53	Coast near Dalat. Heavy fighting 1970-75. 68n 25x 92m 367w 4132Yy
D Quy Nhon	1659	R-Lat	Ps	39	27,000	95,230	42,500	-3.18	Coastal area between Nhatrang and Danang. 37n 4x 5m 261w 1280Yy
M Thanh-Pho Ho Chi Minh City	1844	R-Lat	Ps	51	302,000	475,695	485,584	0.08	Saigon.1975: 3.2 million population, 16% Catholic. 248n 132x 383m 701w 15855Yy
D Can Tho	1955	R-Lat	Ps	115	82,000	80,431	138,594	2.20	Rice-growing Mekong delta. 63,400 Caodaists. 101n 1x 3m 256w 4730Yy
D Da Lat	1960	R-Lat	Ps	188	103,000	77,687	215,973	4.17	High Plateaus, tribes. Many schools, convents. 77n 37x 149m 618w 7463Yy
D Long Xuyen	1960	R-Lat	Ps	237	177,000	106,377	202,100	2.60	Near Cambodia. Mostly refugees from North. 167n 11x 40m 278w 8000Yy
D My Tho	1960	R-Lat	Ps	41	41,000	61,188	86,000	1.37	In Mekong delta; area southwest of Saigon. 67n 1x 1m 186w 2797Yy
D Phan Thiet	1975	R-Lat	Ps	127	61,000	–	114,345	5.00	Formerly part of D Nha Trang. 54n 5x 28m 214w 4498Yy
D Phu Cuong	1965	R-Lat	Ps	40	39,000	64,208	84,994	1.13	Area north of Saigon in mountainous region. 5n 0x 11m 58w 2015Yy
D Vinh Long	1938	R-Lat	Ps	168	110,000	79,613	170,000	3.08	Mekong. 204,800 Caodaists, 90,700 Hoa Hao. 102n 10x 43m 564w 5345Yy
D Xuan Loc	1965	R-Lat	Ps	210	492,000	302,611	762,065	3.76	NE of Saigon. 29% Catholics, refugees from North. 221n 55x 192m 1233w 30209Yy
Church of Christ	c1967	I-3pF	x....	10	1,000	300	2,000	7.88	*INC. Iglesia ni Cristo* (Manalista), HQ Quezon (Philippines). Filipinos.
Church of God	1968	I-Non	.....	10	600	100	1,000	9.65	Small group of indigenous Vietnamese independent congregations.
Ch of Jesus Christ of Latter-day Saints	c1960	m-LdS	x....	100	10,100	7,027	20,200	4.31	*Mormons.* M=CJCLdS(Utah, USA). Leaders prosperous businessmen; schools, hospitals.
Churches of Christ (Non-Instrumental)	1963	I-Dis	x....	1	50	200	100	-2.73	M=CC(Non-Instrumental)(USA). Until 1972 many USA Personnel on military bases. 4f.
Evangelical Church of Viet Nam	1911	P-Hol	xF..E	2	260,000	147,505	450,000	4.56	*ECVN* (before 1975, ECNV). Hoi-thanh Tin-lanh VN. *M=CMA. (1970) 344n,83f,4s,3600Y.*
General Ev (Reformed) Ch of North VN	c1965	I-Ref	.....	275	10,000	2,000	20,000	9.65	*EEGV.* Over 200 house churches.
Hidden Buddhist believers in Christ	c1970	I-Bud	.....	1,400	130,000	–	288,000	65.34	Over 1,000 house churches for converted Buddhists witnessing for Christ.
Isolated radio churches	1952	I-3rV	.....	2,000	60,000	12,600	100,000	8.64	Radio believers in mountains, mostly youths and students. R=4500,T=39000(ICI).
Jehovah's Witnesses	1936	m-Jeh	x....	200	10,050	300	15,083	16.96	Active witnessing under way by 1957. Underground. Strong in Ho Chi Minh City.
Mennonite Church of Viet Nam	1957	P-Men	G...E	1	100	300	200	-1.61	M=EMBMC(USA). Aid and relief. 1 school. 1n,4x,14f,1h,1p,W=30%,22Y,3z.
Montagnard Evangelical Church	1956	I-3nE	.....	400	18,000	14,491	60,000	5.85	*Co-Duc-Truyen-Giao-Hoi.* M=UWM(USA),WEC(1958-68). Among 14 Montagnard tribes.
New Apostolic Church	c1980	I-3aX	.....	10	350	–	483	6.67	*NAC/NAK.* M=Neuapostolische Kirche. HQ Zurich (Switzerland).
Seventh-day Adventist Church	1929	P-Adv	x....	23	4,000	5,000	6,670	1.16	*SDA Mission in Vietnam. Vietnam Mission.* 8nx,105mw,15f,1H,1j,1r,24t(2877),459Y.
United Pentecostal Church	c1960	P-Pe1	.....	70	7,000	1,000	11,000	10.07	*UPC.* M=UPCI(USA). Oneness theology. Clandestine operation.
United Protestant Church	1976	P-Uni	.....	100	9,000	–	15,000	5.26	An attempt to create a church not subject to continued state harassment.
Unregistered house churches	1988	I-3hV	.....	253	38,000	–	95,000	14.29	Rapid growth: 60,000 converts in 1991. Many tribal churches from 62 tribes. Healings.
Vietnam Christ's Church	1964	I-Hol	.v...	4	2,000	5,000	3,000	-2.02	*Co-Doc-Giao. Viet-Nam Inland Mission (VNIM).* Ex CMA. 1969 applied to join WCC. 3n,34m,2h.
Viet Nam Baptist Church	1954	P-Bap	T....	50	2,500	5,000	7,140	1.44	M=FMB-SBC(USA),CSI. Expanding until 1975. 4 schools. 14n,39f,1h,1s,235Y.
Other indigenous churches		I-Non	.....	30	4,000	3,000	7,000	0.05	Chinese Christian Assemblies, Spiritual Food Ch; Philippine Independent Ch, Meo Ch.
Other Protestant denominations		P-	.....	40	2,000	2,000	4,000	0.05	Total about 25 (see list below); including expatriate congregations (ROC, AUCECB).
Totals				**8,807**	**3,599,574**	**3,107,577**	**5,915,359**		

Churches, members, growth, 1900-2025	*Congs*	*Adults*	*Affiliated*	*G%*	*Total denominations*	*6 Megablocs:* O	*R*	*A*	*P*	*I*	*m*
Total churches, members, and denominations (mid-1900)	600	568,000	900,000	1.79	1	0	1	0	0	0	0
Total churches, members, and denominations (mid-1970)	2,985	1,962,269	3,107,577	1.79	37	0	1	1	17	16	2
Total churches, members, and denominations (mid-1990)	5,000	3,159,000	5,190,900	2.60	67	0	1	1	32	31	2
Total churches, members, and denominations (mid-1995)	8,807	3,599,574	5,915,359	2.65	67	0	1	1	32	31	2
Total churches, members, and denominations (mid-2000)	11,000	3,997,000	6,567,922	2.11	68	0	1	1	33	31	2
Total churches, members, and denominations (mid-2025)	16,000	6,894,000	11,329,000	2.20	127	0	1	1	50	70	5

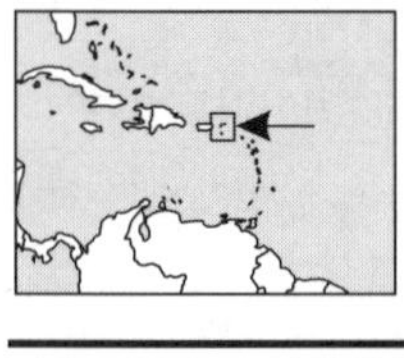

VIRGIN ISLANDS OF THE US

SECULAR DATA, AD 2000

STATE
Official name: The Virgin Islands of the United States.
Short name: Virgin Islands of the US. **Adjective of nationality:** Virgin Islander.
Flag: White field with golden eagle and letters V & I.
Area: 352 sq. km. (136 sq. mi.).
Government: Self-governing unincorporated territory of the USA, since 1954 (1493 Spanish possession, 1716 Danish West Indies colony, 1917 US colony).
Legislature: Senate, 15 members.
Official language: English.
Monetary unit: 1 dollar (U.S.$) = 100 cents. **US$1=** 1.00.
Chief cities: CHARLOTTE AMALIE (Saint Thomas) 34,043.
Political divisions: 3 provinces.

DEMOGRAPHY
Population: 93,000.
Population density: 264.0/sq. km. (683.4/sq. mi.).
Under 15 years: 22,000.
Growth rate p.a.: 1.19% (births 15.26, deaths 5.77).
Mortality: Infant, per 1,000: 7.8; **Maternal per 100,000:** 20.0.
Life expectancy: 78 (male 75, female 82).
Household size: 3.1. **Floor area per person, sq.m:** 35.0.
Major languages: English, Spanish, French Creole, French.
Urban dwellers: 46.43%. **Urban growth rate p.a.:** 1.5%.
Labor force: 47%.

ETHNOLINGUISTIC PEOPLES
61.1% Black; 15.0% USA White; 12.0% Puerto Rican White; 9.0% French Creole; 1.0% British.

ECONOMY
National income p.a. per person: US$11,736; **per family:** US$36,384.

EDUCATION
Adult literacy: 95% (male 96%, female 94%). **Schools:** 20.
Universities: 1. **School enrolment:** female/male: 95%/95%.

HEALTH
Access to health services: 95%. **Access to safe water:** 95%.
Hospitals: 5 (49 beds per 10,000). **Doctors:** 250.
Blind: 20. **Deaf:** 6,500. **Murder rate:** 22. **Lepers:** 100.

LITERATURE
New book titles p.a.: 46 (500 p.a. per million). **Periodicals:** 17.
Newspapers: 2 dailies.

COMMUNICATION (per 1,000 people)
Phones: 597 (30% mobile). **Radios:** 1,029. **TV sets:** 315.
Daily newspaper circulation: 267. **Computers:** 500.

HUMAN LIFE AND LIBERTY (optimum condition=100.0%)
HDI: 87.6. **HSI:** 90.0. **HFI:** 85.0. **EFL:** 60.0.

Country status. The Virgin Islands is group of islands in the Greater Antilles in the Caribbean Sea. Tourism is the main economic activity.

HUMAN LIFE AND LIBERTY

Human rights and freedoms. The US Virgin Islands is an integral part of the United States of America where the Constitutional guarantees of human rights apply.

NON-CHRISTIAN RELIGIONS

Baha'i has a small community, in 7 local spiritual assemblies.

Judaism is also present, with about 300 Jews.

CHRISTIANITY

PROTESTANT CHURCHES. Moravians sent their first missionaries to St Thomas in 1732, and the island was also visited by Zinzendorf in 1739. Lutherans arrived earlier (1666) and British Methodists later (1891), but the Church of God of Prophecy, a Pentecostal body, did not enter until 1926. Other active churches include Adventists, who have grown at over 8% per year since 1970 to become the largest Protestant denomination, Baptists, Salvation Army, and a large number of smaller groups mostly from the USA.

Country Table 1. **Religious adherents in the Virgin Islands of the US, AD 1900-2025.**

Year	1900		1970		mid-1990		Annual change, 1990-2000				mid-1995		mid-2000		mid-2025	
Name	Adherents	%	Adherents	%	Adherents	%	Natural	Conversion	Total	Rate	Adherents	%	Adherents	%	Adherents	%
Christians	**30,500**	**100.0**	**62,400**	**98.3**	**99,200**	**97.3**	**-879**	**-89**	**-968**	**-1.02**	**93,800**	**96.7**	**89,520**	**96.3**	**78,880**	**94.4**
PROFESSION																
professing Christians	**30,500**	**100.0**	**62,400**	**98.3**	**99,200**	**97.3**	**-879**	**-89**	**-968**	**-1.02**	**93,800**	**96.7**	**89,520**	**96.3**	**78,880**	**94.4**
AFFILIATION																
unaffiliated Christians	1,000	3.3	6,476	10.2	4,200	4.1	-37	-47	-84	-2.20	3,600	3.7	3,361	3.6	1,880	2.2
affiliated Christians	**29,500**	**96.7**	**55,924**	**88.1**	**95,000**	**93.1**	**-842**	**-42**	**-884**	**-0.97**	**90,200**	**93.0**	**86,159**	**92.6**	**77,000**	**92.1**
Protestants	14,900	48.9	22,314	35.1	41,600	40.8	-367	207	-160	-0.39	39,916	41.2	40,000	43.0	40,000	47.8
Roman Catholics	6,000	19.7	18,870	29.7	30,500	29.9	-269	119	-150	-0.50	30,000	30.9	29,000	31.2	29,000	34.6
Anglicans	8,600	28.2	9,686	15.3	13,600	13.3	-120	140	20	0.15	13,800	14.2	13,800	14.8	12,000	14.3
Independents	0	0.0	4,354	6.9	12,400	12.2	-109	149	40	0.32	12,604	13.0	12,800	13.8	12,500	14.9
Marginal Christians	0	0.0	700	1.1	1,300	1.3	-11	31	20	1.44	1,400	1.4	1,500	1.6	2,400	2.9
doubly-affiliated	0	0.0	0	0.0	-4,400	-4.3	39	-693	-654	9.54	-7,520	-7.8	-10,941	-11.8	-18,900	-22.6
Trans-megabloc groupings																
Evangelicals	12,200	40.0	10,400	16.4	17,800	17.5	-157	227	70	0.39	18,356	18.9	18,500	19.9	20,000	23.9
Pentecostals/Charismatics	0	0.0	6,800	10.7	23,460	23.0	-207	96	-111	-0.48	22,963	23.7	22,350	24.0	21,700	26.0
Great Commission Christians	**1,500**	**4.9**	**7,600**	**12.0**	**12,800**	**12.6**	**-113**	**26**	**-87**	**-0.70**	**12,330**	**12.7**	**11,931**	**12.8**	**12,540**	**14.9**
Nonreligious	0	0.0	600	0.9	1,620	1.6	-14	59	45	2.48	1,805	1.9	2,069	2.2	3,000	3.6
Baha'is	0	0.0	300	0.5	500	0.5	-4	12	8	1.44	580	0.6	577	0.6	800	1.0
Hindus	0	0.0	0	0.0	300	0.3	-3	12	9	2.66	380	0.4	390	0.4	500	0.6
Jews	0	0.0	200	0.3	300	0.3	-3	3	0	0.03	340	0.4	301	0.3	300	0.4
Muslims	0	0.0	0	0.0	80	0.1	-1	3	2	2.05	95	0.1	98	0.1	120	0.1
World A (unevangelized persons)	0	0.0	0	0.0	408	0.4	-3	6	3	0.80	388	0.4	372	0.4	420	0.5
World B (evangelized non-Christians)	0	0.0	1,100	1.7	2,392	2.3	-22	83	61	2.65	2,812	2.9	3,108	3.3	4,300	5.1
World C (Christians)	30,500	100.0	62,400	98.3	99,200	97.3	-879	-89	-968	-1.02	93,800	96.7	89,520	96.3	78,880	94.4
Country's population	**30,500**	**100.0**	**63,500**	**100.0**	**102,000**	**100.0**	**-904**	**0**	**-904**	**-0.92**	**97,000**	**100.0**	**93,000**	**100.0**	**83,600**	**100.0**

COLUMNS, ROWS.
For meanings and definitions, see Codebook (Part 3). Note that, by definition, total 'Christians' = professing + crypto-Christians, which also = affiliated + unaffiliated Christians, and also = Great Commission Christians + latent Christians. Percentages may not always total exactly, due to rounding.

CENSUSES.
The religion question has not been asked.

NOTES ON RELIGIONS
BAHA'IS. In 3 local spiritual assemblies (1973), increasing to 7 (1996).
INDEPENDENTS. In about 7 denominations in 1995 (see Table 2).
PENTECOSTALS/CHARISMATICS. The Catholic Charismatic renewal became widespread in 1977, spread by citizens who had experienced renewal in Puerto Rico, with 2 large meetings in November 1977: one on St Thomas (300 attenders), and one on St Croix (700). Subsequently expansion has been stimulated by this constant mobility of migrant laborers.

Great Commission Instrument Panel: status of the Virgin Islands of the US (for explanation see start of Part 4)

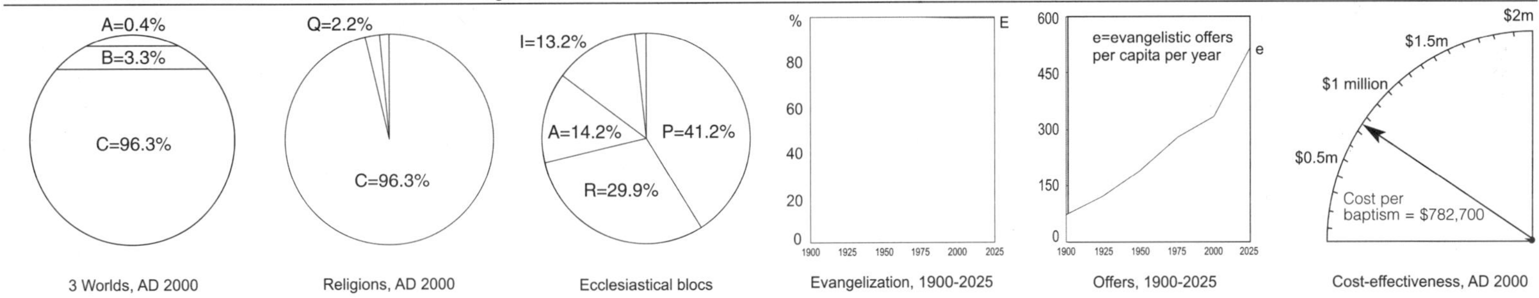

Country summary. **Worlds A, B, C by ethnolinguistic peoples, cities, and major civil divisions in the Virgin Islands of the US.**

	PEOPLES							CITIES							CIVIL DIVISIONS						
World	Num	Pop 2000	C%	Christians	E%	U%	Unevangelized	Num	Pop 2000	C%	Christians	E%	U%	Unevangelized	Num	Pop 2000	C%	Christians	E%	U%	Unevangelized
A	1	307	0.98	3	49	51	157	0	0	0.00	0	0	0	0	0	0	0.00	0	0	0	0
B	1	651	15.05	98	73	27	176	0	0	0.00	0	0	0	0	0	0	0.00	0	0	0	0
C	7	91,997	93.54	86,058	100	0	58	1	34,043	92.00	31,320	99	1	208	3	92,953	92.69	86,159	100	0	389
Total	**9**	**92,955**	**92.69**	**86,159**	**100**	**0**	**391**	**1**	**34,043**	**92.00**	**31,320**	**99**	**1**	**208**	**3**	**92,953**	**92.69**	**86,159**	**100**	**0**	**389**

Methodist Church in the Caribbean & The Americas. Christchurch Methodist Church, St. Thomas.

CATHOLIC CHURCH. There were 30,000 Catholics in the US Virgin Islands in 1995, consisting of either local inhabitants or Puerto Ricans and Americans. There are 3 parishes served by Redemptorist priests, who also make periodic visits to the British Virgin Islands, and 2 congregations of sisters: missionary Sisters of the Immaculate Heart of Mary, and Sisters of Charity. St Thomas is the seat of the prelature of the Virgin Islands, a suffragan of the archdiocese of Washington DC (USA).

The Holy See has no diplomatic relations with Virgin Islands of the US in AD 2000.

ANGLICAN CHURCH. The Church of England began work in the Virgin Islands during the early part of the 18th century, and by 1848 one-third of the population was Anglican. Today the population is only 14.8% Anglican, a proportion slightly lower than that in the British Virgin Islands. In 1916 the mission was transferred to the Episcopal Church in the USA.

INDIGENOUS CHURCHES. Blacks and Puerto Ricans from the USA have been instrumental in the establishment of 6 denominations in the Virgin Islands, 2 being Methodist (AMEC and AME Zion) and 4 others being Pentecostal. No independent churches have arisen from within the territory.

Indigenous missions. Very few Christians have been sent out as missionaries from the Virgin Islands.

CHURCH AND STATE

Freedom of religion is fully guaranteed, but a somewhat rigid separation of church and state is maintained as in all US overseas territories.

BROADCASTING AND MEDIA

Local station WIVH carries Christian programming, including Back to the Bible. Shortwave broadcasts from TWR (Antilles), HCJB (Ecuador), and AWR (Costa Rica) can be received. Christian television programming can be received via satellite.

INTERDENOMINATIONAL ORGANIZATIONS

The St Thomas Inter-Church Council has 6 members: AME, Episcopal, Lutheran, Methodist, Moravian churches, and the Salvation Army.

FUTURE TRENDS AND PROSPECTS

Christians will likely continue to become nonreligious, with Christianity claiming 94.4% by AD 2025.

Christianity is expected to continue to decline slightly but should remain around 90% throughout the next fifty years.

BIBLIOGRAPHY

Bibliography of the Virgin Islands of the United States. C. F. Reid. New York: H. W. Wilson, 1941. 225p.
C. G. A. Oldendorp's history of the mission of the Evangelical Brethren on the Caribbean islands of St. Thomas, St. Croix, and St. John. J. J. Bossart. Trans., A. R. Highfield & V. Barac. Ann Arbor, MI: Karoma Publishers, 1987. 772p.
'Catholic education in the Virgin Islands.' D. Griffith. M.A. thesis, University of the Virgin Islands, St. Croix, USVI, 1986. 96p.
'Developing a course on church administration for the U.S. Virgin Islands: Seminary Extension Center, Southern Baptist Convention.' B. C. Driggers. Paper, Candler School of Theology, Emory University, Atlanta, 1984. 76p.
Frederick Evangelical Lutheran Church, 325th anniversary, 1666–1991: celebrate our past, challenge the future. St. Thomas, USVI: Frederick Evangelical Lutheran Church, 1991. 75p.
Historic churches of the Virgin Islands. W. Chapman & W. Taylor. St. Croix, USVI: Saint Croix Landmarks Society, 1986. 145p.
Praise God: two hundred years (1773–1973): history of the Catholic Church in St. Thomas. J. Gauci (ed). Charlotte Amalie, USVI: Redemptorist Fathers, 1973. 77p.
'Race and ethnicity in the United States Virgin Islands,' K. de Albuquerque & J. L. McElroy, in *Caribbean ethnicity revisited,* p.41–70. S. Glazier (ed). New York: Gordon and Breach, 1985.
'Religious development,' E. Baa, in *Fifty years: commemorating the fiftieth anniversary of the transfer of the Virgin Islands from Denmark to the United States of America March 31, 1967,* p.45–57. E. Downing (ed). Charlotte

Amalie, USVI: Friends of Denmark Society, 1967.

The historical records of the Moravian churches of the United States Virgin Islands in the Moravian archives at Bethlehem, Pennsylvania. A. R. Highfield. Christiansted, USVI: Society of Virgin Islands Historians, 1990. 32p.

'The history of the African Methodist Episcopal Church in the Virgin Islands,' V. Adams-Gordon, *Missionary*, 65, 2 (1963), 10–11.

Virgin Islands. V. Moll. *World bibliographical series*, vol. 138. Oxford, UK: CLIO Press, 1991. 216p. (See especially 'Religion,' p.52-6).

Virgin Islands Christmas–time. ESEA, no. 111. St. Thomas, USVI: Department of Education.

Virgin Islands English creoles. G. Sprave. *Microstate studies*, vol. 1. N.p.: Caribbean Research Institute, 1977, p.8–28.

Virgin Islands story: a history of the Lutheran State Church, other churches, slavery, education and culture in the Danish West Indies, now the Virgin Islands. P. M. J. Larsen. Philadelphia: Muhlenberg, 1950. 250p.

'West Indian immigrants in St. Croix, United States Virgin Islands, 1950–1982: a case study in immigration and changes in religious affiliation.' S. R. Michael. Ph.D. dissertation, Boston University, Boston, 1985. 361p.

Country Table 2. **Organized churches and denominations in the Virgin Islands of the US.**

Official name (bold type = church with over 10% of all affiliated) 1	*Begun* 2	*Type* 3	*Counc* 4	*Congs* 5	*Adults* 6	*Affiliated 1970* 7	*Affiliated 1995* 8	*G%* 9	*Names, notes, and other statistics* (see Codebook, Part 3) 10
African Methodist Episcopal Church		I-Met	VwM.C	4	1,100	1,200	1,470	0.05	*Virgin Islands Annual Conference*, 16th Episcopal District. M=AMEC(USA Blacks).
African Methodist Episcopal Zion Ch	1917	I-Met	Vw...	1	400	600	571	-0.20	M=AMEZC(Black mission from USA). 1919, took over Colored Methodist Episcopal work.
American Orth Cath Ch (AD N&S Amer)	c1965	I-ReO	x....	1	300	500	600	0.73	*Orth Cath=Orthodox Catholic. D Virgin Islands.* Schism in USA ex Ukrainian Orth Ch of USA.
Assemblies of God	c1965	P-Pe2	.....	4	1,000	167	1,670	9.65	M=AoG(USA).
Baptist Convention	c1965	P-Bap	.....	2	125	167	208	0.88	M=SBC. Southern Baptist Convention, USA.
Baptist General Conference	c1970	P-Bap	.....	11	800	–	1,600	34.33	M=BGC(USA).
Baptist International Missions	1964	I-Bap	x....	5	1,800	1,000	3,000	4.49	M=BIM(USA). Fundamentalist Baptists. One school. 14f,1s.
Catholic Church: D Saint Thomas	1648	R-Lat	B...r	10	17,500	18,870	30,000	1.87	C=1+0+2. M=CSSR. (1970) 14nx, 1090Yy. (1990) 9n, 5x, 7m, 21w, 573Yy
Christian Brethren		P-CBr	x....	2	100	100	200	0.05	*Plymouth Brethren. Open Brethren. Gospel Hall.* Small independent congregation.
Church of God Holiness	1947	I-Hol	x....	8	100	200	250	0.90	M=CGH(Overland Park, Kansas, USA). Wesleyan doctrines. 1 school. 5f.
Church of God of Prophecy	1926	P-Pe3	Z....	4	2,100	5,000	2,800	-2.29	M=CGPL(USA). Holiness Pentecostals. Ex CoG (Cleveland). HQ St Thomas. 2f.
Church of God (Cleveland)	1945	P-Pe3	ZF...	5	1,118	700	2,240	4.76	M=CoG(Cleveland)(USA). St Thomas: 3 churches. St. Croix: 1 church. 7n,2f,1p.
Ch of Jesus Christ of Latter-day Saints	c1980	m-LdS	.....	2	140	–	200	6.67	*Mormons.* M=CJCLdS(Utal, USA).
Church of the Nazarene	1961	P-Hol	xF...	4	305	330	699	3.05	M=CoN(USA). Holiness denomination. Growing. 1n,2f,W=68%,13Y,7z.
Damascus Christian Church		I-3pL	x....	30	1,500	200	2,500	0.05	Spanish-speaking pentecostals; Puerto Ricans, Cubans, Central Americans. HQ Bronx (USA).
Episcopal Church: D Virgin Islands	c1700	A-ACa	aw.RC	8	6,875	9,686	13,800	1.43	1963, extra-provincial missionary diocese of PECUSA (now ECUSA). 14n,1x,5f,W=36%,609Yy.
Jehovah's Witnesses	c1940	m-Jeh	x....	8	481	700	1,200	2.18	*Watch Tower.* Active witnessing under way by 1947. (1975) 20Y. (1995) 13Y.
Lutheran Church in America	1664	P-Lut	L.M.C	8	1,540	1,939	2,800	1.48	In Caribbean Synod, LCA. M=LCA(USA). Lutheran Welfare Society (St Croix).
Methodist Ch in Caribbean & Americas	1891	P-Met	VwM.C	8	2,250	3,000	4,500	1.64	In MCCA (1967 union), Leeward Islands district. M=MMS(UK). 2n,1x,1f.
Metropolitan Church Association		P-Hol	x....	4	200	300	400	0.05	M=MCA(USA). Holiness denomination. HQ Christiansted, St Croix.
Moravian Church	1732	P-Mor	xWM.C	8	2,200	5,101	6,290	0.84	*VI Conf*, Eastern WIndies Province. 1968 applied to WCC. 8f,W=63%,209Yy.
Salvation Army		P-Sal	xwM.C	10	600	1,500	1,700	0.05	*Virgin Islands Region*, Caribbean & CAmerica Territory (HQ Jamaica). HQ St Thomas.
Seventh-day Adventist Church	c1926	P-Adv	x....	15	4,500	1,500	7,500	6.65	*SDA*, in East Caribbean Conference, Caribbean Union Conference.
United Methodist Church		P-Met	Vw...	2	200	500	400	0.05	In Puerto Rico Conference, UMC (USA). Only on St Croix. 1t(260),W=81%.
United Pentecostal Church		P-Pel	x....	10	500	500	1,000	0.05	*Jesus Only Church.* Unitarian Pentecostals. M=UPC(USA). 4n.
Wesleyan Church	1911	P-Hol	VF...	7	500	510	909	2.34	Until 1968 Pilgrim Holiness Ch (USA). 1 school. 4n,1f,1j,1k,W=95%,11Y.
Other independent charismatic chs	c1975	I-3cU	.....	18	900	–	1,290	5.00	In about 4 loose networks.
Other independent pentecostal chs	c1965	I-3pU	.....	12	600	154	923	7.43	In 3 loose geographical networks.
Other Protestant denominations		P-	.....	40	3,000	1,000	5,000	0.05	Total about 30 (see list below).
Other Non-White indigenous churches		I-	.....	25	1,000	500	2,000	0.05	Missions from USA, incl Assembly of Christian Chs, Ch of God in Christ, Assembly Hall Chs.
Doubly-affiliated		2-aff			-4,100	0	-7,520		Evangelicals who are also baptized Roman Catholics.
Totals				**276**	**49,634**	**55,924**	**90,200**		

Churches, members, growth, 1900-2025	*Congs*	*Adults*	*Affiliated*	*G%*	*Total denominations*	*6 Megablocs:* *O*	*R*	*A*	*P*	*I*	*m*
Total churches, members, and denominations (mid-1900)	70	15,000	29,500	0.92	5	0	1	1	3	0	0
Total churches, members, and denominations (mid-1970)	164	28,464	55,924	0.92	45	0	1	1	28	14	1
Total churches, members, and denominations (mid-1990)	270	52,200	95,000	2.68	79	0	1	1	46	29	2
Total churches, members, and denominations (mid-1995)	276	49,634	90,200	-1.03	79	0	1	1	46	29	2
Total churches, members, and denominations (mid-2000)	250	47,400	86,159	-0.91	80	0	1	1	46	30	2
Total churches, members, and denominations (mid-2025)	240	42,300	77,000	-0.45	147	1	1	1	60	80	4

NOTES ON TABLE ABOVE
NATIONAL COUNCILS (Column 4, 5th letter).
C = St Thomas Inter-Church Council.
E = St. Croix Evangelical Ministerial Association.
r = member, National Conference of Catholic Bishops, USA (NCCB).

OTHER PROTESTANT DENOMINATIONS. There are numerous groups from the USA, including: Apostolic Faith Mission, Baptist Bible Fellowship International (1972), Bethany Fellowship Missions (1966), Christian Mission, Dutch Reformed Ch, Reformed Ch in America.

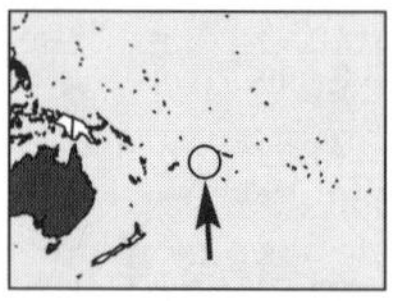

WALLIS & FUTUNA ISLANDS

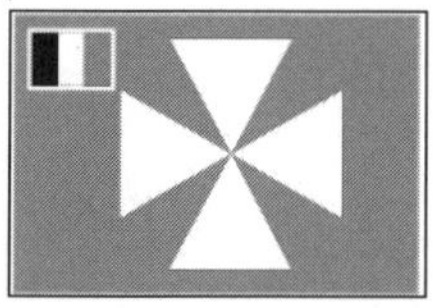

SECULAR DATA, AD 2000

STATE
Official name: Le Territoire de Wallis et Futuna (The Overseas Territory of the Wallis & Futuna Islands).
Short name: Wallis & Futuna Islands. **Adjective of nationality:** Wallis & Futuna Islander.
Flag: That of France.
Area: 240 sq. km. (97 sq. mi.).
Government: Overseas territory of France, since 1961 (kingdoms under French advisers, 1887 French protectorate).
Legislature: Territorial Assembly, 20 members.
Official language: French (Français).
Monetary unit: 1 franc (F) = 100 centimes. **US$1=** F 5.60.
Chief cities: MATA-UTU 1,111.
Political divisions: 1 province.

DEMOGRAPHY
Population: 15,000.
Population density: 60.4/sq. km. (149.6/sq. mi.).
Under 15 years: 6,000.
Growth rate p.a.: 1.85% (births 27.33, deaths 4.64).
Mortality: Infant, per 1,000: 19.3; **Maternal per 100,000:** 70.0.
Life expectancy: 73 (male 71, female 75).
Household size: 5.0. **Floor area per person, sq.m:** 20.0.
Major languages: French, Uvean, Futunan.
Urban dwellers: 0.0%. **Urban growth rate p.a.:** 0.0%.
Labor force: 40%.

ETHNOLINGUISTIC PEOPLES
66.5% Wallisian (East Uvean); 31.9% East Futunan; 0.9% French.

ECONOMY
National income p.a. per person: US$4,684; **per family:** US$23,420.

EDUCATION
Adult literacy: 95% (male 97%, female 93%). **Schools:** 20.
Universities: 0. **School enrolment:** female/male: 85%/85%.

HEALTH
Access to health services: 90%. **Access to safe water:** 90%.
Hospitals: 1 (45 beds per 10,000). **Doctors:** 20.
Blind: 10. **Deaf:** 900. **Murder rate:** 2.
Lepers: 20.

LITERATURE
New book titles p.a.: 4 (250 p.a. per million). **Periodicals:** 1.
Newspapers: 0 dailies.

COMMUNICATION (per 1,000 people)
Phones: 26 (20% mobile). **Radios:** 100. **TV sets:** 80.
Daily newspaper circulation: 30. **Computers:** 20.

HUMAN LIFE AND LIBERTY (optimum condition=100.0%)
HDI: 79.9. **HSI:** 70.0. **HFI:** 70.0. **EFL:** 40.0.

Country status. The Wallis & Futuna Islands, an overseas department of France, is 2 groups of islands in the Pacific Ocean to the west of Samoa.

HUMAN LIFE AND LIBERTY

Human rights and freedoms. The Wallis and Futuna Islands is an overseas territory of France. All human rights and civil liberties are fully respected on the islands.

NON-CHRISTIAN RELIGIONS

Traditional pre-Christian religion has a few remnant adherents, and there are a few other non-Christian religionists.

CHRISTIANITY

CATHOLIC CHURCH. Virtually the entire population has become Catholic, and Catholicism is the only organized denomination represented in the islands. A Marist priest established the first mission on Wallis in 1836, and there are now stations at Matautu, Malaetoli, and Lano. Futuna was reached later and is served by mission centers at Sigave and Alo. In 1972 the bishop, a Frenchman, resided at Lano; while his auxiliary, a national, was stationed in Futuna. However, in 1974 the European bishop withdrew and was replaced by his indigenous auxiliary. During the 1960s the last French bishop effected an *aggiornamento* (renewal) preparing for the departure of French clergy and sisters in order to leave the islands to national workers. Indigenous vocations have been successful, the first national priests being ordained as early as 1886.

The Holy See has no diplomatic relations with Wallis & Futuna Islands in AD 2000, but has an apostolic delegate for the Pacific Ocean residing in Wellington, New Zealand.

Indigenous missions. Several Christians, nearly all Roman Catholics, have served in surrounding islands as missionaries.

Country Table 1. **Religious adherents in Wallis & Futuna Islands, AD 1900-2025.**

Year	*1900*		*1970*		*mid-1990*		*Annual change, 1990-2000*				*mid-1995*		*mid-2000*		*mid-2025*	
Name	*Adherents*	*%*	*Adherents*	*%*	*Adherents*	*%*	*Natural*	*Conversion*	*Total*	*Rate*	*Adherents*	*%*	*Adherents*	*%*	*Adherents*	*%*
Christians	**1,600**	**80.0**	**8,600**	**99.3**	**13,380**	**97.7**	**80**	**1**	**81**	**0.59**	**13,765**	**97.6**	**14,189**	**97.8**	**17,110**	**97.8**
PROFESSION																
professing Christians	**1,600**	**80.0**	**8,600**	**99.3**	**13,380**	**97.7**	**80**	**1**	**81**	**0.59**	**13,765**	**97.6**	**14,189**	**97.8**	**17,110**	**97.8**
AFFILIATION																
unaffiliated Christians	100	5.0	238	2.8	170	1.2	1	-1	0	-0.12	175	1.2	168	1.1	110	0.6
affiliated Christians	**1,500**	**75.0**	**8,362**	**96.6**	**13,210**	**96.4**	**78**	**3**	**81**	**0.60**	**13,590**	**96.4**	**14,021**	**96.7**	**17,000**	**97.1**
Roman Catholics	1,500	75.0	8,362	96.6	13,140	95.9	78	2	80	0.59	13,514	95.8	13,936	96.1	16,830	93.6
Marginal Christians	0	0.0	0	0.0	35	0.3	0	1	1	2.54	40	0.3	45	0.3	90	0.5
Protestants	0	0.0	0	0.0	35	0.3	0	1	1	1.34	36	0.3	40	0.3	80	0.4
Trans-megabloc groupings																
Evangelicals	0	0.0	0	0.0	10	0.1	0	1	1	4.14	10	0.1	15	0.1	30	0.2
Pentecostals/Charismatics	0	0.0	20	0.2	265	1.9	2	5	7	2.22	279	2.0	330	2.2	700	3.9
Great Commission Christians	**80**	**4.0**	**700**	**8.1**	**1,710**	**12.5**	**12**	**6**	**18**	**0.98**	**1,800**	**12.8**	**1,885**	**13.0**	**2,650**	**15.1**
Ethnoreligionists	0	0.0	0	0.0	200	1.4	1	-2	-1	-0.56	200	1.4	189	1.3	150	0.8
Baha'is	400	20.0	100	1.2	100	0.7	1	1	2	1.50	115	0.8	116	0.8	200	1.1
Nonreligious	0	0.0	0	0.0	20	0.1	0	0	0	1.41	20	0.1	23	0.2	40	0.2
World A (unevangelized persons)	40	2.0	43	0.5	14	0.1	0	-1	-1	-6.70	15	0.1	16	0.1	18	0.1
World B (evangelized non-Christians)	360	18.0	17	0.2	306	2.2	2	0	2	2.96	323	2.4	311	2.1	372	2.1
World C (Christians)	1,600	80.0	8,600	99.3	13,380	97.7	80	1	81	0.59	13,765	97.6	14,189	97.8	17,110	97.8
Country's population	**2,000**	**100.0**	**8,661**	**100.0**	**13,700**	**100.0**	**82**	**0**	**82**	**0.69**	**14,088**	**100.0**	**14,500**	**100.0**	**17,500**	**100.0**

COLUMNS, ROWS.
For meanings and definitions, see Codebook (Part 3). Note that, by definition, total 'Christians' = professing + crypto-Christians, which also = affiliated + unaffiliated Christians, and also = Great Commission Christians + latent Christians. Percentages may not always total exactly, due to rounding.

CENSUSES.
The religion question has not been asked.

NOTES ON RELIGIONS
COUNTRY'S POPULATION. The figures on the bottom line of the table are averages, since the population fluctuates considerably between 7,000 and 10,000 due to short-term labor migration of young men to New Caledonia and New Hebrides.
OTHER RELIGIONISTS. Unorganized expatriates who are adherents of non-Christian religions including small number of traditional (tribal) religionists indigenous to the islands.

Great Commission Instrument Panel: status of the Wallis & Futuna Islands (for explanation see start of Part 4)

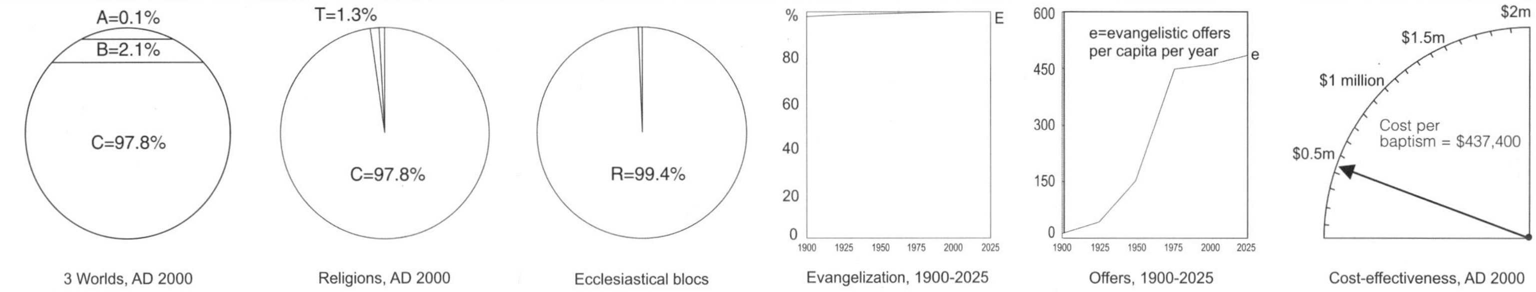

Country summary. **Worlds A, B, C by ethnolinguistic peoples, cities, and major civil divisions in Wallis & Futuna Islands.**

	PEOPLES							CITIES							CIVIL DIVISIONS						
World	*Num*	*Pop 2000*	*C%*	*Christians*	*E%*	*U%*	*Unevangelized*	*Num*	*Pop 2000*	*C%*	*Christians*	*E%*	*U%*	*Unevangelized*	*Num*	*Pop 2000*	*C%*	*Christians*	*E%*	*U%*	*Unevangelized*
A	0	0	0.00	0	0	0	0	0	0	0.00	0	0	0	0	0	0	0.00	0	0	0	0
B	0	0	0.00	0	0	0	0	0	0	0.00	0	0	0	0	0	0	0.00	0	0	0	0
C	4	14,518	96.58	14,021	100	0	5	1	1,111	93.97	1,044	100	0	3	1	14,517	96.58	14,021	100	0	5
Total	**4**	**14,518**	**96.58**	**14,021**	**100**	**0**	**5**	**1**	**1,111**	**93.97**	**1,044**	**100**	**0**	**3**	**1**	**14,517**	**96.58**	**14,021**	**100**	**0**	**5**

Eglise Catholique, Diocèse de Wallis et Futuna. Government postage stamps commemorating 1836 arrival of first French missionaries.

CHURCH AND STATE

An agreement was signed in July 1969 between the bishop and the French government recognizing Catholic education, the only education existent, as the quasi-official educational system of the territory. At the same time provision was made for subsidizing it. As is true with other French overseas departments and territories but unlike France itself, there is no real separation of church and state. Until 1970 the Catholic bishop bore the title 'co-prince' of the kingdom. The king and the mission, with the acquiescence of the French civil authorities, until recently formed a veritable theocracy, where for example failure to attend mass was punishable by fine of a pig.

FUTURE TRENDS AND PROSPECTS

Few changes are expected in the religious situation on the Wallis & Futuna Islands before AD 2025.

Christianity is expected to predominate throughout the next fifty years, if present trends continue.

BIBLIOGRAPHY

'Contemporary healing practices in east Futuna,' B. Biggs, in *Healing practices in the South Pacific*, p.108–28. C. D. F. Parsons (ed). Honolulu, HI: Institute for Polynesian studies, 1985.

Country Table 2. **Organized churches and denominations in Wallis & Futuna Islands.**

Official name (bold type = church with over 10% of all affiliated) 1	*Begun* 2	*Type* 3	*Counc* 4	*Congs* 5	*Adults* 6	*Affiliated 1970* 7	*Affiliated 1995* 8	*G%* 9	*Names, notes, and other statistics* (see Codebook, Part 3) 10
Eglise Catholique: D Wallis & Futuna	1836	R-Lat	PzPY.	5	6,000	8,362	13,514	1.94	M=SM2. (1970) 8n,4x,8m,63w,372Yy. (1990) 4n, 3x, 8m, 43w, 395Yy.
Eglise Evangélique de Futuna	1990	P-Eva	.....	1	20	–	30	20.00	*Futuna Evangelical Church.*
Pentecostal Churches	c1980	P-Pe2	.....	1	2	–	6	6.67	Mainline Pentecostals from France.
Témoins de Jéhova	c1975	m-Jeh	.....	1	4	–	40	5.00	*Jehovah's Witnesses.* In 1995, 4,400 hours of preaching.
Totals				**8**	**6,026**	**8,362**	**13,590**		

Churches, members, growth, 1900-2025	*Congs*	*Adults*	*Affiliated*	*G%*	*Total denominations*	*6 Megablocs:* O	*R*	*A*	*P*	*I*	*m*
Total churches, members, and denominations (mid-1900)	2	770	1,500	2.48	1	0	1	0	0	0	0
Total churches, members, and denominations (mid-1970)	5	4,300	8,362	2.48	1	0	1	0	0	0	0
Total churches, members, and denominations (mid-1990)	7	5,900	13,210	2.31	2	0	1	0	0	0	1
Total churches, members, and denominations (mid-1995)	8	6,026	13,590	0.57	4	0	1	0	2	0	1
Total churches, members, and denominations (mid-2000)	8	6,200	14,021	0.63	4	0	1	0	2	0	1
Total churches, members, and denominations (mid-2025)	20	7,500	17,000	0.77	16	0	1	0	4	10	1

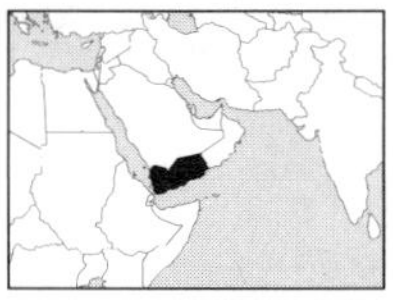

YEMEN

SECULAR DATA, AD 2000

STATE
Official name: Al-Jamhuriya al Yamaniya (The Republic of Yemen).
Short name: Yemen. **Adjective of nationality:** Yemeni, a Yemenite.
Flag: Red, white, and navy stripes.
Area: 472,099 sq. km. (182,278 sq. mi.).
Government: Multiparty republic with one legislative house, since 1990 (885 Rassid dynasty, 1517 Turkish rule, 1918 imamate, 1969 Marxist rule in South, 1974 military junta in North).
Legislature: Council of Representatives, 301 members.
Official language: Arabic.
Monetary unit: 1 Yemeni Rial (YRls) = 100 fils. **US$1=** YRls 133.82.
Chief cities: SAN'A 737,171; ADAN (Aden, Asashaab) 582,132; Ta'izz (Taiz) 307,264; Al-Hudaydah (Hodeida) 267,687; Al Mukalla 106,175.
Political divisions: 17 provinces.
Armed forces: 66,300.

DEMOGRAPHY
Population: 18,112,000.
Population density: 38.3/sq. km. (99.3/sq. mi.).
Under 15 years: 8,748,000.
Growth rate p.a.: 3.47% (births 43.34, deaths 8.72).
Mortality: Infant, per 1,000: 68.5; **Maternal per 100,000:** 1,400.0.
Life expectancy: 61 (male 60, female 61).
Household size: 5.6. **Floor area per person, sq.m:** 10.0.
Major languages: Arabic, Somali, Hindi, Persian in (North Yemen). Arabic, English, Hindi, Somali, Malay, Russian, Persian, Mahari (Mahri), Kharawi, Harsusi, Botahari, Sokotri, and numerous others in (South Yemen).
Urban dwellers: 38.00%. **Urban growth rate p.a.:** 5.6%.
Labor force: 26%.

ETHNOLINGUISTIC PEOPLES
89.3% Yemeni Arab; 3.7% Somali; 1.7% Sudanese Arab; 1.1% Arabized Black; 1.0% Indo-Pakistani.

ECONOMY
National income p.a. per person: US$259; **per family:** US$1,455.

EDUCATION
Adult literacy: 46% (male 68%, female 23%). **Schools:** 7,313.
Universities: 1. **School enrolment:** female/male: 39%/100%.

HEALTH
Access to health services: 38%. **Access to safe water:** 52%.
Hospitals: 75 (8 beds per 10,000). **Doctors:** 3,065.
Blind: 16,000. **Deaf:** 1,087,100. **Murder rate:** 1.
Lepers: 3,600. **Underweight prevalence under 5:** 39%.

LITERATURE
New book titles p.a.: 180 (10 p.a. per million). **Periodicals:** 0.
Newspapers: 3 dailies.

COMMUNICATION (per 1,000 people)
Phones: 12 (10% mobile). **Radios:** 48. **TV sets:** 243.
Daily newspaper circulation: 17. **Computers:** 25.

REFUGEES
Alien refugees from other countries: 53,400.

HUMAN LIFE AND LIBERTY (optimum condition=100.0%)
HDI: 36.1. **HSI:** 25.0. **HFI:** 15.0. **EFL:** 25.0.

Country Table 1. **Religious adherents in Yemen, AD 1900-2025.**

Year	1900		1970		mid-1990		Annual change, 1990-2000				mid-1995		mid-2000		mid-2025	
Name	Adherents	%	Adherents	%	Adherents	%	Natural	Conversion	Total	Rate	Adherents	%	Adherents	%	Adherents	%
Muslims	2,488,850	98.4	6,321,400	99.8	11,462,710	98.9	645,044	626	645,670	4.57	14,860,810	98.9	17,919,414	98.9	38,490,640	98.7
Hindus	2,800	0.1	4,000	0.1	80,000	0.7	4,502	-5	4,497	4.56	103,500	0.7	124,973	0.7	350,000	0.9
Christians	**4,500**	**0.2**	**2,100**	**0.0**	**22,700**	**0.2**	**1,277**	**-328**	**949**	**3.56**	**27,000**	**0.2**	**32,192**	**0.2**	**64,000**	**0.2**
PROFESSION																
crypto-Christians	0	0.0	1,797	0.0	18,500	0.2	1,041	9	1,050	4.60	24,000	0.2	29,000	0.2	60,000	0.2
professing Christians	**4,500**	**0.2**	**303**	**0.0**	**4,200**	**0.0**	**236**	**-337**	**-101**	**-2.71**	**3,000**	**0.0**	**3,192**	**0.0**	**4,000**	**0.0**
AFFILIATION																
unaffiliated Christians	0	0.0	120	0.0	1,525	0.0	86	-85	1	0.07	1,565	0.0	1,536	0.0	700	0.0
affiliated Christians	**4,500**	**0.2**	**1,980**	**0.0**	**21,175**	**0.2**	**1,192**	**-244**	**948**	**3.77**	**25,435**	**0.2**	**30,656**	**0.2**	**63,300**	**0.2**
Orthodox	0	0.0	0	0.0	8,500	0.1	478	-128	350	3.51	10,000	0.1	12,000	0.1	22,000	0.1
Independents	0	0.0	1,400	0.0	5,000	0.0	281	19	300	4.81	6,500	0.0	8,000	0.0	20,000	0.1
Roman Catholics	500	0.0	120	0.0	4,000	0.0	225	-25	200	4.14	5,000	0.0	6,000	0.0	13,000	0.0
Protestants	2,000	0.1	290	0.0	3,500	0.0	197	-99	98	2.49	3,760	0.0	4,476	0.0	8,000	0.0
Anglicans	2,000	0.1	170	0.0	175	0.0	10	-9	1	0.28	175	0.0	180	0.0	300	0.0
Trans-megabloc groupings																
Evangelicals	400	0.0	240	0.0	1,000	0.0	56	4	60	4.81	1,349	0.0	1,600	0.0	2,300	0.0
Pentecostals/Charismatics	0	0.0	1,400	0.0	5,600	0.1	315	-25	290	4.26	7,736	0.1	8,500	0.1	23,500	0.1
Great Commission Christians	**4,000**	**0.2**	**1,800**	**0.0**	**15,800**	**0.1**	**889**	**-168**	**721**	**3.83**	**19,000**	**0.1**	**23,012**	**0.1**	**50,000**	**0.1**
Nonreligious	0	0.0	1,800	0.0	16,500	0.1	928	-54	874	4.34	21,000	0.1	25,236	0.1	60,000	0.2
Atheists	0	0.0	400	0.0	6,000	0.1	338	-161	177	2.62	7,400	0.1	7,772	0.0	17,000	0.0
Jews	33,100	1.3	1,300	0.0	1,100	0.0	62	-63	-1	-0.12	1,100	0.0	1,087	0.0	500	0.0
Baha'is	0	0.0	300	0.0	700	0.0	39	-9	30	3.63	850	0.0	1,000	0.0	2,000	0.0
Jains	0	0.0	0	0.0	140	0.0	8	-2	6	3.47	170	0.0	197	0.0	500	0.0
Buddhists	0	0.0	0	0.0	70	0.0	4	-1	3	3.42	80	0.0	98	0.0	300	0.0
Sikhs	400	0.0	100	0.0	80	0.0	5	-3	2	2.05	90	0.0	98	0.0	60	0.0
Zoroastrians	350	0.0	600	0.0	0	0.0	0	0	0	0.00	0	0.0	0	0.0	0	0.0
World A (unevangelized persons)	2,406,030	95.1	5,065,280	80.0	7,301,700	63.0	410,854	-173,593	237,261	2.85	8,562,390	57.0	9,671,808	53.4	18,283,965	46.9
World B (evangelized non-Christians)	119,470	4.7	1,264,220	20.0	4,265,600	36.8	240,076	173,921	413,997	7.02	6,432,347	42.8	8,408,000	46.4	20,637,035	52.9
World C (Christians)	4,500	0.2	2,100	0.0	22,700	0.2	1,277	-328	949	3.56	27,000	0.2	32,192	0.2	64,000	0.2
Country's population	**2,530,000**	**100.0**	**6,331,600**	**100.0**	**11,590,000**	**100.0**	**652,207**	**0**	**652,207**	**4.57**	**15,021,738**	**100.0**	**18,112,000**	**100.0**	**38,985,000**	**100.0**

COLUMNS, ROWS.
For meanings and definitions, see Codebook (Part 3). Note that, by definition, total 'Christians' = professing + crypto-Christians, which also = affiliated + unaffiliated Christians, and also = Great Commission Christians + latent Christians. Percentages may not always total exactly, due to rounding.

CENSUSES.
1901 Census of the British Empire (Aden, total population 43,974): 76.4% Muslims, 9.0% Christians (3,969 persons), 7.0% Jews, 6.2% Hindus, 0.7% Parsis, 0.4% Jains, 0.2% Buddhists, 0.2% Sikhs. **8.II.1955** (Aden Colony, excluding Perim: population 138,441): 91.3% Muslims, 4.0% Christians (total 5,580), 3.5% Hindus, 0.6% Jews, 0.4% Parsis.

NOTES ON RELIGIONS
ATHEISTS. A small Communist party exists; membership negligible.
BAHA'IS. In 2 local spiritual assemblies (1964, 1973). Little change by 1997.
CHRISTIANS. Since they are not recognized by the state, all Christians exist as crypto-Christians whose presence is tolerated or ignored. Before 1967, Aden used to have thousands of South Indian Protestants teaching in its schools; though these all went at Independence in 1967, a number of Palestinian Arab Christians from Lebanon have replaced them. Although most Christians are expatriate Arabs, Indians and Europeans, there is a small number of Yemeni believers in the main churches.
CRYPTO-CHRISTIANS. Unorganized individual nationals in recognized churches. In addition, for some years Yemen has had a number of Palestinian Arab Christians from Lebanon teaching in schools.
INDEPENDENTS. Isolated Yemeni and other Arab radio believers (see Table 2).
JEWS. In 1948-51, over 50,000 Yemeni Jews emigrated to Israel. In the 1970s the last remnants also were emigrating.
MUSLIMS. 3 distinct groups: 55% Zaydis (a rural Shia sect), 40% urban-dwelling Sunnis (of the Shafiite rite), 5% Ishmaelites (Ismailis). Since 1946, there has been a small Ahmadiya community in Aden (Qadianis; HQ Rabwah, Pakistan). *Hajj pilgrims to Mecca.* (Including South Yemenis, about 10% of the whole); (1968) 31,489; (1969) 54,658; (1970) 50,269; (1971) 60,358; (1972) 60,250; (1973) 54,082; (1974) 75,557; North Yemen only (1975) 113,899; (1976) 61,110.

Great Commission Instrument Panel: status of Yemen (for explanation see start of Part 4)

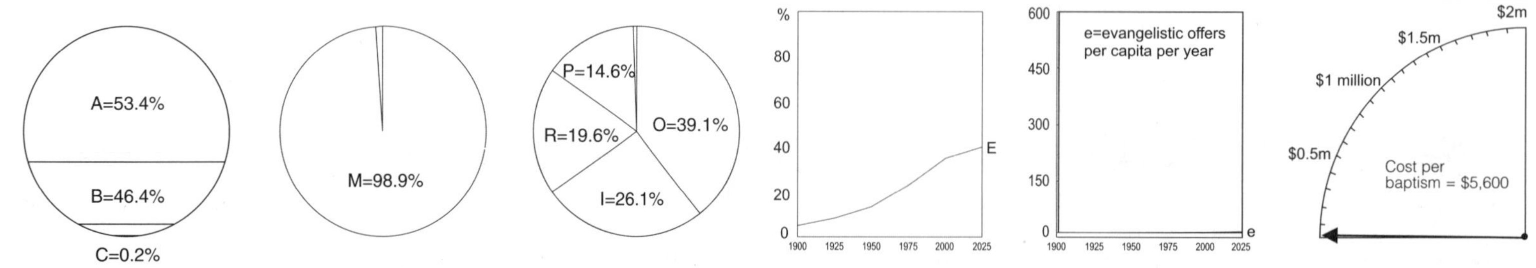

3 Worlds, AD 2000 | Religions, AD 2000 | Ecclesiastical blocs | Evangelization, 1900-2025 | Offers, 1900-2025 | Cost-effectiveness, AD 2000

Country status. Yemen is a desert country in western Asia on the Arabian peninsula bordered by the Gulf of Aden and the Red Sea. Oil is the most important export but fish, coffee, and cotton are also produced.

HUMAN LIFE AND LIBERTY

Human need and development. Yemen does not share the oil wealth of its neighbors in the peninsula, and as a result still remains an undeveloped country mired in poverty. The major economic resource is migration, mostly to other Islamic countries in Asia. The country has suffered at least 2 major civil wars and numerous coups, further depressing its living standards and quality of life. In the former British colony of Aden there are some vestiges of modernity, but the rest of the country has yet to emerge from the Middle Ages. Transportation, medical and

Country summary. **Worlds A, B, C by ethnolinguistic peoples, cities, and major civil divisions in Yemen.**

World	PEOPLES Num	Pop 2000	C%	Christians	E%	U%	Unevangelized	CITIES Num	Pop 2000	C%	Christians	E%	U%	Unevangelized	CIVIL DIVISIONS Num	Pop 2000	C%	Christians	E%	U%	Unevangelized
A	11	17,476,332	0.03	4,432	46	54	9,411,226	5	2,000,429	0.31	6,207	48	52	1,039,817	14	11,880,763	0.09	10,929	41	59	6,962,586
B	7	624,866	2.98	18,619	58	42	262,353	0	0	0.00	0	0	0	0	3	6,231,302	0.32	19,727	56	44	2,711,023
C	4	10,867	69.96	7,603	100	0	33	0	0	0.00	0	0	0	0	0	0	0.00	0	0	0	0
Total	**22**	**18,112,065**	**0.17**	**30,654**	**47**	**53**	**9,673,612**	**5**	**2,000,429**	**0.31**	**6,207**	**48**	**52**	**1,039,817**	**17**	**18,112,065**	**0.17**	**30,656**	**47**	**53**	**9,673,609**

educational services, and communications are primitive, where they exist. The dry harsh climate adds to the general misery of the people which is relieved only by the almost universal consumption of qat, a mild narcotic.

Human rights and freedoms. Concepts of human rights are relatively new to Yemen where medieval notions of torture, retaliation, and punishment hold sway. Prisoners are generally shackled in blood-money cases, and are required to compensate the families of those they have wronged. Over 4,000 persons are reported to be held in jails without any charges, but a certain number of them are pardoned at the end of every Ramadan. Third-country nationals are treated worse than Yemeni nationals, and are often jailed under false charges. The judges are not independent. Since unification, Yemenis have enjoyed greater freedom of speech. The government exercises control over the media through indirect means, such as subsidies or lower tariffs for government-friendly newspapers. Women suffer discrimination under certain Islamic codes.

Human environment. With little rainfall, Yemen has a permanent shortage of surface water. Land degradation is common in the wadis, or the dry river beds, where there is no plant cover. Tihama, a hot, sandy semidesert that separates the Red Sea coast from the less arid inland, is affected by soil salinization.

Muslims. Mullah (in window) hands down answers to petitions presented to him by crowd.

NON-CHRISTIAN RELIGIONS

Islam is the religion of all Yemeni nationals since the emigration of more than 50,000 Jews to Israel during 1948-51. Muslims are divided into 2 principal groups: Zaydis, a Shia sect, in the north, center and west; Sunnis of the Shafiite rite in the south and southwest; and a few Ismailis. The ancient royal family are Zaydis.

CHRISTIANITY

In its early history, Yemen was identified with the ancient biblical kingdom of Sheba. Over the centuries, it was the scene of a series of conflicts between Egyptians, Turks, and Arabians, as well as its own contesting imams. Christians are known to have flourished in North Yemen beginning around AD 500, but all were wiped out by Muslims within 2 centuries.

CATHOLIC CHURCH. Yemen is part of the vicariate of Arabia with headquarters in Abu Dhabi since 1974, having earlier been centered in Aden. The first Catholic priest, a Servite, entered Aden in 1841 and the prefecture of Aden was formed in 1854, becoming a vicariate in 1888. The vicariate was extended to cover all of Arabia in 1889.

Catholic Church. In Taiz, Indian missionary nun (from Mother Teresa's Missionary Sisters of Charity) treats some of the over 1,000 Muslim lepers.

A priest lived briefly in Hodeida towards the end of the last century, and another took up residence in 1963 for a few years in order to serve the Italian embassy and the European community.

In 1972 there were 87 baptized Catholics, all foreigners, served by Capuchins from Aden, who were unable to obtain permission to reside in North Yemen. In early 1973 the authorities officially invited Mother Teresa's Missionaries of Charity from India to take charge of a home for the aged and helpless built in the suburbs of Hodeida, and the first 5 sisters arrived in the country in August. The invitation was made through the USA-based Catholic Relief Services (CRS/USCC) which has been assisting Yemen since 1970. CRS was requested at the same time to seek personnel for other medical and educational posts, especially those financed by CRS and CONCERN, the latter being an Irish Catholic organization providing development assistance. A French White Father, a medical doctor by profession, also entered in 1973 for work at Sana hospital. Although not allowed to engage in proselytism, by 1975 there were 3 White Fathers and 20 sisters resident in Yemen. In addition to their house at Hodeida, the Missionaries of Charity opened another in Taiz in 1974 and a third house, in Sana, in 1975.

The Holy See has no diplomatic relations with Yemen in AD 2000, but has an apostolic delegate residing in Lebanon.

PROTESTANT CHURCHES. At the invitation of the Ministry of Health, the Southern Baptist mission opened a clinic in Taiz in 1964 and another in Jibla in 1968. The Baptists have had a staff of 15 missionaries all engaged in medical work, including surgery at their main hospital. The Red Sea Team (RSMT) entered Yemen in 1969 after persistent efforts. It also operates a clinic at Yarim in co-operating with government. There are a few Yemeni secret believers. A Lebanese Arab Baptist pastor built up a congregation of 12 believing men in Taiz before being expelled in 1974 and has since been replaced by another short-term Arab pastor.

Indigenous missions. There have been few missionaries sent out from Yemen since the church disappeared from there in the 6th century.

CHURCH AND STATE

According to the constitution of December 1970, Islam is the state religion, and the Sharia (Islamic law) is the basis of all legislation. The constitution was suspended following the coup d'etat of 13 June 1974, but the religious situation remains unaltered. In April 1975 the Yemen Arab Republic granted the 'right of return' to Jews who emigrated to Israel after the founding of the Jewish state in 1948.

BROADCASTING AND MEDIA

No Christian programming is permitted to be broadcast from within the country. Shortwave radio programs in Arabic can be received from FEBA (Seychelles) and HCJB (Ecuador). Over 166,000 have heard the 'Jesus' Film via radio broadcasts of the production.

FUTURE TRENDS AND PROSPECTS

Christianity is not expected to grow beyond 0.2% of the population before AD 2025.

Islam will likely continue to claim more than 97% of the population for the indefinite future. Immigrant non-Muslim laborers could cause this percentage to fluctuate.

BIBLIOGRAPHY

A guide to current research on Yemen. C. E. Farah. *Yemen guide series*, no. 3. Portland, OR: American Institute for Yemen Studies, Portland State University, 1987. 33p.

Analytical guide to the bibliographies on the Arabian Peninsula. C. L. Geddes. *Bibliographic series*, 4. Denver, CO: American Institute of Islamic Studies, 1974.

Bibliography on women in Yemen. J. Buringa. Ed., M. Colburn. *Yemen development series*, no. 2. Westbury, NY: American Institute for Yemeni Studies, 1992. 158p.

Brides for sale?: human trade in North Yemen. E. MacDonald. Edinburgh: Mainstream, 1988. 216p.

'Christianity in South–west Arabia,' J. S. Trimingham, chapter 8 in *Christianity among the Arabs in pre–Islamic times*, p.287–308. London: Longman, 1979.

Culture et institutions du Yemen. J. Chelhod. *Islam d'hier et d'aujourd'hui*, no. 25. Paris: G.–P. Maisonneuve et Larose, 1985. 443p.

Economy, society and culture in contemporary Yemen. B. R. Pridham (ed). London: Croom Helm Centre for Arab Gulf Studies, University of Exeter, 1985. 269p.

Egalität und Klassengesellschaft in Südarabien: anthropologische Untersuchungen zur sozialen Evolution. W. Dostal. *Wiener Beiträge zur Kulturgeschichte und Linguistik*, Bd. 20. Horn, Austria: F. Berger & Söhne, 1985. 484p.

Ethnographica jemenica: Auszüge aus den Tagebüchern Eduard Glasers mit einem Kommentar versehen. W. Dostal. Vienna: Verlag der Österreichischen Akademie der Wissenschaften, 1993. 276p.

Island of the phoenix: an ethnographic study of the people of Socotra. V. V. Naumkin. Reading, UK: Ithaca Press, 1993. 432p.

Libraries and scholarly resources in the Yemen Arab Republic. B. Croken, L. Swanson & M. Wenner. *Yemen guide series*, no. 2. DeKalb, IL: American Institute for Yemeni Studies, Northern Illinois University, 1985. 46p. (In English and Arabic).

'Religion and politics in South Arabia,' R. W. Stookey, in *Religion and politics in the Middle East*, p.349–62. M. Curtis (ed). Boulder, CO: Westview Press, 1981.

'Sokotra: die ehemals christliche Insel,' L. Brandl, *Oriens Christianus*, 57 (1973), 162–77.

Source book on Arabian Gulf States, Arabian Gulf in general, Kuwait, Bahrain, Qatar and Oman. S. Kabeel. Kuwait: Kuwait University, Libraries Department, 1975. 427p. (With over 3,000 item bibliography).

The answered prayer, and other Yemenite folktales. S. Gold & M. Caspi. Ill., M. Wunsch. Philadelphia: Jewish Publication Society, 1990. 76p. (Tales from the Jewish communities in Yemen).

The calligraphic state: textual domination and history in a Muslim society. B. M. Messick. *Comparative studies on Muslim societies*, no. 16. Berkeley, CA: University of California Press, 1993. 353p.

The Jews of Aden. R. Burman (ed). London: London Museum of Jewish Life, 1991. 48p.

The Jews of Yemen. S. D. Goitein, in A. J. Arberry (ed), *Judaism and Christianity*, vol. 1 of *Religion in the Middle East.* Cambridge, UK: Cambridge University Press, 1969, p.226–39

The Jews of Yemen in the nineteenth century: a portrait of a Messianic community. B. E. Klorman. *Brill's series in Jewish studies*, vol. 6. Leiden and New York: E. J. Brill, 1993. 217p.

'The mufti, the text and the world: legal interpretation in Yemen,' B. Messick, *Man*, n.s. 21, no. 1 (March 1986), 102–119.

The Yemens: The Yemen Arab Republic and The People's Democratic Republic of Yemen. G. R. Smith. *World bibliographical series*, vol. 50. Oxford, UK: CLIO Press, 1984. 184p. (No separate section on religion).

'Tribe, tribute, and trade: social class formation in highland Yemen.' R. N. Tutwiler. Ph.D. dissertation, State University of New York at Binghamton, Binghamton, NY, 1987. 592p.

'Tribes at the core: legitimacy, structure and power in Zaydi Yemen.' J. R. Meissner. Ph.D. dissertation, Columbia University, New York, 1987. 460p.

Tribes, government, and history in Yemen. P. Dresch. Oxford, UK: Clarendon Press, 1989. 440p.

Country Table 2. Organized churches and denominations in Yemen.

Official name (bold type = church with over 10% of all affiliated) 1	*Begun* 2	*Type* 3	*Counc* 4	*Congs* 5	*Adults* 6	*Affiliated 1970* 7	*Affiliated 1995* 8	*G%* 9	*Names, notes, and other statistics* (see Codebook, Part 3) 10
Anglican Church (D Cyprus & the Gulf)		A-Cen	aw...	2	56	170	175	0.05	In ECJME. Expatriates. International chs in Aden & Saana. Also M=CMS.
Baptist Church	1964	P-Bap	T....	1	30	50	60	0.73	M=Southern Baptist Convention (USA). Temporary Lebanese Arab pastors. 15f,1H.
Catholic Church (VA Arabia)	1841	R-Lat	P..L.	10	3,000	120	5,000	16.09	Decline from 9,640 RCs in 1961, then influx by 1990; all aliens (Cubans, Europeans, Indians).
Christian Brethren		P-CBr	x....	2	50	100	100	0.05	*Gospel Halls*. Indigenous congregations similar to Plymouth (Open) Brethren.
Church of South Arabia	1885	P-Uni	.....	3	200	100	300	4.49	1961 union of Ch of Scotland Mission, Ch of Denmark Mission. 1n,1f,1H,15Yy.
Coptic Orthodox Church	c1970	O-Cop	N....	10	3,000	–	7,000	42.50	Clandestine believers among the 45,000 Egyptian laborers and workers. Under P Alexandria.
Other independent fellowships	c1980	I-3cS	.....	30	600	–	1,000	6.67	Mainly Ethiopian refugees, Indian laborers, Somali secret believers.
Isolated radio churches	c1960	I-3rS	.....	500	3,000	1,400	5,500	5.63	Isolated Arab radio believers (mostly pupils, students) via TWR, RVOG, ICI, &c.
Red Sea Team	1952	P-Non	xC...	3	50	20	100	6.65	M=RSMT(UK, USA). Isolated local believers, adherents and transients.
Other Orthodox churches	c1975	O-	.....	6	1,600	–	3,000	5.00	Total 5, including Greek Orthodox Ch, Ethiopian Orthodox Ch, Russian Orthodox Ch.
Other Protestant denominations		P-	.....	5	1,700	20	3,200	0.05	Including: Evangelical Alliance Mission (TEAM), Sudan Interior Mission (8f), German churches.
Totals				**572**	**13,286**	**1,980**	**25,435**		

Churches, members, growth, 1900-2025	*Congs*	*Adults*	*Affiliated*	*G%*	*Total denominations*	*6 Megablocs:*	*O*	*R*	*A*	*P*	*I*	*m*
Total churches, members, and denominations (mid-1900)	30	2,100	4,500	-1.17	2		0	1	0	1	0	0
Total churches, members, and denominations (mid-1970)	55	936	1,980	-1.17	10		0	1	1	7	1	0
Total churches, members, and denominations (mid-1990)	500	11,100	21,175	12.58	19		6	1	1	10	1	0
Total churches, members, and denominations (mid-1995)	572	13,286	25,435	3.73	20		6	1	1	10	2	0
Total churches, members, and denominations (mid-2000)	600	16,000	30,656	3.80	20		6	1	1	10	2	0
Total churches, members, and denominations (mid-2025)	900	33,100	63,300	2.94	46		8	1	1	30	6	0

YUGOSLAVIA

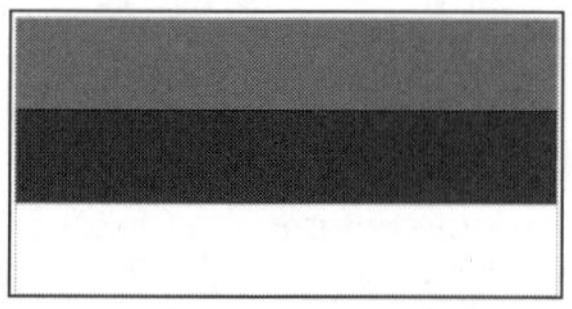

SECULAR DATA, AD 2000

STATE
Official name: Savezna Republika Jugoslavija (The Federal Republic of Yugoslavia).
Short name: Yugoslavia. **Adjective of nationality:** Yugoslavian.
Flag: Blue, white, and red stripes.
Area: 102,173 sq. km. (39,449 sq. mi.).
Government: Federal multiparty republic with two legislative houses, since 1991 (1918 united kingdom, 1921 absolute monarchy, 1941-45 German rule, 1945 republic (Communist).
Legislature: Chamber of Republics, 40 members; Chamber of Citizens, 138 members.
Official language: Serbo-Croatian.
Monetary unit: 1 Yugoslav new dinar (second) = 100 paras. **US$1=** 10.16 Yugoslav.
Chief cities: BEOGRAD (Belgrade) 1,232,000; Novi Sad 286,850; Pristina 263,257; Nis 258,298; Kragujevac 184,525.
Political divisions: 4 provinces.
Armed forces: 127,000.

DEMOGRAPHY
Population: 10,640,000.
Population density: 104.1/sq. km. (269.7/sq. mi.).
Under 15 years: 2,131,000.
Growth rate p.a.: 0.07% (births 12.71, deaths 10.09).
Mortality: Infant, per 1,000: 16.3; **Maternal per 100,000:** 25.0.
Life expectancy: 74 (male 71, female 76).
Household size: 3.0. **Floor area per person, sq.m:** 20.0.
Major languages: Serbo-Croatian, Albanian, Hungarian, Slovak, Romanian.
Urban dwellers: 59.85%. **Urban growth rate p.a.:** 1.0%.
Labor force: 40%.

ETHNOLINGUISTIC PEOPLES
62.0% Serb; 17.0% Kosovar (Gheg Albanian); 4.3% Montenegrin; 4.2% Hungarian; 3.0% Croat.

ECONOMY
National income p.a. per person: US$1,999; **per family:** US$5,999.

EDUCATION
Adult literacy: 93% (male 97%, female 89%). **Schools:** 4,996.
Universities: 146. **School enrolment:** female/male: 66%/63%.

HEALTH
Access to health services: 80%. **Access to safe water:** 85%.
Hospitals: 1,000 (55 beds per 10,000). **Doctors:** 22,000.
Blind: 10,000. **Deaf:** 630,100. **Murder rate:** 7.
Lepers: 100.

LITERATURE
New book titles p.a.: 3,190 (300 p.a. per million). **Periodicals:** 168.
Newspapers: 9 dailies.

COMMUNICATION (per 1,000 people)
Phones: 192 (9% mobile). **Radios:** 256. **TV sets:** 170.
Daily newspaper circulation: 90. **Computers:** 100.

HUMAN LIFE AND LIBERTY (optimum condition=100.0%)
HDI: 63.1. **HSI:** 56.0. **HFI:** 20.0. **EFL:** 35.0.

Country Table 1. Religious adherents in Yugoslavia, AD 1900-2025.

Year	*1900*		*1970*		*mid-1990*		*Annual change, 1990-2000*				*mid-1995*		*mid-2000*		*mid-2025*	
Name	*Adherents*	*%*	*Adherents*	*%*	*Adherents*	*%*	*Natural*	*Conversion*	*Total*	*Rate*	*Adherents*	*%*	*Adherents*	*%*	*Adherents*	*%*
Christians	**3,450,000**	**89.3**	**5,170,000**	**59.5**	**6,538,000**	**64.4**	**31,158**	**37,516**	**68,674**	**1.00**	**6,952,000**	**65.8**	**7,224,736**	**67.9**	**7,858,000**	**72.5**
PROFESSION																
crypto-Christians	0	0.0	964,500	11.1	0	0.0	0	0	0	0.00	0	0.0	0	0.0	0	0.0
professing Christians	**3,450,000**	**89.3**	**4,205,500**	**48.4**	**6,538,000**	**64.4**	**31,158**	**37,516**	**68,674**	**1.00**	**6,952,000**	**65.8**	**7,224,736**	**67.9**	**7,858,000**	**72.5**
AFFILIATION																
unaffiliated Christians	257,000	6.7	85,042	1.0	250,656	2.5	1,195	7,657	8,852	3.07	372,473	3.5	339,179	3.2	7,400	0.1
affiliated Christians	**3,193,000**	**82.6**	**5,084,958**	**58.5**	**6,287,344**	**61.9**	**29,963**	**29,858**	**59,821**	**0.91**	**6,579,527**	**62.3**	**6,885,557**	**64.7**	**7,850,600**	**72.4**
Orthodox	2,688,500	69.6	4,328,772	49.8	5,500,000	54.2	26,211	28,389	54,600	0.95	5,846,600	55.3	6,046,000	56.8	6,700,000	61.8
Roman Catholics	331,000	8.6	577,700	6.7	556,000	5.5	2,650	-3,594	-944	-0.17	458,847	4.3	546,557	5.1	750,000	6.9
Independents	0	0.0	34,800	0.4	125,000	1.2	596	5,404	6,000	4.00	164,050	1.6	185,000	1.7	260,000	2.4
Protestants	173,500	4.5	136,286	1.6	98,244	1.0	468	-392	76	0.08	101,550	1.0	99,000	0.9	130,000	1.2
Marginal Christians	0	0.0	7,000	0.1	7,800	0.1	37	43	80	0.98	8,180	0.1	8,600	0.1	10,000	0.1
Anglicans	0	0.0	400	0.0	300	0.0	1	9	10	2.92	300	0.0	400	0.0	600	0.0
Trans-megabloc groupings																
Evangelicals	37,500	1.0	27,000	0.3	28,400	0.3	135	1,265	1,400	4.09	36,110	0.3	42,400	0.4	72,000	0.7
Pentecostals/Charismatics	0	0.0	32,000	0.4	160,000	1.6	763	8,237	9,000	4.56	216,200	2.1	250,000	2.4	400,000	3.7
Great Commission Christians	**230,000**	**6.0**	**800,000**	**9.2**	**1,265,000**	**12.5**	**6,029**	**7,360**	**13,389**	**1.01**	**1,355,000**	**12.8**	**1,398,890**	**13.2**	**1,700,000**	**15.7**
Muslims	375,000	9.7	984,000	11.3	1,570,000	15.5	7,498	7,780	15,278	0.93	1,666,000	15.8	1,722,775	16.2	1,765,000	16.3
Nonreligious	5,000	0.1	1,470,000	16.9	1,477,050	14.5	7,039	-21,988	-14,949	-1.06	1,401,220	13.3	1,327,557	12.5	1,108,700	10.2
Atheists	3,000	0.1	1,058,000	12.2	560,000	5.5	2,669	-22,952	-20,283	-4.40	540,000	5.1	357,166	3.4	100,000	0.9
Jews	32,000	0.8	7,000	0.1	6,300	0.1	30	-368	-338	-7.41	3,000	0.0	2,918	0.0	2,300	0.0
Ethnoreligionists	0	0.0	500	0.0	1,600	0.0	8	2	10	0.58	1,630	0.0	1,696	0.0	3,000	0.0
Baha'is	0	0.0	200	0.0	1,200	0.0	6	6	12	0.97	1,250	0.0	1,321	0.0	3,000	0.0
Other religionists	0	0.0	1,300	0.0	1,850	0.0	9	4	13	0.69	1,900	0.0	1,981	0.0	4,000	0.0
World A (unevangelized persons)	200,980	5.2	1,077,729	12.4	893,728	8.8	4,265	-23,474	-19,209	-2.39	824,210	7.8	702,240	6.6	422,916	3.9
World B (evangelized non-Christians)	214,020	5.5	2,443,640	28.1	2,724,272	26.8	12,994	-14,042	-1,048	-0.04	2,790,593	26.4	2,713,024	25.5	2,563,084	23.6
World C (Christians)	3,450,000	89.3	5,170,000	59.5	6,538,000	64.4	31,158	37,516	68,674	1.00	6,952,000	65.8	7,224,736	67.9	7,858,000	72.5
Country's population	**3,865,000**	**100.0**	**8,691,370**	**100.0**	**10,156,000**	**100.0**	**48,417**	**0**	**48,417**	**0.47**	**10,566,804**	**100.0**	**10,640,000**	**100.0**	**10,844,000**	**100.0**

COLUMNS, ROWS.
For meanings and definitions, see Codebook (Part 3). Note that, by definition, total 'Christians' = professing + crypto-Christians, which also = affiliated + unaffiliated Christians, and also = Great Commission Christians + latent Christians. Percentages may not always total exactly, due to rounding.

CENSUSES.
31.I.1921: 46.8% Orthodox, 39.8% Roman Catholics (0.4% Greek Catholics), 10.9% Muslims, 1.8% Protestants, 0.5% Jews, 0.2% other religionists. **1928:** 47.3% Orthodox, 38.6% Roman Catholics (0.3% Greek Catholics), 11.5% Muslims, 2.0% Protestants, 0.6% Jews. **1931:** 48.7% Orthodox, 37.9% Roman Catholics, 11.2% Muslims, 1.7% Protestants, 0.5% Jews. **31.III.1953** (de jure): 41.3% Orthodox, 31.7% Roman Catholics, 13.3% termed 'atheists' (i.e. non-religious as well as atheists), 12.3% Muslims, 0.9% Protestants (157,702 persons), 0.4% 'other Christians' (other Protestants, Old Catholics, marginal Protestants; 61,274 persons), 0.015% Jews (2,565 persons).

NOTES ON RELIGIONS
CRYPTO-CHRISTIANS. (1970 only) Christians affiliated to churches but not known as such to the state, of 3 kinds: (1) unorganized individuals in the legal churches, (2) members of the many illegal or underground churches, and (3) isolated radio believers.
JEWS. Decline from 80,000 in 1925 due to mass murders under Nazi rule.
MUSLIMS. Sunnis (of the Hanafite rite). Mainly Bosnians (since the days of their conquest by Turkey); there are also many Albanians, Serbs, Turks, Gypsies and others. *Hajj pilgrims to Mecca.* (1970) 2,211; (1974) 1,845; (1975) 1,048; (1976) 855.
PENTECOSTALS/CHARISMATICS. Pentecostalism began around 1910, but has grown very slowly since. The Catholic Charismatic Renewal began in 1975 through a Yugoslav priest returning from Rome, with prayer groups in Jelsa (diocese of Hvar) and Zagreb university before the end of 1975. By 1977 several hundred clergy, nuns and seminarians were involved. By 1998 total members were still small, but Neocharismatics with no Western affiliations were becoming sizable.

Great Commission Instrument Panel: status of Yugoslavia (for explanation see start of Part 4)

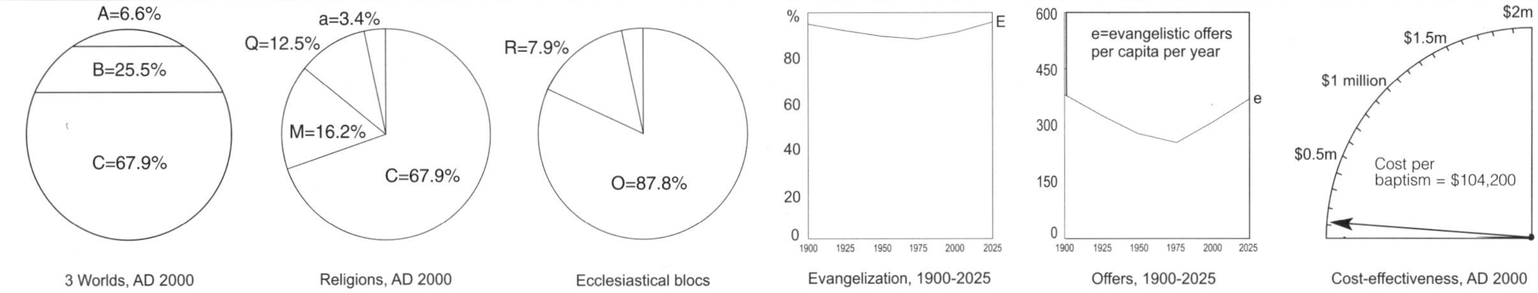

Country status. Yugoslavia, consisting of Serbia and Montenegro in AD 2000, is a country in the Balkan region. Landlocked Serbia occupies the central part of the Balkan Peninsula, and Montenegro forms a bridge southwestward from southern Serbia to the Adriatic Sea. The current federation is the third state to bear the name Yugoslavia, the first and second being the Kingdom of Yugoslavia (1929-World War II) and the Socialist Federal Republic of Yugoslavia (World War II-1991).

HUMAN LIFE AND LIBERTY

Human need and development. The Federal Republic of Yugoslavia, consisting of Serbia and Montenegro was proclaimed as an independent state with the adoption of a constitution on 27 April 1992. As with other former Communist nations, the move to a market economy driven by democratic political order has had drastic effects upon the people and governing bodies. While the lack of internal security, poor economic conditions, and other restructuring woes have had their effect on this new nation, the struggle has been exacerbated by the international isolation which was imposed upon the FRY in the early 1990s. This international boycott, ordered by the UN Security Council because of human rights abuses, forbad UN members every economic and trade activity with the Federal Republic. This lasted from 1992 to 1995. As a result of the boycott, gross domestic product spiraled down in the span of 2 years to one half of its level in 1990. By January 1994 the monetary and fiscal systems were devastated and per capita income had fallen to a level not seen since 1969. Unemployment reached 800,000 and several thousand employees were placed on leave of absence.

A study of the poverty rate prepared in 1994 indicated that 23.5% of the population (2.3 million people) subsisted at the poverty level, with less than a $120 monthly purchasing level. This was 3.1 times greater than that of 1990 with a 22% increase for the urban population.

In the 1970s Yugoslavia's education GDP expenditure was above the level of several western European nations, as well as proportionately higher than in countries of the same level of economic development, thus granting superior educational opportunities than afforded in other European nations. But because of the retarding economic activities of the 1980s and 1990s, GDP expenditure for education decreased and the once highly acclaimed system became in dire need of restructuring.

In Yugoslavia, 8 years of primary education commence at age 7. Four years of secondary education is also afforded between 2 types of schools: secondary schools which are precursors to university study, and vocational schools which lead to 2-year technical training degrees. Ironically, the FRY has the highest illiteracy rate in the world among countries having compulsory education. This rate hovers around 11%, ranging from 6 to 18%, in the Vojvodina and Kosovo regions respectively. Progress is however being made. As of 1994 the GDP expenditure had climbed to 5% and showed signs of climbing back to once exceptional levels.

Housing has also been drastically influenced by the economic upheaval. There are no credit or purchase incentives to buying homes. Apartment rates are high and few are in a position to purchase or rent by means of their personal incomes. Formerly, public housing was the norm, but now construction is almost completely privately financed and 90 % of all state-owned housing has now been privatized.

UN sanctions against the FRY were formally lifted in 1996. Despite this suspension, economic performance has been listless, and unemployment/underemployment remains high as the government has introduced no restructuring programs.

Human rights and freedoms. Until the secession of its 4 other republics, Yugoslavia permitted only one political party, the League of Communists of Yugoslavia (LCY). During the period of the secessions after 1990, branches of the LCY in Serbia and Montenegro adopted the designation Socialist. Other political parties are now permitted, but the Socialist parties remain the dominant force.

Constitutional guarantees are not enforced in the Federal Republic of Yugoslavia. Horrendous human rights abuses continue unabated. Minorities suffer the most but few are immune if they are cause for agitation. The police commit numerous extrajudicial beatings, killings, torture, and arbitrary arrests. Police repression has been directed against the ethnic Albanian population as well as the Muslims of Sandzak. Citizens who protest against the government are also victims of police brutality even though this voicing of opinion is protected by constitutional rights.

Article 21 clarifies the principle separation between the legislature, executive, and judiciary powers but the judicial system is in practice not independent of the government and does not ensure fair trials. The government's infringement negates these freedoms: the right to privacy, police and economic pressure used against the independent press and media, restricted freedom of assembly and association, freedom of worship by minority religions, freedom of movement. Discrimination against ethnic Albanians, Muslims, and Gypsy minorities is widespread.

Federal law provides for freedom of speech and of the press, but in reality the government strongly influences the media. Ethnic Albanian students staged a peaceful protest march in October 1997 only to be accused by state-controlled media as being proponents for violence. Police moved in with tear gas, water cannons, and truncheons on a peaceful march that was media-propagated as violent. Economic pressure is the main vehicle of influence used on the press.

There is no state religion, but the Serbian Orthodox Church receives access to state-run television for major events. Many religious communities are subject to harassment. A Roman Catholic parish in Kilna has the resources and permission to build a church for its 6,000 members, but the local Socialist Party of Serbia has continued to block construction.

Other abuses occurring include: the right of citizens to change their government, and discrimination based on sex and age. For instance, women are not recognized by the FRY as equal to men and domestic violence is extremely high with very few formal complaints ever filed with authorities.

Overall, freedoms that are expressed constitutionally are little more than an outward facade resulting in a bleak outlook for the future.

Human environment The international boycott has had a multifaceted impact upon the Federal Republic of Yugoslavia and the environment has not been immune from its effects. Economic facilities and equipment in various industries are either obsolete or in great disrepair, which has fostered an increase in breakdowns, industrial accidents, and employee hazards.

In an attempt to overcome the lack of energy sources, wood has now become a primary fuel source. This has led to an increase in the degree of deforestation and the fragility in the biological balance of forested areas. Waste water treatment facilities are not adequately developed in either residential areas or industrial sectors, in particular the mining industry. What treatment facilities do exist are seldom used due to the high cost of operation. Air pollution is consistently high with the main contributors being central heating, power plants and stations, individual home heating systems, industrial facilities, and motor vehicles.

In June 1993 the Integrated Policy for the Protection and Enhancement of the Environment was established. It defined the objectives, principles, and the other key elements of the protection policy that should be implemented. But to date, very little has been initiated.

NON-CHRISTIAN RELIGIONS

Islam. Islamization began in the 14th century and was pursued through the Turkish conquest of 1459 and the subsequent settlement of Turkish nomadic tribes and military colonies. Following the Muslim conquest, part of the peasant class, especially in Bosnia, and the Croatian and Bogomil (Cathari) feudal classes converted to Islam. Today, most Muslims are Bosnians living in Serbia or Montenegro.

Judaism has an ancient history in Yugoslavia. Before World War II there were 76,000 resident Jews, of whom some 60,000 died in concentration camps run by Nazis and their local collaborators. After the war about 8,000 emigrated to Israel. Yugoslavia's Jews are organized into 36 communities, united through the League of Jewish Communities of Yugoslavia, which was founded in 1919. There are no professional religious officials, the work of rabbis being done by the laity.

Montenegrin Orthodox Church. At Montenegro's ecclesiastico-historical capital of Cetinje, a church assembly at Cetinje Monastery & Royal Mausoleum.

CHRISTIANITY

The first Christians arrived in Dalmatia and Illyricum near the end of the Apostle Paul's ministry, being probably converted Jews of the Diaspora. Organized Christianity came to Yugoslavia from both Rome and Constantinople by the middle of the 4th century, and the influence of Byzantium grew in the 9th century through the missionary activity of Cyril and Methodius who translated the liturgy into the national language of the people. In 1054 the Great Schism separated the peoples on religious lines, creating divisions which continue until today.

At the same time the autocephalous Orthodox archdiocese of Ohrid was erected in southern Macedonia. A desire for greater autonomy stimulated the formation of an independent Serbian Orthodox Church in 1219 which continued its ties with the ecumenical patriarch, but in 1346 the Serbian archepiscopate was raised to a patriarchate at Pec to the dismay of Constantinople. The Turks favored the rival archepiscopate of Ohrid over the Pec patriarchate, suppressing the latter completely between 1463 and 1557. The 16th century saw the rise of Protestantism, Lutheranism from Germany, and Calvinism from Switzerland, although the Counter Reformation prevented Protestants from gaining a

Country summary. **Worlds A, B, C by ethnolinguistic peoples, cities, and major civil divisions in Yugoslavia.**

World	*PEOPLES* Num	Pop 2000	C%	Christians	E%	U%	Unevangelized	*CITIES* Num	Pop 2000	C%	Christians	E%	U%	Unevangelized	*CIVIL DIVISIONS* Num	Pop 2000	C%	Christians	E%	U%	Unevangelized
A	4	114,764	0.45	517	47	53	60,706	0	0	0.00	0	0	0	0	0	0	0.00	0	0	0	0
B	5	2,092,073	19.56	409,235	70	30	621,455	1	157,672	55.00	86,720	84	16	25,732	1	2,164,457	15.00	324,669	71	29	620,657
C	26	8,433,315	76.79	6,475,806	100	0	20,754	17	3,901,891	66.48	2,593,803	97	3	100,533	3	8,475,694	77.41	6,560,889	99	1	82,258
Total	**35**	**10,640,152**	**64.71**	**6,885,558**	**93**	**7**	**702,915**	**18**	**4,059,563**	**66.03**	**2,680,523**	**97**	**3**	**126,265**	**4**	**10,640,151**	**64.71**	**6,885,558**	**93**	**7**	**702,915**

major foothold. During the same period, in 1557 the Pec patriarchate was re-established and continued to function until 1766, when the ecumenical patriarch succeeded in having it revoked by edict of the sultan. In 1611 the first Uniates of the Byzantine rite passed over to the Roman Catholic Church.

ORTHODOX CHURCH. The Orthodox drive to free itself from the control of Constantinople resulted in 1832 in the granting of internal autonomy to the Serbian Orthodox Church, with the right to elect metropolitans and bishops, followed by the proclamation of complete autocephality and the election of its own patriarch in 1920.

Above. **Serbian Orthodox Church.** Monk at Studenica monastery in southern Serbia. *Below.* Patriarch Pavle in Belgrade.

Prior to World War I, Serbian Orthodox were divided into 3 autocephalous churches nominally under the patriarch of Constantinople: in Serbia, in Montenegro and Dalmatia, and in Austro-Hungary. The political unity achieved after the war stimulated efforts to unify the church; and the united Serbian Orthodox Church was formed in 1919, followed by the institution of the Serbian patriarchate in 1920.

The Serbian Orthodox Church has usually been considered the dominant church of the country. Although never the official state church, prior to World War II it was the church of the ruling dynasty and was widely acknowledged to be the traditional church of the people. The patriarch sat on the royal council, and many Orthodox priests were members of the national assembly. Orthodox holidays took precedence, and parliamentary oaths were celebrated according to Orthodox rites. In addition, the church owned large estates and received important subsidies for its schools and the salaries of its leaders. In Montenegro priests were recognized and paid as civil servants. All of these privileges were swept away by the Communist regime after World War II. Nevertheless, the Serbian Orthodox Church continues to exert an important influence in the country.

The patriarch as head of the church is archbishop of Pec and metropolitan of Belgrade-Karlovci, with his see in Belgrade; and the bishops of the eparchies of Dabar-Bosnia, Montenegro-Coastland, and Zagreb also bear the title of metropolitan. Eparchies outside Yugoslavia include those of Eastern America and Canada (with see in Cleveland, Ohio); Mid-West America (Chicago); Western America (Alhambra, California); Western Europe and Australia (London); Budim (Szentendre, Hungary); and Timisoara (Romania).

The church's main legislative and administrative organs are: (1) the Holy Archiepiscopal Council, composed of the patriarch and all diocesan bishops, which is the supreme legislative and juridical authority; (2) the Holy Archiepiscopal Synod, composed of the patriarch and 4 diocesan bishops, which is the supreme executive authority; (3) the High Ecclesiastical Tribunal, composed of 3 bishops, which is the church's highest court (although appeals may be made to the Holy Archiepiscopal Council); (4) the Patriarchal Council; and (5) the Patriarchal Administrative Board. Each eparchy or diocese in turn, in addition to its bishop, has an Eparchy Ecclesiastical Court, Eparchy Council, and Eparchy Administrative Board.

A striking feature of the church's life is the large variety of church newspapers and journals. These include *Pravoslavni Misionar* (The Orthodox Creed), *Glasnik* (The Messenger), *Pravoslavni Misionar* (The Orthodox Missionary), *Svetosavsko Zvonce* (The Bell of St Sava), *Bogoslovlje* (Divinity), *Vesnik* (The Messenger), *Pravoslavna Misao* (Orthodox Thought), and *Teoloski Pogledi* (Theological Views).

Other Orthodox bodies in Yugoslavia include the Romanian Orthodox Church with 30 parishes in the northeast, Russian Orthodox Church with one parish in Belgrade, and sizeable Albanian Orthodox and Bulgarian Orthodox communities.

CATHOLIC CHURCH. Catholicism in Communist Yugoslavia did not present a uniform outward appearance. In Slovenia it had been under Austrian influence, while on the Dalmatian coast Venetian influence was predominant (although there existed also a secular tradition of resistance by priests against Italian control). In Croatia proper secular nationalism played a major role. The east and south of the country had only 3 dioceses and an apostolic administration. Thus in the former republics of Serbia and Macedonia, it was possible to speak of Catholics of the diaspora, given the fact that they consisted mostly of small minority groups of largely Croatian background. One of the most important of these communities is still the 5,000 inhabitants of the little town of Janjevo, in the autonomous province of Kosovo (diocese of Skopje), who are all Catholics descended from Croatian immigrants of 6 centuries ago. Nevertheless 80% of the Catholics of the diocese of Skopje are Albanians. Other Albanians living dispersed in numerous Yugoslavian towns have generally remained faithful to both their Christian and Albanian traditions. Of note also are the Byzantine-rite Catholics, descendants of Orthodox, who emigrated to Croatia in the 16th century and passed over to the Roman Catholic Church in 1611.

In general one can say that Vatican II has split the Catholic community, with ecclesiastics now divided into progressivist and conservative wings. The episcopate remains for the most part traditionalist and protective of its authority, in part due to conservatism.

The Holy See has diplomatic relations with Yugoslavia and in AD 2000 is represented to government and the Catholic hierarchy by a pro-nuncio residing in Belgrade.

Independents. Group of young Christian activists climb hill then pray and intercede for embattled city of Prizren, Kosovo.

PROTESTANT CHURCHES. The principal Protestant tradition is Lutheranism, which began during the 16th-century Reformation but later suffered severe persecution in the Counter Reformation. The period of tolerance proclaimed by the Austro-Hungarian emperor Joseph II permitted the re-establishment of Lutheran communities which remained largely under the Hungarian Evangelical Church until World War I. In 1918 the Evangelical Church of Yugoslavia came into existence, comprising all but Slovak Lutherans, and this was renamed the German Evangelical Church in Yugoslavia in 1933. Lutheran unity disintegrated during World War II, and the churches were reconstituted as separate entities after 1945. Lutherans are today divided into 4 separate ethnic denominations: (1) the Slovak Evangelical Christian Church, centered in Jovi Sad among descendants of immigrant farmers from Slovakia, whose supreme administrative and legislative authority is vested in a synod of 96 members, chaired jointly by a bishop and a lay-president, and whose theological students are trained in Czechoslovakia and West Germany; (2) the Evangelical Christian Church in Slovenia, with its headquarters in Lendava and the majority of its parishes in the Prekmurje region, which served as a Lutheran refuge during the Counter Reformation; (3) the Evangelical Church in Croatia, Bosnia and Herzegovina, and Vojvodina, with its see at Zagreb; and (4) the Evangelical Church in Serbia, centered in Subotica, which is composed mostly of Hungarians.

The Reformed Christian Church in Yugoslavia also owes its origin to the Reformation, when Calvinism gained a foothold among Croatians and Hungarians in Baranja and Slavonia. Disbanded under Turkish rule, the church was re-established under the Austro-Hungarian empire as part of the Reformed Church of Hungary. Autonomy was proclaimed in 1920 when Yugoslavia was created as a separate state. The Reformed community is still mostly of Hungarian background. The church is organized into 3 seniorates (Backa, Banat, and Baranja-Slavonia) each composed of several parishes. The supreme legislative body is the synod with 2 presidents (a bishop and a layman), with the synodal council acting ad interim. Clergy are educated abroad in Austria and Hungary.

Of the many new Protestant denominations established over the past hundred years, the most successful has been the Christian Adventist Church. Adventists began work in Banat, Backa, Slovenia, Bosnia, and Croatia shortly after the turn of the century, forming their first community in Belgrade, Serbia in 1909 and Prilep, Macedonia in 1923. The church is now organized into 4 districts, with its central headquarters in Belgrade. Educational institutions include a higher divinity school in Rakovica near Belgrade, with 70 students, and a secondary religious school at Marusevac near Varazdin, with 120 students.

Many Pentecostal bodies are active, the largest being the Church of God in Serbia; and there are also a number of other small Protestant denominations: Brethren, Baptists, Nazarenes, Methodists, and others.

INDEPENDENT CHURCHES. This more recent megabloc has large numbers of overseas pentecostals and others.

There has also been a long Old Catholic tradition, although seriously fragmented by the breakup of the Communist state. Reform movements out of Roman Catholicism began in 1919 resulting in the formation of the Croatian Old Catholic Church by 1923 which joined the Utrecht Union of Old Catholic Churches. Prior to World War II internal conflicts produced a division between the Croatian Old Catholic Church and the Croatian National Old Catholic Church. A series of further schisms from the former resulted in the creation of Old Catholic churches in Slovenia in 1946, in Serbia and Vojvodina in 1954, and in Bosnia and Herzegovina in 1965. In 1954 the Union of Old Catholic Churches in Yugoslavia was formed in Belgrade to provide a degree of unity for the divided churches, although only 3 of the 5 denominations have joined: Croatian Nationals, Serbians, and Slovenians. There are no Old Catholic religious schools in Yugoslavia, clergy being trained in Switzerland and Germany. With the breakup of Yugoslavia there are only a handful of Old Catholics left in the present republic.

INDIGENOUS MISSIONS. Christians were sent out from Serbia shortly after the gospel arrived there in the early Christian centuries. Missionary activity increased along with influence from Constantinople. After Cyril and Methodius more missionaries were sent to surrounding countries. This continued through the 20th century, even under Communist rule. In the 1990s Serbian Orthodox missionaries form the bulk of the foreign missionary force sent out from Yugoslavia.

Independents. Charismatics preparing for a mass baptism in Serbia.

CHURCH AND STATE

The constitution of the former Republic of Yugoslavia promulgated on 21 February 1974 proclaimed equality of rights and duties for all citizens without any discrimination especially due to religion (Article 154). Article 174, which was devoted to religious questions, stipulated: 'The manifestation of religion is free; it is the personal affair of each individual. Religious communities are separate from the State; they are free as far as the exercise of religious affairs and worship are concerned. Religious communities may establish confessional schools only for the training of priests. It is anti-constitutional to abuse religion and religious activities by using them for political purposes. The social community may accord material aid to religious communities. Religious communities may have, within the limits fixed by the law, a right of ownership over property.' These 2 articles were reproduced without change from the previous constitutions.

The situation did not remain static throughout the whole period of Communist rule. One can in fact distinguish 4 successive phases. The first, from 1945 to 1950, was characterized by opposition and serious tension between church and state, due principally to the policy of agrarian reform, nationalization and suppression of former privileges. Those most affected were the Catholic Church and the Islamic community. Beginning in 1950, a period of transition ensued during which, although antireligious campaigns continued (especially in 1952 and 1957-58 against Catholics), there was a progressive improvement of relationships between government and Orthodox and Muslims. Following the promotion to the cardinalate of msgr Stepinac, accused by the regime of collaboration with the Ustachis (those seeking the creation of an independent Croatian state) during World War II, Yugoslavia broke off diplomatic relations with the Vatican in 1952. A law concerning religious communities was adopted in 1953 which took up again and considered more fully various matters in the constitution of 1946, thereby providing an opportunity for the state to show that it had a positive attitude towards religion. This law of 1953 expired in 1970 and religious affairs were relegated to the competence of the republics.

The third period began during the 1960s, and became much more evident after 1967, leading to a phase of normalization. It was characterized especially by improvement of relations between the state and the Catholic Church, facilitated by the death of cardinal Stepinac in 1960 and the Vatican's change of attitude towards questions of peace, the Third World and Communism. A protocol was signed between the Holy See and Yugoslavia in 1966 which gave official recognition to the socialist system of government and repudiated the use of religion for political purposes. This was followed in 1970 by the visit of president Tito to the Vatican and by the re-establishment of diplomatic relations, making Yugoslavia and Cuba the only Communist countries maintaining official relations with the Vatican.

The fourth phase, one characterized by a hardening of attitude on the part of the authorities, dates from 1972. The 'Take-Charge' campaign launched in 1971 by the Communist League, which was centered on the purification of party leadership in several republics (Croatia in 1971, Serbia and Slovenia in 1972), as well as the battle against nationalism and liberalism, did not spare the religious milieu, either Orthodox or Catholic. While in no sense returning to the systematic persecution of the earlier period, repression continued to express itself concretely through seizures of newspapers, imprisonment of priests and laity, and loss of jobs for teachers known for their religious convictions. Party leaders criticized the church for having taken advantage of the 'euphoria of nationalism and liberalism' to mix in purely political matters, and this also created fear among the faithful, in some cases leading to conflict. The hierarchies of the Catholic and Serbian Orthodox churches made known their views through direct representation to the authorities in power.

A final phase began after the collapse of the Communist regime. A new constitution was adopted on 27 April 1992. In it, Article 18 states: (1) Church and State shall be separate. (2) Churches shall be free and equal in conducting religious affairs and in the performance of religious rites. As such there is no official state religion but preferential treatment is given to the Serbian Orthodox Church. Access to state run television is afforded the SOC while no other religious organization has been granted this amenity. Article 43 states: (1) Freedom of religion, public or private profession of religion, and performance of religious rites shall be guaranteed. And (2) No one shall be obliged to reveal his religious beliefs. Unfortunately these provisions have in practice been ignored by the Serbian government regime.

INTERDENOMINATIONAL ORGANIZATIONS

The Ecumenical Council of Churches in Yugoslavia was formed in 1968 and counts in its membership the 3 Yugoslav churches belonging as full members to the WCC (Serbian Orthodox, Lutheran, Reformed) and 3 others. There is also a loose Federation of Protestant churches; and the Catholic Episcopal Conference maintains a Commission for Ecumenism. Catholic/Serbian Orthodox relations are still difficult, due to the unresolved problem of the Uniate churches.

BROADCASTING AND MEDIA

The government Jugoslovenska Radiotelevizija permits the broadcasting of occasional Orthodox and Catholic church services. From abroad, Protestant programs are beamed in over Europe 1 in Serbo-Croatian for 15 minutes on Wednesdays, and by TWR (Monaco) for one hour 15 minutes a week in Serbo-Croatian and 15 minutes in Serbian on Saturdays. Radio Vatican beams in Catholic programs in Croatian and Slovenian, each for one hour 45 minutes a week. IBRA programs can be heard over local Serbian stations in Sombor, Temerin, Kragujevac, Subotica, Zrenjanin.

FUTURE TRENDS AND PROSPECTS

The nonreligious and atheists, near 30% of the population in 1970, will probably decline to only 11% by 2025. These losses will be made up by gains among Christians, growing from 60% to over 72% in the same period.

Muslims will likely continue as a significant minority at 17%. Christianity could grow to 80% of the population by AD 2050.

BIBLIOGRAPHY

'A history of Baptists in Yugoslavia, 1862–1962.' J. D. Hopper. Ph.D. dissertation, Southwestern Baptist Theological Seminary, Fort Worth, TX, 1977. 180p.

'A history of the Congregational and Methodist Churches in Bulgaria and Yugoslavia.' P. B. Mojzes. Ph.D. dissertation, Boston University, Boston, 1965. 674p.

'Changing functions of religion in a socialist society: the case of Catholicism in Yugoslavia,' S. Vrcan, *Social compass*, 28, 1 (1981), 43–61.

Church and state in Yugoslavia since 1945. S. Alexander. Cambridge, UK: Cambridge University Press, 1979. 351p.

'Church–state relations in Yugoslavia since 1967,' S. Alexander, *Religion in Communist lands*, 4, 1 (Spring 1976), 18–27.

'Denominational affiliation in Yugoslavia, 1930–1989,' S. Flere, *East European quarterly*, 25 (June 1991), 145–65.

Forced conversions of Croatians to the Serbian faith in history: paper presented to the III World Congress for Soviet and East European Studies, October 30–November 4, 1985, Washington, DC. I. Omrcanin. Washington, DC: Samizdat, 1985. 84p.

God and the villagers: a story of Montenegro. L. A. Vucinich. Buffalo, NY: Buffalo State College Foundation, 1974. 325p.

In the claws of the red dragon: ten years under Tito's heel. W. Gruber. Toronto: St. Michaelswerk, 1988. 208p.

'Islam in Yugoslavia today,' S. Ramet, *Religion in Communist lands*, 18, 3 (Autumn 1990), 226–35.

Istorija Srpske Pravoslavne Crkve (History of the Serbian Orthodox Church). D. M. Slijepcevic. Munich, 1962–1966. 2 vols.

Krsna slava u Srba: porijeklo, obred, zdravice. D. M. Kalezic. *Slovesna sfera*, 5. Belgrade: Sfairos, 1989. 138p. (In Serbo-Croatian).

'La situación religiosa en Yugoslavia,' G. Canders, *Revista de estudios politicos*, 161 (1968), 259–67.

Montenegrin social organization and values: political ethnography of a refuge area tribal adaptation. C. Boehm. *AMS studies in anthropology*, no. 1. New York: AMS Press, 1983. 184p.

Nations and nationalities of Yugoslavia. K. Joncic (ed). Belgrade: Medjunarodna politika, 1974. 549p.

Opci sematizam katolicka crkve u Jugoslaviji, cerkerv Jugoslaviji, 1974 (General survey of the Catholic Church in Yugoslavia). Zagreb: Biskupska konferencija Jugoslavije, 1975. 1,166p. (Parts in Croat, Slovenian, Latin, English, French, German).

'Present day Serbian Orthodoxy,' S. Flere, *Occasional papers on religion in Eastern Europe*, 8 (November 1988), 1–11.

'Recent developments in church–state relations in Yugoslavia,' C. Criic, *Religion in Communist lands*, 1, 1 (Spring 1973), 6–8.

'Recherches nouvelles sur les monuments chrétiens de Serbie et du Monténégro,' I. Nilolajevic, in *Actes du XIe Congrès International d'Archéologie Chrétienne, 3*, p.2441–2462. N. Duval (ed). *Studi di Antichità Cristiana*, 41. Rome: Ecole Française, Pontificio Ist di Archeologia Chr, 1989.

'Religion and nationality in Yugoslavia,' P. Ramet, in *Religion and nationalism in Soviet and East European politics*, p.299–327. P. Ramet (ed). 2nd ed. Durham, NC: Duke University Press, 1989.

'Religion in Yugoslavia: the background,' J. Broun, *America*, 165 (November 30, 1991), 414–16.

Religions in Yugoslavia: historical survey, legal status, church in socialism, ecumenism, dialogue between Marxists and Christians, etc. Z. Frid (ed). Zagreb: Binoza, 1971. 168p.

Serbian Church life. R. M. French. London: Society for Promoting Christian Knowledge, 1942. 64p.

'Skopje from the Serbian to Ottoman Empires: conditions for the appearance of a Balkan Muslim city.' E. Fraenkel. Ph.D. dissertation, University of Pennsylvania, Philadelphia, 1986. 311p.

'Some social expectations of Christians in Yugoslavia with primary emphasis on the Protestant churches,' N. G. Shenk, *Occasional papers on religion in Eastern Europe*, 1 (November 1981), 1–10.

Srpska Pravoslavna Crkva 1920–1970 (The Serbian Orthodox Church, 1920-1970). Belgrade: Holy Episcopal Synod, 1971. 539p.

'The Gypsy population of Yugoslavia,' T. P. Vukanovic, *Journal of the Gypsy Lore Society*, 42, 1/2 (1963), 10–27.

'The position of believers as second–class citizens in Socialist countries: the case of Yugoslavia,' Z. Roter, *Occasional papers on religion in Eastern Europe*, 9 (June 1989), 1–17.

The position of the Church in Yugoslavia. R. Vidic. Belgrade: Izdavac, 1962.

'The Serbian Orthodox Church,' P. Ramet, in *Eastern Christianity and politics in the twentieth century*, p.232–48. P. Ramet (ed). *Christianity under stress*, 1. Durham, NC: Duke University Press, 1988.

'The Serbian Orthodox Church: yesterday, today, tomorrow,' V. Tomic, *Religion in Communist dominated areas*, 25 (Summer 1986), 120–29.

'The social role of religion in contemporary Yugoslavia.' N. G. Shenk. Ph.D. dissertation, Northwestern University, Evanston, IL, 1987. 264p.

Uloga crkve u starijoj istoriji srpskog naroda (The role of the church in the early history of the Serbian people). B. Djurdjev. *Biblioteka drustvo i religija.* Sarajevo: Svjetlost, 1964. 239p.

'Yugoslavia,' A. Fiamengo, in *Western religion: a country by country sociological enquiry*, p.587–99. H. Mol (ed). The Hague: Mouton, 1972.

Yugoslavia. J. J. Horton. 2nd ed. *World bibliographical series*, vol. 1. Oxford, UK: CLIO Press, 1990. 304p. (See especially 'Religion,' p.72f, and 'Nationalities,' p.97–103).

Yugoslavia: a comprehensive English–language bibliography. F. Friedman (ed). Wilmington, DE: Scholarly Resources, Inc., 1993. 547p. (Section on 'Religion,' p.453–61).

Yugoslavia: the church and the state. London: Information Office, Embassy of the Federal People's Republic of Yugoslavia, 1953. 92p.

'Yugoslavie aujourd'hui: une église entre l'est et l'ouest,' *Information catholique internationale* (Paris), 400 (January 1972), 7–15.

Country Table 2. **Organized churches and denominations in Yugoslavia.**

Official name (bold type = church with over 10% of affiliated) 1	*Begun* 2	*Type* 3	*Counc* 4	*Congs* 5	*Adults* 6	*Affiliated 1970* 7	*Affiliated 1995* 8	*G%* 9	*Names, notes, and other statistics* (see Codebook, Part 3) 10
SERBIA									
Albanian Orthodox Church		O-Alb	C....	15	50,000	25,000	100,000	0.05	Related to long-suppressed church in Albania.
Bulgarian Orthodox Church		O-Bul	Mwc..	30	20,000	15,000	35,000	0.05	*Balgarskata Pravoslavna Crkva.* Under P Sofia. Bulgarian residents.
Catholic Church in Serbia:	c 250	R-LEr	B.B.R	171	323,200	546,350	430,147	-0.95	*Rimokatolicka Crkva.* C=16-0-32. 2p,4q,8s. 127n 30x 39m 168w 3463Yy
M Beograd (Belgrade)	c 850	R-Lat	Bs	15	5,000	19,994	8,600	-3.32	Serbia. Serbian. 5 parishes in the capital. W=10%. 8n 11x 12m 41w 100Yy
D Subotica	1923	R-Lat	Bs	116	255,200	411,356	333,312	-0.88	Serbia (Vojvodina). Croatian and Hungarian. 94n 14x 21m 109w 2535Yy
D Zrenjanin (Banat)	1923	R-Lat	Bs	40	63,000	115,000	88,235	-1.05	Serbia. Croatian,Hungarian,Slovenian. HQ Zrenjanin. 25n 5x 6m 18w 828Yy
Christian Adventist Ch in Serbia	1909	P-Adv	x....	69	2,923	20,000	4,500	-5.79	*Adventisticka Crkva. Seventh-day Adventists, Yugoslavian UC.*
Christian Nazarene Community	1871	P-Hol	x....	80	1,500	5,000	4,000	-0.89	From Hungary. Severe persecution up to 1920. Vojvodina; HQ Novi Sad. Declining.
Church of England (D Gibraltar)	c1850	A-plu	awc..	2	150	400	300	-1.14	English-speaking expatriates in Belgrade, Zagreb. Good relations with Serbian OC.
Church of God in Serbia		P-Pe2	.....	30	5,000	7,000	8,000	0.05	*Crkva Bozja u SFRJ.* HQ Vinkovci. Many north of Belgrade; Croatia, Macedonia.
Ch of the Spirit (Foot-washing)	c1930	I-3oW	.....	90	58,600	7,000	75,000	9.95	*Kristova Duhovna Crkva 'Nogoprani'. HQ vrdnik.* Baptism in name of Jesus only.
Ch of the Spirit (Infant-baptizing)	c1930	I-3oW	.v...	60	2,500	5,000	5,500	0.38	*Kristova Duhovna Crkva 'Malkrsteni'. HQ Subotica.* Indigenous Pentecostal church.
Ch of United Brethren in Christ in S	c1900	P-LuR	Rwc..	24	1,000	1,900	2,000	0.21	*Ceskobratrska Cirkev Ev.* Slovaks: 71% Serbia, 21% Croatia, 8% Slovenia. HQ Zagreb.
Evangelical Church in PR of Serbia	c1800	P-Lut	l....	9	2,800	6,000	5,500	-0.35	*Ev Crkva u NR Srbiji.* A=1945. Diaspora Hungarian farmers. 1967, joined SECC.
Free Brethren Congregations	c1905	I-CBr	xv...	25	3,400	10,000	9,500	-0.20	*Slobodna Braca.* 2 rival groups, Open and Closed. 1952, applied to join WCC.
Greek Orthodox Church	c 50	O-Gre	C....	2	5,000	2,000	9,000	6.20	Greek expatriates from Greece, and many Arabs.
Gypsy Evangelical Movement	c1913	I-3pE	.....	100	6,000	2,000	10,000	6.65	Loosely-organized networks of churches. M=GGMS(Switzerland).
Isolated radio churches	c1950	I-rad	.....	900	15,000	500	20,000	15.90	Isolated radio believers in non-religious families across nation, mostly aged 12-25.
Methodist Church in Serbia	c1890	P-Met	Vwc.W	14	1,200	4,000	2,000	-2.73	*Metodisticka Crkva. Provisional Annual Conf.* C&S Europe Central C, UMC(USA). 6n.
Old Cath Ch of Serbia & Vojvodina	1954	I-OCa	U....	3	900	2,000	1,900	-0.20	Separately founded. One vicar administrator. 3 priests.
Pentecostal Chs of Christ in Serbia	c1910	I-3pW	Z....	47	4,000	5,000	6,150	0.83	*Kristova Pentekostna Crkva.* Till 1954, Religious Ch of Christ. German. 54n:1s(18).
Reformed Christian Ch in Serbia	c1550	P-Ref	RWC.W	110	8,500	26,716	21,250	-0.91	*Református Keresztyén Egyház.* Scattered diaspora Hungarians. A=1920. 26n,1s.
Romanian Orthodox Church		O-Rum	Cwc..	50	20,000	10,000	50,000	0.05	*Biserica Ortodoxa Romana.* Under P Bucharest. In northeast. HQ Vojvodina. 30nx.
Russian Orthodox Church		O-Rus	Mwc..	10	7,000	3,000	15,000	0.05	Parish in Belgrade. Under jurisdiction of P Moscow. Russians, Ukrainians.
Serbian Orthodox Church:	c 150	O-Ser	CWc.W	1,115	2,595,000	4,047,281	5,359,000	1.13	*Srpska Pravoslavna Crkva.* P since AD 1346. 13 Dioceses, 36 bishops,1j,6s.
P Beograd (Belgrade) & Karlovci	c 350	O-Ser	Cp	85	140,000	217,994	289,000	1.13	Patriarchal D. 1725, union P Karlovci. 2s(292).
D Backa	c1550	O-Ser	Cb	100	223,000	349,000	462,000	1.13	HQ Novi Sad, northwest of Belgrade.
D Banat	1931	O-Ser	Cb	120	294,000	458,000	607,000	1.13	HQ Vrsac, on border with Romania.
D Branicevo	c 350	O-Ser	Cb	110	307,000	478,280	633,000	1.13	HQ Pozarevac, southeast of Belgrade.
D Nis	c 250	O-Ser	Cb	260	553,000	860,803	1,140,000	1.13	*Pravoslavne Eparhije Niske.* HQ Nis.
D Raska-Prizren	c1150	O-Ser	Cb	60	164,000	255,363	338,000	1.13	Present name from 1789. HQ Prizren. 1s(129).
D Sabac-Valjevo	1831	O-Ser	Cb	140	307,000	478,518	633,000	1.13	HQ Sabac; area west of Belgrade.
D Skopie (part only)	c1250	O-Ser	Cb	20	62,000	98,829	131,000	1.13	Half old diocese is now in Macedonian Orthodox Church.
D Sumadija (Shumadia)	1947	O-Ser	Cb	140	348,000	542,093	718,000	1.13	HQ Kragujevac. SE of Belgrade. Serb heartland.
D Timok	1833	O-Ser	Cb	80	197,000	308,401	408,000	1.13	HQ Zajecar, northeast of Nis on Bulgaria border.
Slovak Evangelical Christian Church	c1680	P-Lut	LWC.W	52	28,700	53,170	41,000	-1.03	*Slovacká ev-kr AV Cirkev.* Rural emigrants from Slovakia, c1800; A=1800. 20n,P=30%.
Union of Baptist Churches in Serbia	1875	P-Bap	T....	51	1,619	7,000	2,000	-4.89	*Savez Baptisticka Crkva u SFRJ. Baptist Union* (1923). M=ABCUSA,SBC. 23n,100Y.
United Jehovah's Witnesses in Serbia	1925	m-Jeh	x....	45	5,000	7,000	8,180	0.63	*Verska Zajednica Jehovinih Svedoka.* HQ Zagreb. Scriptures from Bible Society. 532Y.
Other Protestant denominations		P-	.....	80	3,000	3,000	5,000	0.05	Total about 40 (see list below), mainly incognito or underground bodies.
Other independent Catholic churches		I-CCa	.....	8	700	200	1,000	0.05	Including: Liberal Catholic Ch.
Other Orthodox churches		O-	.....	20	3,000	1,000	4,000	0.05	Including: Ukrainian Orthodox Ch, Macedonian OC, Armenian AC, ROCOR.
Subtotals				**3,212**	**3,175,692**	**4,822,517**	**6,234,927**		
MONTENEGRO									
Albanian Orthodox Church		O-Alb	C....	4	1,000	500	2,000	0.05	*AOC.* Albanians resident but members of home church.
Catholic Ch in Montenegro:		R-Lat	B....	45	19,700	31,350	28,700	0.05	Long history of being harassed, repressed. 18n 13x 13m 91w 380Yy
D Kotor	c 950	R-Lat	Bs	26	8,700	11,356	12,700	0.45	Montenegrins and Croatians. 12n 3x 3m 50w 190Yy
AD Bar (Antivari)	c 850	R-Lat	bs	19	11,000	19,994	16,000	-0.89	*Nadbiskupija Bar.* Montenegrins, Croats, Albanians. 6n 10x 10m 41w 190Yy
Church of God in Yugoslavia		P-Pe2	.....	2	500	1,000	1,000	0.05	*COGY.* Classical Pentecostals.
Greek Orthodox Church		O-Gre	C....	1	500	300	1,000	0.05	Greek residents and labor migrants, some Arabs.
Gypsy Evangelical Movement		I-3pE	.....	50	2,000	1,100	5,000	0.05	*GEM.* Many bands and communities of Gypsies. Harassed continuously.
Isolated radio churches	c1950	I-3rW	.....	300	10,000	2,000	20,000	9.65	During Communist times, large numbers of fervent believers.
Macedonian Orthodox Church		O-Mac	c....	1	800	200	1,600	0.05	*MOC.* Macedonians.
Montenegrin Autocephalous Orth Ch	1766	I-Ser	.....	20	5,000	–	10,000	44.54	HQ Cetinje.Liquidated 1920, revived 1993, elected a Montenegrin, A. Abramovic, as patriarch.4n
Montenegrin Orthodox Church	1219	O-Ser	C....	650	172,000	223,491	250,000	0.45	*SOC, Metropolitanate of Montenegro and Coastland.* Under P Belgrade. Montenegrins, Serbs.
Pentecostal Chs of Christ in Yugoslavia	c1930	P-Pe2	Z....	20	900	500	1,300	3.90	*PCCY.*
Union of Baptist Chs in Yugoslavia	c1900	P-Bap	T....	10	400	1,000	1,000	0.00	*UBCY.*
Other Orthodox churches		O-	.....	30	10,000	1,000	20,000	0.05	About 5, including Bulgarian Orthodox Ch, Russian Orthodox Ch, Ukrainian Orthodox Ch.
Other Protestant churches	c1980	P-	.....	10	1,000	–	3,000	6.67	Total 3 other small denominations.
Subtotals				**1,143**	**223,800**	**262,441**	**344,600**		
Totals for Yugoslavia				**4,355**	**3,399,492**	**5,084,958**	**6,579,527**		

Churches, members, growth, 1900-2025	*Congs*	*Adults*	*Affiliated*	*G%*	*Total denominations*	*6 Megablocs:* *O*	*R*	*A*	*P*	*I*	*m*
Total churches, members, and denominations (mid-1900)	1,100	2,175,000	3,193,000	0.67	17	7	2	1	6	1	0
Total churches, members, and denominations (mid-1970)	3,027	3,463,944	5,084,958	0.67	63	17	2	1	30	12	1
Total churches, members, and denominations (mid-1990)	3,500	3,249,000	6,287,344	1.07	101	26	2	1	55	16	1
Total churches, members, and denominations (mid-1995)	4,355	3,399,492	6,579,527	0.91	101	26	2	1	55	16	1
Total churches, members, and denominations (mid-2000)	4,500	3,558,000	6,885,557	0.91	102	26	2	1	56	16	1
Total churches, members, and denominations (mid-2025)	5,000	4,056,000	7,850,600	0.53	254	30	2	1	80	140	1

NOTES ON TABLE ABOVE

NATIONAL COUNCILS (Column 4, 5th letter).

E = Serbian Evangelical Alliance (SEA).

K = Yugoslav Ecumenical Council (Ecumenical Council of Churches in Yugoslavia, ECCY).

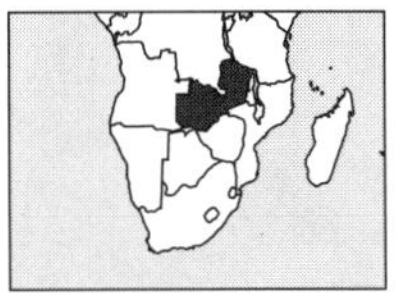

ZAMBIA

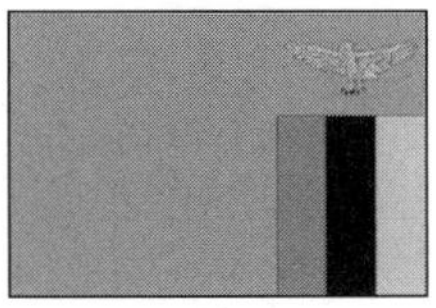

SECULAR DATA, AD 2000

STATE
Official name: The Republic of Zambia.
Short name: Zambia. **Adjective of nationality:** Zambian.
Flag: Green field with red, black, and orange bars on right surmounted by eagle.
Area: 752,614 sq. km. (290,586 sq. mi.).
Government: Multiparty republic, since 1990 (1888 British claims, 1924 British protectorate of Northern Rhodesia, 1953 in Federation of Rhodesia and Nyasaland, 1964 Independence, 1972 one-party republic).
Legislature: National Assembly, 155 members.
Official language: English.
Monetary unit: 1 Zambian kwacha (K) = 100 ngwee. **US$1=** K 2,020.
Chief cities: LUSAKA 1,695,000; Ndola 496,520; Kitwe 446,244; Chingola 221,605; Kabwe (Broken Hill) 219,712.
Political divisions: 9 provinces.
Armed forces: 22,000.

DEMOGRAPHY
Population: 9,169,000.
Population density: 12.1/sq. km. (31.5/sq. mi.).
Under 15 years: 4,331,000.
Growth rate p.a.: 2.05% (births 40.57, deaths 17.85).
Mortality: Infant, per 1,000: 74.0; **Maternal per 100,000:** 940.0.
Life expectancy: 42 (male 41, female 42).
Household size: 4.4. **Floor area per person, sq.m:** 6.4.
Major languages: English, Bemba, Tonga, Nyanja (Chichewa), Lunda, Lamba, Ila, Mambwe, Lozi, Ngoni, Afrikaans, Greek, Gujarati, Chinese, Shona, and over 30 other tribal languages.
Urban dwellers: 44.53%. **Urban growth rate p.a.:** 3.3%.
Labor force: 33%.

ETHNOLINGUISTIC PEOPLES
19.2% Bemba; 6.2% Zambezi Tonga; 5.2% Lozi (Rotse, Tozvi); 5.0% Nsenga (Senga); 4.8% Plateau Tonga.

ECONOMY
National income p.a. per person: US$399; **per family:** US$1,759.

EDUCATION
Adult literacy: 78% (male 85%, female 71%). **Schools:** 3,995.
Universities: 2. **School enrolment:** female/male: 58%/66%.

HEALTH
Access to health services: 75%. **Access to safe water:** 43%.
Hospitals: 965 (29 beds per 10,000). **Doctors:** 713.
Blind: 38,000. **Deaf:** 548,000. **Murder rate:** 9.
Lepers: 50,000. **Underweight prevalence under 5:** 28%.

LITERATURE
New book titles p.a.: 1,100 (120 p.a. per million). **Periodicals:** 56.
Newspapers: 2 dailies.

COMMUNICATION (per 1,000 people)
Phones: 8 (4% mobile). **Radios:** 139. **TV sets:** 64.
Daily newspaper circulation: 13. **Computers:** 3.

REFUGEES
Alien refugees from other countries: 125,400.

HUMAN LIFE AND LIBERTY (optimum condition=100.0%)
HDI: 36.9. **HSI:** 32.0. **HFI:** 22.5. **EFL:** 41.0.

Country Table 1. **Religious adherents in Zambia, AD 1900-2025.**

Year	1900		1970		mid-1990		Annual change, 1990-2000				mid-1995		mid-2000		mid-2025	
Name	Adherents	%	Adherents	%	Adherents	%	Natural	Conversion	Total	Rate	Adherents	%	Adherents	%	Adherents	%
Christians	**2,000**	**0.3**	**2,786,000**	**66.5**	**5,900,800**	**81.5**	**157,322**	**7,739**	**165,061**	**2.50**	**6,707,670**	**81.9**	**7,551,406**	**82.4**	**13,703,000**	**87.8**
PROFESSION																
professing Christians	**2,000**	**0.3**	**2,786,000**	**66.5**	**5,900,800**	**81.5**	**157,322**	**7,739**	**165,061**	**2.50**	**6,707,670**	**81.9**	**7,551,406**	**82.4**	**13,703,000**	**87.8**
AFFILIATION																
unaffiliated Christians	0	0.0	633,456	15.1	474,800	6.6	12,659	-10,206	2,453	0.50	549,092	6.7	499,326	5.5	393,000	2.5
affiliated Christians	**2,000**	**0.3**	**2,152,544**	**51.4**	**5,426,000**	**75.0**	**144,663**	**17,945**	**162,608**	**2.66**	**6,158,578**	**75.2**	**7,052,080**	**76.9**	**13,310,000**	**85.2**
Roman Catholics	1,000	0.1	922,890	22.0	2,350,000	32.5	62,654	9,346	72,000	2.71	2,677,471	32.7	3,070,000	33.5	5,600,000	35.9
Protestants	1,000	0.1	294,554	7.0	1,940,000	26.8	51,723	24,777	76,500	3.38	2,308,304	28.2	2,705,000	29.5	4,997,000	32.0
Independents	0	0.0	392,800	9.4	1,180,000	16.3	31,460	8,540	40,000	2.96	1,369,563	16.7	1,580,000	17.2	3,000,000	19.2
Marginal Christians	0	0.0	452,100	10.8	380,000	5.3	10,131	-10,563	-432	-0.11	375,040	4.6	375,680	4.1	400,000	2.6
Anglicans	0	0.0	85,000	2.0	150,000	2.1	3,999	3,001	7,000	3.90	170,000	2.1	220,000	2.4	500,000	3.2
Orthodox	0	0.0	5,200	0.1	6,000	0.1	160	-120	40	0.65	6,200	0.1	6,400	0.1	10,000	0.1
doubly-affiliated	0	0.0	0	0.0	-580,000	-8.0	-15,463	-17,037	-32,500	4.55	-748,000	-9.1	-905,000	-9.9	-1,197,000	-7.7
Trans-megabloc groupings																
Evangelicals	800	0.1	205,000	4.9	832,000	11.5	22,182	9,218	31,400	3.25	1,237,200	15.1	1,146,000	12.5	2,250,000	14.4
Pentecostals/Charismatics	0	0.0	240,000	5.7	1,447,800	20.0	38,600	18,320	56,920	3.37	1,769,173	21.6	2,017,000	22.0	3,904,000	25.0
Great Commission Christians	**1,900**	**0.3**	**500,000**	**11.9**	**1,122,000**	**15.5**	**29,914**	**8,554**	**38,468**	**2.99**	**1,311,000**	**16.0**	**1,506,682**	**16.4**	**2,967,000**	**19.0**
Ethnoreligionists	748,000	99.7	1,361,200	32.5	1,100,000	15.2	29,327	-8,372	20,955	1.76	1,220,000	14.9	1,309,548	14.3	1,266,000	8.1
Baha'is	0	0.0	10,300	0.3	120,000	1.7	3,170	1,074	4,244	3.07	137,000	1.7	162,443	1.8	360,000	2.3
Muslims	0	0.0	13,000	0.3	80,000	1.1	2,133	-338	1,795	2.04	86,340	1.1	97,949	1.1	180,000	1.2
Nonreligious	0	0.0	10,000	0.2	19,000	0.3	507	-70	437	2.09	20,600	0.3	23,366	0.3	60,000	0.4
Hindus	0	0.0	7,700	0.2	10,000	0.1	267	-13	254	2.29	11,240	0.1	12,537	0.1	25,000	0.2
Atheists	0	0.0	0	0.0	5,800	0.1	155	-20	135	2.11	6,300	0.1	7,147	0.1	13,000	0.1
Buddhists	0	0.0	0	0.0	2,400	0.0	64	8	72	2.65	2,750	0.0	3,117	0.0	7,000	0.0
Jews	0	0.0	800	0.0	1,000	0.0	27	-8	19	1.72	1,100	0.0	1,186	0.0	2,000	0.0
World A (unevangelized persons)	729,750	97.3	418,941	10.0	159,258	2.2	4,237	-8,938	-4,643	-3.37	139,286	1.7	110,028	1.2	124,928	0.8
World B (evangelized non-Christians)	18,250	2.4	984,469	23.5	1,178,942	16.3	31,413	1,141	32,554	2.49	1,346,394	16.4	1,507,566	16.4	1,788,072	11.4
World C (Christians)	2,000	0.3	2,786,000	66.5	5,900,800	81.5	157,322	7,739	165,061	2.50	6,707,670	81.9	7,551,406	82.4	13,703,000	87.8
Country's population	**750,000**	**100.0**	**4,189,411**	**100.0**	**7,239,000**	**100.0**	**192,972**	**0**	**192,972**	**2.39**	**8,193,351**	**100.0**	**9,169,000**	**100.0**	**15,616,000**	**100.0**

COLUMNS, ROWS.
For meanings and definitions, see Codebook (Part 3). Note that, by definition, total 'Christians' = professing + crypto-Christians, which also = affiliated + unaffiliated Christians, and also = Great Commission Christians + latent Christians. Percentages may not always total exactly, due to rounding.

CENSUSES.
None have enumerated religion for African; censuses have been taken for non-Africans only. **15.X.1946** (Europeans): 20,815 Christians (15,199 Protestants and Anglicans, 5,283 Roman Catholics, 134 Orthodox, 199 others), 656 Jews, 229 nonreligious and agnostics, 83 other religionists. **15.X.1946** (Coloured): 552 Christians (294 Protestants, 258 Roman Catholics), 37 nonreligious, 18 Muslims, 73 other religionists. **15.X.1946** (Asiatics): 768 Hindus, 330 Muslims, 18 other religionists. **8.V.1951** (Europeans): 33,571 Christians, 766 Jews, 2,742 other religionists. **8.V.1951** (Coloured): 839 Christians, 74 Muslims, 77 nonreligious, 80 other religionists. **8.V.1951** (Asiatics): 1,658 Hindus, 837 Muslims, 12 others. **8.V.1956** (non-Africans): 62,236 Christians, 3,763 Hindus, 2,878 nonreligious, 1,724 Muslims, 974 Jews, 729 other religionists (28 Spiritists). **26.IX.1961** (non-Africans): 65,280 Christians, 5,490 Hindus, 3,820 nonreligious, 2,390 Muslims, 850 Jews, 6,530 other religionists.

NOTES ON RELIGIONS
BAHA'IS. Rapid growth from 19 local spiritual assemblies (1964) to 69 (1973); in 1970 there were 3,250 adult believers. This early growth was followed by a consolidation of new organization resulting in 105 LSAs (1996).
ETHNORELIGIONISTS. Although tribal religions are also known as traditional religions, they are far from static; since the beginning of colonial times they have embodied and still embody a vast and continuing amount of non-Christian religious innovation, primarily in the form of possession healing movements. It is estimated that over 15% of the modern Zambian population (including numerous Christians) adhere to and are active in the many such movements. Peoples with over 60% traditionalists in 1995: Mashi Bushmen (90% animist), Nyiha (60%), Kwengo (90%). Most other tribes have sizeable numbers of animists also.
HINDUS. 70% of all Indians in Zambia (Gujaratis).
INDEPENDENTS. In about 75 denominations in 1995 (see Table 2).
MARGINAL CHRISTIANS. Jehovah's Witnesses have grown rapidly since their arrival in 1911. By 1943 there were 2,784 active adult publishers; by 1948 peak publishers were 11,606; by 1959, 28,000 active publishers with a total community of 79,500 African and 5,000 European adherents; by 1963, 30,728 peak publishers; and by 1973, 52,339 peak publishers, over 130,000 adult members, 194,133 adult attenders at the annual Memorial services, a total affiliated community of over 500,000. By 1995 these totals had increased to: 84,592 peak publishers, 2,034 congregations, 108,017 Bible studies, 370,622 Memorial attenders. It is estimated that at least one in every 4 adult Zambians (25% in 1970 or 12% in 1995) has been involved in Jehovah's Witnesses (Watch Tower) at some time in his life, either as member or strong sympathizer or regular attender at meetings, i.e. a total professing or self-identifying community including children and infants of around 1,070,000 from 1970-1995. Of these, 50,000 were in independent Watchtower groups (not under Jehovah's Witnesses). At least 280,000 have left the main body and are now affiliated with or adherents of other churches, but it also has successfully won back many from independent Watchtower. This leaves around 750,000 still professing some relation to Jehovah's Witnesses.
MUSLIMS. About 2,000 Indo-Pakistanis, and African Muslims (Sunnis, of the Shafiite rite) from neighboring countries. Hajj pilgrims to Mecca. (1976) 4 persons.
NONRELIGIOUS. Mainly Chinese technicians from People's Republic of China, also Europeans.
PENTECOSTALS/CHARISMATICS. The Catholic Charismatic Renewal was not formally organized by 1975, but many charismatics existed including the archbishop of Lusaka who was widely known as a charismatic healer. The First Inter-Diocesan Conference on the Charismatic Renewal was held in Lusaka in mid-1978, with 200 attenders including the archbishop, 20 priests and 45 sisters. Subsequently he was removed from his post by the Vatican for allegedly introducing pagan practices. By 1996 the CCR was still continuing its rapid growth.

Country status. Zambia is a landlocked country in central Africa bounded by Angola, Zaire, Tanzania, Malawi, Zimbabwe, and Namibia. Its chief exports are copper, cobalt, lead, and zinc.

HUMAN LIFE AND LIBERTY

Human need and development. Zambia is a wealthy country, but its landlocked status is a limiting factor in development. Although designated by the United Nations in 1995 as a least developed country, it is more prosperous than all African countries except 7: Gabon, Mauritius, Namibia, Congo, Cameroon, Senegal, and Ivory Coast. Average life expectancy remains low at 42, but the illiteracy rate has fallen to 22%. A host of tropical diseases, many debilitating but some lethal, continue to pose a burden on the exiguous medical services, and contribute to the low longevity. Malnutrition generally exacerbates the effects of these diseases. In the towns, shortage of housing is a major problem adversely affecting sanitation, availability of water, and living conditions. Nevertheless, Zambia has escaped the kind of political and social upheavals that have rocked neighboring countries, and this has helped to consolidate gains in the economic sector.

Human rights and freedoms. The vestiges of president Kaunda's long authoritarian rule continued to surface under his successor, Frederick Chiluba, who is nevertheless committed to rule of law. A state of emergency was declared briefly in 1993 in response to a purported plot by members of the former ruling party. This resulted in arbitrary detention of opposition leaders and their torture at the hands of the police. During the emergency there was an increase in self-censorship by the press. Constitutional and legal reforms promised by the new president have been beset by political squabbles. In other areas, there are signs of genuine progress toward full freedom, marred only by occasional bureaucratic actions that overstep the boundaries of civil liberties.

Great Commission Instrument Panel: status of Zambia (for explanation see start of Part 4)

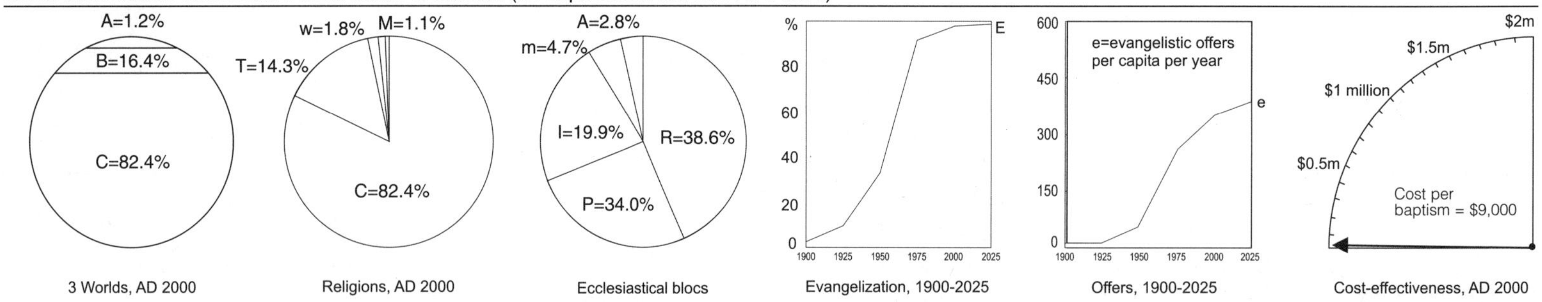

Human environment. Zambia is a poacher's paradise. As a result the black rhino population has been reduced from 65,000 in 1970 to less than 4,000 and the elephant herd has been reduced from over 100,000 in 1970 to about 30,000. The miombo woodland areas around towns are being destroyed by forest fires and the practice of shifting cultivation. Overcrowding of the rangelands by cattle reared by traditional herders is leading to land degradation.

NON-CHRISTIAN RELIGIONS

Traditional African religions are based on belief in a supreme being called Lesa or Mulungu, in ancestor veneration, and in the practice of magic and witchcraft. They are especially strong in the rural areas. Some 15% of the population are still traditionalists, numbering over 60% in the Luvale, Mashi, and Subia tribes. As with all African tribal religions, these are far from static; over the last century they have embodied a vast and continuing among of non-Christian religious innovation. Spirit-possession healing movements or cults known by various names are common among Zambian peoples: Baami (among the Ila), Wamowa and Awayambo (Lamba), Wamukamwami (Lenji), Bamoba and Biciwila (Ambo), Muba (Lozi), Mahamba (Luvale, Luchazi), Ihamba (Ndembu) and Ngulu (Bemba). Zambia has been the meeting place of 2 spirit-possession movements owing their origin to the last century: the Mashave possession cults of the Shona moving northward, and the eastward movement of the Mahamba cults from Angola. The Mchape (Medicine) witchcraft eradication movement which began in Nyasaland in 1930 also spread to Northern Rhodesia.

Hinduism has a small community restricted to urban areas and largely composed of Asians.

Islam has grown dramatically since 1970 primarily due to immigration. Islam has had little success in appealing to the African population, except among the Lozi.

Baha'i has a growing following among Africans, increasing from 10,300 in 1970 to 137,000 in 1995.

Catholic Church in Zambia, Archdiocese of Lusaka. Archbishop Emmanuel Milingo of Lusaka, leader of Zambia's Catholic pentecostals, greets congregation after mass in Lusaka Cathedral. After receiving a vision recently, he found he had charismatic gifts of healing and exorcism, which he then exercised widely; but in 1978 he was forbidden by the Vatican to continue exercising such gifts.

CHRISTIANITY

CATHOLIC CHURCH. Early contacts were made in the 18th century by Portuguese priests. In 1879 the Jesuit Zambezi Mission arrived, and in 1882 Jesuits went to Barotseland; but these attempts all failed. Catholicism came to Zambia definitively with the arrival of the first White Fathers in 1891. The Kasama mission was opened in 1913 and another at Lusaka in 1927, and in 1935 the Episcopal Conference of Northern Rhodesia was founded. The hierarchy was established in 1959 and the first African bishop consecrated in 1963. The Zambian church is divided into 2 archdioceses, Kasama (with 2 suffragan dioceses) and Lusaka (with 5 suffragan dioceses).

The Holy See has diplomatic relations with Zambia and in AD 2000 is represented to government and the Catholic hierarchy by a pro-nuncio residing in Lusaka.

MARGINAL CHURCHES. Jehovah's Christian Witnesses, as they term themselves and are correctly termed, first entered Northern Rhodesia from Nyasaland in 1911, and have had extraordinary success since, and massive influence on Zambia. Over 25% of the population in 1970 or over 12% in 1995 (one million Zambians) are estimated to have been involved in Jehovah's Witnesses at one time or another in their lives, either as members or regular attenders or strong sympathizers. Of these, large numbers have subsequently defected to join Catholic, Protestant or African separatist churches. Each year around 370,000 adults are present at the Memorial of Christ's Death held in April. The large headquarters at Bethel, Kitwe, contains massive archives. At various times in their history, governments have acted against the Witnesses, and all foreign missionaries were deported in 1969.

PROTESTANT CHURCHES. David Livingstone of the LMS journeyed through Zambia on his way to Luanda as early as 1853, and abortive attempts to open work were made by the LMS in 1859 and the Paris Mission in 1878. The first permanent Christians arrived in 1884 and the first permanent Paris Mission station was established in 1885. The LMS, Scottish Presbyterians and British Methodists soon followed, and in 1965 the churches created through the activity of these 4 missions joined together to form the United Church of Zambia. This is now the country's largest Protestant denomination. Three other early arrivals have constituencies of similar size: the Reformed Church, Christian Brethren, and Seventh-day Adventists. Other early and important groups include the Churches of Christ and the Evangelical Church, the latter being related to the Africa Evangelical Fellowship. Some 45 different Protestant denominations are active in Zambia.

Although all primary schools now belong to the state, the Protestant churches continue to operate 10 private secondary schools and are tending to concentrate more of their resources on new educational approaches to teaching religion in the schools.

INDIGENOUS CHURCHES. There are about 70 active African indigenous churches at the present time. Many of these have been brought to Zambia from other countries: South Africa, Malawi, Zimbabwe, and Zaire. Zimbabwe has been the principal source, but the AME Church, a Black denomination from the USA, has the largest constituency. Of groups indigenous to Zambia, the best-known has been the Lumpa Church founded by Alice Lenshina in 1954. By 1958 this church had a total community of 100,000, but it later clashed with the Zambian government and was banned in 1965. Other independent denominations have been formed through schisms within the Brethren, Catholic, Reformed, and United churches.

OTHER CHURCHES. Anglican pioneers of the UMCA entered Zambia in 1909. The church is divided into 3 dioceses and has been part of the Church of the Province of Central Africa since 1965.

One of Zambia's largest denominations is the New Apostolic Church, with world headquarters in Dortmund (Germany), which is in the Catholic Apostolic tradition with over 8 million followers across the world. Outside Germany itself, the Zambia community is their third largest, after that in South Africa.

Lumpa (Visible Salvation) Church. *Top.* Founding prophetess, Alice Lenshina. *Lower.* Banner at headquarters, destroyed and banned in 1965, but still active 30 years later.

Orthodoxy is represented by several small Greek and Syrian Orthodox congregations.

Indigenous missions. Zambian Christians have been involved in foreign missions for several decades, though the vast majority serve in surrounding African countries.

Renewal movements. In the 1990s the Pentecostal/Charismatic Renewal continued to spread rapidly across most older churches, and numbered over 2,017,000 adherents (of whom 15% Pentecostals, 21% Charismatics, and 63% Independents).

Charismatic revivalists in United Church of Christ in Zambia, 1994.

CHURCH AND STATE

The 1964 constitution, Article 13, guarantees freedom of conscience. Article 14.1 specifies that this includes for everyone 'freedom of thought and religion, freedom to change his religion or belief, and freedom, either alone or in community with others, and both in public and in private, to manifest and propagate his religion or belief in worship, teaching, practice and observance'. The constitution defines in Article 14.3 what is meant by freedom of religious teaching; and

Country summary. **Worlds A, B, C by ethnolinguistic peoples, cities, and major civil divisions in Zambia.**

	PEOPLES							CITIES							CIVIL DIVISIONS						
World	Num	Pop 2000	C%	Christians	E%	U%	Unevangelized	Num	Pop 2000	C%	Christians	E%	U%	Unevangelized	Num	Pop 2000	C%	Christians	E%	U%	Unevangelized
A	5	18,449	0.34	62	45	55	10,151	0	0	0.00	0	0	0	0	0	0	0.00	0	0	0	0
B	31	1,682,147	51.03	858,383	95	5	89,646	0	0	0.00	0	0	0	0	0	0	0.00	0	0	0	0
C	50	7,468,106	82.93	6,193,640	100	0	13,770	10	3,782,977	70.02	2,648,695	99	1	24,840	9	9,168,698	76.91	7,052,080	99	1	113,564
Total	**86**	**9,168,702**	**76.91**	**7,052,085**	**99**	**1**	**113,567**	**10**	**3,782,977**	**70.02**	**2,648,695**	**99**	**1**	**24,840**	**9**	**9,168,698**	**76.91**	**7,052,080**	**99**	**1**	**113,564**

from a practical standpoint there is an extensive religious education program in Zambia's schools, in which both government and churches are involved.

The Protection of Fundamental Rights Rule, 1969 (Statutory Instrument No 156 of 1969) allows citizens to introduce petitions at the High Court when they consider their individual liberties endangered. The Education Act in almost the same terms provides for grant-aided and private schools run by church agencies, and the same freedom is allowed for denominationally-run hospitals and other medical institutions.

In 1965 the Lumpa Church was banned on security grounds, after clashes with government troops took 700 lives. Jehovah's Witnesses encountered serious persecution from supporters of the ruling United National Independence Party in Luapula province in 1969 when they refused to vote or take part in political life. Many worship halls were seized or burned and about 1,000 Witnesses fled, some to nearby Zaire. Although missionaries attached to Jehovah's Witnesses were expelled in 1969, Zambian Witnesses are allowed to continue their activities despite the conflict of authority between their views and those of the state. Freedom of conscience and religion is a reality for all other churches.

There is no ministry or governmental department in charge of religious affairs. Churches are required to register with the government's registrar of societies.

In 1974 the government nationalized all confessional primary schools, although secondary schools remain under the control of the churches.

BROADCASTING AND MEDIA

Zambia is a member of UNDA. Catholics broadcast Sunday services in 7 local languages and English, along with daily 'Thought for the Day' programs broadcast each morning, afternoon and evening. In addition, several air-time slots are available for religious broadcasters on special occasions.

Television programs are available both on local channels and via satellite. CBN's *International 700 Club* and Christian drama series *Another Life* are available on Sundays and Wednesdays throughout the country. TBN programs air on ZNBC.

Independents. Opening service at vast New Jerusalem Church, Chingola.

INTERDENOMINATIONAL ORGANIZATIONS

A number of councils and associations are actively promoting interdenominational co-operations, including: (1) Christian Council of Zambia (CCZ) which was founded in 1945 and now has 13 member churches following the withdrawal of Seventh-day Adventists and the Wesleyan Church in 1974 in protest over the AACC's support of liberation movements; (2) Evangelical Fellowship of Zambia (EFZ), with 15 member churches, which is related to the Association of Evangelicals of Africa and Madagascar; and (3) Association of Independent Churches (AIC), with about 10 members, which provides for fellowship between indigenous churches. Catholic concern for ecumenism is fostered through the Catholic Ecumenical Commission.

The most representative council of all has been the Zambia Christian Commission for Development (ZCCD), which flourished particularly around 1973 with 30 member churches including the Roman Catholic Church and indigenous denominations also. After many conferences and widespread activity up to 1974, its role has declined.

Cooperation is also maintained through the work of several other bodies. The Mindolo Ecumenical Foundation, founded in 1958 is a social ecumenism center affiliated with the CCZ and has a board of governors including Catholic and government representatives. It offers programs for training, study, consultation, and worship, at the service of the whole Zambian community and that of neighboring countries, placing its emphasis on what the churches can bring to a society in rapid social change. The Mindolo Foundation serves also as the Sodepax agency in Zambia and is a member of the Regional Sodepax Programme MEND, with headquarters in Malawi. The Churches Medical Association of Zambia (CMAZ), founded in 1970, co-ordinates all Christian medical work in the country.

FUTURE TRENDS AND PROSPECTS

Christians are expected to grow to 87.8% by 2025, with most of these conversions from the continued losses to ethnoreligionists.

Christianity could grow to claim 92% of the population before AD 2050 and remain there around mid-century.

BIBLIOGRAPHY

'A history of Lozi religion to the end of the Nineteenth century,' M. Mainga, in *The historical study of African religion*, p.95–107. T. O. Ranger & I. N. Kimambo (eds). London: Heinemann, 1972.

A short history of the AME Church in central Africa, 1900–1962. J. L. C. Membe. Luanshya, Zambia, 1969.

'A study of how churches grow in Zambia.' C. I. Woodhall. M.A. thesis, Abilene Christian University, Abilene, TX, 1979. 316p.

'A study of the growth of the church of Christ among the Tonga tribe of Zambia.' J. S. Shewmaker. M.A. thesis, Fuller Theological Seminary, Pasadena, CA, 1969. 278p.

'Acts of Jehovah's Witnesses in modern times in Zambia,' in *1972 Yearbook of Jehovah's Witnesses*, p.234–54. Brooklyn, NY: Watch Tower Bible & Tract Society, 1971. (Detailed historical narrative covering 1911–71).

An African church in transition from missionary dependence to mutuality in mission: a case study on the Roman Catholic Church in Zambia. F. J. Verstraelen. Leiden: Development Research Institute, 1975. 2 vols.

Bemba–speaking women of Zambia in a century of religious change (1892–1992). H. F. Hinfelaar. Leiden: E. J. Brill, 1994. 238p. (Revision of author's Ph.D. dissertation, University of London, 1989).

'Charismatic religion as popular protest: the ordinary and the extraordinary in social movements,' K. E. Fields, *Theory and society*, 11 (1982), 321–61.

Christian ethics in an African context: a focus on urban Zambia. D. A. Rader. *American University studies, Series VII: theology and religion*, vol. 128. New York: P. Lang, 1991. 213p.

Christian missionaries and the creation of Northern Rhodesia, 1880–1924. R. I. Rotberg. Princeton, NJ: Princeton University Press, 1965. 240p.

Christians of the Copperbelt: the growth of the church in Northern Rhodesia. J. V. Taylor & D. A. Lehmann. London: SCM Press, 1961. 308p.

'Church and state in Zambia: the case of the African Methodist Episcopal Church,' D. J. Cook, in *Christianity in independent Africa*, p.258–303. E. F. Luke, R. Gray, A. Hastings & G. Tasu (eds). London: R. Collings, 1978.

'Churches and development: directory for Zambia.' C. Woodhall. Mindolo Ecumenical Foundation, Kitwe, Zambia, 1971. 23p.

Coillard of the Zambezi: the lives of François and Christina Coillard of the Paris Missionary Society in South and Central Africa, 1858–1904. C. W. Mackintosh. 2nd ed. London: T. Fisher Unwin, 1909. 484p.

'Conceptions of God amongst the Tonga of Northern Rhodesia,' C. R. Hopgood, in *African ideas of God*, p.61–77. E. W. Smith (ed). London: Edinburgh House Press, 1950.

'Faith healers and folk healers: the symbolism and practice of indigenous therapy in urban Africa,' B. Jules-Rosette, *Religion*, 11 (April 1981), 127–149.

'Independent churches and independent states: Jehovah's Witnesses in East and Central Africa,' S. Cross, in *Christianity in independent Africa*, p.304–315. E. F. Luke, R. Gray, A. Hastings & G. Tasu (eds). London: R. Collings, 1978. (Contains brief account of Jehovah's Witnesses in Zambia).

La chiesa cattolica di Zambia: tra passato e futuro. Simposio di studio per il 50° di presenza dei Frati Minori Conventuali in Zambia. Ancona: Curia Provinciale Frati Minori Conventuali, 1980. 140p.

'L'église du Sacré–Coeur,' Oger L., *Notes et documents* (Rome: White Fathers), 51 (November 1964), 421–30.

Lumpa Church, 1: the genesis and development, 1953–1964. J. L. Calmettes. Chinsali, Zambia: Ilondola Language Centre, 1970. 55p.

Magic, divination and witchcraft among the Barotse of Northern Rhodesia. B. Reynolds. Berkeley, CA: University of California Press, 1963. 181p.

Mainstream Christianity to 1980 in Malawi, Zambia, and Zimbabwe. J. C. Weller et al. Gweru, Zimbabwe: Mambo Press, 1984. 235p.

Ndembu divination: its symbolism and techniques. V. W. Turner. Manchester, UK: Manchester University Press, 1961.

Profile for victory: new proposals for missions in Zambia. M. W. Randall. South Pasadena, CA: William Carey Library, 1970. 204p.

'Reflections on Zambian humanism: Christian perspectives on an African social system.' C. P. Burr. Thesis, Wesley Theological Seminary, Washington, DC, 1980. 275p.

Religious change in Zambia: exploratory studies. W. M. J. Van Binsbergen. *Monographs from the African Studies Centre, Leiden.* London: Kegan Paul, 1981. 423p.

'Some developments in Bemba religious history,' D. Werner, *Journal of religion in Africa*, 4 (1971), 1–24.

Sorcery in its social setting: a study of the Northern Rhodesia Cewa. M. G. Marwick. Manchester, UK: Manchester University Press, 1965. 339p.

Spirit of Africa: the healing ministry of Archbishop Milingo of Zambia. G. ter Haar. London: Hurst, 1992. 295p.

'The Brethren in Christ in Zambia.' G. J. Schwartz. M.A. thesis, Fuller Theological Seminary, Pasadena, CA, 1975. 152p.

'The development of the White Fathers' Mission among the Bemba–speaking peoples.' B. Garvey. Ph.D. dissertation, University of London, 1974. 460p.

The drums of affliction: a study of religious processes among the Ndembu of Zambia. V. W. Turner. Oxford, UK: Clarendon Press, 1968. 326p.

The Korsten Basketmakers: a study of the Masowe Apostles, an indigenous African religious movement. C. M. Dillon–Malone. Manchester, UK: Manchester University Press, 1978. 169p.

'The Lenshina movement of Northern Rhodesia,' R. Rotberg, *Rhodes–Livingstone journal* (Lusaka, Zambia), 29 (June 1961), 63–78.

The life of a Zambian evangelist: the reminiscences of Reverend Paul Bwembya Mushindo. P. B. Mushindo. *Communication*, no. 9. Lusaka, Zambia: University of Zambia, Institute for African Studies, 1973. 60p.

'The Lumpa Church of Alice Lenshina,' A. D. Roberts, in *Protest and power in Black Africa*, p.513–68. R. Rotberg & A. Mazrui (eds). New York: Oxford University Press, 1970.

The media and development: an exploratory survey in Indonesia and Zambia: with special reference to the role of the churches. K. E. Eapen. Leicester, UK: University of Leicester for the World Association for Christian Communication, 1973. 83p.

'The Mwana Lesa movement of 1925,' T. Ranger, in *Themes in the Christian history of Central Africa*, p.45–75. T. O. Ranger & J. Weller (eds). London: Heinemann, 1975.

The plateau Tonga of Northern Rhodesia: social and religious studies. E. Colson. Manchester, UK: Manchester University Press, 1962.

'The significance of dreams and visions among members of the Baptist churches of Zambia with special reference to the Manyika Baptist Association and to selected urban areas.' N. O. Hayashida. Ph.D. dissertation, University of Edinburgh, Edinburgh, Scotland, 1993. 529p.

'The Watch Tower movement in south central Africa, 1908–1945.' S. Cross. Ph.D. dissertation, Oxford University, Oxford, UK, 1973.

Tonga Christianity. S. Shewmaker. South Pasadena, CA: William Carey Library, 1970. 215p.

Towards church union in Zambia: a study of missionary co–operation and church–union efforts in Central–Africa. P. Bolink. Franeker: T. Wever, 1967. 446p.

Zambia. A. M. Bliss & J. A. Rigg. *World bibliographical series*, vol. 51. Oxford, UK: CLIO Press, 1984. 254p. (See especially 'Religion,' p.66–73).

Country Table 2. **Organized churches and denominations in Zambia.**

Official name (bold type = church with over 10% of affiliated) 1	Begun 2	Type 3	Counc 4	Congs 5	Adults 6	Affiliated 1970 7	Affiliated 1995 8	G% 9	Names, notes, and other statistics (see Codebook, Part 3) 10
African Gospel Church	1947	I-3aA	x....	30	30,000	30,000	60,000	2.81	*Basketmakers. Hosannas. Apostles of Johane Masowe.* Shona, some Ndebele. Sabbatarian.
African Methodist Episcopal Church	1929	I-Met	Vw..d	193	42,400	56,000	82,000	1.54	M=AMEC(USA Blacks). 17th Episcopal District. Many development projects. 88n,W=54%.
African National Church		I-Ref	C	10	3,600	10,000	6,000	0.05	M=ANC(Malawi). Copperbelt, Northern, Central. Several attempts to join CCZ.
Anglican Church in Zambia:	1909	A-ACa	AwAVd	400	90,000	85,000	170,000	2.81	1910, D NRhodesia; 1965 in CPCA with 10 Dioceses (4 in Zambia). M=USPG. 65f,4H,P=20%,1s
Apostles in Zion Church		I-3aA	I	20	9,000	5,000	20,000	0.05	Zionists. South African Bantu members, indigenous Black pentecostals.
Apostolic Church in Zambia	1958	P-PeA	Z....	24	1,680	1,000	4,200	5.91	M=Danish missionaries of Apostolic Church (Netherlands). Pentecostals. 5n,2x.
Apostolic Church of Christ	1961	I-3aA	.....	9	500	300	1,000	4.93	Indigenous pentecostals. Begun in Bulawayo (Rhodesia), then later spread to Zambia.
Apostolic Church of Johane Maranke	1952	I-3aA	x....	50	8,000	2,000	16,000	8.67	*AACJM.* Scattered members of large Shona church based on Umtali (Rhodesia).
Apostolic Church of Pentecost	1954	P-Pe1	x....	20	1,200	1,000	3,000	4.49	Scattered groups in Copperbelt and Lusaka. M=ACP(Canada), but aid discontinued.
Apostolic Faith & Acts Church	1965	I-3aA	....b	7	2,100	1,500	4,000	4.00	In Lusaka, Luanshya, Ndola and Kitwe. Originally from Bulawayo (Rhodesia).
Apostolic Faith Church		I-3aA	....b	180	8,200	1,500	18,200	0.05	No buildings; meetings in rooms, under trees. Link with AFC, Bournemouth (UK).
Apostolic Faith Holy Gospel Church	1947	I-3aA	....b	130	25,000	20,000	45,000	3.30	From Rhodesia. Growing. Ndola, Lusaka, Livingstone, 4 community development centers.
Apostolic Faith Mission of Zambia	1947	P-Pe2	Z....	180	9,000	8,000	18,000	3.30	M=AFM(SA),Velberter Mission(Germany). 5n,3x,9f,1p,1s,W=75%,250Y.
Apostolic Faith Star Church	1971	I-3pA	.....	15	1,800	1,500	3,000	4.17	New separatist group of Bantu indigenous pentecostals. HQ in Kitwe.
Apostolic Faith (Born Again) Church		I-3pA	I	5	300	300	600	0.05	Small group of Bantu indigenous pentecostals. In Ndola, Kitwe, Luanshya.
Baptist Association of Zambia	1905	I-Bap	.....	150	7,000	8,000	18,000	3.30	1976 union: Lambaland Baptist Chs, Scandinavian Indep Baptist Union. M=SIBU, Australia.
Baptist Convention of Zambia	1959	P-Bap	T.G.z	500	43,000	4,000	108,000	14.09	M=FMB-SBC(USA). 62% Lamba. 18,000 in mail courses. 12n,12x,36f,1j,1s(11),W=88%,404Y.
Baptist Union of Zambia		P-Bap	T.G.E	20	1,400	3,000	3,200	0.05	British Baptists. Lusaka and the Copperbelt. 12 Zambian pastors, 3 expatriate.
Brethren in Christ Church	1906	P-Men	GFG.z	116	6,632	6,300	16,632	3.96	M=BiCC(USA). Southern Province. Tonga. 4n,8x,6m,50f,1H,3h,1s(5),W=90%,240Y.
Broadsheet Readers' Clubs	c1980	I-3nA	.....	65	1,000	–	2,000	6.67	Readers of Gospel Broadsheets produced by WEC(UK).
Catholic Church in Zambia:	1889	R-Lat	P.SEV	252	1,344,000	922,890	2,677,471	4.35	C=6+4+15 M=WF, SMA, OFM. 241n 398x 621m 895w 54308Yy
M Kasama (Bangueolo)	1913	R-Lat	Ps	15	140,000	171,264	293,000	2.17	Language; 50% Bemba, 45% Bisa, 5% Lungu. 33n 25x 55m 66w 10118Yy
D Mansa (Fort Rosebery)	1952	R-Lat	Ps	15	128,000	138,996	269,409	2.68	Rural. 42% Ngumbo, 39% Aushi, 15% Lunda. 25n 17x 20m 60w 5858Yy
D Mbala-Mpika (Abercorn)	1933	R-Lat	Ps	16	69,000	81,783	136,080	2.06	Rural. 65% Bemba, 19% Lundu, 14% Bisa. M=WF. 23n 22x 28m 58w 4830Yy
M Lusaka	1927	R-Lat	Ps	48	212,000	124,384	402,920	4.81	Urban. 60% Bemba, 30% Nyanja. M=SJ. 1s. 80n 132x 229m 240w 2320Yy
D Chipata (Fort Jameson)	1937	R-Lat	Ps	19	106,000	103,180	212,000	2.92	Rural. 49% Chewa, 20% Nsenga, 19% Ngoni. 14n 29x 36m 111w 6598Yy
D Livingstone (Victoria Falls)	1936	R-Lat	Ps	23	52,000	66,394	104,232	1.82	74% Lozi, 5% Maleya, 4% Luvale. M=SVD,OFMCap. 10n 50x 65m 107w 3156Yy
D Monze	1962	R-Lat	Psj	20	50,000	49,404	101,560	2.92	80% Tonga, 10% Bemba, 8% Nyanja, 5% Lozi. M=SJ. 19n 23x 46m 96w 2438Yy
D Ndola	1938	R-Lat	Ps	82	567,000	181,954	1,109,000	7.50	Copperbelt. Mainly Bemba, Lamba, Ngoni. M=OFM. 30n 90x 126m 135w 17500Yy
D Solwezi	1959	R-Lat	Psma	14	20,000	5,531	49,270	9.14	Rural. Languages: Kaonde, Ndembu. M=SMA,OFM. 7n 10x 16m 22w 1490Yy
Catholic Church of the Sacred Heart	1955	I-CCa	.....	2	600	6,000	1,000	-6.92	*Bana ba Mutimu. Followers of Emilyo.* Split ex RCC. Bemba. 1960 banned.
Central Africa Church	1959	I-CBr	.....	10	3,000	4,000	6,000	1.64	Copperbelt. Ex CMML. Lamba, Luvale. 7,000 also in Zaire (Assemblees des Freres).
Central Africa Pioneer Mission	1958	I-3pA	..G.E	2	250	400	500	0.90	Single congregation in Lusaka served by one tentmaking Australian family.
Central Church of God		I-Non	I	2	100	200	300	0.05	Indigenous body in Central Province. No Buildings, meetings in open air.
Christian Brethren	1897	P-CBr	x.G.E	1,000	37,500	50,000	75,000	1.64	*Open Brethren.* M=CMML(UK,USA,NZ,SA). Mainly Luvale tribe. 114f,7H,3h.
Christian Fellowship of Zambia	c1975	I-3cA	.....	26	5,250	–	10,500	5.00	*CFZ.* A charismatic split from Christian Brethren, founded by a Brethren missionary.
Christian Reformed Church		P-Ref	.....	1	20	50	40	0.05	*Gereformeerde Kerk. Doppers (Baptizers).* White Afrikaners: church disbanding.
Christian Zion Church		I-3zA	.....	10	500	500	1,000	0.05	Central and Eastern provinces: no church building, meetings in open air.
Church of Central Africa Presbyterian		P-Ref	R....	29	10,300	1,000	20,000	0.05	Migrants from CCAP (Malawi), who refused to join UCZ. Lusaka, Kitwe, Chingola.
Church of Christ, Scientist		m-Sci	x....	4	40	100	40	0.05	*Christian Science.* M=CCS(Boston, USA). Whites, Lusaka, Ndola, Kitwe, Chingola.
Church of God of Prophecy	c1980	P-Pe3	.....	12	480	–	1,200	6.67	M=CGP (USA). Holiness Pentecostals.
Church of God Zambia	c1960	I-3pA	.....	33	3,000	1,000	6,000	7.43	African Independent pentecostals.
Ch of JC on Earth thru the Prophet SK	1968	I-3nA	xwi.d	30	8,000	5,000	15,000	4.49	SK=Simon Kimbangu. M=EJCSK(Zaire). Copperbelt. Bemba-speaking ex-Congo Zambians. 9x.
Church of Our Lord Jesus Christ		I-Non	.....	15	1,000	1,000	2,000	0.05	Grouping of indigenous Bantu Christians in Northwestern Province.
Church of the Nazarene	1958	P-Hol	xFG.z	21	2,111	1,000	4,887	6.55	M=CoN(USA). Lozi,Bemba,Tonga: half members in Lusaka. 1x,4m,4f,W=92%,47z.
Churches of Christ (Instrumental)	1962	I-Dis	x.G.E	13	8,780	4,000	17,000	5.96	M=Zambia Christian Mission. CCCC(USA). Ndola, Kitwe, Livingstone, Lusaka. 20f,4i.
Churches of Christ (Non-Instrumental)	1910	I-Dis	x.G.E	909	40,000	20,000	100,000	6.65	Begun by Rhodesian evangelists. 1923, M=CC(USA). 1school. 24m,31f.
Commandments Church	1968	I-3pA	.....	5	1,500	1,000	2,500	3.73	*Malango Ch.* Ex UCZ, traditional medicine, no baptism except Holy Spirit. Bemba.
Dutch Reformed Ch (Mother Church)	1904	P-Ref	F...d	8	200	1,000	500	-2.73	*NGK (Moederkerk).* All White Afrikaners; rapid emigration. HQ Lusaka. W=80%,6y.
Dutch Reformed Church (Reformed)		P-Ref	J....	1	30	100	50	0.05	*Gereformeerde Kerk.* South African Whites, declining fast. Last minister left 1964.
Evangelical Church in Zambia	1910	P-Eva	xMG.E	494	15,200	20,000	31,600	1.85	ECZ. M=AEF(SAGM)(SA,USA,UK,&c). A=1962. Kaonde, Mbunda, Nkoya. 139f,2H,13h,2s.
Evangelical Healing Church of Christ	1972	I-3pA	C	10	700	500	1,500	4.35	One of several indigenous pentecostal churches from Zaire. HQ Kitwe. 2 pastors.
Full Gospel Church of God	1946	P-Pe3	ZFG.a	348	40,736	10,000	74,100	8.34	Begun from Rhodesia. M=CoG(Cleveland) (USA). Nutrition, poultry farm schemse. 37n.
Gospel Seventh-day Church of Zambia		I-Adv	.....	20	5,000	6,000	9,000	0.05	Small Adventist split mainly on Copperbelt and in Southern Province.
Greek Orth Archbishopric of Rhodesia	c1910	O-Gre	Cw...	3	1,700	5,000	3,400	-1.53	Churches in Kitwe and Luanshya. Under P Alexandria. Members Greek settlers. 1s.
Holy Gospel Church	1959	I-3pA	I	5	600	500	1,000	2.81	Split ex Apostolic Faith Holy Gospel Church. Central Province. Local pentecostals.
Independent Brethren Assemblies		I-CBr	.....	4	600	1,000	1,300	0.05	Secession ex CMML in Mufulira, Chingola, Solwezi. Independent congregations.
Independent Methodist Church	1965	I-Met	C	20	10,000	4,000	15,000	5.43	IMC. Migrant Shona (ex USA Methodist), joined UCZ in 1965, then split.
Independent Watchtower	c1940	I-Jeh	.....	5	3,500	5,000	6,000	0.73	Ex Jehovah's Witnesses. 4 collective co-operative villages. Luapuia, Copperbelt.
Intern Ch of the Foursquare Gospel	c1980	P-Pe2	Z....	1	89	–	95	6.67	M=ICFG(USA). Mainline Pentecostals.
Jehovah's Witnesses	1911	m-Jeh	x....	1,800	200,000	450,000	370,000	-0.78	Massive influence. 1973: 194,133 at annual Memorial. HQ Kitwe. (1975) 3797Y. (1995) 5841Y.
Last Church of Christ		I-Non	.....	10	1,000	2,000	2,100	0.05	*Last Church of God. Covenanter Brethren.* Indigenous Bantu Christians.
Lumpa (Visible Salvation) Church	1954	I-mar	.....	5	2,500	20,000	5,000	-5.39	Led by Alice Lenshina: 1958, 100,000; 1965 banned; still active. Bemba, Senga.
Lutheran Church of Central Africa	1953	P-Lut	x....	30	1,800	2,639	6,000	3.34	M=Wisconsin ELS(USA). 45% Chewa, 23% Tonga, 19% Ila. 1n,6x,10f,1h,6p,W=51%,123Y,249y.
New Apostolic Church	c1915	I-3aX	x....	435	376,000	120,000	728,063	7.48	*Zambia-Malawi Church District.* M=NAC(HQ Zurich). Lozi, Bemba. 12n, 4x.
Old Apostolic Church	1963	I-3aX	x....	4	300	500	800	1.90	Split (in UK) from Catholic Apostolic Ch. From South Africa. Kitwe. 4 priests.
Orthodox Syrian Church of India	c1965	O-SyM	Dwe..	1	100	200	300	1.64	D Bahya Kerala. Indians from all over Copperbelt meet in Mindolo chapel. 1 priest.
Pentecostal Assemblies of God of Z	1948	P-Pe2	ZFG.E	311	40,500	6,000	125,000	12.91	PAoC(Canada),AoG(USA). Along railway. 6n,14x,20m,8f,1s(11).
Pentecostal Church of Zambia	1962	I-3oA	C	2	100	100	200	2.81	Split ex ACP(Canada). Central and Southern provinces. Unitarian pentecostals. 1n.
Pentecostal Free Churches	c1968	I-3pA	C	5	1,000	1,000	2,000	2.81	Split ex PAG, aided by Pentecostals from UK. Mufulira. Kitwe, Copperbelt. 4n.
Pentecostal Holiness Association	1934	P-Pe3	ZFG.E	261	25,506	2,000	42,500	13.00	M=IPHC(USA). Copperbelt. Isoka; expansion to Tanzania, Malawi. 16n,4f,1s,W=75%,55Y.
Pilgrim Wesleyan Church	1890	P-Hol	VFG.a	163	4,259	6,882	13,000	2.58	1890 M=Primitive Meth,now WC(USA),RBM(Canada). 8n,9x,29f,4h,1s,W=64%,184Y.
Presbyterian Church of Central Africa	c1955	P-Ref	Rwa.d	17	3,494	3,000	8,000	4.00	*PCSA. Presbytery of Zambia.* Expatriates (Malawi, UK, SAfrica). HQ Lusaka. 2n,1x.
Reformed Church in Zambia	1899	P-Ref	F.A.d	1,695	290,000	50,000	500,000	9.65	*Eklesia wa Cikonzedwe m'Zambia.* M=DRC(SA). 90% Chewa. 22n,3x,6f,2H,1p,1s(6).
Religious Society of Friends	1964	P-Qua	Q...d	2	100	100	300	4.49	2 workers, 2 work camp; (Kafue, Northern Province). Joined UCZ, later left.
Remnant Church of Israel		I-Non	C	10	2,600	3,000	6,000	0.05	Lusaka area. Bishop and 4 pastors. Attempting to join Christian Council of Zambia.
Salvation Army	1924	P-Sal	xwA.d	90	7,500	7,132	15,000	3.02	*Nkondo ya Lufutuko. Zambia Command.* 99% Tonga. 34n,43x,2H,1r,1s,W=79%,65Y.
Salvation Church	1930	I-Non	.....	20	3,000	4,000	6,000	1.64	*Worldwide Missionary Christian Fellowship.* Ex BiCC. Choma. No church buildings.
Serbian Orthodox Church	c1970	O-Ser	C....	1	800	–	1,500	33.98	Serbia immigrants. Under P Belgrade (Serbia).
Seventh-day Adventist Church	1905	P-Adv	x...C	522	120,000	50,000	218,000	6.07	*Zambia Field,* Zambesi Union. 58% Tonga,34% Bemba. 23nx,36f,3H,1r,546t(49597),2816Y.
United Church of Zambia	1884	P-Uni	WWA.d	1,200	300,000	52,351	1,000,000	12.52	*UCZ.* 1958/65 unions M=PEMS,LMS,MMS,CSM. Lozi,Bemba. 57n,28x,87f,3H,7h,5r,1s.9160Yy.
Watchman Healing Mission	1937	I-Jeh	.....	60	25,800	30,000	50,000	2.06	*Mhionda, Bamulonda.* From Malawi. Collective villages. Big non-member attendances.
World Outreach Team Action	1995	I-3pA	.....	7	1,000	–	3,000	100.00	Recent Zambian indigenous mission starting churches in Zambia and Botswana.
Zion Christian Church	c1960	I-3zA	.....	20	10,000	1,000	15,000	11.44	ZCC. Related to ZCC (South Africa, Zimbabwe); also Victory Bible Ch, New Life Ministries.
Other African indigenous churches		I-3pA	.....	100	40,000	15,000	80,000	0.05	Total about 100 (see list below), rising from 55 in 1971, and 70 in 1976.
Other Orthodox churches	c1970	O-	.....	3	600	–	1,000	31.83	Total 5, including Syrian Orthodox Ch (P Antioch).
Other Protestant denominations		P-	.....	60	10,000	8,000	20,000	0.05	Total about 15 (see list below), including WCOG (Radio Ch of God, USA).
Other marginal Protestant bodies		m-	.....	30	3,000	2,000	5,000	0.05	Many European adherents.
Doubly-affiliated		2-aff			-358,000	0	-748,000		Pentecostals and Independents who are also baptized Catholics, Anglicans, or Reformed.
Totals				**12,283**	**2,949,557**	**2,152,544**	**6,158,578**		

Churches, members, growth, 1900-2025	*Congs*	*Adults*	*Affiliated*	*G%*	*Total denominations*	*O*	*R*	*A*	*P*	*I*	*m*
Total churches, members, and denominations (mid-1900)	20	960	2,000	10.49	6	0	1	0	5	0	0
Total churches, members, and denominations (mid-1970)	6,247	1,037,696	2,152,544	10.49	124	2	1	1	31	83	6
Total churches, members, and denominations (mid-1990)	12,000	2,599,000	5,426,000	4.73	201	7	1	1	40	140	12
Total churches, members, and denominations (mid-1995)	12,283	2,949,557	6,158,578	2.57	205	8	1	1	41	142	12
Total churches, members, and denominations (mid-2000)	13,000	3,377,000	7,052,080	2.75	209	9	1	1	42	144	12
Total churches, members, and denominations (mid-2025)	25,000	6,374,000	13,310,000	2.57	388	12	1	1	60	300	14

(The columns O, R, A, P, I, m are headed *6 Megablocs:*)

NOTES ON TABLE ABOVE

NATIONAL COUNCILS (Column 4, 5th letter). The pattern of membership (1974) is complex. Some churches belong to one organization only (code letters C, G, I), but most belong to the ZCCD and also to some other council. The Christian Council of Zambia (CCZ) is affiliated to CWME of WCC. In 1975, 2 members of the CCZ (SDAC, Wesleyan Ch) withdrew in protest against AACC support for liberation movements.

- a = member of EFZ and ZCCD.
- b = member of ZCCD and AIC.
- C = Zambia Christian Commission for Development (ZCCD) (very active in 1973.
- d = member of Christian Council of Zambia (CCZ, 1945) and ZCCD.
- E = Evangelical Fellowship of Zambia (EFZ).
- I = Association of Independent Churches (AIC) (Lusaka area).
- V = Zambia Episcopal Conference (ZEC), and member of ZCCD.
- z = member of ZCCD, CCZ, and EFZ.

Other national councils. Zambia Anglican Council (ZAC).

OTHER AFRICAN INDIGENOUS CHURCHES. These others include (with total adult members in brackets): African Apostolic Faith Mission (50), African Christian Gospel Ch (150), African Covenant Ch, African Doctors Ch (30), African Evangelical Ch (150), African Independent Holiness Ch (30), African Reformed Pentecost Ch, Amos Apostolic Ch (100), Black Mans' Ch (home groups), Christian Holiness Ch (30), Ethiopian Catholic Ch in Zion (from South Africa about 1910), Full Gospel African Ch (100), Israel Ch of God (member of ZCCD), Love (Kutemwa) Ch, Messengers Ch, Modern Ch of God, New African Christian Movement, Nzila movement (a Lozi religious healing movement), Zambia True Gospel Ch (20), Zion Africa Ch, Zion City Ch (200). Indigenous bodies from other countries include the Unification Church, from Korea.

OTHER PROTESTANT DENOMINATIONS. These include: Christian Church (Disciples of Christ) (1960: 2 missionaries), Christian Nationals Evangelism Commission (1972), Dorothea Mission, Elim Missionary Society (UK), Zambesi Mission.

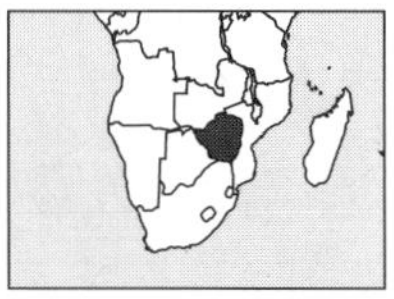

ZIMBABWE

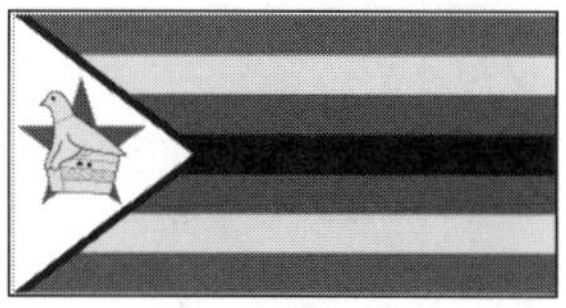

SECULAR DATA, AD 2000

STATE
Official name: The Republic of Zimbabwe.
Short name: Zimbabwe. **Adjective of nationality:** Zimbabwean.
Flag: Bird on red star in white triangle, 7 stripes of green, gold, red, black.
Area: 390,757 sq. km. (150,872 sq. mi.).
Government: Parliamentary republic, since 1980 (1890 British South Africa Company possession, 1923 British colony of Southern Rhodesia, self-governing colony, 1965 Independence declared by White regime, 1970 republic declared, 1980 Independence recognized).
Legislature: House of Assembly, 150 members.
Official language: English.
Monetary unit: 1 Zimbabwe dollar (Z$) = 100 cents. **US$1=** Z$31.75.
Chief cities: HARARE (Salisbury) 1,803,000; Bulawayo 816,198; Chitungwiza 322,129; Gweru (Gwelo) 130,079; Mutare (Umtali) 124,177.
Political divisions: 10 provinces.
Armed forces: 47,000.

DEMOGRAPHY
Population: 11,669,000.
Population density: 29.8/sq. km. (77.3/sq. mi.).
Under 15 years: 4,822,000.
Growth rate p.a.: 0.97% (births 29.70, deaths 20.02).
Mortality: Infant, per 1,000: 67.1; **Maternal per 100,000:** 570.0.
Life expectancy: 41 (male 41, female 41).
Household size: 4.8. **Floor area per person, sq.m:** 7.0.
Major languages: English, Shona, Ndebele, Tsonga, Venda, Tonga, Zulu, Afrikaans, Chewa (Chichewa), Pedi (Sepedi), Tswana (Setswana), Greek, Gujarati, Marathi, Portuguese, and about 15 smaller languages.
Urban dwellers: 35.31%. **Urban growth rate p.a.:** 4.1%.
Labor force: 42%.

ETHNOLINGUISTIC PEOPLES
22.0% Central Shona; 14.7% Karanga (Shona, Rozwi); 13.0% Ndebele (Tabele); 12.7% Zezuru; 6.8% Manyika (Shona, Hungwe).

ECONOMY
National income p.a. per person: US$539; **per family:** US$2,591.

EDUCATION
Adult literacy: 85% (male 90%, female 79%). **Schools:** 6,193.
Universities: 28. **School enrolment:** female/male: 81%/90%.

HEALTH
Access to health services: 85%. **Access to safe water:** 74%.
Hospitals: 1,378 (15 beds per 10,000). **Doctors:** 1,551.
Blind: 15,000. **Deaf:** 745,400. **Murder rate:** 5.
Lepers: 60,000. **Underweight prevalence under 5:** 16%.

LITERATURE
New book titles p.a.: 1,750 (150 p.a. per million). **Periodicals:** 39.
Newspapers: 2 dailies.

COMMUNICATION (per 1,000 people)
Phones: 14 (5% mobile). **Radios:** 113. **TV sets:** 27.
Daily newspaper circulation: 17. **Computers:** 8.

HUMAN LIFE AND LIBERTY (optimum condition=100.0%)
HDI: 51.3. **HSI:** 34.0. **HFI:** 20.0. **EFL:** 26.0.

Country Table 1. **Religious adherents in Zimbabwe, AD 1900-2025.**

Year	1900		1970		mid-1990		Annual change, 1990-2000				mid-1995		mid-2000		mid-2025	
Name	Adherents	%	Adherents	%	Adherents	%	Natural	Conversion	Total	Rate	Adherents	%	Adherents	%	Adherents	%
Christians	**19,000**	**3.8**	**2,760,000**	**52.5**	**6,558,000**	**66.5**	**120,083**	**11,155**	**131,238**	**1.84**	**7,281,000**	**67.0**	**7,870,379**	**67.5**	**11,156,900**	**73.9**
PROFESSION																
professing Christians	**19,000**	**3.8**	**2,760,000**	**52.5**	**6,558,000**	**66.5**	**120,083**	**11,155**	**131,238**	**1.84**	**7,281,000**	**67.0**	**7,870,379**	**67.5**	**11,156,900**	**73.9**
AFFILIATION																
unaffiliated Christians	3,000	0.6	608,237	11.6	837,460	8.5	15,335	-3,779	11,556	1.30	901,000	8.3	953,019	8.2	656,900	4.4
affiliated Christians	**16,000**	**3.2**	**2,151,763**	**40.9**	**5,720,540**	**58.0**	**104,748**	**14,934**	**119,682**	**1.92**	**6,380,000**	**58.7**	**6,917,360**	**59.3**	**10,500,000**	**69.6**
Independents	0	0.0	673,200	12.8	3,649,000	37.0	66,816	38,284	105,100	2.56	4,289,778	39.5	4,700,000	40.3	7,000,000	46.4
Protestants	5,000	1.0	728,574	13.9	1,250,000	12.7	22,889	-3,889	19,000	1.43	1,359,488	12.5	1,440,000	12.3	1,700,000	11.3
Roman Catholics	5,000	1.0	556,789	10.6	910,000	9.2	16,663	4,337	21,000	2.10	1,022,226	9.4	1,120,000	9.6	1,700,000	11.3
Anglicans	6,000	1.2	153,000	2.9	275,000	2.8	5,035	-535	4,500	1.53	300,000	2.8	320,000	2.7	360,000	2.4
Marginal Christians	0	0.0	32,200	0.6	55,000	0.6	1,007	-107	900	1.53	59,700	0.6	64,000	0.6	83,000	0.6
Orthodox	0	0.0	8,000	0.2	6,400	0.1	117	-157	-40	-0.64	6,200	0.1	6,000	0.1	9,000	0.1
doubly-affiliated	0	0.0	0	0.0	-424,860	-4.3	-7,780	-22,998	-30,778	5.60	-657,392	-6.1	-732,640	-6.3	-352,000	-2.3
Trans-megabloc groupings																
Evangelicals	4,000	0.8	250,000	4.8	455,700	4.6	8,344	-1,414	6,930	1.43	499,147	4.6	525,000	4.5	700,000	4.6
Pentecostals/Charismatics	0.	0.0	650,000	12.4	3,770,000	38.2	69,032	46,968	116,000	2.72	4,397,003	40.5	4,930,000	42.3	7,150,000	47.4
Great Commission Christians	**15,000**	**3.0**	**1,052,000**	**20.0**	**2,367,000**	**24.0**	**43,342**	**13,426**	**56,768**	**2.17**	**2,675,000**	**24.6**	**2,934,675**	**25.2**	**4,225,000**	**28.0**
Ethnoreligionists	479,800	96.0	2,421,000	46.0	3,072,600	31.2	56,265	-11,830	44,435	1.36	3,329,140	30.6	3,516,949	30.1	3,500,000	23.2
Nonreligious	0	0.0	8,000	0.2	85,000	0.9	1,556	1,191	2,747	2.84	98,500	0.9	112,474	1.0	200,000	1.3
Muslims	1,000	0.2	50,000	1.0	80,000	0.8	1,465	-922	543	0.66	82,500	0.8	85,433	0.7	100,000	0.7
Baha'is	0	0.0	9,700	0.2	29,000	0.3	531	277	808	2.49	35,000	0.3	37,077	0.3	60,000	0.4
Hindus	0	0.0	3,650	0.1	13,500	0.1	247	91	338	2.26	16,200	0.2	16,880	0.1	30,000	0.2
Atheists	0	0.0	1,000	0.0	13,000	0.1	238	80	318	2.21	15,500	0.1	16,180	0.1	25,000	0.2
Jews	200	0.0	5,200	0.1	9,400	0.1	172	-32	140	1.40	10,400	0.1	10,797	0.1	15,000	0.1
Buddhists	0	0.0	0	0.0	700	0.0	13	-1	12	1.56	780	0.0	817	0.0	1,800	0.0
Spiritists	0	0.0	300	0.0	500	0.0	9	-6	3	0.60	530	0.0	531	0.0	800	0.0
Other religionists	0	0.0	1,150	0.0	1,300	0.0	24	-3	21	1.52	1,450	0.0	1,511	0.0	2,500	0.0
World A (unevangelized persons)	420,000	84.0	315,620	6.0	256,438	2.6	4,688	-9,536	-4,848	-2.08	239,164	2.2	210,042	1.8	120,736	0.8
World B (evangelized non-Christians)	61,000	12.2	2,184,715	41.5	3,048,562	30.9	55,832	-1,619	54,213	1.64	3,350,957	30.8	3,588,579	30.7	3,814,364	25.3
World C (Christians)	19,000	3.8	2,760,000	52.5	6,558,000	66.5	120,083	11,155	131,238	1.84	7,281,000	67.0	7,870,379	67.5	11,156,900	73.9
Country's population	**500,000**	**100.0**	**5,260,336**	**100.0**	**9,863,000**	**100.0**	**180,603**	**0**	**180,603**	**1.70**	**10,871,122**	**100.0**	**11,669,000**	**100.0**	**15,092,000**	**100.0**

COLUMNS, ROWS.
For meanings and definitions, see Codebook (Part 3). Note that, by definition, total 'Christians' = professing + crypto-Christians, which also = affiliated + unaffiliated Christians, and also = Great Commission Christians + latent Christians. Percentages may not always total exactly, due to rounding.

CENSUSES.
These have only been taken for the White and other non-African populations. **1936** (Europeans only; 55,450 persons): 42.9% Anglicans, 40.8% Protestants (17.8% Dutch Reformed, 11.4% Presbyterians, 8.9% Methodists), 8.5% Roman Catholics, 4.0% Jews, 1.0% Greek Orthodox. **1941** (Europeans only; 68,950 persons): 43.3% Anglicans, 38.3% Protestants, 8.7% Roman Catholics, 4.7% Jews, 1.1% Greek Orthodox. **1946** (Europeans only; 82,406 persons): 37.9% Anglicans, 37.8% Protestants, 15.4% Roman Catholics, 4.2% Jews, 1.2% nonreligious and atheists, 1.0% Greek Orthodox. **8.V.1956** (non-Africans): 170,612 Christians, 7,787 nonreligious, 2,941 Jews, 1,379 Hindus, 1,097 Muslims, 567 other religionists. **26.IX.1961** (non-Africans): 209,700 Christians, 10,360 nonreligious, 7,060 Jews, 3,310 Hindus, 3,100 Muslims, 4,970 other religionists. **1969** (Europeans, Asians, and Coloureds only; 252,414 persons): 36.0% Protestants, 32.1% Anglicans, 14.0% Roman Catholics, 2.1% Jews, 2.0% nonreligious and atheists, 1.6% Muslims, 1.5% Greek Orthodox, 1.4% Hindus.

NOTES ON RELIGIONS
ATHEISTS. Europeans.
BAHA'IS. Growth from 13 local spiritual assemblies (1964) to 56 (1973). Including many Indians, formerly Hindus or Muslims; then mushrooming to 282 LSAs (1996).
ETHNORELIGIONISTS. Animists, adherents of traditional religions, especially among the Ndau (50% animist), and the Hiechware Bushmen (88%). All tribes however have numerous traditionalists still; and the largest, the Shona and Ndebele, both still contain traditionalist minorities which are strongly resistant to Christianity. There are several highly-elaborate cults attended by vast crowds of many thousands, notably the Mwari cult in the Matopo hills where annually the voice of God is believed to be heard.
HINDUS. Indians (Asians), with some Europeans and Coloureds.
INDEPENDENTS. In about 232 denominations in 1995 (see Table 2). Although most converts come from tribal religion (paganism), a considerable number of Protestants, Anglicans, and Roman Catholics join these churches each year.
JEWS. The first pioneers arrived in 1869, followed by many from Eastern Europe. These are now congregations in Bulawayo, Gatooma, Que Que, and Salisbury.
MUSLIMS. African Muslims from neighboring countries especially Mozambique and Malawi (Makua, Yao, Swahili et alii) (Sunnis, of the Shafiite rite), also 3,200 Asian traders (Indians, Indo-Pakistanis). *Hajj pilgrims to Mecca.* (1976) 12 persons.
NONRELIGIOUS. Europeans, with some Chinese.
OTHER RELIGIONISTS. Adherents of smaller religions and cults, including Rosicrucians (1 AMORC center).
PENTECOSTALS/CHARISMATICS. The Anglican Charismatic Renewal began in 1973 and by 1977 was involving about 10 Anglican parishes, mainly White. The Catholic Charismatic Renewal began late in 1979 and has grown far less rapidly than in neighboring Zambia.
SPIRITISTS. Mostly Europeans, followers of non-Christian high spiritism.
UNAFFILIATED CHRISTIANS. Africans who regard themselves as Christians having broken with traditional religion, but not yet initiated by the churches.

Great Commission Instrument Panel: status of Zimbabwe (for explanation see start of Part 4)

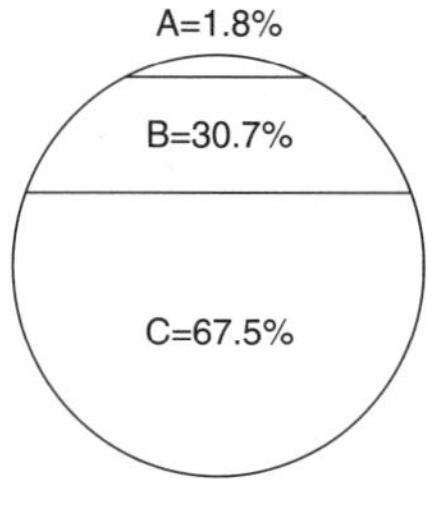

3 Worlds, AD 2000

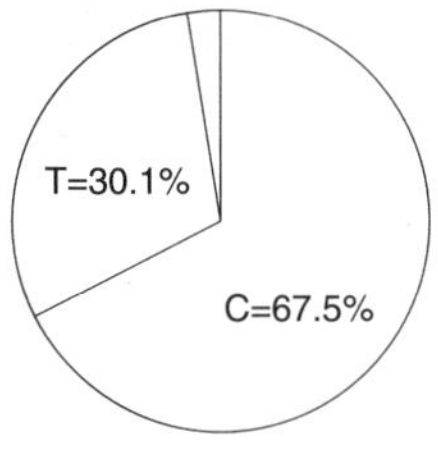

Religions, AD 2000

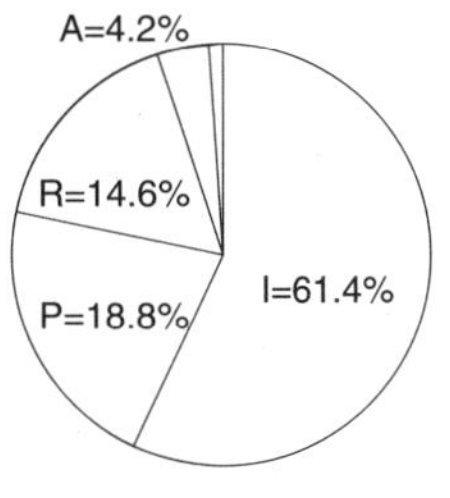

Ecclesiastical blocs

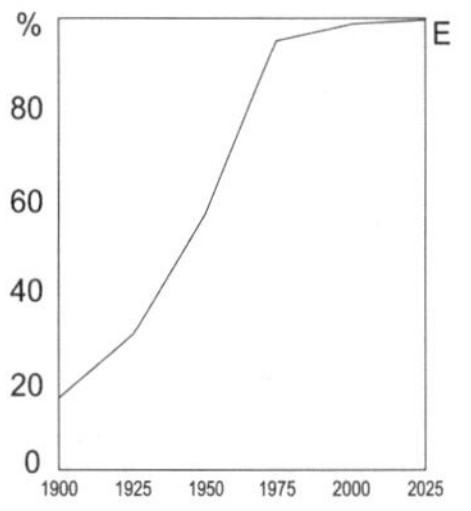

Evangelization, 1900-2025

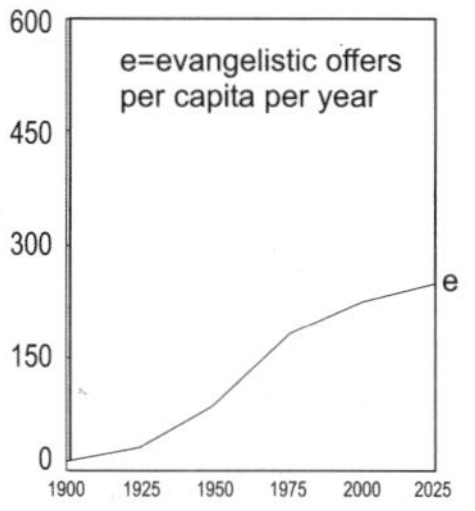

Offers, 1900-2025

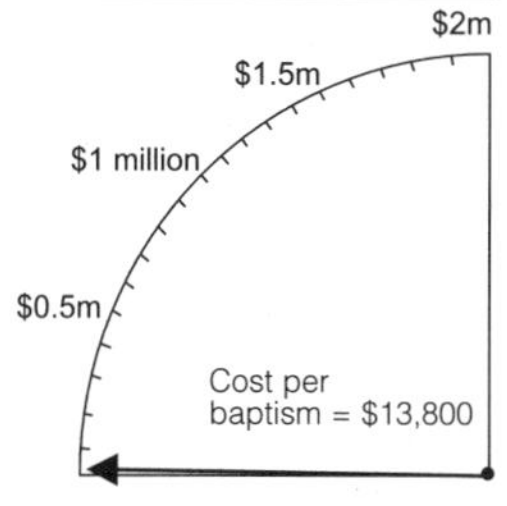

Cost-effectiveness, AD 2000

Country summary. **Worlds A, B, C by ethnolinguistic peoples, cities, and major civil divisions in Zimbabwe.**

	PEOPLES							CITIES							CIVIL DIVISIONS						
World	Num	Pop 2000	C%	Christians	E%	U%	Unevangelized	Num	Pop 2000	C%	Christians	E%	U%	Unevangelized	Num	Pop 2000	C%	Christians	E%	U%	Unevangelized
A	3	19,356	2.42	469	48	52	10,063	0	0	0.00	0	0	0	0	0	0	0.00	0	0	0	0
B	19	3,585,511	47.02	1,685,988	95	5	166,908	3	2,743,375	56.56	1,551,589	95	5	123,516	6	6,566,305	58.62	3,849,086	98	2	149,442
C	20	8,064,161	64.87	5,230,901	100	0	30,545	1	130,079	60.00	78,047	99	1	1,379	4	5,102,725	60.13	3,068,274	99	1	58,075
Total	**42**	**11,669,028**	**59.28**	**6,917,358**	**98**	**2**	**207,516**	**4**	**2,873,454**	**56.71**	**1,629,636**	**96**	**4**	**124,895**	**10**	**11,669,030**	**59.28**	**6,917,360**	**98**	**2**	**207,517**

Country status. Zimbabwe is a landlocked country in southeast Africa south of the River Zambezi. Both minerals and agriculture products are important to the economy. These include gold, asbestos, tobacco, cotton, and sugar.

HUMAN LIFE AND LIBERTY

Human need and development. Zimbabwe has had a mixed record in improving the standard of living for its people since independence. Before independence, it had one of Africa's strongest economies, with mining as the most profitable sector. Since then, periodic droughts, massive increase in population, the flight of white settlers from the country, and economic mismanagement (coupled with a brief flirtation with Marxism) have combined to drag the country down. AIDS, affecting between 10 and 30% of the population, bodes ill for the country. The urban poor live in dormitory towns on the outskirts or major urban settlements. Living conditions in these slums have deteriorated in the past 15 years. The unemployment rate is as high as 45%.

Human rights and freedoms. Although the government is broadly committed to human rights, there are occasional lapses due to party politics and sectional interests gaining the upper hand. In general, police brutality remains a problem for which the government evades responsibility. The jails are overcrowded and their squalid conditions promote cholera, diarrhea, and AIDS. There are significant, politically motivated restrictions on press freedom. Government influences mainstream media through direct ownership, editorial appointments, directives to editors, and firing of who refuse to heed them. The opposition press is small and ineffective. Official policy supports women's rights, but women continue to suffer traditional social disabilities.

Human environment. Zimbabwe has not escaped the environmental problems common to its neighbors. The most serious are land degradation, soil erosion, deforestation, and discharge of raw sewage and industrial pollutants into the lakes and rivers.

Ethnoreligionists. Traditionalists (pagans) number 3.5 million (AD 2000), increasing by 44,000 a year. Preparation for Mukwerere (rain ritual), with millet for sacrificial beer presented to ancestors by senior women.

NON-CHRISTIAN RELIGIONS

Traditional religions are still practiced by over 30% of the population. The eastern Ndau (60% traditionalist) and Hiechware Bushmen (85%) are the most resistant of the indigenous peoples to Christian influence. An unusual feature of Shona traditional religious practice is the Mwari cult of the Matopo Hills. Unlike many African traditional religions which picture God as remote, Mwari, the supreme being of the Shona, continues to speak to his people through the Rozvi priests at Matonjeni. His holy days (*chisi*) are observed at local cult shrines throughout Mashonaland where annual fees are collected and forwarded to Matonjeni as rain offerings to Mwari. Mwari's advice is also sought in times of national crisis. The Shona emphasis on God does not interfere with their traditional belief in the ancestors (Midzimu), for the latter are seen as intermediaries between man and God. Although the high God is not directly involved, the Korekore and Tawara peoples of the Mount Darwin district recognize the cults of Dzivaguru and Karuva as playing a role similar to that of Mwari at Matonjeni. Both were once human and Dzivaguru is said to have been the father of Karuva. The center of both cults is the Chona chiefdom, and both spirits are renowned for their ability to produce rain. The Korekore also attach great significance to the role of lion spirits (Mhondoro) who are the spirits of chiefs ruling the area prior to the Korekore's arrival. The spirits have their abode in lions and speak through their recognized mediums. Spirit-possession cults among the southern Shona also have a long history. The Mashave are the most prevalent and have undergone gradual change from an earlier period when they were regarded as individual guardian spirits to a more recent identification of them as foreign spirits. The Ndebele have 4 spirit-possession types, the most important being the Amatshave. These are spirits of the previous inhabitants of the area and speak through their mediums in Shona.

Islam exists among African Muslims from neighboring countries especially Malawi and Mozambique, and also among Asian traders and Coloureds.

Baha'i has grown rapidly among Africans, from 9,000 in 1970 to 35,000 in 1995. There are also many Indian followers formerly Muslims or Hindus.

Judaism has an ancient history in Zimbabwe. Jewish pioneers from England arrived as early as 1869, followed by others from Eastern Europe. The first organized Jewish congregation, in Bulawayo, dates from 1849. Others are now found at Gatooma, Que Que and Salisbury, the latter with 2 groups including the only Sefardi congregation in the country. The principal co-ordinating agency for the Jewish community is the Central African Jewish Board of Deputies in Bulawayo.

CHRISTIANITY

The first Christian contact was made with the Shona by the Portuguese Jesuit Gonzalo da Silveira in 1561, and there were further efforts in the 1600s; but no permanent Catholic presence resulted until 1879. The pioneer Protestant missionary to Zimbabwe was Robert Moffat who received permission from the Ndebele chief Mziligazi to open a London Missionary Society station at Inyati in 1859. Several missions tried to follow in the footsteps of the LMS but were unsuccessful; and it was not until 1888 that new groups were able to commence work in the country.

White and Black Christians each have their distinctive image and form their own communities, largely separated from each other. White Christianity is urban and bears the imprint of the Whites' country of origin; England for Anglicans and Methodists, Ireland for Catholics, and South Africa for Dutch Reformed. It is plagued by marriage instability, the White community of Zimbabwe having the third highest divorce rate in the world (25%). Christianity has had little social relevance for White Christians. Black Christianity, on the other hand, is mainly rural, characterized by personalistic piety and conservative theology. The churches are predominantly African in membership, though many continue to remain under European leadership. Until 1973, all 5 Catholic bishops were White, as were also the 2 Anglican bishops then. Where church leaders have taken a liberal view on race relations, their ideas have been rejected by the majority of their White adherents; and there are also tensions within the ministry over the race issue. The great majority of African Christians are below the age of 30. The churches are numerically weakest among African men over 40, by far the most active and best-organized lay movement being that of married women.

Methodists. Worship under way in village church near Gweru.

PROTESTANT CHURCHES. The 2 decades after 1888 witnessed a rapid expansion of Protestantism and established patterns of church adherence which have largely continued until today. Zimbabwe is primarily a Protestant country, but there is no single predominant church. Rather there are a number of important churches, the largest of which owe their origin to the end of the last century and the early part of this century.

Methodism is represented by 2 major denominations, one related to British Methodism and the other to the USA's United Methodists. The former, arriving in 1890, has a substantial White constituency (16%); while the latter, which entered from Mozambique in 1896, is almost completely African. Other smaller bodies are the Free Methodist and Wesleyan churches. Taken as a whole, Methodists form the major Protestant church tradition in the country.

The Salvation Army has been at work since 1891. The church is 90% Shona. Other churches with substantial constituencies are the African Reformed Church (Dutch Reformed) since 1891, and Seventh-day Adventists since 1894. A later arrival in 1903 was Swedish Lutherans who laid the foundation for the Evangelical Lutheran Church.

Several Presbyterian groups are active, including the Presbyterian Church of Southern Africa (begun 1896) composed mostly of White settlers, and the Church of Central Africa, Presbyterian (1912) consisting of Malawians.

The United Congregational Church is a product of early LMS work in 1859, while the United Church of Christ traces its history to the outreach of the American Board in 1893. Both are declining. The African Evangelical Church (formerly SAGM) dates from 1897.

British Baptists began work in 1917 but confined their activities to the European community; Southern Baptists from the USA came in 1950 and directed their attention to the African population.

Newer churches, representing for the most part North American Pentecostal and conservative groups, are establishing themselves as rapidly-growing denominations. Among these are the Pentecostal Assemblies of Canada, Assemblies of God, and Church of the Nazarene.

The Protestant churches have played a leading role in education, medicine, and social service. Until 1970, 90% of all African students were educated in government-aided church schools.

CATHOLIC CHURCH. Growth has been substantial since the arrival of Catholic missionaries in

Catholic Church in Zimbabwe, Diocese of Wankie. On Good Friday, school pupils guided by Marist Brothers re-enact Crucifixion.

1879, and today the Salisbury archdiocese has 3 suffragan dioceses. In the 2 main cities of Salisbury and Bulawayo, the Catholic Church has been most closely associated with the White community, which exercises a strong influence on the clergy. On the other hand, clergy of the dioceses of Gwelo and Wankie, as well as German Jesuits in Salisbury, have long been known as progressivist and have been responsible for new impulses in the fields of liturgy and catechetics in recent years. Catholicism in Zimbabwe is characterized by strong lay activity.

Vocations to the priesthood remain a serious problem for the church. Less than 10% of Catholic priests are African, and the same holds true for brothers. African sisters, however, outnumber all others (695 Blacks out of 1,071). Undoubtedly one reason for the latter has been the establishment of 4 indigenous religious congregations: Little Children of Our Blessed Lady (formed in 1932), Sisters of the Child Jesus, Handmaids of Our Lady of Mount Carmel, and Servants of Mary the Queen. Until 1973 all Catholic bishops were Whites. The first Black bishop was consecrated in January 1973 and appointed as auxiliary bishop of Salisbury.

The Holy See has diplomatic relations with Zimbabwe and in AD 2000 is represented to government and the Catholic hierarchy by a nuncio residing in Harare.

ANGLICAN CHURCH. The UMCA entered Zimbabwe in 1888 after receiving a grant of land from the British government. Beginning with the settler community, attention was later directed to the needs of the African population. At the present time Anglican work is divided into 2 dioceses, Mashonaland and Matebeleland, corresponding to the 2 major ethnic groups in the country. Anglicanism in Zimbabwe is part of the Church of the Province of Central Africa.

INDIGENOUS CHURCHES. At the end of the last century, South African independent churchmen attempted to export their new faith to Zimbabwe but were prevented by government and mission hostility. However, Black American missionaries of the African Methodist Episcopal Church working in South Africa were able to obtain entrance in 1900. The first church indigenous to the country was established in 1906, and today there are more than 120 separate denominations with members from every tribe, several of which have very large constituencies. The African Apostolic Church of Johane Maranke, founded in 1932, is the largest with 910,000.

Indigenous missions. Christians in Zimbabwe have been committed to foreign missions since the rise of the African Independent churches in the middle of the 20th century. These churches sent the largest number of missionaries, though most serve in neighboring countries.

Renewal movements. In the 1990s the Pentecostal/Charismatic Renewal continued to spread rapidly across most older churches, and numbered over 4,930,000 adherents (of whom 3% Pentecostals, 5% Charismatics, and 92% Independents).

CHURCH AND STATE

Separation between church and state with freedom of conscience and religion were guaranteed in the illegal Smith regime's republican constitution of 1970, but freedom of expression, assembly, and association were restricted through legal measures. Racial legislation brought churches into conflict with the government, especially since 1962. Between 1964 and 1971, 13 missionaries among whom was the head of the United Methodist Church, bishop Ralph Dodge, were expelled.

The constitution of 2 March 1970 began in its Dedication: 'The peoples of Rhodesia humbly acclaim the supremacy and omnipotence of Almighty God and acknowledge the ultimate direction by Him of the affairs of men'. However, it soon provoked direct confrontation between churches and state. The constitutional proposals were put before the mainly White electorate in June 1969, but were condemned by the 5 Catholic bishops as 'completely contrary to Christian teaching' in their pastoral letter of 5 June 1969, and by the heads of 9 Christian churches (including the Catholic bishops) as a 'potential tool of tyranny' in their statement of 6 June 1970. After this same republican constitution had come into force on 2 March 1970, the Catholic bishops threatened civil disobedience in their pastoral letter of 17 March 1970, a position which was supported in principle by the leaders of 16 Protestant churches in their joint statements of 18 April 1970. These leaders included those of the Salvation Army and the African branch of the Dutch Reformed Church, which have traditionally not spoken out on racial issues. The main argument of the churches centered around the new Land Tenure Act, which imposed severe limitations on the non-racial service of the churches. In essence, the Act divided Rhodesia into 2 areas, European and African, and thus introduced apartheid. Moreover, the Catholic bishops announced on 29 April 1970 that they would prefer to close all Catholic private schools (catering mainly for White children) than comply with the new Act which forbade Africans from attending those schools.

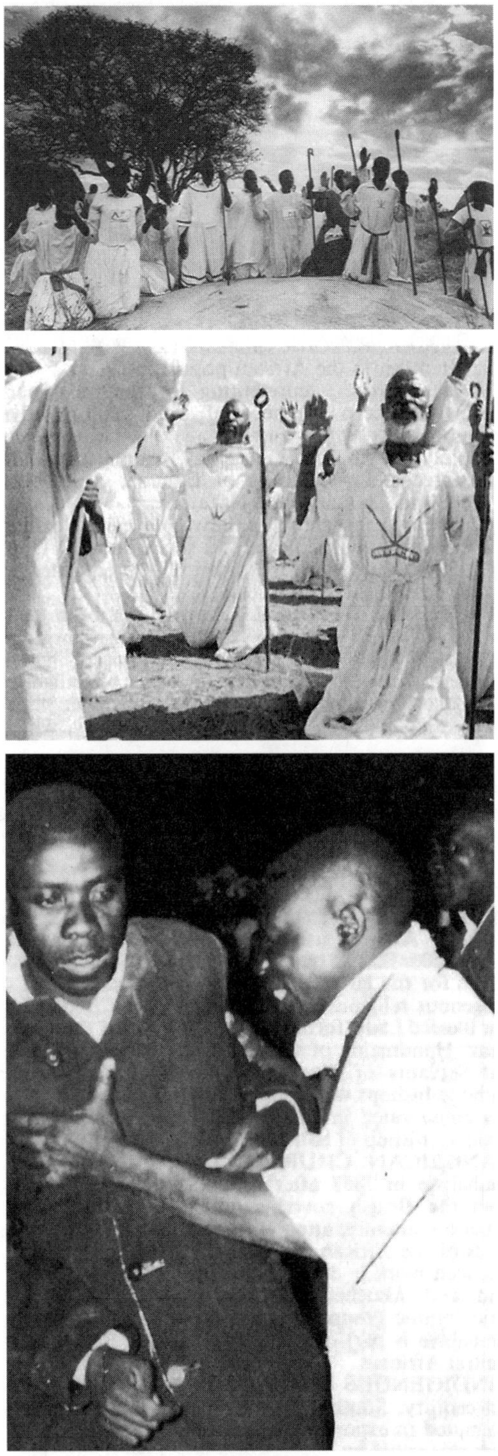

African Apostolic Church of Johane Maranke (AACJM). Largest of 130 indigenous denominations, the Vapostori (Apostles) have created new and striking forms. *Top.* Apostles at corporate prayer. *Center.* Liebauma prophets engaging in simultaneous audible prayer. *Bottom.* Zionist prophet of Mutendi's ZCC (right) detects and intercepts an unconfessed sinner (left) trying to enter sacred enclosure for holy communion.

The Smith regime endeavored to avoid a direct confrontation with the churches by amending those provisions of the Land Tenure Act which restricted the freedom of the churches, especially the requirement that churches register as 'voluntary associations' before being permitted to continue their multiracial work on 'mission land'. However, by a statement on 11 September 1970, the leaders of 11 churches rejected these amendments. The government made a further compromise with the churches, especially with the Catholic Church, when it proposed at the end of 1970 that Africans might continue to attend Catholic private schools located in European areas provided they constituted not more than 6% of the total enrollment of pupils. In February 1971 the Catholic bishops agreed to this condition on a temporary basis and 'under force majeure'. This compromise was heavily criticized within and outside Rhodesia and was partly attributed to the influence of an emissary sent by Rome, at the bishops' request.

In the sphere of public services to the African population, there is a tradition of close co-operation between churches and state, particularly in the fields of public health and education; and ministers of all churches retain the right of entry into schools for the purpose of teaching religion. Government grants for the 75 church-run hospitals cover only a small portion of the cost; but schools, especially primary schools, until 1970 received grants for the total salaries of all teachers. After January 1971, the churches, with the exception of the Anglican diocese of Mashonaland and the Salvation Army, ceased to be responsible authorities for African primary education. They refused to co-operate further in this field because the government decreed that 5% of teachers' salaries should be contributed by African parents, who had already paid for the erection of school buildings, repairs and book fees. African primary schools were after this taken over 'ad interim; by the central government; but for financial reasons and to foster 'separate development' they were placed into the hands of local African authorities.

In 1971 the churches played a major role in influencing the outcome of the Pierce Commission inquiry and thus the decision of the British government to continue its refusal to recognize the minority government of Ian Smith. A key leader of the opposition at the time was bishop Abel Muzorewa, the head of both the United Methodist Church and the African National Council.

On 15 November 1974 the Catholic newspaper, *Moto*, was banned by vote of parliament.

By 1978 bishop Muzorewa was serving on a 4-man executive council with Smith, and a year later became prime minister. By mid-1978, over 40 White missionaries had been murdered by guerrillas.

In 1980 Robert Mugabe, a Marxist Socialist guerrilla leader, was elected to lead a new government and the independence of Zimbabwe was confirmed and recognized.

BROADCASTING AND MEDIA

Over shortwave radio, programs in Shona can be received from FEBA (Seychelles) and in Ndebele and Shona from TWR (Swaziland). Shortwave radio programs from KNLS have seen some response. Zimbabwe is a member of UNDA. The Zimbabwe Broadcast Corp. (ZBC) broadcasts a Sunday Service in English over Radio One, and in Ghona and Ndebele on Radio Two. Other air slots are also available and are shared between denominations. Christian Vision is a local radio broadcaster that airs WEC programs.

Television programs are available both on local channels and via satellite. 'Epilogue' is a 3-minute program aired on a semiregular basis by ZBC over both television and Radio Four. CBN's programs, including animated specials and drama series, can be seen Friday to Monday, and are followed-up from a volunteer ministry center.

INTERDENOMINATIONAL ORGANIZATIONS

The Christian Council of Rhodesia was founded in 1964. It has been active in race relations, taking positions which have been opposed by some Protestant churches. A larger organization, including also the Dutch Reformed Church, Salvation Army and several smaller conservative bodies, is the Rhodesian Christian Conference, which built on the foundations first laid by the Southern Rhodesia Missionary Conference in 1903. A more conservative group is the Evangelical Fellowship of Zimbabwe which is a member of the Association of Evangelicals in Africa and Madagascar. The Episcopal Commission for Ecumenism represents the Zimbabwe Catholic Bishops' Conference in ecumenical relations. Epworth Theological College, sponsored by 5 denominations, illustrates Protestant ecumenism in theological education. Catholic-Protestant co-operation exists through the activities of the Ecumenical Adult Literacy Programme, Christian Publishers' Association, Christian Urban Program and Ecumenical Arts Association. A non-church interracial body in Salisbury, Ranch House College, has played an important role in promoting ecumenical contacts.

In July 1972 the African Independent Churches Conference was formed, with 12 indigenous churches as founding members and 8 others considering membership.

FUTURE TRENDS AND PROSPECTS

Christians are projected to grow to over 73% by 2025. Tribal religions, though waning, could still claim 23% of the population by 2025.

Ethnoreligionists, surprisingly resilient at the end of the 20th century, might decline precipitously after AD 2025. Christianity would probably receive the vast majority of these, perhaps attaining 80% by AD 2050.

BIBLIOGRAPHY

A history of the church in Southern Africa: a select bibliography of published material. J. W. Hofmeyr & K. E. Cross. Pretoria, South Africa: University of South Africa, 1986. 2 vols.

'Adapting to a revolution: a study of the Brethren in Christ in the changing context of Bulawayo, Zimbabwe.' D. R. Climenhaga. D.Miss. thesis, Asbury Theological Seminary, Wilmore, KY, 1993. 312p.

African Apostles: ritual and conversion in the Church of John Maranke. B. Jules–Rosette. Ithaca, NY: Cornell University Press, 1975. 302p.

'Bibliography on peoples of Zimbabwe.' M. F. C. Bourdillon & A. Cheater. Computer database and printout, University of Zimbabwe, Harare, Zimbabwe, 1983.

Catholic directory of Rhodesia, 1972. Gwelo, Rhodesia: Mambo Press, 1972. 75p.

'Christian missions and the British expansion in Southern Rhodesia, 1888–1923.' P. Hassing. Ph.D. dissertation, American University, Washington, DC, 1970.

Christian terror in Southern Africa. A. R. Lewis. Salisbury, Rhodesia: Rhodesia Christian Group, 1978. 80p.

Christianity and the Shona. M. W. Murphree. London: Athlone Press, 1969. 200p.

Christianity and traditional religion in western Zimbabwe, 1859–1923. N. Bhebe. London: Longman, 1979. 204p.

'Christianity, politics, and the Manyika: a study of the influence of religious attitudes and loyalties on political values and activities of Africans in Rhodesia.' N. E. Thomas. Thesis, Boston University, Boston, 1968. 396p.

Church and state in Zimbabwe. Vol. 3 of *Christianity south of the Zambezi.* C. F. Hallencreutz & A. Moyo (ed). Gweru, Zimbabwe: Mambo Press, 1988. 510p.

Church and politics: from theology to a case history of Zimbabwe. E. McDonagh. Notre Dame, IN: University of Notre Dame Press, 1980. 177p.

Fambidzano: ecumenical movement of Zimbabwe's independent churches. M. L. Daneel. Gweru, Zimbabwe: Mambo Press, 1989.

Freedom fighter. S. Lungu & A. Coomes. Crowborough, UK: Monarch, 1994. 187p.

God gave growth: history of the Lutheran church in Zimbabwe 1903–80. H. Söderström. *Studia missionalia*, no. 40. Gweru, Zimbabwe: Mambo Press, 1984. 237p.

History of Christian missions in Zimbabwe. C. J. M. Zvobgo. Gweru, Zimbabwe: Mambo Press, 1996. 412p.

Islam in Zimbabwe. E. C. Mandivenga. Gweru, Zimbabwe: Mambo Press, 1983. 81p.

Mainstream Christianity to 1980 in Malawi, Zambia, and Zimbabwe. J. C. Weller et al. Gweru, Zimbabwe: Mambo Press, 1984. 235p.

Missions in Southern Rhodesia. P. S. King. Cape Town, South Africa: Inyati Centenary Trust, 1959. 80p.

Ndebele religion and customs. W. Bozongwana. Gweru, Zimbabwe: Mambo Press in association with the Literature Bureau, 1983. 56p.

Old and new in Southern Shona independent churches. M. L. Daneel. *Monographs under the auspices of the Afrika–Studiecentrum, Leiden.* The Hague: Mouton Atlantic Highlands, 1971–88. 3 vols.

Rain in a dry land. J. Knight. London: Hodder & Stoughton, 1987. 221p.

'Religion and authority in a Korekore community,' M. F. C. Bourdillon, *Africa* (London), 49, 2 (1979), 172–81.

Serima: towards an African expression of Christian belief = Ein Versuch in afrikanisch–christlicher Kunst. A. B. Plangger & M. Diethelm. Gwelo, Rhodesia: Mambo Press, 1974. 76p.

'Shona independent churches and ancestor worship,' M. L. Daneel, in *African initiatives in religion*, p.160–70. D. B. Barrett (ed). *21 studies from Eastern and Central Africa*, no. 20. Nairobi: East African Publishing House, 1971.

Shona religion: with special reference to the Makorekore. M. Gelfand. Cape Town, South Africa: Juta & Co, 1962. 184p.

Spirits of protest: spirit–mediums and the articulation of consensus among the Zezuru of Southern Rhodesia (Zimbabwe). P. Fry. *Cambridge studies in social anthropology*, no. 14. Cambridge, UK: Cambridge University Press, 1976. 145p.

The Catholic Church and Zimbabwe, 1879–1979. A. J. Dachs & W. F. Rea. Gweru, Zimbabwe: Mambo Press, 1979. 260p.

'The church in Zimbabwe: the trauma of cutting apron strings,' *Pro Mundi Vita: Dossiers*, Africa dossier 20 (January 1982), 1–36.

'The Church of England as an international actor in Southern Africa, 1970–1980.' V. Austin. Ph.D. dissertation, University of Kent, Canterbury, UK, 1991. 302p.

The clash of cultures: Christian missionaries and the Shona of Rhodesia. G. Z. Kapenzi. Washington, DC: University Press of America, 1979. 104p.

The demands of simple justice: a study of the church, politics and violence with special reference to Zimbabwe. E. McDonagh. Dublin, Ireland: Gill and Macmillan, 1980. 177p.

'The early history of independency in Southern Rhodesia,' T. O. Ranger, in *Religion in Africa*, p.52–74. W. N. Watt (ed). Edinburgh, Scotland: 1964.

The God of the Matopo Hills: an essay on the Mwari cult of Rhodesia. M. L. Daneel. The Hague: Mouton, 1970. 95p.

'The impact of Christianity on the political values of Africans in Rhodesia.' N. E. Thomas. Ph.D. dissertation, Boston University, Boston, 1968.

The Korsten Basketmakers: a study of the Masowe Apostles, an indigenous African religious movement. C. M. Dillon–Malone. Manchester, UK: Manchester University Press, 1978. 169p.

The new crusaders: Christianity and the new right in Southern Africa. P. Gifford. London: Pluto Press, 1991. 131p. (Chapter 3 on Zimbabwe).

'The professional preparation of adult religious educators in Zimbabwe using the behavioral contingency management model.' D. A. Mpinga. Ed.D. dissertation, Southwestern Baptist Theological Seminary, Fort Worth, TX, 1979. 124p.

The Shona and the Ndebele of Southern Rhodesia. H. Kuper, A. J. B. Hughes & J. van Velsen. London: International African Institute, 1954. 131p.

The Shona peoples: an ethnography of the contemporary Shona, with special reference to their religion. M. F. C. Bourdillon. 3rd ed. Gwelo, Zimbabwe: Mambo Press, 1987. 359p.

The theology of promise: the dynamics of self–reliance. C. Banana. Harare, Zimbabwe: College Press, 1982. 156p. (By former state president).

The Wesleyan Methodist missions in Zimbabwe, 1891–1945. C. J. M. Zvobgo. Harare, Zimbabwe: University of Zimbabwe Publications, 1991. 169p.

Transfigured night: mission and culture in Zimbabwe's vigil movement. T. L. Presler. Pretoria: UNISA, 1999. 349p.

Zimbabwe. D. Potts. 2nd ed. *World bibliographical series*, vol. 4. Oxford, UK: CLIO Press, 1993. 402p. (See especially 'Religion,' p.99–109).

Zimbabwe Christian art: the first collected exhibition 28th November–13th December held at the Anglican Cathedral, Harare opened by H.E. the Rev Canaan Banana, president of the Republic of Zimbabwe. Harare: Anglican Cathedral, 1986. 24p.

Zionism and faith healing in Rhodesia: aspects of African independent churches. M. L. Daneel. The Hague: Mouton, 1970. 64p.

Country Table 2. **Organized churches and denominations in Zimbabwe.**

Official name (bold type = church with over 10% of all affiliated) 1	*Begun* 2	*Type* 3	*Counc* 4	*Congs* 5	*Adults* 6	*Affiliated 1970* 7	*Affiliated 1995* 8	*G%* 9	*Names, notes, and other statistics* (see Codebook, Part 3) 10
African Apost Ch of Johane Maranke	1932	I-3aA	x...I	500	420,000	260,000	910,000	5.14	*AACJM. VaPostori (Apostles).* Ex USA Methodists. Manyika, Zezuru; since 1950 across Africa.
African Apost Ch St Simon & St Johane	1963	I-3aA	.....	10	3,000	2,000	5,000	3.73	Schism ex AACJM claiming succession after founder's death, by his cousin. Manyika.
African Congregational Church	1930	I-Ref	I	30	12,000	15,000	25,000	2.06	*Chibarirwe (Born for us).* Ex DRC. Returning Ndau laborers from South Africa. 6n.
African Free Presb Ch of Zimbabwe	1953	I-Ref	.....	4	2,100	2,000	4,000	2.81	Schism ex FPCS protesting discrimination in use of mission transport. Shangaan.
African Full Gospel Church	1923	I-3fA	.....	3	500	500	1,000	2.81	Begun by returning miners from Rand. 1947, split ex FGCoG(SA). Mainly Venda.
African Methodist Church in Zimbabwe	1947	I-Met	.vA.d	6	4,000	5,000	7,000	1.35	Schism ex UK Methodists. Ndebele. 1961, applied to WCC, rejected. HQ Selukwe.
African Methodist Episcopal Church	1900	I-Met	Vw..d	120	19,300	40,000	32,150	-0.87	*AMEC, 17th Episcopal District. Ethiopian Church.* Black mission from USA. Declining.
African Orthodox Church	1924	I-ARo	x....	15	11,000	30,000	20,000	-1.61	M=AO(USA). Ex Anglicans. Registered 1924: 1972 Rhodesian African bishop. Ndebele.
Alliance Church of Zimbabwe		I-Non	x.G.E	23	2,300	500	5,750	0.05	M=SAM(Sweden). HQ Bulawayo. HQ and main work in Transvaal, South Africa. 2f.
Anglican Church in Zimbabwe:	1888	A-Hig	AwaVd	900	170,000	153,000	300,000	2.73	In CPCA, Ch of the Province of Central Africa, with 10 Dioceses (4 in Zimbabwe). 103f,1s.
Anglican Orthodox Church of Zimbabwe	1968	I-ReA	x....	10	400	300	700	3.45	M=AOC(USA). Ex Anglican Ch. Whites. Fundamentalists opposing CPCA policies. 1n.
Apostolic Church	1951	P-PeA	ZG...	6	1,000	500	2,000	5.70	Begun from South Africa. Largely Whites. M=ACCM(UK). HQ Chadcombe, Salisbury. 4f.
Apostolic Ch of Pentecost of Z	1951	P-Pe1	.....	10	1,000	500	2,000	5.70	M=ACP (Canada). Oneness Pentecostals, from Saskachewan.
Apostolic Faith		I-3pA	.....	50	15,000	13,000	30,000	0.05	*Apostolic Faith* (Portland). Some aid from M=AF(Portland, USA). Rapid growth.
Apostolic Faith Mission of SAfrica	1918	P-Pe2	Z....	975	40,000	55,000	87,000	1.85	*AFMSA*(Rhodesia). Shona-speaking. M=AFM(SA). 4% White. Static. HQ Bulawayo. 4f.
Assemblies of God International	1970	I-3pA	.....	10	1,000	600	3,000	6.65	Rival body to AoG (USA) claiming half its churches..
Assemblies of God in Zimbabwe	1964	P-Pe2	ZF...	35	2,550	1,045	6,375	7.50	M=AoG(USA,UK,SA). HQ Salisbury. Tent campaigns, up to 8,000 present. 7n,4f.
Assemblies of God (Back to God)	1958	I-3pA	x....	120	20,000	6,000	40,000	7.88	M=AoG (Nicholas Bhengu) (South Africa). Rapid expansion, some splits. Zulu et alii.
Baptist Convention of Zimbabwe	1950	P-Bap	T...C	503	121,678	14,000	150,000	9.95	1956. M=FMB-SBC(USA). 92% Zezuru, 8% Ndebele. 3 schools. 31n,52f,1H,17h,1s,1040Y.
Baptist Union of Zimbabwe	1917	P-Bap	..G.x	32	3,514	3,900	5,500	1.38	*BUCA.* M=British & SA Baptists. Members Whites only. HQ Salisbury.
Bible Pattern Church		I-3pA	.....	20	2,000	2,000	5,000	0.05	Independent Black pentecostals, split ex Elim Ch. Expanding.
Brethren in Christ Church in Africa	1898	P-Men	GFG.x	173	12,039	10,000	26,200	3.93	M=BiCC(USA). A=1964. 98% Ndebele. 7n,55f,2H,1h,W=60%,260Y,2023z.
Broadsheet Readers' Clubs	c1980	I-3nA	.....	384	5,000	–	10,000	6.67	Readers of Gospel Broadsheets produced by M=WEC(UK).
Catholic Church in Zimbabwe:	1561	R-Lat	P.SSs	170	507,000	556,789	1,022,226	2.46	92% Black, 6% White. C=8+3+21. 1p,1s(64). 107n 235x 347m 1120w 41255Yy
M Bulawayo	1931	R-Lat	Pcmm	30	59,000	69,596	117,906	2.13	52% Ndebele, 24% Shona, 13% Kalanga, 11% White. 12n 35x 44m 166w 5241Yy
D Gweru (Gwelo, Fort Victoria)	1946	R-Lat	Ps	46	165,000	177,764	335,942	2.58	60% Karanga, 20% Zezuru, 10% Ndebele, 2% White. 27n 44x 84m 253w 12257Yy
D Hwange (Wankie)	1953	R-Lat	Pieme	19	15,000	26,280	30,156	0.55	46% Shona, 33% Nambia, 14% Ndebele, 2% White. 8n 18x 26m 68w 1602Yy
M Harare (Salisbury)	1879	R-Lat	Ps	33	163,000	211,495	318,691	1.65	85% Shona, 8% White (strong influence). M=SJ. 1s. 33n 84x 122m 400w 14317Yy
D Chinhoyi (Sinoia)	1973	R-Lat	Psj	16	23,000	–	58,668	4.55	Formed in 1973 out of M Salisbury. M=SJ. 9n 18x 28m 89w 3099Yy
D Gokwe	1991	R-Lat	Ps	6	25,000	–	50,863	25.00	Formerly part of D Hwange. M=IEME. 12n 0x 0m 28w 1966Yy
D Mutare (Umtali)	1953	R-Lat	Ps	20	57,000	71,654	110,000	1.73	50% Manyika, 35% Hungwe, 12% Wesa, 2% White. 6n 36x 43m 116w 2773Yy
Christadelphian Ecclesias		m-Ade	x....	2	50	50	100	0.05	*Christadelphian Bible Mission.* 1 ecclesia (church) in Salisbury. Pacifist.
Christian Brethren	c1903	P-CBr	x....	35	4,100	5,000	6,830	1.26	*Open.* Strong in south in Harding district. 1950, M=CMML(UK, USA, Australia). 23f.
Christian Chs and Chs of Christ	1956	I-Dis	.....	51	10,000	5,000	16,700	4.94	Independent Disciples. M=CCCC(USA).
Christian Marching Ch of Central Africa	1954	I-Sal	....W	40	15,000	3,000	27,000	9.19	*CMCCA.* Ex Soldiers of God. 70% Zezuru, 30% Ndebele. 4n,W=39%, 60Y,150y,45z.
Ch of Central Africa, Presbyterian	1912	P-Ref	J...C	70	6,173	18,000	11,937	-1.63	*CCAP, Salisbury Synod.* Malawians: 92% Chewa. 4n,4x,1s,W=61%,371Y,568y.
Church of Christ, Scientist		m-Sci	x....	2	100	370	200	0.05	*Christian Science.* M=CCS(Boston, USA). 90% Whites. Decline from 1,500 in 1960. 6w.
Ch of England in South Africa	c1970	I-ReA	J.G.Z	3	150	300	400	1.16	From SAfrica. Evangelicals, opposing CPCA. Whites. Fort Victoria, Salisbury.
Church of God of Prophecy	1976	P-Pe3	.....	38	6,850	–	9,790	5.26	M=CGP(USA). Holiness Pentecostals.
Ch of Jesus Christ of Latter-day Saints		m-LdS	x....	10	1,040	280	1,600	0.05	*Mormons.* M=CJCLdS(Utah, USA). All Whites. Based in Salisbury.
Church of the Nazarene	1963	P-Hol	xFG.Z	31	2,037	2,000	3,962	2.77	M=CoN(USA). Holiness denomination. HQ Salisbury. 2n,2x,4f,W=83%,75z.
Churches of Christ (NZ)	1898	I-Dis	x...d	120	14,100	10,000	40,300	5.73	M=Associated CCNZ. A=1943. HQ Dadaya. 90% Karanga, 10% Ndebele. 35 schools. 1H,2h.

Continued opposite

Country Table 2–concluded

Official name (bold type = church with over 10% of affiliated) 1	*Begun* 2	*Type* 3	*Counc* 4	*Congs* 5	*Adults* 6	*Affiliated 1970* 7	*Affiliated 1995* 8	*G%* 9	*Names, notes, and other statistics* (see Codebook, Part 3) 10
Churches of Christ (Non-Instrumental)	1921	I-Dis	x....	30	4,000	5,000	10,000	2.81	M=CC(Non-Instrumental) (USA). Independent congregations. 1 school. 32f,2s.
Churches of Christ (USA)	1896	I-Dis	x...C	115	39,600	14,000	70,000	6.65	*Central African Christian Mission.* 1956, M=CCCC(Instrumental) (USA). Bulawayo. 87f.
Dutch Reformed Ch (Mother Church)	1895	P-Ref	F...C	16	2,015	17,000	2,585	-7.26	*NGK Moederkerk (Rhodesie).* Afrikaans-speaking Whites only. HQ Salisbury. 191Yy.
Elim Pentecostal Church	c1960	P-Pe2	ZGG.E	8	1,000	300	2,500	8.85	M=Elim Foursquare Gospel Alliance (EMS,UK). Mozambique border. Schools. 14f,1H,191Y.
Evangelical Church	c1965	P-Eva	.....	25	2,300	1,000	4,600	6.29	Mainline Evangelicals.
Evangelical Church of Zimbabwe	1942	P-Eva	xMG.E	120	7,500	6,000	18,800	4.67	M=TEAM(USA,SA), 99% Korekore. HQ Hatfield. 2 schools. 15n,20x,821,1H,7h,1s,161Y.
Evangelical Lutheran Ch in Zimbabwe	1903	P-Lut	LW.Jd	200	27,200	42,039	60,500	1.47	2 Dioceses. M=SKM(Sweden). 66% Karanga. 24n,5x,4H,4h,1p,1u,w=67%,60Y,317y,3100z.
Faith Ministries	c1975	I-3wA	.....	6	1,000	–	1,820	5.00	African Independents with Word of Faith theology (Prosperity Gospel).
First Ethiopian Church	1926	I-Non	I	4	2,000	5,000	4,000	-0.89	1910 founder joined church in South Africa, 1926 began in Rhodesia. Karanga.
Free Methodist Church	1938	I-Hol	VFG.x	20	4,700	6,000	8,250	1.28	M=FMC(USA), 58% Karanga. 38% Hlengwe. 9n,3x,28f,1H,1h,1s(17),W=33%,100Y.
Free Presbyterian Church of Scotland	1904	P-Ref	.....	30	300	300	400	1.16	M=FPCS(UK). Small mission from Scotland. Shangaan. Schools. 1H,1r.
Full Gospel Ch of God in Southern A	c1950	P-Pe3	ZFG.E	82	7,200	15,000	14,400	-0.16	Branch of South African body. M=CoG(Cleveland) (USA). 7% White. Static. 36n.
Glad Tidings Fellowship	1973	I-3pA	.....	25	3,700	–	7,400	4.55	African Independent pentecostals.
Gospel of God Church in Zimbabwe	1932	I-3aA	x....	100	21,000	30,000	55,000	2.45	*Basketmakers. Hosannas.* Ex Anglican Ch. Shona artisans. Missions in 11 countries.
Greek Orth Archbishopric of Zimbabwe	1905	O-Gre	Cw...	5	3,320	8,000	6,200	-1.01	In P Alexandria. 4,000 Greek settlers from Greece, Egypt, Cyprus. 3x,W=20%,150y.
Independent African Church	1942	I-Met	....W	50	3,000	5,000	9,000	2.38	*Muchakata (Worshippers under trees).* Schism ex Methodists (USA). 80% Manyika.
Jehovah's Witnesses	c1910	m-Jeh	x....	700	18,382	30,000	55,800	2.51	Many from Zambia, Malawi, SAfrica. 94% African, 6% White. (1975) 684Y. (1995) 1939Y.
Mai Chaza Church	1952	I-Met	.....	160	33,900	50,000	60,000	0.73	*Guta ra Jehovah (Cities of God).* Schism ex UK Methodists by Mother Chaza. Manyika.
Methodist Church in Zimbabwe	1890	P-Met	VwA.d	1,116	78,000	112,500	137,669	0.81	M=MMS. 66% Zezuru, 16% White, 14% Ndebele, 49n,29x,340m,60f,6r,1u,1191Y,4748y.
National Baptist Convention	c1975	I-Bap	T....	10	1,513	–	2,800	5.00	M=NBCUSA(Afro-American Blacks).
Netherlands Reformed Church	1900	P-Ref	.....	20	2,200	4,620	3,390	-1.23	*Nederduits Hervormde Kerk.*
New Apostolic Church	c1910	I-3aX	x....	70	13,111	40,000	30,000	-1.14	*Rhodesia Church District.* Begun by Germans and Lozis. World HQ Zurich (Switzerland).
New Covenant Assemblies of God	c1975	I-3cA	.....	14	1,120	–	2,490	5.00	Independent charismatics.
New Life For All	c1970	I-Non	.....	5	400	–	667	29.71	Independent Nondenominationalists.
Pentecostal Apostolic Ch of God	1960	I-3aA	.....	25	15,000	1,000	30,000	14.57	*PACG.* In northern Honde Valley. Led by female prophets. In Zambia, Mozambique, SAfrica.
Pentecostal Assemblies of God in Z	1942	P-Pe2	ZFG.Z	75	2,100	6,000	7,000	0.62	*PAG.* M=PAOC(Canada). Southeast of country. HQ Salisbury. Static. 44n,10x,1p.
Pentecostal Holiness Church	1950	P-Pe3	ZF...	48	3,500	2,000	7,450	5.40	M=IPHC(USA). 27nm,4f,1s.
Presbyterian Church of Southern Africa	1896	P-Ref	Rwa.d	10	5,192	25,000	17,300	-1.46	*PCSA.* 2 Presbyteries. White settlers, some Ndebele. 21nx(16 Whites, 5 Africans).
Reformed Church in Zimbabwe	1891	P-Ref	F.G.x	756	25,000	60,000	80,000	1.16	M=DRC(SA). HQ Morgenster. 60% Karanga, 30% Zezuru. 200f(1972),38f(1977),24n,10x,1s.
Reformed True Methodist Church	1964	I-Met	.....	2	570	2,000	1,000	-2.73	*RTMC.* Schism ex Methodist Ch; mainly Plumtree and Shabani. Declining.
Religious Society of Friends	c1920	P-Qua	Q...d	2	50	70	100	1.44	*Central African General Mtg.* M=FSC(UK). 80% British, Salisbury, Bulawayo. W=70%.
Rhema Bible Churches	1980	I-3wA	.....	27	15,000	–	25,000	6.67	Related to M=RMAI (USA). Prosperity gospel teaching.
Salvation Army: Zimbabwe Territory	1891	P-Sal	xwA.d	687	60,075	140,000	150,000	0.28	*Hondo yo Ruponiso.* 90% Shona. 232n,105x,2H,7h,5r,1s(24),W=64%,2873Y.
Seventh-day Adventist Church	1894	P-Adv	x....	1	166,617	50,000	278,000	7.10	*Zambesi Union.* 69% Ndebele, 30% Shona. 44n,20x,38f,3h,4r,1s,703t(45611),W=90%,2694Y.
Sign of the Apostles Church	c1970	I-3zA	.....	70	20,000	–	40,000	52.79	Ardent advocates of green revolution and AAEC/ZIRRCON earthkeeping.
Soldiers of God	1938	I-Sal	.....	40	14,000	20,000	31,000	1.77	*Soja we Mwari.* Ex Salvation Army. 50% Karanga, 20% Ndebele,20% Nyanja. 4n,84Y,66y.
United Apostolic Faith Church	1920	P-Pe2	x....	30	3,100	5,000	7,750	1.77	M=UAFC(SA,UK), HQ Pretoria. British-Israelite Pentecostals. 10% Whites. 20nx,1p.
United Assemblies of God		I-3pA	.....	29	2,500	2,000	5,000	0.05	*UAOG.* African Independent pentecostals.
United Church of Christ in Zimbabwe	1892	P-Uni	..A.d	160	10,000	4,300	30,000	8.08	M=ABCFM, now UCBWM(USA). A=1963. 99% Ndau. Declining. 11n,17f,1u,W=65%,50Y,22y.
United Baptist Churches of Zimbabwe	1897	P-Bap	TMG.E	44	6,000	6,000	9,000	1.64	M=SAGM(AEF). 90% Ndau, near Mozambique. School. (1970)1n,3x,20f,1h,1p,W=43%,175Y.
United Congr Ch of Southern Africa	1859	P-Con	Rwa.d	160	11,000	20,000	16,700	-0.72	*Zimbabwe Region, UCCSA.* 1859, M=LMS; CCWM. 95% Ndebele. 10n,5x,3h,W=20%,400Y.
United Methodist Church	1896	P-Met	VwA.W	650	65,000	90,000	163,000	2.40	*Z Annual Conf, UMC.* 59% Manyika, 41% Zezuru. 54n,16x,93f,3H,W=35%,1368Y,6443y.
United Pentecostal Church	1967	P-Pe1	x....	30	5,000	2,000	11,000	7.06	*Jesus Only Church.* M=UPC(USA). Unitarian Pentecostals. 4n,1f,2p(37).
Unity of African Apost Faith Ch	1931	I-3aA	.....	70	3,500	2,000	7,000	5.14	*UAAFC. Mugodhi Church.* Practice of *pungue* (night-time prayer vigils).
Victory Fellowship	c1975	I-3wA	.....	8	358	–	651	5.00	African Independents following Word of Faith theology.
Wesleyan Church	1888	P-Hol	VFG.E	15	300	500	750	1.64	Begun by M=WMMS(UK), then 1968 WC(USA). Holiness doctrines. 5 schools. 2f,1h.
Zimbabwe Assemblies of God Africa	1965	I-3pA	.....	1,709	300,000	25,000	600,000	13.56	*ZAOGA (Guti).* Independent Black pentecostals. Growing very rapidly to 50,000 by 1978.
Zimbabwe Christian Fellowship	c1975	I-3cA	.....	18	385	–	700	5.00	African charismatics.
Zion Apostolic Churches	1922	I-3zA	I...I	1,300	430,000	12,000	760,000	18.05	*ZAC. Myriads of Ndaza.* Zionists and related groups. Bishop Masuka's church. Karanga.
Zion Apostolic Faith Mission	1924	I-3zA	.....	10	6,000	7,000	16,000	3.36	*ZAFM. Bishop Shoko's church.* HQ Chibi Reserve. Southern part of country.
Zion Christian Church	1923	I-3zA	I...I	1,400	480,000	25,000	1,044,000	16.10	*ZCC.* Begun by Bishop Mutendi from South Africa. Holy cities. HQ Bikita, Karanga.
Ziwezano Church	c1960	I-Met	....W	15	2,000	3,000	5,000	2.06	*Church of Wisdom.* Ex USA Methodists in Honde valley. Manyika. Industrial schools.
Other African indigenous churches		I-3pA	.....	3,000	135,000	24,000	280,000	0.05	Total about 200 (see list below), 90 belonging to AIC council Fambidzano.
Other Protestant denominations		P-	.....	70	10,000	9,000	25,000	0.05	Total about 40 bodies (see list below), including Tsonga Presbyterian Ch, ICFG.
Other marginal Protestant bodies		m-	.....	40	1,000	1,500	2,000	0.05	Incl: Christian Spiritualist Ch (GWCSL, UK). Whites.
Doubly-affiliated		2-aff			-328,000	0	-657,392		Independents who are also baptized Catholics or Protestants.
Totals				**17,943**	**3,184,689**	**2,151,763**	**6,380,000**		

Churches, members, growth, 1900-2025	*Congs*	*Adults*	*Affiliated*	*G%*	*Total denominations*	*6 Megablocs:* *O*	*R*	*A*	*P*	*I*	*m*
Total churches, members, and denominations (mid-1900)	60	8,300	16,000	7.25	18	0	1	1	13	3	0
Total churches, members, and denominations (mid-1970)	7,914	1,122,325	2,151,763	7.25	187	1	1	1	51	125	8
Total churches, members, and denominations (mid-1990)	16,000	2,855,000	5,720,540	5.01	330	1	1	1	73	240	14
Total churches, members, and denominations (mid-1995)	17,943	3,184,689	6,380,000	2.21	337	1	1	1	74	246	14
Total churches, members, and denominations (mid-2000)	20,000	3,453,000	6,917,360	1.63	348	1	1	1	75	256	14
Total churches, members, and denominations (mid-2025)	35,000	5,241,000	10,500,000	1.68	625	3	1	1	100	500	20

NOTES ON TABLE ABOVE

NATIONAL COUNCILS (Column 4, 5th letter).

- C = Rhodesia Christian Conference (RCC, or ZCC).
- d = member of both CCZ & RCC.
- E = Evangelical Fellowship of Zimbabwe (EFZw).
- I = African Independent Churches' Conference (AICC) (Fambidzano Yamakereke Avatema = Cooperation of Churches of the Black People); about 15 members; 1973 application to Rhodesia Christian Conference as associate member.
- s = Rhodesia Catholic Bishops' Conference (RCBC), or Zimbabwe Catholic Bishops' Conference (ZCBC), and also associate member of CCZ.
- W = Christian Council of Zimbabwe (CCZ, former CCR, 1964), or Zimbabwe Council of Churches (ZCC).
- x = member of both EFR & RCC.

Other national councils. Pentecostal Fellowship of Zimbabwe (PFZ).

OTHER AFRICAN INDIGENOUS CHURCHES. Among the 100 smaller bodies are: African Catholic Ch (Ruponiso rwa Jesu, Moses Ch), African Ch of Israel, African Reformed Ch (ex African Cong Ch), African Zion Collar Church of Jesus ('Only the Bishop shall wear a clerical collar'; begun 1953), Apostolic Faith & Acts Ch, Apostolic Faith African, Apostolic Faith (Fort Victoria), Apostolic Followers, Apostolic Sabbath Ch of God, Assemblies of God (Lekuku), Central African Episcopal Ch, Ch of the Courageous Apostles, Ch of the Holy Cross, Evangelist Soldiers of God, Gospel of Christ Ch (Sande), Mashona United Independent Reformed Ch, National Baptist Assembly of Africa (Holy Trinity Ch; begun c1930 from Nyasaland), New Ch of Africa, Reformed Mai Chaza Ch, Smyrna & Crown of Life Mission, Swazi Christian Ch of SA, United African Apostolic Faith Ch of God, Zimbabwe Ch of the Orphans (c1960), Zion Apostolic Ch of Jesus, Zion Reformed Ch, Zion Sabbath Ch.

OTHER PROTESTANT DENOMINATIONS. Among the 20 are: Apostolic Ch of Pentecost of Canada (1951; 10 missionaries), Assemblies of God International, Cooneyites (Go-Preachers, from Ireland, UK, South Africa), Immanuel Ch (interdenominational), Nederduitsch Hervormde Kerk van Afrika, Pentecostal Ch in Malawi, Pentecostal Protestant Ch, Seventh Day Baptist Ch (113 members), Seventh-day Adventist Reform Movement, United Ev Churches (USA).

Part 5

COUNTRYSCAN

Comprehensive summary table of 167 indicators for all 238 countries

Go and measure the temple of God and the altar, and count the worshipers.

—Revelation 11:1, Revised English Bible, and New International Version

Christian churches and missions worldwide activate every year several hundred scientific measuring devices (instruments). These can be called 'scientific' for 3 reasons: (1) they produce hitherto unknown data, information, and knowledge, (2) other observers can use the same instruments to repeat the investigations to exactly verify the measurements, and (3) the resulting new data fit well into existing knowledge.

Part 5 contains the largest concentration of these instruments and measurements in this Encyclopedia: 167 instruments arranged into 44 instrument panels resulting in 45,090 measurements. Most of Table 5-1's columns report numbers; for the meaning of columns with symbols, consult Part 3 "Codebook".

Table 5-1. Geopolitico-religious data and typologies for all 238 countries and 7 continents, AD 1900-2025.

Notes

1. This table is the original source from which many tables elsewhere in this Encyclopedia have been derived. It summarizes much of the material in the Encyclopedia's Part 4, especially in the footnotes under Country Tables 1 and 2, concerning Christian resources, organizations, institutions, personnel, activities and attributes in the 20th century at various points from AD 1900-2000 and beyond to AD 2025.
2. The table is spread out over 22 pages making up 11 pairs of facing pages. Each pair lists all countries of the world with totals for continents and for the world. Each pair then gives the statistics, codes or values for between 15 and 26 variables (in 15 to 20 columns).
3. To locate specific data for a country, the reader should use a ruler or straight edge. From the listing below, or from Part 3 "Codebook", obtain the column number of the data you require. Locate the country (whose physical position on the pair of pages is exactly the same for all 11 pairs), locate the column number, and read off the data.
4. *Rows.* These list the 227 countries of the world whose AD 2000 population is each over 4,500.
5. *Minicountries.* The 11 smallest countries with population each under 5,000 are combined here in the single line '11 minicountries' in the same position for all 11 pairs of tables. With each's AD 2000 population (in parentheses) they are: Antarctica (4,500), British Indian Ocean Territory (2,000), Christmas Island (3,424), Cocos (Keeling) Islands (726), Falkland Islands (2,255), Holy See (5,000), Niue Island (1,876), Norfolk Island (2,075), Pitcairn Islands (47), Svalbard & Jan Mayen Islands (3,676), Tokelau Islands (1,500).
6. *Columns.* These give the values of 167 variables whose meaning is given below, and in more detail set out in Part 3 "Codebook". The numbers of the columns are given at the top of each column.
7. *Abbreviations.* The abbreviation 'p.m.' throughout means total per million population of the country; 'p.m.a.' means total per million of the country's affiliated church members; 'p.a.' means per annum, per year.
8. *Dating.* All data refer to the year AD 2000 at its midpoint, except (a) columns clearly identified at other dates (columns 6, 7, 58, 59, 60, 61, 62, 116, 152-156, 158), and (b) the analysis in columns 120-146 which is based on a detailed study of empirical numbers in 1995.
9. *Totals.* At the end of the listings for countries, totals are given for each of the 7 continents (UN major areas); for Worlds A, B, C (as countries); and lastly for the entire globe. These totals are compiled from Country Tables 1 in Part 4 "Countries", each being the sum of the 228 figures in the column above. Many totals, for example of foreign missionaries and personnel (column 109, 111), are clear in their meaning and so can immediately be understood and used. Other totals (of percentages, per thousand, per million) require clear thinking, interpreting, and some processing; for example, the totals in many columns will yield average values for a continent or world, if divided by 238 (for the world) or 57 for Africa, 47 for Europe, etc. For columns composed of alphabetic or alphanumeric characters, totals are meaningless and so are omitted, being entered here as '–'. If a global figure 'per million' is wanted, the reader can immediately compute it by dividing the global absolute total given on the last line by the global population in millions for the year required.
10. *Global totals.* The final line contains totals, averages, other figures derived from each column.

BRIEF MEANINGS OF COLUMNS 1-167 IN TABLE 5-1: COLUMN NUMBERS, HEADINGS, AND SUBJECTS

Column	*Heading*	*Subject*
COUNTRY		
1.	*code*	4-letter country code
2.	*short name*	as in Table 5-2
3.	*UN*	UN major area and region
4.	*prov*	major civil divisions (provinces, states)
DEMOGRAPHICS		
5.	*pop 2000*	population, mid-AD 2000
6.	*pop 2010*	population, mid-AD 2010
7.	*pop 2025*	population, mid-AD 2025
8.	*adults*	population age 15 and over
9.	*apop*	adults as % population
10.	*bpop*	birth rate, % per year
11.	*dpop*	death rate, % per year
12.	*npop*	natural increase, % per year
13.	*life*	life expectancy, years
14.	*hom*	household size (adults, children)
15.	*spac*	floor area per person, sq. meters
16.	*den*	density of population per sq. kilometer
17.	*peop*	total ethnolinguistic peoples
18.	*langs*	official and national state language(s)
GEOPOLITICAL TYPOLOGIES		
19.	*dev*	more/less/least-developed
20.	*HDI*	human development index
21.	*HFI*	human freedom index
22.	*HSI*	human suffering index
23.	*liter*	literacy as % population over 15
24.	*literates*	adult literates (over 15)
SOCIETY		
ECONOMICS		
25.	*GNP*	gross national product p.a. per capita
26.	*EFL*	economic freedom level
URBANIZATION		
27.	*rural*	ruralites, country-dwellers (millions)
28.	*urban*	urbanites, town/city dwellers (millions)
29.	*metro*	metropolitan urbanites (millions)
METROSCAN		
30.	*cit50*	cities over 50,000 persons
31.	*cit100*	cities over 100,000 persons
32.	*mega*	megacities over 1 million persons
HEALTH		
33.	*access*	people's access to health services, %
34.	*water*	people's access to safe water, %
35.	*mat-m*	maternal mortality, per 100,000 births
36.	*inf-m*	infant mortality, per 1000 live births
37.	*hosp*	hospitals
38.	*beds*	beds, per 10,000 population
39.	*doct*	doctors
40.	*blind*	nonsighted persons
41.	*deaf*	hearing-impaired persons
42.	*lepers*	persons with leprosy
43.	*murder*	murders per 100,000 per year
EDUCATION		
44.	*educ*	rate % school enrolments, female/male
45.	*schools*	elementary, secondary, high
46.	*univs*	degree-granting colleges, universities
COMMUNICATION		
47.	*news*	daily newspaper copies per 1000 persons
48.	*radios*	radio sets per 1000 persons
49.	*TVs*	TV sets per 1000 persons
50.	*fones*	telephones per 1000 persons
51.	*faxes*	fax machines per 1000 persons
52.	*computers*	general-purpose computers in use
53.	*Internet*	users of Internet, e-mail, www
RELIGIOUS RELATIONS		
RELIGIONS		
54.	*religs*	total major religions in country
55.	*indig*	religions indigenous to this country
RELIGIOUS PERSECUTION		
56.	*liberty*	religious liberty or persecution
57.	*CSI*	Christian Safety Index, 0-100
58.	*martyrs*	martyrs ever (less background martyrs)
59.	*mar-sit*	major martyrdom situations (since AD 33)
CHURCH/STATE RELATIONS: state religion or philosophy		
60.	*1900*	situation in 1900
61.	*1970*	situation in 1970
62.	*1990*	situation in 1990
63.	*2000*	situation in AD 2000
BIBLIOGRAPHY		
64.	*items listed*	total listed in Part 4 after country's text
CHRISTIANITY		
CHURCH MEMBERS		
65.	*affiliated*	affiliated church members
66.	*AC*	affiliated church members, %
FOUR MEGATYPOLOGIES OF RENEWAL		
1. THE GREAT COMMISSION		
67.	*GCCs*	Great Commission Christians
68.	*GCC*	Great Commission Christians, % country
2. ECCLESIASTICAL RENEWAL: 6 MEGABLOCS		
69.	*Megabloc O*	Orthodox, affiliated
70.	*Megabloc R*	Roman Catholics, affiliated
71.	*Megabloc A*	Anglicans, affiliated
72.	*Megabloc P*	Protestants, affiliated
73.	*Megabloc I*	Independents, affiliated
74.	*Megabloc m*	Marginal Christians, affiliated
3. EVANGELICAL RENEWAL		
75.	*Evangelicals*	Evangelicals (linked to Ev councils)
76.	*evangelicals*	evangelicals (all varieties)
4. PENTECOSTAL/CHARISMATIC RENEWAL		
77.	*1st-Wavers*	Pentecostals (Classical denominations)
78.	*2nd-Wavers*	Charismatics (in non-Pentecostal churches)
79.	*3rd-Wavers*	Neocharismatics (Independents)
CHURCHES		
STRUCTURES		
80.	*denom*	denominations
81.	*p.m.*	denominations per million
82.	*worship*	worship centers (churches, congregations)
83.	*p.m.*	worship centers per million
FINANCE, US$		
84.	*personal*	personal income p.a. of all Christians
85.	*church*	churches' income per year
86.	*parachurch*	parachurch income per year
87.	*ecc crime*	ecclesiastical crime p.a. (embezzlements)
MISSION		
STATUS OF MISSIONS		
88.	*stat*	current status of foreign missions, 1-7
89.	*misags*	foreign mission agencies present
90.	*all orgs*	all service agencies
91.	*p.m.*	all organizations per million
MISSION INSTITUTIONS		
92.	*major*	major institutions
93.	*p.m.*	major institutions per million
94.	*minor*	minor institutions
95.	*p.m.*	minor institutions per million
RESPONSE/GROWTH		
96.	*CG%*	annual church growth 1900-2000, % p.a.
97.	*g%*	new Christians per year, %
98.	*bapt p.a.*	newly baptized persons per year
99.	*resp R*	responsiveness to evangelism
100.	*cost-eff, $*	cost-effectiveness: $ cost per baptism
WORLDS A, B, and C		
101.	*A-individuals*	World A individuals
102.	*B-individuals*	World B individuals
103.	*C-individuals*	World C individuals
MINISTRIES		
104.	*peo-ags*	total agencies-in-peoples
CHRISTIAN PERSONNEL		
ALL WORKERS		
105.	*workers*	full-time Christian workers in country
106.	*w.p.m.*	Christian workers per million population
CITIZENS		
107.	*workers*	citizen Christian workers in country
108.	*citw p.m.*	citizen Christian workers per million
GLOBAL MISSION SHARING		
CITIZENS SENT ABROAD		
109.	*total*	citizen missionaries working abroad
110.	*p.m.a.*	citizen missionaries abroad, p.m. affiliated
ALIENS RECEIVED FROM ABROAD		
111.	*total*	aliens at work as missionaries
112.	*p.m.*	aliens at work as missionaries, p.m.
CHRISTIAN LITERATURE		
LIBRARIES		
113.	*total*	Christian or religious libraries
114.	*p.m.*	Christian or religious libraries, p.m.
BOOKS ON CHRISTIANITY IN EACH COUNTRY		
115.	*total*	all books describing this country's Christians
116.	*1970-99*	such books published since 1970
117.	*p.a.*	books published per year in AD 2000
PERIODICALS		
118.	*total*	Christian periodicals
119.	*p.m.*	Christian periodicals, per million
SCRIPTURES		
BIBLE DISTRIBUTION		
120.	*goal*	goal for all Bibles in place
121.	*goal p.a.*	required Bibles distributed p.a.
122.	*UBS p.a.*	UBS Bibles distributed p.a.
123.	*other p.a.*	all other Bibles distributed p.a.
124.	*total p.a.*	total all Bibles distributed p.a.
125.	*T/G%*	ratio Bible total (col 124) to goal (col 121), %
NEW TESTAMENT DISTRIBUTION		
126.	*goal*	goal for all NTs in place
127.	*goal p.a.*	required NTs distributed p.a.
128.	*UBS p.a.*	UBS NTs distributed p.a.
129.	*other p.a.*	all other NTs distributed p.a.
130.	*duplicates*	NTs distributed via Bibles p.a.
131.	*total p.a.*	total all NTs distributed p.a.
132.	*T/G%*	ratio NT total (col 131) to goal (col 127), %
PORTIONS DISTRIBUTION (GOSPELS)		
133.	*goal*	goal for all gospels in place
134.	*goal p.a.*	required gospels distributed p.a.
135.	*UBS p.a.*	UBS portions (gospels) distributed p.a.
136.	*other p.a.*	all other gospels distributed p.a.
137.	*duplicates*	gospels distributed via Bibles & NTs p.a.
138.	*total p.a.*	total all gospels distributed p.a.
139.	*T/G %*	ratio gospel total (col 138) to goal (col 134),%
SELECTIONS DISTRIBUTION		
140.	*goal*	goal for all selections in place
141.	*goal p.a.*	required selections distributed p.a.
142.	*UBS p.a.*	UBS selections distributed p.a.
143.	*other p.a.*	all other selections distributed p.a.
144.	*duplicates*	selections distributed via gospels,N or B p.a.
145.	*total p.a.*	total all selections distributed p.a.
146.	*T/G %*	ratio selection total (col 145) to goal (col 141),%
BROADCASTING		
RADIO/TV AUDIENCES		
147.	*cb aud*	regular audience for Christian programs, %
148.	*cstat*	audience via Christian stations, %
149.	*secstat*	audience via secular stations, %
EVANGELISM		
OFFERS VIA 45 MINISTRIES		
150.	*q per day*	offers (disciple-opportunities) per day
151.	*e p.a.p.c.*	offers per year per capita
EVANGELIZATION		
WHEN BEGUN		
152.	*year begun*	year first Christians resident
STATUS OF EVANGELIZATION, E		
153.	*1900*	E (% population evangelized), 1900
154.	*1970*	E (% population evangelized), 1970
155.	*1990*	E (% population evangelized), 1990
156.	*1995*	E (% population evangelized), 1995
157.	*2000*	E (% population evangelized), 2000
158.	*2025*	E (% population evangelized), 2025
SOURCE OF E IN AD 2000		
159.	*internal*	evangelized by population's Christians
160.	*external*	evangelized by Christians from outside
UNEVANGELIZED, AD 2000		
161.	*U*	U, % population unevangelized
162.	*total*	unevangelized persons
STRATEGIES		
163.	*World*	3-fold trichotomy: A, B, C
164.	*plans*	plans to evangelize globe (less 'other plans')
165.	*target*	total top priority target peoples (T=1)
FUTURES (CHRISTIAN FUTURISTICS)		
166.	*growth index*	growth relative to demographics
167.	*prospects*	outlook during 21st century (+2 to -2)

COUNTRY				DEMOGRAPHICS														GEOPOLITICAL TYPOLOGIES					
																		SCALES, 0–100					
code	short name	UN	prov	pop 2000	pop 2010	pop 2025	adults	apop	bpop	dpop	npop	life	hom	spac	den	peop	langs	dev	HDI	HFI	HSI	liter	literates
1	2	3	4	5	6	7	8	9	10	11	12	13	14	15	16	17	18	19	20	21	22	23	24
afgh	Afghanistan	C3	29	22,720,416	32,901,664	44,934,122	12,782,506	56.3	4.65	1.83	2.82	47	6.2	2	68	70	PD	3	23	5	11	32	4,029,278
alba	Albania	E3	26	3,113,434	3,346,892	3,819,763	2,195,905	70.5	1.81	0.55	1.25	74	4.7	8	132	12	a	1	66	30	53	92	2,016,604
alge	Algeria	A3	48	31,471,278	38,303,706	46,610,551	19,940,202	63.4	2.67	0.51	2.16	70	6.9	7	19	44	A	2	74	20	46	62	12,283,541
amer	American Samoa	P4	3	68,089	94,712	142,680	42,093	61.8	2.73	0.46	2.27	73	7.0	15	716	10	Ew	2	67	80	75	96	40,382
ando	Andorra	E3	7	77,985	108,765	154,335	63,402	81.3	1.19	0.95	0.23	79	3.0	40	329	11	F	1	89	90	80	100	63,402
ango	Angola	A2	18	12,878,188	17,235,659	25,106,861	6,761,049	52.5	4.56	1.65	2.92	49	4.8	7	20	60	P	3	34	30	14	42	2,832,760
angu	Anguilla	L1	1	8,309	9,361	10,984	6,326	76.1	1.53	0.58	0.95	78	4.0	18	120	5	E	2	85	70	80	90	5,690
anti	Antigua	L1	7	67,560	70,919	75,080	51,433	76.1	1.53	0.58	0.95	78	3.5	25	169	6	E	2	89	70	80	90	46,244
arge	Argentina	L3	24	37,027,297	41,467,500	47,150,313	26,763,330	72.3	1.91	0.78	1.13	74	3.2	20	16	64	S	2	88	63	61	96	25,746,324
arme	Armenia	C4	11	3,519,569	3,697,258	3,946,381	2,656,923	75.5	1.40	0.79	0.61	71	4.7	15	132	25	a	2	65	40	55	99	2,623,234
arub	Aruba	L1	1	102,747	154,785	250,376	77,112	75.1	1.53	0.61	0.92	76	3.6	35	1,297	7	D	2	90	80	90	95	73,229
aust	Australia	P1	8	18,879,524	20,608,386	23,090,790	14,982,790	79.4	1.26	0.77	0.49	79	3.0	50	3	133	E	1	93	83	96	100	14,907,876
ausz	Austria	E4	9	8,210,520	8,347,849	8,185,725	6,814,732	83.0	0.94	0.99	-0.05	78	2.6	55	97	36	G	1	93	90	94	100	6,814,732
azer	Azerbaijan	C4	4	7,734,015	8,411,360	9,402,570	5,520,540	71.4	1.57	0.67	0.90	71	4.8	12	108	35	A	2	64	25	25	97	5,375,317
baha	Bahamas	L1	19	306,529	354,213	414,631	213,405	69.6	2.06	0.50	1.56	75	3.8	40	29	9	E	2	89	90	90	98	209,662
bahr	Bahrain	C4	12	617,217	713,145	858,368	434,953	70.5	1.61	0.38	1.23	74	6.5	25	1,236	14	A	2	87	30	71	85	369,376
bang	Bangladesh	C3	6	129,155,152	151,799,126	178,751,214	83,795,863	64.9	2.64	0.86	1.78	61	5.3	5	1,211	61	B	3	37	18	32	38	31,867,231
barb	Barbados	L1	11	270,449	282,304	296,753	213,601	79.0	1.21	0.79	0.43	77	3.7	30	690	11	E	2	91	80	89	97	208,006
belg	Belgium	E4	11	10,161,164	10,135,688	9,917,861	8,420,557	82.9	1.00	1.07	-0.07	78	2.7	50	324	34	DFG	1	93	88	98	100	8,420,557
beli	Belize	L2	6	240,709	294,499	370,035	144,955	60.2	2.73	0.39	2.34	76	4.9	18	16	19	E	2	81	70	75	70	101,545
belo	Belorussia	E1	6	10,236,181	9,973,382	9,495,683	8,322,015	81.3	1.05	1.37	-0.32	68	3.2	19	45	26	BR	1	81	55	50	98	8,121,979
beni	Benin	A5	6	6,096,559	7,902,809	11,109,357	3,303,725	54.2	3.95	1.24	2.72	54	5.4	6	98	58	F	3	37	33	38	37	1,225,342
berm	Bermuda	N1	10	64,590	69,443	75,613	44,968	69.6	2.06	0.50	1.56	75	2.6	45	1,400	7	E	1	92	90	95	97	43,552
bhut	Bhutan	C3	17	2,123,970	2,753,954	3,903,897	1,219,796	57.4	3.50	0.85	2.64	63	5.4	5	83	27	z	3	34	10	27	42	515,858
boli	Bolivia	L3	9	8,328,665	10,229,354	13,131,183	5,028,848	60.4	3.05	0.82	2.23	63	3.8	7	11	58	Syq	2	59	45	32	83	4,184,693
bosn	Bosnia-Herzegovina	E3	8	3,971,813	4,329,808	4,323,818	3,223,921	81.2	1.11	0.81	0.30	74	3.6	12	84	20	Q	1	72	35	20	86	2,786,967
bots	Botswana	A4	19	1,622,220	1,831,933	2,241,857	938,454	57.9	3.18	1.99	1.19	41	5.7	8	3	54	EX	2	67	65	43	70	657,171
boug	Bougainville	P2	1	198,495	229,750	286,097	121,757	61.3	3.04	0.90	2.14	60	4.0	7	28	35	tE	2	48	30	30	80	97,628
braz	Brazil	L3	27	170,115,463	190,875,224	217,929,781	121,037,152	71.2	1.92	0.72	1.20	68	4.2	10	25	224	P	2	78	45	50	83	100,762,679
brit	Britain	E2	64	58,830,160	59,331,486	59,960,856	47,758,324	81.2	1.11	1.07	0.04	78	2.7	50	245	95	E	1	93	80	84	94	45,127,318
briz	British Virgin Is	L1	1	21,366	27,248	36,663	14,734	69.0	2.00	0.56	1.43	76	4.0	45	239	8	E	2	88	90	90	93	13,702
brun	Brunei	C2	4	328,080	384,439	458,972	222,110	67.7	1.88	0.32	1.56	76	5.8	15	79	27	m	2	88	40	55	88	194,855
bulg	Bulgaria	E1	9	8,225,045	7,752,691	7,023,064	6,890,120	83.8	0.88	1.38	-0.50	72	3.3	17	63	35	b	1	78	10	68	98	6,743,906
burk	Burkina Faso	A5	30	11,936,823	15,751,319	23,321,336	6,287,125	52.7	4.43	1.69	2.74	46	6.2	6	84	80	F	3	22	15	27	19	1,215,665
buru	Burundi	A1	15	6,695,001	8,496,970	11,568,648	3,591,199	53.6	3.97	1.82	2.14	44	4.6	7	415	14	yF	3	25	20	25	36	1,279,038
camb	Cambodia	C2	20	11,167,719	13,250,035	16,526,449	6,603,472	59.1	2.97	1.20	1.77	54	5.6	4	90	37	k	3	35	10	16	66	4,369,081
came	Cameroon	A2	10	15,084,969	19,239,891	26,484,402	8,524,516	56.5	3.78	1.26	2.52	54	5.2	9	55	297	EF	2	47	20	23	63	5,411,864
cana	Canada	N1	12	31,146,639	33,928,551	37,896,497	25,247,466	81.1	1.10	0.75	0.35	79	2.7	50	3	152	EF	1	96	85	97	96	24,362,491
cape	Cape Verde	A5	9	427,724	529,110	670,931	259,244	60.6	2.92	0.56	2.36	71	5.1	15	166	7	P	3	55	45	70	72	186,682
caym	Cayman Islands	L1	1	38,371	53,015	77,938	26,461	69.0	2.00	0.56	1.43	76	4.0	40	300	6	E	2	89	85	90	93	24,604
cent	Central African Rep	A2	17	3,615,266	4,333,276	5,703,795	2,078,416	57.5	3.63	1.84	1.80	45	4.7	6	9	95	Fx	3	36	30	27	60	1,251,785
chad	Chad	A2	14	7,650,982	9,887,331	13,908,122	4,165,195	54.4	4.19	1.62	2.58	49	3.9	5	10	136	FA	3	29	12	18	48	2,009,677
chan	Channel Islands	E2	1	152,898	162,284	173,400	124,123	81.2	1.11	1.07	0.04	78	2.0	45	893	6	EF	1	92	85	85	98	121,618
chil	Chile	L3	13	15,211,294	17,010,268	19,547,916	10,883,681	71.6	1.82	0.57	1.24	76	4.1	14	25	25	S	2	89	20	63	95	10,361,051
chin	China	C1	33	1,262,556,787	1,356,939,193	1,462,931,461	949,063,937	75.2	1.46	0.70	0.76	71	4.1	10	152	254	C	2	63	5	39	82	773,923,298
colo	Colombia	L3	26	42,321,361	49,665,304	59,757,874	28,469,580	67.3	2.23	0.55	1.68	72	5.4	11	52	99	S	2	85	35	49	91	25,993,056
como	Comoros	A1	3	592,749	766,305	989,515	343,261	57.9	3.48	0.84	2.64	61	5.6	9	531	11	AFj	3	41	15	37	57	196,722
cong	Congo-Brazzaville	A2	15	2,943,464	3,858,198	5,689,140	1,579,463	53.7	4.13	1.42	2.70	50	4.7	12	16	79	Fb	2	50	20	36	75	1,184,204
conz	Congo-Zaire	A2	11	51,654,496	69,389,334	104,787,601	26,684,713	51.7	4.29	1.29	3.00	53	6.0	11	44	260	FES	3	38	13	12	77	20,562,039
cook	Cook Islands	P4	1	19,522	20,968	23,736	12,069	61.8	2.73	0.46	2.27	73	5.0	20	101	8	E	2	71	70	85	92	11,113
cost	Costa Rica	L2	7	4,023,422	4,856,685	5,928,508	2,721,443	67.6	2.19	0.40	1.79	77	4.2	17	116	22	S	2	89	78	66	95	2,581,230
croa	Croatia	E3	21	4,472,600	4,402,743	4,193,413	3,709,127	82.9	1.04	1.18	-0.14	74	3.1	22	74	31	C	1	76	30	40	97	3,587,957
cuba	Cuba	L1	15	11,200,684	11,516,190	11,798,235	8,823,899	78.8	1.17	0.72	0.44	76	3.7	18	106	15	S	2	72	13	62	96	8,448,963
cypr	Cyprus	C4	5	600,506	647,453	687,811	460,948	76.8	1.36	0.76	0.61	78	3.5	30	116	10	g	2	91	40	50	95	439,268
czec	Czech Republic	E1	8	10,244,177	10,066,401	9,512,292	8,547,741	83.4	0.89	1.08	-0.19	75	2.7	25	120	26	c	1	88	15	75	100	8,547,741
denm	Denmark	E2	16	5,293,239	5,327,432	5,238,499	4,341,515	82.0	1.13	1.17	-0.04	76	2.2	51	121	29	d	1	93	95	99	100	4,341,515
djib	Djibouti	A1	5	637,634	785,170	1,026,235	373,462	58.6	3.47	1.36	2.11	52	5.6	13	44	10	AF	3	32	15	18	46	172,567
domi	Dominica	L1	10	70,714	71,045	73,442	53,835	76.1	1.53	0.58	0.95	78	4.3	15	97	10	E	2	87	45	40	90	48,403
domr	Dominican Republic	L1	30	8,495,338	9,708,026	11,164,412	5,687,629	67.0	2.18	0.52	1.66	72	5.1	14	230	14	S	2	72	53	47	82	4,669,447
ecua	Ecuador	L3	21	12,646,068	14,898,509	17,796,101	8,367,903	66.2	2.32	0.58	1.74	70	4.1	17	65	33	S	2	78	60	42	90	7,540,180
egyp	Egypt	A3	27	68,469,695	80,063,292	95,615,454	44,272,505	64.7	2.35	0.61	1.74	68	4.9	12	95	38	A	2	61	28	41	51	22,745,477
elsa	El Salvador	L2	14	6,276,023	7,440,647	9,062,331	4,041,759	64.4	2.53	0.59	1.94	70	4.9	11	430	15	S	2	59	50	36	74	3,002,804
equa	Equatorial Guinea	A2	7	452,661	575,328	794,724	257,021	56.8	3.88	1.46	2.42	52	4.5	8	28	23	SF	3	46	40	40	79	202,296
erit	Eritrea	A1	6	3,850,388	4,909,569	6,680,653	2,151,597	55.9	3.82	1.33	2.49	52	4.0	9	56	16	gEA	3	27	30	45	20	428,770
esto	Estonia	E2	15	1,396,158	1,260,920	1,131,222	1,152,389	82.5	0.91	1.35	-0.43	70	3.1	21	25	24	E	1	78	35	50	100	1,149,405
ethi	Ethiopia	A1	10	62,564,875	79,943,539	115,382,091	33,691,185	53.9	4.31	1.88	2.43	44	4.5	11	101	145	L	3	24	5	15	35	11,938,930
faer	Faeroe Islands	E2	1	42,749	39,703	36,604	35,063	82.0	1.13	1.17	-0.04	76	3.0	30	26	5	Jd	1	92	80	90	99	34,712
fiji	Fiji	P2	15	816,905	936,229	1,104,141	561,295	63.7	2.10	0.47	1.63	74	6.0	18	60	30	E	2	86	40	60	92	514,073
finl	Finland	E2	12	5,175,743	5,235,338	5,253,863	4,239,451	81.9	1.08	0.99	0.09	78	2.3	45	15	31	fs	1	94	90	92	100	4,239,451
fran	France	E4	96	59,079,709	60,596,993	61,661,804	48,031,803	81.3	1.19	0.95	0.23	79	2.6	50	113	97	F	1	95	88	93	99	47,454,211
freg	French Guiana	L3	2	181,313	264,502	416,191	127,209	70.2	1.88	0.69	1.19	66	3.4	15	4	24	F	2	77	30	60	83	105,509
frep	French Polynesia	P4	5	235,061	272,750	324,439	157,185	66.9	2.11	0.47	1.64	73	4.7	18	81	15	FN	2	87	70	65	95	149,245
gabo	Gabon	A2	9	1,226,127	1,506,584	1,981,233	733,469	59.8	3.48	1.55	1.93	52	4.0	9	7	51	F	2	56	25	45	63	464,945
gamb	Gambia	A5	7	1,305,363	1,651,481	2,150,833	778,910	59.7	3.74	1.58	2.16	49	8.3	7	201	32	E	3	28	20	36	39	301,368
geor	Georgia	C4	13	4,967,561	5,010,697	5,178,116	3,868,737	77.9	1.38	0.97	0.41	74	4.1	18	74	35	G	2	64	40	45	100	3,851,073
germ	Germany	E4	16	82,220,490	82,032,281	80,238,159	69,468,092	84.5	0.84	1.10	-0.26	78	2.3	36	224	79	G	1	92	88	94	100	69,468,092
ghan	Ghana	A5	10	20,212,495	26,366,959	36,876,215	11,488,782	56.8	3.55	0.85	2.70	62	4.9	5	154	108	E	2	47	28	19	65	7,427,323
gibr	Gibraltar	E3	1	25,082	23,454	21,393	20,364	81.2	1.11	1.07	0.04	78	3.2	28	3,565	7	E	1	93	80	80	99	20,160
gree	Greece	E3	13	10,644,744	10,554,397	9,862,572	9,052,290	85.0	0.88	1.03	-0.15	79	3.3	26	74	31	g	1	92	78	81	95	8,627,998
grel	Greenland	N1	6	56,156	57,200	59,634	46,059	82.0	1.13	1.17	-0.04	76	1.8	15	<1	5	Hd	1	86	75	75	100	46,059
gren	Grenada	L1	9	93,717	97,453	104,647	70,269	75.0	1.37	0.60	0.77	75	3.7	16	304	10	E	2	84	60	70	85	59,713
guad	Guadeloupe	L1	3	455,687	509,648	569,216	346,915	76.1	1.53	0.58	0.95	78	3.4	14	319	7	F	2	87	60	70	90	312,601
guam	Guam	P3	1	167,556	193,836	227,634	112,430	67.1	2.07	0.47	1.60	76	4.0	20	154	13	yE	2	90	80	80	99	111,306
guat	Guatemala	L2	22	11,385,295	14,631,050	19,816,134	6,420,168	56.4	3.42	0.68	2.74	66	5.4	15	181	65	S	2	57	50	31	56	3,570,151
guin	Guinea	A5	33	7,430,346	9,427,100	12,496,941	4,160,994	56.0	4.04	1.60	2.44	49	4.7	10	50	44	F	3	27	15	14	36	1,497,292
gunb	Guinea-Bissau	A5	9	1,213,111	1,480,638	1,946,020	696,690	57.4	4.03	1.95	2.07	45	4.1	9	53	32	P	3	29	20	18	55	383,589
guya	Guyana	L3	10	861,334	922,942	1,044,669	604,312	70.2	1.88	0.69	1.19	66	5.1	13	4	24	E	2	65	55	39	98	592,484
hait	Haiti	L1	9	8,222,025	9,669,191	11,988,232	4,874,839	59.3	3.06	1.17	1.88	55	4.4	10	432	9	hF	3	34	23	11	45	2,196,064
hond	Honduras	L2	18	6,485,445	8,202,633	10,656,044	3,784,257	58.4	3.00	0.51	2.49	71	5.7	14	94	27	S	2	58	45	38	73	2,749,248
hung	Hungary	E1	20	10,035,568	9,626,550	8,900,388	8,329,521	83.0	0.93	1.33	-0.40	72	2.9	29	95	23	h	1	86	18	68	99	8,236,792
icel	Iceland	E2	7	280,969	303,644	328,356	215,419	76.7	1.51	0.68	0.83	80	2.9	38	3	10	i	1	94	85	93	100	215,419
indi	India	C3	32	1,013,661,777	1,152,163,518	1,330,448,707	676,011,039	66.7	2.26	0.84	1.42	64	5.6	12	420	439	HE	2	45	35	37	52	351,847,386
indo	Indonesia	C2	26	212,107,385	238,011,716	273,442,120	147,181,314	69.4	2.01	0.70	1.31	67	4.5	14	142	744	X	2	67	13	36	84	123,320,868
iran	Iran	C3	27	67,702,199	76,931,899	94,462,501	43,180,463	63.8	2.12	0.52	1.60	71	5.1	15	57	78	N	2	78	10	44	72	31,172,831
iraq	Iraq	C4	18	23,114,884	30,338,663	41,013,588	13,559,191	58.7	3.38	0.54	2.84	69	8.9	13	94	36	A	2	53	0	35	58	7,873,960
irel	Ireland	E2	4	3,730,239	4,016,447	4,403,843	2,938,309	78.8	1.45	0.81	0.64	77	3.9	48	62	21	iE	1	93	68	89	100	2,938,309
isle	Isle of Man	E2	1	79,166	88,814	100,891	64,275	81.2	1.11	1.07	0.04	78	2.0	42	176	5	E	1	92	80	85	96	61,692
isra	Israel	C4	6	5,121,683	6,017,886	6,926,755	3,701,440	72.3	1.82	0.62	1.20	78	3.7	28	339	53	eA	2	91	48	79	96	3,539,836
ital	Italy	E3	20	57,297,886	55,781,181	51,269,528	49,132,937	85.8	0.85	1.09	-0.24	79	2.8	50	170	60	I	1	92	73	88	97	47,697,971
ivor	Ivory Coast	A5	50	14,785,832	18,200,343	23,345,116	8,364,345	56.6	3.60	1.53	2.07	48	5.4	10	72	103	F	2	37	35	26	40	3,355,871
jama	Jamaica	L1	13	2,582,577	2,815,869	3,244,840	1,780,945	69.0	2.00	0.56	1.43	76	4.2	18	295	14	E	2	74	63	56	85	1,513,460
japa	Japan	C1	47	126,714,220	127,315,474	121,150,001	107,947,844	85.2	1.01	0.90	0.12	80	3.0	38	320	34	J	1	94	80	93	100	107,947,844
jord	Jordan	C4	12	6,669,341	8,797,930	12,062,895	3,871,552	58.1	3.30	0.41	2.89	72	6.0	25	135	20	A	2	73	20	59	87	3,353,965
kaza	Kazakhstan	C3	16	16,222,563	16,492,359	17,698,360	11,751,625	72.4	1.72	0.83	0.89	69	4.0	18	6	49	K	2	71	40	35	98	11,464,897
keny	Kenya	A1	8	30,080,372	35,204,705	41,755,990	17,136,788	57.0	3.20	1.41	1.79	48	6.2	10	71	124	ES	2	46	20	25	78	13,395,752
kirg	Kirghizia	C3	7	4,699,337	5,188,282	6,096,197	3,054,569	65.0	2.31	0.68	1.62	69	4.2	15	30	42	k	2	64	15	30	97	2,961,759
kiri	Kiribati	P3	3	83,387	96,191	119,324	55,953	67.1	2.07	0.47	1.60	76	6.6	20	147	6	E	3	53	60	50	90	50,447
kuwa	Kuwait	C4	5	1,971,634	2,419,713	2,974,454	1,306,996	66.3	2.02	0.24	1.78	77	7.4	25	166	27	A	2	84	20	72	79	1,029,088
laos	Laos	C2	18	5,433,036	6,964,623	9,652,526	3,044,673	56.0	3.70	1.19	2.52	56	6.0	5	40	97	l	3	46	5	13	57	1,735,312
latv	Latvia	E2	33	2,356,508	2,137,362	1,936,009	1,940,113	82.3	0.91	1.40	-0.48	70	3.1	19	29	35	L	1	71	35	55	99	1,929,871
leba	Lebanon	C4	5	3,281,787	3,722,943	4,399,649	2,208,643	67.3	1.98	0.61	1.37	71	5.3	18	430	19	A	2	79	30	39	92	2,041,955
leso	Lesotho	A4	10	2,152,553	2,609,785	3,506,420	1,294,115	60.1	3.39	1.40	1.99	52	4.8	10	115	13	wE	3	46	40	30	72	926,153
libe	Liberia	A5	12	3,154,001	4,443,705	6,617,526	1,824,590	57.9	4.77	1.19	3.58	55	5.0	8	66	47	E	3	31	18	24	38	697,173
liby	Libya	A3	13	5,604,722	6,981,828	8,646,769	3,495,665	62.4	2.78	0.46	2.33	71	5.4	12	4	40	A	2	80	3	49	76	2,652,973
liec	Liechtenstein	E4	2	32,843	36,668	41,252	27,112	82.6	1.01	0.89	0.12	79	3.0	45	257	6	G	1	93	80	85	100	27,112
lith	Lithuania	E2	10	3,670,269	3,565,746	3,398,950	2,964,843	80.8	0.98	1.19	-0.21	71	3.2	16	52	24	e	1	76	55	65	99	2,948,287
luxe	Luxembourg	E4	3	430,615	456,615	463,356	352,932	82.0	1.15	0.94	0.21	77	2.8	40	179	15	OG	1	90	85	93	100	352,932
mace	Macedonia	E3	30	2,023,580	2,142,050	2,257,977	1,559,371	77.1	1.56	0.81	0.75	74	4.4	32	87	24	M	1	75	50	65	89	1,387,759
mada	Madagascar	A1	6	15,941,727	20,691,738	28,963,663	8,854,035	55.5	3.62	0.93	2.69	60	4.7	5	49	55	mF	3	35	40	25	80	7,105,073
mala	Malawi	A1	24	10,925,238	13,912,265	19,958,349	5,773,988	52.9	4.51	2.14	2.37	40	4.3	7	168	31	Ec	3	32	35	21	57	3,275,908
malb	Malaysia	C2	15	22,244,062	25,919,134	30,968,453	14,678,857	66.0	2.15	0.47	1.69	73	4.9	12	93	174	m	2	83	23	60	84	12,282,504

COUNTRY				DEMOGRAPHICS														GEOPOLITICAL TYPOLOGIES					
																			SCALES, 0–100				
code	short name	UN	prov	pop 2000	pop 2010	pop 2025	adults	apop	bpop	dpop	npop	life	hom	spac	den	peop	langs	dev	HDI	HFI	HSI	liter	literates
1	2	3	4	5	6	7	8	9	10	11	12	13	14	15	16	17	18	19	20	21	22	23	24
mald	Maldives	C3	19	286,223	373,116	501,456	163,405	57.1	3.33	0.63	2.70	67	7.1	10	1,682	9	f	3	61	10	30	93	152,218
mali	Mali	A5	8	11,233,821	14,558,463	21,295,460	6,034,809	53.7	4.47	1.44	3.03	55	5.6	7	17	45	F	3	23	10	30	31	1,879,779
malt	Malta	E3	6	388,544	412,587	429,847	309,825	79.7	1.32	0.78	0.54	78	3.6	17	1,360	11	oE	1	89	70	80	96	297,583
mars	Marshall Islands	P3	24	64,220	86,434	127,147	43,092	67.1	2.07	0.47	1.60	76	8.7	15	702	3	dE	2	58	70	70	91	39,327
mart	Martinique	L1	3	395,362	420,797	450,094	306,406	77.5	1.34	0.66	0.68	79	3.3	12	399	9	F	2	91	50	65	93	283,491
maur	Mauritania	A5	13	2,669,547	3,455,905	4,766,399	1,511,231	56.6	3.86	1.20	2.66	56	5.0	4	4	26	A	3	36	5	23	38	572,103
maus	Mauritius	A1	11	1,156,498	1,254,018	1,377,463	863,788	74.7	1.58	0.66	0.92	73	5.3	7	675	24	E	2	83	35	60	83	716,412
mayo	Mayotte	A1	2	101,621	129,559	186,507	58,849	57.9	3.48	0.84	2.64	61	4.9	8	500	10	AF	2	49	20	35	91	53,556
mexi	Mexico	L2	32	98,881,289	112,890,609	130,196,156	66,102,142	66.9	2.22	0.51	1.71	73	5.1	6	66	278	S	2	85	38	47	90	59,212,395
micr	Micronesia	P3	4	118,689	144,265	189,609	79,640	67.1	2.07	0.47	1.60	76	7.0	12	270	22	E	2	56	65	65	77	60,975
mold	Moldavia	E1	50	4,380,492	4,424,179	4,546,842	3,360,713	76.7	1.29	1.07	0.21	69	3.4	18	134	32	OR	1	61	40	60	96	3,240,096
mona	Monaco	E4	1	33,597	36,867	40,692	27,314	81.3	1.19	0.95	0.23	79	2.2	35	20,346	15	F	1	94	85	95	99	27,041
mong	Mongolia	C1	21	2,662,020	3,083,289	3,708,989	1,740,695	65.4	2.09	0.59	1.50	68	4.8	10	2	21	o	2	66	5	57	83	1,443,354
mont	Montserrat	L1	1	10,629	10,502	10,658	8,091	76.1	1.53	0.58	0.95	78	4.0	18	104	8	E	2	84	65	70	82	6,627
moro	Morocco	A3	43	28,220,843	32,682,965	38,529,890	19,034,959	67.5	2.28	0.61	1.67	69	5.8	10	83	32	A	2	57	18	41	44	8,339,748
moza	Mozambique	A1	11	19,680,456	23,116,593	30,611,842	10,845,899	55.1	4.12	2.39	1.73	38	4.4	8	37	57	P	3	28	15	7	40	4,370,576
myan	Myanmar	C2	14	45,611,177	50,902,661	58,120,485	32,885,659	72.1	1.99	0.86	1.13	63	5.2	7	85	133	W	3	48	7	19	83	27,352,910
nami	Namibia	A4	13	1,725,868	1,915,827	2,337,592	1,008,425	58.4	3.42	2.20	1.22	41	4.8	3	2	33	EM	2	57	60	60	76	765,352
naur	Nauru	P3	1	11,519	13,790	17,821	7,728	67.1	2.07	0.47	1.60	76	8.0	10	848	9	nE	2	86	65	65	99	7,651
nepa	Nepal	C3	14	23,930,490	29,715,459	38,010,174	14,123,775	59.0	3.19	0.95	2.23	60	5.5	14	258	118	n	3	35	10	31	28	3,903,191
neth	Netherlands	E4	12	15,785,699	15,972,738	15,781,965	12,926,909	81.9	1.03	0.90	0.13	78	2.4	48	380	46	D	1	94	93	98	100	12,926,909
nets	Netherlands Antilles	L1	5	216,775	236,607	258,459	162,690	75.1	1.53	0.61	0.92	76	3.7	40	323	15	D	2	89	70	80	94	152,580
newc	New Caledonia	P2	3	214,029	245,885	285,515	150,163	70.2	2.06	0.54	1.53	74	4.1	30	15	50	F	2	71	75	80	58	86,854
newz	New Zealand	P1	16	3,861,905	4,207,078	4,694,964	2,986,411	77.3	1.42	0.79	0.63	78	2.9	45	17	48	EI	1	94	90	92	100	2,986,411
nica	Nicaragua	L2	17	5,074,194	6,529,320	8,696,054	2,905,483	57.3	3.28	0.54	2.74	69	6.9	25	66	22	S	2	53	50	34	66	1,906,154
niga	Niger	A5	7	10,730,102	14,485,881	21,495,434	5,559,266	51.8	4.56	1.51	3.05	51	6.4	10	16	37	F	3	21	20	30	14	760,265
nige	Nigeria	A5	31	111,506,095	138,698,398	183,041,179	63,469,269	56.9	3.72	1.44	2.28	50	5.0	12	198	491	E	2	39	33	30	57	36,318,385
nork	North Korea	C1	13	24,039,193	26,451,118	29,387,635	17,399,568	72.4	1.68	0.55	1.13	73	4.8	14	239	7	K	2	77	35	63	95	16,530,077
norl	Northern Cyprus	C4	1	185,045	195,562	212,470	142,041	76.8	1.36	0.76	0.61	78	3.0	18	63	4	T	2	88	25	45	85	120,730
norm	Northern Mariana Is	P3	1	78,356	131,073	245,191	52,577	67.1	2.07	0.47	1.60	76	4.6	15	514	10	E	2	84	70	55	96	50,623
norw	Norway	E2	19	4,461,033	4,643,522	4,812,063	3,585,332	80.4	1.22	1.00	0.23	79	2.2	38	14	32	j	1	94	88	96	100	3,585,332
oman	Oman	C4	8	2,541,739	3,517,471	5,351,885	1,420,578	55.9	3.58	0.39	3.19	72	3.7	24	17	26	A	2	72	20	50	59	843,675
paki	Pakistan	C3	6	156,483,155	199,744,986	262,999,723	91,041,900	58.2	3.29	0.68	2.62	66	6.3	1	330	93	UE	2	45	13	33	38	34,283,164
pala	Palau	P3	1	19,426	24,391	33,228	13,035	67.1	2.07	0.47	1.60	76	6.0	10	20	5	pE	2	67	75	60	97	12,708
pale	Palestine	C4	2	2,215,393	2,845,762	4,132,562	1,070,699	48.3	4.38	0.38	3.99	73	6.0	12	662	21	A	2	79	25	30	72	771,743
pana	Panama	L2	11	2,855,683	3,266,131	3,779,174	1,961,854	68.7	2.03	0.51	1.53	74	4.4	14	50	33	S	2	86	53	62	91	1,781,470
papu	Papua New Guinea	P2	20	4,608,145	5,687,355	7,173,798	2,826,636	61.3	3.04	0.90	2.14	60	4.6	8	15	862	tE	2	53	75	34	72	2,038,801
para	Paraguay	L3	18	5,496,453	6,980,320	9,355,207	3,323,705	60.5	2.96	0.51	2.46	71	4.7	10	23	45	Sg	2	71	25	37	92	3,059,885
peru	Peru	L3	14	25,661,669	29,885,322	35,518,199	17,093,238	66.6	2.26	0.62	1.64	70	5.1	12	27	111	Syq	2	72	40	37	89	15,162,189
phil	Philippines	C2	16	75,966,500	90,544,498	108,251,048	48,094,391	63.3	2.56	0.53	2.03	70	5.7	22	360	183	OES	2	67	25	50	95	45,522,856
pola	Poland	E1	49	38,765,085	39,190,093	39,069,168	31,240,782	80.6	1.11	0.99	0.12	74	3.6	18	124	24	Y	1	83	25	67	99	30,846,308
port	Portugal	E3	20	9,874,853	9,776,944	9,348,354	8,261,302	83.7	1.00	1.09	-0.09	76	3.8	30	101	30	P	1	89	75	75	90	7,405,885
puer	Puerto Rico	L1	7	3,868,602	4,158,727	4,477,962	2,928,145	75.7	1.66	0.81	0.85	75	3.6	40	491	12	SE	2	88	75	85	90	2,625,135
qata	Qatar	C4	9	599,065	692,178	778,537	442,889	73.9	1.81	0.44	1.37	73	6.4	25	68	21	A	2	84	20	68	79	351,850
reun	Reunion	A1	4	699,406	777,722	879,761	507,699	72.6	1.67	0.52	1.14	77	3.8	20	350	17	F	2	84	35	55	78	396,772
roma	Romania	E1	41	22,326,502	21,524,798	19,945,452	18,363,548	82.3	0.92	1.18	-0.26	71	3.1	22	83	29	R	1	75	3	56	97	17,760,820
russ	Russia	E1	21	146,933,847	144,418,309	137,932,932	120,250,660	81.8	1.04	1.44	-0.39	67	3.2	17	8	169	R	1	79	8	69	98	117,920,179
rwan	Rwanda	A1	10	7,733,127	9,534,549	12,426,835	4,223,834	54.6	4.12	2.02	2.10	41	4.7	10	471	13	FrE	3	19	15	24	61	2,559,101
saha	Sahara	A3	1	293,357	386,057	469,946	182,116	62.1	2.86	0.76	2.10	64	5.0	3	1	12	A	2	24	5	5	10	18,172
saih	Saint Helena	A5	1	6,293	6,841	7,756	5,109	81.2	1.11	1.07	0.04	78	3.0	20	63	4	E	2	75	70	75	98	5,007
saik	Saint Kitts & Nevis	L1	2	38,473	36,321	35,052	29,289	76.1	1.53	0.58	0.95	78	4.0	15	130	6	E	2	85	70	75	90	26,361
sail	Saint Lucia	L1	10	154,366	175,541	208,093	117,519	76.1	1.53	0.58	0.95	78	4.0	18	337	7	E	2	84	75	80	80	93,962
saip	Saint Pierre & Miquelon	N1	1	6,567	6,778	7,171	5,340	81.3	1.19	0.95	0.23	79	3.0	22	29	3	F	1	75	75	80	99	5,287
saiv	Saint Vincent	L1	13	113,954	121,403	130,781	86,753	76.1	1.53	0.58	0.95	78	4.0	17	336	13	E	2	84	80	75	96	83,264
samo	Samoa	P4	2	180,073	216,958	271,417	111,321	61.8	2.73	0.46	2.27	73	7.8	14	96	8	wE	3	68	70	60	100	111,321
sanm	San Marino	E3	9	26,514	29,407	32,392	22,736	85.8	0.85	1.09	-0.24	79	2.7	40	531	4	I	1	96	85	95	99	22,529
saot	Sao Tome & Principe	A2	7	146,775	175,794	217,146	84,381	57.5	3.63	1.84	1.80	45	4.0	10	216	7	P	3	53	10	20	54	45,752
saud	Saudi Arabia	C4	5	21,606,691	28,778,495	39,964,965	12,849,499	59.5	3.22	0.38	2.84	73	6.6	15	17	39	A	2	77	15	56	62	7,961,789
sene	Senegal	A5	10	9,481,161	12,166,453	16,742,579	5,244,978	55.3	3.79	1.16	2.63	54	8.8	8	85	58	F	2	33	58	34	33	1,734,634
seyc	Seychelles	A1	5	77,435	85,582	97,962	57,836	74.7	1.58	0.66	0.92	73	4.8	10	215	10	sEF	2	85	10	56	84	48,758
sier	Sierra Leone	A5	4	4,854,383	6,017,780	8,085,454	2,716,513	56.0	4.39	2.23	2.17	41	4.7	6	112	31	E	3	18	35	16	32	857,127
sing	Singapore	C2	1	3,566,614	3,885,328	4,167,756	2,778,749	77.9	1.28	0.53	0.75	78	3.9	25	6,501	47	CmtE	2	90	28	72	89	2,475,686
slok	Slovakia	E1	4	5,387,191	5,456,375	5,392,691	4,326,992	80.3	1.11	0.96	0.15	74	3.0	22	109	19	u	1	87	25	60	100	4,326,992
slov	Slovenia	E3	12	1,985,557	1,950,573	1,817,953	1,669,059	84.1	0.89	1.05	-0.16	75	3.1	21	89	15	W	1	89	25	55	100	1,669,059
solo	Solomon Islands	P2	8	443,643	587,925	816,561	253,542	57.2	3.30	0.37	2.93	73	5.6	18	28	76	E	3	56	30	51	54	136,651
soma	Somalia	A1	13	7,264,500	10,579,797	16,227,263	3,780,446	52.0	4.99	1.67	3.32	49	4.9	4	32	29	vA	3	22	5	8	25	942,117
somi	Somaliland	A1	3	2,832,677	3,550,995	4,984,017	1,474,125	52.0	4.99	1.67	3.32	49	5.0	3	35	11	vA	2	28	15	20	25	367,470
soua	South Africa	A4	9	40,376,579	42,514,924	46,015,286	26,236,701	65.0	2.52	1.81	0.71	47	4.6	27	37	70	ME	2	72	8	39	82	21,461,149
souk	South Korea	C1	15	46,843,989	49,975,564	52,532,789	36,777,216	78.5	1.41	0.66	0.76	74	3.8	25	529	9	K	2	71	13	66	98	36,045,783
spai	Spain	E3	17	39,629,775	39,089,282	36,658,293	33,863,643	85.5	0.89	1.00	-0.11	79	3.5	25	72	36	S	1	93	65	89	97	32,701,002
span	Spanish North Africa	A3	2	130,000	133,911	140,000	87,685	67.5	2.28	0.61	1.67	69	3.0	20	4,242	5	S	2	91	70	70	92	80,672
sril	Sri Lanka	C3	25	18,827,054	20,869,505	23,546,757	13,913,193	73.9	1.72	0.59	1.13	74	5.2	15	358	22	ut	2	71	28	42	90	12,559,041
suda	Sudan	A3	9	29,489,719	36,256,579	46,264,179	17,864,872	60.6	3.17	1.07	2.10	57	5.3	5	18	245	A	3	33	5	11	46	8,250,003
suri	Suriname	L3	10	417,130	452,074	524,642	290,030	69.5	1.89	0.60	1.29	71	3.9	7	3	28	D	2	79	15	45	93	269,822
swaz	Swaziland	A4	4	1,007,895	1,310,450	1,784,790	574,601	57.0	3.51	0.79	2.73	63	5.7	12	102	12	xE	2	58	60	34	77	441,048
swed	Sweden	E2	23	8,910,214	9,039,070	9,096,927	7,288,555	81.8	0.98	1.11	-0.13	79	2.2	50	20	51	s	1	94	95	89	100	7,288,555
swit	Switzerland	E4	26	7,385,708	7,602,762	7,586,992	6,097,641	82.6	1.01	0.89	0.12	79	2.2	50	183	39	GFrI	1	93	85	97	100	6,097,641
syri	Syria	C4	14	16,124,618	20,464,138	26,291,810	9,547,386	59.2	2.92	0.45	2.47	70	6.2	30	141	28	A	2	76	13	36	71	6,769,049
taiw	Taiwan	C1	23	22,401,000	24,033,000	25,730,000	16,838,832	75.2	1.46	0.70	0.76	71	3.8	25	711	30	C	2	90	55	75	94	15,829,482
taji	Tajikistan	C3	6	6,188,201	7,133,677	8,856,904	3,692,500	59.7	2.87	0.63	2.24	69	6.1	20	61	41	T	2	58	5	10	98	3,607,426
tanz	Tanzania	A1	25	33,517,014	42,235,298	57,918,322	18,290,235	54.6	3.90	1.50	2.40	48	5.1	17	61	163	SE	3	36	25	29	68	12,438,289
thai	Thailand	C2	7	61,399,249	66,510,844	72,716,978	45,908,218	74.8	1.58	0.72	0.86	69	5.3	15	141	95	Z	2	83	35	46	94	43,059,485
timo	Timor	C2	1	884,541	1,015,062	1,184,977	540,720	61.1	2.76	1.35	1.41	50	4.0	10	79	22	X	2	52	10	20	90	487,254
togo	Togo	A5	5	4,629,218	5,953,281	8,482,467	2,506,722	54.2	3.95	1.43	2.51	50	5.6	8	149	53	F	3	37	20	29	52	1,300,487
tong	Tonga	P4	5	98,546	101,251	105,126	60,921	61.8	2.73	0.46	2.27	73	6.1	13	140	10	zE	2	63	65	70	93	56,567
trin	Trinidad & Tobago	L1	12	1,294,958	1,374,007	1,493,418	970,960	75.0	1.37	0.60	0.77	75	4.1	14	291	16	E	2	88	63	71	98	950,524
tuni	Tunisia	A3	23	9,585,611	10,928,892	12,843,081	6,678,295	69.7	1.97	0.64	1.34	71	5.1	12	78	25	A	2	75	28	47	67	4,455,919
turk	Turkey	C4	8	66,590,940	76,054,450	87,869,200	47,745,704	71.7	1.98	0.63	1.35	71	4.5	18	112	57	T	2	77	18	47	82	39,220,503
turm	Turkmenistan	C3	6	4,459,293	5,218,906	6,286,522	2,779,923	62.3	2.53	0.65	1.88	67	5.6	10	12	38	Y	2	72	5	10	98	2,715,673
turs	Turks & Caicos Is	L1	1	16,760	23,068	33,769	12,759	76.1	1.53	0.58	0.95	78	3.0	15	67	5	E	2	67	65	70	93	11,861
tuva	Tuvalu	P4	9	11,719	15,022	20,674	7,245	61.8	2.73	0.46	2.27	73	6.4	12	861	7	E	3	57	70	70	96	6,920
ugan	Uganda	A1	38	21,778,450	29,830,737	44,435,310	10,876,158	49.9	4.92	1.72	3.20	45	4.8	10	184	63	E	3	33	30	15	62	6,732,412
ukra	Ukraine	E1	25	50,455,980	48,723,593	45,687,963	41,489,952	82.2	0.97	1.38	-0.41	70	3.2	21	75	66	U	1	69	35	55	98	40,817,060
unia	United Arab Emirates	C4	7	2,441,436	2,851,247	3,283,949	1,757,590	72.0	1.79	0.33	1.46	76	6.8	18	39	39	A	2	87	15	66	79	1,392,552
usa	USA	N1	51	278,357,141	297,988,958	325,572,586	218,593,863	78.5	1.30	0.86	0.44	77	2.6	50	34	307	E	1	94	83	95	95	208,750,843
uuay	Uruguay	L3	19	3,337,058	3,565,821	3,906,674	2,509,801	75.2	1.69	0.93	0.75	75	3.3	22	22	32	s	2	88	20	63	97	2,442,336
uzbe	Uzbekistan	C3	13	24,317,851	28,170,066	33,354,778	15,210,816	62.6	2.57	0.62	1.96	69	5.5	20	74	64	Z	2	66	10	45	97	14,791,263
vanu	Vanuatu	P2	11	190,417	239,668	319,146	111,622	58.6	3.00	0.53	2.46	69	5.1	18	26	123	FEp	3	55	55	55	53	58,669
vene	Venezuela	L3	23	24,169,722	28,715,855	34,775,110	15,942,349	66.0	2.28	0.47	1.82	73	5.3	15	38	70	S	2	86	73	49	91	14,516,250
viet	Viet Nam	C2	7	79,831,650	90,764,274	108,037,101	53,319,559	66.8	1.95	0.63	1.33	69	4.8	12	326	100	V	2	56	13	24	94	50,023,168
virg	Virgin Is of the US	L1	3	92,954	87,198	83,559	70,766	76.1	1.53	0.58	0.95	78	3.1	35	237	9	E	2	88	85	90	95	67,212
wall	Wallis & Futuna Is	P4	1	14,517	15,529	17,500	8,974	61.8	2.73	0.46	2.27	73	5.0	20	72	4	F	2	80	70	70	95	8,533
yeme	Yemen	C4	17	18,112,066	25,366,187	38,985,203	9,363,938	51.7	4.33	0.87	3.46	61	5.6	10	82	22	A	3	36	15	25	46	4,310,408
yugo	Yugoslavia	E3	4	10,640,150	10,762,337	10,844,276	8,508,928	80.0	1.27	1.01	0.26	74	3.0	20	106	35	Y	1	63	20	56	93	7,945,123
zamb	Zambia	A1	9	9,168,700	11,426,935	15,616,246	4,837,406	52.8	4.06	1.79	2.27	42	4.4	6	20	86	E	3	37	23	32	78	3,791,486
zimb	Zimbabwe	A1	10	11,669,029	12,863,136	15,092,435	6,847,386	58.7	2.97	2.00	0.97	41	4.8	7	38	42	E	2	51	20	34	85	5,828,177
	11 minicountries		11	23,079	25,481	30,666	17,447	75.6	1.59	0.79	0.80	76	2.0	21	20	48	-	-	78	77	79	90	15,766
	Africa	A	793	784,445,039	973,315,192	1,298,310,949	451,269,790	57.5	3.59	1.36	2.22	54	3.1	10	25	3,823	-	-	42	22	27	56	252,799,651
	Antarctica	B	1	4,500	6,193	10,000	3,253	72.3	1.91	0.78	1.13	74	0.9	15	0	1	-	-	80	80	70	100	3,253
	Asia	C	666	3,682,550,093	4,135,949,307	4,723,140,220	2,579,677,434	70.1	1.99	0.74	1.25	69	3.7	12	115	3,696	-	-	58	20	40	72	1,860,609,403
	Europe	E	811	728,886,951	724,242,074	702,335,374	601,533,471	82.5	1.01	1.16	-0.15	75	3.0	32	31	1,518	-	-	86	52	78	98	588,366,397
	Latin America	L	531	519,138,048	595,030,371	696,648,086	355,459,810	68.5	2.14	0.64	1.50	73	3.3	11	25	1,555	-	-	79	44	49	87	307,774,051
	Northern America	N	80	309,631,093	332,050,930	363,611,501	243,937,696	78.8	1.28	0.85	0.43	77	2.2	49	14	474	-	-	94	83	95	96	233,208,233
	Oceania	P	149	30,393,391	34,179,316	39,647,012	22,765,535	74.9	1.67	0.76	0.91	73	2.6	39	3	1,516	-	-	85	79	83	95	21,550,015
	World A		**517**	**605,303,996**	**744,275,621**	**953,171,604**	**373,218,956**	**61.7**	**2.95**	**0.77**	**2.18**	**62**	**3.6**	**9**	**32**	**1,448**	**-**	**-**	**55**	**14**	**36**	**58**	**216,596,374**
	World B		**812**	**3,755,011,992**	**4,193,116,856**	**4,783,698,891**	**2,636,973,009**	**70.2**	**2.02**	**0.85**	**1.16**	**64**	**3.6**	**12**	**70**	**5,192**	**-**	**-**	**57**	**21**	**40**	**72**	**1,907,016,671**
	World C		**1,702**	**1,694,733,127**	**1,857,380,906**	**2,086,832,647**	**1,244,455,024**	**73.4**	**1.82**	**0.94**	**0.87**	**71**	**2.9**	**27**	**21**	**5,943**	**-**	**-**	**80**	**55**	**65**	**92**	**1,140,697,957**
	GLOBAL TOTAL		**3,031**	**6,055,049,115**	**6,794,773,383**	**7,823,703,142**	**4,254,646,989**	**70.3**	**2.05**	**0.87**	**1.18**	**68**	**3.4**	**16**	**40**	**12,583**	**-**	**-**	**63**	**30**	**47**	**77**	**3,264,311,003**

COUNTRY		SOCIETY																					
		ECONOMIC		URBANIZATION			METROSCAN			HEALTH											EDUCATION		
code	short name	GNP	EFL	rural	urban	metro	cit50	cit100	mega	acces	water	mat-m	inf-m	hosp	beds	doct	blind	deaf	lepers	murd	educ	schools	univs
1	2	25	26	27	28	29	30	31	32	33	34	35	36	37	38	39	40	41	42	43	44	45	46
afgh	Afghanistan	600	2	17.7	5.0	4.9	10	8	1	29	12	1,700	142	250	3	2,233	200,000	1,535,500	8,000	90.0	36	2,605	5
alba	Albania	670	31	1.9	1.2	0.7	6	1	0	45	50	65	26	895	57	4,467	2,000	209,600	500	50.0	79	2,290	8
alge	Algeria	1,600	35	12.8	18.7	11.3	44	26	2	98	78	160	36	284	22	25,304	25,000	1,895,900	44,000	1.0	84	17,372	40
amer	American Samoa	2,600	50	0.0	0.0	0.0	0	0	0	80	80	30	19	1	27	34	50	3,800	550	8.0	95	38	2
ando	Andorra	16,200	45	0.0	0.1	0.0	0	0	0	95	90	10	5	1	20	110	50	4,900	0	1.6	90	18	0
ango	Angola	410	13	8.5	4.4	3.9	6	6	1	30	32	1,500	112	58	12	662	12,000	766,800	50,000	3.4	45	6,308	1
angu	Anguilla	2,000	40	0.0	0.0	0.0	0	0	0	70	90	30	7	1	50	10	10	500	0	3.0	90	7	0
anti	Antigua	7,690	45	0.0	0.0	0.0	0	0	0	90	95	40	7	2	65	59	120	4,100	200	4.7	90	56	1
arge	Argentina	8,030	47	3.9	33.1	22.7	43	26	3	71	64	100	20	2,000	44	88,800	14,300	2,221,800	40,000	2.3	94	31,735	1,540
arme	Armenia	730	25	1.1	2.5	1.8	5	3	1	50	60	50	24	183	83	14,000	3,000	219,700	1,000	5.4	87	1,443	14
arub	Aruba	15,890	46	0.0	0.1	0.0	0	0	0	90	90	30	12	2	44	74	60	4,400	0	1.2	85	56	1
aust	Australia	18,720	58	2.9	16.0	13.8	25	15	5	90	95	9	5	1,071	50	38,800	18,820	1,129,900	1,800	1.8	96	9,865	95
ausz	Austria	26,890	59	2.9	5.3	3.8	12	6	1	95	100	10	5	324	92	26,121	11,000	497,500	300	2.5	106	6,311	44
azer	Azerbaijan	480	6	3.3	4.4	2.6	7	3	1	30	50	22	32	749	105	29,000	7,000	469,700	10,000	8.1	97	4,578	23
baha	Bahamas	11,940	60	0.0	0.3	0.2	1	1	0	95	97	100	13	5	40	357	110	18,100	60	17.6	98	227	1
bahr	Bahrain	7,840	66	0.0	0.6	0.4	1	1	0	80	100	60	14	12	23	542	62	37,100	100	1.8	106	118	4
bang	Bangladesh	240	27	101.8	27.4	19.8	35	24	3	45	83	850	67	891	3	21,749	200,000	7,698,600	700,000	1.9	46	62,433	1,046
barb	Barbados	6,560	40	0.1	0.1	0.1	1	1	0	90	100	43	10	10	75	312	250	15,900	180	6.8	90	139	1
belg	Belgium	24,710	58	0.3	9.9	4.7	17	13	1	92	89	10	6	363	76	37,792	4,780	615,400	200	3.1	102	6,707	21
beli	Belize	2,630	46	0.1	0.1	0.1	1	0	0	70	89	70	26	7	29	110	80	14,500	1,000	33.2	92	267	4
belo	Belorussia	2,070	29	2.6	7.6	5.3	22	12	1	65	80	37	21	868	122	45,000	9,000	617,100	300	2.9	95	5,047	38
beni	Benin	370	41	3.5	2.6	1.3	4	3	0	18	50	990	80	50	10	323	5,000	373,300	100,000	0.9	40	3,048	13
berm	Bermuda	31,870	50	0.0	0.1	0.0	0	0	0	95	85	30	13	2	42	91	25	3,900	0	5.1	75	36	1
bhut	Bhutan	420	2	2.0	0.2	0.0	0	0	0	65	58	1,600	53	27	12	141	10,000	121,900	9,000	6.0	30	187	2
boli	Bolivia	800	45	2.9	5.4	3.8	8	6	2	67	55	650	55	336	15	3,392	1,070	499,700	6,500	5.0	77	10,529	10
bosn	Bosnia-Herzegovina	300	10	2.3	1.7	1.2	6	6	0	40	50	50	14	200	46	6,929	4,000	260,300	500	2.5	70	2,443	44
bots	Botswana	3,020	44	0.4	1.2	0.3	2	1	0	89	70	250	58	30	25	240	1,880	97,100	6,000	12.7	92	1,025	1
boug	Bougainville	1,400	25	0.2	0.0	0.0	0	0	0	20	30	20	54	5	20	15	200	11,900	7,000	7.0	50	140	0
braz	Brazil	3,640	31	31.8	138.3	92.3	185	143	14	45	72	220	38	35,701	37	208,966	60,700	10,152,100	280,000	12.0	96	208,147	873
brit	Britain	18,700	61	6.2	52.6	36.8	111	65	5	95	100	9	6	2,423	54	87,000	116,414	3,500,200	500	2.5	104	28,169	820
briz	British Virgin Is	8,000	50	0.0	0.0	0.0	0	0	0	90	90	10	19	1	50	60	20	1,300	20	2.0	95	18	1
brun	Brunei	15,800	45	0.1	0.2	0.1	1	0	0	80	90	60	8	10	36	197	300	19,500	500	1.5	89	187	4
bulg	Bulgaria	1,330	30	2.5	5.8	3.9	26	10	1	75	99	27	14	287	106	28,457	3,312	498,300	400	5.9	81	3,881	88
burk	Burkina Faso	230	26	9.7	2.2	1.6	4	2	1	90	78	930	91	78	5	341	90,000	723,400	450,000	0.2	25	2,936	9
buru	Burundi	160	25	6.1	0.6	0.4	2	2	0	80	52	1,300	109	264	19	317	11,000	418,400	70,000	3.3	40	1,531	8
camb	Cambodia	270	5	8.5	2.6	1.1	6	3	0	53	13	900	92	188	16	600	40,000	672,400	47,000	70.0	75	5,044	9
came	Cameroon	650	28	7.7	7.4	4.1	10	8	2	70	41	550	66	629	27	945	15,630	907,700	200,000	0.1	58	6,763	5
cana	Canada	19,380	60	7.1	24.0	21.1	49	34	4	95	100	6	5	1,079	50	60,559	27,184	1,840,700	500	5.2	105	16,231	272
cape	Cape Verde	960	31	0.2	0.3	0.1	2	0	0	80	51	100	49	75	15	112	400	26,200	3,000	7.0	83	367	3
caym	Cayman Islands	5,000	60	0.0	0.0	0.0	0	0	0	95	90	10	19	5	65	50	10	2,200	0	1.0	95	20	1
cent	Central African Rep	340	22	2.1	1.5	1.0	4	2	0	45	18	700	92	133	15	170	27,000	218,400	200,000	1.6	43	976	1
chad	Chad	180	10	5.8	1.8	1.3	4	3	1	30	24	1,500	103	40	7	217	175,000	436,200	25,000	45.0	33	2,610	4
chan	Channel Islands	12,000	60	0.1	0.1	0.1	0	0	0	95	90	10	6	70	50	230	120	9,200	0	1.0	95	50	2
chil	Chile	4,160	51	2.3	12.9	10.3	28	17	1	97	85	65	11	217	32	15,015	2,910	912,700	1,000	11.0	89	8,626	201
chin	China	620	24	829.0	433.6	329.6	491	332	92	92	90	95	36	60,784	24	1,832,000	2,000,000	75,234,000	3,500,000	0.2	86	953,807	1,065
colo	Colombia	1,910	40	10.6	31.7	21.1	35	26	4	60	76	100	25	947	14	36,551	30,000	2,334,300	50,000	81.9	89	44,693	235
como	Comoros	470	25	0.4	0.2	0.0	0	0	0	55	48	950	67	20	25	57	500	36,700	3,000	10.0	49	275	2
cong	Congo-Brazzaville	680	24	1.1	1.8	1.8	4	2	1	83	60	890	85	500	33	613	4,000	178,900	66,000	5.0	40	1,623	124
conz	Congo-Zaire	120	16	36.0	15.6	12.3	30	24	1	26	27	870	76	400	21	2,469	73,000	3,105,000	800,000	1.5	49	12,987	0
cook	Cook Islands	2,000	60	0.0	0.0	0.0	0	0	0	90	90	30	19	18	100	25	20	1,200	700	3.0	90	35	0
cost	Costa Rica	2,610	44	1.9	2.1	1.1	2	1	1	80	92	55	10	33	21	4,027	2,000	227,900	3,000	5.3	82	3,729	6
croa	Croatia	3,250	26	1.9	2.6	2.0	7	7	1	75	96	35	9	98	61	9,280	3,700	269,100	500	7.4	84	2,413	54
cuba	Cuba	1,300	15	2.5	8.7	5.2	19	16	1	98	93	95	8	244	61	46,860	4,600	672,000	11,000	5.0	90	12,233	35
cypr	Cyprus	13,420	48	0.3	0.3	0.3	3	1	0	90	100	5	8	110	18	1,441	1,209	36,500	700	1.9	95	501	30
czec	Czech Republic	3,870	60	3.5	6.8	4.4	23	11	1	85	100	15	6	287	98	31,897	10,000	611,700	500	2.0	95	5,344	23
denm	Denmark	29,890	61	0.8	4.5	2.3	9	4	1	95	100	9	6	163	35	14,497	8,000	316,500	300	4.9	108	2,952	235
djib	Djibouti	850	5	0.1	0.5	0.4	1	1	0	40	90	570	97	8	27	97	300	41,200	9,000	4.4	26	82	1
domi	Dominica	2,990	28	0.0	0.1	0.0	0	0	0	70	77	50	7	53	25	38	60	4,300	400	4.2	70	77	2
domr	Dominican Republic	1,460	31	3.0	5.5	6.5	11	9	2	80	71	110	30	103	20	11,130	2,850	509,700	528	11.9	84	6,207	7
ecua	Ecuador	1,390	37	4.8	7.9	5.5	16	13	2	88	70	150	41	429	16	12,853	10,000	758,800	6,300	10.5	91	18,353	21
egyp	Egypt	790	31	37.0	31.5	24.2	60	29	2	99	64	170	40	6,418	20	101,500	75,000	4,087,100	115,000	1.6	87	19,150	12
elsa	El Salvador	1,610	51	3.3	2.9	1.8	4	3	1	40	55	300	26	78	17	4,525	3,961	379,200	600	25.0	68	3,806	6
equa	Equatorial Guinea	380	22	0.2	0.2	0.1	1	1	0	35	95	820	98	15	29	99	800	27,100	16,000	12.0	40	713	4
erit	Eritrea	570	20	3.1	0.7	0.5	2	1	0	30	25	1,400	81	7	9	68	3,200	228,500	25,000	20.0	33	581	1
esto	Estonia	2,860	53	0.4	1.0	0.8	5	2	0	85	90	41	14	115	84	4,680	1,200	85,100	200	24.3	96	825	22
ethi	Ethiopia	100	26	51.5	11.0	4.1	10	7	1	46	27	1,400	103	86	3	1,466	90,000	3,970,500	400,000	16.4	20	8,120	11
faer	Faeroe Islands	15,000	50	0.0	0.0	0.0	0	0	0	95	90	12	6	3	57	81	20	2,900	0	2.0	95	77	1
fiji	Fiji	2,440	38	0.5	0.3	0.2	1	1	0	75	100	90	17	25	22	426	4,000	50,900	8,000	11.5	97	693	5
finl	Finland	20,580	54	1.8	3.4	2.4	12	5	1	95	100	11	5	317	90	13,344	3,345	310,700	300	0.6	110	5,490	20
fran	France	24,990	54	14.4	44.6	30.2	108	59	3	90	100	15	5	3,834	120	155,896	43,000	3,543,600	400	4.7	106	52,981	1,062
freg	French Guiana	10,580	24	0.0	0.1	0.1	1	0	0	75	60	70	51	6	66	200	150	10,700	8,500	27.2	60	110	1
frep	French Polynesia	16,940	30	0.1	0.1	0.1	1	1	0	80	70	20	10	34	58	323	96	14,400	2,200	0.9	99	316	4
gabo	Gabon	3,490	39	0.5	0.7	0.7	4	2	0	90	67	500	81	27	51	448	1,300	74,100	40,000	1.4	40	1,024	1
gamb	Gambia	320	20	0.9	0.4	0.3	1	1	0	93	76	1,100	112	13	7	61	2,700	74,600	33,000	0.4	44	277	9
geor	Georgia	440	23	2.0	3.0	2.1	7	4	1	80	90	33	18	422	105	30,000	4,500	325,100	500	10.7	75	3,808	19
germ	Germany	27,510	58	10.2	72.0	52.3	137	74	12	95	100	22	4	2,381	80	259,981	15,000	4,961,300	1,000	4.6	100	18,867	314
ghan	Ghana	390	36	12.5	7.8	4.0	7	5	1	60	56	740	58	121	13	628	65,000	1,195,700	120,000	2.1	58	16,653	16
gibr	Gibraltar	6,600	40	0.0	0.0	0.0	0	0	0	90	90	12	6	2	86	29	140	1,700	20	3.7	95	22	1
gree	Greece	8,210	44	4.2	6.4	5.3	15	6	2	95	99	10	7	372	50	40,116	13,000	635,800	5,000	2.6	96	11,317	17
grel	Greenland	15,500	40	0.0	0.0	0.0	0	0	0	80	90	25	6	16	75	78	50	3,600	0	18.1	60	88	2
gren	Grenada	2,980	35	0.1	0.0	0.0	0	0	0	75	85	30	12	3	38	47	90	5,600	50	7.8	95	76	1
guad	Guadeloupe	9,200	40	0.0	0.5	0.2	2	1	0	70	80	20	7	30	80	590	90	27,400	2,500	13.2	90	418	1
guam	Guam	20,300	50	0.1	0.1	0.1	1	0	0	85	90	15	9	1	6	147	150	9,900	800	7.9	95	63	1
guat	Guatemala	1,340	43	6.8	4.6	2.9	3	2	1	34	64	200	41	160	16	7,601	6,000	733,300	1,200	27.4	57	12,670	5
guin	Guinea	550	33	5.0	2.4	2.4	5	4	1	80	62	1,600	114	38	6	773	45,000	471,700	250,000	0.5	30	2,849	10
gunb	Guinea-Bissau	250	20	0.9	0.3	0.2	1	1	0	40	53	910	122	16	13	274	5,000	70,800	35,000	0.5	38	648	4
guya	Guyana	590	32	0.5	0.3	0.2	1	1	0	50	61	500	51	30	33	138	1,300	52,400	4,400	4.5	82	524	1
hait	Haiti	250	16	5.4	2.9	1.9	2	1	1	50	28	1,000	61	87	8	564	9,000	469,000	1,500	18.0	40	6,741	2
hond	Honduras	600	37	3.4	3.0	1.9	5	2	1	64	65	220	31	86	12	3,803	1,000	389,100	1,300	9.4	77	8,838	10
hung	Hungary	4,120	42	3.3	6.7	4.0	20	8	1	70	94	30	9	148	98	36,643	10,000	588,700	1,000	4.3	91	5,094	91
icel	Iceland	24,950	55	0.0	0.3	0.2	1	1	0	95	100	10	5	26	111	726	434	16,900	0	0.9	102	80	5
indi	India	340	25	725.4	288.3	206.1	642	346	33	85	81	570	64	15,067	8	405,253	9,000,000	60,406,200	5,500,000	4.6	73	812,975	7,958
indo	Indonesia	980	43	126.8	85.3	39.3	94	65	6	80	62	650	39	971	6	25,135	1,000,000	12,753,900	200,000	0.8	80	180,604	1,000
iran	Iran	4,700	6	26.0	41.7	31.1	80	65	6	80	83	120	29	609	15	37,000	200,000	4,585,700	30,000	0.5	84	81,134	0
iraq	Iraq	2,000	2	5.4	17.8	12.3	16	16	3	93	44	310	39	177	18	9,366	75,000	1,386,500	7,000	7.1	69	11,045	20
irel	Ireland	14,710	56	1.5	2.2	1.3	3	2	0	95	100	10	6	63	34	6,036	7,000	214,500	0	1.2	108	4,103	26
isle	Isle of Man	10,800	58	0.0	0.1	0.0	0	0	0	95	100	10	6	3	50	86	60	4,700	0	0.7	95	40	1
isra	Israel	15,920	42	0.5	4.7	4.0	9	5	1	80	99	7	7	244	63	24,344	5,285	298,900	500	2.1	92	3,065	7
ital	Italy	19,020	46	18.9	38.4	26.3	107	52	4	40	100	12	6	1,926	68	296,385	110,000	3,431,700	1,000	4.7	87	38,459	50
ivor	Ivory Coast	660	35	7.9	6.9	4.7	7	6	1	30	72	810	79	100	8	2,020	50,000	908,600	250,000	2.5	49	7,249	1
jama	Jamaica	1,510	46	1.1	1.4	1.0	2	2	0	90	70	120	19	30	22	1,589	3,100	155,200	2,500	27.6	86	932	15
japa	Japan	39,640	59	26.8	100.0	83.5	216	108	6	95	95	18	4	9,963	136	219,704	256,455	7,585,700	15,000	1.0	101	48,002	1,207
jord	Jordan	1,510	44	1.7	4.9	2.3	4	3	1	97	89	150	21	53	11	6,395	9,000	379,800	600	2.0	92	3,277	55
kaza	Kazakhstan	1,330	20	6.2	10.0	7.5	34	21	1	80	70	80	30	1,805	134	66,000	15,000	1,015,700	2,000	12.0	89	11,956	61
keny	Kenya	280	39	20.1	10.0	3.9	7	7	1	77	53	650	63	877	14	3,794	65,000	1,820,400	120,000	6.4	72	18,506	14
kirg	Kirghizia	700	15	2.8	1.9	1.4	7	2	0	70	75	110	35	396	99	14,674	4,000	272,600	1,000	10.4	95	3,359	12
kiri	Kiribati	920	30	0.1	0.0	0.0	0	0	0	90	99	300	9	4	40	10	100	5,200	1,000	5.1	90	107	0
kuwa	Kuwait	17,390	52	0.0	1.9	1.5	2	2	1	100	100	29	10	22	26	2,717	1,000	118,000	200	1.7	66	671	1
laos	Laos	350	5	4.2	1.3	0.8	4	1	0	67	39	650	82	1,074	25	1,173	10,000	341,600	20,000	15.0	67	9,250	9
latv	Latvia	2,270	39	0.6	1.8	1.3	4	3	0	90	90	40	15	170	121	7,714	2,000	143,800	200	14.6	85	978	14
leba	Lebanon	2,660	41	0.3	2.9	2.7	4	4	1	95	100	300	25	25	50	6,638	5,000	197,300	1,000	4.3	94	2,100	20
leso	Lesotho	770	27	1.6	0.6	0.2	1	1	0	80	52	610	87	22	15	136	3,000	137,600	40,000	33.9	73	1,397	1
libe	Liberia	770	20	1.6	1.5	1.4	1	1	1	39	30	560	75	92	13	89	15,000	195,400	39,000	20.0	45	2,076	3
liby	Libya	6,510	6	0.7	4.9	3.6	6	6	1	45	30	220	25	75	41	4,749	10,000	383,200	7,700	1.3	105	4,494	10
liec	Liechtenstein	33,000	55	0.0	0.0	0.0	0	0	0	95	95	9	5	1	35	32	30	2,000	50	5.0	100	23	0
lith	Lithuania	1,900	30	0.9	2.7	1.6	6	5	0	90	95	36	14	198	117	14,670	3,000	221,400	100	6.9	87	2,485	14
luxe	Luxembourg	41,210	61	0.0	0.4	0.2	2	1	0	95	95	8	6	34	115	848	204	25,800	50	13.2	81	100	1
mace	Macedonia	860	25	0.8	1.3	0.9	3	3	0	80	80	70	20	61	52	4,528	2,000	134,000	200	3.9	77	1,145	27
mada	Madagascar	230	33	11.2	4.7	2.9	7	7	1	65	29	490	73	250	9	1,392	40,000	1,043,700	120,000	0.6	43	14,766	5
mala	Malawi	170	32	9.2	1.7	0.9	2	2	0	80	45	560	126	395	16	186	18,400	659,000	70,000	3.1	88	3,225	4
malb	Malaysia	3,890	52	9.5	12.7	5.8	21	17	1	70	90	80	10	264	22	7,012	50,000	1,337,900	30,000	2.1	78	8,379	54

COUNTRY		SOCIETY																					
		ECONOMIC		*URBANIZATION*			*METROSCAN*			*HEALTH*											*EDUCATION*		
code	*short name*	*GNP*	*EFL*	*rural*	*urban*	*metro*	*cit50*	*cit100*	*mega*	*acces*	*water*	*mat-m*	*inf-m*	*hosp*	*beds*	*doct*	*blind*	*deaf*	*lepers*	*murd*	*educ*	*schools*	*univs*
1	*2*	*25*	*26*	*27*	*28*	*29*	*30*	*31*	*32*	*33*	*34*	*35*	*36*	*37*	*38*	*39*	*40*	*41*	*42*	*43*	*44*	*45*	*46*
mald	Maldives	990	8	0.2	0.1	0.1	1	0	0	50	89	200	40	5	8	45	128	18,100	100	1.9	90	262	0
mali	Mali	250	38	7.9	3.4	1.7	7	4	1	30	37	1,200	109	15	4	435	110,000	753,600	270,000	6.0	21	1,821	7
malt	Malta	12,000	39	0.0	0.4	0.2	1	1	0	95	100	10	7	7	58	900	570	22,700	500	3.0	98	192	1
mars	Marshall Islands	1,890	40	0.0	0.0	0.0	0	0	0	70	31	100	9	2	14	20	50	3,900	50	7.0	75	115	0
mart	Martinique	10,000	35	0.0	0.4	0.1	1	1	0	75	80	20	7	20	103	625	100	23,900	4,000	5.8	90	361	1
maur	Mauritania	460	24	1.1	1.5	0.4	1	1	0	63	76	930	83	16	7	135	15,000	154,800	9,000	1.8	44	1,696	4
maus	Mauritius	3,380	15	0.7	0.5	0.5	1	1	0	100	98	120	13	23	28	941	250	70,600	400	3.2	80	421	2
mayo	Mayotte	600	20	0.1	0.0	0.0	0	0	0	50	60	600	67	2	11	9	80	6,100	200	11.0	40	95	1
mexi	Mexico	3,320	33	25.3	73.6	56.5	132	85	8	78	83	110	28	1,539	10	149,432	60,000	5,932,900	40,000	7.3	86	112,624	13,000
micr	Micronesia	2,010	35	0.1	0.0	0.0	0	0	0	70	100	700	9	4	31	50	200	8,500	600	6.0	90	193	1
mold	Moldavia	920	31	2.0	2.4	1.4	5	4	0	75	80	60	24	335	122	18,000	3,700	267,500	500	8.8	80	1,700	18
mona	Monaco	25,000	60	0.0	0.0	0.0	0	0	0	95	100	10	5	1	168	112	15	2,000	0	0.5	100	6	0
mong	Mongolia	310	30	1.0	1.7	0.8	2	1	0	95	54	65	44	475	105	5,911	4,000	164,200	200	19.0	68	708	9
mont	Montserrat	12,527	45	0.0	0.0	0.0	0	0	0	90	90	35	7	2	55	10	10	600	0	4.0	90	15	1
moro	Morocco	1,110	46	12.6	15.6	10.6	26	17	2	70	52	610	41	203	11	7,695	35,000	1,731,200	40,000	1.4	59	6,474	50
moza	Mozambique	80	19	11.8	7.9	4.4	10	6	1	39	32	1,500	115	238	9	388	28,000	1,173,800	20,000	4.2	35	4,035	2
myan	Myanmar	1,790	14	33.0	12.6	8.4	29	16	1	60	38	580	69	717	6	12,245	210,000	2,960,500	880,000	4.1	62	38,754	40
nami	Namibia	2,000	25	1.0	0.7	0.2	1	1	0	62	57	370	74	47	45	324	1,400	104,000	1,500	72.4	109	1,064	7
naur	Nauru	8,070	30	0.0	0.0	0.0	0	0	0	70	60	100	9	1	40	5	10	700	100	25.0	70	6	1
nepa	Nepal	200	30	21.1	2.8	0.8	3	2	0	35	44	1,500	70	114	3	1,497	60,000	1,460,800	120,000	2.5	74	26,835	3
neth	Netherlands	24,000	63	1.7	14.1	8.6	38	23	2	85	100	12	5	236	57	39,069	8,000	952,300	500	24.9	110	10,888	206
nets	Netherlands Antilles	10,400	35	0.1	0.2	0.2	1	1	0	85	90	15	12	11	73	291	500	12,100	30	7.0	95	142	1
newc	New Caledonia	8,000	40	0.1	0.1	0.1	1	1	0	70	90	40	9	8	62	370	30	11,700	3,500	5.0	101	342	6
newz	New Zealand	14,340	65	0.5	3.4	2.5	10	6	1	95	100	25	6	330	77	11,413	3,687	225,600	50	3.9	108	2,772	7
nica	Nicaragua	380	28	1.8	3.3	1.9	6	6	1	83	61	160	38	56	12	2,554	1,800	281,700	900	25.6	79	7,544	4
niga	Niger	220	26	8.5	2.2	1.1	5	3	0	32	53	1,200	105	15	5	142	50,000	648,300	75,000	0.2	18	2,768	3
nige	Nigeria	260	35	62.5	49.1	35.7	110	70	2	66	39	1,000	76	11,588	12	17,954	420,000	7,727,100	1,000,000	15.0	63	44,723	31
nork	North Korea	950	2	8.9	15.1	7.0	12	12	1	40	100	70	19	2,500	135	57,690	48,000	1,434,800	40,000	5.0	80	6,122	281
norl	Northern Cyprus	12,402	15	0.1	0.1	0.0	0	0	0	70	100	40	8	25	15	250	150	11,100	500	20.0	90	80	2
norm	Northern Mariana Is	10,500	40	0.0	0.0	0.0	0	0	0	75	70	20	9	1	19	23	40	3,200	100	3.8	90	27	1
norw	Norway	31,250	51	1.2	3.3	1.6	9	4	0	95	100	6	4	350	53	14,497	4,000	264,200	200	1.0	108	4,096	195
oman	Oman	4,820	43	0.4	2.1	0.1	1	0	0	96	63	190	21	180	23	2,095	23,000	163,000	250	0.8	75	568	5
paki	Pakistan	460	39	98.5	58.0	38.7	63	55	8	55	60	340	65	10,905	6	63,033	900,000	9,360,400	150,000	6.4	42	156,450	804
pala	Palau	5,000	40	0.0	0.0	0.0	0	0	0	75	90	20	9	1	45	10	10	1,100	0	5.0	90	32	1
pale	Palestine	14,584	25	0.1	2.1	0.9	5	5	0	70	85	200	20	100	50	9,000	2,000	124,200	500	20.0	85	500	1
pana	Panama	2,750	52	1.2	1.6	1.3	3	2	1	80	83	55	18	60	29	3,168	2,000	171,300	850	13.9	85	3,141	8
papu	Papua New Guinea	1,160	38	3.8	0.8	0.3	2	1	0	96	28	930	54	150	40	301	9,000	276,700	20,000	8.6	51	3,073	2
para	Paraguay	1,690	47	2.4	3.1	1.7	5	3	1	63	8	160	37	100	12	2,924	4,000	329,800	14,000	15.6	79	6,282	2
peru	Peru	2,310	40	7.0	18.7	12.1	24	15	1	75	60	280	37	427	17	23,771	23,000	1,539,700	12,000	9.3	101	63,551	655
phil	Philippines	1,050	42	31.4	44.5	21.9	51	44	3	76	85	280	29	1,723	11	78,445	80,000	4,502,200	67,000	30.1	99	42,228	809
pola	Poland	2,790	39	13.4	25.4	17.6	74	34	3	90	100	19	13	752	63	87,706	21,523	2,323,600	1,000	3.1	98	31,813	140
port	Portugal	9,740	48	6.1	3.8	3.4	5	2	2	95	100	15	8	335	42	24,499	8,225	587,300	4,000	4.2	92	14,140	250
puer	Puerto Rico	7,800	50	1.0	2.9	2.0	4	4	1	95	95	12	11	72	26	6,269	4,500	232,600	1,800	26.8	95	1,989	45
qata	Qatar	11,600	30	0.0	0.6	0.5	1	1	0	90	100	50	15	3	20	758	200	36,000	1,000	1.8	85	197	1
reun	Reunion	4,300	35	0.2	0.5	0.1	1	1	1	80	90	30	8	20	44	1,061	1,000	41,900	1,400	7.8	75	445	1
roma	Romania	1,480	26	9.3	13.0	8.9	48	24	1	60	100	130	19	300	95	42,808	15,918	1,350,300	4,500	3.3	83	16,769	63
russ	Russia	2,240	30	32.8	114.1	78.4	293	152	13	65	90	75	17	12,265	119	612,400	350,000	8,771,700	20,000	21.8	94	72,574	569
rwan	Rwanda	180	20	7.3	0.5	0.3	1	1	0	80	66	1,300	115	220	9	272	7,000	460,400	80,000	85.0	50	1,724	3
saha	Sahara	207	5	0.0	0.3	0.2	1	1	0	25	40	800	53	2	10	50	1,000	17,400	100	25.0	30	45	1
saih	Saint Helena	9,000	40	0.0	0.0	0.0	0	0	0	75	75	40	6	1	30	10	12	400	0	4.0	75	8	0
saik	Saint Kitts & Nevis	5,170	45	0.0	0.0	0.0	0	0	0	90	100	70	7	0	0	0	0	2,500	100	14.0	95	0	0
sail	Saint Lucia	3,370	48	0.1	0.1	0.1	1	0	0	95	100	50	7	4	37	64	200	9,100	100	17.0	90	84	0
saip	Saint Pierre & Miquelon	11,000	45	0.0	0.0	0.0	0	0	0	80	80	40	5	1	40	10	10	400	0	4.0	80	9	0
saiv	Saint Vincent	2,280	46	0.1	0.1	0.0	0	0	0	90	100	40	7	0	44	40	100	7,000	100	10.3	95	60	0
samo	Samoa	1,120	44	0.1	0.0	0.0	0	0	0	80	90	35	19	16	20	50	200	10,500	1,000	7.0	75	206	6
sanm	San Marino	24,700	60	0.0	0.0	0.0	0	0	0	95	100	10	6	5	66	60	100	1,600	0	4.1	100	17	0
saot	Sao Tome & Principe	350	20	0.1	0.1	0.0	0	0	0	30	70	1,200	92	5	10	61	200	8,800	200	4.0	50	64	2
saud	Saudi Arabia	7,040	42	3.1	18.5	9.9	17	16	2	97	93	130	18	229	21	25,543	230,000	1,299,700	2,000	0.9	66	17,338	72
sene	Senegal	600	32	5.0	4.5	3.0	6	6	1	40	50	1,200	58	20	10	520	22,000	569,700	100,000	1.4	38	2,832	18
seyc	Seychelles	6,620	20	0.0	0.0	0.0	0	0	0	70	97	200	13	7	56	72	150	4,600	100	2.7	90	45	1
sier	Sierra Leone	180	25	3.1	1.8	1.1	5	2	0	38	34	1,800	145	219	10	404	28,000	291,900	150,000	12.0	36	2,039	2
sing	Singapore	26,730	74	0.0	3.6	3.6	1	1	1	100	100	10	4	22	36	4,301	427	215,200	12,000	1.7	86	392	7
slok	Slovakia	2,950	41	2.1	3.3	1.4	11	2	0	65	90	17	10	111	91	15,767	4,500	322,300	700	2.4	0	3,386	14
slov	Slovenia	8,200	33	0.9	1.0	0.5	2	2	0	75	95	13	6	24	58	4,086	1,600	114,800	1,000	4.9	90	1,067	28
solo	Solomon Islands	910	30	0.4	0.1	0.0	0	0	0	60	90	70	19	8	53	52	370	26,600	4,000	10.0	64	544	1
soma	Somalia	500	6	5.3	2.0	1.5	3	1	1	27	25	1,600	112	90	7	450	10,000	521,800	14,000	1.5	10	1,125	1
somi	Somaliland	155	2	2.1	0.8	0.2	2	1	0	25	20	1,700	112	10	5	50	2,500	170,000	4,500	2.0	10	200	0
soua	South Africa	3,160	40	20.0	20.3	13.3	15	14	6	75	70	230	63	834	39	25,967	62,000	2,775,400	36,000	8.0	104	22,447	32
souk	South Korea	9,700	54	6.5	40.4	31.2	55	31	5	100	89	130	9	600	29	51,518	110,000	2,813,000	90,000	1.4	98	10,312	645
spai	Spain	13,580	46	8.9	30.8	19.3	69	44	3	90	99	7	6	813	42	159,291	30,000	2,388,100	4,000	2.6	110	42,315	1,415
span	Spanish North Africa	8,000	30	0.0	0.1	0.2	2	0	0	90	57	250	41	3	40	100	150	7,800	100	2.0	80	20	1
sril	Sri Lanka	700	47	14.4	4.4	2.9	7	3	1	93	46	140	15	422	28	3,345	65,000	1,129,200	13,000	8.2	87	18,654	8
suda	Sudan	800	18	18.8	10.7	4.8	12	12	1	70	50	660	64	200	8	2,400	110,000	1,789,400	150,000	4.2	39	10,661	24
suri	Suriname	880	22	0.2	0.2	0.3	1	1	0	40	72	100	25	40	47	329	1,300	27,100	3,700	7.6	70	454	1
swaz	Swaziland	1,170	42	0.6	0.4	0.1	1	0	0	45	43	560	55	24	0	83	1,000	59,000	10,000	88.1	95	705	1
swed	Sweden	23,750	49	1.5	7.4	4.7	21	11	1	95	100	7	5	700	52	22,200	15,716	533,900	200	4.5	100	5,426	100
swit	Switzerland	40,630	64	2.8	4.6	4.0	18	9	0	95	100	6	5	500	78	23,000	9,000	444,700	300	2.3	96	3,000	12
syri	Syria	1,120	16	7.3	8.8	7.1	15	10	2	90	85	180	28	213	12	11,808	12,000	967,600	6,500	1.4	77	10,219	47
taiw	Taiwan	12,400	61	5.4	17.0	10.7	28	23	2	75	80	50	36	810	48	27,288	18,510	1,344,100	55,000	8.2	90	3,654	125
taji	Tajikistan	340	20	4.2	2.0	1.1	4	3	0	60	50	130	51	449	88	13,084	6,000	383,900	1,500	2.5	83	3,350	22
tanz	Tanzania	120	31	24.2	9.3	5.0	13	10	2	80	49	770	74	170	11	1,065	40,000	2,021,200	200,000	6.4	44	10,892	4
thai	Thailand	2,740	54	48.1	13.2	9.0	18	7	1	90	81	200	24	1,097	17	13,398	210,000	3,629,700	500,000	7.7	67	37,409	84
timo	Timor	644	30	0.8	0.1	0.1	1	1	0	40	60	1,000	120	5	5	100	800	53,000	1,000	5.0	75	750	5
togo	Togo	310	22	3.1	1.5	0.8	2	1	0	61	63	640	76	30	16	319	9,000	280,600	80,000	7.0	64	2,594	1
tong	Tonga	1,630	35	0.1	0.0	0.0	0	0	0	80	100	60	19	4	31	46	80	6,000	200	3.0	90	163	1
trin	Trinidad & Tobago	3,770	50	0.3	1.0	0.5	2	1	0	100	82	90	12	31	33	1,051	1,300	80,400	3,000	11.7	87	576	1
tuni	Tunisia	1,820	47	3.3	6.3	3.3	11	6	1	90	99	170	25	138	20	4,670	25,000	590,200	10,000	2.1	86	4,998	0
turk	Turkey	2,780	40	16.4	50.2	32.4	102	48	5	75	92	180	38	857	24	50,639	38,178	3,943,900	50,000	3.6	80	50,701	424
turm	Turkmenistan	920	15	2.4	2.0	1.2	7	5	0	70	85	55	49	368	115	14,000	4,000	268,800	500	5.0	60	1,832	9
turs	Turks & Caicos Is	2,172	45	0.0	0.0	0.0	0	0	0	65	90	40	7	1	20	7	10	1,000	0	4.0	90	20	0
tuva	Tuvalu	800	30	0.0	0.0	0.0	0	0	0	70	100	200	19	8	36	8	10	600	50	3.0	85	11	0
ugan	Uganda	240	43	18.7	3.1	1.4	4	1	1	49	34	1,200	94	89	12	774	209,000	1,347,500	200,000	9.5	47	8,815	9
ukra	Ukraine	1,630	20	13.9	36.6	24.9	87	49	5	75	97	50	15	3,900	130	230,000	43,000	3,048,100	1,000	8.8	90	22,448	159
unia	United Arab Emirates	17,400	58	0.3	2.1	2.0	5	4	0	99	98	26	13	35	21	3,090	400	146,600	50	1.1	103	363	1
usa	USA	26,980	62	63.4	214.9	188.2	344	258	39	85	90	12	6	6,580	46	670,300	482,850	16,669,300	1,000	9.0	103	85,393	5,758
uuay	Uruguay	5,170	44	0.3	3.0	1.7	4	1	1	82	34	85	13	112	45	11,201	3,000	196,500	2,000	4.1	95	2,862	2
uzbe	Uzbekistan	970	25	14.0	10.3	6.5	24	17	1	75	90	55	39	1,388	85	79,000	22,000	1,501,100	1,000	5.5	87	9,347	52
vanu	Vanuatu	1,200	35	0.2	0.0	0.0	0	0	0	70	72	280	31	90	22	12	200	11,500	400	4.0	66	272	1
vene	Venezuela	3,020	30	3.1	21.1	14.0	40	29	4	60	79	120	18	610	26	32,616	18,000	1,450,200	40,000	22.1	85	17,421	99
viet	Viet Nam	240	6	64.1	15.8	12.7	43	29	3	90	38	160	31	12,500	27	28,500	200,000	4,832,900	240,000	6.0	55	19,841	104
virg	Virgin Is of the US	11,740	60	0.0	0.0	0.0	0	0	0	95	95	20	7	5	49	250	20	6,500	100	22.3	95	20	1
wall	Wallis & Futuna Is	4,654	40	0.0	0.0	0.0	0	0	0	90	90	70	19	1	45	20	10	900	20	2.0	85	20	0
yeme	Yemen	260	25	11.2	6.9	2.0	5	5	0	38	52	1,400	68	75	8	3,065	16,000	1,087,100	3,600	1.5	70	7,313	1
yugo	Yugoslavia	2,000	35	4.3	6.4	4.1	18	18	1	80	85	25	16	1,000	55	22,000	10,000	630,100	100	7.0	65	4,996	146
zamb	Zambia	400	41	5.1	4.1	3.8	10	9	1	75	43	940	74	965	29	713	38,000	548,000	50,000	9.8	62	3,995	2
zimb	Zimbabwe	540	26	7.5	4.1	2.9	4	4	1	85	74	570	67	1,378	15	1,551	15,000	745,400	60,000	5.0	86	6,193	28
	11 minicountries	21,015	48	0.0	0.0	0.0	0	0	0	77	89	236	112	11	29	93	142	1,312	120	2.9	85	15	1
	Africa	657	30	489.2	295.2	190.6	493	334	40	63	48	819	75	27,694	15	218,175	2,170,862	49,194,200	6,269,200	7.9	57	302,576	556
	Antarctica	80,000	50	0.0	0.0	0.0	0	0	0	80	100	10	20	1	20	20	10	300	0	1.0	100	0	0
	Asia	2,396	28	2,294.4	1,388.1	972.4	2,199	1,373	195	82	80	338	46	130,113	22	3,316,962	15,357,604	220,900,900	12,319,800	4.0	77	2,674,707	16,186
	Europe	12,714	43	182.8	546.1	371.1	1,361	735	66	78	96	34	11	37,269	88	2,450,000	908,711	43,759,900	52,020	8.5	96	442,546	6,360
	Latin America	3,302	35	127.8	391.3	271.5	594	420	52	63	72	181	31	43,697	26	682,333	273,691	30,881,200	545,418	16.9	89	596,382	16,803
	Northern America	26,214	62	70.6	239.0	209.4	393	292	43	86	91	11	7	7,678	46	731,038	510,119	18,517,900	1,500	8.6	103	101,757	6,033
	Oceania	14,091	54	9.1	21.3	17.4	41	25	6	89	84	160	14	1,789	50	52,183	37,410	1,815,212	52,240	3.7	90	19,043	135
	World A	**1,464**	**26**	**315.0**	**290.3**	**185.2**	**475**	**325**	**36**	**61**	**64**	**496**	**57**	**21,762**	**24**	**429,916**	**2,026,691**	**37,328,710**	**1,404,150**	**8.5**	**63**	**428,932**	**1,855**
	World B	**2,284**	**29**	**2,342.0**	**1,413.0**	**1,000.2**	**2,413**	**1,448**	**197**	**82**	**78**	**378**	**47**	**142,888**	**25**	**3,652,694**	**15,284,994**	**225,955,000**	**15,511,650**	**4.0**	**76**	**2,510,926**	**14,514**
	World C	**11,448**	**44**	**516.8**	**1,177.9**	**847.0**	**2,193**	**1,406**	**169**	**73**	**81**	**174**	**25**	**83,591**	**47**	**3,368,101**	**1,946,722**	**21,785,902**	**2,324,378**	**10.9**	**92**	**1,197,153**	**29,704**
	GLOBAL TOTAL	**4,767**	**33**	**3,173.9**	**2,881.2**	**2,032.3**	**5,081**	**3,179**	**402**	**78**	**77**	**333**	**42**	**248,241**	**31**	**7,450,711**	**19,258,407**	**365,069,612**	**19,240,178**	**6.4**	**79**	**4,137,011**	**46,073**

COUNTRY		SOCIETY (continued)							RELIGIOUS RELATIONS												CHRISTIANITY	
		COMMUNICATION per 1000							RELIGIONS		RELIGIOUS PERSECUTION				CHURCH/STATE RELATIONS				bibliography		church members	
code	short name	news	radios	TVs	fones	faxes	computers	internet	relig	indig	liberty	CSI	martyrs	mar-sit	1900	1970	1990	2000	items listed		affiliated	AC
1	2	47	48	49	50	51	52	53	54	55	56	57	58	59	60	61	62	63	64		65	66
afgh	Afghanistan	11	73.7	10.0	1.4	0.1	25,592	1,000	10	4	9	9	1,000,030	2	RI	RJ	A	RI	17		6,897	0.0
alba	Albania	54	157.0	89.0	12.0	0.3	122,252	20,000	6	1	7	39	12,200	2	RI	A	S	S	18		1,070,390	34.4
alge	Algeria	46	125.0	71.0	42.0	0.2	221,190	25,000	6	4	8	39	30,833	6	RI	RI	RI	RI	22		90,877	0.3
amer	American Samoa	51	330.0	130.0	136.0	15.0	3,134	5,000	5	0	5	67	0	0	S	S	S	S	5		55,240	81.1
ando	Andorra	63	6.0	360.0	438.0	20.0	20,248	4,000	6	0	3	80	0	0	RC	RC	RC	RC	6		70,205	90.0
ango	Angola	11	39.0	51.0	5.6	0.8	127,806	10,000	7	38	7	46	24,300	4	RC	RC	A	A	32		10,934,238	84.9
angu	Anguilla	1	700.0	500.0	350.0	25.0	8,304	500	6	0	4	74	0	0	S	S	S	S	2		7,186	86.5
anti	Antigua	94	778.0	419.0	311.0	7.5	6,791	3,000	6	0	5	68	0	0	S	S	S	S	9		53,713	79.5
arge	Argentina	138	637.0	347.0	160.0	1.6	2,329,017	300,000	14	17	7	56	12,035	3	RC	RC	RC	RC	46		33,985,872	91.8
arme	Armenia	23	250.0	241.0	155.0	0.3	128,163	30,000	6	1	3	73	204,000	9	RO	A	RO	RO	31		2,953,693	83.9
arub	Aruba	757	571.0	471.0	390.0	6.8	5,856	2,000	10	0	5	72	0	0	S	S	S	S	5		95,241	92.7
aust	Australia	255	1,152.0	641.0	510.0	32.0	10,600,000	800,000	16	67	3	81	6,000	2	R	R	R	R	61		12,587,959	66.7
ausz	Austria	465	584.0	497.0	466.0	61.0	2,871,633	100,000	14	1	2	87	8,100	3	R	S	S	S	25		6,909,670	84.2
azer	Azerbaijan	28	200.0	212.0	85.0	0.4	156,561	20,000	6	0	9	29	22,000	2	RI	A	A	RI	6		357,802	4.6
baha	Bahamas	126	282.0	233.0	277.0	2.0	75,487	25,000	6	0	4	73	0	0	RA	RA	RA	RA	17		266,851	87.1
bahr	Bahrain	128	542.0	442.0	242.0	13.0	43,256	25,000	9	0	7	50	0	0	RI	RI	RI	RI	7		62,698	10.2
bang	Bangladesh	6	67.0	7.0	2.4	0.0	384,930	80,000	10	17	4	56	13,000	1	S	RI	RI	RI	40		931,740	0.7
barb	Barbados	159	1,132.0	284.0	345.0	7.0	23,791	10,000	10	0	2	84	0	0	RA	RA	R	R	21		196,858	72.8
belg	Belgium	321	500.0	464.0	458.0	22.0	4,156,023	300,000	13	1	2	87	1,000	1	R	R	R	R	17		8,518,696	83.8
beli	Belize	100	140.0	167.0	134.0	3.3	12,079	5,000	9	2	4	67	0	0	S	S	S	S	20		197,139	81.9
belo	Belorussia	187	311.0	265.0	190.0	0.6	411,376	60,000	8	2	7	51	550,000	1	RO	A	A	RO	10		6,584,077	64.3
beni	Benin	2	73.0	73.0	5.2	0.2	93,323	5,000	7	39	6	50	500	1	RT	S	A	A	17		1,684,195	27.6
berm	Bermuda	254	1,311.0	460.0	900.0	40.0	13,061	12,000	7	0	3	82	0	0	RA	RA	R	R	3		55,675	86.2
bhut	Bhutan	6	28.0	3.0	6.3	0.4	2,032	500	7	5	9	29	40	1	RB	RB	RB	RB	16		9,649	0.5
boli	Bolivia	69	553.0	202.0	47.0	0.8	166,573	50,000	11	29	2	75	902	4	RC	RC	RC	RC	32		7,786,232	93.5
bosn	Bosnia-Herzegovina	131	263.0	111.0	69.0	0.7	151,842	40,000	5	0	8	37	53,333	2	R	A	R	RI	37		1,385,885	34.9
bots	Botswana	29	206.0	24.0	41.0	2.1	24,286	3,000	8	31	4	61	0	0	RR	S	S	S	34		751,073	46.3
boug	Bougainville	15	72.0	163.0	8.0	1.0	1,985	500	4	31	4	64	3,000	1	S	S	S	S	7		185,331	93.4
braz	Brazil	45	340.0	278.0	78.0	3.0	8,500,000	520,000	14	169	7	52	50	1	RC	R	R	R	57		155,475,609	91.4
brit	Britain	351	1,109.0	612.0	502.0	69.0	26,000,000	17,000,000	14	16	3	78	70,933	15	RA	RA	RA	RA	88		39,053,151	66.4
briz	British Virgin Is	250	625.0	234.0	370.0	35.0	6,365	4,000	6	0	5	70	0	0	S	S	S	S	9		14,892	69.7
brun	Brunei	71	417.0	609.0	240.0	7.0	26,063	5,000	10	7	6	51	0	0	RI	RI	RI	RI	10		24,592	7.5
bulg	Bulgaria	141	437.0	359.0	306.0	2.4	646,172	200,000	6	1	8	51	102,000	2	R	A	A	A	25		6,657,950	81.0
burk	Burkina Faso	1	48.0	4.0	2.9	0.5	24,114	10,000	6	52	5	52	100	1	RT	S	S	S	35		1,984,078	16.6
buru	Burundi	3	47.0	7.0	2.7	0.1	6,974	2,000	6	4	3	67	80,003	4	RT	S	S	S	23		5,152,841	77.0
camb	Cambodia	5	150.0	8.0	0.5	0.1	16,811	2,000	10	13	9	14	98,002	4	RB	RB	A	A	12		118,398	1.1
came	Cameroon	4	115.0	75.0	4.5	0.7	30,258	4,000	7	243	4	60	600	1	S	S	S	S	47		7,761,501	51.5
cana	Canada	189	803.0	647.0	590.0	32.7	16,000,000	11,600,000	15	3	3	80	100	1	S	S	S	S	56		20,237,778	65.0
cape	Cape Verde	40	135.0	3.0	55.0	2.6	1,093	500	6	0	7	57	0	0	RC	RC	S	S	15		406,880	95.1
caym	Cayman Islands	700	1,450.0	800.0	700.0	5.0	14,410	10,000	7	0	5	70	0	0	S	S	S	S	4		25,820	67.3
cent	Central African Rep	1	55.0	5.0	2.3	0.1	3,640	1,000	5	59	4	60	3,000	1	RT	S	S	S	14		1,608,999	44.5
chad	Chad	0	240.0	2.0	0.8	0.0	7,270	2,000	5	61	6	36	400	1	RT	S	S	S	8		1,438,014	18.8
chan	Channel Islands	300	900.0	500.0	700.0	30.0	38,223	15,000	8	0	3	78	0	0	RA	RA	RA	RA	2		100,781	65.9
chil	Chile	99	317.0	280.0	132.0	2.0	886,818	20,000	10	6	3	74	2,120	2	RC	S	S	S	40		13,358,340	87.8
chin	China	23	178.0	247.0	34.0	1.0	15,900,000	3,800,000	17	139	9	33	2,753,055	27	RG	A	A	A	148		88,955,347	7.1
colo	Colombia	64	150.0	188.0	100.0	3.0	1,968,576	350,000	12	65	7	38	126,100	4	RC	RC	RC	RC	44		40,935,888	96.7
como	Comoros	100	97.0	5.0	8.2	0.3	1,530	500	5	0	7	41	0	0	S	S	S	S	7		7,061	1.2
cong	Congo-Brazzaville	8	95.0	17.0	8.1	0.1	2,982	1,000	10	51	7	49	400	1	S	A	A	A	18		2,332,878	79.3
conz	Congo-Zaire	3	81.0	41.0	0.8	0.1	113,849	20,000	10	163	6	51	0	0	RC	R	R	R	52		47,151,525	91.3
cook	Cook Islands	100	200.0	700.0	200.0	20.0	1,005	500	3	0	3	81	0	0	S	S	S	S	7		18,492	94.7
cost	Costa Rica	102	224.0	220.0	167.0	0.7	303,816	25,000	10	4	2	82	0	0	RC	RC	RC	RC	24		3,870,161	96.2
croa	Croatia	575	230.0	230.0	269.0	14.5	313,947	50,000	5	1	5	61	33,333	1	RC	A	RC	RC	41		4,256,386	95.2
cuba	Cuba	120	326.0	200.0	32.0	0.1	448,020	10,000	11	4	8	46	15,000	1	RC	A	A	A	34		4,822,909	43.1
cypr	Cyprus	110	288.0	143.0	474.0	16.0	48,630	10,000	6	0	7	54	17,520	5	R	R	R	R	19		551,594	91.9
czec	Czech Republic	219	884.0	406.0	237.0	10.0	1,336,540	300,000	6	1	9	44	19,530	4	R	A	A	RC	31		4,819,136	47.0
denm	Denmark	308	988.0	536.0	612.0	57.0	2,691,014	1,200,000	9	1	2	88	0	0	RL	RL	RL	RL	24		4,751,110	89.8
djib	Djibouti	7	61.0	73.0	13.0	0.2	1,373	400	5	0	4	68	0	0	S	S	S	S	8		28,194	4.4
domi	Dominica	60	875.0	141.0	240.0	5.6	1,067	200	9	1	5	62	0	0	S	S	S	S	6		66,757	94.4
domr	Dominican Republic	35	154.0	87.0	76.0	0.5	84,953	5,000	11	3	2	76	1,500	1	RC	RC	RC	RC	34		8,026,705	94.5
ecua	Ecuador	72	277.0	148.0	65.0	2.6	885,225	50,000	10	16	3	71	3,135	4	R	R	R	R	22		12,307,787	97.3
egyp	Egypt	64	265.0	126.0	46.0	0.9	1,362,372	40,000	7	5	8	39	1,056,263	30	RI	RI	RI	RI	51		10,320,466	15.1
elsa	El Salvador	53	373.0	241.0	53.0	0.8	315,970	45,000	10	4	6	52	20,000	2	RC	RC	RC	RC	22		6,098,022	97.2
equa	Equatorial Guinea	2	488.0	92.0	6.3	0.4	6,777	1,000	7	3	6	54	35,000	1	RC	A	S	S	18		394,698	87.2
erit	Eritrea	5	80.0	6.0	4.8	0.3	95,224	4,000	7	3	4	60	10,000	1	RO	RO	A	S	9		1,934,358	50.2
esto	Estonia	242	400.0	411.0	277.0	14.3	56,706	3,000	6	0	5	54	50,000	1	R	A	A	S	21		529,875	38.0
ethi	Ethiopia	10	167.0	4.0	2.5	0.0	1,654,380	50,000	8	110	8	35	643,350	7	RO	RO	A	S	43		31,161,159	49.8
faer	Faeroe Islands	100	447.0	286.0	400.0	42.0	9,579	1,000	3	0	2	87	0	0	RL	RL	RL	RL	14		39,590	92.6
fiji	Fiji	45	574.0	89.0	83.0	5.9	67,812	10,000	9	2	4	65	0	0	R	R	R	R	40		459,745	56.3
finl	Finland	464	966.0	519.0	547.0	40.0	2,615,352	800,000	10	1	2	87	100	1	RX	RX	RX	RX	32		4,579,451	88.5
fran	France	237	862.0	579.0	558.0	45.0	21,800,000	12,600,000	14	7	4	75	174,616	17	R	S	S	S	47		41,116,959	69.6
freg	French Guiana	11	486.0	170.0	288.0	1.1	5,358	500	12	7	5	60	0	0	S	S	S	S	4		152,736	84.2
frep	French Polynesia	112	488.0	177.0	219.0	4.0	14,424	1,000	7	1	4	71	0	0	S	S	S	S	17		198,725	84.5
gabo	Gabon	16	119.0	76.0	24.0	0.4	24,709	2,000	8	26	4	68	100	1	R	R	R	R	27		1,085,756	88.6
gamb	Gambia	2	125.0	5.0	17.0	0.9	18,653	500	6	5	5	52	0	0	S	S	S	S	14		47,198	3.6
geor	Georgia	703	400.0	220.0	103.0	0.1	162,547	10,000	6	1	5	58	210,000	2	RO	A	A	RO	9		3,008,814	60.6
germ	Germany	317	1,875.0	550.0	494.0	32.0	30,600,000	22,900,000	14	7	5	70	799,546	10	R	S	S	S	41		58,783,222	71.5
ghan	Ghana	18	76.0	16.0	3.5	0.4	498,210	20,000	11	75	4	58	210	2	R	R	R	R	57		8,666,976	42.9
gibr	Gibraltar	214	573.0	275.0	696.0	10.7	2,816	1,000	6	0	2	84	0	0	S	S	S	S	10		21,368	85.2
gree	Greece	156	400.0	442.0	493.0	3.0	1,321,445	800,000	8	3	2	85	5,000	1	RO	RO	RO	RO	25		10,061,020	94.5
grel	Greenland	150	374.0	380.0	305.0	20.3	5,995	1,000	4	1	2	78	0	0	RL	RL	RL	RL	23		39,350	70.1
gren	Grenada	45	489.0	158.0	255.0	4.3	7,525	1,500	7	2	6	62	0	0	R	R	A	A	13		90,745	96.8
guad	Guadeloupe	83	208.0	262.0	378.0	8.1	31,936	3,000	8	0	7	56	66	1	S	S	S	S	10		432,948	95.0
guam	Guam	170	1,827.0	648.0	461.0	10.0	19,736	7,000	8	0	2	84	210	2	R	R	R	R	5		156,656	93.5
guat	Guatemala	23	52.0	122.0	27.0	1.6	733,299	250,000	11	2	3	65	41,000	3	RC	RC	RC	RC	50		10,684,153	93.8
guin	Guinea	2	35.0	9.7	1.6	0.1	23,584	1,000	6	12	8	33	100	1	S	A	A	A	7		231,322	3.1
gunb	Guinea-Bissau	6	36.0	10.0	8.8	0.5	4,719	500	6	13	7	40	0	0	RC	RC	A	A	20		155,645	12.8
guya	Guyana	63	454.0	42.0	63.0	0.3	15,734	2,000	11	9	6	51	950	1	R	R	R	R	16		374,036	43.4
hait	Haiti	7	41.0	5.0	8.4	2.0	117,250	5,000	9	2	8	38	29,500	3	RC	RC	RC	RC	37		7,639,424	92.9
hond	Honduras	44	354.0	80.0	29.0	1.2	194,563	25,000	11	6	6	55	8,020	2	RC	RC	RC	RC	16		6,057,600	93.4
hung	Hungary	228	590.0	444.0	185.0	4.4	1,504,063	200,000	7	2	8	51	71,505	6	R	A	A	A	39		8,749,732	87.2
icel	Iceland	515	733.0	447.0	556.0	17.8	84,571	150,000	9	1	2	88	0	0	RL	RL	RL	RL	17		265,259	94.4
indi	India	21	121.0	61.0	13.0	0.2	6,241,974	600,000	13	280	5	52	866,064	18	S	S	S	S	121		62,243,546	6.1
indo	Indonesia	20	132.0	147.0	17.0	0.8	3,294,753	150,000	11	524	3	63	94,610	8	RR	R	R	S	73		26,364,858	12.4
iran	Iran	20	213.0	134.0	85.0	0.8	3,057,144	300,000	12	11	7	44	227,270	14	RI	RI	RI	RI	40		313,990	0.5
iraq	Iraq	27	630.0	74.0	33.0	0.4	462,180	80,000	8	2	8	36	2,262,300	16	RI	RI	RI	RI	24		724,662	3.1
irel	Ireland	170	610.0	382.0	365.0	32.0	1,444,394	200,000	7	1	5	72	3,950	5	RC	RC	R	R	35		3,355,446	90.0
isle	Isle of Man	300	900.0	500.0	700.0	25.0	11,874	3,000	4	0	3	78	0	0	RA	RA	RA	RA	12		52,438	66.2
isra	Israel	281	481.0	303.0	418.0	25.5	1,598,856	1,000,000	7	11	6	56	5	2	R	RI	RJ	RJ	38		294,078	5.7
ital	Italy	105	801.0	436.0	433.0	4.4	17,500,000	10,600,000	12	3	3	80	236,260	19	RC	RC	RC	RC	25		46,922,140	81.9
ivor	Ivory Coast	7	110.0	59.0	8.1	0.5	227,154	15,000	7	70	3	63	0	0	S	S	S	S	25		4,353,882	29.5
jama	Jamaica	66	747.0	306.0	116.0	0.8	129,334	30,000	11	6	3	65	0	0	S	S	S	S	36		1,121,713	43.4
japa	Japan	576	801.0	619.0	488.0	79.0	49,900,000	21,900,000	13	195	5	64	399,120	8	RS	S	S	S	72		3,436,881	2.7
jord	Jordan	48	234.0	175.0	73.0	8.0	379,811	20,000	5	0	4	62	10,004	2	RI	RI	RI	RI	8		273,522	4.1
kaza	Kazakhstan	400	150.0	275.0	118.0	0.4	507,835	25,000	8	3	8	36	6,000	2	RO	A	S	S	9		2,591,803	16.0
keny	Kenya	13	103.0	18.0	9.0	0.2	758,507	35,000	11	61	4	61	7,333	5	S	S	S	S	49		22,477,365	74.7
kirg	Kirghizia	11	183.0	238.0	77.0	0.1	113,565	15,000	8	2	8	35	0	0	RO	A	RI	RI	7		465,665	9.9
kiri	Kiribati	100	79.0	25.0	26.0	2.3	8,619	2,000	4	0	4	68	200	1	S	S	S	S	10		77,331	92.7
kuwa	Kuwait	387	591.0	373.0	226.0	21.0	167,098	40,000	6	0	8	45	0	0	RI	RI	RI	RI	12		247,535	12.6
laos	Laos	3	121.0	7.0	4.1	0.2	56,927	3,000	11	65	8	30	12,000	2	RB	RB	A	A	27		112,563	2.1
latv	Latvia	228	547.0	482.0	280.0	0.5	95,870	12,000	7	0	6	55	50,500	2	RO	A	S	S	18		1,576,425	66.9
leba	Lebanon	135	601.0	291.0	89.0	1.9	115,104	10,000	6	2	4	62	170,204	8	RI	R	R	R	41		1,734,821	52.9
leso	Lesotho	7	569.0	7.0	9.0	0.5	91,766	3,000	7	1	6	46	0	0	S	S	S	S	22		1,445,329	67.1
libe	Liberia	14	275.0	25.0	2.1	0.3	65,125	2,500	5	28	4	54	15,000	1	RX	RX	RX	RX	24		932,060	29.6
liby	Libya	13	190.0	138.0	59.0	2.0	159,684	5,000	11	1	9	35	12,500	1	RI	RI	RI	RI	14		170,352	3.0
liec	Liechtenstein	581	384.0	371.0	638.0	30.0	5,000	8,000	5	0	2	84	0	0	RC	RC	RC	RC	5		27,051	82.4
lith	Lithuania	136	381.0	364.0	254.0	1.1	147,603	18,000	6	2	5	65	173,030	7	RO	A	S	S	22		3,213,397	87.6
luxe	Luxembourg	384	586.0	593.0	550.0	18.3	107,444	40,000	6	0	2	85	0	0	RC	RC	RC	RC	8		402,674	93.5
mace	Macedonia	21	179.0	179.0	179.0	1.3	100,504	15,000	5	1	5	64	0	0	RO	A	RO	RO	34		1,287,192	63.6
mada	Madagascar	4	173.0	24.0	2.4	0.3	260,922	20,000	10	36	3	65	9,010	5	R	R	S	S	36		7,629,263	47.9
mala	Malawi	2	112.0	70.0	3.6	0.1	54,920	3,000	9	10	4	60	7,000	2	S	S	S	S	31		7,032,260	64.4
malb	Malaysia	142	476.0	226.0	166.0	4.5	2,539,817	800,000	12	111	8	42	0	0	RI	RI	RI	RI	58		1,771,189	8.0

COUNTRY		SOCIETY (continued) COMMUNICATION per 1000							RELIGIOUS RELATIONS RELIGIONS		RELIGIOUS PERSECUTION				CHURCH/STATE RELATIONS				bibliography	CHRISTIANITY church members	
code	short name	news	radios	TVs	fones	faxes	computers	internet	religs	indig	liberty	CSI	martyrs	mar-sit	1900	1970	1990	2000	items listed	affiliated	AC
1	2	47	48	49	50	51	52	53	54	55	56	57	58	59	60	61	62	63	64	65	66
mald	Maldives	12	99.0	40.0	57.0	14.0	4,533	1,000	6	0	5	51	0	0	RI	RI	RI	RI	7	358	0.1
mali	Mali	4	176.0	12.0	1.7	0.1	50,237	5,000	6	17	4	55	30	1	R	S	S	S	18	224,365	2.0
malt	Malta	145	260.0	448.0	459.0	13.2	94,558	35,000	7	0	3	80	5,000	1	RC	RC	RC	RC	16	371,381	95.6
mars	Marshall Islands	20	500.0	20.0	44.2	3.8	13,039	6,000	4	1	5	67	0	0	S	S	S	S	7	60,103	93.6
mart	Martinique	84	187.0	137.0	381.0	9.0	47,878	5,000	11	1	5	66	0	0	S	S	S	S	10	373,372	94.4
maur	Mauritania	0	444.0	58.0	4.1	0.2	7,739	500	6	1	5	49	0	0	RI	RI	RI	RI	14	6,526	0.2
maus	Mauritius	68	353.0	187.0	131.0	18.0	58,833	7,000	11	0	2	75	0	0	S	S	S	S	26	369,432	31.9
mayo	Mayotte	15	427.0	1.0	48.0	1.0	203	100	4	0	5	50	0	0	S	S	S	S	6	1,866	1.8
mexi	Mexico	113	230.0	192.0	96.0	3.5	6,300,000	200,000	12	24	6	57	3,081,550	10	S	S	S	S	54	93,806,927	94.9
micr	Micronesia	25	667.0	21.0	74.0	4.3	9,879	1,500	7	6	5	66	1,510	2	S	S	S	S	17	108,662	91.6
mold	Moldavia	24	358.0	300.0	131.0	0.2	200,629	20,000	6	1	5	62	0	0	RO	A	RO	RO	3	2,798,558	63.9
mona	Monaco	263	987.0	670.0	876.0	61.0	10,080	10,000	5	0	2	88	0	0	RC	RC	RC	RC	12	31,101	92.6
mong	Mongolia	88	121.0	59.0	32.0	0.9	5,472	1,000	8	10	10	28	11,050	3	RB	A	A	A	25	33,393	1.3
mont	Montserrat	150	1,935.0	125.0	350.0	25.0	1,605	500	5	0	5	68	0	0	S	S	S	S	10	10,170	95.7
moro	Morocco	13	194.0	145.0	43.0	0.7	288,536	25,000	6	4	9	33	30,512	3	RI	RI	RI	RI	40	174,476	0.6
moza	Mozambique	5	36.0	3.0	3.4	0.8	156,503	10,000	8	25	8	34	35,200	2	RC	RC	A	A	30	6,460,533	32.8
myan	Myanmar	23	72.0	76.0	3.3	0.0	74,013	1,000	14	75	8	34	41,004	4	R	S	S	S	48	3,741,464	8.2
nami	Namibia	93	136.0	29.0	51.0	8.0	69,335	7,000	6	8	6	45	0	0	R	R	R	R	27	1,349,211	78.2
naur	Nauru	20	577.0	300.0	250.0	5.0	585	200	5	0	4	65	0	0	R	R	R	R	3	8,341	72.4
nepa	Nepal	8	29.0	3.0	3.6	0.0	97,389	1,000	11	67	8	36	50	1	RH	RH	RH	RH	70	576,061	2.4
neth	Netherlands	299	775.0	495.0	525.0	38.0	7,146,914	5,400,000	14	4	3	76	36,333	3	S	S	S	S	39	10,282,853	65.1
nets	Netherlands Antilles	260	1,009.0	325.0	374.0	25.0	30,128	5,000	11	0	2	83	50	1	S	S	S	S	14	184,912	85.3
newc	New Caledonia	123	495.0	380.0	236.0	20.6	38,946	5,000	9	1	4	73	10	1	S	S	S	S	16	161,679	75.5
newz	New Zealand	297	866.0	506.0	479.0	24.0	1,876,902	800,000	14	3	3	79	0	0	S	S	S	S	35	2,562,219	66.4
nica	Nicaragua	30	222.0	170.0	23.0	2.0	70,416	15,000	11	6	6	51	6,150	4	R	R	A	A	35	4,857,432	95.7
niga	Niger	1	48.0	23.0	1.5	0.1	32,415	7,000	5	3	4	56	0	0	R	S	S	S	19	58,270	0.5
nige	Nigeria	18	170.0	38.0	3.6	0.3	1,030,285	120,000	10	450	3	63	231,600	4	S	S	S	S	85	50,965,002	45.7
nork	North Korea	213	211.0	115.0	46.0	0.2	23,913	1,000	8	1	10	32	820,000	7	RG	S	A	A	19	500,213	2.1
norl	Northern Cyprus	90	220.0	100.0	350.0	8.0	9,252	2,000	3	0	9	31	0	0	RO	RO	RI	RI	5	16,106	8.7
norm	Northern Mariana Is	20	190.0	82.0	100.0	38.0	526	200	8	0	5	64	0	0	S	S	S	S	1	69,260	88.4
norw	Norway	498	767.0	561.0	558.0	39.0	2,271,390	1,000,000	12	2	2	88	2,000	1	RL	RL	RL	RL	34	4,201,262	94.2
oman	Oman	30	416.0	61.0	79.0	1.0	108,694	20,000	10	1	6	50	0	0	RI	RI	RI	RI	21	121,916	4.8
paki	Pakistan	22	76.0	22.0	16.0	1.2	780,037	200,000	12	21	4	56	1,200	2	S	RI	RI	RI	54	3,812,245	2.4
pala	Palau	15	536.0	89.0	90.0	3.0	363	100	6	1	5	65	0	0	S	S	S	S	5	18,371	94.6
pale	Palestine	200	300.0	150.0	300.0	10.0	434,679	20,000	6	1	6	43	168,504	11	RI	S	S	S	17	188,289	8.5
pana	Panama	62	200.0	229.0	116.0	2.0	85,670	20,000	13	9	7	53	0	0	RC	RC	RC	RC	10	2,457,064	86.0
papu	Papua New Guinea	15	72.0	163.0	10.0	0.3	46,125	5,000	9	639	3	68	475	4	S	S	S	S	57	3,785,528	82.2
para	Paraguay	42	144.0	144.0	34.0	0.5	192,376	15,000	8	16	2	74	1,550	5	RC	RC	RC	RC	19	5,173,602	94.1
peru	Peru	86	225.0	100.0	47.0	0.6	1,134,246	100,000	11	56	2	75	18,500	4	RC	RC	RC	RC	42	24,702,049	96.3
phil	Philippines	65	116.0	129.0	25.0	0.8	1,583,276	250,000	13	139	3	68	64,000	6	R	R	R	R	53	66,600,057	87.7
pola	Poland	141	421.0	408.0	148.0	1.4	3,686,795	1,000,000	9	3	8	52	1,592,500	4	R	A	A	A	57	37,498,059	96.7
port	Portugal	41	224.0	333.0	362.0	6.1	1,567,058	400,000	10	2	3	78	10,000	1	RC	RC	RC	RC	29	9,080,231	92.0
puer	Puerto Rico	184	666.0	311.0	321.0	140.0	697,935	250,000	11	2	3	76	0	0	S	S	S	S	40	3,722,291	96.2
qata	Qatar	138	311.0	451.0	212.0	33.0	35,970	15,000	7	0	8	44	0	0	RI	RI	RI	RI	7	59,635	10.0
reun	Reunion	83	265.0	205.0	329.0	5.7	20,966	4,000	11	0	5	63	0	0	S	S	S	S	14	607,104	86.8
roma	Romania	297	198.0	201.0	131.0	0.4	1,005,968	120,000	7	2	8	49	155,500	5	RO	A	A	A	39	19,627,363	87.9
russ	Russia	267	341.0	380.0	170.0	0.7	9,200,000	5,000,000	10	57	9	40	24,204,490	18	RO	A	A	A	83	83,618,357	56.9
rwan	Rwanda	0	78.0	2.0	2.5	0.1	61,391	5,000	6	4	4	46	510,000	2	RT	R	R	R	40	6,336,822	81.9
saha	Sahara	1	50.0	10.0	10.0	0.0	289	50	5	0	3	51	0	0	R	S	S	S	11	487	0.2
saih	Saint Helena	0	600.0	150.0	100.0	10.0	4,406	200	3	0	3	78	0	0	RA	RA	RA	RA	3	5,332	84.7
saik	Saint Kitts & Nevis	600	650.0	241.0	355.0	20.0	3,707	1,000	7	0	4	72	0	0	S	S	S	S	10	36,000	93.6
sail	Saint Lucia	700	699.0	172.0	211.0	10.0	10,628	3,000	7	1	2	82	0	0	S	S	S	S	12	144,339	93.5
saip	Saint Pierre & Miquelon	0	900.0	200.0	150.0	15.0	6,691	300	4	0	5	70	0	0	S	S	S	S	1	6,388	97.3
saiv	Saint Vincent	500	565.0	161.0	165.0	8.6	9,333	2,500	7	0	4	70	0	0	S	S	S	S	8	78,439	68.8
samo	Samoa	122	448.0	38.0	47.0	4.6	6,968	1,000	5	0	4	70	0	0	RX	RX	RX	RX	20	169,129	93.9
sanm	San Marino	82	522.0	367.0	571.0	192.0	8,025	4,000	5	0	3	82	0	0	S	S	S	S	2	23,779	89.7
saot	Sao Tome & Principe	20	237.0	154.0	19.0	2.0	2,197	500	5	1	3	67	0	0	RC	RC	A	A	9	132,103	90.0
saud	Saudi Arabia	54	213.0	257.0	96.0	5.8	1,470,808	35,000	11	2	9	36	20,000	1	RI	RI	RI	RI	26	786,985	3.6
sene	Senegal	6	93.0	37.0	9.8	0.1	75,961	10,000	7	25	4	57	0	0	S	S	S	S	38	467,291	4.9
seyc	Seychelles	40	667.0	184.0	187.0	9.1	1,546	500	8	0	4	70	0	0	S	S	S	S	9	71,795	92.7
sier	Sierra Leone	2	221.0	16.0	3.7	0.3	19,463	2,000	8	16	4	52	0	0	S	S	S	S	33	510,494	10.5
sing	Singapore	340	275.0	218.0	478.0	28.5	1,477,954	900,000	14	1	5	60	300	1	S	S	S	S	49	402,936	11.3
slok	Slovakia	256	118.0	216.0	208.0	11.3	602,696	300,000	6	1	5	65	8,300	2	R	A	S	S	33	4,324,186	80.3
slov	Slovenia	183	320.0	374.0	309.0	10.5	191,369	200,000	6	1	5	64	0	0	RO	A	RO	RO	36	1,736,806	87.5
solo	Solomon Islands	15	117.0	16.0	17.0	2.2	22,200	5,000	7	65	4	67	301	2	S	S	S	S	27	403,203	90.9
soma	Somalia	1	41.0	13.0	1.7	0.1	17,394	2,000	7	2	8	31	40	1	RI	RI	RI	RI	17	98,583	1.4
somi	Somaliland	0	20.0	5.0	1.0	0.0	2,833	200	6	0	9	29	0	0	RI	RI	RI	RI	8	8,381	0.3
soua	South Africa	33	273.0	101.0	95.0	2.2	2,118,564	1,200,000	14	37	6	54	10,000	1	R	R	R	R	91	31,800,789	78.8
souk	South Korea	405	928.0	321.0	415.0	13.0	10,600,000	3,200,000	11	160	6	57	20,000	6	RG	RI	S	S	51	18,681,876	39.9
spai	Spain	104	304.0	490.0	385.0	7.5	8,100,000	4,400,000	7	1	2	87	141,402	9	RC	RC	RC	RC	51	37,073,672	93.6
span	Spanish North Africa	90	250.0	400.0	350.0	3.0	23,400	3,000	5	0	2	82	0	0	RC	RC	RC	RC	4	104,324	80.3
sril	Sri Lanka	25	182.0	66.0	11.0	0.8	150,564	20,000	13	6	6	48	1,120	4	RB	RB	RB	RB	45	1,755,120	9.3
suda	Sudan	23	193.0	76.0	2.7	0.3	59,646	5,000	8	111	8	33	810,000	7	RI	RI	RI	RI	49	4,874,391	16.5
suri	Suriname	103	609.0	186.0	123.0	2.2	6,784	1,000	13	11	2	72	10	1	S	S	S	S	24	172,334	41.3
swaz	Swaziland	14	550.0	96.0	21.0	2.0	39,345	6,000	7	1	4	46	0	0	RT	R	R	R	22	680,841	67.6
swed	Sweden	515	844.0	476.0	681.0	56.0	4,528,309	3,700,000	9	1	2	84	1,000	1	RL	RL	RL	RL	24	6,000,356	67.3
swit	Switzerland	415	791.0	370.0	613.0	40.0	3,288,599	1,300,000	9	3	2	88	0	0	R	R	R	R	33	6,445,548	87.3
syri	Syria	18	207.0	89.0	63.0	0.3	1,128,841	110,000	7	2	7	43	145,408	10	RI	RI	S	S	29	1,257,709	7.8
taiw	Taiwan	188	402.0	327.0	467.0	25.0	5,199,272	1,500,000	11	18	6	54	7,000	1	RG	S	S	S	46	1,179,743	5.3
taji	Tajikistan	13	100.0	258.0	45.0	0.3	127,966	2,000	9	0	9	27	0	0	RO	A	RI	RI	7	129,612	2.1
tanz	Tanzania	8	123.0	16.0	3.0	0.2	336,872	25,000	12	107	5	54	0	0	S	S	S	S	43	15,722,778	46.9
thai	Thailand	47	167.0	227.0	59.0	1.6	3,127,602	200,000	14	35	3	63	2,244	4	RB	RB	RB	RB	57	1,345,167	2.2
timo	Timor	15	100.0	100.0	15.0	0.4	4,421	1,000	9	14	3	67	92,000	2	RC	RC	RC	RC	27	815,391	92.2
togo	Togo	2	170.0	12.0	5.2	2.1	37,408	6,000	7	23	7	43	1	1	S	S	S	S	22	1,749,095	37.8
tong	Tonga	73	400.0	20.0	67.0	3.0	3,001	500	6	0	2	83	3	1	RM	RM	RM	RM	22	89,688	91.0
trin	Trinidad & Tobago	135	433.0	328.0	166.0	1.9	67,036	10,000	11	3	2	78	166	2	R	R	R	R	39	795,865	61.5
tuni	Tunisia	46	193.0	156.0	58.0	4.1	98,366	5,000	6	0	5	54	178,933	7	RI	RI	RI	RI	27	50,503	0.5
turk	Turkey	44	141.0	240.0	215.0	1.8	1,801,043	120,000	9	7	8	39	1,369,520	28	RI	S	S	S	37	373,155	0.6
turm	Turkmenistan	250	189.0	189.0	71.0	0.3	35,834	5,000	8	0	9	26	2,600,000	2	RO	A	RI	RI	14	98,883	2.2
turs	Turks & Caicos Is	80	190.0	150.0	127.0	12.5	414	200	8	0	5	66	0	0	S	S	S	S	2	13,262	79.1
tuva	Tuvalu	60	320.0	200.0	165.0	1.0	204	100	5	0	4	72	0	0	S	S	S	S	9	9,745	83.2
ugan	Uganda	2	507.0	26.0	2.3	0.2	224,587	15,000	10	35	7	45	203,095	4	S	S	S	S	51	18,944,173	87.0
ukra	Ukraine	118	346.0	233.0	161.0	0.1	2,301,278	500,000	8	6	5	62	4,170,500	6	RO	A	RO	RO	43	41,669,097	82.6
unia	United Arab Emirates	126	206.0	26.0	283.0	16.6	244,382	80,000	9	0	6	54	0	0	RI	RI	RI	RI	15	262,745	10.8
usa	USA	228	1,976.0	780.0	626.0	108.0	164,100,000	132,300,000	18	123	4	74	600	2	S	S	S	S	119	191,827,627	68.9
uuay	Uruguay	237	591.0	310.0	199.0	3.7	98,234	20,000	9	1	3	73	0	0	R	S	S	S	22	2,161,729	64.8
uzbe	Uzbekistan	264	250.0	176.0	76.0	0.2	875,640	15,000	10	1	8	38	2,000,000	1	RO	A	RI	RI	14	394,334	1.6
vanu	Vanuatu	70	327.0	12.0	250.0	4.0	2,876	500	7	56	3	74	0	0	S	S	RX	RX	22	170,054	89.3
vene	Venezuela	215	372.0	183.0	111.0	1.0	1,488,855	35,000	11	25	2	75	34	1	RC	RC	RC	RC	34	22,735,834	94.1
viet	Viet Nam	8	95.0	163.0	11.0	0.3	966,584	25,000	12	64	8	34	116,670	11	S	S	A	A	35	6,567,922	8.2
virg	Virgin Is of the US	267	1,029.0	315.0	597.0	50.0	54,227	20,000	6	0	4	73	0	0	S	S	S	S	16	86,159	92.7
wall	Wallis & Futuna Is	30	100.0	80.0	26.0	10.0	305	100	4	2	4	73	400	1	S	S	S	S	1	14,021	96.6
yeme	Yemen	17	48.0	243.0	12.0	0.2	452,952	5,000	10	3	8	35	20,000	1	RI	RI	RI	RI	24	30,656	0.2
yugo	Yugoslavia	90	256.0	170.0	192.0	1.6	1,050,206	150,000	8	2	6	56	0	0	R	A	A	A	38	6,885,557	64.7
zamb	Zambia	13	139.0	64.0	8.2	0.1	27,398	5,000	9	53	6	52	700	1	S	R	S	S	44	7,052,080	76.9
zimb	Zimbabwe	17	113.0	27.0	14.0	1.0	99,381	10,000	11	14	6	52	3,055	3	R	R	A	A	46	6,917,360	59.3
	11 minicountries	0	1,054.0	206.0	183.0	43.0	19,692	4,235	10	0	3	73	0	0	–	–	–	–	86	13,876	60.1
	Africa	18	163.0	51.0	17.0	1.0	10,933,293	1,773,450	16	2,141	5	49	3,949,169	114	–	–	–	–	1,627	335,115,750	42.7
	Antarctica	0	2,000.0	200.0	200.0	100.0	9,000	2,000	5	0	3	76	0	0	–	–	–	–	17	3,400	75.6
	Asia	55	184.0	169.0	55.0	4.0	116,150,740	35,656,500	19	2,021	6	45	15,865,294	240	–	–	–	–	1,647	307,288,308	8.3
	Europe	236	698.0	431.0	341.0	19.0	161,425,041	91,179,950	16	139	5	64	32,741,963	151	–	–	–	–	1,319	536,831,571	73.7
	Latin America	83	311.0	223.0	90.0	3.0	27,578,722	2,455,200	15	509	5	57	3,368,389	60	–	–	–	–	1,043	475,658,900	91.6
	Northern America	224	1,858.0	766.0	622.0	100.0	180,125,747	143,913,300	18	127	3	75	700	3	–	–	–	–	202	212,166,818	68.5
	Oceania	205	884.0	500.0	391.0	24.0	12,742,117	1,651,685	16	875	3	77	12,109	17	–	–	–	–	431	21,374,546	70.3
	World A	**41**	**149.0**	**95.0**	**53.0**	**1.0**	**9,235,090**	**885,260**	**19**	**307**	**6**	**42**	**10,696,410**	**106**	–	–	–	–	**744**	**10,026,564**	**1.7**
	World B	**60**	**196.0**	**172.0**	**55.0**	**4.0**	**123,679,836**	**40,336,450**	**19**	**3,295**	**6**	**40**	**32,008,114**	**227**	–	–	–	–	**2,137**	**491,326,295**	**13.1**
	World C	**152**	**739.0**	**377.0**	**283.0**	**28.0**	**376,049,734**	**235,410,375**	**19**	**2,210**	**4**	**66**	**13,233,099**	**252**	–	–	–	–	**3,405**	**1,387,086,434**	**81.8**
	GLOBAL TOTAL	**84**	**343.0**	**222.0**	**118.0**	**10.0**	**508,964,660**	**276,632,085**	**19**	**5,812**	**6**	**51**	**55,941,623**	**585**	–	–	–	–	**6,286**	**1,888,439,293**	**31.2**

COUNTRY		FOUR MEGATYPOLOGIES OF RENEWAL IN GLOBAL CHRISTIANITY, AD 30–AD 2000												
		1. The Great Commission		2. Ecclesiastical Renewal: 6 megablocs						3. Evangelical Renewal		4. Pentecostal/Charismatic Renewal		
code	short name	GCCs	GCC	Megabloc O	Megabloc R	Megabloc A	Megabloc P	Megabloc I	Megabloc m	Evangelicals	evangelicals	1st -Wavers	2nd-Wavers	3rd-Wavers
1	2	67	68	69	70	71	72	73	74	75	76	77	78	79
afgh	Afghanistan	4,081	0.0	100	1,497	100	2,000	3,000	200	800	4,081	48	267	1,985
alba	Albania	614,345	19.7	500,000	521,390	0	20,000	17,000	12,000	6,000	614,345	2,868	40,946	56,186
alge	Algeria	65,098	0.2	1,800	20,277	200	3,400	65,000	200	5,700	65,098	0	1,543	53,457
amer	American Samoa	30,261	44.4	0	9,470	190	35,800	1,780	8,000	5,450	30,261	3,570	5,527	803
ando	Andorra	26,551	34.1	0	69,535	0	140	80	450	20	26,551	0	758	82
ango	Angola	1,545,888	12.0	0	8,000,000	4,000	1,930,238	880,000	120,000	1,227,000	1,545,888	414,526	783,776	846,698
angu	Anguilla	1,098	13.2	0	310	2,650	4,126	0	100	800	1,098	0	1,040	0
anti	Antigua	10,329	15.3	0	7,800	22,613	21,000	1,200	1,100	7,000	10,329	2,249	5,280	891
arge	Argentina	2,739,882	7.4	158,000	33,750,000	19,000	2,295,000	2,050,000	500,000	1,960,000	2,739,882	1,659,492	4,657,566	2,082,942
arme	Armenia	395,380	11.2	2,752,493	160,000	0	12,000	28,000	1,200	1,900	395,380	0	59,228	17,672
arub	Aruba	5,402	5.3	0	84,341	750	7,500	1,350	1,300	4,100	5,402	2,550	4,668	1,232
aust	Australia	6,485,759	34.4	700,000	5,400,000	4,060,000	2,630,000	840,000	220,000	2,598,851	6,485,759	146,247	1,776,680	532,073
ausz	Austria	1,722,957	21.0	155,000	6,200,000	3,100	413,570	73,000	65,000	46,000	1,722,957	17,316	269,594	11,590
azer	Azerbaijan	126,853	1.6	345,302	7,500	0	1,400	3,600	0	450	126,853	0	6,259	3,741
baha	Bahamas	40,536	13.2	380	48,000	27,300	167,171	19,000	5,000	90,600	40,536	28,127	10,937	9,936
bahr	Bahrain	21,414	3.5	2,500	25,000	3,000	5,100	27,058	40	3,700	21,414	0	2,372	26,028
bang	Bangladesh	639,011	0.5	160	235,000	0	160,490	536,000	90	72,000	639,011	17,556	28,804	433,639
barb	Barbados	49,919	18.5	300	11,000	77,300	85,158	17,500	5,600	80,400	49,919	31,428	10,732	6,740
belg	Belgium	4,675,333	46.0	48,500	8,222,396	10,800	125,000	40,000	72,000	27,700	4,675,333	13,310	267,136	22,054
beli	Belize	28,865	12.0	0	136,939	10,500	39,500	5,200	5,000	17,100	28,865	7,082	20,089	4,229
belo	Belorussia	2,162,574	21.1	4,986,077	1,350,000	0	130,000	110,000	8,000	30,800	2,162,574	63,842	22,035	9,123
beni	Benin	1,004,584	16.5	0	1,266,195	0	230,000	175,000	13,000	112,000	1,004,584	84,306	104,526	153,168
berm	Bermuda	11,327	17.5	0	10,384	24,200	19,500	7,000	1,650	7,700	11,327	2,421	8,335	2,644
bhut	Bhutan	8,666	0.4	0	600	0	3,200	5,849	0	1,100	8,666	231	304	4,965
boli	Bolivia	1,724,676	20.7	3,100	7,350,000	1,100	530,000	145,000	135,000	375,000	1,724,676	145,271	951,855	117,874
bosn	Bosnia-Herzegovina	368,217	9.3	700,000	681,135	0	2,700	750	1,300	400	368,217	479	31,631	290
bots	Botswana	384,089	23.7	120	60,000	10,500	178,000	498,253	4,200	51,800	384,089	29,479	26,639	478,882
boug	Bougainville	16,167	8.1	0	148,401	0	22,650	14,000	280	5,200	16,167	0	6,658	2,642
braz	Brazil	24,207,478	14.2	170,000	153,300,000	125,000	30,200,000	25,500,000	1,420,000	27,749,000	24,207,478	25,234,662	33,185,413	21,529,926
brit	Britain	21,120,856	35.9	370,000	5,620,000	26,278,000	5,050,000	2,140,000	550,000	11,560,000	21,120,856	277,128	4,089,776	1,453,096
briz	British Virgin Is	6,229	29.2	0	700	2,800	9,792	1,000	600	3,650	6,229	705	1,607	359
brun	Brunei	18,199	5.6	0	5,600	4,592	6,000	8,300	100	6,350	18,199	0	2,509	6,341
bulg	Bulgaria	493,299	6.0	5,886,450	90,000	0	95,000	580,000	6,500	120,000	493,299	55,894	3,778	80,328
burk	Burkina Faso	1,521,822	12.8	0	1,129,078	0	799,000	54,000	2,000	765,000	1,521,822	635,430	151,853	56,717
buru	Burundi	1,144,771	17.1	1,400	3,827,541	500,000	800,000	23,000	900	850,000	1,144,771	497,639	257,824	19,537
camb	Cambodia	103,375	0.9	0	22,000	40	21,500	74,708	150	20,000	103,375	1,187	2,716	52,097
came	Cameroon	3,388,574	22.5	1,200	3,989,401	900	3,120,000	590,000	60,000	620,000	3,388,574	99,499	554,497	326,004
cana	Canada	12,604,889	40.5	580,000	13,017,945	820,000	5,350,000	1,680,000	450,000	2,540,000	12,604,889	504,551	2,596,361	1,324,088
cape	Cape Verde	55,921	13.1	0	417,000	0	15,500	12,800	4,800	10,900	55,921	499	17,621	13,580
caym	Cayman Islands	7,430	19.4	0	200	500	20,690	4,050	380	5,600	7,430	601	3,683	2,216
cent	Central African Rep	811,638	22.5	0	664,639	0	520,800	418,000	5,560	630,000	811,638	103,705	123,870	257,425
chad	Chad	718,153	9.4	0	502,158	0	782,756	152,000	1,100	653,000	718,153	17,107	149,905	82,988
chan	Channel Islands	40,543	26.5	200	22,300	67,511	10,500	0	270	20,000	40,543	1,419	6,981	0
chil	Chile	2,222,359	14.6	23,750	11,800,000	12,000	382,000	3,820,000	420,000	250,000	2,222,359	90,791	1,635,173	3,811,036
chin	China	81,352,742	6.4	55,000	7,500,000	23,000	640,000	80,708,347	29,000	2,521,500	81,352,742	47,686	629,491	53,597,823
colo	Colombia	2,673,679	6.3	7,200	40,670,000	3,600	1,100,000	535,000	275,000	590,000	2,673,679	512,397	11,522,127	550,476
como	Comoros	3,558	0.6	0	5,751	0	900	400	10	220	3,558	0	198	362
cong	Congo-Brazzaville	567,743	19.3	400	1,451,178	0	500,000	370,000	11,300	195,000	567,743	53,479	195,925	339,595
conz	Congo-Zaire	3,898,238	7.6	8,100	26,300,000	440,000	10,485,000	12,050,000	360,000	4,440,000	3,898,238	78,344	2,780,182	14,891,474
cook	Cook Islands	2,521	12.9	0	3,650	100	14,200	60	1,650	1,530	2,521	1,278	1,816	6
cost	Costa Rica	514,542	12.8	0	3,660,000	1,600	330,000	108,000	75,000	280,000	514,542	223,063	199,841	71,095
croa	Croatia	233,171	5.2	250,000	3,960,000	0	26,000	11,386	9,000	6,700	233,171	2,909	119,765	5,146
cuba	Cuba	2,584,208	23.1	1,400	4,367,909	3,600	190,000	135,000	125,000	134,400	2,584,208	68,215	366,011	136,774
cypr	Cyprus	66,156	11.0	525,294	9,800	3,300	4,600	400	8,200	3,050	66,156	1,398	1,543	260
czec	Czech Republic	2,591,316	25.3	60,000	4,135,936	1,200	320,000	270,000	32,000	127,000	2,591,316	9,451	155,059	91,490
denm	Denmark	682,522	12.9	1,400	33,200	4,800	4,639,710	36,000	36,000	264,000	682,522	27,390	141,621	36,989
djib	Djibouti	11,995	1.9	18,900	8,854	0	240	200	0	70	11,995	0	984	16
domi	Dominica	5,057	7.2	0	56,300	1,320	11,200	2,100	750	4,700	5,057	1,202	2,355	1,443
domr	Dominican Republic	496,611	5.9	0	7,522,305	4,400	360,000	130,000	60,000	267,000	496,611	169,018	770,066	96,916
ecua	Ecuador	646,048	5.1	1,800	11,900,000	1,600	240,000	225,000	185,000	295,000	646,048	129,230	1,218,821	61,949
egyp	Egypt	8,196,488	12.0	9,317,066	225,000	2,500	550,000	225,000	900	408,000	8,196,488	165,338	422,795	164,868
elsa	El Salvador	510,916	8.1	0	5,723,000	400	530,000	710,000	110,000	423,000	510,916	385,343	400,452	694,205
equa	Equatorial Guinea	63,372	14.0	0	391,000	0	15,200	18,000	1,200	11,200	63,372	3,389	10,314	11,197
erit	Eritrea	286,321	7.4	1,774,558	130,000	0	22,000	7,800	0	13,700	286,321	0	34,452	3,348
esto	Estonia	292,255	20.9	230,000	5,875	0	240,000	46,000	8,000	72,000	292,255	6,488	18,862	34,650
ethi	Ethiopia	9,745,644	15.6	22,837,859	450,000	800	8,510,000	860,000	12,500	6,569,000	9,745,644	1,095,426	2,229,221	741,353
faer	Faeroe Islands	11,794	27.6	0	130	0	38,860	400	200	7,500	11,794	691	1,940	349
fiji	Fiji	105,120	12.9	0	85,000	8,300	375,000	86,000	15,000	106,200	105,120	65,206	35,740	84,054
finl	Finland	1,033,772	20.0	55,900	6,400	170	4,635,000	77,700	38,000	740,585	1,033,772	73,741	513,445	79,813
fran	France	24,539,680	41.5	660,000	48,600,000	13,200	910,000	1,325,000	330,000	236,000	24,539,680	161,535	1,114,446	191,019
freg	French Guiana	23,745	13.1	0	145,000	90	7,000	1,700	5,500	3,600	23,745	2,116	6,509	1,775
frep	French Polynesia	32,345	13.8	0	100,000	0	110,000	4,800	25,000	6,130	32,345	1,374	20,188	3,238
gabo	Gabon	102,629	8.4	0	745,000	0	233,000	180,000	7,500	57,500	102,629	12,144	41,662	35,694
gamb	Gambia	30,607	2.3	450	31,238	2,800	3,670	8,950	90	1,200	30,607	197	1,618	9,185
geor	Georgia	742,337	14.9	2,886,814	55,000	0	24,000	42,000	1,000	9,200	742,337	0	20,609	9,391
germ	Germany	26,146,513	31.8	680,000	28,700,000	27,000	30,420,000	728,000	540,000	1,323,000	26,146,513	145,957	1,904,070	549,974
ghan	Ghana	3,925,064	19.4	1,600	1,925,000	250,000	3,360,000	2,920,376	210,000	1,490,000	3,925,064	858,349	889,035	2,732,617
gibr	Gibraltar	2,285	9.1	0	21,200	1,900	380	0	240	340	2,285	0	3,900	0
gree	Greece	262,176	2.5	9,900,000	62,000	3,600	21,400	228,000	40,000	12,300	262,176	3,157	104,249	14,594
grel	Greenland	12,438	22.2	0	110	0	38,880	120	240	2,100	12,438	2,206	3,277	117
gren	Grenada	6,456	6.9	0	52,700	14,400	19,100	3,700	1,400	10,100	6,456	5,684	5,656	2,861
guad	Guadeloupe	65,752	14.4	0	433,000	0	22,500	1,120	19,700	13,650	65,752	4,294	18,236	281
guam	Guam	16,931	10.1	0	139,400	900	17,500	2,900	4,300	8,500	16,931	2,410	6,694	797
guat	Guatemala	974,549	8.6	0	9,600,000	1,800	1,450,000	1,030,000	160,000	1,180,000	974,549	698,717	921,741	869,542
guin	Guinea	169,775	2.3	0	117,000	1,400	69,182	43,000	740	54,100	169,775	8,646	11,841	41,913
gunb	Guinea-Bissau	97,900	8.1	0	141,000	280	9,500	31,000	70	9,400	97,900	347	4,928	29,025
guya	Guyana	104,650	12.2	8,800	86,500	77,000	168,636	27,000	6,100	105,000	104,650	76,242	28,351	21,407
hait	Haiti	535,309	6.5	0	6,520,000	105,000	1,440,000	430,000	50,000	1,170,000	535,309	327,903	973,804	194,293
hond	Honduras	414,293	6.4	7,200	5,590,000	6,000	425,000	180,000	70,000	310,000	414,293	199,438	531,984	128,578
hung	Hungary	1,066,779	10.6	90,000	6,330,000	0	2,560,000	165,000	40,000	455,000	1,066,779	11,202	514,103	164,694
icel	Iceland	30,470	10.8	0	2,900	0	250,459	11,000	900	6,500	30,470	878	18,109	4,013
indi	India	50,364,266	5.0	3,100,000	15,500,000	0	16,826,000	34,200,000	50,000	9,300,000	50,364,266	1,263,041	5,032,741	27,234,219
indo	Indonesia	14,599,219	6.9	100	5,752,358	3,400	12,125,000	8,436,000	48,000	4,030,000	14,599,219	1,395,797	971,415	7,082,789
iran	Iran	129,374	0.2	202,290	16,400	1,200	13,800	80,000	300	20,000	129,374	5,070	3,967	66,963
iraq	Iraq	196,953	0.9	139,485	268,000	200	1,400	315,547	30	69,000	196,953	340	9,050	255,610
irel	Ireland	1,805,772	48.4	1,550	3,159,896	134,000	31,500	19,000	9,500	124,000	1,805,772	3,056	466,998	19,946
isle	Isle of Man	25,633	32.4	0	6,800	33,588	11,200	210	640	17,700	25,633	181	5,625	194
isra	Israel	192,425	3.8	46,878	140,000	2,200	19,000	85,000	1,000	30,600	192,425	2,692	17,668	84,640
ital	Italy	24,220,748	42.3	91,000	55,680,000	10,600	446,000	415,000	420,000	340,000	24,220,748	320,346	3,407,064	452,590
ivor	Ivory Coast	2,035,544	13.8	20,000	2,182,882	0	760,000	1,373,000	18,000	665,000	2,035,544	216,484	191,221	807,294
jama	Jamaica	635,819	24.6	3,300	110,000	103,000	643,413	232,000	30,000	304,000	635,819	169,902	63,604	151,494
japa	Japan	3,116,536	2.5	26,000	460,000	60,000	570,881	1,600,000	720,000	455,140	3,116,536	55,740	152,234	1,552,026
jord	Jordan	228,157	3.4	131,330	48,000	7,200	9,822	77,000	170	29,800	228,157	2,653	8,467	76,879
kaza	Kazakhstan	1,443,467	8.9	1,401,803	510,000	0	25,000	650,000	5,000	10,000	1,443,467	0	43,986	38,014
keny	Kenya	3,693,709	12.3	740,000	7,000,000	3,000,000	6,375,000	6,607,000	30,000	6,750,000	3,693,709	2,077,689	1,730,553	4,541,758
kirg	Kirghizia	225,162	4.8	363,065	1,600	0	30,000	70,500	500	3,000	225,162	4,008	6,042	7,750
kiri	Kiribati	10,228	12.3	0	44,100	50	37,000	1,300	1,700	5,950	10,228	4,246	7,005	1,449
kuwa	Kuwait	163,948	8.3	7,000	175,185	200	1,100	64,000	50	18,000	163,948	0	7,493	60,507
laos	Laos	100,576	1.9	0	32,000	200	34,400	45,613	350	40,000	100,576	0	3,178	46,822
latv	Latvia	471,566	20.0	555,000	490,000	0	560,000	115,000	2,500	168,000	471,566	9,698	73,574	6,728
leba	Lebanon	720,781	22.0	535,000	1,395,000	200	20,000	118,000	8,000	58,000	720,781	1,194	47,802	118,004
leso	Lesotho	510,738	23.7	0	806,529	102,000	279,000	254,000	3,800	76,000	510,738	25,102	68,896	248,003
libe	Liberia	542,686	17.2	0	150,000	34,500	430,000	538,500	8,000	335,000	542,686	152,946	48,602	318,452
liby	Libya	93,153	1.7	106,642	45,000	150	4,500	14,000	60	5,500	93,153	0	4,730	13,270
liec	Liechtenstein	14,173	43.2	0	24,381	0	2,520	40	110	125	14,173	0	763	37
lith	Lithuania	429,935	11.7	114,000	3,105,000	0	44,000	32,000	4,300	8,900	429,935	3,197	35,829	12,274
luxe	Luxembourg	75,421	17.5	1,100	407,000	600	7,500	2,200	3,000	1,100	75,421	223	17,652	1,925
mace	Macedonia	212,563	10.5	1,200,000	70,600	0	7,000	8,192	1,400	3,120	212,563	221	2,171	5,308
mada	Madagascar	2,487,601	15.6	4,400	3,662,363	320,000	4,090,000	510,000	27,500	950,000	2,487,601	15,252	467,847	251,901
mala	Malawi	2,457,034	22.5	4,400	2,697,860	230,000	2,140,000	1,830,000	130,000	940,000	2,457,034	130,999	346,922	1,462,079
malb	Malaysia	1,355,307	6.1	2,300	721,889	205,000	660,000	178,000	4,000	500,000	1,355,307	51,215	328,689	160,096

COUNTRY		FOUR MEGATYPOLOGIES OF RENEWAL IN GLOBAL CHRISTIANITY, AD 30–AD 2000												
		1. The Great Commission		*2. Ecclesiastical Renewal: 6 megablocs*						*3. Evangelical Renewal*		*4.Pentecostal/Charismatic Renewal*		
code	short name	GCCs	GCC	Megabloc O	Megabloc R	Megabloc A	Megabloc P	Megabloc I	Megabloc m	Evangelicals	evangelicals	1st -Wavers	2nd-Wavers	3rd-Wavers
1	2	67	68	69	70	71	72	73	74	75	76	77	78	79
mald	Maldives	300	0.1	0	80	0	258	20	0	60	300	0	29	21
mali	Mali	200,207	1.8	0	125,565	0	82,000	16,300	500	87,900	200,207	1,599	12,156	15,444
malt	Malta	170,064	43.8	130	367,501	1,100	1,000	750	900	550	170,064	523	95,811	666
mars	Marshall Islands	7,300	11.4	0	5,250	0	67,431	8,100	2,500	19,900	7,300	19,189	7,434	3,577
mart	Martinique	42,790	10.8	0	366,000	0	23,700	4,349	8,000	16,000	42,790	4,579	9,080	1,741
maur	Mauritania	3,914	0.2	0	4,216	0	600	1,700	10	600	3,914	0	154	1,946
maus	Mauritius	88,727	7.7	0	310,000	5,000	110,000	3,400	2,500	102,000	88,727	112,576	180,422	3,002
mayo	Mayotte	929	0.9	0	1,256	0	350	160	100	120	929	0	86	114
mexi	Mexico	5,123,454	5.2	100,000	92,770,000	187,800	3,280,000	2,900,000	1,950,000	1,740,000	5,123,454	861,284	9,497,650	2,691,066
micr	Micronesia	22,442	18.9	0	74,578	0	47,000	1,700	3,300	13,900	22,442	1,081	7,480	839
mold	Moldavia	836,487	19.1	1,950,558	73,000	0	78,000	670,000	27,000	20,000	836,487	16,451	31,334	1,214
mona	Monaco	8,786	26.2	90	30,000	330	681	0	0	65	8,786	0	1,060	0
mong	Mongolia	29,582	1.1	1,400	350	0	21,573	10,000	70	1,100	29,582	0	3,093	6,807
mont	Montserrat	1,946	18.3	0	1,400	3,100	5,500	1,050	130	2,650	1,946	1,654	777	1,109
moro	Morocco	109,745	0.4	740	22,076	450	4,100	147,000	110	43,200	109,745	89	775	149,136
moza	Mozambique	3,554,815	18.1	500	3,110,000	110,000	1,750,000	1,422,033	68,000	1,350,000	3,554,815	684,668	241,992	1,398,340
myan	Myanmar	2,257,465	5.0	0	590,000	58,000	2,511,664	575,000	6,800	1,120,000	2,257,465	298,025	249,765	412,210
nami	Namibia	295,226	17.1	0	306,211	31,000	820,000	187,000	5,000	160,000	295,226	23,749	87,174	119,077
naur	Nauru	2,187	19.0	0	2,920	320	5,840	380	40	310	2,187	0	708	392
nepa	Nepal	543,340	2.3	2,500	7,000	0	14,561	551,000	1,000	185,000	543,340	4,865	1,318	501,817
neth	Netherlands	6,515,668	41.3	7,400	5,450,000	8,600	4,238,853	490,000	88,000	614,000	6,515,668	52,390	537,922	449,688
nets	Netherlands Antilles	38,128	17.6	0	150,862	2,550	23,000	2,100	6,400	7,000	38,128	3,229	5,172	1,798
newc	New Caledonia	40,236	18.8	0	116,019	160	30,000	11,000	4,500	10,800	40,236	3,936	4,618	3,246
newz	New Zealand	1,541,611	39.9	6,000	495,000	825,000	931,219	190,000	115,000	660,000	1,541,611	37,262	419,689	133,049
nica	Nicaragua	307,306	6.1	0	4,320,000	8,300	590,000	155,000	51,000	446,000	307,306	378,967	238,016	103,017
niga	Niger	44,186	0.4	0	19,670	0	13,000	25,000	600	12,200	44,186	526	2,087	24,387
nige	Nigeria	11,252,805	10.1	3,100	13,400,000	20,070,000	14,050,000	23,975,000	600,000	22,300,000	11,252,805	3,034,330	9,793,479	23,057,191
nork	North Korea	468,670	2.0	0	55,000	0	10,000	432,413	2,800	20,000	468,670	0	715	449,285
norl	Northern Cyprus	4,479	2.4	13,870	0	0	0	2,236	0	220	4,479	0	0	2,180
norm	Northern Mariana Is	7,226	9.2	0	69,300	0	6,500	6,660	1,870	3,290	7,226	983	6,232	1,085
norw	Norway	1,074,638	24.1	1,600	45,000	2,000	4,200,000	136,000	24,000	485,000	1,074,638	70,742	1,031,297	146,961
oman	Oman	55,517	2.2	16,500	53,000	2,800	5,700	43,916	0	6,600	55,517	0	7,139	39,861
paki	Pakistan	3,520,938	2.3	0	1,165,000	0	1,796,000	850,000	1,245	626,000	3,520,938	77,920	292,012	520,068
pala	Palau	2,814	14.5	0	8,600	0	5,600	4,100	650	1,950	2,814	243	900	127
pale	Palestine	169,540	7.7	48,140	28,000	3,500	3,900	103,349	1,400	13,600	169,540	1,665	3,857	101,478
pana	Panama	445,061	15.6	1,400	2,210,000	23,500	340,000	73,000	42,000	263,000	445,061	225,235	207,163	57,602
papu	Papua New Guinea	523,096	11.4	400	1,380,000	308,000	2,610,000	270,000	15,400	810,000	523,096	238,143	310,060	202,797
para	Paraguay	429,463	7.8	2,000	4,950,000	17,600	200,000	70,800	26,000	159,000	429,463	76,990	107,312	57,698
peru	Peru	968,929	3.8	5,500	24,550,000	2,000	1,480,000	456,000	330,000	1,129,000	968,929	449,618	2,605,445	384,937
phil	Philippines	3,915,959	5.2	0	62,570,000	120,000	3,775,000	14,330,000	670,000	1,825,000	3,915,959	765,813	11,659,457	7,624,730
pola	Poland	2,958,523	7.6	1,030,000	35,743,059	0	195,000	330,000	200,000	140,000	2,958,523	42,155	1,823,326	149,519
port	Portugal	3,570,189	36.2	1,200	8,970,000	3,050	135,000	277,000	98,000	108,000	3,570,189	89,340	256,631	296,030
puer	Puerto Rico	544,610	14.1	1,300	2,900,000	12,400	505,000	249,000	95,000	348,000	544,610	239,572	544,717	240,711
qata	Qatar	30,261	5.1	1,300	36,100	8,000	4,000	10,235	0	4,300	30,261	0	4,019	10,381
reun	Reunion	56,272	8.1	0	611,000	0	31,500	700	6,000	26,900	56,272	23,624	30,727	649
roma	Romania	1,857,773	8.3	19,000,000	3,237,000	450	2,380,000	290,000	150,000	1,395,302	1,857,773	864,250	360,247	125,503
russ	Russia	29,373,498	20.0	75,950,000	1,500,000	3,300	1,630,000	7,800,000	200,000	560,000	29,373,498	140,319	1,001,265	5,333,416
rwan	Rwanda	960,617	12.4	2,000	3,942,000	600,000	1,619,822	165,000	8,000	1,505,000	960,617	636,449	502,657	97,893
saha	Sahara	284	0.1	0	140	0	0	347	0	40	284	0	0	370
saih	Saint Helena	1,167	18.5	0	40	4,412	520	160	200	155	1,167	0	765	165
saik	Saint Kitts & Nevis	2,098	5.5	0	4,850	9,700	22,270	1,500	510	7,100	2,098	2,591	3,570	989
sail	Saint Lucia	9,556	6.2	0	116,000	4,400	20,500	3,239	1,400	10,400	9,556	7,702	3,392	1,657
saip	Saint Pierre & Miquelon	2,251	34.3	0	6,465	0	70	0	40	10	2,251	0	160	0
saiv	Saint Vincent	24,080	21.1	70	10,000	19,715	33,854	13,300	1,500	15,050	24,080	8,551	4,485	10,964
samo	Samoa	85,350	47.4	0	39,500	450	128,000	2,000	17,000	26,830	85,350	18,962	7,849	1,489
sanm	San Marino	12,895	48.6	0	23,509	0	0	0	270	0	12,895	0	485	0
saot	Sao Tome & Principe	21,628	14.7	0	110,553	0	5,450	15,500	600	4,620	21,628	3,974	3,222	13,904
saud	Saudi Arabia	417,623	1.9	36,000	625,875	2,000	38,000	85,000	110	26,000	417,623	0	33,133	83,367
sene	Senegal	300,623	3.2	0	441,031	160	9,800	14,000	2,300	6,000	300,623	3,281	18,139	13,580
seyc	Seychelles	9,236	11.9	0	70,000	5,200	1,950	50	270	2,550	9,236	789	3,212	49
sier	Sierra Leone	389,099	8.0	610	169,140	25,000	171,000	165,000	2,700	86,000	389,099	25,234	23,666	151,100
sing	Singapore	292,499	8.2	1,400	143,000	34,000	126,536	94,000	4,000	118,000	292,499	31,469	51,856	62,675
slok	Slovakia	761,996	14.1	21,000	3,660,186	0	600,000	23,000	20,000	115,000	761,996	5,262	236,722	4,016
slov	Slovenia	264,345	13.3	12,000	1,659,006	0	32,000	31,000	2,800	13,800	264,345	973	36,117	32,409
solo	Solomon Islands	59,890	13.5	0	48,000	169,503	159,000	22,500	4,200	99,400	59,890	4,626	37,230	20,145
soma	Somalia	13,606	0.2	91,753	200	30	1,100	5,500	0	870	13,606	0	120	6,880
somi	Somaliland	3,120	0.1	4,400	31	320	330	3,300	0	550	3,120	0	59	3,621
soua	South Africa	7,717,095	19.1	150,000	3,350,000	2,660,000	12,410,000	18,500,000	190,000	4,522,000	7,717,095	1,772,371	2,331,365	17,096,264
souk	South Korea	13,329,255	28.5	5,000	3,700,000	110,000	8,870,000	7,700,000	850,000	9,142,000	13,329,255	2,393,749	2,020,598	3,165,652
spai	Spain	17,132,496	43.2	2,250	38,080,000	12,000	120,000	320,000	200,000	120,000	17,132,496	18,048	752,763	314,189
span	Spanish North Africa	11,344	8.7	0	102,874	0	650	800	0	300	11,344	66	2,167	767
sril	Sri Lanka	1,402,374	7.5	0	1,260,000	55,000	102,000	331,120	7,000	86,500	1,402,374	53,731	35,836	310,432
suda	Sudan	1,910,208	6.5	155,000	3,148,593	2,320,000	796,000	150,000	900	781,000	1,910,208	7,282	511,678	130,039
suri	Suriname	70,952	17.0	0	93,000	800	71,334	2,800	4,400	11,700	70,952	1,413	7,129	2,558
swaz	Swaziland	271,534	26.9	0	54,000	40,000	153,200	460,000	5,500	123,000	271,534	53,612	16,100	455,288
swed	Sweden	2,499,326	28.1	120,000	175,000	2,880	8,420,000	60,000	56,000	890,000	2,499,326	182,053	382,949	57,999
swit	Switzerland	2,541,157	34.4	26,000	3,260,000	13,300	3,040,000	160,000	122,000	298,500	2,541,157	40,562	313,236	118,702
syri	Syria	791,510	4.9	798,269	325,000	4,000	30,040	100,000	400	40,300	791,510	343	17,346	92,311
taiw	Taiwan	820,752	3.7	0	300,000	1,650	400,000	451,093	27,000	215,000	820,752	26,554	66,246	266,200
taji	Tajikistan	50,711	0.8	93,000	4,412	0	17,000	15,000	200	1,900	50,711	416	1,562	1,221
tanz	Tanzania	5,627,411	16.8	12,500	8,283,000	2,650,000	5,530,000	638,000	18,000	4,860,000	5,627,411	1,464,786	1,328,831	631,383
thai	Thailand	1,187,923	1.9	0	255,000	450	303,000	778,717	8,000	194,000	1,187,923	33,905	52,065	742,930
timo	Timor	39,435	4.5	0	796,000	0	47,000	0	0	4,800	39,435	3,783	42,417	0
togo	Togo	917,794	19.8	0	1,122,995	0	480,000	110,000	36,100	139,000	917,794	87,526	177,221	110,253
tong	Tonga	27,926	28.3	0	13,900	660	42,320	20,798	14,350	7,350	27,926	1,306	3,695	7,300
trin	Trinidad & Tobago	287,827	22.2	8,500	397,865	154,000	179,000	42,000	14,500	164,000	287,827	53,935	47,560	35,505
tuni	Tunisia	36,504	0.4	270	19,000	100	670	30,413	50	7,000	36,504	5	659	15,636
turk	Turkey	198,054	0.3	227,655	30,500	2,100	32,500	78,000	2,400	13,500	198,054	0	8,959	56,041
turm	Turkmenistan	48,002	1.1	74,583	2,100	0	2,800	19,000	400	900	48,002	0	739	10,011
turs	Turks & Caicos Is	3,513	21.0	0	750	2,000	8,112	2,000	400	3,000	3,513	1,141	1,234	1,924
tuva	Tuvalu	2,240	19.1	0	95	0	12,000	250	290	560	2,240	0	1,836	264
ugan	Uganda	3,019,984	13.9	32,000	9,130,000	8,580,000	596,000	815,000	6,000	3,890,000	3,019,984	371,193	3,879,073	759,734
ukra	Ukraine	6,110,588	12.1	27,400,000	5,578,901	0	1,340,000	8,500,000	135,000	1,016,000	6,110,588	399,462	589,113	3,046,426
unia	United Arab Emirates	137,255	5.6	70,000	124,345	8,600	12,800	47,000	0	13,500	137,255	0	8,696	45,304
usa	USA	98,662,079	35.4	5,762,000	58,000,000	2,400,000	64,570,000	78,550,000	10,080,000	40,640,000	98,662,079	4,946,390	19,473,158	50,736,451
uuay	Uruguay	891,482	26.7	26,500	2,608,000	1,200	110,000	52,500	95,000	64,800	891,482	38,878	215,453	49,669
uzbe	Uzbekistan	244,386	1.0	188,934	40,000	0	44,000	120,000	1,400	12,500	244,386	0	13,669	136,331
vanu	Vanuatu	28,820	15.1	0	29,400	34,500	102,254	16,500	1,400	53,300	28,820	27,708	15,111	4,381
vene	Venezuela	1,861,728	7.7	27,000	22,816,000	600	500,000	350,000	300,000	302,000	1,861,728	160,593	3,203,257	306,151
viet	Viet Nam	5,597,118	7.0	0	5,320,822	3,100	580,000	640,000	24,000	628,000	5,597,118	52,101	157,802	588,097
virg	Virgin Is of the US	11,931	12.8	0	29,000	13,800	40,000	12,800	1,500	18,500	11,931	7,149	7,290	7,911
wall	Wallis & Futuna Is	1,885	13.0	0	13,936	0	40	0	45	15	1,885	8	322	0
yeme	Yemen	23,012	0.1	12,000	6,000	180	4,476	8,000	0	1,600	23,012	0	1,388	7,112
yugo	Yugoslavia	1,398,890	13.2	6,046,000	546,557	400	99,000	185,000	8,600	42,400	1,398,890	11,064	78,057	160,879
zamb	Zambia	1,506,682	16.4	6,400	3,070,000	220,000	2,705,000	1,580,000	375,680	1,146,000	1,506,682	311,113	427,400	1,278,487
zimb	Zimbabwe	2,934,675	25.2	6,000	1,120,000	320,000	1,440,000	4,700,000	64,000	525,000	2,934,675	164,858	241,644	4,523,498
	11 minicountries	4,300	18.6	779	4,598	2,128	5,343	730	520	1,185	4,300	0	1,105	44
	Africa	90,820,254	11.6	35,304,168	120,386,235	42,541,902	88,999,928	83,840,642	2,426,550	69,578,305	90,820,254	15,560,021	31,471,122	78,990,057
	Antarctica	1,000	29.4	30	1,400	300	970	700	0	500	1,000	110	300	500
	Asia	191,890,345	5.2	14,113,465	110,480,013	727,212	49,969,501	154,732,021	2,485,605	31,503,970	191,890,345	6,594,195	22,120,550	106,174,783
	Europe	192,462,065	26.4	158,105,154	285,977,773	26,637,479	77,528,973	25,723,708	3,563,880	21,543,577	192,462,065	3,146,171	20,880,430	13,542,099
	Latin America	52,301,448	10.1	557,500	461,220,001	1,089,611	48,131,716	39,706,358	6,595,300	40,341,240	52,301,448	32,698,803	74,226,603	34,507,477
	Northern America	111,292,984	35.9	6,342,000	71,034,904	3,244,200	69,978,450	80,237,120	10,531,930	43,189,810	111,292,984	5,455,568	22,081,291	52,063,300
	Oceania	9,053,891	29.8	706,400	8,227,767	5,408,938	7,392,067	1,504,858	456,965	4,446,081	9,053,891	577,778	2,683,950	1,003,797
	World A	**7,281,018**	**1.2**	**1,891,769**	**2,720,984**	**17,385**	**2,265,910**	**3,140,736**	**15,985**	**1,264,540**	**7,281,018**	**108,775**	**425,007**	**2,553,191**
	World B	**279,101,242**	**7.4**	**117,870,812**	**103,758,713**	**26,909,172**	**95,386,092**	**185,699,067**	**3,382,820**	**73,462,585**	**279,101,242**	**15,324,280**	**29,614,682**	**138,640,023**
	World C	**361,438,727**	**21.3**	**95,366,136**	**950,848,396**	**52,723,085**	**244,349,603**	**196,905,604**	**22,661,425**	**135,875,858**	**361,438,727**	**48,599,481**	**143,424,257**	**145,088,299**
	GLOBAL TOTAL	**647,820,987**	**10.7**	**215,128,717**	**1,057,328,093**	**79,649,642**	**342,001,605**	**385,745,407**	**26,060,230**	**210,602,983**	**647,820,987**	**64,032,536**	**173,463,946**	**286,281,513**

COUNTRY		CHURCHES								MISSION							
		STRUCTURES				FINANCE, US $				STATUS OF MISSIONS				MISSION INSTITUTIONS			
code	short name	denom	p.m.	worship	p.m.	personal	church	parachurch	ecc crime	stat	misags	all orgs	p.m.	major	p.m.	minor	p.m.
1	2	80	81	82	83	84	85	86	87	88	89	90	91	92	93	94	95
afgh	Afghanistan	9	0	49	2	4,138,200	29,381	44,278	4,552	1	29	12	1	0	0	0	0
alba	Albania	51	16	1,010	324	717,161,300	5,091,845	7,673,625	788,877	6	79	0	0	5	2	10	3
alge	Algeria	33	1	1,100	35	145,403,200	1,032,362	1,555,814	159,943	4	37	26	1	70	2	50	2
amer	American Samoa	25	367	130	1,909	143,624,000	1,019,730	1,536,776	157,986	7	18	5	73	10	147	15	220
ando	Andorra	11	141	20	256	1,137,321,000	8,074,979	12,169,334	1,251,053	5	1	2	26	1	13	5	64
ango	Angola	42	3	11,000	854	4,483,037,580	31,829,566	47,968,502	4,931,341	2	68	20	2	350	27	1,000	78
angu	Anguilla	17	2,046	25	3,009	14,372,000	102,041	153,780	15,809	7	3	2	241	0	0	0	0
anti	Antigua	25	370	140	2,072	413,052,970	2,932,676	4,419,666	454,358	2	25	9	133	6	89	25	370
arge	Argentina	193	5	24,000	648	272,906,552,160	1,937,636,520	2,920,100,108	300,197,207	6	207	140	4	1,500	41	7,000	189
arme	Armenia	27	8	300	85	2,156,195,890	15,308,990	23,071,296	2,371,815	2	10	0	0	10	3	20	6
arub	Aruba	25	243	90	876	1,513,379,490	10,744,994	16,193,160	1,664,717	6	3	0	0	2	20	5	49
aust	Australia	267	14	24,000	1,271	235,646,592,480	1,673,090,806	2,521,418,539	259,211,251	5	200	190	10	1,300	69	4,000	212
ausz	Austria	70	9	5,400	658	185,801,026,300	1,319,187,286	1,988,070,981	204,381,128	5	133	195	24	250	30	1,000	122
azer	Azerbaijan	19	2	100	13	171,744,960	1,219,389	1,837,671	188,919	3	4	0	0	0	0	10	1
baha	Bahamas	47	153	1,000	3,262	3,186,200,940	22,622,026	34,092,350	3,504,821	6	39	22	72	25	82	50	163
bahr	Bahrain	22	36	180	292	491,552,320	3,490,021	5,259,609	540,707	6	9	0	0	3	5	15	24
bang	Bangladesh	42	0	9,000	70	223,617,600	1,587,684	2,392,708	245,979	2	116	40	0	250	2	600	5
barb	Barbados	52	192	550	2,034	1,291,388,480	9,168,858	13,817,856	1,420,527	6	37	25	92	20	74	70	259
belg	Belgium	99	10	5,500	541	210,496,978,160	1,494,528,544	2,252,317,666	231,546,675	5	130	330	33	2,100	207	7,500	738
beli	Belize	43	179	600	2,493	518,475,570	3,681,176	5,547,688	570,323	6	61	13	54	40	166	100	415
belo	Belorussia	31	3	2,030	198	13,629,039,390	96,766,179	145,830,721	14,991,943	2	18	0	0	5	1	40	4
beni	Benin	46	8	2,400	394	623,152,150	4,424,380	6,667,728	685,467	2	51	35	6	75	12	350	57
berm	Bermuda	71	1,099	190	2,942	1,774,362,250	12,597,971	18,985,676	1,951,798	7	12	6	93	2	31	10	155
bhut	Bhutan	32	15	200	94	4,052,580	28,773	43,362	4,457	5	20	6	3	3	1	5	2
boli	Bolivia	131	16	7,000	840	6,228,985,600	44,225,797	66,650,145	6,851,884	7	190	90	11	500	60	2,700	324
bosn	Bosnia-Herzegovina	30	8	700	176	415,765,500	2,951,935	4,448,690	457,342	5	13	0	0	5	1	30	8
bots	Botswana	196	121	3,900	2,404	2,268,240,460	16,104,507	24,270,172	2,495,064	7	66	25	15	150	93	300	185
boug	Bougainville	11	55	430	2,166	259,463,400	1,842,190	2,776,258	285,409	6	0	0	0	10	50	10	50
braz	Brazil	1,581	9	220,000	1,293	565,931,216,760	4,018,111,638	6,055,464,019	622,524,338	7	453	250	2	4,500	27	15,000	88
brit	Britain	828	14	66,000	1,122	730,293,923,700	5,185,086,858	7,814,144,983	803,323,316	5	369	1,300	22	2,400	41	10,000	170
briz	British Virgin Is	19	889	45	2,106	119,136,000	845,865	1,274,755	131,049	7	6	3	140	1	47	5	234
brun	Brunei	20	61	140	427	388,553,600	2,758,730	4,157,523	427,408	6	3	0	0	3	9	10	30
bulg	Bulgaria	54	7	5,600	681	8,855,073,500	62,871,021	94,749,286	9,740,580	2	42	10	1	200	24	800	97
burk	Burkina Faso	40	3	4,000	335	456,337,940	3,239,999	4,882,815	501,971	2	54	30	3	100	8	600	50
buru	Burundi	34	5	5,100	762	824,454,560	5,853,627	8,821,663	906,900	2	37	40	6	220	33	800	119
camb	Cambodia	23	2	2,300	206	31,967,460	226,968	342,051	35,164	2	35	4	0	25	2	100	9
came	Cameroon	103	7	17,000	1,127	5,044,975,650	35,819,327	53,981,239	5,549,473	6	120	57	4	400	27	1,500	99
cana	Canada	469	15	35,000	1,124	392,208,137,640	2,784,677,777	4,196,627,072	431,428,951	5	178	350	11	900	29	3,000	96
cape	Cape Verde	12	28	130	304	390,604,800	2,773,294	4,179,471	429,665	7	16	8	19	7	16	40	94
caym	Cayman Islands	25	652	160	4,170	129,100,000	916,610	1,381,370	142,010	6	12	0	0	1	26	5	130
cent	Central African Rep	62	17	4,000	1,106	547,059,660	3,884,123	5,853,538	601,765	6	44	28	8	300	83	1,400	387
chad	Chad	51	7	3,800	497	258,842,520	1,837,781	2,769,614	284,726	2	53	26	3	70	9	300	39
chan	Channel Islands	22	144	120	785	1,209,372,000	8,586,541	12,940,280	1,330,309	5	1	12	79	4	26	20	131
chil	Chile	252	17	23,000	1,512	55,570,694,400	394,551,930	594,606,430	61,127,763	7	147	95	6	2,000	132	10,000	657
chin	China	546	0	520,000	412	55,152,315,140	391,581,437	590,129,771	60,667,546	3	122	0	0	50	0	1,000	1
colo	Colombia	175	4	9,000	213	78,187,546,080	555,131,577	836,606,743	86,006,300	6	188	140	3	2,500	59	9,000	213
como	Comoros	6	10	50	84	3,318,670	23,562	35,509	3,650	5	8	8	14	2	3	10	17
cong	Congo-Brazzaville	65	22	2,200	747	1,586,357,040	11,263,134	16,974,020	1,744,992	6	64	13	4	100	34	500	170
conz	Congo-Zaire	864	17	49,000	949	5,658,183,000	40,173,099	60,542,558	6,224,001	2	218	95	2	2,500	48	11,000	213
cook	Cook Islands	13	666	160	8,196	36,984,000	262,586	395,728	40,682	7	5	0	0	2	102	10	512
cost	Costa Rica	122	30	4,500	1,118	10,101,120,210	71,717,953	108,081,986	11,111,232	7	140	76	19	200	50	1,000	249
croa	Croatia	48	11	2,200	492	13,833,254,500	98,216,106	148,015,823	15,216,579	6	25	0	0	20	5	150	34
cuba	Cuba	69	6	3,900	348	6,269,781,700	44,515,450	67,086,664	6,896,759	1	53	20	2	25	2	120	11
cypr	Cyprus	30	50	750	1,249	7,402,391,480	52,556,979	79,205,588	8,142,630	6	49	10	17	30	50	150	250
czec	Czech Republic	56	5	6,100	595	18,650,056,320	132,415,399	199,555,602	20,515,061	6	69	20	2	50	5	280	27
denm	Denmark	88	17	3,010	569	142,010,677,900	1,008,275,813	1,519,514,253	156,211,745	7	34	90	17	150	28	500	94
djib	Djibouti	6	9	20	31	23,964,900	170,150	256,424	26,361	5	7	0	0	2	3	10	16
domi	Dominica	23	325	120	1,697	199,603,430	1,417,184	2,135,756	219,563	6	16	14	198	8	113	30	424
domr	Dominican Republic	81	10	6,000	706	11,718,989,300	83,204,824	125,393,185	12,890,888	2	102	40	5	250	29	700	82
ecua	Ecuador	122	10	6,200	490	17,107,823,930	121,465,549	183,053,716	18,818,606	2	167	58	5	500	40	2,000	158
egyp	Egypt	68	1	6,500	95	8,153,168,140	57,887,493	87,238,899	8,968,484	2	103	60	1	300	4	1,500	22
elsa	El Salvador	87	14	9,500	1,514	9,817,815,420	69,706,489	105,050,624	10,799,596	2	83	39	6	200	32	650	104
equa	Equatorial Guinea	16	35	620	1,370	149,985,240	1,064,895	1,604,842	164,983	7	28	4	9	90	199	400	884
erit	Eritrea	32	8	1,200	312	1,102,584,060	7,828,346	11,797,649	1,212,842	5	11	0	0	40	10	200	52
esto	Estonia	26	19	580	415	1,515,442,500	10,759,641	16,215,234	1,666,986	6	15	0	0	50	36	270	193
ethi	Ethiopia	52	1	30,000	480	3,116,115,900	22,124,422	33,342,440	3,427,727	2	107	69	1	3,500	56	8,500	136
faer	Faeroe Islands	8	187	90	2,105	593,850,000	4,216,335	6,354,195	653,235	5	4	4	94	0	0	5	117
fiji	Fiji	45	55	4,000	4,897	1,121,777,800	7,964,622	12,003,022	1,233,955	7	48	34	42	40	49	150	184
finl	Finland	56	11	1,740	336	94,245,101,520	669,140,221	1,008,422,586	103,669,611	5	27	55	11	150	29	750	145
fran	France	429	7	43,000	728	1,027,512,805,410	7,295,340,918	10,994,387,017	1,130,264,085	5	252	610	10	4,200	71	13,000	220
freg	French Guiana	15	83	100	552	1,615,946,880	11,473,222	17,290,631	1,777,541	7	16	12	66	10	55	50	276
frep	French Polynesia	15	64	320	1,361	3,366,401,500	23,901,450	36,020,496	3,703,041	7	7	12	51	30	128	180	766
gabo	Gabon	23	19	3,000	2,447	3,789,288,440	26,903,947	40,545,386	4,168,217	2	17	20	16	60	49	250	204
gamb	Gambia	37	28	200	153	15,103,360	107,233	161,605	16,613	6	29	17	13	15	12	80	61
geor	Georgia	31	6	990	199	1,323,878,160	9,399,534	14,165,496	1,456,265	2	7	0	0	50	10	300	60
germ	Germany	342	4	47,500	578	1,617,126,437,220	11,481,597,704	17,303,252,878	1,778,839,080	5	279	0	0	5,000	61	25,000	304
ghan	Ghana	598	30	40,500	2,004	3,380,120,640	23,998,856	36,167,290	3,718,132	6	183	65	3	500	25	3,000	148
gibr	Gibraltar	8	319	20	797	141,028,800	1,001,304	1,509,008	155,131	7	7	3	120	1	40	5	199
gree	Greece	64	6	34,800	3,269	82,600,974,200	586,466,916	883,830,423	90,861,071	2	69	60	6	700	66	1,800	169
grel	Greenland	13	231	130	2,315	609,925,000	4,330,467	6,526,197	670,917	6	11	3	53	2	36	10	178
gren	Grenada	41	437	220	2,347	270,420,100	1,919,982	2,893,495	297,462	7	21	21	224	15	160	50	534
guad	Guadeloupe	14	31	310	680	3,983,121,600	28,280,163	42,619,401	4,381,433	7	11	15	33	35	77	120	263
guam	Guam	47	281	150	895	3,180,116,800	22,578,829	34,027,249	3,498,128	7	30	15	90	30	179	50	298
guat	Guatemala	162	14	17,000	1,493	14,316,765,020	101,649,031	153,189,385	15,748,441	6	159	50	4	700	62	3,500	307
guin	Guinea	51	7	700	94	127,227,100	903,312	1,361,329	139,949	2	43	3	0	5	1	25	3
gunb	Guinea-Bissau	7	6	190	157	38,911,250	276,269	416,350	42,802	6	38	1	1	25	21	120	99
guya	Guyana	76	88	1,500	1,741	220,681,240	1,566,836	2,361,289	242,749	2	50	19	22	80	93	400	464
hait	Haiti	234	28	6,500	791	1,909,856,000	13,559,977	20,435,459	2,100,841	1	169	35	4	300	37	1,200	146
hond	Honduras	100	15	5,200	802	3,634,560,000	25,805,376	38,889,792	3,998,016	2	143	35	5	200	31	1,000	154
hung	Hungary	72	7	6,800	678	36,048,895,840	255,947,160	385,723,185	39,653,785	2	80	24	2	50	5	400	40
icel	Iceland	30	107	410	1,459	6,618,212,050	46,989,305	70,814,868	7,280,033	5	16	20	71	10	36	50	178
indi	India	1,327	1	280,000	276	21,162,805,640	150,255,920	226,442,020	23,279,086	4	720	320	0	7,500	7	35,000	35
indo	Indonesia	276	1	63,000	297	25,837,560,840	183,446,681	276,461,900	28,421,316	2	234	105	1	3,500	17	12,500	59
iran	Iran	36	1	990	15	1,475,753,000	10,477,846	15,790,557	1,623,328	3	26	24	0	40	1	200	3
iraq	Iraq	34	1	5,000	216	1,449,324,000	10,290,200	15,507,766	1,594,256	3	23	15	1	30	1	100	4
irel	Ireland	64	17	2,850	764	49,358,610,660	350,446,135	528,137,134	54,294,471	5	112	105	28	1,000	268	3,000	804
isle	Isle of Man	21	265	119	1,503	566,330,400	4,020,945	6,059,735	622,963	5	2	8	101	0	0	5	63
isra	Israel	109	21	1,700	332	4,681,721,760	33,240,224	50,094,422	5,149,893	7	146	60	12	200	39	1,500	293
ital	Italy	337	6	38,000	663	892,459,102,800	6,336,459,629	9,549,312,399	981,705,013	5	199	850	15	13,500	236	25,000	436
ivor	Ivory Coast	80	5	8,500	575	2,873,562,120	20,402,291	30,747,114	3,160,918	6	96	56	4	200	14	800	54
jama	Jamaica	173	67	5,000	1,936	1,693,786,630	12,025,885	18,123,516	1,863,165	6	127	29	11	150	58	600	232
japa	Japan	262	2	25,000	197	136,237,962,840	967,289,536	1,457,746,202	149,861,759	5	334	250	2	900	7	2,500	20
jord	Jordan	33	5	1,200	180	413,018,220	2,932,429	4,419,294	454,320	3	57	8	1	40	6	200	30
kaza	Kazakhstan	77	5	650	40	3,447,097,990	24,474,395	36,883,948	3,791,807	2	15	0	0	5	0	40	2
keny	Kenya	825	27	55,000	1,828	6,293,662,200	44,685,001	67,342,185	6,923,028	2	345	180	6	1,500	50	7,500	249
kirg	Kirghizia	39	8	530	113	325,965,500	2,314,355	3,487,830	358,562	3	9	0	0	3	1	15	3
kiri	Kiribati	16	192	300	3,598	71,144,520	505,126	761,246	78,258	7	5	4	48	13	156	45	540
kuwa	Kuwait	18	9	2,300	1,167	4,304,633,650	30,562,898	46,059,580	4,735,097	6	5	2	1	5	3	20	10
laos	Laos	24	4	900	166	39,397,050	279,719	421,548	43,336	3	15	15	3	80	15	250	46
latv	Latvia	45	19	1,000	424	3,578,484,750	25,407,241	38,289,786	3,936,333	2	14	0	0	10	4	50	21
leba	Lebanon	69	21	3,100	945	4,614,623,860	32,763,829	49,376,475	5,076,086	7	81	140	43	250	76	500	152
leso	Lesotho	322	150	2,200	1,022	1,112,903,330	7,901,613	11,908,065	1,224,193	2	65	55	26	200	93	1,000	465
libe	Liberia	327	104	5,000	1,585	717,686,200	5,095,572	7,679,242	789,454	6	110	35	11	150	48	700	222
liby	Libya	35	6	370	66	1,108,991,520	7,873,839	11,866,209	1,219,890	2	13	0	0	0	0	10	2
liec	Liechtenstein	16	487	40	1,218	892,683,000	6,338,049	9,551,708	981,951	5	1	3	91	2	61	10	304
lith	Lithuania	28	8	910	248	6,105,454,300	43,348,725	65,328,361	6,715,999	6	9	0	0	15	4	40	11
luxe	Luxembourg	32	74	360	836	16,594,195,540	117,818,788	177,557,892	18,253,615	5	17	45	105	40	93	100	232
mace	Macedonia	38	19	1,000	494	1,106,985,120	7,859,594	11,844,740	1,217,683	2	4	0	0	10	5	50	25
mada	Madagascar	49	3	14,000	878	1,754,730,490	12,458,586	18,775,616	1,930,203	2	57	58	4	450	28	1,200	75
mala	Malawi	401	37	17,000	1,556	1,195,484,200	8,487,937	12,791,680	1,315,032	6	124	50	5	200	18	1,000	92
malb	Malaysia	70	3	6,000	270	6,889,925,210	48,918,468	73,722,199	7,578,917	5	98	41	2	250	11	750	34

COUNTRY		CHURCHES								MISSION							
		STRUCTURES				FINANCE, US $				STATUS OF MISSIONS				MISSION INSTITUTIONS			
code	short name	denom	p.m.	worship	p.m.	personal	church	parachurch	ecc crime	stat	misags	all orgs	p.m.	major	p.m.	minor	p.m.
1	2	80	81	82	83	84	85	86	87	88	89	90	91	92	93	94	95
mald	Maldives	8	28	10	35	354,420	2,516	3,792	389	1	1	0	0	0	0	0	0
mali	Mali	39	3	1,400	125	56,091,250	398,247	600,176	61,700	6	48	17	2	70	6	300	27
malt	Malta	17	44	160	412	4,456,572,000	31,641,661	47,685,320	4,902,229	5	20	48	124	20	52	100	257
mars	Marshall Islands	17	265	400	6,229	113,594,670	806,522	1,215,462	124,954	7	11	0	0	0	0	10	156
mart	Martinique	47	119	290	734	3,733,720,000	26,509,412	39,950,804	4,107,092	7	11	25	63	10	25	50	126
maur	Mauritania	31	12	70	26	3,001,960	21,313	32,120	3,302	1	20	1	0	0	0	0	0
maus	Mauritius	25	22	380	329	1,248,680,160	8,865,629	13,360,877	1,373,548	7	14	41	36	30	26	100	86
mayo	Mayotte	5	49	10	98	1,119,600	7,949	11,979	1,231	1	0	0	0	0	0	5	49
mexi	Mexico	297	3	65,000	657	311,438,997,640	2,211,216,883	3,332,397,274	342,582,897	6	395	205	2	1,500	15	5,000	51
micr	Micronesia	14	118	270	2,275	218,410,620	1,550,715	2,336,993	240,251	7	20	0	0	10	84	50	421
mold	Moldavia	28	6	1,100	251	2,574,673,360	18,280,180	27,549,004	2,832,140	2	7	0	0	15	3	60	14
mona	Monaco	4	119	12	357	777,525,000	5,520,427	8,319,517	855,277	7	6	20	595	7	208	25	744
mong	Mongolia	27	10	350	131	10,351,830	73,497	110,764	11,387	7	23	0	0	2	1	15	6
mont	Montserrat	21	1,976	80	7,527	127,399,590	904,537	1,363,175	140,139	7	8	4	376	2	188	10	941
moro	Morocco	32	1	1,900	67	193,668,360	1,375,045	2,072,251	213,035	5	47	31	1	50	2	250	9
moza	Mozambique	308	16	15,000	762	516,842,640	3,669,582	5,530,216	568,526	2	120	20	1	350	18	1,000	51
myan	Myanmar	118	3	12,000	263	6,697,220,560	47,550,265	71,660,259	7,366,942	3	72	20	0	60	1	300	7
nami	Namibia	104	60	3,100	1,796	2,698,422,000	19,158,796	28,873,115	2,968,264	2	42	12	7	200	116	1,000	579
naur	Nauru	12	1,042	50	4,341	67,311,870	477,914	720,237	74,043	7	2	0	0	2	174	10	868
nepa	Nepal	57	2	4,700	196	115,212,200	818,006	1,232,770	126,733	4	115	50	2	35	2	200	8
neth	Netherlands	393	25	10,000	633	246,788,472,000	1,752,198,151	2,640,636,650	271,467,319	5	125	340	22	1,800	114	4,500	285
nets	Netherlands Antilles	48	221	210	969	1,923,084,800	13,653,902	20,577,007	2,115,393	7	26	20	92	70	323	250	1,153
newc	New Caledonia	12	56	260	1,215	1,293,432,000	9,183,367	13,839,722	1,422,775	7	16	12	56	40	187	150	701
newz	New Zealand	175	45	6,200	1,605	36,742,220,460	260,869,765	393,141,758	40,416,442	5	119	150	39	300	78	1,500	388
nica	Nicaragua	95	19	5,000	985	1,845,824,160	13,105,351	19,750,318	2,030,406	6	108	40	8	250	49	1,250	246
niga	Niger	65	6	1,400	130	12,819,400	91,017	137,167	14,101	5	38	12	1	20	2	100	9
nige	Nigeria	2,079	19	109,000	978	13,250,900,520	94,081,393	141,784,635	14,575,990	5	246	105	1	1,500	14	8,000	72
nork	North Korea	18	1	20,900	869	475,202,350	3,373,936	5,084,665	522,722	1	1	0	0	2	0	20	1
norl	Northern Cyprus	3	16	120	648	199,746,612	1,418,200	2,137,288	219,721	7	0	0	0	0	0	10	54
norm	Northern Mariana Is	23	294	70	893	727,230,000	5,163,333	7,781,361	799,953	6	14	0	0	5	64	25	319
norw	Norway	92	21	3,000	672	131,289,437,500	932,155,006	1,404,796,981	144,418,381	5	36	110	25	80	18	250	56
oman	Oman	37	15	300	118	587,635,120	4,172,209	6,287,695	646,398	2	7	2	1	2	1	10	4
paki	Pakistan	56	0	8,000	51	1,753,632,700	12,450,792	18,763,869	1,928,995	2	150	45	0	300	2	1,500	10
pala	Palau	11	566	60	3,089	91,855,000	652,170	982,848	101,040	7	1	0	0	0	0	10	515
pale	Palestine	71	32	2,300	1,038	2,746,006,776	19,496,648	29,382,272	3,020,607	5	10	40	18	150	68	400	181
pana	Panama	88	31	2,500	875	6,756,926,000	47,974,174	72,299,108	7,432,618	7	87	47	17	100	35	500	175
papu	Papua New Guinea	100	22	13,000	2,821	4,391,212,480	31,177,608	46,985,973	4,830,333	2	140	130	28	700	152	2,500	543
para	Paraguay	96	17	2,800	509	8,743,387,380	62,078,050	93,554,244	9,617,726	6	136	54	10	300	55	1,500	273
peru	Peru	134	5	15,000	585	57,061,733,190	405,138,305	610,560,545	62,767,906	2	237	130	5	600	23	2,500	97
phil	Philippines	598	8	65,000	856	69,930,059,850	496,503,424	748,251,640	76,923,065	2	2,766	190	3	2,000	26	10,000	132
pola	Poland	66	2	17,000	439	104,619,584,610	742,799,050	1,119,429,555	115,081,543	3	91	45	1	400	10	2,000	52
port	Portugal	91	9	9,200	932	88,441,449,940	627,934,294	946,323,514	97,285,594	5	140	130	13	380	39	2,100	213
puer	Puerto Rico	135	35	5,000	1,292	29,033,869,800	206,140,475	310,662,406	31,937,256	7	90	50	13	150	39	700	181
qata	Qatar	35	58	200	334	691,766,000	4,911,538	7,401,896	760,942	3	0	0	0	0	0	10	17
reun	Reunion	17	24	290	415	2,610,547,200	18,534,885	27,932,855	2,871,601	2	16	18	26	20	29	100	143
roma	Romania	55	2	38,000	1,702	29,048,497,240	206,244,330	310,818,920	31,953,346	2	82	20	1	300	13	1,500	67
russ	Russia	470	3	84,000	572	187,305,119,680	1,329,866,349	2,004,164,780	206,035,631	2	112	120	1	400	3	2,500	17
rwan	Rwanda	44	6	7,000	905	1,140,627,960	8,098,458	12,204,719	1,254,690	2	57	38	5	200	26	1,000	129
saha	Sahara	2	7	30	102	100,809	715	1,078	110	1	3	0	0	2	7	10	34
saih	Saint Helena	12	1,907	30	4,767	47,988,000	340,714	513,471	52,786	7	4	2	318	0	0	10	1,589
saik	Saint Kitts & Nevis	38	988	160	4,159	186,120,000	1,321,452	1,991,484	204,732	6	7	8	208	0	0	5	130
sail	Saint Lucia	36	233	180	1,166	486,422,430	3,453,599	5,204,720	535,064	2	13	13	84	7	45	20	130
saip	Saint Pierre & Miquelon	3	457	6	914	70,268,000	498,902	751,867	77,294	7	3	5	761	2	305	10	1,523
saiv	Saint Vincent	42	369	300	2,633	178,840,920	1,269,770	1,913,597	196,725	2	18	7	61	6	53	20	176
samo	Samoa	27	150	640	3,554	189,424,480	1,344,913	2,026,841	208,366	7	16	12	67	18	100	50	278
sanm	San Marino	2	75	14	528	587,341,300	4,170,123	6,284,551	646,075	7	1	0	0	1	38	5	189
saot	Sao Tome & Principe	9	61	140	954	46,236,050	328,275	494,725	50,859	7	7	5	34	2	14	10	68
saud	Saudi Arabia	42	2	4,000	185	5,540,374,400	39,336,658	59,282,006	6,094,411	2	12	0	0	0	0	5	0
sene	Senegal	37	4	450	47	280,374,600	1,990,659	3,000,008	308,412	5	71	35	4	150	16	750	79
seyc	Seychelles	12	155	50	646	475,282,900	3,374,508	5,085,527	522,811	7	7	14	181	20	258	100	1,291
sier	Sierra Leone	67	14	2,000	412	91,888,920	652,411	983,211	101,077	2	82	24	5	100	21	400	82
sing	Singapore	92	26	520	146	10,770,479,280	76,470,402	115,244,128	11,847,527	5	112	60	17	20	6	150	42
slok	Slovakia	49	9	3,100	575	12,756,348,700	90,570,075	136,492,931	14,031,983	2	20	0	0	20	4	100	19
slov	Slovenia	39	20	1,700	856	14,241,809,200	101,116,845	152,387,358	15,665,990	6	17	0	0	10	5	50	25
solo	Solomon Islands	37	83	2,500	5,635	366,914,730	2,605,094	3,925,987	403,606	7	30	9	20	70	158	300	676
soma	Somalia	11	2	250	34	49,291,500	349,969	527,419	54,220	3	22	5	1	10	1	30	4
somi	Somaliland	5	2	80	28	1,299,055	9,223	13,899	1,428	1	0	0	0	0	0	5	2
soua	South Africa	3,364	83	80,000	1,981	100,490,493,240	713,482,502	1,075,248,277	110,539,542	7	271	160	4	2,000	50	8,000	198
souk	South Korea	385	8	45,000	961	181,214,197,200	1,286,620,800	1,938,991,910	199,335,616	5	161	120	3	1,000	21	5,000	107
spai	Spain	315	8	30,000	757	503,460,465,760	3,574,569,306	5,387,026,983	553,806,512	5	303	300	8	4,100	104	9,500	240
span	Spanish North Africa	6	46	30	231	834,592,000	5,925,603	8,930,134	918,051	6	1	5	39	2	15	10	77
sril	Sri Lanka	61	3	3,900	207	1,228,584,000	8,722,946	13,145,848	1,351,442	5	93	45	2	150	8	600	32
suda	Sudan	37	1	4,400	149	3,899,512,800	27,686,540	41,724,786	4,289,464	2	68	27	1	60	2	250	8
suri	Suriname	33	79	250	599	151,653,920	1,076,742	1,622,696	166,819	7	38	24	58	50	120	200	479
swaz	Swaziland	103	102	2,400	2,381	796,583,970	5,655,746	8,523,448	876,242	7	53	18	18	100	99	500	496
swed	Sweden	156	18	9,500	1,066	142,508,455,000	1,011,810,030	1,524,840,468	156,759,300	5	52	90	10	75	8	250	28
swit	Switzerland	182	25	6,900	934	261,882,615,240	1,859,366,568	2,802,143,983	288,070,876	5	106	480	65	220	30	700	95
syri	Syria	29	2	3,800	236	1,408,634,080	10,001,301	15,072,384	1,549,497	4	20	29	2	40	3	200	12
taiw	Taiwan	153	7	4,200	187	14,628,813,200	103,864,573	156,528,301	16,091,694	5	229	90	4	300	13	1,200	54
taji	Tajikistan	26	4	100	16	44,068,080	312,883	471,528	48,474	2	3	0	0	0	0	10	2
tanz	Tanzania	81	2	24,000	716	1,886,733,360	13,395,806	20,188,046	2,075,406	2	183	75	2	500	15	2,500	75
thai	Thailand	58	1	30,000	489	3,685,757,580	26,168,878	39,437,606	4,054,333	2	176	90	2	300	5	1,500	24
timo	Timor	10	11	200	226	525,111,804	3,728,293	5,618,696	577,622	6	3	3	3	15	17	70	79
togo	Togo	45	10	3,200	691	542,219,450	3,849,758	5,801,748	596,441	6	49	32	7	100	22	400	86
tong	Tonga	26	264	600	6,089	146,191,440	1,037,959	1,564,248	160,810	7	15	6	61	25	254	120	1,218
trin	Trinidad & Tobago	97	75	1,400	1,081	3,000,411,050	21,302,918	32,104,398	3,300,452	7	51	30	23	80	62	300	232
tuni	Tunisia	20	2	360	38	91,915,460	652,599	983,495	101,107	3	19	18	2	25	3	100	10
turk	Turkey	56	1	1,370	21	1,037,370,900	7,365,333	11,099,868	1,141,107	3	48	17	0	50	1	200	3
turm	Turkmenistan	23	5	100	22	90,972,360	645,903	973,404	100,069	2	11	0	0	0	0	5	1
turs	Turks & Caicos Is	17	1,014	50	2,983	28,805,064	204,515	308,214	31,685	7	2	3	179	1	60	5	298
tuva	Tuvalu	9	768	30	2,560	7,796,000	55,351	83,417	8,575	7	2	0	0	2	171	10	853
ugan	Uganda	78	4	25,000	1,148	4,546,601,520	32,280,870	48,648,636	5,001,261	2	150	59	3	350	16	1,350	62
ukra	Ukraine	124	2	51,000	1,011	67,920,628,110	482,236,459	726,750,720	74,712,690	2	56	0	0	100	2	500	10
unia	United Arab Emirates	72	29	1,800	737	4,571,763,000	32,459,517	48,917,864	5,028,939	2	12	6	3	5	2	20	8
usa	USA	4,684	17	600,000	2,156	5,175,509,376,460	36,746,116,572	55,377,950,328	5,693,060,314	5	256	2,300	8	9,000	32	25,000	90
uuay	Uruguay	132	40	2,200	659	11,176,138,930	79,350,586	119,584,686	12,293,752	7	105	68	20	150	45	700	210
uzbe	Uzbekistan	80	3	1,000	41	382,503,980	2,715,778	4,092,792	420,754	2	9	0	0	3	0	10	0
vanu	Vanuatu	29	152	1,150	6,039	204,064,800	1,448,860	2,183,493	224,471	6	15	8	42	20	105	100	525
vene	Venezuela	110	5	9,500	393	68,662,218,680	487,501,752	734,685,739	75,528,440	2	124	78	3	450	19	1,500	62
viet	Viet Nam	68	1	11,000	138	1,576,301,280	11,191,739	16,866,423	1,733,931	2	51	62	1	800	10	2,000	25
virg	Virgin Is of the US	80	861	250	2,690	1,011,506,660	7,181,697	10,823,121	1,112,657	7	33	10	108	10	108	50	538
wall	Wallis & Futuna Is	4	276	8	551	65,253,734	463,301	698,214	71,779	7	3	6	413	2	138	10	689
yeme	Yemen	20	1	600	33	7,970,560	56,590	85,284	8,767	3	12	0	0	0	0	10	1
yugo	Yugoslavia	102	10	4,500	423	13,771,114,000	97,774,909	147,350,919	15,148,225	6	16	40	4	400	38	1,800	169
zamb	Zambia	209	23	13,000	1,418	2,820,832,000	20,027,907	30,182,902	3,102,915	2	141	78	9	250	27	950	104
zimb	Zimbabwe	348	30	20,000	1,714	3,735,374,400	26,521,158	39,968,506	4,108,911	6	159	58	5	500	43	2,000	171
	11 minicountries	41	1,777	193	8,363	349,448,200	2,481,079	3,739,091	384,390	4	14	150	6,499	2	87	110	4,766
	Africa	11,680	15	603,662	770	199,617,997,404	1,417,287,750	2,135,912,544	219,579,767	4	4,150	1,994	3	18,192	23	73,375	94
	Antarctica	2	444	20	4,444	272,000,000	1,931,200	2,910,400	299,200	1	1	0	0	0	0	0	0
	Asia	5,378	1	1,145,849	311	588,150,287,072	4,175,867,011	6,293,208,046	646,965,289	3	6,264	1,921	1	18,461	5	79,230	22
	Europe	5,192	7	546,167	749	6,976,591,936,380	49,533,802,725	74,649,533,695	7,674,251,106	4	3,218	5,639	8	38,258	52	115,912	159
	Latin America	5,456	11	461,860	890	1,574,429,913,124	11,178,452,364	16,846,400,051	1,731,872,886	6	4,122	2,068	4	17,504	34	69,942	135
	Northern America	5,240	17	635,326	2,052	5,570,172,069,350	39,548,221,689	59,600,841,140	6,127,189,274	5	460	2,664	9	9,906	32	28,030	91
	Oceania	963	32	54,787	1,803	288,463,899,984	2,048,093,679	3,086,563,715	317,310,277	5	718	593	20	2,629	86	9,311	306
	World A	**1,068**	**2**	**56,222**	**93**	**10,548,883,544**	**74,897,052**	**112,873,033**	**11,603,752**	**3**	**987**	**364**	**1**	**1,024**	**2**	**4,526**	**7**
	World B	**9,769**	**3**	**1,456,811**	**388**	**771,979,359,808**	**5,481,053,425**	**8,260,179,119**	**849,177,266**	**3**	**5,466**	**2,720**	**1**	**26,008**	**7**	**105,582**	**28**
	World C	**23,074**	**14**	**1,934,638**	**1,142**	**14,415,169,859,962**	**102,347,705,941**	**154,242,317,439**	**15,856,686,781**	**5**	**12,480**	**11,795**	**7**	**77,918**	**46**	**265,692**	**157**
	GLOBAL TOTAL	**33,911**	**6**	**3,447,671**	**569**	**15,197,698,103,314**	**107,903,656,418**	**162,615,369,591**	**16,717,467,799**	**4**	**18,933**	**14,879**	**2**	**104,950**	**17**	**375,800**	**62**

COUNTRY		MISSION (continued)									CHRISTIAN PERSONNEL			
		RESPONSE/GROWTH					*WORLDS A,B, and C*			*ministries*	*ALL WORKERS*		*CITIZENS*	
code	*short name*	*CG%*	*g %*	*bapt p.a.*	*resp R*	*cost-eff, $*	*A -individuals*	*B-individuals*	*C-individuals*	*peo-ags*	*workers*	*w.p.m.*	*workers*	*citw p.m.*
1	*2*	*96*	*97*	*98*	*99*	*100*	*101*	*102*	*103*	*104*	*105*	*106*	*107*	*108*
afgh	Afghanistan	3.6	2.0	136	182	30,410	16,000,408	6,712,933	7,075	64	70	3.1	20	0.9
alba	Albania	1.6	3.8	40,396	117	17,753	454,107	1,558,097	1,101,230	23	1,800	578.1	1,000	321.2
alge	Algeria	-1.8	2.0	1,824	110	79,681	15,876,006	15,504,320	90,952	53	620	19.7	120	3.8
amer	American Samoa	2.3	3.9	2,178	71	65,922	252	2,613	65,224	11	350	5,140.3	150	2,203.0
ando	Andorra	2.8	5.0	3,532	87	322,003	734	4,368	72,883	4	30	384.7	20	256.5
ango	Angola	7.0	5.4	593,401	106	7,554	91,226	671,654	12,115,308	98	27,000	2,096.6	25,000	1,941.3
angu	Anguilla	0.6	2.0	144	38	99,157	17	688	7,604	11	30	3,610.5	20	2,407.0
anti	Antigua	0.6	0.9	476	17	866,967	157	3,962	63,441	9	170	2,516.3	100	1,480.2
arge	Argentina	2.1	2.0	685,834	33	397,918	242,999	2,384,300	34,399,998	119	36,000	972.3	24,000	648.2
arme	Armenia	1.9	2.9	85,716	53	25,155	77,944	485,574	2,956,051	47	300	85.2	250	71.0
arub	Aruba	2.0	5.3	5,086	91	297,509	475	3,178	99,094	9	51	496.4	40	389.3
aust	Australia	1.4	1.7	213,365	33	1,104,424	307,968	3,598,791	14,972,765	206	59,400	3,146.3	55,000	2,913.2
ausz	Austria	0.2	1.4	95,629	25	1,942,919	115,508	724,934	7,370,078	42	25,500	3,105.8	24,000	2,923.1
azer	Azerbaijan	0.9	0.8	3,012	58	57,007	4,872,856	2,503,202	357,957	50	150	19.4	50	6.5
baha	Bahamas	1.7	2.2	5,873	39	542,480	859	22,465	283,205	20	720	2,348.9	420	1,370.2
bahr	Bahrain	5.9	3.4	2,110	148	232,917	264,134	288,608	64,475	16	110	178.2	60	97.2
bang	Bangladesh	3.3	3.4	31,231	160	7,159	55,267,877	72,953,499	933,776	103	3,400	26.3	2,400	18.6
barb	Barbados	0.2	1.3	2,496	25	517,350	2,159	6,415	261,875	10	550	2,033.7	350	1,294.1
belg	Belgium	0.3	1.1	95,579	19	2,202,317	219,444	972,518	8,969,202	54	57,600	5,668.6	55,000	5,412.8
beli	Belize	1.9	2.8	5,482	52	94,570	5,155	16,631	218,923	41	800	3,323.5	400	1,661.8
belo	Belorussia	0.0	2.1	136,751	42	99,662	86,904	2,958,209	7,191,068	58	1,700	166.1	1,200	117.2
beni	Benin	5.8	4.5	75,064	158	8,301	1,574,060	2,817,682	1,704,817	104	2,200	360.9	1,600	262.4
berm	Bermuda	1.1	1.3	707	22	2,507,474	121	4,239	60,230	8	250	3,870.6	150	2,322.3
bhut	Bhutan	9.6	2.3	217	297	18,641	1,683,112	431,209	9,649	17	250	117.7	50	23.5
boli	Bolivia	1.7	3.1	245,110	53	25,412	24,406	469,058	7,835,201	135	7,200	864.5	3,000	360.2
bosn	Bosnia-Herzegovina	0.7	1.0	13,858	28	30,000	1,045,717	1,535,294	1,390,802	57	1,050	264.4	500	125.9
bots	Botswana	4.1	5.2	39,311	135	57,699	83,331	566,698	972,191	78	1,400	863.0	1,000	616.4
boug	Bougainville	5.1	2.8	5,263	56	49,295	256	10,063	188,176	57	200	1,007.6	100	503.8
braz	Brazil	2.2	2.0	3,174,811	33	178,256	425,724	14,144,725	155,545,014	461	150,000	881.8	125,000	734.8
brit	Britain	0.1	1.0	402,247	19	1,815,533	1,116,976	9,132,524	48,580,660	244	215,000	3,654.6	200,000	3,399.6
briz	British Virgin Is	1.2	2.8	411	59	289,645	90	2,815	18,461	14	30	1,404.1	20	936.1
brun	Brunei	5.7	2.1	526	127	738,662	180,020	122,877	25,183	32	70	213.4	40	121.9
bulg	Bulgaria	0.8	1.3	84,223	24	105,138	454,079	1,106,963	6,664,003	39	3,200	389.1	3,000	364.7
burk	Burkina Faso	15.6	4.9	97,378	212	4,686	4,406,314	5,542,063	1,988,446	183	7,000	586.4	6,000	502.6
buru	Burundi	12.7	4.0	206,835	79	3,986	54,611	502,751	6,137,639	21	9,200	1,374.2	8,000	1,194.9
camb	Cambodia	1.2	6.3	7,447	350	4,292	5,685,563	5,363,556	118,600	48	600	53.7	300	26.9
came	Cameroon	7.2	4.7	361,608	133	13,951	3,027,138	3,884,172	8,173,659	402	18,500	1,226.4	15,000	994.4
cana	Canada	1.4	1.6	329,875	31	1,188,957	688,856	5,695,795	24,761,988	236	138,000	4,430.7	130,000	4,173.8
cape	Cape Verde	1.8	2.8	11,299	49	34,569	202	20,642	406,880	8	300	701.4	200	467.6
caym	Cayman Islands	1.8	4.1	1,054	86	122,488	749	7,856	29,766	11	120	3,127.4	100	2,606.1
cent	Central African Rep	10.9	4.5	72,018	133	7,596	578,728	586,294	2,450,244	105	6,000	1,659.6	5,000	1,383.0
chad	Chad	15.2	4.7	66,968	250	3,865	3,818,667	2,086,520	1,745,795	167	3,250	424.8	2,500	326.8
chan	Channel Islands	0.2	1.3	1,320	25	916,030	719	20,599	131,580	8	60	392.4	50	327.0
chil	Chile	1.6	2.1	278,387	36	199,616	61,134	1,586,996	13,563,164	39	23,000	1,512.0	15,000	986.1
chin	China	4.2	3.9	3,484,380	165	15,828	444,210,082	729,291,154	89,055,551	369	104,000	82.4	100,000	79.2
colo	Colombia	2.6	2.4	1,002,110	40	78,022	119,613	1,258,792	40,942,956	161	42,000	992.4	35,000	827.0
como	Comoros	4.4	5.0	353	365	9,379	371,333	214,224	7,192	12	60	101.2	20	33.7
cong	Congo-Brazzaville	5.8	4.5	106,006	94	14,964	28,634	232,228	2,682,602	108	7,800	2,649.9	7,000	2,378.2
conz	Congo-Zaire	6.1	4.6	2,160,011	86	2,619	461,513	1,937,082	49,255,901	566	80,000	1,548.8	65,000	1,258.4
cook	Cook Islands	0.8	1.1	198	18	186,219	10	424	19,088	13	130	6,659.2	60	3,073.5
cost	Costa Rica	2.5	3.2	124,154	53	81,359	4,553	133,901	3,884,968	39	5,000	1,242.7	3,600	894.8
croa	Croatia	0.5	1.2	52,098	20	265,522	33,972	179,825	4,258,803	76	2,700	603.7	1,200	268.3
cuba	Cuba	1.1	1.1	53,148	28	117,967	100,633	6,116,018	4,984,033	26	1,750	156.2	1,500	133.9
cypr	Cyprus	1.1	2.4	13,061	40	566,722	1,086	33,820	565,600	10	1,600	2,664.4	1,400	2,331.4
czec	Czech Republic	-0.4	1.2	56,094	27	332,474	59,480	3,727,387	6,457,310	33	5,500	536.9	4,000	390.5
denm	Denmark	0.7	1.3	60,766	21	2,336,982	41,131	405,164	4,846,944	36	4,400	831.2	3,000	566.8
djib	Djibouti	5.8	2.5	699	142	34,274	345,336	263,782	28,516	15	123	192.9	50	78.4
domi	Dominica	0.9	0.4	298	8	668,903	62	3,600	67,052	17	230	3,252.5	150	2,121.2
domr	Dominican Republic	2.7	2.3	184,453	38	63,533	6,278	405,568	8,083,492	20	3,000	353.1	1,000	117.7
ecua	Ecuador	2.2	2.7	328,741	44	52,040	71,415	234,516	12,340,137	94	10,500	830.3	7,000	553.5
egyp	Egypt	1.7	2.3	238,712	81	34,154	15,303,820	42,820,086	10,345,789	47	6,500	94.9	5,000	73.0
elsa	El Salvador	1.8	2.7	163,061	45	60,209	6,319	147,733	6,121,971	27	3,400	541.7	2,000	318.7
equa	Equatorial Guinea	4.2	4.1	16,076	77	9,329	6,462	45,879	400,320	44	800	1,767.3	500	1,104.6
erit	Eritrea	3.5	4.3	82,384	112	13,383	1,017,551	889,321	1,943,516	42	1,000	259.7	800	207.8
esto	Estonia	-0.2	1.6	8,562	41	176,980	26,919	482,686	886,553	59	650	465.6	500	358.1
ethi	Ethiopia	2.5	4.7	1,464,574	124	2,127	9,707,024	16,749,811	36,108,040	211	252,500	4,035.8	250,000	3,995.9
faer	Faeroe Islands	1.0	1.5	593	26	1,000,000	30	766	41,953	10	70	1,637.5	40	935.7
fiji	Fiji	1.6	1.7	8,031	40	139,668	91,621	261,649	463,635	77	2,600	3,182.7	2,000	2,448.3
finl	Finland	0.5	1.3	58,754	22	1,604,053	14,982	357,193	4,803,568	53	3,100	598.9	2,600	502.3
fran	France	0.0	1.2	506,149	23	2,030,056	2,188,393	15,105,381	41,785,935	173	216,000	3,656.1	200,000	3,385.3
freg	French Guiana	2.1	5.1	7,730	93	209,049	2,240	25,711	153,362	32	300	1,654.6	100	551.5
frep	French Polynesia	1.8	2.4	4,759	44	707,306	3,191	25,038	206,832	46	600	2,552.5	200	850.8
gabo	Gabon	4.2	4.2	46,112	82	82,175	23,478	91,756	1,110,893	77	2,400	1,957.4	2,000	1,631.2
gamb	Gambia	2.6	4.8	2,276	295	6,633	730,102	524,794	50,467	55	670	513.3	500	383.0
geor	Georgia	0.5	0.9	26,387	20	50,171	565,806	1,311,275	3,090,480	52	1,000	201.3	900	181.2
germ	Germany	0.4	1.3	763,006	24	2,119,414	1,942,922	17,951,407	62,326,161	133	310,000	3,770.3	300,000	3,648.7
ghan	Ghana	4.8	4.0	348,932	114	9,687	3,106,004	5,911,396	11,195,095	369	27,000	1,335.8	25,000	1,236.9
gibr	Gibraltar	0.1	1.5	320	26	440,000	1,359	2,105	21,618	13	60	2,392.2	20	797.4
gree	Greece	1.4	1.4	140,049	23	589,798	165,750	396,020	10,082,974	36	17,500	1,644.0	17,000	1,597.0
grel	Greenland	1.5	1.2	479	25	1,271,534	166	1,867	54,123	11	260	4,630.0	200	3,561.5
gren	Grenada	0.4	0.9	799	15	338,251	28	2,754	90,935	16	220	2,347.5	100	1,067.0
guad	Guadeloupe	0.9	2.1	9,078	35	438,721	434	20,980	434,273	17	2,400	5,266.8	2,000	4,389.0
guam	Guam	2.8	2.6	4,121	45	771,569	1,708	8,125	157,723	29	550	3,282.5	100	596.8
guat	Guatemala	1.9	3.3	353,324	57	40,520	7,929	253,700	11,123,666	225	7,500	658.7	4,000	351.3
guin	Guinea	5.0	5.1	11,765	334	10,814	4,337,014	2,798,103	295,229	76	450	60.6	350	47.1
gunb	Guinea-Bissau	3.5	4.3	6,742	232	5,771	628,702	424,479	159,930	59	230	189.6	40	33.0
guya	Guyana	1.0	1.3	4,754	34	46,420	161,535	260,619	439,180	42	1,200	1,393.2	900	1,044.9
hait	Haiti	1.8	2.8	215,737	47	8,852	5,934	341,421	7,874,670	21	4,600	559.5	3,100	377.0
hond	Honduras	2.5	3.3	202,808	57	17,921	6,422	187,257	6,291,766	74	3,300	508.8	2,500	385.5
hung	Hungary	0.4	1.1	98,172	19	367,201	65,545	1,206,351	8,763,672	36	8,200	817.1	7,000	697.5
icel	Iceland	1.2	1.5	4,016	26	1,647,952	154	7,726	273,089	12	340	1,210.1	300	1,067.7
indi	India	2.8	3.5	2,158,606	159	9,803	412,122,495	539,198,276	62,341,006	835	308,000	303.8	300,000	296.0
indo	Indonesia	4.0	2.4	633,811	101	40,765	78,805,877	105,497,392	27,804,116	730	56,000	264.0	50,000	235.7
iran	Iran	1.0	2.2	6,841	159	215,695	42,507,292	24,831,853	363,054	61	600	8.9	400	5.9
iraq	Iraq	1.6	2.1	15,399	116	94,117	11,916,962	10,457,144	740,778	70	1,580	68.4	1,500	64.9
irel	Ireland	0.1	1.3	44,526	22	1,108,515	10,277	96,195	3,623,767	55	25,500	6,836.0	25,000	6,702.0
isle	Isle of Man	0.4	1.8	954	35	593,406	292	8,494	70,380	9	124	1,566.3	120	1,515.8
isra	Israel	2.3	4.0	11,683	193	400,704	2,252,726	2,571,811	297,146	58	1,500	292.9	500	97.6
ital	Italy	0.4	1.0	469,221	18	1,902,000	436,987	9,850,473	47,010,426	72	282,000	4,921.6	270,000	4,712.2
ivor	Ivory Coast	9.4	4.2	183,733	146	15,639	4,029,608	6,054,370	4,701,854	235	9,720	657.4	8,000	541.1
jama	Jamaica	0.7	1.2	13,483	31	125,623	27,592	384,458	2,170,527	43	3,700	1,432.7	3,000	1,161.6
japa	Japan	3.0	1.5	50,075	59	2,720,658	41,890,821	80,263,826	4,559,573	58	23,500	185.5	16,000	126.3
jord	Jordan	3.0	4.6	12,669	232	32,599	3,051,282	3,344,170	273,889	32	1,000	149.9	800	120.0
kaza	Kazakhstan	3.2	2.0	51,836	78	66,500	5,799,212	7,713,371	2,709,980	85	500	30.8	300	18.5
keny	Kenya	8.8	4.1	931,911	83	6,753	1,742,085	4,478,448	23,859,839	330	41,000	1,363.0	35,000	1,163.5
kirg	Kirghizia	3.4	3.0	13,970	159	23,333	2,473,100	1,737,992	488,245	68	200	42.6	150	31.9
kiri	Kiribati	1.3	1.8	1,408	32	50,521	60	4,639	78,688	11	550	6,595.8	500	5,996.1
kuwa	Kuwait	7.4	4.7	11,656	193	369,292	700,639	1,021,449	249,546	33	120	60.9	20	10.1
laos	Laos	2.7	3.3	3,697	189	10,654	2,849,470	2,470,957	112,609	82	620	114.1	540	99.4
latv	Latvia	0.3	0.7	10,987	14	325,681	22,603	756,035	1,577,870	78	1,200	509.2	800	339.5
leba	Lebanon	1.7	3.0	52,582	69	87,759	266,666	1,276,767	1,738,354	41	6,600	2,011.1	6,000	1,828.3
leso	Lesotho	4.0	3.2	46,655	64	23,853	8,139	184,442	1,959,972	40	4,250	1,974.4	3,600	1,672.4
libe	Liberia	3.6	4.5	42,194	163	17,009	867,108	1,048,172	1,238,721	152	2,900	919.5	2,400	760.9
liby	Libya	2.9	2.3	3,948	135	280,845	3,019,596	2,409,648	175,478	31	140	25.0	40	7.1
liec	Liechtenstein	1.1	2.0	541	36	1,650,000	538	1,775	30,530	11	50	1,522.4	30	913.4
lith	Lithuania	0.5	1.3	41,742	22	146,266	14,620	441,709	3,213,940	48	1,900	517.7	1,500	408.7
luxe	Luxembourg	0.6	2.2	8,742	37	1,898,203	3,931	22,270	404,414	32	2,040	4,737.4	2,000	4,644.5
mace	Macedonia	0.9	0.6	8,263	13	133,956	241,781	493,480	1,288,319	69	450	222.4	300	148.3
mada	Madagascar	2.2	4.4	332,864	119	5,271	2,712,337	5,339,031	7,890,359	85	16,000	1,003.7	14,000	878.2
mala	Malawi	6.7	3.9	277,282	88	4,311	431,511	2,105,620	8,388,107	82	7,500	686.5	6,000	549.2
malb	Malaysia	4.1	3.0	53,401	128	129,021	8,081,332	12,315,745	1,846,985	231	4,000	179.8	3,000	134.9

COUNTRY		MISSION (continued)									CHRISTIAN PERSONNEL			
		RESPONSE/GROWTH					*WORLDS A,B, and C*			*ministries*	*ALL WORKERS*		*CITIZENS*	
code	*short name*	*CG%*	*g %*	*bapt p.a.*	*resp R*	*cost-eff, $*	*A -individuals*	*B-individuals*	*C-individuals*	*peo-ags*	*workers*	*w.p.m.*	*workers*	*citw p.m.*
1	*2*	*96*	*97*	*98*	*99*	*100*	*101*	*102*	*103*	*104*	*105*	*106*	*107*	*108*
mald	Maldives	6.1	2.8	9	385	35,895	230,137	55,717	369	12	10	34.9	0	0.0
mali	Mali	6.0	4.4	9,869	276	5,683	6,340,283	4,668,098	225,440	108	1,000	89.0	400	35.6
malt	Malta	0.7	1.6	6,046	27	737,100	220	6,285	382,039	29	3,230	8,313.1	3,200	8,235.9
mars	Marshall Islands	2.5	4.2	2,506	74	45,312	42	2,136	62,042	6	130	2,024.3	50	778.6
mart	Martinique	0.6	1.6	5,791	26	644,745	507	11,559	383,296	16	1,200	3,035.2	1,000	2,529.3
maur	Mauritania	5.0	0.6	41	54	71,987	1,818,258	844,720	6,569	31	60	22.5	10	3.7
maus	Mauritius	1.1	1.7	6,446	51	193,696	290,720	488,624	377,154	42	700	605.3	400	345.9
mayo	Mayotte	4.2	4.6	85	303	13,040	60,252	39,147	2,222	8	40	393.6	10	98.4
mexi	Mexico	2.0	2.3	2,117,222	38	147,097	147,917	3,564,338	95,169,034	394	98,000	991.1	90,000	910.2
micr	Micronesia	1.6	2.5	2,761	47	79,102	441	7,720	110,528	34	580	4,886.7	100	842.5
mold	Moldavia	0.8	2.0	55,523	43	46,370	252,923	1,113,616	3,013,953	58	1,200	273.9	700	159.8
mona	Monaco	0.7	2.0	606	33	1,281,394	392	1,892	31,313	17	260	7,738.8	110	3,274.1
mong	Mongolia	4.2	3.2	1,056	202	9,797	1,522,030	1,106,075	33,915	25	500	187.8	100	37.6
mont	Montserrat	-0.1	1.5	152	27	835,133	7	413	10,209	13	30	2,822.5	20	1,881.6
moro	Morocco	1.8	2.5	4,279	158	45,250	16,314,645	11,730,763	175,435	42	1,800	63.8	300	10.6
moza	Mozambique	6.4	5.9	378,135	191	1,366	4,521,300	7,606,979	7,552,177	140	11,200	569.1	8,000	406.5
myan	Myanmar	2.8	2.9	109,662	128	61,071	17,852,271	23,985,544	3,773,362	127	7,700	168.8	7,500	164.4
nami	Namibia	5.2	4.8	64,654	92	41,736	39,161	94,399	1,592,308	63	2,800	1,622.4	1,600	927.1
naur	Nauru	3.4	2.2	186	44	360,107	410	2,472	8,637	14	30	2,604.4	10	868.1
nepa	Nepal	14.2	5.4	31,009	318	3,715	12,866,777	10,487,030	576,683	65	1,500	62.7	600	25.1
neth	Netherlands	0.7	1.3	134,705	26	1,832,061	373,557	2,718,199	12,693,943	74	47,100	2,983.7	45,000	2,850.7
nets	Netherlands Antilles	1.8	1.9	3,570	34	538,581	1,547	10,498	204,730	35	750	3,459.8	150	692.0
newc	New Caledonia	1.5	2.8	4,472	55	289,226	2,965	24,869	186,195	108	600	2,803.4	300	1,401.7
newz	New Zealand	1.3	1.9	48,169	37	762,765	35,988	601,577	3,224,340	154	9,300	2,408.1	6,500	1,683.1
nica	Nicaragua	2.4	3.4	164,472	56	11,222	7,125	181,337	4,885,732	78	5,000	985.4	3,000	591.2
niga	Niger	11.6	4.9	2,850	317	4,497	6,208,244	4,463,281	58,577	97	530	49.4	80	7.5
nige	Nigeria	6.4	4.1	2,072,237	110	6,394	22,559,535	37,823,393	51,123,167	661	55,300	495.9	50,000	448.4
nork	North Korea	3.7	2.5	12,380	135	38,383	12,026,315	11,510,232	502,646	4	170	7.1	150	6.2
norl	Northern Cyprus	4.8	1.7	270	75	739,094	81,374	87,269	16,402	1	90	486.4	50	270.2
norm	Northern Mariana Is	3.4	6.5	4,523	121	160,771	836	7,889	69,631	3	160	2,042.0	40	510.5
norw	Norway	0.7	1.4	59,952	23	2,189,908	61,076	191,843	4,208,114	55	3,700	829.4	2,700	605.2
oman	Oman	9.1	5.3	6,425	302	91,461	1,347,866	1,069,746	124,127	10	90	35.4	50	19.7
paki	Pakistan	3.8	3.8	144,674	222	12,121	83,307,766	69,324,793	3,850,596	153	4,500	28.8	3,000	19.2
pala	Palau	2.2	2.9	525	51	174,764	11	822	18,593	6	40	2,059.1	20	1,029.5
pale	Palestine	1.8	3.3	6,238	127	440,205	650,425	1,375,327	189,641	32	1,600	722.2	400	180.6
pana	Panama	2.6	2.1	52,802	38	127,966	47,114	290,405	2,518,164	97	2,800	980.5	700	245.1
papu	Papua New Guinea	5.0	3.4	127,572	75	34,421	113,957	114,273	4,379,915	932	17,600	3,819.3	14,000	3,038.1
para	Paraguay	2.2	3.2	164,365	53	53,194	10,063	115,564	5,370,826	123	3,500	636.8	2,300	418.5
peru	Peru	2.0	2.3	574,569	38	99,312	68,433	644,093	24,949,143	321	15,800	615.7	9,000	350.7
phil	Philippines	2.4	2.8	1,840,825	50	37,988	4,222,787	3,592,289	68,151,424	532	59,500	783.2	50,000	658.2
pola	Poland	0.6	1.2	464,601	20	225,181	16,713	990,216	37,758,156	45	75,700	1,952.8	75,000	1,934.7
port	Portugal	0.5	1.0	94,162	16	939,247	35,999	717,800	9,121,054	66	14,750	1,493.7	14,000	1,417.7
puer	Puerto Rico	1.4	1.7	63,390	27	458,015	3,864	111,138	3,753,600	32	5,500	1,421.7	3,000	775.5
qata	Qatar	7.0	3.3	1,968	152	351,515	261,389	275,417	62,259	28	40	66.8	30	50.1
reun	Reunion	2.3	1.9	11,735	34	222,452	19,656	65,959	613,791	22	2,640	3,774.6	2,400	3,431.5
roma	Romania	0.7	1.0	202,358	17	143,549	162,918	2,524,231	19,639,353	43	30,000	1,343.7	29,000	1,298.9
russ	Russia	0.4	1.7	1,442,416	36	129,855	9,923,477	52,702,172	84,308,198	183	219,000	1,490.5	200,000	1,361.2
rwan	Rwanda	11.7	3.2	202,017	59	5,646	88,387	1,247,774	6,396,966	43	5,200	672.4	4,000	517.3
saha	Sahara	1.6	1.3	6	147	15,622	221,118	71,752	487	2	10	34.1	0	0.0
saih	Saint Helena	0.6	1.6	84	28	569,620	9	223	6,061	13	30	4,767.2	10	1,589.1
saik	Saint Kitts & Nevis	-0.1	1.5	540	27	344,666	28	1,974	36,471	24	140	3,638.9	100	2,599.2
sail	Saint Lucia	1.1	2.0	2,824	35	172,202	1,573	4,413	148,380	20	300	1,943.4	150	971.7
saip	Saint Pierre & Miquelon	0.2	1.2	74	19	947,459	4	168	6,395	3	55	8,375.2	15	2,284.1
saiv	Saint Vincent	0.6	1.2	907	24	197,061	1,389	10,996	101,569	36	160	1,404.1	80	702.0
samo	Samoa	1.7	1.6	2,662	26	71,156	113	6,032	173,928	24	3,300	18,325.9	2,500	13,883.3
sanm	San Marino	1.1	2.3	542	37	1,083,333	31	2,049	24,434	6	40	1,508.6	20	754.3
saot	Sao Tome & Principe	5.0	3.7	4,935	67	9,368	142	6,074	140,559	11	120	817.6	20	136.3
saud	Saudi Arabia	10.2	3.8	29,763	184	186,144	9,735,310	11,073,316	798,065	38	130	6.0	30	1.4
sene	Senegal	3.5	4.0	18,869	234	14,858	5,118,446	3,840,197	522,518	123	2,000	210.9	800	84.4
seyc	Seychelles	1.4	1.7	1,195	29	397,597	348	2,091	74,996	9	220	2,841.1	70	904.0
sier	Sierra Leone	2.5	5.0	25,356	229	3,623	1,981,739	2,316,971	555,673	95	1,900	391.4	1,200	247.2
sing	Singapore	3.9	2.7	10,899	99	988,170	974,057	2,154,964	437,593	124	1,800	504.7	800	224.3
slok	Slovakia	0.1	1.1	46,830	23	272,391	25,349	751,390	4,610,452	0	2,800	519.8	1,800	334.1
slov	Slovenia	0.7	1.4	24,836	24	573,426	3,933	152,143	1,829,481	52	2,200	1,108.0	1,400	705.1
solo	Solomon Islands	3.5	3.9	15,575	78	23,556	471	18,548	424,624	112	1,700	3,831.9	1,200	2,704.9
soma	Somalia	5.2	0.9	927	57	53,134	4,080,364	3,082,255	101,881	19	80	11.0	30	4.1
somi	Somaliland	9.5	3.7	306	223	4,245	1,566,720	1,257,556	8,401	6	20	7.1	10	3.5
soua	South Africa	3.3	3.8	1,212,882	69	82,852	781,832	6,030,845	33,563,902	169	92,000	2,278.5	80,000	1,981.3
souk	South Korea	6.3	1.8	344,680	48	525,745	560,817	27,185,788	19,097,384	19	52,800	1,127.1	50,000	1,067.4
spai	Spain	0.7	1.0	381,117	16	1,321,011	125,103	2,397,563	37,107,109	81	172,500	4,352.8	170,000	4,289.7
span	Spanish North Africa	1.6	0.5	503	8	1,656,314	8,550	17,126	104,324	6	60	461.5	10	76.9
sril	Sri Lanka	1.5	1.7	30,205	72	40,674	6,670,591	10,392,860	1,763,603	57	4,200	223.1	2,500	132.8
suda	Sudan	7.9	3.4	165,095	163	23,619	13,620,937	10,947,827	4,920,955	177	3,700	125.5	3,000	101.7
suri	Suriname	1.7	0.9	1,478	24	102,564	67,699	139,228	210,203	66	700	1,678.1	300	719.2
swaz	Swaziland	7.2	4.2	28,915	86	27,548	6,491	126,096	875,308	34	2,800	2,778.1	2,000	1,984.3
swed	Sweden	0.2	1.4	83,164	27	1,713,564	140,311	2,718,098	6,051,805	112	9,000	1,010.1	8,000	897.8
swit	Switzerland	0.7	1.5	98,616	26	2,655,555	130,557	727,846	6,527,305	85	20,200	2,735.0	18,000	2,437.1
syri	Syria	1.5	2.4	30,574	103	46,071	6,092,966	8,768,933	1,262,719	54	800	49.6	700	43.4
taiw	Taiwan	5.2	1.6	18,486	61	791,321	6,977,716	14,012,974	1,410,310	73	7,000	312.5	4,000	178.6
taji	Tajikistan	3.3	2.5	3,240	151	13,600	3,457,770	2,599,837	130,594	61	70	11.3	30	4.8
tanz	Tanzania	5.5	4.8	756,108	139	2,495	6,227,819	10,406,634	16,882,561	376	27,500	820.5	23,000	686.2
thai	Thailand	3.7	2.1	28,907	103	127,501	26,509,177	33,528,284	1,361,788	265	4,000	65.1	2,000	32.6
timo	Timor	2.9	3.2	26,386	67	19,901	10,692	57,890	815,959	43	300	339.2	200	226.1
togo	Togo	6.5	4.8	83,326	147	6,507	1,118,285	1,539,323	1,971,610	154	1,800	388.8	1,200	259.2
tong	Tonga	1.5	0.5	478	9	305,243	91	6,867	91,588	22	1,000	10,147.5	600	6,088.5
trin	Trinidad & Tobago	1.4	1.0	8,125	22	369,245	109,423	348,544	836,991	48	1,200	926.7	700	540.6
tuni	Tunisia	-0.9	1.7	840	92	109,309	4,897,282	4,636,763	51,566	27	240	25.0	40	4.2
turk	Turkey	-2.1	1.2	4,533	68	228,806	34,243,536	31,958,647	388,757	78	900	13.5	400	6.0
turm	Turkmenistan	3.1	2.5	2,472	194	36,800	2,918,902	1,438,743	101,648	64	70	15.7	20	4.5
turs	Turks & Caicos Is	1.0	3.8	508	74	56,606	35	1,376	15,349	20	30	1,790.0	20	1,193.3
tuva	Tuvalu	1.4	3.1	300	57	25,940	20	1,238	10,461	18	40	3,413.3	30	2,559.9
ugan	Uganda	5.1	4.8	907,994	89	5,007	195,502	2,261,835	19,321,113	175	32,600	1,496.9	30,000	1,377.5
ukra	Ukraine	0.5	1.4	588,367	25	115,439	752,837	7,834,697	41,868,446	93	10,200	202.2	6,000	118.9
unia	United Arab Emirates	8.9	3.3	8,623	146	530,164	1,028,415	1,142,777	270,244	67	220	90.1	100	41.0
usa	USA	1.3	1.7	3,335,882	32	1,551,466	4,084,367	38,531,122	235,741,652	519	1,533,200	5,508.0	1,500,000	5,388.8
uuay	Uruguay	1.3	1.6	34,198	32	326,801	43,093	1,115,569	2,178,396	66	5,200	1,558.3	2,200	659.3
uzbe	Uzbekistan	3.1	2.0	7,886	112	48,500	12,558,682	11,358,026	401,143	81	250	10.3	50	2.1
vanu	Vanuatu	2.6	3.2	5,431	63	37,570	1,304	11,991	177,122	226	700	3,676.1	400	2,100.7
vene	Venezuela	2.3	2.6	599,771	44	114,480	149,477	1,110,150	22,910,095	126	14,000	579.2	7,000	289.6
viet	Viet Nam	2.0	3.0	197,431	122	7,984	26,516,153	46,729,168	6,586,329	107	17,200	215.5	16,000	200.4
virg	Virgin Is of the US	1.1	1.5	1,292	25	782,666	390	3,044	89,520	35	300	3,227.4	150	1,613.7
wall	Wallis & Futuna Is	2.3	1.1	149	20	437,406	5	323	14,189	5	80	5,510.8	50	3,444.2
yeme	Yemen	1.9	4.6	1,423	272	5,601	9,673,610	8,406,264	32,192	32	230	12.7	80	4.4
yugo	Yugoslavia	0.8	1.9	132,133	40	104,220	702,914	2,712,500	7,224,736	75	9,000	845.9	8,000	751.9
zamb	Zambia	8.5	4.4	313,465	89	8,998	113,566	1,503,728	7,551,406	207	7,200	785.3	4,000	436.3
zimb	Zimbabwe	6.3	3.9	271,298	86	13,768	207,516	3,591,134	7,870,379	153	8,700	745.6	6,000	514.2
	11 minicountries	0.9	1.7	258	57	1,349,544	1,924	6,381	14,774	54	1,221	52,905.2	950	41,163.0
	Africa	2.7	4.1	14,373,418	124	13,888	176,794,822	247,418,035	360,232,182	6,872	798,793	1,018.3	708,330	903.0
	Antarctica	4.0	4.8	162	138	1,677,852	243	857	3,400	0	30	6,666.7	20	4,444.4
	Asia	2.4	3.1	9,630,494	150	61,071	1,423,824,293	1,945,876,370	312,849,430	5,344	681,440	185.0	623,470	169.3
	Europe	0.2	1.3	7,023,145	26	993,371	21,474,187	147,770,219	559,642,545	2,653	1,809,539	2,482.6	1,703,840	2,337.6
	Latin America	1.6	2.3	10,864,866	38	144,910	1,944,600	36,091,075	481,102,373	3,291	462,401	890.7	354,280	682.4
	Northern America	0.9	1.7	3,667,019	32	1,518,991	4,773,514	44,233,191	260,624,388	777	1,671,765	5,399.2	1,630,365	5,265.5
	Oceania	1.3	2.1	454,646	42	634,479	563,298	4,720,573	25,109,520	2,150	99,846	3,285.1	84,080	2,766.4
	World A	**1.7**	**2.4**	**332,049**	**180**	**31,768**	**334,256,241**	**260,720,907**	**10,326,848**	**1,848**	**20,518**	**33.9**	**10,340**	**17.1**
	World B	**2.1**	**2.9**	**16,177,799**	**140**	**47,718**	**1,269,343,426**	**1,972,637,223**	**513,031,343**	**8,181**	**1,309,120**	**348.6**	**1,206,055**	**321.2**
	World C	**1.2**	**2.1**	**29,503,902**	**38**	**488,585**	**25,775,290**	**192,752,190**	**1,476,205,647**	**11,058**	**4,194,176**	**2,474.8**	**3,887,990**	**2,294.2**
	GLOBAL TOTAL	**1.4**	**2.3**	**46,013,752**	**115**	**330,286**	**1,629,374,957**	**2,426,110,320**	**1,999,563,838**	**21,087**	**5,523,814**	**912.3**	**5,104,385**	**843.2**

COUNTRY		GLOBAL MISSION SHARING				CHRISTIAN LITERATURE								SCRIPTURES					
		citizens sent		aliens received		libraries		book on country's Christians			periodicals		Bible distribution						
code	short name	total	p.m.a.	total	p.m.	total	p.m.	total	1970–99	p.a.	total	p.m.	goal	goal p.a.	UBS p.a.	other p.a.	total p.a.	T/G%
1	2	109	110	111	112	113	114	115	116	117	118	119	120	121	122	123	124	125
afgh	Afghanistan	0	0.0	50	2.2	0	0.0	20	8	0	147	7	399	19	40	10	50	250
alba	Albania	50	46.7	800	257.0	0	0.0	72	64	3	200	64	201,647	10,082	8,002	5,334	13,336	132
alge	Algeria	20	220.1	500	15.9	10	0.3	470	230	9	67	2	7,502	375	300	33	333	88
amer	American Samoa	60	1,086.2	200	2,937.3	0	0.0	10	0	0	10	147	6,373	318	1,400	73	1,473	462
ando	Andorra	40	569.8	10	128.2	1	12.8	9	9	0	1	13	19,326	966	1,300	144	1,444	149
ango	Angola	320	29.3	2,000	155.3	12	0.9	122	49	2	38	3	796,991	39,849	70,702	4,593	75,295	188
angu	Anguilla	5	695.8	10	1,203.5	1	120.4	4	0	0	4	481	1,498	74	200	10	210	280
anti	Antigua	2	37.2	70	1,036.1	0	0.0	10	2	0	10	148	13,576	678	700	77	777	114
arge	Argentina	1,800	53.0	12,000	324.1	90	2.4	1,001	591	24	168	5	9,606,646	480,332	145,797	198,876	344,673	71
arme	Armenia	100	33.9	50	14.2	0	0.0	501	260	10	56	16	584,002	29,200	7,819	44,307	52,126	178
arub	Aruba	4	42.0	11	107.1	0	0.0	6	4	0	0	0	20,015	1,000	1,000	666	1,666	166
aust	Australia	5,500	436.9	4,400	233.1	110	5.8	3,195	2,459	98	364	19	4,013,329	200,666	323,195	91,157	414,352	206
ausz	Austria	2,500	361.8	1,500	182.7	190	23.1	2,185	1,093	44	3,534	430	2,613,771	130,688	12,698	52,755	65,453	50
azer	Azerbaijan	15	41.9	100	12.9	0	0.0	18	15	1	69	9	74,505	3,725	18,542	187	18,729	502
baha	Bahamas	20	74.9	300	978.7	2	6.5	45	32	1	17	56	63,559	3,177	2,000	4,666	6,666	209
bahr	Bahrain	5	79.7	50	81.0	0	0.0	10	7	0	4	7	7,132	356	200	600	800	224
bang	Bangladesh	30	32.2	1,000	7.7	20	0.2	68	58	2	57	0	59,688	2,984	3,225	402	3,627	121
barb	Barbados	10	50.8	200	739.5	5	18.5	62	40	2	73	270	50,728	2,536	10,600	2,650	13,250	522
belg	Belgium	10,200	1,197.4	2,600	255.9	260	25.6	1,594	721	29	19,188	1,888	3,125,982	156,299	13,750	50,203	63,953	40
beli	Belize	10	50.7	400	1,661.8	0	0.0	27	23	1	11	46	25,140	1,257	2,000	500	2,500	198
belo	Belorussia	100	15.2	500	48.8	0	0.0	97	66	3	217	21	1,940,202	97,010	35,710	35,710	71,420	73
beni	Benin	50	29.7	600	98.4	13	2.1	60	38	2	21	3	99,188	4,959	29,349	1,544	30,893	622
berm	Bermuda	10	179.6	100	1,548.2	0	0.0	43	14	1	42	650	20,001	1,000	1,000	666	1,666	166
bhut	Bhutan	2	207.3	200	94.2	0	0.0	20	15	1	0	0	692	34	40	2	42	121
boli	Bolivia	2,800	359.6	4,200	504.3	62	7.4	392	242	10	70	8	1,520,924	76,046	81,550	20,771	102,321	134
bosn	Bosnia-Herzegovina	250	180.4	550	138.5	0	0.0	50	3	0	129	33	378,487	18,924	9,000	1,000	10,000	52
bots	Botswana	80	106.5	400	246.6	5	3.1	52	43	2	20	12	79,665	3,983	20,617	1,085	21,702	544
boug	Bougainville	10	54.0	100	503.8	0	0.0	5	3	0	0	0	34,383	1,719	3,000	92	3,092	179
braz	Brazil	20,000	128.6	25,000	147.0	450	2.6	3,280	2,351	94	5,295	31	28,993,076	1,449,653	1,838,680	4,751,570	6,590,250	454
brit	Britain	18,500	473.7	15,000	255.0	480	8.2	18,527	4,662	186	8,971	153	13,701,830	685,091	247,014	855,727	1,102,741	161
briz	British Virgin Is	4	268.6	10	468.0	0	0.0	12	5	0	3	140	3,070	153	400	600	1,000	651
brun	Brunei	2	81.3	30	91.4	0	0.0	12	2	0	21	64	3,509	175	300	75	375	213
bulg	Bulgaria	100	15.0	200	24.3	135	16.4	768	380	15	1,043	127	2,012,363	100,618	22,593	52,717	75,310	74
burk	Burkina Faso	40	20.2	1,000	83.8	14	1.2	41	25	1	52	4	52,537	2,626	15,133	796	15,929	606
buru	Burundi	150	29.1	1,200	179.2	17	2.5	55	28	1	18	3	362,725	18,136	8,927	5,951	14,878	82
camb	Cambodia	4	33.8	300	26.9	0	0.0	29	22	1	4	0	12,052	602	4,927	49	4,976	825
came	Cameroon	400	51.5	3,500	232.0	21	1.4	291	228	9	81	5	801,509	40,075	28,117	2,985	31,102	77
cana	Canada	16,500	815.3	8,000	256.8	250	8.0	5,856	2,578	103	1,960	63	6,940,684	347,034	87,294	300,679	387,973	111
cape	Cape Verde	80	196.6	100	233.8	3	7.0	28	15	1	6	14	50,827	2,541	3,000	157	3,157	124
caym	Cayman Islands	2	77.5	20	521.2	0	0.0	5	3	0	4	104	5,067	253	300	75	375	148
cent	Central African Rep	80	49.7	1,000	276.6	8	2.2	40	33	1	17	5	180,773	9,038	18,724	189	18,913	209
chad	Chad	30	20.9	750	98.0	8	1.0	24	23	1	14	2	154,448	7,722	11,698	118	11,816	153
chan	Channel Islands	15	148.8	10	65.4	5	32.7	30	9	0	14	92	48,809	2,440	4,000	6,000	10,000	409
chil	Chile	1,700	127.3	8,000	525.9	50	3.3	1,160	779	31	584	38	2,898,028	144,901	89,305	124,343	213,648	147
chin	China	5,000	56.2	4,000	3.2	10	0.0	4,645	1,956	78	9,080	7	15,601,316	780,065	3,400,000	600,000	4,000,000	512
colo	Colombia	3,500	85.5	7,000	165.4	120	2.8	910	460	18	112	3	6,315,030	315,751	419,202	553,424	972,626	308
como	Comoros	2	283.2	40	67.5	0	0.0	10	8	0	0	0	617	30	40	17	57	185
cong	Congo-Brazzaville	120	51.4	800	271.8	7	2.4	34	15	1	4	1	320,867	16,043	12,594	29,386	41,980	261
conz	Congo-Zaire	1,000	21.2	15,000	290.4	130	2.5	1,011	600	24	95	2	5,340,910	267,045	294,827	64,718	359,545	134
cook	Cook Islands	10	540.8	70	3,585.7	2	102.4	9	7	0	4	205	3,293	164	600	257	857	520
cost	Costa Rica	700	180.9	1,400	348.0	20	5.0	223	169	7	35	9	771,920	38,596	88,581	124,867	213,448	553
croa	Croatia	300	70.5	1,500	335.4	0	0.0	512	376	15	493	110	1,305,774	65,288	1,800	4,200	6,000	9
cuba	Cuba	20	4.1	250	22.3	11	1.0	441	254	10	224	20	1,224,535	61,226	106,765	11,862	118,627	193
cypr	Cyprus	50	90.6	200	333.1	16	26.6	212	144	6	67	112	141,301	7,065	1,725	3,733	5,458	77
czec	Czech Republic	250	51.9	1,500	146.4	14	1.4	708	291	12	4,057	396	1,756,067	87,803	24,211	6,052	30,263	34
denm	Denmark	600	126.3	1,400	264.5	30	5.7	1,773	681	27	399	75	2,143,367	107,168	29,537	19,691	49,228	45
djib	Djibouti	5	177.3	73	114.5	0	0.0	10	1	0	10	16	2,388	119	100	42	142	119
domi	Dominica	5	74.9	80	1,131.3	1	14.1	14	12	0	8	113	14,040	702	800	88	888	126
domr	Dominican Republic	130	16.2	2,000	235.4	12	1.4	253	191	8	388	46	1,192,644	59,632	68,464	31,629	100,093	167
ecua	Ecuador	400	32.5	3,500	276.8	45	3.6	1,021	348	14	70	6	2,453,197	122,659	95,396	131,197	226,593	184
egyp	Egypt	300	29.1	1,500	21.9	52	0.8	1,211	674	27	372	5	1,002,195	50,109	68,979	12,749	81,728	163
elsa	El Salvador	200	32.8	1,400	223.1	12	1.9	430	381	15	28	5	832,542	41,627	100,940	122,378	223,318	536
equa	Equatorial Guinea	50	126.7	300	662.7	6	13.3	20	13	1	8	18	60,677	3,033	4,000	444	4,444	146
erit	Eritrea	120	62.0	200	51.9	0	0.0	10	9	0	0	0	80,020	4,001	19,485	602	20,087	502
esto	Estonia	40	75.5	150	107.4	0	0.0	105	53	2	350	251	151,944	7,597	4,164	6,246	10,410	137
ethi	Ethiopia	250	8.0	2,500	40.0	60	1.0	553	316	13	4	0	2,161,999	108,099	215,421	26,353	241,774	223
faer	Faeroe Islands	50	1,262.9	30	701.8	0	0.0	20	10	0	8	187	13,686	684	600	200	800	116
fiji	Fiji	100	217.5	600	734.5	8	9.8	83	46	2	21	26	65,575	3,278	23,700	2,633	26,333	803
finl	Finland	1,400	305.7	500	96.6	60	11.6	662	394	16	7,995	1,545	1,968,946	98,447	44,151	3,476	47,627	48
fran	France	30,500	741.8	16,000	270.8	670	11.3	19,811	6,662	266	3,741	63	15,448,745	772,437	71,769	618,317	690,086	89
freg	French Guiana	20	130.9	200	1,103.1	0	0.0	10	5	0	3	17	30,341	1,517	2,000	105	2,105	138
frep	French Polynesia	30	151.0	400	1,701.7	2	8.5	33	16	1	14	60	36,884	1,844	2,100	134	2,234	121
gabo	Gabon	20	18.4	400	326.2	4	3.3	38	24	1	6	5	150,924	7,546	8,452	1,491	9,943	131
gamb	Gambia	4	84.7	170	130.2	0	0.0	18	11	0	14	11	1,916	95	100	5	105	109
geor	Georgia	60	19.9	100	20.1	0	0.0	11	8	0	105	21	753,102	37,655	2,730	4,095	6,825	18
germ	Germany	26,500	450.8	10,000	121.6	0	0.0	20,911	9,677	387	10,963	133	24,772,421	1,238,621	498,426	717,247	1,215,673	98
ghan	Ghana	550	63.5	2,000	98.9	35	1.7	373	288	12	169	8	985,972	49,298	219,339	81,125	300,464	609
gibr	Gibraltar	10	468.0	40	1,594.8	0	0.0	12	3	0	21	837	6,863	343	300	52	352	102
gree	Greece	400	39.8	500	47.0	500	47.0	3,186	1,115	45	433	41	2,863,481	143,174	8,233	12,349	20,582	14
grel	Greenland	2	50.8	60	1,068.5	1	17.8	103	20	1	3	53	21,608	1,080	400	400	800	74
gren	Grenada	10	110.2	120	1,280.5	0	0.0	20	16	1	17	181	20,524	1,026	900	385	1,285	125
guad	Guadeloupe	140	323.4	400	877.8	4	8.8	29	18	1	14	31	106,920	5,346	16,000	4,000	20,000	374
guam	Guam	25	159.6	450	2,685.7	2	11.9	12	10	0	13	78	35,126	1,756	2,000	222	2,222	126
guat	Guatemala	450	42.1	3,500	307.4	60	5.3	628	346	14	56	5	965,826	48,291	117,124	183,965	301,089	623
guin	Guinea	2	8.6	100	13.5	0	0.0	561	304	12	4	1	16,171	808	2,918	153	3,071	379
gunb	Guinea-Bissau	10	64.2	190	156.6	4	3.3	40	25	1	4	3	18,483	924	1,000	111	1,111	120
guya	Guyana	10	26.7	300	348.3	7	8.1	63	31	1	28	33	69,436	3,471	4,000	347	4,347	125
hait	Haiti	30	3.9	1,500	182.4	20	2.4	325	222	9	56	7	723,114	36,155	78,280	11,080	89,360	247
hond	Honduras	200	33.0	800	123.4	19	2.9	177	140	6	28	4	675,930	33,796	70,879	101,157	172,036	509
hung	Hungary	250	28.6	1,200	119.6	45	4.5	1,551	573	23	1,684	168	3,023,496	151,174	86,711	1,769	88,480	58
icel	Iceland	40	150.8	40	142.4	2	7.1	141	64	3	837	2,979	88,006	4,400	3,134	579	3,713	84
indi	India	7,000	112.5	8,000	7.9	580	0.6	5,141	2,003	80	910	1	5,054,462	252,723	762,776	362,262	1,125,038	445
indo	Indonesia	600	22.8	6,000	28.3	150	0.7	1,262	764	31	164	1	4,534,021	226,701	448,218	215,808	664,026	292
iran	Iran	20	63.7	200	3.0	5	0.1	212	90	4	445	7	38,768	1,938	500	190	690	35
iraq	Iraq	40	55.2	80	3.5	8	0.3	271	23	1	21	1	42,821	2,141	18,049	2,117	20,166	941
irel	Ireland	9,300	2,771.6	500	134.0	60	16.1	6,604	2,017	81	360	97	836,770	41,838	6,800	16,567	23,367	55
isle	Isle of Man	20	381.4	4	50.5	0	0.0	30	5	0	21	265	24,131	1,206	400	1,600	2,000	165
isra	Israel	50	170.0	1,000	195.2	32	6.2	4,100	793	32	1,130	221	65,678	3,283	3,997	1,088	5,085	154
ital	Italy	31,500	671.3	12,000	209.4	850	14.8	16,618	9,672	387	14,090	246	16,374,428	818,721	33,213	1,548,358	1,581,571	193
ivor	Ivory Coast	300	68.9	1,720	116.3	13	0.9	40	20	1	25	2	293,344	14,667	44,755	19,180	63,935	435
jama	Jamaica	45	40.1	700	271.0	15	5.8	276	140	6	56	22	219,107	10,955	71,961	2,998	74,959	684
japa	Japan	800	232.8	7,500	59.2	120	0.9	3,157	1,467	59	5,485	43	1,112,518	55,625	184,172	25,591	209,763	377
jord	Jordan	12	43.9	200	30.0	0	0.0	138	93	4	43	6	32,689	1,634	8,051	7,582	15,633	956
kaza	Kazakhstan	30	11.6	200	12.3	0	0.0	20	10	0	123	8	757,244	37,862	51,880	2,730	54,610	144
keny	Kenya	800	35.6	6,000	199.5	28	0.9	651	578	23	168	6	2,524,927	126,246	161,240	34,915	196,155	155
kirg	Kirghizia	30	64.4	50	10.6	0	0.0	10	8	0	70	15	113,496	5,674	5,000	50	5,050	89
kiri	Kiribati	10	129.3	50	599.6	3	36.0	12	9	0	14	168	9,867	493	600	25	625	126
kuwa	Kuwait	10	40.4	100	50.7	0	0.0	20	4	0	102	52	22,180	1,109	800	200	1,000	90
laos	Laos	5	44.4	80	14.7	0	0.0	36	22	1	4	1	9,681	484	500	26	526	108
latv	Latvia	60	38.1	400	169.7	0	0.0	130	62	2	238	101	528,902	26,445	12,662	8,441	21,103	79
leba	Lebanon	200	115.3	600	182.8	55	16.8	560	321	13	84	26	279,000	13,950	10,330	15,495	25,825	185
leso	Lesotho	50	34.6	650	302.0	14	6.5	72	53	2	28	13	194,898	9,744	13,193	408	13,601	139
libe	Liberia	70	75.1	500	158.5	16	5.1	248	132	5	42	13	44,301	2,215	28,679	10,715	39,394	1,778
liby	Libya	5	29.4	100	17.8	0	0.0	11	8	0	3	1	23,129	1,156	100	900	1,000	86
liec	Liechtenstein	25	924.2	20	609.0	0	0.0	6	4	0	111	3,380	8,556	427	60	240	300	70
lith	Lithuania	220	68.5	400	109.0	0	0.0	355	210	8	332	91	991,076	49,553	1,065	1,065	2,130	4
luxe	Luxembourg	120	298.0	40	92.9	10	23.2	71	31	1	711	1,651	135,890	6,794	2,000	3,000	5,000	73
mace	Macedonia	50	38.8	150	74.1	0	0.0	218	147	6	104	51	273,672	13,683	1,763	440	2,203	16
mada	Madagascar	300	39.3	2,000	125.5	23	1.4	212	93	4	88	6	1,111,671	55,583	21,269	1,381	22,650	40
mala	Malawi	400	56.9	1,500	137.3	22	2.0	192	146	6	20	2	807,961	40,398	99,528	10,447	109,975	272
malb	Malaysia	90	50.8	1,000	45.0	10	0.4	218	143	6	2,283	103	268,305	13,415	28,618	1,506	30,124	224

COUNTRY		GLOBAL MISSION SHARING				CHRISTIAN LITERATURE							SCRIPTURES					
		citizens sent		aliens received		libraries		book on country's Christians			periodicals		Bible distribution					
code	short name	total	p.m.a.	total	p.m.	total	p.m.	total	1970–99	p.a.	total	p.m.	goal	goal p.a.	UBS p.a.	other p.a.	total p.a.	T/G%
1	2	109	110	111	112	113	114	115	116	117	118	119	120	121	122	123	124	125
mald	Maldives	0	0.0	10	34.9	0	0.0	8	6	0	90	314	49	2	5	0	5	226
mali	Mali	10	44.6	600	53.4	6	0.5	20	12	0	10	1	10,789	539	4,068	353	4,421	819
malt	Malta	1,000	2,692.7	30	77.2	8	20.6	137	69	3	503	1,295	95,996	4,799	7,500	5,000	12,500	260
mars	Marshall Islands	10	166.4	80	1,245.7	0	0.0	15	3	0	0	0	5,283	264	300	12	312	118
mart	Martinique	80	214.3	200	505.9	2	5.1	18	10	0	6	15	100,747	5,037	10,000	2,500	12,500	248
maur	Mauritania	0	0.0	50	18.7	0	0.0	17	13	1	1	0	491	24	30	0	30	123
maus	Mauritius	40	108.3	300	259.4	2	1.7	58	48	2	87	75	55,050	2,752	8,769	2,634	11,403	414
mayo	Mayotte	0	0.0	30	295.2	0	0.0	7	5	0	0	0	292	14	10	5	15	105
mexi	Mexico	4,500	48.0	8,000	80.9	180	1.8	6,891	2,554	102	255	3	15,178,697	758,934	181,426	134,097	315,523	41
micr	Micronesia	50	460.1	480	4,044.2	0	0.0	43	15	1	0	0	10,762	538	3,711	412	4,123	766
mold	Moldavia	100	35.7	500	114.1	0	0.0	45	23	1	95	22	766,724	38,336	46,874	46,874	93,748	244
mona	Monaco	20	643.1	150	4,464.7	1	29.8	15	8	0	4	119	13,352	667	100	900	1,000	149
mong	Mongolia	5	149.7	400	150.3	0	0.0	29	8	0	63	24	5,080	254	1,261	12	1,273	501
mont	Montserrat	2	196.7	10	940.8	0	0.0	15	6	0	4	376	2,114	105	100	11	111	105
moro	Morocco	15	86.0	1,500	53.2	4	0.1	43	9	0	21	1	12,069	603	399	171	570	94
moza	Mozambique	150	23.2	3,200	162.6	13	0.7	164	99	4	4	0	514,540	25,727	22,266	1,196	23,462	91
myan	Myanmar	250	66.8	200	4.4	33	0.7	241	17	1	28	1	546,104	27,305	4,782	1,195	5,977	21
nami	Namibia	50	37.1	1,200	695.3	5	2.9	195	155	6	35	20	189,744	9,487	17,071	1,896	18,967	199
naur	Nauru	2	239.8	20	1,736.3	0	0.0	3	2	0	3	260	942	47	50	12	62	132
nepa	Nepal	100	173.6	900	37.6	2	0.1	45	30	1	4	0	24,462	1,223	9,344	491	9,835	804
neth	Netherlands	10,200	991.9	2,100	133.0	300	19.0	3,973	1,673	67	514	33	4,231,832	211,591	83,194	194,119	277,313	131
nets	Netherlands Antilles	20	108.2	600	2,767.8	4	18.5	17	9	0	17	78	44,635	2,231	3,302	5,078	8,380	375
newc	New Caledonia	30	185.6	300	1,401.7	4	18.7	30	18	1	10	47	20,818	1,040	1,000	250	1,250	120
newz	New Zealand	2,100	819.6	2,800	725.0	30	7.8	658	331	13	8,103	2,098	852,259	42,612	33,527	12,909	46,436	109
nica	Nicaragua	250	51.5	2,000	394.2	16	3.2	578	501	20	35	7	403,824	20,191	39,717	5,830	45,547	225
niga	Niger	10	171.6	450	41.9	0	0.0	32	20	1	3	0	1,049	52	100	1	101	192
nige	Nigeria	2,500	49.1	5,300	47.5	80	0.7	1,403	1,158	46	129	1	5,139,377	256,968	276,174	31,369	307,543	119
nork	North Korea	2	4.0	20	0.8	0	0.0	150	29	1	0	0	89,788	4,489	1,600	177	1,777	39
norl	Northern Cyprus	2	124.2	40	216.2	0	0.0	10	5	0	0	0	4,406	220	200	133	333	151
norm	Northern Mariana Is	5	72.2	120	1,531.5	0	0.0	2	2	0	0	0	10,911	545	600	66	666	122
norw	Norway	1,800	428.4	1,000	224.2	30	6.7	1,213	481	19	9,814	2,200	1,866,629	93,331	63,542	12,283	75,825	81
oman	Oman	2	16.4	40	15.7	0	0.0	24	13	1	21	8	11,295	564	200	22	222	39
paki	Pakistan	50	13.1	1,500	9.6	15	0.1	258	127	5	395	3	197,826	9,891	34,941	502,612	537,553	5,434
pala	Palau	10	544.3	20	1,029.5	0	0.0	22	16	1	0	0	2,663	133	100	66	166	125
pale	Palestine	250	1,327.7	1,200	541.7	30	13.5	2,700	1,023	41	42	19	20,131	1,006	2,000	1,636	3,636	361
pana	Panama	600	244.2	2,100	735.4	20	7.0	139	65	3	11	4	468,666	23,433	52,016	22,935	74,951	319
papu	Papua New Guinea	100	26.4	3,600	781.2	34	7.4	356	254	10	42	9	525,576	26,278	49,451	6,174	55,625	211
para	Paraguay	450	87.0	1,200	218.3	16	2.9	249	143	6	28	5	890,730	44,536	33,178	23,633	56,811	127
peru	Peru	800	32.4	6,800	265.0	65	2.5	1,039	594	24	63	3	3,946,150	197,307	168,828	127,882	296,710	150
phil	Philippines	2,000	30.0	9,500	125.1	195	2.6	1,692	992	40	2,198	29	9,960,360	498,018	456,758	1,204,180	1,660,938	333
pola	Poland	2,500	66.7	700	18.1	76	2.0	3,716	2,305	92	4,130	107	10,179,134	508,956	46,913	41,269	88,182	17
port	Portugal	5,000	550.6	750	76.0	35	3.5	1,151	563	23	1,312	133	2,073,046	103,652	51,391	75,814	127,205	122
puer	Puerto Rico	900	241.8	2,500	646.2	25	6.5	381	252	10	49	13	892,086	44,604	93,128	41,062	134,190	300
qata	Qatar	4	67.1	10	16.7	0	0.0	10	6	0	266	444	6,975	348	300	33	333	95
reun	Reunion	10	16.5	240	343.1	2	2.9	18	11	0	3	4	117,428	5,871	5,000	2,142	7,142	121
roma	Romania	200	10.2	1,000	44.8	200	9.0	1,622	388	16	1,931	87	6,169,502	308,475	48,724	146,172	194,896	63
russ	Russia	1,000	12.0	19,000	129.3	72	0.5	3,421	1,693	68	3,629	25	25,416,691	1,270,834	303,275	707,641	1,010,916	79
rwan	Rwanda	120	18.9	1,200	155.2	17	2.2	120	80	3	21	3	547,003	27,350	48,493	5,388	53,881	197
saha	Sahara	0	0.0	10	34.1	0	0.0	12	5	0	1	3	9	0	1	0	1	265
saih	Saint Helena	5	937.7	20	3,178.1	1	158.9	25	0	0	3	477	1,707	85	100	42	142	167
saik	Saint Kitts & Nevis	2	55.6	40	1,039.7	0	0.0	15	10	0	8	208	8,442	422	700	77	777	184
sail	Saint Lucia	4	27.7	150	971.7	0	0.0	13	5	0	10	65	26,952	1,347	1,000	428	1,428	106
saip	Saint Pierre & Miquelon	10	1,565.4	40	6,091.1	1	152.3	2	0	0	1	152	2,084	104	100	25	125	120
saiv	Saint Vincent	2	25.5	80	702.0	1	8.8	10	6	0	6	53	18,257	912	1,100	122	1,222	133
samo	Samoa	300	1,773.8	800	4,442.6	3	16.7	54	42	2	20	111	19,845	992	2,000	222	2,222	224
sanm	San Marino	6	252.3	20	754.3	0	0.0	13	10	0	25	943	8,177	408	300	200	500	122
saot	Sao Tome & Principe	20	151.4	100	681.3	0	0.0	11	5	0	1	7	16,268	813	500	214	714	87
saud	Saudi Arabia	10	12.7	100	4.6	0	0.0	28	14	1	81	4	62,002	3,100	3,000	750	3,750	121
sene	Senegal	90	192.6	1,200	126.6	8	0.8	44	29	1	172	18	15,133	756	1,000	176	1,176	155
seyc	Seychelles	15	208.9	150	1,937.1	2	25.8	12	8	0	3	39	11,995	599	700	77	777	129
sier	Sierra Leone	10	19.6	700	144.2	8	1.6	122	60	2	21	4	28,595	1,429	8,368	1,098	9,466	662
sing	Singapore	500	1,240.9	1,000	280.4	10	2.8	180	144	6	35	10	85,945	4,297	32,656	8,164	40,820	949
slok	Slovakia	70	16.2	1,000	185.6	0	0.0	227	139	6	594	110	1,424,158	71,207	7,436	826	8,262	11
slov	Slovenia	150	86.4	800	402.9	0	0.0	267	195	8	675	340	553,570	27,678	14,700	6,300	21,000	75
solo	Solomon Islands	45	111.6	500	1,127.0	5	11.3	103	60	2	11	25	33,104	1,655	2,000	222	2,222	134
soma	Somalia	4	40.6	50	6.9	0	0.0	20	12	0	1	0	5,443	272	600	66	666	244
somi	Somaliland	0	0.0	10	3.5	0	0.0	6	3	0	0	0	379	18	50	2	52	277
soua	South Africa	7,000	220.1	12,000	297.2	150	3.7	2,626	1,644	66	15	0	5,195,286	259,764	664,374	17,734	682,108	262
souk	South Korea	5,500	294.4	2,800	59.8	160	3.4	845	758	30	126	3	4,544,073	227,203	1,209,905	42,584	1,252,489	551
spai	Spain	30,500	822.7	2,500	63.1	300	7.6	7,716	4,578	183	2,797	71	10,162,121	508,106	31,938	1,964,187	1,996,125	392
span	Spanish North Africa	10	95.9	50	384.6	0	0.0	5	3	0	0	0	32,035	1,601	1,800	34,200	36,000	2,247
sril	Sri Lanka	200	114.0	1,700	90.3	25	1.3	249	129	5	238	13	288,151	14,407	29,463	3,716	33,179	230
suda	Sudan	100	20.5	700	23.7	5	0.2	230	150	6	14	1	387,100	19,355	25,681	524	26,205	135
suri	Suriname	25	145.1	400	958.9	2	4.8	25	13	1	7	17	40,596	2,029	16,268	677	16,945	834
swaz	Swaziland	100	146.9	800	793.7	3	3.0	53	41	2	28	28	78,008	3,900	10,270	427	10,697	274
swed	Sweden	2,000	333.3	1,000	112.2	40	4.5	2,025	713	29	64	7	2,705,595	135,279	65,796	1,069	66,865	49
swit	Switzerland	3,400	527.5	2,200	297.9	150	20.3	2,738	1,200	48	4,311	584	2,856,836	142,841	51,238	204,952	256,190	179
syri	Syria	150	119.3	100	6.2	0	0.0	340	163	7	42	3	130,371	6,518	5,294	2,268	7,562	116
taiw	Taiwan	400	339.1	3,000	133.9	60	2.7	404	283	11	5,788	258	277,162	13,858	92,049	18,454	110,503	797
taji	Tajikistan	5	38.6	40	6.5	0	0.0	8	5	0	36	6	22,196	1,109	4,000	40	4,040	364
tanz	Tanzania	300	19.1	4,500	134.3	60	1.8	341	253	10	84	3	1,830,026	91,501	212,278	12,117	224,395	245
thai	Thailand	30	22.3	2,000	32.6	15	0.2	283	202	8	1,810	30	226,129	11,306	25,977	18,051	44,028	389
timo	Timor	40	49.1	100	113.1	0	0.0	29	16	1	3	3	168,386	8,419	5,000	11,666	16,666	198
togo	Togo	80	45.7	600	129.6	5	1.1	41	24	1	14	3	137,059	6,852	22,873	2,541	25,414	370
tong	Tonga	50	557.5	400	4,059.0	2	20.3	121	87	3	11	112	13,541	677	700	175	875	129
trin	Trinidad & Tobago	150	188.5	500	386.1	10	7.7	49	43	2	28	22	187,956	9,397	9,000	2,250	11,250	119
tuni	Tunisia	4	79.2	200	20.9	2	0.2	65	46	2	1	0	6,432	321	200	85	285	88
turk	Turkey	30	80.4	500	7.5	7	0.1	1,338	702	28	1,855	28	66,119	3,305	14,029	769	14,798	447
turm	Turkmenistan	2	20.2	50	11.2	0	0.0	15	11	0	46	10	18,426	921	2,000	20	2,020	219
turs	Turks & Caicos Is	2	150.8	10	596.7	0	0.0	2	2	0	3	179	3,477	173	100	66	166	95
tuva	Tuvalu	2	205.2	10	853.3	0	0.0	10	6	0	3	256	1,279	63	100	42	142	223
ugan	Uganda	500	26.4	2,600	119.4	28	1.3	357	211	8	36	2	2,109,730	105,486	69,473	9,116	78,589	74
ukra	Ukraine	400	9.6	4,200	83.2	0	0.0	1,360	749	30	449	9	12,851,431	642,571	160,476	481,428	641,904	99
unia	United Arab Emirates	10	38.1	120	49.2	0	0.0	18	12	0	112	46	26,997	1,349	2,000	500	2,500	185
usa	USA	118,700	618.8	33,200	119.3	2,700	9.7	41,948	21,067	843	16,230	58	67,674,125	3,383,706	1,989,928	16,100,326	18,090,254	534
uuay	Uruguay	600	277.6	3,000	899.0	20	6.0	219	141	6	651	195	616,295	30,814	17,920	8,549	26,469	85
uzbe	Uzbekistan	5	12.7	200	8.2	0	0.0	15	10	0	85	4	88,595	4,429	40,562	409	40,971	924
vanu	Vanuatu	10	58.8	300	1,575.5	2	10.5	90	51	2	8	42	15,496	774	900	100	1,000	129
vene	Venezuela	900	39.6	7,000	289.6	44	1.8	498	264	11	63	3	3,532,494	176,624	91,241	121,441	212,682	120
viet	Viet Nam	800	121.8	1,200	15.0	65	0.8	110	50	2	42	1	1,154,978	57,748	20,000	10,075	30,075	52
virg	Virgin Is of the US	20	232.1	150	1,613.7	0	0.0	17	10	0	17	183	27,642	1,382	3,000	12,000	15,000	1,085
wall	Wallis & Futuna Is	2	142.6	30	2,066.5	0	0.0	8	5	0	1	69	2,579	128	200	133	333	258
yeme	Yemen	2	65.2	150	8.3	0	0.0	26	17	1	0	0	1,755	87	100	100	200	227
yugo	Yugoslavia	500	72.6	1,000	94.0	280	26.3	769	475	19	168	16	2,046,035	102,301	9,539	38,156	47,695	46
zamb	Zambia	250	35.5	3,200	349.0	33	3.6	198	153	6	56	6	1,094,611	54,730	65,694	6,576	72,270	132
zimb	Zimbabwe	400	57.8	2,700	231.4	25	2.1	310	237	9	39	3	1,131,167	56,558	105,155	39,090	144,245	255
	11 minicountries	176	12,683.8	271	11,742.3	71	3,076.4	31,718	0	0	144	6,239	4,550	227	244	1,049	1,293	568
	Africa	17,406	51.9	90,463	115.3	985	1.3	13,056	8,524	338	2,201	3	36,398,525	1,819,926	2,994,093	481,858	3,475,951	190
	Antarctica	0	0.0	10	2,222.2	1	222.2	15	0	0	0	0	1,450	72	0	0	0	0
	Asia	24,504	79.7	57,970	15.7	1,623	0.4	29,746	13,008	520	33,880	9	47,596,347	2,379,817	6,959,865	3,116,180	10,076,045	423
	Europe	192,346	358.3	105,699	145.0	4,866	6.7	158,802	54,316	2,173	111,400	153	180,180,811	9,009,040	2,178,112	7,957,672	10,135,784	112
	Latin America	41,544	87.3	108,121	208.3	1,412	2.7	21,015	11,433	458	8,623	17	85,206,783	4,260,339	4,135,898	6,892,994	11,028,892	258
	Northern America	135,222	637.3	41,400	133.7	2,952	9.5	47,952	23,679	948	18,236	59	74,658,503	3,732,925	2,078,722	16,402,097	18,480,819	495
	Oceania	8,502	397.8	15,766	518.7	213	7.0	4,920	3,442	136	8,656	285	5,720,961	286,048	451,308	115,404	566,712	198
	World A	**507**	**50.6**	**10,178**	**16.8**	**72**	**0.1**	**3,935**	**1,904**	**73**	**3,688**	**6**	**943,843**	**47,192**	**166,959**	**509,493**	**676,452**	**1,433**
	World B	**29,898**	**60.9**	**103,065**	**27.4**	**1,974**	**0.5**	**35,832**	**16,964**	**680**	**38,073**	**10**	**80,963,360**	**4,048,168**	**8,324,398**	**2,335,117**	**10,659,515**	**263**
	World C	**389,119**	**280.5**	**306,186**	**180.7**	**10,006**	**5.9**	**235,739**	**95,534**	**3,820**	**141,235**	**83**	**347,856,179**	**17,392,808**	**10,306,641**	**32,121,596**	**42,428,237**	**243**
	GLOBAL TOTAL	**419,524**	**222.2**	**419,429**	**69.3**	**12,052**	**2.0**	**275,506**	**114,402**	**4,573**	**182,996**	**30**	**429,763,383**	**21,488,169**	**18,797,998**	**34,966,207**	**53,764,205**	**250**

COUNTRY		SCRIPTURES (continued)														
		NEW TESTAMENT DISTRIBUTION							PORTIONS DISTRIBUTION (Gospels)							
code	short name	goal	goal p.a.	UBS p.a.	other p.a.	duplicates	total p.a.	T/G%	goal	goal p.a.	UBS p.a.	other p.a.	duplicates	total p.a.	T/G%
1	2	126	127	128	129	130	131	132	133	134	135	136	137	138	139
afgh	Afghanistan	1,393	69	100	11	50	161	231.2	3,484,672	348,467	1,000	52	161	1,213	0.3
alba	Albania	668,444	33,422	25,002	6,250	13,336	44,589	133.4	2,056,753	205,675	413,180	413,180	44,589	870,949	423.5
alge	Algeria	32,800	1,640	700	36	333	1,070	65.3	10,933,335	1,093,333	3,500	388	1,070	4,959	0.5
amer	American Samoa	27,580	1,379	1,500	78	1,473	3,052	221.4	33,647	3,364	3,800	3,800	3,052	10,652	316.6
ando	Andorra	47,138	2,356	2,000	150	1,444	3,594	152.5	52,109	5,210	700	175	3,594	4,469	85.8
ango	Angola	2,008,419	100,420	9,097	1,193	75,295	85,585	85.2	2,402,128	240,212	25,655	4,527	85,585	115,768	48.2
angu	Anguilla	4,563	228	3,000	260	210	3,471	1,521.2	5,342	534	500	26	3,471	3,997	748.2
anti	Antigua	36,174	1,808	2,000	222	777	3,000	165.9	45,038	4,503	2,000	105	3,000	5,105	113.4
arge	Argentina	22,219,788	1,110,989	79,137	113,410	344,673	537,221	48.4	24,172,963	2,417,296	748,279	187,069	537,221	1,472,569	60.9
arme	Armenia	2,072,060	103,603	4,394	39,546	52,126	96,066	92.7	2,665,714	266,571	29,985	269,865	96,066	395,916	148.5
arub	Aruba	54,076	2,703	2,000	857	1,666	4,523	167.3	58,109	5,810	1,000	52	4,523	5,576	96.0
aust	Australia	9,554,935	477,746	173,835	305,049	414,352	893,236	187.0	14,165,953	1,416,595	437,470	187,487	893,236	1,518,194	107.2
ausz	Austria	5,640,517	282,025	5,975	28,966	65,453	100,395	35.6	6,640,590	664,059	6,492	1,623	100,395	108,510	16.3
azer	Azerbaijan	255,275	12,763	4,519	45	18,729	23,293	182.5	5,252,575	525,257	23,190	473	23,293	46,957	8.9
baha	Bahamas	168,151	8,407	3,000	7,000	6,666	16,666	198.2	191,691	19,169	2,000	500	16,666	19,166	100.0
bahr	Bahrain	32,672	1,633	1,400	2,975	800	5,175	316.8	334,763	33,476	1,000	52	5,175	6,227	18.6
bang	Bangladesh	205,246	10,262	3,881	12,494	3,627	20,003	194.9	29,320,947	2,932,094	484,740	261,013	20,003	765,757	26.1
barb	Barbados	148,241	7,412	5,000	2,142	13,250	20,392	275.1	203,321	20,332	5,000	555	20,392	25,948	127.6
belg	Belgium	6,994,354	349,717	17,104	62,821	63,953	143,878	41.1	8,276,363	827,636	6,775	15,808	143,878	166,462	20.1
beli	Belize	74,183	3,709	3,000	1,285	2,500	6,785	182.9	90,313	9,031	2,000	222	6,785	9,007	99.7
belo	Belorussia	5,047,631	252,381	3,745	1,248	71,420	76,413	30.3	8,270,737	827,073	54,005	29,079	76,413	159,497	19.3
beni	Benin	290,250	14,512	12,695	1,410	30,893	44,999	310.1	1,069,849	106,984	25,655	10,995	44,999	81,649	76.3
berm	Bermuda	36,204	1,810	2,000	857	1,666	4,523	249.9	41,826	4,182	5,000	5,000	4,523	14,523	347.2
bhut	Bhutan	2,148	107	120	11	42	173	161.9	447,656	44,765	600	12	173	786	1.8
boli	Bolivia	3,489,669	174,483	28,781	360,151	102,321	491,253	281.5	3,719,933	371,993	1,069,216	118,801	491,253	1,679,271	451.4
bosn	Bosnia-Herzegovina	1,105,985	55,299	10,000	2,500	10,000	22,500	40.7	2,370,307	237,030	10,000	10,000	22,500	42,500	17.9
bots	Botswana	262,694	13,134	4,392	488	21,702	26,582	202.4	595,273	59,527	30,339	7,584	26,582	64,505	108.4
boug	Bougainville	84,363	4,218	8,000	333	3,092	11,426	270.9	90,537	9,053	2,000	3,000	11,426	16,426	181.4
braz	Brazil	86,640,011	4,332,000	64,161	2,148,287	6,590,250	8,802,699	203.2	94,440,823	9,444,082	1,541,991	8,737,949	8,802,699	19,082,639	202.1
brit	Britain	30,032,493	1,501,624	55,000	165,000	1,102,741	1,322,741	88.1	44,731,149	4,473,114	729,598	6,566,382	1,322,741	8,618,721	192.7
briz	British Virgin Is	8,469	423	1,500	2,250	1,000	4,750	1,121.7	11,970	1,197	1,000	428	4,750	6,178	516.2
brun	Brunei	13,779	688	800	141	375	1,316	191.0	175,758	17,575	300	33	1,316	1,649	9.4
bulg	Bulgaria	5,562,996	278,149	100,000	150,000	75,310	325,310	117.0	6,970,300	697,030	28,640	28,640	325,310	382,590	54.9
burk	Burkina Faso	171,564	8,578	16,446	865	15,929	33,241	387.5	1,053,188	105,318	57,977	585	33,241	91,803	87.2
buru	Burundi	895,002	44,750	10,634	7,089	14,878	32,601	72.9	1,165,670	116,567	7,516	1,879	32,601	41,996	36.0
camb	Cambodia	39,907	1,995	1,498	15	4,976	6,489	325.2	4,385,473	438,547	13,295	134	6,489	19,919	4.5
came	Cameroon	2,355,250	117,762	7,982	376	31,102	39,460	33.5	4,722,780	472,278	83,258	2,574	39,460	125,293	26.5
cana	Canada	15,190,520	759,526	137,303	446,965	387,973	972,241	128.0	23,191,634	2,319,163	140,860	563,440	972,241	1,676,541	72.3
cape	Cape Verde	157,112	7,855	7,000	216	3,157	10,374	132.1	165,137	16,513	1,000	30	10,374	11,405	69.1
caym	Cayman Islands	13,977	698	900	385	375	1,660	237.6	20,522	2,052	2,000	222	1,660	3,882	189.2
cent	Central African Rep	488,456	24,422	6,508	723	18,913	26,144	107.0	1,134,099	113,409	10,004	526	26,144	36,674	32.3
chad	Chad	327,918	16,395	12,109	247	11,816	24,172	147.4	1,756,395	175,639	25,714	259	24,172	50,146	28.6
chan	Channel Islands	79,246	3,962	5,000	7,500	10,000	22,500	567.8	117,524	11,752	5,000	20,000	22,500	47,500	404.2
chil	Chile	8,501,511	425,075	23,602	57,226	213,648	294,477	69.3	9,679,508	967,950	412,772	766,576	294,477	1,473,825	152.3
chin	China	48,082,788	2,404,139	200,000	85,714	4,000,000	4,285,714	178.3	738,598,894	73,859,889	660,000	220,000	4,285,714	5,165,714	7.0
colo	Colombia	22,939,853	1,146,992	46,611	174,294	972,626	1,193,531	104.1	23,671,296	2,367,129	1,164,809	776,539	1,193,531	3,134,880	132.4
como	Comoros	2,003	100	100	42	57	200	199.6	171,245	17,124	2,000	105	200	2,305	13.5
cong	Congo-Brazzaville	809,234	40,461	4,480	10,453	41,980	56,913	140.7	1,029,167	102,916	19,988	13,325	56,913	90,226	87.7
conz	Congo-Zaire	16,554,686	827,734	54,264	11,911	359,545	425,720	51.4	18,138,147	1,813,814	200,360	35,357	425,720	661,438	36.5
cook	Cook Islands	10,180	509	1,000	428	857	2,285	449.0	10,749	1,074	1,000	111	2,285	3,396	316.0
cost	Costa Rica	2,192,932	109,646	13,643	23,531	213,448	250,622	228.6	2,278,845	227,884	69,413	46,275	250,622	366,310	160.7
croa	Croatia	3,356,924	167,846	128	298	6,000	6,426	3.8	3,603,010	360,301	51,362	27,656	6,426	85,445	23.7
cuba	Cuba	3,569,348	178,467	162,277	8,540	118,627	289,445	162.2	8,266,207	826,620	1,138,930	35,224	289,445	1,463,600	177.1
cypr	Cyprus	379,620	18,981	5,243	5,243	5,458	15,944	84.0	412,138	41,213	262	112	15,944	16,319	39.6
czec	Czech Republic	3,956,208	197,810	18,844	3,325	30,263	52,433	26.5	8,615,436	861,543	7,341	1,835	52,433	61,609	7.2
denm	Denmark	3,867,577	193,378	76,793	19,801	49,228	145,823	75.4	4,285,404	428,540	22,279	3,931	145,823	172,033	40.1
djib	Djibouti	7,834	391	300	128	142	571	145.9	162,542	16,254	2,000	105	571	2,676	16.5
domi	Dominica	45,963	2,298	2,500	131	888	3,520	153.2	48,592	4,859	3,000	61	3,520	6,581	135.4
domr	Dominican Republic	4,072,225	203,611	20,305	42,950	100,093	163,349	80.2	4,300,132	430,013	164,117	70,335	163,349	397,801	92.5
ecua	Ecuador	6,655,449	332,772	105,721	263,932	226,593	596,247	179.2	6,832,409	683,240	135,392	72,903	596,247	804,543	117.8
egyp	Egypt	3,175,296	158,764	74,754	2,872	81,728	159,354	100.4	20,699,453	2,069,945	353,670	10,938	159,354	523,963	25.3
elsa	El Salvador	2,627,170	131,358	18,368	17,437	223,318	259,123	197.3	2,705,076	270,507	247,659	61,914	259,123	568,697	210.2
equa	Equatorial Guinea	155,036	7,751	8,000	888	4,444	13,333	172.0	178,060	17,806	2,000	61	13,333	15,395	86.5
erit	Eritrea	178,860	8,943	19,377	395	20,087	39,860	445.7	356,154	35,615	8,921	90	39,860	48,871	137.2
esto	Estonia	388,785	19,439	2,738	6,388	10,410	19,536	100.5	1,222,597	122,259	4,571	4,571	19,536	28,678	23.5
ethi	Ethiopia	5,239,064	261,953	75,863	19,084	241,774	336,721	128.5	10,581,830	1,058,183	148,379	20,233	336,721	505,334	47.8
faer	Faeroe Islands	33,677	1,683	2,000	857	800	3,657	217.2	36,232	3,623	2,000	222	3,657	5,879	162.3
fiji	Fiji	270,341	13,517	10,000	1,764	26,333	38,098	281.9	483,184	48,318	10,000	1,111	38,098	49,209	101.8
finl	Finland	3,709,357	185,467	4,954	707	47,627	53,289	28.7	4,183,800	418,380	14,280	2,520	53,289	70,089	16.8
fran	France	32,655,557	1,632,777	83,055	399,822	690,086	1,172,964	71.8	46,604,192	4,660,419	150,009	1,350,081	1,172,964	2,673,054	57.4
freg	French Guiana	72,377	3,618	3,000	92	2,105	5,198	143.6	85,461	8,546	3,000	61	5,198	8,259	96.6
frep	French Polynesia	115,922	5,796	3,500	145	2,234	5,879	101.4	136,717	13,671	4,000	123	5,879	10,003	73.2
gabo	Gabon	361,132	18,056	3,874	968	9,943	14,786	81.9	407,277	40,727	13,382	1,486	14,786	29,654	72.8
gamb	Gambia	9,490	474	500	55	105	660	139.3	255,807	25,580	3,000	157	660	3,818	14.9
geor	Georgia	2,404,716	120,235	2,610	3,915	6,825	13,350	11.1	4,047,662	404,766	68,058	29,167	13,350	110,575	27.3
germ	Germany	48,139,504	2,406,975	92,323	112,839	1,215,673	1,420,835	59.0	66,925,488	6,692,548	320,883	1,283,532	1,420,835	3,025,250	45.2
ghan	Ghana	2,746,090	137,304	27,520	27,520	300,464	355,504	258.9	6,470,523	647,052	381,613	163,548	355,504	900,665	139.2
gibr	Gibraltar	17,831	891	1,000	250	352	1,602	179.8	20,884	2,088	1,000	111	1,602	2,714	130.0
gree	Greece	8,035,844	401,792	39,781	92,822	20,582	153,185	38.1	8,491,857	849,185	12,144	48,576	153,185	213,905	25.2
grel	Greenland	31,901	1,595	1,000	1,000	800	2,800	175.5	45,307	4,530	1,000	111	2,800	3,911	86.3
gren	Grenada	56,941	2,847	3,000	1,000	1,285	5,285	185.7	58,720	5,872	1,500	224	5,285	7,009	119.4
guad	Guadeloupe	276,755	13,837	9,500	2,375	20,000	31,875	230.3	291,015	29,101	5,000	1,250	31,875	38,125	131.0
guam	Guam	94,278	4,713	3,100	547	2,222	5,869	124.5	100,370	10,037	6,000	315	5,869	12,185	121.4
guat	Guatemala	2,941,001	147,050	30,630	28,615	301,089	360,335	245.0	3,127,726	312,772	179,876	44,969	360,335	585,180	187.1
guin	Guinea	42,563	2,128	2,577	286	3,071	5,934	278.9	1,437,959	143,795	7,922	416	5,934	14,273	9.9
gunb	Guinea-Bissau	43,521	2,176	95	23	1,111	1,229	56.5	342,417	34,241	10,000	526	1,229	11,756	34.3
guya	Guyana	248,455	12,422	90	15	4,347	4,453	35.9	571,161	57,116	12,000	1,333	4,453	17,787	31.1
hait	Haiti	1,886,432	94,321	4,195	6,137	89,360	99,693	105.7	2,017,143	201,714	74,460	31,911	99,693	206,064	102.2
hond	Honduras	2,248,112	112,405	27,527	58,226	172,036	257,790	229.3	2,398,242	239,824	124,939	31,234	257,790	413,964	172.6
hung	Hungary	7,277,555	363,877	3,904	976	88,480	93,360	25.7	8,394,919	839,491	5,830	647	93,360	99,838	11.9
icel	Iceland	195,676	9,783	7,249	8,076	3,713	19,038	194.6	205,780	20,578	42	42	19,038	19,122	92.9
indi	India	18,876,599	943,829	1,811,385	4,287,554	1,125,038	7,223,977	765.4	323,783,860	32,378,386	19,402,010	41,229,271	7,223,977	67,855,258	209.6
indo	Indonesia	14,157,709	707,885	1,072,504	357,501	664,026	2,094,032	295.8	114,823,272	11,482,327	467,280	116,820	2,094,032	2,678,132	23.3
iran	Iran	126,104	6,305	0	0	690	690	11.0	28,660,089	2,866,008	50,000	1,020	690	51,711	1.8
iraq	Iraq	223,562	11,178	52,012	525	20,166	72,703	650.4	6,836,763	683,676	200,512	2,025	72,703	275,241	40.3
irel	Ireland	2,570,584	128,529	1,750	8,920	23,367	34,038	26.5	2,842,938	284,293	14,000	6,000	34,038	54,038	19.0
isle	Isle of Man	39,184	1,959	2,000	8,000	2,000	12,000	612.5	57,734	5,773	2,000	6,000	12,000	20,000	346.4
isra	Israel	175,623	8,781	9,550	4,391	5,085	19,026	216.7	3,097,409	309,740	37,502	12,500	19,026	69,029	22.3
ital	Italy	39,315,003	1,965,750	17,360	705,973	1,581,571	2,304,904	117.3	47,741,351	4,774,135	2,139	2,139	2,304,904	2,309,182	48.4
ivor	Ivory Coast	896,103	44,805	17,916	746	63,935	82,598	184.3	3,068,848	306,884	65,824	2,035	82,598	150,458	49.0
jama	Jamaica	634,604	31,730	5,918	1,479	74,959	82,356	259.6	1,449,530	144,953	30,000	5,294	82,356	117,650	81.2
japa	Japan	2,843,263	142,163	377,038	397,167	209,763	983,968	692.1	106,889,597	10,688,959	29,272	19,514	983,968	1,032,755	9.7
jord	Jordan	113,856	5,692	52,824	2,780	15,633	71,237	1,251.4	2,882,438	288,243	65,150	2,714	71,237	139,101	48.3
kaza	Kazakhstan	2,194,193	109,709	10,924	574	54,610	66,109	60.3	11,658,836	1,165,883	139,651	4,319	66,109	210,079	18.0
keny	Kenya	8,918,397	445,919	32,516	7,380	196,155	236,052	52.9	12,109,162	1,210,916	60,152	8,988	236,052	305,192	25.2
kirg	Kirghizia	309,845	15,492	600	18	5,050	5,669	36.6	2,882,287	288,228	10,000	309	5,669	15,978	5.5
kiri	Kiribati	43,699	2,184	500	20	625	1,145	52.4	46,897	4,689	2,000	40	1,145	3,186	67.9
kuwa	Kuwait	108,806	5,440	3,000	333	1,000	4,333	79.7	880,313	88,031	5,000	555	4,333	9,888	11.2
laos	Laos	32,551	1,627	1,500	264	526	2,291	140.8	1,514,033	151,403	1,000	52	2,291	3,343	2.2
latv	Latvia	1,349,880	67,494	911	227	21,103	22,242	33.0	2,078,017	207,801	8,640	1,524	22,242	32,406	15.6
leba	Lebanon	995,168	49,758	49,015	73,522	25,825	148,362	298.2	1,870,968	187,096	231,670	154,446	148,362	534,479	285.7
leso	Lesotho	562,429	28,121	188	9	13,601	13,798	49.1	825,766	82,576	12,270	511	13,798	26,580	32.2
libe	Liberia	128,141	6,407	13,447	14,982	39,394	67,823	1,058.6	463,104	46,310	9,595	3,198	67,823	80,616	174.1
liby	Libya	77,898	3,894	200	1,800	1,000	3,000	77.0	2,360,573	236,057	200	1,800	3,000	5,000	2.1
liec	Liechtenstein	21,190	1,059	300	1,200	300	1,800	169.9	25,417	2,541	2,000	1,333	1,800	5,133	202.0
lith	Lithuania	2,561,892	128,094	4,238	1,816	2,130	8,184	6.4	2,961,383	296,138	14,077	3,519	8,184	25,780	8.7
luxe	Luxembourg	311,851	15,592	2,000	3,000	5,000	10,000	64.1	333,495	33,349	10,000	15,000	10,000	35,000	104.9
mace	Macedonia	927,924	46,396	638	70	2,203	2,912	6.3	1,348,139	134,813	1,000	111	2,912	4,023	3.0
mada	Madagascar	2,901,885	145,094	7,246	778	22,650	30,675	21.1	6,122,120	612,212	190,938	10,049	30,675	231,662	37.8
mala	Malawi	1,836,133	91,806	18,813	28,574	109,975	157,363	171.4	2,882,469	288,246	60,074	20,024	157,363	237,462	82.4
malb	Malaysia	867,568	43,378	9,716	1,079	30,124	40,919	94.3	11,080,057	1,108,005	78,486	4,130	40,919	123,536	11.1

COUNTRY		SCRIPTURES (continued)													
		NEW TESTAMENT DISTRIBUTION							PORTIONS DISTRIBUTION (Gospels)						
code	short name	goal	goal p.a.	UBS p.a.	other p.a.	duplicates	total p.a.	T/G%	goal	goal p.a.	UBS p.a.	other p.a.	duplicates	total p.a.	T/G%
1	2	126	127	128	129	130	131	132	133	134	135	136	137	138	139
mald	Maldives	198	9	10	0	5	16	161.8	132,519	13,251	0	1,869	16	16	0.1
mali	Mali	32,457	1,622	2,049	227	4,421	6,698	412.8	1,655,990	165,599	35,521	1,869	6,698	44,088	26.6
malt	Malta	275,571	13,778	4,000	2,666	12,500	19,166	139.1	287,083	28,708	1,500	1,000	19,166	21,666	75.5
mars	Marshall Islands	30,842	1,542	1,900	100	312	2,312	150.0	33,473	3,347	0	0	2,312	2,312	69.1
mart	Martinique	257,661	12,883	15,000	789	12,500	28,289	219.6	271,565	27,156	0	0	28,289	28,289	104.2
maur	Mauritania	1,391	69	200	2	30	232	333.8	497,100	49,710	0	0	232	232	0.5
maus	Mauritius	217,922	10,896	9,490	134	11,403	21,027	193.0	688,538	68,853	259,611	2,622	21,027	283,261	411.4
mayo	Mayotte	828	41	70	37	15	123	297.1	47,897	4,789	0	0	123	123	2.6
mexi	Mexico	51,749,491	2,587,474	142,932	396,434	315,523	854,889	33.0	54,593,830	5,459,383	501,959	2,007,836	854,889	3,364,684	61.6
micr	Micronesia	50,549	2,527	5,595	621	4,123	10,340	409.1	55,191	5,519	1,662	87	10,340	12,089	219.0
mold	Moldavia	1,999,984	99,999	10,721	2,680	93,748	107,149	107.2	3,236,220	323,622	19,572	2,174	107,149	128,895	39.8
mona	Monaco	23,882	1,194	1,000	250	1,000	2,250	188.4	25,605	2,560	0	0	2,250	2,250	87.9
mong	Mongolia	15,946	797	4,561	141	1,273	5,975	749.5	1,328,880	132,888	16,443	335	5,975	22,754	17.1
mont	Montserrat	6,438	321	400	21	111	532	165.3	6,718	671	0	0	532	532	79.2
moro	Morocco	47,217	2,360	201	50	570	821	34.8	7,615,695	761,569	98	10	821	930	0.1
moza	Mozambique	1,247,677	62,383	12,746	9,420	23,462	45,629	73.1	3,842,554	384,255	8,069	1,423	45,629	55,122	14.3
myan	Myanmar	2,047,456	102,372	4,283	225	5,977	10,485	10.2	25,689,540	2,568,954	60,980	2,540	10,485	74,006	2.9
nami	Namibia	532,163	26,608	739	30	18,967	19,737	74.2	683,575	68,357	14,245	440	19,737	34,423	50.4
naur	Nauru	5,061	253	200	22	62	284	112.5	6,974	697	0	0	284	284	40.8
nepa	Nepal	79,407	3,970	15,484	316	9,835	25,635	645.7	3,452,514	345,251	127,512	1,288	25,635	154,435	44.7
neth	Netherlands	8,317,074	415,853	4,951	7,364	277,313	289,629	69.6	12,659,170	1,265,917	87,382	37,449	289,629	414,460	32.7
nets	Netherlands Antilles	123,946	6,197	2,867	2,532	8,380	13,779	222.4	144,443	14,444	26,982	8,994	13,779	49,755	344.5
newc	New Caledonia	59,885	2,994	3,200	355	1,250	4,805	160.5	78,404	7,840	0	0	4,805	4,805	61.3
newz	New Zealand	1,911,252	95,562	14,774	30,824	46,436	92,035	96.3	2,839,055	283,905	73,171	109,756	92,035	274,962	96.9
nica	Nicaragua	1,595,486	79,774	10,591	10,054	45,547	66,192	83.0	1,664,912	166,491	60,962	26,126	66,192	153,280	92.1
niga	Niger	3,481	174	200	2	101	303	174.1	644,737	64,473	0	0	303	303	0.5
nige	Nigeria	14,626,669	731,333	11,312	11,868	307,543	330,723	45.2	32,160,662	3,216,066	222,676	2,004,084	330,723	2,557,483	79.5
nork	North Korea	311,947	15,597	2,000	857	1,777	4,634	29.7	15,291,520	1,529,152	0	0	4,634	4,634	0.3
norl	Northern Cyprus	10,147	507	500	55	333	888	175.2	117,442	11,744	0	0	888	888	7.6
norm	Northern Mariana Is	33,678	1,683	2,300	121	666	3,087	183.4	38,024	3,802	0	0	3,087	3,087	81.2
norw	Norway	3,300,462	165,023	45,241	3,352	75,825	124,419	75.4	3,492,553	349,255	15,450	3,862	124,419	143,732	41.2
oman	Oman	23,359	1,167	600	31	222	853	73.1	493,848	49,384	0	0	853	853	1.7
paki	Pakistan	725,102	36,255	20,129	3,141	537,553	560,824	1,546.9	29,962,913	2,996,291	606,562	31,924	560,824	1,199,310	40.0
pala	Palau	10,723	536	1,000	111	166	1,277	238.3	11,280	1,128	0	0	1,277	1,277	113.3
pale	Palestine	58,376	2,918	5,000	2,142	3,636	10,779	369.3	680,380	68,038	8,275	3,546	10,779	22,600	33.2
pana	Panama	1,416,686	70,834	15,848	26,300	74,951	117,099	165.3	1,641,202	164,120	112,572	28,143	117,099	257,814	157.1
papu	Papua New Guinea	1,482,986	74,149	60,706	3,737	55,625	120,069	161.9	1,823,195	182,319	1,056,637	1,056,637	120,069	2,233,343	1,225.0
para	Paraguay	2,531,535	126,576	21,314	28,023	56,811	106,149	83.9	2,689,117	268,911	205,198	87,942	106,149	399,289	148.5
peru	Peru	13,405,505	670,275	50,326	130,053	296,710	477,089	71.2	13,903,241	1,390,324	400,826	601,239	477,089	1,479,154	106.4
phil	Philippines	35,943,655	1,797,182	1,255,897	6,593,459	1,660,938	9,510,294	529.2	40,938,104	4,093,810	426,158	1,704,632	9,510,294	11,641,084	284.4
pola	Poland	29,532,112	1,476,605	10,226	15,794	88,182	114,202	7.7	30,711,431	3,071,143	43,237	129,711	114,202	287,150	9.3
port	Portugal	6,590,379	329,518	11,164	31,609	127,205	169,979	51.6	7,157,232	715,723	8,253	21,222	169,979	199,454	27.9
puer	Puerto Rico	2,430,792	121,539	21,886	85,398	134,190	241,474	198.7	2,522,353	252,235	213,698	142,465	241,474	597,637	236.9
qata	Qatar	33,003	1,650	1,000	111	333	1,444	87.5	321,670	32,167	0	0	1,444	1,444	4.5
reun	Reunion	323,918	16,195	5,000	2,142	7,142	14,285	88.2	371,764	37,176	0	0	14,285	14,285	38.4
roma	Romania	15,730,688	786,534	2,415	7,245	194,896	204,556	26.0	18,079,173	1,807,917	43,850	102,316	204,556	350,722	19.4
russ	Russia	66,563,265	3,328,163	51,626	120,460	1,010,916	1,183,003	35.5	118,778,132	11,877,813	574,058	5,166,522	1,183,003	6,923,583	58.3
rwan	Rwanda	1,404,233	70,211	22,080	1,162	53,881	77,123	109.8	1,737,698	173,769	156,384	4,836	77,123	238,343	137.2
saha	Sahara	29	1	2	0	1	3	256.6	15,380	1,538	0	0	3	3	0.2
saih	Saint Helena	4,158	207	300	100	142	542	261.1	4,801	480	0	0	542	542	113.1
saik	Saint Kitts & Nevis	25,707	1,285	3,000	658	777	4,436	345.1	27,406	2,740	0	0	4,436	4,436	161.9
sail	Saint Lucia	82,075	4,103	3,000	529	1,428	4,957	120.8	87,762	8,776	0	0	4,957	4,957	56.5
saip	Saint Pierre & Miquelon	5,084	254	300	75	125	500	196.7	5,212	521	0	0	500	500	95.9
saiv	Saint Vincent	55,598	2,779	4,500	500	1,222	6,222	223.8	80,356	8,035	0	0	6,222	6,222	77.4
samo	Samoa	95,691	4,784	6,000	666	2,222	8,888	185.8	101,551	10,155	0	0	8,888	8,888	87.5
sanm	San Marino	18,933	946	1,000	1,000	500	2,500	264.1	20,909	2,090	0	0	2,500	2,500	119.6
saot	Sao Tome & Principe	37,410	1,870	3,000	1,285	714	5,000	267.3	41,296	4,129	0	0	5,000	5,000	121.1
saud	Saudi Arabia	243,359	12,168	2,000	500	3,750	6,250	51.4	6,816,803	681,680	0	0	6,250	6,250	0.9
sene	Senegal	73,672	3,683	3,500	1,166	1,176	5,843	158.6	1,525,319	152,531	0	0	5,843	5,843	3.8
seyc	Seychelles	43,006	2,150	3,000	750	777	4,527	210.6	46,183	4,618	0	0	4,527	4,527	98.0
sier	Sierra Leone	75,209	3,760	3,111	10,015	9,466	22,592	600.8	735,907	73,590	14,820	6,351	22,592	43,764	59.5
sing	Singapore	261,144	13,057	4,353	12,784	40,820	57,957	443.9	2,356,896	235,689	61,414	61,414	57,957	180,785	76.7
slok	Slovakia	3,431,653	171,582	8,276	435	8,262	16,973	9.9	4,300,856	430,085	21,624	901	16,973	39,498	9.2
slov	Slovenia	1,442,526	72,126	3,908	1,302	21,000	26,210	36.3	1,659,411	165,941	9	1	26,210	26,221	15.8
solo	Solomon Islands	105,947	5,297	7,000	291	2,222	9,513	179.6	117,224	11,722	0	0	9,513	9,513	81.2
soma	Somalia	13,881	694	1,000	30	666	1,697	244.6	708,238	70,823	0	0	1,697	1,697	2.4
somi	Somaliland	987	49	60	1	52	113	230.6	329,153	32,915	0	0	113	113	0.3
soua	South Africa	15,529,127	776,456	99,690	32,876	682,108	814,675	104.9	19,916,798	1,991,679	267,718	29,746	814,675	1,112,139	55.8
souk	South Korea	13,556,698	677,834	1,502,864	1,214,792	1,252,489	3,970,146	585.7	34,583,413	3,458,341	1,543,703	435,403	3,970,146	5,949,252	172.0
spai	Spain	30,392,364	1,519,618	26,501	1,125,716	1,996,125	3,148,342	207.2	32,390,881	3,239,088	1,263,734	1,263,734	3,148,342	5,675,810	175.2
span	Spanish North Africa	64,823	3,241	3,000	27,000	36,000	66,000	2,036.3	79,733	7,973	0	0	66,000	66,000	827.8
sril	Sri Lanka	1,107,307	55,365	26,791	53,421	33,179	113,391	204.8	11,945,066	1,194,506	202,937	86,973	113,391	403,301	33.8
suda	Sudan	1,242,880	62,144	125,455	1,267	26,205	152,927	246.1	7,433,496	743,349	239,712	7,413	152,927	400,053	53.8
suri	Suriname	110,083	5,504	11,583	1,838	16,945	30,367	551.7	264,496	26,449	116,616	12,957	30,367	159,940	604.7
swaz	Swaziland	253,494	12,674	2,210	68	10,697	12,976	102.4	381,538	38,153	12,116	247	12,976	25,339	66.4
swed	Sweden	4,868,990	243,449	19,503	175,527	66,865	261,895	107.6	7,198,388	719,838	169,596	638,004	261,895	1,069,495	148.6
swit	Switzerland	5,188,930	259,446	13,162	13,162	256,190	282,514	108.9	5,897,181	589,718	117,101	468,404	282,514	868,019	147.2
syri	Syria	478,595	23,929	7,773	7,773	7,562	23,108	96.6	5,952,677	595,267	54,350	126,816	23,108	204,275	34.3
taiw	Taiwan	791,702	39,585	443,392	617,354	110,503	1,171,249	2,958.8	15,137,715	1,513,771	188,142	438,998	1,171,249	1,798,389	118.8
taji	Tajikistan	80,792	4,039	3,000	30	4,040	7,070	175.0	3,352,401	335,240	0	0	7,070	7,070	2.1
tanz	Tanzania	5,093,091	254,654	54,967	1,064	224,395	280,426	110.1	11,071,938	1,107,193	94,232	951	280,426	375,610	33.9
thai	Thailand	896,108	44,805	15,280	73,043	44,028	132,352	295.4	41,105,910	4,110,591	261,499	2,353,491	132,352	2,747,342	66.8
timo	Timor	411,739	20,586	2,000	3,714	16,666	22,380	108.7	447,786	44,778	0	0	22,380	22,380	50.0
togo	Togo	415,618	20,780	4,729	248	25,414	30,392	146.3	1,136,500	113,650	29,359	908	30,392	60,659	53.4
tong	Tonga	51,064	2,553	3,800	422	875	5,097	199.6	55,740	5,574	0	0	5,097	5,097	91.4
trin	Trinidad & Tobago	577,812	28,890	320	35	11,250	11,605	40.2	926,724	92,672	0	0	11,605	11,605	12.5
tuni	Tunisia	22,857	1,142	400	21	285	706	61.8	4,155,825	415,582	0	0	706	706	0.2
turk	Turkey	213,333	10,666	44,663	10,004	14,798	69,465	651.2	36,158,183	3,615,818	23,471	211,239	69,465	304,175	8.4
turm	Turkmenistan	64,326	3,216	2,000	20	2,020	4,040	125.6	2,483,665	248,366	0	0	4,040	4,040	1.6
turs	Turks & Caicos Is	7,943	397	400	266	166	833	209.8	9,917	991	0	0	833	833	84.0
tuva	Tuvalu	5,062	253	700	233	142	1,076	425.1	6,046	604	0	0	1,076	1,076	178.0
ugan	Uganda	5,057,278	252,863	20,197	8,780	78,589	107,566	42.5	5,843,861	584,386	67,696	22,565	107,566	197,827	33.9
ukra	Ukraine	33,816,743	1,690,837	31,897	74,426	641,904	748,227	44.3	41,615,485	4,161,548	188,796	283,194	748,227	1,220,217	29.3
unia	United Arab Emirates	132,163	6,608	2,000	352	2,500	4,852	73.4	1,259,902	125,990	0	0	4,852	4,852	3.9
usa	USA	138,175,676	6,908,783	1,696,117	32,226,223	18,090,254	52,012,594	752.8	200,254,603	20,025,460	2,188,717	70,768,516	52,012,594	124,969,827	624.1
uuay	Uruguay	1,529,603	76,480	5,267	11,400	26,469	43,137	56.4	2,355,047	235,504	86,680	202,253	43,137	332,070	141.0
uzbe	Uzbekistan	304,789	15,239	27,805	280	40,971	69,057	453.1	13,667,699	1,366,769	73,222	739	69,057	143,019	10.5
vanu	Vanuatu	46,329	2,316	3,000	296	1,000	4,296	185.5	52,355	5,235	0	0	4,296	4,296	82.1
vene	Venezuela	12,349,178	617,458	6,508	58,572	212,682	277,762	45.0	13,126,252	1,312,625	202,647	810,588	277,762	1,290,997	98.4
viet	Viet Nam	3,702,767	185,138	159,300	240,951	30,075	430,326	232.4	46,226,812	4,622,681	0	0	430,326	430,326	9.3
virg	Virgin Is of the US	65,236	3,261	7,000	28,000	15,000	50,000	1,532.9	70,153	7,015	0	0	50,000	50,000	712.7
wall	Wallis & Futuna Is	7,974	398	1,000	428	333	1,761	441.9	8,273	827	0	0	1,761	1,761	213.0
yeme	Yemen	5,083	254	300	33	200	533	209.8	2,990,001	299,000	0	0	533	533	0.2
yugo	Yugoslavia	4,908,643	245,432	9,037	21,086	47,695	77,818	31.7	7,884,104	788,410	185	226	77,818	78,229	9.9
zamb	Zambia	2,541,075	127,053	17,605	18,470	72,270	108,346	85.3	3,380,438	338,043	60,404	90,606	108,346	259,356	76.7
zimb	Zimbabwe	3,186,090	159,304	14,602	29,646	144,245	188,494	118.3	5,428,677	542,867	66,687	92,091	188,494	347,272	64.0
	11 minicountries	9,402	470	621	642	1,293	2,556	543.8	15,113	1,511	471	728	2,556	3,755	497.0
	Africa	103,728,365	5,186,418	870,548	299,425	3,475,951	4,645,925	89.6	225,242,765	22,524,276	3,372,274	2,588,483	4,645,925	10,606,683	94.2
	Antarctica	2,096	104	0	0	0	0	0.0	2,818	281	100	100	0	200	141.9
	Asia	156,012,976	7,800,648	7,227,618	14,111,365	10,076,045	31,415,028	402.7	1,748,880,458	174,888,046	25,654,631	47,787,940	31,415,028	104,857,599	119.9
	Europe	430,315,211	21,515,760	840,470	3,404,343	10,135,784	14,380,597	66.8	584,861,414	58,486,141	4,454,434	17,962,989	14,380,597	36,798,021	125.8
	Latin America	260,148,612	13,007,430	992,208	4,103,718	11,028,892	16,124,818	124.0	285,128,350	28,512,835	9,070,093	14,920,598	16,124,818	40,115,510	281.4
	Northern America	153,439,387	7,671,969	1,836,720	32,675,120	18,480,819	52,992,659	690.7	223,538,585	22,353,858	2,335,577	71,337,067	52,992,659	126,665,304	1,133.3
	Oceania	14,101,655	705,082	313,041	346,727	566,712	1,226,480	173.9	20,300,756	2,030,075	1,597,891	1,363,062	1,226,480	4,187,434	412.5
	World A	**3,241,833**	**162,091**	**193,865**	**19,827**	**676,452**	**890,145**	**549.2**	**195,813,022**	**19,581,302**	**1,211,398**	**255,113**	**890,145**	**2,356,657**	**24.1**
	World B	**234,756,609**	**11,737,830**	**6,606,618**	**7,736,859**	**10,659,515**	**25,002,993**	**213.0**	**1,802,090,967**	**180,209,096**	**28,626,930**	**53,535,419**	**25,002,993**	**107,165,342**	**118.9**
	World C	**879,749,863**	**43,987,493**	**5,280,122**	**47,184,013**	**42,428,237**	**94,892,372**	**215.7**	**1,090,051,160**	**109,005,116**	**16,646,672**	**102,169,708**	**94,892,372**	**213,708,753**	**392.1**
	GLOBAL TOTAL	**1,117,748,305**	**55,887,415**	**12,080,605**	**54,940,701**	**53,764,205**	**120,785,511**	**216.1**	**3,087,955,150**	**308,795,515**	**46,485,000**	**155,960,241**	**120,785,511**	**323,230,753**	**209.3**

COUNTRY		SCRIPTURES (continued)							BROADCASTING			EVANGELISM	
		SELECTIONS DISTRIBUTION							RADIO/TV AUDIENCES			offers via 45 ministries	
code	short name	goal	goal p.a.	UBS p.a.	other p.a.	duplicates	total p.a.	T/G%	cb aud	cstat	secstat	q per day	e p.a.p.c.
1	2	140	141	142	143	144	145	146	147	148	149	150	151
afgh	Afghanistan	999,011	499,505	227,204	11,958	1,213	240,376	48.1	0.1	0.1	0.0	2,040	<1
alba	Albania	620,455	310,227	31,134	31,134	870,949	933,217	300.8	0.4	0.4	0.0	939,481	110
alge	Algeria	2,500,854	1,250,427	314,712	34,968	4,959	354,639	28.4	4.2	4.2	0.0	45,093	<1
amer	American Samoa	7,775	3,887	680	680	10,652	12,014	309.0	74.4	4.4	70.0	83,937	450
ando	Andorra	21,365	10,682	779	194	4,469	5,444	51.0	65.3	5.3	60.0	110,355	516
ango	Angola	953,225	476,612	21,253	3,750	115,768	140,771	29.5	4.6	1.6	3.0	15,268,570	432
angu	Anguilla	1,754	877	83	4	3,997	4,085	465.7	42.3	2.3	40.0	10,310	452
anti	Antigua	16,902	8,451	675	35	5,105	5,816	68.8	51.0	1.0	50.0	74,393	401
arge	Argentina	10,451,094	5,225,547	14,058,031	3,514,507	1,472,569	19,045,108	364.5	64.3	4.3	60.0	55,335,797	545
arme	Armenia	751,322	375,661	65,654	590,886	395,916	1,052,456	280.2	0.0	0.0	0.0	4,426,109	459
arub	Aruba	21,507	10,753	1,027	54	5,576	6,657	61.9	0.0	0.0	0.0	152,671	542
aust	Australia	5,950,081	2,975,040	1,235,596	529,541	1,518,194	3,283,331	110.4	61.5	1.5	60.0	17,396,559	336
ausz	Austria	3,077,196	1,538,598	38,746	9,686	108,510	156,942	10.2	71.8	1.8	70.0	10,294,026	457
azer	Azerbaijan	1,533,043	766,521	2,009	41	46,957	49,007	6.4	0.0	0.0	0.0	140,652	6
baha	Bahamas	72,457	36,228	3,065	766	19,166	22,998	63.5	76.4	1.4	75.0	412,498	491
bahr	Bahrain	73,083	36,541	6,172	324	6,227	12,724	34.8	15.5	15.5	0.0	38,910	23
bang	Bangladesh	8,526,902	4,263,451	608,673	327,747	765,757	1,702,177	39.9	0.4	0.4	0.0	533,701	1
barb	Barbados	69,576	34,788	2,704	300	25,948	28,953	83.2	70.3	0.3	70.0	267,176	360
belg	Belgium	3,698,949	1,849,474	2,094	4,886	166,462	173,442	9.4	56.2	1.2	55.0	13,226,127	475
beli	Belize	30,606	15,303	2,407	267	9,007	11,682	76.3	73.0	3.0	70.0	285,083	432
belo	Belorussia	3,179,096	1,589,548	6,687	3,600	159,497	169,785	10.7	0.0	0.0	0.0	8,829,247	314
beni	Benin	365,603	182,801	142,430	61,041	81,649	285,120	156.0	0.3	0.3	0.0	1,300,872	77
berm	Bermuda	23,106	11,553	645	645	14,523	15,815	136.9	76.6	1.6	75.0	86,413	488
bhut	Bhutan	144,348	72,174	21,239	433	786	22,459	31.1	2.6	2.6	0.0	2,003	<1
boli	Bolivia	1,621,281	810,640	11,246,626	1,249,625	1,679,271	14,175,522	1,748.7	42.1	2.1	40.0	12,508,582	548
bosn	Bosnia-Herzegovina	811,160	405,580	39,718	39,718	42,500	121,936	30.1	0.0	0.0	0.0	1,311,740	120
bots	Botswana	180,525	90,262	8,440	2,110	64,505	75,055	83.2	10.6	5.6	5.0	793,734	178
boug	Bougainville	36,900	18,450	1,984	2,977	16,426	21,388	115.9	0.0	0.0	0.0	255,127	469
braz	Brazil	31,603,528	15,801,764	164,859,596	934,204,377	19,082,639	1,118,146,612	7,076.1	46.1	11.1	35.0	262,023,044	562
brit	Britain	20,407,849	10,203,924	174,712	1,572,408	8,618,721	10,365,841	101.6	60.3	5.3	55.0	56,338,076	349
briz	British Virgin Is	4,339	2,169	213	91	6,178	6,483	298.8	73.2	3.2	70.0	19,016	324
brun	Brunei	44,761	22,380	3,280	364	1,649	5,294	23.7	0.6	0.6	0.0	11,275	12
bulg	Bulgaria	2,521,442	1,260,721	82,250	82,250	382,590	547,090	43.4	1.1	1.1	0.0	9,476,260	420
burk	Burkina Faso	322,515	161,257	110,000	1,111	91,803	202,914	125.8	4.2	0.2	4.0	1,255,326	38
buru	Burundi	472,421	236,210	10,012	2,503	41,996	54,511	23.1	8.7	1.7	7.0	7,154,204	390
camb	Cambodia	1,324,404	662,202	65,426	660	19,919	86,006	13.0	5.5	5.5	0.0	58,157	1
came	Cameroon	1,607,196	803,598	53,175	1,644	125,293	180,113	22.4	8.9	0.9	8.0	7,396,710	179
cana	Canada	10,596,464	5,298,232	5,383,873	21,535,492	1,676,541	28,595,906	539.7	76.2	11.2	65.0	28,268,128	331
cape	Cape Verde	53,423	26,711	4,277	132	11,405	15,814	59.2	3.6	1.6	2.0	621,713	530
caym	Cayman Islands	7,440	3,720	383	42	3,882	4,309	115.8	19.5	19.5	0.0	33,349	317
cent	Central African Rep	419,721	209,860	12,784	672	36,674	50,131	23.9	11.0	3.0	8.0	1,474,165	148
chad	Chad	827,255	413,627	63,370	640	50,146	114,156	27.6	5.7	0.7	5.0	731,518	34
chan	Channel Islands	72,385	36,192	1,528	6,115	47,500	55,144	152.4	73.3	3.3	70.0	142,766	340
chil	Chile	3,299,588	1,649,794	4,718,174	8,762,323	1,473,825	14,954,322	906.4	41.6	1.6	40.0	20,915,153	501
chin	China	239,651,552	119,825,776	17,641,828	5,880,609	5,165,714	28,688,151	23.9	3.0	3.0	0.0	57,687,543	16
colo	Colombia	6,516,386	3,258,193	12,760,796	8,507,197	3,134,880	24,402,873	749.0	51.7	6.7	45.0	67,012,049	577
como	Comoros	52,805	26,402	5,927	311	2,305	8,544	32.4	2.0	2.0	0.0	2,656	1
cong	Congo-Brazzaville	408,072	204,036	45,743	30,495	90,226	166,465	81.6	3.0	1.0	2.0	3,061,436	379
conz	Congo-Zaire	5,851,770	2,925,885	602,800	106,376	661,438	1,370,614	46.8	4.6	1.6	3.0	68,605,469	484
cook	Cook Islands	3,477	1,738	195	21	3,396	3,613	207.8	30.9	0.9	30.0	28,903	540
cost	Costa Rica	802,161	401,080	1,265,112	843,408	366,310	2,474,830	617.0	42.0	2.0	40.0	6,354,804	576
croa	Croatia	1,401,496	700,748	44,726	24,083	85,445	154,254	22.0	0.0	0.0	0.0	7,094,544	579
cuba	Cuba	2,835,884	1,417,942	686,779	21,240	1,463,600	2,171,619	153.2	1.8	1.8	0.0	5,108,908	166
cypr	Cyprus	153,405	76,702	6,005	2,573	16,319	24,897	32.5	31.0	1.0	30.0	877,476	533
czec	Czech Republic	3,824,187	1,912,093	2,280	570	61,609	64,459	3.4	2.5	2.5	0.0	5,667,786	201
denm	Denmark	2,374,922	1,187,461	52,932	9,341	172,033	234,307	19.7	54.9	1.9	53.0	7,667,816	528
djib	Djibouti	49,556	24,778	6,376	335	2,676	9,388	37.9	2.1	0.1	2.0	13,471	7
domi	Dominica	14,843	7,421	707	14	6,581	7,303	98.4	20.5	0.5	20.0	101,404	523
domr	Dominican Republic	1,259,392	629,696	3,699,857	1,585,653	397,801	5,683,311	902.5	42.0	12.0	30.0	12,987,209	558
ecua	Ecuador	2,518,424	1,259,212	2,347,994	1,264,304	804,543	4,416,841	350.8	95.4	35.4	60.0	20,386,618	588
egyp	Egypt	6,533,217	3,266,608	1,025,480	31,715	523,963	1,581,158	48.4	9.1	2.1	7.0	8,055,124	42
elsa	El Salvador	857,230	428,615	2,606,856	651,714	568,697	3,827,267	892.9	31.4	1.4	30.0	9,797,692	569
equa	Equatorial Guinea	69,688	34,844	54,897	1,697	15,395	71,990	206.6	14.0	14.0	0.0	571,996	461
erit	Eritrea	159,339	79,669	22,382	226	48,871	71,479	89.7	0.0	0.0	0.0	2,001,093	189
esto	Estonia	477,812	238,906	13,961	13,961	28,678	56,601	23.7	0.0	0.0	0.0	561,191	146
ethi	Ethiopia	4,366,792	2,183,396	882,126	120,289	505,334	1,507,750	69.1	15.0	15.0	0.0	32,276,728	188
faer	Faeroe Islands	14,724	7,362	427	47	5,879	6,354	86.3	32.6	2.6	30.0	61,677	526
fiji	Fiji	117,203	58,601	8,169	907	49,209	58,285	99.5	22.3	1.3	21.0	539,097	240
finl	Finland	2,220,783	1,110,391	10,905	1,924	70,089	82,918	7.5	53.0	1.0	52.0	7,171,420	505
fran	France	22,047,588	11,023,794	38,032	342,288	2,673,054	3,053,374	27.7	61.5	1.5	60.0	58,324,406	360
freg	French Guiana	35,826	17,913	1,813	37	8,259	10,109	56.4	30.2	0.2	30.0	225,667	454
frep	French Polynesia	43,500	21,750	2,350	72	10,003	12,426	57.1	51.1	1.1	50.0	293,119	455
gabo	Gabon	170,209	85,104	31,000	3,444	29,654	64,099	75.3	21.1	1.1	20.0	1,523,859	453
gamb	Gambia	51,650	25,825	13,053	687	3,818	17,559	68.0	18.4	0.4	18.0	21,088	5
geor	Georgia	1,267,635	633,817	2,000	857	110,575	113,432	17.9	0.0	0.0	0.0	3,565,445	262
germ	Germany	34,439,624	17,219,812	721,556	2,886,224	3,025,250	6,633,030	38.5	0.0	0.0	0.0	86,029,245	381
ghan	Ghana	2,323,214	1,161,607	1,008,423	432,181	900,665	2,341,270	201.6	20.9	3.9	17.0	8,336,764	150
gibr	Gibraltar	8,038	4,019	250	27	2,714	2,992	74.5	21.6	1.6	20.0	32,986	480
gree	Greece	3,025,976	1,512,988	106,447	425,789	213,905	746,143	49.3	51.0	1.0	50.0	16,213,334	555
grel	Greenland	30,688	15,344	561	62	3,911	4,535	29.6	10.4	0.4	10.0	51,450	334
gren	Grenada	21,166	10,583	937	140	7,009	8,087	76.4	50.5	0.5	50.0	145,655	567
guad	Guadeloupe	112,429	56,214	4,556	1,139	38,125	43,821	78.0	30.4	0.4	30.0	698,605	559
guam	Guam	37,396	18,698	1,675	88	12,185	13,948	74.6	83.6	3.6	80.0	246,248	536
guat	Guatemala	1,027,147	513,573	3,800,725	950,181	585,180	5,336,086	1,039.0	44.8	12.8	32.0	16,831,815	539
guin	Guinea	546,337	273,168	2,000	105	14,273	16,379	6.0	0.1	0.1	0.0	96,415	4
gunb	Guinea-Bissau	145,423	72,711	12,131	638	11,756	24,525	33.7	3.8	0.8	3.0	79,426	23
guya	Guyana	159,624	79,812	8,613	957	17,787	27,357	34.3	21.2	0.2	21.0	375,046	158
hait	Haiti	773,219	386,609	940,409	403,032	206,064	1,549,506	400.8	12.0	2.0	10.0	12,359,824	548
hond	Honduras	721,069	360,534	1,029,310	257,327	413,964	1,700,601	471.7	14.1	2.1	12.0	9,596,450	540
hung	Hungary	3,487,710	1,743,855	832	92	99,838	100,762	5.8	52.0	2.0	50.0	13,735,329	499
icel	Iceland	92,551	46,275	36	36	19,122	19,194	41.5	66.0	1.0	65.0	409,772	532
indi	India	86,697,475	43,348,737	108,079,130	229,668,151	67,855,258	405,602,540	935.7	12.3	2.3	10.0	37,196,743	13
indo	Indonesia	36,772,276	18,386,138	3,122,859	780,714	2,678,132	6,581,705	35.8	18.1	3.1	15.0	17,094,974	29
iran	Iran	8,810,952	4,405,476	677,021	13,816	51,711	742,549	16.9	4.0	1.0	3.0	117,464	<1
iraq	Iraq	1,309,539	654,769	348,157	3,516	275,241	626,914	95.7	4.8	4.8	0.0	361,244	5
irel	Ireland	925,426	462,713	37,302	15,986	54,038	107,327	23.2	83.0	1.0	82.0	5,419,381	530
isle	Isle of Man	35,555	17,777	791	2,374	20,000	23,166	130.3	72.0	2.0	70.0	73,733	340
isra	Israel	1,158,347	579,173	1,157	385	69,029	70,572	12.2	5.5	0.5	5.0	165,684	11
ital	Italy	19,883,944	9,941,972	5,126	5,126	2,309,182	2,319,434	23.3	66.3	1.3	65.0	69,060,006	439
ivor	Ivory Coast	1,004,605	502,302	200,500	6,201	150,458	357,159	71.1	18.6	13.6	5.0	3,433,471	84
jama	Jamaica	500,473	250,236	25,825	4,557	117,650	148,034	59.2	30.9	4.9	26.0	1,176,116	166
japa	Japan	41,824,000	20,912,000	4,403,130	2,935,420	1,032,755	8,371,305	40.0	32.0	7.0	25.0	2,304,429	6
jord	Jordan	827,573	413,786	72,506	3,021	139,101	214,628	51.9	9.6	6.6	3.0	149,097	8
kaza	Kazakhstan	4,023,618	2,011,809	162,225	5,017	210,079	377,322	18.8	0.0	0.0	0.0	1,812,189	40
keny	Kenya	3,428,279	1,714,139	136,902	20,456	305,192	462,551	27.0	27.5	2.5	25.0	30,405,132	368
kirg	Kirghizia	1,055,783	527,891	46,993	1,453	15,978	64,425	12.2	0.0	0.0	0.0	240,423	18
kiri	Kiribati	10,589	5,294	833	17	3,186	4,037	76.3	60.5	0.5	60.0	120,466	527
kuwa	Kuwait	179,455	89,727	19,716	2,190	9,888	31,795	35.4	11.2	11.2	0.0	164,982	30
laos	Laos	450,283	225,141	54,330	2,859	3,343	60,533	26.9	0.9	0.9	0.0	53,546	3
latv	Latvia	814,196	407,098	3,545	625	32,406	36,577	9.0	0.0	0.0	0.0	2,137,002	331
leba	Lebanon	524,536	262,268	203,574	135,716	534,479	873,769	333.2	73.0	13.0	60.0	2,081,785	231
leso	Lesotho	286,152	143,076	3,000	125	26,580	29,705	20.8	4.9	1.9	3.0	1,977,210	335
libe	Liberia	160,105	80,052	5,700	1,900	80,616	88,216	110.2	71.0	51.0	20.0	706,315	81
liby	Libya	700,886	350,443	56,047	504,424	5,000	565,472	161.4	1.0	1.0	0.0	80,014	5
liec	Liechtenstein	10,263	5,131	328	218	5,133	5,680	110.7	51.9	1.9	50.0	40,282	447
lith	Lithuania	1,145,620	572,810	15,221	3,805	25,780	44,806	7.8	0.0	0.0	0.0	5,004,866	497
luxe	Luxembourg	145,321	72,660	4,306	6,459	35,000	45,765	63.0	73.6	3.6	70.0	632,883	536
mace	Macedonia	397,606	198,803	20,235	2,248	4,023	26,507	13.3	0.0	0.0	0.0	1,622,634	292
mada	Madagascar	2,345,298	1,172,649	506,259	26,645	231,662	764,566	65.2	31.2	6.2	25.0	7,619,345	174
mala	Malawi	1,268,385	634,192	515,000	171,666	237,462	924,128	145.7	9.2	1.2	8.0	8,591,312	287
malb	Malaysia	3,426,634	1,713,317	1,353,878	71,256	123,536	1,548,671	90.4	6.1	6.1	0.0	1,135,332	18

COUNTRY		SCRIPTURES (continued)							BROADCASTING			EVANGELISM	
		SELECTIONS DISTRIBUTION							RADIO/TV AUDIENCES			offers via 45 ministries	
code	short name	goal	goal p.a.	UBS p.a.	other p.a.	duplicates	total p.a.	T/G%	cb aud	cstat	secstat	q per day	e p.a.p.c.
1	2	140	141	142	143	144	145	146	147	148	149	150	151
mald	Maldives	32,693	16,346	2,862	58	16	2,936	18.0	1.5	1.5	0.0	70	<1
mali	Mali	550,470	275,235	40,000	2,105	44,088	86,194	31.3	6.0	2.0	4.0	97,868	3
malt	Malta	100,006	50,003	3,885	2,590	21,666	28,142	56.3	72.1	2.1	70.0	611,887	574
mars	Marshall Islands	5,734	2,867	642	26	2,312	2,981	104.0	0.0	0.0	0.0	92,559	526
mart	Martinique	106,184	53,092	3,953	439	28,289	32,682	61.6	30.1	0.1	30.0	601,913	555
maur	Mauritania	175,622	87,811	26,695	269	232	27,197	31.0	1.7	1.7	0.0	2,086	<1
maus	Mauritius	173,936	86,968	386,870	3,907	283,261	674,038	775.0	9.1	1.1	8.0	339,914	107
mayo	Mayotte	16,879	8,439	1,016	435	123	1,574	18.7	1.0	1.0	0.0	775	2
mexi	Mexico	16,012,973	8,006,486	3,011,786	12,047,144	3,364,684	18,423,614	230.1	81.5	1.5	80.0	151,910,938	560
micr	Micronesia	11,750	5,875	4,000	210	12,089	16,300	277.4	0.0	0.0	0.0	158,364	487
mold	Moldavia	1,240,653	620,326	43,804	4,867	128,895	177,568	28.6	0.0	0.0	0.0	3,489,522	290
mona	Monaco	14,315	7,157	335	59	2,250	2,645	37.0	83.5	3.5	80.0	50,365	547
mong	Mongolia	423,383	211,691	1,290	26	22,754	24,070	11.4	0.1	0.1	0.0	14,312	2
mont	Montserrat	2,206	1,103	106	1	532	639	58.0	53.0	3.0	50.0	15,272	524
moro	Morocco	1,946,702	973,351	6,072	674	930	7,676	0.8	5.8	5.8	0.0	73,925	1
moza	Mozambique	1,584,662	792,331	2,945	519	55,122	58,587	7.4	0.3	0.3	0.0	5,411,988	100
myan	Myanmar	6,852,006	3,426,003	616,690	25,695	74,006	716,392	20.9	1.7	1.7	0.0	2,332,055	18
nami	Namibia	243,730	121,865	17,258	533	34,423	52,215	42.8	21.8	1.8	20.0	1,919,388	405
naur	Nauru	1,299	649	115	6	284	405	62.5	51.6	1.6	50.0	11,409	361
nepa	Nepal	1,063,588	531,794	709,675	7,168	154,435	871,279	163.8	0.2	0.2	0.0	266,428	4
neth	Netherlands	6,441,145	3,220,572	7,615	3,263	414,460	425,339	13.2	54.1	2.1	52.0	14,171,828	327
nets	Netherlands Antilles	52,016	26,008	303,561	101,187	49,755	454,503	1,747.5	66.4	16.4	50.0	281,861	474
newc	New Caledonia	27,256	13,628	2,140	89	4,805	7,035	51.6	49.1	0.1	49.0	221,953	378
newz	New Zealand	1,265,983	632,991	2,413,210	3,619,815	274,962	6,307,987	996.5	71.3	1.3	70.0	3,543,036	334
nica	Nicaragua	421,396	210,698	746,845	320,076	153,280	1,220,202	579.1	27.5	2.5	25.0	7,920,529	569
niga	Niger	194,441	97,220	107,301	1,083	303	108,687	111.8	5.7	1.7	4.0	24,584	<1
nige	Nigeria	11,300,302	5,650,151	1,002,604	9,023,436	2,557,483	12,583,523	222.7	25.8	10.8	15.0	51,347,240	168
nork	North Korea	4,401,400	2,200,700	240,391	103,025	4,634	348,051	15.8	1.6	1.6	0.0	249,956	3
norl	Northern Cyprus	51,000	25,500	1,850	97	888	2,836	11.1	0.0	0.0	0.0	9,759	19
norm	Northern Mariana Is	12,319	6,159	783	24	3,087	3,895	63.2	0.0	0.0	0.0	101,750	474
norw	Norway	1,975,269	987,634	30,876	7,719	143,732	182,327	18.5	75.5	2.5	73.0	7,113,157	582
oman	Oman	238,813	119,406	25,417	1,059	853	27,330	22.9	2.0	2.0	0.0	58,288	8
paki	Pakistan	8,174,661	4,087,330	9,320,863	490,571	1,199,310	11,010,745	269.4	0.3	0.3	0.0	1,782,987	4
pala	Palau	2,801	1,400	194	3	1,277	1,476	105.4	0.0	0.0	0.0	27,806	522
pale	Palestine	234,630	117,315	221	94	22,600	22,916	19.5	6.6	1.6	5.0	133,986	22
pana	Panama	542,941	271,470	1,929,404	482,351	257,814	2,669,569	983.4	61.6	1.6	60.0	3,770,119	481
papu	Papua New Guinea	646,147	323,073	156,150	156,150	2,233,343	2,545,643	787.9	21.5	1.5	20.0	4,626,672	366
para	Paraguay	946,176	473,088	1,530,794	656,054	399,289	2,586,138	546.7	19.1	4.1	15.0	8,359,506	555
peru	Peru	4,092,667	2,046,333	5,320,872	7,981,308	1,479,154	14,781,334	722.3	32.7	2.7	30.0	40,763,321	579
phil	Philippines	11,344,374	5,672,187	11,099,395	44,397,580	11,641,084	67,138,059	1,183.6	40.5	5.5	35.0	99,946,706	480
pola	Poland	10,585,622	5,292,811	844	2,532	287,150	290,526	5.5	66.0	6.0	60.0	60,660,610	571
port	Portugal	2,251,353	1,125,676	120,657	310,260	199,454	630,372	56.0	41.8	1.8	40.0	15,783,258	583
puer	Puerto Rico	925,688	462,844	2,312,687	1,541,791	597,637	4,452,116	961.9	82.3	2.3	80.0	6,316,728	596
qata	Qatar	67,984	33,992	5,990	315	1,444	7,750	22.8	0.8	0.8	0.0	35,423	21
reun	Reunion	134,774	67,387	6,994	1,748	14,285	23,028	34.2	31.2	1.2	30.0	919,398	479
roma	Romania	7,090,567	3,545,283	223,265	520,951	350,722	1,094,939	30.9	8.0	8.0	0.0	30,911,134	505
russ	Russia	45,354,553	22,677,276	26,579	239,211	6,923,583	7,189,373	31.7	8.1	8.1	0.0	108,009,832	268
rwan	Rwanda	676,900	338,450	29,885	924	238,343	269,153	79.5	5.0	1.0	4.0	9,299,920	439
saha	Sahara	4,955	2,477	2,933	325	3	3,263	131.7	0.1	0.1	0.0	120	<1
saih	Saint Helena	1,971	985	62	15	542	621	63.1	33.0	3.0	30.0	8,235	477
saik	Saint Kitts & Nevis	9,000	4,500	384	42	4,436	4,863	108.1	51.1	1.1	50.0	54,324	515
sail	Saint Lucia	28,820	14,410	1,543	81	4,957	6,582	45.7	60.3	0.3	60.0	217,865	515
saip	Saint Pierre & Miquelon	2,136	1,068	65	7	500	572	53.6	61.0	1.0	60.0	10,232	568
saiv	Saint Vincent	26,387	13,193	1,139	59	6,222	7,421	56.3	55.7	0.7	55.0	101,830	326
samo	Samoa	21,060	10,530	1,800	94	8,888	10,784	102.4	72.0	2.0	70.0	280,111	567
sanm	San Marino	9,031	4,515	265	397	2,500	3,162	70.0	66.1	1.1	65.0	39,994	550
saot	Sao Tome & Principe	17,957	8,978	1,467	366	5,000	6,834	76.1	16.5	1.5	15.0	201,840	501
saud	Saudi Arabia	1,736,756	868,378	216,066	144,044	6,250	366,361	42.2	3.6	3.6	0.0	441,262	7
sene	Senegal	313,325	156,662	94,811	23,702	5,843	124,357	79.4	10.3	0.3	10.0	220,608	8
seyc	Seychelles	12,882	6,441	774	86	4,527	5,388	83.7	26.8	1.8	25.0	112,173	528
sier	Sierra Leone	279,799	139,899	11,187	4,794	43,764	59,745	42.7	6.5	1.5	5.0	302,876	22
sing	Singapore	775,680	387,840	1,015,654	1,015,654	180,785	2,212,093	570.4	19.0	9.0	10.0	299,905	30
slok	Slovakia	1,784,884	892,442	53,871	2,244	39,498	95,615	10.7	0.0	0.0	0.0	5,528,472	374
slov	Slovenia	636,800	318,400	16,729	2,952	26,221	45,902	14.4	0.0	0.0	0.0	2,736,859	503
solo	Solomon Islands	36,628	18,314	4,436	137	9,513	14,087	76.9	31.0	1.0	30.0	544,808	448
soma	Somalia	277,745	138,872	72,645	1,482	1,697	75,825	54.6	0.2	0.2	0.0	44,007	2
somi	Somaliland	126,500	63,250	28,326	286	113	28,726	45.4	0.0	0.0	0.0	3,756	<1
soua	South Africa	6,663,186	3,331,593	3,986	442	1,112,139	1,116,568	33.5	36.4	1.4	35.0	47,484,938	429
souk	South Korea	11,592,024	5,796,012	30,099,374	8,489,567	5,949,252	44,538,193	768.4	33.1	8.1	25.0	19,604,761	152
spai	Spain	10,830,354	5,415,177	73,223	73,223	5,675,810	5,822,256	107.5	61.8	1.8	60.0	62,524,748	575
span	Spanish North Africa	39,403	19,701	1,300	3,033	66,000	70,333	357.0	41.1	1.1	40.0	159,167	446
sril	Sri Lanka	3,108,427	1,554,213	1,620,718	694,593	403,301	2,718,613	174.9	8.5	3.5	5.0	1,136,791	22
suda	Sudan	2,315,197	1,157,598	993,471	30,725	400,053	1,424,250	123.0	8.6	1.6	7.0	2,772,066	34
suri	Suriname	97,540	48,770	681,200	75,688	159,940	916,829	1,879.9	60.2	0.2	60.0	165,234	144
swaz	Swaziland	117,412	58,706	10,078	205	25,339	35,624	60.7	26.6	1.6	25.0	920,157	333
swed	Sweden	3,999,993	1,999,996	88,596	333,289	1,069,495	1,491,381	74.6	64.6	1.6	63.0	8,318,294	340
swit	Switzerland	3,246,774	1,623,387	85,794	343,176	868,019	1,296,989	79.9	71.3	1.3	70.0	10,296,118	508
syri	Syria	1,621,532	810,766	9,735	22,715	204,275	236,725	29.2	1.8	1.8	0.0	810,468	18
taiw	Taiwan	5,299,466	2,649,733	10,174,695	23,740,955	1,798,389	35,714,039	1,347.8	54.4	14.4	40.0	821,337	13
taji	Tajikistan	921,022	460,511	61,882	625	7,070	69,577	15.1	0.0	0.0	0.0	58,442	3
tanz	Tanzania	3,978,318	1,989,159	335,170	3,385	375,610	714,166	35.9	6.0	1.0	5.0	14,876,893	162
thai	Thailand	10,372,919	5,186,459	2,549,517	22,945,653	2,747,342	28,242,512	544.5	13.2	3.2	10.0	764,862	4
timo	Timor	183,128	91,564	8,845	20,639	22,380	51,865	56.6	2.1	0.1	2.0	1,075,256	443
togo	Togo	374,785	187,392	20,000	618	60,659	81,277	43.4	4.2	0.2	4.0	1,544,801	121
tong	Tonga	14,781	7,390	985	51	5,097	6,134	83.0	31.4	1.4	30.0	145,617	539
trin	Trinidad & Tobago	301,454	150,727	12,949	826	11,605	25,381	16.8	56.3	1.3	55.0	975,253	274
tuni	Tunisia	1,169,610	584,805	95,856	5,045	706	101,607	17.4	1.7	1.7	0.0	24,777	<1
turk	Turkey	11,206,627	5,603,313	105,421	948,789	304,175	1,358,385	24.2	0.2	0.2	0.0	182,137	1
turm	Turkmenistan	711,440	355,720	44,592	450	4,040	49,083	13.8	0.0	0.0	0.0	34,777	2
turs	Turks & Caicos Is	4,342	2,171	167	111	833	1,112	51.2	69.5	9.5	60.0	18,690	407
tuva	Tuvalu	1,528	764	117	20	1,076	1,214	158.9	61.7	1.7	60.0	14,256	444
ugan	Uganda	2,437,867	1,218,933	102,278	34,092	197,827	334,198	27.4	11.6	4.6	7.0	27,895,295	467
ukra	Ukraine	15,815,200	7,907,600	504,559	756,839	1,220,217	2,481,616	31.4	0.0	0.0	0.0	64,170,409	464
unia	United Arab Emirates	257,368	128,684	24,414	2,712	4,852	31,980	24.9	1.1	1.1	0.0	161,352	24
usa	USA	98,078,443	49,039,221	57,801,656	1,868,920,210	124,969,827	2,051,691,694	4,183.8	138.0	58.0	80.0	280,931,560	368
uuay	Uruguay	948,877	474,438	1,261,271	2,942,965	332,070	4,536,307	956.1	50.7	0.7	50.0	2,858,670	312
uzbe	Uzbekistan	3,972,879	1,986,439	243,178	2,456	143,019	388,654	19.6	0.0	0.0	0.0	191,686	2
vanu	Vanuatu	17,512	8,756	1,904	100	4,296	6,301	72.0	6.1	1.1	5.0	232,583	445
vene	Venezuela	3,754,777	1,877,388	2,881,434	11,525,736	1,290,997	15,698,167	836.2	54.6	4.6	50.0	36,995,749	558
viet	Viet Nam	14,419,203	7,209,601	798,316	1,197,474	430,326	2,426,117	33.7	1.2	1.2	0.0	4,416,271	20
virg	Virgin Is of the US	29,725	14,862	929	2,788	50,000	53,718	361.4	81.4	1.4	80.0	137,088	538
wall	Wallis & Futuna Is	2,676	1,338	145	36	1,761	1,943	145.2	71.3	1.3	70.0	19,728	496
yeme	Yemen	1,032,744	516,372	181,120	9,532	533	191,186	37.0	0.0	0.0	0.0	14,292	<1
yugo	Yugoslavia	3,286,276	1,643,138	106,401	130,046	78,229	314,677	19.2	21.5	1.5	20.0	9,020,080	309
zamb	Zambia	1,456,181	728,090	34,224	51,336	259,356	344,916	47.4	11.4	1.4	10.0	9,573,904	381
zimb	Zimbabwe	1,927,359	963,679	564,740	779,879	347,272	1,691,891	175.6	21.5	1.5	20.0	8,547,782	267
	11 minicountries	7,126	3,563	231	310	3,755	4,297	1,206.0	392.0	82.0	310.0	17,204	272
	Africa	76,137,742	38,068,871	9,877,176	11,543,963	10,606,683	32,027,823	841.3	716.2	193.2	523.0	397,631,611	185
	Antarctica	1,950	975	45	45	200	290	297.4	0.0	0.0	0.0	3,216	260
	Asia	541,625,705	270,812,852	206,372,348	344,701,530	104,857,599	655,931,478	2,422.1	429.7	146.7	283.0	265,064,772	26
	Europe	245,848,304	122,924,152	2,844,243	8,224,861	36,798,021	47,867,126	389.4	1,906.7	126.7	1,780.0	791,068,562	396
	Latin America	93,659,253	46,829,626	244,074,329	999,901,956	40,115,510	1,284,091,796	27,420.5	2,135.7	189.7	1,946.0	776,662,515	546
	Northern America	108,730,840	54,365,420	63,186,802	1,890,456,418	126,665,304	2,080,308,524	38,265.3	362.2	72.2	290.0	309,347,783	364
	Oceania	8,276,287	4,138,143	3,838,207	4,311,324	4,187,434	12,336,966	2,981.3	1,077.3	62.3	1,015.0	28,990,880	348
	World A	**56,675,257**	**28,337,628**	**13,268,270**	**2,175,763**	**2,356,657**	**17,800,691**	**628.2**	**98.5**	**54.5**	**44.0**	**4,670,919**	**2**
	World B	**577,425,774**	**288,712,887**	**191,690,499**	**309,051,866**	**107,165,342**	**607,907,708**	**2,105.6**	**800.6**	**271.6**	**529.0**	**435,715,991**	**42**
	World C	**440,179,052**	**220,089,526**	**325,234,383**	**2,947,912,469**	**213,708,753**	**3,486,855,605**	**15,842.9**	**5,728.7**	**464.7**	**5,264.0**	**2,128,382,429**	**458**
	GLOBAL TOTAL	**1,074,280,084**	**537,140,042**	**530,193,153**	**3,259,140,099**	**323,230,753**	**4,112,564,005**	**7,656.40**	**6,627.8**	**790.8**	**5,837.0**	**2,568,769,339**	**154**

COUNTRY		EVANGELIZATION												STRATEGIES		FUTURES	
		when begun	status of evangelization, E						source of E		unevangelized						
code	short name	year begun	1900	1970	1990	1995	2000	2025	internal	external	U	total	world	plans	target	growth	prospect
1	2	152	153	154	155	156	157	158	159	160	161	162	163	164	165	166	167
afgh	Afghanistan	c300	3.0	14.0	25.0	27.0	29.6	35.0	2.5	27.1	70.4	16,000,408	A	0	47	1	-2
alba	Albania	c70	39.0	34.0	75.7	81.1	85.4	90.8	43.4	42.0	14.6	454,107	B	0	1	24	2
alge	Algeria	c100	15.0	24.0	43.9	47.1	49.6	55.0	4.4	45.2	50.5	15,876,006	A	2	22	18	-2
amer	American Samoa	1827	100.0	100.0	99.6	99.6	99.6	99.4	91.0	8.6	0.4	252	C	0	0	0	0
ando	Andorra	c600	100.0	100.0	99.1	99.1	99.1	98.7	97.7	1.4	0.9	734	C	0	1	-2	0
ango	Angola	1491	15.0	86.0	99.1	99.2	99.3	99.5	94.1	5.2	0.7	91,226	C	0	0	3	1
angu	Anguilla	c165	100.0	100.0	99.8	99.8	99.8	99.5	96.5	3.3	0.2	17	C	0	0	-2	0
anti	Antigua	1634	100.0	99.9	99.8	99.8	99.8	99.7	89.5	10.3	0.2	157	C	0	0	-1	0
arge	Argentina	1527	99.5	99.7	99.4	99.4	99.3	98.9	96.4	2.9	0.7	242,999	C	2	0	-1	1
arme	Armenia	c35	95.0	93.0	96.5	97.4	97.8	98.9	93.8	4.0	2.2	77,944	C	0	6	10	2
arub	Aruba	c155	100.0	99.9	99.6	99.6	99.5	99.4	98.6	0.9	0.5	475	C	0	2	-1	0
aust	Australia	1788	99.2	99.5	98.6	98.4	98.4	97.7	76.5	21.9	1.6	307,968	C	6	0	-5	-1
ausz	Austria	174	99.8	99.9	98.7	98.6	98.6	97.8	93.9	4.7	1.4	115,508	C	0	1	-3	0
azer	Azerbaijan	60	18.0	25.0	33.8	34.6	37.0	41.5	8.1	28.9	63.0	4,872,856	A	0	14	-16	1
baha	Bahamas	c167	99.8	99.9	99.8	99.7	99.7	99.6	96.9	2.8	0.3	859	C	0	0	-2	0
bahr	Bahrain	c250	8.9	40.1	53.1	55.4	57.2	65.0	16.0	41.2	42.8	264,134	B	0	1	8	1
bang	Bangladesh	1536	15.0	43.0	53.0	55.1	57.2	62.0	5.8	51.4	42.8	55,267,877	B	0	3	17	2
barb	Barbados	1626	100.0	99.8	99.3	99.2	99.2	99.0	82.7	16.5	0.8	2,159	C	0	1	-1	0
belg	Belgium	c200	100.0	99.5	98.2	98.0	97.8	97.2	93.6	4.2	2.2	219,444	C	5	0	-3	-1
beli	Belize	c165	99.0	99.0	98.0	97.9	97.9	97.3	90.6	7.3	2.1	5,155	C	0	0	-1	0
belo	Belorussia	992	99.9	97.8	98.5	99.1	99.2	99.2	74.2	25.0	0.9	86,904	C	0	4	22	1
beni	Benin	1680	12.9	52.2	67.1	71.0	74.2	79.8	36.1	38.1	25.8	1,574,060	B	0	1	24	1
berm	Bermuda	1609	100.0	100.0	99.8	99.8	99.8	99.7	95.9	3.9	0.2	121	C	0	1	-2	0
bhut	Bhutan	1865	0.0	15.5	19.0	20.0	20.8	24.4	4.9	15.9	79.2	1,683,112	A	0	3	-18	-1
boli	Bolivia	1537	96.1	99.0	99.7	99.7	99.7	99.7	98.5	1.2	0.3	24,406	C	1	0	-2	0
bosn	Bosnia-Herzegovina	c150	64.9	65.0	70.8	71.6	73.7	74.6	40.7	33.0	26.3	1,045,717	B	0	0	-27	-1
bots	Botswana	1816	18.0	85.0	91.0	93.0	94.9	96.0	55.7	39.2	5.1	83,331	B	0	0	11	2
boug	Bougainville	1900	5.0	99.6	99.8	99.9	99.9	99.9	98.3	1.6	0.1	256	C	0	0	1	1
braz	Brazil	1500	98.3	99.5	99.7	99.7	99.8	99.8	99.1	0.7	0.3	425,724	C	8	1	-2	1
brit	Britain	61	99.9	99.5	98.2	98.1	98.1	97.7	76.1	22.0	1.9	1,116,976	C	88	0	-3	0
briz	British Virgin Is	1648	100.0	99.8	99.7	99.6	99.6	99.5	79.7	19.9	0.4	90	C	0	0	-2	0
brun	Brunei	c160	6.0	40.2	42.1	44.2	45.1	52.1	13.8	31.3	54.9	180,020	A	0	0	-5	-1
bulg	Bulgaria	c150	90.7	75.0	92.3	93.4	94.5	95.7	88.2	6.3	5.5	454,079	C	1	0	3	1
burk	Burkina Faso	1900	0.0	44.7	55.5	59.0	63.1	72.1	24.5	38.6	36.9	4,406,314	B	0	5	23	1
buru	Burundi	1879	0.1	98.0	98.9	99.0	99.2	99.5	86.9	12.3	0.8	54,611	C	0	2	2	1
camb	Cambodia	1555	7.0	25.0	38.0	44.9	49.1	60.7	6.2	42.9	50.9	5,685,563	A	0	1	32	-1
came	Cameroon	1845	15.7	65.0	78.0	78.4	79.9	83.9	60.3	19.6	20.1	3,027,138	B	1	1	12	1
cana	Canada	1534	99.0	99.5	98.0	97.9	97.8	96.5	74.5	23.3	2.2	688,856	C	11	0	-4	0
cape	Cape Verde	1462	99.9	100.0	100.0	100.0	100.0	99.9	98.8	1.2	0.1	202	C	0	0	0	0
caym	Cayman Islands	1670	100.0	99.9	98.3	98.1	98.1	97.7	77.2	20.9	2.0	749	C	0	0	-2	0
cent	Central African Rep	1894	0.2	78.4	81.6	82.5	84.0	87.7	53.6	30.4	16.0	578,728	B	0	2	5	1
chad	Chad	1663	0.0	45.0	48.1	49.0	50.1	54.0	24.4	25.7	49.9	3,818,667	B	0	40	-1	-2
chan	Channel Islands	c550	100.0	99.9	99.7	99.6	99.5	99.3	75.9	23.6	0.5	719	C	0	0	-10	0
chil	Chile	1541	98.5	99.6	99.6	99.6	99.6	99.7	97.2	2.4	0.4	61,134	C	0	0	-1	1
chin	China	635	18.0	20.0	53.0	57.0	64.8	70.6	13.8	51.0	35.2	444,210,082	B	7	35	31	2
colo	Colombia	1512	83.0	99.1	99.7	99.7	99.7	99.7	99.3	0.4	0.3	119,613	C	0	0	0	1
como	Comoros	1517	1.0	20.2	35.0	36.1	37.4	44.4	4.3	33.1	62.7	371,333	A	0	2	24	0
cong	Congo-Brazzaville	1491	13.9	93.0	98.8	98.9	99.0	99.4	89.0	10.0	1.0	28,634	C	0	0	0	1
conz	Congo-Zaire	1482	17.0	93.0	98.7	98.9	99.1	99.5	96.9	2.2	0.9	461,513	C	0	0	1	1
cook	Cook Islands	1823	100.0	99.9	99.9	100.0	100.0	99.9	99.3	0.7	0.1	10	C	0	0	-2	0
cost	Costa Rica	1514	100.0	99.9	99.9	99.9	99.9	99.8	98.7	1.2	0.1	4,553	C	2	0	-1	1
croa	Croatia	250	99.0	97.0	98.0	98.7	99.2	99.3	97.7	1.5	0.8	33,972	C	0	1	1	1
cuba	Cuba	1512	99.8	65.0	97.7	98.7	99.1	99.2	52.1	47.0	0.9	100,633	B	0	0	7	-1
cypr	Cyprus	46	100.0	99.5	99.8	99.8	99.8	99.9	99.0	0.8	0.2	1,086	C	1	1	-2	-1
czec	Czech Republic	828	99.8	95.0	99.0	99.3	99.4	99.7	56.1	43.3	0.6	59,480	B	1	0	18	1
denm	Denmark	826	100.0	100.0	99.4	99.3	99.2	98.7	98.3	0.9	0.8	41,131	C	2	0	-3	0
djib	Djibouti	1862	5.0	35.0	40.0	43.0	45.8	51.3	9.0	36.8	54.2	345,336	A	0	0	-8	-2
domi	Dominica	1642	100.0	99.9	99.9	99.9	99.9	99.9	99.0	0.9	0.1	62	C	0	0	-2	1
domr	Dominican Republic	1494	99.8	99.9	99.9	99.9	99.9	99.9	99.7	0.2	0.1	6,278	C	0	0	-1	0
ecua	Ecuador	1526	90.0	99.3	99.5	99.5	99.4	99.3	99.1	0.3	0.6	71,415	C	1	0	-1	1
egyp	Egypt	30	34.0	48.0	73.0	75.1	77.7	81.2	22.5	55.2	22.4	15,303,820	B	9	11	-5	0
elsa	El Salvador	1525	99.5	99.8	99.9	99.9	99.9	99.9	99.7	0.2	0.1	6,319	C	0	0	-1	1
equa	Equatorial Guinea	1445	16.7	96.0	98.3	98.4	98.6	98.9	95.4	3.2	1.4	6,462	C	0	1	1	0
erit	Eritrea	c340	35.0	68.0	70.3	71.8	73.6	77.6	57.5	16.1	26.4	1,017,551	B	0	1	1	1
esto	Estonia	c125	99.8	90.0	93.6	96.1	98.1	98.6	47.1	51.0	1.9	26,919	B	0	3	11	1
ethi	Ethiopia	332	51.0	76.0	81.1	83.0	84.5	89.6	58.7	25.8	15.5	9,707,024	B	1	5	3	0
faer	Faeroe Islands	c750	100.0	100.0	100.0	99.9	99.9	99.9	99.9	0.0	0.1	30	C	0	0	-1	0
fiji	Fiji	1804	95.0	75.0	84.4	86.1	88.8	90.9	62.4	26.4	11.2	91,621	B	0	1	-1	1
finl	Finland	c110	100.0	99.9	99.8	99.7	99.7	99.5	98.5	1.2	0.3	14,982	C	0	0	-2	0
fran	France	c80	99.9	98.0	96.4	96.4	96.3	95.1	79.1	17.2	3.7	2,188,393	C	19	0	-4	0
freg	French Guiana	1598	97.1	97.5	98.2	98.5	98.8	99.0	90.5	8.3	1.2	2,240	C	0	1	-2	1
frep	French Polynesia	1659	99.9	98.0	98.5	98.6	98.6	98.8	91.0	7.6	1.4	3,191	C	0	0	-2	0
gabo	Gabon	1673	23.0	97.0	97.8	97.9	98.1	98.5	94.1	4.0	1.9	23,478	C	0	0	-1	1
gamb	Gambia	1651	17.0	25.0	39.1	42.4	44.1	53.5	8.8	35.3	55.9	730,102	A	0	3	-1	-1
geor	Georgia	c500	95.9	65.0	87.9	88.2	88.6	91.1	69.5	19.1	11.4	565,806	C	0	10	8	1
germ	Germany	c90	99.7	96.0	97.2	97.3	97.6	97.2	81.1	16.5	2.4	1,942,922	C	31	0	-3	0
ghan	Ghana	1471	23.0	70.0	82.6	83.4	84.6	89.2	51.8	32.8	15.4	3,106,004	B	0	0	8	1
gibr	Gibraltar	1309	99.9	94.0	94.6	94.6	94.6	94.4	88.0	6.6	5.4	1,359	C	0	0	-4	0
gree	Greece	c40	93.4	99.0	98.5	98.5	98.4	98.0	96.6	1.8	1.6	165,750	C	8	0	-1	0
grel	Greenland	c990	97.4	99.8	99.7	99.7	99.7	99.6	80.1	19.6	0.3	166	C	0	0	-1	0
gren	Grenada	c165	99.9	99.9	100.0	100.0	100.0	100.0	99.2	0.8	0.0	28	C	0	0	-1	0
guad	Guadeloupe	1523	99.8	99.8	99.9	99.9	99.9	99.9	99.3	0.6	0.1	434	C	0	0	-1	1
guam	Guam	1668	100.0	99.7	99.2	99.0	99.0	98.6	97.3	1.7	1.0	1,708	C	0	0	0	1
guat	Guatemala	1524	99.9	99.9	99.9	99.9	99.9	100.0	98.7	1.2	0.1	7,929	C	0	0	-1	1
guin	Guinea	1877	6.6	12.0	35.7	38.5	41.6	45.6	7.8	33.8	58.4	4,337,014	A	0	5	17	-1
gunb	Guinea-Bissau	1445	7.5	29.9	45.0	46.6	48.2	52.2	19.9	28.3	51.8	628,702	A	0	0	15	-1
guya	Guyana	1548	61.8	75.0	76.1	78.9	81.3	85.7	51.9	29.4	18.8	161,535	B	0	1	-5	0
hait	Haiti	1493	100.0	99.9	99.9	99.9	99.9	99.9	99.9	0.0	0.1	5,934	C	0	0	-1	0
hond	Honduras	1524	99.0	99.9	99.9	99.9	99.9	99.9	99.6	0.3	0.1	6,422	C	0	0	-1	1
hung	Hungary	c250	99.8	94.0	99.2	99.2	99.4	99.4	96.9	2.5	0.7	65,545	C	1	1	4	1
icel	Iceland	c740	100.0	99.9	100.0	100.0	100.0	99.9	99.7	0.3	0.1	154	C	0	0	-1	0
indi	India	c52	15.0	35.1	53.0	56.6	59.3	66.2	12.5	46.8	40.7	412,122,495	B	15	32	20	2
indo	Indonesia	c650	24.0	50.0	56.5	59.3	62.9	68.9	18.6	44.3	37.2	78,805,877	B	3	33	20	1
iran	Iran	c50	13.0	25.0	31.6	34.5	37.2	44.4	3.3	33.9	62.8	42,507,292	A	0	31	22	-1
iraq	Iraq	c50	22.0	30.0	42.5	45.0	48.4	56.1	7.8	40.6	51.6	11,916,962	A	0	4	-3	-2
irel	Ireland	350	100.0	99.8	99.8	99.8	99.7	99.7	98.6	1.1	0.3	10,277	C	8	0	-1	1
isle	Isle of Man	442	99.9	99.9	99.7	99.7	99.6	99.5	76.2	23.4	0.4	292	C	0	0	-4	0
isra	Israel	30	23.8	40.0	52.2	54.6	56.0	68.2	10.7	45.3	44.0	2,252,726	B	8	9	19	-1
ital	Italy	30	100.0	99.5	99.3	99.3	99.2	98.7	91.8	7.4	0.8	436,987	C	39	2	-3	0
ivor	Ivory Coast	1637	5.0	50.0	66.9	69.3	72.8	78.6	37.2	35.6	27.3	4,029,608	B	0	1	9	1
jama	Jamaica	1509	99.9	98.0	98.7	98.8	98.9	99.0	52.5	46.4	1.1	27,592	B	2	0	-4	0
japa	Japan	1549	20.0	40.0	62.0	65.0	66.9	75.2	8.7	58.2	33.1	41,890,821	B	6	0	15	0
jord	Jordan	30	16.0	35.0	48.1	51.2	54.3	63.5	9.6	44.7	45.8	3,051,282	B	1	2	29	1
kaza	Kazakhstan	c400	14.3	40.0	59.0	61.0	64.3	68.9	21.3	43.0	35.8	5,799,212	B	0	18	-7	-1
keny	Kenya	1498	6.9	85.0	93.0	93.6	94.2	96.2	83.5	10.7	5.8	1,742,085	C	8	6	3	1
kirg	Kirghizia	c500	10.3	25.0	40.8	45.3	47.4	52.4	13.7	33.7	52.6	2,473,100	A	0	19	-29	-1
kiri	Kiribati	1837	100.0	99.9	99.9	99.9	99.9	99.9	99.8	0.1	0.1	60	C	0	0	-2	0
kuwa	Kuwait	c155	6.7	34.8	50.0	55.0	64.5	68.1	19.0	45.5	35.5	700,639	B	0	1	9	1
laos	Laos	1630	4.0	30.0	43.4	45.5	47.6	49.8	7.5	40.1	52.5	2,849,470	A	0	1	18	-2
latv	Latvia	1185	99.9	94.0	98.7	98.9	99.0	99.4	76.8	22.2	1.0	22,603	C	1	5	16	1
leba	Lebanon	30	82.0	80.0	89.2	90.3	91.9	93.2	62.0	29.9	8.1	266,666	B	0	0	-4	-1
leso	Lesotho	1833	29.5	97.9	99.6	99.6	99.6	99.5	77.1	22.5	0.4	8,139	C	0	0	3	1
libe	Liberia	1822	27.1	45.1	69.8	71.3	72.5	76.7	37.9	34.6	27.5	867,108	B	0	0	10	0
liby	Libya	30	6.3	13.9	43.4	45.0	46.1	49.1	7.9	38.2	53.9	3,019,596	A	0	7	8	-2
liec	Liechtenstein	c450	100.0	99.9	98.8	98.6	98.4	98.1	92.3	6.1	1.6	538	C	0	1	-3	0
lith	Lithuania	1251	100.0	94.9	99.5	99.5	99.6	99.6	96.2	3.4	0.4	14,620	C	0	5	6	1
luxe	Luxembourg	c250	100.0	99.7	99.5	99.3	99.1	98.9	98.5	0.6	0.9	3,931	C	0	0	-1	0
mace	Macedonia	60	95.0	91.0	87.1	87.5	88.1	88.9	72.6	15.5	12.0	241,781	C	0	0	-3	1
mada	Madagascar	1540	55.0	75.0	79.4	80.9	83.0	86.2	56.8	26.2	17.0	2,712,337	B	0	2	5	1
mala	Malawi	1561	16.9	85.0	95.1	95.3	96.1	97.5	74.1	22.0	4.0	431,511	C	2	2	3	1
malb	Malaysia	1511	11.9	40.0	57.7	59.1	63.7	70.9	14.3	49.4	36.3	8,081,332	B	0	9	19	0

COUNTRY		EVANGELIZATION												STRATEGIES		FUTURES	
		when begun	status of evangelization, E						source of E		unevangelized						
code	short name	year begun	1900	1970	1990	1995	2000	2025	internal	external	U	total	world	plans	target	growth	prospect
1	2	152	153	154	155	156	157	158	159	160	161	162	163	164	165	166	167
mald	Maldives	1887	0.0	8.7	19.0	19.3	19.6	21.2	3.2	16.4	80.4	230,137	A	0	1	24	-2
mali	Mali	1895	3.9	25.0	40.1	42.0	43.6	49.8	7.2	36.4	56.4	6,340,283	A	0	10	11	-1
malt	Malta	60	100.0	100.0	100.0	100.0	99.9	99.9	99.2	0.7	0.1	220	C	1	0	-1	1
mars	Marshall Islands	1857	78.0	98.7	99.9	99.9	99.9	100.0	99.0	0.9	0.1	42	C	0	0	0	0
mart	Martinique	c155	100.0	99.9	99.9	99.9	99.9	99.8	99.2	0.7	0.1	507	C	0	0	-1	0
maur	Mauritania	1448	1.0	8.0	26.5	29.2	31.9	37.1	1.6	30.3	68.1	1,818,258	A	0	13	-35	-2
maus	Mauritius	1598	44.4	64.8	69.2	71.0	74.9	80.4	38.7	36.2	25.1	290,720	B	0	0	9	-1
mayo	Mayotte	1517	1.0	20.0	35.0	37.5	40.7	46.5	5.0	35.7	59.3	60,252	A	0	2	20	-2
mexi	Mexico	1518	99.8	99.8	99.8	99.8	99.9	99.9	99.3	0.6	0.2	147,917	C	3	0	-1	1
micr	Micronesia	1668	90.0	99.5	99.5	99.5	99.6	99.6	97.0	2.6	0.4	441	C	0	0	0	0
mold	Moldavia	c300	99.9	90.0	93.0	93.7	94.2	95.7	73.5	20.7	5.8	252,923	C	0	5	19	1
mona	Monaco	c100	99.9	99.8	99.0	98.9	98.8	98.8	96.6	2.2	1.2	392	C	0	0	-2	0
mong	Mongolia	c650	3.8	16.0	32.3	36.5	42.8	49.0	6.8	36.0	57.2	1,522,030	A	1	2	33	1
mont	Montserrat	1632	100.0	99.9	99.9	99.9	99.9	99.9	99.4	0.5	0.1	7	C	0	0	-2	0
moro	Morocco	c150	7.7	28.0	40.1	41.5	42.2	47.6	5.0	37.2	57.8	16,314,645	A	0	8	4	-1
moza	Mozambique	1506	11.0	60.0	73.0	75.0	77.0	82.0	41.6	35.4	23.0	4,521,300	B	0	2	11	1
myan	Myanmar	c920	19.6	35.0	53.1	56.9	60.9	69.0	14.0	46.9	39.1	17,852,271	B	0	3	33	1
nami	Namibia	1805	13.4	97.0	97.6	97.7	97.7	97.9	87.5	10.2	2.3	39,161	C	0	0	-2	1
naur	Nauru	1888	50.0	90.0	95.0	95.5	96.4	96.6	81.6	14.8	3.6	410	C	0	0	-2	0
nepa	Nepal	1715	0.0	23.8	37.9	42.2	46.2	52.4	7.7	38.5	53.8	12,866,777	A	0	45	66	2
neth	Netherlands	c650	99.5	98.0	97.7	97.7	97.6	96.9	74.9	22.7	2.4	373,557	C	12	0	-4	-1
nets	Netherlands Antilles	c155	100.0	99.8	99.4	99.3	99.3	98.8	95.2	4.1	0.7	1,547	C	0	0	-1	0
newc	New Caledonia	1831	79.9	99.5	98.8	98.7	98.6	98.3	84.5	14.1	1.4	2,965	C	0	0	-2	0
newz	New Zealand	1785	99.8	99.5	99.1	99.1	99.1	98.5	76.2	22.9	0.9	35,988	C	0	0	-3	1
nica	Nicaragua	1517	99.0	99.9	99.9	99.9	99.9	99.8	99.0	0.9	0.1	7,125	C	1	1	-1	1
niga	Niger	c650	0.0	15.0	38.2	40.4	42.1	47.4	4.1	38.0	57.9	6,208,244	A	0	12	5	-1
nige	Nigeria	1487	16.7	57.8	75.2	77.3	79.8	84.6	52.1	27.7	20.2	22,559,535	B	9	7	2	1
nork	North Korea	c160	15.0	21.1	45.5	47.2	50.0	60.0	8.1	41.9	50.0	12,026,315	A	0	0	132	-2
norl	Northern Cyprus	46	4.3	20.1	50.6	53.3	56.0	63.9	15.1	40.9	44.0	81,374	B	0	0	4	0
norm	Northern Mariana Is	1668	80.0	99.5	98.6	98.8	98.9	99.0	91.9	7.0	1.1	836	C	0	0	-2	0
norw	Norway	c900	100.0	99.6	98.8	98.7	98.6	98.0	96.7	1.9	1.4	61,076	C	6	0	-2	0
oman	Oman	1508	0.0	13.0	40.6	43.9	47.0	55.2	9.9	37.1	53.0	1,347,866	A	0	4	22	-1
paki	Pakistan	c750	9.6	35.0	42.5	44.3	46.8	50.5	7.4	39.4	53.2	83,307,766	A	0	21	15	-1
pala	Palau	1891	84.4	99.9	99.9	99.9	99.9	99.9	99.2	0.7	0.1	11	C	0	0	-2	0
pale	Palestine	30	31.9	47.7	60.9	67.1	70.6	75.8	15.3	55.3	29.4	650,425	B	24	1	5	-1
pana	Panama	1513	99.0	98.5	98.4	98.4	98.4	97.5	92.7	5.7	1.7	47,114	C	0	0	-3	1
papu	Papua New Guinea	c180	17.0	95.0	97.5	97.5	97.5	98.0	91.7	5.8	2.5	113,957	C	0	0	1	1
para	Paraguay	1524	98.0	99.5	99.8	99.8	99.8	99.8	98.9	0.9	0.2	10,063	C	0	0	0	1
peru	Peru	1532	97.0	99.0	99.7	99.7	99.7	99.7	99.0	0.7	0.3	68,433	C	3	2	-1	1
phil	Philippines	1521	93.0	97.0	94.6	94.5	94.4	94.6	90.7	3.7	5.6	4,222,787	C	6	2	-1	2
pola	Poland	c950	99.0	98.0	99.9	99.9	100.0	100.0	99.8	0.2	0.0	16,713	C	0	1	1	2
port	Portugal	c150	100.0	99.5	99.6	99.6	99.6	99.5	98.8	0.8	0.4	35,999	C	0	0	-2	0
puer	Puerto Rico	1509	100.0	99.8	99.9	99.9	99.9	99.9	99.4	0.5	0.1	3,864	C	0	0	-1	0
qata	Qatar	c210	2.0	34.8	48.5	54.7	56.4	61.5	15.9	40.5	43.6	261,389	B	0	1	16	-1
reun	Reunion	1649	60.0	98.5	97.4	97.3	97.2	96.9	92.6	4.6	2.8	19,656	C	0	0	-3	-1
roma	Romania	c100	99.0	95.0	99.1	99.2	99.3	99.3	97.8	1.5	0.7	162,918	C	1	1	3	2
russ	Russia	c35	90.1	85.0	91.0	92.2	93.3	95.3	66.3	27.0	6.8	9,923,477	B	3	32	21	2
rwan	Rwanda	1889	0.2	90.0	98.2	98.4	98.9	99.0	91.7	7.2	1.1	88,387	C	0	1	5	-1
saha	Sahara	c200	4.0	49.0	20.0	23.0	24.6	31.9	2.3	22.3	75.4	221,118	A	0	6	-10	-2
saih	Saint Helena	1561	100.0	99.9	99.9	99.9	99.9	99.8	94.7	5.2	0.1	9	C	0	0	-1	1
saik	Saint Kitts & Nevis	1623	100.0	100.0	100.0	99.9	99.9	99.8	98.1	1.8	0.1	28	C	0	0	-2	0
sail	Saint Lucia	1648	99.8	99.8	99.1	99.1	99.0	98.8	98.4	0.6	1.0	1,573	C	0	0	-1	0
saip	Saint Pierre & Miquelon	1604	100.0	100.0	100.0	100.0	99.9	99.9	99.7	0.2	0.1	4	C	0	0	-2	1
saiv	Saint Vincent	c165	99.9	99.8	98.9	98.9	98.8	97.9	78.6	20.2	1.2	1,389	C	0	0	-5	0
samo	Samoa	1827	100.0	99.9	99.9	99.9	99.9	99.9	99.7	0.2	0.1	113	C	1	0	-1	1
sanm	San Marino	441	100.0	99.8	99.9	99.9	99.9	99.8	99.3	0.6	0.1	31	C	0	0	-2	0
saot	Sao Tome & Principe	1485	14.0	99.5	99.9	99.9	99.9	99.9	99.3	0.6	0.1	142	C	0	0	-1	-1
saud	Saudi Arabia	100	2.0	18.0	40.0	46.3	54.9	62.5	8.9	46.0	45.1	9,735,310	B	0	4	29	-2
sene	Senegal	1445	10.0	35.0	42.8	44.2	46.0	49.9	9.0	37.0	54.0	5,118,446	A	0	6	13	-1
seyc	Seychelles	1742	99.9	99.9	99.6	99.6	99.6	99.5	98.6	1.0	0.5	348	C	0	1	-1	-1
sier	Sierra Leone	1785	17.6	50.0	54.9	56.4	59.2	62.9	17.5	41.7	40.8	1,981,739	B	0	0	16	-2
sing	Singapore	1511	20.0	48.1	65.2	69.6	72.7	78.4	18.2	54.5	27.3	974,057	B	12	1	29	2
slok	Slovakia	828	99.0	95.0	98.8	99.4	99.5	99.6	90.3	9.2	0.5	25,349	C	0	0	3	1
slov	Slovenia	c550	100.0	96.0	99.8	99.8	99.8	99.9	97.5	2.3	0.2	3,933	C	0	0	2	1
solo	Solomon Islands	1845	24.0	99.5	99.8	99.8	99.9	99.9	97.5	2.4	0.1	471	C	0	0	1	1
soma	Somalia	1881	1.0	5.8	33.0	38.3	43.8	46.2	4.9	38.9	56.2	4,080,364	A	0	11	-47	-2
somi	Somaliland	c189	0.0	10.0	40.0	42.0	44.7	47.8	3.3	41.4	55.3	1,566,720	A	0	1	0	-2
soua	South Africa	1501	52.0	94.9	97.7	97.8	98.1	97.5	87.3	10.8	1.9	781,832	C	0	1	0	1
souk	South Korea	1592	16.0	85.0	98.4	98.6	98.8	99.0	48.8	50.0	1.2	560,817	B	0	0	6	2
spai	Spain	63	100.0	99.8	99.7	99.7	99.7	99.5	99.3	0.4	0.3	125,103	C	11	1	-2	1
span	Spanish North Africa	c400	97.0	95.0	93.7	93.4	93.4	92.1	85.0	8.4	6.6	8,550	C	0	0	-4	0
sril	Sri Lanka	c100	30.0	48.0	60.0	62.0	64.6	70.0	15.4	49.2	35.4	6,670,591	B	0	3	1	-1
suda	Sudan	34	4.0	25.0	49.0	52.0	53.8	60.9	22.1	31.7	46.2	13,620,937	B	0	65	10	-2
suri	Suriname	1580	57.9	75.0	83.5	83.6	83.8	88.6	50.2	33.6	16.2	67,699	B	0	1	4	1
swaz	Swaziland	1825	10.0	95.0	99.3	99.3	99.4	99.6	77.5	21.9	0.6	6,491	C	0	0	3	1
swed	Sweden	829	99.9	99.8	98.6	98.5	98.4	97.8	77.1	21.3	1.6	140,311	C	5	0	-2	1
swit	Switzerland	c200	100.0	99.9	98.4	98.3	98.2	97.5	95.1	3.1	1.8	130,557	C	21	0	-2	1
syri	Syria	30	37.1	46.0	57.5	60.0	62.2	68.8	14.4	47.8	37.8	6,092,966	B	6	0	-1	0
taiw	Taiwan	1621	12.5	40.0	65.0	67.0	68.9	76.7	11.5	57.4	31.2	6,977,716	B	1	2	5	1
taji	Tajikistan	c400	2.0	23.5	39.0	42.0	44.1	49.2	5.5	38.6	55.9	3,457,770	A	0	18	-33	-2
tanz	Tanzania	1502	18.4	60.0	76.4	79.5	81.4	87.1	55.4	26.0	18.6	6,227,819	B	0	2	11	1
thai	Thailand	1554	13.9	35.0	51.8	54.5	56.8	65.6	7.9	48.9	43.2	26,509,177	B	4	4	9	1
timo	Timor	1511	20.8	42.0	98.0	98.4	98.8	99.1	95.4	3.4	1.2	10,692	C	0	0	3	0
togo	Togo	c186	9.6	56.0	71.8	73.9	75.8	81.1	46.7	29.1	24.2	1,118,285	B	0	0	15	1
tong	Tonga	1797	100.0	100.0	99.9	99.9	99.9	99.9	99.5	0.4	0.1	91	C	0	0	-2	0
trin	Trinidad & Tobago	1513	90.0	82.0	89.3	90.5	91.6	93.3	70.9	20.7	8.5	109,423	C	0	0	-7	0
tuni	Tunisia	c80	18.0	25.0	43.6	47.0	48.9	55.6	5.0	43.9	51.1	4,897,282	A	2	9	16	-1
turk	Turkey	c33	46.1	20.0	41.0	45.8	48.6	54.3	4.3	44.3	51.4	34,243,536	A	1	13	-12	-1
turm	Turkmenistan	c600	6.1	20.1	29.1	32.9	34.5	39.6	5.2	29.3	65.5	2,918,902	A	0	16	-35	-2
turs	Turks & Caicos Is	c175	100.0	100.0	99.7	99.8	99.8	99.8	89.1	10.7	0.2	35	C	0	0	-1	0
tuva	Tuvalu	1861	100.0	100.0	99.9	99.9	99.8	99.9	93.1	6.7	0.2	20	C	0	0	-2	0
ugan	Uganda	1875	23.8	92.0	98.5	98.7	99.1	99.5	93.8	5.3	0.9	195,502	C	0	2	4	1
ukra	Ukraine	c35	99.8	90.0	98.0	98.2	98.5	98.8	92.5	6.0	1.5	752,837	C	0	13	6	2
unia	United Arab Emirates	1892	1.0	24.7	50.6	54.8	57.9	63.5	16.9	41.0	42.1	1,028,415	B	0	1	7	1
usa	USA	1526	99.9	99.5	98.6	98.6	98.5	97.8	78.7	19.8	1.5	4,084,367	C	329	1	-5	1
uuay	Uruguay	1616	89.1	95.0	98.4	98.6	98.7	99.0	74.6	24.1	1.3	43,093	C	0	0	-1	0
uzbe	Uzbekistan	c400	6.8	20.0	38.0	44.0	48.4	54.0	6.2	42.2	51.6	12,558,682	A	0	23	-31	-1
vanu	Vanuatu	1830	39.0	94.0	99.0	99.2	99.3	99.4	96.1	3.2	0.7	1,304	C	0	0	2	0
vene	Venezuela	1513	97.1	99.0	99.3	99.3	99.4	99.5	97.9	1.5	0.6	149,477	C	3	1	-1	1
viet	Viet Nam	1530	26.8	52.0	60.0	63.0	66.8	74.9	15.2	51.6	33.2	26,516,153	B	0	0	27	1
virg	Virgin Is of the US	1648	100.0	100.0	99.7	99.6	99.6	99.5	96.6	3.0	0.4	390	C	0	0	-2	0
wall	Wallis & Futuna Is	1836	98.0	99.5	99.9	100.0	100.0	99.9	99.8	0.2	0.0	5	C	0	0	0	0
yeme	Yemen	c350	4.9	20.0	37.0	43.0	46.6	53.1	3.3	43.3	53.4	9,673,610	A	0	2	-8	-1
yugo	Yugoslavia	c60	94.8	87.6	91.2	92.2	93.4	96.1	74.3	19.1	6.6	702,914	C	1	0	7	1
zamb	Zambia	1885	2.7	90.0	97.8	98.4	98.8	99.2	86.7	12.1	1.2	113,566	C	0	0	7	1
zimb	Zimbabwe	1561	16.0	94.0	97.4	97.8	98.2	99.2	69.1	29.1	1.8	207,516	B	1	0	10	1
	11 minicountries	40	88.7	90.9	90.6	91.1	91.7	93.2	68.7	23.0	8.3	1,924	C	1	1	-3	0
	Africa	30	20.6	60.8	74.0	75.8	77.5	81.4	49.9	27.6	22.5	176,794,822	B	35	278	5	0
	Antarctica	1958	0.0	90.0	93.9	94.4	94.6	96.5	85.6	9.0	5.4	243	C	0	0	6	0
	Asia	30	18.3	32.2	53.7	57.0	61.3	66.7	14.4	46.9	38.7	1,423,824,293	B	96	447	22	1
	Europe	30	97.6	93.9	96.3	96.7	97.1	97.2	82.4	14.7	2.9	21,474,187	C	266	78	4	1
	Latin America	1493	97.3	98.3	99.5	99.6	99.6	99.6	97.2	2.4	0.4	1,944,600	C	26	11	-1	1
	Northern America	990	99.8	99.5	98.5	98.5	98.5	97.6	78.3	20.2	1.5	4,773,514	C	340	2	-5	1
	Oceania	1659	82.1	98.3	98.2	98.1	98.1	97.8	79.8	18.4	1.9	563,298	C	7	2	-3	0
	World A	**30**	**14.7**	**25.2**	**39.2**	**42.1**	**44.8**	**50.1**	**5.9**	**38.9**	**55.2**	**334,256,241**	**A**	**6**	**382**	**13**	**-1**
	World B	**30**	**24.2**	**37.7**	**58.7**	**61.9**	**66.2**	**72.1**	**19.8**	**46.4**	**33.8**	**1,269,343,426**	**B**	**114**	**348**	**21**	**2**
	World C	**30**	**94.6**	**97.4**	**98.3**	**98.4**	**98.5**	**98.4**	**89.4**	**9.1**	**1.5**	**25,775,290**	**C**	**650**	**88**	**-1**	**1**
	GLOBAL TOTAL	**30**	**45.7**	**55.6**	**68.4**	**70.4**	**73.1**	**76.4**	**37.9**	**35.2**	**26.9**	**1,629,374,957**	**B**	**770**	**818**	**14**	**1**

SOME TECHNICAL NOTES ON SOURCES, STATISTICS, AND CONCILIARISM

CATHOLIC STATISTICS

In Part 4's Country Tables 2, columns 5-10, and in Part 5's columns 69-74, and numerous other places this Encyclopedia attempts to present variables giving precisely comparable data for Roman Catholics, Orthodox, Anglicans, Protestants, Independents, and marginal Christians. Figures for these megablocs are shown to total exactly to country, continental, and global figures. Likewise, values for Roman Catholic dioceses in most cases total exactly in our Country Tables 2 to the totals for the countrywide Catholic Church. However, in several cases local complexities may prevent this, for a variety of internal reasons.

Country totaling of Roman Catholic dioceses. Roman Catholic statistics are compiled each year at parish level and then are totaled at diocesan level. These diocesan figures are eventually reported year by year in *Annuario Pontificio (AP)* for every diocese, but without country totals in that publication. Totals for each country are then agglomerated, and the resulting national totals for all dioceses and jurisdictions are published each year, firstly in national Catholic yearbooks, and then secondly in the Vatican's official *Annuarium Statisticum Ecclesiae (ASE, Statistical yearbook of the Church)* published every two years, which then gives, definitively, totals at country level, at continental level, and at global level.

Unfortunately, these official publications do not all agree in their listings and totals of all Roman Catholic dioceses and jurisdictions. For many countries, totals derived from dioceses and jurisdictions in *AP* differ, often markedly, from country totals in *ASE*. Various explanations can be advanced, as follows.

Varying dates, methods. Due to divergent census dates (dates of counting or reporting) differing methods of compilation, or different definitions, or varying ways of measurement and counting, totals for all dioceses in a country often display differences at country level.

De jure or de facto. Some parishes and hence dioceses report Catholics who are present in the diocese *de facto*, either as transients, visitors, refugees, illegal immigrants, military of one's own country, or alien military. Other parishes and dioceses may not include such persons, reporting only *de jure* Catholics as understood by local clergy which means those on parish lists in good standing. In horrific situations of social turmoil, or even genocide (such as in Rwanda, Cambodia, Bosnia, Kosovo, Chechnia), uniform counting methods are impracticable or even impossible.

There is also the problem of disaffiliation, which refers to baptized Catholics still on the church's rolls but who individually regard themselves as atheists, agnostics, communists, secularists, or other varieties of non-Christians; or, of course, persons who have recently died or been killed.

Overlap. Listing and variables are not all mutually exclusive but often overlap, duplicating a number of persons involved. One example concerns priests and brothers. In Country Tables 2, column 10 contains the variable n = number of diocesan priests (who are almost always citizens), also x = number of religious priests (in mission countries, usually foreigners). A third variable, m, might appear to be unordained men layworkers (as is the case with m in Protestant or Independent denominations), but in Roman Catholic usage m = members of male religious orders which means unordained religious brothers plus the religious priests already enumerated as x. This distinction is clear to knowledgeable officials but may not be clear to laypersons or non-Catholics or government officials involved at any stage.

Inclusion or exclusion of nondiocesan staff. Although Catholic statistics attempt to be complete within a diocese or country, in numerous cases ordained and/or lay Catholic workers are employed in a diocese's geographical area but are not recorded in diocesan totals (for example, priests in university, ecumenical, relief, medical, broadcasting, UN, other secular or diplomatic posts). This Encyclopedia includes all such full-time workers on specifically church or Christian ministries.

Double counting can be observed to take place in rapidly expanding Catholic missions. When a huge diocese divides off several smaller daughter dioceses, comparison of total Catholics reported in *AP* before and after makes it clear that for 2 or 3 years large numbers of Catholics are being officially claimed (in *AP*) by both the parent diocese and the daughter dioceses.

Differing definitions of 'affiliated Christians'. Other problems arise in any attempt to compare Catholic members with Anglicans, Protestants, or other non-Catholics. In official Roman Catholic usage, 'Catholics' means baptized persons only, excluding catechumens. In this Encyclopedia, however, catechumens (whose catechumente may last only one or 2 months) are always counted with baptized persons as 'affiliated' church members. Thus the definition of 'affiliated Catholics' in Country Tables 2 columns 7 and 8 includes both *baptized* Catholics (adults and children) and also *catechumens.* This is particularly important for those rapidly-growing Catholic dioceses in Africa where there are actually more enrolled catechumens than enrolled baptized Catholics.

All of this means that figures in the tables of a country's Roman Catholic dioceses may not always add up to the country totals shown either here or in *ASE.* The figures given attempt to reconcile these conflicting factors and to provide figures directly comparable to Anglican, Protestant, and Independent statistics. Readers wanting exact Catholic numbers on Catholic definitions should get them from the 2 source yearbooks described above.

CONCILIARISM

In Part 4, Country Tables 2 have a column 4 headed 'Councils' describing the extent of conciliarism which describes for every denomination (Protestant, Catholic, Anglican, Orthodox, Independent) or diocese its conciliar links at 5 levels: confessional, global, continental, regional, national. This part of the World Christian Database is a long-term compilation begun in 1970 and still in process. At present it is therefore incomplete. A much more complete version will be available on the CD *World Christian database* and subsequent revisions.

Part 6

ATLAS

A mini-atlas of human environment, Christianity, and ministries in the global context

The light of Christ illuminates the whole world.
—Liturgy of the Presanctified, Byzantine rite, AD 692

CONTENTS OF PART 6 "ATLAS"

This mini-atlas is divided into 2 sections: an 8-page section with 16 global religious maps, and a 16-page section with 18 secular politico-geographical human environment maps.

A. Global Christianity and world ministries

The data on which Global Maps 1-16 are based come from Country Tables 1 and 2 in Part 4, from Table 5-1, and from other parts of this Encyclopedia. Taken in conjunction with Maps 1-18 below, they contribute to the subject known as the geography of religion, and in particular the geography of Christianity, and the geography of missions. Note that the Global Maps are meant to illustrate only the subjects in the titles; to keep them uncluttered, no names of countries are added except the Top Ten in Global Map 15. For country details, the reader should consult Maps 1-18. Note also that the unit used on these maps is the country—every country is given a single color in each Global Map, corresponding to its value of the variable being depicted. Note carefully that the situation of many countries is fluid, often very fluid, which means that some countries slip into or out of the colored categories, or their exact numerical state, as the months go by. This means that the Global Maps and their colors should be viewed as visual aids, an impressionistic portrait rather than a precise photograph.

B. The modern world: human environment and activity

The 18 maps in this section describe the modern world which forms the context for global Christianity. They are intended to illustrate each country's article and text in Part 4. They are arranged not geographically but chronologically, in approximately the order of the worldwide expansion of Christianity by continents and regions, beginning with the cradle region of the Middle East. All countries are shown except the smaller Pacific islands. In the listing below, after each region a typical or representative country is named for illustrative purposes, followed by the date of the definitive coming of Christianity.

Key to Human Environment maps
These maps portray the secular context for the study of religion. For each country the following 22 subject areas have been quantified and/or depicted (see each map's small key for more detail): topographical features (heights in meters), political boundaries (state and internal), vegetation (forest to desert), land usage (farming, paddy, irrigation), rural population density (4 levels of brown shading), metropolises and cities (each with impressionistic yellow population blocs), motorways, railways, shipping routes, ports, shipping (5 sizes, largest over 70 million tonnage p.a.), airports, air traffic (10 levels, with highest level 10 = over 1.5 million incoming flights p.a.), hydro-electric power stations (HEP), dams, canals, and mining (extraction of 14 major minerals).

Additional secular and religious country variables .

A large number of additional variables describing countries can be found in 2 parallel atlases. For religious data, *The state of religion atlas* (J. O'Brien, M. Palmer, D. B. Barrett, 1993) contains 34 world maps depicting world religions with a wide range of 100 newly–quantified variables. For secular data, *The new state of the world atlas* (M. Kidron, D. Smith, 6th edition 1999) has 50 world maps with a wealth of data on over 100 recently quantified variables (e.g. Map 27 'Human rights').

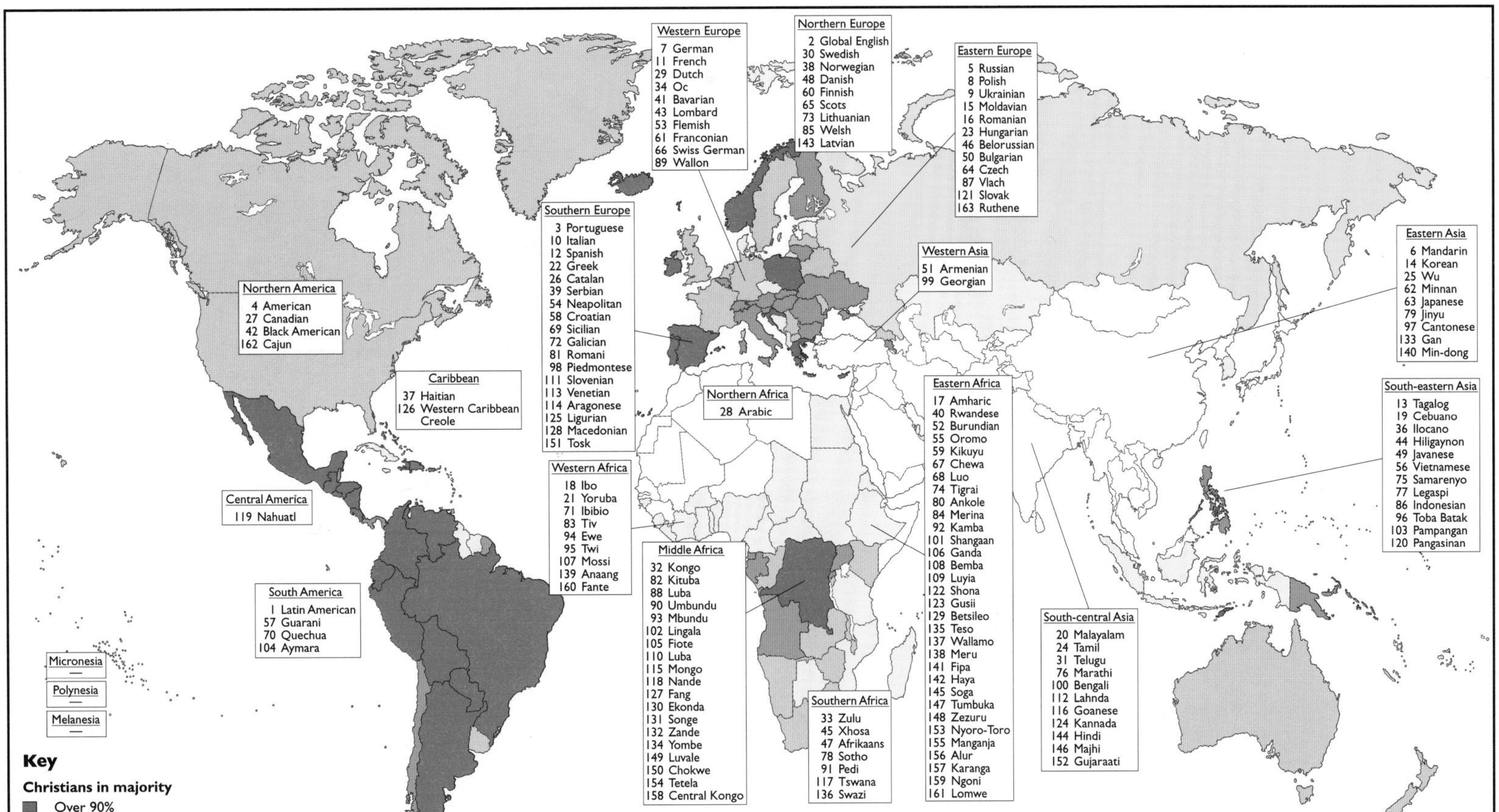

Global Map 1. Christians and million-Christian languages, AD 2000.

Colors = Christians (affiliated church members of all varieties) as per cent of country's population.
Names = languages each with over 1 million native (mother-tongue) speakers who are affiliated church members worldwide, ranked 1–163 in order of global size; each listed above only once, in the region with its epicenter.
Boxes = groupings of languages in size order, in each of the 22 United Nations' regions (4 having none).
Source of data: WCE Part 5, Table 5-1, column 66; Part 9 "LinguaMetrics", Table 9-13, columns 5 and 8.

Global Map 2. Growth of organized Christianity, per cent per year, AD 2000.

Net church growth for each country is measured by the annual growth rate of all affiliated church members there.
Source of data: Country Tables 1, column 'Rate', line 'affiliated'.

Key
- World A = the unevangelized world (countries with evangelized persons E<50%)
- World B = the evangelized non-Christian world (countries with E>=50% but Christians AC<60%)
- World C = the Christian world (countries with AC>=60%)

Global Map 3. Evangelization and christianization in Worlds A, B, and C countries, AD 1900.

Source of data: Country Tables 1, column 'AD 1900'.

Key
- World A = the unevangelized world (countries with evangelized persons E<50%)
- World B = the evangelized non-Christian world (countries with E>=50% but Christians AC<60%)
- World C = the Christian world (countries with AC>=60%)

Global Map 4. Evangelization and christianization in Worlds A, B, and C countries, AD 2000.

The 10/40 Window is a popularized version of World A not amenable to statistical data-gathering or analysis.
Source of data: Country Tables 1, column 'AD 2000'.

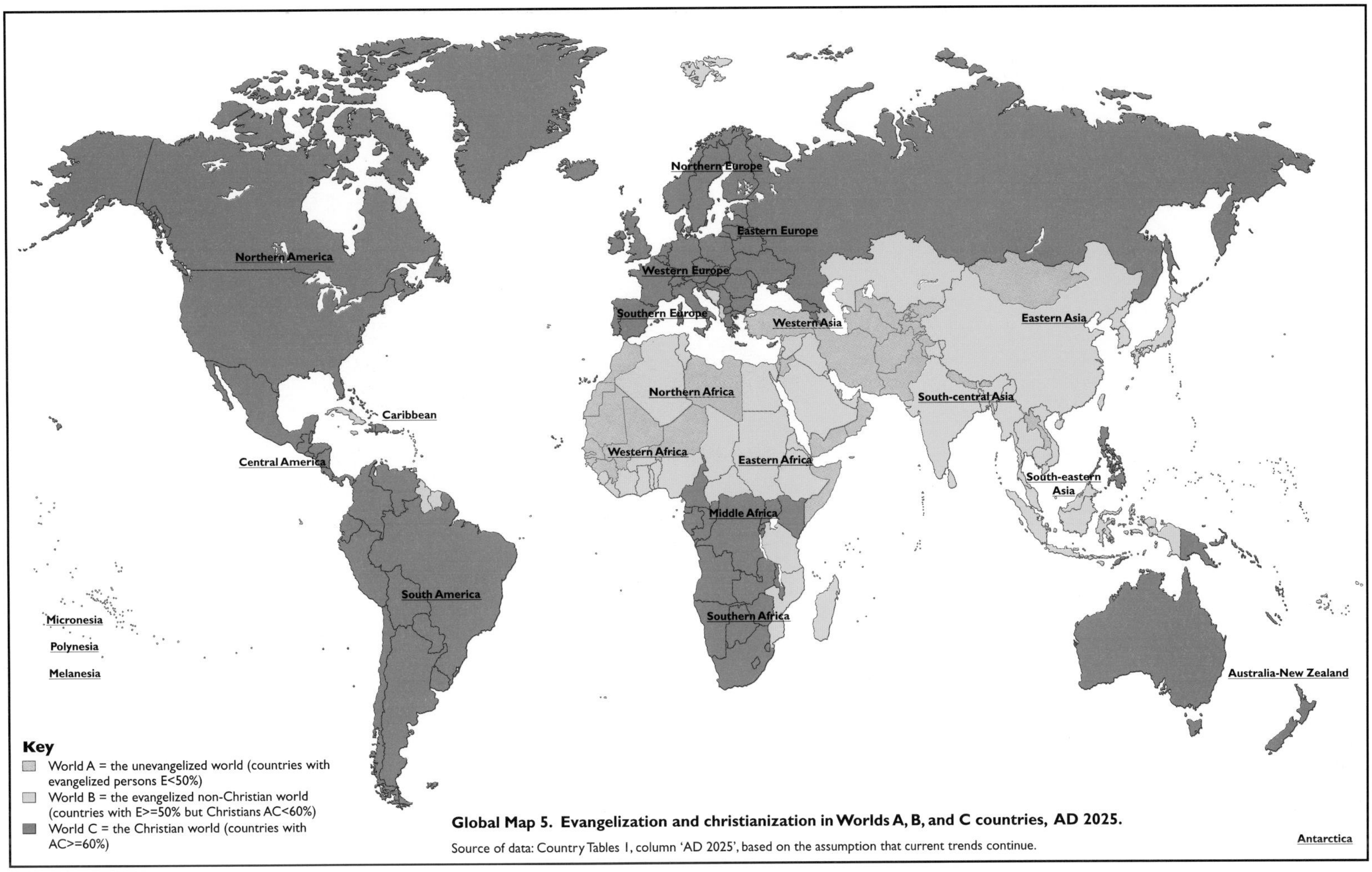

Global Map 5. Evangelization and christianization in Worlds A, B, and C countries, AD 2025.

Source of data: Country Tables 1, column 'AD 2025', based on the assumption that current trends continue.

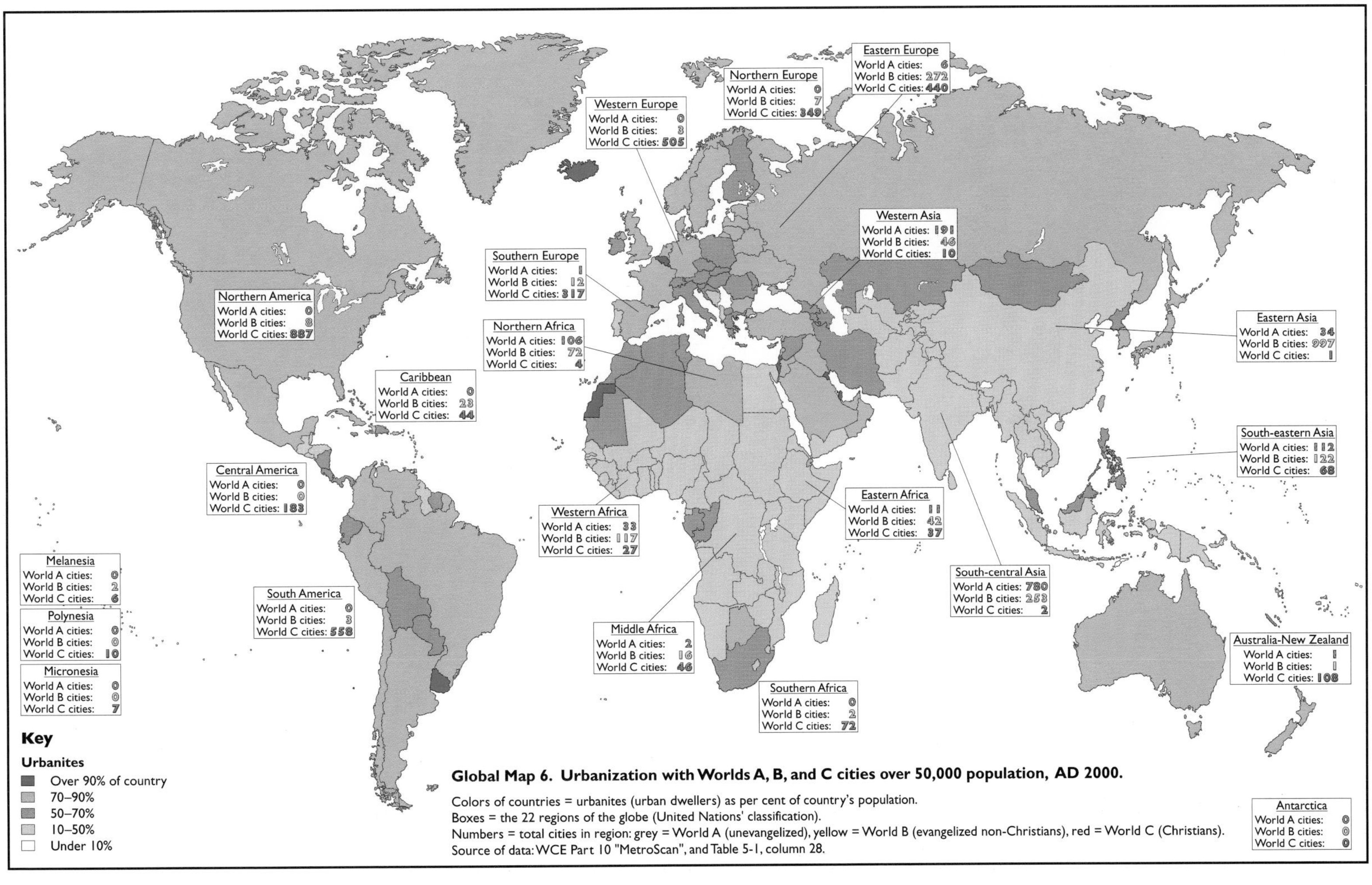

Global Map 6. Urbanization with Worlds A, B, and C cities over 50,000 population, AD 2000.

Colors of countries = urbanites (urban dwellers) as per cent of country's population.
Boxes = the 22 regions of the globe (United Nations' classification).
Numbers = total cities in region: grey = World A (unevangelized), yellow = World B (evangelized non-Christians), red = World C (Christians).
Source of data: WCE Part 10 "MetroScan", and Table 5-1, column 28.

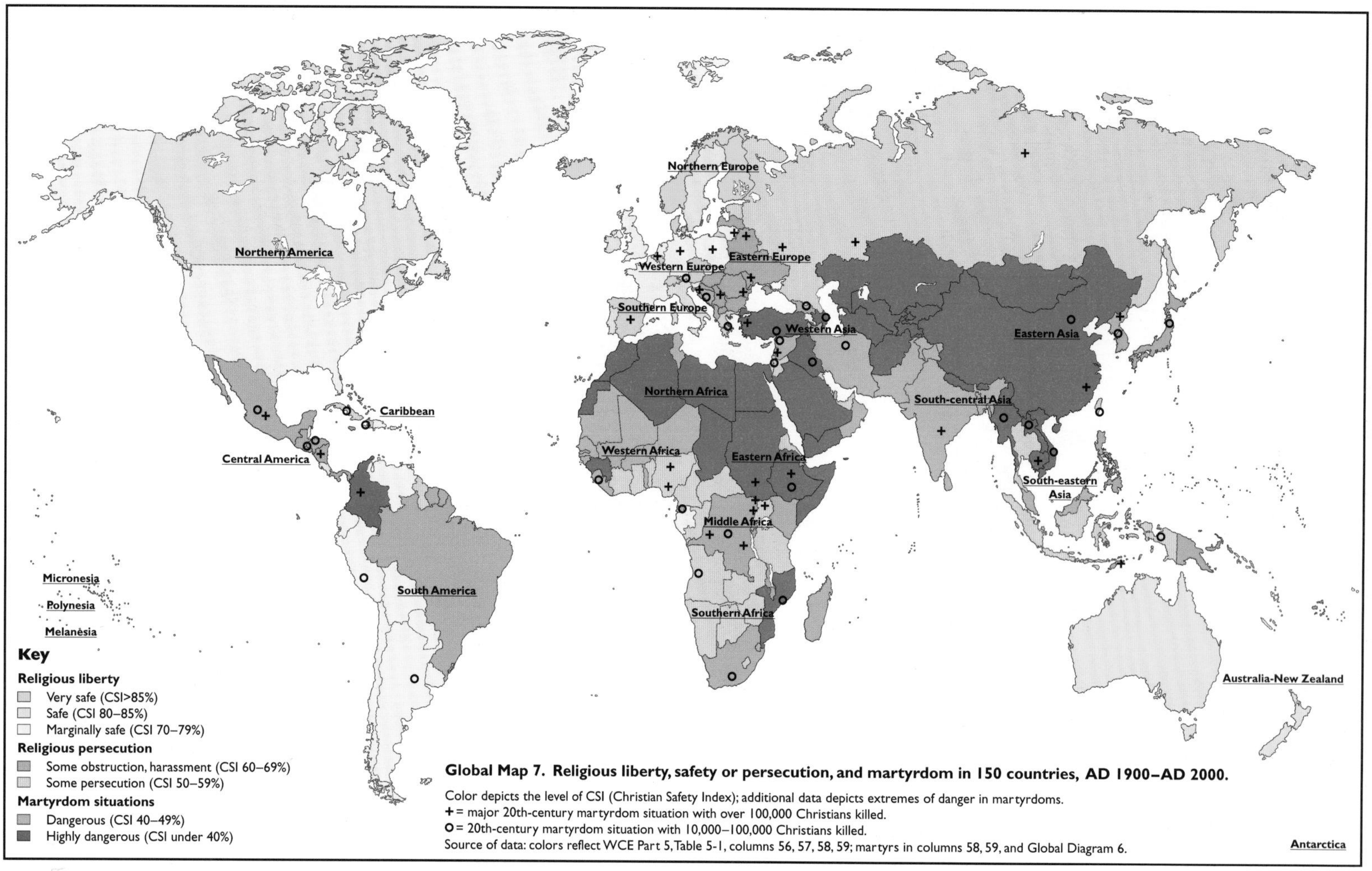

Global Map 7. Religious liberty, safety or persecution, and martyrdom in 150 countries, AD 1900–AD 2000.

Color depicts the level of CSI (Christian Safety Index); additional data depicts extremes of danger in martyrdoms.
+ = major 20th-century martyrdom situation with over 100,000 Christians killed.
O = 20th-century martyrdom situation with 10,000–100,000 Christians killed.
Source of data: colors reflect WCE Part 5, Table 5-1, columns 56, 57, 58, 59; martyrs in columns 58, 59, and Global Diagram 6.

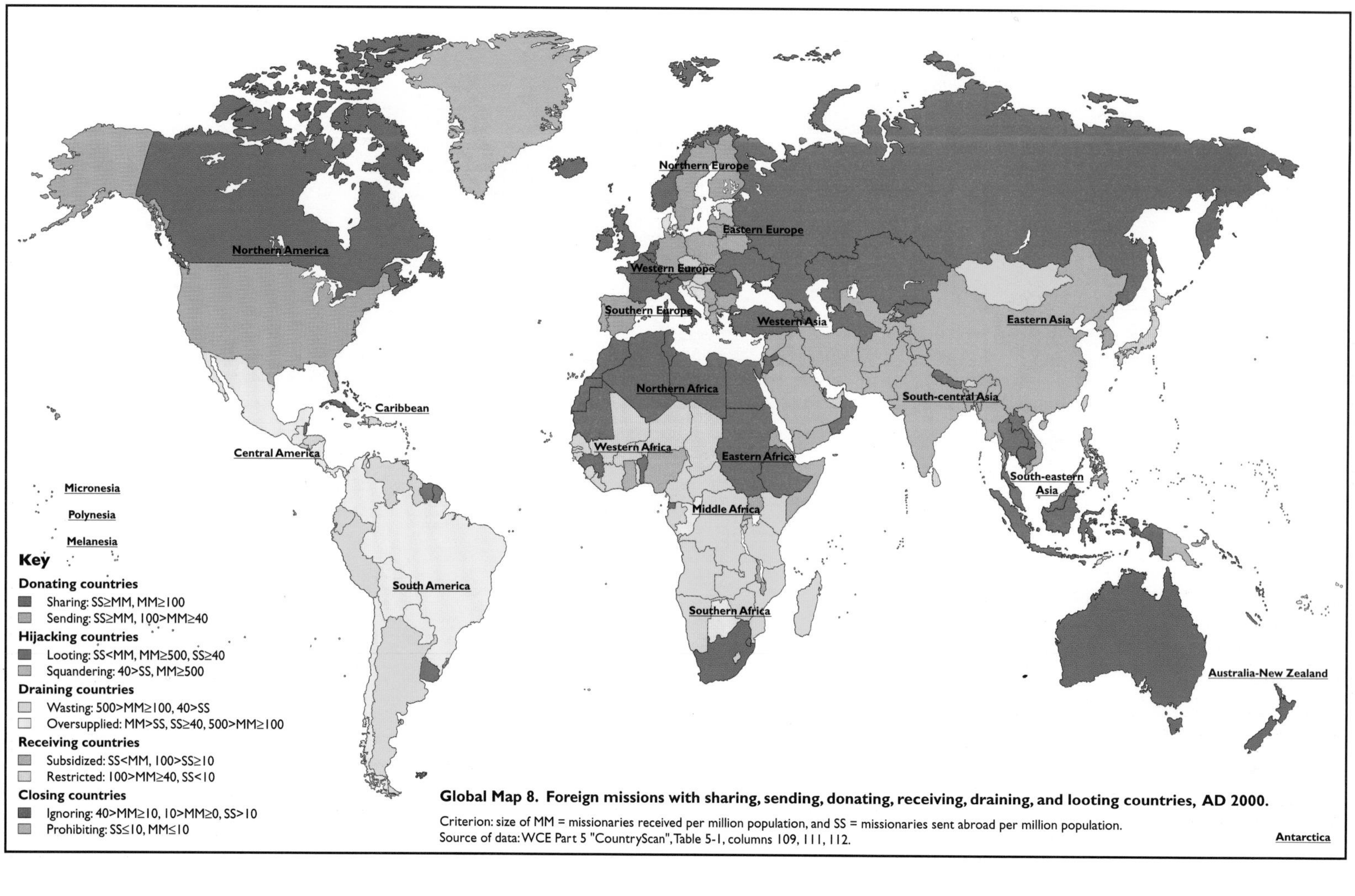

Global Map 8. Foreign missions with sharing, sending, donating, receiving, draining, and looting countries, AD 2000.

Criterion: size of MM = missionaries received per million population, and SS = missionaries sent abroad per million population.
Source of data: WCE Part 5 "CountryScan", Table 5-1, columns 109, 111, 112.

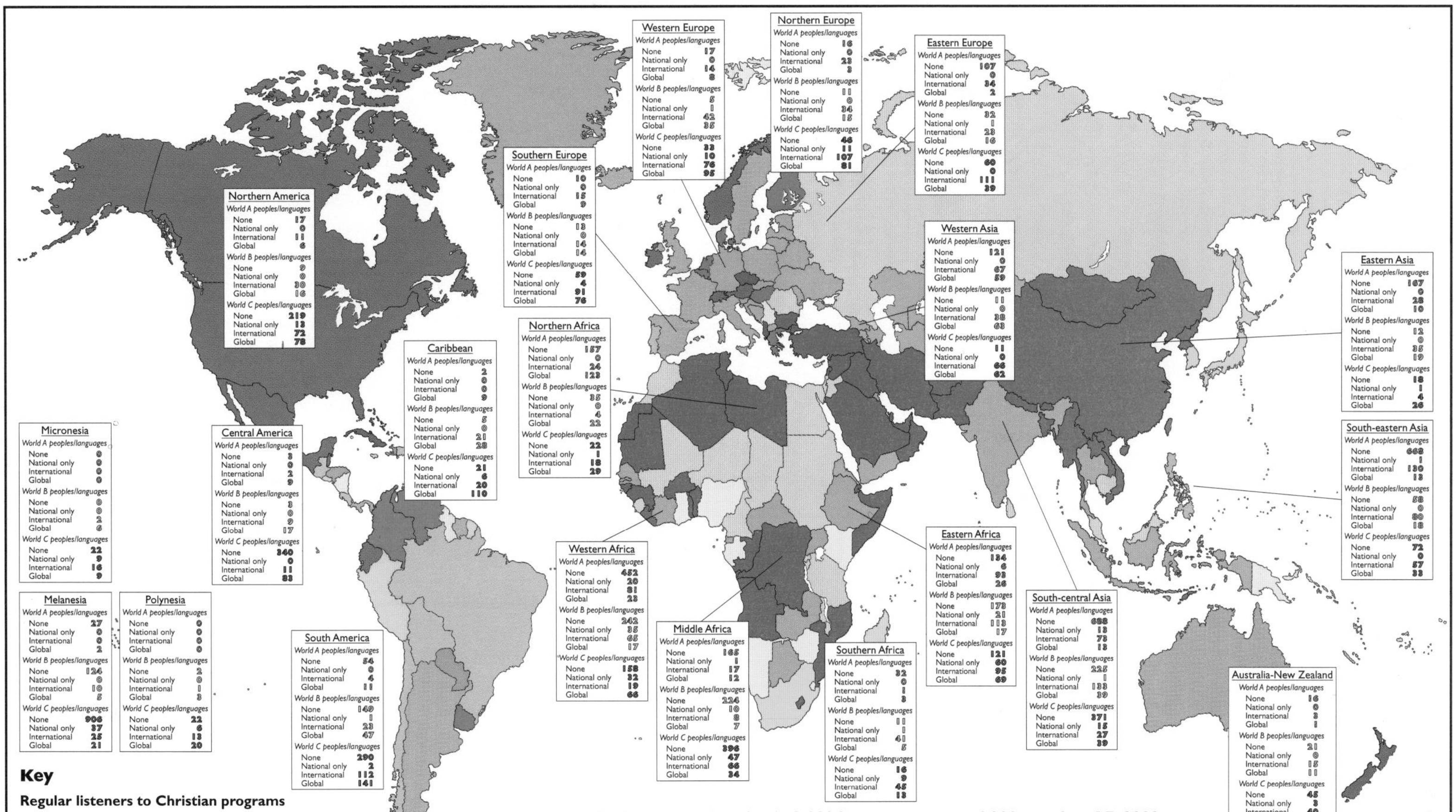

Key

Regular listeners to Christian programs

- Over 70%
- 60–69%
- 50–59%
- 40–49%
- 30–39%
- 20–29%
- 10–19%
- 5–9%
- 0.1–4.9%
- Under 0.1%

Global Map 9. Christian broadcasting in 3,000 languages among 4,800 peoples, AD 2000.

Colors represent percentage of each country's population who listen regularly to Christian radio or TV programs over Christian and/or secular stations. Boxes: For each of the 22 U.N. regions, the box enumerates all its peoples/languages, divided into Worlds A/B/C status, by availability to them of Christian broadcasting. Note that 'International' means broadcasting originating in under 10 foreign countries, and 'Global' in over 10 foreign countries.
Source of data: WCE Part 5 "CountryScan", Table 5-1, column 147, also Part 8 "EthnoSphere" and Part 9 "LinguaMetrics".

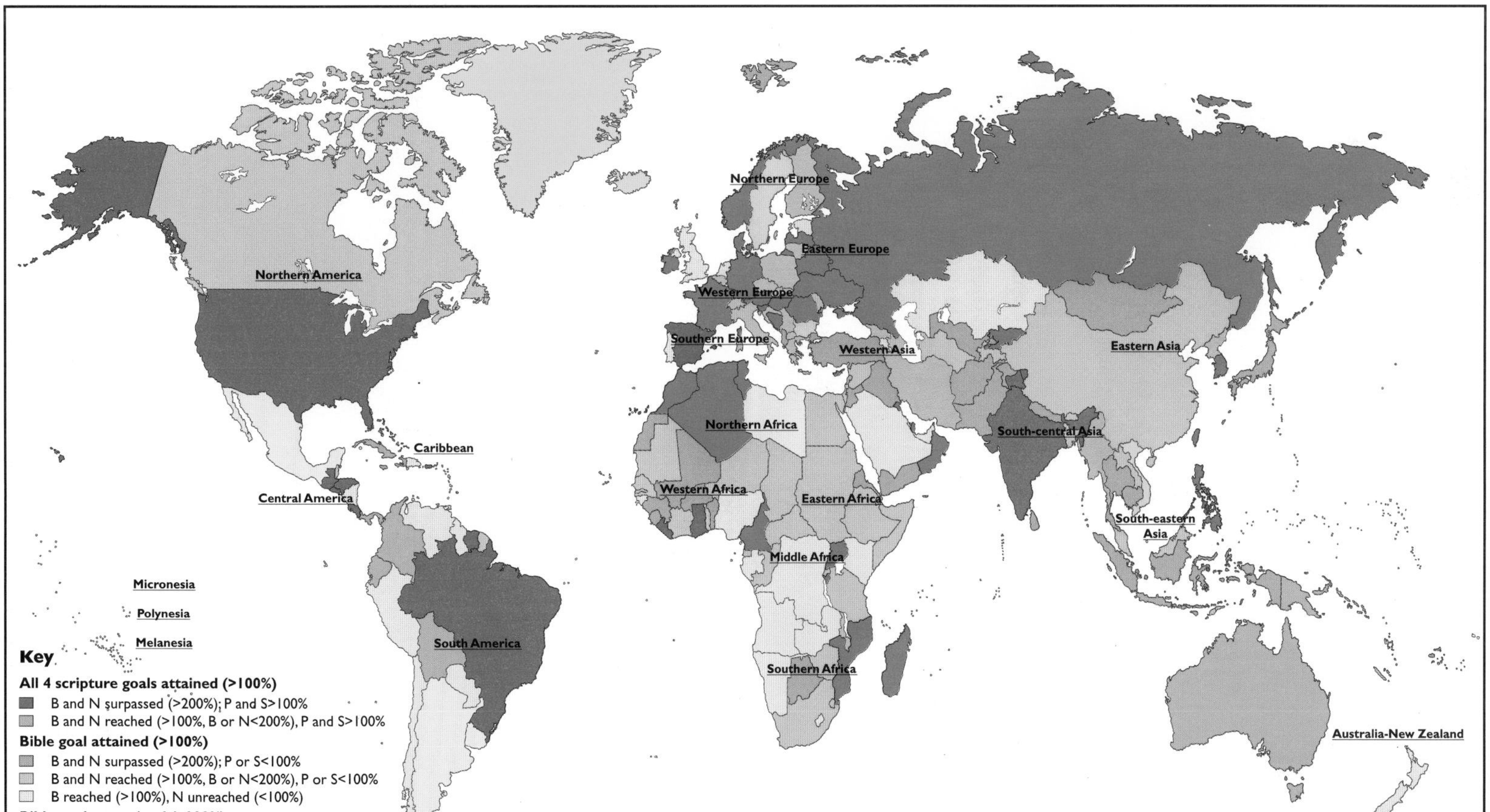

Key

All 4 scripture goals attained (>100%)

- B and N surpassed (>200%); P and S>100%
- B and N reached (>100%, B or N<200%), P and S>100%

Bible goal attained (>100%)

- B and N surpassed (>200%); P or S<100%
- B and N reached (>100%, B or N<200%), P or S<100%
- B reached (>100%), N unreached (<100%)

Bible goal unattained (<100%)

- B unreached (<100%), N reached (>100%)
- B and N unreached (<100%), P and/or S reached (>100%)

None of the 4 goals attained

- B, N, P, S all unreached (<100%, some >50%)
- None of the 4 goals even half reached (all <50%)

Global Map 10. Scripture distribution in 2,500 languages: Bibles, New Testaments, Gospels, and Selections, in AD 2000.

Colors represent each country's attainment or otherwise of the annual distribution necessary to achieve the 4 basic placement or density goals articulated by the United Bible Societies and other agencies ('a Bible for every Christian home, an NT for every Christian adult, a Gospel for every literate adult, a Selection for every family on Earth').
Source of data: WCE Part 5 "CountryScan", Table 5-1, columns 125, 132, 139, 146.

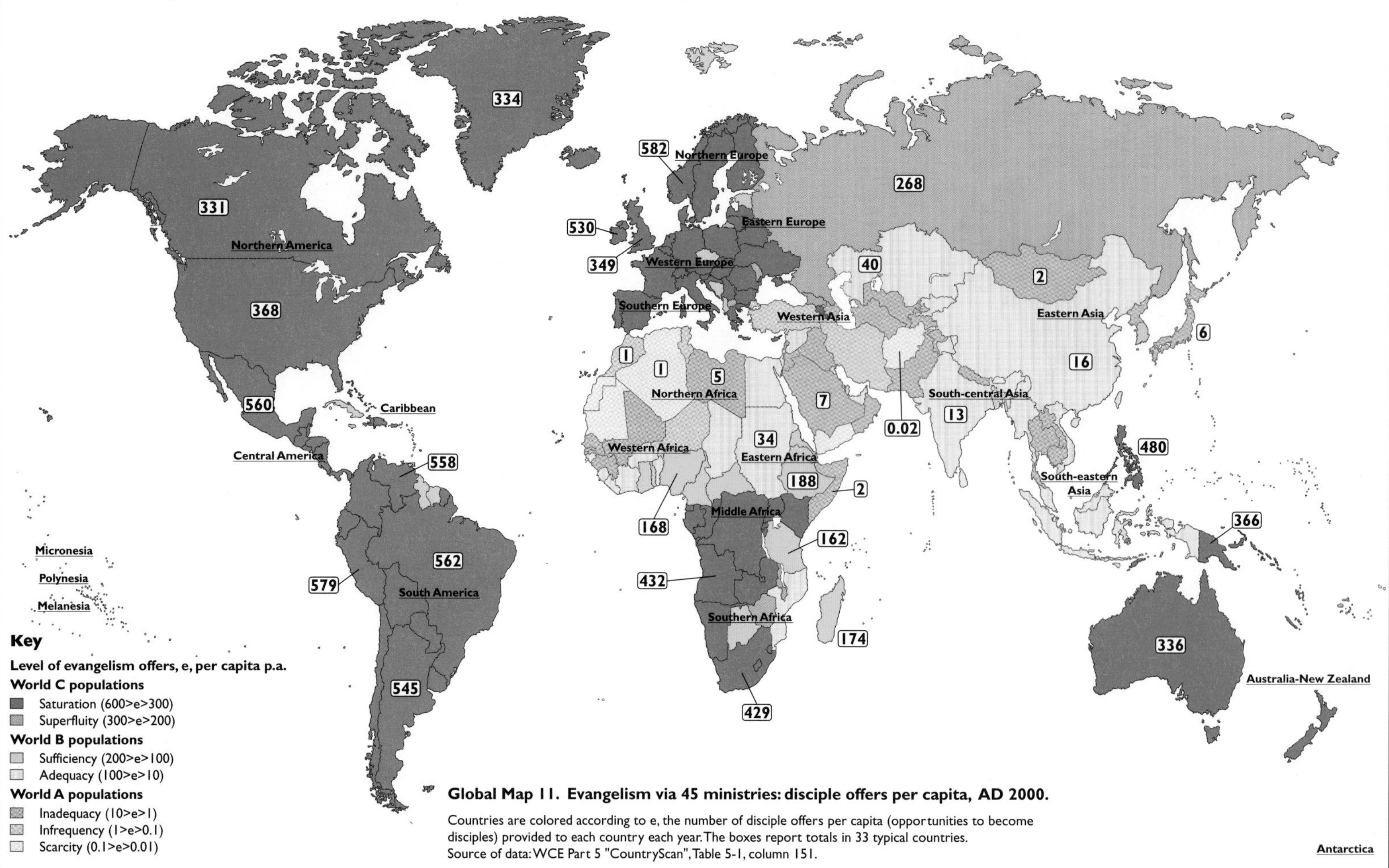

Key

Level of evangelism offers, e, per capita p.a.

World C populations
- Saturation (600>e>300)
- Superfluity (300>e>200)

World B populations
- Sufficiency (200>e>100)
- Adequacy (100>e>10)

World A populations
- Inadequacy (10>e>1)
- Infrequency (1>e>0.1)
- Scarcity (0.1>e>0.01)

Global Map 11. Evangelism via 45 ministries: disciple offers per capita, AD 2000.

Countries are colored according to e, the number of disciple offers per capita (opportunities to become disciples) provided to each country each year. The boxes report totals in 33 typical countries.
Source of data: WCE Part 5 "CountryScan", Table 5-1, column 151.

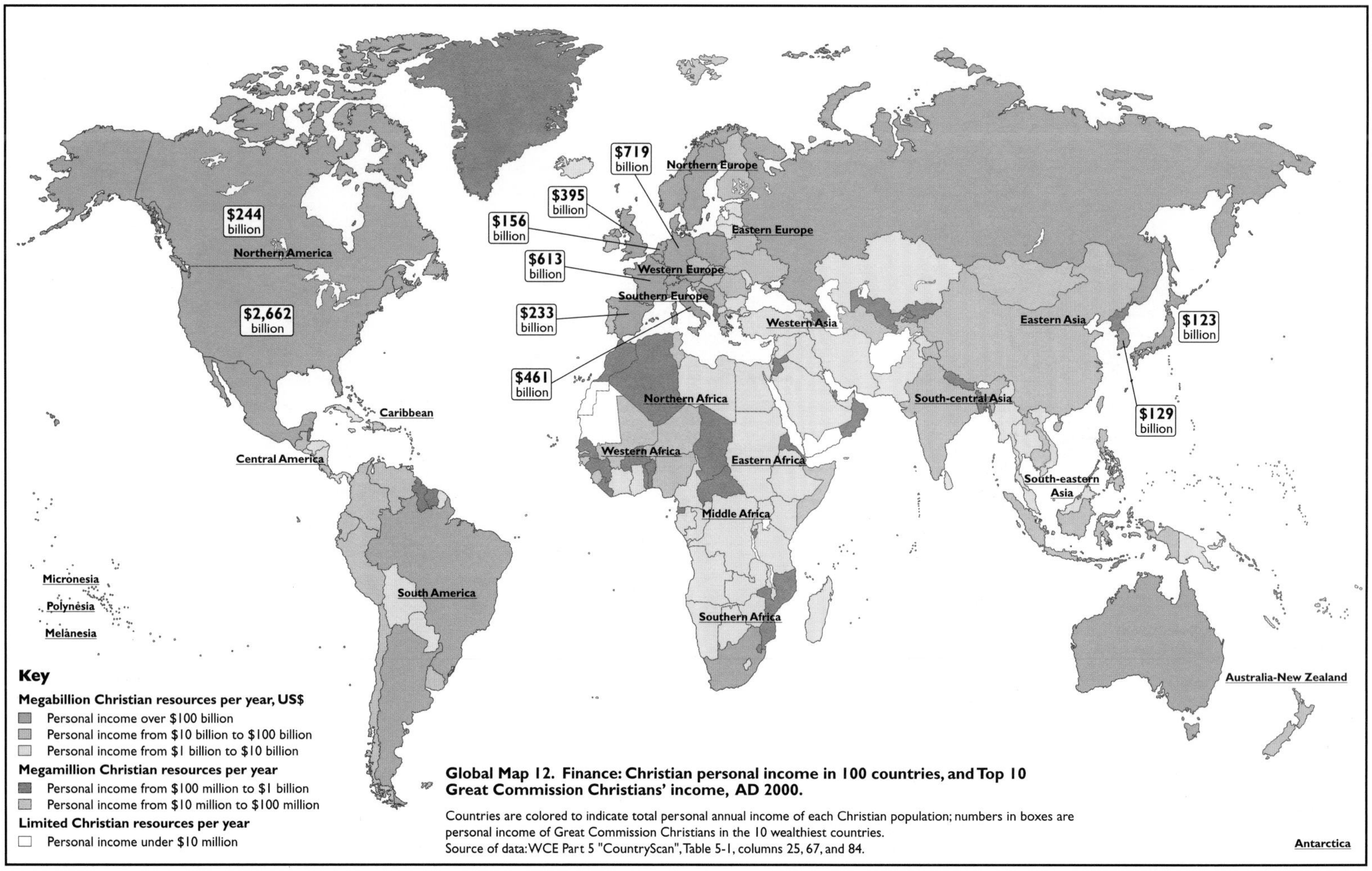

Key

Megabillion Christian resources per year, US$
- Personal income over $100 billion
- Personal income from $10 billion to $100 billion
- Personal income from $1 billion to $10 billion

Megamillion Christian resources per year
- Personal income from $100 million to $1 billion
- Personal income from $10 million to $100 million

Limited Christian resources per year
- Personal income under $10 million

Global Map 12. Finance: Christian personal income in 100 countries, and Top 10 Great Commission Christians' income, AD 2000.

Countries are colored to indicate total personal annual income of each Christian population; numbers in boxes are personal income of Great Commission Christians in the 10 wealthiest countries.
Source of data: WCE Part 5 "CountryScan", Table 5-1, columns 25, 67, and 84.

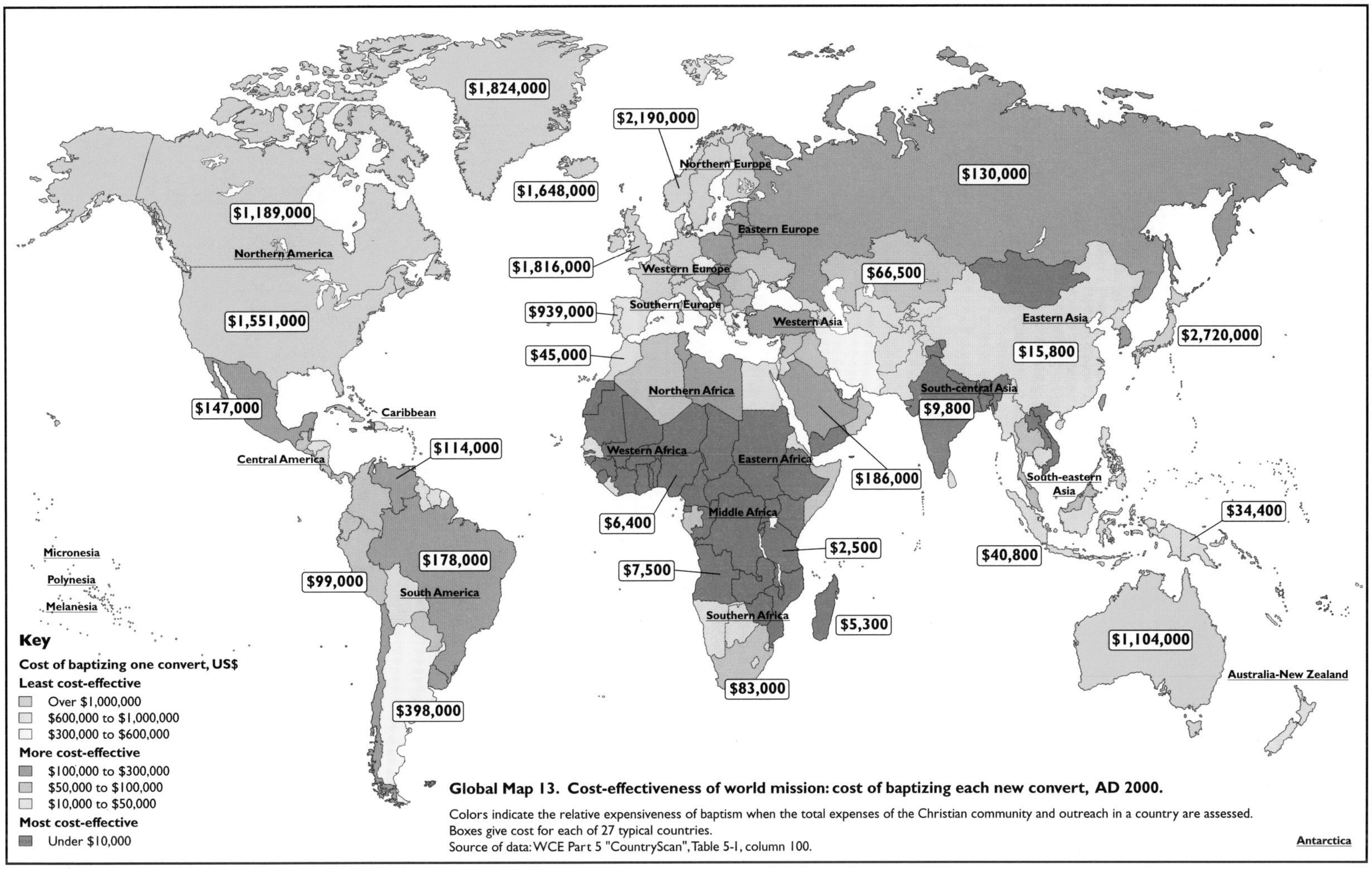

Global Map 13. Cost-effectiveness of world mission: cost of baptizing each new convert, AD 2000.

Colors indicate the relative expensiveness of baptism when the total expenses of the Christian community and outreach in a country are assessed.
Boxes give cost for each of 27 typical countries.
Source of data: WCE Part 5 "CountryScan", Table 5-1, column 100.

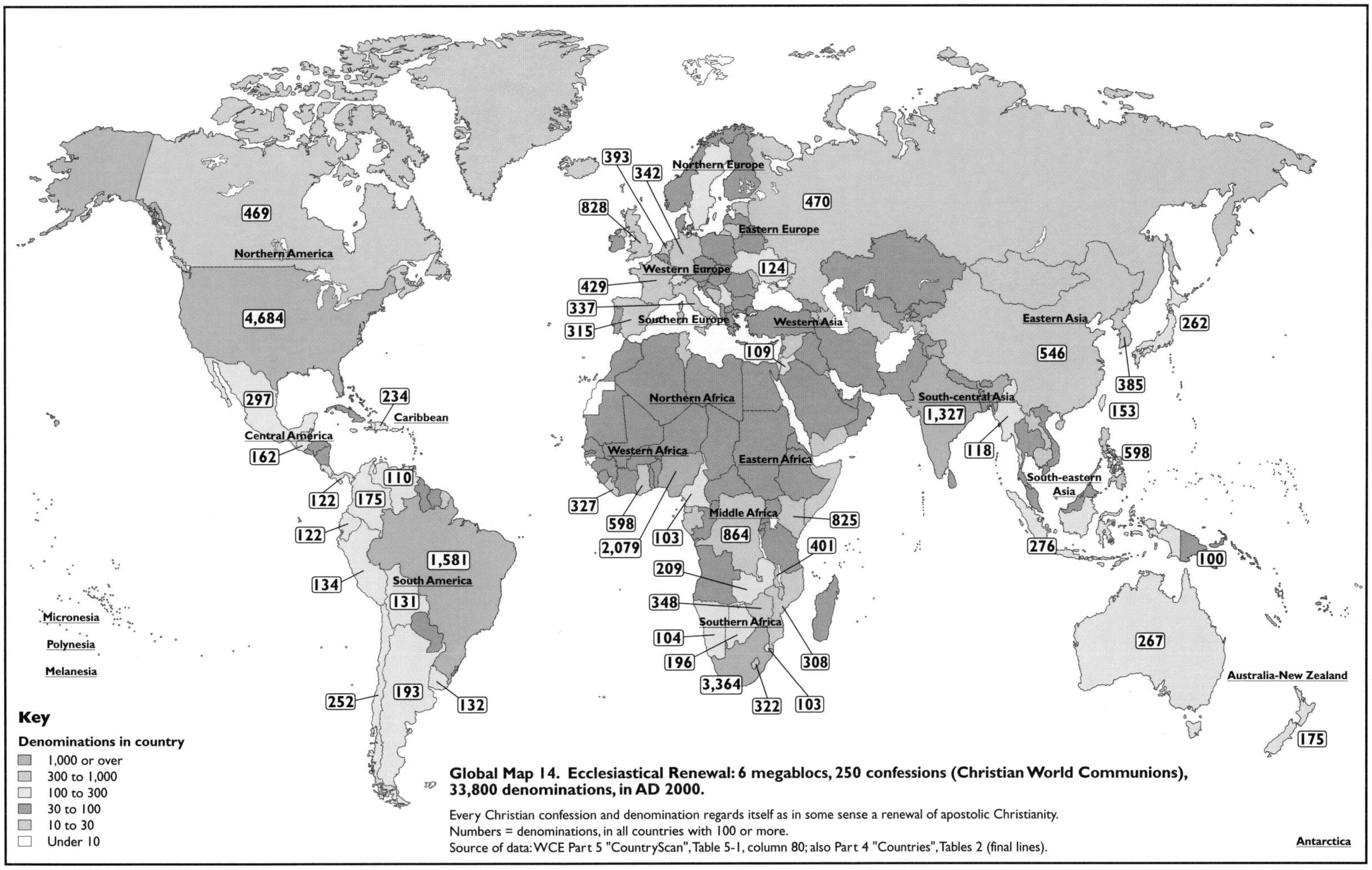

Global Map 14. Ecclesiastical Renewal: 6 megablocs, 250 confessions (Christian World Communions), 33,800 denominations, in AD 2000.

Every Christian confession and denomination regards itself as in some sense a renewal of apostolic Christianity.
Numbers = denominations, in all countries with 100 or more.
Source of data: WCE Part 5 "CountryScan", Table 5-1, column 80; also Part 4 "Countries", Tables 2 (final lines).

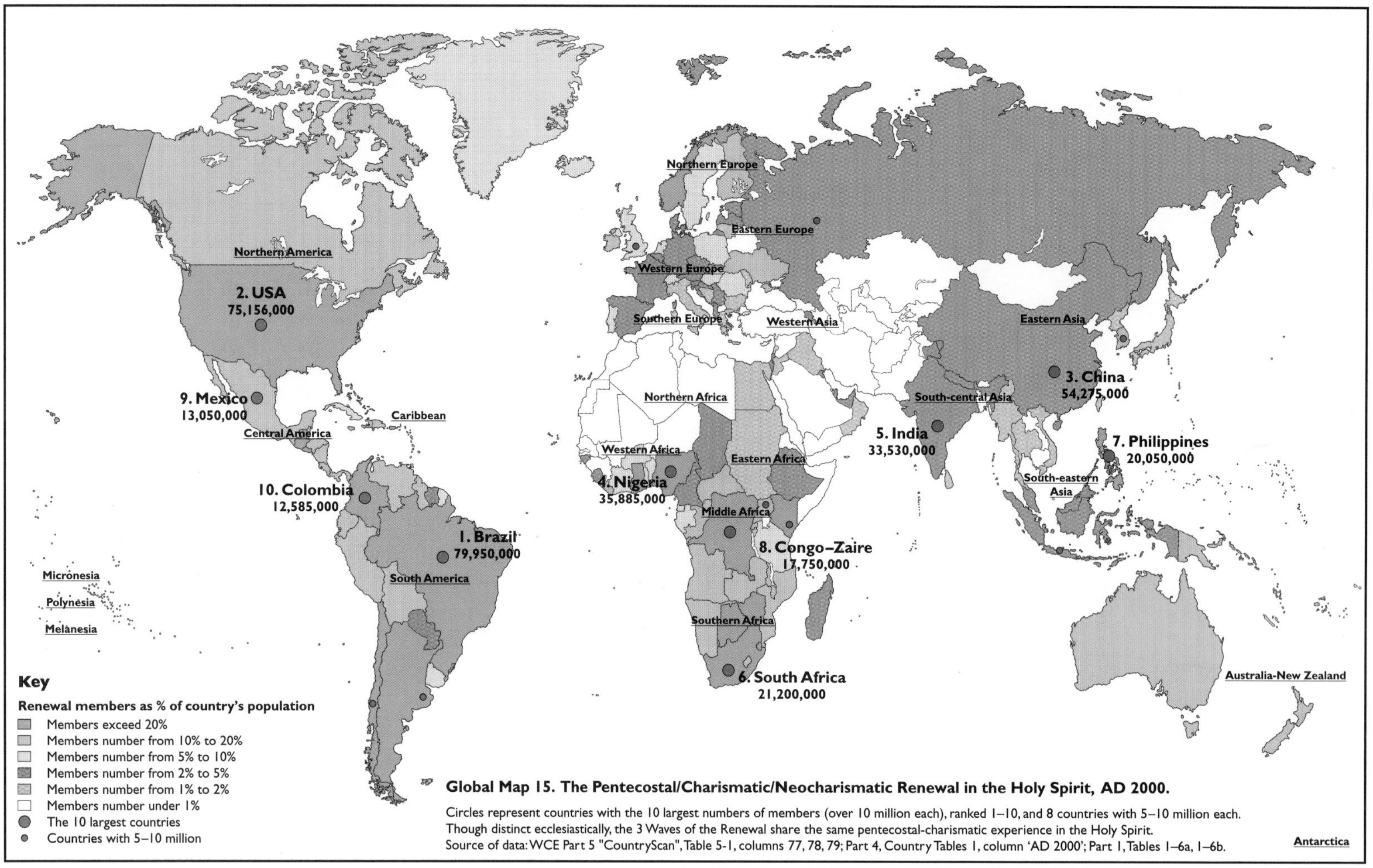

Global Map 15. The Pentecostal/Charismatic/Neocharismatic Renewal in the Holy Spirit, AD 2000.

Circles represent countries with the 10 largest numbers of members (over 10 million each), ranked 1–10, and 8 countries with 5–10 million each. Though distinct ecclesiastically, the 3 Waves of the Renewal share the same pentecostal-charismatic experience in the Holy Spirit.
Source of data: WCE Part 5 "CountryScan", Table 5-1, columns 77, 78, 79; Part 4, Country Tables 1, column 'AD 2000'; Part 1, Tables 1–6a, 1–6b.

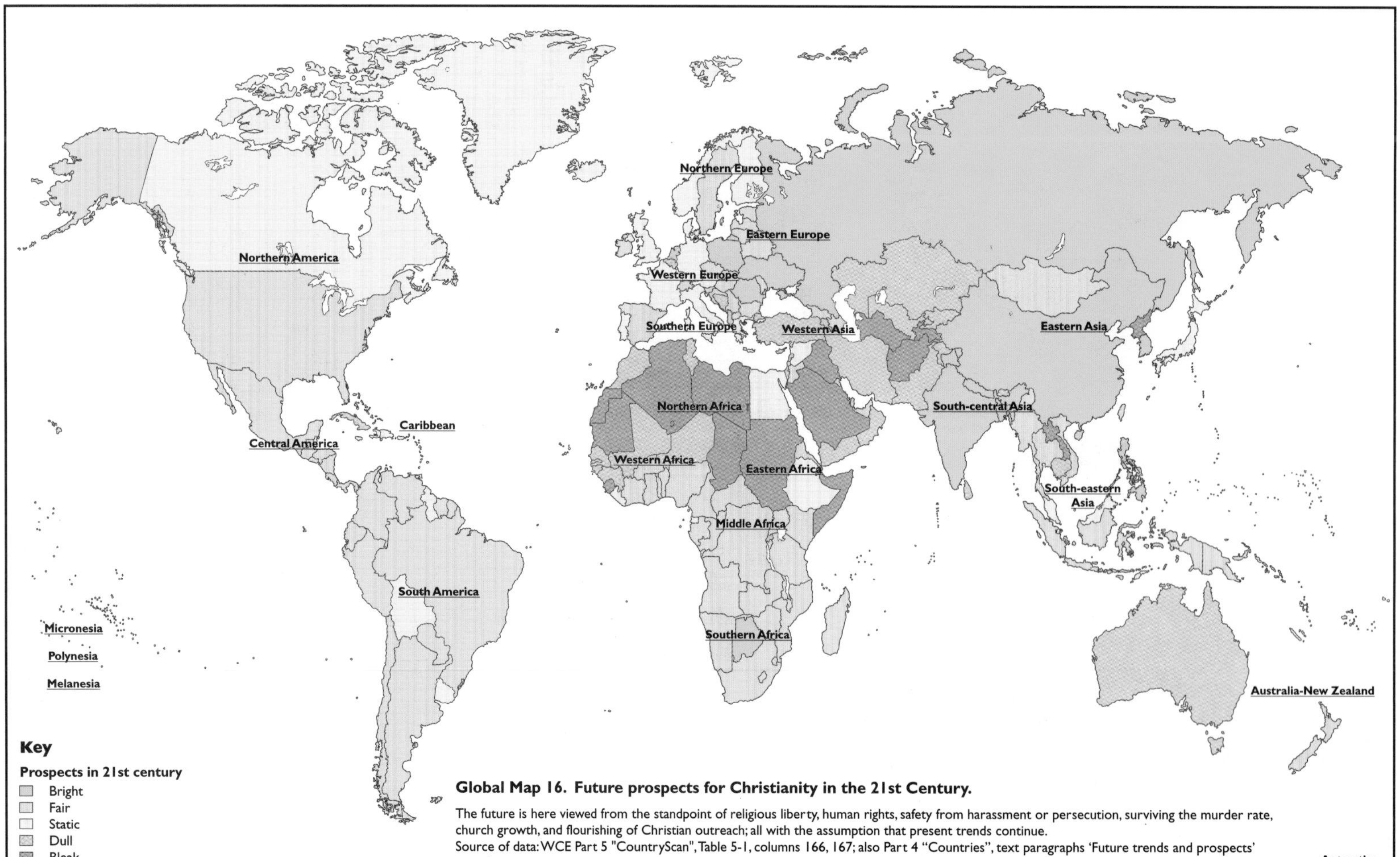

Global Map 16. Future prospects for Christianity in the 21st Century.

The future is here viewed from the standpoint of religious liberty, human rights, safety from harassment or persecution, surviving the murder rate, church growth, and flourishing of Christian outreach; all with the assumption that present trends continue.
Source of data: WCE Part 5 "CountryScan", Table 5-1, columns 166, 167; also Part 4 "Countries", text paragraphs 'Future trends and prospects' in each country.

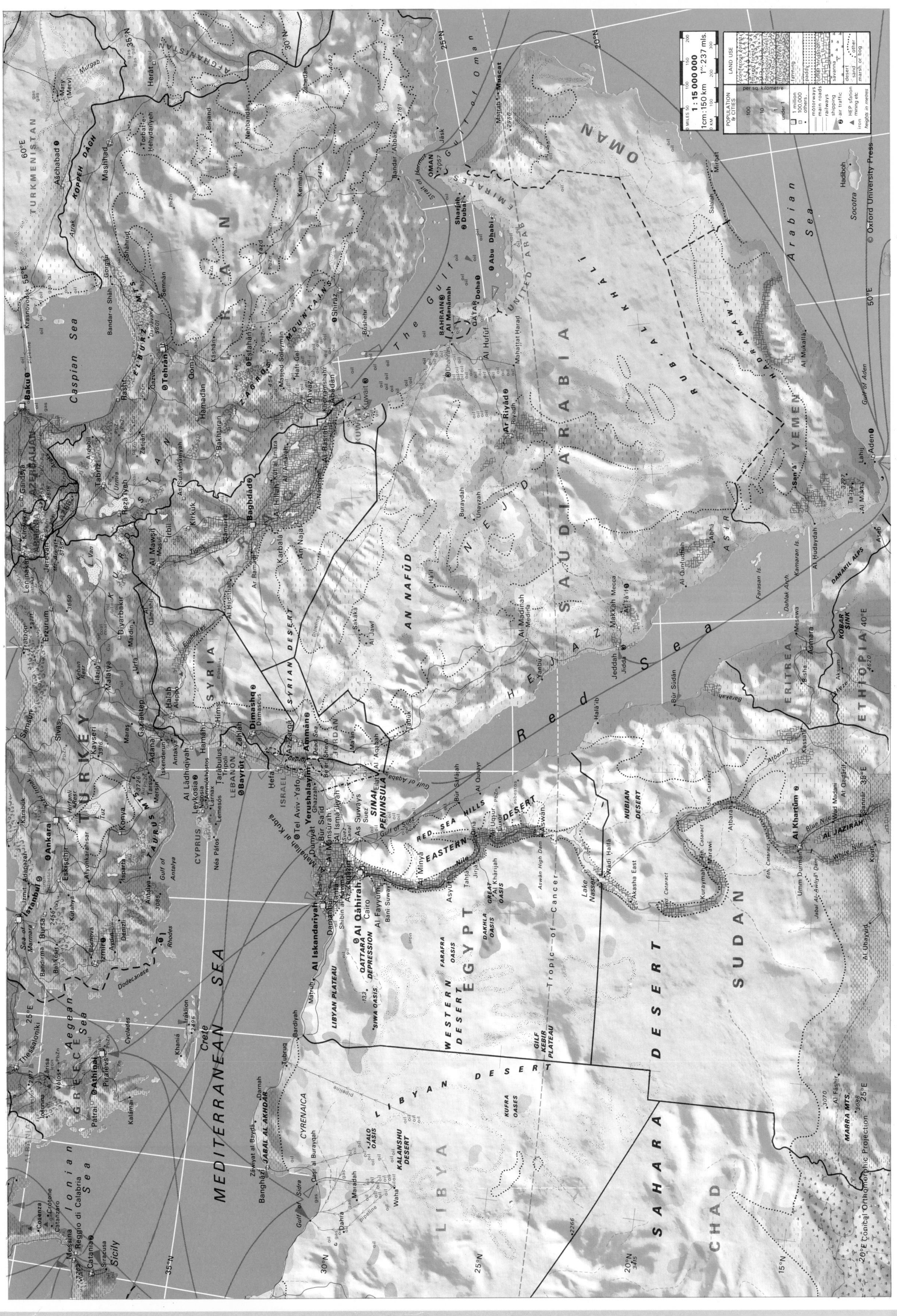
MEDITERRANEAN SEA
Caspian Sea
Red Sea
The Gulf
Gulf of Oman
Arabian Sea
Aegean Sea
Ionian Sea
TURKEY
SYRIA
IRAQ
IRAN
SAUDI ARABIA
OMAN
YEMEN
EGYPT
LIBYA
SUDAN
CHAD
ETHIOPIA
ERITREA
GREECE
CYPRUS
LEBANON
ISRAEL
JORDAN
KUWAIT
QATAR
BAHRAIN
UNITED ARAB EMIRATES
TURKMENISTAN
AFGHANISTAN
AZERBAIJAN
SAHARA DESERT
LIBYAN DESERT
WESTERN DESERT
NUBIAN DESERT
EASTERN DESERT
SYRIAN DESERT
AN NAFŪD
NEJD
HEJAZ
RUB AL KHALI
HADRAMAWT
ZAGROS MOUNTAINS
ELBURZ MTS
TAURUS MTS
KOPPEH DAGH
SINAI PENINSULA
RED SEA HILLS
QATTARA DEPRESSION
LIBYAN PLATEAU
GILF KEBIR PLATEAU
KUFRA OASES
AL JAZIRAH
DANAKIL ALPS
MARRA MTS.
CYRENAICA
JABAL AL AKHDAR
Crete
Rhodes
Socotra
Sicily
Dodecanese
Cyclades
Gulf of Aden
Gulf of Sidra
Tropic of Cancer
Baghdād
Tehrān
Ar Riyād
Al Qāhirah
Dimashq
Ammān
Bayrūt
Ankara
İstanbul
Baku
Muscat
Abu Dhabi
Doha
Al Manāmah
Kuwait
Şan'ā
Aden
Al Khartūm
Athinai
Al Iskandariyah
Yerushalayim
Makkah Mecca
Al Madinah Medina
Jeddah
Sharjah
Dubai
Aschabad
Mashhad
Esfahān
Shirāz
Tabriz
Al Başrah
Al Mawşil
Halab Aleppo
Adana
İzmir
Konya
Aswān
Luxor
Bür Sa'id
Suez
Benghazi
Omdurman
1 : 15 000 000
1cm : 150 km 1" : 237 mls.
POPULATION & CITIES
LAND USE
© Oxford University Press
Conical Orthomorphic Projection

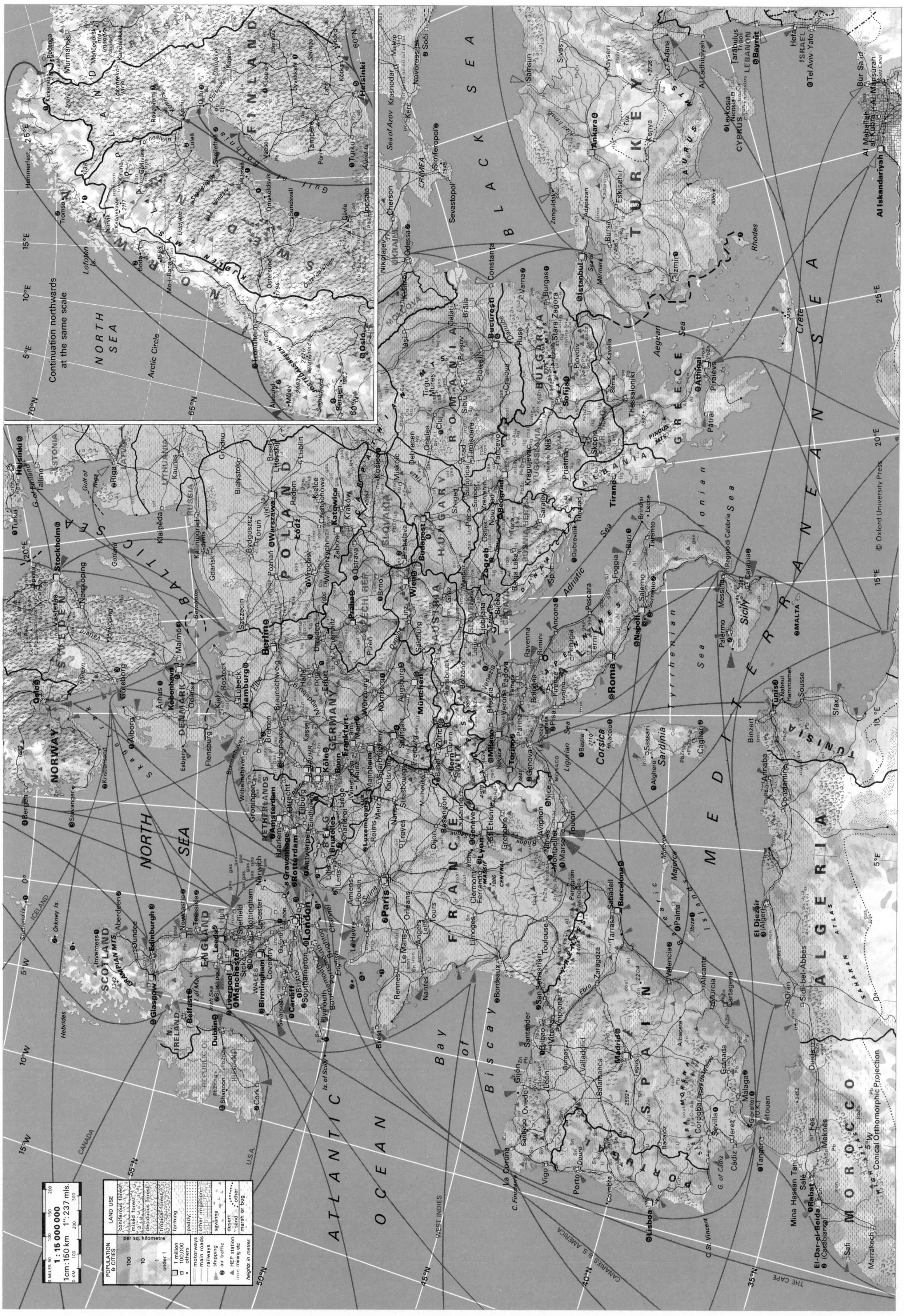
Continuation northwards at the same scale
1:15 000 000
1cm:150 km 1":237 mls.
Conical Orthomorphic Projection
© Oxford University Press
NORTH SEA
BLACK SEA
ATLANTIC OCEAN
MEDITERRANEAN SEA
Bay of Biscay
FRANCE
SPAIN
GERMANY
POLAND
ROMANIA
TURKEY
ALGERIA
MOROCCO

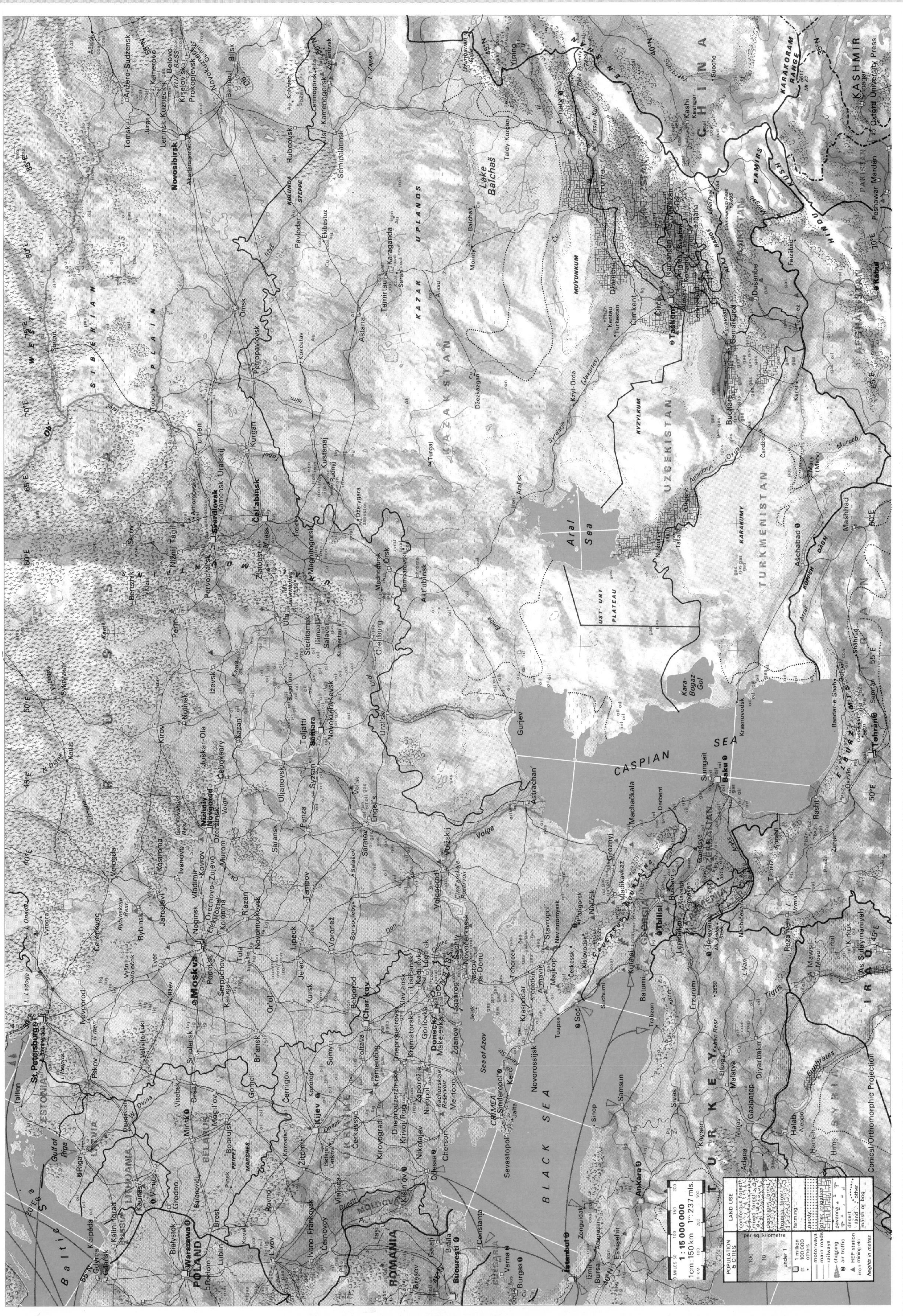
1:15 000 000
1cm:150 km 1":237 mls.
POPULATION & CITIES
per sq. kilometre
LAND USE
coniferous forest
mixed forest
deciduous forest
tropical forest
farming
paddy
other irrigation
1 million
100,000
others
motorways
main roads
railways
shipping
air traffic
HEP station
iron mining etc.
heights in metres
desert
sand
marsh or bog
Conical Orthomorphic Projection
© Oxford University Press
RUSSIA
KAZAKSTAN
UZBEKISTAN
TURKMENISTAN
CHINA
TURKEY
IRAN
IRAQ
SYRIA
AFGHANISTAN
PAKISTAN
KASHMIR
UKRAINE
BELARUS
POLAND
ROMANIA
BULGARIA
MOLDOVA
LITHUANIA
LATVIA
ESTONIA
GEORGIA
ARMENIA
AZERBAIJAN
BLACK SEA
CASPIAN SEA
Aral Sea
Sea of Azov
Lake Balchaš
Moskva
St. Petersburg
Kijev
Tbilisi
Baku
Taškent
Almaty
Ankara
Tehrān
Kābul

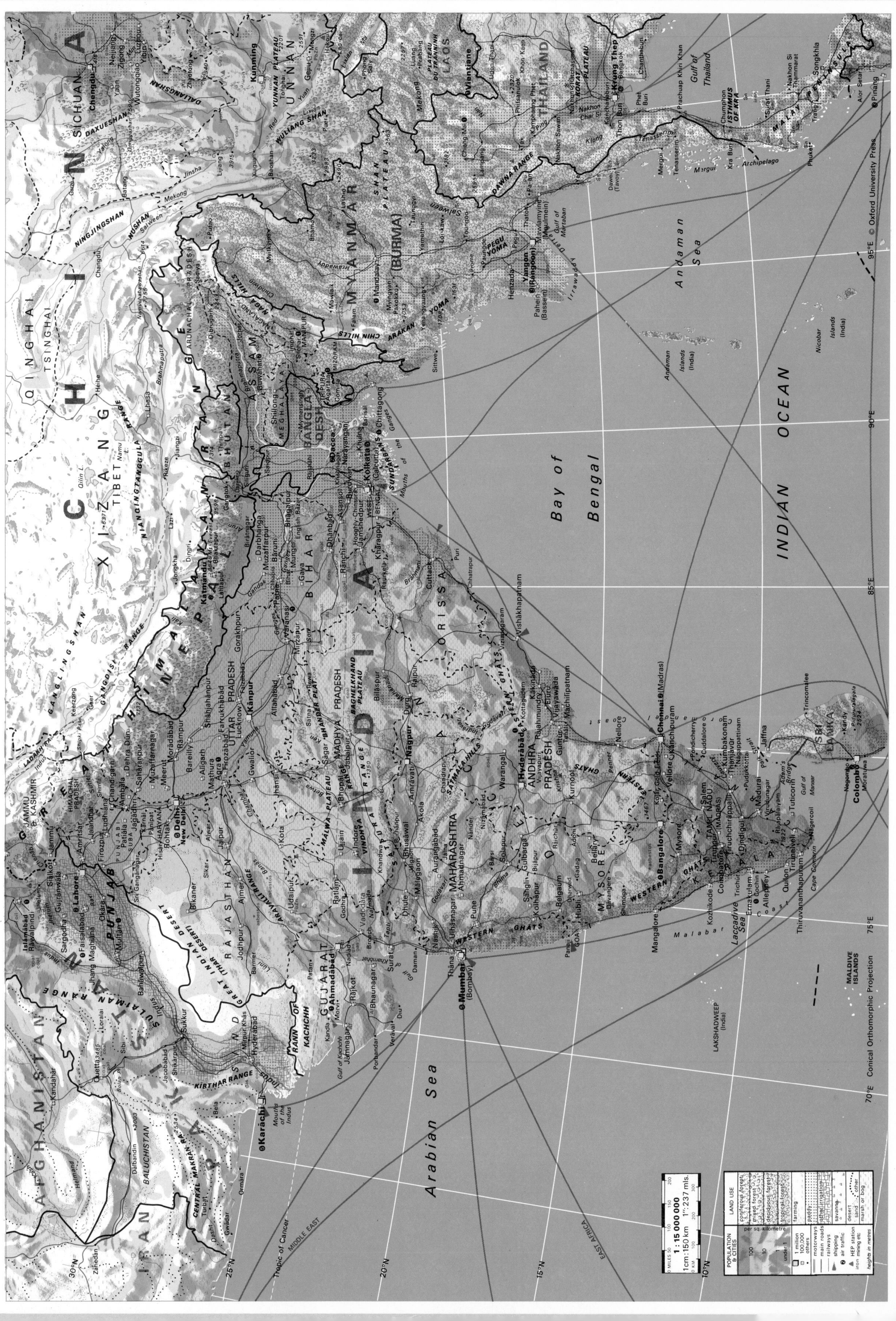

CHINA
XIZANG
TIBET
QINGHAI
TSINGHAI
SICHUAN
YUNNAN
AFGHANISTAN
IRAN
PAKISTAN
INDIA
NEPAL
BHUTAN
BANGLADESH
MYANMAR
(BURMA)
LAOS
THAILAND
SRI LANKA
MALDIVE ISLANDS
Arabian Sea
Bay of Bengal
INDIAN OCEAN
Andaman Sea
Gulf of Thailand
Laccadive Sea
LAKSHADWEEP (India)
Andaman Islands (India)
Nicobar Islands (India)
HIMALAYA
WESTERN GHATS
EASTERN GHATS
GREAT INDIAN DESERT (THAR DESERT)
Tropic of Cancer
MIDDLE EAST
EAST AFRICA
Delhi
New Delhi
Mumbai (Bombay)
Kolkata (Calcutta)
Chennai (Madras)
Karachi
Lahore
Kathmandu
Dhaka
Colombo
Yangon (Rangoon)
Krung Thep (Bangkok)
Kunming
Chengdu
Lhasa
POPULATION & CITIES
per sq. kilometre
over 100
10
1
under 1
1 million
100,000
others
LAND USE
coniferous forest
mixed forest
deciduous forest
tropical forest
farming
paddy
other irrigation
savanna
desert
sand
other
marsh or bog
motorways
main roads
railways
shipping
air traffic
HEP station
mining etc.
heights in metres
1 : 15 000 000
1cm:150 km 1":237 mls.
Conical Orthomorphic Projection
© Oxford University Press

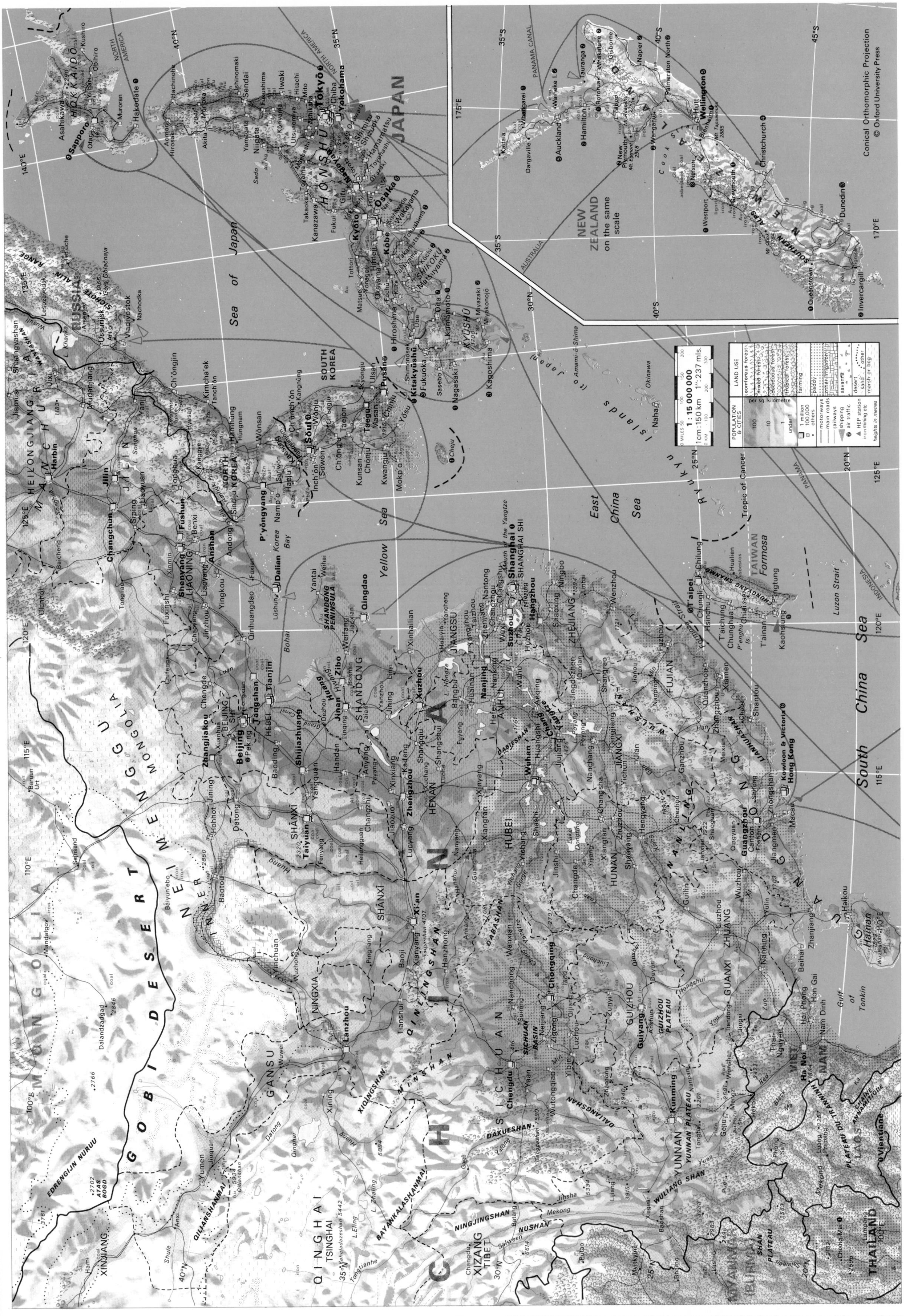
CHINA
JAPAN
MONGOLIA
GOBI DESERT
INNER MONGOLIA
MANCHURIA
NORTH KOREA
SOUTH KOREA
RUSSIA
TAIWAN
Formosa
VIETNAM
LAOS
THAILAND
BURMA
XIZANG
TIBET
QINGHAI
TSINGHAI
SICHUAN
YUNNAN
GUIZHOU
GUANXI
GUANGDONG
FUJIAN
ZHEJIANG
JIANGSU
SHANDONG
HENAN
HUBEI
HUNAN
JIANGXI
ANHUI
SHANXI
SHAANXI
GANSU
NINGXIA
HEBEI
LIAONING
JILIN
HEILONGJIANG
XINJIANG
HONSHU
HOKKAIDO
SHIKOKU
KYUSHU
Sea of Japan
Yellow Sea
East China Sea
South China Sea
Korea Bay
Bohai
Luzon Strait
Gulf of Tonkin
Ryukyu Islands
Tropic of Cancer
Beijing
Peking
Tianjin
Shanghai
Nanjing
Wuhan
Chongqing
Chengdu
Xi'an
Lanzhou
Kunming
Guangzhou
Canton
Hong Kong
Kowloon & Victoria
Macau
Hanoi
Shenyang
Harbin
Changchun
Dalian
Qingdao
Hangzhou
Zhengzhou
Taiyuan
Jinan
P'yŏngyang
Sŏul
Pusan
T'aipei
Kaohsiung
Tokyo
Yokohama
Osaka
Kyoto
Kobe
Nagoya
Sapporo
Hiroshima
Fukuoka
Kitakyushu
Nagasaki
Kagoshima
Naha
Okinawa
NEW ZEALAND
on the same scale
Auckland
Wellington
Christchurch
Dunedin
Invercargill
Hamilton
Napier
Nelson
Cook Strait
SOUTHERN ALPS
1 : 15 000 000
1cm : 150 km 1": 237 mls.
POPULATION & CITIES
per sq. kilometre
100
10
1
under 1
1 million
100,000
others
motorways
main roads
railways
shipping
air traffic
HEP station
ironmining etc
heights in metres
LAND USE
coniferous forest
mixed forest
deciduous forest
tropical forest
farming
paddy
other irrigation
savanna
desert
sand
other
marsh or bog
Conical Orthomorphic Projection
© Oxford University Press

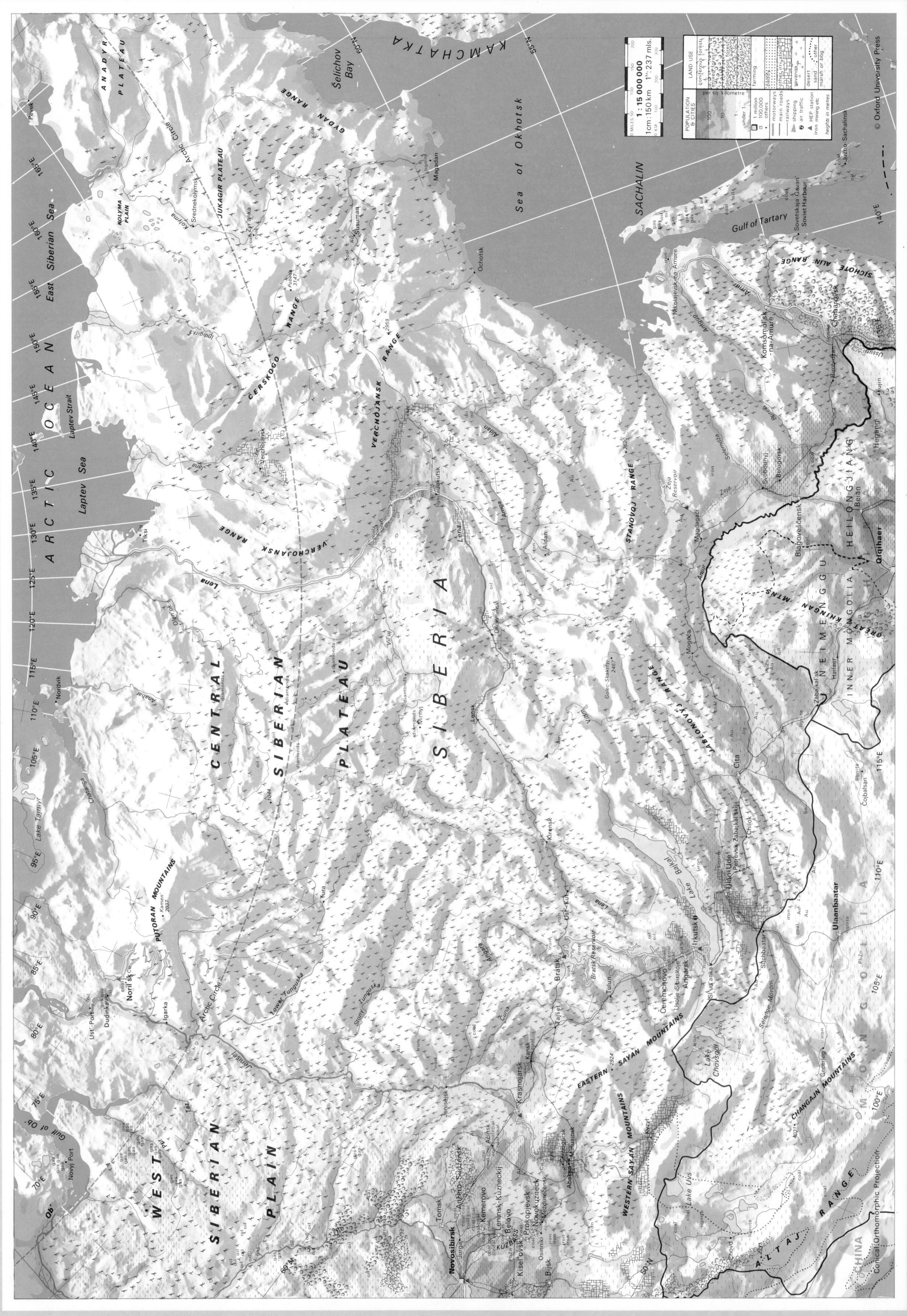
ARCTIC OCEAN
Laptev Sea
Laptev Strait
East Siberian Sea
Sea of Okhotsk
KAMCHATKA
Šelichov Bay
SACHALIN
Gulf of Tartary
Gulf of Ob
WEST SIBERIAN PLAIN
CENTRAL SIBERIAN PLATEAU
SIBERIA
PUTORAN MOUNTAINS
VERCHOJANSK RANGE
ČERSKOGO RANGE
GYDAN RANGE
ANADYR PLATEAU
JUKAGIR PLATEAU
KOLYMA PLAIN
STANOVOJ RANGE
JABLONOVYJ RANGE
SICHOTE ALIN RANGE
GREAT KHINGAN MTNS
EASTERN SAYAN MOUNTAINS
WESTERN SAYAN MOUNTAINS
CHANGAJN MOUNTAINS
ALTAJ RANGE
MONGOLIA
INNER MONGOLIA
HEILONGJIANG
CHINA
Lake Bajkal
Lena
Jenisej
Ob
Amur
Novosibirsk
Krasnojarsk
Irkutsk
Jakutsk
Magadan
Noril'sk
Ulaanbaatar
Chabarovsk
Arctic Circle
1:15 000 000
1cm:150 km 1": 237 mls.
POPULATION & CITIES
LAND USE
heights in metres
© Oxford University Press
Conical Orthomorphic Projection

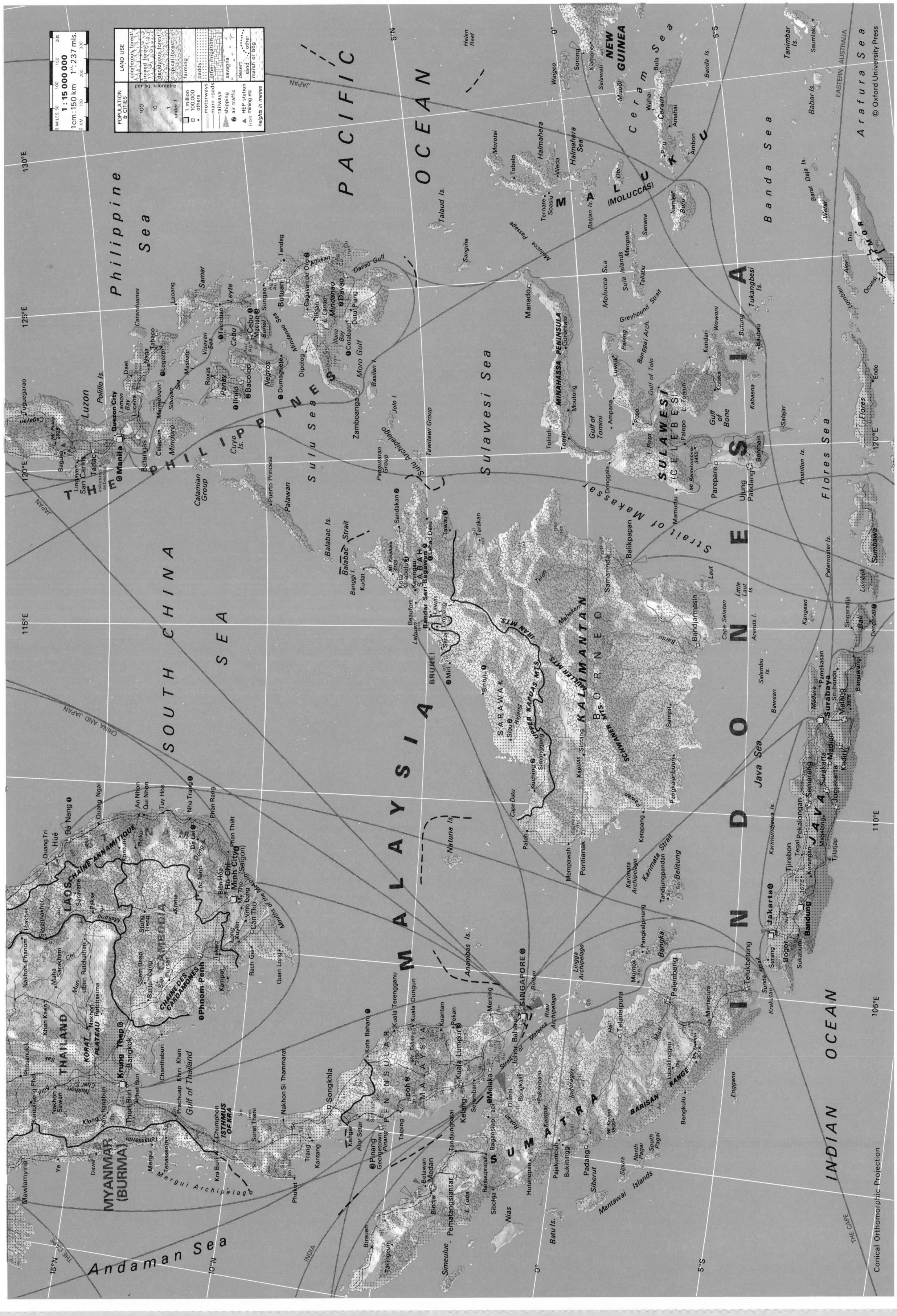
1 : 15 000 000
1cm : 150 km 1": 237 mls.
POPULATION & CITIES
per sq. kilometre
100
10
1
under 1
1 million
100,000
others
LAND USE
coniferous forest
mixed forest
deciduous forest
tropical forest
farming
paddy
other irrigation
savanna
desert
sand
other
marsh or bog
motorways
main roads
railways
shipping
air traffic
HEP station
iron mining etc
heights in metres
PACIFIC OCEAN
Philippine Sea
SOUTH CHINA SEA
Sulu Sea
Sulawesi Sea
Molucca Sea
Banda Sea
Flores Sea
Java Sea
Arafura Sea
Ceram Sea
Andaman Sea
Gulf of Thailand
INDIAN OCEAN
THE PHILIPPINES
MALAYSIA
INDONESIA
THAILAND
MYANMAR (BURMA)
CAMBODIA
LAOS
VIETNAM
BRUNEI
SINGAPORE
SUMATRA
JAVA
BORNEO
KALIMANTAN
SARAWAK
SABAH
SULAWESI (CELEBES)
MALUKU (MOLUCCAS)
NEW GUINEA
Luzon
Mindanao
Mindoro
Palawan
Samar
Leyte
Negros
Cebu
Panay
Halmahera
Ceram
Buru
Timor
Flores
Sumbawa
Lombok
Bali
Madura
Bangka
Belitung
Nias
Siberut
Mentawai Islands
Natuna Is.
Anambas Is.
Sula Islands
Tanimbar Is.
Manila
Quezon City
Bangkok
Krung Thep
Phnom Penh
Ho Chi Minh City (Saigon)
Jakarta
Surabaya
Bandung
Semarang
Medan
Palembang
Kuala Lumpur
Kuching
Balikpapan
Ujung Pandang
Davao
Zamboanga
Manado
Ambon
Dili
Strait of Makassar
Sunda Strait
Strait of Malacca
KORAT PLATEAU
ISTHMUS OF KRA
BARISAN RANGE
CHAÎNE ANNAMITIQUE
CHAÎNE DES CARDAMOMES
IRAN MTS.
MULLER MTS.
SCHWANER MTS.
Mekong
5°N
0°
5°S
10°N
15°N
105°E
110°E
115°E
120°E
125°E
130°E
Conical Orthomorphic Projection
© Oxford University Press

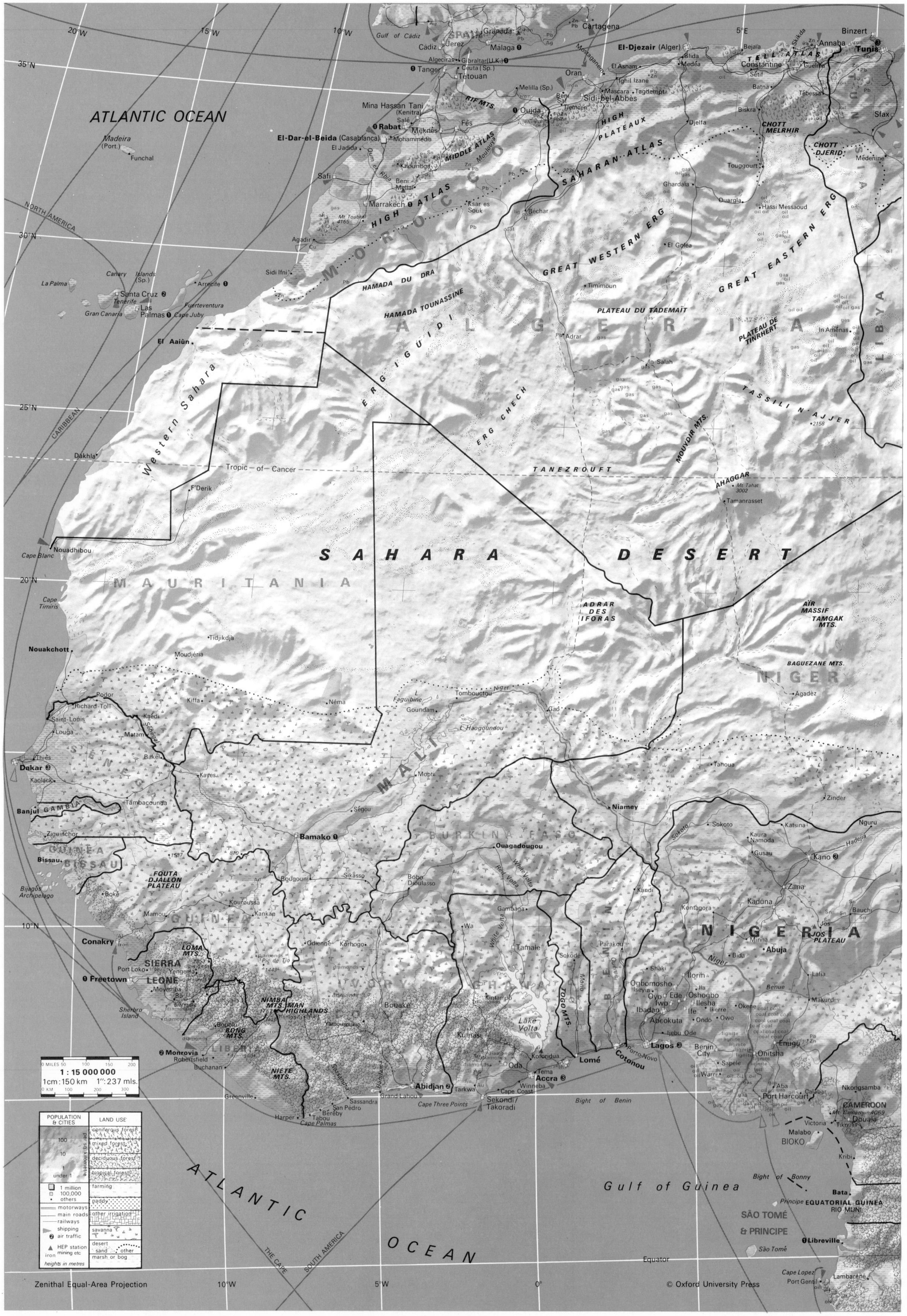
ATLANTIC OCEAN
Madeira (Port.)
Funchal
Canary Islands (Sp.)
La Palma
Santa Cruz
Tenerife
Gran Canaria
Las Palmas
Fuerteventura
Arrecife
Cape Juby
Gulf of Cádiz
SPAIN
Cádiz
Jerez
Granada
Malaga
Cartagena
Algeciras
Gibraltar (U.K.)
Tanger
Ceuta (Sp.)
Tétouan
Melilla (Sp.)
RIF MTS.
Mina Hassan Tani (Kenitra)
Rabat
Salé
Meknès
Fès
Oujda
El-Dar-el-Beida (Casablanca)
Mohammedia
El Jadida
Khouribga
MIDDLE ATLAS
Safi
Beni Mellal
Marrakech
Mt. Toubkal 4165
HIGH ATLAS
MOROCCO
Ksar es Souk
Agadir
Sidi Ifni
Oran
Mostaganem
El-Djezair (Alger)
Blida
Médéa
El Asnam
Tighil Izane
Mascara
Tagdempt
Sidi-bel-Abbès
Tlemcen
Bejaïa
Skikda
Annaba
Constantine
Sétif
Guelma
Batna
Tébessa
TELL ATLAS
Binzert
Tunis
Sfax
Médenine
Biskra
CHOTT MELRHIR
CHOTT DJERID
HIGH PLATEAUX
Djelfa
SAHARAN ATLAS
Touggourt
Ghardaïa
Ouargla
Hassi Messaoud
Béchar
El Goléa
GREAT WESTERN ERG
GREAT EASTERN ERG
HAMADA DU DRA
HAMADA TOUNASSINE
Timimoun
PLATEAU DU TADEMAÏT
ALGERIA
Adrar
In Salah
PLATEAU DE TINRHERT
In Amenas
LIBYA
TUNISIA
ERG IGUIDI
ERG CHECH
TASSILI N'AJJER
2158
MOUYDIR MTS.
TANEZROUFT
AHAGGAR
Mt. Tahat 3002
Tamanrasset
El Aaiún
Western Sahara
Dakhla
Tropic of Cancer
F'Derik
Nouadhibou
Cape Blanc
SAHARA DESERT
MAURITANIA
Cape Timiris
Tidjikdja
Nouakchott
Moudjéria
ADRAR DES IFORAS
AÏR MASSIF
TAMGAK MTS.
BAGUEZANE MTS.
NIGER
Agadès
Podor
Richard-Toll
Saint-Louis
Louga
Kiffa
Néma
L. Faguibine
Goundam
Tombouctou
Niger
Gao
L. Haoggoundou
Thiès
Dakar
SENEGAL
Matam
Bakel
Kayes
Kaolack
MALI
Mopti
Tahoua
Banjul
GAMBIA
Tambacounda
Ségou
Niamey
Zinder
Ziguinchor
GUINEA-BISSAU
Bissau
Bijagós Archipelago
Bamako
BURKINA FASO
Ouagadougou
Sokoto
Katsina
Kaura Namoda
Gusau
Kano
Nguru
Hadejia
FOUTA DJALLON PLATEAU
Boké
Bougouni
Sikasso
Bobo Dioulasso
White Volta
Red Volta
Kandi
Zaria
Kouroussa
Kankan
Mamou
GUINEA
Gambaga
Kontagora
Kaduna
Bauchi
Conakry
LOMA MTS.
Odienné
Korhogo
Wa
Tamale
Parakou
NIGERIA
Minna
Abuja
JOS PLATEAU
SIERRA LEONE
Port Loko
Freetown
Yengema
Moyamba
Bo
Kenema
Sherbro Island
Pic de Tor 1443
diamonds
IVORY COAST
GHANA
TOGO MTS.
BENIN
Sokodé
Bida
Shaki
Ilorin
Lafia
Ogbomosho
Oyo
Ede
Oshogbo
Iwo
Ilesha
Ibadan
Ife
Abeokuta
Ondo
Owo
Ijebu Ode
Benue
Makurdi
Okene
NIMBA MTS.
MAN HIGHLANDS
Bouaké
Kintampo
Lake Volta
Kumasi
Yamoussoukro
Bopolu
BONG MTS.
LIBERIA
Monrovia
Robertsfield
Buchanan
NIETE MTS.
Abidjan
Tarkwa
Oda
Koforidua
Tema
Accra
Winneba
Cape Coast
Sekondi/Takoradi
Lomé
Cotonou
Porto Novo
Lagos
Benin City
Onitsha
Enugu
Sapele
Aba
Port Harcourt
Calabar
Greenville
Harper
Cape Palmas
Sassandra
San Pédro
Bérébi
Grand Lahou
Cape Three Points
Bight of Benin
Bight of Bonny
Gulf of Guinea
ATLANTIC OCEAN
Nkongsamba
CAMEROON
Mt. Cameroun 4069
Douala
Victoria
Tiko
Malabo
BIOKO
Kribi
Bata
Príncipe
EQUATORIAL GUINEA
RIO MUNI
SÃO TOMÉ & PRINCIPE
São Tomé
Libreville
Equator
Cape Lopez
Port Gentil
Lambaréné
NORTH AMERICA
CARIBBEAN
SOUTH AMERICA
THE CAPE
20°W
15°W
10°W
5°W
0°
5°E
35°N
30°N
25°N
20°N
10°N
1 : 15 000 000
1cm : 150 km 1" : 237 mls.
POPULATION & CITIES
per sq. kilometre
100
10
1
under 1
1 million
100,000
others
motorways
main roads
railways
shipping
air traffic
HEP station
mining etc
heights in metres
LAND USE
coniferous forest
mixed forest
deciduous forest
tropical forest
farming
paddy
other irrigation
savanna
desert
sand
other
marsh or bog
Zenithal Equal-Area Projection
© Oxford University Press

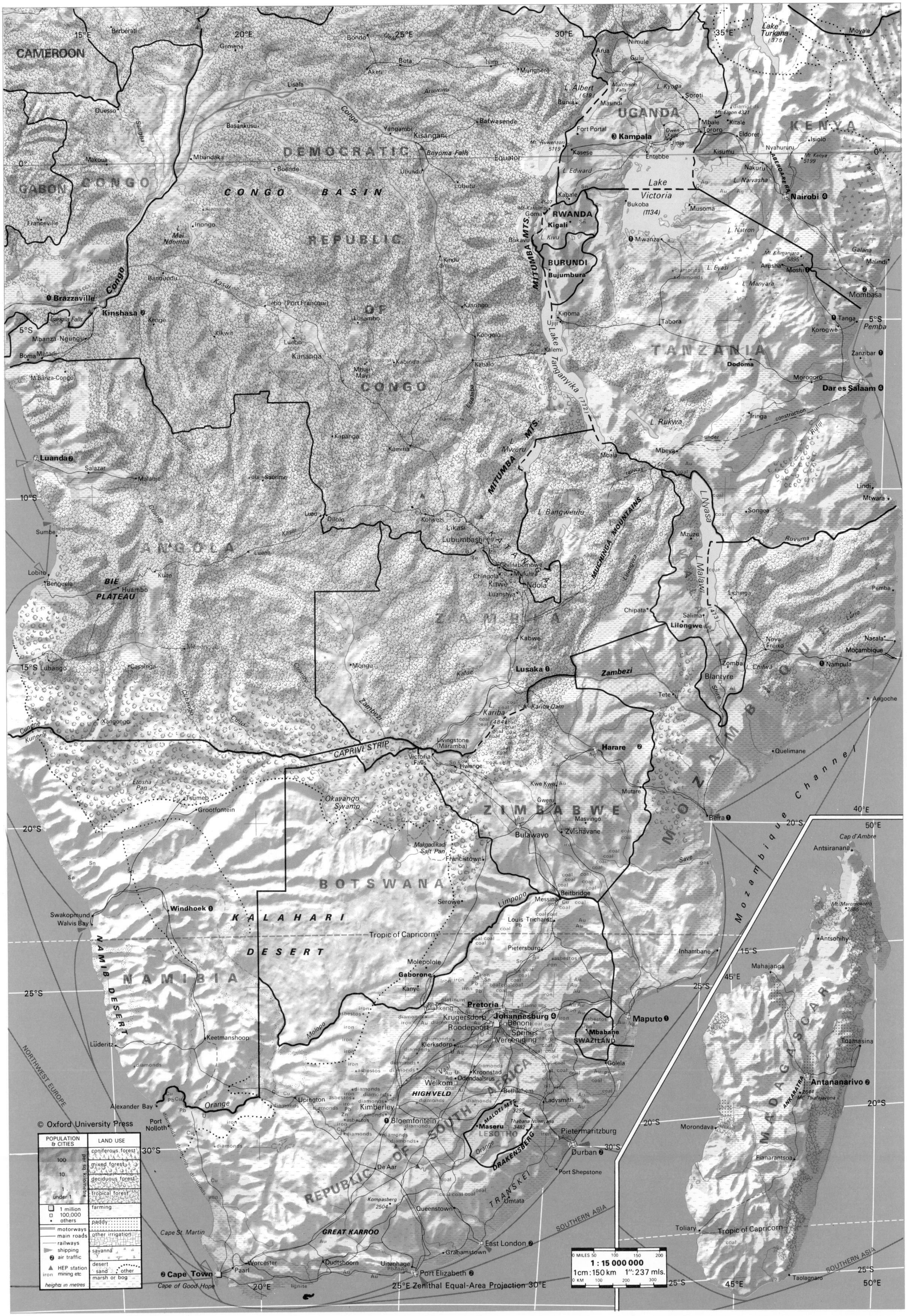
CAMEROON
GABON
CONGO
DEMOCRATIC REPUBLIC OF CONGO
CONGO BASIN
UGANDA
KENYA
RWANDA
BURUNDI
TANZANIA
ANGOLA
BIE PLATEAU
ZAMBIA
MOZAMBIQUE
ZIMBABWE
BOTSWANA
NAMIBIA
KALAHARI DESERT
NAMIB DESERT
REPUBLIC OF SOUTH AFRICA
LESOTHO
SWAZILAND
MADAGASCAR
MITUMBA MTS
MUCHINGA MOUNTAINS
DRAKENSBERG
MALOTI MTS
GREAT KARROO
HIGH VELD
CAPRIVI STRIP
TRANSKEI
Lake Victoria (1134)
L. Albert
L. Edward
L. Kivu
Lake Tanganyika
L. Mweru
L. Bangweulu
L. Rukwa
L. Nyasa
L. Malawi
Lake Turkana
Kariba
Okavango Swamp
Etosha Pan
Makgadikadi Salt Pan
Mozambique Channel
Tropic of Capricorn
Congo
Kasai
Zambezi
Limpopo
Orange
Molopo
Cuando
Cubango
Cunene
Kunene
Ruvuma
Brazzaville
Kinshasa
Kisangani
Mbandaka
Kananga
Lubumbashi
Kolwezi
Likasi
Luanda
Benguela
Lobito
Huambo
Lubango
Kampala
Nairobi
Mombasa
Kigali
Bujumbura
Dodoma
Dar es Salaam
Zanzibar
Tanga
Mbeya
Lusaka
Kitwe
Ndola
Kabwe
Lilongwe
Blantyre
Zomba
Nampula
Moçambique
Beira
Quelimane
Tete
Harare
Bulawayo
Victoria Falls
Livingstone (Maramba)
Gaborone
Francistown
Windhoek
Walvis Bay
Swakopmund
Lüderitz
Keetmanshoop
Pretoria
Johannesburg
Soweto
Bloemfontein
Kimberley
Maseru
Mbabane
Maputo
Durban
Pietermaritzburg
East London
Port Elizabeth
Cape Town
Cape of Good Hope
Antananarivo
Toamasina
Antsiranana
Mahajanga
Fianarantsoa
Toliary
Taolagnaro
Cap d'Ambre
© Oxford University Press
POPULATION & CITIES
LAND USE
coniferous forest
mixed forest
deciduous forest
tropical forest
farming
paddy
other irrigation
savanna
desert
sand
other
marsh or bog
per sq. kilometre
100
10
1
under 1
1 million
100,000
others
motorways
main roads
railways
shipping
air traffic
HEP station
mining etc
heights in metres
1 : 15 000 000
1cm : 150 km 1": 237 mls.
25°E Zenithal Equal-Area Projection 30°E
NORTHWEST EUROPE
SOUTHERN ASIA

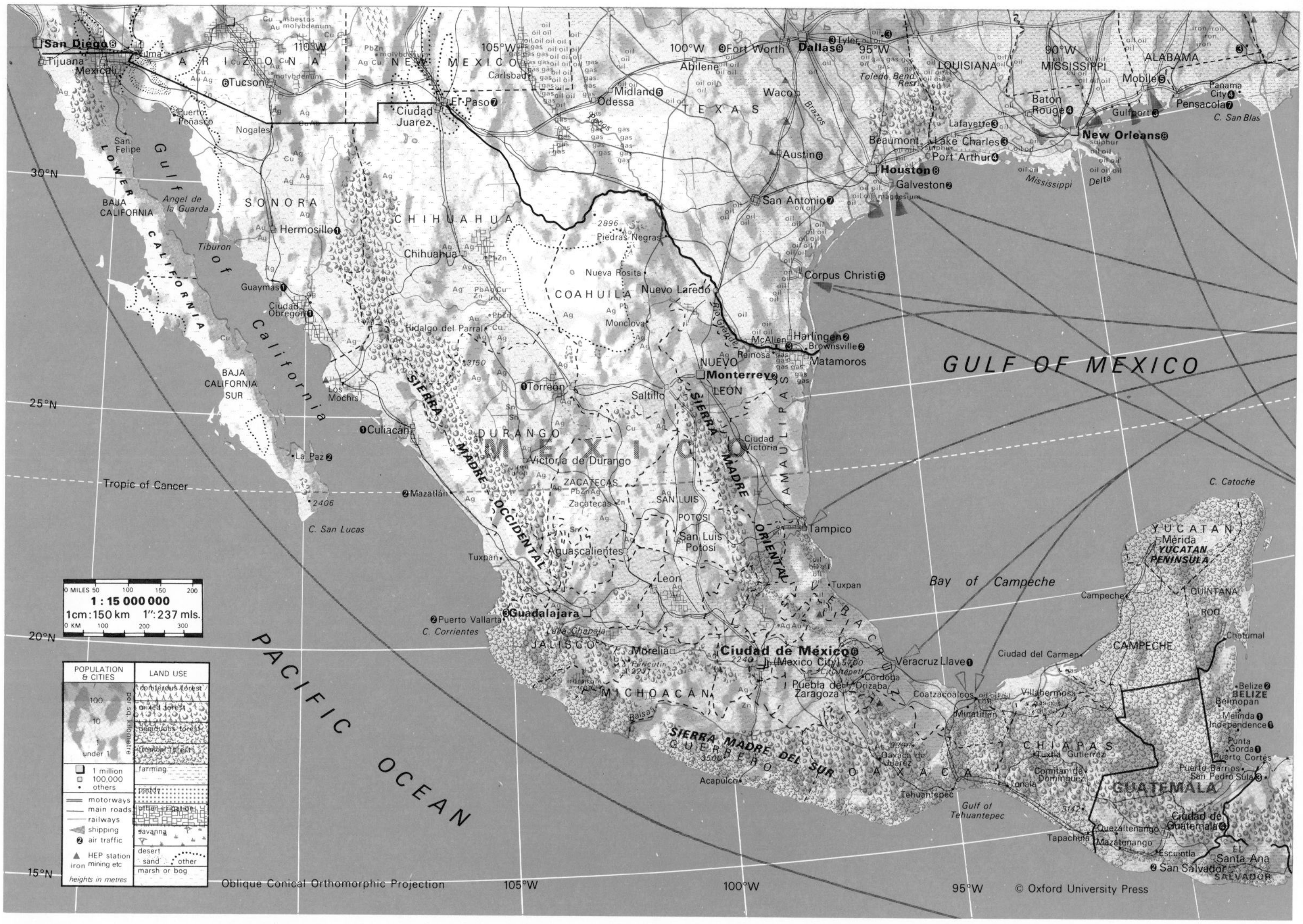

GULF OF MEXICO
PACIFIC OCEAN
MEXICO
Bay of Campeche
Gulf of California
Tropic of Cancer
SIERRA MADRE OCCIDENTAL
SIERRA MADRE ORIENTAL
SIERRA MADRE DEL SUR
LOWER CALIFORNIA
ARIZONA
NEW MEXICO
TEXAS
LOUISIANA
MISSISSIPPI
ALABAMA
SONORA
CHIHUAHUA
COAHUILA
NUEVO LEON
DURANGO
ZACATECAS
SAN LUIS POTOSI
JALISCO
MICHOACAN
GUERRERO
OAXACA
CHIAPAS
CAMPECHE
QUINTANA ROO
YUCATAN
YUCATAN PENINSULA
BELIZE
GUATEMALA
EL SALVADOR
San Diego
Tijuana
Mexicali
Tucson
Ciudad Juarez
El Paso
Odessa
Midland
Abilene
Fort Worth
Dallas
Waco
Austin
San Antonio
Houston
Galveston
Beaumont
Port Arthur
Lake Charles
Lafayette
Baton Rouge
New Orleans
Gulfport
Mobile
Pensacola
Corpus Christi
Hermosillo
Guaymas
Ciudad Obregon
Chihuahua
Nuevo Laredo
Monterrey
Matamoros
Brownsville
Saltillo
Torreon
Culiacan
La Paz
Mazatlan
Victoria de Durango
Zacatecas
San Luis Potosi
Tampico
Aguascalientes
Guadalajara
Leon
Morelia
Ciudad de Mexico
(Mexico City)
Puebla de Zaragoza
Veracruz Llave
Acapulco
Coatzacoalcos
Villahermosa
Merida
Campeche
Ciudad del Carmen
Chetumal
Belize
Belmopan
Tapachula
Quezaltenango
Ciudad de Guatemala
Santa Ana
San Salvador
Gulf of Tehuantepec
C. Catoche
C. San Lucas
C. Corrientes
1 : 15 000 000
1cm : 150 km 1": 237 mls.
POPULATION & CITIES
LAND USE
coniferous forest
mixed forest
deciduous forest
tropical forest
farming
paddy
other irrigation
savanna
desert
sand
other
marsh or bog
1 million
100,000
others
motorways
main roads
railways
shipping
air traffic
HEP station
iron mining etc
heights in metres
Oblique Conical Orthomorphic Projection
© Oxford University Press

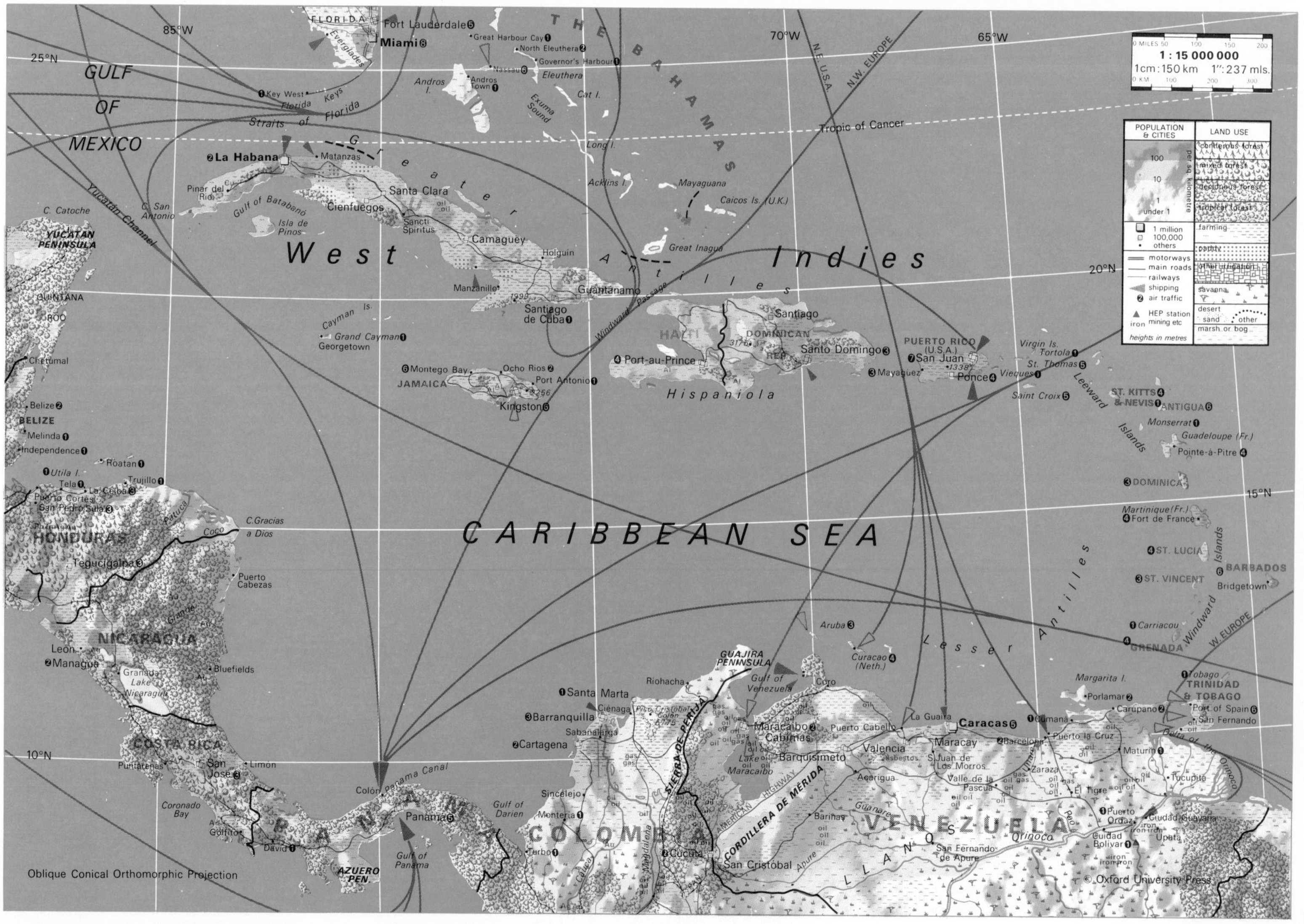

CARIBBEAN SEA
GULF OF MEXICO
West Indies
Greater Antilles
Lesser Antilles
THE BAHAMAS
Tropic of Cancer
FLORIDA
Miami
Fort Lauderdale
Key West
Straits of Florida
Andros I.
Nassau
Eleuthera
Cat I.
Long I.
Acklins I.
Mayaguana
Caicos Is. (U.K.)
Great Inagua
La Habana
Matanzas
Pinar del Rio
Santa Clara
Cienfuegos
Sancti Spiritus
Camaguey
Holguin
Manzanillo
Guantanamo
Santiago de Cuba
Isla de Pinos
Yucatan Channel
Grand Cayman
Georgetown
JAMAICA
Montego Bay
Ocho Rios
Port Antonio
Kingston
HAITI
Port-au-Prince
DOMINICAN REP.
Santiago
Santo Domingo
Hispaniola
Windward Passage
PUERTO RICO (U.S.A.)
San Juan
Mayaguez
Ponce
Vieques
Virgin Is.
Tortola
St. Thomas
Saint Croix
ST. KITTS & NEVIS
ANTIGUA
Monserrat
Guadeloupe (Fr.)
Pointe-a-Pitre
DOMINICA
Martinique (Fr.)
Fort de France
ST. LUCIA
ST. VINCENT
BARBADOS
Bridgetown
Carriacou
GRENADA
Leeward Islands
Windward Islands
TRINIDAD & TOBAGO
Port of Spain
San Fernando
Margarita I.
Aruba
Curacao (Neth.)
GUAJIRA PENINSULA
Gulf of Venezuela
Coro
Maracaibo
Lake Maracaibo
Barquisimeto
Valencia
Maracay
Caracas
La Guaira
Puerto Cabello
Barcelona
Cumana
Maturin
Ciudad Bolivar
Puerto Ordaz
Orinoco
VENEZUELA
LLANOS
San Cristobal
Cucuta
COLOMBIA
Riohacha
Santa Marta
Barranquilla
Cartagena
Sincelejo
Monteria
Gulf of Darien
PANAMA
Colon
Panama Canal
Panama
Gulf of Panama
AZUERO PEN.
David
Golfito
Coronado Bay
COSTA RICA
San Jose
Limon
Puntarenas
NICARAGUA
Managua
Leon
Lake Nicaragua
Bluefields
Puerto Cabezas
HONDURAS
Tegucigalpa
San Pedro Sula
Puerto Cortes
Roatan
Utila I.
Trujillo
C. Gracias a Dios
BELIZE
Belize
Melinda
Independence
Chetumal
YUCATAN PENINSULA
C. Catoche
QUINTANA ROO
CORDILLERA DE MERIDA
SIERRA DE PERIJA
1 : 15 000 000
1cm : 150 km 1": 237 mls.
POPULATION & CITIES
LAND USE
heights in metres
Oblique Conical Orthomorphic Projection
© Oxford University Press

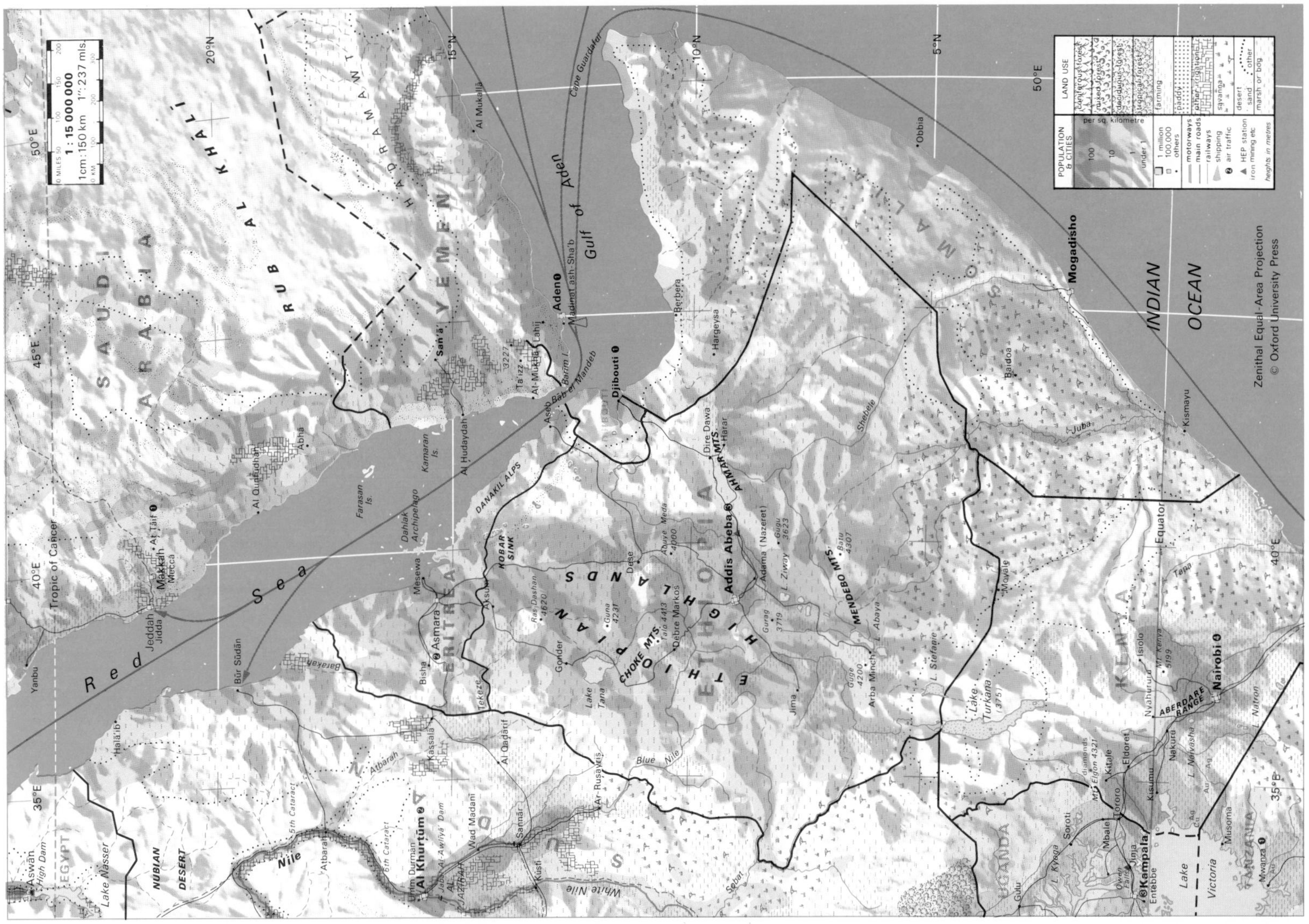
1 : 15 000 000
1cm : 150 km 1" : 237 mls.
SAUDI ARABIA
RUB AL KHALI
YEMEN
HADRAMAWT
Red Sea
Gulf of Aden
Tropic of Cancer
ERITREA
ETHIOPIA
ETHIOPIAN HIGHLANDS
SOMALIA
KENYA
UGANDA
TANZANIA
EGYPT
INDIAN OCEAN
Addis Abeba
Mogadisho
Djibouti
Nairobi
Kampala
Al Khurtum
Asmara
San'a
Aden
Makkah
Jiddah
Lake Victoria
Lake Turkana
Nile
Blue Nile
White Nile
Equator
POPULATION & CITIES
LAND USE
Zenithal Equal-Area Projection
© Oxford University Press

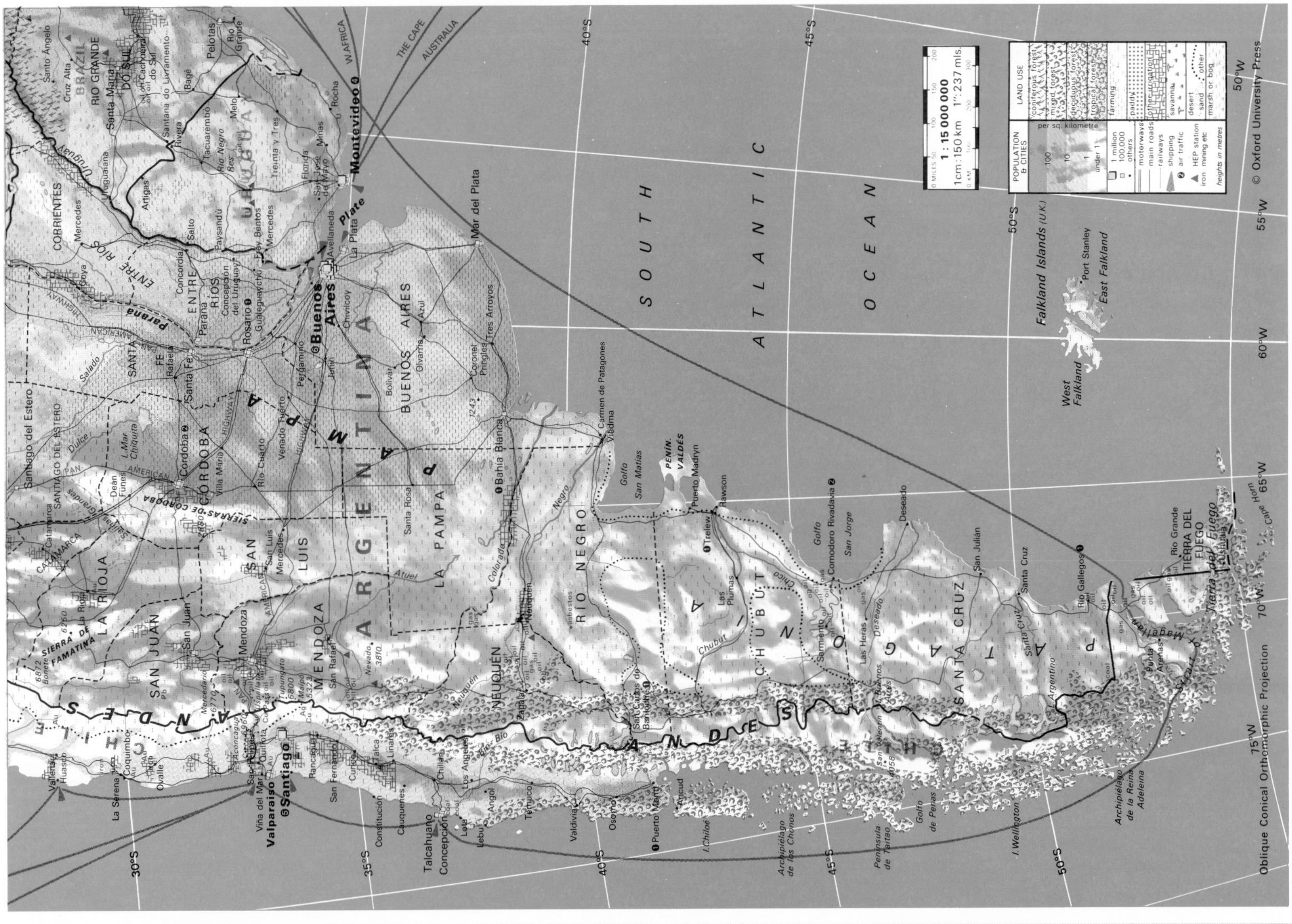
1 : 15 000 000
1cm : 150 km 1" : 237 mls.
ARGENTINA
CHILE
ANDES
URUGUAY
BRAZIL
PATAGONIA
PAMPA
SOUTH ATLANTIC OCEAN
Falkland Islands (U.K.)
East Falkland
West Falkland
Buenos Aires
Montevideo
Santiago
Valparaíso
Córdoba
Mendoza
Tierra del Fuego
Cape Horn
POPULATION & CITIES
LAND USE
Oblique Conical Orthomorphic Projection
© Oxford University Press

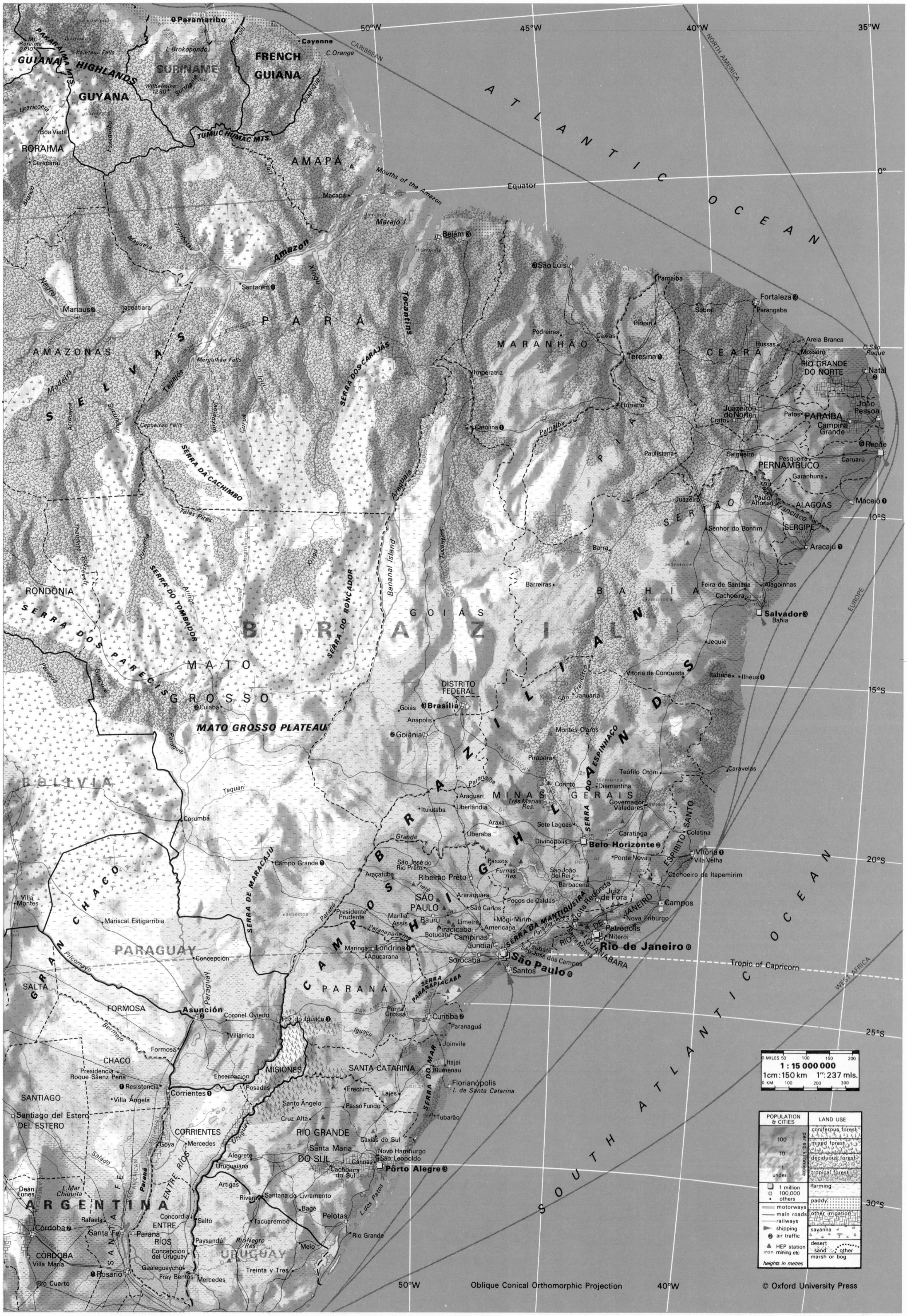
Paramaribo
Cayenne
C. Orange
FRENCH
GUIANA
SURINAME
GUYANA
GUIANA HIGHLANDS
PAKARAIMA MTS.
Mt. Roraima 2810
Kaieteur Falls
L. Brokopondo
Wilhelmina 1280
TUMUC HUMAC MTS.
Boa Vista
RORAIMA
Caracaraí
AMAPÁ
Macapá
Mouths of the Amazon
Equator
Marajó I.
Belém
São Luís
Parnaíba
Fortaleza
Parangaba
Sobral
Amazon
Santarém
Manaus
Itacoatiara
P A R Á
AMAZONAS
S E L V A S
Tocantins
Xingu
Tapajós
Madeira
Negro
Trombetas
Mapuera
SERRA DOS CARAJÁS
Mergulhão Falls
Capoeiras Falls
SERRA DA CACHIMBO
Teles Pires
M A R A N H Ã O
Pedreiras
Caxias
Teresina
Piripiri
Imperatriz
Floriano
Carolina
Parnaíba
C E A R Á
Russas
Areia Branca
Mossoró
C. São Roque
RIO GRANDE DO NORTE
Natal
João Pessoa
PARAÍBA
Campina Grande
Patos
Juàzeiro do Norte
Crato
Recife
Caruaru
Pesqueira
Garanhuns
PERNAMBUCO
Salgueiro
Paulistana
P I A U Í
Juàzeiro
Paulo Afonso
São Francisco
ALAGOAS
Maceió
SERGIPE
Aracajú
Senhor do Bonfim
S E R T Ã O
Barra
Barreiras
B A H I A
Feira de Santana
Alagoinhas
Cachoeira
Salvador
Bahia
Jequié
Itabuna
Ilhéus
Vitória de Conquista
RONDÔNIA
SERRA DOS PARECIS
SERRA DO TOMBADOR
SERRA DO RONCADOR
Bananal Island
Araguaia
G O I Á S
B R A Z I L
MATO GROSSO
Cuiabá
MATO GROSSO PLATEAU
DISTRITO FEDERAL
Brasília
Goiás
Anápolis
Goiânia
Montes Claros
Januária
Pirapora
SERRA DO ESPINHAÇO
BRAZILIAN HIGHLANDS
Teófilo Otôni
Caravelas
Corinto
Diamantina
MINAS GERAIS
Três Marias Res.
Governador Valadares
Araguari
Uberlândia
Ituiutaba
Uberaba
Araxá
Sete Lagoas
Divinópolis
Belo Horizonte
Caratinga
Colatina
ESPÍRITO SANTO
Vitória
Vila Velha
Ponte Nova
Cachoeiro de Itapemirim
BOLIVIA
Taquari
Corumbá
Campo Grande
SERRA DE MARACAJU
CAMPOS
São José do Rio Prêto
Araçatuba
Ribeirão Prêto
Passos
Furnas Res.
São João del Rei
Barbacena
Juiz de Fora
Campos
SÃO PAULO
Araraquara
Poços de Caldas
São Carlos
Presidente Prudente
Marília
Bauru
Assis
Jaú
Mogi-Mirim
Limeira
Americana
Piracicaba
Campinas
Botucatu
Jundiaí
SERRA DA MANTIQUEIRA
Volta Redonda
Petrópolis
Nova Friburgo
Niterói
Rio de Janeiro
GUANABARA
Taubaté
São José dos Campos
Sorocaba
São Paulo
Santos
Tropic of Capricorn
Londrina
Maringá
Apucarana
Paranapanema
PARANÁ
SERRA PARANAPIACABA
Ponta Grossa
Curitiba
Paranaguá
Foz do Iguaçu
Iguaçu
Joinvile
Itajaí
Blumenau
SANTA CATARINA
Florianópolis
I. de Santa Catarina
SERRA DO MAR
Tubarão
Lajes
Erechim
Passo Fundo
Santo Ângelo
Cruz Alta
RIO GRANDE DO SUL
Caxias do Sul
Santa Maria
Novo Hamburgo
São Leopoldo
Canoas
Cachoeira do Sul
Pôrto Alegre
L. dos Patos
Pelotas
Rio Grande
Bagé
Santana do Livramento
Rivera
Alegrete
Uruguaiana
Artigas
Tacuarembó
URUGUAY
Salto
Paysandú
Río Negro Res.
Melo
Treinta y Tres
Mercedes
Fray Bentos
Gualeguaychú
Concepción del Uruguay
GRAN CHACO
Villa Montes
Mariscal Estigarribia
PARAGUAY
Concepción
Asunción
Coronel Oviedo
Villarrica
Encarnación
Posadas
MISIONES
Pilcomayo
Bermejo
SALTA
FORMOSA
Formosa
CHACO
Presidencia Roque Sáenz Peña
Resistencia
Villa Ángela
Corrientes
CORRIENTES
Goya
Mercedes
SANTIAGO
Santiago del Estero
DEL ESTERO
Salado
ARGENTINA
ENTRE RÍOS
SANTA FE
Deán Funes
L. Mar Chiquita
Rafaela
Córdoba
Santa Fe
Paraná
CÓRDOBA
Villa María
Rosario
Río Cuarto
Concordia
A T L A N T I C   O C E A N
SOUTH ATLANTIC OCEAN
CARIBBEAN
NORTH AMERICA
EUROPE
WEST AFRICA
50°W
45°W
40°W
35°W
0°
10°S
15°S
20°S
25°S
30°S
1 : 15 000 000
1cm : 150 km   1": 237 mls.
POPULATION & CITIES
LAND USE
per sq. kilometre
1 million
100,000
others
motorways
main roads
railways
shipping
air traffic
HEP station
mining etc
heights in metres
coniferous forest
mixed forest
deciduous forest
tropical forest
farming
paddy
other irrigation
savanna
desert sand other
marsh or bog
Oblique Conical Orthomorphic Projection
© Oxford University Press

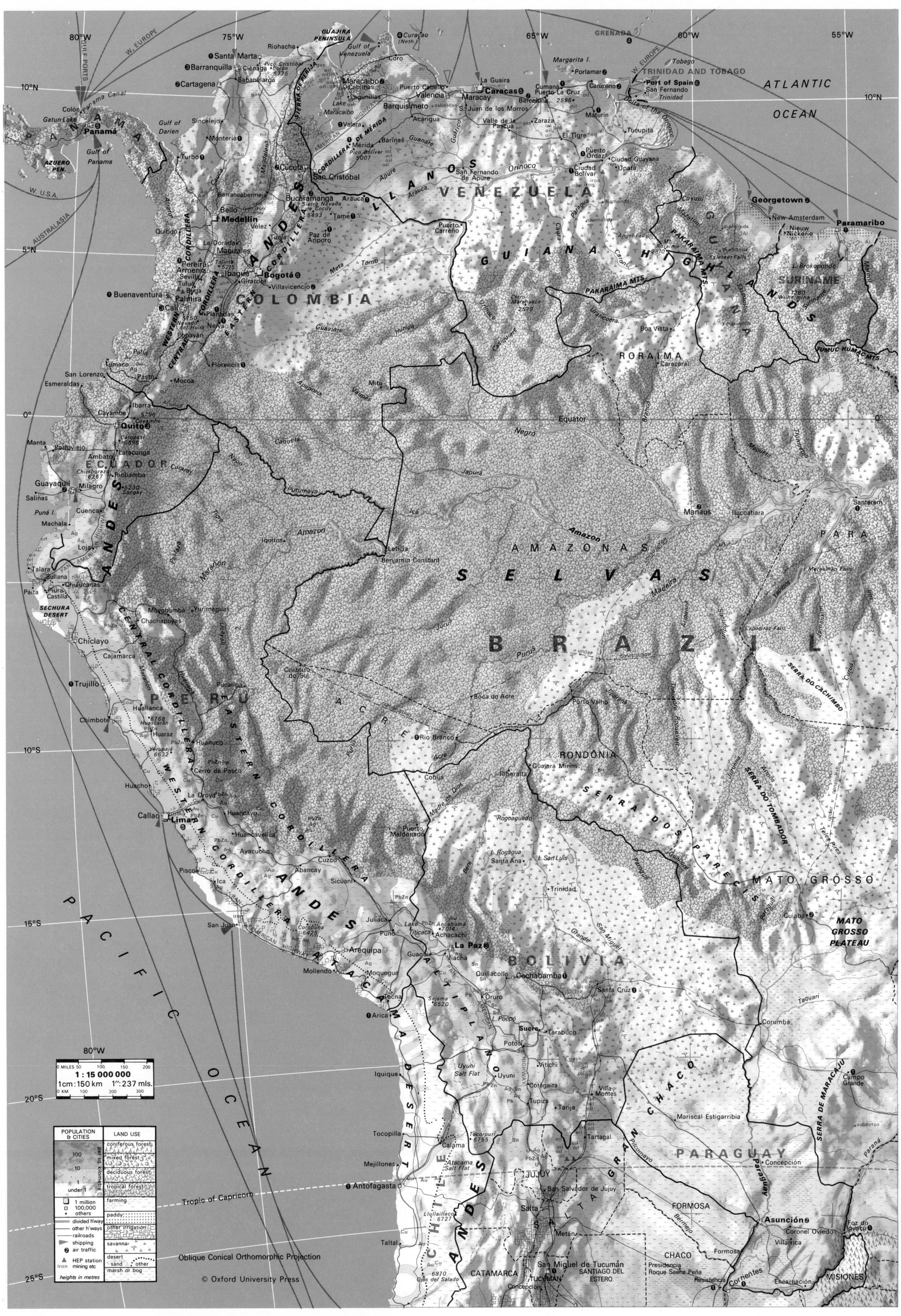
ATLANTIC OCEAN
PACIFIC OCEAN
TRINIDAD AND TOBAGO
VENEZUELA
COLOMBIA
ECUADOR
PERU
BRAZIL
BOLIVIA
PARAGUAY
SURINAME
PANAMA
CHILE
LLANOS
GUIANA HIGHLANDS
SELVAS
AMAZONAS
ANDES
ATACAMA DESERT
ALTIPLANO
GRAN CHACO
MATO GROSSO
MATO GROSSO PLATEAU
SERRA DOS PARECIS
SERRA DO TOMBADOR
SERRA DO CACHIMBO
SERRA DE MARACAJU
PAKARAIMA MTS.
TUMUC HUMAC MTS.
SECHURA DESERT
GUAJIRA PENINSULA
RONDÔNIA
RORAIMA
ACRE
PARÁ
Equator
Tropic of Capricorn
Caracas
Bogotá
Quito
Lima
La Paz
Asunción
Georgetown
Paramaribo
Port of Spain
Panamá
Manaus
Amazon
Orinoco
Negro
Madeira
Lake Titicaca
1 : 15 000 000
1cm : 150 km 1": 237 mls.
POPULATION & CITIES
LAND USE
coniferous forest
mixed forest
deciduous forest
tropical forest
farming
paddy
other irrigation
savanna
desert
sand
other
marsh or bog
1 million
100,000
others
divided h'way
other h'ways
railroads
shipping
air traffic
HEP station
mining etc
heights in metres
per sq. kilometre
Oblique Conical Orthomorphic Projection
© Oxford University Press

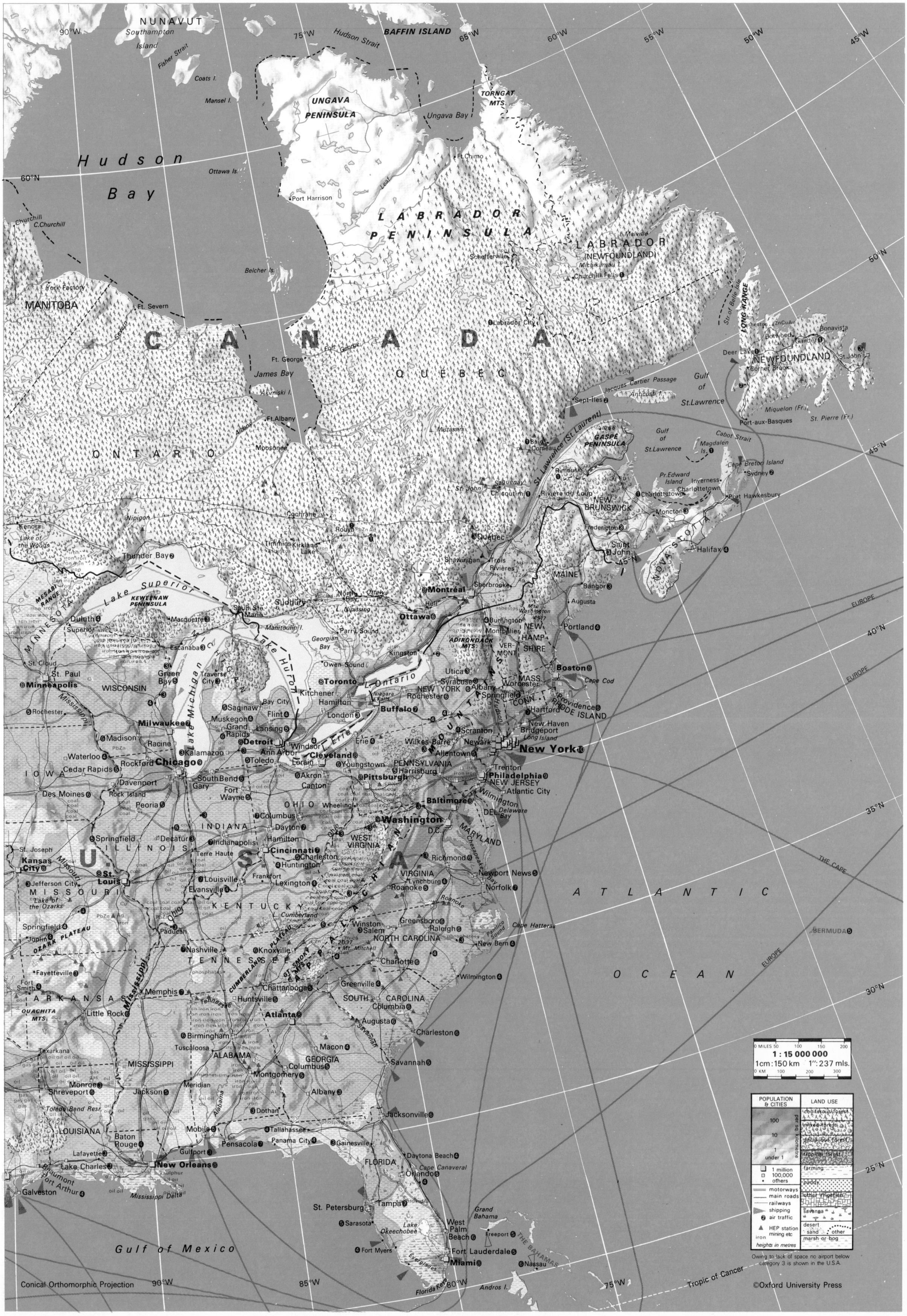
NUNAVUT
Southampton Island
BAFFIN ISLAND
Hudson Strait
Fisher Strait
Coats I.
Mansel I.
UNGAVA PENINSULA
Ungava Bay
TORNGAT MTS.
Hudson Bay
Ottawa Is.
Ft.Chimo
Port Harrison
LABRADOR PENINSULA
LABRADOR (NEWFOUNDLAND)
Churchill
C.Churchill
Schefferville
Churchill Falls
Belcher Is.
York Factory
MANITOBA
Ft. Severn
Labrador City
C A N A D A
QUÉBEC
Ft. George
James Bay
Akimiski I.
Ft. Albany
Moosonee
ONTARIO
NEWFOUNDLAND
Bonavista
Gander
St.John's
Deer Lake
Corner Brook
LONG RANGE
Str. of Belle Isle
Jacques Cartier Passage
Anticosti I.
Gulf of St.Lawrence
Sept-Îles
Port-aux-Basques
Miquelon (Fr.)
St. Pierre (Fr.)
Cabot Strait
Magdalen Is.
GASPÉ PENINSULA
St. Lawrence (St. Laurent)
Baie Comeau
Mistassini
Cape Breton Island
Sydney
Pr.Edward Island
Charlottetown
Port Hawkesbury
Rimouski
Rivière du Loup
Chicoutimi
Saguenay
NEW BRUNSWICK
Moncton
Fredericton
Saint John
NOVA SCOTIA
Halifax
L. Nipigon
Cochrane
Kenora
Lake of the Woods
Thunder Bay
Rouyn
Timmins
Kirkland Lake
Québec
Shawinigan
Trois Rivières
Sherbrooke
Montréal
MAINE
Bangor
Augusta
Lake Superior
KEWEENAW PENINSULA
MESABI RANGE
Sudbury
North Bay
L. Nipissing
Ottawa
Hull
Duluth
Superior
Marquette
Sault Ste Marie
Manitoulin I.
Georgian Bay
Parry Sound
MINNESOTA
Escanaba
Lake Huron
Burlington
Montpelier
NEW HAMPSHIRE
VERMONT
Portland
ADIRONDACK MTS.
Kingston
Owen Sound
St. Cloud
St. Paul
Minneapolis
WISCONSIN
Green Bay
Traverse City
Lake Michigan
Toronto
Lake Ontario
Utica
Syracuse
Albany
NEW YORK
Rochester
Boston
MASS.
Worcester
Springfield
Cape Cod
CONN.
Providence
RHODE ISLAND
Hartford
Rochester
Bay City
Saginaw
Flint
Kitchener
Hamilton
Niagara Falls
Buffalo
London
Milwaukee
Muskegon
Grand Rapids
Lansing
Detroit
Windsor
Ann Arbor
Lake Erie
Erie
Scranton
Wilkes-Barre
Allentown
Newark
New Haven
Bridgeport
Long Island
New York
Madison
Racine
Kalamazoo
Toledo
Cleveland
Lorain
Youngstown
Waterloo
Cedar Rapids
Rockford
Chicago
IOWA
Davenport
South Bend
Gary
Akron
Canton
Pittsburgh
PENNSYLVANIA
Harrisburg
Trenton
Philadelphia
NEW JERSEY
Atlantic City
Des Moines
Rock Island
Peoria
Fort Wayne
OHIO
Wheeling
Baltimore
Wilmington
DEL.
Delaware Bay
Columbus
INDIANA
Dayton
Washington D.C.
MARYLAND
Springfield
Decatur
ILLINOIS
Indianapolis
Hamilton
WEST VIRGINIA
St. Joseph
Kansas City
Terre Haute
Cincinnati
Charleston
Richmond
Huntington
VIRGINIA
St. Louis
Jefferson City
MISSOURI
Lake of the Ozarks
Evansville
Louisville
Frankfort
Lexington
Roanoke
Lynchburg
Newport News
Norfolk
Chesapeake Bay
KENTUCKY
A T L A N T I C
Springfield
Joplin
OZARK PLATEAU
Paducah
Cumberland
Winston Salem
Greensboro
Raleigh
NORTH CAROLINA
Pamlico Sound
Cape Hatteras
BERMUDA
Nashville
Knoxville
TENNESSEE
Mt. Mitchell
New Bern
Fayetteville
CUMBERLAND PLATEAU
GT. SMOKY MTS.
Charlotte
Wilmington
O C E A N
Fort Smith
ARKANSAS
Memphis
Chattanooga
Greenville
SOUTH CAROLINA
Columbia
QUACHITA MTS.
Little Rock
Huntsville
Atlanta
Augusta
Charleston
Birmingham
Tuscaloosa
ALABAMA
Macon
GEORGIA
Columbus
Savannah
Texarkana
MISSISSIPPI
Montgomery
Monroe
Shreveport
Jackson
Meridian
Albany
Toledo Bend Resr.
Dothan
Jacksonville
LOUISIANA
Mobile
Tallahassee
Baton Rouge
Pensacola
Panama City
Gainesville
Lafayette
Gulfport
Lake Charles
New Orleans
FLORIDA
Daytona Beach
Cape Canaveral
Orlando
Beaumont
Port Arthur
Galveston
Mississippi Delta
Grand Bahama
St. Petersburg
Tampa
Sarasota
Lake Okeechobee
West Palm Beach
Freeport
THE BAHAMAS
Gulf of Mexico
Fort Myers
Fort Lauderdale
Miami
Nassau
Everglades
Florida Keys
Andros I.
Tropic of Cancer
EUROPE
THE CAPE
0 MILES 50 100 150 200
1 : 15 000 000
1cm : 150 km 1": 237 mls.
0 KM 100 200 300
POPULATION & CITIES
LAND USE
per sq kilometre
100
10
1
under 1
1 million
100,000
others
motorways
main roads
railways
shipping
air traffic
HEP station
mining etc
heights in metres
coniferous forest
mixed forest
deciduous forest
tropical forest
farming
paddy
other vegetation
savanna
desert
sand
other
marsh or bog
Owing to lack of space no airport below category 3 is shown in the U.S.A.
Conical Orthomorphic Projection
©Oxford University Press